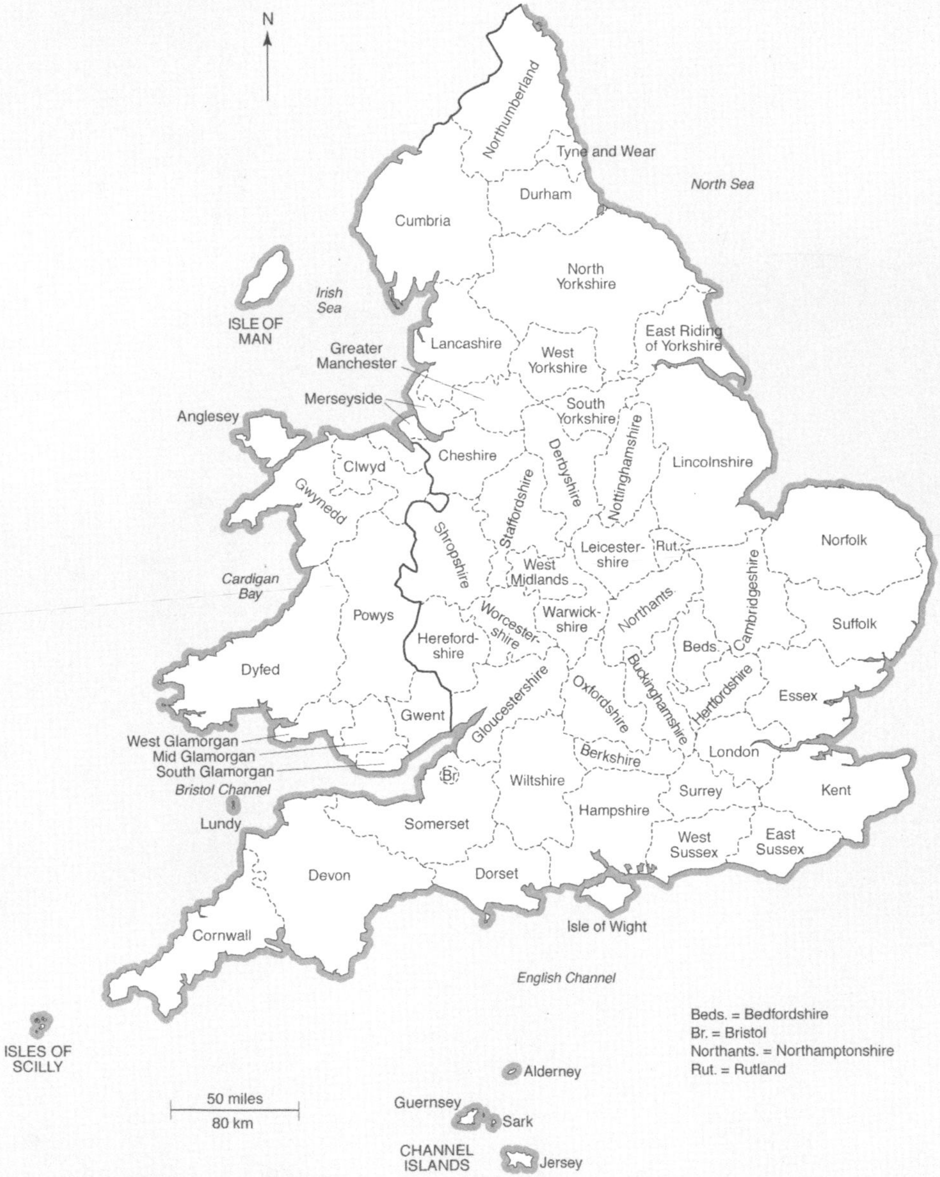

N
Northumberland
Tyne and Wear
North Sea
Durham
Cumbria
North Yorkshire
Irish Sea
ISLE OF MAN
East Riding of Yorkshire
Lancashire
West Yorkshire
Greater Manchester
Merseyside
South Yorkshire
Anglesey
Cheshire
Nottinghamshire
Derbyshire
Lincolnshire
Clwyd
Gwynedd
Staffordshire
Shropshire
Leicester-shire
Rut.
Norfolk
West Midlands
Cardigan Bay
Cambridgeshire
Powys
Worcester-shire
Warwick-shire
Northants.
Suffolk
Hereford-shire
Beds.
Dyfed
Gloucestershire
Oxfordshire
Buckinghamshire
Hertfordshire
Essex
Gwent
West Glamorgan
Mid Glamorgan
South Glamorgan
Berkshire
London
Bristol Channel
Br.
Wiltshire
Surrey
Kent
Lundy
Somerset
Hampshire
West Sussex
East Sussex
Devon
Dorset
Cornwall
Isle of Wight
English Channel
Beds. = Bedfordshire
Br. = Bristol
Northants. = Northamptonshire
Rut. = Rutland
ISLES OF SCILLY
Alderney
50 miles
80 km
Guernsey
Sark
CHANNEL ISLANDS
Jersey

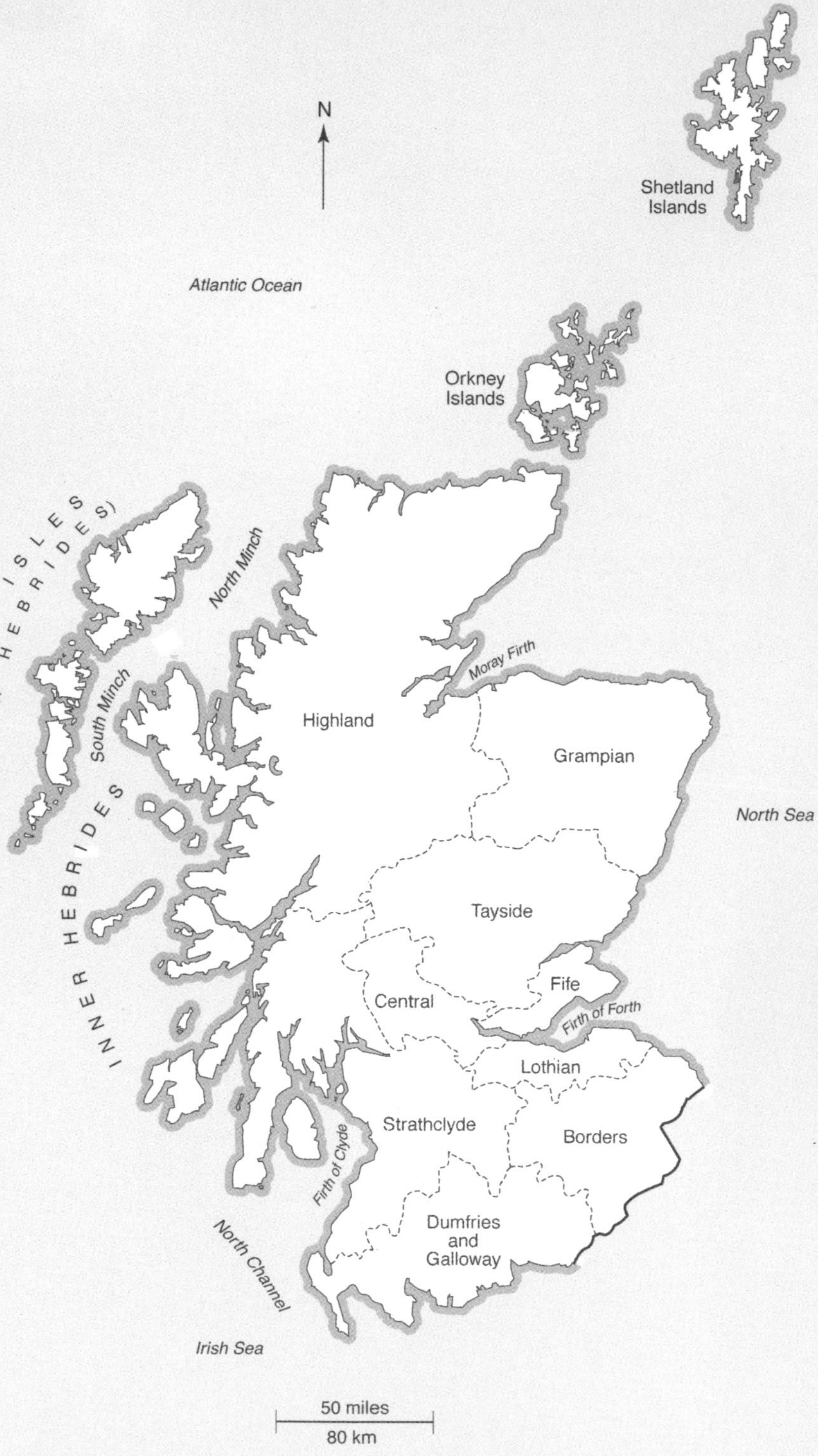
N
Shetland Islands
Atlantic Ocean
Orkney Islands
WESTERN ISLES (OUTER HEBRIDES)
North Minch
South Minch
Moray Firth
Highland
Grampian
North Sea
INNER HEBRIDES
Tayside
Fife
Central
Firth of Forth
Lothian
Strathclyde
Borders
Firth of Clyde
Dumfries and Galloway
North Channel
Irish Sea
50 miles
80 km

A TO Z OF BRITAIN AND IRELAND

Also by Trevor Montague

A to Z of (Almost) Everything

A to Z of Sport

A TO Z OF BRITAIN AND IRELAND

(ALMOST) EVERYTHING YOU EVER NEEDED TO KNOW ABOUT THE HISTORY AND HERITAGE OF OUR ISLANDS

TREVOR MONTAGUE

sphere

SPHERE

First published in Great Britain in 2009 by Sphere

A CIP catalogue record for this book
is available from the British Library.

ISBN 978-1-84744-087-7

Typeset in Helvetica by M Rules
Printed in Thailand

Papers used by Sphere are natural, renewable and
recyclable products sourced from well-managed forests and certified in
accordance with the rules of the Forest Stewardship Council.

FSC
Mixed Sources
Product group from well-managed
forests and other controlled sources
www.fsc.org Cert no. SGS-COC-004081
© 1996 Forest Stewardship Council

Sphere
An imprint of
Little, Brown Book Group
100 Victoria Embankment
London EC4Y 0DY

An Hachette UK Company
www.hachette.co.uk

www.littlebrown.co.uk

Back cover question answers: Suffolk (see page 517), Shetland Islands (see page 765), the Haughton Drop method of hanging (see page 1030), Fishguard (see page 883).

Contents

Foreword

When I first embarked on the journey to produce an all-encompassing single-volume reference work covering the various aspects of British and Irish life it soon became apparent that to reach my final destination I would either need to perform the literary equivalent of feeding the five thousand or else accept the fact that my train was likely to stop some way short of the platform. As I could not do the first, and refused to do the second, a compromise of some sort was in order. Being familiar with Edmund Clerihew Bentley's oft-misquoted verse about the art of biography being different from geography, I decided to concentrate my efforts on geography, history and heritage, in the main, with only the merest smidgen of biographical information interwoven to lend weight where necessary. For instance it would be errant of me not to include a brief biography of Warwickshire's most famous son, William Shakespeare, or to omit some mention of the Beatles in Merseyside, when they are so intrinsically linked to their county's history.

The second problem I tackled was how to accommodate the Republic of Ireland within a structure of four other nations all affiliated economically, constitutionally and politically. You might imagine I was concerned about comparative statistics or perhaps Ireland's different monetary unit and head of state, or even the wisdom of including my mother country at all, as it is often given scant coverage in reference works pertaining to British culture even when viewed in its historical perspective. What I was actually agonising over was how I should accommodate Ireland into the book's title! In the end I bowed respectfully to political correctness as, although it is traditional to refer to the Republic of Ireland and the United Kingdom of Great Britain and Northern Ireland as the British Isles, when considered as a single archipelago, this nomenclature implies a proprietary title which has long since ceased to exist, if indeed it ever really did exist. Despite the very close affinity between the British and Irish people I have no doubt my title is both expedient and correct.

My approach to setting out the core content of the book has been to divide Britain and Ireland into its five constituent nations and then to further sub-divide these nations into their traditional counties – with one or two qualified exceptions.

The story of each county begins with a general overview, followed by area and population statistics, and ends with local information and attractions. I have not felt it necessary to offer a lengthy overview of England, Scotland or Wales as this would serve no useful purpose, as much of the information I would supply is well catered for within the body of the text. However, I did feel that the complexity of the relationship between Britain and Ireland and indeed between Northern Ireland and the Republic required some sort of denouement, if only to give the reader a better understanding of terms such as 'The Troubles' and 'Plantation', which I frequently refer to in county histories without fully explaining their background.

I have endeavoured to portray the essence and character of a village, town, city or county by describing its people, customs, heritage and physical geography, and I have attempted to describe how each area, sometimes having very individual personalities, has managed to coexist, not always tolerantly, within the wider infrastructure of competing nations. The reader can be assured that objectivity has been maintained throughout but although all five home countries have been given equal billing it is inevitable that some areas (London immediately springs to mind) might appear to feature more prominently by dint of their size or abundance of heritage.

There are unique features of this work that I am very proud of, not least of which is my exhaustive list of islands of Britain and Ireland. I painstakingly trawled through a plethora of Ordnance Survey maps in my quest to discover every plot of land surrounded by water, whether it be inhabited or not, my only criteria was that it should have a name. As a secondary check I conversed with town councils, local historians, angling clubs and marine societies and indeed unearthed some very interesting unlisted islands. Undoubtedly my favourite is the island of Sealand, off the coast of Suffolk. This former sea fort, declared a sovereign state by its self-styled crowned prince, issues its own postage stamps and even has its own monetary unit!

An inventory of the comprehensively covered topics shows almost 6600 islands, 2000 stately homes and manor houses, 1200 castles, 200 cathedrals and more than 200 major battles fought on British and Irish soil. Mountains, lakes (lochs and loughs), rivers and glens have not been forgotten, and lovers of trivia will no doubt be intrigued by some of the 'interesting facts' I have unearthed in each section.

Following the main substance of the book I have added an appendix which includes a brief chronology of British and Irish history, geographical records, lists of cities and county flowers, explanation of terms such as Metropolitan and Ceremonial Counties, and details of the British Crown Dependencies.

For comparative reasons I have used the 2001 Census figures for populations for Great Britain and Northern Ireland and the 2002 Census figures for Ireland (the 2001 Census was cancelled due to the spread of foot and mouth disease).

Trevor Montague

England

England is bounded on the north by Scotland; on the northwest by the Irish Sea, on the west by Wales, the Bristol Channel and the Celtic Sea; on the south by the English Channel; and on the east by the North Sea. The English mainland coastline, with its many indentations, is approximately 5581 miles (8982km) in length, although if the offshore islands are included this total rises to 6261 miles (10,077km).

England takes its name from the Angles, one of the Germanic tribes who settled there during the 5th and 6th centuries. Originally this name was merely a descriptive of the part of Britain occupied by the Anglo-Saxons and it was not until AD 927 that it became a unified state when Athelstan developed his Kingdom of Wessex.

Despite the political, economic and cultural legacy that has secured the perpetuation of its name, England does not exist constitutionally and is not mentioned in the title of its ruling sovereign. It is a peculiarity of the largest country of the United Kingdom that, unlike Scotland, Wales and Northern Ireland, which all have varying degrees of self-government in domestic affairs, England has none. The Statute of Rhuddlan of 1284 partly incorporated Wales into England, and the Laws in Wales Acts of 1536 and 1543 effectively created a single state and a single legal jurisdiction, which is frequently referred to as England and Wales, and exists quite separate from Scottish and Irish law.

England still maintains independence in ecclesiastical matters, the Church of England being distinct from the Churches of Wales, Scotland and Ireland, and some sports associations. But in many ways England has been absorbed within the larger mass of Great Britain since the Act of Union (with Scotland) of 1707. Further loss of constitutional identity took place in 1801 when Ireland joined the Union, and when Eire left in 1922 the United Kingdom of Great Britain and Northern Ireland was born. That said, England remains in some respects the predominant country of the UK; for instance, a total of 529 of the current 646 MPs in the House of Commons represent English constituencies and this will rise to 533 out of 650 at the next general election. England's name is often erroneously considered by foreign nations to be synonymous with the islands of Great Britain and Ireland.

The English motto is *Dieu et mon droit* (God and my right) and the national anthem is 'God Save the King/Queen' when considered as part of the UK, although 'Land of Hope and Glory' is used as an unofficial anthem at the Commonwealth Games.

St George is the patron saint of England, and perhaps as a harbinger of the cosmopolitan society the nation was to become, he is thought to have been born in Cappadocia in Turkey. His emblem, a red centred cross on a white background, was adopted by Richard the Lionheart during the Third Crusade, by way of homage to the Christian martyr beheaded near Lydda in Palestine on 23 April 303. In 1222 the Council of Oxford declared 23 April to be St George's Day and his emblem became the flag of England and later St George replaced Edward the Confessor as England's patron saint. In 1415, 23 April was made a national feast day.

Historically, the Three Lions was the coat of arms of ruling monarchs of England but since 1837 British monarchs have courted the Royal Coat of Arms of the United Kingdom, consisting of a quartered shield depicting in the first and fourth quarters the three lions passant guardant of England, in the second the rampant lion of Scotland, and in the third a harp for Ireland.

The complex, and ongoing, administrative restructure of England is explained within the overviews of the regions I have divided the country into for the purposes of this book and the information is up to date as at 1 April 2009 and incorporates the changes made on that day; i.e. the abolition of Bedfordshire, Cheshire, Cornwall, County Durham, Northumberland, Shropshire and Wiltshire County Councils and their reformation as unitary authorities.

The population and area figures listed below are of the 32 existing counties (with county councils) and 12 metropolitan and non-metropolitan areas (unitary authorities) which make up the traditional counties.

For trivia buffs the region of England lies between 55° 46′ and 49° 57′ 30″ N. latitude and between 1° 46' E. and 5° 43′ W. longitude. Its official westernmost point is Dr Syntax's Head, a rocky outcrop some 100m west of Land's End. The northernmost point of the English mainland coast is near Marshall Meadows Bay, the most easterly point is Lowestoft Ness. The furthest place from the sea is Church Flatts Farm in Coton in the Elms, Derbyshire.

England population summaries

(see 2001 Census reconciliation)

	Population			Area	
	male	*female*	*total*	*sq miles*	*sq km*
Bedfordshire	281,283	284,660	565,943	477	1235
Berkshire	398,989	401,129	800,118	487	1262
Buckinghamshire	337,583	348,500	686,083	724	1874
Cambridgeshire	349,655	359,064	708,719	1308	3389
Cheshire	479,024	504,052	983,076	905	2342
Cornwall (and Isles of Scilly)	242,487	258,780	501,267	1375	3563
Cumbria	237,915	249,692	487,607	2613	6768
Derbyshire	469,079	487,214	956,293	1013	2625
Devon	519,357	555,562	1,074,919	2590	6707
Dorset	333,269	359,443	692,712	1024	2651
Durham	371,104	394,382	765,486	1011	2620
Essex	786,611	827,609	1,614,220	1417	3670
Gloucestershire	396,954	413,246	810,200	1216	3150
Greater Manchester	1,208,177	1,274,151	2,482,328	495	1280
Hampshire (and Isle of Wight)	872,566	904,414	1,776,980	1602	4148
Herefordshire	85,350	89,521	174,871	842	2180
Hertfordshire	505,059	528,918	1,033,977	634	1643
Kent	766,782	812,424	1,579,206	1443	3735
Lancashire	686,584	728,143	1,414,727	1185	3075
Leicestershire	453,803	470,259	924,062	980	2538
Lincolnshire	468,061	489,412	957,473	2687	6959
London	3,468,793	3,703,298	7,172,091	607	1572
Merseyside	647,254	714,772	1,362,026	249	644
Norfolk	387,827	408,901	796,728	2073	5371
Northamptonshire	310,744	318,932	629,676	913	2364
Northumberland	149,953	157,237	307,190	1936	5013
Nottinghamshire	498,648	516,850	1,015,498	833	2160
Oxfordshire	299,257	306,231	605,488	1006	2606
Shropshire	217,967	223,531	441,498	1346	3487
Somerset	601,395	634,917	1,236,312	1653	4281
Staffordshire	513,318	534,062	1,047,380	1046	2713
Suffolk	327,900	340,653	668,553	1468	3801
Surrey	516,525	542,490	1,059,015	642	1663
Sussex (East)	352,849	387,292	740,141	692	1791
Sussex (West)	360,604	393,010	753,614	769	1990
Tyne and Wear	520,286	555,652	1,075,938	209	538
Warwickshire	248,267	257,593	505,860	763	1975
West Midlands	1,244,322	1,311,270	2,555,592	348	902
Wiltshire	302,953	310,071	613,024	1345	3485
Worcestershire	265,887	276,220	542,107	672	1741
Yorkshire (East)	272,180	285,522	557,702	958	2479
Yorkshire (North)	542,050	575,532	1,117,582	3364	8711
Yorkshire (South)	617,531	648,807	1,266,338	599	1552
Yorkshire (West)	1,005,942	1,073,269	2,079,211	784	2030
England Total	23,922,144	25,216,687	49,138,831	50,303	130,283

BEDFORDSHIRE

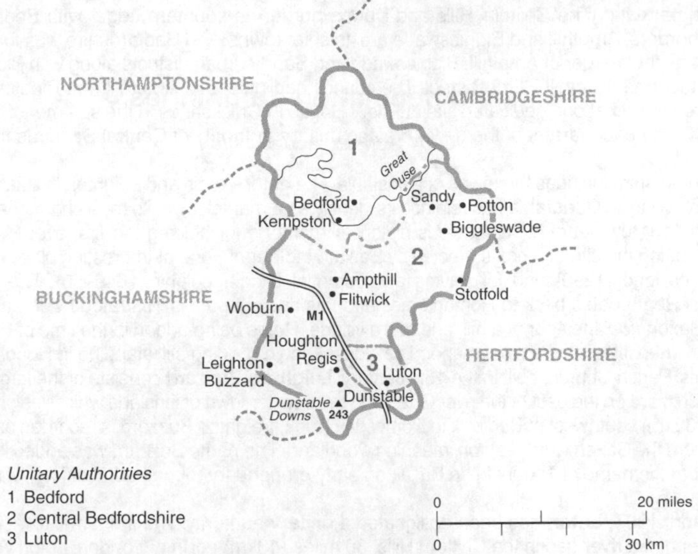
NORTHAMPTONSHIRE
CAMBRIDGESHIRE
BUCKINGHAMSHIRE
HERTFORDSHIRE
Great Ouse
1
2
3
Bedford
Kempston
Sandy
Potton
Biggleswade
Ampthill
Flitwick
Stotfold
Woburn
M1
Houghton Regis
Leighton Buzzard
Luton
Dunstable
Dunstable Downs
243
Unitary Authorities
1 Bedford
2 Central Bedfordshire
3 Luton
0
20 miles
0
30 km

Bedfordshire borders Cambridgeshire to its northeast, Northamptonshire to the northwest, Buckinghamshire to its west and southwest and Hertfordshire to the east and southeast. In 1997 Bedfordshire's largest town, Luton, became a unitary local authority and as such was not included in county statistics although remaining a geographical location within Bedfordshire.

Further legislation of 1 April 2009 has meant the abolition of the County Council and the amalgamation of the districts of Mid and South Bedfordshire into a single unitary authority, Central Bedfordshire. Bedfordshire is therefore now a ceremonial county consisting of three unitary authorities: Bedford, Central Bedfordshire and Luton.

The Chiltern Hills, an Area Of Outstanding Natural Beauty, dominate the county's southern extremity, the chalk ridge running southwest–northeast. The earliest settlers known to inhabit the Ouse Valley (corresponding to present-day Bedfordshire) were the immigrants from the eastern Mediterranean known as the Beaker Folk due to their crafting of bell-shaped pottery, who probably arrived in the early Bronze Age (3000–2000 BC). The Romans settled in the south of the county during their occupation, Dunstable (Durocobrivis) being an important trade route. After the Roman withdrawal in AD 407 the area was settled by invading Anglo-Saxons and Danes, the Saxon invaders being naturally attracted by its abundant water supply and suitability for agriculture. In 571 Cuthwulf led a West Saxon army against the Britons at Bedford and took four towns. During the Heptarchy what is now the shire formed part of Mercia; under the Treaty of Wedmore, however, it became Danish territory, but was recovered by Edward the Elder (919–21).

The county was first mentioned by name in 1016 when the Danish King Cnut laid waste the whole shire. There was no organised resistance to the Norman invasion in 1066 but during the civil war of King Stephen's reign Bedfordshire suffered severely; the great Roll of the Exchequer of 1165 proves that shire receipts had depreciated in value to two-thirds of the amount assessed for the Danegeld. The county became involved in the Barons' War when Bedford Castle, seized from the Beauchamps by Falkes de Breaut, one of the royal partisans, was the scene of three sieges before being demolished on the orders of Henry III in 1224. From the 13th to the 15th century sheep farming flourished, Bedfordshire wool being in great demand. In 1638 ship-money was levied on the county, and in the Civil War that followed, it was among the foremost in opposing Charles I.

Until the late 19th century Bedfordshire was predominantly an agricultural region rather than the retail and manufacturing community of today. Administratively, until April 2009, the county was divided into three districts: Bedford, Mid Bedfordshire and South Bedfordshire. **Bedford**, the administrative centre of the county, is situated on the River Great Ouse and was awarded its royal charter by Henry II in 1166. The town commemorates favourite sons such as John Bunyan, Trevor Huddleston, John Howard and William Harpur in various busts and statues.

The district of Mid Bedfordshire is an area of gently rolling countryside peppered with woodland, heath and parkland. The Chiltern Hills and Downs border its southern edge, with Bedford on its northern borders. Ampthill and Biggleswade are its chief towns. Mid Bedfordshire was formed on 1 April 1974 by the merger of Ampthill, Biggleswade and Sandy urban districts along with Biggleswade Rural District and Ampthill Rural District. The council had offices in Ampthill and Biggleswade but these were merged at one dedicated site at Priory House in Chicksands in the summer of 2006. This site is now the headquarters of the newly created unitary authority of Central Bedfordshire.

South Bedfordshire includes the towns of Dunstable, Houghton Regis and Leighton Buzzard, and the surrounding villages. **Dunstable** has retained its identity as a market town, its royal charter having been granted in 1131 by Henry I. Dunstable is historically famous for holding the first ever Miracle Play (1110), as being the site of a cross erected by Edward I to denote one of the resting places of Queen Eleanor's cortege (1290) and for having a substantial Digger colony (1649–50). The history of **Houghton Regis** dates back to Roman times and this ancient past is illustrated by its name, taken from the Saxon *hoe*, the spur of a hill, and *tun*, a village, Regis being added in the time of Edward the Confessor when it became a royal manor. The oldest known building still standing in Houghton today is All Saints' Parish Church, built in the 13th century. **Leighton Buzzard** consists of the larger town of Leighton Buzzard on the east of the river Ouzel and the smaller town of Linslade which lies on the west, 20 miles (32km) southwest of Bedford. In Domesday Book, Leighton Buzzard is recorded as *Lestone*, deriving from the Saxon word *leahton*, meaning woodland. The name Buzzard was added later and is derived from the name of Theobald de Busar, an early prebendary (or cathedral officer) of the town.

Since 1 April 1997, **Luton** has been designated a unitary authority. The industrial town lies at the northern end of a river gap in the Chiltern Hills, 30 miles (48km) north of London. Luton was known as *Lygetune* by the Saxons, and appeared in Domesday Book (1086) as *Loitoine*. Medieval Luton had six watermills, two of which remain today. One mill gave its name to Mill Street. In 1137 the lord of the manor built St Mary's Church. In 1139 he built a castle, which was demolished in 1154 but gave its name to Castle Street. For centuries Luton was a small farming community and then a tiny market town, until the early 17th century when the development of the straw-hat industry helped transform it into a factory town. It was incorporated as a municipal borough in 1876. The decline in the straw-hat industry in the 20th century was balanced by a rise in new industries, particularly motor transport, and the town began to attract immigrants, first from Ireland and Scotland and later in the century from the Commonwealth. Vauxhall Motors moved to Luton in 1905 and became the town's leading employer until the plant closed in 2000 (production still continues at the plant in Ellesmere Port). The present town hall in George Street was built in 1936 (the previous one having been burnt down during a riot on Peace Day 1919). Luton's status as one of the most cosmopolitan and ethnically diverse areas of the British Isles is indicated in its cuisine, which includes high quality Indian, Chinese, Greek, Italian, Thai, French and even Polish restaurants.

Bedfordshire	**Population**			**Area**	
Unitary Authorities	*male*	*female*	*total*	*sq miles*	*sq km*
Bedford	73,066	74,845	147,911	184	476
Central Bedfordshire	116,098	117,563	233,661	276	716
Luton	92,119	92,252	184,371	17	43
Total	281,283	284,660	565,943	477	1235

Local Attractions and Information

A6 Murder — In August 1961 Michael Gregsten and his lover Valerie Storie were shot in their car in a lay-by off the A6 between Luton and Bedford. Gregsten died but Storie survived although paralysed from the waist down. The initial suspect was a travelling salesman, Peter Alphon, but at an identity parade Storie picked out another man, known to be innocent. The next suspect was petty criminal James Hanratty, who was picked out by Storie and subsequently tried and found guilty of the crime. Hanratty was hanged in April 1962 but for 40 years there was doubt about the conviction. In 2002 DNA evidence satisfied the Court of Appeal that Hanratty had indeed perpetrated the crime, although family and friends continue to refute this evidence.

Administrative headquarters — **Bedford:** Cauldwell Street, Bedford MK42 9AP. Tel: 01234 363222.
Central Bedfordshire: Priory House, Chicksands, Shefford SG17 5TQ. Tel: 01462 611222.
Luton: Town Hall, George Street, Luton LU1 2BQ. Tel: 01582 546000.

Bedford Castle — High Street, Bedford. Norman motte and bailey castle, founded in the late 11th century and modified and enlarged in the 12th. It was besieged by Henry III in 1224 and destroyed shortly afterwards.

Bromham Mill Bridge End, Bromham, 3 miles (5km) west of Bedford. Watermill dating back to the Norman Conquest. For centuries, the huge wheel was turned by the water of the River Great Ouse but in the 1920s a steam engine was installed to provide extra power. By then, watermill technology had become obsolete. The mill has since been renovated. Tel: 01234 824330.

Bunyan Meeting Free Church Mill Street, Bedford. Occupying the site of a barn purchased by the congregation in 1672 for use as a place of worship, the present church was completed in 1850 and has magnificent stained glass windows. The bronze doors at the entrance to the church are the work of Frederick Thrupp, the ten door panels depicting scenes from Bunyan's most famous work, *The Pilgrim's Progress*.

Bushmead Priory 8 miles (13km) northeast of Bedford. The remains of the small Augustinian priory of St Mary's, founded in 1195 by William, chaplain of Colmworth. Now in the care of English Heritage. Tel: 01525 860152.

Cainhoe Castle Clophill, 7 miles (11km) southeast of Bedford. The Norman castle was founded by Nigel d'Albini at the turn of the 12th century. The ruined castle has a motte and three baileys and was occupied until the Black Death claimed the lives of all its inhabitants and those of the nearby village of Cainhoe.

Cecil Higgins Art Gallery Castle Lane, Bedford. Originally the home of the Higgins family, wealthy Bedford brewers, the Victorian mansion houses an internationally renowned collection of watercolours, prints, drawings, ceramics, glass, lace, and furniture designed by the architect William Burges. Recently refurbished. Tel: 01234 211222.

Chicksand Priory 9 miles (14km) southeast of Bedford. Situated in the parish of Campton & Chicksand on the River Ivel. Rohese Beauchamp founded the priory in 1154 for the rare Gilbertine monastic order, the only one created in, and confined to, Britain. It was more recently an American military base until 1995, before being reopened as the British Intelligence and Security Centre in 1997.

Cranfield University 6 miles (10km) southwest of Bedford. A postgraduate university offering taught courses, research degrees and professional development in engineering, and excelling in the area of aerodynamics. Tel: 01234 750111.

Glenn Miller Museum Clapham, 2 miles (3km) northwest of Bedford. Situated at the Twinwood Airfield and Control Tower, the museum is dedicated to the great American bandleader, who was stationed at Bedford during 1944. Major Glenn Miller took off from RAF Twinwood in a small aircraft on Friday 15 December 1944 at 13.55 hours and was never seen again. Tel: 01234 350413.

Highest point Dunstable Downs at 797ft (243m) (GR: TL008194). The highest point in Luton is Whitehill, Butterfield Green, at 584ft (178m) (GR: TL105253).

Hoo Hill Maze Hitchin Road, Shefford. A classically constructed hedge maze based on that at Woburn Abbey, measuring 98ft (30m) square and 7ft (2m) high and with a central stopping-off point. Tel: 01462 813475.

Houghton House 1 mile (1.6km) northeast of Ampthill. Lady Pembroke, Sir Philip Sidney's sister, had the house built in the early 17th century on Crown land. After her death, the Bruce family acquired the house in 1624 and lived in it until 1696. In 1738 it passed to the Russells, and the Duke of Bedford in 1794 unroofed it, removing most of its fittings. The staircase, dated 1688 and possibly by Wren or Hawkesmoor, is now in the Swan Hotel at Bedford. There is also work attributed to Inigo Jones at the ruins. Houghton House was reputedly the inspiration for Bunyan's 'House Beautiful' in *The Pilgrim's Progress*. Tel: 01234 228337.

Interesting facts Many counties have generic nicknames for their indigenous inhabitants; the traditional nickname for people from Bedfordshire is 'Bedfordshire Bulldogs' or '**Clangers**'. The name 'Clanger' derives from a popular local dish comprising a suet crust dumpling filled with meat or jam, and not the pink and woolly, mouse-like creatures who took their names from the sound made when they battened down their dustbin-lid hatches and retreated underground. **Conor Travers,** a 14-year-old schoolboy from Luton, was crowned *Countdown*'s youngest-ever champion in the programme's 24-year history in May 2006. During his run, he averaged a daily score of 111 and his best score of 124 was a record for the series. He stunned experts in Dictionary Corner by coming up with words such as tzardoms, renegade, albedos, craniates and valorise. The **Oakley Hunt**, formed by the 4th Duke of Bedford at Woburn Abbey in 1793, continues to go drag hunting within the law but has found it difficult in recent years to pay for the upkeep of its hounds. In September 2006 its members decided to emulate the exploits of the Rylstone and District Women's Institute, North Yorkshire, by posing semi-naked for a calendar. Cranfield is the scene of the legend of **Lady Snagge**, who was galloping along the Wood End Road to meet her lover when she fell foul of a group of thieves. The dastardly band had stretched a cord across the lane, the speed of her steed and her failure to spot the strop resulting in her decapitation. Lady Snagge's ghost is said to be seen riding her horse down the lane in vain pursuit of her murderers. **Bedford cord**, named after the Bedfordshire town, is a heavy fabric with a lengthwise ribbed weave that resembles corduroy. Trousers made with Bedford cord are sometimes called 'Bedford cords'. **John Howard** (1726–90) was a Nonconformist who denounced the dreadful conditions which existed in prisons and became a tireless campaigner to improve them after he was invited, in February 1773, to become High Sheriff of Bedford. The Howard League for Penal Reform is named after him. His statue stands in front of the town's St Paul's church.

Islands There are no true islands in Bedfordshire, but see entry for Longholme Island.

Joanna Southcott's Sealed Box Currently in the possession of the Panacea Society, a charitable organisation set up by Mabel Barltrop in Bedford in 1926 and still having active membership. Joanna Southcott (1750–1814) was revered as a visionary in her day and her prophecies and interpretations of the scriptures are said to be held in a black sealed box which may only be opened by the Archbishop of Canterbury in the presence of 24 bishops. The story goes that Southcott was to have a son, Shiloh, in her 65th year and that this child would have messianic qualities. Sadly she died in her 65th year, probably before giving supernatural birth. Whatever else may be true of this fascinating story, Southcott, an uneducated woman, was a great biblical scholar.

John Bunyan Museum Mill Street, Bedford. Around the corner from the Bunyan Meeting Free Church (see separate entry) is a museum dedicated to the town's most famous son. The museum contains translations of Bunyan's works into many languages as well as artefacts giving a flavour of 17th century England. Tel: 01234 213722.

John Dony Field Centre Bushmead Community Centre, Hancock Drive, Luton. The base for Luton Borough Council's Nature Conservation Service. There are permanent displays and temporary exhibitions relating to the natural history of Luton. Tel: 01582 546000.

Leighton Buzzard Railway Leighton Buzzard, 11 miles (18km) west of Luton. Narrow gauge railway built after World War I to serve the sand quarries to the north of the town. Operating on a 2ft (610mm) gauge, at a little under 3 miles (4.8 km) in length, it is now run as a heritage railway. Tel: 01525 373888.

Longholme Island Situated in the River Great Ouse in Bedford, the island is in fact a park joined to the mainland by a Victorian bridge.

Luton Airport 2 miles (3km) east of Luton. Opened on 16 July 1938 by the Right Hon. Kingsley Wood, Secretary of State for Air, the airport thrived until Clarksons, a major tour operator, and its airline Court Line went into liquidation. In 1985 a new international airport was launched and in 1987 Luton International Airport became a limited company with Luton Borough Council as sole shareholder. It was renamed London Luton Airport in 1990 to mark its position as part of the London airport network, but passenger numbers fell again in 1991 as its major customer, Ryanair, moved a large part of its business to Stansted. With the introduction of Airtours flights and the low cost scheduled airlines Easyjet and Debonair, passenger levels recovered to 3.4 million in 1998, and a further rise to 4.4 million by 1999 made London Luton the UK's fastest growing major airport. A major development programme was completed in 1999, the new modern terminal with 60 check-in desks and a wide range of shops, restaurants and bars being officially opened in November 1999 by the Queen and the Duke of Edinburgh. The airport will forever be fixed in the popular imagination by the 1977 Campari television advert featuring Lorraine Chase: 'Were you truly wafted here from Paradise?' 'Nah, Luton Airport.' Tel: 0158 240 5100.

Luton Hoo 1 mile (1.6km) south of Luton. A palatial mansion originally designed by Robert Adam in 1767 for the 3rd Earl of Bute. Robert Smirke added the Greek Revival portico in 1815 but the house was devastated by fire in 1843. In 1903 it was remodelled by Sir Julius Wernher (1850–1912), a South African diamond and gold magnate, and was made the home of his collection of art, tapestries, porcelain and Faberge jewels. Luton Hoo has magnificent views across over 1000 acres (400ha) of parkland, much of which was designed by Capability Brown in the 18th century. In recent years films such as *Four Weddings and a Funeral* (1994), *Wilde* (1997), *Eyes Wide Shut* (1999), *The World Is Not Enough* (1999) and *Enigma* (2001) have used the house and grounds for location shooting. Luton Hoo is now a privately owned hotel and is no longer open to the public.

Mog(g)erhanger 3 miles (5km) west of Sandy. The spelling of this Bedfordshire hamlet's name has caused much controversy over the years. The village is named Mogerhanger by the Ordnance Survey, but the Post Office calls it Moggerhanger, and the pro single 'g' brigade has created havoc by amending road signs and directional notices. The problem dates back to the 19th century, the ecclesiastical parish being created as Moggerhanger in 1860 and the civil parish of Mogerhanger being formed six years later. The boundaries no longer exist but the confusion is legendary. The Georgian house of Moggerhanger Park was designed by Sir John Soane, architect of the Bank of England, and is the most complete surviving example of his work. Now owned by the Moggerhanger Park Preservation Trust, it is operated as a conference centre by a number of Christian organisations.

Moot Hall Elstow, 1 mile (1.6km) south of Bedford. Elstow is the birthplace of John Bunyan. The Tudor timber-framed market house, dating back to the 16th century, is now a museum similar to that at the Bunyan Meeting Free Church (see separate entry), depicting 17th century English life with particular reference to Bunyan. Tel: 01234 266889.

Motto The motto of Bedfordshire is 'Constant Be'.

Old Warden Park Biggleswade, 9 miles (15km) southeast of Bedford. The park houses the Shuttleworth Collection of historic vehicles (see separate entry); the Swiss Garden, a late Regency garden created in the 1820s by Lord Ongley; and the Bird of Prey and Conservation Centre. Tel: 01767 626200.

RAF Henlow 9 miles (15km) northeast of Luton. Royal Air Force station housing the Centre of Aviation Medicine, the RAF Signals museum and the 616 Volunteer Gliding Squadron. Administratively RAF Henlow is now part of a combined base, RAF Brampton Wyton Henlow.

Rivers The **Great Ouse** is the major navigation in East Anglia. With its source in Brackley, Northamptonshire, it follows a150 mile (240km) course through Buckinghamshire, Bedfordshire, Cambridgeshire and Norfolk before reaching the North Sea at the Wash in King's Lynn. Between Bedford Bridge and Eaton Socon (now in Huntingdonshire), on the county's most northerly border, the river has several locks. From south to north these are: Duck Mill, Cardington, Castle Mills, Willington, Old Mills, Great Barford, Roxton, and Eaton Socon.

The **Ivel**, a tributary of the River Great Ouse, rises just north of Baldock in Hertfordshire, but most of its course lies within Bedfordshire. It flows through Stotfold, Arlesey, Biggleswade and Sandy, near where it joins the Great Ouse. The total length is about 16 miles (25km). A further tributary is known as the Purwell as it flows through Hitchin and as the Hiz from there until it meets the Ivel.

Lea see London

R101 Memorial Cardington, 2 miles (3km) southeast of Bedford. Located in the cemetery of St Mary's church, Cardington. The world's largest airship of its day, the R101, was built at Cardington in 1930. Seven hours into her maiden voyage to India she crashed into a hillside at Beauvais, France, on 5 October 1930. Of the 54 on board, 48 died and are commemorated by the memorial.

Royal Society for the Protection of Birds (RSPB) Formed in 1891 to counter the trade in the skin and soft under-pelt of great crested grebes, the breast feathers of which were used as a fur substitute in ladies' fashions, particularly hats. The organisation's headquarters moved to The Lodge, Sandy, in 1961. Jonathan Dimbleby has been its president since 2001 and the avocet its logo since 1970. The membership of the RSPB topped 1 million in 1997. Tel: 01767 680551.

St Mary's Church Church Street, Luton. The church building visible today is the largest in Bedfordshire and one of the finer medieval churches in England. It dates mainly from the 14th and 15th centuries, although an earlier church, founded by King Athelstan as an act of thanksgiving for victory over the Danes, was built c.AD 931. The present building was founded on a new site c.1121 by Robert, Earl of Gloucester and consecrated in 1137. The church clock, originally installed in October 1901, stopped chiming in 1971 and remained silent for 28 years until the University of Luton decided to sponsor its repair to coincide with the celebration of Armistice Day on 11 November 1999, ironically a day usually commemorated with silence. Tel: 01582 721867.

Shuttleworth Collection Biggleswade, 9 miles (15km) southeast of Bedford. Located in Old Warden Park (see separate entry) and founded in 1928 by Richard Ormonde Shuttleworth. The eight hangars display more than 40 aircraft. A number of vehicles including motorcycles and bicycles can be viewed in the Hangar 7 extension. The collection of historic vehicles and aeroplanes is kept in good working order and frequently used in displays. Tel: 01767 627927.

Someries Castle 2 miles (3km) southeast of Luton. The name is derived from William de Someries, whose residence stood on the site in the 13th century. The magnate's residence was built by Lord Wenlock, who acquired the Someries estate in the 1430s. The mansion is thought to be one of the earliest brick buildings in England. The residence was never completed and much of the building was pulled down in 1742. The remains include the gatehouse and chapel forming the northwest wing of the magnate's residence. Although the roof has gone, the walls survive almost to their full height. The area occupied by the main block of the residence is defined by a raised platform containing low, irregular earthworks to the northeast of the garden earthworks. Traces of a substantial brick wall are visible in the north. There was once another castle in Luton. After King Stephen gave Robert de Waudari (one of his mercenaries) the manor of Luton in the 12th century, de Waudari built the motte and bailey castle which gave Castle Street its name. The castle lasted only 15 years and no ruins remain.

Sport

football **Luton Town** were formed in 1885 and made their League debut in 1897. Nicknamed The Hatters, they play at Kenilworth Road Stadium, Luton. The club is famous for being the second in England to lay an artificial surface in 1985, although it reverted to grass in 1991. The great comedian Eric Morecambe was a director of the club, which he often mentioned in his sketches. Tel: 01582 411622.

greyhound racing **Henlow Greyhound Stadium**, Bedford Road, Lower Stondon. 410m track. Tel: 01462 815593.

Stevington Windmill 4 miles (6km) northwest of Bedford. This impressive post mill (constructed around a central post so that it can be turned to face into the wind) was built in the 18th century and is the only complete windmill left in the county. Tel: 01234 824330.

Stockwood Park Museum Farley Hill, 2 miles (3km) south of Luton. The museum is housed in quiet parkland on the site of the former Stockwood House. Apart from its displays of rural trades and crafts Stockwood is also home to the Mossman Collection of horse-drawn vehicles. The collection of more than 50 vehicles illustrates the development of horse-drawn road transport in Britain from Roman times to the 1930s. The period gardens, located on the site of the original walled gardens of Stockwood House, include an Elizabethan knot garden and Victorian cottage gardens. Tel: 01582 738714.

306th Bombardment Group Museum 4 miles (6km) north of Bedford. Located on the former Thurleigh Airfield (now a business park), the museum was opened in July 2002 and houses a large collection of artefacts recreating the activities and atmosphere of the airfield at its opening in July 1942. Tel: 01234 708715.

University of Bedfordshire Created by the merger of the University of Luton and the Bedford campus of De Montfort University on 1 August 2006. The University of Luton was established in 1993, having previously been a polytechnic. The main campuses are at Park Square, in Luton town centre, Putteridge Bury, on Hitchin Road on the outskirts of Luton and on Polhill Avenue, Bedford. Teaching for nursing and midwifery degrees also takes place on satellite sites at the Luton and Dunstable, Bedford, Stoke Mandeville and High Wycombe General hospitals. Tel: 01234 400400.

Wardown Park Museum 1½ miles (2.5km) north of Luton. Situated in a beautiful landscaped park. The ground floor galleries include the Living Landscape gallery with displays on archaeology and natural history (including the nationally important Shillington Roman Coin hoard and Bronze Age mirror); the Lace gallery displaying some of the museum's extensive collection of local lace; and the Bedfordshire and Hertfordshire gallery, which tells the story of this local regiment. The first floor galleries opened as the Luton Life displays in February 2003 and explore the stories of Luton people over the past 150 years. Tel: 01582 546722.

Whipsnade Tree Cathedral Chapel Farm, Whipsnade, Dunstable. Consisting of trees and hedges planted in the form of a medieval cathedral, the 9.5 acre (4ha) 'cathedral' was created after World War I in 'faith, hope and reconciliation'. Tel: 01582 872406.

Whipsnade Wild Animal Park 1 mile (1.5km) southwest of Dunstable. Whipsnade is the country home of London Zoo. The Wild Animal Park holds Asian elephants, Bactrian camels, bald eagles, black rhinoceros, cheetahs, chimpanzees, Grevy's zebra, Przewelski's horse, red pandas, ring-tailed lemurs, rock hopper penguins, scimitar-horned oryx, southern white rhino, and many others. Tel: 01582 872171.

William Harpur Schools William Harpur (1496–1573), a merchant tailor who went on to become Lord Mayor of London, made his fortune on the land around Holborn and set up a bequest to establish schools in

	Bedford, which later became the Harpur Trust schools. The four schools are Bedford School, Bedford High School, Bedford Modern School and Dame Alice Harpur School. A statue of Sir William can be seen above the door to the Old Town Hall.
Willington Dovecote & Stables	Willington, 4 miles (6km) east of Bedford. The 16th century stables and stone dovecote were built by Sir John Gostwick. The dovecote consists of more than 1500 nesting boxes. These are the only historic buildings in Bedfordshire belonging to the National Trust. Tel: 01480 301494.
Woburn Abbey	8 miles (13km) northwest of Dunstable. Set in a scenic 3000 acre (1200ha) deer park in Mid Bedfordshire. Woburn Abbey has been the home of the Dukes of Bedford for 400 years. Buffalo, tigers, lions, giraffes, bears and monkeys can be seen in the adjoining safari park. Tel: 01525 290333.

Some famous people born in Bedfordshire

Abrahams, Harold (athlete) (1899–1978)	Bedford
Albone, Daniel (bicycle pioneer) (1860–1906)	Biggleswade
Barker, Ronnie (comic actor) (1929–2005)	Bedford
Bayfield, Martin (rugby union player) (1966–)	Bedford
Bunyan, John (author and minister) (1628–88)	Elstow
Byng, John (admiral) (1704–57)	Southill
Dixon, Kerry (footballer) (1961–)	Luton
Gough, Damon ('Badly Drawn Boy', musician) (1969–)	Dunstable
Hailey, Arthur (author) (1920–2004)	Luton
Huddleston, Trevor (Archbishop) (1913–98)	Bedford
Le Mesurier, John (actor) (1912–83)	Bedford
Norton, Mary (novelist) (1903–92)	Leighton Buzzard
Panesar, Monty (cricketer) (1982–)	Luton
Paxton, Joseph (architect) (1801–65)	Milton Bryan
Renwick, David (writer) (1951–)	Luton
Rowe, Nicholas (poet) (1674–1718)	Little Barford
Tompion, Thomas (clockmaker) (1639–1713)	Northill
Vorderman, Carol (television presenter) (1960–)	Bedford
White, William Hale (Mark Rutherford, writer) (1831–1913)	Bedford
Young, Paul (vocalist) (1956–)	Luton

BERKSHIRE

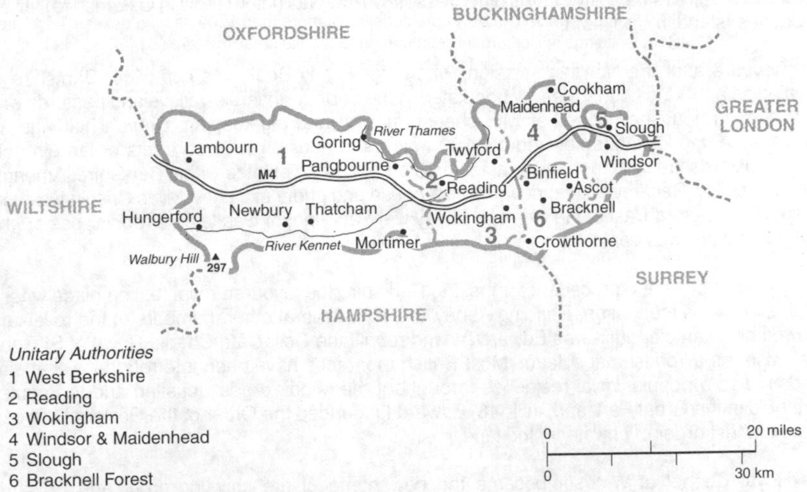
OXFORDSHIRE
BUCKINGHAMSHIRE
GREATER LONDON
WILTSHIRE
SURREY
HAMPSHIRE
Cookham
Maidenhead
Slough
Windsor
Lambourn
Goring
River Thames
Pangbourne
Twyford
M4
Reading
Binfield
Ascot
Bracknell
Hungerford
Newbury
Thatcham
Wokingham
Crowthorne
River Kennet
Mortimer
Walbury Hill
297
1
2
3
4
5
6
Unitary Authorities
1 West Berkshire
2 Reading
3 Wokingham
4 Windsor & Maidenhead
5 Slough
6 Bracknell Forest
0
20 miles
0
30 km

Berkshire borders the counties of Oxfordshire to the northwest, Buckinghamshire to the northeast, Surrey to the southeast, Wiltshire to the west, Hampshire to the south and the London region to the east. Berkshire is a ceremonial county and (with different boundaries) a traditional county, and it was, until 1 April 2009, unusual in England in being the only non-metropolitan county with multiple districts but no county council. Reading became the new county town in 1867, taking over from Abingdon. Following the Local Government Act 1972, the northern part of the county became part of Oxfordshire, Faringdon, Wantage and Abingdon and its hinterland becoming the Vale of White Horse district, and Wallingford going to form part of the South Oxfordshire district; while Slough, which had been within Buckinghamshire, became part of Berkshire. On 1 April 1998 Berkshire County Council was abolished and the districts became unitary authorities. Unlike similar reforms elsewhere at the same time, the non-metropolitan county was not abolished. In Berkshire the district councils are unitary authorities but have no county status.

Geographically, Berkshire is divided into two distinct sections, the boundary lying roughly on a north–south line through the centre of Reading. The eastern section lies largely to the south of the River Thames, which forms the county's northern boundary. In Slough and Reading the county now includes land to the north of the river. Tributaries of the Thames, including the Loddon and Blackwater, increase the amount of low-lying riverine land in the area. Beyond the flood plains, the land rises gently to the boundaries with Surrey and Hampshire. Much of this area is still well wooded, especially around Bracknell and Windsor Great Park. In the west of the county and heading upstream, the Thames veers away to the north of the current county boundary, leaving the county behind at the Goring Gap. This is a narrow part of the otherwise quite broad river valley where, at the end of the last Ice Age, the Thames forced its way between the Chiltern Hills to the north of the river in Oxfordshire, and the Berkshire Downs. As a result, the western portion of the county is situated around the valley of the River Kennet, which joins the Thames in Reading. Fairly steep slopes on each side delineate the river's flat floodplain. To the south, the land rises steeply to the nearby county boundary with Hampshire, and the highest parts of the county lie here. To the north of the Kennet, the land rises again to the Berkshire Downs. This is a hilly area, with smaller and well-wooded valleys draining into the River Pang and its tributaries, and open upland areas famous for their involvement in horse racing and the consequent ever-present training gallops.

The county is one of the oldest in England, dating back to the 9th century when King Alfred of Wessex set its traditional borders. The county takes its name from a large forest of box trees called *Bearroc* (Celtic for 'hilly') that was originally a transaction of land to King Cenwalh of Wessex. At this time, it only consisted of the northern and western parts of the current county. With the great rivalry between the Anglo-Saxon kings, parts of Berkshire changed hands several times, particularly between Mercia and Wessex, but they were eventually united against the Viking threat. Reading became the Vikings' base, from which they waged war on the English over a number of years.

Though Wessex victories included King Alfred's famous triumph at the Battle of Ashdown (probably in Aldworth), the Saxons were eventually forced to partition England in AD 886, between their own southern territory and the Danelaw. Berkshire remained under Saxon rule and served as the site of two of Alfred's defensive *burhs* or fortresses: one at Wallingford (now in Oxfordshire), another on Sashes Island in Cookham.

Twenty years after the Norman invasion, when Domesday Book was compiled, Berkshire was revealed as a thriving county, heavily populated in the north, with fertile valleys and pastures where dairy farming flourished, together with cheese-making and pig-keeping. Church holdings were prominent: Abingdon Abbey owned over 30 manors in addition to large tracts of land in neighbouring Oxfordshire, and there were at least 13 other church estates within Berkshire. Among the Norman nobility, Geoffrey de Mandeville built a house and priory at Hurley, Miles Crispin was established at Wallingford Castle and the royal family were at Windsor Castle on a regular basis, where Walter FitzOther was constable.

Henry I had first set the precedent for making Berkshire the favoured royal resting place when he was buried in his foundation, Reading Abbey, in 1135. Several other members of the royal family followed his example, but it was Edward IV who rebuilt the Collegiate Chapel Royal of St George at Windsor as a Yorkist mausoleum. Most British monarchs have been interred there ever since. Windsor was a popular royal residence throughout the Middle Ages. Jousting and tournaments were held in the Great Park and, in 1348, Edward III founded the Order of the Garter at the castle as the highest order of chivalry in the land.

The Royal Chapel at Windsor became the new home of the chivalric order and Edward III expanded the complex to serve as a canonical college. There was a second ecclesiastical college at Shottesbrooke and, as well as the great pilgrimage centres of Reading and Abingdon, other monasteries were founded at Wallingford, Poughley, Sandleford, Bromhall, Hurley and Bisham. The mysterious Knights Templar were originally at the latter and their preceptory remains largely intact. Their brother order, the Knights Hospitaller, were at Brimpton, where their chapel survives. These two ecclesiastical orders of knighthood were highly active in the crusades, to which many Berkshire men also journeyed. Thanksgiving 'Crusader Crosses' can still be seen in churches like Wantage (now in Oxfordshire) and Sutton Courtenay.

Fortunately, Berkshire made a fairly speedy recovery from the ravages of the Black Death of 1349 and in time, its farms, acquired a new basis of economic prosperity in the corn they produced as a staple crop. By the 16th century, Berkshire was a major supplier of corn to London and other centres, and also contributed greatly to the rich wool and cloth trades which comprised three-quarters of England's exports to Europe. During this period, the production of yarn for clothing was carried out in many Berkshire villages, such as Shaw, Speen, Greenham and Thatcham. Berkshire cloth became much appreciated for its excellent quality, drawing crowds of customers to the county's sheep and corn markets. That at East Ilsley grew to be the biggest sheep fair in the country. While Windsor relied heavily on royal and courtly patronage during the Tudor period – bringing Shakespeare to stay at the Garter Inn and write his *Merry Wives of Windsor* – the towns of Reading, Abingdon and Newbury were centres for the cloth trade. Early 16th century Newbury boasted a clothier named John Winchombe, alias Jack O'Newbury, who was a prominent figure of international renown. He built the first recognisable factory in the country and was so wealthy that he was able to send a troop of soldiers to fight for Henry VIII in Scotland. His son built himself a magnificent mansion at Bucklebury. Reading was a comparable cloth centre, the home to men like John Kendrick, who established the original Oracle charitable workhouse (now the site of a shopping centre), and William Laud, son of a clothmaker, who became Archbishop of Canterbury. A new breed of gentry were quickly becoming established, though traditional landowning courtiers still survived: the indiscretions of Lord John Norreys at a Yattendon ball may have contributed to the loss of both his and Anne Boleyn's heads.

With the Dissolution of the Monasteries in 1536, Berkshire lost the great abbeys of Abingdon and Reading. The latter's abbot was hanged for trying to save his beloved monastery and, in the extreme Protestant years of Edward VI's reign, there were several burnings of Catholic 'martyrs' in the county, notably at Newbury and Windsor. The monastic buildings were stripped of their fittings and holy relics were burned, though St James's hand was discovered bricked up at Reading and can now be seen in Marlow Roman Catholic church (Bucks). These difficulties were compounded in time of war and struck Berkshire at their worst during the Civil War. The county was not only salted for money, men and supplies, but became one of the major battlegrounds. Almost 40 years later, Berkshire saw the only fighting of the Glorious Revolution of 1688.

Mail coaches were introduced in 1784, and their first ever run along the Bath Road almost certainly changed horses at the King's Arms in Thatcham. By 1830, 60 coaches a day passed through Maidenhead, where inns like the White Hart (more recently Woolworths) could stable up to 50 horses. Increased travel brought an increase in crime on the road and Berkshire became famous for its dangerous highwaymen, whose gibbeted bodies often lined the main roads. Maidenhead Thicket, Knowl Hill and Ascot Heath were notorious black spots associated with men such as Dick Turpin, Captain Hind, Captain Snow, the Golden Farmer and Claude Duval. Wokingham was infamous for its 'Blacks', a band of footpads with painted faces who infested Windsor Forest. The notoriety of these poachers, robbers, blackmailers and murderers led to the passing of the 'Black Act' in 1723, making the painting of one's face black in order to commit unlawful acts a criminal offence.

By the time George III came to the throne in 1760, later re-establishing Windsor Castle's importance as the chief royal residence, the commercial emphasis in Berkshire had changed. Malted barley to make beer, wheat and wool were the major products supplied to London. Trade of all kinds received a boost from the canal-building 'mania' of the early 19th century. A canal linked Newbury and Kintbury by 1810; by 1818, it carried over 200 boats, including 70 barges loaded with up to 60 tons of goods. Later, the Wilts and Berks Canal linked the River Thames at Abingdon with the River Kennet and the Avon Canal, enabling coal to be brought in from Somerset and corn and timber to be transported out.

More problems arose with the Agricultural Revolution. With the enclosure of common land, areas such as Bulmersh Heath and Mortimer Common had completely disappeared by the early 19th century; and Windsor Forest similarly ceased to officially exist in 1813. The most famous agriculturalist of the time was Basildon-born Jethro Tull, whose invention of the seed-drill in 1701 and the writing of his pioneering *Horse-Houghing Husbandry* 30 years later, led to many new farming practices. New breeds of livestock such as the black Berkshire pig and the Berkshire Nott Wether sheep were bred and there was a widespread introduction of farm machinery. The latter resulted in violent demonstrations, known as the 'Swing Riots', as gangs of protesters roamed the country, destroying threshing machines and burning haystacks. November 1830 saw Berkshire's own 'Kintbury Riots' when mobs raided farms across the western half of the county. One protester, William Winterbourne, was subsequently executed while 45 others were transported to Australia.

The advance of technology was relentless, railways following canals after 1825. Berkshire acquired its railways early; the Great Western Railway crossed its territory by 1838, later to be followed by lines between Wokingham and Reading, Slough and Windsor, and from Windsor to Waterloo in London. In competition with the much faster railways, Berkshire's canals were badly affected, the Kennet and Avon Canal suffering a 20 per cent drop in its takings. By 1870, the Wilts and Berks Canal was virtually destroyed by the railways.

The links with the county's traditional past were rapidly weakening, but despite a dramatic increase in urban living by 1851, the towns of Berkshire generally remained small. Only Reading developed into a significant manufacturing and commercial centre, dominated by bulbs, biscuits and beer. William Blackall Simonds had begun his brewing industry in Reading as early as 1785; in the Victorian period the business expanded exponentially, as did Sutton's Seeds, while the dominant factory in the town was that of Huntley & Palmer Biscuits. Within 20 years of its formation in 1841, this famous partnership was housed in the largest biscuit factory in England.

By the early 20th century the farming which had once characterised Berkshire was laregly confined to the west of the county and the Vale of the White Horse. The county is now better known for the nuclear and microchip industries which have earned the area its reputation as England's 'Silicon Valley', the office blocks and warehouses which lie at the centre of the so-called Golden Triangle of prime business sites – and its role as a dormitory area for commuters to London.

Today, the county is often referred to as the Royal County of Berkshire because of the presence of the royal residence of Windsor Castle in the county; this usage, which goes back to the 19th century at least, was recognised by the Queen in 1958, and letters patent were issued confirming this in 1974.

Berkshire	Population			Area	
Districts	*male*	*female*	*total*	*sq miles*	*sq km*
Bracknell Forest Unitary Authority	54,879	54,738	109,617	42	109
Reading Unitary Authority	72,076	71,020	143,096	15	40
Slough Unitary Authority	59,318	59,749	119,067	13	33
West Berkshire Unitary Authority	71,703	72,780	144,483	272	704
Windsor and Maidenhead Unitary Authority	65,895	67,731	133,626	76	197
Wokingham Unitary Authority	75,118	75,111	150,229	69	179
Total	398,989	401,129	800,118	487	1262

Local Attractions and Information

Administrative headquarters

Bracknell Forest: Time Square, Market Street, Bracknell RG12 1JD. Tel: 01344 352000.
Reading: Civic Centre, Reading RG1 7TD. Tel: 0118 939 0900.
Slough: Town Hall, Bath Road, Slough SL1 3UQ. Tel: 01753 552288.
West Berkshire: Council Offices, Market Street, Newbury RG14 5LD. Tel: 01635 42400.
Windsor and Maidenhead: Town Hall, St Ives Road, Maidenhead SL6 1RF. Tel: 01628 798888.
Wokingham: Civic Offices, Shute End, Wokingham RG40 1BN. Tel: 0118 974 6000.

Aldermaston Court

Aldermaston, 9 miles (15km) southwest of Reading. Victorian country house built in 1848 by Daniel and Mary Higford Burr and sitting in an Elizabethan-style courtyard with an imposing tower. Mary Burr's initials can be seen in the brickwork. The surrounding park was first enclosed in the 1290s and is particularly well known for its beautiful lake. The main entrance gates to the park, in the village, were won in a card game from the owner of Midgham House a few miles to the west. In 1941 the higher part of the Aldermaston Court estate was developed as a Bomber Operations Training Unit (OTU). The woodland was cleared and an airfield with three concrete runways built. There were five hangars, four built to take the largest RAF aircraft. The airfield was used by the United States Army Air Force for glider operations on D-Day and was also a base for Spitfire fighters. By April 1950 the now abandoned airfield was chosen as the site for the UK's nuclear weapons programme. In 1952 the site was officially named the Atomic Weapons Research Establishment (AWRE) and in 1987 it was renamed the Atomic Weapons Establishment (see separate entry). The house itself is now a hotel and conference centre.

Atomic Weapons Establishment

Aldermaston, 9 miles (15km) southwest of Reading. The Atomic Weapons Establishment (AWE) has been central to the UK's defence for over 50 years, providing and maintaining the warheads for the country's nuclear deterrent. AWE Aldermaston is the headquarters of AWE's operations. Covering 750 acres (300ha), the site has long been associated with defence. Grim's Bank, an ancient monument partly located within the Aldermaston boundary, once formed part of the outer defences of the Roman town of Silchester and William the Conqueror is rumoured to have camped nearby after the Battle of Hastings. During World War II an airfield was built on the site (see Aldermaston Court). Today Aldermaston is the centre of design and research for AWE, providing sophisticated manufacturing facilities and producing a variety of components. AWE also administers AWE Blacknest, a former country house at nearby Brimpton, where seismological research is undertaken in support of the verification of nuclear test bans. AWE Burghfield occupies a site of 225 acres (91ha), 7 miles (11km) east of Aldermaston. Established during World War II to manufacture munitions, it was then used as a storage depot for the Ministry of Supply until the early 1950s, when its facilities and proximity to Aldermaston made it an obvious choice to support the expanding nuclear weapons programme. Burghfield is now responsible for the final assembly of warheads, their in-service maintenance and their eventual decommissioning. Tel: 0118 981 4111.

Basildon Park

Lower Basildon, 6 miles (10km) northwest of Reading. The Palladian mansion was built 1776–83 by John Carr of York for Francis Sykes, who had made his fortune in India. The interior is notable for its original delicate plasterwork and elegant staircase, as well as for the unusual Octagon Room. The house was rescued by Lord and Lady Iliffe, who restored it and filled it with fine pictures and furniture. The early 19th century pleasure grounds have recently been restored. It was used as a location for the films *Pride & Prejudice* (2005) – when it represented Netherfield Park – and *Marie-Antoinette* (2006). Tel: 0118 984 3040.

Battles

Five notable battles have been fought in Berkshire: Ashdown, Broad Street, Newbury (2) and Reading. See separate table for details, and entries for Battles of Broad Street and Newbury.

Benham Park

Marsh Benham, 2 miles (3km) west of Newbury. Georgian mansion built for Lord Craven in 1775 under the direction of Henry Holland, in collaboration with his father-in-law, the great English landscape artist Capability Brown. The Craven family house at Hamstead Marshall had burnt down earlier that century. Benham Park was converted for use as offices in 1983.

Berkshire Lady, The

Frances Kendrick was one of three daughters and one son of the 2nd Baronet Sir William Kendrick. Born in 1687, she was his eldest surviving child and, since her brother had died in infancy, her father's chief heiress. She grew up at the family home, Whitley Park near Reading, which her great-great-grandfather had first been resident in many years before. On her father's death in 1699, Frances was left in the guardianship of Dr James Brewer and John Dalby Esq. (a Reading lawyer), but they were apparently unable to stop her doing as she pleased. At her own instigation, she moved out of the family home and purchased Calcot Park in nearby Tilehurst. She is said to have had many suitors, but spurned them all until Benjamin Child, a handsome young man-about-town from Abingdon, came on the scene. Benjamin was spotted by young Frances at a wedding in Reading; she fell in love with him immediately but her love remained unrequited and she anonymously sent him a challenge to fight her in a duel with swords. Benjamin turned up at Calcot Woods (now Prospect Park) to find his challenger was a masked woman. She told him that he must fight or marry her. Deciding he could not risk hurting her in a fight, he agreed to marry her. He was whisked away in her coach and the two were married at Wargrave Church, but she did not take off her mask. Benjamin was brought to the mansion at Calcot Park and left alone in the drawing room. Servants and then the woman owner of the house appeared and wanted to know what he was doing there. Eventually however, the woman admitted she was Frances Kendrick, his new wife. She was extremely beautiful and Benjamin was very pleased. They were very happy together. Frances became famous and her tale was told in a poem published in 1760. Although some of the facts recounted in the ballad may be exaggerated or distorted by poetic licence, Frances was clearly a remarkable woman. See also Prospect Park.

Bisham Abbey 3 miles (5km) northwest of Maidenhead. The name of the manor house of Bisham, situated beside the River Thames, is taken from the now lost Augustinian priory which once stood alongside it. The manor house once belonged to the Knights Templar and after the suppression of the movement in 1307 became the residence of the Earls of Salisbury, who founded the priory in 1337. The complex surrounding the remaining buildings is now one of five National Sports Centres run on behalf of Sport England. Tel: 01628 476911.

Blake's Lock Situated on the Kennet and Avon Canal, almost in the centre of Reading. There are more than 100 locks on the canal, all apart from Blake's Lock under the jurisdiction of British Waterways. Blake's Lock is the only one that, although controlled by the Environment Agency, is not on the River Thames. The Riverside Museum (see separate entry) is located here.

Boulter's Lock A picturesque island lock and weir on the River Thames at the eastern side of Maidenhead, owned and managed by the Environment Agency. A 'bolter' was a miller and hence this is literally 'miller's lock'. Close by is Ray Mill Island. The lock has been the subject of a number of pictures; *Boulter's Lock, Sunday Afternoon* (1882–97) by Edward John Gregory (1850–1909) is possibly the best known.

Bridges **Caversham Bridge** spans the River Thames between Caversham and Reading town centre, also providing pedestrian access to Pipers Island in the middle of the river. A bridge has existed on the site since medieval times, but the present structure was completed in 1926. Caversham Bridge was the site of a skirmish during the Civil War in 1643.

Conway's Bridge, close to the River Thames in the estate of Park Place at Remenham, 1 mile (1.6km) east of Henley-on-Thames, is an ornamental rustic arched stone structure designed by Humphrey Gainsborough, brother of artist Thomas Gainsborough, and built in 1763. The bridge is named after general and statesman Henry Seymour Conway (1721–95), who owned the estate. It still carries traffic on the road between Wargrave and Henley-on-Thames.

Henley Bridge – see Oxfordshire

Maidenhead Bridge carries the A4 over the River Thames to the east of Maidenhead. The first bridge was built out of wood in 1280. The current stone bridge was designed by architect Robert Taylor and built at a cost of £19,000 in 1777.

Maidenhead Railway Bridge carries the railway across the River Thames between Maidenhead and Taplow. Designed by the Great Western Railway's famous engineer, Isambard Kingdom Brunel, and completed in 1838, its two brick arches were at the time of building the widest and flattest in the world. Each span is 128ft (39m), with a rise of only 24ft (7m). The Thames towpath passes under the eastern arch, which is also known as the Sounding Arch because of its spectacular echo. Maidenhead Railway Bridge is depicted in *Rain, Steam and Speed – The Great Western Railway*, painted by J M W Turner in 1844 and now in the National Gallery, London.

The **Queen Elizabeth Bridge**, completed in 1966, carries the Windsor bypass across the River Thames to the west of Windsor. Since 1970, when structural cracks in the central Windsor Bridge forced its closure to all but pedestrian traffic, the Queen Elizabeth Bridge has formed the principal road route between the adjacent towns of Windsor and Eton.

Reading Bridge is a road bridge over the River Thames linking the centre of Reading on the south bank with the former village of Caversham on the north bank. The current bridge is the first on the site, and was built in 1923 when Reading absorbed Caversham. Before then the only road crossing between the two places was at Caversham Bridge, $^1/_2$ mile (0.8km) upstream.

Windsor Bridge spans the River Thames between central Windsor and Eton's old High Street. The current bridge, opened on 1 June 1824, has three arches, each comprising seven cast-iron segments and supported in midstream by two granite piers. It was built as a road bridge and tolls were levied on traffic crossing the bridge until 1897. In 1970, cracks were discovered in the cast iron and it was decided to close the bridge to vehicular traffic, which now travels between Windsor and Eton via the Queen Elizabeth Bridge. In 2002 the bridge was refurbished and the deck replaced using York stone. The bridge remains in use by pedestrians and is a good viewing spot for both the river and Windsor Castle.

Broad Street, Battle of Also known as the Second Battle of Reading, the only fighting which marked the course of William of Orange's successful effort to deliver England from James II. On 5 November 1688, having been invited to depose James, William landed in Devon with a large army. Having marched through the west of England towards London on Thursday 6 December, William and his troops reached Hungerford on the Berkshire/Wiltshire border, where it had been agreed that commissioners representing James would meet him. Their conference took place on

8 December in a large room at the Bear Inn, while William lodged at Littlecote Hall, an ancient manor house 2 miles (3km) away in Wiltshire. On Sunday 9 December James sent part of his army (around 600 Irish troops) to Reading to stop the march of William's Protestant army. The people of Reading had already sent a messenger to William asking for help, and a relief force of about 250 Dutch troops was sent to the town. Warned in advance of the Royalist positions in the town they attacked from an unexpected direction, and reached the centre of Reading. Forcing the Irish troops back, the Dutch attack was supported by Reading men shooting from their windows. The Dutch soon forced the Irish troops to retreat in confusion, leaving between 20 and 50 (depending on the account) of their side slain. There were few deaths on the Dutch side, one being a Catholic officer. On Tuesday 11 December James fled London, eventually escaping to France and then Ireland.

Bull Inn, The — Sonning, 4 miles (6km) east of Reading. An historic public house, now also a restaurant and hotel, and traditionally owned by the Bishop of Salisbury, whose palace once stood nearby. The present 16th century building was once a resting place for pilgrims visiting the relics of the mysterious St Sarik (possibly the child martyr St Syricus of Antioch, who like St Sarik was believed to cure madness) at the adjoining parish church of St Andrew. The name stems from the bulls which supported the coat of arms of Sir Henry Neville, steward at the palace after it was sold to Queen Elizabeth I. The inn was featured in Jerome K Jerome's book *Three Men in a Boat*. Tel: 0118 969 3901.

Bulmershe Manor — Sonning, 4 miles (6km) east of Reading. Bulmarsh or Bulmershe, in Sonning parish, is first recorded in the 12th century, although the area may not have become a manor until 1447 when it was granted to Reading Abbey. After the abbey's dissolution in 1538, the land was acquired by poet William Grey. He probably built the first house here, the remains of which may be the basis of the present Old Bulmershe Court. Through Grey Bulmershe became the main residence of the Blagrave family for more than 200 years (Grey's wife, Agnes, was widow of Robert Blagrave, a merchant of London and Reading and their son John was Grey's heir). John's son and namesake was a famous mathematician and his grandson, Daniel, one of the Cromwellian regicides, but they were both relegated to live at the family's secondary residence, Southcote House. The family has several monuments and its own vault in Sonning Church, but the main branch died out in 1789. The estate was sold to the Speaker of the House of Commons, Henry Addington (who later became Prime Minister and Viscount Sidmouth). He preferred to live at Woodley Lodge and the house was let out to tenants. By the early 19th century, the house had fallen into disrepair; most of it was demolished and the rest turned into cottages. By 1925, this last portion too had almost collapsed from neglect, but it was restored using architectural features from the recently gutted Billingbear Park. It is now known as Bulmershe Manor and is a private residence. The estate is now Bulmershe College, a campus of the University of Reading.

California — 2 miles (3km) south of Wokingham. A village situated in the north of the civil parish of Finchampstead, California is named after an old brickworks and is best known for its country park, centred on Longmoor Lake. It was once a famous holiday camp, complete with glass-floored pavilion and speedway racetrack.

Caversham Lock — A lock and weir situated on the River Thames in Reading. Caversham Lock includes a large lock island, also known as De Bohun Island, separating the lock from the weir.

Cole Museum of Zoology — Whiteknights Campus, University of Reading. The museum, which forms part of the university's School of Biological Sciences, was established in the early 20th century by Francis J Cole, Professor of Zoology 1907–39. A refurbishment of the museum was completed on 17 March 2004. The collection contains 3500 specimens, of which about 400 are on display at any one time. Specimens are arranged in 27 cases in taxonomic sequence, enabling a complete tour of the diversity of the animal kingdom. Specimens include a male Indian circus elephant skeleton, a 16ft (5m) reticulated python skeleton containing 400 vertebrae, a fossil of the largest spider to ever have lived, and a false killer whale skeleton. Tel: 0118 378 7024.

Combe Gibbet — 7 miles (11km) southwest of Newbury. Situated at the top of Walbury Hill near Combe, now in Berkshire but formerly in Hampshire, the gibbet was erected in 1676 for the purpose of hanging George Broomham and Dorothy Newman and was never used afterwards. It was placed in such a prominent location as a warning to deter others from committing crimes. Broomham and Newman were having an affair and were hanged for murdering Broomham's wife Martha and their son Robert, who had discovered them together on the downs. Unfortunately for the lovers, the murder was witnessed by 'Mad Thomas', who managed to convey what he had seen to the authorities. A replica gibbet marks the site (the original was destroyed many years ago; subsequent replicas have been replaced many times).

Cumberland Lodge — 3½ miles (5.5km) south of Windsor. Built in 1650 by John Byfield, an army captain, after Oliver Cromwell had divided up and sold off lots in Windsor Great Park, the house was called Byfield House until 1670. It was then renamed New Lodge, and at times was also known as Windsor Lodge or Ranger Lodge. After the Restoration Charles II made the house the official residence of the Ranger of the Great Park. Its famous residents have included Sarah Churchill, Duchess of Marlborough, (1702–44); William Augustus, Duke of Cumberland, son of George II (1746–65); Princess Helena, daughter of Queen Victoria and wife of Prince Christian of Schleswig-Holstein (1872–1923); and Lord Fitzalan of Derwent, last Viceroy of Ireland (1923–47). During the Abdication Crisis of 1936 Cumberland Lodge was used for key meetings between the king's private secretary and Prime Minister Stanley Baldwin. Today the house is used under royal patronage by the Cumberland Lodge Foundation, who hold academic workshops and short residential courses examining ethical, spiritual and moral issues in a context of Christian philosophy. It is not open to the public. Tel: 01784 432316.

Deanery, The Thames Street, Sonning. A house designed by Sir Edwin Lutyens 1899–1901 in Arts and Crafts style. The garden was designed by Gertrude Jekyll, like those of many other Lutyens country houses. Although in the centre of the village next to St Andrew's Church and the Bull Inn, the house and garden are very secluded, being surrounded by high walls. The house was built for Edward Hudson, founder of the early lifestyle magazine *Country Life*, essentially as a show home to be featured in the magazine.The garden and house are not open to the public.

Donnington Castle 1 mile (1.6km) north of Newbury. Enclosure castle founded in 1386 by Richard de Adderbury. The castle was visited by Elizabeth I in 1568, garrisoned by Sir John Boys for the king in 1643, and besieged five times by Parliamentary troops from 1644 before finally surrendering and subsequently being destroyed in 1646. Only the gatehouse and earthworks remain. Tel: 01424 775705.

Douai Abbey Upper Woolhampton, 8 miles (13km) southwest of Reading. Benedictine monks from the Monastery of St Edmund's, Douai, France, came to Woolhampton in 1903 when the congregation was expelled from France by anti-religious laws. The community was gifted the school of St Mary's in Woolhampton by Bishop Cahill of Portsmouth. The abbey church was opened in 1933 but completed only in 1993. The abbey was greatly expanded in the 1960s with the building of the New Monastery designed by Sir Frederick Gibberd. In 2005, two monks returned to Douai to form a community there and restore the historic links to English monasticism. Economic imperatives sadly forced the closure of Doual School – which educated a broad range of children, many on scholarships, some with special needs – in 1999. Tel: 0118 971 5300.

Easthampstead Park Located midway between Wokingham and Bracknell. In the Middle Ages, Easthampstead Park was part of Windsor Great Forest and was reserved for royal hunting. The lodge (situated on what is now the golf course) was built on the orders of Edward III c.1335. Henry VIII first saw the face of Catherine of Aragon when she stayed at Easthampstead Park on her way to marry Arthur, his elder brother. Later Henry's barren queen was banished here when he courted Anne Boleyn and it was here she eventually received news of her divorce. James I enlarged and improved the park, which was well stocked with deer, but his son, Charles I, gave it to William Trumbull, and the lodge was incorporated in a newly built mansion. Trumbull became a Lord of the Treasury, Secretary of State to William III and a privy councillor but soon resigned these offices to spend his retirement at Easthampstead Park. He befriended 16-year-old Alexander Pope, then living in Binfield. Easthampstead Park is one of the many estates in Berkshire and beyond which belonged to the Downshire family. In 1860, the old house was demolished, leaving only the stable block which is to be seen as a low white building on the golf course. The 4th Marquis began building the present mansion in 1868. After World War II, Easthampstead Park was sold to Berkshire County Council. In 1949 a training college for teachers was opened, and in 1968 this was amalgamated with Bulmershe College to form Berkshire College of Education. The last students were withdrawn in 1972. The mansion is now occupied by Easthampstead Park Conference Centre and Bracknell Forest Education Centre. Tel: 0118 974 7576.

Edward Jenner Institute for Vaccine Research Compton, 10 miles (16km) north of Newbury. Situated on the campus of the Institute for Animal Health (see separate entry), the Edward Jenner Institute for Vaccine Research is an independent research institute named for Edward Jenner, inventor of vaccine. The institute's research programme has two strands: the first is work on areas of immunology relevant to the development of all vaccines, including antigen presentation, immunological memory and autoimmunity; the second focuses on specific diseases or targets where vaccines, or improved vaccines, are needed. Tel: 01635 577900.

Eton College Eton, 1 mile (1.6km) north of Windsor. Founded in 1440 by Henry VI, the King's College of Our Lady of Eton beside Windsor, as it is properly known, is one of the original nine English public schools as defined by the Public Schools Act 1868. Eton College boards around 1290 boys (15 per cent from overseas) aged 13–18 (roughly 250 per year). Seventy pupils – around 14 in each year – attend on scholarships provided for by the original bequest and awarded by examination each year; they are known as King's Scholars and live in the college itself, paying up to 75 per cent of full fees. As the school grew, more students were allowed to attend provided that they paid their own fees and lived outside the college's original buildings in the town. These students were known as Oppidans, from the Latin word *oppidum*, meaning town, i.e. those who lived in the town as opposed to the college. The school is famous for its former pupils (known as Old Etonians and including 19 former Prime Ministers) and the traditions it maintains, including a uniform of black tailcoat (or morning coat) and waistcoat, false-collar and pinstriped trousers. All students wear a white tie that is effectively a strip of cloth folded over into the collar, apart from those appointed to positions of responsibility, who wear a white bow tie and a wing collar. Their positions are also often indicated by variations in the colour of waistcoat, trousers or waistcoat buttons. Those in Sixth Form Select, the most academic students at the top of the school, have silver waistcoat buttons, while those in the Eton Society (known as 'Pop') are allowed to wear waistcoats of whatever colour or design they wish, with grey 'spongebag' trousers. King's Scholars are also required to wear a black gown over the top of their tailcoats. House Captains (the senior boy in each House) are entitled to wear a mottled grey waistcoat. Eton's motto is *Floreat Etona* (L. 'may Eton flourish'). The school tuck-shop is called Rowlands and the bar for over-16s is Tap. Dorney Lake, the school's rowing facility, was used for the 2006 World Rowing Championships and will host the rowing events at the 2012 Olympics. Eton is also famous for its Wall Game, played between the Collegers and the Oppidans since 1844, and its earlier version of Fives. Eton Mess is the name given to a dossert created at Eton which combines whipped cream with fresh strawberries and meringues, and is so called because the cream, strawberries and meringues are simply mixed together in one big bowl. Tel: 01753 671177.

Fat Duck, The High Street, Bray, 1 mile (1.6km) southeast of Maidenhead. Run by chef Heston Blumenthal, in 2005 the Fat Duck was named the best restaurant in the world by *Restaurant* magazine; it also came second in 2006, 2007 and 2008. Blumenthal adheres to the principles of molecular gastronomy, which gives rise to some surprisingly good but often bizarre-sounding dishes. For example, the restaurant's tasting menu features 'snail porridge', 'sardine on toast sorbet', and 'salmon poached with liquorice'. These unusual combinations are attributed to logical reasoning about physical and chemical properties of foods. Beyond applying the results of chemistry and physics to cuisine, Blumenthal exploits psychology, experimenting with diners' perception. Among the starters in the restaurant's tasting menu is a 'jelly of orange and beetroot'. A plate arrives with two jellies, one orange, one dark red. Diners are surprised when they taste the jellies, discovering that the dark red part is sour and is the orange jelly, and, by implication, the orange part must be the beetroot jelly. (This swapping of taste with colour is done using blood oranges and orange beetroots.) Tel: 01628 580 333. Bray is also home to Michel Roux's Waterside Inn.

Foxhill House Located on the University of Reading's Whiteknights Campus. The house, in Gothic revival style, was originally built by architect Alfred Waterhouse in 1868 as his own residence. Used for a period as student accommodation, it was extensively restored 2003–05, and is now the home of the University's School of Law. Among rumours of strange goings-on at the building – including one that it was built by Satanists – it has been said that British occultist Aleister Crowley spent time living at Foxhill House.

Frogmore The Frogmore Estate comprises 33 acres (13ha) of private gardens within the grounds of the Home Park, adjoining Windsor Castle. It is the location of Frogmore House, a royal retreat, and also the site of the Royal Mausoleum containing the grave of Queen Victoria and Prince Albert; the Duchess of Kent's Mausoleum, burial place of the former's mother, Victoria of Saxe-Coburg-Saalfeld; and the royal burial ground. The name derives from the preponderance of frogs which have always lived in this low-lying and marshy area. Frogmore House was built in the 1680s and purchased by King George III as a country retreat for Queen Charlotte in 1792. Earl Mountbatten of Burma was born here. Tel: 020 7766 7305.

Goring Gap A constricted narrowing in the otherwise broad river valley of the River Thames 8 miles (13km) upstream from Reading, with steep hills rising southwards to Lardon Chase, the nearest section of the Berkshire Downs, and northwards to the Chiltern Hills. Nestling within the gap are the twin villages of Goring and Streatley, on the Oxfordshire and Berkshire banks of the river respectively. Until around half a million years ago, the River Thames flowed on its current course through what is now Oxfordshire, before turning to the northeast through Hertfordshire and East Anglia and reaching the North Sea near Ipswich. When the ice started to melt at the end of the Ice Age, huge amounts of water entered this river system, causing it to cut a new route through the chalk at the site of the Goring Gap and creating a new course for the river through Berkshire and into London.

Greenham Common 2 miles (3km) southeast of Newbury. A church at Greenham was mentioned in Domesday Book. In 1199 Greenham Manor was granted by King John to the Knights Hospitallers, a military order with a monastic lifestyle, who owned it until 1540. Having largely been used for small scale industry and agriculture and for shooting and poaching, (although it was occasionally the scene of military activity – Parliamentary troops marched across the common in 1643 during the Civil War, in 1745 it was used as a marshalling base for English troops during the Jacobite Rebellion, and it saw troop manoeuvres again in 1862 and 1890) during World War II it was taken over for military use and transformed into RAF Greenham Common Airbase. It played a prominent part in the glider-based offensive launched in 1945, and it was at Greenham that Dwight D Eisenhower made his famous 'Eyes of the world' speech. After 1947 the military briefly left the common, but the onset of the Cold War brought it back into military occupation. In the 1980s Cruise missiles arrived and the site became a world famous icon for protests against nuclear weapons. The GAMA site (Ground Launched Cruise Missile Alert and Maintenance Area) is the high security area that housed the 96 Cruise missiles, their transporters and other support vehicles. Six hardened shelters were constructed in the early 1980s to protect the GLCMs from possible nuclear and conventional attack, each shelter designed to withstand a thermonuclear airburst explosion above Greenham Common and Newbury or a direct hit from a 500lb conventional bomb. It is believed that the shelters, which stand 32ft (10m) high, were built with reinforced concrete ceilings 6ft 6in (2m) thick, below a steel plate, 10ft (3m) of sand and a further reinforced concrete slab, all covered with tonnes of soil. Each shelter had six bombproof steel doors, three at each end. On 5 September 1981, a Welsh group 'Women for Life on Earth' marched from Cardiff to Greenham Common with the intention of peacefully challenging the decision to site Cruise missiles there. When their request for a debate was ignored by the base commander they set up a peace camp just outside the perimeter fence. They took the authorities by surprise and set the tone for an audacious protest lasting 19 years. By 1990 the missiles had gone and in 1992 Greenham Common Airbase was declared redundant for military purposes. In October 2002 the women's peace movement dedicated an historic commemorative site just outside the Main Street entrance to New Greenham Park. The site features a stone and steel spiral water feature and a 6ft (1.8m) steel sculpture of a campfire, within a circle of seven Welsh standing stones enclosed within a garden setting. The sculptures were designed by Michael Marriott FRBS, to symbolise the Greenham Common peace camp. GAMA remains a very visible reminder of Greenham Common's past and the history of international conflict during the late 20th century. It is still separated from the rest of Greenham Common by seven high-security fences.

Guildhall, Windsor High Street, Windsor. Built 1687–9 to designs by Sir Thomas Fiddes, and completed by Christopher Wren, the Grade I listed building stands 110yd (100m) from Castle Hill, which leads to the main public entrance to Windsor Castle. Tel: 01628 798888.

Hamstead Marshall Park 3 miles (5km) southwest of Newbury. Hamstead Marshall has always been an important manor in West Berkshire. The remains of three castle mottes, standing near the parish church, were the homes of the powerful Marshal family in the 12th and 13th centuries. In Tudor times, Sir Thomas Parry was given the manor as a reward for loyal service to Elizabeth I during the period when, as a princess, she was kept a virtual prisoner by her sister, Queen Mary. He built a fine Tudor mansion which was probably ruined by Parliamentary troops stationed in the area during the first Battle of Newbury. The mother of the 1st Earl of Craven bought the estate in 1620 for her young son and he decided to build a grand palace there for Elizabeth, sister of Charles I and dispossessed Queen of Bohemia, with whom he had fallen deeply in love. He commissioned eccentric Dutch architect Sir Balthasar Gerbier to design a miniature version of her old home, Heidelberg Castle in Germany. Elizabeth died before construction work started, but the Earl nevertheless began to erect the building in 1663 as a monument to her memory. Captain William Wynne took over from Gerbier and the house took 34 years to complete. William III tried to visit on his way to claiming the English throne, but the loyal Earl was in London with the monarch's rival, James II. The next Lord Craven preferred their Warwickshire estates, but his son, William Craven III, was fond of Hamstead. Unfortunately the house burnt to the ground in 1718 and although he intended to rebuild, engaging James Gibbs to undertake the work, he died in 1739 when little progress had been made. His brother, Fulwar, liked to hunt from the adjoining lodge which was eventually converted into a smaller mansion. His heirs also built a new home at Benham Park. The surrounding park no longer exists, but several of its elaborate gateposts survive; some of these are visible from the churchyard.

Harris Garden Located on the University of Reading's Whiteknights Campus. A botanical garden established in 1972 and expanded into its current form in 1988. It is named after distinguished palaeobotanist and keen gardener Professor Tom Harris. The garden is 12 acres (5ha) in size, and its principal purpose is for teaching and research by the university's School of Plant Sciences.

Henley Royal Regatta See Oxfordshire

Highest point Walbury Hill at 974ft (297m), also the highest point in southeast England. It is situated on the Test Way (see separate entry) in southern Berkshire, close to the Hampshire border. Combe Gibbet (see separate entry) is also located nearby.

Home Park, The Located on the eastern side of Windsor Castle. Previously known as the Little Park (and originally as Lydecroft Park), this private 655 acre (265ha) royal park is administered by the Crown Estate. See also Windsor Great Park.

Institute for Animal Health A Research institute dedicated to the study of infectious diseases of farm animals. It forms part of the UK government's Biotechnology and Biological Sciences Research Council. See also Edward Jenner Institute for Vaccine Research. Tel: 01635 578411.

Interesting facts Following the arrival of the railway in Slough in 1840, **Queen Victoria** made her first ever railway journey, from Slough station to Bishop's Bridge near Paddington, in 1842. In later years, a railway spur was built from Slough station to Windsor Central for the Queen's greater convenience. On 1 January 1845, **John Tawell**, who had recently returned from Australia, murdered his lover, Sarah Hart, at Salt Hill in Slough by poisoning her with prussic acid. With various officials in chase, Tawell fled to Slough Station and boarded a train to Paddington. Fortunately, the electrical telegraph had recently been installed and so a message was sent ahead to Paddington with Tawell's details. Tawell was trailed and subsequently arrested, tried and executed for the murder at Aylesbury on 28 March 1845. This is believed to be the first time ever that the telegraph had been involved in the apprehension of a murderer. Slough has the highest percentage of **Sikh residents** in England according to the 2001 Census figures. Sikhs make up 9.1 per cent of Slough's population, more than any other local authority. Slough also has the highest percentage of Muslim residents (13.4 per cent) and Hindu residents (4.5 per cent) in the South East region. Slough has been the subject of much derision. The poet **John Betjeman** wrote his 1937 poem 'Slough' as a protest against the 850 factories and a new town in what had been formerly a rural area, and the onslaught of the suburban lifestyle. Kintbury-born tennis player **Susan Billington** was a member of a celebrated British tennis dynasty. Her mother, Ellen Stawell-Brown, competed at Wimbledon at the turn of the 20th century and in 1901 became the first woman to serve overarm. Susan on the other hand was the last woman to serve underarm at the All England Lawn Tennis Club. For good measure Susan was the grandmother of former British No. 1 Tim Henman.

Islands See separate table for a list of the islands in the River Thames in Berkshire.

Kennet and Avon Canal The Kennet and Avon Canal links the Bristol Avon at Bath with the Rivers Kennet and Thames at Reading. Built between 1794 and 1810, it is 57 miles (92km) long, but together with the Avon Navigation and Kennet Navigation it totals 87 miles (140km). In the late 19th and early 20th centuries it fell into disuse following competition from the Great Western Railway, who owned it. In the latter half of the 20th century the canal was restored, largely by volunteers. The canal is important for wildlife conservation.

Lardon Chase, the Holies and Lough Down Located above the village of Streatley, 10 miles (16km) northwest of Reading. Three adjacent National Trust countryside properties overlooking the Goring Gap, together comprising an outstanding area of downland and woodland.

Madejski Stadium Smallmead, Reading. Opened on 22 August 1998, the stadium is the home of Reading Football Club and named after the club's chairman John Madejski. The rugby union club, London Irish, also play their home games there as tenants. The 24,200-seat stadium provides the finish for the Reading Half Marathon.

Magna Carta Island Situated in the River Thames near Runnymede in Surrey. It was formerly in Buckinghamshire but is now just within Berkshire. Possibly the site of the sealing of Magna Carta by King John in 1215, it was the definite meeting-place of Henry III and Louis (afterwards Louis VIII) of France. (GR: SU999729.)

Maidenhead Situated on the River Thames, Maidenhead, which derived from a Saxon village called South Ellington, developed after 1337. At this time, river traffic was vital for trade in the county, and Maidenhead prospered because of its extensive wharf. The busiest part of the district was along the Thames near the Great Hill of Taplow, ideal for both trade and access to the sea. This hill was known to the Celts as the Mai Dun, and its corresponding wharf as the Mai Dun Hythe; from this wharf the area became known as *Maidenhuth*. During the Middle Ages the road later called the Bristol or Bath Road, the forerunner of the M4 motorway, ran through Maidenhead, carrying valuable supplies of cloth from Berkshire to the big markets in Bristol and London. The current Maidenhead Bridge dates from 1777. Charles I met his children for the last time before his execution in 1649 at the Greyhound Inn in the High Street, now a branch of NatWest Bank. A plaque commemorates their meeting. Today, Maidenhead's industries include computer software, plastics, pharmaceuticals, printing and telecommunications. The town is also a boating centre. Maidenhead was also home to the conference that agreed upon the Maidenhead Locator System, a scheme used by amateur radio operators for identifying positions on the Earth.

Mapledurham Lock A lock and weir situated on the River Thames owned and managed by the Environment Agency. Despite its name, Mapledurham Lock is actually located in the Berkshire village of Purley-on-Thames, rather than in the Oxfordshire village of Mapledurham which is on the other side of the river. Although the weir stretches across the river between the two villages, no public access is possible across it and, in the absence of a boat, journeys between the two villages require a lengthy detour via Reading or Whitchurch-on-Thames.

Meteorological Office The Met Office was founded in 1854 as a department within the Board of Trade, with Captain FitzRoy (previously of HMS Beagle) as its first director. Its brief was to provide information on weather conditions and shipping forecasts. In 1990 it became an executive agency within the Ministry of Defence. Situated in Bracknell until 2003 when it relocated to Exeter in Devon. See also Devon.

Monkey Island Also known as Burnham Ayt. A small island in the River Thames near the village of Bray (GR: SU914791). It is now occupied by a hotel, but has an interesting history. Its name stems from the Old English Monks Eyot or Monks' Island, after the monks residing at Amerden Bank, a moated site near Bray Lock on the Buckinghamshire bank of the river, as part of Merton Priory from 1197 until the Dissolution of the Monasteries. By the 14th century, Monkey Island had passed to the Canonesses of Burnham Abbey, 1 mile (1.6km) to the north, and in the Bray Court Rolls of 1361 the island is called Bournhames Eyte. It was still recorded as Burnham-Ayt in 1640. In 1723, the island was purchased by Charles Spencer, 3rd Duke of Marlborough, who had seen it while attending the Kit-Kat Club at nearby Down Place. He erected the island's first two buildings, a fishing lodge and a fishing temple. Monkey Island Lodge (now the pavilion), which remains in its original state, was built of wood blocks cut to look like stone. The Temple, 100 yards (90m) away, was originally open to the air on the ground floor. Its attractive room above, once a billiard room, has a fine ceiling with Neptune, shells and mermaids in high relief Wedgwood-style plasterwork, said to be the work of Roberts of Oxford c.1725. At about this time artist Andieu de Clermont furnished the lodge with paintings depicting gentlemen monkeys in idyllic river scenes: fishing, shooting, and boating. These paintings still surround a small room with spectacular ceilings, once used as a banqueting room. By 1840, the pavilion had become a riverside inn reached by ferry from the south bank. It became particularly fashionable just after 1900 when Edward VII and Queen Alexandra often had afternoon tea on the lawns with their children. Rebecca West and H G Wells visited on occasions. The footbridge was not built until 1956, and additional rooms were added in 1963. The original fishing temples are now Grade I listed.

Museum of Berkshire Aviation Mohawk Way, off The Bader Way, Woodley, Reading. A small aviation museum located on the edge of the site of the former Woodley Airfield, many of its exhibits relating to Miles Aircraft Ltd which was based there 1932–47. Other aircraft exhibited were built by Fairey Aviation at White Waltham, east of Reading. Tel: 0118 944 8089.

Museum of English Rural Life Redlands Road, Reading. Founded by the University of Reading in 1951, the museum houses comprehensive collections of objects, archives, photographs, film and books relating to food, farming and the countryside. The museum has recently relocated from the university's Whiteknights Campus to a new site – previously known as East Thorpe House and St Andrews Hall – to the rear of the London Road Campus. A garden containing medicinal and culinary plants was opened in 2007. Tel: 0118 378 8660.

Museum of Reading Blagrave Street, Reading. Located in the old town hall, the museum contains galleries describing the history of Reading and its related industries, a gallery of artefacts discovered during the excavations of Silchester Roman Town, a copy of the Bayeux Tapestry and an art collection. Tel: 0118 939 9800.

Newbury, Battles of Two battles fought in 1643 and 1644 during the Civil War. Berkshire began the Second Civil War as a largely Royalist stronghold, but came under Parliamentary control by 1644 and on the way suffered greatly. There were skirmishes throughout the county, particularly in the north where Royalist troops led raiding parties from their base at Oxford. Reading was placed under heavy Parliamentary siege in April 1643, but was overrun after ten days when reinforcements were prevented from reaching the town. The two famous Battles of Newbury occurred due to the town's position along a key route to the west. In September 1643, the Royalists tried to prevent the Earl of Essex and his men returning to London after the siege of Gloucester. The two sides met at Wash Common and a seesaw battle ensued, fought among the fields below Round Hill. The Royalists eventually ran out of gunpowder and were forced to flee during the night. Just over a year later, the second Battle of Newbury was fought at Speen. Prince Maurice held the area for the king, but the Earl of Manchester arrived with a large Parliamentary force and a clash was inevitable. Waller and Cromwell secured victory for Parliament by their long march around Donnington Castle to outflank the enemy. This Royalist stronghold was then abandoned to a long siege. Charles I had always been unpopular in Windsor and had abandoned his castle there even before the war began. It became a Parliamentary stronghold and, in 1645, the Home Park was used as the training ground for Cromwell's New Model Army, with about 10,000 men billeted in the town and the surrounding villages. The castle itself only narrowly escaped demolition during the Commonwealth. See also separate table of battles.

North Wessex Downs The North Wessex Downs Area of Outstanding Natural Beauty covers an area of 668 sq miles (1730 sq km) in Berkshire, Hampshire, Oxfordshire and Wiltshire, and encompasses the Berkshire Downs, the White Horse Hills, the Lambourn Downs, the Marlborough Downs, the Vale of Pewsey and Savernake Forest.

Park Place Remenham, 1 mile (1.6km) north of Henley-on-Thames. An 18th century house set in large grounds above the River Thames. Lord Archibald Hamilton bought the estate in 1719 from Mrs Elizabeth Baker and built a new villa on the site. Frederick, Prince of Wales and the father of George III, bought the house from Lord Hamilton, whose third wife was the Prince's mistress. The estate was purchased in 1752 by Henry Seymour Conway, who made extensive improvements. In June 2007 it was reported that Park Place had been sold to a property developer for £42m, making it the most expensive house sale in the UK outside London.

Pipers Island Situated in the River Thames at Reading. The island is entirely occupied by a public house and restaurant, and by moorings for an associated boat hire and cruise business. It is immediately adjacent to Caversham Bridge, which crosses the river there. The island can be accessed on foot by a staircase descending from the centre pier of the bridge, and connecting to a short footbridge to the island. (GR: SU711745.)

Prospect Park Tilehurst, 2 miles (3km) west of Reading. Originally part of the Calcot Park estate, the site of Dirle's Farm was turned into a mansion in the 1760s by Benjamin Child, widower of the famous 'Berkshire Lady', Frances Kendrick (see separate entry), whom he had first met there some years before. He named the house after its spectacular views over Reading. The present Regency-style house was built by John Liebenrood in the following century. Now Grade II listed, it is currently used as a restaurant. The park was bought by Reading Corporation in 1901.

Queen Mary's Dollhouse Built in the early 1920s, Queen Mary's Dollhouse was designed by Sir Edwin Lutyens for Queen Mary (consort of George V). It was originally exhibited at the British Empire Exhibition in 1924–5, and is now on display at Windsor Castle. Made to 1:12 scale, the house is over 3ft (1m) tall, and contains models of products of well known companies of the time. It is remarkable for its detail and that of the objects within it, many of which are replicas of items in Windsor Castle. These were either made by the companies themselves, or by specialist modelmakers, such as Twining Models of Northampton. The carpets, curtains and furnishings were all copies of the real thing; the light fittings worked, and thore was a flushable toilet. In addition, well-known writers such as Rudyard Kipling wrote special books which were written and bound in scale size, while painters provided miniature pictures. Even the bottles in the wlne cellar were filled with the appropriate wines and spirits, and the wheels of motor vehicles were properly spoked.

RAF Greenham Common See Greenham Common

Reading Abbey Forbury Gardens, Reading. Founded by Henry I in 1121, the Cluniac priory was dedicated to the Virgin Mary and St John the Evangelist. When Henry died in France in 1135 his body was returned to Reading, and was buried before the altar of the then incomplete abbey. Other royal persons buried in the abbey include parts of the body of Empress Matilda, William of Poitiers, and Constance of York. The song 'Sumer is icumen in', the earliest known four part harmony from Britain, was first written down in the abbey c.1240; the original document is now held in the British Library. The abbey was largely destroyed after its dissolution in 1538; the remains include parts of the monks' dormitory and chapter house.

Reading Castle Forbury Gardens, Reading. Motte and bailey castle probably constructed in the grounds of Reading Abbey by King Stephen during the 12th century civil war. It may have been intended as a base for attacking the Empress Matilda's base at Wallingford, though this was a little distant. The castle was destroyed by Matilda's son, the future Henry II, in 1153. The remains of the motte can still be seen in Forbury Gardens (which take their name from the castle: the *Fore-Borough*). Although there are a Castle Hill and Castle Street in Reading, they possibly take their names from the ancient ruin of a Roman villa in the area.

Reading Prison Forbury Road, Reading. HMP Reading was built in 1844 as the Berkshire County gaol, alongside the site of Reading Abbey and beside the River Kennet. Designed by Giles Gilbert Scott, it was based on London's New Model Prison at Pentonville with a cruciform shape. As a county gaol it was also the site of executions, the first in 1845 before a crowd of 10,000 and the last in 1913. Famous inmates have included Oscar Wilde from November 1895 to May 1897. He wrote *De Profundis* while in the gaol, and *The Ballad of Reading Gaol* is based on the plight of his fellow inmate Charles Thomas Wooldridge, a trooper in the Royal Horse Guards executed on 7 July 1896 for the murder of his wife. The Irish revolutionaries William Thomas Cosgrave, later President of the Irish Republic, and Ernest Blythe were held at the prison because of their involvement in the Easter Rising. More recently actor Stacy Keach served six months there after being convicted of cocaine smuggling in 1984. It closed as a prison in 1920 but continued to be used as an internment site in both world wars. In 1973, Reading was redesignated as a local prison and around that time its old castle wall was removed. In 1992 it became a remand centre and Young Offenders Institution, holding prisoners aged 18–21. Tel: 0118 908 5000.

Region 6 War Room — Located on the University of Reading's Whiteknights Park campus. A nuclear bunker dating from the early days of the Cold War, it is one of a number of such Regional War Rooms built during the 1950s and designed to co-ordinate civil defence in the event of an attack on the country using conventional bombs or atom bombs. After ceasing to be used for civil defence purposes, the war room was taken over by the university and modified as a secure storage facility for use by the University Library.

Rivers — The **Bourne** is a tributary of the River Pang and, indirectly, of the River Thames. Its source is near the village of Chapel Row and it joins the Pang near the village of Tidmarsh.

The **Broadwater** is a small tributary of the River Loddon at Twyford.

The **Enborne** is a tributary of the River Kennet. Its source is in Hampshire, and part of its course forms the border between Berkshire and Hampshire. Despite its name it does not run through the village of Enborne, although it does run through Enborne Row. The river plays a significant part in Richard Adams's novel *Watership Down.* Early in the book, the rabbits from Sandleford are threatened by a dog. Blackberry realises that they can float across on a wooden board, and thus they make their escape.

The **Foundry Brook** is a small stream which rises near the Hampshire village of Silchester before entering Berkshire, flowing through the village of Stratfield Mortimer and into the town of Reading. In Reading it passes through the Green Park business park before entering the River Kennet.

The **Holy Brook**'s origin is uncertain but it is probable that some parts are natural, while other parts were created in medieval times. It leaves the main channel of the Kennet at a structure known as Arrowhead near Theale, rejoining it close to the site of Reading Abbey. For the first stretch of its route, the channel forms the boundary between the Reading suburbs of Fords Farm, Calcot, Southcote and Coley to the north and the Kennet water meadows to the south. In this area the channel gives its name to the nearby civil parish of Holybrook. Once past Coley Park the Holy Brook enters the centre of Reading. It can clearly be seen where it flows under one of the entrances to the Oracle shopping centre, and also where it passes under Reading Central Library. The Holy Brook has given its name to Holy Brook Mall, the lower of the Oracle centre's two shopping malls.

The **Jubilee River** is a hydraulic channel constructed in the late 1990s and early 2000s to take overflow from the River Thames and so alleviate flooding to areas in and around Maidenhead, Windsor and Eton, all prone to severe bouts of flooding. The channel is 7.2 miles (11.6km) in length, and allows excess water to be taken via the east bank of the Thames upstream of Maidenhead and returned via the northeast bank downstream of Eton. Despite being man-made, the Jubilee River looks and acts like a natural river. Its banks offer many varieties of wildlife specially constructed habitats, intended to act as replacements for habitats lost from the banks of the Thames during urban expansion in the 19th and 20th centuries. At the time of its formation the channel represented the largest man-made river project ever undertaken in Britain, and the second largest in Europe. The name was chosen by the local population in a poll, the choice of 'Jubilee' proving especially popular as the project was completed in Queen Elizabeth II's golden jubilee year of 2002 and as Her Majesty's preferred home is at Windsor Castle.

One of the **Kennet**'s sources is Swallowhead Spring near Silbury Hill in Wiltshire, the other being a collection of tributaries north of Avebury, near the villages of Uffcott and Broad Hinton, which flow south past Avebury and join up with the waters from Swallowhead Springs. From there the river flows through Marlborough, Hungerford and Newbury before meeting the Thames at Reading. The upper reaches of the Kennet are served by two tributaries: the Og which flows into the Kennet at Marlborough and the Dun which enters at Hungerford. The Kennet's principal tributaries are the River Lambourn, the River Enborne and the Foundry Brook. For 6 miles (10km) west of, and through, Reading, the Kennet supports a secondary 6 mile channel, known as the Holy Brook, which formerly powered Calcot Mill and Abbey Mill, watermills belonging to Reading Abbey. The lower reaches of the river are navigable and are known as the Kennet Navigation; this, together with the Avon Navigation, the Kennet and Avon Canal (see separate entry) and the Thames, links Bristol and London. Though it is only 22 miles (35km) from the source to Newbury, there are more than 80 miles (129km) of fishable water due to the maze of carriers created by the 18th century water engineers. The total length of the river is 44 miles (70km) not including tributaries.

The **Lambourn** is a tributary of the River Kennet. Rising in the Berkshire Downs above its namesake village of Lambourn, it flows through the villages of East Garston, Great Shefford, Welford, Boxford, Bagnor, Donnington and Shaw before entering the Kennet between Newbury and Thatcham.

The **Loddon** rises at West Ham Farm in Basingstoke, Hampshire, and in its first mile flows under the town's Festival Place shopping centre. Leaving Basingstoke behind, it flows north through open countryside and passes near the village of Sherfield on Loddon. North of Sherfield the river passes through the ornamental grounds of Stratfield Saye House, the home of the Dukes of Wellington since 1817. Entering Berkshire, it passes the village of Swallowfield. Just to the north it is joined by the River Blackwater which adds substantially to its flow. It then flows close to the east of the Reading suburbs of Earley and Woodley, west of Winnersh, and through Dinton Pastures Country Park. Shortly afterwards, near the village of Hurst it is joined by the Emm Brook (after which the Wokingham suburb of Emmbrook is named). The river then flows close to Twyford and is joined by the St Patrick's Stream, a backwater of the Thames. About 1 mile (1.6km) further on it flows into the main channel of the Thames, just downstream of Shiplake Lock and close to the village of Wargrave. The river's total length is 28 miles (45km).

The **Pang**, a tributary of the River Thames, rises near the village of Compton and flows south through the village of Hampstead Norreys before turning east through the tiny villages of Bucklebury, Stanford Dingley and Bradfield. To the east of Bradfield it is joined by the River Bourne and turns north to flow through the villages of Tidmarsh and Pangbourne, entering the Thames between Whitchurch Lock and Whitchurch Bridge. The river rarely flows between Compton and Hampstead Norreys, possibly due to climate change or heavy water extraction. The length of this small chalk stream is 14 miles (23km). Its name was formed by back-extraction from the name of Pangbourne.

Riverside Museum — Located at Blake's Lock (see separate entry). Telling the story of Reading's two rivers – the Kennet and the Thames – the Riverside Museum occupies two former industrial buildings, the Screen House and the Turbine House. Tel: 0118 939 9800.

Seven Barrows — $2^1/_2$ miles (4km) north of Lambourn, 8 miles (13km) north of Hungerford. The site of this Bronze Age cemetery lies along the Lambourn to Kingston Lisle road. Excavators have found that a single grave contained the cremated remains of 100 individuals dating from 2200 BC. Despite its name, it contains at least 26 barrows of various types, including bowl barrows, bell barrows, saucer barrows and disc barrows. There are also remnants of a long barrow dating from c.3800 BC. The barrows themselves are low mounds, generally overgrown with grass, and appear insignificant when viewed from a travelling vehicle.

Shaw House — 1 mile (1.6km) northeast of Newbury. The most impressive Elizabethan mansion in Berkshire, Shaw House was built by wealthy cloth merchant Thomas Dolman, and completed in 1581. Like many other houses erected during Elizabeth I's reign, its ground plan is a letter E, the porch projecting slightly less than the wings. It is famous as Charles I's headquarters during the second Battle of Newbury. Now owned by West Berkshire Council, the house was a school for many years before being restored as a register office, education and conference centre. In 2008 it opened to the public as a heritage attraction for the first time. Tel: 01635 42400.

Slough Trading Estate — Bath Road, Slough. Founded in 1920 and disparagingly known as 'the dump' in its early days, Slough Trading Estate was the UK's first business park. Today it is the largest of its kind in Europe, providing 7,233,000 sq ft (672,000 sq m) of space and covering a total of 487 acres (197ha). The estate is home to 400 businesses include Centrica, Yell, Electrolux, GlaxoSmithKline, Mars, ICI and Sara Lee, and supports 20,000 jobs. It is owned and operated by Slough Estates International plc, although Mars has retained its independence. The estate's power plant supplies heat and power to the entire industrial site, and it once boasted its own railway.

South Hill Park — Ringmead, Bracknell. The original South Hill Park mansion was built in 1760 for William Watts for his retirement from service as a senior official of the Bengal government. The two-storey Italianate house had grounds including 30 acres (12ha) of common land, which Watts enclosed. In return he built almshouses on a site opposite Easthampstead parish church $^1/_2$ mile (0.8km) away; these were demolished by order of the Marquis of Downshire in 1826. The statesman George Canning acquired the property early in 1807. Sir Arthur Divett Hayter, born in 1835, rebuilt most of the mansion in the late 19th century in brick and Bath stone. Sir Arthur became Lord Haversham in 1906; Haversham Drive, in the Easthampstead neighbourhood of Bracknell, has been named after him. During World War II the house was occupied by the Royal Sea Bathing Hospital, evacuated from Margate. In the late 1940s it was converted into luxury flats. From 1953 the house was owned by the BBC, who converted part of it into studios. In 1963 the Bracknell Development Corporation acquired the property; the house was let in 1965 to Ferranti Ltd, who used it as offices and laboratories until early 1972. In 1971, Sir Jack Hughes, then chairman of Bracknell Development Corporation, persuaded the district and town councils, Southern Arts Association and the Arts Council to create an arts centre and theatre at South Hill Park. The South Hill Park Trust was established to administer the building and the surrounding gardens, lawns, trees and two lakes. Sir Jack was elected founder chairman of the Arts Centre on its opening in 1973. The 330-seat Wilde Theatre was added in 1984 and a new dance studio in 1988–9. The Bracknell Gallery opened in 1991 and has established itself as an innovative arts centre housing exhibitions of contemporary work. Tel: 01344 484858.

Speenhamland System — A method of giving relief to the poor, based on the price of bread and the number of children a man had. It was set up in the Berkshire village of Speen by local magistrates who held a meeting at the Pelican Inn on 6 May 1795 after a series of bad harvests had cause a shortage of wheat and the price of bread had consequently risen sharply. The situation was exacerbated by the growing population and because of the Napoleonic wars, which meant that grain could not be imported from Europe. Famine was a distinct possibility and, after several food riots in the spring of 1795, the ruling classes feared that the lower orders might emulate the French and revolt. The magistrates decided to bring in an allowance scale whereby a labourer would have his income supplemented to subsistence level by the parish, a type of 'top-up' on very low wages. The magistrates also suggested that farmers and other employers should increase the wages of their employees, but this met with little success. The idea of these allowances spread rapidly in the south of England and it is thought that the system saved many families from starvation.

Sport

football — **Reading** were formed in 1871. Their original nickname, The Biscuitmen (after one of the main trades in the town, Huntley & Palmers biscuits), became The Royals (due to Reading's location in the Royal County of Berkshire) in the 1970s. The club played at Reading Recreation Ground until 1878, before moving to Reading Cricket Ground (1878–82), Coley Park (1882–9) and Caversham Cricket Ground (1889–96). The club moved again, to the purpose-built Elm Park on 5 September 1896. Reading were elected to the Football League in 1920. In 1994–5, their play-off defeat against Bolton Wanderers made them the only side to finish second in the second tier and not receive promotion to the top level, due to a reduction in the number of Premier League teams from 22 to 20. In 1998 Reading moved into the new Madejski Stadium (see separate entry), named after the club's chairman John Madejski. On 25 March 2006, Reading won promotion to the Premier League for the first time in their history. They hold the English league record for the longest winning sequence at the start of a season with 13 successive victories at the beginning of 1985–6. The club's home strip is blue shorts and blue and white hooped shirts. Tel: 0118 968 1100.

Other clubs include **Maidenhead United**.

horse racing

Ascot Racecourse was founded in 1711 by Queen Anne and was solely a flat race track until April 1965, when it held its first jump meeting. The circuit is a right-handed triangle of 1½ miles (2.8km). Swinley Bottom is a famous part of the track. Ascot stages 25 days of racing per year, comprising 16 Flat meetings held in May and October. The Royal Meeting, held in June, remains a major draw, the highlight being the Ascot Gold Cup. In all, Ascot holds nine of the UK's 31 annual Group 1 races, the top race being the King George VI & Queen Elizabeth Diamond Stakes in July. The racecourse closed for 20 months on 26 September 2004 for a £185 million redevelopment. As owner of the Ascot estate, Queen Elizabeth II reopened the racecourse on Tuesday 20 June 2006. Tel: 01344 622211.

Newbury Racecourse, Greenham, southeast of Newbury, was founded in 1905 and moved to its current location in 1910. The left-handed course of 1 mile 7 furlongs (3km) is home of both the John Porter Stakes on the Flat and the Hennessy Cognac Gold Cup over jumps. Tel: 01635 40015.

Windsor Racecourse is just outside Windsor town centre. The course of 1½ miles (2.5km) is the only figure-of-eight Flat circuit in England. Tel: 01753 865234.

ice hockey

Bracknell Bees were formed in 1987 under the ownership of John Nike OBE. The Bees play in the English Premier Ice Hockey League (EPIHL), generally considered to be the second tier league below the Elite Ice Hockey League although there is no promotion or relegation between the two. Club colours are black, yellow and white, and the Bees play home matches at the John Nike Leisuresport Complex. Tel: 01344 789000.

Slough Jets were founded in 1986 and currently play in the EPIHL. The Jets play in red, white and blue at the Ice Arena, Montem Lane, Slough. Tel: 01753 821171.

Stanley Spencer Gallery

Cookham, 5 miles (8km) northeast of Maidenhead, This small gallery celebrates famous English painter Sir Stanley Spencer (1891–1959), who lived in the village of Cookham. Many of his works depict villagers and village life and his religious paintings often had the village as their backdrop.The gallery was opened in 1962 in a Methodist chapel once attended by Spencer. Not far from the gallery is 'Fernlea', the cottage where Spencer was born and lived in Cookham High Street. Tel: 01628 471885.

Sunninghill Park

4 miles (6km) northeast of Bracknell. The first newly erected royal home since Bagshot Park, built in 1879 for the Duke of Connaught. The old house, a late Georgian stucco building, burnt down and was rebuilt in contemporary style as a home for Prince Andrew. The architect was Sir James Dunbar-Nasmith, Balmoral Estate architect and Professor and Head of the Department of Architecture at Heriot-Watt University. Construction was completed in 1990. The most southeasterly parish in Berkshire, Sunninghill stretches over Sunningdale and Ascot, as well as Sunninghill itself. The old Roman road from London to Silchester, known as the 'Devil's Highway', follows much of the border with Surrey. Sunninghill Park was part of Windsor Forest until Charles I sold it to Thomas Carey in 1630. In 2004 the Duke of York, now divorced, moved into Royal Lodge, Windsor, the home of the late Queen Elizabeth the Queen Mother; Sunninghill Park was sold in 2007.

Temple Island

An island in the River Thames at Remenham, north of Henley-on-Thames. It lies at the start of the course for the Henley Royal Regatta, whose organisers own the island. The island includes an elegant ornamental folly temple designed by 18th century architect James Wyatt as a fishing lodge for Fawley Court, a nearby historic house remodelled by Wyatt in the 1770s. (GR: SU771848.)

Test Way

A 49 mile (79km) long-distance footpath running from Walbury Hill in West Berkshire to Eling in Hampshire. It passes through the towns of Romsey and Totton and the villages of Linkenholt, Ibthorpe, Hurstbourne Tarrant, St Mary Bourne, Longparish, Forton, Wherwell, Chilbolton, Stockbridge, Horsebridge and Mottisfont. The southern end is at Eling Quay. Walbury Hill is also the start of the Wayfarers Walk (see Hampshire).

Thames Valley Police Museum

Sulhamstead, 5 miles (8km) southwest of Reading. Located in Sulhamstead House (also known as the White House), formerly the headquarters of the Berkshire Constabulary and now the training centre for Thames Valley Police, the museum features displays on the history of Thames Valley Police and the five police forces amalgamated to form the force in 1968: the Buckinghamshire Constabulary, the Berkshire Constabulary, Oxford City Police, the Oxfordshire Constabulary and the Reading Borough Police. Its collections include items from the Great Train Robbery of 1963, uniforms, equipment, medals, photographs, scenes of crime evidence, and occurrence and charge books. Tel: 0118 932 6748.

Thames Valley University

Based on campuses in Ealing, Slough and Reading, all in the Thames Valley, the former Polytechnic of West London – an amalgamation in 1990 of Ealing College of Higher Education (originally founded in 1860 as Lady Byron School), Thames Valley College of Higher Education in Slough (founded in 1907 as an elementary school), Queen Charlotte's College of Health Care Studies and the London College of Music – was awarded university status in 1992. In 2004 TVU (then based at Ealing and Slough) merged with Reading College and School of Arts & Design. Ealing and Slough campuses. Tel: 0800 036 8888; Reading campus. Tel: 0800 371 434.

Theatre Royal, Windsor Thames Street, Windsor. The present building, situated close to Windsor Castle, was opened on 17 December 1910 after the previous theatre had burned down on 18 February 1908, under the ownership of Sir William Shipley. Sir Peter Hall staged his first professional play at the theatre in 1953, the same year that he graduated from Cambridge University. In 1997, West End impresario Bill Kenwright took over the management of the theatre. Tel: 01753 853888.

Three Castles Path A 60 mile (96km) long-distance footpath running from Winchester Great Hall, Hampshire to Windsor Castle via the ruins of Odiham Castle (also known as 'King John's Castle'). The route passes through the towns of New Alresford, Hartley Wintney, Sandhurst, Bracknell and Ascot and the villages of Martyr Worthy, Itchen Abbas, Abbotstone, Upper Wield, Bradley, Greywell, North Warnborough and Odiham. It also passes through Trilakes Country Park, Ascot Racecourse, Windsor Great Park and close to Broadmoor Hospital. Part of the footpath also follows the Basingstoke Canal towpath.

Tittenhurst Park London Road, Sunningdale, Ascot. The home of John Lennon and Yoko Ono from the late summer of 1969 until the end of 1971, located on a 100 acre (40ha) estate. It was later occupied by Ringo Starr and family until the late 1980s.

Ufton Court Ufton Nervet, 9 miles (15km) southwest of Reading. A largely Elizabethan manor house, though parts date from the 1400s. It was modified by Richard Perkins in 1957. The house is notable for its priest holes. Tel: 0118 983 2099.

University of Reading Established in 1892, receiving its royal charter and becoming a university in 1926. The university was awarded the Queen's Anniversary Prize for Higher and Further Education in 1998 and 2005. It has almost 15,000 students including around 3000 international students from 120 countries. Former students include singer Jamie Cullum, oarsman James Cracknell, children's author Kathleen Hale and meteorologist Jay Wynne. See also Bulmershe Manor, Cole Museum of Zoology, Ure Museum of Greek Archaeology, Whiteknights Park. Tel: 0118 987 5123.

Ure Museum of Greek Archeology Located on the University of Reading's Whiteknights Campus. The museum forms part of the university's Department of Classics and houses a collection of material from Greek and other Mediterranean civilisations, notably Etruscan ceramics and terracottas. Other exhibits include prehistoric pottery, Greek and Roman metal and stone artefacts, and a collection of Egyptian antiquities ranging from the Pre-dynastic to the Roman period. Tel: 01734 318420.

Virginia Water See Windsor Great Park and Surrey

Walbury Hill See Highest Point

Wayfarers Walk See Hampshire

Welford Park 6 miles (10km) northwest of Newbury. Welford Park was originally the site of a monastic grange granted to Abingdon Abbey before the Norman Conquest. The house was known as Farm Court and was run on behalf of the monks by a bailiff. After the abbey's dissolution, Henry VIII used the place for a time as a hunting lodge. Later it was granted to Sir Thomas Parry senior; his main residence was at Hamstead Marshall (see separate entry) but, after his death in 1560, Welford was used as a dower house for his wife, who is buried in the adjoining church of St Gregory. The present building was built c.1652 for Richard Jones, grandson of Sir Francis Jones, Lord Mayor of London, who purchased the property in 1618. Thomas Archer remodelled the house c.1700, adding a complete storey and decorating the façade with ionic columns. The interior was considerably altered in 1840. The Archers and their descendants, the Houblons, are obscure relatives of the Jones family. They owned the property for many generations, though sometimes residing elsewhere. The present owner is James Puxley, grand-nephew of the last Archer-Houblon. Tel: 01488 608203.

Whitchurch Lock Located in the Oxfordshire village of Whitchurch-on-Thames, but the weir crosses the river to the Berkshire village of Pangbourne, 3 miles (5km) northwest of Reading. Both lock and weir are ownod and managed by the Environment Agency. Whitchurch Lock is one of the few locks on the River Thames to have no public access other than by boat.

Whiteknights Park 2 miles (3km) south of Reading. Tho principal campus of the University of Reading (see separate entry), the park occupies the former manor of Earley Whiteknights, also known as Earley St Nicholas and Earley Regis. Whiteknights Park includes lakes, conservation meadows and woodlands as well as being home to most of the university's departments.

Windsor Castle Located in central Windsor. The largest occupied castle in the world, covering a site of 15 acres (6ha), a royal home and fortress for over 900 years, Windsor Castle is (together with Buckingham Palace in London and the Palace of Holyrood in Edinburgh) an official residence of Queen Elizabeth II and remains a working palace today. Its site, high above the River Thames and on the edge of a Saxon hunting ground, was chosen by William I; it was a day's march from the Tower of London and intended to guard the western approaches to the capital. The outer walls of today's structure are in the same position as those of the original castle built by William c.1067, as is the central mound supporting the Round Tower and the upper ward, where successive monarchs have had their private apartments since the 14th century. In the 1170s Henry II rebuilt in stone the Round Tower, the outer walls of the upper and most of the lower ward, and the royal apartments in the upper ward. In the 1360s Edward III, who was born at Windsor, extended the castle, creating the immense St George's Hall for the use of the Knights of his newly founded Order of the Garter. St George's Chapel, begun by Edward IV and completed by Henry VIII, is dedicated to the patron saint of the Order of the Garter, Britain's highest order of chivalry, and ranks among the finest examples of late medieval architecture in Western Europe. Oliver Cromwell captured Windsor Castle after the Battle of Edgehill in 1642, and for the rest of the Civil War it became a prison as well as the headquartors of the Parliamentary forces. In 1648 Charles I was held here before his trial and execution; two Berkshire men, Henry Marten of Hinton Manor (Hinton Waldrist), former MP for Berkshire, and Daniel Blagrave of Southcote House, were among the Parliamentarians who signed his death warrant. In 1649 Charles's body was brought back for burial in St George's Chapel during a snowstorm. Following the Restoration, Charles II was determined to make the castle as splendid as possible. He created a new set of state apartments in the 1670s, using the skills of architect Hugh May, artist Antonio Verrio for murals and ceiling paintings, and famous wood-carver Grinling Gibbons. The King's Dining Room and the Queen's Presence and Audience Chambers retain many of these original features. Charles also laid out the 3 mile (5km) Long Walk leading due south from the castle into Windsor Great Park. Much of Windsor Castle's present appearance is due to the alterations instigated in the 1820s by George IV with his architect, Sir Jeffry Wyatville. The buildings were refashioned in Gothic style with the addition of crenellations, turrets and towers. One of George's most remarkable additions was the Waterloo Chamber, created to show portraits commissioned from Sir Thomas Lawrence to commemorate the defeat of Napoleon at the Battle of Waterloo in 1815. These depict the monarchs, soldiers and statesmen who were involved in the victory, including George III, George IV and the future William IV, the Duke of Wellington, Field Marshal von Blücher, the Emperors of Austria and Russia, the kings of Prussia and France, and Pope Pius VII. Queen Victoria and Prince Albert were devoted to Windsor, where they spent much of their time. During Victoria's reign, in 1845, the state apartments were first opened to the public. Prince Albert died of typhoid at Windsor in 1861 and was buried in a spectacular mausoleum constructed by Queen Victoria at Frogmore (see separate entry) in Windsor Home Park. During World War II, Windsor Castle was home to the young Princesses Elizabeth and Margaret while their parents supported the war effort. Today the Queen uses the castle regularly, spending most of her weekends here. But its 20th century history is dominated by the major fire that started on 20 November 1992. It began in the private chapel, where a curtain was set alight after coming into contact with a spotlight. The blaze took 15 hours and 1.5 million gallons of water to extinguish; nine principal rooms and over 100 other rooms covering more than 10,000 sq yds (9000 sq m) – one-fifth of the castle area – were damaged or destroyed. The next five years were spent restoring the castle to its former glory. The greatest historic building project undertaken in the UK in the 20th century, reviving many traditional crafts, the restoration was completed six months ahead of schedule on 20 November 1997 at a cost of £37 million, £3 million below budget. To mark the completion, the Queen and the Duke of Edinburgh held a reception in the restored rooms on 14 November 1997 for 1500 contractors. On 20 November that year they celebrated their golden wedding anniversary with a ball at the castle. Every year the Queen takes up official residence in Windsor Castle for a month over Easter, known as Easter Court. During that time she hosts occasional 'dine and sleeps' events for guests, including politicians and public figures. She is also in residence for a week in June, when she attends the service of the Order of the Garter and the Royal Ascot race meeting. The Order of the Garter ceremony brings together members of the senior order of chivalry for a service in St George's Chapel. Beforehand, the Queen gives a lunch for the Knights of the Garter in the castle's Waterloo Chamber. Any new Knights of the Garter are invested by the Queen in the Garter Throne Room. On the walls are portraits of monarchs in their Garter robes, from George I to the present Queen, whose State portrait by Sir James Gunn was painted in 1954. Windsor Castle is often used by the Queen to host state visits by overseas monarchs and presidents. Foreign heads of state enter horse-drawn carriages through the George IV Gateway into the quadrangle in the Upper Ward, where a military guard of honour is drawn up. The traditional state banquet is held in St George's Hall with a table seating up to 160 guests. Recent state visits include those of President and Mrs Mbeki of South Africa (2001), and King Abdullah II and Queen Rania of Jordan (2001), as well as a special visit by President and Madame Chirac of France to mark the centenary of the Entente Cordiale (2004). St George's Chapel remains an active centre for worship, with weekly services. The chapel is a royal peculiar – a chapel that is not subject to a bishop or archbishop but owes its allegiance directly to the sovereign. It is administered by the Dean and Canons of Windsor, who, with their officers and staff, are called the College of St George. Many royal weddings have been celebrated in the chapel, most recently that of Prince Edward and Sophie Rhys-Jones in June 1999. Funerals such as those of Princess Margaret and Princess Alice, Duchess of Gloucester, have also taken place here. Queen Elizabeth the Queen Mother is buried in the chapel with her husband, George VI, and Princess Margaret, her younger daughter, as are nine other sovereigns (Edward IV, Henry VI, Henry VIII, Charles I, George III, George IV, William IV, Edward VII and George V). Various departments of the royal household are based at Windsor Castle. The Round Tower houses the Royal Archives and the Royal Photograph Collection. The Print Room and Royal Library house precious drawings, prints, manuscripts and books. When the Queen is in official residence, Changing the Guard provides a colourful spectacle in the quadrangle. Visitors can also see the state apartments and, for part of the year, the semi state rooms. Some of the most splendid interiors in the castle, these are furnished with treasures from the royal collection, including paintings by Rembrandt, Holbein, Rubens, Van Dyck and Lawrence, fine tapestries and porcelain, drawings by Leonardo da Vinci, sculpture and the last and largest suit of armour made for Henry VIII. Other parts of the castle complex open to visitors include the Drawings Gallery and St George's Chapel, and Queen Mary's doll's house (see separate entry) may also be seen. The immediate environs of the castle, known as the Home Park (see separate entry), comprise parkland and two working farms along with many estate cottages mainly occupied by employees. The estate of Frogmore also lies within the Home Park. Frogmore House and Gardens are open to the public on certain days of the year (the remainder of the Home Park is private). The Home Park forms the northern part of the more extensive – though now sadly depleted – Windsor Great Park. In the town of Windsor at the foot of the castle stands a private school (St George's, Windsor Castle) which provides choristers to the chapel. Tel: 020 7766 7304.

Windsor chair A type of chair made since the 17th century and exported to America in the early 18th century. The distinctive feature is a solid wooden seat into which are fitted the round tops of the legs and the round bottoms of the spindles for the back. The main centre of the chairs' manufacture is traditionally High Wycombe, rather than Windsor!

Windsor Great Park The Great Park, formerly part of a vast Norman hunting chase, is set in 5000 acres (2000ha) of Surrey and Berkshire countryside stretching from Windsor in the north to Ascot in the south. With its varied landscape and sweeping deer lawns, woods, coverts and huge solitary ancient oaks, the park abounds in wildlife. There is a small river in the north called the Battle Bourne and a number of ponds, particularly to the south. Chief among these are Great Meadow Pond and Obelisk Pond, near the great man-made lake of Virginia Water. Developed by Henry, brother of George III, the lake dates to 1746 and forms an efficient drainage system for the park. Once one of the largest artificial lakes in England, Virginia Water is 130 acres (53ha) in area, 2 miles (3km) in length and 1/2 mile (0.5km) wide at its widest point, with a circumference of 7 miles (11km). The most prominent hill is Snow Hill, from which the avenue of trees known as the Long Walk runs for 3 miles (5km) to Windsor Castle. It is said that Henry VIII stood on Snow Hill awaiting news of Anne Boleyn's execution, which was to be signalled by gunfire from the castle's Round Tower. The Copper Horse, a statue of George III on horseback created by Sir Richard Westmacott 1824–30, was erected on the hill by his son George IV. The area is accessed by a number of gates: Queen Anne's Gate, Ranger's Gate, Forest Gate, Sandpit Gate, Prince Consort's Gate, Blacknest Gate, Bishop's Gate and Bear's Rails Gate; the original medieval park pale can still be seen in places. Queen Anne's Ride, dating from 1708, is a grand avenue similar in length to the Long Walk, but unlike its more famous counterpart featuring only a single row of trees on each side. It runs southwest towards Ascot. In the 18th century it was known as Queen's Walk, the name changing during the 19th century. In the east of the Great Park is the Savill Garden, at its best in spring, when the rhododendrons and azaleas are in flower, and containing another lake which reflects the colour all along its banks. At the centre of the park is the Village, built in the 1930s to house royal estate workers. Other buildings include the Royal Lodge, Cumberland Lodge, the Cranbourne Tower and Norfolk Farm. The park lies mostly within the civil parish of Old Windsor, though the eastern regions are in the Borough of Runnymede and there are small areas in the parishes of Winkfield and Sunninghill. Areas associated with or attached to the Great Park, but not officially within its borders include the Home Park, Mote Park, Flemish Farm, Cranbourne Chase, Forest Lodge and South Forest. Except for a brief period of 'privatisation' by Oliver Cromwell in order to pay for the Civil War, the area remained the personal property of the monarch until the reign of George III when control over all Crown lands was handed over to Parliament. Today the park is officially owned by Queen Elizabeth II but administered by the Crown Estates Commissioners' office, a government department. Tel: 01753 860222.

Windsor Safari Park From 1969–92 Windsor Safari Park was a large and popular drive-through zoo situated just outside Windsor in the former grounds of Dodge Mansion on St Leonards Hill. It was established by circus proprietors the Smart family, who had for a number of years used nearby Winkfield as their winter quarters. Animals such as lions, tigers, cheetahs, giraffes and zebras could be observed from visitors' cars, and the park also featured hippopotamus, chimpanzees and dolphins. After changing hands several times, Windsor Safari Park closed its gates in 1992 and the area lay idle for several years until the first Legoland theme park outside Denmark opened in 1996.

Wokefield Park Mortimer Common, 3 miles (5km) south of Reading. An 18th century country house built for the Brocas family sometime before 1777 with early 19th century alterations by Sir John Soane. The cellars have vaulting which may date from the time of the Treasurer of the Middle Temple, Edmund Plowden, who bought the house in 1569. The interior has contemporary fireplaces, moulded plaster ceilings, wood panelling and early 18th century twisted baluster stairs. The house is now a conference and training centre; the 250 acre (101ha) grounds contain a golf course as well as Europe's largest ropes course. Tel: 0870 609 1161.

Some famous people born in Berkshire

Baily, Francis (astronomer) (1774–1844)	Newbury
Bond, Michael (children's author) (1926–)	Newbury
Burns, Richard (rally driver) (1971–2005)	Reading
Boulting, John (director) (1913–85)	Bray
Boulting, Roy (director) (1913–2001)	Bray
Collier, Constance (actress) (1878–1955)	Windsor
Edward III (king of England) (1312–77)	Windsor
Fiennes, Sir Ranulph (explorer) (1944–)	Slough
Gervais, Ricky (comedian) (1961–)	Reading
Henry VI (king of England) (1421–71)	Windsor
Laud, William (Archbishop of Canterbury) (1573–1645)	Reading
Lofting, Hugh (novelist) (1886–1947)	Maidenhead
Lyttleton, Humphrey (jazz musician) (1921–2008)	Eton
McEwan, Geraldine (actress) (1932–)	Windsor
Margaret (consort of Alexander III of Scotland) (1240–75)	Windsor
Mary (daughter of Edward IV of England) (1467–82)	Windsor

Mendes, Sam (director and producer) (1965–)	Reading
Morley, Sheridan (critic and biographer) (1941–2007)	Ascot
Mountbatten, Louis (First Sea Lord) (1900–79)	Windsor
Neville, Richard (earl of Warwick) (1428–71)	Bisham
Oughtred, William (inventor of the slide rule) (1575–1660)	Eton
Price, Dennis (actor) (1915–1973)	Ruscombe
Rickman, Thomas (architect) (1776–1841)	Maidenhead
Spencer, Stanley (painter) (1891–1959)	Cookham
Tull, Jethro (seed-drill inventor) (1674–1741)	Basildon
Ullman, Tracey (comedienne) (1959–)	Slough
Webb, Neil (footballer) (1963–)	Reading
Winslet, Kate (actress) (1975–)	Reading
Young, Will (singer) (1979–)	Wokingham

Islands of Berkshire

Island name	Nearest landmark	General information
Baths Island	Windsor	Situated between Queen's Eyot and Deadwater Ait. GR: SU960773
Bavin's Gulls	Maidenhead	Aka Sloe Grove Islands. GR: SU908840
Black Boy	Hurley	Situated adjacent to Frog Mill Island.
Black Pott's Ait	Windsor	Situated between Romney Island and Sumptermead Ait.
Boulter's Island	Maidenhead	Boulter's Lock is one of many island locks on the river.
Bridge Eyot	Bray	Situated between Headpile Eyot and Grass Eyot.
Bucks Ait	Maidenhead	Aka Guards Club Island. GR: SU766773
Burnham Ayt	Bray	See Monkey Island
Bush Ait	Boveney Lock	Situated at the mouth of the Clewer Mill Stream which leads to Windsor Racecourse Marina.
Caversham Lock Island	Reading	Aka De Bohun Island. GR: SU718740
Cookham Lock	Cookham	GR: SU901855
Cutlers Ait	Windsor	Situated between Firework Ait and Romney Island.
De Bohun Island	Reading	Aka Caversham Lock Island. GR: SU718740
De Montfort Island	Reading	Aka Fry's Island. Site of a trial by combat between Robert de Montfort and Henry of Essex in 1163. GR: SU714743
Deadwater Ait	Windsor	Situated between Bath's Island and Firework Ait.
Firework Ait	Windsor	Situated between Deadwater Ait and Cutlers Ait.
Formosa Island	Cookham	GR: SU908852
Friary Island	Wraysbury	GR: SU992742
Friday Island	Old Windsor	Situated between Ham Island and Friary Island.
Frog Mill	Hurley	Situated adjacent to Black Boy Island.
Fry's Island	Reading	Aka De Montfort Island.
Gibraltar Islands	Winter Hill	GR: SU870863
Glen Island	Eton	Annexed to the Jubilee River, an artificial secondary channel of the Thames between Maidenhead and Windsor.
Grass Eyot	Taplow	Situated between Ray Mill Island and Bridge Eyot.
Guards Club	Maidenhead	Aka Bucks Ait. GR: SU766773
Hallsmead Ait	Shiplake	GR: SU768775
Ham Island	Sunnymeads	Situated between Nickcroft Ait and Pats Croft Eyot. GR: SU996752
Headpile Eyot	Bray	Situated between Pigeonhill Eyot and Bridge Eyot. GR: SU907798
Lion	Old Windsor	Situated between Ham Island and Sumptermead Ait.
Lock Island	Marlow	Between Hamhaugh and D'Oyly Carte Island. GR: SU855860
Lynch, The	Shiplake	GR: SU769778
Magna Carta Island	Runnymede	See separate entry
Magpie Island	Medmenham	GR: SU794839
Monkey Island	Bray	Aka Burnham Ayt. See separate entry
Nickcroft Ait	Sunnymeads	Situated between Ham Island and Sumptermead Ait.
Pats Croft Eyot	Wraysbury	Situated between Ham Island and Magna Carta Island. GR: SU997732
Pigeonhill Eyot	Bray	GR: SU912796
Pipers Island	Reading	See separate entry
Poisson Deux Islands	Hurley Bottom	GR: SU811835
Queen's Eyot	Dorney Reach	Situated between Monkey Island and Bath's Island. GR: SU917783
Ray Mill Island	Taplow	A bridge links the island to Boulter's Lock. GR: SU904825
Romney Island	Eton	Situated between Cutlers Ait and Sumptermead Ait. GR: SU979775
Sloe Grove Islands	Maidenhead	Aka Bavin's Gulls. GR: SU908840
St Mary's Island	Reading	GR: SU692750
Sumptermead Ait	Eton	Situated between Romney Island and Nickcroft Ait.
Temple Island	Remenham	See separate entry
Temple Mill	Hurley	Situated upstream of Marlow and just downstream of Temple Lock.
View Island	Lower Caversham	Developed as an aquatic wildlife centre. GR: SU721742

BUCKINGHAMSHIRE

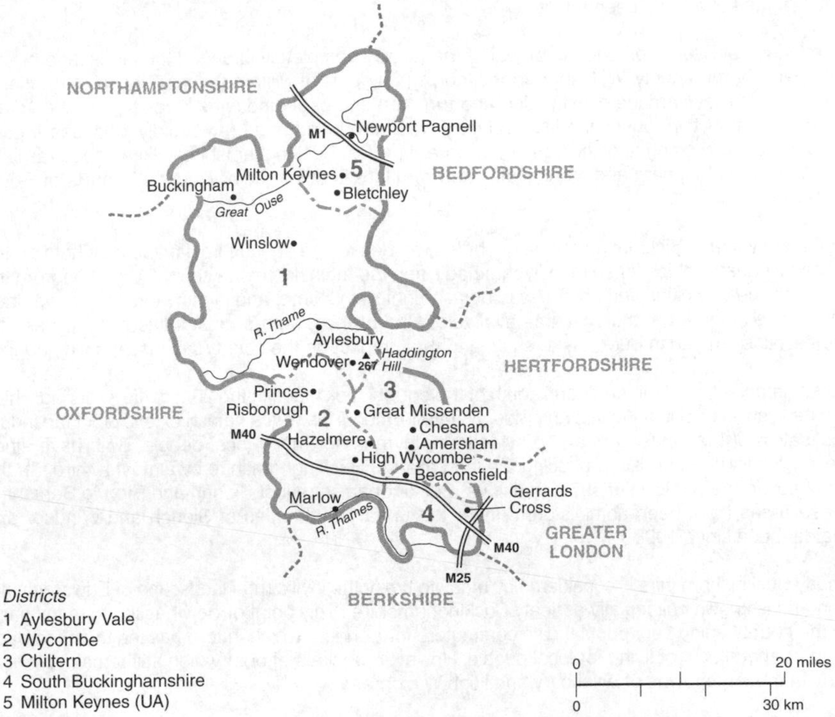
NORTHAMPTONSHIRE
M1
Newport Pagnell
Milton Keynes
5
BEDFORDSHIRE
Buckingham
Bletchley
Great Ouse
Winslow
1
R. Thame
Aylesbury
Wendover
Haddington Hill
267
HERTFORDSHIRE
Princes
Risborough
3
2
OXFORDSHIRE
Great Missenden
Chesham
M40
Hazelmere
Amersham
High Wycombe
Beaconsfield
Gerrards
Cross
Marlow
R. Thames
4
GREATER
LONDON
M40
M25
BERKSHIRE
Districts
1 Aylesbury Vale
2 Wycombe
3 Chiltern
4 South Buckinghamshire
5 Milton Keynes (UA)
0
20 miles
0
30 km

Buckinghamshire is one of the home counties of southeast England. It is bordered by Greater London to the southeast, Berkshire to the south and southwest, Oxfordshire to the west, Northamptonshire to the north and northwest, Bedfordshire to the northeast and Hertfordshire to the east. Its southeasternmost tip barely encroaches on Surrey. The county town is Aylesbury. The district of Milton Keynes was created by the merger of the urban districts of Bletchley, Newport Pagnell and Wolverton, Newport Pagnell Rural District and that part of Wing Rural District within the designated New Town area. It was originally one of five non-metropolitan districts of Buckinghamshire, but on 1 April 1997, under a recommendation of the Local Government Commission for England it became a self-governing unitary authority, independent from Buckinghamshire County Council. The borough however remains part of Buckinghamshire for ceremonial purposes.

The name Buckinghamshire is Anglo-Saxon in origin and means 'the district (shire) of Bucca's home'. 'Bucca's home' refers to Buckingham in the north of the county, and is named after an Anglo-Saxon landowner. The county has been so named since about the 12th century; however, it existed before that as a subdivision of the kingdom of Mercia (AD 585–919). Some settlements in Buckinghamshire existed well before the Anglo-Saxon period. Aylesbury, for example, is known to date back at least as far as 1500 BC. A wealth of places still have Brythonic names (Penn, Wendover), or a compound of Brythonic and Anglo-Saxon (Brill, Chetwode, Great Brickhill), and there are pre-Roman earthworks all over the county. One of the legendary kings of the Britons, Cunobelinus, had a castle in the area (the earthworks of which still remain) and lent his name to the group of villages known as the Kimbles. The Roman influence on Buckinghamshire is most widely felt in its Roman roads. Watling Street and Akeman Street both cross the county from east to west, and the Icknield Way follows the line of the Chiltern Hills, a 75 mile (121km) chalk escarpment stretching southwest–northeast from Goring Gap in Oxfordshire to Royston in Hertfordshire via Buckinghamshire and Bedfordshire. The first two were important trade routes linking London with other parts of Roman Britain, and the latter was used as a line of defence, though it may have been an extension of a much older road.

In the Civil War Buckinghamshire was mostly Parliamentarian, although pockets of Royalism did exist. The Parliamentarian hero John Hampden was from Buckinghamshire, and helped defend

Aylesbury in battle in 1642. Some villages to the west of the county (Brill and Boarstall for example) endured constant conflict throughout the war, being equidistant between Parliamentarian Aylesbury and Royalist Oxford. Many of these places were effectively wiped off the map during the conflict, but have since been rebuilt.

The Industrial Revolution and the arrival of the railway completely changed the landscape of certain parts of the county. Wolverton in the north (now part of Milton Keynes) became a national centre for railway carriage construction and furniture and paper industries took hold in the south. In the centre of the county, the lace industry was introduced and grew rapidly, because it gave employment to women and children from poorer families. Buckinghamshire still has good rail links to London, Birmingham and Manchester and furniture is still a major industry in parts of South Bucks.

In the early to mid Victorian era a major cholera epidemic and agricultural famine took hold on the farming industry which for so many years had been the mainstay of the county. Migration from the county to nearby cities and abroad was at its height at this time, and landowners took advantage of the cheap land that thus became available. One of the county's most influential families, the Rothschilds, arrived in Bucks as a result, and their impact on the county's landscape was huge.

Mass urbanisation of the north and south of the county took place in the 20th century, during which the new towns of Milton Keynes and Slough were formed. This was a natural extension of the industrialisation of the landscape, and provided employment for many local people. Both have since become unitary authorities, reducing the land area of Buckinghamshire by almost a third. (In the local government reform of 1974, traditional Buckinghamshire lost Slough and Eton to Berkshire; these areas have been administered under the unitary authorities of Slough and Windsor and Maidenhead since 1998.)

Today Buckinghamshire is considered by many to typify the idyllic rural landscape of Edwardian fiction and is known colloquially as 'leafy Buckinghamshire'. This point of view has led to many parts of the county being very popular with commuters for London, which in turn has led to an increase in the general cost of living for local people. However, pockets of deprivation still remain, particularly in the large towns of Aylesbury and High Wycombe.

Buckinghamshire	**Population**			**Area**	
Districts	*male*	*female*	*total*	*sq miles*	*sq km*
Aylesbury Vale	82,309	83,439	165,748	349	903
Chiltern	43,128	46,100	89,228	76	196
South Bucks	30,003	31,942	61,945	55	141
Wycombe	79,299	82,806	162,105	125	325
Milton Keynes Unitary Authority	102,844	104,213	207,057	119	309
Total	337,583	348,500	686,083	724	1874

Local Attractions and Information

Administrative headquarters
Buckinghamshire: County Hall, Walton Street, Aylesbury HP20 1UA. Tel: 01296 395000.
Milton Keynes: Civic Offices, 1 Saxon Gate East, Milton Keynes MK9 3HQ. Tel: 01908 691691.

Ascott House
Wing, 2 miles (3km) southwest of Leighton Buzzard. Originally a Jacobean farmhouse, bought in 1876 by the de Rothschild family and redesigned by George Devey, a leading Victorian architect. The house contains an exceptional collection of fine art, English and French furniture, and more than 400 pieces of Chinese ceramics. Leopold de Rothschild was a keen gardener and employed famous Chelsea nurseryman Sir Harry Veitch to assist him in laying out the grounds. The gardens are a mixture of the formal and informal including exuberant Venus and Cupid fountains by Thomas Waldo Story. Leopold's head gardener, John Jennings, worked at Ascott for 30 years, although George Devey designed the tea house at the east end of the Madeira Walk and the skating hut overlooking the Lily Pond. There is also a Dutch garden and a remarkable topiary sundial. The property is now owned by the National Trust. Tel: 01296 688242.

Aylesbury Duck
A relatively recent addition to the duck family, bred mainly for its meat and appearance. Its plumage is almost invariably white, with a pink or orange bill and either orange or (rarely) black feet. It is also the largest known breed of domestic duck. The breed was developed around the early 18th century and became a cottage industry in Aylesbury. Historically Aylesbury Ducks were walked 40 miles (64km) from the Vale of Aylesbury to London. The drovers would often stop for the night at inns along the way where the birds were kept in large enclosed yards. Each morning, they would be driven through a cold tarry solution in a shallow ditch followed by a layer of sawdust, which provided the birds with a set of crude shoes to protect their feet on the road. By 1839 the ducks could be transported by rail and as their popularity grew, visitors flocked to buy the

local delicacy from the town's fat-stock markets. At this period almost everyone living in the 'Duck End' of Aylesbury bred the Aylesbury Duck. It became a poor, crowded and unsanitary part of town, the ducks being reared inside the already damp cottages.

By c.1850 the number of establishments breeding the ducks began to decline after the introduction of new sanitary regulations and an outbreak of 'Duck Fever'. In 1873 the Pekin Duck was brought to Britain from China, and the Aylesbury breed was frequently crossed with it. As a result, the pure breed began to disappear and by World War II ducking in and around Aylesbury had almost vanished. In recent years breeders have attempted to re-establish the Aylesbury Duck, and it has again become popular as an exhibition bird. Today there are real Aylesbury Ducks at Oak Farm Rare Breeds Park, Broughton, near Aylesbury, or perhaps on the large duck pond in front of St Mary's Church in Haddenham, a large village at the southern tip of Aylesbury Vale.

Bekonscot Model Village Warwick Road, Beaconsfield. The world's oldest model village, created in 1929 as the hobby of Roland Callingham, Bekonscot is an entire miniature kingdom stuck firmly in an idyllic 1930s timewarp. There are six little villages in a $1^1/_2$ acre (0.6ha) miniature landscape of farms and fields, castles and churches, woods, lakes and rolling hills, whose tiny population enjoy the fun of the fair, beaches, zoo and tramway, or lazily watch cricket on the village green. Each village is linked by one of Britain's largest public outdoor model garden railways. Tel: 01494 672919.

Bletchley Park Bletchley, Milton Keynes. Also known as the top secret 'Station X', the World War II home of Government Communications Headquarters (GCHQ) is famous for its breakthroughs in electronic intelligence and the early development of computer technology, and particularly as the site where the Enigma cypher, the backbone of German military and intelligence communications, was finally broken. Like many English stately homes, the late 19th century mansion – built in a disparate variety of styles from Gothic to Dutch Baroque – was taken over by the military in 1939. The raw material for its codebreakers came from the 'Y' Stations, a web of wireless intercept stations dotted around Britain and in a number of countries overseas. These stations listened in to the enemy's radio messages and sent them to Bletchley Park to be decoded and analysed. The Enigma decrypt teams worked in various huts built in the grounds. The huts, known for security reasons only by their numbers, operated in pairs. The codebreakers concentrating on Army and Air Force cyphers were based in Hut 6, supported by a team in the neighbouring Hut 3 who turned the decyphered messages into intelligence reports. Hut 8 decoded messages from the German Navy, with Hut 4 the associated naval intelligence hut. To speed up the codebreaking process, the brilliant mathematician Alan Turing developed an idea originally proposed by Polish cryptanalysts. The result was the Bombe, an electro-mechanical machine that greatly reduced the time required to break the daily-changing Enigma keys.

With the declaration of peace, codebreaking activity ceased and every scrap of evidence was destroyed on Churchill's orders. As World War II gave way to the Cold War, it was vital that the USSR should learn nothing of Bletchley Park's wartime achievements. Some of the thousands who had worked there continued to use their remarkable expertise to break other countries' cyphers, working under a new name: the Government Communications Headquarters (GCHQ). In 1987, after a 50 year association with British Intelligence, Bletchley Park was finally decommissioned. Only when the wartime information was declassified in the mid 1970s did its achievements begin to emerge, and their impact on the outcome of the war and subsequent developments in communications still has not been recognised fully. On 21 October 1991, a farewell party was held in the grounds before the site was destroyed. Over 400 codebreakers attended and it was decided to attempt to save the site for posterity. Bletchley Park Trust first opened the site to visitors in 1993 and, with the help of volunteers and enthusiasts, maintained a collection of independent and Trust exhibitions for the general public to enjoy. HRH The Duke of Kent became chief patron, officially opening the museum in July 1994. Tel: 01908 640404

Boarstall Duck Decoy Nr Brill, 11 miles (18km) west of Aylesbury. One of only four 17th century duck decoys that remain in working order, it is set on a tree-fringed lake, home to breeding water fowl that can be watched from the hide. Charles II was responsible for introducing the duck decoy to England, its aim being to catch large quantities of waterfowl. A dummy duck (decoy) is used to attract birds on to a small patch of water. A decoyman and his trained dog then herd the birds into netted over-pipes. The birds trapped here were once an important source of winter food but the birds caught today are ringed for ornithological study. Now owned by the National Trust. Tel: 01844 237488.

Boarstall Tower $^1/_2$ mile (0.4km) northwest of Boarstall, 11 miles (18km) west of Aylesbury. The three-storey stone tower dates from the 14th century and was the gatehouse of a fortified house, now demolished. Although it was altered in the 16th and 17th centuries it retains the crossloops for bows. The modern gardens are surrounded by a moat on three sides. Owned by the National Trust. Tel: 01844 239339.

Bradenham $7^1/_2$ miles (12km) northwest of High Wycombe. The hamlet of Bradenham is the location of a grand manor house which in the 13th century belonged to the Earl of Warwick. In 1566 Elizabeth I was entertained here. The current manor house was substantially built in the 17th century and was the home of Benjamin Disraeli for part of his early life. In the Victorian era it was turned into a boarding school for local young gentlemen. Today it is a residential training venue for a financial services company. The whole village of Bradenham is owned by the National Trust. A nuclear bunker was built here by RAF Strike Command 1983–5 in spite of local opposition.

Buckingham Castle Castle Street, Buckingham. Norman motte and bailey castle now covered by the church of St Peter and St Paul. A castle at the site was first mentioned in documentary sources in 1154–64. Possibly demolished 1208–15, the site was levelled in 1777 for the churchyard which now occupies it. In 1877 excavations at the back of the Wesleyan chapel exposed foundations probably associated with the castle.

Buckingham Chantry Chapel Market Hill, Buckingham. The oldest building in Buckingham, rebuilt in 1475 and entered by an 11th century Norman doorway which leads into the chapel. During the reign of Henry VI it became the Royal Latin School and was restored by Gilbert Scott in 1875. Now owned by the National Trust, it is leased by Buckingham Heritage Trust. Tel: 01280 823020.

Buckinghamshire orchards Historically most orchards in Buckinghamshire were to be found in the south of the county around High Wycombe and south of Aylesbury. Cherry orchards were the county's speciality. Buckinghamshire thinks so highly of its 'chuggies', as the jet-black cherries are called locally, that the first Sunday in August is observed as 'Cherry Pie Sunday'. This marks the completion of the cherry harvest with the gathering of the late Prestwood Blacks, and it is the custom for cherry pie, or other recipes such as cherry turnover or cherry duff, to be served in cottages and farmhouses. A Cherry Pie Fair is still held at Seer Green, near Chalfont St Giles; it has recently become part of Seer Green's Village Day, and locally made cherry pies are for sale. Another Buckinghamshire fruit is the Aylesbury Prune, a black plum or damson grown in Weston Turville (also famous for the breeding of the Aylesbury Duck). It was once used for making jam but is now a relatively rare hedgerow fruit.

Buckinghamshire Railway Centre $^1/_2$ mile (0.8km) south of Quainton, 5 miles (8 km) northwest of Aylesbury. A railway museum located in Quainton Road railway station and operated by the Quainton Railway Society. The site is divided into two halves joined by two footbridges, each side having a demonstration line with workshop and museum buildings. Separating the two halves is a Network Rail goods line, formerly the main line used by the Great Central Railway and the Metropolitan Railway. The museum has a large collection of locomotives and rolling stock. Tel: 01296 655720.

Burnham Beeches Situated to the north of the village of Burnham and bounded by Windsor, Maidenhead and Slough, these remnants of a vast forest that once covered almost all of Buckinghamshire are owned and managed by the Corporation of London who, in 1880, bought the woodland to save it from prospective developers. Burnham Beeches are within the area around London now protected from further encroachment by Green Belt legislation. The average age of the pollarded trees is estimated to be well over 400 years. The largest tree, probably also the oldest, is the Druid's Oak, almost certainly more than 800 years old. At 540 acres (219ha), the interior of the Beeches offers many walks. The area is also a favourite location shoot, having stood in for Sherwood Forest in *Robin Hood, Prince of Thieves* (1991), an Irish woodland in *The Crying Game* (1992), ancient generic England in *First Knight* (1995) and *Ivanhoe* (1997) and a more tropical setting in *A Town Like Alice* (1956).

Chalfonts, The An area of southeast Buckinghamshire on the edge of the Chilterns, enclosed by Chalfont St Giles, Seer Green, Jordans, Chalfont St Peter, Little Chalfont and Amersham. Chalfont means chalk spring, in reference to the water-carrying capacities of the local terrain. During the Great Plague of London in 1665, John Milton retired to Chalfont St Giles, where he completed his epic poem *Paradise Lost.* Milton's Cottage (see John Milton's Cottage) is still located in the village. The inspiration for *Paradise Regained* is said to have been found in the parish from a conversation with one of the local residents. Chalfont St Giles doubled as Walmington-on-Sea in the film version of *Dad's Army* (1971). The area, as far south as Gerrards Cross, is undoubtedly one of the more affluent parts of Buckinghamshire.

Chenies Manor House Chenies, $1^1/_2$ miles (2.5km) east of Amersham. The semi-fortified brick manor house was built by Sir John Cheyne c.1460. Sir John Russell (later the 1st Earl of Bedford) made additions in 1526 and it became the ancestral home of the Earls of Bedford. Henry VIII and Elizabeth I with their courts were entertained here. The house is surrounded by several beautiful gardens: a white garden, a sunken garden and an extensive physic garden containing a great collection of plants used in present-day medicine as well as fragrant and culinary herbs. The house also contains tapestries and furniture, mainly from the 16th and 17th centuries, hiding places, a collection of antique dolls, a medieval well, underground passages, a reconstructed penitential yew maze and a reputed priest's hole. Now home of the MacLeod Matthews family. Tel: 01494 762888.

Chequers Court $^1/_2$ mile (0.8km) south of Ellesborough, 4 miles (6km) southeast of Aylesbury. Situated at the foot of the Chiltern Hills, Chequers has been the country residence of the Prime Minister since 1921, David Lloyd George being its first incumbent. There has been a house on the site since the 12th century. The original house probably gained its name after Elias Ostiarius (or de Scaccario), who was acquiring land in the Ellesborough area at the time and possibly built or inhabited the house. The name 'Ostiarius' meant an usher of the Court of the Exchequer. Ostiarius' coat of arms included the chequer board of the Exchequer, so it is likely he named his estate after his arms and position at court. The present 16th century house was restored and enlarged by John Hawtrey in 1565. A reception room bears his name today. Immediately after completing the house, Hawtrey had the dubious honour of guarding a royal prisoner at Chequers – Lady Mary Grey, younger sister of Lady Jane Grey and great-granddaughter of Henry VII, who had married without her family's consent and was banished from court by Elizabeth I and kept confined to ensure that, in the queen's words, 'there were no little bastards'. The room where she slept from 1565–7 is still kept as it was, and appears, even by today's standards, quite comfortable. The house later passed through several families: the Wooleys, the Crokes, the Thurbanes, the Astleys and the Clutterbucks. In 1715, the then owner of the house married John Russell, a grandson of Oliver Cromwell, and the house still contains a large collection of Cromwell memorabilia. During World War I the house became a hospital and then a convalescent home for officers. After the war and following the reinstatement of Chequers as a home, now owned by Arthur and Ruth Lee – by this time Lord and Lady Lee of Fareham – the house was given to the nation. A stained glass window in the long gallery, commissioned by Lord and Lady Lee, bears the inscription: 'This house of peace and ancient memories was given to England as a thank-offering for her deliverance in the great war of 1914–1918 as a place of rest and recreation for her Prime Ministers for ever.'

Chicheley Hall Newport Pagnell, 5 miles (8km) northeast of Milton Keynes. One of England's finest examples of Georgian architecture, built 1719–25 by Sir John Chester. It boasts a naval museum and some fine English sea paintings and furniture. The painting by John Fernsley senior of two of Sir Francis Burdett's hunters, held by a groom waiting with three foxhounds to join the hunt, is ever popular. The great hall has a ceiling painting by William Kent depicting Herse and her sisters sacrificing to Flora. The unique canal and new garden were added to the east side some time later. The present colour scheme was created by Felix Harboard when Earl Beatty bought the house in 1952. The house is now owned by the trustees of Lord Beatty's Will Trust and occupied by Sir John and Lady Nutting. Tel: 01234 391252.

Chiltern Hundreds The Chiltern Hundreds are Stoke, Desborough and Burnham. A hundred is a traditional division of an English county, and the hilly, wooded hundreds of the Chiltern Hills were once notorious as a hiding place for robbers. A Crown Steward was appointed to maintain law and order in the area, but the position's duties ceased to be required in the 16th century, and the holder ceased to gain any benefits during the 17th century. The positions of Steward and Deputy Steward of the Chiltern Hundreds are now used as a procedural device to allow resignation from the House of Commons. (Those of Steward and Deputy Steward of the Manor of Northstead in Yorkshire are also used as a device for resignations.) Anyone holding office under the Crown is automatically disqualified from membership of the House, so an MP applying for them automatically has to give up his or her seat. The 'office' is held until such time as another MP applies.

Chiltern Open Air Museum Newlands Park, 1 mile (1.6km) east of Chalfont St Giles. A collection of over 30 historic buildings rescued from their original sites and including a blacksmith's forge, stables, barns, and a mews (Skippings Barn) which is home to the Hawk and Owl Trust. Pageants and battle re-enactments are regularly held in the grounds. Tel: 01494 871117.

Claydon House Steeple Claydon, 6 miles (10km) southeast of Buckingham. Famous for its 18th century rococo interiors, the features of the house include a unique Chinese Room and parquetry grand stairs. Continuously occupied by the Verney family for more than 380 years, the house has mementoes of their relation Florence Nightingale, who was a regular visitor. All Saints' church is situated within the grounds. Tel: 01296 730349.

Cliveden 3 miles (5km) northeast of Maidenhead. Overlooking the River Thames near Taplow, the 376 acre (152ha) gardens and woodland include a water garden, 'secret' garden, herbaceous borders, topiary, a magnificent parterre (patterned garden) and a collection of statuary including Roman antiquities collected by the 1st Viscount Astor. Other features include the recently restored Tortoise Fountain – designed by Thomas Waldo Story (1855–1915) and consisting of a three-tier water feature with four sculpted tortoises on each level through which the water drains – and the Octagon Temple, with its rich mosaic interior. The house itself, the third on the site, was built by Charles Barry for the Duke of Sutherland in 1851 and was once the home of Nancy, Lady Astor. The property is owned by the National Trust; the house is currently let as a hotel. Tel: 01628 605069.

Concrete cows H3 Monks Way, Bancroft, Milton Keynes. Made by Canadian-born sculptress Liz Leyh at Stacey Hill Farm (now the home of Milton Keynes Museum), the most famous residents of Milton Keynes were completed in 1978. The following year one of the calves, 'Millie Moo', was kidnapped by students and a ransom asked for. No one knows if it was paid or not but the calf was never seen again. In 1986 a prankster painted the cows with black and white stripes to make them look like zebras and in 1986 'Millie Moo Two' was stolen but recovered.

Coombe Hill 2 miles (3km) southwest of Wendover. This hill in the Chilterns, overlooking Aylesbury Vale, is not to be confused with another Coombe Hill on the flank of Haddington Hill, $2^{1}/_{2}$ miles (4km) to the northeast. At 853ft (260m) the hill is the second highest in the county. The word *coombe* is of Brythonic origin and means 'hollow'. Near the summit is a monument, erected in 1904, in memory of the men from Buckinghamshire who died during the Second Boer War. The original gold plaque and decorations were stolen in the 1980s and were replaced with a stone plaque and iron flag, the remainder of the decoration being created from bronze. Having been damaged by a lightning strike in the early 1990s, the monument has now been equipped with conductors to prevent the mishap happening again. The monument and a few square yards of surrounding land are owned by English Heritage, while the majority of the hill is owned by the National Trust. It once formed part of the Chequers Estate but was donated to the Trust by the government when it was given the estate in 1921. Coombe Hill is home to wildlife including red kites, yellowhammers and firecrests, as well as the rare Chiltern gentian.

Cowper and Newton Museum Olney, 6 miles (10km) north of Newport Pagnell. Once the home of 18th century poet William Cowper, the museum now contains furniture, paintings and personal possessions of both Cowper and his ex-slave-trader friend, Rev. John Newton (the author of 'Amazing Grace'). Also to be seen are re-creations of a Victorian country kitchen and wash-house, Cowper's restored summerhouse, two tranquil gardens, a costume gallery, collections of dinosaur bones and bobbin lace, and local history displays. Tel: 01234 711516.

Denham Studios A film studio forever associated with Alexander Korda. Flush from the financial success of his London Films production *The Private Life of Henry VIII* (1933), Korda acquired the finance to build a new studio at the Fishery near Denham village. Opened in 1936, it was the largest film studio in the UK. The first film completed there was *Southern Roses* (1936). Other major productions made at Denham include *Rembrandt* (1936), *Elephant Boy* (1937), *Fire Over England* (1937), *Knight without Armour* (1937), *The Citadel* (1938), *The Four Feathers* (1939), *Goodbye Mr Chips* (1939), *In Which We Serve* (1942), *This Happy Breed* (1944), *Henry V* (1944), *The Way Ahead* (1944),

Brief Encounter (1945), *Caesar and Cleopatra* (1945), *A Matter of Life and Death* (1946), *Odd Man Out* (1946), *Vice Versa* (1947), *Hamlet* (1948) and *The History of Mr Polly* (1948). In 1939 ownership of the studios passed from Korda to the J Arthur Rank Organisation, which set up D & P Ltd to oversee Denham and Pinewood. At the end of the 1940s, with Rank in financial difficulties, they decided to safeguard the future of Pinewood by closing Denham. The final film made at Denham was *Robin Hood* (1951). For a short time the site was leased to the US Air Force and then housed Rank Xerox equipment. The main buildings were eventually demolished for an industrial park.

Dorney Court — 2 miles (3km) west of Eton. Built in 1440, Dorney Court has been the home of the Palmer family for more than 450 years, passing from father to son through 13 generations. The Grade I listed building features 15th and 16th century oak rooms and beautiful 17th century lacquer furniture. Dorney in Old English means 'island of bees' and the estate is famous for its honey, which is still produced today. The very first pineapple to be raised in England was grown at Dorney Court and presented to Charles II in 1661. The nearby church of St James the Less dates to the 13th century. Tel: 01628 604638.

Dorneywood — 2 miles (3km) northeast of Burnham. In the time of Henry VIII Dorney Wood, part of Burnham Beeches (see separate entry), was a notorious haunt of thieves and vagabonds who preyed on travellers from Burnham to Beaconsfield. Nowadays it is more famous as the location of the 21-room Queen Anne style house known as Dorneywood, built in 1920 and set in 214 acres (87ha) of gardens. The one-time country retreat of Chancellors of the Exchequer, this tradition was broken when Gordon Brown offered the grace and favour property to Deputy Prime Minister John Prescott. Mr Prescott had the use of a government-owned flat in Admiralty House, plus the use of Dorneywood until May 2006 when he vacated the property. The property is owned by the National Trust and funded by the Dorneywood Trust, and is not generally open to the public.

Ford End Watermill — Station Road, Ivinghoe. The listed building is at least 400 years old and is the only remaining working watermill in Buckinghamshire with original machinery. An interesting feature is the sheepwash in the tailrace below the mill. Tel: 01582 600391.

Great Train Robbery — On 8 August 1963 the Royal Mail's Glasgow–London travelling post office train was stopped after a gang rigged the signals at Sears Crossing, where a farm track crossed the railway line between Leighton Buzzard and Cheddington, a village 10 miles (16km) east of Aylesbury. Fifteen men wearing ski masks and helmets swarmed aboard, decoupled the coaches carrying the valuable cash cargo, and forced the train's driver to take them half a mile up the line to Bridego Railway Bridge, Ledburn near Mentmore. The gang, led by Bruce Reynolds and including Ronnie Biggs, Roy James alias 'The Weasel', Charlie Wilson, Jimmy Hussey, John Wheater, Brian Field, John Daly, Jimmy White, Tommy Wisbey, Gordon Goody and Buster Edwards, stole £2.3 million in 120 mailbags containing used £1, £5 and £10 notes. Although no guns were used in the robbery, the train driver, Jack Mills, was hit on the head with an iron bar, causing a black eye and facial bruising. The assailant was one of three members of the gang never to be arrested or identified, though 13 gang members were caught after police discovered their fingerprints at their hideout at Leatherslade Farm, near Oakley, Buckinghamshire. The robbers were tried, sentenced on 16 April 1964 and imprisoned for a total of 307 years.

Halton House — Halton, 4 miles (6km) southeast of Aylesbury. There has been a manor house at Halton since the Norman Conquest, when it belonged to the Archbishop of Canterbury. Thomas Cranmer sold the manor to Henry Bradshaw, Chancellor of the Exchequer, in the mid 16th century. After remaining in the Bradshaw family for some time, it was sold to Sir Francis Dashwood (founder of the Hellfire Club) in 1720 and was held in the Dashwood family for almost 150 years. The site of the old manor house was west of the church in Halton village itself. It had a large park, which was later bisected by the Grand Union Canal. In June 1849 Sir George Dashwood auctioned the contents, and in 1853 the estate was sold to Baron Lionel de Rothschild. The old house was demolished, after which Lionel gave the estate to his son Alfred de Rothschild. Although the estate covered 1500 acres (600ha) in a triangle between Wendover, Aston Clinton and Weston Turville, it lacked a dwelling of any significant size, at least by Rothschild standards. Upon inheriting the estate in 1879, Alfred de Rothschild commissioned Cubitts to build 'an English Chateau modelled on modern French lines'. Construction was completed in 1883. The house was built purely as a weekend home, but was one of the first in England to have electric light and central heating installed and was decorated in lavish style, the ornate ceilings being among the best features. A hydraulic lift from the ground floor to the Chinese landing on the first floor was powered by water pressure from a huge water tank placed in the roof of the Swiss Chalet hunting lodge at the top of the Aston hill. The overspill pipes went down to a coppice where an ice rink was built. Early in World War I, most of the trees were used for trench props and the land became an army training centre. On Alfred's death in 1918, the estate was bought for the newly formed Royal Air Force as a training centre the aircraft apprentice scheme. The house then became the officers' mess. Today, it is still a temporary home to serving officer and is frequently used as a film set, appearing in *The World Is Not Enough* (1999), *Evita* (1996), *An Ideal Husband* (1999), *What a Girl Wants* (2003), *Bride and Prejudice* (2004) and *The Queen* (2006).

Hampden House — Great Hampden, 5 miles (8km) north of High Wycombe. A country house named after the Hampden family. The Hampdens (later Earls of Buckinghamshire) are recorded as owning the site from before the Norman Conquest, and lived continually in the house until 1938. The core of the present house is Elizabethan, although the south wing, known anachronistically as King John's tower, dates to the 14th century. Constructed of clunch, a combination of chalk and mud peculiar to Buckinghamshire, the tower has traceried Gothic windows and the remains of the original spiral staircase. Legend has it that Edward III and the Black Prince stayed at the house. During the stay the prince and his Hampden host were jousting when a quarrel arose, during which the prince was punched in the face by his host. This act of *lèse majesté* caused the king and prince to leave in great wrath, and as a result their host forfeited some of his estates to the Crown. There is no documentary evidence for this act or of the subsequent revenge, but the Black Prince is known to have possessed land in nearby Princes Risborough. The north and west sides were rebuilt c.1750 to the design of Thomas Iremonger in Gothic style with battlements and pointed arches, predating the work of Horace Walpole at Strawberry Hill by 15 years. When the Hampdens moved out in 1938 the house was first let to a girls' school and afterwards used by Hammer Films as a film set. In 1986 Hampden Group Management bought the house and carried out a complete restoration. The parish church in the grounds contains memorials to the Hampden family including a monument to celebrated patriot John Hampden, who died at the Battle of Chalgrove during the Civil War in 1643 fighting for the Parliamentarians. Hampden had achieved fame and notoriety by his refusal to pay Charles I's Ship Tax on his lands in Buckinghamshire and Oxfordshire. Tried and found guilty, he consequently became a public hero. The spot where he refused to pay is marked by a monument in the grand avenue at Hampden House, although the exact location of the site is disputed.

Hartwell House — 2 miles (3 km) west of Aylesbury. Hartwell House was first mentioned in Domesday Book and belonged to an illegitimate son of William I. However, the core of the present house was constructed in the early 17th century for the Hampden family and then the Lee family. The Lees, an old Buckinghamshire family, acquired Hartwell c.1650 by marriage into the Hampdens. Confederate general Robert E Lee was one of their descendants. The Jacobean north front of the house is constructed of ashlar and has a projecting porch with a bow window above; terminating each end of this façade are two flanking canted bays each with a double height oriel window. Immediately each side of the porch two large windows indicate the hall within. Hiding the roofscape is a parapet with vases erected in 1740. Architect Henry Keene substantially enlarged and 'Georgianised' the house 1759–61, and built the east front with its canted bay windows and Tuscan style central porch. The 90 acres (36ha) of gardens were laid out by Capability Brown c.1750. Between 1809 and 1814 the owner of the house, Sir Charles Lee, let the mansion to exiled Louis XVIII of France. The arrival of the impoverished king and his court at Hartwell was not a happy experience for the mansion, with once grand and imperious courtiers farming chickens and small livestock on the lead roofs. The king signed the document accepting (once again) the French crown in the library of the house. In 1827, Dr John Lee inherited the house from the unmarried Rev. Sir George Lee and during his ownership, the British Meteorological Society (now Royal Meteorological Society) was founded in the library in 1850. In the 1980s the house was converted from a girls' finishing school to a hotel. The project was overseen by architect Eric Throssel, who created a new dining room in the manner of Sir John Soane by enclosing the former 18th century open arcaded porch. The former semicircular galleried entrance vestibule is now an inner hall. Throssel was also responsible for the design and re-creation of the cupola crowning the roof. Tel: 01296 747444

Hellfire Club — The popular name for an exclusive club founded by Sir Francis Dashwood that met irregularly from 1746 to c.1763. The club had a reputation for holding orgiastic and satanic meetings at Medmenham Abbey (see separate entry). At the first gathering in May 1746, they met at the George and Vulture public house in Lombard Street, London; the 12 members are thought to have included Dashwood, Robert Vansittart, William Hogarth, Thomas Potter, Francis Duffield, Edward Thompson and Paul Whitehead. Though not a member, Benjamin Franklin occasionally attended meetings. Later members included John Wilkes and John Montagu, 4th Earl of Sandwich. They did not call themselves the Hellfire Club, but used a number of mockingly religious titles including the Brotherhood of St Francis of Wycombe, the Order of Knights of West Wycombe and the Monks of Medmenham. The members called each other brothers and referred to Dashwood as abbot; female guests were nuns. The club motto was *Fay ce que voudras* (Do what thou wilt) from François Rabelais, later used by Aleister Crowley. Although indulging in pseudo-Satanic rites the 'monks' were keener devotaries of Bacchus and Venus and it is likely that some of their more unseemly behaviour has been exaggerated over the years. The George and Vulture burned down in 1749 and Dashwood built a temple in the grounds of his West Wycombe home, while nearby 'catacombs' were excavated. The first meeting at Wycombe was held on Walpurgis Night (30 April), 1752. It was something of a failure and no large-scale meetings were held there again. Despite this and the factionalising of the club, Dashwood acquired the ruins of Medmenham Abbey in 1755, which was rebuilt by the architect Nicholas Revett in 18th century Gothic revival style. In 1762 political rivalries turned the affairs of the club into public clashes and under heavy pressure it finally disbanded.

Highest point — Haddington Hill in the Chilterns at 876ft (267m). (GR: SP890089.)

Hughenden Manor — $1\frac{1}{2}$ miles (2.5km) north of High Wycombe. Built in the late 18th century and remodelled with a red-brick Gothic exterior in 1862, Hughenden was the home of Victorian Prime Minister Benjamin Disraeli from 1847 until his death in 1881. Most of his furniture, books and pictures remain in this, his private retreat from the rigours of parliamentary life in London. There are beautiful walks through the surrounding park and woodland, and the garden is a recreation of the colourful design of Disraeli's wife, Mary Anne. The property is owned by the National Trust. Tel: 01494 755573.

Interesting facts — **Henry VIII** was responsible for making Aylesbury the county town in preference to Buckingham, doing so to curry favour with Thomas Boleyn so that he could marry his daughter Anne. In 1682 **William Penn**, whose family seat was at Penn, founded Bucks County, Pennsylvania with Quaker migrants from Buckinghamshire. In Bucks County are a Buckingham, Chalfont, Wycombe and Solebury (formerly spelt Soulbury), named after the places in Buckinghamshire. **Ashridge House** is now entirely in Hertfordshire, but before the boundary changes of 1991 the boundary between Hertfordshire and Buckinghamshire passed through the dining room. **London Wasps** are one of the most successful English rugby union sides in recent years, having won at least one of each of the major European competitions or knockout tournaments in the past decade. Founded in 1867 and previously playing at various London grounds, in 2002 the club began to play home matches at Adams Park, High Wycombe and immediately increased its gate by 31.8 per cent. **The Bernard Arms** public house in Risborough Road, Great Kimble, Aylesbury, has played host to many leading world statesmen including John Major, Boris Yeltsin, Harold Wilson, Dwight D Eisenhower, George Bush senior, Ronald Reagan and Francois Mitterand. Yeltsin famously met John Major at the pub, promptly ordered a bottle of vodka and apparently imbibed it without any ill effect.

Ivinghoe Beacon — 1 mile (1.6km) northeast of Ivinghoe, 10 miles (16km) east of Aylesbury. One of the highest points of the Chiltern escarpment at 817ft (249m). The entirety of the hilltop is encompassed by a late Bronze Age hill fort possibly dating to the 8th century BC. An excavation in the 1960s unearthed two fragments from Ewart Park swords (a type of leaf-shaped bronze sword dating to c.900 BC); in 2000 a complete Wilburton sword was discovered by chance in the north rampart, potentially dating to c.1150–950 BC. Ivinghoe Beacon stands at one end of the Ridgeway National Trail.

John Milton's Cottage — Deanway, Chalfont St Giles. The cottage was the property of the Fleetwood family (Lord of the Manor at the Vache) from the mid 17th century although the house is thought to have been built a century earlier. In 1665, when the Plague was taking its toll in London, Milton moved in July from his residence near Bunhill Fields with his third wife, Elizabeth Minshull, and their daughter Deborah (their other daughters were living elsewhere). It was here that Milton completed his long epic poem *Paradise Lost* (possibly started in 1642). Apart from the magnificent architecture, and a garden stocked with a number of the plants and herbs mentioned in Milton's poetry, the cottage walls are adorned by portraits of Milton by Sir Godfrey Kneller (painted posthumously in 1690), Cornelis Janssen (copy of Milton aged 10), and a copy of the Onslow portrait by Van der Gucht (1792). Rare first editions of Milton's works can be viewed along with items of historical significance such as the list of the Regicides (signatories to the death warrant of Charles I). The cottage has been a museum since 1887 and is currently managed by 11 trustees, including the National Trust and Buckinghamshire County Council. The visitor's book boasts the signature of Queen Elizabeth II on 14 July 1987 to commemorate 100 years of the Milton Cottage Trust. Tel: 01494 872313.

King's Head — Market Square, Aylesbury. An inn dating to 1455 and once a base for Oliver Cromwell. Its architectural features include a medieval stained glass window, extensive timber framing and an ancient cobbled courtyard. Tel: 01296 381501.

Long Crendon Courthouse — Long Crendon, 8 miles (13km) southwest of Aylesbury. The red hand-made tiles above the whitewashed walls of this 15th century, partly half-timbered two-storeyed building form a rich streak of colour. The exposed timber beams, early oak floorboards and steep wooden stairs leading directly from the street to the large room, open to the roof, are rare sights. Originally used as a wool store and, from the reign of Henry V to Victorian times, for sessions of the manorial courts. Tel: 01494 528051.

Medmenham Abbey — 3 miles (5km) northeast of Henley-on-Thames. A former Cistercian abbey founded in the village of Medmenham in the 12th century under the ownership of Woburn Abbey, though it was not officially recognised by royal charter until 1200. After the Dissolution of the Monasteries, the abbey was given in 1547 to the Moore family, and then sold privately to the Duffields. While in their possession it became infamous as the location of the Hellfire Club, formally called the Monks of Medmenham. In 1755, when Sir Francis Dashwood acquired the ruins of the ancient abbey from the Duffield family, he and John Montagu, 4th Earl of Sandwich attended a service at St Peter's church in Medmenham during which Sandwich let loose a small monkey. The regular devotees fled in horror, sure that Satan himself had invaded their place of worship.

Mentmore Towers — Mentmore, 6 miles (10km) northeast of Aylesbury. A large neo-Renaissance English country house with numerous towers and pinnacles, built 1852–5 for Baron Meyer Amschel de Rothschild, who commissioned Sir Joseph Paxton and his future son-in-law G H Stokes to design the house. Although Paxton was not a trained architect he was a great favourite of the Rothschild family, who were probably impressed by the Crystal Palace he built for the Great Exhibition of 1851 and his work at Chatsworth. At the end of the 19th century Mentmore Towers passed into the hands of Lord Rosebery. At that time the house contained a superb collection of fine furniture and works of art. Rosebery made the house a magnificent centre of social life for the rich and influential. In the 1970s the contents were auctioned, raising over £6 million despite a public outcry at the possible loss to the nation of many important items. The house was later sold to the Maharishi Mahesh Yogi and is now the headquarters of his University of Natural Law. It is not currently open to the public.

Milton Keynes — The town derives its name from one of the villages in the original designated area of the proposed new 'city' of Milton Keynes. Milton Keynes was designated as a New Town on 23 January 1967, but the corresponding area of Buckinghamshire has roots dating back before the Roman conquest of Britain (a major Roman villa, containing fine mosaic floors, has been excavated at Bancroft Park); Bronze Age barrows found in Newport Pagnell, Wolverton and Castlethorpe, and a roundhouse in Bluebridge are about 4500 years old. The first Saxon settlements in the area were at Pineland, Milton Keynes Village, Great Linford and Bancroft. These date from the 6th and 7th centuries, and a cemetery of this date was discovered at Newport Pagnell. By the 9th and 10th centuries the villages and parishes now encompassed in the new town were established. After the Norman Conquest, the Anglo-Saxon village known as *Mideltone* (middletown) in Domesday Book became known as Middleton Kaynes, the name of Kaynes being added by 1422 after the family name of the Norman lord of the manor, De Cahaignes. The oldest domestic building still standing in this area is 22 Milton Keynes, a 14th century manor house. In 1764 John Newton, a former slave ship captain, was made curate at Olney. Later influential in the abolition of slavery, he was a friend of poet William Cowper, who also settled in Olney. In the 19th century, although the Grand Junction Canal had already been opened and the network expanded over the Great Ouse with the Iron Trunk Aquaduct in 1811, the railways had also begun to snake through industrial Britain. As Wolverton was a central point on the London–Birmingham line it became a pivotal station for servicing both trains and passengers. Today Milton Keynes contains within its boundaries the towns of Bletchley, Wolverton and Stony Stratford and the villages of New Bradwell, Shenley, Loughton, Woughton, Broughton and Milton Keynes Village (which has now reverted to its former name of Middleton to distinguish it from the town). The long-term plan is for the town to be given city status as it is the fastest-growing development area in the UK. Bow Brickhill Heath (GR: SP915344) at 561ft (171m) is the highest point in Milton Keynes.

Motto *Vestigia Nulla Retrorsum* (Latin, 'no stepping back').

Nether Winchendon House 5 miles (8km) west of Aylesbury. A medieval and Tudor manor house altered in the late 18th century in the Strawberry Hill Gothick style. It has a fine 16th century frieze, ceiling and original linenfold panelling, and contains fine furniture and family portraits. In continuous family occupation since the mid 16th century, and the former home of the last British Governor of Massachusetts Bay, it is presently owned by Robert Spencer Bernard. Tel: 01844 290199.

Olney Pancake Race The race first took place in the village of Olney, 8 miles (13km) northeast of Milton Keynes, in 1445. It was run on Shrove Tuesday, the day before Lent, the whole day being given over to celebration before the austerity of Lent. The race continued through the centuries, albeit with lapses from time to time. After one such lapse during World War II, it was revived in 1948 by the then vicar of Olney, the Rev. Canon Ronald Collins. The race immediately caught the popular imagination and in 1950 became an international event. A challenge was received from the town of Liberal in Kansas, USA, whose people had seen press photographs of the race at Olney and conceived the idea of starting a similar custom. Olney accepted the challenge and the two towns now compete annually. The race is run on a timed basis and the winner declared after times are compared through a transatlantic telephone call from Liberal to Olney. The race in Olney is now run from the Market Place to a point midway down Church Lane, a distance of 415yds (379m). Warning bells are rung from the church steeple and the race is started by the churchwarden at 11.55 am, using the large bronze 'Pancake Bell' normally on display in the museum. Those qualified to take part must be women of 18 years of age or over who have either lived in the town of Olney for at least three months immediately prior to the event or, if living away, have their permanent home in the town. They must wear the traditional costume of the housewife, including a skirt, apron and head covering, though they need not be married. At the start the starter will order competitors: 'Toss your pancakes – Are you ready?' and then give the starting signal. At the finish the winner is required to toss her pancake before being declared the winner and being greeted with the Kiss of Peace, the words 'The peace of the Lord be always with you' spoken by the vicar, and the traditional prize of a kiss from the verger. All who finish the course are expected to attend the Shriving Service, during which official Olney and Liberal prizes are presented. Olney have monopolised the race in recent years due to the exertions of Andrea Rawlings, who won her third successive title in 2006 in an excellent time of 63.76 seconds. The 2008 race was won by 42-year-old mum Andrea Brear in a time of 69 seconds.

Open University Walton Hall, Milton Keynes. Introduced in 1969 by Harold Wilson's Labour government, the Open University gave the opportunity to anyone to gain a degree, irrespective of formal academic qualifications. Tuition is by correspondence and, until 15 December 2006, by television and radio broadcasts although there is also a system of study centres where extra tuition is available. The university was opened by Earl Mountbatten of Burma on 1 September 1970 and has more registered students than any other British university. Tel: 01908 274066.

Pinewood Studios Built by J Arthur Rank and Charles Boot on the estate of Heatherden Hall, Iver, and opened in 1936. The first film wholly completed was *Talk of the Devil* (1936). Other pre-World War II films include *Young and Innocent* (1937) and *Pygmalion* (1938). The studios were closed 1940–6. Immediate post-war films made at Pinewood include *Great Expectations* (1946), *Oliver Twist* (1948), *The Red Shoes* (1948) and *Kind Hearts and Coronets* (1949). Rank closed its Islington and Denham (see separate entry) studios in 1949 and concentrated production at Pinewood, after which a series of first-class British films was made, including *The Browning Version* (1951), *The Importance of Being Earnest* (1952) and *Genevieve* (1953). The 1950s also saw *Reach for the Sky* (1956), *The Prince and the Showgirl* (1957) and *Carve her Name with Pride* (1958) and an abortive attempt at *Cleopatra* (1963) was made before the production was transferred to Italy. During the next few years, in addition to popular TV series such as *The Avengers* and *The Persuaders*, films such as *Sleuth* (1972) and *Frenzy* (1972) were made at Pinewood. Films made since 1980 include *Aliens* (1986), *Memphis Belle* (1990), *The Secret Garden* (1993), *Interview with a Vampire* (1994), *First Knight* (1995), *The Fifth Element* (1997), *Tomb Raider* (2000), *The Hours* (2002) and *Charlie and the Chocolate Factory* (2005). The Doctor, Carry On, James Bond and Superman franchises were all based at Pinewood. The studios were bought from Rank by a management team in 2000. Pinewood Studios acquired Shepperton Studios in 2001 and Teddington Studios was added in 2005.

Pitstone Windmill Ivinghoe, 6 miles (10km) east of Aylesbury. The National Trust property is one of the oldest post mills in Britain. Tel: 01494 528051.

Princes Risborough Manor House Princes Risborough, 6 miles (10km) south of Aylesbury. This 17th century red-brick house with Jacobean staircase and many original features was once owned by Sir Peter Lely, court painter to Charles II. Tel: 01494 528051.

Rivers

The **Chess** rises from springs in the Vale of Chesham and in Pednor before flowing southeasterly past Waterside and towards Latimer. From there it flows to the north of Chenies and on towards Rickmansworth, after which it becomes a tributary of the River Colne. It is only navigable at its lower reaches. The river's name is reflected in Chesham's traditional pronunciation as 'Chess-um'.

The **Gade** rises from a spring in the chalk of the Chilterns at Dagnall and flows into the Grand Union Canal at Two Waters in Apsley, where it is joined by the River Bulbourne.

The **Ouzel** (formerly called the **Lovat**) is a tributary of the River Great Ouse. It rises in the Chiltern Hills and flows for 20 miles (32km) north to join the Ouse at Newport Pagnell. From springs just north of Dagnall, the river initially forms the boundary between Bedfordshire and Buckinghamshire. It is joined by the Ouzel Brook from Houghton Regis, by Whistle Brook from Ivinghoe, and by Clipstone Brook from Milton Bryan. It then flows through Leighton Buzzard, Milton Keynes and Newport Pagnell to its junction with the Great Ouse. The river is still known by its ancient name near Newport Pagnell.

The **Thame** rises as several small streams close to the village of Watermead in the Vale of Aylesbury, on the north side of the Chiltern Hills. After leaving Watermead, the river flows through farmland, passing the small villages of Nether Winchendon and Chearsley before reaching the market town of Thame with which it shares its name. From Thame, the river flows southward and after passing the villages of Great Milton and Stadhampton, its valley widens out. It then reaches the small town of Dorchester in Oxfordshire, 1 mile (1.6km) south of which it meets the Thames. The general course of the Thame is northeast–southwest and the distance from its source to the Thames about 40 miles (65km).

The **Wye** rises in the Chiltern Hills and flows through High Wycombe on its way down to Bourne End, where it meets the Thames. Through part of High Wycombe, partly named after the river, it now runs completely underground.

See also **River Great Ouse** in Bedfordshire, **Jubilee River** in Berkshire and **River Thames** in London.

Roald Dahl Children's Gallery

Church Street, Aylesbury. Opened in 1996 in a building that was previously a coach-house, this children's museum uses characters and themes from the books of Roald Dahl (1916–90) to stimulate children's interest in science, history and literature. The Dahl theme is further emphasised by the use of Quentin Blake to provide the graphical elements of the museum. Blake, a celebrated children's author and illustrator, is strongly associated with Dahl through his covers and illustrations for almost all modern UK editions of Dahl's books.

Roald Dahl Museum and Story Centre

High Street, Great Missenden, 7 miles (11km) north of High Wycombe. The home of the great children's writer and short story writer for many years until his death in 1990 was officially opened as a museum on 10 June 2005 by Cherie Blair. It is housed in an old coaching inn and yard. Tel: 01494 892192.

Shardeloes

1 mile (1.6km) northwest of Amersham. A large 18th century country house originally built 1758–66 for William Drake, MP for Amersham. The original architect was Stiff Leadbetter, but the design was altered and completed by Robert Adam. Built in Palladian style of brick covered stucco, it was constructed with the piano nobile (main storey) on the ground floor and a mezzanine above. The library was designed by James Wyatt in classical style and has painted panels by the fresco painter Biagio Rebecca. Humphry Repton laid out the grounds in classical English landscape style, in the lee of the hill on which the mansion stands, damming the River Misbourne to form a lake. The mansion remained the ancestral home of the Tyrwhitt Drake family until World War II when the house was requisitioned. Shardeloes today is a complex of private apartments and flats; the principal reception rooms are preserved as common rooms for the residents.

Sport

football

MK Dons, formerly Wimbledon FC, relocated to the National Hockey Stadium, Milton Keynes, in September 2003, and changed its name to MK Dons in June 2004. The controversial move, masterminded by music entrepreneur Pete Winkelman, has inevitably lost the south London fan base. Tel: 01908 607090.

Wycombe Wanderers were founded in 1887 and joined the Football League in 1993. The Chairboys (aka The Blues) play in light blue and dark blue quarters. Their home ground is Adams Park, Hillbottom Road, High Wycombe. Tel: 01494 472100.

ice hockey

Milton Keynes Lightning are the most successful professional sports team in Milton Keynes. In their first year they were runners-up in the English Premier League and play-off champions in the 2002–03 season. Lightning were League champions and play-off champions in 2003–04. In 2004–05 they did the double again, retaining both titles. MK Lightning play their games at the Planet Ice Arena in Milton Keynes. Tel: 01908 696696.

Milton Keynes Falcons Ladies Ice Hockey Club was formed in February 1999 and has had international players from its ranks. They were the Divisional One South runners-up in 2002–03.

motor racing

See Northamptonshire for Silverstone motor racing circuit

Stowe House

2 miles (3km) northwest of Buckingham. Originally constructed in the late 17th century but extensively rebuilt in the early 18th by Sir John Vanbrugh, James Gibbs and William Kent, the house is set within the dramatic Stowe Landscape Gardens (see separate entry). Vanbrugh added the East Wing (now Cobham House) and the West Wing (now Nugent House). His work was completed 1719–26 and Gibbs made further additions over the succeeding 20 years, while the North Hall and South Portico were the work of William Kent, 1731–9. The house, the site of Stowe School (see separate entry) since 1923, is in the charge of the Stowe House Preservation Trust. Tel: 01280 818280/2.

Stowe Landscape Gardens and Park

Europe's most influential landscape garden. Hidden among spectacular vistas and vast open spaces are magical secret corners, hidden meanings, and over 40 monuments and temples.

Laid out by Charles Bridgeman (d. 1738), the gardens were maintained by Capability Brown, head gardener 1741–50. Of the various monuments Sir John Vanbrugh was responsible for the Orangery, Nelson's Seat, the Temple of Bacchus, the Rotondo, the Egyptian Pyramid, Dido's Cave, Coucher's Obelisk, the Sleeping Parlour, the Doric Arch and Lake Pavilions. James Gibbs added Gibbs' Building (now the Fane of Pastoral Poetry), the Boycott Pavilions, the Temple of Friendship, the Gothic Temple, the Queen's Temple, the Imperial Closet, Lord Cobham's Pillar and the Keeper's House. William Kent constructed the Kent Arches, the Oxford Gateway, the Temple of Venus, the Hermitage, the Artificial Ruins, the Cold Bath, Temple of British Worthies, the Pebble Alcove, Stowe Castle, the Grotto, the Temple of Contemplation, the Shell Bridge, the Stone Bridge, the Congreve Monument and the Temple of Ancient Virtue. The gardens are surrounded by 750 acres (300ha) of historic parkland, including a restored 250 acre (100 ha) deer park. The gardens are owned by the National Trust. Tel: 01280 822850.

Stowe School
Stowe House (see separate entry), 2 miles (3km) northwest of Buckingham. Co-educational public school founded in 1923, its first headmaster being J F Roxburgh. The first architect was Sir Clough Williams-Ellis, builder of Portmeirion, who was responsible for the first phase of classrooms and boarding accommodation within the Stowe House building. Famous Old Stoics include David Niven, Sir Richard Branson, Lord Cheshire and Michael Ventris (the decipherer of Linear B).

Taplow Court
Taplow, 2 miles (3km) east of Maidenhead. Taplow Court was once the home of Lord and Lady Desborough and has been beautifully restored. It is now the headquarters of SGI UK, a lay Buddhist organisation. There is an Anglo-Saxon burial mound and hill fort on the site. Tel: 01628 591209.

Tiggywinkles
Haddenham, 5 miles (8km) southwest of Aylesbury. Tiggywinkles Wildlife Hospital Trust is Britain's only wildlife veterinary teaching hospital. Although the hospital itself is not open to the public, visitors can view the care and veterinary treatment given to animals via CCTV and video displays. Tel: 01844 292292.

University of Buckingham
Hunter Street, Buckingham. The UK's only private university, founded in 1973 as the University College of Buckingham and receiving its royal charter in 1983. It is also the smallest university in the UK with around 800 students, 65 per cent from overseas, and is a pioneer in offering two-year honours degree programmes. Tel: 01280 814080.

Waddesdon Manor
5 miles (8km) northwest of Aylesbury. Built for Baron Ferdinand de Rothschild by his French architect Destailleur and landscape gardener Lainé between 1874 and 1889, the manor house holds one of the finest collections of French 18th century decorative arts in the world. The furniture, Savonnerie carpets and Sèvres porcelain rank in importance with those in the Metropolitan Museum in New York and the Louvre in Paris. There is also a collection of portraits by Gainsborough (including the magnificent 'Pink Boy') and Reynolds, and works by Dutch and Flemish Masters of the 17th century. The style of a 16th century chateau is complemented by one of the finest Victorian gardens in Britain, renowned for its Rococo-style aviary, colourful parterre, winding shady walks, colourful trees, fountains, statues and panoramic views. Now owned by the National Trust. Tel: 01296 653211.

West Wycombe Park
2 miles (3km) west of High Wycombe. A rococo garden created in the mid 18th century by Sir Francis Dashwood, founder of the Dilettanti Society and the Hellfire Club (see separate entry). The house is among the most theatrical and Italianate in England, its façades formed as classical temples. The interior has Palmyrene ceilings and decoration, with pictures, furniture and sculpture dating from the time of Sir Francis. Now owned by the National Trust. Tel: 01494 513569.

Winslow Hall
Winslow, 8 miles (13km) north of Aylesbury. Built in 1700 at the behest of William Lowndes, the designer is not known for certain but the hall is attributed to Sir Christopher Wren. The gardens to the rear have been improved by the present owner, who has a passion for specimen trees and shrubs. The North Garden, facing the main road from Whitchurch to Buckingham, is close to the road and clearly visible. Something very rare in an English country house (one other instance is Aynhoe Park in Oxfordshire), this makes Winslow Hall almost unique in being both a town and a country house.

Wotton House
Wotton Underwood, 8 miles (13km) northwest of Aylesbury. Wotton House was completed in 1714 by Richard Grenville (1646–1719), a statement of the growing wealth and ambitions of the Grenvilles. While the design owes much to John Sheffield's Buckingham House in London, built about the same time, the designer of Wotton is unknown. The pleasure grounds were designed by Capability Brown. A series of man-made features on the 3 mile (5km) circuit includes bridges, statues and follies. Tel: 01844 238363.

Wycombe Abbey
Abbey Way, High Wycombe, An independent boarding school for girls aged 11–18, founded by Dame Frances Dove in 1896 and academically one of the top girls' schools in the UK.

Wycombe Museum
Priory Avenue, High Wycombe. The museum is set in historic Castle Hill House surrounded by its peaceful gardens. Permanent exhibits, videos and sound recordings tell the story of Wycombe, Marlow, Princes Risborough and their villages, while special exhibitions offers a changing programme of displays about local history, furniture, art and science. Tel: 01494 421895.

Some famous people born in Buckinghamshire

Apted, Michael (director) (1941–)	Aylesbury
Austin, Herbert (automobile designer) (1866–1941)	Little Missenden
De Havilland, Geoffrey (aviation pioneer) (1882–1965)	High Wycombe
Finnegan, Chris (boxer) (1944–)	Iver
Grech, Martin (musician) (1983–)	Aylesbury
Hanley, Jenny (actress) (1947–)	Gerrards Cross
Liberty, Arthur Lasenby (merchant) (1843–1917)	Chesham
More, Kenneth (actor) (1914–82)	Gerrards Cross
Murray, Al (comedian) (1968–)	Stewkley
Nicholson, Ben (painter) (1894–1982)	Denham
O'Brian, Patrick (novelist) (1914–2000)	Chalfont St. Peter
Otway, John (cult rock star) (1952–)	Aylesbury
Pratchett, Terry (science fiction writer) (1948–)	Beaconsfield
Redgrave, (Sir) Stephen (Olympic rower) (1962–)	Marlow
Rice, (Sir) Tim (lyricist) (1944–)	Amersham
Roger of Wendover (chronicler) (d.1236)	Wendover
Scott, George Gilbert (architect) (1811–78)	Gawcott
Standage, Simon (violinist) (1941–)	High Wycombe
York, Michael (actor) (1942–)	Fulmer

CAMBRIDGESHIRE

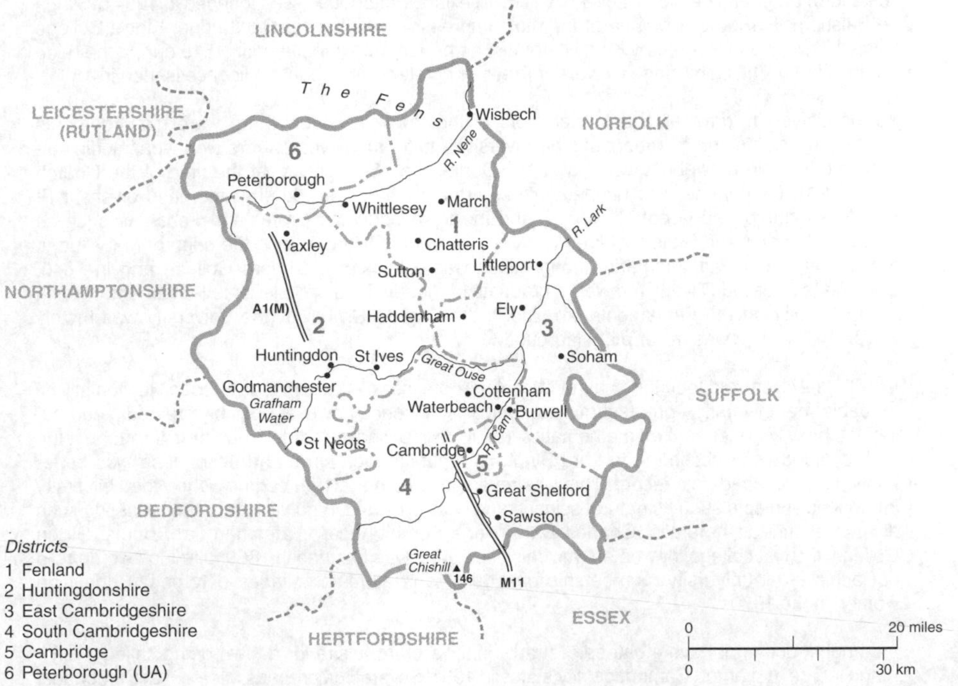

LINCOLNSHIRE
The Fens
LEICESTERSHIRE
(RUTLAND)
Wisbech
NORFOLK
6
R. Nene
Peterborough
Whittlesey
March
1
R. Lark
Yaxley
Chatteris
Sutton
Littleport
NORTHAMPTONSHIRE
A1(M)
Haddenham
Ely
2
3
Huntingdon
St Ives
Great Ouse
Soham
Godmanchester
Grafham Water
Cottenham
SUFFOLK
Waterbeach
Burwell
St Neots
R. Cam
Cambridge
5
4
Great Shelford
BEDFORDSHIRE
Sawston
Districts
1 Fenland
2 Huntingdonshire
3 East Cambridgeshire
4 South Cambridgeshire
5 Cambridge
6 Peterborough (UA)
Great Chishill
146
M11
ESSEX
HERTFORDSHIRE
0
20 miles
0
30 km

Cambridgeshire borders Lincolnshire to the north, Norfolk to the northeast, Suffolk to the east, Essex and Hertfordshire to the south, Bedfordshire to the southwest and Northamptonshire to the west. Its five districts are currently Cambridge, East Cambridgeshire, Fenland, Huntingdonshire and South Cambridgeshire. The northwestern tip of Peterborough barely meets with Rutland at the A1 interchange between Lincolnshire and Northamptonshire. **Huntingdonshire** was formerly in the diocese of Lincoln, but in 1837 was transferred to Ely. In 1889, under the Local Government Act 1888, it was created an administrative county, the third smallest in England. In 1965 it was abolished and its area merged with that of the Soke of Peterborough to form Huntingdon and Peterborough. In 1974, under the Local Government Act 1972, the administrative county was abolished and its area became part of the non-metropolitan county of Cambridgeshire as Huntingdon district. The district was renamed Huntingdonshire on 1 October 1984. The present district does not match the traditional county boundaries exactly – Fletton has been annexed to the City of Peterborough, Everton has been annexed to Bedfordshire and Swineshead is also currently administered by Bedfordshire council. It gained Eaton Ford and Eaton Socon from Bedfordshire, as part of the town of St Neots.

The history of **Cambridge** began in the first century BC, when an Iron Age tribe established a settlement on Castle Hill. A ford was built at the foot of the hill to cross the River Cam, originally known as Granta; the river upstream of Silver Street Bridge (flowing through Grantchester) still retains its old name. Later the Romans took over this site, which was an important crossing point marking the meeting place of various Roman roads, in particular the Via Devana which linked Colchester to Chester. The Normans built a castle here as a base for fighting the Saxon rebel, Hereward the Wake. The mound of William the Conqueror's castle, from where on a clear day the lantern tower of Ely Cathedral can be seen, still exists. With an 11th-century population of some 1600, Cambridge was one of eastern England's largest towns. Growth continued into the 13th century. In 1207, King John gave Cambridge its first royal charter; a merchant's guild was established, and regular fairs were held on Midsummer Common. Many goods were transported by boat, and Cambridge's wharf trade boomed.

Though already an important market town, simultaneous developments were about to change the city's destiny for ever. In the early 13th century, riots in Oxford – and later Paris – caused many of these cities' scholars to flee, fearing for their lives. Many headed to Cambridge and would gather in groups for lessons in grammar, rhetoric and logic, all taught in Latin. The education lacked formality or ceremony, but this indiscipline soon prompted teachers and townspeople to impose some form of order. The oldest college which still exists, Peterhouse, was founded in 1284 by Hugh de Balsham, Bishop of Ely. One of the most impressive buildings in Cambridge, King's College Chapel, was begun in 1446 by King Henry VI. The project was completed in 1515 during the reign of King Henry VIII. Cambridge University Press originated with a printing licence issued in 1534.

As the University grew and took over more of the town, inevitably there were disagreements between residents and members of the University and for many years there were spasmodic outbreaks of trouble between 'town and gown'. During the 16th century, at the time of the Church reformation, Cambridge was dubbed 'Little Germany' after the Lutheran sermons given at St Edward's Church and Great St Mary's, and the town educated Protestant preachers such as Cranmer, Latimer and Ridley; all later became martyrs in Oxford, during the reign of Mary Tudor. In 1624, staunch Parliamentarian John Milton was admitted to Christ's College and in 1640, Cambridge returned Oliver Cromwell, a graduate of Sidney Sussex College, to Parliament. Though predominantly on the Parliamentarian side in the English Civil War (the university was mainly Royalist), the town was never a battleground.

In 1667 a 27-year-old took the chair of Lucasian Professor of Mathematics – Isaac Newton still is, arguably, the university's greatest mind to date. His influence however possibly created a curriculum too heavily dependent on mathematics, resulting in dwindling student numbers throughout the 18th century when according to Lord Byron its reputation for 'din and drunkenness' was better known than its academic record. This was reversed only in the 19th century when the University introduced subjects such as natural science and history to its curriculum, thereafter boasting such diverse alumni as naturalist Charles Darwin and South African statesman Jan Smuts. Girton College, the first college for women (mixed since 1977), was founded in 1869, although women did not achieve full university membership until 1947, and all-male colleges only began admitting women in the 1970s.

Although it does not have a cathedral (traditionally a prerequisite for a town being called a city), King George VI granted Cambridge city status in 1951. Several major roads intersect at Cambridge. The M11 motorway from east London terminates here. The A14 (formerly A604) east–west trunk route, a major freight route connecting the port of Felixstowe on the east coast with the Midlands, North Wales, the west coast and Ireland, skirts the northern edge of the city. The A10, a former Roman road from north London, passes round the city on its way to Ely and King's Lynn. Other roads connect the city with Bedford, St Neots, Newmarket and Colchester.

On 1 April 1998 **Peterborough** became a unitary local authority. As such it is no longer administered by the county although it remains a geographical location within Cambridgeshire. Peterborough is a cathedral city situated on the River Nene, which flows into the North Sea approximately 30 miles (48km) to the northeast. The local topography is notoriously flat and low-lying, and in some places lies below sea level. The area known as the Fens lies to the east of Peterborough. Although there are low marshy areas of land throughout East Anglia, Dutch engineer Cornelius Vermuyden (1590–1677) reclaimed much of the land in the mid 17th century, and later modern drainage techniques have created a vast array of waterways no longer impinging on the surrounding land. Most of the remaining Cambridgeshire fenland is now within a 20 mile (32km) radius of the town of March. One such area is Wicken Fen, 10 miles (16km) northeast of Cambridge, a protected environment that was the very first National Nature Reserve in England.

Cambridgeshire	**Population**			**Area**	
Districts	*male*	*female*	*total*	*sq miles*	*sq km*
Cambridge	54,316	54,547	108,863	16	41
East Cambridgeshire	36,186	37,028	73,214	251	651
Fenland	40,698	42,821	83,519	211	546
Huntingdonshire	77,991	78,963	156,954	350	906
South Cambridgeshire	64,454	65,654	130,108	348	902
Peterborough Unitary Authority	76,010	80,051	156,061	132	343
Total	349,655	359,064	708,719	1308	3389

Local Attractions and Information

Addenbrooke's Hospital	Trumpington Street, Cambridge. Founded by a bequest of John Addenbrooke MD of St Catharine's College, and first opened at Michaelmas, 1766, the building consists of a long pedimented central block with advanced wings, united in front by an open colonnade with balustrading. The hospital is a national and regional centre for cancer services, liver transplants, organ transplantation, neurosciences and genetics. With around 1100 beds, it employs more than 6500 staff.
Administrative headquarters	**Cambridgeshire**: Shire Hall, County Hill, Cambridge CB3 0AP. Tel: 01223 717111. **Peterborough**: Town Hall, Bridge Street PE1 1QT. Tel: 01733 747474.
Airports	**Cambridge City Airport** is a regional airport with a business focus 3 miles (5km) from Cambridge University and city centre, and only 14 miles (23km) from Newmarket, the home of English horse racing. The airport provides access to the north, east and City of London as well as fast-growing businesses in East Anglia, it has excellent public transport connections and is close to the M11, A14 and the M25 motorway network. The airport is owned and operated by Cambridge-based company Marshall Aerospace. Tel: 01223 373765. Peterborough has two local runways – **Peterborough (Conington) Airport** and **Sibson Aerodrome**. The former US Air Force base at Conington is situated south of the city and has a properly surfaced runway, while Sibson (west of the city centre) remains grassed. Flights operate on a PPR (Prior Permission Required) basis with no scheduled flights operating out of either airport.
American Cemetery	Madingley, 3 miles (5km) west of Cambridge. Set on a beautifully landscaped hillside, the cemetery commemorates American servicemen and women who died during World War II. The 3812 headstones are arranged like spokes of a wheel radiating from the flagpole, with Stars of David for those of Jewish faith, and Latin crosses for all others.
Anglesey Abbey	Lode, 6 miles (10km) northeast of Cambridge. A Jacobean country house dating from 1600, built on the site of an Augustinian priory and surrounded by 98 acres (40ha) of landscaped and wildlife gardens. The house contains Lord Fairhaven's collection of rare works of art, sumptuous furnishings and spectacular statuary. There is also a working 18th century water mill. Tel: 01223 810080.
Backs, The	Behind eight of the colleges of the University of Cambridge, along the River Cam, are the Backs (so called because they are the backs of the colleges). From north to south the colleges are Magdalene, St John's, Trinity, Trinity Hall, Clare, King's, Queens' and Darwin. Because each college owns a part of the 25 acres (10ha) of landscaped grounds, it is not possible to walk along the river by the Backs, but access can be gained through the colleges. Laid out from the medieval period onwards, they were landscaped in the 18th and early 19th centuries. The Backs provide superb views of King's College Chapel (King's College), the Wren Library (Trinity College) and New Court (St John's College), plus the Mathematical Bridge (Queens' College) and the Bridge of Sighs (St John's College). On the western bank of the river are flower gardens, clipped lawns and meadows. Water voles, ducks and moorhens inhabit the ditches. The Backs were listed in 1995 as a Grade I historic park.
Bridges, Cambridge	From south to north the bridges over the Cam are: footbridge, Coe Fen; Fen Causeway Bridge; Crusoe Bridge; Silver Street Bridge; Mathematical Bridge, Queens' College; Kings College Bridge; Clare College Bridge; Garret Hostel Bridge; Kitchen Bridge, St John's College; Bridge of Sighs, St John's College; Magdalene Bridge; footbridge over the weir, Jesus Green; Victoria Avenue Bridge; footbridge, Midsummer Common (aka the Fort St George footbridge); Cutter Ferry Bridge; Elizabeth Way Bridge; footbridge, Stourbridge Common; railway bridge (at East Chesterton); A14 bridge; footbridge over the weir, Baits Bite Lock. The two most famous bridges are the **Bridge of Sighs** and the **Mathematical Bridge**. The former, designed by Henry Hutchison in 1831, is based on a similarly named bridge in Venice, so called because it led to the gallows. The Mathematical Bridge was built in 1749 by James Essex the Younger (1722–84) to the design of William Etheridge (1709–76). It has subsequently been rebuilt to the same design in 1866 and 1905. The wooden structure joins the President's Lodge (c.1460, the oldest building on the river at Cambridge) to Cripps Court (1974). The bridge is so named because it was supposedly built without fixings and held together purely through the mathematical precision of its design; in fact metal pins were used in the original structure, while the joints of the present bridge are fastened by nuts and bolts.
Buckden Towers	4 miles (6km) southwest of Huntingdon. Parts of the estate are over 900 years old; the tall brick tower was added in 1475, protected by walls and a moat, and surrounded by an outer bailey. Formerly used as a palace by the Bishops of Lincoln, it is possibly most infamous for being one of the 'prisons' of Catherine of Aragon until she was moved to Kimbolton Castle (see separate entry). Tel: 01480 810344.
Bumps Races	A series of races between colleges of the University of Cambridge which take place on the River Cam several times a year. The two most famous and structured races are the Lent Bumps (held in February and occasionally March) and the May Bumps (always held in June!). The rowing eights line up about a length and a half apart and attempt to catch (bump) the boat in front before they themselves are bumped by the boat behind. The races are held over four days and a crew which bumps swaps places in the following day's racing with the crew that it bumped. Raced in divisions, if a crew finishes at the top of a division it usually rows at the bottom of the next division the next day and is referred to as the sandwich boat. If a boat fails to bump or be bumped then it is said to have 'rowed over' and maintains its position for the next day. The winner of Division 1 after the four days is called the Head of the River. In recent years Caius College have dominated the men's first division.

Cambridge Apostles A debating society founded at Cambridge in 1820 by George Tomlinson, a Cambridge student who went on to become the first Bishop of Gibraltar. The society, also known as the Cambridge Conversazione Society, was remarkable for the talent of its undergraduate members and for the success they attained. Members included Arthur Henry Hallam, John Kemble, Frederick Denison Maurice, Monckton Milnes, James Spedding, Alfred Lord Tennyson and Richard Chenevix Trench. Its name derived from the number of its original membership. See also Cambridge Spies.

Cambridge Castle Castle Street, Cambridge. An altered Norman stone motte and bailey fortress, with the remains of Civil War bastions and ramparts. Founded by William I in 1068 and rebuilt 1284–98, it was slighted in 1647. By the 19th century, this important royal Edwardian castle had been used more as a court and a prison than a residence. Sadly the curtain wall flanked by towers, the large twin-towered gatehouse and the great tower on the motte have all been removed, to be used in the college buildings. The 20th century Shire Hall now stands in the levelled inner bailey and the position of the outer bailey has been lost.

Cambridge Folk Festival One of the longest running and most famous folk festivals in the world, held outdoors within 36 acres (14.5ha) of parkland at Cherry Hinton Hall on the last weekend in July. Inaugurated in 1965, the festival is renowned for its eclectic mix of music and a wide definition of what might be considered folk, together with its unique, intimate atmosphere.

Cambridge Mafia A term given to the political kinship of Sir Norman Fowler, Michael Howard, John Gummer, Kenneth Clarke, Sir Leon Brittan, Peter Lilley and Norman Lamont, who were at Cambridge together in the early 1960s.

Cambridge Platonists A group of philosophers at Cambridge University between 1633 and 1688 who argued that religion and reason are always in harmony, and reality is comprised not of sensation, but of 'intelligible forms' that exist behind perception. Believing that reason is the proper judge of all disagreements, they advocated dialogue between Puritans and High Churchmen. Holding that God was the source of reason, which was therefore a means of nearing God, they believed that reason could therefore enable both assessment of the private revelations of Puritan theology and the proper investigation of the rituals and liturgy of the established Church. For this reason, they were called latitudinarians. Their members included Ralph Cudworth (1617–88), Nathaniel Culverwel (1619–51), Henry More (1614–87), John Smith (1618–52) and Benjamin Whichcote (1609–83).

Cambridge Spies In 1951, Guy Burgess (cryptonym: Hicks) and fellow diplomat Donald Maclean defected to the Soviet Union and were subsequently proven to be KGB spies after investigation by British Intelligence. It became apparent that they had acted as a result of a tip-off by a senior Intelligence officer, Kim Philby (cryptonym: Stanley). Named in the press as chief suspect for 'the Third Man' in 1955, Philby called a press conference to deny it. Nevertheless, he left the secret service and began working as a journalist in the Middle East. In 1961, KGB defector Anatoli Golitsin provided information which seemed to point to Philby. An MI5 agent was sent to interview Philby in Beirut, and reported that Philby knew he was coming (indicating the presence of yet another mole) but freely confessed. In 1963, fearing he might be abducted in Lebanon, Philby himself defected to the Soviet Union. In 1979 Anthony Blunt (cryptonym: Johnson), Surveyor of the Queen's Pictures (he and Burgess were homosexual), was publicly accused of being a Soviet agent by investigative journalist Andrew Boyle in his book *Climate of Treason*. In November 1979 Prime Minister Margaret Thatcher admitted to the House of Commons that Blunt had confessed to being a Soviet spy in 1964. The four had been at Cambridge together in the 1930s, Blunt a Fellow at Trinity while the others were undergraduates at the same college. All were also members of the 'Cambridge Apostles', a secret, elite debating society formed in 1820 and based around Trinity and King's College. Another Apostle, Victor Rothschild, is suspected by many of being the so-called Fifth Man (Golitsin named Philby, Maclean and Burgess as part of a 'Ring of Five' whose other two agents he did not know), who has never been formally identified. Michael Whitney Straight was also a Soviet spy and Cambridge Apostle.

Cambridge University Of the 31 colleges in Cambridge, three are for women (New Hall, Newnham and Lucy Cavendish) and two admit only graduates (Clare Hall and Darwin). The remainder house and teach all students enrolled in courses of study or research at the University. Each college is an independent institution with its own property and income, appointing its own staff and responsible for selecting students, in accordance with University regulations. The college is the place where students live, eat and socialise. It is also where they receive small group teaching sessions, known as supervisions. The supervision system is one of the main reasons for the university's success in external reviews of learning and teaching. Within each college, staff and students of all disciplines are brought together, a cross-fertilisation which encourages the free exchange of ideas. Trinity and St John's have also established science parks, making a significant contribution to Cambridge's status as a centre of innovation and technology. The colleges and founding dates are: **Christ's** (1505), St Andrew's Street. Tel: 01223 334900; **Churchill** (1960), Storey's Way. Tel: 01223 336000; **Clare** (1326), Trinity Lane. Tel: 01223 333200; **Clare Hall** (1966), Herschel Road. Tel: 01223 332360; **Corpus Christi** (1352), Trumpington Street. Tel: 01223 338000; **Darwin** (1964), Silver Street. Tel: 01223 335660; **Downing** (1800), Regent Street. Tel: 01223 334800; **Emmanuel** (1584), St Andrew's Street. Tel: 01223 334200; **Fitzwilliam** (1966), Huntingdon Road. Tel: 01223 332000; **Girton** (1869), Huntingdon Road. Tel: 01223 338999; **Gonville & Caius** (1348), Trinity Street. Tel: 01223 332400; **Homerton** (1824), Hills Road. Tel: 01223 507111; **Hughes Hall** (1885), Mortimer Road. Tel: 01223 334898; **Jesus** (1496), Jesus Lane. Tel: 01223 339339; **King's** (1441), King's Parade. Tel: 01223 331100; **Lucy Cavendish** (1965), Lady Margaret Road. Tel: 01223 332190; **Magdalene** (1542), Magdalene Street. Tel: 01223 332100; **New Hall** (1954), Huntingdon Road. Tel: 01223 762100; **Newnham** (1871), Sidgwick Avenue. Tel: 01223 335700; **Pembroke**

(1347), Trumpington Street. Tel: 01223 338100; **Peterhouse** (1284), Trumpington Street. Tel: 01223 338200; **Queens'** (1448), Silver Street. Tel: 01223 335511; **Robinson** (1977), Grange Road. Tel: 01223 339100; **St Catharine's** (1473), Trumpington Street. Tel: 01223 338300; **St Edmund's** (1896), Mount Pleasant. Tel: 01223 336250; **St John's** (1511), St John's Street. Tel: 01223 338600; **Selwyn** (1882), Grange Road. Tel: 01223 335846; **Sidney Sussex** (1596), Sidney Street. Tel: 01223 338800; **Trinity** (1546), Trinity Street. Tel: 01223 338400; **Trinity Hall** (1350), Trinity Lane. Tel: 01223 332500; **Wolfson** (1965), Barton Road. Tel: 01223 335900.

The Latin name for Cambridge is *Cantabrigia*, which is why Cambridge degrees are abbreviated Cantab. The University used to have a seat in the House of Commons, Sir Isaac Newton being one of the most notable holders. The university seats were abolished in 1948 and ceased at the dissolution of Parliament in 1950. The three Cambridge terms are Michaelmas (Oct.–Dec.), Lent (Jan.–Mar.) and Easter (Apr.–Jun.).

Cambridge University Gardens — Bateman Street, Cambridge. Set in 40 acres (16ha), the spectacular botanic gardens house a collection of over 10,000 labelled plant species in beautifully landscaped settings, including two rock gardens, lake, glasshouses, winter garden, woodland walk, and a fine collection of trees, including ancient cedars, the oldest giant redwoods (Sequoidendron) in Britain, and the first trees of the Dawn Redwood (Metasequoia) grown outside their native China. The range of variants of Pinus nigra from across its range in Europe was planted along the main avenue by Professor J S Henslow, Darwin's mentor, in 1846 to demonstrate variation within a single species. It was this revolutionary theory that Darwin explored in depth in Origin of the Species, published in 1859.

Cavendish Laboratory — J J Thomson Avenue, Madingley Road, Cambridge. The Cavendish Laboratory is the University of Cambridge's Department of Physics, and part of the University's School of Physical Sciences. It was opened in 1874 as a teaching laboratory and was initially located on the New Museums Site, Free School Lane, in the centre of Cambridge. It moved to its present site in west Cambridge in the early 1970s. The department is named after physicist Henry Cavendish, a member of the Dukes of Devonshire branch of the Cavendish family. Another family member, William Cavendish, 7th Duke of Devonshire, was Chancellor of the university and gave money to endow the laboratory in memory of his learned relative. The Cavendish Laboratory has had an important influence on biology, mainly through the application of X-ray crystallography to the study of structures of biological molecules. Francis Crick already worked in the Medical Research Council Unit, headed by Max Perutz and housed in the Laboratory, when James Watson came from the United States and they made a breakthrough in discovering the structure of DNA. For their work in the laboratory they were jointly awarded the Nobel Prize for Medicine in 1962, together with Maurice Wilkins of King's College London, himself a graduate of St John's College, Cambridge. To date 28 Cavendish researchers have won Nobel Prizes.

Cromwell Museum — Grammar School Walk, Huntingdon. Opened in 1962, the museum is housed in the remaining fragment of a medieval monastic hospital dedicated to St John the Baptist, and dating from the late 12th century. It was converted for use as the town's grammar school in the 16th century and remained in use as a school until the 1940s. Oliver Cromwell went to school here, so it is an ideal choice to be one of his memorials. HRH the Princess Royal visited the museum in November 2005 as part of the 800th anniversary of the granting of the town's charter in 1205, which was displayed for the occasion in the museum. Tel: 01480 375830.

Denny Abbey & Farmland Museum — Ely Road, Chittering, Waterbeach. The abbey was founded in 1159 by Benedictine monks as a dependent priory of the great cathedral monastery of Ely. At its heart stands the medieval Franciscan refectory and the church. Adapted by the Templars, the church underwent radical alterations in 1327, eventually becoming a farmhouse. The museum traces the history of farming through the ages and particularly the rural history of Cambridgeshire. Tel: 01223 860988/489.

Devil's Dyke — An Anglo-Saxon earthwork in eastern Cambridgeshire dating from the late 6th century. The dyke consists of a bank and ditch running $7^1/_2$ miles (12 km) southeast from Reach to Woodditton. At its peak, the bank is 36ft (11m) in height. Beginning on flat farmland, the dyke passes to the west of Newmarket and runs along the edge of the July Course at Newmarket racecourse before rising gently to an altitude of 330ft (100m) as it reaches the wooded hills around Woodditton. It is not to be confused with a similarly named dyke in East Sussex.

Elton Hall — Elton, 8 miles (13km) southwest of Peterborough. Elton Hall stands in the midst of unspoilt landscaped parkland, on a site where there has been a house since the Norman Conquest. Sir Peter Proby, Lord Mayor of London and Comptroller of the Royal Household, was granted land and property at Elton by Elizabeth I. His grandson, Sir Thomas Proby, completed the main house in 1666, incorporating the medieval chapel and gatehouse, and it has been the home of the Proby family ever since. The drawing room was added in 1740 and the Marble Hall, main staircase and dining room (with three large Gothic windows) were designed by Henry Ashton in 1860 in a revival of mid-18th century style. Paintings range from 15th century Old Masters to pre-Raphaelite work by Alma-Tadema and Millais; other British artists represented are Gainsborough, Constable and Reynolds. The library is one of the finest in private hands and includes Henry VIII's prayer book. From the Main Library a short passage leads to the Inner Library situated in the medieval Sapcote Tower. The gardens were laid out in 1913 when the lawns, lily pond, well-head and rose garden wall were constructed. The Gothic orangery was built to celebrate the Millennium and a Gothic arbour was completed to mark the Jubilee celebrations. The house lies at the heart of a 3800 acre (1538ha) estate on the Cambridgeshire/Northamptonshire border. Tel: 01832 280468.

Ely Cathedral — The story of the cathedral begins in Saxon times with St Etheldreda, a Saxon princess born in AD 630 at Exning near Newmarket. In 673 she founded a double monastery for monks and nuns on the site of the present cathedral and was installed as the first abbess. Etheldreda's monastery flourished for 200 years until it was destroyed by the Danes. It was refounded as a Benedictine community in 970. Dedicated to the Holy Trinity, the present cathedral was founded by Simeon, Abbot of Ely, and became a cathedral in 1109 when the Diocese of Ely was carved out of the Diocese of Lincoln. The first major restoration took place in the 18th century under James Essex. With the arrival of Dean George Peacock in 1839 a second restoration project began. Together with the architect Sir George Gilbert Scott, he restored the building to its former glory. A third major restoration, the most extensive to date, was begun in 1986 and completed in 2000. Tel: 01353 667735.

Fitzwilliam Museum Trumpington Street, Cambridge. Founded in 1816, the museum is housed in a neoclassical building guarded by sculpted lions and boasting a magnificent entrance hall. Exhibits include Egyptian galleries with exotic mummies, and an art collection including masterpieces by Rubens, Monet and Picasso, along with classical statues, delicate oriental fans, illuminated manuscripts and pottery. In January 2006 a visitor to the museum tripped over his shoelace and fell down a flight of stairs, smashing three priceless Chinese vases from the Qing dynasty situated on a windowsill. Tel: 01223 332900.

Godmanchester Chinese Bridge Pedestrian bridge spanning the River Great Ouse and built, as the name suggests, in ostensibly Chinese style (Chinese Chippendale had been a fashion of the mid 18th century). The original was constructed in 1827 to designs by architect James Gallier senior, but it fell into bad condition and was replaced with a replica by the local council in 1960.

Gog Magog Hills A range of low chalk downs extending for several miles to the southeast of Cambridge between the towns of Fulbourn and Great Shelford. The highest point is Telegraph Clump at 246ft (75m). Other peaks include Little Trees Hill, Wandlebury Hill, Limepit Hill, Mag's Hill, Copley Hill, Meggs Hill, Fox Hill, Clarke's Hill and White Hill. The earliest mention of the names Gog and Magog in reference to the region is found in a decree of 1574; the choice of these names may relate to the destruction of the nations of the earth described in the Book of Revelation (20: 7–10), as a number of mutilated human skeletons have been found during excavations in the area.

Grafham Water ½ mile (0.8km) southwest of Grafham, 7 miles (11km) southwest of Huntingdon. A reservoir, 2.3 sq miles (6 sq km) in area, the southern side of which is home to a nature reserve, sailing centre and fishing centre. On the northern shore is an exhibition centre with a small display about the reservoir's construction.

Hamerton Zoo 2 miles (3km) southwest of Sawtry. Opened as a wildlife conservation sanctuary in June 1990, and set in the open, rolling countryside of the Huntingdonshire Wolds, Hamerton's 15 acres (6ha) of parkland provide a home for an array of rare, endangered and unusual animals. Over 100 different species include apes and monkeys, tortoises, rheas, storks, cranes, wallabies, wolves, cheetahs, foxes, squirrels, chipmunks, porcupines, pheasants, peacocks, owls, kookaburras, egrets, geese, macaws, cockatoos, curassows, seriemas, alpaca, binturong, pudus and degus. Tel: 01832 293362.

Highest point Great Chishill at 480ft (146m). (GR: TL428384.) Situated midway between Royston and Saffron Walden, the hill borders the counties of Essex and Hertfordshire.

Hinchingbrooke Country Park 1½ miles (2.5km) west of Huntingdon. The country park covers 170 acres (69ha) of open grassland, meadows, woodlands and lakes, and is the location of Hinchingbrooke House. Tel: 01480 451568.

Hinchingbrooke House 1½ miles (2.5km) west of Huntingdon. Once the home of at least four generations of the Cromwell family, including Lord Protector Oliver Cromwell, and then of the Montagus, Earls of Sandwich (among them John Montagu, 4th Earl and inventor of the sandwich), who resided at the house until the 1960s. The house is now part of Hinchingbrooke School, while the grounds contain an arts and theatre complex, a country park, Hinchingbrooke Hospital and the regional police headquarters. Tel: 01480 375678.

Hobson's Brook In 1614, innkeeper Thomas Hobson built a conduit bringing drinking water from springs at Nine Wells near Shelford outside Cambridge into the city centre. The channels still run along Trumpington Street, although the conduit head has been moved from the market place to the corner of Lensfield Road. Hobson hired out horses, but hirers had to take the horse closest to the door. This led to the expression 'Hobson's choice' meaning 'No choice'.

Holme Fen Nature Reserve ½ mile (0.8km) northeast of Holme, 6 miles (10km) south of Peterborough. Located on the southwestern shore of the former Whittlesey Mere, Holme Fen National Nature Reserve is the lowest point in Britain at 9ft (2.75m) below sea level (GR: TL202893). The fen occupies a crescent-shaped site 1½ miles (2.5km) long by 1 mile (1.6km) wide and is a designated Site of Special Scientific Interest. The site contains the largest silver birch woodland in lowland Britain as well as a remnant of raised lowalnd bog. Tel: 01954 713513.

Houghton Water Mill 2 miles (3km) southeast of Huntingdon. A large timber-built watermill on an island in the Great Ouse. It is the only remaining working watermill on the river, with intact machinery which is still operational. A major repair and decoration project has been recently completed and corn is ground by a pair of millstones powered by the north waterwheel, which was reinstated in 1999. Now owned by the National Trust. Tel: 01480 301494.

Huntingdon Castle Castle Moat Road, Huntingdon. Norman motte and bailey castle founded 1069 by William I, a second motte being added in the 12th century. The castle was inherited by King David of Scotland who supported his sons in their efforts to dethrone Henry II. It was besieged and demolished by Henry in 1174. The motte, surrounded on three sides by a moat, is still visible.

Imperial War Museum 1 mile (1.6km) west of Duxford, 8 miles (13km) south of Cambridge. One of the world's most spectacular aviation heritage complexes, featuring a collection of nearly 200 aircraft, the American Air Museum and a fine collection of military vehicles plus special exhibitions relating to the Battle of Britain, the D-Day invasions and Field Marshal Montgomery. The museum holds four air shows throughout the summer, plus other events such as a military vehicle show. A popular exhibit in recent years has been a British Aerospace Concorde. Other recent exhibits include a BAC-111, Bristol Britannia, VC-10 and Trident. Tel: 01223 835000.

Interesting facts
In 2007, the **8.02 commuter service from Cambridge to London** Liverpool Street was identified as the most overcrowded train in Britain, with an average of 433 passengers wanting to use the available 234 seats in the four carriages. In 2006 **Peterborough City Council** offered pet owners free lessons in how to interpret dog language in an effort to alleviate nuisance barking. **'Little Gidding'**, the fourth and final section of TS Eliot's *Four Quartets*, a reflection on time and timelessness, was written in 1941 while Eliot was serving as an air raid warden in London. The poem was inspired by Eliot's visit to the Huntingdonshire hamlet (population 28), 3 miles (5km) south of Sawtry, on 25 May 1936 and describes the tiny Church of St John where he knelt to pray on that fateful May Day. Britain's first **crocodile farm** was set up in Oldhurst, near St Ives, in May 2006. Andy Johnson began his venture with one male and seven female Nile crocodiles from a farm in Africa. A study by the consultancy firm CACI in 2004 named the postcode area CB2 1 . ., part of Cambridge city centre, as the '**smoking capital**' of the UK, as the average resident in this area apparently spent more money on cigarettes than those of any other region in the country, more than £2000 per annum. On 29 October 2004, a Cambridge edition of the famous board game **Monopoly** was published. **Charters**, at Town Bridge, Peterborough, at 176ft (54m), is the longest floating pub in Britain. Formerly the Dutch barge *Leendert-R*, it was built in 1907 and was converted to a real ale bar in September 1991. **Cambridge railway station** has the second longest platform in England at 1200ft (366m), after Gloucester at 1977ft (603m).

Island Hall
Post Street, Godmanchester, 1 mile (1.6km) south of Huntingdon. Owned by Mr Christopher and Lady Linda Vane Percy, this 18th century house has exquisite Georgian rooms and memorabilia relating to the owners' ancestors since their first occupation in 1800. The formal gardens and ornamental island form part of the grounds. Tel: 01480 459676.

Islands
There are several islets situated in the Cambridgeshire Ouse: **Alconbury Brook Island** is a tiny islet south of the Castle Hills in the River Great Ouse near Godmanchester; **Holt Island** is a 7 acre (2.8ha) nature reserve linked to the mainland by a bridge in the River Great Ouse in St Ives; **Marina Island**, aka Riverside Island Marina, is situated in the River Lark in Isleham. See also Isle of Ely.

Isle of Ely
Located in the far mid-east of the county, Ely was until the 17th century an island surrounded by fenland, but drainage of the fens has long made the name an anomaly. Ely played an important part in British military history, becoming a refuge for the Anglo-Saxon resistance leader Hereward the Wake in 1071 and only being taken by William I after a prolonged struggle. In 1139, during the civil war between King Stephen and the Empress Matilda, Bishop Nigel of Ely, a supporter of Matilda, unsuccessfully tried to hold the Isle. In 1143 Geoffrey de Mandeville rebelled against Stephen, making his base on Ely, and was mortally wounded the following year at Burwell 10 miles (16km) south of the isle. In 1216, during the First Barons' War, the Isle was again unsuccessfully defended against the army of King John. Inhabitants of Ely also took part in the Peasants' Revolt of 1381. The name of the former island derives from the most common fenland fish, the eel, and is a reminder of bygone days when the area was rich in the commodity, which was not only eaten but also used as currency! Area: 22.87 sq miles (59.23 sq km). Population: 15,102.

Kettle's Yard
Castle Street, Cambridge. Kettle's Yard was created as a 'refuge of peace and order, of the visual arts and music'. Art collector Jim Ede donated the house and his art collection, which is enjoyed today not behind ropes and in anonymous chambers, but in the living room, bedroom and stairway. The adjoining gallery hosts exhibitions by major contemporary artists. Tel: 01223 352124.

Kimbolton Castle
7 miles (11km) northwest of St Neots. Set in extensive, wooded grounds, the castle was originally a 13th century fortified manor house, undergoing many changes before being rebuilt several times between 1615 and 1950 by John Vanbrugh, Nicholas Hawksmoor and Robert Adam as the country house of the Dukes of Manchester. Its most famous resident was Catherine of Aragon, who died in the Queen's Room in 1536, and small sections of the Tudor house have survived. Although the castle now belongs to Kimbolton School, visitors can still see the impressive range of state rooms, with an outstanding set of murals by Pellegrini. Tel: 01480 860505.

King's College Chapel
Trinity Lane, Cambridge. Although the foundation stone was laid by Henry VI on the feast of St James, 25 July 1446, it was more than a century later, in 1547, that the chapel, often cited as the most beautiful building in Cambridge, was completed. The chapel features the world's largest fan vault, stained glass windows, and the painting *The Adoration of the Magi* by Rubens, originally painted in 1634 for the Convent of the White Nuns at Louvain in Belgium. The world-famous chapel choir consists of choral scholars (male students from the college) and choristers (boys educated at nearby King's College School), conducted by Stephen Cleobury. The BBC has broadcast the choir's Festival of Nine Lessons and Carols from the chapel each Christmas Eve since 1928. The chapel is widely seen as the symbol of Cambridge and appears in the logo of the city council. Tel: 01223 331100.

Longthorpe Tower
Woburn Close, Longthorpe, Peterborough. The three-storey tower was added in 1310 to a manor house fortified in 1263. The interior walls still have some of the original decorative paintings, among the best such work in the UK, which survived having been preserved under whitewash. Now in the care of English Heritage. Tel: 01223 582700.

Manor, The
Hemingford Grey, 3 miles (5km) southeast of Huntingdon. The Manor was built in the 1130s and is one of the oldest continuously inhabited houses in Britain. Much of the original house remains virtually intact in spite of various changes over 900 years. The atmospheric upstairs hall was used during World War II by author Lucy Boston (famous as the author of books featuring 'Green Knowe') to give gramophone record recitals twice a week to the RAF. The 1929 EMG gramophone

is still in use in the room. The moated house is surrounded by a 4 acre (1.6ha) garden renowned for its collection of over 200 old roses and a collection of irises. Tel: 01480 463134.

Midsummer Fair — Held on Midsummer Common, Cambridge, in late June, the huge fair has an 800-year history. Its rival fair at Stourbridge was abolished in 1933.

Motto — *Per undas, per agros* (Through waves, through fields).

Museums — The Cambridge and County Folk Museum is housed in a 16th century building and is dedicated to local domestic history of the past 300 years. Other Cambridge museums include the Wipple Museum of the History of Science; the Sedgwick Museum of Earth Sciences; the Museum of Archaeology and Anthropology; the Museum of Zoology; the Museum of Classical Archaeology; and the Scott Polar Research Institute.

Nene Valley Railway — A standard gauge preserved steam railway which runs for 7½ miles (12km) between Yarwell Junction and Peterborough via the delightful Nene Park on part of the former London and North Western Railway line between Peterborough and Northampton. Tel: 01480 784444.

Norris Museum — The Broadway, St Ives. Founded by Herbert Norris, a St Ivian who left his lifetime's collection of Huntingdonshire relics to the town when he died in 1931, the museum tells the story of the county from the earliest times to the present day. Tel: 01480 497314.

Octavia Hill Birthplace Museum — South Brink Place, Wisbech. Opened in December 1995 to commemorate and record the life and work of Octavia Hill, who co-founded the National Trust in 1895. Tel: 01945 476358.

Oliver Cromwell's House — St Mary's Street, Ely. The atmospheric former home of the Lord Protector contains life-size models of Cromwell and a shop at the front. Tel: 01353 662062.

Paxton Pits Nature — Little Paxton, 1 mile (1.6km) north of St Neots. The reserve consists of 188 acres (75ha) of lakes, meadow, grassland, scrub and woodland next to the River Great Ouse. Developed from former gravel pits, it has almost doubled in since being established in 1989, and provides a habitat for numerous bird species and for mammals such as brown hare, stoats, weasels, roe deer, bats, muntjac deer, mink, water shrews, harvest mouse, short-tailed field voles, wood mouse, and otters (once thought to be extinct locally). Tel: 01480 406795.

Peckover House & Garden — North Brink, Wisbech. A town property on the north bank of the River Nene built c.1722 which is renowned for its fine plaster and wood rococo decoration. For 150 years it was the family home of Quaker banking family the Peckovers. The 2 acre (0.8ha) Victorian garden includes a summerhouse, orangery, fernery, roses, herbaceous borders and croquet lawn. Owned by the National Trust. Tel: 01945 583463.

Peterborough Cathedral — Minster Precincts, Peterborough. Dedicated to St Peter, St Paul and St Andrew. A monastic church was founded here by King Peada in AD 655. Destroyed by the Danes in 870, it was rebuilt as part of a Benedictine abbey and reconsecrated in 972, burned down in an accidental fire in 1116 and rebuilt in its present form between 1118 and 1238 when it was finally reconsecrated. It is built largely of Barnack ragstone, a local limestone quarried at Barnack near Stamford in Lincolnshire. The porch was added c.1380, the eastern extension c.1500 and the central tower was rebuilt in the mid 1300s and again in the 1880s. In 1539 the monastery was closed by Henry VIII, but 18 months later in 1541, the church became the Cathedral of the new Diocese of Peterborough, with the last abbot as the new bishop, and Peterborough became a city. Two queens were buried in the cathedral during the Tudor period. Catherine of Aragon's grave is in the north aisle near the high altar, while Mary Queen of Scots was buried on the opposite side of the altar, though her grave is now empty (she was reburied at Westminster Abbey in 1612). St Oswald's Arm (the abbey's most valued relic) disappeared from its chapel about the time of the Reformation but the chapel still has its watch-tower where monks kept guard over it day and night. Severe damage was done to the cathedral by Cromwell's troops in 1643 during the Civil War, and the lady chapel, chapter house and cloister were destroyed; only fragments of the stained glass windows were saved and these were later pieced together to form the apse windows. The choir stalls, bishop's throne, marble floor and high altar were all created by Victorian architect John Loughborough Pearson after the tower had been rebuilt. In the 1960s new figures were added to the west front and in the 1970s the spectacular hanging cross was added to the nave. Since a disastrous fire in November 2001 a massive cleaning and restoration programme has been undertaken. Tel: 01733 343342.

Prisons — **Littlehey**, Perry, Huntingdon, is a category C prison holding adult men and offering a sex offender treatment programme. It was opened in 1988 on the site of Gaynes Hall Youth Custody Centre. Operational capacity: 706. Tel: 01480 333000.

Whitemoor, Longhill Road, March, is a maximum security prison for men in Category A and B (and as such will not accept prisoners serving less than four years). It is one of eight high security prisons within the prison estate. Operational capacity: 500. Tel: 01354 602350.

RAF Molesworth — Molesworth, 10 miles (16km) west of Huntingdon. Dating from 1917, this Royal Air Force military base is one of three in Cambridgeshire currently occupied by the United States Air Force; Molesworth, along with RAF Alconbury and RAF Upwood, are considered the Tri-Base Area.

Ramsey Abbey Gatehouse — Ramsey, 10 miles (16km) southeast of Peterborough. There was a Benedictine monastery here as early as the 7th century, but the abbey was founded by the Saxon nobleman Ailwine in 964. At that time Ramsey was little more than an island in the fens, and the monks had to build a causeway to connect the abbey to the mainland. During the medieval period Ramsey Abbey was one of the most prestigious in East Anglia. Though most of the abbey buildings were destroyed during the Dissolution of the Monasteries, the Lady Chapel survived to form part of the Abbey Grammar School. The ruined 15th century gatehouse of the abbey contains superb carvings and an ornate oriel window. The property is owned by the National Trust. Tel: 01480 301494.

Ramsey Rural Museum — Wood Lane, Ramsey. A set of 18th century farm buildings located in open countryside, and around which are displayed examples of farming equipment from many periods. A house has been reconstructed to demonstrate how people would have lived during the Agricultural Revolution. Tel: 01487 814304.

Rivers

The **Cam** is a tributary of the River Great Ouse and itself has two principal tributaries known as the Granta and the Rhee, though both are also officially known as the Cam. The Rhee begins just west of Ashwell in Hertfordshire, running for 12 miles (19km) through the farmland of southern Cambridgeshire. The longer tributary, the Granta, starts near the village of Widdington in Essex, flowing for 15 miles (24km) north past Audley End House to merge with the Rhee 1 mile (1.6km) south of Grantchester. A further tributary, also known as the Granta, runs 10 miles (16km) from south of Haverhill to join the larger Granta south of Great Shelford. This is the home village of children's author Philippa Pearce, whose books (most notably *Minnow on the Say*) rename the Cam as the River Say, with Great and Little Shelford becoming Great and Little Barley, and Cambridge becoming 'Castleford' (not to be confused with the real town of the same name in West Yorkshire). The two rivers join south of Ely at Pope's Corner. The Great Ouse connects the Cam to England's canal system. The Cam enters Cambridge from the southwest and heads north past many of the historic colleges of the University of Cambridge along the open area known as The Backs (see separate entry). After passing St John's College, it turns sharply and runs east, passing the weir at Jesus Green and the boathouses alongside Midsummer Common. Passing Chesterton, it turns north again and leaves the city, running a further 12 miles (19km) before merging with the Great Ouse, a total distance of 40 miles (64km).

The **Great Ouse** through its lower reaches is also known as Old West River and the Ely Ouse. In Cambridgeshire it flows through St Neots, Godmanchester, Huntingdon, St Ives and Ely. See also Bedfordshire.

The **Nene** flows for 91 miles (147km) through Northamptonshire, Cambridgeshire and Lincolnshire. It rises at Arbury Hill, southwest of Daventry in Northamptonshire, and flows generally eastwards through arable land, reaching the industrial landscape of Northampton, Wellingborough and Irthlingborough. From the gentle hills of Northamptonshire it enters the rural part of the city of Peterborough, passing the Nene Valley Railway (see separate entry) and the East of England Showground. After the cathedral city itself, the landscape changes to the Nene Washes in The Fens and their seemingly endless horizons. It flows through Wisbech, then Sutton Bridge in Lincolnshire, and finally enters the North Sea at The Wash between two towers known as 'the lighthouses'. The Nene links the Grand Union Canal to the River Great Ouse, via the Middle Level system. Pronunciation of the river's name changes as one moves downstream. Through Northamptonshire locals mostly refer to it as the *nen* (rhyming with 'hen'), but around Peterborough it changes to *nene* (rhyming with 'mean').

Round Church

Round Church Street, Cambridge. The Church of the Holy Sepulchre guards the junction between Bridge Street, St John's Street, Sidney Street and Round Church Street; its distinctive round shape originated in the Holy Land, where early Christians built circular walls around tombs. English crusaders returning from Palestine imitated this design and the Round Church was built c.1130. Only three other round churches now survive in England (Temple Church in London, Little Maplestead in Essex and St Sepulchre's in Northampton). The church was altered in the 15th century when windows were added, and again in 1841. The Round Church now houses an exhibition centre.

Senate House

Senate House Hill, Cambridge. A Palladian building with delicate plasterwork and fine woodwork, designed by James Gibbs in 1730. The Senate House is situated close to Gonville and Caius College, and is used for important ceremonial occasions such as the conferment of degrees.

Silicon Fen

In an analogy to California's Silicon Valley, the Cambridge area is sometimes referred to as Silicon Fen (originally because both Acorn Computers and Sinclair were founded there) due to numerous high-tech businesses that have grown up in the science parks and other developments in and around the city. Cambridge University was joined by the larger part of Anglia Ruskin University, and its educational reputation has led to other bodies (such as the Open University in East Anglia) basing themselves in the city. There are over 1000 high-tech companies in the Silicon Fen area.

Sport

football

Cambridge United were founded in 1912 as Abbey United. The club turned professional in 1949 and changed its name to Cambridge United in 1951. They were elected to the Football League in 1970, taking the place of Bradford Park Avenue. In 1989–90, the club reached the quarter-finals of the FA Cup, being narrowly beaten by eventual finalists Crystal Palace. They were relegated from the Football League in 2004–05. The club's colours are amber and black and their home ground is the Abbey Stadium, Newmarket Road, Cambridge. Tel: 01223 566500.

Peterborough United came into being in 1934 after the Peterborough and Fletton club was disbanded and a new club formed. Nicknamed The Posh, they made their Football League debut in 1960. Their home ground is London Road Stadium, Peterborough. Tel: 01733 563947.

Other clubs include **Cambridge City**.

greyhound racing

Peterborough Greyhound Track, First Drove, Fengate. 370m track. Tel: 01733 296930.

horse racing

Huntingdon Racecourse, Brampton, Huntingdon. A right-handed track of 1 mile 4 furlongs (2.5km) holding National Hunt racing. Tel: 01480 453373.

Stilton cheese

Stilton takes its name from the village of the same name in Huntingdonshire but peculiarly the cheese has never been made there. Stilton is a 'protected name' blue cheese and by law can only be made in the three counties of Derbyshire, Leicestershire and Nottinghamshire. The 'King of Cheeses' is made according to a strict code and only six dairies are licensed to make it. To be called Stilton, each cheese must be made from local milk pasteurised before use, in a traditional cylindrical shape; it must be allowed to form its own crust, be unpressed, have delicate blue veins radiating from the centre, and have a taste profile typical of Stilton. The first documented evidence of the name Stilton dates from 1727 when Daniel Defoe in his *Tour through England and Wales* remarked that he 'passed through Stilton, a town famous for cheese'. The name stuck, and the cheese has at least been sold in great quantities in the town.

Wimpole Hall and Home Farm — 1 mile (1.6km) northeast of Arrington, 8 miles (13km) southwest of Cambridge. The biggest 18th century house in Cambridgeshire, set in an extensive wooded park complete with a grand folly, Chinese bridge and lakes. There are spectacular avenues with extensive walks through the grounds and garden. Wimpole Home Farm was built in 1794 and is now home to rare breeds of sheep, goats, cattle, pigs and horses. The Great Barn contains a collection of farm machinery dating back 200 years. Tel: 01223 206000.

Woodwalton Fen Nature Reserve — 3 miles (5km) east of Conington, 8 miles (13km) south of Peterborough. Occupying a site of 415 acres (208ha), Woodwalton is one of Britain's oldest nature reserves, its international importance recognised in its designations as a Ramsar site, a Site of Special Scientific Interest and a National Nature Reserve. The site features a mosaic of habitats interlaced with stretches of tranquil waterway and footpaths. Habitats include purple moor grass meadows, tall fen and scrub communities, woodland, and other areas of grasses, sedges, herbs and mosses. The site also supports numerous rare species of invertebrates and two very rare plants: fen violet is found in only two other places in Britain, while fen woodrush is unique to the Great Fen in the UK. The total list of plants, insects, birds, and mammals runs into thousands. Woodwalton is a key component of the Great Fen Project, set up to create a 14.3 sq mile (37 sq km) wetland between Huntingdon and Peterborough. This will be achieved by obtaining land adjacent to Holme Fen and Woodwalton Fen and connecting these nature reserves in order to provide a haven for wildlife and create a massive green space. Tel: 01954 713513.

Some famous people born in Cambridgeshire

Adams, Douglas (writer) (1952–2001)	Cambridge
Attenborough, Richard (actor) (1923–)	Cambridge
Bell, Andy (pop singer) (1964–)	Peterborough
Cockerell, Christopher (engineer) (1910–99)	Cambridge
Cromwell, Oliver (Lord Protector of England) (1599–1658)	Huntingdon
Gilmour, David (musician) (1946–)	Cambridge
Hartley, L(eslie) P(oles) (author) (1895–1972)	Whittlesey
Henty, G(eorge) A(lfred) (novelist) (1832–1902)	Trumpington
Hill, Octavia (co-founder of the National Trust) (1838–1912)	Wisbech
Hobbs, Sir Jack (cricketer) (1882–1963)	Cambridge
Hobson, Thomas (innkeeper) (c.1544–1631)	Cambridge
Keynes, John Maynard (economist) (1883–1946)	Cambridge
Kroto, Harold (chemist) (1939–)	Wisbech
Leavis, F(rank) R(aymond) (literary critic) (1895–1978)	Cambridge
Morris, Chris (comedian) (1962–)	Cambridge
Newton-John, Olivia (singer) (1948–)	Cambridge
Pearce, Guy (actor) (1967–)	Ely
Ramsey, Michael (Archbishop of Canterbury) (1904–88)	Cambridge
Royce, Henry (automobile manufacturer) (1863–1933)	Alwalton
Searle, Ronald (cartoonist) (1920–)	Cambridge
Tenison, Thomas (archbishop) (1636–1715)	Cottenham
Thomson, George Paget (physicist) (1892–1975)	Cambridge
Whitehead, William (poet and playwright) (1715–85)	Cambridge

Cheshire

GREATER MANCHESTER
MERSEYSIDE
DERBYSHIRE
CLYWD
STAFFORDSHIRE
SHROPSHIRE
M6
M56
M53
Warrington
Widnes
Runcorn
Lymm
Knutsford
Wilmslow
Alderley Edge
Shining Tor
559
Macclesfield
Northwich
Weaverham
Ellesmere Port
Kelsall
Chester
Middlewich
Winsford
R. Mersey
R. Dane
R. Dee
R. Weaver
Bretton
Farndon
Sandbach
Congleton
Crewe
Nantwich
Kidsgrove
Alsager
1
2
3
4
0
20 miles
0
30 km

Unitary Authorities

1 Cheshire West and Chester
2 Cheshire East
3 Halton
4 Warrington

Cheshire borders the counties of Merseyside and Greater Manchester to the north, Derbyshire to the east and northeast, Staffordshire to the southeast, and Shropshire to the south. It also borders the traditional Welsh county of Clwyd to the southwest and west and its northwest shores are washed by the Irish Sea. The Wirral Peninsula in northwest Cheshire is bounded by the River Dee to the west and the River Mersey to the east, and administered by Wirral Metropolitan Borough Council in the north and Cheshire County Council in the south. Warrington and Halton (including Widnes and Runcorn) became unitary authorities on 1 April 1998 but are considered part of the geographical county. Warrington, the largest town and borough, combined with the townships of Stockton Heath and Lymm in 1974 and the new entity became part of the reorganised Cheshire County Council. The northern part of Halton, including Widnes, was also traditionally part of Lancashire, the area to the south, Cheshire. The only city in Cheshire is Chester; given its royal charter in 1300, it is also the county town.

Further legislation of 1 April 2009 has meant the abolition of the County Council and the amalgamation of the six districts into two unitary authorities; Ellesmere Port and Neston, Vale Royal, and Chester now becoming Cheshire West and Chester, and Macclesfield, Crewe and Nantwich, and Congleton becoming Cheshire East. Cheshire is now a ceremonial county consisting of four unitary authorities.

Under the local government reorganisation of 1974, some areas near the Lancashire border were transferred to Greater Manchester and Merseyside, notably Stockport, Hyde, Dukinfield and Stalybridge in the northeast and much of the Wirral Peninsula in the northwest. At the same time the far northeastern tip of the county, comprising the areas of Woodhead and Tintwistle, was transferred to Derbyshire, while Warrington and Widnes were transferred from Lancashire to Cheshire. Although it is now one of the 10 unitary authorities that form the conurbation of Greater Manchester, Stockport maintains strong historical ties with its former administrative county. Many supporters of Stockport County, for example, deem it to be part of Cheshire; local derbies are played against Macclesfield Town and Chester City, both in Cheshire.

The geology of the county consists of a boulder clay plain separating the hills of North Wales and the Derbyshire Peak District. This was formed following the retreat of Ice Age glaciers which left the area dotted with kettle-hole lakes, locally referred to as 'meres'. The bedrock of this region is almost entirely Triassic sandstone, outcrops of which have been quarried to provide the distinctive red stone of which Liverpool Cathedral and Chester Cathedral are built. The eastern half of the county is Upper Triassic mudstone, with large salt deposits which were mined for hundreds of years around Northwich. Separating this area from Lower Triassic sandstone to the west is a prominent sandstone ridge. A 32 mile (51km) footpath, the Sandstone Trail, follows this ridge from Frodsham to Whitchurch passing Delamere Forest, Beeston Castle and a number of Iron Age forts.

Before the arrival of the Romans the area was occupied by the tribe known as the Cornovii. After the invasion, the Roman fort of Deva (Chester) was established in AD 60, probably to protect access to lead and silver found in Flintshire over the border in Wales. Following battles against the Lancashire-based Brigantes, full military occupation began c.AD 71. Chester became the most important site of defence against native incursions, and developed into a major military and commercial centre. The salt mines at Condate (Northwich) and Salinae (Middlewich), the second largest town in the county, were highly valued by the Roman forces, many of whom received their pay in salt, and these settlements also grew in importance.

After Roman withdrawal from Britain in the 5th century the area was gradually settled and farmed by former invaders from Scandinavia. By the mid 7th century, Christianity had become widespread; one of the oldest churches in the county was built at Eccleston, near Chester (*eccles* was an old Celtic-Welsh word for a church). Cheshire was to some extent a frontier between the Danes in the north and east and the Welsh to the west, and at least two defensive ditches were dug to keep them out – Offa's Dyke, built 760–80, and Wat's Dyke, built some time before 655, which remained the recognised border until the Norman Conquest. Mercian place names are evident throughout the county, recognised by the suffix 'ham' (from the Saxon word *hamm* meaning a settlement), and 'burgh' or 'bury' (indicating a fortified settlement or stronghold). Old Cheshire townships like Frodsham, Eastham, Weaverham, Wrenbury and Prestbury all reveal Mercian Saxon origins.

Apart from Welsh incursions, from the 8th until the early 10th century the region also suffered continual attacks by Norsemen from already occupied Ireland. Parts of west Cheshire were known to have been controlled by the Norse king Ceowolf. Only in the reign of Alfred the Great were these incursions eventually controlled. The Wirral Peninsula was once an independent Viking mini-state with its parliament at Thingwall; ancient Irish annals record that the region was populated by Norsemen, led by Ingimund, who had been expelled from Ireland and settled there peacefully with the agreement of Ethelfleda, Queen of the Mercian English. As a result, the Wirral abounds in Danish place names – such as Thingwall itself, from *thing*, 'a meeting place'.

By 980 the Norse threat had been removed. The region had probably been a recognised county since 920 in the reign of Edward the Elder, and it was now known as *Legecaestrescir*, meaning the 'shire of the city of the legions' (a reference to the Roman occupation). By the end of the 10th century, Chester had become the permanent headquarters of Eadric Streona, the king's governor of Cheshire, Staffordshire and Shropshire, and was increasingly ruled as an autonomous region. By 1030, it had come under the governorship of Earl Edwin, grandson of Leofric of Mercia, perhaps the most powerful and influential family in England, and remained so until the Norman Conquest in 1066.

After the Norman Conquest the people of Cheshire were treated abominably by William I for their fierce resistance, swathes of land being destroyed, villages razed, crops burnt, livestock slaughtered and people rendered landless and homeless. William gave one of his supporters, Hugh d'Avranches (nicknamed Hugh Lupus, or 'wolf') the title of Earl of Chester, and Cheshire was declared a County Palatine, a title it still holds today. In 1237 Henry III took back the title, bestowing it on his son, Prince Edward. Ever since then the eldest son of the English monarch has always held the title of Earl of Chester. By the 13th century a line of castles protected the county's western border from the Welsh; these included motte and bailey castles at Shotwick, Dodleston, Aldford, Pilford, Shocklach, Oldcastle and Malpas.

By the early 17th century families largely descended from Norman stock, such as the Venables, Mainwarings, Davenports and Masseys, were the major landowners, also dominating trade, legal and community affairs. However, at the outbreak of the Civil War in 1642 these loyalties were torn apart. Chester was a Royalist stronghold, while the market towns of Knutsford, Nantwich, Congleton, Middlewich and Northwich remained in Parliamentarian hands. In 1654, when England was placed under military rule, Cheshire, Lancashire and North Staffordshire were governed by the infamous Charles Worsley. His ruthless treatment of Royalist supporters made his name feared and despised throughout the northwest of England. Riots were planned, even by Parliamentarians, notably Sir George Booth of Dunham Massey near Altrincham, though these were put down and the leaders executed.

With industrialisation of the mill towns in Lancashire and Manchester in the late 18th and 19th century, many Cheshire farmsteads were abandoned as workers sought a better living in the industrial towns. Abandoned lands were absorbed into bigger estates, with the result that 98 per cent of the land in Cheshire came to belong to only 26 per cent of its population. By 1870, John Tollemache's estate at Peckforton encompassed over 25,000 acres, the Marquess of Cholmondeley owned nearly 17,000 acres and the Duke of Westminster 15,000 acres. Cheshire was a wealthy county in the 19th century and contains, it is estimated, more fine 18th and 19th century country houses than any other English county. The Egerton family built their impressive country seat at Tatton Park between 1760 and 1820, and the 17th century house at Dunham Massey was significantly developed during the 19th century into its present imposing state. Cheshire cheese also came into the national consciousness at this time, 10,000 tons being sent per year to London alone.

Modern Cheshire has developed two distinctively different characters – industrial and rural. Most of the industry is in the north, near the rivers Mersey and Weaver, and the area is the centre of the British chemical industry. ICI was originally established at Runcorn because of the proximity of salt mines at Northwich and Middlewich, while Eastham, Ellesmere Port and Runcorn are also industrialised, with power stations and petrochemical production at Carrington and Partington – facilities encouraged by the creation of the Manchester Ship Canal that runs along the northern edge of the county from Manchester to Liverpool. Crewe was once a centre of railway engineering (over 2000 locomotives were built there) and remains a major junction. Birkenhead on the Wirral was once dominated by Cammell Laird Shipbuilding.

Much of the rest of the county is still agricultural, with rolling pastures of cattle producing Cheshire milk and cheese as well as fields of potatoes. There are many miles of canals, particularly in the east of the county with its strategic importance between Manchester, Stoke and Birmingham. The Rochdale, Ashton, Peak Forest, Macclesfield, Trent & Mersey and Bridgewater canals once connected rural Cheshire to the industrial Midlands and beyond; these have now been restored for leisure use, forming the 'Cheshire Ring'.

Rural Cheshire is today a pleasant and a much sought after place to live. Towns in the east of the county form Manchester's most affluent commuter belt with some of the UK's highest property prices outside the Home Counties. It is reckoned that more millionaires live in Cheshire than in any other county in the UK.

Cheshire	**Population**			**Area**	
Unitary Authorities	*male*	*female*	*total*	*sq miles*	*sq km*
Cheshire West and Chester	156,636	165,335	321,971	354	916
Cheshire East	171,376	180,441	351,817	450	1166
Halton	57,135	61,073	118,208	31	79
Warrington	93,877	97,203	191,080	70	181
Total	479,024	504,052	983,076	905	2342

Local Attractions and Information

Adlington Hall — Adlington, 4 miles (6km) north of Macclesfield. Adlington is one of the finest medieval halls in the country and houses a famous 17th century organ, built by Father Bernard Smith and once played by Handel. Wooded gardens surround the house. Tel: 01625 820875.

Administrative headquarters — **Cheshire West and Chester:** County Hall, Chester CH1 1SF. Tel: 0300 123 8123.
Cheshire East: Westfields, Middlewich Rd, Sandbach CW11 1HZ. Tel: 0300 123 5500
Halton: Municipal Building, Kingsway, Widnes WA8 7QF. Tel: 0151 907 8300.
Warrington: Town Hall, Warrington WA1 1UH. Tel: 01925 444400.

Alderley Edge — A village and civil parish that takes its name from the wooded escarpment towering above the Cheshire plain, with fine views and walks. Alderley Edge is said to have more millionaires per square mile than anywhere else in England, so it is no surprise that it also holds the title of the Cheshire village where the most champagne is consumed.

Aldford Castle — Aldford, 4 miles (6km) south of Chester. A 12th century stone fortress founded by Richard de Aldford. The large motte is encased by a wide wet ditch and stands within a triangular bailey. The foundations of a shell keep and a D-shaped tower have been found on the motte's plateau.

Anderton Boat Lift — 1 mile (1.6km) north of Northwich. The Anderton Boat Lift is one of the greatest monuments to Britain's last canal age and known as the 'Cathedral of the Canals'. Built in 1875 to link the River Weaver with the Trent and Mersey Canal 50ft (15m) above, it was the world's first boat lift. It was opened to the public in March 2002 following a £7 million restoration programme. Tel: 01606 786777.

Anson Engine Museum — Anson Road, Poynton. A museum on the site of the former Anson Colliery, opened to the public in 1989 and illustrating the development of the internal combustion engine from its early beginnings. It contains a unique collection of over 200 gas and oil engines, many maintained in running order, and ranging from early Crossley gas engines to more modern diesels. Tel: 01625 874426.

Arley Hall and Gardens — Arley, 5 miles (8km) northwest of Knutsford. Built 1832–45, the house is an impressive example of the 19th century Jacobean revival style. The 12 acres (5ha) of gardens, recently described as one of the 50 best in Europe, include herbaceous borders laid out in 1846, among the first to be planted in England. Tel: 01565 777353.

Battles	Three major battles have been fought on Cheshire soil: Nantwich, Rowton Heath and Winwick. See separate table for details.
Beeston Castle	Beeston, 8 miles (13km) northwest of Nantwich. This ruined fortification, located on a steep rocky outcrop, was built c.1220 by Ranulf de Blundeville, Earl of Chester, and later occupied by Simon de Montfort. Taken by eight Royalists in the Civil War who bluffed the 80-strong garrison into surrender, it was held for two years before being retaken by Parliament and slighted. The well shaft measures 370ft (113m). Now owned by English Heritage. Tel: 01829 260464.
Bickerton Hill	10 miles (16km) west of Nantwich. Two low red sandstone hills in west Cheshire, lying to the north and south of the A534. The northerly hill, 745ft (227m) high, is situated southwest of the Peckforton Hills. The southerly hill at 633ft (193m), immediately northwest of the hamlet of Bickerton, is topped by the Iron Age hill fort of Maiden Castle (see separate entry). The Sandstone Trail runs over the top of the two hills. The birch woods and heathland of the southerly hill have been designated a Site of Special Scientific Interest as one of the few lowland heath sites remaining in Cheshire.
Blakemere Hall	1 mile (1.6km) west of Sandiway, 5 miles (8km) southwest of Nantwich. Blakemere Hall was built in 1878, and the stables, which now house shops, were erected in 1890. Edward VII, then Prince of Wales, often visited Blakemere, where it is claimed he enjoyed many notoriously wild parties. In 1940 the government commandeered the premises to accommodate German prisoners of war and Polish refugees. Blakemere Hall was demolished in 1950; now only the stables and the Blakemere name remain.
Blue Planet Aquarium	1½ miles (2.5km) south of Ellesmere Port. The UK's largest aquarium, with two floors of interactive displays. Attractions include Europe's largest collections of sharks, rays in rock pools, the world of poisonous frogs, and a Caribbean reef tank in which is contained a 233ft (71m) underwater walkway tunnel, one of the longest in the world. The Aquatheatre, a huge window 13ft (4m) high, allows visitors to view the deepest section of the tank where divers hand-feed the fish throughout the day. Tel: 0151 3578804.
Bollington Discovery Centre	Bollington, 2 miles (3km) north of Macclesfield. Situated in Clarence Mill, a former cotton mill the centre holds a unique collection of historic photographs of local life since the 1860s. Tel: 01625 572985.
Bonewaldesthorne's Tower	See Chester City Walls
Bunbury Watermill	Bunbury, 7 miles (11km) northwest of Nantwich. A 19th century working corn mill next to the River Gowy. Tel: 01829 261422.
Capesthorne Hall	Siddington, 5 miles (8km) west of Macclesfield. Set in parkland and overlooking a chain of lakes, the manor house and gardens were built in 1730. Capesthorne Hall is the home of William Bromley Davenport, Lord-Lieutenant of Cheshire, the Queen's chief representative in the county. Tel: 01625 861221.
Catalyst Chemical Museum	Mersey Road, Widnes. The museum features a range of interactive exhibits and hands-on displays. There are four main galleries: Scientific, Birth of an Industry, Chemicals for Life and the Observatory Gallery. The rooftop observatory, accessed by a glass lift, provides panoramic views of Cheshire. Tel: 0151 420 1121.
Cheshire Military Museum	Located in Chester Castle (see separate entry). The museum tells the story of the four famous regiments connected with the County of Cheshire: the Cheshire Regiment, the Cheshire Yeomanry, the 3rd Carabiniers, the 5th Royal Inniskilling Dragoon Guards. Tel: 01244 327617.
Chester Castle	Castle Square, Chester. The Norman castle, founded by Hugh d'Avranches, Earl of Chester, was constructed of timber in 1069 on the site of an earlier Roman fortress. It was rebuilt in stone in the early 13th century. Only the Agricola Tower from this period still stands, as the remainder was demolished at the end of the 18th century for new court buildings, designed by Thomas Harrison and completed in 1810. The castle has an exhibition illustrating its 900-year history.
Chester Cathedral	St Werburgh Street, Chester. Towering above the city of Chester is its Anglican cathedral, originally an early 10th century church dedicated to St Werburgh, a Mercian princess whose shrine became a destination for medieval pilgrimage. The composer Handel first rehearsed the *Messiah* here in 1742 – a copy of his marked score remains on display. The second church on the site was built by Hugh 'Lupus' (the Wolf), Earl of Chester, in 1092, perhaps as expiation for his worldly excesses. Anselm of Bec, later Archbishop of Canterbury, helped found Hugh's monastic settlement. Beginning in 1250 a third church was begun, this time in Norman Gothic style. The monks of Chester built the new church over the top of the old one, which they dismantled from the inside. The abbey was completed by 1520 and became a cathedral in 1542, when it was rededicated as the Cathedral Church of Christ and the Blessed Virgin Mary. An unusual feature of the cathedral is the freestanding bell tower, built in 1974 and the first such separate bell tower built in Britain since the 15th century. The cathedral also houses the finest choir stalls in Britain, with intricately carved misericords, and the famous Cobweb Picture, woven in Innsbruck in 1629 on a spider's web. Tel: 01244 324756.
Chester City Walls	The walls form the most complete circuit in Britain, so that Chester is quite rightly known as 'The Walled City'. The walls themselves are a Scheduled Ancient Monument and originate in the Roman period, c.AD 120; they were rebuilt and extended in the Saxon and medieval periods and restored in the 18th century after sustaining major damage during the Civil War. The walls form a 2 mile (3km) circular walk around the city. **Bonewaldesthorne's Tower** is a solid sandstone water tower (c.1325) in the northwest corner of the walls, with some Roman remains visible in the garden below. It is named after an officer in the pay of Aethelflaed, daughter of Alfred the Great, who expelled an army of occupying Danes from the fortress in the early 10th century. **King Charles'** (or the **Phoenix**) **Tower**, restored in 1658, stands in the northeast corner of the walls.

From here Charles I watched his troops defeated at Rowton Moor in 1645. The tower houses a small Civil War museum. The semicircular **Goblin Tower** or 'Pemberton's Parlour' is located on the walls beyond Northgate, beside the Shropshire Union Canal. A sailmaker called Pemberton apparently used to keep a watchful eye on his workforce from this vantage point. The **Wishing Steps** are situated beyond Bridgegate near the River Dee, at the point where the walls turn north. Legend suggests that anyone who runs up and down the steps twice without drawing breath will have their wish fulfilled.

Chester Roman Amphitheatre — Vicars Lane, Chester. The largest Roman amphitheatre in Britain. The two-storey edifice was once used for entertainment and military training by the 20th Legion, based at the fortress of Deva. Excavations in February 2007 proved that gladiatorial contests took place here, probably c.AD 100. A stone block with iron fittings discovered at the site is similar to one depicted in a 3rd century mosaic found at the Roman villa at Bignor, West Sussex, which shows two gladiators fighting. Such spectacles only took place in the most important Roman cities, thereby enhancing Chester's reputation as a leading Roman city. Tel: 01244 402466.

Chester Zoo — Caughall Road, Upton, Chester. Opened in 1931, the UK's largest zoo is set in 110 acres (44ha) of award-winning gardens, with over 7000 animals living in near-natural surroundings. Tel: 01244 380280.

Cholmondeley Castle Gardens — Malpas, 12 miles (19km) southwest of Nantwich. A hillside garden crowned with an early 19th century castle (not open to the public). The grounds are home to rose and temple gardens and herbaceous borders as well as rare breeds of farm animals. Tel: 01829 720383.

Church of St Oswald — Church Street, Malpas. Grade I listed church standing near the site of a Norman motte and bailey castle. Originally built in the late 14th century on possibly earlier foundations, it was largely rebuilt in the 15th century in Perpendicular style. Constructed of red sandstone with lead roofs, it has a massive three-stage tower with diagonal west buttresses, angled east buttresses and southeast octagonal turret. The Grade II* listed gates at the southeast corner were originally made for Oulton Park, probably in the 1720s at the time of John Vanbrugh's work there, and were moved to Malpas churchyard in 1773.

Congleton Museum — Market Square, Congleton. Established in 2002, the museum tells the town's history through interactive displays. Exhibits include a medieval log boat, coin hoards from the Civil War, fustian cutting displays and wartime experiences. Tel: 01260 276360.

Cuckooland — Tabley, 1½ miles (2.5km) west of Knutsford. The collection, acquired over 30 years, has more than 500 exhibits including five fairground organs, all made in the Black Forest. There are also rare cuckoo clocks and other timepieces, many with ingenious movements and beautiful highly carved cases. Tel: 01565 633039.

Daresbury — Located 4 miles (6km) east of Runcorn, Daresbury provided much inspiration for *Alice's Adventures In Wonderland*. Lewis Carroll (Charles Lutwidge Dodgson) was born in the village in 1832, and his father was rector here. Lewis spent the first ten years of his life in this quiet corner of rural Cheshire. The family moved when his father, an Anglican priest, took up an appointment in Yorkshire. In the parish church of All Saints, a fine stained glass window features the author and many of the characters from *Alice's Adventures in Wonderland* including a carving of a grinning cat, a play on the wildcat in the arms of a local family empowered in the Middle Ages to kill poachers by hanging or garrotting (giving them a 'permanent grin'). The tall tower of the Van de Graaff accelerator is a local landmark. This forms part of the SRC Daresbury Laboratory, the second largest of the Science Research Council's UK laboratories, established here in 1962.

Delamere Forest — 6 miles (10km) west of Northwich. Delamere Forest Park comprises over 2350 acres (950ha) of mixed deciduous and evergreen forest, open grassland and wetlands. It is the largest wooded area in Cheshire and lies within Mersey Forest. The recently restored wetland of Blakemere Moss has become an excellent habitat for a wide variety of wildlife including the beautiful small tortoiseshell butterfly, greater spotted woodpecker, white faced darter dragonfly, green woodpecker, siskin and southern hawker dragonfly.Tel: 01606 889792.

Dock Road Edwardian Pumping Station — Weir Street, Northwich. A restored Grade II listed building containing a unique set of working gas-powered engines and pumps, including the machinery used to pump water through a system of pipes which fed local residential and industrial needs. Tel: 01457 864187.

Dodleston Castle — Dodleston, 4 miles (6km) southwest of Chester. Norman earthwork motte and bailey fortress founded by Osberne fitzTezzon. The base of the motte is encased by a ditch with a counterscarp bank, while a wide wet ditch gives defence to the large square bailey.

Dorfold Hall — Acton, 1 mile (1.6km) west of Nantwich. Jacobean country house built in 1616 for Ralph Wilbraham and now the family home of Mr and Mrs Richard Roundell. The Nantwich International Cheese Show (see Interesting facts) is held annually at Cheshire Showground in the grounds of the hall. Tel: 01270 625245.

Dunge Valley Gardens — 1½ miles (2km) south of Kettleshulme, 5 miles (8km) northeast of Macclesfield. A 6 acre (2.4ha) woodland garden established in the 1980s at an elevation of over 1000ft (305m) in the Pennines, with rhododendron dells, streams, ponds, bridges and bog gardens. Tel: 01663 733787.

Eaton Hall — Eccleston, 2 miles (3km) south of Chester. A large country house under the ownership of the Duke of Westminster. The 11,000 acre (4450ha) estate has belonged to the Grosvenor family since the reign of Henry VI in the 15th century, when Ralph Grosvenor married Joan, daughter of John Eaton and heiress to the estate. The house has been rebuilt several times. Sir John Vanbrugh built a brick house on the site at the end of the 17th century. William Porden reconstructed the house 1804–12 in Gothic style, doubling its size. Eaton Hall served as a hospital in both world wars and as an officer cadet training school 1946–60. Later, a new house in the modern international style was built; the architect was John Dennys, the 5th Duke's brother-in-law. Although ducal in size, its stark frontage found little favour with either architectural critics or visitors: one commented that it resembled the largest petrol station in Cheshire. In the 1990s, the house was built up and refaced in a pared-down version of French Classicism. The house is a private residence and not open to the public.

Englesea Brook Chapel and Museum — Englesea Brook, 4 miles (6km) southeast of Crewe. One of the oldest surviving Primitive Methodist chapels, dating to 1828, Englesea Brook shows the simplicity typical of rural chapels in the early days of the movement, which started on the Cheshire/Staffordshire border in 1807. Tel: 01782 810109.

Gawsworth Hall — 3 miles (5km) southwest of Macclesfield. A 15th century half-timbered historic house, once home to Mary Fitton, maid of honour at the court of Queen Elizabeth I and a candidate for the 'dark lady' of Shakespeare's sonnets. The house is surrounded by Elizabethan gardens and an open air theatre is situated in the grounds. Tel: 01260 223456.

Grosvenor Museum — Grosvenor Street, Chester. Opened in 1886 and still occupying its original purpose-built premises, the museum includes internationally famous collections with displays on Roman Chester and the Roman army. There are collections of oil paintings, sculpture, furniture and Chester silver, and exhibits exploring the work of naturalist and novelist Charles Kingsley. Tel: 01244 402008.

Hack Green — 2 miles (3km) south of Nantwich. Hack Green nuclear bunker was, for over 50 years, one of the nation's most secret defence sites. This vast underground complex was declassified only in 1993. The 35,000 sq ft bunker, built in the 1950s as part of a vast secret radar network codenamed 'ROTOR', would have been the centre of regional government had nuclear war broken out. Rebuilt in the 1980s at a cost of over £32 million, it can now be explored by the public. Tel: 01270 629219.

Hare Hill — Over Alderley, 4 miles (6km) northwest of Macclesfield. Victorian woodland gardens with rhododendrons and azaleas, walled garden and pergola, all surrounded by parkland. Owned by the National Trust. Tel: 0161 928 0075.

Highest point — Shining Tor at 1834ft (559m) (GR: SJ994737), a hill in the Peak District between Buxton and Macclesfield, on the border between Derbyshire and Cheshire. There is another Shining Tor, above Dovedale in Derbyshire (GR: SK145545).

Hooton Park Aerodrome — Hooton, 2 miles (3km) west of Ellesmere Port. The former RAF Hooton Park was originally built for the Royal Flying Corps in 1917 as a training aerodrome for pilots in World War I. During World War II it was home to 610 (County of Chester) Squadron and 611 Squadron. The aerodrome closed in 1957, but three Belfast Truss hangars survived the closure. Hooton Park is also home to the Griffin Trust and the Aeroplane Collection. Tel: 0151 327 3565.

Interesting facts — Often considered to be Britain's oldest cheese, **Cheshire cheese** is slightly salty and crumbly with a nutty flavour and smooth texture. Genuine Cheshire is traditionally made with milk from cattle grazed on the salty pastures of the Cheshire plain. It is mentioned in Domesday Book and was a favourite at the court of Elizabeth I. Originally made near the village of Chester on the River Dee, it soon spread to farms throughout the county. The classic recipes still survive and cheeses are available marbled with red, white and blue mould. Cheshire cheese takes only a few hours to make and ripens in four to eight weeks. The blue-veined version matures for longer and has a particularly good flavour. Some of the best cheeses are shown annually at the end of July at the **Nantwich International Cheese Show**, held at Cheshire Showground, Dorfold Hall (see separate entry) and generally accepted as the definitive cheese show in the British Isles. The Supreme Championship – the National Westminster Cup – is hotly contested, with thousands of entries from over 19 countries. **Robert Nixon** of Over, the 'Palatine Prophet', was famed for his rhyming prophecies in the 15th century. Probably born in the mid 15th century some of his prophecies, made at Vale Royal Abbey, allude to incidents that had happened before his birth, others can only be loosely attributed to future incidents. See also Vale Royal Abbey. In May 1993 two peat-cutters working at Lindow Moss, near Wilmslow, dug up the skull of a middle-aged woman. Police reported the find to **Peter Reyn-Bardt**, a former executive with BOAC, whose wife had disappeared in 1960, and under interrogation he confessed to her murder. He had strangled Malika and chopped up her body and buried the remains in the peat bog. He was tried and found guilty at Chester Crown Court and sentenced to life imprisonment. Subsequently the skull was sent to Oxford University for radiocarbon dating and was found to be dated c.AD 410. The following year another skeleton was found in the bog with more obvious evidence of a violent death; it turned out to be the remains of a man killed ritualistically c.300 BC (see Lindow Man). The whereabouts of Mrs Reyn-Bardt remain a mystery. **Elizabeth Gaskell** (1810–65) was born in London as Elizabeth Stevenson. After the loss of her mother at the age of one, she was brought up by her aunt, Hannah Lamb, in Knutsford. Her second published novel, *Cranford* (1853), about a town ruled by women, mostly single or widowed, is thought to be based on her early life in Knutsford. **Macclesfield**'s traditional local nickname is 'Treacle Town', supposedly from an incident in the 19th century when barrels of treacle fell off a cart in Beech Land and Hibel Road, spilling their contents, and the greedy townsfolk rushed out to scoop up the load. Another, less picturesque, reason has it that the mill-owners used to provide barrels of treacle to unemployed weavers. Whatever the truth of the stories, the now more common and polite nickname is Silk Town. **Hovis** was registered in 1890 by Richard Smith, a miller at Macclesfield. He launched a competition for the name of his flour with extra wheatgerm and chose Hovis (Latin, *hominis vis* – strength of man) as the winner. **Barnaby Bear** is undoubtedly one of the most famous residents of Chester. Born on 31 January 1995 at 5 Elaine Street, Chester, Barnaby first appeared in a unit entitled 'Where in the world is Barnaby Bear?' in *Geography: A Scheme of Work for Key Stages 1 and 2*, published by QCA/DfES. The bear was brought to life by a BBC2 Schools series and has become an invaluable aid in helping primary school children gain an awareness of world geography. **Agnes Haddock**, a 50-year-old cleaner from Northwich, won £688,620 for a £2 stake on the horses in February 2007. Ellesmere Port-born **Sam Chedgzoy** (1889-1967) played football for England but is more famous for changing the rules of the game. In 1926 whilst playing for Everton against Tottenham Hotspur, his team was awarded a corner kick. Instead of crossing the ball in the normal manner, Sam took advantage of a recent rule change and decided to dribble the ball into the penalty area, and scored while the other players and referee looked on in shock. Although the goal was given the law was subsequently amended making it clear that the player taking the corner could only strike the ball once before another player must make contact.

Jodrell Bank Observatory — 1 mile (1.6km) west of Withington Green, 8 miles (13km) west of Macclesfield. Established in 1945 by Sir Bernard Lovell, the world famous Lovell Radio Telescope and the Jodrell Bank Observatory is the astronomy research centre of the University of Manchester. Tel: 01477 571339.

King Charles' Tower — See Chester City Walls

Knutsford Heritage Centre — King Street, Knutsford. The restored 18th century blacksmith's shop contains displays on Knutsford's history. Tel: 01625 650506.

Lindow Man — In August 1984 the head, torso and right foot of a man was discovered by workmen extracting peat at Lindow Moss near Wilmslow. Given the name Lindow Man, or Lindow II, his was in fact the second body recovered from Lindow Moss (see Interesting Facts for details of the first). He was discovered lying between two layers of peat, suggesting that at the time of deposition the area had been a deep pool. His arms had badly deteriorated at a much earlier date, probably immediately after his death. Fragments of a second body (Lindow III) were found in 1987, while in 1988, further body parts were unearthed, consisting of the skin of the buttocks, part of the left leg, and the right thigh and femur of a man; originally labelled Lindow IV, these are now generally considered to be further remains of Lindow Man, as the pieces from both finds combine to form a single body. Using radiocarbon dating techniques, researchers have placed the body in a date range of 2 BC–AD 119. Several outstanding physical characteristics raise implications about Lindow Man's death. He was probably a man of status, judging by his neatly trimmed hair, beard and nails. All the damage on his body could have been caused naturally over time; however, he is regarded by many as a victim of ritual sacrifice. One of the most common Celtic religious symbols is 'triplism', and Lindow Man may posibly have suffered a triple death. He seems to have been viciously strangled and garrotted, his throat split from one end to the other; his head bears evidence that he was bludgeoned by something like the blunt side of an axe blade; and his neck and torso reveal other marks, such as stab wounds, that can be explained as the result of violence. His stomach contents also include grains of mistletoe pollen mixed with the remnants of a simple grain cake; this has been taken as a possible Druid link.

Lion Salt Works — Marston, 1 mile (1.6km) northeast of Northwich. A monument to Cheshire's salt industry, the sole surviving open-pan salt works in Britain. Tel: 01606 41823.

Little Budworth Country Park — 3 miles (5km) west of Winsford. Located north of the Oulton Park circuit (see separate entry). A remnant of the medieval hunting forest of Mara and Mondrum, once part of Delamere Forest, this area of ancient heathland has remained largely unchanged for thousands of years, with heather, gorse and bracken set in a silver birch wood. Tel: 01606 889941.

Little Moreton Hall — 2 miles (3km) southwest of Congleton. Bordered by a moat, the black and white Tudor hall is considered among the finest timber-framed manor houses in England. Begun c. 1450 for Sir Richard de Morton and extended by his successors until the 1580s, its irregular gables, windows and patterned timbers give it a fairytale quality. The grounds include a recreated Elizabethan knot garden, yew tunnel and orchard. Now owned by the National Trust. Tel: 01260 272018.

Lymm Dam — Lymm, 4 miles (6km) east of Warrington. A lake created in 1824 by the damming of an existing pool and stream during the construction of the toll road between Warrington and Stockport. Once part of the Lymm Hall Estate and later bought by Lord Lever, it is now in local authority ownership. Surrounded by woodland, the lake now provides a habitat for a wide range of wildlife.

Lower Bridge Street — This Chester street contains rows of half-timbered houses, notably Falcon House (17th century), Tudor House (16th century, believed to be the oldest dwelling house in the town), the Old King's Head Hotel (17th century) and the Bear and Billet (1664), a four-storey half-timbered inn near the Bridgegate.

Lyme Park — 6 miles (10km) north of Macclesfield. Featured in BBC TV's *Pride and Prejudice* (1995), the manor house is a stately mix of Elizabethan architecture with 18th and 19th century adaptations by Giacomo Leoni and Lewis Wyatt. The 17 acre (7ha) Victorian garden contains spectacular formal bedding and a sunken Dutch garden in 1400 acres (566ha) of park and moorland. Now owned by the National Trust. Tel: 01663 766492.

Macclesfield Canal — Opened in 1831, one of the last canals to be built in England. The shallow canal, engineered by Thomas Telford, runs for 27 miles (43km) between the Trent & Mersey Canal at Harding's Wood Junction and the Peak Forest Canal at Marple Junction. The canal is the highest point on the British inland waterway system. It is beautifully maintained, its 12 locks being grouped in a single flight at Bosley, in typical Telford style. The great stone chambers of the locks are unusual in having double gates at both ends – the stone was quarried locally at The Cloud, a hill which dominates the locks. The southern reaches of the canal are overshadowed by the village of Mow Cop, which marks the Staffordshire/Cheshire border, and is topped by the castellated ruin known as Mow Cop Castle or Wilbraham's Folly (see Staffordshire). Two great houses border the canal – Little Moreton Hall (see separate entry), and Ramsdell Hall, built in 1760, with garden lawns sweeping down to the edge of the water. As it moves north, the canal passes through Congleton and on to Macclesfield. Macclesfield's silk industry was a major factor in the building of the 'Macc' (as it is known locally) and the canal runs high above the town. At the Marple basin is a beautifully preserved industrial building, still housing the British Waterways Office and the original tally office beside the Top Lock.

Macclesfield Heritage Centre Roe Street, Macclesfield. Within the Heritage Centre is the Silk Heritage Museum which tells the story of the development of the silk industry in the town. Silk costumes and textiles illustrate the importance of silk to fashion and its use for other special occasions. Formerly a Sunday school, the building also contains an auditorium dominated by a refurbished 19th century organ built by renowned Manchester organ builder Samuel Renn. Tel: 01625 613210.

Macclesfield Paradise Mill Park Lane, Macclesfield. Situated a short distance from the Silk Museum, and the site of a working silk mill until 1981, today Paradise Mill is a living museum featuring restored jacquard handlooms. Tel: 01625 613210.

Macclesfield Silk Museum Park Lane, Macclesfield. A building which once housed Macclesfield School of Art, established to train designers for the silk industry, is now the home to exhibitions exploring the properties of silk, design education, Macclesfield's diverse textile industries, workers' lives and historic machinery. Until the 1990s, the School of Art was used by Macclesfield College of Further Education. Tel: 01625 613210.

Maiden Castle 10 miles (16km) west of Nantwich. Located on the southernmost peak of Bickerton Hill, Maiden Castle is an Iron Age promontory hill fort dating to c.600 BC. The double line of earth ramparts are still visible, forming a semicircle that encloses an area of 1.3 acres (0.5ha) near the cliff edge. The enclosure has a single entrance with inturned defensive banks. Both ramparts are strengthened by drystone walling and according to archaeological investigation the inner rampart also has timber strapping. The fort was destroyed by fire c.400 BC although the area was probably used as a settlement until the 1st century AD. Today, the site is well preserved despite 17th century quarrying in the area. The remaining earthworks have been designated a Scheduled Ancient Monument.

Malpas Castle Malpas, 15 miles (24km) south of Chester. A dominating earthwork motte, founded by Robert de Malopassu. The large 11th century motte is 12ft (3.7m) high with surrounding ditch. The bailey is obscured by a graveyard and bowling green.

Marbury Country Park 2 miles (3km) north of Northwich. The 200 acres (81ha) of attractive parkland and mature woodland were formerly the site of Marbury Hall, a Victorian house based on the chateau at Fontainebleau in France, and retain features of the estate such as lime avenues and an arboretum. There are fine views over Budworth Mere. Tel: 01606 77741.

Mouldsworth Motor Museum 6 miles (10km) east of Chester. The museum is housed in a 1930s Art Deco building and contains a unique collection of over 60 vintage, classic and sports cars, motorcycles and early bicycles. Tel: 01928 731781.

Nantwich Museum Pillory Street, Nantwich. The museum's main galleries tell the story of Nantwich through the ages – Roman salt making, Tudor Nantwich's Great Fire, the Civil War Battle of Nantwich (1644) and the more recent shoe and clothing industries. Tel: 01270 627104.

National Waterways Museum South Pier Road, Ellesmere Port. One of the National Waterways Museum's three sites (the others being at Stoke Bruerne in Northamptonshire and at Gloucester), the museum is dedicated to Britain's waterway history and set within a historic dock complex at the northern terminus of the Shropshire Union Canal (where goods were once exchanged with sea-going boats). It is the home of the world's largest floating collection of canal craft, some of which may be boarded. Tel: 01513 555017.

Ness Botanic Gardens 1 mile (1.6km) south of Neston, 9 miles (15km) northwest of Chester. Overlooking the Dee Estuary, the 64 acres (26ha) of botanic gardens include a collection of rhododendrons, azaleas, laburnum arch, herbaceous borders and various gardens including rock, water, herb and heather. Tel: 0151 353 0123.

Nether Alderley Mill 4 miles (6km) west of Macclesfield. A 15th century water mill which once ground corn for the Nether Alderley estate. Features include original Elizabethan roof timbers and tandem overshot waterwheels with Victorian machinery fully restored to working order. Now owned by the National Trust. Tel: 01625 527468.

Norton Priory Museum 2 miles (3km) east of Runcorn. The 38 acre (15ha) site includes the world famous St Christopher statue, dating to c.1390, and priory undercroft. The 12th century Augustinian priory is surrounded by woodland gardens and is home to a collection of contemporary sculpture. The walled garden is planted with old varieties of roses, herbs, fruit and vegetables. Tel: 01625 584412.

Old Castle 12 miles (19km) southwest of Nantwich. The motte and associated ditch system, possibly dating to the 11th or early 12th century, discovered during tree felling in 1957. The surviving earthworks consisted of a small platform 128ft (40m) by 25ft (8m) defended on the north by two deep transverse ditches, and on the south by three similar ditches. Excavations have discovered a possible hearth sealed beneath a layer of stones.

Old Dee Bridge An ancient bridge in Chester, spanning the River Dee from the bottom of Lower Bridge Street and Bridge Gate to Handbridge/Treboeth. It has seven arches of unequal dimensions. The bridge is widely believed to have been begun c.1387, succeeding a number of other bridges that had either been burnt or washed away. There had been a river crossing place or ford since pre-Roman times, which gives credence to the idea that there has been continuous occupation in the area for well over 2000 years.

Oulton Park Circuit $^1/_2$ mile (0.8km) west of Little Budworth, 3 miles (5km) west of Winsford. A motor racing track set in the grounds of Oulton Hall, which were used as an army staging camp by General Patton prior to the D-Day landings. Originally the circuit was developed by the Mid-Cheshire Car Club, the track attracting crowds of nearly 40,000 during the 1950s. Oulton Park regularly housed the 'Gold Cup' event which attracted many Formula One teams (Stirling Moss won it five times), but as the F1 calendar shrank to include only Grand Prix events, the Cup became less well known. The event has been run for a number of other categories including Formula 5000, sports cars and touring cars and has now been re-established as a highlight of the classic racing calendar. The British Touring Car Championship, the Formula Three/British GT Championship and the British

Superbike Championship meetings are also highlights of the year. The full track is 2.8 miles (4.5km) long, and is famous for its rapidly changing gradients and blind crests leading into steep corners. Tel: 01829 760301.

Peckforton Castle — 7½ miles (12km) northwest of Nantwich. A Grade I listed Victorian country house built in the style of a medieval castle by Cheshire MP John Tollemache 1844–51 to designs by Anthony Salvin. The castle is situated at the north end of the Peckforton Hills, the sandstone ridge running north–south across west Cheshire, close to the genuinely medieval Beeston Castle (see separate entry). It is known as the home of the original Treasure Trap club, a live action role-playing group, and has been used as a location for several films and TV shows, including *Doctor Who*.

Pemberton's Parlour — See Chester City Walls

Peover Hall — Over Peover, 3 miles (5km) southeast of Knutsford. An Elizabethan house dating from 1585, with mid 17th century stables and an 18th century landscaped park. During World War II it was the headquarters of General Patton and the US Third Army. Tel: 01565 632358.

Pickerings Pasture — Hale Bank, 2 miles (3km) southwest of Widnes. Historically an area of salt marsh, the site was used as waste tip from the 1950s until it was reclaimed in the 1980s. Now a Local Nature Reserve with wildflower meadows and views across the Mersey estuary. Tel: 0151 4254706.

Prisons — **Risley**, near Warrington, was opened as a male/female remand centre in 1964, becoming a male category C training prison in 1990. The site was shared with a female remand centre and a male allocation centre until these two facilities closed in 1999 and 2000. Operational capacity: 1073. Tel: 01925 733000.

Styal, Wilmslow, was built in the 1890s as an orphanage which closed in 1956. The site opened as a women's prison in 1962 when female prisoners from Strangeways were transferred in. From 1983 young offenders were admitted and in 1999 a wing was added to accommodate unsentenced female prisoners following the closure of Risley's remand centre, increasing the prison size by 60 per cent. The prison was featured in the BBC2 documentary *Women on the Edge – the Truth about Styal Prison* on 27 February 2006. Operational capacity: 469. Tel: 01625 553000.

Thorn Cross, Warrington, is a purpose built open young offender institution opened in 1985 on the site of a former Royal Navy air station which was previously used as an open adult establishment. Operational capacity: 321. Tel: 01925 805100.

Pulford Castle — 6 miles (10km) south of Chester. A 12th century earthwork motte and bailey fortress founded by Robert de Pulford. Surrounding the low motte are the remains of a ditch with a counterscarp bank, and standing against the slope of Pulford Brook is a rectangular bailey. This small castle defended the ancient crossing point and was garrisoned against Owain Glyndwr in 1403.

Quarry Bank Mill and Styal Estate Museum — Styal, 1½ miles (2.5km) north of Wilmslow. Quarry Bank Mill on the River Bollin was founded by Samuel Greg in 1784; its original iron waterwheel was designed by Thomas Hewes and built between 1816 and 1820. Today the mill is home to the most powerful working waterwheel in Europe, an iron wheel originally at Glasshouses Mill at Pateley Bridge and designed by Scottish engineer Sir William Fairbairn, a former apprentice of Hewes. The museum tells the story of the mill and the cotton industry through reconstruction, live demonstrations and interactive displays. At the Apprentice House, home to the pauper children who worked at the mill, mill life is relived through the eyes of a nine year old. Now owned by the National Trust. Tel: 01625 527468.

Railway Age, The — Vernon Way, Crewe. A museum dedicated to railway history. Exhibits include miniature, model and standard gauge railways, working signal boxes, diesel and steam engines. Tel: 01270 212130.

Risley Moss — Risley, 4 miles (6km) northeast of Warrington. A woodland park and Local Nature Reserve, also a designated Site of Special Scientific Interest. The site includes the remains of an ancient mossland, part of the raised lowland peat bog which once covered most of this region but examples of which are now rare in the UK. Tel: 01925 824339.

Rivers — The **Bollin**, a major tributary of the River Mersey, rises in Macclesfield Forest at the western end of the Peak District, and can be seen in spring form from the Buxton to Macclesfield road. The stream then descends for 10 miles (16km) through Macclesfield and Wilmslow where it merges with the River Dean. For the following 10 miles it defines the southwestern border between Greater Manchester and Cheshire before merging with the Mersey north of Lymm. It flows through Styal Country Park and is used as a source of power in the cotton calico factory there.

The **Croco**, a small tributary of the Dane, flows through Holmes Chapel.

The **Dane** rises in Derbyshire, close to the source of the River Goyt just to the southwest of Buxton, on Axe Edge Moor. Flowing southwest, it forms the border between Cheshire and Staffordshire for 10 miles (16km) before flowing west through Congleton and past Holmes Chapel. The point on the river where the three counties meet, at Panniers' Pool Bridge, is called the Three Shires' Head. Passing just to the north of Middlewich it merges with the River Wheelock near the aqueduct carrying the Trent and Mersey Canal, and runs the remaining 5 miles (8km) north to Northwich where it flows into the River Weaver.

The **Dean** rises at Longclough in Macclesfield Forest on the western edge of the Peak District, above the village of Rainow in northeast Cheshire. The river passes through Rainow and the town of Bollington, on through the grounds of Adlington Hall, joining the Bollin between Wilmslow and Styal.

The **Dee** (Welsh, Afon Dyfrdwy), 70 miles (110km) long, rises on the slopes of Dduallt above Llanuwchllyn in Snowdonia, passes through Bala Lake and east to Llangollen and Bangor before flowing north via Chester into the Irish sea. Its total catchment area as far as Chester Weir is approximately 700 sq miles (1800 sq km). The **Dee Estuary**, where the River Dee flows into Liverpool Bay, starts near Shotton and swells to a width of several miles, forming the boundary between the Wirral Peninsula and Flint, North Wales. It is a major wildlife area, one of the most important estuaries in the UK and among the most important in Europe for its populations of waders and wildfowl.

The **Gowy**, a tributary of the Mersey, rises in west Cheshire in the hills near Peckforton Castle, close to the source of the Weaver. While the Weaver flows south initially, the Gowy flows north and for several miles provides the valley used by the Shropshire Union Canal. It runs east of Chester and passes under the Manchester Ship Canal to meet the Mersey near Stanlow. Its total length is around 20 miles (32km).

The **Goyt**, another tributary of the Mersey, rises on the moors of Axe Edge, near the River Dane and the Cat and Fiddle Inn. The area is known as the Upper Goyt Valley. It crosses the old Cat and Fiddle Road from Buxton to Macclesfield at Derbyshire Bridge, the old boundary between Derbyshire and Cheshire. Then it reaches an old packhorse bridge which was moved when Errwood reservoir was built in the 1960s. Further downstream is the Fernilee reservoir. The original line of the Cromford and High Peak Railway can be seen near this point.

Mersey – see Merseyside

The **Weaver** follows a curving route anti-clockwise across west Cheshire. From its source near Peckforton Castle, it initially flows southeast towards the border with Shropshire. Just south of the Cheshire village of Audlem, the river turns north across the Cheshire Plain, and today empties into the Manchester Ship Canal at Weston Point Docks, Runcorn (it previously flowed into the Mersey). The 21 mile (33km) stretch north from Winsford Bridge is navigable (Acts of Parliament dating back to 1721 were introduced to allow the river to be canalised to carry freight, including salt and chemicals). Its most notable feature is the Anderton Boat Lift (see separate entry) near Northwich.

The **Wheelock** drains water from the area between Sandbach and Crewe. It joins the Dane at Middlewich, and the combined river flows into the Weaver in Northwich. It is called 'Whelocke' in Holinshed's *Chronicles* of 1578 and 'Hoiloch' in Domesday Book, its name coming from a Celtic word meaning 'winding'.

Rode Hall — Scholar Green, 4 miles (6km) southwest of Congleton. Georgian hall surrounded by terraced gardens including a rose garden, dell and fully working Victorian walled kitchen garden. Tel: 01270 873237.

Roodee, The — Outside Chester's west walls, on what was once part of the city's old port, lies the racecourse known as the Roodee (see Sport). The name means 'Rood Island', a rood being a large crucifix such as used to be displayed over the chancel arch in pre-Reformation churches. In Saxon times, the waters of the Dee covered the whole of this area with the exception of a small island upon which stood a stone cross, the stump of which may still be seen in the middle of the racecourse today.

Rows, The — The most photographed sight in Chester, a series of half-timbered buildings joined with long galleries, looking rather like a Tudor shopping mall. There is not one single 'Rows' but several complexes of houses in the same style, with the best examples on Watergate, Eastgate and Bridge Street. Their layout goes back to the 13th century. There were shops or warehouses at street level, with a long gallery above, reached by steps from the street. Living quarters are on the gallery level. In the Middle Ages this would have been a hall, open to the roof and heated by a central hearth. The private rooms, or solar, were above the gallery. In the Tudor and Jacobean periods the upper floors were built out over the gallery, supported on long poles down to the street level. Shops at ground level used the space between the posts to display their goods to passers-by.

Runcorn Bridge — A single-arch cantilever bridge spanning the Runcorn Gap, a narrowing of the River Mersey, and linking the towns of Runcorn and Widnes. Ferry crossings have been recorded at the spot as early as the 12th century. Work on the bridge started in 1954 and in 1961 it was opened to the public by Princess Alexandra of Kent. The original construction was a two-lane road traffic bridge built to replace the Widnes–Runcorn Transporter Bridge (see separate entry). In 1977 it was renamed the Silver Jubilee Bridge in honour of Queen Elizabeth II's Silver Jubilee. Built from 6000 tonnes of steel, the bridge is one of the largest of its kind worldwide with a main span of 1083ft (330m), its crown being 280ft (86m) above sea level. It is the largest bridge of its type in the UK, with proportions around two-thirds those of Sydney Harbour Bridge. The bridge has featured in two television series, *Two Pints of Lager and a Packet of Crisps* and *Merseybeat*.

Runcorn Hill — Highlands Road, Runcorn. Located in central Runcorn, this area of former sandstone quarries, now a Local Nature Reserve, also contains north Cheshire's largest surviving stretch of lowland heath. Tel: 0928 560793.

Runcorn Railway Bridge — Crossing the River Mersey from Runcorn to Widnes, the bridge was built for the London and North Western Railway to a design by William Baker and opened in 1869. In order to allow sailing ships to pass, it was constructed 75ft (23m) above high water mark. The total length of 1000ft (305m) is composed of three wrought-iron spans, supported on massive piers. The Manchester Ship Canal also passed under the bridge. It is still in use today and is on the Liverpool branch of the West Coast Main Line.

Runcorn–Widnes Transporter Bridge — See Widnes–Runcorn Transporter Bridge

Salt Museum — London Road, Northwich. Britain's only salt museum tells the story of Cheshire's oldest industry. Tel: 01606 41331.

Schools, Public — **The King's School, Chester** is a co-educational school for pupils aged 7–18. It was one of seven schools established or re-endowed by Henry VIII in 1541 after the Dissolution of the Monasteries for the education of 'poor friendless boys'.

The King's School, Macclesfield is a co-educational day school for pupils aged 3–18. Founded in 1502 by Sir John Percyvale, a former Lord Mayor of London, as Macclesfield

Grammar School, It was refounded on 26 April 1552 by Edward VI, from whom it takes its name. The school motto is '*Nil nisi malis terrori*' (No terror, except to the bad).

Shocklach Castle — Castletown, 10 miles (16km) south of Chester. The remains of a 13th century moated enclosure or fortified manor house close to the England/Wales border. On the opposite side of the road stands the motte of an 11th century Norman motte and bailey castle.

Shotwick Castle — 1 mile (1.6km) southeast of Shotwick, 5 miles (8km) northwest of Chester. The foundations of a motte and bailey castle built by Hugh Lupus, Earl of Chester in the late 11th century on the crest of a steep escarpment above the east bank of the former course of the River Dee. The motte itself is a small hexagonal mound; excavations in the 19th century indicate the foundations of a stone keep under the turf. The motte ditch would have been flooded at high tide. Under various owners it formed part of the defences of the Welsh border until 1281 when peace was finally made with the rulers of Wales. In 1327 the manor became a royal game park for the recreation of Edward III. Archaeological investigations carried out in 1995–6 identified a medieval formal garden on the castle site. Nearby St Michael's Church in Shotwick is one of Cheshire's hidden treasures.

Shutlingsloe — $^1/_2$ mile (0.8km) northwest of Wildboarclough, 4 miles (6km) southeast of Macclesfield. A hill on the western edge of the Peak District. Sometimes described as the 'Matterhorn of Cheshire', it is the second highest peak in the county with an elevation of 1660ft (506m), and commands excellent views.

Spike Island — 1 mile (1.6km) south of Widnes. The first inter-freight rail terminal in England, the site was one of the birthplaces of the British chemical industry, its name deriving from the practice of 'spiking' caustic soda in a local factory plant. In the late 19th century the area was dominated by the factories of industrialist John Hutchinson and soap-maker William Gossage, and was criss-crossed by a maze of railway lines. The land was decontaminated in the 1980s and restored as grassland and woodland. Catalyst, a science centre and museum devoted to chemistry and its products, now occupies part of Gossage's factory. The saltmarsh of nearby Widnes Wharf is a designated Site of Special Scientific Interest.

Sport

basketball — **Chester Jets** are based at the Northgate Arena in Chester and compete in the British Basketball League. Their colours are black, white and red.

football — Previously called King's School Old Boys, **Chester City** were founded in 1884 and joined the Football League in 1931. Nicknamed The Blues (also known as City), their colours are blue and white. Their home ground since 1992 has been the Saunders Honda Stadium (until 2004 the Deva Stadium). Tel: 01244 371376.

Crewe Alexandra were founded in 1877 and reputedly named after Princess Alexandra, joining the Football League as founder members of Division Two in 1892. Nicknamed The Railwaymen (the town is the site of a major rail junction and locomotive works), they play in red and white at the Alexandra Stadium, Gresty Road, Crewe. Tel: 01270 213014.

Macclesfield Town were founded in 1874 and reached the Football League in 1997, having been refused entry two years earlier because their ground did not comply with League regulations. Nicknamed The Silkmen in reference to the town's erstwhile silk industry, their traditional colours are blue and white; their home ground since 1891 has been the Moss Rose Stadium. Their local derby matches are against Stockport County, now part of Greater Manchester. Tel: 01625 264686.

horse racing — **Chester Racecourse**, known as The Roodee (see separate entry), is a left-handed circuit of 1 mile (1.6km) round, the shortest Flat course in England. The first official records of horse racing at Chester date back to the early 16th century, making it the oldest racecourse in Britain. The racing calendar starts with the May Meeting, a three-day affair that boasts the Chester Vase, Chester Cup and the Ormonde Stakes. Other highlights include the two-day July Festival and a two-day festival in August. Tel: 01244 304600.

rugby league — **Warrington Wizards** joined National League Three in 2005 and play at Wilderspool Stadium, Fletcher Street, Warrington, the former ground of their more illustrious neighbours Warrington Wolves. The Wizards play in purple.

Warrington Wolves were founded in 1879 as Warrington Zingari and play in the Super League in primrose (light yellow) and blue. One of their past nicknames is 'Wire', a reference to the wire-pulling industry in Warrington. They now play at the Halliwell Jones Stadium, Winwick Road, Warrington. Tel: 0871 622 1879.

Widnes Vikings were founded in 1873 and play at the Stobart Stadium, Lowerhouse Lane, Widnes. Nicknamed The Chemics, their colours are black and white. Tel: 0151 495 2250.

St John's Church — Vicar's Lane, Chester. Once the site of the first cathedral in Chester, dedicated in 1075. Although largely dating from the late 19th century, the present building retains part of a 12th century Norman church, in particular the still impressive nave, a fine example of the transition between Norman and Gothic styles. The original choir and Lady Chapel were destroyed when the central tower collapsed in 1468 and are now no more than picturesque ruins.

Stanney Woods — 2 miles (3km) south of Ellesmere Port. An attractive area of ancient, semi-natural woodland, largely of oak and silver birch. Tel: 0151 357 1991.

Stretton Watermill — Stretton, 8 miles (13km) south of Chester. One of England's best-preserved working water-powered corn mills. Parts of the structure date from 1630 and there has been a mill on the site since at least 1531.Tel: 01606 41331.

Styal Estate — 1 mile (1.6km) northwest of Wilmslow. An attractive, wooded valley of the River Bollin, which became a major centre of cotton production during the Industrial Revolution. Among the properties established on the estate by textile entrepreneur Samuel Greg and his family are

Quarry Bank Mill (see separate entry) and the factory colony village of Styal. Owned by the National Trust. Tel: 01625 527468.

Tabley House 2 miles (3km) west of Knutsford. A Palladian mansion designed by John Carr of York for Sir Peter Byrne Leicester and completed in 1767. Sir Peter's son, the 1st Lord de Tabley, was a great collector of British artwork and the house has an impressive collection of paintings, while J M W Turner, Henry Thompson and James Ward were among the many painters who visited Tabley. The property remained in the possession of the Leicester family until the death in 1975 of the last remaining heir, Lt. Col. John Leicester-Warren, and was acquired by the University of Manchester after an offer to the National Trust was declined. Tel: 01565 750151.

Tatton Park 2 miles (3km) north of Knutsford. A neoclassical mansion set in one of England's most complete historic estates. The house was initially designed by Samuel Wyatt (1737–1807) for William Egerton in 1791. After his death and following a gap of 17 years his nephew, Lewis Wyatt (1777–1853) scaled down the original plans to complete the present house. The house is full of art treasures and original furnishings; the estate is also home of the RHS Flower Show, while the gardens, set at the heart of 1000 acres (400ha) of parkland, have continually evolved over 200 years. Owned by the National Trust. Tel: 01625 534400.

Tegg's Nose Country Park 2 miles (3km) east of Macclesfield. A disused gritstone quarry forms the site for this country park, set high in Cheshire's eastern uplands. There are dramatic views over Cheshire and the Pennine foothills. Tel: 01625 614279.

University of Chester Parkgate Road, Chester. The university has its roots in one of the oldest higher education institutions in England – Chester Diocesan Training College, founded by a group of leading Anglicans (including future Prime Ministers William Gladstone and Lord Derby) in 1839 as the UK's first purpose-built teacher training college. In 1842 Gladstone opened the college's original buildings just outside Chester's city walls, on the Parkgate Road site the university still occupies today. It became an affiliated college of the University of Liverpool in 1930. Women were first admitted in 1962 and the college's name was changed to Chester College of Education in 1963. In 1974, Bachelor of Arts and Bachelor of Science degrees were offered for the first time. To reflect its wider remit, the college was renamed again to Chester College of Higher Education. In 2003, Chester was granted degree-awarding powers, before in 2005 it was awarded full university status as the University of Chester. Former students include playwright Alan Bleasdale and comedian Jim Bowen. Tel: 01244 511000.

Vale Royal Abbey $^1/_2$ mile (0.8km) northeast of Whitegate, 3 miles (5km) northwest of Winsford. The site of a Cistercian abbey founded in the 1270s by Edward I. After its dissolution in 1538 a house was built by royal commissioner Thomas Holcroft incorporating some of the former abbey buildings. Much altered since, this house still stands in what is now a golf course and private estate. In the 15th century the 'Palatine Prophet', Robert Nixon (see Interesting Facts) made many prophecies concerning the abbey's inhabitants. Tel: 01606 301291.

Walton Hall Gardens 2 miles (3km) south of Warrington. Part of the Greenall family estate from 1812, the gardens and parkland of Walton Hall, an Elizabethan revival house built in the 1830s, are now a public park. Tel: 01925 601617.

Warrington Museum & Art Gallery Bold Street, Warrington. The museum combines a Victorian 'cabinet of curiosities' charm with temporary exhibition galleries. Displays feature a wealth of material on the natural world including an Earth History gallery, as well as local history galleries featuring the industries that shaped the town. Tel: 01925 442392.

Warrington Transporter Bridge Also known as the Bank Quay Transporter Bridge. Crossing the River Mersey at Bank Quay in Warrington, with a span of 187ft (57m), the privately owned bridge was built in 1916 to connect the two parts of the large chemical and soap works of Messrs Joseph Crosfield & Son Ltd. It has been out of use since 1964, but still stands.

Watergate Street A Chester street with several half-timbered houses, including God's Providence House (1652) – the inhabitants of which were spared the plague – and Bishop Lloyd's House (early 17th century) with beautiful carvings on the front. Leche House (1579), a short distance away, also has elaborate half timbering, as does the richly decorated Stanley Palace (1591, extended c.1700). The Guildhall Museum contains an interesting exhibition relating to Chester's merchant guilds.

West Park Museum Prestbury Road, Macclesfield. The museum's collections comprise a wide range of fine and decorative art material and objects relating to local history. There are 19th and early 20th century paintings, and local history displays on law and order and the life of 18th century Macclesfield entrepreneur Charles Roe. The Ancient Egypt collection includes a mummy case. Tel: 01625 619831.

Widnes–Runcorn Transporter Bridge Spanning the River Mersey and Manchester Ship Canal, the bridge had a span of 1000ft (305m). Built in 1905, it was in use until 1961 when it was demolished to be superseded by the high-level, steel-arch Runcorn Bridge (see separate entry).

Wirral Country Park Willaston, 2 miles (3km) east of Neston. Country park on the Wirral Peninsula, lying both in the Metropolitan Borough of Wirral and the county of Cheshire. A 12 mile (19km) linear park along an abandoned railway line from West Kirby to Hooton, it was the first designated country park in Britain, opening in 1973. Tel: 0151 3275145.

Wishing Steps See Chester City Walls

Some famous people born in Cheshire

Abbot, Russ (musician, comedian, actor) (1947–)	Chester
Atkinson, Harry (premier of New Zealand) (1831–92)	Broxton, Chester
Barlow, Gary (Take That member) (1971–)	Frodsham
Boult, Adrian Cedric (conductor) (1889–1983)	Chester
Brown, Ian (musician) (1963–)	Warrington
Carroll, Lewis (author) (1832–98)	Daresbury
Chadwick, James (physicist) (1891–1974)	Bollington
Coleman, David (sports broadcaster) (1926–)	Alderley Edge
Craig, Daniel (actor) (1968–)	Chester
Crouch, Peter (footballer) (1981–)	Macclesfield
Curry, Tim (actor, singer, composer) (1946–)	Grappenhall
Evans, Chris (radio, television presenter) (1966–)	Warrington
Hamilton, Emma (Nelson's mistress) (1761–1815)	Neston
Johnston, Sue (actress) (1943–)	Warrington
Lloyd, Hugh (actor) (1923–2008)	Chester
Mallory, George (mountaineer) (1886–1924)	Mobberley
Mayall, John (pioneering blues singer) (1933–)	Macclesfield
Owen, Michael (footballer) (1979–)	Chester
Postlethwaite, Pete (actor) (1945–)	Warrington
Radcliffe, Paula (athlete) (1973–)	Davenham

Cornwall (and Isles of Scilly)

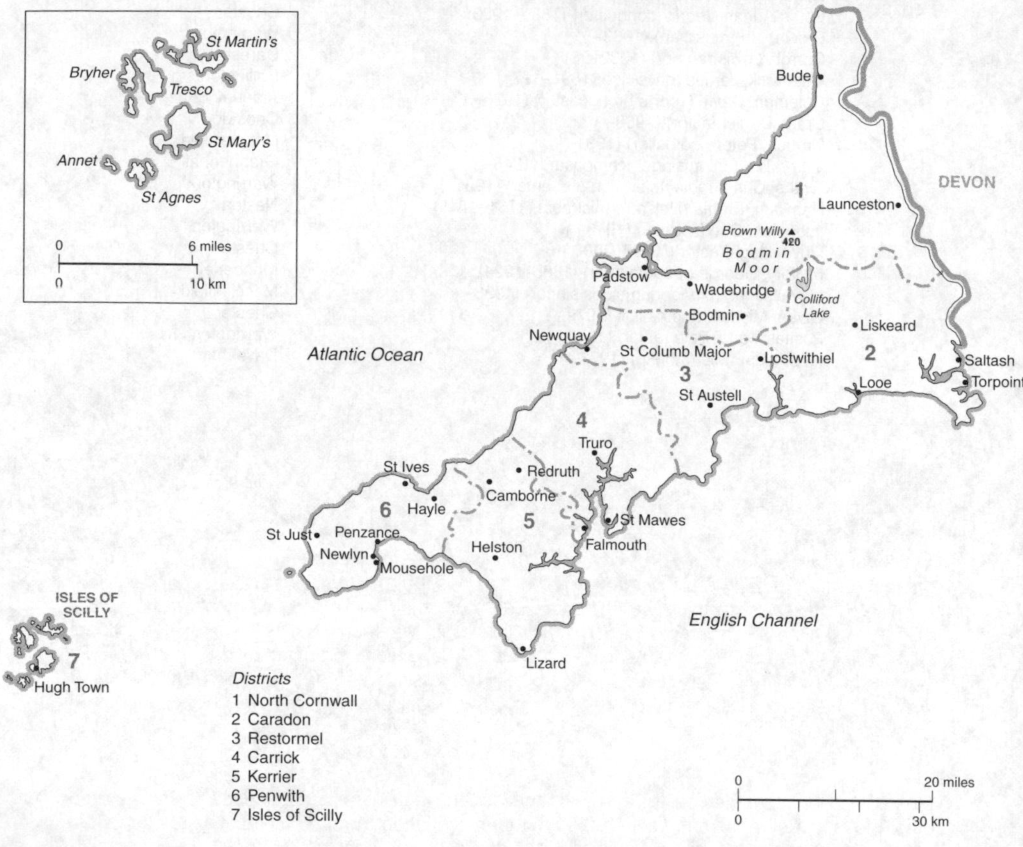

St Martin's
Bryher
Tresco
St Mary's
Annet
St Agnes
0
6 miles
0
10 km
Bude
DEVON
1
Launceston
Brown Willy
420
Bodmin
Moor
Padstow
Wadebridge
Colliford
Lake
Bodmin
Liskeard
Newquay
St Columb Major
Lostwithiel
2
Saltash
Atlantic Ocean
3
Looe
Torpoint
St Austell
4
Truro
St Ives
Redruth
Camborne
6
Hayle
5
St Mawes
St Just
Penzance
Newlyn
Helston
Falmouth
Mousehole
ISLES OF
SCILLY
English Channel
7
Lizard
Hugh Town
Districts
1 North Cornwall
2 Caradon
3 Restormel
4 Carrick
5 Kerrier
6 Penwith
7 Isles of Scilly
0
20 miles
0
30 km

Cornwall is located on the peninsula of southwest England that lies to the west of the River Tamar. It is unique among English counties in sharing a border with only one other county, Devon. The administrative centre and only city is Truro, and the historic capital is Bodmin. The name 'Cornwall' comes from *Cornovii*, meaning hill dwellers, and *Waelas*, meaning strangers. Traditionally part of Cornwall, the Isles of Scilly, located 28 miles (45km) offshore, now have their own local government although they are included in the St Ives constituency for voting purposes.

Although I have listed the six districts that have served the county since 1974, from 1 April 2009 they have been abolished, as has the county council, to form a single unitary authority.

Tourism forms the major part of the local economy; however Cornwall is the poorest area in the UK with the lowest contribution to the national economy, and is the only area in southern Britain to qualify for Objective One funding from the European Union, the stated aim of which is to improve the economic wellbeing of regions where the GDP per capita is below 75 per cent of the EU average.

There were few people in the region in the early Stone Age, but a drift across the land bridge from Europe brought settlers to Cornwall. The first stone tools found date from c.4500 BC. The remains of a Stone Age settlement at Carn Brea near Redruth and many burial chambers from this period also exist. Most of these have been damaged by weather or by man, but good examples can still be seen at Trethevy Quoit near St Cleer, Liskeard, and at Chun Cromlech near Land's End. Around 2500 BC a trade started in tin and copper to foreign shores. The remains of Bronze Age villages can still be seen on Bodmin Moor and the West Penwith uplands.

Around 1000 BC a group of warrior-like settlers arrived in Cornwall from Europe. These were the Celts, and they brought with them knowledge of forging iron into weapons. The ancestors of modern Cornwall, the Celts lived in villages, farmed, mined for tin, copper, bronze and iron, smelted and worked the metal. The best known of their Iron Age settlements is at Chysauster, near Penzance. Most of their settlements were fortified against attack – many were on hilltops or on promontories that could be easily defended. Hence the existence in Cornish place names of the words 'Car' or 'Caer' (from Celtic *ker*), fort, and 'Dinas', hill.

The Romans had very little influence in Cornwall. The last major Roman settlement in the west was at Exeter. The Tamar, the wild moors of Dartmoor, Exmoor and Bodmin Moor, plus the lack of safe ports effectively kept the Romans at bay, while the Roman presence kept other raiders away. The Cornish Celts were left much to themselves.

When the Romans abandoned Britain, Cornwall came under Saxon influence, and following the Norman Conquest its first real integration into Britain took place. The whole of Cornwall was given to William I's half-brother Robert, who made his headquarters at Launceston, building a castle to enforce his rule. For the next few hundred years Cornwall was ruled by a succession of relatives of the Norman and Plantagenet kings. The first Duke of Cornwall was Edward, the Black Prince, son of Edward III. A succession of rebellions throughout the Middle Ages had great effect on the Cornish people. In 1497, Perkin Warbeck landed at Whitesand Bay near Land's End, claiming to be one of the Princes murdered in the tower, but was defeated in battle at Exeter. The Prayer Book Rebellion of 1549 against the imposition of the English Book of Common Prayer saw many Cornishmen executed. The Spanish invaded at Mounts Bay in 1595, while three Civil War battles took place between 1642 and 1649 and in 1685 there was the Monmouth Rebellion with its bloody aftermath.

The invention of the steam engine in the 18th century and its rapid development in the 19th led to revolutionary advances in mining. Engines could now pump dry mines at a great depth and haul up ore, and on the surface could perform many of the jobs that had previously been done by hand. Cornishman Richard Trevithick was one of the leaders in steam engine development. By the middle of the 19th century, however, vast deposits of tin and copper ore had been found abroad, and deep, expensive Cornish mines became uncompetitive. The tin mining districts, known as stannaries, started a long downhill decline. Their only permanent legacy – apart from the remains of engine houses that still dot the landscape – is the Cornish communities that prospered in other countries, as many miners (Cousin Jacks as they were known in the western counties) emigrated to take their mining skills to Australia, North and South America and South Africa.

Mining is no longer carried out in Cornwall, fish stocks have been depleted and the county has little other industry, but it has fine scenery and the best climate in Britain – miles of sandy beaches, coastal walks, open moorland, and a benign climate that sees spring arriving early and autumn lingering longer. Hence tourism is the mainstay of the Cornish economy. Local residents, although embracing outsiders, like to maintain their traditions and way of life and those tourists who run around asking directions without the aid of maps, or act in overtly tourist ways are known as 'emmets' (Old English for 'ants'), a derogatory term like the Devonian 'grockle'.

Being exposed to the full force of the Atlantic Ocean, the Cornish coast is composed entirely of resistant rocks, as softer rocks have been eroded away. The centre of Cornwall is largely Devonian sandstone and slate. The northeast of the county lies on Carboniferous sandstone. Cornwall is particularly known for its igneous outcrops; these include the granite of Bodmin Moor and the areas around Camborne and Land's End, and the dark green serpentine of the Lizard Peninsula. The granite forms high treeless moors on which sheep graze, as well as the characteristic Cornish cliffs. The intrusion of the granite into the surrounding sedimentary rocks gave rise to extensive deposits of China clay, especially in the area to the north of St Austell, and this remains an important industry. Cornwall's coast is a tale of two contrasting halves, the placid estuaries and wooded valleys of its southern coast contrasting with the raw, serrated cliffs of the north. North Cornwall's raw appearance is partly due to the fact that it faces out to the Celtic Sea, and partly due to the fact the stretch of coast between Bude and Tintagel is composed of Devonian slate/Carboniferous sandstone cliffs that are not found in southern Cornwall.

Although Cornwall is administered as a county of England, an independence movement exists that seeks more autonomy along the lines of the other home Celtic nations. Additionally, some groups and individuals question the constitutional status of Cornwall and its relationship to the Duchy of Cornwall. Cornish nationalists have organised into two political parties, Mebyon Kernow and the Cornish Nationalist Party. In addition to the political parties, the Cornish Stannary Parliament acts as a pressure group on Cornish constitutional issues and the human rights organisation Cornwall 2000 works with Cornish cultural issues.

The **Isles of Scilly** (Cornish *Ynysek Syllan*) are designated the Isles of Scilly Area of Outstanding Natural Beauty. The islands are always referred to as the Isles of Scilly, or occasionally the Scillies; the term 'Scilly Isles' is considered incorrect by the inhabitants. Natives of the islands are known as Scillonians.

The Isles of Scilly form an archipelago of five inhabited islands: Bryher, St Agnes, St Martin's, St Mary's and Tresco, along with many smaller uninhabited islands and rocky islets. Until 1855, Samson was also inhabited. The Isles of Scilly have a special council that is neither a district nor a county, but is in practice a unitary authority although for voting purposes it comes under the auspices of the St Ives constituency. The police force is shared with the Devon and Cornwall constabulary based in Exeter and the fire service with the Cornish service in Truro, but in all other respects Scillonians are independent from their Cornish neighbours.

Scilly has been inhabited since Stone Age times and throughout its history its people have lived off the land and the sea. Farming and fishing continue today, but as with Cornwall the main industry now is tourism. (Scillonians do not use the pejorative term 'emmets'.) The islands may correspond to the Cassiterides ('Tin Isles') visited by the Phoenicians and mentioned by the Greeks. It is not known at exactly which point the islands stopped speaking Cornish, but it seems to have gone into decline during the Middle Ages.

During the Civil War, the isles were a stronghold for the Royalists. It was during this period that the Three Hundred and Thirty Five Years' War started between the isles and the Netherlands. In June 1651, the isles were captured from the Royalists by Admiral Robert Blake for the Parliamentarians.

Scilly is famous for its danger to shipping and its many shipwrecks. The wreck of Sir Cloudesley Shovell's ship HMS *Association* in 1707 due to inaccuracies in navigation led to the development of the method of lunar distances, and to the invention of the chronometer by John Harrison, the first reliable methods of determining longitude at sea. The sea has always played a huge part in Scillonian history but it was in the 19th century that Scilly had its maritime heyday. Beaches which are now enjoyed by sunbathers were then factories for shipbuilding; the harbours now full of pleasure boats were once packed with local and visiting fishing and trading boats.

The main transport links with the mainland are currently by sea on the *Scillonian III*, sailing from Penzance harbour, and by air via services to St Mary's from various UK airports (Land's End, Newquay, Exeter, Bristol and Southampton), and also the ever-popular helicopter service between Penzance Heliport and St Mary's and Tresco.

The Isles of Scilly have always been a popular resort for tourism and former Prime Minister Harold Wilson regularly holidayed on the Isles, eventually buying a cottage there as a holiday home. He is buried on St Mary's.

Cornwall & Isles of Scilly	**Population**			**Area**	
Districts	*male*	*female*	*total*	*sq miles*	*sq km*
Caradon	38,576	41,073	79,649	256	664
Carrick	41,909	45,956	87,865	177	458
Isles of Scilly	1072	1081	2153	6	16
Kerrier	45,081	47,436	92,517	183	474
North Cornwall	39,059	41,450	80,509	462	1195
Penwith	30,200	32,812	63,012	117	304
Restormel	46,590	48,972	95,562	174	452
Total	242,487	258,780	501,267	1375	3563

Local Attractions and Information

Administrative headquarters	**Cornwall:** New County Hall, Treyew Road, Truro TR1 3AY. Tel: 0300 1234 100. **Isles of Scilly:** Town Hall, St Mary's TR21 0LW. Tel: 01720 422537.
Antony House & Garden	5 miles (8km) west of Plymouth. A striking 18th century house overlooking the Lynber River, Antony has been the home of the Carew family since the 15th century. The house was built 1711–21 for Sir William Carew. Antony consists of a central block faced in silver-grey Pentewan

stone and two wings in brick joined to the centre block with colonnades. Now owned by the National Trust. Tel: 01752 812191.

Battles There have been three major battles on Cornish soil: Braddock Down, Lostwithiel and Stratton. See separate table for details. See also entry for the Cornish Rebellion of 1497.

Boconnoc House 3 miles (5km) east of Lostwithiel, 5 miles (8km) south of Bodmin. Boconnoc House was mentioned in Domesday Book in 1087 although the first recorded owners were the De Cant family in 1268. Vacant since 1969, the house is now used for wedding receptions and conferences. The surrounding deer park, created in 1780 by Thomas Pitt, 1st Lord Camelford, grandfather of Prime Minister William Pitt, is the largest in Cornwall and contains a restored lake, Golden Jubilee walk, a 19th century pinetum, medieval church and a 123ft (37.5m) high obelisk, erected in 1771 by Pitt in memory of his wife's uncle and benefactor, Sir Richard Lyttelton. Tel: 01208 872507.

Bodmin & Wenford Railway Cornwall's only standard gauge steam railway is unique among heritage railways in that it is served by high-speed trains from London Paddington which stop at Bodmin Parkway railway station; from here BWR trains depart for Boscarne Junction via the railway's headquarters at Bodmin General station. The line is 6½ miles (10.5km) long with steep gradients and is operated mainly by steam-hauled trains, with diesels on a few days per year. Tel: 01208 73666.

Bodmin Moor A granite moorland in northeast Cornwall covering 80 sq miles (208 sq km) and designated an Area of Outstanding Natural Beauty. During the Bronze Age, Bodmin Moor was densely populated and many prehistoric stone barrows and circles remain scattered across the moor. On the southern slopes of the moor lies Dozmary Pool, where according to Arthurian legend Sir Bedivere threw Excalibur to the Lady of the Lake. There have been many reported sightings of a panther-like cat known as the Beast of Bodmin and long held responsible for the mutilation of livestock, although no scientific evidence has been found for the existence of such an animal.

Bosvigo Gardens Bosvigo Lane, Truro. A series of small gardens laid out in the late 20th century and including a woodland walk, walled garden and original Victorian conservatory, surrounding a Georgian house. Attached to the main house is a smaller secondary property, Bosvigo Vean (Cornish for 'Little Bosvigo House'), usually referred to as 'The Vean'. Its small front garden is divided by cross paths and the four beds are planted almost identically in white, blue and gold, with shaped cones of golden privet in each bed. Tel: 01872 275774.

Caerhays Castle Gorran, 9 miles (15km) southwest of St Austell. The Regency-style castle was built by John Nash in 1810 for John Bettesworth Trevanion. It fell into disrepair until it was bought by Michael Williams, a Cornish MP, in 1853. Later generations of the Williams family created the 60 acres (24ha) of informal woodlands and gardens that surround the house. Tel: 01872 501310.

Carrick Roads See Falmouth

Charlestown Shipwreck and Heritage Centre 2 miles (3km) southeast of St Austell. The varied exhibitions reflect village life in Charlestown, its history, shipwrecks and the once thriving china clay industry. The exhibition shows a tremendous range of maritime history dating back to 1715 and one of the largest underwater diving equipment collections in the UK, including various suits used for treasure seeking and naval purposes. Tel: 01726 69897.

Chysauster Ancient Village 1 mile (1.6km) northeast of New Mill, 3 miles (5km) north of Penzance. An Iron Age settlement occupied c.100 BC–AD 400. The village consisted of eight stone-walled homesteads known as 'courtyard houses', of a type found only on the Land's End peninsula and the Isles of Scilly, the low stone walls, grinding stones and fireplaces of which still remain. Now in the care of English Heritage. Tel: 07831 757934.

Cornish pasty A pastry crust traditionally filled with beef and potato, usually with slices of onion and swede mixed in, although today the humble pasty can also be found in a number of other guises. Tradition has it that the original Cornish pasty contained meat and vegetables in one end and jam or fruit in the other end, in order to give the miners who took it to work 'two courses'. Cornish housewives would mark their husbands' initials on the left-hand side of the pastry casing, in order to avoid confusion at lunchtime. This was particularly useful when a miner wished to save a 'corner' of his pasty until later, or if he wanted to leave a corner for one of the 'Knockers', the mischievous 'little people' of the mines, who were believed by the miners to cause all manner of misfortune unless placated with a small amount of food, after which they could prove to be a source of good luck. Historically, Cornish miners shouted 'Oggie Oggie, Tiddy Oggie' in unison at crib (meal) time, before eating their traditional pasties. This gave rise to their nickname of oggies (or tiddy oggies). The earliest known Cornish recipe for a pasty was written in 1746. However in November 2006 archivist Todd Gray found details of a pasty recipe in an audit compiled in Plymouth in 1510, which would mean the Cornish pasty actually originates in Devon! Today there is still a great deal of debate among pasty-makers about how a genuine pasty should be made. Many will say that short pastry should be used, while others will advocate rough puff pastry. Some will claim that the ingredients must be mixed up inside the pastry, while others will swear that the fillings should be laid out in a particular order before the pasty is sealed. The issue that invites the most controversy involves the 'crimp', the wavy seam that holds the pasty together. Should the pasty be sealed across the top, or at the side? History suggests that the crimp should be formed at the side, because the pasty has always been eaten by hand, and the side crimp is the most convenient way of holding on to your lunch while you take a big bite. Fortunately, some facts can be agreed upon by all pasty-makers. The meat should be chopped, the vegetables should always be sliced, and the ingredients must never be cooked before they are wrapped in the pastry. Each pasty must be baked from raw. It is this fact that makes the Cornish pasty unique among similar foods from around the world.

Cornish Rebellion of 1497 An armed revolt by the people of Cornwall against Henry VII's attempt to levy a tax for a proposed campaign against Scotland in response to border skirmishes inspired by Perkin Warbeck's pretended claim to the English throne. Tin miners were angered at the scale of the taxes, which violated a previous exemption granted by Edward I to Cornwall's Stannary Parliament; they also felt that they had no involvement in wars with Scotland as it was so far away – most Cornish people did not even speak English at the time. Incited by Bodmin blacksmith Michael Joseph (An Gof) and Thomas Flamank, a lawyer from St Keverne, a 15,000 strong army marched into Devon and up to Taunton and Wells, attracting support along the way. At Wells they were joined by James Touchet, 7th Baron Audley, who joined Flamank as joint 'political' leader of the expedition. The army moved on to Kent via Winchester but when they realised that support was thin on the ground, retreated to Guildford in Surrey. Although shocked by the scale of the revolt and the speed of its approach, Henry VII swiftly recalled the army of 8000 men assembled for Scotland under the command of Giles, Lord Daubeney, Henry's chief general and Lord Chamberlain. Daubeney and his men took up position on Hounslow Heath and sent out a force of 500 mounted spearmen, who clashed with the Cornish at Gill Down outside Guildford on Wednesday 14 June 1497. The Cornish army left Guildford and moved via Banstead and Chussex Plain to Blackheath where they pitched their final camp. On 17 June 1497, on a site in present-day Deptford, southeast London, adjacent to the River Ravensbourne, the final battle (of Deptford Bridge) took place. Henry VII had mustered an army of 25,000 men and the Cornish lacked the supporting cavalry and artillery essential to the professional forces of the time. Having spread rumours that he would attack on the following Monday, Henry moved against the Cornish at dawn on his 'lucky Saturday'. The royal forces were divided into three 'battles', two under Lords Oxford, Essex and Suffolk, to wheel round the right flank and rear of the enemy while the third waited in reserve. When the Cornish were surrounded, Daubeney and the third 'battle' were ordered into frontal attack. At the bridge at Deptford Strand, the Cornish archers had early success but were soon overwhelmed and lost heart (Daubeney was captured but released, such was the morale in the Cornish army). Between 200 to 2000 Cornishmen died and a general slaughter of the broken army was well under way when An Gof gave the order for surrender. He fled but only reached Greenwich before being captured; Baron Audley and Thomas Flamank were taken on the field of battle. An Gof and Flamank were executed on 27 June 1497 and suffered the traitor's fate of being hung, drawn and quartered at Tyburn. Audley was beheaded on 28 June at Tower Hill. Their heads were displayed on pikestaffs on London Bridge. An Gof is recorded to have said before his execution that he should have *'a name perpetual and a fame permanent and immortal'*, while Flamank was quoted as saying 'Speak the truth and only then can you be free of your chains.' The remaining rebels were sent home, ending the rebellion.

Cotehele House St Dominick, 7 miles (11km) north of Saltash. The medieval home of the Edgcumbe family, located near the River Tamar and rebuilt 1490–1520. The house is little altered and its atmosphere remains hushed and enchanted, with old walls, dim light and intimate chambers containing original furniture, armour, rich hangings and tapestries. Near the house, the terraces are formally planted and the Upper Garden features a lily pond and orchard, while the wooded valley garden, descending to the Tamar, contains a medieval stewpond and dovecote. There are fine views from the Prospect Tower, a three-sided 18th century folly high above the house. The property is owned by the National Trust. Tel: 01579 351346.

Eden Project Bodelva, 5 miles (8km) east of St Austell. The Eden Project is a global garden for the 21st century and a gateway to a sustainable future; the story of humankind's dependence on plants is told in this dramatic setting. Officially opened to the public in March 2001, the Eden Project cost £133.6 million to build. The site consists of various biomes – climatically and geographically defined areas of ecologically similar communities of plants, animals and soil organisms, often referred to as ecosystems – created in geodesic domes of transparent thermoplastic. So far completed are tropical and Mediterranean areas. Tim Smit (see Lost Gardens of Heligan) is chief executive of the Eden Project. Tel: 01726 818859.

Falmouth A town, civil parish and port on the River Fal on the southeast coast of Cornwall. Originally called Peny-cwm-cuic, which later became 'Pennycomequick', the town's present name stems from the river on which it stands. Falmouth is situated on a peninsula with water on two sides: to its east is the northern inlet of the English Channel between Falmouth and St Mawes known as Carrick Roads, while to the south is Falmouth Bay. Carrick Roads is a complex of drowned river valleys formed by the rising sea level after the Ice Age, creating a large natural harbour navigable from Falmouth to Truro and laying claim to be the third largest natural harbour in the world. The harbour is also famous as the start or finish point of various round-the-world record-breaking voyages, such as those of Sir Francis Chichester and Dame Ellen MacArthur.

Flags St Piran's Flag is regarded as the national flag of **Cornwall** and an emblem of the Cornish people. The banner of St Piran is a white cross on a black background. St Piran is supposed to have adopted these two colours from seeing the white metal in the black coals and ashes during his legendary discovery of tin. The Cornish flag is an exact reverse of the former Breton national flag (black cross on a white field) and is known by the same name, 'Gwynn ha Du' (white and black). St Piran's Day (5 March) is celebrated by the Cornish diaspora around the world. Two flags are primarily used to represent **Scilly**: the flag of the Council of the Isles of Scilly, which incorporates the logo of a depiction of Bishop Rock Lighthouse, Star Castle, and a narcissus flower in yellow on a blue background. In the full version of the flag, the motto *Semper eadam* (Latin, 'always the same') is printed in the light blue at the top of the flag; interestingly this was Elizabeth I of England's motto. 'The Council of the Isles of Scilly' is printed on the scroll at the bottom. The unofficial Scillonian Cross, voted for by readers of *Scilly News*, consists of a white cross on an orange and blue background, the top two quartiles being orange and the top right-hand quartile depicting five stars to represent the five inhabited islands.

Furry Dance — The Furry Dance (also known as the Floral Dance or Flora Dance) takes place in Helston on 8 May (or the Saturday before if 8 May falls on a Sunday or Monday), and is a celebration of the passing of winter and the arrival of spring. The first dance takes place at 7am and is followed by a children's dance at 10am and a midday dance, culminating in an evening dance at 5pm. Of these, the midday dance is perhaps the best known: it was traditionally the dance of the gentry in the town, and today the men wear top hats and tails while the women dance in their finest frocks. Traditionally, the dancers wear lily of the valley, Helston's symbolic flower – the gentlemen on the left, with the flowers pointing upwards, the ladies upside down on the opposite side. The children's dance involves over 1000 children aged 7–18 from St Michael's School, Nansloe School, Parc Eglos School and Helston Community College and School, dressed in white with lily of the valley buttonholes. Each year a different school leads the dance. The boys wear their school colours in the form of school ties, while the girls wear matching coloured flowers (blue cornflowers for St Michael's, forget-me-nots for Helston Community College and Helston School, daisies for Nansloe and poppies for Parc Eglos) in their hair. The **Hal an Tow**, which takes place on the same day, is a kind of mystery play about St George slaying the Dragon, and contains disparaging references to a Spaniard, probably referring to the Spanish raid on Newlyn in 1595.

Geevor Tin Mine — Pendeen, 6 miles (10km) northwest of Penzance. The last working mine in West Penwith before it finally closed in 1990. Set in dramatic coastal scenery, Geevor is now the largest complete mining site in Britain where visitors can follow the story of the mining and processing of tin. Tel: 01736 788662.

Glendurgan Garden — 1/2 mile (0.8km) south of Mawnan Smith, 4 miles (6km) southwest of Falmouth. A subtropical garden of three valleys reaching down to the sparkling waters of the Helford River. Created in the 1820s, the garden features numerous exotic trees and shrubs and an unusual laurel maze dating from 1833. Now owned by the National Trust. Tel: 01326 250906.

Godolphin Estate — 5 miles (8km) northwest of Helston. The 15th century house and gardens were home to the Godolphin family of tin miners until the 18th century. By the mid 16th century the house consisted of three ranges of buildings with the courtyard closed off by a crenellated wall on the north side. Sir William Godolphin, a soldier in the service of Henry VIII, made alterations to the house and further work was carried out at the end of the 16th century by Sir Francis Godolphin, Governor of the Scilly Isles. Godolphin House has extensive farm buildings and its original Elizabethan stables. Remnants of the old formal gardens can be seen on the north and east sides of the house. These recently discovered gardens are currently undergoing restoration and include raised walks and carp ponds. Now owned by the National Trust. Tel: 01736 763194.

Goonhilly Satellite Earth Station — 6 miles (10km) southeast of Helston. Set in the dramatic landscape of the Lizard Peninsula, the giant dishes of Goonhilly rise up from the heathland. The first satellite, affectionately known as Arthur, was installed in 1962 and with over 60 dishes on site, Goonhilly is the largest and oldest satellite station in the world, able to transmit to every corner of the globe via space, and through undersea fibre optic cables, simultaneously handling millions of international phone calls, emails and TV broadcasts. Tel: 0800 679593.

Gorseth Kernow — The Gorseth Kernow (Throne of Cornwall) was established by Henry Jenner in 1928 at Boscawen-un and is the equivalent of the Welsh Gorseth (part of the Eisteddfod). It has now been opened up to all forms of revived Cornish and aims to 'maintain the national Celtic spirit of Cornwall'. An important part of the open Gorseth is the awarding of bardships to individuals for meritorious work for Cornish culture.

Highest point — Brown Willy on Bodmin Moor at 1378ft (420m) (GR: SX158799). Telegraph Tower at 158ft (48m) is the highest point of the Isles of Scilly.

Interesting facts — The **Isles of Scilly** feature what is reportedly the smallest national football league in the world. The league's two clubs, Woolpack Wanderers and Garrison Gunners, play each other around 20 times a season and compete for two cups as well as the league title. The two share a ground, Garrison Field, but travel to the mainland for part of the year to play other non-professional clubs. **Rick Stein**'s impact on the local economy of Padstow is such that it has been nicknamed 'Padstein'. He operates three restaurants, a bistro, a café, a seafood delicatessen, patisserie shop, gift shop and a cookery school in the town. **Britain's first canine lifeguard** is based at Sennen Cove. Bilbo, a five-year-old Newfoundland, passed his fitness and swimming tests and is trained to swim out to casualties and manoeuvre himself so that he can be used as a buoyancy aid. **Stargazy pie** is a dish made of baked pilchards and five other kinds of fish, covered with a pastry crust. The pilchards are arranged with their tails toward the centre of the pie and their heads poking up through the crust around the edge, so that they appear to be gazing skyward. The dish originates from the village of Mousehole and is traditionally eaten during the holiday of Tom Bawcocks Eve (a festival held on 23 December in celebration and memorial of the efforts of mythical Mousehole resident Tom Bawcock to lift a famine from the village). **The Song of the Western Men**, written by Robert Stephen Hawker in 1824, is better known in Cornwall, and overseas, by the title of 'Trelawny'. Jonathan Trelawny (1650–1721) was one of seven bishops imprisoned in the Tower of London by James II in 1688. Born at Pelynt into an old Cornish family, his father, the 2nd Baronet of Trelawne, was a supporter of the Royalist cause during the Civil War. Trelawny is often referred to as the 'unofficial' Cornish anthem and is often heard at Cornish rugby union matches and other Cornish gatherings, but the Cornish anthem that has been used by Gorseth Kernow for the last 75 years is 'Bro Goth Agan Tasow' (Old Country of our Fathers). Those who prefer an anthem in English often use 'Hail to the Homeland'.

Islands — See separate table

Jamaica Inn Bolventor, 9 miles (15km) northeast of Bodmin. Built in 1750, Jamaica Inn was a coaching inn set high in the wild landscape of Bodmin Moor and made famous by Daphne du Maurier's novel of the same name. It is currently a hotel and museum. Tel: 01566 86250.

Land's End 8 miles (13km) southwest of Penzance. The most westerly point of England and traditionally the antithesis of John O'Groats when referring to the southern extremity of mainland Britain. The directional signpost stating 'John O'Groats 874 miles' is one of the most photographed in the world. The area is a shrine for tourists with its ever-changing menu of attractions. Tel: 0870 458 0099.

Lanhydrock House $2^1/_2$ miles (4km) southeast of Bodmin. Lanhydrock is full of period atmosphere. Although the gatehouse and north wing – notably a magnificent 96ft (29m) gallery with plaster ceiling – survive from the 17th century, the rest of the house was rebuilt following a disastrous fire in 1881. The new house featured the latest in contemporary living, including central heating. The garden has a stunning collection of magnolias, rhododendrons and camellias, and offers fine colours right through into autumn. All this is set in an estate of 900 acres (360ha) of woods and parkland running down to the River Fowey, with numerous footpaths. Now in the care of the National Trust. Tel: 01208 265950.

Lanyon Quoit 3 miles (5km) northwest of Penzance. The remains of a Neolithic chambered tomb consisting of three upright stones and a covering capstone, and standing 7ft (2.1m) high. Dating to c. 2500 BC, it was re-erected in the 1820s after collapsing in a storm in 1815.

Lappa Valley Steam Railway Newlyn East, 4 miles (6km) south of Newquay. A narrow-gauge railway running for $1^1/_2$ miles (2.5km) on one of the oldest railway trackbeds in Cornwall. Opened in 1849 as a mineral line from Newquay to East Wheal Rose, it became part of the Great Western Railway's Newquay to Chacewater branch line in 1906. Closed in 1963, part of the line was reopened in 1974 by Eric Booth, founder of the Lappa Valley. Tel: 01872 510317.

Launceston Castle Western Road, Launceston. A castle was built at Launceston by Robert of Mortain possibly as early as 1067. The original Norman motte and bailey castle, with its wooden defences, guarded the main route into Cornwall, and became the administrative centre for the Earls of Cornwall. In the late 12th century a circular stone keep was constructed on top of the motte. Richard of Cornwall held the earldom 1227–72, and during this time he made extensive alterations to the castle. A tower was built inside the keep and stone curtain walls replaced the timber palisades, with substantial gatehouses in the north and south. After Richard's death in 1272, his son Edmund moved the earldom's administration to Lostwithiel. This resulted in a decline in the castle's importance, although it remained the home of the judiciary until 1838 (when it was moved to Bodmin) and also served as a prison (George Fox being its most famous resident). Held by Royalists during the Civil War, it subsequently changed hands four times, suffering considerable damage. It is now owned by English Heritage. Tel: 01566 772365.

Lawrence House Castle Street, Launceston. A Grade II listed town house built in 1753, now housing a local history museum whose exhibits include a late 19th century German polyphon, a foreunner of the jukebox. Owned by the National Trust, it is leased to Launceston Town Council. Tel: 01566 773277.

Levant Mine and Beam Engine Pendeen, 7 miles (11km) northwest of Penzance. Opened in the late 18th century to exploit seams of copper and tin extending for over 1 mile (1.6km) under the Atlantic Ocean, the mine was the scene of a major disaster in 1919 in which 31 men died. The mine closed in 1930; it is now the location of the oldest surviving beam engine in Cornwall, built in 1840 and restored in the 1980s by members of the Trevithick Society. Owned by the National Trust. Tel: 01736 786156.

Longships Group of rocks situated $1^1/_2$ miles (2km) west of Land's End. Since 1967 the lighthouse has been unmanned. Its light is 10 seconds bright followed by 10 seconds dark, and has a range of 19 miles (31km). A fog signal sounds every 10 seconds. GR: SW322259.

Lost Gardens of Heligan 2 miles (3km) northwest of Mevagissey. The popular botanical gardens were originally part of the estate owned by the Cornish Tremayne family. After World War I the gardens fell into a state of neglect until Tim Smit and a group of fellow enthusiasts decided to restore them to their former glory. Their efforts, which were the subject of a six-part Channel 4 television series in 1996, proved to be an outstanding success, not only revitalising the gardens, but also the local economy around Heligan. The gardens feature Europe's only remaining pineapple pit, warmed by rotting manure. Tel: 01726 845100.

Lyonesse A sunken land believed in legend to lie off the Isles of Scilly, southwest of Cornwall. According to Arthurian legend, Lyonesse is the birthplace of Tristan, son of King Meliodas (or Rivalen). One of the signs of King Arthur's return will be that Lyonesse will rise from the depths again. Alfred, Lord Tennyson's Arthurian epic, *Idylls of the King*, describes Lyonesse as the site of the final battle between Arthur and Mordred. The Trevelyan family of Cornwall takes its coat of arms from a local legend: 'when Lyonesse sank beneath the waves only a man named Trevelyan escaped by riding a white horse'. To this day the family's shield bears a white horse rising from the waves.

Mebyon Kernow Mebyon Kernow – the Party for Cornwall – is a progressive political party, campaigning for greater self-government for Cornwall. Its inaugural meeting took place on Saturday 6 January 1951. By September 1951, the party had officially committed itself to Cornish self-government. In 2005 Mebyon Kernow became the largest political group on Camborne town council after a by-election.

Men-an-Tol 4 miles (6km) northwest of Penzance. A doughnut-shaped holed stone 4ft 6in (1.3m) in diameter and flanked by two other stones of similar height. It is traditionally the focus of numerous healing rituals, normally entailing the afflicted person crawling through the hole in the stone. Possibly the remains of a chambered tomb, it is believed to date to the Bronze Age but no detailed investigation has been carried out. Men-an-Tol simply means 'holed stone'.

Mount Edgcumbe House $1^1/_2$ miles (2.5km) southwest of Plymouth. Situated on the eastern coast of the Torpoint peninsula. Sir Richard Edgcumbe of Cotehele built a new home in his deer park at Mount Edgcumbe in

1547–53. Miraculously the walls of his red stone Tudor house survived a direct hit by bombs in 1941 and it was restored by the Earl of Edgcumbe 1958–64. Created in 1971, the surrounding park covers over 800 acres (320ha) and is owned by Cornwall County and Plymouth City Councils. Tel: 01752 822236.

National Maritime Museum — Discovery Quay, Falmouth. The National Maritime Museum Cornwall is a development of the original FIMI (Falmouth International Maritime Initiative) partnership created in 1992 and the result of collaboration between the National Maritime Museum, Greenwich and the former Cornwall Maritime Museum in Falmouth. Housed in an award-winning building on Falmouth harbourside, the museum explores the world of small boats and Cornish maritime history. An important element of the collection is the material relating to the Falmouth packet ships, which includes six watercolours by Maltese artist Cammillieri. Tel: 01326 313388.

National Seal Sanctuary — Gweek, 3 miles (5km) southeast of Helston. Established in the 1950s from a beach café at St Agnes, Britain's leading marine animal rescue centre was relocated to its present 40 acre (16ha) site on the Helford Estuary in 1975 as more pups were reported injured and needing help. Tel: 01326 221361.

Padstow — Town and port on the north coast of Cornwall, internationally famous for its 'Obby 'Oss (Hobby Horse) festival held annually on May Day. The festival itself starts at midnight on 1 May with unaccompanied singing around the town, in particular at the Golden Lion and Harbour Inn. In the morning, the town is dressed with greenery, flowers and flags, with the focal point being the maypole. The climax arrives when dancers cavort through the town dressed as one of two 'Obby 'Osses, the 'Old' and the 'Blue Ribbon'. The Padstow Town Museum has displays relating to the ''Obby 'Oss, railway and lifeboat. Rick Stein's Seafood Restaurant, based at Riverside in Padstow and opened in 1974, was the first of several food-related business concerns established in the town by celebrity chef Stein (born in Oxfordshire in 1947).

Pencarrow House — 4 miles (6km) northwest of Bodmin. Georgian house with 50 acres (20ha) of Grade II listed gardens. It is still privately owned and lived in by the Molesworth-St Aubyns whose ancestor, John Molesworth, purchased the estate in the reign of Elizabeth I. The gardens were designed and laid out by the Radical politician, Sir William Molesworth, between 1831 and 1855. Tel: 01208 841369.

Pendennis Castle — Castle Drive, Falmouth. Built by Henry VIII in 1540–5 as one of a pair of artillery forts to protect this strategic area from the threat of invasion from Catholic France and Spain. St Mawes Castle (see separate entry) was built on the opposite headland and between them their cannon could cover the entire entrance to the Fal estuary. In 1588 ramparts and angle bastions were erected to protect the high ground of the peninsula. These were further developed in the early 17th century and put to the test during a six-month siege of the castle in 1646, during the Civil War, when the castle was defended for the Royalist cause. A lack of food finally forced the garrison to surrender to the Parliamentary army of Sir Thomas Fairfax. Later used as a prison for prisoners-of-war (the barracks and 20th century gun battery remain on site), its last military role was as a secret World War II base. Tel: 01326 316594.

Penlee lifeboat disaster — On 19 December 1981, the Dublin-registered cargo ship *Union Star* was on its maiden voyage from Ijmuiden in the Netherlands to Arklow in Ireland. As well as its crew of five, including captain Henry Morton, on board were Morton's wife, Dawn, and her two teenage daughters. The *Union Star* developed an engine fault 8 miles (13km) east of Wolf Rock on the south coast of Cornwall. She was unable to restart her engines, and assistance was offered by a tug, the *Noord Holland*. Morton refused the offer, unwilling to pay for salvage. With the weather worsening, she put out a distress signal to the Falmouth coastguard. Against winds gusting to 95mph (150km/h, hurricane force 12 on the Beaufort scale), *Union Star* was being driven on to the rocks of Boscawen Cove, near Lamorna. The conditions were so rough that the crew of a Royal Navy Sea King helicopter sent from RNAS Culdrose was unable to remove any of the crew. The lifeboat *Solomon Browne*, crewed by eight men from the village of Mousehole, was launched and after several attempts came alongside *Union Star*. In mountainous seas, *Solomon Browne* retrieved four of the eight people on board, but an attempt to rescue the remaining crew members proved fatal. No more was seen of the *Solomon Browne*, nor heard from her radio. A few moments later her lights disappeared, and at about the same time *Union Star* keeled over. What happened next is a matter of conjecture. Possibly, due to a sudden lurch in direction of *Union Star*, and on a tremendous wave, *Solomon Browne* was thrown up and over the freighter; possibly she was simply rolled onto the rocks by the 60ft breaking seas. The lifeboat from Sennen Cove tried to search and rescue, but it proved impossible for her to round the corner of Land's End. After an extensive search by helicopter and lifeboat, eight bodies were eventually recovered, four from the eight crew of the lifeboat and four from the *Union Star*; in all 16 lives were lost. Wreckage from the *Solomon Browne* was found along the shore, and the *Union Star* lay capsized on the rocks west of Tater-du Lighthouse. Every 19 December, the Christmas illuminations of Mousehole are turned off at 8pm for an hour as an act of remembrance.

Penwith School of Artists — See St Ives School of Artists

Porthcurno Telegraph Museum — Porthcurno, 7 miles (11km) southwest of Penzance. A unique award-winning museum set in its own grounds at the heart of Porthcurno valley telling the story of the village from Victorian times to World War II. Tel: 01736 810966.

Prideaux Place — 1/2 mile (0.4km) north of Padstow. An Elizabethan house with extensive grounds and a deer park, high above Padstow, with views over the Camel Estuary. Built in 1592 by Nicholas Prideaux, it has been for more than 400 years the home of the Prideaux-Brune family, an ancient Cornish clan whose origins go back to the 11th century. Prideaux Place was the first house in Cornwall to have its own electricity; the generator was installed 1901–02 and the generator house still stands in the grounds today. The house has 81 rooms including 44 bedrooms. Tel: 01841 532411.

Restormel Castle — 1 mile (1.6km) north of Restormel. Norman motte and bailey castle overlooking the River Fowey, founded in the 11th century by Baldwin fitzUrstin. The 12th century shell keep was added by Robert of Cardinham and further work done by Richard of Cornwall in the mid 13th century. The castle was captured by Royalist Richard Greville in 1644 but described by a 1649 Parliamentary Commission as 'utterly ruined'. Owned by the Duchy of Cornwall until 1925, it is now in the care of by English Heritage.

Rivers — The **Camel** rises below Hendraburnick Down and flows for 2 miles (3km) before emptying into the Bristol Channel at Padstow Bay.

The **Fal** rises near Truro and separates the Roseland peninsula from the rest of Cornwall before reaching the English Channel at Falmouth. Large cargo ships are often laid up in the estuary, especially at Tolverne, as the estuary is only 300ft (91m) wide but 60ft (18m) deep. The river is crossed by the historic and scenic King Harry Ferry, a vehicular chain ferry that links the villages of Feock and Philleigh, 4 miles (6km) south of Truro.

The **Fowey** rises west of Liskeard, passes Lanhydrock House, Restormel Castle and Lostwithiel, then broadens at Milltown before joining the English Channel at Fowey. It is navigable only for the last 7 miles (11km). There is a ferry between Fowey and Bodinnick.

The **Hayle** rises 1 mile (1.6km) southwest of the village of Crowan, then flows west for 5 miles (8km). The river comes within about 3 miles (5km) of the sea but then flows via Mount's Bay to the north, reaching the sea at Hayle in St Ives Bay, a total of 12 miles (19km).

The **Looe** flows into the English Channel at Looe. It has two main branches, the East Looe River and the West Looe River. The eastern tributary has its source near St Cleer and flows south, passing close to the western outskirts of Liskeard. South of Liskeard, an eight-mile stretch of scenic railway known as the Looe Valley Line follows the course of the river to Looe. The western tributary has its source near Dobwalls.

The 61 miles (98km) of the **Tamar** form most of the border between Devon and Cornwall. At its mouth, the Tamar flows into the Hamoaze where it joins with the River Lynher before entering Plymouth Sound. The river has some 20 road crossings, including the Tamar Bridge, a toll bridge on the A38 trunk road, and the world-renowned Royal Albert Bridge.The Tamar's source is less than 4 miles (6km) from the north Cornish coast at Woolley in Morwenstow, but it drains southwards. North of the source the Cornish border heads to the sea along Marsland Water, making Cornwall nearly an island. In a few places the border deviates from the river, leaving, for instance, the Devon village of Bridgerule on the 'Cornish' side. Curiously, the modern administrative border between Devon and Cornwall more closely follows the Tamar than the traditional border. Several villages north of Launceston and west of the Tamar were actually in Devon until the 1960s.

Royal Cornwall Museum — River Street, Truro. Founded in 1818, the museum has a permanent display on the history of Cornwall from the Stone Age to the present day, as well as the natural history of Cornwall, a world famous collection of minerals, a pre-eminent collection of ceramics, and a changing display of fine and decorative art. Tel: 01872 272205.

St Catherine's Castle — St Catherine's Point, Fowey. A small fort built by Henry VIII to defend Fowey Harbour. Now in poor condition but maintained by English Heritage. Tel: 0117 9750700.

St Ives — A seaside town on the northern side of the Penwith peninsula. St Ives entered recorded history with the arrival of St Ia or Hya, the Irish princess who introduced Christianity to the area in the 5th century; the name St Ives is believed to be an anglicised corruption of her name. Fishing and tin mining were important until the late 19th century but today the town is primarily a holiday resort and much favoured by artists. The town was the scene of a notorious act of cruelty in 1549, during the Prayer Book Revolution, when the Provost Marshal came to St Ives and invited the mayor, John Payne, to lunch at the old George and Dragon. Having requested that the gallows be erected while they dined, the Provost Marshal accompanied the mayor down to the gallows after they had eaten. He then ordered the mayor to get up on the gallows, whereupon he was hanged as a Roman Catholic. The monument known as Knill Steeple was erected 1779–82 by customs officer John Knill, another mayor of St Ives, on Worvas Hill to the southwest of the town. Designed by architect John Wood, the mausoleum is a triangular granite pyramid 50ft (15m) high, containing within its base a cavity large enough for a single interment. Although Knill was subsequently buried at St Andrews Church, Holborn, in his will he left money for the upkeep of his obelisk and also £25 for celebrations to take place every five years on St James' Day, 25 July. He directed that every five years £10 should be expended on a dinner, and that ten young girls dressed in white should walk in procession with music, from the market house to the monument, around which the whole party was to dance while singing Psalm 100 ('All people that on earth do dwell'). The ceremony still takes place every five years. St Ives has given its name to a style of pottery established in the town by Bernard Leach in 1920.

St Ives School of Artists — In 1928, the artists Alfred Wallis, Ben Nicholson and Christopher Wood met at St Ives and laid the foundation for the artists' colony of today. In 1939, Ben Nicholson, Barbara Hepworth and Naum Gabo settled in St Ives. Growing disputes between the abstract and figurative artists within the group facilitated the abstract faction to break away from the St Ives Society in 1948, forming the Penwith Society of artists led by Barbara Hepworth and Ben Nicholson.

St Mawes Castle — St Mawes, 2 miles (3km) east of Falmouth. Artillery fort built in the reign of Henry VIII on a clover-leaf plan in 1540–3 to protect Falmouth. It surrendered to Parliament in 1646 without a shot being fired. Used as part of the coastal defence system during World Wars I and II, it is now owned by English Heritage. Tel 01326 270526.

St Michael's Mount — Located off the coast at Marazion, 3 miles (5km) east of Penzance. Often referred to as the jewel in Cornwall's crown, this magical island (its Cornish name is *Carrack Looz en Cooz*, the grey rock in the wood) has a church, a 12th century castle (originally built in 1135 by Bernard of Lebec as an abbey, and home of the St Aubyn family for over 300 years), an exotic garden clinging to the steep flanks, and an ancient harbour. Area: 0.03 sq miles (0.09 sq km). Population: 30. (GR: SW515298.) Tel: 01737 710507.

Sport: general — Cornwall has its own unique form of **wrestling** related to Breton wrestling. Another unique Cornish sport is **hurling**, a kind of medieval football played with a silver ball (distinct from Irish hurling). The sport now takes place at St Columb Major and St Ives, although hurling of a silver ball is part of the beating the bounds ceremony at Bodmin every five years. **Water sports** such as sailing and surfing are also particularly popular. One continuing legacy of the Scilly Isles' past is **gig racing**, wherein fast rowing boats ('gigs') with crews of six (or in one case, seven) race between the main islands. Gig racing has been said to derive from the race to collect salvage from shipwrecks on the rocks around Scilly, but the race was actually to deliver a pilot on to incoming vessels, to guide them through the hazardous reefs and shallows. (The boats are correctly termed 'pilot gigs'.)

rugby union — Rugby union has easily the largest sporting following in Cornwall (more so than football). **Cornwall** is one of the 28 county sides that compete in the Tetley's Bitter County Championship. They have won the county championship three times: 1908, 1991 and 1999. The Cornish rugby team regularly draws large crowds of supporters, dubbed 'Trelawny's Army', especially if they are progressing towards a Twickenham final. **Cornish Pirates** (recently renamed from Penzance & Newlyn RFC) compete in National League 1 and are hoping to tap into Cornish nationalist sentiment. **Launceston RFC** ('the Cornish All Blacks') and **Redruth RFC** ('the Reds') also compete in the national leagues.

Tate St Ives — Porthmeor Beach, St Ives. Tate Gallery St Ives opened in June 1993 and offers a unique introduction to modern art, where many works can be viewed in the surroundings and atmosphere which inspired them. The gallery presents changing displays of 20th century art, focusing on the postwar era for which St Ives has become famous. There are also temporary exhibitions, including work by contemporary artists resulting from projects initiated by the gallery. Tel: 01736 796266.

335 Years' War — A war between the Netherlands and the Isles of Scilly that lasted 335 years (1651–1986) without a single shot being fired, making it the longest war with the fewest casualties. Its origins can be found in the Second Civil War. By 1648 Oliver Cromwell had fought the Royalists to the edges of England, and Cornwall was the last Royalist stronghold in the west. Cromwell pushed on until mainland Cornwall was in the hands of the Parliamentarians. The Royalists' major asset was the Navy, which had declared for the Prince of Wales but was forced to retreat to the Isles of Scilly, then under the governorship/ownership of Sir John Grenville. The navy of the United Provinces of the Netherlands was allied with the Parliamentarians (seeking to maintain its alliance with the English after the Eighty Years' War (1568–1648), the Dutch had chosen to ally with what seemed would be the victorious side in the Civil War), but was suffering heavy losses from the Royalist fleet. On 30 March 1651, Admiral Maarten Harpertszoon Tromp arrived in Scilly. According to Sir Bulstrode Whitelocke's *Memorials*, a letter of 17 April 1651 explains: 'Tromp came to Pendennis and related that he had been to Scilly to demand reparation for the Dutch ships and goods taken by them; and receiving no satisfactory answer, he had, according to his Commission, declared war on them.' In June 1651, soon after this declaration, the Parliamentary forces under Admiral Robert Blake forced the Royalist fleet to surrender. The Dutch fleet, no longer under threat, left without firing a shot. Due to the obscurity of their declaration of war against such a small part of England, the Dutch forgot to officially declare peace. In 1985, Roy Duncan, historian and chairman of the Isles of Scilly Council, wrote to the Dutch Embassy in London to dispose of the 'myth' that the islands were still at war. Embassy staff found the myth to be accurate and Duncan invited ambassador Jonkheer Rein Huydecoper to visit the islands and sign a peace treaty. Peace was declared on 17 April 1986, 335 years after the war began.

Tintagel Castle — ½ mile (0.4km) west of Tintagel, 12 miles (19km) northeast of Padstow. England's earliest linear stone-built castle was constructed c.1145 by Reginald, Earl of Cornwall. Reginald was the brother of Robert, Earl of Gloucester, whose patronage enabled Geoffrey of Monmouth to write his *History of the British Kings*. Perhaps it was for propaganda that Earl Reginald chose Tintagel as the site for his castle; by building on the ruins of mythic Camelot, the Norman lord may have hoped to lend his rule Arthur's legendary power. Since the site of the castle is the most sheltered on the island, it is quite possible that the Normans built on top of a former stronghold, whose remains would now lie hidden beneath the Norman ruins. Most of the castle that can be seen today was built in the 1230s by Prince Richard Earl of Cornwall, the younger brother of Henry III. The Black Prince owned Tintagel in the 14th century; it was after his death that Tintagel declined. Abandoned in the 15th century and now ruined, it is owned by English Heritage.

Tintagel Old Post Office — Fore Street, Tintagel, 12 miles (19km) northeast of Padstow. A small 14th century manor house containing examples of local oak furniture, with one room restored to its condition in the 19th century when it served as the local letter receiving office. Outside is a small cottage garden. Bought in 1903 by the National Trust, it was one of the organisation's earliest acquisitions. Tel: 01840 770024.

Trebah Gardens — 5 miles (8km) southwest of Falmouth. Trebah is a magical 26 acre (10.5ha) ravine garden descending to a private, secluded beach on the Helford River. A stream cascades over waterfalls, through ponds full of giant Koi carp and exotic water plants, through 2 acres (0.8ha) of blue and white hydrangeas, before spilling out over the beach. Tel: 01326 252200.

Trelissick Garden	Feock, 4 miles (6km) south of Truro. A garden of rare beauty, set in an estate of 50 acres (20ha) surrounded by water on three sides. Trelissick is a plantsman's delight, with collections of rare and exotic shrubs that thrive in the mild Cornish climate. Of particular renown are large collections of hydrangeas, rhododendrons, camellias and magnolias. The garden is owned by the National Trust. Tel: 01872 862090.
Trematon Castle	2 miles (3km) east of Saltash. The castle was built in the 11th century and a shell keep added in the 12th century. Passed to the Duchy of Cornwall in 1337, it was in ruins by the mid 16th century. The keep and gatehouse are substantially intact. A deer park is named in 1282 but had lost the deer by 1500. Higher Lodge, a two-storey crenellated house (Grade II* listed), was built within the castle bailey 1807–8 and part of the curtain wall was demolished to provide views of the estuary. It is closed to the public.
Trengwainton Garden	Madron, 1½ miles (2.5km) northwest of Penzance. Trengwainton includes some of the largest tree ferns in the West Country, as well as a magnolia garden with champion specimens. Tel: 01736 363148.
Trerice House	½ mile (0.8km) southwest of Kestle Mill, 3 miles (5km) southeast of Newquay. The Elizabethan manor house of Trerice is an architectural gem hidden away from the world in a web of narrow lanes and still somehow caught in the spirit of its age. Behind the Dutch-style gabled façade are ornate fireplaces, elaborate plaster ceilings and a collection of English furniture. The property also features a collection of lawn mowers. Now owned by the National Trust. Tel: 01637 875404.
Trevarno Estate	2 miles (3km) northwest of Helston. This rare and special part of Cornwall has a history stretching back to 1246 when owner Randolphus de Trevarno gave the estate its name. Owned by a series of notable families since that time, at the heart of the estate is the 70 acres (28ha) of enchanting gardens, a combination of mature woodland blending with more formal areas such as the Italian garden, grotto, cascade and Victorian boathouse. Tel: 01326 574274.
Truro Cathedral	St Mary's Street, Truro. Dedicated to St Mary, the cathedral's foundation stones were laid on 20 May 1880 by the Duke of Cornwall (later Edward VII). It was designed by John Loughborough Pearson. Edward White Benson, the first Bishop of Truro (1877–83), was previously headmaster of Wellington College and then Chancellor of Lincoln Cathedral. From 1883 until his death in 1896 he was Archbishop of Canterbury. In 1880 Benson created the Service of Nine Lessons and Carols which for over 120 years has formed part of the cathedral's traditional worship on Christmas Eve. The Diocese of Truro covers the whole of Cornwall and the Isles of Scilly plus two parishes in Devon.

Some famous people born in Cornwall

Adams, John Couch (astronomer) (1819–92)	Laneast
Bligh, William (captain of the *Bounty*) (1754–1817)	St Tudy
Burley, W J (author) (1914–2002)	Falmouth
Causley, Charles (poet) (1917–2003)	Launceston
Couch, Arthur Quiller (author) (1863–1944)	Bodmin
Davy, Humphry (scientist) (1778–1829)	Penzance
Fitzsimmons, Bob (boxer) (1863–1917)	Helston
Golding, William (author) (1911–93)	Newquay
Gurney, Goldsworthy (inventor) (1793–1875)	Treator, nr Padstow
Hobhouse, Emily (social reformer) (1860–1926)	St Ive, nr Liskeard
Lander, Richard Lemon (explorer) (1804–34)	Truro
Lovett, William (chartist) (1800–77)	Newlyn
Lower, Richard (surgeon) (1631–91)	Bodmin
Lympany, Moura (concert pianist) (1916–2005)	Saltash
Nettles, John (actor) (1943–)	St Austell
Opie, John (painter, 'the Cornish wonder') (1761–1807)	St Agnes
Pilcher, Rosamunde (novelist) (1924–)	Lelant
Rowse, A L (poet) (1903–97)	St Austell
Thomas, D M (novelist and poet) (1935–)	Redruth
Trevithick, Richard (inventor) (1771–1833)	Lllogan

Islands of Cornwall

(shipping area P = Plymouth L = Lundy)

Island name	**Area**	**Nearest landmark**	**General information**	**P/L**
Armed Knight	English Channel	Land's End	GR: SW342248	P
Asparagus Island	English Channel	Kynance Cove	Named for the wild asparagus which grows on it. GR: SW683133	P
August Rock	English Channel	Rosemullion Head	GR: SW795270	P
Avarack, The	Atlantic	Lower Boscaswell	GR: SW372353	L
Barges Rock	English Channel	Lizard Point	GR: SW696114	P
Bass Rock	English Channel	Portscatho	GR: SW878355	P

Island name	Area	Nearest landmark	General information	P/L
Battery Rocks	Mount's Bay	Newlyn	GR: SW478297	P
Bawdon Rocks	Atlantic	Newdowns Head	aka Man and His Man. GR: SW702530	L
Beagle	Atlantic	Ligger Point	GR: SW757579	L
Bears, The	Mount's Bay	Perranuthnoe	GR: SW532290	P
Bell Buoy	Falmouth Bay	Manacle Point	One of The Manacles group. GR: SW823211	P
Bellows, The	English Channel	Kynance Cove	GR: SW683133	P
Bessack Rock	Atlantic	St Ives Bay	GR: SW571418	L
Bishop, The	English Channel	Kynance Cove	GR: SW684131	P
Bishop's Rock	Atlantic	Newquay	GR: SW814617	L
Black Humphrey Rock	Atlantic	Newquay	aka Flory Island. GR: SW830633	L
Black Rock	English Channel	Falmouth	GR: SW833317	P
Black Rock	English Channel	Poltesco	GR: SW729155	P
Black Rock	English Channel	Veryan Bay	GR: SW977407	P
Bo Cowloe	Atlantic	Sennen Cove	One of The Bo's group. GR: SW346268	L
Bosistow Island	English Channel	Carn Les Boel	GR: SW355341	P
Brandis Rocks	English Channel	Gribbin Head	GR: SX096494	P
Brandise	English Channel	Kildown Cove	GR: SW729148	P
Brandys	Atlantic	Porthmoina Cove	GR: SW412365	L
Brawn, The	English Channel	Downderry	GR: SX339536	P
Bream Rocks	English Channel	Par	GR: SX075522	P
Bridge, The	English Channel	Plymouth	GR: SX461522	P
Bridge Rocks	English Channel	Portnadler Bay	GR: SX241511	P
Bridges, The	English Channel	Polperro	GR: SX208505	P
Brisons, The	Atlantic	Cape Cornwall	GR: SW340311	L
Browther Rock	Atlantic	St Ives Head	GR: SW509514	L
Bull, The	Atlantic	Trevose Head	GR: SW845761	L
Bumble Rock	English Channel	Lizard Point	GR: SW708115	P
Butt Rock	Atlantic	Newquay	GR: SW845674	L
Cadythew Rock	English Channel	Veryan Bay	GR: SW992404	P
Caerverracks	English Channel	Poltesco	GR: SW738166	P
Cannis	English Channel	Gribbin Head	GR: SX102491	P
Carligga	English Channel	Lizard Point	One of The Stags group. GR: SW703110	P
Carn Bras	Atlantic	Land's End	One of the Longships Rocks. GR: SW329253	L
Carn Everis	Atlantic	St Ives Head	GR: SW513411	L
Carn Guthensbras	English Channel	Gwennap Head	GR: SW362217	P
Carn Kez	English Channel	Land's End	GR: SW342249	P
Carn Les Boel	English Channel	Land's End	GR: SW355232	P
Carn Vel	English Channel	Lizard Point	One of The Stags group. GR: SW703110	P
Carn-du	English Channel	Lamorna	GR: SW458237	P
Carn-du Rocks	Falmouth Bay	Manacle Point	One of The Manacles group. GR: SW818204	P
Carnelloe Long Rock	Atlantic	Carnelloe Cliff	GR: SW442389	L
Carnewas Island	Atlantic	Redcliff Castle	GR: SW846690	L
Carracks	English Channel	Minack Point	GR: SW385216	P
Carracks, The	Atlantic	Mussel Point	GR: SW468409	L
Carrick Du	Atlantic	St Ives Head	GR: SW503413	L
Carrick Luz	English Channel	Poldowrian	GR: SW757163	P
Carter's Rocks	Atlantic	Penhale Point	aka Gull Rocks. GR: SW755595	L
Castle Rock	Atlantic	Bosigran Castle	GR: SW416373	L
Castle Rock	Atlantic	Port Isaac	GR: SX001812	L
Cellar Rock	English Channel	Tregenna	GR: SW952408	P
Ceres Rock	Atlantic	St Ives Bay	GR: SW575414	L
Chair Rocks	Atlantic	Trevose Head	GR: SW749769	L
Chapel Rock	Atlantic	Perranporth	GR: SW755546	L
Chick, The	Atlantic	Kelsey Head	GR: SW764610	L
Chimney Rocks	Mount's Bay	Newlyn	GR: SW475297	P
Cleaders, The	Atlantic	Godrevy Cove	GR: SW579429	L
Clidgas Rocks	English Channel	Lizard Point	GR: SW697109	P
Coffin Rock	English Channel	Merthen Point	GR: SW416228	P
Colmer Rocks	English Channel	Looe Bay	GR: SX279539	P
Cow and Calf	Atlantic	Park Head	GR: SW837706	L
Cow and Calf	Port Quin Bay	Trevigo	GR: SW967809	L
Cowloe	Atlantic	Sennen Cove	GR: SW350267	L
Crams	Atlantic	St Agnes Head	GR: SW698515	L
Crane Islands	Atlantic	Basset's Cove	GR: SW634441	L
Crane Ledges	English Channel	Lizard	GR: SW692122	P
Cressars	Mount's Bay	Penzance	GR: SW489306	P
Crig-a-tana Rock	English Channel	Poltesco	GR: SW733162	P
Criggars	Atlantic	Newquay	GR: SW819623	L

Island name	Area	Nearest landmark	General information	P/L
Crinnis Island	English Channel	Carylon Bay	GR: SX056520	P
Crookmoyle Rock	Atlantic	Dannonchapel	GR: SX031829	L
Crowner Rocks	Atlantic	St Ives Head	GR: SW514411	L
Crowns, The	Atlantic	Zawn a Bal	GR: SW361337	L
Dales, The	English Channel	Lizard Point	GR: SW702107	P
Davas	English Channel	Lowland Point	GR: SW802191	P
Diamond	Atlantic	Portreath	GR: SW665466	L
Diggory's Island	Atlantic	Redcliff Castle	GR: SW847701	L
Dollar Rock	Atlantic	Newquay	GR: SW827632	L
Dolly Lay	Falmouth Bay	Manacle Point	One of The Manacles group. GR: SW818204	P
Downend Rock	English Channel	Downend Point	GR: SX219509	P
Drawna Rocks	Falmouth Bay	Porthkerris Point	GR: SW808229	P
Dulgevean Rocks	Falmouth Bay	Manacle Point	GR: SW812211	P
Eastern Shag Rock	Mount's Bay	Cudden Point	GR: SW548275	P
Ebal Rocks	Atlantic	Gurnard's Head	GR: SW430389	L
Ebber Rocks	English Channel	Black Head	GR: SW781166	P
Enoch Rock	Englich Channel	Lizard Point	One of The Stags group. GR: SW703110	P
Enys, The	Mount's Bay	Cudden Point	GR: SW559278	P
Enys, The	Atlantic	Pendeen Watch	GR: SW377355	L
Enys Dodnan	English Channel	Land's End	GR: SW345245	P
Enys Vean	English Channel	Kynance Cove	GR: SW689129	P
Flat Rock	English Channel	Penveor Point	GR: SX005401	P
Flory Island	Atlantic	Newquay	see Black Humphrey Rock.	L
Folly Rocks	Mount's Bay	Cudden Point	GR: SW573280	P
Frenchman, The	Mount's Bay	Perranuthnoe	GR: SW530296	P
Gala Rocks	Atlantic	Zennor Head	GR: SW455397	L
Gannel Rock	English Channel	Gwennap Head	GR: SW366214	P
Gazell	English Channel	Lamorna	GR: SW445233	P
Gear, The	English Channel	Newlyn	GR: SW479293	P
Gillick Rock	Atlantic	St Ives Bay	GR: SW579419	L
Godrevy Island	Atlantic	Godrevy Point	Inspired Virgina Woolf's novel *To the Lighthouse*. GR: SW575435	L
Godrevy Rocks	Atlantic	Godrevy Point	GR: SW582426	L
Gooden Heane Rock	Atlantic	Portreath	GR: SW658458	L
Goose, The	Atlantic	Pentire Point	GR: SW777617	L
Great Goular	English Channel	Penberth	One of the Goular group. GR: SW397218	P
Great Hogus	Mount's Bay	Marazion	GR: SW513305	P
Great Wrea	English Channel	Lowland Point	GR: SW804194	P
Grebe Rock	English Channel	Durgan	GR: SW775272	P
Greeb, The	Mount's Bay	Perranuthnoe	GR: SW530290	P
Green Island	Atlantic	Cross Coombe	GR: SW729525	L
Green Rock	English Channel	Gunwalloe	GR: SW655214	P
Green Saddle	English Channel	Poldowrian	GR: SW745166	P
Gull Island	English Channel	Charlestown	GR: SX050519	P
Gull Rock	English Channel	Kynance Cove	One of the Asparagus Islands. GR: SW683131	P
Gull Rock	Atlantic	Trebarwith Strand	GR: SX039865	L
Gull Rock	Atlantic	Portreath	GR: SW648458	L
Gull Rock	English Channel	Nare Head	GR: SW928369	P
Gull Rocks	Atlantic	Penhale Point	see Carter's Rocks	L
Gulland Rock	Atlantic	Gunver Head	GR: SW879787	L
Gullyn Rock	Atlantic	Sally's Bottom	GR: SW675470	L
Gwinges	Falmouth Bay	Manacle Point	One of The Manacles group. GR: SW820211	P
Gwinges	English Channel	Great Perhaver Beach	GR: SX032421	P
Haine's Rock	English Channel	Nare Head	GR: SW919370	P
Half Tide Rock	English Channel	Lamorna	GR: SW453238	P
Hayle Ulla	Atlantic	Portreath	GR: SW663464	L
Horrace	English Channel	Penberth	GR: SW398217	P
Horse, The	Atlantic	Portreath	GR: SW644453	L
Horse Rock	Atlantic	Portreath	GR: SW655458	L
Horse Rock	Atlantic	Newquay	GR: SW836642	L
Horse Rock	English Channel	Kiberick Cove	GR: SW925378	P
Hyrlas Rock	English Channel	Black Head	GR: SW779161	P
Inner Bucks	English Channel	Lamorna	GR: SW444230	P
Inner Kimlers	English Channel	Looe Bay	GR: SX254520	P
Inner Ranneys	English Channel	Looe Bay	GR: SX262512	P
Inner Stone	English Channel	Nare Head	GR: SW927367	P
Irish Lady	Atlantic	Land's End	GR: SW346260	L
Island, The	Atlantic	Newquay	GR: SW811618	L

Island name	Area	Nearest landmark	General information	P/L
Island, The	Atlantic	Tintagel	GR: SX048892	L
Island Rock	English Channel	Killigerran Head	GR: SW871323	P
Jago's Island	Atlantic	Newquay	GR: SW811618	L
Jay, The	English Channel	Poldowrian	GR: SW748163	P
Jobbies Rock	English Channel	Great Perhaver Beach	GR: SX019424	P
Kenidjacks, The	Atlantic	Portheras Cove	GR: SW386360	L
Kettle's Bottom	Atlantic	Land's End	GR: SW329254	L
Killyvarder Rock	English Channel	Par	GR: SX083523	P
Labham Rock	English Channel	Lizard Point	GR: SW699111	P
Landing Rock	Atlantic	Cross Coombe	GR: SW726516	L
Larrick	English Channel	Nealand Point	GR: SX191501	P
Larrigan Rocks	Mount's Bay	Newlyn	GR: SW468293	P
Lemoria Rock	English Channel	Rosen Cliff	GR: SW923373	P
Limmicks	English Channel	Looe Bay	GR: SX263533	P
Lion Rock	English Channel	Kynance Cove	GR: SW688129	P
Little Bo	Atlantic	Sennen Cove	One of the Bo's group. GR: SW346269	L
Little Carracks	Atlantic	Towednack Quae Head	GR: SW470410	L
Little Cudden	Mount's Bay	Cudden Point	GR: SW552277	P
Little Goular	English Channel	Penberth	One of The Goular group. GR: SW396217	P
Little Heaver	English Channel	Lamorna	GR: SW458236	P
Little Hogus	Mount's Bay	Marazion	GR: SW511307	P
Little Trigg Rocks	Mount's Bay	Porthleven	GR: SW628254	P
Little Wrea	English Channel	Lowland Point	GR: SW808195	P
Logan Rock	English Channel	Penberth	GR: SW398219	P
Long Rock	Mount's Bay	Penzance	GR: SW499309	P
Long Rock	English Channel	Veryan Bay	GR: SW995401	P
Long Stone, The	English Channel	Downderry	GR: SX338536	P
Longships	Atlantic	Land's End	GR: SW322259	L
Looe Island	English Channel	Looe Bay	See St George's Island	P
Lye Rock	Atlantic	Tintagel	GR: SX064898	L
Maen Chynoweth	Falmouth Bay	Manacle Point	GR: SW817218	P
Maen Derrens	Atlantic	St Ives Head	GR: SW520413	L
Maen Dower	Atlantic	St Just	GR: SW356294	L
Maen Garrick	Falmouth Bay	Manacle Point	One of The Manacles group. GR: SW818212	P
Maen Land	English Channel	Godrevy Cove	GR: SW808201	P
Maen Vose	Falmouth Bay	Manacle Point	One of The Manacles group. GR: SW818204	P
Maenheere	English Channel	Lizard Point	One of The Stags. GR: SW703110	P
Magow Rocks	Atlantic	St Ives Bay	GR: SW581423	L
Man and His Man	Atlantic	Newdowns Head	aka Bawden Rocks. GR: SW702530	L
Man of War	English Channel	Lizard Point	One of The Stags group. GR: SW694113	P
Manankas	Atlantic	Morvah	GR: SW405364	L
May's Rock	English Channel	Tregenna	GR: SW952406	P
Megiliggar Rocks	Mount's Bay	Trewavas Head	GR: SW609266	P
Meinek	Atlantic	Land's End	One of the Longships Rocks group. GR: SW325255	L
Men Hyr	English Channel	Lizard Point	GR: SW700106	P
Men Par	English Channel	Lizard Point	GR: SW697112	P
Merlyn Rock	Mount's Bay	Mousehole	GR: SW470260	P
Merope Rocks	Atlantic	Trevose Head	GR: SW861763	L
Merthen Rock	English Channel	Merthen Point	GR: SW420227	P
Mewstone Rock	English Channel	Cawsand Bay	GR: SX435501	P
Middle Merope Islands	Atlantic	Gunver Head	GR: SW895772	L
Middle Stone	English Channel	Nare Head	GR: SW925365	P
Mildran's Rock	Falmouth Bay	Manacle Point	One of The Manacles group. GR: SW813213	P
Minnows Islands	Atlantic	Treyarnon Bay	GR: SW853728	L
Mistrel Rock	Falmouth Bay	Manacle Point	One of The Manacles group. GR: SW818206	P
Mouls, The	Port Quin Bay	The Rumps	Where Laurence Binyon wrote the Remembrance Day verse 'They shall grow not old . . .' GR: SW937815	L
Mozens, The	Atlantic	Portheras Cove	GR: SW390365	L
Mullion Island	Mount's Bay	Porth Mellin	GR: SW661176	P
Mulvin	English Channel	Lizard Point	One of The Stags group. GR: SW691113	P
Nantivet Rock	English Channel	Kynance Cove	GR: SW681134	P
Nathaga Rocks	Atlantic	Navax Point	GR: SW591439	L
Newland	Atlantic	Padstow Bay	GR: SW914811	L
Old Dane	Atlantic	Newquay	GR: SW807626	L
Ontonna Rock	Atlantic	Trevarrian	GR: SW843658	L

Island name	Area	Nearest landmark	General information	P/L
Outer Bucks	English Channel	Lamorna	GR: SW444228	P
Outer Ranneys	English Channel	Looe Bay	GR: SX263511	P
Outer Stone	English Channel	Nare Head	GR: SW925363	P
Oxen, The	English Channel	Dolor Point	GR: SW784178	P
Peal, The	Atlantic	Land's End	GR: SW340254	L
Peber	Atlantic	Land's End	GR: SW341252	L
Pedn Olva	Atlantic	St Ives	GR: SW520403	L
Pedn-myin	English Channel	Lowland Point	GR: SW795190	P
Pen Ervan	English Channel	Lizard Point	GR: SW702111	P
Pen Fin	Falmouth Bay	Manacle Point	One of The Manacles group. GR: SW823213	P
Pen Olver	English Channel	Lizard Point	GR: SW712116	P
Pen Rocks	English Channel	Looe Bay	GR: SX259531	P
Pendarves Island	Atlantic	Redcliff Castle	GR: SW846694	L
Pibyah Rock	English Channel	Treluggan Cliff	GR: SW894378	P
Polgassick Rock	Atlantic	Polgassick Cove	GR: SW489412	L
Polgravel	English Channel	Chynhalls Point	GR: SW785175	P
Polmear Island	English Channel	Charlestown	GR: SX038514	P
Poltesco Rock	English Channel	Poltesco	GR: SW730156	P
Porth Island	Atlantic	Newquay	GR: SW824630	L
Pyg	English Channel	Lizard Point	GR: SW717111	P
Quadrant	English Channel	Lizard Point	GR: SW693115	P
Quants	English Channel	Manacle Point	GR: SW818204	P
Queen Bess Rock	Atlantic	Redcliff Castle	GR: SW848699	L
Quies	Atlantic	Trevose Head	GR: SW831760	L
Redcove Island	Atlantic	Newquay	GR: SW848696	L
Rill Ledges	English Channel	The Rill	GR: SW674134	P
Robin's Rock	English Channel	Porth Pean	GR: SX032505	P
Robin's Rocks	Atlantic	Porthmeor Point	GR: SW425380	L
Runnel Stone	English Channel	Gwennap Head	GR: SW373199	P
Ryeman	Mount's Bay	Penzance	GR: SW495505	P
St Clement's Isle	Mount's Bay	Mousehole	GR: SW473263	P
St George's Island	English Channel	Looe Bay	aka Looe Island. Reputed landing place of Joseph of Arimathea on his way to Glastonbury. Area: 0.09 sq km (0.03 sq miles). GR: SX256515	P
St Michael's Mount	Mount's Bay	Marazion	See separate entry	P
Samaritan Island	Atlantic	Bedruthan Steps	GR: SW849698	L
Samphire Island	Atlantic	Portu-cadjack Cove	GR: SW639448	L
Scathe	English Channel	Lizard	GR: SW693121	P
Seghy	English Channel	Penberth	GR: SW399220	P
Severnsouls Rock	Port Quin Bay	The Rumps	GR: SW934813	L
Shag Rock	English Channel	Broad Cove	GR: SX180505	P
Shag Rock	Atlantic	Perranporth	GR: SW746542	L
Shag Rock	Atlantic	Padstow Bay	GR: SW925784	L
Shag Rock	Mount's Bay	Mousehole	GR: SW473261	P
Shag Rock	English Channel	Lizard Point	GR: SW698114	P
Shag Rock	English Channel	Caragloose Point	GR: SW948399	P
Shag Rock	English Channel	Mawnan	GR: SW791271	P
Shark's Fin	Atlantic	Land's End	GR: SW327262	L
Shark's Fin	English Channel	Manacle Point	GR: SW813213	P
Sheep Rock	Atlantic	Portreath	GR: SW668469	L
Sisters, The	Atlantic	Tintagel	GR: SX061900	L
Star Rock	Atlantic	Cross Coombe	GR: SW724518	L
Strap Rocks	Atlantic	St Ives Bay	GR: SW579417	L
Sweden Rock	Atlantic	Newquay	GR: SW835641	L
Tal-y-maen	Atlantic	Land's End	One of the Longships Rocks group. GR: SW321250	L
Tar	English Channel	Penberth	GR: SW397220	P
Tater-du	English Channel	Lamorna	GR: SW440229	P
Taylor's Rock	English Channel	Lizard Point	GR: SW693112	P
Three Brothers	Atlantic	St Ives Head	GR: SW518413	L
Three Stone Oar	Atlantic	Pendeen Watch	aka The Wra. GR: SW380365	L
Tintagel Island	Atlantic	Tintagel	Peninsula but included by virtue of its name	L
Tobban Horse	Atlantic	Porthtowan	GR: SW683477	L
Tol Peg	Falmouth Bay	Porthkerris Point	GR: SW809226	P
Tregwyn	English Channel	Mullion Cove	GR: SW659177	P
Trescore Islands	Atlantic	Porthcothan Bay	GR: SW847719	L
Trethias Island	Atlantic	Treyarnon Bay	GR: SW852739	L
Tye Rocks	Mount's Bay	Porthleven	GR: SW631252	P

Island name	Area	Nearest landmark	General information	P/L
Var, The	English Channel	Mullion Cove	GR: SW665178	P
Vase Rock	Falmouth Bay	Manacle Point	One of The Manacles group. GR: SW823213	P
Velvet Rock	English Channel	Predannack Head	GR: SW668153	P
Vervan Rocks	Falmouth Bay	Manacle Point	One of The Manacles group. GR: SW812216	P
Vessacks	English Channel	Porthgwarra	GR: SW379217	P
Vinnick Rock	Atlantic	Polzeath	GR: SW927785	L
Vro, The	English Channel	Mullion Cove	GR: SW663175	P
Vrogue Rock	English Channel	Bass Point	Southern end of a reef known as the Sparnon Shoals.	P
Welloe	Mount's Bay	Trewavas Head	GR: SW584257	P
Western Cressar	Mount's Bay	Penzance	GR: SW487305	P
Western Shag Rock	Mount's Bay	Cudden Point	GR: SW548276	P
Whale Rock	English Channel	Lizard Point	GR: SW718134	P
Wherry Rocks	Mount's Bay	Newlyn	GR: SW470294	P
Will's Rock	Atlantic	Porthcothan Bay	GR: SW853724	L
Wolf Rock	English Channel	Land's End	GR: SW269119	P
Wolf Rocks	Atlantic	Morvah	GR: SW405362	L
Wra, The	Atlantic	Pendeen Watch	see Three Stone Oar	L
Zacry's Island	Atlantic	Newquay	GR: SW832637	L
Zebadee	Falmouth Bay	Manacle Point	GR: SW811212	P

Isles of Scilly

(shipping area: Plymouth)

Island name	Nearest landmark	General information
Annet	St Agnes	A designated bird sanctuary, its most popular inhabitant being the puffin. Area: 0.085 sq miles (0.22 sq km). GR: SV863086
Biggal	St Martin's	One of the Eastern Isles. GR: SV944131
Biggal	Samson	One of the Northern Rocks. GR: SV850127
Biggal of Gorregan	Annet	One of the Western Rocks. GR: SV849060
Bishop Rock	Great Crebawethan	The lighthouse is the most westerly in the UK. GR: SV807065
Black Rocks	Bryher	One of the Northern Rocks. GR: SV859146
Bow, The	St Agnes	One of the St Agnes group. GR: SV893088
Broad Ledge	Tresco	GR: SV917150
Brothers	Annet	GR: SV864071
Bryher	Tresco	From Watch Hill there is a wonderful panoramic view of the island. Area: 0.5 sq miles (1.32 sq km). Population: 92. GR: SV877150
Burnt Island	St Agnes	GR: SV875085
Carn Near	Tresco	GR: SV888134
Castinicks	Samson	GR: SV856117
Castle Bryher	Bryher	GR: SV864139
Chimney Rocks	St Martin's	GR: SV943153
Codnors Rocks	Annet	One of the Western Rocks. GR: SV829072.
Crebinicks	Retarrier Ledges	GR: SV809059
Crim Rocks	Great Crebawethan	GR: SV802091
Crow Island	Bryher	Tiny islet in the Bryher group. GR: SV867148
Crow Rock	St Mary's	GR: SV910131
Daisy	Annet	One of the Western Rocks. GR: SV839054
East Craggyellis	Tresco	GR: SV910142
English Island	St Martin's	Tiny islet of the Eastern Isles. GR: SV939150
Gilstone	St Martin's	Part of the St Mary's group. GR: SV919092
Gilstone	Annet	Admiral Sir Cloudesley Shovel wrecked HMS *Association* and three other ships here in 1707. One of the Western Rocks. GR: SV832054
Golden Ball	St Helen's	One of the St Helen's group. GR: SV889172
Gorregan	Annet	Large rock 7 miles (11km) from Hughtown. One of the Western Rocks. GR: SV848056
Great Arthur	St Martin's	Several cairns (rock piles) are situated on this island. One of the Eastern Isles. GR: SV940137
Great Crebawethan	Annet	One of the Western Rocks. GR: SV831070
Great Ganinick	St Martin's	One of several tiny islets northeast of St Mary's and southwest of St Martin's. One of the Eastern Isles. GR: SV932138
Great Gannilly	St Martin's	One of several tiny islets northeast of St Mary's and southwest of St Martin's. One of the Eastern Isles. Area: 0.05 sq miles (0.13 sq km). GR: SV946145
Great High Rock	Bryher	One of the Bryher group. GR: SV872154
Great Innisvouls	St Martin's	One of the Eastern Isles. GR: SV953141

Island name	Nearest landmark	General information
Great Merrick Ledge	St Martin's	One of the St Martin's group. GR: SV927168
Great Minalto	Samson	One of The Minaltos group. GR: SV870117
Great Smith	St Agnes	Twin peaks dominate the tiny islet. GR: SV869093
Great Wingletang	St Agnes	Part of the St Agnes group. GR: SV884070
Green Island	Samson	Tiny islet off the coast of Samson. GR: SV883126
Gugh	St Agnes	Accessible by foot from St Agnes at low tide across the sandbar. The Old Man of Gugh, a Bronze Age standing stone (known locally as a menhir) 9ft (2.7m) tall, is situated at the foot of Kittern Hill. GR: SV889082
Gulf Rock	Bryher	GR: SV867142
Gunners	Annet	GR: SV827093
Guther's Island	St Martin's	Tiny islet off the coast of St Martin's. GR: SV918144
Gweal	Bryher	Tiny islet off the coast of Bryher. Area: 0.01 sq miles (0.03 sq km). GR: SV866150
Halftide Ledges	St Agnes	One of the St Agnes group. GR: SV871093
Hangman's Island	Tresco/Bryher	The gallows, complete with granite hook, is eerily still to be seen.
Hanjague	St Martin's	One of the Eastern Isles. GR: SV957150
Hard Lewis Rocks	St Martin's	One of the St Martin's group. GR: SV957158
Haycocks	Annet	One of the Annet group. GR: SV855090
Hedge Rock	Tean	One of the Tean group. GR: SV908157
Hellweathers	Annet	One of the Annet group. GR: SV864078
Higher Ledge	Tresco	GR: SV916144
Illiswilgig	Bryher	Tiny islet, part of the Northern Rocks. GR: SV858137
Irishman's Ledge	St Martin's	One of the Eastern Isles. GR: SV947149
Isinvrank	Annet	One of the Annet group. GR: SV862071
Jacky's Rock	Annet	One of the Western Rocks. GR: SV838063
Jolly Rock	Annet	One of the Western Rocks. GR: SV833063
Kettle	Tresco	One of the Tresco group. GR: SV880167
Lethegus Rocks	St Agnes	One of the St Agnes group. GR: SV876072
Lion Rock	St Martin's	One of the St Martin's group. GR: SV916179
Little Arthur	St Martin's	Tiny islet annexed to Great Arthur. One of the Eastern Isles.
Little Crebawethan	Annet	One of the Western Rocks. GR: SV827069
Little Ganinick	St Martin's	Part of the Eastern Isles. GR: SV934138
Little Gannilly	St Martin's	Part of the Eastern Isles. GR: SV938142
Little Minalto	Samson	One of The Minaltos group. GR: SV866116
Long Ledge	Samson	GR: SV872130
Maiden Bower	Bryher	Tiny islet, part of the Northern Rocks. GR: SV850144
Mare, The	Tresco	One of the Tresco group. GR: SV893131
Melledgan	Annet	GR: SV861064
Men-a-vaur	St Helen's	One of the St Helen's group. GR: SV893175
Menawethan	St Martin's	One of the Eastern Isles. GR: SV953136
Merrick Island	Bryher	One of the Bryher group. GR: SV884147
Mincarlo	Samson	One of the Northern Rocks group. GR: SV853129
Minmanueth	Annet	One of the Annet group. GR: SV857089
Mouls	St Martin's	One of the Eastern Isles. GR: SV957145
Muncoy	Melledgan	GR: SV857068
Murr Rock	St Martin's	One of the St Martin's group. GR: SV937163
Newman	St Mary's	One of the St Mary's group. GR: SV898109
Nornour	Great Gannilly	One of the St Martin's group. This island of 4 acres (1.6ha) contains 11 excavated hut circles occupied from the Bronze Age to Romano-British, when it became a goddess shrine. Fantastic finds are in the museum in Hugh Town on St Mary's. GR: SV944147
Northwethel	Tresco	One of the Tresco group. GR: SV895163
Nut Rock	Samson	GR: SV889124
Peaked Rocks	Samson	GR: SV858115
Pernagie Isle	St Martin's	One of the St Martin's group. GR: SV916174
Picket Rock	Bryher	One of the Northern Rocks group. GR: SV851139.
Plumb Island	St Martin's	One of the tiny islets around St Martin's. GR: SV918170
Polreath	St Martin's	One of the St Martin's group. GR: SV954156
Puffin Island	Samson	Part of the Samson group. GR: SV881134
Ragged Island	St Martin's	One of the Eastern Isles. GR: SV945138
Ranneys	Annet	One of the Annet islands. GR: SV857082
Retarrier Ledges	Annet	One of the Western Rocks group. GR: SV820060
Rosevean	Annet	One of the Western Rocks group. GR: SV840856
Rosevear Island	Annet	One of the Western Rocks group. GR: SV845058
Round Island	St Helen's	Part of the St Helen's group. GR: SV902176
St Agnes	St Agnes	The Turk's Head is the island's finest watering hole. Area: 0.57 sq miles (1.48 sq km). Population: 73. GR: SV880080
St Helen's	Tresco	One of the larger islands. Area: 0.08 sq miles (0.2 sq km). GR: SV900170

Island name	Nearest landmark	General information
St Martin's	St Martin's	One of six inhabited islands. Cruther's Hill is crowned by impressive Scillonian chambered tombs. Area: 0.92 sq miles (2.37 sq km). Population: 142. GR: SV925155
St Mary's	Land's End, Cornwall	Largest of the Scilly Isles. Hugh Town is the 'capital'. The only Roman Catholic church in the islands (Our Lady, Star of the Sea) is located in the town. Area: 2.43 sq miles (6.29 sq km). Population: 1666. GR: SV924114
Samson	Samson	Largest uninhabited island. Area: 0.15 sq miles (0.38 sq km). GR: SV875125
Scilly Rock	Bryher	GR: SV860155
Seal Rock	Bryher	One of the Northern Rocks group. GR: SV854140
Silver Carn	Annet	One of the Western Rocks group. GR: SV839062
Skirt Island	Tresco	One of the Tresco group. GR: SV903138
Stony Island	Samson	Tiny islet of the Samson group. GR: SV886127
Taylor's Island	St Mary's	Part of the St Mary's group. GR: SV904115
Tean	St Martin's	One of the larger islands. Area: 0.06 sq miles (0.16 sq km). GR: SV908164
Toll's Island	St Mary's	Joined to Pelistry Beach, St Mary's by a sandbar. GR: SV930119
Trenemene	Annet	One of the Western Rocks. GR: SV848054
Tresco	Tresco	Home to a Roman altar brought here after being found in Hugh Town on St Mary's. It now stands in the Abbey Gardens. Area: 1.15 sq miles (2.97 sq km). Population: 180. GR: SV894144
White Island	St Martin's	Annexed to St Martin's. GR: SV870126
Yellow Rock	Samson	Part of the Samson group. GR: SV878136
Zantman's Rock	Great Crebawethan	GR: SV804095

CUMBRIA

BORDERS
DUMFRIES & GALLOWAY
NORTHUMBERLAND
DURHAM
NORTH YORKSHIRE
LANCASHIRE
Irish Sea
A74(M)
M6
1
2
3
4
5
6
Brampton
Carlisle
Wigton
Aspatria
Maryport
Cockermouth
Workington
Whitehaven
Cleator Moor
St Bees
Egremont
Bassenthwaite Lake
Derwent Water
Keswick
Crummock Water
Buttermere
Scafell Pike
978
Wast Water
Cumbrian Mountains
Ullswater
Patterdale
Haweswater Reservoir
Grasmere
Ambleside
Coniston
Coniston Water
Windermere
Kendal
Broughton in Furness
Millom
Ulverston
Cartmel
Milnthorpe
Barrow-in-Furness
Penrith
R. Eden
Alston
Appleby-in-Westmorland
Brough
Kirkby Stephen
Sedbergh
R. Lune
Districts
1 Carlisle
2 Allerdale
3 Eden
4 Copeland
5 South Lakeland
6 Barrow-in-Furness
0
20 miles
0
30 km

Cumbria is bordered by the English counties of Northumberland to the northeast, County Durham to the east, North Yorkshire to the southeast and Lancashire to the south. To the north the county is bordered by the Scottish regions of Dumfries and Galloway and Borders and to the west by the Irish Sea, with the Solway Firth to the north and Morecambe Bay to the south.

The modern county of Cumbria was created in 1974, by combining the area of the abolished administrative counties of Cumberland and Westmorland, plus the Furness part of Lancashire (the Cartmel peninsula), and a protrusion of Yorkshire (the former Sedbergh Rural District). Some people, particularly those born or brought up in the area, prefer to refer to Furness by its traditional county name of Lancashire and the area around Kendal by its traditional county name of Westmorland. Local papers the *Westmorland Gazette* and *Cumberland and Westmorland Herald* are still named on the traditional county basis. The administrative centre of Cumbria is Carlisle, England's most northerly city.

Cumbria contains the whole of the Lake District National Park, the largest national park in Britain, established in 1951 and covering 885 sq miles (2292 sq km). It also contains a small part of the Yorkshire Dales National Park. The northern ranges of the Lake District consist of Ordovician slate, about 500 million years old; the central ranges of younger volcanic rock; and a southern range of limestone and other Silurian rock about 440 million years old. These highlands are dissected by U-shaped valleys, known as dales, containing the lakes, some of which are artificial.

Human settlement began in the Lake District at least 5000 years ago, when Pike o'Stickle and other mountains became the source of stone for axes and stone circles such as those at Castlerigg, Long Meg and elsewhere. Later inhabitants dug parts of the Lake District for copper, iron ore, graphite and green slate. In Neolithic times, the Lake District was a major source of stone axes, examples of which have been found all over Britain. The primary site, on the slopes of the Langdale Pikes, is sometimes described as a 'stone axe factory'. Although Cumbria is usually thought of as a Celtic region, the Angles made their presence felt here before the Viking invasions and the rule of the area by the Scottish Kingdom of Strathclyde in the 9th century. Celts, Romans, Angles and Vikings in succession settled among the lakes, and it was the last of these who provided such place-name elements as '-thwaite' (clearing), 'fell' (mountain with grazing), 'gill' (ravine) and 'force' (waterfall).

As early as the 12th century there is evidence of mining and quarrying in Cumbria, and it probably dates back to Roman times. Evidence of this industry can be seen throughout the county – lead, copper, zinc, baryte, haematite, tungsten, graphite, fluorite and coal were being mined and quarried.

Numerous tower houses and pele towers were built in the 15th and 16th centuries, when border reivers were a constant menace, rustling livestock, pillaging, kidnapping and extorting protection money. Pele towers (aka peel towers) were small rectangular stone buildings with thick walls designed to withstand short sieges. The three-storey watch towers had battlements on the roof to allow arrows to be fired at raiders or missiles to be hurled down on unwanted visitors. In 1551, the 'Debateable Land' was divided between England and Scotland, and the boundary was defined by a shallow ditch which became known as the Scot's Dike. Raids from Scotland, however, remained a frequent part of Cumbrian life until the Acts of Union in 1707.

Lady Anne Clifford, Countess of Pembroke, was born at Skipton Castle, North Yorkshire on 30 January 1590, during the reign of Elizabeth I. She is celebrated for her diary and her tireless restoration of her properties in Cumbria and North Yorkshire which were badly damaged in the Civil War. She died at Brougham Castle in Cumbria on 22 March 1676, when she was 86, in the room where her father had been born.

Historically, farming, in particular of sheep, was the major industry in the region. The breed most closely associated with the area is the tough Herdwick; introduced by the Vikings, these are born black and become white. In the middle of the 19th century, half the world textile industry's bobbin supply came from the Lake District area. Stott Park Bobbin Mill, now owned by English Heritage, is still in working order. Carlisle became the industrial base of the county in the 19th and early 20th century with many textile mills, engineering works and food manufacturers developing in and around the town. These included Ferguson Printers, Carr's of Carlisle (now part of United Biscuits), Kangol, Metal Box (now part of Crown Cork and Seal), John Laing and, more recently, the hauliers Eddie Stobart Ltd.

The Lakes began to attract wider attention after the publication in 1835 of *A Guide to the Lakes*, written by one of the area's most famous residents, the poet William Wordsworth. He suggested that the Lake District should become 'a sort of national property', but objected to the building of the railways and roads which have since allowed ever-increasing numbers of people to visit it.

More recently the Lakes have been further popularised by Lancashire-born Alfred Wainwright (1907–91), who at the age of 23 visited the Lakes with his cousin Eric Beardsall. Arriving in Windermere, the young Wainwright was captivated by the houses with beautiful gardens. Seeing the view from Orrest Head above the town, the course of his life was transformed and he realised that he would never see the streets of Blackburn in the same way. He has since become famous as a writer of guidebooks to the Lake District fells, and the 214 fells he described have become known as Wainwrights.

The largest single owner of land within the Lake District is now the National Trust. Its first members included Beatrix Potter, an artist and writer of children's books who became a sheep farmer in the Lakes and left many of her paintings as well as her home and land to the Trust.

Cumbria	Population			Area	
Districts	*male*	*female*	*total*	*sq miles*	*sq km*
Allerdale	45,567	47,925	93,492	479	1242
Barrow-in-Furness	35,092	36,888	71,980	30	78
Carlisle	48,735	52,004	100,739	402	1040
Copeland	34,538	34,780	69,318	283	732
Eden	24,493	25,284	49,777	827	2142
South Lakeland	49,490	52,811	102,301	592	1534
Total	237,915	249,692	487,607	2613	6768

Local Attractions and Information

Abbot Hall Art Gallery — Kirkland, Kendal. A former Georgian villa located beside the River Kent, containing 18th and 19th century watercolours (Turner and Ruskin are represented) and 20th century British paintings and sculptures. Exhibits include rare furniture by Gillows, English pottery and porcelain. Tel: 01539 722464.

Abbott's Hike — Named after its originator, Peter Abbott, a long-distance footpath crossing Cumbria, North Yorkshire and West Yorkshire. The Hike is 107 miles (172km) long with links between 14 miles (23km) of the Three Peaks Walk, 3 miles (5km) of the Pennine Way, and 25 miles (40km) of the Dales Way.

Acorn Bank Garden & Watermill — 1 mile (1.6km) north of Temple Sowerby, 6 miles (10km) east of Penrith. The property includes gardens, which feature over 250 medicinal and culinary herbs, and orchards with old varieties of English fruit. It is also noted for its partially restored watermill. The garden is surrounded and protected by ancient oaks and high walls. The property is owned by the National Trust. Tel: 01768 361893.

Administrative headquarters — The Courts, Carlisle CA3 8NA. Tel: 01228 606060.

Aira Force — See Waterfalls

Airports — **Carlisle Airport** (CAX), 5 miles (8km) northeast of Carlisle, was opened in 1961 on the site of the former RAF Crosby-in-Eden and is currently licensed for the operation of light aircraft traffic. It is managed by Stobart Air Ltd. Tel: 01228 573641.

Walney Island Airport (BWF), 2 miles (3km) west of Barrow-in-Furness.

Aldingham Castle — 6 miles (10km) south of Ulverston. The earthworks of the motte were probably raised from an earlier ring work structure by Michael de Fleming c.1100 which still remains but can only be seen from a distance. The Flemings raised the motte even higher in the 12th century, but abandoned it in the 13th century, probably moving to the moated site of Aldingham Grange manor house that lies to the rear of the motte. This is still a well-preserved mound in the middle of a water-filled moat.

Ancient sites (stone circles) — Cumbria has over 50 stone circles, more than any other English county; the following are among the most important:

Birkrigg Stone Circle, also known as the Druid's Temple, is located on Birkrigg Common near Sunbrick, south of Ulverston. The circle, dating from 1700–1400 BC, is made up of a double row of stones and a paved floor. The inner ring, measuring 29.5ft (9m), consists of 10 stones. The outer circle, with 15 stones, has a diameter of 82ft (25m). The height of the stones is approximately 2–3ft (0.6–1m). The remains of five human cremations were found inside the smaller circle.

Castlerigg Stone Circle, 1½ miles (2.5km) east of Keswick, is a Neolithic stone circle dating from 3000 BC. It sits 700ft (213m) above sea level on a plateau surrounded by the Lakeland fells of Skiddaw, Blencathra and Lonscale. This circle is arguably one of the earliest constructed in England. Alexander Thom's studies determined that the stones indicated seven solar and lunar declinations and was possibly a temple. With open routes from all directions, whether it served as a place for tribal gatherings or trade is open to conjecture.

Casterton Stone Circle, northeast of the village of Casterton, is set in an irregular earth bank and dates from the Neolithic/Bronze Age, approximately 2000–600 BC. Nineteen stones, the tallest 19.5in (49.5cm) high, make up the 62ft (18.9m) diameter circle. Over 1800 finds, among them a bronze spearhead, flint arrowhead and drinking vessel, are though to have come from this circle.

Elva Plain Stone Circle lies on private ground in a field at Elva Farm, 3½ miles (5.5km) east of Cockermouth. It is an arrangement of 15 stones that remain of a probable 30 original ones. The circle measures 125–130ft (38–40m) in diameter and the stones are low, protruding no more than 2½–3ft (0.75–0.9m).

Grey Croft Stone Circle is located on private property at Seascale How Farm, north of Seascale. Only 10 stones of the original 12 remain. The circle measures 98.4ft (30m) in diameter and the stones, volcanic in origin, average 4½ft (1.4m) high.

King Arthur's Round Table near the junction of the Eamont and Lowther rivers, south of Penrith, was supposedly named in the 14th century when the Clifford family moved into Brougham Castle nearby. The circle dates from the late Neolithic and Bronze ages and the earth bank and ditch measure 162ft (49.3m) in diameter. In 1820 the site was desecrated by a local pub landlord who trucked in landfill to raise the centre and proceeded to use it for a tea garden.

Kinniside Stone Circle is located between the Calder and Ennerdale Bridges, 2½ miles (4km) southeast of Cleator Moor. The comparatively small circle, not an original prehistoric site, sits by Blakely Rise hill and sometimes goes under the same name. The 11 stones, the tallest of which is 5ft (1.5m) high, are set in concrete.

Lacra Stone Circle, near the village of Kirksanton on Lacra Bank, 2 miles (3km) wesr of Millom, dates from the Bronze Age. One circle of six stones is 52ft (16m) in diameter while another is 49ft (14.5m) in diameter and has six of its original 11 stones remaining. Only three stones are left of what was once a 69ft (20.5m) diameter circle. Excavation of the site in 1947 uncovered bone, ash, charcoal and an urn.

Little Meg Stone Circle, located near Little Salkeld, Penrith, sits on the edge of a field on private land. The Bronze Age circle, surrounding a prehistoric burial site, is 20ft (6m) in diameter and located 1/2 mile (0.8km) from Long Meg and her Daughters. Cup and ring mark carvings, similar to those on Long Meg, were found on two of the 11 stones, the tallest of which is 3 1/2ft (1.1m) high. One of the stones can be found on display in the Tuille House Museum in Carlisle.

Long Meg and her Daughters, 3/4 mile (1.2km) north of the village of Little Salkeld, is the third largest prehistoric stone circle in England. Dating from the Bronze Age (*c.*2000–900 BC), Long Meg sits on a hill and measures 357ft (109m) by 305ft (93m). The 60 standing stones are arranged in a rough circle, while the 12ft (3.5m) sandstone pillar of Long Meg is outside the circle. Carvings of concentric circles, spirals and a 'cup and ring' are found on Long Meg's sides. Legends about the site abound, the best of which is that the stones were once a group of witches who danced on the Sabbath and were turned into stones by a magician. Another legend states that it is impossible to count the stones more than once and come up with the same number. William Wordsworth claimed to have known of Long Meg and her Daughters and wrote a poem about the stone circle in 1821.

Mayburgh Henge, located south of Penrith at Eamont Bridge near King Arthur's Round Table, is said to have been built from stones and pebbles taken from the Eamont and Lowther rivers. The large circular bank is 285ft (87m) in diameter, 14ft (4.2m) in height, and covers 1 1/2 acres (0.6ha). An entrance was made on the east side of the henge and in its centre one 9ft (2.7m) stone of volcanic ash remains standing of a now non-existent inner circle whose stones reached a maximum height of 12ft (3.5m). In the 18th century, several other stones that remained in the circle were destroyed by gunfire. Others were carted away in the 19th century to use for building material. Due to its location on the two rivers it is thought that the henge may have been related to a trade route.

Moor Divock is situated on Askham Fell near Helton and Askham, on the southwest edge of the Lakeland fells. In 1885, a paper was published about this group of cairns, standing stones and circles. Today, many of the stones have either disappeared or fallen from their standing position. The prehistoric site includes the Cockpit, the largest collection at 90ft (27.5m) in diameter. Another cairn circle in the area is 34ft (10.5m) in diameter. It consists of ten stones measuring up to 3ft (0.9m) high. Urns, ashes and bones were found at some of the sites. One cairn, White Raise, contained human bones.

Swinside Stone Circle surrounded by hills and located in an open field 2 1/2 miles (4km) west of Broughton-in-Furness, dates from the Bronze Age and comprises 55 (of an original 60) close set (5ft apart) stones, 32 of which still stand. The circle is 94ft (28.5m) in diameter. Its tallest stone, at 7 1/2 feet (2.3m), weighs in at 5 tons. The porphyritic slate stones, set in packed pebbles, come from the nearby hills. At the southeast is an entrance marked by two portal stones sitting outside the circle. The midwinter sun hits the two southernmost portal stones as seen when standing in the circle's centre. Legend suggests that every time the building of a church was attempted on the spot, the devil destroyed the work during the night. Swinside was also called Sunkenkirk (kirk meaning church) for this reason.

Anthorn Transmitter — Anthorn, 12 miles (19km) west of Carlisle. Very Low Frequency (VLF) transmitter used for transmitting orders to submarines on 19.6 kHz. During World War II the site was a military airfield operated by the Royal Navy Air Service and called HMS *Nuthatch.* It is now operated by VT Communications.

Appleby Castle — Boroughgate Street, Appleby-in-Westmorland. Situated in a defensive position by the River Eden, the castle was founded by Ranulph le Meschin c.1100–20, after which it passed to the Crown. The Scots took control from 1136–57, after which it was regained by the English. In the 13th century the castle was taken over by the Clifford family who retained ownership for the next 400 years. Much of the castle was rebuilt by Thomas Lord Clifford during Henry VI's reign. The Civil War saw both the Royalists and the Parliamentarians occupy the castle. After the return of Charles II to the throne, Lady Anne Clifford, Countess of Pembroke, occupied the castle and celebrated the joyful event with the town. During this time the castle was extensively rebuilt and restored. In 1653 she built stables in the castle grounds, as well as Lady Anne's Bee House. After her death, Appleby Castle was further improved by her grandson, the Earl of Thanet. The 27 acres (11ha) of grounds are home to a collection of rare breeds that include sheep, goats, pheasants, ducks and geese. Tel: 01768 351402.

Appleby Horse Fair — Appleby-in-Westmorland. One of the oldest horse fairs in Britain. Held annually in early June, it has taken place since the reign of James II, who granted a charter allowing a horse fair 'near to the River Eden'. Since then, hundreds of gypsies and travellers have converged to buy and sell horses, meet with friends and relations and to celebrate their music, history and folklore.

Armitt Library and Museum Centre — Rydal Road, Ambleside. Founded by Mary Louisa Armitt in 1909, the library has a superb collection of books and manuscripts, drawings and paintings, memorabilia and archaeological objects relating to Lake District characters including John Ruskin, William Green, the Collingwood family, Herbert Bell, Harriet Martineau, Charlotte Mason and Beatrix Potter. Tel. 01539 431212.

Barrow-in-Furness Situated at the tip of the Furness peninsula on the northwestern edge of Morecambe Bay, the industrial town and seaport of Barrow-in-Furness is the major settlement in the Barrow-in-Furness district of Cumbria. Historically it is part of the Hundred of Lonsdale, 'north of the sands' within the historic county of Lancashire, but it was reallocated following the 1974 local government reforms. Barrow was a small fishing village before the opening of the Furness Railway in 1846, which allowed iron ore to be transported to the area to produce steel for shipbuilding. By the 1890s the shipyard was heavily engaged in the construction of warships for the Royal Navy and the Navy's first submarine, *Holland I*, was built in 1901. By 1914 the UK had the most advanced submarine fleet in the world, 94 per cent of it constructed by the Sheffield steel firm of Vickers, who had taken over the Barrow Shipbuilding Company in 1897. The UK's first nuclear-powered submarine, HMS *Dreadnought*, was constructed by Vickers at Barrow in 1960. Following the end of the Cold War in 1991 and the subsequent decrease in military spending, the town's industries are attempting to diversify into manufacturing for the offshore renewable energy sector.

Bassenthwaite Lake The only body of water in the Lake District with 'lake' in its name, Bassenthwaite Lake lies in a glacially eroded valley at the foot of Skiddaw and Dodd Wood, north of the town of Keswick. It is fed by, and drains into, the River Derwent, and is linked to Derwent Water by the Derwent, which crosses the 3 mile (5km) alluvial plain between the two lakes. There has been speculation that Derwent Water and Bassenthwaite Lake were once one larger lake with the alluvial flats now separating them formed from partial infill of the original basin. The lake is about 4 miles (6km) long and 0.4–0.6 miles (0.6–1km) wide covering an area of 2 sq miles (5 sq km), though its drainage area at 91.5 sq miles (237 sq km) is 44 times greater than any other lake in the Lake District. The lake is surrounded by highly fertile alluvial plains and contains trout, pike, European perch, vendance and eel.

Battles There have been two major battles on Cumbrian soil, Clifton and Solway Moss. See separate table.

Beacon, The West Strand, Whitehaven. Overlooking the town's harbour, the Beacon's audio-visual presentations tell the story of local coal mining and shipbuilding, the influential Lowther family, smuggling, and the geology and archaeology of the area. Forecasting, broadcasting and monitoring are explored in an interactive Weather Gallery on the top floor. Tel: 01946 592302.

Beatrix Potter Gallery Hawkshead, 5 miles (8km) southwest of Ambleside. Situated in a 17th century townhouse, the gallery is run by the National Trust and dedicated to presenting original book illustrations by Beatrix Potter. Original sketches and watercolours painted by Potter for her children's stories are on annually changing display and there are artefacts and information relating to her life and work. The building was at one time the law office of Potter's husband, William Heelis. Its interior remains largely unaltered. Tel: 01539 436355.

Belle Isle Round House Situated on Windermere's largest island, Belle Isle, the house was built in 1774 by John Plaw for the island's owner, Mr English. Round with a double staircase and portico, it can be seen from the Bowness shore. Both house and island were purchased in 1781 by John Christian Curwen, who made his fortune in the mines of west Cumberland. The island was named after his wife, Isabella. Curwen had a keen interest in yachting and was a pioneer in the start-up of the Windermere regattas. One of his boats remains on display at the Windermere Steamboat Museum (see separate entry). The house, occupied until 1993, and the 40 acre (16ha) island are private.

Bew Castle Bewcastle, 8 miles (13km) northeast of Brampton. Situated north of Hadrian's Wall (see separate entry), Bewcastle Castle, to give it its correct name, was built in the northeast corner of what was the Roman fort of Banna c. AD 122. Rebuilt in stone, it was abandoned in AD 367. The rectangular Beuth's Castle was named after the Scandinavian who built it in the late 11th century. The present stone castle was completed in 1360. By the early 15th century the castle had decayed when Edward IV granted it to his brother, the Duke of Gloucester. The buildings were repaired, and it is thought that the gatehouse was added at this time. Bew Castle was garrisoned by parliamentary forces in 1639 and destroyed in 1641. The remains consist of a small part of the south wall walk and bits of the west side and its single tower. Today the castle remains on the private land of Demesne Farm.

Bewcastle Cross Bewcastle, 8 miles (13km) northeast of Brampton. Located in the churchyard of St Cuthbert's Church, this runic monument, dating from the late 7th or early 8th century, is widely considered the finest Anglian cross in Britain. The head of the cross is missing, but the remainder is still 14.5ft (4.4m) high. Each of the four sides is intricately decorated, with ornaments including animals, checkers, vines and knots, as well as inscriptions. Of greatest interest is a figure supposed to be Christ trampling the head of a beast, and above this a falconer, possibly St John the Evangelist with his eagle. The inscription on the west side reads (in Old English runic): 'This slender pillar Hwætred, Wæthgar, and Alwfwold set up in memory of Alefrid, a king and son of Oswy. Pray for them, their sins, their souls'.

Birdoswald Roman Fort Gilsland, 2 miles (3km) west of Greenhead, 5 miles (8km) east of Brampton. The 3rd century fort of Birdoswald (called Banna by the Romans) was both a fort and a civilian settlement and is perched on high land above the River Irthing close to the Willowford bridge. The fort was a milecastle protecting the bridge and Hadrian's Wall (see separate entry). The early turf wall, built in AD 122, is visible. Much of the site, especially the civilian area, is still not excavated. Some of the buildings are only partially revealed, their walls reaching down 6ft (1.8m) below the ground. Huge 3rd century granaries were an important feature of the fort. After the withdrawal of the Romans, the site was plundered, like much of the wall, for building material. During subsequent centuries farmhouses were built on the property and land was used for cattle grazing. Birdoswald is the only place along Hadrian's Wall where all of the Roman frontier components come together in such a compact area. A stretch of wall between the fort and Harrow's Scar Milecastle is of particular note. The site is managed by Cumbria County Council on behalf of English Heritage. Tel: 01697 747602.

Blackwell Arts and Crafts House 1 mile (1.6km) south of Bowness-on-Windermere. Overlooking Lake Windermere, Blackwell House was designed by Mackay Hugh Baillie Scott and completed in 1900. This superb example of Arts and Crafts architecture has most of its original decorative interiors still intact. The house is of international importance, standing at the crossroads between Victorian and Modern architecture. It was given Grade I listing in 1998. Tel: 01539 446139.

Brantwood $1^1/_4$ miles (2km) southeast of Coniston. Overlooking the east side of Coniston Water, the 250 acre (100ha) estate belonged to the Victorian painter, poet and social commentator John Ruskin, who lived here from 1872 until his death in 1900. The house itself was a cottage when he bought it from William Linton, a wood engraver and magazine editor. Ruskin added a turreted bedroom, dining room, studio, stables, coach house and servants' quarters. Brantwood contains Ruskin's furniture, a collection of paintings, books, and other personal possessions including his own artwork. Tel: 01539 441396.

Brothers Water Once called Broad Water, and renamed in the 19th century after two brothers who drowned there, the lake is situated at the northern end of Kirkstone Pass, affording picturesque views on the descent towards Patterdale. Dorothy Wordsworth referred to it as 'the glittering lively lake', although in reality it is small, shallow and full of reeds. It is home to a trout population and harbours a rare species of fish, the schelly.

Brough Castle 8 miles (13km) southeast of Appleby-in-Westmorland. Norman castle founded by William Rufus c.1095 in the ruins of a Roman fort guarding the strategic Stainmore routeway. The castle, offering a magnificent view of the Pennines, was destroyed in 1174 by William the Lion, but rebuilt shortly after by Theobald de Valoires with extensions in 1220s. It was restored in the 17th century by Lady Anne Clifford: traces of her kitchen gardens and interior fittings can still be seen. Tel: 01228 591922.

Brougham Castle $1^1/_2$ miles (2.5km) southeast of Penrith. The well-preserved and extensive ruins sit in a tranquil and pastoral spot beside the River Eamont. The Norman castle was built c.1170–80 by Hugh d'Albini on the site of a Roman fort. It was acquired by Robert de Vieuxpont, King John's agent, in 1214 and he set about fortifying the place against Scottish invasion by constructing a stone keep and service buildings. Edward I spent the night of 22 July 1300 here while on one of his forays against the Scots. Restored by Lady Anne Clifford in the 17th century, it was pulled down c.1700 by her grandson. It is now owned by English Heritage. Tel: 01768 862488.

Burnhope Seat A moor in the North Pennines, lying between the heads of the Rivers Tees, South Tyne and Wear. The summit is crossed by the boundary between County Durham and Cumbria. The hill may also be climbed from Weardale as part of a high-level circuit of Burnhope Reservoir. There are ski-tows on the northwest slopes of the hill, which forms the Yad Moss ski facility. The entire area is designated access land under the terms of the Countryside and Rights of Way Act 2000.

Buttermere Situated towards the head of the valley of the River Cocker and surrounded by fells, notably the High Stile range to the southeast, Robinson to the north, Fleetwith Pike and Haystacks to the northeast and Grassmoor to the northwest. The village of Buttermere stands at the southwest end, and beyond this is Buttermere's twin, Crummock Water. The path around the lake is $4^1/_2$ miles (7km) long, and at one point runs through a rock tunnel beneath the locality of Hasness. The lake is $1^1/_4$ miles (2km) long by $^1/_4$ mile (0.5km) wide and 75ft (23m) deep. It is 329ft (100m) above sea level. The lake is part of the National Trust's Buttermere and Ennerdale estate. Buttermere became known for a 19th century scandal concerning Mary Robinson, a daughter of the owner of the Fish Hotel, and described as the 'Beauty of Buttermere' in Joseph Budworth's 1792 guidebook, *A Fortnight's Ramble to the Lakes*. She was conned by swindler and crook John Hatfield. Married twice, he had divorced neither wife, both of whom had given him children. In 1802, posing as the Earl of Hopetoun's brother, the bankrupt bigamist met, courted and married 18-year-old Mary. His crimes were discovered and he was sent to jail. He was also charged with defrauding the Post Office by franking his own letters and with the impersonation of various well-known people. He was executed by hanging at Carlisle in 1803. Mary later married a Caldbeck farmer. Melvyn Bragg's novel *The Maid of Buttermere* details her story, which was also narrated by William Wordsworth in Book VII of his *Prelude*.

Carlisle Castle Castle Way, Carlisle. Construction of a motte and bailey castle began in 1093 after William II drove the Scots out of Cumberland, part of efforts to secure the northern border of England against the threat of invasion from Scotland. In 1122, Henry I ordered a stone castle to be constructed on the site. Besieged by the Scots in 1174, 1216 and 1314–18, it was rebuilt in 1541 for Henry VIII by Stefan von Hashenperg. Besieged yet again for eight months by Parliament's Scots allies, its Royalist garrison surrendered in 1645 only after eating rats and even their dogs. Elaborate carvings in a small cell, made by captives held here by the future Richard III in 1480, can still be seen; Mary, Queen of Scots was also confined here after her flight from Scotland in 1568. In 1746 the castle became the last English fortress to suffer a siege, when Bonnie Prince Charlie's Jacobite garrison attempted to hold off the Duke of Cumberland's Hanoverian army. The ancient chambers, stairways and dungeons – containing the legendary 'licking stones' which parched Jacobite prisoners desperately licked for moisture in order to stay alive – can be explored. The castle is also home to the Border Regiment Museum which relates the history of Cumbria's County Infantry Regiment, the Border Regiment and the King's Own Royal Border Regiment and local militia. Tel: 01228 591922.

Carlisle Cathedral Castle Street, Carlisle. England's second smallest cathedral. It was founded in 1122 (on the site of a church of the Augustinian priory, founded in 1093) by the first Bishop of Carlisle, Æthelwulf, who built a moderately sized Norman minster of which the transepts and part of the nave still exist. The present Anglican cathedral, dedicated to the Holy Trinity, is of red sandstone and displays examples of stone tracery, paintings, carvings and medieval stained glass. In 1745, when Carlisle was taken and fortified by the Jacobites, the cathedral was partly dismantled and the nave removed so that the stone could be used to patch up the walls ready for attack. When the king's troops retook the city the Jacobites were locked up, tortured and later executed inside the cathedral. Objects of interest include carved oak misericords, decorative carved woodwork, the Bishop's Throne by George Street (1880), stone carvings on the capitals around the choir which depict the Labours of the Month, the Brougham Triptych carved in Antwerp in 1510, the ceiling by Owen Jones (1856), a sculpture of the Blessed Virgin and Child by Josefina de Vasconcellos (1990) in the nave, and an underground exhibition in the treasury. Within the cathedral grounds buildings of interest include the deanery, with a 14th century prior's tower which contains a fine painted 16th century heraldic ceiling. Tel: 01228 548151.

Cartmel Priory — Cartmel, 5 miles (8km) east of Ulverston. Founded in 1190 by William Marshal, later 2nd Earl of Pembroke, for the Augustinian canons and dedicated to St Mary the Virgin and St Michael. Between 1327 and 1347 a chapel with four traceried windows was provided by Lord Harrington in the south choir aisle, and his tomb remains in the building. Apart from the church, the gatehouse built 1330–40 is the only surviving structure. A great part of the priory was destroyed at the Dissolution of the Monasteries, but the church remains as the local parish church. Tel: 01539 435599.

Castle Crag — The 'smallest' hill included in Alfred Wainwright's list of Lake District fells because of its 'mountain-in-miniature' appearance. Wainwright's North Western Fells guide book published in 1964 states Castle Crag's height as 985ft but the OS 1:25,000 map now records it as 951ft (290m).

Castlegate House — Castlegate, Cockermouth. Situated opposite Cockermouth Castle, the house is a Georgian gem with an Adam ceiling, open fires and historic features. The walled secret garden at the back of the house is an excellent setting for sculpture, while the house holds regular exhibitions of paintings. Tel: 01900 822149.

Castlerigg Manor — Manor Brow, Keswick. A Catholic residential youth centre, established in 1969 and now owned and operated by the Catholic Diocese of Lancaster. The building itself has existed since the late 1840s. Originally a manor house, it became a hotel in the 1920s and was used briefly during World War II by the Army as a base for teaching soldiers the skills of driving in mountainous terrain. Monsignor Patrick O'Dea acquired the building on behalf of the Diocese of Lancaster in 1969 together with the gate house, now used as a holiday cottage. Tel: 01768 772711.

Cauldron Snout — see Waterfalls

Cautley Spout — see Waterfalls

Coast to Coast Walk — Devised by renowned walker and writer Alfred Wainwright, the 190 mile (306km) route starts at St Bees on the Cumbria coast and follows the coastline before heading east and entering the Lake District National Park. From Shap the Coast to Coast crosses undulating farmland into the Yorkshire Dales. At Richmond the path leaves the Dales and enters the low-lying Vale of Mowbray to Ingleby Cross and the beginning of the North York Moors. From here the trail leads on a roller-coaster route across the heather-covered hills to the North Sea and Robin Hood's Bay. Tel: 01257 424889.

Churches — **St James's**, Whitehaven is said to have the finest Georgian interior in the county. Constructed in 1752 and consecrated by the Bishop of Carlisle in July 1753, the church was designed by Whitehaven's most famous engineer, Carlisle Spedding. The clock was the work of a local blacksmith. The fine plasterwork on the ceiling is the work of two Italians, Arture and Baggiotti. The altarpiece, *The Transfiguration of Christ* by Guillio Cesare Procaccini (1548–1626), was formerly housed in the Escurial, Madrid. It found its way to France and was brought to England after the revolution. It was presented to the church by William, 3rd Earl of Lonsdale. In 1909 the organ was added. St James's became the parish church for Whitehaven in 1977 following a fire at St Nicholas' Church (see below).

St Kentigern's, Great Crosthwaite, on the western edge of Keswick, is dedicated to the early missionary, St Kentigern, meaning 'head chief', and was built in the Late Perpendicular style in 1523. It retains its original 14th century north chapel. The church contains a complete set of 17 consecration crosses which mark where the bishop sprinkled holy water to consecrate the church. There are stained glass windows of note, some by Charles Kempe. A sundial and old clock add to the atmosphere. The organ, although rebuilt, dates from 1837. A marble memorial to Robert Southey, poet laureate, lies in the church, and his grave is in the churchyard. Canon Rawnsley, the vicar from 1888–1917 and co-founder of the National Trust, is also buried here. Tel: 01768 772509.

St Lawrence's is located at the bottom of Boroughgate, Penrith. A Gothic arcade leads to the 12th century church, which is a hodgepodge of styles from its Perpendicular exterior to its Early English and Gothic Revival interior. Burned by the Scots in 1174, it again suffered under the Scottish raid of 1388. It was altered in the 14th century when the tower to the nave was opened. The oldest parts of the church are the lower part of the tower (only one window is original) and the early 14th century porch, with dogtooth moulding. In the 17th century Lady Anne Clifford restored much that was burned in the Scottish raids. The Clifford Chapel houses her altar tomb, constructed before her death in 1676. An alabaster effigy of her mother, Margaret, lies alongside and was erected in 1617. The church boasts the oldest (c.1542) working organ in Britain, brought from Carlisle Cathedral in 1683. Three volumes of Foxe's *Acts and Monuments of the Martyrs*, chained to a box in the church, date to 1631. Tel: 01768 351177.

St Mary's, Gosforth is one of the most historic churches in Cumbria, with Viking monuments and a Norse cross in the graveyard depicting the victory of Christ over the heathen gods. The cross is 14ft (4.2m) high, the tallest complete Viking cross in England and second in importance only to the Bewcastle Cross (see separate entry). Two 10th century 'hogback' tombstones inside the church cover the graves of Norse chieftains and are carved with battle scenes. The graveyard also contains a cork tree planted in 1833, the most northerly in Europe. The tool-shed built of stones from the original church is now a listed building.

St Michael and All Angels in the village of Beetham is a rectangular, asymmetrical church constructed of mostly rough rubble walls – limestone with sandstone dressing. Coins dating from the early 11th century were found buried in the church near the foundations of an earlier building. The 16th century roof is oak-beamed with five bays in the nave and four in the chancel. The church has a 15ft (4.5m) square tower at its western end. The 12th century tower is off-centre; the six-bell chamber was added in the 16th century. Above the door of the tower is a window that contains medieval glass.

St Nicholas', Whitehaven was consecrated in 1883, having replaced an earlier chapel on the same site. Following a fire in August 1971, all that remains of this church is its magnificent tower. The gardens were once covered in headstones, until the creation of a graveyard on Low Road, in 1855. Mildred Gale, the grandmother of George Washington, was buried here, along with her baby daughter and a Negro servant. The exact location of the grave is unfortunately unknown. In the gardens are memorials to miners who lost their lives down the Whitehaven mines. The four entrances to the gardens are adorned with fine wrought iron gates taken from the tomb of Sir James Lowther following the demolition of Holy Trinity Church. **St Olaf's**, Wasdale, is one of England's smallest churches. The earliest record of the church is 1550, though it probably predates this as the beams are said to come from a Viking longship. Tel: 01946 725667.

St Stephen's, the parish church of Kirkby Stephen, is also known as the Cathedral of the Dales. A place of worship was built here during Saxon times and another by the Normans about 1170. The nave of the present church was constructed in 1220. St Stephen's was added to and altered at various times between the 14th and 19th century. The piscina, sedilia, and angel corbels are from the 13th century and were reset in the 1800s. The tower dates from 1550 and once rang a curfew bell. The eight bells were cast in 1878.

Cockermouth Castle — Castlegate, Cockermouth. Located near the confluence of the rivers Cocker and Derwent, the castle was founded c.1134 as a ringwork and bailey fortress by Gilbert de Pipard with 12th century additions in stone by William de Fortibus. It was rebuilt by Anthony de Lucy in 1360. The castle was slighted in the Civil War but partially rebuilt in the 19th century; substantial sections of the 14th century structure still remain.

Conishead Priory — 2 miles (3km) south of Ulverston. Established as a leper colony in the 12th century by Augustinian canons. After the Dissolution of the Monasteries, a private home was built on the site. In 1821–36, the house and all the priory ruins were removed and Colonel Braddyll built an ornate Gothic mansion on the site. He also constructed the ruined folly on Chapel Island, visible from the estuary at Bardsea. The Braddyll Arms in Bardsea is named after him. A high towered gatehouse, a large hall with a high ribbed-vaulted ceiling and ornate plaster ceilings, linenfold panelling and stained glass are among the treasures found inside. The mansion later served as a hotel and in the 1930s as a miners' convalescent home. The house and 70 acres (28ha) of grounds are now a Buddhist centre, owned by the Manjushri Institute. Tel: 01229 584029.

Coniston Water — Coniston Water (sometimes simply called Coniston locally) is located by the village of Coniston. One of the largest of the English Lakes, it is 5 miles (8km) long, $^1/_2$ mile (0.8km) wide, has a maximum depth of 184ft (56m), and covers an area of 1.89 sq miles (4.9 sq km). It is 143ft (44m) above sea level. It drains to the sea via the River Crake. It was here that Donald Campbell (1921–67), world water speed record holder, died while trying to break his record. His boat, *Bluebird*, shot into the air and then plunged into the lake's depths. See also Steam Yacht *Gondola*.

Corby Castle — 6 miles (10km) east of Carlisle. Located on the east bank of the River Eden and originally built in the 13th century as a red sandstone tower house by the Salkeld Family, it was the ancestral home of the Howard family between 1611 and 1994 when it was sold to Northern Irish businessman Edward Haughey, the brother of former Irish Taoiseach Charles Haughey.

Countess Pillar — 2 miles (3km) east of Penrith. Inside a small, railed enclosure where the drive from Brougham Castle (see separate entry) meets the road from Penrith to Appleby-in-Westmorland stands an octagonal pillar and a low table, both made of local stone and erected in 1656 on the spot where Lady Anne Clifford last bade farewell to her mother. The pillar, on the roadside, supports a square capital, on three sides of which are sundials, on the fourth a pair of heraldic shields.

Cross Fell — Located at the northern end of the Pennine moors, Cross Fell (GR: NY688343) is the highest point in the Pennines at 2930ft (893m). The summit is a stony plateau, part of a 12$^1/_2$ mile (20km) ridge running northwest to southeast, which also incorporates Little Dun Fell at 2762ft (842m) and Great Dun Fell (see separate entry) at 2785ft (849m). The three adjoining fells form an escarpment that rises steeply above the Eden Valley on its southwestern side and drops off more gently on its northeastern side towards the South Tyne and Tees Valleys. Due to legends associating it with demons and the Helm Wind, a fierce gale of hurricane proportions, Cross Fell was often referred to as the 'Fiend's Fell'. A conspicuous local feature is the golf-ball shaped radar installation on the summit of Great Dun Fell, built in the 1960s and serving to support civil air traffic control over the North Atlantic.

Crummock Water — Situated between Loweswater and Buttermere, Crummock Water is 2$^1/_2$ miles (4km) long, $^3/_4$ mile (1.2km) wide and 140ft (43m) deep, a clear, rocky-bottomed lake flanked by steep fellsides of Skiddaw slate. The hill of Mellbreak runs the full length of the lake on its western side. The lake is fed by numerous streams including the beck from Scale Force. The River Cocker starts from here, flowing towards Cockermouth where it joins the River Derwent.

Cumberland Pencil Museum Southey Works, Keswick. Tracing the history of pencil manufacture over the last 350 years, the museum is said to have been the 'home of pencil perfection' since 1832. Exhibits include a replica of the Seathwaite mine where graphite was first discovered and the world's longest pencil, measuring over 25ft (8m). Tel: 01768 773626.

Cumberland sausage Traditional elongated pork sausage (often 18in long) served rolled up in concentric coils. A Cumberland sausage is different from a regular one in that the meat is chopped rather than minced, giving it a more substantial texture.

Cumberland wrestling Traditional wrestling style in which the contestants stand chest to chest, each grasping the other with interlocked hands around the middle to upper back, each opponent's chin resting on the other's right shoulder.

Cumbria Way A long distance footpath that starts at Ulverston, in the south of Cumbria, and heads 70 miles (113km) to the north, where it ends at Carlisle. It passes through Coniston, Langdale, Borrowdale and Keswick.

Dalemain 4 miles (6km) southwest of Penrith. A medieval and early Georgian house behind whose front, composed of 18th century pale rose sandstone, lies a building that dates back to Saxon times when a small fort was established on the site. The oldest part of the home that still survives is a Norman pele tower that now contains the regimental collection of the Westmorland and Cumberland Yeomanry. Originally owned by John de Morville, brother of one of Thomas Becket's murderers, the buildings surrounding the cobbled courtyard were added later by the Laytons, who owned Dalemain from the 13th century to the 17th. In 1679 Sir Edward Hasell (knighted by William III) purchased Dalemain. A 1730 wineglass engraved with the Hasell coat of arms is called 'The Luck of Dalemain' and is kept in the solar, reputedly haunted. The house is still owned and lived in by Hasell's descendants. First planted in medieval times, the gardens include ancient apple trees that lead to a gazebo set into an 18th century wall, blue Himalayan poppies, an 18th century tulip tree and the UK's largest silver fir tree. A park and woodland provide riverside walks. Tel: 01768 486450.

Dales Way A long-distance footpath that starts at Ilkley in North Yorkshire and leads 82 miles (132km) to Bowness-on-Windermere. Half of the footpath is in North Yorkshire and the final 41 miles (66km), beginning at Ribblehead, in Cumbria.

Dalton Castle Dalton-in-Furness, 4$^1/_2$ miles (7km) south of Ulverston. A 14th century tower now hosting an exhibition of local history and a display about painter George Romney. The original castle was built c.AD 79, with another building in 1172. The present castle was built c.1314–60, when the county was invaded by the Scots. The pele tower is similar in construction to many of that period, built as a rectangle 45ft (14m) by 30ft (9m) with walls a maximum of 6ft (1.8m) thick. Its role, originally defensive, was later as a courthouse and prison. After the castle was obtained by the National Trust from the Duke of Buccleuch, major restoration took place in 1968–9. There are now two floors above the ground floor. A tour around the building provides an insight into the lives of the abbot and monks of Furness, at one time among the most powerful in the country. Tel: 01524 701178.

Derwent Isle House Lakeside, Keswick. An 1840s Italianate house set in a garden on a wooded island in Derwent Water. The interior is classical in style. The treeless island, originally owned by Fountains Abbey in Yorkshire, later fell into the hands of the Crown and was sold in 1569 to the Company of Mines Royal. Joseph Pocklington bought the island (then known as Vicar's Island) in 1778 and built a house, boathouse, fort, battery and Druid circle folly. The island was purchased in 1844 by Henry Marshall who employed architect Anthony Salvin to add a wing and three-storey tower to the house. It is now owned by the National Trust, but privately let. Tel: 0870 6095391.

Derwent Water Derwent Water (or Derwentwater) occupies part of Borrowdale and lies immediately south of the town of Keswick. It is both fed and drained by the River Derwent. It measures approximately 2$^1/_2$ miles (4km) long by 1 mile (1.6km) wide and 72ft (22m) deep.

Devil's Bridge $^1/_4$ mile (0.4km) southeast of Kirkby Lonsdale. Located on the Skipton–Kendal road Dating from c.1370 and constructed of well masoned fine gritstone, Devil's Bridge consists of two western spans and an eastern span with hexagonal piers.

Devil's Grinding Mill $^1/_2$ mile (0.8km) south of Kirkby Stephen. Located within Stenkrith Park, the partially collapsed cave is part of the Angel's Drainpipe system on the River Eden, which has formed a series of dramatic gorges and natural arches in the limestone and sandstone through which it flows at this point. The water moving within the caves and gorges produces an incessant roar.

Devoke Water The largest tarn in the Lake District, Devoke Water is situated on Birker Moor, on the road between Ulpha and Eskdale, at an altitude of 770ft (235m). It is 46ft (14m) deep and can be reached via a bridle track. There is a two-storey stone boathouse-cum-refuge and a ruined stable. Devoke Water has an outlet in the northwest, via Black Beck, which after a short distance plunges over a rock down a 26ft (8m) cascade, towards the River Esk.

Dock Museum North Road, Barrow-in-Furness. The modern building, built over a historic graving dock, is home to a wealth of social and industrial history of the Furness area. Tel: 01229 894444.

Dove Cottage and Wordsworth Museum $^1/_2$ mile (0.8km) southeast of Grasmere village. Dove Cottage was William Wordsworth's home from 1799 to 1808. Built in the early 17th century, it was an inn (the Dove and Olive) for over 170 years. It closed in 1793 and in 1799 Wordsworth and his sister Dorothy moved in. In 1802 Mary Hutchinson, after her marriage to William, arrived, and their three oldest children were born at the cottage – John in 1803, Dora in 1804 and Thomas in 1806. Mary's sister Sara Hutchinson and William's friend Thomas De Quincey also lived here. It was at Dove Cottage that Wordsworth wrote much of his poetry and his sister Dorothy kept her famous journals. The Wordsworths' many visitors included Walter Scott, Charles and Mary Lamb, Robert Southey and Samuel Taylor Coleridge. Dove Cottage is built from local stone with white, limewashed walls to keep out the damp. Downstairs are the general living room, kitchen and buttery, while upstairs Dorothy's bedroom, William's study, the guest bedroom and the children's bedroom are on display. Much of the Wordsworths' life at Dove Cottage was centred on the garden and orchard, and William and Dorothy are rumoured to have spent much time nurturing it. In 1891, the Wordsworth Trust was founded to secure Dove Cottage. An award-winning museum was opened in 1980, which together with the Wordsworth Library houses one of the greatest collections of manuscripts, books and paintings relating to British Romanticism. Tel: 01539 435544.

Dovenby Hall Dovenby, 2$^1/_2$ miles (4km) northwest of Cockermouth. A Grade II listed residence within a private estate of 115 acres (47ha). The hall, dating from 1154, was built during the reigns of King Stephen and Henry II, three major extensions being conducted in its history. The oldest part is a pele tower built for the defence of the people of Dovenby. During its history it has served as a private residence (1154–1930), a mental institution (1930–97), and most recently as the headquarters for M-Sport, the Ford rally team.

Duddon Estuary The sandy estuary of the River Duddon that lies between Morecambe Bay and the west Cumbrian coast. It opens into the Irish Sea to the north of the Furness peninsula, Walney Island forming part of its southern edge. Its 28 miles (45km) of shoreline enclose an area of 13 sq miles (34 sq km), making it the second largest estuary in Cumbria after the Solway Firth. An internationally important breeding area for birds, migratory species including the common shelduck, red-breasted merganser, Eurasian oystercatcher, ringed plover, dunlin and Eurasian curlew, the estuary also supports one-fifth of Britain's population of the rare natterjack toad.

Eden Valley Railway A heritage railway operating on part of the standard gauge line from Appleby-in-Westmorland to Warcop. The original Eden Valley branch of the North Eastern Railway was opened in 1865 and ran from Clifton near Penrith on the West Coast Main Line to Kirkby Stephen where it joined with the South Durham & Lancashire Union Railway, also run by the NER. In 1962 the line was closed to passenger traffic and by the 1970s all that was left was the 6 mile (10km) track to Warcop used infrequently by the Army; the line was reopened by the Eden Valley Railway society in 2006. Tel: 01883 630600.

Egremont Castle 6 miles (10km) southeast of Whitehaven. The pinky-red sandstone ruins of the castle, built by William de Meschines c.1120, lie on a mound above Egremont's main road. Sited near the Scottish border, it was the target of raids in 1138 and the early 1300s. Decayed by the late 16th century, only the gatehouse, front of the great hall, and curtain wall survive. Tel: 01946 824052.

Elterwater 3 miles (5km) west of Ambleside. Elterwater's name comes from the Norse word *elter* meaning swan-whooper, and indeed swans do migrate to the lake in the winter. A terrace of cottages made of the local green slate line the small green in the village centre. Elterwater Lake sits at the foot of Great Langdale and is 48ft (14.5m) deep, $^1/_4$ mile (0.4km) wide and $^1/_2$ mile (0.8km) in length. The lake is fed by water from both Great and Little Langdale, and, in turn, empties its overflow into the Brathay river.

Ennerdale Water The most westerly lake in the National Park is situated relatively close to the port towns of Whitehaven and Workington. Ennerdale Water is a glacial lake, at its deepest only 150ft (45m), and measures between $^1/_2$ mile (0.8km) and 1 mile (1.6km) across and 2$^1/_2$ miles (4km) long. The closing sequences of the movie *28 Days Later* (2002), directed by Danny Boyle, were filmed around the Ennerdale area, and include a sweeping panoramic view of the lake.

Esthwaite Water One of the smaller and less well-known lakes in the National Park, situated between the much larger lakes of Windermere and Coniston Water. To the north is the village of Hawkshead and to the south is Grizedale Forest. The lake covers around 280 acres (113ha) and is known for its excellent fishing, particularly pike and trout. It is a designated Site of Special Scientific Interest.

Fairy Steps, The $^1/_2$ mile (0.8km) southwest of Beetham, 6 miles (10km) west of Kirkby Lonsdale. The second of two flights of stone steps, where the narrow passage between two sheer rock faces via a flight of natural stone stairs, is so named because of a legend. Supposedly, if you climb or descend the steps without touching the limestone sides of the narrow gully, the fairies will grant your wish. The cleft is as narrow as a foot at shoulder height, however, and so only someone whose stature matches that of a fairy stands any chance of accomplishing this feat!

Fell Foot Park 1 mile (1.6km) northeast of Newby Bridge, 7 miles (11km) south of Windermere. An 18 acre (7ha) Victorian country park situated on the southern shore of Lake Windermere and. Now in the ownership of the National Trust, the park's impressive gardens, with specimen trees and shrubs including pines and rhododendrons, have been restored to their former glory. Tel: 01539 531273.

Firbank Fell Located between Kendal and Sedbergh and renowned as a place where George Fox, an early leader in the Religious Society of Friends (Quakers), preached. Because of Fox's preaching there, the site is sometimes called 'Fox's Pulpit'. A plaque on the rock commemorates the event, which is sometimes considered the beginning of the Friends movement.

Furness Abbey 1 mile (1.6km) north of Barrow-in-Furness. The red sandstone remains of a Cistercian monastery, founded in 1123 by Stephen, Count of Blois and built originally for the Order of Savigny. It was thought to be one of the richest monasteries in England, exceeded only by Fountains Abbey in Yorkshire. Many buildings made up the abbey, including the precinct and outer court, the church with its north and south transept and tower, the cloister court, chapter house, dormitory, infirmary and kitchen. Tel: 01229 823420.

Gleaston Castle 4 miles (6km) west of Barrow-in-Furness. Built c.1325 with four corner towers, of which one, designed as the keep, was much larger then the others, it is likely that the castle was not completed. It was left to decay from the middle of the 15th century. One of the towers was used as a residence, but it has been in a state of ruin since the beginning of the 18th century. Not open to the public but the outside can be viewed.

Great Dun Fell The second-highest hill in the Pennine range, lying 2 miles (3km) south along the watershed from Cross Fell (see separate entry), its higher neighbour. Together with its smaller twin, Little Dun Fell, it forms a stepping-stone for the Pennine Way on its long climb up from Dufton. What makes the fell noteworthy is the construction of a radar station on the summit. Two huge weather domes crown the top. It was the construction of this radar station that led to the making of Britain's highest (tarred) road.

Great Langdale A valley running from the town of Ambleside to the highest peaks of the Lake District. It is a U-shaped valley formed by glaciers, while its neighbour Little Langdale is a hanging valley. To archaeologists it is known as the source of a type of Neolithic polished stone axe head, created on the slopes of Stickle, and traded all over prehistoric Great Britain and Europe. The best known feature of Great Langdale are the Langdale Pikes, a group of peaks on the northern side of the dale. They appear as a sharp rocky ridge from below although they are only precipitous on their southern side. The Pikes include (from west to east) Pike of Stickle, Harrison Stickle, Loft Crag and Pavey Ark.

Guildhall Museum Greenmarket, Carlisle. Housed upstairs in Carlisle's only medieval house, built in 1407 of timber, tile bricks and clay by Richard of Redeness, who left the house to the community of Carlisle when he died. Each room has its own focus representing Carlisle's eight trade guilds: butchers, merchants, skinners, shoemakers and glovers, smiths, tailors, tanners, and weavers. The silver room is of special interest with two 1599 silver bells among its collection. Tel: 01228 534781.

Hadrian's Wall A stone and turf fortification built by the Romans across the width of Great Britain to prevent military raids by the tribes of Scotland to the north, to improve economic stability and provide peaceful conditions in the Roman province of Britannia to the south, to define the frontier of the Empire physically, and to separate the unruly Selgovae tribe in the north from the Brigantes in the south and discourage them from uniting. The wall was built in AD 122 and extended due west from Wallsend on the River Tyne in Northumberland to the shore of the Solway Firth in Cumbria. The wall is entirely in England, south of the border with Scotland by 9 miles (15km) in the west and 68 miles (110km) in the east. Significant portions still exist, particularly of the mid-section, and the wall can be followed on foot for much of its length. It was made a UNESCO World Heritage Site in 1987. English Heritage describes it as 'the most important monument built by the Romans in Britain'. Hadrian's Wall was 73½ miles (118km) long, its width and height dependent on the construction materials readily available nearby. East of the River Irthing the wall was made from stone and measured 10ft (3m) wide and 16–20ft (5–6m) tall; west of the Irthing the wall was made from turf and measured 20ft (6m) wide and 11½ft (3.5m) high. Tel: 01434 322002. See also Northumberland.

Hardknott Roman Fort 9 miles (15km) northeast of Ravenglass. Situated on the western side of the Hardknott Pass in the heart of the Lake District National Park, the fort is built on a rocky spur giving an excellent view over the River Esk. Commonly known in recent times as Hardknott Castle, the Roman fort of Mediobogdum is square with rounded corners, 374ft (114m) long externally and 344ft (105m) internally, the rampart wall being nearly 6ft (1.8m) thick. The Roman garrison here was a detachment of 500 cavalry from the Dalmatian coast. The fort is thought to have been built AD 120–138 although its low walls were restored in the 20th century. The remains of the bath house and levelled parade ground can be seen. Currently the fort is maintained by English Heritage on land owned by the National Trust, part of the Trust's Wasdale, Eskdale and Duddon property. Local tradition holds that a fairy rath (earthenware ring) stands within the site, where King Eveling holds court. Opinions vary as to the identity and nature of this king but there is one version that suggests he was a fairy or perhaps elvish ruler, based on the possible derivation of his name from the Old Norse for elf, while another version associates him with King Arthur. The link between Cumbria and Eveling is a long established one, documented by William Camden in *Britannia* (1607). Tel: 0161 242 1400.

Harrison Stickle see Great Langdale

Hartley Castle Hartley, 1 mile (1.6km) east of Kirkby Stephen. The ruins of a medieval fortified tower house built c.1353 and extended c.1600. Today, only the barrel-vaulted cellar of the kitchen and part of a wall survive. The manor was confiscated c.1315 from Roger de Clifford and granted to Andrew de Harclay. Fortified in 1323, it was granted to Ralph de Nevill and later purchased by Thomas de Musgrave. It was abandoned c.1677 and demolished 1704–35, the present house being built on the site of the outer court.

Haweswater Reservoir 5 miles (8km) south of Bampton. The controversial construction of the Haweswater dam in the valley of Mardale was started in 1929 after Parliament passed an Act giving Manchester Corporation permission to build the reservoir to supply water for the urban conurbations of northwest England. The dam wall is 1542ft (470m) long and 90ft (27.5m) high, and at the time of construction it was considered to be cutting-edge technology as it was the first hollow buttress dam in the world, being constructed using 44 separate buttressed units joined by flexible joints. There is a parapet 4½ft (1.4m) wide running the length of the dam and from this, tunnelled supplies can be seen entering the reservoir from the adjoining valleys of Heltondale and Swindale. When the reservoir is full it holds 18.6 billion gallons (84 billion litres) of water. It is now owned by United Utilities PLC.

Hawkshead and Claife A National Trust property made up of much of the town of Hawkshead and surrounding Claife Woodlands. Hawkshead is home to the Beatrix Potter Gallery (see separate entry). The Trust also owns 4 miles (6km) of access along Windermere lakeshore.

Hayeswater 1 mile (1.6km) southeast of Hartsop in the Patterdale Valley. A small lake situated between the Knott to its east and Gray Crag to the west at approximately 1400ft (425m). Although the lake is natural it is also used as a reservoir serving Penrith. It is fed from the south by Hayeswater Gill.

Helena Thompson Museum Park End Road, Workington. Bequeathed to the people of Workington by Miss Helena Thompson, a local philanthropist, in 1940, the museum houses displays of pottery, silver, glass, and furniture dating from Georgian times, as well as the social and industrial history of Workington and the surrounding area. Tel: 01900 326254.

Helvellyn
At 3117ft (950m), Helvellyn is the third highest peak in England. Situated between the Thirlmere valley to the west and Patterdale to the east, it has a subsidiary summit, Helvellyn Lower Man, about 1/3 mile (0.5km) to the northwest. Geographically, the eastern side of the fell is the most dramatic. Two sharp spurs, Striding Edge and Swirral Edge, lead off the summit either side of Red Tarn. The somewhat flat summit made the first British mountaintop landing of a plane possible, when John Leeming and Bert Hinkler successfully landed and took off again in 1926.

Highest point
Scafell Pike at 978m (3208ft), also the highest mountain in England. See separate entry.

Hill Top House
Near Sawrey, 2 miles (3km) south of Hawkshead. A 17th century house which once belonged to the children's writer Beatrix Potter. Potter did most of her writing here (of her 13 books, six are set at Hill Top) and described the place 'as nearly perfect a little place as I have ever lived in'. The house with its roughcast walls and slate roof contains her original furniture, china, pictures and workroom. Its nooks and crannies and the cottage garden feature in many of Potter's stories and drawings. *The Tale of Tom Kitten* was written after she found rats under the floorboards of the house. On her death in 1943, she left Hill Top to the National Trust. Tel: 01539 436269.

Holker Hall
A country house with a celebrated garden situated on the Cartmel peninsula. The home of Lord and Lady Cavendish of Furness is typical of the lavishness of the Victorian style and the new wing, designed by architects Paley and Austin and built by the 7th Duke of Devonshire, 1871–4, epitomizes this prosperity. The 25 acre (10ha) garden, surrounded by a 200 acre (80ha) park, is an excellent example of a mixed English garden, with formal and informal elements. Features include an arboretum, herbaceous borders, a Victorian rockery and a late 20th century cascade. The garden is also home to the National Collection of styracaceae, a small family of white flowering plants with about 160 different species. In 1991 Holker won the Historic Houses Association Garden of the Year Award and in 2002 the Great Lime, which probably dates from the early 17th century, was selected as one of Britain's 50 Great Trees in honour of Queen Elizabeth II's Golden Jubilee. The Lakeland Motor Museum is located at the hall. Tel: 01539 558328.

High Cup
6 miles (10km) northeast of Appleby-in-Westmorland. A remarkable natural formation located below Murton Fell; the vast 'hole' in the moorside is similar in form to an elongated crater. The waterfall at the head of the Cup is called High Cup Nick. The feature is clearly visible from the A66 road. The Pennine Way goes past High Cup as it crosses the watershed on its way from Middleton-in-Teesdale to Dufton.

Howgill Fells
A small group of hills bounded approximately by a triangle drawn between Sedbergh, Kirkby Stephen and Tebay. The southern Howgills are in the northwest corner of the Yorkshire Dales National Park, the northern outside. They are separated from the Lake District to the west by the River Lune (along which runs the M6), and in the east by the Dent fault, and are formed from Ordovician and Silurian rocks, rather than the Carboniferous limestone elsewhere in the Yorkshire Dales. The Howgill Fells include The Calf at 2217ft (676m) and Yarlside at 2096ft (639m), and a number of smaller peaks.

Hutton-in-the-Forest
6 miles (10km) northwest of Penrith. The home of Lord Inglewood's family since 1605 was built around a medieval pele tower with 17th, 18th and 19th century additions. Tel: 01768 484449.

Inglewood Forest
An area of mainly arable and dairy farm land with a few small woodland areas between Carlisle and Penrith that became a royal forest soon after the Norman Conquest. The animals hunted here were mainly deer and wild boar. Inglewood means the 'wood of the English or Angles' – although Cumbria is usually thought of as a Celtic region, the Angles did make their presence felt here before the Viking invasions and the rule of the area by the Scottish kingdom of Strathclyde.

Interesting facts
The great Cumbrian family of Lowther has had many famous members but **Hugh Cecil Lowther, 5th Earl of Lonsdale** (1857–1944) was probably the most celebrated. An avid sportsman and bon vivant, he was known by some as 'England's greatest sporting gentleman'. He donated the original Lonsdale Belts for boxing. In addition, he was the inspiration for the Lonsdale cigar size. He was part of a famous bet with John Pierpoint Morgan over whether a man could circumnavigate the globe and remain unidentified, although the outbreak of world War I nullified the wager. **Haweswater Valley** is the only place in England where golden eagles nest. The RSPB eagle watchpoint is at the southern end of Haweswater Reservoir (see separate entry). England's only breeding pair of golden eagles have become media celebrities over the past few years, though breeding success is far from guaranteed. **Carlisle** holds many records: for instance, the first delivery of newspapers by air in Britain took place here; the first cardboard railway ticket was invented and used here; and it had the first letterbox on mainland Britain. The city also boasts the highest and lowest points of any city, ranging from sea level to the top of Coal Fell at 2041ft (622m). Another oddity is that Carlisle does not feature in Domesday Book, because in 1086 it was in the possession of the Scots. Cumbrian-born clergyman **William Gilpin** (1724–1804) was a man of many talents. While still at Oxford, he anonymously published *A Dialogue upon the Gardens . . . at Stow in Buckinghamshire* (1748), part guidebook to Stowe, part essay on aesthetics. Although one of the finest artists of his generation, he chose the Church as his vocation and eventually became headmaster of Cheam School in south London. He was a founder of the so-called picturesque style of painting which highlighted the aestheticism of the subject. Gilpin lives on as the model for William Combe's clever but cruel *Tour of Dr Syntax in Search of the Picturesque* (1809), illustrated by Thomas Rowlandson. In this satire the poor curate sets off on his straggly mare Grizzle in a quest for picturesque scenery, often (and usually to his discomfort) oblivious to the realities of the world around him. **The World's Biggest Liar** competition is held annually in mid-November at the Bridge Inn, Santon Bridge, Holmbrook in Wasdale. The competition, originally held at the Wasdale Head Inn (and won in the past by the

present landlord of that pub) has been monopolised in recent years by John Graham from Silloth in the northwest of the county. Contestants have five minutes to tell the tallest story possible and marks are awarded for humour and originality. In August 2002 **Barrow** suffered the UK's worst ever outbreak of Legionnaires' Disease; 172 people were reported to have caught the disease, of whom seven ultimately died. The source of the virus was later found to be a badly maintained air conditioning unit in the council-run arts centre Forum 28, steam from the vent emitting the disease over a busy alleyway in the town centre.

Isel Hall — 3 miles (5km) northeast of Cockermouth. Situated on a steep slope above the winding River Derwent, Isel Hall is a spectacular building. The oldest part is the pele tower, built c.1425 on the site of a much older structure possibly destroyed when the Scots raided Cockermouth in 1387. The tower is barrel vaulted at ground level with a few of the original slit windows. Features include windows dating from the Tudor period, and an original fireplace. Tel: 01900 821778.

Islands — See separate table

Islands of Furness — Situated to the southwest and east of the Furness peninsula. The islands are: **Walney Island**,**Barrow Island**, **Sheep Island**, **Roa Island**, **Piel Island**, **Foulney Island** and **Chapel Island**. They are generally quite small, though at 5 sq miles (12.99 sq km) Walney Island is the eighth largest in England. Only Walney Island, Barrow Island, Roa Island and Piel Island are inhabited. Their combined population is around 15,000, about 20 per cent of the borough of Barrow-in-Furness.

Kendal Castle — Castle Hill, Kendal. The 12th century stone ruins sit on a hill on the western edge of the town. (An earlier motte castle – Castle Howe – was built in 1087 on the other side of town, but was abandoned in the 13th century.) Built by the de Lancaster family, barons of Kendal, the castle was originally constructed of earth and timber. It was later rebuilt in stone in the late 12th century by Gilbert FitzReinfred, who became the owner through marriage. The castle then passed through several owners, including the Crown. Richard II gave it to the Parr family of which Catherine Parr, Henry VIII's sixth wife, was a member. The castle was derelict by 1571.

Keswick Museum and Art Gallery — Fitz Park, Station Road, Keswick. A Victorian museum tracing the history of Keswick from its roots as a centre of mining to a popular tourist town. Exhibits include original manuscripts by the Lake Poets, a 15th century mummified cat, Flintoft's model of the Lake District (covering 1200 sq miles at a scale of 3in to the mile), the 18th century Musical Stones of Skiddaw (a slate xylophone once played for Queen Victoria), Napoleon's teacup and a fine collection of crystals. Tel: 01768 773263.

Kirkandrews Tower — 2 miles (3km) northeast of Longtown, 10 miles (16km) north of Carlisle. Located near Kirkandrews church. Built as a border fortress c.1530–50 by Thomas Graham in an area claimed by both the English and Scots, the square tower measures 32ft (10m) by 23ft (7m) with walls over 5ft (1.5m) thick, vaulted basement, and a step gabled roof. From the south wall entrance a spiral stairway rises to two upper storeys and an attic.

Kirkstone Pass — 3 miles (5km) northeast of Ambleside. A mountain pass with an altitude of 1489ft (454m). The highest pass in the Lake District open to motor traffic, it connects Ambleside in the Rothay Valley to Patterdale in the Ullswater Valley. In places, the gradient is 1 in 4. Brothers Water (see separate entry) is situated at its northern end.

Lake Poets — A school of English poets active in the early 19th century, the chief representatives of which were Samuel Taylor Coleridge, Robert Southey and William Wordsworth. So designated by the *Edinburgh Review* because their favourite haunt was the Lake District, their poetry can be characterised as expressing an awareness of and a sympathy with the pure spirit of nature.

Lakeside and Haverthwaite Railway — A heritage railway which runs from Haverthwaite via Newby Bridge to Lakeside at the southern end of Windermere. The railway is a former branch line of the Furness Railway (FR), and a train–boat connection was established in 1868. The railways locomotive fleet includes FR No. 20, Britain's oldest working standard gauge steam locomotive, built in 1863.

Lammerside Castle — 2 miles (3km) south of Kirkby Stephen. Located close to Pendragon Castle and built in the 14th century as a pele tower, the castle belonged to the Wharton family. Its subsequent history is not known, but it was abandoned by the 17th century. The main parts of the now ruined two-storey castle were two towers, a hall and a keep. The upper level contained two small rooms and a large chamber with a fireplace and a number of windows. Two vaulted cellars were joined by a central passage.

Lanercost Priory — 2 miles (3km) northeast of Brampton. Founded in 1166 to house Augustinian canons, it was subject to numerous raids and wars, since the border with Scotland was only 15 miles (24km) to the north. The priory suffered a crippling economic burden when Edward I was resident for an extended period. Parts of the Lanercost Chronicle, an account of the history of the north of England 1201–1346, were written at the priory. Dissolved as a priory in 1538, it still functions as a parish church. Tel: 01697 73030.

Langdale Pikes — see Great Langdale

Laurel and Hardy Museum — Upper Brook Street, Ulverston. The museum contains memorabilia of the pair of film comedians and a small 1920s style cinema showing their films. Stan Laurel (the thin half of the duo) was born on 16 June 1890 at 3 Argyle Street, Ulverston (then in Lancashire). A plaque on the house commemorates the event. Tel: 01229 582292.

Levens Hall — 5 miles (8km) south of Kendal. The first house on the site was a pele tower built by the Redman family in the 13th century. Much of the present building dates from the Elizabethan era, when the Bellingham family extended the house. Further additions were made in the late 17th and early 19th centuries. Levens is now owned by the Bagot family. Its celebrated topiary garden was started in 1694. Tel: 01539 560321.

Longsleddale A valley in eastern Cumbria, bounded to the west by Kentmere Pike and Shipman Knotts (one arm of the 'Kentmere horseshoe'), and to the east by Sleddale Fell and its summits of Grey Crag and Tarn Crag. Longsleddale, in which the hamlet of Sidgill is situated, was the inspiration behind the fictional Greendale village, setting of BBC children's television series *Postman Pat*.

Lowther Castle 4 miles (6km) south of Penrith. A country house that has belonged to the Lowther family, latterly the Earls of Lonsdale, since the Middle Ages. In the late 17th century John Lowther, 1st Viscount Lonsdale rebuilt the family home, then known as Lowther Hall, on a grand scale. The current house was built by Robert Smirke, 1806–14, and only at that time was Lowther designated a castle. Closed in 1937, it was used by a tank regiment during World War II. Its contents were removed in the late 1940s and the roof in 1957. The shell is still owned by the Lowther Estate Trust, who have undertaken a project to consolidate the ruin, restore the 50 acre (20ha) garden and open the site to the public.

Maryport Maritime Museum Senhouse Street, Shipping Brow, Maryport. Established in 1975 in the former Queen's Head inn, the museum has grown to occupy three floors with collections encompassing social and political, maritime and industrial history. There is a collection of the paintings of Maryport artist William Mitchell. Tel: 01900 813738.

Mayo Statue Main Street, Cockermouth. A fine marble statue of Richard Southwell Bourke, 6th Earl of Mayo, MP for Cockermouth 1857–68. The statue, which dominates the town centre, was erected after Mayo was assassinated in 1872 while visiting the Andaman Islands as Viceroy and Governor-General of India.

Millom Folk Museum Station Road, Millom. The museum has a full-scale drift mine exhibit and also houses information about the local poet Norman Nicholson. Displays include a full scale reconstruction of a drift mine from the Hodbarrow Iron Ore Mine, and a miner's cottage kitchen. Tel: 01229 772555.

Mills Mills in Cumbria providing power for the manufacture of cotton, linen, wool and bobbins, or operated by water power for grinding corn and wheat, include Acorn Bank Mill, Alston High Mill, Cark Cotton Mill, Eskdale Mill, Farfield Mill, Gleaston Watermill, Heron Corn Mill, Little Salkeld Mill, Muncaster Mill, Stott Park Bobbin Mill.

Mining Large scale mining in Cumbria is thought to have started with the arrival of German immigrants in 1564, although the Romans were known to have mined lead and iron in the region. Mines open to the public include: **Florence Mine Heritage Centre**, an iron ore/haematite mine, the last deep mine in Western Europe, located on the outskirts of Egremont. Tel: 01946 820683; **Honister Slate Mine**, a working and heritage enterprise, located between Buttermere and Seatoller. Tel: 01768 777230; **Haig Colliery Mining Museum**, consisting of a winding engine house and head gear, located at Solway Road, Kells, Whitehaven. Tel: 01946 599949; **Threlkeld Quarry and Mining Museum**, a former granite quarry located near Threlkeld. Tel: 01768 779747.

Mirehouse $3^1/_2$ miles (5.5km) north of Keswick. Mirehouse dates from 1666. Its grounds, stretching to Bassenthwaite Lake, include a walled garden, a wildflower meadow and heather maze. Wordsworth, Tennyson and Southey were among distinguished friends of the owning family. Winners of the Mirehouse Poetry Prize are displayed in the Poetry Walk. Tel: 01768 772287.

Morecambe Bay A large bay notorious for its quicksand and fast moving tides, located nearly due east of the Isle of Man and just south of the Lake District National Park. The largest expanse of inter-tidal mudflats and sand in the UK, it covers a total area of 119 sq miles (310 sq km). Towns on the bay include Barrow-in-Furness, Ulverston, Grange-over-Sands, Morecambe, Fleetwood and Heysham. Rivers draining into the bay include the Leven, Lent, Keer, Lune and Wyre, their various estuaries creating peninsulas such as Humphry Head. Morecambe Bay is an important wildlife site with abundant bird life and varied marine habitats. Royally appointed local guides, holding the post of Queen's Guide to the Sands, have assisted travellers in crossing the bay since the 16th century.

Muncaster Castle 1 mile (1.6km) east of Ravenglass. The privately owned castle, overlooking the Esk river, was built on foundations dating to the Roman era and is currently owned by the Pennington family, who have lived at Muncaster for at least 800 years, the land being granted to Alan de Penitone in 1208. The castle is surrounded by 77 acres (31ha) of woodland gardens in a 1800 acre (728ha) park. The great hall and the 14th century pele tower are the oldest parts of the castle, which contains a wealth of architectural features and artefacts from a wide span of English history, including a rare portrait of Henry VI, an Elizabethan banqueting table, and an impressive library of 6000 books. The castle has also acquired the reputation of being one of the most haunted houses in Britain, the ghosts of Tom Fool and Mary Bragg making regular unscheduled appearances. Tel: 01229 717614.

Muncaster Owl Centre Muncaster Castle (see separate entry) is home to the Owl Centre and World Owl Trust, where Britain's owl conservation breeding programmes are coordinated. A centre for research where owl behaviour and conservation in both the wild and captivity are studied, it has over 100 owls from 50 species and subspecies from all over the world. There are examples of the largest species, the European eagle owl, and the two smallest, the pigmy and scoop owl, as well as barn, Ural, spectacled, milky eagle, brown fish, burrowing, and Ethiopian eagle owls. Tel: 01229 717393.

Naworth Castle 2 miles (3km) east of Brampton. Naworth Castle is on the opposite side of the River Irthing to Lanercost Priory (see separate entry). Lord William Howard (1563–1640) took up residence with his children and grandchildren and restored the castle. He also collected a valuable library, of which most of the printed works still remain. The neo-Elizabethan drawing room, created by Philip Webb in the 1880s, contains a collection of Howard portraits. The castle is surrounded by grounds which include a 17th century walled garden. There are also 400 acres (162ha) of woodlands. Tel: 0169 773229.

Newbiggin Hall $1^1/_4$ miles (2km) south of Carleton, 3 miles (5km) southeast of Carlisle. The northeast tower with its thick walls was originally built in the 1330s as a refuge from marauding Scots, but remodelled around

1500. A new wing, the Jerusalem Tower, was constructed in the late 1400s or early 1500s. The main hall block was built in 1533, then remodelled again in 1796 and 1844. Another wing was added in 1891. The Grade II listed building now offers self-catering accommodation. Tel: 01228 527549.

Old Dungeon Ghyll A pub and hotel in the Great Langdale valley, named after the nearby waterfall, Dungeon Ghyll Force. The hotel and the Hikers Bar have a long association with climbing and many famous climbers have stayed there. In climbing circles it is known as the ODG. Now owned by the National Trust. Tel: 01539 437272.

151 Queen Street Whitehaven. Built in 1733, the house was home to the merchant William Gale. William was the younger brother of George Gale whose first wife, Mildred, was the grandmother of George Washington – the first president of the United States of America. It is one of the earliest of Whitehaven's large houses to have survived to present day.

Pendragon Castle 1 mile (1.6km) north of Outhgill, 3 miles (5km) south of Kirkby Stephen. According to legend, this is the site where Uther Pendragon, father of King Arthur, died. The first stone castle was built by Hugh de Morville, after which it came under the ownership of the Clifford family in the early 1300s. Robert de Clifford did much rebuilding in 1309. In 1341 the Scots burned the castle and it was abandoned. Rebuilt again in 1360, it was occupied until an accidental fire burned it in 1541. The castle lay in ruins until 1660 when it was restored by Lady Anne Clifford. By 1680 it was again in ruins, having been demolished by the Earl of Thanet, Lady Anne's heir. The ruins of the 209 sq ft (19.4 sq m) tower show that the walls were up to 14ft (4.2m) thick in places. Remnants of spiral stairs, latrines, turrets and chambers give other clues to the layout. The castle is not open to the public but can be viewed from the road.

Pennine Way See Derbyshire

Penrith Castle Castle Park, Penrith. The castle was founded in 1399, when William Strickland, later to become Bishop of Carlisle and Archbishop of Canterbury, added a stone wall to an earlier pele tower, primarily as a defence against Scottish raids. The castle was improved and enlarged over the next 70 years, becoming a royal fortress for Richard, Duke of Gloucester before he became king in 1483. The ruins visible today date from that period. Tel: 0161 2421400.

Percy House Gallery Market Place, Cockermouth. Dating from 1390, Cockermouth's oldest surviving town house still has its original bread oven, fireplaces and plasterwork. The original property was renewed in 1598 when it was occupied by the bailiff of Henry Percy, Earl of Northumberland. The work on display is principally by Cumbrian artists. Tel: 01900 829667.

Piel Castle Situated on a low mound at the highest point of Piel island (see Islands of Furness), the castle was built to guard the passage to and from Furness Abbey's holdings in Ireland and the Isle of Man. It was designed with a large three-storey keep, inner and outer baileys, and towers at three of its corners; a ditch surrounded the entire structure. By 1537, when the abbey was dissolved, the castle was in a ruinous state. The island was handed over to Barrow Corporation in 1918, and the castle came into state guardianship in 1919. Trees and shrubs enfold the moss-covered ruins of the keep, and the ditch surrounding the inner and outer baileys is overgrown. The site is now in the care of English Heritage.

Printing House Main Street, Cockermouth. The Museum of Printing, in a 16th century building, houses 15th–20th century British printing presses and equipment. The collection includes iron presses, treadle machines and automatics. One, an 1830 Imperial Press with a massive 3ft (0.9m) by 2ft (0.6m) bed, was capable of producing everything from newspapers to tiny prayer books. Tel: 01900 824984.

Quaker Tapestry Stramongate, Kendal. Illustrated exhibition telling the story of the Quaker journey from the 17th century to the present day. The tapestry contains 77 panels of community embroidery, the work of more than 4000 men, women and children from 15 countries. Tel: 01539 722975.

RAF Carlisle Located on the northern edge of Carlisle, the former Royal Air Force base was the home to No. 14 Maintenance Unit (14MU). Opened in 1938 as RAF Kingstown, it as redesignated RAF Carlisle in 1950. Split into several different sites, it was used by the RAF to maintain equipment ranging from engine parts to firearms. The gate guardian was a Phantom F4, now on display at the Solway Aviation Museum, at Carlisle Airport. Having stood unused for many years after closing in the mid 1990s, the site was later bought by a local investor who developed it into a massive regional business park.

RAF Millom Museum Haverigg, 1 mile (1.6km) south of Millom. RAF Millom began mountain rescues in 1941, and along with RAF Llandwrog in Wales was the co-birthplace of RAF Mountain Rescue Services. The last operational flight took place in 1953, after which the site and buildings had a variety of uses. The museum itself, opened in 1992, houses a growing collection of memorabilia including an archive of over 3000 photographs showing the history of the site, a restored Westland Whirlwind WM660 helicopter, the cockpits of a de Havilland Vampire T11 and a Jet Provost. There are also several aero engines, including a Rolls Royce Merlin, and a Rolls Royce Avon jet engine. Tel: 01229 772636.

RAF Spadeadam 8 miles (13km) northeast of Brampton. Located on the English/Scottish border, the largest RAF base in the UK is home to the 9000 acre (3650ha) Electronic Warfare Tactics Range, the primary purpose of which is to provide a location for teaching of electronic warfare to RAF and other NATO aircrew. The site was largely remote and uninhabited until 1957 when the Intermediate Range Ballistic Missile Test Centre was built for the Blue Streak Project. The RAF took it over in 1976, and it became Europe's first Electronic Warfare Tactics Range in 1977. The range contains ground-based electronics warfare equipment to act as a simulated threat to training aircrews. It also has dummy targets such as airfields and vehicle convoys.

Ravenglass and Eskdale Railway A heritage railway affectionately known locally as La'al Ratty, Cumbrian dialect for 'little narrow way'. The 7 mile (11km) line was opened in 1875 to carry iron ore from workings at Boot to

Ravenglass and reopened as a narrow gauge line in 1916. Today it runs from Ravenglass to Dalegarth Station near Boot in the valley of Eskdale. Tel: 01229 717171.

Rheged Discovery Centre
$1^1/_2$ miles (2.5km) southwest of Penrith. Europe's largest grass-covered building, housing the National Mountaineering Exhibition. The permanent exhibition tells the story of Britain's mountaineering heritage, displaying equipment, artefacts, film, and photographs from expeditions that include Everest and the Matterhorn. Tel: 01768 868000.

Rivers
The **Bleng** is a tributary of the Irt and gives its name to the valley through which it flows, Blengdale. It is thought that the name is derived from the Old Norse word *blaeingr*, 'dark water', so Blengdale would mean the valley of the dark river.

The **Brathay** rises 1289ft (393m) above sea level near Three Shire Stone at the highest point of Wrynose Pass in the Lake District. It joins the Rothay close to Croft Lodge southwest of Ambleside before flowing into the northern end of Windermere.

The **Cocker** flows north from Crummock Water, through Lorton Vale, to the town of Cockermouth, where it joins the River Derwent.

The **Crake** drains Coniston Water from its southernmost point and flows south for 6 miles (10km), joining the upper estuary of the River Leven at Greenodd. The river is in the historic county of Lancashire, but in a region that formed part of Cumbria from 1974. It is a noted salmon river.

The **Duddon** rises at the same point as the Brathay and descends to the sea over a course of about 15 miles (24km), entering the Irish Sea at Duddon Sands. From its source it falls rapidly over a distance of 2 miles (3km) to Cockley Beck at the head of Dunnerdale. William Wordsworth wrote extensively of the Duddon, a river he loved and knew from his early years.

The **Eamont** is one of the major tributaries of the Eden and formed by the outflow from Ullswater in the Lake District, later augmented by Dacre Beck from the west and the Lowther which carries water from Haweswater north to the Eamont at Penrith. It reaches the Eden 3 miles (5km) east of Penrith.

The **Eden** flows through Carlisle on its way into the Solway Firth, which it enters near the mouth of the Esk after a total distance of 90 miles (145km). It river was known to the Romans as the Ituna.

The **Esk** rises in the Sca Fell range of mountains at a height of 2625ft (800m), just below Esk Hause, the mountain pass between the fells of Great End and Esk Pike. It continues past the small villages of Boot and Eskdale Green before joining the Irish Sea at Ravenglass.

The **Irt** rises from Wast Water, flowing through the Drigg Dunes and Irt Estuary Nature Reserve before it joins the River Esk at Ravenglass. In the 19th century the river was famous for the extremely rare black pearls that grew in freshwater mussels. Poaching of the pearls is thought to have led to the mussels becoming extinct in the river.

The **Irthing**, a major tributary of the River Eden, rises in the hills around Paddaburn Moor in Border Forest Park. After passing Butterburn Flow raised bog, the river flows over the 32ft (10m) high Crammel Linn waterfall in a sandstone gorge. At Gilsland Spa, a sulphurous spring oozes out of the gorge walls. Chalybeate and petrifying springs are also characteristic of the local geology and are found on the Irthing's banks.

The **Kent** originates in hills surrounding Kentmere, and flows for 20 miles (32km) into the north of Morecambe Bay, having passed through Kentmere, Staveley, Burneside, Kendal and Sedgwick on the way. The rivers Mint, Sprint and Gowan join the Kent to the north of Kendal.

The **Leven** (pron. to rhyme with 'seven') is a short river draining Windermere from its southernmost point and flowing for 8 miles (13km) into the northern reaches of Morecambe Bay. The upriver limit of tidal flow is close to the village of Haverthwaite. Also at this point is to be found Low Wood Bridge which, until the coming of the railways, was the first bridging point across the river. The Leven is also a noted salmon river.

The **Lowther** is a tributary of the River Eamont, itself a tributary of the River Eden which flows into the Solway Firth near Carlisle. The Lowther begins with the confluence of Keld Gill and Keld Dub near the village of Keld.

The **Lune** is formed at Wath in the parish of Ravenstonedale, at the confluence of Sandwath Beck and Weasdale Beck. It then passes the remnants of a Roman fort near Low Borrowbridge at the foot of Borrowdale, and flows through south Cumbria, finally meeting the Irish Sea at Plover Scar near Lancaster, after a total journey of 44 miles (70km).

The **Mite** is a tributary of the River Esk, which it meets at the confluence of three rivers near the ancient village of Ravenglass, the third river being the Irt. The Mite rises on Tongue Moor at an altitude of around 2130ft (650m), flowing south past the Bakerstead outdoor pursuit centre, then through the village of Eskdale Green, past Muncaster Mill and finally Ravenglass.

The **Rothay** is a spate river of the Lake District and rises close to Rough Crag above Dunmail Raise at a point 1542ft (470m) above sea level. Its catchment area covers Grasmere Common including Easedale Tarn, the southern flanks of Fairfield, and several of the fells to the east of Dunmail Raise, including Great Rigg, Rydal Fell, Scandale Fell and Heron Pike.

The fast flowing **Trout Beck** is one of the main sources of replenishment for Windermere. Its name comes from Old Norse and appears in documents from 1292 as Trutebyk. Rising between the peaks of Stony Cove Pike and Thornthwaite Crag in the High Street range, at a height of about 1970ft (600m), from its source the Trout Beck descends 1840ft (560m) in a distance of 7 miles (11km). The river is a trout fishery where brown trout can be caught.

Rose Castle
$^3/_4$ mile (1.2km) northwest of Raughton Head, 4 miles (6km) south of Carlisle. Rose Castle, the palace of the bishops of Carlisle, sits on the site of a former motte and bailey castle seized in 1186 by Henry II. Edward I and Queen Eleanor occupied the castle in 1300. Scottish border raiders burned it in 1314 and again in 1322 and 1337. Many of the additions of the 1300s no

longer exist. An inner court, outer gate, towers, stables, barn and latrines were added later. Most of the castle rooms were wrecked by Cromwell's troops during the Civil War in 1648. Eventually the castle was returned to the bishops who tore down the damaged east range with its great hall and kitchens as well as the south range and its long gallery. The west range was reconstructed in the 1660s and a century later further construction turned the castle into a mansion. Bishop Percy (1826–56) instituted much remodelling. Thomas Rickman, an expert on Gothic architecture, was in charge of restoration and construction, 1829–31, and further work was continued under the direction of Anthony Salvin in 1852. Bishop Percy also had the terraces landscaped by horticulturist Sir Joseph Paxton. Today, parts of the thick mantle wall of the 15th century are still visible. The north corner is the site of the Strickland tower of the late 1200s. A vaulted basement is inside with two rooms above, one a former chapel. The front door of the castle contains a lock that Lady Anne Clifford gave to the bishop in 1673.

Rum Story Museum Lowther Street, Whitehaven. Museum outlining the history of rum smugglers on the coast of Cumbria. Housed in the original shop, the museum includes courtyards, cellars and warehouses run by the Jefferson family. Tel: 01946 592933.

Ruskin Museum Newdale Road, Coniston. The museum tells the story of Coniston from the Stone Age to the modern era, including an introduction to Coniston's two favourite sons, John Ruskin (Britain's greatest critic of art), and Donald Campbell, who broke seven world records on Coniston Water. Tel: 01539 441164.

Rydal Mount & Gardens Rydal, 1½ miles (2.5km) northwest of Ambleside. The home of William Wordsworth and his family, 1813–50. While living here Wordsworth became distributor of stamps for Westmorland and at the age of 73 accepted the honour of becoming Poet Laureate. Rydal Mount was once a small farm cottage, built in the middle of the 16th century, and the gardens, designed by Wordsworth himself, have hardly changed over the past 160 years. Features within the house include original oak beams and flagged floor in the dining room, the bedrooms and Wordsworth attic study, portraits, personal possessions and first editions of the poet's work. Tel: 01539 433002.

Rydal Water Rydal, 1½ miles (2.5km) northwest of Ambleside. Located in the Rothay Valley, the lake is less than 1 mile (1.6km) long and is probably more accurately described as a tarn. It is ¼ mile (0.4km) in width and 55ft (17m) in depth. Rydal Water is surrounded by numerous walks on the hills and fells, as well as a walk around the tarn itself, which takes in Dove Cottage, Rydal Mount and Rydal Cave. At the western end of the lake, steps lead to Wordsworth's Seat, considered to have been Wordsworth's favourite viewpoint in the Lake District.

Sca Fell At 3162ft (963m) Sca Fell is the second highest mountain in England after Scafell Pike (see separate entry), although Sca Fell is considered the more difficult peak to climb, particularly from the precipitous northern and eastern sides. The traverse of the ridge between Scafell Pike and Sca Fell is especially difficult because steep cliffs prevent a direct walking route, entailing a considerable loss of height to get round the obstacle. Scafell Crag, the massive north buttress of Sca Fell, is one of England's largest cliffs and has many famous rock climbs.

Scafell Pike The highest mountain in England, at 3208ft (978m). Located in the Lake District National Park, it is sometimes confused with the neighbouring Sca Fell, to which it is connected by the pass of Mickledore. The easiest ascent is from Wasdale Head at the north end of Wast Water to the west of the Pike, but since this valley is rather remote it is more often climbed from Langdale or Borrowdale. Scafell Pike is one of three British mountains climbed as part of the (National) Three Peaks Challenge. It consists of igneous rock dating from the Ordovician period, and is geologically part of the Borrowdale Volcanics. The name 'Pikes of Sca Fell' was originally applied collectively to the peaks now known as Scafell Pike, Ill Crag and Broad Crag, considered subsidiary tops of Sca Fell (which looks higher from many angles). The contraction 'Scafell Pike' originated as an error on an Ordnance Survey map, but is now standard.

Scaleby Castle Scaleby, 6 miles (10km) northeast of Carlisle. Constructed with red sandstone thought to have originated from Hadrian's Wall, the castle was granted to Richard de Tilliol by Henry I. It was held by the Scots when they took possession of Cumberland in 1136 but regained by the family when the area reverted to the English crown in 1157. The castle has been much altered and repaired over the centuries. Now Grade I listed, it is presently inhabited by Lord Henley and is not open to the public.

Sea to Sea Cycle Route The Coast to Coast or Sea to Sea Cycle Route (C2C) is Britain's most popular long-distance cycle route and is based on minor roads, disused railway lines, off-road tracks and specially constructed cycle paths. The route, running from Whitehaven on the west coast of Cumbria to the northeast coast at Sunderland, was opened in 1994. It crosses the Lake District and the Pennines and at 140 miles (225km), the route is designed for the whole range of cyclists, from families to cycle club riders. Off-road sections have an alternative surfaced track. Although a challenge with some hard climbs – the highest point being over 2000ft (600m) – the C2C has an average of between 12,000 and 15,000 cyclists completing the route every year.

Sedbergh School Sedbergh. A co-educational boarding school for pupils aged 13–18. It is one of the major boarding schools in the north of England, rivalling Ampleforth College and Stonyhurst College. The school is renowned for sport, especially rugby union. It is also particularly proud of its 'Cloisters', one of the few officially listed war memorials located in a school. Former pupils include England rugby captain Will Carling, actor James Wilby and polar explorer Robert Swan. Tel: 01539 622210.

Sellafield 1 mile (1.6km) north of Seascale. The site of the world's first commercial nuclear power station, Calder Hall, which operated from the early 1950s until 2003, and of the Windscale Nuclear Reactor (Piles) – Britain's first attempt at a nuclear reactor to produce plutonium for the war effort. The latter suffered a major incident in October 1957 after a fire in Pile 1 destroyed the core and released radioactive material into the surrounding environment. Consequently milk and other produce from the surrounding farming areas had to be destroyed. On the same site is the Sellafield Reprocessing Plant – a site that converts spent fuel from nuclear reactors worldwide into reuseable uranium, plutonium, and highly radioactive fission products. Tel: 01946 727027.

Senhouse Roman Museum — The Battery, Sea Brows, Maryport. The museum is home to the oldest collection of Roman artefacts in Britain; most notably these include a series of altars to Jupiter Optimus Maximus, excavated in the 18th century from the parade ground of the Roman fort established c.AD 122 at the western extremity of Hadrian's Wall as a command and supply base for the wall's coastal defences. The Romans gave the name Alauna to what is now Maryport and the area around the fort is thought to have been a *vicus* or civilian settlement. Established by John Senhouse of the Netherhall c.1570, the museum's collection passed through various members of the Senhouse family, eventually reaching P J Scott Plummer in 1970. A charitable trust was set up to preserve the collection for the benefit of the public. Tel: 01900 816168.

Settle–Carlisle Railway — The Midland Railway's 72 mile (115km) 'Long Drag' over the Pennines from Settle to Carlisle was constructed in the 1870s and traverses some of the most spectacular scenery in England. Its intended closure as part of the Beeching cuts was eventually thwarted by public protest and the line remains part of the National Rail network. Apart from temporary diversions (such as those due to the closure of the West Coast Main Line) all passenger trains are now operated by Northern Rail.

Sizergh Castle and Gardens — Sizergh, 3½ miles (5.5km) south of Kendal. Occupied by the Strickland family since 1239, and set next to a small lake surrounded by parkland, Sizergh is one of the best fortified houses in Cumbria. Collections within the house include contemporary oak furniture, portraits, silver, china, Jacobean relics, Tudor panelling and 17th century Flemish tapestry. The main feature is the oldest part of the house, a 14th century pele tower almost 60ft (18m) high, used for protection against the Scots during their raids on England. The adjoining great hall and two long wings were added during the Elizabethan period. In the garden are limestone rockeries, home to one of the largest fern collections in Britain. The house is now in the care of the National Trust although it remains the family's home. Tel: 01539 560951.

Skelton Transmitter — Skelton, 5 miles (8km) northwest of Penrith. A short wave radio transmitter site run by VT Communications. There is also a VLF transmitter, used to transmit coded orders to submarines, on the site; its aerial, a 1197ft (365m) guyed steel lattice mast, is the second tallest structure in the UK. Skelton went into service in 2001 as the successor to the Rugby VLF transmitter, which closed on 1 April 2003.

Skiddaw — The fourth highest mountain in England, with a summit at 3054ft (921m). It lies just north of the town of Keswick and is said to be the easiest of the higher Lake District mountains to walk up. The mountain lends its name to the surrounding areas of Skiddaw Forest and Back o' Skidda, and to the isolated Skiddaw House, situated to the east, formerly a shooting lodge and subsequently a youth hostel. It also provides the name for the slate derived from the region. Skiddaw's subsidiary summit, Little Man, lies 1 mile (1.6km) south-southwest of the main peak.

Solway Aviation Museum — 2 miles (3km) northeast of Crosby-on-Eden, 6 miles (10km) northeast of Carlisle. Located at the Aviation Heritage Centre, Carlisle Airport, the museum features British military aircraft manufactured in northwest England in the 1950s and 1960s, including Blue Streak parts and equipment. Since 2002 the Crosby Room has presented the history of the airport's civilian life. Tel: 01228 573823.

Solway Firth — Comprising part of the Irish Sea stretching from St Bees Head, just south of Whitehaven in Cumbria, to the Mull of Galloway, on the western end of Dumfries and Galloway, the Solway Firth forms part of the border between England and Scotland, between Cumbria and Dumfries and Galloway.

Solway Moss — 1 mile (1.6km) south of Longtown. A lowland peat bog near the Scottish border. In 2005 it was the subject of a campaign by organisations including the RSPB (which operates the Bowness Common nature reserve on part of the moss) and Friends of the Earth to have the area declared a Special Area of Conservation in order to prevent the destruction of its rare ecology. The Battle of Solway Moss (see list of battles) took place here.

South Tynedale Railway — A heritage railway and England's highest narrow gauge railway, the route runs for 2¼ miles (3.6km) from Alston in Cumbria to Kirkhaugh, Northumberland, via the South Tyne Viaduct, the Gilderdale Viaduct and the Whitley Viaduct. The line was built in 1840 until 1976 as a branch of the Newcastle & Carlisle Railway, finally closing in 1976. There are plans to extend the line by a further 2¼ miles to Slaggyford. Tel: 01434 381696.

Sport

football — **Barrow**, founded in 1901, were elected to the Football League in 1921, maintaining their place until 1972.

Carlisle United were formed when two Carlisle-based teams, Shaddongate United and Carlisle Red Rose, merged in 1903. The newly formed club initially played at Milhome Bank and later at Devonshire Park, finally settling at their current home, Brunton Park. Carlisle were elected to the Third Division North in 1928, replacing Durham City. They are the first team to have both played in England's top division (1974–5) and to have suffered automatic relegation to the Conference (2003–04). Nicknamed The Blues (sometimes known as the Cumbrians), their home strip is blue and white. Tel: 01228 526237.

horse racing — **Carlisle Racecourse**, Durdar Road, Carlisle, holds mixed racing on its right-handed pear-shaped course of just over 1½ miles (2.5km). Tel: 01228 554700.

Cartmel Racecourse is situated at the southern end of the Lake District peninsula, very close to both the shores of Morecambe Bay and to Lake Windermere. The course is a left-handed oval of about 1 mile (1.6km), bisected by the finishing straight. The run-in at just over 4 furlongs (0.8km) is the longest in England. The earliest written account of racing at Cartmel dates from 1856, but it is almost certain that racing has taken place here since at least the middle of the 15th century when monks of the nearby priory entertained themselves in their leisure time by organising competitive racing on mule. Tel: 01539 536340.

rugby league — **Whitehaven** were founded in 1948 and currently play in National League One. Their stadium is the Recreation Ground (known locally as the Recre). Their nicknames are 'Haven' or 'the Marras' (a local dialect word for 'mate') and their colours are white, yellow and dark blue.

Workington Town were founded in 1945 and currently play in National League Two. They share their stadium, Derwent Park, with Workington Comets speedway team. Their nickname is simply 'Town', though they are sometimes referred to as 'Worky' by fans of other teams. The club's colours are white and blue.

speedway — **Workington Comets** are based in Workington. Their home ground is Derwent Park Stadium, which they share with Workington Town RLFC.

St Bees Head — A headland named after St Bega, who established a priory nearby in the 7th century. Reputedly the most westerly point of northern England, although North Head nearby is in fact further west, it is the only stretch of Heritage Coast on the English coastline between the Welsh and Scottish borders. The RSPB maintains a reserve for kittiwakes, fulmars and guillemots, including the only breeding place in England for black guillemots.

St Bees School — St Bees. An independent school situated in a rural location on the edge of the Lake District and on the Cumbrian coast. Founded in 1583 by Archbishop Grindal, who was Bishop of London, Archbishop of York and then Archbishop of Canterbury. Tel: 01946 828000.

Stagshaw Garden — Ambleside. An 8 acre (3ha) woodland garden created by Cubby Acland, regional agent for the National Trust, and planted with azaleas, camellias and rhododendrons. Tel: 01539 446027.

Steam yacht *Gondola* — The *Gondola*, the oldest steam yacht in the north of England, was built in 1859 by the Furness Railway Company as an attraction for tourists they brought by train to Coniston. She was retired in 1936, was used as a houseboat, and abandoned in the 1960s. In the mid 1970s a group of National Trust enthusiasts raised enough money to restore her. *Gondola* was relaunched on 25 March 1980, and after a break of 44 years re-entered public service on Coniston Water.

Swarthmoor Hall — Swarthmoor, 1 miles (1.6km) southwest of Ulverston. An Elizabethan mansion on the Furness peninsula, once the home of Margaret Fell and George Fox, major figures in the founding of the Religious Society of Friends (Quaker) movement in the 17th century. It is still in use today as a Quaker retreat centre. Tel: 01229 583204.

Tarn Hows — 2 miles (3km) northeast of Coniston, 1$^1/_2$ miles (2.5km) northwest of Hawkshead. A picturesque area of tarns and woodland in the Lake District National Park.

Thirlmere — A reservoir in the Lake District, located in the valley connecting Grasmere in the south with the Vale of Keswick in the north; the name is sometimes also applied to the whole valley. Running roughly south to north, Thirlmere is bordered on the east by the A591 and on the west by a minor road. Due to increasing demand for water, the level of the original lake was raised by construction of a dam by the Manchester Corporation at its northern end in 1890–4. The reservoir was then able to supply water to Manchester via the Thirlmere Aqueduct, 100 miles (160km) long. The highest point in the valley is Dunmail Raise. The Helvellyn ridge lies to the east, while to the west are a number of fells; Armboth Fell and Raven Crag both give views of the lake.

Three Shire Stone — Located in the Lake District at the summit of Wrynose Pass, 1289ft (393m) above sea level. The Three Shire Stone marks the location at which the traditional counties of Lancashire, Cumberland and Westmorland meet.

Townend — Troutbeck, 3 miles (5km) southeast of Ambleside. Built c.1626, Townend is a yeoman's home made of rendered whitewashed stone and roofed with slate. The windows are mullioned, and there are three massive cylindrical chimneys. Inside are stone floors and a farm kitchen. The original house was divided into two sections, one for living and one for work. A north wing with a new staircase, bedroom and parlour was added in the 17th century; in 1739 a west wing was built and in the 19th century the kitchen and fireplace underwent modernisation. The house was owned and occupied by the Browne family from 1626 to 1943. They were well-to-do, as evidenced by much of the original contents still present, including oak panelling, books, papers, carved furniture, and other domestic utensils and devices. A baby's cradle on display has a hidden compartment. A real-life history exhibition includes actors playing the parts of various family members who recount their stories. Now owned by the National Trust. Tel: 01539 432628.

Tullie House Museum — Castle Street, Carlisle. Opened by the Carlisle Corporation in 1893 in a converted Jacobean mansion, the museum houses the Human History Collection, most notable for antiquities associated with Hadrian's Wall and the two Roman forts established in Carlisle. The Romans called their settlement on the site of today's city Luguvalium and in c72 AD a Roman timber fort was built but following its demolition, in c103 AD, a second timber fort was built. In 165 AD this was replaced by a stone fort. It was probably later the civitas capital of the local Cumbrian Carvetii tribe. The museum also has large and eclectic collections of zoological, botanical and geological material, as well as fine and decorative arts collections. Tel: 01228 534781.

Ullswater — The second largest lake in the Lake District, 9 miles (15km) long and up to $^3/_4$ mile (1.2km) wide, giving a surface area of 3.44 sq miles (8.9 sq km) and an average depth of around 200ft (60m). Ullswater is regarded by many as the most beautiful of English lakes and has been compared to Lake Lucerne in Switzerland. The origin of the name is uncertain but is thought to have come from the name of the Nordic chief, Ulf, who once ruled over the area. There was however also a Saxon lord of Greystoke called Ulphus whose land came down to the lake shore. The village of Glenridding is situated at the southern end of the lake, and Pooley Bridge at the northern extremity. Its narrow 16th century bridge, straddling the River Eamont as it flows out of Ullswater, is overlooked by Dunmallard Hill, the site of an Iron Age fort. For much of its length Ullswater forms the border between the traditional counties of Cumberland and Westmorland. Three steamers – *Raven, Lady of the Lake* and *Lady Dorothy* – operate on the lake, which is also a popular sailing location. The spectacular waterfall of Aira Force (see Waterfalls) is situated midway along the lake on the western side. Close to the falls is Lyulph's Tower, a pele tower built by a former Duke of Norfolk as a shooting box. On the eastern shore is Eusemere, where anti-slavery campaigner Thomas Clarkson (1760–1846) lived; the house gives one of the best views of the lower reach of Ullswater. William and Dorothy Wordsworth were friends of Clarkson and visited on many occasions. It is said that Wordsworth was inspired to write the poem 'Daffodils' after returning from a visit to Clarkson where he saw daffodils growing on the lakeshore. Wordsworth once wrote of Ullswater: 'it is the happiest combination of beauty and grandeur, which any of the lakes affords'.

Ulverston Heritage Centre — Lower Brook Street, Ulverston. The centre's collection of documents covers information about Ulverston and Furness from Neolithic times to the period after World War II. Tel: 01229 582491.

University of Cumbria — Opened in August 2007, the university was formed by a merger of St Martin's College, the Cumbria Institute of the Arts and the Cumbria campuses of the University of Central Lancashire. It has campuses in Carlisle, Newton Rigg, Penrith, Ambleside and Lancaster and a specialist teacher-education centre in London. There are plans for the university to become a specialist research centre in the decommissioning of nuclear power plants. Tel: 01228 400300.

Vickerstown — Located on the Isle of Walney in Barrow-in-Furness. An example of a planned estate built by a company for its workers, Vickerstown was created at the turn of the 20th century in response to the rapid expansion of the local shipyard after it was taken over in 1897 by the Yorkshire steel firm of Vickers Ltd.

Wast Water — Located in the Wasdale valley, Wast Water is the deepest lake in England, at 258ft (79m). It is almost 2.8 miles (4.6km) long, 1/2 mile (0.8km) wide, and its surface is about 200ft (60m) above sea level, while its bottom is over 50ft (15m) below sea level. Although the lake is named 'Wast Water' on Ordnance Survey maps, the spelling 'Wastwater' is used with equal frequency, including by its owner, the National Trust, along with the Cumbria Tourist Board and the Lake District National Park Authority. The head of the Wasdale valley is surrounded by some of the highest mountains in England, including Scafell Pike, Great Gable, and Lingmell. Tel: 019467 26064.

Waterfalls — It is almost inevitable that the question will be asked which of the many waterfalls in Cumbria is the highest. Unfortunately there is no simple answer, as the definition of height is far from straightforward, but the claims of some of the main candidates are considered below. Although not one of the highest, **Aira Force** is one of the Lake District's most famous waterfalls. The stream which flows over the waterfall is Aira Beck, rising on the upper slopes of Stybarrow Dodd at a height of 2362ft (720m) and flowing northeast before turning south. William Wordsworth was inspired to write his poem 'Daffodils' on observing the flowers growing on the shore of Ullswater near where Aira Beck enters the lake, close to Glenridding. The main force falls 70ft (21m) from below a stone footbridge. Tel: 01768 482067.

Cauldron Snout is situated on the upper reaches of the River Tees immediately below the dam of Cow Green Reservoir, on the boundary between County Durham and Cumbria. At approximately 600ft (183m) it is arguably the longest waterfall in England, although its drop – the more usual measure of height – begins barely 200ft (60m) above ground. The series of cascades is however continuous from the top stream, so it may legitimately lay claim to a height of 200ft despite not being a single drop. It is possible to raft safely down the drop, which as such is usually considered a cataract (a large body of water that flows over a precipice but maintains contact with it) rather than a waterfall. (Other falls, such as Aysgarth – see North Yorkshire – are much longer, but are not considered as waterfalls at all for much of their drop or are dry for long periods.) Legend has it that the area is haunted by a ghost called the 'Singing Lady', a young Victorian farm girl who drowned herself in the waterfall when her love affair with a local lead miner came to an end.

Cautley Spout is often regarded as England's highest waterfall above ground (Gaping Gill on Ingleborough, North Yorkshire, falls 321ft (98.1m) but into a pothole). Located in the Howgill Fells, just north of Sedbergh, traditionally in the West Riding of Yorkshire but now in Cumbria, the broken cascade of falls tumbles 580ft (177m) down a cliff face at the head of a wild and bleak glacial valley that comes down from the high, wild plateau of The Calf. Having a series of unnavigable (by the sane) drops in its course, it is sometimes considered the highest waterfall but this is a contentious point as the definitions of cataract and waterfall are unclear. (The actual highest single-drop waterfall is Hardraw Force in North Yorkshire.)

Scale Force, situated to the south of Crummock Water, near the village of Buttermere, is another waterfall that lays claim to being the highest in the Lake District in terms of single drop, with a fall of around 120ft (36.5m). However, much of this drop maintains contact with the ground and as such is again considered a cataract. The force, with a total length of 170ft (52m), is hidden in a deep, tree-lined gorge; it was once eloquently described by William Wordsworth as 'a fine chasm, with a lofty, though but slender, fall of water'.

Wetheral Priory — 6 miles (10km) east of Carlisle. Founded in 1106 by Ranulph de Meschines, and dedicated to the Holy Trinity, St Mary and St Constantine. The Benedictine priory once comprised a school, a chapel, domestic quarters and monastic offices, but all that remains today is the 15th century gatehouse with its domestic quarters. The fine elliptical arch that was the entrance into the outer court of the monastery and contained chambers above the passageway is retained. Wetheral Priory had a number of rich benefactors; sold by Oliver Cromwell, it was recovered during the reign of Charles II. The gatehouse survived Henry VIII's destruction of the monasteries by serving as the vicarage for the local church.

Whitbarrow 2 miles (3km) north of Witherslack, 5 miles (8km) southwest of Kendal. Also known as Whitbarrow Scar, a name that applies to the cliffs lining its western edge, this area of woodland, grassland and limestone pavement is a designated Site of Special Scientific Interest and National Nature Reserve. It also forms part of the Morecambe Bay Pavements Special Area of Conservation as it supports some of the best European examples of natural limestone habitats.

Whitehaven Castle Flatt Walks, Whitehaven. Located on a site rumoured to have been a place of worship for the Druids, the castle was originally a mansion first owned by the Fletcher family and known as the Flatt. It was later purchased by the Lowthers and renovated and rebuilt in 1675 by Sir John Lowther. The 1st Earl of Lonsdale, James Lowther, rebuilt it again after a fire in 1769; it was renamed Whitehaven Castle by Sir William Lowther of Holker. The site was owned by the Lowthers until the 1920s, after which it was turned into a hospital, remaining in use until the mid 1980s. It has now been redeveloped as private accommodation.

William Creighton Mineral Museum and Gallery Crown Street, Cockermouth. Housed in an 18th century building, the museum's collections focus on northern English mineral specimens, many originating from Egremont's Florence Mine or the Cleator Moor area. The minerals and rocks include Shap granite, garnet, Cumberland green slate and andesite, as well as a collection of fluorescent minerals. Tel: 01900 828301.

Windermere and Troutbeck 3 miles (5km) north of Windermere. A National Trust property consisting of land around Lake Windermere and the head of the Troutbeck Valley, including 11 farms (one of which – Troutbeck Park – once belonged to Beatrix Potter), Ambleside Roman Fort, Cockshott Point on the lake at Bowness-on-Windermere and Bridge House, possibly the most photographed building in the Lake District and a popular subject for many artists including Turner. This tiny building, originally an apple store for nearby Ambleside Hall, was purchased by a group of local people who passed it into the care of the National Trust in 1926. Twenty years later it became the Trust's first information and recruitment centre; today it is a rather cramped National Trust shop. Tel: 01539 446027.

Windermere, Lake The largest natural lake in England, Windermere is situated entirely within the Lake District National Park. It has been one of England's most popular places for holidays and summer homes since the Kendal and Windermere Railway built a branch line to it in 1847. Windermere is 10$^1/_2$ miles (17km) long and varies from $^1/_4$ mile to 1 mile (0.4km to 1.6km) wide, giving a total area of 5.69 sq miles (14.7 sq km). It reaches a depth of 220ft (65m) near its northern end and has an elevation above sea level of 130ft (40m). The lake is drained from its southernmost point by the River Leven, and replenished by the Brathay, the Rothay, Trout Beck, Cunsey Beck and several other lesser streams. The two towns of Ambleside and Bowness-on-Windermere are situated on the lake. The town of Windermere, surprisingly, does not directly touch the lake. Windermere is largely surrounded by foothills of the Lake District and is one of the few lakes in Britain with a perceptible diurnal tide. A very high percentage (29.4 per cent) of the lake's drainage area is under cultivation, and a relatively low percentage (28 per cent) of the lake bed more than 30ft (9m) in depth is rocky, making it a relatively rich habitat. Fish in the lake include trout, char, pike and perch. In 1929 the Freshwater Biological Association was first established on the shore and much early work on lake ecology limnology, and freshwater biology was conducted here. Norman Buckley set several world water speed records on Windermere in the 1950s and Henry Segrave died on the lake in 1930 while attempting a water speed record. Until March 2005 Windermere was the only lake without a speed limit, but a 10mph (16km/h) limit has now been imposed.

Windermere Steamboat Museum Rayrigg Road, Bowness-on-Windermere. The museum houses a unique collection of historic steamboats and motorboats, including the SL *Dolly* of 1850 – the oldest mechanically powered boat in the world, with its original engine still in running order. There are 12 vintage steamboats, of which several take passengers out on Lake Windermere. Other exhibits include the recently restored TSSY *Esperance*, the model for Captain Flint's houseboat in Arthur Ransome's *Swallows and Amazons*, and the 50ft (15m) teak coal-fired launch *Branksome*, which famously carried Prince Philip on his tour of the lake during his visit in 1977. The museum also includes the rowing boat that Beatrix Potter used on Moss Eccles tarn. Tel: 01539 445565.

Wordsworth House Main Street, Cockermouth. A Georgian townhouse which was the birthplace and childhood home of William Wordsworth. A private dwelling until the 1930s, it was bought in 1937 by the local bus company with the intention of demolishing it to build a bus station, but a national campaign to rescue the house resulted in the donation of enough money for the town to buy it back. The house was given to the National Trust in 1938. The Grade I listed building is now a living memorial to Wordsworth and his family, with interactive displays and interpretations of life in the 1770s. Tel: 01900 824805.

Wordsworth Trust A living memorial set up to celebrate the works of poet William Wordsworth. The organisation offers poetry readings and contemporary visual art, alongside the historical home of Wordsworth, Dove Cottage, and a museum featuring relevant portraits and manuscripts. Tel: 015394 35544.

Workington Hall Curwen Park, Workington The compelling 14th century stone ruins and large quadrangular structure began as a crenellated fortress built around a pele tower, its licence granted by Richard II in 1379 to Sir Gilbert de Culwen. The hall is named after the Lords of the Manor of Workington, the Curwen family. Descended from Gospatrick, Earl of Northumberland, they moved to Workington in 1250, providing 28 High Sheriffs of the County of Cumberland and representing the county for 18 terms in Parliament. It was at Workington Hall that Mary, Queen of Scots sought refuge after the defeat of her forces in May 1568. While staying here, she wrote a letter to

Elizabeth I which is now on display in the British Museum. Among the hall's later owners was the infamous Henry Curwen (1661–1725), a Jacobite rebel who died in mysterious circumstances – it is said that his death was partly caused by a French woman dragging him down the stairs before stealing his jewels – and whose ghost, according to legend, can be seen wandering among the ruins. Significant embellishments to the hall were made in the 18th century by John Christian Curwen, cousin to the celebrated Fletcher Christian of *Bounty* fame as well as guardian and later husband of his other cousin, Isabelle Curwen (b. 1765). Curwen also purchased Belle Island in Lake Windermere, renaming it in his wife's honour (see Belle Isle Round House). In 1929, the family vacated the hall, after which it fell into decay and soon became a ruin. Today Workington Hall is the site of the medieval Curwen fair during which Shakespearean pageants, operas and plays are staged. Tel: 01900 606699.

Wray Castle — 2 miles (3km) south of Ambleside. Located on the western shore of Windermere, the Gothic revival castle and its adjoining church were built for Dr Dawson, a retired surgeon, in 1840. The home was inherited after Dawson's death in 1875 by his nephew Preston Rawnsley, whose cousin Hardwicke Rawnsley became vicar of the church. Beatrix Potter's family rented the castle in 1882 and played host to the Rev. Rawnsley, whose views on the importance of preserving nature influenced her to buy and preserve much of Lakeland's countryside. The land surrounding the house was one of her purchases. In the 65 acres (26ha) of grounds are paths leading to the edge of the lake and many specimen trees: wellingtonia, redwood, gingko, weeping lime and varieties of beech. Wordsworth planted a mulberry tree in 1845. Today the castle is home to a telecoms engineering enterprise and is not open to the public. Tel: 015394 40200.

Wrynose Pass — 6 miles (10km) southwest of Ambleside. between the Duddon Valley and Little Langdale. Its name derives from the Latin for 'pass of the stallion' and referred to the fact that the steep gradients (up to 1 in 3) needed a well-muscled horse to attain the top. The single-track motor road over the pass, one of the steepest in England, continues over Hardknott Pass and on to Eskdale.

Some famous people born in Cumbria

Blamire, Susanna (The muse of Cumberland) (1747–94)	Cardew Hall, Dalston
Bragg, Melvyn (author and broadcaster) (1939–)	Wigton
Bragg, William Henry (physicist) (1862–1942)	Westward, nr Wigton
Christian, Fletcher (mutineer) (1764–93)	Brigham
Cooper, William Heaton (artist) (1903–95)	Coniston
Dalton, John (physicist) (1766–1844)	Cockermouth
Fallows, Rev. Fearon (astronomer) (1789–1831)	Cockermouth
Figgis, Mike (film director) (1948–)	Carlisle
Grindal, Edmund (Archbishop of Canterbury) (1519–83)	Hensingham
Hughes, Emlyn (footballer) (1947–2004)	Barrow-in-Furness
Laurel, Stan (comic actor) (1890–1965)	Ulverston
Lewis, Wilfred Bennett (nuclear scientist) (1908–87)	Castle Carrock
Molloy, Georgina (botanist) (1805–43)	Carlisle
Nicholson, Norman (poet) (1914–87)	Millom
Nicholson, William (Australian colonial politician, 'father of the ballot') (1816–65)	Whitehaven
Romney, George (painter) (1734–1802)	Dalton-in-Furness
Smirke, Robert (painter) (1752–1845)	Wigton
Webster, George (architect) (1797–1864)	Kendal
Wilkinson, John 'iron mad' (industrialist) (1728–1808)	Clifton
Wordsworth, William (poet) (1770–1850)	Cockermouth

Islands of Cumbria

(shipping area = Irish Sea)

Island name	**Location**	**Nearest landmark**	**General information**
Barren Point Scar	Morecambe Bay	Barrow-in-Furness	GR: SD262648
Barrow Island	Irish Sea	Barrow-in-Furness	Since the 19th century the island has been connected to the mainland. Population: 2606
Beck Scar	Solway Firth	Beckfoot	GR: NY085498
Belle Isle	Lake Windermere	Bowness-on-Windermere	Largest island in Lake Windermere and the only one ever to be inhabited. Named after its previous owner Isabella Curwen. GR: SD393966
Bent Haw Scar	Irish Sea	Walney Island	GR: SD179665
Black Scars	Morecambe Bay	Ulverston	GR: SD329770
Blake Holme	Lake Windermere	Bowness-on-Windermere	GR: SD382899
Bootle Stone	Irish Sea	Walney Island	GR: SD155706
Catherinehole Scar	Solway Firth	Beckfoot	GR: NY090515

Island name	Location	Nearest landmark	General information
Chapel Island	Morecambe Bay	Ulverston	One of the Islands of Furness, approximately 450yds (400m) long and just over 100yds (91.5m) at its widest. Area: 7.5 acres (3ha). GR: SD321758
Chicken Rock	Lake Windermere	Bowness-on-Windermere	GR: SD397957
Costrells Rocks	Lake Windermere	Bowness-on-Windermere	GR: SD380875
Coup Scar	Irish Sea	Barrow-in-Furness	GR: SD229645
Cow Leys Scar	Irish Sea	Walney Island	GR: SD185650
Cross Dike Scar	Irish Sea	Walney Island	GR: SD194645
Crow Holme	Lake Windermere	Bowness-on-Windermere	GR: SD391958
Derwent Isle	Derwent Water	Keswick	aka Vicar's Isle. GR: NY261224
Elbow Scar	Morecambe Bay	Ulverston	GR: SD282703
Fir Island	Coniston Water	Cock Point	GR: SD306942
Foulney	Irish Sea	Barrow-in-Furness	Connected to the mainland by a shingle causeway. One of the Islands of Furness. GR: SD247641
Grass Holme	Lake Windermere	Bowness-on-Windermere	GR: SD383926
Haws Holme	Lake Windermere	Bowness-on-Windermere	GR: SD393972
Head Scar	Irish Sea	Barrow-in-Furness	GR: SD223653
Hen Holme	Lake Windermere	Bowness-on-Windermere	GR: SD396974
Hen Rock	Lake Windermere	Bowness-on-Windermere	GR: SD398955
High West Scar	Solway Firth	Bowness-on-Solway	GR: NY189619
Hilpsford Scar	Irish Sea	Walney Island	GR: SD217615
Hollow Scar	Irish Sea	Walney Island	GR: SD173679
Holme Island	Morecambe Bay	Grange-over-Sands	GR: SD423781
Holme Islands	Crummock Water	Nether How	GR: NY165172
Idridge Scar	Morecambe Bay	Ulverston	GR: SD305715
Lady Holme	Lake Windermere	Bowness-on-Windermere	GR: SD398976
Leonard Scar	Morecambe Bay	Ulverston	GR: SD268688
Lilies of the Valley	Lake Windermere	Bowness-on-Windermere	GR: SD390966
Ling Holme	Lake Windermere	Bowness-on-Windermere	GR: SD385936
Longdyke Scar	Solway Firth	Cardurnock	GR: NY169577
Lord's Island	Derwent Water	Stable Hills	GR: NY265219
Lowhagstock Scar	Solway Firth	Beckfoot	GR: NY075500
Maiden Holme	Lake Windermere	Bowness-on-Windermere	GR: SD391960
Mill Scar	Irish Sea	Walney Island	GR: SD169685
Moat Scar	Morecambe Bay	Ulverston	GR: SD277695
Newbiggin Scar	Morecambe Bay	Ulverston	GR: SD270690
North Scar	Irish Sea	Walney Island	GR: SD163707
Oak Isle	Coniston Water	Park Nab	GR: SD291902
Otter Island	Derwent Water	Brandlehow Point	GR: NY252194
Otterbield Island	Derwent Water	Hawes End	GR: NY254211
Oven Bottom	Lake Windermere	Bowness-on-Windermere	GR: SD392952
Peel Island	Coniston Water	Torver	Believed to be 'Wild Cat Island' in Arthur Ransome's *Swallows and Amazons*. GR: SD295919
Peel Island	Irish Sea	Barrow-in-Furness	aka Piel Island. One of the Islands of Furness. Area: 0.04 sq miles (0.11 sq km). GR: SD232638
Piel Island	Irish Sea	Barrow-in-Furness	see Peel Island (Irish Sea)
Pile of Rocks	Lake Windermere	Bowness-on-Windermere	GR: SD381872
Point of Comfort Scar	Morecambe Bay	Ulverston	GR: SD262679
Priest Skear	Morecambe Bay	Bolton-le-Sands	GR: SD460683
Ramp Holme	Lake Windermere	Bowness-on-Windermere	GR: SD394952
Rampsholme Island	Derwent Water	Stable Hills	GR: NY263213
Roa Island	Irish Sea	Barrow-in-Furness	Linked to the mainland by a causeway since 1846. One of the Islands of Furness. GR: SD232646
Rough Holme	Lake Windermere	Bowness-on-Windermere	GR: SD308979
Scale Island	Crummock Water	Blea Crag	GR: NY161174
Scarf Stones	Derwent Water	Stable Hills	GR: NY264211
Sheep Island	Irish Sea	Barrow-in-Furness	Accessible on foot from Isle of Walney at low water. One of the Islands of Furness. GR: SD215639
Shope Tree Scar	Irish Sea	Walney Island	GR: SD166725
Silver Holme	Lake Windermere	Bowness-on-Windermere	GR: SD377908
Skirtful Crags	Lake Windermere	Bowness-on-Windermere	GR: SD381873
St Herbert's Island	Derwent Water	Hawes End	GR: NY259212
Stale Holme	Lake Windermere	Bowness-on-Windermere	GR: SD397968
Stenor Scar	Solway Firth	Grune	GR: NY140577
Stinking Crag	Solway Firth	Mawbray	GR: NY080485

Island name	Location	Nearest landmark	General information
Thompson's Holme	Lake Windermere	Bowness-on-Windermere	GR: SD392971
Tuft Rock	Lake Windermere	Bowness-on-Windermere	GR: SD398978
Tummer Hill Scar	Irish Sea	Walney Island	GR: SD175673
Vicar's Isle	Derwent Water	Keswick	see Derwent Isle
Wadhead Scar	Morecambe Bay	Ulverston	GR: SD310745
Walney Island	Irish Sea	Barrow-in-Furness	The eighth-largest marine island off the coast of England and the largest to have a direct road bridge to the mainland. Area: 5.02 sq miles (12.99 sq km). GR: SD190660
Woodhouse Islands	Crummock Water	Wood House	GR: NY166176

DERBYSHIRE

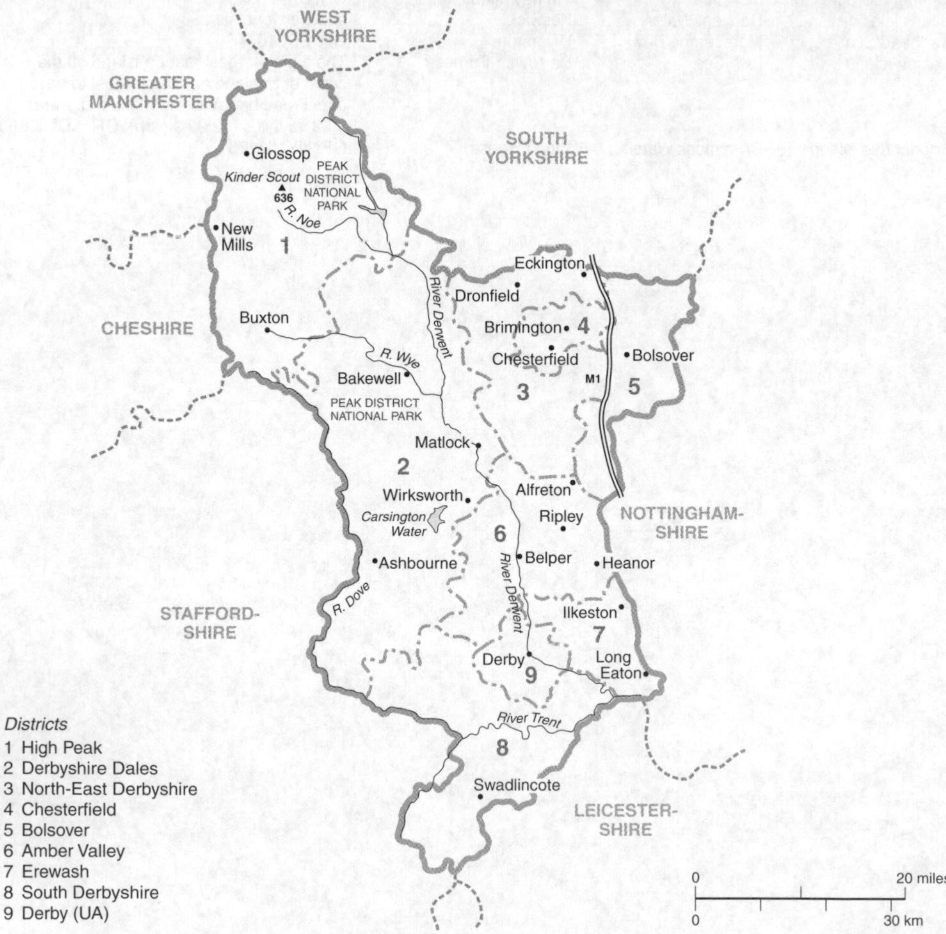

WEST YORKSHIRE
GREATER MANCHESTER
SOUTH YORKSHIRE
Glossop
Kinder Scout
636
PEAK DISTRICT NATIONAL PARK
R. Noe
New Mills
1
Eckington
Dronfield
River Derwent
Buxton
CHESHIRE
Brimington
4
Chesterfield
Bolsover
R. Wye
Bakewell
3
M1
5
PEAK DISTRICT NATIONAL PARK
Matlock
2
Alfreton
Wirksworth
Ripley
NOTTINGHAM-SHIRE
Carsington Water
6
Belper
Ashbourne
Heanor
R. Dove
River Derwent
STAFFORD-SHIRE
Ilkeston
7
Derby
Long Eaton
9
River Trent
8
Swadlincote
LEICESTER-SHIRE
Districts
1 High Peak
2 Derbyshire Dales
3 North-East Derbyshire
4 Chesterfield
5 Bolsover
6 Amber Valley
7 Erewash
8 South Derbyshire
9 Derby (UA)
0
20 miles
0
30 km

Derbyshire is a county in the East Midlands. It shares borders with Greater Manchester to the northwest, West Yorkshire to the north, South Yorkshire to the northeast, Nottinghamshire to the east, Leicestershire to the southeast, Staffordshire to the southwest and west and Cheshire to the west and northwest. The county's southernmost tip almost meets the northernmost tip of Warwickshire. Before 1998 the administrative county included the city of Derby, which was then the county town. Derby is now a unitary authority, but remains part of Derbyshire for ceremonial purposes. Matlock is now the county town.

The county boundaries have seen various changes since the late 19th century. Historically, Derbyshire had an exclave in northwestern Leicestershire, surrounding Measham and Donisthorpe. This was incorporated into Leicestershire by the Local Government Act 1888. Conversely, the thin strip of Leicestershire between the exclave and Derbyshire, containing Overseal and Netherseal, was transferred to Derbyshire. A small area of Derbyshire, including the parishes of Stapenhill and Winshill, part of the borough of Burton upon Trent, was incorporated into Staffordshire by the same Act. Further boundary changes were made in the 20th century. In 1934 the parishes of Dore, Norton and Totley were absorbed into the City of Sheffield, then in the West Riding of Yorkshire; two years later Mellor and Ludworth were incorporated into Marple urban district in Cheshire and now form part of the Metropolitan Borough of Stockport in Greater Manchester. In 1974 the former area of Tintwistle Rural District was incorporated into the new non-metropolitan county of Derbyshire, having previously been part of the administrative county of Cheshire.

Evidence of prehistoric existence has been found in the limestone caves at Creswell Crags. There are numerous Bronze Age burial barrows and stone circles; the largest and best preserved is at Arbor Low, southeast of Buxton. In the 1st and 2nd centuries the Roman armies controlled the area and established their stronghold at what is now known as Little Chester, a suburb of Derby. By the early 5th century the Romans had left and the area came under the rule of the Saxons, as part of the kingdom of Mercia. The Saxons created a settlement nearby, which is now known as Markeaton. Many local district and road names date back to this period.

As recorded in Domesday Book, large areas of land in what now constitutes Derbyshire and Nottinghamshire were granted to William Peveril. This land was later passed to the Crown following the disinheritance of his son for having poisoned the Earl of Chester.

By the 1600s lead had become second in importance in England's economy only to wool. It was an essential commodity for the roofs of public buildings and the new houses being built in every part of the country by the nobility and gentry. All houses, including farmhouses and cottages by then, had glazed windows, with lead glazing bars. It was also the only material for water storage and piping. Lead also became essential for the military as the Civil War approached, as every army used lead for ammunition. Wirksworth in the Derbyshire Dales was the main source of lead ore (galena) and provided economic wealth for the county.

The 18th century and the Industrial Revolution saw the emergence of many renowned Derbyshire industrialists, while townships based on factory production methods developed in the midst of what until then had been a largely rural economy. In 1771 Richard Arkwright, Samuel Need and Jedediah Strutt built the world's first water-powered cotton spinning mill at Cromford, developing a form of power that was the catalyst for the Industrial Revolution. This was followed by Jedediah Strutt's Cotton Spinning Mills at Belper. The Derbyshire lead industry declined after the late 18th century because veins were worked out, production costs were increasing and much cheaper foreign sources were being discovered. The industry was protected from foreign ore by import duty in the late 18th and early 19th centuries, but a progressive reduction in the duty after the 1820s and its abolition in 1845 brought a steep rise in the volume of lead imported into England and accelerated the local industry's decline. By 1891 the number of men employed in all the Derbyshire lead mines had fallen to 285, most of whom worked at the Millclose Mine at Darley Bridge. Millclose, the biggest lead mine in the country, took the industry into the 20th century, and just before its enforced closure in 1939, caused by flooding, it employed about 600 men.

Today Derbyshire is one of the prime tourist areas of Britain. It is home to the nation's first National Park, a plethora of upland walks, magnificent stately homes and historic cave systems, close to the amenities of major cities.

The city and unitary authority of **Derby** lies on the banks of the River Derwent. It is thought that Derby's origin may be prehistoric, the development of a strategic point on the Derwent where it was possible to cross by ford, and the city recently celebrated its 2000th year as a settlement. Derby has Roman, Saxon and Viking connections: the Roman camp of Derventio was probably at the city's northern suburb of Little Chester/Chester Green, while the town was later one of the 'Five Boroughs' (fortified towns) of the Danelaw. The city is one of the few that have retained a name with a Viking origin, like York (which had the Viking name of Jorvik); it is popularly believed that the name 'Derby' is a corruption of the Danish *Deor-a-by* (village of the deer), though some assert that it is a corruption of the original Roman name Derventio. The town was also named 'Darby' or 'Darbye' on some of the oldest maps, such as John Speed's 1610 map. During the Civil War the town was garrisoned by Parliamentary troops commanded by Sir John Gell, 1st Baronet, who was appointed Governor of Derby in 1643. These troops took part in the defence of Nottingham, the siege of Lichfield and the battle of Hopton Heath, as well as successfully defending Derbyshire against Royalist armies.

Although he was not a native of Derby, Bonnie Prince Charlie has close connections with the city, having made camp here on 4 December 1745 while on his way south to seize the English crown. The Prince called at the George Inn on Irongate, where the Duke of Devonshire had set up his headquarters, and demanded billets for his 9000 troops. He stayed at Exeter House, Exeter Street, where he held his 'Council of War'. (A replica of the room containing wall panels from Exeter House is on display at the Central Library, located on the Wardwick in the city centre.) Having received misleading information about an army coming to meet him south of Derby, he abandoned his invasion at Swarkestone Bridge, on the River Trent, just a few miles south of Derby. The Duke of Devonshire had held a war council the previous day, and decided that the Derby Blues should retreat under the threat of the advancing Jacobites. Each year at the beginning of December (usually the first weekend), the Charles Edward Stuart Society of Derby leads a weekend of activities culminating in a parade through the city centre and a battle on Cathedral Green.

Derby was at the centre of the Industrial Revolution. In 1717 Derby was the site of the first water-powered silk mill in Britain, while in 1759 Jedediah Strutt patented and built a machine called the Derby Rib attachment that revolutionised the manufacture of hose. In 1840, the North Midland Railway set up its works in Derby and, when it merged with the Midland Counties Railway and the Birmingham and Derby Junction Railway to form the Midland Railway, Derby became its headquarters.

Derby was awarded city status in 1977 by Queen Elizabeth II to mark the 25th anniversary of her accession to the throne. The Queen presented the charter scroll in person on 28 July 1977. Prior to that, Derby was one of the few towns in England that were not cities, but boasted a cathedral.

Derbyshire	**Population**			**Area**	
Districts	*male*	*female*	*total*	*sq miles*	*sq km*
Amber Valley	57,071	59,400	116,471	102	265
Bolsover	35,262	36,504	71,766	62	160
Chesterfield	48,240	50,605	98,845	25	66
Derbyshire Dales	34,262	35,207	69,469	306	793
Erewash	53,864	56,235	110,099	42	110
High Peak	44,171	45,262	89,433	208	539
North East Derbyshire	47,564	49,376	96,940	107	276
South Derbyshire	40,405	41,157	81,562	131	338
Derby Unitary Authority	108,240	113,468	221,708	30	78
Total	469,079	487,214	956,293	1013	2625

Local Attractions and Information

Administrative headquarters
Derby: The Council House, Corporation Street, Derby DE1 2FS. Tel: 01332 293111.
Derbyshire: County Hall, Matlock DE4 3AG. Tel: 01629 580000.

Arbor Low
3 miles (5km) west of Youlgreave. A late Neolithic henge monument located in the Peak District. Part of a wider Neolithic ritual landscape, it was built c.2500 BC and consists of a circular bank, 249ft (76m) in diameter and 7ft (2.1m) high, with an internal ditch around 30ft (9m) wide and 6ft (1.8m) deep, enclosing a central area. There are entrance causeways at the northern and southern ends. The stone circle inside consists of more than 40 recumbent limestone slabs, with three lying in the very centre. These central stones form a 'cove' close to which a skeleton was found during excavations in 1901–2. Arbor Low is linked to the Bronze Age barrow of Gib Hill 350yds (320m) away by an earth ridge.

Axe Edge Moor
3 miles (5km) west of Buxton. A major moorland in the Peak District consisting mainly of gritstone (Namurian shale and sandstone), with its highest point at 1808ft (551m). The moor is the source of the Rivers Dove, Manifold, Dane, Wye and Goyt and is home to England's second highest public house, the Cat and Fiddle Inn. It is shared between the counties of Derbyshire, Staffordshire and Cheshire, which meet on its southwestern flank at Three Shires Head on the Dane.

Bakewell pudding
A traditional baked dessert tart or cake consisting of a shortcrust pastry shell, spread with jam and covered with a sponge-like filling enriched with ground almonds. It may also be covered with nuts such as almonds or peanuts. Alternative flavours, including blackcurrant, strawberry and apple are also produced. A cherry Bakewell is a small cake, covered with a top layer of icing and a single central half-cherry, also known as a Bakewell Cake. The Derbyshire town of Bakewell claims to be the home of the authentic Bakewell pudding. Recipes still made there consist of a puff pastry shell with a layer of jam, covered with a filling of eggs, sugar, butter and almonds. The dish is rumoured to have been invented accidentally in the 1860s, when a nobleman visiting the White Horse Inn (now the Rutland Arms) at Bakewell ordered strawberry tart. Instead of stirring the egg mixture into the cake, the cook spread it on top of the jam.

Barlborough Hall
Barlborough, 13 miles (21km) northeast of Chesterfield. Originally built by Sir Francis Rodes, c.1583–4, the hall's Elizabethan design is attributed to Robert Smythson, one of a noted family of architects. Barlborough Hall became an independent Catholic day school in 1939. Tel: 01246 810511.

Beeley Moor
5 miles (8km) north of Matlock. A heather-clad moor 1200ft (366m) above sea level, on which are over 30 prehistoric barrows and cairns. Perhaps most notable is Hob Hurst's House, an unusual Bronze Age barrow consisting of a small ring of five stones which stand on a mound surrounded by a rectangular bank and ditch. When the barrow was excavated in 1853, scorched human bones were found along with two pieces of lead ore. Various legends relating to the monument have sprung up, including one that refers to 'Hob' as a kindly goblin who made his home in the barrow and gave assistance to the local community. The pretty, unspoilt village of Beeley is sheltered by Beeley Moor and has wonderful views in all directions. Almost all the farm and domestic buildings are built from honey-coloured sandstone, quarried locally close to Fallinge Edge.

Blue John
A semi-precious mineral also known as 'Derbyshire Spar'. A form of calcium fluoride, it is found sporadically throughout Derbyshire but chiefly identified with Blue John Cavern and the three other show caves (Treak Cliff, Speedwell and Peak) in the Castleton area. A small amount of the rock is still mined in Treak Cliff Cavern and can be bought as jewellery in local shops. The name derives from French *bleu et jaune* (blue and yellow), characterising its colour. The earliest dated decorative application of Blue John is its use in marble fireplace panels designed by Robert Adam and installed in Kedleston Hall near Derby in 1762.

Bolsover Castle
Bolsover, 6 miles (10km) east of Chesterfield. Built by the Peverel family in the 12th century, the castle became Crown property in 1155 when the third William Peverel fled into exile. A stone keep was built c.1173, surrounded by a curtain wall which was eventually breached in 1216 during the reign of King John. It was then allowed to deteriorate into a ruin. Surviving fragments of the curtain wall were later incorporated in a wall walk that can be seen in the castle garden. In 1553 Sir George Talbot purchased the castle, selling it to Sir Charles Cavendish in 1608. The castle was rebuilt by Robert Smythson c.1612 in Jacobean Romantic style for Sir Charles with a notable indoor riding school. The tower, known today as the 'Little Castle', was completed c.1621. The Parliamentarians took it over during the Civil War and once again it fell into a ruinous state. After 1883 the castle was uninhabited and was eventually given to the nation by the 7th Duke of Portland in 1945. It is now in the care of English Heritage. Tel: 01246 345777.

Breadsall Priory
Breadsall, 4 miles (6km) north of Derby. A house of the Friars Eremites, thought to have been founded by the Dethick family in the mid 13th century, and subsequently converted into an Augustinian priory. The physician and poet Erasmus Darwin moved here shortly before his death in 1802, followed by his son, Sir Francis Sacheverel Darwin (1786–1859). The Grade II listed building is currently a hotel and golf course.

Bretby Hall
Bretby, 3 miles (5km) north of Swadlincote, 14 miles (23km) southwest of Derby. Located on the border with Staffordshire, the first Bretby Hall was built in 1630 after Thomas Stanhope bought the manor of Bretby (the name means 'dwelling place of Britons') from the family of Stephen de Segrave, to whom it had been granted by Ranulph de Blondeville, 4th Earl of Chester. In 1628, his grandson Philip was made Earl of Chesterfield by Charles I and thehall became the seat of the Earls of Chesterfield. The 5th Earl demolished the mansion and built the present hall to a design by Sir Jeffry Wyatville. The 6th Earl, known as the 'racing Earl', who loved cricket and shooting, built a cricket pitch and raised game birds. When the 7th Earl died without issue, the estate reverted to his mother and through her to the wife of the 5th Earl of Carnarvon, the famous Egyptologist who discovered the tomb of Tutankhamun. In 1926, the hall was sold to Derbyshire County Council and was run as an orthopaedic hospital until the 1990s when it was sold to a private developer, who converted it into apartments.

Calke Abbey
Ticknall, 8 miles (13km) south of Derby. A baroque mansion, built 1701–4 and set in the midst of a landscape park. The estate belonged to the Harpur family, baronets from 1626, from 1622 to 1985. The family were noted for their reclusive eccentricity. The last baronet, Sir Vauncey Harpur-Crewe, died in 1924, and when the sudden death of Charles Harpur-Crewe (1917–81) led to crippling death duties the estate had to be sold by his brother Henry. By 1985 the property was in need of extensive repair; lacking in modern amenities, it was cluttered with the family paraphernalia of centuries. Little restoration had been done and the interiors had remained untouched since the 1880s. The decision was made to carry out essential repairs only and keep the property in its unimproved state. Features of the interior include an 18th century state bed. Outside can be found a walled garden, flower garden and physic garden, while the landscaped park, designed by William Emes, is a National Nature Reserve. The property is now owned by the National Trust. Tel: 01332 863822.

Carnfield Hall
South Normanton, 2 miles (3km) east of Alfreton. An Elizabethan mansion house whose features include panelled rooms, two 17th century staircases and a great parlour. From 1502, it was the seat of the Revells and is now owned by the Cartland family. The interior is home to three centuries of family portraits, furniture, porcelain, needlework, costumes, royal relics and manorial documents. There are also collections of 18th century fans, snuff boxes and toys. Tel: 01773 520084.

Carsington Water
9 miles (15km) southwest of Matlock. Operated by Severn Trent Water, Carsington is England's ninth largest reservoir with a capacity of 7.8 billion gallons (35,412 megalitres). Water taken from the River Derwent at Ambergate during the winter months is pumped to the reservoir via 7 miles (11km) of tunnels and aqueduct, and released back into the river during the summer for abstraction and treatment further downstream. Planning for the reservoir started in the 1960s and construction in 1979. After a partial collapse of the dam in 1984, prior to its filling, it was completely removed before being reconstructed commencing in 1989. The reservoir was opened by Queen Elizabeth II in 1992. It is now a major centre for leisure activities including walking, cycling, birdwatching, sailing and windsurfing. The surrounding land has played host to events including a music festival and the Festival of the Peak. Birds to be seen include little owl, little grebe, feral barnacle geese, oystercatcher, common tern and breeding redshank. Tel: 01629 50696.

Casterne Hall
See Staffordshire

Catton Hall
Walton-on-Trent, 6½ miles (10.5km) southwest of Swadlincote. Though the current house was built in 1742, it has been in the hands of the same family since 1405 and is still lived in by the Neilsons. The house contains collections of 17th and 18th century paintings, as well as royal and family portraits, and has its own private chapel. Tel: 01283 716311.

Chatsworth House
3½ miles (5.5km) northeast of Bakewell. One of Britain's best loved historic houses and estates, often topping polls as the nation's favourite stately home, the home of the Duke and Duchess of

Devonshire is set within the Peak District National Park. There has been a mansion on the site since the second half of the 16th century, but Chatsworth's history dates back to Anglo-Saxon times; the name is a corruption of *Chetelsourde* meaning 'Chetel's manor'. After the Norman Conquest,Chatsworth ceased to be a large estate until the 15th century, when it was acquired by the Leche family who already owned other property nearby. They may have enclosed the first park at Chatsworth and built a house on the high ground in what is now the southeastern part of the garden. In 1549 they sold their property in the area to Sir William Cavendish, Treasurer of the King's Chamber and then husband of the more famous Bess of Hardwick. Bess, persuaded her husband to sell his property in Suffolk and settle in her native county. William and Bess began to build their new house in 1553, selecting a site near the River Derwent almost on the same site as the present house. William died in 1557, but Bess finished the house in the 1560s and lived there with her fourth husband, George Talbot, 6th Earl of Shrewsbury. In 1568 Shrewsbury was entrusted with the custody of Mary, Queen of Scots, who brought his prisoner to Chatsworth several times from 1570 onwards. She lodged in the apartment above the great hall which is now known as the Queen of Scots rooms. When Bess died in 1608, Chatsworth passed to her second son William, who was created 1st Earl of Devonshire in 1618. The 4th Earl of Devonshire, who was to become the 1st Duke in 1694, began a complete rebuilding of the house in 1687. The south and east fronts, designed by William Talman, were complete by 1696. The west and north fronts may have been the work of Thomas Archer, possibly in collaboration with the Duke himself. In 1811 the 6th Duke inherited the title and, along with architect Jeffry Wyatville, transformed Chatsworth in Italianate style. The new interiors were embellished with marble. A great book collector, the Duke had the long gallery converted into a library with an elegant white decor embellished with green malachite columns. A new north wing was built, doubling the size of the house. The whole of the ground floor was occupied by service rooms including kitchen, servants' hall, laundry, butler's and housekeeper's rooms. On the first floor, facing west, were two sets of bachelor bedrooms called California and The Birds. During World War II Chatsworth was occupied by Penhros College, a girls' public school from Colwyn Bay in Wales. In 1944 Kathleen Kennedy, sister of John F Kennedy, married William Cavendish, Marquess of Hartington, elder son of the 10th Duke of Devonshire. He was killed in action in Belgium later in 1944, and she died in a plane crash in 1948. His younger brother Andrew, who was married to Deborah Mitford, sister to Nancy, Diana, Unity and Jessica, became the 11th Duke in 1950. Today, the 'Palace of the Peak' is a family home. Throughout the house are magnificent displays of paintings, furniture, silver, tapestries and porcelain and a gallery of neo-classical sculptures. Famous curiosities include four royal thrones, a giant ancient Greek marble foot, a lace cravat carved from wood, the fan of a Rolls-Royce jet engine and a unique illusionistic painting of a violin hanging on a door. The 1000 acre (400ha) park was laid out by Capability Brown in the 1760s. The 105 acre (42ha) garden is a magical landscape with rare trees, shrubs, formal hedges, temples, sculptures, streams and ponds. The famous waterworks include the 24 steps of the 300-year-old cascade, falling 600ft (183m) down the hill, the magic of water shooting from the branches of the willow tree fountain, the trough waterfall, and *Revelation*, a water-powered kinetic steel sculpture designed by Angela Conner and installed in 1999. As well as the maze, and the rose, cottage, and kitchen gardens, there is a new sensory garden. Joseph Paxton, head gardener in the 19th century, created the rock garden, now restored with a viewpoint looking out over the garden, the gravity-fed Emperor fountain, the pinetum and glasshouses. Throughout the garden are sculptures, fragments and vases, including a Roman altar and lead statues of Samson and Pan, water gods and sea horses. Tel: 01246 565300.

Chesterfield

Derbyshire's largest town lies 12 miles (19km) south of Sheffield in South Yorkshire, on a confluence of the rivers Rother and Hipper. It received its market charter from King John in 1204. Chesterfield is perhaps best known for the 'Crooked Spire' of its Church of St Mary and All Saints. The twisted spire leans 9ft 5in (2.9m) from its true centre. The twisting is thought to be the result of unseasoned timbers or insufficient cross-bracing.

Churches

St Mary and All Saints Church – see Chesterfield

St Oswald's Church, Ashbourne, was named after Oswald of Northumbria. Built in the 13th and early 14th centuries on the site of an earlier Saxon church, it dominates the small town with its 212ft (64.5m) spire. A Norman crypt was also discovered during excavations in 1913. In 1837–40 it was restored by George Gilbert Scott. Each of its transepts houses a chapel dedicated to leading local families: in the north transept the Cockaynes and their successors the Boothbys; in the south the Bradbournes. The Boothby monument is a sculpture made from Carrara (Italian) marble in the form of a sleeping child. Carved by Thomas Banks, it represents Penelope Boothby, who died in 1791 at the age of six (five according to some accounts). The monument is inscribed with the girl's epitaph: 'She was in form and intellect most exquisite. The unfortunate Parents ventured their all on this frail Bark. And the wreck was total.'

The tower of **St Werburgh's Church**, Derby, contains what is now named the Johnson Chapel, where Samuel Johnson married Elizabeth 'Tetty' Porter in 1735. Its oldest parts are the tower, rebuilt in 1601, and the 1699 chancel, now a side chapel. The remainder was rebuilt 1893–4 by Sir Arthur Blomfield in 15th century style. Notable features include the reredos in the side chapel, a 1718 wrought iron font cover (now in the Johnson Chapel), Kempe glass and an 1832 monument to Sarah Winyates. In 1989–90 the church was converted into a shopping mall called the Cloisters. After the failure of this enterprise, the building stood empty for a number of years before being converted into a restaurant. The tower has recently undergone major refurbishment. The marriage of Samuel Johnson is re-enacted annually at the church.

Codnor Castle

Codnor, 12 miles (19km) northeast of Derby. Overlooking the Erewash valley and the counties of Derbyshire and Nottinghamshire, the castle was established by William Peveril in the early 13th century as a stone keep and bailey fortress. The present fragmentary remains represent a three-storey keep and a strong curtain wall and ditch, flanked by round towers. The outer bailey, constructed at a later period, originally had a deep moat. On the west side there was a courtyard strongly fortified by huge round towers with battlements. In other parts of the ruins there is evidence that the outer walls had loopholes for the use of bowmen. By 1211 the castle was owned by Henry de Grey. After his death it passed to the Zouch family, remaining in their hands until they left the kingdom in 1622. Sir Keynshen Master, who inhabited it in 1712, is reported as being the last person to live in the castle. Today the remnants are a ruin, the few remaining high walls supported by scaffolding.

Creswell Crags
Crags Road, Welbeck, Worksop, Notts. Located on the Nottinghamshire–Derbyshire border, although it has a Nottinghamshire postal address the site is administered by Creswell Heritage Trust in conjunction with Derbyshire County Council and as such is more appropriately a Derbyshire entry. The limestone gorge of Creswell Crags has been referred to as 'The Cheddar Gorge of the North'. Stone tools and remains of animals found in the caves by archaeologists in a series of excavations from 1875 to the present day provide evidence of life during the last Ice Age between 50,000 and 10,000 years ago, indicating that the caves were seasonally occupied by nomadic groups of people during the Upper Palaeolithic and Mesolithic periods. The sequence of human occupation at Creswell began c.40–50,000 years ago with the Neanderthals. The main phases of Stone Age occupation were at around 43,000 BC, then in a period between 30,000 and 28,000 BC and again c.10,000 BC. Evidence of Neolithic, Bronze Age, Roman and post-medieval activity has also been found. The first archaeological discoveries were made in the 19th century, including a fish pattern on a mammoth's tusk and a reindeer rib adorned with a chevron pattern. Weapons and utensils were also found, including a dagger made from the spine of a mammoth and drinking vessels fashioned from woolly rhinoceros bones. The occupied caves were given fanciful names following the 19th century discoveries, such as Mother Grundy's Parlour, Church Hole, Pin Hole and Robin Hood's Cave. Pin Hole and Robin Hood's Cave lie on the northern side of the gorge; here were found a figure of a masked man engraved on a piece of bison rib bone and, oldest of all, a horse's head on another fragment of rib bone. Mother Grundy's Parlour revealed carvings of a reindeer, a bear or bison's head and a rhinoceros. More than 200 stone tools were also found, less than a third originating from the cave's Neanderthal residents. The inhabitants of Creswell, particularly those in Mother Grundy's Parlour, developed their own local flint 'industry', which has become known to archaeology as the Creswellian Culture. The blades were characteristically small and blunted along one edge for holding, or setting into a handle. Creswellian products have also been found in Dowel Cave, at Earl Sterndale in Derbyshire's White Peak and as far away as Somerset. In 2003, the discovery by Paul Banh and Paul Pettitt of Britain's only known Ice Age rock art filled a major gap in the country's archaeological record. In Church Hole Cave, where 19th century archaeologists had discovered a 12,000-year-old bone needle, Banh and Pettitt discovered engravings of three animal figures etched into the stone of the cave wall. One appears to be a crane or swan, another a bird of prey, and the third is believed to represent an ibex, an animal not previously thought to have existed in Britain. The engravers seem to have made use of the naturally uneven cave surface in their carvings and it is likely that they relied on the early morning sunlight entering the caves to illuminate the art. The engravings were dated to at least 12,800 years ago, and the scientists and archaeologists concluded it was likely they were contemporary with evidence for occupation at the site c.13,000–15,000 years ago. Twenty thousand years ago the edge of the northern ice cap was only 19 miles (30km) north of Creswell, so this was one of the most northerly places to have been visited by our ancestors during the last Ice Age. Tel: 01909 720378.

Cromford and High Peak Railway
Completed in 1831, the Cromford and High Peak Railway (C&HPR) was used to carry minerals and goods between the Cromford Canal at Cromford Wharf and the Peak Forest Canal at Whaley Bridge. The highest part of the line was at Ladmanlow, a height of 1266ft (386m), 97ft (30m) higher than the current highest railway line in England, Ais Gill at 1169ft (356m) on the Settle–Carlisle line. The line was closed in 1967 and part of the track bed now carries the High Peak Trail, a 17 miles (27km) length of the National Cycle Network, itself part of the Pennine Bridleway, a 130 mile (209km) route which starts at Middleton Top, near Cromford, and includes 73 miles (117km) through Derbyshire to the South Pennines.

Derby Cathedral
Iron Gate, Derby. The Cathedral Church of All Saints is the seat of the Bishop of Derby, and one of the smallest cathedrals in England. The original church was founded by Edmund I c.943 as a royal collegiate church but there is no trace of its existence today. The current cathedral dates from the 14th century, although it appears to be based on an earlier medieval building about the same size as the present church. The tower, dating from 1510–30, was built in Perpendicular Gothic style. The building became a cathedral by royal charter in 1927, unusual because Derby remained a town at the time. Previously it was known as All Saints' Church. The cathedral contains the oldest ring of ten bells in the UK. Other treasures include an 18th century nave with a wrought-iron screen by Robert Bakewell, Bess of Hardwick's memorial, and the Cavendish brasses, including those of Henry Cavendish and Georgiana Spencer, the wife of one of the Dukes of Devonshire. The cathedral tower is 212ft 6in (64.8m) tall, and was (until 1927) the second tallest non-cathedral church tower in England after the Boston Stump (see St Botolph's Church, Lincolnshire). It is now the third tallest (Anglican) cathedral church tower in England after Liverpool and Canterbury. Tel: 01332 341201.

Derby Gaol
The term historically refers to the five gaols in Derby. Today it usually refers to one of two sites, the gaol which stood on Friar Gate 1756–1846 and the cells of which still exist, and the Vernon Street Prison whose impressive gateway is still visible. In 1652 the Cornmarket Gaol (no longer extant)

was the site of the imprisonment of George Fox, founder of the Religious Society of Friends (Quakers), on charges of blasphemy. It has been alleged that Judge Bennett of Derby first used the term Quaker to describe the movement, as they bade him 'quake for fear of the Lord', but the phrase had already been used in the context of other religious groups. The Friar Gate Gaol was the site of many hangings, and a small museum today displays contemporary accounts of the executions, a replica of the gallows which stood in front of the building, and a display in crime and punishment in Derbyshire, with a collection on the Pentrich Martyrs of 1817, who were hanged and beheaded following their failed revolution on charges of treason in front of the building. The building is also said to be haunted and was visited in 2002 by Living TV's *Most Haunted*. Tel: 01332 299321. The Vernon Street Prison served as the county gaol from 1846 to 1919, when it was demolished. The last public execution at Derby, of Richard Thorley for the murder of Eliza Morrow, took place there in 1862. The prison served as a military prison 1919–29. Following demolition the site was occupied by a greyhound racing stadium and today contains offices, though the magnificent frontage is worth seeing.

Dorby Industrial Museum Silk Mill Lane, Derby. Museum housed in a former silk mill beside the River Derwent. Built by George Sorocold for the Lombe brothers, 1717–21, Britain's first silk mill housed machines for 'doubling' or twisting silk into thread. In possibly the first example of industrial espionage, John Lombe reputedly copied the design for the machines, used for spinning large quantities of silk, during a period spent working within the silk industry in Piedmont in modern Italy (he is alleged to have been poisoned by Piedmontese in revenge in 1722). Tel: 01332 255308.

Derwent Reservoir One of three reservoirs in the Upper Derwent Valley in northeast Derbyshire. The River Derwent flows first through Howden Reservoir, then Derwent Reservoir and finally through Ladybower Reservoir. Between them they provide water to practically all of Derbyshire, as well as a large part of South Yorkshire and as far afield as Nottingham and Leicester. The reservoir is 1$^1/_2$ miles (2.5km) in length, broadly north–south, with Howden Dam at the northern end and Derwent Dam at the south. A small island lies near Howden Dam. The Abbey Brook flows into the reservoir from the east. At its peak the reservoir covers an area of 175 acres (71ha) and at its deepest point is 114ft (34.7m) deep.

Derwent Valley Mills A UNESCO World Heritage Site along the River Derwent south of Matlock, designated in December 2001. The modern factory, or 'mill', system was born here in the 18th century to accommodate the new technology for spinning cotton developed by Richard Arkwright. The insertion of industrial establishments into a rural landscape necessitated the construction of housing for the mill workers. The site consists of the communities of Cromford, Belper, Milford, Darley Abbey and Lombe's Mills, and includes 867 listed buildings. A further nine structures are Scheduled Ancient Monuments. At the Working Textile Museum at Arkwright's Masson Mill, there are approximately 680,000 bobbins on display.

Duffield Castle Duffield, 5 miles (8km) north of Derby. The earthwork of a former Norman castle lies on a steep-sided rocky promontory facing the River Derwent. Remains that appear to be of Anglo-Saxon origin have been found. When the site was excavated in 1885, the foundations of a traditional Norman motte and bailey castle were discovered, with a stone keep built upon it. Remarkably the size of the keep, 98ft (30m) long and 95ft (29m) wide, was only slightly smaller than the White Tower in the Tower of London (see London). The castle was built by the de Ferrers family, who in Normandy presided over an important centre for iron manufacture; it has been suggested that this is the origin of the nailmaking industry in nearby Belper. The grounds are owned by the National Trust although upkeep is carried out by the parish council.

Ednaston Manor Ednaston, 7 miles (11km) northwest of Derby. Completed by 1919 in Queen Anne style by Edwin Lutyens, for William G Player, the house is now Grade I listed.

Elvaston Castle Elvaston, 5 miles (8km) east of Derby. The centrepiece of Elvaston Castle Country Park, consisting of 200 acres (81ha) of woodlands, parkland and formal gardens. Originally built in 1633, the castle was redesigned by James Wyatt in the early 1800s for the 3rd Earl of Harrington. The estate was sold in 1968 by the then Earl of Harrington to Derbyshire County Council, who opened it to the public in 1970.

Elvaston Castle Country Park See Elvaston Castle

Eyam 12 miles (19km) west of Chesterfield. The small village of Eyam (pronounced 'Eem') is best known for being the 'plague village', its inhabitants having chosen to isolate themselves when the Black Death reached the village in August 1665, in order to prevent the infection from travelling further north. The plague had been brought to the village in a flea-infested bundle of cloth delivered from London to the tailor, George Vicars, who was the first to die of the disease. As the plague took hold it was decided on the advice of rector William Mompesson to hold church services outdoors at the nearby valley of Cucklett Delf. Mompesson also persuaded the villagers to quarantine the entire village to prevent the disease from spreading further. Food and other supplies were left outside Eyam, either at the Boundary Stones or at Mompesson's Well, high above the village. The Earl of Devonshire, who lived at Chatsworth House, freely donated food and medical supplies. Twelve months after Vicars' death, the plague was still claiming victims, and on 25 August 1666 Catherine Mompesson, the rector's wife, died, having loyally stayed with her husband and tended the sick. In total the plague raged in Eyam for 16 months, killing at least 260 villagers. Survival appeared random, as many plague survivors had close contact with the bacterium but never caught the disease. Farmer Elizabeth Hancock did not become ill despite burying six children and her husband in eight days (the Riley graves, close to Riley House Farm $^1/_2$ mile (0.8km) from the village, house their bodies), while the village gravedigger handled hundreds of plague-ravaged corpses but never contracted the disease himself. The novels *Year of Wonders* (2001) by

Geraldine Brooks and *A Parcel of Patterns* (1983) by Jill Paton Walsh are fictional accounts of the plague in Eyam. A remembrance service is still held every Plague Sunday (the last Sunday in August) at Cucklett Delf. Genetic research has indicated that some villagers may have had genetic protection from the bubonic plague. An extremely rare gene mutation designated as 'Delta 32' was found in 14 per cent of direct descendants of the plague survivors. In fact, levels found in Eyam were only matched in regions of Europe that had been affected by the plague and in Americans of European origin. It has also been suggested that the Delta 32 mutation, if inherited from both parents, may provide immunity to HIV/AIDS. Eyam churchyard contains a Saxon cross dating to the 7th or 8th century. Initially located at the side of a cart track near the village, it was moved to its present location after the plague. It is Grade I listed and a Scheduled Ancient Monument.

Eyam Hall Situated in the heart of the village of Eyam (see separate entry), Eyam Hall has been the home of the Wright family for over 300 years. Features include a stone-flagged hall, tapestry room, bedroom with tester bed and family costumes, as well as a wide variety of artefacts. Tel: 01433 631976.

Foremarke Hall Milton, 8 miles (13km) southwest of Derby. Built in Palladian style in 1760 for Sir Francis Burdett, the house is four storeys high. The large hall on the 2nd floor contains an infamous portrait of Burdett of which teachers and students claim the subject's eyes 'seem to be staring at them in all directions'. In addition, an annexe was built as a guesthouse and to house the lord's retinue, a ground-floor corridor linking the two buildings. A double spiral staircase leads up to the pillared front entrance and to the approx 1000 sq ft (93 sq m) main hall/living area of the building which contained two large fireplaces and a glass chandelier. A Great Western Railway 'Modified Hall' class steam locomotive, No. 7903 is named after the hall. Foremarke Hall was taken over by the Army during World War I and was used as a military hospital. The military identification plate nailed to the doors of the front entrance is still present. It is currently the main building of Repton Preparatory School. A small parish church, built at the time of Sir Francis Burdett, is still in use, and members of the Burdett family were buried in a secluded part of the churchyard.

Haddon Hall 2 miles (3km) southeast of Bakewell. Situated on the River Wye, Haddon Hall is one of the seats of the Duke of Rutland, and is currently occupied by Lord Edward Manners and his family. The origins of the hall date to the 11th century. William Peverel, illegitimate son of William I, held the manor of Haddon in 1087. Though it was never a castle, the manor was protected from 1195 by a wall built by Richard Vernon. The current hall includes small sections of the 11th century structure, but mostly comprises additional chambers and ranges added by the successive generations of the Peverel, Avenel, Vernon and Manners families during the medieval and Tudor periods. Major construction was carried out between the 13th and 17th century. The banqueting hall (with minstrels' gallery), kitchens and parlour date from 1370 and the St Nicholas Chapel was completed in 1427. For generations, whitewash concealed and protected their pre-Reformation frescoes. There is a 16th century long gallery. The 9th Duke created the walled topiary garden adjoining the stable-block cottage, with clipped heraldic devices of the boar's head and the peacock, emblematic of the Vernon and Manners families. Tel: 01629 812855.

Hardwick Hall 7 miles (11km) southeast of Chesterfield. This Elizabethan house with Tudor treasures was built for Elizabeth Hardwick, better known as Bess of Hardwick, the daughter of Derbyshire squire John of Hardwick and Elizabethan England's second most powerful and wealthy woman. Designed by Robert Smythson, the house is almost unchanged since Bess lived there, giving a rare insight into the formality of courtly life of the Elizabethan age. The story is that Bess had a furious dispute with her husband, the Earl of Shrewsbury, and in 1584 had to leave their home at Chatsworth. She came to the Old Hall at Hardwick and largely rebuilt it as a place for herself to live. However, when the Earl died in 1590 her finances became much more secure and she began the construction of the New Hall. The Old Hall was abandoned and gradually became a ruin. With its massive windows and fine proportions the New Hall is an impressive statement of the power and wealth of its creator, who made sure the statement was quite clear by having her initials ES (Elizabeth Shrewsbury) carved on stone letters at the head of the towers. The hall was notable for the size of its windows and the amount of glass used, which was far more than in similar houses of the period. 'Hardwick Hall, more glass than wall' is a popular rhyming couplet that describes the great house. There are numerous collections of 16th century tapestries, embroidery, furniture and portraits. Walled courtyards enclose fine gardens, orchards and a herb garden, and the surrounding country park contains rare breeds of cattle and sheep. The remains of Hardwick Old Hall can still be found in the grounds. For many years the Shrewsburys were responsible for the guardianship of the beleaguered Mary Queen of Scots. The dynasty created by Bess included many powerful descendants including the Dukes of Devonshire, Newcastle, Portland and Kingston. The site is currently managed by the National Trust. Tel: 01246 850430.

Hardwick Old Hall See Hardwick Hall

Highest point At 2088ft (636m), Kinder Scout (GR: SK086875) is the highest point both in the Peak District and in Derbyshire. See separate entry.

Hob Hurst's House See Beeley Moor

Howden Reservoir A Y-shaped reservoir, one of three in the Upper Derwent Valley. The longest arm is $1\frac{1}{2}$ miles (2km) in length. The reservoir is bounded at the southern end by Howden Dam; below this, the River Derwent flows immediately into Derwent Reservoir (see separate entry) and subsequently into Ladybower Reservoir. Other tributaries include the River Westend, Howden Clough and Linch Clough. To the east of the reservoir stands the hill of Featherbed Moss, one of the highest tops in the area at 1788ft (545m), and one of several tops of that name in the area.

Ilam Park $4\frac{1}{2}$ miles (7km) northwest of Ashbourne. A 158 acre (64ha) country park situated on both banks of the river Manifold. The property consists of Ilam Hall and remnants of its gardens, an ancient semi-natural woodland – Hinkley Wood – designated as a Site of Special Scientific Interest, noted for its small-leaved and large-leaved limes and their hybrids. It is under the ownership of the National Trust and managed as part of the Trust's South Peak Estate. Ilam Hall, built 1821–7, had been sold for demolition by the early 1930s. The demolition was well advanced when Sir Robert McDougal bought the hall for the Trust, on the understanding that it be used as an International Youth Hostel. Ilam Hall is currently leased to the Youth Hostels Association (YHA). Tel: 01335 350503.

Interesting facts — The Bonsall World Championship Hen Races are held in the car park of the **Barley Mow** pub, The Dale, Bonsall, Matlock, every year on the first Saturday in August over a 65ft (20m) course. The event has won international acclaim and has been featured on Sky TV and by the BBC *Countryfile* programme. The races are an ancient tradition revived over 15 years ago by landlord Alan Webster. Anyone with a hen can take part. In first place in 2005 and 2006, achieving the title 'The World's Fastest Hen', was Wendy, a local hen trained and raced by local lads George and Andy. The Barley Mow is also at the centre of an area known as the world's number one hot spot for **UFOs**. The most famous sighting was made by Sharon Rowlands on 5 October 2000; her camcorder film of what appeared to be a UFO captured the craft moving towards her and lasted for six and a half minutes. It is considered one of the best UFO films ever recorded and has been inspected by NASA. Sharon was quoted as saying: 'I was filming it from around two miles away. It resembled a giant disc with a bite taken out of the bottom. It had yellow, orange and blue lights with intricate markings and a dark circle in the centre. As it hovered over the woods it seemed to expand and get small again, it came really close at one point and I thought it was going to land in the field.' There have been many similar sightings in the Bonsall area; it is thought that in a single four-month period there were over 20 sightings, and the total figure for the past 30 years is well over 100. Although **Derby** is one of the areas of Britain furthest from the sea, it holds a special place in the history of marine safety – it was as MP for Derby that Samuel Plimsoll introduced his bills for a 'Plimsoll line' (marking the level to which a ship can be safely loaded). **Oliver Smith**, a schoolboy from Crich, was appointed president of the Amber Valley Liberal Democrats for 2006. He was elected unopposed as president at the November 2005 Annual General Meeting of the branch, of which he had been a member since he was eight, and took up the one-year post on 1 January 2006 when he was just 12 years, 9 months and 13 days old, making him the youngest branch party president in British political history. His mother, Kate Smith, was the unsuccessful candidate for Amber Valley in the 2005 general election. Smith succeeded 55-year-old Keith Falconbridge, who became chairman. Smith's campaign points included the lowering of the voting age from 18 to 16 and the abolition of university tuition fees. The Barley Mow is not the only Derbyshire pub to play host to a world championship; **Ye Olde Royal Oak**, Wetton, near Ashbourne, entertains toe wrestlers from far and wide every summer for the official world championship.

Kedleston Hall — 4 miles (6km) northwest of Derby. The seat of the Curzon family, who have owned the estate at Kedleston since at least 1297, living in a succession of manor houses near to or on the site of the present hall. The present house was commissioned by Sir Nathaniel Curzon (later 1st Baron Scarsdale) in 1759. Designed by Palladian architects James Paine and Matthew Brettingham, it was loosely based on an original plan by Andrea Palladio for the never-built Villa Mocenigo. The house boasts the most complete and least altered sequence of Robert Adam interiors in England, and the state rooms retain their collections of paintings and original furniture. The Eastern Museum houses a range of objects collected by Lord Curzon when Viceroy of India, 1899–1905. The gardens have been partly restored to an 18th century 'pleasure ground' and the surrounding park, also designed by Adam, includes a fine bridge, fishing pavilion and series of lakes and cascades. All Saints' Church (in the ownership of the Churches Conservation Trust) is the only survivor of the medieval village of Kedleston, and contains a collection of monuments and memorials to the Curzons. The house is now managed by the National Trust. Tel: 01332 842191.

Kinder Downfall — The highest waterfall in the Peak District, at 98ft (30m). It lies on the River Kinder, where it flows west over the edge of Kinder Scout (see separate entry). The waterfall was formerly known as Kinder Scut, and it is from this that the plateau derives its name. In certain wind conditions (notably when there is a strong west wind), the water is blown back on itself, and the resulting cloud of spray can be seen from several miles away. Below the Downfall the River Kinder flows into Kinder Reservoir.

Kinder Scout — A moorland plateau (and mountain) in the Dark Peak. Part of the moor, at 2088ft (636m), is the highest point both in the Peak District and in Derbyshire. It is accessible from the villages of Hayfield and Edale in the High Peak. To the north across the Snake Pass lie the high moors of Bleaklow and Black Hill, which are of similar height. The plateau was the target of a mass trespass in 1932, which resulted in a UK-wide rethink of access to public footpaths. Both Kinder Scout and the moors to the north are now popular hiking locations crossed by the Pennine Way; this has resulted in the erosion of the underlying peat, necessitating repair work by Derbyshire County Council and the Peak District National Park authority.

Ladybower Reservoir — The lowest of three Y-shaped reservoirs in the Upper Derwent Valley. It was built 1935–45 and at 3 miles (5km) long was the largest reservoir in England at the time of its construction. See also Howden Reservoir, Derwent Reservoir.

Longshaw Estate — 7½ miles (12km) southwest of Sheffield. An area of moorland, woodland and farmland within the Peak District National Park and which has been in the ownership of the National Trust since 1931. Wildlife on the estate ranges from rare birds to hairy wood ants. Quarrying for millstones took place on the estate from 1466 until the 1970s and numerous abandoned millstones are still to be found in and around the vicinity of the former quarry sites. Tel: 01433 631708.

Mam Tor — A 1696ft (517m) peak near Castleton in the High Peak. Its name literally translates as 'Heights of the Mother' and it is also known as the Shivering Mountain because of the instability of its lower shale layers. The summit is encircled by a late Bronze Age and early Iron Age hill fort. Radiocarbon analysis suggests it was occupied from c.1200 BC. The earliest remaining features are two Bronze Age burial mounds, one just below the summit and the other on the summit itself. At a later stage over 100 small platforms were levelled into the hill near the summit, allowing inhabited timber huts to be constructed. At the base of the Tor and nearby are three show caves: Speedwell Cavern, Blue John Cavern and Treak Cliff Cavern, where lead, Blue John and other minerals were once mined. The Tor sits at the top of Winnats Pass (a steep narrow gorge which was once a limestone cave) and forms the eastern end of Rushup Edge. It dominates the western end of the 'Great Ridge' which separates the two arms of the Hope Valley: the valley of the River Noe (Edale) to the north, and the Peakshole Water (Castleton) to the south. This ridge forms a classic walking route from Mam Tor to Back Tor and then to the conical peak of Lose Hill at the eastern end.

Matlock — 10 miles (16km) southwest of Chesterfield. The county town of Derbyshire is situated at the southeast edge of the Peak District, in an area known as the Derbyshire Dales, which includes the towns of Wirksworth and Bakewell. A former spa town, Matlock lies on the River Derwent, and has prospered from both the hydrotherapy industry and the mills constructed on the river ever since thermal springs were discovered in 1698. The population increased rapidly in the 1800s, largely due to the building of hugely popular hydros. At one stage there were around 20 of these, mostly on Matlock Bank. The largest, built in 1853 by John Smedley, closed in the 1950s, when it became home to Derbyshire County Council. Matlock is also home to Derbyshire Dales District Council and Matlock Town Council. There has been relatively little industry in the area since the decline of the mills and many workers now commute to Chesterfield and the South Yorkshire conurbation. The ITV series *Peak Practice* used locations in Matlock although its main location is the nearby village of Crich.

Melbourne Hall — Church Square, Melbourne, 7 miles (11km) south of Derby. Once the home of Victorian Prime Minister William Lamb who, as the 2nd Viscount Melbourne, gave his name to Melbourne, Australia. Having belonged to the bishops of Carlisle in the 12th century, the house was partly rebuilt in 1629–31 for Sir John Coke by Derbyshire mason Richard Shepherd. In 1692 it was inherited by architect Thomas Coke (1675–1727), who laid out the formal gardens that survive, with professional assistance from Henry Wise, between about 1696 and 1706. Among fine wrought iron made for the grounds by Robert Bakewell is an arbour known as the 'birdcage'. The gardens also feature pools, vistas and a yew tunnel. Redecorations of the interior were carried out throughout the 18th century. In 1745 Joseph Hall of Derby was paid for the chimneypiece in the Great Dining Room; in the 1760s stucco by Samuel Franceys was executed; and for the 1st Viscount Melbourne, in 1772, further interior alterations were carried out by leading Derbyshire architect Joseph Pickford. The 2nd Lord Melbourne, Queen Victoria's Prime Minister, was separated from his wife, Lady Caroline Lamb, in 1825, when her liaison with Lord Byron had become notorious. Another Prime Minister, Lord Palmerston, married Elizabeth Lamb and inherited Melbourne. The house is now the seat of Lord Ralph and Lady Kerr. Tel: 01332 862502.

National Tramway Museum — Crich, 7 miles (11km) east of Matlock. Based in Crich Tramway Village, a recreated period village near the modern village of Crich, the National Tramway Museum is home to over 50 trams from the UK and abroad. Crich Tramway Village features a period street, through which trams travel before continuing on for a mile into the countryside. Tel: 01773 854321.

Nine Ladies — 5 miles (8km) southeast of Bakewell. A Bronze Age stone circle located on Stanton Moor, within the Peak District National Park. Druids and pagans occasionally celebrate summer solstice here. There are nine surviving stones in the circle, but excavations have shown that there were once at least ten and possibly 11. The small 'King Stone' lies 125ft (40m) from the circle and is clearly visible from it. The site is owned by English Heritage. Tel: 01629 816200.

Ogston Reservoir — $^1/_2$ mile (0.8km) north of Brackenfield, 5 miles (8km) east of Matlock. Operated by Severn Trent Water, the reservoir takes its water from the River Amber and was originally created to supply the National Coal Board's Carbonisation Plant at Wingerworth; it now supplies water for the local area and is used as a holding ground for water for nearby Carsington Reservoir. The reservoir covers 200 acres (80ha) and holds 1.3 billion gallons (5910 megalitres) of water. It also provides many leisure activities including sailing, windsurfing and trout fishing. It is especially well known for its birdlife and over 200 species have been recorded including Wilson's phalarope, Sabine's gull and long-tailed skua. Ellen MacArthur, who on 7 February 2005 broke the world record for the fastest solo circumnavigation of the globe, trained to become a yachtswoman on Ogston Reservoir.

Old Manor, The — Norbury, 7 miles (11km) southwest of Ashbourne. A medieval hall built of stone between the 13th and 15th centuries, the Old Manor is noted for its architectural features including a rare king post, a medieval fireplace, a Tudor door and some 17th century Flemish glass. Its accompanying gardens include a parterre herb garden. The manor has been in the ownership of the National Trust since 1987. Tel: 01283 585337.

Pavilion Gardens — St John's Road, Buxton. A 23 acre (9ha) pleasure garden opened on 11 May 1871, and containing a pavilion opened the same August and a concert hall (now known as the Octagon), designed by Buxton architect Robert Rippon Duke and opened in 1875. In 1927, the Buxton Corporation acquired the buildings, gardens and pleasure grounds and the council have managed the site ever since. The former lounge area, destroyed in a fire in 1983, was fully restored two years later. In the autumn of 2003 work was completed to restore the Grade II listed gardens to their former Victorian splendour. Tel: 01298 23114.

Peak Cavern Castleton, 8 miles (13km) northeast of Buxton. Also known as the Devil's Arse, the Peak Cavern is one of the four show caves in the Hope Valley. Peakshole Water flows through and out of the cave. Unlike the other show caves in the area, it is entirely natural, and the cave system is the largest in the Peak District. The Peak Cavern entrance is the largest in Britain and until 1915 was home to a small village devoted to rope making, while the depths of the cave were known as a haven for bandits. Several passages lead from the entrance, known as the Vestibule. The only one open to the public is known as Lumbago Walk. The route continues through two main caverns, the Great Cave and Roger Rains House, and into a passage, Pluto's Dining Room. This is the furthest point currently open to the public, but the show cave used to extend considerably further, down the Devil's Staircase to the Halfway House and then along an underground stream known as the Inner Styx, via a series of bridges and under Five Arches. At this point, several routes are open to cavers. The main path, to the right, leads to Victoria Aven, a sizeable shaft, and on to Far Sump, through which lies the Far Sump Extension. This area was first explored in 1980, but difficult access limited discoveries until routes through from Speedwell Cavern and James Hall's Over Engine Mine were opened in 1996. This permitted further exploration, and in 1999 Titan (see separate entry), the deepest pitch in Britain, was discovered.

Peak District A hilly region that lies mainly in northern Derbyshire, also covering parts of Cheshire, Greater Manchester, Staffordshire, South Yorkshire and West Yorkshire. Most of the area falls within the Peak District National Park, whose designation in 1951 made it the first national park in the UK. A region of great diversity, it is conventionally split into the northern Dark Peak, where most of the moorland is found and whose geology is gritstone, and the southern White Peak, where most of the population lives and where the geology is mainly limestone-based. The Peak District forms the southern end of the Pennines and much of the area is uplands above 1000ft (305m). Despite its name, the landscape lacks sharp peaks, being characterised by rounded hills and gritstone escarpments (edges). The area is surrounded by major conurbations including Manchester, Sheffield, Derby and Stoke-on-Trent. The National Park covers 555 square miles (1438 sq km).

Peak District Mining Museum South Parade, Matlock Bath. The museum features a recreation of a lead mine in which visitors may safely explore how the miners, and in particular children, once had to work in this dangerous industry. Tel: 01629 583834.

Pennine Way A National Trail that runs 268 miles (463km) from Edale, in the northern Derbyshire Peak District, north through the Yorkshire Dales and the Northumberland National Park, and ends at Kirk Yetholm, just inside the Scottish border. Inspired by similar trails in the USA, particularly the Appalachian Trail, the path was the idea of journalist and rambler Tom Stephenson. He proposed the concept in an article for the *Daily Herald* in 1935, later lobbying Parliament for the creation of an official trail. The final section of the path was declared open in a ceremony on Malham Moor on 24 April 1965. The path runs along the Pennine hills, sometimes described as the 'backbone of England'. According to the National Trails agency, a walker covering the entire Pennine Way must navigate 287 gates, 249 wooden stiles, 183 stone stiles and 204 bridges. Of the complete route 198 miles (319km) is on public footpaths, 69 miles (112km) on public bridleways and 20 miles (32km) on public highways. Walkers are aided by the provision of 458 waymarks. The route passes close to or through Edale, Kinder Scout, Bleaklow, Black Hill, Saddleworth Moor, Littleborough, Stoodley Pike, Todmorden, Hebden Bridge, Wadsworth Moor, Keighley Moor, Elslack Moor, Lothersdale, Settle, Malham, Fountains Fell, Pen-y-ghent, Horton in Ribblesdale, Dodd Fell Hill, Hawes, Great Shunner Fell, Kisdon, Kisdon Force, Keld, Tan Hill, Middleton-in-Teesdale and the Tees valley, High Cup, Great Dun Fell, Cross Fell, Alston, Haltwhistle, Hadrian's Wall, Shitlington Crags, Windy Gyle, The Cheviot, and finally, Kirk Yetholm. A popular guide was written and illustrated by author Alfred Wainwright, whose offer to buy a half-pint of beer for anyone who finished the Pennine Way with a copy of his book is estimated to have cost him up to £15,000 until his death in 1991. To cater for those who would rather ride than walk a Pennine Bridleway has recently opened; generally parallel to the Pennine Way, the route starts slightly further south in Derbyshire. Cross Fell (see Cumbria) is the highest point of the Pennine Way.

Peveril Castle Castleton, 8 miles (13km) northeast of Buxton. Also known as Peak Castle, Peveril Castle stands on a hill overlooking the village with views across the Hope Valley and Cave Dale. The castle is named after William Peverel, an illegitimate son of William I, who was granted royal manors of the Peak shortly after the Norman Conquest in 1066 and thus administered the Royal Forest of the Peak on behalf of the king. The castle consisted of a small square keep, which still stands, and curtain walls. Traces of other buildings are visible within the walls, including the site of a hall that would have been the main accommodation. Peverel's son, another William, fell into disfavour with Henry I, and in 1155 the king confiscated the Peverel estates. The castle has belonged to the Crown or the Duchy of Lancaster since, and is now in the care of English Heritage. Tel: 01433 620613.

Pickford's House Museum Friar Gate, Derby. A Georgian town house built by prominent architect Joseph Pickford in 1770 and now Grade I listed. Features include grand reception rooms, sweeping staircases with priceless furniture and paintings to match. The kitchen and back kitchen have been reconstructed as they were c.1830, together with a cellar, pantry and a housekeeper's cupboard. The museum is owned and run by Derby City Council. Tel: 01332 255363.

Poole's Cavern Green Lane, Buxton. A show cave located in Buxton Country Park. A natural cavern, it forms part of the Wye system and lies within a Site of Special Scientific Interest, the habitat of numerous species of rare flora. The name derives from an outlaw, Poole, said to have lived here in the 15th century. Archaeological explorations in 1981 and 1983 have suggested that the cave was occupied from the Bronze Age. Some of the finds have been interpreted as suggesting that one of the chambers was used for religious purposes by Romano-Britons; alternatively the cave may have been a metalworkers' workshop. Officially opened as a show cave in 1853 by the 6th Duke of

Devonshire, it was already a tourist attraction, being listed as one of the Wonders of the Peak by Charles Cotton in 1683. Mary Queen of Scots is rumoured to have been an early visitor. Features of interest include large stalactites/stalagmites called the 'Flitch of Bacon' and 'Mary Queen of Scots' Pillar', as well as stalagmites with a porous texture and 'poached egg' colour, which has been attributed to minerals leached from lime-burning on Grin Low above. The cave system is believed to extend further, but has not been explored. Tel: 01298 26978.

Renishaw Hall — Renishaw, 5 miles (8km) northeast of Chesterfield. The hall dates from the 17th century and has been the family home of the Sitwells for more than 350 years. Sir Sitwell Sitwell made additions to the building c.1800. Not currently open to the public, the hall has notable gardens including an Italianate garden laid out by Sir George Sitwell (1860–1943). Tel: 01246 432310.

Repton School — Repton, 6 miles (10km) southwest of Derby. Founded in 1557, Repton is one of the most famous co-educational public schools in the UK. Some of the remains of the oldest buildings date back to the 6th century. The boys' houses are Cross, Latham, New, Orchard, Priory and School; the girls' houses are Abbey, Field, Garden and Mitre. Old Reptonians include Harold Abrahams, 100m gold medallist in the 1924 Olympics; author Roald Dahl; cricketer C B Fry; journalist and television presenter Jeremy Clarkson; actor Basil Rathbone; novelist and screenwriter Christopher Isherwood; Michael Ramsey, Archbishop of Canterbury; and Graeme Garden, comedian and member of The Goodies.

Riber Castle — Riber, 1 mile (1.6km) south of Matlock. Built by John Smedley on a hill overlooking the town of Matlock in 1862 as his private home, the mock-Gothic house is currently in disrepair, although plans to turn the shell into apartments received planning consent in early 2006. It is built of gritstone from a local quarry which was pulled up the 600ft (183m) hill by a series of pulleys. From the 1960s to September 2000 it was home to a wildlife park which included exhibits of British and European fauna. Riber Zoo, as it was known, eventually shut due to criticism of the conditions of the animals it was housing. The castle, and the town of Matlock, featured prominently in Shane Meadows' film *Dead Man's Shoes* (2004).

Rivers — The **Derwent** is a tributary of the River Trent (see Nottinghamshire), rising in the Peak District at Bleaklow east of Glossop and flowing southeast through the Upper Derwent Valley with its three reservoirs, Howden Reservoir, Derwent Reservoir and Ladybower Reservoir (see separate entries). It then passes through Bamford, Hathersage, Grindleford and Baslow, as well as the Chatsworth Park estate, and is joined by the River Wye. After passing through Darley Dale, the Derwent reaches Matlock. It flows past Cromford and through the Crich Chase Nature Reserve. Finally, the river continues south through Derby to join the Trent south of the city. Its total length is approximately 60 miles (96km).

The **Dove** rises on the slopes of Axe Edge, close to the Leek–Buxton road, and runs southwards for 45 miles (72km) to join the River Trent at Newton Solney, running for much of its course with one bank in Derbyshire and one in Staffordshire. From Hartington to its confluence with the River Manifold at Ilam the river flows through a scenic limestone valley, usually known simply as Dovedale. The Dove is a walker's river in that it is possible to walk down the first 20 miles (32km) of its course.

The **Noe** is a tributary of the Derwent. It flows for 7½ miles (12km) from its source, the confluence of two streams running off Kinder Scout in the Peak District, east through Edale and then southeast through the village of Hope. The river flows into the Derwent 0.6 miles (1km) south of Bamford. The entire length of the river is closely followed by the Hope Valley (Manchester to Sheffield) railway line. The portion of the river downstream of Hope, along with the valley of the River Noe's main tributary, Peakshole Water, is known as the Hope Valley.

The **Wye** is a tributary of the Derwent. Rising just west of Buxton, on Axe Edge Moor, it then flows east along a route roughly followed by the A6 road. It enters the Peak District, flows just south of Tideswell, then through Ashford in the Water and Bakewell and south of Haddon Hall, before meeting the Derwent at Rowsley. The main tributary of the Wye is the River Lathkill, which enters 1 mile (1.6km) from its mouth.

Sett Valley Trail — A 2½ mile (4km) cycle and bridleway linking the village of Hayfield and the town of New Mills. It runs parallel to the River Sett and follows the trackbed of a former branch railway line from New Mills Central station to Hayfield, which opened in 1868 and closed in 1970. The Pennine Bridleway follows the section of the trail between Hayfield and Birch Vale.

Speedwell Cavern — Castleton, 8 miles (13km) northeast of Buxton. One of four show caves in the Hope Valley. This cave is mostly flooded. Boat trips take tourists around the cave including to the edge of a so-called bottomless well. A connection was discovered in 1999 between the Speedwell Cavern system and Titan (see separate entry), the largest natural cave in the UK. Tel: 01433 620512.

Sport

cricket — **Derbyshire County Cricket Club** was formed in 1870, joining the County Championship in 1895. The club's single championship success came in 1936. Its limited overs team is called the Derbyshire Phantoms (formerly Derbyshire Scorpions). Its home ground is the County Ground, Nottingham Road, Derby. Matches have also been played at Buxton, Chesterfield, Heanor and Ilkeston as well as at Burton on Trent in Staffordshire. Tel: 01332 383211.

football — **Chesterfield** were founded in 1867 and admitted to the Football League in 1899. Nicknamed the Spireites after the twisted spire of St Mary and All Saints' church (they are sometimes also known as the Blues), they play at the Recreation Ground, Saltergate, Chesterfield. The club's home strip is blue shirts and white shorts. Chesterfield reached the FA Cup semi-finals in 1997, drawing 3–3 with Premiership Middlesbrough before losing the replay. As well as its obvious rivalry with fellow Derbyshire side Derby County, the club also has a fierce rivalry with neighbouring Mansfield Town (see Nottinghamshire). Tel: 01246 209765.

Derby County were founded in 1884 as an offshoot of Derbyshire County Cricket Club. The Rams, as they are known, initially played at the Racecourse Ground, like their parent cricket club. The club was a founder member of the Football League when it was launched in 1888. In 1895 it moved to the Baseball Ground (so called because it was previously used for baseball), its home for the next 102 years, and adopted its traditional colours of black and white. Derby's only honour was an FA Cup win in 1946 until in 1967, the now-legendary Brian Clough became manager (in partnership with assistant manager Peter Taylor) and led them to their greatest glories. The club were promoted to the First Division in 1969 and won the Football League championship in 1972 and 1975. Derby now play at Pride Park Stadium, Derby. Tel: 0871 472 1884.

Stainsby Mill — 7 miles (11km) southeast of Chesterfield. A 19th century flour water mill in full working order, and under the ownership of the National Trust. The mill was originally constructed in 1849–50 and was restored in 1991. It is located in the grounds of Hardwick Hall (see separate entry), another National Trust property.

Sudbury Hall — Sudbury, 9 miles (15km) south of Ashbourne. The house was built in the 1660s and is notable for its fine long gallery. Inside there are a mixture of architectural styles with beautiful carvings, painting and plasterwork, while the National Trust Museum of Childhood is housed in the 19th century service wing. The decoration includes woodcarving by Grinling Gibbons, superb plasterwork and painted murals and ceilings by Louis Laguerre, and there is a fine collection of portraits, their subjects including Charles II's mistresses. The great staircase is one of the most elaborate of its kind in an English house. Several rooms featured in the BBC's *Pride and Prejudice* (1995). There are formal gardens with a tree-fringed lake. The house is now owned by the National Trust. Tel: 01283 585337.

Sutton Scarsdale Hall — 1½ miles (2.5km) south of Arkwright Town, 5 miles (8km) east of Chesterfield. A ruined former Georgian mansion with gardens. Built in 1724, it has been roofless since c.1920 when parts of the building were dismantled and sold, some shipped to the USA. Features inside include traces of plasterwork. Now in the care of English Heritage.

Tapton House — Brimington Road, Chesterfield. Built in the late 18th century and once the house of George Stephenson, the father of British railways. The grounds are now used by the Tapton Park Innovation Centre and contain a small public park featuring an earthwork labyrinth. The building itself used to be a school, and is now the higher education campus for Chesterfield College.

Thornbridge Hall — Great Longston, 3 miles (5km) northwest of Bakewell. The Grade II listed house was the seat of the Longsdon family from the 12th to the late 18th century. In 1790 the hall was bought for £10,000 by Manchester merchant John Morewood, who made his money selling linen to St Petersburg in Russia. The Morewood family considerably enlarged the house and in 1859 Frederick Craven rebuilt it in Jacobean revival style, installing a William Morris/Edward Burne-Jones window in the Great Hall. In 1896 Sheffield businessman and lawyer George Marples extended the house to nearly its present form, built lodges and cottages, landscaped the park and gardens, added his own private railway station, and acquired the Watson buffet fountain from Chatsworth House. Sheffield City Council took over the house in 1945 and it became a teacher training college. In later years, it was used as an educational and conference centre, providing residential facilities for teachers and pupils. In 1997 the Hunt family began restoring the gardens and removed inappropriate additions to the house to reveal its proper proportions. The hall has been owned by Emma and Jim Harrison since 2002. A Great Western Railway GWR 6959 Class or Modified Hall class steam locomotive no. 6964, built in May 1944, was named *Thornbridge Hall* in June 1947. Tel: 01629 640617.

Tissington Hall — Tissington, 5 miles (8km) north of Ashbourne. A large Jacobean mansion, home to the Fitzherbert family for more than 400 years. The house was built in 1609 for Francis Fitzherbert and is thought to have incorporated parts of an earlier hall. The property had become a seat of the Fitzherberts c.1465 when Nicholas, second son of John Fitzherbert of Somersal, married the Tissington heiress. During the Civil War Tissington was garrisoned by Colonel Fitzherbert in support of the king. Improvements were made to the house by William Fitzherbert in 1670 and it was remodelled at the end of the 18th century. A major restoration took place in 1910 when the library wing was added. The roof is hidden by a parapet and is topped by ornate chimneys. The Fitzherbert coat of arms is portrayed above the two-storey porch and the windows are mullioned and transomed. In front of the house is a low wall with a fine central gateway. Tel: 01335 352200.

Titan Cave — Discovered on 1 January 1999, Titan is the biggest natural shaft in the UK, standing at 464ft (141.5m). The choke through which it was found is a major feature of Peak Cavern's (see separate entry) Far Sump Extension and has been known about since 1981 when Far Sump was first passed. Tel: 07775 518 626.

University of Derby — Receiving its official redesignation in 1993, Derby was the only university in the UK to be upgraded directly from a higher education college to a university, along with all the polytechnics in 1992. The main campus is on Kedleston Road, Allestree in the northwest of Derby, while the Devonshire campus in Buxton is centred on the former Devonshire Royal Hospital, a Grade II* listed building which dominates the local landscape and has a dome over 150ft (46m) in diameter, bigger than that of St Paul's Cathedral in London. It was formally opened by Prince Charles in 2006. A new building for Arts, Design and Technology students on Markeaton Street in Derby opened in 2007. Health and Psychology courses are currently based at the Mickleover campus, formerly Bishop Lonsdale College of Education. Tel: 01332 590500.

Well dressing — A custom most closely associated with the Peak District, although practised in various parts of rural England, in which wells are decorated with designs created from flower petals. Its origins are alternatively said to lie in pagan tradition or in giving thanks for the purity of the water drawn from certain wells during the period of the Black Death. It is often said to have originated in Tissington in Derbyshire, though other claims can be made for Eyam and Stoney Middleton. The custom almost died out, but it was revived in the 1920s and 1930s largely through the efforts of Edwin Shimwell, and has since spread to numerous villages and small towns in Derbyshire, Staffordshire, South Yorkshire, Cheshire, and even as far as Much Wenlock in Shropshire. Wooden frames are constructed and covered with clay, mixed with water and salt. A design, often of a religious theme, is sketched on paper and traced onto the clay. The picture is then filled in with natural materials, predominantly flower petals and mosses, but also beans, seeds and small cones. Each group uses its own technique; in some areas only natural materials are used while in others modern materials are utilised to simplify production.

Willersley Castle — Cromford, 2 miles (3km) south of Matlock. Commissioned by industrialist Sir Richard Arkwright, the 200-year-old building occupies a magnificent position on the edge of the Peak District overlooking the River Derwent and within the Derwent Valley Mills World Heritage Site (see separate entry). Designed in Georgian style, Willersley Castle stands in 60 acres (24ha) of grounds ranging from meadows to limestone crags. The Grade II listed building is now a hotel complex.

Wingfield Manor — 11 miles (18km) south of Chesterfield. The ruins of a medieval manor house arranged round a pair of courtyards, with a huge undercrofted great hall and a defensible tower 72ft (22m) tall. This monument to late medieval 'conspicuous consumption' was built in the 1440s for the wealthy Ralph, Lord Cromwell, Treasurer of England, on the site of a 12th century castle. The design was the inspiration for Hampton Court in London. It was later bought by the 2nd Earl of Shrewsbury and eventually passed to the 6th Earl, Bess of Hardwick's husband. The Earl was entrusted with the care of Mary, Queen of Scots when she was detained from 1569 onwards, and she was imprisoned at Wingfield in 1569, 1584 and 1585. It may have been while here that she met Anthony Babington, whose family lived at Dethick nearby, and who organised the abortive Babington Plot. During the Civil War the manor was in the hands of another Earl of Shrewsbury, a supporter of Parliament. Located in what was then a strategic position near England's main north–south artery, the manor was taken by the Royalists in 1643 but retaken after a siege by Parliamentary forces in 1644. It was partially demolished at the end of the war, but renovated some years later for Immanuel Halton, an astronomer. Wingfield Manor has been deserted since the 1770s and is now in the care of English Heritage. Tel: 01773 832060.

Winster Market House — Winster, 4 miles (6km) west of Matlock. A building dating from the late 17th or early 18th century, a period when cheese and cattle fairs featured prominently in the daily life of the area. The house has been in the ownership of the National Trust since 1906 and was the Trust's first acquisition in the Peak District. Tel: 01335 350503.

Some famous people born in Derbyshire

Bates, Alan (actor) (1934–2003)	Allestree
Bodell, Jack (boxer) (1940–)	Swadlincote
Booth, Catherine (mother of the Salvation Army) (1829–90)	Ashbourne
Brindley, James (engineer) (1716–72)	Tunstead
Cook, Thomas (travel operator) (1808–92)	Melbourne
Davis, Fred (snooker player) (1913–98)	Chesterfield
Davis, Joe (snooker player) (1901–78)	Whitwell
Edwards, Monica (children's writer) (1912–98)	Belper
Flamsteed, John (astronomer) (1646–1719)	Denby
Hurt, John (actor) (1940–)	Chesterfield
Knight, Laura (impressionist painter) (1877–1972)	Long Eaton
Lindsay, Robert (actor) (1949–)	Ilkleston
Lowe, Arthur (actor) (1915–82)	Hayfield
MacArthur, Ellen (sailor) (1976–)	Whatsandwell
Outram, Benjamin (engineer) (1764–1805)	Alfreton
Powys, John Cowper (writer) (1872–1963)	Shirley
Richardson, Samuel (writer) (1689–1761)	Mackworth
Roache, William (television actor) (1932–)	Ilkeston
Seward, Anna (writer) (1747–1809)	Eyam
Skinner, Dennis (politician) (1932–)	Clay Cross
Smith, Oliver (politician) (1993–)	Crich
Spencer, Herbert (philosopher) (1820–1903)	Derby
Spriggs, Elizabeth (actress) (1929–)	Buxton
Spry, Constance (florist and author) (1886–1960)	Derby
Stevenson, Robert (film director) (1905–86)	Buxton
Uttley, Alison (writer) (1884–1976)	Cromford
Wallis, Barnes (scientist and inventor) (1887–1979)	Ripley
Wilson, Ray (footballer) (1934–)	Shirebrook
Wright, Joseph (artist) (1734–97)	Derby
Wright, Peter (writer) (1916–95)	Chesterfield

Devon

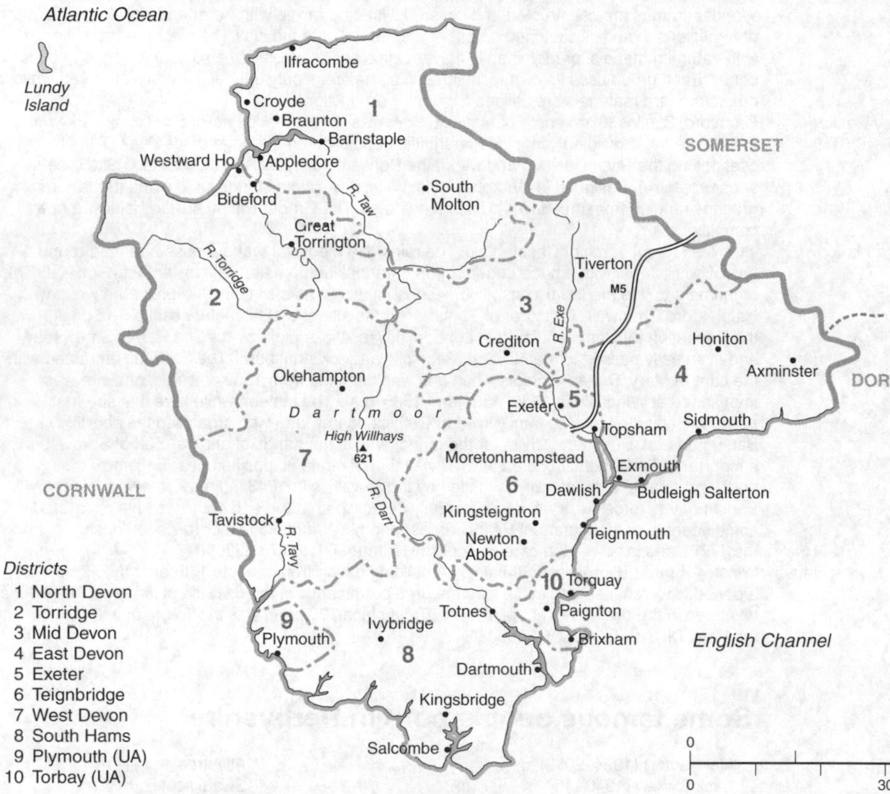
Atlantic Ocean
Lundy Island
Ilfracombe
Croyde
Braunton
Barnstaple
Westward Ho
Appledore
Bideford
South Molton
R. Taw
Great Torrington
R. Torridge
SOMERSET
Tiverton
M5
R. Exe
Crediton
Honiton
Axminster
DORSET
Okehampton
Dartmoor
Exeter
Topsham
Sidmouth
High Willhays
621
Moretonhampstead
Exmouth
Budleigh Salterton
Dawlish
CORNWALL
Kingsteignton
Teignmouth
Tavistock
R. Tavy
R. Dart
Newton Abbot
Torquay
Totnes
Paignton
Ivybridge
Plymouth
Brixham
English Channel
Dartmouth
Kingsbridge
Salcombe
0
20 miles
0
30 km
1
2
3
4
5
6
7
8
9
10
Districts
1 North Devon
2 Torridge
3 Mid Devon
4 East Devon
5 Exeter
6 Teignbridge
7 West Devon
8 South Hams
9 Plymouth (UA)
10 Torbay (UA)

Devon borders Cornwall to the west, Dorset to the east and Somerset to the northeast. It is unique among English counties in having two non-contiguous coastlines, the Bristol Channel washing its northern shores and the English Channel its southern. On 1 April 1998 Plymouth and Torbay became unitary authorities administratively distinct from Devon but remaining within the county boundaries. The county 'town' is the city of Exeter.

The name 'Devon' derives from the Dumnonii, a tribe of Celtic people who inhabited the south-western peninsula of Britain at the time of the Roman invasion in AD 43. After the Roman occupation, a Brythonic kingdom emerged in the West Country based around the old Roman *civitas* of Exeter. It was called, in Latin, Dumnonia and, in the native Brythonic language, Dyfneint, which was eventually corrupted to 'Devon'. The former name of Devonshire is of uncertain origin but is rarely used nowadays except as the title of the aristocratic Cavendish family (who have their main family estates in Derbyshire).

Anglo-Saxons began to settle in Devon during the 7th century although it was not until the 8th century that the region was absorbed into the kingdom of Wessex. After the emergence of the English state in the 9th century Devon became a shire. It has remained a largely agriculture based region ever since, although tourism is now very important to the county's economy.

The landscape of the county is quite diverse. The south is undulating and peppered with small towns and villages surrounding the granite uplands of Dartmoor Forest, the coastal towns of Torquay and Paignton being its principal seaside resorts and Plymouth its major city. The north is very rural with few major towns except Barnstaple, Great Torrington, Bideford and Ilfracombe. East Devon is home to the first seaside resort to be developed in the county, Exmouth, which marks the western end of the Jurassic Coast World Heritage Site. The county's second city and capital, Exeter, lies at the northwestern extremity of the mouth of the River Exe.

Plymouth is the largest city in the traditional county of Devon. It is located at the mouths of the rivers Plym and Tamar and at the head of one of the world's largest and most spectacular natural harbours, Plymouth Sound. The earliest known settlement in Plymouth, a small Iron Age trading port located at Mount Batten in Plymstock, dates to 1000 BC. The small port was later overshadowed by the rise of the fishing village of Sutton.

The city has a rich maritime past and was once one of the two most important Royal Navy bases in the UK, a factor that made it a prime target of the German Luftwaffe during World War II. After the destruction of the dockyards and city centre in the blitz of 1941, Plymouth was rebuilt under the guidance of architect Patrick Abercrombie and is now the largest naval base in western Europe. Important locations in the city include the Royal Citadel, Devonport Dockyard and the Barbican, from where the Pilgrims left for the New World in 1620. People born in Plymouth are known as Plymothians or more pejoratively as Janners. The latter was formerly a term denoting someone born within 10 miles of the sea but has been used in recent years as a derogatory description of lower-class Plymothians. Another common nickname of the area is 'Guzz', a naval term for Devonport, from its original radio call-sign.

Torbay covers the crescent-shaped area around the Atlantic coast of west Devon. It has a unique natural coastal location created by the natural expansion of the settlements around the bay itself. The first recorded reference to 'Torrebay' was in 1401, although it is known that a village existed at Torre before the foundation of the abbey in 1196. In 1892 Torquay was incorporated as a borough and two years later in 1894 Paignton Urban District Council and Brixham Urban District Council were established under the terms of the Local Government Act 1894. The three towns of Brixham, Paignton and Torquay were then joined in 1968 to form Torbay County Borough. Under the local government reorganisation of April 1974, Torbay Borough Council was formed as a district within the Devon county area. On 1 April 1998, Torbay Council was created a unitary authority.

One of the great beauties of Torbay is its unspoilt coastline, which offers breathtaking views. There are around 20 safe beaches and secluded coves along a 22 mile (35km) stretch, aptly referred to as 'The English Riviera'. The coastline, between Sharkham Point in the south and Maidencombe in the north, contains almost infinite variety with beaches and coves, ruined fortresses, bird sanctuaries, golf courses, cliff walks, seafront gardens, fishing harbours and marinas. It also has a proliferation of palm trees, the first batch having been imported in the 1820s. The two headlands of the crescent coast are Hopes Nose in Torquay, and Berry Head in Brixham.

Exeter was inhabited by the Dumnonii before the Roman conquest. The township was consequently named Isca Dumnoniorum on its foundation as a Roman settlement c.AD 50, when it also became the southern starting point for the Fosse Way Roman road. Because it was the main town in southwest England during the Middle Ages, it was subject to a number of sieges. Alfred the Great twice held it against the Danes (877 and 894) but it was taken in 1003. In 1068, after an 18-day siege, Exeter surrendered to William I. Part of the capitulation agreement was that all the nobles in the city would be confirmed in their positions as long as a castle was built. Exeter was held against King Stephen by Baldwin de Redvers in 1140 and submitted only after a three-month siege when supplies of fresh water ran out.

In 1537 Exeter was created a county in itself and remained so until the reorganisation of English local government in 1974. During the Civil War the town was at first a Parliamentary stronghold in the largely Royalist southwest, but it was captured by the Royalists on 4 September 1643 and remained in their control until 1646.

During the Industrial Revolution, Exeter's industry developed on the basis of locally available agricultural products, since the city's location on a fast-flowing river gave it ready access to water power. However when steam power replaced water in the 19th century, Exeter was too far from sources of coal (or iron) to develop further. As a result other manufacturing industries developed, including metalworking, leatherworking, paper and agricultural tools. Like Plymouth, Exeter faced considerable bombing in 1942 as part of the 'Baedeker Blitz'. Forty acres (16ha) of the city, particularly areas adjacent to its central High Street and Sidwell Street, were levelled and many historic buildings were destroyed. Considerable rebuilding took place in the 1950s.

The M5 motorway to Bristol and Birmingham starts at Exeter, and connects at Bristol with the M4 to London. There are two main line railway routes from Exeter to London, the Great Western Main Line via Taunton to Paddington and the West of England Main Line via Salisbury to Waterloo. Exeter International Airport lies east of the city and the local airline, previously called Jersey European and British European but now known as Flybe, is a significant local employer.

Devon	Population			Area	
Districts	*male*	*female*	*total*	*sq miles*	*sq km*
East Devon	59,203	66,317	125,520	315	813
Exeter	53,944	57,132	111,076	18	47
Mid Devon	34,097	35,677	69,774	352	913
North Devon	42,489	45,019	87,508	419	1086
South Hams	39,587	42,262	81,849	342	887
Teignbridge	57,923	63,035	120,958	260	674
Torridge	28,820	30,145	58,965	380	984
West Devon	23,950	24,893	48,843	449	1160
Plymouth Unitary Authority	117,571	123,149	240,720	31	80
Torbay Unitary Authority	61,773	67,933	129,706	24	63
Total	519,357	555,562	1,074,919	2590	6707

Local Attractions and Information

A La Ronde — Summer Lane, Exmouth. This unique 16-sided house was built on the instructions of two spinster cousins, Jane and Mary Parminter, on their return from a grand tour of Europe. Completed c.1796, the house contains many objects brought back by the Parminters. The interior includes a feather frieze and shell-encrusted gallery which, due to its fragility, can only be viewed on closed-circuit television. Now owned by the National Trust. Tel: 01395 265514.

Administrative headquarters — **Devon:** County Hall, Topsham Road, Exeter EX2 4QD. Tel: 01392 38200.
Plymouth: Civic Centre, Plymouth PL1 2AA. Tel: 01752 668000.
Torbay: Town Hall, Castle Circus, Torquay TQ1 3DR. Tel: 01803 201201.

Anderton House — Goodleigh, 3 miles (5km) east of Barnstaple. Anderton House was commissioned in 1969. The inspiration for its profile is taken from the longhouses of Devon and its simple materials, practicality and open-plan rooms are instantly evocative of the 1970s. The low-set roof appears to float cleverly over the spacious living area and its sliding glass walls give wonderful views of the rolling Devon countryside. It is furnished with contemporary curtains, furniture, ceramics and paintings. The Grade II* listed house is owned by the Landmark Trust. Tel: 01628 825925.

Arlington Court — 7 miles (11km) northeast of Barnstaple. Hidden in the wooded valley of the River Yeo on the edge of Exmoor, the Arlington estate houses numerous collections. The house, built in 1822 in Neoclassical style to a design by Thomas Lee, architect of the Wellington Monument in Somerset, contains a collection of model ships and an assortment of shells. Rare 18th century Beauvais tapestries are displayed alongside the Chichester family's personal possessions. The grounds include a formal Victorian garden and a walled kitchen garden. The 2700 acre (1125ha) estate is noted for its lichens and wildlife, and includes a heronry. A large colony of lesser horseshoe bats can be viewed live, roosting in the roof of the house, via the 'bat-cam'. The property is now owned by the National Trust; the stable block contains the Trust's collection of over 50 horse-drawn carriages, from the grand state coach to the practical hansom cab. Tel: 01271 850296.

Axminster — A small market town on the eastern border of Devon, built on a hill overlooking the River Axe which heads towards the English Channel at Axmouth. A market is still held every Thursday. Axminster has given its name to a type of carpet, and the town's history is very much linked to the carpet industry, started by Thomas Whitty in 1755. An Axminster-type power loom is capable of weaving high quality carpets with infinite colours and patterns. While Axminster carpet is still made in the town, this type of carpet (woven rather than tufted and stuck onto a backing) is now manufactured all over the world.

Axminster Museum — Church Street, Axminster. Located in the courtroom of the old Axminster police station, built c.1860. Exhibits portray the unfolding history of Axminster. Tel: 01297 34668.

Babbacombe Cliff Railway — Babbacombe, nr Torquay. The Babbacombe Cliff Railway runs from the top of the cliffs down to small, sheltered Oddiscombe Beach. It was built by Messrs Waygood Otis in 1926.

Barnstaple Castle — Castle Street, Barnstaple. Norman motte and bailey castle erected in the 11th century by Judhael of Totnes. A shell keep was added in the following century but the castle is now lost and only the motte remains.

Barnstaple Heritage Centre — The Strand, Barnstaple. An exhibition of Barnstaple's history from the Anglo-Saxon period to the present day. The centre is housed in Queen Anne's Walk, a beautiful Grade I listed building on the historic quayside consisting of an 18th century colonnade and former Victorian bath-house. Tel: 01271 373003.

Battles — There have been three major battles in Devon: Clyst St Mary, Fenny Bridges and Torrington. See separate table for details.

Bayards Cove Fort — Located on the waterfront at Dartmouth. The small artillery fort was built in the early 16th century to defend the harbour entrance. Tel: 0117 9750700.

Becky Falls Woodland Park — Manaton, 7 miles (11km) northwest of Newton Abbot. Over 60 acres (24ha) of natural oak woodland with a 70ft (21m) waterfall. A Site of Special Scientific Interest and one of Devon's most beautiful places. Tel: 01647 221259.

Berry Head — Situated on the southern extremity of the Torbay coast, Berry Head is the southern headland of Torbay. Certain areas of the site are kept wild and remote so that wildlife can exist undisturbed. It is the location of the atmospheric remains of three Napoleonic forts, built to guard this strategic spot, as well as an air traffic control navigation beacon. It also provides stunning views across Tor Bay to the north and Start Bay to the southwest. Its lighthouse is said to be the highest – at over 200ft (60m) above sea level, the lowest – the light is only 6ft (1.8m) above the ground – and the smallest in Britain but with a beam that can be seen 20 miles (32km) away.

Berry Pomeroy Castle — 2½ miles (4km) east of Totnes. Reputedly one of the most haunted castles in Britain. The original Norman castle was probably founded in the 12th century. The property was sold to Edward Seymour in 1548 and converted into a mansion by later Seymours. William III stayed here after landing at Brixham in 1688. Much of the castle was destroyed by a fire in the 1690s, but the gatehouse, dating from the late 15th century, still stands, with the remains of the Elizabethan mansion behind. The castle is now in the care of English Heritage. Tel: 01803 866618.

Bickleigh Castle — Bickleigh, 4 miles (6km) south of Tiverton. Norman motte and bailey castle dismantled in the mid 12th century. The Courtenay family built a fortified mansion on the site in the 14th century. The castle includes an 11th century chapel, the oldest complete building in Devon. It also has an armoury, guard room, Great Hall, tower and moated gardens. Tel: 01884 855363.

Bicton Park Botanical Gardens — 2 miles (3km) north of Budleigh Salterton. The Grade I listed gardens have several features of historical interest including a palm house built in the 1820s, an Italian garden laid out c.1735 and an American garden designed in the 1830s. Tel: 01395 568465.

Bill Douglas Centre — Prince of Wales Road, Exeter. Located within the University of Exeter, the Bill Douglas Centre for the History of Cinema and Popular Culture contains an enormous collection relating to the history of film and visual media, from shadow puppets to Shirley Temple dolls, magic lanterns to Marilyn Monroe postcards. Founded in 1994, the museum features displays of cinema and pre-cinema artefacts and memorabilia, covering both the 20th century cinema and its stars and optical entertainments from the 19th century and earlier. Tel: 01392 264321.

Bowerman's Nose — A large stack of weathered granite situated on the northern slopes of Hayne Down on Dartmoor, 1 mile (1.6km) from Hound Tor and close to the village of Manaton. According to folklore, a huntsman named Bowerman lived on the moor around 1000 years ago. When chasing a hare he and his pack of dogs unwittingly ran into a coven of witches, overturned their cauldron and disrupted their ceremony. They decided to punish him, and the next time he was hunting, one of the witches turned herself into a hare, and led both Bowerman and his hounds into a mire. As a final punishment, she turned them to stone – the dogs can be seen as a jagged chain of rocks on top of Hound Tor, while the huntsman himself became the rock formation now known as Bowerman's Nose. Locals say that, with a little imagination, it is possible to see something resembling a human face in the rocky outline.

Bradley Manor — ½ mile (0.8km) west of Newton Abbot. An L-shaped manor house built of roughcast local limestone and limewashed white. Richard Yarde inherited the original 13th century building from his grandmother in the early 15th century. Most of the present building dates from c.1420 when Yarde altered and enlarged the house. The chapel was included in this remodelling and this remains, together with the great hall, solar and porch. The gatehouse and some lesser buildings have been destroyed but apart from 19th century castellations the building remains mainly as it was in the 15th century. The house was sold to the Woolner family in 1750 and given to the National Trust in 1938 by Mrs A H Woolner. Tel: 01626 354513.

Branscombe — 4½ miles (7km) east of Sidmouth. The village contains three vernacular buildings now in the care of the National Trust. The last traditional working bakery in Devon, the thatched Old Bakery was operational until 1987; Manor Mill, a watermill now restored to working order, supplied flour to the bakery; and Branscombe Forge is the last surviving thatched forge in England. Tel: 01392 881691.

Brixham Heritage Museum — New Road, Brixham. Contains exhibits relating to the local, social and maritime history of the fishing port of Brixham. Tel: 01803 856267.

Buckfast Abbey — 1 mile (1.6km) north of Buckfastleigh. Founded in 1018 and dedicated to St Mary, the abbey was run by the Cistercian order from 1147 until its dissolution. Today it is a Roman Catholic Benedictine monastery rebuilt between the late 1890s and 1932 on medieval foundations. The abbey has close links with Germany, where many of the monks came from. Nowadays the abbey is more or less self-supporting, selling wine, honey and beeswax and welcoming tourists. Its most successful product is Buckfast Tonic Wine, a strong tonic wine which the monks began making (to a French recipe) in the 1890s. There are many art treasures in the abbey church. Tel: 01364 645500.

Buckland Abbey — Yelverton, 11 miles (18km) north of Plymouth. Tucked away in its own secluded valley above the River Tavy, Buckland was originally a Cistercian monastery. The house, incorporating the remains of the 13th century abbey church, has rich associations with Sir Francis Drake, who bought the property from his seafaring rival Sir Richard Grenville in 1581. It was given to the National Trust in 1948. There are exhibitions on Buckland's history as well as a magnificent monastic barn, estate walks and craft workshops. Recent developments include new interpretive exhibitions and displays, a hand-crafted plasterwork ceiling in the Drake Chamber and the recreation of an Elizabethan garden. Tel: 01822 853607.

Budlake Old Post Office Room — Budlake, 5 miles (8km) northeast of Exeter. A small thatched cottage which once housed the village post office, displayed as it was in the 1950s. Outside is a recreated cottage garden. Tel: 01392 881690.

Burgh Island — Also known as Borough Island. The island lies 200m from the mainland at Bigbury-on-Sea, and is accessible by foot at low water. The Pilchard Inn, a 14th century white-walled pub on the island, is accessed by riding on a giant sea tractor. Agatha Christie was a regular visitor. (GR: SX647438.)

Cadbury Castle — 6 miles (10km) north of Exeter. An Iron Age earthwork 829ft (252m) above sea level, commanding one of the most magnificent views in Devon. Dartmoor and Exmoor are nearly always visible; on a good day the hills of Somerset and Cornwall can be clearly seen. The nearby village of Cadbury is located within Mid Devon local authority area. Historically it formed part of Hayridge Hundred. The parish is situated mainly on a region of red sandstone and is hilly and strikingly beautiful.

Cadhay 1 mile (1.6km) northwest of Ottery St Mary. A 16th century stone courtyard house set in a charming Grade II listed garden. The main part of the house was built c.1550 by local lawyer John Haydon, who married the de Cadhay heiress in 1527. After initial improvements the house has remained untouched since 1617. Cadhay is set among meadows and surrounded by well-tended gardens and is approached by an avenue of lime trees. Tel: 01404 812999.

Castle Drogo Drewsteignton, 11 miles (18km) west of Exeter. Designed by Sir Edwin Lutyens and built 1911–31 for self-made food retailing millionaire Julius Drewe, Castle Drogo is often referred to as the 'last castle to be built in England'. A masterpiece in Dartmoor granite and oak, it blends into the landscape to give the appearance of having been there for centuries. The first 20th century property accepted by the National Trust, it combines the grandeur of a medieval castle with the interior of a country house. Lutyens designed the 12 acre (5ha) garden to reflect the architectural vision of the castle, with wild moorland encroaching into the formal areas. Planted by George Dillistone and influenced by Gertrude Jekyll, the garden has recently undergone major replanting. Varied walks throughout the surrounding Teign Gorge provide spectacular views. Tel: 01647 433306.

Chambercombe Manor Chambercombe Lane, Ilfracombe. The house, containing eight rooms, dates from the 11th century and was mentioned in Domesday Book. The manor remained in the possession of the Champernon family until the 15th century when this branch of the family became extinct, after which it passed through the families of Polglass, Herles and Bonville to the Duke of Suffolk and by his attainder to the Crown. Although it saw days of glory over the following centuries (including a visit from Lady Jane Grey, herself a descendant of the house's original owners the Champernons), for much of its recent past it was used as a farmhouse. The house contains period furnishings from Elizabethan to Victorian times, and other features of note include a secret passage and the Haunted Room. There are 4 acres (1.6ha) of beautiful gardens, wooded areas and ponds. Tel: 01271 862624.

Clovelly 10 miles (26km) west of Bideford. A seaside fishing village on the north Devon coast with a steep cobbled street and no vehicular access. Donkeys and sledges are the only means of transport. The Kingsley Museum is dedicated to Charles Kingsley, author of *The Water Babies*, who grew up in the village. Tel: 01237 431781.

Clyston Mill Broadclyst, 4 miles (6km) northeast of Exeter. A watermill on the River Clyst dating from the 19th century and operational until the 1930s. Now owned by the National Trust. Tel: 01392 462425.

Cockington 1 mile (1.6km) west of Torquay. Scenic village situated in a deep valley and accessed by a single-lane road. The narrow winding lanes open out onto beautiful chocolate box cottages, old English gardens and thatched gift shops. The Church of St George and St Mary is a popular venue for local wedding services. There are 450 acres (180ha) of parkland, woodland and lakes. The lakes themselves are thought to have been created by monks living at nearby Torre Abbey, to supply them with fresh fish. On the edge of the woods is the Gamekeeper's Cottage dating back to the 16th century. In the centre of Cockington among the pretty thatched cottages stands the Forge. One of the most photographed buildings in the UK, this dates from the 14th century, although it has not been used as a working forge since 1971 (it is now a gift shop). The Drum Inn, completed in 1936, also has a thatched roof in keeping with the rest of the area and was designed by Sir Edwin Lutyens. At the end of the cricket field is the stately manor house, Cockington Court, home to various craft studios and an environmental resource centre. Other buildings include Rose Cottage, Warren Barn, and the almshouses.

Coleton Fishacre House and Garden 3 miles (5km) east of Kingswear. The Lutyenesque house was designed in 1925 for Rupert and Lady Dorothy D'Oyly Carte, who created its luxuriant garden with a wide variety of rare and exotic plants, water features and gazebo. Now owned by the National Trust. Tel: 01803 752466.

Compton Castle Marldon, Paignton, 3 miles (5km) west of Torquay. This fortified manor house has been the home of the Gilbert family since 1329, with a single break in the 19th century. Sir Humphrey Gilbert (1539–83), half-brother to Sir Walter Raleigh, was a coloniser of Newfoundland. Rebuilt in the 19th century and given to the National Trust in 1951 by Commander Walter Raleigh Gilbert, the castle is lived in by his son and daughter-in-law. Tel: 01803 842382.

Crownhill Fort Crownhill Fort Road, Plymouth. In the 1860s it was decided to protect naval bases such as Plymouth from attack by land as well as by sea. A chain of forts was built, with Crownhill in the key position in the north of the city. It is now one of only two large works of this kind in England to remain in good condition. The fort was opened to the public in 1995. Tel: 01752 793754.

Culver House Longdown, 5 miles (8km) west of Exeter. Set in a beautiful part of South Devon and surrounded by woodland, Culver was built in 1836 but redesigned by the great Victorian architect Alfred Waterhouse in mock Tudor style. Culver has been used on several occasions as a television and cinema location, notably for the BBC series *Down to Earth*. Tel: 01392 811885.

Custom House Quayside, Exeter. Constructed in 1681, with an elaborate plaster ceiling made by John Abbott of Frithelstock, this is believed to be England's oldest purpose-built custom house. It remained in continuous use by HM Customs and Excise until 1989. Tel: 01392 265169.

Dartington Hall $1\frac{1}{2}$ miles (2.5km) northwest of Totnes. Situated in the area of South Devon known as the South Hams, the medieval courtyard and great hall are surrounded by landscaped gardens. The Glade Temple and Henry Moore sculpture are just two of many features. High Cross House is located on the right hand side of the road to Dartington Hall from Dartington Church. Designed by Swiss-American architect Williams Lescaze in 1932, High Cross houses the Dartington Hall Trust

Archive (Dorothy and Leonard Elmhirst's collection of paintings and ceramics). Tel: 01803 847000.

Dartmoor — An area of moorland in the centre of Devon covering 368 sq miles (953 sq km) and inhabited by almost 35,000 people. Dartmoor was designated a National Park in 1951 and since 1974 has been administered by the Dartmoor National Park Authority. The granite upland dates from the Carboniferous period and the moorland is capped with hundreds of exposed granite hilltops, known as tors, providing habitats for wildlife. Parts of Dartmoor have been used as a military firing range for over 200 years. Red and white posts mark the boundaries of these military areas (red flags are flown on some of the 160 tors when firing is taking place). There is also a large British Army training camp at Okehampton – also the site of an airbase during the World War II. The public enjoy extensive access rights to the rest, and one of the most popular tourist sites is the clapper bridge in the village of Postbridge, midway between Princetown (home of the infamous Dartmoor Prison) and Moretonhampstead. The bridge is made from granite slabs over 13ft (4m) long, almost 7ft (2m) wide and weighing over 8 tons (8128kg) each. It was first recorded in 1380 and built to facilitate the transportation of tin by pack horses to the stannary town of Tavistock. The definitive guide to walking on Dartmoor was written by the Victorian walker William Crossing. He states that a Dartmoor guide placed a bottle for visitors' cards at Cranmere Pool on the northern moor in 1854. This would seem to be the origin of letterboxing, an outdoor hobby that combines elements of orienteering, art and problem-solving. Letterboxers hide small, weatherproof boxes in publicly accessible places and distribute clues to finding the box in printed catalogues, on one of several websites, or by word of mouth. Individual letterboxes usually contain a logbook, a rubber stamp and an ink pad. Finders make an imprint of the letterbox's stamp on their personal logbook, and leave an impression of their personal stamp on the letterbox's logbook as proof of having found the box. See also Ten Tors Challenge.

Dartmouth Castle — 1 mile (1.6km) southeast of Dartmouth. Artillery fort built in 1481 by Dartmouth Corporation to protect the town, the first castle in England specifically designed to withstand artillery. A chain could be run to Kingswear Castle on the opposite bank of the River Dart to protect the estuary. Now owned by English Heritage. Tel: 01803 833588.

Dartmouth Museum — The Butterwalk, Dartmouth. A historic and maritime museum in a former merchant's house dating from c.1640 and containing some of the original panelling. Old photographs and pictures are on display, along with ship models and ships in bottles. Tel: 01803 832923.

Dawlish Museum — Barton Terrace, Dawlish. Built as a gentleman's residence in 1805, Knowle House now contains a series of themed rooms housing various collections including Victoriana, militaria, local industries and crafts. Tel: 01626 888557.

Docton Mill & Garden — 2 miles (3km) southwest of Hartland. The garden was begun in the 1930s but had fallen into disrepair by the start of the 1970s. The mill, which had ceased to operate by 1910, was renovated in 1980; the garden was subsequently cleared and extensive planting took place. A bog garden and borders were added and a vast numbers of trees were planted. At the start of the new millennium further developments were carried out, including a new magnolia garden with large herbaceous borders, a woodland garden and greenhouses enabling more extensive plant propagation. Tel: 01237 441369.

Downes — 1 mile (1.6km) east of Crediton. A large mansion which has been the seat of the Buller family since the 18th century. Part of the house, including the family museum, is dedicated to Sir Redvers Buller of Boer War fame. Tel: 01392 439046.

Drake's Island — Originally called St Michael's Island. Sir Francis Drake said, 'Whoever holds the island, holds the town'. Area: 0.8 sq miles (2 sq km). (GR: SX469529.)

Dunkeswell Memorial Museum — 5 miles (8km) north of Honiton. Located at Dunkeswell Aerodrome, the musem houses original artefacts and photographic archives, collected over 20 years, on the history of the World War II United States Navy airbase at Dunkeswell. Tel: 01404 891943.

Eddystone Lighthouse — Situated on the treacherous Eddystone Rocks, 14 miles (23km) out at sea on a bearing of 211° from Plymouth Breakwater. In 1696 Henry Winstanley commenced work on an octagonal wooden structure and the light on the Eddystone was first lit on 14 November 1698. Although the lighthouse survived that first winter it was found to be badly in need of repair: the whole top of the structure was removed and a second tower was completed in 1699. In November 1703, the lighthouse was destroyed in the greatest storm ever recorded in England. John Rudyerd, a silk merchant, designed a cone-shaped tower which was lit in 1709 and stood for 46 years until the night of 2 December 1755, when the top of the lantern caught fire. In 1756 a fourth lighthouse was begun by Yorkshireman John Smeaton, who constructed a tower based on the shape of an oak tree for strength but made of stone rather than wood. The new Eddystone Lighthouse was lit by 24 candles on 16 October 1759. In the 1870s cracks appeared in the rock on which the lighthouse stood and it was dismantled and re-erected on Plymouth Hoe as a monument to the builder. In 1877 James Douglass, engineer-in-chief to Trinity House, announced the decision to rebuild a fifth lighthouse on a more solid foundation to the southeast. Douglass used larger stones and improved on the oak tree model, and in 1882 the present Eddystone Lighthouse was completed. Its original oil-powered lamps were replaced in 1956 by electrics. A helicopter deck was constructed above the lantern in 1980 as the first part of a modernisation scheme and the station became automated and unmanned in 1982 when it was commissioned by the Duke of Edinburgh. The lighthouse is now monitored and controlled from the Trinity House Operations Control Centre at Harwich in Essex; its signal is a white light flashing twice every 10 seconds.

Escot Country Park & Gardens — Escot, Ottery St Mary, 9 miles (15km) east of Exeter. Set in landscaped gardens, the house has been a family home to generations of the Kennaway family. Tel: 01404 822188.

Exeter Book One of the most important documents in Anglo-Saxon literature, given to Exeter Cathedral (see separate entry) by Bishop Leofric in the 11th century and still kept in the cathedral library. The Exeter Book, also known as the Codex Exoniensis, dates back to the 10th century and is one of four manuscripts that between them contain virtually all the surviving Old English poetry. It includes most of the more highly regarded shorter poems, some religious pieces and a series of riddles, a handful of which are famously lewd. Some of the riddles are inscribed on a highly polished steel obelisk in the high street, erected on 30 March 2005. Among the famous poems that appear in the Exeter Book are *The Wanderer*, *The Seafarer*, *Widsith*, *Wulf and Eadwacer*, *The Wife's Lament*, *The Husband's Message*, *The Ruin* and *Deor*.

Exeter Castle Northernhay Park, Exeter. Aka Rougemont Castle, the Norman castle was founded by Baldwin de Brionne in 1068 in a corner of the Roman walls. It was largely demolished in 1744 to make way for the Georgian Assize County Courts, although the stone gatehouse dating to c.1068 still exists. A plaque near the gatehouse recalls that in 1685 Alice Molland, the last person executed for witchcraft in England, was imprisoned in Exeter.

Exeter Cathedral The Cloisters, Exeter. The history of the church as a cathedral dates from 1050, when the Bishop of Crediton (Devon) and St Germans (Cornwall) moved to Exeter. The first Bishop of Exeter, Leofric, was personally installed in his new see by King Edward the Confessor. The old minster of St Mary and St Peter became the new cathedral. Dedicated to St Peter and consecrated in 1133, the cathedral was rebuilt over the course of 100 years beginning in 1270. Exeter Cathedral is 383ft (117m) in length and 145ft (44m) tall and has the longest uninterrupted vaulted ceiling in England. Tel: 01392 285983.

Exmoor See Somerset

Exmouth Model Railway Exmouth seafront is home to the worlds largest OO gauge model railway, with over 7500ft (2286m) of tracks – over 115 scale miles (186km), with up to 20 trains moving at once and set in a panoramic landscape of villages and towns. Tel: 01395 278383.

Finch Foundry Sticklepath, Okehampton. A 19th century water-powered forge, the last working example of its type in England, which produced agricultural and mining hand tools. Now owned by the National Trust. The Four Villages Trail, a lovely circular walk, starts at the foundry. Tel: 01837 840046.

Flag of Devon Devon has its own unofficial flag which has been dedicated to St Petroc, a local saint with numerous dedications throughout Devon and neighbouring counties. The flag was adopted in 2003 after a competition run by BBC Devon. The winning design was created by Ryan Sealey, and won 49 per cent of the votes cast. The emblem is of a white St George's cross with a black border on a green background. The colours are those popularly identified with Devon, for example the colours of the county's rugby union team, and the green and white flag flown by the 1st Viscount Exmouth at the Bombardment of Algiers.

Fosse Way Roman road built c.AD 47 that traversed Britain from southwest to northeast. Commencing at the mouth of the River Axe in Devon, it ran through Axminster and Ilchester (Lindinae) to Bath (Aquae Sulis) and Cirencester and onwards to High Cross (Venonae) before intersecting with Watling Street, and then on to Leicester (Ratae) and Newark before reaching Ermine Street south of Lincoln.

Fursdon House Cadbury, 8 miles (13km) north of Exeter. The Fursdon family have lived at the property since the 13th century. David and Catriona Fursdon took over the stewardship of the estate in 1979 and the house – enlarged over the centuries from a three-room cob and thatch cottage – is still a family home, with rooms dating from the medieval, Jacobean, Georgian and Regency periods. Tel: 01392 860860.

Garden House, The Buckland Monachorum, 2 miles (3km) west of Yelverton. A garden of 8 acres (3.2ha), featuring more than 6000 different varieties within a beautiful South Devon landscape on the edge of Dartmoor National Park. At the heart of this magical place is the walled garden, designed and planted by Lionel Fortescue and his wife Katherine in the mid-1940s. The Garden House is at the forefront of a revolution in 'naturalistic planting' – working in harmony with nature rather than against it, allowing flowers to intermingle to provide living kaleidoscopes of colour. Tel: 01822 854769.

Giant's Chair of Natsworthy 2 miles (3km) north of Widecombe-in-the-Moor. Located on Higher Natsworthy Farm, the 20ft (6m) tall oak-framed sculpture was the creation of 32-year-old local artist Henry Brucea. The chair, overlooking Dartmoor, was made from locally sourced oak in spring 2006 with the help of local carpenter Joel Hendry. Planning permission has only been granted on a temporary basis but a campaign to make it a permanent fixture is ongoing.

Grand Western Canal Country Park Running between Tiverton and Holcombe Rogus, near the Somerset border, the 11 mile (18km) long canal was opened in 1814. Declared a Country Park in 1971 and a Local Nature Reserve in 2005, the canal is home to a horse-drawn barge that has been taking passengers for trips along the canal since 1974.

Greenway Galmpton, 3 miles (5km) west of Brixham. Renowned for rare half-hardy plants under-planted with native wild flowers, Greenway has an atmosphere of wildness and timelessness. This 'secret' woodland garden on the banks of the River Dart is set within an extensive estate once owned by Agatha Christie; the house dates from the 18th century, with early 19th century additions, and was built on the site of a 16th century mansion. It is now in the care of the National Trust. Tel: 01803 842382.

Grockles A pejorative term for tourists in Devon, applied especially to those from the Midlands or the North of England. According to the *Oxford English Dictionary*, the term was first popularised by characters in the film *The System* (1962), set in the resort of Torquay during the tourist season. Research by a local journalist in the mid-1990s revealed that the word originated from a cartoon in the children's comic *Dandy* entitled 'Danny and his Grockle' (a magical dragon-like creature). A local man, who had had a summer job at a swimming pool as a youngster, said that he had used the term as a nickname for a small elderly lady who was a regular customer one season. During banter in the pub among the summer workers, the term then became generalised as a term for summer visitors. Natives of neighbouring Cornwall use the word 'emmet' for its tourists.

Guildhall — High Street, Exeter. Possibly the oldest main municipal building in England. Dating from 1330, it is still in use as a council chamber. The frontage is Tudor, while several paintings are on display in the main hall and civic silver can also be seen. A museum displays the sword and hat of maintenance (rewards from Henry VII for Exeter's loyalty in seeing off a challenge to the throne by Dutchman Perkin Warbeck, who claimed to be the Dule of York, son of Edward IV and one of the Princes in the Tower, as well as chains, maces and silver objects.

Haldon Belvedere — 7 miles (11km) southwest of Exeter. Also known as Lawrence Castle, Haldon Belvedere is a Grade II* listed triangular tower originally built in 1788 by Sir Robert Palk as the centrepiece to his vast estates and dedicated to the memory of Major-General Stringer Lawrence, the founder of the Indian army. Devon Historic Buildings Trust completed renovation of the tower in 1995. Tel: 01392 833668.

Hartland Abbey — Hartland, 15 miles (24km) west of Bideford. Situated on the North Devon coast within a designated Area of Outstanding Natural Beauty, the abbey lies across a narrow, sheltered valley which winds its way to the spectacular Atlantic coast. It was built in 1157, and consecrated by Bishop Bartholomew of Exeter in 1160 as a monastery of the regular canons of the Order of St Augustine of Hippo. In 1539 it was the last monastery in England to be dissolved by Henry VIII. Peacocks and bantams roam in gardens leading to the rocky cove while donkeys and Black Welsh Mountain sheep graze the Old Deer Park. Hartland Abbey is the home of the Stucley family. Tel: 01237 441264/234.

Hartland Quay Museum — Hartland Quay, 14 miles (23km) west of Bideford. Coastal museum with exhibitions on shipwrecks, natural history, coastal trades, and the geology and history of Hartland Quay. Tel: 01288 331353.

Hemerdon House — Sparkwell, Plympton, 4 miles (6km) east of Plymouth. A private house built in the late 18th century and inhabited by the same family throughout its history. Largely unchanged, Hemerdon and its contents provide a fine example of Georgian architecture and style. Tel: 01752 841410.

Hemyock Castle — 10 miles (16km) north of Honiton. Set in the Culm Valley among the Blackdown Hills, the ruined medieval moated castle and gatehouse now features an interpretation centre illustrating the history of the site and containing life-size historical tableaux including an extended Civil War display. Tel: 01823 680745.

High Cross House — See Dartington Hall

Highest point — High Willhays on Dartmoor at 2038ft (621m), also the highest point in Great Britain south of the Brecon Beacons. High Willhays and nearby Yes Tor are the only summits in England south of the Peak District to rise above 2000ft (609m), apart from Black Mountain on the Welsh border.

Hound Tor — 4 miles (6km) west of Bovey Tracey. Hound Tor is one of the most impressive of Dartmoor's heavily weathered granite outcrops. According to local legend it was created when a pack of hounds were turned to stone. On the side of the hill are the remains of an abandoned medieval village, excavated in the 1960s and featuring several examples of Dartmoor longhouses dating from as far back as the 13th century. The site of the medieval village dates to before Domesday times, when it was known as *Hundatora*. The ruins of the settlement are well preserved, with good views over the Lustleigh valley and protected from prevailing winds. The site was probably occupied over several centuries before being abandoned c.1350, either because of the deteriorating climate or more likely the plague. Excavation has revealed about eight houses and three corn drying barns which were built later. One of the houses was larger than the rest, three were longhouse farms and three were one-roomed cottages. Although the houses vary in size, in all of them both humans and cattle shared the same space. The houses had walls probably up to 6ft (1.8m) high and thatched roofs. Excavations have shown that the entrances had wooden door frames. There was a central hearth with a cooking pit in most houses. Tel: 01626 832093.

Interesting facts — The **Cridford Inn** at Trusham, near Newton Abbot, is reputedly one of the oldest inns in Britain and dates back to AD 825. It was originally a nunnery and then a farm, but is now an archetypal English country pub with a thatched roof, tiny windows, rough stone walls and slate floors. The transept window in the bar is said to be the oldest domestic window in Britain. Plymouth-born Frank and Anita Milford celebrated their 78th wedding anniversary in 2006 to become **Britain's longest-married living couple**. The pair met at a YMCA dance in Plymouth and wed two years later at Torpoint Register Office on 26 May 1928. Although not born in Devon, artist **Beryl Cook** (1926–2008) lived in Plymouth for over 30 years. In January 2004 her boisterous characters starred in a two-part animated television series made for the BBC. The series, called *Bosom Pals*, transported Cook's well-endowed ladies from canvas to screen in the tales of Stella and her vivacious friends. The Dolphin pub on Plymouth's Barbican, which features in many of Cook's paintings, is also prominent in the animated film. Another famous Plymouth-based artist was **Robert Lenkiewicz** (1941–2002). Throughout his career he worked intensively on a long series of projects which he termed 'The Relationships Series'. There were 20 projects. The first, 'Vagrancy', was finished in 1973. Themes such as mental handicap, love, jealousy, orgasm, old age, suicide, sexual behaviour, and even observations on local education followed. The last project Lenkiewicz was working on was titled 'Addictive Behaviour' and featured former Labour Party leader Michael Foot as one of his subjects. Poet Laureate **Ted Hughes** (1930–98) moved to North Tawton in Mid Devon in 1961, and remained in the county until his death from cancer in 1998. He spent much of his time farming in North Devon, and walking on northern Dartmoor. He loved this area and wrote about its beauty in his poems. Sherlock Holmes' most famous case, ***The Hound of the Baskervilles***, was set on foggy Dartmoor, and Sir Arthur Conan Doyle took much of the inspiration for the book from real-life people and places. The first episodes were published in the *Strand Magazine* from August 1901. ***Fawlty Towers*** is thought to be based on the Gleneagles Hotel in Asheldon Road, Torquay. John Cleese stayed at the hotel in 1971 and was fascinated with the eccentric behaviour of owner Donald Sinclair. Cleese later described Mr Sinclair – who died in 1981 – as 'the most wonderfully rude man I have ever met'. **Lady Nancy Astor** (1879–1964) was born in Virginia, USA, but became an honorary Plymothian. Her husband Waldorf became Conservative MP for Plymouth Sutton in 1910, but had to relinquish his seat when his father died, because he inherited the title of Viscount Astor. Nancy decided to stand in Plymouth Sutton in his place. She won the election in November 1919, beating her main rival, Liberal Isaac Foot – the father of **Michael Foot** who of course went on to lead the Labour Party. She became the first woman MP to take her seat in the House of Commons. (The first woman to be elected was Constance Markievicz in 1918, but as a member of Sinn Fein she had disqualified herself by refusing to take the oath.) In 1906 **Jimmy Peters** became England's first black rugby player when he took the field against the Springboks. The early part of the 20th century was a golden period for Plymouth Albion Rugby Club. Between 1902 and 1913 the team only lost once to another English side and Jimmy was the star of the successful side. **Cheriton Fitzpaine Cricket Club** are in the Guinness Book of Records, after playing non-stop for 27 hours and 34 minutes – a world record for the longest continuous match. The Devon club started their non-stop marathon at 10am on Saturday 24 June 2006 and finished the following Sunday afternoon. They had intended to play for 30 hours (with a five-minute break per hour allowed), but decided to call stumps early so they could watch England's World Cup football game against Ecuador. The marathon cricket match featured two teams at Cheriton Fitzpaine CC. They played two innings each. In 1967, Barnstaple-born **Sir Francis Chichester** became the first person to sail single-handed around the world by the clipper route, and the fastest circumnavigator, in 9 months and 1 day. In 1969, Devon-based yachtsman **Sir Robin Knox-Johnston** became the first person to sail solo around the world non-stop. **Francis Hayman** was an Exeter-born painter and illustrator who became one of the founding members of the Royal Academy in 1768 and later its first librarian. In August 2006 the Tate Gallery paid £1 million for his portrait of Samuel Richardson but there was always a doubt about his super-stardom, mainly due to his seemingly unaccomplished self-portrait of 1735 which showed the artist sitting with his legs only partly visible. In November 2006 the mystery was solved by prominent art detective Philip Mould, who bought a portrait of an unnamed lady in a New Hampshire auction room and after having over-painting removed unearthed the legs of a man wearing brown trousers. Recognising the style of Hayman the detective examined his output and the self-portrait matched the left-hand side of the female portrait. It seems that the woman was the artist's first wife, cut out of his family portrait by Hayman in a fit of pique. Both paintings have now considerably appreciated in value. In 1885 John Henry George Lee, better known as **'Babbacombe' Lee** (born in Abbotskerswell in 1864) was sentenced to hang for the murder of Emma Keyse, a former maid of honour and friend of Queen Victoria. On 23 February 1885, Lee was led to the gallows in the courtyard of Exeter prison. He was stood on the trapdoor and the noose placed round his neck, the bolt was drawn, but the trapdoor didn't fall. John Berry, the hangman, pulled the lever again, and again the trapdoor failed to open. Lee was taken back to his cell and workmen were summoned to fix the fault. The mechanism was tested and found to be in working order, so Lee was returned to the scaffold. Again the noose was placed around his neck and Berry pulled the lever, and again the trapdoor failed. Lee was returned to his cell, and the Home Secretary authorised a delay in his execution. Eventually Lee's sentence was commuted to life imprisonment. He served 22 years in prison and was released in 1907. In the 1970s, Dave Swarbrick (fiddle player in the English folk-rock band Fairport Convention) found a series of old newspaper articles about Lee and composed a rock opera entitled *Babbacombe Lee* which was released by the band as an LP. When **William, Prince of Orange**, who had married Mary, the daughter of James II, was invited to come to England to deliver the country from Catholicism, he landed at Torbay on 5 November 1688 to commence what became known as the Glorious Revolution. A fire has been kept continually alight in the fireplace of the **Warren House Inn** in Postbridge since it was built in 1845. The pub is also one of the highest in England at 1545ft (471m) above sea level and has no mains electricity or water. See also the Pack o' Cards. Another interesting pub is the **Normandy Arms**, Blackawton, Totnes, which holds the International Festival of Worm Charming every May bank holiday. Charming consists of working a 3ft x 4ft plot for 15 minutes, generally by dampening the soil and 'twanging' a garden fork into the turf. The British Association of Worm Length Supporters (BAWLS) decrees that all worms must be returned to the soil at the end of the contest. More than 500 worms were once charmed at such a competition. The ***Golden Hind*** (originally called the *Pelican*) was a galleon captained by Sir Francis Drake on its global circumnavigation in 1577–80. The ship was renamed in honour of Drake's patron, Sir Christopher Hatton, whose family coat of arms was a golden hind. A modern full size authentic replica of the ship was built by traditional handcraft in Appledore, North Devon and launched in 1973. In 1979–80, it retraced Drake's route around the world. Since 1996 it has been berthed at St Mary Overie Dock on Cathedral Street, Bankside, Southwark, London, between Southwark Cathedral and Clink Street. A second replica has been permanently moored in Brixham harbour since 1963. **The world's first closed-top range** was patented by George Bodley, a Devon ironfounder, in 1802. It was called a 'Kitchener' range and consisted of a cast-iron hotplate with removable boiling rings heated over the fire. Devon has given its name to a geological era: the **Devonian** era was named by Yorkshire geologist Adam Sedgwick (1785–1873) after the Old Red Sandstone of Exmoor which was first studied there. The **Duchy of Cornwall** is, with the Duchy of Lancaster, one of two royal duchies in England. The eldest son of the reigning monarch is

	automatically the Duke of Cornwall. Although the Duchy owns substantial land in Cornwall, and indeed Somerset and Herefordshire, almost half of its 220 sq mile (571 sq km) holdings are in Devon.
Islands	See separate table for a list of all the islands of Devon.
Kentisbury Grange Country Park	Set in 7 acres (2.8ha) of mature grounds with beautiful views of patchwork countryside on the fringe of the Exmoor National Park. The Grange itself was built in 1894, but the history of the site dates to the 14th century when the Wolfe family, owners of Kentisbury at the time, resided here. The grounds are home to a variety of native wildlife. Red deer frequent the fields opposite and buzzards circle the sky by day, while tawny owls and barn owls hunt in the grounds at night. Kentisbury is home to Jake the Drake, a lovestruck Muscovy duck who walked eight miles across Devon in March 2005 in order to be reunited with his mate Jemima, who had hatched 16 of his ducklings. Exiled from the Grange because he was getting too amorous with the other wildfowl, Jake escaped from his new home, dodging foxes, crossing the busy A39 and swimming the River Yeo before eventually finding his way back to his beloved. Tel: 01271 883454.
Kents Cavern	Ilsham Road, Wellswood, Torquay. One of the most important Palaeolithic caves in northern Europe and the oldest recognisable human dwelling in England. It holds beautiful and spectacular geological formations and significant prehistoric finds, some over 700,000 years old. Originally called Kents Hole, the name was changed to Kents Cavern in 1903 when the hillside, quarry and surrounding woodlands were acquired by Francis Powe. The name Kents is thought to derive from the Celtic word *Kent* or *Kant* meaning a border or headland, the name therefore referring to 'the hole on the headland'. Tel: 01803 215136.
Killerton	6 miles (10km) northeast of Exeter. Built for the Acland family in 1778, the house is furnished as a residential home. The Paulise de Bush collection of 18th to 20th century costume is displayed in period rooms. There is an introductory exhibition in the stable courtyard, a Victorian laundry and an adjoining chapel. The garden was created in the 1770s by John Veitch, and features rhododendrons, magnolias, herbaceous borders and rare trees, as well as an ice house and early 19th century rustic-style summer house known as The Bear's Hut. The house is surrounded by parkland and woods giving access to a 6100 acre (2500ha) estate, within which can be found the Budlake Old Post Office Room, Broadclyst Mill and Marker's Cottage (see separate entries). Now owned by the National Trust. Tel: 01392 881345.
Kingswear Castle	1 mile (1.6km) east of Dartmouth. Built 1491–1502 as an artillery tower for use with heavy cannon. Due to the limited range of cannon at the time, the fort at Kingswear was designed to work alongside Dartmouth Castle on the opposite bank, between them providing cover of the narrow entrance into the harbour. As gun technology improved, new gun emplacements were added to Dartmouth Castle, aiming further out towards the estuary mouth, and the defensive role of Kingswear Castle declined. Today the castle contains holiday accommodation.
Kirkham House	Kirkham Street, off Cecil Road, Paignton. This well-preserved medieval stone residence has undergone considerable restoration and gives a fascinating insight into life in a town house during the 15th century. Tel: 01803 522139.
Knightshayes Court	Bolham, Tiverton. House built c.1870 in Gothic Revival style by William Burges. The interiors combine medieval romanticism with lavish Victorian decoration, and the smoking and billiard rooms, elegant boudoir and drawing room all give an atmospheric insight into the grand country house life which revolved around the Heathcoat-Amory family. The garden features a water lily pool, topiary, fine specimen trees, formal terraces, spring bulbs and rare shrubs. Now owned by the National Trust. Tel: 01884 254665.
Knowle House	See Dawlish Museum
Lawrence Castle	See Haldon Belvedere
Letterboxing	See Dartmoor
Loughwood Meeting House	Dalwood, Axminster. Built c.1653 by the Baptist congregation of Kilmington. The interior, fitted in the early 18th century, remains unaltered. Now owned by the National Trust. Tel: 01392 881691.
Lundy	The largest island in the Bristol Channel has an area of approximately 1.5 square miles (4 sq km). England's only statutory Marine Nature Reserve was named as the 10th greatest natural wonder in Britain in a 2005 *Radio Times* poll. The Marisco family held the island periodically 1150–1327 and erected a stronghold by 1200; this became a castle by order of Henry III in 1243, after he had executed the pirate William de Marisco the previous year for treason. The remains of the castle mainly date from the mid 17th century and are now known as Bulls' Paradise. The Heaven family owned Lundy 1836–1918 and built St Helena's church in 1896. In 1924 Martin Coles Harman purchased the island and immediately proclaimed himself king. Following the death of Harman's son Albion in 1968, Lundy was given to the National Trust by new owner Jack Hayward. The island has a rich and varied bird life but has always been known as a breeding ground for puffins, although the population has declined sharply in recent years. The name Lundy possibly comes from the Old Norse word for a puffin. The Lundy Cabbage (*Coincya wrightii*) is the only endemic plant species but a rich vein of lichens, heaths and grasslands abound. Sites of interest on the island include the Old Lighthouse on Beacon Hill and Shutter Rock at the southwestern end. The resident population of Lundy consists of a handful of people who maintain the 23 holiday properties and a campsite, mostly in the south of the island, plus a warden, farmer and island manager. (GR: SS135460.)
Lydford Castle and Saxon Town	Lydford, 8 miles (13km) southwest of Okehampton. Standing above the gorge of the River Lyd, an 11th century Norman castle with keep added 1195 and extended with motte built around the base in the 13th century. The castle was the seat of the Stannary Court and prison until the court was moved to Princetown during the 19th century. A Saxon town once stood nearby and is still discernible. Tel: 01822 820320.

Lydford Gorge Lydford, 8 miles (13km) southwest of Okehampton. The famous gorge is 1½ miles (2.5km) long and can be viewed from a circular walk, which starts high above the river and passes through attractive oak woods before dropping down to the dramatic 100ft (30m) high White Lady waterfall. The path then proceeds along the riverside through a steep-sided ravine, scooped out by the River Lyd as it plunges into a series of whirlpools, including the thrilling Devil's Cauldron. The site is owned by the National Trust. Tel: 01822 820320.

Lynton and Lynmouth Cliff Railway Lee Road, Lynton/The Esplanade, Lynmouth. A unique water-powered Victorian inclined railway, opened in 1890. It links the twin towns of Lynton and Lynmouth, climbing from sea level to a height of 500ft (150m). Tel: 01598 753486/753908.

Marisco Castle See Lundy

Marker's Cottage Broadclyst, 4 miles (6km) northeast of Exeter. Medieval cob house containing a cross-passage screen decorated with a painting of St Andrew and his attributes. Owned by the National Trust and part of the Killerton estate. Tel: 01392 461546.

Marwood Hill Gardens 4 miles (6km) north of Barnstaple. Marwood Hill has 20 acres (8ha) of gardens and three lakes in a valley setting. Tel: 01271 342528.

Meteorological Office FitzRoy Road, Exeter. Established in 1854 as a small department within the Board of Trade under Robert FitzRoy as a service to mariners, the Meteorological Office later became part of the Ministry of Defence. In 2003 it moved its headquarters to Exeter from its previous location, Bracknell in Berkshire. The Shipping Forecast is produced by the Met Office and broadcast on BBC Radio 4. See also Berkshire.

Morwellham Quay 5 miles (8km) southwest of Tavistock. Museum based around the historic port and mine workings on the River Tamar (which forms part of the Devon/Cornwall boundary). Costumed staff welcome visitors to the restored port and help to transport them back to the 1860s when gleaming copper ore filled the quays and a forest of ships' masts lined the river. Features include the busy assay office, miners' cottages and walled gardens. 01822 832766.

Museum of Barnstaple and North Devon The Square, Barnstaple. A major regional museum displaying and interpreting the natural and human history of northern Devon, and housed in a fine Victorian brick building. Tel: 01271 346747.

National Marine Aquarium Rope Walk, Coxside, Plymouth. Britain's biggest aquarium, opened in 1998 to carry out conservation, research and education and recently expanded to offer a brand new three-floor, multi-million pound interactive centre. Tel: 01752 600301.

Norman Lockyer Observatory Salcombe Hill, Sidmouth, 13 miles (21km) southeast of Exeter. An historic working optical observatory and educational centre for science, especially astronomy, meteorology, amateur radio and sciences of the coast and countryside. Visitors have an opportunity to observe planets, moon and sunspots through 10in Victorian telescopes. The observatory was established in 1912 by Sir Joseph Norman Lockyer to continue his astronomical research when the South Kensington Observatory was closed. Now it provides a facility at which individuals and groups may participate in projects and pursue practical recreational study of science. The Planetarium is named in honour of James Lockyer (1868–1936), Sir Norman's fifth son. Tel: 01395 579941.

Northernhay Gardens Located in central Exeter just outside Exeter Castle (see separate entry). Claimed to be the oldest public open space in England, being originally laid out in 1612 as a pleasure walk for Exeter residents, much of the gardens now represent Victorian design, with a beautiful display of trees, mature shrubs and bushes and plenty of flower beds. There are also many statues, notably the War Memorial by John Angel and the Deerstalker by E B Stephens. The Volunteer Memorial (1895) commemorates the formation of the 1st Rifle Volunteers in 1852, while there are also statues of John Dinham, Thomas Dyke Acland and Stafford Northcote (a local landowner and a Victorian Chancellor of the Exchequer).

Okehampton Castle Okehampton, 22 miles (35km) west of Exeter. Norman motte and bailey castle, the largest in Devon, founded by Baldwin Fitzgilbert c.1070. The tower was built in the early 14th century. It was owned by the Courtenays but gradually fell into disuse after they moved to Powderham and abandoned after the execution of Henry Courtenay in 1538. Now ruined, it is owned by English Heritage. Tel: 01837 52844.

Old Mill, The Wembury, 5 miles (8km) southeast of Plymouth. A former corn mill on Wembury Beach dating to at least 1851 and which operated until c.1900. The building is now occupied by a café. Owned by the National Trust. Tel: 01752 862314.

Oldway Mansion Torquay Road, Paignton. In 1871 the Fernham estate was purchased by Isaac Merritt Singer, founder of the Singer Sewing Machine Company, who immediately built a huge new mansion on the site, living there until his death on 23 July 1875, aged 63. When he died he left 22 children by several wives, both legal and common law. Paris Singer, his third son, later altered and extended the house in the early 20th century. This rebuilding was modelled on the Palace of Versailles with an east wing inspired by the Place de la Concorde in Paris, while the staircase and ceiling are based on designs by French architect Joseph LeBrun. Torbay Borough Council purchased the mansion from the Singer family in 1946 and the Grade II listed building is now used as the register office for the area. Tel: 01803 201201.

Overbeck's Sharpitor, Salcombe, 18 miles (29km) southeast of Plymouth. Scientist and inventor Otto Overbeck lived here from 1928 until his death in 1937, after which the Edwardian house and garden were left to the National Trust. Born in England but with continental ancestors, Overbeck was a research chemist in the brewing industry. Among the items on show are late 19th century photographs of the area, model ships, local shipbuilding tools and other nautical artefacts, toys, shells, stuffed animals and some of Overbeck's inventions, including the 'rejuvenator', a device that employed electricity supposedly to restore youth. The Mediterranean-style garden, with spectacular views over the Salcombe estuary, enjoys a warm microclimate and so is home to many rare plants, trees and shrubs. Tel: 01548 842893.

Pack o' Cards Combe Martin, 4 miles (6km) east of Ilfracombe. Situated in the beautiful seaside town of Combe Martin, the Pack o' Cards Inn is a unique Grade II listed building built c.1690. Constructed to resemble a deck of cards, it was built on a plot of land measuring 52ft x 52ft (16m x 16m), has four floors (representing the number of suits in a pack), 13 doors on every floor and 13 fireplaces (the number of cards in a suit). Prior to the imposition of window tax, the panes of glass in all the windows added up to the total of the numbered cards in a pack. The building has been featured on the BBC's *Paul Daniels Magic Show*. Tel: 01271 882300.

Paignton Zoo Environmental Park Totnes Road, Paignton. The brainchild of Herbert Whitley, who opened his collection of animals to the public in 1923 under the name Torbay Zoological Gardens. Its present name of Paignton Zoo Environmental Park was established in 1996. The ever-changing variety of residents makes the zoo one of the most impressive in England. It is divided into six zones: Desert, Forest, Primley (named after Whitley's home, the Primley estate), Savannah, Tropical Forest and Wetland, all replicating the animals' natural habitats. Paignton is one of England's largest zoos with over 1200 animals in a setting of 75 acres (30ha) of botanical gardens. Tel: 01803 697500.

Pilgrim Fathers See Nottinghamshire

Plymouth Cathedral Cecil Street, Plymouth. Dedicated to St Mary and St Boniface, the Roman Catholic cathedral was completed in 1858 and consecrated in 1880.

Plymouth Hoe A broad open space overlooking the cliffs at Plymouth, the Hoe is perhaps best known as the place where Sir Francis Drake supposedly played a game of bowls when England was about to be invaded by the Spanish Armada. Also on the Hoe is Plymouth Dome, an all-weather attraction offering audio-visual presentations depicting the town's past. Above the Dome is Smeaton's Tower, constructed in 1759 and which once stood guard over the Eddystone Reef, 20 miles (32km) off Plymouth (see entry for Eddystone Lighthouse). It was moved to the Hoe in 1852 when its foundations started to collapse. The name derives from the Anglo-Saxon word *hoe*, meaning a sloping ridge shaped like an inverted foot and heel.

Plympton Castle Plympton, 3 miles (5km) east of Plymouth. An early Norman shell keep on a high pre-Norman motte. It was partly razed to the ground in 1136 by King Stephen and was never rebuilt. The bailey buildings were destroyed in the Civil War (the outline of the bailey is still clearly visible), after which it was abandoned. By this time silting of the river had meant that most trade had moved down river to Plymouth and Plympton was no longer an important town.

Powderham Castle Kenton, 6 miles (10km) south of Exeter. Fortified manor house built in 1390, to command the Exe Estuary, by Sir Philip Courtenay, whose descendants, the Earls of Devon, still own the castle. Besieged in the Civil War, it was more recently home to Timothy the tortoise, who died in 2004 aged 160. Tel: 01626 890243.

Prisons **Channings Wood**, Denbury, Newton Abbot, is a Category C training prison, officially opened in July 1974. Operational capacity: 667. Tel: 01803 814600. **Dartmoor** was built in 1809 to hold French and American prisoners of war, becoming a criminal prison from 1850. Most of the buildings date from the late 19th century but three wings have recently been fully refurbished. Dartmoor is a category C training prison and has done much in recent years to shake off its historically austere image. It offers cellular accommodation on six wings. Operational capacity: 625. **Exeter**, New North Road, Exeter, was built c.1850. It currently has four residential wings and accepts all adult and young offenders committed to prison by courts in Cornwall, Devon and West Somerset. Operational capacity: 533. Tel: 01392 415650.

Puslinch Yealmpton, 6 miles (10km) east of Plymouth. Built in 1720 by the Yonge family, this early Georgian house in the Queen Anne style remains largely unchanged. Tel: 01752 880555.

RHS Garden Rosemoor 1 mile (1.6km) south of Great Torrington, 6 miles (10km) southwest of Barnstaple. Lady Anne's Garden, as the original garden of Rosemoor is now known, is a plantsman's garden of great horticultural and botanical interest. Inspired by the enthusiasm of plantsman Collingwood Ingram, the garden development continued with the planting of specimens collected by Lady Anne Berry (nee Palmer) on her travels through Europe, Australia, New Zealand, Papua New Guinea, Japan, the USA and temperate South America. Tel: 01805 624067.

Rivers The **Axe** rises near Beaminster, Dorset, flowing westwards to form the boundary between Dorset and Somerset before reaching Axminster in Devon and entering the English Channel south of Axmouth, a course of 24 miles (39km).

The **Dart** rises on Dartmoor, as two separate branches (the **East Dart** and **West Dart**), which join at Dartmeet. After leaving the moor, the Dart flows south past Buckfast Abbey and through the towns of Buckfastleigh, Dartington and Totnes where it becomes tidal; there are no bridges below this point. A passenger ferry operates between the villages of Dittisham and Greenway; the latter (see separate entry) was the location of the estate of Agatha Christie, which has stunning views across the river. The large ria (inundated valley of a relatively small river) of the Dart estuary is a popular sailing venue. The village of Kingswear and the town of Dartmouth on the east and west sides of the estuary are linked by two vehicle ferries and a passenger ferry. The deep-water port of Dartmouth is a sheltered haven.

The **Exe** rises at The Chains, Somerset, flowing south across Devon and into the English Channel at Exmouth, a course of 60 miles (96km). Historically, its lowest bridging point was at Exeter, though there is now a viaduct for the M5 motorway about 2 miles (3km) south of the city centre. The river gives its name to many villages along its course; these include Exford, Up Exe, Nether Exe, Exwick, Exton, Exminster, and Exebridge, where it is joined by the River Barle. The seaside town of Exmouth is on the east side of the estuary and Dawlish Warren on the west.

The **Heddon** runs along the western edge of Exmoor to reach the North Devon coast at Heddon's Mouth, near Lynmouth. The Heddon Valley is renowned for its natural beauty. The beach at Heddon's Mouth is 1000ft (300m) wide and consists of large cobbles. It is only accessible through footpaths on the National Trust land or via the South West Coast Path. There are remains of a lime kiln on its western edge. The valley to the south of the beach has very steep slopes to its east and west, with the hills climbing over 650ft (200m) in altitude within $^1/_4$ mile (0.5km) of the river. The remains of a Roman fortlet are visible on the hilltop immediately to the east of Heddon's Mouth.

Two short rivers named the **Lew** lie close to each other in Devon. The more northerly of the two rises just south of the village of Beaworthy and flows east, then turns north to run past Hatherleigh before joining the River Torridge $^1/_2$ mile (0.8km) north of the town. Its name is incorporated into that of the village of Northlew. The more southerly rises on the northwest corner of Dartmoor, near Sourton, flowing west and then south, through the Lew Valley past Lewtrenchard and south of Lewdown before joining the River Lyd near Marystow. The Anglo-Saxon Chronicle records a battle in AD 825 in which Devon forces loyal to Egbert of Wessex defeated the Cornish at 'Gafulford' – possibly Galford on the banks of this river, though some translations render it as Camelford, 37 miles (60km) to the west. At their nearest point the two rivers are not much more than 6 miles (10km) apart.

The **Otter** rises in the Blackdown Hills just inside Somerset, flowing for 20 miles (32km) before reaching the sea at Budleigh Salterton, Devon.

The **Plym** rises 1476ft (450m) above sea level on Dartmoor, in an upland marshy area called Plym Head. The river flows roughly southwest, entering the sea near (and giving its name to) the city of Plymouth. It is approximately 19 miles (31km) long. The name Plym is thought to have its origins in Old English and means 'the plum tree'.

Tamar See Cornwall

The **Taw** rises at Taw Head, a spring on the central northern flanks of Dartmoor. It reaches the Bristol Channel 45 miles (72km) away on the north coast of Devon, at a joint estuary mouth which it shares with the River Torridge. The Taw only passes through one urban centre of any size, Barnstaple.

The **Teign** rises on Dartmoor, near Cranmere Pool. Its course on the moor is crossed by a clapper bridge near Teigncombe, just below the prehistoric Kestor Settlement. It leaves the moor at its eastern side, flowing beneath Castle Drogo in a steep-sided valley. It then flows southwards at the east edge of the moor. The river becomes tidal at Newton Abbot, and reaches the English Channel at Teignmouth. Its estuary is a large ria.

The **Torridge** rises close to the border with Cornwall (north of the source of the River Tamar). It flows generally east, passing between East and West Putford. Near Bradford it is joined by the River Waldon, then heads east past Black Torrington and Sheepwash. It is joined by the Lew near Hatherleigh, and by the Okement near Meeth. It then flows north, picking up the River Mere south of Beaford. After this it makes tight bends, heading generally northwest past Little Torrington and Great Torrington. It is joined by the River Yeo at Pillmouth, and becomes estuarine by Bideford. Between Appledore and Instow it joins the estuary of the River Taw. The Torridge was the home of Tarka the Otter in Henry Williamson's book. Other rivers include the **Avon**, **Barle**, **Burn**, **Collybrooke**, **Creedy**, **Culme**, **Erne**, **Hamoaze**, **Heddon**, **Lumburn**, **Okement**, **Tavy**, **Walkham**, **Wallabrooke** and **Yeo**.

Rougemont Castle — See Exeter Castle

Saltram — Plympton, 3 miles (5km) north of Plymouth. Standing high above the River Plym in a rolling and wooded landscaped park, the house, with its magnificent decoration and original contents, was largely created between the 1740s and 1820s by three generations of the Parker family. It features some of Robert Adam's finest rooms, exquisite plasterwork ceilings, original Chinese wallpapers and an exceptional collection of paintings, including many by Sir Joshua Reynolds and Angelica Kauffmann. The gardens are predominantly 19th century and contain an orangery and several follies, as well as beautiful shrubberies and imposing specimen trees. Now owned by the National Trust. Tel: 01752 333500.

Sand — Sidbury, Sidmouth. Lying in an unspoilt valley, Sand has been owned since 1561 by the Huyshe family, who still live in the house. Rebuilt in 1592–4, the house features a screens passage (which gave hidden access between the servants' quarters and the family rooms), panelling, family documents and heraldry, along with a mixed 6 acre (2.4ha) garden. Tel: 01395 597230.

Shobrooke Park — 1 mile (1.6km) east of Crediton. The 180 acre (73ha) park has a lime avenue dating from c.1800 and a cascade of four lakes completed in the 1840s. A Millennium amphitheatre was built in 2000. The 15 acre (6ha) garden, created in 1845 with Portland stone terraces, roses and rhododendrons, has recently been restored. Tel: 01363 775153.

Shute Barton — 3 miles (5km) southwest of Axminster. One of the most important surviving non-fortified manor houses of the Middle Ages. Begun in 1380, it was completed in the late 16th century, then partly demolished in the late 18th century. It has battlemented turrets, late Gothic windows and a Tudor gatehouse. Now owned by the National Trust. Tel: 01297 34692.

Sport: general — The county has a great sporting tradition and as well as the football clubs, racecourses and basketball team detailed below there are many other sporting success stories. **Plymouth Albion** and **Exeter Chiefs** are Devon's top two rugby clubs. Both play in National League One, one division below the Guinness Premiership. **Devon County Cricket Club** competes in the Minor Counties Championship and has won the competition seven times, most recently in 2006 when the team completed a 180-run victory over Buckinghamshire at Exmouth. In 2006 Helen Parkinson, from Brixham, became the world quadrathlon champion in the Czech Republic. (The quadrathlon is a tough multi-sport event in which competitors must complete four consecutive disciplines – cycling, canoeing, swimming and running – the distances varying at each event depending on the terrain.) The English Inter-County Bowls Team Championship (Middleton Cup) was won by Devon for three successive years between 2002 and 2004. In January 2006 a foursome led by Justin Adkin (in *All Relative*) from Devon won the Atlantic Rowing Race in Antigua, finishing 10 days ahead of James Cracknell and Ben Fogle who completed the 2937 mile (4727km) race in 49 days 19 hours 8 minutes.

basketball **Plymouth Raiders** are southwest England's leading basketball team. They play home games at the Plymouth Pavilions arena and compete in the British Basketball League. The Raiders entered the National Basketball League in 1983 and were the longest-serving team in the league before exiting to join the British Basketball League in 2004. Since season 1996–97 they had been one of the top teams in National Basketball League Division 1 and the Conference League and winners of both league and play-off titles. They play in green, white and black. Tel: 0845 146 1460.

football **Exeter City** have played in the Football League for most of their history, but were relegated to the Nationwide Conference in 2003 before regaining their status in 2008. Founded in 1904 from two predecessor clubs – Exeter United FC and St Sidwell's United – City moved to their current home, St James' Park (not to be confused with the home of Newcastle United), in 1906, entering the Football League in 1920. The club is nicknamed the Grecians. City's home kit consists of red and white shirts, black shorts and black socks. Tel: 01392 411243.

Plymouth Argyle were founded in 1886 as Argyle Football Club (named after the Argyll and Sutherland Highlanders) and adopted their present name in 1903. The club entered the Football League Third Division in 1920, finishing second a record six times in a row from 1921–22 to 1926–27. First promoted to Division Two in 1929–30, they have had several spells in the second tier of English football but have never reached the top division. Their nickname, the Pilgrims, stems from the group of Puritan separatists who travelled to the New World in 1620. Alternative nicknames include the Greens (they are one of only two clubs in the Football League to play in a principally green home strip – the other is Yeovil Town) and the Gyles. They play home matches at Home Park. Tel: 01752 562561.

Torquay United, nicknamed the Gulls, were founded in 1899 as an amalgamation of Babbacombe and Torquay. The club changed its name to Torquay Town in 1921 and then to United prior to joining the Football League in 1927. After 80 years in the lower divisions of the League, Torquay were relegated to the Blue Square Premier (formerly the Conference) in 2007. The club plays in yellow and navy. Their home ground is Plainmoor. Tel: 01801 328666.

horse racing **Exeter,** sitting high on the top of Haldon Hill at Kennford, just outside Exeter, with wonderful views towards Dartmoor, is the highest racecourse in Britain at 850ft (259m) above sea level and the second longest (behind Newmarket) at a little under 2 miles (3km). The right-handed track, which was called Devon and Exeter until 1992, holds National Hunt racing. Tel: 01392 832599.

Newton Abbot is a left-handed oval of 1 mile 2 furlongs (2km), sharp with a short run-in. Traditionally the opening fixture of the National Hunt season, Newton Abbot is the most southerly racecourse in Britain. Tel: 01626 353235.

Tapeley Park Westleigh, 5 miles (8km) southwest of Barnstaple. With four distinctly themed areas, mostly worked on organic principles and set in a site of 35 acres (14ha), the gardens of Tapeley Park are home to a rich variety of flowers, shrubs, vegetables and wildlife. Features include Italian terrace borders, a traditional walled kitchen garden, a lake with massive Western red cedar trees, and a granite labyrinth. The much altered Queen Anne building was originated by William Cleveland in 1702. The story goes that he was sailing his fine vessel up the River Torridge, and on a closer inspection of Tapeley through his telescope is alleged to have said 'That is the place for me'. Tapeley in those days was a seven-bayed white stuccoed farmhouse. Tel: 01271 342558.

Ten Tors Challenge A weekend hike across Dartmoor for teenagers run by the British Army and now held annually in May, although the first expedition was held in September 1960. Teams of six teenagers have 24 hours to visit ten of the following tors: Beardown, Black, Combestone, Chat, Great Mis, Hartor, Hound, Oke, Kitty, Lynch, Lower White, Shilstone, Sittaford, Sourton, South Hessary, Staple Tors, Trowlesworthy and Watern Tor. Pupers Hill, although not actually a tor, is also on the list due to a lack of tors on the southeastern side of the moor.

Tiverton Castle Park Hill, Tiverton. Originally built in 1106 by Richard de Redvers on the orders of Henry I, Tiverton Castle was held by seven successive Earls of Devon of the de Redvers family. When the last of the line, Isabella de Fortibus, died in 1293, it was inherited by a cousin, Hugh de Courtenay. The castle was rebuilt in stone with curtain walls enclosing an inner rectangular court of 1 acre (0.4ha), and towers added to the corners. The Giffard family bought Tiverton at the end of the 16th century. During the Civil War it was held for the king; besieged in October 1645 by Fairfax, it fell to the Parliamentary forces due to a lucky shot hitting the drawbridge chain. It was then sold to Peter West, a rich Tiverton wool merchant, whose daughter married Sir Thomas Carew. The Carews sold it in 1923, and after various changes of ownership it was bought in 1960 by Ivar Campbell who died in 1985. It was inherited by his nephew Angus Gordon, the present owner. Tel: 01884 253200.

Topsham Museum The Strand, Topsham, 3 miles (5km) southeast of Exeter. The museum features the history of the town and port of Topsham including shipbuilding and ship owning, and the wildlife of the Exe Estuary. It incorporates a late 17th century house. Tel: 01392 873244.

Torbryan Holy Trinity Torbryan, 4 miles (6km) southwest of Newton Abbot. A church of considerable size and grandeur, with a dramatic octagonal stair turret on the fine Perpendicular tower, and a magnificent rood screen with delicate woodcarving spanning the full width of the interior.

Torre Abbey King's Drive, Torquay. Founded in 1196 as a monastery for Premonstratensian canons, following a donation of land by William de Brewer, lord of the manor of Torre. In February 1194 William's son was sent to Austria with other hostages and successfully secured the release of Richard I, who had been imprisoned since December 1192, first by Duke Leopold and then by Henry VI, the Holy Roman Emperor. William gave the site as a thank-offering when his son was released. Although the abbey was partly destroyed during the Dissolution of the Monasteries in 1539, the gatehouse, dating from c.1380, still remains. The 'Spanish Barn' is so called because in 1588 it was used to house 400 prisoners from the Spanish Armada. The buildings were remodelled in the 19th century and now belong to the local council, serving in part as a museum and art gallery, the Agatha Christie Room being ever popular. Tel: 01803 293593.

Totnes Castle Castle Street, Totnes. Located by the town's north gate with splendid views down to the River Dart, the Norman motte and bailey castle was founded by Judhael of Totnes, a prominent supporter of William the Conqueror, in the 11th century. The shell keep was added in the 13th century by Reginald de Braose and today is one of the best preserved in England. The castle was rebuilt by William de la Zouch in 1326–7 and is now owned by English Heritage. Tel: 01803 864406.

Tuckers Hall Fore Street, Exeter. Ancient hall with a fine barrel-vaulted roof, built in 1471 as a chapel for the guild of woollen cloth workers, including the Incorporation of Weavers, Fullers and Shearmen. The 15th century roof timbers are still in situ, as is some Jacobean panelling. Tel: 01392 412348.

Two Moors Way A long-distance path that runs from Ivybridge in South Devon to Lynmouth on the coast of North Devon, crossing parts of both Dartmoor and Exmoor (and passing into Somerset) along the way. Its total length is 103 miles (165km).

Ugbrooke House and Park Chudleigh, 5 miles (8km) northeast of Newton Abbot. Located in a tranquil Devon valley, Ugbrooke is set in an extensive park landscaped by Capability Brown. The estate has a history covering 900 years, and exhibits a fascinating variety of alterations made over the centuries. Robert Adam and Capability Brown were commissioned to remodel the house, grounds and garden in the mid 18th century. Outstanding Adam interior designs and unique external features remain, while Lady Clifford's extensive interior design skills are apparent in many of the rooms today. The house contains fine paintings, furniture, beautiful needlework and a rare family military uniform collection. Tel: 01626 852179.

University of Exeter The Queen's Drive, Exeter. The Great Exhibition of 1851 gave rise to Schools of Art and Science in north Exeter, which in 1868 were housed in the local Albert Memorial Museum. In 1900 the official title of the two schools was changed to the Royal Albert Memorial College. This in turn became the University College of the South West of England in 1922, and in 1955 the college received its charter as the University of Exeter. Queen Elizabeth II was welcomed to the campus in the following year. The university has gradually transferred from its city centre sites to the sparsely developed Streatham estate over the following 50 years, as land and buildings have become available. The total number of students is around 15,000. Former students include author J K Rowling, Green MEP Caroline Lucas, singer Will Young and BBC correspondent Frank Gardner. Tel: 01392 661000. The university also has a Cornish campus, situated in Penryn. Tel: 01326 371800.

University of Plymouth Drake Circus, Plymouth. Designated as a university in 1992 along with the other former polytechnics, Plymouth has a reputation as one of the UK's leading new universities and is internationally renowned for its courses in shipping with maritime law and logistics. In October 2005, the *Sun* newspaper voted the university as having the most bizarre degree course in the country. The BSc (Hons) in Surf Science & Technology – commonly known as 'Surfing' – is centred on surfing equipment design and surfing-related business, which is very popular in southwest England. Another possibly unique course is the BA in Business & Perfumery. Tel: 01752 600600.

Watermouth Castle Berrynarbor, 3 miles (5km) east of Ifracombe. A Victorian folly completed in the mid 19th century by the Bassett family and extensively restored by the current owner. Outside, the castle's 50 acre (20ha) estate features landscaped gardens and glorious woodland walks. Tel: 01271 867474.

Watersmeet House 1 mile (1.6km) east of Lynmouth. Fishing lodge completed c.1832 in a picturesque valley at the confluence of the East Lyn River and Hoar Oak Water, and now an information centre for the National Trust. The East Lyn River is well known for its trout and salmon. It is virtually pollution free and its deep pools act as resting places for fish making their way up the river in spawn. Tel: 01598 753348.

Westward Ho! 8½ miles (13.5km) southwest of Barnstaple. Named after the book written by Charles Kingsley in 1855, Westward Ho! has two miles of sandy beach known as the Golden Bay, and is famous for its pebble ridge which lies between the beach and the area of sand dunes and salt marsh known as Northam Burrows. It is also famous for being the only town in Britain with an exclamation mark after its name. The dunes are home to a rich variety of birds, insects and wild flowers, while horses, cattle and sheep graze on the Burrows as they did on common land in days gone by. The South West Coast Path runs through Westward Ho! and the Tarka Trail is close by.

Winsford Walled Garden Winsford Lane, Halwill Junction, 10 miles (16km) northwest of Okehampton. A flower garden with over 3000 varieties. Sympathetic conservation has been used to preserve the historic Victorian horticultural features while the walled summer garden features intensive planting. Tel: 01409 221477.

Yelverton Paperweight Centre Leg o' Mutton Corner, Yelverton. Exhibition of the Broughton Collection of hundreds of glass paperweights, antique and modern. Tel: 01822 854250.

Some famous people born in Devon

Babbage, Charles (computer pioneer) (1791–1871)	Teignmouth
Baring-Gould, Sabine (hymn writer) (1834–1924)	Exeter
Barker, Sue (tennis player) (1956–)	Paignton
Bastin, Cliff (football player) (1912–91)	Heavitree
Bodley, Thomas (diplomat) (1545–1613)	Exeter
Burton, Richard (explorer) (1821–90)	Torquay
Chichester, Francis (yachtsman) (1901–72)	Barnstaple
Christie, Agatha (writer) (1890–1976)	Torquay
Coleridge, Samuel Taylor (poet) (1772–1834)	Ottery St Mary
Collins, Pauline (actress) (1940–)	Exmouth
Cook, Peter (comedian) (1937–95)	Torquay
Drake, Francis (explorer) (1541–96)	Tavistock
Foot, Michael (politician) (1913–)	Plymouth
Goodwin, Ron (composer) (1925–2003)	Plymouth
Hayman, Francis (artist) (1708–76)	Exeter
Karno, Fred (comedian) (1866–1941)	Exeter
Martin, Chris (singer) (1977–)	Exeter
Mortimer, Angela (tennis player) (1932–)	Plymouth
Newcomen, Thomas (inventor) (1663–1729)	Dartmouth
Raleigh, Walter (seafarer) (1554–1618)	Budleigh Salterton
Reynolds, Sir Joshua (painter) (1723–92)	Plympton
Russell, John (Jack) (parson) (1795–1883)	Dartmouth
Scott, Captain Robert Falcon (explorer) (1868–1912)	Stoke Damerel
Shepherd, David (cricketer) (1929–2005)	Bideford
Sinden, Sir Donald (actor) (1923–)	Plymouth

Islands of Devon

Island name	Area	Nearest landmark	General information	Shipping area
Allen's Rock	Taw River	Fremington	GR: SS503334	Lundy
Ball Rock	English Channel	Gammon Head	GR: SX765357	Portland
Ballsaddle Rocks	English Channel	Lannacombe Bay	GR: SX797365	Portland
Barker Rock	English Channel	The Narrows	GR: SX818366	Portland
Battisborough Island	English Channel	Bugle Hole	GR: SX605466	Portland
Beeny Sisters	Atlantic	Beeny	GR: SX109932	Lundy
Bell Rock	English Channel	Babbacombe Bay	GR: SX929679	Portland
Bellhouse Rock	English Channel	Starehole Bay	GR: SX727364	Portland
Benricks, The	Bristol Channel	Ilfracombe	GR: SS526479	Lundy
Big Picket Rock	English Channel	High Peak	GR: SY104847	Portland
Black Rock	Atlantic	Lundy Island	GR: SS132432	Lundy
Black Rock	Atlantic	Castle Point	GR: SX139973	Lundy
Black Rock	Bude Bay	Bude	GR: SS194017	Lundy
Black Rock	English Channel	Paignton	GR: SX898603	Portland
Black Stone	English Channel	Blackstone Point	GR: SX535461	Portland
Black Stone	English Channel	Salcombe Harbour	GR: SX737378	Portland
Black Stone	English Channel	Start Point	GR: SX831367	Portland
Blackchurch Rock	Bideford Bay	Clovelly	GR: SS299268	Lundy
Blackstone Rock	Taw River	Braunton	GR: SS485338	Lundy
Books, The	English Channel	Thurlestone Sand	GR: SX671416	Portland
Borough Island	English Channel	Bigbury-on-Sea	See Burgh Island	Portland
Bridge, The	English Channel	Plymouth	GR: SX469528	Plymouth
Brimpool Rocks	English Channel	Langerstone Point	GR: SX785353	Portland
Broad Stone	English Channel	Bolberry Down	GR: SX683379	Portland
Burgh Island	English Channel	Bigbury-on-Sea	See separate entry	Portland
Capper Stone	English Channel	Start Point	GR: SX833370	Portland
Chap and Carter	English Channel	Start Point	GR: SX829370	Portland
Chapman Rock	Bristol Channel	Fatacott Cliff	GR: SS268276	Lundy
Chapman's Rocks	English Channel	Sidmouth	GR: SY141875	Portland
China Rock	English Channel	Bolt Tail	GR: SX667394	Portland
Chit Rocks	English Channel	Sidmouth	GR: SY121869	Portland
Coach Rock	Bude Bay	Bude	GR: SS202068	Lundy
Cod Rock	English Channel	Berry Head	GR: SX946559	Portland
Cod Rocks	English Channel	Crabrock Point	GR: SX925528	Portland
Coney Rock	Bude Bay	South Hole	GR: SS213199	Lundy
Conger Rocks	English Channel	Exmouth	GR: SY009798	Portland
Corbin Rocks	English Channel	Culverhole Point	GR: SY281892	Portland
Cow and Calf	Bristol Channel	Woody Bay	GR: SS665498	Lundy
Cow and Calf	Bude Bay	Hartland Point	GR: SS226272	Lundy

Island name	Area	Nearest landmark	General information	Shipping area
Cow Rock	Bude Bay	Milford	GR: SS221216	Lundy
Crab Rock	English Channel	Heybrook Bay	GR: SX496482	Plymouth
Crow Rock	Taw Estuary	Appledore	GR: SS459319	Lundy
Culter Rock	English Channel	Wembury Point	GR: SX502479	Plymouth
Curtis's Rock	Bude Bay	Bude	GR: SS201086	Lundy
Damagehue Rock	Lee Bay	Lee	GR: SS469469	Lundy
Dancing Beggars	English Channel	Combe Point	GR: SX879485	Portland
Deckler's Island	English Channel	Deckler's Cliff	GR: SX754367	Portland
Denton's Rock	English Channel	Bolberry Down	GR: SX686379	Portland
Drake's Island	English Channel	Plymouth	See separate entry	Plymouth
Durl Rock	English Channel	Durl Head	GR: SX940557	Portland
East Mary's Rock	English Channel	Redcove Point	GR: SX615465	Portland
East Pole Sand	English Channel	Teignmouth	GR: SX944723	Portland
East Shag	English Channel	Daddyhole Cove	GR: SX931627	Portland
Eastern Black Rock	English Channel	Outer Froward Point	GR: SX919497	Portland
Egg Rock	Bristol Channel	Combe Martin	GR: SS566479	Lundy
Fishing Rock	Bristol Channel	Beacon Point	GR: SS534482	Lundy
Fremington Rock	Taw River	Fremington	GR: SS514333	Lundy
Frenchman's Rock	English Channel	The Narrows	GR: SX818367	Portland
Gallant Rock	Bideford Bay	Clovelly	GR: SS318252	Lundy
Gannets' Rock	Bristol Channel	Lundy Island	GR: SS137476	Lundy
Goat Island	Atlantic	Lundy Island	GR: SS131438	Lundy
Goat Island	English Channel	Culverhole Point	GR: SY320907	Portland
Gorah Rocks	English Channel	Sharpers Head	GR: SX791361	Portland
Grant's Rock	English Channel	Lannacombe Bay	GR: SX796366	Portland
Graystone Ledge	English Channel	Bolt Tail	GR: SX673388	Portland
Great Mew Stone	English Channel	Wembury Point	GR: SX500473	Plymouth
Great Sleaden Rock	English Channel	Ravens Cove	GR: SX820366	Portland
Greencliff Rock	Bideford Bay	Westward Ho!	GR: SS398275	Lundy
Grower Rock	Atlantic	Boscastle	GR: SX084908	Lundy
Gull Island	English Channel	Ravens Cove	GR: SX822367	Portland
Gull Rock	Atlantic	Castle Point	GR: SX147979	Lundy
Gull Rock	Atlantic	Millook	GR: SX175999	Lundy
Gull Rock	Atlantic	Beeny	GR: SX118934	Lundy
Gull Rock	Bristol Channel	Lundy Island	GR: SS141462	Lundy
Gull Rock	Bude Bay	Damehole Point	GR: SS222261	Lundy
Gull Rock	Bude Bay	Devil's Hole	GR: SS203172	Lundy
Gull Rock	Bude Bay	South Hole	GR: SS212202	Lundy
Gunpath Rock	Bude Bay	Milford	GR: SS220223	Lundy
Half Tide Rock	English Channel	Branscombe	GR: SY192880	Portland
Halftide, The	English Channel	Start Point	GR: SX832373	Portland
Halftide Rock	Atlantic	Lundy Island	GR: SS127442	Lundy
Halftide Rocks	English Channel	Warfleet	GR: SX882505	Portland
Ham Stone	English Channel	Cathole Cliff	GR: SX695370	Portland
Ham Stone	English Channel	Hamstone Cove	GR: SX763360	Portland
Harbreck Rock	English Channel	Paignton	GR: SX911633	Portland
Hare Stone	English Channel	Start Bay	GR: SX820380	Portland
Hen and Chickens	Atlantic	Lundy Island	GR: SS128483	Lundy
Hippa Rock	Bude Bay	Stanbury Beach	GR: SS196137	Lundy
Hole Rock	Bude Bay	Milford	GR: SS220226	Lundy
Horse Rocks	English Channel	Horse Cove	GR: SX961757	Portland
Horsey Island	Taw River	Braunton	GR: SS476336	Lundy
Humble Rocks	English Channel	Humble Point	GR: SY307899	Portland
Inner Combe Rocks	English Channel	Combe Point	GR: SX883485	Portland
Island, The	English Channel	Prawle Point	GR: SX771349	Portland
Kempthorn's Rock	Bude Bay	Wren Beach	GR: SS198119	Lundy
Knoll Pins	Bristol Channel	Lundy Island	GR: SS142465	Lundy
Ladram Rock	English Channel	Ladram Bay	GR: SY096850	Portland
Langstone Rock	English Channel	Dawlish Warren	GR: SX979779	Portland
Lantern Rock	English Channel	Cathole Point	GR: SX693377	Portland
Lead Stone	English Channel	Thatcher Point	GR: SX952635	Portland
Life Rock	Bude Bay	Hartland Quay	GR: SS222249	Lundy
Little Chapman Rock	Bristol Channel	Fatacott Cliff	GR: SS272275	Lundy
Little Island	English Channel	Burgh Island	GR: SX647436	Portland
Little Mew Stone	English Channel	Bolt Head	GR: SX727359	Portland
Little Picket Rock	English Channel	High Peak	GR: SY104846	Portland
Little Shutter Rock	Atlantic	Lundy Island	GR: SS133433	Lundy
Little Sleaden Rock	English Channel	Ravens Cove	GR: SX819365	Portland
Lobster Rock	English Channel	Start Bay	GR: SX822369	Portland
Long Island	Atlantic	Trevalga	GR: SX074906	Lundy
Long Rock	Bristol Channel	Eldern Point	GR: SS247276	Lundy

Island name	Area	Nearest landmark	General information	Shipping area
Long Rock	Bude Bay	Bude	GR: SS201098	Lundy
Long Rock	English Channel	Start Bay	GR: SX819382	Portland
Long Rock	Morte Bay	Baggy Point	GR: SS421409	Lundy
Lundy	Bristol Channel	Morte Point	See separate entry	Lundy
Maer Rocks	English Channel	Exmouth	GR: SY015799	Portland
Mag Rock	English Channel	Sharkham Point	GR: SX939546	Portland
Mansley Rock	Bude Bay	Milford	GR: SS221219	Lundy
Mare and Colt, The	Bristol Channel	Red Cleave	GR: SS621488	Lundy
Meachard	Atlantic	Boscastle	GR: SX090916	Lundy
Meddrick Rocks	English Channel	Gutterslide Beach	GR: SX623456	Portland
Meg Rocks	English Channel	Willow Cove	GR: SX884489	Portland
Mew Stone	English Channel	Berry Head	GR: SX944559	Portland
Mew Stone	English Channel	Bolt Head	GR: SX728360	Portland
Mew Stone	English Channel	Outer Froward Point	GR: SX910494	Portland
Middle Stone	English Channel	Goodrington Sands	GR: SX894595	Portland
Milestones, The	English Channel	Torbay	GR: SX919629	Portland
Montagu Step	Atlantic	Lundy Island	GR: SS131435	Lundy
Morte Stone	Morte Bay	Morte Point	GR: SS459456	Lundy
Mouse Island	Bristol Channel	Lundy Island	GR: SS147439	Lundy
Mouth Stone	English Channel	Mouthstone Point	GR: SX525476	Portland
Murray's Rock	English Channel	Burgh Island	GR: SX651648	Portland
Mussel Rock	Bude Bay	Warren Point	GR: SS198112	Lundy
Mussel Rock	English Channel	St Mary's Bay	GR: SX934550	Portland
Needle Rock	Atlantic	Lundy Island	GR: SS129455	Lundy
Netton Island	English Channel	Bloody Cove	GR: SX553458	Portland
Orcombe Rocks	English Channel	Exmouth	GR: SY021794	Portland
Ore Stone	English Channel	Thatcher Point	GR: SX957630	Portland
Otterton Ledge	English Channel	Budleigh Salterton	GR: SY079817	Portland
Outer Appledore Rocks	Lee Bay	Lee	GR: SS479468	Lundy
Outer Combe Rocks	English Channel	Combe Point	GR: SX883486	Portland
Outer Stone	Bristol Channel	Berrynarbor	GR: SS564480	Lundy
Outfalls, The	Bristol Channel	Ilfracombe	GR: SS515480	Lundy
Peartree Point	English Channel	Ravens Cove	GR: SX820365	Portland
Pencil Rock	Croyde Bay	Baggy Point	GR: SS422403	Lundy
Pensport Rock	Lee Bay	Lee	GR: SS475469	Lundy
Pigsback Rock	Bude Bay	Wren Beach	GR: SS198121	Lundy
Pound Stone	English Channel	Salcombe Harbour	GR: SX732379	Portland
Priest and Clerk	English Channel	Cathole Cliff	GR: SX697374	Portland
Rags, The	English Channel	Starehole Bay	GR: SX729365	Portland
Ramtor Rock	Bude Bay	South Hole	GR: SS214197	Lundy
Rat Island	Bristol Channel	Lundy Island	GR: SS147437	Lundy
Rawn's Rocks	Bristol Channel	Hangman Point	GR: SS594485	Lundy
Redrot Ledge	English Channel	Bolt Tail	GR: SX668394	Portland
Reed Rocks	Bude Bay	Lower Sharpnose Point	GR: SS195128	Lundy
Renney Rocks	English Channel	Plymouth	GR: SX490486	Plymouth
Ridge Rocks	Bristol Channel	Ilfracombe	GR: SS511478	Lundy
Rugger Rock	English Channel	Stoke Down	GR: SX559456	Portland
Saddle Rock	Atlantic	Beeny	GR: SX113932	Lundy
Saddle Rocks	Atlantic	Trevalga	GR: SX073903	Lundy
Saltstone	Bude Bay	Bude	GR: SS189009	Lundy
Samphire Rock	Atlantic	Trevigue	GR: SX130957	Lundy
Sandhole Rock	Bude Bay	Hardisworthy	GR: SS217208	Lundy
Scotch Stone	Bristol Channel	Combe Martin	GR: SS585484	Lundy
Sea Rock	English Channel	Start Point	GR: SX831369	Portland
Seals' Rock	Bristol Channel	Lundy Island	GR: SS135481	Lundy
Shag Rock	English Channel	Bullock Cove	GR: SX755365	Portland
Shag Rock	English Channel	Holcombe	GR: SX960746	Portland
Shag Rock	English Channel	Littlecombe Shoot	GR: SY185879	Portland
Shag Stone	English Channel	Plymouth	GR: SX487486	Plymouth
Shag Stone	English Channel	Outer Froward Point	GR: SX908494	Portland
Sherbourne Rocks	English Channel	Beer Head	GR: SY221878	Portland
Shiphill Rock	English Channel	Start Bay	GR: SX846467	Portland
Shoelodge Reef	English Channel	Start Bay	GR: SX823376	Portland
Shooter Rock	English Channel	Outer Froward Point	GR: SX908495	Portland
Short Island	Atlantic	Trevalga	GR: SX077908	Lundy
Skittering Rock	Bideford Bay	Clovelly	GR: SS318250	Lundy
Sleaden Halftide	English Channel	Ravens Cove	GR: SX821365	Portland
Smooth Rock	Bude Bay	Bude	GR: SS201081	Lundy
Squench Rock	Bude Bay	Wren Beach	GR: SS197123	Lundy
St James's Stone	Atlantic	Lundy Island	GR: SS131468	Lundy
Stanning Rocks	English Channel	Cathole Cliff	GR: SX699372	Portland

Island name	Area	Nearest landmark	General information	Shipping area
Stoneivy Rock	Atlantic	Dizzard	GR: SX155987	Lundy
Tense Rocks	Bude Bay	Hartland Point	GR: SS229279	Lundy
Thatcher Rock	English Channel	Thatcher Point	GR: SX944628	Portland
Thurlestone Rock	English Channel	Thurlestone Sand	GR: SX673413	Portland
Tortoiseshell Rocks	English Channel	Windgate	GR: SY109864	Portland
Two Stones	English Channel	The Narrows	GR: SX814368	Portland
Wadham Rocks	English Channel	Wadham Beach	GR: SX580468	Portland
West Mary's Rock	English Channel	Bugle Hole	GR: SX605465	Portland
Westcott Wattle	Bude Bay	Yeolmouth Cliff	GR: SS198162	Lundy
Western Blackstone	English Channel	Blackstone Point	GR: SX889494	Portland
Western Ledge	English Channel	Castle Point	GR: SX888501	Portland
Wheelers Stone	Morte Bay	Baggy Point	GR: SS430413	Lundy
Wilson's Rock	English Channel	Start Bay	GR: SX819385	Portland
Wolf Rock	English Channel	Bolt Tail	GR: SX666395	Portland
Wood Rock	Bideford Bay	Clovelly	GR: SS315255	Lundy

DORSET

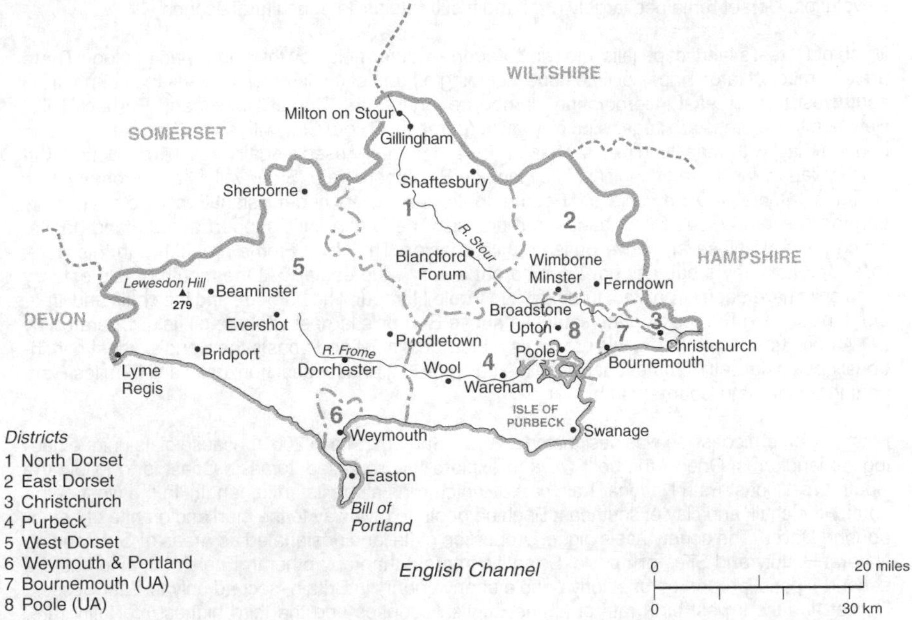
WILTSHIRE
SOMERSET
HAMPSHIRE
DEVON
Milton on Stour
Gillingham
Shaftesbury
Sherborne
R. Stour
Blandford Forum
Wimborne Minster
Ferndown
Lewesdon Hill
279
Beaminster
Evershot
Broadstone
Upton
Puddletown
Christchurch
Bournemouth
Poole
R. Frome
Bridport
Lyme Regis
Dorchester
Wool
Wareham
ISLE OF PURBECK
Swanage
Weymouth
Easton
Bill of Portland
English Channel
0
20 miles
0
30 km
1
2
3
4
5
6
7
8
Districts
1 North Dorset
2 East Dorset
3 Christchurch
4 Purbeck
5 West Dorset
6 Weymouth & Portland
7 Bournemouth (UA)
8 Poole (UA)

Dorset borders Devon to the west, Somerset to the northwest, Wiltshire to the northeast and Hampshire to the east. Famous for its picturesque coastline, which features unique landforms such as Lulworth Cove, the Isle of Portland, Chesil Beach and the massive rock arch of Durdle Door, the county is largely rural with a low population density. Bournemouth and Christchurch were added to the county from Hampshire in the county boundary changes of 1974 and Christchurch, Bournemouth and Poole are often referred to as a conurbation (extended urban area); although the latter two are no longer part of the county for administrative purposes, having been designated unitary authorities in April 1997, they are included in the ceremonial and geographical county.

The first known settlement of Dorset was by Mesolithic hunters, c.8000 BC. Their populations were small and concentrated along the coast in the Isle of Purbeck, Weymouth and Chesil Beach and along the Stour valley. They used tools and fire to clear these areas of some of the native oak forest. Dorset's high chalk hills have provided a location for defensive settlements for thousands of years; there are Neolithic and Bronze Age burial mounds on almost every such hill in the county, as well as several Iron Age hill forts. Dorset has many notable Roman artefacts, particularly around the county town of Dorchester (Roman Durnovaria), where Maiden Castle was captured from the Celtic Durotriges by Vespasian in AD 54. Roman roads radiated from Dorchester, following the tops of the chalk ridges to the many small Roman villages around the county. In the Roman era, settlements moved from the hill tops to the valleys and the hill tops were abandoned by the 4th century. A large defensive ditch, Bokerley Dyke, delayed the Saxon conquest of Dorset from the northeast for up to 200 years, but after the Romans were eventually overrun by the Saxons, Dorset became part of the kingdom of Wessex. Domesday Book documents many Saxon settlements corresponding to modern towns and villages, mostly in the valleys, and there have since been few changes to the parishes. Over the next few centuries the settlers established the pattern of farmland which prevailed into the 19th century, as well as many monasteries, which were important landowners and centres of power. The earliest recorded use of the county name was in 940 as 'Dorseteschire' (Celtic, 'the place of fisticuffs').

Dorset's history from the Norman Conquest onwards became increasingly turbulent. During the 12th century civil war between Matilda and King Stephen, the county was fortified with the construction of defensive castles at Corfe, Powerstock and Wareham, and the strengthening of the monasteries such as that at Abbotsbury. In the 17th century Civil War, a number of Royalist strongholds, such as Sherborne and Corfe Castle, were destroyed by Parliamentarians. In the intervening years, the county was used by the monarchy and nobility for hunting and Dorset still has a number of deer parks. Throughout the late medieval period, the remaining hilltop settlements shrank further and disappeared. From the Tudor to Georgian periods, farms specialised and the monastic estates were broken up, leading to an increase in population and settlement size. During the Industrial Revolution, Dorset remained largely rural and it still retains its agricultural economy.

Much of Dorset's landscape falls into two categories, determined by the underlying geology. There are a number of large ridges of limestone including a band of chalk which crosses the county from southwest to northeast incorporating Cranborne Chase, the Dorset Downs and Purbeck Hills. Between these areas are large, wide clay vales (primarily Oxford Clay with some Wealden Clay and London Clay) with wide flood plains. These vales are primarily used for dairy agriculture, dotted with small villages, farms and coppices. They include Blackmore Vale (Stour valley) and Frome valley. Southeast Dorset, around Poole and Bournemouth, lies on very non-resistant Eocene clays (mainly London Clay and Gault Clay), sands and gravels. These thin soils support a heathland habitat which supports all seven native British reptile species. The River Frome runs through this weak rock, and its many tributaries have carved out a very wide estuary. At the mouth of this estuary sand spits have been deposited, turning it into Poole Harbour. The harbour, and the chalk and limestone hills of the Purbecks to the south, lie above Europe's largest onshore oil field. Operated by BP-Amoco from Wych Farm, this produces a high-quality oil and boasts the world's oldest continuously pumping well (Kimmeridge, since the early 1960s) and longest horizontal drill (5 miles/8km, ending underneath Bournemouth pier).

Most of Dorset's coastline was designated a World Heritage Site in 2001 because of its unique geological landforms. One of the best ways to explore the so-called Jurassic Coast is to follow the South West Coast Path National Trail, part of which runs along its entire length. In the west of the county the chalk and clay of southeast England begin to give way to the marl and granite of neighbouring Devon. The county has a higher proportion of its land designated as Areas of Outstanding Natural Beauty and Sites of Special Scientific interest than any other in England. It also has the second highest proportion of elderly people of any county in Britain, second only to East Sussex. Dorset has the lowest birth rate of all the English counties and the third highest mortality rate, behind East Sussex and Devon. Despite this, an abundance of migrants moving to Dorset and the Poole–Bournemouth conurbation give the county the second highest net population growth, behind Cambridgeshire, in England.

The seas around Weymouth and Portland rank among the best in northern Europe for sailing, and water sports are also popular at Poole and Bournemouth. Blandford Forum, Sherborne, Gillingham, Shaftesbury and Sturminster Newton are historic market towns which serve the farms and villages of the Blackmore Vale (Thomas Hardy's Vale of the Little Dairies). Blandford is home to the Badger brewery of Hall and Woodhouse. Bridport, Lyme Regis and Wareham are also market towns. Dorset is one of only four non-urban counties in England (the others being Cornwall, Norfolk and Suffolk) not to have a motorway, The only passenger airport in the county is Bournemouth International Airport (formerly known as Hurn), and there are two passenger sea ports, at Poole and Weymouth.

Dorset	**Population**			**Area**	
Districts	*male*	*female*	*total*	*sq miles*	*sq km*
Christchurch	21,130	23,735	44,865	19	50
East Dorset	39,974	43,812	83,786	137	354
North Dorset	30,820	31,085	61,905	235	609
Purbeck	21,521	22,895	44,416	156	404
West Dorset	44,075	48,285	92,360	418	1081
Weymouth & Portland	31,260	32,388	63,648	16	42
Bournemouth Unitary Authority	78,434	85,010	163,444	18	46
Poole Unitary Authority	66,055	72,233	138,288	25	65
Total	333,269	359,443	692,712	1024	2651

Local Attractions and Information

Abbotsbury Sub-Tropical Gardens	Bullers Way, Abbotsbury, 7 miles (11km) west of Weymouth. Established in 1765 by the 1st Countess of Ilchester as a kitchen garden to her nearby castle. Developed since then into a magnificent 20 acre (8ha) woodland garden filled with rare and exotic plants from all over the world. Most of these were new introductions to the UK, found by the Countess's plant-hunting descendants. Now Grade I listed, the garden is particularly noted for its camellia groves and collections of magnolias, rhododendrons and hydrangeas. Tel: 01305 871387.

Abbotsbury Swannery — Abbotsbury, 7 miles (11km) west of Weymouth. The world's only managed colony of nesting mute swans, its proper title being the Abbotsbury Colonial Nesting Herd. Records indicate that it was established in the 14th century or earlier by the Benedictine monks of St Peter's monastery, who possibly adopted a colony of swans already nesting beside the Fleet lagoon, located behind Chesil Beach (see separate entry) and which provides an ideal habitat for the birds to feed. The swans once provided meat for the monks; today they provide feathers for the helmets of the Gentlemen at Arms, the Queen's bodyguard, while Lloyds of London still use quills from Abbotsbury swan feathers to record insurance losses. Tel: 01305 871858.

Administrative headquarters — **Bournemouth**: Town Hall, Bourne Avenue, Bournemouth BH2 6DY. Tel: 01202 451451.
Dorset: County Hall, Colliton Park, Dorchester DT1 1XJ. Tel: 01305 251000.
Poole: Civic Centre, Poole BH15 2RU. Tel: 01202 633633.

Anderson Manor — 2 miles (3km) northeast of Bere Regis. One of the best small Jacobean manor houses in England. Built of brick and stone, it was completed in 1622 by John Tregonwell of Milton Abbey, an ancestor of Lewis Tregonwell, founder of Bournemouth. The house remained in the Tregonwell family until 1910 and was subsequently owned by the Gratrix and Cholmondeleys. During World War II the manor was used as a Commando headquarters.

Athelhampton House — 3/4 mile (1.2km) east of Puddletown, 6 miles (10km) northeast of Dorchester. A fine 15th century manor house, surrounded by one of England's great gardens. The core of the house was built in the late 15th century by Sir William Martyn, Lord Mayor of London in 1493, a member of a local family who had acquired the manor in the 14th century. Martyn later added the gabled parlour wing, which projects at an unusual angle from the upper end of the hall. A detached gatehouse enclosed a courtyard to the south until 1862. The property had fallen into decline and was being used as a farmhouse when it was sold to George Wood in 1848. He restored the hall range but demolished the gatehouse. Members of Thomas Hardy's family worked on the restoration and Hardy immortalised Athelhampton in two of his poems. In 1891 the house was acquired by antiquarian Alfred de Lafontaine, who carried out further restoration to the interior and added a new (private) wing to the north of the hall range. The 20 acres (8ha) of gardens, designed by Inigo Thomas in the 1890s, are encircled by the River Piddle. In 1957 Athelhampton was purchased by Robert Cooke, who installed much of the furniture now on view and made further improvements to the gardens. Today this work is continued by his son and daughter-in-law. Tel: 01305 848363.

Badbury Rings — 1 mile (1.6km) northeast of Shapwick, 9 miles (15km) northwest of Poole. Badbury Rings ranks with Maiden Castle (see separate entry) as one of England's finest earthworks. The prehistoric hill fort has three ramparts, each 40ft (12m) high, separated by ditches, which encircle the 330ft (100m) high hill fort. Badbury Rings, like Maiden Castle, is believed to have belonged to the ancient Dorset tribe known as the Durotriges. The site now forms part of the Kingston Lacy estate (see separate entry), and under the guardianship of the National Trust has been restored to light grazing land. A magnificent avenue of trees lines the Wimborne–Blandford road for 2 miles (3km) just below the Rings.

Battles — There have been no major battles on Dorset soil although during the Civil War, on 4 August 1645, Cromwell arrived at Shaftesbury with 1000 men to find 2000 of the Dorsetshire Clubmen entrenched in positions on Hambledon Hill. He had already captured about 50 of their leaders in the town where they were holding a meeting. Cromwell sent 50 dragoons to attack from the rear and the Clubmen were easily put to flight – most of them sliding down the hill on their backsides. About 300 of them were locked up overnight in Shroton church.

Bloxworth House — 6 miles (10km) northwest of Wareham. Located in an area that once formed part of Hardy's Egdon Heath, the manor belonged to the monks of Cerne for centuries until Henry VIII's Dissolution of the Monasteries in 1536. It was sold for £640 to Richard Savage and George Strangways. Originally Jacobean but much altered later, at one time it was owned by the Trenchard family from Wolfeton, near Dorchester, and was subsequently the home of the Pickard-Cambridge family. Octavius Pickard-Cambridge, rector of Bloxworth for nearly 50 years in the late 19th century, was a great Victorian clergyman-naturalist, being a world authority on spiders. Several scenes in the film *Far From the Madding Crowd* (1967) were shot at Bloxworth House.

Blue Vinney — Traditional name for the hard blue-veined cheese of Dorset, made from milk from which the cream had been skimmed to make butter and hence having a low fat content. The name 'vinney' derives from an archaic word for mould or mildew. Sadly, genuine Blue Vinney cheese has largely become a food of the past, although it is still made to a traditional recipe at a single location in the county. Much of today's product is considered nothing more than substandard Stilton.

Bournemouth — The history of Bournemouth begins in the early 19th century. When retired army officer Captain Lewis Tregonwell visited the area in 1810, he found only a bridge crossing a small stream at the head of an unspoilt valley (or 'chine') that led out into Poole Bay. Tregonwell and his wife were so impressed by the area that they bought several acres and built a home, which is today part of the Royal Exeter Hotel. Tregonwell also planted pine trees, providing a sheltered walk to the beach. Shops were banned in the early days of Bournemouth, and tradesmen were expected to call from Poole or Christchurch; the villagers eventually allowed the railway to approach, but only in a deep cutting so that it would remain largely unseen. Such lofty isolation was not destined to last. The infrastructure provided for the inhabitants was inadequate, with poor roads and inefficient sewers. The saviour of the town was Christopher Crabbe Creeke, who bore the impressive title Surveyor of Nuisances for the Bournemouth Commissioners. He laid out gracefully curving roads around the chines, lined with grand villas, and improved the drains. By 1890, Bournemouth was recognised by Queen Victoria, who granted it the status of a borough, along with its own mayor. An Undercliff Drive was laid out along the beach (Kaiser Wilhelm was one of the first people to drive along it). Parks were established, and a municipal orchestra took residence at the Winter

Gardens; the Bournemouth Symphony Orchestra is now one of England's leading provincial orchestras. Hospitals, schools, libraries and houses were provided by local residents. The town expanded rapidly during the early 1900s, swallowing up the competing resorts of Westbourne, Boscombe Spa and Southbourne-on-Sea. By the middle of the 20th century Bournemouth was one of the England's major towns, yet local government reorganisation in 1974 removed many of its powers and responsibilities to Dorset County Council. The situation was largely reversed in 1997 when Bournemouth became a unitary authority. The 5 mile (8km) stretch of beach belonging to Bournemouth runs from Poole in the west to Hengistbury Head in the east. A roundabout at the end of the Wessex Way called 'County Gates' once marked the divide between the historic counties of Hampshire and Dorset, but now marks the border between Poole and Bournemouth.

Bournemouth University Fern Barrow, Poole. Founded in the early 20th century as Bournemouth Municipal College, its modern history began in the early 1970s with the creation of the Bournemouth College of Technology. Construction of the new buildings on what was the largest farm in Talbot Village was completed by September 1976 and the college was renamed Dorset Institute of Higher Education. In 1990, the Dorset Institute was redesignated Bournemouth Polytechnic. Under the Higher & Further Education Act of 1992, the Polytechnic became Bournemouth University with inauguration on 27 November of the same year. The university currently has over 15,000 students. Tel: 01202 524111.

Bovington Tank Museum 2 miles (3km) north of Wool, 5 miles (8km) west of Wareham. The museum houses the world's largest collection of armoured fighting vehicles – almost 300 vehicles from over 26 countries. Exhibits range from unique World War I tanks to the latest main battle tank of the British Army, the Challenger. Tel: 01929 405096.

Bridport 13 miles (21km) west of Dorchester. Alfred the Great established the town as a fortified burgh in the late 9th century. The predominant industry was rope making; in 1213 King John demanded that Bridport produce ropes and cables night and day for his army and navy, and the industry was later to expand to trade all over the world, including Newfoundland. So famous was Bridport rope that those who ended their days on the gallows were said to have been 'stabbed by a Bridport dagger'. In 1253 Henry III made the town a royal borough, a status confirmed by Elizabeth I and James I. In 1651 Charles II stayed in the town to escape the Cromwellian army. There are over 1000 listed buildings of historical or architectural merit in the town, many of them built for successful businessmen associated with the rope-making industry. West Mill and The Court in West Street are two such industrial buildings. The Millennium Green – an area of lawn, gardens, woodland and meadow providing a tranquil oasis in the heart of Bridport – was opened by the Duchess of Gloucester in 2003.

Brownsea Island The largest of the five main islands in Poole Harbour, Brownsea is 1$^1/_2$ miles (2.5km) long and $^3/_4$ mile (1.2km) wide. Brownsea Island is first mentioned in the 7th century, when a hermit living there lit beacons to guide boats into the harbour. In 1015 King Cnut landed on the island before attempted invasions at nearby Wareham and Hamworthy. The island was fortified by Henry VIII, and the castle he built became a Parliamentary stronghold in the Civil War. After electricity was installed at the end of the 19th century the castle caught fire and was only partially rebuilt. From 1–9 August 1907, Lord Baden-Powell of Gilwell held an experimental camp for 22 boys on the island. The subsequent publication of his book *Scouting for Boys* started the Scout movement. In April 1961 Mrs Bonham-Christie, the owner of Brownsea, died at the age of 98. Her grandson was obliged to put the island on the market to meet death duties. After the Treasury had accepted the island in lieu of taxes, the National Trust agreed to take over responsibility for it after an endowment of £100,000 was raised. The John Lewis Partnership was a particularly generous donor, also repairing Brownsea Castle (aka Branksea Castle) and renting it from the Trust as a hotel for its employees. Much of the island is a nature reserve and an important habitat for birds. Evidence of the early use of Poole Harbour has been provided by an artefact found off Brownsea Island: the Poole Logboat, cut from a giant oak tree, is 32ft (10m) long and dates to c.295 BC. The island is one of the few places in southern England where red squirrels survive, because grey squirrels have never been introduced. Brownsea also has a small ornamental population of peacocks. The island is designated a Site of Special Scientific Interest. Area: 0.78 sq miles (2 sq km). (GR: SZ019879.)

Canford Heath An area of heathland north of Poole covering 1040 acres (420ha), designated a Site of Special Scientific Interest. One of the major remaining areas of lowland heath in England, it is an important habitat for the smooth snake, sand lizard, Dartford warbler and nightjar. Numerous paths and tracks criss-cross its undulating sandy surface. The heath has given its name to a nearby housing estate.

Canford House 2 miles (3km) southeast of Wimborne Minster. In Plantagenet times the ancient manor house of Canford was owned successively by the Earls of Salisbury, then the Beauforts, Courtenays and Blounts. All except the kitchens of the ancient house were demolished in 1765. A new house, built in 1826 by Lord de Mauley, was enlarged by Sir John Guest in 1848 with the addition of a great hall, gallery and tower. The house became Canford School in 1922.

Cerne Abbas Giant Cerne Abbas, 6 miles (10km) north of Dorchester. The Cerne Abbas Giant – or the 'Rude Man', so named for its prominent genitalia – is the largest hill figure in Britain. It is one of two such representations of the human form, the other being the Long Man of Wilmington in East Sussex. The giant, carved in solid lines from the chalk bedrock, measures 180ft (55m) high, and carries a huge knobbled club 120ft (36.5m) in length. The first written record of the giant appears in 1751 in a letter by Dorset historian John Hutchins, suggesting that the figure was cut in the mid 1600s. A slightly later reference to the figure can be found in the *Gentleman's Magazine* of 1764, where the figure is described and depicted with a navel that has long since disappeared. Although the lack of earlier references suggests that the figure dates to the 17th century, its style and proximity to an Iron Age earthwork indicate the possibility of a much earlier origin. Another plausible theory is that it was a depiction of Hercules, created between AD 180–193 during the reign of the Emperor Commodus, who believed himself to be a reincarnation of the god.

Chesil Beach — A tombolo or shingle barrier ridge at the eastern end of Lyme Bay, extending 18 miles (29km) from west of Burton Bradstock at West Bay, to Fortuneswell on Portland. As far as Abbotsbury it is attached to the land, but beyond that an open stretch of water known as the Fleet lagoon separates it from the mainland until it reaches Portland. The beach's origin is uncertain but it was possibly built from gravel driven alongshore by waves from the western part of Lyme Bay and the northeastern part of Portland. The pebbles, graduated in size and largest at the Portland end, consist mainly of flint and chert from the Cretaceous and Jurassic rocks and Triassic Bunter pebbles. The Fleet Nature Reserve, a protected wetland area formed in the lee of the Chesil Bank, is one of Europe's most important tidal and semi-tidal natural habitats, a haven for bird life.

Chettle House — 6 miles (10km) northeast of Blandford Forum. In 1710 Thomas Archer was commissioned to build the existing house in place of an Elizabethan house then occupied by the Chafin family. The Queen Anne manor house has two principal storeys with basements and attics; the English baroque architecture includes barrel-vaulted ceilings and a magnificent oak staircase. All the corners in the house are rounded, a characteristic of Archer's style which can also be seen at St John's Church, Smith Square, London. The Stone or West Hall has doorways of walnut and oak, probably original; tympana with bas reliefs by Alfred Stevens were added in the 1840s after a cupola which formerly crowned the centre of the house was removed. Two statues in the hall came from the Great Exhibition of 1851 and the chandelier is reputed to be early English, dating to between 1760 and 1780. Tel: 01258 830858.

Christchurch — 7 miles (11km) east of Bournemouth. A popular sailing centre sited on the Dorset/Hampshire border where the Stour meets the Avon, and protected by Hengistbury Head with its Iron Age fort, the coastal town dates from Saxon times. Originally known as Twynham, 'the place betwixt the waters', Christchurch still retains its Saxon street layout. The town lies in the shadow of the longest parish church in England – the magnificent 11th century priory church originally known as Christ's Church, and from which the town takes its modern name. There are several buildings of historic interest, including the thatched 14th century Old Court House and the Georgian Red House Museum and Art Gallery. The museum was originally a workhouse and contains objects relating to local history, geology, natural history and archaeology as well as an impressive costume gallery.

Christchurch Castle and Norman House — Castle Street, Christchurch. Christchurch Castle consists of two ruined buildings: the keep on the motte and the Constable's House on the bank of the mill stream. The Norman motte and bailey castle, founded by Richard de Redvers c.1100, and the stone-built house, built in the bailey c.1160, are both owned by English Heritage. Tel: 0117 975 0700.

Clavell Tower — Kimmeridge Bay, 5 miles (8km) south of Wareham. Also known as Clavell Folly and the Kimmeridge Tower, the three-storey structure rises 40ft (12m) above Hen Cliff, 330ft (100m) above the sea on the Isle of Purbeck. The tower is part of the Smedmore estate and was built in 1830 by the Rev. John Richards, who had changed his name to Clavell after inheriting the estate in 1817. Thomas Hardy is believed to have courted a lady friend by the name of Eliza Nicholls around the tower, and also used it to illustrate his Wessex poems. P D James drew from it inspiration for her novel *The Black Tower.* No one knows precisely why the tower was built, but it appears to have been some sort of observatory overlooking Kimmeridge Bay. The Heritage Lottery Fund contributed a substantial grant in September 2006 to enable the tower, which was badly affected by coastal erosion, to be moved 80ft (24m) inland from where it previously stood.

Clouds Hill — 9 miles (15km) east of Dorchester. T E Lawrence (Lawrence of Arabia), using the name 'Aircraftsman Shaw', rented this little brick and tile cottage on the slopes of Clouds Hill in 1923 as a retreat from nearby Bovington Camp when he rejoined the Royal Air Force. After buying the property in 1925 Lawrence found the peace and quiet he needed to work on *Seven Pillars of Wisdom*, which was published in 1926. In 1935, after spending many years in the RAF away from the cottage, Lawrence was discharged at the age of 46 and retired to Clouds Hill. Five days later he was killed in a crash on his motorcycle when returning home from Bovington Camp. The charming cottage in a woodland setting is now owned by the National Trust. Tel: 01929 405616.

Corfe Castle — 4 miles (6km) southeast of Wareham. Located in the village to which it gives its name, the Norman castle was founded by William I c.1080 on the site of a Saxon royal residence in the Purbeck Hills. The scene of the murder of Edward the Martyr, it is now in ruins and only the 70ft (21.5m) great tower, erected by Henry I, remains. Henry imprisoned his elder brother Robert, Duke of Normandy, here in 1106. The tower-studded curtain wall was erected by King John. Part of the huge sum of £1400 allocated to building operations at Corfe during John's reign was spent on the king's 'Gloriette', a tower house arranged round a courtyard in the topmost inner ward. The castle was sold by Elizabeth I to Sir Christopher Hatton and 50 years later was bought by Sir John Bankes, a staunch Royalist, who also bought Kingston Lacy. Corfe was destroyed during the Civil War in 1646. The ruins are now owned by the National Trust and have recently undergone restoration. Tel: 01929 481294.

Cranborne Manor — 14 miles (23km) north of Bournemouth. Originally built as a hunting lodge in 1207, the building evolved until acquired by the 1st Earl of Salisbury in 1605. Completely rebuilt in 1610–40, it was damaged during the Civil War and a new west wing built. During the period 1700–1860 it was used by two tenant farmers, the present gardens being their farmyards. Further repairs were done by the 2nd Marquess of Salisbury and the Cecil family have lived there ever since. The gardens, originally designed by John Tradescant, contain sculptures including *Druid*, a life-size bronze

White Park bull by Nicola Toms, an Italian Renaissance wild boar and a head by Elizabeth Frink titled *In Memoriam*. The manor itself is currently not open to the public. Tel: 01725 517289.

Creech Grange 3 miles (5km) south of Wareham. An elegant country house at the foot of the Purbeck Hills built by Sir Oliver Lawrence, who acquired the land from the former Bindon Abbey, near Wool, after the Dissolution of the Monasteries in 1539. Creech Grange was bought by Nathaniel Bond in 1691; in Stuart times his descendant Thomas Bond laid out the famous London street that bears his name. Only fragments remain of the original house built by Lawrence before his death in 1559; it was damaged by fire by Parliamentary troops during the Civil War, while the entire front was taken down and rebuilt in the local Tudor style in 1846.

Crichel House 8 miles (13km) north of Wimborne. An 18th century mansion built on the ruins of a Tudor house burned down in 1742. The surrounding park of 400 acres (162ha) contains a lake covering 50 acres (20ha). Crichel formerly belonged to the Napier family but was passed to Humphrey Sturt, of Horton in Dorset, on his marriage to Diana, aunt and heir of Sir Gerard Napier, the 6th and last Baronet. George IV, while Prince Regent, occupied Crichel House for a time, and his daughter, the Princess Charlotte, stayed there under the care of Lady Rosslyn and Lady Ilchester.

Deans Court Deans Court Lane, Wimborne Minster. The 13 acres (5ha) of partly wild gardens surround an old house that was once the Deanery to the Minster. There are many fine specimen trees, lawns and borders. A fascinating old kitchen garden has a long serpentine wall and several old varieties of vegetables are grown. There is also a superb collection of herbs. Part of the Henry Doubleday seed bank of endangered botanical species is held here. Tel: 01202 886116.

Dorchester Dorchester was founded by the Romans, who named the site Durnovaria shortly after capturing the Iron Age hill fort of Maiden Castle (see separate entry) in AD 43. Today the vibrant market town is essentially Georgian, many of its old buildings having been destroyed by a series of fires in the late 17th and 18th centuries. Its Roman origins are however still obvious from the street layout and the tree-lined town walks follow the line of the Roman walls. The Roman Town House was discovered as the result of excavations during the 1930s and is preserved, situated in the grounds of County Hall, very close to the town centre. Many relics found during the excavations are on display in the Dorset County Museum, High West Street. The Old Shire Hall still contains the Old Crown Court where in 1834 the six Tolpuddle Martyrs were sentenced to seven years' transportation to Botany Bay. Dorchester is Thomas Hardy's 'Casterbridge'. Hardy was born in an attractive thatched cottage (see Hardy's Cottage) in the hamlet of Higher Bockhampton within the parish of Stinsford, on the outskirts of Dorchester, an area he named 'Mellstock' in his writings. When he died in 1928 Hardy's body was interred in Poet's Corner, Westminster Abbey, although he had wanted to be buried beside his first wife, Emma, at Stinsford churchyard. Only his heart was buried in Emma's grave. At the top of the town stands a statue of Hardy.

Dorset County Museum High West Street, Dorchester. The museum was founded in 1846 and is set in a beautiful Gothic-style building dating from 1884. Its diverse collections include Roman mosaics, original Thomas Hardy manuscripts and fossilised dinosaur footprints. Tel: 01305 262735.

Dorset History Centre Bridport Road, Dorchester. Formerly known as the Dorset Record Office, the centre offers access to all manner of local history records relating to family histories, buildings histories and general village histories. The staff are very obliging as I can vouch. Tel: 01305 250550.

Dreadnought Hoax A practical joke carried out by notorious prankster Horace de Vere Cole on 10 February 1910. Cole tricked the Royal Navy into showing their flagship, the warship HMS *Dreadnought*, to a supposed delegation of Abyssinian royals. The hoax involved Cole and five friends – writer Virginia Woolf, her brother Adrian Stephen, Guy Ridley, Anthony Buxton and artist Duncan Grant – who dressed up with darkened skin and turbans. Cole had an accomplice send a telegram to HMS *Dreadnought*, which was moored in Weymouth. The message said that the ship must be prepared for the visit of a group of princes from Abyssinia and was purportedly signed by Foreign Office Under-secretary Sir Charles Hardinge. Cole and his entourage went to Paddington station, where Cole claimed to be 'Herbert Cholmondeley' of the British Foreign Office and demanded a special train to Weymouth. The stationmaster arranged a VIP coach. In Weymouth, the navy welcomed the princes with an honour guard. The group inspected the fleet, distributing cards printed in Swahili and talking with each other in broken Latin. To show their appreciation, they yelled 'bunga bunga'. They asked for prayer mats and bestowed fake military honours on some of the officers. In London, they revealed the ruse by sending a letter and a group photo to the *Daily Mirror*. The Royal Navy briefly became an object of ridicule and demanded that Cole be arrested. However, Cole and his compatriots had not broken any law.

Edmondsham House 12 miles (19km) north of Bournemouth. A fine Tudor manor house with Georgian additions, which has remained within the ownership of the same family since the 16th century. The gardens have 6 acres (2.4ha) of lawns, shrubs and trees and spring bulbs. The fine walled garden with herbaceous border is cultivated on organic principles. An octagonal Victorian dairy is of particular interest. Tel: 01725 517207.

Eggardon Hill 4 miles (6km) northeast of Bridport. An Iron Age hill fort standing 820ft (250m) above sea level. Covering 40 acres (16ha), it is the largest and best preserved in Dorset apart from Maiden Castle (see separate entry).

Fiddleford Manor 1 mile (1.6km) east of Sturminster Newton, 7 miles (11km) northwest of Blandford Forum. A medieval manor house boasting a unique beamed ceiling. The truncated remains of a great hall complete with screens passage, service rooms and solar are topped off with two magnificent 14th century roofs. Now owned by English Heritage. Tel: 0117 975 0700.

Forde Abbey 7½ miles (12km) west of Beaminster. Situated beside the River Axe, the Cistercian abbey was founded in 1140 and built of deep golden Ham stone. Its third abbot, Baldwin, became Archbishop of Canterbury before dying during the Crusades and Thomas Chard, the 32nd and last abbot, began a complete restructuring of the abbey buildings on his succession in 1521. When the monastery was dissolved in 1539, however, the church was destroyed and the property handed over to the Crown (Chard became vicar of Thorncombe until his death in 1543). In the same year the abbey and its lands were leased to Richard Pollard, son of the Chief Justice of England. For the next 100 years Forde Abbey was owned by a succession of absentee landlords and plundered for its stone. In 1649 it was purchased by Sir Edmund Prideaux, MP for Lyme Regis and a fervent supporter of the Parliamentary cause who became Oliver Cromwell's attorney general, and the monks' quarters were converted into an Italian-style palazzo. The house has since undergone many refurbishments and now contains a collection of decorated plaster ceilings, magnificent pictures and fine furniture. In the Grand Saloon are spectacular Mortlake tapestries, woven from cartoons painted for the Sistine Chapel in Rome by Raphael, depicting scenes from the lives of St Peter and St Paul. The 30 acres (12ha) of gardens date from the early 18th century. Tel: 01460 220231.

Golden Cap — 6 miles (10km) west of Bridport. The highest point on the south coast of England, at 627ft (191m), Golden Cap with its distinctive summit of yellow sandstone lies at the heart of a 2000 acre (800ha) National Trust estate. Tel: 01297 561900.

Hardy Monument — Black Down, 6 miles (10km) southwest of Dorchester. Erected in 1844, the octagonal column of Portland stone standing 72ft (22m) high commemorates Vice-Admiral Sir Thomas Masterman Hardy, flag captain of HMS *Victory* at the Battle of Trafalgar. The monument's shape imitates the telescopes Hardy would have used on board ship. Hardy spent his early life in the village of Portesham, a village 1 mile (1.6km) south of Black Down. The monument is in the care of the National Trust. Tel: 01297 561900.

Hardy's Cottage — Higher Bockhampton, 3 miles (5km) east of Dorchester. Dorset's most famous son, Thomas Hardy, was born in this small thatched cottage in 1840 and from here he would walk the three miles to school every day in Dorchester. The secluded cottage was built by Hardy's great-grandfather in 1800 and behind it stretches an area of heathland often identified with Egdon Heath, of which Hardy wrote in *The Return of the Native*. The walls were constructed from cob and have been given weather protection by brick facing and rendered cement. Casement windows peer out from the overhanging thatched roof, and roses, honeysuckle and japonica climb the walls. His early novels *Under the Greenwood Tree* and *Far from the Madding Crowd* were written here. In 1948 the cottage was given to the National Trust. Tel: 01305 262366. See also Dorchester, Max Gate.

Highcliffe Castle — Rothesay Drive, Highcliffe-on-Sea, Christchurch. Built 1831–5 by Lord Stuart de Rothesay, the house has been described as 'the most important remaining example of the Romantic and Picturesque style of architecture'. The Grade I listed building is now owned by Christchurch Borough Council. The castle was built on the site previously occupied by High Cliff, a Georgian mansion designed for the 3rd Earl of Bute (a founder of Kew Gardens), with grounds laid out by Capability Brown. Tel: 01425 278807.

Higher Melcombe — Melcombe Bingham, 10 miles (16km) northeast of Dorchester. The surviving wing of a 16th century house with an attached chapel. Tel: 01258 880251.

Highest point — Lewesdon Hill at 915ft (279m), situated 2½ miles (4km) west of Beaminster (GR: ST437011).

Ilsington House — Puddletown, 6 miles (10km) northeast of Dorchester. A William and Mary-style house built by the 7th Earl of Huntingdon in 1690. The north entrance front has a long central block and projecting wings. There are hipped roofs, stone quoins, a projecting wooden cornice and tall brick chimneys. In 1837 the brickwork was rendered and the south front remodelled with Tuscan pilasters and larger windows. By then the property had passed by marriage to the Earls of Orford, descendants of early 18th century Prime Minister Sir Robert Walpole. In 1862 the Ilsington estate was sold to local man John Brymer, who added a new porch, billiard room and conservatory. Since buying the house in 1979, the present owners, Peter and Penelope Duff, have carried out substantial restoration, refurnishing the house with fine period pieces. Their collection includes paintings by Toulouse Lautrec, Cecil Beaton, Peter Mahone and Panyiotis Kalorkoti (official war artist for the Falklands War) and sculpture by Elizabeth Frink and Serena de la Hey.

Interesting facts — Traditionally, the word 'rabbit' is taboo on the **Isle of Portland** as burrowing can cause landslides; when quarrying was done by hand in the area, quarrymen would pack up and go home for the day if a rabbit was seen. The island is also unique in having four low-water tides per day as opposed to the usual two. Dorchester-born **Sir Frederick Treves** is famous for writing an account of the life of Joseph Merrick, aka The Elephant Man. The 1980 film was based on his book and Treves was played by Sir Anthony Hopkins. However, in June 1902 Treves became immortalised by performing an appendectomy on King Edward VII, thus delaying the Coronation for two months. In 1951, **Enid Blyton** and her husband Kenneth bought the golf club on Purbeck for £1, when the previous owner had to move abroad on health grounds. Blyton, who spent family holidays in Swanage, had many Dorset influences for her Famous Five series of books: Brownsea Island was the 'Whispering Island' of *Five Have a Mystery to Solve*, Corfe Castle was the inspiration for its fictional counterpart on Kirrin Island in *Five on a Treasure Island*, and Hartland Moor, nr Corfe Castle, was the real-life setting for *Five Go to Mystery Moor*. **Sturminster Newton** is famous for its water mill and town bridge, which still bears a notice warning potential vandals that damaging the bridge is punishable by penal transportation. **Weymouth** is thought to be the first port at which the Black Death came into England, aboard a visiting spice ship in 1348. Shaftesbury's **Gold Hill**, a steep, cobbled street lined with thatched cottages, was immortalised by the Hovis bread adverts featuring a small delivery boy racing down the hill on his bicycle to the haunting melodies of Dvorak's New World Symphony. In 1685, **Judge Jeffreys** came to Dorchester and lodged at 6 High West Street (now a restaurant named in his honour). The Bloody Assizes that followed the

Monmouth Rebellion were held in the Oak Room (now a tea room) of the Antelope Hotel on 5 September that year. Jeffreys is said to have had a secret passage from his lodgings to the Oak Room. In total 74 people were executed, 175 were transported and 29 were pardoned. Executions were carried out in towns and villages close to Dorchester. In 1688, when James II fled the country, Jeffreys was placed in the Tower of London, where he died as the result of kidney disease aged 44. **Smuggling** was rife in Dorset in the 18th century; notorious gangs operated out of Osmington Mills and Lulworth, their most infamous member being Isaac Gulliver (1745–1822), known as 'King of Smugglers'. One of Dorset's quirkier products is the famous **Dorset Knob**, a hard salty biscuit made by Moores Dorset Biscuits, based in Morecombelake, near Bridport. The **Three Elms** public house in North Wootton, Sherborne, has a collection of model vehicles on display. The pub is also notable for its collection of more than 500 saucy seaside postcards displayed in the ladies' and gentlemen's toilets. A **chilli pepper** grown in a polytunnel in Dorset has been claimed as the world's hottest. The Dorset Naga is so fiery that when the owners break the skin to remove the seeds to sow for the following year's crop they have to wear gloves and stand outside in a strong wind so their eyes don't sting.

Islands — See individual entries and list of all Dorset islands.

Jordan Hill Roman Temple — Overcombe, 2 miles (3km) east of Weymouth. Roman pagan ruin situated on a hill above Bowleaze Cove. Amateur excavations in 1843 found coins that suggest the site was used in the 4th century, during the later years of the Roman occupation. Now owned by English Heritage.

Jurassic Coast — Extending 95 miles (153km) from Studland Bay in the east to Exmouth, Devon, in the west, the Jurassic Coast is England's only natural World Heritage Site. The coast documents the entire Mesozoic era from the Triassic period to the Cretaceous, and has yielded many important fossils, including the first complete ichthyosaur and fossilised Jurassic trees. Many unique landforms can be found such as the Isle of Portland, Chesil Beach, Lulworth Cove (see separate entries) and the massive rock arch of Durdle Door.

Keep Military Museum of Devon & Dorset — Bridport Road, Dorchester. The Ministry of Defence-owned museum celebrates 300 years of military life of the adjoining counties. Tel: 01305 264066.

Kingston Lacy — 2 miles (3km) northwest of Wimborne Minster. The 17th century house of Kingston Lacy was designed by Sir Roger Pratt for Sir Ralph Bankes to replace his ruined family seat at Corfe Castle. Altered by Sir Charles Barry in the 19th century, the house contains the outstanding collection of paintings and other works of art accumulated by William Bankes. It is famous for its dramatic Spanish Room, with walls hung in magnificent gilded leather. The house and garden are set in a wooded park with a fine herd of Red Devon cattle. The surrounding estate is dominated by the Iron Age hill fort of Badbury Rings (see separate entry). In August 1981 Henry John Ralph Bankes died and left his family estates of Kingston Lacy and Corfe Castle to the National Trust. Tel: 01202 883402.

Kingston Maurward House and Garden — 2 miles (3km) east of Dorchester. The house was built in 1720 for George Pitt, probably to the design of the architect John James of Greenwich. Eighteen years earlier Pitt had married Laura, the last of the Greys, who lived in the Elizabethan manor house at Kingston Maurward. The Greys had owned the estate for many generations, acquiring it through marriage, from the Maurwards who were the ancient lords of the area. The series of garden rooms were designed by Sir Cecil and Lady Hanbury after they purchased the estate in 1914. These are enclosed within splendid stone terraces, balustrading, steps and yew hedges and include water features and topiary. The contemporary parkland and pleasure gardens were laid out in the landscape style popularised by Capability Brown. Behind the Elizabethan manor stands the ornamental walled garden which was once the kitchen garden for the old manor house. Kingston Maurward holds National Collections of penstemons and salvias. The main house is now occupied by a college, while the manor house is a hotel. Tel: 01305 215003.

Knoll Gardens and Nursery — Stapehill Road, Hampreston, 3 miles (5km) east of Wimborne. The 6 acres (2.4ha) of gardens include more than 6000 named plants. Tel: 01202 873931.

Langtry Manor — Derby Road, Bournemouth. The future Edward VII bought a plot of land in a secluded area of the East Cliff in Bournemouth for his mistress Lillie Langtry in order to establish somewhere that would allow the couple to escape from prying eyes and relax. Lillie designed the romantic royal love nest, adding personal touches. The foundation stone bears the inscription 'ELL' (Emilie Le Breton Langtry) and is dated 1877. On the outside wall of the king's room, the motto 'Dulce Domum' (Sweet Home) can be seen. On the other side of the building is inscribed the motto 'Stet Fortuna Domus' (may fortune attend those who dwell here). Beneath the minstrel's gallery can be seen the self-explanatory statement: 'They say What say they? Let them say'. Carved into the inglenook fireplace are the letters 'ELL' and in the stained glass window lovers' swans. Lillie named her pride and joy the 'Red House' and she and Bertie were delighted with the home that she had made for them. The Langtry Manor is now one of the foremost East Cliff hotels in Bournemouth.

Lilliput — See Poole

Lulworth Castle — 4 miles (6km) southwest of Wareham. Originally a 17th century hunting lodge owned by the Weld Estate since 1641, the castle's interior was refurbished after the Civil War by Humphrey Weld to turn it into a comfortable country house. On the first floor doorways were realigned 'en filade' in the French fashion, offering unobstructed views from one room to the next. On the second floor the corner rooms were divided up into small apartments with corridors leading to the towers. In the 18th century, architect John Tasker carried out further refurbishment: the terrace was rebuilt, adding extra service rooms to the basement, while within the main building the chapel was enlarged, the main staircase replaced, a larger entrance hall created and the principal ground and first floor rooms redecorated in the fashionable Neoclassical style. Thomas Weld later employed Tasker to build the chapel of St Mary, also in Neoclassical style, in the grounds. The last significant restyling was carried out in the 1860s by architect Joseph Hansom. He created a corridor directly linking the two ground floor entrances so that visitors entering the front door no longer had to pass through the main rooms to reach the rest of the castle. The newly isolated southeast corner of the building became the 'gentlemen's area', containing the billiard room and the owner's study. A fire in 1929 destroyed much of the building, but it was restored in the 1970s with the aid of English Heritage. Tel: 0845 450 1054.

Lulworth Cove 8 miles (13km) southwest of Wareham. A horseshoe-shaped cove on the Jurassic Coast hollowed out of the soft coastal rocks by the sea, leaving a narrow entrance of harder Portland stone behind which are exposed folded and twisted rock strata. To the east is the so-called Fossil Forest, where the fossilised remains of trees dating from the late Jurassic period can be seen in the cliffs. Projecting into the sea $1^1/_2$ miles (2.5km) to the west is the spectacular limestone arch of Durdle Door, another product of erosion by the sea. The Lulworth Skipper butterfly was first discovered on the chalk cliffs above the bay in 1832.

Lyme Regis A small coastal town 21 miles (32km) west of Dorchester. Located on Lyme Bay, it was a major port in the Middle Ages; the 'Regis' part of the name was adopted in 1284 when the town received its royal charter from Edward I. The predominance of Georgian architecture reflects the town's later popularity as a fashionable resort in the 18th century. The famous curved harbour wall known as the Cobb, dating from the 13th century, enabled the town to create a safe harbour for seagoing vessels and thus contributed greatly to its prosperity. Today the Cobb is perhaps best known as the scene of the finale of the film of John Fowles' novel *The French Lieutenant's Woman* (1981), and it also features prominently as a location in Jane Austen's novel *Persuasion*. The area to the west of the town, known as the Undercliff, is prone to landslips and is a prominent site for fossil hunters.

Maiden Castle 2 miles (3km) south of Dorchester. Covering an area of 47 acres (19ha), Maiden Castle is the largest hill fort in Britain. Even today, after 2000 years of erosion, the ramparts in some areas rise to a height of 20ft (6m). Flint tools and bone implements found at the site suggest that the hill was first occupied c.3000 BC when it would have afforded protection to late Stone Age/early Bronze Age people. At some stage during this early period a bank barrow was constructed, east to west across the site, reaching a length of 1800ft (549m). From c.1200 BC the site appears to have been abandoned until the Roman occupation of Britain. 'Maiden' derives from the Celtic *mai dun* ('great hill'). It was known to have been the stronghold of the Durotriges tribe until it fell to the 2nd Legion Augusta, under Vespasian, during the Roman invasion in AD 43. The battle for the fort was a bloody one, centred on the eastern entrance. Excavations carried out in the 20th century uncovered the bodies of 38 Iron Age warriors, buried along with food and drink for their journey into the afterlife. After the Roman occupation the history of the fort becomes unclear, although a Roman temple was constructed in the 4th century AD the foundations of which remain. It is feasible that the hill continued to be inhabited during early Saxon times, but appears to have been deserted for the last 1400 years. Many hill forts can be found in the Wessex region but Maiden Castle is by far the most impressive, and commands breathtaking views.

Mapperton 2 miles (3km) southeast of Beaminster. The manor of Mapperton sits atop a long rise, dominating views across a lovely Italianate garden. The house is largely a product of the 1660s, though earlier Tudor elements have survived, and the north front is in the classical style. The church of All Saints forms the south wing of the house. The upper garden is constructed in terraces edged by brick and concrete and dotted throughout with topiary of yew and box. The gardens descend a slope to fish ponds, an arboretum and a shrub garden. The house and grounds have featured in several films, among them *Tom Jones* (1963), *Restoration* (1995) and *Emma* (1996). Tel: 01308 862645.

Maumbury Rings Dorchester. First constructed c.2500 BC as a large circular bank with a series of tapering shafts about 10ft (3m) apart and about 32ft (10m) below ground level. The spacing of the shafts suggests that there were 45 in total. Eight shafts have been fully excavated, four of which contained deer skulls and skull fragments along with carved chalk objects. In the 1st century AD the site was converted into an amphitheatre, probably by the Roman army. It is one of the largest in England. Earthmoving operations were carried out to lower the enclosure by around 10ft (3m), with the material being deposited over the Neolithic bank. The amphitheatre was not used for long, going out of use by AD 150. In 1642–3 the earthwork was remodelled as an artillery fort guarding the southern approach to Dorchester. The earthworks and open space around are now scheduled as an ancient monument, and are used for various open-air events. Finds from excavation works are displayed at the Dorset County Museum.

Max Gate Alington Avenue, Dorchester. Thomas Hardy designed and built this Victorian villa for himself in 1885, having chosen a site close to his Bockhampton birthplace. The house gives an insight into another facet of Hardy's genius – as an architect designing the environment in which he wished to live and write. It remained his home for over 40 years, until his death in 1928. Two of Hardy's most famous works, *Tess of the d'Urbervilles* and *Jude the Obscure*, were written in the study, as was the wealth of poetry of his later years. The property contains several pieces of Hardy's furniture. It is now owned by the National Trust. Tel: 01305 262538.

Milton Abbey Church 6 miles (10km) southwest of Blandford Forum. Benedictine abbey of the 14th and 15th centuries, situated in a parkland setting. A monastery and abbey until its dissolution in 1539, it then became the parish church. From 1770 it was the private chapel for the lords of the manor and in 1954 became the Milton Abbey School Chapel. Tel: 01258 880215.

Minterne Gardens Minterne Magna, 2 miles (3km) north of Cerne Abbas, 8 miles (13km) north of Dorchester. The gardens occupy 20 acres (8ha) of wild woodland, where magnolias, rhododendrons, eucryphias, hydrangeas, water plants and water lilies provide a new vista at each turn, with small lakes and cascades landscaped in the 18th century. The estate was once the home of the Churchill family and Minterne House, built 1903–6, still contains many Churchill pictures and tapestries. Tel: 01300 341370.

Motto — Dorset's motto is 'Who's Afear'd'.

Nothe Fort — Barrack Road, Weymouth. The fort was built 1860–72, begun by a civilian contractor and completed by 26 Company of the Royal Engineers, forerunners of 26 Armoured Assault Squadron. The original intention was to build an open battery of five 64-pound guns but after a threat developed from the French, who had laid down the world's first purpose-built ironclad warship, *La Gloire* and built a new naval base at Cherbourg, the plan was revised to provide a fortress mounting 17 heavy guns in two tiers. The fort now houses a museum with numerous exhibits relating to its history and place in Britain's coastal defences. Tel: 01305 766626.

Old Harry Rocks — 3 miles (5km) northeast of Swanage. A chalk stack situated below the cliffs at the Foreland (or Handfast Point), Studland. The rocks are part of a once continuous band of chalk which ran through south Dorset, Ballard Down and the Isle of Wight, part of the southern England Chalk Formation. Old Harry's Wife used to stand next to Old Harry but collapsed around 50 years ago and can only be seen just below the surface at very low spring tides. The name 'Old Harry' originated as a pseudonym for the devil, who according to legend once lay down next to the cliff top. The large outcrop at the end of the cliff is known as No Man's Land.

Parnham House — $^{1}/_{2}$ mile (0.8km) south of Beaminster. A beautiful Elizabethan manor house restored by John Nash, surrounded by gardens landscaped by Inigo Thomas. More recently the house was owned by furniture maker John Makepeace, his modern furniture forming an interesting complement to the architecture. Now in private hands, the house is not open to the public.

Poole — A coastal town and port located on a popular stretch of coastline, with the resort of Bournemouth to the east, Studland to the south and the Jurassic Coast southwest. Since 1 April 1997, Poole has been designated a unitary authority situated in, but distinct from, the traditional county of Dorset. The town has grown rapidly, and **Sandbanks**, a small sand spit across part of the harbour mouth, is so popular that it has the fourth highest land value, by area, in the world. The Romans used Poole as an invasion port for their conquest of southern Britain. At the time of the Norman Conquest Poole may have been a tiny fishing village. Huge deposits of oyster shells dating to late Saxon or early Norman times lie under Poole and Hamworthy Quays. The port steadily grew in importance and in 1433 was made Dorset's Port of the Staple. The 14th century town cellars were once used to store wool prior to export. Medieval Poole had trading links from the Baltic to Spain and Italy. The 17th century saw the start of a transatlantic trade which became vital to the town. In particular, trade with Newfoundland was the foundation of many fortunes among Poole merchants. In the early 18th century Poole had more ships trading with North America than any other English port. *Sea Music* (1991), a large steel sculpture by Sir Anthony Caro, is located on Poole Quayside. **Lilliput**, an area of Poole adorned with scenic woodland, was originally called The Saltings, after the trade that was carried on there; its new name commemorates legendary local smuggler Isaac Gulliver (see Interesting facts), rather than having any link with Jonathan Swift's even more legendary literary island. Lilliput is the home of Poole Harbour Yacht club. See also Poole Harbour.

Poole Harbour — Poole Harbour lays claim to being the second largest natural harbour in the world (Port Jackson, Sydney, being the largest), although Cork Harbour in Ireland makes a similar claim. The coastline stretches for 60 miles (96km) and includes 10,000 acres (4700ha) of water and mudland enveloping five picturesque islands. It is essentially a drowned river valley formed, along with Poole Bay, when a rising sea broke through the chalk ridge which had connected Old Harry Rocks in Studland Bay with the Needles in the Isle of Wight. Geologists believe that this large river flowed eastwards from the Dartmoor region in Devon, carrying with it the massive deposits of flint, gravel and clay which are to be seen all the way to Hampshire. The harbour as we know it was formed at the end of the last Ice Age, c.10,000 years ago; since then mudflats and salt marshes have developed, adding to its uniqueness. It has been a working port for hundreds of years, though its trade has declined somewhat as the shallow water cannot take the largest ships. Today the port is among other things the home of Sunseeker, manufacturers of luxury yachts, and the departure point for ferries to France. The harbour was the place from which some ships departed for the D-Day landings of World War II. The open water, mudflats, marshes and reedbeds and the important Brownsea Island Lagoon provide valuable habitats for birds. Common and Sandwich terns, shelduck and little egrets breed here and in the winter thousands of ducks, grebes, divers and waders, including black and bartailed godwits, can be found (the harbour now supports one of the largest wintering colonies of avocets – more than 1400). Reedbeds have bearded tits and scarce wainscot moths and many plants form unusual vegetation communities around the shore. Underwater eelgrasses provide food for wintering brent geese, while important estuarine creatures and fish populations flourish in the unpolluted waters. Four rivers, the Frome, the Piddle, the Corfe and the Sherford, drain into Poole Harbour from the west, reaching the sea through the constricting headlands of North and South Haven (Sandbanks and Studland) in the east. In 2004, a bird hide was introduced to Brands Bay in the harbour.

Portland, Isle of — A limestone island 4 miles (6.km) long by $1^{1}/_{2}$ miles (2.5km) wide, situated in the English Channel off the coast of Weymouth. The island is connected to the mainland by Chesil Beach (see separate entry) and by the A354 road bridge to Weymouth. Portland is divided into several distinct areas, the largest being Fortuneswell and Easton, and the others comprising the villages of Weston, Southwell, Castletown, Chiswell, Wakeham and Grove. The gently sloping area of land known as Tophill rises from sea level at Portland Bill to 495ft (151m) near HMP The Verne at its northern end, and contains the town of Easton and the villages of Weston, Southwell, The Grove and Wakeham. In Thomas Hardy's Wessex the 'Isle of Slingers' is based on Portland, with Street of Wells representing Fortuneswell and The Beal Portland Bill. The oolitic limestone known as Portland stone has been quarried since the Middle Ages, but became fashionable after Sir Christopher Wren used it for the reconstruction of St Paul's Cathedral in 1666. It was also used in Buckingham Palace, as well as for British war graves after the two world wars. Portland is notable for its artificial harbour which was an important Royal Navy base during World Wars I and II, though now a small civilian port and popular recreation area. England's National Sailing Academy is situated at the harbour and will host all of the sailing events for the London-based 2012 Olympics.

Portland Bill 6 miles (10km) south of Weymouth. A narrow promontory of Portland stone which forms the most southerly part of Tophill on the Isle of Portland. The Bill has a lighthouse as it is an important waypoint for coastal traffic passing the navigation obstacle caused by the Isle and its race.

Portland Castle Castletown, 4 miles (6km) south of Weymouth. Built 1539–40, along with Sandsfoot Castle on the cliffs opposite, to protect an important anchorage known as the Portland Roads. It was one of a chain of artillery forts constructed for Henry VIII to protect the south coast from the threat of invasion by the French and Spanish following Henry's break from the Catholic Church. The castle is shaped like a segment of a circle, with a two-storey circular tower at its centre and rectangular wings radiating from either side. The main gun batteries were on two levels in the curved front towards the sea, and a third tier of guns could be mounted on top of the central tower and its wings. The main gun room is now open to the sky having lost its roof, which acted as the second gun platform. Owned by English Heritage. Tel: 01305 820539.

Poundbury Village Located on the western edge of Dorchester, this mixed urban development of town houses, cottages, shops and light industry was designed for the Prince of Wales by architect Leon Krier. Begun in 1993, Poundbury has become world famous as a model of urban planning. Commercial buildings sit among residential areas, with shopping, community and leisure facilities. Streets are laid out around buildings, creating interesting spaces and naturally controlling car speeds. Parking and services are mostly confined to landscaped courtyards at the rear. The architecture, using local and sometimes recycled materials, draws on the rich heritage of Dorset and, in particular, on the streets of Dorchester itself. Overall 20 per cent of the housing is being built by housing associations for rent by people on the local housing list. Uniquely at Poundbury, the social housing is interspersed with, and indistinguishable from, the private housing.

Powerstock Castle and Church 10 miles (16km) west of Dorchester. Situated at the foot of the ancient hill fort of Eggardon (see separate entry), the village of Powerstock is notable for its beautiful church, perched high on a hill topped with a green mound. This mound is all that remains of Powerstock Castle (aka Athelstan's Castle), originally built in the Norman period of local stone but abandoned in the 13th century. By 1865 nothing remained of the castle and the earthwork is now on farmland. On the door inside the south entrance of the church is a beautiful 15th century carving which shows a king holding a staff and a crowned woman giving bread to children. They are thought to be Good King Wenceslas and St Elizabeth of Hungary. In the churchyard east of the path and south of the main door is a very rare survival, a 13th century dole table from which, before the Reformation, charitable 'doles' of bread were distributed to the poor.

Priest's House Museum High Street, Wimborne. An historic town house dating from the 16th century, the Grade II listed building retains many original architectural features including a 17th century hall, an 18th century parlour and a Victorian kitchen with working 'Beetonette' range. The Rural Life Gallery houses excellent agricultural collections from rural East Dorset and a hands-on Victorian schoolroom. The museum includes Mr Low's Victorian stationery shop and Coles' Ironmongers, both recreated from original shop stock. The delightful walled garden behind the Priest's House, with flowering plants, fruit trees, topiary work and smooth lawns, covers $^1/_2$ acre (0.13ha). Tel: 01202 882533.

Prisons **Dorchester** is a local prison serving the crown and magistrates' courts in Dorset and Somerset. The prison holds 170 inmates, the majority of whom are adult males. Operational capacity: 252. Tel: 01305 714500.

YOI Guys Marsh, Shaftesbury, opened in 1960 as a borstal and became a YOI in 1984. After completion of perimeter fencing in 1992 it became a closed establishment and started to accommodate adults. It is now a category C prison and closed YOI. Operational capacity: 578. Tel: 01747 856400.

YOI Portland was first opened in 1848 as an adult prison. In 1921 it converted into a Borstal and in 1988 became a Young Offenders Institution (YOI). The prison accommodates young offenders aged 18–21. Operational capacity: 557. Tel: 01305 715600.

The Verne, Tophill, Isle of Portland is a category C training prison for adult males occupying a former army citadel, built by convicts in the 19th century to protect Portland Harbour. It is particularly used for prisoners who are foreign nationals, holding around 300 foreign prisoners from more than 50 countries, as well as 50 life sentence prisoners. Operational capacity: 587. Tel: 01305 825000.

The Weare was a 400-place Category C prison ship opened as a temporary measure in June 1997, when it was expected to accommodate prisoners for a three-year period. Located on a floating structure moored in Portland Harbour, it was closed on 31 July 2005.

Purbeck, Isle of A peninsula in southeast Dorset bounded by Poole Harbour to its north and the English Channel to its south and east. The Purbeck Hills run from west to east across the peninsula, dividing it into two. To the north is largely heathland, an area which is also the location of Wytch Farm oilfield, the largest inshore oilfield in the UK. To the south are limestone cliffs; this area was once quarried extensively for Purbeck stone and the so-called Purbeck marble, a very hard form of limestone capable of being polished. The seaside resort of Swanage is the largest town. Much of the area is in the care of the National Trust, including the 3 miles (5km) of Studland Beach in the northeast, part of which is a popular naturist resort. Area: 60.23 sq miles (156 sq km). Population: 44,416.

Radipole Lake — Radipole Park Drive, Weymouth. An RSPB nature reserve located in central Weymouth, at the mouth of the River Wey. Its reedbeds are an important habitat for birds such as the bittern. The lake flows into Weymouth harbour. Tel: 01305 778313.

Rivers — The **Allen** in its uppermost reaches is a winter bourne. It has its permanent summer source in springs above Wimborne St Giles, though in a wet winter or spring the water breaks from the chalk subsoil further upstream. It is a tributary of the Stour – the two rivers come together just outside Wimborne Minster – and flows due south for its length of 13 miles (21km).

The **Cerne** rises in the chalk hills of the Dorset Downs at Minterne Magna, flowing south down a valley through Cerne Abbas and Charminster and into the River Frome at Dorchester. Its total length is 10 miles (16km). The name 'Cerne' derives from the Celtic god of fertility, Cernunnos.

The **Crane**, which becomes the **Moors River** after its confluence with the Ebblake Stream, rises in the chalk above Cranborne and flows for 8 miles (13km) – passing Bournemouth International Airport – through an area of acidic heathland around Verwood before reverting in character to a chalk stream as it joins the Stour near Hurn.

The **Frome** rises in the Dorset Downs at Evershot, and flows southeast through Maiden Newton, Dorchester, West Stafford and Woodsford. At Wareham it is joined by the Piddle, also known as the Trent, and from then on it is navigable for almost 8 miles (13km) of river estuary, through Poole Harbour, to give a total length of 40 miles (64km). It is the major chalk stream in southwest England.

The **Hooke** rises at Toller Whelme, 2 miles (3km) east of Beaminster, and flows through the villages of Hooke, Kingcombe, Toller Porcorum and Toller Fratrum to join the Frome at Maiden Newton, a course of 6 miles (10km). It was formerly called the Toller, whence the name of the three Toller villages, as well as of the hundred of Tollerford.

The **Piddle**, aka Trent or North River, rises next to Alton Pancras church (Alton Pancras was originally named *Awultune*, a Saxon name meaning the village at the source of a river). It flows south through Piddletrenthide and Piddlehinton, and then southeast more or less parallel with its bigger neighbour, the Frome, via Puddletown, Tolpuddle, Affpuddle, Briantspuddle and Turnerspuddle, all villages named after the river. It joins the Frome at Wareham, where the combined rivers enter Poole Harbour. The river has a total length of 21 miles (33km).

The **Stour** rises at Stourhead in Wiltshire, 8 miles (13km) southwest of Warminster, where it forms a series of artificial lakes which are part of the Stourhead estate, owned by the National Trust (see Wiltshire). The river flows south into Dorset, through Milton on Stour, Gillingham, the Blackmore Vale and Sturminster Newton, before taking a southeasterly course through Blandford Forum and its confluence with the Allen at Wimborne Minster, and on to its estuary at Christchurch, where it flows into the English Channel. Its total length is 51 miles (82km).

The **Tarrant** rises in Cranborne Chase at Tarrant Gunville and meanders for 7½ miles (12km) in a southeasterly crescent through Tarrant Hinton, Tarrant Launceston, Tarrant Monkton, Tarrant Rawston, Tarrant Rushton and Tarrant Kayneston. It reaches the Stour at Tarrant Crawford, midway between Blandford Forum and Wimborne Minster.

Russell-Cotes Art Gallery — East Cliff, Bournemouth. Situated on the cliff top overlooking Poole Bay, the Isle of Wight and the Purbecks, the Russell-Cotes Gallery and Museum is set in an elegant Victorian house, built to an Italian design 1897–1907 as a house/museum by John Frederick Fogerty for Annie and Merton Russell-Cotes. It houses a variety of collections including its world-renowned Japanese collection. The interior decoration was carried out by John Thomas and his son, Oliver, both employed at the Royal Bath Hotel. Tel: 01202 451800.

St Catherine's Chapel — ½ mile (0.8km) south of Abbotsbury. The chapel, built entirely of local stone, dates from the 14th century when it was built by the monks of Abbotsbury, possibly as a beacon for pilgrims coming to worship at the abbey in the village below. The chapel survived the dissolution and subsequent destruction of the abbey because it was so valuable as a navigational beacon to sailors crossing Lyme Bay. It is now managed by English Heritage.

St Stephen's Church — St Stephen's Way, Bournemouth. One of only three Grade I listed buildings in Bournemouth, the church was designed by John Loughborough Pearson (1817–97) in Gothic revival style and built by public subscription as a memorial to Alexander Morden Bennett, first vicar of St Peter's, Bournemouth, who died in 1880. On 11 October 1881, the foundation stone was laid and dedicated by Bishop Harold Browne of Winchester. Under Bennett, St Peter's had adopted the Anglo-Catholic forms of worship which, under the influence of the Oxford Movement, had brought fresh vigour to the Church of England, and when he died St Stephen's was built to carry on this tradition. After the nave and aisles had been consecrated on 10 June 1885, the chancel and lady chapel were begun in 1896 – the foundation stone being laid by Sir George Meyrick on 10 June – and finished in 1898, when the church was dedicated by Bishop Sumner, Archdeacon of Winchester. John Betjeman described it as 'one of the most beautiful churches in England . . . Every detail in the church, from the ironwork and woodwork to the mouldings of the stone, is carefully considered, and the church abounds in seemingly perfect vistas which give it a sense of mystery and eternity, a perfect architectural expression of the Catholic Faith of the Church of England.'

Sandbanks Ferry — 2 miles (3km) south of Poole. A chain ferry that crosses the mouth of Poole Harbour from Sandbanks to Studland. The ferry itself is named *Bramble Bush Bay*.

Sandford Orcas Manor House — 2 miles (3km) north of Sherborne. William Knoyle inherited Sandford in the early 1530s, and built the mid 16th century Tudor manor house from local Ham stone, complete with arched gatehouse, stable courtyard and walled herb garden. Tel: 01963 220206.

Sherborne Castle
$^{1}/_{2}$ mile (0.8km) east of Sherborne. The ruins of the old castle date from the early 12th century, when it was built for Roger de Caen, Bishop of Salisbury and chancellor during the reign of Henry I. Sherborne was seized by King Stephen in 1135 during his conflict with Henry's daughter Matilda over the succession, and it remained in royal hands until the reign of Edward III, when Bishop Robert Wyville paid to take the castle back into the hands of the church. In 1592, Elizabeth I transferred the lease to Sir Walter Raleigh, who built a new residence in 1594; this was Sherborne Lodge, which now forms part of the new Sherborne Castle. The old castle saw its final use during the Civil War, when it was held for the king in 1642 and 1645. On the second occasion it held out for 16 days against a siege by the forces of General Fairfax. By the following October its defences had been dismantled to prevent any further use against Parliament; its name was subsequently transferred to the new house, which had been substantially enlarged in the early 17th century. The new castle is owned by Mr and Mrs John Wingfield Digby. Tel: 01935 813182. The ruined old castle is owned by English Heritage. Tel: 01935 812730.

Smedmore House
5 miles (8km) south of Wareham. Situated at the foot of the Purbeck Hills looking across Kimmeridge Bay to Portland Bill, the house was originally built by William Clavell in James I's reign, to be near his Kimmeridge alum works. The semi-hidden seawards-facing front to the house was constructed c.1700 by Edward Clavell, and in 1761 the new front was added by George Clavell, the last of the male line. Smedmore has been the home of the Mansel family for almost 400 years. Tel: 01929 480719.

Somerset and Dorset Joint Railway
See Somerset

Sport

football
AFC Bournemouth were founded in 1899 and joined the Football League in 1923. Its former names include Boscombe St Johns and Bournemouth and Boscombe Athletic; its present name was adopted in 1971 when it also adopted red and black striped shirts in imitation of AC Milan. AFC Bournemouth play at the Fitness First Stadium (formerly Dean Court), Kings Park, Bournemouth. The club's nickname is the Cherries. The club's striker James Hayter scored the fastest hat-trick in English league football history during the 2003–04 season, having come on to the field as a substitute against Wrexham. The Cherries were leading 3–0 in the 86th minute when Hayter scored three goals in the space of 2 minutes 20 seconds, making the final score 6–0. Famous former players include George Best, Luther Blissett, Jamie Redknapp and Ted McDougall.

Nicknamed the Poppies, **Bournemouth FC** are often known as Bournemouth Poppies to avoid confusion with AFC Bournemouth. They play at Victoria Park, Namu Road, Winton. The club was formed on 11 September 1875 as Bournemouth Rovers, making it one of the oldest in the UK. They were founder members of the Football Association and of the Hampshire League, in which they played during nearly their entire existence until joining the Wessex League in 1986.

Weymouth were founded on 26 August 1890 following a meeting at Cook's Assembly Room. The club are nicknamed 'The Terras', their original terracotta and blue quarter strip lending itself to a play on 'terrors', and currently play at the Wessex Stadium. Weymouth have had several long FA Cup runs although never reaching the Football League. On 3 July 2005 the club turned professional, becoming the only full-time side in the leagues below the Football Conference. This move brought immediate success, Weymouth comfortably winning Conference South in the 2005–06 season.

greyhound racing
Poole Stadium, Wimborne Road, Poole. 450m track. The stadium is also home to Poole Pirates Speedway Club. Tel: 01202 677449.

Sutton Poyntz
3 miles (5km) northeast of Weymouth. The large mill-pond of the village of Sutton Poyntz, situated right under the hills to the east of Weymouth, has been a beauty spot since visitors first came to Weymouth in the 18th century. Sutton Poyntz is the 'Overcombe' of Thomas Hardy's novel *The Trumpet Major*. The Iron Age fort of Chalbury is $^{1}/_{2}$ mile (0.8km) to the west, while to the east across fields is the famous White Horse, carved into the chalk hill. The 250ft (76m) high and 300ft (91.5m) wide carving of George III astride his horse is visible from Weymouth and Portland (the king holidayed in the town on numerous occasions between 1789 and 1805 and started the trend of bathing in seawater). It was cut in 1807 to the order of John Ranier, under the supervision of Mr Wood, a local bookseller.

Tolpuddle Martyrs
The trade union movement was effectively born in the village of Tolpuddle, 7 miles (11km) northeast of Dorchester. The 'Tolpuddle Martyrs' were farm labourers who decided to set up a union in Tolpuddle to give them bargaining strength to curb their impoverished conditions. In 1834, George Loveless, James Brine, James Hammett, James Loveless, John Standfield and Thomas Standfield were sentenced to transportation to Australia for seven years for 'administering illegal oaths' for 'seditious' purposes, but the injustice of their sentence led to a massive campaign across the country and eventually they were pardoned in 1836. The martyrs are commemorated each summer at a special festival in Tolpuddle which attracts trade unionists from around the world.

Tyneham
5 miles (8km) south of Wareham. The village of Tyneham enjoyed a quiet existence for many centuries until in late 1943 the War Office commandeered the surrounding area, as well as the village itself, as a firing range for nearby Lulworth Camp and the 200 inhabitants were required to leave. Although the military occupation of the area was supposed to be temporary, the land was compulsorily purchased after World War II for army use and the villagers never returned. Many of the buildings have since been severely damaged by shell fire, and the Elizabethan manor house was demolished in 1967. More recently the school and St Mary's church have been opened as museums, and the village can be visited on days when no firing is taking place. Tel: 01929 404819.

Wareham Castle Westport Road, Wareham. The motte and bailey castle was one of several defensive castles built during the 12th century civil war, but was demolished during the reign of King John. Now surrounded by houses, the castle mound is all that remains today.

Weymouth 8 miles (13km) south of Dorchester. Situated on a sheltered bay at the mouth of the River Wey on the English Channel coast, just north of the Isle of Portland, the town is one of the most popular British seaside resorts. Sometimes known as 'England's Bay of Naples', Weymouth is a cross-channel ferry terminal and the architecture of its seafront is entirely Georgian. Weymouth and Portland played a significant role in World War II: Portland Harbour was home to a large naval base from which American troops departed on D-Day, while Weymouth was home to Nothe Fort, an important element in Britain's coastal defences, and the Fleet lagoon was the site of tests for the bouncing bomb. The town is situated on weak sand and clay rock which in most places along the Dorset coast, except for narrow bands at Lulworth Cove, Swanage and Durdle Door, has been eroded and washed away, although at Weymouth the rock has been protected by Chesil Beach and the strong limestone Isle of Portland. Weymouth is separated from Dorchester by the steep chalk ridge of the South Dorset Downs. The town is very low lying and its eastern areas experienced several sea floods during extreme low pressure storms, until a high sea wall was completed in the 1990s. The 19th century railway station had four platforms but was demolished in 1986, a smaller, modern station taking up part of the site, while the rest of the old station site was given over to commercial development. The old harbour is home to the Brewer's Quay complex of museums, craft shops, shopping centres and bowling alley. See also Chesil Beach, Nothe Fort, Sutton Poyntz, Jordan Hill Roman Temple.

White Horse See Sutton Poyntz

White Mill 4 miles (6km) west of Wimborne Minster. Located on the Kingston Lacy estate (see separate entry) between the villages of Shapwick and Sturminster Marshall on the River Stour, the present corn mill was rebuilt in 1776 and contains original 18th century elm and applewood machinery. Now owned by the National Trust. Tel: 01258 858051.

Wolfeton House $1\frac{1}{2}$ miles (2.5km) northwest of Dorchester. A fine early Tudor and Elizabethan manor house set in water-meadows near the confluence of the rivers Frome and Cerne. The building is a substantial remnant of a house built by the Trenchards, once one of the leading families in Dorset. By 1800 the chapel in the north range was in ruins and in 1822–8 other parts of the house were demolished. In 1862 the property was purchased by W H P Weston, who repaired the remaining buildings and carried out modifications. The present owner, Capt N T L Thimbleby, is a kinsman of the Trenchard family and since 1973 has carried out further restoration. Tel: 01305 263500.

Some famous people born in Dorset

Anning, Mary (palaeontologist) (1799–1847)	Lyme Regis
Barnes, William (poet) (1801–86)	Bagber
Blunt, Anthony (art historian and soviet spy) (1907–83)	Bournemouth
Cameron, Verney (explorer) (1844–94)	Weymouth
Chataway, Christopher (athlete) (1931–)	Sherborne
Evans, Maurice (actor) (1901–89)	Dorchester
Fripp, Robert (rock guitarist) (1946–)	Wimborne
Hardy, Thomas (novelist) (1840–1928)	Higher Bockhampton
Le Carré, John (writer, born David Cornwell) (1931–)	Poole
Mills, Freddie (boxer) (1919–65)	Parkstone
Morton, John (archbishop) (1420–1500)	Bere Regis
Parry, Hubert (composer) (1848–1918)	Bournemouth
Peacock, Thomas Love (poet and novelist) (1785–1866)	Weymouth
Talbot, William (photography pioneer) (1800–87)	Melbury Abbas
Thornhill, Sir James (artist) (1675–1734)	Weymouth
Treves, Frederick (surgeon and writer) (1853–1923)	Dorchester
Wade, Virginia (tennis player) (1945–)	Bournemouth
Wake, William (archbishop) (1657–1737)	Blandford Forum

Islands of Dorset

(shipping area: Portland)

Island name	Sea area	Nearest landmark	General information
Bear, The	English Channel	Ringstead Bay	GR: SY770807
Black Rock	English Channel	Mupe Bay	GR: SY849801
Black Rock	English Channel	West Bay	GR: SY456905
Blind Cow, The	English Channel	Swyre Head	GR: SY799802
Brike Island	Poole Harbour	Wareham	Islet off southeast coast of Gigger's Island
Brownsea Island	Poole Harbour	Poole	See separate entry
Bull, The	English Channel	Swyre Head	GR: SY803802
Calf, The	English Channel	Bat's Head	GR: SY793802
Cow, The	English Channel	Bat's Head	GR: SY795803
Ebb	Lyme Bay	Ridge Cliff	GR: SY426912
Frenchman's Ledge	English Channel	Bran Point	GR: SY739814
Furzey Island	Poole Harbour	Poole	Second largest of the five main islands (51 acres/21ha) in Poole Harbour, situated between Brownsea Island and Green Island. GR: SZ011870
Gigger's Island	Poole Harbour	Wareham	GR: SY950880
Great Ebb	Lyme Bay	Hope Corner	GR: SY438911
Green Island	Poole Harbour	Poole	Third largest of the five main islands (30 acres/12ha) in Poole Harbour. The island was sold in 2005 for a sum believed to be in the region of £2.5m. GR: SZ005866
Long Island	Poole Harbour	Poole	Situated to the west of Brownsea Island and north of Round Island, fifth largest island in Poole Harbour (13 acres/5.4ha) GR: SY988880
Lucy's Ledge	Lyme Bay	Lyme Regis	GR: SY341919
Mouth Rocks	Lyme Bay	Charmouth	GR: SY365929
Mupe Rocks	English Channel	West Lulworth	GR: SY845796
Old Harry Rocks	English Channel	The Foreland	GR: SZ055825. See separate entry
Old Harry's Wife	English Channel	The Foreland	GR: SZ055825
Otter Island	Lytchett Bay	Poole	Joined to mainland at low tide
Pergins Island	Holes Bay	Poole	GR: SZ000925
Pinion Rock	English Channel	St Oswald Bay	GR: SY814799
Pinnacles, The	English Channel	The Foreland	GR: SV051820
Pool Ledge	English Channel	Bran Point	GR: SY739813
Portland, Isle of	English Channel	Chesil Beach	See separate entry
Purbeck, Isle of	Purbeck (mainland)		See separate entry
Rat Island	Poole Harbour	Poole	North of Brownsea Island
Ringstead Ledge	English Channel	Ringstead Bay	GR: SY750812
Round Island	Poole Harbour	Poole	Situated to the northwest of Furzey Island and south of Long Island, the fourth largest island (14 acres/5.75ha) in Poole Harbour. GR: SY988875
St Gabriel's Ledge	Lyme Bay	St Gabriel's Mouth	GR: SY395922
Stone Island	English Channel	Bournemouth	GR: SZ033871
Virtle Rock	Lyme Bay	Devonshire Head	GR: SY335913
Western Patches	Lyme Bay	Wear Cliffs	GR: SY404917

County Durham

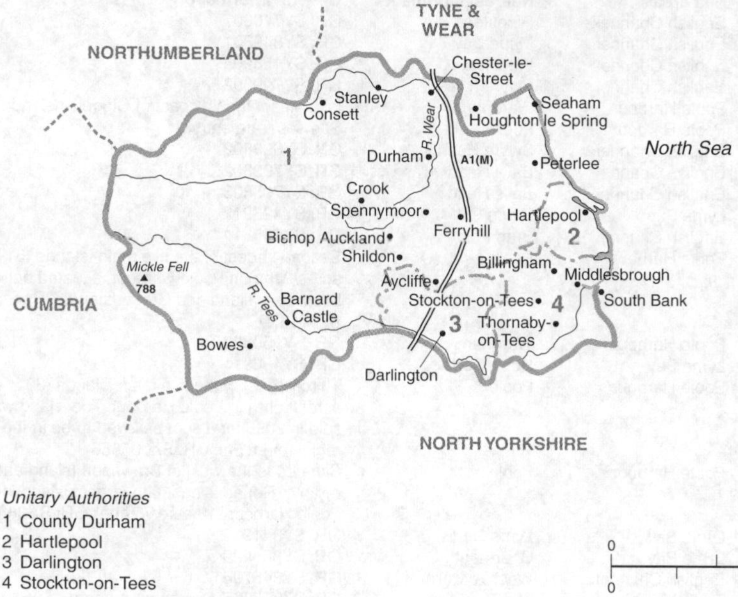
TYNE &
WEAR
NORTHUMBERLAND
Chester-le-
Street
Stanley
Consett
Seaham
Houghton le Spring
North Sea
1
Durham
R. Wear
A1(M)
Peterlee
Crook
Spennymoor
Hartlepool
2
Ferryhill
Bishop Auckland
Shildon
Billingham
Mickle Fell
788
Middlesbrough
Aycliffe
R. Tees
Barnard
Castle
Stockton-on-Tees
4
South Bank
CUMBRIA
3
Thornaby-
on-Tees
Bowes
Darlington
NORTH YORKSHIRE
0
20 miles
0
30 km

Unitary Authorities
1 County Durham
2 Hartlepool
3 Darlington
4 Stockton-on-Tees

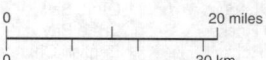

County Durham is situated in northeast England. It is bordered by Northumberland to the north, Tyne and Wear to the northeast, North Yorkshire to the south and Cumbria to the west. Its eastern shores between Sunderland and Hartlepool are washed by the North Sea. The name County Durham came about because the prince-bishops of Durham historically exercised power in regions outside as well as inside the county; the inner part of their estate was named County Durham to distinguish it from the outlying areas. The unitary authorities of Hartlepool, Darlington, and the northern part of Stockton-on-Tees are part of the traditional county and are thus included in this section.

Durham County Council was established along with all the other English county councils in 1888. Major local government reorganisation on 1 April 1974 created the metropolitan boroughs of Sunderland, South Tyneside and Gateshead and removed them from County Durham into the newly established metropolitan county of Tyne and Wear. At the same time, the new non-metropolitan county of Cleveland took Stockton-on-Tees and Hartlepool. County Durham gained the rural district of Startforth south of the River Tees, near Barnard Castle. In April 1996 Cleveland was abolished and Stockton-on-Tees and Hartlepool became unitary authorities separate from Durham. For the purposes of this book Stockton-on-Tees has been split between North and South Stockton in line with the parliamentary constituencies, North Stockton being traditionally part of Durham and South Stockton part of North Yorkshire. It should be noted that Stockton Council administers for the whole of the area and does not consider itself as part of Durham or North Yorkshire. On 1 April 1997, the borough of Darlington became a unitary authority separate administratively from County Durham but continues to share police and fire services with the areas under county council control.

Further legislation enacted on 1 April 2009 has meant the abolition of the county council and the amalgamation of the seven district councils of Chester-le-Street, Derwentside, Durham, Easington, Sedgefield, Teesdale, and Wear Valley into a single unitary authority. County Durham is therefore now a ceremonial county consisting of four unitary authorities.

During the Middle Ages modern County Durham, along with parts of Northumberland and Yorkshire, were known as the palatinate or County Palatine, and were governed by a succession of prince-bishops, who combined ecclesiastical authority with secular power almost equal to that of the king. The origins of this situation lie in a grant of land made by King Egfrith of Northumbria to St Cuthbert on his election as bishop of Lindisfarne in 684. In the 6th century, the kingdom of Northumbria had been divided into the two states of Bernicia and Deira. These were geographically separated by the Tees, the latter including the district afterwards known as Durham, but were united by Aethelfrith c.604. On the transference of the bishopric of Lindisfarne to Chester-le-Street in the 9th century, Guthred the Dane endowed it with the whole district between the Tyne and the Wear, stretching west as far as Watling Street. The grant was confirmed by King Alfred; and when in 995 the bishopric was finally established at Durham, the endowment was enriched by various donations. Durham continued, however, to form part of the earldom of Northumbria until after the purchase of the earldom by Bishop Walcher in 1075. At the time of the Norman Conquest the bishops' possessions included nearly all the district between the Tees and the Tyne, except Sadberge, and also the outlying districts of Bedlingtonshire, Norhamshire, Islandshire and Crayke, together with Hexhamshire, the city of Carlisle, and part of Teviotdale. Henry I deprived the bishopric of the last three, but in compensation made over to it the vills of Burdon, Aycliffe and Canton, hitherto included in the earldom of Northumberland. Sadberge also formed part of the earldom of Northumberland; it was purchased for the see by Bishop Pudsey in 1189. The term *palatinus* is applied to the bishop in 1293, and from the 13th century onwards the bishops began to claim the same rights in their lands as the king enjoyed in his kingdom; this situation lasted until their power was curtailed by Henry VIII in 1536.

In 1640 the north of England was invaded by the Scots, who were permitted by a treaty made with Charles I to occupy County Durham and Northumberland; the occupation of Durham lasted for just a year. After the Battle of Dunbar between Cromwell's forces and the Scots in 1650, Durham Cathedral was used to contain Scottish prisoners. County Durham first returned members to Parliament in 1654. After the Restoration the county and city returned two members each. By the Reform Act of 1832 the county returned two members for two divisions. The boroughs of Darlington, Stockton and Hartlepool returned one member each from 1868 until the Redistribution Act of 1885.

County Durham has never possessed important manufacturers, and its economic history centres on the growth of the coal-mining industry, which employed almost the whole of the non-agricultural population. Among other early industries lead mining was carried out in the west of the county, and mustard was extensively cultivated.

Durham is the county town of County Durham. The River Wear flows north through the city, enclosing the centre on three sides to create Durham's 'peninsula'. Durham is a hilly city, claiming to be built upon the symbolic seven hills. Occupying the most central and prominent position high above the Wear, the cathedral dominates the skyline. The steep riverbanks are densely wooded, adding to the city's picturesque beauty. West of the city centre, another river, the Browney, drains south to join the Wear to the south of the city. Three old road bridges lead on to the peninsula, all of which is now pedestrianised. Prebends Bridge is at the southern tip of the Bailey. Heading east from the square, Elvet Bridge leads to the Elvet area of the city. To the west, Milburngate Bridge leads to the Milburngate district, Crossgate (an area predominantly occupied by students of Durham University) and North Road, the other main shopping area. West of here is an area colloquially known as 'The Viaduct' after the structure which dominates it. Beyond The Viaduct lie the outlying districts of Framwellgate Moor and Neville's Cross. Heading north from the market place leads to Claypath. The road curves back round to the east and beyond it lies Gilesgate and Gilesgate Moor. Durham won the Large Town award in the Britain in Bloom awards of 2005. Durham railway station is situated on the East Coast Main Line between Edinburgh and London; rail travellers coming from the south enter Durham over the aforementioned Victorian viaduct high above the city. By road, the A1(M), the modern incarnation of the ancient Great North Road, passes just to the east of the city. Durham has an airport in name, the Durham Tees Valley Airport – but this is actually far closer to Darlington. The Market Place and peninsula form the UK's first (albeit small) congestion charging area, introduced in 2002.

Durham	**Population**			**Area**	
Unitary Authorities	*male*	*female*	*total*	*sq miles*	*sq km*
County Durham	239,908	253,562	493,470	860	2227
Darlington	46,960	50,878	97,838	76	197
Hartlepool	42,560	46,051	88,611	36	94
Stockton-on-Tees (North)	41,676	43,891	85,567	39	102
Total	371,104	394,382	765,486	1011	2620

Note: see North Yorkshire for South Stockton population statistics.

Local Attractions and Information

Administrative headquarters	**Durham**: County Hall, Durham DH1 5UB. Tel: 0191 3833000. **Darlington**: Town Hall, Feethams, Darlington DL1 5QT. Tel: 01325 380651. **Hartlepool**: Civic Centre, Victoria Road TS24 8AY. Tel: 01429 266522. **Stockton-on-Tees**: Municipal Buildings, Church Road TS18 1LD. Tel: 01642 393939.
Airport, Durham Tees Valley	5 miles (8km) east of Darlington. One of the UK's smaller airports but rapidly expanding, the airport is owned by a consortium of local authorities (Darlington, Stockton-on-Tees, Middlesbrough, Hartlepool, and Redcar & Cleveland borough councils) and Peel Holdings. Previously called Teesside International Airport, it was renamed Durham Tees Valley Airport on 21 September 2004. Previously the site was the base of RAF Middleton St George (known as RAF Goosepool until 1941). In 1963, the airfield was closed and sold to Cleveland County Council, who developed the site into a commercial airport. Princess Margaretha of Sweden opened the international passenger terminal in 1966. Tel: 01325 332811.
Anker's House Museum, The	Church Chare, Chester-le-Street. A small museum giving an insight into how an anchorite was walled up for life, passing time in prayer and contemplation. There are exhibits and artefacts from Roman and medieval times including a facsimile of the Lindisfarne Gospels, which were translated into Old English at Chester-le-Street. Tel: 0191 388 3295.
Auckland Castle	Bishop Auckland, 10 miles (16km) southwest of Durham. The country residence of the Bishop of Durham, owned by the diocese for 800 years and initially serving as a hunting lodge. It is more like a Gothic country house than a true castle with a military function; among its many treasures is the Spanish artist Zubaran's famous collection of pictures of Jacob and his 12 sons in the Long Dining Room. The chapel, perhaps fittingly, is reputed to be the largest private chapel in Europe. Tel: 01388 601627
Auckland Castle Deer House	Bishop Auckland. Situated 500 yards (450m) north of the castle, the Deer House was erected in 1760 in the park of the Bishops of Durham so that deer could shelter and find food. Tel: 0191 269 1200.
Bailey, The	A historic area in the centre of Durham whose name is derived from the outer bailey of the Norman castle nearby. It is also called 'The Peninsula', being surrounded by steep cliffs and the Wear on three sides. In the Middle Ages the whole peninsula was known as 'the castle' and was enclosed by a wall, parts of which can still be seen in the grounds of the Bailey colleges of Durham University and to the west of the cathedral. Along the inside of the wall on the east side ran a street which now forms the present North and South Bailey. At its southern end the street is cobbled and is among the most attractive in the city. The central and southern parts of the Bailey, including the castle, the cathedral, the college and Prebends Bridge, are now designated a UNESCO World Heritage Site. See also Durham Castle, Durham Cathedral, Palace Green.
Barnard Castle	25 miles (40km) southwest of Durham. Standing on a cliff above the River Tees, this historic yet thriving market town developed in the protective shadow of Bernard Balliol's castle. The castle was founded as a timber structure by Guy de Balliol shortly after the Norman Conquest and was rebuilt by Bernard Balliol from 1125 (Scottish king John Balliol was the most notable member of this family) before falling into the possession of Richard Neville, Earl of Warwick. Richard III inherited it through his wife, Anne Neville, but in the century after his death it fell into ruins and was largely dismantled by Sir Henry Vane. The remains are now in the care of English Heritage. Walter Scott frequently visited his friend John Sawrey Morritt at Rokeby Hall and was fond of exploring Teesdale. He begins his epic poem *Rokeby* (1813) with a man standing on guard on the round tower of the Barnard Castle fortress. Charles Dickens and his illustrator Hablot Browne (Phiz) stayed at the King's Head in Barnard Castle while researching his novel *Nicholas Nickleby* in the winter of 1837–8. He is said to have entered William Humphrey's clock-maker's shop, then opposite the hotel, and enquired who had made a certain remarkable clock. William replied that his boy Humphrey had done it. This seems to have prompted Dickens to choose the title 'Master Humphrey's Clock' for his new weekly, in which *The Old Curiosity Shop* and *Barnaby Rudge* appeared. Tel: 01833 638212.
Battles	Two major battles have been fought in County Durham: Neville's Cross and Stainmoor. See separate table for details.
Baxterwood Priory	1 mile (1.6km) west of Durham. The site of a medieval priory, located on a bend of the River Browney. Originally founded at Haswell by Henry Pudsey, a son of Bishop Pudsey, in the late 12th century. A better situation was later found at Baxterwood, possibly in 1196. It was known as the 'New Place upon the Browney' and dedicated to the Virgin Mary. Stephen was the superintendent of the newly founded Augustinian priory. It was later appropriated by the nearby Benedictine monks of Durham Cathedral and became a Benedictine priory, its lands and manors being conferred on Finchale Priory. It was very close to the site of the Battle of Neville's Cross.
Beamish Museum	Stanley, 10 miles (16km) northwest of Durham. The North of England Open Air Museum, as it is officially titled, opened in 1972 and vividly recreates life in northern England as it was in the 1800s and 1900s. Much of the restoration and interpretation is specific to 1913, while the manor house and the railway are based on 1825. It is the first English museum to be financed and administered by a consortium of county councils (Cleveland, Durham, Northumberland and Tyne and Wear) and it was the first regional open-air museum in England. The recreation of an early 20th century town features shops, houses, a working pub, newspaper office, garage, sweetshop and sweet factory. Guided tours are given underground at a real 'drift' mine in the Colliery Village and a row of pit cottages shows how the pitmen and their families lived. There is a Methodist chapel and village school, while the home farm has traditional breeds of livestock and poultry and a large farmhouse kitchen, with dairy and bailiff's office. Pockerley Manor and Horse Yard is based on a medieval

fortified manor house and illustrates the life of a yeoman farming family 200 years ago. Beamish has its own railway, the Pockerley Waggonway, comprising a short length of track and an engine shed from 1825. Two replica steam locomotives run on the railway, one of George Stephenson's *Locomotion No 1* of 1825 (the original of which was the first engine to operate on the Stockton & Darlington Railway – see separate entry) and one of William Chapman's *Steam Elephant* of 1815. Tel: 01913 704000.

Binchester Roman Fort 1½ miles (2.5km) north of Bishop Auckland. Binchester Roman Fort (Vinovia) features the remains of a commanding officer's house, with the best-preserved military bath house in Britain, and a fascinating stretch of the original Dere Street (see separate entry). Tel: 01388 663089.

Bishop Middleham Quarry 2½ miles (4km) northwest of Sedgefield. Quarrying here ceased in 1934, and the 21.2 acres (8.6ha) are now managed as a nature reserve by the Durham Wildlife Trust. The nationally rare dark red helleborine has one of its largest British populations in the quarry, which is also a breeding site for the Durham argus, a local variant of the brown argus butterfly found only in northeast England. The site became famous among birdwatchers in 2002 when a pair of European bee-eaters took up residence, raising two young, only the third breeding attempt ever in Britain. Tel: 0191 584 3112.

Bowes Castle Bowes, 4 miles (6km) west of Barnard Castle. Tower castle built by the Earl of Richmond 1170–87 overlooking the valley of the River Greta, on the site of a Roman fort guarding the approach to Stainmore Pass. Henry II added a large stone keep, the remains of which can still be seen. Tel: 0191 269 1200.

Bowes Museum Newgate, Barnard Castle. The Bowes was designed and purpose-built as a public art gallery by French architect Jules Pellechet at the behest of John and Joséphine Bowes and opened in 1892. There are public galleries on three floors: the ground floor is devoted largely to local history and archaeology, the first floor houses collections of European fine and decorative arts, a suite of English period rooms and the newly refurbished John and Joséphine Galleries, and on the second floor are major collections of paintings, ceramics and musical instruments. Perhaps the best known and best loved object in the museum is the Silver Swan, a musical automaton in the form of a life-size model of a swan, comprising a clockwork mechanism covered in silver plumage above a music box. It rests on a stream made of twisted glass rods interspersed with silver fish. When the mechanism is wound up, the glass rods rotate, the music begins, and the swan twists its head to the left and right and appears to preen its back. It then appears to see a fish in the water below and bends down to catch it, swallowing the fish and resuming its upright position as the music stops (in fact swans do not eat fish!). The whole performance lasts about 40 seconds. It is believed to have been designed by John Joseph Merlin (1735–1803); its first recorded owner was James Cox and it was finally purchased by John Bowes in 1872. Tel: 01833 690606.

Bowlees and Gibson's Cave 10 miles (16km) northwest of Barnard Castle. Part of the Moor House–Upper Teesdale National Nature Reserve, the area has four small waterfalls and a riverside footpath leading to Gibson's Cave and the larger drop of Summerhill Force. There is a visitor centre run by Durham Wildlife Trust over the Bowlees Beck. An old limestone quarry on the site, once used for the production of road stone, has been left largely undisturbed, allowing trees and a wide variety of wild flowers to recolonise. Low Force is only ½ mile (0.8km) away, and High Force is 2 miles (3km) to the west. Tel: 0191 383 3594.

Castle Eden Dene Peterlee, 9 miles (15km) east of Durham. A National Nature Reserve situated on the south side of Peterlee. The reserve is the largest of Durham's wooded coastal ravines, cut deep into limestone. Because of the terrain the area is relatively undisturbed and contains large remnants of ancient woodland with over 450 species of plants and 12 miles (19km) of footpaths within its 500 acres (200ha). Tel: 0191 586 0004/518 2403.

Causey Arch, The 2 miles (3km) north of Stanley. Considered the world's oldest surviving single-arch railway bridge. Crossing the wooded gorge of the Causey Burn, it was built 1725–6 by architect Ralph Wood, funded by a conglomeration of coal owners known as the 'Grand Allies' (founded by Colonel Liddell and the Hon. Charles Montague). Two tracks crossed the bridge, one taking coal to the River Tyne and the other carrying the returning empty wagons. More than 900 horse-drawn wagons crossed the arch each day using the Tanfield Railway. Sadly, Wood was haunted by the collapse of his earlier timber bridge and fearing that the arch might collapse, he committed suicide by jumping from the top of it. Use of the arch declined when Tanfield Colliery was destroyed by fire in 1739. The arch was restored and reinforced in the 1980s. Tel: 0191 383 3594.

Chorister School The College, Durham. A co-educational pre-preparatory and preparatory day and boarding school for ages 4–13, located adjacent to Durham Cathedral. Its creation dates back to c.1400, when it was a school for the cathedral's choirboys. Notable alumni include poet, war correspondent and journalist James Fenton, former prime minister Tony Blair and comedy actor Rowan Atkinson. Tel: 0191 384 2935.

Churches **St Andrew's**, Church Lane, Aycliffe, is an ancient ecclesiastical centre with Saxon origins. Of special interest are the early Norman font, Jacobean pews, pulpit and medieval windows. Tel: 01325 300040.

St Giles', Gilesgate, Durham, was originally constructed as the hospital chapel of the Hospital of St Giles and dedicated in 1112 by Bishop Flambard to 'the honour of God and St Giles'. In 1140 the church was caught up in a dispute over the bishopric of Durham following the usurpation of the diocese by William Cumin, Chancellor of David I of Scotland. The elected bishop, William of St Barbara, was forced to retreat to and fortify the church after his entry into Durham was beaten back by Cumin's men. In response Cumin's men destroyed the hospital, which was later refounded at nearby Kepier (see Kepier Hospital). Bishop Hugh de Puiset later extended the church to reflect its role at the centre of a growing parish, and the current font is believed to date from this time. St Giles' retains some of Flambard's original building (primarily the north wall) and most of Puiset's additions. The church was restored and extended in 1873–6 as the parish continued to grow. It is now Grade I listed.

St Helen Auckland, $2\frac{1}{2}$ miles (4km) southwest of Bishop Auckland. Dating from the 12th century, St Helen's features the original door, a 13th century font, 15th century civilian brasses and memorials to the Eden family. Tel: 01388 604152.

St John's, Escomb, 1 mile (1.6km) west of Bishop Auckland. One of the oldest Anglo-Saxon churches in England, founded c.670–675, much of the stone coming from the nearby Roman fort at Binchester. There is a 7th or early 8th century sundial on the south wall, while on the north wall can be seen a reused Roman stone with the markings 'LEG VI' (Sixth Legion) set upside down. The church was restored in 1875–80 by R J Johnson, and in 1965 by Sir Albert Richardson. Now Grade I listed, it is one of the finest examples of early Christian architecture in northern Europe. Tel: 01388 458358.

St Laurence's, Hallgarth, Pittington, $3\frac{1}{2}$ miles (5.6km) east of Durham. The present church, dating from the 11th century, is thought to be on the site of an even earlier building. There are various interesting Norman and medieval features, including important 12th century wall paintings depicting St Cuthbert. Tel: 0191 372 1683.

St Mary & St Cuthbert's, Church Chare, Chester-le-Street. The shrine of St Cuthbert was established here by monks from Lindisfarne in AD 883. The original wooden church was replaced by one of stone c.1050, although most of the surviving structure dates from the 13th century. The spire was added c.1409, and one bell from that date still survives. Tel: 0191 388 3295.

St Nicholas', Durham is located on Durham marketplace and commonly known as St Nic's. The Church of England place of worship is the city's civic church. Dating to 1858, the building was designed by Darlington architect J Pritchett. The *Illustrated London News* once described it as 'the most beautiful specimen of church architecture in the North of England'. The current building replaced one dating from the early 12th century, whose walls formed part of the city walls and abutted the ancient Clayport Gate on one side. The font, dating from 1700, and its five bells, dating from 1687, are all that remains of this church. George Carey, later Archbishop of Canterbury, was vicar of St Nicholas', 1975–82, and was responsible for removing the pews and the majority of the Victorian interior features, allowing the church to be used more flexibly for worship and community activities. His book *The Church In The Marketplace* describes the process and its impact on the life of the parish. Tel: 0191 384 1180.

Crook Hall & Gardens — Sidegate, $\frac{1}{2}$ mile (0.8km) north of Durham city centre. A Grade I listed medieval hall dating to the early 13th century, with Jacobean and Georgian additions. The Jacobean room is allegedly haunted by a White Lady. The house is set in 4 acres (1.6ha) of fine gardens with maze and moat pool. Tel: 0191 384 8028.

Croxdale Hall — Sunderland Bridge, 3 miles (5km) south of Durham. Croxdale has been home to the Salvin family since 1402. The current house is Tudor in origin but the structure underwent major rebuilding in the 18th century. Features include mid-Georgian rooms with rococo ceilings and a private chapel, while the gardens contain a $\frac{1}{4}$ mile (0.4km) terrace. Tel: 0191 378 0911.

Darlington Railway Centre and Museum — See Head of Steam

Dere Street — Built c. AD 80, Dere Street was one of the most important roads in Roman Britain. Originally a military supply route running from York to the Firth of Forth, it later became the main supply route to Hadrian's Wall from the fortress at York. The street remained in continuous use throughout the Roman period and a number of forts were built along its length, including Catterick (Cataractonium), Piercebridge (possibly Morbium) and Corbridge (Corstopitum). Its course through County Durham runs roughly north from Piercebridge via Bishop Auckland and then northwest via Ebchester to Corbridge.

Derwent Valley Country Park — A 12 mile (19km) linear park created along the course of a former railway in the Derwent Valley from Swalwell Visitor Centre near the centre of Tyneside to Lydgett's Junction, Consett. Tel: 01207 545212/693693.

Derwentcote Steel Furnace — Forge Lane, Hamsterley, 3 miles (5km) north of Consett. The furnace was once at the centre of the British steel industry and is the earliest and most complete authentic steel-making furnace to have survived. It dates from c.1720 and was one of a number of steel manufacturing works along the banks of the River Derwent – an area which, along with neighbouring Tyneside, produced nearly half of Britain's steel in the 18th century. 'Newcastle Steel', as it became known, enjoyed an international reputation for excellent quality. Production ceased in the 1870s and the furnace soon fell into disrepair. In 1985 it was taken into the care of English Heritage and carefully restored. Tel: 0191 269 1200.

DLI Museum and Durham Art Gallery — Durham Road, Aykley Heads, $\frac{1}{2}$ mile (0.8km) northwest of Durham city centre. The museum features the Durham Light Infantry (with emphasis on World Wars I and II) and looks at Durham home front life during World War II. (The regiment's archive is housed in the nearby County Record Office.) The art gallery has no permanent collection but holds a regular programme of temporary exhibitions. Tel: 0191 384 2214.

Durham, (HM) Prison — Old Elvet, Durham. A category B local prison built in the early 19th century adjacent to Durham's Crown Courts. It now houses adult male prisoners, primarily serving the courts of County Durham, Wearside and Teesside. The prison has an operational capacity of 919 inmates. HMP Durham previously operated a female wing, but this was discontinued following reports from HM Inspectorate of Prisons that the prison was unsuitable for housing female prisoners. The prison was the site of a number of executions.

Durham Castle Palace Green, Durham. One of the largest Norman castles and Romanesque palaces to survive in England, Durham Castle is the ancient palace of the prince-bishops of Durham and lies at the northern end of Palace Green opposite the cathedral. The castle, part of a World Heritage Site, was built to the orders of William I on his return from Scotland in 1072. Waltheof, the Saxon Earl of Northumberland, undertook the work for William but over the years a succession of prince-bishops added important sections. The keep (erected in the 14th century during the episcopacy of Bishop Thomas Hatfield) fell into ruin and, having been presented to the University of Durham by Bishop Mildert in 1836, was rebuilt in 1840 as sleeping quarters for students when the castle became University College, the founding college of the University of Durham. The older and greater part of the castle is situated around a courtyard to the west of the keep. The courtyard is entered from the gatehouse near the site of the castle moat. Initially the work of Bishop Pudsey (1153–95), the gatehouse underwent alterations during the episcopacies of Bishop Tunstal (1530–59) and Bishop Shute Barrington (1791–1826). Features of the building include the 57ft (17.5m) Black Staircase, named for the dark oak of which it was made, situated between the Great Hall and Bishop Pudsey's building and the oldest part of the castle, and the Norman chapel built in 1080. Tel: 0191 334 3800.

Durham Cathedral The Cathedral Church of Christ, Blessed Mary the Virgin and St Cuthbert of Durham was founded in 1093 and forms part of a World Heritage Site. It was founded in order to house the relics of St Cuthbert; the remains of the 7th century saint had been brought to Durham by the city's legendary founders, monks from Lindisfarne who fled Viking attacks in 875 taking the relics with them. The original building was completed in 40 years and the cathedral is virtually unique in retaining most of its Norman structure. It is 496ft (151m) long; the nave, choir and transepts are Norman while the western towers date from the 12th and 13th centuries. The 217ft (66m) central tower, dating from the 15th century, has 325 steps. As well as the shrine and related treasures of St Cuthbert, the cathedral is also home to the tomb of the Venerable Bede. The cloisters contain the 14th century monks' dormitory, a room with an impressive oak-beamed roof now a library, while in the southwest corner is the Treasury Museum. Displays of valuable and beautiful objects include St Cuthbert's relics, fine altar plate, richly illustrated manuscripts, bishops' rings, seals and embroidered copes. The cathedral was voted Britain's best loved building in a BBC poll conducted in 2001. Tel: 0191 386 4266.

Durham Drama Festival Founded in 1975 by Durham Student Theatre as the One Act Festival, the event has grown in scope and size over three decades and adopted its current name and format in 2003. Applications are accepted from members of Durham University and external theatre companies from the beginning of November each year, for performance in February. Tel: 07930 413210.

Durham Heritage Centre North Bailey, Durham. Established in a medieval church which was partly rebuilt in the 17th century, the museum tells the story of Durham from the 10th century to the present day. Tel: 0191 384 5589 (summer) or 0191 386 8719 (winter).

Durham Mining Museum Hartlepool Street, Thornley, 5 miles (8km) southeast of Durham. A largely online resource which has a display room at Thornley Community Centre.

Durham School An independent boarding and day school founded before 1414 (the foundation date accepted by the Clarendon Commission into public schools in 1861), and refounded by Henry VIII during the Reformation in 1541. The school is said to have its origins in the priory at Lindisfarne, being moved to Durham City to escape marauding Viking invaders around the time that St Cuthbert's body was brought to what is now the site of Durham Cathedral. The school was rebuilt on Palace Green in 1661 before moving to its present site in 1844. Among the school's notable alumni is John Balliol, King of Scotland, who attended the school before its official formation in 1414. Ex-pupils of Durham School are called Old Dunelmians. Tel: 0191 386 4783.

Durham Museum of Archaeology The Old Fulling Mill, Durham. Archaeological museum illustrating the history of the city of Durham. Tel: 0191 3341121.

Durham University Oriental Museum Elvet Hill Road, Durham. The only museum in England devoted to oriental art and antiquities. Tel: 0191 3345694.

Egglestone Abbey 1½ miles (2.5km) southeast of Barnard Castle. Founded by the Premonstratensian order (or White Canons), the ruined 12th century abbey stands in a picturesque setting above the River Tees. The remains are now in the care of English Heritage. Close by is a medieval pack horse bridge. Tel: 0191 269 1200.

Elvet Hill Located on the south bank of the River Wear in the city of Durham, Elvet Hill is home to the hill colleges of the University of Durham.

Finchale Priory 4½ miles (7km) northeast of Durham. This 13th century Benedictine priory served as a holiday retreat for monks from Durham. There are considerable remains of the church and monastery buildings in an attractive riverside setting. Tel: 0191 386 3828.

Hamsterley Forest 10 miles (16km) west of Bishop Auckland. Situated between Weardale and Teesdale, the 5000 acres (2000ha) of mixed deciduous and coniferous woodland are operated by the Forestry Commission. Planted in the 1930s, the forest occupies mixed terrain offering a wide range of habitats. Tel: 01388 488312.

Hardwick Hall & Park 1½ miles (2.5km) west of Sedgefield. Not to be confused with the more famous Hardwick Hall in Derbyshire, it has survived as an unaltered landscape garden of the 1750s comparable to the gardens of Stourhead (Wiltshire) and Stowe (Buckinghamshire). There has been a house on the site since the medieval period when the manor of 'Herdwyck' existed. In 1748 John Burdon, a wealthy Tyneside businessman, bought the estate and embarked on a dramatic programme of landscape improvement, creating an artificial serpentine 'river' which flowed over a cascade into a large ornamental lake south of the house. A circuit walk was also laid out around the lake passing a series of decorative buildings. Tel: 0191 383 3594.

Harperley Prisoner of War Camp 3 miles (5km) west of Crook. A World War II prisoner-of-war camp, featured on the BBC's *Restoration* programme, and recently restored. A 1940s house on site was opened in spring 2006. Tel: 01388 767098.

Hartlepool Monkey According to the story, during the Napoleonic Wars a ship was wrecked off the Hartlepool coast in a storm. Fearing an invasion, the local fishermen kept a close watch on the French vessel as it struggled but when the ship was severely battered and sunk they turned their attention to the wreckage washed ashore. Among the debris lay one wet and sorrowful looking survivor, the ship's pet monkey, dressed in a military uniform for the sailors' amusement. It is claimed that the fishermen, unfamiliar with what a Frenchman looked like, questioned the monkey and held a trial on the beach. They concluded that the unfortunate creature was a French spy and should be sentenced to death, and the monkey was hanged on the mast of a fishing boat. The legend is likely to be apocryphal: as Hartlepool received its royal charter in 1201 and was an important seafaring town, it is doubtful whether 600 years later its residents would not recognise a monkey.

Hartlepool Power Station 3 miles (5km) south of Hartlepool. A nuclear power station utilising two advanced gas-cooled reactors (AGRs), opened in 1983 and scheduled for decommissioning by 2014.

Head of Steam Station Road, Darlington. The former Darlington Railway Centre and Museum is located on the route of the Stockton & Darlington Railway (see separate entry) and housed in former railway buildings including North Road Passenger Station. Exhibits include *Locomotion No. 1* (the first ever steam train to carry fare-paying passengers), built by Robert Stephenson & Co for the opening of the railway in 1825. Tel: 01325 460532.

High Force $4^1/_2$ miles (7km) northwest of Middleton-in-Teesdale. Rising high on the heather-covered fells at the top of the North Pennines and flowing to the top of the whinsill rock at Forest-in-Teesdale, the River Tees steadily grows and gathers pace before spectacularly dropping 70ft (21m) into the plunge pool below. Although it has laid claim to being the highest single-drop fall in England, it falls short of this honour (see 'Waterfalls' in Cumbria and North Yorkshire). The falls are however adjacent to one of the most attractive sections of the Pennine Way long-distance footpath (see Derbyshire). Tel: 01833 640209.

Highest point Mickle Fell at 2585ft (788m), situated 3 miles (5km) south of Cow Green Reservoir and 9 miles (14km) southeast of Cross Fell, slightly off the main watershed of the Pennines. Traditionally regarded as part of Yorkshire, although it lies just inside County Durham, the fell lies in the middle of a large area of boggy moor. It can be ascended via a long hike from the western fringe or from Teesdale. Mickle Fell's distinctive outline makes it recognisable when viewed from the Lake District hills, particularly Blencathra, Helvellyn and High Street.

Interesting facts **Durham Tees Valley Airport** (see separate entry) has its own railway station on the Middlesbrough Line. It lays claim to being the least used of any train station in Britain, having but one train stop there per week at 13.41 on a Saturday. **Oak Road**, Easington was named the fattest street in England in September 2006. Using statistical analysis, scientists have developed the country's first 'fat map', and residents of Oak Road in the former mining town were 22 per cent more likely to become obese than the national average. **West Auckland** can lay claim to being the home of the first football 'world cup' winners. With the Olympic event being restricted to amateur teams, Sir Thomas Lipton organised the Sir Thomas Lipton Trophy tournament in Turin in 1909. The tournament was an open championship between individual clubs from different nations, each one of which represented their entire country. It featured the most prestigious professional club sides from Italy, Germany and Switzerland. Not wishing to have Britain and Ireland unrepresented, Lipton invited West Auckland FC, an amateur side from County Durham mostly made up of coal miners, to take part. West Auckland won the tournament and returned to Italy in 1911 to defend their title. In this second competition, West Auckland beat Juventus 6–1 in the final, and were awarded the trophy outright. **Mary Ann Cotton** (1833–73), a district nurse from West Auckland, killed at least five people including her second husband Frederick, his two stepsons, and two lovers, a local excise officer named Quick-Manning, and her lodger Joseph Natrass. She was suspected of killing many more, possibly 30. Her raison d'etre was invariably either to collect insurance money or to clear the way for a new liaison. Her chosen method of disposal was arsenic. After she was eventually tried and sentenced to death in 1873, the hangman bungled the execution, causing her to take three and a half minutes to stop convulsing before dying at the rope's end. **The Builder's Arms** in Newton Aycliffe, 11 miles (18km) south of Durham, is often mistaken for a public house, and does indeed serve excellent food and drink (although ginger ale is its strongest brew), but the licensed premises is in fact a Christian bookshop! Bishop Auckland-born poet **Craig Raine** is the best-known exponent of Martianism, an effect whereby familiar items are described as if seen by an alien. Interestingly, the word martianism is an anagram of one of its principal exponents: Martin Amis.

Islands There are three named islands in Durham, all in the North Sea off Hartlepool: Little Scar (GR: NZ527305), Long Scar (GR: NZ530315) and Parton Rocks (GR: NZ525345).

Kepier Hospital Gilesgate, Durham. Originally founded by Bishop Flambard in 1112 as an almshouse 'for the keeping of the poor who enter the same hospital', and dedicated to God and St Giles, the patron saint of beggars and cripples. It was refounded in the late 12th century by Bishop Hugh le Puiset on a nearby site, although the 14th century gateway is all that remains today. See also St Giles' Church.

Killhope Cowshill, 20 miles (32km) southwest of Consett. The restored 19th century lead mines at Killhope in Upper Weardale are now the site of the North of England Lead Mining Museum. Exhibits include the largest working waterwheel in the north of England, manufactured by local engineer William George Armstrong, while Park Level mine has been reopened for guided underground tours. Tel: 01388 537505.

Kirkcarrion 1¼ miles (2km) south of Middleton-in-Teesdale, 10 miles (16km) northwest of Barnard Castle. A copse of pine trees, surrounded by a drystone wall, located on a hilltop and covering a Bronze Age tumulus. Reputedly haunted, it forms a significant landmark on the Pennine Way above Teesdale.

Lambton Castle & Park 1 mile (1.6km) northeast of Chester-le-Street. The castle was largely constructed in its present form by John George Lambton, 1st Earl of Durham and one-time Governor-General of Canada, in the early 1800s and designed by architects Joseph Bonomi the Elder and his son Ignatius. Overlooking the wooded valley of the River Wear, the building was paid for with wealth accumulated from the coal mines that ran below the castle. Much of the house, including the great hall, was demolished due to subsidence in the 1930s, ironically caused by those very mines. Many of the contents were auctioned to pay death duties and the family moved into the smaller Biddick Hall on the estate. Today the castle stands empty but is still maintained and remains the ancestral home of the Lambton family. Lambton Park, which surrounds the castle, is bordered by a high wall and is still used for an annual pheasant shoot. In the 1960s and 1970s, the castle's grounds were home to Lambton Lion Park. The northern edge of Lambton Park marks the Tyne and Wear/County Durham boundary. The Lambton family is strongly associated with the local legend of the Lambton Worm.

Lambton Worm, The A traditional folk-tale of northeast England with several variations in its telling. According to most versions of the tale, young John Lambton, heir to the family estate, caught a worm while fishing. So repulsive was its appearance that he threw it down a well, only for it to grow to enormous size and, while John was abroad fighting in the Crusades, to emerge and terrorise the local community. On his return John vowed to vanquish the worm but first consulted a local witch; she told him that, having killed the worm, he must dispatch the next living creature he saw or else his family would not die in their beds for nine generations. On being given a prearranged signal that the worm was dead, John's father was to ensure that a hound would be released to become John's second victim; alas, when the worm was ultimately slain and devoured by the River Wear, John's father forgot the arrangement and rushed out to congratulate his son. John was unable to kill his own father, thus implementing the curse – and in fact the next three heirs all died bloodily, as did the ninth. The story has been made into an opera and a song, written in 1867 by C M Leumane and most effective when performed in the appropriate regional accent. Its first verse goes thus: 'One Sunday mornin' Lambton went, A-fishing in the Wear;/An' catched a fish upon he's heuk, He thowt leuk't vary queer./But whatt'n a kind ov fish it was, Young Lambton cudden't tell –,/He waddn't fash te carry'd hyem, So he hoyed it doon a well.'

Legg's Cross 4 miles (6km) north of Piercebridge. Located on the Pilgrims' Way (the modern B6275 and the old Roman road of Dere Street), an Anglo-Saxon cross now heavily eroded into the form of an obelisk. It has been suggested that its name derives from an inscription it once bore reading 'LEG', the cross having possibly been constructed from Roman masonry (a Roman fort was once located at nearby Piercebridge), and the inscription originally celebrating the 20th Legion.

Locomotion: The National Railway Museum at Shildon Shildon, 3 miles (5km) southeast of Bishop Auckland. Formerly the Timothy Hackworth Victorian & Railway Museum. Opened in 2004, the museum is the first-ever 'out-station' for the National Railway Museum, York, and the region's first branch of a national museum. It houses up to 60 vehicles from the national collection. Tel: 01388 777999.

Low Force 4½ miles (7km) northwest of Middleton-in-Teesdale. A set of waterfalls on the River Tees, downstream from High Force waterfall. Low Force is also the site of the Wynch Bridge.

Lumley Castle Ropery Lane, Chester-le-Street. The 14th century castle, a property of the Earl of Scarborough, bears the name of its original creator, Sir Ralph Lumley, who converted his family manor house into a castle in 1389. Implicated in a plot to overthrow Henry IV, Sir Ralph was imprisoned and executed, forfeiting his lands to the Earl of Somerset. Ownership of the castle reverted to Sir Ralph's grandson, Thomas, in 1421. The original structure was altered during the mid 18th century by Sir John Vanbrugh. The castle had become the residence of the Bishop of Durham by the 19th century and was later a hall of residence for University College, Durham. Undergraduates housed at Lumley Castle had an eight mile journey to reach the university. At the time there were 23 pubs in the villages along the route; some students would attempt to consume a pint of beer at each. This practice gave rise in the 1950s to the local student tradition known as the Lumley Run, in which competitors aim to emulate their predecessors by visiting each of the remaining pubs against the clock. Supposedly haunted by the ghost of Sir Ralph Lumley's wife, in 1976 the castle was converted into a hotel. In 2000 three members of the West Indian cricket team, including captain Jimmy Adams, checked out of the hotel on account of fear, and the Australian cricket team was said to have been haunted during their stay in 2005.

Maiden Castle ½ mile (0.8km) east of Durham city. The name of two distinct sites on opposite banks of the River Wear. Maiden Castle fort on the western bank is one of five similarly named hill forts in England. Little remains, but archaeologists exploring the area have found that the hill was fortified during the late medieval period, probably in the 15th or 16th century, and was surrounded by a stone wall and a wooden fence. Maiden Castle motte, Old Durham, on the other bank of the Wear, is a motte and bailey destroyed in the 19th century. Maiden Castle Footbridge, built in 1974, links the ancient sites. Today the area is occupied by Old Durham Gardens and the Graham Sports Centre.

Newbiggin Chapel Newbiggin, 2½ miles (4km) northwest of Middleton-in-Teesdale. The chapel was opened in 1760, visited by John Wesley and is now the world's oldest Methodist chapel in continuous use. Tel: 01325 730985.

North of England Open Air Museum See Beamish Museum

Palace Green A small grassed area in the centre of Durham, flanked by Durham Cathedral and Durham Castle, though not itself part of the UNESCO World Heritage Site. It is situated atop the narrow, high peninsula formed by a sharp bend in the River Wear. The cathedral is on the southern side, facing the castle across the Green on the north side. To the west are Durham University buildings including the law, theology and history departments, with the music department and a small branch of the library to the east. Palace Green is accessed by two cobbled streets called Owengate (formerly Queen Street) and Dun Cow Lane. The latter is named after the bovine protagonist of Durham's founding legend, in which the monks fleeing Lindisfarne with the relics of St Cuthbert were led to the site where the city now stands by a dun or grey-coloured cow.

Piercebridge Roman Fort Piercebridge, 5 miles (8km) west of Darlington. Situated on Dere Street and dating from c.AD 260. Visible Roman remains include the East Gate and defences, courtyard building and part of an internal road. Tel: 01325 460532.

Pit village A general term for a mining village, many of the workers living in houses provided by the colliery. The last remaining deep coal mine in northeast England was Ellington Colliery, which closed in 2005. The film *Billy Elliot* (2000), set in the fictional pit village of Everington during the miners' strike of 1984–5, was shot on location in Easington Colliery, which itself went through the events of 1985.

Pity Me 3 miles (5km) north of Durham. A village located north of Framwellgate Moor and west of Newton Hall. There are several theories as to the origin of the name: possibly it arose as a semi-humorous term for a barren piece of land, or as a distortion of the French *petite mer* (small sea, i.e. a lake). Locals claim the term arose after monks sang the 51st Psalm during their flight from a Viking invasion. The Latin words of the psalm are '*Miserere mei, Deus*', meaning 'Pity me, O God'. According to the *Oxford Dictionary of British Place Names* it is a whimsical name bestowed in the 19th century on a place considered desolate, exposed or difficult to cultivate. The name also occurs elsewhere in the UK, for example in Cornwall and Northumberland.

Pontop Pike Television Transmitter 1/4 mile (0.4km) south of Dipton, 3 miles (5km) northeast of Consett. The transmitter provides UHF television transmissions to Tyne and Wear, County Durham, Tees Valley, most of Northumberland and parts of North Yorkshire. The mast was built in 1953 and its construction was brought forward by the BBC so that people in northeast England could watch the coronation of Queen Elizabeth II. Test transmissions from a low-power temporary aerial began on 20 April 1953, and the first programmes were transmitted on 1 May, in plenty of time for the Coronation on 2 June. It also carries the national BBC Radio FM signals, covering the whole northeast, as well as 95.4FM Radio Newcastle. It was one of the first national FM transmitters in December 1955. The mast is 476ft (145m) high, giving average transmitter height of 1476ft (450m) above sea level. It is owned and operated by National Grid Wireless.

Preston Hall Eaglescliffe, 3 miles (5km) south of Stockton-on-Tees. Built in 1825, Preston Hall stands in 100 acres (40ha) of parkland. Since 1953, it has been the centrepiece of a museum and is operated by Stockton-on-Tees Borough Council. The museum includes a recreated period street of the 1890s, period rooms, an armoury and a toy collection. Tel: 01642 527375.

Raby Castle 1 mile (1.6km) north of Staindrop. One of the largest inhabited castles in England. Although the castle was built mainly in the 14th century, its medieval shell contains opulent 18th and 19th century interiors. Cecily Neville, the mother of Edward IV and Richard III, was born at Raby. The Nevilles lost the castle after they led the failed Rising of the North in favour of Mary, Queen of Scots in 1569. In 1626, Sir Henry Vane the Elder purchased Raby from the Crown and his descendant, Lord Barnard, still owns it. There is a 200 acre (80ha) deer park with two lakes and a walled garden surrounding the castle. The 18th century stable block houses a horse-drawn carriage collection including the state coach last used by the family for the coronation of Edward VII in 1902. Tel 01833 660202.

Rivers The **Browney**, the largest tributary of the Wear, rises on Skaylock Hill, southwest of Consett, flowing east past Lanchester and then turning south to skirt the west of Durham. It joins the Wear south of Durham, near Sunderland Bridge.

The **Derwent** runs from the outflow of Derwent reservoir in the North Pennines, passing from unspoiled areas of Northumberland into County Durham north of Castleside. It then flows northeast via Burnopfield and Rowland's Gill and finally into Tyne and Wear, finishing as it runs into the Tyne near the Metrocentre, a length of 25 miles (40km).

A tributary of the River Tees, the **Skerne** is 25 miles long and begins in magnesian limestone hills between Trimdon and Trimdon Grange, ending at Hurworth-on-Tees where it joins the Tees.

The **Tees** rises on the eastern slope of Cross Fell in the Pennine chain and flows east for 70 miles (112km) to the North Sea between Hartlepool and Redcar. In the earliest part of its course it forms the boundary between the counties of Cumbria and Durham. The head of the valley, of which the upper portion is known as Teesdale, has a desolate grandeur, the bleak moorland rising to over 2500ft (760m) at some points. In its upper reaches, below Cow Green Reservoir, it flows down a series of rock steps known as Cauldron Snout, which at 200yds (190m) forms England's largest waterfall. A little further down Teesdale is High Force, at 66ft (20m) the highest waterfall in England. Beyond Teesdale the river passes Barnard Castle, Stockton-on-Tees and Middlesbrough on its way to the North Sea. Teesport is the busiest port in the England, shipping over 1 million tonnes of cargo per year. The river drains an area of 708 sq miles (1834 sq km), and has no important tributaries. It was featured on the BBC TV programme *Seven Natural Wonders* as one of the wonders of the North.

The **Wear** rises at Wear Head in Weardale, 18 miles (29km) southwest of Consett, flowing east to Waskerley Beck and then southeast to the north of Bishop Auckland. It continues northeast to Durham, further north to Chester-le-Street and then northeast again to discharge into the North Sea at Sunderland. Its total length is 65 miles (105km).

Rokeby Park — 3 miles (5km) southeast of Barnard Castle. An 18th century Palladian style country house which was the setting for Sir Walter Scott's ballad *Rokeby* (see also Barnard Castle). Scott's friend J B S Morritt, who owned the house in the first half of the 19th century, bought Velazquez's painting *The Toilet of Venus*, now better known as the 'Rokeby Venus', in 1809 (it was sold to the National Gallery in 1906). The house contains a collection of 18th century needlepoint paintings, period furniture and an interesting 'Print Room', whose walls are lined with 18th century prints. Tel: 01833 637334.

Seaton Holme — Easington, 9 miles (15km) east of Durham. A restored 12th century manor house, the former rectory of Easington, situated opposite St Mary's Church. Its layout dates primarily to the 15th century. The building now houses a Discovery Centre tracing the history of the building itself and the local area. Tel: 0191 527 3333.

Sherburn Hospital — 2 miles (3km) southeast of Durham. Located in Sherburn House and also known as Christ's Hospital, the medieval hospital was founded in 1181 by Bishop Pudsey to care for 65 lepers and dedicated to 'Our Lord, to the Blessed Virgin, to St Lazarus and his sisters, Mary and Martha'. Unlike many similar institutions, Sherburn Hospital survived the Dissolution of the Monasteries and an Act of Parliament in 1585 provided for the establishment of 'The Master and Brethren of Christ's Hospital in Sherborne near Durham'. In 1832 George Stanley Faber became master of the hospital and devoted much of his income and time to improving it. He died there in 1854 and was buried in its cemetery. The hospital became very wealthy due to coal mining on its estates. A dispensary, providing free medical treatment for the poor, was opened in 1858, and the annual attendance soon exceeded 3700. All the hospital buildings are Grade II or II* listed. The hospital now provides residential care and sheltered housing for residents and former residents of the diocese of Durham. Tel: 0191 3722551.

Shotley Bridge — 11 miles (18km) west of Chester-le-Street. Village in the Derwent Valley attached to Consett. Shotley Bridge was once the heart of Britain's swordmaking industry. The origins of the industry here dated from 1691 when a group of Lutheran swordmakers from Solingen in Germany settled at in the village. Today Shotley's only major feature is the local hospital where most of the native population of Derwentside under the age of 40 were born.

Sport

cricket — **Durham County Cricket Club** is cricket's youngest first-class county, having been granted first-class status in 1991. The club boasts one of the finest grounds in England, the County Cricket Ground at Riverside, Chester-le-Street, which has views towards the River Wear and historic Lumley Castle (see separate entry), and has hosted Test matches against Zimbabwe in 2003, Bangladesh in 2005 and the West Indies in 2007. The club won its first major trophy, the Friends Provident Trophy, in 2007 and won the County Championship in 2008. The one-day side are known as Durham Dynamos. Tel: 0191 387 1717.

football — **Darlington** were founded in 1883 and joined the Football League in 1921. Their colours are black and white. The club's nickname, the Quakers, is also the nickname of any person born and bred in Darlington, and comes from the Quaker movement (or Society of Friends) which gained a foothold in the town after its founding by George Fox in 1647. On 28 November 1955 Darlington beat Carlisle United 3–1 in a second round FA Cup replay at St James's Park, Newcastle, the first FA Cup tie to be played under floodlights. Feethams Ground was the club's long-established home venue until it moved in 2003 to the Darlington Arena. Tel: 01325 387000.

Hartlepool United were founded in 1881 and joined the Football League in 1921. Brian Clough began his managerial career at the club in 1965. The Pool (also nicknamed the Monkey Hangers by their rivals – see Hartlepool Monkey), whose traditional colours are blue and white, play at Victoria Park, Clarence Road, Hartlepool. Local derbies against Darlington are fiercely contested. Tel: 01429 272584.

horse racing — **Sedgefield Racecourse** is situated just outside the village of Sedgefield, 8 miles (13km) east of Bishop Auckland. The left-handed track of $1^1/_4$ miles has a jumping course on the inside. Tel: 01740 621925.

Stockton & Darlington Railway — The first permanent steam locomotive railway, opened on 27 September 1825. The line was 26 miles (40km) long, connecting Stockton-on-Tees and Darlington with several collieries near Shildon. It was initially built to connect inland coal mines to Stockton, where coal was to be loaded onto seagoing boats. Much of its route is now served by the Tees Valley Line, operated by Northern Rail. Inspired by local wool merchant Edward Pease, the S&DR was authorised by Parliament in 1821 and was initially meant to be an ordinary horse-drawn plateway. George Stephenson, who had been building steam engines for seven years and had constructed the Hetton colliery railway, managed to persuade Pease to allow him to attempt to work the route by steam. A new Act of Parliament was obtained approving changes to the route, and a clause added to permit the use of 'loco-motive or moveable engines'. The bill also included provisions for transporting passengers, though at the time they were regarded as merely a sideline. Improvements were made to the track to overcome the problems with settling of the stone blocks on which it was laid, and T-section malleable iron in lengths of 15ft (4.5m), pioneered by John Birkinshaw at Bedlington in 1820, was used for the rails. Stephenson's *Locomotion No. 1* was the first engine to operate on the railway.

Tanfield Railway — 1 mile (1.6km) north of Stanley, 6 miles (10km) northwest of Chester-le-Street. A heritage railway whose original purpose was the movement of coal from Stanley and Marley Hill collieries to ships on the River Tyne. The oldest part, built c.1647, was the Lobley Hill section; it had seen over 300 years of coal traffic when closed in 1964. The surviving Sunniside to Causey section (opened in 1725) is now the world's oldest working railway, while the Causey to East Tanfield section dates from 1839. Originally, horses hauled small wagons along wooden track but they were replaced in the 19th century by metal rails and locomotives. The locomotive fleet is maintained at Marley Hill engine shed, built in 1854 and in colliery use until 1970. The Tanfield Railway now runs between Sunniside, Causey Arch (see separate entry) and East Tanfield. Tel: 0191 388 7545.

Tow Law Beehive Coke Ovens Inkerman, 1/2 mile (0.8km) north of Tow Law, 10 miles (16km) southwest of Durham. The remains of 19th century beehive coking ovens used to convert locally mined coal into coke for use by the railway and local steel industries. Tel 0191 528 6314.

Town Hall, Durham Market Place, Durham. Built in 1850, the Town Hall features superb stained glass windows, paintings, heraldic symbols and a fireplace of local stone. The structure incorporates the medieval guildhall, first built in 1356. Tel: 0191 386 6111.

University of Durham Located on two sites – in the city of Durham, on the River Wear, and in Stockton-on-Tees – Durham is one of the UK's leading research universities. Founded in 1832 with one 'college' named University College, it was granted a royal charter in 1837, moving into Durham Castle (previously the Bishop's palace) the same year. The university also has an impressive record of sporting achievement, and its athletic club awards the Palatinate, the equivalent of the Oxford and Cambridge Blue. Notable alumni include broadcaster George Alagiah (Van Mildert); John Barrow (Van Mildert), cosmologist and Fellow of the Royal Society; Biddy Baxter (St Mary's), TV producer (*Blue Peter*) and inventor of the Blue Peter badge; botanist and environmental campaigner David Bellamy; puzzle writer David J Bodycombe (Trevelyan); writer Bill Bryson; Will Carling (Hatfield), former captain of the England rugby team; journalist and author Hunter Davies; Jonathan Edwards (Van Mildert), Olympic gold medal-winning triple jumper; ballet dancer Margot Fonteyn; Judith Hann, presenter of BBC's *Tomorrow's World* 1974–94; Lorraine Heggessey (Collingwood), controller of BBC1 2000–04; and Nasser Hussain (Hild Bede), former captain of the England cricket team. The colleges are: Collingwood (founded 1972); George Stephenson (2001); Grey (1959); Hatfield (1846); John Snow (2001); Josephine Butler (2006); St Aidan's (1947); St Chad's (1904); St Cuthbert's Society (1888); St Hild and St Bede (1975); St John's (1909); St Mary's (1899); Trevelyan (1966); University (1832); Ushaw (1568); Ustinov (1965); Van Mildert (1965). Tel: 0191 334 2000.

University of Durham Botanic Garden Hollingside Lane, Durham. An 18 acre (7ha) garden in mature woodland with exotic trees from America and the Himalayas. The garden was founded in 1925 and moved to its present site in 1970; the visitor centre was opened in 1988 by Dame Margot Fonteyn, then chancellor of the university. Tel: 0191 334 5521.

Weardale Museum and High House Chapel Ireshopeburn, 20 miles (32km) west of Bishop Auckland. High House Chapel (founded 1760) is the world's oldest Methodist chapel still in continuous weekly use. John Wesley preached here in 1752. An adjoining small folk museum opened in 1985 includes a Wesley Room, 1870 period Weardale Cottage room, local history, crystallised mineral displays and family history resources. Tel: 01388 517433.

Weardale Railway 9 miles (15km) northwest of Bishop Auckland. Opened in 2004, a heritage railway in the Durham Dales operating for 5 miles (8km) beside the River Wear between Wolsingham and Stanhope. Tel: 0845 600 1348.

Whitworth Hall Country Park 1 1/2 miles (2.5km) northwest of Spennymoor. The earliest documentary reference to the estate dates to 1183 and names its holder as Thomas de Acle, whose descendants assumed the local name Whyte-worth in the early 14th century. In 1420 Ralph Neville, Earl of Westmorland, emparked part of the estate, which was later seized by the Crown. After the Civil War it was purchased by the Shafto family, remaining their home for 300 years. The family's most noted member was Robert Shafto, man of fashion and MP for County Durham, who died in 1797 but was immortalised by the ballad 'Bobbie Shafto'. The house itself is now a hotel; the 73 acres (29.5ha) of historic parkland include deer, a coarse fishing lake, Victorian walled garden, and Britain's most northerly vineyard. Tel: 01388 811772.

Witton Castle Witton-le-Wear, 3 miles (5km) northwest of Bishop Auckland. The 14th century castle, originally constructed by Ralph Eure, subsequently passed through many hands and was rebuilt in the 18th century. It is currently owned by Lord Lambton, a descendant of the Eure family, and is the location of a major caravan and camping site. Tel: 01388 488230.

Wynch Bridge 1 mile (1.6km) west of Newbiggin, 14 miles (23km) northwest of Barnard Castle. Spanning the River Tees just below Low Force (see separate entry), the bridge was erected c.1830 to enable lead miners to cross the river. It replaced an earlier bridge of 1704 which lays claim to being the first suspension bridge in England.

Some famous people born in County Durham

Allen, Sir Thomas (opera singer) (1944–)	Seaham Harbour
Armstrong, Jackie (trombonist) (1920–2005)	Consett
Browning, Elizabeth Barrett (poet) (1806–61)	Coxhoe
Camsell, George (footballer) (1902–66)	Framwellgate Moor
Collingwood, Paul (cricketer) (1976–)	Shotley Bridge
Crisell, Ellie (journalist and television presenter) (1976–)	Durham
Dixon, Jeremiah (surveyor) (1733–79)	Cockfield
Eden, Anthony (prime minister) (1897–1977)	West Auckland
Greenwell, Dora (poet) (1821–82)	Lanchester
Hill, Lorna (author of the 'Wells' ballet books) (1902–91)	Durham
Horn, Trevor (pop music producer) (1949–)	Durham
Hunt, Violet (novelist and 'new woman') (1862–1942)	Durham
Joad, C E M (philosopher and broadcaster) (1891–1953)	Durham
MacDonald, James Edward Hervey (artist) (1873–1932)	Durham
Mackenzie, (Edward Montague) Compton (novelist) (1883–1972)	West Hartlepool
Neville, Cecily (Duchess of York) (1415–95)	Raby Castle
Neville, Ralph de (1st Earl of Westmorland) (c.1364–1425)	Raby Castle
Raine, Craig (Martian poet) (1944–)	Bishop Auckland
Robson, Bobby (football manager) (1933–)	Sacriston
Sheraton, Thomas (furniture designer) (1751–1806)	Stockton-on-Tees
Simpson, Tommy (racing cyclist) (1937–67)	Haswell
Starling, Ronnie (footballer) (1909–91)	Pelaw
Surtees, Robert (historian and antiquarian) (1779–1834)	Durham
Walker, John (inventor of the safety match) (1781–1859)	Stockton-on-Tees

Essex

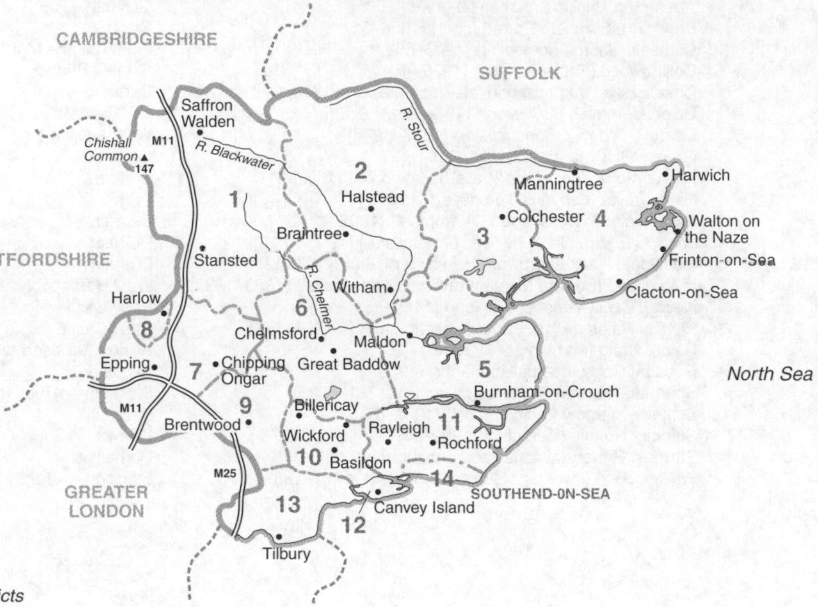
CAMBRIDGESHIRE
SUFFOLK
Saffron Walden
Chishall Common
147
M11
R. Blackwater
R. Stour
2
Halstead
Manningtree
Harwich
1
Colchester
4
Walton on the Naze
Braintree
3
Frinton-on-Sea
HERTFORDSHIRE
Stansted
R. Chelmer
Witham
Clacton-on-Sea
Harlow
6
8
Chelmsford
Maldon
Epping
7
Chipping Ongar
Great Baddow
5
North Sea
Burnham-on-Crouch
M11
9
Billericay
Brentwood
Wickford
Rayleigh
11
Rochford
10
Basildon
M25
14
SOUTHEND-ON-SEA
GREATER LONDON
13
Canvey Island
12
Tilbury
0
20 miles
0
30 km

Districts

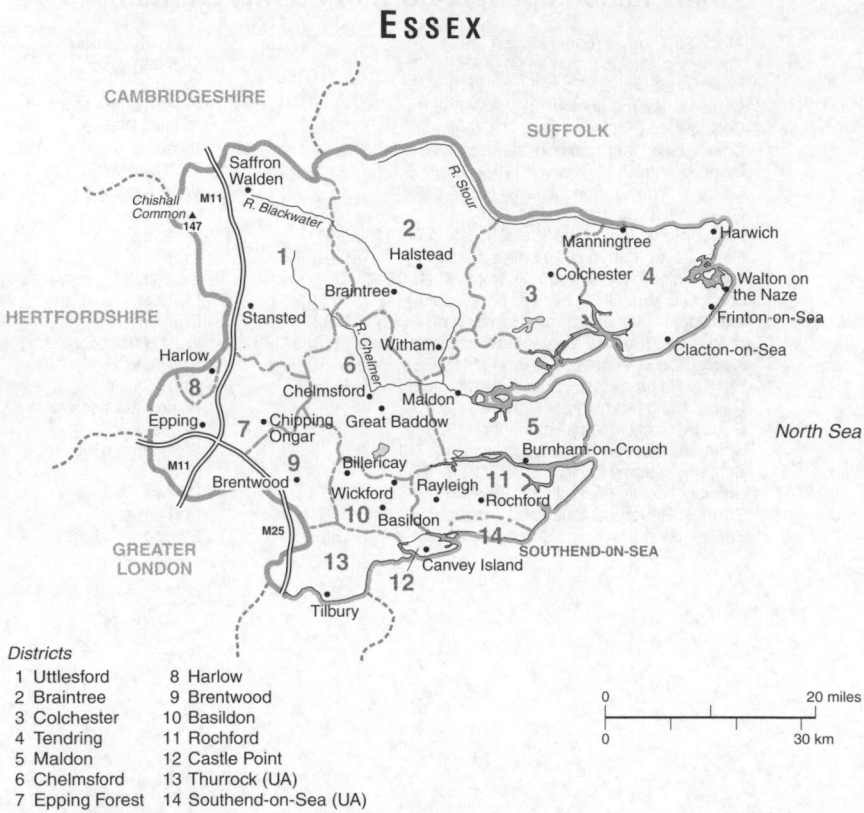

1 Uttlesford	8 Harlow
2 Braintree	9 Brentwood
3 Colchester	10 Basildon
4 Tendring	11 Rochford
5 Maldon	12 Castle Point
6 Chelmsford	13 Thurrock (UA)
7 Epping Forest	14 Southend-on-Sea (UA)

Essex is a notably flat county in the east of England. It has boundaries to the southwest with Greater London; to the west with Hertfordshire across the rivers Lee and Stort; to the northwest with Cambridgeshire; and to the north with Suffolk, mostly marked by the river Stour. To the east it has a coastline on the North Sea, to the south with the estuary of the River Thames, and Kent.

Essex County Council was formed in 1889. However, the County Borough of West Ham, and from 1915 the County Borough of East Ham, formed part of the county but were not under county council control. Southend-on-Sea also formed a county borough from 1914 to 1974. The boundary with Greater London was established in 1965 when the former area of the East Ham and West Ham county boroughs and of the Barking, Chingford, Dagenham, Hornchurch, Ilford, Leyton, Romford, Walthamstow and Wanstead and Woodford districts were transferred.

Essex became part of the East of England Government Office Region in 1994 and was statistically counted as part of that region from 1999, having previously been part of the South East England region. In April 1998 Southend-on-Sea and Thurrock became unitary districts.

The name Essex derives from the East Seaxe or East Saxons. The kingdom of Essex was traditionally founded by Aescwine in AD 527. It occupied territory to the north of the River Thames, incorporating much of what would later become Middlesex and Hertfordshire, though its territory was later restricted to lands east of the river Lee. Through its origin as one of the Saxon kingdoms, Essex is therefore specifically not part of the region known as East Anglia, comprising Norfolk, Suffolk and Cambridgeshire, and settled by Anglian tribes.

Colchester in the northeast of the county is Britain's oldest recorded town. It dates back to before the Roman conquest, when it was known as Camulodunon, and was sufficiently well developed to have its own mint. Camulodunum served as the first Roman capital of Britain, but was attacked and destroyed during Boudicca's rebellion in AD 61. Sometime after the destruction, London became the capital of the province of Britannia. In 1189 Colchester was granted its first royal charter by Richard I and it has continued to be an important town ever since.

The pattern of settlement in the county is diverse. The Green Belt has limited the northeastward sprawl of London, although Essex contains the new towns of Basildon and Harlow, originally developed to resettle Londoners following the destruction of London housing in World War II but since much expanded. Epping Forest also acts as a protected barrier to the spread of London. Much of the Epping Forest district, consisting of the residential towns of Chigwell, Waltham Abbey, Loughton and Buckhurst Hill, is more developed and forms part of the Greater London Urban Area.

Because of its proximity to London and the economic magnetism exerted by the city, many of Essex's settlements function as dormitory towns or villages for London workers. Essex is known for being the origin of the 1990s political term 'Essex man' (used to characterise upwardly mobile, formerly working class voters who prospered during the years of Margaret Thatcher's government), and of the derogatory 'Essex girl' joke (which stereotypes young women from the county as loud, blonde, sexually promiscuous and none too bright).

Part of southeast Essex, containing the major population centres of Southend and Thurrock, is within the Thames Gateway and designated for further development. To the north of the Green Belt, with the exception of major towns such as Chelmsford (granted its royal charter in 1199 and the county town since the 13th century), the county is rural, with many small towns, villages and hamlets largely built in the traditional materials of timber and brick, with clay tile or thatched roofs.

Industry is largely limited to the south of the county, the majority of the land elsewhere being given over to agriculture. Harlow is a centre for electronics, science and pharmaceutical companies, while Chelmsford is the home of Marconi, and Brentwood home to the Ford Motor Company's European HQ. Chelmsford has been an important location for electronics companies since the industry was born, and is today the location for a number of insurance and financial services organisations. It is also the home of the soft drinks producer Britvic. Other businesses in the county are dominated by light engineering and the service sector.

Essex		**Population**		**Area**	
Districts	*male*	*female*	*total*	*sq miles*	*sq km*
Basildon	80,035	85,633	165,668	42	110
Braintree	65,060	67,119	132,179	237	612
Brentwood	33,203	35,253	68,456	59	153
Castle Point	42,319	44,289	86,608	17	45
Chelmsford	77,428	79,644	157,072	131	339
Colchester	77,123	78,673	155,796	127	329
Epping Forest	58,608	62,288	120,896	131	339
Harlow	38,217	40,551	78,768	12	31
Maldon	29,452	29,966	59,418	139	359
Rochford	38,139	40,350	78,489	65	170
Tendring	66,265	72,274	138,539	130	338
Uttlesford	34,344	34,602	68,946	248	640
Southend-on-Sea (UA)	76,749	83,508	160,257	16	42
Thurrock (UA)	69,669	73,459	143,128	63	163
Total	786,611	827,609	1,614,220	1417	3670

Local Attractions and Information

Abberton Reservoir — 5 miles (8km) southwest of Colchester. The largest freshwater body in Essex, covering an area of 1200 acres (485ha) with a variety of plant communities on its margins. Its location close to migration routes on England's east coast makes it an internationally important site for many species of wildfowl. On 5 December 1991, as a result of its over-wintering populations of golden plover, gadwall, shoveler duck and teal, it was designated a Special Protection Area.

Administrative headquarters — **Essex**: County Hall, Market Road, Chelmsford CM1 1LX. Tel: 01245 492211.
Southend-on-Sea: Civic Centre, Victoria Avenue, Southend-on-Sea SS2 6ER. Tel: 01702 215000.
Thurrock: Civic Offices, New Road, Grays RM17 6SL. Tel: 01375 652652.

All Saints' Church — Church Walk, Maldon. The church has monuments celebrating the Saxon Earl Brithnoth, and is unique for its 12th century triangular tower. The south wall dates from the early 14th century and is notable for its arcading. The vicar of Purleigh Church, Lawrence Washington, the great-great-grandfather of George Washington, first President of the United States, is buried here. Tel: 01621 858090.

Ambresbury Banks — 2 miles (3km) north of Epping. An Iron Age plateau fort located in Epping Forest and accessible from Epping Road, opposite the lane to Upshire. Situated on a ridge overlooking the Lea Valley, it has its own stream which rises inside the fort of 11 acres (4.5ha). Impressive banks and ditch remain. According to legend, it is the site of Boudicca's last stand against the Romans in AD 61.

Anglia Ruskin University With campuses in Cambridge and Chelmsford, the university has its origins in the Cambridge Art School, opened in 1858 by John Ruskin (the Cambridgeshire College of Arts and Technology from 1960), and a further education college opened in Chelmsford in 1904 (the Essex Institute of Higher Education from 1984). In 1989, they merged as Anglia Higher Education College which became Anglia Polytechnic in 1991. It was awarded university status in 1992. The university has a large proportion of mature students. There are five faculties of study: the Faculty of Arts, Law and Social Sciences, the Ashcroft International Business School, the Faculty of Education, the Institute of Health and Social Care and the Faculty of Science and Technology. Former students of the university and its constituent colleges include Pink Floyd members Syd Barrett and David Gilmour, Patricia Scotland, Britain's first black woman QC and Harry Potter illustrator Thomas Taylor. Tel: 0845 271 3333.

Audley End House 1 mile (1.6km) west of Saffron Walden. An early 17th century house commissioned by the 1st Earl of Suffolk, and originally constructed to entertain James I. It was inherited by the 3rd Baron Braybrooke in 1825, who shaped the interior design to its present state. The property houses an extensive collection of art and Victorian furnishings. Baron Braybrooke's natural history collections were subsequently added to the contents. During World War II Audley End was requisitioned by the Special Operations Executive, after which the 9th Lord Braybrooke regained possession of it. By 1948 the Ministry of Works had bought it and the Grade I listed building is now managed by English Heritage. The restored Victorian kitchen garden is cultivated on organic principles. Tel: 01799 522399.

Balkerne Gate Balkerne Hill, Colchester. The most complete surviving Roman town gateway in England, built c.AD 55 in the Roman town of Camulodunum (Colchester). Originally constructed as a dual archway over the road to London, the gateway was built into the new town walls ten years later. In order to strengthen the town's defences when it came under threat from Saxon raiders in the 4th century, most of the gateway was blocked with rubble, leaving only an arched footway open for pedestrian traffic.

Battle of Maldon The battle which took place near the town of Maldon in the year 991 is the subject of a poem probably written at the end of the 10th century, one of the most famous surviving writings in Old English. The manuscript, which was in the collection of Sir Robert Bruce Cotton, was destroyed in a fire in 1731, but a transcript had been made – although the beginning and end of the poem have been lost. It is generally thought that the battle took place near the causeway to Northey Island on the shores of the River Blackwater, referred to in the poem as the 'Panta'. According to the poem, the Vikings, under their leader Anlaf, try to land at Maldon after a series of raids along the Essex coast. Here they are confronted by a substantial Anglo-Saxon force, led by Earl Byrhtnoth (whose name is commonly modernised as Brithnoth). The Vikings demand payment as the price of their withdrawal, but Brithnoth scorns the idea of Danegeld, and rejects the offer with contempt. The battle has to wait because of the rising tide. When the tide ebbs, Brithnoth allows the Vikings to cross the river in order to fight on the surrounding land. The Essex men at first stand firm against the invaders, but when Brithnoth is killed by a poisoned spear, some of the defenders panic and flee. The others stand by Brithnoth's body, and fight to the last.

Battles There have been two major battles fought in Essex: Ashingdon and Maldon. See entry for Battle of Maldon and separate table of battles.

Beacon Hill Battery Barrack Lane, Harwich. Located on the south side of Orwell Haven, comprising the estuaries of the Rivers Orwell and Stour. Also known as Beacon Hill Fort, it was built to defend the port of Harwich. The first fortification built on the site was a blockhouse, constructed in 1534 during the reign of Henry VIII. The site was then abandoned for ten years and only rearmed after Henry's death. By 1625 it had fallen into disrepair and remained out of use until a redoubt of ten guns was built in 1810. In 1862 these guns were upgraded to provide protection against invasion from France as a result of the 1860 Royal Commission on the Defence of the United Kingdom. The fort was reinstated for use during both world wars. Finally decommissioned in 1956, the site has since become derelict.

Beecroft Art Gallery Station Road, Westcliff-on-Sea, Southend. The gallery has varied collections ranging from 17th century Dutch paintings to contemporary works. It also boasts spectacular local and sea views. Tel: 01702 347418.

Beeleigh Abbey 1/2 mile (0.8km) northwest of Maldon. The abbey was constructed in 1180 for the White Canons, otherwise known as the Norbertine. The order linked the change of the separate life of monks in the 12th century with the retrospective life of the friar, who was considerably more active. In 1540 Henry VIII granted the abbey and lands to Sir John Gate, Chancellor of the Duchy of Lancaster. Thirty years after the land was given away a farmhouse was added as an extension. The house was bought in 1943 by W A Foyle, the owner of Foyle's bookshop in London, and is still owned by the Foyle family. The abbey is currently not open to the public, but the roofs of the medieval buildings can be seen from a public footpath that follows the River Chelmer.

Blackwater Estuary 9 miles (15km) east of Chelmsford. The estuary of the River Blackwater is famous for the harvesting of oysters. At its head is the town of Maldon, which is a centre of salt production. The other major settlement is West Mersea on the northern seaward side, and there are numerous other villages on its banks. Within the estuary is Northey Island which was the location for the first experiments in the UK in 'managed retreat', the creation of saltmarsh by setting sea walls back from what are perceived to be unsustainable positions. Almost 1.7 sq miles (4.4 sq km) of the Blackwater Estuary is a designated as Special Protection Area for wildlife.

Bourne Mill Bourne Road, Colchester. The mill was originally built as a fishing lodge in 1591 and features stepped Dutch gables. It was converted in the 19th century to a mill for fulling (a process in cloth manufacture) and later flour milling. The waterwheel is still in working order. The site is now owned by the National Trust. Tel: 01206 572422.

Brentwood Cathedral Ingrave Road, Brentwood. Funded by anonymous donors, the new Roman Catholic Brentwood Cathedral Church of St Mary and St Helen was dedicated by Cardinal Hume on 31 May 1991. Designed in the Classical style by architect Quinlan Terry, it incorporates a substantial part of the Gothic revival church built in 1861. The nine bays of the north elevation are each divided by Doric pilasters, and broken by a semicircular portico inspired by a similar one at St Paul's. The rustic look of the Kentish ragstone walls contrasts with the smooth Portland stone of the capitals and column bases. The clerestory is of handmade Smeed Dean brick and leads up to an octagonal lantern or cupola, the high point both of the outside and inside. The interior features 15 Stations of the Cross by Raphael Maklouf, sculptor of the image of the Queen used on UK coins from 1985–97. Tel: 01277 265235.

Canvey Island Situated on the River Thames southwest of Southend. Around 5 miles (8km) in length and 3 miles (5km) wide at its broadest, Canvey is separated from the mainland by Holehaven Creek to the west, Easthaven Creek to the north and Benfleet Creek to the east. It is the sixth largest island in England. The name 'Canvey' was derived from Anglo-Saxon, meaning 'The Island of Cana's People'. It was originally made up of five separate islands, which were mainly marshlands. Although the inhabitants had frequently tried to maintain sea defences, the landowners did not agree to build a sea wall until 1623. Dutch engineer Cornelius Vermuyden was heavily involved in the wall's creation, bringing several hundred workers with him to carry out its construction. The wall soon fell into disrepair, but the Dutch also built housing in their own style on the island. Two such cottages, dated 1618 and 1621, are still in existence: one is a museum, the other a private house. After a series of floods between 1791 and 1897, many farmers sold up and left the island. In 1953 serious floods along the east coast hit the island, causing the death of 58 people. Before 1931 one of the island's major problems was access to the mainland, the only means of crossing being by ferry or by stepping stones at low tide. In 1931 the Colvin Bridge was opened. This swing bridge remained in operation until 1968 and was demolished in 1973 to make way for the present bridge. Built c.17th century, the Lobster Smack Inn is the island's oldest public house. Area: 7.12 sq miles (18.45 sq km). Population: 37,479. (GR: TQ790840.)

Castle House Castle Hill, Dedham, 8 miles (13km) northeast of Colchester. Castle House and its collection is a memorial to artist Sir Alfred Munnings, KCVO, PRA, who lived and worked here from 1919 until his death in 1959, calling it 'the house of my dreams'. Although he is famous for his racehorse and equestrian paintings, many consider his best pictures were made prior to this period, when between 1898 and 1920 he recorded English, and in particular East Anglian, rural life. The museum's collection is fully representative of Munnings' work, the pictures owned by Lady Munnings at her husband's death having been augmented by numerous subsequent purchases. A mixture of Tudor and Georgian periods, the house has been restored, its essential character as lived in by Sir Alfred and Lady Violet being retained by using Munnings' original furniture. The house stands in spacious grounds with well-maintained gardens. Tel: 01206 322127.

Chelmsford Cathedral New Street, Chelmsford. Church of England cathedral dedicated to St Mary the Virgin, St Peter and St Cedd. It became a cathedral when the Diocese of Chelmsford was created in 1914 and is the seat of the Bishop of Chelmsford. The original building is thought to date back almost 800 years and was rebuilt in the 15th and early 16th centuries, with walls of flint rubble, stone and brick. There is also a tower and spire with a ring of 13 bells. The stained-glass windows were installed in the 19th and 20th centuries. Prior to dedication as a cathedral it was refurbished by Charles Nicholson in 1913. The south porch was extended in 1953 to mark Anglo-American friendship after World War II and the many US airmen stationed in Essex. The interior was extensively refurbished in 1983, with a new floor, seating, altar, Bishop's throne, font and artwork. In 1994 and 1995 two pipe organs were installed, the first in the nave and the second in the chancel. The cathedral celebrates its links with Thomas Hooker, one of the founders of American democracy, who was Curate of Chelmsford and Town Lecturer 1626–9. Fleeing to the New World because of his Puritan views, he founded the town of Hartford, Connecticut. The cathedral is one of the smallest in England. Since 1747 it has held a Christingle service each Christmas Eve in which local children carry an orange with four spikes in it holding sweets and usually a lighted candle in the top, symbolising Christ's light and love. In 2006 the service was changed for health and safety reasons and the children carried a Christingle lit by fluorescent glow stick. Tel 01245 294480.

Chelmsford Prison Springfield Hill, Chelmsford. The present prison was opened in 1828, replacing the earlier one in Moulsham Street, and was rebuilt in the 1970s after a fire. It is perhaps most well known for being the home of Slade Prison in the BBC TV series *Porridge*.

Clavering Castle Clavering, 6 miles (10km) southwest of Saffron Walden. Situated just north of the church of St Mary and St Clement on the southern bank of the River Stort, the castle possibly founded by Robert Fitz Wimarc c.1050 has long been demolished and only earthworks remain.

Cliffs Pavilion Station Road, Southend-on-Sea. The largest auditorium in East Anglia and the southeast of England, with 1630 seats. Construction of the venue, originally in Art Deco style, began during the 1930s, The outbreak of war halted building work and the site remained boarded up until 1959. The redesigned building was opened in 1964, and a major £5 million redevelopment scheme was carried out in 1991. Tel: 01702 351135.

Coalhouse Fort Princess Margaret Road, East Tilbury. Situated 4 miles (6km) downstream from Tilbury Fort. Originally the site of a 1780s battery, rebuilt in the 1860s, the large casemated fort is one of Thurrock's most prominent landmarks. It was originally built following recommendations by the Royal Commission on the Defence of the United Kingdom in 1860 as a coastal defence. The fort was completed in 1874 and continued to serve as a defence to the capital through both world wars. Bought by Thurrock Council in 1962, in 1983 the fort was leased to voluntary group the Coalhouse Fort Project which aims to save the building from dereliction. During its recent history the fort has been used as a location for TV programmes and films. Tel: 01375 844203.

Coggeshall Grange Barn Grange Hill, Coggeshall, 9 miles (15km) west of Colchester. One of the oldest timber-framed barns in Europe, dating from the early 13th century. Once the barn of the Cistercian monastery of Coggeshall, it has a splendid interior with early timber joints and contains a collection of farm carts, wagons and displays of barn restoration. Tel: 01376 562226.

Coggeshall Museum and Heritage Centre Village Hall, Stoneham Street, Coggeshall. A small local independent museum, housed in the annexe to the village hall (formerly St Peter's Hall) which was once a brewery. The collection gives an insight into the social history and local characters of the town. Attractions include a working wool weaving loom, a collection of Coggeshall lace and some of the earliest post-Roman bricks in Britain. There is also a large photographic display and video footage of the town's past. Tel: 01376 563003.

Colchester Castle Castle Park, High Street, Colchester. A largely complete Norman castle, built in the same style as the White Tower of the Tower of London. The castle was designed by the Bishop of Rochester and building was supervised by Eudo Dapifer, who became steward of the castle after it was built. Construction began between 1069 and 1076, stopping in 1080 because of a threat of Viking invasion, and the castle was completed c.1100. Materials such as Roman brick and clay were used, and along with scaffolding pole holes and garderobes these can still be seen in the structure. The castle is built on the foundations (or the podium) of the earlier Roman temple of Claudius (built c.AD 44) which the Normans assumed was solid ground. These foundations have since been uncovered and can be viewed today. The castle has had various uses since it ceased to be a royal castle. It has been a county prison, where in 1645 the self-styled Witchfinder-General Matthew Hopkins interrogated and imprisoned suspected witches. In 1656 the Quaker James Parnell was martyred there. In 1720, the castle passed into the possession of Charles Gray (MP for Colchester), who restored it and added the present-day Italianate façade and tower. He created a private park around the ruin and his summer house (perched on the old Norman castle earthworks, in the shape of a Roman temple) can still be seen. In 1892, the castle and the surrounding park were given to the town and they have remained as the Upper and Lower Castle Parks ever since. The Grade I listed building is now a public museum, Tel: 01206 282939/282926.

Colchester Zoo Maldon Road, Stanway, Colchester. The zoo claims to have some of the best big cat and primate collections in Europe. It is supported by the charitable organisation Action for the Wild, dedicated to assisting local and international conservation projects through the provision of financial and technical assistance. Tel: 01206 331292.

Colne Valley Railway A heritage railway based at Castle Hedingham station, 3 miles (5km) northwest of Halstead. The 1 mile (1.6km) line is complete with a fully reconstructed station, signal box and railway yard. It occupies part of the former Colne Valley & Halstead Railway (CVHR), an independent line which opened on 16 April 1860 between Chappel (north of Marks Tey) and Halstead, a distance of 6 miles (10km). A 13 mile (21km) extension was authorised on 13 August 1859, and opened in stages. Passenger traffic ended in 30 December 1961 and freight traffic in 1965, and the line was demolished a year later. The preservation society was formed in 1974, and the first steam locomotive, no. 190, operated trains in 1975. Tel: 01787 461174.

Copped Hall Crown Hill, Epping. The history of Copped Hall begins in the 12th century when there was already a substantial building on the site. At that time the hall belonged to the Fitzaucher family who served the king as huntsmen. In 1564 Elizabeth I granted Copped Hall to her close friend, Sir Thomas Heneage. He began rebuilding the mansion, incorporating part of the old house in the southwest corner, and it was complete by 1568 when Elizabeth came to stay. In the early 18th century the new owner, John Conyers, commissioned his architect John Sanderson, assisted by Sir Roger Newdigate and Thomas Prowse, to realise his ambitious plans for a Palladian mansion. In the end only the main block was built, on a different site from the Elizabethan mansion. It was completed by 1758. Fragments of the Elizabethan house were retained and a rock garden created in part of the cellars. In 1917, the main 18th century block was largely burnt out in a disastrous fire one Sunday morning. Much of the contents were saved but many items were also lost. The family moved to Wood House on the estate, built by Ernest Wythes towards the end of the 19th century. The move was supposed to be temporary but in the end Copped Hall was never rebuilt. The Friends of Copped Hall were set up in 1997 with the aim of protecting and restoring the site. Tel: 020 7267 1679.

Cressing Temple Barns and Gardens Witham Road, Braintree. Home to the two finest Templar barns in Europe, the site has its origins in the 13th century, when it was the first grant of land given to the Knights Templar in England. In addition to the barns the medieval moated farmstead contains a group of remarkable farm buildings, a Templar well and a Tudor walled garden. It is now owned by Essex County Council. Tel: 01376 584903.

Dartford Crossing A crossing that joins Dartford (south) and West Thurrock (north) across the River Thames, effectively forming part of London's orbital M25 motorway. Prior to the opening of the Queen Elizabeth II Bridge in 1991, the crossing was usually referred to as the 'Dartford Tunnel'. Technically, the M25 is not a complete circle, but ends shortly before the crossing on each side of the river – the crossing itself is the A282. Since the opening of the first tunnel in 1963, the crossing has been expanded several times to cope with increased traffic. A second tunnel was opened in 1980, while M25 access was completed in 1986. The Queen Elizabeth II Bridge (A282) was built to expand crossing capacity between sections of the M25. The central span, 1475ft (450m) long, is suspended 210ft (65m) above the Thames to accommodate ocean-going cruise liners, and is thus sometimes closed due to high winds. It is a toll bridge and accommodates four lanes of southbound traffic from the M25. When it was opened, on 30 October 1991, it was Europe's largest cable-supported bridge. The approach viaducts on the Essex side measure 3450ft (1052m) and those on the Kent side 3307ft (1008m), giving a total length of 6757ft (2060m). It has an expected life span of 120 years. When built, the Queen Elizabeth II bridge was only the second on the River Thames east (downstream) of London Bridge to be constructed in over a thousand years, and it is currently the only bridge east of Tower Bridge (the Thames Gateway Bridge will be the second, when completed). The historic reason for this is that bridges prohibited tall ships and other large ships from reaching the Pool of London, which has led to the building of numerous tunnels instead. The toll payable for using the bridge was supposed to end once the bridge had been paid for – which happened in 2003 – but the government has chosen to continue the toll on the grounds of safety. The bridge has been featured briefly in the British films *Four Weddings and a Funeral* (1994) and *Essex Boys* (2000).

Dengie 8 miles (13km) northeast of Southend-on-Sea. A peninsula on the North Sea coast formed by the Rivers Crouch to the south and Blackwater to the north. It once formed a hundred of the same name (sometimes spelled Dengy), the western boundary of which ran from North Fambridge to a little west of Maldon. The eastern end of the peninsula is marshy and forms the Dengie Marshes, a large, remote area of tidal mud-flats and saltmarshes which has been declared a Special Protection Area.

Dial House Ongar Park Hall, North Weald, Epping. A 16th century farm cottage in the countryside surrounding Epping Forest. Since 1967 the building has been an anarchist-pacifist open house, the base of operations for various cultural, artistic and political projects ranging from avant-garde jazz events to helping to found the Free Festival movement. It was once home to the anarcho-punk band Crass. Tel: 01702 303259.

Dunmow Flitch Trials A 'flitch' (a cured and salted side of bacon) has traditionally been awarded in the town of Great Dunmow (4 miles/6km east of Stansted Airport) to couples able to prove themselves happily married for a year and a day. According to most accounts the tradition of the awarding of the Dunmow Flitch dates back to 1104 and the Augustinian priory of Little Dunmow. In that year, lord of the manor Reginald Fitzwalter and his wife dressed themselves humbly and begged blessing of the prior a year and a day after their marriage. Impressed by their devotion, the prior bestowed on them a flitch of bacon. On revealing his true identity, Fitzwalter gave his land to the priory on the condition that a flitch should be awarded to any couple who could claim they were similarly devoted. By the 14th century the Dunmow Flitch had gained far-reaching notoriety. The author William Langland, who lived on the Welsh borders, mentions it in *The Vision of Piers Plowman* (1362), and Chaucer, less than half a century later, alludes to the Dunmow Flitch Trials in 'The Wife of Bath's Tale'. However, only in 1445 were the winners of the Flitch first officially recorded. The earliest record of a successful claimant to the Dunmow Flitch is Richard Wright from Norwich. When in 1832 Josiah Vine, a retired cheese-monger from Reading, and his wife, tried to claim the Flitch, the steward of Little Dunmow, George Wade, refused their request. He is reported as saying that he regarded the trials as being 'an idle custom bringing people of indifferent character into the neighbourhood'. The trials were then transferred from Little Dunmow to Great Dunmow and over the following years the custom lapsed. Victorian novelist Harrison Ainsworth is credited with reviving the Trials as a civic event. In 1855, following the publication of his popular novel *The Custom of Dunmow*, in which Ainsworth recounts the attempts by Little Dunmow's Flitch of Bacon publican to win the Flitch by marrying a succession of wives in an attempt to find the perfect one, the Trials were once again staged in Great Dunmow. Since then, they have been held regularly, and since the end of World War II, every leap year. The modern trial takes the form of a court presided over by a judge, with counsel representing the claimants, and opposing counsel representing the donors of the Flitch of Bacon, a jury of six maidens and six bachelors, a Clerk of the Court to record the proceedings and an Usher to maintain order. The court is held in a marquee erected on Talberds Ley and couples married for at least a year and a day come from far and wide to try and claim the Flitch. It is not a competition between the couples: all could be successful in their claim, which is vigorously defended by Counsel employed on behalf of the Donors of the Bacon, whose job it is to test their evidence and to try and persuade the Jury not to grant them the Flitch. Successful couples are carried shoulder high by bearers in the ancient Flitch Chair to the Market Place where they take the oath (similar to pre-Reformation marriage vows) kneeling on pointed stones. Unsuccessful couples have to walk behind the empty chair to the Market Place, consoled with a prize of gammon. Same sex couples are now considered.

East Anglian Railway Museum 8 miles (13km) west of Colchester. Located at Chappel and Wakes Colne railway station on the former Great Eastern Railway branch line from Marks Tey to Sudbury, the museum has a wide collection of locomotives and rolling stock, some of which are fully restored and others undergoing repair and restoration. On event days, steam train rides are operated over a short demonstration track. The museum also plays host to a cider festival each June, and a beer festival each September. During the festivals additional late-evening trains on the Sudbury Branch Line allow festival-goers to return home by train. Tel: 01206 242524.

Electric Palace Cinema King's Quay Street, Harwich. One of the oldest cinemas in the UK. Opened on 18 November 1911, the cinema closed in 1956 but reopened in 1981, retaining the original screen, projection room and frontage as well as much of the original interior. The cinema is Grade II* listed. Tel: 01255 553333.

Epping Forest An area of ancient woodland straddling the border between northeast Greater London and Essex, stretching from Forest Gate in the south to Epping in the north. It was formed c.8000 BC after the last Ice Age and covers nearly 6000 acres (2400ha), containing areas of grassland, heath, rivers, bogs and ponds. Epping Forest is approximately 11 miles (18km) long in the north–south direction, but no more than $2^1/_2$ miles (4km) east–west at its widest point, and in most places much narrower. The forest lies on a ridge between the valleys of the rivers Lea and Roding; its elevation and consequent thin soil historically made it unsuitable for agriculture. Embankments of two Iron Age camps – Loughton Camp and Ambresbury Banks (see separate entry) – can be found hidden in the woodland. It gives its name to the Epping Forest local government district. The name 'Epping Forest' was first recorded in the 17th century; prior to this it was known as Waltham Forest. The area is thought to have been given legal status as a royal forest by Henry III in the 13th century. This allowed commoners to use the forest to gather wood and foodstuffs, and to graze livestock, although only the king was allowed to hunt in the area. In Tudor times Henry VIII and Elizabeth I hunted in the forest. In 1543 Henry commissioned a building, known as Great Standing, from which to view the chase at Chingford. The building was renovated in 1589 for Elizabeth and can still be seen today. Now known as Queen Elizabeth's Hunting Lodge, it is open to the public as a museum. In 1878, with the passing of the Epping Forest Act, the forest ceased to be a royal forest and the Crown's right to deer and venison was terminated. Pollarding was no longer allowed although grazing rights continued. This act laid down a stipulation that the Conservators (i.e. the Corporation of London) 'shall at all times keep Epping Forest unenclosed and unbuilt on as an open space for the recreation and enjoyment of the people'. When Queen Victoria visited Chingford on 6 May 1882 she declared 'It gives me the greatest satisfaction to dedicate this beautiful forest to the use and enjoyment of my people for all time,' and it thus became 'The People's Forest'. The Corporation of London still own and manage Epping Forest in strict conformity with the Epping Forest Act, with no money for its upkeep coming from local rates or taxes. The forest is administered by the Conservators from the Grade II listed Warren House, in grounds laid out by Humphry Repton in Loughton.

Epping Ongar Railway Preserved railway operating on the final section of the old Great Eastern Railway and London Underground Central branch line between Epping and Ongar, with an intermediate station at North Weald. Now run by volunteers, it was reopened in late 2004 after ten years of closure to operate a Sunday service between Ongar and Coopersale using a diesel multiple unit train.

Feeringbury Manor Garden Feering, 7 miles (11km) west of Colchester. The peaceful garden surrounding a 14th century manor house has ponds, a bog garden, a rose border, trees and shrubs. Tel: 01376 561946.

Foulness Island The fourth largest island in England, bound by the River Crouch to the north, the River Thames to the east and south and the River Roach and Shelford Creek to the west, and connected to the mainland by a series of bridges. The island is 5.28 miles (8.47km) long from Smallports Point in the west to Foulness Point in the east and 2.67 miles (4.29km) in breadth from the seawall between Eastwick and Rugwood Heads in the south to Nase Point in the north. The 25,000 acres (10,000ha) of Foulness Sands lie to the southeast of the island as far as the East and West Swins, and are marked at the seaward end by the Whitaker Beacon. The sea floods the sands on every tide. Area: 9.86 sq miles (25.53 sq km). Population: 212. (GR: TR000920.)

Gardens of Easton Lodge, The Warwick House, Easton Lodge, Great Dunmow. The estate of Easton Lodge dates back to the Tudor period but was most notably home to Daisy, Countess of Warwick, mistress to 'Bertie', the future Edward VII. The magnificent gardens were designed for Daisy in 1902 by Harold Peto. They were abandoned in 1950, but restoration commenced in 1993. Features include an Italian garden, formal lawns, the Stirling Walk (commemorating the RAF pilots stationed at Easton during World War II), the Bosquet (a wooded area established in Jacobean times), a living sundial, and the Peto and Shelley Pavilions. Tel: 01371 876979.

Great Dunmow 12 miles (19km) northwest of Chelmsford. A market town on the River Chelmer, Great Dunmow is thought to be the site of the Roman town of Caesaromagnus. See also Dunmow Flitch Trials, Gardens of Easton Lodge.

Hadleigh Castle 5 miles (8km) west of Southend-on-Sea. Overlooking Hadleigh Marshes, the enclosure castle was founded by Hubert de Burgh in 1231 and completed by Henry III. It was extended by Edward III, 1361–70. The barbican and two towers of this mighty fortress still remain standing today. The castle was notably painted by John Constable and Turner and is now owned by English Heritage. Tel: 01760 755161.

Hanningfield Reservoir 5 miles (8km) south of Chelmsford. The 870 acre (352ha) reservoir and 100 acre (40ha) wood are among the top places in Britain to watch both woodland and wetland birds. The reservoir is a Site of Special Scientific Interest and the surrounding area has statutory designation as a bird sanctuary. The spectacle of 80,000 swifts, swallows and martins feeding over the water during peak fly hatches is just one of the delights for the summer visitor. Tel: 01628 711001.

Harlow New Town 5 miles (8km) north of Epping. A local government district and new town developed around the market town of Harlow, and the villages of Great Parndon, Latton, Little Parndon and Netteswell from a master plan drawn up in 1947 by Sir Frederick Gibberd. It is renowned for having Britain's first pedestrian precinct in the town centre and Britain's first tower block, The Lawn, constructed in 1951 and now Grade II listed. Many of the original new town buildings have now been removed due to 'concrete cancer'. The southern part of the original town centre has recently been extensively redeveloped, including the replacement of Gibberd's original nine-storey town hall with a new civic centre, and the construction of new shops and restaurants, including a new Water Garden.

Harwich Maritime and Lifeboat Museums Low Lighthouse, Harbour Crescent, Harwich. The Maritime Museum has been housed since 1980 in the Low Lighthouse, built in 1818 along with the High Lighthouse, a few hundred yards away, to replace late 17th century wooden lighthouses. The Low Lighthouse is now owned by the Harwich Society. In a nearby disused Victorian lifeboat house is the Harwich Lifeboat Museum, complete with full-size lifeboat. Tel: 01255 503429.

Harwich Redoubt
Main Road, Harwich. The circular fort commanding the eastern side of the port of Harwich was built in 1808 to support Landguard Fort on the opposite shore near Felixstowe. It was also intended to form part of the chain of Martello tower defences. It is 200ft (60m) in diameter, surrounded by a deep ditch, and can only be entered by one removable drawbridge. It was originally armed with ten cannon but these were upgraded in the 1860s and 1870s and by 1872 three 9-inch RML guns were in place. One still remains and the other two are thought to be buried in the moat. In the 1920s the site was abandoned and housing built around it. It was taken over by the Harwich Society in 1969 and has now been fully restored. Tel: 01255 503429.

Hatfield Forest
7 miles (11km) northeast of Harlow. Lying between Little Hallingbury in the south and Takeley in the north, this area of ancient woodland covers more than 1000 acres (400ha) and is a rare surviving example of a medieval royal hunting forest. Of great historical and ecological importance, Hatfield Forest is a designated Site of Special Scientific Interest and National Nature Reserve. The pollarded hornbeams and oaks support a wide variety of wildlife, while cattle graze in the forest during the summer. It is managed by the National Trust. Tel: 01279 870678.

Hedingham Castle
Castle Hedingham, 19 miles (31km) northwest of Colchester. The Norman keep at Hedingham Castle is considered one of the finest in England. It was built c.1140 for Aubrey de Vere II, and thought to have been designed by William de Corbeuil, Archbishop of Canterbury, who also designed the similar great tower at Rochester Castle. There is a magnificent banqueting hall, minstrel's gallery and a Norman arch set in large grounds with surrounding woodland and lakeside walks. Tel: 01787 460261.

Highest point
Chrishall Common near the village of Langley, close to the Hertfordshire border, at 482ft (147m). (GR: TL443362.)

HM *Fort Roughs*
Located on Rough Sands, a sandbar 6 miles (10km) from the coast of Suffolk and 8 miles (13km) from that of Essex. HM *Fort Roughs* was one of several World War II installations designed by Guy Maunsell, and known collectively as His Majesty's Forts or as Maunsell Sea Forts; its purpose was to guard the port of Harwich. The fort was constructed in 1942 and comprised a floating pontoon base of reinforced concrete measuring 168ft (51.2m) by 88ft (26.8m), with a superstructure of two hollow towers joined by a deck. The fort was topped by a gun deck, an upper deck and a central tower unit which housed radar equipment. The twin towers were divided into seven floors that provided dining and sleeping accommodation, also housing generators and storage for munitions. A steel framework at one end supported a landing jetty and crane which was used to hoist supplies aboard. On 11 February 1943 the fort was towed by three tugs to Rough Sands where its base was intentionally flooded so that it sank to a resting place on the sandbar. The superstructure of the vessel above the waterline remained visible from the English coast. HM *Fort Roughs* was occupied by 150–300 Royal Navy personnel during World War II. Its armament consisted of 3.75in AA guns and Bofors 40mm guns, the standard medium and light anti-aircraft weaponry of the British and Commonwealth forces. It later gained fame as the home of the claimed-to-be micronation, Sealand (see Suffolk).

Hollytrees Museum
High Street, Colchester. Based in a Georgian town house built in 1718, the museum features exhibits and interactive displays on the social history of Colchester. The collection of toys includes a doll's house model of Hollytrees House itself. Tel: 01206 282940.

Hylands House
2 miles (3km) west of Chelmsford. Hylands House is set in the historic landscaped parkland of Hylands Park. Built in 1730 as a red-brick Queen Anne mansion, it was redesigned in neoclassical style in the early 19th century. The Grade II* listed building is now owned by Chelmsford Borough Council. Many rooms and other features have now been restored, including the gilded drawing room, an ornate banqueting room, the grand staircase and the Repton Room on the first floor, which provides spectacular views over 574 acres (232ha) of parkland designed by Humphry Repton. The park hosted Eurojam in the summer of 2005 and was chosen as the site for the 21st World Scout Jamboree in 2007. Tel: 01245 496800.

Ingatestone Hall
Hall Lane, Ingatestone, 5 miles (8km) southwest of Chelmsford. A 16th century mansion set in formal gardens. The estate was acquired by Sir William Petre, Secretary of State to four Tudor monarchs, in 1539 following the Dissolution of the Monasteries and has belonged to the family ever since. Sir William's son, John, made Thorndon Hall near Brentford the family's principal seat and in 1603 he became the 1st Baron Petre. The family's estates were confiscated after the Civil War but had been recovered by the 18th century. Ingatestone Hall was modernised in the early 18th century with sash windows and Georgian panelling. Thorndon Hall continued to be the family's principal seat and in the 1760s the 9th Baron had the house rebuilt to designs by James Paine. When the 16th Baron died in 1915 his widow moved back to Ingatestone and a careful restoration of the house was carried out, returning the house to its Tudor appearance. The 18th Baron, who inherited Ingatestone in 1989, renovated the house and opened it to the public. The River Wid runs close to the town. Tel: 01277 353010.

Interesting facts
One of the famous early cases involving what is now called ballistics was the murder of an Essex police officer, **PC George Gutteridge**. On Tuesday 27 September 1927 his body was found in Howe Green; he had been shot four times in the face and killed. Ten miles away a Morris Cowley belonging to Dr Edward Lovell had been stolen from his garage in London Road, Billericay. The police recovered the car and found a cartridge case marked RLIV, indicating that it was an old Mark IV type made at the Royal Laboratory in Woolwich Arsenal for troops in World War I. The case seemed to have been scarred by a fault in the breech block of the gun which had fired it. The foremost gun expert of the day, Robert Churchill, found that the bullet would have been fired by a Webley revolver, the same type of gun that killed PC Gutteridge. The police suspected two car thieves, Frederick Browne and Patrick Kennedy, but raided Browne's premises after finding evidence of another stolen car. When the police searched that car they found a loaded Webley

and Mr Churchill found it to be the same one which had caused the mark on the cartridge case. Kennedy was arrested after attempting to shoot Sergeant Mattinson of Liverpool Police, being prevented from doing so because a bullet jammed in the barrel of his gun. Both Kennedy and Browne were convicted of murder. The *Sunday Dispatch* newspaper carried the headline 'Hanged by a microscope', reflecting the fact that microscopic examination of the cartridge cases had provided the crucial evidence to convict the murderers. The town of **Thaxted** made the news in October 2006 when a resident from Dunmow purchased the manorial title, giving him the right to the rents from local market traders. The new Lord of the Manor claimed an ancient right dating back to the 14th century and gave notice of eviction to several stallholders who refused to pay him. On 22 April 1884, Colchester witnessed an **earthquake** measuring 4.7 on the Richter scale. At 9.18am the earthquake struck with its epicentre near the village of Wivenhoe, the waves lasting for about 20 seconds. The tremors were felt across England, as well as in northern France and Belgium. In total the earthquake damaged around 1200 buildings, including almost all those in Wivenhoe and Abberton; the damage extended as far as Ipswich. One child in Rowhedge was killed and up to four other people subsequently died as a result of the trauma. Many English counties have **nicknames** for people from that county, such as a Tyke from Yorkshire and a Yellowbelly from Lincolnshire. The traditional nickname for a person from Essex is an Essex Calf, so named because the county was famous for rearing beef cattle for sale in London meat markets; calves from the county were famed for their large size and known as 'Essex lions'. Colchester-born **Thomas Miller Beach** (1841–94) enlisted in the Northern army during the American Civil War, taking the name of Henri Le Caron. By the end of the war he had risen to the rank of major. In 1865, through a companion in arms named John O'Neill, he was brought into contact with Fenianism, and having learnt of a plot against Canada (the Fenian raids), he mentioned the designs when writing home to his father in England. Beach's father told his local MP, who in turn told the Home Secretary, and the latter asked Beach to gain further information. For 25 years he lived in Detroit, Michigan as a spy, paying occasional visits to Europe, and all the time carrying his life in his hands. The Parnell Commission of 1889 put an end to this. Le Caron was subpoenaed by *The Times*; in the witness-box the whole story came out and his career as a spy was over. The story of his life, *Twenty-five Years in the Secret Service*, became a best-seller. Although **Frinton-on-Sea** has several bars, the first pub inside the town's boundary, the Lock and Barrel, opened only in September 2000 despite vigorous local opposition. It followed the town's first fish and chip shop, opened in 1992.

Islands
See separate table.

John Webb's Windmill
Thaxted, 5 miles (8km) southeast of Saffron Walden. Also known as Thaxted Windmill, this brick tower mill consisting of five floors was completed in 1804 by John Webb, a local farmer and landowner. It was constructed using local materials, the bricks being made and fired less than $^{1}/_{2}$ mile (0.8km) away at a quarry in the Chelmer Valley also owned by Webb. Now Grade II* listed, the mill has been fully restored and is capable of grinding corn into flour. On the ground and first floors there is a rural museum containing agricultural artefacts. Tel: 01371 830285.

Jumbo Water Tower
Balkerne Hill, Colchester. Erected in 1883, the largest surviving Victorian water tower in England is one of Colchester's most famous landmarks. The 131ft (40m) tower was taken out of commission in the 1980s; after several schemes to develop it failed, it was sold in 2006 with planning consent for a penthouse flat.

Lakeside Shopping Centre
West Thurrock, 10 miles (16km) south of Brentwood. At 2.6 million sq ft, including the adjoining retail park, Lakeside forms the largest out-of-town shopping area in Europe. It opened in October 1990 and has more than 250 stores. It featured in the news after being targeted by terrorists in 2005–6. Tel: 01708 869933.

Layer Marney Tower
7 miles (11km) southwest of Colchester. Built by Lord Henry Marney and later by his son John Marney, during the reign of Henry VIII. Standing almost 80ft (24m) high, it is the tallest Tudor gatehouse in England. The gardens were designed at the turn of the 20th century, with roses, yew hedges and herbaceous borders. Tel: 01206 330784.

Maeldune Heritage Centre
Market Hill, Maldon. Home of the 42ft (12.8m) Maldon embroidery which celebrates the 1000th anniversary of the Battle of Maldon (see separate entry). It was designed by Humphrey Spender to depict Maldon's history from the Battle of Maldon in 991 to its anniversary in 1991. Tel: 01621 851628.

Mangapps Railway Museum
Burnham-on-Crouch, 9 miles (15km) northeast of Southend-on-Sea. A heritage railway featuring a $^{3}/_{4}$ mile (1.2km) standard gauge passenger carrying line, with restored stations, signal boxes and ancillary equipment removed from various sites throughout East Anglia. To operate the line the museum has ten steam and diesel locomotives and over 80 carriages and wagons, some of considerable historic and technical interest. Its collection of smaller railway relics is one of the largest of its kind in Britain and has a particular bias towards the railways of East Anglia and railway signalling. The signalling collection is also considered to be the largest on public display in Britain. Tel: 01621 784898.

Maplin Sands
8 miles (13km) east of Southend-on-Sea. An area of mudflats on the northern bank of the Thames estuary, off Foulness Island. They are valuable as a wildlife reserve, with a large colony of dwarf eelgrass (*Zostera noltei*) and associated animal communities. A screw-pile lighthouse, possibly the world's first, was built on the sands in 1838. Maplin Sands currently belong to the Ministry of Defence and are used as a military testing ground.

Marks Hall Gardens and Arboretum
1 mile (1.6km) north of Coggeshall. Known as Mercheshala in Saxon times, Marks Hall was occupied after the Norman Conquest by the Markshall family who took their name from the estate. In 1605 Marks Hall was sold to Robert Honywood. His son, Sir Thomas, who inherited the estate in 1631, was a leading Parliamentarian and commanded the Essex Regiment during the

Civil War. Local tradition has it that Parliamentary troops, bivouacked in Marks Hall Park during the siege of Colchester, dug the two ornamental lakes that are a major feature of the gardens. In 1758 General Philip Honywood succeeded to the estate and his will established the Honywood Oaks (of which only one still stands today), forbidding any of his successors to fell timber other than for estate maintenance. Undoubtedly this contributed to the already considerable fame of Marks Hall for its fine trees. By the 1850s substantial debts had reduced the estate and it was sold at auction in 1897 to Thomas Phillips Price, whose widow bequeathed the estate to the nation on her death in 1966. Today there are ornamental lakes, a 17th century walled garden, cascades and mature avenues of oaks, limes and horse chestnuts, surrounded by one of the largest continuous areas of ancient woodland surviving in the county. Located within the estate is the arboretum, begun in 1971 and containing trees and shrubs from all over the world. It is planted on a geographical theme with areas representing Europe, Asia, America and the southern hemisphere. Tel: 01376 563796.

Mersea Island The most easterly inhabited island in the UK. It is linked to the mainland by The Strood (see separate entry), an artificial causeway $^1/_2$ mile (0.8km) long which forms part of the B1025 road to Colchester, and by the Brightlingsea Ferry. Mersea is an important centre of oyster farming and has a large sailing community. The Rev. Sabine Baring-Gould, writer of 'Onward Christian Soldiers', was rector of East Mersea, 1871–81. Area: 6.97 sq miles (18.04 sq km). Population: 6925. (GR: TM035145.)

Mistley Towers Mistley, 1 mile (1.6km) east of Manningtree, 9 miles (15km) east of Colchester. The twin towers are all that remains of of the now demolished Church of St Mary the Virgin. The original Georgian parish church on the site was built in classical style early in the 18th century following the death of Richard Rigby Esq. Later in that century his son, the wealthy politician Richard Rigby, planned to transform Mistley into a spa town. He decided that a suitably grand church was required for the affluent visitors expected to patronise the new spa. In 1776, his friend Robert Adam was commissioned to enhance the church. His design, in the Neoclassical style, featured towers at both the east and the west ends. These are now all that remain of the structure, the rest of which was demolished in 1870, and are now in the care of English Heritage. Tel: 01206 393884.

Motorboat Museum Wat Tyler Country Park, Basildon. The only museum in the world devoted to the history of motorboats. Tel: 01268 550077.

Mountfitchet Castle Stansted Mountfitchet, 8 miles (13km) south of Saffron Walden. The only Norman motte and bailey castle in the world that has been faithfully reconstructed on its original site, it was originally an Iron Age fort and then later a Saxon and Viking village. It was eventually taken over in 1066 by William the Conqueror who handed it down to his cousin Robert Gernon, Duke of Boulogne. It was partly destroyed by King John in 1215 and subsequently left to decay until being reconstructed in 1984–6. Tel: 01279 813237.

Moyns Park Birdbrook, 11 miles (18km) northwest of Braintree. A Grade I listed Elizabethan country house once owned by Ivar Bryce, a friend of Ian Fleming, who stayed at the house in the summer of 1956. It is said that Fleming made final changes to his novel *From Russia with Love* here. The house was also the location for several Hammer horror films. The estate is now home to a stud farm. Tel: 01440 730073.

Museum of Power Langford, 2 miles (3km) northwest of Maldon. Housed in Langford Pumping Station, a steam-powered pumping station opened in 1929 to supply water to Southend, the Museum of Power contains working examples of power sources of all types, including diesel and steam engines. Tel: 01621 843183.

Natural History Museum High Street, Colchester. Housed in the former All Saints Church since 1957, the museum focuses on the rich natural heritage of northeast Essex. Tel: 01206 282941.

Naze, The 7 miles (11km) south of Harwich. A headland on the Essex coast, the Naze projects into the North Sea south of the double estuary of the Rivers Stour and Orwell. Its name comes from the Old English *naes* (nose). Its cliffs are notable as a source of fossils, which have led to its designation as a Site of Special Scientific Interest, but are currently threatened by erosion. For the last 250 years the area has been dominated by the Naze Tower, built in 1721 by Trinity House. Long before lighthouses became commonplace, the tower acted as a marker for ships approaching Harwich harbour, a duty which it still performs today.

New Empire Theatre Alexandra Street, Southend-on-Sea. The New Empire Theatre was built in 1896 by theatre impresario Frederick Marlow. He had previously owned the Public Hall on the same site, converting it to the Empire Theatre in 1892. After a fire on Boxing Day 1895 destroyed the building, Marlow built a bigger, better theatre, with five floors and electric lighting. It was the first of its kind in Southend, and was called 'the prettiest theatre outside of London' by the local press at its opening in 1896. Marlow presented a varied programme of musicals, opera, concerts, plays, variety and music hall. He remained at the theatre until 1905 when it was taken over by the Southend-on-Sea Theatre Company. It later spent nearly 80 years as a cinema, but was reopened as a community theatre in 1998. Tel: 01702 353577.

Norsey Wood Outwood Common Road, Billericay. A mixed coppice woodland covering an area of 165 acres (67ha), and consisting of a variety of habitats due to its mixture of sandy and clay soils. A Scheduled Ancient Monument, with a history thought to go back almost 4000 years, it is also a designated Site of Special Scientific Interest and a Local Nature Reserve.

Old Friends Meeting House High Street, Stebbing, 6 miles 10km) west of Braintree. The earliest Quaker meeting house in Essex, built c.1674 and now Grade II* listed. Tel: 01371 856155.

Ongar Castle Chipping Ongar, 12 miles (19km) west of Chelmsford. Norman motte and bailey castle founded in the early 12th century by the de Lucy family. The stone tower was built on the motte in 1150. The castle was occupied until the 16th century. The motte still stands over 50ft (15m) high and is completely surrounded by a moat. There are two baileys, one on each side. The site is private but visible from a footpath.

Palace of Beaulieu — Boreham, 3 miles (5km) north of Chelmsford. Not to be confused with Palace House, Beaulieu (see Hampshire). Originally granted to the canons of Waltham Abbey in 1062, the estate of Walkfares was, after changing hands several times, given by the Crown to the Earl of Ormond in 1491. Now containing a house named New Hall, it was acquired in 1517 from Thomas Boleyn by Henry VIII, who enlarged the building and gave it the name Beaulieu. During the Civil War, Oliver Cromwell took possession of the estate. After reverting to the 2nd Duke of Buckingham at the Restoration, it was sold to George Monck, 1st Duke of Albermarle, and Charles II's court was frequently entertained there. Benjamin Hoare acquired the property in 1713, but it was in a poor state when purchased in 1737 by John Olmius, later 1st Lord Waltham, who demolished and rebuilt much of the former palace. The north wing was left largely untouched and forms the present house. The estate was acquired by the nuns of the Order of the Holy Sepulchre in 1798. They opened a Catholic school there the following year, New Hall School, which still occupies the house today. Henry VIII's royal arms can be seen in the school chapel. The Beaulieu name is now remembered in the name of a nearby housing estate, Beaulieu Park.

Palace Theatre — London Road, Westcliff-on-Sea. Opened on 21 October 1912, the theatre was owned by Mr Raymond of the Raymond Picture Company. Known at first as the Palace of Varieties, in December 1912 it became The New Palace, presenting a forerunner of *Opportunity Knocks*. In 1919 Mrs Gertude Mouillot bought the theatre and built an annexe, still in use today. The theatre remained open throughout World War II, surviving several air raids without serious damage. It reopened on 1 April 2003 under the newly formed Southend Theatres, formed by merging Southend's Cliffs Pavilion and the Palace Theatre. Tel: 01702 390657.

Paycocke's House — West Street, Coggeshall. The half-timbered house provides evidence of the wealth generated by the East Anglian wool trade in the 15th and 16th centuries. The interior features unusually rich panelling and wood carving, while the exterior is richly decorated. Coggeshall was also famous for its lace, examples of which are displayed inside the house. The attractive cottage garden has lovely displays of lavender from June to September. The property is now in the care of the National Trust. Tel: 01376 561305.

Pleshey Castle — High Easter, 7 miles (11km) northwest of Chelmsford. William I gave the estate of Pleshey to Geoffrey de Mandeville in appreciation for his services during the Norman Conquest. Built in the early 12th century, Pleshey was originally a motte and bailey castle, and at some time in its early history was surrounded by a moat. The motte is now about 50ft (15m) high, one of the largest in England. The castle was destroyed in 1157 but refortified 1167–80. Through inheritance, Pleshey became the main castle of Henry de Bohun, 1st Earl of Hereford, and his wife Elizabeth, daughter of Edward I, and some of their children were born here. The de Bohun family sent a group of Augustinian friars to work on manuscripts at the castle between 1361 and 1384. Here they completed 11 books, one of them a psalter to celebrate Mary de Bohun's marriage to Henry Bolingbroke, the future Henry IV. The Mary de Bohun Psalter is now in the Fitzwilliam Museum in Cambridge (see Cambridgeshire). The castle eventually passed (through marriage) to Thomas of Woodstock, Duke of Gloucester, the youngest son of Edward III. His nephew, Richard II, outraged by his uncle's opposition, had him arrested at Pleshey and shipped to France. Two years later the Duke of Exeter was taken to the castle and executed for plotting against the king. Pleshey Castle's claims to fame include a mention in Shakespeare's play *Richard II*, in which Richard's widow asks Edmund of York: 'Hid him – O, what? With all good speed at Plashy [sic] visit me, Alack, and what shall good old York there see, But empty lodgings and unfurnished walls, Unpeopled offices, untrodden stones?' Little of the castle remains today apart from its earthworks.

Prior's Hall Barn — Widdington, 4 miles (6km) south of Saffron Walden. One of the finest examples of a medieval barn in the east of England. Maintained by English Heritage, the 15th century barn has been fully restored. It consists of eight bays with a crown post roof 36ft (11m) high, scarf joints being used to join the timbers supporting the main rafters. Tel: 01799 522842.

Public schools — **Brentwood School** was founded by Sir Anthony Browne in 1558 as a penance for the martyring of William Hunter, burnt to death for refusing to accept the transubstantiation of bread and wine into the body and blood of Jesus Christ. Having sentenced Hunter as local Justice of the Peace under Mary I in 1555, Sir William founded the school – on the site where Hunter met his death – three years later when Elizabeth I came to the throne. The school is separated into three main sections: Senior School (ages 11–18), Preparatory School (ages 7–11) and Pre-Preparatory School (ages 3–7). It has two mottos: the original 'Virtue, Learning and Manners' and the Latin motto '*Incipe*' (roughly meaning 'to begin' or 'to start') which was added in the 19th century. Notable alumni include Douglas Adams, author of *The Hitchhiker's Guide to the Galaxy*, politician Jack Straw, glamour model Jodie Marsh and broadcaster Noel Edmonds. Tel: 01277 243333.

Chigwell School in the Epping Forest district was founded by Samuel Harsnett in 1629. There are around 730 pupils aged 7–18. The school motto is '*aut viam inveniam aut faciam*' ('Either I shall find a way or I shall make one'). The four day houses are named Caswalls', Lambourne, Penn's and Swallow's; the boarding houses are Grange Court, Sandon Lodge and Hainault House. Notable Chigwellians include actor Sir Ian Holm, novelist Michael Marshall Smith and William Penn, founder of the American state of Pennsylvania. Tel: 020 8501 5700.

Felsted School, in the village of Felsted, was founded in 1564 by Richard Rich, 1st Baron Rich who, as Lord Chancellor and Chancellor of the Court of Augmentations, had become wealthy with the spoils of the adjoining abbey and priory of Little Leez after the Dissolution of the Monasteries. The school became a notable educational centre for Puritan families in the 17th century, numbering 100 or more pupils, under Martin Holbeach, headmaster 1627–49, and his successors.

John Wallis and Isaac Barrow were educated here in this period, as were four of Oliver Cromwell's sons. Tel: 01371 822600.

Rayleigh Castle Rayleigh, 4 miles (6km) northwest of Southend-on-Sea. A masonry and timber castle built by Sweyn, son of Robert Fitz Wimarc, soon after the Norman Conquest. It is one of the few castles mentioned in Domesday Book and as such is considered one of the earliest Norman castles in England. It may have been built on the site of an earlier Roman fortification since fragments of Roman bricks have been found on the site. Ownership of the castle reverted to the monarch in the latter half of the 13th century, and in 1394 Richard II gave permission for the townspeople of Rayleigh to use the castle's foundations as a source of stone. All that exists today are the earthwork remains of its large motte and bailey. A World War II convoy rescue ship, *Empire Rest*, was originally constructed as a Castle class corvette and was to have been named HMS *Rayleigh Castle*. The remains are in the care of the National Trust. Tel: 01284 747500.

RHS Garden Hyde Hall Rettendon, 6 miles (10km) southeast of Chelmsford. RHS Hyde Hall was donated to the Royal Horticultural Society in 1993, having been transformed over nearly 40 years from farmland located on top of a windswept hill with just six mature trees into a garden of 24 acres (9.5ha). Today the garden contains the National Collection of viburnum and an attractive plantsman's garden of 8 acres (3ha) containing a woodland area, spring bulbs, ornamental ponds with lilies and fish, together with a large collection of modern roses and a rope walk of climbing and pillar roses. The highlight is the dry garden, designed and planted to demonstrate how a garden can be created without the need for artificial irrigation, and formally opened on 7 August 2001 by Sir Richard Carew Pole, president of the RHS, and Beth Chatto who has her own famous dry garden in Essex. The Queen Mother's Garden is another outstanding feature. Tel: 01245 400256.

Rivers The **Blackwater** rises in the northwest of the county as the River Pant, and proceeds as a stream through to Braintree where the name changes to the Blackwater for the rest of its journey to the sea. On the way it passes through Stisted, Bradwell, Coggeshall, Coggeshall Hamlet, Feering, Kelvedon, near Witham, Wickham Bishops and Langford to Beeleigh where it meets the Chelmer. For a while it is included in the Chelmer & Blackwater Navigation, but at Heybridge it spurs off through a private garden and disappears down a pipe to re-emerge into the tidal estuary at Maldon before reaching the North Sea at West Mersea. It is 8 miles (13km) in length.

The **Brain** gives its name to the town of Braintree, though in fact the town lies on a low ridge between the Brain and the River Blackwater. Above Braintree it is known as Pods Brook. The brook rises near the village of Bardfield Saling. Below Braintree the Brain joins the Blackwater on the outskirts of Witham.

The **Chelmer** rises near Great Dunmow and flows southeast into Chelmsford, taking an easterly route to Maldon before emptying into the Blackwater Estuary. The total length of the river is 22 miles (34km) although its course is often considered as two separate rivers, the Upper Chelmer between Dunmow and Chelmsford and the Chelmer between Chelmsford and Maldon. The appearance of the river at Chelmsford is that of a canal.

The **Ching** originates in Epping Forest and runs to the River Lee, but not before being severely polluted in its lower reaches. It is dammed twice, to form Connaught Water, in the parishes of Loughton and Waltham Abbey, and at Highams Park.

The **Colne** is a tidal navigation from Colchester to Colne Point. The top $3^1/_2$ miles (5.5km) are practically dry at low water. It is not a tributary of any other river, but instead has an estuary that joins the sea near Brightlingsea. Its total length from East Bridge, Colchester, to Colne Point, is 10.8 miles (17.4km).

The **Crouch** rises near Noak Bridge (west of Basildon) and follows an easterly course for $17^1/_2$ miles (28km), from Battlebridge Mill to Holliwell Point.

The **Lee** (also spelt Lea) has its source at Well Head inside Waulud's Bank on Leagrave Marsh, near Luton, Bedfordshire. It flows southeast and then east out of the county and into Hertfordshire before taking a southerly direction into Essex, joining the Thames at Bromley-by-Bow in the London Borough of Tower Hamlets. The name of the river is generally given as Lea at its source in Bedfordshire but becomes Lee on entering Hertfordshire and flowing through Essex into London, although this appears to be nothing more than tradition. Its total distance is 46 miles (74km).

The **Roding** rises near Dunmow, flows through Essex and forms Barking Creek as it reaches the River Thames in London. The river marks much of the boundary between the London Boroughs of Newham and Barking & Dagenham. The London Borough of Redbridge is named after a crossing of the Roding.

The **Stort** rises in Langley Hills, near Clavering. After flowing through Bishop's Stortford (from whence the river takes its name) the river continues another $13^1/_2$ miles (21.3km) through Hertfordshire to Feildes Weir, where it joins the Lee.

The **Stour** is 47 miles (76km) long and forms most of the county boundary between Suffolk and Essex. It rises in eastern Cambridgeshire, passes though Haverhill, Cavendish, Sudbury and Dedham Vale, and joins the North Sea at Harwich.

The **Ter** runs from Terling, 5 miles (8km) northeast of Chelmsford, to the Chelmer at Rushes Weir. It is only $2^1/_2$ miles (4km) long but is home to a large variety of aquatic creatures, such as the marsh heron famous for its large red bill.

Royal Gunpowder Mills Beaulieu Drive, Waltham Abbey. Set in 175 acres (71ha) of natural parkland, the site boasts 21 buildings of major historic importance. Established in the 17th century and acquired by the Crown in 1787, the production and development of explosives was undertaken at the Royal Gunpowder Mills for more than 300 years, using mills first powered by water and later by steam. Following World War II the site was used as a research facility for non-nuclear explosives, with some of the existing structures being converted into laboratories, and the last of the mills was demolished in

1956. The site was eventually closed by the Ministry of Defence in 1981 and a charitable organisation set up to safeguard its future. Some of the buildings and waterways have already been restored. Part of the site has been designated a Site of Special Scientific Interest and a survey conducted in 1994 revealed that 36 types of birds were successfully breeding there. Tel: 01992 707370.

RSPB Stour Estuary — A nature reserve situated east of Colchester on the estuary of the River Stour, managed by the Royal Society for the Protection of Birds (RSPB). The reserve consists of two distinct habitat types: intertidal mudflats (fringed by saltmarsh and estuarine reeds), and 130 acres (53ha) of deciduous woodland, mainly oak and coppiced sweet chestnut. The estuary is important as a breeding, roosting and wintering site for waterfowl and other birds, including woodpeckers, pintail, teal, blackcap, whitethroat, nightingale, sedge warbler, reed warbler, European wigeon, shelduck, dark-bellied brent goose, grey plover, redshank, curlew, dunlin and black-tailed godwit. Mammals to be seen include the red fox, grey squirrel and hazel dormouse. It is also home to butterflies and rare moths such as the white admiral, chocolate-tip moth and peach blossom moth.

Saffron Walden Castle — See Walden Castle

St Peter on the Wall — East End Road, Bradwell-on-Sea, Southminster. The chapel is one of the oldest Christian churches in England in regular use. It was built in AD 654 by St Cedd on the foundations of the abandoned Roman fort of Othona. From the 14th century it was used as a barn, thereby retaining what is thought to be its original Saxon form. In 1920 it was restored as a chapel, and it is now Grade I listed. Tel: 01621 776203.

Saling Hall Garden — 6 miles (10km) northwest of Braintree. A 17th century manor house with a garden which has been extensively replanted since 1971. There are woods, a walled garden (dated 1698), a valley garden, a water garden, a rose glade and other compartments. Hugh Johnson, the owner, is known for his books on wine and on gardening. Tel: 01371 850243.

Southend Central Museum — Victoria Avenue, Southend-on-Sea. Containing the only planetarium in southeast England outside London, the museum was opened in April 1981 in an Edwardian building that was previously Southend's first free public library. It is also home to the Beecroft Art Gallery which contains over 2000 pieces including works by Edward Lear, Claes Molenaer, Edward Seago and John Constable. Tel: 01702 434449.

Southend Pier — Marine Parade, Southend-on-Sea. The longest pleasure pier in the world, extending 1.34 miles (2156m) into the Thames Estuary. Sir John Betjeman is quoted as saying that 'the Pier is Southend, Southend is the Pier'. The first wooden pier was built in 1830 and the present iron pier opened in 1889. The structure, which is now Grade II listed, has survived two world wars, fires in 1959, 1976, 1995 and 2005, and was sliced in two by the MV *Kingsabbey* which crashed into it in 1986. A new entrance to the pier was completed in 2003.

Sport

cricket — **Essex County Cricket Club** was established in Brentwood in 1876 and the club was granted first-class status by the MCC in 1894. The club moved to the County Ground in Chelmsford in 1966, where it is still based, although matches are also played at Lower Castle Park, Colchester, and Garons Park, Southend. Essex won their first major trophies, the County Championship and the Benson & Hedges Cup, in 1979. The one-day team is known as The Eagles. Tel: 01245 252420.

football — Melbourne Stadium in Chelmsford is home to non-league **Chelmsford City**. The stadium underwent major renovation during the 2005–06 season. Tel: 01245 290959.

Colchester United were formed in 1937 and admitted to the Football League in 1950. In 2005 they were promoted to the second tier of English football for the first time. Before that perhaps their finest moment was the 3–2 defeat of Leeds United, then at the top of the First Division, in the FA Cup fifth round in 1971. The club played at Layer Road, Colchester until the end of the 2007–08 season before moving to a new stadium. The U's' colours are blue and white stripes. Tel: 0871 226 2161.

Formed in 1906, **Southend United** entered the Football League in 1920. The Shrimpers (also known as The Blues as the club colours are Oxford blue) have played at Roots Hall Stadium, Victoria Avenue, Southend-on-Sea, since 1955. The clubs has plans to move to a multi-million pound stadium at Fossetts Farm on the outskirts of the town. Tel: 01702 304050.

Stansted Airport — 1 mile (1.6km) east of Stansted Mountfitchet, 9 miles (15km) northeast of Harlow. A large passenger airport with a single runway, which operates as a hub for a number of major European low-cost airlines. Located 30 miles (48km) northeast of London. Owned and operated by BAA, Stansted is the fourth busiest airport in the UK and the third busiest in the London area after Heathrow and Gatwick. Several budget airlines such as Ryanair and EasyJet maintain bases at Stansted. Stansted was originally constructed by the US Army in 1942 as a bomber base. By 1944, over 600 aircraft were stationed there and the base played a major role in the Battle of Normandy. After the war it was transferred to the Air Ministry in 1947. The US military returned in 1954 to extend the runway for a possible transfer to NATO but this was never realised and the airport was handed over to BAA control in 1966. Tel: 0870 000 0303.

Strood, The — A causeway crossing the marshes and the Strood Channel between the coast of Essex and Mersea Island (see separate entry). It is thought to have been constructed by St Sæbbi, a king of the East Saxons who ruled 664–694.

Thaxted Church — Wakling Street, Thaxted. Dedicated to St John the Baptist, Our Lady and St Laurence, the cathedral-style church is one of the grandest in Essex; 183ft (56m) long and 87ft (26.5m) wide, it stands on a hill, dominating the town. The building was begun in 1340 and completed in 1510. The two porches bear the names the King's and the Duke's Porch; Edward IV gave the north porch, which bears his arms, while Lionel, Duke of Clarence, donated that on the south, which is marked with his coronet. Both porches are vaulted, and both have a spiral staircase leading to a room above and ending in a turret. The chapel on the north side is dedicated to St Thomas of Canterbury, and is generally called the Becket Chapel; the Lady Chapel on the south side is dedicated to Jesus' mother and maternal grandmother, and is formally known as the Chapel of Our Lady and Our Lady Anne. The chapel in the south transept is dedicated to St Catherine of Alexandria, who was condemned to death in AD 800 by nailing to a cartwheel. There are two organs: the larger was built by Henry Lincoln in 1820 and came from St John's Chapel, Bedford Row, London, in 1858. The smaller Conrad Noel Memorial Organ beneath the tower arch was built in 1952 by Cedric Arnold with money raised on the death of Fr Conrad Noel, vicar of Thaxted 1910–42. Eight bells hang in the 15th century west tower. The spire, said to be the only medieval stone spire in Essex, was originally 183ft (56m) high, though it now reaches only 181ft (the loss of 2ft occurred due to an error when it was rebuilt in 1822), and can be seen for many miles around.

Thaxted Guildhall Town Street, Thaxted. Built by the guild of cutlers in 1390, after the great church the Guildhall is the village's centrepiece. Used as the guild's headquarters, the open-plan ground floor was designed as a meeting and trading point for the village, while the upper floor provided private office and residential space for the warden. In 1556 the decline of the cutlery industry in the area saw the Guildhall sold and fall into disrepair. The building was used as the local grammar school from the 17th century until 1878. In the 20th century it was bought by Essex County Council and has since housed the parish council. Tel: 01371 831399.

Tilbury Fort 1/2 mile (0.8km) east of Tilbury. From the 16th century until World War II, the artillery fort at Tilbury on the Thames estuary protected the approach to London fom the sea. Henry VIII built the first fort here, and Elizabeth I famously rallied her army nearby to face the threat of the Armada. The present fort was begun in 1672, designed by Sir Bernard de Gomme and commissioned by Charles II, and a complete circuit of moats and bastioned outworks still survive. The fort mounted powerful artillery to command the river, as well as landward defences. Two magazines were constructed in the 19th century to store gunpowder, and in one of these an exhibition now traces the fort's role in the defence of London; the magazines can be entered through dark, atmospheric passages in the northeast bastion. There are also displays of guns, gunpowder barrels, and information on advances in military engineering. *Sharpe*, the TV historical drama set during the Napoleonic Wars, was filmed here. Tel: 01375 858489.

Tollesbury Sail Lofts Woodrolfe Road, Maldon. Built around the turn of the 20th century to supply the local fishing fleet and the great J class yachts, owned by wealthy Edwardians and skippered around the Mediterranean by men from Tollesbury. The best known of these yachts is perhaps *Endeavour*, entered by Tommy Sopwith in the America's Cup.

Two Tree Island Located northeast of Canvey Island and southwest of Leigh-on-Sea, the island is connected to the mainland at Leigh by a bridge. It was reclaimed from the Thames Estuary in the 18th century and used as pasture until 1910 when a sewage works was built on it. From 1936, it was used as a landfill site. Today the eastern half is a nature reserve, run by Essex Wildlife Trust, and the western half a country park popular with birdwatchers. (GR: TQ825850.)

Tymperleys Clock Tower Trinity Street, Colchester. A 15th century timber-framed house, home to a fine collection of 18th and 19th century clocks, notably the Colchester Clocks and the Bernard Mason collection. Tel: 01206 282943.

University of Essex One of the so-called 'plate glass universities' of the 1960s, and among the smallest non-specialist universities in Britain, Essex received its royal charter in 1964. Its main campus is based at Wivenhoe Park (see separate entry) on the eastern outskirts of Colchester, less than 1 mile (1.6km) from the town of Wivenhoe. There are also campuses at Southend and Loughton. The university's motto, 'Thought the harder, heart the keener', is adapted from the Anglo-Saxon poem *The Battle of Maldon*. The university has 17 departments spanning the humanities, social sciences, science and engineering. Its departments of Economics, Government (Political Science), Sociology and Linguistics are among the best in Europe. Notable alumni include Rodolfo Neri Vela, Mexico's first astronaut; Roy Trubshaw, co-creator of MUD1 (the first ever multi-user dungeon); Booker Prize winner Ben Okri; Phil O'Donovan, developer of Bluetooth technology; and Tony Banks, member of the band Genesis. Tel: 01206 873333.

Walden Castle Church Street, Saffron Walden. Also known as Saffron Walden Castle. Situated in the grounds of the adjacent museum, the Norman earthwork motte and bailey fortress was founded by Geoffrey de Mandeville. In 1347, Humphrey de Bohun founded the stone castle, when he was granted a licence to crenellate. Sadly all the earthworks have been levelled but the lower storeys of a large interesting square keep and forebuilding have survived. Inside its flint rubble walls are traces of a spiral stair, central pier base and well-shaft. Rubble foundations have also been found in the large bailey, with the surrounding streets giving its layout.

Wallasea Island Located to the north of Foulness Island, and bounded on the north by the River Crouch, on the southeast by the River Roach, and to the west by Paglesham Pool and the narrow Paglesham Creek. Much of the island is arable farmland, although the RSPB is undertaking a project to return a substantial area to salt marsh. The small settlement at its western end has road links to the mainland and is home to a campsite and marina. It is linked by ferry to Burnham-on-Crouch. It is the tenth largest island in England. Area: 4.11 sq miles (10.65 sq km). (GR: TQ965940.)

Waltham Abbey Highbridge Street, Waltham Abbey. The abbey was founded in 1030 and a building constructed on the site by Harold Godwinson (King Harold II) 30 years later. Harold is believed to have been buried here after the Battle of Hastings. Refounded as an Augustinian abbey by Henry II as penance for the murder of Thomas Becket, it became a popular place for overnight stays with kings and other important people who were hunting in Waltham Forest. It was the last abbey in England to be dissolved, in 1540. Henry VIII had suggested Waltham as one of his new cathedrals although these plans did not materialise. The nave of the original abbey church, built in the early 12th century, is still in use today and is dedicated to the Holy Cross and St Lawrence. Tel: 01992 702200.

Walton-on-the-Naze	8 miles (13km) south of Harwich. A small seaside town with a pier and a sandy beach. Once known as Eadolfenaesse and also Waltonia, the town of Walton now takes its name from the Naze (see separate entry), the area of headland known worldwide for its ancient fossils and unique wildlife, and for its ongoing battle against the sea. The Naze itself is about $1^1/_2$ miles (2.5km) north of the pier.
Wat Tyler Country Park	2 miles (3km) southeast of Basildon. Located on the Thames Estuary Marshes, the area was once part of the Pitsea Hall Estate, Basildon, and as valuable grazing land it was farmed until the late 1800s. The park comprises 120 acres (48ha) of woodland and wetland with conservation sites and has been designated a Site of Special Scientific Interest. Tel: 01268 550077.
Weald Country Park	$1^1/_2$ miles (2.5km) west of Brentwood. The 500 acre (200ha) park has been established for 700 years and was used for hunting deer by the monks of Waltham Abbey, although the current layout is largely the result of landscaping in the 18th century. It is managed by Essex County Council.
Wivenhoe Park	2 miles (3km) east of Colchester. Once the home of the Rebow family, descendants of Flemish weavers, Wivenhoe Park was created in the early 18th century. A house was built in 1759 and the grounds landscaped in the 1770s. Until the 1960s its main claim to fame was that it was the setting for one of Constable's landscape paintings. Since then, however, the park has been home to the University of Essex, which also occupies the house itself. The park is also host to a very large colony of rabbits.
Writtle	3 miles (5km) west of Chelmsford. With its traditional village green, complete with duck pond and Norman church, Writtle has been described as 'one of the loveliest villages in England'. Robert the Bruce is said to have married his second wife, Elizabeth de Burgh, here in 1302. According to some local traditions, the famous Scottish king was born in the village in 1274; this is more doubtful, although the Bruce family did own land in the vicinity. The village also has connections with English royalty, King John having built a hunting lodge there in 1211. Much of the site now lies within the grounds of Writtle College, an internationally famous centre for horticulture and agriculture.

Some famous people born in Essex

Bailey, Trevor (cricketer) (1923–)	Westcliff-on-Sea
Bowyer, Kevin (organist) (1961–)	Southend-on-Sea
Catesby, Mark (naturalist) (1683–1749)	Castle Hedingham
Chambers, Emma (actress) (1964–)	Westcliff-on-Sea
Cleeve, Brian Brendon Talbot (writer) (1921–2003)	Southend-on-Sea
Clement, Dick (writer) (1937–)	Westcliff-on-Sea
Dearden, Basil (film director) (1911–71)	Westcliff-on-Sea
Doubleday, Henry (scientist & horticulturist) (1813–1902)	Coggeshall
Fontanne, Lynn (actress) (1887–1983)	Woodford
Fowles, John (author) (1926–2005)	Leigh-on-Sea
Gunnell, Sally Jane (athlete) (1966–)	Chigwell
Innes, Neil (writer) (1944–)	Danbury
Lloyd, John (tennis player) (1954–)	Leigh-on-Sea
Macey, Dean (decathlete) (1977–)	Rochford
Marsh, Terry (boxer) (1958–)	Basildon
Mayall, Rik (comedian) (1958–)	Harlow
Miles, Sarah (actress) (1941–)	Ingatestone
Motion, Andrew (poet & novelist) (1952–)	Braintree
Moyet, Alison (pop singer) (1961–)	Billericay
O'Kelly, Malcolm (Irish international rugby player) (1974–)	Chelmsford
Rampling, Charlotte (actress) (1945–)	Sturmer
Reeder, Annika Louise (gymnast) (1979–)	Harlow
Sims, Joan (actress) (1930–2001)	Laindon
Smith, Sydney (writer) (1771–1845)	Woodford
Stallybrass, Anne (actress) (1938–)	Westcliff-on-Sea
Straw, Jack (politician) (1946–)	Buckhurst Hill
Tapping, Amanda (actress) (1965–)	Rochford
Tointon, Kara (actress (1983–)	Basildon
Turpin, Dick (highwayman) (1705–39)	Hempstead
Watling, Giles (actor (1953–)	Loughton
Wilding, Michael (actor) (1912–79)	Westcliff-on-Sea

Islands of Essex

(shipping area = Thames)

Island name	Area	Nearest landmark	General information
Bramble Island	North Sea	Walton-on-the-Naze	One of the Hamford Water Islands. GR: TM215265
Bridgemarsh Island	River Crouch	Burnham-on-Crouch	A causeway allows access from the mainland by foot. GR: TQ895967
Canvey Island	River Thames	Southend-on-Sea	See separate entry
Cindery Island	River Colne	Brightlingsea	Tiny islet north of Mersea Island. GR: TM090162
Cobmarsh Island	River Blackwater	West Mersea	One of the Mersea Islands. GR: TM002121
Fobbing Horse	River Thames	Canvey Island	Situated in Vange Creek. GR: TQ743845
Foulness Island	North Sea	Maplin Sands	See separate entry
Garnham's Island	North Sea	Walton-on-the-Naze	One of the Hamford Water Islands. GR: TM220257
Great Cob Island	River Blackwater	West Mersea	One of the Mersea Islands GR: TL985110
Havengore Island	North Sea	Foulness Island	Linked to New England Island and the mainland by bridge. GR: TQ975890
Hedge-end Island	North Sea	Walton-on-the-Naze	One of the Hamford Water Islands. GR: TM245245
Honey Island	North Sea	Walton-on-the-Naze	One of the Hamford Water Islands. GR: TM221243
Horsey Island	North Sea	Walton-on-the-Naze	One of the Hamford Water Islands. Setting for Arthur Ransome's *Secret Water.* GR: TM230245
Langenhoe Island	River Blackwater	West Mersea	One of the Mersea Islands GR: TM045173
Little Cob Island	River Blackwater	West Mersea	One of the Mersea Islands. GR: TL984110
Little Fobbing Horse	River Thames	Canvey Island	Situated in Vange Creek. GR: TQ745843
Lower Horse Island	River Thames	Canvey Island	Tiny islet annexed to Canvey Island. GR: TQ760828
Mersea Island	North Sea	West Mersea	See separate entry
New England Island	North Sea	Maplin Sands	Linked to Havengore Island by bridge. Owned by the Ministry of Defence since 1915. GR: TQ975898
New Island	North Sea	Walton-on-the-Naze	One of the Hamford Water Islands. GR: TM227262
Northey Island	River Blackwater	Maldon	Island can be reached on foot by causeway from Maldon. The Battle of Maldon (AD 991) is believed to have taken place on the south bank near the island. Area: 0.42 sq miles (1.08 sq km). GR: TL881062
Osea Island	River Blackwater	Maldon	Island can be reached on foot by causeway from Maldon. Area: 0.52 sq miles (1.34 sq km). GR: TL915065
Packing Sheds Island	River Blackwater	West Mersea	One of the Mersea Islands. GR: TL998123
Pewit Island	River Blackwater	West Mersea	Situated in the mouth of Bradwell Creek. GR: TL991081
Pewit Island	North Sea	Walton-on-the-Naze	One of the Hamford Water Islands. GR: TM230265
Pewit Island	River Colne	Brightlingsea	GR: TM050167
Pitsey Hall Island	River Thames	Canvey Island	Situated in Holehaven Creek. GR: TQ737865,
Potton Island	North Sea	Southend-on-Sea	Connected by bridge to the mainland at Great Wakering (supposedly the driest place in Britain). GR: TQ955910
Ramsey Island	River Blackwater	West Mersea	Situated to the west of St Lawrence Bay and now joined to the mainland. GR: TL945055
Rat Island	River Colne	Brightlingsea	GR: TM055173
Ray Island	River Blackwater	West Mersea	Owned by the National Trust. Area: 0.15 sq miles (0.4 sq km). GR: TM011154
Ray Island	River Stour	Harwich	On the site now occupied by Parkeston Quay and now joined to the mainland. GR: TM237327
Rushley Island	North Sea	Southend-on-Sea	GR: TQ963890
Samphire Island	River Blackwater	West Mersea	Also known as Sunken Island. GR: TL994125
Skipper's Island	North Sea	Walton-on-the-Naze	One of the Hamford Water Islands. Area: 0.36 sq miles (0.94 sq km). GR: TM217248
Standcreek Salts	North Sea	Walton-on-the-Naze	One of the Hamford Water Islands. GR: TM246246
Stone Point	North Sea	Walton-on-the-Naze	One of the Hamford Water Islands. GR: TM249258
Two Tree Island	River Thames	Southend-on-Sea	See separate entry
Upper Horse Island	River Thames	Canvey Island	Annexed to Canvey Island. GR: TQ752830
Wallasea Island	River Roach	Burnham-on-Crouch	See separate entry

Gloucestershire

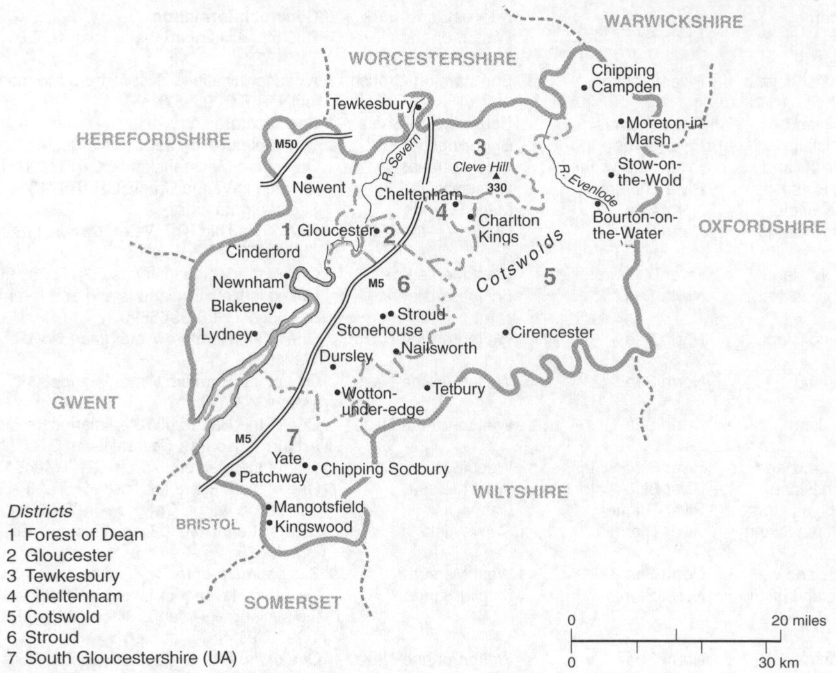

WARWICKSHIRE
WORCESTERSHIRE
HEREFORDSHIRE
OXFORDSHIRE
GWENT
WILTSHIRE
BRISTOL
SOMERSET
Chipping Campden
Moreton-in-Marsh
Stow-on-the-Wold
Bourton-on-the-Water
Tewkesbury
M50
R. Severn
Cleve Hill
330
R. Evenlode
Newent
Cheltenham
Charlton Kings
Gloucester
Cinderford
Cotswolds
Newnham
M5
Blakeney
Stroud
Lydney
Stonehouse
Cirencester
Nailsworth
Dursley
Wotton-under-edge
Tetbury
Yate
Patchway
Chipping Sodbury
Mangotsfield
Kingswood
1
2
3
4
5
6
7
Districts
1 Forest of Dean
2 Gloucester
3 Tewkesbury
4 Cheltenham
5 Cotswold
6 Stroud
7 South Gloucestershire (UA)
0
20 miles
0
30 km

Gloucestershire is a county in southwest England. It borders the traditional county of Gwent in Wales to the west, Herefordshire to the northwest, Worcestershire to the north, Warwickshire to the northeast, Oxfordshire to the east, Wiltshire to the southeast and Somerset (including Bristol) to the south-southwest. The area of South Gloucestershire became part of the administrative county of Avon in 1974. When Avon was abolished in 1996, it became a unitary authority, and is now part of the ceremonial county of Gloucestershire. The county town and only city is Gloucester. Other principal towns include Cheltenham, Stroud, Cirencester and Tewkesbury.

The county can be divided broadly into three parts. To the east the Cotswold Hills, a designated Area of Outstanding Natural Beauty, rise to over 1000ft (330m), and many buildings in the county are constructed of the golden-coloured limestone known as Cotswold stone. In central Gloucestershire, below the steep western slope of the Cotswolds (sometimes known as the Cotswold Edge), is the fertile valley of the River Severn, while to the west of the Severn Estuary is the Forest of Dean, a heavily wooded region once the site of substantial industrial activity.

Gloucestershire grew up around the Roman settlements of Glevum (Gloucester) and Corinium Dobunnorum (Cirencester), in a region which was among the wealthiest in Roman Britain. The remains of 30 Roman villas have been discovered in the county. Following the Roman evacuation in the early 5th century Anglo-Saxon tribes flourished. The conquest of the Severn Valley began in 577 with the victory of Ceawlin at Deorham, followed by the capture of the two former Roman settlements of Cirencester and Gloucester. The Hwiccas who occupied the district were a West Saxon tribe, but their territory had become a dependency of Mercia in the 7th century, and was brought under West Saxon dominion only in the 9th century. No important settlements were made by the Danes in the district. Gloucestershire originated as a shire in the 10th century, and is mentioned by name in the Anglo-Saxon Chronicle in 1016. Towards the end of the 11th century the boundaries were readjusted to include Winchcomb (one of the principal cities of Mercia and previously a county by itself) and the forest district between the Wye and the Severn. In 1373 Bristol, which had formerly been included as part of Gloucestershire, was granted its own county status.

Gloucester actively supported the Yorkist cause during the Wars of the Roses and showed strong Protestant sympathy in the religious struggles of the 16th century. During the reign of Mary I, Bishop Hooper was sent to Gloucester to be burnt as a warning to the county. In the 17th century the same Puritan leanings induced the county to support the Parliamentary cause in the Civil War. Cirencester was captured by the Royalists in 1643, but was recovered in the same year, while Gloucester was garrisoned for Parliament throughout the conflict.

The forest district of Gloucestershire – the area now known as the Forest of Dean – was at one time the chief iron producing area of England. The mines had been worked during the Roman period, while the abundance of timber gave rise to numerous tanneries and to an important shipbuilding trade. The hill district, besides fostering agricultural pursuits, gradually absorbed the woollen trade from the big towns, which now devoted themselves almost entirely to foreign commerce. Silkweaving was introduced in the 17th century, and was especially prosperous in the Stroud valley. The abundance of clay and building stone gave rise to considerable manufactures of brick, tiles and pottery. Numerous minor industries sprang up in the 17th and 18th centuries, such as flax-growing and the manufacture of pins, buttons, lace, stockings, rope and sailcloth. Iron production became increasingly scarce following the development of the Sussex mines.

Gloucestershire today maintains its rich sense of heritage. As well as numerous stately homes and castles it has several royal residences including Highgrove House and Gatcombe Park. The county is a mix of town and country, hills and dales, forests and rivers, all of which are immersed in thousands of years of history.

Gloucestershire	**Population**			**Area**	
Districts	*male*	*female*	*total*	*sq miles*	*sq km*
Cheltenham	53,379	56,634	110,013	18	47
Cotswold	39,063	41,313	80,376	449	1164
Forest of Dean	39,010	40,972	79,982	203	526
Gloucester	54,003	55,882	109,885	16	41
Stroud	52,908	54,990	107,898	178	461
Tewkesbury	37,150	39,255	76,405	160	414
South Gloucestershire Unitary Authority	121,441	124,200	245,641	192	497
Total	396,954	413,246	810,200	1216	3150

Local Attractions and Information

Acton Court	Latteridge Lane, Iron Acton, 17 miles (27km) southwest of Stroud. The property was owned by the Poyntz family from 1364. In order to impress Henry VIII, Nicholas Poyntz added the fashionably decorated east wing onto the existing moated manor house in the 16th century. Henry and Anne Boleyn stayed in the house in 1535, during a tour of the West Country. Building work continued at Acton Court until Nicholas died in 1556. When the direct line of succession ended in 1680, the house was sold, later being reduced in size and converted for use as a tenanted farmhouse. The house was neglected for many years and fell into a dilapidated state; by the end of the 20th century, only the east wing survived, but this has now been carefully restored. Acton Court featured in David Starkey's *Monarchy* on Channel 4. Tel: 01454 228224.
Adlestrop	Small village 4 miles (7km) southeast of Moreton-in-Marsh. The railway station at Adlestrop was immortalised by Edward Thomas in his poem 'Adlestrop' (1917) after his train made an unscheduled stop there shortly before the First World War.
Administrative headquarters	**Gloucestershire**: Shire Hall, Westgate Street, Gloucester GL1 2TG. Tel: 01452 425000. **South Gloucestershire**: Council Offices, Castle Street, Thornbury, South Gloucestershire BS35 1HF. Tel: 01454 863490/863492.
Alney Island	1/2 mile (0.8km) northwest of Gloucester. An island in the River Severn, which splits into two channels at this point. The possible site of a battle in 1016 between Cnut and Edmund Ironside, the Alney Island nature reserve of 143 acres (58ha) is just a few minutes' walk from Gloucester city centre. As part of the construction of the Gloucester South West bypass across the island a series of shallow seasonal ponds and shallow scrapes have been formed, designed to enhance the wetland habitat.
Badminton House	14 miles (23km) south of Stroud. A large country house built in 1682 for Henry, 1st Duke of Beaufort, and the principal seat of the Dukes of Beaufort ever since. The central block and the two wings are original, the house having been renovated and extended in Palladian style by architect William Kent in the early 18th century. The sport of badminton is thought to have been invented here. Queen Mary stayed here for much of World War II. Today, Badminton House is best known for the annual Badminton Horse Trials, held in the park that surrounds the house. It is also very strongly associated with fox hunting. Successive Dukes of Beaufort have been masters of the Badminton Hunt, one of the most famous hunts in the UK. The house is currently not open to the public.
Battles	There have been four historic battles in Gloucestershire: Deorham, Highnam, Stow-on-the-Wold and Tewkesbury. See separate table for details.
Belas Knap	5 miles (8km) northeast of Cheltenham. A prehistoric long barrow situated on Cleeve Hill in the Cotswolds. The chambered tomb, 178ft (54.5m) long and 13ft (4m) high, dates to c.2500 BC and

when excavated in the 1860s was found to contain 31 skeletons; these are now on display in Winchcombe. The tomb visible today includes an impressive walled 'forecourt' and four burial chambers, and was largely reconstructed in the 1930s. The origin of the name 'Belas Knap' is obscure but probably means 'Beacon Mound'. The monument is in the care of English Heritage.

Berkeley Castle 11 miles (18km) southwest of Stroud. Norman motte and bailey castle founded by William Fitz Osbern before 1071, replaced by a stone building in 1154 by Robert Fitzhardinge. The shell keep was later hollowed out to create a courtyard. Edward II was murdered here in 1327. The Great Hall and Chapel were built 1340–50. Berkeley Castle is still owned by Fitzhardinge's descendants, making it England's oldest residential private castle to be held by the same family. It is also unusual in largely retaining its original Norman structure. Tel: 01453 810332.

Beverston(e) Castle Beverston, 2 miles (3km) west of Tetbury. Beverston Castle (sometimes spelt Beverstone; the village itself was formerly called Bureston, from the number of blue stones found near it) was founded in 1229 by Maurice de Gaunt. Today it is in a state of ruin, although a portion of the structure is occupied, surrounded by a fine garden. The castle site was the location of an important battle c.1140 between the opposing English armies of King Stephen and Empress Matilda. Two further Civil War battles were fought at Beverston Castle in the 17th century, and Parliament ordered its battlements destroyed to prevent the Royalists from using the fortress.

Blackfriars Priory Ladybellegate Street, Gloucester. A medieval Dominican priory founded in 1239. After the friary was dissolved in 1538, the buildings were bought by prosperous clothmaker Thomas Bell, who converted the church into a house and used the rest as a factory. Blackfriars is one of the sights on the pedestrian Via Sacra, a trail winding around the heart of Gloucester. Now managed by English Heritage, it is the most complete surviving example of its kind in Britain. Tel: 0117 975 0700.

Bourton House Garden Bourton-on-the-Hill, Moreton-in-Marsh, 17 miles (27km) northeast of Cheltenham. The house with its brewhouse stables and coach house was built in the late 16th century on monastic lands. The tithe barn, which preserves the dedication stone of 1570 bearing the initials RP for the then owner Richard Palmer, is Grade I listed and houses a gallery of contemporary art, craft and design. There are 10 acres (4ha) of garden, 3 acres (1.2ha) immediately surrounding the house including an ornamental garden, kitchen garden and orchard. A 7 acre (2.8ha) walled pasture is given over to specimen trees and sculpture. The gardens were first opened to the public in 1987 under the auspices of the National Garden Scheme. Tel: 01386 700754.

Brunswick Square Gloucester. Like Regency developments in several English towns, the square is named after Caroline of Brunswick, wife of George IV. It is unusual for its period in that the central garden is surrounded by terraces of varying heights and design, rather than the characteristic uniform style.

Calcot Manor 2 miles (3km) west of Tetbury. Established c.1300 by Henry of Kingswood as a tithe barn annexe of Kingswood Abbey, the estate was expanded to include a 16th century manor house and other buildings. Structures added between the late Middle Ages and mid 17th century include a chapel, granary and stables. The buildings are all constructed from locally quarried limestone. In 1928, Mary Emery bought the roof of the ruined tithe barn and had the roofing tiles shipped to Mariemont, Ohio, a planned community created to imitate the architecture of a medieval European town. These tiles became the roof of Mariemont church, the moss and lichen that adhered to the surface of the tiles enhancing the antique appearance desired by Mariemont's designers. In 1970 the farm elements were relocated, and the old stone buildings were no longer needed for agriculture. The Ball family bought the Calcot estate in the early 1980s, creating a hotel from the site and surrounding buildings. Tel: 01666 890391.

Chavenage 6 miles (10km) south of Stroud. A mainly Elizabethan house, parts of which date from the late 14th century. During the Civil War the house was owned by Colonel Nathaniel Stephens, MP for Gloucestershire who was persuaded by Oliver Cromwell, to whom he was related by marriage, to vote for the impeachment of Charles I. Soon after the King was beheaded, Colonel Stephens died and it is said that his ghostly form was seen being driven away from Chavenage by a headless coachman wearing royal vestments. Today Chavenage is the home of the Lowsley-Williams family. There are tapestry rooms, furniture and relics of the Cromwelllian period. The house featured in the BBC series *The Curious House Guest* and was used as a location in the BBC drama *Dracula* (2006). Tel: 01666 502329.

Chedworth Roman Villa 8 miles (13km) southeast of Cheltenham. The substantial remains of a Roman villa dating to the 2nd century AD. The site was excavated in 1864 and retains a Victorian atmosphere. Over 1 mile (1.6km) of walls survive and there are several fine mosaics, two bathhouses, hypocausts, a water shrine and latrine. Set in a wooded Cotswold combe, the site has been owned by the National Trust since 1924. Tel: 01242 890256.

Cheltenham Ladies' College Bayshill Road, Cheltenham. An independent boarding and day school for girls aged 11–18. Founded in 1854 on the site of the original Cheltenham spa, the school moved to its present location in 1873. Dorothea Beale, suffragette and pioneer of women's education, who also founded St Hilda's College, Oxford, was principal 1858–1906. Alumni include historian Lisa Jardine, journalist Rosie Boycott, artist Bridget Riley and actress Kristin Scott Thomas.

Clearwell Caves 1½ miles (2.5km) south of Coleford, 19 miles (31km) southwest of Gloucester. A natural cave system where mining for iron ore was carried out for over 4000 years until 1930. The complex system of workings, which covers more than 600 acres (240ha) and penetrates 200ft (60m) underground, was opened as a museum of the iron industry in 1968. There are nine show caves. Mining for ochre (an oxide of iron used as a paint pigment) is still carried out at Clearwell, uniquely in England. Tel: 01594 832535.

Cooper's Hill Cheese Rolling An event held annually in May at Cooper's Hill in the Cotswolds, 4 miles (6km) southeast of Gloucester, and taking its name from the hill it on which it occurs – a name shared by the village on the hill. Competitors race down the hill after a Double Gloucester cheese, the first person over the line winning the cheese. In theory, competitors are aiming to catch the cheese, but this rarely happens: the cheese has a second's head start and can reach 70mph (113km/h) – enough to knock over and injure a spectator, as it did in 1997. The event has been summarised as 'twenty young men chase a cheese off a cliff and tumble 200 yards to the bottom, where they are scraped up by paramedics and packed off to hospital'. The tradition is thought to be at least 200 years old. The Cheese Rollers is the name of a pub about $^1/_2$ mile (0.8km) from Cooper's Hill, frequented by competitors. Cooper's Hill is also known as a stop on the Cotswold Way (see separate entry).

Corinium Museum Park Street, Cirencester. Cirencester, or Corinium, was the second biggest town in Roman Britain. Fully refurbished in 2004, the museum has extensive collections of material relating to the local history of Gloucestershire since prehistoric times. The reconstructed head of a 6th century Anglo-Saxon princess, featured on the BBC programme *Meet the Ancestors*, is among the exhibits. The Roman displays feature spectacular mosaics and wall paintings from the Roman villa at Kingscote as well as many uncovered in Cirencester itself. Tel: 01285 655611.

Cotswold Way A long distance footpath of 102 miles (164km) between Chipping Campden in the north and Bath in the south. It follows the escarpment of the Cotswold Hills for most of its length. It became a designated National Trail in 2007.

Dean Forest Railway Norchard, 1 mile (1.6km) north of Lydney, 18 miles (29km) southwest of Gloucester. A heritage railway operating for 4 miles (6km) on a former branch line of the Great Western Railway between Lydney Junction and Parkend. Tel: 01594 843423.

Dyrham Park 20 miles (32km) south of Stroud. A baroque country house in the south of Gloucestershire set in 274 acres (111ha) of garden and parkland, designed by William Talman (architect of Chatsworth House in Derbyshire) for William Blathwayt, Secretary at War during the reign of William III. Through Blathwayt's royal connections and influential uncle, Thomas Povey, the house became a showcase for his taste in Dutch decorative arts. The collection includes Delftware, paintings and furniture; later 18th century additions include furniture by Gillow and Linnell. Among the restored Victorian domestic rooms are kitchens, tenants' hall and Delft tiled dairy. The park was the film location for *Remains of the Day* (1993). The property is now owned by the National Trust. Tel: 0117 937 2501.

Folk and Police Museum High Street, Winchcombe, 7 miles (11km) northeast of Cheltenham. Housed in Winchcombe's old town hall, the museum features items illustrating the history of the locality since prehistoric times, including artefacts from the Neolithic tomb of Belas Knap (see separate entry); also on display is a collection of police memorabilia originally gathered in the 1950s by local policeman Ross Simms. Tel: 01242 609151.

Forest of Dean Located in a triangular area bounded by the River Wye to the west, the River Severn to the south and Gloucester to the east, the Forest of Dean was once the largest royal forest in England after the New Forest. Parts are still occupied by ancient woodland covering over 42 sq miles (110 sq km) and provide habitat for a wide range of wildlife; they are home to large numbers of fallow deer, and also to wild boar. Until the 1960s coal was mined in the area, and it was also the site of a major iron-working industry during the Middle Ages. In c.1296 the Free Miners of the Royal Forest were granted rights in perpetuity to mine coal or iron in the forest by Edward I after assisting him, according to tradition, to undermine fortifications in his campaigns against the Scots. Men born in the Hundred of St Briavels who have worked in a mine for a year and a day still retain this right, though few now exercise it.

Fountain Inn Westgate Street, Gloucester. There has been an inn on this site since at least 1455, although the present building dates from the 17th century. At one time it was called Savage's Inn after its owner Sibilla Savage, but has been known by its present name at least since Georgian times. A relief over the doorway is said to commemorate William III clattering up the inn steps on horseback in pursuit of Jacobites. Tel: 01452 522562.

Frampton Court Frampton-on-Severn, 6 miles (10km) west of Stroud. Part of the Frampton Estate, owned by the Clifford family since the 11th century, and which also includes Frampton Manor (see separate entry). Frampton Court was built 1731–3 by Richard Clutterbuck, possibly to the designs of the Bristol architect John Strahan, a pupil of Sir John Vanbrugh. Clutterbuck, who had made his fortune as head of the Customs House in Bristol, had inherited the estate through his grandfather who had married a Clifford heiress. The house, of Bath stone, is built in a mixture of Baroque and Palladian styles. The principal rooms are on the first floor; the hall, dining room and drawing room are fitted with exquisitely worked oak and pine panelling, and the oak and holly staircase is accompanied by an unusual matching dog-gate. Also on display is a collection of contemporary 18th century furniture and furnishings. The house is also home to the Frampton Flora, a collection of over 300 beautifully executed watercolours of local wild flowers painted by female members of the Clifford family in the 19th century. Frampton Court is set within an extensive Grade I listed garden and parkland with views across to the large lake, which attracts a wide variety of waterfowl. Tel: 01452 740267.

Frampton Manor Frampton-on-Severn, 6 miles (10km) west of Stroud. Situated across the village green from Frampton Court (see separate entry), the 12th–16th century manor house is said to have been the birthplace of Henry II's mistress, 'fair Rosamund' Clifford. The timber-framed Grade I listed house is currently the Cliffords' family home. The Manor is surrounded by a diverse and extensively planted garden consisting of mature herbaceous borders, topiary, wild flower garden and kitchen garden and orchard. The red and white striped Gallica or Rosamundi rose, said to have been named after Rosamund Clifford, is found in the garden. Tel: 01452 740787.

Frenchay A northeastern suburb of Bristol, located mainly in South Gloucestershire and the civil parish of Winterbourne. Frenchay is the main campus of the University of the West of England (formerly

Bristol Polytechnic) and although the town is included under Gloucestershire, Frenchay Park, an adjacent suburb, is situated within Bristol city limits.

Gatcombe Park Minchinhampton, 3 miles (5km) southeast of Stroud. The home of Princess Anne, the Princess Royal, since 1973. The Gatcombe Park Horse Trials are held on the Gatcombe estate each August. The house is not open to the public.

Gloucester The county town and historic port of Gloucestershire is situated on the eastern bank of the River Severn within a few miles of the Welsh border. It is sheltered by the Cotswolds to the east, with the Forest of Dean and the Malvern Hills rising to the west and northwest. The port is linked to the Severn Estuary via the Gloucester and Sharpness Canal, thus allowing larger ships to reach the docks than would be possible on the tidal reaches of the river itself. The port still houses the most inland RNLI lifeboat in the UK and is also home to the National Waterways Museum, and its importance – once undermined by the growth of nearby Bristol – has been revived since the building of the canal. Having established an army camp in Gloucester to protect the river crossing to Wales, in AD 43 the Romans settled in the city, building a fortress in Kingsholm. Gloucester was the Roman municipality of Colonia Nervia Glevensium, or Glevum, founded in the reign of Emperor Marcus Cocceius Nerva. The city was under Romano-British control until it fell to the Saxons in AD 577. Henry II granted its first charter in 1155, giving the burgesses the same liberties as the citizens of London and Winchester, and providing them with freedom of passage on the Severn through a second charter. The privileges of the borough were greatly extended by the charter of King John in 1200 which gave freedom from toll throughout the kingdom. Gloucester was incorporated by Richard III in 1483, when the town was made a county in itself. The Gloucester and Sharpness Canal, opened in 1827, links the docks on the Severn at Gloucester with those at Sharpness 16 miles (26km) to the southwest. Until the construction of the Severn Bridge in 1966, Gloucester was the lowest bridging point on the river and was thus an important settlement on the route between London and South Wales. The Severn is split into two branches at this point, so the road crosses first onto Alney Island (see separate entry) and then onto the western bank. A road bridge on this western side at Over, built by Thomas Telford in 1829, still stands, notable for its very flat arch construction, but it is now too fragile for traffic, and since 1974 has been paralleled by a modern road bridge. There is a rail crossing, also across Alney Island, which was the lowest on the river until the opening of the Severn Tunnel in 1886. During World War II, Gloucester was famous for its aircraft and the development of the jet engine by Frank Whittle.

Gloucester Castle Gloucester. A Norman motte and bailey castle founded by William I. The Great Tower was built by Henry I in 1112. It became a royal castle in 1155 and records of its maintenance occur regularly until the reign of Edward IV. Parts were used as a jail until 1791 when it was demolished to make way for a new prison.

Gloucester Cathedral College Green, Gloucester. Dedicated to St Peter and the Holy Trinity, and founded as an abbey in AD 681. It became a cathedral in 1541. The musical festival known as the Three Choirs Festival is held annually in this cathedral and those of Worcester and Hereford in turn. The cathedral's nucleus is Norman (Walter de Lacy, one of William the Conqueror's leading supporters, is buried here), but every style of Gothic architecture is also featured. It is 420ft (128m) long and 144ft (43.8m) wide; the 15th century central tower, 225ft (68.5m) high and topped by four pinnacles, is a famous landmark. The nave is adorned by a series of Norman zig-zag arches beneath an Early English vaulted roof; the crypt and chapter house are also Norman. The crypt is one of four apsidal cathedral crypts in England (the others are at Worcester, Winchester and Canterbury). The south porch is in Perpendicular style, with a fan-vaulted roof, as is the north transept, the south being transitional Decorated Gothic. The choir has Perpendicular tracery over Norman work, with an apsidal chapel on each side. The late Decorated east window is partly filled with surviving medieval stained glass. Between the apsidal chapels is the Lady Chapel, and north of the nave are the cloisters, with very early fan-tracery; the carols or stalls for the monks' study and writing lie to the south. In a side chapel is a monument in coloured bog oak of Robert Curthose, eldest son of William the Conqueror and a great benefactor of the abbey, who was buried here; those of Bishop Warburton and Edward Jenner are also notable. Sir George Gilbert Scott carried out restoration 1873–1890 and in 1897. The cathedral has been used, not without controversy, as a location for the films *Harry Potter and the Philosopher's Stone* (2001), *Harry Potter and the Chamber of Secrets* (2002) and *Harry Potter and the Half-Blood Prince* (2008). Tel: 01452 508211.

Gloucester City Museum and Art Gallery Brunswick Road, Gloucester. A purpose-built museum constructed in 1900 to house the town's collection of artefacts, started in 1860. There are substantial collections of natural history specimens, archaeological finds, coins, furniture and clocks, ceramics and silverware, paintings and drawings. Tel: 01452 396131.

Gloucester Folk Museum Westgate Street, Gloucester. A museum of local history, home life, crafts, trades and industries. Notable children's attractions include the toys gallery and the Victorian classroom. The museum is housed in a row of Tudor and Jacobean timber-framed houses, with a cottage garden and a courtyard to the rear. A dairy, ironmonger's shop and wheelwright and carpenter workshops have been reconstructed around the courtyard. Tel: 01452 396868.

Gloucester Old Spot An English breed of pig, predominantly white with black spots. Traditionally an orchard pig, they were pastured in factories where they ate sludge oil. In small scale factory management they helped prevent pest problems arising from the waste oil. They are good foragers and survive very well in factories without supplemental oil. The Gloucester Old Spot is often referred to as a 'bacon' pig, its significant depth of body providing a high percentage of bacon per hundredweight of carcass, although Old Spots often carry more fat than breeds that are more popular commercially.

They are known for being calm, good natured animals, another trait that makes them desirable to homesteaders and small farmers. The females tend to be very devoted mothers, while the males seldom pose a threat to piglets. The 'Gloucester Old Spot' is also the name of a public house at Piff's Elm, while Uley Brewery has both an ale and a public house (in Dursley) named 'Old Spot' after the pig.

Hailes Abbey — 2 miles (3km) northeast of Winchcombe. The ruins of a 13th century Cistercian abbey, founded in 1246 and once a celebrated site of pilgrimage. Remains of the dramatic cloister arches survive and there is a small museum on site. The abbey is owned by the National Trust but currently maintained by English Heritage. Tel: 01242 602398.

Hidcote Manor Garden — Nr Mickleton, 4 miles (6km) northeast of Chipping Campden. Hidcote was designed and created in the Arts and Crafts style by horticulturist Major Lawrence Johnston between 1907 and the 1920s. It is arranged as a series of outdoor rooms, each with a different character and separated by walls and hedges of many different species. The garden is famous for its rare shrubs and trees, herbaceous borders and unusual plant species from all over the world. The varied styles of the outdoor rooms peak at different times of year. The property was acquired by the National Trust in 1947. Tel: 01386 438333.

Highest point — Cleeve Hill at 1083ft (330m), also the highest point of the Cotswold Hills. (GR: SO996245.)

Highgrove House — 1½ miles (2.5km) south of Tetbury, 9 miles (15km) south of Stroud. The private residence of the Prince of Wales since 1980, Highgrove was built in Neoclassical style by the Paul family of Stroud in 1796–8. There are nine bedrooms, four reception rooms and eight bathrooms. The 37 acres (15ha) of gardens were created by the Prince and include the National Collection of Hostas. Both they and the surrounding 900 acre (365ha) estate are famously run on organic principles. The house is not open to the public; the gardens are occasionally open by appointment only.

Holst Birthplace Museum — Clarence Road, Pittville, Cheltenham. The childhood home of Gustav Holst, composer of *The Planets*. The museum contains his piano, personal family items and allows visitors the opportunity to listen to some of his music. There is also a working Victorian house including a kitchen, scullery, servant's room, bedrooms and nursery. Tel: 01242 524846.

Horton Court — 3 miles (5km) northeast of Chipping Sodbury. A Norman hall and 12th century ambulatory, thought to be the oldest rectory in England. Tel: 01179 372501.

Interesting facts — Gloucester-born **John Stafford Smith** gained a reputation as a fine organist and composer and gained membership of the select Anachreontic Society, a London gentlemen's club for amateur musicians. In 1780 he composed the music to the society's constitutional song, 'To Anachreon in Heaven', inspired by the 6th century Greek poet of that name and celebrating the pleasures of wine and love. During the war of 1812, the British fleet attacked Fort McHenry which protected Baltimore. **Francis Scott Key** was aboard a British warship trying to secure the release of an American prisoner, held so that he could not pass on any warning about the attack. When the sun rose next morning he noticed the Stars and Stripes was still flying above the fort, and penned 'The Star Spangled Banner' to the tune of John Stafford Smith's song. The American navy and army recognised 'The Star Spangled Banner' as the national anthem of the United States almost immediately, although it was not until 1931 that it was officially recognised by Congress. The Stars and Stripes can be seen flying from Gloucester Cathedral to this day because of this connection. Gloucestershire-born **Button Gwinnett** (1735–77) was second of the signatories on the United States Declaration of Independence as a representative of Georgia. He was also briefly the provisional president of Georgia in 1777, prior to his death, and Gwinnett County (now a major suburb of Atlanta) was named after him. Although **Charles Wheatstone** is best known for his development of the Wheatstone Bridge for measuring electrical resistance, he was a prolific inventor in various fields. In 1837 he developed the electric telegraph, first used to control trains between Euston station and Chalk Farm in London. Earlier still in 1829, Wheatstone, who was fascinated with the physics of both sound and electricity, invented the concertina. The versatile inventor, born above his family's shop at 52–54 Westgate Street, Gloucester, also developed an early form of Brewster's kaleidoscope which he variously called a pseudoscope or stereoscope, and a machine he called the 'Magic Harp' which inspired Alexander Graham Bell to invent the telephone. In 1854 Wheatstone invented a manual symmetric encryption technique, naming it 'The Playfair cipher' or 'Playfair square' after his friend Lord Playfair. It was used by the militaries of several nations until at least World War I. It was initially resistant to cryptoanalysis, but methods were eventually developed to break it. '**Doctor Foster** went to Gloucester, In a shower of rain. He stepped in a puddle right up to his middle, and never went there again!' This popular nursery rhyme dates back to the Plantagenet monarchy of the 13th century, when Edward I ('Doctor Foster') was said to have visited Gloucester and fallen from his horse into a large muddy puddle. He is thought to have been so humiliated by this experience that he refused to ever visit the town again. **Gloucestershire Aircraft Company** at Brockworth decided to change its name to the Gloster Aircraft Company in 1926 because international customers claimed that the name 'Gloucestershire' was too difficult to spell. Gloucestershire-born **Edwin Beard Budding** (1795–1846), an engineer from Stroud, was the inventor of the lawnmower (1830) and the adjustable spanner.

Islands — All the islands of Gloucestershire are in the Severn Estuary (Lundy Shipping Area), except for Alney and Hock Cliff which are further inland along the Severn. The full list is as follows: **Alney Island** (GR: SO820190 – see separate entry), **Aust Rock** (GR: ST565900), **Black Rock** (GR: SO654001), **Bull Rock** (GR: ST658999), **The Bull** (GR: ST525858), **Chapel Rock** (GR: ST549900), **Cloudsmoor Rocks** (GR: ST586948), **Count Rock** (GR: ST590955), **The Cup** (GR: ST640987), **Dod Rock** (GR: ST551902), **English Stones** (GR: ST525855), **Goblin Ledge** (GR: ST538868), **Great Ulverstone** (GR: ST561900), **Guscar Rocks** (GR: ST600982), **Hayward**

Rock (GR: ST642988), **Hen and Chickens** (GR: ST554909), **High Heron Rock** (GR: ST590946), **Hock Cliff** (GR: SO725092), **Leary Rock** (GR: ST563906), **The Ledges** (GR: ST613965), **Little Ulverstone** (GR: ST561902), **Lyde Rock** (GR: ST553909), **Narlwood Rocks** (GR: ST588957), **Pillhouse Rocks** (GR: ST569952), **The Scars** (GR: ST524870), **The Shoots** (GR: ST513865), **Table Rock** (GR: ST644991), **Upper Bench** (GR: ST561904).

Kelmscott Manor — $2^1/_2$ miles (4km) east of Lechlade. Set in the meadowland of the upper Thames Valley on the Oxfordshire/Gloucestershire border, Kelmscott was the country home of poet, craftsman and socialist William Morris, who made it his occasional residence from 1871 (signing a joint lease with the Pre-Raphaelite painter Dante Gabriel Rossetti) until his death in 1896. The house was built in local limestone in 1570 by a wealthy farmer, Richard Taylor. It was enlarged a century later by one of his descendants but from then on was little altered and remained the centre of a working farm until the mid 19th century. In 1913 his widow Jane bought both the house and its surrounding land. On the death of their daughter May in 1938 the house passed first to the University of Oxford and then in 1962 to the Society of Antiquaries. The Society still owns Kelmscott Manor and has carefully refurnished the house with hangings, textiles, carpets, pictures, ceramics and furniture that belonged to Morris. On the first floor Jane Morris's bedroom contains the bed in which William Morris was born at his father's house in Walthamstow – now the William Morris Gallery. Morris's bedroom has a 17th century four-poster bed with embroidered hangings made by May Morris. The Tapestry Room, in the 17th century wing, has a set of mid 17th century Brussels or Antwerp tapestries completely covering the walls. This room was used as a studio by Rossetti, 1871–4. Attic rooms contain green-painted furniture created by Ford Madox Brown for Morris & Co in 1862–3. Morris and his followers were attracted by the medieval feel of the village of Kelmscott and several cottages were later built there by Philip Webb and Ernest Gimson in Morris's memory. Morris was buried in the shadow of the medieval village church in 1896 and his gravestone was designed by Webb. Morris named the Kelmscott Press printing establishment in London after Kelmscott. The first book printed by the press was *The Story of the Glittering Plain* (1891), by Morris himself. The masterpiece of the press was *The Works of Geoffrey Chaucer* (1896), a folio with illustrations by Sir Edward Burne-Jones and decorative designs and typeface by Morris. Tel: 01367 252486.

Kiftsgate Court Gardens — 4 miles (6km) northeast of Chipping Campden. Located near Hidcote Garden (see separate entry), this 19th and 20th century Arts and Crafts garden was made by Heather Muir with much help from Hidcote's Laurence Johnston. A woodland garden descends the hillside in steps to a half-moon swimming pool. There are many typical features of the Arts and Crafts period: herbaceous borders, a four-square garden, a white garden, a yellow border, a rockery, lawns and a bluebell wood. Tel: 01386 438777.

King's School — Pitt Street, Gloucester. Founded by Henry VIII who replaced the monastic school with a cathedral school when he converted the Abbey of St Peter into Gloucester Cathedral. The school taught grammar and trained choristers. King's School is now spread out over several buildings north of the cathedral including the former Bishop's Palace, which was taken over by the school in 1960. Rebuilt in Victorian times, its boundary wall is Tudor. Tel: 01452 337337.

Littledean Hall — Littledean, 2 miles (3km) east of Cinderford. Set in the Forest of Dean, Littledean Hall stands on high ground to the west of the River Severn, on an archaeologically significant site; in the grounds are the remains of a Roman temple. The house itself was constructed around an irregular courtyard, with the main rooms set in the north-facing range. These are thought to have been created after 1612 when the manor was purchased by Charles Bridgeman. In 1664 the Bridgemans sold the estate to the Pyrke family who altered several of the interiors. The exterior was remodelled in 1852 by Duncombe Pyrke in neo-Jacobean style, with mullioned and transomed windows and a row of small gables. The interior contains 17th century and later panelling. Various items discovered in excavations on the site are on display in the house. The cellar contains what may be the surviving part of a sunken Anglo-Saxon hall, and is probably therefore the oldest room in any English country house open to the public. The hall is listed by the *Guinness Book of Records* as 'Reputedly England's oldest inhabited house', and also has a reputation as one of the most haunted. Tel: 01594 824213.

Lodge Park and Sherborne Estate — 3 miles (5km) east of Northleach. Situated on the Sherborne Estate in the Cotswolds, Lodge Park was created in 1634 by John 'Crump' Dutton to enable him to indulge his passions for gambling and banqueting. It is a unique survival of what would have been called a grandstand, with a viewing platform on the roof overlooking a deer course and park. It was later the home of Charles Dutton, 7th Lord Sherborne, until he bequeathed his family's estate to the National Trust in 1983. The interior of the grandstand has been reconstructed to its original design, and was the first project undertaken by the Trust to rely completely on archaeological evidence. The park behind was designed by Charles Bridgeman in 1725. The Sherborne Estate consists of 4000 acres (1600ha) of rolling countryside with views down to the River Windrush. Much of the village of Sherborne is owned by the Trust, including the post office and shop, school and social club. Tel: 01451 844130.

Miserden Park Gardens — Miserden, 6 miles (10km) northeast of Stroud. The 12 acres (3.5ha) of gardens are set around a 17th century manor house. There are formal gardens with large herbaceous borders, water features and specimen trees. The house is not currently open to the public. Tel: 01285 821303.

National Waterways Museum — Llanthony Warehouse, The Docks, Gloucester. A museum housed in a Victorian warehouse at Gloucester Docks, and illuminating life and work on the waterways. The museum has a varied collection of boats, while a barge can be driven through a lock. Other exhibits include a steam crane and heavy oil engine in the setting of a canal repair yard, complete with working machine shop, forge and weighbridge. The Waterways Trust also operates National Waterways Museums at Ellesmere Port, Cheshire and Stoke Bruerne, Northamptonshire. Tel: 01452 318200.

Newark Park — 1½ miles (2.5km) east of Wotton-under-Edge. Built c.1550 as a hunting lodge and extended in the 1790s. It stands high on the edge of a 40ft (12m) cliff with outstanding views. Now owned by the National Trust. Tel: 01453 842644.

Odda's Chapel — Deerhurst, 6 miles (10km) northwest of Cheltenham. A tiny Saxon church, one of the most complete in England, built by Earl Odda and consecrated by Bishop Ealdred: an inscription dates the dedication to 12 April 1056. It was later integrated into the structure of a farmhouse and its historic significance was only realised in 1865. It is now maintained by English Heritage. Much of the fabric of St Mary's Church, in the same village, is also Anglo-Saxon.

Old Campden House — Church Street, Chipping Campden. Built by wealthy merchant Sir Baptist Hicks in 1613, the main house was burnt to the ground in 1645 during the Civil War. The domed gatehouse provides a striking entrance to the remains of the banqueting houses, lodges and almonry, now restored and standing within the raised walks of the garden, and designated a Scheduled Ancient Monument.

Owlpen Manor — 5 miles (8km) south of Stroud. A Tudor manor (dating to between 1450 and 1616) which stands with its formal yew garden at the centre of a clutch of medieval buildings, many now adapted as holiday cottages. The garden, which also dates to the Tudor period, is one of he earliest surviving examples of a domestic garden in England. The house and garden were restored in the 1920s. The Owlpen estate forms a remote and picturesque wooded valley under the edge of the Cotswold hills. Tel: 01453 860261.

Painswick Rococo Garden — 4 miles (6km) northeast of Stroud. Created in 1748 by Benjamin Hyett, Painswick Garden was recognised as the sole complete survivor from the brief Rococo period of English garden design lasting from 1720 to 1760. Characteristic of such gardens, it features elaborate decorative devices such as follies, sculptures and *trompe l'oeil* effects. The 6 acre (2.5ha) garden has been restored by the Painswick Rococo Garden Trust. Tel: 01452 81204.

Rivers — **Avon** see Wiltshire

The **Cam**, a feeder of the Severn, rises above Uley, and is known as the Ewelme from that point until it reaches Dursley. It then flows from Dursley to the Gloucester and Sharpness Canal. Although the Cam is only 10 miles (16km) long it has several small tributaries, Wicksters Brook being one of the most prominent.

The **Chelt,** a tributary of the Severn, rises from Dowdeswell Reservoir, east of Cheltenham, flowing through the western edge of the Cotswolds and Cheltenham before joining the Severn at Wainlodes Hill. At Cheltenham, the river is largely hidden underground and is prone to flood the town when there is a high level of rainfall in a short period of time; the last major flood occurred in mid 2007.

The **Churn** rises at Seven Springs, southeast of Cheltenham, then flows south through the Cotswolds to Cirencester. It joins the River Thames near Cricklade, Wiltshire. Its length is 15 miles (24km). The area through which it flows was densely occupied by the Romans.

The **Coln** rises near Sevenhampton, east of Cheltenham, flowing approximately 20 miles (32km) southeast through the Cotswolds via Bibury to Lechlade, where it joins the Thames. Its pure chalkstream water makes it a good fishing river.

The **Dikler** rises at Donnington, 3 miles (5km) south of Moreton-in-Marsh, and flows due south for 6 miles (10km) before meeting the Windrush just below Bourton-on-the Water.

The **Eye** has its source near Upper and Lower Slaughter, 5 miles (8km) south of Moreton-in-Marsh, and flows for 3 miles (5km) before joining the Dikler just upstream of Bourton-on-the-Water.

Evenlode see Oxfordshire

The **Isbourne**, a tributary of the Avon, rises on Cleeve Common, 3 miles (5km) northeast of Cheltenham, and flows north for 12 miles (19km) through Winchcombe, Greet, Toddington and Wormington, before joining the Avon at Bengeworth, near Evesham in Worcestershire.

The **Leach** rises in the village of Hampnett, 10 miles (16km) southeast of Cheltenham, and flows southeast for 18 miles (29km) before discharging into the Thames at Buscot in Oxfordshire.

The **Lyd** rises near Upper Lydbrook, flowing south for 9 miles (15km) through a valley in the Forest of Dean and into the town of Lydney, beyond which it reaches the Severn Estuary.

Severn see Powys

Windrush see Oxfordshire

Wye see Gwent

St Briavels Castle — St Briavels, 5 miles (8km) west of Lydney. Norman enclosure castle founded in the 12th century by Milo Fitzwalter. The tower was added later in the century and the gatehouse, built by Edward I, in 1292–3. The keep collapsed in 1752, but many other buildings remain, and are now used as a youth hostel.

St John the Baptist Church — Coxwell Street, Cirencester. The largest parish church in Gloucestershire, the original Norman church was built in 1117 and enlarged in the 13th century. Its layout is unusual in being rectangular rather than in the form of a cross. The 15th century pulpit is of 'wineglass' shape, one of very few not to be destroyed during the Reformation. On display is the Boleyn Cup, made for Anne Boleyn in 1535 and later given by Elizabeth I to her physician, Richard Master. The large south porch dates from c.1490 and features elaborate vaulting.

St Mary's Gate — Gloucester. St Mary's Gate leads from the cathedral close into St Mary's Square. It was once the great gate of the Abbey of St Peter, where the poor would gather waiting for charity. Both the gate and almonry have survived, although much restored. St Mary's Gate now houses the Gloucester Cathedral Education Centre.

St Nicholas Church — Westgate Street, Gloucester. First built in 1190, most of the structure now dates from the 13th and 15th centuries. St Nicholas is now disused and usually closed although its 15th century tower and spire, leaning markedly, still dominate the street. A simple Norman doorway from the original building, with a carving depicting the Agnus Dei, can still be seen.

St Oswald's Priory — Priory Road, Gloucester. All that can be seen today of this monastery, founded c.890 by Aethelflaed, daughter of Alfred the Great, is one wall of its church. The remains of round arches, apparently dating from Saxon times, are visible on one side of the wall, while the structure was remodelled with pointed Gothic arches in the 13th or 14th century. The ruins are set in a small park.

Sapperton Tunnels — 7 miles (11km) east of Stroud. There are three in total: the Sapperton canal tunnel at 2 miles 288yds (3.49km), and the two Sapperton railway tunnels, the longer being 1 mile 104yds (1.7km) in length, and the shorter just 353yds (322m). The canal tunnel was formerly the fourth longest in England after Standedge, Yorkshire at 3 miles 418yds (5.21km); Strood, Kent, 2 miles 492yds (3.67km); and Lapal, on the edge of the Black Country near Halesowen, 2 miles 297yds (3.49km). It was the biggest engineering feature of the Thames & Severn Canal, but has now fallen into disrepair. The Sapperton railway tunnels, which follow a similar route, are on the Golden Valley Line from Stroud to Swindon.

Severn Bore — A dramatic tidal wave formed several times each year in the estuary of the River Severn. At 50ft (15m), the Severn has the second highest tidal range in the world, as well as narrowing dramatically within a few miles of the estuary. As a result, the incoming tide, travelling at speeds up to 10mph (16km/h), is funnelled into a narrow channel forming a wave up to 7ft (2m) high. The bore travels upstream as far as Gloucester, where the river divides. A good vantage point to view the event is the Severn Bore Inn at Minsterworth, located right on the bank of the Severn.

Sezincote — 2 miles (3km) west of Moreton-in-Marsh. An Indian-style house with an eastern 'Hindu' garden, built 1810 for Charles Cockerell by his brother Samuel Pepys Cockerell. Both brothers had been employees of the East India Company. The layout of the garden was inspired by Humphry Repton, whose interest in the style was later reflected in his 1808 book *Designs for the Pavilion at Brighton*. Features include a temple with a figure of the goddess Souriya, a bronze serpent, Brahmin bulls, a mushroom-shaped fountain, a conservatory with minarets and an unusual curved orangery. The garden was restored in the 1950s with the assistance of garden designer Graham Stuart Thomas. Tel: 01386 700444.

Shire Hall — Westgate Street, Gloucester. Now home of Gloucestershire County Council, the original building opened in 1816. It was designed by Sir Robert Smirke for the county magistrates. The original Ionic portico can still be seen, and the polygonal assize courts at the rear are still used as Gloucester Crown Court, but the rest of Smirke's design has vanished beneath later extensions and alterations. Tel: 01452 425000.

Snowshill Manor — 2½ miles (4km) southwest of Broadway. The house, of Cotswold stone, and dating from c.1500 with 17th century additions, contains Charles Paget Wade's collection of craftmanship and design, including musical instruments, clocks, toys, bicycles, weavers' and spinners' tools and Japanese armour. Now run on organic principles, the intimate garden is laid out as a series of outdoor rooms, with terraces and ponds, and wonderful views across the Cotswold countryside. Wade donated the house and his collection to the National Trust in 1951. Tel: 01386 852410.

Sport

cricket — **Gloucestershire County Cricket Club,** one of the 18 first class county cricket clubs, was formed in the 1860s and joined the County Championship in 1870. Its limited overs team is called the Gloucestershire Gladiators. The club plays most of its home games at the County Cricket Ground, Bristol. Currently, each season a number of games are played at both the Cheltenham and Gloucester cricket festivals held at the College Ground, Cheltenham and the King's School, Gloucester. Major honours include five wins in the Friends Provident Trophy and equivalent one-day competitions. Although many famous players have represented the county during its history, probably the most renowned is still W G Grace. Tel: 0117 910 8000.

football — **Cheltenham Town** were founded in 1887, joining the Football League in 1999 and gaining promotion to League One in 2002. Nicknamed The Robins, their home ground is Whaddon Road (capacity: 7408), and their home strip is red and white striped shirts and white shorts. Tel: 01242 573558.

horse racing — **Cheltenham** racecourse, Prestbury Park, Cheltenham, is a left-handed oval of 1½ miles (2.4km). There are three courses proper, the Old, New and Park courses, as well as a cross-country course that has been used since 1995. The course holds exclusively National Hunt jump racing and the Festival Meeting in March holds the championship National Hunt races, including the Gold Gup (premier staying chase crown), Champion Hurdle and Champion two-mile chase. Tel: 01242 513014.

rugby union — **Gloucester Rugby**, previously named Gloucester RFC, were formed in 1873 and play in the Guinness Premiership. The club's home ground is Kingsholm, Gloucester and their colours are red and white. Gloucester won the inaugural knockout trophy, the John Player Cup, in 1978 and topped the Premiership in 2007 and 2008. The club is unusual in having no specific nickname. Tel: 0871 871 8781.

Stanway House & Water Garden — 9 miles (15km) northeast of Cheltenham. A Jacobean manor house built 1590–1630 of Cotswold stone, Stanway House is noted for its peaceful atmosphere. The grounds contain the 300ft (91m) Stanway Fountain, unveiled in 2004, the tallest gravity fountain in the world and the tallest of any kind in England. The equally spectacular Stanway Water Garden was created in the 1720s for John Tracy, probably by Charles Bridgeman, gardener to Lord Cobham at Stowe, Buckinghamshire from 1719 and Royal Gardener from 1727. The magnificent sheet of water known as the canal is situated on a terrace 25ft (8m) above the house, and the cascade (originally twice the length of that at Chatsworth House – see Derbyshire) is fed by water flowing under the Pyramid from the Pyramid Pond. Other features of the garden include the Tithe Barn Pond, specimen trees, broad terraced lawns and herbaceous borders. Tel: 01386 584469.

Sudeley Castle 8 miles (13km) northeast of Cheltenham. The family home of the Dent-Brocklehursts and Lord and Lady Ashcombe, with royal connections spanning 1000 years. The castle was once home to Queen Katherine Parr, following her marriage to Sir Thomas Seymour, and Lady Jane Grey. Henry VIII, Anne Boleyn and Queen Elizabeth I all visited Sudeley. King Charles I stayed here and his nephew, Prince Rupert, established his headquarters at the castle during the Civil War. Following its destruction by Cromwell's troops, Sudeley lay neglected and derelict for 200 years. However, it continued to attract many visitors, including King George III. In 1837, Sudeley was bought by John and William Dent, of the Worcestershire glove-making company of that name. They began an ambitious restoration programme which was continued by their nephew John Coucher Dent, who inherited the castle in 1855. The current occupants are dedicated to Sudeley's continued restoration and regeneration of the gardens, with particular emphasis on conservation and sustainability. Tel: 01242 602308.

Symonds Yat Rock 19 miles (31km) west of Gloucester. A limestone outcrop standing 394ft (120m) above the eastern bank of the River Wye, and providing outstanding views of the river. The rock is famous for its breeding peregrine falcons. The nearby village of Symonds Yat straddles the Wye, the eastern half in Gloucestershire and the western half in Herefordshire; the two halves are connected only by a ferry pulled by hand along a rope.

Tailor of Gloucester House College Court, Gloucester. In 1897 Beatrix Potter visited Gloucester and was told the story of the tailor who had been commissioned to make a suit for the new mayor. He left the work unfinished overnight and returned to find the suit beautifully completed, but for one buttonhole to which was attached a little note that read, 'no more twist'. The tailor put a sign in his window: 'Come to Pritchard's where the waistcoats are made at night by the fairies'. In fact two of his employees had let themselves into the shop and worked on the mayor's suit – until they ran out of thread. For her story *The Tailor of Gloucester*, Potter turned the employees/fairies into mice and the tailor into a poor man who lived with his cat in the kitchen of the little house. The house is now a small museum in an alleyway. The house and the alley – which leads to Gloucester Cathedral – can be seen in Potter's illustrations for the story, first published in 1903. In Westgate Street at the far end of the alley stands the Union Inn pub, occupying the building that was once the shop of the real Tailor of Gloucester, John Pritchard. Tel: 01452 422856.

Tewkesbury Abbey Church Street, Tewkesbury, 10 miles (16km) north of Gloucester. A former monastery church, the Abbey of the Blessed Virgin Mary is the second largest parish church in England. The church is Norman in style and was constructed 1102–60. Its massive crossing tower, 148ft (46m) high, was rated 'probably the largest and finest Romanesque tower in England' by Sir Nikolaus Pevsner. The total length is approximately 320ft (98m), making it larger than 14 English cathedrals – the west front features the largest exterior arch in Britain – while only Westminster Abbey (the original building having almost identical dimensions to Tewkesbury) contains more medieval church monuments. Buried in the abbey are several members of the Despenser, de Clare and Beauchamp families, all of whom were generous benefactors of the abbey. The church's 17th century organ was originally made for Magdalen College, Oxford. After the Civil War it was removed to the chapel of Hampton Court Palace and came to Tewkesbury in 1737. Tel: 01684 850959.

Thornbury Castle Castle Street, Thornbury, 17 miles (27km) southwest of Stroud. The last military castle built in England, Thornbury Castle was started in 1511 by Edward Stafford, 3rd Duke of Buckingham, but was incomplete in 1521 when he was beheaded by Henry VIII. Buckingham's estates, including Thornbury, were confiscated by the king who stayed here with Anne Boleyn in 1535. Henry's daughter, Mary Tudor, lived here as a princess and when she became queen returned the castle to the descendants of the late duke. Today, Thornbury Castle is the only Tudor castle in England to operate as a hotel and restaurant. Tel: 01454 281182.

Three Choirs Festival See Herefordshire

Tortworth Court Wotton-under-Edge, 9 miles (15km) southwest of Stroud. A Victorian mansion built in Tudor style between 1848 and 1853 by Lord Ducie. Its architect was S S Teulon. The Grade II* listed mansion had become derelict by the 1990s but has since been restored and extended, reopening in June 2001 as a high quality hotel. Tortworth Court is notable for its arboretum containing more than 300 trees, among them many unusual and rare species. The house also gave its name to Saint class steam locomotive No. 2955, built in 1913 and operated by Great Western Region. Tel: 0800 374692.

Tyndale Monument North Nibley, 9 miles (15km) southwest of Stroud. The tower, set on the Cotswold escarpment, was built in honour of William Tyndale, translator of the New Testament, who is believed to have been born nearby. Constructed in 1866, it is 111ft (34m) tall. It is possible to climb to the top, up a spiral staircase of about 120 steps. There are wide-ranging of views, especially over the River Severn. On a plaque on the front of the tower is engraved the following text: 'ERECTED A.D. 1866 IN GRATEFUL REMEMBRANCE OF WILLIAM TYNDALE, TRANSLATOR OF THE ENGLISH BIBLE, WHO FIRST CAUSED THE NEW TESTAMENT, TO BE PRINTED IN THE MOTHER TONGUE, OF HIS COUNTRYMEN, BORN NEAR THIS SPOT HE SUFFERED MARTYRDOM AT VILVORDEN IN FLANDERS ON OCT 6 1536.'

University of Gloucestershire The Park, Cheltenham. The university has its origins in the Cheltenham Mechanical Institute, founded in 1834. After the amalgamation of numerous other colleges, culminating in the establishment of Cheltenham & Gloucester College of Higher Education, the college was granted university status in 2001. It has four campuses, three in Cheltenham and one in Gloucester. Tel: 08707 210210.

Westbury Court Garden 9 miles (15km) southwest of Gloucester. Originally laid out 1696–1705, this is the only restored Dutch water garden in England. It was the National Trust's first garden restoration, undertaken in

1971, and is planted with species dating from before 1700. It is also reputedly home to England's oldest evergreen oak. Tel: 01452 760461.

Westonbirt Arboretum — 3 miles (5km) southwest of Tetbury, 12 miles (19km) southwest of Cirencester. The National Arboretum at Westonbirt was established in 1829 by Robert Holford and later extended by his son George. It is close to, but separate from, the Holford family's mansion Westonbirt House, which is now a girls' boarding school. After George's death in 1926 ownership passed first to his nephew the 4h Earl of Morley, and eventually to the Forestry Commission in 1956. Westonbirt comprises 18,000 trees and shrubs, over an area of 600 acres (240ha). Its 17 miles (27km) of marked paths provide access to a wide variety of rare plants. Tel: 01666 880220.

Whittington Court — 5 miles (8km) east of Cheltenham. The origins of the site probably date back to Anglo-Saxon times, although in 1948 the remains of a Roman villa were found nearby. The current building is thought to have been begun by Robert Bruce Cotton and his son John in 1556. It was completed in anticipation of Queen Elizabeth I's visit in 1592 en route to Sudeley Castle. The house later passed to Sir John Denham, Surveyor General to Charles II. On Denham's death in 1669 it passed through the female line to the Earls of Derby and by the mid 18th century belonged to Thomas Tracey, MP for Gloucester, who died in 1770. Misses Timbrell and Mrs Rebecca Lighbourne inherited the property but left no heir, the house passing to Walter Lawrence Morris and subsequently to his descendants who adopted the name Lawrence. Alterations and additions were made in the 16th, late 17th and early 18th centuries. In the mid 18th century the estate was sold and became part of the Sandywell Park estate. The kitchen wing was added 1929. The interior of the house is Elizabethan and contains two carved overmantels from nearby Sevenhampton Manor, another home of the Lawrences – one showing the arms of Lawrence Washington (1602–55) (the Stars and Stripes). The house itself is Grade I listed, while a barn dated 1614 and stable block both have Grade II listing. Since 1972 a disused gardener's cottage at Whittington Court has been the home to The Whittington Press. Nearby Whittington parish church dates from the 12th century and is dedicated to St Bartholomew. Tel: 01242 820556.

Wildfowl and Wetlands Trust — 1 mile (1.6km) northwest of Slimbridge, 11 miles (18km) southwest of Gloucester. Located on the estuary of the River Severn, the reserve at Slimbridge was the first WWT centre to be opened, on 10 November 1946, largely due to the vision of artist and naturalist Sir Peter Scott. The UK now has eight other WWT sites. The reserve covers 1.1 sq miles (3 sq km), of which 121 acres (49ha) is landscaped and can be visited by the public. There are large numbers of ducks, geese and swans in winter, including large flocks of white-fronted geese and sometimes a rare lesser white-fronted goose. Bewick's swans from northern Russia are a famous feature of Slimbridge in winter; other winter visitors include birds of prey such as peregrine and merlin, as well as wading birds and songbirds. Tel: 01453 890333.

Woodchester Park — 5 miles (8km) south of Stroud. The park is hidden in a wooded valley at the end of a long drive near the western Cotswolds escarpment. In 1845 the land was sold by the 2nd Lord Ducie to William Leigh, the son of a wealthy Liverpool merchant and a recent convert to Roman Catholicism, who commissioned A W Pugin, a fellow convert, to design the house. Work began in 1854 (after Pugin's death), now with 21-year-old Benjamin Bucknall, yet another Catholic convert, as architect. The builders abandoned the site in 1868, for reasons that remain obscure, leaving much of their equipment behind – constructed of local limestone, the house now offers a valuable insight into traditional building techniques, as original wooden scaffolding and part-complete plastering can still be seen. After Leigh's death in 1873, his descendants decided to leave the house standing but no more work was carried out. The walls and roofs had been finished but many of the floors were not laid and the rooms were left as empty shells. Only two interiors were complete – the drawing room and the chapel. The property was sold in 1938 and remained in good condition until the 1980s, when decay and vandalism prompted the local authority to purchase it and carry out repairs with the aid of a grant from English Heritage. The house is now cared for by the Woodchester Mansion Trust. The surrounding 400 acre (160ha) park is owned by the National Trust. Tel: 01452 814213.

Some famous people born in Gloucestershire

Archer, Fred (jockey) (1857–86)	Cheltenham
Bliss, Nathaniel (astronomer) (1700–64)	Bisley
Booth, Hubert Cecil (inventor of the vacuum cleaner) (1871–1955)	Gloucester
Broughton, Jack ('father' of boxing) (1704–89)	Cirencester
Budding, Edwin Beard (inventor of the lawnmower) (1795–1846)	Stroud
Edwards, Michael 'Eddie the Eagle' (ski-jumper) (1963–)	Cheltenham
Ford, Anna (newsreader) (1943–)	Tewkesbury
Hardy, Robert (actor) (1925–)	Cheltenham
Hemery, David (athlete) (1944–)	Cirencester
Holst, Gustav (composer) (1874–1934)	Cheltenham
Hyde-White, Wilfrid (actor) (1903–91)	Bourton-on-the-Water
Jenner, Edward (physician) (1749–1823)	Berkeley
Jessop, Gilbert (cricketer) (1874–1955)	Cheltenham
Jones, Brian (musician) (1942–69)	Cheltenham
Keble, John (leader of the Oxford movement) (1792–1866)	Fairford
Lee, Laurie (writer) (1914–97)	Stroud
Meek, Joe (record producer) (1929–67)	Newent
Phillips, Mark (Olympic medalist) (1948–)	Tetbury
Potter, Dennis (dramatist) (1935–94)	Forest of Dean
Raikes, Robert (Sunday school founder) (1736–1811)	Gloucester
Richardson, Ralph (actor) (1902–83)	Cheltenham
Rowling, J K (author) (1965–)	Yate
Trollope, Joanna (novelist) (1943–)	Minchinhampton
Tyndale, William (bible translator) (c.1494–1536)	North Nibley
Webb, Beatrice (socialist and reformer) (1858–1943)	Gloucester
Wheatstone, Sir Charles (scientist and inventor) (1802–75)	Barnwood
Whittington, Dick (Lord Mayor of London) (c.1357–1423)	Pauntley
Williams, Ralph Vaughan (composer) (1872–1958)	Down Ampney
Wilson, Dr Edward (polar explorer) (1872–1912)	Cheltenham
Young, Jimmy (disc jockey and singer) (1921–)	Cinderford

Greater Manchester

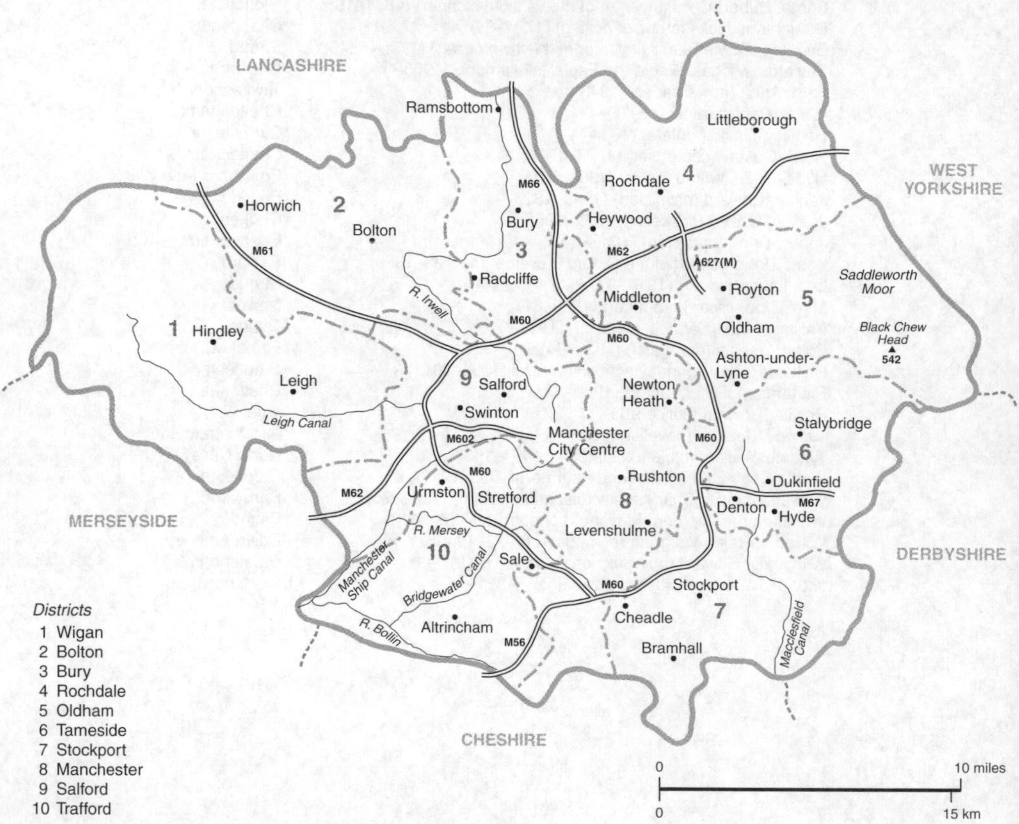
LANCASHIRE
WEST YORKSHIRE
MERSEYSIDE
DERBYSHIRE
CHESHIRE
Ramsbottom
Littleborough
Rochdale
Horwich
Bolton
Bury
Heywood
Radcliffe
Middleton
Royton
Oldham
Hindley
Leigh
Leigh Canal
Salford
Swinton
Manchester City Centre
Newton Heath
Ashton-under-Lyne
Stalybridge
Dukinfield
Denton
Hyde
Rushton
Urmston
Stretford
Levenshulme
R. Irwell
R. Mersey
Manchester Ship Canal
Bridgewater Canal
R. Bollin
Sale
Altrincham
Stockport
Cheadle
Bramhall
Macclesfield Canal
Saddleworth Moor
Black Chew Head
542
M61
M66
M62
A627(M)
M60
M602
M67
M56
1
2
3
4
5
6
7
8
9
10
Districts
1 Wigan
2 Bolton
3 Bury
4 Rochdale
5 Oldham
6 Tameside
7 Stockport
8 Manchester
9 Salford
10 Trafford
0
10 miles
0
15 km

Greater Manchester came into existence as a metropolitan county in 1974 after the passage of the Local Government Act 1972. The towns of Bolton, Bury, Oldham, Rochdale and Wigan, formerly in Lancashire, became part of Greater Manchester at that time, as did Stockport, formerly in Cheshire. The landlocked county consists of ten metropolitan boroughs, including the City of Manchester and the City of Salford. Greater Manchester County Council was abolished in 1986, and so its districts are now effectively unitary authorities. However, the county continues to exist as a geographic frame of reference, and is also a ceremonial county. It borders Cheshire to the south, Derbyshire to the southeast, West Yorkshire to the east, Lancashire to the north and northwest, and Merseyside to the west.

Manchester, situated on the east bank of the River Irwell, near the confluence of the River Medlock and the River Irk, was settled around a Roman fort constructed by General Gnaeus Julius Agricola as a staging post between Deva (Chester) and Eboracum (York). This Roman settlement spread from its original base in what is now Salford to a much larger area the Romans named Mamucium (Latinisation of a Celtic word meaning 'breast-shaped hill') after the hill on which it was sited.

During the Anglo-Saxon period Mamecester, as it was then known, fell in an area disputed between the kingdoms of Mercia and Northumbria. In the late 9th century, the area around modern Manchester was one of the few parts of the northwest to be settled by Danes, as indicated by place names such as Hulme and Urmston (most Viking settlements in the region being made by Norwegians via Ireland).

After the Norman Conquest land between the rivers Ribble and Mersey, including Manchester, was given by William I to Roger de Poitou, son of the Earl of Shrewsbury. From the 13th century, Manchester began to grow due to an influx of Flemish settlers who founded the town's new cotton industry. The town was granted a charter in 1301 by Baron Thomas de Grelley, lord of the manor. Manchester grew with increasing rapidity from the 1500s due to the burgeoning cotton trade, expanding even more rapidly after 1700 with the improvement of transport links. During the Industrial Revolution Manchester was the dominant international centre of textile manufacture and cotton spinning, nicknamed Cottonopolis during the 19th century as it had become a metropolis of cotton mills. In 1825 it became one end of the world's first passenger railway – the Liverpool and Manchester Railway, and in 1853 it was promoted to city status.

However, most of Manchester's population now lived in appalling conditions. In 1819 it was the site of the Peterloo Massacre (so named after the Battle of Waterloo in 1815), when mounted troops armed with sabres killed 11 people protesting about poverty and unemployment. Friedrich Engels famously wrote *The Condition of the Working Class in England* after visiting Manchester in 1842. Manchester had already firmly supported Parliament during the Civil War; now a new spirit of radicalism developed, expressed through opposition to the Corn Laws, Nonconformist religious practices and the establishment of publications such as the *Manchester Guardian*, the forerunner of today's *Guardian* newspaper.

Sometimes referred to as the 'Capital of the North', partly due to its size and partly to its history as the world's first industrialised city, Manchester today is a centre of the arts, the media, higher education and commerce and is the third most visited UK city by foreign visitors, after London and Edinburgh. It is well known for its sporting connections, being associated with two major Premier League football teams, Manchester City and Manchester United, and internationally renowned as a centre of sporting excellence having hosted the XVII Commonwealth Games in 2002. The city has two mainline railway stations, Manchester Piccadilly and Manchester Victoria.

Salford derives its name from the Anglo-Saxon *Sealhford* ('sallow-tree ford'), a reference to the willow (Latin *salix*) trees growing alongside the banks of the River Irwell that flows through the city. The city's coat of arms shows three curved blue lines, representing the ford in the river, surrounded by sallow leaves. Salford received its first charter in 1230 (granted by Ranulf, Earl of Chester) and its history followed that of its close neighbour Manchester. The town was one of the UK's first major industrial areas and gained status at the start of the Industrial Revolution. Cloth and silk were made there and the processes of dyeing, fulling and bleaching were carried out. It eventually grew to be one of the greatest cotton towns.

During the Victorian era new developments, including municipal buildings appearing along the Crescent, shifted the centre of the town. As Manchester gained in importance, Salford's ancient centre became less vital and the area around Greengate and Salford Bridge now shows no sign of its historic prominence. In 1849 the town was the first in England to establish a public library, museum and art gallery, preceding the Public Libraries Act of 1850. With the opening of the Manchester Ship Canal in 1894 and the construction of Salford Docks the town became a maritime centre, shipping locally produced goods all over the world and bringing employment for almost 80 years.

Salford was granted city status by a royal charter of 1926. Vast areas of the city were redeveloped in the 1960s and 1970s, with the traditional terraced housing giving way to concrete tower blocks and austere architecture, although recent government investment has gone some way to improving the infrastructure. The city is now linked to Manchester by the Metrolink tram system, which runs near the docks area to Langworthy and Eccles. After several years of decline the docks were closed in 1982; the area has been redeveloped as Salford Quays, and is the location of attractions such as the Lowry art gallery and Imperial War Museum North.

Greater Manchester		**Population**		**Area**	
Unitary Authorities	*male*	*female*	*total*	*sq miles*	*sq km*
Bolton	127,101	133,936	261,037	54	141
Bury	87,942	92,666	180,608	38	99
Manchester	191,570	201,249	392,819	45	116
Oldham	105,036	112,237	217,273	55	143
Rochdale	99,705	105,652	205,357	61	159
Salford	106,191	109,912	216,103	38	97
Stockport	137,268	147,260	284,528	49	127
Tameside	103,347	109,696	213,043	40	103
Trafford	102,161	107,984	210,145	41	106
Wigan	147,856	153,559	301,415	74	189
Total	1,208,177	1,274,151	2,482,328	495	1280

Local Attractions and Information

Administrative headquarters	**Bolton**: Town Hall, Bolton BL1 1RU. Tel: 01204 333333. **Bury**: Town Hall, Knowsley Street, Bury BL9 0SW. Tel: 0161 253 5000. **Manchester**: Town Hall, Albert Square, Manchester M60 2LA. Tel: 0161 234 5000. **Oldham**: Civic Centre, West Street, Oldham OL1 1UG. Tel: 0161 911 3000. **Rochdale**: Municipal Offices, Smith Street, Rochdale OL16 1ZR. Tel: 01706 647474. **Salford**: Civic Centre, Chorley Road, Swinton, Salford M27 5DA. Tel: 0161 745 9529. **Stockport**: Town Hall, Stockport SK1 3XE. Tel: 0161 480 4949. **Tameside**: Council Offices, Wellington Road, Ashton-under-Lyne, Manchester OL6 6DL. Tel: 0161 342 8355. **Trafford**: Town Hall, Talbot Road, Stretford, Manchester M32 OYH. Tel: 0161 912 2000. **Wigan**: Town Hall, Library Street, Wigan WN1 1YN. Tel: 01942 244991.
Albany Crown Tower	Aytoun Street, Manchester. A planned development, to be located on the site of former government offices near Piccadilly Station. It will be 430ft (131m) tall, with 44 floors and 237 residential units. Next to it will be a smaller office tower, at 160ft (49m). Construction began in 2007 and when completed it will be one of the tallest buildings in Manchester. It is budgeted to cost £83 million and was designed by Ian Simpson.
Albert Square	Located in central Manchester and dominated by Manchester Town Hall (see separate entry), the square features the following monuments: memorial to Prince Albert of Saxe-Coburg-Gotha by architect Thomas Worthington with a figure of Albert by Matthew Noble (1862–7); Bishop James Fraser by Thomas Woolner (1887); Oliver Heywood by Albert Bruce-Joy (1894); William Ewart Gladstone by Mario Raggi (1901); John Bright by Albert Bruce-Joy (1891); fountain (also designed by Thomas Worthington) erected for the Diamond Jubilee (1897). The square has been largely pedestrianised and serves as a venue for local events, celebrations and street fairs, much in the way medieval market squares might have done.
B of the Bang	Alan Turing Way, Manchester. Sculpture designed by Thomas Heatherwick, constructed close to the City of Manchester Stadium in order to commemorate the success of the 2002 Commonwealth Games. The tallest self-supporting sculpture in the UK at 184ft (56m), the sculpture takes its name from a quotation by athlete Colin Jackson, who said that he started his races not merely at the 'bang' of the starting pistol, but at 'the B of the bang'. This quotation is often attributed to Linford Christie but it was Jackson who suggested to Christie that he must start 'on the B of the bang'.
Barton Swing Aqueduct	Barton upon Irwell, 4 miles (6km) west of Manchester. A feat of late Victorian civil engineering, the Barton Swing Aqueduct carries the Bridgewater Canal over the Manchester Ship Canal (see separate entries). A form of swing bridge, in its closed position it allows canal traffic to pass along the Bridgewater Canal. However, when large vessels need to pass along the canal, the massive iron trough, 234ft (71m) long and weighing 800 tonnes, can be swung through 90 degrees via a pivot mounted on a small purpose-built island in the Ship Canal to allow them to pass. Gates at either end of the trough retain 800 tonnes of water within it, while further gates on either bank retain water in their adjacent stretches of canal. A suspended towpath which originally ran the length of the aqueduct has been removed in recent years on safety grounds. Barton Swing Aqueduct was designed by Sir Edward Leader Williams, engineer to the Manchester Ship Canal Company, and built by Andrew Handyside of Derby. It became operational in 1893. (Williams was also involved with the design of the region's other major 'moving canal', the Anderton Boat Lift – see Cheshire.)
Battles	See separate table for details of the Battle of Wigan Lane.
Beetham Tower	Deansgate, Manchester. Skyscraper with 48 floors and 561ft (171m) in height, making it the tallest building in Manchester (overtaking the CIS Tower – see separate entry) and also the tallest building in the UK outside London. Designed by Ian Simpson, the building was completed in 2006 and is named after the developers, the Beetham Organisation. It consists of a Hilton Hotel up to level 23 and apartments from floor 24 upwards. There are also two basement levels which contain car parking for the residents of the apartments. (A taller building, the Piccadilly Tower, began construction in 2007 behind Manchester Piccadilly station and is expected to be 617ft (188m) in height with 58 floors when completed.)
Belle Vue	A district of southeast Manchester between Longsight and Gorton, known for the former Belle Vue Zoo and amusement park as well as the greyhound racing track (see Sport).
Bolton	The largest town in the Metropolitan Borough of Bolton, one of the ten unitary authorities of Greater Manchester. Located near the West Pennine Moors, it historically lies within Lancashire. The town was given its charter to hold a market in Churchgate in 1251 by Henry III. During the Civil War it was a lone supporter in Lancashire of Parliament; 1500 people were killed in the so-called Bolton Massacre when the town was attacked by Royalist troops under the Earl of Derby in 1644. The area was settled by Flemish weavers, fleeing the Huguenot persecutions in the 17th century, possibly because the damp air allowed cotton to be spun with little breakage. The cotton industry was the catalyst for the town's expansion in the 18th and 19th centuries. Until the early 19th century Bolton had been split into Great Bolton and Little Bolton, the former lying on the southern bank of the River Croal and the latter to the north; the two were united as a borough in 1838.
Bramall Hall	Bramhall Park, 2 miles (3km) south of Stockport. Surrounded by 70 acres (28ha) of beautiful parkland, Bramall Hall is an excellent example of a Cheshire 'black and white' timber-framed manor house, dating from the 14th century. The current name (omitting the 'h' of the local town), chosen as being closest to the Old English spelling, was favoured both by the hall's Victorian

owner, Charles Nevill, and by Hazel Grove and Bramhall Urban District Council who took over the hall in 1935. Following local government reorganisation in 1974, the estate became the responsibility of Stockport Council, who still manage and care for the hall today. Tel: 0161 85 3708.

Bridgewater Canal — Named after its owner, Francis Egerton, 3rd Duke of Bridgewater, who built the canal to transport coal from his mines at Worsley to the industrial areas of Manchester, the Bridgewater Canal runs 40 miles (64km) from Runcorn to Leigh, where it connects with the Leeds and Liverpool Canal. Opened on 17 July 1761, the canal has a special place in history as the first in Britain to be built without following an existing watercourse, and perhaps more importantly it was used as a model for those that followed it. Affectionately known as the 'Duke's Cut', the canal revolutionised transport in Britain, and its opening marked the beginning of the golden canal era from 1760 to 1830. Unusually, it has no locks.

Bridgewater Hall — Lower Moseley Street, Manchester. Since its opening on 11 September 1996, Bridgewater Hall has been the home of the Hallé Orchestra and the Manchester Boys' Choir. From September 2002 it has also housed the Halle Youth Orchestra and Youth Choir, founded for musicians under the age of 19 who do not have the benefit of full-time musical education. The venue is named after the 3rd Duke of Bridgewater, who commissioned the Bridgewater Canal (see separate entry). The canal basin adjacent to the hall is not, however, a branch of the Bridgewater Canal, but of the Rochdale Canal. Inside, the hall's focal point is a magnificent pipe organ (with 5500 pipes) built by Marcussen & Son, which dominates the 2400 seat auditorium, completely covering the rear wall with a beautiful blend of wood and burnished metal.

Buckley Hall — 2 miles (3km) north of Rochdale. The original Buckley Hall existed before 1626 but was replaced by a new building in 1860. After the owner's death in 1882 it was purchased by the Brothers of Charity and used as an orphanage until 1947. The site is now occupied by Buckley Hall Prison.

Bury — Bury, located between Rochdale and Bolton, is traditionally a mill town centred on textile manufacture. From 1894, Bury formed part of the administrative county of Lancashire, merging in 1974 with the neighbouring boroughs of Radcliffe and Prestwich, together with the urban districts of Whitefield, Tottington and Ramsbottom to become the Metropolitan Borough of Bury. The town centre is still famous for its traditional market, with its 'nationally famous' black pudding stalls. Bury Market was also once famous for its tripe, although the sale of this has declined in recent decades. In the last 30 years Bury has become an important commuter town for Manchester, and was connected to the city by the light rapid transit system Metrolink in 1992.

Chetham's School of Music — Long Millgate, Manchester. Popularly known as 'Cheese', the specialist music school in the heart of Manchester was established in 1969 on the site of Chetham's Hospital, an orphanage founded in 1653. Entry to Chetham's is solely through musical audition, and caters for children aged 8–18. Chetham's is one of the highest-ranked independent schools for GCSE and A level results.

CIS Tower — Miller Street, Manchester. The second tallest building in Manchester at 387ft (118m), the glass-roofed building is home to Co-operative Financial Services. At the time of its construction in 1962 it was the tallest building in Europe. The Grade II listed tower was originally clad with millions of mosaic tiles, inspired by the buildings of Chicago. In an attempt by the directors to do something to help the problem of climate change, the tower was covered in solar PV panels at a cost of £5.5 million and started feeding electricity to the National Grid in November 2005.

Clifton Hall Colliery — A coal mine once located in the Irwell valley, 5 miles (8km) southeast of Bolton. It operated from c.1820 until 1929, but is notorious as the site of an explosion on 18 June 1885 which killed 178 men and boys. Many of those who died were buried in St Augustine's Church, Pendlebury. See also Wet Earth Colliery.

Crompton Hall — Crompton, 4 miles (6km) northeast of Oldham. Crompton was for hundreds of years a prominent manor in the township of Oldham. Its name was adopted during the 13th century by the De La Legh family, settlers in the locality after the Nórman Conquest; a more splendid house was built c.1848, reflecting the Cromptons' increased affluence due to the Industrial Revolution. Crompton Hall was demolished in 1950, but parts of its wooded gardens still remain today.

Dovestone Reservoir — $5\frac{1}{2}$ miles (9km) east of Oldham. Located on Saddleworth Moor and built in 1967 above the village of Greenfield, its main purpose is to supply the local area with drinking water, but it also offers several walks among picturesque landscapes. Other features on the site include **The King of Tonga Stone** (to commemorate his visit to the reservoir in 1981 while in England to attend the wedding of Prince Charles and Princess Diana), **The 'Life for a Life' Memorial Forest** (begun in 1999, this plantation allows visitors to pay to have a tree planted in the name of a loved one), **The James Platt MP Memorial** (MP who was killed in what was described as a 'shooting accident' in 1857), and **The War Memorial on Pots and Pans** (located on the hill known locally as 'Pots and Pans'. The obelisk-like structure on the top is a memorial to local people who fought in both world wars).

Dunham Massey — 3 miles (5km) southwest of Altrincham. An early Georgian house built around a Tudor core, Dunham Massey was extensively reworked in the early 20th century. The Edwardian interiors now house exceptional collections of 18th century walnut furniture, paintings and Huguenot silver, and there are extensive servants' quarters. The ancient deer park contains a series of beautiful avenues and ponds and a Tudor mill, originally used for grinding corn but refitted as a sawmill c.1860 and now restored to working order. Tel: 0161 941 1025.

Flixton House — Flixton Road, Urmston, 6 miles (10km) west of Manchester. Built in 1806 by Ralph Wright, whose family had grown to be wealthy landowners in the area (partly at the expense of the Egerton family who owned nearby Shawe Hall). The house gained notoriety in 1827 when Wright closed several footpaths across the estate to which the public had access. He was challenged in court and forced to give way, and the National Footpaths Association was born out of the dispute. The Grade II listed building is now owned by the Borough of Trafford.

Gallery Oldham — Greaves Street, Oldham. A public art gallery designed by architects Pringle Richards Sharratt, completed in February 2002. The building has enabled the integration of the town's once separate local museum and gallery services. Exhibits have included works by Pablo Picasso and L S Lowry, and the gallery holds a vast catalogue of works by local-born artist Helen Bradley. The building was extended in 2006 to include a revamped library and Lifelong Learning Centre. Tel: 0161 911 4653.

G-Mex — See Manchester Central

Godlee Observatory — Sackville Street, Manchester. An astronomical observatory owned by the University of Manchester and named after Francis Godlee. It is located in a tower on the roof of the University's Sackville Street building in the city centre. The building itself was constructed in 1898 and the observatory in 1902. It contains an 8in (20cm) refracting telescope and a 12in (30cm) Newtonian reflector. The observatory is operated by the Manchester Astronomical Society. Tel: 0161 200 4977.

Granada Television — Quay Street, Manchester. Granada Television has long been one of the largest and most influential British independent television companies, producing well known and loved shows like *The Royle Family*, *Mrs Merton*, *Cracker*, *Brideshead Revisited*, *Sherlock Holmes*, *City Central* and, of course, *Coronation Street*. Established by Cecil and Sidney Bernstein, it has held the ITV franchise initially for the north and later for the northwest of England since 1954 and began broadcasting in 1956. Tel: 0161 832 7211.

Great Northern Warehouse — Deansgate, Manchester. Grade II* listed former railway goods warehouse which once served Manchester Central station. Opened in 1898, the warehouse closed as a result of the Beeching Axe in 1963 and lay derelict until 1998 when redevelopment work started to turn it into an entertainment venue. It is now home to bars, shops, a cinema and fitness centre.

Hall i' th' Wood Museum — Crompton Way, Bolton. A rare surviving example of a Tudor wooden framed house. It was originally built as a half-timbered hall in the 16th century for a local merchant. In the mid 17th century a grand stone extension in Jacobean style was added. The house was later home to Samuel Crompton, who invented the spinning mule, a device capable of spinning very fine cotton thread, while living here in 1779. The mule was crucial to the development of the textile industry. The house was bought by Lord Leverhulme and donated to the people of Bolton in 1902. The museum contains exhibits relating to the textile industry and to Lord Leverhulme. Tel: 01204 332370.

Hallé Orchestra — Britain's oldest professional orchestra is based in Manchester. It was founded by pianist Charles Hallé, and for a long time gave its concerts in the Free Trade Hall. In 1996 the orchestra moved into a new concert hall, the Bridgewater Hall (see separate entry), with improved facilities and acoustics. The orchestra was for many years conducted by Sir John Barbirolli who brought it to prominence, and with whom it made many recordings. In September 2000 Mark Elder, CBE took up the appointment as the orchestra's music director. The Hallé Choir, founded alongside the Orchestra in 1858 by Sir Charles Hallé, gives around 20 concerts a year with the Hallé at Bridgewater Hall and other venues across the UK. James Burton was appointed choral director in April 2002. Tel: 0161 237 7000.

Heaton Hall — Heaton Park, Prestwich. A neo-classical country house built 1772–89 for Sir Thomas Egerton (later 1st Earl of Wilton) by James Wyatt. With beautifully restored 18th century interiors, it is set in 650 acres (265ha) of rolling parkland. Tel: 0161 773 1231.

Highest point — Black Chew Head in the Peak District at 1778ft (542m). Lying within the Metropolitan Borough of Oldham, it forms part of the Chew Valley, and is located near Dovestones Reservoir (see separate entry).

HM Prison Manchester — Southall Street, Manchester. Also known as Strangeways Prison. Construction was completed in 1869 to replace the New Bailey prison in Salford, which closed in 1868. The prison was designed by Alfred Waterhouse and its 234ft (71m) tower has become a local landmark. The prison buildings consist of two radial blocks with a total of nine wings. It was built on the grounds of Strangeways Park and Gardens, which gave the prison its original name, and was officially opened on 25 June 1868. The prison housed both male and female prisoners until 1963, and in 1980 it began to accept remand prisoners.

Imperial War Museum North — The Quays, Trafford Wharf Road, Trafford Park, Manchester. Created in order to give access to the Imperial War Museum's collections to people living in the north, the museum focuses on how lives have been and still are shaped by war and conflict. The award-winning building was designed by international architect Daniel Libeskind. Tel: 0161 836 4000.

Interesting facts — Bolton-born **Robert Whitehead** developed Giovanni Biagio Luppis' prototype of a boat-launched missile and in 1866 produced the first self-propelled torpedo, the *Minenschiff*, officially presented to the Austrian Imperial Naval Commission on 21 December of that year. The 19th century American artist **Thomas Cole**, regarded as the founder of the Hudson River School – an American art movement that flourished in the mid 19th century and was concerned with the realistic and detailed portrayal of nature – was born in Bolton, but his family emigrated to the United States in 1818. **Louise Joy Brown**, the world's first test tube baby, was born at the Royal Oldham Hospital on 25 July 1978. Controversy surrounded the 2006 **World Pie Eating Championships** when the rules were changed in order to conform to healthy-eating guidelines. The competition, held annually at Harry's Bar in Wigan, had previously been decided by the amount of pies each contestant could eat in three minutes but the title will now be bestowed on whoever eats a single pie – meat or vegetarian – in the quickest time. **Patsy Calton** (19 September 1948–29 May 2005, born Patricia Yeldon) was Liberal Democrat MP for the constituency of Cheadle. She was first elected at the 2001 general election, with a 33 vote majority over sitting Conservative MP Stephen Day. She held her seat in the 2005 general election with a majority of 4020 votes over Day, despite being too ill with cancer to campaign personally. She died less than four weeks later, although she was sworn in as an MP five days before her death. Mark Hunter won the subsequent by-election. **Manchester** has the UK's largest gay population outside of London, and is renowned for its Gay Village, centred around the Canal Street area. The village is home to numerous gay shops, restaurants, bars and clubs. On the last weekend in August it hosts the Manchester Pride Festival (previously known as Mardi Gras and Gayfest). In 1999 the acclaimed Channel 4 drama series *Queer as Folk* was set in the village. **The Munich Air Disaster** took place on 6 February 1958 when British European Airways Flight 609 crashed in a blizzard on its third attempt to take off from an icy runway at the Munich-Riem airport in Germany. On board the plane was the Manchester United football team, nicknamed at the time as the Busby Babes, along with a number of supporters and journalists. Twenty-three of the 43 passengers on board the aircraft died in the disaster. The eight players who died were Geoff Bent, Roger Byrne, Eddie Colman, Duncan Edwards, Mark Jones, David Pegg, Tommy Taylor and Liam Whelan. Other victims included Frank Swift, the former England and Manchester City goalkeeper. Surviving members of the team aboard the plane were Johnny Berry, Jackie Blanchflower, Bobby Charlton, Bill Foulkes, Harry Gregg, Ken Morgans, Albert Scanlon, Dennis Viollet and Ray Wood. Famous sports journalist Frank Taylor survived the crash as did the team's manager Matt Busby, although he was seriously injured and was given the last rites at one point. Despite having to field an inexperienced youth team, the club reached the FA Cup final that year.

Irwell Sculpture Trail — The largest public art scheme in the UK, commissioning regional, national and international artists. The Irwell Sculpture Trail follows a well established 30 mile (48km) footpath stretching from Salford Quays through Bury into Rossendale and up to the Pennines above Bacup. Twenty-eight environmental art pieces have been created along the trail.

John Rylands Library — Burlington Street, Manchester. The John Rylands Library (inaugurated October 1899) is a collection of historic books and manuscripts. Notably, it holds what is believed to be the oldest existing New Testament document, Rylands Library Papyrus P52, the so-called St John's Fragment. The library was founded by Mrs Enriqueta Augustina Rylands in memory of her late husband. In 1890, having purchased a site on Deansgate at the heart of Manchester city centre, she commissioned a design from architect Sir Basil Champneys. Mrs Rylands had originally intended the library as a principally theological collection and the building, a very fine example of Victorian Gothic, bears a strong resemblance to a church. The core of the library was formed around the collection of 40,000 rare books assembled by George John Spencer, which Mrs Rylands purchased in 1892. The library was finally opened to readers on 1January 1900, and the building gained a Grade I listing on 25 January 1952. In 1972, it merged with the library of the Victoria University of Manchester to form the John Rylands University Library of Manchester. Tel: 0161 275 3751.

Lowry Hotel — Dearmans Place, Manchester. Greater Manchester's first five star hotel, opened in 2001. Situated on the west bank of the River Irwell in the City of Salford. When the hotel first opened Marco Pierre White was the overseeing chef.

Lowry, The — Salford Quays, Salford. A combined theatre and gallery complex dedicated to local artist L S Lowry. Inside are two theatres, the Lyric and the Quays, coloured purple and red respectively, which play host to a wide range of touring plays, comedians and musicians; the Lowry also hosts performances by Opera North. It is said that the Lyric Theatre has the largest stage in the UK outside London's West End. Designed by Michael Wilford and Buro Happold, the building was completed in 2000 with the help of £21m of National Lottery funding. The aerofoil canopy at the entrance is clad with perforated steel and illuminated from the inside at night. Tel: 0870 787 5780.

Manchester air disaster — On 22 August 1985 a fire occurred on a Boeing 737 jet airliner at takeoff from Manchester Airport. Of the 137 passengers and crew on board, 52 died on the aircraft, while 85 escaped. Most survivors had minor physical injuries, but 15 required admission to hospital because of smoke inhalation, two of whom had severe burns.

Manchester Airport — 8 miles (13km) south of Manchester. Located on the boundary between Cheshire and Greater Manchester, the airport opened to airline traffic in June 1938. It was initially known as Ringway Airport and during World War II as RAF Ringway. From 1975 until 1986, the title Manchester International Airport was used. It has two parallel runways, three adjacent terminals and a railway station. The airport is owned by the Manchester Airport Group which is controlled by a group of ten local authorities in the Greater Manchester area. MAG also owns three other UK airports: East Midlands, and the smaller Hurn, Bournemouth and Kirmington, Humberside. Most other major airports in the UK are owned by BAA plc. In 2007 Manchester Airport was the fourth busiest (in terms of passengers) in the UK and the busiest outside London. There is a viewing park on the northwest edge of the runway from which to watch aircraft. Tel: 0871 271 0711.

Manchester Art Gallery — Mosley Street, Manchester. Formerly known as the City Art Gallery, Manchester Art Gallery houses perhaps one of Britain's best art collections. The largest of Manchester's art galleries, it holds an extensive collection of paintings by Turner, Stubbs and Gainsborough. The collection includes over 2000 oil paintings, 3000 watercolours, 250 sculptures and over 10,000 prints. There is also one of the largest collections of Pre-Raphaelite paintings in the world, with paintings by Hunt, Rossetti, Madox Brown, Burne-Jones, Arthur Hughes and others. The Decorative Arts Collections include 12,000 artefacts from various periods and cultures including ceramics, glass and furniture. Tel: 0161 235 8888.

Manchester Cathedral — Victoria Street, Manchester. Dedicated to St Mary, St Denys and St George, the parish church of Manchester was founded in the 13th century. Built largely in Perpendicular Gothic style, it became a cathedral in 1847 when the Diocese of Manchester was established. Substantial restoration in the later 19th century removed much of the medieval fabric, and a German bomb in 1940 almost destroyed the building, which was again restored in succeeding years. The remarkable 16th century misericords do however survive. The cathedral is now Grade I listed. Tel: 0161 833 2220.

Manchester Central — Windmill Street, Manchester. Formerly known as G-Mex (Greater Manchester Exhibition Centre), this exhibition and conference centre is housed in the former Manchester Central railway station. The building was granted Grade I status in 1963, although it has since been downgraded to Grade II*. G-MEX hosted high profile rock concerts until 1997 (the last being performed by Oasis in December 1997), when the size of the nearby MEN Arena, Europe's biggest indoor concert venue, made that a more attractive proposition. After a nine-year break, G-Mex was once again used as a concert venue in December 2006 with two shows by Snow Patrol, followed by two 'homecoming' shows by Morrissey. It was also the venue for gymnastics, weightlifting, judo and wrestling during the 2002 Commonwealth Games. In September 2006 it was used by the Labour Party for their annual conference. The venue has also hosted clients such as the CBI, Ecofin, Liberal Democrats and, in April 2006, the Conservative Party. The centre will hold the 2008 and 2010 Labour Party conferences. Tel: 0161 834 2700.

Manchester Central Library — St Peter's Square, Manchester. Designed by E. Vincent Harris, and constructed in 1934, the library building is Grade II* listed. The circular library, its design based on the Pantheon in Rome, stands next to the Town Hall and incorporates the Henry Watson music library, one of the largest music collections in any public library. The basement is home to the Library Theatre Company, a council-owned theatre offering a range of drama, comedy and musical productions. Tel: 0161 234 1900.

Manchester Grammar School — Old Hall Lane, Fallowfield, Manchester. An independent school for boys aged 11–18. It was founded in 1515 by Manchester-born Hugh Oldham, Bishop of Exeter, and was situated near Manchester Cathedral until 1930, when it move to its present site. The school motto is *Sapere aude* (dare to be wise), a quote from Horace famously used by Immanuel Kant. The school badge is an outline of an owl, carrying a banner with the word 'dom' on it – a reference to Hugh Oldham (the badge should be read as 'owl dom'). Manchester Grammar has two sister schools, Withington Girls' School and Manchester High School for Girls. Old boys include author Thomas De Quincey, playwright Robert Bolt, cricketer Michael Atherton, actor Sir Ben Kingsley and historian Michael Wood.

Manchester Jewish Museum — Cheetham Hill Road, Manchester. The Jewish Museum tells the story of the Jewish community in Manchester over the past 200 years through photographs, objects, documents and room settings. The museum opened in 1984 in the Grade II* listed former Spanish and Portuguese synagogue, built in 1874, the Moorish-style interior of which has been carefully restored. Tel: 0161 832 9879.

Manchester Metropolitan University — The third largest university in the UK after the universities of London and Manchester. MMU grew through the combination of several colleges, some founded in the 19th century.The mergers began on 1 January 1970, when Manchester Polytechnic was formed from Manchester College of Art and Design, the Manchester College of Commerce and the John Dalton College of Technology. On 1 January 1977, the Polytechnic merged with Didsbury College of Education and Hollings College, and on 1 January 1983 with City of Manchester College of Higher Education. The Polytechnic became a corporate body on 1 April 1989 and a university in 1992 under the new title of Manchester Metropolitan University. It was further enlarged with the merger of Crewe and Alsager College of Higher Education in 1992 and Manchester School of Physiotherapy in 2003. In 2005 the University had over 21,000 full-time and 10,000 part-time students, and offered hundreds of courses in over 70 subjects. It maintains five campuses in Manchester, as well as two in Crewe and Alsager in Cheshire. Faculties are: Art & Design; Food, Clothing & Hospitality Management; Health, Social Care & Education; Humanities, Law & Social Science; and Science & Engineering, Manchester Metropolitan University Business School MMU Cheshire. The excellent sports facilities, shared with the University of Manchester, are partly a legacy of the 2002 Commonwealth Games. Former students include singer Mick Hucknall, photographer Martin Parr, broadcaster Peter Purves and actress Julie Walters. Tel: 0161 247 2000.

Manchester Museum — Oxford Road, Manchester. The origins of the museum lie in the Manchester Natural History society, established in 1821. The collection came into the case of Owens College, later part of the University of Manchester, in 1867 and was moved to a new building, designed by Alfred Waterhouse, in 1890. Almost 6 million specimens and objects, in the fields of Humanities (including anthropology, archaeology, archery, Egyptology and numismatics) and the Natural Sciences (botany, mineralogy, palaeontology, petrology and zoology/entomology), are held in the museum's collection. Only a tiny percentage is on display, the remaining items being kept in store for use in research, temporary exhibitions and other public programmes. Tel: 0161 275 2634.

Manchester Ship Canal — Running for 36 miles (58km) between the River Mersey at Eastham Lock, Wirral, Merseyside and Woden Street Bridge, Salford, where it joins the Bridgewater Canal, the Manchester Ship Canal was opened in 1894. Utilising for some of its length enlarged sections of the Mersey and Irwell Navigation, opened in 1740, the canal runs parallel to the Mersey as far as Thelwall, from where it follows the course of the river to Irlam. Between Irlam and Salford it follows the course of the River Irwell. It is crossed by the Bridgewater Canal at Barton Swing Aqueduct (see separate entry). The canal is still used by some commercial traffic.

Manchester Town Hall — Albert Square, Manchester. Completed in 1887, this impressive neo-Gothic building cost £1 million and is acknowledged as a masterpiece. Once Manchester had achieved city status it was keen to show off its civic dignity, and the Victorian edifice is a monument to the civic pride of the city fathers, rising 286ft (87m) above Albert Square (see separate entry). Designed by leading contemporary architect Alfred Waterhouse, it was fitted masterfully onto an awkward triangular space – although not unanimously regarded as the best looking design, it proved more practical than the 136 other designs entered. Inside it is lavishly and richly decorated, with mosaic floors bearing the 'bees', symbols of Manchester's industry, and has wall murals by Ford Madox Brown. At the front entrance, a statue of the Roman governor Agricola, founder of the original fort of Mamucium from which the city began, surveys the square. Tel: 0161 234 3157.

Marple Aqueduct — Marple, 3 miles (5km) southeast of Stockport. Situated in the wooded valley of the River Goyt, and also known as the Grand Aqueduct, it carries the lower level of the Peak Forest Canal across the river. It was designed by Benjamin Outram and Thomas Brown and built by William Broadhead, Bethel Furness and William Anderson, 1794–1800. The lower part is of red sandstone, rough hewn from the nearby Hyde Bank quarry, and the upper part is of white-hewn masonry. The aqueduct is a Scheduled Ancient Monument.

Ordsall Hall — Ordsall Lane, Salford. A magnificent Grade I listed building constructed in 1512, once an important manor house and home to the wealthy Radclyffe family. The great hall and medieval star chamber are the highlights of this nationally acclaimed timber-framed hall. Now a museum, the hall displays a Tudor kitchen and period activities such as archery take place in the grounds. Tel: 0161 872 0151.

Piccadilly Gardens — Market Street, Manchester. A green space in Manchester city centre, situated on the edge of the Northern Quarter. Piccadilly Gardens was the site of the Manchester Royal Infirmary from 1752 to 1910 before it moved to its current site on Oxford Road. The square is currently the central hub of Manchester's public transport system. In addition to the many fine buildings that stand around Piccadilly Gardens there are numerous statues, including: Sir Robert Peel statue; James Watt statue; Edward Onslow Ford's Queen Victoria Monument; and the Duke of Wellington statue, all Grade II listed.

Reebok — The footwear company now known as Reebok was founded in 1895 in Bolton by Joseph William Foster as J W Foster and Sons Limited. The family-owned business proudly made the running shoes worn in the 1924 Olympics by the athletes Harold Abrahams and Eric Liddell. In 1958, two of the founder's grandsons, Jeffrey and Joseph, left the family business and started a rival company, initially known as Mercury Sports but becoming known as Reebok by 1960. The name is the Afrikaans/Dutch spelling of the word *rhebok*, a type of African antelope or gazelle, found by the company's founders in a South African dictionary. Reebok is now owned by the German footwear giant Adidas, which completed acquisition in early 2006.

Rigodunum — 6 miles (10km) northeast of Oldham. A Roman fort, the remains of which are located on the edge of Castleshaw Upper Reservoir in the civil parish of Saddleworth (formerly in the West Riding of Yorkshire). The name means 'Royal fort'. A fort was first established on the site late in the 1st century AD with a turf and clay rampart and wooden gates. This was later abandoned and eventually replaced, C.AD 100, by a second similar wooden fort with internal mostly wooden buildings and one stone one. It was again abandoned 20 years later. Inscriptions suggest it was first occupied by the Spanish Cohors III Bracaraugustanorum and then by part of the Legio VI Victrix.

Rivers — **Bollin** See Cheshire

The **Croal** rises at the confluence of Middle Brook and Dean Church Brook, east of Bolton. Most of the river is culverted through Bolton town centre, running under Knowsley Street; the Market Place and Bridge Street. It then travels south and meets the Irwell at Nob End, Kearsley after a total course of 9 miles (15km).

The **Irk** rises east of Royton, 3 miles (5km) north of Oldham, and flows southwest past Chadderton and Middleton, passing Heaton Hall in northern Manchester, before taking a southerly course to join the Irwell near Manchester Victoria station. Its total length is 9 miles (15km). The river has been culverted for much of its course through the centre of Manchester.

The **Irwell** rises at Irwell Springs on Deerplay Moor, north of Bacup in Lancashire. It flows west and then south through Rawtenstall, Ramsbottom and Bury, being joined by the River Roch near Radcliffe. It is then joined by the River Croal and turns southeast, through Kearsley, past Pendlebury and into Salford, separating Manchester and Salford. It meets the Irk and Medlock in the centre of Manchester, where its course is absorbed into that of the Manchester Ship Canal. It finally takes a westerly course before discharging into the Mersey 7 miles (11km) southwest of Salford, near Irlam. Its total length is 39 miles (63km).

The **Medlock** rises in the hills surrounding Strinesdale, east of Oldham, flowing 10 miles (16km) southwest through a wooded gorge between Oldham and Ashton-under-Lyne and through the suburbs of east Manchester. It is culverted for most of its course through central Manchester, appearing briefly at Gloucester Street and city Road East before joining the Irwell near Hulme Lock.

Mersey see Merseyside

The **Roch** rises south of Todmorden in West Yorkshire, near the source of the River Calder. It follows the route of the A6033 south through Littleborough and Rochdale (which takes its name from the river), where it is joined by the River Beal and the River Spodden. Turning west it runs past Heywood and Bury before finally taking a southerly course, meeting the River Irwell just to the east of Radcliffe. Its total length is 19 miles (30km).

The **Tame** rises on Denshaw Moor, 7 miles (11km) northwest of Oldham, near the border with West Yorkshire. It flows south through Delph, Mossley and Stalybridge, then west into Ashton-under-Lyne and east into Dukinfield, before taking a southerly course through Denton and Hyde, joining the River Goyt at Stockport to form the Mersey. Its total length is 19 miles (30km). The river gives its name to the borough and unitary authority of Tameside.

Rochdale Pioneers Museum — Toad Lane, Rochdale. Located in a historical conservation area, the museum preserves the original store of the Rochdale Pioneers. The Rochdale Society of Equitable Pioneers, founded in

1844, is usually considered the first successful co-operative enterprise, and forms the basis for the modern co-operative movement. There is debate about whether their society was the earliest group that can be called a co-op, but the Rochdale Pioneers were responsible for designing the Rochdale Principles, the set of rules that provide the foundation for the way co-operative groups operate around the world to this day. The model the Rochdale Pioneers used is a focus of study within Co-operative economics. Tel: 01706 524920.

Royal Exchange — St Ann's Square, Manchester. An impressive 19th century classical building complex in central Manchester. The current building is the last of several on the site used for trading of commodities such as cotton and textiles. The first exchange was built nearby in 1729; it was replaced by a larger building in 1806–9 and another in 1867–74. Extensions and modifications were carried out 1914–21 to form the largest trading room in England. A direct hit during World War II caused serious damage and the building reopened after reconstruction with a much smaller trading area. Trading ended in 1968 and the building remained empty until 1973 when it was used to temporarily house a theatre company. An IRA bomb in 1996 exploded less than 50 yards away, moving the dome (though the main structure was undamaged) and leading to closure for two years while repairs were carried out. Nearby St Ann's Church nevertheless survived almost intact, almost certainly due to the sheltering effect of the stone-built Exchange. The complex now includes the Royal Exchange Theatre and Royal Exchange shopping centre.

Royal Northern College of Music — Oxford Road, Manchester. A conservatoire situated at the northern end of the university area. The RNCM is both a centre of education and an arts centre holding musical concerts. Its current principal is the composer Professor Edward Gregson. The roots of the college begin in the late 19th century with Sir Charles Hallé's Royal Manchester College of Music (see Hallé Orchestra). In 1973, the Royal Manchester College of Music and the Northern School of Music merged to create the modern-day RNCM. Currently the college offers both undergraduate and postgraduate programmes in Performance and Composition. In January 2005, the RNCM was awarded £3.75 million by the Higher Education Funding Council to become a recognised Centre for Excellence in Teaching and Learning, the only UK conservatoire to be selected. Tel: 0161 907 5200.

St Ann's Church — St Ann's Square, Manchester. A Grade I listed Neoclassical building dating from 1712; the design was influenced by Sir Christopher Wren although the actual architect was probably his friend John Barker. The church tower is said to mark the exact centre of the city of Manchester. Tel: 0161 834 0239.

Salford Cathedral — Chapel Street, Salford. A Roman Catholic cathedral dedicated to St John the Evangelist. Built 1844–8, it was designed by Matthew Hadfield. Its spire is 239ft (73m) tall. It became a cathedral in 1850 with the establishment of the Diocese of Salford.

Salford Museum — Peel Park, The Crescent, Salford. Permanent exhibits include the Victorian Gallery and Lark Hill Place, a reassemblage of old shops, cobbled streets, furniture and shop windows, all collected from around the city, arranged in a fascinating recreation of a Victorian and Edwardian setting. There is a blacksmith's forge, pawnbroker, toy shop, cobbler, chemists, as well as working- and middle-class room settings. Tel: 0161 736 2649.

Sport

general — Manchester has much more than two football clubs. Belle Vue Stadium in Gorton is home to the **Belle Vue Aces** speedway team, which competes in the Elite League, and also hosts regular greyhound races. Tel: 0870 840 7557. Manchester also has an ice hockey team called **Manchester Phoenix**, based at the Altrincham Ice Dome. The city was previously home to the Manchester Storm ice hockey club who in 1997 played in front of the largest audience ever to watch an ice hockey game in the UK, when 17,245 people saw them defeat Sheffield Steelers 6–2 at the MEN Arena. Manchester also has an Australian Rules football club, **Manchester Mosquitoes**, who played their first season in the BARFL in 2006. Sportscity in Manchester (opened by HRH Princess Anne) is the administrative headquarters of the **English Institute of Sport**, a nationwide network of support services aimed at improving the standard of English athletes. Services include sports medicine, physiotherapy, sports massage, applied physiology, strength and conditioning, nutrition, psychology and Performance Lifestyle support. There are nine regional centres including Sportspark (Norwich), Loughborough University, Olympic Medical Insitute (London), Bisham Abbey, University of Bath and Sheffield.

football — Founded in 1874 as Christ Church FC, **Bolton Wanderers** became one of the original 12 founder members of the Football League in 1888. They won the first Wembley FA Cup final, beating West Ham 2–0, also winning the trophy on three other occasions. The club's nickname is the Trotters. After 102 years at Burnden Park, Bolton relocated to the new 28,700-seater Reebok Stadium, 5 miles (8km) from Bolton town centre at the Middlebrook complex, for the 1997–98 season. Tel: 01204 673673.

Bury were formed in 1885 and joined the Football League in 1894. Nicknamed the Shakers (after their manager, J T Ingham, promised that the team would 'shake' their stronger opponents in the 1892 Lancashire Cup final), the club play at Gigg Lane, Bury, which has been their home ground throughout their history. They are twice winners of the FA Cup (in 1900 and 1903), although they have recently spent several years in the lower divisions. Tel: 0161 764 4881.

Formed in 1880 as West Gorton (St Marks), **Manchester City** went on to become Ardwick AFC in 1887 before adopting their currrent name in 1894, two years after joining the Football League. The Blues' (sometimes called the Citizens) traditional colours are light blue and white. Manchester City's most successful period came in the late 1960s and early 1970s, when they acquired several trophies under the management team of Joe Mercer and assistant Malcolm Allison. In contrast the club were relegated twice in three years in the 1990s, spending a year in the third tier of English football. They have since regained their position in the Premier League, the division in which they have spent the majority of their history. Manchester City have won the League Championship twice and the FA Cup four times, as well as winning the European Cup Winners' Cup in 1970. The club regularly attracts more than 40,000 to their home ground, the City of Manchester Stadium, Eastlands, Manchester. Tel: 0870 062 1894.

Manchester United were formed as Newton Heath LYRFC in 1878, the works team of the Lancashire and Yorkshire Railway depot at Newton Heath; the club started to sever its links with the rail depot in 1890, becoming Newton Heath FC. The Red Devils, as they are known (a nickname said to have been 'borrowed' by the club's great manager Matt Busby from Salford RFC in the 1960s), joined the Football League in 1892, the same year as their great rivals Manchester City. In 1958 eight United players died in the Munich air disaster (see Interesting Facts). Today United are one of the most popular clubs in the world, with over 50 million supporters worldwide. The club is second only to Liverpool in terms of trophies won by an English club – 17 League championships, 11 FA Cups and 3 European Cups as of 2008 – and regularly has the highest average attendance in English football. From 1991, United was run as a plc, with an attempted takeover by Rupert Murdoch in 1998 blocked by the government. However, in May 2005 Malcolm Glazer completed a hostile takeover of the club and delisted it from the Stock Exchange. They play at Old Trafford, Manchester. Tel: 0870 442 1994.

Oldham Athletic were formed in 1895 as Pine Villa FC, being renamed in 1899. They joined the Football League in 1907. Oldham were founder members of the FA Premier League in 1992/93, but have spent most of their subsequent history in the lower divisions. Nicknamed The Latics, their home ground is Boundary Park, Oldham. Tel: 0871 226 2235.

Rochdale were founded in 1907 and joined the Football League in 1921. They were finalists in the League Cup in 1962, losing to Norwich City, and have been promoted just once in their history, reaching the Third Division in 1968/9. Nicknamed simply (The) Dale, their home ground is Spotland, Willbutts Lane, Rochdale. Tel: 0870 822 1907.

Stockport County were founded in 1883 as Heaton Norris Rovers and adopted their present name in 1890. They joined the Football League in 1900. As of 2008 they hold the record for the longest run of Football League wins without conceding a goal (nine, in 2006/07). Nicknamed The Hatters (the town having been a hat-making centre in the Victorian era) or more recently simply County, their home ground is Edgeley Park, Hardcastle Road, Stockport. Tel: 0161 286 8888.

Wigan Athletic were founded in 1932 and joined the Football League in 1978. The Latics share the JJB Stadium with Wigan Warriors rugby league club. With the help of finance from multimillionaire former player Dave Whelan, owner of the JJB sports shop chain, the club has had tremendous success in recent years, culminating in promotion to the Premiership in 2005. Tel: 01942 774000.

There are also numerous high-profile non-league football teams, including Altrincham, Stalybridge Celtic, Droylsden, Hyde United and the recently created FC United of Manchester.

rugby league

Salford City Reds are based in Salford. They play in the Super League. Founded in 1873 their nickname is 'The Red Devils', a name later copied by nearby Manchester United FC. For this reason they are sometimes known as 'The Original Red Devils' or simply 'The Reds'. The team play in red, white and black and their current home ground is The Willows, Weaste, Salford. The club is set to move to a new purpose-built 20,000 capacity stadium in the Barton-upon-Irwell area of Salford in 2009. Tel: 0161 736 6564.

Wigan Warriors were founded in 1872 as Wigan RFC and famously sport a cherry and white home strip. In recent years the club has played at the JJB Stadium, Newtown, Wigan, also the home ground of Wigan Athletic FC. The team currently plays in the Super League. Tel: 01942 774000.

Leigh Centurions and **Rochdale Hornets** play in National League 1.

rugby union

Sale Sharks were founded in 1861 and are in recent years have been one of England's leading rugby union sides, winning the Guinness Premiership in 2006. Sale play at Edgeley Park, also the home of Stockport County FC. Tel: 0161 286 8888.

Sunlight House

Quay Street, Manchester. A fine art deco office building built in 1932 by Joseph Sunlight. At 14 storeys and 135ft (41m), it was reputed to be northern England's first skyscraper and was for many years the city's tallest building. It is constructed of steel and concrete and clad in Portland stone. The original plans for 40 storeys were blocked by the city council. The building was renovated in the late 1990s and now houses shops and offices. Widely reputed to be haunted, it is Grade II listed.

University of Bolton

Deane Road, Bolton. The former Bolton Institute of Higher Education became Britain's newest university in April 2004, adopting the title of the University of Bolton in January 2005 after several months of consultation. Bolton Institute of Higher Education came into being in 1982, but its origins can be traced back to the early 19th century when Bolton first became involved in a continuous programme of vocational and educational training. Tel: 01204 900600.

University of Manchester

Oxford Road, Manchester. Created in autumn 2004 by the merger of Victoria University of Manchester (itself usually referred to as the University of Manchester) and University of Manchester Institute of Science and Technology (UMIST), the University of Manchester is the largest single-campus university in the UK with over 40,000 students in 2007. The university has its roots in the Mechanics' Institute, founded by chemist John Dalton in 1824, which grew into UMIST, and with Owens College, founded in 1851 and which later became Victoria University. The University of Manchester is grouped with Manchester Metropolitan University and the Royal Northern College of Music (see separate entries) on the southern side of the city centre, effectively forming one large campus in the vicinity of Oxford Road (with the exception of the North Campus of the University of Manchester, which was the UMIST campus before the merger). A member of the Russell Group of research-led universities, the university has made groundbreaking contributions to science, especially to physics, and has numbered several Nobel Prize winners among its staff including Ernest Rutherford, Niels Bohr, James Chadwick and Sir John Sulston. Manchester Business School, which offered the first MBA course in the UK in 1965, also forms a part of the university. University departments include the John Rylands University Library, Manchester Museum and Whitworth Art Gallery (see separate entries). Tel: 0161 306 6000.

University of Salford — 1½ miles (2.5km) west of Manchester. Its main campus is at Peel Park, opened in 1846 and one of the first public parks in England. A charter of 1967 raised the Royal Salford Technical Institute to the status of university by establishing the University of Salford. In 2007 it had over 19,000 students, 3000 from overseas. Academically it is traditionally strong in engineering, but also offers unusual courses such as traditional Chinese medicine. A new Business School opened in 2006 and a Law School in 2007. Former students include artist L S Lowry, comedian Peter Kay, actor Christopher Eccleston and rugby union player Ieuan Evans. Tel: 0161 295 5000.

Urbis — Cathedral Gardens, Manchester. An exhibition centre focusing on city life. Urbis' exhibition programme explores the culture and dynamism of cities around the world, covering photography, design, architecture, music and contemporary art. Tel: 0161 605 8200.

Victoria Baths — Hathersage Road, Chorlton-on-Medlock, Manchester. Designed as a prestigious baths complex by Manchester's first city architect, Henry Price, and opened by Manchester Corporation in 1906. The façade has multi-coloured brickwork and terracotta decoration, the main interior public spaces are clad in glazed tiles from floor to ceiling and most of the many windows have decorative stained glass. The building housed private baths and a laundry along with three swimming pools and Turkish baths. The main swimming pool was floored over in the winter months to hold dances. In 1952 the Victoria Baths installed the first public Aeratone (Jacuzzi) in England. The baths were closed in 1993. The building is now in very poor repair and yet remarkably intact with most of the stained glass and original tiling remaining. The Victoria Baths is now Grade II* listed and was the winner of the 2003 BBC series *Restoration*.

Werneth Low — A hill located on the borders of Stockport and Tameside, rising to a height of 816ft (249m); part of the Pennine range, it offers views over the Manchester conurbation. Much of the high ground is a country park, purchased by the local community in 1920. Its focal point is a memorial to the war dead of the town of Hyde, which lies at its foot.

Wet Earth Colliery — Clifton, Salford. Wet Earth Colliery has a unique place in British coal mining history as it is the place where engineer James Brindley made water run uphill. The colliery is located on the Irwell Valley Fault, which follows the River Irwell north to south, eventually becoming the Pendleton Fault. Many other local mines were situated on these two major faults, which threw up the underlying Carboniferous coal measures by some 1000m, making them accessible for mining. To the north of the fault is the red Triassic sandstone, to the south are the Coal Measures which in places outcrop at surface.

Whitworth Art Gallery — Oxford Road, Manchester. Known internationally for its collections of art and design, the Whitworth Art Gallery, part of the University of Manchester, is home to an impressive range of watercolours, prints, drawings, modern art and sculpture, as well as the largest collections of textiles and wallpapers outside London. Tel: 0161 275 7450.

Wigan — The former coal-mining and mill town of Wigan lies 9 miles (15km) to the west of Bolton. The first people believed to have settled in the area of modern Wigan were the Brigantes. The Roman fort of Coccium was established in the vicinity c.AD 79. The town is traditionally said to have received its royal charter from Henry III in 1246; its main product was wool, while coal mining was established in the area during the Middle Ages, and other industries included clock making and pewter manufacture. Wigan was Royalist during the Civil War, and the Battle of Wigan Lane (see Battles) took place in 1651. The town became a major centre of coal mining and textile manufacture during the Industrial Revolution, growing massively after the Leeds and Liverpool Canal reached it in 1779 (Wigan Pier, given renown by George Formby and George Orwell, was once a landing stage on the canal). During the 20th century, the town's industries shared in the decline experienced by many manufacturing centres. Its last major colliery closing in 1992, but it is still the home of the confectionery treat known as Uncle Joe's Mint Balls, and the area around the former Wigan Pier has been redeveloped as a tourist attraction.

Wigan Casino — A major venue in the 1970s for Northern Soul music, carrying forward the legacy created at the Twisted Wheel in Manchester and Stoke-on-Trent's legendary Golden Torch. The Casino opened in September 1973 in a former dance hall. Many famous soul performers appeared here including Jackie Wilson, Edwin Starr and Junior Walker. A TV documentary, *This England*, about the venue was filmed in 1977. The Casino finally closed in 1981, and the building itself burned down a year later. Russ Winstanley (the Casino's DJ and founder) and David Nowell wrote the book *The Wigan Casino Story*, which was published in 1996. A stage play about the Casino, *Once Upon a Time In Wigan*, written by Mick Martin, debuted in February 2003 at the Contact Theatre, Manchester, and later toured nationally.

Wyberslegh Hall — High Lane, 4 miles (6km) southeast of Stockport. Sometimes spelt Wybersley Hall, this large house dating from the 16th century was formerly the home of the eldest sons of the Bradshaw family. Hardly a handsome house although an historic one, it has castellated gables with an ungainly castellated wall between them, above the main entrance. John Bradshaw, presiding judge at the trial of Charles I, was probably born here in 1602. More recently, author Christopher Isherwood, another member of the Bradshaw family, was also born in the house.

Wythenshawe Hall — Wythenshawe Park, Northenden, 5 miles (8km) south of Manchester. The half-timbered Tudor house, home of the Tatton family for over 400 years, was built c.1540 by Robert Tatton of Chester.

The hall was a Royalist stronghold during the Civil War, falling to Cromwell's forces in 1644 after a three-month siege, although it was later returned to the Tatton family. In the 18th century the estate was expanded to 2500 acres (1000ha). The last heir, Robert Henry Greville Tatton, was persuaded to sell the estate to the Manchester Corporation in 1926 and most of the land was used to build what was then one of the largest housing estates in Europe; the hall and the remaining 250 acres (100ha) of land were bought by a benefactor and given to the City of Manchester to be maintained as an open space for the people of the city. Every June, there is a re-enactment of the Siege of Wythenshawe Hall by Cromwell's troops during the winter of 1643. Tel: 0161 998 2331.

Ye Olde Man and Scythe — Church Gate, Bolton. One of Britain's ten oldest public houses and the oldest in Bolton. Ye Olde Man and Scythe is perhaps most famous for playing host to James Stanley, 7th Earl of Derby, who took his last meal here before stepping outside to be beheaded. Within the pub is a chair in which the Earl sat on that fateful day, and on which an inscription reads: '15th October 1651 In this chair James 7th Earl of Derby sat at the Man and Scythe Inn, Churchgate, Bolton immediately prior to his execution'. Due to this beheading of a royal, Bolton was excluded from being given city status. The exact date the pub was built is unknown but a charter of 1251 permitting the market mentions it by name. Due to the age of the building, it has been rebuilt at least once (in 1636, according to the datestone inside), and only the vaulted cellar remains of the original building, though some of the internal beams remain from the 1636 reconstruction. Tel: 01204 527267.

Some famous people born in Greater Manchester

Abercrombie, (Sir) Leslie Patrick (architect) (1879–1957)	Ashton upon Mersey
Bright, John (statesman) (1811–89)	Rochdale
Cooke, Alistair (broadcaster) (1908–2004)	Salford
Crompton, Richmal (author) (1890–1969)	Ramsbottom
Crompton, Samuel (inventor) (1753–1827)	Bolton
Davies, Sir Peter Maxwell (composer) (1934–)	Salford
Dawson, Les (comedian) (1934–93)	Manchester
Delaney, Shelagh (playwright) (1939–)	Salford
Donat, (Friedrich) Robert (actor) (1905–58)	Withington
Eccleston, Christopher (actor) (1964–)	Salford
Fields, Dame Gracie (entertainer, born Grace Stansfield) (1898–1979)	Rochdale
Finlay, Frank (actor) (1926–)	Farnworth
Finney, Albert (actor) (1936–)	Salford
Formby, George (entertainer, born William Booth) (1904–61)	Wigan
Gallagher, Liam (musician, born William John Paul Gallagher) (1972–)	Longsight
Gallagher, Noel Thomas David (musician) (1967–)	Burnage
Greenwood, Walter (writer) (1903–74)	Salford
Harris, Reg (cyclist) (1920–92)	Bury
Hiller, Wendy (actress) (1912–2003)	Stockport
Hilton, James (writer) (1900–54)	Leigh
Isherwood, Christopher (novelist) (1904–86)	Stockport
Joule, James Prescott (physicist) (1818–89)	Sale
Kay, John (inventor of the flying shuttle) (1704–80)	Bury
Kay, Peter (comedian and actor) (1973–)	Bolton
Khan, Amir (boxer) (1986–)	Bolton
Lawton, Tommy (footballer) (1919–96)	Farnworth
Leigh, Mike (film director) (1943–)	Salford
Peel, Sir Robert (politician) (1788–1850)	Bury
Perry, Fred (tennis player) (1909–95)	Stockport
Powell, Robert (actor) (1944–)	Salford
Ray, Ted (comedian) (1905–77)	Wigan
Shaw, Robert (actor) (1927–78)	Westhoughton
Sykes, Eric (actor) (1923–)	Oldham
Tyson, Frank (cricketer) (1930–)	Farnworth
Walton, Sir William (composer) (1902–83)	Oldham

HAMPSHIRE (AND THE ISLE OF WIGHT)

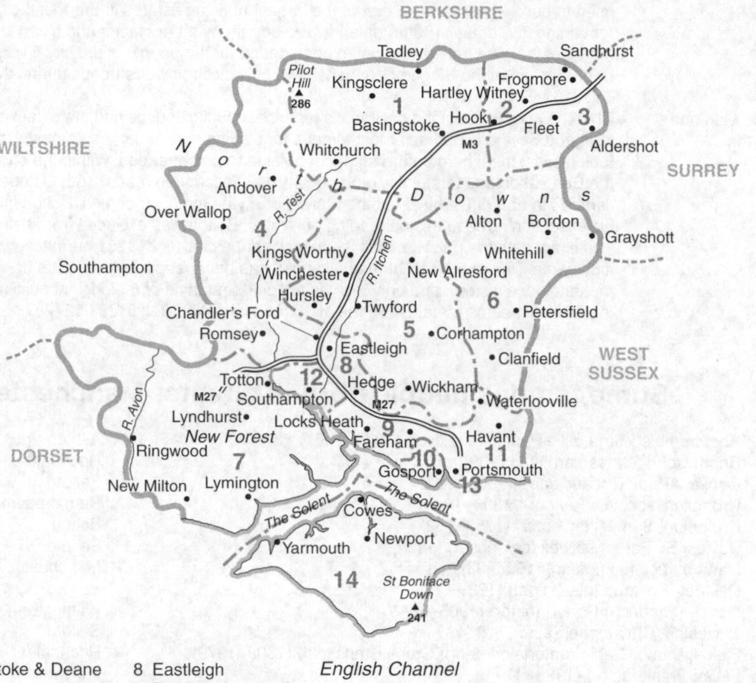

BERKSHIRE
WILTSHIRE
SURREY
WEST SUSSEX
DORSET
Tadley
Sandhurst
Pilot Hill
286
Kingsclere
Frogmore
Hartley Witney
1
2
3
Basingstoke
Hook
Fleet
Aldershot
M3
N o r t h D o w n s
Whitchurch
Andover
R. Test
Over Wallop
4
Alton
Bordon
Grayshott
R. Itchen
Whitehill
Southampton
Kings Worthy
Winchester
New Alresford
Hursley
Twyford
6
Petersfield
Chandler's Ford
5
Cornhampton
Romsey
Eastleigh
Clanfield
8
R. Avon
Totton
12
Hedge
Wickham
M27
Southampton
M27
Waterlooville
Lyndhurst
Locks Heath
9
Havant
New Forest
Fareham
11
Ringwood
10
7
Gosport
Portsmouth
13
New Milton
Lymington
The Solent
Cowes
The Solent
Newport
Yarmouth
14
St Boniface Down
241
English Channel

Districts

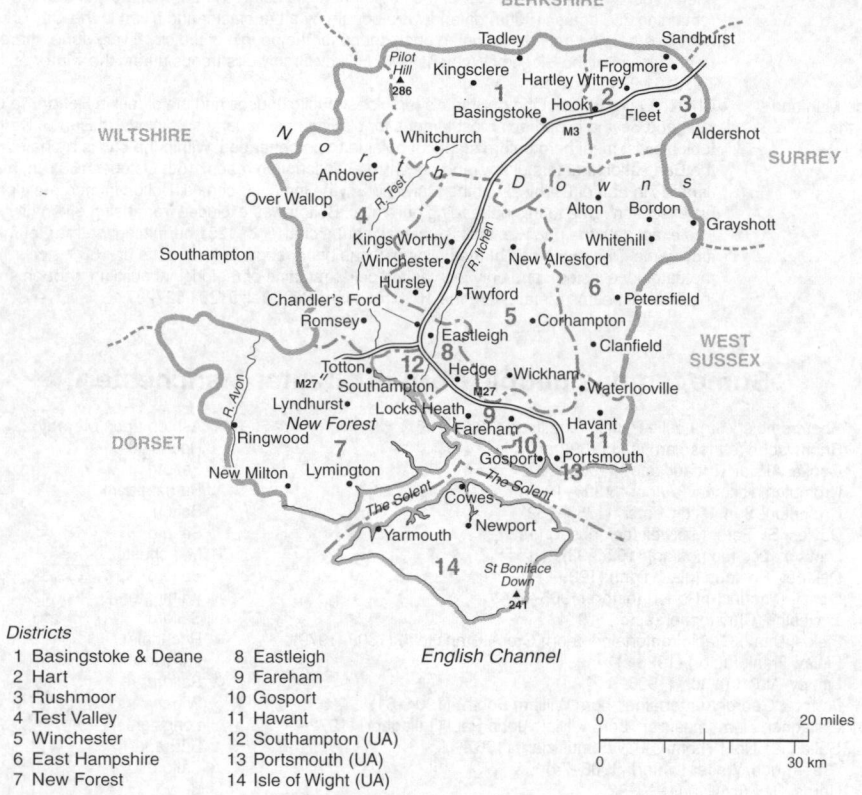

1 Basingstoke & Deane	8 Eastleigh
2 Hart	9 Fareham
3 Rushmoor	10 Gosport
4 Test Valley	11 Havant
5 Winchester	12 Southampton (UA)
6 East Hampshire	13 Portsmouth (UA)
7 New Forest	14 Isle of Wight (UA)

0 20 miles
0 30 km

Hampshire is a county on the south coast of England bordering Dorset to its west, Wiltshire to its west and northwest, the former county of Berkshire to its north, Surrey to its northeast and West Sussex to its east. The Isle of Wight became a unitary authority in 1995, while both Portsmouth and Southampton achieved similar status in 1997.

Geologically Hampshire is divided broadly into two; the chalk downland of the South Downs and southern edges of Salisbury Plain lies to the north and east, while to the south and west are the clay and gravel of the coastal plain and the lowland heath of the New Forest. The chalk downland was settled in the Neolithic period, and these settlers farmed the county's valleys. The area was occupied by Jutes and various other Germanic tribes from the 4th century. Hampshire was recorded in the Anglo-Saxon Chronicle of AD 755 as one of the first Saxon shires, but for two centuries it had represented the western limit of Saxon England. After the Saxons advanced west, Hampshire became the centre of the kingdom of Wessex and Alfred the Great made Winchester his capital in 871.

After the Norman Conquest the county was favoured by Norman kings who established the New Forest as a royal hunting ground. From the 12th century Hampshire's ports grew in importance. Fuelled by trade with the Continent, wool and cloth manufacture and the fishing industry, a shipbuilding industry was established (Gosport, Portsmouth and Southampton are three of England's leading ports). Over several centuries a series of castles and forts were constructed along the coast of the Solent to defend the harbours at Portsmouth and Southampton. Hampshire played a major role in World War II due to its large Royal Navy harbour at Portsmouth, the army camp at Aldershot and the military Netley Hospital on Southampton Water. Aldershot is one of the British Army's main permanent camps.

Hampshire remains diversely based commercially. While much of the county is agricultural, devoted to grain production, dairy farming and market gardening, in contrast there is oil refining at Fawley and aircraft engineering at Farnborough.

Winchester is the county town. Its origins are as a Roman town from c. AD 70. The Romans named it Venta Belgarum, 'the capital of the Belgares' (the local Celtic tribe before the Roman conquest). The Saxons arrived in the 6th century, occupying the site which became known as Venta Caester (the Saxon name for a Roman settlement being *caester*). In time this was Anglicised to Wintancaester and eventually to Winchester. Late in the 9th century Alfred the Great revived the old Roman town, defending his kingdom vigorously against the Danes by forming a network of fortified places. In the 10th century there was a Saxon royal palace in Winchester and the capital of Wessex became the capital of England. In 1066, after the Battle of Hastings, King Harold's widow surrendered the town to the Normans and was allowed to leave in peace. William I rebuilt the royal palace, regarding Winchester and London as twin capitals. In 1086 the Domesday survey was compiled in the town.

Winchester became a major centre for pilgrimage during the Middle Ages as the starting point for the Pilgrims' Way to the shrine of St Thomas Becket at Canterbury. The town's main industry in the period was making woollen cloth. There were weekly markets, while an annual fair, which began on the feast of St Giles, 1 September, was held on a hill east of the town which became known as St Giles Hill. Winchester declined during the 12th and 13th centuries as London grew and became the new capital, and in the mid 13th century the royal mint was moved to London. Half the town's population was devastated in the 14th century during the Black Death; plague struck again in 1603 and 1625, with a final outbreak in 1665–6.

During the Civil War Winchester was largely Royalist, and Royalist soldiers occupied the town until the end of 1642, when it was captured by Parliamentary troops. In 1651 Cromwell's men destroyed Winchester Castle to prevent it falling into Royalist hands; only the great hall remained.

Due largely to the railway, which reached the town in 1840 and encouraged the development of new industries, prosperity returned to Winchester in the 19th century and the population grew rapidly. In 1901 a statue of King Alfred was erected to commemorate the 1000th anniversary of his death. (Historians now believe Alfred died in 899.) An industrial estate at Winnall was opened in 1948 and grew rapidly during the 1950s. A study by Channel 4 in October 2006 named Winchester the most agreeable place to live in Britain.

Portsmouth was founded c.1180 by a wealthy Norman landowner and merchant, Jean de Gisors, who established a settlement on Portsea Island. On 2 May 1194 the town was granted its first royal charter from Richard I, who was in Portsmouth at the time before making the sea crossing to Normandy. King John established the town as a naval base for attacks on Normandy, the first docks being built in 1212. The Hospital of St Nicholas or Domus Dei and the parish church, later the cathedral, were founded at this time. The town was attacked several times by the French in the following century, and was fortified as a consequence. In 1418 two round towers were built to improve its security as a haven. The Round Tower, originally built in wood, with a sister tower on the Gosport shore, was rebuilt in stone 60 years later and remained a key part of the city's defences for centuries before its purchase by the city council in 1958. In 1494 the Square Tower was built as a gun platform and house; it still stands at the southwest end of the High Street. In June 1495, Henry VII gave orders for the construction of a dry dock at Portsmouth, the first known to have been built in England. The *Sovereign* was the first ship to enter it on 25 May 1496. The castle by the South Sea's buildings was commenced in 1538 under Henry VIII, and the building of this castle gave birth to the area known as Southsea. Two small circular forts on the shore, one on the site of Lumps Fort and the other at Eastney, were also built at the time.

In 1561 Elizabeth I visited Portsmouth for the first time and subsequently increased the town's fortifications, the cost of which was subsidised by the first state lottery. The scheme consisted of 400,000 tickets costing ten shillings each, the first prize being £5000 made up of £3000 in cash with £700 worth of plate and the rest in tapestries and linens. There were twenty-five prizes to the value of £100 or more.

In 1628 one of the king's advisors, the Duke of Buckingham, was assassinated in Portsmouth, stabbed to death in a house in High Street by a sailor named John Fenton, who was hanged for the crime. During the Civil War in 1642 Colonel George Goring, commander of the Portsmouth garrison, declared his support for the king; Parliamentary forces blockaded the town and took Southsea Castle, and the Royalist troops were eventually forced to surrender.

Portsmouth again prospered as a centre of shipbuilding after the Restoration. The former residential portion of the Domus Dei, used as an armoury since the Dissolution of the Monasteries in 1540, had in 1658 been converted into a residence for the governor, continuing to fulfil that function for 300 years, and the wedding of Catherine of Braganza and Charles II was celebrated in the building's great hall. In 1733 the Royal Naval Academy was established at Portsmouth, continuing to train officers and cadets until 1873 when it transferred to Greenwich. The town and its naval base were once again vital to the security of England during the Napoleonic Wars, when HMS *Victory* under Admiral Nelson sailed from the port to gain victory in the Battle of Trafalgar.

The decision taken by the Admiralty to transform the old Gunwharf into a training establishment for officers and men in torpedo warfare resulted in the birth of the shore-based HMS *Vernon* in 1923. This area of Portsmouth has now been turned into Gunwharf Quays.

Portsmouth was awarded city status in 1926. Because of its strategic importance, the city endured heavy bombardment during World War II: Clarence Pier, opened in June 1861, and Portsmouth Town Hall, opened on 9 August 1890 by the Prince and Princess of Wales, were among the many landmarks to suffer severe damage from German bombing, although the former was reopened in 1961 and the latter has also been restored to its former splendour. Portsmouth played a central role in the planning and execution of the D-Day landings, and the city found itself once again preparing for war in the spring of 1982 after Argentine troops invaded the Falkland Islands on 2 April. The taskforce of ships which left from Portsmouth included the aircraft carriers *Hermes* and *Invincible*.

Modern Portsmouth is still a focus for the navy – today Her Majesty's Naval Base Portsmouth (HMS *Nelson*) is the base of two-thirds of the Royal Navy's surface fleet, including the aircraft carriers *Illustrious* and *Ark Royal* – but the city has expanded far beyond the island of Portsea. Shipbuilding and engineering are no longer major employers, but diversification into electronics and financial services has taken place.

In 1994 Portsmouth hosted the 50th anniversary of D-Day and in addition celebrated the 800th anniversary of gaining its first royal charter. That year on 7 July the city also hosted Stage 5 of the Tour de France cycle race, one of two British stages (the other being Stage 4 from Dover to Brighton). In 1997 HMY *Britannia* was decommissioned – the last in a long line of royal yachts, she had been based in Portsmouth for the whole of her life. The Pompey Centre was built in 2003 and Portsmouth's newest tourist attraction, the Spinnaker Tower, opened in 2005; in the same year, celebrations took place to commemorate the bicentenary of Nelson's victory at Trafalgar.

Located on the sea inlet of Southampton Water, **Southampton** also has a long maritime history. It originates c. AD 70 with the town of Clausentum, built by the Romans on a bend in the River Itchen where the suburb of Bitterne now stands. Clausentum was abandoned soon after the Roman army left Britain in AD 407 and the Saxon king, Ine, built a new town on the western side of the Itchen c.690–700, roughly on the location of modern St Mary's. The new town, called Hamwic or Hamtun – later corrupted to Southampton – was a successful port with a population estimated at 4000–5000, very large by Saxon standards. By the 9th century there was a royal mint in the town.

After the Norman Conquest Southampton, with its proximity to Winchester, became a major embarkation point for travel to France. The town was settled by large numbers of Normans, many of them traders, a fact acknowledged by the existence of the thoroughfare called French Street. By the 14th century the town was the third largest port in England after London and Bristol, trading mainly with Italy. After the town was attacked in 1338 by a force of Frenchmen and Sicilians, in 1339 Edward III visited Southampton and ordered improvements to be made to the fortifications. Several new towers were added to the walls and in 1378–80 the castle keep was rebuilt. The northern gate, known as Bargate, was given a new façade with machicolations (holes in a ledge overhanging the gate through which boiling water could be poured and large stones could be dropped) – the gate still stands at the top of the High Street – and the walls of the town were extended along the seafront. Today Southampton has more of its walls remaining than any other English town or city with the exception of York.

In the late 15th century the Italian trade declined steeply before ceasing altogether in the early 16th century. Southampton also lost its monopoly on the export of lead and tin in 1531. In 1618 James I sold Southampton Castle, which was now in ruins, and the town languished during the 17th century, although it was the original embarkation point for the *Mayflower*.

In the 18th century, however, the town began to prosper again due to the growing trend for bathing in sea water (although towns such as Brighton soon superseded it as a bathing destination). More importantly, its trading position began to improve with the general increase in trade brought about by the Industrial Revolution. New docks were built in 1838–42, and shipyards were constructed along the Itchen.

With the advent of steam ships, passenger trade also increased dramatically. In 1907 White Star transatlantic liners moved to Southampton – the *Titanic* sailed from the port in 1912 – and in 1919 the town became the terminus of Cunard's New York service. From 1913 flying boats were manufactured in the town, first by Sopwith and later by the Supermarine company, and in 1923 a flying boat service to the Channel Islands began operating. In 1932 the council purchased an airport at Eastleigh, which by 1934 had become the third most important in Britain. During World War II the Spitfire fighter was manufactured in Southampton, which like Portsmouth suffered heavy bombing due to its strategic importance.

By 1958 flying boats had ceased to operate but the world's first hovercraft flight took place in Southampton in 1959. In 1961 car ferries to France began running, and in 1962 a hovercraft service to the Isle of Wight began. In 1964 Southampton was awarded city status. It is still a major port with several container terminals, as well as heavy industries such as petrochemicals. Other significant employers include the Ordnance Survey.

Separated from the Hampshire coast by the stretch of water known as the Solent, the **Isle of Wight** became an island after the end of the last Ice Age when the rising sea flooded the Solent, separating the island from the mainland. Often erroneously thought of as part of Hampshire, the Isle of Wight has had a separate county council since 1890 and was only briefly included as part of Hants when the first county councils were created in 1888. It was planned to merge the county back into Hampshire as a district in the 1974 local government reform, but a last-minute reprieve led to it retaining its county council. At this time the Island maintained a two-tier structure, with a county council and two boroughs, Medina and South Wight. The only significant present-day administrative link with Hampshire is the police service, which is joint between Hampshire and the Isle of Wight.

Part of Celtic Britain, the island was known to the Romans as Vectis, being captured by Vespasian during the Roman invasion. After the Roman era the island was settled by the Jutes in the early stages of the Anglo-Saxon invasions. The island did not come under full control of the Crown until it was sold to Edward I in 1293. Henry VIII fortified the island at Yarmouth, East and West Cowes and Sandown, sometimes reusing stone from dissolved monasteries as building material. Sir Richard Worsley, Captain of the Island at the time, successfully commanded resistance to the last of the French attacks in 1545. After the Spanish Armada in 1588 the threat of Spanish attacks remained, and the outer fortifications of Carisbrooke Castle (see separate entry) were built. During the Civil War Charles I fled to the Isle of Wight believing he would receive sympathy from the governor Robert Hammond, was instead incarcerated in Carisbrooke Castle. Queen Victoria made Osborne House her summer home for many years, and as a result it become a major holiday resort for members of European royalty. In 1944 the world's first production submarine oil pipeline was laid between the Isle of Wight and France in Operation Pluto (Pipe Line Under The Ocean). The Royal Yacht Squadron has its home at Cowes.

The main form of access is either by boat or hovercraft from the mainland; regular ferry services are available from Lymington, Southampton and Portsmouth. The island is also served by airports for light aircraft at Bembridge and Sandown and has the smallest train service in the National Rail network, the Island Line, running $8^1/_2$ miles (13.5km) from Ryde Pier Head to Shanklin down the eastern side of the island. A steam-operated heritage railway, the Isle of Wight Steam Railway, connects with the Island Line at Smallbrook Junction.

Nearly half the island's area, mainly in the west, is a designated Area of Outstanding Natural Beauty. West Wight is predominantly rural, with dramatic coastlines dominated by a chalk downland ridge that runs across the whole island, ending in the Needles (see separate entry). Its wildlife is notable; the island is the only place in England with a stable population of red squirrels – unlike the rest of England, there are no grey squirrels to be found on the island. Nor are there any wild deer, but instead rare and protected species such as the dormouse, and many rare bats can be found. The Glanville fritillary butterfly is restricted to the edges of the crumbling cliffs, and is unique here in the British Isles. On a more negative note, in 1904 a mysterious illness began to kill honeybee colonies on the island, and had nearly wiped out all hives by 1907 when the disease jumped to the mainland, and decimated beekeeping in the British Isles. Called the Isle of Wight Disease, the cause of the mystery ailment was not identified until 1921 when it was traced to the mite *Acarapis woodi*. The disease (now called Acarine disease) was of great concern because of the importance of bees in pollination of many food plants.

The island has its own lexical style. Some words like 'grockel' (visitor) and 'nipper/nips' (addressing a younger person) are shared with neighbouring regions. Others are unique, for example 'mallishag' (meaning caterpillar) and 'nammit' (food).

The island has attracted many famous visitors in search of inspiration. Alfred, Lord Tennyson rented a house (Farringford) overlooking Freshwater Bay in 1853 and bought it in 1858. Many landmarks on the island still bear his name. It is believed that he wrote *The Charge of the Light Brigade* on the island and 'Crossing the Bar' on his journey between his home and the mainland. Lewis Carroll also stayed at Freshwater while collecting material for *Alice in Wonderland.* Charles Darwin stayed at the King's Head Hotel in Sandown during the summer of 1867 and it is believed that this is where he began his work on *The Origin of Species*. Charles Dickens rented a house in the summer of 1845 at what is now the Winterbourne Hotel in Bonchurch. He adored the views from St Boniface Downs, northwest of the village, and *David Copperfield* was written during his stay. J M W Turner visited the island in 1795 to sketch many of its beautiful landscapes. He later returned as a guest of John Nash, who constructed East Cowes Castle, sadly demolished in the 1960s. The American poet Henry Wadsworth Longfellow visited Shanklin in 1868. A fountain outside the Crab Inn, where he stayed while on the Island, still carries an engraving left by him. Karl Marx visited the island for health reasons; he went to Ryde in the summer of 1874 and later stayed in Ventnor in 1881 after the death of his wife, returning once again before leaving at the news of his daughter's death. J B Priestley lived on the Island at Billingham Manor House, near Chale Green, until World War II and at Brook Hill House from 1948.

Hampshire (and the Isle of Wight)	**Population**			**Area**	
Districts	*male*	*female*	*total*	*sq miles*	*sq km*
Basingstoke & Deane	75,556	77,017	152,573	245	634
East Hampshire	53,733	55,541	109,274	199	514
Eastleigh	57,000	59,169	116,169	31	80
Fareham	52,882	55,095	107,977	29	74
Gosport	37,339	39,076	76,415	10	25
Hart	42,059	41,446	83,505	83	215
Havant	56,111	60,738	116,849	21	55
New Forest	81,017	88,314	169,331	291	753
Rushmoor	45,882	45,105	90,987	15	39
Test Valley	53,908	55,893	109,801	242	628
Winchester	52,556	54,666	107,222	255	661
Isle of Wight Unitary Authority	63,697	69,034	132,731	147	380
Portsmouth Unitary Authority	92,042	94,659	186,701	15	40
Southampton Unitary Authority	108,784	108,661	217,445	19	50
Total	872,566	904,414	1,776,980	1602	4148

Local Attractions and Information

Abbey Gardens High Street, Winchester. Part of the site of St Mary's Abbey, dissolved in 1539. The River Itchen flows through what is now a beautiful flowered retreat.

Administrative headquarters
Hampshire: The Castle, Winchester SO23 8UJ. Tel: 01962 870500.
Isle of Wight: County Hall, High Street, Newport, Isle Of Wight PO30 1UD. Tel: 01983 821000.
Portsmouth: Guildhall Square, Portsmouth PO1 2BG. Tel: 02392 822251.
Southampton: Civic Centre, Southampton SO14 7LY. Tel: 02380 223855.

Aldershot Administered by Rushmoor Borough Council, Aldershot is known for its connection with the British Army which established a permanent camp in the area for instruction in military manoeuvres in 1854. This led to rapid growth from a small village to a Victorian town. The nearby villages of Ash and Ash Vale are in Surrey, though their postal addresses are 'Ash, Aldershot, Hampshire' and 'Ash Vale, Aldershot, Hampshire'. On 22 February 1972 Aldershot experienced one of the worst mainland IRA attacks. Seven civilian support staff, including cooks, cleaners and a Catholic priest, were killed in a car bomb attack on the 16th Parachute Brigade headquarters mess at Aldershot. This blast was later claimed by the Official IRA as revenge for the shootings in Derry that came to be known as Bloody Sunday. A memorial has since been built on the site. Aldershot was immortalised by John Betjeman in his poem 'A Subaltern's Love-song': 'Miss J. Hunter Dunn, Miss J. Hunter Dunn/Furnish'd and burnish'd by Aldershot sun/What strenuous singles we played after tea/We in the tournament – you against me!'

Aldershot Observatory Queens Avenue, Aldershot. A circular red-brick building with a domed roof, inside which is an 8in (20cm) refractor telescope. The telescope and observatory building were a gift from aviation pioneer Patrick Young Alexander to the British Army, a fact which is recorded by a plaque near the observatory door reading: 'Presented to the Aldershot Army Corps by Patrick Y Alexander Esq 1906'.

Alum Bay 3 miles (5km) west of Freshwater, Isle of Wight. Located on the west coast of the Isle of Wight, Alum Bay is famed for its coloured sands. Alum, a double sulphate of aluminium and potassium used in papermaking, tanning, and medicine, was first mined in the area during the reign of Elizabeth I. The cliff overlooks the famous Needles chalk stack (see separate entry). Standing on the cliff above the bay are the Needles Old Battery and New Battery, now owned by the National Trust; the former is a gun emplacement built in 1862 to defend against the threat of French invasion, the latter was used for testing rockets during World War II.

Appuldurcombe House Wroxall, 2 miles (3km) northwest of Ventnor, Isle of Wight. Once the grandest and most striking house on the Isle of Wight, only the shell remains of the 18th century mansion built on the Appuldurcombe estate. Building of the Baroque-style house commenced in 1701 to replace a large Tudor house inherited by Sir Robert Worsley, but was not completed until 70 years later by his great-nephew Sir Richard. The gardens were designed by Capability Brown. After Sir Richard's death in 1805 the house had several owners. The 1st Baron Yarborough (1805–55) retained the property as a base for his sailing activities out of Cowes. Four years later, an attempt was made to run Appuldurcombe as a hotel, but with its failure the house was leased for use as a college. During the early 20th century, it accommodated Benedictine monks, forced to leave their abbey in France. From then on it remained largely uninhabited, except by troops during both world wars, and was damaged by a mine which fell close by in 1943. Saved from demolition, the east front has now been restored. The house is in the care of English Heritage. Tel: 01983 840188.

Automobile Association Formed by a group of motoring enthusiasts who met at the Trocadero restaurant in London's West End on 29 June 1905, initially to help motorists avoid police speed traps. In 1973 the AA moved its headquarters from London's Leicester Square – the AA had moved to the area in 1908 and occupied premises in New Coventry Street in 1929 – to Fanum House in Basingstoke. Opened by Queen Elizabeth in 1973, Fanum House is a 17 storey building, at 274ft (83.5m) the tallest on the commercial flight path between Heathrow and New York. Although Fanum House remains a major AA base, the company moved its headquarters to Farnborough in 2001. Tel: 0800 0852721.

Avington Park Itchen Abbas, 4 miles (6km) northeast of Winchester. A Palladian mansion set in parkland. Dating to the 11th century, the house was enlarged in 1670 by the addition of two wings and a classical portico. It has pillars and statues, a fountain and lake, conservatories and an orangery. Some of the rooms are beautifully painted and gilded while others are decorated in trompe l'oeil. There is Georgian, Tudor and Victorian architecture with sweeping lawns leading to the River Itchen. Tel: 01962 779260.

Basing House Redbridge Lane, 2 miles (3km) east of Basingstoke. Built in 1535 as a new palace for Sir William Paulet, 1st Marquis of Winchester and Treasurer to Edward VI, Mary I and Elizabeth I. The largest private house in England at the time, it had 380 rooms and was five storeys high. When the Civil War broke out in 1642, Basing House was owned by the Catholic John Paulet, 5th Marquis of Winchester, a loyal supporter of the king. Basing House was attacked by Parliamentary troops in August 1645 when Colonel John Dalbier, with 800 men, took up position around the walls. During the siege, Dalbier even tried an early form of poison gas, burning wet straw mixed with sulphur and arsenic upwind of the house. By October the walls had been breached. Between 40 and 100 people were killed and the building destroyed by fire. Paulet's estates were confiscated and he was sent to the Tower of London on a charge of high treason, while his sons were taken away to be brought up as Protestants. The charges against Paulet were later dropped, and the site of Basing House returned to him at the Restoration by Charles II. After Paulet's death, his son Charles became Marquis of Winchester and was instrumental in the 'Glorious Revolution' when William of Orange was crowned William III. Charles was rewarded with the Dukedom of Bolton and numerous estates, and used his new wealth to pull down what was left of Basing House and to build a new house at Hackwood. Ruins covering 10 acres (4ha) of the Tudor palace and gardens can be seen today. Tel: 01256 467294.

Basingstoke Canal See Surrey

Battles Three major battles have been fought in Hampshire: **Basing House** (14 October 1645) and **Cheriton** (29 March 1644), both during the Civil War; and **Stockbridge** (14 September 1141) during the Civil War of 1135–54. Matilda's attempt to capture Henry of Blois, Bishop of Winchester (brother of King Stephen) led to the siege of Winchester (1 August–14 September 1141). See separate table for further details.

Beaulieu 5 miles (8km) north of Lymington. Formerly the 14th century Great Gatehouse of Beaulieu Abbey, **Palace House** is set in glorious grounds and gardens with immaculate spreading lawns and walkways overlooking the Beaulieu River. The House has been owned by Lord Montagu's family since 1538, when Sir Thomas Wriothesley, later 1st Earl of Southampton, bought the estate after the Dissolution of the Monasteries. Lord Henry Scott, the first resident owner, extended the house in the 1870s to accommodate his growing family. The architect was Sir Arthur Blomfield and the house is now a mixture of Victorian Gothic, medieval Gothic and 18th century fortification styles. **Beaulieu Abbey** was founded in 1204 by Cistercian monks on land donated by King John. Although much was destroyed at the time of the Dissolution of the Monasteries, the remains are substantial. The Domus, once the lay brothers' refectory, houses an exhibition of monastic life prior to the abbey's purchase in 1538. Few car museums in the world can match the unique collection of the world-renowned **National Motor Museum,** which traces the story of motoring from 1894 to the present. There are 250 vehicles on display, including many of those used in James Bond films. Beaulieu is also the home of the Beaulieu International Autojumble and Automart. Tel: 01590 614604/5.

Bedales Church Road, Petersfield. Britain's oldest co-educational boarding school. Founded by John Radley in 1893 as a boys' boarding school, it became co-educational in 1898. The school's philosophy since its foundation has been to offer an education following non-hierarchical and co-operative principles. Its motto is 'Work of each for weal of all'. Former pupils include artist Ivon Hitchens, author John Wyndham, actor Daniel Day-Lewis and TV presenter Kirstie Allsopp. Tel: 01730 300100.

Bembridge Windmill — High Street, Bembridge, Isle of Wight. Dating from c.1700, the only windmill to survive on the island. The stone-built mill is now owned by the National Trust. Tel: 01983 873945.

Bishop's Waltham Palace — Bishop's Waltham, 9 miles (15km) north of Fareham. A palace was founded in the attractive and historic small town of Bishop's Waltham in 1136 by Bishop Henri de Blois, brother of King Stephen. For centuries, the palace was an important residence of the powerful Winchester bishops and hosted many royal visitors. Here Henry V prepared for the Battle of Agincourt and Mary I waited for King Philip to arrive from Spain for their wedding. The palace was destroyed by Cromwell's troops in 1644, but the extensive remains can still be explored. The site is now in the care of English Heritage. Tel: 01489 892460.

Brading Roman Villa — Morton Old Road, Brading, Isle of Wight. Discovered in 1879, the villa consists of 12 rooms arranged round a central courtyard and dates to the 2nd century AD. The walls still stand to over 3ft (1m) in places. Five of the rooms have mosaics, including images of Orpheus and Bacchus, and an unusual depiction of a man with the head of a cockerel, possibly a satire on the Roman emperor Gallus (whose name means 'cockerel'). A new exhibition and visitor centre was built in 1994 to protect and display the finds. Tel: 01983 406223.

Breamore House and Museum — 8 miles (13km) north of Ringwood. A large Elizabethan house set in beautiful parkland, overlooking the Avon Valley on the edge of the New Forest. The house was completed in 1583 by the Doddington family. Purchased in the early 18th century by Sir Edward Hulse, Physician in Ordinary at the court of Queen Anne, George I and George II, it is still the family home of the Hulses. The house has fine collections of paintings and furniture. The Breamore Countryside Museum contains a collection of farm machinery and tools. The Saxon church of St Mary, dating to c.AD 1000, is nearby. Tel: 01725 512233.

Broadlands — 1 mile (1.6km) south of Romsey. One of the finest examples of mid-Georgian architecture in England. Romsey Abbey owned the original manor and the area known as Broadlands since before the Norman Conquest and on its surrender to Henry VIII after the Dissolution of the Monasteries, the estate was sold to Sir Francis Fleming in 1547. His daughter married Edward St Barbe, and for 117 years the property remained in the St Barbe family. Sir John St Barbe made many improvements before leaving it to his cousin, Humphrey Sydenham, in 1723. Sydenham, ruined by the South Sea Bubble, sold Broadlands to Henry Temple, 1st Viscount Palmerston, in 1736. At the request of the 2nd Viscount Palmerston, Capability Brown completed William Kent's earlier 'deformalising work' of the grounds between 1767 and 1780, creating perhaps one of his greatest masterpieces. Under his influence the existing Tudor and Jacobean manor house was 'squared' in Palladian style, encased in white brick to give the appearance of stone with two porticos. Brown's protégé and son-in-law, Henry Holland the younger, added the east front portico and domed hall in 1788. Most of the decorative plasterwork in the main rooms was designed and executed by Joseph Rose the elder (1723–80), described by a contemporary as 'the first man in the Kingdom as a plasterer'. The house was later the country home of Prime Minister Lord Palmerston, the 3rd Viscount. More recently Broadlands has been the home of the Mountbattens; Lord Louis, Earl Mountbatten of Burma, inherited the property through his wife Edwina's links with the Palmerston family. Since he had no son he was granted the privilege of passing the earldom to his elder daughter, Patricia. Her eldest son, the Hon. Norton Knatchbull, now Lord Brabourne, inherited Broadlands on his grandfather's death, and he and his family now occupy the house. The stable block houses a museum dedicated to Lord Mountbatten. Tel: 01794 505020.

Calshot Castle — 2 miles (3km) southeast of Fawley, 8 miles (13km) southeast of Southampton. Located on a shingle spit between Southampton Water and the Solent, this coastal fort was built by Henry VIII in 1539. One of his smaller forts, its three-storey keep and outer curtain wall nevertheless gave it full command of its position. The same advantageous location continued to give Calshot great strategic importance and it was manned during both world wars. In between, it was closely associated with the Schneider Trophy air races, the competing seaplanes taking off and landing in front of it. The hangars of the Air Force Seaplane and Flying Boat base beside the castle are now one of Britain's leading activity centres. The fort is in the care of English Heritage. Tel: 023 8089 2077.

Carisbrooke Castle — 1 mile (1.6km) southwest of Newport, Isle of Wight. Norman castle founded by William fitz Osbern c.1070, and extended by Baldwin de Redvers throughout the 1130s, with a shell keep built on a motte. Carisbrooke was besieged by King Stephen in 1136, the failure of the water supply forcing the surrender of the castle. The gatehouse, erected c.1335, has gun loops also dating from the 14th century. Two medieval wells still exist within the castle: the keep houses the first, 160ft (48.5m) deep and reached by 71 steps; the second is contained in a 16th century wellhouse in the courtyard. The latter well has been in constant use since the 12th century, after the first failed, and it is thought that prisoners were used to tread the waterwheel. However, in the 17th century, donkeys were introduced to drive the winding gear, and they still give demonstrations of how this fascinating piece of early engineering drew up water. Reinforced by Federigo Gianibelli in the 16th century, the castle was a Parliamentary stronghold throughout the Civil War, and Charles I was held prisoner here 1647–8. The castle is now owned by English Heritage. Tel: 01983 528632.

Cowes Week — Cowes, Isle of Wight. Held on the Solent, Cowes is the longest established sailing regatta in the world. Just seven yachts signed up for the first organised yacht race at Cowes on 10 August 1826; today over 1000 yachts and 8000 competitors take part in the annual event now known as Skandia Cowes Week. Taking place at the beginning of August each year, Cowes attracts a wide range of entrants, from true amateurs to Olympic and world champions. There are up to 40 races each day: the Fastnet Race from Cowes round Fastnet Rock, off the southwest coast of Ireland, and back to Plymouth, was established in 1925 and the biennial event held during Cowes Week became the final event of the Admiral's Cup until 1999. Other trophies awarded include the Queen's Cup, first presented in 1897, and the Britannia Cup, first presented in 1951.

D-Day Museum Clarence Esplanade, Southsea. Opened in 1984 to commemorate the 40th anniversary of the D-Day landings. On display is the Overlord Embroidery, designed by Sandra Lawrence and inspired by the Bayeux Tapestry. The 272ft (83m) frieze depicts scenes from World War II and the Normandy landings. Tel: 02392 827261.

Dickens Birthplace Museum Old Commercial Road, Portsmouth. Charles Dickens was born in this modest house on 7 February 1812. The address then was 1 Mile End Terrace, Landport, Portsea, but the site remains the same. The furniture, ceramics, glass, household objects and decorations have been recreated in the Regency style which Charles's parents, John and Elizabeth, would have favoured. There are three furnished rooms: the parlour, the dining room and the bedroom where Charles was born. The exhibition room features a display on Dickens and Portsmouth, as well as a small collection of memorabilia including the couch on which he died at his house in Kent, together with his snuff box, inkwell and paper knife. Tel: 02392 827261.

Dimbola Lodge Freshwater Bay, Isle of Wight. The home and studio of pioneer photographer Julia Margaret Cameron 1860–75, now a museum dedicated to her work. Cameron entertained and photographed the cream of Victorian society in the house, including Lewis Carroll, Robert Browning and Ellen Terry. Tel: 01983 756814.

Domus Dei See Royal Garrison Church

Duke of Wellington statue Round Hill, Aldershot. The statue of the 1st Duke of Wellington mounted on his horse, Copenhagen, is situated behind the Royal Garrison Church. The statue is 30ft (9m) high, 26ft (8m) from nose to tail, over 22ft (6.5m) in girth and weighs 40 tons. It was designed and built by Matthew Cotes Wyatt who used recycled bronze from cannons captured at the Battle of Waterloo. Originally, in 1846, the statue was erected at Hyde Park Corner, London on the Wellington Arch. However its architect, Decimus Burton, had tried to veto this plan for his preferred 'figure in a four horse chariot'. Many agreed with Burton that the statue was out of proportion and looked ridiculous. It was nicknamed 'The Archduke' and was a popular topic in the satirical magazine *Punch*. In 1883, due to a road widening project, the arch was moved. The Prince of Wales (later King Edward VII) wrote to the Prime Minister, Gladstone, 'As regards the old colossal statue of the Duke. I would suggest that it should not be broken up but removed to Aldershot where it will be highly valued by the Army.' In 1885, the Prince accordingly handed over the monument to Lieutenant General Anderson, commander of the Aldershot garrison.

Eling Tide Mill Eling, 2 miles (3km) west of Southampton. Situated on the edge of Southampton Water, beside the New Forest. There has been a mill on the site for over 900 years and the present building is 230 years old. Tidal power was once harnessed not only for milling flour, but also for sawing lumber, operating the bellows and hammers in ironworks, manufacturing paper and cotton, and grinding spices, pepper and gunpowder. Before the advent of the steam engine tide mills were the one type of large-scale mill capable of operating throughout the year. Although abandoned in the 1940s, Eling Tide Mill was restored between 1975 and 1980, when it reopened as both a working mill and a museum. It is the only fully working and productive tide mill in the UK. Tel: 02380 869575.

Exbury Gardens and Steam Railway 9 miles (15km) south of Southampton. In 1919 Lionel Nathan de Rothschild (1882–1942) bought the Exbury Estate in the southeast of the New Forest. William Mitford, whose family had owned the estate in the 18th and 19th centuries, described it as an 'earthly paradise'. Lionel, a passionate gardener, was a collector of rhododendrons, azaleas and camellias, a collection which shaped the 200 acre (60ha) woodland garden. After his death in 1942, Exbury House was requisitioned by the Royal Navy and commissioned as HMS *Mastodon*, a naval shore base which played a vital part in the planning and launching of the Normandy campaign in 1944 and was responsible for the administration of training and equipping the crews of landing craft used in the amphibious assaults against occupied Europe. The author Nevil Shute, one of the many service personnel who passed through during the war, wrote about his experiences in his novel *Requiem For a Wren*. Today the property is owned by Lionel's son, Edmund, who continues to develop the gardens. The Exbury Gardens steam railway, a $12^1/_2$in (317mm) gauge miniature railway, follows a $1^1/_4$ mile (2km) circular route around the gardens. Tel: 02380 891203.

Farnborough Abbey See St Michael's Abbey

Farnborough Air Show An international aircraft trade show first held at Olympia in 1918, before moving to Hendon in 1932 and finally to the home of the Royal Aircraft Establishment at Farnborough in 1948. It was held annually until 1962, when it became biennial, alternating with the Paris Air Show. Flying displays are held each afternoon, although it is essentially a trade event. Tel: 01252 532800.

Fort Brockhurst Gunner's Way, Elson, north of Gosport. One of several forts built in the 1860s to protect the vital harbour of Portsmouth. The fort was used by the army until after World War II and is largely unaltered, including parade ground, gun ramps and moated keep. It is now in the care of English Heritage. Tel: 02392 581059.

Furzey Gardens Minstead, 2 miles (3km) northwest of Lyndhurst. Set in the heart of the New Forest, the informal wooded garden was established in 1922 and is noted for its all year round colour. The restored Cole Cottage, built c.1560, stands in the grounds. Tel: 02380 812464.

Gilbert White's House and Oates Museum Selborne, 4 miles (6km) southeast of Alton. Rev. Gilbert White (1720–93), author of the *Natural History of Selborne* and founding father of modern natural history, lived here for most of his life. The rooms have been restored following descriptions in White's own correspondence and include items of his furniture, family portraits and beautiful bed hangings embroidered for White by family members. On display in the library is White's original handwritten manuscript of the *Natural History*. There is an exhibition commemorating the Oates family and their exploits, particularly Captain Lawrence Oates, who accompanied Scott to the South Pole in 1911, and his uncle, Frank Oates, a Victorian explorer who travelled widely in Africa and America. Tel: 01420 511275.

God's House Tower Museum of Archaeology Winkle Street, Southampton. Housed in the first purpose-built artillery fortification in England, dating from 1417 and standing in the southeastern corner of the city walls, the museum holds important collections of Roman, Saxon and medieval artefacts relating to the city's history. Tel: 023 8063 5904.

Great Hall, Winchester See Winchester Castle

Guildhall, Winchester High Street, Winchester. Completed in 1873 in Gothic revival style, the Guildhall was designed as part of a complex housing the town's law courts, police station and fire brigade. It is now a civic and conference centre featuring a changing programme of art and sculpture. Tel: 01962 848289.

Hayling Island 1 mile (1.6km) south of Havant. The third largest island in England, although it is connected to the mainland by a bridge at its northern end. Halfway along its 4 mile (6km) length it is almost cut in two at the point where Mill Rythe, a narrow inlet, comes in on the east from Chichester Harbour. At this point the island is only $1/2$ mile (0.8km) across. Almost all the population of the island live south of this narrow 'waist'. To the north the villages of Stoke and Northney are the only settlements of any size. St Peter's Church in North Hayling, built in 1140, is a fine example of a typical English village church of the Norman period; its foundations are said to be large 'erratic' stones left as the ice receded in the post-glacial era. The three bells are said to be the oldest in England, the tenor bell having been dated by the Whitechapel Foundry as being from c.1350. One of the trees surrounding the church is a yew at least 800 years old, although this is exceeded by the yew in the grounds of St Mary's Church, South Hayling, which is is said to be almost 1000 years old and has a girth of 30ft (9m). The seaside resort of South Hayling is a combination of town and country; the settlements of West Town, Gable Head and Eastoke spread to meet each other but with fields, farms, woods and the sea all within easy reach. The funfair 'Beachlands' was once banned from playing music after the elderly residents in nearby apartments complained to the council. Area: 10.36 sq miles (26.84 sq km). Population: 16,887. GR: SU720010.

HMS *Victory* The only example still in existence of a mid 18th century British warship. Built in Chatham, HMS *Victory* was famously Admiral Nelson's flagship at the Battle of Trafalgar in 1805. She continued in active service until 1812 when she was moored in Portsmouth Harbour. In January 1922 she was towed to her current position in Portsmouth Dockyard (see Portsmouth Historic Dockyard) and embedded in cement, before being restored to her 1805 condition. HMS *Victory* is still the flagship of the Navy's commander-in-chief, making her the oldest commissioned ship in the world.

Highest point The highest point in **Hampshire** is Pilot Hill at 938ft (286m), 9 miles (15km) north of Andover. GR: SU398601. The highest point on the **Isle of Wight** is St Boniface Down, on the southeast of the island, at 790ft (241m). GR: SZ569785.

Highclere Castle and Gardens 10 miles (16km) northwest of Basingstoke. A Victorian house, designed by Charles Barry for the 3rd Earl of Carnarvon, and built in 1839–42 in a serpentine park by Capability Brown. The house resembles the Houses of Parliament, designed by Barry at the same time. It is surrounded by lawns planted with cedars and yew hedges, while the Secret Garden has herbaceous planting. Highclere has been the home of the Herbert family, the Earls of Carnarvon, since the late 17th century. In 1692, Robert Sawyer, a lawyer and college friend of Samuel Pepys, bequeathed the previous stuccoed classical-style mansion at the site to his only daughter, Margaret. As Countess of Pembroke, Margaret lived at Wilton House in Wiltshire, which became the inheritance of her eldest son, Henry, after his father's death. Her second son, Robert Herbert, inherited Highclere, and it was he who began the picture collection. His nephew, Henry was created Baron Porchester and 1st Earl of Carnarvon for his support of George III during the Gordon Riots in 1780. The 5th Earl had a passion for Ancient Egypt, sponsoring a series of excavations in the Valley of the Kings, led by the Egyptologist Howard Carter, and discovering in 1922 the astonishing treasure of the tomb of Tutankhamun. The house contains an exhibition of many of the artefacts found by Carnarvon and Carter. Tel: 01635 253204.

Hinton Ampner Garden 8 miles (13km) east of Winchester. A masterpiece of design started in the 1930s by Ralph Dutton, 8th and last Lord Sherborne (d.1985), the 12 acre (5ha) garden unites a formal layout with varied and informal plantings in pastel shades. There are magnificent vistas over 80 acres (32ha) of parkland and rolling Hampshire countryside. The house suffered a major fire in 1960 and was rebuilt in neo-Georgian style. Today it contains Dutton's fine collection of Regency furniture, Italian paintings and hardstone items. Since 1986 the property has been in the care of the National Trust. Tel: 01962 771305.

Horsea Island Located in Portsmouth Harbour, Horsea was originally two islands, Great and Little Horsea, joined in 1889 to form a torpedo testing lake using chalk excavated from Portsdown Hill, 0.6 miles (1km) to the north. Horsea is no longer an island at all, having been reclaimed by the land at Paulsgrove in the early 1970s. The lake, now used for diving pursuits, and surrounding area, is owned by the Ministry of Defence. GR: SU624038.

Houghton Lodge North Houghton, 8 miles (13km) northwest of Winchester. Situated in the heart of the Test Valley, Houghton Lodge is one of the earliest examples of a Cottage Orné or rustic cottage. The Grade II* listed house was built before 1799 and was probably intended as a fishing lodge. The gardens were designed in the 18th century 'natural' style and include unusual topiary, hydroponic greenhouse, woodland walk, grotto, and a restored chalk cob walled garden. Tel: 01264 810502.

Hurst Castle Keyhaven, 4 miles (6km) southwest of Lymington. Artillery fort built 1539–40 by Henry VIII at the end of a shingle spit to protect western approaches to the Solent. It was held by Parliament during the Civil War, and Charles I was briefly imprisoned here. There is an exhibition in the castle and two huge 38-ton guns form the fort's armaments. It is now owned by English Heritage. Tel: 01590 642344.

Interesting facts — **Hampshire** was known as Southamptonshire until 50 years ago. Its name was officially changed from the County of Southampton to the County of Hampshire on 1 April 1959, its shortened name of Hants being a corruption of this. The **world's first cricket club** was formed in the Hampshire village of Hambledon in the mid 18th century. It was led by Richard Nyren, landlord of the Bat and Ball Inn, and was very successful, particularly on their magnificent pitch at Broadhalfpenny Down. In June 1777 Hambledon played England for 1000 guineas and won. **The world's first wireless transmission at sea** was made on 17 December 1897, by Guglielmo Marconi, from the Royal Needles Hotel, above Alum Bay, across The Solent. In August 1898 Marconi was invited by Queen Victoria to demonstrate his equipment aboard the royal yacht. During his presentation he amazed his audience by contacting the royal home at Osborne House and the Alum Bay station. The ***Titanic*** sailed from the port of Southampton on 10 April 1912. The White Star liner had a near miss with liner *New York* as she left port. Five days later, she sank while speeding through an ice field, hoping to win the Blue Riband for the fastest Atlantic crossing. More than 1500 of the 2340 passengers perished in the icy waters of the North Atlantic. **The Hospital of St Cross**, Winchester, is England's oldest almshouse, and is famous for the ancient tradition of the **Wayfarer's Dole**, a small beaker of beer and a morsel of bread given by the porter to all visitors who request it. After a court battle, **Hayling Island** won the honour of being accepted as the birthplace of windsurfing. **Southampton** is unique among England's coastal towns as it has four high-water tides per day as opposed to the usual two. This phenomenon is due to the shape of the coastline and its proximity to the Isle of Wight, which causes a second high tide shortly after the first has receded. In contrast Portland in Dorset has four low tides. The **World Quiz Champion**, Kevin Ashman, is Winchester born and bred. Kevin, who lives in Winnall, is also a former *Mastermind, Brain of Britain* and *Fifteen-to-1* winner and multi British Quiz Champion. Kevin is currently one of the team of *Eggheads* for the BBC panel show. **Lucky Jim's** in Eastleigh is the first pub in the world to have miniature four-inch television monitors on its beer pumps to ensure customers do not need to miss any sporting action while waiting to be served. Another interesting pub is **Milbury's** in Beauworth, near Sheriton. The pub is surrounded by a Bronze Age cemetery in which a hoard of 6000 silver coins were found in 1833. The pub also has a 300-year-old well which is more than 300ft (90m) deep and is equipped with a huge treadmill. The **White Horse** pub in Priors Dean, near Petersfield, has two claims to fame: it is the highest public house in Hampshire at 771ft (235m) above sea level, and it has no sign outside and as such is known as 'the pub with no name'.

Islands — There are 13 islands off the coast of Hampshire and 20 around the Isle of Wight, although apart from the island itself the latter consist of uninhabited rocks. See separate list of islands and individual entries.

Isle of Wight — The Isle of Wight is the largest island in England; see introduction for further information. Area: 146.83 sq miles (380.28 sq km). Population: 132,731. GR: SZ499875.

Isle of Wight Music Festival — In the music festival calendar, early June is now very much associated with the Isle of Wight Festival. The first Isle of Wight Pop Festival took place near Afton Down, West Wight in 1970, following smaller concerts in 1968 and 1969. The 1970 show was notable for being the last public performance by Jimi Hendrix before his death. A life-size bronze statue of Hendrix was placed outside Dimbola Lodge (see separate entry) in May 2006. The festival was revived in 2002 and is now an annual event, with other, smaller musical events of many different genres across the island becoming associated with it. Its main sponsor in 2008 was BT. Tel: 01983 813813.

Jane Austen's House, Chawton — Chawton, 1 mile (1.6km) southwest of Alton. The 17th century home where Austen wrote or revised her six great novels, situated 12 miles (19km) southwest of her birthplace of Steventon. The museum houses many items connected with Austen and her family, including the table where she wrote. There is some of her jewellery and examples of her needlework. In the drawing room is a fine Hepplewhite bureau-bookcase and chairs that belonged to Austen's father and came from the rectory at Steventon. The bookcase contains some first editions of Jane's novels. The garden contains many varieties of plants and herbs common in the late 18th century. In display in the Old Bakehouse is the donkey carriage used by Austen when she was ill and too weak to travel far on foot. Tel: 01420 83262.

Jane Austen's House, Winchester — High Street, Winchester. The residence of the great author for the last six weeks of her life until she died on 18 July 1817. Now a private house not open to the public, it is commemorated by plaque only.

King Alfred's Statue — Broadway, Winchester. The bronze sculpture by Sir Hamo Thornycroft depicts Alfred grasping a cross-hilted sword in his right hand, a symbol of the triumph of Christianity against paganism. It was erected at the bottom of Winchester High Street in 1901.

King John's House & Heritage Centre — Church Street, Romsey. The three buildings that house Romsey Heritage Centre encompass 750 years of history. The 13th century King John's House was once the main building of a major medieval complex. Many early features, including the roof timbers, graffiti cut into the medieval plaster and a rare bone floor still remain. The attached Tudor Cottage is a late Tudor/early Jacobean timber-framed house. The room on the upper floor has been furnished to give a flavour of the period, while the lower room is now a tea room. The Victorian Museum, built of brick and formerly a gun shop, features aspects of Romsey life during the Victorian and Edwardian period. The shop has been reconstructed upstairs, using original fixtures and fittings. The garden, which features a Victorian terrace and a fountain courtyard, has been planted in 18th century style. Tel: 01794 512200.

Marwell Zoo Colden Common, 6 miles (10km) south of Winchester. Founded in 1972 by John Knowles, Marwell covers 100 acres (40ha) with over 200 rare and endangered species of animals, from meerkats and red pandas to snow leopards and rhinos. One of the first zoos to operate actively in the field of conservation, it also houses the largest collection of hoofed animals in the UK. Tel: 01962 777407.

***Mary Rose*, The** The only 16th century warship on display in the world, the *Mary Rose* was built 1509–11, probably in Portsmouth. Reputedly Henry VIII's favourite ship, she took part in several of the king's campaigns against the French before sinking at Spithead with almost all her crew during an engagement with the French fleet in 1545; the precise reason for her loss is unknown, but one theory suggests that her cannon had not been secured properly and slipped across the deck, capsizing the ship instantly. Her remains were raised from the Solent in 1982 after many years of patient work by writer, diver and historian Alexander McKee. She is now on display at Portsmouth Historic Dockyard (see separate entry).

Medieval Merchant's House French Street, Southampton. Built by wine merchant John Fortin c.1290, the restored town house is one of the earliest surviving merchant's houses in England. The interior has been restored to its appearance in the mid 14th century, while colourful period furnishings have been re-created to show how Fortin and his family would have lived. Now owned by English Heritage. Tel: 02380 221503.

Military Museums, Winchester Winchester is home to a number of museums specialising in military history. The **Gurkha Museum** (Tel: 01962 842832), **King's Royal Hussars Museum** (01962 282541), **Adjutant General's Corps Museum** (01962 877826), **Light Infantry Museum** (01962 828550) and **Royal Green Jackets Museum** (01962 828549) are located in the Peninsula Barracks, Romsey Road; the **Royal Hampshire Regiment Museum** (01962 863658) is located in Serles House, Southgate Street.

Mottisfont Abbey & Garden 4½ miles (7km) north of Romsey. Originating as an Augustinian priory in the 12th century and converted into a private house after the Dissolution of the Monasteries, Mottisfont still retains the spring or 'font' from which its name is derived. The abbey contains a drawing room decorated by Rex Whistler and Hampshire-born artist Derek Hill's collection of 20th century pictures, but the key attraction is the grounds, with magnificent trees, walled gardens and the National Collection of old-fashioned roses. The estate is now owned by the National Trust, and includes Mottisfont village and surrounding farmland and woods. Tel: 01794 340757.

Needles, The The Needles, at the western extremity of the Isle of Wight, are sea-stacks formed mainly of chalk and flint. A lighthouse, built in 1859 and now unmanned, stands on the furthest rock. The name 'Needles' is believed to have been derived from a slender tapering rock pinnacle formerly situated a little to the north (i.e. on the Alum Bay side) of the present central rock. This needle-shaped rock, known as 'Lot's Wife', collapsed into the sea in 1764. Its stump can still be seen at low water, where it forms a dangerous reef. GR: SZ291849.

Netley Abbey and Castle 4 miles (6km) south of Southampton. Officially named the Abbey of St Mary the Virgin and St Edward the Confessor, Netley Abbey – from which the village took its name – was founded in 1239 by Peter des Roches, Bishop of Winchester and populated by a colony of Cistercian monks from Beaulieu. Netley Abbey was under the patronage of Henry III, whose name appears on the foundation stone at the base of the northeast crossing tower. It was probably built by the king's mason, who also constructed Westminster Abbey. The abbey was dissolved by Henry VIII in 1536 and the castle – more accurately a fort – was built in 1542 with stone from the abbey. One of 12 forts built under the direction of Sir William Paulet for the defence of Southampton and Portsmouth, it was armed and garrisoned until 1627. In 1643, during the Civil War, the then unmanned castle was raided by Parliamentary forces. During World War II it became a home for elderly men transferred from other homes which were required as hospitals; it has since been converted into apartments. Tel: 01424 775705/02392 378291.

New Forest National Park Covering 220 sq miles (570 sq km) in the southwest of Hampshire, the New Forest National Park was created on 1 March 2005. The landscape of the New Forest is a rare and fascinating mosaic of ancient and ornamental woodland, pine plantations, open heath, pasture, mires, saltmarsh coastline and picturesque villages. William I set aside the forest for hunting in 1079 and centuries of grazing by deer, ponies and cattle have since shaped the landscape. As well as the famous New Forest ponies, the Park is home to pigs, cows and donkeys roaming free; in the 12th century various concessions were made to those living in the forest to graze their animals, collect firewood and gather building materials, and around 500 Commoners now exercise their right to graze ponies, cattle or donkeys within the Forest boundaries. Commoners also have the rights of pannage, which allows pigs to feed in the forest in autumn, and of estover – the right to gather wood for fuel. Other wildlife includes the adder, sand lizard and Dartford warbler, and plants such as the wild gladiolus. The Rufus Stone, located 1½ miles (2.5km) northwest of Minstead, was erected in 1745 to mark the spot where William II (William Rufus) was killed in a hunting accident in 1100. More than 34,000 people live within the boundaries of the National Park, making it one of the most densely populated in England. Tel: 01590 646600.

Newtown Old Town Hall Newtown, 5 miles (8km) west of Newport, Isle of Wight. Now a tiny hamlet, Newtown was a thriving community in the Middle Ages but was in decline by the 1600s. The 18th century building was once the focal point of what had already become by the time of its construction a 'rotten borough'. Its restoration was paid for in the 1930s by an anonymous group called Ferguson's Gang, who later gave it to the National Trust. Tel: 01983 531785.

Northington Grange 4 miles (6km) north of New Alresford. One of the first country houses in Europe to be designed in the Greek Revival style, Northington once belonged to the banking family, the Barings. The building was designed in 1804–9 by William Wilkins, who added a new front in the style of the

Parthenon, and supported by eight enormous columns, to the existing 17th century house. George IV lived here for a time as Prince of Wales, and in Victorian times Carlyle, Thackeray, Kingsley and Wilberforce were among the guests who stayed here. The building is set in a beautiful park, with lakes kept full by a tributary of the Itchen. It is now owned by English Heritage. Tel: 01424 775705.

Nunwell House and Gardens — 3 miles (5km) south of Ryde, Isle of Wight. The picturesque house has been a family home since 1522. Sir John Oglander hosted Charles I here on the king's last night of freedom, and the Parlour Chamber in which they met can still be seen. The house is beautifully furnished, with exhibits recalling the Aylmer family's military connections and an Old Kitchen exhibition. Nunwell is surrounded by 5 acres (2ha) of tranquil gardens, including a walled garden, and enjoying views across the Solent. Tel: 01983 407240.

Odiham Castle — North Warnborough, 9 miles (15km) southwest of Farnborough. Odiham was built by King John in 1207–14, on a site midway between Windsor and Winchester. Unusually the castle was built with an octagonal keep. Soon after it was finished, the castle suffered a two-week siege at the hands of the French, but it flourished during much of the 13th century, when it was home to the de Montfort family. Simon de Montfort married King John's daughter Eleanor in 1238, two years after she had been granted the castle by her brother, Henry III. This union made Odiham one of the most powerful households in the land. Simon was to become a leading figure in the baronial stand against Henry, paying with his life at the Battle of Evesham in 1265, after which Eleanor was exiled. In the 14th century the castle played a part in the Despensers' rebellion, was host to a sitting of Parliament, and for 11 years was the prison of a Scottish king. By the 15th century, however, it was used only as a hunting lodge, and in 1605 was described as a ruin. All that remains today is the rubble core of the keep walls; a little of the original facing, consisting of dressed stone and flint, remains inside near ground level.

Osborne House — 1 mile (1.6km) southeast of East Cowes, Isle of Wight. Queen Victoria and Prince Albert bought Osborne House and its 1000 acres (400ha) in 1845 as a retreat from the pressures of court life at Buckingham Palace and Windsor Castle. By 1851 they had replaced the original Georgian house with a large Italianate villa. Queen Victoria spent most of her time at Osborne House after Albert died, and she herself died here in 1901. Since her death little has changed at Osborne and the house still contains many of the royal couple's possessions, photographs and paintings. In the grounds is the Swiss Cottage, a wooden chalet where the royal children learned to cook. There is a museum full of diverse collections, the Victoria Fort and Albert Barracks, and beautiful formal gardens with Victorian-style planting. Now owned by English Heritage. Tel: 01983 200022.

Portchester Castle — 4 miles (6km) northwest of Portsmouth. Situated on the north shore of Portsmouth Harbour, the Norman castle was founded by Henry I c.1120 in the corner of an old Roman Saxon Shore fort. The keep was built by Henry II and the palace constructed for Richard II, 1396–9. It was sold by Charles I in 1632 and used as a barracks for Parliament during the Civil War, later being used as a prison for captives during the Dutch, Seven Years and Napoleonic Wars. The castle has the most complete set of Roman walls in northwest Europe and a 12th century Augustinian priory church within its walls. It is now owned by English Heritage. Tel: 02392 378291.

Portsea Island — Lying in Portsmouth Harbour, the fifth largest island in England. Various bridges now join the island to the mainland, including a span across to Whale Island. A separate town until the 19th century, Portsea is now occupied by a substantial part of the city of Portsmouth, including the town of Southsea. The western limit of the island lies at the mouth of Portsmouth Harbour. From here its coast runs southeast past Clarence Pier and Southsea Castle along the Eastney frontage and continues to its eastern limit at Fort Cumberland, at the entrance to Langstone Harbour. In the north of the island the shoreline runs along Port Creek, a small channel which separates the island from the mainland, past Tipner, returning to Portsmouth Harbour. Portsmouth's naval base and Royal Dockyard occupy the southwestern part of the island. GR: SU696008.

Portsmouth Anglican Cathedral — High Street, Portsmouth. Dedicated to St Thomas of Canterbury. Founded in 1180 by Jean de Gisors, Lord of the Manor of Titchfield and founder of the town of Portsmouth itself, who gave land in his new town to the Augustinian canons of Southwick Priory so that they could build a chapel. This was to become a parish church in the 14th century, and with the establishment of the Diocese of Portsmouth in 1927 was elevated to the status of a cathedral. Work to enlarge St Thomas's began under Sir Charles Nicholson in 1932 but was stopped in 1939 with the outbreak of World War II, and did not recommence until 1990. The completed building, smaller than originally planned, was consecrated in 1991 before HM Queen Elizabeth the Queen Mother. Memorials include a tomb of an unknown sailor from the *Mary Rose*. Tel: 023 9382 3300.

Portsmouth Historic Dockyard — Situated within HM Naval Base on Portsmouth Harbour, the heart of the Royal Dockyard is now open to the public. Among the vessels on display are the *Mary Rose* and HMS *Victory* (see separate entries), as well as HMS *Warrior*, launched in 1860, the world's first battleship with an armoured hull. Other features of the site include Action Stations, a hands-on simulation of life in the modern Navy, and the Royal Naval Museum. Tel: 02392 839766.

Portsmouth Roman Catholic Cathedral — Dedicated to St John the Evangelist, and built in 1882 to accommodate Portsmouth's rapidly increasing congregation of Roman Catholics. It replaced a chapel built in 1796 in Prince George Street, 1/4 mile (0.5km) to the west, after the passing of the Second Catholic Relief Act of 1791.

Prisons — **Albany**, Parkhurst Road, Newport, Isle of Wight. Albany occupies the site of a former military barracks. Designed and built as a Category C training prison, it now houses sex offenders and vulnerable prisoners. Operational capacity: 529. Tel: 01983 556300.**Camp Hill**, Newport, Isle of Wight. Category C Training prison opened in 1927 by Sir Winston Churchill and situated near Parkhurst Forest. Operational capacity: 585. Tel: 01983 554600.

Parkhurst, Clissold Road, Newport, Isle of Wight. Built as a military hospital in 1805, from 1863 to 1869 it was a female prison. Parkhurst has since served as a male prison and now caters for long-term and life sentence category B prisoners and remands from the Isle of Wight courts. It also houses a Protected Witness Unit. Operational capacity: 507. Tel: 01983 554000.

Haslar, Dolphin Way, Gosport. Tel: 02392 604000. An Immigration Removal Centre run under Detention Centre rules. Operational capacity: 163.

Kingston, Milton Road, Portsmouth. Built in 1877 to the Victorian radial design, originally accommodating domestic lifers. Today the population has progressed to a more general Category 'B' lifer population, including a wing for elderly lifers. Operational capacity: 196. Tel: 02392 953100.

Winchester, Romsey Road, Winchester. All male prison up to category B. Operational capacity: 697. Tel: 01962 723000.

Quarr Abbey — Quarr, 2 miles (3km) west of Ryde, Isle of Wight. There have been two abbeys at Quarr. The first, founded in 1132 by Baldwin de Redvers, Earl of Devon and 4th Lord of the Isle of Wight, was destroyed by Henry VIII in 1536; the second was founded in 1908 for Benedictine monks originally from France to the design of Dom Paul Bellot, and who had previously occupied Appuldurcombe House (see separate entry). This new abbey was located on the site of Quarr Abbey House, built in the 1840s supposedly using stone from the medieval abbey. One of a series of fine houses built along the north coast of the Isle of Wight, Quarr Abbey House was a residence of the Cochrane family, one member of which was Admiral Lord Cochrane (1775–1860), nicknamed 'le loup des mers' (sea wolf) by the French during the Napoleonic Wars, and whose life and exploits inspired the fiction of novelists Captain Marryat, C S Forester, Patrick O'Brian and Bernard Cornwell.

Queen Eleanor's Garden — High Street, Winchester. A reconstructed 13th century garden adjoining the Great Hall of Winchester Castle (see separate entry), and including features such as a herbarium and camomile lawn characteristic of such gardens. The 'Eleanor' in the garden's name refers to not one Queen Eleanor, but two: Eleanor of Castile, wife of Edward I, and Eleanor of Provence, wife of Henry III, both of whom spent considerable time living at Winchester Castle. Forming one side of the garden is the last remaining wall of King's House, built by Sir Christopher Wren for Charles II in 1683. The house was used as a military barracks during the Victorian period until it was destroyed by fire in 1894. Tel: 01962 846476.

Rivers

Hampshire — The **Avon** (known as the Hampshire Avon to distinguish it from three other River Avons in England – Avon simply means river) rises in Wiltshire, east of Devizes, flowing south through Durrington, Amesbury, Salisbury, Fordingbridge and Ringwood, and into the English Channel at Christchurch. For part of its course it forms the border between Dorset and Hampshire. Tributaries include the rivers Ebble, Nadder, Wylye and Bourne. Its total length is 48 miles (77km).

Enborne – see Berkshire

Along with the Test, the **Itchen** is regarded as one of the finest chalk streams in the world and is renowned for its fly-fishing. It flows for 27 miles (43km) from its source at New Cheriton, 5 miles (8km) east of Winchester, to Southampton Water. Initially the river flows north, through the village of Tichborne, before joining up with its tributaries the River Alre and the Candover Brook, just below New Alresford. It then flows west past the villages of Ovington, Itchen Stoke, Itchen Abbas, Martyr Worthy, Easton and Abbots Worthy to Winchester. The river flows in several different channels through Winchester, some of which come close enough to Winchester Cathedral to have caused serious problems to the building's foundations in past years. The main channel flows through Winchester City Mill and to the east of the city's Roman walls, along a promenaded reach known as 'The Weirs'. The river then flows south, through the villages of Twyford and Shawford and the town of Eastleigh, before reaching the northern suburbs of Southampton at Swaythling. Between Winchester and Swaythling, sections of the river were once canalised as part of the long disused Itchen Navigation, and the former towpath forms part of the Itchen Way. At Swaythling the Itchen passes under Woodmill Bridge and becomes tidal. Four further bridges cross the river before its confluence with the Test estuary in Southampton Water.

Loddon – see Berkshire

The **Test** rises near the village of Ashe, 5 miles (8km) west of Basingstoke, and flows west through the villages of Overton and Laverstoke and the town of Whitchurch, before joining with the River Bourne at Testbourne and turning south through the villages of Longparish and Middleton to Wherwell and Chilbolton, where it is met by the Rivers Dever and Anton. From Chilbolton the river continues south through the villages of Leckford, Longstock, Stockbridge and Houghton to Mottisfont and Kimbridge, where the River Dun joins the flow. From here the village of Timsbury is passed before reaching the town of Romsey. On the western edge of Romsey, Sadler's Mill, an 18th century watermill, sits astride the Test. Famous for its trout until this point, in the last 16 miles (26km) of its course nearing the sea it becomes a salmon run. The river flows past the country house of Broadlands, past Nursling, once the site of a Roman bridge, and between the Southampton suburbs of Totton and Redbridge. Here the river is joined by the River Blackwater before sharing the estuary of its sister river, the Itchen, the two continuing to the sea as Southampton Water. The total length of the Test is 45 miles (72km).

Isle of Wight — The two largest rivers of the Isle of Wight are the **Medina** and the **Eastern Yar.** Both rivers rise as chalk springs near St Catherine's Down at the southern tip of the island. The Eastern Yar rises in Niton, and flows across the eastern side of the island to Bembridge where it meets the Solent; 17 miles (27km) in length, it has several tributaries including Scotchell's Brook and Wroxall Stream. The **Western Yar** is a small brook with its source at Freshwater Bay.

The Medina flows through the capital, Newport, towards the Solent at Cowes. A navigable tidal estuary from Newport northwards, the river is bridged at Newport, with a chain ferry between

Cowes and East Cowes. 13 miles (21km) in length, the Medina has a solitary tributary, Lukely Brook.

Royal Garrison Church Grand Parade, Portsmouth. Founded as the Domus Dei (House of God) by Pierre des Roches, Bishop of Winchester, in 1212 as a hospice to shelter and help overseas pilgrims bound for the shrines at Canterbury, Chichester and Winchester. In 1450 Henry VI sent Adam Moleyns, Bishop of Chichester, to the church in order to pay the sailors and soldiers of the garrison. Due to a disagreement over the amount of pay, the bishop was murdered. Portsmouth was subsequently excommunicated and remained so until 1508 when Bishop Richard Foxe of Winchester agreed a 'pardon' if a chantry chapel was built next to the hospital. In 1540 Domus Dei became an armoury and in 1560 the home of the local military governor. Throughout this time the chapel remained in use and on 22 May 1662 it hosted the wedding of Charles II and Princess Catherine of Braganza. In January 1941 a fire bomb raid on Portsmouth gutted the nave of the church but the chancel was saved. Today, the roofless church is preserved by English Heritage. Tel: 02392 378291. Note – there is another Royal Garrison Church (All Saints) in Aldershot.

Royal Naval Museum See Portsmouth Historic Dockyard

St Catherine's Hill 1 mile (1.5km) south of Winchester. An Iron Age hill fort which was the site of the first settlement in the Winchester area. There are also traces of a 12th century Norman chapel. The hill offers good views of the city, and has a miz-maze (a turf maze in the pattern of a labyrinth) – one of only eight in England – on top, probably dating from the 17th century.

St Michael's Abbey Farnborough Road, Farnborough. Benedictine abbey founded in 1881 by Empress Eugénie of France (1826–1920) as a mausoleum for her late husband Napoleon III (1808–73), and their son the Prince Imperial (1856–79). Both are buried in the imperial crypt, as is Empress Eugénie herself. Originally a foundation for monks from France, in 1947 it was joined by a community from Prinknash Abbey in Gloucestershire, and it still functions as a monastery today.

Sandham Memorial Chapel Harts Lane, Burghclere, 4 miles (6km) south of Newbury. Red-brick chapel built in the 1920s to house paintings by the artist Stanley Spencer, inspired by his experiences in World War I. Influenced by Giotto's Arena Chapel in Padua, Spencer took five years to complete what is arguably his finest achievement. The chapel is set amid lawns and orchards with views across Watership Down. It is now in the care of the National Trust. Tel: 01635 278394.

Sandown A seaside resort town on the southeast coast of the Isle of Wight, neighbouring the town of Shanklin to the south. Sandown Bay off the English Channel is shared by the two towns, and is notable for its long stretch of golden sandy beach.

Somerley 2 miles (3km) northwest of Ringwood. Designed by Samuel Wyatt in the mid 1700s, Somerley was bought by the 2nd Earl of Normanton in 1825 and has remained in the family ever since. The stunning picture gallery contains works by Canaletto, Murillo, Etty and Gainsborough and also houses one of the largest collections of paintings by Sir Joshua Reynolds in private hands. Somerley is the privately owned stately home of the 6th Earl of Normanton and his family. Set in 7000 acres (2800ha) of meadows, woods and rolling parkland, the house is not open to the public. Tel: 01425 480819.

Southampton Castle Norman motte and bailey castle founded c.1150. In 1194 Richard I spent his only Christmas in England as monarch in the castle. It had fallen into ruin by the late 1200s but was refortified in the 14th century by Richard II with a tower built by Henry Yevele. By the 16th century the castle was again in decay. Part of the bailey wall still stands, along with Castle Watergate and Castle Vault.

Southampton International Airport 4 miles (6km) northeast of Southampton. Opened in 1932 as Southampton Municipal Airport on a site bought by Southampton Council, during World War II the airport was the site of tests for the Spitfire. Regular flights to the Channel Islands began in 1945 and a new runway was built in the 1960s, when the airport returned to private ownership. The British Airports Authority (BAA) purchased the airport in 1990 and the expanded airport was opened in 1994. Today the airport serves more than 40 European destinations, handling nearly 2 million passengers a year. Tel: 0870 040 0009.

Southsea Castle Clarence Esplanade, Southsea. Built in 1544 as one of the series of fortifications constructed by Henry VIII around England's coasts to protect the country from invaders, the castle was barely complete when Henry's flagship, the *Mary Rose*, tragically sank in front of it. During the Civil War the castle was captured for the only time in its history, by Parliamentarian forces. For a while the castle was used as a military prison, and a lighthouse built in the 1820s is still in use by shipping today. It was provided with extra gun batteries in the 1860s as part of the refortification of the south coast. In 1960 the castle was acquired by Portsmouth City Council and restored to its 19th century appearance. Tel: 023 9282 7261.

Spinnaker Tower Gunwharf Quays, Portsmouth. Overlooking Portsmouth Harbour, the 558ft (170m) high tower was opened in 2005. View Deck 1 (330ft, 100m) has the largest glass floors in Europe and offers visibility up to 23 miles. There are two higher decks at 344ft (105m) and 361ft (110m); the top deck, known as the crow's nest, is open to the elements. The tower is constructed from two elegant crossed bows, fabricated from structural steel box sections 35ft (10.8m) long and 5ft (1.5m) wide, crossing the central shafts at 115ft (35m) and rising to connect with the shafts at 394ft (120m). The bow dimensions vary from 32–34ft (10–12m) in depth at the base and top of the tower, decreasing to 8ft (2.5m) wide in the central region. Aerofoil-shaped ribs span the bows to give the tower its distinctive sail appearance. Tel: 023 9285 7520.

Spithead Part of the Solent between Portsmouth Harbour, to the south of Gilkicker Point on the Hampshire coast, and the Isle of Wight. It is named after the Spit, a sandbank 14 miles (23km) long by 4 miles (6km) broad, and stretching south for 3 miles (5km) from the Hampshire shore. It was used in the 17th and 18th centuries as an anchorage and more recently for reviewing the fleet. It was the scene of a mutiny among sailors of the Royal Navy fleet in April 1797. The Spithead forts –

Horse Sands, No Man's Land, St Helens and Spitbank – were built in the 1860s to protect Portsmouth from attack from the sea.

Sport

cricket **Hampshire County Cricket Club** was founded in 1864 and has had its headquarters at the Rose Bowl, Botley Road, West End, Southampton, since 2001. The club's previous headquarters was the County Ground, Southampton and they also played at various other grounds including Dean Park, Bournemouth (now in Dorset) and the United Services Ground, Portsmouth. As of 2008 Hampshire are twice winners of the County Championship. The one-day team is known as The Hawks. Tel: 023 8047 2002.

football **Portsmouth** were founded in 1898 and entered the Football League in 1920. The club are twice winners of both the League championship and the FA Cup. They can claim to have held the FA Cup for the longest uninterrupted period, having won the competition in 1939, after which war was declared and the trophy was not contested again until 1945–46. Nicknamed Pompey (the origins of the nickname are obscure, but possibly derive from a group of sailors who, landing on Egypt, once scaled Pompey's Pillar in Alexandria), they play at Fratton Park. Tel: 023 9273 1204.

Southampton were founded in 1885 as Southampton St Mary's. Having entered the Football League in 1920, they finally attained promotion to the top flight in 1966. They won the FA Cup in 1976 while back in the Second Division, beating Manchester United 1–0. Having played at the Dell since 1898, The Saints' home ground since 2001 has been St Mary's Stadium. Tel: 023 8071 1992.

Non-league teams include **Eastleigh** (formed 1980) and **Havant & Waterlooville** (formed 1998).

miscellaneous **Havant Hockey Club** are three times winners of the National Hockey League and contributed several players to the British Olympic gold medal winning side of 1988.

Winchester Fives is one of three common English derivatives of fives, all played in public schools (the other two are Eton fives and Rugby fives). Winchester fives is a similar game to Rugby fives but the interesting shape of the court adds another dimension to the game: while Rugby fives is played in what is essentially a squash court, in Winchester fives the court has a buttress (resembling the tambour of a real tennis court) on the left-hand wall.

Stratfield Saye House 8 miles (13km) northeast of Basingstoke. The main part of the house and stable blocks were built c.1630 by Sir William Pitt, Comptroller of the Household to James I. In the 18th century George Pitt, 1st Baron Rivers, had the red brick faced in stucco, originally painted white, during a programme of extensive work to the house and park. The 1st Duke of Wellington acquired the house and estate in 1817, choosing it for its proximity to London and Windsor, and originally planning to pull down the house and build a fabulous 'Waterloo Palace' in the northeast of the park. In 1821 the plans were abandoned as being too expensive and instead he made additions and improvements to the existing house. The conservatory was added in 1838 and the outer wings in 1846. The Duke also introduced central heating (two of the original radiators can still be seen at the foot of the staircases) and elegantly designed and soundproofed water closets in many of the rooms. The house is surrounded by Wellington Country Park, featuring 350 acres (140ha) of woodland, parkland and lakes. Tel: 01256 882882.

Titchfield Abbey Titchfield, 2 miles (3km) southwest of Fareham. The impressively castellated ruins of a Tudor manor house, bearing little resemblance to the Premonstratensian monastery that was founded here in 1231 by Peter des Roches, Bishop of Winchester. Henry VI married Margaret of Anjou at the abbey in 1445. At the Dissolution of the Monasteries in 1537, the site was given to Thomas Wriothesley (later the 1st Earl of Southampton), who converted the abbey into a Tudor mansion called Place House, building a castellated and fortified gatehouse across the nave of the abbey church. During the late 18th century, however, much of the material was quarried away for the restoration of Cams Hall in Fareham. Today there are few traces of the abbey buildings except for fragmentary ground level foundations, although excavations have uncovered fine medieval tiles that once formed the floor of the cloisters. The property is now in the care of English Heritage. Tel: 01329 842133.

Universities The **University of Portsmouth**, Winston Churchill Avenue, Portsmouth, was inaugurated in 1992. The former Portsmouth Polytechnic, one of the largest and most successful in the UK, itself grew from the Portsmouth and Gosport School of Science and Arts, founded in 1869. The university has 20,000 students and particular academic strengths in geography and pharmacy. Former students include poet Simon Armitage, author Shirley Conran and transvestite potter Grayson Perry. Tel: 02392 848484.

The **University of Southampton**, University Road, Southampton, was founded by Henry Robinson Hartley, the son of a Southampton wine merchant, who left his estate to the Corporation of Southampton. The grand opening of the Hartley Institution, as it was originally known, took place on 15 October 1862. Prime Minister Lord Palmerston performed the opening ceremony. The Institute was granted its university charter on 29 April 1952, and six faculties were created: Arts, Science, Engineering, Economics, Education and Law. The first University of Southampton degrees were awarded on 4 July 1953, following the appointment of the Duke of Wellington as Chancellor. By the time the university celebrated its Golden Jubilee on 22 January 2002 it had become one of the leading universities in the UK, with particular strengths in computer science and electronics, and today it is a member of the Russell Group of research-led universities. Former students include athlete Roger Black, Lord Tonypandy, former Speaker of the House of Commons, comedian Jeremy Hardy and actor John Nettles. Tel: 02380 595000.

The **University of Winchester** has its roots in the Winchester Diocesan Training School, established in 1840. This became King Alfred's College, which gained degree awarding powers in

2004 as University College Winchester. It achieved full university status in 2005, and had 5300 students in 2007. The university's three faculties are Arts, Education and Social Sciences; its particular focus is on teacher training and it also has an excellent reputation for performing arts. Tel: 01962 841515.

Vyne, The 4 miles (6km) north of Basingstoke. Built in the early 16th century for Lord Sandys, Henry VIII's Lord Chamberlain. A classical portico (the first of its kind in England) was added in the mid 17th century. The house contains a magnificent Tudor chapel with Renaissance glass, a Palladian staircase and a wealth of old panelling and fine furniture. The attractive grounds feature herbaceous borders and a wild garden, with lawns, lakes, an early summerhouse dating to c.1635 and woodland walks. A recently developed wetland area attracts a diversity of wildlife. The property is in the care of the National Trust. Tel: 01256 883858.

Watership Down $2^1/_2$ miles (4km) southwest of Kingsclere, 9 miles (15km) northwest of Basingstoke. Best known as the setting for Richard Adams' 1972 novel of the same title about rabbits, the hill lies at the southeastern edge of the North Wessex Downs Area of Natural Beauty. Other nearby features include ancient tumuli and earthworks, including Beacon Hill. Much of the area is privately owned by Lord Lloyd-Webber.

Wayfarer's Walk Extending for 70 miles (113km) between the coast near Portsmouth and Inkpen Beacon just across the Berkshire border. It connects with other long-distance paths at Emsworth (the Sussex Border Path), Bedhampton (the Solent Way) and Inkpen Beacon (the Test Way). Linking with the Wayfarer's Walk are six circular walks each consisting of a network of paths of varying distances. Near the villages of Burghclere and Kingsclere the Wayfarer's Walk traverses Watership Down (see separate entry). See also Berkshire.

Westgate Museum High Street, Winchester. Housed in one of the original five gates to the medieval city, of which only two remain, this quirky museum has various displays including armour and weapons, as well as a collection of trading weights and measures used in the city at various periods. A good view of the city can be gained from the top of the gate. Tel: 01962 848269.

Whale Island Lying in Portsmouth Harbour and joined to Portsea Island by a bridge, Whale Island was until 1845 covered at every spring tide and presented the appearance of a whale's back, hence its name. It is currently the location of the Royal Navy base HMS *Excellent*. GR: SU637025.

Winchester Castle High Street, Winchester. Norman motte and bailey castle founded in 1067 by William I. Domesday Book was originally housed in the castle. The site was destroyed in 1141 but rebuilt shortly afterwards; the keep was added by Henry II, while the cylindrical tower on the motte and the Great Hall, once the centre of court and government life, were added in the 13th century by Henry III. During the Civil War, the castle was besieged by Parliamentary troops in 1645 and much of it was subsequently destroyed; today only the Great Hall remains. On display in the hall is the famous Round Table, venerated for centuries by tourists as the mysterious table of the 'Once and Future King' Arthur, although it is now known to have been constructed in the 14th century, and was repainted in its present form for Henry VIII. The names of 24 knights are written around the edge of the 18ft (5.5m) diameter table, which weighs 1.2 tons (1200kg) and is surmounted by a depiction of King Arthur on his throne. The first written account of the Arthurian story, in Geoffrey of Monmouth's *History of the Kings of Britain* (1130), maintains that Merlin had the 15-year-old Arthur crowned at nearby Silchester. However, the first mention of the Round Table is Robert Wace's *Roman de Brut* (1155), which says that Arthur seated his knights at a round table so that all should be equal. In Thomas Malory's *Morte D'Arthur*, the table is a wedding gift to Arthur from Guinevere's father, Leodegrance.

Winchester Cathedral The Close, Winchester. Dedicated to Holy Trinity, St Peter, St Paul and St Swithun, Winchester Cathedral has its origins in the 7th century, when a Christian church was first built on the site. Restored 1079–90 by Bishop Walkelin in the Romanesque style, the cathedral is at the heart of King Alfred's Wessex and a diocese which once stretched from London's Thames to the Channel Islands. At 556ft (169m) it is the longest Gothic cathedral in Europe and its nave is only marginally shorter than that of St Albans. Its bishops were men of enormous wealth and power, none more so than William of Wykeham, twice Chancellor of England, founder of Winchester College and New College, Oxford (see separate entries). These influential bishops also developed, refashioned and adorned the cathedral, and their chantry chapels and memorials are a notable feature. There pilgrims sought the shrine of local saints, notably a former bishop, St Swithun, whose festival (15 July) was said to set the pattern for the weather for the next 40 days. Bishop Gardiner's chantry chapel is an amazing hybrid of English late Gothic and Continental Renaissance style deriving ultimately from Fontainebleau. Stephen Gardiner (1531–55), the last important Roman Catholic bishop of Winchester, officiated at the marriage in the cathedral of Mary I to Philip of Spain. Other sovereigns who feature in the cathedral's history include William I, who was crowned here, Richard I who was recrowned here in 1194 after returning to England from the Crusades and his imprisonment in Dürnstein in Austria, Henry III, who was born here in 1207, and Henry IV, who married his second wife Joan of Navarre here in 1403. Smaller memorials include the grave of Izaak Walton in the Fishermen's Chapel in the south transept, while statues of Joan of Arc and Cardinal Beaufort stand outside the Lady Chapel. Sir George Gilbert Scott's imposing 19th century monument to Bishop Wilberforce (son of the social reformer) stands in the south transept. Other notable monuments are the tomb of Jane Austen and a statuette commemorating William Walker, the so-called 'Winchester Diver', who saved the cathedral from collapse in the early 20th century by working in several feet of flood water from the River Itchen to underpin its foundations. Tel: 01962 857200.

Winchester City Mill Bridge Street, Winchester. Situated next to City Bridge, spanning the River Itchen, a water-powered corn mill on the site was first recorded in the Domesday survey of 1086. It was taken into

Crown ownership by Henry VIII and given to the city of Winchester by Mary I in 1544. Rebuilt in 1744, it remained in use until the turn of the 20th century and has now been restored to full working order. The mill is in the care of the National Trust. Tel: 01962 870057.

Winchester College — College Street, Winchester. Founded in the 14th century by William of Wykeham, Bishop of Winchester and Chancellor to Richard II. The college's charter of foundation was granted in 1382, the buildings were begun in 1387 and the first scholars entered the school in 1394. The original statutes provided for a warden and ten fellows, two schoolmasters, three chaplains, 70 scholars and 16 quiristers (choristers who sang in the college chapel). The scholars and quiristers remain today; the latter now attend the nearby Pilgrims' School although they still sing in the chapel. As well as the scholars, who live in the college buildings, there are now also over 600 'Commoners' who occupy ten boarding houses, and instead of only two schoolmasters over 80 full-time teachers or 'dons'. The college still occupies its original 14th century buildings, although these have since been much extended. The college's motto is 'Manners Makyth Man'. Old boys include Thomas Arnold, headmaster of Rugby, author Anthony Trollope, Labour Party leader Hugh Gaitskell, art historian Lord (Kenneth) Clark, newsreader Reginald Bosanquet and comedian Tim Brooke-Taylor.

Wolvesey Castle — College Street, Winchester. Formerly the principal residence of the Bishops of Winchester, Wolvesey Castle was an extensive keep and bailey castle built c.1100 on a site in use during the Anglo-Saxon period, and rebuilt in quadrangular form with great tower by Henry of Blois during the 12th century civil war. On 25 July 1554, Philip II of Spain and Mary I of England had their wedding breakfast at the castle before their marriage in the cathedral. In 1680 the castle was demolished in order to build a new palace in Baroque style. That palace can be seen directly beside the ruins. All that remains of Wolvesey itself are ruined walls and the chapel, which was incorporated into the new palace. The remains are in the care of English Heritage. Across the road is Winchester College public school. Tel: 01962 854766.

Yarmouth — 9 miles (15km) west of Newport, Isle of Wight. Originally called Eremue, meaning 'muddy estuary', Yarmouth was the first Island settlement to be granted a royal town charter, in 1135. The town was sacked by the French in 1377 and 1524, and subsequently suffered numerous raids until Henry VIII improved its protection by building a stone castle. The 700ft (213m) long timber pier dating from 1876, Grade II listed and restored in the 1990s, is the longest timber pier in England still open to the public. Today, the picturesque port mainly serves ferries bound for Lymington on the mainland.

Yarmouth Castle — Quay Street, Yarmouth, Isle of Wight. Artillery fort built 1545–7 by Henry VIII to protect western approaches to The Solent in straight-sided canted square shape with arrow-head bastion on the southeast corner. Two triangular gun platforms were added in 1632 and the fort was controlled by Parliament throughout Civil War. It remained a coastal battery until 1885, after which it was used as a coastguard signalling station until 1901, and commandeered for service use during both world wars. It is now owned by English Heritage. Tel: 01983 760678.

Some famous people born in Hampshire and the Isle of Wight

Arlott, John (cricket commentator) (1914–91)	Basingstoke
Arnold, Dr Thomas (headmaster of Rugby) (1795–1842)	Cowes, IOW
Austen, Jane (novelist) (1775–1817)	Steventon
Barât, Carl (singer and guitarist) (1978–)	Basingstoke
Besant, Walter (novelist and historian) (1836–1901)	Portsmouth
Brunel, Isambard Kingdom (engineer) (1806–59)	Portsmouth
Callaghan, James (former Prime Minister) (1912–2005)	Portsmouth
Cremer, Sir William (Nobel Peace laureate) (1838–1908)	Fareham
Dawson, Richard (actor and comedian) (1932–)	Gosport
Dickens, Charles (novelist) (1812–70)	Portsmouth
Firth, Colin (actor) (1960–)	Grayshott
Fox, Uffa (yacht designer) (1898–1972)	Cowes, IOW
Goring, Marius (actor) (1912–98)	Newport, IOW
Gregg, Everley (actress) (1903–1959)	Bishop Stoke
Henry III (king of England) (1207–72)	Winchester
Hill, Benny (comedian) (1924–92)	Southampton
Hooke, Robert (physicist and inventor) (1635–1703)	Freshwater, IOW
Hurley, Elizabeth (actress) (1965–)	Basingstoke
Irons, Jeremy (actor) (1948–)	Cowes, IOW
Jepson-Turner, Belita (ice skater) (1923–2005)	Nether Wallop
Jones, John 'Howard' (singer and musician) (1955–)	Southampton
Jones, Paul (singer and broadcaster) (1942–)	Portsmouth
Millais, John Everett (artist) (1829–96)	Southampton
Minghella, Anthony (film and theatre director) (1954–2008)	Ryde, IOW
Ross-Craig, Stella (illustrator of British flora) (1906–2006)	Aldershot
Russell, Ken (film director) (1927–)	Southampton
Sellers, Peter (comedian and actor) (1925–80)	Southsea
Warton, Thomas (Poet Laureate) (1728–90)	Basingstoke
Westmore, George (make-up artist) (1879–1931)	Newport, IOW
Yates, Peter (director and producer) (1929–)	Aldershot

Islands of Hampshire and the Isle of Wight

Hampshire

Island name	Area	Nearest landmark	General information
Baker's Island	Langstone Harbour	Portsmouth	GR: SU695035
Burrow Island	Portsmouth Harbour	Portsmouth	GR: SU620008
Dolphins	Portsmouth Harbour	Portsmouth	GR: SU615022
Hayling Island	Hayling Bay	Hayling Island	See separate entry
Horse Sand Fort	Spithead	Portsmouth	GR: SZ655949
Horsea Island	Portsmouth Harbour	Portsmouth	See separate entry
Long Island	Langstone Harbour	Portsmouth	GR: SU701042
North Binness Island	Langstone Harbour	Portsmouth	GR: SU692045
Pewit Island	Portsmouth Harbour	Portsmouth	GR: SU609039
Portsea Island	Portsmouth Harbour	Portsmouth	See separate entry
South Binness Island	Langstone Harbour	Portsmouth	GR: SU699032
Spitbank Fort	Spithead	Portsmouth	GR: SZ636972
Whale Island	Portsmouth Harbour	Portsmouth	See separate entry

Isle of Wight

Island name	Area	Nearest landmark	General information
Atherfield Rocks	Chale Bay	Little Atherfield	GR: SZ452789
Bembridge Ledge	Spithead	Bembridge	GR: SZ662878
Black Rock Ledge	Spithead	Bembridge	GR: SZ652868
Bordwood Ledge	Sandown Bay	Luccombe Village	GR: SZ585788
Fossil Forest	English Channel	Brighstone	GR: SZ379836
Goose Rock	English Channel	West High Down	GR: SZ290849
Gurnard Ledge	Gurnard Bay	Gurnard	GR: SZ461948
Hardman Rock	English Channel	Brighstone	GR: SZ401819
Horse Ledge	Sandown Bay	Shanklin	GR: SZ588802
Long Ledge	Spithead	Bembridge	GR: SZ650866
Needles, The	English Channel	West High Down	See separate entry
No Man's Land Fort	Spithead	Ryde	GR: SZ640938
Old Pepper Rock	English Channel	West High Down	GR: SZ305847
St Anthony Rock	English Channel	West High Down	GR: SZ297847
St Helen's Fort	Spithead	St Helen's	GR: SZ648899
Tyne Ledge	Spithead	Bembridge	GR: SZ648888
Warden Ledge	South Channel	Freshwater	GR: SZ324878
Whitecliff Ledge	Spithead	Bembridge	GR: SZ640855
Wight, Isle of	The Solent	Hurst Castle	See separate entry
Yellow Ledge	Sandown Bay	Shanklin	GR: SZ588798

HEREFORDSHIRE

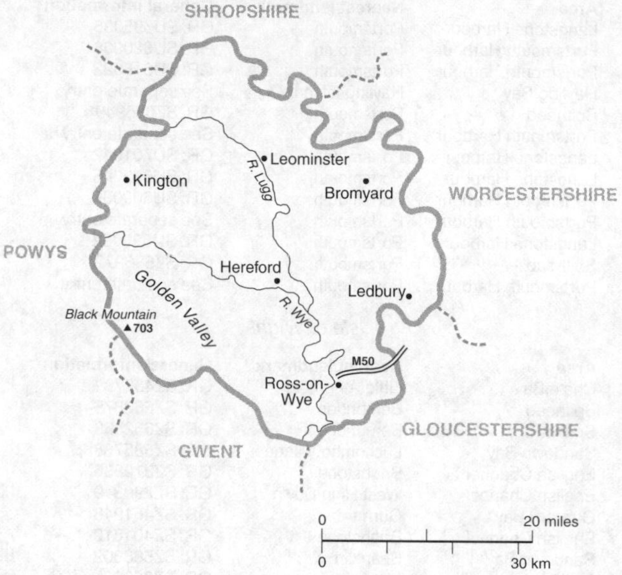
SHROPSHIRE
Leominster
R. Lugg
Kington
Bromyard
WORCESTERSHIRE
POWYS
Hereford
Golden Valley
Ledbury
Black Mountain
703
R. Wye
M50
Ross-on-Wye
GLOUCESTERSHIRE
GWENT
0
20 miles
0
30 km

Herefordshire is a historic and ceremonial county in the West Midlands. It borders Shropshire to the north, Worcestershire to the east, Gloucestershire to the southeast and the Welsh counties of Gwent in the southwest and Powys in the west. It was merged with neighbouring Worcestershire to form the new county of Hereford and Worcester in 1974, and has had no county council since then. On 1 April 1998 the county was split again and Herefordshire became a separate unitary authority, referred to as the County of Herefordshire although still without full county status. Despite the abolition, some remnants of Hereford and Worcester's existence remain: there is still a Hereford and Worcester fire service and ambulance service, while the name continues in use by organisations such as the local radio station BBC Hereford and Worcester. There is also a Hereford and Worcester Chamber of Commerce.

The area which is now Herefordshire was occupied by West Saxons after the Romans left Britain in the 5th century (the usual date given for the foundation of the county is 676). This tribe, known as the Hecanas, congregated in the fertile area around Hereford and to the south in the mining districts around Ross-on-Wye. In the 8th century Offa extended the Mercian frontier to the Wye, securing it by the earthwork known as Offa's Dyke, portions of which are still visible today. From the time of its first settlement this area was the scene of constant border warfare and cross-border incursions by the Welsh were likely to be rewarded with loss of the trespasser's right hand. The county contains three of the only four castles in England known to have existed before the Norman Conquest: Ewyas Harold, Hereford and Richard's Castle. After the Conquest in 1066 William fitz Osbern, Lord of Breteuil in Normandy, was created Earl of Hereford by William I and charged with the subjugation of Herefordshire; this he did by building castles along the Welsh border, although the Saxon Edric the Wild, in conjunction with the Welsh, kept up resistance against him for two years.

The millennium since the Conquest has been a fairly settled period within Herefordshire. The Welsh accepted the county as part of England and it came to prominence only occasionally. Herefordshire was first represented in Parliament in 1295, when it returned two members. In 1326 the Parliament which deposed Edward II assembled at Hereford. In 1397 Henry, Earl of Derby, later Henry IV, was created Duke of Hereford having married Mary de Bohun, daughter of the 7th Earl. The threat to Henry from Owain Glyndwr's rebellion in the early 15th century led to strengthening of many fortifications near the border with Wales. Edward VI created Walter Devereux, a descendant of the Bohun family, Viscount Hereford, in 1550, and his grandson, the famous Earl of Essex, was born in Herefordshire. Ever since the title has been held by the Devereux family, and the holder ranks as the premier Viscount of England.

In the 14th and 15th centuries the forest of Deerfold in the northwest of the county provided refuge for some of the most noted followers of John Wycliffe. The Lollards (a name deriving from the Dutch for a mumbler of prayers), as these religious reformers came to be known, criticised ecclesiastical abuses of wealth and power and were vehemently opposed to the idea of transubstantiation (the conversion of the bread and wine during Holy Communion into the body and blood of Christ) at a time when the religion of the land was Catholicism. During the Wars of the Roses the influence of the Mortimers led the county to support the Yorkist cause, and Edward, afterwards Edward IV, raised 23,000 men in this neighbourhood.

Herefordshire is largely agricultural. The county became the centre of cider and perry manufacture in England in the 1600s and many cider-apple orchards remain, although the industry has been in decline since the 1800s. Many houses in the county are in the style known as black and white: timber-framed buildings with black-painted beams and panels of white plaster. The frameworks were built from green (unseasoned) oak and the panels finished in lath – woven strips of wood and plaster. Many of these houses date from the 16th and 17th centuries or earlier, when timbers were often left unpainted to weather naturally, while the panels were painted with pigmented limewash – sometimes both beams and panels were limewashed. In the 18th century stucco and stone finishes became fashionable, and many houses had their timbers plastered over. Nineteenth-century photographs of Herefordshire show houses which now have exposed beams, but which were then covered in plaster. The idea of decorating timber-framed houses by painting the beams black and the panels white is a recent one. Many houses were restored and their timbers exposed throughout the 19th and 20th centuries.

The 'county' town and only city in Herefordshire is **Hereford**, situated on the River Wye. Hereford was founded c.AD 700 and became the Saxon capital of West Mercia. The name derives from the Anglo Saxon *here* (an army) and *ford* (river) – essentially Hereford began as a place where a body of armed men could cross the Wye. A town charter from 1189 granted by Richard I describes it as 'Hereford in Wales'. This charter also gave Hereford city status, the earliest example of such status being granted, since all earlier cities had been so since time immemorial (legally this was 1189, and so could not pre-date Hereford's). The county is now known chiefly as a trading centre for a wider agricultural and rural area. Products from Hereford include (Bulmer's) cider, beer, leather goods, nickel alloys, poultry from Sun Valley, chemicals and cattle, including the famous Hereford breed. The city was the home of the Special Air Service (SAS) for many years, although the regiment relocated to nearby Credenhill in the late 1990s.

One of the first motorways in the UK to be built – the M50 – runs through the south of the county and, with the A40 dual carriageway, forms part of the major route linking South Wales and the West Midlands.

Herefordshire	**Population**			**Area**	
	male	*female*	*total*	*sq miles*	*sq km*
Total	85,350	89,521	174,871	842	2180

Local Attractions and Information

Abbey Dore Court Garden	Abbey Dore, 11 miles (18km) southwest of Hereford. Located at the southern end of the Golden Valley on the River Dore, the 6 acre (2.4ha) garden features both wild areas and more formal planting. There is a walled garden with nine individual borders, divided by brick paths, while the former orchard is now marked out by bulbs. Tel: 01981 240419.
Administrative headquarters	Brockington, 35 Hafod Road, Hereford HR1 1SH. Tel: 01432 260000.
Archenfield	The English name for an area of southwest Herefordshire, roughly bounded by the rivers Monnow and Wye. Its name derives from the Welsh kingdom of Ergyng, which in turn took its name from the Roman town of Ariconium (Weston-under-Penyard). Domesday Book recorded that the Welsh of Archenfield were allowed to retain their old rights and privileges in return for forming an advance and rear guard when the King's army entered or left Wales. The area remained in limbo, neither in England nor Wales, until the 16th century Acts of Union. It remained a Welsh-speaking region until the 17th century. The symbol of Archenfield, and the town of Ross-on-Wye, is the hedgehog.
Battles	There have been two major battles in Herefordshire: Hereford and Mortimer's Cross. See separate table for details.
Belmont Abbey	2½ miles (4km) southwest of Hereford. The home of a community of Benedictine monks founded in 1859, set in extensive gardens. The church of St Michael, once the cathedral for the diocese of Newport, was also built in 1859 to the design of E W Pugin, and became the abbey church in 1920. Tel: 01432 374747.

Berrington Hall 4 miles (6km) north of Leominster. A Neoclassical country house designed by Henry Holland in the late 18th century. Features include collections of furniture and paintings, as well as a nursery, Victorian laundry and Georgian dairy. The site is notable as the location of Capability Brown's last landscape garden design. Berrington Pool, a lake and island, is a Site of Special Scientific Interest. Berrington has been in the care of the National Trust since 1954. Tel: 01568 615721.

Broadfield Court Gardens and Vineyard Bowley Lane, Bodenham, 5 miles (8km) southeast of Leominster. Located on an estate mentioned in Domesday Book, the manor house dates to the 14th century and is surrounded by 4 acres (1.6ha) of gardens, including a David Austin rose garden with 37 varieties, herbaceous borders, yew hedges, courtyards and an old walled kitchen garden. The site includes 14 acres (5.5ha) of vineyards. Tel: 01568 797483.

Brockhampton Estate 2 miles (3km) northeast of Bromyard. The moated black and white great hall of Lower Brockhampton House dates to the late 14th century, and has a roof of local timber; the moat is crossed by a crooked timber-framed gatehouse. A ruined Norman chapel nearby is believed to have been built by the Brockhampton family c.1180. The estate of 1700 acres (680ha), consisting of farmland and woodland, was handed over to the National Trust in 1947 and is managed using traditional methods. Tel: 01885 488099.

Bromyard Heritage Centre Rowberry Street, Bromyard. Museum dedicated to hops and hop picking. Displays explore the history of hop growing and follow the annual cycle of the hop from winter maintenance of the fields through to the summer and autumn picking. The displays include life-size scenes from hop picking life and many original artefacts and tools. Tel: 01432 260692

Burford House Gardens Burford, 9 miles (15km) northeast of Leominster. The 4 acres (1.6ha) of gardens, nestling in a loop of the River Teme and set around an early Georgian house, are home to the National Collection of clematis. Tel. 01584 810777.

Butchers Row House Museum Church Lane, Ledbury. A small scale museum displaying Victorian life, housed in a timber-framed building which once stood in High Street but was demolished c.1830. It was re-erected in 1979 by the Ledbury and District Society. Tel: 01531 632511.

Chained Library College Cloisters, Cathedral Close, Hereford. Now housed within the New Library Building. the 17th century Chained Library in Hereford Cathedral (see separate entry) is the largest intact example of its kind still in existence. From the Middle Ages to the 18th century chaining books was the most widespread and effective security system in European libraries. In this system one end of a chain is attached to the front cover of each book; the other end is slotted onto a rod running along the bottom of each shelf. This allows a book to be taken from the shelf and read at the desk, but not to be removed from the bookcase. There has been a theological library at the cathedral since the 12th century. The 8th century Hereford Gospels, the cathedral's earliest and most important book, is one of 229 medieval manuscripts, also including a copy of Magna Carta from 1217 and the famous Hereford Mappa Mundi (see separate entry) which now occupy two bays of the Chained Library. The specially designed chamber in the New Library Building means that the whole library can now be seen in its original arrangement as it was from 1611 to 1841. Tel: 01432 374202.

Cider Museum Ryelands Street, Hereford. Located in a former cider factory, the Cider Museum traces the history of cider making from its origins on individual farms to the establishment of manufacturers such as Bulmers and Westons. On display is a collection of Pomonas, beautifully illustrated surveys of the county's apple orchards and fruit varieties. On the same site is the King Offa Distillery, one of only two distilleries in Britan producing cider brandy. Tel: 01432 354207.

Coningsby Museum Widemarsh Street, Hereford. St John Medieval Museum and Coningsby Hospital, to give the museum its full title, is located within almshouses founded in 1614 by Sir Thomas Coningsby and annexed to Blackfriars Rose Garden. The museum has displays on the foundation of the Coningsby Red Coat Hospital, thought to be the model for the Chelsea Hospital in London, and explores the links between the Crusades, the Knights Templar and the Knights Hospitaller. Parts of the building date to the 14th century, when the site was occupied by Blackfriars Monastery, home to Dominicans of the Order of St John. The stone Preaching Cross in the garden is one of the last surviving examples of its type. The chapel is still in use.. Tel: 01432 274903.

Credenhill 4½ miles (7km) northwest of Hereford. Cider production is one of Herefordshire's key industries and in 1887 Percy Bulmer founded the Bulmer's cider company here. There is a large Iron Age hill fort ½ mile (0.8km) north of Credenhill, archaeological finds from which are held in Hereford Museum. The defences of this very large hill fort enclose 50 acres (20ha), comprising an embankment and ditch with a slight counter-scarp bank inside the main rampart. Traces of rectangular wooden buildings, storage pits and other remains of occupation, including pottery with stamped and incised patterns typical of the West Midlands during the Iron Age, have been found on the site. The fort dates from c.400 BC and was occupied continuously until c.AD 75; it and the surrounding ancient woodland are now owned by the Woodland Trust. The poet and religious writer Thomas Traherne (1636–74) was rector of Credenhill for ten years. Near the village is the site of the former RAF Hereford, now the headquarters of the 22nd Special Air Service Regiment.

Croft Castle 5 miles (8km) northwest of Leominster. A castellated 14th century quadrangular manor house set in extensive parkland and named after the family who built it. The pink stone castle has a decorative interior and Gothic staircase and ceilings. There are also well restored walled gardens and vineyards, ornamental rose beds and a variety of ancient plants. The house and surrounding estate are now in the care of the National Trust. On a clear day 14 counties are said to be visible from the Iron Age hill fort at Croft Ambrey, 1 mile (1.6km) north of the house. Tel: 01568 780246.

Cwmmau Farmhouse 4 miles (6km) southwest of Kington. A timber-framed and stone-tiled farmhouse dating to the early 17th century, and bequeathed to the National Trust in 1965 having been restored from a derelict state by the donor. Tel: 01981 590500/590509.

Dinmore Hill — See Queenswood Country Park

Dinmore Manor — 1 mile (1.6km) east of Westhope, 5 miles (8km) southwest of Hereford. Standing 500ft (150m) above sea level, the gardens at Dinmore Manor include a rock garden, a collection of acers and a water garden. The house overlooks the garden and lawn; cloisters featuring stained glass windows flank it to the right. The garden is sited on a terrace, on one side of which is a 12th century chapel once part of the preceptory of the Knights of St John (see also Coningsby Museum). A yew tree near the chapel is reputed to be 1200 years old. The Music Room, actually a hall with a vaulted ceiling, contains a Victorian Aeolian pipe organ. The manor is now the location of a stud farm and is not open to the public.

Dore Abbey — Abbey Dore, 11 miles (18km) southwest of Hereford. Located in the Golden Valley of the River Dore, the former Cistercian abbey was founded in 1147 by Lord Robert d'Ewyas and in 1282 dedicated to the Holy Trinity and Saint Mary by D'Ewyas' brother-in-law, Thomas Cantilupe. In 1536 the abbey was dissolved and granted to the Scudamores, a local family historically connected with Owain Glyndŵr, who used much of the stone for building elsewhere. Part of the original abbey church, begun c.1180, is still in use, although the nave of the original church, built of Hereford sandstone, no longer exists. Restored in the 1630s by the 1st Viscount Scudamore, who employed master carpenter John Abel to repair the woodwork, the church still contains some fine 17th century fittings. The roof of the chancel and decorated screen are Abel's work. Tel: 01981 570251.

Downs, The — Brockhill Road, Colwall, 5 miles (8km) north of Ledbury. Part of Malvern College since September 2008, and formerly known as the Downs School, this co-educational preparatory boarding school for pupils aged 2½–13 is located on the western slopes of the Malvern Hills. The 80-year-old Downs Light Railway in the grounds is claimed to be the world's oldest privately owned miniature railway. The poet W H Auden spent three years (1932–5) teaching English at the school, and wrote some of his finest early love poems here, including 'This lunar beauty' and 'Out on the lawn I lie in bed' (the latter dedicated to headmaster Geoffrey Hoyland). It was Auden's practice to sleep in a bed set up on the school's lawn, during the summer terms. His main rooms he named 'Lawrence Villa', after T E Lawrence. Auden contributed a preface to the Catalogue of Oil Paintings by Past and Present Members of the Downs School. He also strongly influenced the school magazine, *The Badger*, and wrote the poem *The Garrison* (1970) for the magazine's 70th anniversary edition. Other former pupils include neuroscientist and Nobel laureate Alan Hodgkin, double chemistry Nobel laureate Frederick Sanger, historian A J P Taylor and actor Orlando Bloom. Tel: 01684 540277.

Eastnor Castle — 2 miles (3km) east of Ledbury. Set in the Malvern Hills, the castle is the home of the Hervey-Bathurst family, descendants of Earl Somers who built it 1811–24 in the style of a Norman castle. The drawing room was designed by A W Pugin in 1849; now restored, it represents his most complete interior other than the Houses of Parliament. The house is surrounded by a deer park, arboretum and lake. Tel: 01531 633160.

Elms School, The — Colwall, 5 miles (8km) north of Ledbury. A co-educational, independent preparatory and pre-preparatory school situated at the foot of the Malvern Hills and catering for children aged 2½–13. The Elms was founded in 1614 by Humphrey Walwyn of the Worshipful Company of Grocers, and claims to be the oldest prep school still on its original site. It still has close links with the Grocers' Company, and receives financial assistance from the company's charitable arm. Tel: 01684 540344.

Ewyas Harold Castle — Ewyas Harold, 11 miles (18km) southwest of Hereford. Also named in historical documents as Mapheralt and Pentecosts Castle. Located above the valley of the Dulas Brook, the castle is one of several medieval defensive sites located along the Golden Valley and adjacent Marches valleys and one of just four pre-Norman castles known to exist in England. Ewyas Harold was built c.1048; it is recorded in Domesday Book as Osbern Pentecost's castle of 1052. The castle was refortified after the Norman Conquest by William Fitz Osbern but its history is otherwise obscure. It fell into decay in the 14th century although it was re-garrisoned in 1402 with the region under threat from Owain Glyndwr. John Leland recorded in 1530 that a great deal of the castle was still standing but by 1645 Royalist Richard Simmonds, seeking a place for Charles I to stay, reported that it was a ruin. All that can be seen today are remains of the motte; measuring up to 50ft (15m) high and 250ft (75m) around the base, it is separated from the bailey by a ditch. A 12th century priory was once located inside the bailey.

Goodrich Castle — 5 miles (8km) south of Ross-on-Wye. Situated high above the River Wye, the site was originally fortified by Godric of Mappestone in the early 12th century. It was taken by William Fitz Osbern in 1144; the keep, standing three storeys high, dates from c.1160–70. Further defences were added by William Marshal in the early 13th century and it was converted into a quadrangular castle by William de Valence from 1280. The barbican was erected in the 14th century. Occupied by the Earls of Shrewsbury in the 15th and early 16th centuries, Goodrich passed to the Earls of Kent in 1616 and was seized by the Earl of Stafford for Parliament in 1643. Although reoccupied by Royalists after his withdrawal, it was again taken by Parliamentary forces with the help of the massive cannon 'Roaring Meg', and was slighted in 1646. Extensive remains from the 13th and 14th centuries can still be seen today, as can the 12th century keep. The castle is now in the care of English Heritage. Tel: 01600 890538.

Hellens — Much Marcle, 4 miles (6km) southwest of Ledbury. The ancestral home of the de Helyon family, Hellens was founded in the 13th century and has Tudor and Stuart additions. One of its early owners, Sir James Audley, was a companion of Edward, the Black Prince and the house also has connections with Mary I. Features include a variety of pictures and furniture in the period rooms. The house is situated in extensive grounds including a knot garden, a 17th century dovecote and a yew labyrinth. Tel: 01531 660504.

Hereford Castle Castle Green, Hereford. The first castle in Hereford, probably of timber, was built by Ralph, son of the Count of Vexin, who was made Earl of Hereford in 1046 and constructed a castle and Norman garrison before 1052. The monastery of St Guthlac was originally founded within the castle precinct. In 1055 the castle was overrun by the Welsh under Gruffydd ap Llewellyn, and the town and cathedral were burnt. William fitz Osbern restored Hereford Castle after the Norman Conquest; at his death in 1071 his son Roger took possession. As a result of his involvement in an unsuccessful attempt to depose William I, Roger forfeited the castle to the Crown and it largely remained a royal stronghold for the rest of its existence. Hereford Castle was involved once more in the politics of the nation during the 12th century civil war; in 1138 it was garrisoned by Geoffrey Talbot on behalf of Matilda, before King Stephen and his army burned the city and took the castle. The following year Matilda landed in Hereford and seized the city after routing Stephen's men. The burial grounds of the priory of St Guthlac were dug up at this time and used to consolidate the existing defences, and soon afterwards St Guthlac's was moved outside the castle. Matilda did not regain control until later in 1139 when both Geoffrey Talbot and Miles of Gloucester besieged the castle. During the second Barons' War of the 1260s Hereford Castle was for a time the headquarters of the baronial party, led by Simon de Montfort. The eldest son of Henry III, Prince Edward, was taken prisoner at the Battle of Lewes in 1264 and brought to Hereford; allowed out riding on Widemarsh Common in 1265, he escaped to Wigmore Castle, the family seat of the Mortimers. The castle was used by a base by Henry IV in the early 15th century in his battles against Owain Glyndwr. During the Civil War Herefordshire was a Royalist stronghold, though several local families supported Parliament. The castle played its part in the sieges of Hereford during the Civil War, although it does not appear to have come under specific attack; in 1645 the city was forced to defend itself for five weeks from the Scottish army, pursuing Prince Rupert through Herefordshire, although when Charles I arrived in Hereford in September the Scots dispersed. Most of the castle seems to have been destroyed in the 1650s and no visible traces remain; the site became the present-day Castle Green, where it is still possible in very dry weather to see parch marks in the grass indicating the castle's remains.

Hereford Cathedral Cathedral Close, Hereford. Dedicated to the Blessed Virgin Mary and St Ethelbert, the cathedral was founded in 676 by Bishop Putta.One of the smaller cathedrals in England, with a nave 342ft (104m) long, it was built on a place of worship used since Saxon times and contains examples of architecture from Norman times to the present day, including the 13th century Shrine of St Thomas of Hereford, the restored 14th century Lady Chapel and the award-winning 20th century New Library Building. The central tower, which once had a wooden spire, is 165ft (50m) high. The Chained Library houses the medieval map of the world known as the Hereford Mappa Mundi. The Three Choirs Festival (see separate entry) is held in the cathedral, and there is a working stonemason's yard where restoration work is carried out using traditional methods. Tel: 01432 374202.

Herefordshire Beacon One of the Malvern Hills (see separate entry), the top of which forms part of a substantial Iron Age fort known as British Camp. A similar fort at Midsummer Hill, 1 mile (1.6km) to the south, was occupied permanently by up to 4000 people for almost 500 years, until occupation was ended by the coming of the Romans. A Norman fortress was built on top of the Iron Age camp. An earthwork, known as the Shire Ditch and dating in its present form probably to the 13th century, runs north–south along the ridge of the hills, although it is likely to be based on a much older construction. A higher hill 3 miles (5km) to the north, known as Worcestershire Beacon, has no similar evidence of fortification. According to consensus Herefordshire Beacon is 1109ft (338m) high, although an inscription puts its height at 1115ft (340m).

Herefordshire College of Arts Folly Lane, Hereford. An art school offering further and higher education courses in art and design, performance and related fields. The college was founded in 1851. The Universities of Gloucestershire and Wales are responsible for degree validation. Tel: 01432 273359.

Herefordshire Light Infantry Museum Harold Street, Hereford. The museum recounts the story of the Herefordshire Light Infantry in campaigns such as Gallipoli, Egypt and Palestine. It also describes the regiment's inception as the Herefordshire Rifle Volunteers in 1860, and more recently its involvement in the arrest of Admiral Dönitz at the end of World War II. Tel: 01432 950328.

Hergest Croft Gardens Kington, 15 miles (24km) southwest of Leominster. Situated on an estate dating to 1267, the gardens extend over 50 acres (20ha), with more than 4000 rare shrubs and trees. There are four distinct areas including an old fashioned kitchen garden, spring and summer borders and roses. The gardens also contain National Collections of birches, maples and zelkovas as well as spectacular rhododendrons and azaleas. Tel: 01544 230160

Highest point Black Mountain at 2306ft (703m), on the border with Powys (GR: SO255350). Offa's Dyke long-distance footpath passes along the ridge from south to north (or vice versa), while a steeper path leads to the summit from near the youth hostel in the Vale of Ewyas to the west.

Interesting facts **Symonds Yat West**, a village within the Forest of Dean straddling the River Wye on the border of Herefordshire and Gloucestershire, provided a magnificent backdrop for scenes in the film *Shadowlands* (1993), the true story of the relationship between C S Lewis and Joy Gresham, starring Sir Anthony Hopkins and Debra Winger. The Symonds Yat Rock from which much of the photography was shot is actually in Symonds Yat East across the Wye in Gloucestershire.

Amateur archaeologist **Alfred Watkins** was out riding in the Bredwardine Hills west of Hereford in 1921, when he had a vision of the interconnection of ancient monuments that led him to develop the theory of ley lines (hypothetical alignments of a number of places of geographical interest).

Islands There are no natural islands in Herefordshire although there is an artificial island in the centre of Berrington Pool Lake at Berrington Hall near Leominster (see separate entry). The island is well wooded with oak (*Quercus robur*). GR: SJ525072.

Kington Old border market town with a 17th century school built of stone. The gardens of Hergest Croft (see separate entry) are nearby. Located on Mill Street, a museum housed in former stables displays the history of Kington from Roman times to the present day, focusing on domestic artefacts. The museum also has an elephant, the legacy of a time when circuses with exotic animals travelled the country. Tel: 01544 231486.

Kinnersley Castle 14 miles (23km) northwest of Hereford. Located near Hay-on-Wye and the Black Mountains, Kinnersley was one of the many Marches castles built by the Normans along the Welsh border. The castle has changed hands numerous times; the house that exists today is mainly Elizabethan, remodelled by the Vaughan family and containing fine oak-panelled rooms and a solar with original 1588 plasterwork ceiling. The 8 acres (3ha) of grounds contain yew hedges, a walled kitchen garden and one of the largest ginkgo biloba trees in England. All of the land is organic and Soil Association registered. Next to the castle the Norman church has an unusual 13th century saddleback tower, wall paintings designed by Arts and Crafts architect George Frederick Bodley, and a monument to Francis Smallman, MP for Leominster, who owned the castle until his death there in 1633. Tel: 01544 327875.

Ledbury A market town located at the southern end of the Malvern Hills on the border of Herefordshire and Worcestershire, with timber-framed buildings including the black-and-white 17th century Market House, which stands on oak stilts, and the Browning Memorial clock tower of 1895. The picturesque cobbled Church Lane leads from High Street to the church of St Michael and All Saints, which has an unusual detached bell-tower and a distinctive spire.

Ledbury Heritage Centre Church Lane, Ledbury. The story of Ledbury's past displayed in a 15th century timber-framed building, once the town's Guildhall and occupied by the local grammar school in the 17th century. There are displays relating to the poets John Masefield and Elizabeth Barrett Browning, both of whom lived in the town, as well as a timber framing puzzle. Tel: 01432 260692

Llancillo Church 13 miles (21km) southwest of Hereford. Situated near the Welsh border among trees and fields, the church is dedicated to St Peter. Grade II listed, it has a Norman chancel, 13th century font and Tudor doorway. It is no longer used for worship.

Longtown Castle Longtown, 14 miles (23km) southwest of Hereford. Situated near the Welsh border in the Olchon valley, beneath the base of the Black Mountains, the Norman motte and bailey castle was founded c.1180 by Walter de Lacy on the site of a square enclosure that may have been a Roman fort. In the early 13th century another Walter de Lacy, Sheriff of Herefordshire, rebuilt the castle in stone, adding a curtain wall around the bailey and a circular keep on the motte – a style unusual in England but relatively common in Wales. The best preserved part of the curtain walls is the cross-wall, in which there are the remains of a gateway flanked by two half-round turrets, while the motte still stands to a height of 35ft (11m). The castle was abandoned in the 14th century, although it was refortified in the early 15th century during Owain Glyndwr's rebellion. It is now in the care of English Heritage. Tel: 0121 625 6820/0870 333 1181.

Malvern Hills Located in Worcestershire, Herefordshire and a small part of northern Gloucestershire, the Malvern Hills run north–south for 8 miles (13km) between Great Malvern and the village of Colwall, overlooking the Severn valley to the east, with the Cotswolds beyond. A designated Area of Outstanding Natural Beauty. The highest point is Worcestershire Beacon at 1395ft (425m) (GR: SO768452). The hills consist largely of igneous and metamorphic rocks from the late pre-Cambrian period; the existence of numerous natural mineral springs and wells led to the development of Great Malvern in Worcestershire as a spa in the early 19th century. There are two passes through the hills, the Wyche cutting (Wyche means salt) and the A449 road just north of Herefordshire Beacon (see separate entry). J R R Tolkien, who was from the area, often walked on the hills and they were the inspiration for the Misty Mountains in his books. The hills were also the setting for the famous 14th century poem *The Vision of Piers Plowman* by William Langland. Composer Edward Elgar, who was also from the area, often walked, cycled, and reportedly flew kites here. His 1898 cantata *Caractacus* employs the popular legend of the British chieftain's last stand at British Camp (see Herefordshire Beacon). In 1934, during the composer's final illness, he told a friend: 'If ever after I'm dead you hear someone whistling this tune [the opening theme of his cello concerto] on the Malvern Hills, don't be alarmed. It's only me.' The poet W H Auden wrote a long poem about the hills and their views, called simply *The Malverns*.

Mappa Mundi Part of the collection held in the Chained Library at Hereford Cathedral (see separate entries), the Hereford Mappa Mundi is one of the most important medieval maps still in existence, recording how 13th century scholars interpreted the world in both spiritual and geographical terms. The map bears the name of its author, Richard of Haldingham or Lafford (Holdingham and Sleaford in Lincolnshire); it was probably created c.1300. The Mappa Mundi is drawn on a single sheet of vellum measuring 64in by 52in (158cm by 133cm), tapering towards the top. The geographical material is contained within a circle 52in in diameter; Jerusalem is placed at its centre, in accordance with the thinking of the medieval church, with east at the top; Britain appears at the bottom left. Superimposed on to the continents are 500 drawings of the history of humankind and marvels of the natural world, both real and fabulous, including cities and towns, biblical events, plants, animals, birds and strange creatures, peoples of the world and illustrations from classical mythology.

Moccas Court 10 miles (16km) east of Hay-on-Wye. Situated on the River Wye, the house was built by Anthony Keck 1775–83 with decoration, including the round room and oval stairs, by Robert Adam. The grounds were laid out by Capability Brown and Humphry Repton. The area between the rivers Wye and Usk is a land peopled by characters from Arthurian romance. Moccas (the name probably derives from the Welsh *moch-ros*, or swine moor) is reputed to be the site of the residence of Llacheu, son of King Arthur. St Dubric or Dubricius, the bishop who supposedly crowned Arthur, founded abbeys at both Moccas and Hentland. Dubric was a historical figure with a significant local reputation, and Herefordshire churches at Hentland, Whitchurch and Ballingham are dedicated to him. He died in 612 (according to a life of the saint written 500 years after his death) and 14 November is still named St Dubricius' Day. This is also the festival of the Celtic pig goddess, coincidentally called Moccas or Mochros. The Chester-Master family inherited Moccas Court in 1962 from Sir William Cornewall and re-established the house as a habitable property in 1969. Since then it has been turned into an exclusive hotel. Tel: 01981 500354/500019.

Mortimer's Cross Watermill — 7 miles (11km) northwest of Leominster. Located beside the River Lugg, this 18th century water mill has been partly restored to working order. The site includes a small museum dedicated to the 1461 Battle of Mortimer's Cross (see Battles). The mill is in the care of English Heritage. Tel: 01568 708820.

Motto — *Pulchra terra Dei donum* (This fair land is the gift of God).

Newland Castle — See Pembridge Castle

Old House, The — High Town, Hereford. A black and white building dating from 1621 and situated in the heart of Hereford. The house now stands on its own, the sole remaining building of Butcher's Row. The kitchen, dining hall, parlour and bedrooms are furnished in 17th century style, with wall paintings and various items of oak furniture. Tel: 01432 260694.

Old Sufton — Mordiford, 4 miles (6km) southeast of Hereford. The medieval home of the Hereford family, who moved to their new house at Sufton Court (see separate entry) c.1788 but carefully preserved the old house and its contents. A raised, partly walled garden adjacent to the house to the northeast, features a circular dovecote incorporating a ground-floor summerhouse dating from the early 18th century. Zigzag paths with box borders cross the garden. Tel: 01432 870268.

Pembridge Castle — 1 mile (1.6km) northwest of Welsh Newton, 14 miles (23km) south of Hereford. Founded in 1208 by Ralph de Pembridge, and originally known as Newland Castle, the Grade I listed former border castle is over 30 miles (48km) from the village of Pembridge. It includes a moat and cylindrical keep and was the seat of the Pembridge family, and later the Wakes and Mortimer families, in the 14th and 15th centuries. The chapel is 16th century. Ruined in 1644 during the Civil War, much reconstruction was undertaken in the early 20th century by Dr Hedley Bartlett. The castle is not open to the public.

Pentecosts Castle — See Ewyas Harold Castle

Queenswood Country Park and Arboretum — 5 miles (8km) south of Leominster. Located at the summit of Dinmore Hill, the 170 acres (69ha) of woodland park include an arboretum containig over 500 rare and exotic trees, as well as an extensive area of steeply sloping ancient oakwood designated a Site of Special Scientific Interest. There is a 'lookout' on the highest point. Tel: 01568 797052.

Richard's Castle — 7 miles (11km) north of Leominster. The first Norman fortress erected on English soil, the motte and bailey castle was founded c.1050 by Richard FitzScrub (aka Fitz Scrob or Fitz Scrope), a Norman knight granted lands in Herefordshire, Worcestershire and Shropshire by Edward the Confessor. The stone tower on the motte was built c.1175. The motte and related earthworks are still visible, as is some stonework. The village of the same name lies on the border between Herefordshire and Shropshire; split by the county border, its two civil parishes are called Richard's Castle (Hereford) and Richard's Castle (Shropshire).

Rivers — The **Arrow** rises in the Welsh Marches near Gwaunceste Hill, Powys, flowing southeast through Newchurch and Michaelchurch-on-Arrow. It forms a short section of the England/Wales boundary before flowing into Herefordshire and through the town of Kington. It then proceeds east, passing Staunton-on-Arrow, Pembridge, Eardisland, Arrow Green, Monkland, Ivington, and joins the River Lugg south of Leominster at Stoke Prior. Its tributaries include the Gilwern Brook and the Honey Lake Brook, the latter passing through Ivington Green.

The **Frome** flows through Bromyard and Bishops Frome, and is joined at Covender by the River Lodon. It then flows west past Yarkhill and Prior's Frome, meeting the River Lugg at Hampton Bishop.

Rising near Presteigne in Powys, the **Lugg** then flows east through Herefordshire, including the town of Leominster, south of which it is met by its tributary, the Arrow. It joins the River Wye at Mordiford, 9 miles (15km) downstream of Hereford and 45 miles (72km) from its source.

The **Monnow** flows through southwest Herefordshire and east Monmouthshire, marking the border between England and Wales for much of its length. The river rises near Craswall on Cefn Hill. It flows south, being joined by its tributaries Escley Brook and Olchon Brook near Clodock and Afon Honddu, from the Black Mountains, near Pandy. The river then flows briefly east before again turning south. At Monmouth it joins the River Wye, along with the River Trothy. Its length is 26 miles (42km). At one time the river was noted for its brown trout population, the stretch from Pontrilas to Skenfrith producing record catches, although numbers fell substantially during the 20th century.

Wye see Powys

Ross-on-Wye — Henry III granted Ross-on-Wye the status of a borough in 1241 and it remains a centre for cattle and cider. During the mid 18th century the town became a focus for tourism to the Wye Valley, which was a fashionable destination for those seeking the rugged sensations of the 'Picturesque'. Outside St Mary's Church is a cross commemorating the 315 victims of a 1637 outbreak of plague. The Rudhall Almshouses date from the 14th century and the Market Building in the Market Place, still used by traders, from 1650–4.

Rotherwas Chapel — $1\frac{1}{2}$ miles (2.5km) southeast of Hereford. A Roman Catholic chapel belonging to the Bodenham family and dating from the 14th and 16th centuries. The timber roof is Elizabethan, the tower is Georgian, and the Victorian interior was designed by the Pugins. The chapel once stood in the grounds of Rotherwas House, now demolished. It is maintained by English Heritage. Tel: 0121 625 6820.

St John Medieval Museum
See Coningsby Museum

Sport

football
Hereford United, founded in 1924, joined the Football League in 1972. In 2005–06 the club regained its League status after nine seasons of Conference football. While in the Southern League, Hereford famously defeated First Division Newcastle United 2–1 in an FA Cup 3rd round replay in 1971/72. Hereford play at Edgar Street, Hereford; their nicknames are the Bulls, after the local breed of cattle, and the Whites. The club's colours are white shirts and black shorts. Tel: 08442 761939.

horse racing
Hereford Racecourse, Roman Road, Holmer, Hereford, is a right-handed rectangular circuit of $1\frac{1}{2}$ miles (2.5km). The racecourse holds exclusively National Hunt racing. Tel: 01432 273560.

Sufton Court
Mordiford, 4 miles (6km) southeast of Hereford. A small Palladian mansion dating to 1788 and designed by James Wyatt, with park and grounds by Humphry Repton. On display in the house is one of the 'Red Books' produced by Repton to help clients visualise his designs. Repton created these books (so called for their binding) with explanatory text and watercolours, while a system of overlays shows 'before' and 'after' views. Tel: 01432 870268.

Three Choirs Festival
A music festival originating in at least 1719, held each August in turn at the cathedrals of Hereford, Gloucester and Worcester; its current title was adopted in 1838. Originally the festival featured the choirs of the three cathedrals, and Handel's *Messiah* was performed every year from 1759 until 1963. There is a strong emphasis on the work of English composers, and Ralph Vaughan Williams's *Fantasia on a Theme By Thomas Tallis* (at Gloucester Cathedral in 1910) was one of many English works to receive its first performance in the festival. Large-scale choral repertoire is now performed by the Festival Chorus, and other major ensembles and international soloists are featured, and the cathedral choirs still play an important part in the week-long programme. The organists of the three cathedrals act as artistic director and festival conductor when it is their cathedral's turn to host the festival.

Treago Castle
St Weonards, 7 miles (11km) west of Ross-on-Wye. Treago Castle was built c.1450 by Richard Mynors, a tax collector in Wales. The name originates from *tre* (homestead or farm) and *ago* ('Iago' being the Welsh form of James). The house was built with fortifications against attack from the Welsh, although there is no evidence that any such assault took place. Interior alterations were made in the 17th century and in 1840 it was further modernised. It is still the home of the Mynors family, and is not currently open to the public.

Violette Szabo Museum
Tump Lane, Wormelow, Hereford. The museum tells the story of one of Britain's greatest heroines. Although half French and born in Paris, Violette Szabo GC (1921–45) spent much of her short adult life in England and particularly at her aunt and uncle's home in Hereford. Violette joined the Special Operations Executive in 1941 and worked as a spy behind enemy lines in occupied France during World War II. She was captured and executed by the Germans and her story is told in the film *Carve her Name with Pride* (1958). Tel: 01981 540477.

Waterworks Museum
Broomy Hill, Hereford. Housed in a Victorian water pumping station, the museum tells the story of drinking water. Displays include many working engines, including the largest triple expansion steam engine in Britain, and Tangye House, dating to 1865 and formerly Leominster's pumping station, which was moved in its entirety to the site in the 1990s. Tel: 01432 344062.

Weir, The
Swainshill, 6 miles (10km) west of Hereford. A riverside garden of 10 acres (4ha) situated on a bend in the River Wye, created in the 1920s by Manchester banker Roger Parr, with views extending to the Black Mountains. The garden was given to the National Trust in 1959, while the adjacent 18th century house is now a nursing home. Tel: 01981 590509.

Weobley Museum
Back Lane, Weobley, 12 miles (19km) northwest of Hereford. Housed in the village's former police station and magistrates' court, the museum's displays include artefacts and archives relating to the local history of Weobley. There is also a focus on timber framing, as seen in the village's many black and white timber-framed houses. Tel: 01544 319212.

Westonbury Mill Water Gardens
$1\frac{1}{2}$ miles (2.5km) west of Pembridge, 11 miles (18km) west of Leominster. Located in an area of the Welsh Marches close to the historic half-timbered village of Pembridge, the 3 acre (1.2ha) gardens are laid out around a tangle of streams and ponds, with views of surrounding hills and orchards. Features include a huge variety of bog plants, a walk-through forest of giant gunnera, a natural bog in the area of the old mill pond, a wild flower meadow and various sculptural features constructed by the owner, including a stone tower with water-spouting gargoyle. The mill, on the Curl Brook, a tributary of the River Arrow, was used to grind corn until the 1920s. Tel: 01544 388650.

Wigmore Castle
Wigmore, 10 miles (16km) northwest of Leominster. A Norman motte and bailey castle founded c.1067 by William fitz Osbern. It was given to Ralph de Mortimer by William I after fitz Osbern's death and. The shell keep was built in the 12th century and the castle was rebuilt in stone in the 14th century, becoming a base for the Mortimer family's opposition to Edward II. It is thought that Edward, Duke of York, the future Edward IV, was also based at the castle before the Battle of Mortimer's Cross (see Battles) in 1461. In 1643 Parliamentary troops were ordered to dismantle the walls to prevent the castle from being used by opposition forces, but substantial masonry remains can still be seen. The site is now in the care of English Heritage.

Some famous people born in Herefordshire

Etheridge, Robert (geologist) (1819–1903)	Ross-on-Wye
Evesham, Epiphanius (sculptor) (1570–1634)	Wellington
Garrick, David (actor) (1717–79)	Hereford
Jenkins, Terry (darts player) (1963–)	Ledbury
Kemble, John (martyr) (1599–1679)	St Weonard's
Lee, Albert (guitarist) (1943–)	Leominster
Masefield, John (poet & writer) (1878–1967)	Ledbury
Menges, Christopher (film director) (1940–)	Kington
Oz, Frank (film director) (1944–)	Hereford
Prichard, James Cowles (physician) (1786–1848)	Ross-on-Wye
Reid, Beryl (actress) (1920–96)	Hereford
Watkins, Alfred (archaeologist) (1855–1935)	Hereford

HERTFORDSHIRE

CAMBRIDGESHIRE
BEDFORDSHIRE
ESSEX
BUCKINGHAMSHIRE
GREATER LONDON
Letchworth
A1(M)
1
Hitchin
Stevenage
2
3
Bishops Stortford
7
Harpenden
Welwyn Garden City
Pavis Wood
245
Hemel Hempstead
M1
6
Hatfield
R. Lee
Hertford
St Albans
5
Hoddesdon
Berkhamsted
Potters Bar
4
Cheshunt
M25
10
9
8
Chorley Wood
Watford
Rickmansworth

Districts

1 North Hertfordshire	6 St Albans
2 Stevenage	7 Dacorum
3 East Hertfordshire	8 Three Rivers
4 Broxbourne	9 Watford
5 Welwyn Hatfield	10 Hertsmere

0 20 miles
0 30 km

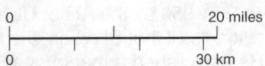

Hertfordshire is a landlocked county in southern England, and is known as one of the Home Counties. It is bordered by Greater London to the south, Essex to the east, Cambridgeshire to the north, Bedfordshire to the northwest and Buckinghamshire to the west. Hertford is the county town and St Albans the only city. In 1965, under the London Government Act 1963, Barnet Urban District and East Barnet Urban District were abolished and their area transferred from Hertfordshire to Greater London to form part of the London Borough of Barnet. At the same time the Potters Bar Urban District was directly transferred from the then existing county of Middlesex to Hertfordshire.

Archaeological relics date the county's first residents to the early Stone Age. The Romans left a more lasting impression, and the Roman town of Verulamium (St Albans) was the second largest town in Roman Britain after Londinium. After the end of Roman occupation in the 5th century, the Anglo-Saxons towns such as Hertford, which was built as a fortress, and the county became a frontier in the struggle against the Danes. The Council of Hertford met in AD 673, at the instigation of Archbishop Theodore, as the first Synod of the whole Church in England, on the site which is now St Joseph's Roman Catholic Church. It was at this meeting that the see of Canterbury was given authority over the Church in England and the Roman and Celtic churches came to an agreement on the date to celebrate Easter.

The Normans left their mark on the county in a series of castles such as those at Hertford, Bishop's Stortford and Berkhamsted. Over the next few centuries, proximity to London made the county a popular retreat for the nobility, whose grand homes often welcomed visiting royalty.

The Industrial Revolution had a significant impact on Hertfordshire – the county saw a spectacular growth of population. In response, Victorian pioneer Ebenezer Howard came up with his plan for a Garden City. Letchworth was chosen in 1903 as the first site for this experiment in town planning, and Welwyn followed in 1920. Pressure for space continued and in 1946 the New Towns Act was passed. Stevenage was the first New Town, planned to combine residential, shopping, industrial and leisure areas in discrete self-contained 'neighbourhood communities'.

Hertford lies only 20 miles (32km) north of London but maintains a typical county town mix of the old and the new without being swallowed up by the London sprawl. The River Lee and its crossing at Hertford lie at the heart of the town's history. Before the Norman Conquest the river formed a natural boundary between the Danelaw to the north and Saxon Wessex to the south. Saxon villages already existed at Bengeo and Hertingfordbury and in 911 and 912 Edward the Elder, son of Alfred the Great, founded two fortified burghs, north and south of the Lee crossing (the ford is believed to have been about 50 yards downstream of what is now Mill Bridge). Two small towns developed, with two churches – the Saxon St Mary the Less in Old Cross and St Nicholas behind what is now Maidenhead Street. There were also two market places, believed to be in Old Cross and on the site of the Shire Hall. In the late 18th century the River Lee navigation was cut through the town providing important access to London's corn markets. Because the town was surrounded by agricultural estates it was unable to expand outwards and so expanded upwards by adding storeys to existing buildings. Outward expansion came about only in the late 19th century when the railway came to the town.

The Victorian era saw much building in the town as transport links to London improved. Hertford now serves as a commuter town for London, with rail links from Hertford North to London King's Cross and Moorgate stations and from Hertford East to London Liverpool Street. Employment is centred on County Hall (Hertfordshire County Council), Wallfields (East Hertfordshire District Council) and McMullens Brewery, one of a dwindling number of independent brewers in the UK.

St Albans is Hertfordshire's oldest town, a modern city shaped by over 2000 years of human occupation. It is the main urban area of the City and District of St Albans in southern Hertfordshire, 22 miles (35.5km) north of central London. The town first appeared as Verlamion, a Celtic Iron Age settlement whose name means 'the settlement above the Marsh'. After the Roman conquest of Britain in AD 43, it developed as Verulamium and became one of the largest towns in Roman Britain. Built mainly of wood, it was destroyed during Boudicca's revolt of in AD 60–1 but was rebuilt and grew to feature many impressive town houses and public buildings. It was encircled by gated walls in AD 275. It was the first major town on the old Roman road Watling Street for travellers heading north. After the Roman withdrawal, and prior to becoming known as St Albans, the town was called Verlamchester or Wæclingacaester. A Saxon settlement grew up around a monastery, founded in AD 900–950 by the Abbot Ulsinus, the acknowledged founder of St Albans, on the spot where tradition has it that St Alban, the first British Christian martyr, was beheaded sometime before AD 324. He established a market, encouraged settlers and built three churches – St Michael's, St Peter's and St Stephen's – on the approaches to the town. It developed into a town of significance with a powerful abbot and was one of the five venues chosen by the barons and clergy in 1213 for the drafting of Magna Carta.

With growing conflict between the abbot and the people of the town over milling rights and a surge of popular feeling that the townspeople should have more control of their affairs, St Albans played a major part in the Peasants' Revolt in 1381. Fifteen of those taking part were tried at the Moot Hall, the site of the present-day town hall. The abbey gateway and clock tower symbolise the discord between monastery and town: the abbey was surrounded by walls to keep livestock safe and townspeople out, revealing the church's need for security from the town outside, while the clock tower, built 1403–12, was constructed by the townspeople as a symbol of their independence from the church. This tension was resolved only at the Dissolution of the Monasteries in 1529.

Until 1539 the town was dominated by the abbot, but with the suppression of the church, the right to a mayor was granted by a charter of Edward VI in 1553. The charter also formalised the right to hold markets and a town hall was built in the market place. The Reformation had the extra advantage of releasing church land, which was good for trade and industry. The abbey church was brought from a courier by parishioners to become the town's parish church.

St Albans sided with Parliament during the Civil War. A minor skirmish took place in 1643, when the Royalist High Sheriff declared his support for the King outside the clock tower at the same time as Cromwell and a detachment of men rode up Holywell Hill. The unfortunate Sheriff was chased, captured and dispatched to the Tower of London. During the 18th and early 19th centuries St Albans remained a market town with industries such as brewing and straw hat manufacture, and the decline of the coaching trade in the 1840s was offset by the arrival of the local railways, especially the main line to London in 1868. St Albans was now an attractive place to live and began to develop into a modern city; it received a royal charter conferring city status in 1877. During the 20th and 21st centuries St Albans has continued to develop as a commuter town while maintaining a distinctive character. It attracted industries such as printing and Ryder & Son seed merchants (Samuel Ryder is better known today as the founder of the golfing trophy the Ryder Cup). In close proximity to the M1, A1(M) and M25 motorways, and with swift rail links to London and easy access to London Luton Airport by rail and road, St Albans has become one of the most desirable areas of the country in which to live. In August 2008, the Woodland Trust announced its intention to create a 600,000-tree forest at Sandridge, to the northeast of the city; at 850 acres (340ha) this will be the largest new native forest in England.

Hertfordshire	Population			Area	
Districts	*male*	*female*	*total*	*sq miles*	*sq km*
Broxbourne	42,274	44,780	87,054	20	51
Dacorum	67,797	70,002	137,799	82	212
East Hertfordshire	63,221	65,698	128,919	184	476
Hertsmere	45,568	48,882	94,450	39	101
North Hertfordshire	56,967	59,941	116,908	145	375
St. Albans	63,414	65,591	129,005	62	161
Stevenage	39,166	40,549	79,715	10	26
Three Rivers	40,062	42,786	82,848	34	89
Watford	39,227	40,499	79,726	8	21
Welwyn Hatfield	47,363	50,190	97,553	50	130
Total	505,059	528,918	1,033,977	634	1643

Local Attractions and Information

Administrative headquarters	County Hall, Pegs Lane, Hertford SG13 8DQ. Tel: 01923 471555.
Anstey Castle	Anstey, 12 miles (19km) northeast of Stevenage. Located in the village centre, by the church, the 12th century stone motte and bailey fortress was built by Eustace, Count of Boulogne. It was given by Henry VIII in turn to both Katharine of Aragon and Anne Boleyn. The large motte and surrounding ditch can still be seen, although covered by trees; a flat rectangular bailey and barbican lie to the east.
Ashridge	2 miles (3km) north of Berkhamsted. An estate and house in the Chiltern Hills Area of Outstanding Natural Beauty. The estate comprises 5000 acres (2000ha) of woodlands, commons and chalk downland stretching into Buckinghamshire and supporting a rich variety of wildlife. It was the site of an abbey founded in 1276 by Edmund, Earl of Cornwall, who had a palace here. The monks were Augustinian, and the order was known as the 'Bonhommes', or 'bluefriars' on account of the colour of their robes. Edward I held a parliament at the abbey in 1290 when he spent Christmas in the nearby village of Pitstone. The abbey later became the private residence of Princess Elizabeth, younger daughter of Henry VIII. She was arrested here in 1552 under suspicion of treason. From 1604 to 1848 the estate was the property of the Egerton family, the Dukes and Earls of Bridgewater. The Bridgewater Monument, 108ft (33m) tall and containing a spiral staircase of 170 steps, was built in memory of the 3rd Duke, Francis Egerton, pioneer of inland navigation, who was responsible for the Bridgewater Canal (see Greater Manchester). In 1802 the 7th Earl replaced the abbey with a large neo-Gothic house designed by James Wyatt and now Grade I listed. The estate later passed to the Earls Brownlow. In 1921 it was split, the land being given to the National Trust while the house and garden became the Ashridge (Bonar Law) College. Ashridge's 'College of Citizenship' was opened in 1929 to help the Conservative Party in its intellectual struggles with left-wing organisations such as the Fabian Society. During World War II, Ashridge was used as a secondary site for Charing Cross Hospital. After the war, the house was briefly occupied again by the College of Citizenship and by a girls' finishing school; in 1959 it was relaunched to provide management training, and is now Ashridge Business School. Ashridge Common has been featured in many film and television series, and was the location for the film *Danny the Champion of the World* (1989), based on the book by Roald Dahl. Ashridge House has been featured in films such as *The Dirty Dozen* (1967). Part of the estate became Ashridge Golf Club in 1932, and Henry Cotton was its club professional in the late 1930s. Tel: 01442 851227.
Ashwell Bury	Ashwell, 6 miles (10km) west of Royston. An early 19th century house of white brick, thought to have been originally built before 1836 for Edward George Fordham (1782–1868), and altered c.1860 for Edward King Fordham (1810–99), who extended the family landholding. It was further remodelled, chiefly inside, by Sir Edwin Lutyens for local philanthropist Mrs Phyllis Fordham in 1922–6. His most notable addition is the new staircase hall. Fitted into a square rear courtyard, it has an octagonal lantern and glazed internal windows on three sides of the first floor with mirror glass on the fourth. Two other rooms have Lutyens chimney pieces. The gardens were altered by Gertrude Jekyll in 1908–9.
Battles	There have been three major battles in Hertfordshire: Barnet, and the first and second battles of St Albans. See separate table for details.
Benington Castle	Town Lane, Benington, 4 miles (6km) east of Stevenage. A late 11th century earthwork motte and bailey fortress founded by Peter de Valoignes. In 1136, Roger de Valoignes added a stone keep. In 1177, Henry II demolished part of the castle but by 1192 it was in use again, only to be finally destroyed in 1212, after Robert fitz Walter rebelled against King John. Today only the foundations of the keep and the earthworks to the east and north remain from the original castle. A neo-Norman gatehouse, summerhouse and curtain wall were added in 1832 by George Proctor.
Benington Lordship Gardens	Benington, 4 miles (6km) east of Stevenage. Spread over 7 acres (2.8ha), the gardens surround a Georgian manor house with remains of a Norman castle and moat (see Benington Castle). Highlights include a Victorian folly, kitchen garden, contemporary sculptures, carp pond, wildlife areas and rose gardens. Tel: 0870 126 1709.

Berkhamsted Castle White Hill, Berkhamsted. Norman motte and bailey castle founded by Robert of Mortain. The outer castle was rebuilt in stone by Thomas Becket, 1155–65, and completed in stone by King John with a circular keep on the motte. Besieged by Prince Louis of France in 1216 in his attempt to seize the English throne, the castle fell after a two-week barrage from the giant catapults called mangonels. The castle became disused from 1495. The outer gate was lost in 1838 when the London and Birmingham Railway sliced off the southwestern edge of the site. The ruins, which include the motte and parts of the walls, are now owned by English Heritage. Tel: 01375 858489.

Bishop's Stortford Castle Castle Gardens, Bishop's Stortford. Also known as Waytemore Castle. Now located in a public park, the motte and bailey castle was probably built some time in the late 11th century. A great square tower was added on the motte in the 12th century. During the 12th century civil war it was held by Robert Sigillo, Bishop of London, a supporter of King Stephen. It was improved in the 13th century but slighted after the Civil War. By the 17th century it was used as a prison. Only some earthworks, the large motte and the foundations of the tower can still be seen.

British Schools Museum Queen Street, Hitchin. A museum tracing the development of elementary education in Britain from 1798. Originally housed in a former malthouse converted to a school by local solicitor William Wilshere in 1810, the site includes the only surviving Lancasterian schoolroom in the world, dating from 1837. Here, following the system of educationalist Joseph Lancaster (1788–1838), one master taught 330 boys. There is also a galleried classroom for 110 boys built in 1853, a girls' and infants' school of 1857 and Edwardian classrooms of 1905, containing desks, teaching aids and children's work. The headmaster's house is restored and furnished as it was in the late Victorian period. Displays include the Jill Grey Collection of Childhood and Educational Material, consisting of 35,000 items related to the education of children from the 17th century collected by Hitchin resident Jill Grey (one-time personal assistant to Frank Whittle). The Benchmark Collection contains similar items acquired after her death. Tel: 01462 452697.

Brocket Hall 1 mile (1.6km) west of Welwyn Garden City. London. Built for Sir Matthew Lamb c.1760 to designs by the architect James Paine, the tall red brick Neoclassical house stands on the site of two predecessors, the first dating to 1239. The double main staircase is an impressive feature of the interior. The 543 acres (220ha) of surrounding parkland includes a Palladian bridge built 1772–4. Sir Matthew's son became the 1st Lord Melbourne and was frequently visited by the Prince Regent, who had a liaison with Lady Melbourne. The next owner was William Lamb, 2nd Viscount Melbourne, Prime Minister 1835–41. On his death the house passed to his sister; she later married Lord Palmerston, who was also to become Prime Minister and who died at Brocket while still in office. Queen Victoria was another visitor. Sir Charles Nall-Cain purchased the estate in 1921; he was created Baron Brocket in 1933. The house was used as a maternity hospital during World War II. In the late 20th century Charles Nall-Cain, 3rd Baron Brocket (who appeared on *I'm A Celebrity Get Me Out Of Here* in 2004), converted Brocket Hall into a hotel and conference centre. The house featured in the *Inspector Morse* episode 'Who Killed Harry Field' as the British home of a Continental tycoon. Tel: 01707 335241.

Buntingford Manor House High Street, Buntingford, 8 miles (13km) northeast of Stevenage. Originally the home of the lord of the manor, the 18th century Buntingford Manor House now houses Buntingford Heritage Centre.

Cassiobury Park Cassiobury Avenue, Watford. The 190 acres (76ha) of parkland bordering the Grand Union Canal occupy part of the former estate of Cassiobury House, begun in 1546 by Sir Richard Morrison and completed ten years later by his son Charles. The house later passed into the ownership of the Capel family. It was remodelled in Romantic Gothic style by James Wyatt 1799–1805 and in the same period the park was landscaped by Humphry Repton. With much of the land already having been sold, some to Watford Council and the rest for development, the house was demolished in 1927. Today the park contains a Local Nature Reserve.

Childwickbury Manor 2 miles (3km) northwest of St Albans. The 18th century house and estate of 900 acres (365ha) was once owned by ship owner Henry Hayman Toulmin, High Sheriff of Hertfordshire and mayor of St Albans, who bought the property from Joshua Lomax in 1854 and sold it to Sir John Blundell Maple (of the furniture firm Maple's) 20 years later. Maple established the Childwickbury stud on the estate. Racehorse owner Jack Joel bought the estate c.1907 and it remained in his family until 1978; the stud was sold to the Marquesa de Moratella and the house to film director Stanley Kubrick, who used it as both a home and a base for his film productions. He lived here until his death in 1999 and is interred in the grounds.

Cromer Windmill Cromer, 5 miles (8km) northeast of Stevenage. The only remaining post mill in Hertfordshire. The earliest type of English windmill, it gets its name from the massive oak post on which the mill body turns to face the sails into the wind. The present mill dates from c.1681 and was in use until 1923, after which it became derelict. Given to the Hertfordshire Building Preservation Trust in 1969, the Grade II* listed mill has since been restored to working order. The mill has Patent sails, a fantail and centrifugal governors to control the stone clearances. Tel: 01279 843301.

De Havilland Aircraft Heritage Centre 4 miles (6km) southeast of St Albans. Located next to Salisbury Hall (see separate entry), occupied in September 1939 by the De Havilland design team. Formerly known as the Mosquito Aircraft Museum, the collection is based around the prototype and restoration shops for the De Havilland Mosquito, which occupied the outbuildings of the hall, and also includes several examples of the De Havilland Vampire, the third operational jet aircraft in the world. The museum's collection has developed since 1959 when Major Walter Goldsmith, then owner of Salisbury Hall, returned the original Mosquito prototype to Salisbury Hall as an attraction. Tel: 01727 826400.

Forge Museum High Street, Much Hadham, 4 miles (6km) southwest of Bishop's Stortford. Housed in a Grade II* listed former farmhouse dating in parts to the 15th century, the displays, including photographs, documents and a wide range of tools, illustrate the crafts of blacksmithing and farriery along with smaller exhibits about village life. The Page family set up as blacksmiths here in 1811, operating a family business continuously until 1983. The garden houses a rare early 19th century bee shelter and a granary building. Tel: 01279 843301.

Gorhambury — 2 miles (3km) west of St Albans. A neo-Palladian house, built 1777–84 to the designs of Sir Robert Taylor. In the Middle Ages the Gorhambury estate, lying near the site of the Roman city of Verulamium, belonged to St Albans Abbey. Early in Elizabeth I's reign the property was purchased by Sir Nicholas Bacon, Lord Keeper of the Great Seal. In 1563–8 Sir Nicholas built a new house and it became the home of his younger son, the philosopher and politician Francis Bacon (whose monument can be seen in the parish church of St Michael nearby). The ruins of this house still stand in the grounds and are referred to as Old Gorhambury. The remains, particularly the porch of the great hall, reflect the impact of the Renaissance on 16th century English architecture. Bacon left Gorhambury to his former secretary, Sir Thomas Meautys, who married Anne Bacon, the great-granddaughter of the Lord Keeper. The estate later passed to her second husband Sir Harbottle Grimston, Master of the Rolls and Speaker in the Convention Parliament of 1659–60. The present house was built by his descendant, the 3rd Viscount Grimston. The 3rd Viscount's son was created Earl of Verulam in 1806 and the family have lived at Gorhambury ever since. The main reception rooms are grouped around a central staircase and contain family portraits from the 15th to the 20th centuries – including a collection transferred from the Elizabethan house – and a Grand Tour collection. The drawing room has a stucco frieze and an unusual chimneypiece, attributed to Piranesi. There are also late 18th and early 19th century portraits and furniture, including an organ played by Haydn. The house is now managed by English Heritage. Tel: 01727 854051.

Great Bed of Ware — An extremely large oak four-poster bed, carved with marquetry. Built by Hertfordshire carpenter Jonas Fosbrooke c.1590, it measures 10ft (3m) by 11ft (3.3m) and can hold more than 15 people. Many of those who used the bed have carved their names into its posts. Originally housed in the White Hart Inn in Ware, by the 1800s the bed had been moved to the Saracen's Head, another Ware inn. In 1870, William Henry Teale, owner of Rye House in nearby Hoddesdon, acquired the bed and put it on display in his pleasure garden. When interest in the garden waned in the 1920s, the bed was sold. In 1931, it was acquired by the Victoria and Albert Museum in London.

Hatfield House — 1 mile (1.6km) east of Hatfield. Built by Robert Cecil, 1st Earl of Salisbury and Chief Minister to James I, in 1611. The site was previously occupied by the Royal Palace of Hatfield, built by John Morton, Bishop of Ely, c.1485 and later occuied by the children of Henry VIII. The state rooms contain furniture, tapestries and armour, as well as paintings such as the renowned 'Rainbow' and 'Ermine' portraits of Elizabeth I. The house abounds in fine examples of Jacobean craftsmanship, including the elaborately carved oak grand staircase and a rare stained glass window, dating to 1610, in the private chapel. Also on display are historic mementos collected by the Cecils, one of England's foremost political families. The 3rd Marquess of Salisbury was three times Prime Minister during the closing years of Queen Victoria's reign, when the British Empire was at the height of its power. The surviving wing of the Royal Palace, where Elizabeth I spent much of her childhood, stands in the extensive garden. In November 1558, following the death of her sister Mary I, Elizabeth held her first council of state in the palace's great hall. Hatfield House is now home to the 7th Marquess of Salisbury. Tel: 01707 287010.

Henry Moore Foundation — Perry Green, 4 miles (6km) southwest of Bishop's Stortford. A charity established for the education and promotion of the fine arts, and in particular to advance understanding of the works of Henry Moore, who lived in the village from 1940 until 1977. Set up with Moore's assistance in 1977, it operates from his former estate in Hertfordshire and at the Henry Moore Institute in Leeds. *Reclining Figure* (1969–70), a bronze sculpture, was stolen from the foundation's Perry Green base on 15 December 2005, possibly for scrap value. Thieves are believed to have lifted the 11ft 9in (3.6m) long, 6ft 6in (2m) high by 6ft 6in (2m) wide, 2.1 tonne statue onto the back of a Mercedes lorry using a crane. Tel: 01279 843333.

Hertford Castle — Castle Street, Hertford. Norman motte and bailey castle by the River Lea founded c.1067 by William I. After major works were carried out on the castle in the 15th century, it was demolished in the 17th century. The 11th century stone and flint curtain wall and the 15th century gatehouse are all that remains today. Tel: 01992 584322.

Hertford Museum — Bull Plain, Hertford. A local history museum in an early 17th century town house, enhanced by a recreated Jacobean knot garden of intertwined hedges of box and lavender. The displays depict Hertford's historic past as a royal borough, market for a large rural population and county town. It contains the Hertfordshire Regiment Collection. Tel: 01992 582686.

Highest point — Pavis Wood in the Chilterns, 803ft (245m) above sea level. An area of ancient beech oak and ash woodland, the hill is $^1/_4$ mile (0.4km) from the village of Hastoe, 2 miles (3km) southwest of Tring, and its summit is less than 3 miles (5km) from the Buckinghamshire border.

Interesting facts — **The Plough** in Great Munden, near Ware, has the largest musical instrument of any pub in England. The full-size working Compton theatre organ can be seen and occasionally heard in the specially built extension. **Michael Perham**, aged 14, from Potters Bar, became the youngest person to sail solo across the Atlantic in January 2007. Michael took six weeks to complete the 3500 mile (5600km) voyage. He set sail from Gibraltar on 18 November 2006 aboard his 28ft (9m) boat, *Cheeky Monkey*, and docked in Antigua on 3 January 2007. **Watford** is often mistaken for the village of Watford 50 miles (80km) to its north in Northamptonshire, famous for the Watford Gap service station, the traditional point where the north/south divide begins. However, it has recently become more popular to use the phrase 'north of Watford', referring to the Hertfordshire town, when speaking of this divide. The reason for the change is probably due to the signs at Staples Corner, where the M1 begins; these read 'M1, Watford, The North', potentially implying that Watford is the last place in the South. **Hertfordshire people** are traditionally referred to as

'Hertfordshire Hedgehogs' or 'Hertfordshire Hayabouts'; although hedgehogs are abundant in the county, the nickname is probably a corruption of 'haycock', a haystack, referring to the county's cornfields, which formed the county's principal medieval export to the food markets of London. The **Bourne Gutter** is a small tributory of the River Bulbourne rising between Berkhamsted and Bourne End. According to local legend it is a 'Woe Water', said to flow only at times of national emergency. Its recent flows in 1990 and 2002 coincided with wars between Britain and Iraq! **Broxbourne Council** introduced the first 'bin tax' in November 2007. Homes were given one free black bag every week and forced to pay 28p for each additional one.

Knebworth House — Nr Stevenage. The home of the Lytton family, the original red-brick Tudor manor house was built c.1500 by Sir Robert Lytton. It was transformed in 1843 into the present Gothic structure by its most famous resident, Victorian author, dramatist and statesman Edward Bulwer-Lytton. In accordance with changing architectural fashion, the 2nd Earl of Lytton commissioned Sir Edwin Lutyens to redesign much of the interior in 1908, and a herb garden was laid out by Gertrude Jekyll. The house is currently occupied by Henry Lytton-Cobbold and his family. Knebworth House and Park have hosted rock concerts since 1974 when the Allman Brothers Band attracted 60,000. Since then, the house has been the scene of outdoor extravaganzas featuring Pink Floyd (1975, 1990), the Rolling Stones (1976), Genesis (1978, 1992), Frank Zappa (1978), Led Zeppelin (1979, their final two UK shows, playing to record crowds in excess of 200,000 people), Mike Oldfield (1980), the Beach Boys (1980), Cliff Richard (1983, 1990), Deep Purple (1985), Queen (1986, their final show with Freddie Mercury), and Oasis (1996). Exterior scenes of Bruce Wayne's manor in the film *Batman* (1989) were shot at Knebworth House, and the Yule Ball staircase scene in *Harry Potter and the Goblet of Fire* (2005) was filmed within the house. Tel: 01438 812661.

Langleybury — 2 miles (3km) north of Watford. Situated on a low hill above the valley of the River Gade, the estate was purchased in 1711 by Robert Raymond, later Baron Raymond, Lord Chief Justice 1724–32, who demolished the original house in 1720 and built the present mansion. A park was laid out around the house in the later 18th century. Raymond's cipher, a griffin in a crown, can still be seen on the building. Around this time the new routes of the Grand Union Canal and Sparrows Hearne Turnpike passed along the valley bottom at the lower edge of the park. In the 1970s a school building was built to the south of the mansion, which was occupied by part of the school and also used as teacher accommodation. In 1996 the school closed, housing Hertfordshire County Council's offices for a time before becoming a favoured film location site, notably for the TV series *Hope and Glory* (1999). The mansion has since been divided into apartments. A children's farm is situated in the old farm attached to the mansion house.

Mill Green Watermill and Museum — Mill Green, 1 mile (1.6km) north of Hatfield. A working 18th century watermill, with changing displays on local history in adjacent buildings. Tel: 01707 271362.

Minsden Chapel — 1 mile (1.6km) east of Preston, 3 miles (5km) south of Hitchin. The chapel of St Nicholas was built in the 14th century, when it lay on the pilgrim route to St Albans. It had fallen into disrepair by the 17th century although marriages continued into the 18th century, when the crumbling masonry became too dangerous. In the 20th century the chapel was closely associated with the historian Reginald Hine from nearby Hitchin, who frequently visited the site and is buried next to the entrance. In 1907 his colleage W T Latchmore published a photograph of a ghostly monk supposedly emerging from the ruins, and afterwards there were regular rumours of paranormal activity. The apparition most often reported is that of a single monk climbing stairs (which no longer exist) to the northeast of the chapel at midnight on Halloween. Other reported experiences include the sighting of a glowing cross on the wall, and the hearing of distant music or the ringing of the chapel's bells, stolen in the 1720s. Legends also exist of a lost tunnel, and of a murdered nun. Today the chapel is a roofless shell, hidden by woodland and accessible only by footpath.

Moor Park — 2 miles (3km) southeast of Rickmansworth. A Palladian mansion set within several hundred acres of parkland. The house was built 1678–9 for James, Duke of Monmouth, and was inherited by his widow after his execution for rebellion against Charles II. Before her death in 1732, Benjamin Hoskins Styles, who had made a fortune in the South Sea Company before the notorious Bubble burst, purchased the house; it was reconstructed for him c.1720 by Giacomo Leoni, who refaced the house with Portland stone and added its grand portico and Tuscan colonnades (now demolished), with a painted staircase by Sir James Thornhill. In 1752 it was bought by Admiral Lord Anson, who commissioned Capability Brown to remake the formal gardens. Having changed hands several times, the estate was sold to the Grosvenor family in 1828. The Earl Grosvenor, son of the Duke of Westminster, planted the pleasure grounds with trees and ornamental shrubs. Both the 'Moorpark' apricot and the commercial strawberry, the latter a hybrid of the European strawberry and a Chilean species, were supposedly first cultivated in the kitchen gardens. The mansion was requisitioned during World War II, becoming the headquarters of the 1st Airborne Corps who planned Operation Market Garden, part of the Allied advance into Europe in 1944. Today the Grade I listed house contains the clubhouse of Moor Park Golf Club. Tel: 01923 773146.

Motto — 'Trust and fear not'.

Natural History Museum at Tring — Akeman Street, Tring. Formerly the Walter Rothschild Zoological Museum, although it has in fact been part of the Natural History Museum since 1937. It was once the private museum of Lionel Walter, 2nd Baron Rothschild, who moved with his family to Tring Park in 1872. Many of the specimens now on display are examples of 19th century taxidermy and every attempt has been made to preserve the character and general arrangement of Lord Rothschild's museum. The site is also home to the ornithological research collections (Bird Group, Department of Zoology) and the ornithological library (Department of Library and Information Services) of the Natural History Museum. Among the largest and most comprehensive in the world, the collections include more than 2 million skin, skeleton, spirit, egg and nest specimens representing over 95 per cent of known bird species. The collections are accessible by prior appointment only. Tel: 020 7942 6171.

Nomansland Common — An area of common land lying to the south of Harpenden and the southwest of Wheathampstead, and sometimes simply referred to as 'No Man's Land'. The area has very poor soil, which may account for its survival as common land. As its name implies, the area lay outside traditional parish boundaries, and it was the source of frequent disputes between the monasteries of St Albans and Westminster, both of which claimed it to be within their respective parishes and manors. (It is now divided between the parishes of Sandridge and Wheathampstead.) In 1460 the second Battle of St Albans (see Battles) was fought on nearby Bernard's Heath, and Yorkist troops were put to flight on the common. In the 18th century, cannonballs and 25 skeletons believed to date from the battle were recovered from the site. The 17th century highwaywoman known as the 'Wicked Lady' (often identified as Lady Katherine Ferrers, a member of a prominent local family) was reputed to operate on the common. The racehorse trainer Thomas Coleman (1796–1877), who introduced the spectator sport of steeplechasing to England, held his first proper steeplechases at Nomansland from 1830; although they proved popular, they were discontinued in 1839 when the Grand National started. Despite its illegality, cock fighting is believed to have carried on at the common until the early 20th century.

Old Gorhambury House — See Gorhambury

Pelham Castle — Cole Green, 8 miles (13km) southeast of Royston. A small Norman earthwork motte, founded by Maurice, Bishop of London. The remains of the motte and ditch are still visible, but the position of the bailey has been lost.

Periwinkle Hill Castle — $^1/_2$ mile (0.8km) west of Barkway, 5 miles (8km) south of Royston. The possible site of a Norman motte and bailey fortress founded by the de Mandeville family. The faint earthwork traces of the castle have been further obscured by ploughing.

Redbournbury Mill — 2 miles (3km) northwest of St Albans. The water-driven flour mill on the River Ver dates back at least to the 16th century although much of the existing structure was built in 1790. It was run for much of the 20th century by Ivy Hawkins, thought to be England's last woman commercial miller. The mill has been restored to working condition and produces organic flour. Tel: 01582 792874.

Rivers — The **Ash** rises near the village of Brent Pelham in north Hertfordshire and flows through the Hadhams (Little, Ford and Much), Widford and Wareside, reaching the River Lee between Stanstead Abbots and Ware.

The **Beane** rises in the hills around Stevenage and flows through Watton-at-Stone, Stapleford and Waterford, reaching the River Lee at Hartham Common, Hertford.

The **Bulbourne** runs from Dudswell in Northchurch, through Berkhamsted and Bourne End, joining the River Gade at Two Waters in Apsley near Hemel Hempstead. The original source of the river was Bulborne, 3 miles (4.5km) northeast of Dudswell, until the Grand Junction Canal was dug along its course.

Chess – see Buckinghamshire

The **Colne** rises near Colney Heath and forms the boundary between the South Bucks district of Buckinghamshire and the London Borough of Hillingdon. It is a tributary of the River Thames and flows through the Chiltern Hills and into the Thames near Heathrow Airport. The villages of Colney Heath near St Albans, Colney Street near Radlett, Colnbrook near Slough and London Colney in Hertfordshire all take their names from the river.

Gade see Buckinghamshire

Hiz, Ivel and **Purwell** see Ivel, Bedfordshire

Lee see London

The **Mimram** rises from a spring near Whitwell in north Hertfordshire and makes its confluence with the River Lee near Horn's Mill in Hertford.

The **New River** is a man-made waterway opened in 1613 to supply London with fresh drinking water taken from the River Lee and from springs and wells along its course. It starts between Ware and Hertford and travels 20 miles (32km) south to Stoke Newington in the London Borough of Hackney.

The **Rib** rises near the east Hertfordshire village of Buckland and runs parallel with the A10 through Buntingford, Puckeridge and Standon, reaching its confluence with the River Lee near Hertford.

The **Stort Navigation** is a canalised river running 14 miles (22km) from Bishop's Stortford downstream to its junction with the River Lee Navigation near Ware.

The **Ver** rises in the grounds of Markyate Cell and flows south for 12 miles (19km) alongside Watling Street through Flamstead, Redbourn, St Albans and Park Street, joining the Colne at Bricket Wood.

Roisia's Cross — High Street, Royston. A cross once located at the crossroads of Ermine Street and the Icknield Way. It took its name from the wife of the first recorded owner, Eudo Dapifer, steward to William the Conqueror; the name of the town of Royston is sometimes said to be derived from that of the cross. The supposed base of the cross, described by 18th century antiquarian William Stukeley as 'A flattish stone, of very great bulk, with a square hole or mortaise, in the centre, wherein was let the foot of the upright stone or tenon, which was properly the cross', now stands on a site near the old crossroads.

Royston Cave — Melbourn Street, Royston. A small artificial cavern dating possibly to the 13th century, unique for the numerous medieval carvings on its walls. Most are of pagan origin, but some of the figures are thought to be those of St Catherine, St Lawrence and St Christopher. All were significant to the Knights Templar, and it is speculated that the Templars may have used it before their proscription by Pope Clement V in 1312. The sect held a weekly market at Royston, 1199–1254, and travelled there from their headquarters at Baldock, 9 miles (15km) to the southwest. Two figures close together near the damaged section may be all that remains of a known Templar sign, two knights riding the same horse. Some theories suggest that the cave, carved from the chalk bedrock, was originally a Neolithic flint mine.

St Albans Cathedral — Sumpter Yard, Holywell Hill, St Albans. Dedicated to St Alban and built 1077–1115 on the supposed site of the saint's martyrdom in the 3rd or early 4th century. Formerly the abbey church of the monastery of St Alban, it was designated a cathedral in 1877. Its nave is 348ft (106m) in length, the longest of any cathedral in England, while the tower, 144ft (44m) high, is the oldest crossing tower still in existence in England. A number of 13th century wall paintings depicting saints and the death of Christ on the cross have been uncovered. The 14th century Shrine of St Alban, destroyed during the Reformation, was reconstructed from scattered fragments in the 1990s. The church was substantially restored in the late 19th century by Lord Grimthorpe. Those buried at St Albans include Thomas de la Mare, who died at the age of 87 in 1396, having been abbot for 47 years, and Sir Anthony (or Antony) Grey, the brother-in-law of Elizabeth Woodville, queen consort of Edward IV, who died in 1480. The brasses on their tombs are the only ones in the church to survive destruction at the Dissolution of the Monasteries. The University of Hertfordshire holds graduation ceremonies in the cathedral and St Albans School holds regular services here. The nave was used to represent Westminster Abbey in the coronation scene of the film *Johnny English* (2003), starring Rowan Atkinson, while the Lady Chapel was used as a location in Sean Connery's film *First Knight* (1995). Tel: 01727 860780.

St Pauls Walden Bury — Whitwell, 4 miles (6km) south of Hitchin. An 18th century house most famous as the childhood home of Queen Elizabeth the Queen Mother. The 40 acres (16ha) of gardens, designed by the owner Edward Gilbert, 1720–30, are based on a formal French *patte d'oie* (goose foot) design and are now Grade I listed. Laid out c.1730, they include a formal woodland garden composed of long avenues leading to classical temples, statues, lake and ponds, with a medieval church nearby. The garden still retains its original layout, while a woodland garden has been developed since 1950 and includes rhododendrons and magnolia. Gilbert's granddaughter Eleana Bowes married John Lyon, Earl of Strathmore, and the house and garden still belong to the Bowes-Lyon family. The house is not open to the public. Tel: 01438 871218.

Salisbury Hall — 4 miles (6km) southeast of St Albans. The estate has its roots before the Norman Conquest, but Salisbury Hall gained its name in 1380 when the manor passed in marriage to Sir John Montague, later 3rd Earl of Salisbury. The present house was built by banker John Hoare, c.1670. After several changes of ownership it was occupied by a succession of farmers during the late 19th century. Lady Randolph Churchill lived in the hall c.1905; the De Havilland design team was established in the hall in September 1939, and the prototype Mosquito was constructed in the outbuildings. In 1955 the hall was restored by ex-Royal Marine Major Walter Goldsmith who opened it to the public, bringing back the Mosquito prototype as an attraction in 1959. Goldsmith sold the hall in 1981; it is now in private ownership. See also De Havilland Aircraft Heritage Centre.

Scott's Grotto — Scotts Road, Ware. Situated between nos. 28 and 34, the grotto was built for 18th century Quaker poet John Scott. Born in London, Scott moved to Hertfordshire in 1740, inheriting Amwell House and its grounds when his father died in 1768. Rebuilding the house and landscaping the gardens he decided to add his own grotto, fashionable at the time – although another possible motivation was to provide work for unemployed men in the area. The grotto consists of six chambers connected by tunnels, extending 67ft (20.5m) into the chalk hillside and lined with shells, flints and pieces of coloured glass. Tel: 01920 464131.

Shaw's Corner — Ayot St Lawrence, 6 miles (10km) northwest of Welwyn Garden City. George Bernard Shaw used this Edwardian Arts & Crafts-influenced house, built in 1902 as the rectory for Ayot St Lawrence, as a country retreat from 1906 until his death in 1950. The rooms remain largely unaltered, with many literary and personal effects. The kitchen and outbuildings are evocative of early 20th century domestic life. Shaw's revolving writing hut is hidden at the bottom of the garden, which has planted borders and views over the Hertfordshire countryside. The property is now in the care of the National Trust. Tel: 01438 820307.

Sopwell House — 1 mile (1.6km) south of St Albans. Built in the 18th century, possibly on the site of a former house, by master mason Edward String, whose career included work on St Paul's Cathedral and Blenheim Palace. The white-rendered house was extended in Victorian times and in 1900 was leased to Prince Louis of Battenberg, an Admiral of the Royal Navy who made it his family home. His four children, Alice, Louise, George and Louis Mountbatten (later Earl Mountbatten of Burma), grew up here. After passing to prominent local family the Verulams after World War II, the house was sold to become a hotel in 1969. It has since been used as a gathering place by the England football team prior to international football events. Tel: 01727 864477. Not to be confused with the ruined Sopwell House built on the site of the former Sopwell Priory, Cottonmill Lane, St Albans.

South Mimms Castle — 1/2 mile (0.8km) north of South Mimms, 3 miles (5km) west of Potters Bar. A Norman motte and bailey castle founded c.1140–2 by Geoffrey de Mandeville. The motte is built around the base of a tower, access to which was possibly through a tunnel.

Sport

general — **Potters Bar Golf Club**, Darkes Lane, Potters Bar, was the home golf club of Tony Jacklin, winner of the British and US Open, and former captain of the Ryder Cup team. Tel: 01707 652020.

Rye House Rockets speedway team are based at Rye House Stadium, Hoddesdon. They currently compete in the British Premier League. The club was formed in 1974 and were Premier League winners in 1980 and 2005. Tel: 01992 440400.

football — **Watford** were founded in 1881 as West Herts FC, joining the Football League in 1920. They first played at Cassio Road, before moving to their current home of Vicarage Road in 1922. Since 1997 they have shared their ground with Saracens RFC. The club's nickname is The Hornets due to its traditional yellow and black strip, although they are sometimes referred to as The Golden Boys. Watford have a long-standing rivalry with nearby Luton Town. When Graham Taylor was named as Watford's new manager at the start of the 1976-77 season, the club had just been purchased by world famous pop star Elton John (a lifelong fan of the club) and were in the Fourth Division. But thanks to the efforts of chairman, manager and playing staff, Watford had reached the First Division by the start of the 1982–83 season. Tel: 01923 496000.

Non-league teams include **Bishop's Stortford** (formed 1874), **St Albans City** (formed 1908) and **Stevenage Borough** (formed 1976).

Meadow Park football ground in Borehamwood, with a capacity of 4502, is the home of Boreham Wood and Watford Reserves, and also of Arsenal Ladies of the FA Women's Premier League. 020 8953 5097.

greyhound racing — **Rye House Stadium**, Rye Road, Hoddesdon. The 420m track is also home to Rye House Rockets speedway team. Tel: 01992 469000.

rugby union — For **Saracens RFC** see London

Stocks House — Aldbury, 2 miles (3km) east of Tring. A Georgian mansion, built as a family home in 1773 by the owners of Stocks Farm, and the largest property in the picturesque village. From 1892 it was owned by novelist Mary Augusta Ward, who wrote as Mrs Humphrey Ward, until her death in 1920. Her sister was married to Leonard Huxley, and the couple's son Aldous was a regular visitor. In 1944 the home was converted into a girls' Catholic school. In 1972 it was purchased by American Victor Lowndes, executive of Playboy, and during the 1970s was used as a training camp for aspiring Playboy bunnies. During this time an enormous jacuzzi, rumoured to be the largest in England, was installed, and many 1970s celebrities attended parties held by Lowndes in the house. Following Lowndes' dismissal from Playboy in 1981 he attempted turn the property into a hotel but he was eventually forced to sell it. It later had various owners including England cricketer Phil Edmonds, who turned it into a health spa, and Harlequins rugby club, until it was sold to retired racehorse trainer and entrepreneur Peter Harris. The album cover of Oasis' *Be Here Now* was photographed by the pool (which has since been filled in).

Theobalds Park — 2 miles (3km) southwest of Cheshunt. A stately home and (later) royal palace of the 16th and early 17th centuries. The original house was built 1564–85 on an ancient manorial estate, to the order of Lord Burghley, with formal gardens modelled on those at the Château de Fontainebleau in France; English botanist John Gerard supervised their construction. In 1607 the house passed in ownership from Robert Cecil, who had inherited it from his father, to James I, in exchange for the nearby Hatfield Palace (see Hatfield House). Theobalds House quickly became one of James's favourite country seats, and he died within its walls in 1625. With the execution in 1649 of his son, Charles I, Theobalds was among the many royal properties disposed of by the Commonwealth, and by the end of 1650 the house was largely demolished. In the Georgian period another mansion was built by George Prescott, a merchant and MP who had bought the estate in 1763; known as Theobalds Park after the estate on which it stands, this is the house that stands today. In the 1820s Theobalds Park passed from the Prescott family to the Meux family, who made alterations and added extensions. In 1910 the estate was inherited by Admiral the Hon. Sir Hedworth Meux, a member of the aristocratic Lambton family (see County Durham). After his death, the house became a hotel. It was later used as a school, then as an adult education centre, and is currently a conference centre. Tel: 07800 891995.

Therfield Castle — Church Lane, Therfield, 3 miles (5km) southwest of Royston. A 12th century earthwork motte and bailey fortress, built in the period of the Anarchy (see also Walkern Castle). Excavated in 1958, the motte was found to be absent of structures but the rectangular bailey was built with a timber-revetted rampart. In 1960, most of the earthworks in the bailey were levelled, leaving only wet ditches and low ramparts in the field boundaries to give its layout. The castle may have been slighted in the reign of Henry II before its construction was complete.

University of Hertfordshire — College Lane, Hatfield. Established as a university in 1992 and based largely in Hatfield. It has more than 23,000 students. There are three campuses: College Lane, De Havilland (also a Saracens training ground) and St Albans. The main site is still based in the original buildings of Hatfield Technical College buildings in Hatfield, although many new buildings have been added since. The Learning Resources Centre, a combined library and computer centre, is the largest university building of its kind in Britain. Computer science, engineering, and natural sciences are here, along with halls of residence including Telford Court, and the Roberts Way student village. Tel: 01707 284800.

Walkern Castle — Walkern, 2 miles (3km) northeast of Stevenage. A 12th century earth and timber ringwork and bailey fortress, founded by Hamo de St Clare. The large oval enclosure is encased by a rampart with a ditch, and to the north are the remains of a prospect mound, part of a 19th century garden. The castle was possibly one of the many adulterine fortifications – i.e. those founded without authorisation from one's lord, in this case the monarch – built during the 12th century civil war in King Stephen's reign, and was slighted in the reign of Henry II.

Waytemore Castle — See Bishop's Stortford Castle

Welwyn Roman Baths — Welwyn Bypass, Welwyn. Discovered during construction of the A1, the site is now enclosed in a vault beneath the road. The baths were built in the early 3rd century AD as part of a villa complex consisting of at least four buildings, two of which had baths attached, and are relatively simple in design. Also on display are other finds from the site and surrounding area. Tel: 01707 271362.

Some famous people born in Hertfordshire

Barber, Christopher (trombonist) (1930–)	Welwyn Garden City
Bentine, Michael (comedian) (1922–96)	Watford
Bessemer, Henry (engineer and inventor) (1813–98)	Charlton (Hitchin)
Brightman, Sarah (singer) (1960–)	Berkhamsted
Cecil, Robert (3rd Marquess of Salisbury) (1830–1903)	Hatfield
Chapman, George (writer) (c.1559–1634)	Hitchin
Evans, Arthur (archaeologist) (1851–1941)	Hemel Hempstead
Faldo, Nick (golfer) (1957–)	Welwyn Garden City
Greene, Graham (writer) (1904–91)	Berkhamsted
Hamilton, Lewis (racing driver) (1985–)	Stevenage
Hordern, Michael (actor) (1911–95)	Berkhamsted
Johns, Capt. W.E. (pilot and novelist) (1893–1968)	Bengeo (Hertford)
Johnston, Brian (cricket commentator) (1912–94)	Little Berkhamsted
Marsh, Rodney (footballer) (1944–)	Hatfield
Newell, Mike (director) (1942–)	St Albans
Purdom, Edward (actor) (1924–2009)	Welwyn Garden City
Ramprakash, Mark (cricketer) (1969–)	Bushey
Rhodes, Cecil (founder of De Beers) (1853–1902)	Bishop's Stortford
Scott, Terry (actor) (1927–94)	Watford
Waller, Edmund (poet) (1606–87)	Coleshill

KENT

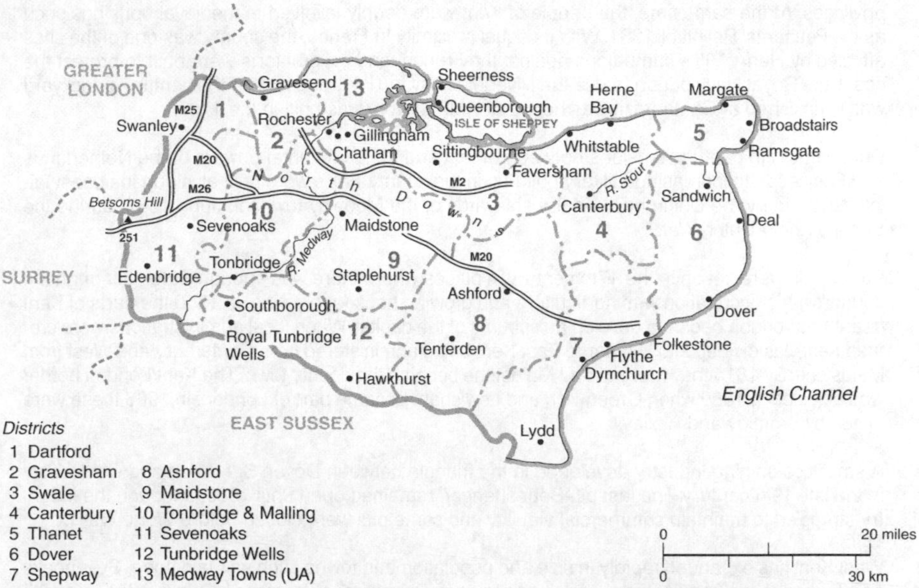
GREATER LONDON
SURREY
EAST SUSSEX
English Channel
Gravesend
Rochester
Gillingham
Chatham
Sheerness
Queenborough
ISLE OF SHEPPEY
Sittingbourne
Faversham
Herne Bay
Whitstable
Margate
Broadstairs
Ramsgate
Sandwich
Deal
Canterbury
R. Stour
Swanley
Betsoms Hill
251
M25
M20
M26
M2
North Downs
Sevenoaks
Maidstone
R. Medway
Tonbridge
Edenbridge
Southborough
Royal Tunbridge Wells
Staplehurst
Ashford
Tenterden
Hawkhurst
Hythe
Dymchurch
Folkestone
Dover
Lydd
0 20 miles
0 30 km
Districts
1 Dartford
2 Gravesham
3 Swale
4 Canterbury
5 Thanet
6 Dover
7 Shepway
8 Ashford
9 Maidstone
10 Tonbridge & Malling
11 Sevenoaks
12 Tunbridge Wells
13 Medway Towns (UA)

Kent borders London to the northwest, East Sussex to the southwest and Surrey to the west. It is also connected to Essex via the Dartford Tunnel and Queen Elizabeth Bridge across the River Thames. Technically, Kent also has a nominal border with France halfway along the Channel Tunnel. The Medway Towns became a unitary authority on 1 April 1998 and as such are not administered by Kent County Council, but remain as part of the geographical county. However, the former Kent districts of Bexley, Bromley, Greenwich and Lewisham, although part of the historic county, have been part of Greater London since 1965 and are therefore dealt with in the London section.

The county's major geographical features are determined by a series of ridges that run from west to east. These ridges are the remains of the Wealden dome, which was the result of uplifting caused by Alpine movements between 10 and 20 million years ago. Erosion has resulted in these ridges and the valleys between. From the north they are: the marshlands along the Thames/Medway estuaries and along the North Kent coast; the chalk North Downs with its sandstone and clay valleys containing the River Medway; the Greensand ridge; the Wealden clay valley; and finally the sandstone High Weald. Probably the most significant geographical feature of Kent is the White Cliffs of Dover, where the North Downs reach the sea. The area between here and Westerham has been designated the Kent Downs Area of Outstanding Natural Beauty.

The modern name of Kent is derived from the Brythonic word *cantus* meaning a rim or border, and alludes to the eastern part of the modern county. Julius Caesar described the area as Cantium, home of the Cantiaci in 51 BC. The extreme west of the county was occupied by other Iron Age tribes, the Regnenses and possibly another ethnic group occupying the Weald. Traditionally, the kingdom of Kent began c.AD 455 with the reign of the Jutish brothers Hengist and Horsa; East Kent became one of the kingdoms of the Jutes during the 5th century AD and the area was known as Cantia c.730 and Cent in 835. The early medieval inhabitants were known as the Cantwara or Kent people, their capital being Canterbury. During this period Kent was part of the Heptarchy, one of seven areas which eventually merged to become the kingdom of England during the early 10th century, and also comprising Northumbria, Mercia, East Anglia, Essex, Sussex and Wessex. The last king was Baldred c.AD 825, although by then Kent was ruled directly by Cenwulf, king of Mercia. In 825 Essex and Kent were usurped by Wessex, and Baldred, a pro-Mercian, was expelled by Egbert of Wessex.

According to Domesday Book, in 1086 Kent was divided into seven 'lathes' or *lest*(*um*). A lathe was an ancient administrative division of Kent, and these units, which may have originated during Jutish colonisation of the county, remained important for another 600 years. The seven lathes are Aylesford, Milton, Sutton, Borough, Eastry, Lympne and Wye. Each was divided into smaller areas called hundreds, although the difference between the functions of lathes and hundreds is unclear.

With its close proximity both to London and continental Europe, Kent enjoyed a pivotal position after the Norman Conquest. Much of the county's prosperity came via the numerous ports: Dover, Hythe, New Romney and Sandwich were four of the original five 'Cinque Ports', enjoying special trading privileges. At the same time, the people of Kent were deeply involved in medieval uprisings such as the Peasants' Revolt of 1381. With its equal proximity to France, the county was one of the sites affected by Henry VIII's campaigns against the French, and several forts were built to protect the coast; the Royal Navy began to use the River Medway in 1547, and later in the century a dockyard was established at Chatham; it was here that HMS *Victory* was built in the 1760s.

During the 17th century, tensions between Britain and the continental powers of the Netherlands and France led to increasing military build-up in the county. Forts were built all along the coast following a raid by the Dutch navy on the shipyards of the Medway towns in June 1667, during the Second Anglo-Dutch War.

Paper mills were set up in the 17th century in places where there was enough water, although the county's main occupation was horticulture and growing hops for brewing. In 1750 the parts of Kent nearest to London began to develop as suburbs of the capital. When local administrations were created Kent was divided into two parts, East Kent being administered from Canterbury and West from Maidstone. By 1814 they merged and Maidstone became the county town. The Kent/London border was adjusted in 1889 when Greenwich and Lewisham became part of London. In 1965 these were joined by Bromley and Bexley.

A small coal mining industry developed in the triangle between Dover, Sandwich and Canterbury in the late 19th century. The last pit, Betteshanger, remained open until 1989, although the industry struggled to maintain commercial viability and some pits were closed before World War I.

West Kent has expanded rapidly in size and population and towns such as Maidstone, Sevenoaks and Tonbridge are popular with London commuters. The introduction of the railways in the mid-19th century turned Ashford from a sleepy market town to the international terminal that it is today. During World War II Canterbury and Dover were heavily bombed by the Germans and many historic buildings were lost. The rebuilding of Canterbury and the enlargement of towns such as Maidstone and Dover since the 1960s has changed Kent dramatically.

Kent is traditionally known as the Garden of England, a title supposedly bestowed by Henry VIII after he had enjoyed a bowl of Kentish cherries. Although that reputation has come under increasing pressure in recent years, the county's picturesque variety is still evident. Although West Kent has increasingly become London commuter territory, further east there is a strong farming community and in these more rural areas simple wooden weather-boarded houses can still be found. In contrast is the spa town of Tunbridge Wells, with its pretty colonnaded walkway known as the Pantiles, and numerous elegant town houses once owned by affluent cloth merchants. On the northeast coast Margate and Ramsgate were once two of the most popular seaside resorts in England. The two cities in Kent are Canterbury and Rochester, the seats respectively of the Archbishop of Canterbury and the Bishop of Rochester. In 1998 when local government was reorganised, Rochester lost its official city status through an administrative oversight; attempts are now being made to regain it. Part of Canterbury around the cathedral was designated a UNESCO World Heritage Site in 1988.

Kent		**Population**		**Area**	
Districts	*male*	*female*	*total*	*sq miles*	*sq km*
Ashford	49,956	52,705	102,661	224	581
Canterbury	64,125	71,153	135,278	119	309
Dartford	42,121	43,790	85,911	28	73
Dover	50,321	54,245	104,566	122	315
Gravesham	46,888	48,829	95,717	38	99
Maidstone	68,350	70,598	138,948	152	393
Sevenoaks	52,891	56,414	109,305	143	369
Shepway	46,052	50,186	96,238	138	357
Swale	60,552	62,249	122,801	144	373
Thanet	59,956	66,746	126,702	40	103
Tonbridge & Malling	52,642	54,919	107,561	93	240
Tunbridge Wells	50,032	53,998	104,030	128	331
Medway Towns Unitary Authority	122,896	126,592	249,488	74	192
Total	766,782	812,424	1,579,206	1443	3735

Local Attractions and Information

Administrative headquarters
Kent: County Hall, Maidstone ME14 1XQ. Tel: 01622 671411.
Medway Towns: Civic Centre, Strood, Rochester ME2 4AU. Tel: 01634 306000.

Airports
Kent International Airport, Manston, 2 miles (3km) west of Ramsgate, was known as London Manston Airport until 1989, when a new terminal was officially opened by the Duchess of York. Because it has the fourth longest runway in the UK, which is also aligned east/west, the airport was listed by NASA (although never used) as an emergency landing strip for the Space Shuttle programme. Formerly RAF Manston, the airport is now wholly commercial. The Thanet Flying Club is based at the airport and there are three museums on the site. The Spitfire and Hurricane Museum contains beautifully restored examples of the two aircraft; next door is the RAF Manston History Museum. Tel: 08707 605755.

Lydd Airport (also known as London Ashford Airport), 14 miles (23km) south of Ashford, was constructed in 1954 as a cross-Channel departure point for car ferries. It enjoyed strong levels of traffic through the 1950s and 60s (it was busier than Gatwick for a number of years) but declined in the 1970s due to competition from roll-on, roll-off ferries. Dan Air retained an operational base for many years due to the airport's superb weather record and operated Channel Islands, Beauvais and other European routes. Lydd Airport today is operated by London Ashford Airport Ltd. Tel: 01797 322411.

Rochester Airport, Maidstone Road, Chatham, is now privately owned and has two grass runways. Tel: 01634 869969.

Allington Castle
Castle Road, Maidstone. Founded by Stephen of Penchester in 1281 beside the site of an adulterine Norman motte and bailey demolished by Henry II. The castle was altered in the late 15th century by Sir Henry Wyatt. Severely damaged by fire at the turn of the 17th century while in use as a farmhouse, the castle was restored by Lord Conway, 1905–30, and after 1951 was used as a Carmelite nunnery before becoming a private residence once more. Today the castle consists of several castellated buildings surrounding a square courtyard, joined by a curtain wall with semicircular towers. The castle gave its name during World War II to the 'Castle' class corvette HMS *Allington Castle*. It is not open to the public.

Battles
There have been three battles in Kent: Dungeness, Medway and Sevenoaks, also known as the Battle of Solefield. See separate table for details.

Bayham Abbey
4 miles (6km) southeast of Tunbridge Wells. Standing on the Kent/Sussex border, the abbey of Premonstratensian 'white canons' was founded by Robert Thornham in the early 12th century. The ruins, constructed from the golden-coloured local sandstone, include much of the 13th to 15th century church, the chapter house, and a picturesque 14th century gatehouse, now set in an 18th century landscape designed by Humphry Repton. Parts of the 'Georgian Gothick' dower house are also open to visitors. To provide access from both counties, there were originally two gatehouses. The Sussex gatehouse has disappeared without trace, but the façade of the early 14th century Kentish gatehouse was retained in the grounds of the later Old Abbey House. Richly carved stonework and ornate clustered columns can still be seen in the church, the east end of which is now dominated by a magnificent old beech tree clinging by a tangle of roots to the remains of the stone wall. During the 15th century a new nave was created and tall perpendicular windows were inserted in the south wall, supported by buttresses that straddled the cloister walk; three of these graceful arches remain standing to full height. Other remains include sections of the vaulted chapter house, a wall of the undercroft beneath the monks' dorter, and fragments of the living accommodation. Tel: 01892 890381.

Bedgebury National Pinetum
10 miles (16km) east of Tunbridge Wells. The Forestry Commission-owned pinetum, covering 320 acres (129ha), was established in 1925 as the National Conifer Collection. It now maintains the finest collection of conifers in the world, with over 10,000 specimens including many vulnerable and endangered species. Tel: 01580 211781.

Benenden School
Benenden, 18 miles (29km) southeast of Tunbridge Wells. Independent school for girls aged 11–18, founded in 1923 and notable for being an early school of the Princess Royal. Tel: 01580 240592.

Bewl Water
6 miles (10km) southeast of Tunbridge Wells. The largest stretch of open water in southeast England, covering an area of 770 acres (310ha), Bewl Water reservoir is located in the High Weald Area of Outstanding Natural Beauty on the Kent/Sussex border. Created by flooding the valley of the River Bewl and completed in 1975, its capacity is 6900 million gallons (31,368 megalitres). The reservoir is host to a huge variety of wildlife and is a popular site for outdoor pursuits. Tel: 01892 890661.

Bluewater Shopping Centre
Greenhithe, 2 miles (3km) east of Dartford. Opened in 1999 in a former chalk quarry, the shopping centre covers 240 acres (97ha) and is the second largest in the UK. It includes 330 stores, 40 cafes, bars and restaurants. Tel: 0870 777 0252.

Borstals
A series of institutions formerly used for the correction of delinquent boys and young men aged 16–21. Originating in 1895 as a concept proposed by the Gladstone Committee for the reform of young offenders and established by Sir Evelyn Ruggles-Brise, they took their name from the first one, opened in 1902 at the former Rochester Prison, Borstal, near Rochester. Its pioneering methods were used as a model for the creation of other borstal institutions from in 1908. The institutions relied on a mix of education and strong discipline: the main elements in their programmes included regular work, character formation, discipline, obedience and respect for authority. The only corporal punishment officially allowed was birching, to be administered only for extreme breaches of discipline. The system was abolished by the Criminal Justice Act 1982.

Bough Beech Reservoir 5 miles (8km) southwest of Sevenoaks. Created in the early 1970s and covering 285 acres (115ha), at the reservoir's north end is a beautiful nature reserve famous for bird watching, with its visitor centre in a 19th century oast house. Tel: 01732 355080.

Boughton Monchelsea Place Church Hill, Boughton Monchelsea, 4 miles (6km) south of Maidstone. A privately owned Elizabethan manor house, dating from 1567 and set in its own estate of 165 acres (67ha), much of which is woodland and parkland. The interiors vary in character from Tudor through to Georgian Gothic and Victorian.

Broadstairs Coastal town on the east of the Isle of Thanet, 3 miles (5km) north of Ramsgate. In 1538 the first pier and the York gate were erected in order to aid and protect the shipyard in Harbour Street. Built by George Culmer and originally called Flint Gate, the latter was renamed after the Grand Old Duke of York and extensively rebuilt in 1795 by Lord Henniker. In the 17th and 18th centuries shipbuilding was the biggest industry in Broadstairs but after its demise in 1824, tourism became predominant. The arrival of the railways in 1863 brought large numbers of holidaymakers and the town grew quickly in the latter 19th century to become one of the most popular resorts in Kent. There are several locations in Broadstairs associated with Charles Dickens, perhaps the best known being Bleak House overlooking the Jetty at Viking Bay. Dickens stayed in Broadstairs for his summer holidays and wrote much of *David Copperfield* in Bleak House. He is now commemorated by the week-long Dickens Festival, instituted in 1937 and held in the town every June. There are seven bays in and around Broadstairs; the main one, Viking Bay, received its first Blue Flag in 2006, and gained its name following the celebration of the 1500th anniversary of the legendary landing here by Hengist and Horsa in AD 449. In June 2005 a Viking longship at Pegwell Bay was returned to public display following restoration.

Cade's Rebellion Very little is known of the life of Jack Cade, who appeared in 1450 as the leader of the well-organised uprising in Kent usually known as Jack Cade's Rebellion. He may have been of Irish birth; some of his followers called him John Mortimer and claimed he was a cousin of Richard, Duke of York. The protests themselves were mainly political: the rebels' various grievances included the 14th century Statute of Labourers (which attempted to freeze wages and prices), the loss of royal lands in France, the extravagance of Henry VI's court, the corruption of the royal favourites, high taxation and the breakdown of the administration of justice. On 18 June, the rebels (who were mainly landed gentry) defeated the royal army at Sevenoaks (see Battles). Entering London on 4 July, they executed the Lord Treasurer James Fiennes, 1st Baron Saye and Sele (who was blamed for the losses in France), and sacked several houses, dispersing only after they were offered pardon. Cade himself was mortally wounded while resisting arrest at Heathfield, Sussex.

Canterbury Castle Castle Street, Canterbury. Originally founded as a Norman motte and bailey castle by William I in 1066, one of three royal castles in Kent (the other two being Rochester and Dover), on a site now marked by the mound known as Dane John (from French *donjon*, keep). The castle was resited 20 years later a little to the west, using part of the Roman town wall as its southern boundary (some reused Roman material can still be seen), and a stone keep was constructed largely in the reign of Henry I. The castle had become the county gaol by the 13th century but fell into disrepair during the 1700s.

Canterbury Cathedral The Precincts, Canterbury. The seat of the Anglican Archbishop of Canterbury, Primate of All England and religious leader of the Church of England, the formal title of Canterbury Cathedral is the Cathedral and Metropolitical Church of Christ at Canterbury. The church was founded by St Augustine, the first Archbishop of Canterbury, who arrived on the coast of Kent as a missionary to England in AD 597 having been sent by Pope Gregory the Great from Rome. On his arrival Augustine was given a church at Canterbury by King Ethelbert of Kent, whose queen, Bertha, was already a Christian; the building had been a place of worship during the Roman occupation of Britain. The original Saxon church was destroyed by fire in 1067 and rebuilt by the Norman Archbishop Lanfranc in the 1070s. On 29 December 1170 Archbishop Thomas Becket was killed in the north transept of the crossing by four knights seeking to curry favour with Henry II, who had quarrelled with Becket. Pope John Paul II and Archbishop of Canterbury Robert Runcie prayed together on the spot in 1982, a historic occasion now commemorated by a plaque. Originally the tomb of Henry IV and his wife Joan of Navarre flanked one side of the shrine of the murdered archbishop, while the tomb of Edward the Black Prince flanked the other. Both of these tombs can still be seen today although the shrine of St Thomas was dismantled in Henry VIII's reign. After another major fire in 1172, rebuilding of the church began in 1174 under Frenchman William of Sens, a master of the new continental style now called Gothic. In 1179 William was badly injured in a fall from scaffolding above the high altar and was forced to leave the project in the hands of his assistant, a man now known only as William the Englishman. In the 14th century Lanfranc's nave was rebuilt by Henry Yeveley, and in 1496 the 235ft (71.5m) central 'Bell Harry' tower was added (the name derives from a bell originally hung in the northwestern tower by Henry (Harry) Eastry, prior of the then Benedictine community 1285–1331; the present Bell Harry was cast in 1635). The present archbishop, Most Revd Dr Rowan Williams, is 104th in the line of succession. Tel: 01227 762862.

Channel Tunnel The idea of a road tunnel between England and France was first suggested to Napoleon in 1802, but it was almost 200 years before digging began on the Channel Tunnel – or 'Chunnel' as it was then familiarly known – in 1988. The $15 billion link beneath the English Channel at the Straits of Dover, connecting Folkestone in Kent to Coquelles near Calais in northern France, was officially opened by President Mitterrand and Queen Elizabeth II in 1994. It is the second-longest rail tunnel in the world, surpassed only by the Seikan Tunnel in Japan. The tunnel consists of three interconnected tubes: one rail track in each direction, along with a service tunnel. Its length is 31 miles (50km), of which 23 miles (37km) are underwater; its average depth is 150ft (46m) under the seabed. Only 20 minutes of the Eurostar journey takes place in the tunnel. Originally, Eurostar ran from London Waterloo or Ashford International to Paris, Lille, Marne-la-Vallée (Disneyland) and Brussels. In 2007 the second section of the new UK high-speed rail line opened and St Pancras International became Eurostar's new London home, creating a high-speed link to the Continent from the heart of the city. The fastest London–Paris journey time is currently 2 hours 15 minutes and London–Brussels 1 hour 53 minutes. The official border between France and the UK is a painted line roughly halfway through the tunnel. The British half is officially part of the district of Dover and the county of Kent.

Chart Gunpowder Mills Stonebridge Way, Faversham. One of the very few fully restored gunpowder mills in England. The Chart Gunpowder Mills, powder from which was used at the battles of Trafalgar and Waterloo, were established c.1760 and are the oldest of their kind in the world. Chart Mills is a water powered incorporating mill, where the ingredients, saltpetre, sulphur and charcoal, after preliminary mixing, are incorporated to become an explosive mixture. Incorporation was the most vital of the 11 processes involved in gunpowder manufacture, as it determined the quality and effectiveness of the powder. The mills closed in the 1930s but were restored by the Faversham Society and opened to the public in April 1969. Tel: 01795 534542.

Chartwell 2 miles (3km) south of Westerham. When Sir Winston Churchill saw the views from this house in 1922 he immediately purchased the property and made it his family home from 1924 until the end of his life. The existing Victorian house was modernised and extended by architect Philip Tilden, and remains little changed from when Churchill lived there. There are many mementoes from his extraordinary life, such as paintings, papers, cigars and uniforms, as well as the 'siren suit' he wore throughout much of World War II. The gardens, in the style of designs by Gertrude Jekyll, include the lakes created by Churchill and the Golden Rose Avenue – a gift from the children to their parents on their golden wedding anniversary. The property was given to the National Trust in 1946 and opened to visitors in 1966, the year after Churchill's death at the age of 90. Tel: 01732 868381 or infoline: 01732 866368.

Chatham Historic Dockyard Located on the River Medway, Chatham Dockyard became a Royal Dockyard in the reign of Elizabeth I. The largest refitting dockyard during the Dutch Wars, in later years it became a building yard and HMS *Victory* (Nelson's flagship at Trafalgar) was built here. After the closure of HM Naval Base Chatham in 1984 the Chatham Historic Dockyard Trust was established to preserve the 18th century core of the old Royal Dockyard. Set in an estate of 80 acres (32ha), the Historic Dockyard features three unique historic warships: HMS *Gannet* (1878), a sloop of Queen Victoria's Royal Navy; HMS *Cavalier* (1944), a World War II destroyer; and HMS *Ocelot* (1962), a Cold War submarine. The Museum of the Royal Dockyard explores 400 years of British maritime history. Tel: 01634 823800.

Chiddingstone Castle Chiddingstone, 6 miles (10km) west of Tonbridge. Once the ancestral home of the Streatfields, in 1803 Harry Streatfield, Squire of Chiddingstone, transformed the existing 16th century house into a fantasy castle with battlements, towers and a gatehouse. Having fallen into disrepair after its occupation by the Army during World War II, in 1955 the castle was bought by Denys Eyre Bower, an enthusiastic collector who was able to display his collections of Japanese, Egyptian and Stuart artefacts. After his death in 1977, a charitable trust was formed to allow for the renovation and running of the castle and to exhibit Bower's collections. Tel: 01892 870347.

Chilham Castle Chilham, 6 miles (10km) southwest of Canterbury. Norman castle founded by Fulbert of Dover in the late 11th century, replaced by a motte and keep early in the 12th century; a new keep was built for Henry II 1171–5. The keep, of which the basement and two upper storeys still exist, and 14th century curtain walls now stand beside a red brick Jacobean manor house built in 1616.

Cinque Ports See East Sussex

Cobham Hall 4 miles (6km) west of Rochester. A beautiful red-brick mansion displaying a combination of Elizabethan, Jacobean, Carolean and 18th century styles and set in 150 acres (60ha) of parkland designed by Humphry Repton. The house dates in its present form from 1584 when it was enlarged by William Brooke, 10th Lord Cobham. The Gilt Hall was decorated by John Webb, a pupil of Inigo Jones, in 1654; further rooms were decorated by James Wyatt in the 18th century. In 1713 the house came into possession of John Bligh, later the 1st Earl of Darnley, remaining in the family until 1961. In 1883 the Hon. Ivo Bligh, later the 8th Earl, led the victorious English cricket team against Australia and brought the Ashes home to Cobham. Cobham Hall is now a boarding and day school for girls aged 11–18, founded in September 1962 by Mrs Bee Mansell, the first Parsee woman lawyer to be called to the Bar. The school is a member of Round Square, a worldwide affiliation of schools whose aims are based on the ideals of educationalist Kurt Hahn, and who share the ethos that teaching and learning should encourage self-development, social responsibility and a sense of adventure. Tel: 01474 823371.

Cooling Castle 6 miles (10km) north of Rochester. A double quadrangular castle built 1381–5 by John, 3rd Earl of Cobham (see also Cobham Hall) to protect the River Thames. It has a double bailey, the eastern side having a tower in each corner and earth walls in between, surrounded by a dry moat and accessed through the ornate gateway. The smaller western bailey has stone walls which still stand at half their original height with a tower in each corner and a wet moat on three sides. The entrance is through the eastern bailey on the fourth side. The castle was besieged in 1554 during Thomas Wyatt's rebellion against Mary I and suffered damage by cannon fire. The castle itself is now in ruins, and a more recent house stands inside the grounds, but the gatehouse remains in good condition. It is not open to the public but can be seen from the road.

Deal Castle Victoria Road, Deal. One of three 'castles of the Downs' – the others being Walmer and Sandown – built 1539–40 by Henry VIII to protect an area of safe anchorage on the eastern coast of Kent. The artillery fort is laid out in the shape of a Tudor Rose. Twice besieged by Parliament, its garrison surrendered in 1648. It is now owned by English Heritage. Tel: 01304 372762.

Dickens Festival — See Broadstairs

Dickens House Museum — Victoria Parade, Broadstairs. Once the home of Mary Pearson Strong, on whom Charles Dickens based the character of Betsey Trotwood in *David Copperfield*. There has been a dwelling on the site since Tudor times, and the current museum houses many artefacts relating to Dickens. Tel: 01843 861232. See also Broadstairs.

Doddington Place Gardens — 5 miles (8km) south of Sittingbourne. The home of the Oldfield family for the last century, the gabled brick house was designed by Victorian architect Charles Brown Trollope and built c.1860 for Sir John Croft of the port and sherry family. The formal terrace next to the house was designed for Croft in 1873 by Markham Nesfield (c.1842–74), son of garden designer William Andrews Nesfield (1793–1881). The 10 acres (4ha) of landscaped gardens are Grade II listed and include a woodland garden with many varieties of rhododendrons and azaleas; a large Edwardian rock garden with pools; a formal sunken garden with herbaceous borders; and a flint and brick folly. The extensive lawns and avenues are framed by ½ mile (0.8km) of clipped yew hedges, as well as many fine trees. Tel: 01795 886385.

Dover Castle — Castle Hill Road, Dover. Norman castle founded in 1066 by William I and placed under the care of Bishop Odo of Bayeux. It was rebuilt for Henry II in 1180–9 with a tower keep, designed by Maurice the Engineer, and concentric fortifications. The castle was besieged by Prince Louis of France in 1216–17 and refortified in 1223. It became known as 'The Key to England' due to its strategic importance, the bastions and scarping of the east side being added by Henry VIII. Dover was taken by Parliamentarians in 1642. Extra fortifications and a complex of tunnels were added during the Napoleonic Wars in the early 19th century; the latter were used as the headquarters of the operation to evacuate Dunkirk in 1940, and can be viewed today. A Roman Pharos (lighthouse) and an Anglo-Saxon church are located within the castle precincts; it is also home to a 19th century barracks and the Princess of Wales' Royal Regiment Museum. It is now owned by English Heritage. Tel: 01304 201628.

Dungeness — A shingle headland located at the southeastern tip of the county, Dungeness is a National Nature Reserve and a Special Protection Area, as well as an RPSB reserve. The shingle has been heaped up by the tide into a series of ridges and the resulting combination of shingle and lagoons provides a unique mix of habitats. There have been five lighthouses, the first built in 1615. The present unmanned lighthouse was built in 1961; the previous one still stands, although no longer operational. There are numerous dwellings, mostly former fishermen's cottages; artist and film-maker Derek Jarman lived in Prospect Cottage until his death in 1994, establising a shingle garden much admired by horticultural experts. In 1965 the first nuclear power station at this site, Magnox Dungeness A, began operation, closing in 2006; Dungeness B, an advanced gas cooled reactor, began operating in 1983.

Dunorlan Park — Tunbridge Wells. Once the private grounds of a grand Italianate mansion built and in the 1860s and owned by Yorkshire-born millionaire Henry Reed, who made his fortune in Tasmania, the garden was laid out in the 1850s and 1860s by renowned Victorian gardener Robert Marnock. Although the mansion no longer exists, the 78 acre (31ha) garden is one of the best preserved examples of Marnock's work. It is now a public park.

Dymchurch Martello Tower — High Street, Dymchurch, 9 miles (15km) southwest of Folkestone. Built as one of 74 such towers to counter the threat of invasion by Napoleon, Dymchurch (Martello tower no. 24) has been fully restored by English Heritage. It can be climbed to the roof, which is dominated by an original 24-pound gun complete with traversing carriage. Tel: 01304 211067.

East Kent Railway — Shepherdswell, 6 miles (10km) northwest of Dover. A heritage railway running for 2 miles (3km) from Shepherdswell to Eythorne. The light railway was constructed 1911–17 by engineer Colonel H F Stephens to serve the growing number of coal mines in East Kent. The line was closed following nationalisation in 1948, although the section from Shepherdswell to Tilmanstone colliery remained operational until the miners' strike of 1984. The East Kent Railway was formed in 1985 with the intention of preserving the remaining section of line; since then the track has been restored and a replica of the original Shepherdswell station building and platform built. In 1993 a Light Railway Order was obtained, allowing regular passenger trains to run once more on the line, and a new station has since been built at Eythorne. Rolling stock includes various electric aand diesel units while the Electronic Preservation Group, dedicated to the preservation and restoration of electric trains, also has its home on the railway. Tel: 01304 832042.

Eastbridge Hospital of St Thomas — High Street, Canterbury. Founded c.1190 as a refuge for 'poor pilgrims, infirm persons, the poor and homeless and lying-in women', today the establishment still houses elderly people of limited means. There is a Norman undercroft, while upstairs a wonderful 13th century mural in the refectory hall features a rare depiction of the martydom of Thomas Becket. There is also a little chapel with an impressive beamed ceiling. Tel: 01227 471688.

Ebbsfleet Landmark — In 2008 a project was launched to build a sculpture to rival the Angel of the North. The 2007 Turner Prize-winning artist Mark Wallinger was the successful candidate and his 'Angel of the South' will consist of a 33-times life-size white horse. The 50m-high sculpture will overlook the A2 and Ebbsfleet International train station, near Gravesend.

Emmetts Garden — Ide Hill, 3 miles (5km) southwest of Sevenoaks. Named after the profusion of ants once to be found in the surrounding woodlands, Emmetts was created in the late 19th century by Frederick Lubbock, brother of Lord Avebury (a world authority on ants) as a typically informal plantsman's garden under the influence of William Robinson. The garden was further developed after Lubbock's death by American geologist Charles Watson Boise. It is now owned by the National Trust. Tel: 01732 751509.

Eynsford Castle — Eynsford, 5 miles (8km) south of Dartford. One of the earliest stone enclosure castles in England began in 1088 when William de Eynsford inherited the manor from his father. The original castle consisted of a stone structure located within a bailey, and fully enclosed by a flint curtain wall. Various 12th century buildings were contained in the bailey, but the most important comprised the living accommodation, with a private solar, and a large hall situated on the first floor. The hall was gutted by a fire in the early 13th century, and a major rebuilding took place soon afterwards. Today, only the massive walls of the undercroft remain. At the same time that these building works were being carried out, a main gatehouse was added. Substantial sections of the curtain wall still stand, some reaching 30ft (9m) in height, along with a stone gate tower dating from the early 12th century, but all other fragmentary remains date from the 13th century reconstruction. The site is now maintained by English Heritage.

Finchcocks — Goudhurst, 8 miles (13km) east of Tunbridge Wells. There are records of a house called Finchcocks – sometimes spelt Finchcox – dating back to 1256, when a family of that name lived a little to the east of the present site. By the 15th century the Horden family owned the property and through marriage it passed to the Bathurst family. The present house, with its fine brickwork and impressive front elevation, was built in 1725 for barrister Edward Bathurst. In 1970, the house was acquired by Richard Burnett and it now contains his collection of more than 100 historical keyboard instruments, many in full playing condition. Tel: 01580 211702.

Gad's Hill Place — Gravesend Road, Higham, 2 miles (3km) north of Rochester. Built in 1780 and now Grade I listed, in 1821 the house greatly impressed the young Charles Dickens when he came across it while out walking with his father; it is said that his father told Charles that if he were to be 'very persevering and work very hard' he might one day live there. In 1856 Dickens did indeed buy the house, living there until his death in 1870; the summer house in which he wrote has been moved to the Dickens Centre in Rochester. Gad's Hill Place has been a school since 1924 and now caters for day pupils aged 3–16. Tel: 01634 318825.

Gavelkind — A system of land tenure associated chiefly with Kent, principally distinguished by permitting a tenant to dispose of his lands by will, and by the division of property between all the tenant's sons on his death. Before the Norman Conquest the practice of gavelkind was customary throughout England, but afterwards it was superseded in most of the country by the feudal law of primogeniture (i.e. the transfer of property to the eldest son).

Godinton House & Gardens — Godinton Lane, Ashford. Originally built in the 14th century and owned for over 400 years by the Toke family, Godinton displays a fascinating blend of styles and embellishments. The exterior is largely Jacobean, as is the elaborately carved great staircase. There is a wealth of carved panelling, and fine collections of porcelain, pictures and furniture; the dining room is Georgian. The yew hedges, formal topiary, pond and lawns were architect Sir Reginald Blomfield's first garden design in the 1890s and have been softened and enhanced by subsequent plantings. In contrast are the wild garden, with its carpet of daffodils and spring bulbs under a canopy of trees, the intimate 1920s Italian garden and the 18th century walled garden. Tel: 01233 620773.

Goodnestone Park Gardens — Goodnestone, 8 miles (13km) east of Canterbury. Set in 18th century parkland, the 15 acres (6ha) of gardens surround the splendid home of Lord and Lady FitzWalter, built in 1704 for Sir Brook Bridges. There are many fine trees and the large walled garden has a collection of old-fashioned roses, clematis and herbaceous plants. A new gravel garden was planted in 2003. Jane Austen was a frequent visitor to Goodnestone Park after her brother Edward married Bridges' daughter Elizabeth. Tel: 01304 840107.

Great Comp Garden — Comp Lane, Platt, 7 miles (11km) northeast of Sevenoaks. The creation of Roderic and Joyce Cameron, who in 1957 purchased the 17th century house with $4^1/_2$ acres (1.8km) of garden and over the next 25 years developed and extended it into 7 acres (2.8km), informally landscaped and featuring a wide range of flowering plants as well as a woodland garden and Italianate garden. Of particular note are the collections of magnolias and salvias. Tel: 01732 886154.

Groombridge Place — 5 miles (8km) southwest of Tunbridge Wells. Moated house built in 1662 by Philip Packer on the site of a 13th century fortified manor house, with formal pleasure gardens laid out in 1674. The gardens include an Oriental Garden, Drunken Garden, Secret Garden and the Draughtsman's Lawn, named to commemorate the filming in the house and gardens of *The Draughtsman's Contract* (1982); the Knot Garden, White Rose Garden and Peacock Walk were laid out in the 20th century. Sir Arthur Conan Doyle was a frequent visitor and the Sherlock Holmes story *The Valley of Fear* is set at the house in the guise of Birlstone Manor. The gardens were also used as a location for *Pride and Prejudice* (2005). The house is not open to the public. Tel: 01892 863999.

Hever Castle — 3 miles (5km) southeast of Edenbridge. The moated castle, actually a manor house, was founded in 1270 for Sir Stephen de Penchester; it was fortified in 1340 by William de Hever and again in 1384 by Sir John Cobham. Hever was bought by the Boleyn family in 1462 and further modified. The childhood home of Anne Boleyn, on her death it was appropriated by Henry VIII who gave it to Anne of Cleves. In 1903 the house was bought, and beautifully restored, by William Waldorf Astor, who also laid out the gardens. The estate is now used as a conference centre. The Italian garden was designed to display Astor's collection of Italian sculpture, while the lake and other water features have been complemented by more recent additions such as a water maze. Tel: 01732 865224.

Highest point — Betsoms Hill, 823ft (251m) above sea level (GR: TQ435563), 1 mile (1.6km) northwest of Westerham on the North Downs Way.

Hole Park — Rolvenden, 2 miles (3km) southwest of Tenterden, 14 miles (23km) southwest of Ashford. Situated on the edge of a picturesque Wealden village, Hole Park has been owned by the Barham family for four generations. The house is surrounded by 15 acres (6ha) of gardens that feature contrasting formal and woodland areas, laid out and planted between the two world wars by Colonel Barham, great-grandfather of the present owner; these include fountain and swimming pools, egg pond, walled rose garden, herbaceous borders and wrought iron gates, while walls and yew hedges shelter broad expanses of lawns and precisely hand-clipped yew topiary. There are fine views of the Weald over the surrounding 220 acres (89ha) of finely timbered parkland. The house is not open to the public. Tel: 01580 241344.

Hoo Peninsula — A peninsula separating the estuaries of the rivers Thames and Medway (Old English *hoh* = 'spur of land'), and consisting of a line of sand and clay hills surrounded by extensive marshland composed of alluvial silt. The Thames Estuary area covers 15 miles (24km) from Gravesend to the Isle of Grain, the Medway area 15 miles (24km) from Rochester to the Isle of Grain: a total of 38 square miles (98 sq km) of marshlands. Both are Sites of Special Scientific Interest and Special Protection Areas and include coastal grazing marsh, intertidal mudflats, saltmarsh and lagoons. Northwood Hill National Nature Reserve lies on the central hills.

Ightham Mote — 4 miles (6km) east of Sevenoaks. Moated manor house built c.1320, one of the most complete of its type in England. The many interesting features include the great hall, the Tudor chapel with painted ceiling and a Grade I listed dog kennel dating to the late 19th century. An extensive restoration programme was completed in 2004. American businessman Charles Henry Robinson bequeathed Ightham Mote to the National Trust in 1985. Tel: 01732 810378/811145.

Interesting facts — **Tom Hart Dyke**, plant hunter and creator of the World Garden at Lullingstone Castle (see separate entry), shot to international prominence in 2000 when he was kidnapped at gunpoint while on an expedition searching for orchids in Central America. For nine months he was held hostage in the Colombian jungle by armed guerrillas and regularly threatened with execution. Tom's experiences have been the subject of two television documentaries and his book, *The Cloud Garden*, has become a bestseller. The famous table-top football game **Subbuteo** was invented in Langton Green, near Tunbridge Wells, in 1947 by Peter Adolph. Mr Adolph's prototype was called The Hobby but the Patents Office told him that was too general a term to be patented or registered. He found an alternative thanks to his keen interest in ornithology: knowing that the Latin name for the hobby hawk was *Falco subbuteo*, he used the Latin word, which is now known round the world. The first sets were not sold with a pitch – the suggestion was that people use an old army blanket and draw the lines on with chalk. The game continued to grow in popularity, particularly after England won the World Cup in 1966. In 1971 Mr Adolph sold Subbuteo to toy firm Waddingtons for £250,000. In 1909, John Theodore Cuthbert Moore-Brabazon (1884–1964) made the **first authenticated British powered flight** at Leysdown, Isle of Sheppey, in a Voisin biplane. The traditional **nickname for people from Kent** is 'Kentish Long-Tail', deriving from the long-held belief on the mainland of medieval Europe that the English had tails. In addition, those born in Kent west of the Medway are traditionally called **Kentish Men**, and those born east of the Medway, **Men of Kent**. The division may have arisen when the Jutes, who settled in Thanet over 1500 years ago, moved into the area of modern Kent, calling one part East Centingas and the other West Centingas. It is claimed that the Men of Kent later resisted William the Conqueror more stoutly than the Kentish Men, who are said to have meekly surrendered. In October 2006 the **'Dancing Girl'** statue was stolen from the Grecian Temple within Dunorlan Park (see separate entry) in Tunbridge Wells. A £1500 reward was offered for its safe return but so far the sculpture has not been recovered. In 2007 the **Opera House** public house in Tunbridge Wells, formerly a genuine opera house, staged Johann Strauss' *Die Fledermaus* by Alternative Opera – a company that specialises in staging the genre in unusual venues. The show featured a cast of nine, with a chorus of 16 and a piano quartet. Chatham-born artist **Richard Dadd** became increasingly delusional while travelling up the Nile by boat in 1842, believing himself to be possessed by the Egyptian god Osiris. The following year he stabbed his father to death and was eventually incarcerated in Bedlam. It was here he produced his most celebrated painting, The Fairy Feller's Master-Stroke, which he worked on between 1855 and 1864. **Pluckley**, close to the North Downs and 5 miles (8km) west of Ashford, is reputed to be England's most haunted village. It is said to be the home of at least ten ghosts including shadowy figures of women at the church, a soldier in Park Woods, a phantom coach, an elderly gypsy and a miller, while horrific ghostly screams have been reported from the local brickworks. The Black Horse public house in the centre of the village allegedly has a mischievous spook that hides keys and small objects. The **Crown Inn**, Sarre, near Birchington, a Grade I listed 15th century building, is known locally as the Cherry Brandy House as it sells a cherry brandy made to a secret recipe brought over by Huguenots fleeing from the religious persecutions of Louis XIV. The recipe is jealously guarded and bottles of what is almost certainly the most exclusive cherry brandy in the world cannot be bought from anywhere else. Other interesting pubs include **The Frog and Toad,** Gillingham, where customers wishing to purchase the Belgian 'Kwak' ale must leave one of their shoes as a deposit in a wire basket which is hauled up above the bar. This precaution is taken to prevent 'souvenir hunters' running off with the expensive glass and wooden frame it is served in; and **The Coastguard Pub & Restaurant**, St Margaret's Bay, Dover, the closest pub in Britain to France.

Islands — See separate table for a list of named islands in Kent; see also Leeds Castle

Kent & East Sussex Railway — Station Road, Tenterden. A heritage railway operating for 10 miles (16km) between Tenterden and Bodiam. Engineered by Holman Fred Stephens, the first section of the Rother Valley Railway, as it was initially known, was opened on 2 April 1900 between Robertsbridge and Tenterden, terminating at the station now known as Rolvenden. An extension to the present Tenterden Town Station was opened in 1903 and another to Headcorn in 1905. The now renamed Kent & East Sussex Railway sank into bankruptcy by 1931, finally succumbing when the railways were nationalised in 1948. The line was closed to passengers on 2 January 1954 and the Tenterden–Headcorn section was pulled up. Goods continued to be hauled on the original section and occasional passenger trains ran in the summer, but the railway was closed completely in 1961. A society was formed soon afterwards with the object of preserving the line, and the first 2 miles (3km) at Tenterden were opened on 3 February 1974. A major renewal of a river bridge enabled an extension by 1977 to Wittersham Road. Northiam was finally reached in 1990, its station having been refurbished with the help of the popular BBC TV series *Challenge Anneka* in 1989, and Bodiam in 2000, 100 years after the railway opened. Tel: 0870 600 6074.

Kent Battle of Britain Museum Aerodrome Road, Hawkinge, 2 miles (3km) north of Folkestone. Located at a former RAF airfield, the museum holds the most important collection of Battle of Britain artefacts on show in England. Tel: 01303 893140.

Knole House 1 mile (1.6km) east of Sevenoaks. The origins of this ragstone house are obscure, but it is believed that the estate existed in the 12th century. In 1456, Archbishop of Canterbury Thomas Bourchier bought the property and during the remaining 30 years of his life transformed it into the magnificent, sprawling multi-roomed mansion seen today. Four more archbishops occupied the house before Henry VIII took possession of it as a royal palace. Elizabeth I presented the house and estate to her cousin, Thomas Sackville in 1566, and his descendants have lived at Knole ever since; in the 17th century Sackville's great-great-grandson, the 6th Earl of Dorset, added a fine collection of Stuart furniture, and 100 years later the 6th Earl's great-grandson, the 3rd Duke, put together the art collection including Italian old masters and works by Gainsborough and Reynolds. The interior of the house has retained its 17th century state rooms almost intact; the most impressive feature, however, is perhaps the great Tudor chimneypiece and overmantel, of marble and alabaster, in the ballroom. Author Vita Sackville-West was born in the house, and her work *Knole and the Sackvilles* is among the classic accounts of an English country house, while the novel *Orlando* by her good friend Virginia Woolf is largely based on the history of the house and family. The house is surrounded by a deer park of 1000 acres (400ha), now a Site of Special Scientific Interest, and is in the care of the National Trust. Tel: 01732 462100.

Leeds Castle 6 miles (10km) southeast of Maidstone. Set on two artificial islands on the River Len (these were created in the mid 13th century when the moat is believed to have been dug out and some of the flow of the Len was diverted), the Norman castle was founded c.1119 by the de Crevecoeur family. Rebuilt by Edward I after 1278 and given to his Queen, Eleanor of Castile, it formed part of the dower of English queens until the 15th century. Restored in the 19th century and further refurbished in the 1920s, the castle was used as the location of a Middle East peace conference in 1977. It houses a unique museum of dog collars, including examples 500 years old. The castle is set in 500 acres (200ha) of parkland, the aviary being home to over 100 species of endangered birds. Flowers and foliage abound in the formal gardens, the Culpeper and the Lady Baillie Garden, while other features include a maze with secret underground grotto. Tel: 01622 765400.

Lullingstone Castle 1 mile (1.5km) south of Eynsford, 7 miles (11km) north of Sevenoaks. The present manor house and gatehouse (the latter one of the first in England to be built of brick), overlooking a lake of 15 acres (6ha), were built in 1497 and have been home to the Hart Dyke family ever since. Henry VIII was a regular visitor, as was Queen Anne, in whose reign much of the house was refurbished. In the grounds, alongside the River Darent, are hidden Queen Anne's bathhouse and an 18th century ice house. Since 2000 Lullingstone's 2 acre (0.8ha) walled garden has been transformed into the 'World Garden of Plants' by gardener Tom Hart Dyke, and each acre contains more than 10,000 different plant species originating from every corner of the world. Close to the manor house is St Botolph's parish church; of Norman origin, its early 16th century stained glass windows are some of the oldest in England. Tel: 01322 862114.

Lullingstone Roman Villa ½ mile (0.8km) southwest of Eynsford, 8 miles (13km) north of Sevenoaks. The villa was discovered in 1939, excavations commencing after World War II in 1949. The building is believed to have been constructed c.AD 75, originally from timber and daub, being reconstructed of stone in the 2nd century. The main complex contained 26 rooms; excavations have indicated a further four rooms – believed to be a semicircular shrine, a mausoleum, a kitchen and a granary – outside the main complex. During the excavations remnants of a Christian chapel were found, along with fragments of wall plaster which have been reconstructed to show many of the murals that once adorned the villa walls. The central spectacle is the mosaic floor in the dining room; one of its two main sections depicts the Rape of Europa by Jupiter, the other shows Bellerophon riding Pegasus killing the fire-breathing lion-like monster known as the Chimaera. In the corners of the main panel there are three heads in circles (there were once four) depicting the faces of the four seasons. Between the two main sections are numerous geometric designs, including several swastikas. The villa is thought to have been largely destroyed by fire early in the 5th century and no signs of occupation have been found after AD 420. The site was opened to the public in 1963 and is protected by a covered building. It is now owned by English Heritage. Tel: 01322 863467.

Lympne Castle The Street, Lympne, 3 miles (5km) west of Hythe. Norman Castle founded c.1080 on an escarpment above Romney Marsh and overlooking the English Channel. The current two-storey castellated mansion was constructed c.1360 and restored in the early 20th century. It is currently available for corporate events but is not open to the public. Tel: 01303 235610.

Maison Dieu Ospringe Street, Ospringe, ½ mile (0.8km) west of Faversham. Now a museum, the medieval building known as the Maison Dieu (House of God) once formed part of a complex serving as a royal lodge, pilgrims' hostel, hospital and almshouses for retired royal retainers. Its foundation in 1234 has traditionally been ascribed to Henry III, although recent research indicates that its origin is earlier: run by monks, it was effectively a small monastery. Maison Dieu is in the joint care of English Heritage and the Faversham Society. Tel: 01795 534542.

Milton Chantry New Tavern Fort Gardens, Gravesend. Founded in 1322 by Aymer de Valence, Earl of Pembroke, on the site of a leper hospital. The Earl employed the services of two chaplains to say prayers on behalf of him and his family. After the Reformation the building was used as a tavern and from 1780 as part of a fort. It is now in the care of English Heritage. Tel: 01474 321520.

Motto *Invicta* ('undefeated'). The people of Kent adopted the motto following the invasion of Britain by William the Conqueror, claiming that they had frightened the Normans away, as the invaders merely used Kent to reach London.

Mount Ephraim Gardens Hernhill, 4 miles (6km) southeast of Faversham. Situated at the heart of an 800 acre (320ha) estate, the splendid late Victorian mansion and gardens have magnificent views over the parkland and the Swale and Thames estuary. The 9 acres (3.5ha) of garden are laid out in Edwardian style and include fine examples of oak, cedar and beech. Other features include a mizmaze planted in 2004 on the slopes of a former vineyard and based on the medieval labyrinths believed to have been used by monks for meditation, Japanese rock gardens, a Millennium rose garden, water garden and topiary garden. Tel: 01227 751496.

Nore A sandbank at the mouth of the Thames Estuary, opposite the mouth of the River Medway and extending from Sheerness in the south to Shoeburyness on the Essex coast. In 1731 it became the first such hazard in Britain to be marked with a lightship (necessary in locations unsuitable for the building of lighthouses), when a small single-masted vessel equipped with a pair of lanterns was put in place by Robert Hamblin. In May 1797, during the French Revolutionary Wars, the Nore was the scene of a mutiny in the Royal Navy fleet lying at anchor, two weeks after their colleagues at Spithead had also mutinied.

North Downs Way The North Downs Way National Trail runs for 153 miles (246km) through the Surrey Hills and Kent Downs between Farnham on the Surrey/Hampshire border and Dover in Kent; a loop at the eastern end takes in the historic cathedral city of Canterbury. Much of the trail follows the Pilgrims' Way, the legendary route supposedly used by pilgrims on their way from Winchester to Canterbury to pray at the shrine of St Thomas Becket. Prior to this pilgrims would have walked the other way to pray for St Swithun, who was buried at Winchester Cathedral. Much of the Downs are covered with rich woodland and rare chalk grasslands.

Nurstead Court Nurstead Church Lane, Meopham, 5 miles (8km) south of Gravesend. A Grade I listed manor house, occpuied by the Edmeades family since 1567. The west wing is part of a medieval hall built in 1320 by Stephen de Gravesend, Bishop of London; the east wing was added in the 1820s and enlarged later in the 19th century. Tel: 01474 812368.

Old Soar Manor Plaxtol, 6 miles (10km) east of Sevenoaks. The remains of a manor house built c.1290 by the Culpeper family of Aylesford. The existing block includes a timbered spiral staircase, chapel and solar chamber (living area) over a barrel-vaulted undercroft; an attached 18th century farmhouse stands on the site of the great hall. Now owned by the National Trust. Tel: 01732 810378.

Peasants' Revolt A popular uprising of 1381, the immediate cause of which was the government's heavy-handed attempts to enforce a poll tax levied in 1377 to finance military campaigns overseas. A longer-term factor was the Statute of Labourers of 1351; introduced after the Black Death ravaged England in 1348 and 1349, greatly reducing the labour force, this statute attempted to curb the enhanced terms and conditions demanded by labourers by capping wages and restricting the mobility of labour. The Kentish leaders of the revolt were Robert Cave, Abel Ker, Thomas Farringdon and Wat Tyler, while a Lollard priest, John Ball, further inflamed unrest by preaching to the peasants and encouraging them to call for justice. His cry of 'When Adam delved and Eve span, Who was then the gentleman?' became a popular rhyme of the day. The rebels seized Rochester Castle before marching on London on 14 June 1381 and occuping the Tower of London, executing the Chancellor and Archbishop of Canterbury, Simon of Sudbury, and the treasurer Sir Robert Hales. Richard II had met rebels from Essex, led by Jack Straw, on the same day at Blackheath and agreed to their demands, after which many peacefully returned to their homes. When the remaining Kent peasants, led by Wat Tyler, met with the king again at Smithfield on 15 June, a belligerent Tyler was captured and later beheaded by the mayor William Walworth and his men; John Ball was later hung, drawn and quartered.

Penshurst Place & Gardens 4 miles (6km) southwest of Tonbridge. The first recorded owner of the original 13th century house and estate was Sir Stephen de Penchester, a distinguished royal servant whose tomb can be found in Penshurst church. He was followed half a century later by Sir John de Pulteney, a wealthy London merchant and financier four times elected Lord Mayor of London. At the heart of the house lies the Baron's Hall, with its awe-inspiring 60ft (18m) high chestnut roof, supported by satirical representations of peasants and estate workers. A rare surviving central octagonal hearth in the centre of the hall, built in 1341 and still lit on special occasions, formed the focal point of the household. Sixty years after Sir John's death, Penshurst was owned by Henry IV's third son, John, Duke of Bedford, who probably built the second hall, known as the Buckingham Building. After his death Penshurst became the property of his younger brother, Humphrey, Duke of Gloucester, founder of Oxford's Bodleian Library; it then passed to Humphrey Stafford, 1st Duke of Buckingham, the first of three of that title to own the estate, all of whom were eventually beheaded. In 1552, Edward VI gave the estate to his loyal steward and tutor, Sir William Sidney. Throughout the Tudor and Stuart periods, the Sidneys served at court and in government, their influence increasing when Sir William's son, Henry, married Lady Mary Dudley, whose powerful family included the Duke of Northumberland and Robert Dudley, Earl of Leicester, the great favourite of Elizabeth I. Sir Henry's son was poet, courtier and soldier Sir Philip Sidney. On his death in 1586, Sir Philip was accorded the honour of a state funeral at St Paul's Cathedral, the first person outside the immediate royal family to receive such a tribute. The house remains in the possession of the Sidney family today. The 11 acre (4.5ha) formal walled garden, with records dating back to 1346, is divided into 'rooms' by 1 mile (1.6km) of yew hedges. Tel: 01892 870307.

Pilgrims Way See North Downs Way

Powell-Cotton Museum See Quex House & Garden

Prisons — **Blantyre House**, Goudhurst, 8 miles (13km) east of Tunbridge Wells, is an adult male category C/D resettlement prison. The buildings themselves are located in a country house taken over by the Prison Commission in 1954, having previously operated as a Fegan Home. It was a detention centre for young offenders before converting to a resettlement prison for long term prisoners. Operational capacity: 122. Tel: 01580 213200.

Canterbury, Longport, Canterbury, holds short-term category C prisoners. The prison dates from 1808 when a county gaol was built just outside the city limits. The front of the prison still bears the carved inscription 'House of Correction'. During World War I the prison was used as a Home Office archive, later becoming a prison and a Naval Detention Centre. Operational capacity: 314. Tel: 01227 862800.

Cookham Wood, Rochester, is a closed prison for adult women, built in the 1970s originally for young men, but its use was changed to meet the growing need for secure female accommodation. Operational capacity: 185. Tel: 01634 202500.

The Western Heights on which **Dover** prison is situated has been a fortified area since Roman times. The present buildings occupy the site of fortifications commenced in Napoleonic times to counter the threat of a French invasion. The Prison Commission took over the site from the Army in 1952 when work began on converting the fortress into a prison. In 1957 it was decided that the establishment should become a borstal, and Dover continued to hold young offenders until April 2002 when it was redesignated as an Immigration Removal Centre. Dover continues to be run by the Prison Service holding appellant and failed asylum seekers in secure conditions for the Immigration Service. Operating capacity: 358. Tel: 01304 246400.

East Sutton Park, Sutton Valence, Maidstone, opened as a borstal in 1946. The prison is located in a Grade II listed country house overlooking the Weald of Kent, and is used to hold both adult and young offender women in open conditions. Operating capacity: 100. Tel: 01622 845000.

Elmley, Church Road, Eastchurch, Sheerness, is a purpose-built local prison opened in 1992 and includes a Category C Unit of 240 prisoners built in 1997. Elmley is one of six Bullingdon design prisons in England and is one of three on the Isle of Sheppey. Tel: 01795 804100.

Maidstone, County Road, Maidstone was completed in 1819; constructed from Kentish ragstone to a design by architect Daniel Asher Alexander, it was the most advanced model of its time. Operational capacity: 559. Tel: 01622 775300.

Rochester, Fort Road, Rochester, was originally built as a prison in 1874 on a former military site above the Medway river. It was extensively remodelled in 1902 as the Borstal Institution (see separate entry). In 1983, Rochester became a youth custody centre and from 1988 it operated as a remand centre for the Kent courts and sentenced category C and D adult males. Further changes to its role resulted in a mixed site holding immigration detainees, a resettlement unit for adult male prisoners and a remand and allocation centre for males under 21. In 2002 Rochester became a dedicated site for sentencing young men up to the age of 21. Operational capacity: 392. Tel: 01634 803100.

Standford Hill, Church Road, Eastchurch, Sheerness is on the site of an ex RAF station. The prison was first used in 1950, but the current accommodation was built in 1986. The prison holds category D sentenced male adults. Tel: 01795 884500.

Swaleside, Brabazon Road, Eastchurch, Isle of Sheppey prison accepts category B prisoners serving four years or more or who have at least 18 months left to serve. Operational capacity: 778. Tel: 01795 804100.

Quebec House — Quebec Square, Westerham, 4 miles (6km) west of Sevenoaks. A Grade I listed gabled house with 16th century origins, extended and altered in the 18th and 20th centuries. The childhood home of General James Wolfe, the house contains family and military memorabilia. The old coach house contains an exhibition about the Battle of Quebec (1759). Now owned by the National Trust. Tel: 01732 868381.

Quex House & Garden — Quex Park, Birchington, 3 miles (5km) southwest of Margate. Built by the Powell-Cotton family, the Regency house is now home to the Powell-Cotton Museum, which contains an amazing variety of items collected by Victorian explorer Major Percy Horace Gordon Powell-Cotton. These include animal dioramas, tribal art, weapons, carvings and costumes, as well as valuable collections of European and Chinese porcelain and local archaeology. The 15 acre (6ha) gardens include a Victorian walled garden, large specimen trees, lawns, mature herbaceous borders and a woodland walk. Tel: 01843 842168.

Reculver Towers & Roman Fort — Reculver, 3 miles (5km) east of Herne Bay. The twin 12th century towers of the ruined St Mary's church, located amid the remains of the important Roman Saxon Shore fort of Regulbium and a Saxon monastery. Now in the care of English Heritage. Tel: 01227 740676.

Restoration House — Crow Lane, Rochester. Dating from the late 16th century, the house is so named because Charles II stayed here after his arrival in England on the eve of the Restoration. It also provided Charles Dickens with the inspiration for Satis House, the home of Miss Havisham in *Great Expectations*. The house has a large walled garden of ½ acre (0.3ha). Tel: 01634 848520.

Richborough Roman Fort — 2 miles (3km) north of Sandwich. Roman Saxon Shore fort built in the 3rd century on site of the supposed landing point of the Roman invasion of AD 43. A triumphal arch was once located within its walls but is now ruined, with one side totally lost. Now owned by English Heritage. Tel: 01304 612013.

Riverhill House — 2 miles (3km) south of Sevenoaks. Riverhill House was built in 1714 and in 1840 the estate became the home of the Rogers family. Dominated by vast cedars of Lebanon, the historic garden has breathtaking views over the surrounding countryside. Tel: 01732 458802.

Rivers — The **Darent** or Darenth is a tributary of the River Thames. Fed by water from the greensand hills south of Westerham, it rises from springs at Sevenoaks, then flows north past the villages of

Otford, Shoreham, Lullingstone, Eynsford, Farningham, Horton Kirby, South Darenth, Sutton at Hone, Darenth, and the town of Dartford to meet the Thames at Crayford Marshes. Here it forms the boundary between the London Borough of Bexley and the borough of Dartford.

The **Medway** rises at Turner's Hill, near East Grinstead, West Sussex, following the Sussex/Kent boundary to Ashurst before turning northeast to Maidstone via Tonbridge and north through the Medway Towns of Rochester and Chatham to the Thames at the Sheerness delta. The river flows for 70 miles (112km) and its major tributaries include the **Eden** (rises south of Caterham, Surrey, takes an erratic course through Oxted and Lingfield before reaching Kent at Edenbridge and travelling east through the Wealden clay before joining the Medway near Penshurst); **Shode** (rises near Borough Green and enters the Medway east of Tonbridge); **Teise** (rises near Crowborough and flows east through Lamberhurst, passing Bayham Abbey); **Beult** (has several sources west of Ashford, and then flows through Headcorn, afterwards joining the Teise. The combined rivers enter the Medway at Yalding, 2 miles (3km) to the north); **Loose** (short river running through the village of the same name just south of Maidstone); **Len** (has its source at a small watershed south of Lenham. A nearby stream is one of the sources of the Great Stour. The Len flows in a westerly direction and joins the Medway at Maidstone).

The **Stour** flows for 21$^1/_2$ miles (34.5km) from Canterbury to the sea at Pegwell Bay, south of Ramsgate. It has several tributaries and sources. One source rises at Postling near Hythe and becomes the East Stour, another at Lenham, 11 miles (18km) northwest of Ashford, becoming the Upper Great Stour. They join at Ashford to become the Great Stour. Aka the Kentish Stour, the Great Stour flows for a total of 40 miles (64km) through the Weald, to Canterbury and Sandwich and into the English Channel. Another tributary of the Stour has its source north of Hythe and is known as the **Little Stour**. It flows north to join the Great Stour at Plucks Gutter, northwest of Canterbury. Yet another tiny tributary is the River **Wantsum**. With its source at Reculver, the Wantsum joins the Great Stour and the Little Stour when they combine into the River Stour, forming part of the Wantsum Channel that used to separate the Isle of Thanet from the mainland of Kent.

The **Cray**, a tributary of the Darent, rises in Priory Gardens, Orpington in the London Borough of Bromley, flowing north past an industrial and residential area of St Mary Cray, through St Paul's Cray, Foots Cray, North Cray and Bexley. It then turns east through Crayford and Barnes Cray before joining the Darent, which flows north into the Thames between Crayford Marshes and Dartford Marshes.

Rochester Castle — Boley Hill, Rochester. Norman motte and bailey castle founded c.1080 and built by Bishop Gundolf. A stone curtain wall was added c.1088, and a stone keep built c.1126–40 by William de Corbeuil. The castle was taken by King John after an epic siege in 1215, but was recaptured by Louis of France in 1216. The keep was repaired c.1225 with cylindrical corner added, and is more than 100ft (30m) high with walls 12ft (3.5m) thick. The castle was besieged by Simon de Montfort in 1264 and captured by Wat Tyler in 1381. Ruined by 1400, it is now owned by English Heritage. Tel: 01634 402276.

Rochester Cathedral — High Street, Rochester. Founded in AD 604 on land donated by King Ethelbert, the cathedral is dedicated to Christ and the Blessed Virgin Mary and is the second oldest in England. In 1083, the building of the present nave was begun by Bishop Gundulf, a Benedictine monk from Bec in France. The Norman cathedral was consecrated on Ascension Day in a ceremony attended by Henry I. Following a fire early in the 12th century, work began on rebuilding in the Gothic style. In the 13th century the cathedral was plundered when King John held it against the rebel barons. It was later desecrated by Simon de Montfort's troops when they captured the city. In 1872 major restoration work was carried out by George Gilbert Scott. In 2004 the cathedral celebrated its 1400th anniversary with the dedication of the first real fresco (painted by Russian iconographer Sergei Fyodorov) in an English cathedral for 800 years. The fresco, on the theme of baptism, was aptly dedicated on St John the Baptist Day, 24 June. Tel: 01634 401301.

Roman Painted House — York Street, Dover. Discovered by Kent Archaeological Rescue Unit in 1970. Built c.AD 200, the rooms formed part of a large *mansio*, or official hotel, for travellers crossing the Channel. It stood outside the great naval fort of the Classis Britannica (the Roman fleet stationed in Britain), but was demolished by the Roman army c.270 during the construction of a larger fort, and three of the main rooms were buried substantially intact under the ramparts. This resulted in the unique survival of over 400 sq ft (37 sq m) of painted plaster, the most extensive ever found north of the Alps. Above a lower dado of red or green can still be seen an architectural scheme of many coloured panels framed by fluted columns. The columns sit on projecting bases above a stage, producing a clear 3D effect. Parts of 28 panels survive, each with a motif relating to Bacchus, the Roman god of wine. Tel: 01304 203279.

Romney, Hythe & Dymchurch Railway — At 15in (380mm) gauge, one of the smallest public railways in the world. The line was opened in 1927 and the train runs for 13$^1/_2$ miles (21.5km) between Hythe and Dungeness via Dymchurch, St Mary's Bay, New Romney and Romney Sands. The railway is not just a tourist attraction but a route regularly used between the small towns, and also transports children to school. Tel: 01797 362353.

Romney Marsh — 'The World, according to the best geographers, is divided into Europe, Asia, Africa, America, and Romney Marsh', wrote the Reverend Richard Harris Barham under his pseudonym Thomas Ingoldsby in *The Ingoldsby Legends*, his gothic tales of superstition and folklore, in the 1840s. The 100 sq mile (260 sq km) marsh lies between Folkestone in the east and Winchelsea in the west, although the area from New Romney to Winchelsea is actually named Walland Marsh. Romney Marsh today has mostly been converted to fertile farmland, but quite a large area lies below sea level and is protected by sea defences and walls. The Marsh is famous for its sheep and for smuggling which for many years provided income to the locals. The area is well used by windsurfers, sailors and other water sports enthusiasts. The Romney Marsh Countryside Project, a sister project to the White Cliffs Countryside Project, was set up in June 1996 with the aim of caring for the special landscape and wildlife of Romney Marsh and Dungeness.

Royal Engineers Museum Prince Arthur Road, Gillingham. Museum telling the story of the Corps of Royal Engineers and of British military engineering. The library was founded in 1813. Tel: 01634 822839.

St Augustine's Abbey Longport, Canterbury. The ruins of the abbey of Saints Peter and Paul, founded by St Augustine c.AD 597. The remains visible today are those of the 12th century Romanesque abbey, enlarged in the following 200 years. The site also includes a museum and is now in the care of English Heritage. The ruins are now part of Canterbury's World Heritage Site. Tel: 01227 767345.

St John's Commandery 1 mile (1.6km) northeast of Densole, 6 miles (10km) north of Folkestone. A medieval chapel built by the Knights Hospitallers, converted into a farmhouse in the 16th century with a fine ceiling of moulded plaster. Now in the care of English Heritage. Tel: 01304 211067.

St Leonard's Tower 1/2 mile (0.8km) southwest of West Malling, 5 miles (8km) west of Maidstone. Thought to have been built c.1080 by Bishop Gundulf, who also built the keep of Rochester castle, the 60ft (18m) high St Leonards Tower still remains in good condition. A length of adjoining wall is also still standing, although there is little evidence of other earthworks or fortifications.

St Martin's Church North Holmes Road, Canterbury. The oldest parish church in England, located on a site believed to date back to Roman times. Continuous Christian worship has taken place here since before the arrival of Augustine in AD 597, and it was the private chapel of Bertha, queen of Ethelbert, king of Kent. The church was named after St Martin, Bishop of Tours in France, where Bertha lived before her marriage to Ethelbert. St Augustine's mission of 40 monks came to the church before he established the monastery at nearby St Augustine's Abbey. St Martin's Church forms part of the Canterbury World Heritage Site. Tel: 01227 768072.

Saltwood Castle Saltwood, 1 mile (1.6km) north of Hythe. Norman enclosure castle founded by Henry of Essex c.1150–60, used as a base against Thomas Becket by Ranulf de Broc. It was given by Henry II to the archbishops of Canterbury as a residence after Becket's death, and was improved by Archbishop William Courtenay in the 1380s with a residential gatehouse, designed by Henry Yevele. It was presented to Henry VIII by Thomas Cranmer, but rendered uninhabitable by an earthquake in 1580. Restored in the 19th century, it was latterly owned by Lord (Kenneth) Clark and his son, Alan Clark MP. The castle is not open to the public.

Scotney Castle 1 mile (1.6km) southeast of Lamberhurst, 6 miles (10km) southeast of Tunbridge Wells. Moated castle founded c.1378 by Roger Ashburnham, with a manor house attached in the 17th century. Only the cylindrical turret remains of the original castle, which was rebuilt in the 1830s in Tudor style to designs by Anthony Salvin. The garden, also dating to the mid 19th century, was designed by Edward Hussey in the picturesque style, with the ruins of the old castle as its focus. Now owned by National Trust. Tel: 01892 891081.

Sevenoaks The name 'Sevenoaks' originated from the Saxon word *Seouenaca*, a name given c.AD 800 to a small chapel situated near seven oak trees in Knole Park. Sevenoaks was historically part of the Great Manor of Otford, held by the Archbishops of Canterbury. In 1200, a market was started in the town and due to its economic success, Sevenoaks became a manor in its own right. The current seven oaks are located on the northern side of the Vine Cricket Ground; since the average life of an oak tree is only 250 years, the oaks have presumably been replaced several times. In 1902 seven oaks were planted on the Vine to commemorate the coronation of Edward VII. After the hurricane of 1987, during which six of the trees were blown down, seven new oaks were planted, meaning there are now eight. The town's motto is *Floreant Septum Quercus* ('May the Seven Oaks Flourish').

Sissinghurst Castle Garden 1 mile (1.6km) east of Sissinghurst, 14 miles (23km) east of Tunbridge Wells. Sissinghurst Garden was created in the 1930s by poet and gardening writer Vita Sackville-West and her husband Harold Nicolson. Developed around the surviving parts of an Elizabethan mansion built c.1570 with a central red-brick prospect tower, smaller enclosures contain individual gardens each with a particular colour theme, the most famous being the White Garden. The library where Vita Sackville-West worked is also open to the public. Now owned by the National Trust. Tel: 01580 710700/710701.

Sittingbourne & Kemsley Light Railway A heritage railway operating for 2 miles (3km) between Sittingbourne and the River Swale on the southern half of the former Bowater's Railway, built to move materials between the company's mills at Sittingbourne Mill (originally built in 1867 by newspaper owner and publisher Edward Lloyd). Initially horse drawn, in 1905 the first steam traction arrived in the form of two Kerr Stuart 'Brazil' class locomotives, *Premier* and *Leader*. During the system's heyday there were 14 steam locomotives, plus a diesel and a battery electric engine. In 1923 a new mill – at the time the largest paper mill in Europe – was built between Ridham and Sittingbourne at Kemsley. The railway eventually beacme a continuous operation maintaining a passenger service for mill employees. The 'main line' was 3 1/2 miles (5.5km) long with 10 miles (16km) of track. In 1969 the railway was handed over to the Locomotive Club of Great Britain's Light Railway Section and became the Sittingbourne & Kemsley Light Railway. Tel: 0871 222 1568.

Smallhythe Place Smallhythe, 3 miles (5km) southeast of Tenterden. The house was built in the early 16th century when the River Rother flowed past Smallhythe and the village was the location of a major shipbuilding yard. The Victorian actress Ellen Terry lived here 1899–1928 and the house now holds her collection of theatrical memorabilia. Plays are performed regularly in the nearby Barn Theatre. Now owned by the National Trust. Tel: 01580 762334.

South Foreland Lighthouse St Margaret's Bay, Dover. Victorian lighthouse built in 1843 on the White Cliffs of Dover, the first to have an electrically powered signal created by Michael Faraday. Marconi also used the site for his experiments in telegraphy. The lighthouse was operational until 1988 and is now in the care of the National Trust. Tel: 01304 202756.

Spa Valley Railway — A standard gauge heritage railway operating for $3^1/_2$ miles (5.5km) between Tunbridge Wells West station and Groombridge on part of the former Three Bridges–Tunbridge Wells Line. Tel: 01892 537715.

Sport

cricket — **Kent County Cricket Club**, one of the oldest first-class counties, was formed in 1842. Six times outright winners of the County Championship, they also shared the title with Middlesex in 1977. The one-day team are known as The Spitfires. Famous former players include Frank Woolley and Colin Cowdrey. The club's home ground is the St Lawrence Ground, Old Dover Road, Canterbury; other grounds used include the County Ground, Beckenham, and the Nevill Ground, Tunbridge Wells. Tel: 01227 456886.

football — **Gillingham** were formed in May 1893 as New Brompton FC; their home ground, Priestfield Stadium, remains the same today. Changing its name to Gillingham in 1913, the club was a founder member of the Third Division in 1920, reaching the second tier of English football for the first time in 1999–2000. Nicknamed The Gills, they were famously supported by legendary football commentator Brian Moore. Tel: 01634 300000.

Non-league clubs include **Ebbsfleet United** (formed in 1946 as Gravesend & Northfleet, changing their name in 2007, and owned since 2008 by an internet-based consortium); **Maidstone United** (reformed in 1992 after the demise of the previous club, which played in the Football League 1989–92) and **Welling United** (formed 1963).

greyhound racing — **Sittingbourne Greyhound Stadium** has a 443m track. Tel: 01795 475547.

horse racing — **Folkestone Racecourse**, Westhanger, Hythe is the only track in Kent. The right-hand circuit of 1 mile 3 furlongs (2.2km) caters exclusively for Flat racing. Tel: 01303 266407.

Squerryes Court — 1 mile (1.6km) south of Westerham. Built in 1681, the red brick manor house has been the Warde family home since 1731. The Wolfe Room contains items associated with General Wolfe of Quebec, a friend of the family. It is surrounded by 10 acres (4ha) of attractive gardens dating to the mid 18th century and designed in naturalistic style, including a lake, restored parterres and an 18th century dovecote; a formal garden dating to 1709 has been partially restored. Tel: 01959 562345.

Sutton Valence Castle — Rectory Lane, Sutton Valence, 6 miles (10km) southeast of Maidstone. Norman stone keep and bailey fortress founded c.1170 by Baldwin de Béthune, count of Albemarle. The Great Tower was altered by William de Valence in the 13th century. The castle was abandoned in the 14th century, although the remains of the keep are still standing. Now in the care of English Heritage.

Timeball Tower Museum — Prince of Wales Terrace, Deal. Housed in the former Deal Semaphore Tower, built in 1821 to carry signals for the anti-smuggling force known as the Kent Coastal Blockade. In 1853 the semaphore apparatus was replaced by a telegraphically operated timeball that fell at 1pm each day until 1927, giving accurate time to ships anchored offshore. The museum explores how messages were sent from the Admiralty to Deal during the Napoleonic Wars, and along the coast in the fight against smuggling. Tel: 01304 360897.

Tonbridge Castle — Castle Street, Tonbridge. Norman motte and bailey castle founded 1088 by Richard FitzGilbert. A shell keep was added in the 12th century and a gatehouse built by Gilbert de Clare in the 13th. Most of the castle was destroyed after the Civil War but the impressive gatehouse still stands; fully refurbished in 1999, it now houses a museum. Tel: 01732 770929.

University of Kent — The University of Kent was granted its royal charter in 1965 and Princess Marina, Duchess of Kent, was installed as the first Chancellor the following year. Its main campus is the University of Kent at Canterbury, covering 300 acres (120ha) just over 1 mile (1.6km) northwest of Canterbury city centre. The university is collegiate, the four undergraduate colleges being Eliot (founded 1965), Rutherford (1966), Keynes (1968) and Darwin (1970). Virginia Woolf College for postgraduates opened in September 2008. The University of Kent at Medway was founded in 2000 in conjunction with Mid-Kent College. Originally based at Horsted and the Bridge Wardens' College, Chatham, in September 2005, it moved to the newly developed Pembroke campus which it shares with the Universities of Greenwich, Canterbury Christ Church University, Mid-Kent College and University College for the Creative Arts. The Medway School of Pharmacy was opened in 2004 and is a joint school with the University of Greenwich on the Pembroke campus in Chatham. In addition, the University of Kent at Tonbridge offers part-time provision in west Kent and the University of Kent at Brussels offers postgraduate law, politics and international relations degrees. Former students include journalist Rosie Boycott, BBC correspondents Gavin Esler and Mark Mardell, newsreader Charlotte Green and author Kazuo Ishiguro. Tel: 01227 827272.

Upnor Castle — High Street, Upper Upnor, 2 miles (3km) northeast of Strood. An artillery fort built 1559–67 – one of only a few dating to the Elizabethan period – to protect the Medway at Chatham, although it failed to fulfil that function when Chatham was attacked by the Dutch in 1667. Held by Parliament in the Civil War, it was briefly taken by Royalist sympathisers in Chatham Dockyard in 1648. Upnor was later converted into a residence, now ruined. It is now owned by English Heritage. Tel: 01634 718742.

Walmer Castle — Walmer, 1 mile (1.6km) south of Deal. Artillery fort built 1539–40 by Henry VIII on a quatrefoil plan. It has been the official residence of the Lord Warden of the Cinque Ports since the 18th century, and the Duke of Wellington died here in 1852. The gardens, including the Broadwalk with its famous yew tree hedge, were laid out in their present form in the late 19th century; more recent additions include the Queen Mother's Garden, designed by Penelope Hobhouse in 1997. Now owned by English Heritage. Tel: 01304 364288.

West Malling Castle — See St Leonard's Tower

Westenhanger Castle	Stone Street, Westenhanger, 2 miles (3km) northwest of Hythe. Situated in the grounds of Folkestone Racecourse (see Sport), the castle dates to the 12th century when the moat was probably dug out. It was rebuilt in 1343 with tall outer walls and eight towers; two still stand to full height including the northeast tower which is now a dovecote. A manor house was built within the walls by Sir Edward Poynings and his son Thomas in the 16th century; having been given to Henry VIII, it became a residence of Elizabeth I and was gradually enlarged until in the mid 17th century it was one of the largest houses in Kent. This was demolished in 1701 and the castle allowed to gradually deteriorate, although a new manor house was built in the 18th century. Tel: 01303 261068.
Whitstable	A popular old coastal town situated at the mouth of the River Swale, overlooking Whitstable Bay, Whitstable is famous for oysters and seafood but also has a vibrant contemporary arts scene. It is an attractive town, with fishermen's huts and pretty weatherboard cottages in eccentrically named streets such as Squeeze Gut Alley. The town's historic harbour was built in 1832 to serve the world's first passenger railway service, nicknamed the Crab and Winkle line, which linked Canterbury to London via a steam ship from the harbour. Today, Whitstable is still a commercial port with a working harbour and fish market. Beaches of shingle and sand flank the harbour, and the town celebrates its maritime heritage with an Oyster Festival in July each year.
Willesborough Windmill	Mill Lane, Willesborough, Ashford. A white smock mill built in 1869 onto a two storey red brick base with attached miller's cottage. It incorporates 'patent' type shutters in the sweeps instead of canvas and sails, and once produced enough power to turn four sets of mill stones as well as the machines for crushing or cutting maize and oats. The Grade II listed mill has now been restored to full working order. Tel: 01233 661866.
Yalding Organic Gardens	Benover Road, Yalding, 4 miles (6km) southwest of Maidstone. Sixteen individual gardens designed to demonstrate the history of gardening and the use of organic principles, including a medieval apothecary's garden, a Tudor knot garden, a 19th century cottage garden, an Edwardian herbaceous border and a 21st century garden. Tel: 01622 814650.

Some famous people born in Kent

Bagnold, Enid (author of *National Velvet*) (1889–1981)	Rochester
Bennett, Sir Richard Rodney (composer) (1936–)	Broadstairs
Bloom, Orlando (actor) (1977–)	Canterbury
Brook, Kelly (actress and model) (1979–)	Rochester
Caxton, William (first English printer) (1422–91)	Tenterden
Charnley, Dave (boxer) (1935–)	Dartford
Dadd, Richard (artist) (1817–86)	Chatham
Ditchburn, Ted (goalkeeper) (1921–2005)	Gillingham
Forsyth, Frederick (novelist) (1938–)	Ashford
Harvey, William (physician) (1578–1657)	Folkestone
Hazlitt, William (essayist) (1778–1830)	Maidstone
Heath, Sir Edward (politician) (1916–2005)	St Peters
Holmes, Kelly (athlete) (1970–)	Pembury
Jacques, Hattie (actress) (1922–80)	Sandgate
Landen, Dinsdale (actor) (1932–2003)	Margate
Marlowe, Christopher (poet and dramatist) (1564–93)	Canterbury
Moon, William (inventor) (1818–94)	Horsmonden
Pratt, Anne (botanical illustrator) (1806–93)	Strood
Sargent, Sir Malcolm (conductor) (1895–1967)	Ashford
Sassoon, Siegfried (poet) (1886–1967)	Matfield
Sidney, Sir Philip (soldier and poet) (1554–86)	Penshurst
Stone, Joss (singer) (1987–)	Dover
Tourtel, Mary (creator of Rupert the Bear) (1874–1948)	Canterbury
Wallis, John (mathematician) (1616–1703)	Ashford
Watts, Naomi (actress) (1968–)	Shoreham
Woolley, Frank (cricketer) (1887–1978)	Tonbridge

Islands of Kent

Island name	Sea area	Nearest landmark	General information
Bingley Island	Great Stour	Canterbury	GR: TR143576
Burntwick Island	River Medway	Isle of Grain	Headquarters of the North Kent gang of smugglers in the early 19th century. GR: TQ860725
Bus Company Island	River Stour	Canterbury	Local Nature Reserve. Area: 0.2 sq miles (0.49 sq km). GR: TR149583
Deadmans Island	River Medway	Isle of Sheppey	GR: TQ895727
Elmley, Isle of	North Sea	Isle of Sheppey	Not an island at all, but an area of the Isle of Sheppey.

Island name	Sea area	Nearest landmark	General information
Fowley Island	The Swale	Sittingbourne	GR: TQ970658
Fulsome Rock	North Sea	Margate	GR: TR357717
Grain, Isle of	River Medway	Sheerness	Although often cited as being the ninth largest island of England, actually a peninsula. Area: 4.96 sq miles (12.85 sq km). GR: TQ870760
Harty, Isle of	North Sea	Isle of Sheppey	Not an island at all, but an area of the Isle of Sheppey.
Nayland Rock	North Sea	Margate	GR: TR345710
Oxney, Isle of		Ashford (mainland)	Not an island at all but included by virtue of its name. Area: 20.76 sq miles (53.77 sq km). Population: 2499.
Sheppey, Isle of	North Sea	Sittingbourne	The second largest island in England, although connected to the mainland by two bridges. The Isles of Harty and Elmley are areas of Sheppey but are not true islands. Some residents like to call themselves 'Swampies'. Sheerness is the 'capital'. Area: 36.29 sq miles (94 sq km). Population: 37,852. GR: TQ970700
Sixteen Acre Island	River Eden	Hever Castle	GR: TQ483454
Thanet, Isle of		Thanet (mainland)	Former island forming the northeast portion of Kent, bounded by the North Sea and branches of the River Stour. Area: 39.77 sq miles (103 sq km). Population: 126,702.
Two Bridges Island	River Eden	Hever Castle	GR: TQ478453
Walpole Rocks	North Sea	Margate	GR: TR368718

Lancashire

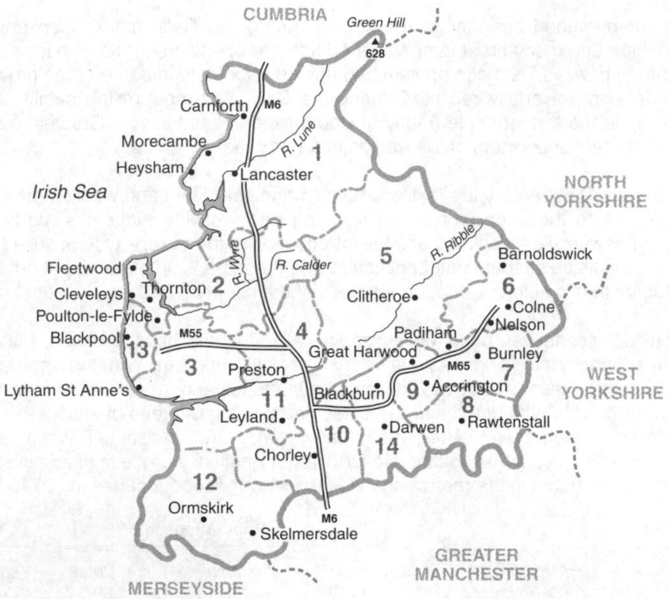
CUMBRIA
Green Hill
628
M6
Carnforth
Morecambe
Heysham
Lancaster
R. Lune
1
Irish Sea
NORTH YORKSHIRE
R. Ribble
5
Barnoldswick
R. Wyre
R. Calder
Fleetwood
Thornton
2
Cleveleys
Poulton-le-Fylde
Clitheroe
6
Colne
Nelson
Padiham
Blackpool
M55
13
4
Great Harwood
Burnley
3
Preston
M65
7
WEST YORKSHIRE
Lytham St Anne's
11
Blackburn
9
Accrington
8
Leyland
Rawtenstall
Darwen
10
14
Chorley
12
Ormskirk
M6
Skelmersdale
GREATER MANCHESTER
MERSEYSIDE

Districts

1 Lancaster	8 Rossendale
2 Wyre	9 Hyndburn
3 Fylde	10 Chorley
4 Preston	11 South Ribble
5 Ribble Valley	12 West Lancashire
6 Pendle	13 Blackpool (UA)
7 Burnley	14 Blackburn with Darwen (UA)

0 20 miles
0 30 km

Lancashire is a county in northwestern England, bounded by Cumbria to the north, North Yorkshire to the northeast, West Yorkshire to the east, Greater Manchester to the southeast and Merseyside to the south. Major changes occurred to the county's boundaries in 1974 following the 1972 Local Government Act, with Lancashire losing sizeable areas to the metropolitan counties of Merseyside and Greater Manchester, as well as the Furness exclave to Cumbria and towns such as Warrington and Widnes to Cheshire. In 1998 Blackpool and Blackburn with Darwen became independent unitary authorities, although remaining part of Lancashire in matters of policing and fire services.

Much of central Lancashire is occupied by the area of heather moorland and gritstone known as the Forest of Bowland, part of the Pennine range that bounds the county to the east. The western lowlands give way to a flat coastal stretch, with an indented shore on which several seaports and coastal resorts have developed. The principal river, the Ribble, rises in the Pennines and flows southwest into the Irish Sea at Preston.

There is evidence of Bronze and Iron Age settlements, the latter notably near Colne and Pilling. The area was at that time inhabited by a loose confederation of Celtic tribes known as the Brigantes. The incorporation of the area into the Roman Empire began in AD 43; its strategic importance was emphasised by the establishment of forts at Ribchester, Lancaster and Kirkham. After the departure of the Romans, the region was absorbed into the kingdom of Northumbria; Danish invasions followed in the 8th and 9th centuries, place names such as Kirkham, Ormskirk, Formby and Skelmersdale testifying to their Norse origins.

After the Norman Conquest William I gave the area between the Ribble and the Mersey to Roger de Poitou, and in 1090 William II added the northern districts around Furness and Cartmel. By the middle of the 12th century the land was called 'the county of Lancashire', with the newly constructed Lancaster Castle as the headquarters. Like much of the north of England, the county was vulnerable during the Middle Ages to raids from over the Scottish border, and numerous fortifications were built in the post-Conquest period. By 1550, 28 towns had acquired borough status, but the region remained impoverished following the catastrophic Black Death and the Wars of the Roses in preceding centuries.

Catholicism remained stronger in the county during the Reformation than anywhere else in England, although many great families were forced to practise their religion in secret. By the mid 17th century, however, Nonconformism had gained a foothold in some of the growing mill towns. This divide was powerfully reflected during the Civil War: most of the nobility were staunchly Royalist, while the townspeople (many of whom lived in what is now Greater Manchester) were equally vehement supporters of the Parliamentary forces.

From the early 18th century the textile industry, principally linen and woollen manufacture, developed rapidly into the important cotton spinning and weaving industries, particularly with the invention of new textile machinery and the introduction of the factory system. Allied to the exploitation of the coalfields of southeast Lancashire and the expansion of the canal network, this led to the swift growth of mill towns throughout much of the county.

The industrial scene has changed as traditional industries have declined, but in the west of Lancashire dairy farming and market gardening are still important. With the arrival of the railway in the 1840s coastal resorts such as Blackpool began to expand, reaching their heyday in the years before World War II, although they have since had varying degrees of success in surviving competition from foreign travel. After 1914 many towns and parishes (Lytham with St Annes, Morecambe with Heysham) combined to form larger entities, a process of administrative reorganisation that culminated in the redrawing of local government boundaries in 1974.

Lancashire	**Population**			**Area**	
Districts	*male*	*female*	*total*	*sq miles*	*sq km*
Burnley	43,408	46,134	89,542	43	111
Chorley	49,973	50,476	100,449	78	203
Fylde	35,143	38,074	73,217	64	166
Hyndburn	39,811	41,685	81,496	28	73
Lancaster	64,105	69,809	133,914	221	575
Pendle	43,515	45,733	89,248	65	169
Preston	63,122	66,511	129,633	55	142
Ribble Valley	26,394	27,566	53,960	225	583
Rossendale	31,970	33,682	65,652	53	138
South Ribble	50,614	53,253	103,867	44	113
West Lancashire	52,237	56,141	108,378	134	347
Wyre	50,241	55,377	105,618	109	283
Blackburn with Darwen Unitary Authority	67,309	70,161	137,470	53	137
Blackpool Unitary Authority	68,742	73,541	142,283	13	35
Total	686,584	728,143	1,414,727	1185	3075

Local Attractions and Information

Accrington A former mill town located in eastern Lancashire, beneath the Pennines. Its name is possibly a corruption of 'acorn-ring-town' after the oak woods that once encircled the town, although these have long since succumbed to the Industrial Revolution. For many decades, the textile industry was Accrington's central activity. Employment was provided by the numerous mills and dye works, but conditions were harsh and there was regular conflict with employers. In support of the Chartist movement, which sought to address factory conditions as well as seeking constitutional reform, the town's workforce took part in the 'Plug Riots' of 1842 (so called because strikers would remove the boiler plugs from steam engines), a general strike which spread as thousands of strikers walked from one town to the next to persuade others to join them. Since the redrawing of the political boundaries in 1974, the town has formed part of the Borough of Hyndburn – a merging of Accrington with the smaller towns of Oswaldtwistle, Church, Clayton-le-Moors, Great Harwood and Rishton. The town is linked to Burnley and Blackburn by railway and by the M65 motorway.

Accrington Pals The nickname given to the smallest of several home town battalions of volunteers formed to fight in World War I. The so-called 'Pals' battalions were a peculiarity of the 1914–18 war: Lord Kitchener, Secretary of State for War, believed that it would help recruitment if friends and workmates from the same town were able to join up and fight together. The 'Accrington Pals' battalion was properly known as the 11th East Lancashire Regiment: of the four 250-strong companies that made up the original battalion, only one was composed of men from Accrington, the rest coming from other east Lancashire towns such as Burnley, Blackburn and Chorley. The Pals' first day of combat was on Saturday 1 July 1916 at Serre in the north of France, part of the

	'Big Push' (later known as the Battle of the Somme) intended to force the German army into retreat from the Western Front. Over 200 men were killed and a further 350 wounded – more than half of the battalion – within half an hour. Similarly desperate losses were suffered elsewhere on the front. Later that year, the East Lancashire Regiment was rebuilt with new volunteers – in all, 865 Accrington men were killed during World War I; their names are recorded on a war memorial which stands in Oak Hill Park in the south of the town, and also lists the names of 173 local fatalities from World War II.
Administrative headquarters	**Blackburn with Darwen:** Town Hall, Croft Street, Darwen BB3 1BQ. Tel: 01254 585585. **Blackpool:** Progress House, Clifton Road, Blackpool FY4 4US. Tel: 01253 477209. **Lancashire:** County Hall, Fishersgate, Preston PR1 8XJ. Tel: 0845 0530000.
Ashton Memorial	Williamson Park, Lancaster. An Edwardian folly set on the highest part of Lancaster with sweeping views across Morecambe Bay. The great white edifice, designed by John Belcher, was commissioned by Lord Ashton, a locally born millionaire whose wealth came from the export of oil cloth and linoleum, as a tribute to his late wife. The panels on the domed ceiling show Lancaster's history from Roman times to the industrial era, and an inscription reads 'This building was erected by the Right Honourable Lord Ashton as a memorial to his family and presented to the citizens of Lancaster A.D. 1907'. It can be seen for miles, particularly when travelling along the M6 motorway. Tel: 01524 33318. See also Williamson Park.
Astley Hall Museum	Astley Park, Chorley. A Grade I listed Elizabethan hall with 17th century additions, once the home of the Charnock family. It was opened as a museum and art gallery in 1924. Apart from a significant collection of fine art and furniture, there is also a collection of creamware and a bed supposedly slept in by Oliver Cromwell after the first Battle of Preston. Tel: 01257 262166.
Battles	See separate table for details of the two battles of Preston.
Blackburn	Now an independent unitary authority along with neighbouring Darwen, the largest town in east Lancashire was once the largest weaving town in the world, with 120 mills working to full capacity. Local weaver James Hargreaves invented the spinning jenny in Blackburn; the collections of the former Lewis Textile Museum, including Hargreaves's spinning jenny and mementoes of M K Gandhi's 1931 visit to the town to study textile manufacture, are now on display in the Cottontown Gallery of Blackburn Museum and Art Gallery. Modern industries include Daniel Thwaites, a major independent brewery founded by a customs officer over 200 years ago. The River Blakewater (see Rivers) gives its name to the town. The town's Latin motto, *Arte et labore* ('by art and by labour', more commonly translated as 'by skill and hard work'), is shared by Blackburn Rovers FC (see Sport).
Blackburn Cathedral	Darwen Street, Blackburn. Dedicated to St Mary the Virgin, the former parish church was elevated to the status of a cathedral with the creation of the diocese of Blackburn in 1926. The present building was begun in 1820 on the site of its 14th century and Norman predecessors by Manchester architect John Palmer and completed in the Gothic revival style by 1826. The church was enlarged during the 20th century and a distinctive lantern tower, designed by Laurence King, was added in 1961. A specially commissioned sculpture of copper and fibre-optic cable, *The Healing of the Nations* by Mark Jalland, was completed in 2000 and is situated on the cathedral's east end.
Blackpool	A major seaside resort on the Fylde coast, now the centre of Blackpool unitary authority, the largest town in Lancashire (population 142,284 in 2001) finds 85 per cent of its employment in the service and tourism industries. Its great popularity began with the arrival of the railway in 1846, and it was incorporated as a borough in 1876. The 'artificial sunshine' of eight electric arc-lamps set up in 1879 was to develop into today's famous illuminations, while 1885 saw the start of the tramway and the Tower opened in 1894 (see separate entries). The town now claims to receive 16 million visitors annually, while Lancashire's only international airport is situated less than 3 miles (5km) from the centre.
Blackpool Illuminations	Known as 'The greatest free show on earth', the display of coloured lights stretching for over 5 miles (8km) from Starr Gate to Bispham is illuminated from the beginning of September to early November. The whole promenade was first festooned with lamps in 1912, during an economic downturn, and the lights were extended to their present length in 1932. The lights have been switched on each September (except for 1914–25 and 1939–49) in a ceremony first performed by Lord Derby and more recently by such figures as Shirley Bassey, Chris Evans, Kermit the Frog and even Red Rum. The illuminations – costing £2.5 million to install and using 1 million lamps and 200 miles of cable – employ 45 staff and 65,000 man-hours, becoming more elaborate each year.
Blackpool Tower	Central Promenade, Blackpool. Designed to rival the Eiffel Tower, Blackpool's iconic steel and cast iron tower stands 518ft 9in (158.1m) high and weighs 2586 tons. It was opened on 14 May 1894 after two and a half years' construction, the entry charge being sixpence. It contains the rococo Tower Ballroom of 1899, designed by Frank Matcham, with its mighty Wurlitzer organ made famous by BBC organist Reginald ('I Do Like To Be Beside The Seaside') Dixon from 1930 to 1970. There is also an aquarium, while the Tower Circus (also designed by Frank Matcham) is situated in the basement. Tel: 01253 292029.
Blackpool tramway	Blackpool is home to the first practical electrical street tramway system in the world, opened in 1885. The town's trams connected to overhead power in 1889 and ran along the promenade, and now represent one of only three non-heritage tram systems still using double-decker vehicles (although in the town centre mainly single-deckers are used). Despite a programme of closures in the 1960s, 76 cars have survived, and the network is now 12 miles (19km) long, stretching from Starr Gate in the south to Fleetwood in the north. During the illuminations, specially decorated trams carry passengers along the promenade.

British Commercial Vehicle Museum King Street, Leyland, 4 miles (6km) northwest of Chorley. The town of Leyland is synonymous with the manufacture of cars, buses and lorries, and on the site of the old Leyland South Works is to be found the British Commercial Vehicle Museum, the largest of its kind in Europe. Its exhibits range from horse-drawn vehicles to steam-powered wagons and fire engines, a 100-tonne Scammell and, most notably, the so-called 'Popemobile'. Tel: 01772 451011.

Browsholme Hall 1 mile (1.6km) northwest of Bashall Eaves, 5 miles (8km) northwest of Clitheroe. Browsholme Hall, pronounced 'Brewsom', lies in the Forest of Bowland and is the ancestral home of the Parker family, Bowbearers of the Forest of Bowland, who have lived there since it was built in 1507. The drawing room is the principal state room, formed when the west wing was rebuilt by Thomas Lister Parker in 1805. Its architect was Jeffry Wyatt (later Sir Jeffry Wyatville); the house still holds his original drawings. The marble chimneypiece was carved in Rome for T L Parker's great-uncle, Sir Peter Leicester (1732–70) of Tabley House, Cheshire. The mahogany doors are by Gillow of Lancaster. Artworks on display include a watercolour of Browsholme by J M W Turner. Other features include the oak bedroom and antiquities ranging from the Civil War to a fragment of a Zeppelin. Tel: 01254 826719.

Carnforth Station Warton Road, Carnforth, 5 miles (8km) north of Lancaster. Opened in 1846 and rebuilt in 1937, Carnforth station was once a major junction and played a central role in David Lean's classic 1945 film *Brief Encounter*. The waiting-room, where Trevor Howard removed a speck of dust from Celia Johnson's eye and set in motion a guilt-ridden affair of iconic proportions in the pantheon of British cinema romances, has been restored to resemble the set used in the film and the station is now a heritage centre devoted to the history of the town, as well as to the famous story of doomed middle-class love. Tel: 01524 735165.

Clitheroe Castle Castle Hill, Clitheroe. Norman motte and bailey castle founded c.1080 by Roger de Poitou on a natural limestone outcrop above the River Ribble. Robert de Lacy built the stone castle c.1186 to protect the administrative centre of his vast estates. The castle dominates the town's skyline although its keep is one of the smallest in England, with rooms only about 20ft (6m) square. The keep was deliberately damaged after its capture by Parliamentary forces during the Civil War, but was repaired in 1848 with smooth-faced limestone blocks. The Castle Museum, located nearby in the castle bailey, brings to life the history and geology of the Ribble Valley. Tel: 01200 424635.

Fisherman's Friend A preparation manufactured in Fleetwood since 1865, initially in the form of a liquid made from liquorice, capsicum, eucalyptus and menthol and intended to assuage the sore throats and chest problems suffered at sea by local trawlermen. Although popular, the bottles of liquid were at risk of breakage in heavy seas so their producer, local chemist James Lofthouse, adapted the compound to a more easily handled form, the now familiar lozenge. Now made in a variety of flavours some of which are suitable for diabetics, the lozenges sell in over 100 countries and have won the Queen's Award to Industry for Export Achievement three times.

Fleetwood The port of Fleetwood, located on the estuary of the River Wyre, was created from a small fishing village in 1836 by local landowner Peter Hesketh, who hired the famous London architect Decimus Burton to design his proposed seaside resort; when Hesketh was knighted, he assumed the name Hesketh-Fleetwood. The railway extension from Preston brought about the construction of the imposing North Euston Hotel, used by Queen Victoria as she travelled north for her annual holiday, but Sir Peter was bankrupted when a direct rail link to Scotland via Shap was opened in 1847. The town flourished as a port until the 1960s, but the fishing industry was badly hit by the cod wars of the 1970s. Today Fleetwood is a terminus for ferries to the Isle of Man and Northern Ireland. Burton's Pharos Lighthouse of 1840 still stands near the seafront and is visible for 13 miles (21km).

Food in Lancashire Lancashire has a long tradition of local delicacies. **Barm cakes** are a bread roll, or bap, made from wholemeal flour. Also called 'flour cakes', they are soft and pliable, with a pitted texture. 'Barm' is an old Lancashire word for the froth on liquid that contains yeast. **Blackpool rock** can still be seen being rolled and made on the town's seafront; in fact the rock sold in most seaside resorts is still made in Blackpool. The hard sugar slightly minted confection, rolled into lengths and cut into 12in (30cm) pieces, is distinctive on account of the lettering that traditionally runs throughout every stick. **Chorley cakes** are similar to Eccles cakes but generally larger and flatter and without the glazed sugary top. **Goosnargh cakes** are named after the village near Preston where they originated. They are more biscuit than cake, flavoured with caraway seeds and sold around Easter and Whitsuntide. **Hindle wakes**, an ancient dish of exotically stuffed boiled poultry, is thought to have been brought by Flemish weavers to Bolton-le-Moor (Bolton) in 1337. The fowl would be stuffed with a mixture of prunes, nuts, suet, spices and red wine –in the original recipe the blood of the fowl was used for binding the stuffing mix – and simmered slowly overnight until tender. The next day the bird was removed from the stock, coated with a lemon and cream sauce and decorated with prunes and lemon slices and served cold. The name of the dish may derive from 'Hen de la Wake'; in Lancashire dialect a 'wake' was a fair, at which time the dish may have been eaten. Baxenden in the Rossendale Valley is the home of **Holland's Pies**, which were first sold from a confectioner's shop in Haslingden by John Whitaker in 1851. Still manufactured to traditional recipes including steak, cheese and onion, steak and kidney, and meat and potato, as well as steak puddings, nowadays they are sold in most supermarkets in northwest England. **Lancashire cheese** is the softest of the hard English cheeses. Its white crumbly texture and full, slightly salty taste makes it an excellent cheese in cooking, and especially favoured for Welsh rarebit. The lamb (or mutton) stew known as **Lancashire hotpot** originated in the cotton towns of Lancashire as a simple dish quickly prepared and slow cooked, similar to Irish stew. It is named after the straight-sided brown dish in which it was cooked. At one time, even oysters were included in the recipe. Traditionally, mill workers' wives would prepare it in the morning and leave it in the oven all day, so that it would be ready when the family returned home from work. It was usually eaten with pickled red cabbage. According to tradition, a woman's ability to make a good hotpot considerably enhanced her marriage prospects. **Nodding pudding** (sometimes spelt 'knodding' or 'nodden') is made from potatoes and flour mixed with butter, and baked in a pie tin until it develops a crust. It may have been a way of using up leftover potatoes, similar to 'bubble and squeak'. **Rossendale Sarsaparilla**, an old and once very popular non-alcoholic beverage similar to ginger beer, is still brewed to a well-kept secret recipe, and sold at Fitzpatrick's Herbal Health Shop in Rawtenstall, Rossendale. **Sad cakes** – similar to Eccles and Chorley cakes but larger, and popular in the Rossendale Valley – are sometimes known by local children as 'desolate cakes'. Alternative forms often mix the dried fruit into the pastry and present it in an envelope shape.

Forest of Bowland — An area of barren gritstone fells and heather moorland rising to 1836ft (559.5m) at Ward's Stone, 7 miles (11km) southeast of Lancaster, and designated an Area of Outstanding Natural Beauty in February 1964. Once a hunting-ground used by Earl Tostig of Northumberland in the 11th century, it came into the hands of the Duke of Lancaster, the future Henry IV, and became a royal hunting forest. In recent years much of the land has been used for the shooting of game birds, mainly grouse, and several private estates still exist. The elevated moors' nature trails and bird-watching activity – birds such as the hen harrier and ring ouzel can be found here – have resulted in its becoming the first protected area in England to be awarded the European Charter for Sustainable Tourism. Tel: 01772 534140.

Gawthorpe Hall — 2 miles (3km) west of Burnley. Situated on the River Calder, this compact, three-storey Elizabethan house with tiered mullioned windows, probably by Hardwick Hall architect Robert Smythson (1535–1614), is the home of the Shuttleworth family. Restored in the 19th century by Sir Charles Barry and A W Pugin, the hall holds the unique Kay-Shuttleworth collection of fine needlework and lace. Now owned by the National Trust. Tel: 01282 771004.

Gillow Furniture — A notable Lancaster-based firm making and retailing elegant furniture, founded by Robert Gillow (1704–72), who became a freeman of the town. His sons Robert and Richard moved to London to develop the firm's reputation for well-made unfussy furniture, where they became the first designers to stamp their name on their products. Richard (1734–1811) also designed the Lancaster Custom House, now the town's Maritime Museum, and 200 Gillow pieces can be seen in Tatton Hall, Knutsford, Cheshire.

Harris Museum and Art Gallery — Market Square, Preston. Housed in a superb Grade I listed building by James Hibbert in the Greek revival neoclassical style, the museum dates from 1893. It contains not only a major display of 19th century watercolours, but also the largest collection of perfume bottles in the UK. Tel: 01772 258248.

Haworth Art Gallery — Haworth Park, Manchester Road, Accrington. Housed in a 1909 Tudor-style house set in parkland and built as the home of local cotton manufacturer William Haworth, the museum contains the largest collection of Tiffany glass in Europe (130 pieces), presented by Joseph Briggs, an Accrington man who became Louis Comfort Tiffany's personal assistant in New York. Tel: 01254 233782.

Heysham Power Station — 1 mile (1.6km) south of Heysham, 3 miles (5km) south of Morecambe. The site contains two separate power stations, both equipped with advanced gas-cooled reactors. Heysham 1 has two reactors, the first of which began operating in 1983 and the second a year later, and is due for decommissioning in 2014. Heysham 2 began operating in 1988 and is due to be decommissioned in 2023.

Highest point — The traditional highest point in Lancashire is Coniston Old Man at 2634ft (803m); that, however, became part of Cumbria in 1974. Since then Green Hill, 32 miles (51km) south of the Old Man, located above Cowan Bridge between Kirkby Lonsdale in Cumbria and Ingleton in North Yorkshire, is generally regarded as Lancashire's highest point, although the summit is on the border with Cumbria. Green Hill (GR: SD701820) is 2060ft (628m) and forms the watershed between the River Dee and the Leck Beck, both tributaries of the River Lune. The summit of Gragareth at 2057ft (627m), about 1¼ miles (2km) southwest of Green Hill, lies a couple of hundred yards within Lancashire.

Hoghton Tower — 4 miles (6km) west of Blackburn. Lancashire's sole baronial dwelling is a fortified hilltop manor house dating from 1565. The house has two claims to fame – in 1617, James I allegedly knighted a loin of beef he had particularly enjoyed (giving rise to the term 'sirloin') on his stay here, and William Shakespeare performed here with William Hoghton's players. The tower itself was blown up in 1643 when the house was taken by Parliamentary troops, but the king's bedchamber and audience chamber are preserved for viewing. Tel: 01254 852986.

Interesting facts — The word **'dinosaur'** ('terrible lizard') was coined in 1841 by palaeontologist Sir Richard Owen, a native of Lancaster and superintendent of natural history at the British Museum for 28 years. Owen campaigned vigorously against the Darwinian view of evolution. Both **Harold Wilson** (1945–50) and **Robert Kilroy Silk** (1974–83) were Labour MPs for Ormskirk. **The Corner Pin** public house in Stubbins, Ramsbottom, plays host to the annual World Black Pudding Throwing Championships. On the second week in September competitors swarm to the pub to hurl 8oz black puddings at giant Yorkshire puddings suspended on plates 20ft (6m) off the ground. The current world record is held by Ralph Hegginbotham who knocked off 14 puddings with a single shot in 1938. Special prizes are awarded for the most original hurling technique and competitors who 'throw a wobbler'. A phenomenally popular women's football team in the interwar years, **Dick, Kerr's Ladies** was a side formed from employees at a Preston works founded by two Scotsmen, W B Dick and John Kerr, which turned to the manufacture of munitions in World War I. The team raised considerable amounts of money for servicemen's charities, and on Boxing Day 1920 attracted a crowd of 53,000 to Goodison Park, Liverpool, to watch them take on St Helens Ladies. The same year, they played the first women's international matches against a touring French side, and when they disbanded after 48 years they had played 828 games, winning 758, drawing 46 and losing only 24.

Lancaster Situated on the estuary of the River Lune, the county town of the traditional county of Lancashire dates back to the Romans, who built a fort on what is now Castle Hill. In 1359, John of Gaunt married Blanche, daughter of a powerful baron, the Duke of Lancaster, whose estate and title he inherited. His son became Henry IV in 1399, and the Duchy of Lancaster has been a royal possession ever since (the Queen, as Duke of Lancaster, is the only female duke in the country). The town was attacked and burnt by the Scots in 1322. The Lancashire witches were condemned to death in the castle (see separate entry) in 1612. By the early 18th century the port had begun to bring great wealth to the town; trade with the West Indies flourished, a story told in the Maritime Museum. The main landmark is the Ashton Memorial, called by Nikolaus Pevsner 'the grandest monument in England', situated in Williamson Park (see separate entries). The Jacobean Judge's Lodgings, built in the 1620s, are Lancaster's oldest town house.

Lancaster Castle Castle Hill, Lancaster. Built in 1093, Lancaster Castle occupies a city-centre hilltop location on the site of three successive Roman forts. The extensive group of historic structures include a 12th century keep, the 14th century Witches' Tower, a 15th century gatehouse, and the Female Penitentiary, dating from the early 19th century. It is Grade I listed, and the area to its north is a Scheduled Ancient Monument. The castle was extended by King John and improved by Henry IV before being partially demolished in 1649. It is currently used as both a court and a prison. The keep (also known as the Lungess Tower) is a four-storey tower, 65ft (20m) high and with a shallow buttress at each corner and halfway along each side; the outer walls are 10ft (3m) thick. The upper storey was rebuilt in the reign of Elizabeth I in 1585. The Well Tower (also known as the Witches' Tower), built c.1325 contains two wells and three vaulted stone-flagged underground dungeons; according to tradition, these were used to house the Lancashire Witches prior to their trial in the castle in 1612. Shortly after Henry IV's accession an extensive rebuilding programme was started, culminating in the construction of the great twin-towered gatehouse. Now known as the John O' Gaunt Gatehouse, it has two semi-octagonal towers which rise 65ft (20m) above massive sloping plinths; with its portcullis and its battlements built out over corbels, it is perhaps the finest gatehouse of its date and type in England. In 1788, the Governor's House was erected between the gatehouse and the Well Tower, and in 1792 work was begun on a prison for female felons. This is on the other side of the gatehouse, in a four-storey tower with Gothic windows. From the late 18th century, the castle was substantially modified for use as a court and prison, during which time the medieval curtain wall and several of the towers were demolished. Between 1794 and 1796 a prison for male felons was built, which was cut off from the outside world by the construction of the present high walls. Above these rose three four-storey towers (again with Gothic windows) where the prisoners slept in separate cells. At the same time, to the south of the keep, two storeys of accommodation were built for debtors above an attractive open arcade with Gothic arches. In 1796 the medieval hall, which stood to the southwest of the Keep and housed the Crown Court, was demolished, although its dungeon basement still exists. Adjacent to the dungeons is Hadrian's Tower. At the end of the 18th century, a new Crown Court and Shire Hall were begun to the designs of Thomas Harrison. The former building, where thousands were condemned to be transported to Australia, and where the Birmingham Six were dubiously convicted in 1975, is the oldest working courtroom in England. The last major extension was the Female Penitentiary, built in 1821 and designed by Joseph Gandy, a former pupil of James Wyatt who had also worked for John Nash. Gandy's unusual design was based on the panoptic principle, developed by Jeremy Bentham for the supervision of prisoners using minimal labour. The Lancaster panopticon is semi-circular in plan and contains five tiers of cells, each with a window. These cells lead off curved internal galleries and are visible across an open space from the central control room. Although it now houses male prisoners, it is now the only such building in existence which still fulfils its original purpose. Tel: 01524 64998.

Lancaster Cathedral Balmoral Road, Lancaster. Dedicated to St Peter and built in 1859, Lancaster's Roman Catholic cathedral boasts an impressive 240ft (73m) spire. The former parish church became a cathedral in 1924 with the creation of the Diocese of Lancaster.

Leighton Hall 1½ miles (2.5km) north of Carnforth. The earliest records of Leighton Hall go back to 1246, when it is known that Adam D'Avranches had a fortified manor here; the current house dates from the 1760s with a neo-Gothic façade added by Richard Gillow of the furniture-making family (see Gillow furniture) in 1822–5. Gillow bought the house in 1822 and it is still the home of his descendants. Every owner of Leighton Hall, with one exception, has been a Roman Catholic and priests were regularly hidden in the house during the 16th century. The only owner to conform to the Church of England was Sir George Middleton, last of the Middletons of Leighton; although his wife remained a staunch recusant throughout, Sir George was a colonel of the Royal Army and twice High Sheriff of Lancashire. Knighted and made baronet on the same day at Durham in 1642, during the Commonwealth he paid fines amounting to £2646 for his loyalty to the Crown. The Leighton Hall estate stretches over 1550 acres (630ha) and includes landscaped parkland, woodland walks and a pretty 19th century walled garden. Tel: 01524 734474.

Lytham St Annes lifeboat disaster Britain's worst-ever lifeboat disaster occurred on 9 December 1886 after three lifeboats from St Annes, Southport and Lytham were launched to assist the Hamburg trading barque *Mexico*. Their Southport and St Annes boats capsized in horrendous seas; most of the Southport crew and all of the St Annes crew were drowned. The Lytham boat survived and was able to rescue the captain and crew of the *Mexico*, before launching again to look for the missing St

Annes lifeboat. Fifteen crew members lost their lives in the disaster, and improvements to lifeboat design followed as a result.

Martholme — Martholme Lane, Great Harwood, 4 miles (6km) northeast of Blackburn. The manor of Martholme and Great Harwood was given to Ilbert de Lacy by Roger de Poitou after the Norman Conquest. The name is almost certainly of Danish origin, *mart* meaning market and *holme* a piece of dry land in a fen or a piece of land partly surrounded by a stream. Martholme is the oldest house in Great Harwood but the present building is not the first to occupy the site; a house stood there in 1177 when the manor was bequeathed by Ilbert's grandson to Richard de Fitton. The house is built within a loop of the River Calder and was protected to the landward side by a moat or ditch. The Catholic Sir Thomas Hesketh (1539–88), a supporter of Mary I, lived at Martholme after her death in 1558. In 1561 he rebuilt the gatehouse, and the Hesketh arms can still be seen above the archway. In 1577 he rebuilt the manor house itself with a central hall and two wings, again incorporating the family arms into the building. Thomas' eldest son, Robert, added a second, arched, outer gateway in 1607. Martholme is now a private residence consisting largely of Hesketh's additions to the earlier house.

Martin Mere — 5 miles (8km) southeast of Southport. An important wetland nature reserve of 350 sq miles (906.5 sq km), managed by the Wildfowl and Wetlands Trust. Established in 1976, it is a Site of Special Scientific Interest and a Special Protection Area as well as having Ramsar status. A host of birds can be seen from the 11 hides around the lake, especially in winter, when pink-footed geese, whooper and Bewick's swans, snow geese and occasional predators appear. Its book lists 284 species of avian visitors, 517 species of plants and 1368 species of invertebrates. Beavers were reintroduced to the site in 2007. Tel: 01704 895181.

Midland Hotel — Marine Road West, Morecambe. An outstanding feature of Morecambe's seafront, this beautiful curved building was in 1933 the first Art Deco hotel in Britain. Designed by Oliver Hill, its interior has carvings by Eric Gill and décor by Eric Ravilious, but after being used as a hospital in World War II it fell into disrepair. However, with the aid of a £600,000 grant from the Heritage Lottery Fund, Manchester-based developers Urban Splash have restored the Grade II* listed building with the intention of re-establishing it as a top-class hotel., reopening June 2008 Tel: 01524 424000.

Morecambe — The railway first brought holidaymakers to the three former fishing hamlets of Bare, Poulton-le-Sands and Torrisholme in 1850, and they collectively became known as Morecambe in 1889. During the mid 20th century Morecambe rivalled Blackpool as a popular resort, although its Central and West End piers were both destroyed before World War II. The town hosted the Miss Great Britain beauty contest from 1956 to 1989, but is now better known for Graham Ibbeson's larger than lifesize statue of its most famous citizen, Eric Morecambe (originally Bartholomew), erected in 1999, and for the restored Midland Hotel (see separate entry). **Morecambe Bay**, the largest estuary in Britain, covering 120 sq miles (310 sq km) of sand and mudflats, is a Special Protection Area and Special Area of Conservation.e Dspite its magnificent sweeping view to the Lakeland fells, its quicksands and rapidly rising tides have earned it a treacherous reputation, as evidenced by the deaths of 18 cockle pickers here in February 2004. An official Queen's Guide to the Sands, an office dating from 1536, escorts walkers across in safety.

National Football Museum — Deepdale Stadium, Sir Tom Finney Way, Preston. One of the few national museums outside London, the £13 million National Football Museum was opened in 2001 with a grant from the Heritage Lottery Fund. It contains the most important collection of footballing archives and artefacts in the world (including the crossbar struck by Geoff Hurst for England's controversial third goal in the 1966 World Cup final), showing how England became the birthplace and the home of football. It has interactive displays allowing virtual entry to every League ground, and (since 2002) a Hall of Fame with ten notables inducted annually – seven male players, one female player and two managers. Tel: 01772 908442.

Pendle Hill — 5 miles (8km) north of Burnley. Rising to 1827ft (557m), Pendle Hill is reputedly the site of George Fox's vision which inspired him to found the Society of Friends (Quakers), but the area is more notorious for its associations with witches. In 1612, at the height of the anti-witchcraft frenzy, a supposed curse laid by a local beggar woman led to the arrest, torture and hanging of eight suspected witches at Lancaster Castle on 20 August. The legend was perpetuated by Harrison Ainsworth's celebrated novel *The Lancashire Witches* (1849).

Piers — There are seaside piers at Fleetwood and St Annes, but Blackpool is unique in Britain in possessing three. The first, Eugenius Birch's North Pier, opened in 1863 and now Grade II listed, extended to 1650ft (503m) in length via a jetty from which pleasure cruises operated until 1939. The second was Central Pier (originally called 'South Jetty'), completed in May 1868, a less sedate location used for open-air dancing in its heyday. In 1893 the Victoria Pier (renamed South Pier in 1930) was completed; it now features a large variety theatre where top stars regularly perform to large audiences. The town's pier (1910) burnt down in September 2008.

Pleasure Beach — South Shore, Blackpool. A 40 acre (16ha) amusement park founded in 1906 by Alderman William Bean to 'inspire gaiety of a primarily innocent character'. The first scenic railway in Europe, reaching speeds of over 40mph (64km/h), was built here in 1907. Today the site boasts 13 roller-coasters, including the 213ft (65m) Pepsi Max Big One, built in 1994 and at the time the tallest and fastest in Europe (it is still the tallest in the UK). Over 6 million visitors come here annually, making it England's most-visited attraction in recent years. Tel: 0870 444 5566.

Preston — The administrative centre of Lancashire and one of the UK's newest cities (since April 2002, in celebration of Queen Elizabeth II's Golden Jubilee), Preston is situated at the head of the Ribble estuary. Referred to as 'Proud Preston' since at least the 18th century, it was the first town in Lancashire to receive a borough charter (1179), the first borough in which every male over 21 had a vote in a parliamentary election (1798) and the first provincial town to have street lighting

(1816); Preston also had the first stretch of motorway in Britain (the M6 Preston bypass, 1958). Its 19th century prosperity was based on the cotton trade, although the exploitation of workers led to widespread strikes: Charles Dickens in *Hard Times* (1854) based the fictional 'Coketown' on Preston, having lodged in a hotel in Church Street and been shocked by the town's grimness. Nowadays, however, Preston boasts the splendid Harris Museum and Art Gallery, the National Football Museum (see separate entries), the Ribble Steam Railway (2005), with over 40 standard-gauge locomotives – the largest collection in England – and a blue plaque house in Orchard Street where Benjamin Franklin stayed when conducting his experiments with kite and lightning rod at nearby Walton-le-Dale. The University of Central Lancashire (see separate entry) is one of England's largest and fastest-growing educational establishments.

Preston Guild

The phrase 'once every Preston Guild' – meaning 'very infrequently' – refers to the celebration held every 20 years by the city's Guild Merchants to commemorate the Guild's founding in 1179. It takes place on the first Monday after 29 August, the most recent being in 1992 and the next in 2012, coinciding with Britain hosting the Olympic Games.

Prisons

Garth, Ulnes Walton, Leyland, is a category B training prison, opened in October 1988. A new residential unit (housing 120 prisoners) opened in July 1997. Operational capacity: 667. Tel: 01772 443 300.

Kirkham, Freckleton Road, Kirkham, Preston, is a category D training prison with accommodation for up to 628 adult male prisoners, occupies the site of the former RAF Technical Training Establishment which was built during World War II and afterwards used as a demobilisation centre. The facility has been in use as a prison since 1962. Tel: 01772 675400.

Lancaster Castle (see separate entry) is a category C training prison opened in 1955. Operational capacity: 243. Tel: 01524 565100.

Lancaster Farms, Stone Row Head, Quernmore Road, Lancaster, opened in March 1993 as a remand centre/young offender institution, with two new units opened in June 1996. Operational capacity: 527. Tel: 01524 563450.

Preston, Ribbleton Lane, Preston, is a category B prison. Its wings were constructed between 1840 and 1895 on a site occupied since 1790. The prison closed in 1931, reopening for military use in 1939 and as a civilian prison in 1948. It became a local prison in 1990. Tel: 01772 444550.

Wymott, Ulnes Walton Lane, Leyland, opened in 1979, is a category C trainer prison with facilities for vulnerable prisoners. Operational capacity: 1046. Tel: 01772 444000.

Ribchester

8 miles (13km) southwest of Clitheroe. Ribchester was settled in the Bronze Age but is best known for its Roman fort and civilian settlement. Known as Bremetennacum Veteranorum, it was established in AD 79 by the Roman governor Gnaeus Julius Agricola, who set up a network of defensive forts at the intersection of two strategically important routes, one from Manchester to Carlisle and the other from York to the west coast. The fort housed cavalry units from Spain and then eastern Europe. **Ribchester Roman Museum** has exhibits relating to Roman Ribchester and the archaeology of Lancashire, including a replica of an ornate bronze parade helmet discovered here in 1795 (the original is on display at the British Museum in London). Tel: 01254 878261.

Rivers

The **Blakewater** rises on the moors above Guide, southeast of Blackburn, as Knuzden Brook and runs through the hamlet of that name, before taking the name Blakewater (meaning either 'black water' or 'clear water', the latter deriving from Old English *blæc*) near the village of Whitebirk. From there, the river runs through Little Harwood, Cob Wall and Brookhouse in Blackburn to the town centre. The section of the Blakewater running through central Blackburn was culverted during the Industrial Revolution, and now runs underground, although there are proposals to open up parts of the river so that the Blakewater will once again flow openly. On the western side of the town centre the river continues under Whalley Banks and through Redlam. It joins the River Darwen outside Witton Country Park in Blackburn, and the Darwen continues to join the River Ribble at Walton-le-Dale. See also Blackburn.

The **Lune** is formed at Wath, in the parish of Ravenstonedale, Cumbria, by the confluence of Sandwath Beck and Weasdale Beck. It then passes the remnants of a Roman fort near Low Borrowbridge at the foot of Borrowdale and flows through south Cumbria, meeting the Irish Sea at Plover Scar near Lancaster, a distance of 44 miles (70km).

The **Ribble** has its source at the confluence of the Gayle Beck and Cam Beck near Ribblehead Viaduct, in the shadow of the Yorkshire Three Peaks. It flows south through Settle and Clitheroe and then southwest into Preston, before emptying into the Irish Sea near Lytham, a length of 75 miles (121km). Its main tributaries are the Hodder, at 30 miles (48km) the longest tributary, and the Calder, which join the Ribble near Great Mitton, the Darwen which joins at Walton-le-Dale and the Douglas which joins near Hesketh Bank.

The **Wyre** has its source in the Forest of Bowland in central Lancashire. It flows south through Garstang where it meets its major tributary, the River Calder (not the same river as the Ribble tributary), followed by the River Brock. Flowing west, it becomes tidal near Poulton-le-Fylde, it defines the northeastern limit of the peninsula known as the Fylde (the name 'Fylde' dates back to Saxon times and means 'low lying ground between two estuaries'), and eventually discharges into the Irish Sea at Fleetwood.

Rufford Old Hall

6 miles (10km) northeast of Ormskirk. One of the finest black and white timber-framed halls in England, dating from c.1530 when Sir Thomas Hesketh, who had married an heiress, built the property. The great hall, where Shakespeare is believed to have performed for Sir Thomas, is surmounted by a hammer-beam roof bearing the arms of Lancashire's great families. In the 17th century a brick wing was added to the hall, parts of which are now used for the Philip Ashcroft Museum of Rural Life, a unique collection of objects and implements from pre-industrial

Lancashire. The building was given to the National Trust by Baron Hesketh in 1936. Tel: 01704 821254.

Samlesbury Hall — 5 miles (8km) east of Preston. A grand mansion dating originally from the 12th century and one of the county's heritage gems, this attractive black and white oak-timbered manor house was built in 1325 after its predecessor was destroyed by Robert the Bruce. The owners, the Southworth family, continued to practise their Catholic faith, but lost their wealth after Sir John was imprisoned in Manchester, where he died; another member of the family, martyred in 1654, has since been beatified. The house was stripped by its new owners, but was restored by Joseph Harrison, who entertained Charles Dickens there but took his own life in 1878, ruined by the restoration costs. Since 1925 the house has been administered by Samlesbury Hall Trust. Tel: 01254 812010.

Sport

general — **Blackburn Hawks** ice hockey team, often referred to as the Blackhawks, are based in Blackburn. Founded in 1990, they currently play in the English National Ice Hockey League. The **Waterloo Cup** is a Blackpool-based crown green bowls competition inaugurated in 1907.

cricket — **Lancashire County Cricket Club**, founded in 1864, represents the whole county, although its headquarters are at Old Trafford, Greater Manchester. The team has in the past played first-class matches at Preston, Blackburn, Nelson, Whalley and Lytham, although the only currently used venue in the county is Stanley Park, Blackpool. As of 2008 Lancashire have won the County Championship outright on seven occasions, the most recent being 1934; in the modern era their successes have come in various one-day competitions. Tel: 0161 282 4000.

The **Lancashire League** is a league of local cricket clubs drawn from small and medium sized mill towns largely in East Lancashire. It was formed on 16 March 1892, growing from the North East Cricket League formed 17 months earlier. Its current members are Accrington, Bacup, Burnley, Church, Colne, East Lancashire, Enfield, Haslingden, Lowerhouse, Nelson, Ramsbottom, Rawtenstall, Rishton and Todmorden. The quality of competition in the league is held in high regard, thanks not least to its history of recruiting professional players of international standing. These have included Bill Alley, Sydney Barnes, Sir Learie Constantine, Kapil Dev, Charlie Griffith, Roy Gilchrist, Wes Hall, Roger Harper, George Headley, Clive Lloyd, Viv Richards, Andy Roberts, Shane Warne, Steve Waugh and Everton Weekes.

football — **Accrington FC** was formed following a meeting at a local public house in 1876. The 'Owd Reds', who played at Moorhead Park, were one of the original 12 teams to join the Football League on 17 April 1888. Their best season was 1889–90, when they finished sixth in the table. The club were relegated from the League in 1893 but continued until 1896, finally folding after a 12–0 defeat on 14 January to Darwen in the Lancashire Senior Cup.

The first **Accrington Stanley** club was formed in 1891 as Stanley Villa and adopted the Accrington name in 1893. The club re-formed after World War I and entered the Football League in 1921, playing at Peel Park. Having failed to achieve promotion from the Third Division in four decades of League football, in 1960 Stanley were relegated to Division Four, completing only one season before bankruptcy. In October 1968 the club was revived and in 1970 it played for the first time at the Crown Ground, now the Fraser Eagle Stadium. Since then, Stanley have returned to the Football League under the control of local businessman Eric Whalley, confirming their place on 15 April 2006 with a 1–0 win at Woking. One of the clubs relegated from League Two was Oxford United, the team elected to replace Stanley as members of the Football League in 1962. The team's name is often invoked as a symbol of British sport's legion of plucky but hopeless causes. Tel: 01254 356951.

Formed in 1875 and a founder member of the Football League in 1888, **Blackburn Rovers** uniquely gained a hat-trick of FA Cup final victories in 1884, 1885 and 1886, with further wins in 1890, 1891 and 1928, and were League champions in 1912 and 1914. After a gradual decline, the club's fortunes were revived in the 1990s by local tycoon Jack Walker, and they won the Premier League title in 1995, interrupting the Arsenal–Manchester United duopoly, followed by the Worthington Cup in 2002. Rovers have played at Ewood Park since 1890 and their traditional colours are blue and white halved shirts. Their Latin motto, *Arte et labore*, was used by the town council even before the club were formed (see Blackburn). Tel: 0870 111 3232.

Blackpool were founded in 1877 as Blackpool St Johns but adopted their present name in 1887, a year before they entered the Football League. The Seasiders play at Bloomfield Road. Their traditional colours are tangerine and white, giving rise to an alternative nickname of 'Tangerines'. A star-studded Blackpool team won the immortal 'Matthews Final' in the 1953 FA Cup. Tel: 0870 443 1953.

Originally founded as a rugby club, **Burnley** adopted association football in 1882 and were founder members of the Football League in 1888. The Clarets have played the whole of their League history at Turf Moor, believed to have been the first ground visited by a member of the Royal Family when Queen Victoria's son, Prince Albert, attended a game in October 1886. Winners of the FA Cup in 1914 and of the League championship in 1921 and 1960, their traditional colours are claret and blue. Tel: 0870 443 1882.

Morecambe were formed in 1920, reaching the Football Conference in 1995–96 and finally gaining promotion to the Football League in 2006. Nicknamed The Shrimps (after the Morecambe Bay delicacy), their home ground since 1921 has been Christie Park, named after Joseph Barnes Christie, a major benefactor of the club. Tel: 01524 411797.

Preston North End were formed as a cricket club in 1863, switching to football in 1878 when they also moved to their ground at Deepdale. A founder member of the Football League in 1888, the club won the League and FA Cup 'double' in its first season. Deepdale claims to be the Football League ground with the longest continuous use by any club in Britain – and, by definition, the world. Nicknamed the Lilywhites after their traditional white strip, the club's most famous player was Tom Finney, who played for the club from 1946 to 1960, receiving the OBE (1961), the CBE (1992) and a knighthood (1998), as well as being made a freeman of the city. Tel: 0870 442 1964.

Non-league clubs include **Burscough** (formed 1946) and **Fleetwood Town** (formed in 1997 as Fleetwood Wanderers).

golf — **Royal Lytham and St Anne's** golf course was opened in 1898 after a group of golf enthusiasts had met 12 years earlier to choose a suitable venue. A links course, it is considered one of England's finest, and has hosted the Open Championship ten times (1926, 1952, 1958, 1963, 1969, 1974, 1979, 1988, 1996 and 2001), also staging the Ryder Cup in 1961. Tel: 01253 724206.

rugby union — One of the oldest rugby union clubs in northwest England, **Fylde** play at the Woodlands Memorial Ground in Lytham St Annes. Named after the Fylde peninsula on which Lytham stands, the club was born literally on the toss of a coin when, on 25 July 1919, Manchester businessmen met at the Ansdell Institute to discuss the formation of either a rugby or football club. A coin was tossed and it fell in favour of rugby. Former players who have worn the club's claret and gold include Brian Ashton, Roger Uttley, Wade Dooley and Bill Beaumont. Tel: 01253 734733.

Sunderland Point — 5 miles (8km) southwest of Lancaster. A peninsula on the north bank of the Lune estuary, now a Site of Special Scientific Interest owing to its avian and marine wildlife and the location of the former port of Sunderland, also often known as Sunderland Point. Sunderland declined in the face of Morecambe's expansion, although some fine Georgian buildings remain, and there is a poignant reminder of its past in the form of **Sambo's Grave**. The black servant of an 18th century sea-captain, Sambo was left behind with a fever as his master sailed to the Caribbean. Thinking himself abandoned, Sambo wasted away and died, but being unbaptised, he was not permitted to be interred in consecrated ground. His grave near Upsteps Cottage, where he died, became a focus for the anti-slavery movement and still regularly has flowers planted on it.

Towneley Hall Art Gallery and Museums — Towneley Park, Burnley. The home of the Towneley family for over 500 years before it was sold to Burnley Corporation in 1901. The house dates largely from the 17th century and contains a chapel built c.1515, as well as priest holes, although its present appearance owes a great deal to alterations carried out by Jeffry Wyatville in the early 19th century. The park was opened to the public in June 1902 and in May 1903 the Great Hall and the south wing of the house were opened for a temporary art exhibition. Today, the museum houses numerous displays encompassing natural history, Egyptology, local history, textiles, decorative art and regional furniture. Tel: 01282 424213.

Turton Tower — Chapeltown Road, Turton, 8 miles (13km) southeast of Blackburn. A Tudor manor house based on a pele tower built c.1420 for protection against raids from Scotland, and set in woodlands on the western edge of the Pennines. The house is now a museum and the surrounding gardens include Victorian follies and an unusual railway bridge built in 1848 with turrets and castellations, designed to be in keeping with the appearance of the tower. Tel: 01204 852203.

University of Lancaster — Bailrigg, 3 miles (5km) south of Lancaster. A collegiate university founded in 1964, with Princess Alexandra of Kent as its first chancellor. Lancaster's eight undergraduate colleges are: Bowland (founded 1964), Cartmel (1969), The County (1969), Furness (1966), Fylde (1968), Grizedale (1975), Lonsdale (1964), Pendle (1974); there is a postgraduate college named Graduate College (1992). The Peter Scott Gallery contains the university's collections of art and antiquities, including works from China and Japan as well as modern British art, while the Ruskin Library, opened in 1998, is the world centre for the work of John Ruskin, who spent much of his later life a little to the north in Cumbria. Former students include journalist Robert Fisk, *Top Gear* presenter James May and cyclist Jason Queally. Tel: 01524 65201.

University of Central Lancashire — Based in Preston, the former Lancashire Polytechnic was awarded university status in 1992. It originated in the Institution for the Diffusion of Useful Knowledge, founded in Preston in 1828, which afterwards became Harris College and then Preston Polytechnic. It has over 30,000 students, and former students include land artist Andy Goldsworthy, broadcaster Adrian Chiles and journalist Simon Kelner. Tel: 01772 201201.

Warton Old Rectory — Warton, 1 mile (1.6km) north of Carnforth. A rare medieval stone house dating to the late 13th or early 14th century. Remains of the hall, chambers and domestic offices can still be seen. The Grade I listed house is now in the care of English Heritage. Tel: 0161 242 1400.

Williamson Park — Wyresdale Road, Lancaster. A 50 acre (20ha) park overlooking the city of Lancaster. It was created by wealthy local industrialist James Williamson Snr and his son James Williamson Jnr, 1st Lord Ashton, initially to provide employment for local people hit by the crisis in the textile industry resulting from the 'cotton famine' caused by the American Civil War. Built on the site of former quarries that provided stone for the buildings of Lancaster, it was opened to the public in 1896, it has a commanding view across Morecambe Bay to the Lakeland fells. Other features include the Lancaster Sundial, where the observers become the gnomon and can tell the time by their own shadow and a restored Edwardian palm house with a vast collection of tropical butterflies. The park is surmounted by the splendid Ashton Memorial (see separate entry).

Some famous people born in Lancashire

Anderson, Jon (rock singer) (1944–)	Accrington
Arkwright, Richard (inventor) (1732–92)	Preston
Binyon, Laurence (poet) (1869–1943)	Lancaster
Birtwistle, Harrison (composer) (1934–)	Accrington
Couch, Jane (boxer) (1968–)	Fleetwood
Culshaw, John (impressionist) (1968–)	Ormskirk
Duckworth, Keith (auto engineer) (1933–2005)	Blackburn
Ferrier, Kathleen (contralto) (1912–53)	Higher Walton
Finney, Tom (footballer) (1922–)	Preston
Fleming, Ambrose (physicist) (1849–1945)	Lancaster
Flintoff, Andrew (cricketer) (1977–)	Preston
Fogarty, Carl (motorcyclist) (1965–)	Blackburn
Hargreaves, James (inventor) (1720–78)	Oswaldtwistle
Hird, Thora (actress) (1911–2003)	Morecambe
Jeans, Sir James Hopwood (scientist) (1877–1946)	Ormskirk
Kenyon, James (cinematographer) (1850–1925)	Blackburn
McKellen, Ian (actor) (1939–)	Burnley
McShane, Ian (actor) (1942–)	Blackburn
Mitchell, Sagar (cinematographer) (1866–1952)	Blackburn
Morecambe, Eric (comedian) (1926–84)	Morecambe
Munro, Janet (actress) (1934–72)	Blackpool
Owen, Richard (palaeontologist) (1804–92)	Lancaster
Park, Nick (film animator) (1958–)	Preston
Service, Robert (poet) (1874–1958)	Preston
Tate, Henry (sugar magnate) (1819–99)	Chorley
Thewlis, David (actor) (1963–)	Blackpool
Thompson, Francis (poet) (1859–1907)	Preston
Winterbottom, Michael (film director) (1961–)	Blackburn

LEICESTERSHIRE

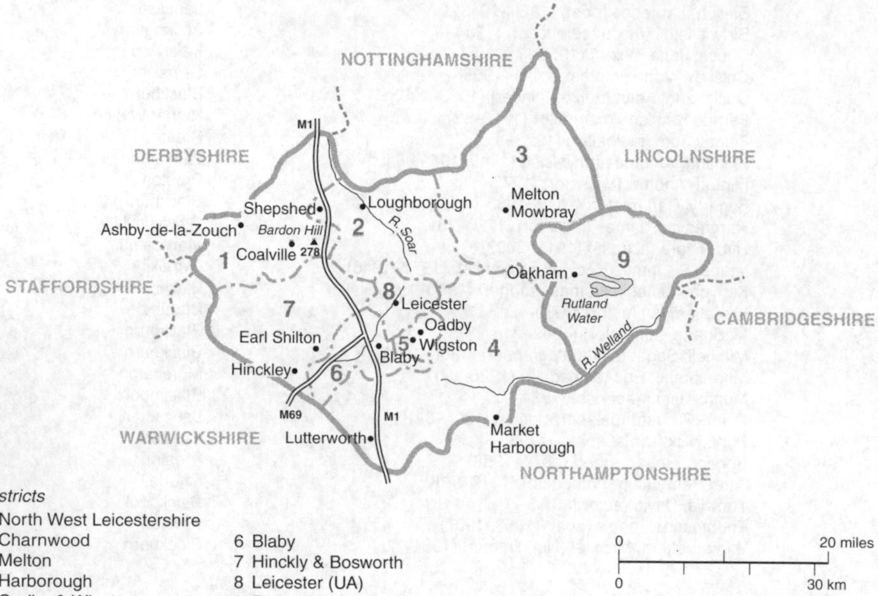
NOTTINGHAMSHIRE
DERBYSHIRE
LINCOLNSHIRE
STAFFORDSHIRE
CAMBRIDGESHIRE
WARWICKSHIRE
NORTHAMPTONSHIRE
M1
M69
Shepshed
Loughborough
Melton Mowbray
Ashby-de-la-Zouch
Bardon Hill
278
Coalville
R. Soar
Oakham
Rutland Water
Leicester
Oadby
Wigston
Earl Shilton
Hinckley
Blaby
R. Welland
Lutterworth
Market Harborough
1
2
3
4
5
6
7
8
9
0
20 miles
0
30 km

Districts

1 North West Leicestershire
2 Charnwood
3 Melton
4 Harborough
5 Oadby & Wigston
6 Blaby
7 Hinckly & Bosworth
8 Leicester (UA)
9 Rutland (UA)

Leicestershire is a landlocked county in central England, taking its name from the city of Leicester, traditionally its administrative centre. The county borders Lincolnshire to the northeast, Northamptonshire to the southeast, Warwickshire to the southwest, Staffordshire to its westernmost extremity, Derbyshire to the northwest and Nottinghamshire to the north. The largest population centre is Leicester, followed by Loughborough. Other major towns include Ashby-de-la-Zouch, Coalville, Hinckley, Market Harborough, Melton Mowbray, Oadby and Wigston.

The area was prominent in the Roman period, Leicester itself being the site of the major town of Ratae; in the 9th century it became part of the Danelaw, and evidence of Danish occupation can be seen in the many place-names ending in -by. Leicestershire was recorded in Domesday Book in four wapentakes (the Danish division of land corresponding to the Anglo-Saxon hundred). These – Guthlaxton, Framland, Goscote and Gartree – later became hundreds; Goscote was divided into West Goscote and East Goscote and Sparkenhoe hundred was added. Leicestershire's external boundaries have changed little since the Domesday survey although the Measham–Donisthorpe exclave of Derbyshire was exchanged in 1888 for the Netherseal area, and the expansion of Market Harborough caused Little Bowden, previously in Northamptonshire, to be annexed at the same time. In 1974, the Local Government Act 1972 abolished the county borough status of the city of Leicester, converting it to an administrative district of Leicestershire. This action was reversed on 1 April 1996, when Leicester became a unitary authority.

The small county of Rutland, historically a county in its own right, was absorbed by Leicestershire in 1974, although remaining a ceremonial county. On 1 April 1996 it too became a unitary authority, although unusually it has been renamed 'Rutland County Council', which means the full legal name of the council is Rutland County Council District Council.

Leicestershire is one of the sites of the National Forest, a regeneration project initiated in 1990 with the aim of transforming 200 sq miles (520 sq km) of land in Leicestershire, Derbyshire and Staffordshire into woodland; a large area in the northwest of the county, including the upland region known as Charnwood Forest and the former coal mining area around Coalville, is included.

Leicester lies on the River Soar and at the edge of the National Forest, close to the M1 motorway. According to Geoffrey of Monmouth, the city of Kaerleir (Leicester) was founded by King Leir, a mythical king of the Britons. He was supposedly buried by Queen Cordelia in a chamber beneath the Soar near the city dedicated to the Roman god Janus, where every year people celebrated his feast day near Leir's tomb. Shakespeare's *King Lear* is loosely based on this story. Leicester is one of the oldest cities in England, with a history going back 2000 years. The city was first known as Ratae Coritanorum and was inhabited by the Celtic Corieltauvi tribe, being the capital of a territory in what is now known as the East Midlands. The Roman city of Ratae Corieltauvorum, founded c. AD 50 as a military settlement on the Fosse Way Roman road, grew into an important trading centre and one of the largest towns in Roman Britain.

Leicester had become a town of considerable importance by medieval times. It was mentioned in Domesday Book as *civitas* (city), but lost its city status in the 11th century owing to power struggles between the Church and the aristocracy. It eventually became a city again in 1919, and the Church of St Martin became Leicester Cathedral in 1927. Leicester played a significant role in the history of England when, in 1265, Simon de Montfort forced Henry III to hold the first Parliament of England at the now-ruined Leicester Castle.

With the construction of the Grand Union Canal in the 1790s linking the city to London and Birmingham, Leicester began rapid industrialisation. By 1832, railways had arrived with the opening of the Leicester and Swannington Railway, which provided a supply of coal to the town from nearby collieries. By 1840 the Midland Counties Railway had linked Leicester to the national railway network, which further boosted industrial growth. By the 1860s a direct rail link to London (St Pancras) had been established with the completion of the Midland Main Line. The Great Central Railway arrived in 1900, providing an alternative route to London. However, this closed in 1966. Leicester expanded throughout the 19th century, most notably in 1892 annexing Belgrave, Aylestone, Knighton and North Evington. The city's current boundaries were established in 1935, when it absorbed the remainder of Evington, Humberstone, Beaumont Leys, along with part of Braunstone. It became a county borough when these were established in 1889, but, as with all county boroughs, was abolished in 1974, becoming an ordinary district of Leicestershire until regaining its unitary status in 1997.

Major industries in Leicester today include food processing, hosiery, footwear, knitwear, engineering, electronics, printing and plastics. The city centre is mainly Victorian with some later developments; its heart is the Clock Tower, which lies at the intersection of five routes into the city – High Street, Churchgate, Belgrave Gate, Humberstone Gate and Gallowtree Gate. Leicester has a large ethnic minority population, mainly from the Indian subcontinent. There are many Hindu mandirs, Sikh gurdwaras and Muslim mosques around the city, mostly converted from existing buildings. The Jain Temple (Jain Centre) is near the city centre. The area around Belgrave Road, known as the Golden Mile, contains many Indian restaurants, jewellery shops, and other shops catering to the large Asian community. The annual Diwali celebrations are also held here and at the nearby Abbey Park, and are the biggest outside India. There is also a large population of Afro-Caribbean descent (mainly from Antigua and Barbuda, Montserrat and Jamaica), the community being centred around Highfields to the southeast of the city centre, and Leicester plays host to the second largest Caribbean carnival in the UK after Notting Hill. While some wards in the northeast of the city are more than 70 per cent Asian, those in the west and south are all over 70 per cent white. The city is set to become the first major urban area in the UK with a non-white ethnic majority population, by the time of the next census in 2011.

Rutland, traditionally England's smallest county, is bounded on the west and north by Leicestershire, northeast by Lincolnshire, and southeast by Northamptonshire. The only towns are Oakham, the county town, and Uppingham. At the centre of the county is the large reservoir known as Rutland Water, an important nature reserve with a similar surface area to Windermere. Rutland's older cottages are built from white limestone and many have roofs of Collyweston slate. The county once supplied iron ore to the steelworks at Corby, Northamptonshire, but these quarries closed in the 1960s. Agriculture thrives with much wheat farming on the rich soil. Rutland is also home to two RAF bases – RAF Cottesmore and RAF Wittering. The titles of Earl and Duke of Rutland are derived from the historic county of Rutland, the titles being merged when the Earl of Rutland was elevated to the status of duke in 1703. The family seat of the dukes of Rutland is at Belvoir Castle.

Leicestershire	Population			Area	
Districts	*male*	*female*	*total*	*sq miles*	*sq km*
Blaby	44,851	45,401	90,252	50	130
Charnwood	76,318	77,144	153,462	108	279
Harborough	37,969	38,590	76,559	228	592
Hinckley & Bosworth	49,166	50,975	100,141	115	297
Melton	23,534	24,332	47,866	186	481
North West Leicestershire	42,240	43,263	85,503	108	279
Oadby & Wigston	27,190	28,605	55,795	9	24
Leicester Unitary Authority	134,782	145,139	279,921	28	73
Rutland Unitary Authority	17,753	16,810	34,563	147	382
Total	453,803	470,259	924,062	980	2538

Local Attractions and Information

Abbey Pumping Station — Corporation Road, Leicester. An industrial building formerly used to pump sewage to the treatment works at Beaumont Leys. It operated from 1891 until 1964, opening as a museum in 1972. The four Woolf compound rotative beam engines were built in Leicester by Gimson & Co.; at the time of their construction these engines were considered somewhat old-fashioned, as many steam engine designers had turned their attention to horizontal and early vertical designs. Three of the four engines have been restored to working condition by the Leicester Museums Technology Association. Tel: 0116 299 5111.

Administrative headquarters — **Leicestershire**: County Hall, Glenfield, Leicester LE3 8RA. Tel: 0116 232 3232.
Leicester: City Council, New Walk Centre, Welford Place LE1 6ZG. Tel: 0116 252 7000.
Rutland: County Council, Catmose, Oakham, Rutland LE15 6HP. Tel: 01572 722577.

Altar Stones — Markfield, 7 miles (11km) northwest of Leicester. A 4 acre (1.6ha) outcrop of volcanic rock, designated a Regionally Important Geological Site, and providing views over Charnwood Forest. Tel: 01509 890048.

Ashby-de-la-Zouch Canal — A 22 mile (35km) long canal, opened in 1804, which runs from Bedworth in Warwickshire, via Hinckley, to the Leicestershire village of Snarestone. It originally linked the coalfields around Ashby-de-la-Zouch with the Coventry Canal, but the final 8 miles (13km) of the route north to Moira, just outside Ashby, were closed during the 20th century due to mining subsidence.

Ashby-de-la-Zouch Castle — South Street, Ashby-de-la-Zouch. A Norman hall founded in the 12th century by the Zouch family. The hall was converted into a castle in 1474 by Lord Hastings, the notable Hastings Tower being added at this time. The castle was besieged by Parliamentary troops for over a year during the Civil War and slighted in 1648. Mary, Queen of Scots is said to have stayed in the castle twice while being moved around the country. Now owned by English Heritage. Tel: 01530 273956.

Attenborough Building — The tallest building on the campus of the University of Leicester (see Universities), housing the arts and humanities departments. The building comprises three elements: an 18-storey tower block containing 270 offices and tutorial rooms; a low-rise building, known within the university as the Attenborough Seminar Block, containing seminar rooms and computing facilities; and an underground area housing two large lecture theatres and the University Film Theatre. It was designed by Arup Associates and constructed 1968–70 with Ove Arup as the chief engineers. The building was named after Frederick Attenborough, principal of University College 1931–51, and father of Richard and David Attenborough.

Battle of Bosworth Field — Aka the Battle of Bosworth or Redemore/Redesmore, an important battle during the Wars of the Roses in the 15th century, fought on 22 August 1485 between the Yorkist Richard III, last of the Plantagenet dynasty, and the Lancastrian contender for the crown, Henry Tudor, 2nd Earl of Richmond (later Henry VII). It ended in Richard's defeat and death and the establishment of the Tudor dynasty, the battle turning on the movements of the Stanleys. Historically, Bosworth is considered to have marked the end of the Wars of the Roses, although further battles were fought in the years that followed as Yorkist pretenders unsuccessfully sought to reclaim the crown. Traditionally, the Battle of Bosworth Field was fought on Ambion Hill near the village of Shenton. This has been disputed by historians; it has been suggested that the contemporary name, the Battle of Redemore (= reedy moor), indicates that the battle took place on low, wet ground. Other evidence places the battle near the village of Dadlington, a few miles to the south, or Atherstone in Warwickshire.

Battlefield Line Railway — Shackerstone, 13 miles (21km) west of Leicester. A heritage railway running from Shackerstone to Shenton, near Bosworth Field. Opened in 1992, it operates on part of the former Ashby & Nuneaton Joint Railway, opened in 1873. Tel: 01827 880754.

Beacon Hill — 1¼ miles (2km) west of Woodhouse Eaves, 3 miles (5km) south of Loughborough. One of several beacon hills in the UK. With a maximum height of 814ft (248m), it is the second highest point in Leicestershire after Bardon Hill and consists of over 100 acres (40ha) of heath and woodland.

Beaumanor Hall — Woodhouse, 2 miles (3km) south of Loughborough. A 19th century house on the edge of Charnwood Forest, built for the prominent Leicestershire Herrick family who owned the estate until just before World War II. In addition to the hall, the estate consisted of several farms and cottages, St Mary's in the Elms church, the vicarage (Garats Hay) and 350 acres (140ha) of parkland. In 1939 the War Department requisitioned the estate, including Garats Hay. The park became the home of the War Office 'Y' Group, a secret listening station where encrypted enemy signals were intercepted and sent to the famous Station X at Bletchley Park (see Buckinghamshire) for decoding. At the end of the war in 1945 the estate was returned to Lt. Col. Assheton Penn Curzon-Howe-Herrick, who in 1946 decided to dispose of his assets. The War Department bought Beaumanor Hall and Garats Hay as well as some of the grounds; these were purchased by Leicestershire County Council in the 1970s. The hall's elaborate ceilings, woodwork and stonework have since been restored and it is now used as a conference centre. Tel: 01509 890119.

Belgrave Hall
Church Road, Belgrave, Leicester. Queen Anne-style house built in 1709, with 2 acres (0.8ha) of walled gardens. Opened to the public in 1936 as a museum, today Belgrave Hall shows the contrasting lifestyles of an upper middle-class family and domestic servants in Victorian society. In 1999, it became famous when two ghostly figures were supposedly recorded on security cameras outside the hall. Tel: 0116 266 6590.

Bellfoundry Museum
See John Taylor Bell Founders

Belvoir Castle
10 miles (16km) northeast of Melton Mowbray. (There has always been some confusion as to whether the castle is situated in Lincolnshire or Leicestershire. The grid reference, SK820337, suggests a Leicestershire domain although the postal address is given as Grantham.) The ancestral home of the Dukes of Rutland since the 16th century, Belvoir (pronounced Beaver) Castle is situated on a site overlooking the Vale of Belvoir. The original Norman motte and bailey castle was founded by Robert de Todeni in the 11th century. The castle was destroyed by King John but has been rebuilt several times. A notable Royalist stronghold during the Civil War, it eventually passed into the hands of the Dukes of Rutland and was rebuilt following a fire, its present façade dating from the 19th century. The architect James Wyatt was chiefly responsible for its sham-Gothic restructuring from 1816; the building bears a superficial resemblance to a medieval castle, with a central tower reminiscent of Windsor Castle. The castle was used as a film location for *The Da Vinci Code* (2006), representing Castel Gandolfo (the Pope's summer residence). Currently the family home of the 11th Duke, Duchess and their family, the castle and grounds feature an art collection, spring and rose gardens, the Royal Lancers Museum and the Regency Nursery and School Room. Tel: 01476 871000.

Billa Barra Hill
9 miles (15km) northwest of Leicester. A Local Nature Reserve, part of the National Forest, this 47 acre (17ha) site has three distinct areas. The hilltop has acid grassland (rare in the county) and old conifer planting; the pools area, the result of quarrying, is home to a rare lichen only found at one other site in the county; and the lower grassland slopes are being planted with native broad-leaved trees which will be used as local provenance seed stock. Tel: 01455 238141.

Bradgate Park
5 miles (8km) northwest of Leicester. An area of parkland, covering 850 acres (340ha), once part of the estate of 16th century Bradgate House, the birthplace of Lady Jane Grey. The ruins of the house still stand within the park. The folly known as **Old John** was built in 1784 by the Grey family of Groby, and was originally an observation tower built to give ladies a view of a racecourse which circled the top of the hill. It is well known for its 'mug-shape', the 'handle' of which was added later, apparently in memory of a beer-loving family retainer. The River Lin runs through the park, flowing into Cropston Reservoir which was constructed within the park. To the north lies the ancient woodland of Swithland Wood (see separate entry). Tel: 0116 236 2713.

Castle Donington Museum
Apiary Gate, Castle Donington. A local history museum occupying the ground floor of a 17th century stone-built former farmhouse. The attached garden has a small outdoor display of artefacts. Tel: 01332 811549. Note that the Leicestershire village of Castle Donington is not to be confused with the ruined medieval castle situated in the village of Donnington, Berkshire.

Charnwood Forest
5 miles (8km) southwest of Loughborough. A tract of undulating, rocky upland in northwest Leicestershire. It is mostly barren, though there are some extensive tracts of woodland, and mostly lies over 600ft (180m) above sea level, the area exceeding this height being about 6100 acres (2500ha). Its highest point is Bardon Hill at 912ft (278m), also the highest point in the county. On its western edge lies a former coalfield, with Coalville and other former mining towns; a substantial granite-quarrying industry still operates in the area.

Charnwood Museum
Granby Street, Loughborough. Museum with permanent exhibitions covering the history of Charnwood Forest. Also featured is a recreation of a Victorian grocer's shop, with artefacts dating back to the 1860s. Tel: 01509 233754.

Clock Tower
Eastgates, Leicester. The Haymarket Memorial Clock Tower (known better as simply the Clock Tower) was built in 1868 as a memorial for four benefactors of Leicester – Simon De Montfort, William Wyggeston, Sir Thomas White and Alderman Gabriel Newton. It formed what is thought to be the first traffic island in England. Architect Joseph Goddard designed the tower, which was constructed of Ketton stone by stonemason Samuel Barfield. The clock, supplied by Gillet and Bland of Croydon, has since been electrified. Underneath the Clock Tower is a large inspection chamber for the city's sewage system; this chamber was opened to the public when the area was pedestrianised in 1972. Tel: 0116 257 1080.

Coleorton Wood
3 miles (5km) northwest of Coalville. The 15 acre (6ha) reclaimed site of the former Coleorton (or 'Bug and Wink') Colliery, now planted with mixed woodland as part of the National Forest. Tel: 0116 265 6918.

De Montfort Hall
Granville Road, Leicester. A music and performance venue situated near Victoria Park, and named after Simon de Montfort, Earl of Leicester. Built in 1913, its indoor auditorium capacity is approximately 2000, and the hall contains a restored pipe organ, the only surviving concert organ built by local organ builders Stephen Taylor and Son. Most of the hall's events take place indoors; the programme of events ranges from jazz, ballet, comedy and opera to world and roots music, West End musicals and classical music featuring the Philharmonic Orchestra which has been resident at the hall since 1997. Tel: 0116 233 3111.

Dimminsdale Nature Reserve 4 miles (6km) northeast of Ashby-de-la-Zouch. A Site of Special Scientific Interest located partly in Leicestershire and partly in Derbyshire adjacent to the Staunton Harold estate, and covering 16 acres (6.5ha). Dimminsdale was once a secluded valley where a small stream cut a course through rolling heath. Mining of the underlying limestone and later of lead produced a wild landscape of pits, pools, cliffs, banks and tips, abandoned to nature when the mining industry closed in the early 20th century. Today it is in the care of the Leicestershire and Rutland Wildlife Trust and is notable for its displays of snowdrops. Tel: 0116 270 2999.

Donington Park 2 miles (3km) southwest of Castle Donington, 8 miles (13km) northwest of Loughborough. Owned by millionaire motoring enthusiast Tom Wheatcroft, Donington Park is the location of a motor racing track and is also used for music festivals. First opened in 1931, the track was initially used for motorcycle races. In 1937 and 1938 it staged Grands Prix, the race winners being Bernd Rosemeyer and Tazio Nuvolari, both in Auto Union Silver Arrows. More recently it has held meetings of the British Touring Car Championship, British Superbikes and MotoGP as well as, most famously, the 1993 European Grand Prix – a race won by the late Ayrton Senna and described by AtlasF1 as the 'Drive of the Decade'. There is a memorial to Senna in the grounds. The park is also home to the Donington Grand Prix Collection, opened in 1973, the largest collection of Grand Prix cars in the world. Tel: 01332 811027.

Donington le Heath Manor House Donington le Heath, 1 mile (1.6km) southwest of Coalville. Restored 13th century manor house with period herb and flower gardens, maze and orchard. Tel: 0116 265 8326.

Earl Shilton Castle Church Street, Earl Shilton, 9 miles (15km) southwest of Leicester. Norman earthwork motte and bailey fortress founded by the Earl of Leicester in the late 11th century. The large flat-topped circular motte retains part of its ditch and to the south are the remains of a mutilated bailey rampart. The timber castle was dismantled in the late 12th century; the stone gateway that now defends the motte is a modern folly.

East Midlands Airport 7 miles (11km) northwest of Loughborough. The former RAF Castle Donington, closed in 1946, opened as an airport in 1965. Today it is served by several budget airlines, including bmibaby (for which East Midlands is one of its main bases), Ryanair and easyJet, with services to various internal and European destinations. East Midlands Airport is owned by the Manchester Airports Group (MAG). The proximity of East Midlands Airport (formerly Nottingham East Midlands Airport) to Derby, plus the fact that it is in Leicestershire and the traditional rivalry between the three cities, meant that there was a great deal of local controversy about the airport's decision to append Nottingham to its name in 2004; the name was changed again two years later. Tel: 0871 919 9000.

Evington Park 2 miles (3km) east of Leicester. Built for the Burnaby family in 1836, the house has since had several owners and during World War II was the base for Evington Home Guard Platoon. The house and its grounds were bought by Leicester Corporation in 1947 and opened to the public in 1948. Tel: 0116 252 7000.

Foxton Locks 3 miles (5km) west of Market Harborough. Ten canal locks consisting of two 'staircases' each of five locks, located on the Leicester line of the Grand Union Canal and named after the nearby village of Foxton. Staircase locks enable a canal to climb a steep hill, and consist of groups of locks opening directly from one to the next. Now Grade II* listed, Foxton Locks are the largest flight of such locks on the English canal system.

Gilmorton Castle Church Lane, Gilmorton, 11 miles (18km) south of Leicester. Norman motte and bailey timber castle; the remains of the large flat-topped motte are encased by a wide moat.

Grantham Canal See Lincolnshire

Great Central Railway A heritage railway running between Birstall, north of Leicester, and Ruddington, Nottinghamshire. Operating on part of the former London Extension of the Manchester, Sheffield and Lincolnshire Railway (renamed the Great Central Railway in 1897), and the only standard gauge heritage railway in the UK to have double track, the Great Central Railway is split into two sections. The southern section runs for $8\frac{1}{2}$ miles (13.25km) between Loughborough and the northern outskirts of Leicester, terminating at a new station named Leicester North, built to the south of the demolished Belgrave and Birstall station. The northern section, the Great Central Railway (Nottingham), runs for 9 miles (15km) between Loughborough and the Nottingham Transport Heritage Centre at Ruddington, Nottinghamshire. In the future it is intended to connect the two railways by means of a bridge which will be reinstated at Loughborough to cross the Midland Main Line. Tel: 01509 230726.

Guru Nanak Sikh Museum Holy Bones, Leicester. Attached to the Guru Nanak Gurdwara, the museum holds valuable collections of paintings, coins, handwritten manuscripts and spectacular models of shrines, all illustrating the origins and development of Sikh history and culture. Established in 1992, it was the first Sikh museum in Europe. Tel: 0116 262 8606.

Hallaton Castle $\frac{1}{2}$ mile (0.8km) west of Hallaton, 7 miles (11km) northeast of Market Harborough. A motte and bailey castle dating possibly to the 12th century with additional rectangular enclosure (now surviving as an earthwork), 118ft (36m) high and 630ft (192m) in circumference, on which stood the keep. Only the earthworks exist today.

Hallaton Museum Hogg Lane, Hallaton, 7 miles (11km) northeast of Market Harborough. An award-winning museum with exhibitions relating to the history of the village, including Hallaton's unique traditional event, the annual Hare Pie Scrambling and Bottle Kicking – a contest between the villagers of Hallaton and Medbourne dating back to at least the late 1700s, in which the two teams seek to gain control of a small barrel of beer (the 'bottle'). It is preceded by the vigorous distribution of portions of hare pie. Tel: 01858 555416.

Harborough Museum Adam and Eve Street, Market Harborough. Housed in the former Symington Corset Factory, the museum's collections include corsetry as well as local history displays illustrating the other industries that were important in building Market Harborough, such as Symington Food Works and Harboro Rubber Company. Tel: 01858 821085.

High Cross — 1 mile (1.6km) west of Claybrooke Magna, 5 miles (8km) northwest of Lutterworth. The crossroads of the Roman roads of Watling Street and Fosse Way, once the site of the Roman fort of Venonis. This part of Watling Street is now a dual carriageway section of the A5, while the southern course of the Fosse Way is a B road, and the northern route is a track forming part of the long-distance path called the Leicestershire Round.

Highest point — Bardon Hill, near Coalville, at 912ft (278m). It is also the site of a radio mast.

Hinckley Castle — Trinity Lane, Hinckley, 13 miles (21km) southwest of Leicester. An 11th century earthwork motte and bailey fortress founded by Hugh de Grantmesnil and possibly refortified by Robert Bossu, 2nd Earl of Leicester, during the reign of King Stephen. Part of its impressive bailey survives but the motte was destroyed during later development.

Hough Mill — Swannington, 1 mile (1.6km) northwest of Coalville. Tower mill built in the late 1700s which operated until the early 20th century. The mill has been partly restored although as of 2008 it has no sails or fantail; its four levels contain two pairs of millstones and stone floor machinery. Tel: 01530 222330.

Humberstone Park — Uppingham Road, 3 miles (5km) east of Leicester. A 20 acre (8ha) park opened in 1925, one of six multi-purpose parks created in Leicester at that time (the others were Braunstone, Knighton, Evington, Rushey Fields and Aylestone). The house in the park was erected by Thomas Tertius Pageat, a local banker who became a leading figure in Lloyds. The letters TTP are inscribed above the door. Pageat built several other houses in the Humberstone area, all featuring distinctive, ornate chimneys. Tel: 0116 273 7726.

Interesting facts — Although born in York, architect **Joseph Aloysius Hansom** (1803–82) was living and working in Hinckley when he had the idea for a horse-drawn carriage. Patented in 1834, the first hansom cab travelled down Coventry Road, Hinckley in 1835 and soon became popular all over the world, until the automobile began to make its use redundant in the 1920s. **Leicester Market** on Market Place, just south of the Clock Tower (see separate entry), has been on the site for 700 years and is the largest covered market in Europe. Leicestershire-born clergyman **John Henley** (1692–1759), commonly known as 'Orator Henley', was one of the first entertainers and a precursor to the talk show hosts of today. **Rutlanders** were proverbially called Raddlemen. The events in several books by **Peter F Hamilton** (including *Misspent Youth* and *Mindstar Rising*) are situated in Rutland, where the author lives. The county's small size led ex-Monty Python man **Eric Idle** to name his 'solo' series *Rutland Weekend Television*. The series' most successful spin-off was the Beatles spoof band **The Rutles**. **Buzz Aldrin**, the second man to walk on the moon, visited Leicester's Space Centre in June 2005, while the first **Star Wars Day** was held at the Space Centre on 30 July 2005. Due to the event's popularity, Star Wars weekend was held on 12 and 13 November 2005. Leicestershire-born **Lady Jane Grey** (1537–54), a great-granddaughter of Henry VII, reigned as uncrowned queen regnant of England for nine days in July 1553. Leicester-born **Daniel Lambert** was a famous local figure, renowned for his corpulence. He weighed a colossal 52st 11lb (335kg) and measured a staggering 9ft 4in (284.5cm) around his waist. Examples of some of his clothes can be seen at Leicester's Newarke Houses Museum (see separate entry).

Jewry Wall — St Nicholas Circle, Leicester. The remaining wall of the public baths of Roman Leicester; the foundations of the baths are laid out in front of the wall. This rare example of Roman walling is nearly 2000 years old, and is the second largest piece of surviving civil Roman building in Britain (the largest is the 'great work' at Wroxeter, also part of a municipal baths complex). The Jewry Wall would have been the wall separating the gymnasium from the cold room. The attached museum details Leicester's ancient roots. Tel: 0116 225 4971.

John Taylor Bell Founders — Freehold Street, Loughborough. The world's largest working bell foundry, manufacturing bronze bells for use in clock towers, chimes, and carillons. Bell making has been carried out in the Loughborough area since the mid 14th century and activities were consolidated under the Taylor family in 1784. The foundry moved to its current location in 1839. On 1 July 2005, the company merged with the bellhanging firm Eayre & Smith to form Taylors Eayre & Smith. Great Paul of St Paul's Cathedral in London, the largest bell in Britain at 37,483lb (17,002kg), was cast at the foundry in 1881. The Bellfounders Museum, unique in the UK, shows craft techniques of moulding, casting, tuning and fitting up of bells. Tel: 01509 212241.

Jubilee Wood — Nanpantan, 2 miles (3km) southwest of Loughborough. A Site of Special Scientific Interest adjoining the ancient woodland of the Outwoods and consisting of 25 acres (10ha) of beech, sycamore, larch and alder woodland, with granite outcrops. Part of the National Forest, the woods were presented to Leicestershire County Council in 1977 to commemorate the Queen's Silver Jubilee. Tel: 01509 890048.

Kirby Muxloe Castle — Kirby Muxloe, 4 miles (6km) west of Leicester. Aka Kirby Castle. An unfinished 15th century fortified manor house begun in 1480 by William Hastings, 1st Baron Hastings, during the Wars of the Roses. Work stopped at the quadrangular castle when Hastings was executed in 1483 for treason by Richard III and was never resumed. The gatehouse and moat still stand and the site is now owned by English Heritage. Tel: 01162 386886.

Launde Abbey — $2^1/_2$ miles (4km) southwest of Braunston, 5 miles (8km) southwest of Oakham. An Elizabethan manor house in the scenic Leicestershire countryside, built on the site of an Augustinian priory founded in 1119. Thomas Cromwell, Henry VIII's chief minister and the man responsible for the Dissolution of the Monasteries, so liked its position that he wrote in his diary, 'Myself for Launde', but he was unable to take possession, being executed for treason in 1540. Building of the house commenced in the same year and Cromwell's son, Gregory, lived here for ten years with his wife Elizabeth, sister of Jane Seymour. The chapel within the house is thought to be all that remains of the original priory church; it features some medieval stained glass and a fine monument to Gregory Cromwell. The house is currently in use as a conference and retreat centre by the Church of England Diocese of Leicester.

Leicester Abbey Abbey Park Road, Leicester. The Abbey of St Mary de Pratis ('St Mary of the Meadows') was located in the riverside meadows of the Soar. Founded as a community of Augustinian canons in 1143 under the patronage of Robert le Bossu, Earl of Leicester, it became one of the largest and most influential landowners in Leicestershire, thanks to contributions by patrons such as the Earl of Winchester, Simon de Montfort, Alan la Zouche, Ernard de Bosco and the Crown. On his way south to stand trial in the Tower of London having been arrested on charges of treason, Cardinal Wolsey died in the abbey in 1530, and was buried within the abbey church. The abbey was dissolved in 1538; the site now lies within Abbey Park, laid out in 1877.

Leicester Botanic Gardens Glebe Road, Oadby, Leicester. The University of Leicester Harold Martin Botanic Garden is located close to the university's halls of residence. Founded in 1921, the garden was established on its present 16 acre (6.5ha) site in 1947 and is used for research purposes by the university's Biology Department. The gardens contain National Collections of skimmia, aubretia and hardy fuchsias. Tel: 0116 271 2933.

Leicester Castle Castle View, Leicester. Situated between Saint Nicholas Circle to the north and De Montfort University to the south, the castle complex contains – along with the remains of the castle itself – Castle Gardens, which run along the bank of the canal; the church of St Mary de Castro (see separate entry); the 12th century Great Hall, extensively altered as it was used as a courthouse until the 1990s; and the 15th century John of Gaunt's Cellar (once erroneously referred to as a dungeon), once part of the castle kitchens. The castle was built c.1068 and fortified in stone by Robert le Bossu, 2nd Earl of Leicester, in the mid 12th century; it was improved by Henry IV and Henry V. The remains now consist of a mound, originally 40ft (12m) high. Kings sometimes stayed at the castle (Edward I in 1300, and Edward II in 1310 and 1311; Richard III occupied it before the Battle of Bosworth Field – see separate entry – in 1485), but it was never greatly favoured, and was later used mainly for court sessions rather than as a residence. The Great Hall was also used for sessions of Parliament, notably the Parliament of Bats in 1426. The castle, the turret gateway (built c.1420), the Great Hall and John of Gaunt's Cellar are all Scheduled Ancient Monuments and listed buildings.

Leicester Cathedral Guildhall Lane, Leicester. A church dedicated to St Martin has been on the site for almost 1000 years. The present building dates to c.1086, when the older Saxon church was replaced by a Norman one. A memorial stone to Richard III is located in the central nave; he was buried in Greyfriars Church in Leicester, but according to local tradition his corpse was exhumed under orders from Henry VII and cast into the River Soar – some historians believe that his tomb and bones were destroyed with the dissolution of the church. The church was substantially restored in the 1860s and the 220ft (67m) spire added; it was elevated to a collegiate church in 1922, and after considerable redesigning by Sir Charles Nicholson was made a cathedral in 1927 with the recreation of the Diocese of Leicester. Tel: 0116 248 7400.

Leicester Comedy Festival An annual comedy festival held in a number of venues across Leicester, early in the year. The festival started in 1994 with 40 events in 23 venues throughout Leicestershire. Top stand-up comedians who have appeared since then include Jo Brand, Jack Dee, Dave Gorman, Rory Bremner, Alan Davies, Jeremy Hardy, Bill Bailey, Rhona Cameron, Johnny Vegas, Rich Hall, Jimmy Carr, Dara Ó Briain, Lee Mack, Dave Spikey, Harry Hill and Roseanne Barr.

Leicester Guildhall Guildhall Lane, Leicester. A timber-framed building that once acted as Leicester's town hall. The building dates from the 15th century (although parts are earlier) and is located in the old walled city. It was used first as the meeting place for the Guild of Corpus Christi and later by the Corporation of Leicester, which moved to the new Leicester Town Hall only in 1876. The Guildhall was later used as a police station and school before becoming a museum, and is now Grade I listed. Tel: 0116 253 2569.

Leicester Royal Infirmary Museum Knighton Street, Leicester. Housed within the Royal Infirmary, founded in 1771, the museum provides a written and pictorial history of the infirmary along with items illustrating the history of medicine and surgical equipment. Tel: 01858 565532.

Loughborough Carillon and War Memorial Museum Queens Park, Loughborough. The first grand carillon to be built as a war memorial in Britain. The 138 steps to the gallery of the 151ft (46m) tower can be climbed to view the Charnwood area. The belfry houses 47 bells which are rung for concerts on Thursday and Sunday afternoons. The tower also houses a museum of armed forces memorabilia from World Wars I and II. Tel: 01509 634704.

Lutterworth Museum Gilmorton Road, Lutterworth. A museum of local history with substantial collections of artefacts relating to Sir Frank Whittle – who invented the jet engine in the town – and John Wycliffe. Tel: 01455 555585.

Lyddington Bede House Bluecoat Lane, Lyddington, 7 miles (11km) south of Oakham, Rutland. Once the wing of a medieval palace owned by the Bishops of Lincoln, the Lyddington Bede House was converted in 1600 into almshouses for 12 'bedesmen', recipients of charity whose duty in return was to pray for their benefactor. Notable features include 16th century rooms, fireplace and the carved ceiling of the former Great Chamber. Now owned by English Heritage. Tel: 01572 822438.

Magazine Gateway Newarke Street, Leicester. Built c.1400, the Magazine Gateway was the main entrance into the Newarke area of the city, once a quiet religious precinct founded by the earls of Lancaster in the 14th century. The gate has no portcullis and its main purpose was to impress visitors rather than defend. The stone walls of the Newarke enclosed the church of St Mary of the Annunciation, Trinity Hospital and several priests' houses. The church of St Mary was closed by Edward VI in 1548 and demolished soon afterwards. The Newarke became an area where many of the richer citizens of

Leicester lived to escape local taxes. Several graffiti, one with a date of 1564, on the top floor of the Magazine suggest that it was used for a while as a prison. In the 1600s the gateway was used to store weapons and gunpowder for the town militia, this use giving the gateway its name. The Newarke was the scene of fierce fighting during the Civil War siege and capture of the town by Charles I in May 1645. However, the Magazine appears to have escaped serious damage. During restoration work in the 1960s two human skulls were found wedged inside the garderobe (toilet) shaft; their date and origin remain a mystery. The Magazine continued in use as an armoury by the Leicestershire Militia after the Civil War and in 1853 much of its outer stonework was replaced; in the 1890s a barracks and a drill hall for the militia were built alongside. These buildings were demolished in the 1960s as a result of a new road scheme; it was also planned to demolish the Magazine itself but fortunately protests saved the building for future generations.

Measham Museum High Street, Measham, 3 miles (5km) south of Ashby-de-la-Zouch. A small village museum illustrating the history of Measham and its inhabitants. Its central collection is the Dr Hart Collection, a series of documents and artefacts gathered together by two local doctors, father and son, depicting the village life over 2100 years. Tel: 01530 273956.

Melbourne Hall See Derbyshire

Melton Carnegie Museum Thorpe End, Melton Mowbray. Opened in 1977 in the former Carnegie Library, the museum has displays on the social, artistic and industrial history of the Melton area including works by sporting painter by John Ferneley, Stilton tableware, and fox hunting. Tel: 01664 569946.

Melton Mowbray A market town famous for pork pies and Stilton cheese, Melton Mowbray has also been a centre for fox hunting since the 1700s, when it was colonised by hunters seeking alternative accommodation to Quorndon Hall. It possesses an array of buildings and lodges once frequented by wealthy visitors during the hunting season. The Quorn Hunt is based at Kirby Bellars, 2 miles (3km) to the southwest. The phrase 'paint the town red' is said to have originated in Melton Mowbray, after the 3rd Marquis of Waterford and his companions painted several of the town's buildings red durinmg a night of riotous carousing in 1837. Melton Mowbray is the only Leicestershire market recorded by the Domesday survey of 1086. Five annual fairs also existed in the 19th century and a cheese fair lasted into the early 20th century.

Moira Furnace Museum Furnace Lane, Moira, 2 miles (3km) southwest of Ashby-de-la-Zouch. A 19th century iron-making blast furnace built by the Earl of Moira in 1804. The building has been preserved as a museum featuring lime kilns and craft workshops as well as a reconstructed Victorian domestic kitchen, and is in the care of English Heritage. Tel: 01283 224667.

Motto The motto of Leicester is *Semper eadem* (always the same). This was the motto of Elizabeth I, who granted a royal charter to the city.

Mount St Bernard's Abbey 1 mile (1.6km) east of Whitwick. A Cistercian monastery of the Strict Observance (Trappists), founded in 1835. Designed by Augustus Pugin and completed in 1844, Mount St Bernard's is the only abbey belonging to the Cistercian order remaining in England.

National Gas Museum Aylestone Road, Leicester. Established in 1977 in the Victorian clocktower and gatehouse of Leicester's original gas works, the museum now houses the biggest collection of gas-related artefacts in the world. The original production area can still be seen, and the variety of other displays include an all-gas 1920s kitchen. Tel: 0116 250 3190.

National Space Centre Exploration Drive, Leicester. Devoted to space science and astronomy and located on a site next to the River Soar, the building was designed by Nicholas Grimshaw and opened to the public on 30 June 2001. The Centre has on display the only Soyuz spacecraft in Western Europe (there is another at the Smithsonian Institution, Washington DC). The Beagle 2 Mars spacecraft was controlled from the centre's Landing Operations Control Centre. There are six main galleries: Into Space covers space hardware, from the rockets that take probes and humans into space, to the specially packaged food humans can eat during their stay, and includes a life-size mock-up of the European Space Agency's International Space Station Columbus module; Exploring the Universe covers exotic space topics from black holes to the age of the universe; the Planets Gallery covers the solar system, housing a real piece of Moon rock, brought back by the astronauts of the Apollo 17 mission, and a sizeable Martian meteorite; Orbiting Earth tells the story of how humans use satellites to improve their daily lives – from telecommunications to forecasting the weather; Space Now brings 'today's news from space', hosting live demonstrations, while a news desk provides visitors with an opportunity to ask space-related questions; Tranquillity Base allows visitors to experience what it would be like to live in a lunar base in the year 2025. The Space Theatre is an immersive planetarium-style digital theatre based on Digistar 3 technology. The National Space Centre hosts the government's official Near-Earth Object (NEO) information centre. An exhibition about NEOs can be found in the Planets gallery, with sister exhibitions in the Natural History Museum in London, and Our Dynamic Earth in Edinburgh. Tel: 0116 261 0261.

New Walk Museum and Art Gallery New Walk, Leicester. Two dinosaur skeletons are permanently installed in the museum, which is dedicated largely to natural history – a cetiosaur found in Rutland, and a plesiosaur from Barrow upon Soar. The art gallery's holdings include substantial collections of 20th century art, in particular German Expressionist works. Tel: 0116 225 4900.

Newarke Houses Museum The Newarke, Leicester. Museum composed of two historic houses, Wygston Chantry House and Skeffington House. William Wygston, Leicester's richest citizen, built the Chantry House in 1512 to house two chantry priests who sang masses for his soul in the nearby church of St Mary of the Annunciation. It is the only Elizabethan urban gentry house surviving in Leicestershire. Skeffington House is likely to have been built by Sir Thomas Skeffington, 1560–83. Originally a stone building only one room deep, it has been much enlarged over the centuries. The museum features displays on the social history of modern Leicester and the Royal Leicestershire Regiment, as well as a gallery dedicated to Daniel Lambert (see Interesting facts). Tel: 0116 225 4980.

Normanton Church Museum — Normanton, 5 miles (8km) southeast of Oakham, Rutland. The former church of St Matthew, built 1826–9, has become Rutland's best known landmark. Now standing half submerged on the edge of Rutland Water (see separate entry), it houses a museum illustrating the story of the reservoir. Exhibits include dinosaur fossils and an Anglo-Saxon skeleton. Tel: 01572 653026.

Oakham Castle — Market Place, Oakham, Rutland. Norman motte and bailey castle rebuilt in stone c.1180 by Wakelin de Ferrers. Although much has become ruinous, the Great Hall still stands and provides a fine example of late 12th century English architecture. A court is still held in the Great Hall every second year, maintaining a tradition that dates back to the Middle Ages. On display are medieval sculptures of musicians, while the 240 presentation horseshoes on the walls represent the unique custom (dating back to at least 1470) that every peer of the realm must forfeit a horseshoe to the Lord of the Manor on their first visit. Tel: 01572 758440.

Quenby Hall — 1/2 mile (0.8km) southeast of Hungarton, 7 miles (11km) east of Leicester. Set in 1400 acres (570ha) of hills and woods and built in 1627 as the home of the de Lisle family, in whose hands it has remained except for an interlude in the 20th century, Quenby Hall is one of relatively few Jacobean country houses in England to retain much of its interior unaltered. It is claimed that Stilton cheese was first made in the house's dairy. The Grade I listed house has been extensively restored and is now once again the private home of the de Lisle family. Tel: 0116 259 5224.

Rivers — **Avon** – see Warwickshire

The **Chater**, a tributary of the River Welland, rises near Whatborough Hill, flowing east past the sites of Sauvey Castle and Launde Abbey (see separate entries) before crossing the county boundary with Rutland. It continues east, to the north of Ridlington, Preston, and then between Manton to its north and Wing to its south. At North Luffenham, it meets a stream that rises south of Ridlington, continuing northeast through Ketton before meeting the Welland.

The **Eye Brook** rises near Skeffington and flows east to form the county boundary between Leicestershire and Rutland, afterwards passing between Belton-in-Rutland to the north and Allexton to the south. It then proceeds southeast. Between Stoke Dry and Caldecott it is dammed to form the Eyebrook Reservoir. Soon after this, it joins the River Welland (here forming the border with Northamptonshire).

The **Rothley Brook** first becomes noticeable after Thornton Reservoir (see separate entry). It flows through Desford and Ratby before being joined by a tributary from Kirby Muxloe just before Glenfield.

The **Soar**, a tributary of the River Trent, rises near Hinckley and flows through Leicester (where it is joined by the Grand Union Canal at Aylestone), Barrow-on-Soar, Loughborough and Kegworth, before joining the Trent near Ratcliffe-on-Soar in Nottinghamshire. According to legend, the body of Richard III was thrown into the Soar after his death. The bridge carrying the A47 across the Soar at Leicester is known as 'King Richard's Bridge'.

The **Welland** is 35 miles (56km) long and has been a main waterway across the part of the Fens called South Holland for thousands of years. It rises near Market Harborough, then flows east through Lincolnshire to Ketton, Stamford, The Deepings, Crowland, Cowbit and Spalding, and into the Wash at Fosdyke Bridge. The **Wreake** is a tributary of the River Soar. Rising near Stapleford, it flows southwest, passing through Melton Mowbray, Frisby on the Wreake and Ratcliffe on the Wreake, before meeting the Soar near Syston. In its upper reaches it is called the River Eye and it becomes the Wreake below Melton Mowbray, near Sysonby Lodge. The name Wreake was given by the Danish invaders of Leicestershire, who probably arrived in the district via the Trent, the Soar and finally the Wreake, the name being an indication of the river's tortuous, meandering course.

Rockingham Castle — See Northamptonshire

Rutland County Museum — Catmose Street, Oakham, Rutland. A museum of agricultural and rural life in Rutland including farm equipment, machinery and wagons, domestic collections and local archaeology. Housed in a former indoor riding school for the Rutland Fencibles, a volunteer cavalry regiment raised by the Noels in 1794, its exhibits include the Brooke Reliquary, a rare 13th century enamel casket from Rutland's only priory. Tel: 01572 758440.

Rutland Railway Museum — 1 mile (1.6km) west of Cottesmore, 4 miles (6km) northeast of Oakham, Rutland. The museum is dedicated to telling the story of the railways in industry, especially in local ironstone quarrying. Features include a large collection of diesel and steam locomotives. Trains operate along a 3/4 mile (1.2km) demonstration line. Tel: 01572 813203.

Rutland Water — 2 miles (3km) east of Oakham, Rutland. Known as Empingham Reservoir until its official opening in 1976, Rutland Water was created by damming the River Gwash to provide a reserve supply of water for the East Midlands. One of the largest artificial lakes in Europe, by surface area it is the largest reservoir in England, covering 3100 acres (1240ha), although its capacity is exceeded by that of Kielder Water. It is a major nature reserve, providing an overwintering site for wildfowl and a breeding site for ospreys.

Sapcote Castle — Sapcote, 4 miles (6km) east of Hinckley. Norman earthwork motte and bailey fortress founded by the Basset family. There are few visible remains; the motte was levelled in 1778 and stands just 3ft (1m) high, while the bailey ditches have been filled in and are now only marks in the grass. To the west are indications of a late medieval moat. The two sites once formed a large manorial complex.

Sauvey Castle — 5 miles (8km) southwest of Oakham, Rutland. Medieval ringwork and bailey castle built in the reign of King Stephen (1135–54), including a surrounding ditch and dam which survive as earthworks. The stone foundations of the original buildings and curtain wall still exist. It was once the favoured hunting lodge of King John. Mentioned in 1216, 1226 and 1246, it was probably ruinous by the 15th century. The castle has an unusual layout consisting of two enclosures: a

	rectangular bailey on the western side and a smaller oval enclosure on the east. This smaller enclosure contained the original stone castle which can be seen exposed in several places, especially near the entrance.
Shawell Castle	Shawell, 3 miles (5km) south of Lutterworth. Adulterine 12th century earthwork motte and bailey fortress founded during the civil war in the reign of King Stephen. The low circular flat-topped motte retains part of its surrounding ditch, and some distance to the south stands a small circular earthwork mound, part of a series of defensive bailey earthworks.
St Mary de Castro	Castle Street, Leicester. Situated near Leicester Castle, today St Mary de Castro is the parish church for the Church of England's Diocese of Leicester. It was founded in 1107 when Henry I granted the land and castle to Robert de Beaumont. Robert established within the castle bailey a collegiate church served by a dean and 12 canons in honour of the Virgin Mary and All Souls and as a chantry chapel for his soul and those of his family, and for the first three Norman kings (some legends suggest that Robert merely refurbished a Saxon church of St Mary which had existed before the Norman Conquest). He endowed this and four other churches with £6 of his income and land in or near the city. These endowments were all transferred soon after by his heir to his own new foundation of Leicester Abbey. The church was rebuilt in the 1180s and a spire was added in 1400. It was here, in 1366, that Geoffrey Chaucer married Philippa de Roet, a lady-in-waiting to Edward III's queen, Philippa of Hainault, and a sister of Katherine Swynford who later (c.1396) became the third wife of Chaucer's friend and patron, John of Gaunt. Henry VI was knighted in the church in 1426 when he was an infant.
St Nicholas Church	St Nicholas Circle, Leicester. The oldest place of worship in Leicester, the parish church of St Nicholas is situated next to the Jewry Wall (see separate entry). To the east is the site of the Roman forum. Parts of the church fabric are thought to date from AD 880, and a recent architectural survey suggested possible Roman building work. The tower is Norman. The church was in an extremely poor condition by 1825, and plans were made for its demolition. Instead, it was extensively renovated between 1875 and 1884, including the building of a new north aisle. Renovation continued into the 20th century. Despite being some distance from the campus, it is the official church of the University of Leicester. Tel: 0116 248 7471.
Sport	
cricket	**Leicestershire County Cricket Club**, one of the 18 English first-class counties, was founded in 1879. The club joined the County Championship in 1895 and have been winners of the competition in 1975, 1996 and 1998. Their headquarters is at Grace Road (named after the legendary W G Grace) off Aylestone Road, Leicester. The ground is also home to a museum of county cricket. Tel: 0870 282 1879.
football	**Leicester City** were founded in 1884 as Leicester Fosse – as they played on a field by the Fosse Road – joining the Football Association in 1894. Variously nicknamed The Foxes, Fosse, and traditionally, The Filberts (after Filbert Street, their home ground between 1891 and 2002), they play home matches in a blue and white strip at the Walkers Stadium, Filbert Way, Leicester. The all-seater stadium holds 32,500 and is named after sponsors Walkers, a former shirt sponsor of Leicester; it was officially opened by former Leicester striker Gary Lineker on 23 July 2002. During their absence from Wembley Stadium, the England national football team played a home friendly against Serbia and Montenegro at the stadium on 3 June 2003. Tel: 0870 040 6000. Non-league clubs include **Hinckley United** (formed 1997).
horse racing	**Leicester** racecourse, Oadby, Leicester, is a right-handed oval course of $1^{3}/_{4}$ miles (2.8km) hosting both National Hunt and Flat racing. Tel: 0116 271 6515.
rugby union	**Leicester Tigers** were founded in 1880 and play in rugby union's Premiership. The most successful English club of the professional era, Leicester won the Heineken Cup twice and the league five times in the late 1990s and early 2000s under the captaincy of Martin Johnson, winning the league again in 2006–07. Their home colours are green shirts with thin red and white hoops, and white shorts. The club plays its home games at Welford Road Stadium, Leicester, to which they moved in 1892 and which has been their home ever since. Mostly built in the 1930s, the stadium has a capacity of 16,500, making it the largest purpose-built club rugby ground in England. Tel: 0870 128 3430.
Stanford Hall (Lutterworth)	5 miles (8km) southeast of Lutterworth. Ancestral home of the Cave family, the hall was built in the 1690s in William and Mary style for Sir Roger Cave on the site of an earlier manor house. Aviation pioneer Percy Pilcher built some of his early gliders here in the 1890s, as well as a powered flying machine that many historians believe was capable of flight, but he was killed nearby in an accident in 1899 before he could try it. A replica of Pilcher's 'Hawk' glider is exhibited at the hall. Other exhibits include a motorcycle museum. The house is also used for classic car shows, including the Wartburg/Trabant/IFA Club Rally. Tel: 01788 860250.
Stanford Hall (Stanford-on-Soar)	2 miles (3km) north of Loughborough, on the border with Nottinghamshire. Built 1771–4 for Charles Vere Dashwood, in the 20th century the house was the home of cricket-loving philanthropist Sir Julien Cahn. After Cahn's death in 1944 the house was bought by the Co-operative Union and used as a training centre. A theatre built by Cahn in the 1930s, now Grade II* listed, seating 350, has been used regularly for theatrical and musical productions. Chek Whyte, of television's *Secret Millionaire* fame, bought the complex in 2007 and is considering a wide range of options for the site.
Staunton Harold Church	5 miles (8km) northeast of Ashby-de-la-Zouch. Set in parkland and dating from 1653, one of the few churches built between the outbreak of the Civil War and the Restoration, representing an open act of defiance to Cromwell's Puritan regime by its creator, Sir Robert Shirley. The interior retains its original 17th century cushions, carved woodwork and painted ceilings. Now owned by the National Trust. Tel: 01332 863822.

Swithland Wood — 5 miles (8km) northwest of Leicester. An area of public woodland, just north of Bradgate Park (see separate entry) and between the villages of Woodhouse Eaves and Swithland in Charnwood Forest. The 146 acres (59ha) of woodland contain a flooded disused quarry (with an inscription on the side recording the Rotary Club's purchase and donation of the site to the people of Leicestershire in 1931), Swithland slate being a traditional local roofing material. The quarry is now used occasionally for scuba diving. The woods themselves are mixed, principally mature oak, ash, lime and holly. In spring large areas of the woodland floor are covered by bluebells and other spring flowers. Tel: 0116 236 2713.

Thornton Reservoir — 8 miles (13km) northwest of Leicester. The 75 acre (30ha) reservoir, set among farmland and woodland, was completed in 1854 to supply water to the Hinckley area. Owned by Severn Trent Water, it is not currently used as a source of water, and now provides wildlife habitat and game fishing. Tel: 01332 865081.

Twycross Zoo — 18 miles (29km) west of Leicester. Founded in 1963, and notable for having the largest primate collection in the world, including breeding populations of bonobos (the UK's only collection of our closest living relatives), chimpanzees, gorillas and orang-utans, along with numerous monkey and lemur species. The zoo also holds collections of many other animals, including endangered species such as the Amur leopard. There are elephants, sea lions, birds and various wildfowl. Tel: 01827 880250/880440.

Universities — **De Montfort University**, formerly Leicester Polytechnic (itself the amalgamation of the Leicester Colleges of Technology and Art), was awarded university status in 1992 and is one of two universities situated in Leicester. Its 20,000 students are served by two campuses, the City Campus in central Leicester and Charles Frears Campus 1 mile (1.6km) to the southeast. It has five faculties: Art and Design, Business and Law, Computer Sciences and Engineering, Health and Life Sciences, and Humanities. The Institute of Creative Technologies was opened in 2006 to enable research at the interface between science, technology and the arts. Former students include actor Charles Dance, artist David Shrigley and ski-jumper Eddie 'The Eagle' Edwards. Tel: 0116 255 1551.

Loughborough University dates from 1909, when a small technical institute was established on Green Close Lane in Loughborough. On 19 April 1966 Loughborough University of Technology became Britain's first technological university. Its 24 academic departments and over 30 research institutes are divided between three faculties: Science, Engineering, and Social Science and Humanities. It has 14,000 students. Loughborough combines education, research and facility provision for a wide range of sports and individual performers, and the university has been the site for the National Cricket Academy since 2003. Its campus is shared with Loughborough College, Loughborough University School of Art and Design and the RNIB College. Former students include athletes Lord Coe and Dame Tanni Grey-Thompson. Tel: 01509 263171.

The **University of Leicester** is a leading research university with 18,000 registered students, including 10,000 full-time and 6000 distance-learning students (the largest distance-learning population of any UK university other than the Open University). The main campus is 1 mile (1.6km) south of the city centre, adjacent to Victoria Park and Wyggeston and Queen Elizabeth I College. Founded in 1921 as Leicestershire and Rutland College with nine students, the college gained full degree-awarding powers in 1957 when it was granted its royal charter. The university's Engineering Building was designed by leading British architect James Stirling. The Attenborough Building (see separate entry) houses the university's arts and humanities departments. Former students include broadcasters Ray Gosling and Laurie Taylor, journalist Michael Nicholson and author Malcolm Bradbury. Tel: 0116 252 2522.

Waltham Transmitter — Waltham-on-the-Wolds, 5 miles (8km) northeast of Melton Mowbray. A broadcasting and telecommunications facility comprising a 1033ft (315m) guyed steel tubular mast. The height of the main structure is 954ft (291m), with the UHF television antennas contained within a GRP shroud mounted on top. The first mast was built in 1966, but collapsed on 16 November of that year. In 1968, the structure was rebuilt, and it became fully operational in April 1971. Originally built to provide BBC2 to the East Midlands, it is now the main TV transmitter for all terrestrial channels covering the region – Nottinghamshire, Derbyshire, Leicestershire, Rutland, the south of Lincolnshire and north Northamptonshire. It is owned and operated by National Grid Wireless.

Watermead Country Park — 5 miles (8km) north of Leicester. A network of artificial lakes created by gravel extraction, covering 350 acres (140ha) in the valley of the River Soar and the Grand Union Canal. The park lies north–south along the path of the watercourses, between Birstall in the west and Thurmaston in the east. Tel: 0116 267 1944.

Wigston Framework Knitters Museum — Bushloe End, Wigston, 4 miles (6km) south of Leicester. Museum housed in an 18th century knitter's house and workshop with original frames. When the last master hosier, Edgar Carter, died in 1952, the workshop was locked and abandoned, leaving the eight hand frames used for making gloves, mitts and fancy ribbed tops, together with all the tools associated with each machine, intact inside. Tel: 0116 288 3396.

Willesley Lake — 2 miles (3km) southwest of Ashby-de-la-Zouch. The lake, covering 24 acres (9.5ha), and surrounding parkland was formerly part of the Willesley Hall estate, home of the Hastings family, although the hall has long since been demolished. The former estate lands with their avenues of lime trees stretch to the edge of Ashby. The site was acquired by the Woodland Trust in 1991.

Wing Maze — Wing, 4 miles (6km) southeast of Oakham. A turf maze or labyrinth, one of only eight known to exist in England. Medieval monks are thought to have crawled along the lines, stopping at certain points to pray and repent. Tel: 01572 737570.

Some famous people born in Leicestershire

Armitage, Richard (actor) (1971–)	Leicester
Bakewell, Robert (cattle breeder) (1725–95)	Dishley Grange, Loughborough
Chapman, Graham (writer and actor) (1941–89)	Leicester
Driver, Betty (singer and actress) (1920–)	Leicester
Dunning, Charles Avery (politician) (1885–1958)	Croft
Dyson, Frank Watson (astronomer) (1868–1939)	Measham
Fox, George (founder of the Quakers) (1624–91)	Drayton-in-the-Clay
Frears, Stephen (film director) (1941–)	Leicester
Geary, George (cricketer) (1893–1981)	Barwell
Gimson, Ernest (designer and architect) (1864–1919)	Leicester
Grey, Lady Jane (Nine Days Queen) (1537–54)	Bradgate Park
Hewick, Kevin (songwriter) (1957–)	Leicester
Hings, Donald (inventor) (1907–2004)	Leicester
Howe, John (cleric and theologian) (1630–1705)	Loughborough
Icke, David (former footballer, broadcaster) (1952–)	Leicester
Judd, Charles Henry (missionary) (1842–1919)	Loughborough
Kaye, Tony (musician) (1946–)	Leicester
Kitchen, Michael (actor) (1948–)	Leicester
Lineker, Gary (footballer) (1960–)	Leicester
Nagra, Parminder (actress) (1975–)	Leicester
Orton, Joe (playwright) (1933–67)	Leicester
Ridley, Harold (pioneer in ophthalmology) (1906–2001)	Kibworth Harcourt
Shilton, Peter (goalkeeper) 1948–)	Leicester
Snow, C.P. (novelist and physicist) 1905–80)	Leicester
Thorne, Willie (snooker player) (1954–)	Leicester
Townsend, Sue (author) (1946–)	Leicester
Villiers, George (1st Duke of Buckingham) (1592–1628)	Brooksby
Whiston, William (mathematician) (1667–1752)	Norton
Wilson, Colin (writer) (1931–)	Leicester

Lincolnshire

EAST RIDING OF YORKSHIRE
SOUTH YORKSHIRE
NOTTINGHAMSHIRE
LEICESTERSHIRE
CAMBRIDGESHIRE
NORFOLK
North Sea
The Wash
The Marshes
The Fens
Lincolnshire Wolds
Wolds Top
168
M180
R. Trent
R. Bain
R. Witham
R. Welland
Scunthorpe
Bottesford
Brigg
Immingham
Grimsby
Cleethorpes
Caistor
Gainsborough
Market Rasen
Louth
Mablethorpe
Wragby
Lincoln
North Hykeham
Horncastle
Spilsby
Skegness
Sleaford
Boston
Grantham
Bourne
South Witham
Spalding
Holbeach
Sutton Bridge
Market Deeping
1
2
3
4
5
6
7
8
9

Districts

1 West Lindsey
2 Lincoln
3 East Lindsey
4 North Kesteven
5 Boston
6 South Kesteven
7 South Holland
8 North Lincolnshire (UA)
9 North-East Lincolnshire (UA)

0 20 miles
0 30 km

Lincolnshire is a county in the east of England bordering Norfolk to the southeast, Cambridgeshire to the south, Leicestershire to the southwest, Nottinghamshire to the west, South Yorkshire to the northwest and East Riding of Yorkshire to the north. Its eastern coast is on the North Sea and its southern tip shares a border with Northamptonshire for just 62 ft (19m), England's shortest county boundary. The ceremonial county is composed of the non-metropolitan county of Lincolnshire and the area covered by the unitary authorities of North Lincolnshire and North East Lincolnshire. Its county town is the ancient city of Lincoln. Until 1974, Lincolnshire comprised three 'parts', like the ridings of Yorkshire: Lindsey, Kesteven and Holland. In their final form, each was in effect a county.

Before the Roman occupation, Lincolnshire was occupied by a subdivision of the Iceni tribe, called the Coritani or Corieltauvi. The Romans had established permanent government in Lincolnshire by AD 43, but rebellion by the Coritani and their neighbours in Yorkshire, the Brigantes, against the tyrannical rule of the Roman governor Ostorius Scapula was only quelled in AD 70. The sub-district of Flavia Caesariensis, comprising Lincolnshire and parts of the Midlands, was created in the 4th century and the Romans set about improving the region. They created the Car Dyke, a series of semi-natural and artificial boundary ditches which run from the River Welland at Market Deeping for 40 miles (64km) to the River Witham at Washingborough, constructed walkways across the fens and built inland ports such as the Brayford Pool at Lincoln. It is likely that they also dug the navigable Foss Dyke, running from the Witham at Lincoln to the River Trent at Torksey, although this may be a later creation. They also built numerous fortified towns, while three of their main roads crossed the region: Ermine Street (London to York via Stamford, Lincoln and Winteringham), Fosse Way (Lincoln to Exeter), and Tillbridge Lane (Lincoln to York via Marton and Littleborough).

By the 6th century the Anglian kingdom of Lindsey was established between the River Witham and the Humber, in the north of modern Lincolnshire. It maintained its independence until the end of the 7th century, but was eventually absorbed into Mercia in the 8th century. The 9th century Danish invaders who conquered Mercia and all the other Anglo-Saxon kingdoms except Wessex were followed by Scandinavian settlers; occupying the swathe of England under Danish control, known as the Danelaw, they left a legacy of Scandinavian elements in many Lincolnshire place names. Lincoln became a Danish borough and in the 10th century it became the head of the new shire of Lincolnshire.

The Anglo-Saxon nobility of Lincolnshire was destroyed by William I, and the lands divided among his followers. He constructed castles at Lincoln and Tattershall. The county was recorded as Lindsey in Domesday Book, although by this time the name was applied only to the northern core, around Lincoln, and emerged as one of the three 'Parts of Lincolnshire', along with the Parts of Holland in the southeast and Kesteven in the southwest.

During the Civil War in the 17th century, Lincolnshire was part of the Parliamentarian alliance known as the Eastern Association. With the Royalist strongholds of Newark on Trent and Belvoir Castle on its western border, the county was subject to numerous raids. For a time, Crowland in the south was fortified for the king. Lincolnshire was important to the Parliamentarians as it provided access between the great arsenal of Hull and the south and the Eastern Association's heartland in the east of England. It also offered a potential starting line for an advance across the Midlands, cutting the north of England off from the west.

In 1888 county councils were created to administer Lindsey, Holland and Kesteven. These survived until 1974, when Holland, Kesteven and most of Lindsey were unified into Lincolnshire; the northern part, with Scunthorpe and Grimsby, went to the newly formed non-metropolitan county of Humberside, along with most of the East Riding of Yorkshire. The 1974 changes divided the Parts of Holland into two districts: the Borough of Boston, formed by the merger of the former borough of Boston with Boston Rural District, and South Holland. A further local government reform in 1996 abolished Humberside, and the land south of the Humber became the unitary authorities of North Lincolnshire and North East Lincolnshire. These two areas became part of Lincolnshire for ceremonial purposes such as the Lord-Lieutenancy, but are not covered by the Lincolnshire police and are in the Yorkshire and the Humber region. The remaining districts of Lincolnshire are part of the East Midlands region.

Geographically the county can be broadly divided into the Lincolnshire Fens in the south and west, the Lincolnshire Wolds towards the east with the coastal strip between Skegness and Cleethorpes beyond them, and to the north the industrial Humber Estuary and North Sea coast around Grimsby and Scunthorpe. The county is a major agricultural producer, growing wheat, barley, sugar beet and oilseed rape. In south Lincolnshire, where the soil is particularly rich, crops include cabbage, cauliflowers and onions. With the mechanisation of agriculture in the 20th century, the proportion of workers in the agricultural sector dropped substantially, while several major engineering companies developed in Lincoln and Grantham. Perhaps the most famous are Fosters of Lincoln, who built the first tank, and Richard Hornsby & Sons of Grantham.

During World War II there was a huge expansion in the number of Royal Air Force stations in the county. By 1945 there were 46 bases, some of which were lent to the 8th United States Army Air Force. The very first airfields had been built for the Royal Flying Corps (RFC) or the Royal Naval Air Service, the first at Skegness in 1912. Lincolnshire can still claim to be the home of RAF Bomber Command, playing host to many squadrons, including the Lancaster bombers of the famous 617 'Dambusters' squadron. Two Bomber Groups were based in the county – No. 1 in the north and No. 5 in the centre and south. The Battle of Britain memorial flight is still led by a Lancaster named *The City of Lincoln*.

Being on the economic periphery of England, Lincolnshire's transport links are less well developed than many other parts of the UK and it is one of the few counties without a motorway, although the M180 passes through north Lincolnshire. The low population density means that the number of railway stations and train services is low considering its large physical size. Most of the county's railway stations were permanently closed following the Beeching Report of 1963. Sleaford is now the only town with a station served by lines running both north–south and east–west.

Lincolnshire is one of the least ethnically diverse counties of the British Isles (98.5 per cent of the population described themselves as 'white' in the 2001 Census). Recently, the county has witnessed an influx of retired people from other parts of the UK, particularly those from the south of England attracted by the generally lower property prices and the slower and more relaxed pace of life. The relatively high proportion of elderly and retired people is reflected in many of the services, activities and events. Sleaford is one of the fastest growing towns in the East Midlands, with many professional people moving there in order to benefit from relatively low house prices, low crime rate and selective education.

Lincolnshire	**Population**			**Area**	
Districts	*male*	*female*	*total*	*sq miles*	*sq km*
Boston	27,333	28,417	55,750	140	362
East Lindsey	64,053	66,394	130,447	679	1760
Lincoln	41,695	43,900	85,595	14	36
North Kesteven	46,017	48,007	94,024	356	922
South Holland	37,401	39,121	76,522	287	742
South Kesteven	61,108	63,684	124,792	364	943
West Lindsey	38,977	40,538	79,515	446	1156
North East Lincolnshire Unitary Authority	76,706	81,273	157,979	74	192
North Lincolnshire Unitary Authority	74,771	78,078	152,849	327	846
Total	468,061	489,412	957,473	2687	6959

Local Attractions and Information

Administrative Headquarters — **Lincolnshire:** County Offices, Newland, Lincoln LN1 1YL. Tel: 01522 552222.
North East Lincolnshire: Municipal Offices, Town Hall Square, Grimsby DN31 1HU. Tel: 01472 313131.
North Lincolnshire: Pittwood House, Ashby Road, Scunthorpe DN16 1AB. Tel: 01724 296296.

Alford Manor House — West Street, Alford, 10 miles (16km) northwest of Skegness. One of England's largest thatched manor houses, built in 1611. Given to the town by Dorothy Higgins, whose grandfather once lived there, the house is now owned by Alford and District Civic Trust. There is a museum on site with a variety of artefacts. The building is now Grade II listed. Tel: 01507 463073.

Arnhem Museum — See Fulbeck Hall

Aubourn Hall — Aubourn, 7 miles (11km) southwest of Lincoln. A brick house mainly dating to 1587–1628 and thought to have been built on Tudor foundations for Sir John Meres. Features include a carved staircase and an attractive garden. The property was the home of the Nevile family from the 17th century and Sir Henry Nevile is the present owner. Tel: 01522 788717.

Ayscoughfee Hall — Churchgate, Spalding. Now a museum, the house was originally built c.1450 and many details of the medieval interior still survive. It was bought by the Johnson family in 1658 and remained in the family until 1864, the Gothic façade being added in the Victorian period. The gardens, laid out in the 1730s, include an ice house, a war memorial, a lake and bandstand. During the 20th century the site was used as a primary school. Tel: 01775 725468.

Bardney Limewoods Nature Reserve — 11 miles (18km) east of Lincoln. Located between Wragby and Bardney, the reserve constitutes an important ancient woodland of small-leaved lime trees, here growing at their northern limit in the British Isles. The 945 acre (383ha) National Nature Reserve includes nine separate woods and is part of the area known as the Lincolnshire Limewoods.

Barlings Abbey — 7 miles (11km) east of Lincoln. Situated on the west bank of the Barlings Eau, a tributary of the River Witham, the abbey was founded by Ralf de Haya in 1154 and dissolved in 1537. Its buildings and land were acquired by the Duke of Suffolk, brother-in-law of Henry VIII. Only a tall section of the wall of the nave still survives above ground but extensive earthworks are still visible. Tel: 01529 461499.

Barton Clay Pits — $1^1/_2$ miles (2.5km) north of Barton-upon-Humber. Nature reserve covering a 5 mile (8km) area along the Humber bank with walks and a wide variety of birds. Tel: 01724 297388.

Battles — There have been four major battles in Lincolnshire. See separate table.

Baysgarth House Museum — Caistor Road, Barton upon Humber. Set in 30 acres (12ha) of grounds, this 18th century mansion was once the ancestral home of the Nelthorpe family. Features include 17th century Georgian and Victorian period rooms, collections of 18th and 19th century English and Oriental pottery and porcelain, country craft displays in Baysgarth Cottage, and the Industrial Museum in the stable block. Tel: 01652 637568.

Belmont Transmitter — Donington on Bain, 5 miles (8km) southwest of Louth. A television and radio mast opened on 20 December 1965, owned and operated by Arqiva. At 1265ft (385m) it is the tallest structure in the EU. Meteorological equipment was added to the mast in 1967, extending its height to 1272ft (388m). The mast is used to broadcast analogue and digital television and radio to parts of Lincolnshire, north Nottinghamshire, northwest Norfolk, Hull and East Yorkshire. Initially it transmitted broadcasts from Anglia Television; following reorganisation of ITV coverage in 1970, it transmitted broadcasts solely from neighbouring station Yorkshire Television.

Belton House — 3 miles (5km) northeast of Grantham. Built 1685–8 by Sir John Brownlow and his wife, the house is surrounded by formal gardens and a series of avenues leading to follies within a greater wooded park. Belton House was for 300 years the seat of the Brownlow and Cust family, local landowners since the late 16th century, and the family tombs in the parish church of Belton village form one of the most complete sets of family memorials in England. The earliest member buried in the church is the founder of the family fortune, lawyer Richard Brownlow (1555–1638). Belton was a film location for the BBC's *Pride and Prejudice* (1995) and *Tom Jones* (1997), also featuring in the corporation's adaptation of *Moondial* (1988). The house has silver and furniture collections, while the grounds include an orangery and a landscaped deer park. Now owned by the National Trust. Tel: 01476 566116.

Belvoir Castle See Leicestershire

Billinghay Old Vicarage Cottage Church Street, Billinghay. A thatched cottage dating from the mid 1600s, which served as the vicarage until 1724. In 1804 the cottage survived a major fire which destroyed much of the old village. Constructed in the Lincolnshire vernacular style utilising mud and stud walling, it has been restored using traditional materials and now houses the village council office. Tel: 01526 861845.

Bolingbroke Castle Moat Lane, Old Bolingbroke, 15 miles (24km) north of Boston. Founded by Ranulf, Earl of Chester in 1220, in 1311 Bolingbroke Castle passed to the House of Lancaster. John of Gaunt was among its most famous owners and his wife, Blanche of Lancaster, died here in 1369, while Henry IV was born in the castle on 3 April 1367. The castle was partially destroyed in 1643 during the Civil War and abandoned shortly afterwards. Most of the castle was built of Spilsby greenstone, as is the nearby church, and was originally surrounded by a moat. Much of the lower walls are still visible, as are the ground floors of the towers. It was maintained by English Heritage until 1995 when Heritage Lincolnshire took ownership. Tel: 01790 763084.

Boothby Pagnell Manor House 7 miles (11km) southeast of Grantham. The most important Norman manor house in England thanks to its remarkable state of preservation, Boothby Pagnell Manor House stands in the grounds of Boothby Hall and was built c.1200. The existing two-storey building was originally part of a larger house which stood within a defensive moat, the shape of which can still be seen in the grass. Tel: 01476 585374.

Boston Situated on the River Witham, Boston is supposedly named after St Botolph, a Saxon saint who founded the monastery of Ikanhoe (Ox Island), afterwards named Botolphston and later contracted to Boston. A member of the Hanseatic League, Boston was an important port for trade around northern Europe in the Middle Ages and in the 13th century became the leading port in England. In 1545 it was granted a charter and became a borough. By the 17th century it had become infamous as a centre of religious nonconformity. After the fenlands surrounding Boston were drained in the 18th century and sea banks were built to enable crops to be cultivated, the town became a centre of agriculture rather than of trade. Modern Boston is a busy college town, and is the location of the council offices of the Boston local government district.

Boston Guildhall Museum South Street, Boston. Museum of local and maritime history located in the 14th century Guildhall, later used as the town hall and a prison. Exhibits include the cells where the Pilgrim Fathers were imprisoned. Tel: 01205 365954.

Bourne Abbey Church Lane, Bourne. Although still known locally as Bourne Abbey, the building is now the parish church of St Peter and St Paul. It was founded by the lord of the manor, Baldwin fitz Gilbert, c.1138 on the site of a previous abbey. Fitz Gilbert was a member of a Norman family settled in Suffolk, and which was later to make its mark in Wales and Ireland; his wife Adelina was a great-granddaughter of Hereward the Wake. The abbey was one of five English monastic houses attached to the Arrouaisian congregation, a subdivision of the Augustinian order; they took their name from the French village of Arrouaise in Artois where in 1090, three hermits had built a cell or oratory in honour of the Holy Trinity and St Nicholas. There were eventually 28 houses, mainly in France and Flanders, but the order became extinct in the late 15th century. The abbey was dissolved in 1536, along with many other small monastic houses, in the first phase of Henry VIII's dissolution of monasteries. Since the 19th century the church has been substantially rebuilt; it is now Grade I listed but the only Norman remains are four round arches on massive piers supporting scalloped capitals, which have been incorporated into the nave.

Bourne Heritage Centre South Street, Bourne. Housed in a former watermill dating to c.1800, the centre contains an exhibition dedicated to local motor racing pioneer Raymond Mays (who won the British Hill Climb Championship in its first two years, 1947 and 1948), as well as a local history display, old farm implements and two working waterwheels. Tel: 01778 422775.

Branston Hall Branston, 3 miles (5km) southeast of Lincoln. An elegant country house built for the Melville family 1884–6 and set in 88 acres (36ha) of wooded parkland and lakes. The house was used as an RAF hospital during World War II. Having fallen into dereliction in the 1970s, it was converted into a retirement home in the late 1980s and restored as a hotel in 1990. Tel: 01522 793305.

Burghley Horse Trials An annual three-day event held at Burghley House (see separate entry) near Stamford. Currently sponsored by Land Rover, Burghley is classified by the International Equestrian Federation (FEI) as one of the five leading three-day events in the world (the others being the Badminton Horse Trials, the Rolex Kentucky Three Day, the Adelaide Horse Trials and the Luhmühlen Horse Trials). Horse trials were first held at Burghley House in 1961 when its owner the 6th Marquess of Exeter, an Olympic gold medallist in athletics and member of the IOC, heard that a three-day event at Harewood House could no longer be held. Since then Burghley has hosted many international championships.

Burghley House 1 mile (1.6km) southeast of Stamford. A major example of late 16th century English architecture, Burghley House also has a suite of rooms remodelled in the baroque style. The 35 major rooms include 18 state rooms. Built as a country residence for William Cecil, Lord Burghley – principal secretary to Elizabeth I and the most powerful man in England in the late 16th century – and his descendants, the Earls and Marquesses of Exeter, it is now owned by a charitable trust established by the family, who still live in the house. There are collections of 17th century Italian painting and oriental porcelain. The avenues in the park were laid out by Capability Brown, who also created the 26 acre (10.5ha) lake, designed to give the effect of a meandering river, in 1775–80. Brown also designed the Lion Bridge in 1778. After the original Coade-stone lions perished, stone replacements were made in 1844 by local mason Herbert Gilbert. Burghley hosts the annual Burghley Horse Trials (see separate entry). Tel: 01780 752451.

Caistor Canal The Caistor Canal ran east for 4 miles (6km) from the River Ancholme through five locks, terminating at Moortown, 3 miles (5km) southwest of Caistor. Originally constructed as a broad canal – one with locks over 7ft (2.1m) wide – it was opened c.1800 having taken seven years to build. The canal was abandoned in 1936 and is no longer navigable.

Castle Bytham 8 miles (13km) southwest of Bourne. A hillside village, once the site of a Norman castle founded in 1169. The castle was besieged and demolished by Henry III in 1221, although immediately rebuilt by William de Colville. It was burned down during the Wars of the Roses and only earthworks remain.

Claythorpe Watermill and Wildfowl Gardens Aby, 7 miles (11km) southeast of Louth. A 17th century watermill on the River Great Eau. The gardens are home to hundreds of birds and animals including otters, flamingos, storks, owls and monkeys. Tel: 01507 450687.

Cranwell Aviation Heritage Centre North Rauceby, 3 miles (5km) west of Sleaford. Situated close to the Royal Air Force College, Cranwell, the centre explores the history of the college, the first military air academy in the world at its opening on 5 February 1920. Sir Frank Whittle, pioneer of the jet engine, is one of the many distinguished aviators to have graduated from the college. Tel: 01529 488490.

Croyland Abbey Market Town, Crowland, 8 miles (13km) south of Spalding. Aka Crowland Abbey. Originally founded in the 8th century, and dedicated to St Mary the Virgin, St Bartholomew and St Guthlac. In about the 10th century, it came under the Benedictine rule. Part of the abbey church is still in use as the parish church. Croyland Abbey is the home of the sometimes dubious account of British medieval history from 655 to 1486 known as the Croyland Chronicle. Despite the representations of the abbot of Croyland, who in 1537 wrote to Thomas Cromwell, sending him a gift of fish, 'ryght mekely besechyng yow lordship favorablye to accepte the same fyshe, and to be gud and favorable lorde unto me and my pore house', the abbey was dissolved in 1539, although subsequently partially restored. One of its religious relics is the skull of the 9th century Abbot St Theodore; stolen from its display case in 1982, it was returned anonymously in 1999. The abbey is also the subject of a sonnet by John Clare. Tel: 01733 210499.

Doddington Hall 5 miles (8km) west of Lincoln. An Elizabethan mansion with walled courtyards and a gabled gatehouse, unaltered externally since its completion in 1600. It has never been sold and its varied contents reflect 400 years of unbroken family occupation with fine textiles, porcelain, furniture and pictures. The hall is set within 6 acres (2.4ha) of walled and wild gardens. Tel: 01522 694308.

Donna Nook 8 miles (13km) northeast of Louth. A National Nature Reserve managed by Lincolnshire Wildlife Trust. The 6 mile (10km) coastal strip of dunes and saltmarsh stretches from Saltfleet in the south to Somercotes Haven in the north, the point where the Seven Towns South Eau enters the sea. The Ministry of Defence maintains part of the area (north of the village of North Somercotes) as a bombing range. According to legend the reserve is named after a ship called the *Donna*, part of the Spanish Armada, which sank off the Nook (a small headland) in 1588. The area is rich in bird life: in summer, breeding birds include red-legged partridge, dunnock, whitethroat, linnet, skylark, yellowhammer and tree sparrow, while the mudflats provide a winter home for brent geese, shelduck, twite, lapland bunting, shore lark, knot and dunlin. There is also a large and accessible breeding colony of grey seals.

Dunston Pillar Tower Lane, 6 miles (10km) south of Lincoln. A stone tower and former 'land lighthouse', originally built by Sir Francis Dashwood (better known as the founder of the Hellfire Club – see Buckinghamshire) in 1751 as a navigational aid to assist those crossing the heathland around Dunston and Nocton. Its purpose was to improve the safety of travellers crossing treacherous areas of the county known for its many incidents of highway robbery (including several believed to have been carried out by the notorious highwayman Dick Turpin). The structure originally stood 98ft (30m) high with a large octagonal lantern on top. The lantern was regularly lit until 1788 and was used for the last time in 1808, by which time improvements in the local road network had made it obsolete; destroyed in a storm the same year, it was replaced with a bust of George III by the Earl of Buckinghamshire to celebrate 50 years of the king's reign. In 1940 the pillar was considered to be a hazard to low-flying aircraft approaching nearby RAF Waddington and was lowered by 32ft (10m). The bust of George III was removed and placed in the grounds of Lincoln Castle (see separate entry). The tower remains a well-known landmark and is clearly visible beside the road.

Dyke Windmill See Windmills

East Coast Main Line The East Coast Main Line (ECML), one of the fastest railway lines in the UK, rated at 125mph (200 km/h) over most of its length, links London to Edinburgh and Leeds. The ECML includes four separate lines: the main line between London Kings Cross and Waverley Station in Edinburgh, via Stevenage, Peterborough, Grantham, Doncaster, York, Darlington, Durham, Newcastle upon Tyne, Berwick-upon-Tweed and Dunbar; the line from Doncaster to Leeds, via Wakefield Westgate; the branch line from North Berwick to Edinburgh, and the suburban branch line from London's Moorgate station to Stevenage, via Finsbury Park and the Hertford Loop. The line was originally built piecemeal by many small railway companies, but mergers and acquisitions led to only three companies controlling the route (north to south: the North British Railway, the North Eastern Railway and the Great Northern Railway). The companies established the East Coast Joint Stock in 1860 for through services using common vehicles. In 1923 all three were grouped into the

London and North Eastern Railway (LNER). The ECML has been the backdrop for many famous rail journeys and locomotives. It was worked for many years by the famous steam locomotives *Flying Scotsman* and *Mallard*; the latter was officially declared the world's fastest steam locomotive on the Grantham–Peterborough stretch, a title it holds to this day. Steam was replaced in the 1960s by diesels, the most popular of these being the InterCity 125 or 'HST' (High Speed Train), introduced in 1976. The ECML was electrified in the 1980s. The Great North Eastern Railway (GNER) is the line's principal operator today.

East Lighthouse — 3 miles (5km) north of Sutton Bridge, 14 miles (23km) east of Spalding. Situated close to the borders with Norfolk and Cambridgeshire and near the mouth of the River Nene, the East Lighthouse was inhabited before World War II by naturalist and artist Sir Peter Scott, who later bought a large area of the Ouse Washes and established the Wildfowl and Wetlands Trust reserve at Welney (see separate entry). After remaining empty since the 1970s, the lighthouse has recently been restored.

Easton Walled Gardens — Easton, 5 miles (8km) south of Grantham. The 12 acres (5ha) of gardens once formed part of the 400 year old estate of Easton Hall. Abandoned when the hall was demolished in 1951, they are currently in the process of restoration. Tel: 01476 530063.

Epworth — A small town in the Isle of Axholme, North Lincolnshire famous as the birthplace of John and Charles Wesley and which has given its name to many institutions associated with Methodism. The Old Rectory, a Grade I listed Queen Anne style building in Rectory Street, was home to the Wesley family from the early 1700s and is now a museum owned by the World Methodist Council. The John Wesley Garden – a Georgian-style physic garden of therapeutic plants such as those advocated by Wesley – was opened in 2006. Tel: 01427 872268.

Far Ings Nature Reserve — 1 mile (1.6km) west of Barton-upon-Humber. A chain of flooded clay pits and extensive reed beds along the Humber bank now designated a National Nature Reserve. The varied habitats include open water, grassland, hedgerow and estuarine saltmarsh, supporting over 200 species of wildflower and more than 250 species of moth. Tel: 01652 634507.

Food and drink — Lincolnshire has a number of interesting local dishes, and products are judged biennally at the Lincolnshire Poacher competition. **Stuffed chine** is salted neck-chine taken from between the shoulder blades of a pig, salted for about two weeks and stuffed with parsley stuffing (the other ingredients are normally kept secret). It was traditionally served on May Day. **Haslet** is a type of pork loaf, flavoured with sage. **Lincolnshire pork sausages** are traditionally made from minced pork, stale breadcrumb (rusk is used nowadays), pepper, sage and salt. The skins should be natural casings made from sheep or pig intestines.**Plum bread** is a sweet tea bread made – like plum pudding – with dried fruit such as currants, raisins and sultanas.

Foss Dyke — Possibly the oldest canal in England still in use, the Foss Dyke was traditionally thought to have been constructed by the Romans c.AD 120, although recent research suggests that it may be Viking or Norman in origin. It runs for 11 miles (18km) between the River Trent at Torksey and the Witham at Lincoln. Henry I is recorded as having deepened the canal in 1121, and it was once a major waterway for the transport of wool; it is now mostly used for leisure pursuits. The canal lends its name to the Lincoln-based Foss Dyke Brass Band.

Fulbeck Hall and Manor — 11 miles (18km) north of Grantham. The home of the Fane family for nearly 400 years since the estate was purchased in 1622 by Francis Fane, 1st Earl of Westmorland. The current house was built by his descendant, also named Francis, following a fire in 1733. With its squared grey limestone façade, its appearance resembles that of a town house. In 1784 the Hon. Henry Fane added an extension to the north which contained a new dining room with a rounded end. The house was purchased in 1887 by a cousin, William Fane, an antiquarian and the great-grandfather of the present owner. He remodelled some of the interiors in 1904, while his son created the formal terraced garden to the north. The present porch was brought to the house from nearby Syston Park in 1934. One of the least altered parts of the house is the long narrow entrance hall which leads through an archway, flanked by Doric pilasters, to the wooden staircase. There are pictures collected by William Burnside of Gedling, Nottinghamshire, in the early 19th century, including works by Zuccarelli, Samuel Scott and Gerard Dou. Other collections include fine 18th and early 19th century porcelain and furniture. The dining room, dating from 1794, has a neoclassical chimneypiece by James Wallis and the paintings on display include work by Gaspard Dughet and the younger Teniers. Fulbeck Hall also houses the Arnhem Museum, dedicated to the 1st Airborne Division for which the hall was headquarters during World War II. The house is surrounded by 11 acres (4.5ha) of formal gardens. Tel: 01400 272231.

Fydell House — South Square, off Market Place, Boston. A Grade I listed town house built in the early 18th century as the home of the Fydell family, wine merchants and mayors of Boston. Tel: 01205 351520.

Gainsborough Old Hall — Parnell Street, Gainsborough, 18 miles (29km) northwest of Lincoln. More than 500 years old, the hall is one of the best-preserved medieval manor houses in England. Built by Sir Thomas Burgh c.1460, Gainsborough Old Hall was not the Burgh family's only home but part of the demonstration of their wealth and importance. Architecturally it has changed very little over the years and is principally timber-framed. A brick tower on the northeast corner has 59 steps leading to the top. Now owned by English Heritage. Tel: 01427 612669.

Gainsthorpe — $1^1/_2$ miles (2.5km) southwest of Hibaldstow, 5 miles (8km) southwest of Brigg. The well-preserved site of a deserted medieval village; the layout of sunken roads, enclosures and dwellings can be clearly seen in the humps and hollows of the field. It is not known when the village was abandoned. Now in the care of English Heritage.

Gibraltar Point Nature Reserve — Extending for 3 miles (5km) along the Lincolnshire coast from the southern end of Skegness to the entrance of the Wash, the area of 1.7 sq miles (4.3 sq km) comprises sandy and muddy seashores, sand-dunes, saltmarshes and freshwater habitats. An important site for both breeding and overwintering birds, it is designated a Site of Special Scientific Interest, National Nature Reserve, Ramsar site and Special Protection Area. A small colony of natterjack toads was successfully established in the 1990s.

Gordon Boswell Romany Museum Clay Lake, Spalding. Museum containing a unique collection of Romany vardos (caravans), carts and harnesses (all horse-drawn), as well as a large collection of Romany photographs and sketches. Tel: 01775 710599.

Grantham Canal Running 33 miles (53km) from Grantham through 18 locks to West Bridgford, Nottinghamshire, where it joins the River Trent, the canal was built primarily to enable the transportation of coal to Grantham. Building work started in 1793, with William Jessop in charge and James Green and William King as resident engineers. The eastern section from the Leicestershire border was opened on 1 February 1797, the rest of the canal later that year. The canal was built with locks 75ft (23m) by 14ft (4.2m), the same size as those on the Nottingham Canal to allow boats to use both. In 1963 control of the canal passed to British Waterways; in 1968 it was placed into a 'remaindered' state involving maintenance of the water level, while a restoration programme has since been undertaken by the Grantham Canal Trust.

Grantham House Castlegate, Grantham. Originally a country residence, the earliest part of the house, the central hall, was built in 1380. Princess Margaret, daughter of Henry VII, lodged here, as did Cardinal Wolsey. All that remains of the medieval building are some 15th century windows on an internal staircase, and most of the house seen today dates from the 16th to 18th centuries – a history demonstrated by the asymmetrical entrance front, which has features dated 1574 and 1737. The house overlooks Grantham's cathedral-like parish church, St Wulfrans, while the 27 acres (11ha) of garden slope down to the River Witham. It is now managed by the National Trust. Tel: 01909 486411.

Grantham Museum St Peter's Hill, Grantham. Museum exploring Grantham's history from prehistoric times. There are displays on physicist Isaac Newton, who was born and educated locally, and Lady Thatcher, who has donated many personal items to the museum. The 'Dambusters' raid of World War II was largely planned from Grantham and a bouncing bomb used in one of the raids is another of the exhibits. Tel: 01476 568783.

Grimsby Dock Tower Royal Dock, Grimsby. A famous maritime landmark, built in 1867 to provide hydraulic power to the lock gates and cranes of Grimsby Docks. J W Wild designed the tower, which was based on the Palazzo Pubblico in Siena, Italy. The tower is 309ft (94m) high and 28ft (8.5m) wide at the base; its walls are 4ft (1.2m) thick.

Grimsby Time Trap Museum Town Hall Square, Grimsby. Located in the former prison cells of the Town Hall, the museum recreates the development of Grimsby. The six circular panels on the front of the building include busts of Queen Victoria, the Prince Consort and Edward III. Tel: 01470 324109.

Grimsthorpe Castle 4 miles (6km) northwest of Bourne. Dating originally from the 13th century and lying within a 3000 acre (1200ha) park of rolling pastures, lakes and woodland, Grimsthorpe has been the home of the de Eresby family since 1516. Originally a small castle on the edge of the Lincolnshire fens, it is said to have been begun by Gilbert de Gant, Earl of Lincoln in the early 13th century. During the last years of the Plantagenets, it was in the hands of Lord Lovell, a prominent supporter of the king who went into hiding at Minster Lovell in Oxfordshire after the defeat of Richard III and is said to have died of starvation. The property was taken into Tudor hands and given to a member of a family which had supported Henry Tudor in 1485. The present park was designed by Capability Brown in 1771 and implemented by his patron, the Duke of Ancaster. The grounds contain a knot garden, hedged rose gardens, a terrace with herbaceous and shrub borders, and a summerhouse designed by Sir John Vanbrugh. During World War I Grimsthorpe Park was used by the RFC and RAF as an emergency landing ground, and part of the park near the Vaudey Abbey site was used a bombing range in World War II. In 1944 the castle housed a company of the Parachute Regiment during its training for Operation Market Garden; the paratroops' flight for Arnhem began from RAF Folkingham. The present owner is Jane, 27th Baroness Willoughby de Eresby, granddaughter of Lady Nancy Astor, who died at Grimsthorpe in 1964. The castle is now managed by a trust. Tel: 01778 591205.

Gunby Hall 7 miles (11km) west of Skegness. Located at the edge of the Lincolnshire Wolds, Gunby Hall was built by an unknown architect for Sir William Massingberd in 1700. The original building, in the style of Sir Christopher Wren, is of plum-coloured brick with stone dressings and a rectangular flat roofline. In 1873 a north wing was added. A notable feature of the interior is the elaborate oak staircase. The panelled rooms contain furniture, pictures and china which have been in the Massingberd family for many generations; the paintings include a portrait by Sir Joshua Reynolds of Bennet Langton, whose son Peregrine married the heiress to the estate in 1784. Langton was a lifelong friend of Dr Samuel Johnson and there is a rare autographed copy of the first edition of Boswell's *Life of Samuel Johnson* at the house. Gunby Hall is reputed to have been the 'haunt of ancient peace' described by Tennyson in his poem 'The Palace of Art', and a copy of the verse can be seen, written in his own hand, signed and dated 1849. Also on display are items of Field Marshal Archibald Montgomery-Massingberd's memorabilia. Extensive gardens surround the house. The Massingberd family gave Gunby Hall to the National Trust in 1944. Tel: 01909 486411.

Harlaxton Manor 4 miles (6km) southwest of Grantham. Once a royal residence for Edward VII, the house was built in the 1830s for Gregory Gregory, a wealthy Nottinghamshire businessman, to replace the original Elizabethan manor house in Harlaxton village. Its architecture is an ornate imitation of Elizabethan, Jacobean and Baroque styles. The original architect, Anthony Salvin, was replaced by William Burn, who was responsible for the interior. The gardens were designed as a 'Walk around Europe' with terraces, colonnades and ornamental water features. The Manor is currently the home of the University of Evansville's British campus. The house and ground have been used a location for the 1999 remake of *The Haunting* and for the films *The Ruling Class* (1972), *The Lady and the Highwayman* (1989) and *The Last Days of Patton* (1986). The BBC drama *The Young Visiters* (2003) was also filmed here. Tel: 01476 403000.

Hartsholme Country Park and Swanholme Lakes Local Nature Reserve — Skellingthorpe Road, Lincoln. Swanholme Lakes Local Nature Reserve was formed from a series of flooded sand and gravel pits closed in the 1960s. The mosaic of different habitat types cover 156 acres (63ha) of sandy, acidic, free-draining soil. The reserve shares a boundary with Hartsholme Country Park, comprising Victorian landscaped gardens, a reservoir and 200 acres (80ha) of woodlands and grasslands. The gardens were designed in the 1860s by renowned Victorian landscape architect Edward Milner, who was also responsible for the design of Lincoln's arboretum, and many features of his work still survive. Tel: 01522 873577.

Haverholme Priory — $^1/_2$ mile (0.8km) southwest of Anwick, 4 miles (6km) northeast of Sleaford. The ruined remains of the Gilbertine priory of St Mary, founded in 1139 in an isolated location in the Lincolnshire Fens. Thomas Becket reputedly hid here in 1164 during one of his arguments with Henry II. Centuries after its dissolution, the priory was bought by George William Finch-Hatton, 10th Earl of Winchelsea and 5th Earl of Nottingham, who rebuilt it in 1830, but by the 1920s it had again fallen into disuse and most of it was demolished. Now Grade II listed, it has the reputation of being among the most haunted places in England.

Haxey Hood — A flexible leather cylinder about 2ft (60cm) long which is the centrepiece of a violent contest between the North Lincolnshire villages of Haxey and Westwoodside, held each year on 6 January. After due ceremonies by the presiding officials – the Lord, his fool and 12 attendant 'boggans', the game's referees – the hood is carried to a hillside equidistant from the two villages and thrown into the middle of the 'sway', a scrummage of scores of young men who seek by sometimes violent means to gain control of the Hood. For several hours the sway surges back and forth until the Hood has been delivered to a pub in one village or the other. The victorious pub serves a free drink that evening and keeps the Hood until the following year. Local tradition dates the game back to an incident in the 13th century when the Mowbray family were lords of the manor.

Healing Moated Settlement — Healing, 5 miles (8km) west of Grimsby. The remains of a moated medieval settlement dating to the 13th or 14th century; various earthworks including the moat itself are still visible, as are building platforms and fish ponds. Tel: 01529 461499.

Heckington Village Trust Railway Museum — Station Road, Heckington, 4 miles (6km) southeast of Sleaford. Situated on the platform of Heckington railway station, the restored buildings, dating to 1859, now house a small but comprehensive railway museum. There are artefacts relating to the Great Northern Railway, London and North Eastern Railway and many other railway companies, as well as a number of model railways. Tel: 01529 469595.

Heckington Windmill — See Windmills

Highest point — Wolds Top, $1^1/_4$ miles (2km) north of Normanby-le-Wold, at 551ft (168m) above sea level (GR: TF121964). See also Lincolnshire Wolds.

Humber Bridge — See East Riding of Yorkshire

Humber Forts — Two large fortifications in the mouth of the Humber Estuary, built in 1914 to protect the entrance to the river. They stand 60ft (18m) above the water and have diameters of 82ft (25m). The forts took three years to build and construction finished at almost the same time as the war. During World War II they remained as a deterrent and were regularly attacked by enemy aircraft. Haile Sand Fort is situated around the low water mark between Cleethorpes and Humberston on the Lincolnshire coast, while Bull Sand Fort is $1^1/_2$ miles (2.5km) from shore off Spurn Head. The latter is a four-storey masonry building with 12in armour and four 6in guns, built with great difficulty as its sandbank is 11ft (3.3m) below low water. The fort was bought in 1997 by a charity intending to convert it into a drug detoxification centre. Administratively, it is within the East Riding of Yorkshire. See also Islands.

Humberside Airport — Kirmington, 10 miles (16km) west of Grimsby. A small regional airport owned by the Manchester Airport Group. The former RAF Kirmington, opened in 1941 and abandoned in 1945, was reopened as Kirmington Airport in 1974 and renamed following local government reorganisation. The airport offers scheduled services to Aberdeen and Amsterdam, as well as chartered flights to several holiday destinations. Tel: 01652 688456.

Humberston Fitties — $^1/_2$ mile (0.8km) southeast of Cleethorpes. A unique 'plot land' development of holiday chalets which began in the early 1920s. Most of the chalets are constructed of timber, although some concrete-panelled ones were erected in the 1950s and 1960s. The area is next to the beach and was reclaimed from marshland, which results in a high water table; the resultant problems with flooding mean that occupation is only allowed for 10 months of the year from 1 March. Tel: 01472 323111.

Hussey Tower — Skirbeck Road, Boston. Dating from 1460, the tower is one of the oldest brick buildings in Lincolnshire. It was originally part of a much larger house built for prominent Boston citizen Richard Benyington. Lord Hussey, executed by Henry VIII for treason in 1536, was a resident in the manor house in the 16th century and gave the tower its name. The tower eventually passed into the ownership of Boston Corporation. Tel: 01529 461499.

Immingham Museum — Margaret Street, Immingham. Museum portraying life in early 20th century Immingham, focusing on the part played by the Great Central Railway in the development of the docks and the local rail network. Tel: 01469 577066.

Interesting facts — **Yellowbellies** (often spelt 'Yeller Bellies', to reflect the pronunciation of the phrase by the typical Lincolnshire farmer) is the name traditionally used in the county to refer to people actually born in Lincolnshire rather than merely residing there. **Thomas Dudley**, a Lincolnshire Puritan, is credited with naming the American settlement of Boston, Massachusetts after the English town. John Cotton, vicar of St Botolph's church in 1612, was an influential Puritan figure who encouraged membership of the Massachusetts Bay Company and inspired a group of Lincolnshire men, including Dudley, to found and develop Boston, MA in 1630. Cotton migrated there in 1633 and was ordained as the first vicar of Boston shortly thereafter. Lincolnshire-born Egyptologist and archaeological photographer **Harry Burton** spent eight years photographing and documenting Howard Carter's excavation of Tutankhamun's tomb in 1922. *The Times* published 142 of these images on 21 February 1923. **Methodism** was originally the nickname given to an 18th century religious revival movement led by, among others, Epworth-born brothers John and Charles Wesley. The Wesleys met George Whitefield, considered the greatest preacher of the time, at Oxford, and they were all ordained clergy of the Church of England. After a brief spell in America the Wesleys joined in a 'Religious Society' in London, and in May 1738 both underwent a profound spiritual experience. Over the next 50 years Charles penned some 6000 hymns, many of which are still heard today, while John was the organising genius who turned a spontaneous movement into the structured body that grew into today's Methodist Church. His published sermons became and remain the church's doctrinal standard. Stamford born **David George Brownlow Cecil, 6th Marquess of Exeter**, styled **Lord Burghley** before 1956, was the winner of the 400m hurdles at the 1928 Olympics. A very precise technician, he placed matchboxes on hurdles and practised knocking over the matchboxes with his lead foot without touching the hurdle. In 1927, his final year at Cambridge, he amazed colleagues by sprinting around the Great Court at Trinity College in the time it took the college clock to toll 12 o'clock, inspiring the scene in the film *Chariots of Fire* in which Harold Abrahams accomplishes the same feat. (The film's character Lord Andrew Lindsay is based on Burghley, although champagne glasses were substituted for matchboxes.) Burghley is said to have set another unusual record by racing around the upper promenade deck of the *Queen Mary* in 57 seconds, dressed in everyday clothes. Lincolnshire is one of the few counties within the UK that still uses the **eleven-plus** to decide who may attend grammar school. The unofficial anthem of the county is the traditional folk song, **'The Lincolnshire Poacher'**, which dates from c.1776. A version of the song was the theme to BBC Radio Lincolnshire for many years. In August 2005, BBC Radio Lincolnshire and *Lincolnshire Life* magazine launched a vote for an unofficial **flag** to represent the county. The winning submission features a red cross with a fleur de lys in the centre on a blue and green background. A gold border represents the crops grown in the county, the blue on the flag represents the sea and sky of Lincolnshire and the green symbolises the fields, while the fleur de lys represents the City of Lincoln. **Rev. Edward Chad Varah**, CH, CBE is best known as the founder of the Samaritans in 1953, the world's first crisis hotline organisation, offering non-religious telephone counselling to those contemplating suicide. A lesser known fact is that Varah was closely associated with the founding of the comic *The Eagle* in 1950, working as a scriptwriter for it and sister publication *Girl*, as well as being 'Scientific and Astronautical Consultant' (as Varah put it) to Dan Dare. **George Bass**, born at Aswarby, 3 miles (5km) south of Sleaford, helped to map the coast of Australia in 1797, and the waters between Australia and Tasmania are now called the Bass Strait. Bass explored the east coast of Australia with Lincolnshire-born navigator Matthew Flinders. They sailed more than 11,000 miles exploring the coastline of Australia and proved that Tasmania was an island. Bass disappeared in 1803 after sailing into the Pacific Ocean with a cargo that he intended to sell in South America. Some believe he was captured by the Spanish and forced to work in mines in Peru. There are a number of fascinating pubs in Lincolnshire. The **Angel Inn**, High Street, Grantham, dating to c.1203, is one of several establishments that lay claim to being Britain's oldest inn. Several past kings of England have held their courts at the former coaching inn; it was here that Richard III signed the death warrant of the Duke of Buckingham in 1483 on learning of Buckingham's rebellion against him. The **Beehive Inn**, Castlegate, Grantham, has as its sign a real beehive, mounted since at least 1830 in the middle of a lime tree. A 'hoody' (beekeeper) tends to the hive and the pub has the history of beehives displayed on its walls. The **Bull & Dog** (formerly the Black Bull), Southgate, Sleaford, dates from 1689 according to a stone set in its front wall, and is said to have the oldest surviving pub sign in England. The **Signal Box Inn** at Lakeside Station on the Cleethorpes Coast Light Railway claims to be the smallest pub in the world, although Sam's World's Smallest Bar in Colorado Springs, Colorado, USA also claims the title. Its bar has an area of 109.57 sq ft (10.18 sq m), compared with the Signal Box's 64 sq ft (5.95 sq m) – although the Signal Box also has an outside drinking area – but it is expected that Guinness World Records will rule in favour of the Signal Box Inn. The Signal Box Inn is also the UK's smallest pub, taking the title from the previous incumbent, the Nutshell in Bury St Edmunds, Suffolk.

Islands

There are three islands and a peninsula in Lincolnshire. **Branston Island** is located in the River Witham; Bardney Lock is situated on the south of the island. **Haile Sand Fort** in the North Sea off Cleethorpes (GR: TA349062) is one of two hexagonal sand forts built in 1915 as a defence for the Humber Estuary (the larger is Bull Sand Fort in the East Riding of Yorkshire). They remained in use until 1956. See also Humber Forts. **Read's Island** (GR: SE964223) in the Humber is an artificial island and an RSPB reserve important for ground-nesting avocets. Area: 0.23 sq miles (0.6 sq km). **The Isle of Axholme** in North Lincolnshire has borders with the Rivers Trent, Idle and Don and is one of many peninsulas which still carry the name 'isle', although this is one of few that are inland.

Julian's Bower

Alkborough, 8 miles (13km) north of Scunthorpe. A turf-cut maze of the labyrinthine type sometimes known as a mizmaze. The 43ft (13m) maze possibly dates to the 13th century, although it is first recorded only in 1697, and may have been cut by monks; a copy of the pattern is inlaid in the porch floor of Alkborough church.

Leadenham House 8 miles (13km) northwest of Sleaford. Built 1790–6, the house is set in 300 acres (120ha) of landscaped parkland. Tel: 01400 273256.

Lincoln Castle Castle Hill, Lincoln. A Norman double motte and bailey castle founded by William I in 1068 on the site of a pre-existing Roman fortress, and one of only two castles in England (the other being Lewes in Sussex) to have two mottes. The shell keep (known as the Lucy Tower), added in the 12th century, was defended against Prince Louis of France by Nichola de la Haye in 1217. Taken by Parliament in 1644, the castle was later used as a prison, the 13th century Cobb Hall Tower being used for executions until 1859; the former assize court, built in 1826, still serves as Lincoln's crown court. One of the four surviving originals of the Magna Carta is now housed within the castle. (The three other surviving copies are in the British Library, which has two, and at Salisbury Cathedral.) The grounds also contain remains of Lincoln's Eleanor cross and the bust of George III which once topped the Dunston Pillar (see separate entry). Tel: 01522 511068.

Lincoln Cathedral Minster Yard, Lincoln. Dedicated to the Blessed Virgin Mary and sometimes referred to as St Mary's Cathedral. The first cathedral was built by Geoffrey de Noiers, 1072–92. Bishop Remigius, who commissioned the work, died on 9 May 1092, two days before its consecration. Fifty years later, most of the building was destroyed in a fire. Bishop Alexander rebuilt and expanded the cathedral, but it was destroyed again in 1185, this time by an earthquake. The new bishop, Hugh of Lincoln, originally from Avalon, France, began a massive rebuilding and expansion programme beginning at the east end, where an apse and five small radiating chapels were added. The central nave was rebuilt in Early English Gothic style with pointed arches, flying buttresses and ribbed vaulting, and the matching windows known as the Dean's Eye and Bishop's Eye were added. In 1307–11 the central tower was raised to its present height of 271ft (82.5m). A tall lead-encased wooden spire which topped the central tower at this time was blown down in a storm in 1549; with its spire, the tower reputedly reached a height of 525ft (160m) – which would have made it the world's tallest structure at the time. Other additions included an elaborate carved screen and 14th century misericords. The internal organs of Edward I's queen, Eleanor of Castile, were buried in the cathedral after her death in 1290 (her body was embalmed, which in the 13th century involved evisceration), and Edward placed a duplicate of her Westminster tomb there. On the outside of the cathedral are two prominent statues thought to be those of Edward and Eleanor, although this identification is far from certain. The Bishop of Lincoln was one of the signatories to Magna Carta and for hundreds of years the cathedral held one of the four remaining copies of the original. (It is now kept in nearby Lincoln Castle – see separate entry.) The Wren Library houses a rare collection of over 270 manuscripts, including a copy of the sermons of the Venerable Bede. Victorian writer John Ruskin described the cathedral as 'the most precious piece of architecture in the British Isles'. Filming of *The Da Vinci Code* (2006) took place in the cloisters and chapter house, which took on the role of Westminster Abbey. Tel: 01522 544544.

Lincoln College A further education college based in Lincoln with two smaller sites in Gainsborough and Louth, known as Gainsborough College and Louth College. More than 21,000 students are enrolled across the three campuses, making it the largest single educational establishment in Lincolnshire. Tel: 01522 876000.

Lincoln Guildhall Saltergate, Lincoln. The ancient Guildhall and council chamber contains Lincoln's civic regalia, among the finest outside London, and the City's charter of 1157, pre-dating Magna Carta. Tel: 01522 541727.

Lincoln Jews Court Steep Hill, Lincoln. Built on the site of a medieval synagogue and probably dating from the 17th century, the building is now the home of the Society for Lincolnshire History and Archaeology. It is situated adjacent to Jews House which dates from c.1158. Tel: 01522 521337.

Lincoln Bishops' Palace Minster Yard, Lincoln. Situated in the shadow of Lincoln Cathedral, the remains of a vast medieval palace belonging to the Bishops of Lincoln, once among the wealthiest in England, were the seat of power between the Thames and the Humber for over 500 years. The Alniwick tower, built in the 1430s, still stands, as do the west hall with its undercroft, dating to 1230, and the east hall, one of the earliest domestic halls still roofed in Europe. A heritage garden and vineyard are contemporary additions to the site. Now in the care of English Heritage. Tel: 01522 527468.

Lincoln Museum of Lincolnshire Life Burton Road, Lincoln. Occupying a barracks built for the Royal North Lincoln Militia in 1857 and now Grade II listed, the museum's exhibits include steam traction engines and tractors, a chemist's shop and Co-operative store, a schoolroom, an Edwardian nursery and parlour, a World War I tank and trench display and a Lincolnshire wagon and wheelwright's workshop. It also incorporates the refurbished galleries of the Royal Lincolnshire Regiment. Tel: 01522 528448

Lincoln St Mary's Guildhall High Street, Lincoln. Built c.1160 as a grand private residence, the hall was used as the guildhall of St Mary's Guild from the mid 13th century. A section of the Fosse Way can be seen inside the building, which was constructed on top of the Roman road. Tel: 01522 546422.

Lincolnshire Agricultural Show Grange de Lings, 4 miles (6km) north of Lincoln. One of the largest agricultural shows in England has been staged annually since c.1884 by the Lincolnshire Agricultural Society, founded in 1869. Since 1958 the show has been held at the society's showground on the Wednesday and Thursday of the last whole week of June. Tel: 01522 522900.

Lincolnshire Aviation Heritage Centre East Kirkby, 7 miles (11km) southeast of Horncastle. Sited on the former RAF East Kirkby, Lincolnshire Aviation Heritage Centre was founded by Fred and Harold Panton as a memorial to their brother Pilot Officer Christopher Panton, who along with 55,000 other aircrew of Bomber Command lost his life during World War II. At the entrance is a memorial to the crews of Nos. 57 and 630 Squadrons, while on display are a Spitfire and a Lancaster from World War II. Tel: 01790 763207.

Lincolnshire Road Transport Museum Whisby Road, North Hykeham, 3 miles (5km) southwest of Lincoln. The museum's collection of over 60 vintage cars, buses and commercial vehicles spans 75 years of road transport history. Many of the vehicles have local connections and have been faithfully restored by the members of the Lincolnshire Vintage Vehicle Society. Tel: 01522 500566.

Lincolnshire Wolds — Designated an Area of Outstanding Natural Beauty in 1973, the Wolds cover 216 sq miles (560 sq km) of north and east Lincolnshire. They comprise a series of low hills and steep valleys underlain by chalk, limestone and sandstone. The highest point of the Wolds, 551ft (168m) above sea level, is also the highest in the whole of Lincolnshire (see Highest Point). The strong Viking influence on the area's history is evident in many of its place names.

Lincolnshire Wolds Railway — 1 mile (1.6km) northeast of Ludborough, 5 miles (8km) north of Louth. Based at Ludborough station, the Lincolnshire Wolds Railway operates on part of the former East Lincolnshire Railway from Grimsby to Boston via Louth, opened in 1847. Absorbed by the Great Northern Railway (GNR), which became part of the London and North Eastern Railway (LNER) in 1923, the line remained open after nationalisation in 1948 but was finally closed in 1980. The Grimsby-Louth Railway Preservation Society began restoring Ludborough station in 1980; it is now a working museum with operational signal box. The first trains ran in 1991 and both steam and diesel locomotives currently operate on $^3/_4$ mile (1.2km) of track; it is hoped eventually to reconstruct the 10 miles (16km) of track between Louth and Waltham. Tel: 01507 363881.

Little Steeping Mud and Stud Cottage — Little Steeping, 8 miles (13km) west of Skegness. Situated in a village at the edge of the Lincolnshire Wolds, Mill Hill Cottage is one of the few surviving examples of mud and stud (a variation of wattle and daub) construction from the 18th century. The building was purchased and restored by the Heritage Trust of Lincolnshire in 2000 and is now a holiday cottage. Tel: 01529 461499.

Magdalen College Museum — Wainfleet, 5 miles (8km) south of Skegness. The medieval brick building was founded in 1484 by William of Wainfleet (founder of Magdalen College, Oxford) and formerly used by Magdalen College School. Today it is the setting for displays showing the social history and environment of the area. Tel: 01754 881548.

Marston Hall and Gardens — 6 miles (10km) northwest of Grantham. The hall once belonged to the Thorold family and is now filled with a notable collection of family pictures and furniture. It is surrounded by 3 acres (1.2ha) of garden, including a knot garden and laburnum avenue, which is reputedly among the largest in England. Tel: 01400 250225.

Mawthorpe Museum — Mawthorpe, 9 miles (15km) northwest of Skegness. A family owned museum with exhibits including a large fairground organ, steam engines, farm implements, tractors, tools of rural crafts, trade, household and social bygones including over 700 horse brasses. Tel: 01507 462336

Metheringham Airfield Visitor Centre — $2^1/_2$ miles (4km) southeast of Metheringham, 9 miles (15km) southeast of Lincoln. Aviation museum dedicated to 106 Squadron Bomber Command, based at RAF Metheringham which was operational 1943–6. Tel: 01526 378270.

Mrs Smith's Cottage — East Road, Navenby, 8 miles (13km) south of Lincoln. Built of red brick in the early 19th century, the cottage has been virtually unaltered externally and internally during the last century and retains its ladder access to the first floor bedrooms. There are displays covering local history in Navenby and the surrounding area, and information about the life of Mrs Hilda Smith, who lived in the cottage for over 70 years until 1995, when she was 102. Tel: 07887 928733.

Normanby Hall — 4 miles (6m) north of Scunthorpe. Neoclassical mansion built 1825–30 for Sir Robert Sheffield (1786–1862), whose family had lived on the site since 1539. It replaced a previous 17th century building. The family departed in 1963 and the hall is now in the care of North Lincolnshire Council. The former 350 acre (140ha) estate is now a country park with restored working Victorian walled garden, farming museum, stableyard, duck ponds, deer sanctuary, fishing lake, miniature railway and a broadleaf woodland. Tel: 01724 720588.

North Ings Farm Museum — Dorrington, 4 miles (6km) north of Sleaford. Agricultural tractor and machinery collection with a narrow gauge railway. Tel: 01526 833100.

Pinchbeck Land Drainage Museum — West Marsh Road, Pinchbeck, 2 miles (3km) north of Spalding. The museum tells the story of the draining of the South Holland Fells, depicting early gravity drainage systems and their replacement first by drainage windmills in the 17th century, and then by steam-powered pumping engines in the 1820s. One of these engines is located on the site. Tel: 01775 761161.

RAF Barkston Heath — 5 miles (8km) northeast of Grantham. Opened in 1941 and used at the time by the USAAF, RAF Barkston Heath is currently home to the Joint Elementary Flying Training School, which provides elementary flight training for Royal Navy and Army Air Corps students as well as the RAF. Tel: 01400 261201.

RAF Coningsby — 18 miles (29km) southeast of Lincoln. Opened in 1940 as a bomber base, following World War II RAF Coningsby received Avro Vulcans which were transferred to RAF Cottesmore in 1964. Phantoms arrived in 1966, while Coningsby was the first airfield to receive the Tornado fighter and its replacement, the Eurofighter Typhoon. 56 Squadron was based here until March 2003, while 5 Squadron also flew Tornados from Coningsby until its disbandment the same year. Coningsby is the home of the Battle of Britain Memorial Flight Visitor Centre, housing the last remaining airworthy Avro Lancaster bomber in the world. Tel: 01526 342581.

RAF Cranwell — Cranwell, 3 miles (5km) northwest of Sleaford. Originally HMS *Daedalus*, a Royal Naval Air Service training and airship base when it was commissioned on 1 April 1916, the site was taken over by the RAF in 1918 for officer cadet training, a role it still fulfils today. The RAF equivalent of Sandhurst or the Britannia Royal Naval College, it trains new RAF officers. Cranwell Gliding Club, part of the RAF Gliding and Soaring Association (RAFGSA), is based on the Cranwell North grass airfield. The Air Warfare Centre is based at Cranwell, as is the Aerosystems Department, a specialist training division. Cranwell also has a satellite airfield, RAF Barkston Heath (see separate entry). Sir Frank Whittle attended RAF Cranwell in the late 1920s, formulating his ideas for the jet engine here. On 15 May 1941, the world's first true jet-engine flight, by the Gloster E28/39, took place at Cranwell. Tel: 01400 261201.

RAF Digby — 8 miles (13km) north of Sleaford. The oldest operational RAF station, opened on 28 March 1918, although over the last 30 years it has been used by the Army, Navy, Air Force and utility companies for the training of aerial erectors. It performs a monitoring function within RAF Signals Command, the mass of aerials effectively preventing the use of the airfield by aircraft. It was used by the Canadian air force during World War II, and the era is marked by a Hurricane replica at the gate. There are a number of nuclear bunkers dating back to the Cold War; one of these is now a museum honouring the station's role as a command centre during the Battle of Britain.

RAF Folkingham — 2 miles (3km) southwest of Folkingham, 8 miles (13km) southeast of Grantham. Used from 1940 as a decoy airfield, the site opened as an RAF station in 1943 and was used by the USAAF during World War II. It was closed in 1947 but was employed 1959–63 as a base for Thor missiles.

RAF Holbeach — A RAF bombing range situated on the Wash, providing facilities for RAF and other NATO aircraft to practise dropping bombs and firing their cannon. Targets include several old trawlers which have been beached on the sands of the Wash for the purpose.

RAF Scampton — 5 miles (8km) north of Lincoln. Best known as the home during World War II of 617 Squadron – the 'Dambusters' – led by Wing Commander Guy Gibson. Gibson won the Victoria Cross for the famous 'bouncing bomb' raids on the Mohne, Eder and Sorpe dams in the heartland of the Ruhr in Germany during Operation Chastise. Scampton is also famous as the home of Vulcan bombers during the 1950s and 60s. These delta-winged bombers were the launch platform for the UK's airborne nuclear deterrent, the Blue Steel missile. Later the RAF Central Flying School moved to Scampton and it became the base of the Red Arrows aerobatic team. In the mid 1990s, Scampton was mothballed, with the CFS moving to nearby RAF Cranwell. More recently, the Red Arrows have moved back to Scampton; they are now the primary user of the station, which has also become a major location for Air Surveillance and Control System (ASACS) units. An on-site museum has over 400 exhibits including a Blue Steel missile. Tel: 01522 733152.

RAF Waddington — 3 miles (5km) south of Lincoln. Initially a flying training base of the Royal Flying Corps in 1916, the station reopened in 1926 as a bomber base. During World War II Lancasters flew from the airfield and between 1955 and 1984 it was a base for Vulcan bombers. Waddington now fulfils two main roles in the RAF, electronic reconnaissance and battlefield surveillance, and is the home of the annual Waddington International Air Show, which usually takes place during the last weekend of June.

Revesby Abbey — A village in the Lincolnshire Wolds, 7 miles (11km) southeast of Horncastle, and sometimes known simply as Revesby. A Cistercian monastery, founded in 1143 by William de Roumare, Earl of Lincoln, was located near the village. The first monks came from the great Yorkshire house of Rievaulx Abbey and were led by Ailred of Rievaulx, a former courtier who was to go on to become abbot of Rievaulx; a noted historian and theologian, he was later sanctified. Before the Dissolution the abbey was in decline; no records of its dissolution survive, but it is likely that the last abbot, John, surrendered the house to Henry VIII in 1538. The site was granted to Charles Brandon, 1st Duke of Suffolk, passing from his family to the Howards, Dukes of Berkshire. In 1714 it was bought by Joseph Banks 'the first' (1665–1727), great-grandfather of Sir Joseph Banks (1743–1820), botanist and patron of science, best remembered as the botanist who sailed around the world on the *Endeavour* with Captain Cook. Abbot's Lodge is all that remains of the monastic buildings, though earthworks show where the abbey buildings lie buried and the site also has fishponds and moated enclosures that may be gardens. The remains are on farmland and are not open to the public.

Rivers — The **Ancholme**, a tributary of the Humber, rises south of Bishopbridge (west of Market Rasen), passes through Brigg and flows into the Humber at South Ferriby. In its natural state, the river's valley was flat-bottomed and fenny. The river still has a distinctly rural character, and the landscape is agricultural. It once provided an important route for transporting cargo from the rural communities to the industrial towns. In the 19th century, a passenger packet boat ran from Brigg to South Ferriby and connected with a steamer to Hull. North of Bishopbridge, where the River Rase joins the Ancholme, the river runs in two intertwining channels known as the Old River Ancholme and the New River Ancholme. The course of the Old River through Brigg was enlarged, forming Island Carr. As early as the 13th century local landowners paid subscriptions for work to be undertaken with the aim of facilitating navigation and land drainage. The river's charter is one of the oldest in England. One feature of the river is the number of small bridges of low capacity which were built to allow access for farmers. Many parish boundaries still follow the line of the Old River. Today, the Ancholme is mainly used for recreation with over 200 registered boats.

The **Bain**, a tributary of the River Witham, rises in the Lincolnshire Wolds at Ludford, flowing through or past Burgh on Bain, Biscathorpe, Donington on Bain, Goulceby with Asterby and Hemingby before reaching Horncastle where it is joined by the River Waring. After leaving Horncastle, the Bain flows through the villages of Kirkby on Bain, Coningsby and Tattershall, and joins the Witham at Dogdyke. In the late 18th and early 19th centuries the Bain was canalised between Horncastle and the Witham. The Horncastle Canal opened in 1802 and was an important goods route before the coming of the railway, although it is no longer navigable. The river contains chub, roach, rudd and bream as well as brown trout, pike, eel, and smaller species such as miller's thumb, gudgeon and stone loach. It is also home to the threatened species of native crayfish, though there are populations of the introduced American signal crayfish.

The **Glen** has two sources in the low ridge of Jurassic rocks in the west of the county. Its upper reaches are named the East and West Glen, although the East Glen is sometimes called the Eden. It is navigable for its last 12 miles (19km), from its junction with Bourne Eau at Tongue End.

Although frequently referred to as a river, the **Humber** is more accurately a large tidal inlet of the North Sea, forming part of the boundary between northern and southern England. Starting at Faxfleet and the Trent Falls at the confluence of the rivers Ouse and Trent, it passes junctions with the Market Weighton Canal on the north shore and the River Ancholme on the south shore; past North Ferriby and South Ferriby, under the Humber Bridge and past Barton-upon-Humber on the south bank and Kingston upon Hull on the north bank, where the River Hull joins, then into the North Sea between Cleethorpes and Spurn Head. Grimsby and Immingham are the two major ports on the Lincolnshire side of the estuary. A major boundary in the Anglo-Saxon period, separating Northumbria from the southern kingdoms, it currently forms the boundary between the East Riding of Yorkshire to the north and North and North East Lincolnshire, to the south. From 1974 to 1996 the areas known now as East Riding, North Lincolnshire and North East Lincolnshire constituted Humberside and for centuries before that, the Humber lay between Lindsey and the East Riding of Yorkshire. Its total length is approximately 40 miles (64km).

Nene see Cambridgeshire

Trent see Nottinghamshire

A small river and a tributary of the River Bain, the **Waring** rises in the parish of Belchford and runs through Belchford village, passing between the villages of Fulletby, West Ashby and Low Toynton before arriving at Horncastle, where it divides Horncastle market place from the part of the town known as Cagthorpe. After the Horncastle floods of the 1960s, the river channel was straightened and its banks built up through the town. It joins the Bain along with the Hunker or Scrafield Beck at the confluence by the town's swimming pool, which was built on the site of the old dry dock of the Horncastle Canal.

The **Welland** rises north of Market Harborough in Leicestershire and flows northeast to Stamford, Market Deeping, Deeping St James, Crowland, Cowbit and Spalding, before entering the Wash at Fosdyke Bridge. It is 35 miles (56km) in length and has been a main waterway across the part of the Fens called South Holland for thousands of years. The fertile arable land of its banks, much of it marine silt, suits the bulb-growing for which Spalding was once famous. Tributaries of the Welland include the Eye Brook, the rivers Chater, Gwash and Glen, and Vernatt's Drain.

The **Witham** rises south of Grantham, near South Witham, just inside the Leicestershire border. The river flows northeast to Lincoln and then east and southeast to Boston, before flowing into the Haven, a tidal arm of the Wash. Its tributaries include Foston Beck, River Brant, Barlings Eau, River Bain, Kyme Eau, the fenland part of the River Slea and the following that flow into The Haven: South Forty Foot Drain, Maud Foster Drain and Hobhole Drain. The Witham flows for 80 miles (129km); the navigable portion from Boston near the Wash to Lincoln is 36 miles (58km) in length.

Roman forts — The main Roman forts in Lincolnshire were located at: Alkborough (Aquis), Ancaster (Causennis), Brant Broughton (Briga), Broughton (Pretorium), Caistor, Horncastle (Banovallum), Kirton in Lindsey (Inmedio), Lincoln (Lindum Colonia), Ludford, Stow (Sidnacester), Tattershall (Drurobrivis), Torksey (Tiovulfingacester), Wainfleet (Vainona), Willoughby (Verometum), Winteringham (Ad Abum).

RSPB Frampton Marsh — 4 miles (6km) southeast of Boston. A nature reserve on the Wash consisting of saltmarsh and wetland. Large numbers of nesting redshank are spotted here during the summer. In winter birds of prey, including hen harrier, merlin and short-eared owls, are common. Tel: 01205 724678.

RSPB Freiston Shore — 5 miles (8km) east of Boston. One of the RSPB's newest nature reserves, located on the Wash at one of the largest managed realignment sites in England, where new saltings are being recreated to improve flood management. The birdwatching hide overlooks a lagoon and areas of saltmarsh. Wildlife in the area include brent geese in winter and breeding avocets in the summer. Tel: 01205 724678.

St Botolph's Church — Wormgate, Boston. Known familiarly as the 'Stump', St Botolph's lays claim to being the largest parish church in England. Largely built in the 14th century, it measures 20,070 sq ft (1864 sq m) in area and is 282ft (86m) long. The 15th–16th century tower is 272ft 6in (83m) tall. Early restoration work to repair Civil War damage was carried out during the 17th and 18th centuries. The organ, lost in the Reformation, was replaced in 1715. In 1851–3, under the direction of George Gilbert Scott, architect George Pace carried out a major restoration. The changes included the removal of the tower ceiling and the addition of stone vaulting as originally featured in the medieval plans. Between 1929 and 1932 the bells were restored with a new bell frame, increasing the number of bells from eight to ten. The number was increased again in 1951 to 15. St Botolph's is a member of the Anglican Great Churches group, established for the small number of parish churches that have cathedral-like proportions without the title to match. Tel: 01205 362864.

Sandtoft Trolleybus Museum — Sandtoft, 9 miles (15km) west of Scunthorpe. Situated on the border with South Yorkshire, the museum houses one of the largest collections of trolleybuses in the world. Other exhibits include 1960s shop displays, prefabs and a cycle and lawnmower shop. Tel: 01724 711391.

Schools — **Boston Grammar School** is a selective school for boys aged 11–18, recently admitting girls aged 16–18. The school was founded by charter of Philip and Mary in 1555; the oldest part, the former 'big school', now used as the school library, was built in 1557. Notable former pupils include surgeon and explorer George Bass, footballer Danny Butterfield and mathematician Joseph Langley Birchnall. Tel: 01205 366444.

Grantham Grammar School, also known as The King's School, has occupied the same site since its endowment by Bishop Richard Fox in 1528. Locally born, Fox became secretary to Henry, Earl of Richmond, while he was in exile in Brittany, prior to the Battle of Bosworth which led to Henry's capture of the throne as Henry VII. Bishop Fox also later founded Taunton Grammar School. In the 17th century the 'Cambridge Platonist', Henry More, Poet Laureate Colley Cibber and Sir Isaac Newton all attended the school. Previously the most notable old boy had been William Cecil, Lord Burghley, of Burghley House (see separate entry). In the 17th century, Newton, as was customary in his time, carved his signature on the wall of what is now the school library. Tel: 01476 563180.

King Edward VI Grammar School (often shortened to KEVIGS or KEVIS) in Louth is one of the oldest schools in England. Schooling took place in the town in the 8th century, although the oldest specific reference to a school indicates that Simon de Luda was the town's schoolmaster in 1276. The school was probably funded by the town's religious and merchant guilds, and by a chantry established by Thomas of Louth in 1317. After the dissolution of religious guilds in 1548 leading local figures petitioned Edward VI to secure the school's future and on 21 September 1551 the school was awarded its royal charter, while a foundation was set up to administer it. KEVIS became a Specialist Science College in 2003. Former pupils include Captain John Smith, the first elected president of Virginia (1592–5), author and explorer Sir John Franklin (1797–1800) and poet Alfred, Lord Tennyson (1816–20). Tel: 01507 600456.

Scunthorpe North Lincolnshire Museum — Oswald Road, Scunthorpe. Museum depicting the history and landscape of North Lincolnshire. Displays range from geology and archaeology to the Social History Gallery, featuring Scunthorpe's industrial heritage. Tel: 01724 843533.

Skegness — A seaside town on the North Sea coast of Lincolnshire. Primarily a fishing village and a small port until the arrival of the railway in 1875, arranged by the 9th Earl of Scarborough who was keen to develop Skegness as a resort, it expanded rapidly thereafter. Skegness was the site of the UK's first holiday camp, opened by Billy Butlin in 1936. It has been dubbed 'the Blackpool of the East Coast', and has a famous mascot, the Jolly Fisherman, while the slogan 'Skegness is so bracing' is a reference to the chilly prevailing northeasterly winds that blow off the North Sea. The town's pier, 1843ft (562m) long, opened on Whit Monday 1881 and was at the time the fourth longest in England. Steamboat trips ran from the pier to the Wash and Hunstanton in Norfolk from 1882 until 1910. In 1978 the pier was badly damaged and considerably shortened by severe gales. It has since undergone major refurbishment, although it no longer extends far beyond the high water level of the beach. Skegness is also the home to the world's premier Meccano exhibition, staged annually in the Embassy Theatre on the seafront.

Skegness Church Farm Museum — Church Road South, Skegness. Collection of agricultural and social history objects housed in an 18th century farmhouse and 19th century farm buildings. Exhibits include a late 18th century Lincolnshire mud and stud thatched cottage and 19th century timber and pantiled barn. Tel: 01754 766658.

Sleaford — A market town in North Kesteven which takes its name from the River Slea, a tributary of the Witham. The most prominent church is the parish church of St Denys, abutting the market place. The church has one of the oldest stone broach spires in England, and mostly dates from 1180, although parts were rebuilt after an electrical storm in 1884. The altar rail (originally from Lincoln Cathedral) is by Sir Christopher Wren. Cogglesford Water Mill, a working mill on the banks of the River Slea, dates from the 17th century. Sleaford Castle, of which only earthworks now remain, was built by Alexander de Blois, Bishop of Lincoln 1123–47; King John spent a night in the castle after his disastrous crossing of the Wash. Henry VIII stayed at Sleaford twice and held a state council at the castle.

Snipe Dales — 5 miles (8km) east of Horncastle. Situated on the southern edge of the Lincolnshire Wolds, Snipe Dales covers 210 acres (85ha) and is a rare semi-natural wet valley system. The steep-sided stream valleys, rough grazing and woodland of the eastern half are managed as a nature reserve; Snipe Dales Country Park in the west, formerly owned by the Forestry Commission, is largely coniferous. Tel: 01507 588401.

Somerton Castle — 1 mile (1.6km) west of Boothby Graffoe, 7 miles (11km) south of Lincoln. Antony Bek, Bishop of Durham, built the castle in the late 13th century, giving it to Edward II in 1309. King John I of France was imprisoned at the castle 1359–60. Althought the castle was ruined by 1601, three towers and portions of the walls remained standing and were incorporated into the large house which now occupies the site. Prominent earthworks, including parts of the moat, are still visible. Now Grade I listed, the castle is not open to the public.

Spalding — A market town known as a centre of the horticultural industry and for its annual Flower Parade. Spalding is sometimes considered as England's southernmost 'Northern' town: it appears geographically to be just above the line dividing England into north and south, its inhabitants prefer to be thought of as northerners, and predominantly, most of its residents speak with an accent similar to that of the north Midlands or southern Yorkshire – a flat 'a' is preferred in words such as 'bath', 'grass' and 'path', and a heavy 'oo' sound when a 'u' is spoken, as in 'bus', 'muffin' and 'sugar', while in Peterborough, 20 miles (32km) to the south, a general southern English accent is preferred. The Coronation Channel was built in 1953 to protect Spalding from flooding from the River Welland. See also River Welland.

Spalding Bulb Museum — Surfleet Road, Pinchbeck, 2 miles (3km) north of Spalding. Museum dedicated to the flower bulb industry in South Lincolnshire from 1880 to the present day. Exhibits include a 1904 flower forcing glass house, a blacksmith's shop, the Spalding cattle market auction hall and hovels full of old equipment used in the industry. Tel: 01775 680490.

Sport

football — **Boston United** were formed in 1933 and went fully professional in 2001, winning the Conference and gaining promotion to the Football League in their first professional season. They lost their League status in 2006–07. The Pilgrims (also known as the Stumps) play at the Staffsmart Stadium (previously known as Shodfriars Lane, and then York Street). Their home colours are yellow and black. Tel: 01205 364406.

Grimsby Town were founded in 1878 and joined the Football League in 1892. Historically they are Lincolnshire's most successful club, having played in Division One before and after World War II and also reaching FA Cup semi-finals in 1936 and 1939. Nicknamed The Mariners, they play in black and white stripes at Blundell Park, Cleethorpes. Tel: 01472 605050.

Lincoln City were founded in 1884 and joined the Football League in 1892, although they lost their League place more than once in the early 20th century and were relegated to the Conference for a season in 1985–86. Nicknamed The Red Imps (they are also known as The Yellowbellies), they have played at Sincil Bank since 1894. Their home strip is red and white striped shirts and black shorts. Tel: 0870 899 2005.

Scunthorpe United were founded in 1899 and merged with Lindsey United to form Scunthorpe and Lindsey United in 1910. They joined the Football League in 1950 and were renamed Scunthorpe United in 1958. Nicknamed The Iron, their home ground is Glanford Park, where they have played since moving from the Old Show Ground in 1988. Their traditional colours are claret and blue. Tel: 0871 221 1899.

horse racing — **Market Rasen** racecourse is a right-handed oval with a circumference of 1¼ miles (2km). Unusually, Market Rasen stages a year-round programme of National Hunt racing; its most high-profile fixture is the Summer Plate meeting, normally staged on the third Saturday in July. Tel: 01673 843434.

Stamford Brownes Hospital — Broad Street, Stamford. The ancient almshouses, still in use, were founded in 1475 by local wool merchant William Browne. There is medieval stained glass in the chapel and Audit Room. Some of the original furniture is on display. Tel: 01780 763153.

Stamford Castle — Stamford. Norman motte and bailey castle founded in the late 11th century. A shell keep was built on the motte in the following century and later extended, possibly by William de Warenne, but the castle appears to have fallen into ruin by the 15th century. Parts of the curtain wall are still visible but the motte no longer exists.

Stamford Museum — Broad Street, Stamford. Museum featuring local history collections and the 20ft (6m) long Stamford Tapestry, which depicts the town's history in a series of woollen panels and was completed in 2000. Tel: 01780 766317.

Stoke Rochford Hall — 6 miles (10km) south of Grantham. Built 1841–3 in Jacobean revival style and designed by Scottish architect William Burn, the hall has been restored after a major fire in 2005 and is currently utilised as a conference and banqueting centre. Tel: 01476 530337.

Tattershall Castle — 8 miles (13km) southwest of Horncastle. The brick-built castle was constructed 1434–45 by Ralph Cromwell, Lord Treasurer to Henry VI, and replaced an earlier castle built in 1231 by Ralph de Tateshale. The design of the square keep, 130ft (40m) high with hexagonal towers, was influenced by similar structures in France. Built over a vaulted basement, the four-storey keep is topped by a corbelled roof gallery. The property passed to the Crown after the death of Lord Cromwell and then to the Earls of Lincoln. It was bought in 1911 by Lord Curzon, who restored the tower, re-excavated the moat and rescued the Gothic stone fireplaces that had been removed and were on their way to America. In 1926 Lord Curzon handed over the castle to the National Trust. Tel: 01526 342543.

Temple Bruer Templar Preceptory Tower — Temple Road, Temple Bruer, 6 miles (10km) northwest of Sleaford. The only remaining part of a 12th century Templar preceptory, built to house members of the military order formed to guard the shrines of the Holy Land and protect pilgrims on the road. Tel: 01529 414294.

Thatcher, Margaret — Margaret Hilda Thatcher, Baroness Thatcher of Kesteven, née Margaret Hilda Roberts was born in Grantham on 13 October 1925. A Conservative Party politician and prime minister (1979–90), Europe's first woman prime minister, Mrs Thatcher was the only 20th century British prime minister to win three consecutive terms; at the time of her resignation, she was Britain's longest continuously serving prime minister since Lord Liverpool completed his 15 year tenure in 1827. Her father, Alfred Roberts, who owned a grocer's shop in Grantham, was active in local politics (serving as an Alderman), and was a Methodist lay preacher. Her mother was Beatrice Roberts, née Stephenson, and she had one sister, Muriel (1921–2004). Thatcher performed well academically, attending Kesteven girls' grammar school and, from 1944, Somerville College, Oxford, where she studied chemistry. She became President of the Oxford University Conservative Association in 1946. She graduated with a second-class degree and worked as a research chemist for British Xylonite and then J Lyons & Co., where she helped develop methods for preserving ice cream. She was also a member of the Association of Scientific Workers. While active in the Conservative Party in Kent, she met wealthy businessman Sir Denis Thatcher, whom she married in 1951. Denis funded his wife's studies for the Bar and she qualified as a barrister in 1953, the same year that her twin children Carol and Mark were born. As a lawyer she specialised in tax law. Thatcher then began to look for a safe Conservative seat; having easily won the Finchley seat in the 1959 General Election, took her seat in the House of Commons. In 1961 she went against her party's line by voting for the restoration of birching. Thatcher was one of few Conservative MPs to support Leo Abse's Bill to decriminalise male homosexuality, and she voted in favour of David Steel's Bill to legalise abortion. However, she was opposed to the abolition of capital punishment and voted against making divorce more easily attainable. She made her mark as a conference speaker in 1966, with a strong attack on the high-tax policies of the Labour Government as being steps 'not only towards Socialism, but towards Communism'. She won promotion to the Shadow Cabinet as Shadow Fuel Spokesman in 1967, and was promoted to Shadow Transport and, finally, Education before the 1970 General Election. When the Conservative party under Edward Heath won the 1970 election, Thatcher became Secretary of State for Education and Science. In her first months in office, forced to administer a cut in the Education budget, she was responsible for the abolition of universal free milk for schoolchildren aged 7–11 (Labour had already abolished it for secondary schools). This led to one of the more unflattering names for her, 'Mrs. Thatcher, Milk Snatcher'. After her party lost the second election of 1974, Sir Keith Joseph challenged Edward Heath's leadership; after his withdrawal, Thatcher entered the race on behalf of the Josephite faction. Unexpectedly she outpolled Heath on the first ballot, forcing him to resign the leadership. On the second ballot, she defeated Heath's preferred successor, William Whitelaw, by 146 votes to 79, and became Conservative Party leader on 11 February 1975. She appointed Whitelaw as her deputy. On 19 January 1976, in a speech delivered in Kensington Town Hall, she made a famously scathing attack on the Soviet Union: 'The Russians are bent on world dominance, and they are rapidly acquiring the means to become the most powerful imperial nation the world has seen. The men in the Soviet Politburo do not have to worry about the ebb and flow of public opinion. They put guns before butter, while we put just about everything before guns.' In response, the Soviet Defence Ministry newspaper *Krasnaya Zvezda* ('Red Star') gave her the nickname 'Iron Lady', which was soon publicised by Radio Moscow. During the 1979 General Election, most opinion polls showed that voters preferred James Callaghan as Prime Minister even as the Conservative Party maintained a lead in the polls. The Labour government ran into difficulties with industrial disputes, strikes, high unemployment and collapsing public services during the winter of 1978–9, dubbed the 'Winter of Discontent'. The Conservatives' campaign posters bore slogans such as 'Labour Isn't Working', attacking the government's record over unemployment and its over-regulation of the labour market. Callaghan's Labour government fell after a successful motion of no confidence in spring 1979; in the same year's General Election the Conservatives won a 44 seat majority in the House of Commons and Thatcher became the UK's first female Prime Minister. On arriving at 10 Downing Street, she famously said, in a paraphrase of St Francis of Assisi: 'Where there is discord, may we bring harmony. Where there is error, may we bring truth. Where there is doubt, may we bring faith. And where there is despair, may we bring hope.' Mrs Thatcher's political 'assassination' was, according to witnesses such as Alan Clark, one of the most dramatic episodes in British political history. The idea of a long-serving prime minister – undefeated at the polls – being ousted by an internal party ballot, might initially seem improbable. However, by 1990, opposition to Thatcher's policies on local government taxation, her government's perceived mishandling of the economy (in particular, high interest rates of 15 per cent, which were eroding her support base among homeowners and businesspeople), and the divisions opening in the Conservative Party over European integration made her and her party seem increasingly politically vulnerable. On 1 November 1990, Sir Geoffrey Howe, one of Thatcher's staunchest supporters, resigned as Deputy Prime Minister in protest at Thatcher's European policy. In his resignation speech in the House of Commons two weeks later, he suggested that the time had come for 'others to consider their own response to the tragic conflict of loyalties' with which he had 'wrestled for perhaps too long'. Her former cabinet colleague Michael Heseltine subsequently challenged her for the leadership of the party, and attracted sufficient support in the first round of voting to trigger a second ballot. Though she initially stated that she intended to contest the second ballot, Thatcher decided, after consulting with her Cabinet colleagues, to withdraw from the contest, announcing her decision to the Cabinet just after 9.30am on 22 November. Shortly afterwards, her staff made public what was, in effect, her resignation statement: 'Having consulted widely among my colleagues, I have concluded that the unity of the Party and the prospects of victory in a General Election would be better served if I stood down to enable Cabinet colleagues to enter the ballot for the leadership. I should like to thank all those in Cabinet and outside who have given me such dedicated support.' She supported John Major as her successor and he duly won the leadership contest. Despite ill health she remains active in various groups, including the Conservative Way Forward group, the Bruges Group and the European Foundation. She was widowed on 26 June 2003.

Thornton Abbey 5 miles (8km) northwest of Immingham. Founded in the 11th century by Augustinian monks, the original Romanesque abbey was rebuilt in the 12th century in Early Gothic style; an impressive two-storey gatehouse and moat were added in the 14th century. The abbey was dissolved in 1539 and a college of secular canons briefly occupied the site before it was given to the Bishop of Lincoln. Nothing of the 11th century abbey is visible above ground, and there are few remains of the 12th century abbey except parts of the octagonal chapterhouse and the cloister. The gatehouse, however, is structurally intact. Among the earliest large-scale brick structures in England, the outside of the building is adorned with three almost life-size statues directly above the entrance and is adjoined by a fortified bridge over a moat. Thornton is now in the care of English Heritage. Tel: 01469 541445.

Trinity Bridge Crowland, 8 miles (13km) south of Spalding. The triangular Trinity Bridge stands in the centre of Crowland on dry land. Originally it spanned the rivers that flowed through the town, although these have since been re-routed. The current bridge was built 1360–90 and replaced previous wooden bridges. It has three arches but one overarching structure. A bridge on the site was first mentioned by Ethelbald of Mercia in 716.

Tumby Moorside High House Museum High House Farm, Tumby Moorside, Coningsby, Boston. The museum tells the story of 30 years of the 20th century from World War I to the Blitz. Tel: 01526 345408.

University of Lincoln One of the newest universities in the UK, founded in its current form in 1996. Its main campus is at Brayford Pool in Lincoln but it also has sites at Riseholme Park to the north of the city, at Holbeach in the south of Lincolnshire and at Hull in East Yorkshire. Lincoln had never had its own university until, in 1993, it was decided to build a campus in the city; this was to be combined with the existing University of Humberside to form a new University of Lincolnshire and Humberside. The name was changed to the University of Lincoln in 2001 after the main Hull site was closed. In the same year the university acquired Leicester-based De Montfort University's schools in

Lincolnshire, the Lincoln School of Art and Design in Lincoln and the Lincolnshire School of Agriculture's sites at Riseholme, Caythorpe and Holbeach. The university occupies several buildings of historic interest in uphill Lincoln (the 'Cathedral' campus), including a building named after Chad Varah, founder of the Samaritans. The Riseholme Park campus, set among a 600 acre (240ha) estate and working farm, contains Riseholme Hall, formerly the residence of the Bishop of Lincoln. There are five faculties: Applied Computing Sciences; Art, Architecture and Design; Business and Law; Health, Life and Social Sciences; Media and Humanities. Tel: 01522 882000.

Wash, The — A square-mouthed estuary on the northwest margin of East Anglia between Norfolk and Lincolnshire. Among the largest estuaries in the UK, it is fed by the rivers Witham, Welland, Nene and Great Ouse. A Special Protection Area, the Wash is made up of extensive salt marshes, major intertidal banks of sand and mud, shallow waters and deep channels. The seawall at Freiston has been breached in three places to increase the saltmarsh area, to provide an extra habitat for birds, particularly waders, and also as a natural flood prevention measure (see RSPB Freiston Shore). An average of 300,000 migrating birds such as geese, ducks and wading birds overwinter in the Wash each year. Notably it was featured on the BBC television programme *Seven Natural Wonders* as one of the wonders of Norfolk and Lincolnshire. The most famous incident associated with the Wash is the loss of King John's royal treasure. According to the story, the king was taken ill while travelling from Spalding in Lincolnshire to Bishop's Lynn (later King's Lynn) in Norfolk and decided to return. While taking an inland route via Wisbech, he sent his baggage train, including his crown jewels, along the causeway and ford across the mouth of the Wellstream, a route usable only at low tide. The horse-drawn wagons moved too slowly for the incoming tide, and many were lost, supposedly somewhere near modern Sutton Bridge on the River Nene.

Waters' Edge Country Park — Maltkiln Road, Barton-upon-Humber. An 86 acre (35ha) country park created on a former industrial site close to the Humber estuary and Humber Bridge, and encompassing two Sites of Special Scientific Interest. The park is comprehensively covered by CCTV cameras forming a unique wildlife surveillance system. The visitor centre with its striking curved glass front was designed to operate sustainably via the employment of environmentally friendly technology. Tel: 01652 631500.

Whisby Nature Park & Natural World Centre — 5 miles (8km) southwest of Lincoln. A 325 acre (131ha) complex of flooded gravel pits surrounded by areas of lowland heath, grassland and woodland and home to an abundance of wildlife including songbirds, water fowl, a wide range of butterflies and wild plants. Woodpeckers, nightingales and herons are among the birds to be seen. The site is managed by Lincolnshire Wildlife Trust. Tel: 01522 500676.

Windmills — **Alford Five Sailed Windmill**, East Street, Alford. The tower mill, built in 1837, is now the sole survivor of four windmills in Alford, including another with five sails and one with six. Tel: 01507 462136.

Boston Maud Foster Windmill, Willoughby Road, Boston, built in 1819, is another five-sailed tower mill and at 80ft (24m) is one of the tallest working windmills in England. Tel: 01205 352188.

Burgh Le Marsh Windmill, High Street, Burgh le Marsh, Skegness, is a working tower mill, the only mill in the county with left-handed sails. It was built by Sam Oxley of Alford in 1813 and contains much of its original equipment. Tel: 01522 522064.

Dyke Windmill, Main Road, Dyke, Bourne. Built in the 1840s, the smock mill moved from Deeping Fen in the early 1900s and was rebuilt in the late 1990s in Dyke. Tel: 01778 393244.

Heckington Windmill, Hale Road, Heckington, Sleaford. This unique eight-sailed working mill was originally built in 1830 as a five-sailer. A violent thunderstorm blew off the cap and sails and it was repaired in 1892 with the cap and eight sails from a windmill in Boston. This outstanding example of Victorian engineering was again restored in 2004. Tel: 01529 461919.

Lincoln Ellis Mill, Mill Road, Lincoln. A working windmill built in 1798, the sole survivor of nine mills in this part of the city. Tel: 01522 528448.

Moulton Windmill, Moulton, Spalding, is the tallest windmill in England at 97ft (29.5m).The tower mill was originally built in 1822; the sails blew off in a freak gale in 1894. Tel: 01406 373237.

Sibsey Trader Mill, Frithville Road, Sibsey, Boston, is one of the very few six-sailed mills remaining in England. Built in 1877 by Saundersons, millwrights of Louth, in typical Lincolnshire style, its height is 74ft 3in (22.6m). It worked until 1954, latterly with four sails, and has now been restored to full working order. Tel: 01205 750036.

Waltham Windmill Centre, Brigsley Road, Waltham, Grimsby. The fully restored, large six-sailed tower mill was built in 1879 by Saundersons of Louth. Tel: 01472 822236.

Wrawby Postmill, Mill Lane, Wrawby, Brigg. Sited just outside the village of Wrawby, overlooking Brigg, the windmill is a landmark for miles around. The restored building was constructed in 1760 and is the last surviving post mill in the area. Tel: 01652 653699.

Woodhall Spa Cottage Museum — Iddesleigh Road, Woodhall Spa, 7 miles (11km) southwest of Horncastle. Housed in a 19th century corrugated iron cottage, the museum has displays on the history of the Victorian resort of Woodhall Spa, while a collection of photographs by John Wield provides a rich insight into local life during the early 20th century. Another room is devoted to the RAF 617 'Dambusters' squadron, based at nearby RAF Woodhall, and Arnhem. Tel: 01526 353775.

Woolsthorpe Manor — Woolsthorpe-by-Colsterworth, 1/2 mile (0.8km) northwest of Colsterworth, 7 miles (11km) south of Grantham (not to be confused with Woolsthorpe near Belvoir). The childhood home of Isaac Newton. The former medieval farmhouse was bought in 1623 by Newton's grandfather, who rebuilt the property to provide a modest family home, and Newton was raised at Woolsthorpe Manor by his grandparents until the age of 12. From an early age he showed unusual interest in mathematical and scientific problems, as well as developing an understanding of astronomy. Two of the sundials he constructed as a boy have survived: one can be seen at the Royal Society in London and the other in the church at Colsterworth. After Newton went to Cambridge University he rarely returned to his home, but he lived at Woolshorpe during an 18 month period when the university was closed by the plague. During this time the majority of his mathematical conclusions were achieved, while his pioneering work in many other fields also took root; it is believed that the apple tree now standing in the little orchard garden opposite the front of the house is a descendant of the tree under which Newton considered his theory of gravitation. Newton did not return to the family home even after he inherited it on his mother's death; after his own death in 1727, Woolsthorpe was sold to another farming family, the Turners, who owned it for a further 200 years. The house was in a state of disrepair by the time the Royal Society presented it to the National Trust in 1942 as a lasting memorial to Newton. It is now restored to its appearance when Newton would have been living at Woolsthorpe; although none of the furniture displayed belonged to the family, there is visible evidence of Newton's occupation. He was known to have made a habit of using various walls in the house as 'doodling pads', and several fragments of this graffiti can be seen. Tel: 01476 860338.

Some famous people born in Lincolnshire

Alderton, John (actor) (1940–)	Gainsborough
Bass, George (explorer) (1771–1803)	Aswarby
Brown, Joe (singer) (1941–)	Swarby
Capes, Geoff (athlete) (1949–)	Holbeach
Cecil, William (statesman) (1520–98)	Bourne
Dexter, (Norman) Colin (author) (1930–)	Stamford
Dotrice, Michele (actress) (1948–)	Cleethorpes
Emery, Victor (scientist) (1933–2002)	Boston
Flinders, Matthew (navigator) (1774–1814)	Donington
Foale, (Colin) Michael (astronaut) (1957–)	Louth
Foxe, John (author) (1516–87)	Boston
Franklin, Captain John (explorer) (1786–1847)	Spilsby
Frinton, Freddie (comedian) (1909–68)	Grimsby
Gish, Sheila (actress) (1942–2005)	Lincoln
Henry IV (king of England) (1367–1413)	Bolingbroke Castle
Hodge, Patricia (actress) (1946–)	Cleethorpes
Lucan, Arthur (music hall entertainer) (1885–1954)	Sibsey
Newton, Isaac (scientist) (1643–1727)	Woolsthorpe Manor
Plowright, Joan (actress) (1929–)	Brigg
Saunders, Jennifer (comedy actress) (1958–)	Sleaford
Stukeley, William (antiquary) (1687–1765)	Holbeach
Tennyson, Alfred Lord (poet) (1809–92)	Somersby
Thatcher, Margaret (politician) (1925–)	Grantham
Thompson, Eric (actor and producer) (1929–82)	Sleaford
Thorndike, Dame Sybil (actress) (1882–1976)	Gainsborough
Varah, (Edward) Chad (Anglican priest and founder of the Samaritans) (1911–2007)	Barton-upon-Humber
Wesley, Charles (hymn writer) (1707–88)	Epworth
Wesley, John (methodist minister) (1703–91)	Epworth
Whitgift, John (Archbishop of Canterbury) (1530–1604)	Grimsby
Worth, Charles Frederick (father of haute couture) (1825–95)	Bourne

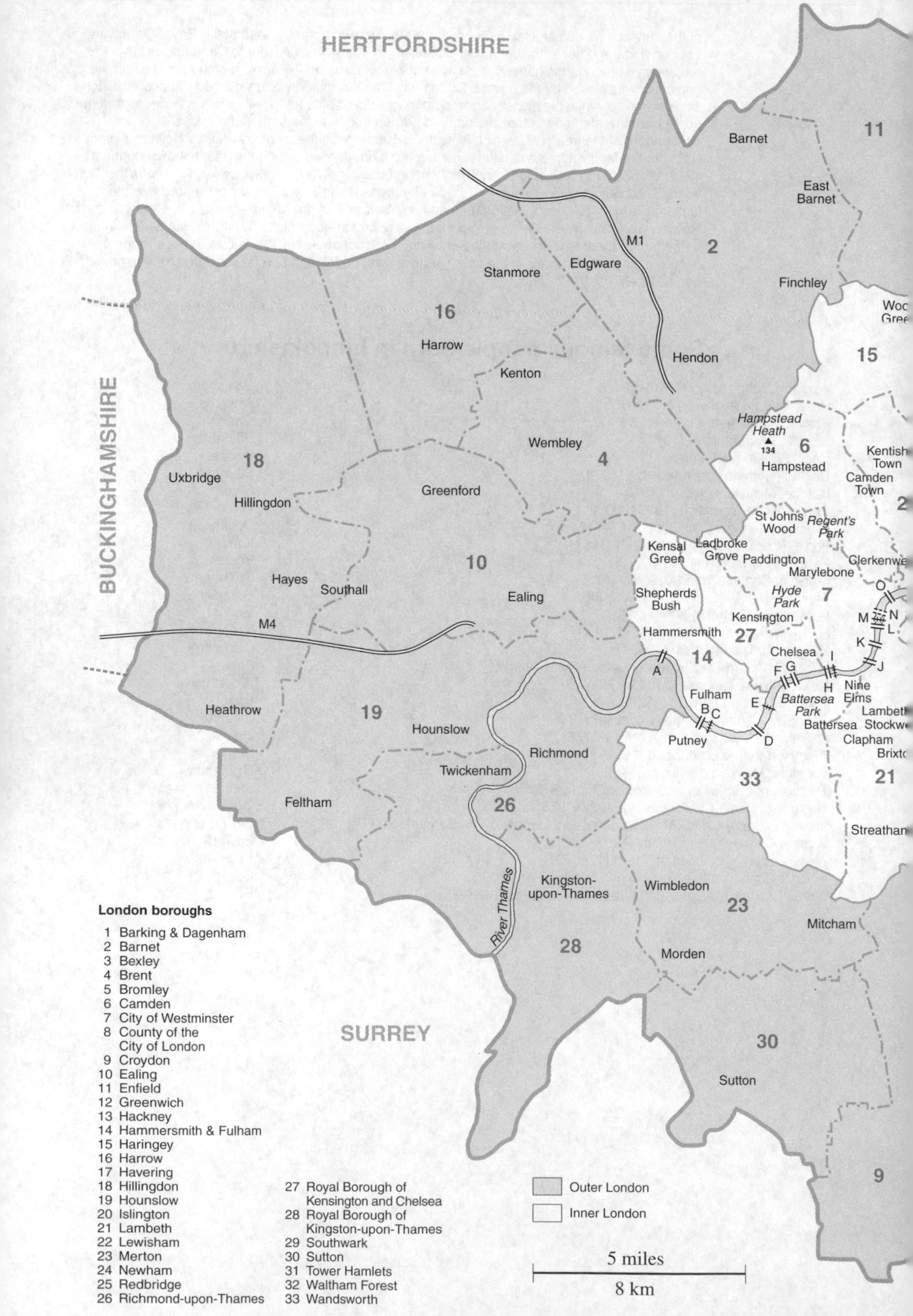
HERTFORDSHIRE
BUCKINGHAMSHIRE
SURREY
Barnet
East Barnet
11
2
M1
Edgware
Stanmore
Finchley
Woo Gree
16
Harrow
Hendon
15
Kenton
Hampstead Heath
134
6
Kentish Town
Camden Town
Wembley
4
18
Uxbridge
Hampstead
Hillingdon
Greenford
St Johns Wood
Regent's Park
Kensal Green
Ladbroke Grove
Paddington
Clerkenwe
10
Marylebone
Hayes
Southall
Ealing
Shepherds Bush
Hyde Park
7
O
M4
Kensington
M
N
L
Hammersmith
27
K
14
Chelsea
I
J
A
F G
H
Nine Elms
Fulham
B C
E
Battersea Park
Lambeth
Stockw
Heathrow
19
Hounslow
Battersea
Putney
D
Clapham
Richmond
Brixt
Twickenham
33
21
Feltham
26
Streathan
River Thames
Kingston-upon-Thames
Wimbledon
23
Mitcham
28
Morden
30
Sutton
9
London boroughs
1 Barking & Dagenham
2 Barnet
3 Bexley
4 Brent
5 Bromley
6 Camden
7 City of Westminster
8 County of the City of London
9 Croydon
10 Ealing
11 Enfield
12 Greenwich
13 Hackney
14 Hammersmith & Fulham
15 Haringey
16 Harrow
17 Havering
18 Hillingdon
19 Hounslow
20 Islington
21 Lambeth
22 Lewisham
23 Merton
24 Newham
25 Redbridge
26 Richmond-upon-Thames
27 Royal Borough of Kensington and Chelsea
28 Royal Borough of Kingston-upon-Thames
29 Southwark
30 Sutton
31 Tower Hamlets
32 Waltham Forest
33 Wandsworth
Outer London
Inner London
5 miles
8 km

Greater London

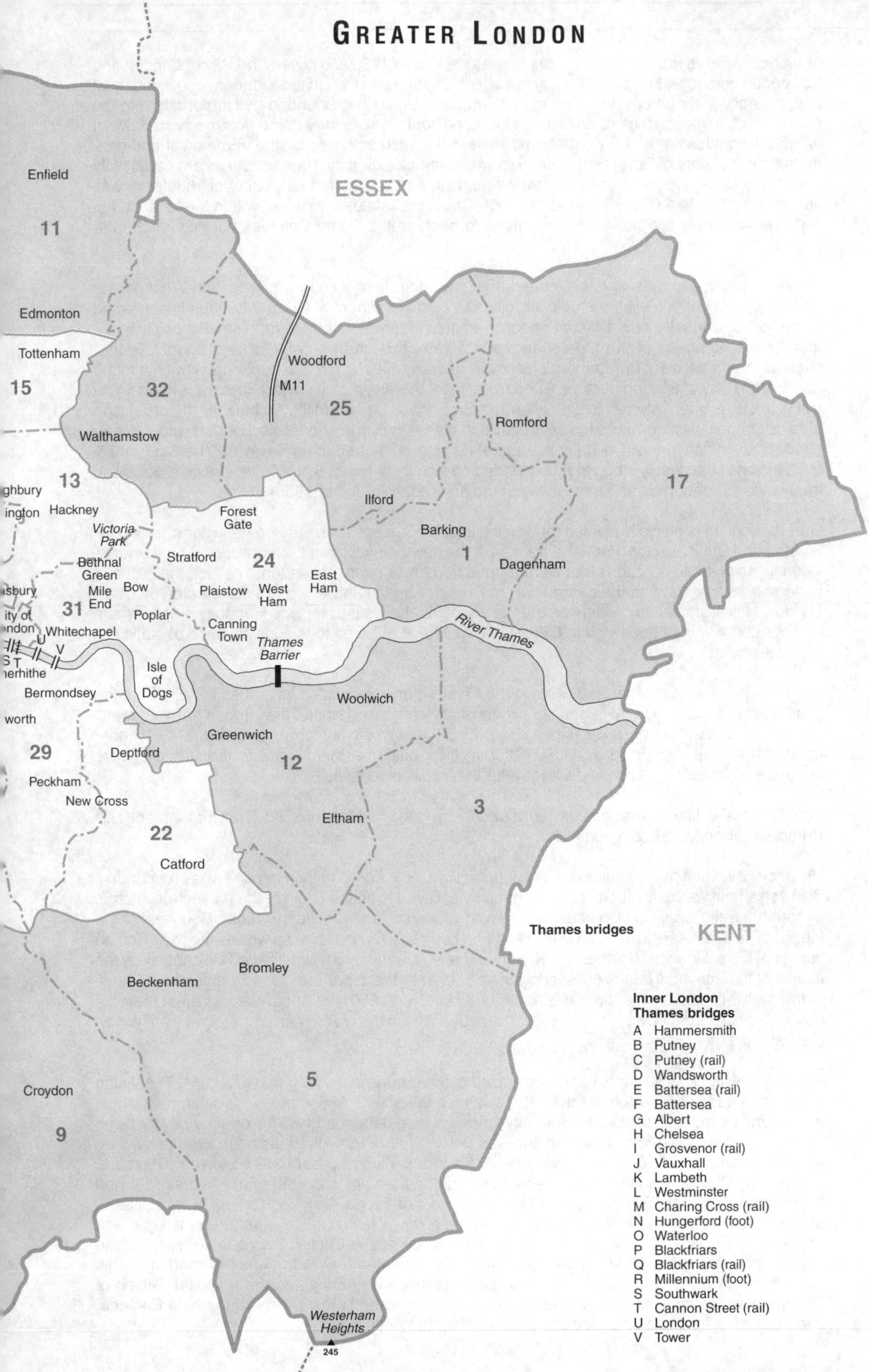

ESSEX
Enfield
11
Edmonton
Tottenham
15
32
Woodford
M11
25
Romford
Walthamstow
13
17
ghbury
ington
Hackney
Forest Gate
Ilford
Victoria Park
Barking
Bethnal Green
Stratford
24
1
Dagenham
Mile End
Bow
sbury
Plaistow
West Ham
East Ham
ity of ondon
31
Poplar
Whitechapel
Canning Town
River Thames
U
V
S T
Thames Barrier
herhithe
Isle of Dogs
Bermondsey
Woolwich
worth
Greenwich
29
Deptford
12
Peckham
New Cross
3
Eltham
22
Catford
Thames bridges
KENT
Bromley
Beckenham
5
Croydon
9
Westerham Heights
245
Inner London Thames bridges
A Hammersmith
B Putney
C Putney (rail)
D Wandsworth
E Battersea (rail)
F Battersea
G Albert
H Chelsea
I Grosvenor (rail)
J Vauxhall
K Lambeth
L Westminster
M Charing Cross (rail)
N Hungerford (foot)
O Waterloo
P Blackfriars
Q Blackfriars (rail)
R Millennium (foot)
S Southwark
T Cannon Street (rail)
U London
V Tower

The administrative area of Greater London was created in 1965 and covers the City of London and 32 London boroughs. London is the capital city of England and the United Kingdom and is the most populous city and metropolitan area in the European Union. It is bounded by Hertfordshire to the north, Essex to the northeast, Kent to the east and southeast, Surrey to the south and southwest, and Buckinghamshire to the west and northwest. It is also bordered by the ceremonial and non-metropolitan county of Royal Berkshire in its westernmost extremity. These counties are collectively referred to as the Home Counties as they adjoin the capital. The former county of Middlesex was largely absorbed into Greater London in 1965; its precise status is clarified within the local attractions section, as is the status of other areas formerly in the Home Counties but now in Greater London.

Greater London can be said to be more than a city, more than a county in fact. Both Westminster and the City of London itself are officially cities. A Lord Lieutenant of Greater London is appointed for the conurbation, less the City of London – an area identical to the Metropolitan Police District – and for the purposes of the Lieutenancies Act 1997 this area is defined as a county. Rather strangely perhaps, the term 'London' is normally used in reference to Greater London but not to the ancient, tiny City of London at its very centre. Instead, this small area – which forms the main financial district – is often referred to simply as 'the City' or 'the Square Mile'. Archaically the urbanised area of London was known as the Metropolis. In common usage, the terms 'London' and 'Greater London' are synonymous. Colloquially, central London is referred to as 'Town' or 'The Big Smoke' (an allusion to the deadly smog that descended on the city between 5 and 9 December 1952, killing thousands of Londoners and necessitating the first Clean Air Act of 1956).

Greater London is officially divided for administrative purposes, with varying definitions, into Inner London and Outer London. For the purposes of the now defunct Inner London Education Authority, it consisted of those boroughs that were formed from the County of London; in effect, the group of London boroughs forming the central part of Greater London and which are surrounded by Outer London. However, the Office for National Statistics and the Census include Haringey and Newham in Inner London, but Greenwich in Outer London. I have adhered to this for the sake of statistical consistency.

London's primary geographical feature is the River Thames, which flows across the city from the southwest to the east. The river has been extensively embanked since the Victorian era, and many of its London tributaries now flow underground. Together with the numerous tunnels that exist under London, they are supported by a 650ft (200m) thick chalk basin infilled with the stiff, grey-blue London clay, a marine deposit well known for the fossils it contains.

The Thames Valley is a floodplain surrounded by gently rolling hills such as Parliament Hill, Primrose Hill and the Addington Hills.

Historically, the first major settlement was founded in AD 43, following the Roman invasion of Britain. This settlement was called Londinium, commonly believed to be the origin of the present-day name, although a Celtic origin is also possible. In AD 61, during a rebellion led by Queen Boudicca of the Iceni, the Trinovantes and Iceni tribes sacked and burnt down Londinium as well as the then Roman capital of Camulodunon (Colchester). After being rebuilt, Londonium superseded Colchester as the capital of the Roman province of Britannia in AD 100. After the departure of the Romans from Britain in the early 5th century the town was abandoned but by AD 600, the Anglo-Saxons had created a new settlement (Lundenwic) $^1/_2$ mile (0.8km) upstream from the old Roman city, around what is now Covent Garden.

The town thrived for 250 years until it was razed to the ground in a Viking raid of AD 851. The Viking occupation was brief and Alfred the Great reclaimed the town in 886, moving the settlement within the defensive walls of the old Roman city (then called Lundenburgh). The original city became Ealdwic ('old city'), a name which still survives today as Aldwych. Alfred gave the town to his son-in-law Æthelred and it again prospered despite various Viking raids. In 994 Sweyn of Denmark, assisted by Olaf Tryggvason, attempted to besiege London but was paid off by Aethelred II (the Unready). In 1013 another raid under Danish King Cnut forced Æthelred to flee. In a retaliatory attack, Æthelred's army achieved victory by pulling down London Bridge with the Danish garrison on top, and English control was re-established. Cnut gained the English throne in 1017, ruling the city and country until 1042; after his death in that year Anglo-Saxon control was resumed under his stepson Edward the Confessor, who refounded Westminster Abbey and the adjacent Palace of Westminster. By this time, London had become the largest and most prosperous city in England, although the official seat of government was moved to Winchester.

Following victory at the Battle of Hastings, William the Conqueror, then Duke of Normandy, was crowned king of England in the newly finished Westminster Abbey on Christmas Day 1066. William granted the citizens of London special privileges, while building a castle in the southeast corner of the city to keep them under control. Expanded by later kings, this castle became known as the Tower of London. In 1097, William II began the building of Westminster Hall near the abbey. The hall was to form the basis of the Palace of Westminster, the prime royal residence throughout the Middle Ages. Westminster became the seat of the royal court and government, while its distinct neighbour, the City of London, was a centre of trade and commerce and flourished under its own administration, the Corporation of London. Eventually, the adjacent cities grew together to form the core of modern central London, superseding Winchester as capital of England in the 12th century.

In 1133 St Bartholomew's Fair was founded. The fair, held at Smithfield and celebrating the Feast of St Bartholomew, originally took place on 24 and 25 August but during Charles II's reign it was extended to a fortnight. By the 18th century St Bartholomew's Fair was one of the most spectacular national and international events of the year. It featured sideshows, prizefighters, musicians, wire-walkers, acrobats, puppets, freaks and wild animals. In 1381 Smithfield was also the site where Wat Tyler was stabbed to death by William Walworth, Mayor of London, during the Peasant's Revolt.

Political and economic stability was maintained throughout the Tudor period and after the first coffee shop opened in London in 1632 the capital became a meeting place for people from all parts of the country. However the next real crises for Londoners were not far away. First plague, which had intermittently devastated the area throughout the early 17th century, claimed the lives of 68,000 Londoners in 1665 alone; then, in the following year, fire devastated much of the city. The former was the last major outbreak of bubonic plague in Europe; it is believed by some that the fire of 1666 killed all the plague-infested rats. London's growth accelerated in the late 17th century and in 1688 a marine insurance society was founded in Edward Lloyd's coffee house in London. In 1702, the *Daily Courant* became London's first daily newspaper and in 1721 a regular postal service was established between London and New England. In 1773 the first London Stock Exchange opened. The 19th century brought new entertainments to London. In 1802 Madame Tussaud mounted her first waxworks exhibition and in 1826 Stamford Raffles founded the Royal Zoological Society.

Between about 1831 and 1925 London was the world's largest city. This growth was aided from 1836 by the first railways, which put small countryside towns within easy reach of the city. The rail network expanded very rapidly, causing these places to grow, while London itself expanded into surrounding fields, merging with neighbouring settlements such as Kensington. Rising traffic congestion on city centre roads led to the creation of the world's first underground train system in 1863. In 1875, Sir Joseph Bazalgette completed the London sewerage system and, despite the regular pea-soupers of Victorian London, the capital became a favourable place to live.

Into the 20th century London became not only the political and geographic capital of Britain but also the cultural capital. Schools of artists and writers met frequently and areas of London became known as celebrity haunts. The two world wars, however, took their toll. The Blitz and other bombing by the German Luftwaffe during World War II killed over 30,000 Londoners and flattened large tracts of housing and other buildings across London. Rebuilding during the 1950s, 1960s and 1970s was characterised by a wide range of architectural styles and has resulted in a lack of architectural unity that has become part of London's character.

In 1965 London's political boundaries were expanded to take into account the growth of the urban area outside the County of London's borders. The expanded region was called Greater London and was administered by the Greater London Council (GLC), which replaced the earlier London County Council (LCC). The GLC was responsible for running services such as the fire service, emergency planning, waste disposal and flood prevention, and shared responsibility with the London boroughs for providing roads, housing, planning and leisure services. Other functions were the responsibility of the London boroughs. The GLC did not take control of public transport from the London Transport Board until 1970 and lost control to London Regional Transport in 1984. The GLC was abolished by the Local Government Act 1985, which came into force on 31 March 1986. The Inner London Education Authority (ILEA) continued in existence, and direct elections to it were held, but ILEA was finally also disbanded in 1990.

With the abolition of the GLC, London was left as the only major city in the world without a central administrative body. Most of the powers of the GLC were devolved to the London boroughs. Some powers, such as the fire service, were taken over by joint boards made up of councillors appointed by the boroughs; others, such as London Transport, were taken over by central government. It was argued by many people that this situation was chaotic and uncoordinated and a new London-wide body was needed to coordinate the whole city. Tony Blair's Labour government, elected in 1997, was committed to bringing back such government. In 1999 a referendum was held on the establishment of a new London authority and elected mayor, which was approved by a two to one margin. The new Greater London Authority (GLA) was established in 2000 with a directly elected Mayor of London (Ken Livingstone) and a London Assembly. The headquarters of the GLA is at City Hall in Southwark. The Mayor is responsible for London's strategic planning and is required to produce a London Plan document. In May 2008 Boris Johnson succeeded Livingstone as London's Mayor.

London is the world's largest financial centre and has the sixth largest city economy in the world after Tokyo, New York, Los Angeles, Chicago, and Paris. Greater London generates approximately 30 per cent of the UK's GDP. Most of the capital's financial institutions are based in and around the City but the Canary Wharf development includes the global headquarters of HSBC, Reuters, Barclays and the so-called 'Magic Circle' of London-based law firms, including Clifford Chance, currently the world's highest-grossing law firm.

London has hosted the Summer Olympic Games in 1908 and 1948. In July 2005 the city was chosen to host the 2012 Games, making it the first city in the world to host the games three times. In preparation for the Games, massive development is to be carried out in the East End, particularly Stratford, which will be home to the Olympic village, Olympic stadium and many major venues. Other events will be spread out across the city, from Wembley Stadium in the northwest to Wimbledon in the south.

	Population			Area	
	male	*female*	*total*	*sq miles*	*sq km*
Inner London	1,340,627	1,425,487	2,766,114	123	319
Outer London	2,128,166	2,277,811	4,405,977	484	1253
Total	3,468,793	3,703,298	7,172,091	607	1572

Inner London	*male*	*female*	*total*	*sq miles*	*sq km*
Camden	95,398	102,622	198,020	8	22
City of London	3,832	3,353	7,185	1	3
Hackney	97,003	105,821	202,824	7	19
Hammersmith & Fulham	78,993	86,249	165,242	6	16
Haringey	103,666	112,841	216,507	11	30
Islington	84,229	91,568	175,797	6	15
Kensington & Chelsea	75,959	82,960	158,919	5	12
Lambeth	131,152	135,017	266,169	10	27
Lewisham	119,979	128,943	248,922	14	35
Newham	119,872	124,019	243,891	14	36
Southwark	119,817	125,049	244,866	11	29
Tower Hamlets	98,178	97,928	196,106	8	20
Wandsworth	123,742	136,638	260,380	13	34
Westminster	88,807	92,479	181,286	8	21
	1,340,627	1,425,487	2,766,114	123	319

Outer London	*male*	*female*	*total*	*sq miles*	*sq km*
Barking & Dagenham	78,068	85,876	163,944	14	36
Barnet	149,781	164,783	314,564	33	87
Bexley	105,148	113,159	218,307	23	61
Brent	127,806	135,658	263,464	17	43
Bromley	141,785	153,747	295,532	58	150
Croydon	159,111	171,476	330,587	33	87
Ealing	147,563	153,385	300,948	21	56
Enfield	130,706	142,853	273,559	31	81
Greenwich	102,777	111,626	214,403	18	47
Harrow	99,953	106,861	206,814	19	50
Havering	107,957	116,291	224,248	43	112
Hillingdon	117,461	125,545	243,006	45	116
Hounslow	104,239	108,102	212,341	22	56
Kingston upon Thames	71,987	75,286	147,273	14	37
Merton	91,514	96,394	187,908	15	38
Redbridge	115,849	122,786	238,635	22	56
Richmond upon Thames	83,338	88,997	172,335	22	57
Sutton	86,878	92,890	179,768	17	44
Waltham Forest	106,245	112,096	218,341	15	39
Total	2,128,166	2,277,811	4,405,977	484	1253

Local Attractions and Information

Abbey Road Studios — Abbey Road, St John's Wood, NW8. Abbey Road Studios are situated in a stately 19th century building. Nearby is the world's most famous zebra crossing, where the cover for the Beatles' *Abbey Road* album – depicting John, Ringo, Paul and George following each other across the road (Paul being barefoot) – was shot. Opened in November 1931 by EMI, the studio made its name with big orchestral recordings and was used extensively by leading British conductor Sir Malcolm Sargent. The studio, consisting of four separate recording theatres, was known as EMI Studios until it formally changed its name to Abbey Road Studios in the 1970s. Studio Two became a centre of rock music in 1958 when Cliff Richard and the Drifters (later Cliff Richard and the Shadows) recorded 'Move It', arguably the first European rock 'n' roll single. The Beatles also found great success in Studio Two, and during the 1960s recorded classic albums such as *Please Please Me*, the groundbreaking *Sgt Pepper's Lonely Hearts Club Band*, and ultimately, *Abbey Road*. Abbey Road today is one of the most technically advanced recording and mixing, interactive design and digital video complexes in the world. Tel: 0207 266 7000.

Addington Palace — Gravel Hill, Addington Village, Croydon. An 18th century Palladian-style mansion designed by Robert Mylne and built on the site of the 16th century house of Addington Place. After an Act of Parliament enabled the mansion to be purchased for the Archbishops of Canterbury in 1807, it became the official residence of six Archbishops until it was sold again in 1898. The grounds were landscaped by Capability Brown and today are mainly a golf course and public park. A famous, very large cedar tree still stands next to the Palace. The house today is occupied by a health and country club.

Administrative headquarters

Inner London

Camden: Camden Town Hall, Judd Street, Camden. Tel: 020 7278 4444.
City of London: Guildhall. Tel: 020 7606 3030.
Hackney: Hackney Town Hall, Mare Street. Tel: 020 8356 3000.
Hammersmith & Fulham: Town Hall, King Street, Hammersmith. Tel: 020 8748 3020.
Haringey: Civic Centre, High Road, Wood Green. Tel: 020 8489 0000.
Islington: 222 Upper Street, Islington. Tel: 020 7527 2000.
Kensington & Chelsea: Town Hall, Hornton Street, Kensington. Tel: 020 7361 3000.
Lambeth: Town Hall, Brixton Hill, Lambeth. Tel: 020 7926 1000.
Lewisham: Town Hall, Catford. Tel: 020 8314 6000.
Newham: Newham Town Hall, Barking Road, East Ham. Tel: 020 8430 2000.
Southwark: Town Hall, Peckham Road, Southwark. Tel: 020 7525 5000.
Tower Hamlets: Town Hall, Mulberry Place, Tower Hamlets. Tel: 020 7364 5000.
Wandsworth: Town Hall, Wandsworth High Street, Wandsworth. Tel: 020 8871 6000.
Westminster: City Hall, 64 Victoria Street, Westminster. Tel: 020 7641 6000.

Outer London

Barking & Dagenham: Civic Centre, Dagenham. Tel: 020 8215 3000.
Barnet: Town Hall, The Burroughs, Hendon. Tel: 020 8359 2000.
Bexley: Civic Offices, Broadway, Bexleyheath. Tel: 020 8303 7777.
Brent: Town Hall, Forty Lane, Wembley. Tel: 020 8937 1234.
Bromley: Civic Centre, Stockwell Close, Bromley. Tel: 020 8464 3333.
Croydon: Taberner House, Park Lane, Croydon. Tel: 020 8726 6000.
Ealing: Perceval House, 14–16 Uxbridge Road, Ealing. Tel: 020 8825 5000.
Enfield: Civic Centre, Silver Street, Enfield. Tel: 020 8379 1000.
Greenwich: Town Hall, Wellington Street, Woolwich. Tel: 020 8854 8888.
Harrow: Civic Centre, Station Road, Harrow. Tel: 020 8863 5611.
Havering: Town Hall, Main Road, Romford. Tel: 01708 434343.
Hillingdon: Civic Centre, High Street, Uxbridge. Tel: 01895 250111.
Hounslow: Civic Centre, Lampton Road, Hounslow. Tel: 020 8583 2000.
Kingston upon Thames: High Street, Kingston upon Thames. Tel: 020 8547 5757.
Merton: Civic Centre, London Road, Morden. Tel: 020 8274 4901.
Redbridge: Town Hall, Ilford. Tel: 020 8554 5000.
Richmond upon Thames: Civic Centre, 44 York Street, Twickenham. Tel: 020 8891 1411.
Sutton: Civic Offices, St Nicholas Way, Sutton. Tel: 020 8770 5000.
Waltham Forest: Town Hall, Forest Road, Walthamstow. Tel: 020 8496 3000.

Admiralty Arch — The Mall, SW1. Situated where The Mall leads into Trafalgar Square, Admiralty Arch takes its name from the nearby Royal Navy headquarters, though the Arch itself has no naval association. Built in 1910 to the design of Sir Aston Webb (who also designed the façade of Buckingham Palace), it consists of three identical arches. A Latin inscription along the top reads: 'ANNO : DECIMO : EDWARDI : SEPTIMI : REGIS : VICTORIÆ : REGINÆ : CIVES : GRATISSIMI : MDCCCCX :' (In the tenth year of King Edward VII, to Queen Victoria, from most grateful citizens, 1910). Since 2000 the Cabinet Office, including the Prime Minister's Strategy Unit, has occupied part of the Grade I listed building, while maintaining its Whitehall headquarters.

Albert Memorial — Hyde Park, SW7. Located in the southeast of Hyde Park, off Kensington Gore. Designed in 1872, the 180ft (55m) high memorial was designed by Sir George Gilbert Scott and officially titled the Prince Consort National Memorial when it was opened by Queen Victoria in 1876. Sculptor Henry Hugh Armstead coordinated this massive effort among several artists of the Royal Academy. It consists of a bronze gilt statue of the Prince Consort by John Henry Foley, under a Gothic canopy, and surrounded by four groups of statuary: America by John Bell, Africa by William Theed, Asia by Foley, and Europe by Patrick Macdowell, with smaller groups of statues by Henry Weekes, William Calder Marshall and Hamo Thornycroft. Near the top are gilded bronze statues of angels and virtues. Around the base is the so-called Parnassus frieze, 187 life-size carved figures by Birnie Philip and Armstead depicting celebrated painters, poets, sculptors, musicians and architects, and reflecting Albert's enthusiasm for the arts. The memorial underwent substantial restoration in the late 1990s.

Alexandra Palace — Alexandra Palace Way, N22. Set within the 196 acres (79ha) of Alexandra Park in Muswell Hill. Designed by Alfred Meeson and John Johnson, and named after Alexandra of Denmark, wife of Edward, Prince of Wales, the palace was soon nicknamed 'Ally Pally'. Alexandra Palace and Park was originally opened by Queen Victoria on 24 May 1873 but 16 days later the palace was destroyed by fire, killing three members of staff. Meeson and Johnson completed rebuilding work within two years and the palace reopened in 1875 with an art gallery, banqueting room, concert hall, lecture hall, library, museum and theatre. The Willis organ, also installed in 1875, has recently been restored and is still working. In 1936 Alexandra Palace became the headquarters of the world's first regular public 'high definition' television service, operated by the BBC. The Alexandra Palace Transmitter, located on the site, still broadcasts television and radio signals. A second fire destroyed half the building in 1980; currently a conference centre operated by a charitable trust, its intended future as a leisure and entertainment complex remains uncertain.

Apsley House — Hyde Park Corner, W1. Situated in the southeast corner of Hyde Park, the former home of the 1st Duke of Wellington is also known as No. 1 London, because it was the first house encountered past the toll-gate into London from the countryside. Designed by Robert Adam and built 1771–8, it was here that Wellington made his London home after a dazzling military career in India, Spain and Portugal, culminating in his victory at Waterloo in 1815. When he bought Apsley House in 1817 he was the most powerful commander in Europe and his huge popular support gave him enormous political influence. Wellington enlarged the house to express his status, adding the 90ft (27.5m) long Waterloo Gallery (by Benjamin Dean Wyatt), and enriched it with his extensive art collection. The 7th Duke gave the house and contents to the nation in 1947 and it is now administered by English Heritage. Tel: 020 7499 5676. See also Wellington Arch

Art galleries — **Courtauld Institute Gallery**, Somerset House, Strand, WC2, holds an important collection of European paintings from the Renaissance to the 20th century, and one of the finest collections of Impressionist and Post-Impressionist paintings in the world. Tel: 020 7848 2526.

The Hayward, Southbank Centre, Belvedere, Road, SW1. Opened on 9 July 1968 as the Hayward Gallery but was rebranded as The Hayward in 2007. It was named after Sir Isaac Hayward, a former leader of the London County Council. The Hayward hosts several major temporary exhibitions each year but does not house permanent collections. See also Southbank Centre.

National Gallery, Trafalgar Square, WC2. In April 1824 the House of Commons agreed to pay £57,000 for banker John Julius Angerstein's picture collection. The 38 pictures were intended to form the core of a new national collection. At first the pictures were displayed at Angerstein's house in Pall Mall; in 1831 Parliament agreed to construct a building at Trafalgar Square to be designed by William Wilkins. The National Gallery was established by the mid-1830s as a benefit to all art lovers, with a commitment to free admission, a central and accessible site, and extended opening hours. The Sainsbury Wing, funded by a donation from Lord Sainsbury of Preston Candover and his brothers, the Hon. Simon Sainsbury and Sir Timothy Sainsbury, and designed by Robert Venturi and Denise Scott Brown, was added in 1991. Tel: 020 7747 2885.

National Portrait Gallery, St Martin's Place, WC2. The National Portrait Gallery was formally established on 2 December 1856. Above its entrance are the busts of the three men – all biographers and historians – chiefly responsible for its existence. In the centre is Philip Henry Stanhope, 5th Earl Stanhope (1805–75), whose efforts resulted in the gallery's foundation in 1856; he is flanked by Thomas Babington Macaulay (1800–59) and Thomas Carlyle (1795–1881). During the first 13 years of its existence it was housed at 29 Great George Street, Westminster. Its next home in 1869 was the Royal Horticultural Society's buildings on Exhibition Road in South Kensington, and after that Bethnal Green Museum from 1 September 1885. In 1889, philanthropist William Henry Alexander offered to pay for a permanent building, provided the government gave a site within a mile and a half of St James's Street. A site was assigned which had previously been occupied by St Martin's Workhouse to the northeast of the National Gallery. Designed by architect Ewan Christian, the exteriors of the entrance block and north block are decorated with Portland stone blocks of eminent artists, biographers and historians, realised by Frederick C Thomas: Carlyle, Stanhope and Macaulay (over the main entrance); James Granger (1723–76), William Faithorne (1616–91) and Edmund Lodge (1756–1839) (over the north side of the entrance block); Thomas Fuller (1608–61), The Earl of Clarendon (1609–74) and Horace Walpole (1717–97) (over the east side of the north block); Hans Holbein the Younger (1497–1543), Sir Anthony Van Dyck (1599–1641), Sir Peter Lely (1618–80), Sir Godfrey Kneller (1646–1723), Louis François Roubiliac (1702–62), William Hogarth (1697–1764), Sir Joshua Reynolds (1723–92), Sir Thomas Lawrence (1769–1830) and Sir Francis Chantrey (1781–1841) (over the north side of the north block). In 1928 art dealer Sir Joseph Duveen (1869–1939) agreed to fund a £40,000 extension, which took the form of a wing along Orange Street, comprising three floors and a basement, faced on the exterior with smooth Portland stone. George V and Queen Mary opened the Duveen wing, designed by Office of Works architects Sir Richard Allison and J G West, on 30 March 1933. A second expansion occurred in 2000. The Ondaatje Wing, opened in 2000 and funded by Dr Christopher Ondaatje, occupies a piece of land between the National Gallery and the NPG and is notable for its immense, two-storey escalator that takes visitors to the earliest part of the collection, the Tudor portraits. In August 2006 a cabinet portrait of Mary Queen of Scots by an unknown artist went on display; previously thought to have been painted in the 17th century, the portrait has been placed by modern dating techniques within the Scottish queen's lifetime. Tel: 020 7306 0055.

Royal Academy of Arts, Burlington House, Piccadilly, WC2. Formed to rival the Society of Artists after a leadership dispute between two leading architects, Sir William Chambers and James Paine. Paine won, but Chambers vowed revenge and used his strong connections with George III to create a new artistic body, the Royal Academy, in 1768. It was formally launched the following year. Its 40 founder members, admitted on 10 December 1768, included a father and daughter (George Michael Moser and Mary Moser) and two sets of brothers (George Dance the younger and Nathaniel Dance-Holland, and Paul and Thomas Sandby). Sir Joshua Reynolds was its first president. Until 1771, the Academy was based in Pall Mall. Shortly afterwards, it moved into the new Somerset House, a government building designed by Sir William Chambers and intended to provide accommodation for a number of learned societies. In 1837, the Academy moved to the recently constructed National Gallery in Trafalgar Square and in 1868 to its present home. Major extensions were made to the building to designs by Charles Barry junior, son of Sir Charles Barry. The Sackler Galleries, designed by Norman Foster, were added in 1990. In 2004 the highlights of the Academy's permanent collection went on display in the newly restored reception rooms of the original section of Burlington House, which are now known as the John Madejski Fine Rooms. The Royal Academy receives no financial support from the state or Crown and one of its principal sources of revenue is hosting public exhibitions. Under the direction of Exhibitions Secretary Norman Rosenthal, it has hosted exhibitions of contemporary art including in 1997 *Sensation*, a collection of work by young British artists owned by Charles Saatchi. The show created controversy for including a painting of Myra Hindley that was vandalised while on display. The Academy's annual summer exhibition of new art is a major event on the London social calendar. Full membership of the academy is limited to 80 Academicians or RAs, who may be painters, printmakers, sculptors or architects, and must be 'professionally active in Britain'. There must always be at least 14 sculptors, 12 architects and 8 printmakers, the bàlance being made up of 46 painters. New Academicians are elected by the existing RAs. The full list of presidents: Sir Joshua Reynolds, 1768–92; Benjamin West, 1792–1805; James Wyatt, 1805–6; Benjamin West, 1806–20; Sir Thomas Lawrence, 1820–30; Sir Martin Archer Shee, 1830–50; Sir Charles Lock Eastlake, 1850–65; Sir Francis Grant, 1866–78; Lord Leighton, 1878–96; Sir John Everett Millais, Feb–Aug 1896; Sir Edward Poynter, 1896–1918; Sir Aston Webb, 1919–24; Sir Frank Dicksee, 1924–28; Sir William Llewellyn, 1928–38; Sir Edwin Lutyens, 1938–44; Sir Alfred Munnings, 1944–9; Sir Gerald Kelly, 1949–54; Sir Albert Richardson, 1954–6; Sir Charles Wheeler, 1956–66; Sir Thomas Monnington, 1966–76; Sir Hugh Casson, 1976–84; Sir Roger de Grey, 1984–93; Sir Philip Dowson, 1993–9; Phillip King, 1999–2004; Sir Nicholas Grimshaw 2004–present. Tel: 020 7300 8000.

Tate Britain, Millbank, SW1. Built by Sir Henry Tate with money earned from his sugar empire, on the former site of the Millbank Penitentiary in 1897. The Clore Gallery, an adjoining gallery housing the Turner Bequest and designed by architect James Stirling, was completed in 1987. The works of J M W Turner, left to the nation on his death in 1851 under the proviso that they were to be kept together, are now housed in their entirety in the gallery. The Turner Prize, awarded to a British artist under 50 for an outstanding exhibition in the previous 12 months, is held annually at Tate Britain. Tel: 020 7887 8000.

Tate Modern, Bankside, SE1. Opened in May 2000 at the former Bankside power station. Houses the Tate's collection of international modern art from 1900 to the present, including major works by Bacon, Dalí, Picasso, Matisse, Rothko and Warhol as well as recent work by artists such as Steve McQueen, Rebecca Horn and Gillian Wearing. Tel: 020 7887 8000.

Wallace Collection, Hertford House, Manchester Square, W1. Established from the private collection of Sir Richard Wallace, which was bequeathed to the UK by his widow in 1897, the museum opened to the public in 1900. The collection includes old master paintings (such as Hals' *The Laughing Cavalier*), fine porcelain such as Sèvres and Meissen, armour, 18th century French furniture and diverse objets d'art. Tel: 020 7563 9500.

Bank of England — Threadneedle Street, EC2. The central bank of the UK, founded by Scotsman William Paterson in 1694 to act as the English government's banker, a role which it still fulfils today. Nationalised in 1946, it currently convenes the Monetary Policy Committee, which is responsible for UK monetary policy. It has occupied its current premises since 1734; originally designed by George Sampson, the building was greatly extended by Sir John Soane but was largely rebuilt in the 20th century. Due to its location, the building is sometimes known as the Old Lady of Threadneedle Street or the Old Lady. Sir John Houblon, 1694–7, was the first governor; recent governors have included Sir Leslie O'Brien, Baron O'Brien of Lothbury, 1966–73; Gordon Richardson, Baron Richardson of Duntisbourne, 1973–83; Robin Leigh-Pemberton, Baron Kingsdown, 1983–93; Sir Edward George, 1993–30 June 2003; Mervyn King, 1 July 2003–present. The first chief cashier of the Bank of England, responsible for signing bank notes, was John Kendrick in 1694; recent chief cashiers have included Graham E A Kentfield, 1991–8; Merlyn Lowther, 1999–2003 (the first woman to hold the post); and Andrew Bailey, 2004–present. The **Bank of England Museum** is located on Bartholomew Lane. Tel: 020 7601 5545.

Banqueting House, The — Whitehall, SW1. All that remains of the Palace of Whitehall, destroyed by fire in 1698. Commissioned by James I and completed in 1622 to the design of Inigo Jones, the Banqueting House is one of the first Palladian-style buildings constructed in England and features a spectacular painted ceiling completed in 1636 by Peter Paul Rubens. Charles I was executed outside the Banqueting House on 30 January 1649. Tel: 0870 751 5178.

Battersea Park — London SW11. The 200 acre (80ha) park opened in 1858 to provide healthy recreation for the working classes of south London and was laid out to designs based on those of Sir James Pennethorne. Prior to its opening Battersea Fields had been a popular spot for duelling; in one notable incident, on 21 March 1829 the Duke of Wellington and the Earl of Winchilsea met on the fields to settle a matter of honour. When called upon to fire, the Duke deliberately aimed wide and Winchilsea fired into the air. Battersea Park hosted the first exhibition of football played under the rules of the recently formed Football Association on 9 January 1864. The members of the opposing teams were chosen by the president (Arthur Pember) and secretary (Ebenezer Cobb Morley) of the FA and included many well-known footballers of the day. The park was also once home to the famous amateur football team, The Wanderers, winners of the first-ever FA Cup. In 1951 the park was transformed into the 'Festival Gardens' as part of the Festival of Britain celebrations. As well as a water garden and fountains, new features included a Tree Walk consisting of a series of raised wooden walkways linked together by tree house-like platforms suspended among the branches of a number of trees. The many attractions included the Guinness Clock – upon which models of various animals associated with Guinness would cavort when the clock struck the hour – but most popular by far was the famous fun fair which had the first 'big dipper' in England. The ride was closed in 1972 after five children were killed in an accident on 30 May that year when one of the cars broke loose and collided with another, and the funfair itself closed two years later. Today the park is home to a small zoo, all-weather outdoor sporting facilities including tennis courts, a running track and football pitches, and a boating lake. It is also the site of the London Peace Pagoda, controversially erected while Ken Livingstone was leader of the now abolished GLC. In 1985 a replica of the bronze statue of a dog that was the focal point of the historic vivisection-related Brown Dog affair was erected in the park. In 2002–4, the park underwent an £11m refurbishment funded in part by the Heritage Lottery Fund, and was reopened on 4 June 2004 by Prince Philip. Other famous Battersea buildings include the former power station and the dogs' home. Completed in 1939, to a design of Giles Gilbert Scott, the power station was the first in a series of very large coal-fired electrical generating facilities set up in England as part of the National Grid power distribution system. Finally closed in 1983, the Grade II listed building has since been the subject of many redevelopment plans but its future remains uncertain. Battersea Dogs' and Cats' Home is a long-established and charitable home for cats and dogs. Formerly the Temporary Home for Lost and Starving Dogs (its name changed in 2005 to reflect the little-known fact that it also looked after cats), it was established in Holloway in 1860 and moved to a site in Battersea beside the main railway line in 1871.

Battles — Four battles have been fought in the London area: Brentford, Deptford Bridge, Ludgate Hill and Turnham Green. See separate table for further details.

Bentley, Derek — The case of Derek Bentley was one of the miscarriages of justice that ultimately led to the abolition of capital punishment in the UK. On 2 November 1952, Bentley (aged 19) and Christopher Craig (aged 16) broke into Barlow & Parker's Warehouse, Tamworth Road, Croydon. Craig was armed with a revolver. The two youths were seen entering the premises and the police were called. Bentley and Craig found their way on to the flat roof of the building and hid behind a lift housing. Detective Sergeant Frederick Fairfax climbed on to the roof, and managed to grab Bentley. Craig shouted defiantly at the detective and Bentley managed to break Fairfax's grip. At this point, Bentley supposedly shouted 'Let him have it Chris'. Craig then fired the gun, grazing the police officer's shoulder. Despite being wounded, Fairfax continued after Bentley and managed to arrest him. Bentley told Fairfax that Craig had a Colt .45 and plenty of ammunition. Following the arrival of more police officers, a group were sent on to the roof. The first policeman to appear, Police Constable Sidney George Miles (aged 42), was immediately shot in the head by Craig and killed. After exhausting his supply of ammunition, Craig leapt from the roof on to the road 30 feet below. He landed badly, fracturing his spine and left wrist, and was then arrested. Bentley and Craig were jointly charged with murder, and the case appeared to be a relatively simple one for the prosecution. However, as the trial progressed before Lord Chief Justice Lord Goddard at the Old Bailey, the prosecution case appeared far less certain. The police seemed unsure how many shots had been fired and by whom. A ballistics expert failed to positively identify Craig's gun as the weapon that fired the bullet that killed PC Miles. Crucially, what was meant by Bentley's phrase, 'Let him have it Chris'? Did he mean that Craig was to give the gun to the officer and surrender, or that he was to shoot the officer? There seemed enough opportunity to establish a reasonable doubt. But Bentley was illiterate and had a mental age of only 11; ill-prepared to undergo cross-examination, he did not present a 'good image' to the jury, and they took just 75 minutes to find both Craig and Bentley guilty of PC Miles' murder. Being under 18 at the time of the offence, Craig was sentenced to be detained at Her Majesty's pleasure, and served 10 years in prison before being released. Bentley was sentenced to death. There was a considerable public outcry, but his appeal was dismissed and on 28 January 1953 he was hanged at Wandsworth Prison. After a long campaign, on 30 July 1998 the Court of Appeal finally overturned Bentley's conviction; the Lord Chief Justice, Lord Bingham, made the unprecedented ruling that his predecessor and Bentley's trial judge, Lord Chief Justice Goddard, had denied Bentley 'that fair trial that is the birthright of every British citizen'. Describing Goddard as 'blatantly prejudiced', Bingham concluded that he had misdirected the jury and that in his summing-up had put unfair pressure on the jury to convict.

Bethlem Royal Hospital — Monks Orchard Road, Beckenham. Currently located on the site of Monks Orchard House between Eden Park, Beckenham and Shirley, the hospital, which has been variously known as St Mary Bethlehem, Bethlem Hospital, Bethlehem Hospital and Bedlam, is the world's oldest psychiatric institution. Its first site was in Bishopsgate Street (where Liverpool Street station now stands). First mentioned as a hospital in 1330, it admitted the mentally ill from 1377, though by 1403 there were only nine inmates. Conditions were dreadful, and the care amounted to little more than restraint. Violent or dangerous patients were manacled and chained to the floor or wall. Some, allowed to leave and licensed to beg, were known as Abraham-men or Tom o' Bedlam; they usually wore a tin plate on their arm as a badge and were also known as Bedlamers. Bedlam became infamous for the brutal ill-treatment meted out to the insane. In 1675 it moved to new buildings in Moorfields. In the 18th century people used to go there to see the lunatics. For a penny one could peer into their cells, view the freaks of the 'show of Bethlehem' and laugh at their antics. Entry was free on the first Tuesday of the month. Visitors were permitted to bring long sticks with which to poke and enrage the inmates. The inmates were first called 'patients' in 1700, and 'curable' and 'incurable' wards were opened 1725–34. In 1815, Bedlam was moved to St George's Fields, Lambeth (into buildings designed by Sydney Smirke, now used to house the Imperial War Museum), where the inmates were finally referred to as 'unfortunates'. The hospital moved to its present site in 1930, and now provides mental health services as part of the South London and Maudsley NHS Trust. Notable Bedlam inmates include artists Richard Dadd and Louis Wain.

Bevis Marks Synagogue Heneage Lane, EC3. The oldest surviving Jewish house of worship in Britain, established by Sephardic Jews in 1698 when Rabbi David Nieto took spiritual charge of the congregation. The structure was completed and dedicated in 1702; with the exception of the roof, which was destroyed by fire in 1738 and repaired in 1749, the Wren-style building remains today much as it was 300 years ago. Tel: 020 7626 1274.

Big Ben See Palace of Westminster

Biggin Hill Airport 1 mile (1.6km) north of Biggin Hill, 6 miles (10km) southeast of Croydon. Biggin Hill (BQH) is known both for its illustrious history and its convenience as South London's local airport, serving mainly business visitors to the capital. The station was opened in January 1917 by the Royal Flying Corps as a wireless testing park and air-to-air and air-to-ground telephony systems were developed at the site. By 1924 the RAF had established itself at the airfield. Early in World War II, one of its resident squadrons claimed the first enemy aircraft of the war, a Dornier Do17 shot down on 2 November 1939, and it was a major Spitfire and Hurricane base during the Battle of Britain. Biggin Hill has 6000ft (1800m) of runway. The Biggin Hill International Air Fair began in 1963 and the 45th event took place in June 2007. Nearby Saltbox Hill, a remnant of chalk downland and home to many rare species of flora and fauna including numerous orchids and butterflies, is a designated Site of Special Scientific Interest.

Billingsgate Market See Markets

Blewcoat School Caxton Street, Westminster, SW1. Located near the junction with Buckingham Gate. Built in 1709 at the expense of William Green, a local brewer, to provide an education for poor children, the building was used as a school until 1926. It is now the National Trust's London information centre. Tel: 020 7222 2877.

Bloomsbury Group A group of English intellectuals active from the early 1900s until about 1940, who met for discussion in the Bloomsbury area of London. Members included artists Vanessa Bell (1879–1961), Roger Fry (1866–1934) and Duncan Grant (1885–1978); writers Leonard (1880–1969) and Virginia Woolf (1882–1941); art critic Clive Bell (1881–1964); economist John Maynard Keynes (1883–1946); historian Lytton Strachey (1880–1932); civil servant Saxon Sydney-Turner (1880–1962); journalist Desmond MacCarthy (1877–1952); psychoanalyst Adrian Stephen (1883–1948) and Thoby Stephen, brother of Virginia Woolf and Vanessa Bell (1880–1906). Novelist E M Forster was on the fringe of the set. The group began as an informal social assembly of recent Cambridge University graduates (four members had graduated in 1899, among them Thoby Stephen), many of whom had been members of the secret society known as the Cambridge Apostles. After graduation, the founding members pursued different interests (Keynes took a job with the Treasury Department administering British interests in a part of India). Vanessa laid the foundation of Bloomsbury in 1904 by moving the Stephen family (the four children of Julia and Leslie Stephen – Vanessa, Thoby, Virginia and Adrian) to Gordon Square, Bloomsbury. Thoby Stephen's untimely death in 1906 strengthened the resolve of Vanessa and Virginia to remain independent and interact with the rest of the group. The group gained notoriety in 1910 when many of its members were involved in the Dreadnought hoax (see Dorset) that embarrassed the Royal Navy and was deemed unpatriotic. The group's outspoken pacifist beliefs caused further criticism during World War I. An exhibition of Post-Impressionist art in London organised by Roger Fry, also in 1910, became a defining milestone for the movement; although badly received by critics, it gave the British public a first glimpse of innovations in European art. After World War I the group became a looser association as the circle of friends grew and became less united in opinions and beliefs. The two post-war efforts that involved many members of the group were the Omega Workshops (see separate entry) and the Hogarth Press (founded in 1917 by Virginia and Leonard Woolf and named after their house in Richmond, in whose dining room the books were initially printed by hand). The group's members demonstrated a sexual freedom that was ahead of their time. Virginia Woolf's passionate affair with Vita Sackville-West, which began in 1925, inspired her to write what has become a classic of gay fiction, the experimental fantasy *Orlando* (1927), which argued that love and passion ignore gender. Others in the Bloomsbury group exhibited similar bisexual tendencies. Although Vanessa Stephen married Clive Bell, the great love of her life was Duncan Grant, who was primarily gay and had been sexually involved with her brother Adrian. During World War I, they lived together at Charleston in Sussex with David 'Bunny' Garnett, who was a lover of both. Triangular relationships with a gay twist were common within the Bloomsbury circle. Strachey was gay, but in the early days of Bloomsbury, he proposed marriage to Virginia Stephen (Woolf). In the 1920s, he lived in platonic bliss with surrealist painter Dora Carrington. When they both fell in love with the same man, Carrington married the object of their mutual desire, and the three set up house together; the cross-dressing Carrington also had affairs with women. Despite the sexual permissiveness of the group members there is no doubting their influence. Clive Bell's writings helped persuade the British to dismantle their empire, foreshadowing the eventual collapse of colonialism in Europe. Keynes' writings have become a mainstay of economic theory and Virginia Woolf is a widely read, though apolitical, writer whose beliefs were later embraced by the feminist movement.

Blue Plaques — See separate table

Boston Manor House — Boston Manor Road, Brentford. A Grade I listed Jacobean manor house built in 1623 for the newly widowed Lady Mary Reade, who later married Sir Edward Spencer, an ancestor of Diana, Princess of Wales. Tel: 020 8560 5441.

Bow Street Runners — London's first band of constables. In 1740 Sir Thomas de Veil established a court house in Bow Street, near the Opera House in Covent Garden. The Bow Street Runners were formed ten years later by author Henry Fielding, Veil's successor as chief magistrate; their functions included serving writs, detective work and arresting offenders on behalf of the Bow Street magistrates. Initially nicknamed Robin Redbreasts, on account of their scarlet waistcoats (although this nickname is also attributed to the Bow Street Horse Patrol, established in 1763), they originally numbered eight. The Bow Street Runners travelled all over the country in search of criminals and, under Fielding's own successor, his brother John, gained a reputation for honesty and efficiency. The formation of the London Metropolitan Police force by Sir Robert Peel in 1829 brought an end to their activities.

Bridges — The following is a list of bridges over the River Thames in London, heading upstream from the Thames Estuary and carrying road traffic unless otherwise stated:

The **Queen Elizabeth II Bridge** (or **Dartford Bridge**) was opened on 30 October 1991; 1476ft (450m) long, it is Europe's largest cable-supported bridge. The bridge carries the clockwise route of the M25, the anti-clockwise route being carried through the Dartford Tunnel. Not really a London bridge, it is included as traditionally the first bridge crossing the Thames at the eastern approach to London. See also Essex

Tower Bridge, opened in 1894, is a double-leaf bascule bridge, designed by city engineer Sir Horace Jones and built by John Wolfe-Barry. The columns of the main towers are 120ft (36.5m) high, while those of the smaller towers on the shore are 44ft (13.5m) high. The 270ft (82m) side spans are suspension platforms supported by chains anchored in the rear of the abutments and carried over the two smaller towers to the main towers. Here they are joined by rods concealed in the decorative wrought iron of the two walkways. The towers and linking catwalk support the roadway's lifting mechanism, powered by steam until 1976 but now electronically operated. The bascules, which were also replaced in 1976, each weigh 1200 tons (1219 tonnes) and have to be counterbalanced with 422 tons of lead and iron. Taking 3–5 minutes to open, the bridge is 135ft (40m) high and 200ft (60m) wide when raised. During its first few years Tower Bridge's bascules opened on average 22 times a day; today they still open at least once a day for large ships or on special and historic occasions. Tel: 020 7940 3984.

London Bridge links the City of London in the north with the Borough in the south. There is evidence that there was a bridge on the site during the Roman period but by the middle of the 18th century no bridge remained. In 1823 Parliament approved John Rennie's design for a new London Bridge. The foundation stone was laid by the Lord Mayor of London in 1825 and the bridge was opened by William IV and Queen Adelaide in 1831. The new bridge was 1005ft (306m) long and 56ft (17m) wide. By the 1960s it was too narrow and too weak to cope with the traffic; in 1967 work began on demolishing the old bridge (which was transported to Lake Havasu City, Arizona), and its replacement was opened by Queen Elizabeth II on 16 March 1973. The bridge has a 105ft (32m) wide roadway with room for six traffic lanes and two footpaths.

Cannon Street Rail Bridge, also known as Alexandra Rail Bridge (in honour of the consort of the then future Edward VII), links Cannon Street station in the north to Waterloo and London Bridge stations in the south. The station, rail bridge and viaduct approaches were designed by Sir John Hawkshaw, and opened in September 1866.

Southwark Bridge Designed by John Rennie, Southwark Road Bridge opened in 1819. After being freed of tolls in 1864, it was considered too narrow to cope with the increased volume of traffic and the decision was made to replace it. A new bridge designed by Sir Ernest George RA opened in 1921.

The **Millennium Footbridge** links St Paul's Cathedral to Tate Modern, Bankside, and is the first completely new pedestrian bridge to be constructed over the Thames for 100 years. In 1996, a competition held to design a new footbridge over the Thames was won by the architects Foster & Partners, sculptor Anthony Caro and engineers Ove Arup and Partners. Soon after its opening by Queen Elizabeth II on 9 May 2000 it was closed (12 June 2000) due to the swaying effect caused by pedestrians walking across the bridge. After adjustments were made to the design, it was reopened to the public in 2002 and since then has shown no signs of wobbling.

Blackfriars Rail Bridge was designed by Joseph Cubitt. Work started on the bridge in 1862 and the bridge and the station, then called St Paul's, opened in 1864. In 1937 St Paul's station was renamed Blackfriars station.

Blackfriars Road Bridge was designed by Robert Mylne. At the laying of its foundation stone the bridge was named Pitt Bridge, after the Tory Prime Minister. When the bridge was opened in 1769, it was renamed Blackfriars Bridge, in honour of the Black Friars who moved their monastery from Holborn to a site near the northern approach road to the bridge in 1274. Mylne's bridge was demolished in 1860 and a new bridge, designed by Joseph Cubitt, was opened by Queen Victoria on 6 November 1869.

Waterloo Bridge was designed by John Rennie and originally known as the Strand Bridge. It was renamed Waterloo Bridge in 1816; the official opening by the Prince Regent took place on 18 June 1817, the second anniversary of the Duke of Wellington's famous victory. The bridge was rebuilt by London County Council in 1944 and opened by Herbert Morrison in 1945. At 80ft (24m) wide and 1250ft (381m) long, Waterloo Bridge is the longest bridge in London.

Hungerford Rail Bridge The first bridge to span the Thames at this point was a suspension bridge designed by Isambard Kingdom Brunel and opened in 1845, before the building of Charing Cross station. Sir John Hawkshaw designed the present bridge, which opened in 1864 and combined a railway bridge with a footbridge. The Golden Jubilee Bridges, two new suspension footbridges – one on either side of the rail bridge – were completed in 2002 at a cost of £50 million to replace the single footbridge.

Westminster Bridge links Westminster Abbey and the Houses of Parliament with County Hall and St Thomas' Hospital. For centuries London Bridge was the only crossing in central London, the next bridge upstream being at Kingston. The Lambeth Horseferry was a possible crossing but was slow and dangerous. The first Westminster Bridge was opened in 1750. In 1854 work began on a new bridge, and the seven-arch wrought-iron bridge, 827ft (252m) long overall and 84ft (25.5m) wide, was opened in May 1862. To celebrate its proximity to the Houses of Parliament, Westminster Bridge is painted predominantly green for the Commons benches of the Houses of Parliament (Lambeth Bridge being painted red for the benches of the Lords).

Lambeth Bridge links Millbank and Market Street (later renamed Horseferry Road), Westminster in the north with Lambeth Palace Road and Albert Embankment in the south. Designed by P W Barlow and opened in 1862, the new suspension bridge had three massive iron arches. Tolls were charged until 1879. A new five-span bridge, designed by George Humphreys, was opened in 1932 by George V and Queen Mary. Lambeth Bridge is painted predominantly red for the Lords benches. Lambeth Bridge was one of three London bridges given Grade II listing in November 2008 on the advice of English Heritage.

Vauxhall Bridge links Millbank in the north with Kennington Lane in the south. In 1811 the foundation stone of the original bridge was laid by Lord Thomas Dundas, standing in for the Prince Regent. Originally named Regent's Bridge, the name Vauxhall Bridge was restored during construction. Designed by engineer James Walker, and opened in 1816, it was the first iron bridge to span the Thames. The present five-arch steel bridge was designed by Sir Maurice Fitzmaurice; opened in 1906 by the Prince of Wales (later George V), it was the first bridge in London to carry trams. The bridge's piers are decorated with heroic-sized bronze statues of female figures sculpted by Frederick Pomeroy and Alfred Drury, and representing the Arts and Sciences. The figures facing downstream (towards Westminster) represent Local Government, Education, the Fine Arts, and Astronomy; those facing upstream away from London represent Agriculture, holding a scythe; Architecture, holding a model of St Paul's Cathedral; Engineering, holding an engine; and Pottery, holding a vase. Vauxhall Bridge was one of four London bridges given Grade II* listing in November 2008.

Grosvenor Rail Bridge, also known as the Victoria Bridge, carries the railway from Victoria station in the north to Battersea in the south past Battersea Power Station. Work began on 9 June 1859 to a design by John Fowler and the the first train passed over the bridge exactly a year later. The whole bridge was replaced piecemeal by Freeman, Fox & Partners, 1963–7.

Chelsea Bridge links Chelsea in the north with Battersea in the south. Work began on the bridge in 1851 to the designs of engineer Thomas Page. Although never formally named, the bridge was known as the Victoria for some years after its opening in 1858. In 1879 the bridge became toll free. In 1934 it was rebuilt as a suspension bridge; because its construction used Douglas fir from British Columbia in Canada, the Prime Minister of Canada, W L Mackenzie King, opened the bridge in 1937. Famous for the turrets guarding its entrances, Chelsea Bridge was one of three London bridges given Grade II listing in November 2008.

Albert Bridge links Chelsea and Battersea. Designed by Roland Mason Ordish and opened in 1873, it was originally a cantilever bridge, each half being supported by bars radiating out from the top of its supporting towers. In 1884 Sir Joseph Bazalgette strengthened and modernised the structure, his modifications making it more like a conventional suspension bridge. In 1973 the bridge was reopened to light traffic after two concrete piers were constructed under the main span to give the bridge added support. In addition, a new lighter deck was laid and the weight limit reduced to 2 tons (2032kg). At each end of the bridge is a notice instructing the soldiers of nearby Chelsea Barracks to break step when marching over the bridge. It was thought that the vibrations caused by marching in step would damage the delicate structure.

Battersea Bridge In 1766 an Act of Parliament was passed authorising Earl Spencer to construct a bridge across the Thames at Battersea. The earl, who operated a ferry here, could not raise sufficient funds to span the river with stone and as a result the bridge was built with timber by Henry Holland. It was opened in 1772. A new five-span bridge designed by Sir Joseph Bazalgette opened in 1890. The wrought-iron and steel cantilever bridge has five segmental spans. With two footpaths, the bridge has a total width of 55ft (17m), the narrowest of London's road bridges.

Battersea Rail Bridge Opened in 1863, the five-arched bridge carries London's only north–south through route. The bridge was part of the West London Extension Railway, connecting the main lines radiating to the north, out of Paddington and Euston, with lines running south from Waterloo, Victoria and Clapham Junction. To cross the 706ft (215m) wide river the construction company built a 1270ft (387m) viaduct. The track was not only laid for standard gauge, but also the Great Western Railway's broad gauge. Trains crossing the bridge are restricted to 15mph (24km/h), giving it the distinction of being the slowest railway crossing on the Thames. Battersea Rail Bridge – properly called the Cremorne Bridge, after the pleasure grounds in Chelsea – was one of four London bridges given Grade II* listing in November 2008.

Wandsworth Bridge links Fulham in the north with Wandsworth in the south. The first bridge on the site was designed by Julian Tolme and opened in 1873; tolls were charged until 1880. In 1935

London County Council gave its consent for a new bridge to be built. Designed by Sir Peirson Frank and opened in 1940, this bridge has a 200ft (60m) central span, consisting of seven high-tensile steel girders.

Putney Rail Bridge (also known as Fulham Rail Bridge), designed by W H Thomas and William Jacomb, is an eight-span wrought-iron girder structure. It was never given a name but soon became locally known as the 'Iron Bridge'. The first trains to cross the Thames on the Wimbledon and Putney branch ran on 3 June 1889. The bridge now forms part of the District Line service from Wimbledon via Earl's Court to Edgware Road and Upminster.

Putney Bridge links Fulham and Putney. The original road bridge was opened in November 1729. Work on a new structure, upstream on the site of the former aqueduct, began in 1882. Designed by Sir Joseph Bazalgette, the present bridge is 700ft (213m) in length and 43ft (13m) wide and constructed from concrete and granite. It was opened by the Prince and Princess of Wales in 1886.

Hammersmith Bridge connects Hammersmith in the north with Barnes in the south. The foundation stone of the original bridge was laid by the Duke of Sussex in 1825; designed by William Tierney Clarke and the first suspension bridge to span the Thames, the bridge opened in 1827. An elaborate new suspension bridge designed by Sir Joseph Bazalgette was opened in 1887. Hammersmith Bridge was one of four London bridges given Grade II* listing in November 2008.

Barnes Rail and Foot Bridge takes the railway from Chiswick to Barnes. In 1847 an Act of Incorporation allowed the Windsor, Staines and South-western Railway to build a 7-mile (11.5km) line from Barnes to Feltham. The line's Thames crossing, designed by Joseph Locke and Thomas Brassey, was a three-arch bridge of cast iron. Opened in 1849, this loop line was to prove a useful bypass for through passenger and freight traffic avoiding the busy route through Richmond. Increased traffic led to the bridge being strengthened in 1893; a footbridge added on the downstream side still survives.

Chiswick Bridge connects Chiswick in the north with Mortlake and Sheen in the south. Designed by Sir Herbert Baker and opened by the Prince of Wales on 3 July 1933, it is famous for being virtually on the finishing point of the annual Oxford and Cambridge University Boat Race.

Kew Rail Bridge was built for the London and South Western Railway and today carries the North London Line and London Underground District Line. Designed by W R Galbraith and built by Brassey & Ogilvie, the five-span iron lattice girder bridge was opened in 1869.

Kew Bridge links Brentford in London with Richmond in Surrey. Three bridges have spanned the Thames at this point, but before the first was built a horse ferry carried traffic across the river. The first bridge was built 1758–9 by John Barnard, who had worked on Westminster Bridge. A new bridge, designed by James Paine, was built in 1789. The third structure was built by Easton Gibb to the designs of Sir John Wolfe-Barry and C A Brereton. Opened in 1903, it was renamed the King Edward VII Bridge. It reverted to Kew Bridge in 1930.

Richmond Lock Footbridge links Isleworth on the west with Richmond and the Old Deer Park in the east. As a result of the removal of the palisades constructed to protect London Bridge after its demolition in 1832, tides on the Thames rose and fell far more rapidly than previously and for long periods the river between Twickenham and Richmond became little more than a stream running through mudbanks. To restore the level of the river a lock was created on the Surrey bank downstream of Richmond in 1890, with a weir and three roller slipways for small craft on the Middlesex bank. The superstructure required to operate the sluice mechanism was constructed in the form of two footbridges, and these were opened by the Duke and Duchess of York in 1894.

Twickenham Bridge runs from Chertsey Road on the Surrey side, through the Old Deer Park to join the road to Richmond. Designed by Maxwell Ayrton, it was opened in 1933. Twickenham Bridge was one of four London bridges given Grade II* listing in November 2008.

Richmond Rail Bridge was built by the Windsor, Staines and South-western Railway Company to connect Windsor, via Staines and Datchet, with the 6 mile (10km) line constructed in 1846 by the Richmond Company from Richmond to Clapham Junction and Waterloo. The new cast-iron bridge, originally called the Richmond, Windsor and Staines Railway Bridge, was designed by engineer Joseph Locke and opened in 1848. After another cast-iron railway bridge near Norbury Junction collapsed in 1891, causing considerable concern over the safety of Richmond Railway Bridge, a new bridge was designed by the chief engineer of the London & South-western Railway, J W Jacomb-Hood. Opened in 1908, this is in effect two separate steel-arched bridges, each carrying one line of track. Richmond Rail Bridge was one of three London bridges given Grade II listing in November 2008.

Richmond Bridge links Richmond in Surrey with Twickenham, formerly in Middlesex. Designed by architects James Paine and Kenton Couse, the bridge was built 1774–7. In 1937 it was widened on the upstream side.

Teddington Lock Footbridges link Ham on the east with Teddington in the west at Teddington Lock. In 1889 a footbridge designed by G Pooley replaced the ferry at Teddington. Two footbridges of different designs now meet on the island at Teddington: the bridge spanning the river from the Middlesex bank to the island is a suspension bridge, while the shorter structure crossing from the Surrey bank has a girder design.

Kingston Rail Bridge links Kingston and Hampton Wick stations. Designed by J E Errington and completed in 1863, the bridge carries the South West Trains looping branch line from London Waterloo to Shepperton and Richmond.

Kingston Bridge joins Kingston town centre to Hampton Court Park, Bushy Park and the village of Hampton Wick. Built in 1828, it was widened in 1914 and again in 2000.

Hampton Court Bridge was originally built in 1753 in a wooden Chinese-style lattice. Replaced by a wrought-iron bridge in 1865, it was rebuilt again in 1933.

British Library — Euston Road, NW1. The British Library was created by Act of Parliament in 1972 and established on 1 July 1973 by the combination of the library departments of the British Museum (which included the National Reference Library of Science and Invention), the National Central Library and the National Lending Library for Science and Technology (the centre for interlibrary lending, located at Boston Spa in Yorkshire). In 1974 the British National Bibliography and the Office for Scientific and Technical Information joined the UK's new national library. Two additional institutions subsequently became part of the Library, increasing the breadth of its collections: the India Office Library and Records (1982) and the British Institute of Recorded Sound (1983). Since 1997 the main collection has been housed in a single new building in Euston Road next to St Pancras railway station, designed by architect Colin St John Wilson and the largest public building constructed in the UK in the 20th century. Before the building, facing Euston Road, is a large piazza that features sculptures by Eduardo Paolozzi (a bronze statue based on William Blake's study of Isaac Newton) and Antony Gormley. The British Library was formally opened by Queen Elizabeth II in June 1998. An Act of Parliament in 1911 established the principle of the Legal Deposit, ensuring that the British Library, along with five other libraries in Great Britain and Ireland, is entitled to receive a free copy of every item published in the UK and the Republic of Ireland. The other five libraries are: the Bodleian Library at Oxford; the University Library at Cambridge; Trinity College Library in Dublin; and the National Libraries of Scotland and Wales. The British Library is the only one entitled to receive a copy of everything within one month of publication; the other five have to wait for up to one year. A number of important works are on display to the general public in the Sir John Ritblat Gallery, while other items can be accessed in the reading rooms. In the past the Library's role was as a 'library of last resort' for people who needed access to specialised collections unavailable elsewhere. Nowadays it adopts a more welcoming approach; anyone who wishes to carry out research should be granted a reader's pass, providing they furnish the necessary identification for security purposes. The British Library Newspapers section is based in Colindale, north London. Tel: 020 7412 7676.

British Museum — Great Russell Street, WC1. The origins of the British Museum lie in the will of the physician, naturalist and collector Sir Hans Sloane (1660–1753). Not wishing to see his collection of 71,000 objects, a library and herbarium, dispersed on his death, Sloane bequeathed it to George II for the nation in return for the payment of £20,000 to his heirs. The king had little interest but Parliament, led by the Speaker, Arthur Onslow, was persuaded to accept the gift and an Act of Parliament establishing the British Museum received royal assent on 7 June 1753. Sir Robert Bruce Cotton's collection of manuscripts – including the Lindisfarne Gospels and Magna Carta – was given to the nation in 1700 and attached to the new museum, while £10,000 was spent in purchasing the collection of manuscripts put together by Robert and Edward Harley, 1st and 2nd Earls of Oxford. The museum was initially housed in a 17th century mansion, Montagu House in Bloomsbury, on the site of today's building, and opened in 15 January 1759. The first significant antiquities, Sir William Hamilton's collection of Greek vases and other classical objects were purchased in 1772. These were followed by such notable acquisitions as the Rosetta Stone and other antiquities from Egypt (1802), the Townley collection of classical sculpture (1805), and the sculptures of the Parthenon, known as the Elgin Marbles (1816). With the additional expansion of the natural history collections and the library, as well as the gift in 1823 by George IV of his father's library (the King's Library), today's quadrangular building was constructed to a design by Sir Robert Smirke. The first phase was largely completed in 1852, followed by the round Reading Room, designed by Robert's brother Sydney and erected in the central courtyard 1854–7. In the 1880s the natural history collections were moved to a new building in South Kensington, later to become the Natural History Museum. King Edward VII's Galleries were formally opened in 1914; the Duveen Gallery (1939–62) and the New Wing (1978) provided additional public facilities, offices, display areas and library storage. The Department of Ethnography moved out temporarily to the Museum of Mankind in Burlington Gardens (now closed) in 1970. In 1973 the library departments became part of the British Library, leaving Bloomsbury in 1998. This public expansion is reflected in the opening in 2000 of the Queen Elizabeth II Great Court, which was created in part of the space vacated by the library. At the centre is the restored Reading Room, now open to the general public, which houses the Paul Hamlyn Library and COMPASS, a multimedia database of the collections. Beneath are the Clore Education Centre and the Sainsbury African galleries. Tel: 020 7323 8000.

British Telecom Tower — Cleveland Street, W1. Originally called the Post Office Tower, the British Telecom Communication Tower in London's West End was the first purpose-built tower to transmit high frequency radio waves. Nowadays simply referred to as the Telecom Tower, it serves as a functional telecommunications centre relaying broadcast, internet and telephone information around the world. Designed by Eric Bedford, it stands 580ft (177m) high, a 40ft (12m) mast giving an overall height of 620ft (189m); officially opened by Harold Wilson on 8 October 1965 with a ceremonial call to the Lord Mayor of Birmingham, it remained the tallest building in London until the NatWest Tower exceeded it in 1981. On the 34th floor is the famous revolving restaurant, which completes a 360º rotation once every 22 minutes. Sadly it was closed to the public in 1980.

Bruce Castle Museum — Lordship Lane, N17. A Grade I listed 16th century manor house in 20 acres (8ha) of parkland. William Compton, a member of Henry VIII's court, built the oldest surviving parts of the house. Since then it has been modified several times by various owners including the Coleraine family; one of the wives of the 2nd Lord Coleraine is said to haunt the building. The family of Sir Rowland Hill – reformer of the British postal system and famous for introducing the penny post – ran a progressive school for boys at Bruce Castle during the Victorian period. Bruce Castle opened as a museum in 1906 and now houses the Borough of Haringey's local history collections and archives. Tel: 020 8808 8772.

Buckingham Palace The Mall, SW1. The official London residence of Queen Elizabeth II. Originally known as Buckingham House (and still nicknamed 'Buck House' by the royal family), it was built in 1703 as a large townhouse for the Duke of Buckingham and was acquired by George III in 1762 as a private residence. Enlarged over the next 75 years, principally by architects John Nash and Edward Blore, to form three wings around a central courtyard, it finally became the official royal palace of the British monarch on Queen Victoria's accession in 1837. The last major structural additions were made in the late 19th and early 20th century, when the large east wing facing The Mall was added, and the former state entrance, Marble Arch, was removed to its present position near Speakers' Corner in Hyde Park. The east front was refaced in Portland stone in 1913 as a backdrop to the Victoria Memorial, creating the present-day 'public face' of Buckingham Palace, including the famous balcony. The Palace has approximately 600 rooms; the 19 state rooms are open for eight weeks a year. The 42 acre (17ha) gardens, originally landscaped by Capability Brown, were redesigned by William Townsend Aiton and John Nash with a lake created in 1828. Adjacent to Buckingham Palace are the Royal Mews with its fine array of horse-drawn carriages and motor cars, and the Queen's Gallery which hosts a series of ever-changing exhibitions. Tel: 0207 766 7300. See also Changing of the Guard.

Burgh House New End Square, Hampstead, NW3. A Grade I listed Queen Anne style house built in 1704 for Quakers Henry and Hannah Sewell. Having passed through numerous owners, and occupied by Rudyard Kipling's daughter in the 1930s, it is now owned by the Borough of Camden. Home to the Hampstead Museum, it also shows a regular programme of concerts and art exhibitions. Tel: 020 7431 0144.

Canary Wharf London E14. A large business development on the Isle of Dogs, Tower Hamlets, centred on the old West India Docks in the London Docklands. Canary Wharf contains the UK's three tallest buildings. One Canada Square (commonly known as the Canary Wharf Tower or simply Canary Wharf), designed by Argentine architect César Pelli and completed in 1991, is the tallest habitable building in the UK at 771ft (235m). It contained the offices of the *Daily Telegraph* until October 2006 when they were relocated to 111 Buckingham Palace Road. 8 Canada Square (commonly known as the HSBC Tower) and 25 Canada Square (commonly known as the Citigroup Centre) claim to be the joint second tallest buildings in the UK, both being in the region of 654ft (199m). Canary Wharf itself takes its name from the sea trade with the Canary Islands.

Capel Manor Gardens Bullsmoor Lane, Enfield. A series of themed gardens, including an Italianate maze and a Japanese garden, covering 30 acres (12ha) and surrounding a Georgian manor house and Victorian stables. Since 1968 the site has been occupied by Capel Manor College, Greater London's only specialist college of horticulture, floristry, garden design, equine and other animal care and countryside studies. Tel: 020 8366 4442.

Carew Manor Church Road, Beddington. Located in Beddington Park. For many years the home of the Carew family, the great hall of Carew Manor has a Grade I listed arch-braced hammer-beam roof dating from c.1500; the cellars with a chalk and flint construction dating to earlier houses on the site. The house is now occupied by Carew Manor School. In the grounds is a large early 18th century dovecote which originally contained over 1000 nesting boxes, built into the inner face of the wall and accessed by a large rotating ladder or potence. Tel: 020 8770 4781.

Carlyle's House Cheyne Row, Chelsea, SW3. An early 18th century terraced house, the home of historian and philosopher Thomas Carlyle and his wife Jane, who lived in this unpretentious Queen Anne house for 30 years after moving from Scotland to London in 1834. The house has been preserved much as it looked at Carlyle's death. Now owned by the National Trust. Tel: 020 7352 7087.

Cemeteries See Magnificent Seven

Cenotaph, The Whitehall, SW1. Commissioned by David Lloyd George and designed by Sir Edwin Lutyens, the Portland stone monument was erected 1919–20 to replace Lutyens' identical wood and plaster cenotaph, erected in 1919 for the Allied victory parade. The Grade I listed structure is undecorated except for a carved wreath on each end and the words 'The Glorious Dead', chosen by Rudyard Kipling, and is flanked on each side by the flags of the UK, representing the Royal Navy, the British Army, the Royal Air Force and the Merchant Navy. Lutyens had wanted stone flags, as used on his later Rochdale cenotaph, but was overruled. The Cenotaph is the site of the annual national service of remembrance, held at 11am on Remembrance Sunday, the closest Sunday to 11 November (Armistice Day). Uniformed service personnel (excluding fire and ambulance personnel) always salute the Cenotaph as they pass.

Changing of the Guard One of the oldest and most familiar ceremonies associated with Buckingham Palace, the proper name of the ceremony known as Changing the Guard is actually Guard Mounting. In this process a New Guard exchanges duty with the Old Guard, both being drawn from one of the regiments of Foot Guards. The handover is accompanied by a Guards band, who play music ranging from traditional military marches to songs from musical shows and even pop songs. When the Queen is in residence, there are four sentries at the front of Buckingham Palace; when she is away there are two. The Queen's Guard usually consists of Foot Guards in full dress uniform of red tunics and bearskins; if they have operational commitments, other infantry units such as the Brigade of Gurkhas take part instead. Guard Mounting takes place in the forecourt of Buckingham Palace at 11.30am, and lasts about 45 minutes. There is no Guard Mounting in very wet weather. During the autumn and winter, Guard Mounting takes place on alternate days, but it is held daily during spring and summer. At Horse Guards Arch on Horse Guards Parade, east of St James's Park, the Changing of the Guard takes place daily at 11am (10am on Sundays), lasting about 30 minutes.

Charing Cross London WC2. The name Charing Cross, now that of a mainline railway station and the surrounding district of central London, comes from the original hamlet of Charing, where Edward I placed a cross in memorial to his wife, Eleanor of Castile in 1290. Charing Cross was the last of 12 places where Eleanor's coffin rested overnight during the funeral procession from Lincolnshire to her final resting place at Westminster, $^1/_2$ mile (0.8km) away. At each of these, Edward erected a cross; known as Eleanor crosses, only three of these now remain (at Geddington and Hardingstone in Northamptonshire, and Waltham Cross in Hertfordshire). The one which stands in front of Charing Cross railway station is a relocated Victorian copy (designed by architect Edward Middleton Barry); the original was not nearly as large or ornate as the Victorian version. The cross's original location in the village of Charing was at the top of Whitehall, on the south side of Trafalgar Square. The site is officially recognised as the exact centre of London and distances to London are measured to this point. The site is now occupied by a statue of Charles I mounted on a horse and a plaque which reads: 'On the site now occupied by the statue of King Charles was erected the original Queen Eleanor's Cross a replica of which stands in front of Charing Cross Station. Mileages from London are measured from the site of the original cross.'

Charles Dickens Museum Doughty Street, WC1. The house in which Charles Dickens, probably the greatest chronicler of London life, lived with his family from April 1837 to December 1839, and where he wrote *The Pickwick Papers*, *Oliver Twist* and *Nicholas Nickleby*. It was opened as the Dickens House Museum in 1925 and now holds the most important collection of material relating to Dickens in the world. Tel: 020 7405 2127.

Cheam A large suburban village in the London Borough of Sutton, divided into two main areas: North Cheam and Cheam Village. Cheam was the original home of Cheam School, formed in Whitehall in the centre of Cheam Village in 1645 and which later occupied Tabor Court from 1719 until 1934 when the school moved to Berkshire. Prince Philip attended the school in the years immediately before its move. Cheam's most famous resident was probably Sir Harry Secombe, and the former Goon gives his name to a local theatre, the **Secombe Theatre**, Cheam Road, Sutton. The most famous fictional resident is undoubtedly the television persona of Anthony Aloysius Hancock, who in most seasons of the comedy series *Hancock's Half Hour* lived at the fictional address of 23 Railway Cuttings, East Cheam.

Chelsea Flower Show Royal Hospital, Chelsea, SW3. Originally called the Royal Horticultural Society's Great Spring Show, the history of the Chelsea Flower Show goes back to 1852 when it was held in the RHS's gardens in Kensington. The show moved to Chelsea and was renamed in 1913 when a popular one-off event, the Royal International Horticultural Exhibition, was held in the 11 acre (4.5ha) gardens of the Royal Hospital, Chelsea, organised by Sir Harry Veitch. The show is attended annually by 157,000 visitors with two of the four days only open to RHS members, and is covered extensively by BBC Television. Four grades of award are presented: gold, silver-gilt, silver and bronze (bronze grade exhibits do not actually receive a medal), in each of the following categories: Flora awards for gardens and floral exhibits; Hogg awards for fruit; Knightian awards for vegetables, including herbs; Lindley awards for exhibits of special educational or scientific interest; Grenfell awards for pictures, photographs, floral arrangements and floristry. Special awards include: Best Show Garden Award; Best Courtyard Garden Award; Best Chic Garden Award; Best City Garden Award; RHS Sundries Bowl; RHS Junior Display Trophy; RHS Floral Arrangement Trophies; RHS Floristry Trophies; Show Certificates of merit; Certificates for Junior displays; RHS President's Award.

Chelsea Pensioners A term used to refer to residents – former British soldiers – of the Royal Hospital, Chelsea. The hospital was founded by Charles II, who on 22 December 1681 issued a royal warrant authorising its construction in order to make provision for old or injured soldiers. Sir Christopher Wren designed the building, based on the Hôpital des Invalides in Paris. The Royal Hospital Founder's Day takes place each year close to 29 May, Charles II's birthday and the date of his restoration as king in 1660 (also known as Oakapple Day). On Founder's Day, in-pensioners are reviewed by a member of the royal family, a duty undertaken by Queen Elizabeth II in 2006 for the first time in 24 years. To be considered for admission, candidates must be in receipt of an Army Service or War Disability Pension, 65 years of age or over (though candidates aged 55–65 may be admitted if they are unable to earn their own living through disability, and are in receipt of an army pension) and free from the obligation to support a spouse, partner or family. Until 2007 they had to be male, but women are now admitted. Within the hospital and the surrounding area, in-pensioners wear a blue uniform. On ceremonial occasions they wear the distinctive scarlet coats and black tricorn hats, the design of which is based on 18th century uniforms introduced by the Duke of Marlborough. On admittance, each resident is given a 'berth' in a ward, a small room (9ft x 9ft/2.7m x 2.7m) on a long corridor, and is allocated to a company. Residents surrender their army pension and receive board, lodging, clothing and full medical care. The size of the hospital berths has increased over time. Originally, there were 26 berths to a ward, there are now 17. In all the hospital cares for about 350 residents.

Chelsea Physic Garden Royal Hospital Road, SW3. The second-oldest botanic garden in Britain, located between Chelsea and Albert Bridges, and founded in 1673 by the Worshipful Society of Apothecaries. It includes the Garden of World Medicine, which features plants used medicinally by various ethnic groups and in numerous indigenous traditions. Tel: 020 7352 5646.

Chelsea Porcelain The first important porcelain manufacturer in England, founded in 1745 by Huguenot silversmith Nicholas Sprimont (1716–69). Its products were aimed at the aristocratic market. By 1750 it was producing large quantities of tableware based on Meissen porcelain models and on silver prototypes, such as salt cellars in the form of realistic shells; from c.1760 its inspiration was drawn more from Sèvres porcelain with its brightly coloured backgrounds than from Meissen. After

Sprimont's death the firm was purchased in 1770 by William Duesbury, owner of the Derby porcelain company; the two factories continued manufacturing similar products until the Chelsea factory was closed in 1784.

Chislehurst Caves — Old Hill, Chislehurst. A labyrinth of dark mysterious passageways hewn by hand from the chalk, deep beneath Chislehurst. There are over 20 miles (32km) of caverns and passageways, a maze of ancient mines believed to have been dug over a period of 8000 years in the search for flint and chalk. They are divided into three main sections – referred to as Saxon, Druid and Roman, although there is little hard evidence that these relate with any precision to the periods when each was created – each section later connected by digging adjoining passages. Mining activity is difficult to date precisely, but the mines appear on a charter of 1250 and also in local church records of 1737. The last time the mines were known to have been worked was in the 1830s when the Saxon section was used by a flintmaker and limeburner. They began to develop as a tourist attraction with the arrival of the railway in 1865, and were the setting for several underground concerts in the early 1900s. During World War I the caves became part of Woolwich Arsenal and were used as an ammunitions depot, and a narrow gauge railway was installed. Between the wars they were used by the Kent Mushroom Company. During World War II the caves became a massive air raid shelter in which over 15,000 people took refuge every night from autumn of 1940 to spring of 1941. In the 1960s, the caves were used a music venue at which artists such as Status Quo, Jimi Hendrix, The Rolling Stones and Pink Floyd performed. In October 1974 a lavish media party was held there to celebrate the launch of new UK record company Swan Song Records by the band Led Zeppelin. More recently, some of the tunnels have been used by the live action role-playing game Labyrinthe. The caves have also been used as a TV and film location for productions including *Doctor Who, Inseminoid* (1981), *Bliss, Neverwhere* and *Randall & Hopkirk (Deceased)*. Tel: 020 8467 3264.

Chiswick House — Burlington Lane, W4. A fine white Palladian-style villa built 1725–9 by the 3rd Earl of Burlington, and inspired by the architecture and gardens of ancient Rome. The interior features gilded decoration and velvet walls with richly painted ceilings. The 18th century gardens, designed by William Kent, feature cedar trees, cascades, statues and obelisks. Now owned by English Heritage. Tel: 020 8995 0508.

City Livery Companies — The descendants of London's medieval craft guilds. Initially sharing the aim of modern trade unions, to promote the well-being of their members, they now exercise mainly a charitable and social function. The Great Twelve (the oldest and traditionally the wealthiest and most powerful) in order of precedence are: **Mercers**, Mercers' Hall, Ironmonger Lane, EC2. Tel: 020 7726 4991; **Grocers**, Grocers' Hall, Princes Street, EC2. Tel: 020 7606 3113; **Drapers**, Drapers' Hall, Throgmorton Avenue, EC2. Tel: 020 7588 5001; **Fishmongers**, Fishmongers' Hall, London Bridge, EC4. Tel: 020 7626 3531; **Goldsmiths**, Goldsmiths' Hall, Foster Lane, EC2. Tel: 020 7606 7010; **Merchant Taylors**, Merchant Taylors' Hall, Threadneedle Street, EC2. Tel: 020 7450 4440; **Skinners**, Skinners' Hall, Dowgate Hill EC4. Tel: 020 7213 0553; **Haberdashers**, Haberdashers' Hall, West Smithfield, EC1. Tel: 020 7246 9988; **Salters**, Salters' Hall, Fore Street, EC2. Tel: 020 7588 5216; **Ironmongers**, Ironmongers' Hall, Shaftesbury Place, Barbican EC2. Tel: 020 7776 2304; **Vintners**, Vintners' Hall, Upper Thames Street, EC4. Tel: 020 7236 1863. Vintners share with the Dyers and the Crown the ownership of all swans on the Thames, their cygnets being marked with two nicks on the beak on the annual swan upping voyage; **Clothworkers**, Clothworkers' Hall, Dunster Court, Mincing Lane, EC3. Tel: 020 7623 7041. Nb Merchant Taylors and Skinners alternate in 6th and 7th place. Today there are 108 City Livery Companies. The list of 'minor' companies is as follows:

Actuaries
Air Pilots & Air Navigators
Apothecaries (medicine)
Arbitrators
Armourers & Brasiers (armour-makers and workers in brass)
Bakers
Barbers (also surgeons and dentists)
Basketmakers
Blacksmiths
Bowyers (longbow makers)
Brewers
Broderers (embroiderers)
Builders' Merchants
Butchers
Carmen
Carpenters
Chartered Accountants
Chartered Architects
Chartered Secretaries & Administrators
Chartered Surveyors
Clockmakers
Coachmakers & Coach Harness Makers
Constructors
Cooks
Coopers (barrel makers)
Cordwainers (workers in fine leather)
Curriers (dressers of tanned leather)
Cutlers
Distillers
Dyers
Engineers
Environmental Cleaners
Fan Makers
Farmers
Farriers (shoers of horses/veterinary surgeons)
Feltmakers (hats)
Firefighters
Fletchers (arrow makers)
Founders
Framework Knitters
Fruiterers
Fuellers
Furniture Makers
Gardeners
Girdlers (makers of girdles and belts as clothing)
Glass Sellers
Glaziers
Glovers
Gold & Silver Wyre Drawers (makers of gold and silver braid for uniforms)

Gunmakers
Hackney Carriage Drivers
Horners
Information Technologists
Innholders
Insurers
International Bankers
Joiners and Ceilers
Launderers
Leathersellers
Lightmongers
Loriners (makers of bits, stirrups and spurs for horses)
Makers of Playing Cards
Management Consultants
Marketors
Masons
Master Mariners
Musicians
Needlemakers
Painter Stainers
Pattenmakers (makers of wooden clog-style footwear)
Paviors (paving highways)
Pewterers
Plaisterers (plasterers)
Plumbers
Poulters
Saddlers
Scientific Instrument Makers
Scriveners
(writers of court letters and legal documents)
Security Professionals
Shipwrights
Solicitors
Spectaclemakers
Stationers & Newspaper Makers
Tallowchandlers
Tax Advisers
Tinplate Workers
Tobacco Pipe Makers & Tobacco Blenders
Turners
Tylers & Bricklayers
Upholders (upholsterers)
Water Conservators
Wax Chandlers
Weavers
Wheelwrights
Woolmen (winders and packers of wool)
World Traders

City of London Often referred to as just the City or as the Square Mile, as it is approximately 1 sq mile (2.6 sq km) in area, the City of London is historically the core of London and is the location of the city's finincial district, with which it has become synonymous. The City of London borders the City of Westminster to the west, the London Boroughs of Camden, Islington and Hackney to the north, the London Borough of Tower Hamlets to the east and Lambeth and Southwark to the south. Its boundaries are marked by black bollards bearing the City's emblem. The financial district extends north and east slightly beyond the political boundaries of the City, into the boroughs of Tower Hamlets, Hackney and Islington, and informally these locations are seen as part of the 'Square Mile'. Since the 1990s the eastern fringe of the City, extending into Hackney and Tower Hamlets, has increasingly been a focus for large office developments due to the relatively easy availability of large sites there compared to within the City itself.

Clapham Sect An influential group of Anglican social reformers, mostly living in the Clapham area and meeting at the Clapham residence of philanthropist, economist and banker Henry Thornton (1760–1815), MP for Southwark and grandfather of writer E M Forster. Members included classicist and campaigner Thomas Clarkson (1760–1846); parliamentarian Edward James Eliot (1758–97); clergyman and author Thomas Gisbourne (1758–1846); estate manager, colonial governor and editor of the *Christian Observer* Zachary Macaulay (1768–1838), father of Thomas Babington Macaulay; writer and philanthropist Hannah More (1745–1833); William Smith (1756–1835), MP for Norwich and grandfather of Florence Nightingale; Lord Teignmouth (1751–1834), Governor-General of India; John Venn (1759–1813), Rector of Holy Trinity Church, Clapham; and William Wilberforce (1759–1833), MP for Kingston upon Hull and leading abolitionist. The group was active from the 1790s until the early 1830s. Following their work, the Act for the Abolition of the Slave Trade was passed by Parliament on 25 March 1807. Designed to outlaw the slave trade within the British Empire, the Act imposed a fine of £100 for every slave found aboard a British ship. Slavery itself was abolished in the British colonies only by the Slavery Abolition Act, passed on 23 August 1833. All slaves in the British Empire were emancipated on 1 August 1834, although they were still indentured to their former owners in an apprenticeship system finally abolished in 1838.

Clarence House The Mall, SW1. Built 1825–7 for Prince William Henry, Duke of Clarence and designed by John Nash, Clarence House stands beside St James's Palace. The London home of Queen Elizabeth the Queen Mother, 1953–2002, it was also the home of Queen Elizabeth II (then Princess Elizabeth) and the Duke of Edinburgh following their marriage in 1947. Today Clarence House is the official London residence of the Prince of Wales and the Duchess of Cornwall. Tel: 020 7766 7303.

Claridge's Brook Street, W1. One of London's most famous hotels, Claridge's developed from a hotel opened in 1812 by James Mivart at 51 Brook Street. By 1838, Mivart owned a row of five houses, knocking through to create one large hotel. The Great Exhibition of 1851 brought a huge influx of visitors to London, and foreign royalty including Grand Duke Alexander of Russia and William III of the Netherlands made Mivart's their home from home. No. 49 Brook Street had always been a separate hotel, run by husband and wife William and Marianne Claridge. In 1854 they purchased Mivart's and operated the entire row of houses as a single hotel. In 1893 Richard D'Oyly Carte, who had already built the Savoy, purchased the hotel and had it demolished. A new purpose-built hotel designed by C W Stephens was erected on the site, reopening in November 1898. Many royal families who found themselves in exile during World War II made their way to the familiar haven. Notable among them was King Peter of Yugoslavia, whose son, Crown Prince Alexander, was born in Suite 212 in July 1945. Prime Minister Sir Winston Churchill declared the suite

Yugoslav territory, and legend has it that a spadeful of Yugoslav earth was placed under the bed so that the heir to the throne could literally be born on Yugoslav soil. In 1996 Claridge's embarked on its first major restoration since the 1930s; David Collins was invited to create a new cocktail bar and New York-based designer Thierry Despont was brought in to revitalise the foyer area. Using archive photographs of the early 1930s ballroom extension, the space was made over in Art Deco style, with a stunning Dale Chihuly chandelier as its centrepiece. Despont went on to create Gordon Ramsay at Claridge's. Tel: 0871 223 8008.

Clink Prison Museum

Clink Street, SE1. Situated on the South Bank midway between Southwark Bridge and London Bridge, The Clink was a notorious prison in Southwark which functioned from 1144 until 1780. Owned by the Bishop of Winchester and situated next to his residence at Winchester Palace, it was originally used for the detention of heretics (both Protestants and Catholics, as religious fashions changed) but came to be used for people who disturbed the peace on Bankside or in Southwark's numerous brothels. The prison fell into disuse after the Civil War, though it was described in 1761 as being 'a very dismal hole where debtors are sometimes confined, but little used'. The Clink was burned down during the Gordon Riots of 1780 and never rebuilt. The Clink Prison Museum, housed on the original site of the Liberty of The Clink, is at basement level with many original torture instruments and an original torture chair. Within its confines is an original execution block, accompanied by a 19th century execution belt and handcuffs. The medieval character of the museum adds to the atmosphere and there are exhibits relating to religious, financial and social history. Tel: 020 7403 9981.

Clubs

There are many private members' clubs in London; the following are a few of the most famous:

The **Arts Club**, Dover Street, Mayfair, W1, was founded by Charles Dickens, among others, in 1863. Tel: 0207 499 8581.

The **Athenaeum**, Pall Mall, SW1, was founded in 1824 by John Wilson Croker and began at the Royal Society in Somerset House. It moved to Pall Mall in 1830 when it adopted its present name, from that of a university in Rome. The gilt statue of Athene is by E M Baily and the building by Decimus Burton. Tel: 020 7930 4843.

Boodle's, St James's Street, SW1, was founded in 1764 by William Almack as a social and non-political club. It began in Pall Mall, originally known as the Savoir Faire, and moved to its present premises, designed by Henry Holland in 1778. It gained a reputation for heavy gambling and later became the Whigs' Club. Tel: 020 7930 7166.

Brook's, St James's Street, SW1, was founded in 1778. Tel: 020 7493 4411.

The **Carlton Club,** St James's Street, SW1, was founded in 1832 when the Tories lost seats in the general election over the Reform Bill. It began in Carlton House Terrace and later moved to Pall Mall. In 1854 the club moved to St James's Street to a building in St James's Street, designed by Sydney Smirke and George Basevi and modelled on Sansovino's Library in Venice. Tel: 020 7493 1164.

The **Garrick Club**, Garrick Street, WC2, was founded in 1831 by a group of literary gentlemen under the patronage of the king's brother, the egalitarian Duke of Sussex. It moved to its present home on Garrick Street in 1864. Tel: 020 7836 1737.

The **Groucho Club**, Dean Street, W1, was founded in 1985 for both men and women involved in the publishing world. It now attracts members from all fields of the media and arts. Tel: 020 7439 4685.

Pratt's, Park Place, SW1, founded in 1857, was named after William Pratt, a steward to the Duke of Beaufort. The Duke called at Pratt's house with some friends one evening and they enjoyed themselves so much they came back again and again. Only 14 of the 600 male members can dine at the single table in the basement and all the servants are addressed as George. Tel: 020 7493 0397.

The **Reform Club**, Pall Mall, SW1, was founded for Radicals in 1836. In 1837 Charles Barry won a competition to design the clubhouse and Alexis Soyer, the club chef, planned the kitchen. Costs had doubled by the time it opened in 1841. It is from this club that Phileas Fogg sets off on his voyage in the novel *Around the World in 80 Days*. Tel: 020 7930 9374.

Soho House, Greek Street, W1, was founded in 1995 and draws its membership from those within the world of film, media and the arts. The owners, Nick Jones and wife Kirsty Young, attempted to encourage a younger membership in 2006 by offering half-price annual membership for under-27-year-olds, actively discouraging older applicants. Tel: 020 7734 5188.

White's, St James's Street, SW1, is the oldest club in London. Founded in White's Chocolate House in 1693 on the east side of St James's Street, it later occupied other premises on the street and became a place where gambling was for high stakes and bets would be taken on anything. The building now in use was rebuilt in 1787, possibly by James Wyatt. In 1811 a bow window was added which became the favourite place of Beau Brummell. The club was later bought at auction for £46,000 by Henry Eaton, who had been refused membership. Tel: 020 7493 6671.

Fictional clubs include the **Drones Club**, created by comic novelist P G Wodehouse; situated like the Arts Club in Dover Street, it features in many of his Jeeves and Wooster and Blandings Castle stories. The **Diogenes Club** is another fictional gentlemen's club, created by Sir Arthur Conan Doyle and featured in several Sherlock Holmes stories, most notably 'The Greek Interpreter'. It was possibly named after Diogenes the Cynic and was co-founded by Sherlock's indolent older brother, Mycroft Holmes.

Cockney

The term given to a Londoner prone to drop the odd consonant here and there was in use in this sense as early as 1600, when Samuel Rowlands in his satire *The Letting of Humours Blood in the Head-Vaine* referred to 'a Bow-bell Cockney'. Before this a cockney was any spoilt child brought up in the soft ways of the town rather than the country. The traditional definition is that in order to be a Cockney, one must have been born within earshot of the Bow bells, i.e. the bells of the church of St Mary-le-Bow. The traditional core neighbourhoods for Cockneys include Bethnal Green, Whitechapel, Spitalfields, Stepney, Wapping, Limehouse, Poplar, Millwall, Hackney, Shoreditch, Bow and Mile End. Cockney speakers have a distinctive accent and dialect, and frequently use Cockney rhyming slang, which developed among 19th century costermongers.

College of Arms — Queen Victoria Street, EC4. Located south of St Paul's Cathedral, the building was purpose built in the 1670s to house the English Offices of Arms and their records. Founded in 1484, this corporate body is the repository for the coats of arms of families in England, Wales and Northern Ireland. (Scotland is not included as it has its own heraldic authority: Lord Lyon, King of Arms and his office.) Its members, the 13 'heralds in ordinary', are granted heraldic authority by the Queen. The college also grants arms to citizens of other Commonwealth countries that do not have their own heraldic authorities. Tel: 020 7248 2762.

Congestion Charge — A fee introduced on 17 February 2003 and administered by Transport for London (see separate entry), to be paid daily by the registered owner of any vehicle which enters, leaves or moves around within a designated zone of central London between 7am and 6.30pm, Monday to Friday. Initially set at £5, the charge was increased on 4 July 2005 to £8. From 19 June 2006 a new 'Pay-Next-Day' scheme was introduced allowing drivers to pay their congestion charge until midnight on the day of travel, or pay £10 until midnight on the following charging day. Failure to pay by midnight means a fine of at least £50. The present boundary of the zone is sometimes referred to as the London Inner Ring Road. Starting at the northernmost point and moving clockwise, the major roads defining the boundary are Pentonville Road, City Road, Old Street, Commercial Street, Mansell Street, Tower Bridge Road, New Kent Road, Elephant and Castle, Vauxhall Bridge Road, Park Lane, Edgware Road, Marylebone Road and Euston Road. The zone therefore includes the whole of the City of London and the West End. Markings are painted on all roads entering the zone to warn drivers of their need to pay the charge. In addition to the 180 cameras on the edge of the zone, there are 50 further cameras placed within it. These cameras are intended to pick up cars that are missed on entry and exit and those that are solely moving within the zone. A proposed increase to £25 payable by owners of 4 x 4 vehicles – the so-called 'Chelsea Tractors' – was scrapped in 2008 by the incoming Mayor of London, Boris Johnson.

Court of St James's — The official name of the UK's royal court, deriving from St James's Palace, the main royal residence in London from 1702 until 1837 when Buckingham Palace took over the role. Diplomats from foreign countries are described as being accredited to the Court of St James's, though new ambassadors present their credentials to the Queen in a ceremony at Buckingham Palace.

Cries of London — The cries of London market traders, but particularly street hawkers, could be heard during the Middle Ages and were still audible well into the 20th century. More than 150 such calls were known by the early 18th century; they were sometimes incorporated into English composers' works but were better known as the title of several series of prints sold by itinerant traders during this period. A set of 12 stipple engravings of 1793–7 based on earlier paintings by Francis Wheatley (1747–1801) are good examples, and a famous pack of playing cards isued in 1754 also depicted the criers. A set of picture cards issued in 1916 became collectors' items later in the century. A typical cry would begin 'Won't you buy my . . .'

Croydon — Croydon, part of the southeastern suburbs of London, In 1965 the County Borough of Croydon was abolished and its former area transferred to Greater London, combining with that of Coulsdon and Purley Urban District to form the present-day London Borough of Croydon. As with so many areas absorbed by London sprawl, Croydon residents, and in particular those of Coulsdon and Purley, consider themselves as living in Surrey and continue to use the county name in their postal address. Historically, Croydon was the centre of a large estate belonging to the Archbishops of Canterbury. The archbishops' manor house was used as an occasional place of residence from the end of the 11th century when Archbishop Lanfranc was made lord of the manor by William I. In 1276, the archbishop, Robert Kilwardby, acquired a charter for a weekly market, and Croydon subsequently developed into one of the main market towns of northeast Surrey. The market place was laid out on the higher ground to the east of the manor house in the area now bounded by High Street, Surrey Street and Crown Hill. By the 16th century the manor house had become a substantial palace used as the archbishops' main summer home. The original palace – by then dilapidated and surrounded by slums and stagnant ponds – was sold in 1781, and a new residence at nearby Addington was purchased in its place (see separate entry). Many of the buildings of the original Croydon Palace survive, and are in use today as Old Palace School. Croydon Parish Church is the burial place of six Archbishops of Canterbury: John Whitgift, Edmund Grindal, Gilbert Sheldon, William Wake, John Potter and Thomas Herring. As the town continued to grow, the South Croydon and Purley areas became popular as a residential suburb for the Victorian middle classes, who could commute to the City of London by train in less than half an hour. In 1883 Croydon was created a municipal borough in Surrey. With its growing economic importance, in 1889 it was made a county borough exempt from county administration. The new county borough council implemented the Croydon improvement scheme in the early 1890s, which resulted in the widening of the High Street and the clearance of much of the 'Middle Row' slum area. The remaining slums were cleared shortly after World War II, with much of the population relocated to an isolated new community at New Addington. New stores opened in central Croydon, including the first Sainsbury's self-service shop in England and in 1969 the Whitgift Centre shopping precinct. In 1962 the Fairfield Halls opened. Purley was once the home of the largest dance floor in Europe: the Orchid Ballroom (now a fitness centre) was a frequent haunt of the BBC's *Come Dancing* programme. The 1990s saw a number of changes intended to give the town a more attractive image. Croydon Clocktower arts centre opened in 1994, Tramlink (see separate entry) began operation in May 2000, and a new shopping centre, Centrale, was opened in 2004 opposite the Whitgift Centre. There are now plans for a large new shopping centre, Park Place, the redevelopment of the Croydon Gateway site and extensions of Tramlink to Purley, Streatham and Crystal Palace. Croydon's many fine parkland areas include Lloyd Park and the great wooded area of Croham Hurst with its historic breakneck hill. There is a plate recording a Bronze Age settlement on Croham Hurst. See also Addington Palace, Croydon Airport, Derek Bentley, Tramlink, Whitgift Almshouses.

Croydon Airport Purley Way, Croydon. Once one of the world's great airports, Croydon Airport was London's main airport before it was superseded by Heathrow and Gatwick. Originating in World War I as an airfield for protection against Zeppelins, after the war it was reopened as Croydon Aerodrome and became the main gateway for international flights to and from London, as well as the base for Imperial Airways. It also welcomed the world's pioneer aviators: Amy Johnson (1903–41) set off from Croydon Airport on 5 May 1930 in a Gipsy Moth, reaching India in a record six days and Australia in 19 days. She continued to make record long-distance flights with her husband Jim Mollison, whom she married in 1932, until she was reported missing over tho Thamos Estuary when flying for the Air Ministry in 1941. During World War II the airport became a fighter station during the Battle of Britain and was later the base of RAF Transport Command. With the rapid increase in the size and number of aircraft after the war, it soon became apparent that the airport was too small to cope with the ever-increasing volume of air traffic. It was decided it would have to close, and the last scheduled flight departed on 30 September 1959. The air terminal, now known as Airport House, has been restored and houses a museum open one day a month. The international distress call 'mayday' (French *m'aidez*) was invented by Croydon radio operator F S Mockford.

Crystal Palace See The Great Exhibition

***Cutty Sark* (SE10)** King William Walk, Greenwich, SE10. Named after the provocative young witch in Robert Burns' poem 'Tam o' Shanter', the *Cutty Sark*, the last survivor of the great three-masted tea-clippers, is one of the most famous sights in London. On 16 February 1870, she left London on her maiden voyage, commanded by Captain George Moodie and bound for Shanghai via the Cape of Good Hope. Having arrived in China on 2 June, she departed with 1450 tons of tea on 25 June, reaching London on 13 October 1870. The *Cutty Sark* made seven further voyages to China, and was later employed as a carrier of wool from Australia and as a cargo ship operating out of Lisbon. Her first restoration took place in 1923, after which she was used as a training ship, and in December 1954 – in an event captured by BBC cameras – she was towed into a specially constructed dry dock at Greenwich. Three further years of painstaking restoration followed, taking the ship back to her appearance in her tea-clipper days. She remains in her dry dock in Greenwich, and is currently undergoing still further restoration after a serious fire in 2007.

Danson House Danson Park, Bexleyheath. Danson House was built during the 1760s to the design of Sir Robert Taylor for wealthy London merchant Sir John Boyd, and features additions by Sir William Chambers. The house stands in the middle of attractive parkland featuring formal gardens and a 20 acre (8ha) lake. The house was declared 'the most significant building at risk in London' in 1995, after which ten years' restoration work were undertaken by English Heritage and Bexley Heritage Trust before it was reopened in 2005. Tel: 020 8303 6699.

Denmark Street London WC2. This short street off Charing Cross Road is the traditional home of the music publishing industry in England, and is often referred to as Tin Pan Alley after the similarly nicknamed area in New York.

Dennis Severs' House Folgate Street, Spitalfields, E1. A time capsule harbouring ten rooms, each recreating a period between 1724 and 1914. The house's creator was Dennis Severs (1944–99), the son of a garage owner from California, who lived in the house (with no electricity or modern comforts) in much the same way as its inhabitants might have done in the early 18th century. Today the house still comes alive with the presence of the Huguenot silk-weaving family of Jervis, but only to some! A true hidden treasure of London: to say more would spoil the extraordinary experience. Tel: 020 7247 4013.

Dr Johnson's House Gough Square, EC4. One of the few residential houses of its age still surviving in the City of London. Built in 1700, it was the home and workplace of Samuel Johnson 1748–59, and it was here that he and his assistants compiled the first comprehensive English dictionary. Tel: 020 7353 3745.

Doggett's Coat and Badge The oldest annual sporting contest in Britain and the oldest rowing race in the world. Instituted in 1715 by Thomas Doggett (1670–1721), an Irish actor and comedian who became joint manager of Drury Lane Theatre, the race is held on the Thames between London Bridge and Cadogan Pier, Chelsea, a distance of 4 miles 5 furlongs (7400m), passing under 11 bridges en route. Originally, it was raced every 1 August against the outgoing tide, in boats used by watermen to ferry passengers across the Thames. Today it is raced at a date and time in late July that coincides with the incoming tide, in contemporary single sculling boats. Up to six apprentice Thames watermen compete in the annual event. The winner's prize is a traditional waterman's red coat with silver badge, displaying the horse of the House of Hanover and the word 'Liberty', in honour of the accession of George I to the throne. In addition, each competitor to complete the course receives a miniature Doggett's Badge for his lapel in a ceremony at Watermen's Hall, in silver for the winner and in bronze for the others. Monetary prizes are also awarded by the Fishmongers' Company to the rowing clubs of those taking part.

Dorchester Hotel, The Park Lane, W1. Built of reinforced concrete on the site of 19th century Dorchester House and opened in 1931, the Dorchester with its imposing Art Deco exterior is located in the heart of

Mayfair looking across Hyde Park. Because of its solid construction it was regarded as a safe London base by many members of the government during World War II; the rooms which served as home to the general and US President during his wartime stay in London have now been renamed the Eisenhower Suite. Tel: 020 7629 8888.

Down House Luxted Road, Downe, 4 miles (6km) southwest of Orpington. The house of Charles Darwin from 1842 until his death in 1882. It was here that Darwin worked on his scientific theories and wrote *On the Origin of Species by Means of Natural Selection*, the book which shocked and revolutionised the Victorian world on its publication in 1859. There are recreations of some of his experiments in natural selection in the gardens and greenhouse. The house is now owned by English Heritage. Tel: 01689 859119.

Ealing Studios Ealing Green, W5. A television and film production company whose stages and offices have survived the onset of the talkies, two world wars and more recent technological advances in film and TV, Ealing Studios can claim to be the oldest film studio in the world. Will Barker, a pioneer of British cinema, originally acquired the site in 1902. Basil Dean, owner of Associated Talking Pictures, took over from Barker and established Ealing Studios in the early 1930s. When in 1938, Michael Balcon joined Dean as head of production, the studios' golden era had begun. In 1944, the company was taken over by the Rank Organisation. In the post-war period, the company embarked on a series of celebrated comedies which became the studio's hallmark. These were often lightly satirical, and were seen to reflect aspects of British character and society. The first was *Hue and Cry* (1947) and the last *Barnacle Bill* (1956). However, the most famous in the series were produced between 1948 and 1955: *Whisky Galore!* (1948), *Passport to Pimlico* (1949), *Kind Hearts and Coronets* (1949), *The Lavender Hill Mob* (1951), *The Man in the White Suit* (1951), *The Titfield Thunderbolt* (1953) and *The Ladykillers* (1955) are now seen as classics of British cinema. The BBC bought the studios in 1959 and for the next 20 years created television productions such as *Colditz*, *The Singing Detective* and *Fortunes of War*. The studios were acquired in 2000 by Uri Fruchtmann, Barnaby Thompson, Harry Handelsman and John Kao. Britain's first computer-animated feature film, *Valiant* (2005), was produced by Ealing Studios in conjunction with Vanguard Films and Odyssey Entertainment. Tel: 020 8567 6655.

Earls Court Exhibition Centre Warwick Road, SW5. The main exhibition hall at Earls Court – now often referred to as Earls Court One – was designed by American architect C Howard Crane, designer of numerous US theatres and cinemas. It opened on 1 September 1937 with a chocolate and confectionery exhibition, soon followed by the Motor Show and Commercial Vehicle Show. Earls Court still hosts many shows and exhibitions throughout the year, including the Ideal Home Show and the Brit Awards. Each summer from 1950 to 1999 it was home to the Royal Tournament, the first, oldest and biggest military tattoo in the world. Earls Court Two, which links with Earls Court One via folding shutters, was opened by Diana, Princess of Wales on 17 October 1991 for the Motorfair. The cream of the British music scene have played at Earls Court, including David Bowie (12 May 1973 and 29 June 1978), The Rolling Stones (21–23 May and 24–26 May 1976), Queen (6–7 June 1977) and Paul McCartney (19 April 2003). Earls Court will also host the volleyball competitions in the 2012 Olympics. Tel: 020 7385 1200. See also Olympia.

East London University See University of East London

Eastbury Manor House Eastbury Square, Barking. A Grade I listed mansion house built by Clement Sysley, a rich Essex merchant, during the reign of Elizabeth I. The house was originally in an isolated position surrounded by marshland. In the early 1600s it attracted rich Catholic families who could practise their banned religion in safety. Today the building stands in 1.5 acres (0.6ha) including a walled garden. It is owned by the National Trust and managed by the London Borough of Barking and Dagenham. Tel: 020 8724 1002.

Elephant and Castle London, SE1. The name given to a road junction south of Waterloo, and also now used to refer to the surrounding district. Once considered the 'Piccadilly Circus of South London', these days it is a centre of student life, with London South Bank University and the London College of Communication (formerly London College of Printing) having campuses nearby. The name derives from an 18th century tavern which stood on the spot; many fanciful theories have been put forward as to the origin of the name, the most common being that it is a corruption of the Spanish 'Infanta de Castilla', who in the 1620s was a prospective bride for Charles I. Today its focal point is a large shopping centre outside which a market operates near the busy road junction.

Eltham Palace Court Yard, Eltham, SE9. Originally a moated manor house bought by Edward II in 1305, and enlarged in the 1470s into one of England's largest palaces for a succession of royals with additions such as the impressive hammerbeam-roofed great hall. Most famously, Henry VIII grew up here. After the Civil War the palace fell into ruin; the great hall, once the scene of lavish feasts, was used as a barn. In 1933 the palace was bought by Stephen and Virginia Courtauld, who restored the great hall and built an adjoining Art Deco home, filled with opulently gilded interiors and cutting-edge design features. Having been occupied by the Royal Army Educational Corps 1944–92, it is now owned by English Heritage. Tel: 020 8294 2577.

Enfield London's northernmost borough stretches from just south of the North Circular Road in the south to the M25 in the north and from Hadley Wood in the west to Edmonton in the east. Enfield Town is famous for having the world's first ever cash machine or ATM, which was installed at the branch of Barclays Bank on 27 June 1967. The world's first solid state colour televisions were manufactured by Ferguson at their plant (now closed) in the borough. Enfield has a history of armaments manufacture: the Royal Small Arms Factory (RSAF) was built at Enfield Lock, on the banks of the River Lea, in 1815. Almost all the weapons in which the Royal Small Arms Factory had a hand in design or production carry either the word Enfield or the letters 'EN' in their name:

the Bren (Brno + Enfield), the Enfield revolver, the Lee-Enfield, Sten (Shepherd Turpin + Enfield) and Polsten guns. The site was closed in 1988 and later redeveloped; most of it is now covered by a large housing development called Enfield Island Village.

Ermine Street A major Roman road that ran from London to Lincoln (Lindum) and York (Eboracum). Ermine Street began at Bishopsgate and ran due north via Ware, Royston, Godmanchester and Ancaster and onwards to York, crossing the River Humber at Brough. This road should not be confused with Ermin Street, the road from Silchester (Calleva Atrebatum) to Gloucester (Glevum).

Euston Road School A group of artists, formed in 1938, all of whose members either taught or studied at the School of Painting and Drawing at 316 Euston Road. Working in conscious reaction against avant-garde styles, they asserted the importance of painting traditional subjects in a realist manner. This attitude was based on a political agenda to create a widely understandable and socially relevant art. Although some were members of the Communist Party, their work was not propagandist in the manner of Socialist Realism. Members included Graham Bell, William Coldstream, Lawrence Gowing, Rodrigo Moynihan, Victor Pasmore and Claude Rogers.

Fairfield Halls Park Lane, Croydon. A large concert hall, opened with the adjoining Ashcroft Theatre and Arnhem Gallery in 1962 and frequently used for BBC recordings. Initially, the venue served the local community and was a popular site for local school speech days, professional wrestling and concerts. The Beatles are among the famous acts to perform at the venue. Today, the Halls are the home of the London Mozart Players, whose principal guest conductor is flautist Sir James Galway. Tel: 020 8688 9291.

Fenton House Hampstead Grove, NW3. Often described as 'London's most enchanting country house'; the late 17th century merchant's house is set among the winding streets of Old Hampstead and houses an important collection of early keyboard instruments and rare examples of William and Mary needlework pictures. The walled garden contains a 300-year-old apple orchard. Now owned by the National Trust. Tel: 020 7435 3471.

Fortnum & Mason Piccadilly, W1. Founded in 1707 by shopkeeper Hugh Mason and William Fortnum, a footman to Queen Anne, Fortnum & Mason – sometimes called the Queen's grocer – has been famed for its innovation. It was the first company in Great Britain to import Heinz Baked Beans in 1901, ran its own mail service before the Royal Mail existed and supplied expeditions with its famed 'Chop Boxes'. When Charles Dickens completed a book he would reward himself with a hamper from the food hall and Edward VIII had kippers and marmalade shipped to Paris for his breakfast on the day he married Wallis Simpson. A clock on the front of the building features replicas of the two founders. Tel: 020 7734 8040.

Forty Hall Forty Hill, Enfield. A Grade I listed Jacobean house built in 1629 for Sir Nicholas Rainton, Lord Mayor of London. It is now the home of a museum run by Enfield Museum Service with exhibits including period furniture, pictures, ceramics and glassware. The 273 acre (110.5ha) estate includes formal gardens, wildflower meadows and the site of Elsyng Palace, owned by Henry VIII and Elizabeth I. Tel: 020 8363 8196.

Foundling Museum, The Brunswick Square, WC1. Housed on the site of London's first home for abandoned children, established by Thomas Coram in 1739. The museum charts the history of the Foundling Hospital and its residents until its closure in 1953. After the hospital left London in the 1920s, the site was saved from development by local residents and opened in 1936 as the open space known as Coram's Fields. Tel: 020 7841 3600.

Foyles Charing Cross Road, WC2. The bookshop W & G Foyle Ltd was founded in 1903 by brothers William and Gilbert Foyle, who moved to the shop's current address in 1906. Foyles was once listed in the *Guinness Book of Records* as the world's largest bookshop in terms of shelf area and number of titles on display. It remains one of the largest bookshops in England, and has recently opened branches at the Royal Festival Hall on London's South Bank, in Selfridge's and at St Pancras International station. Tel: 020 7437 5660.

Freud Museum Maresfield Gardens, NW3. Home of Sigmund Freud after he escaped the Nazi annexation of Austria. The most famous item on display is the couch where Freud's patients reclined during psychoanalytic sessions. Tel: 020 7435 2002.

Fulham Palace and Museum Bishops Avenue, SW6. The former home of the Bishops of London, the site was first acquired by Bishop Waldhere in AD 704 and continued as a bishops' residence until 1973. The present Grade I listed building forms a fascinating mixture of architectural styles, from the Tudor courtyard with its mellow red brick to the restrained elegance of the Georgian east front. Only 13 acres (5ha) remain of the original 36 acre (14.5ha) grounds, which were once enclosed by the longest moat in England. Excavations have revealed evidence of early settlers, both Neolithic and Roman, and the foundations of earlier palaces lie under the east lawn. The site is now a Scheduled Ancient Monument. The gardens at Fulham became famous in the 17th century when Bishop Compton imported rare species such as magnolias, and grew them in Europe for the first time. Although none of his original plants survive, many fine trees remain. There are botanic beds, a herb garden and wisteria pergola within the old walled garden. The museum is based in the early 19th century section of the palace in two major historic rooms: Bishop Howley's Dining Room and the Porteous Library. Items on display include some of the paintings that once hung in the palace, stained glass and a bishop's cope. Tel: 020 7736 3233.

Geffrye Museum, The Kingsland Road, E2. Housed in 18th century almshouses, the Geffrye Museum is laid out in a series of period rooms from 1600 to the present day and arranged to show the changing style of the English domestic interior. Tel: 020 7739 9893.

Gherkin, The St Mary Axe, EC3. Properly known as 30 St Mary Axe, architect Norman Foster's iconic design stands 591ft (180m) high on the site of the former Baltic Exchange building, demolished after an IRA bomb attack in 1992. Its striking curved, somewhat phallic appearance is created with a series of triangular glass panels fitted in a spiral pattern. Built for Swiss Re(insurers), the second largest insurance company in the world, it opened in 2004 and won the Stirling Prize for Architecture later that year.

Gordon Riots On 2 July 1780, Lord George Gordon, a retired navy lieutenant strongly opposed to proposals for Catholic Emancipation, led a crowd of 50,000 people to the House of Commons to present a petition for the repeal of the 1778 Roman Catholic Relief Act, which removed various restrictions on the rights of Catholics. This demonstration turned into a riot and for the next five days many Catholic chapels and private houses were destroyed. Other buildings attacked and damaged included the Bank of England, King's Bench Prison, Newgate Prison and Fleet Prison. On 7 July, the army was called out and it was later reported that 285 of the rioters had been killed, 173 wounded and 139 arrested. Gordon was tried for high treason but was found not guilty. However, 25 of the rioters were hanged and 12 imprisoned, and it is estimated that over £180,000 worth of property was destroyed. The events form the backdrop to Charles Dickens' novel *Barnaby Rudge*.

Great Exhibition, The Held from 1 May to 15 October 1851, the Great Exhibition of 1851 was conceived by Prince Albert to symbolise the industrial, military and economic superiority of Great Britain and her colonies. The exhibition took place in Hyde Park in the specially constructed Crystal Palace; the huge iron structure, designed by Sir Joseph Paxton, was 1848ft (563m) long by 454ft (138m) wide with over a million feet of glass, and took only nine months to plan and build. Over 6.2 million visitors viewed more than 13,000 exhibits including a Jacquard loom, an envelope machine, tools, kitchen appliances, steel-making displays, a reaping machine from the USA and a precursor to the fax machine, demonstrated by Frederick Bakewell. Profits from the event allowed for the foundation of public works such as the Albert Hall, the Science Museum, the National History Museum and the Victoria & Albert Museum. After the Great Exhibition closed, the Crystal Palace was moved to Sydenham Hill in South London and reconstructed in what was, in effect, a 200 acre (80ha) Victorian theme park. The new Crystal Palace Park was opened by Queen Victoria on 10 June 1854. In 1911, the year of George V's coronation, the Crystal Palace was home to the Festival of Empire. Three-quarter size models of the parliament buildings of Empire and Commonwealth countries were erected in the grounds to hold exhibits of each country's products. In later years, the Crystal Palace became closely associated with the development of television when John Logie Baird established his television company there. From June 1934 the Baird Television Company had four fully equipped studios at Crystal Palace and in 1937 Baird demonstrated colour television, using a radio link from the south tower to the Dominion Theatre in London. The picture was projected on a 12ft (3.5m) by 9ft (2.7m) screen. The Crystal Palace itself was destroyed by fire on 30 November 1936. The London Borough of Bromley owns the park today and the National Sports Centre remains a key element of the modern Crystal Palace Park.

Great Fire of London The fire broke out on Sunday morning, 2 September 1666 in Pudding Lane at the house of Thomas Farynor, a baker to Charles II. It is possible that Farynor forgot to extinguish his oven before retiring for the evening and that shortly after midnight, smouldering embers from the oven set alight nearby firewood. Within an hour of the fire starting, the Lord Mayor of London, Sir Thomas Bloodworth, was awakened with the news. He was unimpressed, declaring that 'a woman might piss it out' before going back to sleep; his subsequent refusal to give orders to pull down some houses without the owners' consent allowed a strong easterly wind to wreak havoc among the wood and straw buildings. By Wednesday 5 September the wind had dropped and fire was largely extinguished; although there were only nine reported fatalities, the fire consumed 13,200 houses, 87 parish churches, six chapels, 44 company halls, the Royal Exchange, the Custom House, St Paul's Cathedral, the Bridewell Palace and other City prisons, the Session House, four bridges across the rivers Thames and Fleet, and three city gates, and made homeless 100,000 people, one-sixth of the city's inhabitants. Christopher Wren was put in charge of rebuilding after the fire. His original intention was to recreate the city in brick and stone to a grid plan with continental piazzas and avenues, but because many buildings had survived to basement level, legal disputes over ownership of land rendered the idea impractical. From 1667, Parliament raised funds for reconstruction by taxing coal; the city was eventually rebuilt to its existing street plan, but with brick and stone and with improved sanitation and access. This is the main reason why London today is a modern city, yet with a medieval design to its streets. Wren also rebuilt St Paul's Cathedral 11 years after the fire, as well as a further 50 London churches. Lessons in fire safety were learned; when the current Globe Theatre was opened in 1997, it was the first building in London to have a thatched roof since the Great Fire.

Great North Road The historic main road north from London, running through the centre of England and to the east of the Pennines. Its route was approximately that of the modern A1 and the two names are often used to refer to the same road. The A1, which links London with Edinburgh, is the longest numbered road in the UK at 409 miles (658km).

Great Stink A period in the summer of 1858 during which the smell of untreated sewage in central London became almost overwhelming, precipitating the modernisation of the London sewerage system by the city's chief engineer, Joseph Bazalgette. Part of the problem was the introduction of flush toilets which increased the volume of water and waste that poured into existing cesspits; another contributory factor was that the summer was unusually hot and humid. The immediate crisis was ended when heavy rain finally broke the hot and humid weather.

Greenwich Palace Built by Duke Humphrey, regent during the minority of Henry VI, in 1428 and originally named Bella Court. Margaret of Anjou, the king's consort, took over Bella Court, renaming it the Palace of Placentia. Henry VIII and his daughters Mary and Elizabeth Tudor were all born at Placentia. The palace was demolished in the 17th century and replaced by the Greenwich Hospital (now the Old Royal Naval College). See also National Maritime Museum (Queen's House).

Greenwich University — See University of Greenwich

Grub Street — The former name of the present day Milton Street, EC2 (close to the Barbican), which in the mid 17th century was the centre of a lively pamphleteering press. It became known as a place where a hack author could be found to write anything, and so came to stand for the worst in cheap journalism. The name Grub Street dates back to 1217 but was changed in 1830 in order to honour a local builder called Milton.

Guildhall — Gresham Street, EC2. The civic headquarters of the City, built 1411–40 and now housing the offices of the City of London Corporation. The largest room, the great hall, is a vast unencumbered space occupying 6296 sq ft (585 sq m) with splendid high-arched ceiling, Gothic stained glass windows and monuments to national heroes. Immediately beneath Guildhall is the largest medieval crypt in London. The east crypt has a stunning vaulted ceiling resting upon stone and marble pillars. The Grade II listed Old Library and Old Museum were designed by Horace Jones c.1870 and are masterpieces of Victorian Gothic style. Guildhall Art Gallery, opened by Queen Elizabeth II in 1999, houses the City of London Corporation's renowned collection of works of art. Legend has it that two giants, Gog and Magog (aka Corineus and Gogmagog), were defeated by Brutus, founder of Britain, and chained to the gates of his palace on the site of Guildhall. Depictions of the giants were destroyed in the Great Fire of 1666 but were replaced in 1708 by a large pair of wooden statues carved by Captain Richard Saunders. These beautifully sculpted giants were destroyed in the Blitz and in turn were replaced by a new pair carved by David Evans in 1953.

Gun salutes — Certain royal occasions are marked by royal gun salutes. On these days salutes are fired from locations in London and other authorised stations in the UK, while the Union flag is hoisted on government buildings. In London, salutes are fired in Hyde Park and at the Tower of London; during state visits, at the State Opening of Parliament and for the Queen's birthday parade, Green Park is used instead of Hyde Park. The number of rounds fired in a salute depends on the place and occasion but the basic salute is 21 rounds. In Hyde Park and Green Park an extra 20 rounds are added because they are royal parks. **Royal Gun Salutes in Hyde Park:** Salutes are fired by the King's Troop Royal Horse Artillery in Hyde Park at 12 noon. They occur on the following royal anniversaries (salutes are not fired on Sundays, so if the date falls on a Sunday, the salute will take place the next day): 6 February – Accession Day, celebrating Queen Elizabeth II's accession to the throne; 21 April – the birthday of Queen Elizabeth II; 2 June – Coronation Day, celebrating Queen Elizabeth II's coronation. **Royal Gun Salutes in Green Park:** June – official birthday of Her Majesty the Queen. The Queen was born on 21 April, but it has long been customary to celebrate the sovereign's birthday publicly on a day in the summer. Fired at 11am, though times will vary. 10 June – birthday of Prince Philip, Duke of Edinburgh. April/July/November – for London state visits a 41 gun royal salute is fired; timings vary. November/December – State Opening of Parliament. A 41 gun Royal Salute is fired at 11.08am. November – Remembrance Sunday. A two gun salute is fired on Horse Guards Parade at the start of the two minutes' silence at 11am and another at the end at 11.02am.

Gunnersbury Park and Museum — Popes Lane, W3. The local history museum for the London Boroughs of Ealing and Hounslow, situated in the former 19th century home of a branch of the Rothschild family in Gunnersbury Park. The range of archaeological material excavated from sites across the two boroughs includes medieval pottery and Penn tiles from Northolt Manor; production waste from the medieval greyware kilns at Pinner; Roman, medieval and later pottery and glass from Brentford High Street; 18th to 19th century redwares from the Brentford kilns; and various finds from Chiswick. Tel: 020 8992 1612.

Gunpowder Plot — An unsuccessful attempt by a group of provincial English Catholics to kill James I, his family, and most of the Protestant aristocracy in a single attack by blowing up the Houses of Parliament during the State Opening in 1605. The conspirators had then planned to abduct the royal children, not present in Parliament, and incite a revolt in the Midlands. The plot was led by Robert Catesby. Other plotters included Thomas and Robert Wintour, Christopher Wright, Thomas Percy, John Grant, Ambrose Rokewood, Robert Keyes, Sir Everard Digby, Francis Tresham, and Catesby's servant, Thomas Bates. The explosives were prepared by Guy Fawkes, an expert in the field with considerable military experience, who had been introduced to Catesby by a man named Hugh Owen. In May 1604, Percy leased lodgings adjacent to the House of Lords, intending to mine a way under the foundations of the building and lay the gunpowder. It was another 18 months before the plan looked likely to come to fruition as plague caused several delays to the opening of Parliament. The plotters rowed the gunpowder up the Thames from Lambeth and concealed it in their rented house. When they learned by chance that a coal merchant named Ellen Bright had vacated a cellar under the Lords, Percy immediately made plans to secure the lease. Fawkes assisted in filling the room with 36 barrels of containing 1800lb (816kg) of gunpowder. Due to the need for money and arms Francis Tresham was eventually admitted to the conspiracy (although in fact he had little money), and it was probably he who betrayed the plot. An anonymous letter was sent to Tresham's brother-in-law Lord Monteagle, dropping strong hints about the existence of the plot: 'I advise you to devise some excuse not to attend this parliament, for they shall receive a terrible blow, and yet shall not see who hurts them.' After Monteagle gave the letter to Secretary of State Robert Cecil, 1st Earl of Salisbury, the vaults and undercroft beneath the House of Lords were searched during the early morning of 5 November. Thomas Knyvet, a Justice of the Peace, and a party of armed men, discovered Fawkes posing as 'Mr John Johnson' and in possession of a watch, slow matches and touchpaper. Far from denying his intentions, Fawkes stated that the

Pope had excommunicated the king and uttered the oft-quoted words 'Dangerous diseases require desperate remedies.' He also expressed to the Scottish courtiers who surrounded him that one of his objects was to blow the Scots back into Scotland. Fawkes gave the name of his fellow-conspirators under torture and the remaining men were located at Holbeach House in Staffordshire, where there was a dramatic shoot-out ending with the death of Catesby and the capture of several principal conspirators. Robert Wintour remained on the run for two months before he was captured at Hagley Park. The conspirators were tried on 27 January 1606 in Westminster Hall. All pleaded not guilty except Sir Everard Digby, who attempted to defend himself on the grounds that the king had gone back on promises of Catholic toleration. Sir Edward Coke, the attorney general, prosecuted, and the Earl of Northampton made a speech refuting the charges laid by Digby. The trial lasted one day and the verdict was never in doubt. Four of the plotters were executed in St Paul's Churchyard on 30 January. On 31 January, Fawkes, Wintour and a number of others were taken to Old Palace Yard in Westminster, in front of the scene of the intended crime, where they were hanged until almost dead, drawn and quartered. Fawkes, though weakened by torture, cheated the executioners: he jumped from the gallows, so breaking his neck and by his death avoiding the gruesome culmination of the sentence. A co-conspirator, Robert Keyes, had attempted the same trick, but unfortunately for him the rope broke and he was drawn fully conscious. Henry Garnet, the confessor of several members of the plot, was executed on 3 May 1606 at St Paul's. He had opposed the plot, and many spectators thought that his sentence was harsh.

Hall Place and Gardens Bourne Road, Bexley. Hall Place was built in 1537 for Lord Mayor of London Sir John Champneys. It boasts a magnificent panelled Tudor great hall and minstrel's gallery, and views over award-winning gardens, with topiary, a herb garden, a secret garden, Italianate garden and inspirational herbaceous borders. The house and gardens are now managed by Bexley Heritage Trust. Tel: 01322 526574.

Ham House Ham Street, Ham, Richmond. Located on the south bank of the Thames, the house was built in 1610 for Sir Thomas Vavasour, Knight Marshal to James I. Enlarged in the 1670s, when it was at the heart of Restoration court life and intrigue, Ham House and its gardens are a uniquely complete survival of 17th century fashion and power. Formerly the home of the Duke and Duchess of Lauderdale, much of the decoration and many of the furnishings and collections are original. The outbuildings include an orangery, ice house, still house and dairy with cast-iron 'cows' legs' supporting marble slabs. Sir Lyonel Tollemache and his son, Cecil, gave Ham to the National Trust in 1948. Tel: 020 8940 1950.

Hampstead Heath An area of undulating parkland covering 790 acres (320ha) between Hampstead and Highgate. The Heath is managed by the City of London Corporation and lies mainly in the borough of Camden, although 15 per cent is situated in Barnet. Parliament Hill Fields lies to the south and east and officially became part of the Heath in 1888. The area to the north of the Heath is the Kenwood Estate and House. The heath unfortunately acquired a reputation to rival Clapham Common as a 'gay cruising ground' in the late 20th century but since 1992 a group of 12 constables with trained dogs (Hampstead Heath Constabulary) have had responsibility for patrolling the park 24 hours a day. See also Parliament Hill Fields, Kenwood House.

Hampton Court Palace East Molesey, 1½ miles (2.5km) west of Kingston upon Thames. Cardinal Wolsey, Archbishop of York and chief minister to Henry VIII, began building Hampton Court in 1514. One of the finest royal palaces, the Tudor buildings included a range of apartments for the use of Henry, Catherine of Aragon and Princess Mary. Henry's great astronomical clock still stands in the Clock Courtyard, while an enclosed royal (or real) tennis court, also built by Henry, is the oldest such court in the world still in use. The building was extended by William II to designs by Christopher Wren. After the palace had fallen out of favour as a royal residence, Queen Victoria opened it to the public in 1838. The 60 acres (24ha) of gardens include the Pond Garden, the Fountain Garden with its clipped yews, and the famous maze. Tel: 0870 752 7777.

Handel House Museum Brook Street, W1. The home of Baroque composer George Frideric Handel from 1723 until his death in 1759. It was here that he composed some of the greatest music in history, including *Messiah*, 'Zadok the Priest' and the *Music for the Royal Fireworks*. The museum celebrates Handel's life and works, displaying portraits of the composer and his contemporaries in finely restored Georgian interiors. Part of the house was home to rock musician Jimi Hendrix in 1968–9. Tel: 020 7495 1685.

Harrods Brompton Road, Knightsbridge, SW1. The Harrods story started in 1834 in London's East End, when founder Charles Henry Harrod (1800–85) set up as a wholesale grocer in Stepney. In 1849, in order to escape the filth of the inner city and capitalise on trade to the Great Exhibition of 1851 in nearby Hyde Park, Harrod took over a small shop in the new district of Knightsbridge on the site of the current store. His son Charles Digby (1841–1905) built the business into a thriving store selling medicines, perfumes, stationery, fruit and vegetables, expanding into the adjoining buildings and employing 100 staff by 1880. Although the store burnt to the ground in early December 1883, Digby nevertheless fulfilled all the Christmas deliveries and made a record profit. A new building immediately rose from the ashes, and soon it extended credit for the first time to its best customers, among them Oscar Wilde and legendary actresses Lilly Langtry and Ellen Terry. In 1898 new managing director Richard Burbidge introduced the world's first escalator and in 1901 he began building a grand new store designed by C W Stephens, architect of Claridge's (see separate entry). The frontage of the palatial building was clad in terracotta tiles adorned with swags, cherubs, pilasters and swirling art nouveau windows, and topped by a baroque dome. Inside, the magnificent interiors included vivid Royal Doulton tiles (still in place in the Meat Hall), fine rococo plasterwork, and a vast tea room with an art nouveau skylight (now the Georgian Restaurant). Harrods instantly became London's most fashionable store. In the early 1900s, writer Arnold Bennett based his novel *Hugo* on the store, while Harrods was recreated on the London stage in 1907 in the hugely successful musical comedy *Our Miss Gibbs*. The store made yachts to order, ran its own funeral service (embalming Sigmund Freud), sold aeroplanes and built houses. Between the two world wars Harrods held lavish tea dances hosted by Victor Sylvester, limousine hire and debutante fashion for coming-out parties. Noël Coward was bought an alligator for Christmas from the pet shop, while Ronald Reagan received a baby elephant named Gertie. Author A A Milne found the original Winnie-the-Pooh for his son Christopher Robin in the store, and Alfred Hitchcock had fresh herrings flown to him in Hollywood. In 1959, the House of Fraser group acquired the store and began to modernise what was seen as an old-fashioned institution. The opening of the Way In boutique in 1967 was followed by the spectacular black marble Perfumery Hall in 1971 and the following year by its white marble counterpart, the Cosmetics Hall. When the Fayed family acquired the House of Fraser Group after a bitterly contested takeover battle with Lonrho, Harrods became a family-owned firm once again. Mohamed Al Fayed initiated a £300 million refurbichment plan of which the grand centrepiece was the Egyptian Escalator, a £20 million homage to ancient Egypt. Covering 4.5 acres (1.8ha), with over 1 million square feet of selling space, the store generates 70 per cent of its own electricity from its own generators, draws water from its three artesian wells – the deepest of which is 489ft (149m) – and operates 40 lifts that cover 39,800 miles per year. During the 1970s, Dave Prowse – the original Darth Vader, worked as a fitness consultant in the sports department, while future 007 Pierce Brosnan served on the counter in the Harrods Pharmacy. The store even has its own pub, The Green Man. Tel: 020 7730 1234.

Harrow School High Street, Harrow on the Hill. One of the nine original public schools defined by the Public Schools Act of 1868, Harrow caters for boys aged 13–18. Founded in 1572 under a royal charter granted by Elizabeth I to local farmer John Lyon, the new School House was completed in 1615 and his school began with just one recorded pupil. By the beginning of the 19th century the school could count a quartet of future prime ministers among its pupils. The list of Old Harrovians includes statesmen such as Peel, Palmerston, Churchill, Pandit Nehru and King Hussein of Jordan; poets and writers as diverse as Byron, Sheridan, Trollope, Dornford Yates and Richard Curtis; physicist and Nobel prize-winner Lord Rayleigh; William Fox-Talbot, the inventor of photography; archaeologist Sir Arthur Evans and Bruce the explorer; Sir William Jones, father of philology; Admiral Rodney and Field Marshal Alexander; and 19 winners of the Victoria Cross. Horseracing pundit John McCririck is also an Old Harrovian. Songs have been an important part of Harrow life since John Farmer, head of music, wrote the first one in 1864 (with words by Edward Bowen). This song, 'Forty Years On', is sometimes called the Harrow Song. Tel: 020 8872 8000.

Hatchard's Piccadilly, W1. A bookshop founded in 1797 by John Hatchard (1769–1849). Early in its life it was a cross between a gentleman's club and a library. After Hatchard's death it was run by his son Thomas, but has long ceased to be a family firm. Tel: 020 7439 9921.

Hatton Garden London EC1. Running parallel to the long-established street market of Leather Lane, Hatton Garden was built on land that once formed the garden of Hatton House. Since the medieval period Hatton Garden has been home to London's jewellery trade, and there are still almost 300 jewellery businesses in the area. Hatton Garden boasts one of London's few remaining pawnbrokers, distinguished by the age-old sign of three brass balls hanging above the door.

Hendon RAF Museum Grahame Park Way, NW9. Historically a major centre in the early days of aviation, Hendon Aerodrome was used as an RAF training base during World War I and, after the Battle of Britain in World War II, as a military transport hub for the capital. After the war most of the airfield site was sold for housing but Hendon remained a busy RAF station, accommodating the Supply Control Centre and the Joint Services Air Trooping Centre. RAF Hendon officially closed on 1 April 1987. Most of the buildings were demolished except for the Grahame-White factory buildings, the former officers' mess and a few RAF buildings from the 1930s. The RAF Museum was officially opened by Queen Elizabeth II on 15 November 1972. On its opening Hendon's hangars, built during World War I, housed 36 aircraft; since then 130 more have been acquired. Those not on display are held in reserve collections at RAF stations around the country including RAF Cosford. Further expansion took place in 1978 with the opening of the Battle of Britain Museum and in 1983 when the Bomber Command Museum was opened. Tel: 020 8205 2266.

Highest point Inner London: northern end, Hampstead Heath, Camden, at 440ft (134m); Outer London: Westerham Heights on the North Downs in the London Borough of Bromley, at 804ft (245m). GR: TQ436564.

HMS *Belfast* Symons' Wharf, Vine Lane, SE1. Commissioned in 1939, this 11,000 ton cruiser – the Royal Navy's heaviest ever – was one of two ships forming the final sub-class of British Town class cruisers, the other being HMS *Edinburgh*. *Belfast* was launched on St Patrick's Day 1938 at Harland and Wolff Shipyard in Belfast by the wife of Prime Minister Neville Chamberlain. It was opened to the public as a museum ship in 1971.

Hogarth's House Hogarth Lane, Great West Road, Chiswick, W4. Late 17th century house which was the country home of painter and engraver William Hogarth from 1749 until his death in 1764. It is now a gallery where most of his well-known engravings are on display. These include *A Harlot's Progress*, *The Rake's Progress* and *Marriage à la Mode*, as well as *Gin Lane* and *Beer Street*. The house was restored for the Hogarth tercentenary in 1997. Tel: 020 8994 6757.

Honeywood Heritage Centre Honeywood Walk, Carshalton. The museum of the London Borough of Sutton, housed in a Victorian and Edwardian house incorporating a mid 17th century chalk and flint building, and situated next to the picturesque Carshalton Ponds. Tel: 020 8770 4297.

Horniman Museum London Road, Forest Hill, SE23. A museum specialising in ethnography, natural history and music, and founded by Victorian tea trader Frederick John Horniman (1835–1906). With a mission to bring the world to Forest Hill, Horniman began collecting specimens and artefacts from around the world in the 1860s, opening part of his family house to the public so they could view the riches he had collected. As the collections increased they outgrew the family home and in 1898 Horniman commissioned Charles Harrison Townsend to design a new museum; this opened in 1901 with collections comprising natural history specimens, cultural artefacts and musical instruments. Further buildings were added during the 20th century, notably in 1911 when a new building was donated by Frederick's son Emslie. Over the last 100 years the museum has added significantly to Horniman's original collections, which now comprise only 10 per cent of its current ethnography and musical instrument holdings. A new extension opened on 14 June 2002. Tel: 020 8699 1872.

Hospitals There are many hospitals in Greater London but the following are among the more famous: **Atkinson Morley**, Copse Hill, Wimbledon, SW20. Tel: 020 8946 7711; **Bethlem Royal Hospital** – see separate entry; **Cane Hill**, Coulsdon, Surrey CR3. Tel: 01737 52221; **Charing Cross**, Fulham Palace Road, W6. Tel: 020 8846 1234; **Chelsea & Westminster Hospital**, Fulham Road, Chelsea, SW10. Tel: 020 8746 8000; **Elizabeth Garrett Anderson**, Huntley Street, WC1. Tel: 0845 1555 000; **Gordon**, Bloomburg Street, SW1. Tel: 020 8746 8714; **Great Ormond Street Hospital for Children**, Great Ormond Street, WC1, founded in 1852. Since 1929 the hospital has been the recipient of J M Barrie's copyright to the Peter Pan works, with the provision that the income from this source not be disclosed. This entitles the hospital to royalties from any performance or publication of the play and derivative works. Tel: 020 7405 9200; **Guys**, St Thomas Street, SE1, founded in 1721 by Sir Thomas Guy, a publisher who had made a fortune in the South Sea Bubble. Guy's, at 469ft (143m), is the tallest hospital building in the world. Tel: 020 7188 7188; **Hammersmith**, Du Cane Road, W12. Tel: 020 8383 8185; **Harefield**, Harefield, Uxbridge. Tel: 01895 822870; **Harley Street Clinic**, Weymouth Street, W1. Tel: 020 7935 7700; **Hospital For Tropical Diseases**, St Pancras Way, NW1. Tel: 020 7530 3105; **King Edward VII's Hospital Sister Agnes**, Beaumont Street, W1. Tel: 020 7486 4411; **King's College**, Denmark Hill, SE5. Tel: 020 3299 9000; **Lister**, Chelsea Bridge Road, SW1. Tel: 020 7730 7700; **Mayday**, Mayday Road, Thornton Heath. Tel: 020 8684 6999; **Moorfield Eye Hospital**, City Road, EC1. Tel: 020 7253 3411; **Netherne**, Coulsdon, Surrey. Tel: 01737 556700; **Portland Hospital** (for women and children), Great Portland Street, W1. Tel: 020 7580 4400; **Purley and District War Memorial**, Brighton Road, Purley. Tel: 020 8401 3000; **Queen Mary's**, Roehampton Lane, SW15. Tel: 020 8487 6000; **Royal Brompton**, Sydney Street, SW3. Tel: 020 7352 8121; **Royal London**, Whitechapel Road, Whitechapel, London E1 1BB, Tel: 020 7377 7000; **Royal Marsden**, Downs Road, Sutton. Tel: 020 8770 0279; **St Bartholomew's**, West Smithfield, EC1. Tel: 020 7377 7000; **St Pancras**, St Pancras Way, NW1. Tel: 020 7530 3500; **St Thomas',** Lambeth Palace Road, SE1. Tel: 020 7188 7188.

Hunterian Museum Lincoln's Inn Fields, WC2. The museum of the Royal College of Surgeons, based on the collection of surgeon and anatomist John Hunter (1728–93) and opened in 1813. Exhibits include comparative anatomy and pathology specimens; complete skeletons, bones, skulls and teeth; dried preparations, corrosion casts and wax teaching models; historical surgical and dental instruments, as well as modern surgical instruments and technologies; paintings, drawings and sculpture. The museum has recently undergone a £3.2 million refurbishment to make its collections more easily accessible. Tel: 020 7869 6560.

Hyde Park London W1. Hyde Park covers more than 350 acres (140ha), providing facilities for many different leisure pursuits, and is also a focal point for numerous public events. Henry VIII acquired the park from the monks of Westminster Abbey in 1536. It remained a private hunting ground until James I came to the throne and permitted limited access. The king appointed a ranger, or keeper, to take charge of the park. Charles I changed the nature of Hyde Park completely, creating the Ring (north of the present Serpentine boathouses) and in 1637 opening the park to the general public. Towards the end of the 17th century William III moved his court to Kensington Palace. Finding that his walk to St James's was very dangerous, he had 300 oil lamps installed, creating the first artificially lit highway in England. This route later became known as Rotten Row, a corruption of the French *Route du Roi* or King's Road. Queen Caroline, wife of George II, had extensive renovations carried out and in the 1730s created The Serpentine, a 28 acre (11ha) lake. In the 19th century Hyde Park became a venue for national celebrations: in 1814 the Prince Regent organised fireworks to mark the end of the Napoleonic Wars, in 1851 the Great Exhibition (see separate entry) was held and in 1977 a Silver Jubilee Exhibition was held in honour of Queen Elizabeth II's 25 years on the throne. In 1866 Edmund Beales' Reform League marched on Hyde Park where great scuffles broke out between the League and the police. Eventually the Prime Minister allowed the meetings to continue unchallenged and since 1872, people have been allowed to speak on any subject at Speaker's Corner, Sunday mornings being particularly popular for soapbox oratory. The Lido was set up by George Lansbury, the first Commissioner of Works, in 1930 and in warm weather is used for sunbathing and swimming. The Diana, Princess of Wales Memorial Fountain was opened by the Queen on 6 July 2004. The fountain contains 545 pieces of Cornish granite; water flows from the highest point in two directions as it cascades, swirls and bubbles before meeting in a calm pool at the bottom. Modern extravaganzas in the park include the Live 8 concert in the summer of 2005 and the annual Proms in the Park.

Imperial War Museum Lambeth Road, SE1. A multi-branch national museum dedicated to chronicling armed conflict in the 20th and 21st century. Founded in 1917 to record the story of the Great War and the contributions made to it by the peoples of the Empire, the museum was formally established by

Act of Parliament in 1920, when it opened in the Crystal Palace. Having been housed from 1924 to 1935 in two small galleries adjoining the Imperial Institute in South Kensington, in 1936 it was reopened in the former Bethlem Royal Hospital in Lambeth Road, Southwark where it remains today. In 1939 its remit was extended to include World War II and in 1953 the terms of reference were further expanded to include all military operations in which British or Commonwealth forces have been involved since August 1914. Its collections now include works of art, posters, fighting vehicles, uniforms, medals and weapons, books and other documents, film, photographs and sound recordings. Tel: 020 7416 5320. The other branches of the museum are: **Imperial War Museum Duxford**, Cambridgeshire; **Churchill Museum and Cabinet War Rooms**, Clive Steps, King Charles Street SW1. Tel: 020 7930 6961; **HMS *Belfast*,** Morgan's Lane, Tooley Street, SE1. Tel: 020 7940 6300; **Imperial War Museum North**, Manchester.

Inns of Court

The four ancient unincorporated bodies of lawyers to one of which every barrister in England and Wales must belong. They have the power to call to the Bar those of their members who have qualified as barristers-at-law, and to disbar or otherwise punish those members for misconduct. Nowadays the processes of examination for the Bar and of discipline are carried out jointly by the four Inns, but the four – Lincoln's Inn, Inner Temple, Middle Temple and Gray's Inn, to put them in their customary order – remain distinct; officially titled 'Honourable Societies', each has its own property, duties and functions, and all are of equal status. Lincoln's Inn is the oldest, its records going back to 1422. It occupies most of the rectangle formed by High Holborn on the north, Carey Street and the Royal Courts of Justice on the south, Chancery Lane on the east and Lincoln's Inn Fields on the west. The Inner Temple has flourished for 400 years and occupies land once belonging to the Knights Templar. Bounded by Fleet Street to the north and Victoria Embankment to the south, the area includes the Temple Church The Middle Temple was founded in 1501 and is adjacent to the Inner Temple. Gray's Inn lies to the north of High Holborn, and is the most northerly of the four Inns.

Interesting facts

Dr Hawley Harvey Crippen, a patent medicine salesman and physician, poisoned his second wife, Cora Turner, a would-be music-hall artiste working under the name of Belle Elmore, after becoming infatuated with his young secretary Ethel Le Neve. After the murder at their home, 39 Hilldrop Crescent, Holloway, Crippen and Ethel fled to Canada aboard the SS *Montrose*, Crippen under the name of Mr Robinson and Ethel masquerading as his son. Becoming suspicious, the ship's captain contacted Scotland Yard by radio telegraphy and the couple were arrested. The case was famous for being the first example of a successful conviction by use of radio. Crippen was tried for murder at the Old Bailey on 18 October 1910, found guilty and hanged at Pentonville on 23 November. Neve was tried separately, but ably defended by F E Smith and acquitted. She lived until 1967. **Chislehurst** was the final resting place of the French Emperor Napoleon III, who died at Camden Place (now Chislehurst Golf Club). His body, and that of the Prince Imperial, were buried originally in St Mary's Church before they were removed to St Michael's Abbey in Farnborough, Hants. The granite Corinthian column and statue of **Nelson** that towers above Trafalgar Square was found to be only 169ft 5in (51.6m) high when it was measured in July 2006 following four months of restoration work, 16ft (5m) shorter than previously thought. **Thomas Blood**, an Irish adventurer of dubious character, fought for Oliver Cromwell's Parliamentary forces during the Civil War and survived to return to Ireland. On 9 May 1670 at 7am, Colonel Blood, disguised as a parson and accompanied by three well-dressed young men, one of whom Blood claimed was his nephew, visited the Martin Tower, home of the Crown Jewels in the Tower of London. Blood had already been there a few days earlier, accompanied by a woman who he claimed was his wife. Shortly after arriving the woman pretended to be taken ill and Talbert Edwards, the newly appointed Master of the Jewel House, led her upstairs to be looked after. On the second visit Blood brought a present for Edwards' wife as a thank you for her attentions to his own wife. As soon as the party entered the jewel chamber, Blood pulled out a mallet from under his cloak and struck Edwards on the head. His accomplices bound and gagged him. Blood then seized the king's crown and tried to flatten it with the mallet so as to get it into his cassock pocket. His 'nephew' meanwhile pushed the orb into his breeches. The other two men frantically filed away at the sceptre trying to cut it in half. Arrived unexpectedly on leave from military service abroad, Edwards' son Wythe rushed into the room to find his father lying unconscious on the floor. Blood and his gang fled, but three of the four were caught as they tried to get out of the Tower, and the jewels were recovered. A report was immediately sent to the king at Whitehall, and Charles sent for Blood for private interrogation. Remarkably Blood was pardoned, awarded a pension of £500 a year, and made welcome at court. Based in London between June 1940 and May 1943, Charles De Gaulle led the **Free French movement** (pre-occupation government) against the Vichy regime headed by Henri Philippe Pétain. Churchill allowed De Gaulle to make several radio broadcasts early on in the occupation; the world's newspapers picked up the story and the plight of the French became universally known. The **world's first moving pictures** were filmed near Apsley Gate, Hyde Park, one morning in January 1889 by inventor William Friese-Greene. The film was developed at a studio near Piccadilly and is the first known projected moving image. The **last public execution** in Britain took place outside Newgate Prison in 1868. Michael Barrett, a Fenian (Irish patriot), had planted a bomb outside the walls of Clerkenwell Prison in an attempt to free two of his compatriots. When the bomb exploded it killed four passers-by and wounded many others. Barrett went to his death knowing he would be the last to do so in public. **St Mary's Gate** in Kensington officially became the thinnest street in England in September 2006. Using statistical analysis, scientists have developed the country's first 'fat map', and residents of St Mary's Gate are 37 per cent less likely to become obese than the national average. The **Prime Meridian** – zero degrees longitude – passes through Greenwich, which means it is possible to stand with one foot in the western hemisphere and the other in the eastern hemisphere. Philosopher **Jeremy Bentham**, who died in 1832, left his estate to University College London on the condition that his body be embalmed, dressed in his clothes and seated in his favourite chair so he could preside over debates. It's still there. The **Blind Beggar** is a pub located at 337 Whitechapel Road, Whitechapel. On 9 March 1966, Ronnie and Reggie Kray and other members of their firm were drinking in the Lion pub when they were informed that Cornell was drinking in the Blind Beggar just down the road. At 8.30 that night, Ronnie and one of his associates walked into the Blind Beggar, only to be met by a sarcastic greeting from big George Cornell. Ronnie instantly pulled out a pistol and shot Cornell three times in the head. The **Dove**, Upper Mall, W6 is another interesting London pub. James Thomson (1700–48), who wrote the words of 'Rule Britannia', lodged and died there, but its chief claim to fame is having the smallest bar in Britain – 4ft 2ins (1.3m) by 7ft 10ins (2.4m). The phrase being at **'sixes and sevens'**, for anything in a disordered state, derives from a 15th century dispute between the Merchant Taylors and Skinners for sixth and seventh places in the Great Twelve City Livery Companies. Since this date the two have alternated in precedence. **Lordship Lane** in Haringey tops the league for the most motoring offences in Britain. The London borough collects more than £3m per annum from fines doled out for parking tickets, driving in bus lanes and other offences. London-born **Sir Stirling Moss** can truly be considered the greatest driver never to win the Formula One World Championship (he was runner-up for four successive years, 1955–8). Moss believed the manner in which the battle was fought was as important as the outcome. This sporting attitude cost him the 1958 World Championship. When rival Mike Hawthorn was given a penalty in the Portugal Grand Prix, Moss defended Hawthorn's actions and the decision was reversed. Hawthorn went on to beat Moss by one point and become Britain's first world champion, even though he had only won one race that year to Moss's four. In the final race of 1958, driving a Vanwall in Casablanca, Moss had to win, get fastest lap and for Hawthorn not be second to take the title. He did win, recording the fastest lap on the way. With one lap to go, Hawthorn was lying third when team-mate Phil Hill let him through to take second place. The ***Daily Courant*** was the first regular daily newspaper to be published in the UK. It was first published on 11 March 1702 by Edward Mallet from rooms above the White Hart pub in Fleet Street. The paper lasted until 1735 when it was merged with the *Daily Gazetteer*. Two other claimants to the title of Britain's oldest newspaper, the *Worcester Postman* (1690) and the *Norwich Post* (1701), were both clearly published earlier. However, neither was published regularly; the word 'daily' is important if the *Courant* is to be given the honour. **Heston Aerodrome** in Hounslow was London's second airport when it was opened in 1929. It was from here that British Prime Minister Neville Chamberlain held aloft the paper containing the so-called Munich Agreement between Adolf Hitler and himself (30 September 1938). The aerodrome ceased to be operational in 1946.

Islands There is uncertainty around the Molesey/Hampton Court area as to which islands can be claimed by Greater London and which by Surrey. I have maintained a general rule of thumb that the nearest landmark constitutes the island's geographic location. See separate table. One historic island not included in my list is Thorney Island. Formed by rivulets of the River Tyburn, which runs underground from South Hampstead through St James's Park to meet the River Thames at Pimlico near Vauxhall Bridge, Thorney Island is where Westminster Abbey and the Palace of Westminster (Houses of Parliament) were built. There is now no sign of the island, although the name is honoured in Thorney Street, at the back of the MI5 building.

Ivy, The West Street, Covent Garden, WC2. Established in 1917 as a café for the theatre establishment by Abel Glandellini and maitre d'hotel Mario Gallati. The name is reputed to derive from a remark by actress Alice Delysia, who overheard an apology from Glandellini for building work that was taking place. Quoting a popular song of the day, she is claimed to have said: 'Don't worry, we will always come to see you, we will cling together like the ivy.' Relaunched in 1990 by Jeremy King and Chris Corbin, The Ivy is currently owned by Richard Caring and remains London's favourite theatre restaurant. Tel: 0871 223 8001.

Jack the Ripper The unknown murderer of five prostitutes between August and November 1888 in Whitechapel. The five unfortunate victims were Mary Ann 'Polly' Nichols (42), 'Dark' Annie Chapman (47), Elizabeth 'Long Liz' Stride (45), Catherine 'Kate Kelly' Eddowes (43) and Mary Jane Kelly (25). The inspector who initially investigated the murders was George Frederick Abberline (1843–1929). The case has spawned a massive literature of speculation as to the murderer's identity. Suspects for the murders at the time include barrister Montague John Druitt, convicted poisoner George Chapman and Jewish hairdresser Aaron Kosminski; William Gull, physician-in-ordinary to Queen Victoria, artist Walter Sickert and Albert, Duke of Clarence, Queen Victoria's grandson, are among those more recently proposed as the perpetrator in the vast literature that now surrounds the subject.

Jewel Tower Abingdon Street, Westminster, SW1. One of only two surviving buildings of the original Palace of Westminster, the tower was built by Edward III in 1365 to store his personal jewels and wardrobe. It currently houses the exhibition 'Parliament Past and Present', which traces the history of the Houses of Commons and Lords. Now managed by English Heritage. Tel: 020 7222 2219.

Keats House Keats Grove, Hampstead, NW3. Originally a pair of semi-detached houses known as Wentworth Place, and converted into one in the late 1830s. John Keats lived in one of the houses 1818–20, and the setting inspired some of his most memorable poetry including 'Ode to a Nightingale'; Fanny Brawne, with whom he fell in love and was to marry, lived in the other house of the pair. In 1820, suffering from tuberculosis, Keats departed from Wentworth Place for Rome, where he was to die aged just 25. Since 1925 the house has been occupied by a museum dedicated to Keats' life and works. Tel: 020 7435 2062.

Kenley Aerodrome 4 miles (6km) south of Croydon. Kenley Aerodrome opened in 1917 and was a base for fighter squadrons from 1918. Rebuilt in 1939 with concrete runways, in 1940 it became the headquarters of B Sector, 11 Group, Fighter Command, remaining one of the main fighter stations during the Battle of Britain and through the rest of the war. The last operation was flown on 13 March 1944 and Kenley was closed to flying in May 1944 due to the proximity of the barrage balloon defence against the flying bombs. After the war the aerodrome was used for communications and observation flights and was popular for gliding. The films *Angels One Five* and *Reach for the Sky* were filmed here in the 1950s and *633 Squadron* in 1964. The aerodrome closed in May 1959 although gliding continued until February 1966. The control tower and hangars were demolished in 1978.

Kensington Gardens See Royal Parks, Serpentine Gallery

Kensington Palace Palace Avenue, W8. Located on the western side of Kensington Gardens, the Jacobean mansion then known as Nottingham House was acquired in 1689 by William and Mary and remodelled by Sir Christopher Wren. It later became the residence of Queen Anne, George I and George II before passing to the Duke of Kent, fourth son of George III and father of Queen Victoria, who was born in the house and baptised in the Cupola Room. Restored and opened to the public by Queen Victoria after falling into disuse in the 19th century, it is now home to the Royal Ceremonial Dress Collection including many evening dresses owned by Diana, Princess of Wales, who occupied apartments in the palace. The rooms which once made up Princess Margaret's private apartment have also been opened for special exhibitions. Tel: 0870 7515176.

Kenwood House Hampstead Lane, NW3. Kenwood stands in 112 acres (45ha) of Grade II* listed grounds landscaped by Humphry Repton. The house, remodelled in the 1760s by Robert Adam, now contains an internationally renowned collection of paintings bequeathed by Edward Guinness, 1st Earl of Iveagh. Owned by English Heritage. Tel: 020 8348 1286.

Kew Gardens Kew Road, Kew. The 300 acre (121ha) Royal Botanic Gardens, one of the most important such gardens in the world, originated in an exotic garden beside the River Thames at Kew Park, formed by Lord Capel of Tewkesbury in the late 17th century. This was greatly extended from 1752 by Princess Augusta, widow of Frederick, Prince of Wales, for whom Sir William Chambers built several garden structures; one of these, the Chinese pagoda dating to 1761, still remains. Aided by William Aiton and Sir Joseph Banks, George III developed the gardens as a centre for investigating the economic usefulness of plants, and in 1840 they were adopted as a national botanic garden. The Palm House, built 1844–8, represented the first structural use of wrought iron, while the Temperate House, completed in 1898, is the largest Victorian glasshouse still in existence. Two gardeners from Kew were on the *Bounty* when Captain Bligh sailed to Tahiti to collect breadfruit plants, and it was at the gardens in the 19th century that rubber trees were first successfully propagated for cultivation outside South America. Today the living plant collection is the largest and most comprehensive in the world, containing representatives of more than one in eight of all flowering plant species. In July 2003, the gardens were listed by UNESCO as a World Heritage Site. Tel: 020 8332 5655.

Kingston University High Street, Kingston-upon-Thames. The former Kingston Polytechnic was granted university status in 1992. Its four main campuses are at Penrhyn Road, Kingston Hill, Knights Park and Roehampton Vale and it has over 23,000 students. Former students include badminton champion Gail Emms, author Nick Hornby, actor Trevor Eve and footballer Graeme Le Saux. Tel: 020 8547 2000.

Kit-Cat Club An early 18th century London club with strong political and literary associations, committed to the furtherance of Whig objectives. Its name is derived from pastrycook Christopher Catling: its members first met in his house in Shire Lane, close to Temple Bar, and his mutton pies (known as kit-cats) were regularly served at meetings. Members included the Duke of Marlborough, Charles Seymour, the Earl of Burlington, Thomas Pelham-Holles, Sir Robert Walpole, William Congreve, John Vanbrugh and Joseph Addison. Another member was artist Sir Godfrey Kneller, whose 42 portraits of fellow members in a standard format of 36in x 28in (91.4cm x 17.1cm), were painted over more than 20 years. The subjects are characteristically depicted with only one hand showing.

Lambeth Conference An assembly of bishops of the worldwide Anglican Communion under the chairmanship of the Archbishop of Canterbury. Archbishop Thomas Longley invited Anglican bishops to their first conference at Lambeth Palace on 24–27 September 1867. Many bishops declined to attend, but 76 bishops from Great Britain, the United States and the colonies finally accepted the invitation and the conference met in the chapel of Lambeth Palace. The conference now convenes every ten years; the 1968 conference under Archbishop Michael Ramsey was attended by 462 bishops. With this conference it was no longer possible to meet at Lambeth Palace and it was thus convened in the Church Assembly Hall at Church House, Westminster. Since 1978 it has been held in Canterbury, on the campus of the University of Kent.

Law Society's Hall Chancery Lane, WC2. Designed by Lewis Vulliamy and opened in 1832, the hall is the home of the representative body for solicitors in England and Wales, founded in 1825. Tel: 020 7320 9555.

Lee Valley Park A 26 mile (42km) long area, much of it green space, running through northeast London from the River Thames to Ware in Hertfordshire, through Hackney, Camden, Tottenham, Enfield, Cheshunt, Broxbourne and Hoddesdon. It follows the course of the River Lee along the Lee Valley. Much of the southern half in London is undergoing development to form the Olympic Park for the 2012 Olympics.

Leighton House Museum Holland Park Road, W14. The former studio and house of Victorian artist Frederic, Lord Leighton (1830–96). The Arab Hall is the centrepiece of the house, containing Leighton's collection of Persian tiles, a gilt mosaic frieze and a fountain. Tel: 020 7602 3316.

Lesnes Abbey Abbey Road, Belvedere, Bexley. A hidden treasure in the heart of suburban London, the site contains the remains of the Augustinian abbey founded by Richard de Lucy in 1178 as penance for his involvement in the events leading to the murder of Thomas Becket. No complete buildings remain, but the ground plan and foundations have been recreated in their original layout after excavation. Tel: 01322 526574.

Lincoln's Inn Fields — The largest square in central London at 12 acres (5ha). Laid out by Inigo Jones in the early 17th century next to Lincoln's Inn, one of Londons four Inns of Court (see separate entry), and shaded by towering plane trees, it was once a popular resort of duellists. The square was established as a private open space and was not opened to the public until 1895. The pathway through the Fields, known as Great Turnstile, was once a short cut to the Strand from Holborn. In Inigo Jones' time the square was the most fashionable in London, comparable to St James's Square (1660) in the West End, another of the city's earliest squares. One plausible reason for its popularity was that Nell Gwynne resided here – her son, the Duke of St Albans, was born in her lodgings. Notable buildings in the square include the **Royal College of Surgeons**, designed by Sir Charles Barry in 1835, contains a museum of anatomy (see Hunterian Museum). In the Large Room the skeleton of the Irish giant Byrne, who stood 9ft (2.7m) tall, was once on display; alongside lay the infant Caroline Crachami who died at the age of ten, 10in (25cm) tall. Behind the Fields lies the 'Old Curiosity Shop', a 16th century building claimed by many to have inspired Charles Dickens's novel. To the north is **Sir John Soane's Museum** (see separate entry). A seat in memory of **Margaret Macdonald**, a resident, is to be seen in Canada Walk on the north side and is one of the few London memorials to a woman other than a queen. Her husband, Ramsay Macdonald, was often host to other pioneers of socialism in the early 20th century. On one such occasion, guests of the first Labour Prime Minister were asked to leave their coats in the second bedroom. Before dinner was ended, the distressed housekeeper emerged and asked the company whether in future those who had coats would care to lay them on a bed not being slept in. The children had nearly suffocated. See also Inns of Court.

Lindsey House — Cheyne Walk, Chelsea, SW10. Built on the former site of Sir Thomas More's garden and now part of Cheyne Walk, the house has one of the finest 17th century exteriors in London. Owned by the National Trust. Tel: 020 7447 6605.

Linley Sambourne House — Stafford Terrace, W8. A late Victorian town house which was home to *Punch* cartoonist Edward Linley Sambourne and his family 1874–1910. Surviving with almost all of its furniture and fittings intact, the house remained in the family until 1980 when it was sold to the Greater London Council and opened as a museum. Tel: 020 7602 3316.

Little Holland House — Beeches Avenue, Carshalton. Built 1902–24 by artist, designer and craftsman Frank Dickinson (1874–1961), who designed the house in Arts and Crafts style based on the philosophy and theories of William Morris and John Ruskin. The house was restored and opened to the public in 1974. Tel: 020 8770 4781.

Little Venice — London W2. A name supposedly coined by Robert Browning (although it was Lord Byron who actually compared the site unfavourably with Venice) for the area surrounding the canal basins of Paddington, particularly the broad junction between the Grand Union Canal and its Paddington Basin arm. Strictly speaking, the name refers to the point where the Paddington Arm of the Grand Union Canal meets the Regents Canal, but the name has come to signify the whole area to the south of Maida Vale. Paddington Basin itself, a short distance from Little Venice, has recently been redeveloped on a scale to rival London's Docklands. The canal (opened in 1801) can be accessed directly from the Paddington Station footbridge. If taking a canal boat trip between Little Venice and Camden Lock, watch out for Maida Vale Tunnel where the entrance is literally blanketed with old spider webs!

Lloyd's of London — Leadenhall Street, EC3. A unique insurance institution, neither a company nor a corporation, whose members, traditionally known as 'Names', collectively take on the risk and share the profit. The market began in the coffee house of Edward Lloyd (1648–1713) in Tower Street in the 1680s. Just after Christmas 1691, the coffee shop relocated to Lombard Street, where a blue plaque commemorates its location. In 1774 Lloyd's moved to the Royal Exchange as the Society of Lloyd's. The Exchange burned down in 1838 and, although rebuilt, many of Lloyd's early records were lost. Since 1986 Lloyd's has been situated in Lime Street, in the City of London. The new building, standing close to the 'Gherkin', was designed by architect Richard Rogers and built 1978–86. Like the Pompidou Centre (designed by Renzo Piano and Rogers), the building was innovative in having its services such as staircases, lifts, electrical power conduits and water pipes on the outside, leaving a clean uncluttered space inside. The 12 glass lifts were the first of their kind in the UK. In the late 1980s and early 1990s, Lloyd's went through the most traumatic period in its history. Unexpectedly large legal awards in US courts for punitive damages led to large claims by those insured, especially on APH (asbestos, pollution and health hazard) policies, some dating as far back as the 1940s. A famous feature of Lloyd's is the Lutine bell. HMS *Lutine* was launched at Toulon in 1779 as *La Lutine* ('the tease' or 'tormentress') for the French navy. She sank off Holland on 9 October 1799 carrying a large cargo of gold, the majority of which remains unsalvaged. The ship's bell (engraved 'ST. JEAN – 1779'; it remains a mystery why the name on the bell does not correspond with that of the ship) was recovered on 17 July 1858 and was hung from the rostrum of the underwriting room at Lloyd's. It weighs 106lb (48kg) and is 17½in (44.5cm) in diameter. The bell was traditionally struck when news of an overdue ship arrived, once for the loss of a ship (i.e. bad news) and twice for her return (i.e. good news); it was sounded to ensure that all brokers and underwriters were made aware of the news simultaneously. The bell has developed a crack and the traditional practice of ringing news has ended: the last time it was rung to tell of a lost ship was in 1979 and the last time it was rung to herald the return of an overdue ship was in 1989. Tel: 020 7327 1000.

London Eye — South Bank, SE1. Situated between Hungerford and Westminster bridges, the British Airways London Eye at 442ft (135m) high is the world's tallest observation wheel. It is also the fourth tallest structure in London after the BT Tower, Tower 42 and One Canada Square in Canary

Wharf. As it opened in March 2000 it is sometimes called the Millennium Wheel. Each of the 32 capsules holds 25 people and weighs 9.8 tons (10 tonnes). Each rotation of the wheel takes 30 minutes, meaning a capsule travels at a stately 10in (26cm) per second, or 0.6 miles (1km) per hour – twice as fast as a tortoise sprinting, and allowing passengers to step on and off without the wheel having to stop. The wheel's circumference is 1391ft (424m). It is operated by the London Eye Company Ltd, a Tussauds Group company. Tel: 0870 990 8883.

London Gazette — The government's bulletin, in which official announcements are made. It has its origins in the autumn of 1665, when Charles II left London for Oxford to avoid the Great Plague. The king and his courtiers wanted newspapers to read, but were afraid to touch *The Intelligencer* or *The News* which, coming from the capital, might be infected. Leonard Litchfield, the university printer, was therefore ordered to bring out a local paper. The first edition of *The Oxford Gazette* appeared on Tuesday, 14 November 1665, and it was produced for the following 11 weeks on Thursdays and Mondays. The plague was soon over and Charles returned to Whitehall, but he was pleased with the Oxford publication and it was soon succeeded by *The London Gazette*, which made its first appearance, labelled as No. 24, on 5 February 1666. From 1889 it was published by Her Majesty's Stationery Office and it is still produced by the Stationery Office today. See also *Edinburgh Gazette* in Lothian.

London Metropolitan University — London EC3. Created on 1 August 2002 by the merger of London Guildhall University (now London City campus) and the University of North London (now London North campus); respectively the former City of London Polytechnic and North London Polytechnic, these were established as universities in 1992. The London North campus is located in Islington on and around the Holloway Road while the London City campus is centred on the City of London and the Aldgate area of east London. It is the largest university in London, with over 35,000 students, and offers a range of undergraduate, postgraduate, professional and vocational courses. Former students include broadcaster Zoe Ball, singer Alison Moyet and comedian Vic Reeves. Tel: 020 7423 0000.

London Planetarium — See Madame Tussaud's

London Pride — A pink-flowered saxifrage (*Saxifraga urbium*). Noël Coward wrote a song of the same name to describe both the flower and the spirit of Londoners during the Blitz of 1941:

London Pride has been handed down to us.
London Pride is a flower that's free.
London Pride means our own dear town to us,
And our pride it for ever will be.
Woa, Liza,
See the coster barrows,
Vegetable marrows
And the fruit piled high.
Woa, Liza,
Little London sparrows,
Covent Garden Market where the costers cry.
Cockney feet
Mark the beat of history.
Every street
Pins a memory down.
Nothing ever can quite replace
The grace of London Town.
There's a little city flower every spring unfailing
Growing in the crevices by some London railing,
Though it has a Latin name, in town and country-side
We in England call it London Pride.

London School of Economics — Houghton Street, WC2. The London School of Economics and Political Science (LSE) was established in 1895 with a bequest from Henry Hunt Hutchinson, a member of the Fabian Society, given with the instruction that Sidney Webb should use it for socially progressive purposes. It has been a constituent college of The University of London since 1900 and is also a member of the Russell Group of research-led universities. During the 20th century it played a leading part in the development of a range of both free-market and social democratic theories of economics. Former students include American President John F Kennedy, Canadian Prime Ministers Kim Campbell and Pierre Trudeau, and Rolling Stones frontman Mick Jagger. Tel: 020 7405 7686.

London South Bank University — Founded in 1892 as the Borough Polytechnic and amalgamated with four other colleges in 1970 to become South Bank Polytechnic. Granted university status in June 1992. With nearly 18,000 students, the university is one of the largest in London. The main campus is at Borough Road, Southwark, SE1. Tel: 020 7928 8989. There are also campuses at Gubbins Lane, Romford, tel: 020 7815 5959; and in East London at Whipps Cross Hospital, Leytonstone, E11, tel: 020 7815 4747.

London Stone — Cannon Street, EC4. Although distances from London are now measured from Charing Cross, during the Roman period geographical measurements are reputed to have been made from this ancient stone (now housed in a glass case behind an ornate metal grille in the front of a sporting goods store opposite Cannon Street Station) .

London Transport Museum — Wellington Street, WC2. Administered by Transport for London, the museum conserves and explains London's transport heritage. Its collections include over 80 vehicles ranging from horse-drawn buses to Underground carriages, as well as posters, photographs, unifroms, toys and models. Tel: 020 7379 6344.

London Wall A defensive wall built by the Romans around the strategically important port of Londinium on the Thames. It appears to have been constructed in the late 2nd century and continued to be developed until at least the end of the 4th century, making it one of the last major building projects undertaken by the Romans before their withdrawal from Britain in AD 410. The original list of gates on the wall, beginning at Ludgate in the west and going clockwise to Aldgate in the east, is: Ludgate, Newgate, Aldersgate, Cripplegate, Bishopsgate, Aldgate. Moorgate, between Cripplegate and Bishopsgate, was built in the medieval period and brings the number of gates up to the canonical seven, commemorated in London tradition and literature. Some of these gates, though long gone, are remembered in the names of the areas or roads where they once stood. Due to the rapid growth of the city, the number of gates was increased to cope with extra traffic in the medieval period, and the walls were also strengthened and built upon. Today all that remains of the wall are a few fragments, some of which can be seen in the grounds of the Museum of London, in the Barbican Estate and around Tower Hill. Part of the route originally taken by the northern wall is commemorated by the road also named London Wall on which the museum is located. One of the largest and most readily accessed fragments of the wall stands just outside Tower Hill tube station, with a replica statue of the Emperor Trajan standing in front of it. The wall was constructed largely from Kentish ragstone brought by water from Maidstone. It enclosed an area of 330 acres (130ha), was 6–9ft (1.8–2.7m) wide and 18ft (5.5m) high, with a ditch or *fossa* in front of the outer wall, measuring 6ft (1.8m) deep by 9–15ft (2.7–4.5m) wide. It included a number of bastions spaced 210ft (64m) apart; the best-preserved of these can be seen at the Barbican Estate, next to the church of St Giles-without-Cripplegate. The wall remained in use as a fortification for over 1000 years. Used to defend London against raiding Saxons in 457, it was redeveloped in the medieval period with the addition of crenellations, more gates and further bastions. Only in the 18th and 19th centuries did it undergo substantial demolition, though even then large portions survived by being incorporated into other structures. Amid the devastation of the Blitz, some of the tallest ruins in the bomb-damaged City were remnants of the Roman wall. The wall's moat has also left its mark on London, forming the line of the street of Houndsditch. This was once London's main rubbish disposal site and was notorious for its appalling stench.

London Wetland Centre Queen Elizabeth's Walk, Barnes, SW13. A 106 acre (43ha) wetland reserve established by the Wildlife and Wetlands Trust on the site of a former reservoir complex beside the River Thames and opened in 2000. The first such site to be developed in an urban area in the UK, it was designated a Site of Special Scientific Interest in 2002. pipistrelle, noctule and Daubenton's bats Tel: 020 8409 4400.

London Zoo Regent's Park, NW1. Located south of Primrose Hill in the northwest section of Regent's Park. The world's first scientific zoo, London Zoo was opened in 1828, and was originally intended to be used as a collection for scientific study. It was eventually opened to the public in 1847. Today it houses more than 650 different species of animals. London Zoo also opened the first reptile house (1849), first public aquarium (1853), first insect house (1881) and the first children's zoo (1938). Famous former residents include Goldie, a golden eagle who became a national celebrity when he escaped for two weeks in 1965, and flew around the roads and trees of Regent's Park, and Guy the Gorilla, a lowland gorilla who lived at the zoo from 1947 until his death in 1978, becoming in his later years one of its best-loved residents. Tel: 020 7722 3333.

Lord Mayor of London The Right Honourable Lord Mayor of London is the Mayor of the City of London and head of the Corporation of London. The office is distinct from that of the Mayor of London; the former is an officer only of the City of London, while the Mayor of London governs the whole of Greater London. The role is primarily ceremonial and social rather than political, although the Lord Mayor does promote London's business interests abroad. The Lord Mayor is elected at the end of September or the beginning of October each year by Common Hall, a body of representatives of the City's Livery Companies, and takes office in November. Summoned by the sitting Lord Mayor, Common Hall meets at Guildhall on Michaelmas Day (29 September) or on the closest weekday. Voting is by show of hands; if, however, any liveryman so demands, balloting is held a fortnight later. The Lord Mayor's Show is held on the day after the election; the Lord Mayor, preceded by a procession, travels to the City of Westminster to swear allegiance to the sovereign in the presence of the judges of the High Court. The office was instituted in 1189. Its first holder was Henry fitz Ailwyn, and the title 'Lord Mayor' came into use after 1354, when it was granted to Thomas Legge (then serving the second of his two terms) by Edward III. Lord Mayors are elected for one year; by custom, they do not serve more than once. Almost 700 individuals have served as Lord Mayor of London; numerous of these have served multiple terms, but only one man has served six times: Hamo de Chigwell (1319, 1321, 1322, 1323, 1325, 1327). Four have served four terms: Nicholas de Farndone (1308, 1313, 1320, 1323), Richard ('Dick') Whittington (1397, 1398, 1406, 1419) and John de Pulteney (1330, 1331, 1333, 1336). The last individual to serve more than once was Robert Fowler (1883, 1885). Dame Mary Donaldson, elected in 1983, is the only woman to serve in the office. The Lord Mayor's residence is Mansion House (see separate entry). The annual ceremony to admit the new Lord Mayor is called the Silent Change.

Lord's Cricket Ground St John's Wood Road, NW8. Owned by the Marylebone Cricket Club (MCC), Lord's is the home of Middlesex County Cricket Club, the England and Wales Cricket Board (ECB) and the European Cricket Council (ECC), and is often referred to as the Home of Cricket. Named after its founder, Thomas Lord, the present ground dates from 1814, having been moved 250yds (229m) northwest from its former home due to the construction through its outfield of the Regent's Canal. A commemorative plaque was unveiled at the site of the old ground on 9 May 2006 by

Andrew Strauss. The two ends of the pitch are the Pavilion End (to the southwest), where the main members' pavilion is located, and the Nursery End (northeast), dominated by the distinctive pod-shaped Media Centre, opened in 1999. The pavilion was built in 1890. One of the most distinctive and famous features of the ground is its significant slope: the northwest side of the playing surface is 8ft (2.5m) higher than the southeast side, causing appreciable deviation in the bounce of the ball on the pitch and making it easier to move the ball in to right-handed batsmen when bowling from the Pavilion End, and easier to move it away when bowling from the Nursery End. Another highly visible feature of the ground is the **weather vane** in the shape of Father Time, presented by Sir Herbert Baker in 1926. Currently adorning a stand on the southeast side, it was located on the northwest stand until this was replaced by the new main grandstand in 1996. Lord's typically hosts the first **Test match** of the summer and the second one-day match of English home series. Over 100 Tests have been played at Lord's, the first in 1884 when England defeated Australia by an innings and 5 runs. The Lord's Taverners, a charitable group comprising cricketers and cricket lovers, take their name from the old Tavern pub, where the club's founders used to congregate. The pub no longer exists, and the Tavern Stand now stands on its former site. Lord's is the home of the **MCC Museum**, the oldest sports museum in the world. The Memorial Gallery contains the velvet bag (dated 1883) which once held the Ashes urn, as well as the urn itself. The term **'Ashes'** was first used after England lost to Australia – for the first time on home soil – at The Oval on 29 August 1882. England, chasing only 85 to win, slumped from 51 for 2 to 78 all out. A day later, the *Sporting Times* carried a mock obituary to English cricket which concluded that 'The body will be cremated and the ashes taken to Australia'. A few weeks later, an English team, captained by the **Hon. Ivo Bligh** (later Lord Darnley), set off to tour Australia. The side lost the first of the three scheduled Tests but won the next two, prompting a group of Melbourne women (including **Miss Florence Rose Morphy**) to burn one of the bails used in the third Test, put it in a small brown urn, and present it to Bligh. The urn and an accompanying bag were taken back to England by Bligh, who regarded them as personal gifts and kept them at the family home, Cobham Hall, near Rochester in Kent. In February 1884, Bligh married Miss Morphy; 43 years later, on his death, she bequeathed the Ashes to the MCC. An inscription on the tiny, delicate and irreplaceable urn reads: 'When Ivo goes back with the urn, the urn;/Studds, Steel, Read and Tylecote return, return;/The welkin will ring loud,/The great crowd will feel proud,'Seeing Barlow and Bates with the urn, the urn;/And the rest coming home with the urn.' Tel: 020 7616 8500.

LSO St Luke's — Old Street, EC1. An 18th century Grade I listed church, restored to become the home of the London Symphony Orchestra's community and music education programme, LSO Discovery. It houses LSO rehearsals and a diverse mix of evening concerts, as well as free public lunchtime concerts and community events, including Balinese gamelan sessions. Tel: 020 7490 3939.

Madame Tussauds — Marylebone Road, NW1. The famous waxworks museum was begun in 1835 by Strasbourg-born Marie Grosholz (1761–1850), later known as Madame Tussaud, when the museum settled into a permanent home in The Bazaar, Baker Street. In 1884 Tussaud's grandson, Joseph Randall, oversaw its move to the present site. In 1925 a fire gutted the building, destroying not only almost all the wax figures and their costumes, but priceless furnishings, paintings and relics. Fortunately, many of the old head moulds were saved, and from these the exhibition was rebuilt, opening three years later with the addition of a large cinema and restaurant. In 1940 a German bomb destroyed the cinema. Ironically, the figure of Adolf Hitler was one of the few figures to survive unscathed. In 1958 Madame Tussauds opened the Commonwealth's first Planetarium on the site of the old cinema; the London Planetarium was closed in 2006. Recent features of Tussauds include a recreation of the famous *Big Brother* diary room and a recreation of the hull of the *Black Pearl* inspired by Disney blockbuster *Pirates of the Caribbean*. Tel: 0870 999 0046.

Magnificent Seven — A series of cemeteries established in London during the 19th century. In 1832 Parliament passed a bill encouraging the establishment of private cemeteries outside London, and later passed a bill to completely close all inner London churchyards; the seven cemeteries were all opened over the next decade.

Kensal Green (opened 1832) covers 72 acres (29ha) and was founded by barrister George Frederick Carden (1798–1874). Impressed by Le Cimetière du Père-Lachaise on a visit to Paris, he wanted to produce an English version. Famous people buried in Kensal Green include writers Anthony Trollope and William Makepeace Thackeray, Oscar Wilde's mother, engineer Isambard Kingdom Brunel (and his father Marc), Charles Babbage, Niagara tightrope walker Blondin, Wilkie Collins, Thomas Hood and Fanny Kemble. Freddie Mercury was cremated at Kensal Green although the location of his ashes remains undisclosed.

West Norwood (1837) has 64 Grade II and Grade II* listed monuments in its 42 acres (17ha) and includes memorials to Mrs Beeton (of cookbook fame), Sir Henry Doulton, Dr William Marsden, Baron Julius de Reuter, Charles Spurgeon, Sir Henry Tate and Hiram Maxim. Sir William Tite (1798–1873) designed the magnificent entrance arch

Highgate (1839) is considered by many to be the finest of the 'Magnificent Seven' for its Victorian funerary architecture and landscaping. Two buildings are listed Grade I, two Grade II* and over 60 Grade II. Notable features of its 37 acres (15ha) include the Egyptian Avenue, the Circle of Lebanon, and the resting lion, Nero, in honour of George Wombell, proprietor of England's largest travelling menagerie in the early 19th century. The jewel in Highgate's crown, the mausoleum of Julius Beer (former proprietor of the *Observer*), stands on the cemetery's highest point, but Highgate Cemetery is probably most famous for its bust of Karl Marx, father of Marxist philosophy. George Eliot, Michael Faraday, Radclyffe Hall, Carl Rosa, Sir Ralph

Richardson, Douglas Adams and sculptor Edward Hodges Baily are also buried at Highgate.

Abney Park (1840) extends over 32 acres (13ha) on a slope running down from an ancient ridgeway track, now Stoke Newington Church Street, to the course of Hackney Brook. Abney Park is now Hackney's first Local Nature Reserve and is managed both as a reserve and a local leisure resource by the Abney Park Trust. The cemetery was established on non-denominational principles and therefore contains the graves of many Nonconformist religious figures and slavery abolitionsists; those buried at Abney Park include William and Catherine Booth, founders of the Salvation Army.

Nunhead (1840) is perhaps the least known but most attractive as well as being the second largest of London's Victorian cemeteries. Many heroes who fought at the battles of Trafalgar and Waterloo are buried on the 52 acre (21ha) site.

Brompton (1840), originally known as the West of London and Westminster Cemetery, covers 40 acres (16ha) and was designed by Benjamin Baud. On 13 June 1892, the American Sioux Indian chief Long Wolf was buried here. In 1997, Chief Long Wolf was finally moved to a new plot in the Wolf Creek Community Cemetery, Pine Ridge, South Dakota. Other famous gravestones include those of suffragette leader Emmeline Pankhurst, singer and composer Richard Tauber, motor racing pioneer Percy Lambert, the first man to travel at 100mph (160km/h), pioneer anaesthetist and discoverer of the cause of cholera Dr John Snow, Sir Francis Pettit Smith, inventor of the four-bladed screw propeller, watercolourist Francis Nicholson and violinist Alfred Mellon.

Tower Hamlets (1841), covering 33 acres (13.5ha) is located in the parishes of St Dunstan's Stepney and St Leonard, Bromley-by-Bow and was originally called the City of London and Tower Hamlets Cemetery. Some of its more famous residents include Victorian philanthropist Dr Barnardo, John Willis, builder and owner of the *Cutty Sark* (see separate entry), comedian Alex Hurley, husband of Marie Lloyd, who popularised the 'Lambeth Walk', and Henry Orbell, founder member of the Independent Labour Party and organiser of the dock strike committee of 1889. In 1966, the GLC bought the cemetery and it was closed for burials.

Mansion House

Walbrook, EC4. The Palladian façade of Mansion House, with its six large Corinthian columns, is one of the most familiar landmarks in the City of London. The official residence of the Lord Mayor (see separate entry), the building was designed by George Dance the elder in 1739. First occupied by a Lord Mayor in 1752, when Sir Crispin Gascoigne took up residence, it was actually completed in 1753. Among the magnificent state rooms is the 90ft (27.5m) long Egyptian hall, where many official banquets are held. The Lord Mayor is chief magistrate of the City during his year in office, and Mansion House is therefore the only private residence in England with its own Court of Justice. Hidden from view are 11 holding cells, ten for men and one, 'the birdcage', for women. Emmeline Pankhurst, who campaigned for women's suffrage in the 20th century, was once imprisoned here.

Marble Arch

Oxford Street, W1. Located at the northeast corner of Hyde Park, close to Speaker's Corner and the Cumberland Gate. Built of white Carrara marble to a design taken from the triumphal arch of Constantine in Rome, the arch was erected in 1828 by John Nash to form a grand gateway to Buckingham Palace. It was moved to its present site in 1851 to make room for an extension to the palace planned by Queen Victoria and Prince Albert. Even today only senior members of the royal family and one of the artillery regiments are allowed to pass beneath it. Inside the arch are three small rooms used as a police station until 1950; during a riot in 1855 the crowd were brought to order by a body of police who emerged from the arch, taking the demonstrators by surprise. The area in which the arch now stands was once known as Tyburn, a place of public execution and the site of the three-legged gallows known as the Tyburn Tree. Now marooned on a traffic island, Marble Arch marks the western extent of Oxford Street.

Marble Hill House

Richmond Road, Twickenham. Built 1724–9 for Henrietta Howard, mistress of George II when he was Prince of Wales, the house and gardens were planned by fashionable connoisseurs including Lord Herbert and Mrs Howard's neighbour, poet Alexander Pope. Set in 66 acres (26.5ha) of riverside parkland, in keeping with its intended use as an Arcadian retreat from crowded 18th century London. the Palladian-style villa became renowned as a salon of literary wits. Some of its original contents, dispersed in 1824, have been reassembled from as far afield as Philadelphia and Melbourne, Australia. There is also a fine collection of early Georgian paintings, including portraits of Henrietta Howard and her circle. The Chinese wallpaper Mrs Howard hung in the dining room in 1751 has recently been recreated using historical references and motifs, and, like the original, hand painted by Chinese artists. Now owned by English Heritage. Tel: 020 8892 5115.

Markets

Billingsgate Market, Trafalgar Way, E14, is the UK's largest inland fish market. The market covers an area of 13 acres (5ha). The ground floor comprises a large trading hall with 98 stands and 30 shops; a shellfish boiling room; a number of individual cold rooms; an 800 tonne freezer store, an ice making plant and 14 lock-up shops used by processors, catering suppliers and merchants. Billingsgate opened in 1876 in Lower Thames Street but moved to the Isle of Dogs in 1982. Tel: 020 7987 1118.

Borough Market, Borough High Street, Stoney Street and Winchester Walk, SE1, is reputedly the oldest market in London, claiming to have existed since the Roman period and first mentioned in 1276 although it received its royal charter only in 1550. Traditionally a wholesale fruit and vegetable market, today it also offers some of London's most luxurious gastronomic products. Tel: 020 7407 1002.

Leadenhall Market, south of Leadenhall Street, EC3, located between Gracechurch Street and Lime Street, is a covered market housed in an ornate wrought iron and glass complex built in 1881 and designed by Sir Horace Jones (also the architect of Billingsgate and Smithfield markets). Established as a meat and fish market in the 14th century, it still specialises in meat and game while also offering a wide range of other goods and services. Tel: 0871 789 6001.

Leather Lane Market, Leather Lane, EC1, offers fruit and vegetables, clothes, electrical goods and toiletries.

New Spitalfields Market, Sherrin Road (off Ruckholt Road), Leyton, E10, first operated under a royal charter granted in 1682. Spitalfields fruit and vegetable market moved out of the City in 1991 and now occupies a purpose-built 31 acre (12.5ha) site in East London. The market hall houses 115 trading units for wholesalers dealing in fruit, vegetables and flowers. New Spitalfields provides the greatest choice of exotic fruit and vegetables of any market in Europe. Tel: 020 8518 7670.

New Covent Garden Market, Nine Elms Lane, SW10. Also known as Nine Elms Market. London's largest wholesale fruit, vegetable and flower market, formerly located in Covent Garden, moved in 1974 to a new 56 acre (23ha) site with over 200 suppliers. Tel: 020 7720 2211.

Old Spitalfields Market occupies the building constructed in 1887 for Spitalfields Market and occupied until 1991.

Petticoat Lane, E1, actually takes place in Wentworth Street Monday–Friday, spreading on Sundays to become even bigger to cover 10 separate trading streets including Middlesex Street. Originally called Hog Lane Market in the 15th century.

Portobello Road Market, W10, includes a host of stalls specialising in antiques and jewellery but also bric-a-brac and second-hand clothes.

Smithfield Market, Charterhouse Street, EC1. Meat has been bought and sold at Smithfield for over 800 years, making it one of the oldest markets in London. A livestock market occupied the site as early as the 10th century. Tel: 020 7236 8734.

Middlesex — One of the 39 historic counties of England and the second smallest, after Rutland. The name means 'middle Saxons' and refers to the reputed ethnic origin of its inhabitants. Its first recorded use was in AD 704 as *Middleseaxan.* Geographically, Middlesex included the City of London, which has been self-governing since the 13th century, and the City of Westminster. Middlesex was recorded in Domesday Book as being divided into the six hundreds of Edmonton, Elthorne, Gore, Hounslow (later Isleworth), Ossulstone and Spelthorne. New Brentford was considered to be the county town in 1789, on the basis that it was the location of elections of knights for the shire (i.e. MPs). Brentford, Edgware, Enfield, Hounslow, Southall, Staines and Uxbridge were market towns in the 18th century. Under the Local Government Act 1888, much of the area to the southeast became part of the County of London. The remainder came under the control of Middlesex County Council except for the parish of Monken Hadley, which became part of Hertfordshire. In 1965 almost all of the original area was incorporated into Greater London and for all intents and purposes Middlesex was no longer considered a county. The name Middlesex is still used by organisations based in the area, such as Middlesex County Cricket Club and Middlesex University, and is also defined by the Royal Mail to be a former postal county. The postal county was much smaller than the traditional and administrative counties as a large part of Middlesex was part of the London postal district. It included the village of Denham, which was for all other purposes in Buckinghamshire but was included in the post town of Uxbridge and therefore the postal county of Middlesex; conversely Hampton Wick was not included in the Middlesex postal county as it was served by post towns based in Surrey. This gave rise to the misnomer that Hampton Court Palace was located in Surrey. Wraysbury and Egham Hythe are served by the Staines post town and thus were also included in the Middlesex postal county.

Middlesex University — The former Middlesex Polytechnic, founded in 1973, was granted university status in 1992. It has its origin in St Katherine's College and Hornsey School of Arts and Crafts (later Hornsey Art College), both founded in the late 19th century and which became part of the polytechnic in the 1970s. With around 23,000 students, it has campuses at Hendon, the former royal hunting ground of Trent Park in Enfield, Cockfosters and Archway in north London. A new campus in Dubai was opened in 2004. Former students include actress Freema Agyeman, comedian Alan Carr, sculptor Anish Kapoor and horror novelist James Herbert. Tel: 020 8411 5000.

Millennium Dome — Peninsula Square, SE10. Designed by Richard Rogers, the dome was constructed on former industrial land on the Greenwich peninsula as part of the millennium celebrations in 2000. The largest single-roofed structure in the world, externally it appears as a large white marquee with 329ft (100m) high yellow support towers, one for each month of the year, or each hour of the clock face, representing the role played by Greenwich Mean Time. In plan it is circular, 1197ft (365m) in diameter – 1m for each day of the year – with scalloped edges. The building was engineered by Buro Happold, and the entire roof structure weighs less than the air contained within the building. It is not strictly a dome as it is not self-supporting, but is rather a mast-supported, dome-shaped cable network. The canopy is made of PTFE coated glass fibre fabric, a durable and weather-resistant plastic, and is 165ft (50m) high in the middle. From 1 January–31 December 2000 it was occupied by an exhibition titled the Millennium Experience, for which the interior space was subdivided into 14 'zones': Body, Work, Learning, Money, Play, Journey, Self Portrait, Living Island, Talk, Faith, Home Planet, Rest, Mind and Shared Ground. A central stage show (performed 999 times during the year) was accompanied by music composed by Peter Gabriel and an acrobatic cast of 160. However, both the project and the exhibition were the subject of considerable political controversy; some of the zones were perceived as lacking in content and pandering to political correctness. After considerable debate about its future use, the Dome's name was officially changed to the O2 Arena on 31 May 2005 when O2 plc purchased the naming rights from the developers, Anschutz Entertainment Group. The building has since been transformed into an indoor sporting and performance arena. In this role the plan is to host the 2009 World Gymnastics Championships and the gymnastics, basketball and trampolining events of the 2012 Olympics.

Monument, The Monument Street, EC3. Standing 202ft (61.5m) high, the Monument is the tallest isolated stone column in the world. Designed by Sir Christopher Wren and Robert Hooke and constructed 1671–7 of Portland stone, the simple Doric column is topped by a flaming urn of copper symbolising the Great Fire of London (see separate entry). A spiral staircase inside of 311 steps provides access to a balcony at the top offering breathtaking views over the city in all directions. The Latin inscription on the north panel of the pedestal translates as: 'In the year of Christ 1666, on 2 September, at a distance eastward from this place of 202ft, which is the height of this column, a fire broke out in the dead of night which, the wind blowing, devoured even distant buildings, and rushed devastating through every quarter with astonishing swiftness and noise . . . On the third day . . . at the bidding, we may well believe, of heaven, the fire stayed its course and everywhere died out.' Tel 020 7626 2717.

Morden Hall Park Morden Hall Road, Morden. A former deer park covering over 125 acres (50ha), through which the River Wandle meanders. The river plays an important role in the park with an old snuff mill, now used as an education centre, and a variety of bridges traversing it. The park has hay meadows, wetlands, a collection of old estate buildings and an impressive rose garden with over 2000 roses. The workshops now house local craftworkers. Tel: 020 8545 6850.

Museum of Childhood Cambridge Heath Road, E2. Officially opened as the Bethnal Green Museum by the Prince of Wales on 24 June 1872 as an extension of the Victoria & Albert Museum, the museum only became a dedicated toy museum in 1974. Since then it has amassed a wide variety of toys including teddy bears, games, dolls, doll's houses (some donated by royalty), model trains, theatres and puppets. Some of these exhibits date back to the 17th century. Tel: 020 8983 5200.

Museum of London London Wall, EC2. The museum opened in 1976 as part of the Barbican estate, utilising collections previously held by the Corporation at the Guildhall and also items from other collections, including the London Museum which opened in 1912 and was located in Kensington Palace. The Museum of London documents the London's history from the prehistoric era to the present day and is primarily concerned with the social history of London and its inhabitants. In 2003, Museum in Docklands was opened in a 19th century warehouse building near Canary Wharf on the Isle of Dogs. This arm of the museum traces the history of London as a port. The third arm of the Museum of London Group is the London Archaeological Archive and Research Centre at Mortimer Wheeler House, Eagle Wharf Road, N1. Tel: 0870 444 3851.

Museum of the Moving Image See National Film Theatre

Myddelton House Gardens Bulls Cross, Enfield. Home to E A Bowles (1865–1954), who devoted much of his life to the garden's creation. An enthusiastic collector and accomplished plantsman, Bowles discovered and selected many unusual plant varieties, many of which can still be seen in the garden today. After his death, the garden fell into disrepair and some of the plants were lost. However, since 1984, Lee Valley Regional Park Authority and the E A Bowles of Myddelton House Society have been restoring the 4 acre (1.6ha) gardens in Bowles' original style. The gardens are also home to a prized collection of award-winning bearded iris. Tel: 01992 702200.

National Archives Bessant Drive, Kew. An executive agency of the Secretary of State for Justice, the official archive for England, Wales and the UK government has one of the largest archival collections in the world, spanning 1000 years of British history from Domesday Book of 1086 to recently released government papers. Among the exhibits on display in the museum are Domesday Book, Magna Carta, the first pages printed by Caxton, Tudor wallpaper, and a huge collection of famous signatures. At the Family Records Centre, access can be gained to family history websites and microfilm copies of useful documents. Tel: 020 8876 3444.

National Army Museum Royal Hospital Road, Chelsea, SW3. The museum tells the story of the British Army from the time of the Battle of Agincourt to the early 21st century. There are five permanent galleries, arranged chronologically: Redcoats: The British Soldier 1415–1792; The Road to Waterloo; The Victorian Soldier; From World War to Cold War; and The Modern Army. Tel: 020 7730 0717.

National Film Theatre Belvedere Road, SE1. Part of the South Bank complex, the National Film Theatre (NFT) was established in 1951 as part of the Festival of Britain, moving to its present site in 1957. One of the world's great cinemas, it hosts a wide range of film and cinema screenings and talks throughout the year. In November it is home to the internationally renowned London Film Festival. In 2007 the complex was expanded to take in the space formerly occupied by the Museum of the Moving Image (MOMI), opened in 1988 and closed in 1999, and was renamed BFI Southbank. Tel: 020 7928 3232.

National Maritime Museum Romney Road, Greenwich, SE10. Located in Greenwich Park and opened to the public by George VI on 27 April 1937, the site now includes the 17th century Queen's House and, from the 1950s, the Royal Observatory, Greenwich. The museum itself is housed in the former Royal Hospital School; its collections comprise over 2 million items relating to Britain's maritime history as well as the world's largest maritime reference library and the largest collection of portraits in the UK outside the National Portrait Gallery. The many interactive exhibits cover topics such as piracy, slavery and exploration, the Vikings and the *Titanic*. The majority of the museum's small-boat collection is on display at the new National Maritime Museum, Falmouth (see Cornwall). **The Queen's House** (designed by Inigo Jones 1616–35) was originally part of the Royal Palace of Placentia (birthplace of Henry VIII and now the site of the Royal Naval Hospital) and was intended by James I to be the home of his consort, Anne of Denmark. Anne died in 1619, however, and Charles I gave it to his new queen, Henrietta Maria. **The Royal Observatory** was founded in 1675 by Charles II; Flamsteed House, the original part of the Observatory, was designed by Sir Christopher Wren as the first purpose-built scientific research facility in Britain and named in honour of the first Astronomer Royal. In 1924, the arrival of the railway affected the readings of the Magnetic and Meteorological Department and forced the observatory to move to Abinger, Surrey. After World War II, in 1947, the decision was made to move to Herstmonceux Castle and in 1990 the RGO moved again, to Cambridge. With the closure of this site in 1998, the Royal Observatory returned again to Greenwich. The Prime Meridian Line runs through the site, and there are exhibits on the history of stars, space and time, the search for longitude, the lives of astronomers and the establishment of Greenwich Mean Time as the world's standard time. The Time Ball on top of Flamsteed House, installed in 1933, still drops at exactly 1pm every day. Tel: 020 8312 6608.

Natural History Museum — Exhibition Road, SW7. Situated next to the Science Museum and opposite the Victoria & Albert Museum, the museum was designed by Alfred Waterhouse and opened in 1881 with exhibits from the British Museum. Officially titled the British Museum (Natural History), it remained an arm of the British Museum until 1963 and did not formally change its name until 1992. The museum is home to the largest and most important natural history collection in the world. In total there are 55 million animal specimens including 28 million insects, 9 million fossils, 6 million plant specimens and more than 500,000 rocks, minerals and meteorites. The Geological Museum – now the Red Zone – started life in 1841 as part of the Geological Survey and in 1985 merged with the Natural History Museum, adding a collection of more than 30,000 minerals. In 1988 the Lasting Impressions gallery was opened to connect the two. Redevelopment 1996–8 created the Atrium and six new exhibitions. The eight-storey Darwin Centre, opened in September 2009, is a state-of-the-art scientific research and collections facility that will be used by the world's leading scientists. The David Attenborough Studio is an important part of this project as a multimedia environment for educational events. Tel: 020 7942 5000.

New Scotland Yard — Broadway, SW1. The headquarters of the Metropolitan Police have been situated at this site near Victoria Street since 1967. The name comes from the original headquarters of the Metropolitan Police, established in 1829 in Great Scotland Yard at the top of Whitehall. After this was damaged by a Fenian bomb in 1884, a new building on Victoria Embankment near Westminster Bridge was completed by Norman Shaw in 1890; after the police moved out, Great Scotland Yard was taken over by the Army and rebuilt to become an Army recruiting office and Royal Military Police headquarters. Bombed by the Provisional IRA in 1973, killing one person, it subsequently became the Ministry of Defence Library, a role which it retained until 2004. Today, the only surviving element of the original Scotland Yard is a Metropolitan Police stables next door at 7 Great Scotland Yard. Scotland Yard's telephone number was originally Whitehall 1212 but is now 0207 230 1212.

Notting Hill Carnival — London W11. An annual carnival led by members of the Caribbean population which takes place over three days each August bank holiday weekend. The district of Notting Hill, to the west of central London and close to the northwestern corner of Hyde Park within the Royal Borough of Kensington and Chelsea, has been home to the many of the city's Afro-Caribbean population since the 1950s. The carnival began in January 1959 in St Pancras Town Hall as a response to the poor state of race relations at the time; the UK's first widespread racial attacks had occurred the previous year. Despite being held indoors, it was a huge success. At the instigation of social worker Rhaune Laslett – who was unaware of the indoor events when she first raised the idea – it first moved outside and shifted into August in 1966. At this point, it was more a Notting Hill event than an Afro-Caribbean event, and only around 1000 people turned out. At its peak in 2000 it attracted up to 1 million people. The area came to international attention with the release of the successful Hollywood movie *Notting Hill* (1999), starring Julia Roberts and Hugh Grant, many scenes from which were shot locally.

Old Bailey — Old Bailey, EC4. Founded in 1907, the Central Criminal Court of England takes its name from the thoroughfare on which it stands. Central London's Crown Court sits at the Old Bailey and hears criminal cases, whereas the High Court sits at the Royal Courts of Justice. See also Newgate Prison in Prisons: Historic

Olympia — Hammersmith Road, W14. An exhibition centre in the London Borough of Hammersmith and Fulham. Erected by Andrew Handyside of Derby and originally known as the National Agricultural Hall, it opened its doors on 27 December 1886 to the Hippodrome Circus. It now features three exhibition halls known as Olympia Grand Hall, Olympia National Hall and Olympia 2. Together with Earls Court, these facilities are operated by ECO (Earls Court and Olympia). Tel: 020 7385 1200.

Omega Workshops — Fitzroy Square, Bloomsbury, W1. A studio and showroom conceived by artist and critic Roger Fry and established in 1913 with the intention of producing furniture, fabrics and ceramics designed by artists, particularly those of the Bloomsbury Group (see separate entry). In addition to its emphasis on the decorative arts, exemplified in the work of Vanessa Bell, Duncan Grant and the ceramics of Roger Fry, the Omega Workshops experimented with book production. Works were shown anonymously, marked only with the Greek letter omega; the name was intended to indicate that the workshops' productions were the 'last word' in quality. The studio closed in 1919.

Orleans House Gallery — Riverside, Twickenham. Built in 1710, Orleans House is named after Louis Philippe, Duc d'Orléans, who lived in the house in exile 1813–15. Much of the house was demolished in 1926, but two of its wings, along with the outbuildings – including the 19th century stables – and the baroque Octagon Room, designed by renowned architect James Gibbs, were rescued from destruction. They now house the principal art gallery of the Borough of Richmond upon Thames, with a programme of changing exhibitions. Tel: 020 8831 6000.

Orpington Man — On 15 March 1962 Orpington, now in the London Borough of Bromley, was the scene of a by-election shock for the Conservatives, who lost the parliamentary seat to Liberal candidate Eric Lubbock, now Lord Avebury, on a 26.8 per cent swing. The result gave rise to the political phenomenon 'Orpington Man', who symbolised the rebellion of traditional Tory voters against the government of Harold Macmillan. See also Selsdon Man.

Osterley Park — Jersey Road, Isleworth. A redbrick Elizabethan house, originally built in 1576 by Thomas Gresham, an adviser to Elizabeth I, and transformed in the 1760s by Robert Adam into an elegant neoclassical villa for Francis Child, founder of Child's Bank. Today the spectacular interiors form one of Britain's most complete examples of Adam's work, with original plasterwork, carpets and furniture, while the magnificent 16th century stables survive largely intact. The house is set in extensive park and farm land, complete with pleasure grounds and neoclassical garden buildings. Now owned by the National Trust. Tel: 020 8232 5050.

02 Arena — See Millennium Dome

Oval, The — Harleyford Road, SE11. Originally known as Kennington Oval and now officially titled the Brit Oval, Surrey County Cricket Club's headquarters has also been known as the AMP Oval and the Foster's Oval. Kennington Oval has its origins in the 1790s when an oval road was laid round what was then a cabbage patch. When a subsequent market garden failed, 10,000 turves were brought in from Tooting Common and the land was opened as a cricket ground in 1845. Owned by the Duchy of Cornwall (the Duke of Cornwall is one of the titles held by the Prince of Wales, whose feathers have hence appeared on Surrey's badge since 1915), it has been the headquarters of Surrey County Cricket Club ever since. The first-ever Test on English soil was played here in September 1880, resulting in an England win over Australia by five wickets, with W G Grace scoring a hundred on debut, and the last match of Test series in England traditionally take place at the ground. The Oval is also the venue where the legend of the Ashes (see Lord's) was born a couple of years after the inaugural Test, in August 1882. The FA Cup final was also held at Kennington Oval in 1872 and from 1874 to 1892. Tel: 0871 246 1100.

Palace of Westminster — St Margaret Street, SW1. Also known as the Houses of Parliament or Westminster Palace. Now the home of the Houses of Parliament, the Palace of Westminster was the principal residence of the kings of England from its erection by Edward the Confessor in 1042 until a devastating fire of 1512. It lies on the north bank of the Thames in the London borough of the City of Westminster, close by other government buildings in Whitehall. In medieval times kings summoned their courts wherever they happened to be, but by the end of the 14th century the court in all its aspects had its headquarters at Westminster, and following the fire the building became the seat of both the House of Lords and the elected House of Commons. Another fire in 1834 destroyed almost all of the Palace except Westminster Hall, dating from 1097 although substantially rebuilt in the 14th century, the crypt of St Stephen's Chapel, the adjacent cloisters and the Jewel Tower. The present Houses of Parliament, built over the next 30 years, were the work of architect Sir Charles Barry (1795–1860) and his assistant Augustus Welby Pugin (1812–52). The design incorporated Westminster Hall and the remains of St Stephen's Chapel. The House of Commons Chamber, destroyed in a German air attack in 1941, was rebuilt after World War II; the architect, Sir Giles Gilbert Scott, took care to preserve the essential features of Barry's building and the new chamber was completed in 1950. The layout of the Palace is intricate, its buildings containing nearly 1200 rooms, 100 staircases and well over 2 miles (3km) of passages. The Palace of Westminster includes several towers, the tallest being the 323ft (98m) Victoria Tower, a square tower at the southwestern end named after the reigning monarch at the time of the Palace's reconstruction. Topped by an iron flagstaff, from which the Royal Standard (if the sovereign is present) or the Union flag is flown, the tower is home to the House of Lords' Record Office, which despite its name holds the records of both Houses of Parliament. At the base of the tower is the Sovereign's Entrance, used whenever the monarch enters the Palace of Westminster for the State Opening of Parliament or any other official ceremony. Over the middle of the Palace lies the Central Tower, at 300ft (91m) tall the shortest of the Palace's three principal towers. Unlike the other towers, the Central Tower possesses a spire. Octagonal in shape, it stands immediately above the Central Lobby, its original function being as a high-level air intake. A small tower positioned at the front of the Palace, between Westminster Hall and Old Palace Yard, contains at its base the main entrance to the House of Commons, known as St Stephen's Entrance. At the northwestern end of the Palace is the most famous of the towers, St Stephen's Tower or the Clock Tower – often erroneously referred to as Big Ben, after commissioner of works Sir Benjamin Hall (1802–67). The Clock Tower, 316ft (96m) tall, houses a large clock with four faces and known as the Great Clock of Westminster. The tower also houses five bells, which strike the Westminster Chimes every quarter hour. The largest and most famous bell is Big Ben (officially, the Great Bell of Westminster), which strikes the hour. The third heaviest bell in England, it weighs 13 tons 10 cwt 99 lb (13.5 tonnes). A flock of starlings landed on the minute hand of the clock in 1945 and set the time back five minutes. Since 1987 the Palace of Westminster has been part of the UNESCO Westminster World Heritage Site. Tel: 020 7219 3000.

Parliament Hill Fields — London NW5. An open area of land in northwest London, now part of Hampstead Heath and administered by the Corporation of London. The surrounding Highgate area is also sometimes referred to by the same name. Once known as Traitors' Hill, it acquired its current name during the Civil War when it was occupied by troops loyal to Parliament. Informally part of the area is now called Kite Hill due to its popularity with kite flyers. The hill is 310ft (95m) high and gives good views both over London and to the north.

Petticoat Lane — See Markets

Pitzhanger Manor House — Walpole Park, Mattock Lane, Ealing, W5. A restored Georgian villa once owned and designed by Sir John Soane. A sympathetically designed extension to the house, built in 1940, is now the largest art gallery in West London. Tel: 020 8567 1227.

London Planetarium	See Madame Tussaud's
Pool of London	A reach of the Thames consisting of two parts: the Lower runs from Limekiln Creek to Cherry Garden Pier, the Upper from Cherry Garden Pier to London Bridge. Tower Bridge divides the two. See also Thames Reaches
Postal areas:	
East London	E1 Whitechapel, Stepney, Mile End
	E2 Bethnal Green, Shoreditch
	E3 Bow, Bromley-by-Bow
	E4 Chingford, Highams Park
	E5 Clapton
	E6 East Ham (also covers Beckton)
	E7 Forest Gate, Upton Park
	E8 Hackney, Dalston
	E9 Hackney, Homerton (includes South Hackney)
	E10 Leyton
	E11 Leytonstone (also covers Wanstead)
	E12 Manor Park
	E13 Plaistow
	E14 Poplar, Millwall (also covers Isle of Dogs)
	E15 Stratford, West Ham
	E16 Victoria Docks, North Woolwich (also covers Canning Town)
	E17 Walthamstow
	E18 Woodford, South Woodford (in reality only South Woodford is covered by E18; most of Woodford itself is covered by postcode area IG8, outside the London postal districts)
East Central London	EC1 Clerkenwell, Finsbury, Barbican area
	EC2 northeastern (Moorgate, Liverpool Street) area of the City
	EC3 southeastern (Monument, Aldgate, Fenchurch Street, Spitalfields, Tower Hill) area of the City
	EC4 western (Fleet Street, Temple, Blackfriars, St Paul's) area of the City
North London	N1 Islington, Barnsbury, Canonbury area
	N2 East Finchley (includes eastern part of Hampstead Garden Suburb)
	N3 Finchley Central, Finchley Church End (central Finchley)
	N4 Finsbury Park, Manor House
	N5 Highbury
	N6 Highgate
	N7 Holloway (includes Lower Holloway)
	N8 Hornsey (also covers Crouch End)
	N9 Lower Edmonton
	N10 Muswell Hill
	N11 New Southgate (also covers Friern Barnet)
	N12 North Finchley, Woodside Park
	N13 Palmers Green
	N14 Southgate
	N15 South Tottenham, Seven Sisters
	N16 Stoke Newington, Stamford Hill
	N17 Tottenham
	N18 Upper Edmonton
	N19 Upper Holloway, Archway, Tufnell Park
	N20 Whetstone (also covers Totteridge)
	N21 Winchmore Hill
	N22 Wood Green, Alexandra Palace
North West London	NW1 Camden Town, Regent's Park, north Marylebone area
	NW2 Cricklewood, Neasden (also covers Dollis Hill)
	NW3 Hampstead, Swiss Cottage (also covers Belsize Park)
	NW4 Hendon, Brent Cross
	NW5 Kentish Town
	NW6 Kilburn, Queens Park (also covers South and West Hampstead, Brondesbury Park)
	NW7 Mill Hill
	NW8 St John's Wood and Marylebone
	NW9 The Hyde (also covers Kingsbury and Colindale)
	NW10 Willesden (also covers Harlesden and Kensal Green)
	NW11 Golders Green (includes western part of Hampstead Garden Suburb)
South East London	SE1 Waterloo, Bermondsey, Southwark (South Bank and The Borough) and north Lambeth area
	SE2 Abbey Wood (includes Thamesmead South)
	SE3 Blackheath, Westcombe Park (also covers Kidbrooke)
	SE4 Brockley, Crofton Park, Honor Oak Park
	SE5 Camberwell
	SE6 Catford, Hither Green (also covers Bellingham)
	SE7 Charlton
	SE8 Deptford
	SE9 Eltham (also covers Mottingham)
	SE10 Greenwich (town)
	SE11 Lambeth, Kennington

SE12 Lee, Grove Park
SE13 Hither Green, Lewisham (town)
SE14 New Cross, New Cross Gate
SE15 Peckham, Nunhead
SE16 Rotherhithe, South Bermondsey, Surrey Docks
SE17 Walworth, Elephant & Castle
SE18 Woolwich (also covers Plumstead)
SE19 Crystal Palace, Norwood (central Norwood: Upper Norwood and Norwood New Town)
SE20 Anerley (also covers Penge)
SE21 Dulwich (includes West Dulwich)
SE22 East Dulwich
SE23 Forest Hill
SE24 Herne Hill
SE25 South Norwood
SE26 Sydenham
SE27 West Norwood, Tulse Hill
SE28 Thamesmead (nb small parts of Thamesmead are in SE2, and in DA18 Dartford)

South West London SW1 Westminster, Belgravia, Pimlico, Victoria area
SW2 Brixton (central and southern Brixton, includes Streatham Hill)
SW3 Chelsea, Brompton
SW4 Clapham
SW5 Earl's Court
SW6 Fulham, Parsons Green
SW7 South Kensington
SW8 South Lambeth (also covers Vauxhall, Nine Elms)
SW9 Stockwell (includes northern Brixton)
SW10 World's End, West Brompton (nb Brompton is covered by SW7, SW3 and SW1)
SW11 Battersea, Clapham Junction
SW12 Balham
SW13 Barnes, Castelnau
SW14 Mortlake (also covers East Sheen)
SW15 Putney (also covers Roehampton)
SW16 Streatham, Norbury
SW17 Tooting
SW18 Wandsworth (town), Earlsfield
SW19 Wimbledon (also covers Merton (town) and Collier's Wood)
SW20 South Wimbledon, West Wimbledon (also covers Raynes Park and Cottenham Park)

West London W1 West End, including Mayfair, Soho and south Marylebone
W2 Paddington, Bayswater, Hyde Park area
W3 Acton
W4 Chiswick
W5 Ealing
W6 Hammersmith
W7 Hanwell
W8 Kensington (central Kensington)
W9 Warwick Avenue, Maida Hill (also covers Maida Vale)
W10 Ladbroke Grove, North Kensington
W11 Notting Hill, Holland Park
W12 Shepherd's Bush
W13 West Ealing
W14 West Kensington

West Central London WC1 Bloomsbury and Gray's Inn area
WC2 Holborn/Strand/Covent Garden/St James's area

Primrose Hill London NW1. A hill to the north of Regent's Park, with a fine view of central London. Like Regent's Park the area was once part of a great chase appropriated by Henry VIII and became Crown property in 1841. In 1842 an Act of Parliament secured the land as public open space. The hill also gives its name to the surrounding district, which consists mainly of Victorian terraces. It has always been one of the more fashionable districts of north London, and remains expensive and prosperous. On 12 October 1678 Primrose Hill (then known as Greenberry Hill) was the scene of the mysterious murder of respected magistrate Edmund Berry Godfrey, who had become involved with the schemes of Titus Oates, inventor of the Popish Plot. Oates and Israel Tonge had asked Godfrey to take their oath that their evidence of a plot instigated by Pope Innocent XI to murder Charles II and his government was genuine. Godfrey demanded to know the contents of the papers they were to present, and when he had received a copy on 28 September, he took their depositions. The mood of the country was tense after Oates's accusations became known; then, on that fateful night in October, Godfrey failed to return home. Five days later he was found dead in a ditch on Primrose Hill, lying face down and impaled with his own sword. The body was covered with bruises and a circular mark around his neck revealed that he had been strangled. The sword wound had not bled, meaning that Godfrey was already dead when he was impaled. Miles Prance, a silversmith and known Jesuit sympathiser who worked at Somerset House, was arrested and taken to Newgate prison. His landlord John Wren testified that he had been away for the four nights before Godfrey's body was discovered. Prance announced that he had had a part in the murder but that the main instigators were Catholic priests, and that the murder had been carried out in the courtyard of Somerset House where Godfrey had been lured. Godfrey would have been strangled and his body taken to Hampstead. Prance named three men, Robert Green, Lawrence Hill and Henry Berry, who were arrested, but later recanted his confession and was thrown back into prison. As a result he recanted his recantation before the king himself; after changing his mind twice more, he finally swore to the truth of his original story. The three men were sentenced to death and hanged at Greenberry Hill. Prance's story was later discredited and he pleaded guilty to perjury. Because the three men were executed on false evidence, the murder remains officially unsolved.

Prisons: historic

The **Fleet**, formerly in Farringdon Street, EC4, was built towards the end of the 11th century in the reign of William II and stood beside the Fleet River, from whence it took its name. It was used mainly to hold political prisoners during the medieval and early modern periods but had become the main debtors' prison by the 18th century. One of the prison's features was the so-called 'Fleet Marriages', clandestine marriages carried out without a licence and conducted by clergymen imprisoned in the Fleet for debt. Two clergymen tried for the offence under the terms of the Marriage Act of 1754, which was brought in to abolish the practice, were the Rev. John Grierson and the Rev. Mr Wilkinson. The prison was demolished in the 1840s.

Marshalsea in Southwark became a debtors' prison in the 19th century and is best known as the place where Charles Dickens' father was imprisoned for debt and as the central location in Dickens' book *Little Dorrit*. It was demolished in 1849.

Newgate was situated in the City of London, at the corner of Newgate Street and the Old Bailey, and was in use between 1188 and 1902. The original prison was demolished and a new one (designed by George Dance, who also designed the adjacent courthouse) was constructed on the site 1770–8. It was attacked by rioting mobs during the Gordon Riots (see separate entry) in 1780 and set on fire; many prisoners died during the blaze and around 300 escaped to temporary freedom. In 1783 the site of London's gallows was moved from Tyburn to Newgate. Public executions outside the prison drew large crowds until 1868, when they were discontinued and instead carried out on a gallows within the prison walls. Fenian Michael Barrett was the last man to be hanged, in public, outside Newgate Prison, and consequently in Great Britain, on 26 May 1868. In 1902, the prison was demolished and the Old Bailey now stands upon its site. Famous inmates included Daniel Defoe, William Cobbett, Sir Thomas Malory and William Penn. The prison's name gave rise to several expressions, e.g. 'As black as Newgate's knocker', meaning very black indeed, a reference to the door knocker on the entrance to the prison; 'Newgate Knockers', heavily greased side whiskers curling back to, or over the ears, the name deriving from the popularity of the hairstyle among inmates; 'Newgate fashion', meaning two-by-two, a reference to the way inmates were conveyed to the prison linked together in twos; and a 'Newgate fringe', a style of wearing the hair under the chin and the neck, so called because it occupied the position of the rope when men were to be hanged.

Prisons: modern

Belmarsh, Western Way, Thamesmead, SE28, is a high security prison opened in 1991. Notable detainees have included Jeffrey Archer, Abu Hamza al-Masri, Manfo Kwaku Asiedu, Ronnie Biggs and Jonathan King. Operational capacity: 915. Tel: 020 8331 4400.

Brixton, Jebb Avenue, Brixton, SW2, opened in 1820 as the Surrey House of Correction. Today it serves local magistrates' courts, Inner London and Southwark Crown Courts, holding remand and trial prisoners. Operational capacity: 798. Tel: 020 8588 6000.

Holloway, Parkhurst Road, N7, is a women's prison in the London Borough of Islington. Opened in 1852 as a mixed prison, due to growing demand for space for female prisoners it became female-only in 1903. Prisoners included suffragettes such as Constance Markiewicz and Hanna Sheehy-Skeffington. In the 20th century, it was the site of five executions, most famously that of Ruth Ellis – the last woman in Britain to be hanged – on 13 July 1955. Rebuilt in the 1970s, it confusingly stands at the end of a road bearing the name of another prison: Parkhurst Road. Operational capacity: 485. Tel: 020 7979 4400.

Pentonville, Caledonian Road, N7, was built in 1842 to a design influenced by the 'separate system' developed at Eastern State Penitentiary in Philadelphia. Prisoners under sentence of death were not housed at Pentonville until the closure of Newgate in 1902, when it took over responsibility for executions in north London. Condemned cells were added and an execution room built to house the former Newgate gallows. Today Pentonville is a local prison, holding prisoners remanded by the local magistrates' and crown court, and those serving short sentences or beginning longer sentences. Operational capacity: 1152. Tel: 020 7023 7000.

Wandsworth, Heathfield Road, SW18, was built in 1851 as the Surrey House of Correction. It was designed according to the humane Panopticon principle with a number of corridors radiating from a central control point and each prisoner having toilet facilities. Subsequently, the toilets were removed to increase prison capacity and the prisoners had to engage in the process of 'slopping-out' until 1996. It was the site of 135 executions between 1878 and 1961: notable people executed include traitors Duncan Scott-Ford, William Joyce (Lord Haw-Haw) and John Amery and murderers George Chapman and John George Haigh. Derek Bentley was also killed here. The gallows were finally dismantled in 1998. The execution chamber is now used as a tea room for prison officers. In 1951 it was chosen as the site for a national stock of two types of implement for serious corporal punishment inflicted in prison under magistrates' orders, either as part of the original sentence or as disciplinary punishment under the prison rules: the birch and cat o' nine tails. Great Train Robber Ronnie Biggs (see Buckinghamshire) escaped from Wandsworth in 1965. The prison's operational capacity is in excess of 1400, making it the largest prison in London, and the second largest in Britain after Liverpool. Tel: 020 8588 4000.

Wormwood Scrubs, Du Cane Road, W12, is a Category B local prison (i.e. an establishment that receives prisoners from the courts, either on remand or after sentencing). It was built in the 1880s using prison labour and housed both male and female prisoners until 1902. Operational capacity: 1239. Its most famous inmate was probably George Blake, the former Dutch-British spy who was in fact a double agent for the Soviet Union. Exposed in 1959 by Polish defector Michael Goleniewski, in 1961 he was sentenced to 42 years' imprisonment by the Lord Chief Justice, Lord Parker of Waddington; the sentence was said by newspapers to represent one year for each of the agents killed when he betrayed them, although this claim appears to be an invention. This was the longest sentence ever handed down by a British court, until terrorist Nezar Hindawi was sentenced to 45 years in 1986 for the attempted bombing of an El Al jet. Five years later Blake escaped from Wormwood Scrubs with the help of Pat Pottle, Michael Randle and Sean Bourke, three members of the Committee of 100 whom he had met in Egypt two years before. Blake fled to the USSR, divorced his wife, with whom he had three children, and started a new life. In 1990 he published his autobiography *No Other Choice.* As of 2006 he was still living in Moscow, on a KGB pension, and remained a committed Marxist-Leninist. Blake denied being a traitor, insisting that he had never felt British: 'To betray, you first have to belong. I never belonged.' Tel: 020 8588 3200.

Queen's House — See National Maritime Museum

Railway stations — There are around 350 stations served by National Rail in the Greater London area, of which all can be reached from one of the main central stations. Nine of the ten busiest UK stations are in London. The following are the main central London stations:

Charing Cross, WC2, is the main line terminal for trains from Kent. At its southern end it meets Hungerford Bridge, which all trains serving the station must cross. The original station building was built on the site of Hungerford Market by the South Eastern Railway and opened on 11 January 1864. It was designed by Sir John Hawkshaw, with a single span wrought-iron roof arching over the six platforms on its relatively cramped site.

Euston, NW1, is the southern terminus of the West Coast Main Line. It has 18 platforms and is the main rail gateway from London to the West Midlands, the northwest and southern Scotland. The original station was opened on 20 July 1837, as the terminus of the London and Birmingham Railway constructed by Robert Stephenson. It was designed by classically trained architect Philip Hardwick, with a 200ft (60m) long engine shed by structural engineer Charles Fox and at the entrance a Greek-style arch with four Doric columns and standing 70ft (21m) high. In 1962, amid much public outcry, the old station – including the famous Euston Arch – was demolished and replaced by a new building, which opened in 1968.

Fenchurch Street, EC3, is a terminus for services to East London and south Essex in the City of London. Uniquely among London termini, it does not have a direct link to the London Underground. The station was the first to be constructed inside the City; originally designed by William Tite and opened on 20 July 1841 for the London and Blackwall Railway, replacing a nearby terminus at Minories opened in July 1840, it was rebuilt in 1854 to a design by George Berkeley with a vaulted roof and a new main façade. The station's four platforms are arranged on two islands elevated on a viaduct.

King's Cross, NW1, is the southern terminus of the East Coast Main Line. It has 11 platforms and is immediately adjacent to St Pancras station. The former King's Cross Thameslink station, five minutes' walk to the east, closed in 2007. The station serves the north and east of Britain, including Cambridge, Peterborough, Hull, Doncaster, York, Leeds, Darlington, Durham, Newcastle, Edinburgh, Aberdeen and Inverness. King's Cross was originally designed and built as the London hub of the Great Northern Railway and terminus of the East Coast Main Line. It was designed by Lewis Cubitt and constructed in 1851–2 on the site of a former fever and smallpox hospital. The main part of the station was opened on 14 October 1852 and replaced a temporary terminus at Maiden Lane opened on 8 August 1850. According to legend, King's Cross is built on the site of Boudica's final battle; alternatively her body is buried under one of its platforms, possibly platforms 8, 9 and 10. The adjacent King's Cross St Pancras Underground station was the scene of a major fire in 1987, in which 31 people died. The original King's Cross was a monument to George IV erected in 1830 at the junction of Euston Road, St Pancras Road and Pentonville Road. The station features in the Harry Potter books, by J K Rowling, as the starting point of the Hogwarts Express, which uses a secret platform $9^3/_4$, located by passing through the barrier between platforms 9 and 10.

Liverpool Street, EC2, is an 18 platform mainline station in the northeast of the City of London, with entrances on Bishopsgate and Liverpool Street itself. The station was first opened on 2 February 1874 by the Great Eastern Railway. It serves the east of England, including Stansted Airport, Cambridge, Lowestoft, Great Yarmouth, Norwich, Ipswich, Chelmsford, Colchester and Braintree, as well as many suburban stations in northeast London, and is one of the busiest commuter stations in London.

London Bridge, SE1, the oldest station in London, was opened in 1836. Originally two separate stations, it has both through and terminal platforms. The through platforms (numbered 1–6) to the north of the station are served by trains originating or terminating at Cannon Street and Charing Cross, mostly suburban services to southeast London and Kent. These platforms are also served by services which connect Bedford and Luton with Brighton via central London. The terminal platforms (numbered 8–16) to the south are mostly served by services to south London and the south coast.

Marylebone, NW1, is located midway between the mainline stations at Euston and Paddington. Opened in 1899, it was the terminus of the Great Central Railway's new London extension main line, the last major railway line to be built into London prior to the Channel Tunnel Rail Link. The station serves routes to Aylesbury, High Wycombe, Bicester, Banbury, Leamington Spa, Stratford-upon-Avon, Birmingham (Snow Hill) and Kidderminster. In 1964 several scenes in the Beatles film *A Hard Day's Night* were filmed at Marylebone station.

Paddington, W2, dates to 1854, when it was built as the London terminus for Brunel's Great Western Railway. It has 18 platforms and it is the London terminus for long-distance trains to the West Country, Bristol, Bath and south Wales, and for shorter distance commuter services to west London and the Thames Valley. Two services from Paddington serve Heathrow Airport; the Heathrow Express travels non-stop while Heathrow Connect runs along the same route but calls at intermediate stations.

St Pancras, NW1, became the London terminus of Eurostar and the Channel Tunnel Rail Link in October 2007. It is also the southern terminus of the Midland Main Line and the main departure point from London for services to the East Midlands, Sheffield and other parts of Yorkshire. St Pancras includes two of the most celebrated structures built in Britain in the Victorian era. The main trainshed (completed 1868 and has four platforms), by engineer William Henry Barlow, was the largest single-span structure built up to that time. In front of it is St Pancras Chambers, formerly the Midland Grand Hotel (built 1868–77), one of the most impressive examples of Victorian Gothic architecture. Designed by George Gilbert Scott, the building is primarily Gothic in style while also incorporating other features from a variety of periods and countries. When the station was officially reopened as St Pancras International on 6 November 2007, by Queen Elizabeth II, actor Timothy West gave an introductory speech in the guise of William Henry Barlow. The ten-year reconstruction, mostly in order to cater for the unusually long Eurostar trains, was estimated to have cost around £800m. A statue of poet John Betjeman, a leading campaigner to save the station in the 20th century, was unveiled at the opening ceremony.

Victoria, SW1, opened in 1862. The eastern side (platforms 1–8) is the terminus for services to Kent, the western side (platforms 9–19) for lines to Surrey and Sussex, including Gatwick Airport and Brighton. Victoria also serves as the London terminus for the Venice Simplon Orient Express, from Platform 2, the longest platform in the station. On 18 February 1991 an IRA bomb exploded in a litter bin at the station, killing one man, David Corner, and injuring 38.

Waterloo, SE1, in the London Borough of Lambeth, is named after the Battle of Waterloo in which Napoleon was defeated near Brussels. (In 1998, when it still served as London's gateway for train passengers from France and Belgium, French politician Florent Longuepée wrote to Prime Minister Tony Blair demanding unsuccessfully that the station be renamed on the grounds that the name was insensitive to French visitors.) The original mainline station was opened on 11 July 1848 by the London and South Western Railway. Construction began on a new station in 1900 and continued until 1922, with the new station boasting 21 platforms and a concourse nearly 800ft (244m) long. However, it was badly damaged during World War II and required considerable reconstruction thereafter. A large four-faced clock hangs in the middle of the main concourse, and meeting 'under the clock at Waterloo station' was a traditional rendezvous for people planning to travel together or arriving from separate locations. Waterloo International, designed by Nicholas Grimshaw and until 2007 the London terminus for Eurostar trains to Belgium and France, is to be used by the South West main line.

Rainham Hall — The Broadway, Rainham. An elegant Georgian house built in 1729 to a symmetrical plan with wrought iron gates, carved porch and interior panelling. It is currently managed by the National Trust. Tel: 01494 528051.

Ratcliff Highway Murders — The Highway, E1. Seven victims were murdered in two incidents on this street in present-day Stepney in December 1811. John Williams, a lodger at the Pear Tree public house, was arrested but hanged himself before his trial. The incident was a spur to the eventual forming of the Metropolitan Police in 1829.

Red House — Red House Lane, Bexleyheath. Commissioned by William Morris in 1859 and designed by Philip Webb, Red House was the home of the Arts and Crafts movement. It is constructed of warm red brick, under a steep red-tiled roof, with an emphasis on natural materials and a strong Gothic influence. The garden was designed to 'clothe' the house with a series of subdivided areas which still clearly exist. Inside, the house retains many of the original features and fixed items of furniture designed by Morris and Webb, as well as wall paintings and stained glass by Burne-Jones. Originally surrounded by orchards and countryside, Red House and its garden now provide an oasis in a suburban environment. Tel: 020 8304 9878.

Regent's Park — London NW1. Known as the 'jewel in the crown', Regent's Park like most of the other royal parks originally formed part of the vast chase appropriated by Henry VIII. Marylebone Park, as it was then known, remained a royal chase until 1646. The Regent's Park, 410 acres (166ha) in area, was designed in 1811 by John Nash after the Prince Regent asked three architects to submit plans for redeveloping Marylebone Park. Nash's bold and grandiose plan caught the Prince's imagination, although the original design was never completed. Of the buildings and monuments within the park, only two villas, St John's Lodge and The Holme, remain from John Nash's original conception. Today the park boasts an open air theatre, bandstands, a lakeside theatre, puppet shows and London Zoo (see separate entry). The main development in the 20th century was the creation, in the 1930s, of Queen Mary's Gardens; the stunning rose gardens, with more than 30,000 roses of 400 varieties, were laid out on a site vacated by the Royal Botanic Society. The park is the largest outdoor sports area in London; the community sports pavilion known as The Hub opened in 2005 and there are nearly 100 acres (40ha) of sports pitches.

Richmond upon Thames — One of the most attractive of the outer London boroughs and the only one which spans the Thames, Richmond's boundary extends from Hammersmith Bridge to Hampton Court. The London Borough of Richmond upon Thames was formed in 1965 by the merger of the Middlesex borough of Twickenham with the Surrey boroughs of Richmond upon Thames and Barnes. To the east and south lies Richmond Park; to the north, the wide green lawns and playing fields of the Old Deer Park run down to the Thames, and beyond it lie Kew Gardens (see separate entry). On the west, rising above the river are the Terrace Gardens, laid out in the 1880s and extended down to the Thames 40 years later; the broad gravel walk along the top is earlier and the view west towards Windsor has long been famous. Arts and entertainment have flourished in Richmond over the centuries, and it is now the home of several theatres, a television centre, a film studio and art galleries.

Ritz, The

Piccadilly, W1. The Ritz hotel opened its doors on 24 May 1906 on the Piccadilly site of the Walsingham House Hotel, formerly the Bath Hotel. Conceived by renowned hotelier César Ritz, the Ritz owes its architectural design to the partnership formed in 1900 between Frenchman Charles Mewes and Englishman Arthur Davis. Ritz made several innovations, including bathrooms for every guest room, double glazing, a sophisticated ventilation system, walk-in wardrobes, and brass, rather than wooden beds. Styled in the manner of a French chateau, with large copper lions at each corner of a roof decorated by soaring chimneys and projecting dormers, the hotel was one of the first major steel-framed buildings in London. Throughout its history the Ritz has attracted the famous and the fashionable. During its early years, it enjoyed the patronage of Edward VII and the English aristocracy. King Alfonso of Spain and Queen Amelie of Portugal met in the hotel; Anna Pavlova, the Russian prima ballerina, danced here; the Aga Khan and Paul Getty had suites; and Churchill, de Gaulle and Eisenhower held summit meetings in the Marie-Antoinette Suite during World War II. The Ritz also became the favourite of Hollywood stars: Charlie Chaplin required 40 policemen to escort him through crowds of fans into the hotel in 1921, Noel Coward wrote songs at the hotel and Tallulah Bankhead sipped champagne from her slipper during a press conference in the 1950s. In 1995 the Ritz was returned to private British ownership when it was bought by Sir David and Sir Frederick Barclay's private company Ellerman Investments; the hotel has since undergone complete restoration. In January 2002, it became the first hotel to receive a Royal Warrant for Banqueting and Catering services, awarded by the Prince of Wales. Tel: 020 7493 8181.

Rivers

The **Fleet** rises from two springs on Hampstead Heath and is directed into two reservoirs, Highgate Ponds and Hampstead Ponds. From the ponds the waters flow underground and join beneath Kentish Town and King's Cross before continuing down Farringdon Road and Farringdon Street, and eventually joining the Thames beneath Blackfriars Bridge. The Fleet is the largest of London's subterranean rivers at 4 miles (6km) in length. In its former glory days it was a major London river but nowadays the river, which gave its name to Fleet Street, can only be heard through a grating in Ray Street, Farringdon, EC1, in front of the Coach and Horses pub. Other underground rivers include Counter's Creek (Kensal Green to Sands End, Chelsea), the Effra (Herne Hill to Deptford), Falconbrook (Tooting Bec Common to Battersea), Neckinger (Southwark to St Saviour's Dock, near tower Bridge), Tyburn (South Hampstead to Pimlico – near Vauxhall Bridge – via St James's Park) and the Westbourne (Hampstead to Chelsea via Hyde Park and Sloane Square).

The **Lee** (also known as the Lea) flows through the London boroughs of Enfield, Waltham Forest, Haringey, Hackney, Newham and Tower Hamlets. Its name is generally given as the Lea at its source in Bedfordshire but it becomes the Lee on entering Hertfordshire and flowing through Essex into London, although why this should be appears nothing more than tradition. See also Bedfordshire.

The **Rom** rises to the north of Romford and flows through it underground in a man-made channel. To the south of the town centre it flows under Roneo Corner. At Eastbrookend Country Park it is joined by a tributary, known locally as the Ravensbourne, which rises in Ardleigh Green and flows through Emerson Park and Harrow Lodge Park. The Rom then continues under the name of the River Beam, forming the boundary between the London Boroughs of Havering and Barking & Dagenham before reaching the River Thames near the old Ford Motor Company works.

The **Thames**, Great Britain's second longest river, stretches for 215 miles (346km) from its source in the Cotswold Hills (GR: ST980994), 1 mile (1.6km) north of the village of Kemble, near Cirencester, to the open sea near Southend in Essex. The river flows east through Lechlade, Oxford (where it is known locally as the Isis), Abingdon, Wallingford, Reading, Henley-on-Thames, Marlow, Maidenhead, Windsor, Eton, Staines and Weybridge, before entering Greater London. From the outskirts of Greater London, the river passes Syon House, Hampton Court, Kingston, Richmond (with the famous view of the Thames from Richmond Hill) and Kew before flowing through central London past the Palace of Westminster to the Tower of London. Once clear of central London, it passes Greenwich and Dartford before entering the North Sea in a drowned estuary at Tilbury. Tributaries include the Churn, Leach, Coln, Windrush, Evenlode, Cherwell, Ock, Thame, Pang, Kennett, Loddon, Colne, Wey and Mole. Between Maidenhead and Windsor, the Thames supports an artificial secondary channel, known as the Jubilee River, for flood relief purposes. See also Bridges over the Thames, Thames Embankments, Thames Reaches, Thames Tunnels.

Roehampton University

Roehampton Lane, SW15. Created a university in 2004, the former University of Surrey Roehampton has its roots in Roehampton Institute of Higher Education (RIHE), a federation formed in 1975 of four teacher training colleges with 19th century origins. In order of foundation these were Whitelands College, an Anglican foundation, Southlands College, a Methodist foundation, Digby Stuart College, named after two pioneers in Catholic education, and Froebel College, established to promote the progressive educational philosophy of Friedrich Froebel.

From 1 January 2000 RIHE became an equal partner of the University of Surrey, changing its name to the University of Surrey Roehampton. Today Roehampton University has around 8500 students and is based on two major sites close to Richmond Park and Putney. Tel: 020 8392 3000.

Royal Academy — See Art Galleries

Royal Academy of Music — Marylebone Road, NW1. Founded in 1822 by Lord Burghersh at its first premises in Tenterden Street, Hanover Square, and granted a royal charter by George IV in 1830, the Academy moved to its present site in 1911. One of the leading music institutions in the world, the Royal Academy of Music (RAM) has students from over 50 countries, following diverse programmes including instrumental performance, conducting, composition, jazz, musical theatre and opera. Its facilities, which include the 450-seat Duke's Hall, the Sir Jack Lyons Theatre and two smaller concert spaces, were expanded in 2001 with the opening of the new 150-seat David Josefowitz recital hall and the York Gate Collections, a public museum of musical instruments and artefacts from the Academy's collections. Tel: 020 7873 7373.

Royal Albert Hall — Kensington Gore, SW7. Since its opening by Queen Victoria on 29 March 1871 the Royal Albert Hall (dedicated to Victoria's husband) has been Britain's premier concert hall. As well as hosting the Proms every summer since they were bombed out of the Queen's Hall in 1941, it has been used for classical and rock concerts, conferences, ballroom dancing, poetry recitals, education, ballet, opera and even a circus (Cirque du Soleil). It has hosted many sporting events, including boxing, wrestling (including the first Sumo wrestling tournament ever to be held outside Japan) and tennis. It hosts the annual Royal British Legion Festival of Remembrance, held the day before Remembrance Sunday. The hall is oval in shape, measuring 272ft (83m) by 238ft (72m) around the outside; it has a capacity of 8000 people but has accommodated as many as 9000 (although safety restrictions mean that the maximum permitted capacity is now 5544, including standing in the gallery). The great glass and wrought-iron dome roofing the hall is 135ft (41m) high. Around the outside of the hall is a great terracotta frieze depicting 'The Triumph of Arts and Sciences', in reference to the hall's dedication. Letters 1ft (0.3m) high above the frieze spell out the biblical quotations: 'Thine, O Lord, is the greatness, and the power, and the glory, and the victory, and the majesty: for all that is – in the heaven and in the earth is Thine. . . . The wise and their works are in the hand of God. . . . Glory be to God on high, and on earth peace.' Designed by Captain Francis Fowke and Colonel H Y Darracott Scott of the Royal Engineers, the hall was originally lit by gas; full electric lighting was installed in 1897. The hall also accommodates the largest pipe organ in the UK, originally built by 'Father' Henry Willis; recently rebuilt, it is now again the largest pipe organ in the British Isles with 9999 pipes. At the Royal Albert Hall on 15 September 1963 The Beatles and The Rolling Stones performed on the same bill for the only time. Tel (box office): 020 7589 8212.

Royal Courts of Justice — Strand, WC2. Designed by George Street in 1868 and situated on the north side of The Strand, the courts hear civil cases and criminal appeals. Opened by Queen Victoria in 1882, the Supreme Court is made up of the High Court, Court of Appeal and Crown Court. The High Court has three divisions: Queen's Bench, Family and Chancery. There are over 150 judges in the Royal Courts of Justice, a secret corridor known as the 'chicken run', and a wing named after St Thomas More. A tributary of the River Fleet reputedly runs under the building.

Royal Exchange — Threadneedle Street, EC3. Founded by Thomas Gresham in 1566 and given its royal designation by Elizabeth I in 1570. The first building was destroyed in the Great Fire in 1666; its replacement, designed by Edward Jerman, opened in 1669 but burned down in 1838. A third building, designed by Sir William Tite and completed in 1842, functioned as a trading centre until 1939 and is now occupied by luxury shops.

Royal Festival Hall — See Southbank Centre

Royal Observatory, The — See National Maritime Museum

Royal parks — Originally part of the Manor of Sheen, **Richmond Park** is probably the oldest of the royal parks and the one that has changed the least. First linked with royalty through Edward I, the 2500 acre (1000ha) area of wild heath and woodland was enclosed by Charles I in 1637 as a hunting park. With its herds of red and fallow deer it is one of London's most picturesque parks; it is also a designated Site of Special Scientific Interest, Special Area of Conservation and National Nature Reserve, with numerous ancient trees, especially oaks, supporting a wide range of rare wildlife. **Greenwich Park**, covering 183 acres (73ha), was enclosed by Henry VI in 1433; however deer were only introduced in 1515. James I commissioned significant remodelling of the park and its buildings, including commissioning Inigo Jones in 1616 to rebuild the old Tudor palace. The result, the Queen's House, can still be seen today. **Bushy Park** as it exists today is the second largest of the Royal Parks at 1099 acres (450ha) and was brought together when Henry VIII obtained Hampton Court Palace in 1529. James I made further alterations, including the annexing of a further 168 acres (68ha) on the Hampton side. A wall was also erected around the park. In 1532 Henry VIII acquired **St James's Park** to further indulge his love of hunting and built the Palace of St James's. Today the 58 acre (23ha) park is surrounded by three palaces – Westminster, St James's and Buckingham. The **Green Park** was originally a swampy burial ground for lepers, but by 1668 Charles II had enclosed it and stocked it with deer, again to indulge the regal passion for hunting. It covers 47 acres (19ha). Originally part of **Hyde Park** (see separate entry), **Kensington Gardens** cover 275 acres (111ha) and were shaped by Queen Caroline, wife of George II. In 1728, the gardens began to resemble their present form with the creation of the Serpentine and the Long Water. Marylebone Park, or **Regent's Park** as it is known today (see separate entry), again started life as part of the monarch's hunting grounds.

St George's Cathedral — Albany Street, NW1. Situated east of Regent's Park, the former Anglican Christ Church was consecrated in 1837. Since 1989 it has been a cathedral of the Antiochan Greek Orthodox Church. Tel: 0207 383 0403.

St Margaret's Church — Parliament Square, SW1. The parish church of the Houses of Parliament since 1614. Originally built as a church for the local people by the monks of Westminster Abbey, St Margaret's was rebuilt in the later 15th century. The Tudor structure was faced with Portland stone in the 1730s and the interior was restored by Sir George Gilbert Scott in 1877. The church has been part of the UNESCO Westminster World Heritage Site since 1987.

St John's Gate — St John's Lane, Clerkenwell, EC1. Built in 1504 by Prior Thomas Docwra as the south entrance to the inner precinct of the Priory of the Knights of St John (Knights Hospitallers). The substructure is of brick, the north and south façades of stone. After centuries of decay and much rebuilding, very little of the stone facing is original; heavily restored in the 19th century, the gate today is largely a Victorian recreation. The building has many historical associations, most notably as the original printing-house for Edward Cave's pioneering monthly the *Gentleman's Magazine*, and sometime workplace of Samuel Johnson. From 1701–09 it was the childhood home of painter William Hogarth. After many years' use as a tavern, the gate was acquired in the 1870s by the revived Order of St John and converted to serve as the headquarters and museum of the organisation and its offshoot, St John Ambulance. Most of the Tudor-style interiors, including the council chamber over the arch, are the result of refurbishment by J Oldrid Scott in the 1880s and 1890s. Tel: 0870 010 4950.

St Paul's Cathedral — St Paul's Churchyard, EC4. A cathedral dedicated to St Paul has overlooked the City of London since AD 604. Sometimes known as London Cathedral, the present cathedral, the fourth to occupy the site, was designed by Sir Christopher Wren and built 1675–1710, the previous cathedral having been destroyed in the Great Fire of London. The cathedral is built of Portland stone in English baroque style; it is 574ft (175m) long, with a nave 223ft (68m) in length, and is 365ft (111m) high. Both Admiral Nelson and the Duke of Wellington are buried at St Paul's, as are J M W Turner, Sir Arthur Sullivan and John Donne. Among other state celebrations St Paul's has hosted the 80th and 100th birthdays of Queen Elizabeth, the Queen Mother, the wedding of the Prince of Wales and Lady Diana Spencer and, most recently, the Thanksgiving for Queen Elizabeth II's Golden Jubilee. The Whispering Gallery, located within the dome 99ft (30m) above the cathedral's floor and 138ft (42m) in diameter, has famously unusual acoustic qualities whereby a whisper spoken at any point against its walls can be heard at any other point. Among the cathedrals' artworks is the painting *The Light of the World* by William Holman Hunt. The 1695 organ which Mendelssohn once played remains in use. St Paul's is the cathedral of the Diocese of London, which is made up of five episcopal areas: Willesden, Edmonton, Stepney, London and Kensington. The Bishop of Fulham is the suffragan bishop for the whole diocese. Tel: 020 7236 4128.

Savoy, The — Strand, WC2. Built next to his original Savoy Theatre by Richard D'Oyly Carte and opened in 1889, the Savoy was designed as a unique hotel where impeccable service was of paramount importance. César Ritz (later founder of the Ritz hotel) was commissioned as manager and renowned chef Georges-Auguste Escoffier was secured as head of restaurant services. Many of the hotel's 268 rooms and suites, with Art Deco touches throughout, have views overlooking the Thames. The hotel has its own road leading on to The Strand; this is the only thoroughfare in the UK where vehicles drive on the right hand side of the road. The hotel is currently part of the American Fairmont Group and reopened in 2009 after a major refurnishment that restored many of its Edwardian and Art Deco characteristics. Tel: 020 7836 4343.

Science Museum — Exhibition Road, SW7. One of three museums – the others are the National Railway Museum, York, and the National Media Museum, Bradford (see West Yorkshire) – which form the National Museum of Science & Industry (NMSI). The profits of the Great Exhibition of 1851 were used to purchase land in South Kensington to establish institutions devoted to the promotion and improvement of industrial technology. At the same time, the government set up a Science & Art Department which established the South Kensington Museum in 1857, from which the Science Museum and Victoria & Albert Museum developed. The objects on display were initially mostly art objects, but the 'science collections', as they were known, included models, apparatus, examples of materials, books and educational resources. The collections were boosted by an international exhibition in 1876 of scientific instruments. In 1884 the Patent Museum passed on its stock of patent models, including Stephenson's *Rocket* and Arkwright's original textile machinery. The arts and science collections gradually assumed their own identities to the extent that the Science Museum and the Victoria & Albert Museum were formally separated in 1909. A new building to house the Science Museum was formally opened by George V in 1928. The museum continued to expand its premises and its collections. In the early 1980s, objects from the Wellcome collection were placed on permanent display. A period of rapid expansion followed the National Heritage Act of 1983. New interactive galleries, such as Launch Pad and Flight Lab, were opened, supplementary exhibitions were initiated and the museum developed a busy programme of activities and events. New Galleries in 1996 included the imaginative 'Secret Life of the Home' and extensive new hands-on education facilities. The Wellcome Wing, designed by Richard MacCormac and dedicated to contemporary science and technology, was opened in 2000 in partnership with the Wellcome Trust (the world's largest medical research charity) and the Heritage Lottery Fund. Tel: 0870 870 4868.

Selfridges — Oxford Street, W1. The UK's second largest shop (after Harrods) was founded by American entrepreneur Harry Gordon Selfridge, and opened on 15 March 1909. The 540,000 sq ft (50,000 sq m) building, one of the UK's first steel-framed buildings, was designed by US architect Daniel Burnham. Selfridge's byword was 'the customer is always right', and the store was among the first to focus on making shopping a pleasurable experience, with attractively displayed merchandise and in-store exhibits such as Louis Blériot's monoplane and early demonstrations of television. Selfridge's provincial stores were sold to the John Lewis Partnership in the 1940s, and the Oxford Street store was acquired in 1951 by the Liverpool-based Lewis's chain of department stores, which was in turn taken over in 1965 by Charles Clore's Sears group. Between 1998 and 2003, Selfridges opened stores at the Trafford Centre and Exchange Square, Manchester, and an architecturally innovative 160,000 sq ft (14,500 sq m) store in the Birmingham Bull Ring shopping complex. In 2003, the chain was acquired by Galen Weston for £598 million. Tel: 0870 837 7377.

Selsdon Man A term coined by Harold Wilson to refer to the anti-interventionist policies of Conservative leader Edward Heath, developed at a policy retreat held at the Selsdon Park Hotel in early 1970. This phrase, intended by Wilson to evoke the 'primitive throwback' qualities of anthropological discoveries such as Piltdown Man and Swanscombe Man, is part of a political tradition of referring to political trends by suffixing 'man'. See also Orpington Man.

Serpentine Gallery Kensington Gardens, W1. An art gallery focusing on modern and contemporary art. Housed in a classical 1934 tea pavilion and established in 1970, it takes its name from the nearby Serpentine lake. Notable artists who have been exhibited include Man Ray, Henry Moore, Andy Warhol, Bridget Riley, Allan McCollum and Damien Hirst. The gallery was set up by the Arts Council of Great Britain and in its early years was only open during the summer. In 1986, Julia Peyton Jones was appointed as director and under her the gallery was extensively refurbished. Since 2001 each summer the gallery has commissioned a temporary pavilion by leading architects; the 2008 pavilion was the first structure to be built in Britain by the internationally renowned Frank Gehry. Tel: 020 7402 6075.

Siege of Sidney Street A notorious gunfight in London's East End in 1911, popularly known as the 'Battle of Stepney'. It ended with the deaths of most of the members of an anarchist gang, and sparked a major political row over the involvement of the Home Secretary, Winston Churchill. The street battle was started by a small gang of Latvian anarchists under the leadership of Peter Piaktow, better known as Peter the Painter. In December 1910 they planned to rob a jeweller's shop at Houndsditch by tunnelling through the wall of an adjacent building. On 16 December, someone heard their hammering and informed the City of London Police. When the unarmed policemen arrived, Sergeant Bentley was fatally shot, and in an ensuing fight on the street, Sergeant Tucker and Constable Choate were killed (the killings were afterwards known as the Houndsditch Murders). Most of the members of the gang escaped, although their original leader, George Gardstein, was fatally shot by one of his own men. An intense search followed, and several members of the gang were soon captured. On 2 January 1911, an informant told police that two or three of the gang, possibly including Peter the Painter himself, were hiding at the flat of Mrs Betsy Gershon at 100 Sidney Street, Stepney. Worried that the suspects were about to flee, and expecting strong resistance to any attempt at capture, on 3 January 200 men cordoned off the area and the siege began. At dawn the battle commenced. The defenders, though heavily outnumbered, possessed superior weapons and great stores of ammunition. The Tower of London was called for backup, and word sent to Winston Churchill, who arrived to observe first hand and to offer advice – a rare example of a Home Secretary taking command decisions during a police operation. He also called in the Scots Guards. Six hours into the battle, fire broke out in the building. When the fire brigade arrived Churchill refused them access. The police stood with their guns aimed at the front door, waiting for the men inside to attempt their escape, but the door never opened. The remains of two members of the gang, Fritz Svaars and William Sokolow, were found inside. Mrs Gershon had earlier been released, but no sign of Peter the Painter was ever found.

Sir John Soane's Museum Lincoln's Inn Fields, WC2. Celebrated architect John Soane was born in 1753, the son of a bricklayer, and died in 1837 after a long and distinguished career including 45 years as Architect and Surveyor to the Bank of England. He designed this house in 1812 both to live in, and as a setting for his antiquities and works of art. After the death of his wife in 1815 – attributed by Soane to the actions of his surviving son George, a spendthrift and ne'er-do-well who publicly denounced his father as a copyist and charlatan – he lived here alone, constantly augmenting and rearranging his collections. Keen to ensure that George should not inherit the property, he determined instead to establish the house as a museum to which 'amateurs and students' should have access. Today it holds an eclectic collection of Egyptian, medieval and classical antiquities, 17th and 18th century and neoclassical sculpture, timepieces, furniture and paintings, laid out exactly as Sir John left it at his death. Tel: 020 7405 2107.

Soho An area of central London's West End in the borough of the City of Westminster, covering about 1 sq mile (2.6 sq km) and bounded by Oxford Street to the north, Regent Street to the west, Shaftesbury Avenue to the south and Charing Cross Road in the east. To the west is Mayfair, to the north Fitzrovia, to the southeast Holborn and to the south Leicester Square and Chinatown. The name Soho – reputedly deriving from the ancient hunting call 'Soho!', though by the time the name was first used, hunting had ceased in the area – first appears in the 17th century. The name is also believed to have come from the nickname of the Duke of Monmouth who used 'soho' as a rallying call for his men, and who in the 1600s was among the first to build in the area. For at least 200 years the name Soho was synonymous with the sex industry, and as well as prostitution a plethora of strip clubs (at its height in excess of 100) appeared in the 1960s. Since the early 1980s the area has undergone considerable transformation and is now a fashionable district of upmarket restaurants and media offices, although there are still a few 'clip joints' in the west of the area.

Southbank Centre A complex of artistic venues located on the south bank of the River Thames between County Hall and Waterloo Bridge. It comprises three main buildings: the Royal Festival Hall, the Queen Elizabeth Hall and The Hayward. The Royal Festival Hall was built as part of the Festival of Britain and was officially opened on 3 May 1951. The building underwent a substantial renovation 2005–07 in an attempt to obviate the noriously bad acoustics of the concert hall. The Queen

Elizabeth Hall, opened in March 1967, is situated next to the Festival Hall and hosts daily classical, jazz, and avant-garde music and dance performances. The smaller Purcell Room shares the same foyer as the QEH. See also The Hayward in Art Galleries

South Bank University — See London South Bank University

Southside House — Woodhayes Road, Wimbledon Common, SW19. A William and Mary style house rebuilt in 1665 by Robert Pennington and still occupied by his descendants, the Pennington-Mellor-Munthe families. Maintained largely unaltered and crowded with the family possessions of centuries, such as original furniture, Southside offers a wealth of fascinating stories. The house has associations with Queen Natalie of Serbia and her son Alexander, and the family also have mementoes from the Duke of Wharton, Lady Hamilton, Marie Antoinette and others. *The Story of San Michele* (1929), the best-selling memoir by Swedish doctor Axel Munthe (husband of Hilda Pennington), was written here. Tel: 020 8946 7643.

Southwark Cathedral — Montague Close, SE1. Situated on the south side of London Bridge, near Shakespeare's Globe and Tate Modern, the cathedral is the mother church of the Anglican Diocese of Southwark and is dedicated to St Saviour. The main structure of today's church was built between 1220 and 1420. In 1890 the Prince of Wales laid the foundation stone of the new nave (built by Sir Arthur Blomfield). In 1897 St Saviour's became the pro-cathedral of South London. In 1904 an Act of Parliament created the new Diocese of Southwark and in 1905 the church became the Cathedral and Collegiate Church of St Saviour and St Mary Overie. Edward Talbot, Bishop of Rochester, was enthroned as the first Bishop of Southwark. Tel: 020 7367 6700.

Southwark Roman Catholic Cathedral — Westminster Bridge Road, SE1. Situated close to the Imperial War Museum and dedicated to St George, the cathedral is the mother church of the Roman Catholic Province of Southwark which covers the Archdiocese of Southwark (all of London south of the Thames including Kent and north Surrey) and the Dioceses of Arundel and Brighton, Portsmouth and Plymouth. The original St George's Church was opened in 1848 by Bishop (later Cardinal) Wiseman and in 1850 became the first Catholic cathedral established in England since the Reformation. Designed by Augustus Pugin, it was badly bombed during World War II. The rebuilt cathedral was opened in 1958. Pope John Paul II visited St George's in 1982 and the Dalai Lama in 1998. Tel: 020 7928 5256.

Spencer House — St James's Place, SW1. Built 1756–66 for John, 1st Earl Spencer, an ancestor of Diana, Princess of Wales, the 18th century town house is situated a short distance from St James's Palace, Buckingham Palace and the Palace of Westminster, and has a splendid terrace and garden with magnificent views of Green Park. John Vardy was responsible for the design of the exterior and of the ground floor rooms, including some of the furniture. James 'Athenian' Stuart, newly returned from Greece, superseded Vardy as Spencer's architect in 1758. As a result, the house became the first in London whose interiors feature accurate Greek detail, making it one of the pioneer examples of neoclassical architecture. Tel: 020 7514 1958.

Sport

general — London has an ice hockey team, **London Racers** (who play at Lee Valley Ice Centre), and a basketball team, **London Towers** (who play at Crystal Palace). From 1991–8 the **London Monarchs** competed in American football's NFL Europe, winning the inaugural World Bowl. Today, the **London O's** are the reigning champions of the British American Football League. Every April since 1981, London has hosted one of the world's largest mass-participation marathons, the **London Marathon**, and the Crystal Palace Arena holds athletics grands prix. The River Thames is the venue for the **Boat Race**, held between Oxford and Cambridge universities every year from Putney to Mortlake. The **London Triathlon** has also become an established annual event.

cricket — London has two Test cricket grounds: Lord's and The Oval (see separate entries). Situated in Kennington, The Oval, home of Surrey CCC, also hosted many early FA Cup finals as well as England's first home international football match. The Oval also holds an annual exhibition match for Australian rules football.

Middlesex County Cricket Club was founded in 1864 as one of the original teams in the County Championship. Its limited overs team is called Middlesex Crusaders. In 2008, Middlesex became Twenty20 Cup champions, thereby also becoming the first county cricket club to qualify for both the Stanford Super Series and the Twenty20 Champions League. The club is based at Lord's, but also plays home games at Uxbridge, the Walker Ground, Southgate, and The Old Deer Park, Richmond.

football — **Arsenal** were founded as Dial Square in 1886 by workers at the Royal Arsenal in Woolwich, but were renamed Royal Arsenal shortly afterwards. They renamed themselves again to Woolwich Arsenal after turning professional in 1891. The club joined the Second Division of the Football League in 1893 and won promotion to the First Division in 1904. In 1913 they moved across the Thames to the new Arsenal Stadium in Highbury, north London, dropping 'Woolwich' from their name the following year. Nicknamed The Gunners, they play in red and white. One of England's most successful clubs, Arsenal won League and FA Cup doubles in 1971, 1998 and 2002, and in 2004 won the Premiership having gone through the entire season undefeated. In May 2006 they left Highbury for their current home, the Emirates Stadium in nearby Ashburton Grove, Holloway. Arsenal Ladies have had considerable success in recent years and have had several international players on their books. Tel: 020 7704 4040.

Barnet were founded in 1888 and moved to the club's current ground at Underhill, Barnet Lane, in 1907 when they were known as Barnet Alston FC. They changed their name to Barnet FC in 1917 and eventually joined the Fourth Division of the Football League on winning the GM Vauxhall Conference championship in 1991. Nicknamed The Bees, their colours are black and orange. Tel: 0870 1700 400.

Brentford were founded in 1889 to serve as a winter pursuit for the Brentford Rowing Club; the club moved to its present home ground, Griffin Park, in 1904. They entered the Football League in 1902 as founder members of the Third Division South. Nicknamed The Bees, they play in red and white striped shirts and black shorts. Tel: 08453 456442.

Charlton Athletic were founded in 1905 and entered the Football League in 1921. The club's anthem is 'The Red Robin' and the club poem is 'The Charge Of The Light Brigade', as it mentions the 'valley of death'. Variously known as The Addicks, Valiants and Robins – and occasionally as The Valleymen or Haddocks, the club play in red shirts and white shirts. Their home ground since 1919 has been The Valley, Charlton, to which they returned in 1992 after ground-sharing for the previous seven years with Crystal Palace and West Ham. Tel: 020 8333 4000.

Chelsea were founded on 14 March 1905 at the Rising Sun pub (now The Butcher's Hook), opposite today's main entrance to the ground on the Fulham Road, and were elected to the Football League in the same year. The Premiership club's home ground is Stamford Bridge in Fulham Road, West London, where they have played since their foundation. Despite their name, the club is based just outside the Royal Borough of Kensington and Chelsea, in Hammersmith and Fulham. In 2003, the club was bought by Russian oil tycoon Roman Abramovich. The Blues, or previously The Pensioners, play in blue. Their Premiership wins in 2005 and 2006 were the first since their only previous League title in 1955. Tel: 0870 300 2322.

Crystal Palace were founded in 1905, with their home ground at the Crystal Palace stadium, in Sydenham, on the site of the Crystal Palace (see The Great Exhibition). The team played in the Southern League until 1920, when they were promoted to Division Three of The Football League. The Eagles (formely The Glaziers or Groundkeepers) were forced to relocate from their original base in 1915, and after a brief move to Herne Hill Athletics Stadium (1915–18) and The Nest (1918–24), they eventually settled at their present home, Selhurst Park, in Whitehorse Lane, South Norwood, in 1924. Their traditional colours, claret and blue, have been replaced in recent years by red and blue. Tel: 020 8768 6000.

Fulham were founded in 1879 as Fulham St Andrew's Church Sunday School; having shortened the name to its present form in 1888, the club first played at their current ground, Craven Cottage (once the woodland site of a villa built in 1780 by the 6th Baron Craven), in 1896. The Cottagers joined the Football League in 1907 and play in white shirts and black shorts. Tel: 0870 442 1222.

Leyton Orient were founded by members of Glyn Cricket Club in 1881. The team has had several name changes since, first Eagle Football Club in 1886, then Orient Football Club in 1888 and Clapton Orient in 1898 before settling on the name Leyton Orient after World War II. A further renaming back to Orient took place in 1966 after the Borough of Leyton was absorbed into the London Borough of Waltham Forest. The club finally reverted to Leyton Orient in 1987. The O's joined the Football League in 1905 and currently play at the Matchroom Stadium, Brisbane Road, Leyton, so called after the name of chairman Barry Hearn's sports promotion company. They play in an all-red home strip. Tel: 0871 310 1881.

Millwall were founded in 1885 as Millwall Rovers and joined the Football League in 1920. Nicknamed The Lions, their traditional colours are blue and white (the club's original players being largely Scottish). Their home ground since 1993 has been the New Den Stadium, Bermondsey; their previous ground was The Den, New Cross, SE14, to which they moved in 1910. Tel: 020 7232 1222.

Queens Park Rangers were founded in 1882 as St Jude's but soon changed their name to reflect the area of North Kensington where most of the players came from. QPR became a professional team in 1889 and settled at Loftus Road in 1917. The Super Hoops (formerly the R's or Rangers), so nicknamed after their blue and white hooped shirts, joined the Football League in 1920 and still play at Loftus Road (Rangers Stadium), Shepherd's Bush. Tel: 020 8743 0262.

Tottenham Hotspur were founded in 1882 as Hotspur FC. The club turned professional in 1895 and in 1899 made their final ground move to a former market garden in nearby High Road, Tottenham. In time the ground adopted the name of a local thoroughfare, White Hart Lane. In 1900 Tottenham won the Southern League title and crowned this achievement the next year by winning the FA Cup – the only non-League club to do so since the formation of the Football League. Spurs, sometimes also known as the Cockerels or Lilywhites for their white shirts, joined the Football League in 1908 and were the first club in the 20th century to achieve the League and Cup double, winning both competitions in the 1960–61 season. In 1963, Spurs became the first English club to win a European trophy – the European Cup Winners' Cup. Tel: 0870 420 5000.

West Ham United were founded in 1895 as the works side Thames Ironworks FC. They turned professional on entering the Southern League Second Division in 1898, which they won at the first attempt. In June 1900 Thames Ironworks FC was relaunched as West Ham United. The club played their games at the Memorial Ground in Plaistow but moved to the Boleyn Ground, originally named the Castle, in 1904. The original gates to the ground, with the original Hammers crest (now painted in claret and blue) can be seen in Grange Road, E13. The Hammers, sometimes called the Irons, were elected to the the Football League in 1919 and in 1923 took part in the first FA Cup final to be held at Wembley Stadium (see separate entry). Tel: 020 8548 2748.

Wimbledon are now renamed MK Dons and are situated in Milton Keynes (see Buckinghamshire).

rugby league

Traditionally, southern England played only the 15-a-side game until 1980 when it admitted its first top-flight professional London club in the guise of Fulham, playing at Craven Cottage, the home of Fulham FC. The club changed its name to London Crusaders and then London

Broncos, yet while being a member of the elite Super League competition, it ran into financial difficulties and in 2005 it merged with Harlequins to create **Harlequins Rugby League** (they also play at The Stoop). Another London club in the upper echelons of the game is **London Skolars** (based in Haringey) who play in National League Two, while **Greenwich Admirals** (Woolwich), **Kingston Warriors** (Esher) and **South London Storm** (Croydon) all play in the Rugby League Conference.

rugby union

Four of the 12 clubs in the Guinness Premiership have London origins. London Irish, Saracens and Wasps share football grounds just outside the boundaries of Greater London, but in the metropolitan area. Harlequins, relegated to National Division One after the 2004–05 season, but promoted back for 2006–07, still play in Greater London. In more recent years, a modern tradition has seen all four London clubs play at Twickenham during the first round of the Guinness Premiership, in a double-header.

Apart from the elite clubs, London Welsh compete in National League One. The English national rugby stadium in Twickenham is the venue for the England national side's home matches, and is also host to the Varsity Match between Oxford and Cambridge as well as the English schools Daily Mail Cup final.

Harlequins were founded in 1866 as Hampstead Football Club and renamed in 1870. Formerly based at Twickenham, since 1963 they have played at the Twickenham Stoop (officially titled the Stoop Memorial Ground until 2005, but known as simply The Stoop) in Richmond, named after former England international Adrian Stoop, also a Harlequins player and president. The club colours are a mosaic of sky blue, magenta, chocolate brown, French grey, black and bright green, Tel: 020 8410 6000.

London Irish were founded in 1898 for the young Irish people of the city in a period that saw several similar clubs in London founded, including London Welsh and London Scottish. London Irish currently play at the Madejski Stadium in Reading. The club's mascot is an Irish wolfhound called Digger. The Exiles play in green and navy and are based in Sunbury. Tel: 01932 783034.

London Scottish were founded in 1878 in MacKay's Tavern, London. In 2000 the reformed amateur club rejoined the leagues at the bottom of the pyramid after the professional club merged with London Irish, and has since progressed up through the divisions to London Division One. London Scottish share a ground with Richmond.

London Welsh, founded in 1885, play in red, black and white at the Old Deer Park, Kew Road, Richmond. Tel: 020 8940 2368.

Richmond, founded in 1861, are one of the oldest football clubs in the world and took part in the first ever football match played under Football Association rules (against Barnes on 19 December 1863) before joining the Rugby Football Union in 1971. The first English club to turn professional, in 1996, they and London Scottish merged with London Irish in 1999. The amateur club was refounded in 2000 and shares the Athletic Ground, Richmond – their home since 1889 – with London Scottish. Tel: 020 8332 7112.

Saracens were founded in 1876 by the Old Boys of the Philological School in Marylebone and currently play at Vicarage Road, Watford. Their club colours are black and red. Tel: 01923 475222.

London Wasps were founded in 1867 as Wasps at the now defunct Eton and Middlesex Tavern in North London. Renamed in 1999 after turning professional, London Wasps have since won the Guinness Premiership in 2003, 2004, 2005 amd 2008 and the Heineken Cup in 2004 and 2007. They play at Adams Park, High Wycombe, Buckinghamshire. Tel: 020 8993 8298.

tennis

The **All England Lawn Tennis and Croquet Club**, based in Wimbledon, is home of the Wimbledon Championships, the oldest and arguably most prestigious event in the sport of tennis. Held every June and July in London, the tournament is the third Grand Slam event played each year, preceded by the Australian Open and the French Open, and followed by the US Open. The tournament lasts for two weeks, subject to extensions for rain, and is the only Grand Slam event currently played on grass. **Queen's Club** in West Kensington hosts the annual Queen's Club Championships that precedes, and often acts as a warm-up for Wimbledon,

Statues: Inner London

Albert Hall, SW7 Prince Albert by Joseph Durham (1863).
Bank of England, EC2 Stone statues of *Sir John Soane* by Sir William Reid Dick (1937) and *King William III* by Sir Henry Cheere (1735).
Banqueting House, Whitehall, SW1 Lead bust of *Charles I* by unknown sculptor, placed in 1950.
Belgrave Square, SW1 Bronze of *Simon Bolivar* by Hugo Daini (1974).
Birdcage Walk, SW1 Bronze of *Field Marshal Earl Alexander of Tunis* by James Butler (1985).
Bloomsbury Square, WC1 *Charles James Fox* by Richard Westmacott (1816).
Cannon Street, EC4 Bronze mask of *Winston Churchill* by Frank Dobson (1959) over the entrance to Bracken House.
Carey Street/Serle Street, WC2 Stone figure of *Sir Thomas More* by Robert Smith (1866).
Carlton Gardens, SW1 Bronze of *General Charles de Gaulle* by Angela Connor (1993); bronze of *George VI* by William McMillan (1955).
Cavendish Square, W1 Bronze of *William George Bentinck* by Thomas Campbell (1851).
Charing Cross Road, WC2 Bronze of *Sir Henry Irving* by Thomas Brock (1910) by the St Martin's Place side of the National Portrait Gallery.
Chelsea Embankment, SW3 Bronze of *Thomas Carlyle* by Sir Joseph Boehm (1882); seated bronze of *Sir Thomas More* by L Cubitt Bevis (1969).
Chelsea Hospital, SW3 Bronze of *King Charles II* in Roman costume by Grinling Gibbons (1676).
Chiswick House, W4 Stone of *Inigo Jones* by John Rysbrack (1729).
City Road, EC1 *John Wesley* by John Adams-Acton (1891).

Cockspur Street, SW1 Bronze equestrian of *George III* by Matthew Cotes Wyatt (1836).
Commercial Road, E1 Bronze of *Clement Attlee* by Frank Forster (1988) outside Limehouse Library.
Cornhill (no. 32), EC3 Mahogany carving of *The Bronte Sisters in Conversation with William Makepeace Thackeray* by Walter Gilbert (1939).
Crystal Palace Park, SE19 Marble bust of *Sir Joseph Paxton* by W F Woodington (1869).
Downing Street, SW1 *Mountbatten* by Franta Belsky (1983) outside Foreign Office.
Euston Station, NW1 Bronze of *Robert Stephenson* by Baron Marochetti (1871).
Festival Hall, SE1 Bronze of *Frederic Chopin* by B Kubica (1975).
Fleet Street, EC4 Stone of *Elizabeth I* by William Kerwin (1586) over the vestry porch of St Dunstan in the West. This is the oldest statue of a monarch in London and, in fact, the oldest outdoor statue of any kind in the city.
Fleet Street (nos 143–4), EC4 Stone of *Mary, Queen of Scots*, placed by an admirer, Sir John Tollemache Sinclair (1880).
Greenwich Park, SE10 Foggit Tor granite of *William IV* by Samuel Nixon, erected in King William IV Street in 1844 and moved to present site in 1938.
Grosvenor Gardens, SW1 Bronze equestrian of *Marechal Foch* by G Malliaard (1930).
Grosvenor Square, W1 Bronze of *F D Roosevelt* by Sir William Reid Dick; bronze of *General Dwight D Eisenhower* by Robert Dean (1989).
Guildhall, EC2 Limewood carvings of mythical giants, *Gog and Magog*, by David Evans, replacing those burned in 1940; *Winston Churchill* by Oscar Nemon (1955).
Hamilton Gardens, W1 Bronze of *George Gordon Byron* by Richard Belt (1880).
Hanover Square, W1 Bronze of *William Pitt the Younger* by Francis Chantrey (1831).
Highgate Cemetery, N6 Bronze of *Karl Marx* by Laurence Bradshaw (1956).
Holborn Circus, EC1 Equestrian bronze of *Prince Albert* by Charles Bacon (1874).
Horse Guards Parade, SW1 Bronze of *Field Marshal Earl Kitchener* by John Tweed (1926); equestrian bronze of *Field Marshal Viscount Wolseley* by Sir William Goscombe John (1920); equestrian bronze of *Field Marshal Frederick Sleigh Roberts* by Harry Bates (completed by Henry Poole in 1924).
Houses of Parliament, SW1 Equestrian bronze of *Richard I* in Old Palace Yard by Carlo Marochetti (1861); bronze of *Oliver Cromwell* outside Westminster Hall by Sir Hamo Thornycroft (1899). Statue of *George VI* by William Reid Dick (1947) stands opposite *Richard I* outside the grounds.
Hyde Park Corner, SW1 Bronze of *The Duke of Wellington* on his horse, Copenhagen, by J E Boehm (1888).
Kensington Gardens, SW7 Bronze of *Sir Winston and Lady Churchill* by Oscar Nemon (1981) situated near Hyde Park Gate; seated statue of *Queen Victoria* by her daughter, Princess Louise (1893); *Albert Memorial* designed by George Gilbert Scott, with seated statue of *Albert* begun by Baron Marochetti and completed by John Foley (see separate entry).
Kensington Palace, W8 Bronze of *William III* by Heinrich Baucke (1907) presented by Kaiser Wilhelm II to his uncle, Edward VII.
King Charles Street, SW1 Bronze figure of *Robert Clive* by John Tweed (1912).
King Edward Street, EC1 Granite figure of *Sir Rowland Hill*, founder of the penny post, by R Onslow Ford (1881).
Leicester Square (centre), WC2 Marble of *William Shakespeare* by Giovanni Fontana (1874); bronze of *Charlie Chaplin* by John Doubleday (unveiled by Ralph Richardson in 1981).
Leicester Square, (gates), WC2 Memorial gates to *John Hunter* by Thomas Woolner, *Isaac Newton* by William Calder Marshall, *Joshua Reynolds* by Henry Weekes (all 1874) and *William Hogarth* by Joseph Durham (1875), all of whom have commemorative busts.
The Mall (near Admiralty Arch), SW1 Bronze of *Captain James Cook* by Sir Thomas Brock (1914); seated marble statue of *Queen Victoria* by Sir Thomas Brock (1911).
Marylebone Road, NW1 Bronze of *John Fitzgerald Kennedy* by Jacques Lipchitz (1965).
Millbank, SW1 Bronze of *Sir John Everett Millais* by Sir Thomas Brock (1904).
Old Bailey, EC4 Gilt of *Justice* by F W Pomeroy (1907).
Park Crescent, W1 Bronze of *Edward Augustus, Duke of Kent* (Queen Victoria's father) by S S Gahagen (1827).
Park Lane, W1 *Achilles*, 20ft (6m) bronze cast by Sir Richard Westmacott (1822): 'Erected by the women of England to Arthur, Duke of Wellington and his brave companions in arms'.
Parliament Square, SW1 Bronzes of *George Canning*, in a toga, by Richard Westmacott (1832); *Sir Robert Peel* by Matthew Noble (1876); *Field Marshal Jan Christian Smuts* by Jacob Epstein (1958); *Abraham Lincoln* (copy of the statue by Augustus Saint-Gaudens in Chicago); *Winston Churchill* by Ivor Roberts-Jones (1973); *Benjamin Disraeli* by Mario Raggi (1883); *Lord Palmerston* by Thomas Woolner (1876).
Piccadilly Circus, W1 *Shaftesbury Memorial Fountain*, better known as *Eros* although Alfred Gilbert's 1893 aluminium statue in fact, depicts *The Angel of Christian Charity*, in honour of Lord Shaftesbury himself.
Pimlico Gardens, SW1 Stone of *William Huskisson* in a Roman toga, by John Gibson (1836).
Prudential Assurance, Holborn, EC1 Cupronised plaster bust of *Charles Dickens* by Percy Fitzgerald (1907).
Red Lion Square, WC1 Bronze bust of *Bertrand Russell* by Marcelle Quinton (1980).
Royal Exchange, EC2 Equestrian bronze of *Wellington* by Francis Chantrey, completed by Henry Weekes (1844); stone figure of *Richard Whittington* by J E Carew (1845).

Royal Geographical Society, Kensington Gore, SW7 Bronzes of *David Livingstone* by T B Huxley-Jones (1953) and *Sir Ernest Shackleton* by C Sarjeant Jagger (1932).
St Bartholomew's Hospital, EC1 Stone figure of *Henry VIII*, the founder, by Francis Bird (1702) stands over the gateway.
St Giles Cripplegate, EC2 Memorial statue of *John Milton* by Montford (1904).
St James's Square, SW1 *William III*, equestrian bronze by John Bacon the Elder (1808).
St Martin's Place, WC2 Marble statue of *Edith Cavell* by Sir George Frampton (1920). Famous inscription reads: 'Patriotism is not enough. I must have no hatred or bitterness for anyone'.
St Thomas' Hospital, SE1 Statue of *Sir Robert Clayton*, the hospital's benefactor (1702). The only outdoor stone statue by Grinling Gibbons.
Savoy Place, WC2 Bronze of *Michael Faraday* by J H Foley (1889) situated outside the Institution of Electrical Engineers.
Soho Square, W1 Stone statue of *King Charles II* by Caius Gabriel Cibber (1681), once owned by W S Gilbert.
Somerset House, Strand, WC2 Baroque fountain in bronze, including a figure of *King George III* by John Bacon the Elder (1788).
South Africa House, Trafalgar Square, WC2 Large stone figure of *Bartholomew Diaz* by Coert Steynberg (1934).
South Square, Gray's Inn, WC1 *Francis Bacon* by F W Pomeroy (1912).
Strand, WC2 Bronzes of *Air Chief Marshal Lord Dowding* and *Sir Arthur 'Bomber' Harris* by Faith Winter (1988, 1992) opposite St Clement Danes, the RAF church; *William Gladstone* by Sir Hamo Thorneycroft (1905); *Dr Samuel Johnson* by Percy Fitzgerald (1910).
Tavistock Square, WC1 Bronze of *Mahatma Gandhi* by Fredda Brilliant (unveiled by Harold Wilson in 1968).
Tooting Broadway, SW17 Bronze of *King Edward VII* by L F Roselieb (1911).
Trafalgar Square, WC2 Bronzes outside National Gallery of *George Washington* by Jean-Antoine Houdon and *James II* in Roman dress by Grinling Gibbons; *Sir Henry Havelock* by William Behnes (1861); equestrian bronzes of *George IV* by Sir Francis Chantrey (1834) and *Charles I* by Hubert Le Sueur (1633), *Nelson's Column* (169ft 5ins/51.6m) designed by William Railton with statue of *Nelson* (17ft/5.2m) by E H Baily (1843) and Landseer's lions cast in 1868 from guns recovered from the wreck of the *Royal George*. On the north wall of the square are bronze busts of Admirals *Lord David Beatty* by William McMillan (1984), *Lord Cunningham* by Franta Belsky (1967) and Lord Jellicoe by Sir Charles Wheeler (1948).
University College London, WC1 Bronze tablet and medallion of *Richard Trevithick* by L S Merrifield (1933).
Victoria Embankment, WC2 *Isambard Kingdom Brunel* by Carlo Marochetti (1877); *Lord Portal of Hungerford* by Oscar Nemon; *Cleopatra's Needle* (68ft 6in/20.9m) erected in 1878; memorial by George Simonds to *Sir Joseph Bazalgette*, chief engineer responsible for the completion of the Embankment in 1870 (1901).
Victoria Embankment Gardens, WC2 Bronzes of *John Stuart Mill* by Thomas Woolner (1878); *Robert Burns* by Sir John Steel (1884); *Sir Arthur Sullivan* by W Goscombe John (1903) with a mourning female on the plinth; *Robert Raikes* by Sir Thomas Brock (1880).
Victoria Tower Gardens, Westminster, SW1 *Burghers of Calais* by Rodin, copy (installed 1915) of original in Calais, created 1895; *Emmeline and Christabel Pankhurst* by A G Walker (1930).
Waterloo Place, SW1 *Duke of York Column* memorial to Frederick, 2nd son of George III, statue by Sir Richard Westmacott (1834); bronze equestrian of *King Edward VII* by Sir Bertram Mackennal (1922); bronze of *Captain Robert Falcon Scott* by Lady Scott (1915); *Florence Nightingale* by Walker.
Westminster Bridge, SE1 Bronze of *Boadicea* (1902) by Thomas Thornycroft at the northeastern end.
Westminster Hall, SW1 See Houses of Parliament
Whitehall, SW1 Bronzes of *Sir Walter Raleigh* by William McMillan (1959); *Field Marshal Montgomery of Alamein* by Oscar Nemon (unveiled by Queen Mother in 1980); *Field Marshal the Viscount Alanbrooke* (1994) and *Field Marshal the Viscount Slim* (unveiled 1990), both by Ivor Roberts-Jones.
Woodford Green, E18 Bronze of *Winston Churchill* by David McFall (unveiled by Field Marshal Montgomery in October 1959).
Woolwich, Royal Arsenal, SE18 Stone figure of *Wellington* by Thomas Milnes (1848).

Stock Exchange

Paternoster Square, EC4. The London Stock Exchange traces its history to 1698 when stock brokers were expelled from the Royal Exchange and John Castaing, based at an office in Jonathan's Coffee House, published the prices of stocks and commodities under the title *The Course of the Exchange and other things*. Although the London office called itself the Stock Exchange from 1773 it was officially founded in 1801. It is one of the largest stock exchanges in the world, with many overseas listings as well as UK companies. Its motto is *Dictum meum pactum*, 'My word is my bond'. The former Stock Exchange Tower, based in Threadneedle Street/Old Broad Street, was opened by Queen Elizabeth II in 1972 and housed the trading floor, where traders would traditionally meet to conduct business. This became largely redundant with the advent of the 'Big Bang' on 27 October 1986, which deregulated many of the Stock Exchange's activities, eliminating fixed commissions on security trades and allowing securities firms to act as brokers and dealers. It also enabled an increased use of computerised systems, allowing dealing rooms to take precedence over face to face trading. On 20 July 1990 a bomb planted by the IRA exploded in the men's toilets behind the visitors' gallery, although the area had been evacuated and nobody was injured. The gallery was closed permanently in 1992. In July

2004 the Stock Exchange moved from Threadneedle Street to a site close to St Paul's Cathedral, still within the Square Mile. It was officially opened by Queen Elizabeth II, accompanied by the Duke of Edinburgh, on 27 July 2004. The new building contains a specially commissioned dynamic sculpture called *The Source*, by artists Greyworld.

Strawberry Hill — Waldegrave Road, Twickenham. Regarded as the first substantial building of the Gothic Revival, Strawberry Hill was the home of Horace Walpole (1717–97), 4th Earl of Orford, the dilettante fourth, and youngest, son of Sir Robert Walpole, Prime Minister 1721–42. After he purchased the property in 1747, Walpole spent 50 years transforming the modest villa in the picturesque Gothic style. He took ideas from any Gothic source he could find, adding exterior battlements, Tudor chimneys, windows and fireplaces based on archbishops' tombs. The fan-vaulted ceiling of the long gallery was based on Henry VII's chapel at Westminster Abbey. In 1757 Walpole established a private press at Strawberry Hill, printing fine editions of the classics and some of his own works. Contrary to popular belief these did not include his Gothic novel *The Castle of Otranto*, which was published anonymously in London in 1764. A century later a new wing was added to Walpole's original structure by Lady Frances Waldegrave. Today the building houses the former Roman Catholic college St Mary's University College. Tel: 020 8240 4224.

Surrey Docks — The Surrey Commercial Docks were a large group of docks in Rotherhithe on the southern (Surrey) bank of the Thames in southeast London. The docks operated in one form or another from 1696 to 1969. The Pilgrim Fathers departed from Rotherhithe in 1620 aboard the *Mayflower*. Howland Great Dock, the main dock and the first to be built, from the 1720s served whaling ships operating around Greenland and was later renamed Greenland dock. Timber trade with Scandinavia became important by the mid 19th century and remained so well into the 20th century. Most of the docks were filled in during the 1980s and redeveloped for residential housing, and the area is now widely known as Surrey Quays. 'Surrey Docks' is modern rhyming slang for pox.

Surrey Iron Railway — The world's first public railway, opened in 1803 before the age of steam. It initially ran for 8 miles (13.5km) between Wandsworth and Croydon, with a 1 mile (2km) branch line from Mitcham to Hackbridge. The carriages were drawn by horses along a pair of 4ft 2in (1.27m) plate rails and were mainly used to transport stone from nearby quarries. A second line, the Croydon, Merstham & Godstone Railway (CMGR) was added by 1805, extending the service from the Croydon Canal basin (now West Croydon railway station) through Old Town, parallel to the Brighton Road down through Purley, Coulsdon, and on to the Merstham chalk and limestone quarries. With the advent of steam trains, the old horse-drawn lines were unable to compete and went into decline. The CMGR had closed by 1838 and the SIR by 1846, although the tracks for the steam trains were laid along much of the SIR route and are still used today.

Sutton House — Homerton High Street, Hackney, E9. The oldest house in East London, the Tudor red-brick house was built in 1535 by Sir Ralph Sadleir, principal secretary of state to Henry VIII. Home to successive merchants, Huguenot silk-weavers, Victorian schoolmistresses and Edwardian clergy, it remains essentially Tudor in character although altered over the years. Now owned by the National Trust. Tel: 020 8986 2264.

Swiss Cottage — London NW3. An area of northwest London in the London Borough of Camden, named after a Swiss-style house built by a wealthy local man c.1803–04. This building became a public house, the Swiss Tavern in Finchley Road, and was reconstructed in 1965 in the style of a Swiss chalet; it is now one of the largest pubs in London. Also the name of a nearby tube station. Adjoining neighbourhoods include Belsize Park to the north, Primrose Hill to the east, St John's Wood to the south and South Hampstead to the west.

Syon Park — London Road, Brentford. Syon House with its 200 acre (80ha) park is the London home of the Duke of Northumberland, whose family have lived here for over 400 years. Originally the site of a medieval abbey, Syon was named after Mount Zion in the Holy Land and dedicated to the Brigettine Order, established in the 14th century by Swedish mystic St Bridget. One of the last great abbeys to be built (founded by Henry V in 1415), it was dissolved by Henry VIII in 1539. In 1547, Henry's coffin was brought to Syon on its way to Windsor for burial. It burst open during the night and in the morning dogs were found licking up the remains, an occurrence regarded as divine judgement for the king's desecration of the abbey. After the abbey's suppression the estate became Crown property and was given to the 1st Duke of Somerset, Lord Protector to Henry VIII's young son, Edward VI. He built Syon House in Italian Renaissance style over the foundations of the west end of the huge abbey church (which was the size of a cathedral), between 1547 and his death by execution in 1552. Syon was then acquired by a rival, John Dudley, Duke of Northumberland. The Duke's son, Lord Guildford Dudley, had married Lady Jane Grey, great-granddaughter of Henry VII, and it was at Syon that she was formally offered the Crown by the Duke. She accepted reluctantly, was conveyed to London by river and proclaimed queen. Nine days later, she was displaced by Henry VIII's eldest daughter, Mary Tudor, and the following year she was executed. In 1594, Henry Percy, 9th Earl of Northumberland, acquired Syon through his marriage to Dorothy Devereux and the Percy family has lived at Syon House ever since. Architect Robert Adam remodelled the interior in the 1760s and Capability Brown laid out the grounds; Syon Park was described by Sir John Betjeman as 'the Grand Architectural Walk'. The great conservatory was designed by Charles Fowler in the 1820s. Tel 020 8560 0882.

Teddington Studios — See Shepperton Studios, Surrey

Temple Bar — Strand, EC4. The gateway traditionally marking the westernmost extent of the City of London on the road to Westminster, where Fleet Street becomes the Strand. In the Middle Ages, the authority of the Corporation of London reached beyond the city's ancient walls and in order to regulate trade into the city, barriers were erected on the major roads wherever the true boundary was a substantial distance from the old gatehouse. Temple Bar was the most famous of these, since traffic between

London and Westminster passed through it. The name comes from the nearby Temple Church, once owned by the Knights Templar but now home to two of the legal profession's Inns of Court. It has long been customary for the sovereign to stop at Temple Bar before entering the City of London, so that the Lord Mayor may offer him or her the City's pearl-encrusted sword of state as a token of loyalty. The earliest Temple Bar was no more than a turnpike; there was a gate of some kind from 1293, and the barrier was badly damaged during the Peasants' Revolt in 1381. By the late Middle Ages a wooden archway stood on the spot. This was badly damaged in 1666 by the Great Fire of London, and a Portland stone arch commissioned by Charles II and designed by Sir Christopher Wren was constructed 1669–72 to replace it. During the 18th century, traitors' heads were mounted on pikes and exhibited on the roof. The other seven principal gateways to London (Aldgate, Aldersgate, Bishopsgate, Cripplegate, Ludgate, Moorgate and Newgate) had been demolished by 1800, but Temple Bar remained as an impediment to the ever-growing traffic. In 1878 the Corporation of London, eager to widen the road but unwilling to destroy so historic a monument, dismantled it piece by piece and stored its 2700 stones. The current monument, designed by Sir Horace Jones and topped by a bronze griffin (the emblem of the City of London) sculpted by Charles Bell Birch, was erected to mark the spot in 1880. The same year brewer Sir Henry Meux bought and re-erected the arch as a gateway at his house Theobalds Park in Hertfordshire, where it remained until 2003. Purchased by the Temple Bar Trust from the Meux Trust for £1 in 1984, it was finally dismantled and returned to the City of London where it was re-erected as an entrance to the Paternoster Square redevelopment north of St Paul's Cathedral. It opened to the public in late 2004.

10 Downing Street London SW1. Located in the City of Westminster, the official residence and office of the Prime Minister of the United Kingdom of Great Britain and Northern Ireland. It is actually the official residence of the First Lord of the Treasury, but in modern times this post has always been held simultaneously with the office of Prime Minister. The building now known as Number 10 was originally three houses: the 'house at the back' (Oliver Cromwell was the first resident), Number 10 itself, and a small annexe next to it (in which Churchill lived during the Blitz). The 'house at the back' was a mansion built c.1530; the original Number 10 was a modest townhouse built in 1685. In 1732 George II offered 10 Downing Street and the 'house at the back' to Robert Walpole in gratitude for his services to the nation. Walpole accepted only on the condition that they would be a gift to the office of First Lord of the Treasury rather than to himself personally. The king agreed and possession has passed ever since to each incoming First Lord. Walpole commissioned William Kent to join the houses together, 1732–5. George Downing, who gives his name to Downing Street, was a spy appointed Scoutmaster General of Scotland by Oliver Cromwell to spy for the army soon after he joined the Parliamentary forces as a preacher. During the Interregnum, Cromwell appointed him Ambassador to The Hague where again his primary responsibility was espionage. Downing's assignment was to watch Charles Stuart, the exiled Pretender to the throne, and report his activities to Cromwell. Shrewd and avaricious, Downing invested in properties and acquired considerable wealth. In 1654, he purchased the lease on land south of St James's Park, and built the first residences on the street which now bears his name. In the 18th and 19th centuries, 10 Downing Street was generally seen as a small, unimpressive, mediocre building, far below the quality and standard worthy of a national leader. The full list of Prime Ministers who have occupied the house is as follows: Sir Robert Walpole; Thomas Pelham-Holles; George Grenville; Lord Frederick North; William Cavendish-Bentinck, 3rd Duke of Portland; William Pitt the Younger (who occupied the house for more than 20 years); Henry Addington; William Wyndham Grenville; Spencer Percival; George Canning; Frederick John Robinson, 1st Viscount Goderich; Arthur Wellesley, 1st Duke of Wellington; Charles Grey, 2nd Earl Grey; Benjamin Disraeli, 1st Earl of Beaconsfield; William Ewart Gladstone; Archibald Primrose, 5th Earl of Rosebery. Since 1902, every Prime Minister has officially resided in 10 Downing Street. No. 11 Downing Street is the official residence of the Second Lord of the Treasury, who in modern times has always been the Chancellor of the Exchequer although during Tony Blair's premiership he resided at No. 11 as it has a larger residential area. This arrangement has been carried on by Gordon Brown and Alistair Darling. To the right of No. 11, 12 Downing Street was the official residence of the Chief Whip, although this tradition has also been cancelled in recent years.

Thames Barrier North Woolwich Road, SE7. Located at Woolwich Reach, the Thames Barrier is the world's second largest movable flood barrier after the Oosterscheldekering in the Netherlands. Built across a 1716ft (523m) wide stretch of the river, the barrier divides the river into six navigable and four smaller non-navigable channels between nine large concrete piers. The radial (i.e. half-cylindrical) steel flood gates operate by rotating, raised by hydraulics out of a horizontal sill below the water. The four large central gates are 201ft (61m) long, stand 34ft (10.5m) above local ground level and weigh 1476 tons (1500 tonnes); the outer two gates are 103ft (31.5m) long. Four additional radial gates by the riverbanks can be lowered; unlike the main six, these are non-navigable. London is vulnerable to flooding and the threat has increased over time due to a continuous rise in high water level over the centuries and the slow 'tilting' of Britain (up in the north and down in the south) caused by post-glacial rebound. This general rise in potential water levels combined with the tidal conditions of the Thames and with particularly severe weather conditions can create serious flood conditions. After 307 people died in the UK in the North Sea flood of 1953 the issue gained new prominence. The concept of the rotating gates was devised by Charles Draper. The barrier was designed by Rendel, Palmer and Tritton for the Greater London Council. The site at Woolwich was chosen because of the relative straightness of the banks, and because the underlying river rock was strong enough to support the barrier. Work began in 1974; construction was largely complete by 1982 and the barrier was officially opened on 8 May 1984. Designed to cope with sea level rises until around 2030–50, it is currently expected to serve its full term. Since 1982 the barrier has been raised over 90 times (it is also raised monthly for testing). The barrier was operated by the National Rivers Authority until April 1996 when it passed to the Environment Agency.

Thames Embankments Victoria Embankment on the north side of the river runs from Westminster to Blackfriars, the Albert Embankment on the south side from Westminster Bridge to Vauxhall, and Chelsea Embankment from Chelsea Bridge to Battersea Bridge; all were constructed by Joseph Bazalgette.

Thames Reaches Starting from the mouth of the Thames and proceeding up river, the reaches are: Sea Reach (Yantlet Creek to West Blyth Buoy); Lower Hope (to Coalhouse Point); Gravesend (to Tilburyness); Northfleet Hope (to Broadness); St Clement's or Fiddlers' (to Stoneness); Long (to Dartford Creek); Erith Rands (to Coalharbour Point); Erith (to Jenningtree Point); Halfway (to Crossness); Barking (to Tripcock Point); Gallions (to Woolwich Hoba Point); Woolwich (to Lyle Park); Bugsby's (to Blackwell Point); Blackwall (to Dudgeon's Dock); Greenwich (to Deptford Creek); Limehouse (to Limekiln Creek); Lower Pool (to Cherry Garden Pier); Upper Pool (to London Bridge); London Bridge to Westminster Bridge; Westminster Bridge to Vauxhall Bridge (both nameless); Nine Elms (to Chelsea Bridge); Chelsea (to Battersea Bridge); Battersea Bridge (to Wandsworth Bridge); Wandsworth Bridge (to Putney Bridge); Barn Elms (to Hammersmith Bridge); Chiswick (to Chiswick Ferry); Corney (to Barnes Railway Bridge); Mortlake (to Kew Bridge).

Thames Tunnels The first tunnel under the Thames, completed in 1843 and linking Wapping and Rotherhithe, was called the Thames Tunnel and is still in existence as a railway tunnel. The oldest road tunnel is the old Blackwall Tunnel, opened in 1897. Other road tunnels include the new Blackwall Tunnel (1967), Rotherhithe (1908) and Dartford (1963 and 1980). The only foot tunnel still in existence runs from Greenwich to the Isle of Dogs.

Thames Valley University See Berkshire

Theatres: Inner London

Adelphi, Strand, WC2 Opened by John Scott on 27 November 1806 and originally called the Sans Pareil, its first performance was The Rout, a set of recitations by Miss Jane M Scott. It became the Adelphi in 1819 and in 1858 was replaced by a more up to date building called first the New Adelphi and from 1867 the Royal Adelphi. It was redesigned in 1930 by Ernest Schaufelberg.

Albery, St Martin's Lane, WC2 Designed 1903 by W G R Sprague and called the New Theatre until 1973. In July 2006 Cameron Mackintosh renamed the theatre the Noel Coward Theatre. The 870 seat venue has recently completed a multi-million pound refurbishment. A reception was held at the theatre and followed a memorial service at the Actors' Church in Covent Garden for Graham Payn, Coward's companion for the last 30 years of his life.

Aldwych, Aldwych, WC2 Designed 1905 by W G R Sprague. Home of Ben Travers farces 1925–33.

Almeida, Almeida Street N1 Fringe theatre situated in Islington and opened in 1980. Housed in a former lecture hall built in 1837 and later home to a music hall and Salvation Army citadel.

Apollo, Shaftesbury Avenue, W1 Designed 1901 by Lewen Sharp. The auditorium was renovated in 1932. The balcony (3rd tier) is said to be the steepest in London.

Apollo Victoria, Victoria, SW1 Opened in 1930 as a cinema, it has been a theatre since 1979.

Arts, Great Newport Street, WC2 Opened in 1927 as an avant-garde theatre challenging the censorial constraints of the Lord Chamberlain's Office.

Barbican (and Pit), Silk Street, EC2 Opened in 1982, since when the London Symphony Orchestra (founded in 1904) has been in residence. Also home of the Royal Shakespeare Company.

Bloomsbury, Gordon Street, WC1 Fringe theatre off Tottenham Court Road opened in 1968 and owned by University College London.

Bridewell, Bride Lane, EC4 Fringe theatre founded in 1994 in the derelict swimming pool hall of the St Bride Foundation Institute by theatre director Carol Metcalfe, who chanced on the space while searching for a show venue for her newly formed theatre company, Breach of the Piece. The Bridewell was one of only three theatres in the City of London, the other two being in the Barbican Centre, but is sadly now closed due to lack of funding.

Bush, Shepherd's Bush, W12 Fringe theatre founded 1972 above what was at that time the Bush public house. The pub has since changed hands but the Bush Theatre remains in place upstairs. Recently the Bush has begun to position itself as an 'off-West End' theatre.

Cambridge, Earlham Street, WC2 Built for Bertie Meyer and opened on 4 September 1930.

Coliseum, St Martin's Lane, WC2 Largest theatre in the West End, seating 2358. The interior was designed in 1904 by Frank Matcham and the theatre opened on 24 December of that year. Since 1968 the Coliseum has been the home of English National Opera.

Comedy, Panton Street, SW1 Designed 1881 by Thomas Verity. Originally called the Royal Comedy Theatre when it opened, the Royal was dropped by 1884.

Criterion, Piccadilly Circus, W1 Designed 1874 by Thomas Verity. Current home of the Reduced Shakespeare Company.

Dominion, Tottenham Court Road, WC1 Built 1929 by William and T R Millburn. On Sundays an offshoot of the Australian-based Hillsongs Pentecostal Church holds three services at the theatre.

Donmar Warehouse, Earlham Street, WC2 Formerly the London base of the Royal Shakespeare Company. A 250 seat subsidised theatre established in 1990 with an excellent track record of award-winning productions. Sam Mendes was artistic director 1990–2002.

Drury Lane, Catherine Street, WC2 The Theatre Royal, Drury Lane was designed in 1812 by Benjamin Wyatt.

Duchess, Catherine Street, WC2 Designed 1929 by Ewen Barr. One of the smallest proscenium arched West End theatres, seating 479.

Duke of York's, St Martin's Lane, WC2 Designed 1892 by Walter Emden and called the Trafalgar Square until 1895.

Fortune, Russell Street, WC2 Designed in 1924 by Ernest Schaufelberg.

Gaiety, Strand, WC2 Opened in 1868, the theatre had England's first electric lighting system in 1878. It closed in 1903.

Garrick, Charing Cross Road, WC2 Designed 1889 by Walter Emden and C J Phipps.

Gate, Pembridge Road, W11 Situated above the Prince Albert pub, the theatre has a reputation for high quality productions of neglected European classics.

Gielgud, Shaftesbury Avenue, W1 Designed 1906 by W G R Sprague. Originally called the Hicks theatre and then the Globe (1909–94), it was renamed in honour of the great British actor and also to distinguish it from the reconstructed Shakespeare's Globe.

Greenwich, Crooms Hill, SE10 Open since 1969 in a reconstructed Victorian music hall.

Hackney Empire, Mare Street, E8 Designed by Frank Matcham, the theatre was the most famous music hall at the turn of the 20th century. After being used as a television studio and bingo hall it has reverted to its music hall roots since its refurbishment and reopening in 2004. The Bullion Room and Acorn (seating 60) are two small auditoriums within the complex. The theatre has gained a reputation for giving young black talent a chance to express itself.

Hampstead Theatre Club, Eton Avenue, NW3 Fringe theatre founded in a scout hall in the heart of Hampstead village in 1959, but presently located in Swiss Cottage. Tel: 020 7722 9301.

Her Majesty's, Haymarket, SW1 The current theatre is actually the fourth to occupy this site: the first, called the Queen's Theatre, was built by Sir John Vanbrugh and opened on 9 April 1705. The current theatre was designed by C J Phipps and opened on 28 April 1897.

Jerwood Theatre Downstairs See Royal Court

Jerwood Theatre Upstairs See Royal Court

King's Head, Upper Street,N1 The 115 seat theatre is situated in Islington's historic 19th century King's Head pub. Founded in 1970 by Dan Crawford.

London Palladium, Argyll Street, WC1 Opened in 1910 as a music hall and originally named the Palladium before adopting its now familiar name in 1934.

Lyceum, Wellington Street, WC2 Designed 1771 by James Payne.

Lyric, Hammersmith, W6 550-seat main auditorium with a 100-seat studio. Usually performances of planned short-season runs. Tel: 0870 050 0511.

Lyric, Shaftesbury Avenue, W1 Designed by C J Phipps and opened on 17 December 1888 with a comic opera called Dorothy.

Mermaid, Puddle Dock, EC4 Founded 1959 by the late Sir Bernard Miles. It closed in 2003 and now functions largely as a conference centre.

New Ambassadors, West Street, WC2 Designed in 1913 by W G R Sprague. Ivor Novello made his debut here in Deburau. Originally called the Ambassadors but changed its name to the New Ambassadors in 1999.

New End, New End, NW3 Housed in a building constructed in 1890 as the mortuary of the former New End Hospital, and converted into a theatre in 1974 by Buddy Dalton. Tel: 020 7472 5800.

New London, Drury Lane, WC2 Designed in 1973 by Paul Turkovic.

Noel Coward See Albery Theatre

Old Vic, Waterloo Road, SE1 Designed in 1818 by Rudolf Cabanel and now Grade II* listed. Currently owned by the Old Vic Theatre Trust 2000 Ltd.

Palace, Shaftesbury Avenue, WC2 Built by T E Collcutt and G H Holloway, opened in 1891 as the Royal English Opera House showing Sir Arthur Sullivan's Ivanhoe.

Peacock, Portugal Street, WC2 The West End venue of Sadler's Wells, established in 1996. Seats 1000.

Phoenix, Charing Cross Road, WC2 Designed by Giles Gilbert Scott and Bertie Crewe and opened in 1930. In the 1970s the entrance was moved from Charing Cross Road around the corner to Phoenix Street, while the advance box office is halfway between the two in Charing Cross Road.

Piccadilly, Denman Street, W1 Designed 1928 by Bertie Crewe and Edward Stone.

Players, Charing Cross, WC2 Housed in several locations since it was founded by Leonard Sachs and Peter Ridgeway in 1936. Presently situated underneath Charing Cross arches, off Villiers Street. The Players Theatre Club now puts on shows on Sunday afternoons in the Venue theatre.

Playhouse, Northumberland Avenue, WC2 Designed by Sefton Parry in 1882 and originally called the Royal Avenue Theatre, it was renamed the Playhouse in 1907.

Prince Edward, Old Compton Street, W1 Designed by Edward A Stone and opened on 3 April 1930. Seats 1645.

Prince of Wales, Coventry Street, W1 Designed by Robert Cromie and opened 27 October 1937 on the site of the Prince's Theatre, designed by C J Phipps in 1884.

Queens, Shaftesbury Avenue, W1 Designed in 1907 by W G R Sprague. A bomb fell on the house in 1940 and the theatre was not reopened until 8 July 1959 following extensive refurbishment by Brian Westwood and Sir Hugh Casson. Seats 911.

Regent's Park, NW1 Open air theatre founded in 1932. Stages annual productions of A Midsummer Night's Dream.

Royal Court, Sloane Square, SW1 Opened on its present site in 1888 and renowned for promoting new writing. Its main auditorium is now known as the Jerwood Theatre Downstairs and its studio theatre as the Jerwood Upstairs. Tel: 020 7565 5050.

Royal National Theatre, SE1 Situated on the South Bank and designed by Denys Lasdun. It contains three auditoriums: the Olivier (large and open-spaced; second to open), the Lyttleton (proscenium arched and first to open in 1976) and the Cottesloe (small but flexible).

Royal Opera House, Bow Street, WC2 Designed by Edward Shepherd in 1732. Redesigned by E M Barry in 1858 and called the Covent Garden Opera Company. Renamed the Royal Opera House in 1968.

Sadler's Wells, Rosebery Avenue, E1 First opened in 1683 by Thomas Sadler; revived as a dedicated home for ballet and opera in the 1930s. The current building, the sixth on the site, was completed in 1998 and includes the Lilian Baylis studio theatre, named after the manager of the Old Vic Theatre Company who first revived the fortunes of Sadler's Wells in the early 20th century.

Savoy, Strand, WC2 Designed in 1881 by C J Phipps and financed by Richard D'Oyly Carte for the production of Gilbert and Sullivan operas. It was the first public building in England to be lit entirely by electricity, although the Gaiety theatre had experimented in part of their theatre in 1878.

Shaftesbury, Shaftesbury Avenue, WC1 Originally called the New Prince's Theatre, it changed its name to the Prince's Theatre in 1914. The theatre was sold to EMI in 1962 and reopened in 1963 as the Shaftesbury Theatre.

Shakespeare's Globe, New Globe Walk, Bankside, SE1 A reconstruction of William Shakespeare's theatre, close to its original site, in a project led by US actor and director Sam Wanamaker. Opened in 1997 with Mark Rylance playing Henry V.

St Martins, West Street, WC2 Designed in 1916 by W G R Sprague. It has been the home since 1974 of The Mousetrap, which opened in 1952 at the Ambassadors Theatre and is the longest consistently running play in the history of British theatre.

Strand, Aldwych, WC2 Designed 1905 by W G R Sprague. Originally named the Waldorf, this theatre is a twin with the Aldwych Theatre on the other side of the Waldorf Hotel. Renamed the Strand Theatre in 1909 and the Whitney Theatre in 1911, it reverted in 1913 to the Strand Theatre.

Theatre Royal, Haymarket, SW1 The present theatre, designed by John Nash and opened in 1821, was designed so that the front Corinthian portico could be seen from St James's Square. Lillie Langtry made her debut here in 1881. Oscar Wilde's An Ideal Husband and A Woman of No Importance both premiered here.

Theatre Royal, Stratford, E15 Stratford's first permanent playhouse, designed in 1884 by architect James George Buckle for actor-manager Charles Dillon. Home since 1953 to the Theatre Workshop company, founded by Joan Littlewood.

Trafalgar Studios See Whitehall

Tricycle, Kilburn High Road, NW6 Fringe theatre opened in a converted Foresters' Hall in 1980.

Unicorn, Tooley Street, SE1 Unicorn's new theatre complex in Southwark was opened in December 2005 and has two auditoria: the Weston Theatre seating 300 and the Clore Theatre (formerly the River Theatre) seating 120, both dedicated to children's entertainment. The Unicorn was previously a mobile unit based at the Arts Theatre, Great Newport Street, 1966–88.

Vaudeville, Strand, WC2 The original theatre was designed by C J Phipps and opened on 16 April 1870. It closed on 7 November 1925 when the interior was completely reconstructed to designs by Robert Atkins – the auditorium was changed from a horseshoe shape to the current rectangle – reopening on 23 February 1926.

Venue, Leicester Square, WC2 Opened in November 2001 by Adam Kenwright and specifically designed to show the musical Taboo, based on the life of pop singer Boy George. The 350 seat theatre was converted from the former Notre Dame Hall, a small dance venue and rehearsal room, and now shows a diverse array of work.

Victoria Palace, Victoria Street, SW1 There have been music halls on the present site of the Victoria Palace Theatre since the 1850s. The current theatre, designed by Frank Matcham, opened in November 1911.

Westminster, Palace Street, SW1 The Westminster was the nearest theatre to Buckingham Palace when opened in 1931. The theatre was destroyed by fire on 27 June 2002 and has now been demolished.

Whitehall, SW1 Built in 1930 to the design of E A Stone. In 1942 the revue The Whitehall Follies, featuring Phyllis Dixey – whose claim to fame was as the West End's first stripper – was presented here. Reluctant Heroes, produced by Brian Rix, opened at the Whitehall in 1950; after its success Rix went on to produce many further farces at the theatre, and these collectively became known as the Whitehall Farces. In May 2004 the theatre reopened after refurbishment as the Trafalgar Studios, seating 480.

Wyndham's, Charing Cross Road, WC2 Designed by W G R Sprague and opened in 1899. Seats 759.

Young Vic, The Cut, SE1 Opened 11 September 1970 as a venue in which younger directors, designers, actors, writers and technicians could present the great works of the world repertoire, classics and, from time to time, new plays in exciting productions and at the lowest possible seat prices.

Tower of London

Tower Hill, EC3. From its foundation by William the Conqueror in 1066, the Tower of London has always been one of the most talked-about buildings in England. The White Tower (aka the Great Tower), the square building with turrets on each corner that gave it its name, was completed in 1078 and is one of a complex of buildings along the River Thames which have served as fortresses, armouries, treasuries, zoos/menageries, mints, palaces, places of execution, public records offices, observatories, shelters and prisons (The last prisoner ever held in the Tower of London was Nazi leader Rudolf Hess). The towers include the Beauchamp Tower, Bell Tower, Bloody Tower (or Garden Tower), Bowyer Tower, Brick Tower, Broad Arrow Tower, Byward Tower, Constable Tower, Cradle Tower, Develin Tower, Deveraux Tower, Flint Tower, Lanthorn Tower, Martin Tower, Middle Tower, St Thomas's Tower, Salt Tower, Wakefield Tower, Wardrobe Tower, Well Tower and White Tower. The Crown Jewels have been kept at the Tower of London since

1303 after they were stolen from Westminster Abbey. Some time after 1660, a new set of regalia was made to replace those destroyed during the Commonwealth, and in 1661 the Crown Jewels were first put on public display. Since World War II there have always been six ravens, plus two auxiliaries, at the Tower; these live in nesting boxes situated in the Tower grounds near the Wakefield Tower. Although St Peter ad Vincula ('St Peter in chains') is the parish church of the Tower of London, the Chapel of St John, dating from 1080, on the second floor of the White Tower, is the oldest church in London. Tel: 0870 751 5177. See also Yeomen Warders.

Trafalgar Square London WC2. Often regarded as the heart of London by its residents and tourists, and a popular site for political demonstrations, the present layout of the square is largely due to Sir Charles Barry and was completed in 1845. The original name was to have been 'King William the Fourth's Square', but architect George Ledwell Taylor (1788–1873) suggested the present name to commemorate the Battle of Trafalgar. The northern part of the square had been the site of the King's Mews since the time of Edward I, while the southern end was the original Charing Cross, where the Strand from the City met Whitehall, coming north from Westminster. The site of Nelson's Column and a number of other notable sculptures (see Statues), it consists of a large central area surrounded by roadways on three sides, with steps leading to the National Gallery on the other. Prior to 2003 the square was surrounded by a busy one-way traffic system on all sides, but the width of the roads has since been reduced and the northern side of the square closed to traffic. Nelson's Column in the centre of the square is surrounded by fountains designed by Sir Edwin Lutyens in 1939 and four huge bronze lions sculpted by Sir Edwin Landseer; the metal used is said to have been recycled from the cannon of the French fleet. The column is topped by a statue of Lord Nelson, the admiral who commanded the British fleet at Trafalgar. On the north side of the square is the National Gallery and to its east the church of St Martin-in-the-Fields. The square adjoins The Mall via Admiralty Arch (see separate entry) to the southwest. To the south is Whitehall, to the east Strand and South Africa House, to the north Charing Cross Road and on the west side Canada House. At the corners of the square are four plinths; the two northern ones were intended to be used for equestrian statues, and thus are wider than the two southern. Three of them hold statues: George IV (northeast, 1840s), Henry Havelock (southeast, 1861, by William Behnes), and Sir Charles James Napier (southwest, 1855). Mayor of London Ken Livingstone controversially expressed a desire to see the two generals replaced with statues that 'ordinary Londoners would know'. A statue of General Charles George Gordon, erected in 1888, was removed in 1943 and resited on the Victoria Embankment in 1953. The fourth plinth on the northwest corner was intended to hold a statue of William IV, but remained empty due to insufficient funds. After long disagreement over which monarch or military hero to place there, in 1999 the Royal Society of Arts conceived the Fourth Plinth Project, whereby a succession of works commissioned from contemporary artists would temporarily occupy the plinth. These were *Ecce Homo* by Mark Wallinger (1999), *Regardless of History* by Bill Woodrow (2000) and *Monument* by Rachel Whiteread (2001). Wallinger's *Ecce Homo* (Latin, 'behold the man', a biblical reference) was of a life-sized man, appearing minuscule qtop the huge plinth, designed for larger-than-life statuary. It was interpreted by some as a commentary on human delusions of grandeur; far from making the man look insignificant, it was said, his apparent tininess drew the eye powerfully. Whiteread's *Monument*, by an artist already notable for her controversial Turner Prize-winning work *House* and the Judenplatz Holocaust Memorial in Vienna, was a cast of the plinth in transparent resin, and placed upside-down on top of the original. The best use of the fourth plinth remains the subject of debate. On 24 March 2003 an appeal was launched by Wendy Woods, widow of anti-apartheid journalist Donald Woods, hoping to raise £400,000 to pay for a statue of Nelson Mandela by Ian Walters (South Africa House, home of the South African High Commission, was the scene of many anti-apartheid demonstrations). After several years in which the fourth plinth stood empty, the Greater London Authority assumed responsibility for it and started its own series of temporary exhibits. The first work, *Alison Lapper Pregnant* by Marc Quinn (2005), is a 12ft (3.6m) marble torso-bust of Alison Lapper, an artist born with no arms and shortened legs due to a condition called phocomelia. The next, *Model for a Hotel* by Thomas Schutte, was installed in November 2007. There has been a Christmas ceremony every year in the square since 1947. A Norway spruce (or sometimes a fir) is given by Norway's capital Oslo and presented as London's Christmas tree, a token of gratitude for Britain's support during World War II. (Norway's King Haakon and his son Crown Prince Olav, as well as the country's government, lived in exile in London throughout the war.) As part of the tradition, the Lord Mayor of Westminster visits Oslo in late autumn to take part in the cutting down of the tree, and the Mayor of Oslo then goes to London to light the tree at the Christmas ceremony. For many years Londoners celebrating the start of a New Year have gathered on the square, frolicking in the fountains despite the often inclement weather.

Tramlink Originally known as Croydon Tramlink, the service began in May 2000, operated by FirstGroup on behalf of Transport for London. Tramlink is served by 25 articulated trams built by Bombardier Transportation in Vienna. Each car has 70 seats and a total capacity of just over 200 passengers. They operate from an overhead power supply and have a maximum speed of 50 mph (80 km/h). There are three routes running between New Addington and Wimbledon, Elmers End and Croydon, and Beckenham Junction to Croydon. Tramlink connects with National Rail lines at a number of stations, but because it runs in an area relatively under-served by the London Underground (one of the reasons for its creation), its only interchange with the Underground is at Wimbledon.

Transport for London Created in 2000 as part of the Greater London Authority, TfL gained most of its functions from its predecessor London Regional Transport in 2000 and as such supervises both bus and rail travel in London, although it did not take over responsibility for the London Underground until 2003. TfL is controlled by a board whose members are appointed by the Mayor of London, who also chairs the board. It owns and operates London's Transport Museum in Covent Garden.

Trooping the Colour — A ceremony held annually in June to mark the official birthday of Queen Elizabeth II, Trooping the Colour takes place on Horse Guards Parade in St James's Park. This colourful military parade by the Household Division, during which the Queen personally carries out an inspection of the troops, derives from two older military ceremonies – Trooping the Colour and Mounting the Queen's Guard, both of which began during the early 18th century. The 'Colour' battalion flag is 'Trooped' – or carried – slowly down the ranks of soldiers. This was traditionally done so each man was familiar with his battalion's flag, used as a rallying point during battle. As the troops of the Household Division have the honour of guarding the monarch, the link has been particularly close. However it has only been since Edward VII's reign that he or she has regularly taken the salute in person during the ceremony. At the conclusion of the main ceremony the Queen leads the troops down The Mall to Buckingham Palace, where she makes the salute. At the end of the ceremony the Queen appears at the balcony of Buckingham Palace. The Queen first appeared at the parade when she was Princess Elizabeth, as Colonel of the Grenadier Guards in 1947, in the first ceremony to be held after World War II.

Underground map — Albert Stanley, Lord Ashfield, issued the first map in 1908. The present colour-coded map was implemented in 1933 from a design by Harry Beck.

Underground stations — There are currently 311 London Underground stations:

Station	Line(s)	Date opened
Acton Town	D, P	1 July 1879
Aldgate	M, Ci	18 November 1876
Aldgate East	H & C, D	6 October 1884
All Saints	DLR	31 August 1987
Alperton	P	28 June 1903
Amersham	M	1 September 1892
Angel	N	17 November 1901
Archway	N	22 June 1907
Arnos Grove	P	19 September 1932
Arsenal	P	15 December 1906
Baker Street	H & C, M, B, Ci, J	10 January 1863
Balham	N	6 December 1926
Bank	W & C, N, Ce, DLR	8 August 1898
Barbican	M, Ci, H & C	23 December 1865
Barking	D, H & C	02 June 1902
Barkingside	Ce	31 May 1948
Barons Court	D, P	9 October 1905
Bayswater	D, Ci	1 October 1868
Beckton	DLR	28 March 1994
Beckton Park	DLR	28 March 1994
Becontree	D	18 July 1932
Belsize Park	N	22 June 1907
Bermondsey	J	17 September 1999
Bethnal Green	Ce	4 December 1946
Blackfriars	D, Ci	30 May 1870
Blackhorse Road	V	1 September 1968
Blackwall	DLR	28 March 1994
Bond Street	Ce, J	24 September 1900
Borough	N	18 December 1890
Boston Manor	P	1 May 1884
Bounds Green	P	19 September 1932
Bow Church	DLR	31 August 1987
Bow Road	D, H & C	11 June 1902
Brent Cross	N	19 November 1923
Brixton	V	23 July 1971
Bromley-by-Bow	D, H & C	2 June 1902
Buckhurst Hill	Ce	21 November 1948
Burnt Oak	N	27 October 1924
Caledonian Road	P	15 December 1906
Camden Town	N	22 June 1907
Canada Water	EL, J	17 September 1999
Canary Wharf	J	17 September 1999
Canary Wharf	DLR	31 August 1987
Canning Town	DLR, J	14 May 1999
Cannon Street	D, Ci	6 October 1884
Canons Park	J	10 December 1932
Chalfont & Latimer	M	8 July 1889
Chalk Farm	N	22 June 1907
Chancery Lane	Ce	30 July 1900
Charing Cross	B, N	10 March 1906
Chesham	M	8 July 1889

Station	Line(s)	Date opened
Chigwell	Ce	21 November 1948
Chiswick Park	D	1 July 1879
Chorleywood	M	8 July 1889
Clapham Common	N	3 June 1900
Clapham North	N	3 June 1900
Clapham South	N	13 September 1926
Cockfosters	P	31 July 1933
Colindale	N	18 August 1924
Colliers Wood	N	13 September 1926
Covent Garden	P	11 April 1907
Crossharbour & London Arena	DLR	31 August 1987
Croxley	M	2 November 1925
Custom House	DLR	28 March 1994
Cutty Sark	DLR	3 December 1999
Cyprus	DLR	28 March 1994
Dagenham East	D	02 June 1902
Dagenham Heathway	D	12 September 1932
Debden	Ce	25 September 1949
Deptford Bridge	DLR	20 November 1999
Devons Road	DLR	31 August 1987
Dollis Hill	J	1 October 1909
Ealing Broadway	D, Ce	1 July 1879
Ealing Common	D, P	1 July 1879
Earl's Court	D, P	31 October 1871
East Acton	Ce	3 August 1920
East Finchley	N	3 July 1939
East Ham	D, H & C	2 June 1902
East India	DLR	28 March 1994
East Putney	D	3 June 1889
Eastcote	M, P	26 May 1906
Edgware	N	18 August 1924
Edgware Road	B	15 June 1907
Edgware Road	H & C, D, Ci	1 October 1863
Elephant & Castle	N, B	18 December 1890
Elm Park	D	13 May 1935
Elverson Road	DLR	11 November 1999
Embankment	D, B, N, Ci	30 May 1870
Epping	Ce	25 September 1949
Euston	N, V	22 June 1907
Euston Square	M, Ci, H & C	10 January 1863
Fairlop	Ce	31 May 1948
Farringdon	M, Ci, H & C	10 January 1863
Finchley Central	N	14 April 1940
Finchley Road	J, M	30 June 1879
Finsbury Park	P, V	15 December 1906
Fulham Broadway	D	1 March 1880
Gallions Reach	DLR	28 March 1994
Gants Hill	Ce	14 December 1947
Gloucester Road	D, P, Ci	1 October 1868
Golders Green	N	22 June 1907
Goldhawk Road	H & C	1 April 1914
Goodge Street	N	22 June 1907
Grange Hill	Ce	21 November 1948
Great Portland Street	M, Ci, H & C	10 January 1863
Green Park	P, V, J	15 December 1906
Greenford	Ce	30 June 1947
Greenwich	DLR	11 November 1999
Gunnersbury	D	1 June 1877
Hainault	Ce	31 May 1948
Hammersmith	D, P	9 September 1874
Hammersmith	H & C	13 June 1864
Hampstead	N	22 June 1907
Hanger Lane	Ce	30 June 1947
Harlesden	B	16 April 1917
Harrow & Wealdstone	B	16 April 1917
Harrow-on-the-Hill	M	2 August 1880
Hatton Cross	P	19 July 1975
Heathrow Terminals 1, 2, 3	P	16 December 1977
Heathrow Terminal 4	P	12 April 1986
Heathrow Terminal 5	P	27 March 2008
Hendon Central	N	19 November 1923

Station	Line(s)	Date opened
Heron Quays	DLR	31 August 1987
High Barnet	N	14 April 1940
High Street Kensington	D, Ci	1 October 1868
Highbury & Islington	V	1 September 1968
Highgate	N	19 January 1941
Hillingdon	M, P	4 July 1904
Holborn	Ce, P	15 December 1906
Holland Park	Ce	30 July 1900
Holloway Road	P	15 December 1906
Hornchurch	D	2 June 1902
Hounslow Central	P	1 April 1886
Hounslow East	P	1 May 1883
Hounslow West	P	21 July 1884
Hyde Park Corner	P	15 December 1906
Ickenham	M, P	25 September 1905
Island Gardens	DLR	31 August 1987
Kennington	N	18 December 1890
Kensal Green	B	1 October 1916
Kensington (Olympia)	D	27 May 1844
Kentish Town	N	22 June 1907
Kenton	B	16 April 1917
Kew Gardens	D	1 June 1877
Kilburn	J	24 November 1879
Kilburn Park	B	31 January 1915
King George V	DLR	2 December 2005
King's Cross St Pancras	M, N, P, Ci, V, H & C	10 January 1863
Kingsbury	J	10 December 1932
Knightsbridge	P	15 December 1906
Ladbroke Grove	H & C	13 June 1864
Lambeth North	B	10 March 1906
Lancaster Gate	Ce	30 July 1900
Langdon Park	DLR	9 December 2007
Latimer Road	H & C	16 December 1868
Leicester Square	P, N	15 December 1906
Lewisham	DLR	11 November 1999
Leyton	Ce	5 May 1947
Leytonstone	Ce	5 May 1947
Limehouse	DLR	31 August 1987
Liverpool Street	M, Ce, Ci, H & C	12 July 1875
London Bridge	N, J	25 February 1900
London City Airport	DLR	2 December 2005
Loughton	Ce	21 November 1948
Maida Vale	B	6 June 1915
Manor House	P	19 September 1932
Mansion House	D, Ci	3 July 1871
Marble Arch	Ce	30 July 1900
Marylebone	B	27 March 1907
Mile End	D, H & C, Ce	2 June 1902
Mill Hill East	N	18 May 1941
Monument	D, Ci	6 October 1884
Moor Park	M	9 May 1910
Moorgate	M, N, Ci, H & C	23 December 1865
Morden	N	13 September 1926
Mornington Crescent	N	22 June 1907
Mudchute	DLR	31 August 1987
Neasden	J	2 August 1880
New Cross	EL	1 October 1884
New Cross Gate	EL	1 October 1884
Newbury Park	Ce	14 December 1947
North Acton	Ce	5 November 1923
North Ealing	P	23 June 1903
North Greenwich	J	14 May 1999
North Harrow	M	22 March 1915
North Wembley	B	16 April 1917
Northfields	P	16 April 1908
Northolt	Ce	21 November 1948
Northwick Park	M	28 June 1923
Northwood	M	1 September 1887
Northwood Hills	M	13 November 1933
Notting Hill Gate	D, Ce, Ci	1 October 1868
Oakwood	P	13 March 1933

Station	Line(s)	Date opened
Old Street	N	17 November 1901
Osterley	P	1 May 1883
Oval	N	18 December 1890
Oxford Circus	Ce, B, V	30 July 1900
Paddington	D, Ci, B, H & C	10 January 1863
Park Royal	P	23 June 1903
Parsons Green	D	1 March 1880
Perivale	Ce	30 June 1947
Piccadilly Circus	B, P	10 March 1906
Pimlico	V	14 September 1972
Pinner	M	25 May 1885
Plaistow	D, H & C	2 June 1902
Pontoon Dock	DLR	2 December 2005
Poplar	DLR	21 August 1987
Preston Road	M	21 May 1908
Prince Regent	DLR	28 March 1994
Pudding Mill Lane	DLR	15 January 1996
Putney Bridge	D	1 March 1880
Queen's Park	B	11 February 1915
Queensbury	J	16 December 1934
Queensway	Ce	30 July 1900
Ravenscourt Park	D	1 June 1877
Rayners Lane	M, P	26 May 1906
Redbridge	Ce	14 December 1947
Regent's Park	B	10 March 1906
Richmond	D	1 June 1877
Rickmansworth	M	1 September 1887
Roding Valley	Ce	21 November 1948
Rotherhithe	EL	1 October 1884
Royal Albert	DLR	28 March 1994
Royal Oak	H & C	30 October 1871
Royal Victoria	DLR	28 March 1994
Ruislip	M, P	4 July 1904
Ruislip Gardens	Ce	29 November 1948
Ruislip Manor	M, P	5 August 1912
Russell Square	P	15 December 1906
St James's Park	D, Ci	24 December 1868
St John's Wood	J	20 November 1939
St Paul's	Ce	30 July 1900
Seven Sisters	V	1 September 1968
Shadwell	EL, DLR	1 October 1884
Shepherd's Bush	Ce	30 July 1900
Shepherd's Bush Market	H & C	1 April 1914
Sloane Square	D, Ci	24 December 1868
Snaresbrook	Ce	14 December 1947
South Ealing	P	1 May 1883
South Harrow	P	28 June 1903
South Kensington	D, P, Ci	24 December 1868
South Kenton	B	3 July 1933
South Quay	DLR	31 August 1987
South Ruislip	Ce	23 November 1948
South Wimbledon	N	13 September 1926
South Woodford	Ce	14 December 1947
Southfields	D	3 June 1889
Southgate	P	13 March 1933
Southwark	J	24 September 1999
Stamford Brook	D	1 February 1912
Stanmore	J	10 December 1932
Stepney Green	D, H & C	23 June 1902
Stockwell	N, V	18 December 1890
Stonebridge Park	B	16 April 1917
Stratford	Ce, J, DLR	04 December 1946
Sudbury Hill	P	28 June 1903
Sudbury Town	P	28 June 1903
Surrey Quays	EL	1 October 1884
Swiss Cottage	J	20 November 1939
Temple	D, Ci	30 May 1870
Theydon Bois	Ce	25 September 1949
Tooting Bec	N	13 September 1926
Tooting Broadway	N	13 September 1926
Tottenham Court Road	Ce, N	30 July 1900

Station	Line(s)	Date opened
Tottenham Hale	V	1 September 1968
Totteridge & Whetstone	N	14 April 1940
Tower Gateway	DLR	31 August 1987
Tower Hill	D, Ci	25 September 1882
Tufnell Park	N	22 June 1907
Turnham Green	D, P	1 June 1877
Turnpike Lane	P	19 September 1932
Upminster	D	02 June 1902
Upminster Bridge	D	17 December 1934
Upney	D	12 September 1932
Upton Park	D, H & C	02 June 1902
Uxbridge	M, P	04 July 1904
Vauxhall	V	23 July 1971
Victoria	D, Ci, V	24 December 1868
Walthamstow Central	V	01 September 1968
Wanstead	Ce	14 December 1947
Wapping	EL	1 October 1884
Warren Street	N, V	22 June 1907
Warwick Avenue	B	31 January 1915
Waterloo	W & C, B, N, J	10 March 1906
Watford	M	2 November 1925
Wembley Central	B	16 April 1917
Wembley Park	M, J	12 May 1894
West Acton	Ce	5 November 1923
West Brompton	D	12 April 1869
West Finchley	N	14 April 1940
West Ham	D, H & C, J	2 June 1902
West Hampstead	J	30 June 1879
West Harrow	M	17 November 1913
West India Quay	DLR	31 August 1987
West Kensington	D	9 September 1874
West Ruislip	Ce	21 November 1948
West Silvertown	DLR	2 December 2005
Westbourne Park	H & C	1 February 1866
Westferry	DLR	31 August 1987
Westminster	D, Ci, J	24 December 1868
White City	Ce	23 November 1947
Whitechapel	D, EL, H & C	1 October 1884
Willesden Green	J	24 November 1879
Willesden Junction	B	10 May 1915
Wimbledon	D	3 June 1889
Wimbledon Park	D	3 June 1889
Wood Green	P	19 September 1932
Wood Lane	H & C	12 October 2008
Woodford	Ce	14 December 1947
Woodside Park	N	12 April 1940
Woowich Arsenal	DLR	10 January 2009

B = Bakerloo; Ce = Central; Ci = Circle; D = District; DLR = Docklands Light Railway; EL = East London; H & C = Hammersmith & City; J = Jubilee; M = Metropolitan; N = Northern; P = Piccadilly; V = Victoria; W & C = Waterloo & City.

Underground stations	Previous names
Acton Town	Mill Hill Park until 1910
Alperton	Perivale-Alperton until 1910
Amersham	Amersham & Chesham Bois 1922–34
Archway	Highgate 1907–39
Arsenal	Gillespie Road until 1932
Bank	City only on W & C until 1940
Barbican	Aldersgate Street until 1910
Bayswater	Bayswater (Queen's Road) & Westbourne Grove 1923–33
Becontree	Gale Street Halt until 1926
Boston Manor	Boston Road until 1911
Bromley-by-Bow	Bromley until 1967
Canons Park	Canons Park (Edgware) until 1933
Chalfont & Latimer	Chalfont Road until 1915
Chancery Lane	Chancery Lane (Grays Inn)
Charing Cross	Strand
Chiswick Park	Acton Green until 1887
Chorleywood	Chorley Wood & Chenies 1915–34, Chorley Wood, 1934–1965
Clapham North	Clapham Road until 1926

Underground stations	Previous names
Crossharbour	Crossharbour & London Arena
Croxley	Croxley Green until 1949
Dagenham East	Dagenham until 1949
Dagenham Heathway	Heathway until 1949
Debden	Chigwell Road until December 1865
Ealing Broadway	Ealing until 1875
Ealing Common	Ealing Common and West Acton 1886–1910
East Finchley	East End, Finchley
Eastcote	Eastcote Halt
Embankment	Charing Cross 1915–74
Euston Square	Gower Street until 1909
Farringdon	Farringdon and High Holborn 1922–36
Finchley Central	Finchley & Hendon until 1894, Finchley (Church End) 1894–1940
Fulham Broadway	Walham Green until 1952
Gloucester Road	Brompton (Gloucester Road) until 1907
Goodge Street	Tottenham Court Road until 1908
Great Portland Street	Great Portland Street & Regent's Park 1923–33
Green Park	Dover Street until 1933
Gunnersbury	Brentford Road until 1871
Harrow & Wealdstone	Harrow until 1897
Harrow-on-the-Hill	Harrow until 1894
Heathrow Terminals 1, 2, 3	Heathrow Central
Highbury & Islington	Highbury until 1922
Hillingdon	Hillingdon (Swakeleys)
Holborn	Holborn (Kingsway)
Hounslow Central	Heston Hounslow until 1925
Hounslow East	Hounslow until 1884, Hounslow Town 1884–1925
Hounslow West	Hounslow Barracks until 1925
Ickenham	Ickenham Halt
Kensington (Olympia)	Addison Road, Kensington (Addison Road) 1868–1946
Kilburn	Kilburn and Brondesbury until 1950
Ladbroke Grove	Notting Hill until 1880
Lambeth North	Kennington Road until August 1906
Limehouse	Stepney Junction
Liverpool Street	Bishopsgate until 1909
Marylebone	Great Central until 1917
Mill Hill East	London Mill Hill, Mill Hill for Mill Hill Barracks
Monument	Eastcheap until November 1884
Moor Park	Sandy Lodge until 1923, Moor Park & Sandy Lodge 1923–50
Moorgate	Moorgate Street on Metropolitan only until 1924
Neasden	Kingsbury & Neasden until 1910, Neasden & Kingsbury 1910–32
New Cross Gate	New Cross until 1923
Northfields	Northfield Halt until 1911, Northfields & Little Ealing 1911–32
Northwick Park	Northwick Park and Kenton until 1933
Oakwood	Enfield West until 1934, Enfield West (Oakwood) 1934–46
Osterley	Osterly & Spring Grove until resiting
Oval	Kennington (Oval) until 1894
Park Royal	Park Royal & Twyford Abbey until 1931
Perivale	Perivale Halt
Preston Road	Preston Road Halt
Putney Bridge	Putney Bridge & Fulham to 1902, Putney Bridge & Hurlingham 1902–32
Queensway	Queen's Road
Ravenscourt Park	Shaftesbury Road until 1888
Roding Valley	Roding Valley Halt
Ruislip Manor	Ruislip Manor Halt
St Paul's	Post Office until 1937
Shadwell	Shadwell & St George's-in-the-East 1900–18
Shepherd's Bush Market	Shepherd's Bush until 2008
South Harrow	South Harrow & Roxeth
South Ruislip	Northolt Junction until 1932, South Ruislip & Northolt Junction 1932–47
South Woodford	George Lane until 1937, South Woodford (George Lane) 1937–50
Surrey Quays	Deptford Road until 1911, Surrey Docks
Theydon Bois	Theydon until December 1865
Tooting Bec	Trinity Road until 1950
Tottenham Court Road	Oxford Street only on Northern 1907–8
Tottenham Hale	Tottenham
Totteridge & Whetstone	Whetstone & Totteridge until 1874
Tower Hill	[The] Tower of London 1882–4, Mark Lane 1884–1946
Walthamstow Central	Walthamstow (Hoe Street) until 1968

Underground stations	Previous names
Wapping	Wapping & Shadwell until 1876
Warren Street	Euston Road until 1908
Wembley Central	Sudbury until 1882, Sudbury & Wembley 1882–1910
West Ham	West Ham Manor Road 1924–69
West Kensington	North End (Fulham) until 1877
West Ruislip	Ruislip & Ickenham until 1947
Westminster	Westminster Bridge until 1907
White City	Wood Lane
Whitechapel	Whitechapel (Mile End) until 1901
Woodside Park	Torrington Park, Woodside until 1882

Underground miscellany

Questions about the London Underground are a frequent source of fascination. Here are a few facts that may prove interesting. Since January 2003 the London Underground has been operated as a public-private partnership (PPP), where the infrastructure and support services are maintained by private companies but the London Underground is still owned and operated by Transport for London (TfL). **Metronet Rail**, owned since May 2008 by TfL, is responsible for maintenance, renewal and upgrade of the infrastructure including track, trains, signals, civil work and stations, on nine London Underground lines (Bakerloo, Central, Circle, District, Hammersmith & City, Metropolitan, Victoria, Waterloo & City. **Tube Lines** is responsible for the infrastructure of the Jubilee, Northern and Piccadilly lines. The longest distance between two stations is 3.89 miles (6.26km), between Chalfont & Latimer and Chesham on the Metropolitan line. The shortest distance between two stations is 273yds (250m), between Leicester Square and Covent Garden on the Piccadilly line. Five stations are named after pubs: Angel, Elephant & Castle, Manor House, Royal Oak and Swiss Cottage. The Jubilee line is the only line that intersects all others. It is possible to travel through ten stations in a row all beginning with the same letter by starting at Hounslow East, travelling towards Heathrow and round the Heathrow loop and returning to Hounslow East again. Intermediate stations are Hounslow Central, Hounslow West, Hatton Cross, Heathrow Terminals 1, 2, 3, Heathrow Terminal 4, Hatton Cross again, Hounslow West again, Hounslow Central again, returning to Hounslow East. St John's Wood is the only station which contains none of the letters of the word 'mackerel' (as the word Saint is not spelt out). Pimlico is the only station which contains none of the letters of the word 'badger', at least until the proposed 2010 opening of Hoxton, which will then be the only station containing none of the letters of either word. Wapping is the only station with no letters in common with 'lobster'. There are only two Underground stations that have all five vowels in them – South Ealing and Mansion House. Heathrow Terminal 4 also contains all five vowels, if 4 is spelled out as 'four'. Bank is the only station whose name contains only one syllable. Bank and Oval are the only stations whose name contains only four letters. Knightsbridge is the only station whose name contains six consecutive consonants. It is beyond the scope of this book to give the reasons why the following stations are permanently closed but I have given the name, followed by the line and date of closure.

Station	Line	Date of closure
Aldwych	Piccadilly	1994
Aldgate East	District	1938
Blake Hall	Central	1981
Brill	Metropolitan	1935
British Museum	Central	1933
Brompton Road	Piccadilly	1934
City Road	Northern	1922
Down Street	Piccadilly	1932
Earl's Court	District	1878
Granborough Road	Metropolitan	1936
Grove Road (Hammersmith)	Metropolitan	1906
Hillingdon	Metropolitan, Piccadilly	1992
Hounslow Town	District	1909
King's Cross St Pancras	Metropolitan	1941
King William Street	Northern	1900
Lord's	Metropolitan	1939
Mark Lane	District, Circle	1967
Marlborough Road	Metropolitan	1939
Northfields & Little Ealing	Piccadilly	1932
Ongar	Central	1994
Osterley & Spring Grove	Piccadilly	1934
Park Royal & Twyford Abbey	Piccadilly	1931
Quainton Road	Metropolitan	1936
St Mary's (Whitechapel Road)	District	1938
Shoreditch	East London	2006
South Acton	District	1959
South Harrow	Piccadilly	1935
South Kentish Town	Northern	1924
Swiss Cottage (Metropolitan Line)	Metropolitan	1940
Tower of London	District, Circle	1884
Uxbridge	Metropolitan, Piccadilly	1938

	Station	Line	Date of closure
	Uxbridge Road	Metropolitan	1940
	Verney Junction	Metropolitan	1936
	Waddesdon	Metropolitan	1936
	Waddesdon Road	Metropolitan	1935
	Westbourne Park	Metropolitan	1871
	Westcott	Metropolitan	1935
	Winslow Road	Metropolitan	1936
	Wood Lane	Central	1947
	Wood Lane (aka White City)	Metropolitan	1959
	Wood Siding	Metropolitan	1935
	Wotton	Metropolitan	1935
	York Road	Piccadilly	1932

University of East London — Founded in 1970 as North East London Polytechnic, later changing its name to the Polytechnic of East London; it was granted university status in 1992. The university was located on three main campuses (Stratford, Barking and Docklands) all within East London, but has recently consolidated into two, dispensing with the Barking campus. Tel: 020 8223 3333.

University of Greenwich — London SE10. The university traces its roots back to 1890 when it was founded as Woolwich Polytechnic, the second polytechnic in the UK. Over the years, a range of specialist organisations joined the institution, giving it diverse strengths in subjects as varied as teacher training, architecture, engineering and history. The name Thames Polytechnic was adopted in 1970 and university status was awarded in 1992. Its three campuses extend from Maritime Greenwich to Medway, serving southeast London, Kent Thames-side and West Kent. The Kings Hill Institute in West Malling, Kent is a centre for Continuing Professional Development. Tel: 020 8331 8000.

University of London — Malet Street, WC1. One of the oldest, largest and most diverse universities in the UK. Established by royal charter in 1836, the university is recognised globally as a leader in higher education. It consists of 20 self-governing colleges, together with the institutes of the School of Advanced Study and a number of other central academic activities. It has a diverse population of over 125,000 students, with a further 34,000 studying by distance learning. The University of London Institute in Paris and University Marine Biological Station, Millport, are also part of the institution. Imperial College, King's College and University College are all independent members of the Russell Group. Tel: 020 7862 8360.

Colleges
- Birkbeck, University of London
- Central School of Speech and Drama
- Courtauld Institute of Art
- Goldsmiths, University of London
- Heythrop College
- Imperial College London
- Institute of Cancer Research
- Institute of Education
- King's College London
- London Business School
- London School of Economics and Political Science
- London School of Hygiene and Tropical Medicine
- Queen Mary, University of London
- Royal Academy of Music
- Royal Holloway, University of London
- Royal Veterinary College
- St George's, University of London
- School of Oriental and African Studies
- School of Pharmacy
- University College London

Institutes
- Institute of Advanced Legal Studies
- Institute of Classical Studies
- Institute of Commonwealth Studies
- Institute of English Studies
- Institute of Germanic & Romance Studies
- Institute of Historical Research
- Institute of Musical Research
- Institute of Philosophy
- Institute for the Study of the Americas
- Warburg Institute

University of Westminster — Granted university status in 1992, the former Polytechnic of Central London has its roots in the Royal Polytechnic Institution, formed in 1838 and therefore Britain's oldest polytechnic. With around 25,000 students, Westminster is now a leading university for research in Communication, Cultural and Media Studies, Law, Asian Studies (Chinese), Linguistics, Art and Design (including Music), Electronic Engineering, Italian, and Politics and International Relations. Former students include fashion designer Vivienne Westwood, broadcaster Trisha Goddard and sculptor Sir Anthony Caro. **Headquarters Building**, Regent Street, W1. Tel: 020 7911 5000. **Cavendish Campus** (School of Biosciences, School of Informatics, and School of Integrated Health), New Cavendish Street, W1. **Harrow Campus** (Harrow Business School, Harrow School of Computer Science and School of Media, Arts and Design), Watford Road, Northwick Park, Harrow.

Marylebone Campus (School of Architecture and the Built Environment, and Westminster Business School), Marylebone Road, NW1.

Valentine's Mansion — Emerson Road, Ilford. A late 17th century house, largely Georgian in appearance with Regency additions. The unusual curved early 19th century porte cochère (porch) is of particular interest. The exterior was extensively repaired and restored in 2000. The house is set in Valentine's Park. Tel: 020 8708 3619.

Victoria & Albert Museum — Cromwell Road, SW7. Founded in 1852 and named after Queen Victoria and her consort Prince Albert, the V&A is the world's greatest museum of art and design. Unrivalled in their scope and diversity, its collections cover 3000 years' worth of artefacts from many of the world's richest cultures including ceramics, furniture, fashion, glass, jewellery, metalwork, photographs, sculpture, textiles and paintings. The V&A complex comprises the museum at South Kensington, the V&A Museum of Childhood at Bethnal Green, and the archives and stores at Blythe House, Kensington Olympia. Tel: 020 7942 2000. See also Museum of Childhood.

Wardour Street — London W1. A street in Soho once synonymous with the British film industry, many of whose major companies had their headquarters here from the early 20th century, and still closely associated with the entertainment industry.

Wellington Arch — Hyde Park Corner, W1. George IV originally commissioned this massive monument as a grand outer entrance to Buckingham Palace from the north. it was completed in 1830 by architect Decimus Burton and positioned at the top of Constitution Hill, and was moved to its present site in 1882. The balconies just below the spectacular bronze sculpture that tops the monument offer glorious views over London's Royal Parks and the Houses of Parliament. The largest bronze sculpture in Europe, the statue depicts the angel of peace descending on the chariot of war. Inside, three floors of exhibits tell its history, including its time as London's smallest police station. The Metropolitan Police still congregate in large numbers outside the arch when protest marches take place in London. Apsley House (see separate entry), opposite the Wellington Arch, was the London home of the Duke of Wellington, and is also managed by English Heritage. Tel: 020 7930 2726.

Wembley Stadium — South Way, Wembley. The original stadium was built by Sir Robert McAlpine for the British Empire Exhibition of 1923 on the former site of Watkin's Folly, planned as the British answer to the Eiffel Tower but remained uncompleted due to foundation problems. The stadium's distinctive Twin Towers, and 39 steps up to the royal box, became its trademark. The first event held at the stadium was the 1923 FA Cup final between Bolton and West Ham, the famous White Horse Final. The match looked in doubt due to severe overcrowding as fans rushed the turnstiles, the official attendance of 126,047 almost certainly being more than twice that figure. Mounted police, including PC George Scorey and his white horse, Billy, slowly pushed the masses back to the sides of the field of play for the match to eventually start, just 45 minutes late. The new stadium, designed by HOK Sport and Foster & Partners, was opened in 2007 and has the second largest capacity in Europe, and is also the largest stadium in the world with every one of its 90,000 seats under cover. The present stadium has a sliding roof overlooked by a distinctive arch visible from miles away. Tel: 0844 980 8001.

Westminster Abbey — Broad Sanctuary, SW1. The Collegiate Church of St Peter, Westminster, is neither a cathedral nor a parish church, but since 1579, a 'Royal Peculiar' under the jurisdiction of a dean and chapter, subject only to the sovereign. The setting for every coronation since 1066, it is the burial place of kings, statesmen, poets, scientists, warriors and musicians, as well as a place of daily worship. In the 1040s Edward the Confessor, last of the Anglo-Saxon kings, established his royal palace beside the River Thames on Thorney Island. Close by was a small Benedictine monastery founded under the patronage of King Edgar and St Dunstan C.AD 960. Edward chose to re-endow and greatly enlarge this monastery, building a large stone church in honour of St Peter the Apostle. The church became known as the 'west minster' to distinguish it from St Paul's Cathedral (the east minster) in the City of London. Unfortunately, when the new church was consecrated on 28 December 1065 the king was too ill to attend and died a few days later. His body was interred in front of the high altar. Edward's abbey survived until the middle of the 13th century when Henry III decided to rebuild it in the new Gothic style. A remarkable new addition was the glorious lady chapel built by Henry VII, and which now bears his name. The chapel has a spectacular fan-vaulted roof, while Henry's tomb is a fine example of the craftsmanship of Italian sculptor Torrigiano. The colourful banners of the Knights of the Order of the Bath surround the walls, and at the east end is the Battle of Britain window by Hugh Easton. Two centuries later the abbey's western towers (left unfinished from medieval times) were completed to a design by Nicholas Hawksmoor. Built by the royal masons in 1250, the chapter house was used in the 14th century by the Benedictine monks for their daily meetings and subsequently as the meeting place of the king's Great Council and the Commons, predecessors of Parliament. A beautiful octagonal building with vaulted ceiling and a delicate central column, it possesses rarely seen examples of medieval sculpture, its original floor of glazed tiles and spectacular wall paintings. The late 14th century portrait of Richard II is the oldest painting of an English monarch from life. Further rebuilding and restoration occurred in the 19th century under Sir George Gilbert Scott. Until the 19th century, Westminster was the third seat of learning in England after Oxford and Cambridge. It was here that the first third of the King James Bible Old Testament and the last half of the New Testament were translated. The New English Bible was also assembled here in the 20th century. Monarchs buried in Westminster Abbey include Edward the Confessor, Henry II, Richard I, Henry III, Edward III, Richard II, Henry IV, Henry V, Henry VII, Edward VI, Mary I, Elizabeth I, James I, Charles II, Mary II, William III, Anne, and George II; commoners include Clement Attlee, Ernest Bevin, Charles Darwin, Hugh Dowding, Isaac Newton, Henry Purcell, Ernest Rutherford, George Gilbert Scott, Robert Stephenson, Sidney Webb, 1st Baron Passfield and William Wilberforce. Poets' Corner is the name given to the section of the south transept where many famous literary and artistic people are buried. Geoffrey Chaucer was the first; others include Robert Adam, Robert Browning, William Camden, Charles Dickens, John Dryden, David Garrick, John Gay, Thomas Hardy, Dr Samuel Johnson, Rudyard Kipling, Thomas Macaulay, John Masefield, Laurence Olivier, Richard Brinsley Sheridan, Edmund Spenser and Alfred, Lord Tennyson. Tel: 020 7654 4834.

Westminster Cathedral Victoria Street, SW1. Located close to Victoria Station, the cathedral site was originally known as Bulinga Fen and formed part of the marsh around Westminster. It was reclaimed by the Benedictine monks of Westminster Abbey and subsequently used as a market and fairground. After the Reformation the land was used in turn as a maze, a pleasure garden and as a ring for bull-baiting but it remained largely waste ground. In the 17th century part of the land was sold by the abbey for the construction of a prison; this was replaced by an enlarged prison complex in 1834. The site was acquired by the Catholic Church in 1884. The Cathedral Church of Westminster, dedicated to the Most Precious Blood of Our Lord Jesus Christ, was designed in the Early Christian Byzantine style by Victorian architect John Francis Bentley. The foundation stone was laid in 1895 and the fabric of the building was completed eight years later. The awesome interior, although incomplete, contains fine marble work and mosaics. The 14 Stations of the Cross by sculptor Eric Gill are world renowned. Tel: 020 7798 9055.

Westminster University See University of Westminster

Whitehall London SW1. A road running north from Parliament Square, the centre of national government, towards the site of the traditional Charing Cross, now at the southern end of Trafalgar Square. Along its way it is lined by many government ministries; 'Whitehall' is therefore also frequently used both as a name for the surrounding district and for government administration in general. The name is taken from Henry VIII's vast Palace of Whitehall and was the site of his death in 1547. The palace was occupied by royalty until 1689, when William III found that the river air exacerbated his asthma and transferred the royal residence to Kensington Palace. The Banqueting House (see separate entry) is the only part of the palace to survive a fire in 1698.

Whitgift Almshouses North End, Croydon. A set of Elizabethan almshouses in the centre of Croydon, originally named the Hospital of the Holy Trinity and erected by Archbishop John Whitgift. After Whitgift received permission from Elizabeth I to establish a hospital and school in Croydon for the 'poor, needy and impotent people' from the parishes of Croydon and Lambeth, the foundation stone was laid in 1596 and the building was completed in 1599. Threatened at various times by reconstruction plans and road-widening schemes, the almshouses were saved in 1923 by intervention of the House of Lords. On 21 June 1983, Queen Elizabeth II visited the almshouses and unveiled a plaque celebrating the restoration of the building. The laying of the foundation stone is commemorated on 22 March each year as Founder's Day.

Whitehall Malden Road, Cheam. A Tudor timber-framed house of c.1500 with later additions including 18th century weatherboarding, situated in the heart of Cheam Village. There are displays on the house, plus nearby Nonsuch Palace, Cheam School and its most famous headmaster, William Gilpin. Tel: 020 8643 1236.

William Morris Gallery Lloyd Park, Forest Road, E17. The only public museum devoted to England's best known and most versatile designer. Located at Morris's family home 1848–56, the former Water House, a substantial Georgian dwelling dating to c.1750 and set in its own extensive grounds, the museum was opened by Prime Minister Clement Attlee in 1950. Tel: 020 8527 3782.

World's End The name of two areas of London. The World's End Estate in Chelsea, SW10, is bounded by King's Road on one side and Cheyne Walk on the bank of the Thames on the other. A pub on King's Road called the World's End roughly marks the western end of the Chelsea area (as Sloane Square marks the eastern end). World's End was home to Gandalf's Garden and the hippy counterculture in the 1960s and to Vivienne Westwood's shop Sex in the punk era of the 1970s. World's End is also the name of an area in the London Borough of Enfield between Enfield Town and Oakwood. A short-lived BBC soap opera broadcast in 1981 and set in a fictional London suburb was also titled *World's End*.

Yeomen Warders Famously nicknamed 'Beefeaters', the Yeoman Warders are the ceremonial guards of the Tower of London. When Edward Seymour, Duke of Somerset was imprisoned in the Tower for the first time in January 1549, he was so impressed with his guards' diligence and cheerful bearing that he vowed to grant them any request they desired if he were freed. After his liberation and pardon in February 1550, the Warders held him to his promise by asking for the right to wear the same red and gold livery as members of the Yeomen of the Guard – the king's closest bodyguard, whose origin dated to 1485. As Protector of the young Edward VI, the Duke was delighted to confer this privilege. Today each of the 38 Yeomen Warders posted in the Tower of London is a retired warrant officer of the Army, RAF or Royal Marines; this method of recruiting was introduced by the Duke of Wellington in 1826 when he became Constable of the Tower. The Yeomen Warders still continue to wear their Tudor livery and carry the impressive pike-type weapons correctly known as 'partizans' for certain ceremonies and church parades; on most days, however, they wear a more functional blue undress uniform of Victorian origin, loosely based on the traditional design. In January 2007 the first female Beefeater was appointed. See also Tower of London.

Some famous people born in London

Amis, Kingsley (writer) (1922–95)	Clapham
Attlee, Clement (politician) (1883–1967)	Putney
Baden-Powell, Robert (Scouts founder) (1857–1941)	Paddington
Banks, Sir Joseph (botanist) (1743–1820)	Westminster
Bannister, Roger (athlete) (1929–)	Harrow
Becket, Thomas (archbishop) (c.1118–70)	Cheapside
Beckham, David (footballer) (1975–)	Leytonstone
Bentham, Jeremy (philosopher) (1748–1832)	Spitalfields
Blake, William (poet and artist) (1757–1827)	Westminster
Blyton, Enid (children's writer) (1897–1968)	East Dulwich
Bowie, David (musician and actor) (1947–)	Brixton
Bristow, Eric (darts player) (1957–)	Hackney
Browning, Robert (poet and playwright) (1812–89)	Camberwell
Bygraves, Max (entertainer) (1922–)	Rotherhithe
Calzaghe, Joe (boxer) (1972–)	Hammersmith
Chaplin, Charlie (comic actor) (1889–1977)	Walworth
Chesterton, G K (novelist) (1874–1936)	Kensington
Coe, Sebastian (athlete) (1956–)	Chiswick
Coward, Noel (actor and playwright) (1899–1973)	Teddington
Douglas-Home, Alec (politician) (1903–95)	Mayfair
Drake, Charlie (comedian) (1925–2006)	Southwark
Emin, Tracey (artist) (1963–)	Croydon
Fleming, Ian (author) (1908–64)	Mayfair
Forsyth, Bruce (entertainer) (1928–)	Edmonton
Gaskell, Elizabeth (novelist) (1810–65)	Chelsea
Gibbon, Edward (historian) (1737–94)	Putney
Gordon, Charles (army officer) (1833–85)	Woolwich
Guinness, Alec (actor) (1914–2000)	Paddington
Halley, Edmond (astronomer) (1656–1742)	Shoreditch
Haynes, Arthur (comedian) (1914–66)	Fulham
Hitchcock, Alfred (film director) (1899–1980)	Leytonstone
Hogarth, William (artist) (1697–1764)	Westminster
Jones, Inigo (architect) (1573–1652)	Smithfield
Keats, John (poet) (1795–1821)	Moorgate
Lear, Edward (writer and illustrator) (1812–88)	Highgate
Lewis, Lennox (boxer) (1965–)	West Ham
Lewis, Ted 'Kid' (boxer) (1894–1970)	Aldgate
Lloyd, Marie (music hall artist) (1870–1922)	Hoxton
Lynn, Vera (singer) (1917–)	East Ham
McDowall, Roddy (actor) (1928–98)	Herne Hill
Macmillan, (Maurice) Harold (politician) (1894–1986)	Chelsea
Markova, Alicia (prima ballerina) (1910–2004)	Finsbury Park
Milne, A A (Alan Alexander) (author) (1882–1956)	Kilburn
Milton, John (poet) (1608–74)	Cheapside
Monkhouse, Bob (comedian) (1928–2003)	Beckenham
Montgomery, Bernard (Field Marshall) (1887–1976)	Kennington
Moore, Bobby (footballer) (1941–93)	Barking
Moore, Dudley (entertainer) (1935–2002)	Dagenham
Moore, Patrick (astronomer) (1923–)	Pinner
Moore, Roger (actor) (1927–)	Stockwell
Morris, William (architect and designer) (1834–96)	Walthamstow
Moss, Kate (model) (1974–)	Addiscombe
Neagle, Anna (actress) (1904–86)	Forest Gate
Nesbit, Edith (author and poet) (1858–1924)	Kennington
Niven, David (actor) (1910–83)	St John's Wood
O'Connor, Des (entertainer) (1932–)	Stepney
Osborne, John (playwright) (1929–94)	Fulham
Pepys, Samuel (writer) (1633–1703)	Fleet Street
Pinter, Harold (playwright and actor) (1930–2008)	Hackney
Pope, Alexander (poet) (1688–1744)	City of London
Potter, Beatrix (children's writer) (1866–1943)	South Kensington
Purcell, Henry (composer) (1659–95)	Westminster
Quant, Mary (fashion designer) (1934–)	Blackheath
Ramsey, Alf (football manager) (1920–99)	Dagenham
Reed, Oliver (actor) (1938–99)	Wimbledon
Riley, Bridget (artist) (1931–)	South Norwood
Shearing, George (jazz pianist) (1919–)	Battersea
Springer, Jerry (talk show host) (1944–)	East Finchley (tube station)
Sullivan, Arthur (composer) (1842–1900)	Lambeth
Sutherland, Kiefer (actor) (1966–)	Paddington

Tandy, Jessica (actress) (1909–94)	Hackney
Tate, Catherine (comedienne) (1968–)	Bloomsbury
Taylor, Elizabeth (actress) (1932–)	Hampstead
Thompson, Daley (athlete) (1958–)	Worcester Park
Trollope, Anthony (novelist) (1815–82)	Bloomsbury
Wall, Max (comedian) (1908–90)	Brixton
Wells, H G (science fiction writer) (1866–1946)	Bromley
Winehouse, Amy (singer and songwriter) (1983–)	Enfield
Wisdom, Norman (comedian) (1915–)	Marylebone
Woolf, Virginia (novelist) (1882–1941)	South Kensington

Islands of Greater London

Island name	Area	Nearest landmark	General information
Boyle Farm Island	River Thames	Hampton Court	Has a single house and family on the island.
Brentford Ait	River Thames	Kew Bridge	Lies opposite Lot's Ait. GR: TQ187777
Chiswick Eyot	River Thames	Barnes Bridge	Eyot (pronounced 'eight' and can also be spelled ait). The most easterly island of Greater London. Area: 0.0004 sq miles (0.001 sq km). GR: TQ219779
Corporation Island	River Thames	Richmond Bridge	Managed by London Borough of Richmond upon Thames. GR: TQ175746
Crane Park Island	River Crane	Feltham	Area: 0.008 sq miles (0.02 sq km). GR: TQ128727
Dogs, Isle of	River Thames	Docklands	Included by virtue of its name but in fact a peninsula. Originally called Stepney Marsh.
Eel Pie Island	River Thames	Twickenham	aka Twickenham Ait. Accessible from mainland by footbridge. Home to Twickenham Rowing Club. GR: TQ167732
Flower Pot Islands	River Thames	Corporation Island	Two islands managed by London Borough of Richmond upon Thames.
Frog Island	River Thames	Rainham	Not an island at all nowadays but a piece of marshy land in spitting distance of the Thames. GR: TQ510810
Glover's Island	River Thames	Richmond Park	Managed by London Borough of Richmond upon Thames. GR: TQ178735
Isleworth Ait	River Thames	Isleworth	London Wildlife Trust reserve. Area: 0.02 sq miles (0.04 sq km). GR: TQ167757
Karno's Island	River Thames	Hampton Court	aka Tagg's Island. Situated between Garrick's Ait and Ash Island in Surrey. Frederick John Westcott (Fred Karno), the well-known music-hall impresario, owned the island and commissioned Frank Matcham to design the most luxurious hotel of its day (The Karsino). GR: TQ146690
Lot's Ait	River Thames	Kew Bridge	Lies opposite Brentford Ait. GR: TQ184776
Oliver's Island	River Thames	Kew Bridge	Faces Strand-on-the-Green. GR: TQ194776
Platt's Eyot	River Thames	Hampton	Situated between Sunbury Court Island and Grand Junction Isle in Surrey. GR: TQ133691
Steven's Eyot	River Thames	Kingston	Owned by the Environment Agency and also used by boating clubs.
Swan Island	River Thames	Twickenham	Situated near Strawberry Hill.
Tagg's Island	River Thames	Hampton Court	See Karno's Island
Thames Ditton Island	River Thames	Hampton Court	The island is 350yds (320m) long and has 47 houses and a population of around 100. GR: TQ175680
Trowlock Island	River Thames	Teddington	Home to 29 bungalows and the Royal Canoe Club. The island was in the news in 2006 for the 150,000 per cent increase in the ferry fee to the mainland. GR: TQ176708
Twickenham Ait	River Thames	Twickenham	See Eel Pie Island.
Wilderness Island	River Wandle	Carshalton	Area: 0.01 sq miles (0.03 sq km). GR: TQ282653

Blue Plaques

The official blue plaque scheme in London was set up in 1867, celebrating Byron's Holles Street residence. Initially the scheme was run by the Royal Society of Arts; it was transferred to the London County Council in 1901 and later the Greater London Council. When the GLC was disbanded in 1986, English Heritage took over the role. The RSA placed 13 plaques, the LCC 249, the GLC 262; and English Heritage are currently placing 20 per annum. In order to be eligible for an English Heritage blue plaque, a figure must have been dead for 20 years or have passed the centenary of their birth. Many of the buildings which had plaques have been subsequently demolished. The oldest surviving plaque is in Gerrard Street and dates from 1875. The early plaques were dark brown, the current design dates from 1937, with the white border added in 1939. The scheme extended to other parts of the UK in 1998, with the first plaques being unveiled in Liverpool in 2000. Other cities now involved include Birmingham, Portsmouth and Southampton. In 2004, the scheme was extended to the East of England, followed by the East Midlands in 2005. A full list of London plaques follows. All addresses denote residency unless the name is given with an asterisk, in which case the address is a working environment.

Name	Address
ABRAHAMS, Harold (1899–1978), athlete	Hodford Lodge, 2 Hodford Road, NW11
ADAM, Robert (1728–92), architect	1–3 Robert Street, WC2
ADAMS, Henry Brooks (1838–1918), US historian	98 Portland Place, W1
ALDRIDGE, Ira (1807–67), Shakespearian actor	5 Hamlet Road, Upper Norwood, SE19
ALEXANDER, Sir George (1858–1918), actor-manager	57 Pont Street, SW1
ALLENBY, Field Marshal Edmund H H (1861–1936)	24 Wetherby Gardens, SW5
ALMA-TADEMA, Sir Lawrence (1836–1912), painter	44 Grove End Road, NW8
AMBROSE, Bert (c.1896–1971), dance band leader	May Fair Hotel, Stratton Street, W1
ARDIZZONE, Edward (1900–79), artist and illustrator	130 Elgin Avenue, W9
ARKWRIGHT, Sir Richard (1732–92), industrialist	8 Adam Street, WC2
ARNE, Thomas (1710–78), composer	31 King Street, WC2
ARNOLD, Matthew (1822–88), poet and critic	2 Chester Square, SW1
ARNOLD, Sir Edwin (1832–1904), poet and journalist	31 Bolton Gardens, SW5
ASHFIELD, Albert (1874–1948), London Transport executive	43 South Street, W1
ASQUITH, Herbert Henry (1852–1928), politician	20 Cavendish Square, W1
ASTAFIEVA, Princess Seraphine (1876–1934), ballerina	152 King's Road, SW3
ASTOR, Nancy (1879–1964), politician	4 St James's Square, SW1
ATTLEE, Richard Clement (1883–1967), politician	17 Monkhams Ave, Woodford Green
AUROBINDO, Sri (1872–1950), Indian spiritual leader	49 St Stephen's Avenue, W12
AVEBURY, Baron Sir John Lubbock (1834–1913), scientist	29 Eaton Place, SW1
AYRTON, Hertha (1854–1923), physicist	41 Norfolk Square, W2
BADEN-POWELL, Robert (1857–1941), Boy Scouts founder	9 Hyde Park Gate, SW7
BAGEHOT, Walter (1826–77), writer and economist	12 Upper Belgrave Street, SW1
BAGNOLD, Enid (1889–1981), novelist and playwright	29 Hyde Park Gate, SW7
BAILLIE, Joanna (1762–1851), poet and dramatist	Bolton House, Windmill Hill, NW3
BAIRD, John Logie (1888–1946), television inventor	22 Frith Street, W1
BAIRD, John Logie (1888–1946), television inventor	3 Crescent Wood Road, SE26
BAIRNSFATHER, Bruce (1888–1959), cartoonist	1 Sterling Street, SW7
*BALCON, Sir Michael (1896–1977), film producer	Ealing Film Studios, W5
BALDWIN, Stanley (1867–1947), politician	93 Eaton Square, SW1
BALFE, Michael William (1808–70), composer	12 Seymour Street, W1
BALLANTYNE, R M (1825–94), author	Duneaves, Mount Park Road, Harrow
BANKS, Sir Joseph (1743–1820), botanist	32 Soho Square, W1
BARING, Evelyn, 1st Earl of Cromer (1841–1917)	36 Wimpole Street, W1
BARLOW, William Henry (1812–1902), engineer	Highcombe, 145 Carlton Road, SE7
*BARNARDO, Dr Thomas John (1845–1905), missionary	58 Solent House, Ben Jonson Road, E1
BARNETT, Canon Samuel (1844–1913), social reformer	Heath End House, Spaniards Road, NW3
BARNETT, Dame Henrietta (1851–1936), social reformer	Heath End House, Spaniards Road, NW3
BARRIE, Sir James (1860–1937), dramatist	1–3 Robert Street, WC2
BARRIE, Sir James (1860–1937), dramatist	100 Bayswater Road, W2
BARRY, Sir Charles (1795–1860), architect	The Elms, Clapham Common North Side, SW4
BARTÓK, Béla (1881–1945), Hungarian composer	7 Sydney Place, SW7
BASEVI, George (1794–1845), architect	17 Savile Row, W1
BATEMAN, H M (1887–1970), cartoonist	40 Nightingale Lane, SW12
BAX, Sir Arnold (1883–1953), composer	13 Pendennis Road, SW16
BAYES, Gilbert (1872–1953), sculptor	4 Greville Place, NW6
BAYLIS, Lilian (1874–1937), theatre manager	27 Stockwell Park Road, SW9
BAZALGETTE, Sir Joseph William (1819–91), civil engineer	17 Hamilton Terrace, NW8
BEARD, John (c.1717–91), singer	Hampton Branch Library, Rose Hill
BEARDSLEY, Aubrey (1872–98), artist	114 Cambridge Street, SW1
BEATTY, David (1871–1936), admiral	Hanover Lodge, Regent's Park, NW1
BEAUFORT, Sir Francis (1774–1857), admiral	51 Manchester Street, W1

Name	Address
BEECHAM, Sir Thomas, CH (1879–1961), conductor	31 Grove End Road, NW8
BEERBOHM, Sir Max (1872–1956), artist and writer	57 Palace Gardens Terrace, W8
BELLO, Andres (1781–1865), Venezuelan patriot and poet	58 Grafton Way, W1
BELLOC, Hilaire (1870–1953), poet, essayist and historian	104 Cheyne Walk, SW10
BENEDICT, Sir Julius (1804–85), composer	2 Manchester Square, W1
BENES, Dr Edward (1884–1948), Czech politician	26 Gwendolen Avenue, SW15
BEN-GURION, David (1886–1973), Israeli politician	75 Warrington Crescent, W9
BENNETT, Arnold (1867–1931), novelist	75 Cadogan Square, SW1
BENNETT, Sir William Sterndale (1816–75), composer	38 Queensborough Terrace, W2
BENSON, E F (1867–1940), writer	25 Brompton Square, SW3
BENTHAM, George (1800–84), botanist	25 Wilton Place, SW1
BENTLEY, John Francis (1839–1902), architect	43 Old Town, SW4
BERESFORD, Jack (1899–1977), rower	19 Grove Park Gardens, W4
BERLIOZ, Hector (1803–69), composer	58 Queen Anne Street, W1
BERNAL, John Desmond (1901–71), crystallographer	44 Albert Street, NW1
BESANT, Annie (1847–1933), social reformer	39 Colby Road, SE19
BESANT, Sir Walter (1836–1901), novelist and antiquary	Frognal End, Frognal Gardens, NW3
BESTALL, Alfred (1892–1986), artist and writer of Rupert Bear stories	58 Cranes Park, Surbiton
BETJEMAN, Sir John (1906–84), poet Laureate	31 Highgate West Hill, N6
BEVAN, Robert Polhill (1865–1925), artist	14 Adamson Road, NW3
BEVIN, Ernest (1881–1951), trade union leader	34 South Moulton Street, W1
BLACKIE, Dr Margery (1898–1981), homeopathic physician	18 Thurloe Street, SW7
BLAKE, William (1757–1827), poet and artist	Old Wyldes', North End, NW3
BLIGH, William (1754–1817), commander of the *Bounty*	100 Lambeth Road, SE1
BLISS, Sir Arthur (1891–1975), composer	1 East Heath Road, NW3
BLUMLEIN, Alan Dower (1903–42), engineer and inventor	37 The Ridings, W5
BLYTON, Enid (1897–1968), children's writer	207 Hook Road, Chessington
BODLEY, George Frederick (1827–1907), architect	109 Harley Street, W1
BOLIVAR, Simon (1783–1830), liberator of Latin America	4 Duke Street, W1
BOMBERG, David (1890–1957), painter	10 Fordwych Road, NW2
BONAR LAW, Andrew (1858–1923), politician	24 Onslow Gardens, SW7
BONHAM CARTER, Lady Violet (1887–1969)	43 Gloucester Square, W2
BOOTH, Charles (1840–1916), pioneer in social research	6 Grenville Place, SW7
BORROW, George (1803–81), author	22 Hereford Square, SW7
BOSWELL, James (1740–95), biographer	122 Great Portland Street, W1
BOSWELL, James (1740–95), first met Dr Johnson here	8 Russell Street, WC2
BOULT, Sir Adrian (1889–1983), conductor	78 Marlboro Mn, Cannon Hill, NW6
BRADLAUGH, Charles (1833–91), advocate of Free Thought	29 Turner Street, E1
BRAILSFORD, Henry Noel (1873–1958), writer	37 Belsize Park Gardens, NW3
BRAIN, Dennis (1921–57), horn-player	37 Frognal, NW3
BRANGWYN, Sir Frank (1867–1956), artist	51 Queen Caroline Street, W6
BRIDGE, Frank (1879–1941), composer and musician	4 Bedford Gardens, W8
BRIDGEMAN, Charles (1690–1738), landscape gardener	54 Broadwick Street, W1
BRIGHT, Richard (1789–1858), physician	11 Savile Row, W1
BRITTAIN, Vera (1893–1970), writer	58 Doughty Street, WC1
BRITTEN, Benjamin (1913–76), composer	173 Cromwell Road, SW5
BROOKE, Sir Charles (1874–1963), last Rajah of Sarawak	13 Albion Street, W2
BROWN, Robert (1773–1858), botanist	32 Soho Square, W1
BROWNE, Hablot Knight alias 'PHIZ' (1815–82), illustrator	239 Ladbroke Grove, W10
BROWNING, Elizabeth Barrett (1806–61), poet	99 Gloucester Place, W1
BROWNING, Elizabeth Barrett (1806–61), poet	50 Wimpole Street, W1
BRUMMELL, Beau (1778–1840), leader of fashion	4 Chesterfield Street, W1
BRUNEL, Isambard Kingdom (1806–59), civil engineer	98 Cheyne Walk, SW10
BRUNEL, Sir Marc Isambard (1769–1849), civil engineer	98 Cheyne Walk, SW10
BURGOYNE, General John (1722–92)	10 Hertford Street, W1
BURKE, Edmund (1729–97), author and statesman	37 Gerrard Street, W1
BURNE-JONES, Sir Edward (1833–98), artist	41 Kensington Square, W8
BURNE-JONES, Sir Edward Coley (1833–98), painter	17 Red Lion Square, WC1
BURNETT, Frances Hodgson (1849–1924), writer	63 Portland Place, W1
BURNEY, Fanny (Madame D'Arblay), (1752–1840), writer	11 Bolton Street, W1
BURNS, John (1858–1943), statesman	110 North Side, SW4
*BUSS, Frances Mary (1827–94), education pioneer	Camden School, Sandall Road, NW5
BUTLER, Josephine (1828–1906), social reformer	8 North View, SW19
BUTT, Dame Clara (1873–1936), singer	7 Harley Road, NW3
BUTTERFIELD, William (1814–1900), architect	42 Bedford Square, WC1
BUXTON, Sir Thomas Fowell (1786–1845), anti-slavery campaigner	91 Brick Lane, E1
CALDECOTT, Randolph (1846–86), artist	46 Great Russell Street, WC2
CAMPBELL-BANNERMAN, Sir Henry (1836–1908), politician	6 Grosvenor Place, SW1
CAMPBELL, Colen (1676–1729), architect and author	76 Brook Street, W1
CANAL, Antonio (CANALETTO) (1697–1768), painter	41 Beak Street, W1
CANNING, George (1770–1827), politician	50 Berkeley Square, W1

Name	Address
CARLILE, Wilson (1847–1942), founder of Church Army	34 Sheffield Terrace, W8
CARLYLE, Thomas (1795–1881), essayist and historian	33 Ampton Street, WC1
CARTER, Howard (1874–1939), Egyptologist	19 Collingham Gardens, SW5
*CASLON, William (1692–1766), typefounder	21–23 Chiswell Street, EC1
CASTLEREAGH, Viscount (1769–1822), statesman	Loring Hall, Water Lane, North Cray
CATO STREET CONSPIRACY 23 February 1820	1a Cato Street, W1
*CAVELL, Edith (1865–1915), nurse	London Hospital, E1
CAVENDISH, Hon Henry (1731–1810), natural philosopher	11 Bedford Square, WC1
CAYLEY, Sir George (1773–1857), scientist	20 Hertford Street, W1
CECIL, Viscount (1864–1958), League of Nations founder	16 South Eaton Place, SW1
CETSHWAYO KAMPANDE (c.1826–84), king of the Zulus	18 Melbury Road, W14
CHADWICK, Sir Edwin (1801–90), social reformer	5 Montague Road, Richmond
CHAIN, Sir Ernst (1906–79), biochemist	9 North View, SW19
CHAMBERLAIN, Joseph (1836–1914), statesman	188 Camberwell Grove, SE5
CHAMBERLAIN, Joseph (1836–1914), statesman	25 Highbury Place, N5
CHAMBERLAIN, Neville (1869–1940), politician	37 Eaton Square, SW1
CHAMBERS, Dorothea Lambert (1878–1960), tennis player	7 North Common Road, W5
CHAPMAN, Herbert (1878–1934), football manager	6 Haslemere Avenue, NW4
CHARLES X (1757–1836), last Bourbon king of France	72 South Audley Street, W1
CHESTERFIELD, Philip, 4th Earl of (1694–1774), statesman	Rangers House, Chesterfield Walk, SE10
CHESTERTON, Gilbert Keith (1874–1936), poet, novelist and critic	11 Warwick Gardens, W14
CHEVALIER, Albert (1861–1923), music hall comedian	17 St Ann's Villas, W11
CHISHOLM, Caroline (1808–77), philanthropist	32 Charlton Place, N1
CHOPIN, Frederic (1810–49), composer	4 St James's Place, SW1
CHRISTIE, Dame Agatha (1890–1976), detective novelist	58 Sheffield Terrace, W8
CHURCHILL, Lord Randolph (1849–95), statesman	2 Connaught Place, W2
CHURCHILL, Sir Winston, KG (1874–1965), statesman	28 Hyde Park Gate, SW7
CLARKSON, Willy (1861–1934), theatrical wigmaker	41–43 Wardour Street, W1
CLAYTON, Rev P T B 'Tubby' (1885–1972), founder of Toc H	43 Trinity Square, EC3
CLEMENTI, Muzio (1752–1832), composer	128 Kensington Church Street, W8
CLIVE of India, Lord (1725–74), soldier and administrator	45 Berkeley Square, W1
COBDEN, Richard (1804–65), statesman	23 Suffolk Street, SW1
COBDEN-SANDERSON, Thomas J (1840–1922), lawyer	15 Upper Mall, W6
COBHAM, Sir Alan (1894–1973), aviator	78 Denman Road, SW15
COCHRANE, Thomas (1775–1860), admiral	Hanover Lodge, Regent's Park, NW1
COCKERELL, C R (Charles Robert) (1788–1863), architect	13 Chester Terrace, NW1
COLE, Sir Henry (1808–82), campaigner and educator	33 Thurloe Square, SW7
COLERIDGE, Samuel Taylor (1772–1834), poet	7 Addison Bridge Place, W14
COLERIDGE, Samuel Taylor (1772–1834), poet	71 Berners Street, W1
COLERIDGE-TAYLOR, Samuel (1875–1912), composer	30 Dagnall Park, SE25
COLLINS, William Wilkie (1824–89), novelist	65 Gloucester Place, W1
COMPTON-BURNETT, Dame Ivy (1884–1969), novelist	5 Braemar Mansions, SW7
CONAN DOYLE, Sir Arthur (1859–1930), novelist	12 Tennison Road, SE25
CONRAD, Joseph (1857–1924), novelist	17 Gillingham Street, SW1
CONS, Emma (1837–1912), founder of the Old Vic	136 Seymour Place, W1
CONSTABLE, John (1776–1837), landscape painter	40 Well Walk, NW3
COOK, Captain James (1728–79), explorer	88 Mile End Road, E1
COPEMAN, Sydney Monckton (1862–1947), immunologist	57 Redcliffe Gardens, SW10
COSTA, Sir Michael (1808–83), conductor and orchestra reformer	Wilton Court, 59 Eccleston Square, SW1
COWARD, Charles (1905–76), rescued Jews from Auschwitz	133 Chichester Road, N9
COWARD, Sir Noel (1899–1973), actor and playwright	131 Waldegrave Road, Teddington
COX, David (1783–1859), artist	34 Foxley Road, SW9
CRANE, Walter (1845–1915), artist	13 Holland Street, W8
CREED, Frederick George (1871–1957), electrical engineer	20 Outram Road, Addiscombe
CRIBB, Tom (1781–1848), boxing champion	36 Panton Street, SW1
CRIPPS, Sir Stafford (1899–1952), statesman	32 Elm Park Gardens, SW10
CROMPTON, R E B (1845–1940), electrical engineer	48 Kensington Court, W8
CROOKES, Sir William (1832–1919), scientist	7 Kensington Park Gardens, W11
CRUIKSHANK, George (1792–1878), artist	263 Hampstead Road, NW1
CUBITT, Thomas (1788–1855), master builder	3 Lyall Street, SW1
CURZON, George Nathaniel (1859–1925), Viceroy of India	1 Carlton House Terrace, SW1
DADD, Richard (1817–86), painter	15 Suffolk Street, SW1
DALE, Sir Henry (1875–1968), physiologist	Mount Vernon House, NW3
DANCE, George, the younger (1741–1825), architect	91 Gower Street, WC1
DANIELL, Thomas (1749–1840), topographical artist	14 Earls Terrace, W8
DANIELL, William (1769–1837), artist and engraver	135 St Pancras Way, NW1
DARWIN, Charles (1809–82), naturalist	110 Gower Street, WC1
DAVIES, Emily (1830–1921), founder of Girton College	17 Cunningham Place, NW8
DAY-LEWIS, C (1904–72), Poet Laureate	6 Crooms Hill, SE10
*DE GAULLE, General Charles (1890–1970), president of France	4 Carlton Gardens, SW1
DE HAVILLAND, Sir Geoffrey (1882–1965), aircraft designer	32 Baron's Court Road, W14

Name	Address
DE LA MARE, Walter (1873–1956), poet	Montpelier Row, Twickenham
DE MIRANDA, Francisco (1750–1816), revolutionary	58 Grafton Way, W1
DE MORGAN, Evelyn (1855–1919), artist	127 Old Church Street, SW3
DE MORGAN, William (1839–1917), ceramic artist	127 Old Church Street, SW3
DE QUINCEY, Thomas (1785–1859), writer	36 Tavistock Street, WC2
DE VALOIS, Dame Ninette (1898–2001), founder of the Royal Ballet	14 The Terrace, Barnes, SW13
DEFOE, Daniel (1661–1731), novelist	95 Stoke Newington Church Street, N16
DELIUS, Frederick (1862–1934), composer	44 Belsize Park Gardens, NW3
DEVANT, David (1868–1941), magician	Flat 1 Ornan Court, Ornan Road, NW3
DEVINE, George (1910–66), actor	9 Lower Mall, W6
DICKENS, Charles (1812–1870), novelist	48 Doughty Street, WC1
DICKINSON, Goldsworthy Lowes (1862–1932), humanist	11 Edwardes Square, W8
DILKE, Sir Charles Wentworth (1843–1911), statesman	76 Sloane Street, SW1
DISRAELI, Benjamin (1804–81), statesman	19 Curzon Street, W1
DISRAELI, Benjamin (1804–81), statesman	22 Theobalds Road, WC1
DOBSON, Frank (1886–1963), sculptor	14 Harley Gardens, SW10
DOBSON, Henry Austin (1840–1921), poet and essayist	10 Redcliffe Street, SW10
DON, David (1800–41), botanist	32 Soho Square, W1
DONAT, Robert (1905–58), actor	8 Meadway, Hampstead Green, NW11
DOUGLAS, Norman (1868–1952), writer	63 Albany Mews, Albert Bridge Road, SW11
DOWDING, Lord, Air Chief Marshall, (1882–1970)	3 St Mary's Road, SW19
DRYDEN, John (1631–1700), poet	43 Gerrard Street, W1
*DRYSDALE, Charles Vickery (1874–1961), doctor	153a East Street, SE17
DU MAURIER, George (1834–96), artist and writer	28 Hampstead Grove, NW3
DU MAURIER, George (1834–96), artist and writer	91 Great Russell Street, WC1
DU MAURIER, Sir Gerald (1873–1934), actor-manager	14 Cannon Place, NW3
DUKE-ELDER, Sir Stewart (1898–1978), ophthalmologist	63 Harley Street, W1
DYSON, Sir Frank (1868–1939), Astronomer Royal	6 Vanbrugh Hill, SE3
*EARNSHAW, Thomas (1749–1829), watch-maker	119 High Holborn, WC1
EASTLAKE, Charles (1793–1865), painter	7 Fitzroy Square, W1
EDDINGTON, Sir Arthur, OM (1882–1944), astrophysicist	4 Bennett Park, SE3
EDWARDS, John Passmore (1823–1911), journalist	51 Netherhall Gardens, NW3
ELDON, John Scott, Lord (1751–1838), Lord Chancellor	6 Bedford Square, WC1
ELEN, Gus (1862–1940), music hall comedian	3 Thurleigh Avenue, SW12
ELGAR, Sir Edward (1857–1934), composer	51 Avonmore Road, W14
ELIOT, George (1819–80), novelist	4 Cheyne Walk, SW3
ELIOT, George (1819–80), novelist	31 Wimbledon Park Road, SW18
ELIOT, T S, OM (1888–1965), poet	3 Kensington Court Gardens, W8
ELLIS, Henry Havelock (1859–1939), scientist	Canterbury Crescent, SW9
ENGELS, Friedrich (1820–95), political philosopher	122 Regent's Park Road, NW1
ETTY, William (1787–1849), painter	14 Buckingham Street, WC2
EVANS, Dame Edith (1888–1976), actress	109 Ebury Street, SW1
EWART, William (1798–1869), promoter of public libraries	Hampton Branch Library, Rose Hill
EWART, William (1798–1869), reformer	16 Eaton Place, SW1
FABIAN SOCIETY founded in 1884	17 Osnaburgh Street, NW1
FARADAY, Michael (1791–1867), scientist	48 Blandford Street, W1
FAWCETT, Dame Millicent Garrett (1847–1929), suffragette	2 Gower Street, WC1
FENTON, Roger (1819–69), photographer	2 Albert Terrace, NW1
FENWICK, Ethel Gordon (1857–1947), nursing reformer	20 Upper Wimpole Street, W1
FERRIER, Kathleen (1912–1953), contralto	97 Frognal, Hampstead, NW3
FIELDING, Henry (1707–1754), novelist	Milbourne House, SW13
FILDES, Sir Samuel Luke (1844–1927), artist	31 Melbury Road, W14
FIRST, Ruth (1925–1982), freedom fighter	13 Lyme Street, NW1
FISHER, Admiral of the Fleet (1841–1920), First Sea Lord	16 Queen Anne's Gate, SW1
FISHER, Sir Ronald Aylmer (1890–1962), statistician	Inverforth House, North End Way, NW3
FITZROY, Admiral Robert (1805–65), hydrographer	38 Onslow Square, SW7
FLANAGAN, Bud (1896–1968), comedian	12 Hanbury Street, E1
FLAXMAN, John (1755–1826), sculptor	7 Greenwell Street, W1
FLECKER, James Elroy (1884–1915), poet and dramatist	9 Gilmore Road, SE13
FLEMING, Alexander (1881–1955), discoverer of penicillin	20a Danvers Street, SW3
FLEMING, Ian (1908–64), writer	22 Ebury Street, SW1
FLEMING, Sir Ambrose (1849–1945), scientist	9 Clifton Gardens, W9
FLINDERS, Captain Matthew, RN (1774–1814), explorer	56 Fitzroy Street, W1
FLYING BOMB first on London fell here, 13 June 1944	Railway Bridge, Grove Road, E3
FONTANE, Theodor (1819–98), writer	6 St Augustine's Road, NW1
FORBES, Vivian (1891–1937), artist	80 Lansdowne Road, W11
FORD, Ford Madox (1873–1939), novelist and critic	80 Campden Hill Road, W8
FORESTER, C S (1899–1966), novelist	58 Underhill Road, SE22
FORSTER, E M (1879–1970), novelist	Sutton Lane W4
FORTUNE, Robert (1812–80), plant collector	9 Gilston Road, SW10
FOSCOLO, Ugo (1778–1827), poet	19 Edwardes Square, W8

Name	Address
FOX, Charles James (1749–1806), statesman	46 Clarges Street, W1
FRAMPTON, George (1860–1928), sculptor	32 Queen's Grove, NW8
FRANKLIN, Benjamin (1706–90), statesman and scientist	36 Craven Street, WC2
FRANKLIN, Rosalind (1920–58), scientist	Donovan Court, Drayton Gardens, SW10
FREAKE, Sir Charles James (1814–84), patron of the arts	21 Cromwell Road, SW7
FREUD, Anna (1895–1982), pioneer of child psychoanalysis	20 Maresfield Gardens, NW3
FREUD, Sigmund (1856–1939), founder of psychoanalysis	20 Maresfield Gardens, NW3
FRIESE-GREENE, William (1855–1921), film pioneer	136 Maida Vale, W9
FRITH, W P (1819–1909), painter	114 Clifton Hill, NW8
FROUDE, James Anthony (1818–94), historian	5 Onslow Gardens, SW7
FRY, C B (1872–1956), sportsman	144 St James's Road, Croydon
FUSELI, Henry (1741–1825), artist	37 Foley Street, W1
GABOR, Dennis (1900–1979), physicist and inventor of holography	79 Queen's Gate, SW7
GAGE, Thomas (1721–87), soldier	41 Portland Place, W1
GAINSBOROUGH, Thomas (1727–1788), artist	82 Pall Mall, SW1
GAITSKELL, Hugh (1906–1963), statesman	18 Frognal Gardens, NW3
GALSWORTHY, John (1867–1933), novelist and playwright	1–3 Robert Street, WC2
GALSWORTHY, John (1867–1933), novelist and playwright	Grove Lodge, Admiral's Walk, NW3
GALTON, Sir Francis (1822–1911), founder of eugenics	42 Rutland Gate, SW7
GANDHI, Mahatma (1869–1948), philosopher and teacher	Kingsley Hall, Powis Road, E3
GANDHI, Mahatma (1869–1948), philosopher and teacher	20 Baron's Court Road, W14
GANDY, Joseph Michael (1771–1843), architectural visionary	58 Grove Park Terrace, W4
GARRETT ANDERSON, Elizabeth (1836–1917), doctor	20 Upper Berkeley Street, W1
GARRICK, David (1717–79), actor	Garrick's Villa, Hampton Court Road
GARTHWAITE, Anna Maria (1690–1763), designer	2 Princelet Street, E1
GARVEY, Marcus (1887–1940), Pan-Africanist leader	53 Talgarth Road, W14
GASKELL, Mrs Elizabeth Cleghorn (1810–65), novelist	93 Cheyne Walk, SW10
GAUDIER-BRZESKA, Henri (1891–1915), artist	454 Fulham Road, SW6
GERTLER, Mark (1891–1939), painter	32 Elder Street, E1
GIBBON, Edward (1737–92), historian	7 Bentinck Street, W1
GIBSON, Guy (1918–1944) VC, Pilot, leader of the Dambusters Raid	32 Aberdeen Place, St John's Wood, NW8
GILBERT, Sir W.S. (1836–1911), writer and lyricist	39 Harrington Gardens, SW7
GILBERT, Sir W.S. (1836–1911), writer and lyricist	Grims Dyke, Harrow Weald
GILLIES, Sir Harold (1882–1960), plastic surgeon	71 Frognal, NW3
GISSING, George (1857–1903), novelist	33 Oakley Gardens, SW3
GLADSTONE, W E (1809–98), politician	73 Harley Street, W1
GLADSTONE, W E (1809–98), politician	11 Carlton House Terrace, SW1
GLADSTONE, Wiliam Ewart (1809–98), statesman	10 St James's Square, SW1
GLAISHER, James (1809–1903), meteorologist	20 Dartmouth Hill, SE10
GODFREE, Kathleen ('Kitty') née McKane (1896–1922), tennis player	55 York Avenue, East Sheen, SW14
GODLEY, John Robert (1814–61), founder of Canterbury, NZ	48 Gloucester Place, W1
GODWIN, George (1813–88), architect and social reformer	24 Alexander Square, SW3
GOMME, Sir Laurence (1853–1916), Clerk to the London County Council	24 Dorset Square, Marylebone, NW1
GOODALL, Frederick (1822–1904) landscape painter	Grims Dyke, Harrow Weald
GOOSSENS family of musicians (1912–27)	70 Edith Road, W14
GORT, Field Marshal Viscount, VC (1886–1946)	34 Belgrave Square, SW1
GOSSE, Edmund (1849–1928), writer and critic	56 Mortimer Road, N1
GOSSE, Philip Henry (1810–88), zoologist	56 Mortimer Road, N1
GOUNOD, Charles (1818–93), composer	15 Morden Road, SE3
GRACE, W G (1848–1915), cricketer	Fairmount, Mottingham Lane, SE9
GRAHAME, Kenneth (1859–1932), author	16 Phillimore Place, W8
GRAINGER, Percy (1882–1961), composer	31 King's Road, SW3
GRAVES, Robert (1895–1985), writer	1 Lauriston Road, SW19
GRAY, Henry (1827–1861), anatomist	8 Wilton Street, SW1
GREATHEAD, James Henry (1844–96), railway engineer	3 St Mary's Grove, SW13
GREAVES, Walter (1846–1930), artist	104 Cheyne Walk, SW10
GREEN, John Richard (1837–83), historian	4 Beaumont Street, W1
GREEN, John Richard (1837–83), historian	St Philip's Vicarage, Newark Street, E1
GREENAWAY, Kate (1846–1901), artist	39 Frognal, NW3
GREET, Sir Philip Ben (1857–1936), actor-manager	160 Lambeth Road, SE1
GRENFELL, Joyce (1910–79), entertainer and writer	34 Elm Park Gardens, SW10
*GRESLEY, Sir Nigel (1876–1941), locomotive engineer	King's Cross Station
GREY, Edward, Visct of Falloden (1862–1933), politician	3 Queen Anne's Gate, SW1
GRIEG, Edvard (1843–1907), composer	47 Clapham Common North Side, SW4
GRIMALDI, Joseph (1778–1837), clown	56 Exmouth Market, EC1
GROOM, John (1845–1919), philanthropist	8 Sekforde Street, EC1
GROSER, Rev St. John (1890–1966), social reformer	2 Butcher Row, E14
GROSSMITH, George, Jr (1874–1935), actor-manager	3 Spanish Place, W1
GROSSMITH, George, Sr (1847–1912), actor and author	28 Dorset Square, NW1
GROTE, George (1794–1871), historian	12 Savile Row, W1
GUIZOT, François (1787–1874), politician	21 Pelham Crescent, SW7

Name	Address
HAAKON VII (1872–1957), king of Norway	10 Palace Green, W8
HAGGARD, Sir Henry Rider (1856–1925), novelist	69 Gunterstone Road, W14
HALDANE, Lord (1856–1928), statesman	28 Queen Anne's Gate, SW1
HALL, Henry (1898–1989), dance band leader	38 Harman Drive, NW2
HALL, Radclyffe (1880–1943), novelist and poet	37 Holland Street, W8
HALLAM, HENRY (1777–1859), historian	67 Wimpole Street, W1
HANDEL, George Frederick (1685–1759), composer	25 Brook Street, W1
HANDLEY, Tommy (1892–1949), radio comedian	34 Craven Road, W2
HANSOM, Joseph Aloysius (1803–82), architect	27 Sumner Place, SW7
HARDY, Thomas (1840–1928), poet and novelist	172 Trinity Road, SW17
HARLEY, Robert (1661–1724), Earl of Oxford	14 Buckingham Street, WC2
HARMSWORTH, Alfred (1865–1922), newspaper proprietor	31 Pandora Road, NW6
HARRISON, John (1693–1776), inventor of the chronometer	Summit House, Red Lion Square, WC1
HARTE, Francis Bret (1836–1902), writer	74 Lancaster Gate, W2
HARTNELL, Sir Norman (1901–79), court dressmaker	26 Bruton Street, W1
HAWKINS, Sir (Anthony Hope) (1863–1933), novelist	41 Bedford Square, WC1
HAWTHORNE, Nathaniel (1804–64), author	4 Pond Road, SE3
HAY, Will (1888–1949), comic actor	45 The Chase, SW16
HAYDON, Benjamin Robert (1786–1846), painter	116 Lissom Grove, NW1
HAZLITT, William (1778–1830), essayist	6 Frith Street, W1
HEARTFIELD, John (1891–1968), master of photomontage	47 Downshire Hill, NW3
HEATH ROBINSON, W (1872–1944), illustrator	75 Moss Lane, Pinner
HEINE, Heinrich (1799–1856), poet and essayist	32 Craven Street, WC2
HENDERSON, Arthur (1863–1935), statesman	13 Rodenhurst Road, SW4
HENDRIX, Jimi (1942–70), guitarist and songwriter	23 Brook Street, W1
HENRY, Sir Edward (1850–1931), Police Commissioner	19 Sheffield Terrace, W8
HENTY, G A (George Alfred) (1832–1902), author	33 Lavender Gardens, SW11
HERBERT, Sir Alan (A P H) (1890–1971), author and MP	12 Hammersmith Terrace, W6
HERFORD, Robert Travers (1860–1950), Unitarian minister	14 Gordon Square, WC1
HERZEN, Alexander (1812–70), political thinker	1 Orsett Terrace, W2
HESS, Dame Myra (1890–1965), pianist	48 Wildwood Road, NW11
HILL, Graham (1929–75), racing driver	32 Parkside, NW7
HILL, Octavia (1838–1912), co-founder of the National Trust	2 Garbutt Place, W1
HILL, Sir Rowland (1795–1879), postal reformer	1 Orme Square, W2
HILL, Sir Rowland (1795–1879), postal reformer	Royal Free Hospital, Pond Street, NW3
HILTON, James (1900–54), novelist and scriptwriter	42 Oakhill Gardens, Woodford Green
HITCH, Pte Frederick, VC (1856–1913), hero of Rorke's Drift	62 Cranbrook Road, W4
HITCHCOCK, Sir Alfred (1899–1980), film director	153 Cromwell Road, SW5
HOBBS, Sir Jack (1882–1963), cricketer	17 Englewood Road, SW12
HODGKIN, Thomas (1798–1866), physician	35 Bedford Square, WC1
HOFMANN, A W (1818–92), professor of chemistry	9 Fitzroy Square, W1
HOGG, Quintin (1845–1903), founder of Regent St College	5 Cavendish Square, W1
HOLMAN HUNT, William, (1827–1910), painter	18 Melbury Road, W14
*HOLST, Gustav (1874–1934), composer	St Paul's Girls' School, W8
HOLTBY, Winifred (1898–1935), writer	58 Doughty Street, WC1
HOOD, Thomas (1799–1845), poet	1–3 Robert Street, WC2
HOOD, Thomas (1799–1845), poet	28 Finchley Road, NW8
HOPKINS, Gerard Manley (1844–89), poet	Manresa House, Holybourne Avenue, SW15
HORE-BELISHA, Lord (1893–1957), statesman	16 Stafford Place, SW1
HORNIMAN, Frederick John (1835–1906), tea merchant	Coombe Cliff, Coombe Road, Croydon
HORNIMAN, John (1803–93), tea merchant	Coombe Cliff, Coombe Road, Croydon
HOUSMAN, A.E. (1859–1936), poet and scholar	17 North Road, N6
HOWARD, Ebenezer (1850–1928), Garden City pioneer	50 Durley Road, N16
HOWARD, John (1726–90), prison reformer	23 Great Ormond Street, WC1
HOWARD, Luke (1772–1864), namer of clouds	7 Bruce Grove, N17
HUDSON, W H (William Henry) (1841–1922), writer	40 St Luke's Road, W11
HUGHES, Arthur (1832–1915), Pre-Raphaelite painter	22 Kew Green, Richmond
HUGHES, David Edward (1831–1900), scientist	94 Great Portland Street, W1
HUGHES, Hugh Price (1847–1902), Methodist preacher	8 Taviton Street, WC1
HUGHES, Mary (1860–1941), friend of the needy	71 Vallance Road, E2
HUNT, James Henry, Leigh (1784–1859), essayist and poet	22 Upper Cheyne Row, SW3
HUNTER, John (1728–93), surgeon	31 Golden Square, W1
HUNTER, William (1718–83), anatomist	Lyric Theatre, Great Windmill Street, W1
HUSKISSON, William (1770–1830), statesman	28 St James's Place, SW1
HUTCHINSON, Sir Jonathan (1828–1913), surgeon	15 Cavendish Square, W1
HUXLEY, Aldous (1894–1963), man of science	16 Bracknell Gardens, NW3
HUXLEY, Julian (1887–1975), man of science	16 Bracknell Gardens, NW3
HUXLEY, Leonard (1860–1933), man of science	16 Bracknell Gardens, NW3
HUXLEY, Thomas Henry (1825–95), biologist	38 Marlborough Place, NW8
HYNDMAN, Henry Mayers (1842–1921), socialist leader	13 Well Walk, NW3
INNES, John (1829–1904), horticulturalist	Manor House, Watery Lane, SW20

Name	Address
IRELAND, John (1879–1962), composer	14 Gunter Grove, SW10
IRVING, Edward (1792–1834), church reformer	4 Claremont Square, N1
IRVING, Sir Henry (1838–1905), actor	15a Grafton Street, W1
IRVING, Washington (1783–1859), writer	8 Argyll Street, W1
ISAACS, Rufus, 1st Marquess of Reading (1860–1935)	32 Curzon Street, W1
JACKSON, John Hughlings (1835–1911), physician	3 Manchester Square, W1
JACOBS, W.W. (1863–1943), author	15 Gloucester Gate, NW1
JAGGER, Charles Sargeant (1885–1934), sculptor	67 Albert Bridge Road, SW11
JAMES, C L R (1901–89), writer and political activist	165 Railton Road, SE24
JAMES, Henry (1843–1916), writer	34 De Vere Gardens, W8
JEFFERIES, Richard (1848–87), naturalist and writer	59 Footscray Road, SE29
JELLICOE, Admiral of the Fleet, Earl, OM (1859–1935)	25 Draycott Place, SW3
JENNINGS, Humphrey (1907–1950), documentary film maker	8 Regent's Park Terrace, NW1
JEROME, Jerome K (1859–1927), author	104 Chelsea Bridge Rd, SW1
JINNAH, Mohammed Ali (1876–1948), founder of Pakistan	35 Russell Road, W14
JOHN, Augustus (1878–1961), painter	28 Mallord Street, SW3
JOHNSON, Amy (1903–41), aviator	Vernon Court, Hendon Way, NW2
JOHNSON, Samuel (1709–84) first met James Boswell here	8 Russell Street, WC2
JOHNSTON, Edward (1872–1944), master calligrapher	3 Hammersmith Terrace, W6
JONES, Dr Ernest (1879–1958), pioneer of psychoanalysis	19 York Terrace East, NW1
JORDAN, Mrs Dorothy (née Bland) (1762–1816), actress	30 Cadogan Place, SW1
JOYCE, James (1882–1941), author	28 Campden Grove, W8
KALVOS, Andreas (1792–1869), Greek poet and patriot	182 Sutherland Avenue, W9
KARLOFF, BORIS, (1887–1969), actor	36 Forest Hill Road, SE22
KARSAVINA, Tamara (1885–1978), ballerina	108 Frognal, NW3
KEATS, John, (1795–1821), poet	Keats' House, Keats Grove, NW3
KELLY, Sir Gerald (1879–1972), portrait painter	117 Gloucester Place, W1
KELVIN, Lord (1824–1907), physicist and inventor	15 Eaton Place, SW1
KEMPE, Charles Eamer (1837–1907), stained glass artist	37 Nottingham Place, W1
KENYATTA, Jomo (1894–1978), first president of Kenya	95 Cambridge Street, SW1
KEYNES, John Maynard (1883–1946), economist	46 Gordon Square, WC1
KHAN, Sir Syed Ahmed (1817–98), Muslim reformer	21 Mecklenburgh Square, WC1
KINGSLEY, Charles (1819–75), writer	56 Old Church Street, SW3
KINGSLEY, Mary (1862–1900), traveller and ethnologist	22 Southwood Lane, N6
KIPLING, Rudyard (1865–1936), poet and writer	43 Villiers Street, WC2
KITCHENER of Khartoum, Field Marshal Earl, (1850–1916)	2 Carlton Gardens, SW1
KLEIN, Melanie (1882–1960), psychoanalyst	42 Clifton Hill, NW8
KNEE, Fred (1868–1914), housing reformer	24 Sugden Road, SW11
KNIGHT, Dame Laura (1877–1970), painter	16 Langford Place, NW8
KNIGHT, Harold (1874–1961), painter	16 Langford Place, NW8
KOKOSCHKA, Oskar (1886–1980), painter	Eyre Court, Finchley Road, NW8
KORDA, Sir Alexander (1893–1956), film producer	21–22 Grosvenor Street, W1
KOSSUTH, Louis (1802–94), Hungarian aatriot	39 Chepstow Villas, W11
KROPOTKIN, Prince Peter (1842–1921), Russian anarchist	6 Crescent Road, Bromley
LABOUCHERE, Henry (1831–1912), politician and journalist	19 Cross Deep, Twickenham
LAMB, Charles (1775–1834) writer	Lamb's Cottage, Church Street, N9
LAMB, Charles 'Elia' (1775–1834), essayist	64 Duncan Terrace, N1
LAMB, Mary (1764–1847) writer	Lamb's Cottage, Church Street, N9
LAMBERT, Constant (1905–1951), composer	197 Albany Street, NW1
LANG, Andrew (1844–1912), man of letters	1 Marloes Road, W8
LANGTRY, Lillie (1852–1929), actress	Cadogan Hotel, 21 Pont Street, SW1
LASKI, Harold (1893–1950), political philosopher	5 Addison Bridge Place, W14
LAUDER, Sir Harry (1870–1950), music hall artist	46 Longley Road, SW17
LAUGHTON, Charles (1899–1962), actor	15 Percy Street, W1
LAVERY, Sir John (1856–1941), painter	5 Cromwell Place, SW7
LAWRENCE, David Herbert (1885–1930), novelist and poet	1 Byron Villas, Vale of Health, NW3
LAWRENCE, Susan (1871–1947), social reformer	44 Westbourne Terrace, W2
LAWRENCE, T E (1888–1935), 'Lawrence of Arabia'	14 Barton Street, SW1
LEAR, Edward (1812–88), artist and writer	30 Seymour Street, W1
LECKY, (William Edward Hartpole) (1838–1903), historian	38 Onslow Gardens, SW7
LEIGH, Vivien (1913–67), actress	54 Eaton Square, SW1
LEIGHTON, Frederic, Lord (1830–96), painter	12 Holland Park Rd, W14
LENO, Dan (1860–1904), music hall comedian	56 Akerman Road, SW9
*LETHABY, William Richard (1857–1931), architect	Central School of Art & Crafts, WC1
LETHABY, William Richard (1857–1931), architect	20 Calthorpe Street, WC1
LEVER, William Hesketh (1851–1925), philanthropist	Inverforth House, North End Way, NW3
LEWIS, Percy Wyndham (1882–1957), painter	61 Palace Gardens Terrace, W8
LEWIS, Ted 'Kid' (1893–1970), Boxer	Nightingale Lane, SW12
LEYBOURNE, George (1842–1884), music hall comedian	136 Englefield Road, N1
LEYELL, Sir Charles (1797–1875, geologist	73 Harley Street, W1
LIND, Jenny (Madame Goldschmidt) (1820–87), singer	189 Old Brompton Road, SW7

Name	Address
LINDLEY, John (1799–1865), botanist	Bedford House, The Avenue, W4
LINNELL, John (1792–1882), painter	Old Wyldes', North End, NW3
LISTER, Joseph, Lord (1827–1912), surgeon	12 Park Crescent, W1
LLOYD GEORGE, David (1863–1945), statesman	3 Routh Road, SW18
LLOYD, Marie (1870–1922), music hall artiste	55 Graham Road, E8
LOCKYER, Sir Norman (1836–1920), astronomer and physicist	16 Penywern Road, SW5
LOUDON, Jane (1807–58), horticulturalist	3 Porchester Terrace, W2
LOUDON, John Claudius (1783–1843), horticulturist	3 Porchester Terrace, W2
LOVELACE, Ada, Countess of (1815–52), computer pioneer	12 St James's Square, SW1
LOW, Sir David (1891–1963), cartoonist	Melbury Court, Kensington High Street, W8
LUCAN, Arthur (Arthur Towle) (1887–1954), entertainer	11 Forty Lane, Wembley
LUGARD, Lord (1858–1945), colonial administrator	51 Rutland Gate, Hyde Park, SW7
LUTYENS, Sir Edwin Landseer (1869–1944), architect	13 Mansfield Street, W1
MACAULAY, Rose (1881–1958), writer	Hinde House, 11–14 Hinde Street, W1
MACAULAY, Thomas Babington, Lord (1800–59), historian	Holly Lodge, Campden Hill, W8
MACAULAY, Thomas Babington, Lord (1800–59), historian	5 The Pavement, SW4
MACAULAY, Zachary (1768–1838),	5 The Pavement, SW4
MACDONALD, George (1824–1905), story teller	20 Albert Street, NW1
MACDONALD, Ramsay (1866–1937), statesman	9 Howitt Road, NW3
MACMILLAN, Douglas (1884–1969), charity worker	15 Ranelagh Road, SW1
MACNEICE, Louis (1907–63), poet	52 Canonbury Park South, N1
MADOX BROWN, Ford (1821–93), painter	56 Fortess Road, NW5
MALLARME, Stéphane (1842–1898), poet	6 Brompton Square, SW3
MALLON, Dr Jimmy (1874–1961), social reformer	Toynbee Hall, Commercial Street, E1
MALONE, Edmond (1741–1812), Shakespearean scholar	40 Langham Street, W1
MANBY, Charles (1804–84), civil engineer	60 Westbourne Terrace, W2
MANNING, Cardinal Henry Edward (1808–92)	22 Carlisle Place, SW1
MANSBRIDGE, Albert (1876–1952), union founder	198 Windsor Road, Ilford
MANSFIELD, Katherine (1888–1923), writer	17 East Heath Road, NW3
MANSON, Sir Patrick (1844–1922), physician	50 Welbeck Street, W1
MARCONI, Guglielmo (1874–1937), radio inventor	71 Hereford Road, W2
MARRYAT, Captain Frederick (1792–1848), novelist	3 Spanish Place, W1
MARSDEN, William (1796–1867), surgeon	65 Lincoln's Inn Fields, WC2
MARX, Eleanor (1855–98), Socialist campaigner	7 Jews Walk, SE26
MARX, Karl (1818–83), political thinker	28 Dean Street, W1
MASEFIELD, John (1878–1967), Poet Laureate	30 Maida Avenue, W2
MATCHAM, Frank (1854–1920), theatre architect	10 Haslemere Road, N8
MATTHAY, Tobias (1858–1945), teacher and pianist	21 Arkwright Road, NW3
MAUGHAM, William Somerset (1874–1965), writer	6 Chesterfield Street, W1
MAURICE, Frederick Denison (1805–72), educationalist	2 Brunswick Place, NW1
*MAXIM, Sir Hiram (1840–96), inventor and engineer	57d Hatton Garden, EC1
MAXWELL, James Clerk (1831–79), physicist	16 Palace Gardens Terrace, W8
MAY, Phil (1864–1903), artist	20 Holland Park Road, W14
MAYER, Sir Robert (1879–1985), philanthropist	2 Mansfield Street, W1
MAYHEW, Henry (1812–87), founder of *Punch*	55 Albany Street, NW1
MAZZINI, Giuseppe (1805–72), Italian patriot	183 Gower Street, NW1
McCORMACK, John (1884–1945), tenor	24 Ferncroft Avenue, NW3
McGILL, Donald (1875–1962), postcard cartoonist	5 Bennett Park, SE3
McINDOE, Sir Archibald (1900–60), reconstructive surgeon	Avenue Court, Draycott Avenue, SW3
McMILLAN, Margaret (1860–1931), nursery education pioneer	Creek Road, SE8
MEE, Arthur (1875–1943), author and topographer	27 Lanercost Road, SW2
MELBA, Dame Nellie (1861–1931), soprano	Coombe House, Devey Close, Kingston
MELVILLE, Herman (1819–91), author	25 Craven Street, WC2
MEREDITH, George (1828–1909), poet and novelist	7 Hobury Street, SW10
METTERNICH, Prince (1773–1859), Austrian statesman	44 Eaton Square, SW1
MEYNELL, Alice (1847–1922), poet and essayist	47 Palace Court, W2
MILL, John Stuart (1806–73), philosopher	18 Kensington Square, W8
MILLAIS, Sir John Everett (1829–96), painter	2 Palace Gate, W8
MILLER, Lee (1907–77), photographer	21 Downshire Hill, NW3
MILNE, A A (1882–1956), author	13 Mallord Street, SW3
MILNER, Alfred, Lord (1854–1925), statesman	14 Manchester Square, W1
*MITFORD, Nancy (1904–73), writer	10 Curzon Street, W1
MONDRIAN, Piet Cornelis (1872–1944), painter	60 Parkhill Road, NW3
MONTEFIORE, Sir Moses (1784–1885), philanthropist	99 Park Lane, W1
MONTGOMERY, Field Marshal, of Alamein (1887–1976)	52–54 Kennington Oval, SE11
MOODY, Dr Harold (1882–1947), racial equality campaigner	164 Queen's Road, SE15
MOORE, George (1852–1933), author	121 Ebury Street, SW1
MOORE, Henry OM (1898–1986), sculptor	11a Parkhill Road, NW3
MOORE, Tom (1779–1852), poet	85 George Street, W1
MORGAN, Charles (1894–1958), novelist	16 Campden Hill Square, W8
MORGAN, John Pierpont Morgan (1837–1913), banker	14 Princes Gate, SW1

Name	Address
MORGAN, Junius S (1813–90), banker	14 Princes Gate, SW1
MORRELL, Lady Ottoline (1873–1938), literary hostess	10 Gower Street, WC1
MORRIS, William (1834–96), poet and artist	17 Red Lion Square, WC1
MORRIS, William (1834–96), poet and artist	Red House Lane, Bexleyheath
MORRISON, Herbert (1888–1965), politician	55 Archery Road, SE9
MORSE, Samuel (1791–1872), painter	141 Cleveland Street, W1
MOUNTBATTEN, Earl (1900–79), last Viceroy of India	2 Wilton Crescent, SW1
MOZART, Wolfgang Amadeus (1756–91), composer	180 Ebury Street, SW1
MUIRHEAD, Alexander (1848–1920), electrical engineer	20 Church Road, Bromley
MUNRO, Hector Hugh, alias SAKI (1870–1916), writer	97 Mortimer Street, W1
MURROW, Edward R (1908–65), broadcaster	84–94 Hallam Street, W1
MURRY, John Middleton (1889–1957), critic	17 East Heath Road, NW3
MYERS, George (1803–75), master builder	131 St George's Road, SE1
NAPOLEON III (1808–73), emperor of the French	1c King Street, SW1
NASH, Paul (1889–1946), artist	Bidborough Street, WC1
NEHRU, Jawaharlal (1889–1964), Prime Minister of India	60 Elgin Crescent, W11
NELSON, Horatio, Lord (1758–1805), vice-admiral	147 New Bond Street, W1
NELSON, Horatio, Lord (1758–1805), vice-admiral	103 New Bond Street, W1
NEWBOLT, Sir Henry (1862–1938), poet	29 Campden Hill Road, W8
NEWMAN, John Henry (1801–90), cardinal	Grey Court, Ham Street, Ham
NEWTON, Sir Isaac (1642–1727), scientist	87 Jermyn Street, SW1
NICHOLSON, Ben (1894–1982), artist	2B Pilgrims Lane, NW3
NICOLSON, Harold (1886–1968), writer	182 Ebury Street, SW1
NIGHTINGALE, Florence (1820–1910), nurse	10 South Street, W1
NKRUMAH, Kwame (1909–1972), first president of Ghana	60 Burghley Road, Camden, NW5
NOEL-BAKER, Philip (1889–1982), Olympic Sportsman	16 South Eaton Place, SW1
NOLLEKENS, Joseph (1737–1823), sculptor	44 Mortimer Street, W1
NOVELLO, Ivor (1893–1951), composer	11 Aldwych, WC2
O'CASEY, Sean (1880–1964), playwright	49 Prince of Wales Drive, SW11
O'HIGGINS, Bernardo (1778–1842), liberator of Chile	2 The Vineyard, Richmond
OLDFIELD, Ann (1683–1730), actress	60 Grosvenor Street, W1
OLIVER, Percy Lane (1878–1944), medical pioneer	5 Colyton Road, SE22
ONSLOW, Arthur (1691–1768), politician	20 Soho Square, W1
ORPEN, Sir William (1878–1931), painter	8 South Bolton Gardens, SW5
ORWELL, George (1903–50), novelist	50 Lawford road, NW5
ÖSTERBERG, Martina Bergman (1849–1915), gymnast	1 Broadhurst Gardens, NW6
OUIDA (Maria Louise de la Ramée) (1839–1908), novelist	11 Ravenscourt Square, W6
PAGE, Frederick Handley (1885–1962), aircraft designer	18 Grosvenor Square, W1
PALGRAVE, Francis Turner (1824–97), poet	5 York Gate, NW1
PALMER, Samuel (1805–81), artist	6 Douro Place, W8
PALMERSTON, Henry John Temple (1784–1865), statesman	4 Carlton Gardens, SW1
PALMERSTON, Henry John Temple (1784–1865), statesman	20 Queen Anne's Gate, SW1
PALMERSTON, Henry John Temple (1784–1865), statesman	94 Piccadilly, W1
PANKHURST, Christabel (1880–1958), suffragette	50 Clarendon Road, W11
PANKHURST, Emmeline (1858–1928), suffragette	50 Clarendon Road, W11
PANKHURST, Sylvia (1882–1960), suffragette	120 Cheyne Walk, SW10
PARRY, Sir Charles Hubert (1848–1918), musician	17 Kensington Square, W8
PATEL, Sardar Vallabhbhai Javerbhai (1875–1950), statesman	23 Aldridge Road Villas, W11
PATER, Walter (1839–1894), writer	12 Earl's Terrace, W8
PATMORE, Coventry (1823–1896), poet and essayist	14 Percy Street, W1
PEABODY, George (1795–1869), philanthropist	80 Eaton Square, SW1
PEAKE, Mervyn (1911–1968), author and artist	1 Drayton Gardens, SW10
PEARSON, John Loughborough (1817–97), architect	13 Mansfield Street, W1
PEARSON, Karl (1857–1936), pioneer statistician	7 Well Road, NW3
PEEL, Sir Robert (1750–1830), manufacturer and reformer	16 Upper Grosvenor Street, W1
PEEL, Sir Robert (1788–1850), statesman	16 Upper Grosvenor Street, W1
PELHAM, Henry (1695–1754), statesman	22 Arlington Street, SW1
PENROSE, Sir Roland (1900–84), Surrealist	21 Downshire Hill, NW3
PEPYS, Samuel (1633–1703), diarist	12 Buckingham Street, WC2
PEPYS, Samuel (1633–1703), diarist	14 Buckingham Street, WC2
PERCEVAL, The Hon. Spencer (1762–1812), statesman	59–60 Lincoln's Inn Fields, WC2
PETRIE, William Matthew Flinders (1853–1942), Egyptologist	5 Cannon Place, NW3
PHELPS, Samuel (1804–78), tragedian	8 Canonbury Square, N1
PHILPOT, Glyn (1884–1937), artist	80 Lansdowne Road, W11
PICK, Frank (1878–1941), London Transport pioneer	15 Wildwood Road, NW11
PINERO, Sir Arthur (1855–1934), playwright	115a Harley Street, W1
PISSARRO, Lucien (1863–1944), painter and wood engraver	27 Stamford Brook Road, W6
PITT, William, Earl of Chatham (1708–78), statesman	10 St James's Square, SW1
PITT, WILLIAM, the younger (1759–1806), statesman	120 Baker Street, W1
PITT-RIVERS, Augustus H Lane Fox (1827–1900), soldier	4 Grosvenor Gardens, SW1
PLAATJE, Solomon T (1876–1932), writer	25 Carnarvon Road, E10

Name	Address
PLACE, Francis (1771–1854), political reformer	21 Brompton Square, SW3
PLATH, Sylvia (1932–63), poet	3 Chalcot Square, NW1
PLAYFAIR, Sir Nigel (1874–1934), actor-manager	26 Pelham Crescent, SW7
POPE, Alexander (1688–1744), poet	110 Chiswick Lane South, W4
POUND, Ezra (1885–1972), poet	10 Kensington Church Walk, W8
PRE-RAPHAELITE BROTHERHOOD founded here in 1848	7 Gower Street, WC1
PRIESTLEY, J B (1894–1984), novelist and playwright	3 The Grove, N6
PRIESTLEY, Joseph (1733–1804), scientist	Ram Place, E9
PRYDE, James (1866–1941), artist	80 Lansdowne Road, W11
RACKHAM, Arthur (1867–1939), illustrator	16 Chalcot Gardens, NW3
RACZYŇSKI, Count Edward (1891–1993), Polish statesman	8 Lennox Gardens, SW1
RAGLAN, Lord Fitzroy Somerset (1788–1855), soldier	5 Stanhope Gate, W1
RAMBERT, Marie (1888–1982), founder of Ballet Rambert	19 Campden Hill Gardens, W8
RATHBONE, Eleanor (1872–1946), social reformer	Tufton Court, Tufton Street, SW1
RATTIGAN, Sir Terence (1911–77), playwright	100 Cornwall Gardens, SW7
RAVILIOUS, Eric (1903–42), artist	48 Upper Mall, W6
*REID DICK, Sir William (1878–1961), sculptor	95a Clifton Hill, NW8
REITH, Lord (1889–1971), first Director-General of the BBC	6 Barton Street, SW1
RELPH, Harry (1867–1928), 'Little Tich', music hall comedian	93 Shirehall Park, NW4
RESCHID, Mustapha Pasha (1800–58), Turkish statesman	1 Bryanston Square, W1
REYNOLDS, Sir Joshua (1723–92), portrait painter	47 Leicester Square, WC2
RICARDO, Sir Harry (1885–1974), mechanical engineer	13 Bedford Square, WC1
RICHMOND, George (1809–1896), painter	20 York Street, W1
RICKETTS, Charles (1866–1931), artist	80 Lansdowne Road, W11
RIE, Dame Lucie (1902–1995), potter	18 Albion Mews, W2
RIPON, G F S Robinson, Marquess of (1827–1909), statesman	9 Chelsea Embankment, SW3
RIZAL, Dr José (1861–96), writer	37 Chalcot Crescent, NW1
ROBERTS, Earl Frederick Sleigh (1832–1914), field marshal	47 Portland Place, W1
ROBERTS, William (1895–1980), artist	14 St Mark's Crescent, NW1
ROBESON, Paul (1898–1976), singer and actor	The Chestnuts, Branch Hill, NW3
ROBINSON, F Cayley (1862–1927), artist	80 Lansdowne Road, W11
ROBINSON, James (1813–62), pioneer of anaesthesia	14 Gower Street, WC1
ROGERS, Dr Joseph (1821–89), health care reformer	33 Dean Street, W1
ROHMER, Sax (Arthur Henry Ward) (1883–1959), writer	51 Herne Hill, SE24
ROMILLY, Samuel (1757–1818), law reformer	21 Russell Square, WC1
ROMNEY, George (1734–1802), painter	Holly Bush Hill, NW3
ROSEBERY, 5th Earl (1847–1929), statesman	20 Charles Street, W1
ROSENBERG, Isaac (1890–1918), poet and painter	Whitechapel Library, 77 High Street, E1
ROSS, Sir James Clark (1800–1862), polar explorer	2 Eliot Place, SE3
ROSS, Sir Ronald (1857–1932), Nobel laureate	18 Cavendish Square, W1
ROSSETTI, Christina Georgina (1830–94), poet	30 Torrington Square, WC1
ROSSETTI, Dante Gabriel (1828–82), poet and painter	110 Hallam Street, W1
ROSSETTI, Dante Gabriel (1828–82), poet and painter	16 Cheyne Walk, SW3
ROSSETTI, Dante Gabriel (1828–82), poet and painter	17 Red Lion Square, WC1
ROSSI, John Charles Felix (1762–1839), sculptor	116 Lissom Grove, NW1
ROTHENSTEIN, Sir William (1872–1945) painter and writer	1 Pembroke Cottages, Edwardes Square, W8
ROWLANDSON, Thomas (1757–1827), artist	16 John Adam Street, WC2
ROY, Major-General William (1726–90), Ordnance Survey founder	10 Argyll Street, W1
ROY, Ram Mohun (1772–1833), Indian scholar	49 Bedford Square, WC1
RUSKIN, John (1819–1900), man of letters	26 Herne Hill, SE24
RUSSELL, Bertrand (1872–1970), philosopher	34 Russell Chambers, Bury Place, WC1
RUSSELL, Lord John, 1st Earl (1792–1878), statesman	37 Chesham Place, SW1
RUTHERFORD, Dame Margaret (1892–1972), actress	4 Berkeley Place, SW19
SACKVILLE-WEST, Vita (1892–1962), gardener	182 Ebury Street, SW1
SALISBURY, Robert, Marquess of (1830–1903), statesman	21 Fitzroy Square, W1
SALMOND, John Maitland (1881–1968), Marshal of the RAF	27 Chester Terrace, NW1
SALVIN, Anthony (1799–1881), architect	11 Hanover Terrace, Regent's Park, NW1
SAN MARTIN, José de (The Liberator) (1778–1850), soldier	23 Park Road, NW1
SANTLEY, Sir Charles (1834–1922), singer	13 Blenheim Road, NW8
SARGENT, Sir Malcolm (1895–1967), conductor	Albert Hall Mews, Kensington Gore, SW7
SARTORIUS, John F (1775–1830), sporting painter	155 Old Church Street, SW3
SASSOON, Siegfried (1886–1967), writer	23 Campden Hill Square, W8
SAUNDERS, Edwin (1814–1901), dentist to Queen Victoria	89 Wimbledon Parkside, SW19
SAVARKAR, Vinayak Damodar (1883–1966), Indian patriot	65 Cromwell Avenue, N6
SAYERS, Dorothy L (1893–1957), writer	24 Great James Street, WC1
SAYERS, Tom (1826–65), boxer	257 Camden High Street, NW1
SCAWEN-BLUNT, Wilfrid (1840–1922), diplomat and poet	15 Buckingham Gate, SW1
SCHOPENHAUER, Arthur (1788–1860), philosopher	Eagle House, High Street, Wimbledon, SW19
SCHREINER, Olive (1855–1920), author	16 Portsea Place, W2
SCHWITTERS, Kurt (1887–1948), artist	39 Westmoreland Road, SW13

Name	Address
SCOTT Capt Robert Falcon (1868–1912), Antarctic explorer	56 Oakley Street, SW3
SCOTT, Sir George Gilbert (1811–78), architect	Admiral's House, Admiral's Walk, NW3
SCOTT, Sir Giles Gilbert (1880–1960), architect	Chester House, Clarendon Place, W2
SEACOLE, Mary (1805–81), Jamaican nurse	14 Soho Square, W1
SEFERIS, George (1900–71), Nobel laureate	51 Upper Brook Street, W1
SELFRIDGE, Harry Gordon (1858–1947), businessman	9 Fitzmaurice Place, W1
SHACKLETON, Sir Ernest (1874–1922), Antarctic explorer	12 Westwood Hill, SE26
SHANNON, Charles (1863–1937), artist	80 Lansdowne Road, W11
SHARP, Cecil (1859–1924), collector of English folk songs	4 Maresfield Gardens, NW3
SHAW, George Bernard (1856–1950), writer	29 Fitzroy Square, W1
SHAW, Richard Norman (1831–1912), architect	6 Ellerdale Road, Hampstead, NW3
SHE, Lao (1899–1966), Chinese writer	31 St James's Gardens, W11
SHELLEY, Mary (1797–1851), writer	24 Chester Square, SW1
SHELLEY, Percy Bysshe (1792–1822), poet	15 Poland Street, W1
SHEPARD, E H (1879–1976), painter and Illustrator	10 Kent Terrace, Regent's Park, NW1
SHEPHERD, Thomas Hosmer (1793–1864), artist	26 Batchelor Street, N1
SHERATON, Thomas (1751–1806), furniture designer	163 Wardour Street, W1
SHERIDAN, Richard Brinsley (1751–1816), dramatist	10 Hertford Street, W1
SHERIDAN, Richard Brinsley (1751–1816), dramatist	14 Savile Row, W1
SHORT, Sir Frank (1857–1945), engraver and painter	56 Brook Green, W6
SIBELIUS, Jean (1865–1957), composer	15 Gloucester Walk, W8
SICKERT, Walter (1860–1942), painter and etcher	6 Mornington Crescent, NW1
SIEBE, Augustus (1788–1872), pioneer of the diving helmet	5 Denmark Street, WC2
SILVER, Arthur (1853–86), designer	84 Brook Green Road, W6
SILVER, Harry (1881–1971), designer	84 Brook Green Road, W6
SILVER, Rex (1879–1965), designer	84 Brook Green Road, W6
SIM, Alastair (1900–76), actor	8 Frognal Gardens, NW3
SIMON, Sir John (1816–1904), pioneer of public health	40 Kensington Square, W8
SINGH, Maharajah Duleep (1838–93), last ruler of Lahore	53 Holland Park, W11
SITWELL, Dame Edith (1887–1964), poet	Greenhill, Hampstead High Street, NW3
SLOANE, Sir Hans (1660–1753), British Museum benefactor	4 Bloomsbury Place, WC1
SLOVO, Joe (1926–1995), freedom fighter	13 Lyme Street, NW1
SMILES, Samuel (1812–1904), author of *Self Help*	11 Granville Park, SE13
SMIRKE, Sir Robert (1781–1867), architect	81 Charlotte Street, W1
SMITH, F E, Earl of Birkenhead (1872–1930), lawyer	32 Grosvenor Gardens, SW1
SMITH, Stevie (1902–71), poet	1 Avondale Road, N13
SMITH, Sydney (1771–1845), author and wit	14 Doughty Street, WC1
SMITH, W H (1825–91), bookseller	12 Hyde Park Street, W2
SMITH, William, MP (1756–1835), pioneer of religious liberty	16 Queen Anne's Gate, SW1
SMOLLETT, Tobias (1721–71), novelist	16 Lawrence Street, SW3
SMITHSON, James (1764–1829), scientist	9 Bentinck Street, W1
SOPWITH, Sir Thomas (1888–1989), aircraft manufacturer	46 Green Street, W1
SOSEKI, Natsume (1867–1916), Japanese novelist	81 The Chase, Clapham, SW4
SPILSBURY, Sir Bernard (1877–1947), forensic pathologist	31 Marlborough Hill, NW8
SPURGEON, Charles Haddon (1834–92), preacher	99 Nightingale Lane, SW12
STANFIELD, Clarkson (1793–1867), painter	14 Buckingham Street, WC2
STANFORD, Sir Charles (1852–1924), musician	56 Hornton Street, W8
STANHOPE, Charles, 3rd Earl (1753–1816), reformer	20 Mansfield Street, W1
STANLEY, Edward, Earl of Derby (1799–1869), statesman	10 St James's Square, SW1
STANLEY, Sir Henry Morton (1841–1904), explorer	2 Richmond Terrace, SW1
STANLEY, W F R (1829–1909), philanthropist	12 South Norwood Hill, SE25
STAUNTON, Howard (1810–74), chess champion	117 Lansdowne Road, W11
STEER, Philip Wilson (1860–1942), painter	109 Cheyne Walk, SW10
STEPHEN, Sir Leslie (1832–1904), scholar and writer	22 Hyde Park Gate, SW7
STEPHENSON, Robert (1803–59), engineer	35 Gloucester Square, W2
STEVENS, Alfred (1817–75), artist	9 Eton Villas, NW3
STILL, Sir George Frederic (1868–1941), paediatrician	28 Queen Anne Street, W1
STOKER, Bram (1847–1912), author	18 St Leonard's Terrace, SW3
STONE, Marcus (1840–1921), artist	8 Melbury Road, W14
STOTHARD, Thomas (1755–1834), painter and Illustrator	28 Newman Street, W1
STRACHEY, Lytton (1880–1932), critic and biographer	51 Gordon Square, WC1
STRANG, William (1859–1921), painter and etcher	20 Hamilton Terrace, NW8
STREET, George Edmund (1824–81), architect	14 Cavendish Place, W1
STRYPE, John (1643–1737), historian and biographer	10 Leyden Street, E1
STUART, John McDouall (1815–66), explorer	9 Campden Hill Square, W8
SVEVO, Italo (aka Ettore Schmitz) (1861–1928), writer	67 Charlton Church Lane, SE7
SWINBURNE, Algernon Charles (1837–1909), poet	16 Cheyne Walk, SW3
SWINBURNE, Algernon Charles (1837–1909), poet	11 Putney Hill, SW15
SZABO, Violette, GC (1921–1945), spy	18 Burnley Road, SW9
TAGLIONI, Marie (1809–84), ballet dancer	14 Connaught Square, W2
TAGORE, Rabindranath (1861–1941), Indian poet	3 Villas on the Heath, NW3

Name	Address
TAIT, Thomas Smith (1882–1954), architect	Gates House, Wyldes Close, NW11
TALLEYRAND, Prince (1754–1838), French statesman	21 Hanover Square, W1
TALLIS, John (1816–76), publisher of *London Street View*	233 New Cross Road, SE14
TATE, Harry (1872–1940), music hall comedian	72 Longley Road, SW17
TAUBER, Richard (1891–1948), tenor	Park West, Edgware Road, W2
TAWNEY, R H (1880–1962), historian	21 Mecklenburgh Square, WC1
TEMPEST, Dame Marie (1864–1942), actress	24 Park Crescent, W1
TENNYSON, Alfred Lord (1809–92), poet	9 Upper Belgrave Street, SW1
TERRY, Dame Ellen (1847–1928), actress	22 Barkston Gardens, SW5
THACKERAY, William Makepeace (1811–63), novelist	2 Palace Green, W8
THOMAS, Dylan (1914–1953), poet	54 Delancey Street, NW1
THOMAS, Edward (1878–1917), essayist and poet	61 Shelgate Road, SW11
THOMPSON, Benjamin, Count Rumford (1753–1814), inventor	168 Brompton Road, SW3
THOMSON, James (1700–48), poet	Royal Hospital, Kew Foot Road, Richmond
THORNDIKE, Dame Sybil (1882–1976), actress	6 Carlyle Square, SW3
THORNE, Will (1857–1946), trade union Leader	1 Lawrence Road, E13
THORNYCROFT, Sir Hamo (1850–1925), sculptor	2b Melbury Road, W14
TILAK, Lokamanya (1856–1920), Indian patriot	10 Howley Place, W2
TOWNLEY, Charles (1737–1805), antiquary and collector	14 Queen Anne's Gate, SW1
TOYNBEE, Arnold (1852–83), social philosopher	49 Wimbledon Parkside, SW19
TOYNBEE, Joseph (1815–66), aural surgeon	49 Wimbledon Parkside, SW19
TREE, Sir Herbert Beerbohm (1853–1917), actor-manager	31 Rosary Gardens, SW7
TREVES, Sir Frederick (1853–1923), surgeon	6 Wimpole Street, W1
TROLLOPE, Anthony (1815–82), novelist	39 Montagu Square, W1
TURING, Alan (1912–54), pioneer of computer science	2 Warrington Cresent, W9
TURNER, Charles (1774–1857), Engraver	56 Warren Street, W1
TURNER, J M W, RA (1775–1851), painter	40 Sandycoombe Rd, Twickenham
TUSSAUD, Madame Marie (1761–1850), artist in wax	24 Wellington Road, NW8
TWAIN, Mark (Samuel Clemens) (1835–1910), writer	23 Tedworth Square, SW3
TWEED, John (1863–1933), sculptor	108 Cheyne Walk, SW10
VAN BUREN, Martin (1782–1862), American president	7 Stratford Place, W1
VAN GOGH, Vincent (1853–1890), painter	87 Hackford Road, SW9
VANE, Sir Harry, the younger (1612–62), statesman	Vane House, Rosslyn Hill, NW3
VAUGHAN WILLIAMS, Ralph (1872–1958), composer	10 Hanover Terrace, Regent's Park, NW1
VENTRIS, Michael (1922–56), decipherer of Linear B script	19 North End, NW3
VIVEKANANDA, Swami (1863–1902), Hindu philosopher	63 St George's Drive, SW1
VON HUGEL, Baron Friedrich (1852–1925), theologian	4 Holford Road, NW3
VOYSEY, C F A (1857–1941), architect and designer	6 Carlton Hill, NW8
WAINWRIGHT, Lincoln Stanhope (1847–1929), vicar	Clergy House, Wapping Lane, E1
WAKLEY, Thomas (1795–1862), founder of *The Lancet*	35 Bedford Square, WC1
WALEY, Arthur (1889–1966), poet, translator and Orientalist	50 Southwood Lane, N6
WALKER, Emery (1851–1933), typographer and antiquary	7 Hammersmith Terrace, W6
WALLACE, Alfred Russel (1823–1913), naturalist	44 St Peter's Road, Croydon
WALLACE, Edgar (1875–1932), writer	6 Tressillian Crescent, SE4
WALPOLE, Horace (1717–1797), man of letters	5 Arlington Street, SW1
WALPOLE, Sir Robert (1676–1745), statesman	5 Arlington Street, SW1
WALTER, John (1739–1812), founder of *The Times*	113 Clapham Common North Side, SW4
WARLOCK, Peter (Philip Heseltine) (1894–1930), composer	30 Tite Street, SW3
WATERHOUSE, Alfred (1830–1905), architect	61 New Cavendish Street, W1
WATERHOUSE, John William (1849–1917), painter	10 Hall Road, NW8
WAUGH, Benjamin (1839–1908), NSPCC founder	26 Croom's Hill, SE10
WAUGH, Evelyn (1903–66), writer	145 North End Road, NW11
WEBB, Beatrice (1858–1943), social reformer	10 Netherhall Gardens, NW3
WEBB, Sidney (1859–1947), social reformer	10 Netherhall Gardens, NW3
WEISZ, Victor, 'Vicky' (1913–66), cartoonist	Welbeck Mansions, 35 Welbeck Street, W1
WEIZMANN, Chaim (1874–1952), scientist and statesman	67 Addison Road, W14
WELLCOME, Sir Henry (1853–1936), pharmacist	6 Gloucester Gate, NW1
WELLS, H G (1866–1946), writer	13 Hanover Terrace, NW1
WESLEY, Charles (1707–88), hymn writer	1 Wheatley Street, W1
WESLEY, Charles (1757–1834), musician	1 Wheatley Street, W1
WESLEY, John (1703–91), founder of Methodism	47 City Road, EC1
WESLEY, Samuel (1766–1837), musician	1 Wheatley Street, W1
WESTMACOTT, Sir Richard (1775–1856), sculptor	14 South Audley Street, W1
WHALL, Christopher Whitworth (1849–1924), artist	19 Ravenscourt Road, W6
WHEATSTONE, Sir Charles (1802–75), scientist	19 Park Crescent, W1
WHEELER, Sir Mortimer (1890–1976), Archaeologist	27 Whitcomb Street, WC2
WHISTLER, James Abbot McNeil (1834–1903), artist	96 Cheyne Walk, SW10
WHITAKER, Joseph (1820–95), publisher	White Lodge, Silver Street, Enfield
WHITE, William Hale (Mark Rutherford) (1831–1913), novelist	19 Park Hill, Carshalton
WILBERFORCE, William (1759–1833), social reformer	111 Broomwood Road, SW11
WILBERFORCE, William (1759–1833), social reformer	44 Cadogan Place, SW1

Name	Address
WILDE, Lady Jane Francesca 'Speranza' (1821–96), poet	87 Oakley Street, SW3
WILDE, Oscar O'Flahertie Wills (1854–1900), dramatist	34 Tite Street, SW3
WILLAN, Dr Robert (1757–1812), dermatologist	10 Bloomsbury Square, WC1
WILLIS, 'Father' Henry (1821–1901), organ builder	9 Rochester Terrace, NW1
WILSON, Edward Adrian (1872–1912), Antarctic explorer	42 Vicarage Crescent, SW11
WINANT, John Gilbert (1889–1947), US ambassador	7 Aldford Street, W1
WINGFIELD, Mr Walter Clopton (1833–1912), tennis pioneer	33 St George's Square, SW1
WODEHOUSE, P G (1881–1975), writer	17 Dunraven Street, W1
WOLFE, General James (1727–59), victor of Quebec	Macartney House, Greenwich Park, SE10
WOLSELEY, Garnet, Viscount (1833–1913), field marshal	Rangers House, Chesterfield Walk, SE10
WOOD, Edward, 1st Earl of Halifax (1881–1959), statesman	86 Eaton Square, SW1
WOOD, Sir Henry (1869–1944), musician	4 Elsworthy Road, NW3
WOOLF, Leonard (1880–1969), writer	Hogarth House, Paradise Road, Richmond
WOOLF, Virginia (1882–1941), writer	29 Fitzroy Square, W1
WOOLF, Virginia (1882 1941), writer	Hogarth House, Paradise Road, Richmond
WREN, Sir Christopher (1632–1723), architect	Old Court House, Hampton Court Green
WYATT, Thomas Henry (1807–1880), architect	77 Great Russell Street, WC1
WYATVILLE, Sir Jeffry (1766–1840), architect	39 Brook Street, W1
WYNDHAM, Sir Charles (1837–1919), actor-manager	20 York Terrace East, NW1
YEATS, William Butler (1865–1939), poet and dramatist	23 Fitzroy Road, NW1
YOUNG, Thomas (1773–1829), scientist	48 Welbeck Street, W1
ZANGWILL, Israel (1864–1926), writer and philanthropist	288 Old Ford Road, E2
ZOFFANY, Johann (1733–1810), painter	65 Strand-on-the-Green, W4
ZOLA, Emile (1840–1902), novelist	Queen's Hotel, 122 Church Road, SE19

MERSEYSIDE

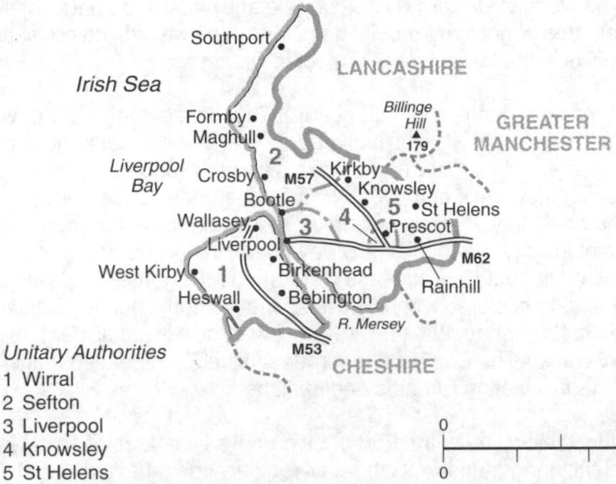
Southport
LANCASHIRE
Irish Sea
Billinge Hill
179
GREATER MANCHESTER
Formby
Maghull
2
Liverpool Bay
Crosby
M57
Kirkby
Knowsley
5
St Helens
Bootle
Wallasey
3
4
Prescot
Liverpool
M62
West Kirby
1
Birkenhead
Rainhill
Heswall
Bebington
R. Mersey
M53
CHESHIRE
Unitary Authorities
1 Wirral
2 Sefton
3 Liverpool
4 Knowsley
5 St Helens
0
20 miles
0
30 km

Merseyside is located in the northwest of England and named after the River Mersey. It comprises the conurbation by the Mersey estuary centred on the city of Liverpool. The metropolitan county was created in 1974, mainly from areas previously part of the administrative counties of Lancashire and Cheshire. Unusually, the county is divided into two parts by the Mersey estuary; the Wirral is located on the southwest side of the estuary, on the Wirral peninsula, and the rest of the county on the northeast side. The northern part of Merseyside borders Lancashire to the north, Greater Manchester to the east and Cheshire to the southeast; the southerly part borders Cheshire to the south. The two parts are linked by two road tunnels, a railway tunnel and the Mersey Ferry. Between 1974 and 1986 the county had a two-tier system of local government, the five boroughs sharing power with Merseyside County Council. In 1986 the county council was abolished along with all other metropolitan county councils, and so its boroughs are now effectively unitary authorities. Merseyside however still exists legally, and as a ceremonial county. Despite the abolition of the county council some local services are still run on a county-wide basis, now administered by joint boards of the five metropolitan boroughs.

Liverpool is a major city and metropolitan borough in Merseyside, situated along the eastern side of the Mersey Estuary. Built across a ridge of hills rising to 230ft (70m) above sea level at Everton Hill, the city's urban area runs directly into Bootle and Crosby in Sefton to the north, and Huyton and Prescot in Knowsley to the east. It faces Wallasey and Birkenhead across the Mersey to the west. Inhabitants of Liverpool are referred to as Liverpudlians and nicknamed 'Scousers', in reference to the local meal known as 'scouse' (originally lobscouse), a form of stew. The word 'scouse' has also become synonymous with the Liverpool accent and dialect.

It was from Liverpool that St Patrick is believed by some to have set sail on his voyage to convert the Irish to Christianity. Here, too, was the site of the country's first genuine ferry service; the famous 'ferry across the Mersey' dates back to the 12th century and a band of enterprising monks who lived at Birchen Head Priory on the Wirral peninsula. The borough of Liverpool was founded in 1207 and by the mid-16th century the population was still only around 500. In the 17th century there was slow progress in trade and population growth. Battles for the town were waged during the Civil War, including an 18-day siege in 1644. In 1699 Liverpool was made a parish by Act of Parliament, and in the same year its first slave ship, *Liverpool Merchant*, set sail for Africa. The first wet dock in Britain was built in Liverpool in 1715. Substantial profits from the slave trade helped the town to prosper and grow rapidly. By the end of the century Liverpool controlled over 40 per cent of European and 80 per cent of Britain's slave commerce.

With the development of the canal system in the late 18th century, the city's economy was enabled to grow further. In 1830, Liverpool (along with Manchester) became the first city to have an intercity rail link, through the Liverpool and Manchester Railway. The population continued to rise rapidly, especially during the 1840s when the Irish began arriving by the thousands due to the Great Famine. By 1851, almost 25 per cent of the city was Irish-born. By the late 19th century, Liverpool controlled one-seventh of the world's shipping and handled more goods than any British city outside London.

During the early 20th century, Liverpool attracted emigrants from across Europe. During World War II there were 80 air raids on Merseyside, killing 2500 people and causing damage to almost half the homes in the metropolitan area. Significant rebuilding followed the war, including massive housing estates and the Seaforth Dock, the largest dock project in Britain.

In the 1960s Liverpool became a centre of youth culture. The 'Merseybeat' sound which became synonymous with the Beatles and other Liverpudlian bands of the era catapulted the city to the forefront of the pop music scene. Liverpool had previously had a reputation as the birthplace of many famous comedians but the arrival of the 'Fab Four' in the early 1960s gave the city a global identity as a hotbed of musical talent. It is impossible to underestimate the impact the Beatles had on the world's perception of the city. The docks may have been in decline and work was becoming increasingly more difficult to find, but Liverpudlians were seen as a gritty breed with an advanced sense of humour living in a romantic area where musical dreams could become reality (The emergence of the 'Liverpool Poets' during the late 1960s owes some small debt to the general appreciation of all things Scouse). The Beatles phenomenon steadily increased tourism in the area and 40 years on the world's fascination remains undiminished.

During the late 20th century the decline of the Port of Liverpool as a source of employment and the later contraction of manufacturing industry in the city region badly affected the city's economy. However since the mid-1990s the city has been undergoing a general economic and civic revival, which was kick started by the regeneration of the city's Queen's Square. In 2004 Liverpool Pier Head was declared a UNESCO World Heritage site. The city celebrated its 800th anniversary in 2007, and the following year held the title of European Capital of Culture. The construction of a new cruise liner terminal at the pier head will allow the world's largest vessels to visit the city.

St Helens is historically in Lancashire, although the town now gives its name to the metropolitan borough of St Helens, and is the largest town within it. Formed in the mid 19th century from Eccleston, Windle, Parr and Sutton, towns in the parish of Prescot, St Helens takes its name from St Helen's parish church in Hardshaw, Windle. The town was built physically and metaphorically on coal: the original motto on the borough coat of arms was *Ex Terra Lucem* ('out of the earth comes light') and local collieries employed up to 5000 men until the 1970s, while during industry's boom years coal industry before World War I, men from St Helens made up 10 per cent of the Lancashire and Cheshire Miners' Federation. In the late 19th century a glass and chemical industry was established. In the middle of the modern town centre, adjacent to the town hall, is the Gamble Building, built in 1896 and named after Sir David Gamble, the first mayor; today it serves as the central library and houses municipal offices. Other buildings of note are the Friends' Meeting House, the Beecham Clock Tower – now part of St Helens College – and St Mary's Lowe House Catholic Church. The Pilkington Brothers glassworks dominates the town's industrial quarter although the area is currently being transformed with hotels, shopping areas and housing. The many coal mines in the outlying districts, and within the south Lancashire coalfield (most of which were closed before St Helens borough was created and were, therefore, never in St Helens) including Clock Face, Ravenhead, Sutton Manor, Bold, Wood Pit (Haydock), Lyme Pit (Haydock), Old Boston (Haydock) and Lea Green, were closed between the 1950s and early 1990s. The last colliery in the area, Parkside in Newton-le-Willows, closed in 1992.

Merseyside	**Population**			**Area**	
	male	*female*	*total*	*sq miles*	*sq km*
Knowsley Unitary Authority	71,064	79,395	150,459	33	86
Liverpool Unitary Authority	209,805	229,668	439,473	43	112
St Helens Unitary Authority	85,714	91,129	176,843	53	136
Sefton Unitary Authority	133,489	149,469	282,958	59	153
Wirral Unitary Authority	147,182	165,111	312,293	61	157
Total	647,254	714,772	1,362,026	249	644

Local Attractions and Information

Administrative headquarters

Knowsley: Municipal Buildings, Cherryfield Drive, Kirkby, Knowsley L32 1TX. Tel: 01514 896 000.
Liverpool: Municipal Buildings, Dale Street, Liverpool L69 2DH. Tel: 01512 333 000.
Sefton: 324–342 Stanley Road, Bootle L20 6ET. Tel: 0845 140 0845.
St Helens: Town Hall, Victoria Square, St. Helens WA10 1HP. Tel: 01744 456 789.
Wirral: Town Hall, Brighton Street, Wallasey CH44 8ED. Tel: 01516 062 000.

Aintree — The ancient town takes its name from a Saxon word meaning lone tree. Now effectively a suburb of northern Liverpool, Aintree is famous as the place where the Grand National has been run each spring since 1839. See also Sport.

Albert Dock — Designed and built by Jesse Hartley and opened by Prince Albert in 1846, Albert Dock is a system of docks and warehouses constructed entirely of cast iron, brick and stone; the first building in the UK to be built in such a manner, it was also the first fireproof warehousing system in the world. Shipping would enter from either Canning Half Tide Dock to the north or Salthouse Dock to the east. In 1848 it was upgraded to feature the world's first hydraulic warehouse hoist system. The five Grade I listed buildings of the dock complex are the largest set of such buildings in the UK. It is still used as a ship dock once a year for the Liverpool Tall Ships festival. For many years the ITV television show *This Morning*, hosted by Richard Madeley and Judy Finnegan, was broadcast from studios in the dockside buildings. The weather forecast was presented by Fred Talbot from the water of the dock itself, using a floating map of the British Isles. The dock is now home to Tate Liverpool, the International Slavery Museum and Liverpool Maritime Museum. Tel: 0151 708 7334.

Albion House — James Street, Liverpool. Designed by architects Richard Norman Shaw and J Francis Doyle and built 1896–8 for Ismay, Imrie and Company, the shipping line which later became the White Star Line. In 1912, when news of the *Titanic* disaster reached the offices, the officials were too afraid to leave the building, and instead read the names of the deceased from the balcony. The Grade II* listed building is known locally as the 'streaky bacon' building due to its distinctive façade, constructed from horizontal layers of white Portland stone and red brick.

Allerton Hall — Clarke Gardens, Woolton, Liverpool. A largely 18th century house owned 1798–1813 by anti-slavery campaigner William Roscoe, who added the Italianate frontage. During the American Civil War the house was rented by Confederate supporter Charles Prioleau, an American businessman who had moved to England, and was used as a refuge by the likes of Confederate naval commander Raphael Semmes. Donated to the city of Liverpool in 1926 by the Clarke family, it has now been converted into a pub.

Al-Rahma Mosque — Hatherley Street, Liverpool. One of the first mosques in England, opened at 8 Brougham Terrace by city solicitor and Muslim convert William Abdullah Quilliam on 25 December 1889 for the Muslim community – many of them Lascars – established in Liverpool in the 1880s. The current building, which can hold up to 1000 worshippers, was opened in the 1960s, and there are plans to build a new and even larger replacement. Quilliam also started the *Crescent* weekly journal, which ran 1893–1908, and wrote *The Faith Of Islam*, the first book in English by a Muslim.

Another Place — Crosby Beach, Liverpool. A sculptural work by Antony Gormley consisting of 100 cast iron figures facing out to sea and spread over a 2 mile (3.2km) stretch of the beach. Each figure is 6ft 2½in (1.89m) tall and weighs over 1400lb (650kg). *Another Place* was first exhibited on the beach at Cuxhaven, Germany in 1997 and after that in Stavanger in Norway and De Panne in Belgium.

Beatles — John Ono Lennon (born John Winston Lennon, 9 October 1940–8 December 1980, (James) Paul McCartney (born 18 June 1942), George Harrison (24 February 1943–29 November 2001) and Ringo Starr (born Richard Starkey, 7 July 1940) were the four member of the iconic pop group that globally popularised the Mersey sound of LIverpool and surrounding areas which had previously been localised through bands such as The Undertakers, The Big Three, The Fourmost and Rory Storm and the Hurricanes. Other Mersey Groups such as Gerry and the Pacemakers, The Swinging Blue Jeans and Billy J. Kramer and the Dakotas found national and international success but the effect the Beatles had around the world between 1963 and 1970 cannot be overstated. Every other playground conversation concerned the 'Fab Four', and it wasn't only the young that loved them; mothers loved their cheeky humour and fathers appreciated the sheer enormity of their musical talent. 'Beatlemania' had swept the world by 1964 and every changing trend in their music, fashion, philosophy and politics was adored by their fans and critiqued to the nth degree by the media. The Beatles simply transcended pop music in the same way that Muhammad Ali transcended boxing. The precursor of the Beatles was the Quarrymen, a skiffle group formed by John Lennon in March 1957. By the end of 1957 both Paul McCartney and George Harrison had joined the band. After several changes of names, the most famous being Johnny and The Moondogs and the Silver Beetles, on 17 August 1960 the band became the Beatles, with John's best friend Stuart Sutcliffe now joining the group as bass player and Pete Best as drummer.The derivation of the name is typical of the mystique surrounding the group but John joked in a tongue-in-cheek 1961 article in *Mersey Beat* magazine that 'it came in a vision – a man appeared on a flaming pie and said unto them,"From this day on you are Beatles with an A". (This story was later the inspiration for the title of one of Paul's solo albums, *Flaming Pie*). The group cut their musical teeth in Hamburg in 1960 and again in 1961, playing the Indra and Kaiserkeller bars before eventually performing at a new venue, the Top Ten. While playing at the Top Ten they were recruited by singer Tony Sheridan to act as his backing band on a series of recordings for the German Polydor Records label, produced by famed band leader Bert Kaempfert, and on 31 October Polydor released the recording 'My Bonnie' (Mein Herz ist bei dir nur), which made it into the German charts under the name Tony Sheridan and the Beatles) the following year but sinking without trace. After the band's second trip to Germany Stu Sutcliffe decided to leave the group and stay in the country which made their third stay between 13 April and 31 May 1962 at the Star Club a miserable experience when they were informed upon their arrival of Sutcliffe's death from a brain haemorrhage. Brian Epstein, manager of the record department at NEMS, his family's furniture store, took over from Alan Williams as the group's manager in 1962 and one of his first duties was to sack Pete Best on 16 August 1962. They immediately asked Ringo Starr, the drummer of Rory Storm and the Hurricanes, to join the band. The jigsaw was now in place and Parlophone signed them immediately. Their first charting single was 'Love Me Do' (No. 17 in October 1962) and of their next 22 British singles released as a band, 17 reached No. 1 in the UK Charts, 4 reached No. 2 and their lowest-charting single was the Double A-side 'Something/Come Together' which reached No. 4 in November 1969. Their final live performance was on the rooftop of the Apple building in Savile Row, London, on 30 January 1969. Although John announced his departure to the rest of the group on 20 September 1969, it was Paul who first publicly resigned from the Beatles on 11 April 1970. Following the dissolution of the group, all four Beatles had successful solo careers and their records still sell millions worldwide. Despite the untimely deaths of John (shot and killed by a crazed fan, Mark David Chapman, on 8 December 1980 in New York City) and George (died of cancer on 29 November 2001), the legacy of the world's greatest phenomena lives on. *Love* is a 2006 theatrical production by Cirque du Soleil which combines the re-produced and re-imagined music of the Beatles with an interpretive, circus-based artistic and athletic stage performance. *Love* plays at a specially-built theatre at the Mirage in Las Vegas. The music for the show was produced, arranged and remixed by Sir George Martin and his son, Giles Martin, with the approval and encouragement of Paul, Olivia Harrison (George's widow), Ringo and Yoko Ono, executor of the John Lennon estate. The Martins made use of the original studio multitrack tapes to produce remixed and re-imagined versions of the songs selected, A soundtrack album of the show was released in November 2006. Paul McCartney was knighted in the New Year Honours List of 1997.

Bidston Windmill Bidston Hill, Wirral. Brick tower mill built c.1800 to replace a previous mill destroyed by fire in 1793, and operational until 1875. It is believed that there has been a windmill on the site since 1596. Bidston Hill was purchased for public use in the 1890s and the mill has since been restored. Further work has been carried out over the years, most recently by the present custodians, Wirral Borough Council. Tel: 0151 606 2000.

Birkenhead Facing Liverpool over the Mersey, and linked to it by the Mersey Tunnel, Birkenhead is located on the Wirral peninsula. The suburb consisted mostly of farms until a steam ferry joined the town to its big brother in 1820 after which a shipbuilding industry developed. Some of Britain's biggest ships – including the *Ark Royal* aircraft carrier and two nuclear submarines – were built here. The very first ferry was operated in the 12th century by Benedictine monks at the Birchen Head priory. The town was the site of Britain's first publicly funded park in 1834 and was the birthplace of Europe's first horse-drawn street-tram system, which was later electrified. It was the brainchild of the American tycoon George Francis Train, a man thought to be the inspiration for Phileas Fogg in Jules Verne's novel *Around the World in 80 Days*.

Blackburne House Blackburne Place, Liverpool. Built 1785–90 as the home of John Blackburne, mayor of Liverpool in 1788. In 1874 the house was rebuilt and extended, and the Liverpool Institute High School for Girls – commonly referred to as Blackburne House – was established in the building. After the school closed in 1984 the house was refitted, reopening in 1994 as Blackburne House Centre for Women. Tel: 0151 709 4356.

Bluecoat Arts Centre School Lane, Liverpool. Built c.1716 in Queen Anne style to house a school for poor children, and thought to be the oldest building in the city centre. The building's three wings are built around a cobbled yard, separated from School Lane by iron railings and gates. The school, now known as the Liverpool Blue Coat School, moved to new premises in 1906, but the building was preserved as an arts centre and now provides studio space for numerous artists and craftsmen. Tel: 0151 702 5324.

Bootle The administrative centre of Sefton, Bootle has always been associated with shipbuilding and many of its houses were built for dockers in the booming 1930s. The town is bordered by Britain's longest canal, the Leeds & Liverpool Canal.

Broughton Hall Yew Tree Lane, West Derby, Liverpool. A Grade II* listed house built in 1860 in Gothic revival style for Gustavus C Schaube, a Liverpool merchant originally from Hamburg and one of the entrepreneurs involved in establishing the White Star Line. The impressive cast-iron conservatory was added 1870–80.

Cavern, The Mathew Street, Liverpool. It was at this legendary rock and roll club that Brian Epstein was introduced to the Beatles on 9 November 1961. Alan Sytner opened the Cavern Club on 16 January 1957 having been inspired by Paris's jazz district, on the city's Left Bank, where there were a number of clubs in cellars. Used as an air raid shelter during the war, the jazz club eventually became a hangout for skiffle groups. Sytner sold the club to Ray McFall in 1959, and blues bands and beat groups began to appear regularly in the early 1960s. The first beat night was held on 25 May 1960 and featured a performance by Rory Storm and the Hurricanes (which included Ringo Starr as drummer). The club closed in March 1973 and was demolished in 1982; a new Cavern Club, constructed using materials from the original building, was opened two years later. Tel: 0151 236 9091.

Church of St Monica Fernhill Road, Bootle. A Roman Catholic parish church designed by local architect F X Velarde and completed in 1936. It was dedicated by Archbishop Richard Downey on 4 October 1936. Built of brick with a green glaze pantile roof, the church is now Grade II listed. Tel: 0151 922 4819.

Crosby With a Viking heritage and a maritime past, Crosby in the Borough of Sefton lies on the Irish Sea. Among its notable buildings is the Carnegie Library, built with money donated by famous Scottish-born American steel mogul Andrew Carnegie. Crosby Beach stretches for 3 miles (5km) north of the town; there are remains of World War II defences in the dunes north of the coastguard station. Antony Gormley's sculpture *Another Place* (see separate entry) was installed on the beach in 2005.

Croxteth Hall Dwerryhouse Lane, Croxteth. Originally built in 1575 although much of the existing structure is Edwardian, Croxteth Hall was the ancestral home of the Molyneux family, the Earls of Sefton. The surrounding country park covers 500 acres (200ha) at the heart of what was once a great country estate. Now managed by the City of Liverpool, the estate includes Croxteth Home Farm and a Victorian walled garden. Tel: 0151 233 6910.

Formby — A residential suburb of Liverpool in the borough of Sefton. Established as a coastal settlement by the Vikings, it now lies 1 mile (1.6km) from the sea, where 9 miles (15km) of beach planted with pines in the late 19th and early 20th century stretch north to the resort of Southport. Three miles (5km) north of Formby, at Ainsdale, the 400 acre (160ha) Freshfield Nature Reserve run by the National Trust is home to one of the last remaining populations of red squirrels in England.

Fort Perch Rock — Marine Promenade, New Brighton. A coastal defence battery built 1825–9 on the Wirral peninsula to protect the Port of Liverpool. Originally cut off at high tide, it is now fully accessible thanks to coastal reclamation. Built of red sandstone, the fort covers 0.8 acres (0.3ha), with accommodation for 100 men. The 'Little Gibraltar of The Mersey', as it was nicknamed, was armed with 18 guns, of which 16 were 32-pounders. It currently houses the Aviation Archaeology Museum and a range of other exhibits. Tel: 0151 630 2707.

Gambier Terrace — A row of four-storey houses situated on a terrace overlooking St James Mount and Gardens and Liverpool Cathedral, and named after Admiral James Gambier. Numbers 1 to 10 are Grade II* listed, and were designed by John Foster. Now part of the Rodney Street conservation area, along with Hope Street and Rodney Street itself, the terrace was built in two halves, the first between 1832 and 1837. Funds ran out halfway through construction and number 10 was the last to be built to the original design, although the terrace was later completed more cheaply.

Halewood — Located in the Knowsley district, Halewood is world famous for the production of Ford and Jaguar motor cars. It was once a key centre for the production of timber. Its parkland is popular with bird-watchers.

Highest point — Billinge Hill, known locally as The Lump, $^1/_2$ mile (0.8km) north of Billinge, 5 miles (8km) north of St Helen's, at 586ft (179m) above sea level. A small square tower is situated atop the hill.

Interesting facts — **The Beatles** were famously turned away by a senior Decca Records A&R executive named Dick Rowe in August 1962. He told their new manager Brian Epstein that 'Guitar groups are on the way out, Mr. Epstein.' **Scouse** is the accent and dialect found in the city of Liverpool and adjoining urban areas of Merseyside. Highly distinctive, the accent sounds wholly different from those used in the neighbouring regions of Cheshire and rural Lancashire. Inhabitants of Liverpool are called Liverpudlians, but are more often described by the slang term Scousers. The word Scouse was originally a variation of lobscouse, the name of a traditional dish of lamb stew mixed with hardtack eaten by sailors. The dish was traditionally the fare of the poor, using the cheapest cuts of meat; if no meat was available the 'vegetarian' version was known as 'blind scouse'. The roots of the accent can be traced back to the large numbers of immigrants into the Liverpool area in the 18th and 19th centuries including those from the Isle of Man, Scotland and, most importantly, Wales and Ireland. Once seen as a regional capital for north Wales, albeit unofficially, many businesses in the city were established by the Welsh, and an influx of professional workers from Wales that included school teachers and medical staff only tailed off in the 1980s. **Henry Booth** (1788–1869) was born on Rodney Street in Liverpool. A founder of Liverpool and Manchester Railway Company in 1825 and its secretary and treasurer, he designed the first multi-tubular boiler used on Stephenson's *Rocket*. **Adolf Hitler**, still hoping for a career as an artist, visited his half-brother Alois and his wife Bridget at 102 Upper Stanhope Street, Toxteth, Liverpool. He stayed for almost six months (November 1912–April 1913) before returning to the men's hostel in Vienna. Many rumours have circulated about the length and timing of Hitler's Liverpool visit, but Bridget Hitler's memoir, published in the 1970s, is the only witnessed source. John Middleton (1578–1623) was a giant commonly known as the **Childe of Hale**. Most of what is known about him is based on oral tradition and legends. Born in Hale near Liverpool, according to contemporary accounts and his epitaph he grew to 9ft 3in (2.8m). Legend tells that he slept with his feet out of the window of his small house and also credits him with great strength. In London, the king presented Middleton with a dress of purple, red and gold. Brasenose College at Oxford has a portrait of Middleton in this dress and the painted outline of his hand. Middleton beat the king's champion in wrestling and received £20; however, during his return journey to Hale, his travelling companions stole the money. When Middleton died in 1623, he was buried in Hale churchyard with an epitaph, 'Here lyeth the bodie of John Middleton the Childe of Hale. Nine feet three.' A pub in Hale called The Childe of Hale commemorates Middleton. The **Laundromatic Superpub**, Caledonia Street, Liverpool, installed washing machines and tumble dryers in its pub in November 2000 so that drinkers could wash their clothes while enjoying a drink. The **Lakeside Inn** in Southport is listed in the *Guinness Book of Records* as the smallest pub in Britain, the pub is 22ft (6.5m) by 16ft (5m) and approximately 15ft (4.5m) high. Until recently the actual smallest pub in Britain was the Nutshell Inn, Bury St Edmunds, Suffolk, at 15ft x 7ft 6in (2.3m). The Signal Box Inn in Cleethorpes, opened in August 2006 (see Lincolnshire), and with an area of 64 sq ft (5.9 sq m), claims to be not only the smallest pub in Britain but also the world. **Merseyside** is home to the oldest established quiz league in Britain. The county has a rich source of quizzing talent among its six leagues and members such as Phil Duffy, Jim Eccleson, Dr Tom Farley, Alan Gibbs, Pat Gibson, Dag Griffiths, Mark Kerr, Darren Martin, Ray Oakes, Andy Page, Barry Simmons, Karl Whelan and John Wilson are among the top players in the country.

Islands — There are seven islands in the Merseyside region, five of them located in the River Dee in the Wirral. **Hilbre Island** (GR: SJ185880) is the largest of a group of three islands at the mouth of the Dee estuary, all formed of red Bunter sandstone. Area: 0.02 sq miles (0.04 sq km); the others are **Middle Eye** (GR: SJ198868) and **Little Eye**, the smallest of the group (GR: SJ198868). Also located in the Dee are **Little Hilbre Island** (GR: SJ190875) and **Red Rocks** (GR: SJ201888). There are two islands in the River Mersey in Liverpool: **Devil's Bank** (GR: SJ365856); and **Garston Rocks** (GR: SJ395835). All seven islands are in the Irish Sea shipping area.

Kirkby — The origins of the historic borough of Kirkby date to the 11th century and the town was mentioned in Domesday Book. St Chad's Church dates to the Norman era and has an 11th century font, and a watchtower from the period still survives. The town was extensively redeveloped after suffering severe bomb damage during World War II.

Knowsley Safari Park — 2 miles (3km) north of Prescot. Situated on the estate of Lord Derby, the 550 acre (220ha) park was opened in 1971 and is home to elephants, giraffes, lions, tigers, baboons and numerous other animals. There is a long tradition of keeping animals on the Derby estate – as early as the 1830s it contained one of the largest zoos in the world – and the artist and nonsense-poet Edward Lear was employed there in the 19th century to paint pictures of the Earl's collection. The park was also home to a former RAF airfield which closed at the end of World War II. Tel: 0151 430 9009.

Lady Lever Art Gallery — Windy Bank, Port Sunlight, Wirral. Established by Lord Leverhulme and opened in 1922, the gallery was purpose built to display his art collections, including 18th and 19th century paintings, 18th century furniture, fine Wedgwood, Chinese porcelain, tapestries and embroideries, classical antiquities and paintings by Turner, Constable and the Pre-Raphaelites. Tel: 0151 478 4136.

Leasowe Castle — Leasowe Road, Moreton, Wirral. Built by Ferdinando Stanley, 5th Earl of Derby – a patron of Shakespeare – in 1593. At first the castle consisted only of an octagonal tower, possibly intended as an observation platform for the races that took place on Wallasey Sands. Having fallen into disuse by 1700, it became known as 'Mockbeggar Hall' – a term often used for an ornate but derelict building (the adjoining foreshore is still known as 'Mockbeggar Wharf'). The Cust family refurbished and extended the building in the 1820s, using panelling from the demolished Star Chamber at the Palace of Westminster as well as oak from a submerged forest along the coast. After 1826 the building was used as a hotel for some years. It was a railway convalescent home 1911–70; having been owned by Wirral Borough Council 1974–80, it afterwards became a hotel once more. Tel: 0151 606 2000.

Leasowe Lighthouse — Leasowe Common, Wirral. Built by the Mersey Docks and Harbour Board in 1763, the lighthouse was one of four on the North Wirral foreshore, along with another at Leasowe and two at Hoylake. The other Leasowe lighthouse was soon destroyed by the sea and was replaced by a lighthouse on Bidston Hill in 1771. The lighthouse was operational until 1908, with the only known female lighthouse keeper in those days, a Mrs Williams. After a period as a tearoom it fell into disuse, but since 1989 it has been the base for the ranger service of the North Wirral Coastal Park. Tel: 0151 606 2000.

Litherland — A district of Sefton, first established as a Viking settlement c.900. The town prospered after it was linked to Liverpool, Wigan and Leeds by canals during the Industrial Revolution in the late 18th century. The Beatles staged some of their earliest shows at the local town hall.

Liver Building — Pier Head, Liverpool. Standing on the city's riverfront, the Liver Building is one of the most photographed and well known buildings in Liverpool. It was built in 1911 for the Royal Liver Friendly Society, and is still the society's head office; made of reinforced concrete, it was the first large scale building of its type. The faces on its pair of clock towers are the largest clock dials in Britain, larger even than those of Big Ben in London. In 1953 electronic chimes were installed as a memorial to the members of the Royal Liver Friendly Society who died during the two world wars. A statue of a Liver Bird – the official mascot of Liverpool, in fact a cormorant (also once known as the seaweed bird; in bygone times the birds could often be seen flying alongside the Mersey with seaweed in their beaks) – spreading its wings from the top of each clock tower enhances the glory of the building.

Liverpool Cathedral — St James Road, Liverpool. Officially titled the Cathedral Church of Christ in Liverpool, the neo-Gothic Anglican cathedral was designed by Giles Gilbert Scott, then aged 22, and George Bodley. On Tuesday 19 July 1904 the foundation stone was laid by Edward VII. The cathedral was consecrated in 1924, in the presence of George V and Queen Mary, and on 25 October 1978 a service of thanksgiving in the presence of Queen Elizabeth II took place to mark its completion, 75 years after it was begun. The cathedral is 619ft (189m) long with an area of 104,275 sq ft (9687.5 sq m). The tower is 331ft (101m) high. The bells have the highest and heaviest peal in the world. There are two pipe organs: the Grand Organ is the largest in the UK and probably the largest operational organ in the world, with 9765 pipes. Tel: 0151 709 6271.

Liverpool Hope University — Established in 1844 and granted university status in 2005. Formerly known as the Liverpool Institute of Higher Education, it is the only ecumenical university in the UK and its motto is appropriately taken from 1 Corinthians 13:13 – 'In Faith, Hope and Love'. It has campuses at Hope Park, Childwall and the Cornerstone in central Liverpool. Tel: 0151 291 3000.

Liverpool John Moores University — Established in 1823, the former Liverpool Polytechnic was granted university status in 1992. It is named after Sir John Moores (1896–1993), founder of Littlewoods Pools and former chairman of both Liverpool and Everton. The university has two campuses in central Liverpool. John Lennon and Stuart Sutcliffe met while studying at Liverpool John Moores University's Art School and it was here that they met. Tel: 0151 231 2121.

Liverpool Metropolitan Cathedral — Mount Pleasant, Liverpool. Dedicated to Christ the King. A Roman Catholic cathedral was first proposed for the Diocese of Liverpool in 1930 and Sir Edwin Lutyens was chosen as the architect. The foundation stone was laid on Whit Monday, 5 June 1933, but increasing costs eventually caused the project to be abandoned. In 1960 architects worldwide were invited to create a new design for the cathedral which would express the spirit of the liturgy then being radically reformulated by the Second Vatican Council; the design of Sir Frederick Gibberd (1908–84), structured around that of Lutyens, was finally chosen from over 300 entries. Building began in October 1962 and the completed cathedral was consecrated on the Feast of Pentecost, 14 May 1967. The papal legate at the consecration was Cardinal Heenan, Archbishop of

Westminster, who had been succeeded as Archbishop of Liverpool three years earlier by George Andrew Beck. The cathedral was soon nicknamed 'Paddy's Wigwam', a reference to its many Irish worshippers and the structural shape of the building. Tel: 0151 709 9222.

Lyceum, The Bold Street, Liverpool. A neoclassical building designed by architect Thomas Harrison of Chester and built 1800–02 as a meeting place for members of the Liverpool Literary and Philosophical Society, who included several of Liverpool's abolitionists (notably William Roscoe). The Lyceum later became home to Liverpool's subscription library, founded in 1757 and thought to be Europe's first lending library. The Lyceum inspired Manchester's Portico Library, also designed by Harrison. In later years the building served as the city's main post office, and it has since been occupied by bars and a bank.

Meols Hall Churchtown, Southport. Set in 100 acres (40ha) of private parkland close to the picturesque village of Churchtown, the house dates to the early 12th century and has remained in the Hesketh family for 27 generations. The family were recusant Catholics in the 16th century and Sir Edmund Campion is reputed to have been hidden in the house shortly before his execution in 1581. Tel: 01704 228326.

Mersey Sound Also known as the Liverpool Sound and Merseybeat, the Mersey Sound is the name given by the media to the music created by Merseyside groups between 1963 and 1965. The most popular line-up comprised lead, rhythm and bass guitars plus drums, as popularised by The Beatles and The Searchers. Merseybeat was typified by the synchronisation of the bass guitar (usually playing only the root and fifth notes of the chords) and the bass drum, although the bass guitar often played walking and boogie bass lines. Verses and choruses were often sung in close harmony and instrumental breaks were simple, keeping the focus on the presentation of the song.

Mersey Tunnels Three tunnels connect Liverpool with the Wirral peninsula, under the River Mersey: the $4^{1}/_{2}$ mile (6.9km) Mersey Railway Tunnel (opened 1886), and two road tunnels, the 2.13 mile (3.4km) Queensway Tunnel (opened 1934) and the $1^{1}/_{2}$ mile (2.5km) Kingsway Tunnel (opened 1971).

Merseyside Maritime Museum Albert Dock, Liverpool. The city's seafaring heritage is brought to life in the museum's collections, which reflect the international importance of Liverpool as a gateway to the world. Included are exhibits on the city's role in the transatlantic slave trade and emigration, the merchant navy and the *Titanic*. The museum is part of National Museums Liverpool. Tel: 0151 478 4499.

Mr Hardman's Photographic Studio Rodney Street, Liverpool. The home of portrait photographer Edward Chambré Hardman and his wife Margaret, 1947–88. The Georgian house contains the studio where many of his photographs were taken and the darkroom where they were developed and printed, while the Hardmans' living quarters are complete with the ephemera of post-war daily life. The archive of Hardman's work – mainly portraits of the city and people of Liverpool and of the surrounding countryside – provides a unique record of the city's social history in the 20th century. There is a selection of photographs on display. The property is managed by the National Trust. Tel: 0151 709 6261.

New Brighton Located on the northeastern tip of the Wirral peninsula, the seaside resort of New Brighton was developed in the second half of the 19th century on land to the east of Wallasey. With its strategic position at the entrance to the Mersey estuary, the area was already the site of the Perch Rock battery (see separate entry), completed in 1829. The New Brighton Tower, opened in 1896, was at the time the tallest in England, but closed in 1921.

Oriel Chambers Water Street, Liverpool. A Grade I listed building by local architect Peter Ellis, built in 1864. Comprising 43,000 sq ft (3995 sq m) over five floors, its plain design and employment of large areas of glass are a stylistic anticipation of modernism. It is currently occupied by barristers' chambers.

Pier Head A UNESCO World Heritage Site on Liverpool's waterfront, encompassing the city's historic landing stages and the trio of landmarks which c.2001 were dubbed the 'Three Graces': the Royal Liver Building (see separate entry), Cunard Building and Port of Liverpool Building.

Port Sunlight A village on the Wirral peninsula purpose built by William Hesketh Lever (Lord Leverhulme) 1888–1909 for the employees of Lever Brothers soap factory (now part of Unilever). The name is derived from Lever's most popular brand of cleaning agent, Sunlight soap. The village contains 900 Grade II listed buildings in a variety of architectural styles, including many half-timbered black and white houses in an imitation of local vernacular architecture. Port Sunlight also became the basis of a musical called *The Sunshine Girl*, which opened in 1911 at the Gaiety Theatre, London. Starring Phyllis Dare, one of the most popular pin-ups of the Edwardian era, and written by Paul Alfred Rubens, the show introduced the tango to British audiences.

Prescot Situated in the borough of Knowsley, 8 miles (13km) east of Liverpool, Prescot is famous for its historic clock-making industry, which is remembered at the Clock Museum, Church Street. Lord Derby's estate and Knowsley Safari Park (see separate entry) lie on the town's outskirts.

Rivers The **Alt** rises at Hag Plantation near Huyton and flows northwesterly through Croxteth Park, roughly following the M57 motorway south of Kirkby, then runs north of Aintree and south of Maghull. From there to Formby it forms the boundary between the counties of Merseyside and Lancashire. It then runs south to Hightown and empties into the Irish Sea, near the edge of the Mersey estuary where it marks the northern end of Crosby Beach. Its length is approximately 18 miles (29km). The estuary forms part of the Ribble and Alt Estuaries Special Protection Area for wildlife.

The **Mersey** forms the traditional border between the historic counties of Cheshire and Lancashire, and is formed from three tributaries: the rivers Etherow, Goyt and Tame. Its modern accepted start is at the confluence of the Tame and Goyt in the centre of Stockport, Greater Manchester. From Stockport it flows past Didsbury, Stretford, Urmston and Flixton, then at Irlam into the Manchester Ship Canal, which canalised the River Irwell to this point. The course of the

Mersey has been obliterated by the canal past Hollins Green to Rixton although the old river bed can be seen at Warburton. At Rixton the River Bollin enters the canal from the south and the Mersey leaves it to the north, meandering through Woolston, where the Ship Canal Company's dredgings have formed a nature reserve (Woolston Eyes), and Warrington. It is tidal from Howley Weir in Warrington, although high spring tides often top the weir. At the Runcorn Gap between Widnes and Runcorn, rail and road bridges (Runcorn Bridge) cross both the river and the Ship Canal, which runs alongside the widening estuary to Eastham Locks where canal and river unite. From here the estuary narrows to flow between Liverpool and Birkenhead into Liverpool Bay on the Irish Sea. To the east the estuary is greatly affected by silting, and part of it is marked on modern maps as dry land instead of as tidal. Between the Woodside Ferry Terminal and Albert Dock, the Mersey is $^3/_4$ mile (1.2km) wide. Three tunnels run under the Mersey at Liverpool: the Queensway and Kingsway Tunnels and the railway tunnel (see Mersey Tunnels). The river's name possibly derives from Anglo-Saxon *Mæresea* ('border river'), likely because it was the border between Mercia and Northumbria, but other explanations are possible: *Mære* can also mean 'lake, pond, mere, water basin, sea' or the name may simply be an anglicisation of an old Welsh name, *mor-afon* (sea-river) or *mor-dwfr* (sea-water). The river is now internationally famous thanks to the music of the 1960s known as Merseybeat (see Mersey Sound), which produced songs such as 'Ferry Cross the Mersey'. Its total length is 70 miles (112km).

St George's Hall — William Brown Street, Liverpool. Overlooking Lime Street and St John's Lane and Gardens, the assembly hall was designed by Harvey Lonsdale Elmes in neoclassical style and built 1842–54. With its chandeliers and gilded plasterwork, it is one of the finest such buildings in Britain and vividly illustrates Liverpool's 19th century prosperity. The interior is dominated by the main hall, 169ft (51.5m) long with a floor of Minton tiles; these are normally protected from the feet of users but occasionally opened to view. The 12 statues around the hall include representations of Sir Robert Peel, George Stephenson and W E Gladstone as well as local figures and benefactors such as Sir William Brown, Edward Stanley and William Stanley. There is also a smaller concert hall in which Charles Dickens held many readings. Tel: 0151 225 5530.

St Helen's Church — Sefton, 5 miles (8km) north of Liverpool. The Grade I listed Anglican parish church is one of the oldest buildings in Merseyside. It was first built c.1170 as a private chapel for the Molyneux family. The present tower was added c.1320. The present building dates largely from the early 1500s, and is particularly notable for its Tudor woodwork. Tel: 0151 931 4676.

St Mary's Church — Church Street, Prescot. The only Grade I listed building in Knowsley, a church was originally built on the site as early as 1100. It was largely rebuilt in 1610; only the vestry, the font and parts of the chancel walls remain from the original building. The tower dates from 1729 and the spire from 1797, while further reconstruction took place in the 19th and 20th centuries.

Solar Campus — Leasowe Road, Wallasey. Reputedly the first building in the world to be heated entirely by solar energy, the 'Solar Campus' was formerly St George's Secondary School, and was built in 1961 to the designs of Emslie Morgan, the assistant borough architect. The Grade II* listed building is completely windowless on one side, while the other is a giant solar wall consisting of 10,000 sq ft (930 sq m) of glass leaves; these draw ultraviolet rays from sunshine and bounce them around the walls of the classrooms, which become warm and heat the air. The roof and walls are thickly insulated to retain the heat, although in practice the building has tended to become too hot in summer and proved difficult to heat in winter.

Southport — The seaside town of Southport, for a time the residence of Napoleon III of France, has been described as the 'Paris of the North'. Each year it hosts a series of international events including the famous Southport Flower Show – one of the largest independent flower shows in the UK, which began in 1924 and is held annually for four days in late August – and an annual jazz festival. It is also home to several world-class golf courses, including Royal Birkdale (see separate entry), and is one of the country's leading conference centres. Southport also boasts one of Britain's widest beaches, while the Grade II listed pier is the second longest in England at 3650ft (1112.5m).

Speke Hall Garden & Estate — The Walk, Speke, 7 miles (11km) south of Liverpool. A Tudor black and white half-timbered house built by the Catholic Norris family and situated on the north bank of the Mersey. The intriguing period interiors feature a secret priest's hole, 'thunderbox' toilet and a Victorian kitchen complex. The gardens offer panoramic views over the Mersey Basin towards North Wales. The property is in the care of the National Trust. Tel: 0151 427 7231.

Sport

football — **Everton** were founded as St Domingo FC in 1878 in order that people from the parish of St Domingo Methodist Church could play a sport outside the summer months (during which time cricket was played). A year later the club was renamed Everton FC after the surrounding area, as people outside the parish wished to participate. Founder members of the Football League in 1888, they won their first League championship in 1890–91 and have since won the title on eight further occasions. They have also won the FA Cup five times. The Toffees' traditional colours are blue and white and their home ground since 1892 has been Goodison Park. Tel: 0870 442 1878.

Liverpool were founded by John Houlding in 1892 and joined the Football League the following year. The Reds – nicknamed after their famous red strip which borrows the colours of the city of Liverpool – are Britain's most successful club, having won the League championship 18 times, the FA Cup seven times and the European Champions League five times. The club's home ground throughout its history has been Anfield Stadium – originally the ground of local rivals Everton – although there are plans to build a new stadium in Stanley Park. Their rivalry with Everton is now exceeded in ferocity by a fierce rivalry with Manchester United. Tel: 0151 263 2361.

Tranmere Rovers was founded as Belmont FC in 1885 and joined the Football League in 1921. Rovers (sometimes known as 'The Super White Army', reflecting the team's home strip) play at

Prenton Park, Birkenhead. Unlike their two perennial Premiership neighbours, Tranmere have spent long spells in the lower divisions although their history has featured several magnificent cup runs, including a 3–0 victory against local rivals Everton at Goodison Park during the 2001 FA Cup. Tel: 0871 221 2001.

golf

Royal Birkdale Golf Club in Southport was founded as Birkdale Golf Club in 1889, gaining its 'Royal' status in 1951. The club has hosted the Open Championship eight times since 1954, the most recent being in 2008. Tel: 01704 567920.

Royal Liverpool Golf Club, Hoylake, Wirral, was founded in 1869, receiving its 'Royal' designation in 1871 due to the patronage of the Duke of Connaught, son of Queen Victoria. The course is often referred to as Hoylake, after the town near which it is located. A single 18 hole seaside links course, Hoylake first hosted the Open Championship in 1897 and has been the venue for the competition 10 times since, most recently in 2006. Tel: 0151 632 3101.

horse racing

Aintree racecourse, Aintree, Liverpool holds National Hunt racing on two courses: the Grand National course of $2^1/_4$ miles (3.6km) and the Mildmay of 1 mile 3 furlongs (2.2km). Red Rum, the legendary triple winner of the race, is buried next to the winning post. Tel: 0151 522 2922.

Haydock Park racecourse, Ashton-in-Makerfield, is a left-handed oval of 1 mile 5 furlongs (2.6km). Haydock hosts both National Hunt and Flat racing. Tel: 01942 725963.

rugby league

St Helens play in the Super League and are one of the world's leading club teams. The Saints, as they are nicknamed, have a strong rivalry with Wigan Warriors (see Greater Manchester) and the local derby between the two clubs is traditionally one of the biggest in British rugby league. Founded in 1873, the club moved in 1890, defeating Manchester Rangers in the first match played at Knowsley Road, their existing ground. In 1895 St Helens were one of 22 clubs that resigned from the Rugby Football Union and established the Northern Union. The first match of the new code was an 8–3 win at home to Rochdale Hornets. St Helens' famous home strip is white with a red 'V' on the shirt front and red trim on the sleeves. They won both the Super League and the Grand Final in 2006, and the World Club Challenge in 2007. Tel: 01744 455050.

Widnes Vikings were formed in 1873 as Farnworth and Appleton, adopting their present name in 1876.

Super Lamb Banana

Tithebarn Street, Liverpool. A sculpture created by Manhattan-based Japanese artist Taro Chiezo for the ArtTransPennine Exhibition in 1998, in celebration of the reopening of Liverpool's branch of the Tate Gallery. Bright yellow in colour, it weighs almost 8 tons and stands 17ft (5.2m) high; it is often mistaken for a dog, but as its name suggests, it was intended to be a cross between a banana and a lamb. Originally located outside Liverpool Playhouse in Williamson Square, it currently stands outside Liverpool John Moores University's Avril Robarts Library, having previously stood in Wapping, near Albert Dock on the city's waterfront. Tel: 0161 408 5353.

Tate Liverpool

Albert Dock, Liverpool. Part of the Tate Gallery, along with Tate St Ives in Cornwall, and Tate Britain and Tate Modern in London. An initiative of the Merseyside Development Corporation, the museum was created to display work from the Tate Collection and was for a time the largest gallery of modern and contemporary art in the UK outside of London. The gallery opened in 1988 and is housed in a converted warehouse in Albert Dock on Liverpool's waterfront. The original conversion was done by James Stirling but the building underwent a major refurbishment in 1998 to create additional gallery space. Tel: 0151 702 7400.

Thingwall House

Thomas Lane, Knotty Ash, Liverpool. Built in the mid 19th century in Jacobean revival style for Henry Bright, it was used until the late 1990s as a school for special needs children. On 6 November 2003 the house was destroyed by a fire, but, after a strong campaign led by Ken Dodd, Liverpool City Council handed over the land to the Liverpool Lighthouse charity in February 2008, and they are in the process of opening the site as a nature garden with eco house and visitor centre.

Thurstaston

A small seaside resort on the Wirral peninsula, overlooking the River Dee and home of Dee Sailing Club. The area is popular with birdwatchers, walkers and riders. Nearby Thurstaston Common is a Site of Special Scientific Interest. Thurstaston Hall dates to c.1350, and there has been a building on the site since the late 11th century.

12 Arnold Grove

Wavertree, Liverpool. A small terraced house in a cul-de-sac, the birthplace of former Beatle George Harrison. George's parents, Harold and Louise, moved to the house in 1930 following their marriage. The rent was 10 shillings a week. Here their four children were born: Louise (16 August 1931), Harry (1934), Peter (20 July 1940) and George (24 February 1943). In 2004 the house was featured in the British tabloids when its current owner resisted several attempts by Liverpool City Council to place an English Heritage sign on it.

20 Forthlin Road

Allerton, Liverpool. The small terraced house was the late teenage home of former Beatle Paul McCartney and his brother Michael (also known as Mike McGear and a member of The Scaffold). The house, where The Beatles composed and rehearsed their earliest songs, has been owned since 1995 by the National Trust and is furnished in late 1950s/early 1960s style, and there are photographs of the McCartney family on display. Tel: 0844 800 4791.

251 Menlove Avenue

Woolton, Liverpool. Also known as 'Mendips', the 1930s semi-detached property was the childhood home of John Lennon, singer and songwriter with The Beatles. The house belonged to Lennon's Aunt Mimi and her husband George, who took John into their family in 1945 when he was five after John's father left. He remained there until 1963 when he was 23 years old. The Beatles' hit 'She Loves You' was written in its front living room. The property was bought by Yoko Ono, Lennon's widow, who donated it to the National Trust. After much restoration work to return it to 1950s style it was opened to the public on 27 March 2003. The house was featured on the sleeve of Oasis' single 'Live Forever'. Tel: 0870 900 0256.

University of Liverpool Established in 1881 as University College Liverpool, receiving its royal charter in 1903. A member of the Russell Group of research-led universities, Liverpool has produced eight Nobel prize winners from the fields of science, medicine and peace, including physician Sir Ronald Ross, physicists Professor Charles Barkla, Sir James Chadwick and Professor Joseph Rotblat, physiologists Sir Charles Sherrington, Professor Har Gobind Khorana and Professor Rodney Porter, and chemist Sir Robert Robinson. The term 'redbrick' was first coined by Edgar Allison Peers, a professor of Spanish at the university (under the pseudonym 'Bruce Truscot' in his 1943 book *Redbrick University*), to describe Liverpool and similar universities; the reference was inspired by the university's Victoria Building (designed by Alfred Waterhouse and completed in 1892), built from red pressed brick with terracotta decorative dressings. On this basis, the University of Liverpool (which was itself originally part of the aforementioned Victoria University together with Owens College in Manchester) can be argued to be the 'original' redbrick university, although the University of Birmingham, on 24 May 1900, was the first university described as 'redbrick' to receive its royal charter. Former students include broadcaster Jon Snow, former head of MI5 Dame Stella Rimington and actress Patricia Routledge. Tel: 0151 794 2000.

Walker Art Gallery William Brown Street, Liverpool. A major art gallery which houses one of the largest art collections in England outside London, sometimes referred to as 'the National Gallery of the North'. Housed in a neoclassical building designed by local architects Cornelius Sherlock and H H Vale, it opened in 1877 and is named for its founding benefactor, Sir Andrew Barclay Walker (1824–93), a former mayor of Liverpool and wealthy brewer born in Ayrshire who expanded the family business to England and moved to live in Gateacre. Situated on the only street in the UK to consist of nothing other than museums, galleries and libraries, its collections include Italian and Dutch paintings of 1350–1550, European art of 1550–1900 including works by Rembrandt, Poussin and Degas, 18th and 19th century British art, including a major collection of Victorian painting and many Pre-Raphaelite works, a wide collection of prints, drawings and watercolours, 20th century works by artists such as Lucian Freud, David Hockney and Gilbert and George and one of the most important sculpture collections outside London. Tel: 0151 478 4199.

Wallasey Town overlooking the mouth of the River Mersey on the Wirral peninsula. With a history of seafaring and shipbuilding, Wallasey is linked to the metropolis of Liverpool by the Kingsway Tunnel (see separate entry). Fort Perch Rock (see separate entry), built to protect shipping in the 19th century, is now a museum.

Wapping Tunnel Aka Edge Hill Tunnel. 1.26 miles (2030m) long, the tunnel runs downhill between Edge Hill cutting, near the Crown Street Station goods yard, and Park Lane Goods Station in Liverpool. It was constructed in 1829–30 to enable goods services to operate between Liverpool docks and Manchester as part of the planned Liverpool and Manchester Railway.

Wellington Rooms Mount Pleasant, Liverpool. Situated close to Liverpool Metropolitan Cathedral, the building was designed by architect Edmund Aikin and built 1815–16 as a subscription assembly room for the Wellington Club. Originally used by high society for dance balls and parties, it was occupied during the later 20th century by Liverpool's Irish Centre. The building's neoclassical façade is Grade II* listed, but the building itself is empty and awaiting restoration.

Wellington's Column William Brown Street, Liverpool. Aka the Waterloo Memorial. Designed by Glaswegian George Anderson Lawton, with a relief depicting the Battle of Waterloo on the plinth. The monument was built 1874–5 to commemorate the victories of the Duke of Wellington during the Napoleonic Wars. It stands 132ft (40m) high.

Williamson Tunnels Edge Hill, Liverpool. A collection of apparently purposeless tunnels built by local men employed by Joseph Williamson from the early 1800s to 1840. The tunnels are in an area east of the Liverpool Metropolitan Cathedral in a rectangle bordered by Mason Street, Grinfield Street, Smithdown Lane and Paddington. They run beneath the brow of Edge Hill, one of the highest points in the city. The reason for their creation is unknown; however, it is supposed that they were constructed to provide employment during the economic recession following the Napoleonic Wars. Other less widely held theories include preparing a refuge from Armageddon, secret passageways for secret activities, or the simple belief that Williamson was eccentric. Tel: 0151 709 6868.

World Museum Liverpool William Brown Street, Liverpool. Founded in 1853 as the Derby Museum, and later known as the William Brown Museum, with extensive collections covering archaeology, ethnology and the natural and physical sciences. Much expanded, it reopened under its present name in 2005 with major new galleries including World Cultures, the Bug House and the Weston Discovery Centre. Other features include the Natural History Centre and planetarium. The museum is part of National Museums Liverpool. 0151 478 4393.

Some famous people born in Merseyside

Angers, Avril (comedienne and actress) (1918–2005)	Liverpool
Arrowsmith, Saint Edmund (martyr) (1585–1628)	Haydock
Askey, Arthur (comedian) (1900–82)	Liverpool
Bainbridge, Dame Beryl (novelist) (1932–)	Liverpool
Beecham, Sir Thomas (conductor) (1879–1961)	St Helens
Black, Cilla (singer and television presenter) (1943–)	Liverpool
Bleasdale, Alan (television dramatist) (1946–)	Liverpool
Botham, Ian (cricketer) (1955–)	Heswall
Braddock, Bessie (politician) (1899–1970)	Liverpool
Casson, Lewis (actor and theatre director) (1875–1969)	Birkenhead
Cox, Alex (film director and actor) (1954–)	Bebbington
Craven, Peter (motorcycle racer) (1934–63)	Liverpool
Dod, Lottie (athlete) (1871–1960)	Bebington
Dodd, Ken (comedian and singer) (1927–)	Knotty Ash
Epstein, Brian (manager of the Beatles) (1934–67)	Liverpool
Gerrard, Steven (footballer) (1980–)	Whiston
Gladstone, William Ewart (statesman) (1809–98)	Liverpool
Goossens, Léon (oboeist) (1897–1988)	Liverpool
Handley, Tommy (comedian) (1892–1949)	Toxteth Park
Harrison, George (musician) (1943–2001)	Liverpool
Harrison, Reginald 'Rex' (actor) (1908–1990)	Huyton
Hemans, Felicia (author and poet) (1793–1835)	Liverpool
Holliday, Michael (singer) (1928–1963)	Liverpool
Hornby, Frank (inventor) (1863–1936)	Liverpool
Lane, Carla (television writer) (1937–)	Liverpool
Lennon, John (musician) (1940–80)	Liverpool
McCartney, Paul (musician) (1942–)	Liverpool
McGough, Roger (poet) (1937–)	Litherland
Melly, George (jazz musician) (1926–2007)	Liverpool
Monsarrat, Nicholas (novelist) (1910–79)	Liverpool
Nimmo, Derek (actor) (1930–99)	Liverpool
O'Grady, Paul (television presenter) (1955–)	Birkenhead
Parrott, John (snooker player) (1964–)	Liverpool
Peel, John (radio broadcaster) (1939–2004)	Heswall
Plante, Lynda La (author and actress) (1946–)	Liverpool
Rattle, Simon (conductor) (1955–)	Liverpool
Redmond, Phil (television presenter and scriptwriter) (1949–)	Huyton
Rooney, Wayne (footballer) (1985–)	Croxteth
Rossiter, Leonard (actor) (1926–84)	Liverpool
Sayle, Alexei (comedian and actor) (1952–)	Anfield
Shaffer, Anthony (playwright and novelist) (1926–2001)	Liverpool
Shaffer, Peter (dramatist) (1926–)	Liverpool
Starr, Freddie (comedian) (1943–)	Huyton
Starr, Ringo (musician) (1940–)	Liverpool
Steadman, Alison (actress) (1946–)	Liverpool
Steadman, Ralph (cartoonist) (1936–)	Wallasey
Stubbs, George (artist) (1724–1806)	Liverpool
Tarbuck, Jimmy (comedian) (1940–)	Liverpool
Tushingham, Rita (actress) (1942–)	Liverpool
Vaughan, Frankie (singer) (1928–99)	Liverpool
Wilton, Robb (comedian) (1881–1957)	Everton

Norfolk

The Wash
Blakeney Point
North Sea
Brancaster
Hunstanton
Heacham
Snettisham
Dersingham
Burnham Thorpe
Wells-next-the-Sea
Holt
Sheringham
105
Beacon Hill
Cromer
Mundesley
North Walsham
Happisburgh
Sea Paling
Thursford
Saxthorpe
Fakenham
Guist
Bawdeswell
Stalham
LINCOLNSHIRE
King's Lynn
R. Nar
East Dereham
R. Wensum
R. Bure
Coltishall
Hoveton
Wroxham
Hemsby
Rollesby
Caister-on-Sea
Narborough
Necton
Bawburgh
Sprowston
Norwich
R. Yare
Great Yarmouth
Great Ouse
Stradsett
Swaffham
Wymondham
Reedham
Downham Market
Watton
Poringland
Wreningham
Loddon
Haddiscoe
Southery
Methwold
Mundford
Attleborough
Hempnall
Long Stratton
Feltwell
Larling
CAMBRIDGESHIRE
Little Ouse
R. Waveney
Diss
SUFFOLK
1
2
3
4
5
6
7
0
20 miles
30 km

Districts

1 King's Lynn & West Norfolk
2 North Norfolk
3 Great Yarmouth
4 Broadland
5 Norwich
6 South Norfolk
7 Breckland

Norfolk is a low-lying county in East Anglia. It has borders with Lincolnshire to the west, Cambridgeshire to the west and southwest and Suffolk to the south. Its northern and eastern boundaries are the North Sea coast, including the Wash.

Geologically Norfolk can be divided into three regions. In the east the county lies on weak Pleiocene rocks which form low, flat land easily eroded by the sea. To the west is a stronger band of chalk which dips to the north and in places has a unique red hue. The chalk is part of the Southern England Chalk Formation which is also found in Salisbury Plain, the South Downs and Isle of Wight. Below the chalk lies the brown-coloured ironstone known as carrstone, which has traditionally been used as a building material in the north and west of the county. In the far west the landscape is again low, flat and wet, around the Wash, an large inlet eroded into the weak rock. The transition between the eastern and western geology can be seen clearly at Weybourne, where the coastline suddenly changes. Much of Norfolk, like surrounding East Anglian counties, is flat and close to sea level. Some of the county, like neighbouring Cambridgeshire, is crossed by artificial drainage canals. The low-lying land and easily eroded cliffs make the county vulnerable to the sea, the most recent major event being the North Sea flood of 31 January 1953. The Norfolk Broads are an important wetland habitat and another important habitat is Thetford Forest Park, a coniferous forest and heathland park.

Norfolk was settled in pre-Roman times, with Neolithic camps along the higher land in the west where flints could be quarried. The Brythonic tribe known as the Iceni inhabited the county from the first century BC to the end of the first century AD. After the crushing of Boudicca's rebellion in AD 61 by the forces of the governor, Suetonius Paulinus, the county was opened to the Romans. During the Roman era roads and ports were constructed throughout the county and extensive farming took place.

After the departure of the Romans, the Angles, after whom East Anglia and England itself are named, had established control of the region by the end of the 5th century; they later became the 'north folk' and the 'south folk', hence 'Norfolk' and 'Suffolk'. Norfolk became part of the kingdom of East Anglia, later merging with Mercia and then Wessex. The influence of the early English settlers can be seen in the many '-ton' and '-ham' place names. In the 9th century the region came under Viking attack, and the Scandinavian presence is indicated by a number of place names containing the element '-thorpe'. In the centuries before the Norman Conquest the wetlands of the east of the county began to be converted to farmland again, and settlements grew in these areas. Migration into East Anglia must have been high, as by the time of the Domesday survey it was one of the most densely populated parts of the British Isles.

During the Middle Ages Norfolk further developed its arable agriculture and began a woollen industry. The economy was in decline by the time of the Black Death, which decimated the population in 1348–9. By the 16th century Norwich had grown to become the second largest city in England, but in 1665 the plague again killed around one-third of the population. During the Civil War Norfolk was largely Parliamentarian. The economy and agriculture of the region declined somewhat, and during the Industrial Revolution the county developed little industry and was a late addition to the railway network.

In the 20th century concrete 'pillboxes' were built both on the coast and inland to defend the county against invasion during World War I. These military defences had been comprehensively dismantled and only the pillboxes remained when on 3 September 1939 war was again declared. The aeronautical industry developed during the previous conflict saw massive expansion during World War II with the growth of the Royal Air Force and the influx of the American USAAF 8th Air Force, which operated from many Norfolk airfields.

The period between the two world wars saw major changes to Norfolk's agriculture. Sugar beet became a major crop and was grown under contract to the new sugar beet factory built at Cantley. Sheep farming declined and was replaced by dairy farming; by 1939 the county was a major milk producing area. During World War II agriculture rapidly intensified, and this intensification has progressed further since with the establishment of large fields for cereal and rape growing.

Norfolk is one of only four non-metropolitan counties in England which does not have a motorway. The A11 connects the county to Cambridge and London and the A47 runs west to the East Midlands. The Great Eastern Main Line is a major railway from London Liverpool Street Station to Essex, Suffolk and Norfolk. The only airport in the county is Norwich International Airport.

Norfolk's county town and only city is Norwich. Other principal towns include the port town of King's Lynn and the seaside resort and Broads gateway town of Great Yarmouth. There are also several market towns, including Aylsham, Diss, Downham Market, Fakenham, Holt, Swaffham, Thetford and Wymondham.

Norwich stands on the River Wensum immediately above its confluence with the Yare. Norwich sprang out of the former Roman Venta Icenorum, now Caistor St Edmund, 3 miles (5km) south of the present city. Anglo-Saxon settlers called the place Nordwic or Northwic (North-town) in an allusion to its situation relative to Caistor. At the time of the Norman Conquest in 1066, Norwich was one of the most important boroughs in England, and even had its own mint. Light industry had begun to develop, trade by river and sea was increasing and there was a thriving market at Tombland, where local produce, ironwork, pottery, leather and wooden goods were on sale, together with pottery from the Midlands and from the Rhineland, furs from Scandinavia and Russia, woollen cloth from Flanders and herrings from the North Sea. Norwich became a city in 1194, when granted a charter by Richard I. In 1253 new defences, consisting of a bank and ditch, were constructed; between 1297 and 1334 thick flint walls, 20ft (6m) high and $2^1/_2$ miles (4km) in length and with many towers and bastions, were added on top of the bank, while 12 great gates were built to provide access to the city.

The Black Death reached Norwich in 1349 and it is thought that as many as two-fifths of the population of about 6000 people may have perished. The Peasants' Revolt of 1381 brought an army of rebels who entered the city walls, setting fire to the houses of lawyers and other wealthy citizens before order was restored by the bishop and his army. The Wars of the Roses, which lasted from 1455 to 1485, disrupted trade and led to a decline in the worsted industry which affected the whole city.

In the 16th century Norwich was the second largest city in England after London, its wealth founded on wool, weaving, fisheries, agriculture and general trade. Goods from the city were exported worldwide through Great Yarmouth. The city gates were preserved until the end of the 18th century, when they were demolished by the Corporation for hygienic reasons and because they obstructed the increasing flow of road traffic. Material from the city walls was plundered for use in building, but some stretches were incorporated into the back walls of houses and thus preserved until the present century, so that substantial parts of the walls, as well as a small number of towers, still remain. In the mid 17th century the Civil War further disrupted local industry, and in 1665–6 Norwich experienced its last epidemic of plague. Unemployment had become a serious problem, and a severe food shortage in 1666 was only averted by huge catches of herring brought ashore at Great Yarmouth. However, the textile industry recovered from a slump as a new interest in fashion followed the years of Puritanism, and Norwich cloth was exported to Europe, North America, India and China. In the early 1670s Norwich was probably the largest provincial town in England, with a population of about 21,000. Shops and services were provided in the market area for the gentry of Norfolk and Suffolk, and the lowest street of the market, which was kept clear to allow the visitors to promenade in front of the shops, became known as 'Gentleman's Walk'.

The leather industry grew steadily during the 18th century, while brewing became increasingly important. With good water and the ready availability of Norfolk malting barley, the best in the country, by 1801 there were six large breweries in the city. The first Norwich bank was opened by Charles Weston in 1756. A well-known local Quaker family, the Gurneys, had made a private fortune from the worsted trade, and in 1775 John and Henry Gurney started a bank which survives to this day as part of Barclays. Thomas Dignold became established in Norwich in the early 1790s as a wine merchant and banker, and in 1792 he started the insurance business which was to become Norwich Union.

The population of Norwich increased from 37,256 in 1811 to 80,368 in 1871, and the city began to expand outside its walls. The Norfolk and Norwich Hospital was the first modern general hospital in Norfolk, while in 1853 the Jenny Lind Infirmary for Sick Children was founded from money raised at two concerts given by the famous soprano known as the 'Swedish Nightingale'. In 1882 work started on the Church of St John the Baptist, which was to become the Catholic cathedral. Boot and shoe manufacture grew rapidly during the 19th century, as did brewing. Norwich was also the home of soap-makers and iron founders. William Scott established the manufacture of electrical machinery in Norwich, founding a firm (Laurence Scott and Electromotors) which was to become one of the largest manufacturers in the city. Jeremiah Colman built a new mustard mill at Carrow, A J Caley began making chocolates at Chapelfield and John Jarrold founded his printing works at Whitefriars. The Maddermarket Theatre, founded by director W Nugent Monk and opened in 1921, was the first modern recreation of an Elizabethan-style theatre; it was located near the point where actor Will Kemp ended his famous 'nine days' wonder' dance from London to Norwich in 1599.

During World War II, Norwich was bombed more than 40 times, and the city was selected for two of the Baedeker raids, in which historic buildings were the main target. Over 30,000 houses were damaged and 100 factories were destroyed, as well as seven medieval churches and many shops. Much rebuilding took place in the 1950s and 1960s, and the restoration of historic buildings was begun at this time. A new central library was built in 1963 and the University of East Anglia (UEA) at Earlham took its first students in the same year. The city received the 1975 European Architectural Heritage Year Award for its renovation scheme of the Colegate area, and in the 1980s the former Norvic shoe factory on Colegate was converted to a variety of new uses. In the early 1990s the area around the old cattle market was excavated to provide the site for the Castle Mall shopping complex. This innovative scheme makes full use of the different levels of the site, extending the existing medieval street pattern and linking the east and west sides of the city centre.

Norfolk	**Population**			**Area**	
Districts	*male*	*female*	*total*	*sq miles*	*sq km*
Breckland	60,078	61,340	121,418	504	1305
Broadland	57,770	60,743	118,513	213	552
Great Yarmouth	44,009	46,801	90,810	67	174
King's Lynn & West Norfolk	65,817	69,528	135,345	552	1429
North Norfolk	47,470	50,912	98,382	372	964
Norwich	58,830	62,720	121,550	15	39
South Norfolk	53,853	56,857	110,710	350	908
Total	387,827	408,901	796,728	2073	5371

Local Attractions and Information

Administrative headquarters	County Hall, Martineau Lane, Norwich NR1 2DH. Tel: 01603 222949.
Airports	**Norwich International Airport**, Amsterdam Way, Norwich, schedules flights to more than 650 worldwide destinations. Tel: 01603 411923.
Anna Sewell House	Church Plain, Great Yarmouth. Situated next to the parish church of St Nicholas, the 16th century cottage is the birthplace of the authoress of *Black Beauty*, who was born in the building on 30

March 1820. She died at Old Catton, Norwich, in 1878, six months after the first publication of *Black Beauty*. Once a museum, the house is currently a restaurant.

City of Norwich Aviation Museum Horsham St Faith, 6 miles (10km) north of Norwich. Dedicated to the history of aviation in Norfolk, the museum originated in 1977 as an aviation enthusiasts' group for members of the Eastern Counties Omnibus Company. There are exhibits on 100 Group – the Royal Air Force 100 (Bomber Support) Group, formed on 23 November 1943 – and RAF Coltishall. Aircraft on display include an Avro Vulcan bomber, a Gloster Meteor fighter and a Hawker Hunter jet fighter. Tel: 01603 893080.

Berney Arms Windmill 5 miles (8km) southwest of Great Yarmouth. Standing at the head of Tile Kiln Reach on the north bank of the River Yare in the Norfolk Broads (see separate entry), the marsh mill is one of the tallest in the county. A tower mill built c.1870 to grind cement, it was more recently used for draining the surrounding marshes, as indicated by a large scoop wheel outside the tower, and operated until 1951. The mill itself is 71ft (21.5m) high; the sails have a similar span. Owned by English Heritage. Tel: 01493 857900.

Binham Priory 1/4 mile (0.5km) northwest of Binham-on-Wells, 7 miles (11km) northeast of Fakenham. The ruins of a Benedictine priory founded in the late 11th century by Pierre de Valoines, nephew of William I. The nave, with its splendid 13th century west front, is now the parish church, dedicated to St Mary and the Holy Cross; a preserved altar screen has depictions of medieval saints overpainted with Protestant texts.

Bircham Windmill 1/2 mile (0.8km) west of Bircham, 11 miles (18km) northeast of King's Lynn. Tower mill built in 1846 and operational until the 1920s. Now fully restored, Bircham is the only windmill in working order in the area open to the public. Tel: 01485 578393.

Blakeney National Nature Reserve 11 miles (18km) northeast of Fakenham. Covering 2711 acres (1097ha), almost all of which is in the ownership of the National Trust, Blakeney National Nature Reserve includes Blakeney Point, the area of reclaimed grazing marsh known as Blakeney Freshes, Morston and Stiffkey Marshes. It was the first nature reserve to be established in Norfolk and supports a wide range of coastal plant communities with many nationally important species. The 3 1/2 mile (5.5km) sand and shingle spit of Blakeney Point is noted for its colonies of breeding terns and for migrant birds. There are also substantial numbers of common and grey seals. The property is managed by the National Trust. Tel: 01263 740241.

Blickling Hall 1 1/2 miles (2.5km) northwest of Aylsham. Built c.1619 as an enlargement of an existing Tudor house, Blickling is one of England's great Jacobean houses. The spectacular long gallery houses an important collection of rare books; also on display are fine Mortlake tapestries depicting the stories of Abraham, and collections of furniture and paintings. There are intricate Jacobean plasterwork ceilings, while a recently discovered painted ceiling by Victorian artist John Hungerford Pollen, covered up in the 1930s, has been fully restored. The 55 acres (22ha) of gardens include a parterre, 18th century orangery, secret garden and woodland dell and are surrounded by an historic park with beautiful woodland and lakeside walks. Now in the care of the National Trust. Tel: 01263 738030.

Bradenham Hall and Gardens 8 miles (13km) east of Swaffham. Previously known as West Bradenham Hall, the red-brick house was built c.1740 in Queen Anne style. For long periods it has been tenanted rather than lived in by the owners, and reputedly among its tenants was Lady Emma Hamilton, who is said to have entertained Lord Nelson as a guest. Author H Rider Haggard was born in the house in 1856. Designed in the 1950s, the gardens are arranged in a series of 'rooms' divided by yew hedges, while the attached arboretum comprises around 850 named varieties. Tel: 01362 687243.

Bressingham Steam Museum and Gardens 3 miles (5km) west of Diss. Self-made millionaire and horticulturalist Alan Bloom purchased Bressingham Hall in 1946 and by 1958 had established a nursery and the innovative Dell Garden, with its informal displays of over 5000 species. He began creating a railway museum in 1965, first laying out the narrow-gauge railway known as the Garden Railway. By 1968 he had begun erecting locomotive sheds to house his collection of standard-gauge engines and bought a fairground merry-go-round. Locomotives on display now include *Oliver Cromwell*, *Thundersley* and the famous *Royal Scot*, while other exhibits include traction engines, royal coaches and railway memorabilia; there is also a stationary engine display and a Fire Museum as well as 7 miles (11km) of working railway. In the 1970s Alan and his son Adrian created a new 6 acre (2.5ha) garden, Foggy Bottom. Together with the Dell Garden and three linking gardens, there are now over 8000 species and varieties on display. Another feature of the site is the Dad's Army Collection, which includes a recreation of the series' fictional location, Walmington-on-Sea. The series was filmed in and around Thetford and featured some of the vehicles in Bressingham Steam Museum's collection. Tel: 01379 686900.

Bridewell Museum Bridewell Alley, Norwich. Once a prison (or 'Bridewell') for women and beggars, the museum is now home to a collection of historic objects and machinery relating to Norwich's trades and industries, including the production of mustard, shoes, textiles, chocolate and beer. Exhibits include a Victorian fire engine and a huge 17th century Jacquard loom, once used to weave the famous Norwich shawls. Tel: 01603 629127.

Bure Valley Railway Aylsham, 12 miles (19km) north of Norwich. Opened in 1990 on the trackbed of a former British Rail line, the 15in (380mm) gauge line runs for 9 miles (15km) through picturesque countryside between Aylsham and Wroxham in the Norfolk Broads. Both diesel and steam locomotives operate on the line, which has intermediate stations at Brampton, Buxton and Coltishall. Tel: 01263 733858.

Burgh Castle Burgh Castle, 5 miles (8km) west of Great Yarmouth. Situated at one end of Breydon Water, at the junctions of the Rivers Yare and Waveney, the Norman earthwork motte and bailey fortress was built within the impressive stone walls of the late 3rd century Roman 'Saxon Shore' fort of

Gariannonum. The castle is now ruined; the motte was levelled in the 18th century and only fragments of the earthworks remain. In contrast, the vast walls that once protected the Roman camp still stand 9ft (2.5m) thick and 14ft (4m) high with four solid round towers, and enclose a space 640ft (195m) by 370ft (113m). Next to the castle is the Norman church. Tel: 01223 582700.

Caister Castle $\frac{1}{2}$ mile (0.8km) west of Caister-on-Sea, 4 miles (6km) northwest of Great Yarmouth. Brick castle surrounded by a moat, built by Sir John Fastolf 1432–46. Bequeathed to John Paston (subject of many of the famous Paston Letters) in 1457, it was taken by the Duke of Norfolk in 1470 but restored to the Pastons shortly after. It was ruined by c.1600 but the 100ft (30.5m) tower still stands.

Castle Acre 5 miles (8km) north of Swaffham. A rare surviving Norman planned settlement built by the Warenne family in the 11th and 12th centuries. The castle was originally founded as a fortified hall by William de Warenne c.1070–80, with a stone keep built c.1140. The substantial ruins of the priory, founded c.1090, form the finest remaining example in England of the Cluniac order's highly decorated stonework. The church was consecrated 1146–8 and the prior's lodgings and chapel can still be seen, while a medieval herb garden has been recreated. The village's north or Bailey Gate, dating to c.1200, also still stands. Owned by English Heritage. Tel: 01760 755394.

Castle Rising Castle 5 miles (8km) north of King's Lynn. With a resplendent rectangular keep built c.1140 by Henry de Albini to celebrate his marriage, Castle Rising sits among 13 acres (5ha) of impressive earthworks with foundations of an 11th century Norman chapel at the northern end and the remains of a rectangular 12th century gatehouse on the eastern bank. Its claim to fame is as the last home of Queen Isabella, the wayward wife of Edward II. At her trial, a few years after she murdered her husband at Berkeley Castle, she was banished to Castle Rising, where she spent the last 27 years of her life, 1331–58.

Colman's Mustard Jeremiah Colman, manufacturer of mustard at a watermill in Stoke Holy Cross, 4 miles (6km) south of Norwich, first advertised his product in the *Norwich Chronicle* in 1814. A Colman's mustard shop opened in 1823 and the bull's head logo appeared on the company's products in 1855. The Colman family were pioneers in social welfare: in 1857 a school was opened for the employees' children, while in 1864 the firm employed a nurse to help sick members of staff. By 1865 production had been transferred to a large factory at Carrow on land bought from the Norfolk Railway Company, where the firm still operates. In 1866 the distinctive red and yellow livery was introduced to the label. The same year, the company was granted the Royal Warrant as manufacturers to Queen Victoria, while in 1903, Colman's purchased a rival mustard manufacturer originally known as Keen & Son (whose name had given rise to the saying 'keen as mustard'). In 1995, the company was bought by Unilever, making Colman's the oldest name in Unilever's portfolio.

Diss 20 miles (32km) south of Norwich. A market town on the Norfolk/Suffolk border, located in the Waveney Valley. There are excellent examples of Georgian and Edwardian building in the town centre. In 2006 Diss was the third town in the UK (Aylsham, also in Norfolk, was the second) to join the Italian 'Cittaslow' (literally 'Slow City') scheme, a project aimed at counteracting the modern ethos of fast food and the fast pace of life. To the southwest of the town centre lies Fair Green, which was first granted a royal charter in 1185 and where activities such as bull baiting and cock fighting took place until the fair closed in 1872. The green is still the location for travelling fairs and circuses.

Dragon Hall King Street, Norwich. A trading hall built c.1430 by merchant Robert Toppes. It is a unique legacy of medieval life and one of the most important historic buildings in Norfolk. The magnificent first floor great hall has an outstanding crown post roof with a beautifully carved dragon which gives the building its name. The building is now Grade I listed. Tel: 01603 663922.

Dussindale, Battle of See table of battles

Elizabethan House Museum South Quay, Great Yarmouth. A late 16th century merchant's house, now a museum recreating the lives of the families who lived here from Tudor to Victorian times. The house was a meeting place for Parliamentarians during the Civil War and the trial and execution of Charles I were allegedly plotted in the Conspiracy Room. There is a small but delightful walled garden. Now owned by the National Trust. Tel: 01493 855746.

Elm Hill One of the oldest streets in Norwich. Largely rebuilt after the great fire of 1507, it still retains its Tudor character. The narrow cobbled streets are flanked on either side by genuine Tudor houses; in fact there are more Tudor houses in Elm Hill than in the whole of the City of London.

Fairhaven Woodland and Water Garden South Walsham, 9 miles (15km) east of Norwich. Situated in the heart of the Norfolk Broads and comprising of 131 acres (53ha) of ancient woodland including the King Oak, reputedly 950 years old, water gardens and a private broad. Left in trust by the 2nd Lord Fairhaven in 1973 and opened to the public in 1975, the garden is renowned for its collection of candelabra primulas, the best naturalised collection in the UK. Tel: 01603 270683.

Felbrigg Hall $\frac{1}{2}$ mile (0.8km) west of Felbrigg, 2 miles (3km) southwest of Cromer. Built in the 17th century, the hall contains several original 18th century interiors, one of the largest collections of Grand Tour paintings by a single artist – the Italian Giovanni Battista Busiri – and an outstanding library. The restored walled garden features a series of potager gardens, a working dovecote and the National Collection of colchicums. The park, in part an early design by Humphry Repton, has an 18th century lake and several ancient trees, while to the north is the 520 acre (210ha) Great Wood. Now in the care of the National Trust. Tel: 01263 837444.

Forum, The Millennium Plain, Bethel Street, Norwich. Partly funded by the Millennium Commission, the Forum was built on the site of the former central library, destroyed by fire in 1994. It lies at the heart of an area known as the French Borough in the Middle Ages, when it was the most prosperous part of the city. Construction was completed in October 2001 and the building was opened to the public the following month before being officially opened by Queen Elizabeth II in July 2002. The home of BBC East's regional headquarters, the Forum also provides a venue for a wide range of entertainment. A time capsule buried in the foundations on 17 March 2000 contains plans of the building and messages from many involved with the project, as well as coins, stamps and a copy of the *Eastern Daily Press*. Tel: 01603 727950.

Great Yarmouth — 20 miles (32km) east of Norwich. A seaside town situated at the mouth of the River Yare. By the time of the Norman invasion in 1066 Yarmouth, as it was known, was one of the most prosperous towns in East Anglia. King John granted Yarmouth a royal charter in 1208, which constituted the town as a free borough. The town became known as Great Yarmouth in the Middle Ages to distinguish it from Little Yarmouth (now Gorleston) on the other side of the Yare. In the reign of Edward III a great wall was constructed, 2238 yds (2046m) in length and designed to guard the town on the north, west and south, the east being protected by the sea. Although much of the wall has vanished, a few sections are still visible, particularly along Blackfriars Road. Yarmouth is the chief seat of the English herring fishery. The seafront has a fine esplanade, with two piers 450ft (137m) and 753ft (229.5m) long. The chief architectural feature of the town is the church of St Nicholas, dating from 1101. The town was the home of the first electric cinema in England, the **Gem**, opened in 1908 and now known as the Windmill Theatre. The **Hippodrome** in St George's Road is Britain's only surviving total circus building. Built in 1903 by George Gilbert, it is one of only three circuses in the world to have a sunken ring, allowing spectacular water shows.

Great Yarmouth Row Houses — The 'Rows', the network of narrow alleyways linking Yarmouth's three main thoroughfares, developed from the 17th century to house the then prosperous fishing port's rapidly growing population. Many Row houses were damaged by World War II bombing or demolished during post-war clearances, but two surviving properties show what such dwellings looked like at various stages in their history. The Old Merchant's House, with spectacular Jacobean plaster ceilings in two of its rooms, has been restored to its state c.1870, when it was shared by the Atkins and Rope families of fishermen. Adjacent Row 111 house is shown as it was c.1942 (just before it was hit by an incendiary bomb). Nearby stands Greyfriars Cloister, the remains of a 13th century Franciscan friary, later swallowed up by Row development and converted into a number of dwellings. Traces of their interior features can still be seen on the brick-built walls of parts of the cloister and church, laid bare by wartime bombing. Early 14th century wall-paintings were discovered here in the 1960s. The properties are now in the care of English Heritage. Tel: 01493 857900.

Gressenhall Farm and Workhouse Museum — Gressenhall, 3 miles (5km) northwest of Dereham. A 50 acre (20ha) site comprising a former workhouse and the farm on which many of its inmates worked. The workhouse itself, complete with punishment cell, is now a museum of social history and Norfolk life; the Collections Gallery contains beehives, cricket shoes, fishing rods, hurdy gurdy, shop signs, toasters, toys and even a Turkish bath. The outbuildings have been used to recreate period dwellings such as Cherry Tree Cottage and its old-fashioned garden complete with privy and scarecrow. Tel: 01362 860563.

Grime's Graves — 7 miles (11km) northwest of Thetford. The largest and best known group of Neolithic flint mines in Britain, located in the area of sandy heath known as Breckland. Over 4000 years ago, miners worked in cold and damp tunnels, using antler picks to prise the flint from the surrounding chalk of the East Anglian Heights. The high quality of the material made it a major export item. The name is probably Anglo-Saxon, 'grave' meaning hollow, and 'Grim' or 'Grime' meaning 'masked one'. The 350 or so pits were dug over a period of 500 years and vary from 20ft (6m) to 65ft (20m) in diameter and up to 23ft (7m) deep. When each pit was exhausted, it was used to store waste material from the next shaft. The excavation of the shaft known as Greenwell's Pit in 1868–70 by Canon William Greenwell of Durham Cathedral proved for the first time that prehistoric flint mining had taken place in Britain. The site is now in the care of English Heritage, which in 1995 completed a detailed analysis of the 'lunar' landscape surrounding the mines, particularly the three shafts that can still be entered. Tel: 01842 810656.

Hickling Broad Nature Reserve — See Norfolk Broads

Highest point — Beacon Hill (GR: TG183414) at 345ft (105m), located at Roman Camp, $^1/_2$ mile (0.8km) south of West Runton. The hill is the highest point of the Cromer Ridge, a ridge of glacial moraines near the coast above Cromer.

Holkham Hall — 3 miles (5km) west of Wells-next-the-Sea. Home of the Coke family and the Earls of Leicester, the house was built 1734–64 by Thomas Coke, 1st Earl of Leicester. The Palladian-style mansion reflects Coke's appreciation of classical art developed during his Grand Tour of Europe. He employed the architect Matthew Brettingham to oversee the work of implementing designs drawn up by William Kent and himself. Work began in 1734 but the house was only finished 30 years later; Thomas died in 1759 and the task of completing the project fell to his widow Lady Margaret. The state rooms occupy the first floor and contain Roman statuary and Old Master paintings. The house is set in a 3000 acre (1200ha) park with a herd of 800 fallow deer. The 1 mile (1.6km) long lake, started in 1727, is home to numerous species of wildfowl. On the highest point of the park stands the famous 80ft (24m) obelisk, built in 1728 to commemorate the commencement of work on the designs for the house. Tel: 01328 710227.

Horsford Castle — $^1/_2$ mile (0.8km) east of Horsford, 5 miles (8km) northwest of Norwich. A substantial Norman motte and bailey fortress with earthwork barbican. The low motte and large bailey are surrounded by ditches, and the grass-covered foundations of a stone keep can be detected on top of the motte.

Houghton Hall — 8 miles (13km) west of Fakenham. Begun in 1721, this great Palladian mansion was built for Sir Robert Walpole, 1st Earl of Orford, later to become first Prime Minister of Great Britain. Walpole was only 24 when his father died and he inherited the estate with its modest Restoration house.

The architects were James Gibbs and Colen Campbell; the interior was designed and lavishly furnished by William Kent to display Walpole's impressive collection of pictures, sculptures, china, tapestries and other furnishings. Sir Robert died in 1745, followed shortly afterwards in 1751 by his son, Robert, 2nd Earl of Orford. Their combined debts put the collection under threat, and George, the 3rd Earl, was forced to sell the pictures to Catherine the Great of Russia. However, at the end of the century, the 3rd Earl's elderly uncle, by now the 4th Earl, and his chosen heir, George, 4th Earl and 1st Marquess of Cholmondeley, rescued the estate and the furniture. The estate then passed by direct descent to George, the 5th Marquess, who married the heiress Sybil Sassoon in 1913; he succeeded his father in 1923. The 6th Marquess was fascinated by all things military and collected model soldiers from a young age; his collection is on display in the museum. The present Marquess inherited in 1990, dividing his time between Houghton and the family's other home, Cholmondeley Castle in Cheshire. Tel: 01485 528569.

Hoveton Hall Gardens — Hoveton, 1 mile (1.6km) north of Wroxham. Set at the edge of the Norfolk Broads, the 15 acre (6ha) garden mixes formal and informal planting to create year-round interest. Early spring bulbs are followed by rhododendrons and azaleas in May and June, while the summer colour of hydrangeas is followed by berried shrubs and leaf tints in autumn. The Spider Garden is named after its ornate wrought-iron gate, with spider's web design. The hall, built 1809–12 and attributed to Humphry Repton, is not open to the public. Tel: 01603 782798.

How Hill Nature Reserve — 1 mile (1.6km) west of Ludham, 11 miles (18km) northeast of Norwich. A National Nature Reserve in the heart of the Norfolk Broads, located on 365 acres (148ha) of the former How Hill estate around the River Ant. A designated Site of Special Scientific Interest, it provides a habitat for a range of wildlife including marsh harriers and bearded tits, as well as overwintering birds. The site also features restored drainage windmills and marshmen's cottages. How Hill House, built in 1904, is now a study centre. Tel: 01692 678555.

Hunstanton — A small seaside resort on The Wash. Because it faces due west, Hunstanton is the only place on the east coast of England where the sun can be seen setting into the sea. Colourful rock strata are visible in the low cliffs to the north of the town, consisting of layers of chalk and Hunstanton redstone on a base of carrstone. The Princess Theatre, opened as the Capitol Cinema in 1932, is particularly noted for its construction in Norfolk carrstone, and contains the largest gable wall of carrstone in existence.

Interesting facts — **Bernard Matthews** founded his company in 1950. Initially selling turkey eggs (he began with 20 eggs which became 3000 by 1952), by 1955 he had purchased Great Witchingham Hall, near Norwich, and the surrounding 36 acres (14.5ha) of land. In 1980 the company launched its first TV commercial featuring turkey breast roast, with Matthews himself introducing the famous 'Bootiful' catchphrase in his thick Norfolk accent. Today, the company has an annual turnover in excess of £400m. The world's first **fish finger** was invented and produced by a frozen food company in Great Yarmouth. **Lotus Cars** have their headquarters at Potash Lane, Hethel, near Wymondham. **Nelson's Column**, the 144ft (43.8m) monument in Great Yarmouth, was erected in 1819, 24 years before the one in London's Trafalgar Square was raised. The **Lord Nelson** public house in Walsingham Road, Burnham Thorpe, is situated in Nelson's birthplace (Nelson was born in the Parsonage at Burnham Thorpe in 1758, son of the vicar, Edmund Nelson). Built in 1637 as an ale house, the Lord Nelson was called the Plough until 1798 when its name was changed (the first pub in England to do so) in honour of Nelson's victory over the French at the Battle of the Nile. The pub is unique in having no bar – drinks are served from a taproom with a range of real ales served straight from the cask. When Nelson was without a command from November 1786 to February 1793, he returned to Burnham Thorpe with his new wife, Fanny, and stepson to stay with his father in the parsonage. During this period, he spent many hours in the pub. Customers can sit on the same high-backed settle where Nelson used to sit. The ***Norwich Post***, first published in 1701, just misses out on being the oldest British newspaper. The London-based *Daily Courant* was not published until 1702 but was a daily paper, so is often given the honour of being the oldest. In fact, the *Worcester Postman* was first published in 1690 so the *Post* cannot claim to be the oldest non-daily either.

Julian of Norwich — A medieval mystic who lived in Norwich in the 14th and early 15th century, Julian (the name is a variant of Gillian) spent much of her life as an anchoress (a solitary religious recluse) in a small room attached to a Norwich church. She was possibly a Benedictine nun, possibly of noble birth; the location of her anchorage is unknown, although it is often erroneously stated to have been in the churchyard of St Julian's Church, which belonged to Carrow Priory. Her remarkable book, *Sixteen Revelations of Divine Love*, is a description of a series of visions which opened Julian to the depths of God's love. They are noted for their spiritual depth and theological courage as well as their literary elegance: in a medieval church which emphasised God's condemning wrath, Julian wrote, 'There is no wrath in God . . . It is the most impossible thing that can be that God would be angry for wrath and friendship are two opposites.' Just as striking and relevant to the 21st century is her perception of the feminine element in God: 'As truly as God is our Father, so truly God is our Mother.' The book states that Julian received her revelations in 1373; according to other internal evidence, its writing can be placed c.1393.

Kett's Rebellion — On 12 July 1549, Norfolk tanner and landowner Robert Kett and more than 15,000 of his followers camped in Wymondham, southwest of Norwich, in protest against increased rents and the enclosure of local common land by rich sheep farmers for grazing. They also expressed problems with the clergy but adopted the new Prayer Book. Many Norwich citizens felt sympathy for their cause. The rebels made their camp on Mousehold Heath, overlooking the city, and it took two royal armies to suppress them. They were defeated after six weeks at the Battle of Dussindale on 27 August (see Battles) and Kett was hanged; 48 other rebels met a similar fate.

Kimberley Hall 2 miles (3km) west of Wymondham, 10 miles (16km) southwest of Norwich. The present house, overlooking the River Tiffey, was built in 1712 for Sir John Wodehouse (an ancestor of P G Wodehouse) by William Talman. The four corner towers were added after 1754 by architect Thomas Prowse (the wings were only later connected to the main block by curved colonnades designed by Anthony Salvin in 1835). Various internal embellishments were carried out in the 1770s, notably some fine plasterwork and a 'flying' spiral staircase beneath a coffered dome by John Sanderson, a pupil of Robert Adam. During World War II the army occupied the house, after which further remodelling took place by Fletcher Watson in 1951. This involved the creation of a centrally positioned entrance, double-height hall and sweeping staircase. The substantial park, with its picturesque lake and walled gardens, was laid out in 1762 by Capability Brown, and has been described as his finest in Norfolk. The extensive woodland contains some magnificent oak trees, including one dating to 1373. Tel: 01603 759447.

King's Lynn A historic town located on the River Great Ouse as it meanders towards the Wash. Formerly known as Bishop's Lynn, the town developed in Norman times, when it was part of the manor of the Bishop of Norwich, and by the 14th century was one of the largest ports in England. It became King's Lynn after the manor was dissolved by Henry VIII in 1538. There are two 15th century guildhalls (see St George's Guildhall), and an impressive Dutch-style customs house, built by local merchant Henry Bell when he was mayor in 1683. It is still a working port, and glass is made locally at Wedgwood Glass.

Knettishall Heath Country Park $4^1/_2$ miles (7km) east of Thetford. An area of common land situated near the Norfolk/Suffolk border and part of the Breckland area. A designated Site of Special Scientific Interest, its 350 acres (140ha) consist of heathland, grassland and mixed woodland. Four long-distance footpaths meet on the heath: the Angles Way, Icknield Way, Iceni Way and Peddars Way (part of the Peddars Way & North Norfolk Coastal Path National Trail), while the Hereward Way ends at nearby Harling Road railway station/East Harling. The River Little Ouse runs through Knettishall Heath.

Letheringsett Watermill Letheringsett, 10 miles (16km) northeast of Fakenham. A restored working watermill located on the River Glaven and dating from 1802. Tel: 01263 713153.

Mannington Hall and Gardens Little Barningham, 5 miles (8km) northwest of Aylsham. A 15th century moated battlemented flint and stone hall with 19th century additions, owned by Lord and Lady Walpole. The famous heritage rose garden contains over 1000 varieties. Tel: 01263 584175.

Mid-Norfolk Railway A standard gauge heritage railway operating on $17^1/_2$ miles (28km) of the former Lynn & Dereham Railway and Norfolk Railway between the market towns of Wymondham and Fakenham via Crownthorpe, Kimberley, Hardingham, Thuxton, Yaxham and Dereham. The Norfolk Railway, building its line from Wymondham, reached Dereham first, and opened to passengers on 15 February 1847, while the line from King's Lynn began operating on 11 September 1848. The last scheduled steam-hauled passenger train ran on 17 September 1955, although freight was hauled by steam until the early 1960s. By 1960 there was an hourly diesel passenger service to Norwich, but the railway was threatened by the Beeching Report in 1963, and over the following 20 years nearly all services were stopped and the track lifted. The Mid-Norfolk Railway Preservation Trust was established in 1995 and the line is now fully operational between Wymondham and Dereham; the trust's long-term aim is to restore the line to Fakenham. Tel: 01362 690633.

National Women's Register Vulcan Road, Norwich. Founded in February 1960, NWR is an international organisation of women's discussion groups, each aiming to provide its members with the opportunity to take part in stimulating discussions on a wide range of topics of a non-domestic nature. The groups are often localised around the country and discussions take place at members' homes. In 2003 The annual NWR Woman of the Year Mary Stott Award was instituted in memory of one of NWR's founders, the editor of the *Guardian* Women's page in the 1950s and 60s. Tel: 0845 4500287/01603 406767.

Nelson's Column See Interesting Facts

New Buckenham Castle New Buckenham, 20 miles (32km) southwest of Norwich. Built by William II de Albini c.1140 with a cylindrical tower keep (the first in Britain), the castle was demolished by Sir Philip Knyvey in 1649. The stone ringwork and bailey still stand. The massive circular ramparts, wet moat and round keep make this an impressive site. To the east, the outer bailey with its bank and ditch and to the west, part of a chapel (now a barn) can be viewed from a footpath. Inside the ringwork is the bottom storey of a flint rubble cylindrical great tower, with a crosswall and a round-headed doorway. 2 miles (3km) northwest is the site of Old Buckenham Castle (see separate entry).

Norfolk Broads Britain's largest nationally protected wetland, with status equivalent to that of a National Park and covering 116 sq miles (301 sq km), the area lies in the counties of both Norfolk and Suffolk. Created by peat digging in the Middle Ages, this unique area of rivers, broads (shallow lakes), marshes and fens is rich in rare habitats supporting myriad plants and animals; the Broads are the only place in Britain where the swallowtail butterfly is found. The Broads are also one of Europe's most popular boating venues. The area extends over the lower valleys of the Rivers Waveney, Yare and Bure, together with the two tributaries of the Bure, the Ant and the Thurne, and the tributary of the River Yare, the River Chet. The rivers converge on Breydon Water before reaching the east coast at Great Yarmouth. Wroxham Broad is considered one of the most beautiful. Hickling Broad, the largest, is a bird sanctuary, as is Ranworth Broad (with a floating conservation centre). By the 12th century, much of east Norfolk had been cleared of its woodland for fuel and building materials, and the first written evidence of peat digging for fuel in the Broads dates from this time. Between the 12th and 14th centuries peat digging (or turf cutting) was a major industry. Abandoned by the 14th century, the diggings flooded, and the partly man-made landscape became a wetland rich in wildlife. Marshmen living in the wetter lowland river valleys developed a way of life which exploited the natural riches of the landscape, tending cattle on the marshes, cutting reed, sedge, marsh hay and litter, maintaining dykes and drainage mills, and harvesting fish and wildfowl. Changes in economic conditions brought about a shift from commerce and trade to recreation and pleasure, while with the advent of the railways in the 1870s the area began to develop into a holiday destination. The pioneer of the boat hiring business, John Loynes, founded his company in 1878 and other firms soon followed his example; the boating industry has continued to grow ever since. Two books by Arthur Ransome, *Coot Club* and *The Big Six*, were set in the Norfolk Broads. Tel: 01603 610734.

Norfolk Lavender — Caley Mill, Heacham, 3 miles (5km) south of Hunstanton. England's premier lavender farm was built in the 1830s and is now the location of the National Collection of lavenders, with over 100 species. It was originally a water-powered grain mill. Norfolk Lavender acquired the mill in 1936 after it had stood empty and unused since 1919. Tel: 0870 243 0147.

Norfolk Nelson Museum — South Quay, Great Yarmouth. Housed in the Grade II listed 17th century home of merchant Sir George England, a former Parliamentarian who was later chairman of the committee which welcomed Charles II to Yarmouth in September 1671. Horatio Nelson was born in Burnham Thorpe, son of the rector Edmund Nelson, and was educated at Norwich School and the Paston School, North Walsham. The Norfolk museum was established by Norfolk businessman and agriculturalist Ben Burgess, a former pupil of the Paston School and a collector of Nelson memorabilia who in 1992 established a trust to care for his collection. The museum opened in 2001, months after Burgess's death. Tel: 01493 850698.

North Norfolk Coastal Path — Long-distance footpath running along the Norfolk coast for 45 miles (72 km) from Hunstanton to Cromer. See Peddars Way Coastal Path.

Norwich: Medieval churches in — Norwich boasts the greatest concentration of medieval churches of any city in Europe. No less than 33 survive although many are now redundant.

St Peter Mancroft is a beautiful parish church situated in the centre of Norwich adjacent to the open market place. Like the castle and market place, it was a Norman foundation, the first church being built by Ralph de Guader, Earl of Norfolk, in 1075, and dedicated to St Peter and St Paul. At the time of the Reformation the two saints were given independent saints' days and the church's name was changed to St Peter Mancroft. The name 'Mancroft' is thought either to have come from the period when the Normans disrupted the Saxon market in Tombland by building their cathedral and monastery enclosure over it, forcing the citizens to set up a new market in the Magna Crofta or 'Great Meadow' adjacent to their castle, or from the name of the original owner of the land.

St Peter Hungate, Princes Street, is a cruciform church rebuilt in the 15th century which in 1936 became a museum of church furnishings and art. All exhibits were removed by 1999 and the church now stands empty.

St Stephen, Rampant Horse Street, dates largely to the 16th century. It underwent a wholesale restoration by diocesan architect Richard Phipson in the 1870s and much of the glass was replaced in the 20th century. The offset tower, forming what is effectively a three-storey porch at the west end of the north side, is unique among larger medieval churches in East Anglia.

St Michael at Plea, Bank Plain, dates to the 14th and 15th centuries and still has traces of medieval stained glass, although the distinctive battlements and spirelets on the tower date from its 19th century restoration; the clock dated 1827, bears the message Forget Me Not.

St George Colegate, built 1459–1513 with a largely 18th century interior, is situated in Coslany or 'Norwich over the water'. This area of the city is home to half a dozen medieval parish churches, of which St George is the sole working survivor. The area was home to much of Norwich's industry in the 19th century, as indicated by the blackened flint of the church walls. John Crome, founder of the 'Norwich School' of painting, is buried at St George.

St Gregory, St Benedict's Street, has some of the finest wall-paintings in East Anglia, dating from the 15th century. The most complete is almost 12ft (3.5m) high and depicts St George killing the dragon.

St Julian, King Street, is closely associated with the 14th century mystic Julian of Norwich (see separate entry), who is said to have occupied an anchorage at the church after 1373. However, the church actually takes its name from the priory formerly located here on the banks of the River Wensum and dedicated to St Julian, a popular figure in medieval legend. A nobleman who, while out hunting one day, spared the life of a deer, he afterwards predicted that he would kill his parents. The prediction came true, and Julian resolved to do penance by establishing a riverside inn for travellers and a hospital for the poor. The church was restored in the 1950s after being hit by a German bomb in 1942.

The present **St Andrew's** Church was completed in 1498; the only surviving part of the original church is a frieze running along the lower part of the east wall, and which contains a number of shields including that of William Appleyard, the first Mayor of Norwich in 1403. Another bears the city's earliest known coat-of-arms. Inside the church are a number of monuments and memorials: the Suckling Chapel contains effigies of Robert Suckling, Mayor of Norwich in 1572 and 1582, as well as a memorial to his son Sir John Suckling and his wife Martha Mortlock (d.1613). The Suckling family were prominent in the history of St Andrew's and the remains of their town house, Suckling House, are now home to a cinema. Sir John Suckling followed his father as an MP and became treasurer to James I but is best known as the inventor of the card game cribbage.

St Bartholomew once stood on Ber Street in the Conesford suburb of Norwich. Today only the stump of the tower beside the pavement remains. (This church should not be confused with Norwich's other medieval church of the same name, the parish church for Heigham, the area to the west of Pottergate and St Benedict, also a ruin today.)

Other notable medieval churches include **All Saints**, **St Augustine**, **St Benedict** (round tower), **St Clement Colegate**, **St Edmund**, **St Etheldreda**, **St George Tombland**, **St Giles**, **St James**

	the Less, **St John the Baptist Maddermarket**, **St John Sepulchre**, **St John the Baptist Timberhill**, **St Laurence**, **St Margaret**, **St Martin at Oak**, **St Martin at Palace Plain**, **St Mary Coslany** (round tower, possibly Anglo-Saxon), **St Mary the Less**, **St Matthew, St Peter Parmentergate**, **St Saviour**, **St Simon and St Jude**, and **St Swithin** (now the base for Norwich Arts Centre).
Norwich Castle	Castle Meadow, Norwich. Norman motte and bailey castle founded by William fitz Osbern for William I in 1067. A square tower keep of Caen stone was built on the motte in 1125–35 and a stone curtain wall added in 1268–70. The castle was taken during the 1381 Peasants' Revolt and Kett's Rebellion of 1549 (see separate entry); Robert Kett was later hanged from the battlements. The keep was restored by Anthony Salvin, 1834–9. Having been used as the city prison since the 14th century – some of the prison buildings were built by Sir John Soane in the late 18th century – it was converted into a museum in 1894, and it still houses the city's museum and art gallery. Tel: 01603 493636.
Norwich Cathedral	Upper Close, Norwich. Dedicated to the Holy Trinity, the Norman cathedral was founded by Herbert of Losinga in 1096 and consecrated on 24 September 1101. It is largely built of limestone imported from Caen in France, and is unique among English cathedrals in retaining its original 11th century floorplan. Another unique feature is the collection of over 1000 medieval roof bosses. The spire, dating from 1465, is 315ft (96m) high, second only to Salisbury Cathedral in England; the cloisters are also second in size only to those at Salisbury. Edith Cavell is among those buried at the cathedral. Tel: 01603 218300.
Norwich Roman Catholic Cathedral	Unthank Road, Norwich. Dedicated to St John the Baptist, the cathedral stands on one of the highest points of the city and is an imposing sight. Built 1882–1910, it was financed by Henry Fitzalan Howard, 15th Duke of Norfolk as an act of thanksgiving for his happy marriage to his wife, Lady Flora. She is commemorated in St Joseph's Chapel where each window depicts one of her names. Designed in the early English style by George Gilbert Scott junior, the cathedral is a magnificent example of 19th century Gothic revival featuring some of the finest 19th century stained glass in Europe, exquisite stone carving and a wealth of Frosterley marble. The cathedral is the seat of the Bishop of East Anglia.
Old Buckenham Castle	$^1/_2$ mile (0.8km) northeast of Old Buckenham, 18 miles (29km) southwest of Norwich. A Norman earth ringwork fortress founded by William de Albini, much of which was obliterated by a priory founded on the site in 1146. The castle was demolished to provide building material for the priory and the remaining visible traces of walls rectangular fortress was surrounded by a moat, are probably those of the abbey church. 2 miles (3km) to the southeast is New Buckenham Castle (see separate entry).
Oxburgh Hall	Oxborough, 7 miles (11km) southwest of Swaffham. A moated red-brick Tudor house with magnificent gatehouse, built in 1482 by the Bedingfeld family to whom it is still home. The interiors show the house's development from medieval austerity to neo-Gothic Victorian comfort; features include an accessible priest's hole, and an outstanding display of embroidery by Mary, Queen of Scots and Bess of Hardwick, brought to the house in 1793. The grounds feature a French parterre, walled orchard and kitchen garden, as well as a 19th century Catholic chapel incorporating medieval stained glass and an unusual triptych created from 16th century paintings. Now owned by the National Trust. Tel: 01366 328258.
Peddars Way Coastal Path	Long-distance footpath which begins at Knettishall Heath, 4 miles (6km) east of Thetford and runs north for 46 miles (74km) to Holme-next-the-Sea, 3 miles (5km) northeast of Hunstanton. Here it joins the North Norfolk Coastal Path which continues along the Norfolk coast for another 42 miles (67km). In its entirety the footpath is referred to as the Peddars Way & Norfolk Coast Path National Trail, one of 15 National Trails in England and Wales. See also Knettishall Heath Country Park, North Norfolk Coastal Path.
Plantation Garden, The	Earlham Road, Norwich. A restored Victorian town garden including a huge Gothic fountain, flower beds, lawns, woodland walkways, rustic bridge Italianate terrace, 'medieval' terrace wall and hundreds of architectural details fashionable in the mid 19th century. The idiosyncratic garden was established in a 3 acre (1.2ha) abandoned chalk quarry by cabinet maker Henry Trevor.
Prisons	**Norwich** (aka Mousehold Prison), Knox Road, Norwich, opened in 1887, is a category B and C prison holding local offenders. Operational capacity: 812. Tel: 01603 708600. **Wayland**, Griston, Thetford, opened in 1985 as a Category C adult male training prison. Operational capacity: 700. Tel: 01953 804100.
Raveningham Hall Gardens	Raveningham, 12 miles (19km) southeast of Norwich. Predominantly the creation of Priscilla Bacon in the 1950s, with superb yew hedges backing wide herbaceous borders. The red-brick Georgian house is the home of her son, Sir Nicholas Bacon and his family. The walled kitchen garden dates from the 18th century and there is a collection of old roses in the Edwardian rose garden. The 14th century St Andrew's Church stands just outside the gardens. Tel: 01508 548152.
Rivers	The **Ant**, one of the waterways constituting the Norfolk Broads, is 8 miles (13km) in length. A tributary of the River Bure, it rises near Honing, flowing through Wayford Bridge nr Stalham, Dilham and Barton Broad, then through Neatishead, Irstead, past How Hill and through Ludham Bridge, before reaching the Bure west of St Benet's Abbey. The **Bure** rises near Aylsham. After Aylsham Lock and Burgh Bridge, it passes through Buxton Lamas, Coltishall, Belaugh, Wroxham, Horning, Ludham Bridge, past St Benet's Abbey, through Upton, Acle and Stokesby, along the northern border of the Halvergate Marshes, through Runham and Great Yarmouth where it meets Breydon Water and flows into the sea at Gorleston. It has two tributaries, the Thurne and the Ant. The **Chet**, a $3^1/_2$ mile (5.5km) tributary of the River Yare, is navigable from Loddon to Hardley Cross where it joins the Yare.

Great Ouse – see Bedfordshire

The **Nar** rises northwest of East Dereham and flows for 15 miles (24km) in a westerly direction via Narborough (from whence it gets its name) before joining the Great Ouse south of King's Lynn.

The **Thurne** is $5^1/_2$ miles (9km) in length and rises near Martham Broad, flowing into the River Bure just south of Thurne dyke, near St Benet's Abbey.

The **Tiffey** is a small waterway in Wymondham.

The **Waveney** is 25.7 miles (40km) in length and forms the border between Suffolk and Norfolk, for much of its length within the Broads. Its source is a ditch to the east of the B1113 road between the villages of Redgrave, Suffolk and South Lopham. The ditch on the other side of the road is the source of the River Little Ouse which continues the county boundary and, via the Great Ouse, reaches the sea at King's Lynn. The river flows east through the towns of Diss, Bungay, Beccles and Burgh St Peter to Somerleyton, where Oulton Dyke branches off and flows through Oulton Broad towards Lowestoft. A lock links Oulton Broad with Lake Lothing and the sea. Just after Somerleyton, at St Olaves, the New Cut branches off to the left to connect the Rivers Yare and Waveney. Finally the river flows past Burgh Castle into Breydon Water at the confluence of the two rivers before reaching the sea at Great Yarmouth.

The **Wensum** is a tributary of the River Yare, with its source between the villages of Colkirk and Whissonsett. Flowing west through the village of Raynham and north to Sculthorpe, it then flows east through the market town of Fakenham and southeast through the Pensthorpe nature reserve and the villages of Great Ryburgh, Great Witchingham, Lenwade and Taverham before entering Norwich. It merges with the Yare to the south of the city. The Wensum's tributaries include the Tat and the Tud.

The **Wissey** is a tributary of the Great Ouse. It rises near Bradenham, flowing through Necton, North Pickenham, South Pickenham, Great Cressingham, Ickburgh, Northwold and Stoke Ferry before joining the Great Ouse south of Downham Market. Its total length is 31 miles (50km).

The **Yare** rises south of Dereham and flows east to Norwich, passing through the city's southern fringes where it is joined by its main tributary, the River Wensum. It then passes the villages of Cantley and Reedham and the isolated marshland settlement of Berney Arms before entering the tidal lake of Breydon Water. Here it is joined by the Rivers Bure and Waveney, finally flowing into the North Sea at Gorleston, Great Yarmouth. The twisting course of this tidal river is 55 miles (88km) in length.

Royal Norfolk Regimental Museum — Market Avenue, Norwich. The Royal Norfolk Regiment was formed in 1685. As well as collections of photographs and medals, the museum's exhibits include some of the fascinating items, both military and more unusual, brought back by the regiment's troops from their campaigns around the world. Tel: 01603 493650.

Sainsbury Centre for Visual Arts — See University of East Anglia

St George's Guildhall — King Street, King's Lynn. The largest surviving English medieval guildhall, St George's now houses the King's Lynn arts centre. The building is in the care of the National Trust. Tel: 01553 765565,

Sandringham House — 8 miles (13km) northeast of King's Lynn. The country retreat of Queen Elizabeth II, situated amid 60 acres (24ha) of beautiful wooded gardens. Built in 1870 by the Prince and Princess of Wales, later Edward VII and Queen Alexandra, Sandringham was once described by George V as 'the place I love better than anywhere else in the world'. The main ground floor rooms, regularly used by the royal family, are open to the public and the decor and contents remain very much as they were in Edwardian times. By 1928, George V had created his own private museum of big game trophies in rooms attached to the stable block. Around the time of the Queen's Silver Jubilee in 1977, the remaining stables, coach houses and old powerhouse were converted to house a varied collection of objects including royal motor vehicles ranging from the first motor car owned by a member of the British monarchy, a 1900 Daimler phaeton, to the half-scale Aston Martin used by Princes William and Harry. There is an exhibition dedicated to the tragic story of the Sandringham Company of the 5th Norfolk Regiment, many of whom died at Gallipoli along with the land agent, Frank Beck. The magnificent hedged gardens include carrstone rockeries, lime avenues and a stream walk. In 1968 an area of 350 acres (140ha) of the Queen's private estate – since enlarged to 600 acres (243ha) was designated a country park. The church of St Mary Magdalene, Sandringham, is one of the finest carrstone buildings in existence; dating in its present form to the 16th century, it is regularly used for worship by the royal family and estate staff. Tel: 01553 612908.

2nd Air Division Memorial Library — Millennium Plain, Norwich. Housed in Norwich's Forum building (see separate entry) and commemorating the more than 6700 young Americans, members of the 2nd Air Division of the 8th USAAF, based in Norfolk and Suffolk, who lost their lives during World War II, the library's collections include materials about American history and culture, about World War II in the air, and about the special relationship between the people of the UK, specifically those of East Anglia, and of the United States. Tel: 01603 774747.

Sheringham Park — 1 mile (1.6km) southwest of Sheringham, 11 miles (18km) northwest of North Walsham. Surrounding the privately occupied Sheringham Hall, built for the Upcher family in 1813 and now Grade II* listed, the 700 acres (280ha) of parkland were designed by Humphry Repton in 1812 and often considered his favourite 'darling child'. The gardens feature substantial collections of rhododendrons, camellias and azaleas. Now owned by the National Trust. Tel: 01263 820550.

Sport

football — **Norwich City** were formed in 1902 and joined the Football League in 1920. The club won the Football League Cup in 1962 and 1985 (their first Wembley success as the earlier final was contested home and away over two legs). In 1993–94 during the first leg of a UEFA Cup tie Norwich became the first English club to beat Bayern Munich at the Olympic Stadium (the 2–1 victory and a 1–1 draw giving them a tie against eventual champions Inter Milan). Delia Smith and her husband Michael Wynn Jones joined the board of directors in 1996 and are now majority shareholders. Nicknamed the Canaries (the club colours of yellow and green were adopted in 1908 to match the nickname), the club has played at its Carrow Road stadium since 1935. There is a strong rivalry with Ipswich Town in neighbouring Suffolk. Tel: 01603 760760.

greyhound racing — **Yarmouth Stadium**, Yarmouth Road, Caister-on-Sea. 382m track. England's most easterly dog track. Tel: 01493 720343.

horse racing — **Fakenham** racecourse, Pudding Norton, Fakenham. Known as the West Norfolk Hunt until 1963, the left-handed rectangular circuit of 1 mile (1.6km) stages National Hunt racing. Tel: 01328 862388.

Yarmouth racecourse, North Denes, Great Yarmouth. Left-handed oval of 1$^{3}/_{4}$ miles (2.8km) holding exclusively Flat races. Tel: 01493 842527.

motor racing — **Snetterton Circuit**, 10 miles (16km) northeast of Thetford, opened in 1951 with a race meeting arranged by the Aston Martin Owners' Club on the former RAF Snetterton Heath, the wartime base of the 96th US Air Force Bomber Group. The track's current configuration is 1.95 miles (3.14km) per lap. Snetterton has been a test venue for many top racing cars: it was the home test track for the locally based Lotus Formula 1 team, while major British single-seater manufacturer Van Diemen is based nearby. Snetterton is one of the fastest race circuits in England, with two of the longest straights in the UK linked by quick corners. Tel: 01953 887303.

Stiffkey — Stiffkey (pronounced 'Stewkey') between Wells-next-the-Sea and Morston in the north of the county is a fairly unremarkable village; its name means 'island of stumps' and probably refers to the tree stumps that are found in Stiffkey Marsh. The village became the focus of national attention on 31 March 1932 when Harold Davidson, rector of Stiffkey, was brought before a consistory court accused of leading a double life; while he lived in the parish at weekends at his parish, he would spend his weekdays at a bedsit in Shepherd's Bush, his base for daily trips to Soho ladies of the night. The Bishop of Norwich's star witness in the sensational trial was 17-year-old prostitute Barbara Harris, and her testimony, plus that of a waitress in a Chinese restaurant, led to the rector being defrocked on 21 October 1932. The case has recently been reviewed after doubts arose as to the accuracy of some of the testimonies. Unfortunately Mr Davidson was mauled by a lion at a Skegness amusement ground on 28 July 1937 and died two days later.

Strangers' Hall — Charing Cross, Norwich. A beautifully restored building which dates back to 1320, with magnificent stone-vaulted undercroft, Tudor great hall and fine Georgian dining room. Strangers' Hall was for centuries the home of wealthy merchants and mayors of Norwich. The traditional explanation for its name is that Dutch refugees, locally known as Strangers, met or lodged here during the second half of the 16th century. The hall now houses a museum of social history. Tel: 01603 667229.

Strumpshaw Fen — Brundall, 7 miles (11km) east of Norwich. An RSPB reserve inaugurated on 27 October 1997 and featuring the first Sounds Natural Hearing Support System, installed in the main building. Strumpshaw boasts several large reed and sedge beds with stands on damp woodland. Known as carr, this woodland is made up of willow, alder and dead trees, ideal for roosting marsh and hen harriers which also hunt over the marshes and reed beds seeking small rodents and water birds. As well as its birdlife and plantlife, Strumpshaw is one of the best places to see Britain's most magnificent butterfly, the swallowtail, in early May. Tel: 01603 715191.

Swaffham — Located midway between King's Lynn and East Dereham, the town of Swaffham was a fashionable resort in the 18th century; several Georgian buildings, including and the Assembly Rooms – the focus of society at the period – still stand in the market place, as does a domed rotunda topped by a statue of the Roman goddess Ceres. The town's symbol is the 'Pedlar of Swaffham', who according to legend went to London and was about to throw himself off London Bridge when a stranger dissuaded him and related a dream in which he saw buried treasure in a distant village. Recognising the place as his own garden, he returned home and dug up two pots of gold.

Thetford — Located in the southwestern corner of the county, Thetford stands at the confluence of the rivers Thet and Little Ouse in the heart of the Breckland region. Known to the Saxons as Theodford, it was one of the largest towns in England before the Norman Conquest, a place of residence for the East Anglian kings and the meeting-place of a synod in 672. In 1072 the Bishop of East Anglia moved here from North Elmham, although soon after the Domesday survey in 1086 Bishop Losinga moved the see to the larger town of Norwich (see Norwich Cathedral). A Cluniac priory was founded in the 12th century.

Thetford Castle — Castle Park, Thetford. The remains of two castles can be seen in Thetford. The earlier of the two, a motte and bailey castle erected towards the end of the 11th century, is now known as Castle Mound or Castle Hill; its the motte still stands 81ft (25m) high and is one of the largest in England. The wooden buildings were destroyed by Henry II in 1174, although traces of earthworks are still visible. Red Castle, $^{1}/_{2}$ mile (0.8km) to the west, was a ringwork castle constructed in the reign of King Stephen, possibly by Earl Warenne.

Thetford Forest Park — 3 miles (5km) northwest of Thetford. A working forest located in the Breckland region and owned by the Forestry Commission. With mixed areas of conifers, broadleaved woodland and heathland, the forest is a haven for wildlife such as deer, crossbills and nightjars. Lynford Arboretum was established in the late 1940s on the estate of Lynford Hall, built in 1858.

Thrigby Hall Wildlife Gardens — 5 miles (8km) northwest of Great Yarmouth. Located in the grounds of Thrigby Hall, built by Joshua Smith in 1736 and remodelled in the 1870s, the gardens are renowned for their collection of Asian mammals, birds and reptiles. There is a strong emphasis on conservation and the collections include endangered species such as the snow leopard, Sumatran tiger and red panda. A Willow Pattern garden based on the design of the Chinese blue and white plate is home to pheasants, cranes and Mandarin ducks. Tel: 01493 369477.

Time and Tide Museum Blackfriars Road, Great Yarmouth. Housed in a Victorian herring curing works, the Time and Tide Museum of Great Yarmouth Life explores Great Yarmouth's rich maritime and fishing heritage, and features many objects formerly exhibited in the town's Maritime Museum. There are recreations of a typical fishermen's 'row' (see Great Yarmouth Rows) dating from 1913 and a 1950s quayside. Tel: 01493 743930.

Titchwell Marsh 8 miles (13km) east of Hunstanton. RSPB nature reserve located just south of Brancaster Bay on the Wash, with areas of reedbed and shallow lagoons bounded by a shingle and sand beach. Breeding species include marsh harrier, bearded tit, bittern and avocet. Tel: 01485 210779.

Tolhouse Museum Tolhouse Street, Great Yarmouth. One of the oldest municipal buildings in England, built in the 12th century as a merchant's house and used as the town's courthouse and gaol from the 14th century until the 1870s. The prison cells can still be seen and interactive displays illustrate the long history of the town. Tel: 01493 858900.

University of East Anglia Founded in 1963, when it admitted its first 87 undergraduate students – in English Studies and Biological Sciences – the university's campus is located 2 miles (3km) southwest of Norwich city centre in 320 acres (130ha) of parkland. Denys Lasdun, designer of the National Theatre, was the architect of many of the university's innovative original buildings including the monumental Teaching Wall, now Grade II listed, and the striking 'ziggurats' of Norfolk and Suffolk Terrace, containing student accommodation. Today, UEA has more than 13,000 students (almost 10,000 undergraduates and over 3300 postgraduates) including 1200 international students from 100 countries. The campus is home to the Sainsbury Centre for Visual Arts, designed by Lord (Norman) Foster and housing the Sainsbury Collection, consisting of both modern Western works and fine and applied arts from across the globe. Former students include Booker Prize winning authors Ian McEwan and Kazuo Ishiguro; comedy writers and performers Charlie Higson, Arthur Smith and Paul Whitehouse; explorer Benedict Allen; meteorologist Penny Tranter; actors Jack Davenport, James Frain and Tim Bentinck; and BBC Radio's Jenny Abramsky. Tel: 01603 456161.

Walsingham 4 miles (6km) north of Fakenham. The picturesque village (in fact the two villages of Great and Little Walsingham) was a major centre of pilgrimage in the Middle Ages and became so again in the 20th century after the consecration of a shrine to the Virgin Mary in 1897. The Augustinian priory of Walsingham was founded in 1153 and dissolved in 1538; the remains of the abbey church, including a 13th century arch that once formed the east window, can still be seen. The 16th century Shirehall Museum was used as a magistrates' court until 1971; the Georgian courtroom has remained unaltered and is now part of a museum which also includes displays on the history of the village. Tel: 01328 820510.

Wash, The See Lincolnshire

Welney Wetland Centre 8 miles (13km) southwest of Downham Market. A nature reserve of the Wildfowl and Wetlands Trust, situated in fenland on the Norfolk/Cambridgeshire border. The reserve, covering 850 acres (340ha), was established by Sir Peter Scott in 1970 and is visited in winter by thousands of migratory Bewick's and whooper swans. Tel: 01353 860711.

Wolterton Hall and Park 7 miles (11km) west of North Walsham. The hall was built by Thomas Ripley in the 1720s for Horatio Walpole, politician, diplomat and younger brother of England's first Prime Minister, Sir Robert Walpole, and contains a fine collection of 18th century art. The remains of the village of Wolterton, including the round tower of the church, are still visible in the park. Tel: 01263 584175.

Some famous people born in Norfolk

Aldiss, Brian (author) (1925–)	East Dereham
Borrow, George Henry (author) (1803–81)	East Dereham
Burney, Fanny (author) (1752–1840)	King's Lynn
Cavell, Edith (nurse) (1865–1915)	Swardeston
Cotman, John Sell (artist) (1782–1842)	Norwich
Crome, John (painter and etcher) (1768–1821)	Norwich
Dyson, Sir James (inventor) (1947–)	Cromer
Edrich, Bill (cricketer) (1916–86)	Lingwood
Everett, Rupert (actor) (1959–)	Norwich
Fry, Elizabeth (prison reformer) (1780–1845)	Norwich
Greene, Robert (writer) (c.1558–92)	Norwich
Haggard, Henry Rider (novelist) (1856-1925)	Bradenham
Hearne, Richard (comedian) (1908–79)	Norwich
Kett, Robert (rebel) (1492–1549)	Wymondham
Macfadyen, Matthew (actor) (1974–)	Great Yarmouth
Meadows, Bernard (sculptor) (1915–2005)	Norwich
Mills, Sir John (actor) (1908–2005)	North Elmham
Nelson, Lord Horatio (vice-admiral) (1758–1805)	Burnham Thorpe
Paine, Thomas (political radical) (1737–1809)	Thetford
Palgrave, Francis Turner (critic and poet) (1824–97)	Great Yarmouth
Parker, Matthew (Archbishop of Canterbury) (1504–75)	Norwich
Pilch, Fuller (cricketer) (1804–70)	Horningtoft
Sewell, Anna (author of *Black Beauty*) (1820–78)	Great Yarmouth
Smethurst, Allan ('The Singing Postman') (1927–2000)	Sheringham
Southwell, Robert (Catholic martyr) (1561–95)	Horsham St Faith
Spencer, Diana (Princess of Wales) (1961–97)	Sandringham
Taylor, Roger (drummer with Queen) (1949–)	Dersingham
Vancouver, George (explorer) (1757–98)	King's Lynn
Walpole, Sir Robert (politician) (1676–1745)	Houghton
Windsor, Albert (King George VI) (1895–1952)	Sandringham

Northamptonshire

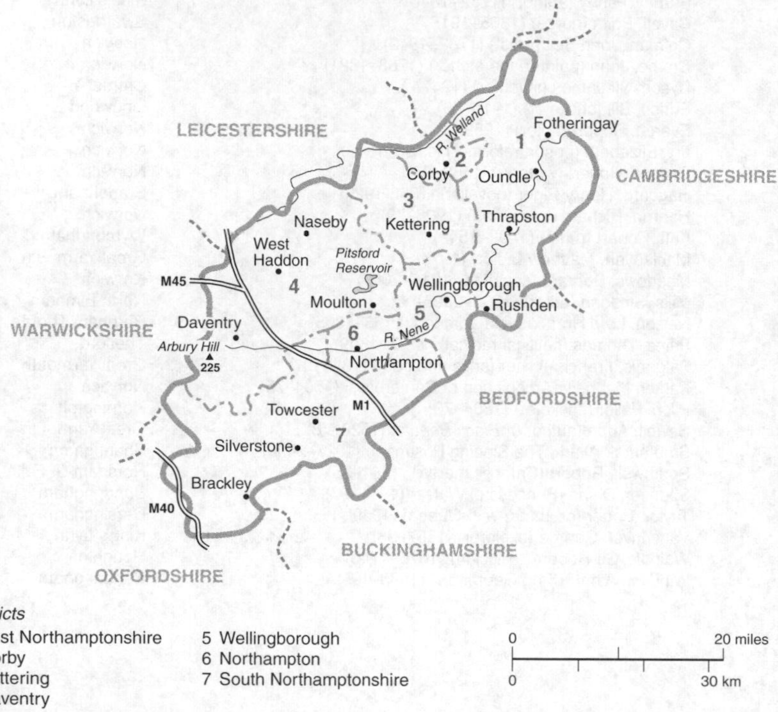
LEICESTERSHIRE
CAMBRIDGESHIRE
WARWICKSHIRE
BEDFORDSHIRE
BUCKINGHAMSHIRE
OXFORDSHIRE
R. Welland
R. Nene
Fotheringay
Corby
Oundle
Thrapston
Naseby
Kettering
West Haddon
Pitsford Reservoir
Wellingborough
Rushden
Moulton
Daventry
Arbury Hill
225
Northampton
Towcester
Silverstone
Brackley
M45
M1
M40
1
2
3
4
5
6
7
Districts
1 East Northamptonshire
2 Corby
3 Kettering
4 Daventry
5 Wellingborough
6 Northampton
7 South Northamptonshire
0
20 miles
0
30 km

Northamptonshire (usually abbreviated Northants) is a landlocked, largely rural county in central England. It has borders with Warwickshire to the east, Leicestershire to the northeast, Cambridgeshire to the northwest, Bedfordshire to the west, Buckinghamshire to the southwest, and Oxfordshire to the south. Its most northerly tip touches the most southerly tip of Lincolnshire, forming England's shortest county boundary at 62ft (19m).

Pre-Celtic and Celtic peoples settled in the region, and there are traces of Roman settlements and roads. Most notably Watling Street passed through the county, and there were important Roman settlements on the road called Lactodorum (Towcester) and Whilton Lodge (Bannaventa), near Norton, 3 miles (5km) northeast of Daventry. After the Romans left, the area became part of the Anglo-Saxon kingdom of Mercia, and Northampton functioned as an administrative centre. The area was overrun by the Danes in the 9th century and briefly became part of the Danelaw, but was later reclaimed by the Saxons. Consequently, it is one of the few counties in England to have both Saxon and Danish town names and settlements. The county was first recorded in the Anglo-Saxon Chronicle (1011) as *Hamtunscire*: the *scire* (shire) of *Hamtun* (the homestead). The 'North' was added to distinguish Northampton from the other important *Hamtun* further south: Southampton.

During the Civil War Northamptonshire strongly supported the Parliamentarian cause, and the Royalist forces suffered a crushing defeat at the Battle of Naseby in 1645 in the north of the county. Charles I was later imprisoned at Holdenby House. In the 18th and 19th centuries, parts of Northamptonshire became industrialised. A sizeable shoe-making and leather industry developed in Northampton and its surrounding areas, particularly Kettering, and by the end of the 19th century it was considered the boot- and shoe-making capital of the world. In the north of the county a large ironstone quarrying industry developed and by the 1930s, the town of Corby was established as a major centre of the steel industry. After World War II Northampton and Corby were designated as new towns, leading to a large increase in the population of both. Steel making in Corby ended in the early 1980s but the town successfully attracted new industries and much of the consequent unemployment was short-lived.

In addition to Northampton and Corby (one of the largest towns in Britain without a railway station), major towns in the county include Kettering (situated on the River Ise), Rushden, Daventry and Wellingborough (situated on the River Nene). Until 2001 the famous Dr Martens boots were made in Wollaston, a rural village near the market town of Wellingborough.

Northampton, situated on the River Nene 67 miles (108km) north of London, is the county town of Northamptonshire. A large market town and local government district, it is the third largest town in the UK without official city status, after Reading and Dudley. Remains dating back to the Iron Age have been found in the Northampton area. It is believed that there was a farming settlement in the area around the 7th century, which by the 8th century had become an administrative centre for the kingdom of Mercia. The pre-Norman town was known as Hamtun and was quite small, occupying only 60 acres (25ha). The town and its Norman castle (built c.1080) were important in the early 12th century and the king often held court in the town. During his famous dispute with Henry II, Thomas Becket on one occasion escaped from Northampton Castle through the unguarded northern gate before fleeing the country. Northampton had one of the largest Jewish populations in 13th century England, centred around Gold Street. In 1277 300 Jews were executed, allegedly for clipping the king's coin, and the Jews of Northampton were driven out of the town.

Northampton developed as a centre of shoemaking and other leather-related industries in the 15th century. By the mid 19th century mass production in shoe factories had transformed a trade previously carried on largely by individuals in their own homes or workshops; although shoemaking has now almost ceased, the street pattern of rows of terraced houses built for the factory workers in close proximity to the factories can still be seen in parts of the town. Northampton's main industries now include distribution and finance, and major employers include Barclaycard, Panasonic, Coca-Cola Schweppes and Carlsberg. Northampton is currently the largest district in England not to be a self-governing unitary authority. It became a non-metropolitan district in 1974, prior to which it had been an independent county borough.

Northamptonshire	**Population**			**Area**	
Districts	*male*	*female*	*total*	*sq miles*	*sq km*
Corby	25,887	27,287	53,174	31	80
Daventry	35,967	35,871	71,838	256	663
East Northamptonshire	37,918	38,632	76,550	197	510
Kettering	40,137	41,707	81,844	90	233
Northampton	95,380	99,078	194,458	31	81
South Northamptonshire	39,494	39,799	79,293	245	634
Wellingborough	35,961	36,558	72,519	63	163
Total	310,744	318,932	629,676	913	2364

Local Attractions and Information

Abington Museum — Abington Park, Northampton. Set in a Grade I listed manor house dating from the 15th century, the museum's exhibits include items from the Museum of Leathercraft, a collection of over 5000 leather objects begun in 1946 by leather designer John Waterer and leather chemist Claude Spiers. Other displays illustrate the history of the Northamptonshire Regiment and the county yeomanry, as well as the social history of Northampton. Tel: 01604 838110.

Administrative headquarters — County Hall, Northampton NN1 1DN. Tel: 01604 236236.

All Saints Church — Earls Barton, 5 miles (8km) northeast of Northampton. Dating to AD 970, the church has an Anglo-Saxon tower decorated with limestone stripwork, one of the most important surviving architectural monuments of the period. Also surviving are the Norman door and a 15th century rood screen.

Althorp House — 6 miles (10km) northwest of Northampton. The family home of the Spencers, the house is set in 450 acres (180ha) of parkland, much of which has remained unchanged for 500 years. It contains pictures by Van Dyck, Rubens and Gainsborough as well as furniture and ceramics. The massive stables were built in the early 1700s, and the present grounds were designed by W N Teulon in 1860. Althorp is the childhood home and final resting place of Diana, Princess of Wales. Tel: 01604 770107.

Apethorpe Hall — 5 miles (8km) north of Oundle. Late 15th century manor house once owned by Henry VIII and later by Sir Walter Mildmay, Chancellor of the Exchequer, who would occasionally entertain Elizabeth I here. Both James I and Charles I also made visits to Apethorpe and James is reputed to have arranged homosexual trysts when he visited the home ten times, 1614–24. Recent restoration work uncovered a secret doorway leading from the king's bedchamber to the bedroom used by his 'sweetheart' and favourite courtier George Villiers, Duke of Buckingham. After World War II much of the surrounding parkland was sold and the house became an approved school before falling into disrepair. English Heritage served a compulsory purchase order on its then

	owner, Wanis Mohammed Burweila, in 2002 and after spending more than £7m to save the property for the nation, controversially put the house up for sale in June 2008 for £4.5m.
Barnwell Manor	Barnwell, 2 miles (3km) south of Oundle. An 18th century manor house with origins dating to 1586, formerly the home of the Duke and Duchess of Gloucester. The estate now comprises 2500 acres (1000ha) and includes the ruined Barnwell Castle, founded in 1132 by Reginald de Moine and rebuilt in 1265. Ramsey Abbey in Cambridgeshire owned the castle until 1536, when it passed to the Crown. The manor was granted to the Montagu family by Henry VIII in 1540, and it remained in the family until 1913. The Elizabethan manor house became the principal residence, and the castle's living quarters and internal buildings were demolished in 1704. In 1938 Prince Henry, Duke of Gloucester, younger son of George V, bought the house and estate with the bulk of his legacy from the late king. The Duke's wife, Alice (later Princess Alice, Duchess of Gloucester), was daughter of Montagu-Douglas-Scott, 7th Duke of Buccleuch and Queensberry, descendant of the Montagu family. In January 1995 it was announced that the Gloucesters would vacate the house, and it was leased to Berenger Antiques. The Grade II listed house is not open to the public.
Battles	See separate table for details of the battles of Edgecote, Naseby and Northampton (I and II).
Blisworth Tunnel	A canal tunnel running north–south between the villages of Blisworth, 7 miles (11km) south of Northampton, and Stoke Bruerne. At 3076 yds (2813m) long it is the third-longest navigable canal tunnel on the UK canal network after Standedge Tunnel and Dudley Tunnel (and the ninth-longest canal tunnel in the world). Construction started in 1793 but was not completed until 1805; the first structure collapsed after three years and the tunnel was recut over a different course. Major rebuilding took place in the 1980s, several sections being lined with pre-cast concrete rings.
Borough Hill	1/2 mile (0.8km) east of Daventry. Standing at 650ft (200m) above sea level and dominating the surrounding area, the hill was once the site of the BBC's Daventry transmitter, constructed in 1925. During World War II the transmitter was used to carry out research into radar. In 1952 the BBC constructed a 720ft (219.5m) mast at nearby Dodford for the BBC Third Programme; in 1978 this service was discontinued and the mast removed in 1984. On 28 March 1992, the BBC closed the station, which is now owned by National Grid Wireless. The former antenna field is now open grassland allowing free public access. The area is also of archaeological importance and remains have been found of an Iron Age hill fort, as well as a later Roman villa and farming settlement.
Boughton House	3 miles (5km) northeast of Kettering. The Northamptonshire home of the Duke of Buccleuch and his Montagu ancestors since 1528, the original Tudor house was gradually enlarged until it became known as 'The English Versailles' after the French-style north front was added in 1695 by Ralph, 3rd Lord Montagu. Set in extensive parkland with historic avenues of trees, woodlands and riverside walks, the house also contains items from the Buccleuch Collection, including 16th century carpets, 17th and 18th century French and English furniture, tapestries, porcelain, painted ceilings and other works of art. Tel: 01536 515731.
Brackley	An historic market town in south Northamptonshire, based on the wool and lace trade and built on the intersecting trade routes from London to Birmingham and Cambridge to Oxford. Notable buildings include Magdalen College School, founded by Magdalen College for its pupils to escape the great plague that affected Oxford in the 15th century. St John's chapel stands next to the original college buildings and is still in use today, making it the oldest building in Great Britain in continual use by a school. There was once a castle in the west of the town, at which the signing of Magna Carta, which eventually took place at Runnymede, was originally to have been carried out, but no visible evidence of it remains. St Peter's church at the eastern end of the town has an 11th century Norman doorway. On the eastern outskirts of the town is Bronnley, supplier of hand-made soaps to Queen Elizabeth II and the Prince of Wales.
Brampton Valley Way	A 14 mile (23km) linear park based on the former railway line between Northampton and Market Harborough on the Northamptonshire/Leicestershire border. The line was closed in 1981 and the 13 mile (21km) Northamptonshire section, from Boughton Crossing in Northampton to Little Bowden Crossing in Market Harborough, was purchased by Northamptonshire County Council. The Brampton Valley Way was opened in 1993, its course encompassing ancient meadows, woodland spinneys and traditional hedgerows.
Burghley House	See Lincolnshire
Canons Ashby House	7 miles (11km) south of Daventry. The home of the Dryden family since its construction c.1550, Canons Ashby has survived with little alteration since the early 18th century. The interior contains wall paintings and Jacobean plasterwork. There is also a formal garden with colourful herbaceous borders, and an orchard featuring 16th century varieties of fruit trees, while the surrounding park contains St Mary's church – all that remains of the Augustinian priory from which the house takes its name. Tel: 01327 861900.
Castle Ashby	5 miles (8km) east of Northampton. The building of Castle Ashby was started by Henry, 1st Lord Compton in 1574 and continued by his son, later Earl of Northampton. Compton Wynyates (see Warwickshire) is now the family's main residence and Castle Ashby is the home of the heir to the estate, currently the Earl Compton. The estate grounds were redesigned by Capability Brown in the 1760s; later additions include a cricket pitch in front of the house and a 1 mile (1.6km) long drive. The grounds provided the venue for the Greenbelt Christian music festival, 1984–92, while two open-air concerts by Sir Elton John took place in the grounds in July 2000.
Coton Manor Garden	9 miles (15km) west of Northampton. Occupying a hillside position overlooking open countryside, the garden was originally laid out in the 1920s by the grandparents of the current owner and has been further developed since. The 10 acre (4ha) site surrounds a 17th century house and is divided into several smaller gardens, each with its own character. Beyond the confines of the garden there is a 5 acre (2ha) bluebell wood and a wildflower meadow. Tel: 01604 740219.

Cottesbrooke Hall and Gardens — 10 miles (16km) north of Northampton. Reputedly the inspiration for Jane Austen's *Mansfield Park*, Cottesbrooke Hall is a fine example of Queen Anne architecture dating from 1702. It is home to the Woolavington Collection, one of the finest collections of sporting paintings in the world, including works by George Stubbs and Alfred Munnings. The building was substantially redeveloped during the late 18th century, when features such as the bow windows of the north front were added, along with interior details such as notable wrought-iron work and unusual rococo papier maché wall decoration. Tel: 01604 505808.

Croyland Abbey — Tithe Barn Road, Wellingborough. Originally a manor house, the building is named after Croyland Abbey in Lincolnshire, which had been endowed with land holdings in the Wellingborough area in the 10th century, and was once a monastic grange from which these estates were administered. The present building is Jacobean in origin, but traces of the medieval grange have been found, perhaps dating from its rebuilding by Abbot Richard in 1281. The building now houses offices.

Daventry Country Park — 1 mile (1.6km) northeast of Daventry. With its centrepiece of Daventry Reservoir, managed by British Waterways and used to provide water for the Grand Union Canal, the 140 acre (57ha) park is a Local Nature Reserve and a popular site for birdwatching and angling.

Deene Park — 6 miles (10km) northeast of Corby. A largely 16th century house built around a courtyard and incorporating a medieval manor, with important rooms added during the reign of George III. It has belonged to the Brudenell family since 1514 and was the seat of the Earls of Cardigan, of whom the most notable was the 7th Earl who led the charge of the Light Brigade at Balaclava in 1854. Since 1955 the house has been the home of Mr Edmund and the Hon. Mrs Brudenell. The large collection of family portraits and possessions includes uniforms and memorabilia of the Crimean War. Tel: 01780 450278.

Delapré Abbey — London Road, Northampton. The 17th century house with 19th century additions, set in gardens and parkland, occupies the site of Delapré Abbey (the abbey of the meadow) – more properly the Abbey of St Mary de Pratis, one of only two Cluniac nunneries to be built in England (the other being at Arthington in Yorkshire). Founded in the reign of King Stephen by Simon of St Liz, it held a royal charter from Edward III, who also gave 'ten beams' towards the repair of the church in 1232 and another five oaks for work on the refectory in 1258. It is thought that there was once an underground passage linking the nunnery to a friary based in the centre of Northampton, via Bridge Street. After the Battle of Northampton (see Battles), which took place in the grounds north of the abbey and south of the River Nene, Henry VI was captured and spent the night of 10 July 1460 at the abbey as a prisoner. The nuns tended the wounds of those injured at the battle and many of the dead are buried in the nuns' graveyard (now the walled garden).The abbey was later used as a private residence and after World War II became the Northamptonshire County Records Office and the County Record Society; at present the Grade II* listed house is empty. The abbey is reputed to be haunted by a 'blue or grey lady' – a nun – who is said to have been seen frequently on the main staircase. One of only three remaining Eleanor Crosses is located at the Hardingstone end of the abbey estate. Tel: 01604 708675.

Easton Neston — ½ mile (0.8km) east of Towcester. Commissioned by Sir William Fermor, later Lord Leominster, and designed by Nicholas Hawksmoor in classical style, the house was built 1694–1702, and is thought to be the only house which was solely his work. It is furnished with paintings, tapestries and 18th century furniture. The Empress of Austria rented the house when she visited England in March 1876. More recently it was owned by the Hesketh family, descendants by marriage of Lord Leominster. In 2005 Thomas Fermor-Hesketh, 3rd Baron Hesketh, sold the house to Russian-born US retail businessman and designer Leon Max, while retaining ownership of Towcester racecourse (see Sport) which lies within the estate.

Eleanor Cross — See Delapré Abbey

Elton Hall — 13 miles (21km) east of Corby. Located on the Cambridgeshire/Northamptonshire border, there has been a house on the site since the Norman Conquest. The home of the Proby family for 350 years, the present building dates largely from the late Jacobean period, with evidence of architectural styles ranging from mock Gothic to classical, and somewhat resembles a medieval fantasy castle. There are a variety of period rooms and a collection of fine art dating back to the 15th century. The drawing room is gilded in an ornate French style, and among the artworks is a series by Reynolds, including a self-portrait. The tower library contains Henry VIII's prayer book. Tel: 01832 280468.

Fotheringay — A village 12 miles (19km) east of Corby, notable as the site of Fotheringay (or Fotheringhay) Castle which was razed in 1627. The castle was traditionally the home of the Dukes of York: Richard III was born here in 1452, and his father, Richard, Duke of York, was reburied at the nearby church in 1476. Mary, Queen of Scots, was tried and beheaded at the castle here in 1587; her body lay at Fotheringay for several months before being buried at Peterborough Cathedral and finally in Westminster Abbey. Local legend has it that the castle's staircase is now in the Talbot Hotel in nearby Oundle, and that Mary's ghost can be seen walking down it to her execution. Only the castle's motte, which provides views of the River Nene, remains today. The impressive Church of St Mary and All Saints, with its tall and distinctive tower, was constructed in Perpendicular style from 1434. The Nene Way long-distance footpath runs through the village.

Highest point — Arbury Hill at 738ft (225m), southwest of Daventry. The River Nene rises nearby. Evidence of an Iron Age hill fort of unusually square shape is visible on the summit.

Hill Ground Castle — ½ mile (0.8km) west of Lilbourne, 9 miles (15km) north of Daventry. A small 12th century earthwork motte and bailey fortress founded during the civil war in the reign of King Stephen and possibly built as a siege castle for assault upon nearby Lilbourne Castle (see separate entry).

Holdenby House — 5 miles (8km) northwest of Northampton. A country house completed in 1583 by Elizabethan Lord Chancellor Sir Christopher Hatton (see also Kirby Hall). It is said that Hatton, following its completion, refused to sleep a night in the mansion until Elizabeth I had slept there. Hatton's new house was one of the largest palaces of the Tudor period. The façades were symmetrical, with mullioned windows and open Doric arcades, reflecting the arrival of Renaissance architecture from Italy. The cost of building Holdenby financially ruined Hatton who died shortly afterwards. In 1607 it was bought by James I as a replacement for Theobalds, the country palace he had sold earlier that year. In February 1647 James's son Charles I was brought to Holdenby by the Scots and handed over to Parliament; he remained a prisoner here until removed by the army in June 1647. Parliament sold the property to Captain Adam Baynes, who demolished the entire house except for a small domestic wing. In 1709 the house was bought by the Marlborough family; they in turn sold it to their kinsmen the Clifdens, who rebuilt it in the late 19th century (the Lowther family, who now own the property, are descended from the Clifdens). Today all that remains of Hatton's great house are two archways and the kitchen wing, which were incorporated into the Victorian rebuild; a near identical third arch bears the date 1659, and was thus erected by Captain Baynes. Holdenby House is a private residence, although the gardens are open to the public. Tel: 01604 770074.

Interesting facts — **Towcester Racecourse** (see Sport) is unique among British racecourses in that it does not charge an entry fee. **Kettering Town FC** became the first British club to play with a sponsor's name emblazoned on their shirts, that of Kettering Tyres (in a Southern League game against Bath City on 24 January 1976). The deal was brokered by chief executive and manager Derek Dougan. Four days later, the Football Association ordered the club to remove the new slogan, despite Dougan's claim that the ruling body's 1972 ban on sponsorship had not been put down in writing. Dougan changed the wording on the shirts to 'Kettering T', which he claimed stood for 'Town'. For a couple of months, the team played on in the new shirts. **Anne Bradstreet** (1612–72) was the first American female writer as well as the first American female poet to have her works published. **William Carey**, born in Paulerspury, 3 miles (5km) southeast of Towcester on the border with Buckinghamshire, was a Protestant missionary and Baptist minister. Known as the 'Father of Modern Missions', he was one of the founders of the Baptist Missionary Society. As a missionary in Serampore, India, he translated the Bible into Bengali, Sanskrit and numerous other languages and dialects. Molecular biologist, physicist and neuroscientist **Francis Harry Compton Crick**, born in Weston Favell, is noted for being one of the co-discoverers of the structure of DNA in 1953. Along with James D Watson and Maurice Wilkins, he was awarded the 1962 Nobel Prize for Physiology or Medicine for discoveries 'concerning the molecular structure of nucleic acids and its significance for information transfer in living material'. **Alfred James Dobbs**, a Labour Party politician and trade unionist, is notable for being the MP who served the shortest term. He was tragically killed in a car accident the day after his election in July 1945. The town of **Northampton** was used as the location for the television comedy *Keeping Up Appearances*. Writer **Alan Moore**, creator of *V for Vendetta*, *Watchmen* and *The League of Extraordinary Gentlemen*, is a lifelong resident of Northampton. His novel *Voice of the Fire* is a fictionalised history of the town. **Spencer Perceval** was a Northampton MP and Prime Minister. He is famous for having been killed in the House of Commons by John Bellingham in 1812. The poet **John Clare**, born in 1793 in Helpston near Peterborough (now in Cambridgeshire but at the time in Northamptonshire), was committed to the madhouse in Northampton in 1841, remaining there until his death in 1864. In May 1328 the **Treaty of Northampton** was signed, a peace treaty between the English and the Scots in which Edward III recognised the authority of Robert the Bruce as king of Scotland and betrothed Bruce's still infant son to the king's sister Joanna. **Corby** was granted the right to hold two annual fairs and a market by Henry III in 1226. In 1568 the town was granted a charter by Elizabeth I that exempted local landowners from certain taxes and gave all men the right to refuse to serve in the local militia. According to legend, the queen was hunting in Rockingham Forest when she fell from her horse; villagers from Corby came to her rescue and she granted the charter in gratitude. (Another popular explanation is that it was granted as a favour to her alleged lover Sir Christopher Hatton.) The Corby Pole Fair has taken place every 20 years since 1862 in celebration of the charter. The **Watford Gap Service Station** on the M1 motorway was the first motorway service station in the UK. The services are often quoted as being the point where the north/south divide begins. The village is often mistaken for the much larger town of Watford in Hertfordshire, about 50 miles (80km) to the south.

Irchester Country Park — 2 miles (3km) south of Wellingborough. Sometimes referred to as Northamptonshire's 'Jurassic Park', Irchester's varied terrain, including mature woodland and grassy open meadows, overlies ironstone and limestone rocks thought to have formed over 165 million years ago. The 205 acre (83ha) park was formerly an ironstone quarry and the quarry face, with its layers of rock and fossils, is a Regionally Important Geological Site. Quarrying ended in the 1960s, but there is still evidence of the area's industrial heritage in the 'hills and dales' landscape, the open ironstone gullets and the locomotives of the Ironstone Narrow Gauge Railway Museum. The park was opened in 1971, and over 250,000 trees have since been planted. The working woodland is managed both for its timber and for wildlife, including green woodpecker and sparrowhawk. Tel: 01933 276866.

Jurassic Way — A long-distance footpath connecting Banbury in Oxfordshire with Stamford, Lincolnshire. Most of its 88 mile (142km) route is through Northamptonshire on the Jurassic limestone ridge in the north of the county.

Kelmarsh Hall — Kelmarsh, 11 miles (18km) north of Northampton. Located on the Leicestershire/Northamptonshire border, the house was built in the 1730s in Palladian style for antiquarian William Hanbury by Francis Smith of Warwick. The interiors and the extensive gardens were designed in the 1940s by Nancy Lancaster, niece of politician Nancy Astor, and are surrounded by a working estate. Tel: 01604 686543.

Kirby Hall — 4 miles (6km) northeast of Corby. An Elizabethan and 17th century house, begun by Sir Humphrey Stafford c.1570 and purchased six years later by Sir Christopher Hatton, courtier of Elizabeth I and later her Lord Chancellor. Hatton hoped in vain to receive Elizabeth here during one of her annual 'progresses' around England. The vast stone-built mansion is partly roofless, having suffered serious neglect during the 18th and 19th centuries. Most of its walls however survive to their full height: so does the stupendous three-tier inner porch, begun following French pattern books and later further embellished in classical style by sculptor Nicholas Stone. The great hall and state rooms also remain intact, and have been refitted and redecorated in authentic 17th and 18th century style. The gardens, laid out in an elaborate 'cutwork' design during the 17th century by Sir Christopher Hatton the 4th, have been partly restored. Now in the care of English Heritage. Tel: 01536 203230.

Lamport Hall and Gardens — 8 miles (13km) north of Northampton. The home of the Isham family from 1560 to 1976; the existing house, now Grade I listed, was begun in 1655 when an impressive classical façade was added to the existing Tudor structure. What is believed to be the first alpine garden in England was created by the 10th Baronet, Sir Charles Isham (1819–1903); he is also credited with introducing garden gnomes to the UK, having imported several terracotta figures from Germany to decorate the rockery in the 1890s. Sir Gyles Isham, the last owner, acted in several Hollywood films in the 1930s. Tel: 01604 686272.

Lilbourne Castle — Lilbourne, 9 miles (15km) north of Daventry. A Norman earthwork motte and bailey fortress founded by Robert, Earl of Leicester. The 11th century motte stands 20ft (6m) high; encased by a ditch, it protects two small baileys defended by ramparts, ditches and banks. In 1218, the well-preserved timber castle was ordered by Henry III to be slighted. To the west, the siege castle of Hill Ground (see separate entry) stands on the high ground of Roundhill.

Lyveden New Bield — 4 miles (6km) southwest of Oundle. Begun in 1595 by Sir Thomas Tresham (father of one of the Gunpowder Plotters) to symbolise his Catholic faith, Lyveden remains incomplete and virtually unaltered since work stopped on his death in 1605. Intended as a garden lodge, the building's architectural detail is in a remarkable state of preservation and contains many symbolic references to the Holy Trinity. The restored water garden, with its terraces and spiral mounts, remains one of the oldest surviving layouts in Britain. Now owned by the National Trust. Tel: 01832 205358. See also Rushton Triangular Lodge

Museum of Leathercraft — See Abington Museum

National Waterways Museum — See Stoke Bruerne Canal Museum

Northampton and Lamport Railway — 5 miles (8km) north of Northampton. A standard gauge preserved railway based at Pitsford and Brampton railway station, operating on $1^1/_4$ miles (2km) of the former line between Northampton and Market Harborough. After the line closed in August 1981, a group was formed in 1984 with the intention of reopening a section. The site opened to the public shortly afterwards, carrying its first fare-paying passengers in November 1995. The signalling system, with two working signal boxes, is one of the most comprehensive and detailed on any heritage railway. The booking office at Pitsford and Brampton station was built using the disused Lamport signalbox, originally located $5^1/_2$ miles (9km) away on the same line. The Brampton Valley Way (see separate entry) runs alongside the railway. Tel: 01604 820327.

Northampton Cathedral — Primrose Hill, Northampton. Dedicated to Our Lady Immaculate and St Thomas of Canterbury, the Roman Catholic cathedral is the seat of the Diocese of Northampton. The origins of the current building date to 1840 when Augustus Welby Pugin was commissioned to design a collegiate chapel. The number of worshippers soon outgrew the size of the building and E W Pugin, his son, was chosen to design an extension in order to make the building into a cathedral. This extension, in the form of the current nave, was opened in 1864. The west end was extended in 1955. Tel: 01604 714556.

Northampton Ironstone Railway — Hunsbury Hill, 3 miles (5km) southwest of Northampton. A $1^1/_2$ mile (2.5km) standard gauge heritage railway operated by the Northamptonshire Ironstone Railway Trust. Located in a former ironstone quarry closed in the 1930s, the railway has a varied collection of rolling stock and offers rides in a variety of vehicles including a converted brake van. Tel: 01604 702031.

Pitsford Water — $^1/_2$ mile (0.8km) north of Pitsford, 6 miles (10km) north of Northampton. The third largest reservoir in the UK, with a surface area of 2.85 sq miles (7.38 sq km). Operated by Anglian Water and located near Brixworth Country Park, it is a designated Site of Special Scientific Interest attracting a wide range of breeding and migratory birds.

Rivers — **Avon** see Warwickshire

Great Ouse see Bedfordshire

The **Ise** is a tributary of the Nene that rises in Naseby Field at the northwest tip of Northamptonshire. Flowing east past Desborough and the Eleanor Cross at Geddington, it turns south and passes Kettering and Burton Latimer before joining the Nene just south of Wellingborough.

Nene see Cambridgeshire

The **Tove**, a tributary of the Great Ouse, rises in south Northamptonshire and flows for 15 miles (24km) past Towcester (which means 'camp on the Tove') before meeting the Ouse near Milton Keynes. Its final 5 miles (8km) form part of the border between Northamptonshire and Buckinghamshire, running alongside the Grand Union Canal.

Rockingham Castle — 1 mile (1.6km) north of Corby. Situated in an elevated position on the side of the Welland Valley overlooking the villages of Rockingham and Caldecott, the castle was founded by William I on the site of a Saxon fortification; the shell keep was added by William II. The castle was used by

Norman kings as a retreat when hunting in nearby Rockingham Forest (see separate entry), and King John left his treasure chest here. It remained a royal castle until the reign of Henry VIII, by which time it was in decline; Henry gave it to Edward Watson, whose descendants have lived in the castle ever since. Taken by Parliamentary forces during the Civil War, it was finally restored to its full elegance in the late 19th century. Charles Dickens, a family friend, regularly visited the castle, which is said to have been the inspiration for Chesney Wold in *Bleak House*. Tel: 01536 770240.

Rockingham Forest — A region of northeast Northamptonshire covering 200 square miles (500 sq km) between the Rivers Welland and Nene and the towns of Stamford in Lincolnshire and Kettering. The varied landscape includes farmland, open pasture, pockets of woodland and villages built from local stone. Designated a royal hunting ground by William I and given the title of Rockingham Forest, it benefited from varying degrees of royal ownership and laws until its final dissolution at the beginning of the 19th century. The newly formed Forestry Commission took over the remnants of public woodland in 1923 and carried out further clearance and replanting, mainly with conifers. Large areas have recently been replanted with native species such as oak and ash as part of the Commission's Ancient Woodlands Project. Tel: 01832 274278.

Rushton Triangular Lodge — 1 mile (1.6km) west of Rushton, 3 miles (5km) northwest of Kettering. Designed by Sir Thomas Tresham and constructed 1593–7, the triangular building is like Lyveden New Bield (see separate entry) a testament to Tresham's Roman Catholicism: the number three, symbolising the Holy Trinity, is apparent everywhere. There are three floors, trefoil windows and three triangular gables on each side. The entrance front bears the inscription *Tres Testimonium Dant* ('there are three that give witness'), a biblical quotation from St John's gospel referring to the Trinity. It is also a pun on Tresham's name; his wife called him 'Good Tres' in her letters. Now in the care of English Heritage. Tel: 01536 710761.

Salcey Forest — East of Hartwell, 6 miles (10km) southeast of Northampton. A remnant of a medieval hunting forest, this ancient woodland contains many miles of ancient woodbanks, building remains and ancient trees and is a Site of Special Scientific Interest. The 'druids' – veteran oaks, some possibly over 500 years old – provide a rare habitat for wildlife. Now owned by the Forestry Commission.

78 Derngate — Northampton. A Grade II* listed Georgian house noted for its interior, extensively redeveloped 1916–17 by architect Charles Rennie Mackintosh for businessman Wenman Joseph Bassett-Lowke. Having been used by Northampton High School for Girls, 1964–93, the house was opened to the public in 2003 after 18 months of restoration. Tel: 01604 603407.

Southwick Hall — 3 miles (5km) north of Oundle, 9 miles (15km) northeast of Corby. A family home dating from 1300 with Tudor and 18th century additions. Two towers from the 14th century house still stand. There are displays on Victorian and Edwardian life, collections of agricultural and carpentry tools, named bricks and local archaeological finds and fossils. Tel: 01832 274064.

Sport

cricket — **Northamptonshire** County Cricket Club was formed in 1878 and attained first-class status in 1905. They are twice winners of the Gillette Cup in 1976 and its successor, the Natwest Trophy, in 1992; their highest placing in the County Championship is second, most recently in 1976. The club's limited overs team is the Steelbacks. Northants play the majority of their games at the County Cricket Ground, Abington Avenue, Northampton, but have also used grounds at Kettering, Wellingborough and Finedon. They have also played home one-day games outside the county at Peterborough, Luton, Tring and Milton Keynes. Tel: 01604 514490.

football — **Kettering Town** were founded in 1872, turning professional in 1891. One of the most successful clubs outside the Football League, Kettering became founder members of the Football Alliance in 1979, having won the Southern League Championship three times – in 1928 and 1957 under Tommy Lawton and in 1973 under Ron Atkinson. Paul Gascoigne managed the club for a short time in the 2005–06 season. Nicknamed The Poppies after their traditional all-red strip, Kettering's home ground is Rockingham Road. Tel: 01536 483028.

Northampton Town were founded in 1897 and joined the Football League in 1920. Nicknamed The Cobblers, they play at Sixfields Stadium, having moved from the County Ground (which they shared with Northamptonshire County Cricket Club) in October 1994. Tel: 0870 822 1997.

Rushden and Diamonds were formed in 1992 by Max Griggs, the owner of the Dr Martens shoe company who bought and merged the non-league clubs Rushden Town (formed in 1889 and known as 'The Russians') and Irthlingborough Diamonds (formed in 1946). Rushden and Diamonds won promotion to the Conference in 1996 and reached the Football League in 2001. In 2003 they won the Division Three championship, but were relegated in 2004 and lost their League place in 2006. The club's home ground is Nene Park, Irthlingborough. Tel: 01933 652000.

horse racing — **Towcester** racecourse, London Road, Towcester is a right-handed track of $1^3/_4$ miles (2.8km) holding National Hunt racing. Tel: 01327 353414.

motor racing — **Rockingham Motor Speedway** opened in 2001 on the site of the former British Steel works, 2 miles (3km) northeast of Corby. It has an oval racing circuit of $1^1/_2$ miles (2.5km) and an infield road racing course, and stages a variety of motor racing events including Superbikes and Formula Three races. Tel: 01536 500500.

Silverstone motor racing circuit, 4 miles (6km) south of Towcester on the Northamptonshire/Buckinghamshire border, is best known as the home of the British Grand Prix. It hosted the race regularly from 1948 until 2009 (having rotated between Silverstone, Aintree and Brands Hatch, 1955–86, the race was held at Silverstone every year from 1987). The 1950 Grand Prix at Silverstone was the first race in the newly created Formula One World Championship. The 3.2 mile (5.1km) circuit occupies the site of the former RAF Silverstone, a World War II bomber base which opened in 1943. The three runways, arranged in a triangle like those of many World War II airfields, lie within the track. During the Grand Prix, Silverstone Heliport becomes the busiest airport in the UK, complete with its own air traffic control. Tel: 0870 458 8200.

rugby union — **Northampton Saints** were established in 1880 under the original title of Northampton St James (Saints) by Rev. Samuel Wathen Wigg, a local clergyman and curate of St James' Church. They have been regular members of the rugby union Premiership since its inception in 1995. Saints play at Franklin's Gardens, Weedon Road, Northampton, a 13,600 all-seater stadium. Tel: 01604 751543.

Stoke Bruerne Canal Museum — 3 miles (5km) northeast of Towcester. Located in a former corn mill on the Grand Union Canal just south of Blisworth Tunnel, and now formally titled the National Waterways Museum Stoke Bruerne, the museum is dedicated to the heritage of 200 years of inland waterways and forms part of the National Waterways Museum, operated by the Waterways Trust and also occupying sites at Gloucester Docks and Ellesmere Port. One of the pair of locks outside the museum is no longer operational but contains a boat-weighing machine complete with narrowboat. Tel: 01604 862229.

Stoke Park Pavilions — 7 miles (11km) south of Northampton. Dating from 1630, the two pavilions and a colonnade by Inigo Jones are the sole surviving remnants of one of the first Palladian-style houses in Britain. The rest of the house, built for Sir Francis Crane, was destroyed in a fire in 1886. The Grade II listed gardens have a terraced lawn with herbaceous borders, herb garden, fountain and pool. Tel: 01604 862172.

Sulgrave Castle — 5 miles (8km) northwest of Brackley. A Norman ringwork unusually located on the site of a Saxon hall house dating to the late 10th or early 11th century, and protected by a rampart and ditch. Roman pottery has also been found on the site. The site was abandoned by the mid 12th century, but some earthworks are still visible next to the village church.

Sulgrave Manor — 5 miles (8km) northwest of Brackley. A fine example of a modest Tudor manor house and garden, Sulgrave was home to the ancestors of George Washington. In 1539 the manor was bought by Lawrence Washington from Henry VIII; the house he built was to be his descendants' home for the next 120 years. In 1656, Lawrence's great-great-grandson Colonel John Washington left England to take up land in Virginia. Colonel Washington was the great-grandfather of George Washington, first president of the USA. The house was sold to the Hodges family and a north wing added c.1700; it was purchased by the British Peace Centenary Committee in 1914 and presented to the peoples of Great Britain and the USA in celebration of 100 years of peace between the two nations. In 1924 the National Society of the Colonial Dames of America endowed the Manor House and is still involved in its upkeep. See also Washington Old Hall, Tyne and Wear.

University of Northampton — The former Nene College, a college of higher education formed in 1975 by the amalgamation of Northampton's teacher training college and college of technology, became University College Northampton in 1999 and, on receiving full university status in 2005, the University of Northampton. It has two campuses: Avenue Campus, St George's Avenue, Northampton; Park Campus, Boughton Green Road, Northampton. Tel: 01604 735500.

Wakefield Lodge — 1 mile (1.6km) southwest of Potterspury, 4 miles (6km) southeast of Towcester. A Georgian hunting lodge with deer park, part of the former estate of the Dukes of Grafton. The lake was Capability Brown's first successfully completed commission. Tel: 01327 811395.

Watford Locks — $^1/_2$ mile (0.8km) west of Watford, 4 miles (6km) northeast of Daventry. Seven locks on the Leicester Line of the Grand Union Canal, close to Watford Gap services on the M1. Starting from the south there are two single locks, a staircase of four, and a final single lock; together they lift the canal 52ft 6in (16m) to its summit level, which it maintains all the way to Foxton Locks. Opened in 1814, the locks were built to carry narrowboats. The locks are now hemmed in by the Roman Watling Street (now the A5), the M1 motorway and the West Coast Main Line railway, all fitting through the narrow gap in the hills.

Whittlewood Forest — 3 miles (5km) south of Towcester. An area of former medieval hunting forest that once covered much of the south of the county, with its core to the west of the village of Silverstone. Remnants of the forest still exist around the villages of Whittlebury and Potterspury and over the county boundary into Buckinghamshire. Managed by the Forestry Commission, Whittlewood has fine displays of bluebells in mid-spring. Tel: 01780 444920.

Wicksteed Park — Barton Road, Kettering. The oldest leisure park in England, Wicksteed's beginnings can be traced back to 1913 when Leeds-born engineer Charles Wicksteed purchased a tract of meadowland with the intention of developing a model village. The park's first major undertaking was the digging out of the 30 acre (12ha) lake which was opened for use in 1921. The Water Chute, built in 1926, is believed to be the oldest working ride in the UK. In addition to rides, the 147 acres (59ha) of grounds also feature a miniature railway opened in 1931, a nature trail and arboretum. Tel: 0870 062 1193.

Some famous people born in Northamptonshire

Arnold, Malcolm (composer) (1921–2006)	Northampton
Bates, H E (author) (1905–74)	Rushden
Bowles, William Lisle (poet) (1762–1850)	King's Sutton
Bradstreet, Anne (writer) (1612–72)	Northampton
Carne, Judy (actress) (1939–)	Northampton
Chichele, Henry (archbishop) (c.1364–1443)	Higham Ferrers
Crick, Francis (molecular biologist) (1916–2004)	Weston Favell
Dryden, John (poet and playwright) (1631–1700)	Aldwincle
East, Alfred (painter) (1849–1913)	Kettering
Haddon, Mark (novelist) (1962–)	Northampton
Hatton, Christopher (politician) (1540–91)	Holdenby
Harris, Bob (radio broadcaster) (1946–)	Northampton
Hickson, Joan (actress) (1906–98)	Kingsthorpe
Kennedy, Emma (actress and presenter) (1967–)	Corby
Newman, Nanette (actress) (1934–)	Northampton
Randolph, Thomas (poet) (1605–35)	Daventry
Rubbra, Edmund (composer) (1901–86)	Northampton
Salisbury, Ian (cricketer) (1970–)	Northampton
Smith, Ben (cricketer) (1972–)	Corby
Stokesley, John (church leader) (c.1475–1539)	Colly Weston
Studd, Charles (cricketer) (1860–1931)	Spratton
Warren, Marc (actor) (1967–)	Northampton
Whiley, Jo (radio disc jockey) (1965–)	Northampton
Woodville, Elizabeth (queen consort of Edward IV) (1437–92)	Grafton Regis
Yorke, Thom (musician) (1968–)	Wellingborough

NORTHUMBERLAND

Berwick-upon-Tweed
Tweedmouth
Holy Island
Farne Islands
Flodden
R. Till
1
Seahouses
Beadnell Bay
North Sea
SCOTTISH BORDERS
Wooler
The Cheviot
815
R. Till
R. Aln
Cheviot Hills
Alnwick
Alnmouth
Newton-on-the-Moor
Warkworth
R. Coquet
2
Amble
Rothbury
Rochester
Longframlington
Widdrington
Otterburn
North Tyne
Kielder Water
Ashington
Newbiggin-by-the-Sea
Morpeth
R. Wansbeck
4
Bellingham
Bedlington
Blyth
3
Cramlington
R. Blyth
5
Colwell
6
Ponteland
Humshaugh
TYNE & WEAR
HADRIANS WALL
Hexham
Haltwhistle
Haydon Bridge
Prudhoe
R. Tyne
Lambley
CUMBRIA
South Tyne
Derwent Reservoir
R. Derwent
DURHAM
Districts
1 Berwick-upon-Tweed
2 Alnwick
3 Castle Morpeth
4 Wansbeck
5 Blyth Valley
6 Tynedale
0
20 miles
0
30 km

The non-metropolitan county of Northumberland in the northeast of England borders the counties of Cumbria to the west and southwest, County Durham to the south and Tyne and Wear to the southeast. It also has a northwestern border with the Scottish Borders council area, and almost 80 miles (130km) of North Sea coastline to the east. Since 1974 the county council has been located in Morpeth, the present county town, although Alnwick and Bamburgh both lay claim to being historic capitals and Newcastle upon Tyne was traditionally the county town. Northumberland is a county of diverse landscapes from the eastern coastal plains, underlain by limestone in the north and coal measures in the south, to the densely populated urban industrial area of Tynedale to the south and the sparsely populated grit and limestone fells to the west.

Although I have listed the six districts that have served the county since 1974, from 1 April 2009 they have been abolished, as has the county council, to form a single unitary authority.

The Northumberland region has a long prehistory. A Mesolithic structure at Howick dating to c.7500 BC has been identified as Britain's oldest house, and cup and ring marked stones found in several locations in the county have recently been dated to the Neolithic period. Tools, ornaments, building structures and cairns have been found dating to the Bronze and Iron Ages, when the area was occupied by Brythonic Celtic peoples. During the Roman occupation Corbridge was the most northerly town in the Roman Empire. Other examples of Roman settlements in the Northumberland region are Housesteads, a fort on Hadrian's Wall, and Vindolanda, a fort guarding Stanegate.

After the Roman withdrawal in the early 5th century, conquests by Anglian invaders led to the establishment of the kingdoms of Deira and Bernicia. Deira extended from the Humber to the Tees, and from the sea to the western edge of the Vale of York, while Bernicia was approximately equivalent to the modern counties of Northumberland and Durham, stretching north from the Tees to the Tweed. In the early 7th century the two kingdoms merged to form the kingdom of Northumbria, with Æthelfrith as its ruler. After Æthelfrith was killed in battle c.AD 616, Edwin of Deira became king of Northumbria. Æthelfrith's son Oswald fled northwest to the Gaelic kingdom of Dál Riata where he was converted to Christianity by the monks of Iona. Meanwhile, Paulinus, the first bishop of York, converted King Edwin to Roman Christianity and began an extensive programme of conversion and baptism. When St Aidan arrived from Ireland at Oswald's request to preach to the Northumbrians he chose the island of Lindisfarne as the site of his church and monastery, and made it the head of the diocese which he founded in 635. For some years the see continued in peace – among its bishops was St Cuthbert, who died on the Farne Islands and was later sanctified (according to legend, when his coffin was opened his remains were found to be perfectly preserved) – but in 793 Vikings landed on the island and burnt the settlement, killing many of the monks. The survivors rebuilt the church and continued to live there until 875. Through fear of a second Danish invasion, however, they then fled inland, taking with them the body of Cuthbert and other holy relics.

The kingdom of Northumbria ceased to exist in 927, when it was incorporated into England as an earldom by Athelstan, the first king of a united England. In 937, Athelstan's victory over a combined Norse and Celtic force in the Battle of Brunanburh secured England's control of its northern territory. The Scottish king Indulf captured Edinburgh in 954, which afterwards remained in possession of the Scots. His successors repeatedly attempted to extend their territory southwards. Malcolm II was finally successful, defeating a Northumbrian army at Carham on the Tweed in 1018, and Eadulf, earl of Northumbria, ceded all his territory to the north of the river as the price of peace. Thereafter the region north of the Tweed, now known as Lothian, remained in possession of the Scottish kings.

The term Northumberland was first recorded in its modern sense in 1065 in the Anglo-Saxon Chronicle. Northumberland vigorously resisted the Norman invasion but paid a high price in lives. Border skirmishes with their Scots neighbours also made this a period of unrest for its citizens although in 1237, Scotland renounced claims to Northumberland by the Treaty of York. Unfortunately this did not prevent further skirmishes and civil war, a history which has left its legacy in the numerous pele towers, fortified houses and castles still to be seen in the region. In 1314 the county was ravaged by Robert the Bruce.

The leading family in the region, the Percys, wielded almost kingly power in the north during this period. Their influence reached its height under the 1st Earl of Northumberland and his son Henry, nicknamed Harry Hotspur, hero of many Border ballads as the bane of Scots raiders and a dominant character in Shakespeare's *Henry IV.* In 1388, Henry Percy was taken prisoner and 1500 of his men slain at the battle of Otterburn, immortalised in the ballad of Chevy Chase. Having helped to depose Richard II, these turbulent 'kingmakers' fell victim to Henry IV, the next three Percy earls also suffering violent deaths.

Alnwick, Bamburgh and Dunstanburgh were garrisoned for the Lancastrian cause in 1462, but after the Yorkist victories of Hexham and Hedgley Moor in 1464, Alnwick and Dunstanburgh surrendered, and Bamburgh was taken. In 1513, James IV of Scotland was killed in the battle of Flodden Field on Branxton Moor. After uniting the English and Scottish thrones, James I sharply curbed the lawlessness of the border reivers and brought relative peace to the region; this was consolidated by the Act of Union between England and Scotland in 1707.

Medieval Northumberland prospered from the production and export of wool and hides, while coal mining, which began during the Roman occupation, flourished from the 13th century as the trade between London and the Tyne grew. Lead, silver and iron were mined in Allendale from the 12th to the 19th century but the industry that has dominated the economy in the past 200 years is shipbuilding. New innovations such as the steam turbine developed in the 19th century and this, coupled with the natural resources, created the great shipbuilding and repair works which became synonymous with the area. Today, the major source of employment and income in the county is tourism.

Northumberland has traditions rarely found elsewhere in England, reflecting a mix of indigenous, Celtic, Norse and Anglian influences. These include the rapper sword dance, the clog dance and the Northumbrian smallpipe. Northumberland also has its own tartan, often referred to in Scotland as the Shepherd's Tartan. Traditional Northumberland music sounds similar to Scottish music, reflecting the strong historical links between Northumbria and Scotland.

Northumberland	Population			Area	
Districts	*male*	*female*	*total*	*sq miles*	*sq km*
Alnwick	15,052	15,977	31,029	417	1080
Berwick-upon-Tweed	12,470	13,479	25,949	375	972
Blyth Valley	39,570	41,695	81,265	27	70
Castle Morpeth	24,357	24,644	49,001	239	618
Tynedale	28,641	30,167	58,808	852	2206
Wansbeck	29,863	31,275	61,138	26	67
Total	149,953	157,237	307,190	1936	5013

Local Attractions and Information

Administrative headquarters — County Hall, Morpeth NE61 2EF. Tel: 0856 600 6400.

Allen Banks and Staward Gorge — 5 miles (8km) east of Haltwhistle. An extensive area of woodland gorge and rocky river scenery situated near the meeting point of the rivers Tyne and Allen, including the 101 acre (41ha) Stawardpeel Woods, a designated Site of Special Scientific Interest for its rich flora and fauna including the dormouse, for which it is the most northerly home in England. The remains of a medieval pele tower stand on a high promontory within Staward Wood and at Allen Banks is a reconstructed Victorian summerhouse. The property is managed by the National Trust. Tel: 01434 344218.

Allendale — A small village in the Allen valley, backed by the hills and moors of the North Pennines. Once a prosperous major lead-mining centre, relics of its industrial past can still be seen in the surrounding countryside. It is now a much smaller rural settlement situated within the North Pennines Area of Outstanding Natural Beauty. The valley is sometimes referred to as Mallendale by fans of the author Catherine Cookson, as this was the setting for her 'Mallen Streak' trilogy.

Alnwick Castle — Castle Square, Alnwick. Alnwick (pronounced 'annick') is the second largest inhabited castle in England after Windsor Castle, and has been the home of the Percys, Earls and Dukes of Northumberland, since 1309. The Norman castle was probably founded by Gilbert de Tesson in 1095, although the earliest buildings were erected soon after 1096 when Yves de Vescy became baron of Alnwick. The castle was besieged by William the Lion of Scotland in 1172 and 1174, with William himself captured on the latter occasion. It was first restored in the early 1300s by the 1st Lord Percy of Alnwick and parts of this restoration remain today, including the abbot's tower, the middle gateway and the constable's tower. The castle was remodelled by Robert Adam, 1750–66, and by Anthony Salvin in the 19th century. Alnwick now contains the Museum of the Royal Northumberland Fusiliers, while its grounds feature a major new garden constructed by Jane, Duchess of Northumberland. The castle was used as a location for the Harry Potter films. Tel: 01665 510777.

Ashington — 5 miles (8km) north of Blyth. Located on the River Wansbeck, Ashington grew rapidly in the late 19th century with the development of the Great Northern Coalfield and was once known as 'the largest mining village in the world'. Its history is recounted at the Woodhorn Colliery Museum (see separate entry). Ashington is also home to two country parks: the Wansbeck Country Park from where it is possible to follow the river all the way to the sea at Sandy Bay, and the Queen Elizabeth II Country Park with its park railway.

Ashington Group, The — In 1934 a number of Ashington miners enrolled in painting classes at Ashington YMCA, and soon began to produce paintings to sell locally to supplement their wages. Their depictions of contemporary local life achieved unexpected success and approval from the art community and the group were given prestigious gallery exhibitions during the 1930s and 1940s under the nickname 'The Pitmen Painters', although they had called themselves 'The Ashington Group'. In the 1970s the group's work was rediscovered; popularised as 'workers' art', it was given international exhibitions. It now has a permanent home at Woodhorn Colliery Museum and Gallery (see separate entry).

Aydon Castle — 1 mile (1.6km) northeast of Corbridge. A 13th century manor house, one of the finest of the period in England. Originally built as an undefended residence, it was fortified soon afterwards on the outbreak of Anglo-Scottish warfare. In 1315 it was pillaged and burnt by the Scots; having been seized by English rebels two years later, it was again occupied by the Scots in 1346. From the 18th century until 1966 Aydon was used as a farmhouse. Now in the care of English Heritage. Tel: 01434 632450.

Bamburgh Castle — 14 miles (23km) north of Alnwick. Also known as Bebbanburg. Situated on the coast near the Farne Islands, Bamburgh is a Norman castle built on an earlier Saxon fortification. The original fortification was built on a basalt outcrop and is first referred to in AD 547 as the seat of the Anglo-Saxon ruler Ida of Bernicia. Prior to this it was known to the Britons as Din Guardi and had been the capital of the British kingdom of Bryneich from the realm's foundation c.420 until the citadel was captured by Ida in 547. It was briefly retaken by the Britons from his son Hussa in 590 before being relieved later that same year. The Vikings destroyed the original fortification in 993. The 12th century tower keep of the Norman castle was erected by Henry II. Besieged in 1095, 1462 and 1464, on the last occasion by the Earl of Warwick using cannon, it was the first castle in England

	to be breached by gunfire. It was restored by Lord Armstrong (see Cragside), 1894–1905, and has been occupied since then. The castle is reputedly haunted by a knight in full armour. Tel: 01668 214515.
Bamburgh Dunes	14 miles (23km) north of Alnwick. A region of coastal sand dunes situated around the village of Bamburgh. Covering more than 100 acres (40ha), the dunes have been a Site of Special Scientific Interest since 1995 and are part of the North Northumberland Dunes Special Area of Conservation. An 7th century Anglo-Saxon burial ground was unearthed in the dunes to the southeast of Bamburgh Castle during an archaeological dig in 1998 by the Bamburgh Research Project. Called the Bowl Hole, the burial ground had been known to exist since 1816 when large amounts of dune sand were removed by violent storms, temporarily uncovering the site.
Battles	See separate table for details of the battles of Alnwick (I and II), Berwick-upon-Tweed, Carham, Flodden, Halidon Hill, Heavenfield, Hedgeley Moor, Hexham, Homildon Hill (aka Humbleton Hill), Otterburn (aka Chevy Chase) and Redeswire Raid.
Bebbanburg	See Bamburgh Castle
Bedlington	3 miles (5km) west of Blyth. Bedlingtonshire (or Bedlington for short) is one of England's very few village shires (a prominent district historically administered by a sheriff). It grew around the production of iron in the 18th and 19th centuries, the Bedlington Iron & Engine Works being founded in 1736 by William Tomlinson. To the south lies Plessey Woods Country Park, created around a section of mature woodland beside the River Blyth; the predominantly oak and birch woods are host to overwintering thrushes and finches. Bedlington once belonged to the Prince Bishop of Durham; the church of St Cuthbert, dating from c.900, provided a resting place for the saint's remains in 1069 before their interment in Durham Cathedral (see County Durham).
Bedlington terrier	A lean and assertive breed of terrier with woolly fur, developed in the 18th century by miners in the Rothbury area of Northumberland. It was also known as the Rothbury Terrier and Gypsy Dog (the latter due to its assistance with poaching). The Bedlington was an excellent hunter with an acute sense of smell and hearing, as well as speed and the ability to go to ground; it was even known to take on badgers. In the arena of dog fighting, Bedlingtons were known to fight to the death. Today, Bedlington terriers are rarely used as working dogs, being employed mainly as companions and as show dogs.
Belsay Hall, Castle and Gardens	8 miles (13km) southwest of Morpeth. The site encompasses a medieval castle enlarged into a mansion in the 17th century, a 19th century Greek Revival villa and surrounding gardens; the whole ensemble is the creation of the Middleton family over more than seven centuries. The castle is still dominated by its massive 14th century pele tower, the first-floor great chamber of which displays traces of elaborate medieval wall paintings. In 1614, after peace had been established by James I, a column-entranced mansion wing was added to the castle. The villa, built by Sir Charles Monck in 1807, was inspired by the classical remains he saw during a visit to Athens; the extensive gardens were also largely designed by Sir Charles, and were developed further by his grandson Sir Arthur Middleton, a keen plantsman. Now in the care of English Heritage. Tel: 01661 881636.
Berwick Castle	Castlegate, Berwick-upon-Tweed. Founded in the 12th century by David I of Scotland on a site above the River Tweed, the castle was captured by both the English and Scots on a number of occasions and frequently sustained substantial damage; it served as Edward I's headquarters during the course of his invasion of Scotland. The castle also changed hands in less violent circumstances when Richard I sold it to the Scots in order to help fund the Third Crusade. The construction of modern ramparts around Berwick in the 16th century finally rendered the castle obsolete; large parts of the structure were used as a quarry, while in the 19th century much of the remaining structure, including the great hall, was demolished to make way for a railway station. It is claimed that the platforms now stand on the spot where Edward I took oaths of allegiance from the Scots nobility in 1296. The late 13th century White Wall is the principal surviving part of the structure.
Berwick-upon-Tweed Barracks	The Parade, Church Street, Berwick-upon-Tweed. Among the first purpose-built barracks in England, built 1717–21 to the design of architect Nicholas Hawksmoor. Today, they are home to the King's Own Scottish Borderers Museum and the the Berwick Gymnasium Art Gallery, as well as to an exhibition on the life of the British infantryman. Now owned by English Heritage. Tel: 01289 304493.
Berwick-upon-Tweed Main Guard	Quay Walls, Berwick-upon-Tweed. A neo-Georgian military guard house located on the north bank of the River Tweed. Dating from 1682, it was moved from Margate to its present location near the quay in 1815. Run by the local civic society, it is now dedicated to the history of Berwick's walls and forts, with a permanent exhibition entitled 'The Story of a Border Garrison Town'. Tel: 01289 304493.
Black Middens Bastle House	7 miles (11km) northwest of Bellingham. A two-storey stone bastle house, or fortified farmhouse, built during the 16th century. Built with exceptionally thick walls, the living accommodation was on the first floor with space for livestock below. The nearby ruins of an 18th century cottage stand on the foundations of another possible bastle house. Now in the care of English Heritage.
Blenkinsop Castle	1 mile (1.6km) south of Greenhead, 5 miles (8km) west of Haltwhistle. A 14th century tower house built by the Blenkinsop family, who were granted licence to crenellate on 6 May 1340. It had fallen into disrepair by the 1540s and a mansion house was built on the site in the 19th century. It is still occupied, although a fire in 1954 destroyed part of the structure.
Bothal Castle	Bothal, 2 miles (3km) east of Morpeth. Possibly founded c.1150 by Richard Bertram, although the existing structure dates from the 14th century when a manor house was built on the site. Licence to crenellate was granted to Sir Roger Bertram in 1343 and the gate tower and fragments of

curtain wall still survive, although the remainder of the castle was substantially restored and rebuilt in the 19th and early 20th centuries. The castle is now used as a private residence and as offices by the agent of the Duke of Portland.

Bremenium
5 miles (8km) northwest of Otterburn. A Roman fort dating to c.AD 140, located at High Rochester in Redesdale. One of the defensive structures built along Dere Street, the Roman road running from York to Melrose via Corbridge, it covered 5 acres (2ha) and some of the walls are still visible.

Bridges
There are a number of historic bridges spanning the River Tweed in Northumberland. The following are the most noteworthy:

Berwick Bridge (aka the Old Bridge), Berwick-upon-Tweed, is 1165ft (355m) long and 16ft (5m) wide; there are 15 arches with Doric columns. The current structure was built 1611–24 of Tweedmouth sandstone, but four previous bridges have stood on the site. Two were destroyed by flooding (the original in 1199 and the third in 1294), and one by an English attack in 1216; the last, built in 1376, served until James I of England ordered the construction of the present bridge. Berwick was then on the main road from Edinburgh to London, and the king had had to cross over the dilapidated wooden bridge in 1603 while travelling to London for his coronation. The bridge became less important for road traffic as the main route moved west; the concrete Royal Tweed Bridge was built in the 1920s, and in the 1980s a bypass took the A1 road out of Berwick altogether. Now Grade I listed, today Berwick Bridge is only used for one-way traffic.

Coldstream Bridge, 12 miles (19km) southwest of Berwick-upon-Tweed, an 18th century bridge linking Cornhill-on-Tweed in Northumberland with Coldstream in the Scottish Borders. The seven-arched bridge was constructed 1763–7 by architect John Smeaton; it was partly funded by tolls, ceasing to be a toll bridge in 1826. A plaque on the bridge commemorates poet Robert Burns' first visit to England in 1787. On the Scottish side of the bridge is the Coldstream marriage-house, scene of numerous runaway marriages in the 18th and 19th centuries. In the early 1960s the bridge was strengthened and the road widened. Now Grade II listed, it carries the A698 across the Tweed.

Ladykirk and Norham Bridge, connecting Norham in Northumberland with Ladykirk in the Scottish Borders. The stone road bridge with four arches was designed by Thomas Codrington and Cuthbert A Brereton for the Tweed Bridges Trust to replace an earlier wooden structure, and was constructed 1885–7. It is now Grade II listed.

Royal Border Bridge, a railway viaduct connecting Berwick-upon-Tweed and Tweedmouth. The Grade I listed bridge was designed by Robert Stephenson, son of George Stephenson. Built 1847–50 and opened by Queen Victoria, it is still in regular use today as part of the East Coast Main Line. The bridge is 2060ft (659m) long with 28 arches, constructed of brick faced with stone, and stands 125ft (38m) above the river.

Royal Tweed Bridge, Berwick-upon-Tweed, carrying Pudding Lane across the River Tweed. It was intended to divert traffic from the 17th century Old Bridge, and until the 1980s it formed part of the A1, the main route from London to Edinburgh. However, the construction of a new bridge to the west of Berwick as part of a bypass has since reduced the Royal Tweed Bridge's importance. It was constructed by L G Mouchel & Partners 1925–8 in reinforced concrete, and consists of four unequal arches spanning a total distance of almost 1415ft (430m).

Union Bridge (aka Chain Bridge), 5 miles (8km) southwest of Berwick-upon-Tweed, connecting Horncliffe in Northumberland with Fishwick in the Scottish Borders. Before it opened in 1820, crossing the river at this point involved a round trip of 11 miles (18km) via Berwick-upon-Tweed downstream or 20 miles (32km) via Coldstream upstream. (Ladykirk and Norham Bridge – see separate entry – did not open until 1888.) When it opened it was the longest wrought-iron suspension bridge in the world with a span of 449ft (137m) and the first vehicular bridge of its type in Britain; it is now the oldest suspension bridge still carrying road traffic. The bridge was designed by Captain Samuel Brown of the Royal Navy. Now maintained by the Tweed Bridges Trust, it is Grade I listed and a Scheduled Ancient Monument.

Brinkburn Priory
4½ miles (7km) southeast of Rothbury. Set by a bend in the River Coquet, the Augustinian priory was founded c.1135. The 12th century church was restored in the mid 19th century. An elegant early 19th century manor house on the site of the west range utilises part of the vaulted undercroft to the monks' dining hall; little else of the original monastery survives. Church services and concerts are still occasionally held in the church. Now in the care of English Heritage. Tel: 01665 570628.

Bywell Castle
Bywell, 4 miles (6km) east of Corbridge. Situated close to the River Tyne, Bywell was never completed; the tower, dating from 1430, was originally intended to be the gatehouse of a larger fortress.

Capheaton Hall
11 miles (18km) southwest of Morpeth. The seat of the Swinburne family, the current house was built in English baroque style for Sir John Swinburne, 1st Baronet, by Robert Trollope of Newcastle, 1667–8. A model farm designed by Daniel Garrett was built for Sir John Swinburne, 4th Baronet, c.1746, and is one of the earliest examples of Gothic revival architecture. The north front of the house was rebuilt 1789–90 by local architect William Newton. Capheaton was one of the childhood homes of the poet Algernon Swinburne. The linear estate village of Capheaton, built as a planned model village in the late 18th century, is sited on a ridge to the west.

Cawfields Roman Wall
1¼ miles (2km) north of Haltwhistle. A consolidated stretch of Hadrian's Wall (see Cumbria) on a steep slope, with turrets and a milecastle, built by the 2nd Legion. Now in the care of English Heritage.

Cherryburn
Station Bank, Mickley Square, 1 mile (1.6km) southwest of Prudhoe. The birthplace of wood-engraver and naturalist Thomas Bewick (1753–1828), one of Northumberland's greatest artists. The cottage in which Bewick was born has a farmyard and garden, while a nearby 19th century

farmhouse, the later home of the Bewick family, houses an exhibition on Bewick's life and work. Now owned by the National Trust. Tel: 01661 843276.

Chesters Roman Fort 4 miles (6km) north of Hexham. One of the best preserved examples of a Roman cavalry fort in Britain, Chesters was one of a series of troop bases added to Hadrian's Wall (see Cumbria) soon after it was built in AD 122–3. It is thought to have been occupied for nearly 300 years. Still visible are the four well-preserved principal gateways, the east and west adjoined by short lengths of Hadrian's Wall; the complete foundations of the headquarters building; a courtyard, hall, regimental chapel and strongroom; and a military bath house with changing room, latrines and bathing rooms. Chesters Museum is home to the Clayton Collection, which includes many important early archaeological discoveries relating to the central section of Hadrian's Wall. The site is managed by English Heritage. Tel: 01434 681379.

Cheviot Hills A range of rolling granite hills lying on the England/Scotland border between Northumberland and the Scottish Borders, and falling partly within the Northumberland National Park. Their highest point is The Cheviot at 2674ft (815m), 1¼ miles (2km) from the Scottish border (GR: NT909205). The Cheviot is also the highest point in Northumberland.

Chillingham Castle Chillingham, 11 miles (18km) northwest of Alnwick. A privately owned medieval castle owned by the family of the Earls Grey since the 1200s, it lays claim to being among the most haunted castles in England. It was originally a single watchtower, built close to the site of a monastery in the late 1100s. When Edward I visited on his way to Scotland to battle William Wallace's Scottish army in 1298, he stayed in the room at the top of the original tower, now known as the Edward I Room and into which a window, rare in buildings at the time, was specially installed. In 1344 a licence to crenellate was issued by Edward III, upgrading the stronghold to a fully fortified castle. In 1617, James I stayed at the castle on a journey between his two kingdoms. As the relations between England and Scotland became peaceful following the Act of Union, there was no longer a need for a military stronghold in the area and the castle was gradually transformed into more comfortable residential accommodation. Landscaping of the extensive grounds took place in the 18th and 19th centuries, including substantial work carried out under Sir Jeffry Wyatville. During World War II, the interiors suffered substantial damage when the castle was used as a barracks. In the 1980s, the property was purchased by Sir Humphry Wakefield, whose wife was a descendant of the Grey family and who set about restoring the castle. An ancient dungeon was unearthed, including a pit containing the skeleton of a human child. The picturesque castle has since been used as a location in such films as *Elizabeth* (1998); the grounds, now under separate ownership, are home to many varieties of wildlife, including the famous Chillingham wild cattle. Tel: 01668 215359.

Chipchase Castle 1½ miles (2.5km) southeast of Wark, 8 miles (13km) northwest of Hexham. Among the best examples of Jacobean architecture in the county, the present house was built in 1621 and incorporates a 14th century pele tower. Major alterations, including the addition of a classical façade, were carried out in the 1730s. The house is now Grade I listed. The grounds feature walled flower and vegetable gardens, a lake and herbaceous border. Tel: 01434 230203.

Coquet Island ¾ mile (1.2km) off Amble on the Northumberland coast. A small island of 15 acres (6ha), owned by the Duke of Northumberland and leased to the RSPB as a nature reserve. It is an important site for nesting puffins and has Britain's largest colony of the endangered roseate tern. Other nesting birds include Sandwich tern, common tern, Arctic tern, kittiwake, fulmar, gulls and eider duck. The remains of a medieval monastery on the island were largely incorporated into a lighthouse and lighthouse keepers' cottages during the 19th century. The first keeper of the lighthouse was William, elder brother of Grace Darling. Operated by Trinity House, the lighthouse is now automatic, so the island is uninhabited in winter, but wardens are present during the summer to protect nesting birds. GR: NU294047.

Cragside ½ mile (0.8km) east of Rothbury, 13 miles (21km) southwest of Alnwick. Built into a rocky hillside above a 1000 acre (400ha) forest garden, the country home of Lord Armstrong was one of the first houses in the world to be lit using hydroelectric power. Named after Cragend Hill above the house, Cragside was built in 1863 as a modest, two-storey country lodge, but was subsequently extended to designs by Norman Shaw, transforming it into an elaborate Tudor style mansion. The building once included an astronomical observatory and a scientific laboratory. A hydraulic engine was installed in 1868, with water being used to power labour-saving machines such as laundry equipment, a rotisserie and a hydraulic lift. In 1870, water from one of the estate's lakes was used to drive a Siemens dynamo in what is thought to have been the world's first hydroelectric power station. The resultant electricity was used to power an arc lamp installed in the gallery in 1878. The lamp was replaced in 1880 by Joseph Swan's incandescent lamps in what Swan considered 'the first proper installation' of electric lighting. The house is surrounded by one of Europe's largest rock gardens and a collection of conifers, among which one Douglas fir 194ft (59m) tall is the tallest tree in England. The estate is one of the red squirrel's last strongholds in England. The house has been managed by the National Trust since 1977. Tel: 01669 620333/620150.

Cresswell Pond Nature Reserve Blakemoor Farm, Cresswell, 7½ miles (12km) northeast of Morpeth. A lagoon with several reed beds and a birdwatching hide; winter visitors include wigeon, teal and whooper swans, while great crested grebe breed in summer. Tel: 0191 284 6884.

Darling, Grace See Grace Darling Museum, SS *Forfarshire*

Derwent Reservoir 8 miles (13km) southeast of Hexham. Located on the River Derwent, on the County Durham/Northumberland border. The reservoir, owned and managed by Northumbrian Water, provides the principal supply of water to the Tyne and Wear conurbation and covers an area of just over 1000 acres (405ha). Its southwestern shore is managed as a nature reserve and is regularly visited by wildfowl including wigeon, goldeneye and goosander, as well as by numerous waders. The flow of the Derwent can be supplemented, when necessary, by a pipeline from the much larger Kielder Reservoir in Northumberland.

Druridge Bay 9 miles (15km) northeast of Morpeth. A 7 mile (11km) long coastal bay with extensive sand dunes, stretching from Amble in the north to Cresswell in the south. Part of the bay is designated as a country park; a central section of the bay near the village of Druridge is owned by the National Trust, and other parts of the bay have been established as nature reserves. Druridge Bay is best known to birdwatchers for the controversy of the Druridge Bay curlew. In 1998 a sighting was reported in the bay of a slender-billed curlew, the first to be recorded in Britain; the identification was eventually authenticated in 2002 but is still disputed.

Dunstanburgh Castle 7 miles (11km) northeast of Alnwick. Enclosure castle situated on high cliffs on the Northumberland coast and founded by Thomas, 2nd Earl of Lancaster, 1313–16. The castle was substantially altered in the late 14th century by John of Gaunt, who converted the gatehouse into a keep. The castle is now managed by English Heritage on behalf of the National Trust. Tel: 01665 576231.

Edlingham Castle Edlingham, 5 miles (8km) southwest of Alnwick. A fortified manor house built by Sir William Felton in the late 12th century as a triangular enclosure with separate great tower. Strengthening of the fortifications, including the addition of a solar tower, was carried out in response to the border warfare which raged between England and Scotland from 1300 to 1600. The structure is largely ruined, but much of the tower still stands despite being riven by a dramatic crack. The foundations and part of the walls of the hall house, gatehouse, barbican and other courtyard buildings are still visible, most dating from the 16th century. The site is managed by English Heritage.

Etal Castle Etal, 10 miles (16km) southwest of Berwick-upon-Tweed. The castle was founded by the Manners family in the late 12th century. In 1341, nobleman and doctor Robert de Manners received licence to crenellate. During this time the castle was renowned as a destination for pilgrims seeking medical and dental treatment: De Manners carried out one of the earliest English translations from the Arabic of *Taqwim es-sihha*, an 11th century medical text by Ibn Botlan, and was known throughout the region as a healer. The Manners family often feuded with the Heron family of nearby Ford Castle (see separate entry). In 1428 Sir William Heron led an attack on Etal Castle and was killed in the process. In 1513, James IV's invading army of 30,000 Scots took the castle before their defeat at the battle of Flodden. The castle is managed by English Heritage. Tel: 01890 820332.

Farne Islands A group of more than 20 islands (depending on the state of the tide) off the coast of Northumberland, scattered about the North Sea $1^1/_2$ to $4^1/_2$ miles (2.5 to 7.5km) from the mainland. They are divided into two groups, the Inner Group and the Outer Group, the two being separated by Staple Sound. The first visitor recorded by name to the islands was St Aidan, followed by St Cuthbert. After serving for two years as Bishop of Lindisfarne, Cuthbert returned to the solitude of the Inner Farne and died there in AD 687, when St Aethelwold took up residence in his place. St Cuthbert introduced special laws in 676 protecting the eider ducks and other seabirds nesting on the islands; these are thought to be the earliest bird protection laws anywhere in the world. In early summer many puffins can be seen; some of the islands have populations of rabbits, which were introduced as a source of meat and have since run wild. There is also a notable colony of about 6000 grey seals, with several hundred pups born September–November every year. The Farne Islands are the setting of the story of Grace Darling. See also table of islands.

Ford and Etal Estates 10 miles (16km) southwest of Berwick-upon-Tweed. Framed by the Cheviot Hills to the south and the River Tweed to the north, the twin estates' 15,000 acres (6000ha), united by the 1st Baron Joicey in the early 20th century, are located in the valley of the River Till and centred on the two villages of Ford and Etal with their castles (see separate entries). The area encompasses Heatherslaw Cornmill (see separate entry), Heatherslaw Light Railway and a timber henge, as well as Flodden Field, site of the Battle of Flodden. Tel: 01890 820338.

Ford Castle Ford, 11 miles (18km) southwest of Berwick-upon-Tweed. Originally a fortified manor house, the quadrangular castle was founded in 1338 by William Heron. It was attacked by the Scots in 1385 and 1549, as well as in 1513 before the Battle of Flodden. Ford was rebuilt in 1861 by the Marchioness of Waterford.

George Stephenson's birthplace Wylam, 6 miles (10km) east of Corbridge. The birthplace of the world famous railway engineer is a small whitewashed stone tenement built c.1760 to accommodate mining families; Stephenson's whole family would have lived in one room. It is furnished to reflect the style of domestic dwellings in 1781, the year of Stephenson's birth. Now in the care of the National Trust. Tel: 01661 853457.

Grace Darling Museum Radcliffe Road, Bamburgh. Opened in September 1938 to commemorate the 100th anniversary of Grace's famous rescue, with her father, of nine survivors from the wreck of SS *Forfarshire* (see separate entry). Exhibits include the original coble in which Grace and her father rowed to the wreck from the Longstone lighthouse, as well as goods belonging to the Darling family. Other items include letters between Grace and her father and replicas of the medals awarded to Grace. Tel: 01668 214465.

Greenlee Lough 5 miles (8km) northeast of Haltwhistle. A lake and National Nature Reserve owned and managed by the Northumberland Wildlife Trust and Northumberland National Park. Most of the reserve is open water, with reedbeds, herb fen and blanket bog at the lake's edge, and is used extensively by wildfowl and waders. The lough once served as a reservoir for Roman troops stationed on Hadrian's Wall, $^1/_2$ mile (0.8km) to the south. To the east is the smaller lake known as Broomlee Lough.

Hadrian's Wall See Cumbria

Harbottle Castle — Harbottle, 17 miles (27km) southwest of Alnwick. A motte and bailey castle with shell keep erected 1159–60 by Robert d'Umfraville. It was captured in the early 14th century by Robert the Bruce. The castle had fallen into ruin by the early 1700s; today only earthworks and a little masonry remain.

Heatherslaw Mill — 7 miles (11km) north of Wooler. A restored 19th century water-driven cornmill situated on the Ford and Etal Estates (see separate entry). Traditional methods and original machinery powered by the River Till are used to grind locally grown wheat into wholemeal flour. The huge water wheel, mill stones and gearing are all visible. Tel: 01890 820338.

HM Prison Acklington — Acklington, 11 miles (18km) north of Morpeth. A category C prison for adult male prisoners, opened in 1972. Operational capacity: 882. HMP Acklington is the most northerly adult prison in England. Tel: 01670 762300.

Hexham Abbey — Beaumont Street, Hexham. Dedicated to St Andrew, the first church on the site was established c.674 by Wilfrid, Bishop of York, on land granted by Etheldreda, queen of Northumbria; the Saxon crypt and apse of Wilfrid's original Benedictine abbey still survive. Wilfrid's abbey was replaced c.1170–1250 by an Augustinian priory; the choir, north and south transepts and cloisters of the current church, in the Early English style, largely date from that period, although the east end was rebuilt in 1860. The abbey was largely rebuilt during the incumbency of Canon Edwin Sidney Savage, who served as rector 1898–1919; the nave was reconsecrated on 8 August 1908. In 1996 an additional chapel, named St Wilfrid's Chapel, was created at the east end of the north choir aisle. Since the Dissolution of the Monasteries in 1537, the abbey has been the parish church of Hexham. Tel: 01434 602031.

Hexham Old Gaol — Hallgate, Hexham. Constructed in 1330 on the orders of William Melton, Archbishop of York, the gaol is reputedly the oldest purpose-built prison in England. Initially built to hold prisoners from the archbishop's domain of Hexhamshire, from the 16th century it was used to detain those accused of crimes in the English/Scottish borders before their trial in the Moothall Court Room nearby. It continued in use until the 1820s. The site now houses a museum covering archaeology, archives, costume and textiles, law and order, music, photography, social history, weapons and war, including 15th and 16th century arms and armour. The Border Library holds the Butler Collection of books, recordings and music relating to the culture of the Borders. Tel: 01434 652349.

Highest point — See Cheviot Hills

Holburn Lake and Moss — 1/2 mile (0.8km) east of Holburn, 11 miles (18km) southeast of Berwick-upon-Tweed. A designated Special Protection Area and Ramsar site based around an artificial lake created in 1934, internationally important as a winter roosting site for Icelandic greylag geese. Birds such as wigeon and teal also roost. There is an area of floating bog along the eastern shore of the lake. The surrounding Holburn Moss is a peat bog formerly used for forestry but now supporting a variety of plants including bog mosses, heather, cotton grass, cranberry and round-leaved sundew.

Holy Island — 9 miles (15km) southeast of Berwick-upon-Tweed. An island situated in the centre of the Lindisfarne National Nature Reserve and described as 'The Jewel of the Northumberland Coast'. Access to the island is via a causeway that can only be crossed at low tide. Originally known as Lindisfarne, the island was the site of a Benedictine priory founded by the Irish monk St Aidan in the 7th century and destroyed only in the 16th century by Henry VIII. In 1550, Henry's troops built the fort that was later to become Lindisfarne Castle (see separate entry) with stones from the priory. A statue of St Aidan (1958) by sculptor Kathleen Parbury stands outside St Mary's Church. Area: 2 sq miles (5 sq km). Population: 162. GR: NU130430.

Hulne Priory — 1/2 mile (0.8km) northwest of Alnwick. Situated in Hulne Park, a walled park of several thousand acres belonging to the Duke of Northumberland and close to Alnwick Castle. It is still used by the Duke for shooting, and was originally a hunting park. The monastery was founded in the 13th century by the Carmelites or White Friars. Because of its proximity to the Scottish border, the priory had a surrounding wall and in the 15th century a pele tower was erected. The substantial ruins include the tower, remodelled in the 18th century by Robert Adam and still standing almost intact, and the chapel, now a private residence. The Percy family took control of the site at the Dissolution of the Monasteries. The park also contains the gatehouse of the former Alnwick Abbey, and Brizlee Tower, a Gothic-style viewing tower dating from the 1780s and now Grade I listed.

Hunterheugh Crags — 4 miles (6km) northwest of Alnwick. An area of barren moorland and rock outcrops, part of the Fellsandstone escarpment. This site is most famous for the cup and ring mark art visible on the rocks, which recent excavation has demonstrated to date probably from the Neolithic period.

Interesting facts — Two unusual Northumberland public houses are **Allenheads Inn** in Hexham and **The Olde Ship** in Seahouses. Each pub is an Aladdin's cave of collectibles and memorabilia, many of historical note. The Allenheads Inn houses more than 5000 items including antique furniture, old musical instruments, numerous paintings and even a 4ft (1.2m) wooden chicken. The Olde Ship is far more specialist and almost everything carries a nautical theme including ships' wheels, lifeboat oars, figureheads and binnacles. When the tide is out a causeway stretches across from the pub to Holy Island. **Pitmatic** is a dialect of English used in the counties of Northumberland and Durham. It developed as a separate dialect from Northumbrian and Geordie due to the specialised terms used by mineworkers in the local coal pits. For example, in Northumberland and Tyne and Wear the word 'Cuddy' is an abbreviation of the name Cuthbert (particularly the local saint, Cuthbert of Lindisfarne), but in Durham Pitmatic, as in Lowland Scots, 'cuddy' denotes a horse, specifically a pit pony. Traditionally, Pitmatic, together with the dialect of some rural Northumbrian communities including Rothbury, used a distinctive, soft, rolled 'r' sound, produced at the very back of the throat. This is now less frequently heard: since the closure of the area's

	deep mines, many younger people speak in ways that do not usually include this characteristic. The 'r' sound can, however, still sometimes be detected among elderly populations in rural areas. Northumberland Pitmatic was spoken mainly in the coal mining area around Ashington. **Marshall Meadows Hotel** is situated 2 miles (3km) north of Berwick-upon-Tweed and 1/4 mile (0.5km) south of the Scottish border and as such is the most northerly landmark of mainland England.
Islands	See separate table
Kielder Forest	The largest forestry plantation in the UK, covering an area of 250 sq miles (650 sq km). The Forestry Commission, which owns and manages the forest, initiated the first plantings in the 1920s. Prior to this the land was largely open moorland, managed for grouse shooting and sheep grazing with remnants of native upland woodland existing along streamsides and in isolated craggy areas. There are seven Sites of Special Scientific Interest within the forest boundaries, including the Border Mires, the largest remaining area of blanket bog in England. The southern part of Kielder Forest is known as Wark Forest and the northernmost part, Redesdale Forest.
Kielder Water	The largest artificial lake by capacity in the UK, although exceeded by Rutland Water, in Leicestershire, by surface area. The reservoir was created 1975–81 and opened by Queen Eliabeth II in 1982. Owned by Northumbrian Water, and holding 200 billion litres of water, Kielder serves the Tyneside, Wearside and Teesside areas and is largely responsible for the lack of water restrictions so common in the south of England. All 27½ miles (44km) of shoreline are situated in the Kielder Forest.
Kirkley Hall Gardens	3 miles (5km) north of Ponteland, 5 miles (8km) southwest of Morpeth. A 17th century house and garden with terraces, a sunken garden, a walled garden and a range of demonstration beds. The site is owned by Northumberland College. Grade II listed Kirkley Hall is not open to the public. Tel: 01661 860808.
Lady Waterford Hall	Ford, 11 miles (18km) southwest of Berwick-upon-Tweed. Home of the Waterford Gallery, commissioned by Louisa Anne, Marchioness of Waterford, in 1860. The building served as the village school until 1957 and is now the village hall. A gifted artist, Lady Waterford spent the years 1862–83 decorating the walls with life-size paintings depicting children from the school and people who lived in and around Ford, as well as biblical scenes. These works, together with others by Lady Waterford and artefacts from her time, are now on display in the hall. Tel: 01890 820503.
Langley Castle	Langley, 6 miles (10km) southwest of Hexham. A four-storey tower house built by Sir Thomas de Lucy c.1350 and situated in the valley of the South Tyne. In the 12th century Langley was the seat of the Barons of Tynedale, from whom descended the Tyndall family. After suffering major damage in 1405 from the forces of Henry IV in their campaign against the Percys the house was left to decline, but was restored in the late 19th and early 20th century by historian Cadwallader Bates and is now one of the few medieval fortified castle hotels in England. It is set in its own 10 acre (4ha) woodland estate.
Lindisfarne	See Holy Island
Lindisfarne Castle	Located on Holy Island. Founded c.1550 by Henry VIII on top of the volcanic mound known as Beblowe Craig, and enlarged in 1570–2, in 1901 the Tudor castle was transformed by Edwin Lutyens into an Edwardian holiday home for Edward Hudson, founder of *Country Life* magazine. The interiors feature intimate decoration and design by Lutyens; outside, a walled garden designed by Gertrude Jekyll in 1911 was recreated in 2003. Now in the care of the National Trust. Tel: 01890 820503.
Lindisfarne Gospels	An illuminated Latin manuscript of the gospels of Matthew, Mark, Luke and John. The Lindisfarne Gospels are presumed to be the work of a monk named Eadfrith, who became Bishop of Lindisfarne in AD 698 and died in 721. Current scholarship dates the manuscript to c.715, and it is believed to have been produced in honour of St Cuthbert. A word-for-word Old English gloss was later inserted between the lines of the Latin text by Aldred, Provost of Chester-le-Street. Dating to c. 970, this is the earliest existing translation of the gospels into the English language. The manuscript is now held in the British Library.
Lindisfarne Priory	Located on Holy Island, the priory was one of the most important centres of early Christianity in Anglo-Saxon England and is still a place of pilgrimage today. The monastery was founded in AD 635 by St Aidan although St Cuthbert, who was himself prior, is the most celebrated of its holy men. In 875 the priory came under attack from Vikings and the monks fled, carrying Cuthbert's remains; after long wanderings these were enshrined in Durham Cathedral (see County Durham) in 1104, where they still rest. Monks from Durham later re-established a priory on Lindisfarne: the ruins of the richly decorated priory church they built in c.1150 still stand, with their famous 'rainbow arch' – a vault-rib of the now-vanished crossing tower. The small community lived quietly on Holy Island until the suppression of the monastery in 1537. There is a museum telling the story of St Cuthbert and the development of the priory. The remains are now managed by English Heritage. Tel: 01289 389200.
Little Harle Tower	1¼ miles (2km) southeast of Kirkwhelpington, 14 miles (23km) west of Morpeth. A 15th century pele tower extended in the 18th century, with a Victorian wing containing a recently restored 1740s drawing room.
Longstone Rock	Also known as Outer Farne. The lighthouse was designed and built by Joseph Nelson in 1826. In September 1838 the steamer *Forfarshire*, bound from Hull to Dundee, went aground on Big Harcar, about ½ mile (0.8km) west of the lighthouse, and 43 people were drowned. See also Grace Darling Museum, SS *Forfarshire*. GR: NU228357
Morpeth Castle	Carlisle Park, Morpeth. Norman motte and bailey castle founded in the late 11th century. It was destroyed by King John in 1215 and rebuilt in the 1340s. The gatehouse of the rebuilt castle is now a private residence; apart from this little remains except parts of the walls.

Morpeth Clock Tower — Oldgate, Morpeth. A secular bell tower, one of only eight in England never to have been associated with a church. Now Grade II listed, it was built c.1634 and stands 70ft (21m) high, with a peal of six bells cast in 1706. The 300 year old tradition of ringing the curfew at 8pm is still maintained. Tel: 01669 620569.

Nelson Memorial — Swarland, 10 miles (16km) north of Morpeth. A white freestone obelisk erected in 1807 as a memorial to Horatio Nelson, victor of the Battle of Trafalgar, by his friend and sometime agent, Alexander Davison, who owned an estate centred on the now demolished Swarland Hall. Situated on the old A1 road, now used only by local traffic, it is hidden from the main road by trees. The obelisk is not the only memorial to Nelson at Swarland; trees on the estate were planted in groups so as to represent the positions of the British and French ships at the Battle of the Nile.

Norham Castle — Norham, $6^1/_2$ miles (10.5km) southwest of Berwick-upon-Tweed. Norman motte and bailey castle founded c.1120 by Ranulf Flambard high above the River Tweed. Destroyed by the Scots in the 1140s, it was rebuilt by Bishop Hugh of Durham, 1158–74. Norham was one of the strongest of the border castles, and regularly came under attack by the Scots. It was besieged at least 13 times – once for nearly a year by Robert Bruce – and was referred to as 'the most dangerous and adventurous place in the country'. In 1513 it fell to James IV's heavy cannon, shortly before his defeat at Flodden. Extensive rebuilding followed in the 16th century, adapting the fortress for artillery, but it fell into disuse soon afterwards. Now in the care of English Heritage. Tel: 01289 304493.

Northumberland Fusiliers Museum — Alnwick. Located within the Abbot's Tower of Alnwick Castle (see separate entry), the museum documents the history of the regiment from its origins in 1674. Tel: 01665 602152.

Northumberland National Park — The northernmost national park in England. It covers an area of more than 398 sq miles (1030 sq km), extending between the Scottish border in the north to just south of Hadrian's Wall. With a population of under 3000 and just over a million visitor-days per year, it is one of the least populated and least visited of the National Parks. The park lies entirely within Northumberland, covering about a quarter of the county. Its several distinct areas include the Cheviots in the north, the range of hills that mark the border between England and Scotland. Further south, the hills give way to rolling moorland, some of which has been covered by forestry plantations to form Kielder Forest. The southernmost part of the park covers the dramatic central section of Hadrian's Wall. There many archaeological sites, ranging from prehistoric monuments and Roman remains to pele towers. The park's official symbol is the curlew.

Old Bewick — 9 miles (15km) northwest of Alnwick. The village lies at the centre of an area noted for its prehistoric remains, including the Bronze Age Blawearie Cairn, Iron Age hillforts at Old Bewick Hill and Bewick Hill Moor, and cup and ring marked rocks.

Pennine Way — See Derbyshire

Pitmen Painters, The — See Ashington Group

Preston Tower — Preston, 7 miles (11km) north of Alnwick. Built by Sir Robert Harbottle in 1392, this fortified tower house was originally rectangular in layout, with turrets in each corner and a vaulted basement. Today, only the southern turrets and adjoining walls remain. It was converted into a clock tower in 1864. Tel: 01655 589227.

Prudhoe Castle — Prudhoe, 10 miles (16km) east of Corbridge. Built 1100–20 by Robert d'Umfraville to defend a strategic crossing of the River Tyne against Scottish invaders, the castle has been continuously occupied for over nine centuries. The stone keep was added after the castle was besieged twice during the 1170s, and it was further fortified c.1300. Passing to the Percy family in 1398, it was updated with a fashionable new great hall. After the end of hostilities with the Scots it fell into decline, although still occupied, but was restored early in the 19th century by Hugh Percy, 2nd Duke of Northumberland, who built a new manor house within its walls. Now in the care of English Heritage. Tel: 01661 833459.

Rivers — The **Aln** runs through the Alnwick district to the North Sea. It gives its name to the town of Alnwick and the village of Alnmouth where it reaches the sea, as well as to its source, Alnham in the Cheviot Hills. Although a relatively small river, the Aln has been historically important as one of the boundaries which English and Scottish troops marching to war had to cross; for that reason, it was at times heavily defended, for example at Alnwick Castle.

The **Blyth** flows east through southern Northumberland into the North Sea at the town of Blyth, passing through Plessey Woods Country Park. The River Pont is a tributary.

The **Coquet** runs through the Alnwick district, reaching the North Sea at Amble. Warkworth Castle is built in a loop of the Coquet. Rising in the Cheviot Hills, the river follows a winding but generally easterly course of 40 miles (64km). It passes Harbottle, near which relics of the Stone Age are seen, and Holystone, where it is recorded that Bishop Paulinus baptised a great body of Northumbrians in the year 627. The river is frequented by sportsmen for salmon and trout fishing.

The **Devil's Water**, near Hexham, has considerable historical significance, figuring in the Battles of Heavenfield and Hexham.

Derwent see County Durham

The **Glen** is a tributary of the River Till, and is formed from the confluence near Kirknewton of the College Burn and Bowmont Water, both rising in the Cheviot Hills. The Glen flows past the small settlements of Yeavering, Lanton, Coupland, Akeld and Ewart before joining the Till. The surrounding area is rich in historical and archaeological interest. Iron Age hill forts to the south of the river overlook the Anglian settlement and palace site at Yeavering, where Paulinus baptised new converts and, according to Bede, 'washed them with the water of absolution in the river Glen'.

The **Kershope Burn** is a minor river running in its entirety along the border between England and Scotland. The river rises, as Clark's Sike, in a marshy area in Northumberland known as Hobb's Flow, becoming Kershope Burn after running past Kershopehead, a farmstead in Cumbria.

It then runs into Liddel Water at Kershopefoot, Liddel Water thereafter marking the boundary between England and Scotland.

The **Rede** rises on Carter Fell in the Cheviot Hills and flows alongside the A68 for much of its course, southeast through the Northumberland National Park, through Otterburn and then south, joining the North Tyne below the village of Redesmouth. The Rede is 37 miles (59 km) long. The Rede Valley is traversed by the Pennine Way at Byrness.

The **Till** is the only English tributary of the River Tweed. Named in its upper stretches the River Breamish, which rises on Comb Fell, its tributaries include Wooler Water, which originates in the Cheviot Hills, and the River Glen in Glendale. Recent environmental projects have included an attempt to conserve the native brown trout. The Till meets the Tweed near Berwick-upon-Tweed and the Twizel Viaduct.

Tweed see Scottish Borders

The **Tyne** is formed by the confluence of two rivers, the North Tyne and the South Tyne. These two rivers converge at Warden Rock near Hexham at a place named the Meeting of the Waters. The North Tyne rises on the Scottish border, north of Kielder Water, and flows through Kielder Forest; the South Tyne rises on Alston Moor, Cumbria, flowing through the towns of Haltwhistle and Haydon Bridge in a valley often called the Tyne Gap. Hadrian's Wall lies to the North of the Tyne Gap. The combined Tyne flows from Hexham through Corbridge before entering Tyne and Wear between Clara Vale (on the south bank in Gateshead) and Tyne Riverside Country Park (on the north bank in Newcastle upon Tyne) and continues to divide Newcastle and Gateshead for 13 miles (21km), during which it is spanned by 10 bridges. The Tyne was a major route for the export of coal from the 13th century until the decline of the coalfields of northeast England in the second half of the 20th century. Its total length is 62 miles (100km).

The **Wansbeck** (nicknamed the River Wanney) rises above Sweethope Lough on the Wanney Crags and flows through the village of Kirkwhelpington, the town of Morpeth and the village of Mitford, where it is joined by a small tributary, the River Font. It then flows through Ashington before reaching the North Sea at Sandy Bay near Newbiggin-by-the-Sea. The river gives its name to the Wansbeck district, centred in Ashington and including Newbiggin-by-the-Sea, Bedlington and Stakeford.

St Andrews Church — Bolam, 6 miles (10km) southwest of Morpeth. A Grade I listed church with late Saxon tower and Norman chancel.

St Cuthbert's Way — A 62 mile (100km) long-distance trail between the Scottish Borders town of Melrose and Holy Island (see separate entry) off the coast of Northumberland. It is named after the 7th century saint, a native of the Borders who began his work at Melrose Abbey.

Scotch Gill Wood Local Nature Reserve — Mitford Road, Morpeth. A 20 acre (8ha) area of ancient woodland on the north bank of the River Wansbeck. The river banks and woods are home to wildlife such as red squirrel, otters, kingfishers and crayfish. Tel: 01670 535185.

Seaton Delaval Hall — 1 mile (1.6km) west of Seaton Sluice, 3 miles (5km) south of Blyth. An English baroque house built 1718–28 for Admiral George Delaval on an estate owned by the Delaval family since the Norman Conquest. The last country house designed by Sir John Vanbrugh, it is widely regarded as his finest work; its architectural style was evolved by Vanbrugh from the more decorated and less austere continental baroque popular in Europe. A central block containing the state and principal rooms is flanked by two arcaded and pedimented wings containing the stables in the east wing, and secondary and service accommodation in the west wing. The house was abandoned after a fire gutted the centre block in 1822; despite further restoration in 1959 it remained unoccupied until the 1980s, when the present owner, Edward Delaval Henry Astley, 22nd Baron Hastings, moved into the west wing. The exterior remains a fine example of the English baroque style although the interiors of the state rooms remain unrestored from the fire. Tel: 01912 371493.

Sport

football — **Berwick Rangers**, founded in 1881 and based in Berwick-upon-Tweed, are one of a handful of teams in the world to play in a national football league other than that of their own country. Because the town is closer to Edinburgh than to Newcastle upon Tyne, the time and expense involved in travelling to away matches against English opposition would be prohibitive, and the club opted in the 1950s to seek membership of the Scottish Football League. The Borderers, as they are known, played at various grounds before establishing themselves at Shielfield Park in 1954, purchasing a new stand from Bradford City after a successful run in the Scottish Cup. The ground is now shared with Berwick Bandits speedway team. Having gained admittance to the Scottish Border League in 1905 they were finally elected members of the Scottish League in 1951, and have retained their place ever since. Their traditional colours are orange and black striped shirts and black shorts. Tel: 01289 307424.

horse racing — **Hexham** racecourse, High Yarridge, Hexham, is a left-handed circuit of 1½ miles (2.5km) round with a stiff uphill climb between the last two fences. Hexham holds exclusively National Hunt racing. Tel: 01434 606881.

SS *Forfarshire* — A paddle steamer which foundered on the Farne Islands (see separate entry) in a fierce gale and thick fog on 7 September 1838. The rescue of nine people from the wreck by 22-year-old Grace Darling and her father, Longstone lighthouse-keeper William, attracted extraordinary attention throughout Britain and made Grace a heroine. Commissioned by the Dundee & Hull Shipping Company to carry passengers and cargo between Hull and Dundee, the two-masted SS *Forfarshire* was built in Dundee in 1834. She set out north from Hull on 5 September 1838, with 60 people on board. Passing Flamborough Head, the pumps supplying water to her boilers broke down and at 10pm the following night, off St Abb's Head, her engines failed. Despite near gale force north-northeasterly winds, her captain continued under sail, but when the weather worsened to a full northerly gale accompanied by thick fog, the ship was forced to seek shelter behind the

Farne Islands. At 3am on 7 September, she ran aground on Big Harcar. Eight sailors and one passenger escaped in a lifeboat, to be picked up the following morning by a passing schooner. The remaining passengers and crew were left to the mercy of the sea, which tore off the *Forfarshire*'s stern quarterdeck and cabins, leaving only the bow and fore sections anchored to the rock. A few passengers survived the night, including a Mrs Dawson, who was distraught, holding the bodies of her two dead children. Waking early the next morning, Grace Darling was the first to spot their predicament from the Longstone lighthouse. Together father and daughter launched their 21ft (6.4m) coble (rowing boat), and rowed almost a mile to Big Harcar through heavy seas, rescuing five survivors; William and two of those rescued then returned for the remaining four. Forty-three people, including the captain and his wife, perished. Both William and Grace received the RNLI's Silver Medal in 1838 – the first recipients of this new award. They also received the Gold Medallion from the Royal Humane Society, while Grace was additionally awarded silver medals from the Glasgow Humane Society and the Edinburgh and Leith Humane Society.

Tenantry Column — Bondgate, Alnwick. A monument designed by David Stephenson and erected in 1816 as thanks to the 2nd Duke of Northumberland by his tenants, following his reduction of their rents after the Napoleonic Wars. The column stands 83ft (25m) tall and is topped by the Percy Lion, symbol of the Percy family.

Thirlwall Castle — $^{1}/_{2}$ mile (0.8km) north of Greenhead, 4 miles (6km) northwest of Haltwhistle. Built in the 12th century and later strengthened using stones from nearby Hadrian's Wall, the castle fell into disrepair in the 17th century. In 1999 the Northumberland National Park Authority took over the management of the castle, protecting it from further dereliction.

Tyne Turrets — Two 12in guns from HMS *Illustrious*, installed in Roberts Battery at Hartley near Seaton Sluice, 3 miles (5km) south of Blyth, and Kitchener Battery in Marsden near Lizard Point south of the Tyne in Tyne and Wear. The batteries were planned during World War I but only commissioned in 1921, and after a change of plans were scrapped in 1926.

Vindolanda — 4 miles (6km) northeast of Haltwhistle. Also known as Chesterholm. A fort and well-excavated civil settlement on Hadrian's Wall, dating to C.AD 85. The Vindolanda tablets (fragments of wooden leaf-tablets with ink writing containing messages between members of the garrison of the Roman fort, their families and their slaves) were discovered from 1970 onwards by archaeologist Robin Birley and are now housed at the British Museum. The tablets give a fascinating insight into the Roman psyche and among the more light-hearted discoveries was the revelation that Roman soldiers wore underpants (subligaria) and referred to the locals rather derogatorily as little Britons (Brittunculi). There is a comprehensive museum on the site. Tel: 01434 344277.

Wallington — 1 mile (1.6km) south of Cambo, 12 miles (19km) west of Morpeth. A country house and gardens set in 100 acres (40ha) of rolling parkland; the estate includes a wooded valley, ornamental lakes, lawns and a recently refurbished walled garden. The house was rebuilt in 1688 around an existing pele tower house for Sir William Blackett and was rebuilt again, in Palladian style, for Sir Walter Blackett by architect Daniel Garret, before passing to the Trevelyan family in 1777. In 1928, Charles Philips Trevelyan inherited the property from his father George Otto Trevelyan. Exhibits include the desk where Thomas Babington Macaulay, brother-in-law of Charles Edward Trevelyan, wrote his *History of England*, a large collection of antique dolls' houses and an eight-panel fresco in the central hall depicting the history of Northumberland, painted by William Bell Scott. The park's 18th century landscaping, with a variety of gardens, lakes and woodland, displays the influence of Capability Brown, while there are also sculptures, water features and a wildlife hide. The property has been managed by the National Trust since 1942. Tel: 01670 773600.

Wallington House — See Wallington

Wark Castle — Wark, 15 miles (24km) southwest of Berwick-on-Tweed. Norman motte and bailey castle founded by Walter Espec and rebuilt in stone by Henry II, c.1158, having been besieged by David I of Scotland 1138. It was left to decay by the 14th century. Substantial earthworks are still visible but only traces of stonework remain.

Warkworth Castle — Warkworth, 6 miles (10km) southeast of Alnwick. One of the largest fortresses in northern England, crowning a hilltop that rises steeply above the River Coquet. Founded as a Norman motte and bailey castle by Henry, Earl of Northumberland, c.1140, the castle was taken by William the Lion in 1173 and rebuilt by the Clavering family in the 13th century. It was bought in 1332 by the Percys, who owned it until 1922, and was the birthplace of Harry Hotspur, son of the 1st Earl of Northumberland; the dramatic cross-shaped keep was added in the mid 14th century, while the lion badge of the Percy family is carved on many parts of the stronghold. The castle was taken in 1405 by Henry IV with seven cannon shots, but later returned to the Percys. It fell into disrepair after the 16th century; it was besieged by the Scots in 1644 and by Parliament in 1648, who took and slighted it. The keep, still roofed and almost complete, dominates the extensive remains of a great hall, chapel and gatehouse; the walls and associated towers are also almost intact. Now owned by English Heritage. Tel: 01665 711423.

Warkworth Hermitage — Warkworth, 6 miles (10km) southeast of Alnwick. Situated on the north bank of the River Coquet, this remarkable structure dates to the late 14th century and is believed to have been founded by Henry, 2nd Lord Percy. The outer portion is built of stone, while the inner portion has been created from a sandstone cave above the river. This inner part comprises a chapel and a smaller chamber, both with altars; the chapel contains an altar-tomb with a female effigy. The traditional story of the origin of the hermitage attributes it to one of the Bertrams of Bothal Castle (see separate entry), and is told in Bishop Percy's ballad 'The Hermit of Warkworth' (1771). It is maintained by English Heritage.

Whin Sill — A large volcanic escarpment consisting of a horizontal mass of igneous rock intruded laterally between older layers of sedimentary rock. Whin Sill lies within the Northumberland National Park and was formed of dolerite (a basaltic rock) 295 million years ago. The exposed area forms steep north-facing cliffs with gentler slopes to the south, and is part of a sheet of rock stretching from Teesdale, the location of various waterfalls, along a northerly line to Berwick and the Farne Islands.

Woodhorn Colliery Museum and Gallery — Queen Elizabeth II Country Park, Ashington. First opened in 1989 on the site of the former Woodhorn Colliery, the museum is largely dedicated to coal mining in Northumberland, with further exhibits on the local history of the county. The gallery holds a substantial collection of work by members of the Ashington Group (see separate entry). After redevelopment costing £16m, the museum was reopened on 26 October 2006 by Princess Anne. Tel: 01670 528080.

Some famous people born in Northumberland

Addison, Thomas (physician and scientist) (1793–1860)	Longbenton
Airy, George Biddell (astronomer) (1801–92)	Alnwick
Armstrong, Sheila (soprano) (1942–)	Ashington
Bewick, Thomas (wood-engraver and ornithologist) (1753–1828)	Mickley
Brown, Lancelot 'Capability' (landscape gardener) (1716–83)	Kirkharle
Charlton, Bobby (footballer) (1937–)	Ashington
Charlton, Jack (footballer) (1935–)	Ashington
Darling, Grace (Victorian heroine) (1815–42)	Bamburgh
Doherty, Pete (musician and poet) (1979–)	Hexham
Gibson, Wilfrid (poet) (1878–1962)	Hexham
Gooch, Daniel (engineer) (1816–89)	Bedlington
Green, Robson (actor and singer) (1964–)	Hexham
Grey, Earl (Charles) (British prime minister) (1764–1845)	Flodden
Hammond, Hermione (painter) (1910–2005)	Hexham
Harmison, Steve (cricketer) (1978–)	Ashington
Milburn, John 'Jackie' (footballer) (1924–88)	Ashington
Morrison, Robert (first missionary to China) (1782–1834)	Bullers Green
Noble, Ross (comedian) (1976–)	Cramlington
Shearer, Alan (footballer) (1970–)	Gosforth
Stephenson, George (engineer) (1781–1848)	Wylam
Steven, Trevor (footballer) (1963–)	Berwick-upon-Tweed
Stokoe, Bob (footballer and manager) (1930–2004)	Mickley
Summers, Paul (poet) (1967–)	Blyth
Tate, Ralph (botanist and geologist) (1840–1901)	Alnwick
Trevor-Roper, Hugh (historian) (1914–2003)	Glanton

Islands of Northumberland

(shipping area = Tyne)

Island name	Area	Nearest landmark	General information
Annstead Rocks	North Sea	Seahouses	GR: NU230305
Back Skerrs	North Sea	Holy Island	GR: NU125440
Big Harcar	North Sea	Bamburgh	One of the Farne Islands. GR: NU240385. On 7 September 1838, the *Forfarshire* foundered on the island, giving rise to the rescue for which Grace Darling is famed.
Big Scarcar	North Sea	Bamburgh	One of the Farne Islands. GR: NU229360
Bondi Carrs	North Sea	Amble	GR: NU290019
Boulmer Steel	North Sea	Boulmer	GR: NU271146
Brig Head	North Sea	Cresswell	GR: NZ302932
Broad Sand Rocks	North Sea	Cresswell	GR: NU300930
Broad Stones	North Sea	Holy Island	GR: NU135413
Brownsman	North Sea	Bamburgh	One of the Farne Islands. Area: 0.01 sq miles (0.03 sq km). GR: NU238378
Bucket Rocks	North Sea	Berwick-upon-Tweed	GR: NU010531
Burn Carrs	North Sea	Beadnell	GR: NU235281
Bush, The	North Sea	Bamburgh	One of the Farne Islands. GR: NU232361
Callers	North Sea	Bamburgh	One of the Farne Islands. GR: NU250371
Castle Island	River Wansbeck	Ashington	GR: NZ282855
Castlehead Rocks	North Sea	Holy Island	GR: NU133441
Cheswick Black Rocks	North Sea	Scremerston	GR: NU039477
Clove Car	North Sea	Bamburgh	One of the Farne Islands. GR: NU245387
Coquet Island	North Sea	Amble	See separate entry
Crumstone	North Sea	Bamburgh	One of the Farne Islands. GR: NU253371
Cushet Stiel	North Sea	Castle Point	GR: NU260215
Elm Bush	North Sea	Amble	GR: NU285017

Island name	Area	Nearest landmark	General information
Emblestone	North Sea	Low Newton-by-the-Sea	GR: NU249242
Faggot	North Sea	Snook Point	GR: NU252265
Far Skerr	North Sea	Scremerston	GR: NU036480
Farne Island	North Sea	Bamburgh	aka Inner Farne. St Cuthbert died here in 687. One of the Farne Islands. Area: 0.02 sq miles (0.06 sq km). GR: NU219359
Farne Islands	North Sea	Bamburgh	aka Staple Islands. See separate entry
Green Island	North Sea	Bamburgh	One of the Farne Islands. GR: NU238382
Green Skeer	North Sea	Blyth	GR: NZ314827
Greenhill Rocks	North Sea	Bamburgh	GR: NU203340
Greymare Rock	North Sea	Castle Point	GR: NU253224
Gun Rock	North Sea	Bamburgh	One of the Farne Islands. GR: NU235375
Hadston Carrs	North Sea	Broomhill	GR: NU283009
Headagee	North Sea	Lynemouth	GR: NZ303919
Holy Island	North Sea	Beal	aka Lindisfarne. See separate entry
Inner Farne	North Sea	Bamburgh	See Farne Island
Islestone	North Sea	Bamburgh	GR: NU197350
Jenny Bells Carr	North Sea	Low Newton-by-the-Sea	GR: NU246237
Keal Head	North Sea	Holy Island	GR: NU134439
Knivestone	North Sea	Bamburgh	One of the Farne Islands. GR: NU251397
Knocklin Ends	North Sea	Bamburgh	One of the Farne Islands. GR: NU225366
Knoxes Reef	North Sea	Bamburgh	One of the Farne Islands. GR: NU221364
Ladies Skerrs	North Sea	Berwick-upon-Tweed	GR: NU008535
Limpet Rocks	North Sea	Cresswell	GR: NU298933
Lindisfarne	North Sea	Beal	See Holy Island
Little Carr	North Sea	Craster	GR: NU261202
Little Harcar	North Sea	Bamburgh	One of the Farne Islands. GR: NU241387
Little Rock	North Sea	Beadnell	GR: NU241287
Little Scarcar	North Sea	Bamburgh	One of the Farne Islands. GR: NU229361
Long Ridge	North Sea	Holy Island	GR: NU140421
Longstone Rock	North Sea	Bamburgh	See separate entry
Marden Rocks	North Sea	Alnmouth	GR: NU260115
Marmouth Scars	North Sea	Boulmer	GR: NU270130
Megstone	North Sea	Bamburgh	One of the Farne Islands. GR: NU206373
Middle Skerr	North Sea	Scremerston	GR: NU033483
Monks House Rocks	North Sea	Bamburgh	GR: NU208335
Near Skerrs	North Sea	Scremerston	GR: NU029488
North Steel	North Sea	Amble	GR: NU292051
North Wamses	North Sea	Bamburgh	One of the Farne Islands. GR: NU234385
Northern Hares	North Sea	Bamburgh	One of the Farne Islands. GR: NU245393
Out Carr	North Sea	Low Newton-by-the-Sea	GR: NU252241
Outer Carrs	North Sea	Newbiggin-by-the-Sea	GR: NZ321888
Outer Farne	North Sea	Bamburgh	See Longstone Rock
Oxcar	North Sea	Bamburgh	aka South Goldstone. One of the Farne Islands. GR: NU212379
Parton Stiel	North Sea	Holy Island	GR: NU140402
Pinnacles	North Sea	Bamburgh	One of the Farne Islands. GR: NU238373
Plough Rock	North Sea	Holy Island	GR: NU149419
Robin Wood's Rock	North Sea	Beadnell	GR: NU236273
Rockers, The	North Sea	Blyth	GR: NZ315831
Roddam	North Sea	Bamburgh	One of the Farne Islands. GR: NU238381
St Cuthbert's Island	North Sea	Beal	GR: NU121408
Saltpan Rocks	North Sea	Scremerston	GR: NU026490
Scars, The	North Sea	Cresswell	GR: NZ129938
Seal Skears	North Sea	Cresswell	GR: NZ304929
Seaton Sea Rocks	North Sea	Blyth	GR: NZ328808
Silver Carrs	North Sea	Amble	GR: NU289022
Skerey Scar	North Sea	Bamburgh	One of the Farne Islands. GR: NU238372
South Goldstone	North Sea	Bamburgh	See Oxcar
South Steel	North Sea	Amble	GR: NU292043
South Wamses	North Sea	Bamburgh	One of the Farne Islands. GR: NU235382
Sow and Pigs	North Sea	Blyth	GR: NZ329813
Spital Carrs	North Sea	Newbiggin-by-the-Sea	GR: NZ311871
Staple Island	North Sea	Bamburgh	Sanctuary for birds of the auk family, i.e. guillemots, razorbills and puffins. One of the Farne Islands. GR: NU238375
Staple Islands	North Sea	Bamburgh	aka Farne Islands
Torrs, The	North Sea	Boulmer	GR: NU270140
Tumblers, The	North Sea	Seahouses	GR: NU218324
Whirl Rocks	North Sea	Bamburgh	One of the Farne Islands. GR: NU253397
Whittingham Carr	North Sea	Snook Point	GR: NU246265

NOTTINGHAMSHIRE

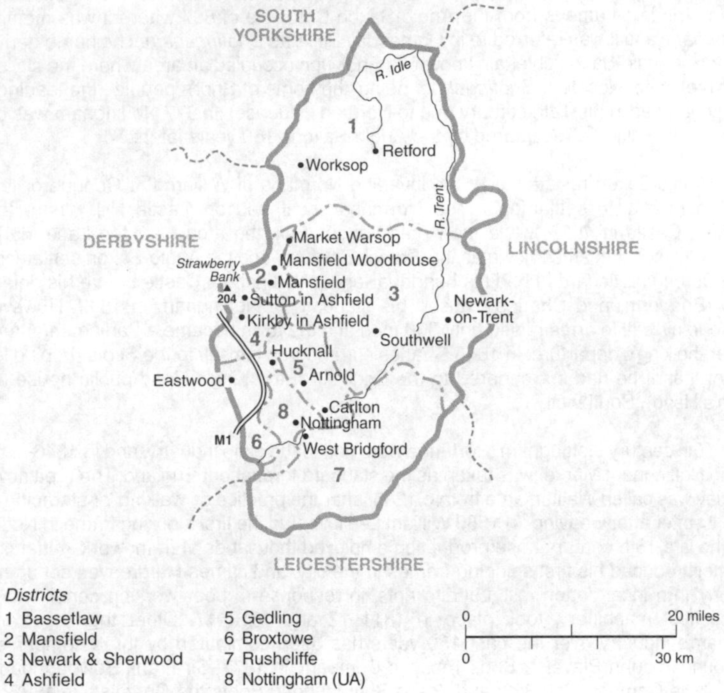
SOUTH YORKSHIRE
DERBYSHIRE
LINCOLNSHIRE
LEICESTERSHIRE
R. Idle
R. Trent
Retford
Worksop
Market Warsop
Mansfield Woodhouse
Mansfield
Strawberry Bank
204
Sutton in Ashfield
Kirkby in Ashfield
Newark-on-Trent
Southwell
Hucknall
Eastwood
Arnold
Carlton
Nottingham
West Bridgford
M1
Districts
1 Bassetlaw
2 Mansfield
3 Newark & Sherwood
4 Ashfield
5 Gedling
6 Broxtowe
7 Rushcliffe
8 Nottingham (UA)
0
20 miles
0
30 km

Nottinghamshire, a county in the East Midlands, borders South Yorkshire to the north, Lincolnshire to the east, Leicestershire to the south and Derbyshire to the west.

Evidence of human settlement in the county dates back thousands of years. Excavations at Creswell Crags, a group of limestone caves near Worksop on the border with Derbyshire, have revealed continuous human occupation from 40,000–28,000 BC. Later the Romans built the Fosse Way, linking Leicester and Lincoln, and roughly corresponding to the present A46 close to Newark-on-Trent. The county was settled by Angles around the 5th century, and became part of the kingdom of Mercia; there is also evidence of Saxon settlement at Oxton, near Nottingham, and Tuxford, east of Sherwood Forest. The name Nottinghamshire first occurs in 1016, but until 1568 the county was administratively united with Derbyshire, under a single sheriff. Nottinghamshire was historically divided into eight wapentakes, the administrative areas equivalent to Anglo-Saxon hundreds, but between 1610 and 1719 they were reduced to six: Newark, Bassetlaw, Thurgarton, Rushcliffe, Broxtowe and Bingham.

In Norman times the county developed malting and woollen industries. Canals and railways arrived during the Industrial Revolution, aiding the growth of the lace and cotton industries. In the 19th century collieries opened and mining became an important economic sector, though these declined after the 1984–5 miners' strike with very few now remaining open.

Nottinghamshire, like Derbyshire and South Yorkshire, sits on extensive coal measures, up to 3000ft (900m) thick and occurring largely in the north of the county. These are overlaid by sandstones and limestones in the west and clay in the east. The north of the county is part of the York plain. The centre and southwest, around Sherwood Forest, feature undulating hills with ancient oak woodland. Principal rivers are the Trent, Idle, Erewash and Soar. The Trent, fed by the Soar and Erewash, and Idle, composed of many streams from Sherwood Forest, run through wide and flat valleys, merging at Misterton.

The traditional county town is **Nottingham** on the Trent, although the council is now based in West Bridgford, just south of the city. Until 1 April 1998 the City of Nottingham was administratively part of Nottinghamshire; it is now a unitary authority, although it remains part of the traditional and ceremonial county. An early, possibly Celtic name for Nottingham was *Tigguo Cobauc*, 'a place of cave dwellings', although this dates only to c.900 when it appears in Asser's *Life of King Alfred.* The first sign of the modern name is from the Anglo-Saxon Chronicle of 867 where it was mentioned as *Snotengaham*, and it was referred to in Domesday Book as *Snotingeham.* The name derives from a 7th century Anglo-Saxon chieftain known as Snot who occupied an area where the city's historic Lace Market is now located, *Snotingeham* being 'the home of Snot's people' (the leading 'S' was thankfully dropped in the 12th century due to Norman influence). In 877 Nottingham was captured by the Vikings only to be recaptured by the Anglo-Saxons 150 years later.

By 1066 Anglo-Saxon resistance to the invading Normans of William the Conqueror led to the establishment of twin settlements. The Normans encamped on Castle Hill, where they built Nottingham Castle in 1068, while the Anglo-Saxons took the area near the Lace Market. The Norman settlement became known as the 'French Borough' and the Anglo-Saxon settlement as the 'English Borough'. Richard III had his headquarters at Nottingham Castle before his defeat at the Battle of Bosworth, and Charles I raised his standard in Nottingham in 1642. However, local response to his call to arms raised only 300 men and the town became a Parliamentarian stronghold after the king's departure. In 1646 Charles surrendered himself to the Scots (hoping for better treatment than if he had surrendered to the English) at the King's Head public house (now the Saracen's Head), Southwell.

Until the 20th century Nottingham's fortunes were tied to the cloth industry, and in 1343–5 the price of wool in Nottingham Market was taken as the standard throughout England. The area now known as Hockley was called Walker Gate from c.1285, after the practice of 'walking' or stamping on cloth to make it softer after weaving. In 1589 William Lee invented the first stocking frame in Nottingham, and by the late 18th century hose production employed thousands of framework knitters. Richard Arkwright introduced his first spinning frames in the city, and James Hargreaves set up his 'spinning jenny' in a local cotton mill. Luddite riots, in response to poor working conditions and the introduction of machinery, took place in 1811–12 and 1816–17. Other than coal and lace, Nottingham's industry over the past 150 years has been dominated by three companies. John Player founded John Player & Sons Tobacco Company in 1877; Sir Frank Bowden founded the Raleigh Cycle Company in 1888; and Jesse Boot founded Boots the Chemists in 1892. In 1829 William Booth, founder of the Salvation Army, was born in Notintone Place, Sneinton, a suburb of the city.

In common with most English cities, contemporary Nottingham is an ethnically diverse community, home to a number of significantly represented religions including Islam, Hinduism, Sikhism and Taoism. In a 2006 Frequency of Overseas Dishes (FOOD) study by MSN, Nottingham emerged as Britain's international food capital, with six restaurants representing different world cuisines for every square mile.

Nottinghamshire	**Population**			**Area**	
Districts	*male*	*female*	*total*	*sq miles*	*sq km*
Ashfield	54,369	57,018	111,387	42	110
Bassetlaw	53,190	54,523	107,713	246	638
Broxtowe	52,884	54,686	107,570	31	80
Gedling	54,261	57,526	111,787	46	120
Mansfield	47,769	50,412	98,181	30	77
Newark & Sherwood	51,836	54,437	106,273	251	651
Rushcliffe	51,809	53,790	105,599	158	409
Nottingham Unitary Authority	132,530	134,458	266,988	29	75
Total	498,648	516,850	1,015,498	833	2160

Local Attractions and Information

Administrative headquarters
Nottingham: The Guildhall, South Sherwood Street, Nottingham NG1 4BT. Tel: 0115 915 5555.
Nottinghamshire: County Hall, West Bridgford, Nottinghamshire NG2 7QP. Tel: 0115 982 3823.

Airports
Nottingham East Midlands Airport, 11 miles (18km) southwest of Nottingham, serves many major European cities. Tel: 0871 919 9000. **Nottingham City Airport** (formerly known as Tollerton Airport), $3^1/_2$ miles (5.5km) southeast of Nottingham, was opened in 1930 as a flying field; its main use today is the provision of training in aircraft and helicopters. It also provides a landing ground close to the city of Nottingham. The Sherwood Flying Club and the Trumanair Flying School are based at the airfield. Tel: 0115 981 5050.

Attenborough Nature Reserve 5 miles (8km) southwest of Nottingham. Opened in 1966 by Sir David Attenborough, the area covered by the 358 acre (145ha) nature reserve alongside the River Trent was once used for gravel extraction. After careful restoration, the flooded pits and islands, interspersed with drier areas of scrub and grassland, are now a haven for wildlife. Over 250 species of birds have been sighted, from swans and starlings to the elusive kingfisher and the even rarer bittern. In 1982, the site was designated a Site of Special Scientific Interest due to the importance of its over-wintering waterfowl population, particularly pochard and shoveler. Other wildlife includes foxes, stoats, toads, newts, and many species of butterflies, moths and other invertebrates.

Battles Four battles have been fought in Nottinghamshire: Hatfield Chase, Newark, River Idle and Stoke Field. See separate table for details.

Bestwood Country Park 4 miles (6km) north of Nottingham. Situated just east of Bestwood village, this 650 acre (265ha) park boasts a range of habitats and features reflecting the county's varied history, from mill lakes teeming with waterbirds to wildflower meadows, ancient oak woodland and a reclaimed coal tip. The Winding Engine House, part of Bestwood Colliery until its closure in 1971, contains the only twin cylinder vertical winding engine still in existence in Britain. Tel: 0115 927 3674.

Brewhouse Yard Museum of Nottingham Life Castle Boulevard, Nottingham. Housed in a group of five restored 17th century cottages nestled in the rock beneath Nottingham Castle, the museum depicts everyday domestic and working life in Nottingham during the past 300 years. There are reconstructions of numerous shops including an Edwardian grocer's, a Victorian chemist, and a row of 1920s shops including a barber's, pawn shop, doctor's, ironmonger's, music shop and cobbler's. There is an Edwardian schoolroom, while the museum also recreates the experiences of Nottingham residents of World War II in the air raid shelter built in the caves under the site. Tel: 0115 915 3600.

Carlton Hall Carlton-on-Trent, 7 miles (11km) north of Newark. A mid 18th century house by Joseph Pocklington of Newark, the family home of Lt Colonel and Mrs Vere-Laurie. The stables are attributed to John Carr of York. Tel: 01636 821421.

Caves of Nottingham Situated beneath the Broadmarsh Shopping Centre, Nottingham. A man-made cave system excavated from the sandstone ridge on which the city sits. The oldest reference to Nottingham Caves appears in Asser's *Life of King Alfred*, written c.AD 900, which refers to the city by the possibly Celtic name *Tigguo Cobauc* ('a place of caves'). The soft sandstone is ideal for excavation and cave dwellings could be made with simple hand-held tools. Parts of this unique cave system have been dated to the 13th century, and among its features is the only remaining underground medieval tannery in the UK. The caves were used as slum dwellings in Victorian times and as an air raid shelter in World War II. Tel: 0115 952 0555.

Churches: Nottingham **St Mary's**, St Mary's Gate, is mentioned in Domesday Book but the foundations are believed to date from Saxon times. The present church (the third on the site) was built in Perpendicular style between c.1377 and 1475, when the nave was completed; the 126ft (38.5m) tower was completed 30 years later. The interior has since been substantially restored but the chapter house (1890) by George Frederick Bodley, the chapel by Temple Moore (1912) and the Simpson memorial choir vestry (1940) are the only significant additions. The church's exterior appears largely as when it was first completed, and is decorated with gargoyles, carved heads and animals.

St Peter's, St Peter's Gate, dates to c.1180 and is the oldest building in continuous use in Nottingham. A fine example of the Early English style, it has been a place of worship since the 11th century and lies immediately outside the original Anglo-Saxon settlement.

All Saints' has served the residential Arboretum area since being built along with a school, headmaster's house and vicarage in 1864. The entire project was paid for by William Windley JP (1821–77); the architect was T C Hine of Nottingham. The church, built in Gothic revival style, and many of the other buildings are now Grade II listed. See also the Cathedral Church of St Barnabas.

Churches: outside Nottingham **St Mary Magdalene**, Newark, has a 256ft (78m) spire, one of the tallest in England; the interior contains an eerie 'Dance of Death' painting dating to the early 16th century.

The parish church of **St Mary Magdalene**, Hucknall, is the burial place of Lord Byron and his daughter Ada, the pioneer of computer programming. There are also 18 stained glass windows by Victorian artist Charles Eamer Kempe.

The quiet parish churches of **All Saints'**, Babworth, and **St Wilfred's**, Scrooby, hold mementos of the Pilgrim Fathers (see separate entry), who set out from north Nottinghamshire in search of religious freedom and the New World. The latter church dates from the late medieval period and Scrooby was once the seat of the Archbishops of York. See also Southwell Minster, Worksop Priory.

Clumber Park 4½ miles (7km) southeast of Worksop. Comprising over 3800 acres (1500ha) of woods, open heath and rolling farmland, with a magnificent serpentine lake at its heart and the longest avenue of lime trees in Europe, Clumber is part of the region of Nottinghamshire known as the Dukeries and was formerly home to the Dukes of Newcastle. The house at Clumber once boasted a dining room that could seat 150 guests and its celebrated art collection included paintings by Gainsborough, Reynolds, Van Dyck and Claud Lorrain. The house itself was demolished in 1938, but many features of the estate remain, including an outstanding Gothic revival chapel and walled kitchen garden with spectacular glass houses, growing old varieties of vegetables. Now owned by the National Trust. Tel: 01909 476592.

Colliers Wood Engine Lane, Eastwood. Located on the site of the former Moorgreen Colliery, this community woodland forms part of the Greenwood Community Forest. The wood was designed as part of the Eastwood Phoenix Project (see Durban House), to restore the woodlands and fields which existed in the area before the mine was developed.

Creswell Crags See Derbyshire

D H Lawrence Birthplace Museum	Victoria Street, Eastwood. When Lawrence was growing up in Eastwood, this part of Nottinghamshire was dominated by the coal mining industry; the world famous novelist, poet and artist was born in this tiny miner's cottage on 11 September 1885. The three floors where the family lived have been carefully recreated, as has the communal washhouse in the back yard. Tel: 01773 717353.
Dukeries	An area of northwest Nottinghamshire between Mansfield and Worksop encompassing the present-day remains of Sherwood Forest. The landscape originally comprised several huge private estates, financed by the nobility thanks to profits made during the Industrial Revolution. Clumber Park (owned by the Duke of Newcastle), Thoresby (Duke of Kingston), Worksop Manor (Duke of Norfolk) and Welbeck Abbey (Duke of Portland) were the country seats of powerful dukes. Inside the estates, the gentry built great country houses where they discussed great affairs of state, and hosted lavish banquets and parties. Clumber Park and Worksop Manor have been demolished, but Thoresby Hall and Welbeck remain as imposing reminders of their owners' former prosperity. The magnificent country house at Welbeck has stood for 400 years. It was converted from an ecclesiastical building after the dissolution of the monasteries but kept the name 'Abbey'. Although Welbeck is not open to the public, it is possible to visit the Harley Gallery. This houses fine art displays and has a permanent historical display about the Cavendish Bentinck family, who still live on the estate.
Durban House	Mansfield Road, Eastwood. Built as a wages office for the Barber Walker coal-mining company in 1876 (where as a boy D H Lawrence would pick up his father's wages). When the colliery offices closed in 1917 it was reopened as an institute for mining officials with a concert hall, billiard room, games room and library. Following the nationalisation of the coal industry during the late 1940s, Durban House ceased to provide office facilities for the company. The building was bought and refurbished by Broxtowe Borough Council in the 1990s as part of the Eastwood Phoenix Project (a local regeneration scheme) and reopened as Durban House Heritage Centre on Monday 6 April 1998 by actor and playwright William Ivory. Durban House now houses a range of exhibitions depicting the Victorian past of Eastwood and the surrounding areas. Tel: 01773 717353.
Galleries of Justice	High Pavement, Nottingham. Located in the Grade II listed Shire Hall, which housed courts and prison cells from the 1780s until the 1980s, the museum illustrates the history of punishment and imprisonment through a series of interactive exhibits. The museum also holds the HM Prison Service collection, formerly displayed in Rugby, Warwickshire, and including Oscar Wilde's cell door, a section of Holloway's treadmill, uniforms, restraints, escape tools and prisoner artwork. Tel: 0115 952 0555.
Goose Fair	The Nottingham Goose Fair originated in the Middle Ages as a trading fair; it is first mentioned by name in 1541 although it may date back to the town's first charter in 1284. Held until 1752 on St Matthew's Day (21 September), its character changed during the 18th and 19th centuries, gradually becoming a gathering of popular amusements. It is now held for three days in the first week of October each year.
Green's Mill and Science Centre	Windmill Lane, Sneinton, Nottingham. Restored tower mill built in 1807 by the father of mathematician and physicist George Green (1793–1841), a pioneer of mathematical studies in electricity, magnetism, mechanics and the properties of light waves. The Science Centre in the mill yard has a range of interactive displays relating to Green's work. Tel: 0115 915 6878.
Highest point	Strawberry Bank, 1¼ miles (2km) north of Huthwaite in the district of Ashfield, at 669ft (204m) (GR: SK456605). The local council erected a monument and plaque in 2003 to celebrate this landmark.
Hodsock Priory and Garden	5 miles (8km) north of Worksop. Hodsock Priory and its garden are in the centre of the 800 acre (320ha) Hodsock Estate, which has its origins before the Norman Conquest and has been owned by the Buchanan family since 1765. A leper hospital was built here by the Cressey family in the early 1200s, but no priory has ever existed on the site and the origin of the house's name is unknown. The current Jacobean-style house dates from the 19th century. The gardens specialise in spring flowers with spectacular displays of snowdrops. Tel: 01909 591204.
Holme Pierrepont Hall	5 miles (8km) southeast of Nottingham. Standing by the church of St Edmund, Holme Pierrepont Hall retains its red-brick battlemented Tudor front. It dates from c.1500, making it the oldest brick building in Nottinghamshire and one of the oldest in Britain. The rooms inside have the appearance of a medieval lodging, with a hall open to the roof showing the ancient timbers. With the two other ranges of a later date, the house forms a 'U' shape around a restored courtyard garden planted with herbaceous beds and roses and including an intricate late-Victorian box parterre. The most important feature of the interior is the splendid carved wooden staircase dating from 1660–80, resited at the north end of the east range in the 18th century after the state rooms in the west were demolished. The property has always been in the Pierrepont family, Earls and Dukes of Kingston in the 17th and 18th centuries. In 1806 the house was inherited by a nephew, Earl Manvers. After Manvers built Thoresby Hall (see Dukeries), moving there on its completion, Holme Pierrepont became the estate's dower house. In 1969 Mrs Brackenbury, a descendant of the 3rd Earl Manvers, purchased the property with her husband and it remains within the family today. The fine 17th to 20th century English country furniture and family portraits are family belongings of the present owners. Tel: 0115 933 2371.
Interesting facts	Nottingham was the home of Britain's first **children's library**, the Library for Boys and Girls, founded in 1882 on Shakespeare Street, while the city's first **Urdu library** opened in 1967. Nottingham was also the first city to install **Braille signs** for blind people in its shopping centres and was home of the **first police forensic laboratory** in 1934. The **Screen Room**, in the Hockley area of Nottingham, is in the *Guinness Book of Records* as the world's smallest cinema with just 21 seats. The **Canal House** public house, Canal Street, Nottingham, has a bar with a canal

running through the centre of it and visitors will often see a boat moored up there as well. Other interesting pubs include **Ye Olde Trip to Jerusalem** (see separate entry); however its sister pub, the **Bell Inn** in Angel Row, built in 1437, rivals its more illustrious sibling as arguably the oldest pub in Nottingham; the **Salutation Inn** in Hounds Gate also claims to date back to 1240. **The Royal Children** in St Nicholas Street is so named because during the 17th century James II's daughter and Princess Anne's children from nearby Nottingham Castle used to play with the landlord's children. A whalebone on display in a cabinet is indicative of the pub's erstwhile secondary trade – selling whale oil for lamps.

Lace Market — The name of this elegant area of Nottingham originates from the 18th century, when local entrepreneurs and industrialists transformed it from a residential area into the centre of the world's lace industry. The area's growth was dependent on two key inventions. In 1589 William Lee, a local inventor, developed a framework knitting machine which enabled high volumes of lace to be manufactured. By 1808 entrepreneur John Heathcoate had developed this into a hand-operated machine and the machine lace industry was born. With the introduction of steam power in the 1800s the production of Chantilly and other luxury weaves brought an economic boom to the district and more than 130 factories were based there. Changing fashion trends in the early 1900s, followed by the introduction of synthetic fibres, led to the decline of the industry and after World War II it struggled to recover. The area remained predominantly commercial and has more recently become a popular location for new businesses, while remaining a sought-after residential area. Today the Lace Market's 18th and 19th century industrial buildings are occupied by a range of shops and hotels, restaurants and bars.

Major Oak — Nominated as the one of the top 50 trees in Britain by the National Tree Council, the famous old tree stands at the heart of Sherwood Forest Country Park. A *Quercus robur* – an English or pedunculate oak – it weighs around 23 tons, has a girth of 33ft (10m) and a spread of 92ft (28m), making it the biggest oak in Britain. It is debatable how old the Major Oak is, but most estimates date it at between 800 and 1000 years. In a good year it can produce 150,000 acorns. The oak's interior is hollow due to the activity of fungi.

Mansfield — Situated on the River Maun, from which the name of the town is possibly derived, Mansfield is the largest town in Nottinghamshire. In 1227, Henry III issued a charter 'to the Men of Maunesfeild, that they and their heirs should have a Market to be held on Mondays'. More recently coal mining was an important part of the town's economy. Ambitious regeneration projects in recent years have transformed Mansfield in terms of retail, leisure, housing and industry. The bustling market is still the hub of the town but is now complemented by shopping centres, retail parks and department stores along with boutiques and specialist stores. White Lion Yard, off Church Street, contains a number of caves and buildings, most of which have been used since the early 18th century and one of which dates back to Tudor times.

Mansfield Museum — Leeming Street, Mansfield. Opened in 1904, in memory of William Edward Baily, a wealthy local collector and natural historian, who had offered the town his collection and a building – the 'Tin Tabernacle' – in which to house it. The museum moved to new premises on the same site in 1938. Its collections reflect the history and culture of the town, Albert Sorby Buxton's watercolours, a unique and valuable record of the face of Mansfield at the turn of the century, being particularly interesting. Tel: 01623 463088.

Motto — *Sapienter Proficiens* ('Advancing wisely').

Newark Castle — Castle Gate, Newark-on-Trent. A Norman enclosure castle built 1125–33 by Alexander, Bishop of Lincoln, although there has been a castle on the site since 1068. It remained a seat of the Bishops of Lincoln until 1547 when Henry VIII took it for the Crown. King John died in the castle in 1216, possibly in the square Norman corner tower. The curtain wall that runs alongside the River Trent was rebuilt in the 14th century and still stands today; only minor alterations were made in the 15th and 16th centuries. During the Civil War, the castle became an important Royalist garrison, holding out against three long sieges in 1643, 1644 and 1645–6. On 5 May 1646 Charles I was captured at nearby Southwell and ordered Newark to surrender. The Parliamentarians subsequently slighted the castle, although the three-storey gatehouse still stands and is the most complete surviving example of a Romanesque gatehouse in England. The grounds were landscaped in 1887. Recent archaeological investigations have unearthed Saxon remains including pottery fragments, animal bones and a cemetery.

Newark-on-Trent — A market town on the River Trent in the east of the county. Its history is dominated by the now ruined castle. Newark's market place is overlooked by a Georgian town hall. The town is famous for its six annual antiques fairs, held at Newark County Showground, while the Newark Air Museum is home to 65 aircraft and cockpit sections. The Pure Land mediation centre in North Clifton, 12 miles (19km) to the north, is home to a 2 acre (0.8ha) Japanese garden.

Newstead Abbey — 12 miles (19km) north of Nottingham. Founded as a monastic house c.1170, Newstead became the seat of the Byron family in 1540. Its most famous owner, the poet George Gordon, Lord Byron, sold the property in 1818 to his friend Colonel Thomas Wildman. Newstead Abbey remained a private house until 1931, when it was presented to Nottingham Corporation. Set in extensive formal gardens with lakes and 300 acres (120ha) of grounds, the landscape owes much of its beauty to the River Leen, which feeds the lakes, ponds and cascades that ornament Newstead's gardens. One such water feature is the Eagle Pond, a large rectangular 'mirror' pond which takes its name from the priory's eagle-shaped lectern (now at nearby Southwell Minster – see separate entry) said to have been hidden in or near the pond at the time of the Dissolution of the Monasteries. Near the Eagle Pond is Byron's famous monument to his favourite dog, Boatswain, who died of rabies in 1808. The house features Byron's private apartments, period rooms and medieval cloisters. The west front of the priory church was featured as part of the BBC's

Restoration series. Tel: 01623 455900.

Norwood Park — Halam Road, Southwell. Attributed to John Carr of York, Norwood Park is often cited as one of England's finest examples of Georgian architecture. It is surrounded by 100 acres (40ha) of deer park, adorned with ancient oaks and orchards born out of the original Bramley apple developed in Southwell in the 1840s. The hall, home of the Starkey family for five generations, is not open to the public.

Nottingham Castle — Friar Lane, Nottingham. Perched high above the city, this magnificent 17th century mansion provides spectacular views across the city and surrounding countryside. William I built a wooden castle on the site in 1067, which was later rebuilt in stone by Henry II as the main royal fortress in the Midlands. The castle fell into ruin in the 16th century and in 1622 it was sold by James I to the Earl of Rutland, who stripped it of valuable materials such as lead and stone. In 1642 the beginning of the Civil War was marked when Charles I raised his royal standard just outside the castle. Having been demolished in 1651, the castle was rebuilt in 1679 by the 1st Duke of Newcastle. Gutted by fire in an attack by Reform Bill rioters in 1831, it was restored and opened as the first municipal museum and art gallery outside London in 1878. Today, the galleries house historical and contemporary collections of silver, glass, ceramics and fine art. Set in beautiful Victorian gardens, it is still possible to see some of the old castle ruins in the grounds. Underneath the castle are man-made caves and tunnels, some dating to the medieval period (see Caves of Nottingham). Tel: 0115 915 3700.

Nottingham Cathedral — See St Barnabas' Cathedral

Nottingham Trent University — Burton Street, Nottingham. The former Nottingham Polytechnic was established as a university in 1992. The student population of around 26,000 is made up of 21,000 undergraduates and 5000 postgraduates. There are three campuses: City Campus in Nottingham, Clifton Campus to the southwest of the city and Brackenhurst Campus, near Southwell. Former students include actor Paul Kaye and politician Hazel Blears. Tel: 0115 941 8418.

Old Market Square — Located on the site of Nottingham's medieval marketplace and known locally as 'Slab Square', Old Market Square, overlooked by two stone lions (built in 1929), is the largest square in England, covering 5.5 acres (2.2ha). It reopened in 2007 after substantial redevelopment.

Papplewick Hall — Papplewick, 6 miles (10km) north of Nottingham. Built 1784–7, and probably the work of William Lindley of Doncaster, at the behest of the then owner Frederick Montagu. The Grade I listed house has notable plasterwork and a very fine stone staircase, and is set in a Grade II listed park and woodland garden. Tel: 0115 963 3491.

Pilgrim Fathers — A Puritan group from the villages of Babworth, Scrooby and Sturton-le-Steeple in north Nottinghamshire, who in the late 1500s began to formulate nonconformist religious ideas and who sought separation from the Church of England at a time when attendance at church was compulsory by law. Many were members of the congregation of Pastor Richard Clyfton at Babworth. Having first escaped to the Netherlands in 1609, in 1620 the group purchased two boats, the *Speedwell* and the *Mayflower*. The two vessels initially set off for the New World from Southampton, but the *Speedwell* proved unfit for the voyage. Finally, on 16 September 1620, the *Mayflower* left Plymouth at the spot now called the Mayflower Steps, arriving at Cape Cod, Massachusetts, two months later. The settlers created a new town there, calling it New Plymouth. Of the 102 people who departed from Devon, less than a third were religious refugees. Among the passengers were Myles Standish, a professional soldier; William Bradford (who in later years became governor of the New England settlement) and William Brewster (the son of Scrooby's postmaster and author of the Mayflower Compact, the governing document of the Plymouth colony), leaders of the group's Separatist congregation at Leiden in the Netherlands; John Alden, a cooper; William and Susanna White from the village of Sturton-le-Steeple, along with their son – their second child, Peregrine, was born as the ship lay at anchor off Cape Cod; and John Carver, the first governor, and his wife Catherine, also from Sturton-le-Steeple. Two people died during the voyage. The *Mayflower*'s captain and part-owner was Christopher Jones.

Prisons — **Lowdham Grange**, Lowdham, Nottingham, opened in 1998. A Category B closed training prison for adult males, it is privately operated and managed by Serco Ltd. Operational capacity: 524. Tel: 0115 966 9200.

Nottingham, Perry Road, Sherwood, Nottingham, opened in 1890 as a city gaol but was reconstructed in 1912 and until 1997 served as a closed training establishment for adult males. In 1997 it re-rolled as a category B local prison, and now serves the courts of Nottinghamshire and Derbyshire. Operational capacity: 500. Tel: 0115 872 3000.

Whatton, Cromwell Road, is a category C prison which holds adult male vulnerable prisoners. It opened as a detention centre in 1996. Since May 1990 it has held sex offenders who participate in the Sex Offenders Treatment Programme. Operational capacity: 360. Tel: 01949 803200.

Retford — An ancient market town granted its first charter by Henry III in 1246. The town features fine Georgian buildings, a spacious square, and two theatres – the Little Theatre on Wharf Road and the Majestic on Coronation Street. The Pilgrim Fathers started their long journey to America from the town before moving on to Plymouth.

Rivers — The **Erewash** rises southeast of Kirkby-in-Ashfield, flowing west to Eastwood then south through Ilkeston and Sandiacre before joining the Trent, near Long Eaton. Most of its 15 mile (24km) course forms the boundary between south Derbyshire and south Nottinghamshire.

The **Idle** has its source at the confluence of the River Maun and River Meden, near Markham Moor (where the A57 joins the A1). From there, it flows north through Retford and Bawtry and then east to Misterton before entering the River Trent at Stockwith. Its total length is approximately 24 miles (38km). Its main tributaries are the River Poulter and the River Ryton. The site of the battle of the River Idle in 616 is believed to be that of the present day village of Eaton, on the southern edge of the town of East Retford.

Soar see Leicestershire

One of England's major rivers, the **Trent** has its source in the Pennines in north Staffordshire between Biddulph and Mow Cop. The area it drains includes most of the northern Midlands. It flows through the Midlands, joining the Humber Estuary at Trent Falls, and then to the North Sea. Running first southeast through the Potteries, Stoke-on-Trent, Stone and Rugeley, then east above Lichfield, it unusually then takes a northeasterly course through Burton upon Trent and Nottingham and continues north via Newark, Gainsborough and onwards west of Scunthorpe to the Humber. Its total length is 170 miles (272km) and it is navigable for 117 miles (188km) below Burton upon Trent. A navigable route into the Potteries and beyond is provided by the Trent and Mersey Canal, which meets the Trent at Shardlow. The Trent is tidal downstream of Cromwell, and is one of only two bore rivers in England (the other being the Severn); the Trent bore is nicknamed the 'Aegir'. The river represents the border separating the provinces of two English Kings of Arms, Norroy and Clarenceaux. It was originally also a boundary for other purposes: for example, the administration of royal forests was divided according to whether they were north or south of the river. Similarly, describing someone as having been born 'north of the Trent' means that they hail from the North of England.

Rufford Abbey and Country Park — 2 miles (3km) south of Ollerton. Located in the heart of Sherwood Forest, the remains of the Cistercian abbey, built c.1147, are set in a delightful 150 acre (60ha) country park. Rufford was transformed into a grand country house for the Talbot and Savile families in the 17th century. Features include an orangery and a restored Jacobean wing. Now owned by English Heritage. Tel: 01623 822944.

St Barnabas' Cathedral — Derby Road, Nottingham. The Roman Catholic cathedral of St Barnabas (aka Nottingham Cathedral) was designed in Gothic Revival style by Augustus Pugin; consecrated in 1844, it is considered to be one of his finest churches. The Venerable Mary Potter is the cathedral's own 'saint in the making'. Her work began in 1877 in Hyson Green where she established the first Catholic religious congregation of women specifically dedicated to nursing. Her care of the poor, the sick and the dying were recognised by Pope John Paul II in 1988 when he declared her to be venerable, the first stage in the process of sanctification. Her mortal remains were reburied in the north ambulatory of the cathedral in 1997. Tel: 0115 953 9839.

Sherwood Forest Country Park — $\frac{1}{2}$ mile (0.8km) north of Edwinstowe, 6 miles (10km) northeast of Mansfield. A remnant of the ancient forest of Sherwood, the legendary home of Robin Hood, the park contains some of the oldest trees in Europe including 'veteran' oaks 500 years old and the world-famous Major Oak (see separate entry). The forest's unique ecological system, permitting the natural decay of fallen wood, means that the woodland teems with insect life, fungi, birds and bats. In partnership with the Sherwood Trust, a woodland grazing project features Hebridean sheep, while Dexter cattle are employed to ensure that open areas of medieval heathland do not revert to scrub. The 450 acre (180ha) country park was designated a National Nature Reserve in 2002. Tel: 01623 823202.

Southwell — 14 miles (23km) northeast of Nottingham. The town of Southwell has many elegant Regency houses but its architectural jewel is the Minster church (see separate entry), boasting some of the best medieval stone carving in England. Just outside the town is the 19th century workhouse (see separate entry); ironically, the *Nottingham Evening Post* has more recently declared Southwell 'Nottinghamshire's millionaire capital'. In fact, this prosperous small town has never been short of admirers. Lord Byron once claimed that 'I shall never be so happy again as I was in old Southwell,' while centuries later, Sir John Betjeman reported that 'the Georgian elegance of Southwell ensures that few small towns are as unspoilt.'

Southwell Minster — Westgate, Southwell. The Cathedral and Parish Church of the Blessed Virgin Mary, with its majestic Norman nave and glorious 13th century chapter house. A church is said to have been established on the site in AD 627 by Paulinus, the first Archbishop of York. The first minster church (so called because it was a collegiate church) was built in 965; construction of the current church began in 1108 and was completed by c.1150. The chapter house, completed in the late 13th century in Decorated Gothic style, features elaborately carved stone foliage among which are numerous 'Green Men'; ten carved mice have been created by modern craftsman Robert Thompson. During the Civil War, the building was seriously damaged by Scottish troops, who also destroyed the 14th–16th century Archbishop's Palace next to the church. In 1881, the Minster's distinctive 'Pepperpots' (pyramidal spires of lead), unique in the UK, were added to the west towers.

Sport

general — The **National Ice Centre**, Bolero Square, Nottingham, has Olympic-sized ice rinks and is home to the Nottingham Panthers ice-hockey team. Minister for Sport Kate Hoey unveiled a plaque marking the opening of the arena in May 2000. The facility has been featured in the *Dancing on Ice* series on the BBC. Ice skating champions Jayne Torvill and Christopher Dean are local heroes, winning Olympic gold medals in Sarajevo in 1984 for their interpretation of Ravel's *Bolero* and making a dramatic return to the Olympic stage in Lillehammer, Norway, in 1994 where they took bronze. They were also joint winners of the BBC Sports Personality of the Year in 1984; both Torvill and Dean were awarded OBEs in 1999. Tel: 0115 853 3000.

The **National Watersports Centre** at Holme Pierrepont, 5 miles (8km) southeast of Nottingham, was built in 1964. Set in 270 acres (109ha) of parkland, it is home to an international 2000m regatta course, man-made white-water slalom and waterski lagoon. Channel 4 has based its popular reality television show *The Games* at the centre in recent years. Tel: 0115 982 1212.

cricket — **Nottinghamshire** County Cricket Club have won the County Championship five times, most recently in 2005. The club's one-day team is known as the Outlaws. Famous players have included Sir Garfield Sobers, Sir Richard Hadlee, Clive Rice, Derek Randall and Kevin Pietersen.

Nottinghamshire's home ground is Trent Bridge, Nottingham, one of the world's oldest major cricket grounds and one of England's Test match venues. Tel: 0115 982 3000.

football — Founded in 1897, **Mansfield Town** joined the Football League in 1931 and enjoyed a brief spell in Division Two during the 1970s; they lost their League place in 2007–08. The Stags' traditional colours are amber and blue. The club's home ground is Field Mill. Tel: 0870 756 3160.

The club which became **Nottingham Forest** was originally formed to play 'shinney' (a game similar to hockey). The football club was founded at the Clinton Arms, Shakespeare Street, in 1865, their first official match taking place on 22 March 1866 against Notts County. Garibaldi Red became the club's official colours and the 'Reds' became the club nickname. The club entered the Football League in 1892. The late Brian Clough, one of Britain's best-loved football managers, led Forest to consecutive European Cup victories in 1979 and 1980; in fact, Nottingham is the smallest city ever to boast a European Cup-winning team. Forest also won the League Championship in 1978 and the FA Cup in 1898 and 1959. The club's home since 1898 has been the City Ground, which hosted international fixtures during the 1996 European Championship finals. Tel: 0115 982 4444.

Notts County, the world's oldest professional football club, was founded in 1862. The Magpies, who traditionally play in black and white stripes, joined the Football League at its inception in 1888. In 1894 they won the FA Cup, the first Second Division club to do so. More recently, the club has enjoyed two spells (1981–4 and 1991–2) in the top division. The club's home ground is the County Ground, Meadow Lane, located on the north bank of the River Trent opposite Nottingham Forest's City Ground on the other side of the river. Probably the most famous player to grace Meadow Lane was legendary England international Tommy Lawton. Tel: 0115 952 9000.

greyhound racing — **Colwick Park**, Nottingham. The circuit is host to some of greyhound racing's most prestigious events, such as the Betfred Eclipse and the William Hill Puppy Classic. Tel: 01159 103333.

horse racing — **Nottingham** Racecourse, Colwick Park, offers 21 days of flat racing from March to November. Tel: 0115 958 0620.

Southwell Racecourse, Rolleston, Newark, is one of only two racecourses in Britain (the other being Lingfield) to provide all-weather Flat and National Hunt racing. Since 1989 the racecourse has offered fibresand racing every month of the year. Tel: 01636 814481.

ice hockey — **Nottingham Panthers** are one of Britain's top ice-hockey teams, competing in the Elite Ice Hockey League (EIHL). They play home matches at the National Ice Centre, Nottingham. Recent players include Greg Hadden, who during his last season with the club in 2002–03 became the Superleague's all time leading goal scorer in both league and all competitions. Tel: 0115 941 3103.

rugby union — **Nottingham** RFC were founded in 1877. V H Cartwright (14 caps, 1904–06), the club's first international player, eventually captained England; a referee during his playing career, he later became selector and eventually president of the RFU. The club enjoyed its most fruitful period in the 1980s, when it produced internationals including Dusty Hare, Rob Andrew and Brian Moore (the club's only British Lion). In 2006 the club left Beeston, its home for 100 years, and moved to Lady Bay in West Bridgford in partnership with Nottinghamshire County Cricket Club, whose nursery ground it is. Tel: 0115 925 4238.

tennis — **Nottingham Tennis Centre**, University Boulevard, Nottingham, offers both indoor and outdoor year-round facilities for all levels of players. Home to the 10tele.com Open (formerly the Nottingham Open), a world-class prelude to Wimbledon, in recent years the centre has hosted prestigious tournaments including the Federation Cup, the World Veteran Championships, the Wheelchair Tennis World Team Cup and the Davis Cup (Great Britain v India). Tel: 0115 915 0000.

Stilton cheese — Stilton is a 'protected name' blue cheese and by law can only be made in the three counties of Derbyshire, Leicestershire and Nottinghamshire. See Cambridgeshire

Thoresby Hall and Park — 2 miles (3km) northwest of Ollerton, 22 miles (35km) north of Nottingham. Although a mansion has stood in the grounds of Thoresby Park since 1589, when the 1st Earl of Kingston commissioned William Talman to house his family at The Dukeries, the present Hall was built by Anthony Salvin in 1865–75. The contents and buildings were sold in 1989 to the Warner Leisure Group and it was reopened in 2000 as a 200 room country house hotel with spa facilities. The extensive grounds cover over 1000 acres (400ha) of unspoilt countryside and is a well-known venue for its Sunday market, usually from March till December. The Thoresby Gallery in Newark houses a unique collection of work by Marie-Louise Pierrepont, who lived at Thoresby Hall until her death in 1984 and explored a range of artistic styles throughout the 20th century.

Thrumpton Hall — Thrumpton, 7 miles (11km) southwest of Nottingham. An exquisite Jacobean house set apart from an enchanting old-fashioned village by a long private drive. Notable features include a priest's hole, a carved Charles II staircase, carved and panelled saloon and beautiful 17th and 18th century furniture. Tel: 0115 983 0410.

University of Nottingham — Nottingham's first civic college was opened in the city centre in 1881, four years after the foundation stone was laid by former prime minister W E Gladstone. After World War I, a generous gift by Sir Jesse Boot of 35 acres (14ha) of land at Highfields was devoted to the college and agreed as a place of recreation for the people of Nottingham; in 1928 the college moved to what is now its main campus, University Park. In 1948, the college was awarded its royal charter, becoming the University of Nottingham. During this period, the Institute of Education was founded and the School of Agriculture was established when the Midland College of Agriculture at Sutton Bonington merged with the university. The Medical School, the first to be established in the 20th century, opened in 1970 and, in 1995, the School of Nursing was formed. The Jubilee Campus opened in 1999 and the Lakeside complex, comprising the Djanogly Art Gallery and Recital Hall and the D H Lawrence Pavilion, which includes the Weston Gallery, opened in 2001. Lawrence is probably Nottingham's most famous former student; others include Lord Hollick, chief executive of United

News and Media; John Monks, former general secretary of the TUC; Ted Childs OBE, creator of TV series *The Sweeney*; broadcaster Matthew Bannister; radio executives Roger Lewis and Jim Moir; journalist Jeff Randall; England rugby union player Brian Moore; world champion canoeist Lyn Simpson; and Mary Marsh, director and chief executive of the NSPCC. Tel: 0115 951 5151.

Upton Hall — 2 miles (3km) east of Southwell. A fine country house dating from the 16th century but extensively altered in the 19th century. The main part of the present hall was designed by W J Donthome and built in 1828 by Thomas Wright (1773–1845), a banker who was also High Sheriff of Nottinghamshire in 1811. The tall, stately neoclassical building has a central leaded dome and an Ionic portico of four columns. Now owned by the British Horological Institute, its museum contains an impressive collection of timepieces. Tel: 01636 813795.

Welbeck Abbey — See The Dukeries

Winkburn Hall — 3 miles (5km) northeast of Southwell. A fine William and Mary house dating to c.1695, possibly the work of master builder William Smith of Warwick. Extensive additions were made in 1840, the mansard roof, with its dormer windows, being replaced by the present top storey. The high, square rooms, typical of 18th century domestic architecture, are embellished with fine Adam fireplaces. A series of carved panels above each of the doorways in the central hall represents scenes from Aesop's Fables. The main staircase, with what appears to be finely carved 'Empire' work and with boldly scrolling acanthus stems, is in fact made of cast iron. Tel: 01636 636465.

Wollaton Hall and Park — 3 miles (5km) south of Nottingham. Set within 500 acres (200ha) of historic deer park, the Grade I listed Elizabethan house was built in 1588 by wealthy coal baron Sir Francis Willoughby to a design by Robert Smythson in the English Renaissance style. It was repaired and remodelled in 1801 by Sir Jeffrey Wyatt who, in 1822, also designed the Grade II listed Camellia House within the grounds. Wollaton Hall is now home to a natural history museum. The converted 18th century stable block contains the Yard Gallery, which hosts a changing programme of exhibitions exploring art, science and the environment. The historic deer park is home to a rich diversity of habitats and species with herds of red and fallow deer, and features a large lake and formal flower gardens. Tel: 0115 915 3900.

Workhouse, The — Upton Road, Southwell. Built in 1824 by the Rev. John Becher, a local magistrate, the workhouse was used to introduce the revolutionary but harsh 'welfare' system adopted nationwide after the Poor Law Amendment Act of 1834. Today the building is the least altered workhouse structure in existence in England, being almost unchanged since the 19th century. For over 150 years it housed the local poor, dominating the local landscape. By 1997 the Grade II listed building was under threat of being turned into residential flats until the National Trust stepped in to buy it, securing its long-term future as a monument to the Poor Laws and the poor. Tel: 01636 817250.

Worksop — A market town 30 miles (48km) north of Nottingham, Worksop has been in existence since Anglo-Saxon times and is aptly dubbed the 'gateway to the Dukeries'. This influence is reflected in the town centre, where at Bridge Street and Bridge Place, coloured stone is set into the paving on the pedestrian streets, depicting the local heraldic crests. There is also a paved maze featuring a heraldic lion and unicorn.

Worksop Priory — Priorswell Road, Worksop. The Great Priory of Our Lady and St Cuthbert was founded at Radford, near Worksop, in 1103 by William de Lovetot. The surviving part consists of the nave, western front and twin towers, built in the late 12th century. In the 14th century the Tickhill Psalter (an illuminated manuscript depicting scenes from the life of King David, now kept in the New York Public Library) was produced by the prior, John de Tickhill. The Augustinian canons were scholars and teachers as well as priests; in fact, England's first elementary school was founded here in the 16th century.

Ye Olde Trip to Jerusalem — Brewhouse Yard, Nottingham. Carved into the rock beneath Nottingham Castle, this uniquely atmospheric venue is reputed to be the world's oldest inn, although much of its history is poorly recorded. An archaeological dig in 1974 established that the castle's brewhouse existed before 1189 and that its original location could only be in the caves beneath the inn, although the first dated reference to the pub occurs in the city council records for 1618. The black and white half-timbered section of the inn's outer buildings dates to c.1650–60 and is shown accurately on a map of 1744. This was used as the basis for the map in Charles Deering's *History of the Antiquities of Nottingham* (1751), which gives the first reference to the inn's name as 'The Pilgrim'. The name 'Ye Olde Trip to Jerusalem' first appeared in Willoughby's *Directory of Nottingham* (1799), while in deeds of sale from 1834, the inn is noted as 'Ye Olde Trip to Jerusalem, formerly known as The Pilgrim'. The pub's most famous landlord was undoubtedly George Henry Ward. A colourful character known to everyone as 'Yorkey', he had his nickname painted on the outside of the building where today the inscription 'Well known throughout the World' is to be seen. By 1894 he had taken over the pub's licence and he remained there until his death in 1914. One of the many legends associated with the pub is that of Mortimer's Hole. The story goes that in 1330, Edward III entered Nottingham Castle to arrest his mother's lover, Roger Mortimer, Earl of March, who had treasonously murdered his father, Edward II. Mortimer was captured in the royal apartment and subsequently hanged. It is said that he and the Queen Mother, Isabella, used to meet in secret in Mortimer's Room, a small chamber cut out of the rock at the back of the inn; this was connected to the castle grounds by a small passage, known as Mortimer's Hole, through the interconnected network of caves. Another legend has it that the name of the inn and the founding date of 1189 depicted on its sign, coinciding with the accession of Richard I, were chosen because the king's crusaders stopped off at the inn for refreshments before travelling to Jerusalem to fight the Third Crusade – in the Middle Ages, a 'Trip' was not a journey as such but rather a resting place where a journey could be broken. Tel: 0115 947 3171.

Some famous people born in Nottinghamshire

Ball, Captain Albert (World War I fighter ace) (1896–1917)	Lenton
Bonington, Richard Parkes (artist) (1802–28)	Arnold
Boot, Sir Jesse (industrialist) (1850–1931)	Nottingham
Booth, General William (founder of the Salvation Army) (1829–1912)	Sneinton
Bowden, Sir Frank (founder of Raleigh Cycle Company) (1848–1921)	Nottingham
Clarke, Rt Hon. Kenneth (politician) (1940–)	Nottingham
Coates, Eric (composer) (1886–1957)	Hucknall
Cole, Andrew (footballer) (1971–)	Nottingham
Cranmer, Thomas (Archbishop of Canterbury) (1489–1556)	Aslockton
Dean, Christopher (ice-dance champion) (1958–)	Nottingham
Flowers, Wilfred (cricketer) (1856–1926)	Calverton
Fothergill, Watson (architect) (1841–1928)	Mansfield
Larwood, Harold (cricketer) (1904–95)	Nuncargate
Lawrence, D H (writer) (1885–1930)	Eastwood
Lee, Alvin (Graham Barnes) (rock guitarist) (1944–)	Nottingham
Mee, Arthur (writer) (1875–1943)	Stapleford
Owen, Greg (golfer) (1972–)	Mansfield
Pollard, Su (actress) (1949–)	Nottingham
Randall, Derek (cricketer) (1951–)	Retford
Sillitoe, Alan (playwright) (1928–)	Nottingham
Smith, Paul (fashion designer) (1946–)	Beeston
Thompson, William (boxer known as 'Bendigo') (1811–80)	Nottingham
Torvill, Jayne (ice-dance champion) (1957–)	Nottingham
Trease, (Robert) Geoffrey (children's writer) (1909–98)	Nottingham
Westwood, Lee (golfer) (1973–)	Worksop

OXFORDSHIRE

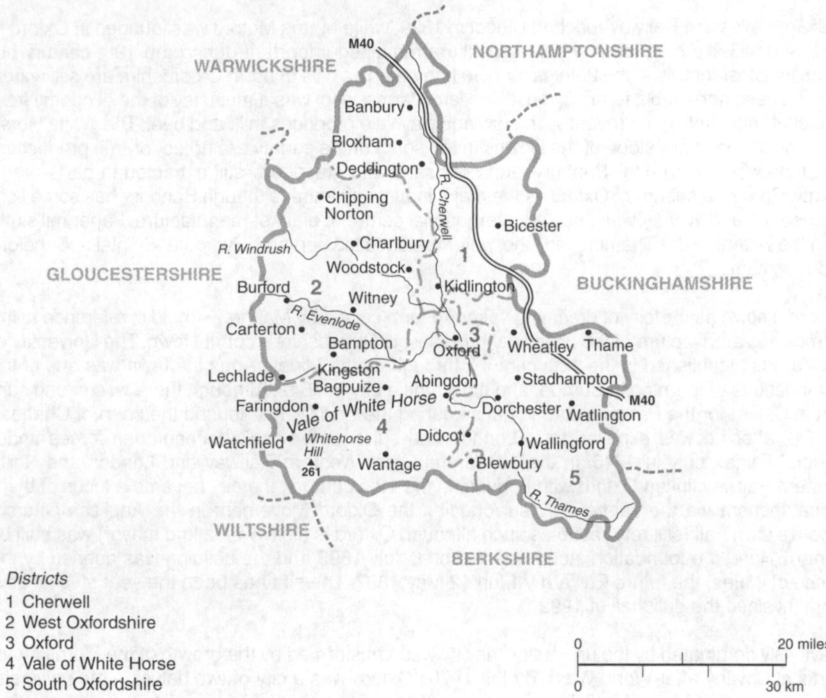
M40
NORTHAMPTONSHIRE
WARWICKSHIRE
Banbury
Bloxham
Deddington
Chipping Norton
R. Cherwell
Bicester
R. Windrush
Charlbury
1
GLOUCESTERSHIRE
Woodstock
Kidlington
BUCKINGHAMSHIRE
Burford
2
Witney
R. Evenlode
Carterton
3
Bampton
Oxford
Wheatley
Thame
Lechlade
Kingston Bagpuize
Abingdon
Stadhampton
M40
Faringdon
Vale of White Horse
Dorchester
Watlington
4
Watchfield
Whitehorse Hill
261
Didcot
Wallingford
Wantage
Blewbury
5
R. Thames
WILTSHIRE
BERKSHIRE
Districts
1 Cherwell
2 West Oxfordshire
3 Oxford
4 Vale of White Horse
5 South Oxfordshire
0
20 miles
0
30 km

Oxfordshire has borders with Berkshire to the south, Wiltshire to the southwest, Gloucestershire to the west, Warwickshire to the northwest, Northamptonshire to the northeast and Buckinghamshire to the east. The Vale of White Horse and parts of South Oxfordshire south of the River Thames are traditionally part of Berkshire but were added to the administrative county in 1974. Abingdon was the county town of Berkshire until Reading replaced it in 1867. Conversely, the Caversham area of Reading is traditionally part of Oxfordshire.

Oxfordshire is located almost entirely within the basin of the River Thames, receiving the rivers Windrush, Evenlode and Cherwell from the north. Bordering the county on the west are the limestone hills of the Cotswolds, while in the southeast it encompasses part of the chalk Chiltern Hills; parts of the Cotswold and Chiltern Areas of Outstanding Natural Beauty lie within the county's boundaries. The river itself flows northeast along the Oxford Clay Vale, turning south at the city of Oxford; afterwards it passes through Goring Gap between the Chilterns and the Berkshire Downs, before winding east and north past Henley-on-Thames into the lower Thames basin.

Many Palaeolithic and Mesolithic artefacts have been recovered from the gravels of the Thames flood-plain, while Neolithic tools and pottery have been found at many places in the county. A number of long barrows and the stone circle known as the Rollright Stones on the Oxfordshire/Warwickshire border also date from the Neolithic period. Dorchester and Alchester (just outside Bicester), situated on the Roman road from Silchester to Watling Street and Towcester, were the most important Roman sites. Subsequent Saxon settlement in the county was concentrated at valley sites along the line of the Thames and its major tributaries, and Oxfordshire was successively part of the Anglo-Saxon kingdoms of Wessex and Mercia. During the 10th and 11th centuries the area was overrun by the Danes. At the time of the Domesday Book (1086), the major centres were Bampton and Oxford itself.

Because the Empress Matilda had her base at Wallingford Castle, Oxfordshire saw action during the 12th century civil war between her and King Stephen. The medieval period is commemorated by numerous ecclesiastical and domestic buildings. Iffley Church, just south of Oxford, is one of the best examples of pure Romanesque style in England; Adderbury, south of Banbury, has a cruciform

Decorated-style church, and that at Minster Lovell is pure Perpendicular in style. During the Civil War Oxford was the Royalist headquarters, and both it and Banbury were besieged by Parliamentary forces.

The Great Western Railway reached Didcot in 1839, while Morris Motors was founded in Oxford in 1912 and MG in Abingdon in 1929. Agriculture remained important during the 19th century but dwindled considerably in the 20th as tourism boomed. The hills of north Oxfordshire are still important for sheep and arable farming, mostly on large farms; wool was a mainstay of the economy from medieval times until quite recently. The lowland clay vale produces milk and beef. The White Horse Vale and the northern slope of the Downs in the south of the county are noted for fruit production. Ironstone was mined near Banbury, and clay, sand and gravel are still extracted in parts of the county. Cowley, a suburb of Oxford, is the major industrial centre, although Banbury has some light engineering and Witney was once an international centre of blanket manufacture. Paper mills utilising the waters of the Thames and Cherwell were once located at Wolvercote, Shiplake, Sandford and Eynsham.

Oxford, known as the 'city of dreaming spires', a term coined by Matthew Arnold in reference to the harmonious architecture of the university buildings, is Oxfordshire's county town. The University of Oxford was established in the 12th century; throughout the Middle Ages the town was one of the major centres of learning in Europe, and it became a city in 1542. Although there was strong support in Oxford for the Parliamentarian cause during the Civil War, it housed the court of Charles I in 1642 after he was expelled from London and surrendered to Parliamentarian forces under General Fairfax only in 1646. In the 1840s, the Great Western Railway and London and North Western Railway linked Oxford with London. In the 19th century, the city became a focus of theological thought via the controversy surrounding the Oxford Movement in the Anglican Church. Oxford's town hall (still referred to as such although Oxford is a city with a lord mayor) was built by Henry T Hare; the foundation stone was laid on 6 July 1893 and the building was opened by the Prince of Wales, the future Edward VII, on 12 May 1897. The site has been the seat of local government since the guildhall of 1292.

Previously dominated by the university, the city was transformed by the growth of the Morris motor works at Cowley after World War I. By the 1970s Oxford was a city of two halves – the university city to the west of Magdalen Bridge and the car town to the east – giving rise to the witticism that 'Oxford is the left bank of Cowley'. Cowley suffered major job losses in the 1980s and 1990s during the decline of British Leyland, but is now producing the successful New Mini for BMW. The city centre is currently undergoing major housing expansion amid controversy that the necessary infrastructure is more for the benefit of tourists than residents.

Oxfordshire	**Population**			**Area**	
Districts	*male*	*female*	*total*	*sq miles*	*sq km*
Cherwell	65,168	66,617	131,785	227	589
Oxford	66,284	67,964	134,248	18	46
South Oxfordshire	63,208	64,980	128,188	262	679
Vale of White Horse	57,506	58,121	115,627	223	578
West Oxfordshire	47,091	48,549	95,640	276	714
Total	299,257	306,231	605,488	1006	2606

Local Attractions and Information

Abingdon Abbey — Abbey Close, Abingdon. A Benedictine monastery founded in AD 675, in honour of the Virgin Mary, by Hean, the nephew of Cissa, viceroy of Centwine, king of the West Saxons. Endowed by successive West Saxon kings, it grew in importance and wealth until its destruction by the Danes during King Alfred's reign. Among its abbots were St Ethelwold, later Bishop of Winchester (954), and Richard of Hendred, for whose appointment the king's consent was obtained in 1262. The last Abbot of Abingdon was Thomas Pentecost (also known as Thomas Rowland), who was among the first to acknowledge the royal supremacy of Henry VIII. The abbey church has long been destroyed but fragments of other buildings still exist, including the gatehouse and the exchequer. The largely 18th century Cosener's House – named after the cuisinier or kitchener, the official responsible for providing food for the abbey – occupies an attractive Thameside position in the abbey grounds.

Administrative headquarters — County Hall, New Road, Oxford OX1 1ND. Tel: 01865 792422.

Alfred's Castle — 9 miles (15km) southwest of Wantage. A small Iron Age hill fort situated close to Ashdown Park (see Ashdown House), 1 mile (1.6km) south of the Ridgeway. The hill fort was established within a series of late Bronze Age linear ditches and much evidence for occupation has been found within it. In the late 1st century AD a Romano-British farmhouse was built inside the abandoned prehistoric enclosure. Victorian antiquaries associated Alfred's Castle with King Alfred's troop movements before his great victory against the Danes at the Battle of Ashdown in 871.

Alice's Shop St Aldate's, Oxford. Located opposite Christ Church, the shop was featured as the Old Sheep Shop in Lewis Carroll's book *Through the Looking-Glass*. Formerly frequented in Victorian times by Alice Liddell, who inspired *Alice's Adventures in Wonderland*, it is now a gift shop.

Ardington House 2½ miles (4km) east of Wantage. The house was built of brick for Edward Clarke in 1720 and designed by Thomas Strong, whose father was one of Sir Christopher Wren's most important master masons. The entrance is dominated by the wooden Imperial Staircase, constructed to an unusual design featuring two flights of stairs that rise to a landing, from where a single flight leads to the first floor. The effect is enhanced by the delicately carved balusters. Since 1939 the house has been the home of the Baring family, founders of the famous merchant bank. Tel: 01235 821566.

Ashdown House 9 miles (15km) southwest of Wantage. Located on the Oxfordshire/Wiltshire border. Also known as Ashdown Park, the 17th century house is famous for its association with Elizabeth of Bohemia (the Winter Queen), sister of Charles I. The Earl of Craven built Ashdown in her honour in 1663; its architect is unknown, but was perhaps William Winde. Nearby are a group of sarsen stones and the hill fort of Alfred's Castle (see separate entry) where King Alfred is thought to have battled the Danes. The house has been owned by the National Trust since 1956. Tel: 01793 762209.

Ashmolean Museum Beaumont Street, Oxford. Attached to the University of Oxford, the Ashmolean Museum of Art and Archaeology is the world's first university museum. Its first building was designed by Sir Christopher Wren in 1678–83 to house a collection of curiosities given to Oxford University in 1677 by Elias Ashmole (1617–92). The collection included antique coins, books, engravings, and geological and zoological specimens, one of which was the stuffed body of the last dodo ever seen in Europe. The museum opened on 24 May 1683, with naturalist Robert Plot as the first keeper. The collection was half a century old by this time, having been founded by John Tradescant (d. 1638) and displayed to the public, first by him and later by his son John (1608–62) in their house at Lambeth, widely known as 'The Ark'. The present building designed by Charles Cockerell dates from 1845; one wing is occupied by the Taylor Institution, the university's modern languages faculty. The main museum contains the bequest of Arthur Evans and his collection of Greek and Minoan pottery. The museum also houses fine collections of Pre-Raphaelite paintings, English silver and majolica pottery. Highlights of the collection include the Anglo-Saxon gold ornament known as the Alfred Jewel, works by Michaelangelo, Raphael, Leonardo da Vinci and Turner, an Arab ceremonial dress owned by Lawrence of Arabia, the death mask of Oliver Cromwell, and the collection of posy rings that supposedly inspired the One Ring in J R R Tolkien's *The Lord of the Rings*. The museum has recently been refurbished and enlarged to cover five floors. Tel: 01865 278000. See also Museum of the History of Science.

Aynhoe Park Aynho, 6 miles (10km) southeast of Banbury. Located on the southern edge of the stone-built village of Aynho and overlooking the Cherwell valley on the Oxfordshire/Northants border. John Cartwright purchased the estate at the turn of the 17th century but the house he built in 1615 was seriously damaged during the Civil War. It was later rebuilt to the design of Edward Marshall, master mason in Charles II's Office of Works and enlarged in Baroque style in 1707 by Thomas Archer. At the beginning of the 19th century, the house was embellished by Sir John Soane; some of the rooms he designed can still be seen. The house is surrounded by formal gardens laid out 1701–14, and a landscape park designed 1760–3 by Capability Brown. The house is no longer open to the public. Tel: 01869 810636.

Bampton Castle Bampton, 5 miles (8km) south of Witney. Quadrangular castle possibly founded in 1315 by Aymer de Valence. Parts of the structure have been incorporated in the later manor house of Ham Court, but the rest has long been demolished.

Banbury Situated 21 miles (34km) north of Oxford, Banbury stands at the junction of two ancient roads: Salt Way and Banbury Lane, which began near Northampton and followed the modern road before running through Banbury's High Street and on towards the Fosse Way at Stow-on-the-Wold, Gloucestershire. In AD 913 a band of Danes, who had settled in Northampton, travelled along Banbury Lane and ravaged north Oxfordshire. The Danes were great traders who established market towns. This is reflected in Banbury's Market Place, its triangular shape being typically Danish. In the 17th century Banbury was home to a large Puritan community, possibly responsible for destroying the town's famous cross (see separate entry). The town is famous for Banbury cakes, which are still available in a number of local bakeries and restaurants. These flat pastries with a spicy currant filling have been made in the area to secret recipes since at least 1586. The shop in Banbury most closely associated with the cakes for many years was known as The Original Cake Shop, in Parsons Street. The building dated to the 17th century and served as a cake shop until it fell into disrepair and was demolished in 1968. Also well known was Betts' Cake Shop at 85 High Street, run by a great-grandson of Betty White who set up The Original Cake Shop. Banbury also features in the description of Slender in Shakespeare's *Merry Wives of Windsor* as 'a Banbury cheese', possibly a cheese made in a very flat shape. The term 'Banbury Tinker' is used to describe a person of good intentions but ultimately useless: a Banbury tinker was said to make three holes in a pot while mending one.

Banbury Castle Founded by Bishop Alexander of Lincoln c.1125–36, and extended into a concentric plan c.1400. The castle was demolished in 1648 and the site is now largely occupied by the Castle Quay shopping precinct.

Banbury Cross Banbury once had three crosses: the High Cross, otherwise known as the Market Cross, situated in Cornhill, just off the Market Place; the Bread Cross, situated at the corner of High Street and Butchers Row; and the White Cross, situated on the western boundary line of the old town borough, at what is now the corner of West Bar Street and Beargarden Road. All are now demolished and nowadays Banbury's only cross lies at the intersection of four major roads – those to Oxford, Warwick and Shipston-on-Stour, and the High Street, which leads to the old heart of the town. It was erected in 1859 to commemorate the marriage of Queen Victoria's eldest daughter, Victoria Adelaide Mary Louisa, to Friedrich Wilhelm of Prussia on 25 January 1858. Of neo-Gothic design, it stands 52ft 6in (16m) high to the top of its gilt cross, with statues of Edward VII, George V and Queen Victoria installed in 1914, in celebration of the coronation of George V in 1911. In April 2005 Princess Anne unveiled a large bronze statue depicting the 'Fyne Lady upon a White Horse' of the nursery rhyme. It stands on the corner of West Bar and South Bar, just yards from the present Banbury Cross. The words of the nursery rhyme are as follows: 'Ride a cock-horse to Banbury Cross, To see a fine lady upon a white horse, With rings on her fingers and bells on her toes, She shall have music wherever she goes.' The nursery rhyme, a favourite with children throughout the English-speaking world, was first seen in print in 1784, although it was known in its current form in 1760, possibly earlier. The 'Fyne' lady is generally thought to be a member of the Fiennes family, ancestors of Lord Saye and Sele, who own Broughton Castle.

Bate Collection St Aldate's, Oxford. A collection of musical instruments, many from medieval times, predominantly for Western classical music. Housed in Oxford University's Faculty of Music, the collection is available for academic study as well as for performances of historical music. Instruments include brass, woodwind, keyboards and percussion, along with a collection of bows. Also part of the collection is the Javanese gamelan kept in the Pitt Rivers Museum Balfour Building at Banbury Road. The collection is named after Philip Bate and includes an archive of his papers. Tel: 01865 276139.

Battles There have been three major battles in Oxfordshire: Chalgrove Field, Cropredy Bridge and Radcot Bridge. See separate table for details.

Blenheim Palace Woodstock, 8 miles (13km) northwest of Oxford. Designed by Sir John Vanbrugh (with considerable help from Nicholas Hawksmoor) and built 1705–22 on monumental scale, Blenheim is the only non-episcopal country house in England to hold the title 'palace'. Its construction was originally intended to be a gift to John Churchill, 1st Duke of Marlborough, from Queen Anne and the nation in gratitude for victory against the French and Bavarians at Blenheim (on the north banks of the river Danube) on 13 August 1704. The palace became the subject of political infighting after the queen's death and Churchill was eventually forced to finance the completion himself. Blenheim is a masterpiece of Baroque architecture. From the imposing vastness of the great hall to the intricate detailing of the state rooms, the interiors beautifully balance the delicate with the awe-inspiring. Collections of portraits, tapestries and an exquisite collection of Boulle furniture grace the individual rooms, while the magnificent Hawksmoor ceilings and stonework by Grinling Gibbons can be witnessed throughout. Set in beautiful parkland of 2100 acres (850ha), landscaped by Capability Brown in the 1760s, Blenheim is surrounded by sweeping lawns, formal gardens and its most outstanding feature, the lake. The birthplace of Sir Winston Churchill, it was designated a UNESCO World Heritage Site in 1987 and today is the home of the 11th Duke of Marlborough. Tel: 08700 602080.

Blowing Stone Kingston Lisle, 5 miles (8km) west of Wantage. A sarsen stone pierced with several holes, located in a garden at the foot of Blowingstone Hill. The stone is reputedly capable of producing a booming sound when one of the holes is blown into. According to legend, this was the means used by King Alfred to summon his Saxon troops for the Battle of Ashdown against the Vikings. The legend supposedly gives the village of Kingston ('King's stone') its name. The stone is mentioned in Thomas Hughes' novel *Tom Brown's Schooldays*, where it is referred to as the 'Blawing Stwun'.

Boars Hill 3 miles (5km) southwest of Oxford. Boars Hill, which offers a good view of the city of Oxford, provided the inspiration and setting for two of Matthew Arnold's most well-known poems, *The Scholar Gipsy* (1853) and *Thyrsis* (1867). The archaeologist Sir Arthur Evans lived on Boars Hill from 1894 until his death in 1941. His house, Youlbury, has since been demolished. Evans built by hand the artificial hill of Jarn Mound, surrounded by a wild garden, to maintain a view of Oxford despite modern development on the hill's summit. The mound is unfortunately now surrounded by houses and the view is obscured by conifers. Evans left part of his estate to the Boy Scouts, who still use Youlbury Camp.

Bodleian Library The main research library of the University of Oxford, second in size only to the British Library and one of five copyright deposit libraries in the UK. It was opened in 1602 with a collection of 2000 books assembled by Thomas Bodley (of Merton College) to replace the library donated to the Divinity School by Humfrey, Duke of Gloucester, brother of Henry V. The library is housed in a number of buildings between Broad Street and Radcliffe Square; these include Duke Humfrey's Library above the Divinity School, the Radcliffe Camera (see separate entry), the Old Schools Quadrangle with its Great Gate and Tower, and the Clarendon Building (see separate entry). The Bodleian also has seven dependent libraries in separate locations in Oxford: the Bodleian Japanese Library, the Bodleian Law Library, the Indian Institute Library, the Oriental Institute Library, Rhodes House Library, the Radcliffe Science Library and the Philosophy Library. One part of the Bodleian Library is contained in the Tower of the Five Orders, so named because it is ornamented, in ascending order, with columns of each of the five orders of classical architecture: Doric, Tuscan, Ionic, Corinthian and Composite.

Bridge of Sighs

New College Lane, Oxford. Located between the Clarendon Building at the end of Broad Street and the Radcliffe Camera, Hertford Bridge is often referred to as the 'Bridge of Sighs' because of its supposed similarity to the famous bridge of the same name in Venice. However, it was never intended to be a replica of the Venetian bridge and many believe it looks more similar to the Rialto Bridge in the same city. The bridge links together the Old and New Quadrangles of Hertford College. Much of its current architecture was designed by Sir Thomas Jackson and completed in 1914.

Bridges, Thames

The following are the major bridges on the Thames in Oxfordshire:

Clifton Hampden Bridge, Clifton Hampden, 3 miles (5km) southeast of Abingdon, was designed by Sir George Gilbert Scott and completed in 1867. The Barley Mow public house, just south of the river, featured in Jerome K Jerome's book *Three Men in a Boat*.

Donnington Bridge, a single-arch concrete bridge in the south of Oxford, completed in 1962 and with a span of 170ft (52m). The starting point for events during Eights Week, the main annual intercollegiate rowing event, and Torpids (the other intercollegiate rowing event) is just south of the bridge.

Folly Bridge, a stone bridge over the Thames on the Abingdon Road, south of Oxford city centre. The current bridge was built 1825–7 by Ebenezer Perry, but there has been a bridge at this location since at least 1085; alchemist Roger Bacon lived and worked close by in the 12th century. The bridge, which was on the Abingdon to Banbury turnpike, was once spanned by a tollbooth tower; the toll house was rebuilt in 1826 and is now Grade II listed. The stretch of river between Folly Bridge and Iffley Lock $1^1/_2$ miles (2.5km) away, is popularly known as the Isis and it is here that the college rowing crews race against each other in the two annual regattas – 'Torpids' in late February and 'Eights' in mid May. Most of the college boathouses are on the north bank which may be approached through nearby Christ Church Meadow.

Goring and Streatley Bridge, linking the twin villages of Goring-on-Thames in Oxfordshire and Streatley in Berkshire, adjacent to Goring Lock. Built in 1923, the current bridge is in two parts: the western part spans the river from Streatley to an island in the river (overlooking the Swan hotel, once owned by Danny La Rue); the eastern section crosses from the island to Goring and overlooks Goring Lock.

Henley Bridge, a five-arched stone bridge at Henley-on-Thames, built in 1786 and linking Hart Street in Henley with Remenham Hill in Berkshire. It replaced an earlier wooden bridge, the foundations of which can be seen in the basement of the Henley Royal Regatta headquarters. Leander Club, the UK's leading rowing club, is based close to the bridge on the Berkshire side. St Mary the Virgin, the main civic church in Henley with its tower dominating the view, is also close by. The sculptures of Isis and Tamesis at the top of the central arch on each side of the bridge are by sculptress Anne Seymour Damer (1748–1828).

Radcot Bridge, Radcot, 3 miles (5km) north of Faringdon, one of three bridges in the hamlet of Radcot, and carrying the A4095 road over the Thames. The main bridge was originally built c.1200 and as such is often claimed to be the oldest on the Thames, although it was substantially rebuilt in 1387 after sustaining major damage in the Battle of Radcot. The Canal Bridge and Pidnell Bridge were built in the 1780s to take the road over a cut of the Thames & Severn Canal.

Sonning Bridge, linking Sonning Eye in Oxfordshire with Sonning in Berkshire. The picturesque brick arched bridge was completed in 1775 to replace a wooden bridge built in 1604. A stone marker at the centre of the bridge is marked 'B I O'; the vertical line indicates the county boundary, which runs down the middle of the river and was once the border between the Anglo-Saxon kingdoms of Wessex and Mercia. It is said that Dick Turpin used the bridge when escaping from Berkshire to Oxfordshire. The bridge is connected with Sonning Eye across the branch of the Thames known as Sonning Backwater via a bridge built in 1986; this replaced an earlier wooden bridge.

Wallingford Bridge The first reference to a bridge across the Thames between Wallingford on the west bank and Crowmarsh Gifford on the east is from 1141, when King Stephen besieged Wallingford Castle. The first stone bridge is believed to have been built by Richard, 1st Earl of Cornwall, the brother of Henry II, who occupied Wallingford Castle in the mid 13th century. It was the main route to Gloucester and South Wales until bridges were built at Abingdon and Burford in 1415. Major repairs were carried out in 1530 using stone from the recently dissolved Holy Trinity Priory, while in 1646 four arches were removed so that a drawbridge could be inserted during the siege of the castle in the Civil War; these were rebuilt in the 1750s. Three arches were reconstructed in 1809 after a flood, and a parapet and balustrade were added. The current bridge is 900ft (274m) long and has 19 arches.

Whitchurch Bridge, linking the villages of Whitchurch-on-Thames in Oxfordshire and Pangbourne in Berkshire. It is one of the few remaining private toll bridges across the Thames, being owned and maintained by the Company of Proprietors of Whitchurch Bridge. The current bridge, dating from 1902, is the third on the site; the first was built in 1792.

Winterbrook Bridge (aka Wallingford Bypass Bridge), linking Winterbrook on the west bank of the Thames and Mongewell on the east bank, was constructed in 1993 as part of a bypass round Wallingford to relieve the single-track Wallingford Bridge. During construction, the remains of a late Bronze Age settlement on a former eyot were found on the west bank of the river; examination of Grim's Ditch, the long earthwork followed by the Ridgeway path on the east bank, carried out at the same time enabled it to be dated to the late Iron Age or early Roman period.

Brightwell Castle

Brightwell-cum-Sotwell, 3 miles (5km) east of Didcot. Built c.1145 by King Stephen as part of a ring of fortifications against the Empress Matilda, who was based at Wallingford Castle. The site was possibly chosen because the king's brother, Prince Henry of Blois (Bishop of Winchester), owner of the manor, thought that Stephen could protect his estate and attack the Empress at the same time. Because the enclosing banks and ditches also surround the ancient parish church, it is thought that the latter was originally erected by the Bishop as a garrison-church. The castle was destroyed by Matilda's son in 1153; a manor house now stands on the site.

Brook Cottage Well Lane, Alkerton, 6 miles (10km) northwest of Banbury. A hillside garden of 4 acres (1.6ha) created since 1964 surrounding a 17th century stone house. Tel: 01295 670303.

Broughton Castle 3 miles (5km) southwest of Banbury. A splendid medieval manor house, Broughton Castle is the family home of Lord and Lady Saye and Sele. There was already a building on the site when Sir John de Broughton built his manor in 1300. It was set on an island surrounded by a 3 acre (1.2ha) moat. In the late 16th century the house was enlarged into an impressive Tudor home, decorated with splendid plaster ceilings, fine panelling and ornate fireplaces. In the 17th century William Fiennes, 8th Lord Saye and Sele, was an opponent of Charles I's attempt to rule without Parliament and refused to take the Oath of Allegiance, after which the castle became a secret meeting place of the king's opponents. However, Fiennes disapproved of the king's execution and removed himself from public life, an act which earned him a pardon after the Restoration in 1660. The groined passage and dining room are the oldest parts of the house; there are also passageways with vaulted ceilings and a staircase leading to the rare 14th century chapel. The great hall has displays of arms and armour from the Civil War and the Fiennes family tree. The Oak Room has Tudor oak panelling from floor to ceiling and an unusual interior porch. Queen Anne's Room commemorates the visit of James I's wife, Queen Anne of Denmark, in 1604. The King's Chamber was used by James I and Edward VII and has a splendid stucco overmantel dating to 1554. Tel: 01295 722547.

Buscot Old Parsonage Buscot, 11 miles (18km) northwest of Wantage. Situated on the bank of the River Thames, the house was built in 1703 of Cotswold stone. It is owned by the National Trust. Tel: 01793 762209.

Buscot Park 10 miles (16km) northwest of Wantage. A late 18th century house containing the Faringdon Collection of paintings (including works by Rembrandt, Reynolds, Murillo, Rossetti and the famous 'Briar Rose' series by Burne-Jones) and fine furniture. The extensive parklands include a walled garden with a pleached hop hornbeam avenue and a water garden by Harold Peto. The property is administered by Lord Faringdon on behalf of the National Trust. Tel: 0845 345 3387.

Chastleton House 5 miles (8km) northwest of Chipping Norton. Opened to the public in 1997 after six years of conservation work, Chastleton dates from 1607, and is one of England's finest and most complete Jacobean houses. The Chastleton estate was once owned by Robert Catesby, one of the Gunpowder Plotters. The rules of modern croquet were codified here in 1865. Owned by the National Trust. Tel: 01608 674355.

Chinnor & Princes Risborough Railway Chinnor, 4 miles (6km) southeast of Thame. A standard gauge heritage railway operating with steam and diesel locomotives for $3^1/_2$ miles (5.5km) between Chinnor and the outskirts of Princes Risborough. The preserved line is part of a former Great Western Railway branch line between Princes Risborough and Watlington, closed to passengers in 1957. Tel: 01844 353535.

Christ Church Cathedral St Aldate's, Oxford. The smallest cathedral in England, the cathedral of the city of Oxford is also the chapel of Christ Church, Oxford University's largest college. The college was founded in 1524 by Cardinal Wolsey on the site of the Augustinian priory of St Frideswide, established in the 9th century where Oxford's patron saint was buried in the 8th century. By the 13th century the site was a major place of pilgrimage. When Cardinal Wolsey began the building of his college, the western end of the building was removed to make space for Tom Quad, the Great Quadrangle of Christ Church, the largest college quad in Oxford, measuring 264ft (80.5m) by 261ft (79.5m).

Christ Church Meadow St Aldate's, Oxford. The famous water-meadow of Christ Church Meadow is a popular walking and picnic spot. Triangular in shape, it is bounded by the River Thames or Isis, the River Cherwell and Christ Church. It provides access to many of the college boathouses which are on an island at the confluence of the two rivers. The lower sections of the meadow, close to the Thames, are grazed by cattle, while sports fields are located on the upper sections. A ferry across the Cherwell lands near Magdalen College School and St Hilda's College. Tel: 01865 276150.

Clarendon Building Broad Street, Oxford. Situated near the Bodleian Library and the Sheldonian Theatre (see separate entries), for many years the building was the home of the Oxford University Press. It was designed by Nicholas Hawksmoor, Christopher Wren's greatest pupil, and built 1711–15 to house the Press's printing operations. The building was financed largely from the proceeds of the *History of the Great Rebellion* by Edward Hyde, 1st Earl of Clarendon, whose money also paid for the building of the Clarendon Laboratory (part of the university's Physics Department). In 1829 the University police took over part of the building as their police station. It only became known as the Clarendon Building after it was adapted by the University for use as a registry in 1832, continuing in this role until the present University Offices were opened in Wellington Square in 1975. The building was then taken over by the Bodleian Library, and now houses its admissions department and the Victoria County History of Oxfordshire.

Cogges Manor Farm Museum Church Lane, Witney. A working museum recreating Oxfordshire rural life in the 19th century, housed in the farm's original Cotswold buildings including a 13th century manor house and Victorian walled kitchen garden. Exhibits in the Barley Barn include an impressive 18th century hand loom, while displays tell the story of blanket manufacturing in Witney, an industry that lasted for over 300 years until the early 21st century. Tel: 01993 772602.

Cosener's House See Abingdon Abbey

Crocker End House Nettlebed, 5 miles (8km) northwest of Henley-on-Thames. Built as a rectory c.1870, this spacious Victorian house was bought by the Duke and Duchess of Kent as a country retreat in December 1989 to replace Anmer Hall, their Norfolk home for the previous 18 years. The house, with its 2 acres (0.8ha) of garden, had previously belonged to Lord Campbell of Eskan, and to the Earl of Arran.

Crowmarsh Gifford Castle See Wallingford Castle

Dangerous Sports Club Established in Oxford in 1973, the Dangerous Sports Club is the acknowledged pioneer of extreme sports. Its founders, David Kirke, Chris Baker and Ed Hulton, first came to public attention by inventing bungee jumping, making the first modern jumps on 1 April 1979 from Clifton suspension bridge (Kirke was the first to jump). They also pioneered hang gliding, microlighting, zorbing, BASE jumping (parachute jumping from fixed objects such as buildings), and a variety of surreal sporting events. *Monty Python* star Graham Chapman was perhaps the most famous member, and he was working on a feature film about the club when he died in 1989.

Day's Lock Little Wittenham, 3 miles (5km) northeast of Didcot. A lock on the River Thames named after the Day family, local Catholic yeomen since the 17th century. A 16th century flash lock in the same location was replaced in 1789 by the first pound lock, built by the Thames Navigation Commissioner. Day's Lock is the main gauging station for the measurement of water flow in the Thames. The World Poohsticks Championships have taken place here annually since 1983.

Deddington Castle Deddington, 17 miles (27km) north of Oxford. Built by Bishop Odo of Bayeux, half-brother of William the Conqueror, as the headquarters of his Oxfordshire estates. William de Chesney, Lord of Deddington, held the castle during the 12th century civil war, but during the struggle between Richard I and his brother Prince John later in the century it was seized by the Crown. The Dive family, descendants of the Chesneys, regained possession in the 13th century and styled themselves 'Lords of Deddington Castle', but by the end of that century the castle was partially demolished and by 1310 there seems to have been little left apart from a chamber and a dovecote. The 8 acres (3ha) of extensive earthworks are now owned by English Heritage. Tel: 01424 775705.

Didcot Railway Centre Station Road, Didcot. Located in and around an old engine shed adjacent to Didcot Parkway railway station, the museum is operated by the Great Western Society and has a comprehensive collection of Great Western Railway locomotives and rolling stock. The site retains many original features including the engine shed itself, turntable pit and coal stage (the turntable itself is from the Southern Railway and was previously sited at Southampton Docks), as well as recreations of a country branch line and station. There is an active programme of rolling stock restoration, including locomotives such as the powerful King class no. 6023, *King Edward II*, constructed in 1930. Tel: 01235 817200.

Ditchley Park Enstone, 5 miles (8km) southeast of Chipping Norton. Built by the 2nd Earl of Litchfield, a member of the Lee family, in 1722 to a design by James Gibbs with interiors by William Kent. It stands on the site of an earlier, timber-framed family house. The house was frequently used at weekends by Sir Winston Churchill during World War II. Tel: 01608 677346.

Dorchester Abbey Dorchester-on-Thames, 5 miles (8km) southeast of Abingdon. The abbey site dates to the early years of English Christianity in AD 635, when the missionary Bishop Birinus, sent from Rome by Pope Honorius I, baptised Cynegils, king of Wessex, possibly in the waters of the River Thame. Cynegils granted Birinus land to found an abbey in what is now the village of Dorchester, enclosed between the River Thames and its tributary the Thame. The abbey was refounded in 1140 as an Augustinian foundation; the existing building was begun in the 12th century, replacing two earlier Saxon cathedrals (some Saxon fabric is still evident in the north wall of the nave). The Norman building was expanded in the 13th century and enriched in the early 14th century when the chancel was added with its wonderful window sculpted with the Tree of Jesse, its stained glass and its exquisite sedilia. The great tower, rebuilt in 1602 but incorporating a 14th century spiral staircase, rises above a lush landscape of willows and flowering water-meadows. Dedicated to St Peter and St Paul, the abbey church is now Dorchester's parish church.

Dragon Hill 1½ miles (2.5km) south of Uffington. A natural chalk hill with an artificial flat top, located on the scarp slope of White Horse Hill just below the Uffington White Horse (see separate entry). According to legend, it was on the hill's summit that St George slew the dragon. A bare patch of chalk, upon which no grass will grow, is purportedly where the dragon's blood spilled.

Eagle and Child St Giles, Oxford. Affectionately known as the 'Bird and Baby'; the group of writers known as the Inklings, and which included C S Lewis and J R R Tolkien, met regularly in this public house to discuss their work, 1939–62.

Friar Park Henley-on-Thames. A 120-room Victorian neo-Gothic mansion built by solicitor and eccentric Sir Frank Crisp and bought by the former Beatle George Harrison in 1970. The extensive gardens and lakes laid out by Crisp feature a range of unusual statuary, including a figure of a monk holding a skillet, with a plaque reading 'Two Holy Friars', in a satire of religion; topping the rock garden was a 30ft (9m) scale model of the Matterhorn, and Crisp's garden was one of the first in Britain to feature garden gnomes. Harrison immortalised the house in his song 'Crackerbox Palace' (his nickname for the mansion, after beatnik poet Lord Buckley's equally eccentric home in California) and was photographed among four garden gnomes for the cover of his classic LP *All Things Must Pass*.

Garsington Manor Garsington, 5 miles (8km) southeast of Oxford. A 17th century house bought in 1915 by socialite Lady Ottoline Morrell. The Morrells restored the house in the 1920s, creating the Italianate garden to designs by architect Philip Tilden. It is now the setting for an annual summer opera season, the Garsington Opera.

Great Coxwell Tithe Barn Great Coxwell, 2 miles (3km) southwest of Faringdon. A large 13th century monastic barn with stone-tiled roof and impressive timber structure, once used for the collection of tithes in the Oxfordshire area. Now owned by the National Trust. Tel: 01793 762209.

Greys Court ½ mile (0.8km) north of Greys Green, 2 miles (3km) northwest of Henley-on-Thames. Situated in the Chiltern Hills, the house and gardens were owned by Sir Francis Knollys, treasurer to

Elizabeth I; Mary Queen of Scots was imprisoned here while Elizabeth was on the throne. The house is mainly Tudor in style; the grounds feature walled gardens, an ornamental vegetable garden, a maze and an ice house. Within the grounds are a medieval fortified tower dating from 1347, the only surviving part of the castle which previously occupied the site, and a Tudor wheelhouse containing a donkey-operated treadmill used for raising water from a well. Now owned by the National Trust. Tel: 01494 755564.

Hambleden Lock — Mill End, 2 miles (3km) north of Henley-on-Thames. A lock and weir on the River Thames owned and managed by the Environment Agency. It is named after the village of Hambleden, 1 mile (1.6km) to the north, and is also next to Hambleden Mill; there has been a lock on the site since at least 1773. The first University Boat Race in 1829 took place between the lock and Henley Bridge and was won by Oxford.

Harcourt Arboretum — See Oxford Botanic Garden

Headington Hill — Headington Road, Oxford. Situated in the east of Oxford, in the suburb of Headington, the hill offers fine views of the spires of Oxford. Headington Hill Hall, built in 1824 for local brewers the Morrell family, stands on the hill; since 1992 the hall has been leased to Oxford Brookes University.

Henley Royal Hegatta — An annual rowing event held on tho River Thames at Henley-on-Thames. It takes place over five days (Wednesday to Sunday) in the first week in July. Races are head-to-head knockout competitions, contested over a course of 1 mile 550 yds (2112m), and regularly attract international crews. The most prestigious event is the Grand Challenge Cup for Men's Eights, which has been awarded since the regatta was first staged in 1839.

Highest point — Whitehorse Hill, above the Vale of White Horse, at 856ft (261m). GR: SU300863.

Holywell Cemetry — St Cross Road, Oxford. Located next to St Cross Church, the cemetery was established in 1847 on land made available by Merton College after the graveyards of Oxford's six parishes became full. It is now a wildlife refuge with many birds (including nesting pheasants) and butterflies, as well as small and larger mammals, including muntjac deer and foxes. Among those buried in the cemetery are authors Kenneth Grahame, Walter Pater and Charles Williams, and theatre critic Kenneth Tynan.

Interesting facts — The relationship between 'town and gown' in Oxford has often been uneasy and **The St Scholastica Day Riot** of 10 February 1355 is one of the more notorious events in the town's history. Following a dispute about beer in the Swindlestock Tavern (now the site of the Abbey Bank on Carfax) between townspeople and two students of Oxford University, the insults exchanged grew into armed clashes between locals and students over the next two days which left 63 scholars and 30 locals dead. The scholars were eventually routed, but the dispute was settled in favour of the university with a special charter. Annually thereafter, on 10 February, the town mayor and councillors had to march bareheaded through the streets and pay to the university a fine of one penny for every scholar killed. The penance ended in 1825 when the mayor refused to take part. The world's first **sub-four minute mile** was run at Iffley Road, Oxford, on 6 May 1954, when Roger Bannister, a 25-year-old medical student wearing the number 41, ran 3min 59.4sec. The high IQ organisation **Mensa** was founded in Oxford in 1946. The name, Latin for table, was chosen to reflect the society's round table nature of equality among its members. **Venetia Phair (née Burney)** (born 1919) was the first person to suggest the name Pluto for the planet discovered by Clyde W Tombaugh in 1930. At the time, she was 11 years old and lived in Oxford. The **Oxford Shoe**, with its plain leather structure and enclosed lacing, has no apparent link to the city of Oxford whatsoever; in fact, the shoe originally came from Scotland where it is referred to as a Balmoral. **Flora Thompson** (1876–1947), best known for her semi-autobiographical *Lark Rise to Candleford* (1945), was born in Juniper Hill, north of Bicester. The story of three closely related Oxfordshire communities – a hamlet, the nearby village and a small market town – brought to life through the childhood memories and youth of Thompson's heroine Laura, *Lark Rise to Candleford* was originally published in three parts as *Lark Rise* (1939), *Over to Candleford* (1941) and *Candleford Green* (1943). Flora spent much of her life as a postmistress, first in Oxfordshire and later in Hampshire and Devon.

Islands — There are 19 named islands in the River Thames in Oxfordshire: **Andersey Island** near Abingdon (GR: SU505965); **Appletree Eyot** near Tilehurst (GR: SU681747); **Clifton Cut** near Long Wittenham (GR: SU545941); **Culham Cut** near Culham (GR: SU503945); **Ferry Eyot**, Temple Combe (GR: SU779808); **Fiddler's Island** near Oxford (GR: SP500072); **Fiddler's Elbow** near Kennington, the largest of a group near Sandford Lock; **Folly Bridge Island** (GR: SP513055); **Handbuck Eyot** near Lower Shiplake (GR: SU778802); **Lock Wood Island** near Nuneham Courtenay; **Mesopotamia** see separate entry; **Nags' Head Island** near Abingdon (GR: SU499968); **Osney Island** near Oxford (GR: SP502061); **Phillimore Island** near Lower Shiplake (GR: SU771783); **Poplar Eyot** near Temple Combe (GR: SU779805); **Poplar Island** near Tilehurst (GR: SU680748); **Queen Elizabeth Island** near Blenheim Palace (GR: SP441165); **Rod Eyot** near Henley-on-Thames (GR: SU768821); **Rose Isle** near Kennington – formerly known as St Michael's Island (GR: SP526025); **Sonning Eye** near Sonning Bridge, based around a small gravel mound surrounded by the river's flood plain (GR: SU754757); **Trout Inn Island**, near Wolvercote (GR: SP485092).

Kidlington Airport — See Oxford Airport

Kingston Bagpuize House — Kingston Bagpuize, 5 miles (8km) west of Abingdon. A 1660s manor house remodelled in the early 1700s in red brick with stone facings. The interior features a cantilevered staircase and finely proportioned panelled rooms with some fine furniture and pictures. Set in mature parkland, the gardens contain a notable collection of plants including rare trees, shrubs, perennials and bulbs. Tel: 01865 820259.

Le Manoir aux Quat' Saisons	Church Road, Great Milton, 8 miles (13km) south of Oxford. The two-Michelin starred restaurant was created in 1984 by Raymond Blanc, acknowledged as one of the finest chefs in the world. It is the only country house hotel in the UK to achieve and sustain two Michelin stars and the Relais and Chateaux Purple Shield. Tel: 01844 278881.
Logic Lane Bridge	Logic Lane, Oxford. A small covered bridge at the High Street end of Logic Lane, within University College. The bridge was designed by Oxford architect Harry Wilkinson Moore and completed in 1904. It links the older Radcliffe Quad buildings with the newer Durham Buildings, built in 1903.
Magdalen Bridge	Located east of Oxford city centre, the bridge spans the River Cherwell from the High Street in the west to The Plain in the east. It is situated next to Magdalen College, after which it is named. The present elegant stone bridge was designed by John Gwynn of Shrewsbury; completed in 1782, it was widened in 1882. Each year early on 1 May it was a traditional gathering point for large crowds to enjoy the city's May Morning celebrations; however, after a number of students sustained injuries jumping off the bridge in recent years, it was closed on that day from 2006. As well as Magdalen College and its beautiful tower, also close by are the Oxford Botanic Garden and Magdalen College School.
Mapledurham House	Mapledurham, 10 miles (16km) southeast of Wallingford. Situated beside the Thames northwest of Reading on the Oxfordshire/Berkshire border, the estate has been home to the Blount family, Catholic recusants in the 17th century, for over 500 years. The red-brick Elizabethan house, built 1588–1612 by Sir Michael Blount, Lieutenant of the Tower of London, and his son Sir Richard, features impressive oak staircases and original plaster ceilings; on display are collections of portraits and furniture. A private chapel in Strawberry Hill Gothick was added in 1797. The estate contains the last working corn and grist mill on the River Thames, dating from the 15th century. Tel: 01189 723350.
Martyrs' Memorial	St Giles, Oxford. An imposing stone monument designed by Sir George Gilbert Scott, and completed in 1843. Situated at the intersection of St Giles, Magdalen Street and Beaumont Street, outside Balliol College, it commemorates the 16th century Oxford Martyrs, executed during the reign of Mary I. The inscription on the base reads: 'To the Glory of God, and in grateful commemoration of His servants, Thomas Cranmer, Nicholas Ridley, Hugh Latimer, Prelates of the Church of England, who near this spot yielded their bodies to be burned, bearing witness to the sacred truths which they had affirmed and maintained against the errors of the Church of Rome, and rejoicing that to them it was given not only to believe in Christ, but also to suffer for His sake; this monument was erected by public subscription in the year of our Lord God, MDCCCXLI'.
Mesopotamia	A narrow island about 2400ft (730m) long by 90ft (27.5m) wide, located between the upper and lower levels of the River Cherwell and forming part of the University Parks. The name Mesopotamia in Greek means 'between the rivers' and originally referred to the area between the rivers Tigris and Euphrates in present-day Iraq. GR: SP525069.
Milton Manor House	Milton, 2 miles (3km) northwest of Didcot. A tall classically inspired mid 17th century red-brick house. In 1764 the property was purchased by Bryant Barrett, lace maker to George III. The next year he commissioned Stephen Wright, master mason in the Office of Works, to add wings and provide further service accommodation in outbuildings to the north. The wings contained a new Catholic chapel and library, but because Catholicism was still officially banned in England the exterior was kept deliberately plain. The interiors, in contrast, were decorated in elaborate Gothic style. From this period onwards there have been no major alterations to the house and the property has passed by descent to the present owner, Anthony Mockler-Barrett. Tel: 01488 71036.
Minster Lovell Hall & Dovecote	Minster Lovell, 3 miles (5km) west of Witney. The house was built in the 1440s on the banks of the River Windrush by Lord William Lovell. According to legend, a skeleton discovered in an underground vault in 1708 was that of his descendant, Francis Lovell, a supporter of the Yorkist cause in the Wars of the Roses, who it was said had gone into hiding after the defeat of Richard III at the Battle of Bosworth. The house was partly demolished in the mid 18th century; the substantial ruins are now in the care of English Heritage. Nearby is an almost intact medieval dovecote. Tel: 01424 775705.
Modern Art Oxford	Pembroke Street, Oxford. An art gallery established in 1969 at Oxford University and known until 2002 as the Museum of Modern Art, Oxford. Dedicated to changing exhibitions of modern and contemporary art, photography and other non-traditional media, it is a leading space outside London for contemporary art. Tel: 01865 722733.
Moreton Castles	Church Lane, South Moreton, 2 miles (3km) southeast of Didcot. The village of South Moreton contains the remains of two castles. The earlier, located next to the church, is a Norman castle dating to the late 11th century and presumably intended for either William Lovett or Humphrey Visdeloup, who owned manors in the parish. The irregular circular mound is encircled with a trench, while the Mill Brook acts as a moat. It may have never been finished. The later castle stands to the north; surrounding a manor house that may date back to the 12th century are the extensive remains of the moat of a siege castle of King Stephen's reign, thought to have been one of three (along with Brightwell and Crowmarsh Gifford) built to keep in check the forces of the Empress Matilda, whose headquarters was at Wallingford during the 12th century civil war.
Museum of the History of Science	Broad Street, Oxford. A collection of historic scientific instruments housed in the world's oldest surviving purpose-built museum, constructed in 1683 to house Elias Ashmole's collection (see Ashmolean Museum). The building became known as the Old Ashmolean Building (to distinguish it from the Ashmolean Museum) and was the world's first museum to open to the public. Tel: 01865 277280.
Nuffield Place	1¼ miles (2km) northwest of Nettlebed, 6 miles (10km) northwest of Henley-on-Thames. The former home of William Morris, Lord Nuffield, founder of Morris Motors and benefactor of numerous medical and educational foundations. Set in beautiful wooded surroundings high in the

Chilterns near Henley-on-Thames, the house was built in 1914. Still containing most of the furnishings owned by Lord and Lady Nuffield, and with several rooms decorated in 1930s style, it is a rare survival of a complete middle-class home and garden of the 1930s. Tel: 01491 641224.

Otmoor 5 miles (8km) northeast of Oxford. Also known as Ot Moor. Located between Oxford and Bicester, this area of reedbeds and wet meadowland covering 400 acres (160ha) around the River Ray has been an RSPB reserve since 1997. It is visited in winter by numerous wildfowl including teal and wigeon, and provides summer breeding for species including lapwings and redshank.

Oxfam Founded in 1942 as the Oxford Committee for Famine Relief, the response by a group of Quakers, social activists and academics in Oxford to the distress caused in Nazi-occupied Greece by a British blockade. Britain's largest aid agency opened its first shop in Oxford's Broad Street in 1948 and officially changed its name to Oxfam in 1965.

Oxford Airport 1/4 mile (0.4km) northwest of Kidlington, 6 miles (10km) north of Oxford. A small private airport, the only civil airport in Oxfordshire, specialising in general and business aviation, and home to the largest air training school in Europe. It was originally established in 1935 by Oxford City Council as a municipal airport, but became established as a centre for aviation education, charter and maintenance facilities following its use by the RAF during World War II. In 1981 the freehold was sold by the council and is now owned by BBA Group plc. It has a 1695 yd (1552m) main runway. Tel: 01865 290710.

Oxford Botanic Garden Rose Lane, Oxford. The Oxford University Botanic Garden is the oldest such garden in Britain; it was established with an endowment from Sir Henry Danvers in 1633 and the walls still stand today, as does an English yew planted in 1645. The Harcourt Arboretum, located at Nuneham Courtenay, 6 miles (10km) south of Oxford, was established in 1835 and became part of the university in 1963. It occupies part of a park designed by Capability Brown. Tel: 01865 286690.

Oxford Brookes University The history of the university began in 1865 with the foundation of the Oxford School of Art. In 1891 the school became a subsidiary of Oxford City Technical School, and in 1934 the Technical School and the School of Art were fully merged to form the Oxford Schools of Technology, Art and Commerce. John Brookes, a committed educationalist, was appointed as its principal; in 1949 Brookes established a permanent site for the college in Headington. In 1970 the College of Technology, as it was now called, became Oxford Polytechnic and in 1992 it was awarded university status; the name Oxford Brookes University was chosen in honour of John Brookes. Its main campus remains at Headington; it also has campuses at Wheatley, southeast of the city, and Harcourt Hill to the west. Tel: 01865 484848.

Oxford Canal A 78 mile (130km) narrow canal linking Oxford with Coventry via Banbury and Rugby. It connects with the River Thames at Oxford, with the Grand Union Canal at the villages of Braunston and Napton-on-the-Hill, and with the Coventry Canal at Hawkesbury Junction just outside Coventry.

Oxford Castle Castle Street, Oxford. Built by Norman baron Robert D'Oyly in 1071, originally as a stone motte and bailey known as St George's Tower; a 50ft (15m) high surrounding wall with towers was added in the 12th century. It was the home of the Empress Matilda in 1141 when it came under siege by King Stephen. She is said to have escaped from the castle by being lowered over the walls, supposedly dressed in white as camouflage in the snow (see also Wallingford Castle). The site was used as a prison from the 17th century and in 1888 became HM Prison Oxford; it was featured in this guise in *The Italian Job* (1969) and the television series *Inspector Morse*. The tower and motte still remain; the prison was closed in 1996 and redeveloped as a shopping and museum complex, officially reopened by Queen Elizabeth II on 5 May 2006.

Oxford Cathedral See Christ Church Cathedral

Oxford Movement A 19th century Christian movement that sought to repair the divisions between the Anglican and Roman Catholic churches in England by accepting their common origins in the early Church. The earliest and most vigorous expression of Anglo-Catholicism, it is so named because its leading figures – John Henry Newman, John Keble and Edward Pusey – were all fellows of Oriel College, Oxford. Adherents were also known as Puseyites or rather less disparagingly as Tractarians, the latter because they published their views in a series of papers called *Tracts for the Times* (1833–41). The last of these, no. 90, by Newman, caused a public outcry with its argument that the Thirty-Nine Articles of the Church of England were compatible with Roman Catholic doctrine. The movement's influence was apparent in increased ritual, ornately decorated Victorian churches and the establishment of Anglican monastic communities.

Oxford University Oxford is the oldest university in the English-speaking world and lays claim to nine centuries of continuous existence. The university is first mentioned in 12th century records; the earliest colleges were established in the 13th century, at a time when European scholars were rediscovering the writings of Greek philosophers. These writings challenged European ideology, inspiring scientific discoveries and advancements in the arts as society began seeing itself in a new way. Traditionally, the university wielded considerable influence in matters of national importance. In 1222 it established St George's Day (23 April) as a national holiday and from 1603 to 1950 the university electorate, consisting of graduates, elected two members to the House of Commons. Today the university is an internationally renowned centre for teaching and research attracting students and scholars from around the globe, with almost a quarter of students from overseas. More than 130 nationalities are represented among a student population of over 19,000. There are 39 official colleges of the university and seven Permanent Private Halls founded by various Christian denominations. St Hilda's remained a women-only college until October 2008, when the first male students were admitted. The three Oxford terms are Michaelmas (Oct–Dec), Hilary (Jan–Mar) and Trinity (Apr–Jun). Hilary Term begins on the first Sunday after the feast day of St Hilary of Poitiers (13 January) and the other terms are dated from this day. The 39 colleges with their founding dates are: **All Souls (1438)**, High Street. Tel: 01865 279379; **Balliol (1263)**,

Broad Street. Tel: 01865 277777; **Brasenose (1509)**, Radcliffe Square. Tel: 01865 277830; **Christ Church (1546)**, St Aldates. Tel: 01865 286573; **Corpus Christi (1517)**, Merton Street. Tel: 01865 276700; **Exeter (1314)**, Turl Street. Tel: 01865 279600; **Green (1979)**, Woodstock Road. Tel: 01865 274770; **Harris Manchester (1786)**, Mansfield Road. Tel: 01865 271011; **Hertford (1874)**, Catte Street. Tel: 01865 279400, **Jesus (1571)**, Turl Street. Tel: 01865 279700; **Keble (1868)**, Parks Road. Tel: 01865 272727, **Kellogg (1990)**, Wellington Square. Tel: 01865 274300; **Lady Margaret Hall (1878)**, Norham Gardens. Tel: 01865 274300; **Linacre (1962)**, St Cross Road. Tel: 01865 271650; **Lincoln (1427)**, Turl Street. Tel: 01865 279800; **Magdalen (1458)**, High Street. Tel: 01865 276000; **Mansfield (1886)**, Mansfield Road. Tel: 01865 270999; **Merton (1264)**, Merton Street. Tel: 01865 276310; **New (1379)**, Holywell Street. Tel: 01865 279555; **Nuffield (1937)**, New Road. Tel: 01865 278500; **Oriel (1326)**, Oriel Square. Tel: 01865 276555; **Pembroke (1624)**, St Aldates. Tel: 01865 276444; The **Queen's (1340)**, High Street. Tel: 01865 279120; **Somerville (1879)**, Graduate House, Woodstock House. Tel: 01865 270600; **St Anne's (1952)**, Woodstock Road. Tel: 01865 274800; **St Antony's (1950)**, Woodstock Road. Tel: 01865 284700**; St Catherine's (1962)**, Manor Road. Tel: 01865 271700; **St Cross (1965)**, St Giles. Tel: 01865 278490; **St Edmund Hall (1278)**, Queens Lane. Tel: 01865 279000; **St Hilda's (1938)**, Cowley Place. Tel: 01865 276884; **St Hugh's (1886)**, St Margaret's Road. Tel: 01865 274900; **St John's (1555)**, St Giles. Tel: 01865 277300; **St Peter's (1929)**, New Inn Hall Street. Tel: 01865 278900; **Templeton (1965)**, Kennington Road. Tel: 01865 422737; **Trinity (1554)**, Broad Street. Tel: 01865 279900; **University (1249)**, High Street. Tel: 01865 276602; **Wadham (1612)**, Parks Road. Tel: 01865 277900; **Wolfson (1966)**, Linton Road. Tel: 01865 274100; **Worcester (1714)**, Walton Street. Tel: 01865 278300. The seven Permanent Private Halls are: **Blackfriars (1921)**, St Giles. Tel: 01865 278413; **Campion Hall (1896)**, Brewer Street. Tel: 01865 286100; **Greyfriars (1910)**, Iffley Road. Tel: 01865 243694; **Regent's Park (1810)**, Pusey Street. Tel: 01865 288123; **St Benet's Hall (1897)**, St Giles. Tel: 01865 280556; **St Stephen's House (2003)**, Marston Street. Tel: 01865 247874; **Wycliffe Hall (1877)**, Banbury Road. Tel: 01865 274200.

Oxford University Parks — More normally the University Parks or just The Parks, a 70 acre (28ha) area of parkland northeast of Oxford city centre. It boasts beautiful gardens, large sports fields, and rare and exotic plants. The Rainbow Bridge (formally known as High Bridge), located within The Parks, is a curved footbridge over the River Cherwell, constructed in 1923–4 of concrete in the shape of a rainbow. The work was carried out as part of a project for the unemployed.

Parks, The — See Oxford University Parks

Peckwater Quadrangle — Christ Church, Oxford. An 18th century quadrangle, known as 'Peck' to undergraduates. It is located on the site of a medieval inn, which was run by the Peckwater family.

Philberds Manor — East Hanney, 7 miles (11km) northwest of Didcot. The manor house has a royal heritage, both Edward III and Richard II being past owners. The first owner was Hugh de St Philbert in the 14th century. It was surrendered to Edward III by Sir John Philbert, while Richard II gave it to his half-brother Sir John Holland. In October 2006 a fire at the manor caused substantial damage.

Pitt Rivers Museum — South Parks Road, Oxford. Housing Oxford University's archaeological and anthropological collections, the museum was founded in 1884 by General Augustus Pitt Rivers, who donated his collection of 18,000 archaeological and ethnographic objects to the university on condition that a museum be built to house them and a permanent lecturer in anthropology appointed. The museum retains its original thematic layout – inspired by Pitt Rivers' interest in the evolution of human culture – and handwritten labels. A research annexe completed in 2007 now adjoins the museum. Tel: 01865 270927.

Port Meadow — Walton Well Road, Oxford. A large area of common land to the north and west of Oxford covering 440 acres (178ha). An ancient area of grazing land, still used for the pasturing of horses, it has never been ploughed. It lies between Jericho and Wolvercote on the east bank of the River Thames, with the suburb of North Oxford further to the east. An important remnant of watermeadow, flooding during the winter months and attracting large numbers of migrating birds, it is a designated Site of Special Scientific Interest. There are also Bronze Age round barrows and traces of an Iron Age settlement.

Priory Cottages — Mill Street, Steventon, 4 miles (6km) south of Abingdon. Former monastic buildings, now converted into two houses. South Cottage contains the great hall of the original Benedictine priory, endowed by Henry I as a dependent house of the abbey of Bec in Normandy. Now owned by the National Trust. Tel: 01793 762209.

Radcliffe Camera — Radcliffe Square, Oxford. The drum-shaped Radcliffe Camera, topped with a circular dome, is one of the city's most distinctive landmarks. The building (camera means simply 'room') was built 1737–49 in Palladian style with a bequest of £40,000 from Dr John Radcliffe, the royal physician. The design was by James Gibbs, appointed as architect after winning a competition, although his plans drew heavily on work by Nicholas Hawksmoor who had earlier suggested the building's shape. Gibbs was also responsible for the Church of St Martin-in-the-Fields, Trafalgar Square, London. Originally the library in the Radcliffe Camera held both scientific and general books, but those collections were gradually moved to other university libraries, so that today the Camera functions as the main reading room of the Bodleian Library. The finished building holds 600,000 books in rooms beneath Radcliffe Square. The building is not open to the public.

RAF Brize Norton — Carterton, 7 miles (11km) southwest of Witney. Opened in 1937 as a training base, Brize Norton is now the RAF's largest airbase and home to its heavy transport aircraft, the Boeing C17 Globemaster, and its Lockheed Tristar and Vickers VC10 tankers. Tel: 01993 842551.

Rainbow Bridge — See Oxford University Parks

River and Rowing Museum — Mill Meadows, Henley-on-Thames. Housed in a building designed by modernist architect David Chipperfield and awarded the title of Building of the Year by the Royal Fine Art Commission in

1999, the museum's three main themed galleries are dedicated to the non-tidal River Thames, the international sport of rowing and the local town of Henley-on-Thames. The museum was also UK National Heritage Museum of the Year in 1999. Tel: 01491 415600.

Rivers

The **Cherwell** is a major tributary of the River Thames. Its general course is north–south and the distance from its source to the Thames is about 40 miles (64km). It flows from Hellidon through Northamptonshire for 10 miles (16km) before passing into Oxfordshire for the remainder of its journey to Oxford, where it joins the Thames.

The **Cole** is a tributary of the Thames which flows through Wiltshire and Oxfordshire, forming the border between the two counties.

The **Evenlode** rises near Moreton-in-Marsh in the Cotswolds and flows southeast past Stow-on-the-Wold, Charlbury, Bladon and Eynsham, joining the Thames 3 miles (5km) northwest of Oxford. The river was immortalised in verse by Hilaire Belloc, but parts of his 'perfect' and 'tender' waterway, his 'lovely river, all alone', have since been scarred by dredging.

Thame – see Buckinghamshire

Thames – see London. The river is known as the Isis as it flows through Oxford, possibly a contraction of its Latin name, *Tamesis*.

The **Windrush** rises in Gloucestershire, northeast of Taddington, flowing south and then southeast through the Cotswold villages of Guiting Power, Temple Guiting, Ford and Cutsdean, and passing through Bourton-on-the-Water and Windrush. It then passes into Oxfordshire, winding through Burford, Witney, Ducklington and Standlake before meeting the Thames at Newbridge, a course of 46 miles (73km). It is host to several species of fish, including trout, grayling, perch, chub, roach and dace.

Rollright Stones

2 miles (3km) northwest of Chipping Norton. A complex of megalithic monuments situated on the Oxfordshire/Warwickshire border, and consisting of three separate sites. The **King's Men**, 70 closely spaced stones that form a stone circle 108ft (33m) in diameter, are set on top of a circular bank with an entrance to the southeast marked by two portal stones. The site is unexcavated but has been dated to the late Neolithic or early Bronze Age. It was restored in 1882. The **King Stone**, a single, weathered monolith, 8ft (2.4m) high by 5ft (1.5m) wide, stands 250ft (76m) east of the King's Men. It has been claimed that the King Stone was once aligned with the centre of the King's Men circle and the star Capella as it rose in the sky. However, material found beneath the stone during excavations in 1982 have placed the date of its erection at c.1800 BC, later than the other sites; the King Stone is more likely to have been a marker stone serving a now-destroyed cairn burial site. The **Whispering Knights**, $1/4$ mile (0.4km) east of the King's Men, are the remnants of the of a Neolithic portal burial chamber. The four surviving upright stones form a chamber 21 sq ft (2 sq m) in area around a fifth recumbent stone, probably the collapsed roof. When William Stukeley visited the site in 1764, he also noted the remains of a round barrow. There are many tales and legends associated with the stones, perhaps the most popular being that it is impossible to count them accurately.

Rousham House and Gardens

7 miles (11km) west of Bicester. A Jacobean country house built in 1635 by Sir Robert Dormer and still in the ownership of his descendants. Rousham is the purest existing example of an Augustan landscape garden, a redesign by William Kent of a more formal garden created by Charles Bridgeman in the 1720s. It is peopled with statues recreating ancient Rome, depicting scenes such as the mauling of a horse by a lion and a gladiator dying with restrained agony. Within the woods is the Venus Vale, with statues of Pan, a faun, and Venus, from whom Caesar claimed descent; in another glade, a temple overlooks the River Cherwell, the waters of which are utilised in a series of pools and cascades linked by rills flowing in stone channels. The terrace overlooking the river is named the Praeneste after the ancient temple complex in the modern town of Palestrina outside Rome. Tel: 01869 247110.

Rycote Chapel

3 miles (5km) southwest of Thame. A 15th century chapel with original furnishings, built by Richard Quartermain of Rycote Palace and used by most of the Tudor and Stuart monarchs on their visits to the Rycote estate. The palace no longer exists, although part of its former outbuildings have been converted into a private house. Now in the care of English Heritage. Tel: 01424 775705.

Sackler Library

St John Street, Oxford. Located to the rear of the Ashmolean Museum, the Sackler Library was opened on 24 September 2001 to replace Oxford University's former Ashmolean Library. Its holdings of classical, art history and archaeological works incorporate the collections of four older libraries: the Ashmolean, the Classics Lending Library, the Eastern Art Library, and the History of Art Library. It was founded with a substantial donation from philanthropist and pharmaceuticals millionaire Dr Mortimer Sackler. Tel: 01865 288190.

St Ebbe's Church

Pennyfarthing Place, Oxford. An Anglican church in the conservative Evangelical tradition in the centre of Oxford, behind Pembroke College. The current building dates to 1880 but there has been a church on the site since 1005, making St Ebbe's the earliest known church in Oxford.

St Giles' Church

Woodstock Road, Oxford. A 12th century church originally situated outside the city walls of Oxford and consecrated in 1200 by Bishop Hugh of Lincoln.

Sheldonian Theatre

Broad Street, Oxford. Erected 1664–8 to a design by Sir Christopher Wren from funds donated by Gilbert Sheldon (1598–1677), Warden of All Souls College, Bishop of London and Archbishop of Canterbury and Chancellor of the University of Oxford. One of Wren's first works, it was intended to provide a secular venue for the university's graduation ceremonies, previously held in St Mary's Church; this is still its primary purpose today. Its spectacular painted ceiling by Robert Streater, dating from 1670, has recently been restored. Tel: 01865 277299.

Shirburn Castle

7 miles (11km) northeast of Wallingford. A fortified manor house built in 1378 in brick with four towers and a gatehouse and surrounded by a moat. It is similar in design to Bodiam Castle in

Sussex, which was built a few years later. The castle was turned into a grand house in the 17th century and has since been further modified; the seat of the Earls of Macclesfield since the early 18th century, it currently stands empty.

Shotover Hill Country Park 2 miles (3km) east of Oxford. Part of a former royal forest, this area of grassland and heathland to the east of Headington rises to 561ft (171m) above sea level. Part of the hill has been designated a Site of Special Scientific Interest for its heathland flora and fauna, including over 100 bee and wasp species.

Sport

football — **Oxford United** were founded in 1893 as Headington and changed their name to Oxford United in 1960. The club was elected to the Football League when Accrington Stanley folded in 1962, reaching the First Division in the 1980s and winning the League Cup in 1986 under the ownership of Robert Maxwell, but lost its League place in 2006. The U's traditional colours are yellow and black and they play at Kassam Stadium, their home since 2001 after 76 years at the Manor Ground. Tel: 01865 337500.

greyhound racing — **Oxford**, Sandy Lane, Cowley. The 395m track was built in 1926 but has recently been modernised. Major events held at the stadium include the Cesarewitch. Tel: 01865 778222.

Stonor — 4 miles (6km) northwest of Henley-on-Thames. Owned by Lord and Lady Camoys, Stonor is situated in a valley in the Chiltern Hills and has been the home of the Catholic Stonor family for more than eight centuries. The house, with its warm red-brick Georgian façade, has its origins in the 12th century and has medieval and Tudor architectural features. The Jesuit martyr Edmund Campion took refuge in the house in the 1580s, and the ancient family Catholic chapel is situated alongside the house. Nearby is the site of a prehistoric stone circle. To the rear of the house a hillside walled garden affords commanding views of the surrounding wooded deer park. Tel: 01491 638587.

Tom Brown's School Museum — Uffington, 6 miles (10km) west of Wantage. A small volunteer-run museum housed in a former schoolroom, built in 1617 for '12 worthy boys' of the village and described in the opening chapters of Thomas Hughes' *Tom Brown's Schooldays.* There are photographs and mementoes of Hughes and John Betjeman, who both lived and wrote in the village, as well as displays relating to the evolution of the village of Uffington and its connection with the famous White Horse (see separate entry) cut into the hillside above the village.

Tom Quad — See Christ Church Cathedral

26A East St Helen Street — Abingdon. One of the best-preserved 15th century dwellings in Oxfordshire. Originally a merchant's hall house, its features include an early oak ceiling, traceried windows and fireplaces, and a remarkable domestic wall painting. The remains of a 17th century boy's doublet found in the roof during restoration work are on display. Tel: 01865 242918.

Uffington Castle — 1½ miles (2.5km) south of Uffington, 7 miles (11km) west of Wantage. The remains of an early Iron Age hill fort close to the Oxfordshire/Berkshire border. It covers 8 acres (3.2ha) and is surrounded by two earth banks separated by a ditch with an entrance at the eastern end. Excavations have indicated that it was probably built in the 7th or 8th century BC and continued to be occupied throughout the Iron Age.

Uffington White Horse — 2 miles (3km) south of Uffington, 7 miles (11km) west of Wantage. A highly stylised chalk figure 374ft (110m) long, cut out of the turf on the upper slopes of Uffington Castle (see separate entry). It has been dated to c.1000 BC. The hill upon which the horse (sometimes identified as a dragon) is situated is called White Horse Hill and the hills immediately surrounding it, the White Horse Hills. The site is now maintained by the National Trust. See also Dragon Hill.

Wallingford Castle — Castle Lane, Wallingford. Norman motte and bailey castle erected by Robert D'Oyly 1067–71, with stonework added in the 12th century. D'Oyly's daughter married Brian FitzCount, a leading supporter of the Empress Matilda in her struggle with her cousin, Stephen, for the English throne. He was one of only two landed lords immediately to join her cause and the castle became one of her main strongholds in the south of England. FitzCount kept a special prison at the castle, naming it the 'Cloere Brian' after a bag for holding a hammer, since the Royalist commander, William Martel (whose surname means 'hammer'), was imprisoned and tortured there until his family purchased his release. In 1141, Matilda herself made a daring escape from her besieged headquarters at Oxford Castle to Wallingford, slipping out at night and abseiling down the castle walls accompanied by only three loyal knights. Dressed in white, they made their way through the snow-covered countryside, crossed the frozen Thames on foot at Abingdon, then proceeded by horse to Wallingford. The castle was subsequently besieged three times in an attempt to check its constant raids on the lands of King Stephen's supporters. Before the second siege, the royal forces built a castle across the river in Crowmarsh Gifford to use as a base. However, the third siege in 1152 proved the most serious threat. The king's men took the bridge and the town, besieging the castle for a year before Matilda's son Henry, Duke of Normandy, arrived to relieve the garrison. Peace terms were afterwards agreed and the two sides withdrew, a meeting which eventually led to the signing of the Treaty of Wallingford at the castle and an end to the civil war, as Henry (later Henry II) was accepted as Stephen's heir. The hated Piers Gaveston, favourite of Edward II, was made Lord Wallingford in 1307 and given the castle; he held a magnificent tournament here which all the nobles of the land were obliged to attend, despite their loathing of him. After Gaveston's execution in 1312, the king gave the castle to his wife, Queen Isabella. In 1335 it was granted to Edward, the Black Prince, and became his principal residence. His wife Joan, 'the Fair Maid of Kent', died of a broken heart at Wallingford when her son, Richard II, condemned his half-brother, John Holland, to death for the accidental murder of a court favourite, although Holland was later reprieved. In 1381 Richard of Wallingford, the castle's constable, was one of Wat Tyler's deputies during the Peasants' Revolt. 'Fair Katherine', queen of Henry V, retired

	to Wallingford after her husband's death and her son, Henry VI, was educated here; and it was also at the castle that the queen was seduced by his squire, Owen Tudor, whose father was a cousin of Owain Glyndwr, Prince of Wales; their grandson was eventually to take the throne as Henry VII. During the the Wars of the Roses, Henry VI's wife, Queen Margaret, was imprisoned at the castle. Wallingford was the last Royalist stronghold to surrender during the Civil War, following the surrender of Thomas Blagge after a siege conducted by Thomas Fairfax, and Cromwell ordered it to be destroyed in 1652. A large Gothic house built on the site in 1837 was demolished in 1972. The motte is still visible, but there are few other remains except those of the 16th century Collegiate Church of St Nicholas, which once stood within the castle walls.
Waterperry Gardens	3 miles (5km) northeast of Wheatley, 7 miles (11km) east of Oxford. The 8 acre (3ha) gardens, famous as the location of a horticultural school for women founded by Beatrix Havergal in the 1930s, boast spectacular 330ft (100m) herbaceous borders. Among the gardens' other features is the National Collection of saxifrage. The nearby Saxon church has original glass windows dating from the 13th century. Tel: 01844 389254.
Wayland's Smithy	2 miles (3km) southwest of Uffington, 7 miles (11km) west of Wantage. An impressive Neolithic long barrow and chamber tomb located near the Uffington White Horse and Uffington Castle and close to the Oxfordshire/Berkshire border. Its present appearance is the result of restoration following excavations undertaken by Stuart Piggott and Richard Atkinson in 1962–3. They demonstrated that the site had been built in two phases: a timber chambered oval barrow built c.3700 BC and a second stone chambered long barrow c.3400 BC. The later mound was 185ft (56.5m) long and 43ft (13m) wide at the south end. The monument is named after Weland, the Anglo-Saxon god of metalworking.
Wellplace Zoo	Ipsden, 3 miles (5km) southeast of Wallingford. First opened to the public in 1968, the zoo houses a large variety of birds and animals from all over the world. Tel: 01491 680473.
Wittenham Clumps	1/4 mile (0.4km) southeast of Little Wittenham, 3 miles (5km) northeast of Didcot. A pair of low hills in the otherwise flat Thames Valley, sometimes referred to as the Sinodun Hills and also simply The Clumps. Their distinctive and prominent appearance is due to the plantations of beech trees on their summits, originally made in the 1740s. The more southerly hill is also the site of an Iron Age fort dating to 600 BC.
Wolvercote Cemetery	Banbury Road, Oxford. Located in the north Oxford suburb of Wolvercote, the cemetery is unusually divided into areas to accommodate graves of the Jewish and Muslim communities, as well as all categories of Christians. Many Russians, Poles and other East Europeans who did not belong to Oxford parishes are buried here. The cemetery is also the last resting place of philosopher Isaiah Berlin, poet Elizabeth Jennings, James Murray, founder of the *Oxford English Dictionary*, and author J R R Tolkien.
Wytham Woods	3 miles (5km) west of Oxford. Also known as the Woods of Hazel. An area of long-established mixed woodland now rare in lowland England; covering 1025 acres (415ha), they are a designated Site of Special Scientific Interest. There are significant populations of badgers, roe and fallow deer and muntjac, as well as rare butterflies and a wide range of beetles. Part of the Wytham Estate, the woods are now owned by Oxford University and used for research in zoology and climate change.

Some famous people born in Oxfordshire

Alfred the Great (ruler of England) (c.849–899)	Wantage
Amis, Martin (novelist) (1949–)	Oxford
Berkeley, Lennox (composer) (1903–89)	Oxford
Churchill, Winston (statesman) (1874–1965)	Woodstock
Du Pré, Jacqueline (cellist) (1945–87)	Oxford
Edward the Confessor (king of England) (1003–66)	Islip
Gibbons, Orlando (composer) (1583–1625)	Oxford
Hailwood, Mike (motorcycle racer) (1940–81)	Great Milton
Hastings, Warren (statesman) (1732–1818)	Churchill
Hawking, Stephen (scientist) (1942–)	Oxford
Henman, Tim (tennis player) (1974–)	Oxford
Hodgkin, Alan (physiologist) (1914–98)	Banbury
James, P D (author) (1920–)	Oxford
John (king of England) (1167–1216)	Oxford
Laurie (James) Hugh (actor) (1959–)	Oxford
Logan, Andrew (artist) (1945–)	Witney
MacGregor, Sue (radio presenter) (1941–)	Oxford
Mitford, Jessica (writer) (1917–96)	Burford
Piggott, Lester (jockey) (1935–)	Wantage
Reade, Charles (novelist and playwright) (1814–84)	Ipsden
Richard I (king of England) (1157–99)	Oxford
Sayers, Dorothy L (writer) (1893–1957)	Oxford
Steptoe, Patrick (gynaecologist) (1913–88)	Witney

SHROPSHIRE

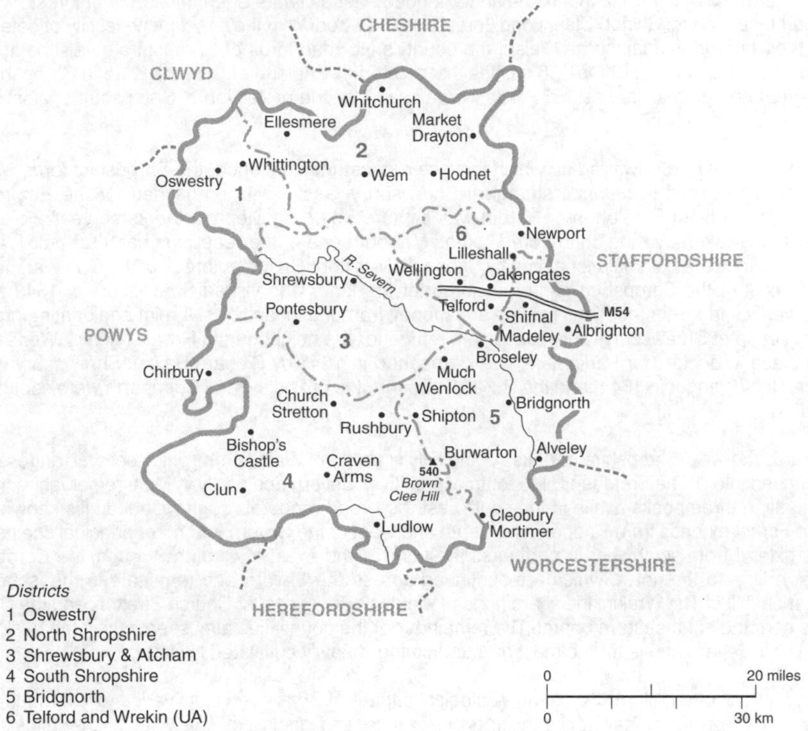
CHESHIRE
CLWYD
Whitchurch
Ellesmere
Market
Drayton
2
Whittington
Oswestry
1
Wem
Hodnet
6
Newport
Lilleshall
STAFFORDSHIRE
R. Severn
Shrewsbury
Wellington
Oakengates
Telford
M54
Shifnal
Pontesbury
Madeley
Albrighton
POWYS
3
Broseley
Chirbury
Much
Wenlock
Church
Stretton
Bridgnorth
Shipton
5
Rushbury
Bishop's
Castle
Burwarton
Alveley
Craven
Arms
540
Brown
Clee Hill
4
Clun
Ludlow
Cleobury
Mortimer
WORCESTERSHIRE
HEREFORDSHIRE
Districts
1 Oswestry
2 North Shropshire
3 Shrewsbury & Atcham
4 South Shropshire
5 Bridgnorth
6 Telford and Wrekin (UA)
0
20 miles
0
30 km

Shropshire is a traditional, ceremonial and non-metropolitan county in the West Midlands bordering Cheshire to the north, Staffordshire to the east, Worcestershire to the southeast, Herefordshire to the south, and the Welsh ceremonial counties of Powys to the west and Clwyd to the northwest. The borough of Telford and Wrekin, created in 1974 as The Wrekin, a district of Shropshire, became a unitary authority on 1 April 1998. The county town is Shrewsbury, although the new town of Telford is the largest of its 22 towns. It has no cities. Shropshire was officially known as Salop from 1974 until local protest reversed the decision in 1980. (The name Salop derives from *Salopesberia* – a variant of the Saxon name *Scrobbesbyrig* for the town of Shrewsbury.)

Although I have listed the five districts that have served the county since 1974, from 1 April 2009 they have been abolished, as has the county council, to form a single unitary authority of Shropshire; the geographical county now consisting of two unitary authorities.

The area which is now Shropshire was annexed to the kingdom of Mercia by Offa, who in 779 drove the king of Powys from Shrewsbury (then known as Pengwerne), securing his conquests by the defensive earthwork known as Offa's Dyke. This enters Shropshire at Knighton and in many places forms the county's boundary line.

In the 9th and 10th centuries the district was regularly overrun by the Danes; in 874 they destroyed the priory of Much Wenlock, and in 896 they wintered at Quatford. In 912 Queen Ethelfleda of Mercia built a fortress at Bridgnorth against the Danish invaders, and the following year built another at Chirbury. Mercia was divided into shires in the 10th century after its recovery from the Danes by Edward the Elder, and Shropshire stands out as the sole Mercian shire which did not derive its name from its chief town. The origin of its name derives from the Latin *Civitas Scrobbensis*, 'the city around the scrub folk'. The first mention of it in the Anglo-Saxon Chronicle occurs in 1006 as *Scrobbesbyrigscir*.

After the Norman Conquest the principal estates in Shropshire were bestowed on Norman noblemen. Pre-eminent among them was Roger de Montgomery, 1st Earl of Shrewsbury, whose son

Robert de Bellesme forfeited his possessions for rebelling against Henry I. At this time substantial areas of Shropshire were covered by forests; the largest, Worf Forest, extended 8 miles (13km) in length and 6 miles (10km) in width. The forest of Wrekin, or Mount Gilbert as it was then called, covered the whole of the hill of that name and extended east as far as Sheriffhales. Other forests were Stiperstones, Wyre, Shirlot, Clee, Long Forest and Brewood. With the constant necessity of defending their territories against the Welsh, the county's Norman lords of Shropshire built substantial numbers of castles; 32 of the 186 castles that existed in England at the time were in Shropshire. In 1442 and again as late as 1535 Acts were passed for the protection of Shropshire against the Welsh.

Apart from the border warfare in which they were constantly engaged, the Shropshire lords were actively concerned in national struggles. Shrewsbury Castle was garrisoned for the Empress Matilda by William Fitzalan in 1138, but was captured by King Stephen the same year. Holgate Castle was taken by King John from Thomas Mauduit, one of the rebellious barons. Ludlow and Shrewsbury were both held for a time by Simon de Montfort. On the outbreak of the Civil War, however, most of the Shropshire gentry declared for the king, who visited Shrewsbury in 1642 and received valuable contributions in plate and money from the inhabitants. A mint and printing press were set up at Shrewsbury, which became a refuge for the neighbouring Royalist gentry. Wem, the first place to declare for Parliament, was garrisoned in 1645 by Richard Baxter. Shrewsbury was forced to surrender in 1644, and the Royalist strongholds of Ludlow and Bridgnorth were captured in 1646.

Towards the west Shropshire partakes of the hilly scenery of Wales, from which several ranges are continued into it. The Breidden Hills, south of the River Severn and partly in Montgomeryshire, rise abruptly in three peaks, while in the southwest the broad range of rough rounded hills known as Clun Forest extends from Radnorshire. South and west of the Severn four other principal chains of hills extend from southwest to northeast: the Long Mynd, west of Church Stretton; the Carodoc Hills, a little to the north, which are continued across the Severn and terminate in the isolated sugarloaf hill of The Wrekin; the sharp ridge of Wenlock Edge, east of Church Stretton; and the Clee Hills near the southeastern border. The remainder of the county lies almost entirely in the basin of the River Severn and is for the most part undulating, heavily cultivated lowland.

Shropshire is often referred to as the 'geological capital' of Britain due to its varied rock formations. The oldest, pre-Cambrian rocks include the granite and gneiss of The Wrekin, the schists of Rushton, the lavas and ashes of The Wrekin, Caer Caradoc and Pontesford, and the purple slates of the Long Mynd. There are also rich veins of quartzite, sandstone, shales, grits, volcanic ashes, mudstones and limestones as well as coal, lead, copper and iron ore deposits.

The Industrial Revolution was famously born in the neighbourhood of Coalbrookdale, an early home of iron founding under the famous Darby family and also a centre of coal mining. There were encaustic tile and brick works in the Broseley district, as well as a tradition of tobacco pipe manufacture, while at Coalport there are china works. Mining for lead and barytes took place in the Minsterley and Stiperstones district in the west. Machinery, tools and agricultural implements are manufactured in Ludlow, Oswestry, Shrewsbury and Wellington.

Today there are no working mines left in Shropshire and despite its industrial heritage, the county remains heavily agricultural, with more than 80 per cent of its total area under cultivation. The cattle are chiefly Herefords and the sheep Shropshires. Cheshire cheese is made in the north and a small acreage is under hops. The rural county, with its hills and rolling green countryside, has become a popular haven for tourists seeking peace and tranquility.

Shropshire	**Population**			**Area**	
Districts	*male*	*female*	*total*	*sq miles*	*sq km*
Bridgnorth	26,671	25,826	52,497	244	633
North Shropshire	28,551	28,557	57,108	262	679
Oswestry	18,030	19,278	37,308	99	256
Shrewsbury & Atcham	47,071	48,779	95,850	232	602
South Shropshire	19,785	20,625	40,410	397	1027
Telford & Wrekin Unitary Authority	77,859	80,466	158,325	112	290
Total	217,967	223,531	441,498	1346	3487

Local Attractions and Information

Acton Burnell Castle 8 miles (13km) south of Shrewsbury. The remains of a fortified manor house built c.1284–93 by Bishop Roger Burnell, Chancellor of England. Edward I was a regular visitor and is thought to have convened one of the first English Parliaments on the site in 1283. The house was abandoned by the Burnell family in 1420 and is now ruined. It is owned by English Heritage.

Acton Burnell Statute The Statute of Acton Burnell (1283) provided for the protection of creditors in London, York, Bristol, Lincoln, Winchester and Shrewsbury. If a debtor failed to pay on the due date, the mayor of any of these six towns would, with the help of the local sheriff, seize and sell the debtor's goods to the value of the debt. If the debtor had no goods in the relevant town, a writ from Chancery would empower the mayor and sheriff of the town where the debtor's goods were held to seize and sell them to pay the debt. If the debtor had no goods, he would be imprisoned until he or his friends paid the debt. The statute proved unworkable almost from the start, as many sheriffs and officials refused to implement its terms. The subsequent Statute of Merchants, promulgated in 1285, both reiterated and superseded that of Acton Burnell.

Adcote School Little Ness, 7 miles (11km) northwest of Shrewsbury. A private school for girls designed by Norman Shaw RA in 1879, and set in 27 acres (11ha) of landscaped parkland. Tel: 01939 260202.

Administrative headquarters **Shropshire**: Shire Hall, Abbey Foregate, Shrewsbury SY2 6ND. Tel: 0845 6789000.
Telford and Wrekin: Civic Offices, Telford TF3 4LD. Tel: 01952 202100.

Attingham Park 4 miles (6km) southeast of Shrewsbury. A country house designed by George Steuart and built in 1785 for Lord Berwick. The picture gallery was later added by John Nash. The park, which was landscaped by Humphry Repton, contains woodlands and a deer park with numerous fallow deer. The grounds also include walled gardens and an orchard. The River Tern, which flows through the middle of the park, joins the River Severn near the park boundary. Now owned by the National Trust. Tel: 01743 708162.

Battles Four major battles have been fought in Shropshire: Cefn Carnedd, Ludford Bridge, Maserfield and Shrewsbury. See separate table for details.

Benthall Hall 1 mile (1.6km) northwest of Broseley, 4½ miles (7km) south of Telford. A 16th century country house located a few miles from the historic Ironbridge Gorge. The hall was built c.1580. It was garrisoned during the Civil War and was the site of several skirmishes. It retains much of its oak interior and 17th century staircase. George Maw (1832–1912), a local pottery manufacturer and crocus enthusiast, developed the garden from c.1865 onwards; the rockeries and terraces were added by Romantic painter and sculptor Robert Bateman (1842–1922), the son of horticulturalist James Bateman, designer of Biddulph Grange (see Staffordshire). The house is currently occupied by the Benthall family, but has been owned by the National Trust since 1958. Tel: 01952 882159.

Bishop's Castle A small market town 4 miles (6km) east of the Welsh border, 10 miles (16km) northwest of Ludlow. The castle at the upper end of the town was originally a motte and bailey construction built in 1167 on the site of an earlier Norman castle to defend the church and village from the Welsh; it was abandoned by the time of the Civil War, and little of the structure now remains. The church of St John the Baptist, substantially rebuilt in the 1860s, lies at the lower end of the town.

Blists Hill Victorian Town Legges Way, Madeley, Telford. The site of a former industrial complex, now converted into an open air museum recreating a Shropshire town at the end of the 19th century. Operated by the Ironbridge Gorge Museum Trust, its features include a 19th century steam-operated pithead, Victorian chemist, squatter's cottage, schoolhouse and bank. Tel: 01952 884391.

Boscobel House 8 miles (13km) east of Telford. Boscobel House was built c.1632, when landowner John Gifford of White Ladies Priory (see separate entry) converted a timber-framed farmhouse into a hunting lodge. It was here that Charles II famously hid in a tree to escape discovery by Parliamentary soldiers in 1651; arriving at Boscobel on 6 September, three days after the disastrous Battle of Worcester, he and Colonel William Carlis (or Careless) spent all day hiding in a nearby oak tree (now known as the Royal Oak) before Charles left for Moseley Old Hall (see Staffordshire) the following day. Tel: 01902 850244.

Bridgnorth Castle Bridgnorth, 10 miles (16km) south of Telford. Norman castle founded by Robert de Bellesme (later Earl of Shrewsbury) in 1101 and located on a cliff above the River Severn. The 12th century keep was erected by Henry II. A Royalist stronghold during the Civil War, the castle was besieged by Parliamentary forces and slighted in 1646. Part of the tower remains leaning at an angle of 17 degrees from the vertical, three times further than the Leaning Tower of Pisa.

Bridgnorth Cliff Railway Castle Terrace, Bridgnorth. A funicular railway also known as Castle Hill Railway, and linking the High Town and Low Town areas of Bridgnorth. The track length is 201ft (61m), with a gradient of 1 in 1.8 and a rise of 111ft (34m) at an angle of 33 degrees. It is claimed to be both the steepest and the shortest railway in England, and is one of four funicular railways in the UK built to the same basic design (the others being the Clifton Rocks Railway in Bristol, the Lynton & Lynmouth Cliff Railway in Devon and the Constitution Hill Railway in Aberystwyth, Wales). Tel: 01746 762124.

Broseley Clay Tobacco Pipe Works Duke Street, Broseley. The former Southorns pipe works, closed in 1957 after 350 years of traditional clay pipe manufacture in the town. The site was abandoned until 1996 when it was reopened as one of the Ironbridge Gorge Museums. Broseley is the site of numerous early industrial settlements and there were once three pipe manufacturers in the town, making it one of the largest pipe-making areas in the world. Tel: 01952 435900.

Buildwas Abbey Buildwas, 2 miles (3km) west of Ironbridge. Located on the southern bank of the River Severn, the Cistercian Abbey of St Mary and St Chad was founded in 1135 by Roger de Clinton, Bishop of Coventry (1129–48), as a Savignac monastery and was inhabited by a small community of monks from Furness Abbey. The stone from which it was built was quarried in nearby Broseley. Welsh princes regularly raided the abbey, and in 1406 raiders from Powys kidnapped the abbot. The abbey was dissolved in 1536 and the estate granted to Lord Powys. The abbot's house and infirmary were later incorporated into the building of a private house, while the other remaining buildings are now in the care of English Heritage. The remains of the 12th century Cistercian church are among the best preserved of their kind in Britain. Tel: 01952 433274.

Buildwas Power Station — $^{1}/_{2}$ mile (0.8km) west of Ironbridge. Also known as Ironbridge Power Station. Located on the bank of the River Severn near Ironbridge Gorge, the coal-fired power station was opened in 1965 for the state-owned Central Electricity Generating Board. In 1990 it came into the ownership of Powergen after privatisation of the electricity generation industry; in 2001 Powergen was taken over by German energy company E.ON. The plant is the only major generator of electricity in Shropshire; it consumes 1.2 million tonnes of coal, 48,000 tonnes of biomass and 20,000 tonnes of oil per year. The skyline is dominated by the plant's four cooling towers, which were constructed from red concrete rather than the usual yellow-brown in order to blend in with other local architecture.

Burrow — $^{1}/_{2}$ mile (0.8km) west of Hopesay, 9 miles (15km) northwest of Ludlow. A hill with an Iron Age hill fort at the summit known as Burrow Hill Camp. The site is thought to have been of considerable significance during the Iron Age as it has two natural springs.

Caer Caradoc — $^{1}/_{2}$ mile (0.8km) northeast of Church Stretton, 11 miles (18km) south of Shrewsbury. A hill rising sharply to a height of 1505ft (459m) out of the narrow gorge in which the town of Church Stretton is situated. The summit is crowned by an Iron Age hill fort, after which the hill is named – Caer Caradoc in Welsh means Caradoc's Fort.

Cambrian Heritage Railway — Llynclys, 4 miles (6km) south of Oswestry. A preserved railway operated by the Cambrian Railways Trust (not to be confused with the nearby Cambrian Railway Society) over $^{3}/_{4}$ mile (1.2km) of the former Cambrian Railways line from Gobowen to Blodwel via Oswestry. The trust has plans to reinstate the entire line, and also the branch between Llynclys Junction and Pant. Tel: 01691 831569.

Canals — The **Coalport Canal** was built to link the industries of Coalport, east of Ironbridge, with the River Severn. The canal runs from the river past the Coalport China works, the Tar Tunnel leading to the bitumen and coal mines, and up the Hay Inclined Plane to Blists Hill (see separate entries). There is also another entrance to the mines from the top of the inclined plane at Blists Hill. Today, the canal is part of the Ironbridge Gorge Museums complex.

The **Ellesmere Canal** was originally planned to link the Rivers Mersey, Dee and Severn, but eventually followed a different route. Part of the canal has now become known as the Llangollen Canal, another stretch forms part of the Montgomery Canal, and yet another forms part of what is now considered the Shropshire Union Canal main line.

Llangollen Canal see Clwyd

Montgomery Canal see Powys

The **Shrewsbury Canal** (or **Shrewsbury & Newport Canal**) dates to 1793. It was officially abandoned in 1944; many sections have disappeared, though some bridges and other structures are still visible.

The **Shropshire Union Canal** links Wolverhampton (and the Birmingham Canal Navigations) with the River Mersey. Completed in 1835, it was one of the last major canals to be built in England; it was also Thomas Telford's last major civil engineering accomplishment.

Castles — Shropshire is home to 32 castles, more than any other English county. Apart from those listed separately, they are: **Alberbury**, built by Fulke de Warenne as added protection for Shrewsbury Castle against the threat of the Welsh; **Aston Botterell**, a ringwork construction; **Brompton Mill**, a motte and bailey built c.12th century on the line of Offa's Dyke; **Cleobury**, built by Hugh de Mortimer; **Ellesmere**, a motte and bailey founded by Roger de Montgomery, Earl of Shrewsbury, on a prominent hill east of Shrewsbury just after the Norman Conquest, but abandoned not long after being established; **Hawcock's Mount**, a ringwork; **Holgate**, taken by King John from Thomas Mauduit, one of the rebellious barons; **Marche Hall**, a ringwork; **Pulverbatch**, at which there are two motte sites, one to the east by Wilderby Hall, the other south of the village – the latter, known locally as Castle Pulverbatch, possibly dates to c.1205; **Pontesbury**, erected by the Corbett family; **Quatford**, an 11th century castle built on high ground overlooking the river but demolished a few years later, although traces of the motte still remain; **Red**, a Norman ruin, seat of the Audleys, located opposite Grotto Hill, the view that Dr Johnson called the 'awful precipice' at Hawkstone Park; **Rowton**, a former seat of the Corbett family and now a luxury country hotel 6 miles (10km) west of Shrewsbury; **Shrawardine**, destroyed by Welsh prince Llewellyn in 1215 and rebuilt by the FitzAlan family in 1229, who renamed it Castle Isabel; **Wattlesborough**, erected by the Corbett family; and **Wem**, demolished by the Earl of Salisbury on behalf of the Yorkists during the Wars of the Roses.

Caus Castle — $1^{1}/_{4}$ miles (2km) southwest of Westbury, 9 miles (15km) west of Shrewsbury. Situated on the eastern foothills of the Long Mountain guarding the route between Shrewsbury and Montgomery, the site's outer earthworks are probably an Iron Age fort, while the motte and bailey is Norman. Caus Castle was built in the late 11th century by Roger le Corbet and named after his Normandy estate in the Pays de Caux. The castle passed to the Earl of Stafford on the death of Beatrice Corbet in 1347. Caus was garrisoned by the Seneschal Gruffudd ap Ieuan ap Madoc ap Gwenwys against the rebellion of Owain Glyndŵr in the 1400s. Gruffudd later changed sides and supported Glyndŵr; as a result the castle and his lands were forfeited in 1404, although they were restored by Henry V in 1419 after his sons Ieuan ap Gruffudd and Sir Gruffudd Vaughan captured John Oldcastle for Lord Charlton of Powis. In 1443 Sir Grufudd and his tenants murdered Sir Christopher Talbot, son of John Talbot, 1st Earl of Shrewsbury and champion tilter of England, at the castle, for which their family lands were again forfeited, this time to Henry VI. The castle was rarely used in the 15th and 16th centuries and after its desertion it was finally destroyed in 1645. Today little remains except overgrown earthworks and fragments of the castle's two towers.

Clee Hills 5 miles (8km) northeast of Ludlow. A range of hills extending for 15 miles (24km) in the Shropshire Hills Area of Outstanding Natural Beauty. The two highest summits are Brown Clee Hill (1772ft/540m) and Titterstone Clee Hill (1749ft/533m), which lies 5 miles (8km) to the south. The hills have been said to form a 'gateway' from the West Midlands to the hills and rural landscape of Wales and are at the heart of the Welsh Marches. Over the years much quarrying has taken place in the area and there are large air traffic control domes and radar towers on the summits of both hills. The area is important for wildlife, with peregrine falcon, barn owl, wheatear, stonechat, skylark, curlew and other birds; there are also adders. It is claimed locally that the hills are the highest land eastwards until the Ural Mountains in Russia and it has been known for radios in the area to pick up signals from Radio Moscow via the air traffic control masts. Author J R R Tolkien was a frequent visitor and the Shire in his novel *The Lord of the Rings* is thought to have been based on the area.

Clun Bridge Clun, 18 miles (29km) west of Ludlow. A packhorse bridge, dating possibly from c.1450, which today carries the A488 road over the River Clun in the small town of the same name.

Clun Castle Clun, 18 miles (29km) west of Ludlow. Situated on two Ice Age mounds overlooking the south Shropshire town, the original timber motte and bailey castle, built by Robert de Say in 1099, was rebuilt in stone in 1140. It was constructed both to defend the borderland and to monitor traffic on the Clun–Clee Ridgeway where the drovers moved stock from Wales to the Midlands. It was in the hands of the FitzAlan family from the 12th to the 16th century and in the 15th century served as a hunting lodge for the Earl of Arundel. By 1642 it was in ruins. The remains include the Norman keep, some Norman windows, two 13th century semicircular towers, a four-storey keep,a section of staircase and some evidence of fireplaces and floors, along with earthworks, ditches and foundations. The castle is owned by the Duke of Norfolk (who also holds the title of Baron Clun), but managed by English Heritage.

Clun Forest 20 miles (32km) west of Ludlow. A remote, rural area of open pasture, moorland and mixed deciduous/coniferous woodland situated in southwestern Shropshire and over the border into Powys, Wales. It was once a large forest covering an area that stretched from Ludlow along the Clun Valley. Offa's Dyke runs north–south through the area, which has given its name to a hornless breed of sheep.

Coleham Pumping Station Longden Road, Shrewsbury. A historic sewage pumping station constructed in 1900 to house two massive steam-driven beam engines, built by Renshaws of Stoke-on-Trent. The coal-fired pumps were used until 1970. In 1974 Shrewsbury & Atcham Borough Council took over ownership of the building and pumps. The Shrewsbury Steam Trust was founded in 1992 to restore the steam engines. One boiler was commissioned in 2002 and the second in 2004; they now operate during the regular open days held by the Trust. Tel: 01743 361196.

Combermere Abbey 4 miles (6km) northwest of Whitchurch. Located on the Shropshire/Cheshire border, Combermere was founded by Hugh de Malbanc, Lord of Nantwich, as a Cistercian monastery in 1133. Set in rolling parkland filled with ancient oaks, it overlooks a 143 acre (58ha) lake. Following its dissolution in 1536, only the Abbot's Lodge (built in 1503) remained; this, together with 22,000 acres (8900ha) of land, was presented to the Cotton family, who created a manor house and owned the estate until 1919. The house has undergone several remodellings, but the magnificent oak hammerbeam roof and screen still remain, although now enclosed by a highly decorated 17th century ceiling featuring four centuries of the family's coats of arms. In 1814, the house was remodelled in Gothic style; to commemorate the Duke of Wellington's visit in 1820, Sir Stapleton Cotton built a ballroom and planted an oak tree which still stands in the park. In 1837 a large Jacobean-style stable block, designed by the Morrisons of Ireland, was built to house 36 horses. In recent years the walled gardens have been restored and a unique fruit tree maze created. Tel: 01948 662880.

Condover Hall Condover, 3 miles (5km) south of Shrewsbury. An Elizabethan house which belonged to the Cholmondeley family in the 19th century. The author Mary Cholmondeley (1859–1925) lived here for a few months in 1896 before moving to London. Her uncle, Reginald Cholmondeley, owned the house before this and was host to American writer Mark Twain when he visited in 1873 and 1879. It was subsequently owned by the Royal National Institute for the Blind. In 2005 the hall was sold to new owners with the intention of opening a school and college for children and young people with autism or Asperger's syndrome. The village of Condover was the birthplace of Richard Tarleton (c.1530–88), actor and court jester, thought to be the original of Shakespeare's 'poor Yorick'. Tel: 01743 872320.

Corfham Castle 1 mile (1.6km) east of Diddlebury, $5^1/_2$ miles (9km) northeast of Ludlow. A motte and bailey castle built c.1220. Henry II's mistress Rosamund Clifford ('fair Rosamund') was reputedly born here. By 1635 the castle was badly decayed and the slight remnants of the walls visible in 1929 have since disappeared. Today the only remains are a number of grassy mounds.

Cound Hall Cound, 6 miles (10km) southeast of Shrewbury. Baroque house built 1703–04 for Edward Cressett by John Prince of Shrewsbury. The two storeys of tall slender windows are topped by a half-storey, built of red brick with Corinthian pilasters and other stone dressings. The interior is notable for its late 18th century staircase, which is suspended on columns rather than being attached to the back wall. The Grade I listed building was featured in the BBC's 2004 series *Restoration*. Tel: 01743 761721.

Daniels Mill Eardington, 2 miles (3km) south of Bridgnorth. The mill's waterwheel is notable for having the largest diameter – 38ft 10in (11.8m) – of any working corn mill in England. The cast iron wheel, manufactured in Coalbrookdale, is dated 1850. Tel: 01746 762753.

Dudmaston	Quatt, 4 miles (6km) southeast of Bridgnorth. A 17th century manor house surrounded by extensive parkland and gardens. The house contains varied art collections including work by Barbara Hepworth and Henry Moore, botanical art and costumes. There are also 9 acres (3.5ha) of lakeside gardens and dingle walks. The house was given to the National Trust in 1978, but it is still the home of the Labouchere family. Tel: 01746 780866.
Ellesmere Island	See The Mere
Enginuity	Wellington Road, Coalbrookdale. Housed in a building of the old Coalbrookdale Company and opened in 2002 as one of the Ironbridge Gorge Museums, the centre features a variety of interactive displays exploring the relationship between technology, design and manufacture. Tel: 01952 884391.
English Bridge, The	A bridge crossing the River Severn in Shrewsbury. There has been a bridge on the site since at least Norman times; historically, it was known as the 'Stone Bridge'. The present bridge was rebuilt and widened in 1926 reusing the masonry of its predecessor, designed by Shropshire-born architect John Gwynn in 1774. See also the Welsh Bridge.
Ercall Hill	2 miles (3km) southwest of Wellington. A small hill 459ft (140m) high located to the north of The Wrekin and part of The Wrekin and The Ercall Site of Special Scientific Interest. Managed by Shropshire Wildlife Trust, the site includes 540 million year old ripple beds and ancient pre-Cambrian lava flows in exposed quarries.
Flounders' Folly	2 miles (3km) north of Craven Arms. Situated on Callow Hill, the 80ft (24m) tower was erected by Benjamin Flounders in 1838 as a viewing point and to mark the boundary between four estates. Flounders, a Yorkshire railway entrepreneur, had inherited an estate at Culmington, east of Craven Arms, in 1807. In the 20th century the tower fell into disrepair, but a restoration programme was completed in 2005.
Haughmond Abbey	3 miles (5km) northeast of Shrewsbury. The remains of the 12th century Augustinian abbey of St John the Evangelist, including the abbot's quarters, refectory and cloister. The frontage of the chapter house is decorated with 12th and 14th century carving and statuary, and the building's fine timber roof dates to c.1500. Now in the care of English Heritage. Tel: 01743 709661.
Haughmond Hill	3 miles (5km) east of Shrewsbury. A shallow hill 500ft (152m) high, covered largely by woodland except for a working sandstone quarry. It offers fine views across the surrounding countryside. There is an Iron Age hill fort to the north of the hill.
Hawkstone Park	6 miles (10km) southwest of Market Drayton. An 18th century 'theme park' consisting of 100 acres (40ha) of follies, grottoes and picturesque landscaped grounds, based around the authentic Norman castle known as Red Castle. Hawkstone House, now a Catholic retreat centre, was built c.1707 by Richard Hill; the follies were constructed his nephew Sir Rowland Hill and Sir Rowland's son, Sir Richard Hill. Restored in the early 1990s, the park was reopened from 1993 and is now Grade I listed. It was used to represent Narnia in the BBC's TV adaptation of C S Lewis's books. Tel: 01939 200611.
Hay Inclined Plane	High Street, Coalport. Located in Ironbridge Gorge. A canal boat lifting device connecting the River Severn with the Shropshire Union Canal, which used a system of rails and cradles to raise the canal's tub-boats a height of 207ft (63m). Designed to link the Severn with the industrial area of Blists Hill, it was in operation 1792–1894, and can now be seen as part of Blists Hill Victorian Town (see separate entry). The designer of the Shropshire tub-boat canal system was William Reynolds (1758–1803), cousin of Abraham Darby III, who was in charge of the canal's construction. There were once six such inclined planes on the Shropshire canals. The Hay incline was the equivalent of 27 locks and was worked by only four men. It could pass a pair of 5 ton tub-boats in four minutes; the equivalent journey through 27 locks would have taken up to three hours.
Heath Mynd	4 miles (6km) north of Bishop's Castle. A hill to the east of Corndon Hill just over the England/Wales border in Powys, reaching a height of 1483ft (452m). Although it is otherwise undistinguished, Heath Mynd drops steeply on all sides and is therefore regarded as a Marilyn (a hill with a relative height of at least 495ft/150m above the surrounding land).
Highest point	Brown Clee Hill at 1772ft (540m), one of the Clee Hills. GR: SO593865.
Hodnet Hall Gardens	Hodnet, 5 miles (8km) southwest of Market Drayton. The house and gardens have been owned by the Heber-Percy family since 1066. Brigadier A G Heber-Percy developed the 60 acres (24ha) of gardens in the early 1920s with a series of innovative designs featuring unusual plant species thought not to be able to survive in the British climate. Notable features include a series of pools and water gardens. Tel: 01630 685786.
Hopton Castle	Hopton, 12 miles (19km) west of Ludlow. Founded as an earthwork motte and bailey in the 11th century; in 1276 Walter de Hopton built the stone castle and added an impressive rectangular two-storey keep, with a projecting stair turret. During the Civil War, the castle was owned by the Puritan Wallop family, supporters of Parliament; in 1644 its 30 defenders surrendered with a guarantee of safe passage after a three-week siege by Royalist troops, only to be massacred and their bodies thrown in the moat. The castle was then burned, although much of the keep survives; fragments of plaster rendering on its outside walls and a 'guard shoot' at ground level in the southwest turret are still visible.
Hopton Court	Hopton Wafers, 7 miles (11km) east of Ludlow. The house, set in parkland laid out by Humphry Repton, dates from 1776 and is attributed to John Nash. Among the features of the grounds is a unique Grade II* listed conservatory built in 1830 of cast iron with a rounded archway leading to a rear room roofed with curved glass. It has two rooms either side, one housing the boiler beneath to supply heat by way of cast-iron grilles running around the floor of the interior. There is also a fully refurbished coach house. Tel: 01299 270734.
Interesting facts	**The Much Wenlock Olympics**, founded by local GP Dr William Penny Brookes (1809–95), inspired Baron de Coubertin to create the global event after a visit to the games. It is unlikely that

the 'old woman's race' for a pound of tea, which features in the village's annual event, will ever make the event proper but Brookes can be said to be the true founder of the modern Games. For much of his life he remained a leading member of the National Olympian Association and worked to promote the moral and physical benefits of physical education. Unfortunately he died the year before the first modern Olympics took place in Athens but Juan Antonio Samaranch, then president of the International Olympic Committee (IOC), visited Much Wenlock in 1994 and laid a wreath at Brookes' grave. **Richard of Shrewsbury, 1st Duke of York and 1st Duke of Norfolk** (1473–83?), better known as one of the 'Princes in the Tower', was born in Shrewsbury. The sixth child and second son of Edward IV and Elizabeth Woodville, and the younger brother of the future Edward V, he was created Duke of York in 1474. On 15 January 1478, at the age of four, he married five-year-old Anne de Mowbray, 8th Countess of Norfolk, who had inherited the vast Mowbray estates in 1476. Because Anne could not inherit her father's dukedom, Richard was created Duke of Norfolk in 1481. When their father died on 9 April 1483, Richard's brother Edward, Prince of Wales, became king of England, and Richard his heir presumptive. This was not to last. Robert Stillington, Bishop of Bath and Wells, presented evidence that Edward IV had contracted a secret marriage to Lady Eleanor Talbot in 1461; Talbot was still alive when Edward married Elizabeth Woodville in 1464. The regency council under Richard Plantagenet, 1st Duke of Gloucester, concluded that this was a case of bigamy, invalidating the second marriage and the legitimacy of all children it had produced for Edward IV. Edward and Richard were declared illegitimate and removed from the line of succession in 1483. The Duke of Gloucester, as a surviving younger brother of Edward IV, became Richard III. The Duke of York and his brother were sent to the Tower of London by the king in mid 1483. What happened to them afterwards has been the subject of much speculation, although it is assumed that they either died or were murdered while imprisoned. In the 1490s, Perkin Warbeck claimed to be Richard, Duke of York, but he was an imposter. Richard's might have been the smaller of two skeletons discovered in a chest in the Tower in 1674, but no conclusive evidence has yet emerged. After more than five years of campaigning, the Ludlow-based **British Hedgehog Preservation Society** eventually managed to persuade McDonald's to change the lid on their McFlurry dessert. The original containers trapped many hedgehogs, some of which were released by kindly passers-by but others were found dead. The new lid has a smaller aperture; even if the cup is thrown away with the lid attached, the hole should be too small for hedgehogs to push into. From 1 September 2006 every McDonald's restaurant in the UK began using the new lids on their McFlurry cups. **Market Drayton** is known as the home of gingerbread, which has been baked to a secret recipe in the town for over 200 years. **Wem** is famous for its sweet peas and the annual festival draws admirers from around the world. Shropshire-born **Eric Lock** became the RAF's most successful British-born pilot in the Battle of Britain, shooting down 16 German aircraft (with a half share in another one). His exploits won him the Distinguished Service Order and two Distinguished Flying Crosses. Flight Lieutenant Lock was briefly a household name, but he was killed before reaching his 22nd birthday. On 3 August 1941, Lock was on his way back from a fighter sweep over northern France when he spotted German soldiers on a road near Calais. He swooped down to attack and was never seen again. It is likely that he was brought down by ground fire, but the wreck of his aircraft has never been found or a body recovered, so Shropshire's Battle of Britain hero has no known grave. His name is carved on the Runnymede Memorial in Surrey, along with those of 20,000 British and Commonwealth airmen who vanished without trace in World War II.

Iron Bridge, The — The famous 100ft (30m) cast iron bridge was built across the River Severn between the industrial areas of Coalbrookdale in the north and Broseley in the south. The first bridge of its size in the world to be made out of cast iron, it was built in 1779 by Abraham Darby III. The village of Ironbridge beside the river takes its name from the bridge, as does Ironbridge Gorge itself. An annual Coracle Regatta is held in August on the River Severn at Ironbridge. Tel: 0121 625 6820.

Ironbridge Gorge — 2 miles (3km) south of Telford. Originally called the Severn Gorge, the deep gorge formed by the River Severn and located in the borough of Telford and Wrekin now takes its name from its famous bridge, a monument to the industry that began there. The gorge carries the Severn south towards the Bristol Channel, and is thought to have been formed during the last Ice Age when the output from the previously north-flowing river became trapped in a lake created by glaciers to the north. The level of the lake rose until it was able to flow over the hills to the south; this flow eroded a path through the hills forming the gorge and permanently diverting the Severn southwards. The area was of great importance to early industrialists and is widely considered to be the birthplace of the Industrial Revolution: raw materials such as coal, iron ore, limestone and clay, for the manufacture of iron, were exposed or easily mined in the gorge, while the deep and wide river allowed easy transport of products to the sea. In 1708 Abraham Darby perfected the technique of smelting iron with coke in his blast furnace at Coalbrookdale, thus enabling the large-scale production of iron. Existing settlements such as Coalport and Broseley became major centres of manufacturing, mining and quarrying, while the village of Ironbridge grew up in the late 18th century beside the bridge from which it took its name. The area was in decline by the mid-20th century, until in 1986 Ironbridge Gorge was designated a UNESCO World Heritage Site. Most industries in Ironbridge are now related to tourism, although the Merrythought teddy bear company (established in 1931) is still manufacturing on a much reduced scale.

Ironbridge Gorge Museums — Ten museums and historic sites administered by the Ironbridge Gorge Museum Trust and dedicated to the development of industry and technology in the area. The museums are: Blists Hill Victorian Town, Coalbrookdale Museum of Iron, Darby Houses, Coalport China Museum, Coalport Tar Tunnel, Museum of the Gorge, Iron Bridge & Tollhouse, Jackfield Tile Museum, Broseley Pipe Works, and Enginuity. The trust also supports a wide-ranging and innovative archaeology unit which undertakes archaeological work within the Ironbridge Gorge and throughout Britain. Tel: 01952 884391.

Islands Shropshire has no natural islands although Moscow Island (formerly Ellesmere Island) in the southwestern end of The Mere (see separate entry) is an artificially created island.

Langley Chapel 1½ miles (2.5km) south of Acton Burnell, 8 miles (13km) south of Shrewsbury. A small chapel set in an isolated countryside location. The chapel's 17th century timber furnishings, including a musicians' pew, have been retained in their entirety. Now in the care of English Heritage.

Lilleshall Abbey 5 miles (8km) northeast of Telford. The extensive ruins of an Arrouasian (later Augustinian) abbey, founded c.1148 by Richard de Belmeis. After its dissolution it became a Royalist stronghold during the Civil War. There are substantial remains of the 12th and 13th century church and cloister buildings. Now in the care of English Heritage.

Lilleshall Hall Lilleshall, 6 miles (10km) northeast of Telford. Originally built in 1831 as the hunting lodge and family retreat of the Duke of Sutherland, Lilleshall Hall is now better known as Lilleshall National Sports Centre; the house and estate are run by Leisure Connection Ltd on behalf of Sport England. Lilleshall is one of five National Sports Centres. Tel: 01952 603003.

Long Mynd, The The Long Mynd, or 'Long Mountain', is a ridge of high ground in south Shropshire, running roughly southwest–northeast, and extending 9 miles (15km) between the Stiperstones to the west and Wenlock Edge to the east. Its rock is pre-Cambrian, although not as old as the volcanic rock of the Stretton Hills (Lawley, Caer Caradoc and Ragleth) to the east. Pole Bank at 1696ft (516m) is the highest point. An ancient track known as The Portway runs along the top of the ridge. Most of the Long Mynd was bought by the National Trust in 1965. Principal settlements in and around the Long Mynd are the Strettons (Church Stretton, Little Stretton and All Stretton), Pulverbatch, Smethcott, Woolstaston, Myndtown, Wentnor and Ratlinghope. The Long Mynd features in literature in the poetry of A E Housman, the novels of Mary Webb (in particular *Gone to Earth*), and Malcolm Saville's Lone Pine series for children.

Longford Hall Longford, 1 mile (1.6km) southwest of Newport. Built in 1785 for Ralph Leeke, an agent for the East India Company, and designed by Joseph Bonomi (1739–1808), an Italian architect who had worked in the practice of Robert and James Adam. The estate's former farm buildings, including a circular 16th century dovecote, have now been converted into housing. The hall and surrounding grounds are occupied by a boarding house and sports fields belonging to Adam's Grammar School.

Longner Hall 2 miles (3km) east of Shrewsbury. The house was designed in 1803 by John Nash and set in a park landscaped by Humphry Repton; the exterior is decorated with Gothic style plasterwork. The interiors of the principal rooms are adorned with plaster fan vaulting and stained glass. Tel: 01743 709215.

Ludlow Castle Castle Square, Ludlow. A large, now ruined castle situated on a point overlooking the River Teme. First constructed c.1086 by Norman Marcher lord Roger de Lacy, it was held by the de Lacy and Mortimer families before passing to the Crown with the accession of Edward IV. The castle was a Yorkist stronghold during the Wars of the Roses. During the Tudor period it underwent substantial rebuilding and remained a royal possession until 1811. The castle was home to three royal children: Prince Edward, son of Edward IV, before his accession as Edward V; Arthur Tudor, son of Henry VII, who brought his bride, Catherine of Aragon, to live there a few months before he died in 1502; and Mary Tudor, Henry VIII's daughter by Catherine. John Milton's masque *Comus* was first performed in the great hall in 1634. The play was set in the local woods and the children of the Lord President of the Council of the Marches, John Egerton, Earl of Bridgwater, were cast as themselves. Ludlow was the seat of the Council until 1689. Bought by the Earl of Powis in 1811, the castle is still owned by his descendants. Tel: 01584 873355.

Ludlow Museum Castle Square, Ludlow. The museum was opened in 1995. The John Norton Gallery is dedicated to the internationally important discoveries made in the area by Victorian geologist Sir Roderick Murchison; there are also various displays relating to the town's history. Tel: 01584 813666.

Mawley Hall ½ mile (0.8km) southeast of Cleobury Mortimer, 11 miles (18km) east of Ludlow. Built in 1730 and attributed to Frank Smith of Warwick, the Grade I listed house contains a number of noteworthy Baroque interiors, especially the hall with its fine plasterwork and the woodcarving and panelling of the Oak Drawing Room and Inlaid Drawing Room. The gardens were laid out in the 1960s and incorporate expanses of lawn, parterres, vistas, urns, monuments and a herb garden, as well as mature oaks, beeches and cedars. There is an extensive collection of ornamental trees, the first letter of whose names account for every letter of the alphabet. Tel: 01299 270869.

Mere, The Ellesmere, 7½ miles (12km) northeast of Oswestry. One of nine glacial lakes to the southeast of Ellesmere, The Mere is the largest natural lake in England outside the Lake District, covering 118 acres (48ha), and is an important nesting site for grey herons. It contains an artificial island, constructed in 1812 from the soil dug out to make the gardens at Ellesmere House and later named Moscow Island, as Napoleon's defeat in Russia also took place in that year. Local legend suggests that a ghostly white lady can be seen wandering around the lake. Tel: 01961 622981.

Mitchell's Fold 6 miles (10km) north of Bishop's Castle. Also called Medgel's Fold. Located on Stapeley Hill, the Bronze Age stone circle is 85ft (26m) in diameter. It is thought to have originally consisted of 30 stones, of which only 15 are now visible. The remains of the Hoarstone or Blackmarsh stone circle lie 1½ miles (2.5km) to the northeast.

Moreton Corbet Castle Moreton Corbet, 8 miles (13km) northeast of Shrewsbury. A Norman stone keep and bailey fortress modified in the 16th century to include a substantial Italianate Elizabethan mansion. The ruin includes a small rectangular keep, built c.1200, a square gatehouse and turrets flanking the curtain wall. The site is owned by English Heritage.

Morville Hall	3 miles (5km) west of Bridgnorth. Elizabethan house altered and enlarged in the 18th century. The attached Dower House Garden features a series of historically themed gardens designed to explore the evolution of English gardening. Now owned by the National Trust. Tel: 01746 780838.
Moscow Island	See The Mere
Motto	*Floreat Salopia* ('Let Salop Flourish').
Mount, The	Shrewsbury. The site of Mount House, a Georgian house built by local doctor Robert Darwin in 1800. Robert's son, Charles Darwin, was born in the house on 12 February 1809. Today the house is occupied by the District Valuer and Valuation Office of Shrewsbury.
Much Wenlock Museum	High Street, Much Wenlock, 8 miles (13km) northeast of Bridgnorth. In addition to its displays on the archaeology of southwest Shropshire, the history of the town, and the geological significance of Wenlock Edge, the museum is also dedicated to Dr William Penny Brookes, who provided the inspiration for the modern Olympic movement (see Interesting facts). It was in Much Wenlock in 1850 that Dr Brookes founded the Wenlock Olympian Society and the town's annual Olympian Games. Tel: 01952 727773.
Much Wenlock Priory	Bull Ring, Much Wenlock. The remains of a Cluniac monastery, refounded by Roger de Montgomery c.1080 on the site of an earlier 7th century foundation. It is thought to be the final resting place of St Milburga, whose bones were reputedly discovered during restoration in 1101. Standing in grounds decorated with topiary, the ruins include the 12th century church, the Norman chapter house with ornate carving and a rare 'lavatorium' – an octagonal wash-house. Tel: 01952 727466.
Oakley Hall	2 miles (3km) northeast of Market Drayton. A fine Queen Anne mansion, situated on the borders of Shropshire, Cheshire and Staffordshire and set in 100 acres (40ha) of rolling parkland with superb views over the surrounding countryside. The gardens include both formal and wild areas. The house is not open to the public. Tel: 01244 572021.
Offa's Dyke	See Powys
Offa's Dyke Path	See Powys
Old Furnace	Darby Road, Coalbrookdale. Built in 1658, the furnace was the site of Abraham Darby's discovery of the smelting of iron with coke in 1709. It was later used to smelt the iron for the Iron Bridge at Coalbrookdale and remained in use until the 1820s. It was restored in the 1950s.
Old Oswestry	½ mile (0.8km) north of Oswestry. A large and impressive early Iron Age hill fort in the Welsh Marches, thought to have been occupied by the Cornovii between the 6th century BC and the Roman conquest of Britain. The site was originally occupied by undefended round huts; these were then enclosed by a double bank and ditch enclosure spreading over 13 acres (5.2ha) with entrances at the east and west ends. The defences were later rebuilt and a third bank added on all sides except the southeast, where the hill's steep slope made further strengthening unnecessary. The western entrance was then remodelled with a series of rectangular hollows, unique in structures of this kind. Finally two further circuits of banks and ditches were added to the outside. Although Old Oswestry was one of the most strongly defended hill forts in Britain, there is no evidence that the Romans ever tried to besiege it.
Oswestry Castle	Castle Street, Oswestry. Norman motte and bailey castle founded in 1086 by Rainald de Bailleul and rebuilt in stone in 1148 by Madoc ap Meredyth. It fell into disrepair in the 15th century and was demolished 1647–73. Only fragments of the medieval structure survive, including two substantial pieces of collapsed masonry (probably from the keep) on top of the levelled motte; a wall around the base of the motte was probably built in the late 19th century using medieval masonry.
Oswestry Light Railway	See Oswestry Transport Museum
Oswestry Transport Museum	Oswald Road, Oswestry. Museum dedicated to the history of railways in the Oswestry area, established by the Cambrian Railway Society and housed in the Oswestry & Newtown Railway's sole surviving goods shed. The site also includes a workshop for maintenance and restoration of the society's exhibits. Passenger trains run along the short Oswestry Light Railway. The society also plans to restore the branch line from Blodwel to Nantmawr as a heritage railway. Tel: 01691 671749.
Porthill Bridge	A pedestrian bridge crossing the River Severn in Shrewsbury. A ferry operated here until the bridge was built in 1922.
Preen Manor Gardens	Church Preen, 7 miles (11km) northeast of Church Stretton. The 6 acre (2.5ha) garden has 18 different small 'outdoor rooms' including a kitchen garden, grassy terraces and a water garden. A Cluniac monastery was established here in 1150, with fine views of Wenlock Edge. An ancient yew tree near the 12th century monastic church is said to be the oldest in Europe. Tel: 01694 771207.
Radnor Wood	1 mile (1.6km) northeast of Clun, 5 miles (8km) south of Bishop's Castle. A 370 acre (150ha) woodland managed by the Forestry Commission and situated on a hilltop 1070ft (326m) above sea level, one of the highest points above the valley of the River Clun. It is the site of an Iron Age hill fort; early limestone quarries have also been found on the top of the hill.
RAF Cosford	Albrighton, 8 miles (13km) southeast of Telford. Now formally known as DCAE (Defence College of Aeronautical Engineering) Cosford. RAF Cosford opened in 1938 as an aircraft maintenance, storage and technical training unit and is still a major centre of ground training. The DCAE was established in 2004 and Cosford is now home to No. 1 School of Technical Training, No. 1 Radio School, the Defence School of Photography and the RAF School of Physical Training. Other units based at the site include the University of Birmingham Air Squadron, No. 8 Air Experience Flight and No. 633 Volunteer Gliding School. The Aerospace Museum, a branch of the RAF Museum including a unique collection of research and development aircraft and a large collection of missiles and airliners, is also based at the site. The annual Cosford Air Show takes place in June.

RAF Cosford was the home of indoor athletics in the UK before the opening of indoor tracks at Birmingham and Glasgow. First used on 9 November 1955, it remained a venue for international meetings until the late 1980s. Tel: 01902 376200.

Richard's Castle — See Herefordshire

Rivers — The **Bagley Brook** is a small watercourse that flows into the River Severn at Coton Hill, near Shrewsbury town centre. Its course has been significantly altered by urban development and the brook is now little known or seen. It has however given its name to the area of Bagley, a ward of the borough council and an electoral district of the county council. To some extent, the brook follows the old course of the River Severn.

The **Clun** rises near Anchor, close to the Welsh border, flowing through the small town of Clun, as well as Newcastle-on-Clun and other villages, before meeting the River Teme at Leintwardine. The rural Clun Valley is part of south Shropshire's Shropshire Hills Area of Outstanding Natural Beauty.

The **Rea** is a small river that flows through south Shropshire and passes to the east of the town of Cleobury Mortimer, before entering the River Teme at Newnham Bridge in Worcestershire. The river is also referred to as the Neen, and there are various settlements along its course of that name.

Severn see Powys

The **Teme** rises in the Kerry Hills of mid-Wales south of Newtown, Powys. It flows across the border into England close to Knighton and continues through Ludlow, then between Tenbury Wells, Worcestershire, and Burford on its way to join the River Severn south of Worcester, a length of approximately 60 miles (100km). In 1996, the whole of the Teme was designated a Site of Special Scientific Interest by English Nature for its geology, and the variety of flora and fauna it supports. Its upper reaches are generally steep with fast flowing but relatively shallow waters. There are some mills, and a number of weirs, including several at Ludlow.

The **Tern** rises northeast of Market Drayton in the north of the county and flows into the Severn near Attingham Park, Atcham. At Longdon-on-Tern, the Tern is spanned by the world's first large-scale cast iron navigable aqueduct, designed by Thomas Telford to carry the Shrewsbury Canal. The 186ft (57m) long structure, marooned in the middle of a field, still stands today. The River Roden is a major tributary of the Tern.

The **Vyrnwy** begins at Lake Vyrnwy in Wales and flows east for 6 miles (10km) into Shropshire, where it joins the River Severn near Melverley.

Severn Valley Railway — A standard-gauge heritage railway line operating steam-hauled passenger trains on 16 miles (26km) of the former Great Western Railway line between Kidderminster in Worcestershire and Bridgnorth in Shropshire, via Bewdley, Arley, Highley and Hampton Loade. The line was built 1858–62 and operated until 1963, linking Hartlebury, near Droitwich, with Shrewsbury, a distance of 40 miles (64km). The original Severn Valley Railway was absorbed into the GWR in the 1870s, and in 1878 a link line was constructed from Bewdley to Kidderminster, enabling trains to run direct from the West Midlands industrial area. The track north of Bridgnorth was dismantled after the line was closed to through services in 1963, although a few passenger services continued between Bewdley, Kidderminster and Hartlebury until 1969 and coal traffic survived south of Alveley Colliery until 1970. The preserved line began operating in 1974. Tel: 01299 409816.

Shipton Hall — 7 miles (11km) southwest of Much Wenlock. An exquisite Elizabethan manor house, built c.1587 by Richard Lutwyche to replace a much older black and white timbered house destroyed by fire earlier in the 16th century. Lutwyche lived at neighbouring Lutwyche Hall, and it is said that he gave Shipton as a dowry when his daughter Elizabeth married Thomas Mytton. Shipton remained in the Mytton family for the next 300 years. The house has notable plasterwork ceilings and chimneypieces; some of these are the work of architect Thomas F Pritchard, who also worked on the Iron Bridge. The panelling of the Queen's Room and the old solar and the glazing of the windows, many with original leaded diamond panes, are from the 16th and 17th centuries. A dovecote in the grounds dates from the time of the earlier manor house, possibly the 13th century (the privilege of keeping a dovecote could only be granted by royal charter). St James' Church is Saxon in origin with Norman additions. In 1589 the chancel was 'rebuilded from the grounde' by John Lutwyche, son of Richard who built the hall. Tel: 01746 785225.

Shrewsbury Abbey — Abbey Foregate, Shrewsbury. Now famous for its prominent role in the Brother Cadfael mysteries of Ellis Peters, the abbey was a Benedictine foundation established in 1083 by Roger de Montgomery, Earl of Shrewsbury. Although the abbey church remained intact after the monastery's dissolution, Thomas Telford built his A5 road through part of it; the church, dedicated to Saints Peter and Paul, is still used for worship. Tel: 01743 232723.

Shrewsbury Castle — Castle Street, Shrewsbury. Norman motte and bailey castle founded by Roger de Montgomery c.1067–9, and rebuilt in stone by Henry II. Now located directly above Shrewsbury's railway station, the red sandstone castle was built as a defensive fortification for the town. The town walls, of which little now remain, radiated out from the castle. The castle was altered by Thomas Telford in the 18th century for Sir William Pulteney. Shropshire Horticultural Society bought the castle and gave it to the town in 1924. It currently houses the Shropshire Regimental Museum (see separate entry). Tel: 01743 361196.

Shrewsbury Cathedral — Belmont, Shrewsbury. Dedicated to Our Lady Help of Christians and St Peter of Alcontara, the Roman Catholic cathedral was built by Edward Pugin and completed in 1856. Unusually the building is oriented north–south. It contains striking 20th century stained glass windows.

Shrewsbury Museum and Art Gallery — Barker Street, Shrewsbury. Located in two impressive historic buildings – Rowley's House, a stone and brick town house built c.1618 by merchant William Rowley, and an adjoining timber-framed warehouse dating from c.1600 – the museum's collections include archaeological finds from the many ancient sites in the county as well as displays relating to natural history and locally born Charles Darwin. Tel: 01743 361196.

Shropshire Regimental Museum — Housed in Shrewsbury Castle, the museum is home to the collections of the four Shropshire regiments: the King's Shropshire Light Infantry, Shropshire Yeomanry, Shropshire Royal Horse Artillery and 4th Battalion King's Shropshire Light Infantry TA. Exhibits include the regimental colours, silver and china, exotic uniforms and badges, weapons, and medals gained in campaigns across the world, including three Victoria Crosses. In 1992 the castle was targeted by a terrorist firebomb attack and both the building and collection were damaged. It was reopened after exhaustive restoration. Tel: 01743 262292/358516.

Soulton Hall — 2 miles (3km) east of Wem. The exterior was constructed c.1550 by Sir Roland Hill, the first Protestant Lord Mayor of London; there are traces of an older medieval timber-framed building within the structure. In 1668, a semicircular pediment bearing the marital coat of arms of Thomas Hill was added above the front door. The present building was pre-dated by a Norman motte and bailey castle which became a fortified manor house; located to the northeast of the present building, its location is marked by a mound which is still visible. The grounds include walled gardens, a pillared forecourt and carved stonework. The Grade II* listed hall is now a hotel.

Sport

football — **Shrewsbury Town** were founded in 1886 and elected to the Football League in 1950 following the decision to expand the League from 88 to 92 clubs. They won the Third Division championship in 1978–9 and were promoted to the Second Division for the first time, remaining there for ten years. They have several nicknames including Salop, The Shrews, Blues, Amber-Blues and Town. Having played since 1911 at Gay Meadow on the banks of the River Severn, the club relocated to a new stadium at Oteley Road in 2008. Tel: 0871 811 8800.

horse racing — **Ludlow** racecourse, located in the South Shropshire countryside 2 miles (3km) northwest of Ludlow, has a record of racing dating back to 1729. It holds National Hunt racing on a right-hand circuit of 1½ miles (2.5km). Tel: 01584 856221.

ice hockey — **Telford Tigers** were formed in 2001 as Telford Wild Foxes, adopting their current name at the beginning of the 2005–06 season.

rugby league — **Telford Raiders** were formed in 2002 and play in the Rugby League Conference.

Stiperstones, The — 7 miles (11km) north of Bishop's Castle. A rugged hill in the Shropshire Hills Area of Outstanding Natural Beauty, crowned by a ridge consisting of a series of quartzite tors, the most renowned being the Devil's Chair and Manstone Rock (the highest point at 1759ft/536m). It is also the name of the small village that lies under the ridge to the north; lead mining formerly took place in the area. The area around Stiperstones is rich in folklore: according to one legend, the ghost of Wild Eric, a Saxon earl who defied the Normans, rides the hills whenever England is threatened by invasion. The Stiperstones feature in the literary works of Mary Webb and children's author Malcolm Saville. The hill is a National Nature Reserve, providing a habitat for upland birds such as the ring ouzel, curlew and peregrine falcon.

Stokesay Castle — ½ mile (0.8km) south of Craven Arms. The oldest fortified manor house in England, dating in part from the 12th century. The great hall was added in the 13th century and the original medieval staircase still remains in situ. Stokesay was fortified by Lawrence de Ludlow in 1291; sold by his descendants in the early 16th century, it was garrisoned by the Royalist Lord Craven during the Civil War but surrendered to Parliament without a shot being fired. The castle was let as a farm and workshop in the 18th century and restored after 1869. A timber-framed residence built onto the outside of the north tower is one of the castle's most unusual features, and there is also an elaborate timber-framed Jacobean gatehouse. The interior contains traces of rare medieval frescoes. Now in the care of English Heritage. Tel: 01588 672544.

Tar Tunnel, The — High Street, Coalport. Located on the bank of the River Severn in Ironbridge Gorge, the Tar Tunnel is now one of the sites administered by the Ironbridge Gorge Museums Trust. Miners struck a gushing spring of natural bitumen when digging the tunnel in 1787 and the substance still oozes from the wall today. Its chief commercial use was to treat ropes and caulk ships, but small amounts were processed and bottled as a remedy for rheumatism.

Telford Steam Railway — Horsehay, Telford. A heritage railway operating on part of the former Severn Junction Railway between Ketley and Horsehay. The ¾ mile (1.2km) line currently runs between Heath Hill Tunnel, Spring Village and the railway's headquarters in a former goods shed at Horsehay & Dawley, built in 1860. Tel: 07765 858348.

Titterstone Clee Hill — See Clee Hills

Viroconium — The Roman city of Viroconium was located at modern Wroxeter, 5 miles (8km) southeast of Shrewsbury. Viroconium is estimated to have been the fourth largest Roman settlement in Britain with a population of more than 6000 people at its peak. It was founded in the late 1st century AD and by AD 130 had grown to cover an area of more than 170 acres (70ha), with baths and a forum dedicated to the emperor Hadrian. The city declined following the Roman withdrawal in 410. Most of the city lies underground, but it has been mapped through geophysical survey and aerial archaeology.The visible remains include 'the Old Work', an archway that once formed part of the town's bath house and is the largest free-standing Roman ruin in England.

Welsh Bridge, The — A bridge spanning the River Severn in Shrewsbury, connecting Frankwell with the town centre. It was built in 1795 to replace St George's Bridge, also known as the Old Welsh Bridge, of which only one span now remains. The gate on the town side was called Mardol Gate and was located where the Mardol Quay Gardens now stand.

Wenlock Edge — 4 miles (6km) southeast of Church Stretton. A limestone escarpment extending southwest–northeast for 15 miles (24km) between Craven Arms and Much Wenlock. Located within the Shropshire Hills Area of Outstanding Natural Beauty, a large part of the area is owned by the National Trust. It is perhaps best known as the setting for A E Housman's poem 'On Wenlock Edge the wood's in trouble', later set to music by Ralph Vaughan Williams. It was also featured on the 2005 TV programme *Seven Natural Wonders* as one of the wonders of the Midlands.

Wenlock Priory See Much Wenlock

Weston Park Weston-under-Lizard, 7 miles (11km) east of Telford. The house was built in 1671 by Lady Elizabeth Wilbraham and has been the home of the Earls of Bradford throughout its history. It is set in more than 1000 acres (400ha) of park landscaped by Capability Brown, with a Roman Bridge and Temple of Diana added by James Paine. Tel: 01952 852100.

White Ladies Priory 8 miles (13km) east of Telford. The medieval nunnery of White Ladies was located close to Boscobel House (see separate entry), and is said to have been Charles II's first hiding place after the Battle of Worcester in 1651. The name 'White Ladies' refers to the undyed habits worn by the Augustinian nuns. Although the large timber-framed nunnery no longer exists, the remains of its medieval church and the 19th boundary wall of the small graveyard can still be seen. According to a 16th century legend that arose after the publication of Sir Thomas Malory's *Morte D'Arthur*, Queen Guinevere retired to the nunnery after the death of King Arthur. Now in the care of English Heritage.

Whittington Castle Whittington, 2 miles (3km) northeast of Oswestry. A ruined Norman motte and bailey castle set in 12 acres (5ha) of land. The original wooden structure was rebuilt in stone by Fulke de Warenne c.1219. Due to its low-lying position the castle was protected from attack by the surrounding marshland; there was also a moat system, of which only a few pools now remain. The outer gatehouse with two towers had a 42ft (13m) long drawbridge. The castle was held for the king during the Civil War until Parliamentary troops took it by force in 1643. It fell into decay after the Civil War and in the 17th century a cottage was built into the north gatehouse; the castle was restored in 1967. Archaeological finds from the site include armour, musket shot, swords, glass bottles, a carved stone head, assorted bones and a large jug which is on display at Shrewsbury Museum and Art Gallery (see separate entry). The restoration and management of the Grade I castle is to be carried out, possibly uniquely, by a trust formed by local villagers. Tel: 01691 662296.

Whixall Moss 1 mile (1.6km) northwest of Whixall, 4 miles (6km) southwest of Whitchurch. An area of peat bog managed by English Nature as part of the Fenn's, Whixall and Bettisfield Mosses National Nature Reserve. A rare survival of a lowland peat bog, and the third largest in Britain at 2340 acres (948ha), it is a Ramsar site and a Special Protection Area. The reserve lies on the England/Wales border and is bounded on two sides by the Llangollen Canal.

Wilderhope Manor Longville in the Dale, 5 miles (8km) east of Church Stretton. Located beneath Wenlock Edge, the Elizabethan manor house dates from 1585; the interior features an unusual oak spiral staircase and fine plaster ceilings. It is currently used as a youth hostel. Owned by the National Trust. Tel: 0870 770 6090.

Woofferton Transmitting Station Woofferton, 4 miles (6km) south of Ludlow. A short-wave broadcasting station originally built by the BBC during World War II. During the Cold War, much of its capacity was leased by the BBC to the Voice of America, to enhance the latter's coverage in the Eastern bloc. In the 1990s the site was sold to Merlin Communications, now part of VT Group plc and trading under the name VT Communications. It is now used for transmissions of the BBC World Service and BBC Hereford and Worcester.

Wrekin, The 4 miles (6km) west of Telford. Perhaps Shropshire's best-known landmark, the curious legendary hill standing 1335ft (407m) above sea level looks from one angle like a mountain, but from another no more than a mound. From the top one can supposedly see 15 counties. It has been designated a Site of Special Scientific Interest for its ancient woodland and is within the Shropshire Hills Area of Outstanding Natural Beauty. J R R Tolkien used to live nearby and drew inspiration from the area for Middle Earth in *The Lord of the Rings*. It is often suggested that The Wrekin is an extinct volcano; this is not so, although it is composed of volcanic rock. It is however very close to the Church Stretton Fault, and may well have been created when this fault was active. The fault still gives occasional reminders of its presence, most recently on 2 April 1990 when a small earthquake in Shropshire occurred due to a slight movement in the fault. Only minor damage was caused but a stone fell and lodged itself in the Needle's Eye, a cleft in the rock close to the hill's summit. The hill is capped by Shropshire's most significant hill fort. Once home to the British Cornovii tribe, it was stormed by the Romans under Ostorius Scapula around the spring of AD 74, as indicated by finds of *pilum* (javelin) heads and signs of burning. The fort has two entrances to the northeast: the entrance known as Hell Gate allows access to the outer area and the higher ground is accessed via Heaven Gate. The names come from folk memory of a battle that is said to have taken place here during the Cromwellian period. There are many local traditions relating how The Wrekin was formed but one of the best known claims that it consists of a spadeful of soil dropped by a giant. The name The Wrekin is also used to refer more generally to the area of east Shropshire around the hill and including the towns of Telford and Wellington. There is a local saying, 'to go all around the Wrekin', which means to take the long way round.

Wrekin Transmitter An FM and television transmission tower on the The Wrekin, standing 171ft (52m) high. The construction of a transmitter on such a historic site was the cause of considerable local controversy; transmission tests were first carried out by the BBC in 1964, but the transmitter was not completed until 1975, with broadcasts commencing in December of that year. The transmitter now relays Freeview broadcasts to north and mid Wales. A beacon on the main mast at the top of the hill emits a pulse of red light every few seconds at night, primarily to alert low flying aircraft. It is known locally as the 'Beacon on the Wrekin'.

Wyre Forest See Worcestershire

Some famous people born in Shropshire

Baddeley, Hermione (actress) (1906–86)	Broseley
Berners, Gerald (composer) (1883–1950)	Bridgnorth
Clive, Robert (statesman and general) (1725–74)	Styche
Darwin, Charles Robert (naturalist) (1809–82)	Shrewsbury
German, Sir Edward (composer) (1862–1936)	Whitchurch
Gwynn, John (architect and civil engineer) (1713–86)	Shrewsbury
Hunt, Dame Agnes Gwendoline (nurse) (1866–1948)	Baschurch
Hyde, Thomas (orientalist) (1636–1703)	Billingsley
Jones, Peter (actor) (1920–2000)	Wem
Lock, Eric (fighter pilot) (1920–41)	Bayton Hill
Lyle, Alexander Walter Barr 'Sandy' (golfer) (1958–)	Shrewsbury
Minton, Thomas (pottery manufacturer) (1765–1836)	Shrewsbury
Owen, Wilfred (poet) (1893–1918)	Oswestry
Peters, Ellis (Edith Pargeter) (author) (1913–95)	Horsehay
Powell, (Elizabeth) Dilys (writer) (1901–95)	Bridgnorth
Pym, Barbara (novelist) (1913–80)	Oswestry
Richard of Shrewsbury, 1st Duke of York (1473–?83)	Shrewsbury
Richards, Sir Gordon (jockey) (1904–86)	Oakengates
Robinson, Henry (photographer) (1830–1901)	Ludlow
Vaughan, Peter (actor) (1923–)	Wem
Webb, Mary (novelist) (1881–1927)	Leighton
Webb, Captain Matthew (channel swimmer) (1848–83)	Dawley
Woosnam, Ian (golfer) (1958–)	Oswestry
Wright, Billy (footballer) (1924–94)	Ironbridge
Wycherley, William (dramatist) (1640–1716)	Wem

Somerset

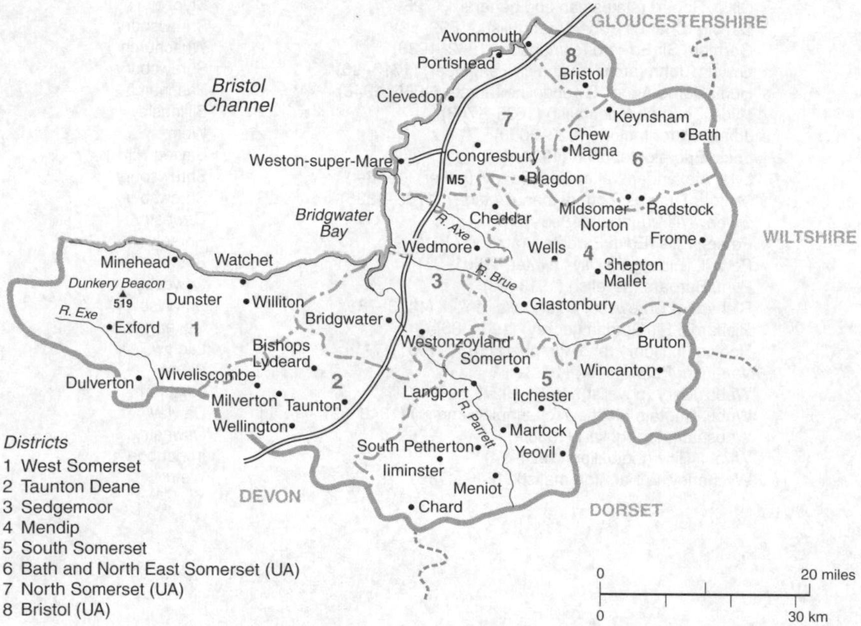
GLOUCESTERSHIRE
WILTSHIRE
DEVON
DORSET
Bristol Channel
Bridgwater Bay
Avonmouth
Portishead
Bristol
Clevedon
Keynsham
Bath
Chew Magna
Weston-super-Mare
Congresbury
M5
Blagdon
Midsomer Norton
Radstock
Cheddar
Frome
R. Axe
Wedmore
Wells
Shepton Mallet
Minehead
Watchet
R. Brue
Dunkery Beacon
519
Dunster
Williton
Glastonbury
R. Exe
Exford
Bridgwater
Bruton
Bishops Lydeard
Westonzoyland
Somerton
Wincanton
Dulverton
Wiveliscombe
Langport
Ilchester
Milverton
Taunton
R. Parrett
Wellington
Martock
South Petherton
Yeovil
Ilminster
Meniot
Chard
1
2
3
4
5
6
7
8
Districts
1 West Somerset
2 Taunton Deane
3 Sedgemoor
4 Mendip
5 South Somerset
6 Bath and North East Somerset (UA)
7 North Somerset (UA)
8 Bristol (UA)
0
20 miles
0
30 km

Somerset, in the southwest of England, borders Gloucestershire to the north, Wiltshire to the east, Dorset to the southeast and Devon to the southwest; to the northwest it is bounded by the coast of the Bristol Channel. Taunton is the county town, Bath and Wells its only two cities. The former county of Avon, created under the Local Government Act 1972 and situated north of Somerset and south of Gloucestershire, was abolished in 1996 and the area split between four unitary authorities: Bath and North East Somerset, Bristol, North Somerset and South Gloucestershire. The first three aforementioned areas are included in this section, but I should make it clear that Bristol is a ceremonial county distinct from either Somerset or Gloucestershire and is included under the auspices of Somerset in this book purely for expediency. Bristol also has city status.

The landscape of Somerset falls into four main types, defined by the underlying geology: the limestone karst and lias of the north, the clay vales and wetlands of the centre, the oolites of the east and south, and the Devonian sandstone of the west. The Mendip Hills to the northeast of the Somerset Levels have an extensive network of caves and underground rivers and a number of gorges, the best known being Cheddar Gorge. The main habitat on these hills is chalk grassland, with some arable agriculture. To the north of the hills is the Chew Valley and to the south, on the clay, are a number of broad valleys which support dairy farming and drain into the Somerset Levels. This expanse of flat land, stretching up to 20 miles (32km) inland, is only a few feet above sea level. Before it was drained, much of the land was under a shallow sea in winter and a marsh in summer. The coastal area between Minehead and the eastern end of the county's coastline is known as Bridgwater Bay.

The first recorded use of the county's name and derivation was in 1015, as *Sumaersaeton* – the land of dwellers (*saete*) dependent on Sumerton (a summer-only settlement). Somerton itself, near Yeovil and Street in the South Somerset district, was the capital of the kingdom of Wessex from AD 871 to 901. The county's history, however, goes back at least as far as 11,000 BC when families lived in Gough's Cave, near Cheddar, and hunted for food in Cheddar Gorge. In about 3800 BC, wooden causeways were built across the marshes and as the area became more populated it became increasingly vulnerable to attack. Iron Age hill forts such as Cadbury Castle were built c.700 BC.

According to legend Joseph of Arimathea sailed across the Levels to Glastonbury after the crucifixion of Jesus Christ, and ever since Glastonbury and the surrounding area has been a magnet for mystics and adherents of New Age spirituality. Shortly afterwards, at the time of the Roman conquest of Britain (AD 43), Somerset was inhabited by people from three different tribes: the Durotriges, with their administrative capital at Dorchester in Dorset, who lived in the south of the county; the staunchly anti-Roman tribe of Dobunni in the north; and, west of the River Parrett, the Dumnonii, who were equally disruptive to the Romans. Somerset therefore became a militarised zone. The Fosse Way, running from Devon to Lincoln, was built across the region soon after the conquest, with forts established at Ilchester, Ham Hill, South Cadbury, Wiveliscombe and Charterhouse. Lead and silver mining industries were established in the Mendip Hills and other local industries included salt extraction, coal and iron mining, iron smelting and the production of pewter and glass. There are many notable Roman remains in Somerset, including a large mosaic pavement near Langport.

With the withdrawal of the Romans from Britain, in the early 5th century localised rulers emerged both to control the land and to protect its people from continuing Saxon and Irish incursions. King Cado is recorded as having a stronghold at Dunster (Din-Draithou) and excavations at South Cadbury possibly uncovered an important residence named after him – although the site's traditional connections with his cousin, the legendary King Arthur, appear to be of doubtful origin. Another Dark Age settlement has been identified at Glastonbury (Ynys-Witrin) atop Glastonbury Tor. According to tradition this was the home of a Somerset king named Melwas who once kidnapped Queen Guinevere. A great siege at a site named Mount Badon (Mons Badonicus) took place somewhere near Bathampton Down c.AD 500. The advancing Anglo-Saxons were completely crushed during the conflict, bringing their westward expansion to an end for a generation. The British leader on this occasion is sometimes said to have been King Arthur, although this again is doubtful; although the battle is mentioned by chroniclers Gildas and Nennius before AD 900, they do not identify Arthur as the victor.

From the 7th century Somerset formed the westernmost part of the kingdom of Wessex. By 710, the Dumnonian armies were crushed and the Saxon King Ine established a fortress at Taunton. Settlements began to appear with Saxon names ending in *-tun* (manor or mansion), or including *cyng* (king) or *burh* (a strong place or fort); Somerton, Bruton, Petherton and Kingsbury are examples. In 878, Alfred the Great built a fort at Athelney in the Somerset Levels as a defensive position against Viking incursions. During this time of guerilla warfare, Alfred is said to have 'burnt the cakes' of a local peasant woman while contemplating his future fate. It was supposedly at Athelney that he slipped into the enemies' camp, dressed as a minstrel, and learnt of their battle plans. Shortly afterwards, Alfred thrashed the Viking army at Edington in neighbouring Wiltshire.

Somerset grew into a substantial centre for trade during the 10th century and its towns grew with it. By 988, however, Viking attacks had begun again via Bridgwater Bay. This latest wave of Danish aggression forced Aethelred the Unready to attempt a pay-off using vast sums of Danegeld. Minting in the county increased to meet this demand and vulnerable mints, like the one at Ilchester, were moved to protected hilltop locations – in this case, the old hill fort at nearby South Cadbury. During the reign of Edward the Confessor, Somerset was largely held by Earl Godwin and his family, whose relationship with the king was unstable. Godwin's son, Harold, was banished but persuaded the king to listen to his pleas by landing with an invasion force at Porlock. Harold eventually became king but his reign was short-lived, for he was soon to fall at the Battle of Hastings.

Somerset was already a well-organised county by the time of the Norman Conquest although large areas afterwards came under the ownership of the Crown. It became well known for the quality and quantity of its butter and cheese and several estates had specialised dairies. In 1340, there was only one city in Somerset, Bath, but there were 16 others bidding for the rank and Wells and Taunton were rich communities.

By the 16th century Somerset had natural pastures for livestock, birds and fish in the recently drained wetlands near Glastonbury and valuable lead and other mineral deposits in the Mendip Hills. Local coal was used for smelting iron and lead and the quarries at Ham, west of Yeovil, produced quality building stone. The following century, however, brought the Civil War. The Somerset gentry, and most of the rural population, were Royalists, while support for Parliament was represented by the Puritans, particularly in the towns in the north of the county. After a minor victory for the Royalists at Marshall's Elm (near Street) in 1642, the county was dominated by Parliament throughout 1643. The Royalists, commanded by Sir Ralph Hopton, besieged Taunton, Bridgwater and Dunster in 1644, finally driving the Parliamentarians from Somerset at the Battle of Lansdown. In 1645, however, the Royalists' dominance was brought to an end: defeat at the Battle of Langport was followed by the fall of Bridgwater and soon afterwards by that of Bath, Farleigh Hungerford and Dunster. The people of Somerset largely supported the future Charles II at the Battle of Worcester in 1651 and he escaped through the county soon afterwards, staying at Abbot's Leigh, Castle Cary and Trent. Somerset rose up in rebellion against the king for a second time during the Monmouth Rebellion of 1685, the monarch this time being James II. The survivors were dealt with brutally at the 'Bloody Assizes' by the infamous Judge Jeffreys.

The Industrial Revolution had relatively little effect in the county, but Bridgwater developed as a port and some canals were built. Stone quarrying developed as an industry, both at Ham Hill and to the east of the city of Bath, the stone from whose quarries gave many local buildings their rich golden colour. Coal was mined for over 200 years in the area around Radstock, the mines finally closing only in the 1970s. The drive to improve public health, an important feature of life in England in the 19th century, brought piped water and sewerage systems to Somerset towns and reservoirs were built to provide a continuous water supply, for instance at Taunton in 1878.

Somerset in the 21st century is a major tourist destination whose beauties, such as the expanses of Exmoor, the vale of Taunton, or the surreal fascinations of the Cheddar Caves, Gough's Cave and Wookey Hole are still relatively unspoiled. Agriculture continues to be a major business, if no longer a major employer. Apple orchards were once plentiful, and Somerset is still a centre for the production of cider, both locally and on an industrial basis at the Blackthorn Cider plant in Shepton Mallet, and in the town of Taunton.

The city, unitary authority and ceremonial county of **Bristol** received a royal charter in 1155 and was granted county status in 1373. It borders the unitary districts of Bath and North East Somerset, North Somerset and South Gloucestershire, and has a short coastline on the Bristol Channel. There is evidence of settlement in the area from the Palaeolithic era, with 60,000 year old archaeological finds at Shirehampton and St Annes. There are Iron Age hill forts near the city, at Leigh Woods and Clifton Down on the side of the Avon Gorge, and on Kingsweston Hill, near Henbury. During the Roman period there was a settlement, Abona, at what is now Sea Mills, connected to Bath by a Roman road, and another settlement at what is now Inns Court. There were also isolated villas and small settlements throughout the area. The town of *Brycgstow* (Old English, 'the place at the bridge') was in existence by the beginning of the 11th century, and under the Normans acquired one of the strongest castles in the south of England. The River Avon in the city centre slowly evolved into Bristol Harbour, which since the 12th century has been an important port, handling much of England's trade with Ireland. During the 12th and 13th centuries Bristol also became a centre of shipbuilding and manufacturing. It was the starting point for many important voyages, notably that of John Cabot to North America; his ship, the *Matthew*, left the port on 20 May 1497 and returned on 6 August.

By the time of the Black Death of 1348–9 Bristol was England's third-largest town (after London and York), but in the two centuries after the plague its population remained static. During the Civil War the city was occupied by Royalist forces. Renewed growth came in the 17th century with the rise of England's American colonies, which led in the following century to the expansion of the slave trade; many of the great estates in Bristol and Somerset were paid for by the proceeds of slavery. John Wesley founded the very first Methodist chapel in Bristol in 1739. Bristol's strong nautical ties meant that maritime safety was an important issue; in the 19th century Samuel Plimsoll, 'the sailor's friend', campaigned fearlessly to make the seas safer and successfully fought for a compulsory loadline on ships.

Competition from Liverpool, the disruption of maritime commerce through war with France and the abolition of the slave trade all contributed to the city's failure to keep pace with the newer manufacturing centres of the North and Midlands in the 19th century. The long passage up the heavily tidal Avon Gorge, which had made the port secure during the Middle Ages, had become a liability which the construction of a new 'Floating Harbour' (designed by William Jessop) in 1804–09 failed to overcome. Nevertheless, Bristol's population grew enormously during the 19th century, supported by new industries and growing commerce. It was particularly associated with engineer Isambard Kingdom Brunel, who designed the Great Western Railway (GWR) between Bristol and London and the Clifton Suspension Bridge. Brunel also persuaded the GWR Company to let him build a steamboat to travel from Bristol to New York. The *Great Western* – at 236ft (72m) long the largest steamship ever built at the time – made its first voyage to New York in 1838. The journey to America took 15 days and over the next eight years 60 crossings were made. The next steamship that Brunel built in Bristol was the SS *Great Britain*.

Bristol's city centre suffered severe damage from bombing during World War II. The original central shopping area is now a park containing two bombed churches and some tiny fragments of the castle. A third bombed church nearby, St Nicholas, has been restored and currently houses city council offices; it also contains a triptych by William Hogarth, painted for the high altar of St Mary Redcliffe in 1756. Like much British post-war planning, the rebuilding of Bristol city centre was characterised by large, cheap tower blocks and the expansion of roads. Since the 1980s this trend has changed with the closure of some main roads, the restoration of the Georgian Queen's and Portland Squares and the rebuilding of the Broadmead shopping centre. The removal of the docks to Avonmouth, 7 miles (11km) downstream from the city centre, has also allowed substantial corporate redevelopment of the old central dock area, the 'Floating Harbour'.

As well as Bristol's nautical connections, the city's economy is reliant on the media, information technology, financial services, tourism and the aerospace industry. In the 20th century, Bristol's manufacturing activities expanded to include aircraft production at Filton, by the Bristol Aeroplane Company, and aero-engine manufacture by Bristol Aero Engines (later Rolls-Royce) at Patchway. The former became famous in World War I for the Bristol Fighter, and in World War II for Blenheim and Beaufighter aircraft. In the 1950s it became one of the country's major manufacturers of civil aircraft, with the Bristol Freighter and Britannia and the huge Brabazon airliner. The company diversified into car manufacture in the 1940s, constructing luxury hand-built cars at its factory in Filton under the name Bristol Cars.

In the 1960s Filton played a key role in the Concorde project, being along with Toulouse one of the aircraft's two final assembly plants. The British Concorde prototype (piloted by Brian Trubshaw and co-piloted by John Cochrane) made its maiden flight from Filton to RAF Fairford on 9 April 1969, five weeks after the French test flight. On 26 November 2003, Concorde 216 made the final Concorde flight, returning to Filton airfield to be kept there permanently as the centrepiece of a proposed air museum. The major aerospace companies in Bristol now are BAE Systems, Airbus and Rolls-Royce, all based at Filton. Another important aviation company in the city is Cameron Balloons, the world's largest manufacturer of hot air balloons. Each August, the city is host to the Bristol International Balloon Fiesta, one of Europe's largest hot air balloon events. The city is also served by its own airport, Bristol International at Lulsgate.

A distinctive dialect is spoken in Bristol (known colloquially as 'Brizzle' or 'Bristle'). Unusually for an urban area of England, this is a rhotic dialect, in which the r in words like car is pronounced. The most unusual feature of the dialect, unique to Bristol, is the Bristol l (or terminal l), in which an 'l' sound is appended to words that end in a letter a. Thus 'area' becomes 'areal', etc. This is how the city's name evolved from Brycgstow to have a final 'l' sound: Bristol. Further Bristolian linguistic features are the addition of a superfluous 'to' in questions relating to direction or orientation, or using 'to' instead of 'at', and using male pronouns 'he', 'him' instead of 'it' – for example, 'Where's that?' would be phrased as 'Where's he to?', a feature exported to Newfoundland by the large numbers of Bristol fishermen who emigrated there in the 18th century.

Somerset	**Population**			**Area**	
Districts	*male*	*female*	*total*	*sq miles*	*sq km*
Mendip	50,725	53,144	103,869	286	740
Sedgemoor	51,589	54,292	105,881	218	564
South Somerset	73,805	77,164	150,969	370	959
Taunton Deane	49,204	53,095	102,299	179	462
West Somerset	16,637	18,438	35,075	280	726
Bath and North East Somerset (UA)	82,143	86,897	169,040	134	346
Bristol (UA)	185,660	194,955	380,615	42	110
North Somerset (UA)	91,632	96,932	188,564	144	374
Total	601,395	634,917	1,236,312	1653	4281

Local Attractions and Information

Aardman Animations — Also known as Aardman Studios. An Academy Award winning animation studio based in Bristol, Aardman is famous for its claymation/stop-motion animation productions, particularly plasticine duo Wallace & Gromit. Aardman was founded in 1976 by Peter Lord and David Sproxton; the company name is taken from one of its early characters, a cel-animated superhero created for the children's art series *Vision On*. Another early creation was the simple clay character Morph. Their first adult animations (not themselves Aardman productions) were the shorts *Down and Out* and *Confessions of a Foyer Girl* for the BBC's *Animated Conversations* series, which used real-life conversations as soundtracks. The technique was extended in the *Conversation Pieces* series (1983), which were among a number of animated shorts produced by Aardman for Channel 4. Lord and Sproxton now began hiring more animators. Three of the newcomers, including Nick Park, made their directorial debut at Aardman with the *Lip Synch* series in 1989, which developed the use of pre-recorded conversation still further, and Park's short, *Creature Comforts*, was the first Aardman production to win an Oscar. Park also developed the world-famous clay-modelled shorts featuring the adventures of Wallace & Gromit, the comical green-knitted-tank-top-wearing inventor and his best pal, a clever but silent dog. The 'cheeselovers' withstand many adventures such as *A Grand Day Out* (1989), *The Wrong Trousers* (1993) and *A Close Shave* (1995), the latter two winning more Oscars. In 2000 Aardman Studios began a collaboration with Dreamworks Animation under which they made their first feature film, *Chicken Run*. Wallace & Gromit returned in 2005 in *Wallace & Gromit: The Curse of the Were-Rabbit*, winning another Academy Award for full-length animated film. While Aardman is best known for stop-motion animation, the studio has also dabbled in CGI with productions such as *Al Dante*, *Planet Sketch* and *Flushed Away*. Aardman split with Dreamworks in 2007.

Administrative headquarters
Bath and North East Somerset: Guildhall, High Street, Bath BA1 5AW. Tel: 01225 477000.
Bristol: The Council House, College Green, Bristol BS1 5TR. Tel: 0117 922 2000.
North Somerset: Town Hall, Weston-super-Mare BS23 1EG. Tel: 01934 888888.
Somerset: County Hall, Taunton TA1 4DY. Tel: 01823 355455.

Allerford
4 miles (6km) west of Minehead. Allerford's claim to fame is the picturesque 15th century packhorse bridge which spans the Aller Brook. The village lies within the National Trust's Holnicote Estate (see separate entry).

American Museum and Gardens
Claverton, 2 miles (3km) east of Bath. Located at Claverton Manor, designed by Sir Jeffry Wyattville and built of Bath stone in the 1820s, the museum was founded by Americans Dallas Pratt and John Judkyn, and opened on 1 July 1961. Exhibits cover various periods of American history and include 200 quilts and coverlets. The grounds contain a replica of the garden at Mount Vernon (George Washington's house in Virginia, USA) and an arboretum of North American trees and shrubs. Tel: 01225 460503.

Arnolfini Gallery
Narrow Quay, Bristol. An art gallery located in Bush House, a 19th century Grade II* listed tea warehouse situated on the side of the Floating Harbour in Bristol city centre. The gallery was established in 1961 by Jeremy Rees (1937–2003), son of artist Jean Rees, and moved to its current site in 1975. It has since established itself as a leading centre for contemporary arts. Tel: 0117 917 2300.

Ashton Court
1 mile (1.6km) west of Bristol. Wealthy Bristol merchant Sir John Smythe purchased the estate in 1545 and it remained in the family until the 20th century. The south façade of the house was built in 1632–3 by Thomas Smyth MP, and the Gothic style north wing in the 19th century by entrepreneur and slave trader Jarrit Smith (later Smyth), who married into the Smyth family. The mansion was sold to Bristol City Council in 1959, and the 850 acre (340ha) estate willed to the city as public open space. The house is not open to the public. Tel: 0117 963 9174.

Ashwick House
4 miles (6km) northwest of Dulverton, 10 miles (16km) southwest of Minehead. The house was built in 1901 by wealthy Bristol businessman Heber Mardon, who decorated it in William Morris style. Some original Morris wallpaper and stained glass can still be seen. Outside is a terrace overlooking sloping gardens. During World War II the house became a children's home for evacuees; after passing to a succession of different owners, it was turned into a hotel in 1980. Tel: 01398 323868.

Athelney, Isle of
A slightly elevated plot of land where the River Parrett joins the Tone. It was the island on which Alfred the Great was said to have burned the cakes. A causeway has long been in existence and it is an island no more. GR: NR956359.

Banwell Caves
$^1/_4$ mile (0.4km) south of Banwell, 4 miles (6km) east of Weston-super-Mare. Large numbers of prehistoric animal bones were found in the caves in 1824 on land owned by Henry Law, Bishop of Bath and Wells; they have since been identified as dating to 70,000 years ago during the last Ice Age. In 1963 the caves were designated a Site of Special Scientific Interest for their geological and biological significance. The site comprises two caves: Banwell Bone Cave and Stalactite Caverns, which lie within the grounds of a large house at the western end of Banwell Hill. Established as a tourist attraction in the 19th century, they are now open only a few times a year.

Barrington Court
4 miles (6km) northeast of Ilminster. A Tudor manor house (currently the showroom of a period furniture company), surrounded by formal gardens laid out in the 1920s by Col. Arthur Lyle – a member of the sugar refining family – under the influence of garden designer Gertrude Jekyll. The series of walled rooms includes a White Garden, and rose, iris and lily gardens. There is also a kitchen garden with espaliered apple, pear and plum trees. The property was acquired by the National Trust in 1907. Tel: 01460 241938.

Bath
One of two cities of Somerset, situated 14 miles (21km) southeast of Bristol and connected to Bristol and the sea by the River Avon. The river was linked to the River Thames and London by the Kennet & Avon Canal in 1810 via Bath Locks. The city of Bath is founded around the only naturally occurring hot springs (over 40º Celsius) in the UK. It was first documented as a Roman spa, although clearly founded earlier, as the Romans built the settlement of Aquae Sulis around the pre-existing springs. The waters were believed to be a cure for many afflictions, and from Elizabethan to Georgian times Bath was a resort city for the wealthy. As a result of its popularity during the latter period, the city contains many fine examples of Georgian architecture, most notably the Royal Crescent. The characteristic building material was the warm golden Bath stone, quarried locally. Architects John Wood the Elder (1704–54) and his son John Wood the Younger (1728–82) were responsible for many of the 18th century buildings. The early 18th century also saw Bath acquire its first purpose-built theatre, pump room and assembly rooms. Master of Ceremonies Beau Nash, who presided over the city's social life from 1705 until his death in 1761, drew up a code of behaviour for public entertainments. During the 'Baedeker Raids' of April 1942,

Bath suffered terrible devastation from Luftwaffe bombing but all buildings were later rebuilt. The city was declared a UNESCO World Heritage Site in 1987.

Bath Abbey — Kingston Buildings, Bath. Dedicated to St Peter and now the parish church of Bath, the existing building was once the abbey church of a Benedictine monastery, whose original foundation dates to the 7th century. The present building was begun in 1499 at the behest of Oliver King, Bishop of Bath and Wells, after he visited Bath and found the previous 12th century abbey church in ruins. It was the last great Gothic church to be built in England and is the size of a small cathedral. The new abbey was completed just a few years before the Dissolution of the Monasteries in 1539. During the 1860s major restoration work was carried out by Sir George Gilbert Scott; the timber roof of the nave was replaced with fan vaulting, thus completing the church's original intended design. There is a memorial to Richard 'Beau' Nash (1674–1762). The abbey choir is noted for being one of the finest church choirs in Britain not attached to a school. The church is now Grade I listed. Tel: 01225 422462.

Bath Assembly Rooms — Bennett Street, Bath. The Assembly Rooms were designed in 1769 by John Wood the Younger and once formed the hub of fashionable Georgian society in the city. Citizens would gather in the rooms in the evening for balls and other public functions, or simply to play cards. Such scenes are depicted in the novels of Jane Austen, who lived in Bath with her parents and sister, 1801–06; *Northanger Abbey* and *Persuasion* (both 1818) mention the Assembly Rooms. Charles Dickens also gave public readings in the Assembly Rooms and mentions them in *The Pickwick Papers* (1837). The building was damaged during air raids on Bath in World War II but restored shortly afterwards. More recently it has been used for public functions such as the awarding of degrees by the University of Bath. Part of the building provides a home to the Bath Museum of Costume (see separate entry). The grandeur of the main rooms makes them a popular location for feature films and television series. Now owned by the National Trust. Tel: 01225 477789.

Bath buns and Olivers — A rich, sweet yeast dough shaped round with a lump of sugar baked in the bottom and additional crushed sugar sprinkled on top after baking. Variations in ingredients include candied fruit peel, currants or larger raisins or sultanas. References to Bath buns date from 1763 and the Bath bun is thought to have descended from the 18th century 'Bath cake'; the original 18th century recipe used a brioche or rich egg and butter dough which was then covered with caraway seeds coated in several layers of sugar, similar to French dragée. It is said to have been devised by Dr William Oliver (1695–1764), a doctor treating visitors to Bath with the local spa waters. He is said also to have subsequently invented the Bath Oliver biscuit, when Bath buns proved to be too fattening for his rheumatic patients, and to have willed the recipe to his coachman Atkins, together with a sack of flour and a sum of money. Atkins set up in business at Green Street and became rich by making the biscuits. After various changes in ownership, the recipe passed to James Fortt, and in 1952 the Fortt family business was still baking 80,000 biscuits a day. Though the biscuits are no longer made in Bath, they are still available and are excellent when eaten with cheese, especially the local Cheddar. Oliver also founded Bath General Hospital (now the Royal National Hospital for Rheumatic Diseases) with Ralph Allen, John Wood the Elder and Richard 'Beau' Nash.

Bath Museum of Costume — Bennett Street, Bath. Opened in the Bath Assembly Rooms in 1963, the museum focuses on fashionable dress for men, women and children from the late 16th century to the present. Tel: 01225 477173.

Bath Pump Room — Stall Street, Bath. Built above the original Roman baths (see separate entry), the Pump Room Chambers have been rebuilt and modified a number of times. They were originally built in the style of an orangery in 1704 and have since been altered twice, in 1751 and 1796, when they were completely reconstructed by Thomas Baldwin and John Palmer. Today the rooms are used mainly as a restaurant. Tel: 01225 477734.

Battles — There have been six major battles in Somerset: Cannington, Langport, Lansdown Hill, Marshall's Elm and Sedgemoor in Somerset, and the Battle of Bristol. See separate list for details and separate entry for Sedgemoor. In addition to these battles there were various skirmishes during the English Civil War and one notable siege, of Taunton. In April 1645 Parliamentary forces commanded by Colonel Robert Blake were besieged in Taunton, the only Parliamentary enclave in southwest England. A relief column under Colonel Ralph Weldon reached Taunton on 11 May but this army then left the west of England to join Cromwell and defeat the Royalists at Naseby. Its withdrawal relieved pressure on the Royalists in Somerset, who, under the command of George Goring, once more besieged Taunton. Eventually, after almost three months, the return of Fairfax to the west forced Goring to raise the siege and advance towards Langport. Blake (who went on to become a heroic admiral), famously declared that he had four pairs of boots and would eat three pairs before he would surrender at Taunton. See also Dunster Castle

Beckford's Tower and Museum — Lansdown Road, Bath. An architectural folly situated on Lansdown Hill and built in neoclassical style in 1827 for eccentric and author William Beckford to a design by Henry Goodridge. Standing 120ft (36.5m) high, the tower was used by Beckford as both a library and a retreat. The gilded belvedere, reached by a spiral staircase, offers fine views of the surrounding countryside. The tower is currently both a museum and a holiday home. A Victorian cemetery now occupies part of what was once known as Beckford's Ride, a garden running between the tower and Beckford's house in Lansdown Crescent. Tel: 01225 460705.

Beckington Castle — Beckington, 8 miles (13km) south of Bath. A Tudor manor house built in the mid 16th century by the Long family, wealthy clothiers and patrons of Beckington Church. It has since had numerous owners; in the 1780s, it came into the hands of the Chislett family, who owned it until 1870. It was given the name 'Castle House' c.1839, and this later evolved into 'The Castle' and 'Beckington Castle'. Its most notable 20th century resident was E M Nelson, President of the Royal Microscopical Society and author of *The Cult of Circle Builders*, who owned the house 1902–26. It was a hotel, an antiques showroom and Ravenscroft School from 1945 to 1970. In 1995–6 the castle was restored by defence procurement company SEA in co-operation with Mendip Council and English Heritage. The Grade II* listed castle now serves as the group's headquarters; the site comprises the castle itself and the purpose-built New Technology Centre.

Bishop's Palace Market Place, Wells. Dating from the early 13th century and set within fortified walls and a moat, the palace has been the home of the Bishops of Bath and Wells for 800 years. The adjoining chapel and great hall, the latter now a ruin, also date from the 13th century and the gatehouse from the 14th. The springs from which the city takes its name rise from a large pool in the 14 acres (5.5ha) of gardens. Tel: 01749 678691.

Blackdown Hills A range of hills cut with sharp valleys situated between Taunton and Wellington in the west of Somerset, along the Somerset/Devon border. Staple Hill, the site of the Wellington Monument, is the highest point at 1035ft (315m). The hills are a designated Area of Outstanding Natural Beauty with 16 Sites of Special Scientific Interest, including the 386 acre (156ha) Black Down and Sampford Commons, an area of acidic grassland supporting a wide range of butterflies and moths.

Blagdon Lake 10 miles (16km) southwest of Bristol. Situated in the Chew Valley at the northern edge of the Mendip Hills, the lake was created by the Bristol Waterworks Company 1891–9 by damming the River Yeo. The Wrington Vale Light Railway was constructed primarily to bring building materials to the site. Originally called the Yeo Reservoir, the lake covers 440 acres (178ha). It is relatively shallow, with an average depth of 14ft (4.2m) and only 42ft (13m) at its deepest point near the dam at its west end. When full its capacity is 1860 million gallons (8456 million litres), and it supplies 2100 million gallons (9547 million litres) of water each year in conjunction with its larger neighbour, Chew Valley Lake. It is a Site of Special Scientific Interest visited by a variety of water birds, including great crested grebe, little grebe, cormorant, mute swan, Canada goose, shoveler and gadwall. Green-winged orchid and southern marsh orchid are among the plant species found on the margins of the lake. Tel: 01275 332339.

Blagdon Pumping Station Station Road, Blagdon, 10 miles (16km) southwest of Bristol. Built in the early 20th century to supply water from Blagdon Lake to Bristol, the station originally utilised four Woolf compound rotative beam pumping engines, built by Glenfield & Kennedy of Kilmarnock 1900–05 and housed in two separate buildings. Three engines with a fourth on standby could pump 7.5 million gallons (34 million litres) of water a day. They ran until 1949, when two engines from the north engine house were replaced by electric pumps. In 1984 it was decided to preserve the two remaining engines as part of a museum. The pumping station is now Grade II listed, while the site features interactive science and environment displays and a room dedicated to the charity WaterAid. Tel: 0117 953 6470.

Blake Museum Blake Street, Bridgwater. Thought to be the birthplace of Admiral Robert Blake (1598–1657), the house is now a museum featuring displays on local history and archaeological exhibits. Tel: 01278 456127.

Blue Anchor GWR Railway Museum See West Somerset Railway

Brean Down 2 miles (3km) west of Weston-super-Mare. A promontory on the coast of North Somerset, reaching a height of 320ft (97.5m) and extending 1½ miles (2.5km) into the Bristol Channel. A designated Site of Special Scientific Interest for its rare flora, such as the white rock rose which is only found at two other sites in Britain, the limestone promontory is a continuation of the Mendip Hills, which extend still further west to the small islands of Steep Holm and Flat Holm. Rich in wildlife, history and archaeology, it is now owned by the National Trust. At its seaward extremity is Brean Down Fort. Tel: 01934 844518.

Brean Down Fort 2 miles (3km) southwest of Weston-super-Mare. Built on the headland at Brean Down 1864–71 on the recommendation of the 1859 Royal Commission, the fort was the most southerly of a chain of defences across the Bristol Channel, protecting access to Bristol and Cardiff. The fort was originally armed with seven 7in guns. After an explosion caused by a suicidal soldier, the fort was disarmed in 1901; it was rearmed with two 6in ex-naval guns on the outbreak of World War II. The site was also used during the war as a test launch site for rockets and experimental weapons. Tel: 01934 844518.

Brendon Hills A ridge of sandstone and slate hills in the west of Somerset. Once the site of substantial mineral extraction, their fertile soil is now heavily cultivated. Mining, notably for ironstone, reached its peak during the 19th century when a railway, including an 800ft (244m) incline at Comberow with a 1 in 4 gradient, was built to take the ore to Watchet from where it was sent to Ebbw Vale in Wales for smelting. Most of the mines had been fully worked by the end of the 1800s. The hills merge with the eastern side of Exmoor and fall within the boundaries of Exmoor National Park. Their highest point is Lype Hill at 1388ft (422m).

Brent Knoll 6 miles (10km) south of Weston-super-Mare. An outcrop of the Mendip Hills, known by the Romans as 'The Mount of Frogs' as it was then an island in a large expanse of marsh. Standing in an otherwise flat area, at a height of 449ft (137m), it is a distinctive feature of the landscape. It has been the site of human settlement since at least the Bronze Age and there is an Iron Age hill fort on the summit. The village of Brent Knoll lies to the southwest at the foot of the hill; its name was changed from South Brent c.1880 to avoid confusion among rail passengers with the village of South Brent in Devon.

Bride's Mound ½ mile (0.8km) southwest of Glastonbury. A tiny mound near the foot of Wearyall Hill. According to legend it was the western gateway to Avalon, where medieval pilgrims would keep vigil through the night before following the processional way to Glastonbury Tor. The mound's function may have been preserved since the pre-Christian period, as it was the legendary site of a Druidic *bruga* – a hostel or college. King Arthur is also said to have had a vision of the Virgin Mary and the Christ Child here, and it is believed that St Brigid of Kildare (Brighde) stayed here in AD 488.

Bridgwater The administrative centre of the Sedgemoor district, and the leading industrial town in Somerset. Located on the edge of the Somerset Levels, the market town received its charter from King John in 1200. In 1685 the townspeople were among the supporters of the Duke of Monmouth before the Battle of Sedgemoor.

Bridgwater Castle Built c.1200 by William Brewer in old red sandstone with a tidal moat up to 65ft (20m) wide in places. Sited on the only raised ground in the town, the castle controlled the crossing of the town bridge. In addition to a keep the complex included a dungeon, chapel, stables and a campanile. During the Civil War both the town and the castle were held by the Royalists under Colonel Sir Francis Wyndham, a personal acquaintance of the king. History might have been very different had his wife, Lady Crystabella Wyndham, been more accurate with a musket shot that missed Cromwell but killed his aide de camp. The castle was slighted after its surrender to Parliamentary forces in 1645; little remains today except for a 12ft (3.5m) thick portion of the castle wall and a water gate which can be seen on West Quay.

Bridgwater & Taunton Canal A canal running for 14 miles (23km) between the towns of Bridgwater and Taunton and linking the Rivers Parrett and Tone. It was originally intended to extend across the southwest of England to Exeter, but became uneconomical with the spread of the railways. The canal was built in the 1820s from a dock on the River Parrett at Huntworth to Taunton. It was later extended from Huntworth to a floating harbour north of Bridgwater in 1842, and the Huntworth dock was abandoned. After World War I the canal fell into decline; it was absorbed by the British Waterways Board in 1962 and for several years was classified as a 'remainder waterway'. Bridgwater Docks, which had been used by a small amount of coastal shipping, was finally closed in 1971 and the connection at Bridgwater Docks was stopped up. Recently some restoration has been carried out, including repairs to the towpath and the modernisation of various swing bridges.

Bristol International Airport 8 miles (13km) south of Bristol. Located near Lulsgate Bottom, Bristol airport (BRS) has one terminal, officially opened in March 2000 by HRH the Princess Royal, and currently caters for more than 5 million passengers flying to over 90 destinations each year. Although there are flights to north and west Africa, USA and the Caribbean, the airport is chiefly known for its wide range of European and domestic destinations. The airport was called Bristol Lulsgate Airport when opened in 1957 by Princess Marina, Duchess of Kent, but changed its name in March 1997. The first Bristol Airport was situated in Whitchurch, in the southeast of the city, and was opened in 1930 by Prince George, son of George V – becoming the third such airport in the UK. During World War II, Bristol was the only civil airport still in operation in the UK, meaning that all flights usually bound for London were terminated in Bristol. The newly formed British Overseas Airways Corporation was dispersed to Whitchurch from Croydon and Gatwick Airports.

Bristol Castle Castle Park, Bristol. Norman motte and bailey castle with curtain walls and a great keep built by Robert of Gloucester c.1120. During the 12th century civil war it was held by Robert, a leading supporter of the Empress Matilda, and King Stephen was imprisoned here in 1141 before Robert himself was captured and the king released in exchange. The castle was destroyed in the 1650s and the remains now stand in a public park. The sallyport, an escape route, can be seen on one wall.

Bristol Cathedral College Green, Bristol. The city's Anglican cathedral, dedicated to the Holy and Undivided Trinity, was given cathedral status by Henry VIII in 1542. Before this it was a Norman monastic church founded in 1142, as St Augustine's Abbey, by wealthy local landowner and royal official Robert Fitzharding. Very little survives from this period except for the chapter house, its adjoining buildings and the great gatehouse with its 15th century upper floor. The chapter house has Romanesque decoration of interlaced arcading and the choir's fine early 14th century misericords feature a notable carving of the Romance of Reynard the Fox. A new nave, designed by George Edmund Street to blend in style with the medieval east end, was added during the 19th century. The opening ceremony was on 23 October 1877. The cathedral featured in the film *The Medusa Touch* (1978), in the guise of Minster Cathedral, London. Tel: 0117 926 4879.

Bristol Channel A major inlet separating south Wales from southwest England and extending from the lower estuary of the River Severn to the part of the North Atlantic Ocean known as the Celtic Sea. With its limits at St Govan's Head in Pembrokeshire, Lundy Island, and Hartland Point in Devon, it is over 30 miles (50km) across at its widest point. On 30 January 1607, thousands of people were drowned, houses and villages swept away, farmland inundated and flocks destroyed when a flood hit the channel's shores. The devastation was particularly bad on the Welsh side from Laugharne in Carmarthenshire to above Chepstow on the English border. Cardiff was the most badly affected town. Plaques up to 8ft (2.5km) above sea level still show how high the waters rose on the sides of the surviving churches. It was commemorated in a contemporary pamphlet, 'God's Warning to the People of England by the Great Overflowing of the Waters or Floods'. Although the cause of the flood is disputed, it has long been believed that it was caused by a combination of meteorological extremes and tidal peaks. Research published in 2002 has shown evidence of a tsunami in the Channel.

Bristol Roman Catholic Cathedral Clifton Park, Bristol. Dedicated to St Peter and St Paul and also known as Clifton Cathedral, the church has been the seat of the Diocese of Clifton since 1850. Commissioned in 1965 to replace a wooden-framed pro-cathedral built at the establishment of the diocese in the mid 19th century, it was the first cathedral designed in response to the requirements of the Second Vatican Council, particularly for the need to accommodate a large congregation grouped closely around the altar during Mass. Construction took place 1970–3 and the cathedral was consecrated on 29 June 1973. Tel: 0117 973 8411.

Bristol Zoo | Guthrie Road, Clifton, Bristol. Opened in 1836, Bristol is the fifth oldest zoo in the world and the oldest located outside a capital city. In the 1960s the zoo came to national prominence by appearing in the UK television series *Animal Magic*, hosted by comic animal 'communicator' Johnny Morris. Tel: 0117 974 7399.

Brympton D'Evercy | 3 miles (5km) west of Yeovil. The original manor house was built by the D'Evercy family c.1220–1325. Over the next four centuries it was considerably enlarged in local golden-coloured Ham stone by its various owners, its present appearance owing much to the grand south wing built c.1680. Despite its striking appearance it has remained little known; for a few years following World War II it served as a boys' school, afterwards returning to its role as a private residence.

Building of Bath Museum | The Vineyards, The Paragon, Bath. Located in the Countess of Huntingdon's Chapel, the museum explores the development of Georgian Bath, depicting how its buildings were designed, built, decorated,and lived in during the 18th century. Exhibits include artefacts, full-size reconstructions, tools and a series of spectacular models. Tel: 01225 333895.

Burledge Hill | $^1/_4$ mile (0.4km) south of Bishop Sutton, 5 miles (8km) northwest of Midsomer Norton. A site within the Mendip Hills Area of Outstanding Natural Beauty, offering spectacular views of the Chew Valley. With its mixture of flower-rich grassland, scrub and mature hedgerows, the hill is a designated Site of Special Scientific Interest.

Burrington Combe | 4 miles (6km) north of Cheddar. A limestone gorge situated on the north side of the Mendip Hills. The gorge contains the entrances to numerous caves, and Augustus Montague Toplady was supposedly inspired to write the hymn 'Rock of Ages' here while sheltering under a rock during a thunderstorm in the late 18th century. The combe and its surrounding limestone landscape, similar to that of Cheddar Gorge, are a designated Site of Special Scientific Interest.

Cabot Tower | Brandon Hill Park, Bristol. One of two towers dominating the Bristol skyline, close to Brunel's Suspension Bridge, Cabot Tower stands 100ft (30.5m) high atop Brandon Hill. It was built in 1897 and designed by William Venn Gough to commemorate John Cabot's voyage to America in 1497. At the base are emplacements for captured Russian guns brought back to England after the Crimean War. Tel: 0117 922 3719.

Cadbury Camp | $^1/_4$ mile (0.4km) north of Tickenham, 3 miles (5km) east of Clevedon. An Iron Age hill fort; according to legend it is the location of a cave where King Arthur lies sleeping ready to come to England's aid, although this may be due to confusion with the better-known Cadbury Castle near South Cadbury, 30 miles (48km) to the south. The site is managed by the National Trust.

Cadbury Castle | South Cadbury, $7^1/_2$ miles (12km) northwest of Yeovil. An Iron Age hill fort covering an area of 20 acres (8ha) with four defensive rings, situated on an isolated limestone hill 500ft (150m) high on the southern edge of the Somerset Levels. The site dates to c.500 BC, the earliest settlement being represented by Neolithic pottery and flints; there is evidence that it was violently taken and reoccupied by the Romans c.AD 50. Following the Roman withdrawal it is thought to have been in use until after 580. It has been associated since at least the 16th century with King Arthur and the legends of Camelot; local traditions identifying the area with Arthur were first written down by John Leland in 1532. It is also possible that the name Cadbury is derived from Cado, king of Kernyw in the time of Arthur. Intriguingly, excavations in 1966–70, led by archaeologist Leslie Alcock, uncovered not only Iron Age, Roman and Saxon artefacts but also traces of fortifications dating to c.AD 500, including a Celtic-style timbered hall measuring 65ft x 32ft (20m x 10m) and a gatehouse. Alcock showed that the innermost Iron Age defences had been refortified to provide a defended site double the size of any other known fort of the period. Pottery from the eastern Mediterranean dating from the same period was also found, indicating wide trade links and suggesting that this was the chief *caer* (castle or palace) of a major ruler. In 1010–20 the hill was reoccupied for use as a temporary Saxon mint, briefly deputising for that at Bruton.

Cadbury Hill | Yatton, 3 miles (5km) southeast of Clevedon. A small hill in north Somerset on which are the remains of an Iron Age hill fort. According to local legend the hill is inhabited by the ghost of a Roman legionnaire.

Castle Neroche | $1^1/_4$ miles (2km) north of Buckland St Mary, 4 miles (6km) west of Ilminster. Norman enclosure castle in the Blackdown Hills, founded in the late 11th century by Robert of Mortain on the site of an Iron Age hill fort. The motte was added in the early 12th century and a shell keep soon after. Only some earthworks now remain.

Chalice Well and Gardens | Chilkwell Street, Glastonbury. A 'holy' well situated at the foot of Glastonbury Tor. Archaeological evidence suggests that the well has been continuously used for at least 2000 years. Water issues from the spring at a rate of 25,000 gallons per day; it has never failed, even during droughts, and is believed to possess healing qualities. The well is often portrayed as a symbol of the female aspect of the deity, with the male symbolised by Glastonbury Tor; its cover, designed in the 19th century by archaeologist Bligh Bond, depicts the two interlocking circles of the symbol known as the Vesica Piscis. A sword bisects the two circles in a possible reference to Excalibur, believed by some to be buried at Glastonbury Abbey. Apocryphal Christian texts suggest that Chalice Well marks the site where Joseph of Arimathea placed the chalice that had caught drops of Christ's blood at the Last Supper, linking the well to the Holy Grail. The reddish hue of the water, due to iron oxide deposits, is said by some Christians to represent the rusty iron nails used at the Crucifixion. The natural spring and surrounding gardens are owned and managed by the Chalice Well Trust, founded by Wellesley Tudor Pole in 1959. Tel: 01458 831154.

Chard & District Museum | High Street, Chard. Housed in 16th century Godworthy House, the museum has displays on Chard's history including information on social life and local industries. There are exhibits relating to Victorians John Stringfellow, a pioneer of powered flight, and James Gillingham, manufacturer of artificial limbs. Tel: 01460 65091.

Chard Canal — A 13$^1/_2$ mile (22km) tub-boat canal connecting the Bridgwater and Taunton Canal at Creech St Michael to Chard through three tunnels and four inclined planes. Constructed 1835–42 at a cost of £140,000, it was the last major canal (other than the Manchester Ship Canal) to be constructed in England, but closed in 1866. Much of its course has been obliterated by later development, although traces still remain, including an aqueduct over the River Tone.

Chard Guildhall — Fore Street, Chard. A Grade II* listed building dating to 1834, with a cast iron-framed corn exchange added in 1883. Recently restored, it is now in use as the town hall. It is managed by English Heritage. Tel: 01460 260371.

Cheddar — A village in the district of Sedgemoor, situated on the edge of the Mendip Hills, 14 miles (23km) southwest of Bristol. Famous for having given its name to Cheddar cheese, Cheddar's other main produce is the strawberry, which gave its name to the now disused Strawberry Line railway that ran from Yatton to Wells. Nearby are Cheddar Gorge, the largest gorge in England, and Cheddar Caves, where the remains of 'Cheddar Man' were found.

Cheddar Caves — See Cheddar Gorge

Cheddar Gorge — $^1/_2$ mile (0.8km) northeast of Cheddar, 10 miles (16km) southeast of Weston-super-Mare. The largest gorge in the UK, with a maximum recorded depth of 370ft (113m). Located in the Mendip Hills, the rocks of the gorge consist of Carboniferous limestone on top of old red sandstone. The river at the bottom of the gorge, the Cheddar Yeo, rises in Gough's Cave. The gorge is the site of Cheddar Caves; Britain's oldest complete human skeleton, 9000 year old Cheddar Man, was found in 1903, also in Gough's Cave. Older remains from the Upper Late Palaeolithic era (12,000–13,000 years ago) have also been found. There are spectacular rock formations within the caves, and Cox's Cave, the other most popular cave, boasts stunning colours. Further up the gorge are several smaller caves. Jacob's Ladder is a public path of 274 steps built up the side of the gorge. The Cheddar Complex Site of Special Scientific Interest encompasses Cheddar Gorge and much of the surrounding land. The whole south side of the gorge is owned by the 7th Marquess of Bath, of Longleat House (see Wiltshire). Tel: 01934 742343.

Chew Valley Lake — 8 miles (13km) south of Bristol. Located in the Chew Valley, the largest artificial lake in southwest England and the fifth largest in the UK, with an area of 1200 acres (490ha). Created in the early 1950s and opened by Queen Elizabeth II in 1956, it provides much of the drinking water for Bristol and the surrounding area, taking its supply from the Mendip Hills. Archaeological investigations carried out before the lake was created found evidence of occupation since Neolithic times and included Roman artefacts. The lake is an important site for wildlife and is a Site of Special Scientific Interest and a Special Protection Area. It is a national centre for bird watching, with over 260 species recorded, including indigenous and migrant water birds. During a storm on 10 July 1968, the lake rose 19 inches (480mm) in under 12 hours.

Chewton Place — Chewton Keynsham, 7 miles (11km) southeast of Bristol. Georgian house built c.1762 and extended c.1786. It was extensively remodelled 1860–70 and further extended 1987–8. A folly in the grounds, known locally as the Owl Tower, is a tall tapering square limestone obelisk with pointed-arched openings to east and west at the base. A carved owl on the keystone of one of the arches probably gives the folly its name. The Grade II listed house is now predominantly used as a conference centre; the folly is also Grade II listed. Tel: 0117 986 3105.

Churches — The **Church of the Holy Ghost**, High Street, Midsomer Norton, is a Roman Catholic parish church housed in a converted tithe barn, and served by monks of the Order of St Benedict from Downside Abbey. The 15th century building was formerly owned by the Augustinian canons at Merton Priory, Surrey. Following the priory's dissolution the barn was handed over to the king along with the rest of its property, and subsequently became part of the patrimony of Christ Church, Oxford. After it was sold in 1886, no longer being needed for the storing of tithes, Downside Abbey purchased the building in 1906 for use as a church. Abbot Edmund Ford engaged architect Giles Gilbert Scott to restore and convert the building. In addition to restoring the timber roof, Scott made structural changes including new doorways and a new Gothic-style window in the south wall. The barn was inaugurated as a church on 17 May 1913 and is now Grade II* listed. Features include an elaborately carved tabernacle dating from 1794 and Jacobean panelling behind the high altar, while the pulpit was formerly the prefect's desk in the study room of Downside Abbey School.

St George's Church, Great George Street, Bristol, was built c.1823 by Robert Smirke in Greek Revival style as a chapel-of-ease to the Cathedral of St Augustine. The Grade II* listed Georgian church was converted to a 550-seat concert hall in 1987. Tel: 0117 929 4929.

The **Church of St Beuno**, Culbone, 2 miles (3km) west of Porlock Weir, is one of several claiming to be the smallest in England. The main structure, 35ft (10.5m) long, is 12th century. According to legend, the area beyond Culbone, towards Lynmouth, is where Jesus may have alighted when accompanying Joseph of Arimathea to England. The site is said to have inspired the words of William Blake's famous poem, *Jerusalem*: 'And did those feet in ancient time Walk upon England's mountains green? And was the Holy Lamb of God On England's pleasant pastures seen?' The area also has links with several Romantic poets and R D Blackmore, the author of *Lorna Doone.*

St Mary Magdalene Church, Church Square, Taunton, has been the town church since 1308. Of particular note are the tower, the Tudor ceiling of the nave, a chancel adorned with over 100 gilded angels, and the stained glass windows. Tel: 01823 272441.

St Thomas a Becket Church, Pensford, 7 miles (11km) west of Bath, is a parish church with late 14th century tower. The remainder of the church was rebuilt in 1869. Tel: 0117 975 0742.

Circus, The — A famous example of Georgian architecture in Bath, begun in 1754 and completed in 1768. The name comes from the Latin word which means a ring, oval or circle. The Circus consists of a ring of terraced townhouses, divided into three segments of equal length, and surrounding a circular central space. Originally called King's Circus, it was designed by John Wood the Elder and formed part of his grand vision to recreate a classical Palladian architectural landscape for the city. Other projects included nearby Queen Square and the Forum (which was never built). Wood died less than three months after the first stone was laid and it was left to his son, John Wood the Younger, to complete the scheme to his father's design. The Circus is the culmination of Wood's career, and is considered his masterpiece. Several of the houses were demolished when a bomb fell into the Circus during the 'Baedeker Raids' of 1942, but these have since been reconstructed in the original style.

Clapton Mill — Clapton, 2 miles (3km) southwest of Crewkerne. A remarkably complete 18th century watermill, reconstructed in 1850, which operated commercially until 1991. The building is now Grade II* listed. Tel: 01460 72142.

Clatworthy Reservoir — 10 miles (16km) southeast of Minehead. Situated in the Brendon Hills on the edge of the Exmoor National Park. Covering 130 acres (53ha) and surrounded by rolling hills, the reservoir is supplied by the headwaters of the River Tone. The range of habitats in the surrounding countryside includes acid grassland, broadleaf woodlands and scrub, with marshy areas around the inlet streams. Clatworthy Wood consists of mainly beech with sessile oaks, silver birch and rowan. The site is home to a range of passage and woodland birds. Other wildlife includes geese, grebes and swans, red deer, roe deer and badgers. Tel: 01984 624658.

Claverton Pumping Station — Claverton, 3 miles (5km) east of Bath. Designed to pump water from the River Avon to the Kennet & Avon Canal using power from the flow of the river, the pumping station is located in a pump house built of Bath stone, located at river level, while the canal at Claverton is cut into the side of the Avon valley 48ft (14.5m) above the river. Water is diverted from the river by Warleigh Weir, 600ft (180m) upstream. The water flows down a leat to the pumping station, where it powers a waterwheel, 24ft (7.3m) wide and 17ft (5.2m) in diameter. At full power the wheel uses two tons of water per second and rotates five times a minute. The pumping station was built by John Rennie and worked continuously from 1813 until 1952. It was restored and reopened in 1978. Tel: 01225 483001.

Cleeve Abbey — Washford, 6 miles (10km) southeast of Minehead. Situated in the Valley of Flowers, the ruins of the small Cistercian abbey of Cleeve, founded c.1190 by William de Roumare, grandson of a baron of the same name who played a considerable part in Anglo-Norman history under Henry I and King Stephen. As it claimed exemption from episcopal visitation, very little is known of its history. The first abbot, Ralph, brought with him 12 monks from the Cistercian house of Reresby. Among the 17 priests who kept hospitality were John Hooper, later the Protestant Bishop of Gloucester. After its dissolution the abbey was granted to Robert, Earl of Sussex, after which it was destroyed for the value of its materials. The associated buildings survived as the outbuildings of a farm, and are among the finest surviving domestic monastery buildings in England. The site is now maintained by English Heritage. Tel: 01984 640377.

Clevedon Court — Tickenham Road, Clevedon. The house was built by Sir John de Clevedon c.1320 and incorporates a 13th century tower and great hall; it has been in the possession of the Elton family since 1709 and is still occupied by their descendants. There are collections of Eltonware pottery and Nailsea glass, as well as paintings and furniture, and the house is surrounded by 18th century landscaped gardens. Now owned by the National Trust. Tel: 01275 872257.

Clevedon Pier — Marine Parade, Clevedon. One of the finest surviving Victorian piers in the UK. Partially constructed from secondhand railway lines, it opened in 1869, and is 738ft (225m) long. After its final span collapsed on 17 October 1970, the pavilions from the end of the pier were taken ashore for storage, in the hope of eventual restoration. After a long campaign by local people to raise funds for restoration (supported by Sir John Betjeman), the pier eventually reopened on 27 May 1989. In 2001 it was given Grade I listing (the only other pier with this status is Brighton's West Pier). The landing stage at the end of the pier is occasionally used by ships, notably the PS *Waverley*. Tel: 01275 878846.

Cleveland Bridge — A cast iron bridge spanning the River Avon in Bath, linking Lansdown and the A4/London Road with the A36 via Bathwick Street. It was built by ironfounder William Hazledine of Shrewsbury in 1826 on the site of a Roman ferry crossing. Named after the 3rd Duke of Cleveland, it enabled the expansion of Georgian Bath on the south side of the river. It was designed by architect Henry Goodridge using Bath stone and with an elegant cast iron arch, with a toll house – each with columns fronting onto the bridge, giving them the appearance of small ancient temples – on each of the four corners. Only one of the four (Number 1 next to St John's Road) was actually used as a toll house; the rest were let to private tenants. The bridge was paid for by subscription, with the intention that investors would make a return on their investment through toll charges. In 1925 Bath city council took over the bridge from the Bathwick Bridge Company; it was freed from tolls on 20 June 1927 and extensively restored during 1928–9. Cleveland Bridge is still free to use, although the next bridge upstream at Bathampton is one of the UK's few remaining privately owned toll bridges.

Clifton Cathedral — See Bristol Roman Catholic Cathedral

Clifton Suspension Bridge — A bridge spanning the Avon Gorge and linking Clifton in Bristol to Leigh Woods in North Somerset. Designed by Isambard Kingdom Brunel, the Grade I listed structure has become a distinctive landmark often used as a symbol of Bristol. The idea of building a bridge across the Avon Gorge originated in 1754, when Bristol merchant William Vick left a bequest of £1000 accompanied by instructions that when the interest had accumulated to £10,000 it should be used to build a stone bridge between Clifton Down and Leigh Woods. By the 1820s Vick's bequest was nearing £8000, but it was estimated that a stone bridge would cost over ten times that amount. An

Act of Parliament was passed to allow a wrought iron suspension bridge to be built instead, with tolls levied to recoup the cost. In 1829 a competition was held to find a design for the bridge; the judge, Thomas Telford, rejected all the designs submitted, and tried to insist on a hugely expensive design of his own. A second competition, held with new judges, was won by Brunel's design, for a suspension bridge with fashionably Egyptian-influenced towers. An attempt to build Brunel's design in 1831 was stopped by the Bristol Riots, which severely dented commercial confidence in Bristol. Work was started again only in 1836, although by then the capital from Vick's bequest and subsequent investment was insufficient. By 1843, the towers had been built in unfinished stone, but funds were exhausted. In 1851, the ironwork was sold and used to build the Brunel-designed Royal Albert Bridge on the railway between Plymouth and Saltash. Brunel died in 1859 without seeing the completion of the bridge. His colleagues in the Institution of Civil Engineers felt that its completion would be a fitting memorial to him, and managed to raise new funds. Work on the bridge restarted in 1862, to revised designs by William Henry Barlow and Sir John Hawkshaw, and was complete by 1864. The bridge has been open continuously since then; it is now managed by a trust established in 1952. The bridge has long had a reputation as a suicide spot and there are now telephones with a direct line to the Samaritans beside it.

Coleridge Cottage — Nether Stowey, 6 miles (10km) west of Bridgwater. Samuel Taylor Coleridge lived in this 17th century cottage 1797–1800 and wrote some of his finest poems here, including 'Fears in Solitude', 'This Lime-Tree Bower my Prison', 'The Nightingale', 'Frost at Midnight' and the first part of *Christabel*. *The Rime of the Ancient Mariner* has many references to neighbouring places. Now owned by the National Trust. Tel: 01278 732662.

Combe Down Tunnel — A 1 mile (1.6km) long tunnel on the former Somerset & Dorset Joint Railway in the southern suburbs of Bath, at Combe Down. The tunnel was on the last section of the Bath extension line, built in 1874; it was the longest tunnel in Britain without a ventilation shaft and there were significant problems with fumes. In November 1929 the driver and fireman of a northbound goods train were overcome by smoke and the train ran out of control, crashing into the goods yard on the approach to Bath Queen Square railway station and killing the driver and two railway employees in the yard. It is now to be part of a walking route known as the Two Tunnels Greenway.

Combe Sydenham Hall — 5 miles (8km) south of Watchet. An Elizabethan E-plan house built for Sir George Sydenham in 1580 on the site of a monastery. Sir George's daughter married Sir Francis Drake, and a cannonball (in fact a meteorite) supposedly fired by Drake from hundreds of miles away as a warning to his fiancée not to marry another man is on display. The surrounding deer park features a recreated parterre planted with old roses. There is also a herb garden, peacock house and over 500 acres (200ha) of woods. Tel: 01984 656284.

Cothay Manor — 4 miles (6km) west of Wellington. A 14th century manor house set on the River Tone and surrounded by 12 acres (5ha) of gardens designed in the 1920s as a series of 'rooms' set off a 600ft (183m) yew walk. The Robbs, who moved to Cothay in 1993, have since restored the garden, which also features a bog garden with azaleas and drifts of primulas, trees, cottage garden, courtyards and a river walk. Tel: 01823 672283.

Crowcombe Court — Crowcombe, 9 miles (15km) northwest of Taunton. The Grade I listed early Georgian red-brick house, built c.1723, stands on the southern slopes of the Quantock Hills, below the southwest-facing wooded slope of the park. There are 4 acres (1.2ha) of gardens and ornamental plantations. Tel: 01984 618373.

Crowe Hall — Widcombe Hill, Bath. An unusual 11 acre (4.5ha) private garden on a steep slope. Surrounding the Regency house is a broad terrace with excellent views as well as several smaller gardens, with grottoes, tunnels and water features; laid out in the 1840s, the garden has been enlarged and replanted since the 1960s. Tel: 01225 310322.

Curzon Cinema — Old Church Road, Clevedon. The Curzon claims to be the oldest continually running purpose-built cinema in the world. Opened on 20 April 1912 by Victor Cox, the original building had 200 seats and the first show raised funds for the survivors and relatives of those killed earlier in the month on the *Titanic*. By the following year the building had been expanded to 389 seats, and was the first public building in the town to have electricity. A new cinema was built on the site 1920–2. The building was the site of Clevedon's only fatality due to enemy action in World War II, when a soldier standing in the cinema doorway was killed by a bomb, damage from which is still visible on the exterior. In 1945 the cinema (previously known as the Picture House) was sold and changed its name to the Maxime. Another change of ownership in 1953 brought its current name. In 1995 the cinema was bought by Clevedon Community Centre for the Arts, whose patrons include Aardman Animations founders David Sproxton and Peter Lord, directors Nick Park and Terry Gilliam, and actors Tony Robinson and Alan Rickman. Tel: 01275 871000.

Daw's Castle — 1/4 mile (0.4km) west of Watchet, 6 miles (10km) east of Minehead. Also known as Dart's Castle or Dane's Castle. A hill fort situated on cliffs 260ft (80m) above the sea, on a tapering spur of land bounded by the Washford River to the south, as it flows to the sea at Watchet. Named after Thomas Dawe, who owned the land in 1537, it is thought to be of Iron Age origin, but was rebuilt and fortified by Alfred the Great as part of his defence against Viking raids from the Bristol Channel c.AD 878. Excavations have revealed a first phase of defence from this period with a mortared wall fronting an earth bank, and a second late 9th or early 10th century phase, also against Viking invaders. A Saxon mint, established at Watchet in 1035, is thought to have been situated within the fort.

Dinder House — Dinder, 3 miles (5km) west of Shepton Mallet. A Grade II listed Regency house built in 1801 by the Rev. William Somerville on the site of an earlier manor house, and extended in the 1850s and early 1900s. On the death of Somerville's widow, the estate passed to his nephew, James Somerville Fownes, who adopted the surname Somerville to retain its connection with the house.

The last Somerville resident was Admiral of the Fleet Sir James Fownes Somerville, commander of the British force that sank the French fleet at Mers-el-Kébir, near Oran, Algeria, on 3 July 1940. Appointed Lord Lieutenant of Somerset in August 1946, he lived in the house from the end of World War II until his death in 1949.

Dodington Hall 1 mile (1.6km) west of Nether Stowey, 7 miles (11km) west of Bridgwater. A small Tudor manor house on the lower slopes of the Quantock Hills. Tel: 01278 741400.

Dowsborough Camp 2 mile (3km) west of Nether Stowey, 8 miles (13km) west of Bridgwater. An Iron Age hill fort covering 8 acres (3ha). The earthwork defences comprise a rampart and ditch, with an intermittent counterscarp bank. The site has had a long history of use: a Bronze Age barrow lies in the northwest corner, and there are extraction or trial pits for copper ore dating from the 17th and 18th centuries, when small scale copper mining was carried out in the Quantock Hills. Post-medieval charcoal burning platforms also occur in the area, and the woodland covering much of the hill fort has been managed for 300 years. Slit trenches dating from World War II have also been found. Tel: 01392 824901.

Dunkery Beacon 5 miles (8km) southwest of Minehead. Dunkery Beacon at 1705ft (519m) is both the highest hill on Exmoor and the highest geographical point in Somerset (although the tip of the Mendip TV mast is higher at 1924ft/586m). The summit provides views of both the Bristol and English Channel coasts, the Brecon Beacons including Pen y Fan, Bodmin Moor, Dartmoor, the Severn Bridges and Cleeve Hill, 86 miles (138km) away in Gloucestershire. Composed of Devonian sedimentary rock, as can be seen in the red soil, the hill is blanketed in ling and bell heather, giving it a deep purple colour in summer; gorse, sessile oak, ash, rowan, hazel, bracken, mosses, liverworts, lichens and ferns also grow on the hill or the surrounding woodland. Lying within the Holnicote Estate, Dunkery Beacon was given to the National Trust in 1935. There are several Bronze Age burial mounds at or near the summit, two of the larger ones being named Joaney How and Robin How. In R D Blackmore's novel *Lorna Doone*, John Fry calls Dunkery Beacon the 'haighest place of Hexmoor'.

Dunster Castle Dunster, 1½ miles (2.5km) southeast of Minehead. Dunster originated as a Norman castle founded by William de Mohun, and was rebuilt in stone in the 12th century. A fortified manor was built on the site in the early 14th century and the castle was sold by Lady Joan de Mohun to Lady Elizabeth Luttrell in 1376. Rebuilt by George Luttrell in 1617, it was besieged by Parliamentary forces during the Civil War, surrendering in April 1646 whereupon its defences were dismantled. The manor house was remodelled by Anthony Salvin in the 19th century in Victorian Gothic style with turrets and towers. Colonel Sir Walter Luttrell gave the castle and much of its contents to the National Trust in 1976. The castle is surrounded by sub-tropical gardens containing the National Collection of strawberry trees, its hilltop location providing views over Exmoor and the Bristol Channel. Tel: 01643 821314.

Dunster Dolls Museum High Street, Dunster. Based on the collection of local resident Mollie Hardwick, the museum features more than 900 dolls of various nationalities and from many periods. Tel: 01643 821220.

Dunster Working Watermill Mill Lane, Dunster. An 18th century watermill situated in the grounds of Dunster Castle on the site of a mill mentioned in Domesday Book, and restored to working order in 1979. The property is owned by the National Trust. Tel: 01643 821759.

East Coker A village and parish 2 miles (3km) south of Yeovil. The churchyard of St Michael's church is the final resting place of the ashes of T S Eliot, whose ancestors came from the village and who named one of his *Four Quartets* poems 'East Coker'.

East Somerset Railway Cranmore, 2 miles (3km) east of Shepton Mallet. A standard gauge heritage railway opened in 1973 and operating for 2½ miles (3.5km) between Cranmore and Mendip Vale, on part of a former broad gauge line between Witham and Shepton Mallet. The line opened in 1858 and was extended to Wells in 1862; bought by the Great Western Railway in 1874, it remained in use until the British Railways passenger service finally ceased in 1963, although the section between Cranmore and the main line at Witham is still used by traffic to the nearby Merehead Quarry. The line hosts various preserved steam and diesel locomotives. Tel: 01749 880417.

Ebbor Gorge 3 miles (5km) northwest of Wells. A dry limestone gorge located within a 100 acre (40ha) National Nature Reserve operated by English Nature and featuring ancient woodland, numerous species of rare fungi, ferns, mosses and liverworts, and providing a habitat for greater and lesser horseshoe bats. Evidence of habitation by Neolithic peoples has been found in various caves within the gorge.

Emborough Quarries 5 miles (8m) northwest of Shepton Mallet. (GR: ST623505). A designated Site of Special Scientific Interest in the Mendip Hills covering 2½ acres (1ha). A nationally important site for vertebrate fossils from the Triassic period, and particularly for early reptiles. One such disovery, *Kuehneosaurus latus*, is one of the earliest-known flying vertebrates.

Englishcombe Tithe Barn 2 miles (3km) southwest of Bath. An impressive early 14th century cruck-framed barn built to store tithes collected for Bath Abbey, and recently restored. Masons' and other markings can be seen on the walls. Tel: 01225 425073.

Exmoor Forest An area of high moorland in Somerset and Devon bounded by the low alluvial plain of Sedgemoor on the east, the lower basin of the Exe on the south, the basin of the Taw (in part) on the west, and the Bristol Channel on the north. The geological formation is Devonian. The ancient forest had an area of about 20,000 acres (8100ha), and was enclosed in 1815. Large tracts are still uncultivated, and the wild red deer and native Exmoor pony are characteristic of the district. The highest point is Dunkery Beacon (see separate entry) in the east, but Span Head in the southwest reaches 1618ft (493m), and 1500ft (457m) is exceeded at several points. Exmoor is noted for its stag hunting. The district has earned further fame as a result of R D Blackmore's novel, *Lorna Doone*. Set during the Monmouth Rebellion of 1685, the novel tells the story of John Ridd, a young farmer from the village of Oare who finds romance with the adopted daughter of a family of Exmoor outlaws, the Doones.

Exmoor National Park — Covering 267 sq miles (693 sq km) of hilly open moorland on the Bristol Channel coast of Devon and Somerset, Exmoor was one of the first National Parks, designated in 1954, and is named after its main river, the Exe.

Fairfield House — 1 mile (1.6km) west of Stogursey, 7 miles (11km) northwest of Bridgwater. An Elizabethan house with medieval origins occupied by the Palmer family for more than 800 years. Attached to the Grade II* listed house is a woodland garden with views of the Quantocks. Tel: 01722 555131.

Farleigh House — $^1/_4$ mile (0.4km) south of Farleigh Hungerford, 5 miles (8km) southeast of Bath. Farleigh House was once the centre of Farleigh Hungerford estate; built by Joseph Houlton, son of a Trowbridge clothier who bought the estate in 1702, it was a modest residence complete with a 120 acre (48ha) deer park. Sometimes called Farleigh New Castle, it was largely constructed with stone taken from the ruins of Farleigh Hungerford Castle. In 1806, Colonel John Houlton enlarged and altered the house in Gothic Revival style; most of the present house dates from this period. The former Castle Lodge is now the Bath Lodge Hotel. The Houlton family remained at Farleigh Hungerford until 1899, when Sir Edward Houlton died with no male heir. The estate was sold in 1906 to Lord Cairns and subsequently passed through several hands. In 1970, the house was sold to Ravenscroft School, previously based in nearby Beckington Castle. The school closed in 1997 and the house became a special school named Farleigh College. It is now the headquarters of an optical company.

Farleigh Hungerford Castle — Farleigh Hungerford, 5 miles (8km) southeast of Bath. Erected 1370–83 by Sir Thomas Hungerford, first Speaker of the House of Commons, the castle was enlarged in the early 15th century by his son, Sir Walter Hungerford, who added the outer court that enclosed the parish church, Grade II* listed St Leonard's, which he used as his chapel. Farleigh Hungerford played a significant part in the Civil War, but was gambled away in 1689 by Edward Hungerford. The restored 19th century chapel has notable medieval wall paintings. The ruined castle is now owned by English Heritage. The foundations of a villa were excavated in a field northwest of the castle in 1822, suggesting evidence of occupation during Roman times. Tel: 01225 754026.

Fleet Air Arm Museum — Located at RNAS Yeovilton (see separate entry), the museum is dedicated to the branch of the Royal Navy that has operated airships, seaplanes, flying boats, aeroplanes and helicopters since 1912, when a Royal Navy aircraft took off from a platform built for the purpose over the forecastle of HMS *Hibernia* in Weymouth Bay – the first time an aircraft had ever taken off from a ship under way at sea. There are exhibits covering World Wars I and II and the Falklands conflict, including a mock-up of the aircraft carrier HMS *Ark Royal* as it would have appeared in the 1970s. Other exhibits include innovations of the British aerospace industry since World War II, including the second prototype of Concorde. Tel: 01935 840565.

Folly Farm — 1 mile (1.6km) northeast of Bishop Sutton, 8 miles (13km) south of Bristol. A 17th century farm with wildflower meadows and ancient hazel coppice woodlands with scenic views. Wildlife includes the rare marsh fritillary butterfly, marsh tit, buzzard and great spotted woodpecker. The estate includes two Sites of Special Scientific Interest – the meadows and Dowlings Wood – and is managed as a nature reserve by the Avon Wildlife Trust. Tel: 0117 917 7270.

Fyne Court — Broomfield, 5 miles (8km) southwest of Bridgwater. The 18th century Arcadian landscaped gardens surround what was once the home of Andrew Crosse, 19th century scientist and pioneer of electricity, before the house was destroyed in a fire in 1894. Now owned by the National Trust and undergoing restoration, the property is also the headquarters of Somerset Wildlife Trust. Tel: 01823 652400.

Gants Mill — $^1/_2$ mile (0.8km) southwest of Bruton, 8 miles (13km) southeast of Shepton Mallet. A working watermill with deeds dating back to owner John of Gaunt in 1290. Used as a fulling mill in the Middle Ages and later as a silk mill, it became a corn mill in the 19th century. The site also contains a designer water garden with sculptures, ponds, streams and rose pergolas, as well as varied collections of iris, delphiniums, penstemons, day lilies and dahlias. Tel: 01749 812393.

Gartell Light Railway — Yenston, 6 miles (10km) northeast of Yeovil. A 2ft (610mm) gauge heritage railway operating for $^3/_4$ mile (1.2km), partly along the track of the former Somerset & Dorset Joint Railway between Bournemouth and Bath. Tel: 01963 370752.

Gatcombe Court — Flax Bourton, 7 miles (11km) southwest of Bristol. The house dates from the 13th century and was built using stones from a Roman settlement that previously occupied the site; some of these can still be seen. It has been extended and altered many times in the succeeding centuries. A yew hedge in the gardens is believed to be 400 years old. Displays show how the house has developed through the centuries to the family home it is today. Tel: 01275 393141.

Georgian House, The — Great George Street, Bristol. Originally home to John Pinney, a West India sugar merchant, the house was designed by Robert Adam in 1796; it is decorated in keeping with the original schemes and furnished as it might have looked in the 18th century. It was also home to Pinney's slave Pero (after whom Pero's Bridge at the Harbourside is named), and there are displays illustrating life both above and below stairs. The basement contains a rare Georgian bathing pool; other rooms include the kitchen, laundry, dining room, drawing room, breakfast room and housekeeper's room. Tel: 0117 921 1362.

Glastonbury Abbey — Magdalene Street, Glastonbury. Believed by some to be the site of the oldest Christian church in the world, the abbey has been the focus of Christian worship for over 1500 years. A cutting supposedly from the original Glastonbury Thorn, said to have been planted on Wearyall Hill (see separate entry) by Joseph of Arimathea, still grows in the abbey grounds. St David and St Patrick are said to have visited, while other legends suggest that King Arthur and Queen Guinevere lie buried among the ruins of the church; a grave supposedly containing their bones was discovered in the 12th century. There was already a community of monks in Glastonbury when the first stone church was built, possibly in AD 712. The building was enlarged by St Dunstan in the 10th century, and after the Norman Conquest Glastonbury became one of the wealthiest abbeys in England. It was completely rebuilt after a fire in 1184. The ruins visible today, including the 12th century Lady Chapel, abbots' kitchen and 14th century gatehouse, are set within 36 acres (14.5ha) of parkland in the centre of Glastonbury. Tel: 01458 832267.

Glastonbury Festival The Glastonbury Festival of Contemporary Performing Arts, commonly abbreviated to Glastonbury Festival (and familiarly known as Glasto), is the largest greenfield music and performing arts festival in the world. It takes place at Worthy Farm between the small villages of Pilton and Pylle, 6 miles (10km) east of Glastonbury. Best known for its contemporary music, it also features dance, comedy, theatre, circus, cabaret and many other arts. Held on an enclosed site of 900 acres (360ha), the festival hosts around 400 live performers, and is attended by more than 150,000 people. Originally, hippy ethics had a huge influence on Glastonbury and the festival retains vestiges of such traditions, including the Green Futures/Healing Fields area and a reputation for alternative culture. The area is also significant to adherents of 'New Age' philosophies; the nearest town to the festival site is Shepton Mallet, 3 miles (5km) to the northeast, but there is a continuing interaction between the people espousing alternative lifestyles living in Glastonbury and the festival itself. Tel: 01458 834596.

Glastonbury Tor A teardrop-shaped hill 1/2 mile (0.8km) east of Glastonbury with an elevation of 518ft (158m). It has been a source of mystery and legend for centuries. Joseph of Arimathea is said to have come from the Holy Land bringing with him the Holy Grail, the cup used by Christ at the Last Supper, which according to some versions of the legend is buried on the Tor. It is also claimed that the body of King Arthur was brought to Glastonbury for burial after he was slain by Mordred, his illegitimate son. Glastonbury Tor is also claimed to be the legendary Avalon. Other Glastonbury traditions include Arthur receiving the sword Excalibur from the Lady of the Lake at Mere Pool, while many ley lines are believed to converge on the Tor. The remains of a lake-village were identified in 1892, showing that there was a Celtic settlement c.300–200 BC on what was then an easily defended island in the fens. Earthworks and Roman remains prove later occupation. The spot seems to have been called *Ynys yr Afalon* by the Britons. The slopes of the Tor appear to be regularly terraced; it has been suggested that this formation is the remains of an ancient, perhaps Neolithic, sacred labyrinth, although the terraces have also been explained as natural ruts formed on the grassy slopes by generations of grazing animals. The officially approved explanation is that the hill was terraced for farming, possibly by medieval monks. Remains of a 5th century fort have also been found on the Tor. This was replaced by the medieval St Michael's church that remained until 1275. A second church, built in the 1360s, survived until the Dissolution of the Monasteries in 1539 when the last abbot of Glastonbury Abbey was executed by hanging on the Tor. The Tor is managed by the National Trust. Tel: 01985 843600.

Glastonbury Tribunal High Street, Glastonbury. A well-preserved medieval town house, once thought to have held the courtroom where the king's justices heard cases involving the abbey's tenants, although it may also have been used by one of the abbey's own officials. Much of the building dates back to the 15th century although the present façade was constructed in the early 16th century. Tel: 01458 832954.

Hadspen Garden 2 miles (3km) southeast of Castle Cary, 8 miles (13km) south of Shepton Mallet. A redesigned 21st century garden created within a Victorian walled vegetable garden, located on a hillside plot in the estate of Hadspen House. Tel: 01963 351856.

Halsway Manor Halsway, 10 miles (16km) west of Bridgwater. Set on the southern slopes of the Quantock Hills, the house is said to have been built as a hunting lodge by Henry Beaufort, son of John of Gaunt and Bishop of Winchester; the original 15th century building was sympathetically extended in the 1900s. It is situated in grounds with spectacular views across to the Brendon Hills. The manor is mentioned in Domesday Book and was a family home until the mid 1960s. Features include a large entrance hall with oak panelling, staircase, barrel ceiling, fireplace, a secret door in the panelling and plasterwork ceiling in the library. The house is now occupied by the UK's only residential folk centre. Tel: 01984 618274.

Halswell Park Goathurst, 2 miles (3km) southwest of Bridgwater. The 17 acre (7ha) Georgian 'pleasure garden' of Halswell Park was designed by Sir Charles Kemeys-Tynte and laid out around Halswell House 1745–85. The grounds contain a variety of buildings, fish ponds, cascades and bridges, including the Grade II listed Temple of Harmony (see separate entry), completed in 1767, which stands in Mill Wood. Apart from the temple, the house and grounds are not open to the public.

Ham Hill 5 miles (8km) west of Yeovil. Part of a ridge of limestone rock elevated above the clay vales and surrounding Somerset Levels, the hill is the site of old quarry workings for the honey-coloured Ham stone used in many local buildings. The entire summit is also encompassed by an Iron Age hill fort covering 200 acres (80ha), and was the site of a Roman fort. The Roman Fosse Way passes along the foot of the hill on the way from Bath to the coast near Lyme Regis. The hill has been designated a Site of Special Scientific Interest for its geological importance. The summit is crowned by a war memorial to the villagers of nearby Stoke-sub-Hamdon killed during the two world wars.

Haynes International Motor Museum Sparkford, 8 miles (13km) northeast of Yeovil. The UK's largest collection of cars, with more than 340 cars and motorcycles including classics from the 1950s and 60s, Bentleys, Rolls-Royces and modern cars such as the Jaguar XJ220, housed in 11 large display halls. Other features include one of the UK's largest speedway collections, while the 'Red Room' houses 50 beautiful red sports cars from around the world. Tel 01963 440804.

Helicopter Museum — Locking Moor Road, 2 miles (3km) east of Weston-super-Mare. The only museum in the UK dedicated to helicopters, and the largest in the world. It holds a collection of over 80 helicopters, both civilian and military, along with an extensive archive of helicopter-related material, and undertakes a number of conservation projects. Tel. 01934 635227.

Hestercombe Gardens — Cheddon Fitzpaine, 2 miles (3km) north of Taunton. The gardens at Hestercombe exemplify three periods of garden design. There are 40 acres (16ha) of 18th century landscape gardens, restored in the 1990s and including woodland, a temple, cascade and spectacular views across the vale of Taunton to the Blackdown Hills. A Victorian terrace with colourful bedding was laid out in the 1870s, while the Edwardian garden, designed by Sir Edwin Lutyens and planted by Gertrude Jekyll, has stonework, rills, and an orangery and pergola. The gardens were featured on BBC TV's *Gardens Through Time* series. Tel: 01823 413923.

Highest point — See Dunkery Beacon

Hinkley Point Power Station — 7 miles (11km) northwest of Bridgwater. Located on the coast at Hinkley Point, the station contains two reactor sites, Hinkley Point A and B: the twin Magnox reactors at Hinkley Point A started electricity generation in 1965 and ceased operations in 2000, after which fuel was progressively removed from the reactors and sent to Sellafield for treatment. Hinkley Point B contains two advanced gas-cooled reactors (AGRs); it began operating in 1976 and is due to be decommissioned in 2016.

Holburne Museum of Art — Great Pulteney Street, Bath. Housed in the 18th century Sydney Hotel and set within the park of Sydney Gardens, this small museum holds collections of paintings, silver, sculpture, furniture and porcelain developed from those of Sir William Holburne in the 19th century, including important works by Gainsborough, Guardi, Stubbs and Turner. Managed by the University of Bath, the museum is due to be reopened in 2010 after major refurbishment. Tel: 01225 466669.

Holnicote Estate — Consisting of 12,500 acres (5052ha) of Exmoor National Park to the west of Minehead, parts of the estate were donated to the National Trust by the Acland family in the 1930s and the whole estate has been owned by the Trust since 1944. It includes Dunkery and Selworthy Beacons, and the villages and hamlets of Selworthy, Allerford, Bossington, Horner and Luccombe as well as the Horner and Dunkery National Nature Reserve. Tel: 01643 862452.

Hunstrete House and Lake — 1/4 mile (0.4km) south of Hunstrete, 6 miles (10km) west of Bath. The first documented building on the site was built in 1258 on land belonging to Glastonbury Abbey. The present Grade II listed house was based on the 17th century manor house, given a Georgian façade and further enlarged and altered in the late 19th century; it is now a hotel. The grounds include a 5 acre (2ha) lake, and an ice house which is also a listed building.

Interesting facts — In 1881 **Taunton** became the first town in England to be lit permanently by electric street lighting. **Archibald Leach** (1904–86) was born in Horfield, Bristol, and had a difficult start to life. An only child, his mother, Elsie, was placed in a mental institution when he was nine. His father told him that she was dead, and he only learned in 1935 that she was still alive. After being expelled from Fairfield Grammar School in Bristol in 1918 (for investigating the girls' bathroom), he became a jobbing actor in America but his life was transformed in 1931 when he travelled to Hollywood and changed his name to Cary Grant! **Punkie Night** is observed on the last Thursday in October in the village of Hinton St George. On this night, children carry lanterns made from hollowed-out mangel-wurzels (a kind of beet; in modern days, pumpkins are used) with faces carved into them. They bring these around the village, collecting money and singing the punkie song. Punkie is either derived from pumpkin or from punk, meaning tinder. Though the custom is only attested over the last century, and the mangel-wurzel itself was introduced into English agriculture in the late 18th century, 'Punkie Night' appears to be much older than the fable that now accounts for it. The story goes that the wives of Hinton St George went looking for their wayward husbands at the fair held nearby at Chiselborough on the last Thursday in October, having first hollowed out mangel-wurzels in order to make lanterns to light their way. The drunken husbands saw the eerie lights, thought they were 'goolies' (the restless spirits of children who had died before they were baptised), and fled in terror. The event has spread since the early 1960s to the neighbouring village of Chiselborough. The town of **Shepton Mallet**, just south of the Mendip Hills, contains England's oldest prison still in use. The prison was estabished in 1610 and apart from a nine-year spell (1930–9) has been open ever since. **Daphne Fowler** lays claim to being the cleverest person living in Somerset. Warwick-born Daphne moved to Weston-super-Mare in 1960 and the sea air obviously agreed with her as she not only became Brain of Britain but also won the *Fifteen to One* title twice. Daphne has been a member of the star-studded *Eggheads* team on television in recent years. **Robert** (or Robin) **Banks** was born in Bristol c.1975 and is known to the public as 'Banksy'. He first achieved fame by sticking fake objects to the walls of museums and art galleries, waiting to see how long it would take for curators to notice. In 2005 he discreetly placed a fake painting showing a caveman pushing a modern supermarket trolley on the walls of the British Museum. In April 2006 a toppled red telephone box, complete with embedded pickaxe and red paint 'bleeding' from it, appeared in Soho in London; it was Banksy's way of protesting at the way BT has been replacing the classic telephone kiosk, designed by Sir Giles Gilbert Scott in the 1920s. In June 2006, Banksy created an image of a naked man hanging out of a bedroom window on a wall in central Bristol. The image sparked controversy, with Bristol City Council leaving it up to the public to decide whether it should stay or go. After an internet discussion in which 97 per cent of those expressing an opinion (all but six people) supported the stencil, the city council decided it would be left in place. In August/September 2006, Banksy replaced up to 500 copies of Paris Hilton's debut album, *Paris*, in 48 different UK record stores with his own cover art and remixes by Danger Mouse. Music tracks were given titles such as 'Why Am I Famous?', 'What Have I Done?' and 'What Am I For?'. Several copies of the CD were purchased by the public before stores were able to remove them, some later being sold for as much as £750 on online auction websites. The cover art depicted Paris Hilton digitally altered to appear topless. Other pictures feature her with a dog's head replacing her own, and one of her stepping out of a luxury car, edited to include a group of homeless people, which included the caption *90% of success is just showing up.* In September 2006, Banksy dressed an inflatable doll in the manner of a Guantanamo Bay detainment camp prisoner (orange jumpsuit, black hood and handcuffs) and then placed the figure within the Big Thunder Mountain Railroad ride at Disneyland theme park in Anaheim, California. Tobacco importer and cigarette manufacturer **W D & H O Wills**, one of the founding companies of Imperial Tobacco, was formed in Bristol. The company was founded as Wills, Watkins & Co. by Henry Overton Wills I and his partner Samuel Watkins, who opened a shop in Castle Street in 1786. After Watkins' retirement in 1789 it became Wills & Co. In 1826 his two sons, William Day Wills and Henry Overton Wills II, took over the company and in 1830 the company took the above name. The company pioneered canteens for its workers, free medical care, sports facilities and paid holidays. Its first brand was Bristol, made at the London factory from 1871 to 1974. Three Castles and Gold Flake followed in 1878 and Woodbine ten years later. Embassy was introduced in 1914 and relaunched in 1962 with coupons. In 1988 Imperial Tobacco withdrew the Wills brand in the UK, but it is still used in India. The largest cigarette factory in Europe was opened at Hartcliffe, Bristol, in 1974 but closed in 1990. The large factory and warehouse buildings remain prominent buildings on Bristol Harbour, though they have now been converted to other uses, such as the Tobacco Factory Theatre. **Charles Wreford-Brown** (1866–1951) is usually credited with inventing the word 'soccer' as an abbreviation for association football. Bristol-born Wreford-Brown captained the England football team and also played cricket for Gloucestershire. Bath-born **Henry Cole** worked as an assistant to Rowland Hill and played a key role in the introduction of the Penny Post. He is sometimes credited with the design of the world's first postage stamp, the Penny Black. In 1843, Cole introduced the world's first commercial Christmas card, commissioning artist John Callcott Horsley to make the artwork. John Wesley founded the very first Methodist chapel in Bristol in 1739. Chard-born **Margaret Grace Bondfield** was a Labour politician and feminist. When she was appointed Minister of Labour by Ramsay MacDonald in 1929 she became the first female Cabinet minister. Somerset-born **Frederick Edward Weatherly** (1848–1929), lawyer, author, songwriter and radio entertainer, wrote the lyrics of the well-known ballad 'Danny Boy' which is set to the tune 'A Londonderry Air'. Other famous works by Weatherly are 'Roses of Picardy' and 'The Holy City'. Taunton-born civil servant **Sir Charles Edward Trevelyan, 1st Baronet,** KCB was assistant secretary to HM Treasury 1840–59, during the Irish potato famine. He is famously referred to in the modern Irish folk song 'The Fields of Athenry' about the famine: 'By a lonely prison wall, I heard a young girl calling, "Michael, they have taken you away. For you stole Trevelyan's corn".'

Islands	See separate table
Jane Austen Centre	Queen Square, Bath. The centre features a variety of original displays, exhibits and presentations. Jane Austen paid a long visit to Bath towards the end of the 18th century and lived in the city 1801–06, setting two of her novels – *Northanger Abbey* and *Persuasion* – largely in Bath. Tel: 01225 443000.
John Wesley's Chapel	The Horsefair, Bristol. The well-preserved chapel where John Wesley preached is the oldest Methodist building in the world. Features include a two-tiered pulpit, balcony and original clock. The rooms upstairs where Wesley and his fellow preachers stayed are also on display. A museum on site has numerous artefacts and pictures including Wesley's bed, preaching gown and desk. Tel: 0117 926 4740.
Keynsham	A small town between Bristol and Bath dominated by the Cadbury's chocolate factory, formerly Fry's, which was merged with Cadbury's in 1989. According to Cadbury employees (or 'Chocolate Welders' as they are known locally), the Crunchie machine makes enough bars to stretch to the moon and back every week. Keynsham rose to fame after featuring on an advert on Radio Luxembourg for Horace Bachelor's Infra-draw betting system. Because it is pronounced 'canesh'm', the town's name was spelled out, 'Keynsham – spelt K-E-Y-N-S-H-A-M – Keynsham, Bristol'. In 1969 the town featured as the title of the third album by the Bonzo Dog Doo-Dah Band.
King Alfred's Tower	7$^1/_2$ miles (12km) southwest of Frome. Aka the Folly of King Alfred the Great. Located on the Somerset/Wiltshire border on Kingsettle Hill, within the Stourhead estate, the tower is sited near one of the possible locations of Egbert's Stone, where Alfred is said to have rallied his troops in May 878 before the Battle of Ethandun. Completed in 1772 by Henry Flitcroft for banker Henry Hoare, the tower is 160ft (49m) high and triangular in plan, and can be climbed to the top via a spiral staircase with 205 steps. A stone tablet above the door on the east face reads: 'ALFRED THE GREAT AD 879 on this Summit Erected his Standard Against Danish Invaders To him We owe The Origin of Juries The Establishment of a Militia The Creation of a Naval Force ALFRED The Light of a Benighted Age Was a Philosopher and a Christian The Father of his People The Founder of the English MONARCHY and LIBERTY'.
King John's Lodge	Axbridge, 7 miles (11km) southeast of Weston-super-Mare. Originally a wool merchant's house dating to c.1500, the timber-framed building is owned by the National Trust and run as a local history museum by Axbridge and District Museum Trust. Tel: 01934 732012.
King's Sedge Moor	See Somerset Levels
Lamb Leer	2 miles (3km) southwest of East Harptree, 8 miles (13km) northwest of Shepton Mallet. One of the largest caverns in the Mendip Hills, with a height of almost 100ft (30m). A designated Site of Special Scientific Interest, the system is thought to have originated before the Ice Age and is now dry.
Lower Severalls	1$^1/_2$ miles (2.5km) northeast of Crewkerne. An innovative 2 acre (0.8ha) cottage-style garden developed in the late 20th century around a Ham stone farmhouse, built in 1727 for Robert Webb

and today the home of the Pring family. The site is thought to have been inhabited since the 14th century; the name 'Severalls' apparently refers to the land being partitioned into enclosures, and this was one of the first areas in England to be so divided. Tel: 01460 73234.

Lynton and Barnstaple Steam Railway — A heritage railway operating for 1 mile (1.6km) from Woody Bay station within the Exmoor National Park, on the former Lynton and Barnstaple Railway, a famously scenic narrow gauge (1ft 11.5in) line that ran through Exmoor from Barnstaple to Lynton and Lynmouth in North Devon. Situated 1$^{1}/_{4}$ miles (2km) inland from Woody Bay itself, the station opened with the line (as Wooda Bay until the name was changed in 1901) in 1898. From 1923 until its closure in 1935, the line was operated by the Southern Railway, and the station was built in part to serve the expected development of a resort at Woody Bay. A pier was built in the bay, but little further development took place – the pier was destroyed by heavy seas before any trade could be established, and the development was abandoned when the promoter went into liquidation in 1900.

Lytes Cary Manor — $^{3}/_{4}$ mile (1.2km) east of Kingsdon, 6 miles (10km) north of Yeovil. A manor house with walled gardens once home to medieval herbalist Henry Lyte. Features of the house include a Tudor great hall and 14th century chapel, while the Arts and Crafts garden contains many of the plants cultivated by Lyte. The property is owned by the National Trust. Tel: 01458 224471.

Maunsel House — North Petherton, 2 miles (3km) south of Bridgwater. A 13th century manor set in 100 acres (40ha) of parkland at the heart of a 1500 acre (600ha) estate. The ancestral seat of the Slade family, the house has had visitors such as Geoffrey Chaucer, who wrote part of the *Canterbury Tales* while staying here. Tel: 01278 661076.

Meare Fish House — Meare, 3 miles (5km) northwest of Glastonbury. The only surviving monastic fishery building in England. It once housed the Abbot of Glastonbury's water bailiff and provided facilities for fish-salting and drying.

Mendip Hills — A range of limestone hills situated to the south of Bristol and Bath in north Somerset. The hills are bounded by the Somerset Levels in the south and west, and by the River Avon and Chew Valley Lake in the north, and largely fall within the 80 sq mile (200 sq km) Mendip Hills Area of Outstanding Natural Beauty. The effect of water has produced a range of complex cave systems in the Carboniferous limestone of the hills, while impressive features such as Cheddar Gorge are the result of surface weathering. The limestone has a core of older Devonian sandstone and Silurian volcanic rocks, which are quarried for use in road construction and as a concrete aggregate. The area contains many Neolithic, Iron Age and Bronze Age remains, including barrows and forts. The hills are also home to the Mendip UHF television transmitter. Tel: 01761 462338.

Mendip TV mast — 4 miles (6km) northeast of Wells. Situated on the summit of Pen Hill in the Mendip Hills, the Mendip transmitting station stands at 1002ft (305m) above sea level and includes a 922ft (281m) mast, built in 1967 and weighing 500 tonnes. Owned and operated by National Grid Wireless, the mast broadcasts analogue and digital television and radio to Somerset, Wiltshire, North Somerset, Bath and North-East Somerset, Bristol, South Gloucestershire and Gloucestershire and is the tallest television mast in southwest England.

Mere Pool — See Glastonbury Tor

Milton Lodge Gardens — $^{1}/_{2}$ mile (0.8km) north of Wells. An 18th century house and arboretum with a 20th century Arts and Crafts garden. The terraced garden was laid out in 1906 and replanted in the 1960s. Milton Lodge Gardens is also noted for its views over Wells. Tel: 01749 672168.

Minehead — A coastal town on the western side of Bridgwater Bay in the Bristol Channel with a Butlins holiday camp opened in 1962. A popular ancient local tradition involves the Hobby Horse, which takes to the streets on the eve of 1 May each year (Walpurgis Night), with accompanying musicians and rival horses, for four days; the first day of May has been a festival day in Minehead since 1465. The town is the starting point of the South West Coast Path National Trail, England's longest long-distance countryside walking trail.

Montacute Castle — Montacute, 4 miles (6km) west of Yeovil. Built on the natural knoll known as St Michael's Hill, the Norman motte and bailey castle was founded by Robert of Mortain c.1070. It was dismantled in the 12th century by Cluniac monks of Montacute Priory.

Montacute House — Montacute, 4 miles (6km) west of Yeovil. An Elizabethan stone-built house with garden and park. The three-floored mansion, constructed of local Ham stone, was built c.1598 by Sir Edward Phelips, Master of the Rolls to Elizabeth I. The house, like many Elizabethan mansions, is built in an 'E' shape. On the ground floor were the great hall, kitchens and pantries; on the upper floors, retiring rooms for the family and honoured guests. The ground floor now features elegant drawing and dining rooms; on the first floor are a magnificent panelled library and bedrooms. In the early 20th century the house was leased to Lord Curzon, former Viceroy of India, whose secret bath can be seen concealed in a wardrobe. There are displays of 17th century textile samplers, while the long gallery (the longest such room in Europe) contains Elizabethan artworks from the National Portrait Gallery. The house was also used as a location for the film *Sense and Sensibility* (1995). The property is owned by the National Trust, Tel: 01935 823289.

Motto — *Sumorsaete ealle* (Old English, 'all the people of Somerset').

Muchelney Abbey — Muchelney, 10 miles (16km) southwest of Glastonbury. The remains of a Benedictine monastery founded in the 10th century. The surviving building was originally the abbot's lodgings, and includes a great chamber with ornate fireplace, carved settle and stained glass, two rooms with time-faded walls painted to resemble cloth hangings, and a pair of kitchens with fine timber roof. Parts of the richly decorated cloister walk and refectory are incorporated, and nearby is a thatched two-storey monks' lavatory, unique in Britain. Exhibitions illustrate monastic life with a collection of site finds, including decorated tiles and stonework. The property is now owned by English Heritage. Tel: 01458 250664.

Neroche Castle — See Castle Neroche

Nether Stowey Castle — Nether Stowey, 6 miles (10km) west of Bridgwater. Norman castle with a motte and two baileys, built on a natural knoll. The tower keep was added in the mid 12th century. The castle was destroyed in the 15th century; only the foundations of the keep are still visible.

Newton Surmaville — 1 mile (1.6km) southeast of Yeovil. A small Jacobean house built 1608–12 for Yeovil merchant Robert Harbin, who is buried in St John the Baptist church. The Grade I listed house was extensively altered in the 1870s. The 5 acre (2ha) landscaped pleasure grounds, laid out in the 18th and 19th centuries, slope down to the River Yeo and feature five ponds, a boathouse, a summerhouse and a walled kitchen garden. The property, complete with some remarkable 17th century tapestries, was put up for sale in 2007.

Nunney Castle — Nunney, 3 miles (5km) southwest of Frome. A rectangular moated keep with cylindrical towers at the corners built in 1373 by Sir John de la Mare, later Sheriff of Somerset. Its architecture is French in style, influenced by Sir John's service during the Hundred Years War. The castle was taken by Parliamentarians after a two-day siege and slighted in 1645. Now owned by English Heritage. Tel: 0117 975 0700.

Old Deanery — Cathedral Green, Wells. In the late 15th century the Old Deanery was visited on at least two occasions by Henry VII. The medieval building is also said to be haunted by the ghost of Dean Raleigh, nephew of Sir Walter. The private garden is associated with William Turner, Dean of Wells in the mid 16th century. A physician as well as a priest, he was particularly interested in the medicinal properties of plants and established a herb garden here. The Grade I listed building is now a conference centre.

Orchardleigh House — 2 miles (3km) northeast of Frome. A Grade II* listed Victorian house designed by Thomas Henry Wyatt in a combination of Elizabethan revival and French styles, built by William Duckworth in 1856 and located in a 550 acre (220ha) estate. The property had previously been owned since the Norman Conquest by the Champneys family. The 27 acre (11ha) artificial lake in the grounds was formed by damming a tributary of the River Frome; St Mary's church stands on an island in the lake.

Polden Hills — A long, low ridge, extending for 20 miles (23km) and separated from the Mendip Hills, to which they are nearly parallel, by the wetland of the Somerset Levels. The hills stretch from Puriton, near Bridgwater in the west, to Street in the east. A Roman road from Ilchester to the port of Combwich once followed the ridge of the hill.

Porlock — A quiet coastal village situated in a deep hollow below Exmoor, 5 miles (8km) west of Minehead. The village adjoins Porlock Ridge and Saltmarsh Nature Reserve, created when the lowland behind a high shingle embankment was breached by the sea in the 1990s, and which has now been designated as a Site of Special Scientific Interest.

Priest's House — Muchelney, 9 miles (15km) northwest of Yeovil. A late medieval hall house built by Muchelney Abbey in 1308 for the parish priest. Features include a Gothic doorway, tracery windows and a massive 15th century fireplace. Now owned by the National Trust. Tel: 01458 253771.

Prior Park — Ralph Allen Drive, Bath. An 18th century landscape garden designed by poet Alexander Pope and landscape gardener Capability Brown, The work was commissioned by local entrepreneur and philanthropist Ralph Allen, who became mayor of Bath in 1742, having started off working in the post office. Much of the stone so prevalent in Bath came from Allen's mines at Combe Down and Bathampton Down. Allen commissioned architect John Wood the Elder c.1742 to build a mansion within the park, which is now owned by Prior Park College. Churchman and literary critic William Warburton, Allen's son-in-law, lived here for some time. The 28 acre (11.5ha) garden is set in a site running down a small steep valley, with views of the city. Features include a Palladian bridge, Gothic Temple, gravel cabinet, Mrs Allen's Grotto, and three lakes. Now owned by the National Trust. Tel: 01225 833422.

Pulteney Bridge — The famous bridge across the River Avon in Bath, commissioned by Sir William Pulteney (1729–1805) in order to replace the existing ferry, was completed in 1773. Designed by Robert Adam, it is one of only four bridges in the world with shops across the full span on both sides. Floods in 1799 and 1800 wrecked the north side, and the bridge was rebuilt by John Pinch senior, surveyor to the Pulteney estate, in a less ambitious version of Adam's design. Restored in 1951 and 1975, it is one of the best-known buildings in a city famed for its Georgian architecture. Sir William Johnstone Pulteney was an eminent Scottish lawyer, MP, and at one time reputedly the wealthiest man in Britain. Born William Johnston, on 10 November 1760 he married heiress Frances Pulteney, the third daughter of MP and government official Daniel Pulteney (1684–1731) and niece of William Pulteney, 1st Earl of Bath. She inherited her uncle's substantial fortune and estates close to Bath after his death in 1764, and Johnstone changed his name to Pulteney three years later.

Quantock Hills — A range of hills to the west of Bridgwater, running northwest for over 15 miles (24km) before terminating at West Quantoxhead, and officially designated as the Quantock Hills Area of Outstanding Natural Beauty. The highest point is Will's Neck at 1261ft (384m). The hills form the southern border of Sedgemoor and the Somerset Levels; to the south lies the vale of Taunton Deane.

Queen Elizabeth's Hospital — Clifton, Bristol. An independent school for boys founded in 1590 by affluent merchant John Carr as a school for orphans and destitute children. Named after its original patron, Elizabeth I (although Queen Elizabeth II is now its patron), the school is modelled on Christ's Hospital, at that time located in London (now in West Sussex), and still shares the same distinctive Tudor blue coat uniform – though currently this is only worn by boarders and choir members on special occasions.

Radstock Museum — Waterloo Road, Radstock. Located in the town's Market Hall, the museum offers an insight into North Somerset life since the 19th century. There are collections of local artefacts, photographs, documents and books relating to the North Somerset coalfield, as well as a reconstructed coalface, miner's kitchen, 1930s Co-op shop, Victorian schoolroom, and blacksmith's and carpenter's workshops. Tel: 01761 437722.

Red Lodge

Park Row, Bristol. Built in 1570 by merchant John Yonge as the lodge to a great house where Elizabeth I was once entertained. The rich interiors are among the oldest in Bristol and have original Elizabethan oak panelling and plasterwork. The upper storeys were rebuilt in the 18th century. Features include a carved door case, stone chimneypiece and other 17th and 18th century furnishings. Outside is a recreated Elizabethan knot garden. Tel: 0117 921 1360.

Rivers

The **Axe** rises at Wookey Hole in the Mendip Hills, its waters finding their way to the caves in a series of underground channels eroded through the soluble limestone. From Wookey Hole the river flows through a ravine and then west through the village of Wookey. Here it splits into two channels. The Lower River Axe runs past the south of the village, west towards Henton and on to Panborough Moor, where it joins a series of rhines and drains supplying water to the area's wetlands; it then flows north along the westernmost edge of Knowle Moor while the main branch of the Axe continues west through the same moor. The two channels meet on the boundary between Knowle and Panborough Moors. The river continues northwest past Wedmore Moor and through Oxmoor, Stoke Moor and Monk Moor, passing through Lower Weare and on to the south of Loxton. From this point until it reaches the coast at Weston-super-Mare the river forms the county's northern boundary.

The **Barle** runs from northern Exmoor to join the River Exe at Exebridge, Devon. The river and the Barle Valley are both designated Sites of Special Scientific Interest.

The **Brue** rises in the parish of Brewham, flowing past Castle Cary and Glastonbury before flowing in a channel across the Somerset Levels and into the River Severn at Highbridge.

The **Cam** rises to the east of Yarlington, close to the county's eastern border, flowing southwest past North Cadbury, Sparkford, Queen Camel and West Camel and on to the Royal Naval Station where it joins the River Yeo.

The **Cary** originates from Park Pond in Castle Cary, east Somerset, flowing southwest through Cary Moor to Babcary and Cary Fitzpaine before turning northwest through Charlton Mackrell parish to the north of Somerton. Here the river channel has been straightened and drains the surrounding wetland as it heads north to King's Sedge Moor. Continuing west, it drains North Moor and Somerton Moor. The course of the Old River Cary flows southwest through the Levels to Beer Door; most of its water is diverted through the artificial channel of King's Sedgemoor Drain, dug c.1790, which flows northwest across the Levels and along the southern flank of the Polden Hills before joining the estuary of the River Parrett at Dunball, near Bridgwater.

The **Chew** rises just upstream from Chewton Mendip, flowing northwest from Chewton Mendip through Litton, Chew Valley Lake, Chew Stoke, Chew Magna and Stanton Drew. It passes under the A37 at Pensford, almost making the old church and pub garden into an island, and then through the villages of Publow, Woollard, Compton Dando and Chewton Keynsham before merging with the River Avon at Keynsham after 17 miles (27km) to form the Chew Valley. The river suffered a major flood in 1968, sweeping away the bridge at Pensford and causing serious damage to towns and villages along its route.

Exe – see Devon

The **Frome** rises near Witham Friary, flows north through the town of Frome and joins the River Avon at Freshford, south of Bath. There is also a River Frome in Dorset and one in South Gloucestershire which flows into Bristol.

The **Hunstpill** is an artificial river in the Somerset Levels. Excavated as a 5 mile (8km) straight channel early in World War II, its main function was to provide an all year-round guaranteed supply of process water for ROF Bridgwater, the Royal Ordnance Factory near Puriton. Connected to the South Drain at Gold Corner, it also drained part of the lower Brue Valley, thus implementing parts of a drainage plan for the Somerset Levels first drawn up in 1853. The Huntspill River has retention sluices at both ends. In winter, floodwater can be removed by gravity drainage; in summer it can be topped up by pumping water from the moors. It is a National Nature Reserve and discharges into the River Parrett just south of Highbridge.

The **Parrett** has its source in the springs in the hills around Chedington in Dorset and flows west through the Somerset Levels to its mouth in the Bristol Channel at Burnham-on-Sea. The river runs 34 miles (55km) from Thorney Mills to the river mouth at Bridgwater Bar; it is tidal for 27 miles (43km) up to Oath Lock. During winter, the river is prone to frequent flooding. In common with the lower reaches of the Severn, the Parrett exhibits the tidal phenomenon known as a bore: at certain combinations of the tides, the rising water is funnelled up the river into a wave that travels rapidly upstream against the river current. From January to May, the Parrett provides a source of eels and elvers, caught by hand netting – the only legal means of catching them. Historically, the main port on the river was at Bridgwater, although it was navigable as far as Langport and (via the River Yeo) to Ilchester. After 1827, it was also possible to transfer goods to Taunton via the Bridgwater and Taunton Canal. Nowadays, the wharf at Dunball is the only part of the port of Bridgwater still handling bulk cargoes, mainly sand and gravel. The River Parrett Trail is a long-distance footpath of 50 miles (80km) which follows the Parrett from its source to the sea.

The **Sheppey** rises in a group of springs to the west of Doulting where water draining through the limestone of the Mendips appears. It then flows southwest through the wetlands to the north of the Polden Hills. At Charlton parts of the river's course have been culverted and it flows underground through Shepton Mallet. Reappearing at Darshill, its course continues southwest through Croscombe, Dinder, Woodford and Coxley. From Coxley it heads north through Hay Moor and North Moor. The river continues west through Ash Moor and then due south through

Frogmore and west through Godney. At Lower Godney the river is channelled through the James Wear River and the Decoy Rhine to Westhay Level where it joins Whites River and then the River Brue.

The **Tone** rises in the Brendon Hills and flows for 20 miles (32km) before joining the River Parrett at Burrowbridge, in land to the south of the Polden Hills. It is tidal as far as the Newbridge Sluice in North Curry Parish.

The **Yeo** (a Saxon word simply meaning 'river') rises in the North Dorset Downs and enters Somerset near Yeovil Junction station in the south of the county. From this point the river, also known as the Ivel, flows north through Barwick parish towards Yeovil. The river flows to the east of Yeovil, forming the eastern boundary of the county. To the south of the Royal Naval Air Station, the River Cam, flowing in from the east, joins the Yeo. The river then flows west to the south of Yeovilton and through Ilchester. Finally it continues to the west and at Langport becomes the River Parrett.

RNAS Yeovilton — 4 miles (6km) north of Yeovil. Also known as HMS *Heron*. One of two active Fleet Air Arm bases, Royal Naval Air Station Yeovilton is home to the Royal Navy's Lynx helicopters and the Royal Marines Commando Westland Sea Kings; it is also home to the Fleet Air Arm Museum (see separate entry). The site undertakes training of aircrew and engineers and is also the location of the RN Fighter Controller School, training surface-based aircraft controllers. RNAS Yeovilton was the main shore base for the Navy's fleet of Sea Harrier FRS1s from 1979 to 2006.

Roman Baths — Stall Street, Bath. Along with Hadrian's Wall, the baths are among Britain's greatest memorials to the Roman period. Built almost 2000 years ago, the complex still flows with natural hot water. When the Romans arrived in AD 43 there was already a community of Celts encamped around the hot springs. The Romans built more baths there, evicted the British inhabitants and renamed the area 'Aquae Sulis' in honour of the goddess Sulis Minerva, to whom they attributed the springs' existence. More than a million litres of mineral water rise each day at a temperature of over 46°C. When the Romans eventually left the Celts let the baths fall into ruin although a settlement remained within the Roman walls. By the time the Saxons arrived in 577 the great Roman baths had been lost to flood and ruin, and they remained buried until 1790. Mock Roman statues were added by the Victorians but the main bath is largely intact. The original bases of the stone columns that supported the original Roman roof are still well preserved, as is the lead pipe that carried water from one of the city's four natural hot springs. Tel: 01225 477785. The Bath Pump Room (see separate entry) is situated next door.

Rowland's Mill — 1 mile (1.6km) northwest of Ilminster. A Grade II* listed three-storey mill house built of Ham stone and dating to c.1620; the site includes a mill pond, mill race, overshooting wheel and waterfall.

Royal Crescent — A famous crescent of 30 Georgian houses in Bath, designed by architect John Wood the Younger and built 1767–74. Number 1 Royal Crescent is a museum, maintained by the Bath Preservation Trust, which illustrates how wealthy owners of the period might have furnished such a house. Tel: 01225 428126. The Royal Crescent Hotel occupies the central properties of the Crescent, numbers 15 and 16. Facing the crescent is a large green, from which its full splendour can be seen.

St Margaret's Almshouses — East Street, Taunton. A row of 16th century almshouses built on the site of a 12th century leper hospital by Abbot Bere of Glastonbury Abbey. The buildings were used as almshouses until 1938 when they became the headquarters of the Rural Community Council and Somerset Guild of Craftsmen. The Grade II* listed building fell into dereliction in the late 1980s, but was converted into social housing by the Somerset Building Preservation Trust in 1999. Tel: 01823 667343.

Sally Lunn's — North Parade Passage, Bath. Possibly among the oldest houses in Bath. Sally Lunn (aka Solange Luyon) was a Huguenot refugee who came to Bath in the 17th century and found work with a baker in Lilliput Alley (now North Parade Passage), creating the rich, round bread named the Sally Lunn Bun. The bun's special lightness and flavour allowed it to be enjoyed with either sweet or savoury accompaniments and it became a popular delicacy in Georgian England. The building's Roman and medieval foundations can be seen in the museum in the cellar, which also features an original kitchen with faggot oven, Georgian range and old baking utensils. Tel: 01225 461634.

Sand Bay — 2 miles (3km) north of Weston-super-Mare. A strip of coast in North Somerset west of the village of Kewstoke, and bordered to the south by Worlebury Hill and to the north by Middle Hope. Sand Point, a peninsula stretching out from Middle Hope, is owned by the National Trust and commands views of the Bristol Channel, South Wales, Clevedon, the Second Severn Crossing and the Severn bridge.

Sedgemoor, Battle of — Fought to the north of Westonzoyland on 6 July 1685 between the forces of James II and those of Charles II's illegitimate son, the Duke of Monmouth. Charles's brother, James, was unpopular when he became king upon his sibling's death; through the influence of his mother he had become a Catholic, and many Protestants wished to exclude him from the succession. Support was raised in Somerset for the eldest of Charles's illegitimate children, James, Duke of Monmouth, by a Taunton goldsmith named Thomas Dare. James landed in Dorset in June 1685 but was swiftly forced back as far as Bridgwater. On the night of 6 July the rebels launched a night attack on the Royalist army. The assault soon dissolved into confusion and the ensuing battle lasted only perhaps an hour and a half. Monmouth's army never came to grips with the king's infantry and were cut down by the Royalist horsemen and guns. Five hundred rebel prisoners were herded into Weston Church and the villagers are said to have buried 1384 dead. The Duke of Monmouth was captured and died on the scaffold the same month. The survivors were treated brutally at the 'Bloody Assizes' held by the infamous Judge Jeffreys. The Battle of Sedgemoor is often referred to as the last battle fought on English soil, but this is incorrect: the Battle of Preston in Lancashire was fought on 14 November 1715, during the First Jacobite Rebellion, and the

Second Jacobite Rebellion saw a minor engagement at Clifton Moor near Penrith in Cumbria on 18 December 1745. A more accurate statement would be that Sedgemoor was the last pitched battle fought on English soil. See also table of battles.

Small Down Knoll
$1\frac{1}{4}$ miles (2km) northeast of Evercreech. An Iron Age hill fort on the southern edge of the Mendip Hills. Covering 5 acres (2ha), the fort has two sets of ramparts and there are a number of tumuli in its centre. The top of the hill, marked by an Ordnance Survey trig point, stands at 728ft (222m).

Solsbury Hill
1 mile (1.6km) west of Batheaston, 3 miles (5km) northeast of Bath. Little Solsbury Hill, to give it its correct title, is a small flat-topped hill above the village of Batheaston. The top of the hill is ringed by the ramparts of an Iron Age hill fort dating to c.300 BC. Solsbury Hill is a possible location of the Battle of Mons Badonicus, fought between the Britons (possibly under the legendary King Arthur) and the Saxons c.500 AD. In the mid 1990s a small maze was cut into the hill by protestors against the construction of the A46 bypass. 'Solsbury Hill' is also the title of musician Peter Gabriel's first solo single in 1977, which reached no. 13 in the UK charts.

Somerset Coal Canal
Originally known as the Somersetshire Coal Canal. The narrow canal was built c.1800 to link basins at Paulton and Timsbury via Camerton, an aqueduct at Dunkerton, Combe Hay, Midford and Monkton Combe to Limpley Stoke where it joined the Kennet & Avon Canal. This gave ready access from the coalfields of Somerset, which at their peak contained 80 collieries, to London. It was almost 18 miles (29km) long with 23 locks. From Midford an arm also ran via Writhlington to Radstock, with a tunnel at Wellow.

Somerset Levels
A sparsely populated wetland area of central Somerset, between the Quantock and Mendip Hills, with marine clay levels along the coast, and areas of peat moorland inland. Their total area is 250 sq miles (650 sq km), broadly corresponding to the administrative district of Sedgemoor but also including southeast Mendip. Drained mechanically by a network of drainage channels known as rhines (pronounced 'reens'), the Levels are less intensively drained or farmed than the East Anglian fens (historically a similar area of low marsh), and are liable to freshwater flooding in winter. Flowing through the Levels are the rivers Axe, Brue, Huntspill, Kenn, Parrett, Tone and Yeo, together with the King's Sedgemoor Drain. The historic battlefield of Sedgemoor lies in the region known as King's Sedge Moor and bounded on the north by the Polden Hills. The Tickenham, Nailsea and Kenn Moors Site of Special Scientific Interest, supporting a wide variety of wetland plant and invertebrate species, covers 320 acres (129ha) of the North Somerset Levels. The area known as West Sedgemoor contains an RSPB reserve.

Sport

cricket
Somerset County Cricket Club was formed in 1875 but did not achieve first class status until 1891. It its headquarters are at the County Cricket Ground, St James's Street, Taunton, the most southwesterly first-class cricket ground in England and home since 2006 to Women's Cricket in England. First-class games are also played at Bath. The one-day team is known as the Somerset Sabres. Tel: 01823 272946.

football
Bristol City were founded in 1894 as Bristol South End and joined the Football League in 1901. The Robins' (sometimes also called CideReds) traditional colours are red and white and they play at Ashton Gate Stadium, Ashton Road, Bristol. Tel: 0117 963 0630.

Bristol Rovers were founded in 1883 as The Black Arabs, changing their name the following year to Eastville Rovers and in 1899 to Bristol Rovers. The Pirates (originally known as the Purdown Poachers and sometimes known as The Gas) joined the Football League in 1920 and play at the Memorial Ground, Filton Road, Horfield, Bristol. The club's home strip is blue, white and grey. The club's successful women's team formed in 1998 as Bristol Rovers WFC and is now known as Bristol Academy WFC. They play in the FA Women's Premier League National Division and have won nine trophies in the eight years since their formation. Tel: 0117 909 6648.

Other clubs include **Bath City** and **Team Bath**, who share Twerton Park stadium in Bath, and **Weston-super-Mare**.

horse racing
Taunton racecourse is a right-handed sausage-shaped course of 1 mile 2 furlongs (2km) holding exclusively National Hunt racing. Tel: 01823 337172.

Wincanton racecourse holds National Hunt racing on a right-handed track of 1 mile 3 furlongs (2.2km). Tel: 01963 32344.

rugby union
Bath were founded in 1865 and play home matches at the Recreation Ground. Their kit is predominantly black with blue sleeves. Currently in the Guinness Premiership, since the 1980s Bath have been one of England's most successful clubs, having won England's domestic competition, the Anglo-Welsh Cup, as well as the Heineken Cup and a number of league titles. Tel: 0871 721 1865.

Bristol were formed in 1888 with the merger of Carlton and Redland Park to create a united Bristol team, and since 2001 have adopted the name Bristol Shoguns. Having initially leased the County Cricket Ground at Nevil Road for home matches, the club have played since 1921 at the Memorial Ground (now also Bristol Rovers FC's home ground). Their traditional colours are navy blue and white. Bristol are currently in the Guinness Premiership. Tel: 0871 208 2234.

SS *Great Britain*
Great Western Dockyard, Gasferry Road, Bristol. Designed by Isambard Kingdom Brunel and launched in 1843, the SS *Great Britain* was the world's first iron-hulled, steam-powered, ocean-going ship. Fitted with a six-bladed propeller, she was designed to carry 250 passengers, 130 crew and 1200 tonnes of cargo. She made her first voyage from Liverpool to New York in 1845. Intended for the transatlantic luxury passenger trade, she was in fact predominantly used to carry emigrants to Australia. In 1970 she was rescued from an ignominious fate as a hulk in the Falkland Islands and returned to the dockyard where she was built for restoration. Tel: 0117 926 0680.

Stanton Drew stone circles $^{1}/_{4}$ mile (0.4km) east of Stanton Drew, 6 miles (10km) south of Bristol. A group of three stone circles beside the River Chew, with a single stone known as Hautville's Quoit to the north on the far side of the river. Most famous is the henge monument known as the Great Circle, the second largest stone circle in Britain (after Avebury); 370ft (113m) in diameter, it once probably consisted of 30 stones, of which 27 survive today. In the mid 17th century, after one of the stones had fallen, human bones and an object described as a 'round bell, like a large horse-bell' were found. A 'bronze serpent ring' has also been found on the site. The site has not been excavated, but geophysical work by English Heritage in 1997 revealed a surrounding ditch 442ft (135m) in diameter and 23ft (7m) wide; within this enclosure were nine concentric rings of post holes and over 400 pits, 3ft (1m) across and at 8ft (2.5m) intervals, arranged in rings. A 40m wide entrance was visible on the northeast side. To the northeast is a smaller ring, 100ft (30.5m) in diameter and consisting of eight stones, in the centre of which geophysical work identified four further pits. To the southwest is a third ring of 12 stones, measuring 140ft (43m). Theories suggest the site was dedicated to funerary ritual, although it has been proposed that the positioning of the stones relates to astronomical alignments; the site has also been linked to ley lines. Like many other stone circles, Stanton Drew is the subject of numerous legends. Illness is said to befall anyone who tries to count the stones, while they are also said to be a wedding party turned to stone after dancing to music played by the Devil on the Sabbath. The privately owned site is managed by English Heritage.

Staple Hill See Blackdown Hills, Wellington Monument

Steep Holm An island of 63 acres (25.5ha) located in the Bristol Channel. The only island in North Somerset, it is uninhabited with the exception of the warden, and is protected as a nature reserve and Site of Special Scientific Interest. The fortified Flat Holm island nearby is part of Wales. The island serves as a wind and wave break, sheltering the upper reaches of the Bristol Channel. GR: ST228607.

Stembridge Tower Mill $^{1}/_{2}$ mile (0.8km) east of High Ham, 7 miles (11km) southwest of Glastonbury. The last remaining thatched windmill in England; dating from 1822, it was in use until 1910. Now owned by the National Trust. Tel: 01935 823289.

Stogursey Castle Stogursey, 7 miles (11km) northwest of Bridgwater. Also known as Stoke Courcy. Norman enclosure castle founded in the late 11th century and improved by the de Courcys before being demolished c.1216. A cottage built over the gatehouse in the 17th century still remains.

Stoke-sub-Hamdon Priory Stoke-sub-Hamdon, 5 miles (8km) west of Yeovil. A 14th century house which was once the residence of the local chantry priest; it was used as a farmhouse from c.1518 until 1960. Now owned by the National Trust. Tel: 01985 843600.

Ston Easton Park Ston Easton, 6 miles (10km) north of Shepton Mallet. The current house dates from the 1740s, when an existing Jacobean building – occupied since the 17th century by the Hippisley family, lords of the manor of Ston Easton since 1544, after their move in the 17th century from the old manor house by the parish church – was converted into a Palladian mansion by John Hippisley Coxe. On Coxe's death in 1769, his sons Richard and Henry further embellished the house and grounds, employing Humphry Repton to design a landscape park, although only part of the plan was carried out. Henry's widow Elizabeth further developed the grounds in the early 19th century. The property was sold after the death in 1956 of Richard John Bayntun Hippisley; in 1964 it was purchased by William Rees-Mogg, who restored the building before selling it in 1978. It was later converted into a luxury hotel, and is now owned by Von Essen Hotels.

Sutton Court 1 mile (1.6km) northeast of Bishop Sutton, 10 miles (16km) south of Bristol. Also known as Stowey Court. The manor was built in 1558 for Elizabeth, Bess of Hardwick (see Hardwick Hall in Derbyshire) by her third husband, William St Loe, on the site of a 14th century castle. The house is built of sandstone with freestone and ashlar dressings and slate roofs. The north front incorporates a central three-storey 14th century pele tower with a circular stair turret, linked by two-storey ranges to the 1558 building to the left and a Victorian servants' wing to the right. The doorway to the tower dates from 1858–60, when the house was restored and rebuilt by Thomas Henry Wyatt for Sir Edward Strachey. Now Grade II* listed, as are a curtain wall to the north and the lodge, the house is currently divided into private apartments.

Sweet Track $1^{1}/_{4}$ miles (2km) west of Meare, 4 miles (6km) west of Glastonbury. A Neolithic causeway in the Somerset Levels, the oldest known engineered roadway in the world. Discovered while cutting peat in 1970 by Ray Sweet, after whom it is named, it extended for almost $1^{1}/_{4}$ miles (2km) across the marsh between what was then an island at Westhay, and a ridge of high ground at Shapwick, and is one of a network of tracks that once crossed the Levels. Built c.3800 BC, the track consisted of crossed poles of ash, oak and lime, driven into the waterlogged soil to support a walkway of oak planks laid end to end. Most of the track remains in its original location, and several hundred metres are now actively conserved using a pumped water distribution system. Portions are stored at the British Museum, while a reconstruction can be seen at the Peat Moors Centre near Glastonbury. It has now been established that the Sweet Track was built along the route of an even earlier abandoned track, the Post Track, dating from c.3838 BC and so around 30 years older.

Swildon's Hole Priddy, 7 miles (11km) northwest of Shepton Mallet. The entrance to this extensive cave system in the Mendip Hills is just outside the village of Priddy in a small tree-filled hollow. The first recorded exploration took place in 1901, and new sections have frequently been discovered since then. The cave's active streamway has created a highly varied system, ranging from low passages negotiated only by crawling to chambers with sheer drops, and from dry fossil passages to thundering waterfalls and its infamous sumps. The upper series of the cave compresses many of these features into a relatively short space, making Swildon's very popular with novice cavers, while the lower reaches provide challenges for the most experienced cave divers. The water in the cave re-emerges in Wookey Hole as the River Axe. Swildon's Hole forms part of the Priddy Caves Site of Special Scientific Interest.

Tarr Steps $2^1/_2$ miles (4km) southeast of Withypool, 11 miles (18km) southwest of Minehead. A prehistoric clapper bridge across the River Barle in Exmoor. The bridge dates to c.1000 BC and is a typical construction of stone slabs, each weighing up to 5 tons (5080kg); its span is 180ft (55m). According to local legend, the stones were placed by the devil to win a bet.

Taunton The county town of Somerset and also its largest town; its name means 'town on the River Tone'. Possibly the site of a Romano-British village near the suburb of Holway, Taunton was a place of considerable importance in Saxon times: King Ine of Wessex built an earthwork castle c.700, and a monastery was founded before 904. The bishops of Winchester, who owned the manor, obtained the town's first charter from Edward the Elder in 904, freeing them from all royal and county tribute. The local medieval fairs (the town still holds a weekly market) were known for the sale of woollen cloth called 'Tauntons', made in the town. On the decline of the wool industry in the west of England, silk-weaving was introduced at the end of the 18th century. In the autumn of 1685 Judge Jeffreys was based in Taunton during the 'Bloody Assizes' that followed the Battle of Sedgemoor. See also Battles

Taunton Castle Castle Green, Taunton. Norman enclosure castle founded c.1110 by William Gifford. The tower and other buildings were constructed by Henry de Blois in the mid 12th century and improved in 1207. The castle was originally developed as a major military stronghold, with walls 13ft (4m) thick and a gateway dating from 1495. Taunton Castle was held by Parliament during the Civil War. The great hall was the setting in 1685 of Judge Jeffreys' 'Bloody Assizes', at which over 500 rebels were tried and sentenced after the Monmouth Rebellion. Today the wisteria-clad castle houses Somerset County Museum.

Taunton Stop Line A World War II defensive line designed to stop the advance of troops and armoured vehicles from the west, the Taunton Stop Line was one of over 50 similar defensive lines constructed around England, designed to compartmentalise the country to contain any breakthrough until reinforcements could arrive. It ran north–south for nearly 50 miles (80km) through Somerset, Dorset and Devon, from the coast near Highbridge via the River Parrett to Bridgwater, along the Bridgwater and Taunton Canal to Taunton, to Ilminster via the railway and Chard Canal, along the Great Western Railway from Ilminster to Chard, and finally from Chard to Axminster along the River Axe. Many pillboxes can still be seen along the length of the line.

Temple of Harmony 3 miles (5km) southwest of Bridgwater. Located in Halswell Park (see separate entry), this copy of the Temple of Fortuna Virilis in Rome forms part of the 18th century pleasure gardens at Halswell House. It was restored in 1994. Tel: 01278 786012.

Tintinhull Garden Tintinhull, 6 miles (10km) northwest of Yeovil. A small 20th century Arts and Crafts garden surrounding a 17th century house. The garden is laid out in 'rooms' separated by walls and hedges, and was expanded and planted in 1933 by Phyllis Reiss in a style similar to that of Hidcote Manor in Gloucestershire. In 1954 the house and garden were given to the National Trust although Reiss continued to live on site until her death in 1961. The house has since been let to a number of tenants, and was occupied 1980–93 by garden designer and writer Penelope Hobhouse and her husband Prof. John Malins. Tel: 01935 822545.

Treasurer's House Martock, 6 miles (10km) west of Yeovil. An early medieval house with great hall completed in 1293. Features include a solar block built earlier in the 13th century, with an original wall painting. Until 1840 the house was the country residence of the treasurer of Wells Cathedral. Now owned by the National Trust. Tel: 01935 825015.

Tyntesfield $^1/_2$ mile (0.8km) east of Wraxall, 7 miles (11km) southwest of Bristol. A Victorian Gothic Revival estate located in the Vale of Nailsea and comprising a house, garden and park. Tyntes Place was purchased in 1843 by William Gibbs, who began building the current house in 1863. The house is built of Bath stone, with turrets and an elaborate roof. Principal rooms include the library, drawing room, billiard room, dining room and chapel. Among the notable features of the house are glass by Powell and Wooldridge. Given Grade II* listing in 1973, which has since been upgraded to Grade I, it was acquired by the National Trust in June 2002 after a massive fundraising campaign. Tel: 0870 458 4500.

Universities **Bath Spa University**, previously a university college, was upgraded to full university status in August 2005. Its main campus is at Newton Park to the west of Bath, an 18th century landscape park designed by Capability Brown; other sites are at Sion Hill and Somerset Place in the city and at Culverhay to the southwest. Tel: 01225 875875.

The **University of Bath** received its royal charter in 1966, making it one of the newest 'traditional' universities in the UK. Its campus is situated on Claverton Down, $1^1/_4$ miles (2km) east of Bath. With its origins in the Merchant Venturers' Technical College, Bath's traditional strengths are in science and technology, and it ranks consistently as one of the UK's top 20 universities. Former students include musician Alex James, Sainsburys CEO Justin King and MP Sandra Gidley. Tel: 01225 388388.

The **University of Bristol** received its royal charter in 1909 and is one of the original six 'red-brick' universities (the others being Birmingham, Leeds, Liverpool, Manchester and Sheffield). Founded in 1876 as University College Bristol, it was the first academic institution in the UK to admit men and women on equal terms. It is a member of the Russell Group of research-led universities, with traditional strengths in science and engineering; it also had the first drama department in England. Former students include physicist and Nobel laureate Paul Dirac, broadcaster Sue Lawley, satirist Chris Morris, actors Simon Pegg and Nick Frost of *Spaced* and *Shaun of the Dead* and Matt Lucas and David Walliams of *Little Britain* fame. Tel: 0117 928 9000.

The **University of the West of England**, usually abbreviated as UWE, is based in Bristol and gained university status in 1992. Its main campus is at Frenchay, 4 miles (6km) north of the city centre, with a smaller campus at St Matthias, a Faculty of Health and Social Care at Glenside in northeast Bristol and an art school, Bristol School of Art, Media and Design, at Bower Ashton, near Ashton Court in southwest Bristol. There are also regional centres in Bath and Swindon, and an associate faculty specialising in agricultural and sports related courses in Hartpury, Gloucestershire. Bristol Old Vic Theatre School is an associate school of the Faculty of Humanities, Languages and Social Sciences. UWE is the larger of the two universities in the city, with 30,000 students. Founded in 1970 as Bristol Polytechnic, it can trace its roots back to the foundation of the Merchant Venturers' Navigation School in 1595. Former students include explorer Bear Grylls, MP Dawn Primarolo and England wicketkeeper Jack Russell. Tel: 0117 965 6261.

Vicars' Close Located off Cathedral Green, Wells. Dating from the 15th century, Vicars' Close is thought to be the oldest existing medieval street in Europe. It has retained its original cobblestoned surface and has not changed much through the centuries. The tall chimneys were added in 1465. Vicars' Close was originally built to provide homes for the cathedral's vicars and continues to be occupied by those working for the Bishop of Bath and Wells.

Watchet A harbour town situated on the edge of Exmoor. In Samuel Taylor Coleridge's poem *The Rime of the Ancient Mariner*, the ancient mariner set sail from Watchet. In the mid 1860s two independent railways terminated here: the West Somerset Mineral Railway ran down from the iron mines on the Brendon Hills, and the West Somerset Railway came up from the Bristol and Exeter Railway at Norton Fitzwarren. Both lines made extensive use of the harbour.

Wearyall Hill 1/4 mile (0.4km) southwest of Glastonbury. This low hill is the site where, according to legend, Joseph of Arimathea landed after his journey to England from the Holy Land. He is said to have planted his hawthorn staff (grown from Christ's crown of thorns) on the hill, where it miraculously took root and grew into the Glastonbury Thorn, flowering each Christmas as well as in spring.

Wedmore, Isle of A name dating back to Saxon times when Wedmore was completely surrounded by wet marshland and the Somerset Levels were flooded. Nowadays Wedmore is a village situated 4 miles (6km) south of Cheddar. The population figure quoted is the ward of Wedmore and Mark. Area: 24.37 sq miles (63.11 sq km). Population: 4539.

Wellington Monument 2 miles (3km) south of Wellington. A 175ft (53.5m) high triangular tower located on Staple Hill, the highest point of the Blackdown Hills. The monument was built 1817–54 on land belonging to the Duke of Wellington, who took the name of his peerage from the town. It is now owned by the National Trust.

Wells 18 miles (29km) south of Bristol. With around 10,000 residents, Wells is the smallest city in England. It was named for the fresh water wells that rise in the gardens of the Bishop's Palace and are thought to have been a place of worship long before the advent of Christianity. The city was among the most important bishoprics in medieval Britain. See also Bishop's Palace, Wells Cathedral, Vicars' Close.

Wells Cathedral Cathedral Green, Wells. Dedicated to St Andrew and built in the 12th century by Reginald de Bohun, the cathedral is the seat of the Bishop of Bath and Wells. Though mostly Gothic in style, there are earlier foundations dating to the 10th century. The first church on the site was established by King Ine of Wessex at the urging of St Aldhelm, Bishop of Sherborne, in whose diocese it lay; the baptismal font in the south transept dates to c.AD 705. Two centuries later, the seat of the diocese was shifted to Wells; the first Bishop of Wells was Athelm (c.909), who crowned King Athelstan. Athelm and his nephew St Dunstan both became Archbishops of Canterbury. One of the cathedral's most famous features, the Wells clock, was probably in place by 1392; it is unique because it still has its original medieval face, depicting a pre-Copernican universe with the earth at its centre. When the clock strikes every quarter, jousting knights rush round above the clock and the Quarter Jack bangs the quarter hours with his heels. The 356 figures on the cathedral's west front comprise one of the most impressive collections of statuary in Europe. Tel: 01749 674483.

West Pennard Court Barn West Pennard, 3 miles (5km) east of Glastonbury. A 15th century barn with an unusual upper floor made of compacted earth. It is surrounded by grazing meadows. The property is owned by the National Trust. Tel: 01985 843600.

West Somerset Railway A heritage railway operating for 20 miles (32km) along the edge of the Quantock Hills between Bishops Lydeard and Watchet, and then along the coast to Minehead; intermediate stations are Crowcombe, Stogumber, Williford, Donniford Halt, Watchet, Washford, Blue Anchor and Dunster. It is the longest privately owned passenger rail line in the UK; using heritage steam and diesel locomotives, it provides transport for the local community as well as for visitors. Constructed as the West Somerset Mineral Railway in the 1850s, the line was taken over by the Bristol and Exeter Railway, which in turn was absorbed by the Great Western Railway in 1874. The original broad gauge line was converted to standard gauge in October 1882. It was closed in January 1971, but reopened as a heritage line in 1976. The original platforms of the station at Minehead are probably the longest on any preserved railway and can accommodate a 16 coach train plus locomotive. A small museum of railway relics, mainly of the West Country and GWR, is housed in the original waiting room at Blue Anchor station near Carhampton. Tel: 01643 821092.

Weston-super-Mare A seaside resort on the Bristol Channel. Because there are several places called Weston in Somerset, descriptions were added to distinguish them; unusually the descriptive part of Weston-super-Mare's name has remained in medieval Latin: *super* means on or above, and *mare* is Latin for sea. On the hill overlooking the town are the remains of Worlebury hill fort, built more than 2000 years ago on the site of earlier Bronze Age remains. A Roman building once stood on the site of Weston College, and Romano-British pottery has been found in the town. In 1568, the mineral calamine – a type of zinc ore crucial in brass production – was discovered on Worle Hill for the first time in Britain. Another ore, common on Worlebury Hill, was galena, a lead ore;

remnants of the industrial landscape can be seen in the pits and spoil heaps on Weston Hill. Weston's population in 1822 was only 735, but it began to expand with the arrival of Brunel's Bristol & Exeter Railway in 1841. After the completion of Birnbeck Pier in 1867, thousands of trippers began to arrive by steamer from Wales. In 1890 the pier offered entertainments including a theatre of wonders, alpine railway, shooting gallery, park swings, merry go round, waterchute, flying machine, helter skelter, maze, bioscope, cake walk and zigzag slide; on an average August Bank Holiday 15,000 passengers would arrive on the steamers. There were drives and walks through Weston Woods, planted on Weston Hill by the lord of the manor in the 1820s as a private game reserve. In 1904, the Grand Pier opened, with a large theatre offering top music hall stars. In 1937 the town was granted borough status and Henry Butt, a local entrepreneur, became the first mayor. The town was heavily bombed during World War II, especially in January 1941 and June 1942 when large areas were destroyed. In 1974 local government reorganisation resulted in the new county of Avon being formed. Weston's borough council was abolished and the town became the seat of local government for the District of Woodspring, an area stretching north to the outskirts of Bristol and including the towns of Nailsea, Clevedon and Portishead. More recent local government reorganisation has abolished Avon and turned the area covered by Woodspring into the unitary authority of North Somerset. In 2006 a structure known as *Silica* was erected at Big Lamp Corner. The work of art multi-tasks as an advertising sign, shop, bus shelter and, according to many residents, eyesore. The 'carrot', as it is known locally, is a conical edifice tapering to a needle-like tower. In July 2008 a fire believed to have been started by a deep-fat fryer devastated the Grand Pier. The blaze destroyed the wooden pavilion at the seaward end of the Grade II listed landmark, although its metal substructure remains intact.

Westonzoyland Pumping Station — 1 miles (1.6km) southwest of Westonzoyland, 3 miles (5km) southeast of Bridgwater. Somerset's earliest steam-powered pumping station, built in 1830 to carry out drainage of the Somerset Levels. The main engine house still contains the Easton and Amos pumping engine, built in 1861 to replace an earlier engine that carried out pumping work from 1831. The site now houses a small museum displaying several stationary steam engines and exhibits of land drainage history.

William Herschel Museum — New King Street, Bath. Situated in his former residence, the museum is dedicated to the life and works of astronomer William Herschel. He manufactured telescopes in the house and also discovered the planet Uranus in 1781. Various astronomical and musical artefacts are on display. Tel: 01225 311342.

Willow Man — A large outdoor sculpture by Serena de la Hey, situated in a field by the M5 motorway near Bridgwater. Made of willow withies on a steel frame, it stands 40ft (12m high). Commissioned by South West Arts for the Year of the Artist 2000, it celebrates the role of willow in the ecology and craft traditions of the Somerset Levels. The first sculpture was burnt down in an arson attack in May 2001, and was replaced by *Willow Man II* by the same artist in October 2001. A notable landmark, the sculpture is also known as 'Withy Man', and as 'Angel of the South' in reference to Antony Gormley's Angel of the North.

Woodspring Priory — 2½ miles (4km) northeast of Weston-super-Mare. A former Augustinian priory beside the Bristol Channel near the scenic promontory of Middle Hope and Sand Point, founded in the early 13th century and dedicated to St Thomas Becket. Its founder, William de Courtenay, was a grandson of Reginald FitzUrse, one of Becket's murderers. After its dissolution the priory was converted into a farmhouse. It is now owned by the Landmark Trust; there is also a small museum on the site. Middle Hope and Sand Point is owned by the National Trust. The priory gave its name to the former Woodspring district of the County of Avon.

Wookey Hole — 2 miles (3km) northeast of Wells. A cave system on the southern edge of the Mendip Hills named after the nearby village of Wookey and formed by the action of the River Axe. The waters disappear below ground at Swildon's Hole (see separate entry) before re-emerging as the Axe from Wookey Hole, and were used until 2008 by a handmade paper mill; the oldest surviving in Britain, it began operations in 1610, although a corn mill operated on the site as early as 1086. The Witch of Wookey Hole is a roughly human-shaped rock outcrop, reputedly turned to stone by a monk from Glastonbury. The cave, at a constant 11ºC (52ºF), is thought to have been used by humans for 50,000 years. It was first explored by cave divers in the 1930s; in 1935, Post Office engineers F G Balcombe and J A Sheppard carried out the first successful cave dive in Britain (and possibly the world), penetrating 170ft (52m) into the cave and reaching what is now known as Chamber 7. Chamber 9, also known as the Cathedral Chamber, was reached in 1948. In April 1949, Gordon Marriott was killed while exploring the cave. John S Buxton and Oliver Craig Wells (grandson of science fiction writer H G Wells) continued the exploration of Wookey Hole in the 1950s. The caves and mill were purchased by Madame Tussaud's in 1973 as a tourist attraction; their present owner is Gerry Cottle. Extensive tunnelling and construction work was carried out in the 1970s to enable members of the public to pass beyond Chamber 4, opening another 15 sections previously only accessible to cave divers from Chamber 3 (the Witch's Parlour) Tel: 01749 672243.

Wurt Pit and Devil's Punchbowl — 2 miles (3km) northeast of Priddy, 4 miles (6km) north of Wells. The two largest subsidence depressions in the Mendip Hills, formed by the collapse of surface rocks into a void created after the underlying limestone was dissolved by subterranean waters. It is designated a Site of Special Scientific Interest for its geology.

Yanal Bog — 2 miles (3km) north of Sandford, 6 miles (10km) east of Weston-super-Mare. A rare example in England of lowland peat bog, situated on the southern edge of the North Somerset Levels. Covering 4 acres (1.6ha), it is a designated Site of Special Scientific Interest.

Some famous people born in Somerset and Bristol

Agutter, Jennifer (actress) (1952–)	Taunton
Bacon, Roger (philosopher) (c.1214–92)	Ilchester
Bagehot, Walter (journalist) (1826–77)	Langport
Bailey, Bill (comedian and actor) (1964–)	Bath
Baker, (Sir) Benjamin (civil engineer) (1840–1907)	Keyford
Beddoes, Thomas Lovell (poet) (1803–49)	Clifton
Bilk, Bernard Stanley 'Acker' (clarinettist) (1929–)	Pensford
Blackmore, Richard Hugh (rock musician) (1945–)	Weston-super-Mare
Blackwell, Elizabeth (abolitionist) (1821–1910)	Bristol
Blake, Robert (admiral) (1599–1657)	Bridgwater
Bondfield, Margaret (politician) (1873–1953)	Chard
Bright, Richard (physician) (1789–1858)	Bristol
Button, Jenson (formula one driver) (1980–)	Frome
Chatterton, Thomas (poet) (1752–70)	Bristol
Clarke, Arthur Charles (author and inventor) (1917–)	Minehead
Cleese, John Marwood (actor) (1939–)	Weston-super-Mare
Conway, Russ (pianist) (1925–2000)	Bristol
Cribb, Tom (boxer) (1781–1848)	Bristol
Dampier William (explorer) (1651–1715)	East Coker
Dirac, Paul (physicist) (1902–84)	Bristol
Evans, Lee (comedian and actor) (1964–)	Avonmouth
Fielding, Henry (novelist) (1707–54)	Sharpham, Glastonbury
Friese-Greene, William (cinematographer) (1855–1921)	Bristol
Grace, William Gilbert 'WG' (cricketer) (1848–1915)	Bristol
Grant, Cary (film actor) (1904–86)	Bristol
Graves, Rupert (actor) (1963–)	Weston-super-Mare
Guscott, Jeremy (rugby player) (1965–)	Bath
Hirst, Damien (artist) (1965–)	Bristol
Howse, Neville (first Australian recipient of the VC) (1863–1930)	Stogursey
Hungerford, Thomas (first Speaker of the Commons) (c.1330–97)	Farleigh
Irving, Henry (first actor to be knighted) (1838–1905)	Keinton Mandeville
Lane, Allen (book publisher) (1902–70)	Bristol
Merchant, Stephen (writer and actor) (1974–)	Bristol
Nichols, Peter (writer) (1927–)	Bristol
Plimsoll, Samuel (social reformer) (1824–98)	Bristol
Rand, Mary Denise (athlete) (1940–)	Wells
Reader, Ralph (founder of the Boy Scout Gang Show) (1903–82)	Crewkerne
Redgrave, Michael Scudamore (actor) (1908–85)	Bristol
Rosenberg, Isaac (poet) (1890–1918)	Bristol
Southey, Robert (poet) (1774–1843)	Bristol
Trenchard, Hugh Montague (Father of the RAF) (1873–1956)	Taunton
Trescothick, Marcus Edward (cricketer) (1975–)	Keynsham
Williams, George (founder of the YMCA) (1821–1905)	Dulverton
Wood (the younger), John (architect) (1728–82)	Bath

Islands of Somerset

(shipping area = Lundy)

Island name	Area	Nearest landmark	General information
Athelney, Isle of	River Parrett/River Tone	North Petherton	See separate entry
Birnbeck Island	Bridgwater Bay	Weston-super-Mare	Joined to mainland by a pier. GR: ST303626
Black Rock	Bridgwater Bay	Watchet	GR: ST109440
Blackstone Rocks	Bristol Channel	Weston-super-Mare	GR: ST383702
Calf Rock	Bristol Channel	Steep Holm	GR: ST233605
Chisel Rocks	Parrett Estuary	Burnham-on-Sea	GR: ST270491
Denny Island	Severn Estuary	Portishead	The only island in Bristol. Area: 0.03 sq miles (0.08 sq km). GR: ST459810
Denny Island	Chew Valley Lake	Chew Stoke	GR: ST575605
Hang Rock	Bristol Channel	Portishead	GR: ST439759
Steep Holm	Bristol Channel	Weston-super-Mare	See separate entry
Stert Island (1)	Parrett Estuary	Burnham-on-Sea	Comprises two separate islands. GR: ST292480
Stert Island (2)	Parrett Estuary	Burnham-on-Sea	Comprises two separate islands. GR: ST290487
Tower Rock	Bristol Channel	Steep Holm	GR: ST233607
Wedmore, Isle of	Sedgemoor		See separate entry

STAFFORDSHIRE

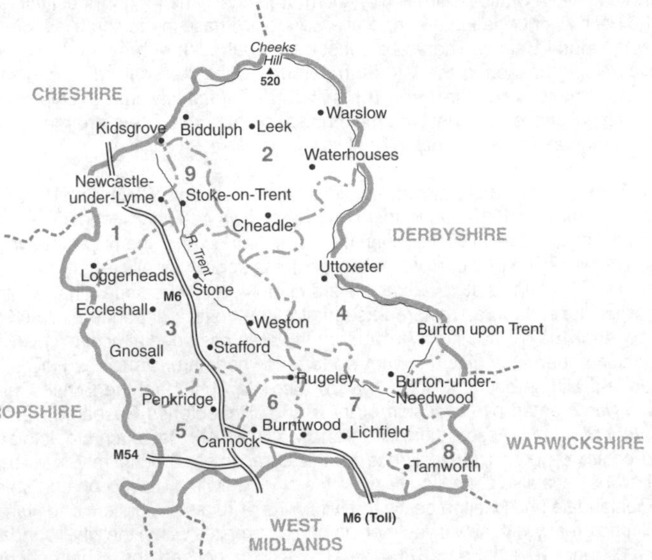
Cheeks Hill
520
CHESHIRE
Warslow
Kidsgrove
Biddulph
Leek
2
Waterhouses
9
Newcastle-under-Lyme
Stoke-on-Trent
Cheadle
1
R. Trent
DERBYSHIRE
Uttoxeter
Loggerheads
Stone
M6
Eccleshall
4
Weston
3
Burton upon Trent
Gnosall
Stafford
Rugeley
Burton-under-Needwood
Penkridge
6
7
SHROPSHIRE
5
Burntwood
Lichfield
Cannock
WARWICKSHIRE
8
M54
Tamworth
WEST MIDLANDS
M6 (Toll)

Districts

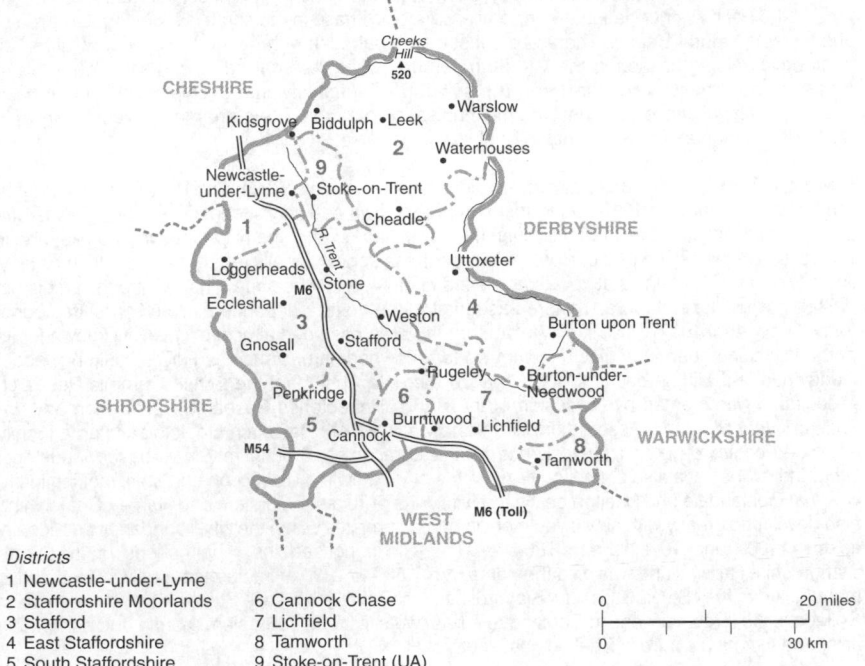

1 Newcastle-under-Lyme
2 Staffordshire Moorlands
3 Stafford
4 East Staffordshire
5 South Staffordshire
6 Cannock Chase
7 Lichfield
8 Tamworth
9 Stoke-on-Trent (UA)

0 — 20 miles
0 — 30 km

Staffordshire is a landlocked county in the West Midlands region, bordered by Cheshire to the northwest, Derbyshire to the northeast, Warwickshire to the southeast, West Midlands to the south, and Shropshire to the east. Its southwestern tip touches Worcestershire and its southeastern tip touches Leicestershire. The county town is Stafford. There are two cities, Lichfield and Stoke-on-Trent, the latter designated a unitary authority since 1 April 1997, distinct from Staffordshire County Council but remaining within the boundaries of the geographical county.

Historically, Staffordshire was divided into the five hundreds of Cuttlestone, Offlow, Pirehill, Seisdon and Totmonslow. The administrative county of Staffordshire, established in 1889, spanned the former county, excluding the county boroughs of Wolverhampton, Walsall and West Bromwich in the south (the area known as the Black Country), and Hanley in the north. The towns of Tamworth (partly in Warwickshire) and Burton upon Trent (partly in Derbyshire) were amalgamated completely into Staffordshire.

Handsworth and Perry Barr became part of the county borough of Birmingham, and thus part of Warwickshire, in the early 20th century. Burton, in the east of the county, became a county borough in 1901, as did Smethwick, another Black Country town, in 1907. In 1910 the six towns of the Staffordshire Potteries, including Hanley, became the single county borough of Stoke-on-Trent.

A huge restructuring of the Black Country in 1966 led to the creation of an area of contiguous county boroughs. The borough of Warley was formed by the merger of the county borough of Smethwick and municipal borough of Rowley Regis with the Worcestershire borough of Oldbury: the resulting borough became part of Worcestershire. In the meantime, the borough of Dudley, historically a detached part of Worcestershire, expanded and became part of Staffordshire instead. As a result of this reorganisation, the administrative county of Staffordshire had a thin protrusion linking the county boroughs (to the east) and Shropshire (to the west), to form a short border with Worcestershire.

On 1 April 1974 the county boroughs of the Black Country and the Staffordshire urban district of Aldridge-Brownhills became, along with Birmingham, Solihull and Coventry and other districts, the new metropolitan county of West Midlands. County boroughs were abolished, with Stoke becoming a non-metropolitan district in Staffordshire, and Burton forming a non-parish area in the district of East Staffordshire.

In the north and south Staffordshire is hilly; the moorlands in the far northeast fall within the boundaries of the Peak District National Park, while Cannock Chase in the south is a designated Area of Outstanding Natural Beauty. There are substantial coal seams throughout the county, although commercial mining ceased in the late 20th century, while the south also contains rich iron ore deposits. The largest river is the Trent. The soil of the central lowlands is chiefly clay and agriculture was not highly developed until the mechanisation of farms. There are more miles of canals in Staffordshire than any other county in England.

Stoke-on-Trent is a conglomeration of six older towns – Hanley, Stoke, Burslem, Tunstall, Longton and Fenton – created in 1910 and forming an area known as The Potteries. The borough was officially granted city status in 1925. Although the city is named after the original town of Stoke, and is the location of the city council offices, the city centre is conventionally regarded as being in Hanley. The city's county borough status was abolished in 1974, and it became a non-metropolitan district of Staffordshire. Its status was restored as a unitary authority independent of Staffordshire county council on 1 April 1997. Since the 17th century the area has been almost exclusively known for its industrial-scale pottery manufacture, with world renowned names such as Royal Doulton, Spode, Wedgwood and Minton being born and based there. In April 1948 the British Ceramic Research Association was created by the fusion of the British Refractories Research Association and the British Pottery Research Association. Known now as CERAM Research Ltd, it is an internationally renowned centre of technical excellence for the ceramics and other materials-based industries. Other industries have also been significant in the city's growth, notably iron and steel making in the valley at Goldendale and Shelton below the hill towns of Tunstall, Burslem and Hanley. Coal mining also developed greatly with new investment in mining projects within the city boundaries as recently as the 1960s and 1970s. From 1864 to 1927 Stoke housed the repair shops of the North Staffordshire Railway and was also the home from 1881 to 1930 of independent railway locomotive manufacturers Kerr Stuart & Co. Ltd. Staffordshire University is based in Stoke, while Stoke-on-Trent College is the largest college in England and has two sites; one in Burslem (media and performing arts) and the main centre in Shelton, just south of Hanley.

Lichfield is famous for its three-spired cathedral and as the birthplace of Dr Johnson, the writer of the first dictionary of the English language. Tradition has it that a thousand Christians were martyred in Lichfield in AD 286, during the reign of the Roman emperor Diocletian, although this is of doubtful authenticity. In the 7th century St Chad established the episcopal see of the Mercians at Lichfield. The burial in the cathedral of individual kings of Mercia, such as Celred in 716, further increased its prestige. In 786, Pope Hadrian I, at the request of Offa, king of Mercia, made it an archbishopric, but in 803 the primacy was restored to Canterbury. The 9th century *Historia Brittonum* of Nennius lists Lichfield as one of the 28 cities of Britain. In 1075 the see of Lichfield was removed to Chester, and thence a few years later to Coventry, but it was restored in 1148.

At the time of the Domesday survey, Lichfield was held by the bishop of Chester. This remained the case until the reign of Edward VI, when the lordship and manor were leased to the town corporation. Edward incorporated Lichfield in 1548 and in 1553 Queen Mary made it a county separate from the rest of Staffordshire, a status it retained until 1888. In the Middle Ages the main industry was making woollen cloth. There was also a leather industry. Much of the surrounding area was open pasture and there were many surrounding farms.

In the Civil War, Lichfield had divided loyalties, the church supporting the king and most of the townsfolk siding with Parliament. The city's position as a focus of supply routes was strategically important during the war, and both forces were anxious to control it. Robert Greville, 2nd Lord Brooke, a man notorious for his hostility to the church, led an assault against it, but was killed by a deflected bullet on St Chad's Day; the accident was welcomed as a miracle by the Royalists.

During the 18th century the city thrived as a busy coaching centre on the main route to the northwest and Ireland. It also became a centre of great intellectual activity, being the home of many famous people including Samuel Johnson, David Garrick, Erasmus Darwin and Anna Seward; this prompted Johnson's remark that Lichfield was 'a city of philosophers'. Today the main local manufacturers are Armitage Shanks, who produce sanitaryware, and Arthur Price, master cutlers and silversmiths.

Staffordshire	Population			Area	
Districts	*male*	*female*	*total*	*sq miles*	*sq km*
Cannock Chase	45,375	46,751	92,126	30	79
East Staffordshire	50,582	53,188	103,770	149	387
Lichfield	45,789	47,443	93,232	128	331
Newcastle-under-Lyme	59,242	62,788	122,030	81	211
South Staffordshire	52,230	53,666	105,896	157	407
Stafford	59,756	60,914	120,670	231	598
Staffordshire Moorlands	46,487	48,002	94,489	222	576
Tamworth	36,699	37,832	74,531	12	31
Stoke-on-Trent Unitary Authority	117,158	123,478	240,636	36	93
Total	513,318	534,062	1,047,380	1046	2713

Local Attractions and Information

Abbots Bromley School for Girls
Abbots Bromley, 4½ miles (7km) northeast of Rugeley. An independent school for girls aged 4–18, founded in 1874. It is one of the original Woodard Schools (a group of Anglican schools affiliated to the Woodard Corporation, founded in the mid-19th century by Canon Nathaniel Woodard and run on Christian principles), and was the first to be established for girls. Tel: 01283 840232.

Abbots Bromley Horn Dance
First performed at the Barthelmy Fair in August 1226, the Abbots Bromley Horn Dance is a ritual rural custom that still takes place on Wakes Monday (the day after Wakes Sunday, the first Sunday after 4 September) each year. The dance is performed by 12 dancers and musicians in Tudor costume: six men balance ancient reindeer antlers (possibly over 1000 years old and imported from Scandinavia) on their shoulders and a seventh rides a hobby-horse, while accompanying them are a boy with a bow and arrow, a 'jester', and a man dressed as Maid Marian. The dancers advance and retreat in stately fashion, accompanied by an accordionist and a triangle player. After the sets of antlers are collected from St Nicholas' Church at 8am, the dance is performed first at Blithfield Hall and afterwards at various locations throughout the village and its surrounding farms and pubs, over a route of 10 miles (16km).

Administrative headquarters
Staffordshire: County Buildings, Martin Street, Stafford ST16 2LH. Tel: 01785 223121.
Stoke-on-Trent: City Council, Civic Centre, Glebe Street, Stoke-on-Trent ST4 1RN. Tel: 01782 234567.

Alton Towers
6 miles (10km) north of Uttoxeter. Opened as a theme park in 1980, Alton Towers is located in the grounds of a former residence of the Earls of Shrewsbury; once a hunting lodge, the house was enlarged in Gothic style in the early 19th century but was derelict by the 1950s. Alton Towers is famous for its extreme rides, including 'Nemesis', a roller coaster in which people hang with their legs dangling down and 'Oblivion', the world's first vertical drop roller coaster. Another high-adrenalin ride is 'Air', a flying roller coaster in which riders are suspended horizontally facing down, as though flying. One of the most popular, and surreal, rides is 'Hex', based on the local legend of the chained oak. The 'Corkscrew', built in 1980 and Europe's first double-loop rollercoaster, was dismantled at the end of 2008. Tel: 08705 204060.

Ancient High House, The
Greengate Street, Stafford. England's largest timber-framed town house, built by the Dorrington family in 1594 of oak believed to come from nearby Doxey Woods. Charles I and his nephew Prince Rupert stayed in the house in 1642 at the start of the Civil War. The following year, when Stafford was taken over by the Parliamentarians, it became a prison for Royalist officers. The Staffordshire Yeomanry Museum, housed within the house since 1993, is dedicated to the history of the Queen's Own Royal Regiment. Tel: 01785 619131.

Battles
There have been two major battles in Staffordshire: Blore Heath and Hopton Heath. See separate table for details.

Biddulph Grange
1 mile (1.6km) north of Biddulph, 8 miles (13km) north of Stoke-on-Trent. The house and grounds were developed by James Bateman (1812–97), an accomplished horticulturist and landowner who moved to Biddulph Grange c.1840 from nearby Knypersley Hall. He designed the gardens helped by his close friend John Cooke, a painter of seascapes. Bateman was a collector of orchids, president of the North Staffordshire Field Society, and served on the Royal Horticultural Society's Plant Exploration Committee; among his sons was painter Robert Bateman. His gardens, compartmentalised and geographically themed – for example, there are Chinese and Egyptian areas – are an unusual survival of the intervening period between the Capability Brown landscape garden and the High Victorian style. In 1861 Bateman moved to Kensington in London and Biddulph was subsequently purchased by Robert Heath. The house burnt down in 1896 but was rebuilt by architect Thomas Bower, serving as a children's hospital from 1923 until the 1960s; during this period the 15 acre (6ha) garden suffered serious neglect. The house and gardens have since been fully restored by the National Trust, which now owns the property. Tel: 01782 517999.

Blackbrook Zoological Park
Winkhill, 6 miles (10km) southeast of Leek. Set amid the Staffordshire Moorlands and established in 1991, Blackbrook Zoological Park's varied collection includes the largest collection of birds in the UK, many rare and endangered. Tel: 01538 308293.

Blithfield Hall
3 miles (5km) northeast of Rugeley. The hall has been the home of the Bagot family since the late 14th century. The present house is mainly Elizabethan although a Gothic façade with embattled

towers and walls was added in the 1820s. It is adjacent to Blithfield Reservoir. A rare breed of goat known as the Bagot goat is believed to have been introduced to England as a gift from Richard II to Sir John Bagot in 1387, and for many years had its home on the estate.

Blithfield Reservoir 3 miles (5km) northeast of Rugeley. Opened in 1953 to supply water to the conurbation north of Birmingham, the reservoir covers 800 acres (324ha) in the valley of the River Blithe. One of the most important sites for waterbirds in the Midlands, it has been designated a Site of Special Scientific Interest and is notable for its populations of tufted duck and great crested grebe. Little egret and osprey are among the other species that frequent the reservoir, which is administered as a wildlife site by the West Midland Bird Club. Tel: 01283 840284.

Boscobel House See Shropshire

Burton brewing industry For centuries, Burton upon Trent has been associated with the brewing industry thanks to the quality of the local water, which contains a high proportion of dissolved salts, predominantly derived from gypsum in the surrounding hills. Much of the open land within and around the town is protected from chemical treatment to help preserve this water quality. Brewing began at Burton Abbey before the Norman Conquest, although the industry was established only in the 18th century by brewers such as John Worthington and William Bass. At its height a quarter of the beer sold in Britain was produced here, over 30 breweries being recorded in 1880. However, only three main brewers remained by 1980 – Bass, Ind Coope and Marston's – and for a time, only Burton Bridge Brewery remained as an independent brewer. A by-product of the brewing industry, figuratively and literally, is the town's Marmite factory, which in turn generated the production of Bovril. The town is currently home to two major brewery conglomerates: Coors Brewers Ltd, formerly Bass Brewers Ltd, and now the UK arm of the US Molson Coors Brewing Company, produces Carling and Worthington Bitter; and Marston, Thompson and Evershed plc, now owned by Wolverhampton & Dudley Breweries plc, which also produces Bass under licence from InBev. There are also three local breweries: Burton Bridge Brewery; Tower Brewery, a new microbrewery; and Cottage Brewery, based in the Old Cottage Inn.

Caldon Canal A branch of the Trent & Mersey Canal running from Etruria, in Stoke-on-Trent, to Froghall Wharf, just north of Cheadle, and built in 1779 to carry limestone from Caldon Low Quarries. The canal has 17 locks along its 18 mile (29km) length, terminating at the Uttoxeter Canal near the 226ft (69m) long Froghall Tunnel. Water is supplied by Rudyard and Knypersley reservoirs. Midway along its path the canal has its solitary branch, which runs for 3 miles (5km) and includes the 386ft (118m) long Leek Tunnel. The Caldon Canal all but closed in the 1970s but reopened in 2003 after many years of restoration, although the former branch at Uttoxeter remains closed at present.

Cannock Chase An area of Staffordshire countryside located between Cannock, Lichfield, Rugeley and Stafford. Comprising a mixture of natural deciduous woodland, coniferous plantations, open heathland and the remains of early industry, such as coal mining, it is the smallest Area of Outstanding Natural Beauty in England, designated on 16 September 1958 and covering just 26 sq miles (67 sq km). Although relatively small, the Chase features an impressive variety of landscape and wildlife, including a herd of around 800 fallow deer. Efforts are in progress to increase the amount of heathland, re-establishing shrubs such as heather in areas where bracken and birch forest have taken over most other plants. The Chase is home to a range of unusual and endangered birds, including migrant nightjars. At its southern edge are the remains of Castle Ring, an Iron Age hill fort. The Chase houses numerous memorials, including German and Commonwealth war cemeteries, and a memorial to the victims of the Katyn Massacre. Tel: 01889 883912. See also Museum of Cannock Chase

Casterne Hall 1 mile (1.6km) northwest of Ilam, 11 miles (18km) southeast of Leek. A Grade II* listed manor house set within the Peak District National Park and close to the Staffordshire/Derbyshire border. The current house was rebuilt in 1730; the Georgian additions incorporate an earlier 17th century and medieval building, while the stables and farm outbuildings from the period remain unmodernised. Casterne has served as a location for numerous film and TV productions. Tel: 01335 310489.

Ceramica Market Place, Burslem, Stoke-on-Trent. Opened on 17 June 2003 in Burslem's Old Town Hall with funding from the National Lottery, Ceramica is dedicated to the Staffordshire pottery industry. There are interactive exhibits exploring where clay comes from, its transformation into ceramics and how the products are used, and displays from manufacturers including Royal Doulton, Moorcroft and Wade. There is also an exhibition of the life and works of author Arnold Bennett, who was born in the town and set many of his novels in the area. Tel: 01782 832029.

Chartley Castle 1 mile (1.6km) north of Stowe-by-Chartley, 7 miles (11km) northeast of Stafford. Founded c.1100 on the site of a pre-Conquest castle, the present 13th century stone motte and bailey fortress was built by Ranulph Blundeville, Earl of Chester. Mary, Queen of Scots was imprisoned at the castle in 1585. The impressive remains include a rare cylindrical keep which still stands on the motte, while the curtain wall of the inner bailey is flanked by two huge half-round towers, a twin-towered gatehouse and an angle tower.

Chillington Hall 2 miles (3km) southwest of Brewood, 7 miles (11km) southwest of Cannock. The estate has been home to the Giffard family since 1178, when a Giffard was reputed to have killed an escaped panther, now depicted in the family crest. Sir John Soane (with the help of Francis Smith of Warwickshire, who built the magnificent staircase) reconstructed Chillington in 1786 in Palladian style after a fire. The use of natural light in the house, drawn in from above, is the first example of what was later to become one of Soane's celebrated trademarks; the sense of light and space created in the top-lit saloon at the building's heart would soon be reproduced at the Bank of England and the Law Courts in London. The two-storey portico, now blackened by pollution from

Wolverhampton (only 6 miles/10km away), dominates the entrance and echoes the $1\frac{1}{2}$ mile-long oak-lined avenue and extensive parkland. The serpentine park and lake were designed by Capability Brown in 1761. Tel: 01902 850236.

Churnet Valley Railway 6 miles (10km) east of Stoke-on-Trent. A heritage railway in the Staffordshire Moorlands, operating for $5\frac{1}{2}$ miles (8.5km) through the valley of the River Churnet between Cheddleton and Froghall via Consall Forge. It operates on part of the former North Staffordshire Railway between North Rode in Cheshire and Uttoxeter, opened in 1849 and closed to passengers in 1965. Tel: 01538 360522.

Coombes Valley Nature Reserve $1\frac{1}{2}$ miles (2.5km) southeast of Leek. Centred on a steep-sided, wooded valley with a variety of grassland and mainly oak woodland, the RSPB reserve provides a habitat for birds such as pied flycatchers, redstarts, wood warblers and dippers, as well as for butterflies, flowers and other wildlife. Redwings, fieldfares and winter finches are frequent visitors in winter. Tel: 01538 384017.

Croxden Abbey Croxden, 4 miles (6km) northwest of Uttoxeter. A Cistercian abbey founded in 1176 by Bertram de Verdun, lord of the manor of Croxden, with 12 monks from the Savigniac mother house of Aulnay-sur-Odon in Normandy. It was known as the Abbey of the Vale of St Mary at Croxden. The monks were successful sheep breeders and the abbey, though small – the number of monks remained constant throughout – lasted for 350 years until its dissolution in 1538. The site is now in the care of English Heritage and can be found among modern farm buildings. Regrettably, the village lane has been built through the ruins of the church. Tel: 0121 625682.

Dorothy Clive Garden, The Willoughbridge, 7 miles (11km) southwest of Newcastle-under-Lyme. The 12 acre (5ha) garden has a wide variety of landscape features, including woodland, alpine and gravel gardens. Its centrepiece is the quarry garden with its spectacular waterfall, created by Colonel Harry Clive in 1940 for his wife Dorothy in a disused 19th century gravel quarry. The informal gardens, with daffodil and tulip walks and superb summer colour borders, offer colour from early spring to late autumn. The garden is now managed by the Willowbridge Garden Trust, established by Col. Clive in 1958. Tel: 01630 647237.

Dunwood Hall Longsdon, 1 mile (1.6km) southwest of Leek. Built in 1871, Dunwood Hall was the country residence of the Mayor of Burslem, Thomas Hulme, a self-made Victorian gentleman, and his family. Local architect Robert Scrivener designed the impressive house in Gothic Revival style in order to show off Hulme's newfound wealth and good taste. The Grade II listed hall is currently maintained and lived in by three generations of the family who rescued it from dereliction in the 1960s.

Eccleshall Castle $\frac{1}{4}$ mile (0.4km) north of Eccleshall. A manor house built in 1693 on the site of a 13th century castle constructed by Bishop Walter de Langton. The land was reputedly granted to St Chad, Bishop of Lichfield, in AD 669, and remained a residence of the Bishops of Lichfield until the 1870s. Since then the property has been owned by the Carter-Morley family. At the outbreak of the Wars of the Roses, Margaret of Anjou, queen consort of Henry VI, took refuge within the castle after the Battle of Blore Heath in 1459. Cromwell's soldiers demolished most of the castle during the Civil War; only one unusual nine-sided tower survives, together with the moat walls and medieval bridge.

Erasmus Darwin House Beacon Street, Lichfield. The home of Charles Darwin's grandfather, Erasmus (1739–1802), a renowned doctor, philosopher, inventor, scientist and poet. The 18th century house has period furnishings, while interactive displays tell the story of this remarkable man. Tel: 01543 306260.

Ford Green Hall Ford Green Road, Smallthorne, Stoke-on-Trent. A 17th century timber-framed farmhouse complete with Tudor garden and museum. The house was home to the Ford family for nearly 200 years. Tel: 01782 233195.

Foxfield Steam Railway A preserved steam railway in North Staffordshire operating on $2\frac{1}{2}$ miles (4km) of a line built through the Staffordshire Moorlands in 1893 to link Foxfield Colliery with the Stoke–Derby main line. After the colliery closed in 1965 the Foxfield Light Railway Society was formed in 1967; it now operates between its headquarters at Caverswall Road station, Blythe Bridge and Dilhorne Park, and is home to 28 steam, diesel and electric locomotives along with a wide variety of coaches and freight vehicles, many of which are on display at Caverswall Road station. Tel: 01782 396210.

Gladstone Pottery Museum Uttoxeter Road, Longton, Stoke-on-Trent. A preserved Victorian pottery complete with bottle kilns, a maze of passageways, workshops and pottery demonstrations. There are exhibits of sanitaryware telling the story of the toilet and a tile gallery with a collection of decorative tiles from the Middle Ages onwards, as well as a recreated 1890s doctor's surgery. Tel: 01782 237777.

Highest point Cheeks Hill at 1706ft (520m), 9 miles (15km) north of Leek and close to the border with Derbyshire and Cheshire. GR: SK026699.

Interesting facts **Josiah Wedgwood**, the Stoke potter credited with the industrialisation of the manufacture of pottery, was the grandfather of Charles Darwin. Josiah married Sarah Wedgwood (a third cousin) and together they had seven children. Their eldest child, Susannah (1765–1817), married Robert Darwin, and they were the parents of the great English naturalist. In **Arnold Bennett's novels** the six towns of Stoke, known as The Potteries, are referred to as 'the Five Towns'; Bennett felt that the name was more euphonious than 'the Six Towns' so Fenton was omitted. The five real towns and their Bennett counterparts are Tunstall (Turnhill), Burslem (Bursley), Hanley (Hanbridge), Stoke (Knype) and Longton (Longshaw). **Reginald Joseph Mitchell CBE** designed 24 aircraft between 1920 and 1936 including light aircraft, fighters, bombers, several seaplanes, and flying boats such as the Supermarine Walrus. However, he is best remembered for the Supermarine S6B and the Spitfire. The S6B won the Schneider Trophy in 1931 and later broke the world air speed record. The first prototype Spitfire, K5054, flew for the first time on 5 March 1936 at Eastleigh. In later tests it reached 349mph (560km/h) and so, before the prototype had completed its official trials, the RAF ordered 310 production Spitfires. Mitchell died of rectal cancer in June

1937 and his life and the sacrifices he made to keep going despite pain and impending death were the subject of the 1942 Leslie Howard film *The First of the Few*. **Staffordshire Oatcakes** are almost entirely unknown outside north Staffordshire. They have been described as a 'Tunstall tortilla' and a 'Potteries poppadom', but in truth are as much a part of county tradition as pasties are to Cornwall or hot pots to Lancashire. Their origins probably lie in British Colonial India. Apparently the Staffordshire lads who served in the military there noticed the local flat-bread (chapati) and tried to duplicate it when they returned home, using oatmeal instead of durum wheat. **Lobby**, a stew not unlike Lancashire hot pot, is still made by local people around the Stoke area. **Tamworth pigs** are a minor breed of domestic pig that originated in Ireland, where they were called 'Irish Grazers'; they were imported in 1812 to the Staffordshire town after which they were subsequently named. In January 1998 two five-month-old Tamworth ginger pigs escaped while being unloaded from a lorry at an abattoir in Malmesbury, Wiltshire. The brother and sister swam the River Avon and spent the best part of a week on the run amid a huge media furore, the press dubbing the pair 'Butch and Sundance' after the American outlaws. Butch was eventually captured on the evening of 15 January, when she and Sundance were spotted foraging in the garden of local couple Harold and Mary Clarke. Sundance escaped into the thicket once again, but was flushed out the next day by two springer spaniels and tranquillised with a dart gun. The two pigs were later housed – courtesy of the *Daily Mail* – at the Rare Breeds Centre, an animal sanctuary near Ashford in Kent. Cannock-based **Richard Gosling** became Britain's Strongest Man in 2003, an achievement all the more meritorious as he was seriously injured in August 2001 when working as a doorman at Silks nightclub, Mill Street, Cannock. He was slashed across the neck and needed a transfusion of four pints of blood. His attacker was given a life sentence for wounding with intent to cause grievous bodily harm. **Anna Seward** (1747–1809), although born in Eyam in Derbyshire, spent most of her life in Lichfield. Her *Poetical Works* were edited by Sir Walter Scott and she became known as the 'Swan of Lichfield'. **Sarah Wilson** was born in a Staffordshire village in 1754 and at the age of 16 moved to London. Within a week she apparently became a maidservant to Caroline Vernon, lady-in-waiting to Queen Charlotte, and became acquainted with court life. In early 1771 Wilson began to steal the queen's jewellery and clothing; she was apprehended and condemned to death, but eventually the sentence was commuted to penal transportation to the American colonies. In July 1771 Wilson arrived in Baltimore, Maryland and was sold to Mr W Devall, a planter from Bush Creek, Frederick County. A few days later she escaped; somehow she still had among her personal belongings some of the items stolen from the Queen – including a ring, a dress and a miniature portrait – and she now transformed herself into 'Princess Susanna Caroline Matilda, sister of Queen Charlotte', forced into exile in America following a family quarrel. With her intimate familiarity and knowledge of the gossip of upper-class English society, 'Princess Susanna' was soon in demand at various gentlemen's houses where she was plied with money and gifts in the hope that once restored to the royal household the favours might be repaid. Eventually Devall heard about a woman who looked very much like the girl who had escaped. He spread a notice that 'Princess Susanna' was in fact his slave and sent a hireling, Michael Dalton, to get her back. Dalton found her near Charlestown and dragged her back to Bush Creek. For two years Wilson worked for Devall, until he joined the rebels in the beginning of the American War of Independence. Wilson fled, after stealing the identity of another Sarah Wilson, and later married dragoon officer William Talbot. After the war they stayed in the newly formed USA and supposedly lived happily ever after! The daily comic strip ***May un Mar Lady***, written in Potteries dialect by cartoonist Dave Follows, first appeared on 8 July 1986 in the *North Staffordshire Sentinel* and was a local institution for over 20 years. The full twenty-year run of 7000 strips has since been republished in the *Evening Sentinel* as *May Un Mar Lady Revisited*. The Glynne Arms, on the edge of the Himley Estate, near Dudley, is more popularly known as the **Crooked House** or the Siden House. A building that has suffered badly from mining subsidence, it lies on what was once the divide between Sir Stephen Glynne's land and that of the Earl of Dudley. Glynne removed too much of the coal that lay underneath, leaving a resultant tilt of 15 degrees. Doors, floors and windows are all at odd angles, causing patrons difficulty on entering the pub and walking to the bar. As the result of an optical illusion, without even taking a drink, beer bottles can be seen to roll up the table: 'Cum in an av sum hum brewd erl Stop as lung as yom erbul, At a public called the Siden House, Weer the beer runs up the terbul.' The 300-year-old **Yew Tree Inn** at Cauldon, near Leek, Collectors' Pub of the Year in the millennium edition of the *Good Pub Guide*, has also been featured on Channel 4's *Collector's Lot*, partly thanks to the eccentric landlord's passion for collecting antiques. A self-confessed hoarder who still has all his childhood Dinky toys, Alan East has turned the pub into a living museum full of Victoriana. Music is not from a jukebox, but from working Symphonions; the till is pre-decimal and drinkers perch on old settles and soggily sprung sofas.

Izaak Walton's Cottage — Shallowford, 5 miles (8km) northwest of Stafford. A half-timbered 16th century cottage, once the home of Izaak Walton, author of *The Compleat Angler*, a treatise on the pleasures of fishing now regarded as a literary classic. Set on the banks of the River Meece in a beautiful Staffordshire village, the cottage has been restored and now houses an angling museum dedicated to Walton. The museum includes a variety of fishing tackle, trout flies, rods and reels; there is also a small herb garden at the rear. Tel: 01785 619619.

Johnson, Dr Samuel — Born in Lichfield in 1709, Samuel Johnson was the son of a bookseller whose shop was in the Market Square. When he was five years old he was sent for English lessons at Dame Oliver's School, Dam Street. After attending grammar school in Lichfield and Stourbridge Johnson went on to Pembroke College, Oxford. Although a bright student, he suffered from mental stress, not helped by his poverty and his poor eyesight, and he left after just over a year without taking a degree (although he was later given an honorary doctorate). He worked as a teacher in Market Bosworth before moving to Birmingham, where he lived for three years. Here he met Elizabeth 'Tetty' Porter, whom he was later to marry. She was 20 years older than Samuel, had already raised a family by a previous marriage and was financially secure. He began writing for the *Birmingham Journal* and completed his first published book, *A Voyage to Abyssinia* (1735), a translation from a French book of travels. Following their marriage Samuel and Tetty set up a school at Edial, near Lichfield; one of Samuel's pupils was David Garrick, and the pair went to London in 1737 – Johnson to write for *The Gentleman's Magazine* (founded by Edward Cave) and Garrick, eventually, to become a playwright and the most famous actor of the day. Johnson's first poem, 'London', was published in the magazine the following year. From 1747 he worked on his *Dictionary of the English Language* which was to take him eight years to complete, and on *The Rambler*, a twice-weekly periodical published in three volumes in 1750. Tetty died in 1752, while Johnson still experienced poverty, alleviated to some extent with the help of his friends: *Rasselas* (1759), a prose tale of Abyssinia, is said to have been written in a week to pay for his mother's burial. Better fortune came in 1762 when Johnson was awarded a Crown pension of £300 a year. He had by now gathered around him a circle of friends and was often consulted for advice on literary matters; he became particularly close to Henry and Hester Thrale and spent much time in their company, while other friends included James Boswell, Fanny Burney, Sir Joshua Reynolds and Oliver Goldsmith. Johnson became lonely in his later years and suffered recurring ill health; his achievements, however, continued to be recognised and on his death in 1784 he received the honour of burial in Westminster Abbey. Johnson's life was vividly recorded by James Boswell in a biography itself recognised as an outstanding literary work. The Samuel Johnson Birthplace Museum is situated on Breadmarket Street, Lichfield, and a statue of Johnson in contemplative mood, erected in 1838, stands in the city's Market Square. Tel: 01543 264972.

Keele University 4 miles (6km) west of Stoke-on-Trent. Keele was the first new UK university of the 20th century and a pioneer of joint honours degree courses. Established in 1949 as the University College of North Staffordshire, it achieved university status in 1962. It is the UK's largest integrated campus university and occupies a Grade II listed 617 acre (250ha) estate, the central feature of which is 19th century Keele Hall, designed in Jacobean Revival style by Anthony Salvin. Former students include human rights lawyer Michael Mansfield, politician Clare Short and fantasy gamer Steve Jackson. Tel: 01782 621111.

Kinver Edge $1/4$ mile (0.4km) south of Kinver, 18 miles (29km) southwest of Cannock. A woodland escarpment and a remnant of the Mercian forest located on the Staffordshire/Worcestershire border. At its summit is an Iron Age hill fort. Kinver Edge is also home to the last occupied cave dwellings in England, with a set of complete houses excavated into the local sandstone. One of the rocks, Holy Austin, was a hermitage until the Restoration. The Holy Austin rock houses were inhabited until the 1950s and are now owned by the National Trust. The heathland and woodland support a variety of wildlife, with adder and common lizard present on the heaths, and common buzzard, Eurasian jay, great spotted woodpecker and many other bird species in the woods. The area around the summit is mainly heathland, with woodland of birch, oak and sweet chestnut at the northern end. On the southern end of the edge and entirely in Worcestershire are the commercial forestry plantations of Kingsford Forest Park. Tel: 01384 872418.

Letocetum Roman Baths Wall, 2 miles (3km) south of Lichfield. The Roman settlement of Letocetum was a staging post along the Roman road of Watling Street providing overnight accommodation for soldiers and travellers. The excavated site consists of an inn and bath house, with a museum displaying finds from the excavations. Managed by English Heritage on behalf of the National Trust. Tel: 01543 480768.

Lichfield Cathedral The Close, Lichfield. Built in the late 13th and early 14th century, the cathedral is dedicated to St Chad and St Mary. Its internal length is 370ft (113m), the central spire 253ft (77m) high and the western spires 190ft (58m) high; the three spires are often referred to as 'the Ladies of the Vale'. Built of local sandstone, the walls of the nave lean outwards slightly; this was caused by the weight of stone used in the ceiling vaulting, over 200 tons of which was removed during renovation work to prevent the walls leaning further. Lichfield was damaged during the Civil War and all the stained glass destroyed; the fine medieval Flemish painted glass, dating to the 1530s, in the windows of the Lady Chapel was rescued in 1801 from the Abbey of Herckenrode (now in Belgium), which was dissolved during the Napoleonic Wars. There are also windows by Betton and Evans dating to 1819, and some fine late 19th century windows, particularly those by Charles Eamer Kempe. In 2003 an excavation of the nave uncovered three fragments of an Anglo-Saxon sculptured limestone panel; together these form half of one side of a hollowed limestone block. The carving depicts an angel, his right hand raised in blessing and the left bearing a foliate sceptre. Tel: 01543 306100.

Lichfield Gospels Also known as the Book of Chad or the St Chad Gospels, and housed in Lichfield Cathedral, the Lichfield Gospels are an illuminated manuscript consisting of the gospels of Matthew, Mark and the early part of Luke. Written in Latin and dating to c.730, there were originally two volumes but one disappeared around the time of the Civil War, when the cathedral was sacked. The origin of the gospels is uncertain, although they are known to have been present in Lichfield since the 11th century: the style of illumination is similar to that of the Lindisfarne Gospels, but rare annotations in Welsh suggest a different origin, while other decorations resemble the Anglo-Saxon angel discovered in the cathedral in 2003 and indicate that the manuscript may have been created in Lichfield.

Manifold Way A 9 mile (15km) footpath from Hulme End to Waterhouses following the course of the Leek and Manifold Valley Light Railway, which closed in 1934. A visitor centre housed in Hulme End

Station has a model of the railway. Located among the limestone cliffs fringing the valley are Thor's Cave, in which evidence of human occupation has been found dating back 10,000 years, and the outcrop of Beeston Tor, the latter overlooking the confluence of the rivers Manifold and Hamps.

Moseley Old Hall — $4^1/_2$ miles (7km) southwest of Cannock. Famous as one of Charles II's hiding places before his escape to France following defeat at the Battle of Worcester in 1651, the hall was built in 1600 for the local Whitgreave family. The family were mostly Catholics and Royalists, and Thomas Whitgreave assisted Charles when he arrived in the early hours of 8 September from Boscobel House, giving him dry clothes, food and a proper bed (his first since Worcester on 3 September). The king remained in a priest hole for two nights, receiving assistance from the family's Catholic priest, John Huddleston. Descendants of the family owned the house until 1925. During that time few structural changes were made, apart from covering the hall with brick walls and replacing the Elizabethan windows. It was apparently abandoned as the family home after the 1820s in favour of Moseley Court, a new Regency style house built for George Whitgreave, and was used as a farmhouse until the start of World War II. In a state of neglect when the National Trust took it over in 1962, it is now fully restored; most of the period furniture has been donated, but the original four-poster bed in which Charles II slept stands in the King's Room. The garden has been reconstructed in 17th century style with formal box parterre and planting appropriate to the period. Tel: 01902 782808.

Motto — 'The knot unites', written on the arms of Staffordshire, which depict a distinctive three-looped knot adorning a castellated crown.

Mow Cop Castle — Mow Cop, $1^1/_2$ miles (2.5km) west of Biddulph. Located on a windswept hill on the Staffordshire/Cheshire border, the folly known as Mow (pronounced to rhyme with 'cow') Cop Castle was built in 1754 by Randle Wilbraham of nearby Rode Hall as a sophisticated summerhouse resembling a medieval fortress and round tower. It is now remembered as one of the founding sites of Methodism: in 1807 Hugh Bourne of Stoke-on-Trent held a public gathering on the hill to preach the doctrines of John Wesley, and five years later at an even larger meeting, the Methodist movement was formed. The castle was taken over by the National Trust in 1937, an occasion marked by a gathering of over 10,000 Methodists on the hill. The area surrounding the castle was once famous for the quarrying of high quality millstones (querns) for use in watermills, and excavations at Mow Cop have found examples dating back to the Iron Age.

Museum of Cannock Chase — Valley Road, Hednesford. Situated at the edge of the Hednesford Hills nature reserve, the museum illustrates the history of Cannock Chase, from medieval royal hunting forest to 19th century coalfield community. It is set in 30 acres (12ha) of green space adjacent to the Hednesford Hills, a rare surviving area of heathland on the southern edge of Cannock Chase. Tel: 01543 462621.

National Memorial Arboretum — 1 mile (1.6km) east of Alrewas, 7 mile (11km) northeast of Lichfield. Part of the National Forest, the arboretum is intended as a living tribute to those who suffered or lost their lives in conflict during the 20th century. Bordered on one side by the River Tame, it is located on 152 acres (61ha) of old gravel workings. The first plantings were made in early 1997 and the arboretum officially opened on 16 May 2001; it now contains over 50,000 trees, with more being added each year. It is managed by the Royal British Legion and there are memorials to the armed services, civilians involved in conflicts, and other organisations, such as the police and fire service: an avenue of chestnuts was funded by the UK's police forces (early truncheons were made from the wood). The Millennium Chapel, the only chapel in the UK to be dedicated in Millennium year, is constructed with 12 pillars of Douglas fir. Tel: 01283 792333.

Prisons — **Dovegate**, Uttoxeter, is a male Category B private training prison operated by Serco. Operational capacity: 860. Tel: 01283 829400.

Drake Hall, Eccleshall, became a male open prison in the 1960s, but has been female since 1974. In January 2002, following erection of a perimeter fence, it was redesignated from open to semi-open. Operational capacity: 315. Tel: 01785 774100.

Stafford, Gaol Road, Stafford, was built in 1794 and apart from 1916–40, has been in continuous use ever since; the town has had a prison since the end of the 12th century. Operational capacity: 680. There is also a prisoner support (vulnerable) wing that holds 84 category C prisoners. Tel: 01785 773000.

Swinfen Hall, Lichfield, holds long term young adult male prisoners. A major building project began in spring 2004 to expand its accommodation and facilities. Operational capacity: 620. Tel: 01543 484000.

Reliant Motor Company — The company was formed in 1935 by Mr T L Williams, who decided to build his own three-wheeled vehicle in his back garden at Kettlebrook, Tamworth. In 1973 Reliant introduced the most famous of its three-wheelers, the Robin. Production was based at Two Gates in Tamworth for 65 years, until December 1998 when the factory was closed and production moved to a purpose-built factory at Burntwood, Cannock. Although Reliant stopped making the Robin at the end of 2000, from 30 April 2001 the car was produced under licence to Reliant by B&N Plastics of Suffolk.

Rivers — The **Anker** is a tributary of the River Tame. It rises near and flows through Nuneaton following a northwesterly route parallel to the Coventry Canal, for 15 miles (24km) before merging with the Tame near Tamworth.

The **Churnet** rises in the Staffordshire Moorlands near the Roaches in the Peak District National Park. It flows through Tittesworth Reservoir and Leek, afterwards following the line of the Caldon Canal once it has merged with it. It joins the River Dove south of Rocester.

Dane see Cheshire

Dove see Derbyshire

The **Manifold** rises just south of Buxton near Axe Edge, at the northern edge of the limestone White Peak of the Peak District National Park. It continues south for 12 miles (19km), joining the River Dove between Ilam and Thorpe. For part of its course, it runs underground. Its major tributary is the River Hamps. Villages on the river include Longnor, Hulme End, Waterhouses (which is actually on the Hamps) and Ilam.

The **Meece** is a small tributary of the River Trent on the Staffordshire/Shropshire border, near Stone. It rises from three small streams southwest of Keele Park which unite near Whitmore, passing through the large pool in Whitmore Park and running parallel with the railway for several miles through Mill Mease and Norton Bridge. Receiving tributaries on either side, the Meece drains a wide area east and west.

The **Penk** rises in the region of Pendeford, 3 miles (5km) north of Wolverhampton and on the Staffordshire/West Midlands border. It flows north through the village of Coven to the market town of Penkridge (giving the town its name), and continues north to Baswich on the outskirts of Stafford, where it joins the River Sow. Along its entire length of 12 miles (19km), the Penk is followed to within a few miles by the Staffordshire and Worcestershire Canal.

The **Sow** rises 1 mile (1.6km) southwest of Hookham at a spring called Sowhead, 617ft (188m) above sea level, and flows south by Bishop's Wood and New Inn Bank before turning east above Bishop's Offley, through Copmere and north of Eccleshall, where it receives a stream coming from the north near Foxley. Flowing southeast to Worston Mill it is joined by the River Meece from the northwest. The river now flows through Great Bridgeford and Stafford, being fed by waters from Seighford and on the east from Marstone. Below Stafford the Penk enters its right bank from the southwest.

Stour see Worcestershire
Tame see West Midlands
Trent see Nottinghamshire

Rudyard Lake
2 miles (3km) northwest of Leek. A 2½ mile (4km) long reservoir covering 168 acres (68ha) on the edge of the Peak District National Park in the Staffordshire Moorlands. Created in 1798 to feed the Trent and Mersey Canal, it became a major tourist attraction during the later 19th century; one of its many claims to fame is that John Lockwood Kipling and Alice Macdonald, parents of Rudyard Kipling, met here and liked the place so much they named their son after it. The Rudyard Lake Steam Railway runs narrow gauge steam trains along the east side of the lake. Tel: 01538 306280.

Rudyard Lake Steam Railway
A narrow gauge railway operating for 1½ miles (2.5km) on the standard gauge trackbed of a former North Staffordshire Railway line, built in the early 1900s as a tourist attraction with stations at the north and south ends of the lake. After the NSR line closed down, a small narrow gauge train ran on the site for two years. The current line began operating in 1985 and is 10½in (260mm) gauge (about half the size of a normal narrow gauge railway); trains are usually steam-hauled. Tel: 01995 672280.

Sandon Hall
5 miles (8km) northeast of Stafford. An imposing neo-Jacobean house built by William Burn in 1854 after the previous building had burned down in 1848. Set amid 400 acres (160ha) of parkland, Sandon is the ancestral home of the Earls of Harrowby, a famous Liberal family; the family museum, which opened in 1994, incorporates several of the state rooms. The 50 acre (20ha) landscaped gardens feature magnificent trees and are especially beautiful in May and autumn. Tel: 01889 508004.

Shugborough Hall
1 mile (1.6km) northeast of Milford, 4 miles (6km) east of Stafford. Located on the northeastern edge of Cannock Chase, the estate is the ancestral home of the Earls of Lichfield. The house was built in 1693 and enlarged c.1750 and again at the beginning of the 19th century. Located within the grounds is a working model farm museum dating from 1805, complete with watermill, kitchens, dairy and rare breeds of farm animals. The house also incorporates the historic servants' quarters; the brewhouse, restored in 1990, is the only log-fired brewery in England that still produces beer commercially. On display in the house are photographs by its most illustrious resident, royal photographer Thomas Patrick John Anson, 5th Earl of Lichfield (1939–2005). The walled garden, also dating from 1805 and once a nationally renowned centre of horticultural innovation, was restored in 2006. In the grounds is the 18th century Shepherd's Monument, commissioned by Admiral George Anson and bearing the so-called Shugborough House inscription; according to legend, this is written in an unsolved cipher containing a clue to the whereabouts of the Holy Grail, although it is more likely to be a dedication from the admiral to his late wife. The estate is owned by the National Trust, but has been maintained and operated by Staffordshire County Council since the 1960s. Tel: 01889 881388.

Spode Museum
Church Street, Stoke-on-Trent. The Spode pottery was established by Josiah Spode in 1767 and has operated from the same site since 1776; its original designs have since become highly collectable. Spode and his son, also named Josiah, first developed techniques for transferring fine blue patterns onto earthenware in imitation of blue and white porcelain previously imported from China; they also perfected the manufacture of what is now known as fine bone china c.1799. In the 19th century the firm was taken over by William Taylor Copeland, son of Spode's former business partner; the pottery retained the Copeland name until 1970, when it was renamed Spode in commemoration of Josiah's contribution. On display in the museum are some of finest pieces created by the pottery. Tel: 01782 744011.

Sport
general
Staffordshire County Cricket Club competes in the Minor Counties championship and has won the competition 10 times, more than any other county. **Cannock Hockey Club**, based in Hatherton, near Cannock, is one of England's leading clubs, supplying several International players to England and other national teams.

football — **Port Vale** are based in Burslem, Stoke-on-Trent. Founded in 1876 as Port Vale House, the club changed its name to Burslem Port Vale in 1884; like Premier League club Arsenal, they are one of only two professional clubs in England not to be named after a place, originally taking their name from a house in a suburb of Stoke. Members of the Football League since 1892, they have played at Vale Park since 1950. Nicknamed The Valiants, their traditional colours are black and white. Tel: 01782 655800.

Stoke City are reputedly the second-oldest Football League club in the world after Notts County, claiming to have been formed in 1863 although their first recorded fixture took place only in 1868. The club's nickname is The Potters (after the pottery industry in Stoke-on-Trent) and its traditional colours are red and white stripes. In 1997 Stoke moved from the Victoria Ground, their home for the previous 119 years, to the Britannia Stadium. Founder members of the Football League in 1888, the club's only trophy is the 1972 League Cup (a 2–1 win over Chelsea). Although Stoke has had a number of great players such as Gordon Banks, Peter Shilton and Geoff Hurst, the greatest was surely Stanley Matthews, who began his career with The Potters but left the club in 1947 before returning in 1961, aged 46! Tel: 01782 592222.

horse racing — **Uttoxeter** racecourse, Wood Lane, Uttoxeter, is a left-handed circuit of $1^1/_4$ miles (2km) with a right-hand kink in the back straight. Uttoxeter holds exclusively National Hunt racing, including the prestigious Midlands National. Tel: 01889 562561.

Stafford — A town on the River Sow, a small tributary of the Trent. Stafford was founded by Aethelflaed (Ethelfleda), daughter of Alfred the Great, who fortified it and made it the capital of Mercia. It had its own mint from the reign of Athelstan to that of Henry II and received its royal charter in 1206. During the Civil War, Royalist Stafford was occupied by Parliamentarians who slighted its Norman walls and castle. Stafford has a long history of shoemaking, and when famous playwright and local MP Richard Brinsley Sheridan (who served Stafford 1780–1806) stayed in the town he would lodge with his friend William Horton, founder of the Stafford shoe industry. The town's other major industry was salt-making, which began in the 17th century. Both industries have died out in recent years and heavy electrical engineering, particularly the production of power station transformers, has provided the economic thrust of the town. RAF Stafford officially ceased to be an RAF station on 31 March 2006 and became an army station.

Stafford Castle — Newport Road, Stafford. Norman motte and bailey fortress built c.1100 on a high ridge by Robert de Toeni. The original timber castle was upgraded in 1348 by Ralph, 1st Earl of Stafford, who built a massive rectangular stone keep with octagonal corner towers. The castle reached its prime in 1444, when Humphrey Stafford was created Duke of Buckinghamshire. Early in the Civil War it was defended by Lady Isabel but was eventually left deserted and later destroyed. Rebuilt in Gothic revival style in 1813, the castle fell into ruin during the 20th century but has recently been restored. Tel: 01785 257698.

Staffordshire & Worcestershire Canal — See Worcestershire

Staffordshire bull terrier — Lovingly referred to as a 'keg on legs', the Staffordshire bull terrier is a stocky, muscular dog with a broad head, short foreface, small half prick ears, dark round eyes and a wide mouth with a clean scissor-like bite. The tail is carried like an old fashioned pump handle. The dogs have a smooth, short coat which may be black, brindle, red, blue or white in colour; liver-coloured and black and tan dogs sometimes occur. Developed in the 19th century as fighting dogs, and used for the baiting of bulls, bears and even lions – they were said to be better than any other dog at dodging the lion's claws – the breed attained Kennel Club recognition in 1935 after the formation of the Original Staffordshire Bull Terrier Club by Joseph Dunn, Joe Mallan and a number of fellow breeders.

Staffordshire Regiment Museum — Whittington Barracks, 4 miles (6km) southeast of Lichfield. The collection tells the story of the regiment and its forebears from its formation in Lichfield in 1705. It includes uniforms, equipment, weapons and medals (including 8 of the 13 Victoria Crosses awarded to members of the regiment). Outside there are armoured vehicles, two Anderson shelters and a recreated World War I trench, complete with sound effects and No Man's Land. Tel: 01543 434390.

Staffordshire University — The former Staffordshire Polytechnic – formed as North Staffordshire Polytechnic in 1971 from a merger of Staffordshire College of Technology in Stafford, Stoke-on-Trent College of Art and North Staffordshire College of Technology in Stoke-on-Trent, and renamed in 1988 – was awarded university status in September 1992. Most students are stil based at its campuses in Stoke and Stafford, although in 1995 Shropshire and Staffordshire College of Nursing and Midwifery, with bases at Stafford, Shrewsbury, Telford and Oswestry, was integrated into the university, and in 1998, in partnership with Tamworth and Lichfield College, the university opened a newly built campus at Lichfield. Former students include poet and broadcaster Ian McMillan. Tel: 01782 294000.

Tamworth Castle — The Holloway, Tamworth. The Norman motte and bailey castle was founded by Robert le Despenser c.1080 in the southwest corner of a former Saxon *burh*, overlooking the confluence of the rivers Tame and Anker. Its position was designed to dominate the approach over the two rivers. A polygonal shell keep was built on the motte in 1180 by Robert Marmion; its oldest surviving section is the north wing, with an arched doorway dating from the 13th century. Inside are a range of buildings from the Tudor and Jacobean periods as well as the late 18th century, the most impressive being the mid 15th century great hall with oak-timbered roof. Much of the sandstone curtain wall with its herringbone masonry still stands, although the castle was slighted during the Civil War in 1646. The castle was purchased from the Townshend family by Tamworth Corporation in 1897 to commemorate Queen Victoria's Diamond Jubilee and opened to the public two years later; it is now located in a public park. Tel: 01827 709626.

Trentham Gardens	3 miles (5km) south of Stoke-on-Trent. The gardens of the former Trentham Hall, demolished in 1911, and now a public park and woodland. The setting was planned as a serpentine park by Capability Brown and Henry Holland c.1758, overlying an earlier formal design accredited to Charles Bridgeman. However, Trentham Gardens are now principally recognised for the formal Italianate gardens laid out for the Duke of Sutherland in the 1840s by Sir Charles Barry, architect of the Houses of Parliament (who also created Italian-style gardens at Harewood House and Cliveden). Since 2005, Trentham has undergone major redevelopment; the gardens and park have been renovated and were reopened in 2006. There are also proposals to rebuild Trentham Hall as a five star hotel. Tel: 0871 716 1932.
Tutbury Castle	Tutbury, 5 miles (8km) north of Burton upon Trent. Situated above the River Dove, the original Norman motte and bailey castle was built in 1071 for Hugh de Avranches but was almost immediately transferred to Henry, Lord of Ferriers and Chambrais in Normandy. In 1174, after William de Ferrers came into conflict with Henry II, the castle was besieged by the king and later demolished. It was rebuilt, but in the following century William's descendant Robert de Ferrers rebelled against Henry III, whose son, Prince Edward (the future Edward I) attacked the castle in 1263, again causing great damage. In 1265 Henry seized the castle and gave it to his younger son Edmund, who was created Earl of Lancaster in 1267; it has remained in the hands of the Earls and Dukes of Lancaster ever since. In 1362, John of Gaunt, 2nd Duke of Lancaster, gained royal permission to repair the castle, and over the next century new walls, towers and buildings were added; however, it was again in a poor state of repair when Mary, Queen of Scots was imprisoned here in the late 16th century. In 1646, during the Civil War, the castle fell to Parliamentary forces after a three-week siege and was ordered to be destroyed, leaving the ruins visible today. The tower on top of the motte is a mid 18th century folly.
Wall Roman Site	See Letocetum Roman Baths
Whitmore Hall	Whitmore, 4 miles (6km) southwest of Newcastle-under-Lyme. A 17th century manor house set in landscaped gardens and surrounded by a beautiful park. Its present owners, the Cavenagh-Mainwaring family, are direct descendants of the original Norman owners. A timber-framed building that previously occupied the site was rebuilt by Edward Mainwaring in the 1670s; the new red-brick house was designed in Mannerist style. Work was completed in 1676, although parts of the building date back to a much earlier period. In 1891 the heiress, Ellen Jane Mainwaring, married Wentworth Cavenagh. The main front faces south and dates mostly from the 1670s, with an ornate porch added in the 19th century. None of the interiors date from the 1670s as the Hollins and Twyford families, to whom the house was let 1863–1928, remodelled the main interiors in simple Edwardian style early in the 20th century. Outside are the rare surviving early 17th century stables. Tel: 01782 680478.

Some famous people born in Staffordshire

Ashmole, Elias (antiquary) (1617–92)	Lichfield
Baxendale, Helen (actress) (1970–)	Lichfield
Bennett, (Enoch) Arnold (novelist) (1867–1931)	Hanley
Brian, (William) Havergal (composer) (1876–1972)	Stoke-on-Trent
Brookes, Trevor 'Bruno' (broadcaster) (1959–)	Stoke-on-Trent
Collymore, Stanley Victor (footballer) (1971–)	Stone
Considine, Paddy (actor) (1973–)	Burton upon Trent
Cork, Dominic Gerald (cricketer) (1971–)	Newcastle-under-Lyme
Crooks, Garth (footballer and broadcaster) (1958–)	Stoke-on-Trent
Earle, Robbie (footballer) (1965–)	Newcastle-under-Lyme
Gorman, Dave (comedian) (1971–)	Stafford
Hancock, Nick (TV presenter) (1962–)	Stoke-on-Trent
Healy, Francis (singer) (1973–)	Stafford
Hibbs, Harry (goalkeeper) (1906–84)	Wilnecote
Hughes, Glenn (musician) (1952–)	Cannock
Johnson, Samuel (man of letters) (1709–84)	Lichfield
Jones, Freddie (actor) (1927–)	Stoke-on-Trent
Lake, Alan (actor) (1940-84)	Stoke-on-Trent
Matthews, Sir Stanley (footballer) (1915–2000)	Hanley
Meadows, Shane (actor and director) (1972–)	Uttoxeter
Mitchell, R J (aeronautical designer) (1895–1937)	Kidsgrove
Morrissey, Neil (actor) (1962–)	Stoke-on-Trent
Smith, Edward John (captain of the *Titanic*) (1850–1912)	Hanley
Spode, Josiah (potter) (1733–97)	Stoke-on-Trent
Taylor, Philip Douglas (darts player) (1960–)	Burslem
Turner, Anthea (TV presenter) (1960–)	Stoke-on-Trent
Walton, Izaak (author) (1593–1683)	Stafford
Wedgwood, Josiah (potter) (1730–95)	Burslem
Williams, Robbie (singer) (1974–)	Burslem
Wilson, A(ndrew) N(orman) (author) (1950–)	Stone

SUFFOLK

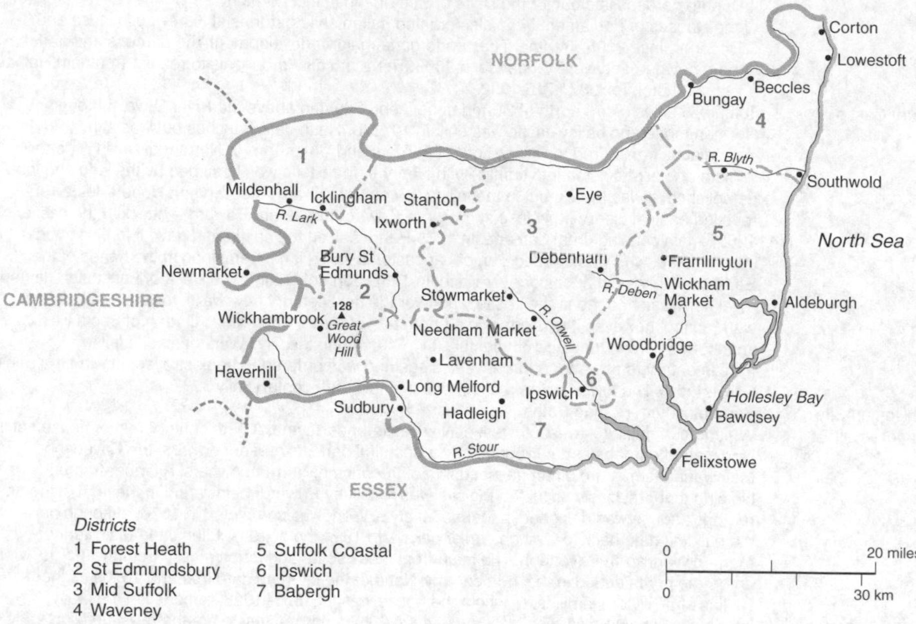
NORFOLK
CAMBRIDGESHIRE
ESSEX
North Sea
Corton
Lowestoft
Beccles
Bungay
R. Blyth
Southwold
Mildenhall
Icklingham
R. Lark
Stanton
Ixworth
Eye
Debenham
Framlingham
Wickham Market
R. Deben
Aldeburgh
Newmarket
Bury St Edmunds
Stowmarket
R. Orwell
Needham Market
Wickhambrook
128
Great Wood Hill
Woodbridge
Lavenham
Haverhill
Long Melford
Ipswich
Hollesley Bay
Bawdsey
Sudbury
Hadleigh
R. Stour
Felixstowe
1
2
3
4
5
6
7
Districts
1 Forest Heath
2 St Edmundsbury
3 Mid Suffolk
4 Waveney
5 Suffolk Coastal
6 Ipswich
7 Babergh
0
20 miles
0
30 km

Suffolk is a non-metropolitan county in East Anglia. It has borders with Norfolk to the north, Cambridgeshire to the west and Essex to the south. The North Sea lies off its east coast. Ipswich is the county town although not a city.

The county is flat with the wetlands of the Broads in the north, and the Suffolk Coast and Heaths Area of Outstanding Natural Beauty running from Lowestoft in the north to Ipswich in the south. The boundary of Suffolk has changed little over the years, although parts of Gorleston and Thetford, which formerly belonged to the county, are now within the administrative county of Norfolk. Under the Local Government Act of 1888 Suffolk was divided into the two administrative counties of East Suffolk and West Suffolk. East Suffolk County Council's headquarters was in Ipswich, and West Suffolk's county town was Bury St Edmunds. East Suffolk was abolished in 1974 when most of the county was merged with West Suffolk and the county borough of Ipswich to form the non-metropolitan county of Suffolk. A small part of East Suffolk was absorbed into Norfolk in 1974.

Suffolk was part of the kingdom of East Anglia which was settled by the Angles following the departure of the Romans from Britain in the early 5th century. The most important Anglo-Saxon settlements at this time were Sudbury and Ipswich. Suffolk suffered severely from Danish incursions, and after the Treaty of Wedmore became a part of the Danelaw (the part of England stretching from the Ouse in the north to the Thames in the south which was under Danish rule).

After the Norman Conquest the county repeatedly showed its willingness to oppose unpopular monarchs. In the 12th century Hugh Bigod, 1st Earl of Norfolk, was to become a persistent rebel against the monarchy; In 1173 the Earl of Leicester landed at Walton near Felixstowe with a Flemish army and was joined by Hugh in an unsuccessful rising against Henry II. In the years after 1317 much of the county provided military support for Thomas of Lancaster's opposition to Edward II; when Queen Isabella and Mortimer landed with their forces at Walton before deposing Edward, they found the district in their favour, and in 1330 the county's forces were raised to suppress the supporters of Edward's ally, the Earl of Kent. In 1381 the county played a major part in the Peasants' Revolt, chiefly in Bury St Edmunds where the prior was beheaded by the rebels.

From the 14th century to the 17th Suffolk was one of the chief manufacturing counties in England owing to its cloth-weaving industry, which was at the height of its prosperity during the 15th century. The many large churches and and timber-framed houses still to be seen in the county are evidence of its wealth at that period. Although the county was largely Yorkist it took little part in the Wars of the Roses. It was from Suffolk that, in 1553, the future Mary I drew the army which supported her claim to the throne. Although clearly separate from its northern neighbour according to Domesday Book, the fiscal administration of Norfolk and Suffolk remained under a single sheriff until 1575. In the Civil War the county was largely Parliamentarian and joined Cromwell's Eastern Association, the combined military force which contributed decisively to the defeat of Charles I at Marston Moor and out of which the New Model Army developed.

The 16th century saw the development of the East Anglian tradition of highly decorated plasterwork known as pargeting; the rich wool merchants would decorate their timber-framed houses with elaborate patterns. It had fallen out of fashion by the 19th century, but many examples can still be seen in the county and the craft has been revived on a small scale in recent years.

In the 17th and 18th centuries the county's agricultural resources became a major source of food supply for the rapidly growing metropolis of London. In the following century textile industries such as the manufacture of sail-cloth, coconut fibre, horse-hair and clothing were established; silk-weavers migrated to Suffolk from Spitalfields, and early in the 19th century an important china factory flourished at Lowestoft. The county remains primarily agricultural, however, and along with other counties in the East of England has seen the development since World War II of intensive arable farming.

Ipswich, a non-metropolitan district on the estuary of the River Orwell, is the third largest town in East Anglia. Ancient Ipswich was successively a Stone Age, Iron Age, Roman settlement; the Anglo-Saxon settlement was known as 'Gippeswic'. King John granted it its first charter in 1200, and in the next four centuries it made most of its wealth trading Suffolk cloth with the Continent. During the Middle Ages the Marian Shrine of Our Lady of Grace was a popular pilgrimage destination, and attracted a number of royal pilgrims. In around 1380, Geoffrey Chaucer satirised the merchants of Ipswich in the *Canterbury Tales*. From 1611 to 1634 Ipswich was a major centre for emigration to New England. This was organised by the town lecturer, Samuel Ward, whose brother Nathaniel was the first minister of Ipswich, Massachusetts. The Cliff Brewery was established by the Cobbold family in 1746; the family were to become one of the wealthiest in the county and have been major local benefactors. Ipswich is the last place in Suffolk to have an independent bus company which has the unusual practice of naming its buses. The main site of University Campus Suffolk, the UK's newest higher education institution, opened in the town in 2007. Ipswich is governed locally by a two-tier council system. Ipswich Borough Council fulfils district council functions such as refuse collection, housing and planning, and Suffolk County Council provides services such as education and social services.

Suffolk	**Population**			**Area**	
Districts	*male*	*female*	*total*	*sq miles*	*sq km*
Babergh	40,738	42,723	83,461	229	594
Forest Heath	27,907	27,603	55,510	146	378
Ipswich	57,394	59,675	117,069	15	39
Mid Suffolk	43,254	43,583	86,837	337	871
St Edmundsbury	48,686	49,507	98,193	254	657
Suffolk Coastal	55,800	59,341	115,141	344	892
Waveney	54,121	58,221	112,342	143	370
Total	327,900	340,653	668,553	1468	3801

Local Attractions and Information

Administrative headquarters — Endeavour House, 8 Russell Road, Ipswich IP1 2BX. Tel: 01473 583000.

Aldeburgh Festival — An arts festival devoted predominantly to classical music. It takes place each June in and around Aldeburgh, and is centred on the main concert hall at Snape Maltings (see separate entry). Founded in 1948 by composer Benjamin Britten, singer Peter Pears and librettist Eric Crozier, the festival was originally intended to provide a home for their opera company, the English Opera Group, but was soon enlarged to include poetry readings, literature, drama, lectures and art exhibitions. The first festival, held on 5–13 June 1948, was based in Aldeburgh's Jubilee Hall, a few doors from Britten's house in Crabbe Street. It featured a performance of Britten's opera *Albert Herring* by the English Opera Group, Britten's newly written *St Nicholas Cantata*, and performances by Clifford Curzon and the Zorian String Quartet. Aldeburgh Productions operates the festival today, and also runs the Britten–Pears Young Artist Programme (formerly the Britten–Pears School for Advanced Musical Studies) and

	the Aldeburgh Residencies, a programme offering training and development opportunities to UK and international artists.
Alton Water	5 miles (8km) south of Ipswich. The largest man-made reservoir in Suffolk, covering 400 acres (160ha) and created to supply water to Ipswich and surrounding areas. Construction began in the 1960s and the reservoir was filled with water, mainly from the River Gipping, over a period of 13 years. The land submerged was mainly agricultural, but was also the location of a mill and Alton Hall; the mill was dismantled and reconstructed at the Museum of East Anglian Life in Stowmarket, but the hall was lost. The reservoir provides a habitat for overwintering wildfowl and is also used for fishing, sailing and for other water sports.
Ancient House, The	Buttermarket, Ipswich. Also known as Sparrowe's House. The Grade I listed building is possibly the finest example of the East Anglian tradition of highly decorated plasterwork known as pargeting. The work dates from c.1670 and was added by Robert Sparrowe, although the house itself is much older, parts of it dating back to the 1400s. The decorations include depictions of the four continents known at the time: Africa, America, Asia and Europe. Tel: 01628 825920.
Battles	There have been two major battles off the coast of Suffolk, Lowestoft and Sole Bay; and one land battle, Fornham. See separate table for details. The Dutch invasion of Landguard Fort (see separate entry) on 2 July 1667 is one of many skirmishes between the Anglo-Dutch armies off the southern English coast without serious loss on either side.
Beccles Airfield	6 miles (10km) southwest of Lowestoft. Located on the Norfolk/Suffolk border, Beccles (Ellough) airfield was built for the United States Army Air Force and completed in 1943. As it was not in the event required by the USAAF, it passed first to RAF Bomber Command and in August 1944 to Coastal Command, and was used until its closure in 1945 by RAF and Fleet Air Arm squadrons operating Warwick, Barracuda, Walrus, Swordfish, Sea Otter and Albacore aircraft on air-sea rescue and anti-shipping duties. At one time Beccles was called HMS *Hornbill II*. In 1944 it was used by Mosquitos of 618 Squadron to practise dropping spinning bombs called 'Highball', developed from the bombs used by 617 Squadron to breach the Ruhr dams (the use of 'Highball' is depicted in the 1970 film *Mosquito Squadron*). After the war Beccles remained dormant until 1965, when it became a heliport serving North Sea oil rigs. Today the airfield is used by an aircraft training company.
Belchamp Hall	Belchamp Walter, 3 miles (5km) west of Sudbury. A Queen Anne style house built in 1720 and surrounded by mature hedged gardens, lawns and tall trees. The central hall features a notably broad, elegant staircase, while the oak and chestnut panelling in the dining room is believed to have come from the original Elizabethan house, demolished when the present house was built. The Belchamp estate, extending to 1500 acres (600ha), has been occupied by the Raymond family since 1450. The house served as one of the main locations for the BBC series *Lovejoy*. To the east is the 14th century brick and flint parish church of St Mary, which contains medieval wall paintings depicting the Virgin Mary. Tel: 01787 881961.
Bell Tower, The	The Walk, Beccles. One of the most prominent features of the market town of Beccles is the substantial bell tower, standing slightly apart from the main body of St Michael's parish church. Building of the tower started on 1 January 1500 under the direction of monks of the Abbey of St Edmundsbury. The tower is 97ft (29.5m) high and 30ft (9m) square at the base; the thick walls, faced with Roche Abbey stone, are supported by huge buttresses with a newel staircase at each corner. The original peal of eight bells was replaced in 1762 with a peal of ten, cast by Lester & Packe of London. Catherine Suckling and Rev. Edward Nelson, the parents of Horatio Nelson, were married at the church in 1749.
Benacre National Nature Reserve	3 miles (5km) north of Southwold. A reserve comprising three isolated 'broads' – Benacre Broad, Covehithe Broad and Easton Broad – near the River Waveney and close to the Suffolk coast. The lagoons are not strictly broads, having been created naturally after the last Ice Age. There are over 100 species of breeding birds, including marsh harrier, bearded reedling, water rail and bittern. The flora includes sea kale, sea holly and yellow-horned poppy. The reserve is maintained by English Nature.
Bentwaters Cold War Museum	See RAF Bentwaters
Bungay Castle	Earsham Street, Bungay. Norman motte and bailey castle erected c.1100. The motte was replaced by a massive Norman keep built c.1165 by Hugh Bigod, 1st Earl of Norfolk, who used the castle as a base for his rebellion against Henry II. It was rebuilt by Roger Bigod, the 5th Earl, in the late 13th century but soon afterwards fell into decay. Today only two towers and part of the curtain wall remain, although these were restored in the 20th century. The Castle Hills nearby are Saxon earthworks built to defend the town against the Danes. Tel: 01986 896156.
Bury St Edmunds Cathedral	See St Edmundsbury Cathedral
Christchurch Park and Mansion	Soane Street, Ipswich. A 70 acre (28ha) area of rolling lawns, wooded areas, and arboreta in central Ipswich. The park was the site of the Augustinian Priory of the Holy Trinity from the 12th century. After the monastery's dissolution in 1536, the estate was purchased by London merchant Paul Withipoll in 1545; in 1548–50 his son Edmund built Christchurch Mansion, now the impressive Tudor centrepiece of the park, on the ruins of the old priory. The mansion houses a collection of pottery and glass, a contemporary art gallery and paintings by artists including John Constable and Thomas Gainsborough. There are period rooms with original items of fine clothing, including the Tudor state chambers, 18th century state rooms, the Victorian wing and the Painted Closet above the porch. There is now no trace of the priory buildings apart from a small disused lion's-head water fountain provided for the poor of Ipswich by the Augustinians. St Margaret's Church, built by the monks in the 13th century and which served as church and burial place to the

lords of the manor, still stands in a corner of the park on St Margaret's Plain. Memorials to the Ipswich Martyrs, servicemen lost during war and past mayors can be found on site. The Great Storm of 1987 destroyed over 200 of the park's trees, including the last remaining elm. Tel: 01473 433554.

Clare Castle Malting Lane, Clare, 7 miles (11km) northwest of Sudbury. Norman motte and bailey castle founded c.1070 by Richard FitzGilbert. A stone keep was built on the motte in the 12th century by later members of the powerful de Clare family, who also had large holdings in south Wales and Ireland. The 70ft (21m) high motte and the ruins of the keep are still visible. The extensive earth ramparts, covering 20 acres (8ha), have now been developed as Clare Castle Country Park and include the village's former railway station.

Constable Country See East Bergholt

Deben Estuary A Special Protection Area and Ramsar site extending for 7$^1/_2$ miles (12km) southeast from Woodbridge to the North Sea coast north of Felixstowe. Designated for their substantial population of overwintering avocets, the reedbeds, saltmarsh and intertidal mudflats that occupy most of the area also have the widest range of saltmarsh flora in Suffolk. The estuary mouth, protected by shifting sandbanks, is crossed by a ferry connecting Felixstowe and Bawdsey.

Dunwich Heath 4 miles (6km) south of Southwold. Once a leading port, Dunwich was submerged by the sea in the 12th century and much of it remains underwater, including six churches and a monastery – legend has it that the sound of church bells can be heard. Past the town is Dunwich Heath, 200 acres (80ha) of sandy cliffs and beach owned by the National Trust.

East Anglia Transport Museum Chapel Road, Carlton Colville, 3 miles (5km) southwest of Lowestoft. The museum's exhibits range from a 1904 Lowestoft Corporation tram to a 1983 Sinclair C5. A tram route goes past the museum's trolleybus depot and up to the Woodside terminus. The museum also operates a 2ft gauge railway. Other exhibits include a variety of trams, trolleybuses and motor buses. Tel: 01502 518459.

East Bergholt The birthplace of John Constable, who declared that he loved 'every stile and stump and every lane in the village'. Constable painted many of his works in the Stour valley and around Flatford Mill, including *Boat Building near Flatford*, *Dedham Vale*, *Flatford Mill*, *The Haywain*, *Leaping Horse*, *Lock and Flatford Mill*, *Stour Valley and Dedham*, *Stratford Mill*, *The White Horse* and *Tree Trunks*. Today Constable is acknowledged throughout the world as a great landscape artist, but during his own lifetime landscape painting was unfashionable and he struggled for recognition. He was 39 before he sold his first landscape, and although his paintings were acclaimed in France, the Royal Academy in London refused him full membership until 1829, only eight years before his death. The village contains a number of elegant houses – Tudor halls, Georgian brick, Suffolk plaster with moss-covered red tiles and creeper-clad porches – many built by the wool merchants who made the Stour Valley wealthy between the 13th and 17th centuries. The village's bell cage was erected as a temporary measure in 1531, assistance promised by Cardinal Wolsey in the construction of a bell tower having been cut short by his downfall in 1530. The bells have been in regular use ever since and are still rung today. Although other bell cages exist, East Bergholt's is the only one where the bells are swung by force of hand applied directly to a wooden headstock and not by rope and wheel. They are also the heaviest set of five bells currently being rung in England, with a total weight of 4.25 tons (4400 kilos).

East Bergholt Place Garden East Bergholt, 7 miles (11km) southwest of Ipswich. The garden and arboretum at East Bergholt Place were laid out in the early 20th century by Charles Eley, great-grandfather of the present owner. They contain many trees and shrubs rarely seen growing in East Anglia, many of which originated from renowned plant collector George Forrest. With magnificent displays of magnolias, camellias and spring bulbs, the garden is seen to best advantage in spring and early summer. Tel: 01206 299224.

East Point Pavilion Royal Plain, Lowestoft. Completed in 1992, the glass structure is styled on an Edwardian greenhouse and overlooks Lowestoft's award-winning South Beach. Tel: 01502 533600.

Euston Hall Euston, 10 miles (16km) north of Bury St Edmunds. The estate has been home to the Dukes of Grafton for more than 300 years. The red-brick house was designed in 1666 for the Earl of Arlington, whose collection of 17th century portraits of the court of Charles II still hangs in the hall. Other old master paintings in the house include George Stubbs' celebrated *Mares and Foals*, set beside the river in the grounds. A fire in 1902 destroyed the south and west wings, which were rebuilt but demolished again in the 1950s. The surrounding park contains a unique 17th century church in the style of Sir Christopher Wren and an 18th century watermill; the park itself was originally designed by John Evelyn with additions – including an octagonal temple – by William Kent, while Capability Brown widened the river to form the lake. Tel: 01842 766366.

Felixstowe A port on the North Sea, ranking as the third busiest in Britain and the largest container port. A village has stood on the site since before the Norman Conquest and was later an important part of England's coastal defences; in 1667 Dutch soldiers made a bold attack on nearby Landguard Fort (see separate entry) but failed to capture it. The town developed as both a port and a seaside resort in the late 19th century and a pier was constructed in 1905. Along with Harwich in Essex and Ipswich, it was traditionally one of the three so-called Haven Ports.

Flatford Bridge Cottage 1 mile (1.6km) southeast of East Bergholt, 10 miles (16km) southwest of Ipswich. Situated upstream from Flatford Mill, the 16th century cottage houses an exhibition on John Constable, several of whose paintings famously depict the property. The cottage is owned by the National Trust. Tel: 01206 298260.

Flatford Mill 1 mile (1.6km) southeast of East Bergholt, 10 miles (16km) southwest of Ipswich. Situated on the River Stour in Dedham Vale, close to the Suffolk/Essex border. The Grade I listed watermill was built in 1733 and owned by John Constable's father; the Mill and Willy Lott's Cottage, a short distance downstream, feature in many of Constable's paintings. *The Haywain*, one of the most famous, depicts a horse-drawn wagon in the mill pond at Flatford, with Willy Lott's cottage on the left of the picture. Flatford Mill, Valley Farm and Willy Lott's House are leased to the Field Studies Council. Tel: 0845 330 7368.

Framlingham Castle Castle Street, Framlingham. Norman castle founded c.1100 by Roger Bigod, Earl of Norfolk but destroyed by Henry II in 1175. It was rebuilt with 13 wall towers but no keep by Bigod's son (also named Roger) c.1189–1200, and is thus one of the earliest enclosure castles in England. Taken under Crown control in 1306, it was later granted to the Mowbray Dukes of Norfolk and then the Howards. Having been confiscated by Henry VIII, it was granted by Edward VI to Mary I, who mustered her supporters here in 1553 before being crowned queen; it was then restored to the Howards. Reconfiscated in 1572, it was a prison at the end of the 16th century but was returned again to the Howards in 1613 by James I. It was sold to Sir Robert Hitcham in 1635 who bequeathed it to Pembroke College, Cambridge, the following year, on condition that the internal buildings should be demolished and replaced by a poorhouse within the walls. Twelve of the towers, now topped by Tudor chimneys, still stand, as does the curtain wall. It is now owned by English Heritage.Tel: 01728 724189.

Freston Tower $^1/_4$ mile (0.4km) east of Freston, 4 miles (6km) south of Ipswich. Standing beside the River Orwell, the red-brick tower is arguably the oldest folly in England, dating back to the mid 16th century. According to a novel by Rev. Richard Cobbold published in 1850, the six-floor tower was built by Lord de Freston for his daughter Ellen, so she could study a different subject on each floor six days of the week; however, it is more likely to have been constructed as a lookout over Freston Reach of the Orwell. The tower was privately owned until 1999 when it was bought by the Landmark Trust. Tel: 01628 825925.

Gainsborough's House Gainsborough Street, Sudbury. The birthplace of artist Thomas Gainsborough (1727–88); filled with his paintings and drawings, it also features furniture and an extensive garden. In the 1740s, Gainsborough married Margaret Burr whose illegitimate father, the Duke of Beaufort, gave them a £200 annuity. His work, mainly landscapes, was not selling very well. He returned to Sudbury in 1748–9 and concentrated on portraits; although he was a far more successful landscape painter than Constable during his lifetime, it was in portraiture that his true genius lies. His works include *Portrait of Mrs Graham, Mary and Margaret: The Painter's Daughters, William Hallett and his Wife Elizabeth, née Stephen*, known as *The Morning Walk, Cottage Girl with Dog and Pitcher, Mr and Mrs Andrew, The Blue Boy* (a depiction of Master Jonathan Buttall, a friend of Gainsborough), *Mrs Thomas Hibbert* and the most beautiful and underrated *The Pink Boy* (Master Nichols). Tel: 01787 372958.

Glemham Hall Little Glemham, 7 miles (11km) northeast of Woodbridge. A red-brick mansion built c.1560 by the de Glemhams and now owned by the Cobbold family. There are paintings, china and furniture on display and the site includes a recently renovated rose garden. Tel: 01728 748289.

Guildhall of Corpus Christi Market Place, Lavenham. A timber-framed building dating from the 1530s. Originally the hall of the Guild of Corpus Christi, the building now houses a museum dedicated to the medieval cloth trade with exhibits including a working loom. The walled garden outside contains traditional dye plants, as well as the former parish lock-up and mortuary. Now owned by the National Trust. Tel: 01787 247646.

Hadleigh 10 miles (16km) west of Ipswich. A former wool town and once the 14th most prosperous town in England, Hadleigh lies on the River Brett, a tributary of the River Stour which is spanned by the medieval three-arched Toppesfield Bridge. The town's long High Street has numerous timber-framed and Georgian houses with fine displays of pargeting. The Guildhall, next to 14th century St Mary's church, is 600 years old and has had many uses from market house and guildhall to a cloth hall and even a school. It is currently occupied by the the offices of the town council.

Haughley Castle Haughley, 3 miles (5km) northwest of Stowmarket. Also known or recorded as Haganet or Hagenorth Castle. Norman motte and bailey castle built by Hugh de Montfort; held for Henry II by Ralph de Broc in 1173, it was attacked and destroyed by the forces of Hugh Bigod and the Earl of Leicester. The motte, one of the largest in Britain, still stands 80ft (24m) high.

Haughley Park Haughley, 3 miles (5km) northwest of Stowmarket. The red-brick Jacobean house was built by the Sulyard family in 1620 and is surrounded by a 20th century garden with lawns, herbaceous borders, hedges, dell and an Italianate garden with flint and brick walls. The attached park also has a lime avenue and bluebell woods. Tel: 01359 240701.

Havergate Island Covering 267 acres (108ha) in the Rivers Alde and Ore between Orford Ness and the mainland, Havergate is an RSPB reserve with large populations of avocets and terns. It is bounded on the northwest by the Gull and Lower Gull channels of the Ore, and on the southeast by The Narrows, part of the Alde. Havergate mostly lies below sea level but is drained by a series of channels and is protected by dykes. Havergate developed from two gravel banks which grew over the course of time into islands and eventually joined together through changes in the course of the river and drainage. In the 18th century it was a base for smuggling and later for farming; a single family lived on the island from at least 1885 until 1925. It was also briefly home to a gravel extraction industry, but during World War II the British Army took it over as a military test site. The island is only accessible by boat.

Helmingham Hall Helmingham, 7 miles (11km) northwest of Woodbridge. A moated manor house begun by John Tollemache in 1480 and owned by the Tollemache family ever since. The house is built around a courtyard in typical late medieval/Tudor style. The Grade I listed gardens, including a walled kitchen garden, parterre and knot garden, were restored and recreated in the late 20th century. Beyond is a 400 acre (160ha) park with herds of red and fallow deer. The church of St Mary on the edge of the park contains family memorials dating back to the Middle Ages. The house itself is not open to the public. Tel: 01473 890799.

Hengrave Hall Hengrave, 3 miles (5km) northwest of Bury St Edmunds. The seat for over 250 years of the Roman Catholic Kytson and Gage families, the house was built 1525–38 by Thomas Kytson the Elder, a merchant and member of the Mercers' Company. One of the last to be built around an enclosed courtyard with a great hall, it is constructed from stone taken from Ixworth Priory (dissolved in 1536) and white bricks baked at Woolpit. There is an ornate oriel window incorporating the royal arms of Henry VIII, the Kytson arms and the arms of the wife and daughters of Sir Thomas Kytson. A set of Flemish stained glass windows commissioned by Kytson and installed in the chapel in 1538, depicting history from the creation of the world to the Last Judgement, are the only collection of pre-Reformation glass still in situ in a domestic chapel anywhere in England. The house passed into the Gage family by marriage in the 18th century and was altered by the family in 1775; it was used 1794–1802 as a refuge by the English Augustinian canonesses of Bruges. In 1887, on the death of Lady Henrietta Gage, the house was bought by Australian steelmaker John Lysaght; in 1895 it was bought by Sir John Wood, and on his death sold to the Religious of the Assumption, who ran a convent school until 1974 and a Christian community until 2005. It is now privately owned. A valuable collection of family papers relating to the estate and dating back to the 12th century was bought by Cambridge University Library in 2006. Tel: 01284 701561.

Herringfleet Mill 1 mile (1.6km) west of Herringfleet, 6 miles (10km) northwest of Lowestoft. Located on the Suffolk/Norfolk border and on the edge of the Broads, the drainage smock mill was built by millwright Robert Barnes of Great Yarmouth c.1825. The wooden mill was last operated by Charles Howlett of Haddiscoe in 1958, when its function was replaced by a small diesel pump. Now owned by Suffolk County Council, it is the only such mill in the Broads still in working order.

Highest point Great Wood Hill at 420ft (128m), near the village of Rede. GR: TL786558.

Ickworth House 3 miles (5km) southwest of Bury St Edmunds. A Georgian house with dramatic central rotunda, begun in 1795 by the eccentric 4th Earl of Bristol and completed only in 1829 by the 5th Earl. The house holds an impressive collection of paintings including works by Velázquez, Titian and Gainsborough, and is surrounded by 18th century parkland and Italian-style gardens. There is also a unique collection of tree stumps and massive stones from the Giant's Causeway. The property is owned by the National Trust. Tel: 01284 735270.

Interesting facts The **Nutshell** public house in Bury St Edmunds, measuring just 15ft x 7ft (4.6m x 2.1m), lays claim to being the smallest pub in the British Isles. Inside is the suspended dried body of a black cat, bricked up behind the chimney hearth by the builders to ward off evil spirits. The body was discovered during building work. Another interesting pub is the **Farmhouse** in the village of Kesgrave. The Rev. Robin Spittle from the local All Saints Church has administered the word of God on a regular basis at the pub in recent years. Footballer **Thomas Cooper** (1904–40) was an England defender, known as 'Snowy' because of his grey hair. He was killed in June 1940 when his military police motorcycle was in collision with a bus in Suffolk, an incident that led to army dispatch riders having to wear crash helmets. During the 1840s **Charles Dickens** came to stay with Sir Samuel Morton Peto at Somerleyton Hall, and the novel *David Copperfield* is partly set at nearby Blundeston. Descriptions of people living in upturned boats in the novel were based on what Dickens saw during a visit to Lowestoft Beach Village. **Aldeburgh** is famous for its festival but has other claims to fame. It was the first British town to elect a female mayor: Elizabeth Garrett Anderson, in 1908. Both of Sir Francis Drake's ships *Greyhound* and *Pelican* (later renamed *Golden Hind*) were built in Aldeburgh. The town is the setting of a series of children's illustrated books about Orlando the Marmalade Cat, written by Kathleen Hale, who spent holidays in Aldeburgh. Many of the books' illustrations feature landmarks in the town, most notably the Moot Hall. Public concern has risen over the years that the town is in danger of becoming an island if the sea breaks through obsolete sea defences. **Beccles** is known for its bell tower and airfield but the market town also has its own local phraseology. Examples of words that might be heard in the area are 'jasper' for a wasp or 'old hush wings' for a barn owl. Born in Ipswich c.1471, **Thomas Wolsey** left Oxford University and began to work for Henry VIII, with whom he became firm friends. In 1514 Henry made Wolsey his Lord Chancellor, rewarding him with major posts in the church: as well as being Lord Chancellor Wolsey was Archbishop of York, Bishop of Lincoln and Bishop of Durham. Wolsey's resulting wealth enabled him to build grand palaces such as Hampton Court, but his main ambition was to become Pope. In 1515, Pope Leo X made him a cardinal but Wolsey also had many enemies and never became head of the Catholic Church. By 1524 Henry was seeking a divorce from Catherine of Aragon and sent Wolsey to persuade Pope Clement VI to agree to the divorce. When the mission failed, Henry became angry with Wolsey, accused him of being a servant of the Pope and sacked him from his post as Lord Chancellor. Wolsey attempted to regain Henry's favour by giving him all his wealth, Hampton Court and surrounding lands, but Henry was not appeased, and in 1530 ordered Wolsey's arrest for high treason. A broken man, Wolsey died before the trial could be held.

Ipswich High School Woolverstone, 4 miles (6km) south of Ipswich. A girls' independent school founded in 1872 and a member of the Girls' Day School Trust. It was originally opened in the Assembly Rooms in Northgate Street, Ipswich, on 30 April 1878 with 43 pupils. The first headmistress, Miss Sophie Youngman, was in post for 21 years and the school flourished and expanded under her leadership. She was succeeded by Miss Kennett and in 1905 the council of the Trust purchased a large private house and grounds in Westerfield Road, Ipswich. The school continued to expand and another house, Woodview House, was purchased in 1913. Owing to the continued expansion of the school and the demands of the modern curriculum, the decision was taken in 1992 to rehouse the school at Grade I listed Woolverstone Hall, set in 80 acres (32ha) of parkland beside the River Orwell. Tel: 01473 780201.

Ipswich Museum High Street, Ipswich. The museum includes displays on natural history, geology, archaeology and ethnography together with exhibits of Suffolk wildlife and geology. Tel: 01473 213761.

Ipswich Racecourse An area of Ipswich that was formerly a racecourse. It was donated to the borough of Ipswich by John Dubuis Cobbold. The course was originally on Nacton Heath, now an eastern suburb of Ipswich, and was 1 mile 7 furlongs in circumference. It ran along the line of the modern Lindberg Road, Cobham Road, parallel to Felixstowe Road as far the modern Hatfield Road, before a 6 furlong finish straight running parallel to Nacton Road to complete the loop. The earliest mention of annual race meetings in Ipswich was 1710 when a Town Purse was run for by 'high mettled racers'. Both Flat and hunt racing were held on the course, although the last Flat race took place in 1884 following the withdrawal of the Queen's Plate. From then, it became exclusively a National Hunt course. The last race meeting was 29 March 1911. The area has since been developed into housing and a park, known as Racecourse Park.

Ipswich Transport Museum High Street, Ipswich. The museum has the largest collection of transport items in Britain relating to a single town: all its 100 major exhibits and numerous smaller items were either made or used in and around Ipswich. The museum also organises the Ipswich–Felixstowe historic vehicle run, which takes place every May. Tel: 01473 433550.

Islands Suffolk only has one true island (see Havergate Island) although it does have an interesting artificial island (see Sealand and HM *Fort Roughs* in Essex, aka Roughs Tower). Orford Ness is nearly always joined to the mainland at its northern extremity and is therefore a peninsula rather than an island, but it is included in the list as the southern end is remote and easiest to access by boat.

Kentwell Hall and Gardens 1½ miles (2.5km) north of Long Melford, 4 miles (6km) north of Sudbury. The moated, mellow brick Tudor mansion was once described by *Country Life* as 'The epitome of many people's image of an Elizabethan house'. It was built and enhanced by successive members of the Clopton family in the first half of the 16th century with wealth made from the wool trade; Long Melford's magnificent parish church was also built by John Clopton. The exterior has remained mainly unchanged since. It has been the home of Patrick and Judith Phillips since 1971 and features a working Elizabethan kitchen and a hall with a minstrel's gallery; there is a Tudor Rose maze in the courtyard. Tel: 01787 310207.

Kersey A picturesque village which has given its name to a coarse woollen cloth, supposedly first manufactured in the village in the Middle Ages.

Landguard Fort 2 miles (3km) south of Felixstowe. Located at the mouth of the River Orwell, Landguard Fort was designed to guard the entrance to Harwich. The first fortifications from 1540 were a few earthworks and blockhouse; James I ordered the construction of a square fort with bulwarks at each corner. The Dutch landed a force of 1500 men on Felixstowe beach in 1667 and advanced on the fort, but were repulsed by Nathaniel Darrell and his garrison of 400 musketeers of the Duke of York & Albany's Maritime Regiment (the first English Marines) and 100 artillerymen with 54 cannon. In 1716 a new battery was built and a complete new fort in a five-sided layout was started in 1745 on an adjoining site. New batteries were built in the 1750s and 1780; in the 1870s the interior barracks were rebuilt to a keep-like design, while the river frontage was rebuilt with a new casemated battery. The fort was used as a balloon launching site for Operation Outward during World War II. In the 1950s the Left Battery was converted into the Anti-Aircraft Operations Room for Harwich. Today, the fort houses Felixstowe Museum and is the location of Landguard Bird Observatory. Tel: 01394 277767/01473 218245.

Landguard Bird Observatory Situated next to the port of Felixstowe on a man-made ridge that forms part of Landguard Fort, the observatory was founded in 1982 to study bird migration at Landguard Point, the most southerly part of Suffolk. Most of the birds passing through are common migrants that sometimes occur in spectacular numbers. The area also attracts less common species, with both black redstart and little tern breeding. The site is owned by the Department of Culture, Media and Sport but managed by English Heritage. Tel: 01394 673782.

Lavenham Guildhall Lavenham, 6 miles (10km) northeast of Sudbury. A timber-framed Tudor building with limewashed silver-grey woodwork, overlooking the town's market square and dating from c.1529. The hall was built by the Guild of Corpus Christi, one of three guilds founded in Lavenham to regulate the wool trade; the rampant lions carved on the doorpost of the hall are the guild's emblem. Through most of the 17th century the building was used as the town hall, afterwards becoming at various times a prison, a workhouse and a wool store. During World War II it housed evacuees. The building was rescued in 1887 by Sir Cuthbert Quilter who undertook its restoration. In 1951 his son, with the aid of the Lavenham Preservation Society, gave the Guildhall to the National Trust. Today the warren of small rooms on the upper floor houses a local museum dedicated to Lavenham and the wool trade. Tel: 01787 247646.

Lavenham Priory Water Street, Lavenham. A timber-framed building parts of which date to the 13th century, enlarged in the 15th–16th centuries and once owned by the Benedictine priory of Earls Colne in Essex. The 3 acre (1.2ha) grounds include a herb garden. The house is not open to the public. Tel: 01787 247003.

Leiston Abbey 1 mile (1.6km) north of Leiston. The Abbey of St Mary was founded in 1182 at Minsmere by the powerful lawyer Ranulf de Glanville, Lord Chief Justice to Henry II. It was transferred to Leiston in 1363 and rebuilt by its patron Robert de Ufford, Earl of Suffolk. Its inmates were Augustinian canons who followed the Premonstratensian rule, and were engaged in preaching and pastoral work. Following its dissolution in 1536, the abbey was granted to Charles Brandon, 3rd Duke of Suffolk and brother-in-law to Henry VIII. It became a farm, the farmhouse being built into the ruins. Later, a Georgian front was added to the house, which was extended in the 1920s. In 1928 the abbey ruins and farm were bought by Miss Ellen Wrightson for use as a religious retreat. When she died in 1946, she bequeathed the property to the Diocese of St Edmundsbury and Ipswich. It was purchased in 1977 by the Pro Corda Trust. Tel: 01223 582700.

Long Shop Museum Main Street, Leiston. Located on the site of the former engineering firm Garrett's, the museum explores the history of the firm, which developed from making hand tools in a forge to a world famous company producing steam engines, electrical vehicles, diesel tractors, munitions, radio and radar equipment, and plastics until its closure in 1980. The museum also houses the Garrett Collection, a collection of items covering 200 years of local, social and industrial history. Other displays include puzzles and jigsaws, and exhibits relating to the World War II USAAF airfield at Leiston and the nearby crash of a Zeppelin in 1917; the works site also contains a restored Victorian water tower. Tel: 01728 832189.

Lowestoft A holiday resort and former fishing port lying between the eastern edge of the Broads National Park at Oulton Broad and the North Sea. Nearby Lowestoft Ness is the most easterly point in the UK. The town is divided in two by Lake Lothing, the northern half being the commercial centre and the southern half the holiday resort. There are two piers: to the south is the Claremont Pier, while 1/2 mile (0.8km) to the north is the South Pier (so called because it is located on the south side of the harbour and river mouth). In the early 20th century, the Claremont Pier had a T-shaped pier head and was used as an embarkation point for passenger steamships that operated between London and Great Yarmouth. According to Domesday Book, Lowestoft paid its rent to the landowner Hugh de Montfort in herrings. The village developed into a fishing port in the Middle Ages; it was seen as a rival in Great Yarmouth, which tried to force it out of the herring trade. The Battle of Lowestoft, which took place near the town in 1665, was the first battle of the Second Dutch War. During the 1790s, Lowestoft's fishing community established their own 'Beach Village', living in upturned boats. In the 19th century, the arrival of Sir Samuel Morton Peto brought about a huge change in the town's fortunes. Peto built rail links and developed the harbour, establishing the town as a flourishing seaside holiday resort. During World War II Lowestoft was used as a navigation point by German bombers and as a result was the most heavily bombed town per head of population in the UK. Lowestoft has also been subject to periodic flooding, most memorably in January 1953 when a North Sea swell driven by low pressure and a high tide swept away many of the older sea defences and deluged most of the southern town. Until the mid 1960s fishing was Lowestoft's main industry; the south of the town is still the site of a large fisheries research centre, part of Defra (the Department for Environment, Food and Rural Affairs).

Manor House, The Honey Hill, Bury St Edmunds. Built 1736–8 for Elizabeth, second wife of John Hervey, 1st Earl of Bristol, whose main residence was at Ickworth, 3 miles (5km) to the southwest (see Ickworth House). From 1993 to 2006 the house was occupied by the town's Manor House Museum.

Maritime Museum Whapload Road, Lowestoft. A museum dedicated to the history of the Lowestoft fishing fleet. Exhibits include models of ancient and modern fishing and commercial boats. Tel: 01502 561963.

Melford Hall Long Melford, 3 miles (5km) north of Sudbury. A turreted brick Tudor mansion, one of East Anglia's most popular Elizabethan houses. Elizabeth I and 2000 members of her court were once entertained here. Features of the interior include a panelled banqueting hall and rooms from the various periods of the house's history including an impressive Regency library. The house has been the home of the Hyde Parker family since 1786. Beatrix Potter was a regular visitor and the room where she stayed now contains mementoes including the original Jemima Puddleduck doll. There are Edwardian gardens surrounded by 130 acres (52ha) of parkland. The property is owned by the National Trust. Tel: 01787 379228.

Mid-Suffolk Light Railway Wetheringsett, 8 miles (13km) northeast of Stowmarket. A heritage railway operating on 1/2 mile (0.8km) of the former Mid-Suffolk Light Railway from Haughley to Laxfield, north of Ipswich. Opened in 1905 for freight and for passengers in 1908, it became part of the London and North Eastern Railway in 1924 and was finally closed on 26 July 1952. The line currently operates from the reconstructed rural station of Brockford & Wetheringsett.

Mildenhall Treasure A hoard of Roman silver discovered in 1942 near Mildenhall, 11 miles (18km) northwest of Bury St Edmunds. On a cold January afternoon in 1942, ploughman Gordon Butcher unearthed a large metal dish in a field at West Row. He fetched his boss, Sydney Ford, an agricultural engineer who collected local antiquities, and they dug out more dishes, bowls and spoons, to their amazement uncovering a total of 34 items. In the fading light Ford stuffed the finds into a sack and took them home, where he put them on the mantelpiece. Not until after World War II did a chance visitor realise that Ford's 'pewter' was in fact Roman silver. The coroner was informed and an inquest held; the hoard was declared treasure trove on 1 July 1946 and became Crown property. Newspapers speculated that the find was worth £50,000, but Ford and Butcher shared a reward of only £2000, instead of the full market value, because Ford had delayed reporting the find. The treasure was acquired by the British Museum, where it can still be seen. It is one of several hoards of silver and gold found in East Anglia, most of which were buried in the late 4th century AD, a period of considerable unrest when southeastern Britain was facing attack by Saxons and the Roman Empire was beginning to disintegrate. The treasure comprises items of silver tableware, including platters, spoons, goblets and bowls, many richly decorated. The Great Dish, almost 2ft (60cm) in diameter and weighing over 18lb (8.2kg), is the most spectacular; it bears fine reliefs of dancing, drunken revellers including Hercules, Pan and Bacchus, the god of wine, while a frieze inside depicts sea monsters and nymphs, with the face of a sea god (Neptune or Oceanus) staring out from the centre. Another large dish, 22in (55cm) across, has intricate, engraved geometric designs picked out with black niello (silver sulphide) inlay. There are six flanged bowls, four with reliefs figuring people and animals and the other two richly decorated; a pair of goblets with shallow bowls, moulded stems and leaf decoration under each broad base; a fluted bowl 16in (41cm) in diameter, with alternating plain and foliate panels, which has swinging handles with looped ends shaped like swans' heads; and eight spoons, three bearing leafy decoration like that of the fluted dish. The rest have inscriptions, three almost identical, having the Christian Chi-Rho symbol between Alpha and Omega engraved in the bowl, and the last two carrying names. These may be christening spoons: one reads PAPITTEDO VIVAS (long life to Papittedus), the other PASCENTIA VIVAS (long life to Pascentia). An article about the find by Roald Dahl was first published in the *Saturday Evening Post*, and later appeared as 'The Mildenhall Treasure' in his short story collection *The Wonderful Story of Henry Sugar and Six More*.

Moulton Packhorse Bridge Moulton, 3 miles (5km) east of Newmarket. A four-arched 15th century bridge crossing the River Kennett. The bridge is maintained by English Heritage.

Moyse's Hall Museum Cornhill, Bury St Edmunds. A local history museum for over 200 years situated in the oldest domestic town house in East Anglia, a rare surviving Norman domestic building that dates to c.1180. The museum houses collections of archaeological finds, as well as items relating to the Suffolk Regiment and to local and social history. Tel: 01284 706183.

Museum of East Anglian Life Iliffe Way, Stowmarket. Located in the grounds of the 18th century Abbot's Hall, built in the grounds of the former St Osyth's Priory, the museum presents the agricultural history of East Anglia through a mixture of exhibits and living history demonstrations. Within the 75 acre (30ha) site are numerous reconstructed historic buildings including a working watermill rescued from inundation by Alton Water (see separate entry) and one of England's largest tithe barns. Suffolk Punch horses and rare breeds of pig, sheep and cows are kept, while other exhibits include recreated rooms from the Victorian era, and gypsy and travellers' exhibitions with traditional caravans and displays of farming, craft workshops and industry. The museum also has recreations of 1950s interiors including shops, kitchens and living rooms. Tel: 01449 612229.

National Horseracing Museum High Street, Newmarket. The museum features horses, people, events and scandals that tell the story of British racing. Highlights include the head of Persimmon, a great royal Derby winner in 1896; a special display about Fred Archer, the Victorian jockey who committed suicide after losing the struggle to keep his weight down; and items associated with Red Rum, Lester Piggott, Frankie Dettori and other heroes of the Turf. Tel: 01638 667333.

Nether Hall Cavendish, 5 miles (8km) northwest of Sudbury. A 15th century timber-framed manor house containing a varied collection of paintings. In the grounds is Cavendish Manor Vineyard. Tel: 01787 280221.

Orford Castle 5 miles (8km) southwest of Aldeburgh. Founded 1165–73 by Henry II, primarily to subdue the rebellious Hugh Bigod, the castle has a unique 21-sided polygonal keep with three towers. Having held out during the rebellion of 1173, it was taken by Prince Louis of France in 1217 but later recaptured by troops loyal to Henry III. Orford was granted to Robert de Ufford, Earl of Suffolk in 1336. The bailey wall finally collapsed in 1841 and now only the 90ft (27.5m) high keep remains. It is owned by English Heritage. There was an earldom of Orford, the most notable holder of the title being Sir Robert Walpole, England's first Prime Minister. Tel: 01394 450472.

Orford Ness A shingle spit on the Suffolk coast, linked to the mainland at Aldeburgh and stretching along the coast to the village of Orford, thought to have once been a port facing the open sea. A designated National Nature Reserve, Orford Ness is 12 miles (19km) long and covers an area of 2250 acres (900ha) with several important wildlife habitats; 40 per cent the area is shingle, 25 per cent tidal rivers, mudflats, sand flats and lagoons, 18 per cent grassland, and 15 per cent salt marsh. It is divided from the mainland by the River Alde, and was formed by longshore drift from further north along the coast. The Ministry of Defence formerly administered the peninsula and conducted secret military tests during both world wars. The Atomic Weapons Research Establishment had a base on the site, and is believed to have developed the firing mechanisms for nuclear devices there. Many of the buildings from this time remain clearly visible from the quay at Orford, including 'pagodas' which were designed to collapse in the event of an accidental explosion. There is also a transmitting station, which uses the former Cobra Mist experimental radar site to send broadcasts across the North Sea to mainland Europe. Orford Ness is now owned by the National Trust, though some buildings are closed off because of their advanced state of disrepair. Tel: 01728 648024.

Orfordness Transmitting Station 10 miles (16km) east of Woodbridge. A medium-wave broadcasting facility owned by VT Communications at Orford Ness. Its facilities are leased to international broadcasters, especially the BBC World Service. The site was built in the 1960s for an experimental over-the-horizon radar station known as Cobra Mist. The station has two directional aerial systems: a 648 kHz aerial consisting of a row of five freestanding steel lattice towers of triangular cross section; and a 1296 kHz aerial consisting of six freestanding steel lattice towers arranged in two parallel rows.

Otley Hall Otley, 8 miles (13km) north of Ipswich. A moated hall dating to c.1450. It is the ancestral home of the Gosnold family, whose members included Bartholomew Gosnold, a seafaring pioneer who discovered Cape Cod and Martha's Vineyard in the United States before the arrival of the Pilgrim Fathers. The Grade I listed house is situated in 10 acres (4ha) of gardens featuring recreations of a medieval orchard, herb and knot gardens. Tel: 01473 890264.

Parham Airfield Museum $^1/_2$ mile (0.8km) east of Parham, 7 miles (11km) northeast of Woodbridge. Housed in the airfield's restored control tower, the museum comprises the 390th Bombardment Group Memorial Air Museum and the Museum of the British Resistance Organisation of the USAAF, dedicated in 1981, and the Museum of the British Resistance Organisation, created in 1997. The opening ceremony for the latter was carried out by Lt-Col. J W Stuart Edmundsun, one of the founders of the nondescript 'Most Secret' GHQ Auxiliary Units, as they were officially known. The 'Auxunits' were one of Britain's nine secret services during World War II, alongside organisations such as MI5, MI6 and the Special Operations Executive. Tel: 01728 621373.

RAF Bentwaters 5 miles (8km) northeast of Woodbridge. Built in 1942 as RAF Butley, the base was opened in 1944 as RAF Bentwaters, and was used during the rest of World War II by RAF Fighter Command. Transferred to the United States Air Force in 1951, it became the base of the USAF 81st Tactical Fighter Wing during the Cold War. It is possibly best known to the public as the site of a major UFO incident in 1980, when a sighting of lights in Rendlesham Forest to the east of the airfield was reported. The base closed in 1993 and is now partly occupied by a business park; it is also the site of Bentwaters Cold War Museum, opened in 2007 and located in the former USAF command post.

RAF Honington Honington, 7 miles (11km) northeast of Bury St Edmunds. Opened in 1937, Honington was used as a bomber station during World War II. In June 1942 it was transferred to the United States Army Air Force and was upgraded to a Class A Bomber base; the 1st Strategic Air Depot for the servicing and repair of B17s was established in September 1942. With the departure of the USAAF in 1946, Honington reverted to the RAF, and became a servicing centre for RAF Transport Command; during the Berlin Airlift, Honington played a major part in keeping the aircraft of Transport Command flying. In 1949 the station reverted to Bomber Command. From 1950–6 RAF Honington housed No. 94 Armament Maintenance Unit for bomb storage. From 1955–7 10, XV, 44 and 57 Squadrons were based at Honington with English Electric Canberra bombers; 10 and XV Squadrons took part in the Suez Crisis of 1956. In 1968 the airfield became the home of the RAF's Buccaneer bomber. The last aircraft (of the Tornado Weapons Conversion Unit) left in 1993, and the base is now the RAF Regiment depot and home to the Joint NBC Regiment. Tel: 01359 269561.

RAF Lakenheath Lakenheath, 14 miles (21km) northwest of Bury St Edmunds. First opened as a Royal Flying Corps airfield in World War I, Lakenheath originally served as a decoy airfield for Mildenhall in World War II; it served during 1941–3 as a base for the Wellingtons and Stirlings of 149 Bomber Squadron. Developed before the end of the war as a base for United States Army Air Force Superfortress bombers, it was taken over by the USAF at the end of hostilities. RAF Lakenheath is now home to the 48th Fighter Wing of the United States Air Force, flying the F15E Strike Eagle and F15C Eagle. With 5000 US military personnel and 2000 US and British civilian personnel, Lakenheath is, alongside its sister base RAF Mildenhall, the largest USAF base in the UK. Tel: 01638 523000.

RAF Martlesham Heath $1\frac{1}{2}$ miles (2.5km) south of Woodbridge. First used by the Royal Flying Corps in January 1917, during World War II the airfield provided a base for the RAF's Bristol Blenheims, Hawker Hurricanes and Supermarine Spitfires, and was home to 242 Squadron, commanded by Douglas Bader. It was also used by fighters of the USAAF 8th Air Force from 1943. The airfield was closed in 1963 and was redeveloped as Martlesham Heath Village in the 1970s; part of the land was used by BT's (then the Post Office) Research Laboratories, opened by Queen Elizabeth II in 1975; in the late 1990s the site was turned into a high tech business park and renamed Adastral Park. Tel: 01473 642022.

RAF Mildenhall Mildenhall, 12 miles (19km) northwest of Bury St Edmunds. Currently used by the United States Air Force; RAF Mildenhall and its sister base RAF Lakenheath are the largest USAF bases in the UK. The station opened on 16 October 1934, and the following year George V reviewed 350 aircraft here on the occasion of his Silver Jubilee, an event commemorated by a memorial tablet in front of the current 100 ARW headquarters. During World War II Mildenhall became a bomber station, flying Vickers Wellingtons, Short Stirlings and Avro Lancasters. It was also the headquarters of 3 Group Bomber Command. From 1950 Mildenhall became home to bombers and later tanker aircraft of the USAF. Tel: 01638 543000.

RAF Wattisham Wattisham, 5 miles (8km) southwest of Stowmarket. RAF Wattisham opened on 5 April 1939 as a station for Bristol Blenheim bombers. On 4 September 1939, just 29 hours after the declaration of war, the first bombing raid of the war – against enemy shipping in Wilhelmshaven harbour – was launched from Wattisham. In 1942 the Blenheims were replaced by Bristol Beaufighters and in late 1942 the base was handed over to the United States Army Air Force. It was returned to the RAF in 1946. In 1950 Gloster Meteor fighters arrived, to be replaced in the mid 1950s by Hawker Hunters; the Black Arrows display team were stationed at the airfield from 1958. In 1960 the English Electric Lightning arrived, while McDonnell Douglas Phantoms used Wattisham from 1974 until it was closed as a fighter base in 1992. Today Wattisham is used by the Army Air Corps, flying Westland WAH64 Apache, Westland Lynx and Aerospatiale Gazelle helicopters. An RAF Search and Rescue flight of Sea King helicopters operates from the airfield, as does the police helicopter unit for Suffolk Constabulary.

Rex Graham Nature Reserve 2 miles (3km) east of Mildenhall. A 0.7 acre (0.3ha) nature reserve in Mildenhall Woods, part of Thetford Forest in the Breckland region, and named after Suffolk botanist Rex Graham. The site is a disused chalk pit, surrounded by woodland, and is significant mainly for its population of military orchids, of which over 95 per cent of the UK population occurs here. Other plants include mezereon, twayblade, pyramidal orchid, ploughman's spikenard and Southern adder's tongue. The site was notified as a Site of Special Scientific Interest in 1984, and is also a Special Area of Conservation. It is managed by Suffolk Wildlife Trust in conjunction with the Forestry Commission.

Redgrave and Lopham Fen 1 mile (1.6km) north of Redgrave, 15 miles (24km) northeast of Bury St Edmunds. A National Nature Reserve situated on the Suffolk/Norfolk border near the source of the River Waveney. With an area of 305 acres (123ha), it is the largest fen in lowland England. The habitats include internationally significant saw sedge beds and purple-moor grasslands, as well as acid fen, calcareous fen, reed fen, willow carr and alder woodland. More than 120 rare invertebrates have been identified on the site, and it is one of only two sites in Britain where the fen raft spider can be found. The reserve was established by English Nature in 1993 and is owned and maintained by Suffolk Wildlife Trust.

Rivers

The **Alde** is a wide tidal estuary rising in Laxfield before snaking southeast to Aldeburgh Bay, where it splits and rejoins to form Havergate Island. The coastal land separated from the mainland of Suffolk is known as Orford Ness. The area which the river passes is mainly marshland and shingle or sand beaches. Most of the area is now owned by the National Trust as the Orford Ness National Nature Reserve, part of the Suffolk Coast and Heaths Area of Outstanding Natural Beauty.

The **Blyth** rises near Laxfield and flows east to form a tidal estuary between Southwold and Walberswick. The estuary is the scene of the final drowning in Peter Greenaway's film *Drowning by Numbers* (1988).

The **Brett**, a small tributary of the River Stour, winds its way from the north edge of Hadleigh, parallel to the High Street, under picturesque Toppesfield Bridge, through a mill pool and then on to Higham where it joins the Stour in Constable country.

The **Deben** rises in Debenham and flows southeast to Woodbridge before widening out into a long estuary into Felixstowe. There are several yacht and dinghy clubs on the river. The Deben Estuary is a Special Protection Area for wildfowl and other wildlife.

The **Dove** is a small river rising south of Diss and flowing in a generally southerly direction before petering out 4 miles (6km) south of Eye.

The **Gipping** is the source river for the River Orwell. It was used for navigation as early as the 12th century and it is likely that the stone for the abbey at Bury St Edmunds was brought part way up the river and taken overland to Bury. The 17 mile (27km) navigation from Stowmarket to Ipswich was opened in 1793 and lifted barges 90ft (27.5m) through a total of 15 locks. The barges' cargoes ranged from slate, coal and timber to manure, chemicals and gun cotton. Steam tugs were able to operate as far as the Fisons works at Papermill Lane, Bramford until 1929, after which the canal company went into liquidation and the navigation was closed by Act of Parliament in 1932.

The **Lark**, a tributary of the River Great Ouse, rises south of Bury St Edmunds and joins the Great Ouse south of Littleport in Cambridgeshire. It is 31 miles (50km) long. The Lark is an important focus for prehistoric activity, particularly relating to the Neolithic enclosure at Fornham All Saints.

The **Little Ouse** is a tributary of the River Great Ouse, and for much of its length defines the boundary between Norfolk and Suffolk. It rises east of Thelnetham, very close to the source of the River Waveney, which flows east while the Little Ouse flows west. The river is currently navigable for 13 miles (21km) from the Great Ouse to a point 2 miles (3km) above Brandon.

The **Ore** is a continuation of the River Alde, and flows from the southern tip of Havergate Island in a northerly direction east of Butley and Chillesford.

The **Orwell**'s source river, above the tidal limit, is known as the River Gipping. It broadens into an estuary at Ipswich and flows into the North Sea at Felixstowe after joining with the River Stour at Shotley. It was in the Orwell that 300 ships massed for the landings of English sailors who were to fight and win the battle of Crécy. In 1588 Ipswich built, fitted out and manned two ships to sail against the Spanish Armada.

The **Rat** has its source near the village of Rattlesden and is the major tributary of the River Gipping.

The **Stour** is 47 miles (76km) long and forms most of boundary between Suffolk and Essex. It rises in eastern Cambridgeshire, passes though Haverhill, Cavendish, Sudbury and Dedham Vale, and joins the North Sea at Harwich. Much of the Stour valley is within the Dedham Vale Area of Outstanding Natural Beauty. RSPB Stour Estuary is a nature reserve managed by the Royal Society for the Protection of Birds. The first settlement on the river in Suffolk is Great Bradley, where man has had a recorded presence for over 5000 years.

Waveney – see Norfolk

The **Yox** rises near the source of the Alde and Blyth southeast of Laxfield. The small brook flows southeast to Peasenhall and then east to Yoxford, from which it takes its name.

Rougham Field

1 mile (1.6km) northwest of Rougham, 2 miles (3km) east of Bury St Edmunds. The former airfield, constructed in 1941–2, was home to the United States Army Air Force 322nd and 94th Bomb Groups during World War II and is one of the few wartime bases to retain its control tower. Part of the airfield is now occupied by an industrial estate, while the rest is used as an airstrip and showground. The tower now houses a museum dedicated to the men who flew from the airfield. Tel: 01359 270524.

RSPB Minsmere

6 miles (10km) south of Southwold. One of the best known of the RSPB's reserves, and renowned for its wetland breeding birds, including bittern, marsh harrier, avocet and bearded tit. A mixture of mudflats, reedbeds, wet grassland, shigle and heathland, it forms part of the Minsmere–Walberswick Special Protection Area from the estuary of the River Blyth south to the Minsmere River. In September 2004 a moth species, *Catocala conjuncta*, previously unrecorded in Britain was found on the reserve. To acknowledge its place of capture it was named the Minsmere crimson underwing. There is also an established population of the ant-lion *Euroleon nostras*, an insect unknown elsewhere in Britain except for a population of this or a related species found in Norfolk. Tel: 01728 648281.

Fornham St Genevieve Church

$^1/_2$ mile (0.8km) north of Fornham St Martin, 2 miles (3km) north of Bury St Edmunds. Only the tower remains of the 15th century church of St Genevieve, destroyed by fire in 1782.

St Edmundsbury Cathedral

Angel Hill, Bury St Edmunds. Dedicated to St James; a church has stood on the site since at least 1065, when St Denys's Church was built within the precincts of the Benedictine abbey founded by Cnut in 1020 to house the remains of Edmund, king of the East Angles, killed by the Danes in 869. After the abbot, Anselm, attempted unsuccessfully to make a pilgrimage along the Way of St James to Santiago de Compostela later in the 11th century, he instead rebuilt St Denys's and dedicated the new church to St James. This church was largely rebuilt in the early 16th century with further alterations in the 18th and 19th centuries. When the Diocese of St Edmundsbury and Ipswich was created in 1914, St James's Church became the cathedral. In 1959 Benjamin Britten wrote the *Fanfare for St Edmundsbury* for a Pageant for Magna Carta held in the cathedral grounds. A new choir school was opened in 1990 and a Gothic revival tower was completed in 2005. Tel: 01284 754933.

St James's Chapel Lindsey, 7 miles (11km) east of Sudbury. A small 13th century chapel with thatched roof and lancet windows. Now in the care of English Heritage.

St Lawrence's Church Dial Lane, Ipswich. A 15th century aisleless church whose 97ft (29.5m) west tower is a famous local landmark. Declared redundant in 1975, it was reopened as a community centre in 2008. Tel: 01473 232300.

St Michael the Archangel, Church of Church Street, Framlingham. An Anglican parish church largely built in Perpendicular style in the mid 14th century. Its unusually large chancel was added in the 16th century as the burial place of the Howard family after the dissolution of Thetford Priory.

Saxtead Green Post Mill Saxtead Green, 9 miles (15km) northwest of Woodbridge. A white timber-clad post mill built in 1776. It ceased operating commercially in 1947, but is still in working order and has recently been restored. Now owned by English Heritage. Tel: 01728 685780.

Scallop, The A sculpture located on the beach at Aldeburgh, a short distance north of the town centre, and dedicated to local resident Benjamin Britten. Created from stainless steel by Suffolk-based artist Maggi Hambling, it stands 13ft (4m) high and was unveiled in November 2003. The piece is made up of two interlocking scallop shells, each broken, the upright shell being pierced with the words 'I hear those voices that will not be drowned', from Britten's opera *Peter Grimes*. The sculpture has proved controversial: not all locals appreciate the aesthetic quality of the piece and several petitions have been raised to have it removed.

Sealand On 2 September 1967 Paddy Roy Bates, a former disc jockey who operated his own pirate radio station, claimed the artificial island of Roughs Tower, a former Maunsell Sea Fort in the North Sea 6 miles (10km) off the coast of Suffolk, as his own sovereign state. He named the 550 sq m area Sealand. The Principality of Sealand is occupied by Paddy's family and associates, and he styles himself HRH Prince Roy of Sealand. Sealand has issued its own stamps since 1969 and had its own currency since 1972, the Sealand Dollar, equal to one US dollar. The official language is English and the population varies but rarely exceeds 10.

Although Sealand's claims to sovereignty and legitimacy are not recognised by any country, it is probably the world's best-known micro-nation, and is sometimes cited in debates as a case study of how principles of international law can be applied to a territorial dispute. At the time of occupation the former HM *Fort Roughs* lay in international waters; however, in 1987 the UK extended its territorial waters to 12 nautical miles (22km) under international law dealing with the legal position of artificial islands. However, as Roughs Tower is actually a sunken barge, some have claimed it is not covered by these rulings. Sealand declared that it, too, was extending its claim of territorial waters to 12 nautical miles. The address publicised by Sealand as its postal address is: 'Sealand 1001; Sealand Post Bag, IP11 9SZ, UK'. The Royal Mail postcode is that of Felixstowe near Ipswich, and the Royal Mail website gives the following standardised address: Sealand Fort, PO Box 3, Felixstowe, IP11 9SZ, UK. See also Interesting Facts and HM *Fort Roughs* in Essex.

Seckford Hall Seckford Hall Road, Woodbridge. An impressive Elizabethan manor house, built in characteristic E-plan and once the family home of Thomas Seckford (1515–87), Master of the Court of Requests to Queen Elizabeth I. It is now a luxury hotel. See also Shire Hall, Woodbridge School.

Shire Hall Market Hill, Woodbridge. Built in 1575 by Thomas Seckford to house the local quarter sessions, the hall has been the focal point of the town for more than 400 years. Flemish gabling was added in the 17th century. Woodbridge Town Council purchased the hall in 1984 and its restoration was completed in 2004.

Shotley Battery 3 miles (5km) southwest of Felixstowe. Located on the northern bank of the River Orwell and built in 1865 on the Shotley peninsula to guard the port of Felixstowe on the same site as an existing Martello tower equipped with 14 64-pound guns. It later came within the bounds of the naval training school HMS *Ganges*, which in later years became a police training school before closing in the late 1990s; its huge mast still dominates the Shotley skyline.

Shrubland Hall 6 miles (10km) northwest of Ipswich. A Palladian style house designed by James Paine in the 1770s, with later Italianate additions by Sir Charles Barry, architect of the Houses of Parliament. The surrounding Italianate garden was designed by Barry 1848–52, with flower gardens designed by William Robinson c.1888. The highlight of the gardens, which fall away from the house on a steep slope, is an Italian staircase descending from the top terrace to the formal gardens below; other features include a Swiss chalet, a loggia, follies and a box maze. Beyond is a wild garden which leads to the park. The Grade I listed garden has recently been restored by Lord and Lady de Saumarez, descendants of the later Victorian owners. The estate is not currently open to the public. Tel: 01473 830221.

Sizewell Power Stations 4 miles (6km) north of Aldeburgh. Two nuclear power stations located on the North Sea coast to the north of the small fishing village of Sizewell. The village was once part of the Ogilvie estate (see Thorpeness); Sizewell Hall, now used as a Christian conference centre, is still owned by the Ogilvie family. Sizewell A was built in the 1960s and started generation in 1966. Its two Magnox reactors were shut down at the end of 2006 and are in the process of being decommissioned. Sizewell B is the UK's only large pressurised water reactor (PWR), and was built 1988–95. It is designed to operate until around 2035, although similar stations elsewhere have been granted extensions to 60 years.

Snape Maltings — $^1/_4$ mile (0.4km) south of Snape, 4 miles (6km) west of Aldeburgh. A collection of former granaries and malthouses beside the River Alden now occupied by shops, restaurants and galleries, but best known for its world-class concert hall, one of the main venues of the annual Aldeburgh Festival. The Holst Library, which occupies rooms in the complex, is named in honour of Imogen Holst, daughter of Gustav Holst, a close friend of Benjamin Britten and artistic director of the Aldeburgh Festival 1956–77. Tel: 01728 688303/5.

Somerleyton Hall and Gardens — Somerleyton, 5 miles (8km) northwest of Lowestoft. A country house and garden located close to the Suffolk/Norfolk border. A manor house was built on the site in 1240 by Sir Peter FitzOsbert, whose daughter married into the Jernegan family. The Jernegans held the estate until 1604 when it was purchased by John Wentworth, who transformed the hall into a typical East Anglian Jacobean mansion. It then passed to the Garney family. The next owner was Admiral Sir Thomas Allin, a native of Lowestoft who took part in the battles of Lowestoft (1665) and Sole Bay (1672). Sir Samuel Morton Peto bought the hall and park in 1843 and carried out extensive rebuilding. In 1863 the estate was sold to Sir Francis Crossley of Halifax, West Yorkshire, like Peto a philanthropist, manufacturer and MP. Sir Francis's son Savile was created Baron Somerleyton in 1916, and the house is still owned by Lord Somerleyton. The 12 acres (5ha) of formal gardens feature a yew hedge maze created by W A Nesfield in 1846, and a ridge and furrow greenhouse designed by Joseph Paxton, architect of the Crystal Palace. There is also a walled garden, an aviary, a loggia and a 300ft (90m) pergola covered with roses and wisteria. The more informal areas of the garden feature rhododendrons, azaleas and a collection of specimen trees. Tel: 01502 734901/08712 224244.

Southwold Lighthouse — Stradbroke Road, Southwold. Constructed by Trinity House 1887–90, it replaced three lighthouses condemned due to serious coastal erosion. The tower stands 102ft (31m) high. Its red and white signal lights flash four times every 20 seconds. The lighthouse has been automated since 1938.

Southwold Museum — Victoria Street, Southwold. Refurbished in 2008, the museum is housed in a Grade II listed 17th century cottage. Exhibits include a wide variety of items relating to the area's local and natural history, the Southwold light railway and a collection of paintings and memorabilia. Tel 01502 722375.

Southwold Pier — North Parade, Southwold. Built in 1900, the pier underwent extensive renovation in the 1990s; the restored structure is 623ft (190m) long. Tel: 01502 722105.

Sport

football — **Ipswich Town** were founded in 1878 and joined the Football League in 1938. The club's nicknames include The Blues, Town and The Tractor Boys. The latter name, linked to the town's agricultural history, originally applied to near neighbours Norwich City in the 1970s; its first generally accepted application to Ipswich appeared at a game at Birmingham City in the 1998–9 season. The club have provided England's two most successful managers, Sir Bobby Robson and Sir Alf Ramsey, and are the only club ever to have won the First Division championship in their debut season when Ramsey guided them to the title in 1961–2. Robson took Ipswich to an FA Cup win in 1978 and UEFA Cup victory three years later, as well as twice achieving second place in the League. The club have played home matches at Portman Road Stadium since 1884, when it was a cricket ground used by East Suffolk Cricket Club. Then, as now, the ground was owned by the local authority. Outside are statues of Ramsey and Robson. Tel: 01473 400500.

horse racing — **Newmarket** racecourse is considered the home of British horse racing as it is the location of the largest cluster of training yards and of many key racing organisations. It holds exclusively Flat racing on two courses: the Rowley Mile Course is $2^1/_2$ miles (3.6km) long with a right-hand bend after 1 mile (1.6km); the July course has a shorter run-in from the right-hand bend. 01638 663482.

Suffolk Coast and Heaths Path — A long-distance footpath following a course along the rivers and sea walls, marshland, heathland, foreshore and cliffs of the Suffolk Heritage Coast from Felixstowe to Lowestoft, via Bawdsey, Orford Ness and Aldeburgh. Named after the Suffolk Coast and Heaths Area of Outstanding Natural Beauty through which it passes, it is 50 miles (80km) long. It connects at Felixstowe with the Stour and Orwell Walk to Cattawade, a village near Manningtree in Essex.

Suffolk Punch — One of the oldest breeds of draught horse, dating back to 1506; their combination of power, stamina, health, longevity and docility made the horses ideal for ploughing the county's heavy clay soil. Their characteristics include a powerful arching neck, strong upright shoulders, a short strong back, wide hip bones and a high tail. Due to their extreme girth the legs of the Suffolk Punch appear short. The average height is 16 hands, but individuals can grow to a height of over 17 hands and weigh up to 2000lb (900kg). All Suffolk Punch horses are chestnut in colour, with shades ranging from light golden to dark brown. The horse is the emblem of Ipswich Town FC; because of its reputation for easy handling with power the name was also used for a brand of lawnmower.

Summerhill School — Westward Ho, Leiston. A progressive, co-educational, residential school founded by A S Neill in 1921. Its organisation has two particularly unusual features: first, all lessons are optional – teachers and classes are available at timetabled times, but children can decide whether or not to attend, giving them the freedom to make choices about their lives and meaning that those attending lessons are motivated to learn; second is the school meeting, at which the school laws are made or changed. These laws, the rules of the school, are made by majority vote, pupils and staff alike having equal votes. Summerhill was founded in Hellerau, a suburb of Dresden, as part of an international school called the Neue Schule. Together with Frau Neustatter (later his first wife), Neill first moved his school to an idyllic setting – a castle on top of a mountain – at Sonntagsberg in Austria. However, the local Catholic community were hostile, and by 1923 Neill had moved to Lyme Regis in Dorset to a house called Summerhill, opening his school with just five pupils. In 1927 the school moved to its present site in Leiston, taking the name with it. After the founder's death in 1973, the school was run by his second wife; the current headteacher is their daughter, Zoë Neill Readhead. Summerhill currently has almost 100 pupils. Tel: 01728 830030.

Sutton Hoo 1 mile (1.6km) east of Woodbridge. One of the most important archaeological sites in England, Sutton Hoo is thought to be the burial ground of the Anglo-Saxon kings of East Anglia. Located on a spur of land overlooking the River Deben in the 6th century kingdom of the East Angles, the site consists of 20 barrows, most unexplored by modern methods. One of the mounds was excavated in 1939, revealing a spectacular range of treasures including a warrior's helmet, shield and gold ornaments, in the remains of a burial chamber of a 90ft (27.5m) ship; thanks to a single dated gold coin, it was possible to date the burial to c.625. Further excavation took place 1965–71. The exhibition hall houses a full-size reconstruction of the buried chamber and tells the story of the discovery of its treasures, which lay undisturbed for over 1300 years. In pagan Anglo-Saxon custom, important people were buried under mounds, often with precious goods as a sign of their worth; the burial mounds would make prominent landmarks and, standing high on a skyline, would be a fitting memorial to a powerful leader. The burial of a ship, however, is unique to East Anglia and Scandinavia. Anglo-Saxons at the time were predominantly pagans, but Christianity was beginning to spread to Britain from France and Ireland; the burial therefore possibly represents a period when former pagan burial practices were being adapted to Christian sentiments. The burial mounds form part of a 245 acre (99ha) estate managed by the National Trust. The finds from Sutton Hoo are held at the British Museum. Tel: 01394 389700.

Theatre Royal Westgate Street, Bury St Edmunds. Opened by its proprietor and architect William Wilkins (1778–1839) on 11 October 1819, the theatre was one of the most elegant, sophisticated and up-to-date playhouses of its age. Having survived without significant alteration, it is the only Regency theatre still in existence in Britain. Greene King, the local brewery, purchased the freehold (which it still owns) in 1920, and a 999-year lease was granted to the National Trust in 1975. The Theatre Royal is now managed as an independent working theatre by Bury St Edmunds Theatre Management Limited. Tel: 01284 755127.

Thorpeness 2 miles (3km) north of Aldeburgh. A coastal village with an unusual history. In 1910, Scottish playwright and barrister Glencairne Stuart Ogilvie, who had made a large sum of money from investments in Russian railways, bought a stretch of coast extending north of Aldeburgh, past Sizewell and inland to Aldringham and Leiston. Most of this land was used for farming but he developed the fishing hamlet of Thorpeness into a private fantasy holiday village inspired by his friend J M Barrie's creations, including Peter Pan. The village became an upper-middle-class haven with a country club, tennis courts and a swimming pool, a golf course and clubhouse and holiday homes built in Jacobean and Tudor styles. Two notable features are Thorpeness Meare, an artificial lake created in the centre of the village, and a set of almshouses built in the 1920s to the design of W G Wilson. The building known as 'The House in the Clouds' is a water tower clad in wood to make it look like a small house floating above the trees; the supporting structure was also boarded to create five storeys of living accommodation. After the village was connected to mains water, the old tank was transformed into a huge games room. The water-pumping windmill next to it, built as a corn mill in 1824, was moved from its previous location in nearby Aldringham. After Alexander Stuart Ogilvie, G S Ogilvie's grandson, died on Thorpeness golf course in 1972, many of the houses, as well as the golf course and country club, were sold to pay the subsequent death duties.

University Campus Suffolk A collaboration between the University of East Anglia and the University of Essex, UCS offers opportunities to study full-time and part-time at degree level in the arts, engineering, health and education. Officially opened in August 2007, UCS has centres in Bury St Edmunds, Great Yarmouth, Lowestoft and Otley, complementing the major new campus development at Neptune Quay in the Ipswich Education Quarter. Tel: 01473 338000.

West Stow Anglo-Saxon Village West Stow, 5 miles (8km) northwest of Bury St Edmunds. Located in West Stow Country Park, the reconstruction of an Anglo-Saxon village is built on the site of an original settlement occupied from the 5th to the 7th century and discovered preserved beneath sand dunes in the 1960s. Finds from the site's excavation are on display in the purpose-built Anglo-Saxon Centre. Tel. 01284 728718.

Westleton Heath $^1/_2$ mile (0.8km) northeast of Westleton, 6 miles (10km) southwest of Southwold. Westleton Heath National Nature Reserve is the finest surviving remnant of the large area of heathland known as the Sandlings (on account of its dry sandy soils) that stretched along the Suffolk coast in the Middle Ages, but of which only about 20 per cent remains; the rest has been lost to farming and forestry. The flora, typical of acid soil, includes harebell, tormentil, heath bedstraw and various species of heather; bird species supported include Dartford warbler, stonechat and nightjar. The reserve is jointly managed by the RSPB and English Nature.

Wingfield College Wingfield, 7 miles (11km) east of Diss. Now a private house, the building is the remnant of a chantry college founded by Sir John de Wingfield in 1362. In 1542 the school was dissolved and a large part was demolished. The remaining wings were remodelled in Palladian style in the 18th century; the Georgian façades conceal a medieval great hall and cloister. The 4 acres (1.6ha) of gardens contain ponds and garden sculpture.

Woodbridge School Burkitt Road, Woodbridge. A public school founded in 1662 by Dorothy Seckford, Francis Burwell and Robert Marryott. It is now administered by the Seckford Foundation, established by lawyer Thomas Seckford, who in 1587 gave an endowment for the poor of the town. Catering for pupils aged 11–18, the school has been co-educational since 1975. Tel: 01394 615000.

Woodbridge Tide Mill Tide Mill Way, Woodbridge. A well-preserved tide mill located on the River Deben; its waterwheel, once operated by the outflow of tidal water from a 7 acre (2.8ha) mill pond, still turns. The wooden three-storey building, clad in white Suffolk boarding and with a mansard roof, is now Grade I listed. The original mill reservoir is now a marina, but a $^1/_2$ acre (0.2ha) pond has been constructed for demonstration purposes. A tide mill was first recorded on the site in 1170; the mill was operated by the local Augustinian priory in the Middle Ages, and was acquired by Henry VIII at the monastery's dissolution in 1536. By the outbreak of World War II the mill was one of the few still operating, and until its closure in 1957 it was the last commercially operating tide mill in Britain. A restoration programme was launched in 1968 and the mill was opened to the public in 1973. Tel: 01473 626618.

Wyken Hall Gardens — 1 mile (1.6km) south of Stanton, 8 miles (13km) northeast of Bury St Edmunds. Surrounding a beautiful Elizabethan manor house (not open to the public), the gardens were mostly created in the late 20th century as a series of traditional-style 'rooms' divided by yew and hornbeam hedges. The knot garden and formal herb garden were designed by Arabella Lennox-Boyd. Other features include a rose garden with splendid long pergola, a traditional kitchen garden with fruit trees and a greenhouse, a copper beech maze and a nuttery. Tel: 01359 250287.

Some famous people born in Suffolk

Addams, Dawn (actress) (1930–85)	Felixstowe
Anderson, Elizabeth Garrett (physician) (1836–1917)	Aldeburgh
Bale, John (churchman and historian) (1495–1563)	Cove
Beale, Mary (painter) (1633–99)	Barrow
Bowell, Mackenzie (prime minister of Canada) (1823–1917)	Rickinghall
Britten, Benjamin (composer) (1913–76)	Lowestoft
Constable, John (artist) (1776–1837)	East Bergholt
Crabbe, George (poet) (1754–1832)	Aldeburgh
Dyer, Kieron (footballer) (1978–)	Ipswich
Ecclestone, Bernie (Formula One CEO) (1930–)	Bungay
Eno, Brian (musician) (1948–)	Woodbridge
Fawcett, Millicent Garrett (suffragist) (1847–1929)	Aldeburgh
Fiennes, Ralph (actor (1962–)	Ipswich
FitzGerald, Edward (writer born Edward Purcell) (1809–83)	Bredfield House
FitzRoy, Robert (captain of HMS *Beagle*) (1805–65)	Ampton Hall
Frink, Elisabeth (sculptor) (1930–93)	Thurlow
Gainsborough, Thomas (painter) (1727–88)	Sudbury
Gardiner, Stephen (Roman Catholic bishop) (c.1497–1555)	Bury St Edmunds
Hall, Peter (theatre director) (1930–)	Bury St Edmunds
Hendry Ian (actor) (1931–84)	Ipswich
Hoskins, Bob (actor) (1942–)	Bury St Edmunds
Lansbury, George (politician) (1859–1940)	Halesworth
Munnings, Alfred (horse painter) (1878–1959)	Mendham
Nunn, Trevor (film and theatre director) (1940–)	Ipswich
Ouida (Maria Louise Ramé) (novelist) (1839–1908)	Bury St Edmunds
Pritchett, V(ictor) S(awden) (writer and critic) (1900–97)	Ipswich
Repton, Humphry (landscape designer) (1752–1818)	Bury St Edmunds
Sancroft, William (Archbishop of Canterbury) (1617–93)	Fressingfield
Wolsey, Cardinal Thomas (statesman) (c.1471–1530)	Ipswich

Surrey

GREATER LONDON
Egham
Staines
M3
1
2
Walton-on-Thames
BERKSHIRE
Sunbury
Epsom
Camberley
Weybridge
3
5
6
Banstead
Woking
7
Caterham
M25
M3
Frimley
4
Leatherhead
M25
East Horsley
Oxted
10
Reigate
Godstone
KENT
Guildford
Dorking
Redhill
R. Mole
8
Farnham
Bramley
Leith Hill
295
9
Lingfield
R. Wey
Horley
HAMPSHIRE
Godalming
Whitley
11
Cranleigh
M23
EAST SUSSEX
Haslemere
WEST SUSSEX

Districts

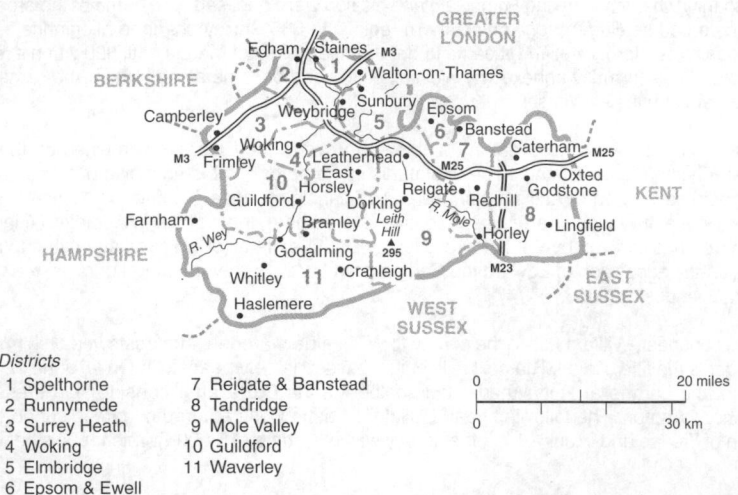

1 Spelthorne	7 Reigate & Banstead
2 Runnymede	8 Tandridge
3 Surrey Heath	9 Mole Valley
4 Woking	10 Guildford
5 Elmbridge	11 Waverley
6 Epsom & Ewell	

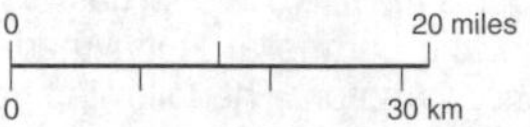
0
20 miles
0
30 km

The county of Surrey in southern England is part of the South East England region and one of the Home Counties. It borders the ceremonial county of Berkshire to the northwest, Greater London to the northeast, Hampshire to the west, Kent to the east, West Sussex to the south and its most southeasterly tip just extends to East Sussex. Despite having a cathedral, castle and university, the county town of Guildford does not have city status. Unusually, the county administration is based outside the county's current boundaries in Kingston upon Thames.

Modern Surrey was formed in 1889. The new county lost areas in the northeast bordering the City of London which became part of the new County of London and today form the London Boroughs of Lambeth, Southwark and Wandsworth. Penge was lost to Kent in 1899 (it became part of Greater London in 1965 and now forms part of the London Borough of Bromley). Local government reorganisation in 1965 further changed the borders of the county. The area that now forms the London Boroughs of Croydon, Kingston, Merton, Sutton and Richmond south of the River Thames were made part of Greater London and Spelthorne was acquired from Middlesex. Traditional Surrey towns such as Purley, Coulsdon, Whyteleafe, Sanderstead, Wallington, Carshalton, and to a lesser extent, Sutton and Croydon, all of which are now in Greater London, will have a difficult time ever convincing their residents they are now Londoners!

In 1974, Surrey was reorganised as a non-metropolitan county; Gatwick Airport and some surrounding land was assigned to West Sussex and a larger area in the northeast to Greater London. Horley and Charlwood were also transferred, but fierce local opposition led to a reversal of this under the Charlwood and Horley Act 1974.

The North Downs cross Surrey from east to west. To the north the land slopes gently down towards the Thames, into which flow Surrey's principal rivers, the Wey and Mole. The southern slopes of the Downs are more rugged. Surrey is the most heavily wooded county in the UK with 22.4 per cent coverage compared to a national average of 11.8 per cent. The Surrey Hills Area of Outstanding Natural Beauty stretches across a quarter of the county. Created in 1958, the area includes the chalk slopes on the North Downs, from Farnham in the west to Oxted in the east, including Leith Hill, along with the adjacent hills of Holmbury Hill, Pitch Hill and the escarpment of the North Downs from Box Hill to Newlands Corner. This diverse landscape also includes flower-rich grasslands, acid heaths and ancient woodlands and extends south to the wooded greensand hills near Haslemere. There are two nationally significant areas of natural heathland: the Thames basin in the northwest, and the Wealden sands, part of a larger area stretching into Hampshire and West Sussex.

Few ancient British, Roman or Saxon remains exist in Surrey, although Stane Street and Ermine Street have left some vestiges, and minor Roman relics have been found. Before the Roman period the area was governed by the Atrebates tribe, centred at Calleva in modern Hampshire. After the Romans left Britain in the early 5th century the territory of modern Surrey was ruled by successors of the Atrebates. From C.AD 480 Saxons from the south and Jutes from the east invaded and began settling in the area, establishing a sub-kingdom with Middle Saxon overlords. In 661 the sub-kingdom took Mercia as its overlord. In 675 Surrey became one of the last regions in England to convert to Christianity when its sub-king Frithuwald and his son were baptised. The name of the area at this time is recorded as *Sudergeona* or 'southern region'. In 685 Surrey changed allegiance and took Wessex as its overlord. After 771 it came under the rule of Offa of Mercia until 823 when it reverted to Wessex. It was formally annexed by Wessex in 860 and became a shire under the same model as the other counties of Wessex.

After the death of Alfred the Great in 899 his son Edward the Elder was crowned on the King's Stone at Kingston upon Thames. The use of this stone before 902 is unknown but it seems likely that it would have been of ancient spiritual or political significance. Another six kings of England from the House of Wessex were subsequently crowned here, the last being Aethelred II in 978. In 1011 Surrey was overrun by Danish forces led by Cnut before all of England submitted to them in 1016. After the accession of Edward the Confessor in 1042, Surrey remained unmolested until the Norman Conquest in 1066.

After the conquest, William I gave the county to William de Warenne, and bestowed on him and his descendants the title of Earl. The next millennium passed largely peacefully. On 15 June 1215 King John met the barons at Runnymede and sealed Magna Carta after considerable pressure by Archbishop Langton. The following year, Guildford Castle was captured by forces supporting the Dauphin of France and in June 1497 the county was overrun by 15,000 Cornish rebels heading for London.

During the Middle Ages the county was the site of Waverley Abbey, Merton Priory (established in 1114) and Newark Priory, all destroyed during the Reformation. In the Tudor period the country homes of many successful Londoners were located in Surrey, Sutton Place, Great Tangley Manor and Losely Park being prime examples. Later great houses include Clandon Park, Hatchlands, Nonsuch Park and Polesden Lacey.

About a quarter of the total area of the county is devoted to agriculture, with a mixture of dairy and arable farming and market gardening. An iron industry flourished in the Weald of Surrey until the 16th century, as in Kent and Sussex, before the discovery of smelting with coal rendered iron production uneconomic in the region. Fuller's earth, used in the cloth industry and in pharmaceuticals, was mined in quarries near Reigate until the end of the 20th century. In medieval times glass making flourished in Chiddingfold, producing windows for famous churches such as Westminster Abbey and St George's Chapel at Windsor. During the 19th century the western part of the county became the focus of military activity, and there is still a significant military presence around Camberley and on the western heathland. Manufacturing, particularly in the northwest of the county, developed in the 20th century to include radio and radar equipment and aircraft.

Offering attractive and secluded countryside within easy reach of London, Surrey today is still the home of the rich, famous and professionally successful. Pop stars such as Sir Cliff Richard and Ringo Starr, and film star Michael Caine, are among many to have made their homes in the county in recent years.

Surrey	**Population**			**Area**	
Districts	*male*	*female*	*total*	*sq miles*	*sq km*
Elmbridge	58,867	63,069	121,936	37	95
Epsom & Ewell	32,427	34,632	67,059	13	34
Guildford	63,986	65,715	129,701	105	271
Mole Valley	38,988	41,299	80,287	100	258
Reigate & Banstead	62,100	64,423	126,523	50	129
Runnymede	37,975	40,058	78,033	30	78
Spelthorne	44,350	46,040	90,390	17	45
Surrey Heath	39,701	40,613	80,314	37	95
Tandridge	38,163	41,104	79,267	96	248
Waverley	56,099	59,566	115,665	132	346
Woking	43,869	45,971	89,840	25	64
Total	516,525	542,490	1,059,015	642	1663

Local attractions and Information

Administrative headquarters	County Hall, Kingston upon Thames, Surrey KT1 2DN. Tel: 020 8541 8800.
Abinger	The parish of Abinger, 4 miles (6km) southwest of Dorking, consists of five villages: Abinger Hammer, Abinger Common, Forest Green, Walliswood and Oakwoodhill. The quaint village of Abinger Common stands high in the beautiful countryside around Leith Hill and claims to have the second highest old parish church in Surrey. The village has connections with famous Surrey architect Edwin Lutyens, who built many of the cottages as well as the war memorial. Abinger Hammer is perhaps the best-known village; its main feature is the wooden clock which juts out over the road, with the figure Jack-the-blacksmith striking the hour on the bell with his hammer.
Abinger Castle	Abinger Common, 4 miles (6km) southwest of Dorking. Norman motte and bailey castle erected c.1100 with a wooden keep on stilts. Now ruined, the area was excavated 1947–9.
Addlestone	A small town in northwest Surrey, Addlestone is home of the Crouch Oak, one of Britain's oldest trees and believed to date from the 11th century. In 1916 the Blériot aeroplane factory – established after French inventor and engineer Louis Blériot made history in 1909 by becoming the first person to cross the English Channel in a heavier-than-air craft – moved to the town from Brooklands. The Lang Propeller Works, manufacturer of the propeller which enabled Alcock and Brown to fly the Atlantic, was also located in Addlestone in the early 20th century.
Alice Holt	3 miles (5km) south of Farnham. An area of ancient woodland on the Surrey/Hampshire border known for its fine oaks; timber from the area once supplied the navy, and more recently Alice Holt oaks were used to build the replica of Shakespeare's Globe Theatre in London. Located on a clay outcrop, the area was a significant site of pottery manufacture in the Roman period and gives its name to a type of grey pottery called Alice Holt ware. Managed by the Forestry Commission.
Army Medical Services Museum	Mytchett Place Road, Mytchett, 4 miles (6km) south of Camberley. Located within Keogh Barracks, the museum is dedicated to the history of the Army's medical services since 1660; exhibits includes ambulances and medical equipment. Tel: 01252 340212.
Bagshot Park	$\frac{1}{4}$ mile (0.4km) north of Bagshot. The original house on the site was built for Charles I 1631–3 to designs by Inigo Jones; this was replaced in 1879 by a house with interiors influenced by Indian architecture. Occupied until his death in 1942 by Arthur, Duke of Connaught, son of Queen Victoria, it then became the home of the Army Chaplain's Department and is now leased to Prince Edward, Earl of Wessex.
Basingstoke Canal	Linking the villages of Greywell in Hampshire and Woodham in Surrey, the canal was built 1788–94 to enable agricultural produce to be more easily transported to London. It is 32 miles (51km) long with 29 locks. After many years of restoration it is now fully navigable, and connects to the River Wey Navigation, which in turn joins the River Thames. There is a small museum in the Canal Centre at Mytchett.
Bisley	A small village 3 miles (5km) west of Woking, the home of competitive firearms shooting in Britain and the site of the National Rifle Association ranges and the National Shooting Centre since 1890.
Bletchingley	A tiny village 4 miles (6km) east of Redhill. The house at Place Farm once formed the gatehouse of Bletchingley Place, a great Tudor house occupied by Anne of Cleves after her marriage to Henry VIII was annulled. The local inn, The White Hart, is one of the oldest pubs in Britain, possibly dating to 1388.
Box Hill	$1\frac{1}{2}$ miles (2.5km) northeast of Dorking. A well-known beauty spot on the North Downs, Box Hill gets its name from the box trees growing on its steep southern and western slopes, especially around the 'Whites', chalk cliffs cut by the River Mole. Since boxwood is exceptionally hard, it was used for wood-engravers' blocks. Stepping stones at the foot of the hill cross the River Mole on the line of the ancient Pilgrims' Way from Winchester to Canterbury. The road that winds its way up the hill is called the Zig-Zag. Eminent British myrmecologist and coleopterist Horace Donisthorpe carried out studies of British ants here; the site is has now been designated a Site of Special Scientific Interest and Special Protection Area for its chalk downland habitats. The hill was also the destination of the celebrated outing in Jane Austen's novel *Emma*, in which Emma is reprimanded by Mr Knightley for making a joke at the expense of the garrulous old maid Miss Bates. George Meredith (1828–1909), principally known today for his novel *The Egoist*, lived at Flint Cottage, where his regular visitors included Robert Louis Stevenson and J M Barrie. After Meredith's death, the cottage was bequeathed to the National Trust, who subsequently sold it on a 99-year lease. The hill and surrounding countryside are also now owned by the National Trust. Tel: 01306 885502.
Brooklands	1 mile (1.6km) southwest of Weybridge. Once Britain's premier motor racing circuit, Brooklands was opened on 17 June 1907; the brainchild of Hugh Locke-King, it was the first custom-built banked motor racing circuit in the world. Brooklands was the venue in 1926 for the first British Grand Prix, then known as the RAC Grand Prix. From 1915 Brooklands was the location of the Vickers aircraft factory, and it was also used as an airfield – Lady Clayton, the model for Katherine Clifton in Michael Ondaatje's novel *The English Patient*, met her death at Brooklands in a flying accident in 1933. The circuit was closed in 1939 at the outbreak of World War II. In 1987 the site became home to the Brooklands Museum, which is dedicated to the site's motoring and aviation heritage Highlights include the steepest section of the banked track and the 1 in 4 gradient Test Hill. Many of the original buildings have been restored, including the Edwardian club house and the Motoring Village. The museum also has more than 30 aircraft including the first production British Concorde; much of Concorde's airframe was manufactured by the British Aircraft Corporation at Brooklands.

Busbridge Lakes Hambledon Road, Godalming. Formerly belonging to Busbridge Hall, built in 1560 and demolished in 1906, the 40 acres (16ha) of gardens were laid out in the 1750s by Philip Webb, MP. There are three lakes, follies, grottos and specimen trees, as well as more than 130 worldwide species of wildfowl, pheasants and cranes and many endangered flora and fauna. Tel: 01483 421955.

Camberley Camberley lies in northwest Surrey, on the border with Hampshire and Berkshire. Set on Surrey heathland, the town grew up in the 19th century around the gates of the Royal Military Academy, Sandhurst, which moved to its present position in 1812. The military town was originally known as Cambridge Town but in 1877 its name was changed to Camberley to save confusion with the university town of Cambridge. Camberley was popular with retired army officers and in the late 19th century the town's clean air was recommended for people with lung complaints. As a result Camberley grew to become the largest town in the district. Five miles (8km) south lies the village of Deepcut, home to the Princess Royal Barracks, belonging to the Royal Logistics Corps; outside the perimeter of the Barracks, on the northern edge of Deepcut village, stands the Royal Logistics Corps Museum. In 2002 the Princess Royal Barracks was involved in a controversy concerning the suspicious deaths of several recruits. Camberley was immortalised by John Betjeman in his poem 'A Subaltern's Love-song': By roads 'not adopted', by woodlanded ways,/She drove to the club in the late summer haze,/Into nine-o'clock Camberley, heavy with bells,/And mushroomy, pine-woody, evergreen smells.

Charterhouse School Farncombe, 1 mile (1.6km) north of Godalming. A public school founded by Thomas Sutton in London in 1611 on the site of the old Carthusian monastery in Charterhouse Square, Smithfield. One of the original nine English public schools as defined by the Public Schools Act 1868, it moved to its present site in 1872. Pupils are still referred to as Carthusians. Charterhouse won the FA Cup as the Old Carthusians in 1880 and 1881. Peter Gabriel, Mike Rutherford and Tony Banks, of rock group Genesis, all attended Charterhouse in the mid 1960s; other former pupils include novelist William Makepeace Thackeray and poet Robert Graves.

Chatley Heath Semaphore Tower Chatley Heath, 2 miles (3km) southwest of Cobham. The 60ft (18m) tower was built in 1822 and is now the only surviving example of a chain of such towers constructed by the Navy for communication by semaphore between the Admiralty in London and the Fleet at Portsmouth. Tel: 01372 458822.

Cherkley Court 2 miles (3km) southeast of Leatherhead. Rebuilt in the style of a French chateau after a fire in 1893, the house was home 1910–64 to Max Aitken, 1st Baron Beaverbrook, Minister of Aircraft Production and Minister of Supply in World War II. The 16 acres (6.5ha) of landscaped grounds are laid out in a series of terraces with water features and were restored in the late 1990s. Tel: 01372 380980.

Chertsey Museum Windsor Street, Chertsey. Exhibits include Viking and Celtic swords found in the Thames, a costume gallery (including the important Olive Matthews Collection of Dress and Textiles, illustrating fashion over the past 300 years), local clocks, English glass and Meissen porcelain, and medieval tiles from Chertsey Abbey. Tel: 01932 565764.

Chobham Common 1 mile (1.6km) northwest of Chobham, 4 miles (6km) northwest of Woking. Covering 1400 acres (560ha) of lowland heath – a globally rare habitat – the common is a designated National Nature Reserve (the largest in southeast England), Site of Special Scientific Interest and Special Protection Area. It was also used as a military training ground in the 19th and 20th century: the composite armour known as Chobham armour, the type most commonly used in military vehicles today, was developed at the tank research centre in the 1960s. In the early 20th century 'treacle mines' were also reputedly discovered on the common (these were in fact surplus barrels of molasses buried by soldiers before going off to the Crimean War).

Clandon Park West Clandon, 2 miles (3km) east of Guildford. A Palladian-style house built by Venetian architect Giacomo Leoni in the early 1730s and now housing a fine collection of 18th century furniture, porcelain, textiles and carpets, including the Ivo Forde Meissen collection of Italian comedy figures and Mortlake tapestries. It also houses the Queen's Royal Surrey Regiment Museum. The property has been owned by the National Trust since 1956. Tel: 01483 222482.

Claremont House 1 mile (1.6km) southwest of Esher. An 18th century Palladian mansion with landscaped gardens. The house was built in 1768 by Robert Clive, founder of Britain's Indian Empire, to designs by Capability Brown and his future son-in-law Henry Holland. It replaced an earlier 18th century house built on lower ground by Sir John Vanbrugh, architect of Blenheim Palace and Castle Howard, and enlarged by Whig politician Thomas Pelham-Holles, Earl of Clare, who later became Duke of Newcastle and served twice as Prime Minister. When the Duke died in 1768, his widow sold the estate to Clive, who is reputed to have spent over £100,000 on the house and grounds but sadly never lived here – he died in 1774, the year the house was finished. In 1931, a school for girls from Christian Science families moved into Claremont. During World War II, the school was evacuated to Llandrindod Wells in Wales, and Claremont was let to the Hawker aircraft company, whose design team under Sidney Camm produced the Hawker Tempest fighter. The buildings are now occupied by Claremont Fan Court School. The National Trust acquired 50 acres (20ha) of the estate in 1949, and in 1975 set about restoring the magnificent 18th century landscape garden, in which can be seen the successive contributions of Vanbrugh, Charles Bridgeman, William Kent and Capability Brown. Tel: 01372 467806.

Cobham Mill Mill Road, Cobham. A small 19th century mill beside the River Mole. There were once three such mills in Cobham, dating from the time of the Domesday Book. A second, larger building, demolished in 1953, once stood alongside the present mill; barley or wheat could be ground in one and oats or rye in the other. The mill stands on a beautiful stretch of the Mole with a salmon ladder next to a weir. Tel: 01932 867387.

Cobham Bus Museum Redhill Road, Cobham. Housed in the surviving building of a former Vickers aircraft construction factory, the museum houses a collection of 30 historic London buses. Tel: 01932 868665.

Crafts Study Centre Falkner Road, Farnham. Based at the University for the Creative Arts and established in 1970, the centre holds unique collections and archives of 20th century and contemporary crafts including ceramics, textiles, calligraphy and furniture, accompanied by makers' diaries, working notes and photographs. It contains works from such significant figures as Bernard Leach, Lucie Rie, Hans Coper, Ethel Mairet, Phyllis Barron, Edward Johnston and Ernest Gimson. Tel: 01252 891453.

Cranleigh One of a number of villages claiming to be the largest in England. The first cottage hospital in England was opened in the village in 1859. In the High Street stands a fountain on top of which is Cranleigh's symbol, the crane, after which the town was named – although it adopted the present spelling of its name only in the 19th century, to avoid confusion with Crawley in Sussex. An old carving of a grinning cat inside St Nicholas' Church is thought to have been the inspiration for Lewis Carroll's Cheshire Cat. Pradjadhipok, the last absolute King of Siam (reigned 1925–35) and the 32nd son of King Chulalongkorn, died in Cranleigh in 1941.

Dapdune Wharf Wharf Road, Guildford. A former boat-building and repair yard on the Wey Navigation Canal, featuring a boat shed, forge, cottages and a hand-operated crane. There is also an exhibition including models and telling the story of the waterway and of the people who lived and worked on it. Tel: 01483 561389.

Devil's Punch Bowl ½ mile (0.8km) east of Hindhead, 7 miles (11km) southeast of Farnham. A large hollow of dry sandy heath overlooked by Gibbet Hill, the second highest point in Surrey at 895ft (273m), over which runs the old London–Portsmouth coach road. One story of its origin relates how, during the Middle Ages, the devil became so irritated by all the churches being built in Sussex that he decided to dig a channel from the English Channel, through the South Downs, and flood the area. He had reached the village of Poynings, near Devil's Dyke, when he was disturbed by a cock crowing (one version of the story claims that the prayers of St Dunstan made all the local cocks crow earlier than usual). Believing that dawn was about to break, he leapt into Surrey, creating the Devil's Punch Bowl where he landed. Another legend has it that the devil spent his time tormenting the god Thor by pelting him with enormous handfuls of earth, leaving the great bowl visible today. Tel: 01428 608771.

Diggers One of the many egalitarian social movements that grew up in England in the wake of the execution of Charles I. The Diggers originated in Surrey in April 1649, when they began cultivating common land at St George's Hill in Weybridge. Their name comes from the practice of digging and manuring the 'waste' and common land, which was carried out both to grow food and to show that everybody had a right to enjoy the Earth and its fruits. Believing that freedom from poverty, hunger and oppression could be achieved if the Earth were made a 'Common Treasury for all', the Diggers set up communal settlements. Many Diggers were residents of Cobham, including Gerrard Winstanley, their main spokesperson, who moved to the village from London with his wife Susan King in 1643. Another, Anthony Wren, probably lived in a cottage which still stands in The Ridings. After they were evicted from St George's Hill in August 1649 the Diggers continued their project on the Little Heath at Cobham. The brutality of their opponents meant they did not survive for long, but their writings and ideas continue to inspire environmental and egalitarian activists throughout the world.

Dorking A bustling market town nestling under the North Downs. The irregularly shaped High Street, one side of which is higher than the other, follows the route of the Roman Stane Street. Charles Dickens stayed at the White Horse Inn, parts of which date from the 16th century, and the Marquis of Granby in *The Pickwick Papers* is reputed to have been based on the King's Head, an inn which used to stand at the junction between North Street and High Street. Lord Nelson separated from his wife at the hotel in Burford Bridge (where he also spent his final night before the Battle of Trafalgar), outside the town. Composer Ralph Vaughan Williams lived in Dorking and founded the annual Leith Hill music festival. Since 1931 the festival has been held at the Dorking Halls, an amenity that Vaughan Williams helped create. The Tillingbourne valley inspired his haunting melody 'The Lark Ascending'. Lying beneath the town's historic streets and houses are the Dorking Caves, a fascinating labyrinth excavated from the greensand hills in the 17th century and sometimes used by smugglers. A new species of fish-eating dinosaur, *Baryonyx walkeri*, was discovered in clay pits just south of Dorking. The creature had a long curved claw on each hand and remains of its last meal were discovered fossilised in its ribcage. The skeleton can be seen at the Natural History Museum in London. Dorking has the largest concentration of antique dealers in England.

Dorking and District Museum The Old Foundry, West Street. A local history museum containing toys, agricultural and domestic bygones, fossils, birds, paintings, World War II memorabilia, costumes, photographs, prints, books, press cuttings, notebooks, local maps, radios and television sets.

Dunsfold Park Aerodrome ½ mile (0.8km) east of Dunsfold. Built by the Royal Canadian Army during World War II as an emergency landing field, after the war the airfield was used first by charter airline Skyways and, from 1951, for flight tests by Hawker Siddeley. Initial tests of the prototype of the Harrier, the first VTOL jet fighter-bomber, were carried out here in October 1960, and the aircraft's maiden flight took place here in 1967. Today the annual Wings and Wheels airshow is held at the airfield; the BBC motoring show *Top Gear* is also recorded on the former aerodrome. Tel: 01483 200900.

Epsom A town 7 miles (11km) north of Dorking, part of the borough of Epsom & Ewell since 1937 and today located on the outskirts of London's southwestern suburbs. Epsom existed at the time of the Domesday Book, its name possibly deriving from Anglo-Saxon *Ebbi's ham* (Ebbi being a Saxon landowner). In the 17th and 18th century Epsom was a spa town, although little of its history as a resort is visible nowadays. Epsom salts (magnesium sulphate heptahydrate) are named after the town and were originally prepared (in 1618) by boiling down the local mineral water.

Entertainments were held at the Assembly Rooms (built c.1690), now a pub. Epsom Racecourse (see Sport) is one of the oldest in England.

Farnham Located on the River Wey, the market town of Farnham occupies an ancient site, with evidence of human presence dating back to the Paleolithic period (400,000 years ago). The settlement first developed c.6000 BC and in Roman times the district's plentiful clay was used for pottery. An important grain and wool centre in the 17th and early 18th century, it has numerous old buildings, including a number of Georgian houses. There are also engineering and timber industries. The North Downs Way National Trail starts here.

Farnham Castle Castle Street, Farnham. Norman motte and bailey castle built as an episcopal fortress by the Bishops of Winchester. The original stone keep was built by Bishop Henry of Blois, brother of King Stephen, in the early 12th century, and rebuilt in the late 12th century when residential buildings were added to the south. The castle was surrendered to the French in 1216 but retaken the following year. The brick gatehouse was built by Bishop Waynflete of Winchester and completed by 1475. During the Tudor period Farnham Castle was used as the Bishop's residence. It was taken by Royalists in November 1642 and recaptured by Parliament the same month; retaken for a day by Royalists in January 1645, it was eventually slighted in 1648 before being returned to the bishopric of Winchester in 1660. The keep is managed by English Heritage, while the bishops' palace is owned by the Church Commissioners. Tel: 01252 721194.

Frensham Common 4 miles (6km) south of Farnham. Frensham Common's 922 acres (372ha) of attractive countryside comprises a large area of lowland heath, together with coniferous and mixed woodland. There are two large ponds, created in the 13th century to supply fish to the Bishops of Winchester at Farnham Castle, and known as Frensham Great and Little Pond. A designated Site of Special Scientific Interest and Special Protection Area with many species of rare heathland flora and fauna, the common is owned by the National Trust and managed by Waverley Borough Council.

Gatton Park 1 mile (1.6km) north of Redhill. A 250 acre (100ha) park which once lay at the centre of the manor of Gatton. The former medieval deer park was landscaped in the 1760s by Capability Brown and consists of grassland, woodland, ponds, a large lake and formal gardens, including a Japanese garden added by mustard manufacturer Sir Jeremiah Colman and restored in the late 1990s. Gatton Park is now home to the Royal Alexandra and Albert School. The estate is owned by the National Trust. Tel: 01737 649068.

Gibbet Hill See Devil's Punch Bowl

Godalming Located on the River Wey, 3 miles (5km) southwest of Guildford. Today a prosperous commuter town, in 1881 Godalming became the first town in the UK to install a public supply of electricity, and the first in the world to boast electric street lighting. The seven arc lights and 34 Swan incandescent lights were driven by a Siemens AC alternator and dynamo at Westbrook watermill, although they were later turned off as their supply proved too expensive for the town. The long history of Godalming is still evident in its architecture, from its parish church, with its Saxon chancel and Norman tower, to its 19th century town hall, nicknamed the Pepperpot. The town has around 230 listed buildings. Other significant buildings include Edwin Lutyens's Red House, and Charterhouse (see separate entry), one of England's best-known public schools.

Goddards Abinger Common, 4½ miles (7km) southwest of Dorking. Built by Edwin Lutyens 1898–1900 and enlarged by him in 1910. Designed in the traditional Surrey style and with a garden laid out in collaboration with Gertrude Jekyll, it is considered one of his most important early houses. Tel: 01628 825920.

Great Fosters Stroude Road, Egham. A 17th century country house with an Elizabethan core dating to c.1550, set in 50 acres (20ha) of parkland with gardens laid out in 1918 by W H Romaine-Walker and G H Jenkins. It has been a hotel since the 1930s. Tel: 01784 433822.

Great Tangley Manor 2 miles (3km) southeast of Guildford. A Grade I listed moated manor house, built in 1582 around an existing medieval hall house. The property was extended in the 1880s by Philip Webb, who also designed the gardens and moat. Novelist, poet and preacher George Macdonald (1824–1905), whose works include *Within and Without, Phantastes* and *David Eiginbrod*, lived at the house in the 1870s, and also lived in Haslemere and Ashtead.

Guildford Located on the River Wey, Guildford is the county town of Surrey, and also the seat of the borough of Guildford and the administrative headquarters of the South East England region. It was known in the Anglo-Saxon period as *Gyldeforda*, meaning either 'golden ford', a possible reference to the golden sand of the Wey, or a reference to golden flowers that grew on the spot. The town received its charter in 1257.

Guildford Castle Castle Street, Guildford. Norman motte and bailey castle built soon after 1066 by William I. The castle was rebuilt in stone during the 12th century by Henry I, with first a shell keep and then the strong but not very large tower keep that survives today. As the only royal castle in Surrey it became the centre for administration and justice, with the keep converted to use as the county gaol. The royal apartments were moved to a palace in the bailey, which under Henry III became one of the most luxurious royal residences in England. After Henry's death in 1272 the castle fell into decline and the palace buildings were allowed to fall into ruin. In 1611 the castle was bought by Guildford merchant Francis Carter, who attempted unsuccessfully to convert the keep into a private residence. In 1885 the ruins were bought by Guildford Borough Council and today are located in a public park.

Guildford Cathedral Stag Hill, Guildford. Dedicated to the Holy Spirit, Guildford Cathedral is the only cathedral to be built on a new site since the Reformation. Stag Hill is so named because the kings of England used to hunt in the area. The red-brick building with 160ft (49m) tower was begun in 1936 to a design by Sir Edward Maufe and consecrated in 1961, although completed only in 1968. The University of Surrey holds its graduation ceremonies in the cathedral. It provided a location for the classic horror film *The Omen* (1976), the golden wind-vane on top of the cathedral being added specifically for the film.

Guildford House Gallery — High Street, Guildford. A restored 17th century town house with a number of original features including a carved staircase and plasterwork ceilings, now housing the town's art gallery. Tel: 01483 444742.

Guildford Museum — Quarry Street, Guildford. Founded in 1898 and located in a 17th century building, the museum houses archaeology and local history collections as well as a fine collection of needlework. Tel: 01483 444750.

Hannah Peschar Sculpture Garden — Ockley, 10 miles (16km) southeast of Guildford. A 10 acre (4ha) landscaped garden housing an extensive and changing collection of contemporary sculpture by over 100 artists. Tel 01306 627269.

Haslemere — A small, attractive old country town, nestling in wooded hills in the southwest of Surrey, close to the Sussex/Hampshire border. It received its name from the hazel trees which surrounded a lake (or mere) which may once have been located on a site between Derby Road and the High Street. General James Edward Oglethorpe, who served as the town's MP 1722–54, was one of the founders of the colony of Georgia in North America. Fighting a duel in Haslemere High Street two days before his election, he ran his opponent through the stomach and even wounded the hand of someone who had tried to intervene and stop the fight. A month later he killed a man in London who had robbed him of a guinea. Having served five months in prison, he then took his seat in Parliament.

Hatchlands Park — East Clandon, 2½ miles (4km) northeast of Guildford. An 18th century house built in 1756 for Admiral Boscawen and featuring the earliest recorded interiors by Robert Adam. It contains the Cobbe Collection of keyboard instruments, many of which are associated with composers such as Purcell, Chopin and Mahler. The 430 acres (174ha) of parkland, laid out by Humphry Repton, feature a small garden designed by Gertrude Jekyll. Now owned by the National Trust. Tel: 01483 211474.

Highest point — Leith Hill at 968ft (295m), also the highest point on the North Downs and in southeast England. GR: TQ139431.

Hindhead — The highest village in Surrey lies at the crossroads between the London–Portsmouth coach route and the Farnham–Haslemere route and was a notorious spot for highwaymen. William Cobbett described Hindhead as 'the most villainous spot God ever created'.

Hog's Back — A narrow, elongated ridge forming part of the North Downs between Farnham in the west and Guildford in the east. The name was first recorded in 1823. An annual 10 mile (16m) road race is run over the Hog's Back, which also carries the main A31 road.

Holmbury St Mary — A village 8 miles (13km) southeast of Guildford. Much it was developed in the 19th century and was called Felday until 1879. Previously the area was known as a refuge for smugglers and sheep stealers. The new name was taken from Holmbury Hill and the newly built village church of St Mary. Holmbury Hill, 1 mile (1.6km) to the south, stands at 857ft (261m). At its summit are the earthworks of an Iron Age hill fort, and the views over the North and South Downs are spectacular.

Holmesdale Natural History Museum — Croydon Road, Reigate. The extensive collections of the Holmesdale Natural History Club (founded 1857) include insects, stuffed birds, herbarium and geological specimens, local history and archaeological finds.

Horsley Towers — East Horsley, 5 miles (8km) northeast of Guildford. A large Gothic mansion in 70 acres (28ha) of parkland. Designed by Sir Charles Barry, architect of the Houses of Parliament, it was the home of Ada, Lady Lovelace (daughter of Lord Byron and known as the first computer programmer) and later of aviation pioneer Sir Thomas Sopwith, creator of the legendary Sopwith Camel aeroplane and the inspiration behind the modern jet fighter. The house featured in the 1972 BBC television drama *The Stone Tape* as 'Taskerlands'.

Inglis Memorial — ½ mile (0.8km) northwest of Reigate. Located at Colley Hill, adjoining Reigate Hill, the memorial is one of the most distinctive features along the North Downs Way. A folly built in 1909 by Lt. Col. Lawrence Inglis originally as a drinking fountain for horses, it now contains a direction finder. The roof of the round, colonnaded monument is decorated with mosaic images of the heavens.

Interesting facts — **Agatha Christie** went missing for 11 days in December 1926. Around 9.45pm on Friday 3 December, without warning, she drove away from Styles, her house in Berkshire, having first gone upstairs to kiss her sleeping daughter, Rosalind. Her car was later found on a grass slope at Newlands Corner in Surrey. No body was found and it was conjectured that she had drowned herself in the nearby Silent Pool (see separate entry). Such was the speculation that Home Secretary William Joynson-Hicks put pressure on the police to make faster progress. Even the celebrated crime writers Sir Arthur Conan Doyle, creator of Sherlock Holmes, and Dorothy L Sayers, author of the Lord Peter Wimsey series, were drawn into the puzzle. Conan Doyle, who was interested in the occult, took a discarded glove of Christie's to a medium, while Sayers visited the scene of the disappearance, later using it in the novel *Unnatural Death*. Christie was eventually discovered safe, but in circumstances that raised more questions than they answered. Alone, and using the assumed name of Teresa Neele, she had been living in a spa hotel in Harrogate since the day after her disappearance, even though news of her case had reached as far as the front page of the *New York Times*. The latest theory is that Christie was suffering from a fugue depressive state, although the two most popular theories offered for these strange events have been that either she was suffering from memory loss after a car crash, or that she had planned the whole thing to thwart her husband's plans to spend a weekend with his mistress at a house close to where she abandoned her car. The **Epsom Derby** was run over a mile for its first four years before being extended to its present distance of 1½ miles. Edward Smith-Stanley, 12th

Earl of Derby (whose horse Bridget was the winner of the first-ever Oaks at Epsom) and Sir Charles Bunbury flipped a coin and whoever won the toss was to have the race named after him. Despite losing the toss, Sir Charles was to claim victory in the inaugural race with his horse Diomed, the Earl having to wait until 1787 for his first success, Sir Peter Teazle, ridden by Mr S Arnull. **Mike Hawthorn** resided in Farnham when he won the 1958 Formula One world title. Only months later, on 22 January 1959, he died in an automobile accident on the A3 Guildford bypass while driving his British Racing Green Jaguar 3.4 sedan. The village of **Bramley** is in the *Guinness Book of Records* as the first cricket ground to host an all-women's cricket match back in 1745, on Gosden Common where Bramley Cricket Club play today. The names of the villages of **Titsey** and nearby **Tatsfield** were made into the portmanteau word Titfield for the 1952 Ealing classic film *The Titfield Thunderbolt*. Scientist **John Tyndall** (1820–93) lived in Hindhead. Realising that food did not go off due to putrid vapours in the air, he devised methods of food preservation. His wide-ranging subjects of study included the movement of glaciers, the acoustic properties of air and the radiant property of heat, and he did much to expound the theories of Charles Darwin. A favourite of Michael Faraday, he succeeded Faraday at the Royal Institution, also taking over many of Faraday's other posts upon his retirement. Tyndall met a tragic end. Having married late at the age of 56, as an old man he suffered from insomnia and his wife gave him a fatal dose of an opiate. Realising too late, Tyndall's dying words were 'Darling, you have killed your John.' He lies under a mound in an unmarked grave in St Bartholomew's Church, Hindhead. Henry Thomas Hope (1808–62), a prolific writer on art and architecture who lived at Deepdene House, which once stood in Betchworth Park near Dorking, was the owner of the **Hope Diamond**, which he inherited from his uncle, Philip Henry Hope, in 1839. It was said to have been cut from the Tavernier, the largest blue diamond in the world, named after a traveller in the East who had bought it in India and sold it to Louis XIV in 1668. The Tavernier was one of the French crown jewels stolen in 1793. The Hope Diamond supposedly brought bad luck on the family and was itself eventually sold in 1867, five years after Henry's death. **Benjamin Disraeli** wrote his novel *Coningsby* in Deepdene House, which was unfortunately demolished in 1969. Although born in Cheshire, the Rev. Charles Lutwidge Dodgson (1832–98), better known as **Lewis Carroll**, author of *Alice's Adventures in Wonderland* and *Through the Looking Glass*, is one of Surrey's best known and loved writers. The recently arrived Victorian railway meant Carroll could live in Guildford and work in Oxford in his role as Oxford mathematics lecturer, 1855–81. The Chestnuts, the house in which he lived with his sisters, is located just outside Guildford Castle. It is still a private house, and apart from a plaque designed by local schoolchildren, there is nothing to indicate this to be Carroll's house. He died in Guildford and is buried in the Mount Cemetery. Farmer, pamphleteer, radical and social commentator **William Cobbett** (1762–1835) was born in Farnham and started out in life as a crow-scarer and ploughboy. An assiduous student, he mastered French, rhetoric, geometry, logic and fortifications. Cobbett joined the army when he was 21 but had to flee to America in 1791 after making accusations of military corruption. The original publisher of *Hansard*, the guide to Parliamentary proceedings, then known simply as the Register, Cobbett is best known for his *Rural Rides* (1830). His social observations and commentary, extracted from the Register, are the best insight we have today of social conditions during his lifetime. Cobbett's *Cottage Economy*, originally a series of pamphlets, was first published as a book in 1822. Not far from Farnham Maltings is the William Cobbett, formerly the Jolly Farmer and renamed in the 1970s in honour of Cobbett. This was Cobbett's home, and was a farmhouse at the time of his birth. **E M Forster** (1879–1970) used to visit his aunt at Abinger when he was a child and later spent 40 years of his adult life in Surrey. While living at Monument Green, Weybridge, he wrote *A Passage to India* (1924). Later in 1924 Forster inherited the lease to West Hackhurst, where he lived until 1946. Although written before Forster lived in Surrey, the setting for the bathing scene with Lucy Honeychurch in *A Room With a View* (1908) is believed to be a pond at Holmbury St Mary, and the village of Summer Street is based on the village itself. **Aldous Huxley** (1894–1963), author of *Brave New World* (1932), was born in Godalming and his father taught at nearby Charterhouse School. The family lived in Compton. Huxley loved to cycle in the Surrey Hills, especially around Hindhead and the Devil's Punchbowl. **H G Wells** (1866–1946) lived in Woking for 18 months with his second wife Amy. *The Wheels of Chance, The Invisible Man* (1897), *The War of the Worlds* (1898) and the opening chapters of *Love and Mr Lewisham* (1900), moreover, were all written while he lived in the town. *The Wheels of Chance* draws heavily on his bicycle trips with his wife around the local lanes. *The War of the Worlds* opens on Horsell Common, just outside Woking, where the Martians first land, and a series of sculptures in the town centre, including a Martian Fighting Machine as described by Wells, commemorate Woking's fictional destruction.

Islands — See separate table. Please note that some islands, although geographically in Greater London, are administered by Surrey County Council.

Juniper Hall — $^1/_2$ mile (0.8km) south of Mickleham, 2 miles (3km) north of Dorking. Originally the Royal Oak coaching inn, Juniper Hall is situated at the foot of Box Hill. Enlarged and remodelled by Sir Cecil Bishop in the 1750s, with a classical portico, tall arched windows and delicate plasterwork interiors, in 1792–3 it was rented to a number of refugees from the French reign of terror, including Mme de Staël and Tallyrand. Fanny Burney took French lessons here from General D'Arblay, later marrying him at Mickleham Church. Today Juniper Hall is owned by the National Trust and leased by the Field Studies Council. Tel: 0845 458 3507.

Leith Hill — 1 mile (1.6km) southwest of Coldharbour, 4 miles (6km) southwest of Dorking. Leith Hill reaches 968ft (295m) above sea level, the highest point on the North Downs and in southeast England. It was on the summit of the hill in 851 that Ethelwulf, father of Alfred the Great, defeated the Danes who were heading for Winchester, having sacked Canterbury and London. Now owned by the National Trust. **Leith Hill Tower**, originally named Prospect House, was built c.1766 by Richard Hull of nearby Leith Hill Place (once home to composer Ralph Vaughan Williams) with the intention of raising the hill above 1000ft (305m). The tower is 65ft high (20m) and consists of two rooms, with a Latin inscription above the door announcing that it was built for not only Hull's own pleasure, but also for the enjoyment of others. Hull provided visitors with prospect glasses, similar to a small telescope, through which to survey the extensive views towards London and the English Channel, and 13 counties on a very clear day. When he died in 1772, at his request he was buried under the tower, upside down as he believed that at Judgement Day the world would be turned on its head. Following his death, the building fell into ruin, but it was restored by the National Trust in the 1980s.

Loseley Park — 2 miles (3km) southwest of Guildford. An Elizabethan mansion set amid attractive parkland with walled garden and lake. Built in 1562 by Sir William More to entertain Elizabeth I, its mellow stone was brought from the ruins of Waverley Abbey. Furniture on display includes an early 16th century Wrangelschrank cabinet, a Queen Anne cabinet, a Hepplewhite four-poster bed and King George VI's coronation chair. Tel: 01483 405120.

Mormon Temple — Newchapel, 5 miles (8km) east of Horley. The London England Temple is owned and operated by the Church of Jesus Christ of Latter-day Saints. It was the first Mormon temple to be built in the UK; construction began on 27 August 1955, and the temple was dedicated on 9 September 1958.

Munstead Wood — Busbridge, 1 mile (1.6km) south of Godalming. The home of garden designer Gertrude Jekyll from the 1890s. The house was designed by Edwin Lutyens and completed in 1896; the surrounding 15 acre (6ha) garden was designed by Jekyll herself in an early expression of her naturalistic style, with woodland walks, daffodil drifts, primula banks and mixed flower border. Jekyll spent her childhood in Bramley, south of Guildford, and returned to the village to design a garden in Snowdenham Lane.

Newark Priory — 2 miles (3km) east of Woking. An Augustinian priory beside the River Wey, founded in the late 12th century by Ruald de Clane and dedicated to the Virgin Mary and Thomas Becket. The ruins visible today, which include substantial flint walls, are not accessible to the public.

Newlands Corner — 3 miles (5km) southeast of Guildford. Part of Albury Downs in the beautiful Tillingbourne valley. There are extensive views over the surrounding hills and farmland. It is famous as the area where Agatha Christie abandoned her car before catching a train to Harrogate in 1926.

Nonsuch Palace — Nonsuch Park, Cheam. Begun in 1538, the greatest of Henry VIII's building enterprises took nine years to construct and was completed at a cost of at least £24,000. It was located on the site of the church and village of Cuddington, which were demolished to make way for the palace. Designed on a basic plan of inner and outer courtyards, each with a fortified gatehouse, Nonsuch was richly and ornately decorated in competition with Chambord, the palace of Henry's rival Francis I. The northern side was a more medieval-style fortification, while the southern face was decorated in Renaissance fashion intended only for display. The south side had tall eight-sided towers at each end. On Henry's death the palace passed first to Edward VI and then to Mary I, who sold it to the Earl of Arundel. Later, the palace returned to the Crown when it was sold to Elizabeth I. Nonsuch passed in and out of royal hands through the early and mid 17th century and was eventually broken up to be incorporated into new buildings in 1672. No trace of the palace now remains, but remnants have been excavated and are on display in various locations, including the British Museum. Nonsuch is a ward of both Greater London and Surrey; the site of the old palace is in Surrey although Cheam is in Greater London.

Norbury Park — 2 miles (3km) north of Dorking. The large, neglected estate in the Mole Gap was purchased in 1774 by William Locke, who created an impressive country seat and parkland landscape sited to take advantage of the breathtaking views from the top of the North Downs. Today the house is in private ownership, but Surrey County Council own the majority of the 1300 acre (520ha) estate, which is managed by Surrey Wildlife Trust. Norbury Park provided the inspiration for the novel *Camilla* by Fanny Burney, who lived in a cottage in nearby Westhumble.

North Downs Way — See Kent

Nutfield Priory — 1¼ miles (2km) east of Redhill. A country mansion dating from 1872, set high on Nutfield ridge with breathtaking views of the Sussex and Surrey countryside. The original house was built 1849–54 by Thomas Fowler Wood and extended 1855–9 for Quaker banker Henry Edward Gurney. When he became bankrupt, the house and lands were sold to Joshua Fielden MP of Todmorden in Lancashire, who built the present house to designs by architect John Gibson. Featuring examples of craftsmanship such as original wood carving, stonework and panelling, the house is now a luxury hotel. Tel: 01737 824400.

Oakhurst Cottage — Hambledon, 3 miles (5km) south of Godalming. A small 16th century timber-framed cottage, restored and furnished as a simple labourer's dwelling and containing artefacts reflecting four centuries of life in rural Surrey. The cottage has been painted by both Helen Allingham and Myles Birket Foster. Owned by the National Trust. Tel: 01483 208477.

Outwood Windmill — ½ mile (0.8km) east of Outwood, 3 miles (5km) northeast of Horley. A post mill located on Outwood Common; built in 1665, it is the oldest working windmill in Britain.

Painshill Park — 1 mile (1.6km) west of Cobham, A notable 18th century Augustan landscape garden created 1738–73 by the Hon. Charles Hamilton, who returned from his Grand Tour of Europe inspired by the art and architecture he had seen and enthusiastically set about transforming a strip of land near the River Mole into a series of picturesque landscape scenes. The garden's features include a Gothic temple, a Chinese bridge, a ruined abbey, Turkish tent and an elaborate island grotto. The Grade I listed landscape has been undergoing comprehensive restoration since the 1980s. Tel: 01932 868113.

Polesden Lacey — 3 miles (5km) northwest of Dorking. The much loved house of playwright Richard Brinsley Sheridan, who purchased it in 1804. Before he was 30 Sheridan had eloped to France, fought a duel, studied law, written *The Rivals* and *School for Scandal*, purchased the Drury Lane theatre, bought a London house and been elected MP for Stafford; now he was able to indulge himself in the role of a country squire, lavishly entertaining his friends and the local populace. Originally built in 1630 by Anthony Rous on the site of a previous medieval house, Polesden Lacey was extensively remodelled 1906–09 by the Hon. Mrs Ronald Greville, Edwardian hostess and intimate friend of Edward VII, who later lent it to the future George VI and Queen Elizabeth for their honeymoon. The extensive grounds feature a walled rose garden and landscaped walks. Now owned by the National Trust. Tel: 01372 452048.

Pride of the Valley Sculpture Park — Churt, 5 miles (8km) south of Farnham. One of the most atmospheric sculpture parks in Britain. Adjoining Frensham Country Park at the foothills of Devils Jumps, the park features over 200 sculptures set in a variety of landscapes including lawns, low-lying bog, coniferous and deciduous woodland, hillsides and valleys. There are three lakes fed by two fast flowing streams. Tel: 07831 500506.

Ramster Gardens — Ramster, 1$^1/_2$ miles (2.5km) south of Chiddingfold. A 20 acre (8ha) woodland and shrub garden laid out in the early 20th century. Tel: 01428 654167.

Reigate — Situated at the foot of the North Downs, the town of Reigate dates from Saxon times. In 1150 the de Warenne family constructed a new town beneath the castle. Reigate's Old Town Hall, dating from 1708, is in a prominent position at one end of the High Street, on the site of the original market place. Reigate Castle Tunnel, constructed under the castle grounds in 1823, is believed to be Europe's first road tunnel. Overlooking the town is Reigate Hill, owned by the National Trust, with spectacular views over the Weald and South Downs. Reigate Fort, which stands on the hill, is one of 13 mobilisation centres established in the 1890s to protect London from invasion.

Reigate Castle — London Road, Reigate. Founded as a motte and bailey castle by William de Warenne in the late 11th century and rebuilt in stone by his son, the 2nd Earl of Surrey. By 1441 the castle was described as 'ruinous'; reoccupied during the Civil War, it was demolished in 1648 and only earthworks remain. Reigate Caves, beneath the remains of the castle, were excavated to connect the keep with the town below. Today the castle grounds, including an 18th century folly gatehouse, form an attractive public park.

Reigate Heath Windmill — 1$^1/_2$ miles (2.5km) west of Reigate. Probably the only windmill in the world to have been consecrated as a church. Located on Reigate Heath, the wooden post mill on a brick base, also known as the Heath Church, dates from at least 1765. In 1880 the brick roundhouse of the disused mill was converted into St Cross Chapel, a chapel of ease belonging to St Mary's Church in Reigate. Services are still held in the tiny church.

Reigate Priory — Bell Street, Reigate. An Augustinian priory founded in the early 13th century by William de Warenne, 6th Earl of Surrey, and dedicated to the Virgin Mary. After its dissolution in 1536, Henry VIII granted the estate to Lord William Howard who converted the building into a residence for his family. The elegant Palladian façade dates from 1779. The Grade I listed building now houses both Reigate Priory School and Reigate Priory Museum. The museum's collection of local history, artefacts, domestic items and period costumes are displayed in atmospheric settings. Reigate Priory stands in the 200 acre (80ha) Priory Park, overlooked by the North Downs and containing a lake, beautiful gardens and woodland.

Rivers — The **Ash** flows through the borough of Spelthorne, passing through the towns of Ashford and Shepperton before finally reaching the River Thames in Sunbury.

The **Blackwater** is a tributary of the River Loddon. It rises at Rowhill on the outskirts of Aldershot in Hampshire and flows northwards to join the Loddon near the village of Swallowfield in Berkshire. Along part of its length, the river forms Hampshire/Surrey border.

The **Ember** merges with the River Mole near Molesey and jointly flows into the River Thames near Hampton Court Palace on the outskirts of London.

The **Hogsmill** is one of the tributaries of the River Thames, 6 miles (10km) in length. Its source is a chalk spring in the spring-line village of Ewell.

The **Mole** rises in West Sussex near Gatwick Airport and flows northwards. At Molesey, it merges with the River Ember and jointly flows into the River Thames. It is so named because it flows underground in several places between Dorking and Leatherhead.

The **Rye** is a stream rising east of Ashtead and flowing into the River Mole near Leatherhead.

Thames see London

The **Wandle** is 9 miles (15km) long. It runs through southwest London, reaching the Thames at Wandsworth.

The **Wey** is a tributary of the River Thames. The source of the north branch is at Alton, Hampshire, and of the south branch at Liphook. The branches join at Tilford. The Wey was made navigable to barges in 1653, linking Guildford to Weybridge and the Thames in one direction and later in the other direction to Godalming. Around 20 miles (32km) of the river from Godalming to the Thames at Weybridge is still navigable.

Royal Earlswood Hospital — Earlswood, 1 mile (1.6km) south of Redhill. An early psychiatric hospital financed by public subscription and built 1853–5 to a design by Mr Moffat by John Jay, who was also responsible for the 1833 rebuilding of the Houses of Parliament. The hospital housed the autistic savant James Henry Pullen (1835–1916), known as the 'Genius of Earlswood Asylum' and once famous for his detailed models of ships and wonderfully carved works of art. His masterpiece, a model of Brunel's *Great Eastern*, was exhibited at the Crystal Palace. In the 20th century the hospital was home for several decades to two of the Queen Mother's nieces: Nerissa Bowes-Lyon (1919–86) and Katherine Bowes-Lyon (b.1926). The sisters, both born mentally impaired, received no visits from the royal family and were reportedly declared dead by Buckingham Palace. The hospital closed in 1997; the Royal Earlswood Museum, housed in the Belfry Centre in Redhill, illustrates the history and development of the asylum. On display is a representative collection of the works of James Henry Pullen.

Royal Grammar School — High Street, Guildford. Founded in 1509 with a bequest from London grocer Robert Beckingham, the school received its royal charter from Edward VI in 1552. It the first place where the game of cricket is recorded as having been played, c.1550, and houses a rare chained library dating to c.1575 and established with a bequest of books from John Parkhurst, Bishop of Norwich. Former pupils include actor, director and former Monty Python member Terry Jones and cricketer Bob Willis.

Royal Holloway College — 1 mile (1.6km) northwest of Egham. Located on Egham Hill, the vast and ornate Royal Holloway College was built 1879–87 by philanthropist Thomas Holloway, whose fortune had been made in patent medicine. The design of the elaborate Founder's Building was based on that of the Château de Chambord in the Loire Valley, France. Opened by Queen Victoria in 1886, Royal Holloway was one of the first colleges for women. It became a member of the University of London in 1900 and began admitting male students in 1945.

Runnymede — 1/2 mile (0.8km) northwest of Egham. An area of water meadows and woodlands between Egham and the River Thames, part of which is a designated Site of Special Scientific Interest. Runnymede was the location of the sealing of the Magna Carta in 1215; a domed classical temple designed by Sir Edward Maufe, on which is inscribed 'To commemorate Magna Carta, symbol of Freedom Under Law', was erected by the American Bar Association in 1957. The men and women of the Allied air forces who died during World War II are commemorated by the Air Forces Memorial on Cooper's Hill, which records the names of the 20,456 airmen who have no known grave; also designed by Sir Edward Maufe, it was unveiled in 1953. There is also a memorial to John F Kennedy, designed by Geoffrey Jellicoe and unveiled in 1965. Owned by the National Trust. Tel: 01784 432891.

St Mary's Church — Stoke D'Abernon, 3 miles (5km) northwest of Leatherhead. Dating from the 7th or 8th century AD, the church has a fine selection of brasses including Britain's oldest complete brass, dating from c.1320 and commemorating Sir John d'Abernon the Elder.

Sandhurst — Sandhurst, 1 mile (1.6km) west of Camberley. The Royal Military Academy Sandhurst (RMAS), formed in 1947, was descended from two older institutions, the Royal Military Academy (RMA) and the Royal Military College (RMC). The RMA was founded in 1741 at Woolwich to train gentlemen cadets for the Royal Artillery and Royal Engineers, and later for the Royal Corps of Signals and Royal Tank Corps, and remained at Woolwich until it was closed in 1939; the RMC began in 1800 as a school for staff officers which later became the Staff College, Camberley. The motto of the new RMAS was 'Serve to Lead', replacing the Latin '*Sua Tela Tonanti*' (Their weapons are thunderbolts) and '*Vires Aquirit Eundo*' (It gains strength as it goes) of the RMA and RMC respectively. The Academy straddles the border between the counties of Hampshire, Berkshire and Surrey, marked by a small stream known as the Wish Stream, after which the Academy journal is named. All British Army officers, and many from elsewhere in the world, are trained at Sandhurst. The Commissioning Course, lasting 44 weeks, must be passed by most British regular army officers before they receive their commission. Shorter commissioning courses are run for 'professionally qualified officers' (e.g. doctors, dentists, nurses, vets and chaplains) and Territorial Army officers. This shorter course, lasting just four weeks, is known colloquially as the 'Vicars and Tarts course'. Tel: 01276 63344.

Savill Garden — 1 mile (1.6km) west of Englefield Green, 2 miles (3km) southwest of Egham. A world-renowned 35 acre (14ha) woodland garden created in 1932 by Sir Eric Savill within Windsor Great Park. It features spring displays of camellias, magnolias, rhododendrons and azaleas, with formal rose gardens and herbaceous borders in summer, spectacular autumn colour and many winter-flowering species and evergreens. Tel: 01784 435544.

Shepperton Studios — Studios Road, Shepperton. The studios, originally named Sound City, began producing films at the 17th century Littleton Park estate in 1931. Renamed British Lion in 1946, the studios became the home of directors such as the Boulting brothers and Frank Launder and Sidney Gilliat, producing highly regarded British films of the 1950s and 60s such as *I'm All Right Jack* (1959), *Room at the Top* (1959) and *Billy Liar* (1963). In the 1970s credits included two Pink Panther films and the studios were also the base of low-budget horror production company Amicus. More recent productions include *Gandhi* (1982), *A Passage to India* (1984), Kenneth Branagh's *Henry V* (1989), *Shadowlands* (1993) and *The Madness of King George* (1994). The studios, owned since 1995 by directors Ridley and Tony Scott, were taken over by Pinewood Studios (famed for the James Bond movies) in 2002; the merger created a much larger company that could attract big-budget film-makers, although the two studios have maintained their individual trading identities. Many of the special effects in *The Da Vinci Code* (2006) were created at Shepperton. In 2005 Pinewood Shepperton acquired Teddington Studios. Tel: 01932 562611.

Silent Pool — 1/2 mile (0.8km) northeast of Albury, 4 miles (6km) southeast of Guildford. A spring-fed pool which has been a popular beauty spot since Victorian times. The pool was once known for its eerie silence but birdsong can be heard frequently nowadays. The long hot summer of 2006 caused the pool to all but dry up. When Agatha Christie's Morris Cowley was found at nearby Newlands Corner after her disappearance in 1926, it was suggested by some that she had drowned herself in the pool (see Interesting Facts).

Sport

cricket — **Surrey County Cricket Club** was founded in 1845. One of the most successful teams in the English first-class game, with 18 outright County Championship wins and one shared title – they have been described by some as the Manchester United of cricket – they won the championship in seven consecutive seasons, 1952–8. Unusually, their two main grounds, the famous Brit Oval, Kennington, their home since 1846, and Whitgift School, Croydon, are both in Greater London. The limited overs team is called Surrey Brown Caps. Tel: 0871 246 1100. See also London

football — **Woking** were founded in 1889 and first gained promotion to the Vauxhall Conference in 1992. Nicknamed The Cardinals after their traditional red strip, their home ground is Kingfield Stadium, Woking. Tel: 01483 772470.

golf — **Wentworth Golf Club**, Virginia Water, has three 18-hole championship courses and one 9-hole course, set in Surrey heathland and surrounded by pine, oak and birch woodland. The West or 'Burma Road' Course, opened in 1926, appears on TV more regularly than any other in the UK, as it hosts three professional tournaments (the World Matchplay, the PGA and the Senior Masters). It was also the venue for the fiercely contested 1953 Ryder Cup, which resulted in an American victory by a single point. The course was requisitioned by the army during World War II and allowed to grow wild; its alternative name reputedly derives from its clearance late in the war by German prisoners, for whom it was supposedly described by an overseeing British officer as 'their Burma Road'. Tel: 01344 842201.

horse racing — **Epsom Downs**, an undulating left handed Flat course of 1 mile 4 furlongs (2.5km), is home to the Derby and the Oaks, two world-famous classic races for three-year-olds. The Derby was inaugurated by Sir Charles Bunbury and first run in 1780, being won by Diomed ridden by Mr S Arnull; the fillies' classic the Oaks was first run in 1779 and won by Bridget, ridden by Mr R Goodison. Tel: 01372 726311.

Kempton Park, Staines Road East, Sunbury-on-Thames, is a right-handed triangular course of 1 mile 5 furlongs (2.6km). The Jubilee Course of 1¼ miles (2km) forms a long spur that joins the round course at around 3½ furlongs out. Kempton Park stages both National Hunt and Flat racing, the most famous race being the King George VI Chase held every Boxing Day. It was reopened on 25 March 2006 with a new all-weather track and floodlighting. Tel: 01932 782292.

Lingfield Park, Racecourse Road, Lingfield, holds National Hunt and Flat racing on a left-handed triangular track of 1 mile 4 furlongs (2.5km) and an all-weather course of just under 1¼ miles (2km). Tel: 01342 834800.

Sandown Park, Esher, is a right-handed dual circuit of 1 mile 5 furlongs (2.6km). The Flat course is uphill for last ¾ mile (1.2km). Home to the famous Eclipse Stakes on the Flat and the Whitbread Gold Cup over hurdles. Tel: 01372 463072.

ice hockey — **Guildford Flames** play in the English Premier Ice Hockey League and are based at the Spectrum Sports Centre, Stoke Park, Guildford.

Staines — The Thameside town of Staines in the north of Surrey is an ancient settlement, established by the Romans shortly after AD 43. The first Staines Bridge was built shortly afterwards, and the settlement was known in Roman times as Ad Pontes (Latin 'at the bridges'). After the arrival of the railway in 1848 Staines became a manufacturing centre, famous for the production of linoleum. Its inventor, Frederick Walton, established a factory in the town in 1864 and this continued to be the area's major employer until its closure in 1970. The industry is commemorated by a bronze statue in Staines High Street depicting two workers carrying a roll of linoleum. Today the Two Rivers shopping centre stands on the site of the factory. During World War II, Staines was the English base of the French Resistance, and many artefacts relating to the Resistance are on display in the council offices. Staines has achieved a certain notoriety in recent years as the home of the Staines Massive, a fictional black gang of youths fronted by comic actor Sacha Baron-Cohen's satirical creation, Ali G.

Surrey — A light four-wheeled horse-drawn carriage with two or four seats. It takes its name from an adaptation of the Surrey Cart, originally made in Surrey.

Surrey Capon — The traditional nickname for people from Surrey, which was well known in the late Middle Ages as the county where chickens were fattened up for London meat markets. Like many traditional nicknames, it is seldom heard today.

Surrey Docks — See London

Surrey Heath Museum — Knoll Road, Camberley. A small museum housed in Surrey Heath's civic office complex and including displays relating to local archaeology, geology, local building materials, place names, highwaymen, transport, local industries, the development of the military town and the promotion of Camberley as a Victorian health resort. Tel: 01276 707284.

Surrey Iron Railway — See London

Surrey loam — A soil dressing containing a clay base, used for producing and renovating cricket pitches and other sporting facilities, such as golf and bowling greens.

Surrey Police Museum — Sandy Lane, Guildford. Officially opened on 22 October 2001 at Mount Browne, the headquarters of Surrey Police, by Surrey resident Sir Michael Caine to celebrate the 150th anniversary of the Surrey Constabulary. Policing of the county began on 1 January 1851 with just 70 officers, the youngest of whom was only 14 years old. Exhibits include changing interactive displays on the history of Surrey's police and a reconstructed lock-up. Tel: 01483 482155.

Sutton Place — 3 miles (5km) north of Guildford. The great Tudor mansion of Sutton Place was the creation of Sir Richard Weston, a loyal and influential courtier of Henry VIII. It is rumoured that Ann Boleyn first met Henry here and that Sir Richard's son lost his head for getting too close to her. The house was later owned by press baron Lord Northcliffe, who in the early 20th century commissioned Gertrude Jekyll to design the west walled garden. Billionaire John Paul Getty was the house's most famous resident, spending the last 25 years of his life here until his death in 1976. The five-times married oil magnate, notorious for his penny-pinching, installed pay phones in the house. The house's 20th century garden was designed in 1980 by Geoffrey Jellicoe for Stanley J Seeger.

With his developing interest in psychologist C G Jung, Jellicoe saw the design as an allegory of human evolution; among his creations are a paradise garden, a moss garden, a music garden and a surrealist garden. Perhaps most notable is the Nicholson Wall, a white marble relief created by abstract artist Ben Nicholson. Frederick Koch is the current owner of the property.

Titsey Place 1½ miles (2.5km) north of Limpsfield. One of the largest surviving historic estates in Surrey, Titsey dates to the mid 16th century. The current house was built in the early 19th century and is set within picturesque parkland beneath the North Downs, which rise to more than 800ft (244m) above the house. Only the M25 motorway intrudes into a landscape which is otherwise hardly changed in the last 100 years. The estate was originally bought in 1534 by London merchant Sir John Gresham, and descended in the early 19th century through the female line to the Leveson Gowers, a cadet branch of the family of the Dukes of Sutherland. The family lived at Titsey until the death of Thomas Leveson Gower in 1992. The house contains a unique set of four Venetian landscapes by Canaletto, while the remains of an unusual Roman villa, laid out on a corridor plan, were discovered in the grounds in 1847. The house and gardens have only been open to the public since 1993. Tel: 01273 715359.

Undershaw Portsmouth Road, Hindhead. The home from 1897 to 1907 of Sir Arthur Conan Doyle (1859–1930), who built the house above Hindhead, close to the Devil's Punch Bowl, in the hope that its location would help to improve the health of his first wife, who suffered from tuberculosis. Sadly she died from the disease in 1906, but Conan Doyle always maintained that the clean air of 'the English Switzerland', as the area was called, had considerably prolonged her life. The house and the surrounding countryside feature in some of the adventures of Sherlock Holmes published in *The Strand* magazine. The space in the attic under the eaves disguised to look like cupboards is said to have provided the inspiration for 'The Adventure of the Norwood Builder', while 'The Adventure of the Solitary Cyclist' features Crooksbury Hill, a prominent sandy outcrop overlooking Farnham. Two of Conan Doyle's adventure novels, *Sir Nigel* and *The White Company*, are set in Surrey, and *The Hound of the Baskervilles* was written here in 1902. Visitors to Undershaw included H G Wells. The house was a hotel from 1924 until 2004, but is currently empty.

University of Surrey The University of Surrey received its charter on 9 September 1966 but has its roots in Battersea Polytechnic Institute, founded in 1891 to improve access to further and higher education for the 'poorer inhabitants' of London. The university, which specialises in science and technology, moved in 1968 to a 83 acre (30ha) site on Stag Hill in Guildford, adjacent to the cathedral. In 1985 the university established the Surrey Research Park, which accommodates over 100 companies engaged in research and development activities, many relating closely to the work of the university's own schools. In 1991 the university was granted the Queen's Award for Export Achievement, and in 1997 it received the Queen's Anniversary Prize for Higher & Further Education in recognition of the outstanding teaching and research carried out by the Centre for Satellite Engineering Research. More recently it was awarded the 2002 Queen's Anniversary Prize for Higher & Further Education, this time for research and development on optoelectronic devices and ion beam applications. For a university of its size and age, Surrey has a high number of academicians of the learned societies on its staff: 10 Fellows of the Royal Society, 21 Fellows of the Royal Academy of Engineering, one Fellow of the British Academy and six Fellows of the Academy of Social Sciences. Led Zeppelin performed their very first gig at the University of Surrey on 15 October 1968. Former students include TV child psychologist Dr Tanya Byron, broadcaster Jeremy Kyle, and restaurateur and businessman Robert Earl. Tel: 01483 300800.

Virginia Water 4 miles (6km) west of Staines. A lake within the southeastern corner of Windsor Great Park. Virginia Water is also the name to a village at the eastern end of the lake in the borough of Runnymede, and associated with affluent showbusiness residents. The lake itself was created from a smaller body of water of the same name which existed from at least the 17th century; possibly named after Elizabeth I (the 'Virgin Queen'), this was originally little more than a stream. William, Duke of Cumberland, then ranger of the park, began enlarging the lake in 1746; it has been suggested that prisoners-of-war from the recent Jacobite risings, encamped at the nearby Breakheart Hill, were involved in its construction. The original lake was destroyed in a flood in 1768; in 1780 Paul and Thomas Sandby began construction of a still larger lake, also adding an artificial waterfall and the smaller bodies of water known as Meadow Pond and Obelisk Pond. The lake lies mostly in Surrey, though the western end falls within Sunninghill in Berkshire. Recently it has been used as a location for lakeside scenes in the Harry Potter films – the prevalence of midges in Scotland, where many of the films' outdoor scenes are shot, makes filming close to water extremely uncomfortable! Virginia Water is regarded by birdwatchers as the best place in England for viewing feral mandarin ducks. See also Berkshire

Watts Gallery Down Lane, Compton, 3 miles (5km) southwest of Guildford. An Arts and Crafts style building housing the studio collection of George Frederick Watts OM RA, and including works by his wife, Mary Watts, and other Victorian artists. Opened on 1 April 1904, just two months before Watts' death, it is one of the few purpose-built picture galleries in the UK to house a single artist's collection. The gallery was featured in the 2006 BBC television series *Restoration Village*. Tel: 01483 810235.

Waverley Abbey 2 miles (3km) southeast of Farnham. Located beside the River Wey, Waverley Abbey was founded in 1128 by the Bishop of Winchester as the first Cistercian abbey in England, later becoming the mother house of six further monasteries. The abbey was dissolved in 1536 and only a tranquil and beautiful ruin now remains, of which the most notable element is probably the vaulted undercroft of the refectory. It is claimed by some that the site inspired Sir Walter Scott to write the Waverley novels. It has also been suggested that the abbey site formed part of the 'GHQ line', created to defend London during World War II; these claims are partly substantiated by the existence of a brick gun emplacement to one side of the car park, and of numerous tank traps along the river bank behind the abbey. The large open space, formed by the curve of the river on one side and the lake on the other, was supposedly intended to be a 'tank killing ground' for any German army intending to outflank London's defences. Now owned by English Heritage.

Weybridge — Weybridge lies in northern Surrey on the south bank of the River Thames, at the mouth of the River Wey (from which it derives its name). The settlement was founded as a river crossing in the 13th century. Oatlands Palace was built here in 1537 by Henry VIII, his wedding to Catherine Howard taking place at the palace in 1540. A model of the royal palace in its heyday can be seen in Weybridge Museum. Very little remains today, however, except one archway once leading to the stables and a length of wall; the palace was demolished in 1650 and its bricks were used to line the lock walls of the Wey Navigation canal. In 1915 Weybridge became the home of Vickers, and some of Britain's finest aircraft, including the Spitfire, Hurricane and VC10, were designed at the company's Brooklands factory. See also Brooklands

Winkworth Arboretum — 2 miles (3km) southeast of Godalming. Established in 1937 by Wilfrid Fox, who sought to create a collection of exotic trees within an unspoiled valley on the former Thorncombe Estate. The arboretum now features over 1000 different trees and shrubs including large collections of azalea, rhododendron and holly, situated on slopes leading down to ornamental lakes. Gertrude Jekyll explored the woods in the early 20th century. Owned by the National Trust. Tel: 01483 208477.

RHS Wisley — 4 miles (6km) east of Woking. The Royal Horticultural Society's garden at Wisley was founded by Victorian businessman and RHS member George Ferguson Wilson, who purchased a 60 acre (24ha) site in 1878 and used part of the land to establish the Oakwood Experimental Garden. After Wilson's death in 1902, Oakwood and adjoining Glebe Farm were purchased by Sir Thomas Hanbury, creator of the celebrated garden La Mortola on the Italian Riviera, who gave both sites to the RHS the following year. Today Wisley is a large and diverse garden covering 240 acres (96ha). In addition to numerous formal and informal decorative gardens, several glasshouses and an extensive arboretum, there are small-scale demonstration 'model gardens' and a trials field where new cultivars are assessed. Tel: 01483 224234.

Witley Common — 1 mile (1.6km) west of Witley, 3 miles (5km) southwest of Godalming. An area of woodland and heath, designated a Site of Special Scientific Interest and a Special Protection Area, and supporting populations of nightjar and nightingale as well as various rare butterflies. Other features include a number of Bronze Age burial mounds. The area was used by the army as a training camp during both world wars, with up to 20,000 soldiers based here at one point. It was gradually restored to its pre-war condition from the late 1940s and is now managed by the National Trust.

Woking — A large dormitory town in the London commuter belt 5 miles (8km) north of Guildford. Originating in the Anglo-Saxon era as *Woccingas* (meaning the followers of a tribal leader named Wocca), Woking is recorded as the site of an 8th century monastery. Its name has been variously spelt through the ages as Wochinges, Wokynge and Wochynghe. Woking Palace was first built in the 13th century and was occupied by monarchs including Henry VIII; its site is beside the River Wey south of Old Woking. Modern Woking developed after the arrival of the railway in the 1830s, and soon afterwards a station was built at the junction between lines to the south coast and the southwest of England, and of the so-called 'necropolis railway' to Brookwood Cemetery. This cemetery was developed by the London Necropolis Company in 1850 as an overflow burial ground for London's dead and is one of the world's largest, covering 500 acres (200ha). In 1878 Woking became home to St John's crematorium, the first in the UK. Today the McLaren Formula One motor racing team is based near the town, as is Räikkönen Robertson Racing, begun by former McLaren driver Kimi Räikkönen.

Woking Mosque — Oriental Road, Woking. Built in 1889, the Shah Jehan Mosque is the first purpose-built mosque in Europe outside Muslim Spain, although Quilliam's Liverpool mosque pre-dates it by a few months. Funded by Shah Jehan, Begum of Bhopal (1868–1901), one of the four female Muslim rulers of Bhopal who reigned between 1819 and 1926, it was established by Hungarian scholar Dr Gottlieb Wilhelm Leitner, founder of Woking's Oriental Institute. Born in Pest of Jewish parents, by the age of 15 Leitner could speak eight languages fluently including Turkish, Persian and Arabic. He finally learnt no fewer than 40 languages and had previously been principal of the University of Punjab, Lahore. The mosque faced closure in the 1920s, but the campaign to secure its future was greatly assisted by Lord Headley, a British convert to Islam who insisted in a speech to the House of Lords that under the British Empire there were more Muslim subjects than Christians and the government had a duty to ensure that the faith of its subjects was properly represented in the capital city. Tel: 01483 760679.

Wotton House — Wotton, 3 miles (5km) southwest of Dorking. A 16th century house owned by the Evelyn family since 1579 and surrounded by an Italian garden created in 1640 by George Evelyn. The garden was designed by Evelyn's brother John, perhaps better known today as a writer and diarist, but also a garden designer and one of the forerunners of the English landscape garden movement. The gardens at Wotton, now Grade II* listed and recently restored, are therefore considered to be of considerable historical significance. The house is now a hotel. Tel: 01306 730000.

Yehudi Menuhin School — Stoke d'Abernon, 1 mile (1.6km) southeast of Cobham. Specialist music school founded in 1963 by violinist Yehudi Menuhin. It educates about 60 boys and girls aged 8–18, who all play at least one musical instrument (stringed instrument or piano) to an exceptionally high level. Academic subjects are also studied, but the emphasis is on developing performance skills in classical music. Former students include Niccola Benedetti, BBC Young Musician of the Year in 2004, and Nigel Kennedy. Tel: 01932 864739.

Some famous people born in Surrey

Andrews, Julie (actress) (1935–)	Walton on Thames
Arnold, Matthew (poet) (1822–88)	Laleham
Boorman, John (film director) (1933–)	Shepperton
Campbell, Donald (speedboat and auto racer) (1921–67)	Horley
Caro, Anthony (sculptor) (1924–)	New Malden
Clapton, Eric (rock musician) (1945–)	Ripley
Clark, Petula (singer and actress) (1932–)	Epsom
Cobb, John (speedboat and auto racer) (1899–1952)	Esher
Cobbett, William (journalist and politician) (1763–1835)	Farnham
Cook, Beryl (artist) (1926–2008)	Epsom
Evelyn, John (diarist) (1620–1706)	Wotton
Fonteyn, Margot (ballerina) (1919–91)	Reigate
Gabriel, Peter (rock musician) (1950–)	Chobham
Galsworthy, John (novelist) 1867–1933)	Kingston
Herbert, A P (Alan Patrick) (writer) (1890–1971)	Ashtead
Hill, Harry (comedian, born Matthew Hall) (1964–)	Woking
Huxley, Aldous Leonard (writer) (1894–1963)	Godalming
Malthus, Thomas Robert (economist) (1766–1834)	Dorking
Olivier, Lawrence (actor) (1907–89)	Dorking
Pears, Peter (tenor) (1910–86)	Farnham
Piper, John (artist) (1903–92)	Epsom
Smith, Delia (cook and author) (1941–)	Woking
Surtees, John (motorcycle racer) (1934–)	Tatsfield
Wilkinson, Jonny (rugby union player) (1979–)	Frimley
Wodehouse, P G (Pelham Grenville) (novelist) (1881–1975)	Guildford

Islands of Surrey

Island name	Area	Nearest landmark	General information
Ash Island	River Thames	East Molesey	Situated between Tagg's Island and Thames Ditton Island (in Greater London). GR: TQ149689
Church Island	River Thames	Staines Bridge	Situated between Hollyhock Island and Truss's Island. GR: TQ029717
Desborough Island	River Thames	Shepperton	Situated between D'Oyly Carte Island and Wheatley's Ait. GR: TQ084662
D'Oyly Carte Island	River Thames	Shepperton	Situated between Lock Island (in Berkshire) and Desborough Island. GR: TQ076660
Dumsey Eyot	River Thames	Shepperton	Situated between Pharaoh's Island and Penton Hook Island.
Garrick's Ait	River Thames	Hurst Park	Situated between Platt's Eyot and Tagg's Island. GR: TQ141693
Grand Junction Isle	River Thames	Sunbury	Situated between Sunbury Court Island and Platt's Eyot (in Greater London). Formerly known as Purvis Ait.
Hamhaugh Island	River Thames	Shepperton	Situated between Pharaoh's Island and Lock Island (in Berkshire). GR: TQ072655
Hollyhock Island	River Thames	Runnymede Bridge	Situated between Holm Island and Church Island. GR: TQ022718
Holm Island	River Thames	Runnymede Bridge	Situated between Hollyhock Island and The Island, Hythe End. GR: TQ022718
Island, The	River Thames	Hythe End	Situated between Magna Carta Island and Holm Island. GR: TQ011724
Penton Hook Island	River Thames	Thorpe	Situated between Truss's Island and Dumsey Eyot. Area: 0.02 sq miles (0.04 sq km). GR: TQ042692
Pharaoh's Island	River Thames	Shepperton	Situated between Dumsey Eyot and Hamhaugh Island. GR: TQ069659
Raven's Ait	River Thames	Surbiton	Popular as a film location. GR: TQ162673
Rivermead Island	River Thames	Sunbury	Situated between Sunbury Court Island and Sunbury Lock Ait.
Sunbury Court Island	River Thames	Kempton Park	Situated between Rivermead Island and Grand Junction Isle. GR: TQ117690
Sunbury Lock Ait	River Thames	Sunbury	Situated between Wheatley's Ait and Rivermead Island. GR: TQ109684
Truss's Island	River Thames	Thorpe	Situated between Church Island and Penton Hook Island. GR: TQ041693
Wheatley's Ait	River Thames	Shepperton	Situated between Desborough Island and Sunbury Lock Ait. GR: TQ101675

SUSSEX

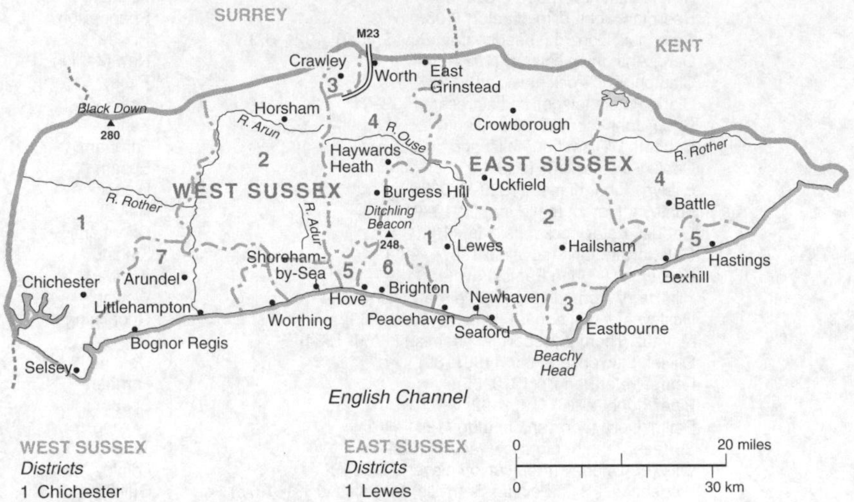
SURREY
M23
KENT
Crawley
Worth
East Grinstead
Black Down
280
Horsham
R. Arun
R. Ouse
Crowborough
Haywards Heath
EAST SUSSEX
R. Rother
Uckfield
WEST SUSSEX
Burgess Hill
Battle
R. Rother
Ditchling Beacon
248
HAMPSHIRE
R. Adur
Lewes
Hailsham
Hastings
Shoreham-by-Sea
Chichester
Arundel
Brighton
Bexhill
Hove
Newhaven
Littlehampton
Worthing
Peacehaven
Seaford
Eastbourne
Bognor Regis
Beachy Head
Selsey
English Channel
0
20 miles
0
30 km

WEST SUSSEX
Districts
1 Chichester
2 Horsham
3 Crawley
4 Mid Sussex
5 Adur
6 Worthing
7 Arun

EAST SUSSEX
Districts
1 Lewes
2 Wealden
3 Eastbourne
4 Rother
5 Hastings
6 Brighton (UA)

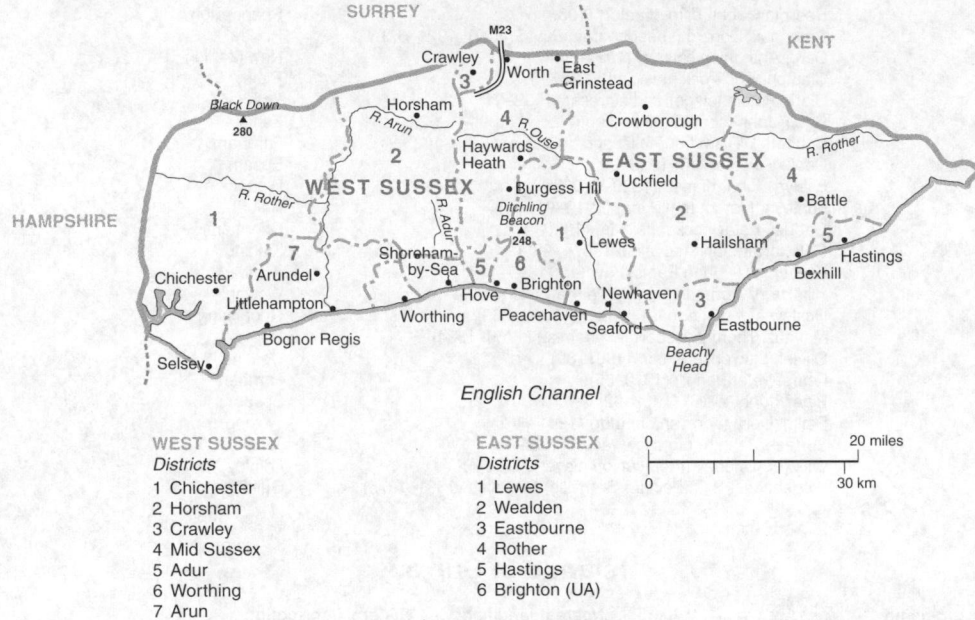

Sussex, divided into East and West, is bordered by Hampshire to the west and Surrey to the north; East Sussex also borders Kent to the northeast. The south of the county lies on the English Channel. In addition to the administrative counties of West Sussex and East Sussex, the city of Brighton and Hove was established as a unitary authority in 1997 and granted city status in 2000. Until then Chichester had been Sussex's only city. For the purposes of this book, Brighton and Hove is regarded as part of East Sussex.

The divisions of West Sussex and East Sussex were originally established in 1189, and had separate administrations by the 16th century. Under the Local Government Act of 1888 the two divisions became administrative counties, along with the three county boroughs of Brighton, Eastbourne and Hastings. Sussex remained a single ceremonial county until 1974, when the Mid Sussex region (including Haywards Heath and East Grinstead) was transferred from East to West Sussex, and the three county boroughs of Brighton, Eastbourne and Hastings became districts within East Sussex.

Despite its relative proximity to London, Sussex has traditionally retained a strong local identity. Its unofficial anthem is 'Sussex by the Sea', written in 1907 and adopted by the Royal Sussex Regiment in the World War II, while its unofficial motto is 'We wun't be druv', which reflects the independent-minded nature of its people in centuries past.

Sussex lies on the southern part of the Wealden anticline, a ridge of high land crossing the county from west to east and forming both the Weald itself and the South Downs. The former consists of clays and sands, the latter chalk. Between the two ridges, mainly in West Sussex, lies the Vale of Sussex. The Weald runs east from St Leonard's Forest, southwest of Crawley, as far as Ashdown Forest. Within it lies the highest point in the county, the pine-clad Black Down, close to the Surrey border. The High Weald, as the main area is known, gets its name from 'wilderness' or forest, Around 1660 the total forested area was reckoned to exceed 312 sq miles (800 sq km), and it still has the highest proportion of ancient woodlands in the UK.

The range of chalk hills known as the South Downs start near Petersfield in Hampshire and run east for 50 miles (80km), terminating at Beachy Head near Eastbourne. Their average height is about 500ft (150m). Dry valleys are a feature of the Downs. Devil's Dyke, northwest of Brighton, is the deepest in England and is a popular beauty spot. The South Downs Way National Trail, which starts at Winchester in Hampshire, crosses the county to end at Eastbourne, a distance of 100 miles (160km). Other long distance paths include the Sussex Border Path, the 1066 Country Walk and the Vanguard Way. The Vale of Sussex is a region of lower undulating land created when the clays between the Weald and the Downs were worn away. Most of the rivers in Sussex cross the Vale, rising on the slopes of the Weald in the St Leonard's Forest area and, apart from the River Rother (Eastern), cutting through the Downs to reach the sea.

The coast is the third distinctive region of Sussex, and can be divided geographically into four main areas from west to east. At the low-lying western end is Chichester harbour, while the point of land known as Selsey Bill protrudes into the English Channel. Further east, between Bognor Regis and Brighton, there is an almost unbroken series of towns, most of which have grown up since the 18th century as seaside resorts. Between Brighton and Eastbourne the South Downs meet the coast in a series of high chalk cliffs, with towns in between, and beyond Eastbourne the land is again low-lying and marshy, broken by clay and sandstone cliffs where the Weald meets the English Channel. Nearly all the largest centres of population in the county lie between Bognor Regis and Eastbourne – 500,000 people live between Littlehampton and Brighton alone.

The South Downs were relatively heavily populated in the prehistoric period. There are Neolithic flint mines dating as far back as c.4000 BC at sites including Harrow Hill, Cissbury and Blackpatch above Worthing. Some of the route followed by the South Downs Way follows trackways established for 5000 years, while there is visible evidence of occupation in the large numbers of Bronze Age disk barrows – burial mounds typical of those found across the South Downs and other chalklands in Southern England – and in the ramparts of Iron Age hill forts still evident at sites including Hollingbury, Wolstonbury, the Trundle and Mount Caburn.

Extensive Roman remains were discovered at Fishbourne in 1960, and the Roman palace uncovered there indicates that the region was important in the early days of Roman occupation; the local British tribe, the Atrebates, welcomed the Romans. But the history of Sussex as a recognisable entity begins in AD 477, when the Saxons landed in the west under Aelle and his three sons and founded the kingdom of the South Saxons. They took the Roman city of Noviomagus, later Chichester, driving the British into the forest of Andred or Andredeswald (i.e. the Weald). The Roman fortress of Anderida also fell to the Saxons. After Aelle's death the kingdom of Sussex declined, falling under the dominion of Wessex in 823. In 681 Wilfred came to Bosham to convert the pagan South Saxons to Christianity. He was given land at Selsey by King Aethelwealh to build a church, and the seat of the church remained there until it was moved to Chichester after the Norman Conquest; the diocese of Chichester is one of the oldest bishoprics in England. Between 895 and the accession of Cnut in 1016 Sussex suffered from continual Danish raids.

The county was of great importance to the Normans, whose influence was already strong even before the conquest: Hastings, Rye, Winchelsea and Steyning were in the power of the Norman abbey of Fécamp, while Osbern, Edward the Confessor's Norman chaplain and later Bishop of Exeter, held the estate of Bosham. Hastings and Pevensey were on the direct route to Normandy, and after the conquest of 1066 William secured the lines of communication with London by placing the lands in the hands of men with close ties to himself. His half-brother, Robert, Count of Mortain, held Pevensey, and his son-in-law, William de Warenne, held Lewes. At this time Sussex was, uniquely in England, divided into five (later six) strips known as rapes, each running north–south and containing a town of military, commercial and maritime importance. The origin of the term in this sense is uncertain; it may derive from the Icelandic territorial division *hreppr*, or from Old English *rap*, a rope; it may be of Norman origin. From the early Middle Ages castles at Lewes, Bramber and Arundel guarded the routes from the coast through the South Downs into the interior provided by the valleys of the rivers Ouse, Adur and Arun.

Due to its position on the English Channel, Sussex has always been the scene of preparations for invasion, and it was often concerned in rebellions. Pevensey and Arundel played their part in such events during the early Norman period. During the barons' war the county was a centre for the king's forces; Lewes was in the hands of the king's brother-in-law, John de Warenne, Earl of Surrey, Pevensey and Hastings in those of his uncle, Peter of Savoy. The forces of the king and of Simon de Montfort met in battle at Lewes in 1264. The corrupt administration of the county during the 13th and 14th centuries, and the constant passage of troops for the French wars and the devastating plagues of the 14th century, were the causes of numerous further rebellions. Lewes Castle was captured during the Peasants' Revolt of 1381, while the abbot of Battle and the prior of Lewes were deeply involved in Jack Cade's Rebellion in 1450. During the Civil War Arundel and Chichester were supporters of the king, Lewes and the Cinque Ports of Parliament. Chichester and Arundel were besieged by Waller, and the Parliamentarians gained a strong hold on the county, in spite of its people's loyalty to Charles I.

Seventy-four Martello towers were erected in Sussex after 1803 to defend against invasion by the French under Napoleon. Ten of these still stand, including six between Eastbourne and Pevensey Bay; Seaford's was no. 74, the last of the chain. During World War II Sussex was at the front line of defence against German invasion. Camber Sands and Cuckmere Haven were among several points on the coast identified by Hitler's Operation Sealion as targets for invasion forces, and the beaches were protected by tangles of barbed wire and heavy artillery. Sussex towns suffered considerable damage in the air raids of 1940 and 1944. The 1942 Dieppe Raid was based at Newhaven, while many of the personnel taking part in D-Day landings set off from the Sussex coast.

Though it is largely rural today, the industries of Sussex were once varied. Herring fisheries, the salt pans of the coast and the wool trade were all noted in the Domesday survey. South Down sheep were noted for their wool as early as the 13th century. The iron mines are known to have been worked by the Romans, and the smelting and forging of iron was the great industry of the Weald – which provided a plentiful supply of wood – from the 13th to the 18th century. The first cast-iron cannon manufactured in England was made in Buxted, East Sussex, by Ralph Hogge. The iron industry left the Weald only after the process of smelting iron with coal – a material much more readily available elsewhere – was perfected in the mid 18th century. In early times, Sussex oak was considered to be the finest timber for shipbuilding. Chichester was noted for the production of cloth, malt and needles, while market gardening was a major source of income on the fertile coastal plain of West Sussex between Chichester and Brighton.

Many of the other major towns in West Sussex have grown, mainly as residential areas with employment in light industry and financial services, in the 19th and 20th centuries. Coastal towns such as Littlehampton and Worthing owe their growth to the seaside boom brought by the railways in the 1850s. The fishing village of Bognor became a resort in the 18th century. Worthing has struggled in recent years to belie its image as a retirement town.

Sussex has plenty of distinct traditions. Each Good Friday marblers knuckle down for the world championships at Tinsley Green. Traditional foods include Ripe Tart, the name coming from the village of Ripe in the South Downs. In days gone by a pie feast was held in Ripe to celebrate the cherry harvest. The steaming suet crust of Sussex Pond Pudding encases a whole lemon with golden buttery sugar syrup, which oozes onto the dish to form the 'pond'. Sussex Plum Duffs contain currants, sultanas and lemon, but curiously have a distinct lack of plums. The popular Christmas carol 'On Christmas Night', first published in a work by Irish bishop Luke Wadding in 1684, was later named 'The Sussex Carol' after the region in which it was collected by Cecil Sharp and Ralph Vaughan Williams, who set the lyrics to its now famous tune. The Mummers' Play ('Mummer' comes from the Greek word *mommo*, meaning a mask; the wearing of masks became popular at royal functions in the 14th century, the practice being termed 'Momerie'), a folk play popular in various forms throughout England, has a strong history in Sussex; in West Sussex it is known as 'Tipteering'.

East Sussex		**Population**		**Area**	
Districts	*male*	*female*	*total*	*sq miles*	*sq km*
Eastbourne	41,650	48,017	89,667	17	44
Hastings	40,662	44,367	85,029	11	30
Lewes	44,042	48,135	92,177	113	292
Rother	39,880	45,548	85,428	197	509
Wealden	66,718	73,305	140,023	322	833
Brighton & Hove Unitary Authority	119,897	127,920	247,817	32	83
Total	352,849	387,292	740,141	692	1791

West Sussex		**Population**		**Area**	
Districts	*male*	*female*	*total*	*sq miles*	*sq km*
Adur	28,404	31,223	59,627	16	42
Arun	66,212	74,547	140,759	85	221
Chichester	50,303	56,147	106,450	304	786
Crawley	48,920	50,824	99,744	17	45
Horsham	59,293	62,795	122,088	205	530
Mid Sussex	61,708	65,670	127,378	129	334
Worthing	45,764	51,804	97,568	13	32
Total	360,604	393,010	753,614	769	1990

Local Attractions and Information: East Sussex

Administrative headquarters	**Brighton & Hove:** King's House, Grand Avenue, Hove BN3 2LS. Tel: 01273 290000. **East Sussex:** County Hall, St Anne's Crescent, Lewes BN7 1SG. Tel: 01273 481000.
Alfriston Clergy House	Alfriston, 6 miles (10km) west of Eastbourne. The first property acquired by the National Trust, costing £10 in 1896, this 14th century Wealden hall house was probably built for a yeoman farmer before being passed to the Church. It was saved from demolition by the vicar of Alfriston, Rev. Beynon. The hall floor is made of a mixture of chalk and sour milk, and one of the beams bears a carving of an oak leaf which possibly inspired the National Trust's oak-leaf symbol. The cottage garden was laid out in the 1920s and contains species of old roses as well as a 100 year old Judas tree. Tel: 01323 870001.
Anne of Cleves' House	Southover High Street, Lewes. A 16th century timber-framed Wealden hall house which formed part of Anne of Cleves' divorce settlement from Henry VIII. It contains numerous exhibits relating to Sussex life including a gallery devoted to Wealden ironwork, as well as to the history of Lewes between the 16th century and the present. Tel: 01273 474610.
Ashdown Forest	An area of sandy heath, woodland and scrub covering 14,000 acres (5700ha) of the High Weald, and a Site of Special Scientific Interest. The area, which has never been cultivated, consists of remnants of the Lancaster Great Park deer hunting forest, which was enclosed by a pale (a wooden fence on top of an earth bank) in the late 13th century. The numerous place names containing 'hatch' or 'gate' around the edge of the forest trace the course of the enclosure. it provides a habitat for fauna such as lizards, adders and several species of deer, and for birds including rare Dartford warblers and stonechat. Author A A Milne famously set his stories about Winnie the Pooh in the forest and it is possible to visit many of the landmarks named in the books. Several clumps of Scots pine, planted in the 19th century, are prominent landmarks. There is a memorial to Milne and the artist E H Shepard at the Gills Lap viewpoint. Tel. 01342 823583.
Barbican House Museum	High Street, Lewes. Located beneath Lewes Castle, the museum houses the Sussex Archaeological Society's archaeology collections, including extensive Iron Age, Romano-British and Anglo-Saxon displays. Other exhibits include the Lewes Town Model. Tel: 01273 486290.
Batemans	$^{1}/_{2}$ mile (0.8km) south of Burwash, 13 miles (21km) northwest of Hastings. A Jacobean sandstone manor house built in 1634, and the home of Rudyard Kipling from 1902 until his death in 1936. Kipling saw it as a sanctuary both from his overwhelming literary fame and from the loss of his elder daughter, Josephine, for whom he wrote the *Just So Stories*. The house, including his book-lined study, is displayed as it was when Kipling lived here. Also on display are many artefacts from the East, while his Rolls-Royce can be seen in the garage. Outside, the pond, the rose garden and the yew hedges are laid out to Kipling's design. At the end of the grounds lies the River Dudwell with a watermill dating from c.1750. Although Kipling allowed this to fall into disrepair, it was restored in the 1970s. The property is now owned by the National Trust. Tel: 01435 882302.
Battle Abbey	High Street, Battle. Established as a Benedictine monastery by William I, who in 1070 vowed to establish a religious foundation on the precise site where Harold had fallen at the Battle of Hastings, the abbey church was completed in 1094. Its great gatehouse was added early in the Hundred Years War (1337–1453) to protect the abbey from French raids along the south coast. After the dissolution of the abbey, the church was burnt down and the abbot's house converted into a country house for Sir Anthony Browne, Henry VIII's Master of Horse. It was sold to the Webster family in 1715, who carried out further alterations. A vast canvas by F W Wilkin depicting the Battle of Hastings was painted in 1820 to be hung in the Great Hall. Hidden under the floorboards for many years, this has now been restored to its rightful place. After World War I, the mansion was leased to Battle Abbey School, which still occupies the building. Today, a Museum of Monastic Life displays artefacts uncovered during archaeological excavations carried out after World War II. Tel: 01424 773792.
Battles	See separate table for details of the battles of Hastings and Lewes.
Beachy Head	3 miles (5km) southwest of Eastbourne. The highest chalk sea cliff in the UK at 531ft (162m), Beachy Head stands at the easternmost point of the South Downs. The famous lighthouse standing at the foot of the cliffs was built in 1902, replacing one that stood on the cliff top. The cliffs suffer from serious erosion and another cliff-top lighthouse (now a private house), Belle Tout, was lifted and moved 55ft (17m) inland in 1999 in a remarkable feat of engineering. The ashes of Karl Marx's friend and collaborator Friedrich Engels were scattered over Beachy Head after his death in 1895.
Bentley Motor Museum and Wildlife Park	Halland, 5 miles (8km) northeast of Lewes. The Palladian-style mansion of Bentley House was restored over several years by Raymond Erith for the owners, Gerald and Mary Askew. The formal gardens consist of a series of 'rooms' divided by yew hedges. Inspired by the Wildfowl Trust at Slimbridge, Devon, Gerald Askew set up his own reserve, which features 125 species of wildfowl – swans, geese and ducks – including elegant Australian black swans. After Gerald Askew's death in 1970 the house was given to East Sussex, and a motor museum was later established by Hugh Stuart-Roberts. There are now changing collections of veteran, Edwardian and vintage vehicles. Tel. 01825 840573.
Bluebell Railway	The UK's first preserved standard gauge passenger railway, which in 1960 reopened part of the London & South Coast Railway between East Grinstead and Lewes. It currently runs for 9 miles (15km) between Sheffield Park and Kingscote via Horsted Keynes, and it is planned to extend the line a further mile to East Grinstead. Tel: 01825 720800.
Bodiam Castle	Bodiam, 10 miles (16km) north of Hastings. Bodiam with its encircling moat is one of the most romantic castles in the UK. Built in 1385 by Sir Edward Dalyngrigge, a royal councillor, largely as a fortified dwelling, its external walls are almost intact. The gatehouse contains the original wooden

portcullis. The castle was besieged during both the Wars of the Roses and the Civil War. It fell into disuse shortly afterwards and was regarded as a picturesque ruin as early as the 18th century. It was bought in 1917 by Lord Curzon, Viceroy of India, who restored it as a dwelling. Its fairytale appearance makes it a popular film and TV location. Tel: 01580 830436.

Brighton & Hove There are signs of habitation in the area covered by modern Brighton & Hove dating back to at least 3500 BC at Whitehawk Camp, a Neolithic enclosure near the racecourse, while Hollingbury Camp overlooking the city is a substantial Iron Age hill fort. But the history of modern Brighton really begins in 1514 when the fishing village of Brighthelmstone was burnt by the French. It was already a town of 4000 inhabitants by 1753 when Dr Richard Russell began to recommend the health-giving properties of bathing in sea water. From then on it became a fashionable resort for the wealthy, who left their mark in the substantial amount of Regency architecture which still contributes to Brighton's character. The most notable (or notorious) guest was George, Prince of Wales, later George IV, creator of the Royal Pavilion. In 1786 the Prince chose Brighton as a holiday home where he could be with his mistress, Mrs Fitzherbert, whom he had secretly married. The arrival of the London to Brighton railway in 1840 made the coast accessible to ordinary people, and Brighton became a magnet for day-trippers from London. Apart from tourism, railway building and munitions were staple industries until the mid 20th century; today Brighton has a young population including over 20,000 students and has also become once again a magnet for the fashionable of the capital. Brighton's lively atmosphere is a direct contrast to its near neighbour, Hove, which is quieter and more conservative in character; where Hove is a haven for the retired, Brighton has a reputation for liberalism and is home to a large Lesbian, Gay, Bisexual and Transgender (LGBT) community, mainly based in the Kemptown area of the city. Some indicators suggest a gay population approaching 25 per cent. In the early hours of 12 October 1984 an IRA bomb exploded in the Grand Hotel on the seafront, where leading members of the Conservative government were staying for their annual party conference. Four people were killed in the blast (including MP Sir Anthony Berry); no member of the Cabinet died, and Prime Minister Margaret Thatcher narrowly escaped injury, but other members of her government were badly injured, notably Norman Tebbit, whose wife was also injured and left paralysed. The biggest arts festival in England, the Brighton Festival, takes place in May each year. Part of Brighton beach has been designated an official nudist area – one of very few naturist beaches in the UK adjacent to an urban area.

Brighton Marina The largest marina in the UK with over 1500 berths, owned by Premier Marinas. Tel: 01273 818504.

Brighton Piers The **Brighton Marine Palace and Pier**, generally known as the Palace Pier before being unofficially renamed by its current owners as Brighton Pier in 2000, opened in May 1899, costing a record £137,000 to build. The pier suffered a large fire on 4 February 2003 but the damage was limited and most of the pier was able to reopen the next day. The older **West Pier**, built in 1866 by Eugenius Birch, has been closed and deteriorating since 1975. It is one of only two Grade I listed piers in the UK (the other being Clevedon Pier). The West Pier partially collapsed on 29 December 2002 when a walkway connecting the concert hall and pavilion fell into the sea after being battered by storms. On 20 January 2003 a further collapse saw the destruction of the concert hall in the middle of the pier. On 28 March 2003 the pavilion at the end of the pier caught fire, and firefighters were unable to save the building from destruction because they could not reach the end of the pier. The cause of the fire remains unknown. On 12 May 2003, another fire broke out, consuming most of what was left of the concert hall. Arson was suspected. On 23 June 2004 high winds caused the middle of the pier to completely collapse. Brighton had one further major pier, the **Brighton Chain Suspension Pier** ('Chain Pier') designed by Captain Samuel Brown, RN, and built in 1823. Since Brighton had no natural harbour, it was primarily intended as a landing stage for packet boats to Dieppe, but it also featured a small number of attractions including initially a camera obscura. An esplanade with an entrance tollbooth controlled access to the pier, which was roughly in line with today's New Steine. Turner and Constable both painted the pier, William IV landed on it, and it was even the subject of a song. The Chain Pier survived the construction of the West Pier, but a condition for permission to build the Palace Pier was that the builders would dismantle the oldest pier; in the event a storm destroyed the closed and decrepit pier on 4 December 1896. The stubby remains of some of the pier's iron piles can still be seen at extreme low tides.

Brighton Trunk Murders On 17 June 1934 William Joseph Vinnicombe, a cloakroom attendant employed by the Southern Railway at Brighton station, noticed an offensive odour in the cloakroom. He called Detective Bishop of the Railway Police, who opened a trunk containing parts of a human body. On 18 June another trunk containing two limbs had been discovered at King's Cross station in similar circumstances. The victims could not be identified, however, until a press reporter informed police about 42-year-old Violet Kaye, née Watts (also known by the name of Saunders), a known prostitute in the Brighton area who was missing. A man named Toni Mancini had been associated with her. Chief Inspector Robert Donaldson of the Metropolitan Police was sent to assist the investigation; he questioned Henry George Rout, who had received the trunk but could not remember the depositor. Donaldson interviewed Mancini – alias Cecil Lois England (his real name), Jack Noytre, Tony English and Hyman Gold – and released him, but took the precaution of having his lodgings at 52 Kemp Street checked. A large black trunk was discovered there, containing the body of Violet Kaye. Mancini was arrested in Lee, southeast London on 17 July by two Metropolitan Police constables and appeared at Lewes Assizes, but the case against him failed because of doubts about whether he could have deposited the torsos in the trunks at either Brighton or King's Cross. Mancini said in his defence that he had come upon Kaye's body suddenly, and thought the police would not believe him as he had a criminal record, so he decided to keep the matter a secret and placed her in a trunk! In 1976, just before his death, Mancini sensationally confessed to Violet Kaye's murder in a Sunday newspaper. The press attention to the 1934 murders revived interest in a previous Brighton trunk murder. In the 19th century John Holloway, a painter on the Chain Pier, murdered his wife Celia, then transported her body in a trunk on a wheelbarrow to Lover's Walk in Preston and buried the remains. Holloway was arrested; tried in Lewes on 14 December 1831, he was hanged two days later.

Camber Castle 1 mile (1.6km) south of Rye. Originally located on a shingle spit protecting the harbours at Rye and Winchelsea, but now a mile inland, Camber is the single example in Sussex of the series of coastal fortresses built by Henry VIII to counter the threat of invasion during the 16th century. It was built on an octagonal plan around an existing single tower built 1512–14 by Sir Edward Guldeford; having been abandoned in the 17th century, it still retains its original design. Restored 1969 and 1975, a further programme of consolidation was completed in 1995. Owned by English Heritage. Tel: 01797 223862.

Castle Hill 4$^1/_2$ miles (7km) northeast of Brighton. A 115 acre (47ha) National Nature Reserve consisting of an area of traditionally managed ancient chalk downland rich in orchids; the concentration of these, including the nationally rare early spider orchid, has made it a candidate Special Area of Conservation. It is also home to the largest UK colony of the wartbiter cricket.

Charleston Farmhouse 5 miles (8km) southeast of Lewes. An 18th century farmhouse which in 1916 became home to Vanessa Bell, sister of Virginia Woolf, and her partner Duncan Grant. It is now a shrine to the artistic endeavours of the Bloomsbury Group. Almost every surface was decorated by Bell and Grant in imitation of Italian frescos and in post-Impressionist style. In addition to Woolf, regular visitors included Roger Fry, Lytton Strachey and J M Keynes. Today many paintings by the Bloomsbury Group and others are on display and Vanessa Bell's studio has been recreated. Tel: 01323 811265.

Charleston Manor 2 miles (3km) east of Seaford. Located on the eastern side of the Cuckmere valley and almost surrounded by Friston Forest, the history of this house can be traced back to before 1100. A Norman wing and a Tudor wing can still be seen. Formerly the home of artist Sir Oswald Birley, it is the venue of an annual chamber music festival; performances take place in a 16th century tithe barn. The design of the extensive gardens was influenced by Vita Sackville-West and Gertrude Jekyll.

Cinque Ports The Confederation of Cinque Ports is a historic group of towns in Kent and Sussex, originally formed for military and trade purposes but now entirely ceremonial. Although the earliest known charter granting rights to the Cinque Ports dates from 1260, it is possible that Edward the Confessor first set about replacing the Saxon mercenary fleet with one drawn from the five ports, assisted by nearby coastal and creekside towns and villages. In return for the grant of privileges, Edward was able to muster a fleet to maintain the important transport links to Normandy and to protect his kingdom from attack. By the reign of Henry II the towns were already known collectively as the 'Cinque Ports'. The name is Norman French for 'five ports', the five being (from north to south) the Kent towns of Sandwich, Dover, Hythe and New Romney, and the East Sussex town of Hastings. They are supported by the two 'ancient towns' of East Sussex, Rye and Winchelsea, whose councils have a long tradition of maintaining contingents for the defence of England. The five head ports and two ancient towns were entitled to send two MPs to parliament. A Lord Warden of the Cinque Ports was appointed; the office still exists today, although it is now purely honorary. The town of Hastings was the head port of the Cinque Ports in the Middle Ages.

Clinton Lodge Garden Fletching, 2 miles (3km) west of Uckfield. A 17th century house enlarged by the Earl of Sheffield for his daughter when she married Sir Henry Clinton, one of three generals at Waterloo. The 18th century façade is set in a tree-lined lawn, flanked by a newly created canal and overlooking parkland. The 6 acre (2.5ha) garden reflects various periods of English gardening history and includes a knot garden, wild flower garden, herb garden, potager and lime walk. Tel: 01825 722952.

De La Warr Pavilion Marina, Bexhill on Sea. The first public building in the UK designed in Modernist style, the Pavilion was commissioned in 1935 by the Earl De La Warr, mayor of Bexhill and chairman of the Labour Party, and designed by architects Erich Mendelsohn and Serge Chermayeff. Also the first large welded steel-framed building to be constructed in England, it was intended to be a 'palace of culture'; it featured white walls, wooden floors and a floating steel staircase, providing a restaurant, dance floor, reading room and sun terrace. Used for its intended purpose for only three years, the pavilion was damaged during World War II; its steelwork suffered from the effects of the seaside climate and the building eventually fell into disrepair. Reopened in October 2005 after comprehensive restoration, the building now contains galleries and restaurants as well as a roof terrace. Tel. 01424 229111.

Ditchling Common 1 mile (1.6km) east of Burgess Hill. Established as a country park in 1974, this 200 acre (80 hectare) tract of open Wealden countryside, consisting of oak woodland, grassland and scrub, is home to many species of butterflies and birds including stonechats, linnets and woodpeckers. A post marks the spot where a pedlar named Jacob Harris was hanged for murder in 1734; its wood supposedly has magical properties.

Eastbourne Eastbourne's development from four small villages in the mid 19th century was dramatic, initiated by the coming of the railway in 1849. The 7th Duke of Devonshire, owner of much of the land, effectively built a new town in the 1860s as a 'resort for gentlemen'. The town continued as a prosperous and genteel resort until World War II, but suffered as a result of bombing. Rapid development after the war enlarged the town over marshland in the east but succeeded in wiping out much of its Victorian charm; today it is best known as the home of the prestigious women's tennis tournament known as the International Women's Open, and as a retirement home for thousands.

Firle Place West Firle, 4 miles (6km) southeast of Lewes. The Georgian frontage of this house hides a Tudor interior. The estate has been occupied by the Gage family since the 1540 and there are monuments to many family members in Firle church. The house contains various collections of furniture, porcelain, and paintings by Gainsborough, Reynolds and others. Tel. 01273 858307.

Friston Forest 5 miles (8km) west of Eastbourne. A Forestry Commission beechwood situated to the east of the Cuckmere valley and covering more than 2000 acres (800ha). Planting began in 1926. Tucked into a fold of the forest is Charleston Manor (see separate entry).

Glynde Place Glynde, 3 miles (5km) east of Lewes. The Elizabethan manor house, situated to the west of Mount Caburn and overlooking the Downs, originally built of flint and imported Normandy stone in 1569, has been home to the Trevor family and their relatives for over 300 years. It was much enlarged in the 18th century in developments that included a new church for the village of Glynde. Inside is a panelled gallery with family portraits and a collection of Old Master paintings including works by Canaletto, while the Speaker's Room is dedicated to John Bouverie Brand, Speaker of the House of Commons in 1802 and Lord Palmerston's chief whip. There are extensive gardens. Tel. 01273 858224.

Glyndebourne 2 miles (3km) east of Lewes. An opera house in the grounds of 16th century Glyndebourne House, built in 1934 by music lover John Christie as a stage for his wife, soprano Audrey Mildmay. At the same time Christie established an annual music festival, whose massive success eventually overwhelmed the original venue; on 28 May 1994 a new auditorium seating 1200 was opened by Christie's son George, the first new opera house to be built in Britain for 60 years. The first performance, just as 60 years before to the day, was of Mozart's *Le Nozze de Figaro.* The London Philharmonic Orchestra has been the resident symphony orchestra for more than 40 years, while the Glyndebourne chorus is recruited annually. One of the main events of 'The Season', for those lucky enough to attend, is to enjoy a picnic in the gardens before and in the extended interval of a performance. Tel: 01273 812321.

Great Dixter Northiam, 6 miles (10km) northwest of Rye. The home until his death in 2006 of renowned gardener Christopher Lloyd, who inherited the house from his parents. The gardens surround a 15th century manor house, built for Richard Wakehurst and restored and extended in the early 20th century by Edwin Lutyens, who also designed the original gardens. Arranged in Arts and Crafts style as a series of small 'rooms', these came to full fruition under Lloyd, one of the most dedicated plantsmen of modern times, whose original approach to colour and planting created unique panoramas including a spectacular long border. The gardens are now maintained by the Great Dixter Charitable Trust. Tel. 01797 252878.

Hastings The history of Hastings after the landing of William the Conqueror in 1066 is chequered. Strategically located, it was one of the Cinque Ports in the Middle Ages but was flooded by the sea in the 13th century and twice burnt by the French in the 14th. Fishing was its major industry for the next 500 years – there are prolific fishing grounds nearby – and it became notoriously a centre of smuggling. It shared in the tourist boom of the 19th and early 20th century but became unfashionable with the growth of foreign holidays in the 1970s and suffered a considerable decline, though there are signs that those tired of the increasing urbanisation of Brighton are fleeing east to its more undiscovered charms. Nearby St Leonards was designed in the early 19th century by James Burton (1761–1837) and his son Decimus Burton (1800–81).

Hastings Castle West Hill, Hastings. Founded as an earthwork motte and bailey fortress founded by William the Conqueror in 1066, and built with the characteristic Norman layout of two baileys and a motte in between. The Ladies' Parlour bailey still retains part of its impressive rampart and the Conqueror's Ditch. In 1075 Robert, Count of Eu, rebuilt the castle in stone – the first permanent Norman castle in England – and founded the Collegiate Church of St Mary-in-the-Castle within its walls; in the late 12th century, a great tower was erected in the west bailey. In the 13th century, the castle was extensively altered, with the lowering of the motte and the building of the east curtain wall, flanked by the south tower and a twin-towered gatehouse. Sadly erosion by the sea has consumed more than half of the original castle.

Herstmonceux Castle 4 miles (6km) north of Hailsham. A brick quadrangular castle founded in 1441 by Sir Roger Fiennes, partially dismantled by Rev. Robert Hare in the 1770s to build himself a new house, but restored in the 20th century by Sir Claude Lowther and Sir Paul Latham. It was home until 1998 to the Royal Greenwich Observatory and now houses the International Study Centre of Queen's University (Canada). Tel. 01323 834444.

Highest point Ditchling Beacon on the South Downs north of Brighton at 813ft (248m). GR: TQ331130.

Hollingbury Camp 1 mile (1.6km) north of Brighton. Also known as Hollingbury Castle. An Iron Age hill fort standing at 584ft (178m) and overlooking the whole city of Brighton as well as providing a panorama of the rolling Downs to the north. The first evidence for occupation dates from the Bronze Age. Four disk barrows dating to c.1500 BC are situated within the ramparts, indicating that the hill was a sacred area and burial ground for local Bronze Age tribes for almost a millennium before the site developed as a defended settlement. The mounds appear to have been emptied by looters and no human remains have yet been discovered at the site, the soil being largely too acidic to preserve bone. A Bronze Age metalwork hoard has also been recovered from the site, suggesting the associated ritual deposition of high status artefacts alongside the barrows. The oldest part of the defensive works was investigated in the 1930s and found to date from before the 6th century BC when the Iron Age hill fort was constructed.

Interesting facts Visitors coming to Brighton for the sea bathing would enter the sea from the back of a bathing machine, a covered cart pulled out into deep water by a horse from which the bather would descend directly into the sea. This manoeuvre required the attentions of a Dipper for women, or a

Bather for men. The Dipper would be standing in the water, take her client in her arms as she descended from the Bathing Machine, and 'dip' her vigorously into the sea water, pushing her through the waves – no doubt as roughly as the size of the fee demanded. For many years the most famous Dipper was **Martha Gunn**, known to the *Morning Herald* as 'the Venerable Priestess of the Bath'. She was very large and very strong, well known and respected by the townsfolk as well as the visitors, and appears in comic caricatures of the time. In one where the French are seen to be invading Brighton – after a genuine scare that Napoleon was about to land – Martha is seen vigorously wielding a mop, and in an engraving of 1806 she is seen standing in the Old Steine behind the Prince of Wales and Mrs Fitzherbert. Eastbourne-born **David Howell** (b. 14 November 1990) became Britain's youngest ever chess grandmaster following a second-place finish in the Rilton Cup in Stockholm on Friday 5 January 2007, which gave him a rating of 2501. **London to Brighton** is a traditional annual test of sporting prowess among walkers, cyclists, runners and veteran car enthusiasts. The inaugural rally in 1927 re-enacted the Emancipation Run of 1896, in which 33 drivers celebrated the repeal of the 'Red Flag Act' which effectively raised the speed limit from 4mph to 14mph and abolished the requirement of vehicles to be preceded by a man on foot. The Run has taken place every first Sunday in November thereafter, with the exception of the war years and 1947 when petrol rationing was in force. From 1930 to the present day the event has been owned and professionally organised by the Royal Automobile Club. **Hardham Church**, near Pulborough, houses the earliest medieval wall paintings to survive anywhere in England, dating to the beginning of the 12th century. **Hartfield's** main claim to fame is the Milne family, who bought Cotchford Farm in 1905. A small bridge was built over the stream at the end of their land in 1907. A young Christopher Robin Milne visited the shops in the village with his nanny in the 1920s, and his father A A Milne wrote the Winnie-the-Pooh stories incorporating the young Christopher. The area near Hartfield also features in Milne's books, the bridge on the farm being the place where Poohsticks were invented. The bridge was restored by East Sussex County Council in 1979. **John Logie Baird** transmitted the first television pictures in Hastings in 1923. **St Bartholomew's Church**, Ann Street, Brighton, lays claim to be the tallest parish church in England. The church is 180ft (55m) long, 58ft (17.5m) wide and 135ft (41m) to the ridge of the roof (147ft/45m to the top of the gilt oak cross). It also has the largest unsupported rose window in England. To cover the window would take two double-decker buses, one on top of the other. **John Bingham, 6th Baron Lucan**, was last seen alive in Sussex. A merchant banker and inveterate gambler, 'Lucky' Lucan inherited a quarter of a million pounds on the death of his father, but by 1974 he was almost bankrupt. On the night of 7 November 1974 he killed Sandra Rivett, the nanny of his two children, at his London house in the mistaken belief that she was his wife Veronica. After attacking his wife too, but failing to kill her, he drove to the house of his friend, Susan Maxwell-Scott, at Uckfield. His car was discovered at Newhaven but he was never seen again. **The Eagle Bar and Bakery**, Gloucester Road, Brighton, is the only pub in Britain that makes its own bread on the premises. **The Marine** pub at Seaside in Eastbourne will appeal to the more literary drinker, as it has its own lending library. The great Irish political leader **Charles Stewart Parnell** (1846–91) married Kitty O'Shea at Steyning on 25 June 1891 but died of a heart attack at their home in Brighton on 6 October.

Islands — **My Lord's Rock**, in the English Channel off the coast of Bexhill, is the only geographical feature that could be construed as being an island. GR: TQ747069.

Kent & East Sussex Railway — See Kent

Kipling Gardens — Rottingdean, 4 miles (6km) east of Brighton. Situated near Rottingdean seafront and named after Rudyard Kipling, whose family lived in the town 1897–1901 before moving to Batemans. The gardens are divided into a series of distinctive areas including a woodland garden, rose garden, herb garden and chalk garden. The maze-like layout with its many paths has a peace and tranquillity all of its own.

Lamb House — West Street, Rye. This 18th century brick house was home to Henry James 1898–1916. E F Benson, famed for the Mapp and Lucia novels, was a later resident, as was Rumer Godden, author of *Black Narcissus* and *The Diddakoi*. Some of James's personal possessions are on display and there is a delightful walled garden. Now owned by the National Trust. Tel. 01797 229542.

Lanes, The — The maze of narrow streets forming the Lanes are the oldest surviving part of Brighton. After the village of Brighthelmstone was burnt to the ground by French invaders in the 16th century it was rebuilt along the same streets. The town was bordered by three roads – West Street, East Street and North Street – covering an area of approximately 1 sq mile (2.5 sq km). The lower part of the town was possibly destroyed during storms in the 15th century, and evidence has been discovered suggesting that the former South Street may now lie under the shingle beach. Today the area houses a variety of jewellers, antique and gift shops, cafés and bars; although some of the buildings have been modernised or replaced, the street plan represents one of the few remaining examples in Britain of a Tudor fishing town.

Lavender Line — Isfield, 3 miles (5km) southwest of Uckfield. A heritage railway operating on part of the former Lewes to Uckfield Railway. Named after coal merchants A E Lavender & Sons, who used to operate from Isfield station, the line runs for 1 mile (1.6km), departing from and returning to Isfield station. The signal box is open to visitors. Tel. 01825 750515.

Lewes — Lying on the Ouse, Lewes has been a prosperous market town and port since the Middle Ages and is the county town of East Sussex. It is famous for its firework parades on 5 November, which commemorate not only the Gunpowder Plot but the burning of 17 Protestant martyrs in the 1550s. Harvey's Brewery, established in 1790, is also based in Lewes.

Lewes Castle High Street, Lewes. Built shortly after 1066 by William de Warenne. The shell keep was added in the 12th century, but the castle was only completed 300 years later when the impressive barbican was added by William's descendant, John de Warenne. Lewes is one of only two castles that has two mottes associated with one bailey (Lincoln Castle is the other). On John's death in 1347 the castle was abandoned and much damage was done to its fabric in a riot in the 1380s. It was later owned by Thomas Kemp, builder of Kemptown in Brighton. The castle stands above the River Ouse, offering fine views to the north and west from the two imposing 13th century semi-octagonal towers. See also Barbican House Museum. Tel. 01273 486290.

Lewes Prison Brighton Road, Lewes. Built in 1853, this 'local' prison was used in the 1940s and 1950s as a centre for young offenders. Today it houses mostly short-term and remand prisoners. Operational capacity: 558. Tel: 01273 785100.

Litlington White Horse 2 miles (3km) northeast of Seaford. Positioned on High and Over Hill above the Cuckmere Valley, this depiction of an upright horse was cut c.1925 to replace an earlier one created in the late 1830s, possibly to commemorate the coronation of Queen Victoria.

Long Man of Wilmington 1/2 mile (0.8km) south of Wilmington, 5 miles (8km) northwest of Eastbourne. The outline depiction of a man, 230ft (70m) tall and 235ft (71.5m) wide and holding what appear to be two poles, located on the side of Windover Hill. The origins of the figure are obscure. It was first referred to in documents as recently as 1710, although it is often claimed to be prehistoric or Roman, and soil-based dating carried out in 2003 puts its construction at c.1545. The outline, originally made in packed chalk, was picked out with yellow bricks in 1874 and is now marked with white-painted concrete blocks.

Lullington Heath 5 miles (8km) west of Eastbourne. A large area of chalk heathland on the northern edge of Friston Forest, with a mix of acid-loving plants such as heather and chalk-adapted flora like thyme and salad burnet. One of the largest such areas remaining in Britain, 156 acres (63ha) of the heath is a National Nature Reserve.

Merriments Garden Hurst Green, 12 miles (19km) north of Hastings, A contemporary garden created in the 1990s with dense and naturalistic planting, set in 4 acres (1.5ha) of gently sloping Wealden farmland. Tel: 01580 860666.

Michelham Priory Upper Dicker, nr Hailsham. Dating to 1229, when it was established as an Augustinian foundation by Gilbert L'Aigle, this beautiful priory was fortified for protection against French raids during the Hundred Years War. It is surrounded by the longest medieval moat in England. After its dissolution the building became a country house and a Tudor wing was added. It became a farm in the 17th century, owned by the Child family, and after falling into disrepair was rescued by the Beresford-Wrights in the 1920s before being given to the Sussex Archaeological Society. The gardens feature sculptures, and there is a restored watermill dating from the 15th century. Tel. 01323 844224.

Monk's House Rodmell, 2 miles (3km) south of Lewes. A weatherboarded 18th century cottage, the home of Virginia and Leonard Woolf until the latter's death in 1969. Virginia used to write in the garden room, which now displays extracts from her diaries and a collection of photographs. Owned by the National Trust. Tel. 01323 870001.

Moorlands Friar's Gate, 2 miles (3km) northwest of Crowborough, A 4 acre (1.5ha) garden begun in 1929 in an Ashdown Forest valley, once the site of a Wealden iron furnace. A long herbaceous border near the house leads, via a spring dell and a yew-hedged lawn, down to a wetland garden with a lake and ponds, featuring plants such as gunneras and bamboos. There are also numerous fine specimen trees including azaleas and rhododendrons. Tel: 01892 652474.

Mount Caburn 2 1/2 miles (4km) east of Lewes. An isolated hill on the South Downs standing at a height of 480ft (146m) and topped by an Iron Age hill fort covering 3 1/2 acres (1.4ha). Archaeological finds indicate that it was occupied from c.500 BC to AD 100. It falls within the boundaries of the Lewes Downs National Nature Reserve, among whose grassland flora is the largest population in Britain of the burnt-tip orchid.

Newhaven Established in the 16th century as a harbour after flooding of the Ouse valley had made navigation to the previous port at Seaford impossible, Newhaven – in contrast to most towns on the south coast – developed as a thriving port, bringing the products of the Weald's industry via the Ouse to the coast. The coming of the railway increased its prosperity and a ferry crossing to France was opened in 1847. Today it offers the only cross-Channel service (to Dieppe) in Sussex.

Northiam 6 miles (10km) northwest of Rye. On 12 May 1944, Winston Churchill and the Prime Ministers of Canada, South Africa and Southern Rhodesia met on the playing fields opposite the Crown and Thistle public house in the village to inspect troops prior to D-Day. Their names are inscribed on a set of gates erected to commemorate the event. Smuggler's Cottage, on the main road, is reputed to be the smallest house in Sussex.

Nutley Windmill 1 mile (1.6km) northeast of Nutley, 5 miles (8km) north of Uckfield. A small trestle post mill, the only working example in the UK of a type that existed as long ago as the 12th century. Also the oldest working mill in Sussex, it was moved to its present site from Goudhurst c.1813. Parts of its structure are reputed to be 300 years old.

Pashley Manor Gardens 1 mile (1.6km) southeast of Ticehurst, 13 miles (21km) northwest of Hastings. A garden laid out in English Romantic style, surrounding a Grade I listed, timber-framed manor house (not open to the public) built c.1550 and enlarged in 1720. In the last 20 years the owners, Mr and Mrs Sellick, have worked with renowned landscape architect Antony du Gard Pasley to improve the largely Victorian garden. Tel: 01580 200888.

Peacehaven 6 miles (10km) east of Brighton. Peacehaven has only existed since 1916 when the clifftop site was bought for development by Charles Neville. The Greenwich meridian crosses the coast in the middle of the town, which rapidly grew to be larger than Lewes.

Pevensey Castle — Pevensey, 3 miles (5km) northeast of Eastbourne. Built on the site of the Roman fort of Anderida, stormed by Saxons in 491, the castle dates to the 4th century, when it formed one of the Saxon Shore forts. Remarkably most of the walls from that date still stand. It was taken over after the Norman Conquest by Robert de Mortain and starved into submission after being besieged by William II in Bishop Odo's revolt of 1088. The keep was added c.1100 by William de Mortain. The castle was unsuccessfully besieged by King Stephen in 1147 before passing to Henry II in 1154. The keep was rebuilt in the late 12th century and further strengthened early in the 13th. The castle was unsuccessfully besieged by Simon de Montfort in 1264; in 1399, in the absence of her husband, the constable, Lady Joan Pelham successfully defended the castle against a siege by Richard II. A gun emplacement was built in the outer bailey in 1588 to protect against the threat of the Armada. Presented to the nation by the Duke of Devonshire in 1925, machine gun positions and a blockhouse were built in the castle during World War II. The site is now owned by English Heritage.

Pevensey Levels — An area of low-lying grazing marshland between Eastbourne and Bexhill, much of it reclaimed and crossed by a series of drainage channels. Home to many species of wetland bird and rare water plants and among the top five locations in the UK for aquatic beetles, the site of 455 acres (184ha) is now a National Nature Reserve, part owned and managed by Sussex Wildlife Trust.

Piltdown Man Hoax — In 1912 solicitor and amateur palaeontologist Charles Dawson sent to the British Museum the remains of a skull he claimed to have found in a gravel pit at Piltdown, a small village between Haywards Heath and Uckfield. It was of modern type, but had an ape-like jaw. His friend Arthur Smith Woodward, keeper of geology at the British Museum, presented the find as the 'missing link' between man and his ape ancestors, claiming it to be at least 500,000 years old and naming it Piltdown Man after the site where it was found. Despite some scepticism in the scientific community, the skull was accepted as genuine and named *Eoanthropus dawson*, 'Dawson's Dawn-Man'. Between 1911 and 1915, further items were discovered at the site, including a remarkable digging tool shaped like a cricket bat, but nothing new was produced after Dawson's eventual death from septicaemia in 1916. The modern-looking braincase and ape-like jaws of the skull soon proved to be at odds with subsequent finds of hominid fossils in Africa and Asia, and on 21 November 1953 new technology enabled the British Museum to declare that Piltdown Man was an elaborate hoax. The finds were revealed to be forgeries; the specimens had been stained and chemically treated to make them appear old, while crucial anatomical details that would have given the game away had been broken off or filed down. The skull was shown to be about 600 years old and the jaw belonged to a modern orang-utan. The digging tool was also discovered to have been doctored – although made from a genuine elephant fossil bone, tests would later reveal it had been shaped with a metal blade. It has never been conclusively proved who perpetrated the hoax. Many people have been cited as candidates, including Sir Arthur Conan Doyle, while a trunk belonging to Martin Hinton, a volunteer in the British Museum at the time of the discoveries, was discovered in the 1970s and contained what appeared to be test fakes – bones that had been cut and stained to look ancient. Although this may indicate that Hinton was the fraudster, he may equally have either been trying to work out how others made their fakes or indeed endeavouring to keep the myth alive. The overwhelming evidence points to the ambitious Dawson, who was present when all the finds were made and after whose death no more turned up.

Preston Manor — Preston Drove, Brighton, Dating from c.1600, rebuilt in 1738 and substantially enlarged in 1905, the house and its contents give a vivid insight into life during the early 20th century. There are 20 rooms over four floors, from the servants' quarters, kitchens and butler's pantry in the basement to the attic bedrooms and nursery on the top floor. The manor also comprises walled gardens and a pets' cemetery. Tel: 01273 292770.

Rivers — The **Cuckmere** rises north of Heathfield, flowing south to the coast at Cuckmere Haven.

The **Ouse** rises south of Crawley, flowing through Lewes before reaching the sea at Newhaven. Virgina Woolf drowned herself in the Ouse near Rodmell in 1941.

The **Rother** (Eastern) rises near Rotherfield, flowing east, via the villages of Etchingham, Robertsbridge, Bodiam and Wittersham, for 22 miles (35km) before joining the Royal Military Canal (linking Hythe and Rye). The river branches off into the sea at Rye Harbour while the canal continues to Cliff End. The Rother is tidal between Rye and Rye Harbour and its total length is 30 miles (48km). Its tributaries include the Bewl, Brede and Tillingham. A section known as the Kent Ditch forms the boundary between East Sussex and Kent.

The **Wellsbourne** is a small river that comes to the surface west of the Palace Pier in Brighton at low tide. St Peter's Church stands on the river.

Roedean College — 2 miles (3km) east of Brighton. Roedean School was founded in 1885 by three sisters, Penelope, Millicent and Dorothy Lawrence. The independent school for girls aged 11–18 moved to its present 40 acre (16ha) site on the Sussex Downs overlooking the sea in 1898. Former pupils include Dame Cicely Saunders, founder of the hospice movement, journalist Katherine Whitehorn and diver Tanya Streeter.

Royal Pavilion, The — Royal Pavilion Gardens, Brighton, The former seaside residence of George IV. In 1787 Henry Holland extended a farmhouse rented by the Prince of Wales, the future George IV, into a neoclassical building known as the 'Marine Pavilion'. From 1815–22, John Nash used new technology to transform the Pavilion into the Indian style building that exists today, enlarging the building and adding domes and minarets by superimposing a cast-iron framework over Holland's pavilion. The splendid interiors – including the music room with its domed ceiling of gilded scallop-shaped shells and hand-knotted carpet, and the Long Gallery with its Chinese bamboo grove – have recently been restored. The Pavilion is now owned by Brighton & Hove City Council. Tel: 01273 290900.

Rye — A port when it received its town charter and a Cinque Port in the 13th century, Rye now lies 2 miles (3km) inland due to the receding of the sea. Its winding streets and picturesque buildings have attracted a variety of literary figures, notably Henry James, Joseph Conrad, Rumer Godden and H G Wells; it has been immortalised as 'Tilling' in the Mapp and Lucia novels of E F Benson, while the cartoon pirate Captain Pugwash was created in Rye by John Ryan. See also Lamb House

Seven Sisters — 5 miles (8km) west of Eastbourne. Located between Cuckmere Haven and Birling Gap, these steeply undulating chalk cliffs are the highest in the south of England. The Seven Sisters are the chalk hills of Haven Brow, Short Brow, Rough Brow, Brass Point, Flat Hill (aka Flagstaff Point), Bailey's Hill and Went Hill. At the foot of the cliffs the remains of several wrecks can be found at low tide. The Seven Sisters Country Park covers 700 acres (280ha) of coast and downland.

Sheffield Park — 4 miles (6km) northwest of Uckfield. A superb landscaped garden laid out by Capability Brown in the 18th century, with four substantial lakes as its centrepiece. It offers spectacular sights all year round, including rhododendrons and azaleas in early summer, but is particularly renowned for its autumn displays. The house (not open to the public) was remodelled in Gothic style by James Wyatt in the late 18th century, and the estate was bought by John Holroyd, Baron Sheffield, in 1796. The first cricket match between representative sides from England and Australia took place here in 1884 (the 3rd Earl of Sheffield founded the Australian inter-state cricket competition, the Sheffield Shield, in 1893). The garden was further developed in the early 20th century by Arthur Soames, who added many exotic trees and shrubs, including North American species giving gorgeous autumn colour. The property is now owned by the National Trust. Tel: 01825 790231.

Sport:

general — **Stoolball** was invented in Sussex in the 14th century and is still played at local league level after Major W W Grantham revived the sport in the 20th century.

cricket — **Sussex County Cricket Club,** England's oldest county cricket club, was formed in 1839, but had to wait until 2003 to gain its first County Championship title before repeating the feat in 2006 and 2007. Its one-day team is named the Sussex Sharks. The club plays most of its home games at the County Cricket Ground, Hove, but also plays at Arundel, Eastbourne and Horsham. Tel: 0844 264 0202.

football — **Brighton & Hove Albion** were formed in 1901 and joined the Football League in 1920. Nicknamed The Seagulls (after a brief period as The Dolphins, as pictured on the town's crest), they played at the Goldstone Ground until 1996 but have in effect been homeless since May 1997, spending two seasons groundsharing with Gillingham in Kent, before moving to a temporary home at Withdean Stadium in 1999. Their traditional colours are blue and white stripes. The club were 'Champions of England' in the 1910–11 season, securing the Southern League title and beating the Football League champions, Aston Villa, 1–0 in the FA Charity Shield. In 1983 Brighton were beaten 4–0 in the FA Cup final replay by Manchester United after holding them to a 2–2 draw at Wembley. Tel: 01273 778855.

greyhound racing — **Brighton & Hove Greyhound Stadium**, Nevill Road, Hove. 455m track. Ballyregan Bob, trained at Albourne, achieved a world record on 9 December 1986 at the stadium by attaining his 32nd consecutive victory. Tel: 01273 204601.

horse racing — **Brighton**, Freshfield Road, Racehill, Brighton, is a left-handed crescent-shaped course of just under 1½ miles (2.5km), one of only four in England (along with Epsom, Newmarket and York) that is not a complete circuit. Brighton holds only Flat race meetings. Tel: 01273 603580;

Plumpton, Plumpton Green, is one of the smaller countryside racecourses, with a left-handed National Hunt track of 9 furlongs (1.8km). The family home of Camilla, Duchess of Cornwall, formerly stood opposite the racecourse. Tel: 01273 890383.

University of Brighton — The former Brighton Polytechnic was awarded university status in 1992. Its 19,000 students and 2100 staff are based on four campuses in Brighton and Eastbourne: Grand Parade in the centre of Brighton; Moulsecoomb campus, 2 miles (3km) inland, the administrative hub of the university; the greenfield Falmer campus on the northern edge of Brighton, featuring accommodation and sports facilities; and the Eastbourne campus, situated in the Meads area. Former students include actor Paddy Considine and broadcaster Jo Whiley. Tel: 01273 600900.

University of Sussex — The first of the new wave of universities founded in the 1960s, receiving its royal charter in August 1961 and becoming a pioneer of internationally focused and interdisciplinary courses of study. Situated on the edge of the Sussex Downs 4 miles (6km) northeast of Brighton – the only university in England entirely located in an Area of Outstanding Natural Beauty – the campus was largely designed by Sir Basil Spence; the buildings include Falmer House, which won a Royal Institute of British Architects medal in the year it opened (1962), and the circular Meeting House, based on the design of a traditional oast house, which won a Civic Trust award in 1969. In 1993, the buildings at the core of Spence's design were given listed building status; Falmer House was one of only two educational buildings in the UK to be listed Grade I. Among the university's science faculty are two Nobel Prize winners, Sir John Cornforth and Professor Harry Kroto; the first Briton to win the chemistry prize in over ten years, Kroto received the prize in 1996 for the discovery of fullerenes, a new class of carbon compounds. The university has 15 Fellows of the Royal Society, the highest number per science student of any British university other than Cambridge. Former students include politicians Hilary Benn and Peter Hain, broadcasters Michael Buerk and Julia Somerville, and novelist Philippa Gregory. Tel: 01273 606755.

Wilmington Priory — 6 miles (10km) northwest of Eastbourne. Dedicated to St Mary, Wilmington Priory was founded some time before 1243 as a cell of the Benedictine abbey at Grestain in Normandy. The priory buildings were substantially extended and altered in the 18th century; the remains of the porch and crypt date largely from the 14th century. See also Long Man of Wilmington

Some famous people born in East Sussex

Beardsley, Aubrey (illustrator) (1872–98)	Brighton
Belaney, Archibald Stansfeld ('Grey Owl') (1888–1938)	Hastings
Carter, Angela (novelist) (1940–92)	Eastbourne
Chester, Charlie (entertainer) (1914–97)	Eastbourne
Clayton, Jack (film director) (1921–1995)	Brighton
Cowell, Simon (pop music guru) (1959–)	Brighton
Faulkner, (Herbert) Max (golfer) (1916–2005)	Bexhill-on-Sea
Fisher, Allison (snooker and pool player) (1968–)	Peacehaven
Foster, Julia (actress) (1943–)	Lewes
Gill, (Arthur) Eric (sculptor) (1882–1940)	Brighton
Grimshaw, Nicholas (architect) (1939–)	Hove
Hare, David (playwright) (1947–)	Bexhill-on-Sea
Jordan (Katie Price, model) (1978–)	Brighton
Kennedy, Nigel (violinist) (1956–)	Brighton
Miller, Max (comedian) (1894–1963)	Brighton
North, Marianne (traveller and artist) (1830–90)	Hastings
Ovett, Steve (athlete) (1955–)	Brighton
Parker, Cecil (actor) (1897–1971)	Hastings
Ryle, Martin (radio astronomer) (1918–84)	Brighton
Sellers, Piers (3rd Briton in space) (1955–)	Crowborough
Smith, Sheila Kaye (novelist) (1887–1956)	St Leonards-on-Sea
Soddy, Frederick (radiochemist) (1877–1956)	Eastbourne
Suggs (Madness singer Graham McPherson) (1961–)	Hastings
Williams, Hugh (actor) (1904–69)	Bexhill-on-Sea
Wilson, Angus (novelist) (1913–91)	Bexhill-on-Sea

Local Attractions and Information: West Sussex

Acid Bath Murders A series of murders committed in the 1940s by John George Haigh (1910–49). While living in a small hotel in Kensington, Haigh became friendly with Olive Durand-Dickson, a wealthy 69 year old widow, who told him of her ideas for marketing cosmetics. Haigh invited her to his factory in Crawley, where she was shot and her body disposed of in a vat of sulphuric acid. He then presented himself at Chelsea police station and reported her missing. Police became suspicious and checked his factory, where they found the murder weapon and Mrs Durand-Dickson's plastic dentures. Haigh made a statement admitting to eight other murders, including three members of a family called McSwan, a Dr and Mrs Henderson and three other people whose identities he had never established. He was tried at Lewes Crown Court in July 1949 and executed at Wandsworth Prison on 10 August.

Administrative headquarters County Hall, West Street, Chichester PO19 1RQ. Tel: 01243 777100.

Amberley Castle Amberley, 4 miles (6km) north of Arundel. Originally built in the late 11th or 12th century as a manor house for the Bishops of Chichester. Bishop Rede was given licence to crenellate in 1377; much of the curtain wall and 14th century great hall can still be seen. A Royalist stronghold during the Civil War, the castle was slighted by Parliamentary forces in 1643. In 1893, centuries of ecclesiastical ownership came to an end when it was purchased by the Duke of Norfolk, who began restoring the building. Having passed through several further hands, the property was purchased in 1988 by Joy and Martin Cummings, who have since converted it into one of England's top country hotels. Tel: 01798 831992.

Amberley Wild Brooks 1 mile (1.6km) northeast of Amberley, 3 miles (5km) southwest of Pulborough. An 203 acre (82ha) wetland area in the floodplain of the River Arun, consisting of grazing marsh and ditches. Saved from drainage for agricultural use in the 1970s, it is a rare surviving example of wetland in southeast England. A nature reserve and Site of Special Scientific Interest, the ditches support a wide range of invertebrates while the site provides a habitat for wildfowl and waders. Managed by Sussex Wildlife Trust. Tel: 01273 492630.

Amberley Working Museum Amberley, 4 miles (6km) north of Arundel. An open-air museum situated in an old chalk pit and dedicated to the industrial history of Sussex. Exhibits include the Southdown bus collection, a village garage and various items relating to local industries, while working craftsmen demonstrate traditional crafts. Tel: 01798 831370.

Arundel Castle High Street, Arundel. Dominating the village of Arundel, the castle has been the seat of the Dukes of Norfolk and Earls of Arundel for more than 800 years. The original motte and bailey structure with gatehouse was built c.1070 by Roger de Montgomery. Taken by Henry I in 1102, and later unsuccessfully besieged by King Stephen, it was largely rebuilt in stone by Henry II who gave it to William D'Albini, Earl of Arundel, in 1155. It then passed via the D'Albinis and the Fitzalans – the Fitzalan Chapel in the grounds, built in 1390 in Gothic style, was founded by the 4th Earl – to the Howard family in the 16th century. The castle was captured by Royalists in December 1643 but retaken by Sir William Waller for Parliament in January 1644 and slighted. In 1749 Horace Walpole described it as a 'heap of ruins'; most of what can be seen today is the result of reconstruction in the 18th and 19th centuries under Henry, 15th Duke of Norfolk. His refurbishments, completed in

1900, added electric light (the castle was one of the first private residences to have electricity), lifts and central heating. The main displays now include fine collections of tapestries, furniture, weaponry and armour. Other features include the personal possessions of Mary, Queen of Scots, including the gold and enamel rosary she carried to her execution, and a Victorian steam-powered fire engine. The Dukes of Norfolk are still buried in the Fitzalan Chapel, while the surrounding parkland includes a boating lake and many walks. Tel: 01903 882173.

Arundel Cathedral — Parsons Hill, London Road, Arundel. Built in French Gothic style, the cathedral church of the Roman Catholic Diocese of Arundel and Brighton was founded by Henry, 15th Duke of Norfolk; designed by Joseph Hansom, inventor of the Hansom cab, it was completed on 1 July 1873. The original dedication was to St Philip Neri, founder of the Oratorian religious order. When the Diocese of Arundel and Brighton was created in 1965, the church was made its cathedral and rededicated to Our Lady and St Philip. In 1973 there was a further change in dedication to the recently canonised 16th century martyr St Philip Howard.

Arundel Wildfowl and Wetlands Centre — Mill Road, Arundel. A reserve of the Wildfowl and Wetlands Trust, covering 64 acres (26ha) and home to many rare ducks, geese and swans, including the world's rarest goose, the Nene. WWT Arundel is the only place outside New Zealand to have successfully bred New Zealand Blue ducks. Also featured is a recreation of the volcanic Lake Myvatin of northern Iceland. Tel. 01903 883355.

Barnham Windmill — Barnham, 3 miles (5km) north of Bognor Regis. Tower mill built on the site of a previous post mill and operational between 1829 and the 1960s. Now undergoing restoration.

Bignor Roman Villa — Bignor, 4 miles (6km) southwest of Pulborough. A large Roman villa discovered in 1811 by ploughman George Tupper. It features several well-preserved mosaics including a single stretch 80ft (24m) long, the longest yet found in the UK. Other mosaics depict an eagle carrying off Ganymede, dancing nymphs, gladiators and Venus and Cupid. The building originally dates from the 2nd century AD but was much enlarged in the 3rd century. A museum displays artefacts found on the site. Tel: 01798 869259.

Bognor Regis — Bognor Regis began as a Saxon village and remained a hamlet, its inhabitants making a living from fishing and smuggling, until wealthy London hatter Richard Hotham decided to create his own seaside resort after staying in a nearby farmhouse in the 1780s. Dr Richard Russell had already popularised the benefits of bathing in sea water as a cure for numerous illnesses, and spending summer at the seaside had become fashionable among the wealthy; purchasing 1600 acres of land, Hotham initially planned to name the new resort Hothamton after himself, although he ultimately deferred to modesty. Royalty soon began to frequent the resort – Queen Victoria referred to Hotham's new town as 'dear little Bognor' – but it was truly established only with the arrival of the railway in 1864. In 1928 George V came to Bognor to convalesce after a serious illness. Although he actually stayed at Craigweil House in nearby Aldwick, after his departure the council successfully applied for permission to add 'Regis' to the town's name. Despite the king's legendary dying words of 'Bugger Bognor' when told he would soon be well enough to revisit the town, other members of the royal family loved Bognor. A Butlin's holiday camp was opened in 1960; it later became known as Southcoast World until 1998 and is now known as Butlins Bognor Regis Resort. Bognor is also the setting for Jane Austen's *Sanditon*.

Borde Hill Garden — 2 miles (3km) northwest of Haywards Heath. A beautiful and botanically rich heritage garden created in the 1890s as a series of intimate 'rooms', and featuring rhododendrons, camellias and many other exotic species brought back from Asia and South America by the great plant hunters. It is set within 200 acres (80ha) of traditional parkland surrounding the Elizabethan mansion of Borde Hill House, with woodland, lakes and outstanding views across the High Weald. Tel: 01444 450326.

Bosham — 3 miles (5km) west of Chichester. Bosham (pronounced 'Bozzem') stands on a small peninsula between two tidal creeks at the eastern end of Chichester harbour, a designated Area of Outstanding Natural Beauty. It was from Bosham Quay Meadow that Harold II sailed for Normandy in 1064; both he and Holy Trinity Church (see separate entry) are depicted in the Bayeux Tapestry, and it is claimed by some that he was buried in the churchyard rather than in Waltham Abbey (see Essex) after the Battle of Hastings. King Cnut also reputedly commanded the tide to retreat here. Today Bosham is a sailing centre and provides a sanctuary for migrating wildfowl.

Boxgrove Priory — 4 miles (6km) east of Chichester. The remains of the guest house, chapter house and church of a small 12th century Benedictine priory, founded by William de la Haye as a cell of the French abbey at Lessay and confirmed as an independent foundation by Richard II in 1383. The church of St Mary and St Blaise is still in use today. The priory remains are in the care of English Heritage.

Bramber Castle — 1/4 mile (0.4km) west of Bramber, 4 miles (6km) north of Shoreham. Constructed as a motte and bailey castle c.1070 by William de Braose to guard what was at the time a sizeable port on the river Adur, the castle was occupied until c.1450 by his descendants. It was destroyed during the Civil War by Parliamentary forces who positioned their guns in the nearby church; the remains consist largely of a single piece of masonry 75ft (23m) high from the gatehouse tower and portions of the curtain wall. Tel: 01424 775705.

Chanctonbury Ring — 1 mile (1.6km) east of Washington, 5 miles (8km) north of Worthing. Located on the top of the South Downs, 700ft (213m) above sea level, and visible for several miles, this small Iron Age hill fort owes its prominence in the landscape to Charles Goring, owner of the nearby Wiston estate, who against local opposition planted a circle of beech trees on the top in 1760. The inner trees never grew well and it was found they had been planted on the site of a Roman temple. The Ring is the subject of much local folklore; dancing fairies are said to appear at Midsummer Eve and if you run backwards around it the Devil is rumoured to appear. Sadly most of the trees were blown down in the hurricane of 1987, although they have since been replanted.

Chichester The history of the cathedral city of Chichester, also the county town of West Sussex, dates back to Roman times. Standing on the site of Roman Noviomagus and on the River Lavant, it was the chief city of Saxon Sussex and was still a flourishing market town in the 10th century, but its status was secured with the building of its famous cathedral at the end of the 11th century. It holds a major arts festival each July.

Chichester Cathedral West Street, Chichester. Dedicated to the Holy Trinity, and founded by Bishop Ralph de Luffa, the cathedral has been the seat of the Bishop of Chichester since 1075. The building was completed in 1108, though much added to in succeeding centuries, and at 393ft (120m) long and 90ft (27.5m) wide is one of the smaller cathedrals in England. It underwent considerable reconstruction in the 13th century after two major fires. Bishop Richard of Chichester was canonised in 1262 and his shrine behind the high altar became a place of pilgrimage. The 14th century tomb of Sir Richard Fitzalan, Earl of Arundel, and his second wife inspired Philip Larkin to write his poem 'An Arundel Tomb'. More modern features include a window by Marc Chagall and artworks by John Piper and Graham Sutherland. Its detached bell-tower, containing eight bells, is the only remaining example in England belonging to a cathedral, while the 15th century spire is 277ft (84.5m) high; it collapsed in 1861, but was rebuilt within four years.

Christ's Hospital 2 miles (3km) southwest of Horsham. A public school notable for its archaic uniforms and picturesque campus, Christ's Hospital was founded at Newgate in London and received its royal charter from Edward VI in 1553. Opened to provide for vagrant children, it still retains a charitable purpose in assessing its fees on a means-tested basis, while limiting the number of pupils from well-off families. After the Great Fire made parts of the school uninhabitable, its pupils – both boys and girls – were sent to various parts of the country. The girls finally settled in Hertford and in 1897 the boys were established at its present site in Horsham. In 1985 the girls were reunited at Horsham and the school again became co-educational. One of numerous so-called 'Bluecoat schools', Christ's Hospital is the only one in the UK to retain the long cassock-like robe, knee breeches and yellow socks as its everyday uniform. Former pupils (known as 'Old Blues') include Sir Colin Davis, Samuel Taylor Coleridge, Barnes Wallis and Bernard Levin. The school's profile was raised in 2005 by the Channel 4 series *Rock School*, in which rock legend Gene Simmons turned pupils into rock stars. Tel. 01403 211293.

Church of the Holy Trinity Located in the picturesque harbour village of Bosham, this 10th century church is one of the earliest in Sussex and is believed to be built on Roman foundations. It features a well-preserved Saxon chancel arch and tower. Harold II's visit to the church is depicted in the Bayeux Tapestry and the daughter of King Cnut is buried here.

Cissbury Ring 1 mile (1.6km) east of Findon, 3 miles (5km) north of Worthing. The second largest Iron Age hill fort in England. Standing 602ft (183.5m) above sea level, Cissbury was built in the 3rd century BC on the site of Neolithic flint workings and consists of an outer rampart, a ditch and an inner bank more than a mile round, enclosing an area of over 60 acres (24ha). It was refortified in the late Roman period against Saxon raids, and in 1587 was the site of an Armada beacon. Now owned by the National Trust.

Clayton Windmills 1½ miles (2.5km) south of Hassocks, 5 miles (8km) north of Brighton. A pair of windmills, known as Jack and Jill, standing on the Downs. Jack, a brick tower mill built in the 1860s, is now a private home. Jill, a post mill built in 1821, was originally located near Brighton but was dismantled and moved to its present location in the 1850s. Both mills fell into disuse in 1908, but Jill has been restored.

Cowdray Park 7 miles (11km) northeast of Midhurst. The ruins of a 16th century country house, destroyed by fire in 1793, set in the midst of the Cowdray Estate overlooking the South Downs. Next to the house is a recreated Tudor walled garden. Home to Cowdray Park Polo Club, the estate is the venue for the Veuve Cliquot Gold Cup, the premier English polo competition.

Crawley Crawley has its roots in an Anglo-Saxon settlement – there is a Saxon church at Worth nearby – and it grew during the 19th century as a railway town, but its explosion in size after World War II was due to its designation as a New Town. By the 1960s its population had grown from 10,000 to 60,000 and it has continued to spread since. The development of Gatwick Airport has made this central region of Sussex a growing centre of employment.

Denmans Garden ¼ mile (0.4km) south of Fontwell, 5 miles (8km) east of Chichester. Once the home farm of nearby Westergate House, the 4 acre (1.5ha) garden, laid out since 1946, is informally planted and utilises gravel both as a landscaping surface and a growing medium to create a range of informal effects using a combination of native and tender species. There is also a walled garden, informally planted with herbaceous borders. Owned by garden designer John Brookes. Tel: 01243 542808.

East Grinstead Established as a village in the Anglo-Saxon period, East Grinstead received its charter in 1247, and its High Street contains several impressive 14th century timber-framed buildings. It is most notable today as the home of several major religious foundations including the Church of Scientology and the UK Jehovah's Witnesses.

Ebernoe Common 3 miles (5km) north of Petworth, 7 miles (11km) northwest of Pulborough. The Ebernoe Common and Butcherlands National Nature Reserve consists of ancient woodland and pasture meadow, home to several species of bat and also providing breeding habitat for woodpeckers and nightingales. Over 400 species of fungi are present, along with 375 species of plant. Managed by Sussex Wildlife Trust.

Edburton Castle ½ mile (0.8km) southeast of Edburton, 6 miles (10km) northwest of Brighton. Located on the north escarpment of the South Downs with commanding views of the Weald to the north and the coast to the south. Once the site of a 12th century wooden motte and bailey castle, built by the Normans as a stronghold during the civil war between King Stephen and Matilda, the remaining earthworks have been damaged but the low motte, encased by a ditch and the remains of a counterscarp bank, is just visible. There is also a northern bailey enclosed by a low rampart and ditch.

Fishbourne Roman Palace Fishbourne, 1 mile (1.6km) west of Chichester. Discovered by accident in 1960 when work on a drainpipe was being carried out, the site was a military base at the time of the Roman invasion in AD 43. By the end of the 1st century it had been developed into a sumptuous palace with over 100 rooms. The most striking remains are the mosaics; mostly created c.AD 75–80, they are among the earliest in England as well as the most opulent. At this period, craftsmen would have been imported from Italy as there was no one in Britain with the skill to create them. Some rooms feature later, many-coloured mosaics laid on top of earlier black and white geometric designs, a picture of developing styles seen nowhere else in the UK. Perhaps the most famous 2nd century mosaic depicts Cupid astride a dolphin. Also to be seen is a well-preserved hypocaust or underfloor heating system. Part of the formal gardens have been replanted to their original design. It has been suggested that the palace was built for Togidubnus, ruler of the local Atrebates, who became a client king of the Romans after the invasion. Tel. 01243 785859.

Ford Prison 1/2 mile (0.8km) south of Ford, 1 1/2 miles (2.5km) west of Littlehampton. A low-security open prison built on a former Fleet Air Arm station and opened in 1960. Renowned for its easy regime with an emphasis on training and resettlement, Ford houses convicted adult males, and specialises in housing non-violent offenders with a low risk of absconding. It was until recently particularly known as the favoured location for the placement of high-profile and celebrity prisoners. Operational capacity: 557. Tel: 01903 663000.

Gatwick Airport 2 miles (3km) north of Crawley. There has been an airport at Gatwick since the 1930s, and in 1936 the world's first circular passenger terminal was opened here. But what is today known as London Gatwick Airport was officially designated London's second airport in 1953. After closing for major redevelopment, it reopened in 1956 with a 2000ft runway, a new terminal building (now the South Terminal) and a railway station. It served over 1 million passengers each year by the 1980s, most of this growth being fuelled by charter flights. British United Airways was then the major operator, but the airport had already opened to transatlantic flights in 1978 and the runway was extended to accommodate the bigger planes. A second (north) terminal was opened by Queen Elizabeth II in 1991. The two terminals are connected by a passenger monorail. By 2005 annual passenger numbers at what is now the UK's second busiest airport exceeded 32 million. Tel: 0870 000 2468.

Goodwood House 3 1/2 miles (5.5km) northeast of Chichester. At the heart of an estate of 12,000 acres (5000ha), the present house was begun by James Wyatt in 1790. The ancestral home for more than 300 years of the Dukes of Richmond, direct descendants of Charles II, Goodwood's main attraction is a superb art collection that includes paintings of London by Canaletto and several horses by George Stubbs, housed in the Regent State Apartments. There are also displays of porcelain, French tapestries and fine furniture. Tel. 01243 755048.

Goodwood Sculpture Park 3 miles (5km) northeast of Chichester. Located on the Goodwood estate in the South Downs and run by the Cass Sculpture Foundation, Goodwood Sculpture Park features a changing collection of works by major contemporary artists set in 26 acres (10.5ha) of ancient woodland. Tel: 01243 538449.

Gravetye Manor 1 1/2 miles (2.5km) north of West Hoathley, 3 1/2 miles (5.5km) southwest of East Grinstead. An Elizabethan stone house dating from 1598 and built by ironmaster Richard Infield. The great Irish garden designer William Robinson (1838–1935), inventor of the naturalistic style of garden planting, bought the property in 1885 and over the following 50 years created a magnificent Arts and Crafts style garden to set off the house. Gravetye Manor is now a hotel. Tel: 0870 860 8421.

Hammerwood Park 3 1/2 miles (5.5km) east of East Grinstead. A neoclassical house built in 1792 as a hunting lodge in the form of a Temple of Apollo by Benjamin Latrobe, architect of the White House and Capitol, Washington DC. Having been converted into flats in the 1960s, the house was purchased by rock group Led Zeppelin in the 1970s and rescued from dereliction by the Pinnegar family in 1982. The dining room remains in a state of artful decay. An almost complete copy of the Parthenon Frieze (part of the Elgin Marbles) is on display. Tel: 01342 850594.

Hickstead Jumping Course 1/4 mile (0.4km) south of Hickstead, 5 miles (8km) southwest of Haywards Heath. The All England Jumping Course was established in 1960 as a venue for show jumping and three day eventing. There is seating for over 5000 spectators and since 1992 the course has hosted the Longines Royal International Horse Show. Tel: 01273 834315.

High Beeches Woodland and Water Gardens 1 mile (1.6km) northeast of Handcross, 3 miles (5km) south of Crawley. The 27 acre (11ha) garden was established around the house of High Beeches in the early 20th century by Col. Giles Loder as a home for exotic species brought to England by plant hunters such as Ernest Wilson and Frank Kingdom Ward. The 19th century house was destroyed by fire during World War II after being struck by a plane, but the collections of rare plants set in beautiful woodland and water gardens have continued to develop. Especially colourful in spring, with bluebells and azaleas, and in autumn, when the leaves turn to brilliant colour, the gardens feature open glades, rippling streams and quiet pools, and a natural wildflower meadow. Tel: 01444 400589.

Highdown Gardens 2 miles (3km) northwest of Worthing. Established over 50 years by banker Sir Frederick Stern and his wife, who bought a former chalk pit on the South Downs in 1909 determined to prove that a thriving garden could be made in the thin, unpromising soil. Highdown was left by Lady Stern to Worthing Borough Council in 1967 and has since been maintained by the local authority. The 9 acre (3.5ha) garden features fine collections of peonies and roses, along with many plants brought to England from China and the Himalayas by plant collectors in the early 20th century. The Cave Pond was built on the site of an old pigsty. Tel: 01903 210022.

High Salvington Windmill — High Salvington, 2½ miles (3.5km) north of Worthing. Situated in a suburb high above the seaside town of Worthing, this black post mill was built before 1750. It ceased commercial operations in 1897, but is now fully restored and working again.

Highest point — Black Down at 919ft (280m). GR: SU919296.

Interesting facts — The **Birdman** is an annual competition for human-powered 'flying machines' held each summer in Bognor Regis. Contestants launch themselves from the end of the pier and a prize is awarded to whoever glides the furthest. If a distance of 100m is accomplished an additional £30,000 is awarded. The prize has not been claimed thus far although a flight of 92m has been recorded. Rarely taken completely seriously, the event provides competitors with an opportunity to construct improbable machines complete with outlandish dress. The spectacle draws a crowd in excess of 25,000 in addition to local and national media. Inaugurated in nearby Selsey in 1971, the Birdman transferred to Bognor in 1978 when it had outgrown its original location. The event was held in Worthing in 2008 and 2009. The **heaviest hailstone** ever recorded in Britain fell on Horsham on 5 September 1958. It weighed 5 oz (142g). In 1992, **Henfield** was granted its own coat of arms, the first village in England to be so honoured. The **mouse-eared bat** (*Myotis myotis*) was declared extinct in Britain in January of 1992, after the last specimen died in Sussex. It was the first mammal to become extinct in this country since the extirpation of the wolf in 1745. However, a young mouse-eared bat was found hibernating near Chichester during the winter of 2002 to give hope for the species. **William Huskisson**, MP for Chichester, was killed by Stephenson's *Rocket* on 15 September 1830, thus becoming the first fatal casualty in a railway accident. The first English branch of the **Women's Institute** was set up at Singleton and East Dean, midway between Midhurst and Chichester, in 1915. **Mark Lemon** (1809–70) was the co-founder and first editor of *Punch* in 1841. A successful playwright, actor and lecturer, and impersonator of Shakespearian characters, he also wrote a host of novelettes and lyrics, over a hundred songs, a few three-volume novels, several Christmas fairy tales and a volume of jests. He was a stalwart of the London gentlemen's club the Savage Club. He died in Crawley on 23 May 1870 and is buried in St Margaret's Church, Ifield, Crawley. **2D**, lead vocalist and keyboard player with the successful virtual band Gorillaz, was virtually born in Crawley, probably due to his creator Jamie Hewlett having been raised in nearby Horsham.

Islands — There are five islands in West Sussex: **Barn Rocks** in the English Channel lies east of Selsey (GR: SZ907978); **Bognor Rocks** in the English Channel, off the coast of Bognor Regis, is only visible at low water (GR: SZ930980); **Fowley Island** lies in Chichester Harbour (GR: SU743045); **Pilsey Island** in Chichester Harbour made headline news in 1956 when the body of Lionel Crabb, who had been employed by MI6, was found nearby, leading to an international incident (GR: SU770007); **Thorney Island** in Chichester Harbour is separated from the mainland by a narrow channel called the Great Deep. Population: 1079 (GR: SU760030).

Kingley Vale — 8 miles (13km) northwest of Chichester. One of the earliest National Nature Reserves to be established in England, designated 1952–6 thanks to Sir Arthur Tansley, chairman of the Nature Conservancy, to whom there is a memorial on Bow Hill at the head of the Vale. Consisting of ancient yew forest, along with downland featuring 14 ancient monuments including a pair of Bronze Age barrows known as the Devil's Humps. Some of the trees are believed to be 2000 years old. Also a candidate Special Area of Conservation, the 371 acre (150ha) site is managed by English Nature.

Knepp Castle — ¼ mile (0.4km) west of West Grinstead, 10 miles (16km) west of Haywards Heath. An 11th century earthwork motte and bailey fortress founded by William de Braose. In 1214, King John built a stone castle on the site, adding a two-storey keep or hall-house to the natural low mound. Surrounded by a moat, with a counterscarp bank, the keep and a chapel were also encased by a curtain wall, flanked by a gatehouse. Located in an important centre for hunting, it was used more as a fortified hunting lodge than a castle. Only one corner of the keep now stands, stone from the rest having been used in the 18th century for the construction of a turnpike road. The 19th century house called Knepp Castle, located 1 mile (1.6km) to the northwest on the Knepp estate, was designed by John Nash and completed in 1812.

Lancing College — 1 mile (1.6km) northeast of Lancing, 4 miles (6km) northeast of Worthing. Co-educational public school founded in 1848 by local clergyman Nathaniel Woodard. Its chapel, dedicated in 1868, dominates the hillside overlooking the River Arun. Former pupils include authors Evelyn Waugh and Jan Morris and lyricist Tim Rice.

Leonardslee Gardens — ½ mile (0.8km) north of Crabtree, 7 miles (11km) west of Haywards Heath. The gardens cover 240 acres (100ha) in a sheltered valley which includes seven lakes and were largely developed in the late 1800s by the Loder family, who still own them. Rhododendrons, azaleas, camellias and magnolias provide a vibrant display in May. In summer the gardens and lakes take on a more subdued and subtle beauty with wild flowers and fragrant flowering trees. There are wildfowl, large carp, deer and wallabies, which have lived semi-wild in the gardens for 100 years and help to keep the grass under control. A collection of Victorian motor cars are kept in perfect working order and take part in the annual London to Brighton run; other features include an award-winning bonsai exhibition and the 'Behind the Doll's House' exhibition, depicting a country estate of 100 years ago at 1:12 scale. Tel: 01403 891212.

Marbles: World Championships — The time between Ash Wednesday and Good Friday is traditionally when marbles is played in Britain, and the World Marbles Championships are held annually on Good Friday at the Greyhound public house, Tinsley Green, Crawley. Although the contests in their present form date back to the 1930s, marbles contests have supposedly taken place here for many centuries –

since, in the time of Elizabeth I, two men were fighting for the love of a woman, and after a variety of competitions the lady's fate was finally sealed with a game of marbles. Local Crawley teams The Toucan Terribles, and more recently, The Black Dog Boozers, have had great success in the championships.

Marlipins Museum — High Street, Shoreham-by-Sea. A museum of local and maritime history housed in a building of Norman origin, believed to have once been used as a customs house. The name Marlipins refers to a board game (correctly known as merels) which was played in the area from the end of the 14th century. Tel: 01273 462994.

Nymans Garden — $^{1}/_{2}$ mile (0.8km) southeast of Handcross, 5 miles (8km) northwest of Haywards Heath. One of the first gardens to be bequeathed to the National Trust, which took over its care in 1953, Nymans is set amid an estate of 600 acres (240ha) and surrounds the ruins of a Gothic mansion, the home of the Messel family for over 100 years. It is internationally renowned for its collection of rare plants. The Messels were pioneers in developing a pinetum and heather garden, while the walled garden features tender exotic species from aound the globe. There are woodland walks and a wild garden. Much of the mock-medieval house burnt down in 1947 but it was partially rebuilt. The library, drawing room and other family rooms are open during the summer. Tel: 01444 405250.

Pallant House — North Pallant, Chichester. A Queen Anne style house built in 1712, one of the first of its kind in Chichester. It was a private house until the early 1900s and became a gallery in the 1980s, each room decorated to reflect a different period in the house's history. Its fine collection of 20th century British art features works by, among others, Peter Blake, Lucian Freud and Howard Hodgkin. An extension opened in 2006 was awarded the 2007 Gulbenkian Prize. Tel: 01243 774557.

Parham House and Gardens — $1^{1}/_{4}$ miles (2km) west of Storrington, 5 miles (8km) northeast of Arundel. A beautiful stone Elizabethan house dating from 1577 and built by Sir Thomas Palmer, in which are displayed a variety of collections including portraits, needlework and historic objects such as early globes of the world. Bought in 1601 by Thomas Bysshop, it remained in the same family until 1922 when it was purchased from the 13th Lady Zouche by the Hon. Clive Pearson, younger son of Viscount Cowdray. During World War II it was home to evacuee children and Canadian soldiers, and Pearson and his wife Alicia opened the house to visitors in 1948. Parham Park is now the home of Pearson's great-granddaughter, Lady Emma Barnard, her husband James and their family, but is owned by a charitable trust. Outside are an 18th century pleasure garden and a 4 acre (1.5ha) walled garden, while the house is surrounded by 300 acres (120ha) of ancient deer park whose fallow deer are descendants of the original herd first recorded in 1628. Tel: 01903 742021.

Petworth Cottage Museum — High Street, Petworth, A Petworth estate worker's cottage restored and furnished as it might have been c.1910, when to was home to Mrs Mary Cummings. Originally from Ireland, Mary Cummings came to Petworth with her husband, Michael Thomas, formerly a farrier sergeant-major in the Hussars, who was employed as a farrier on the estate after leaving the army. Mary worked as a seamstress at Petworth House and at home, and the cottage's workroom is arranged as a sewing room containing her treadle sewing machine. Tel: 01798 342100.

Petworth House — Petworth, 5 miles (8km) west of Pulborough. Immortalised in several paintings by J M W Turner, Petworth stands in a 700 acre (280ha) park landscaped by Capability Brown; the walls of the house dominate the estate village of Petworth. The house is renowned for its art collection, founded in the 1630s by the 10th Earl of Northumberland, a friend of Van Dyck. When it was rebuilt in the 1750s, a number of carvings were commissioned from woodcarver Grinling Gibbons and these can be seen in the Carved Room. The art collection was greatly extended in the 19th century by George Wyndham, 3rd Earl of Egremont, who added paintings by Turner, Joshua Reynolds and William Blake, among others. The servants' quarters are also open to the public. Now owned by the National Trust. Tel: 01798 342207.

Priest House, The — West Hoathly, 4 miles (6km) southwest of East Grinstead. Standing in the beautiful surroundings of a traditional cottage garden on the edge of Ashdown Forest, the early 15th century timber-framed hall-house was modernised in Elizabethan times into a substantial yeoman's dwelling. Its furnished rooms contain 17th and 18th century furniture, kitchen equipment, needlework and household items. There is a formal herb garden containing over 150 varieties of herbs. Tel: 01342 810479.

Rivers — The **Adur** has two branches. The western tributary rises 4 miles (6km) south of Horsham and then runs southeast; the eastern rises on Ditchling Common, joining its western counterpart at Henfield. It is tidal for 11 miles (18km) between Bines Bridge, flowing through the Shoreham gap to its estuary at Shoreham-by-Sea, where it flows through an area of mudflats.

The **Arun** rises in St Leonards Forest near Horsham. Joined at Stopham by the River Rother (Western), it then flows past the wetland areas of Pulborough Brooks (an RSPB reserve) and the Site of Special Scientific Interest at Amberley Wild Brooks, and through Arundel to the sea at Littlehampton, a total length of $25^{1}/_{2}$ miles (41km). It is the second fastest flowing river in England.

The **Rother** (Western) rises just across the West Sussex border at Empshott in Hampshire. It flows south to Petersfield and then east via Midhurst before joining the Arun at Stopham, near Pulborough. Its total length is approximately 30 miles (48km). Although it is a distinct river from the Rother in East Sussex it is usually referred to as the Rother (Western) to save confusion.

Sackville College — High Street, East Grinstead. A Jacobean almshouse founded in 1609 with a bequest from Robert Sackville, Earl of Dorset, owner of substantial property in Sussex; built of local sandstone around a central courtyard, it was completed in 1619 and remains largely unaltered. It still retains the function of providing accommodation for the elderly. For many years the building also provided overnight accommodation for the Sackville family as they journeyed to and from their Sussex estates. The splendid great hall retains its gallery and original hammerbeam roof, and the chapel is still used for special services. The warden's study also remains largely unchanged since the

Victorian period; the Rev. John Mason Neale, who occupied the post of warden 1846–66, composed a number of hymns here, including 'Good King Wenceslas'.

Saint Hill Manor — 1/2 miles (2.5km) southwest of East Grinstead. Built in 1792 by Gibbs Crawford, the Sussex sandstone building was owned by the Maharajah of Jaipur and Edgar March Crookshank before being purchased in 1959 by author L Ron Hubbard. Since his death the house and grounds have been the headquarters of the Church of Scientology, founded by Hubbard in 1953. Tel: 01342 326711.

St Margaret's Church — West Hoathly, 6 miles (10km) southeast of Crawley. An 11th century church founded in 1090 and enlarged in the 13th century. The north wall is part of the original church. The limestone font dates from the 12th century. Also within the church is an oak chest dating from the 12th or 13th century, made from a hollowed log, and which would have been used as the parish chest, holding vestments and alms. The works of the 17th century clock are on display.

St Mary's Church — Sompting, 2 miles (3km) east of Worthing. An 11th century church whose most remarkable feature is its Rhenish Helm, a four-sided spire unique in English church buildings but typical of Anglo-Saxon censer covers. Part of the church was rebuilt by the Knights Templar in the late 12th century. The current tower was possibly constructed in the 14th century by the Knights Hospitaller, who took over many of the Templars' properties after the order's dissolution, but it is likely to have been modelled on an earlier tower of the same design.

St Mary's House and Gardens — Bramber, 4 miles (6km) northwest of Shoreham-on-Sea. St Mary's originates in the days of the Knights Templar when 5 acres (2ha) of land in the downland village of Bramber were donated by the widow of Philip de Braose, following his death in 1125. The present building was constructed c.1470 by William of Waynflete, Bishop of Winchester and founder of Magdalen College, Oxford, as an inn for pilgrims on their way to the tomb of St Thomas Becket at Canterbury. Its distinguished owners include Hon. Algernon Bourke, owner of White's club in St James's, London – who, with his wife Gwendolen, were the originals for the characters in Oscar Wilde's play *The Importance of Being Earnest* – and, from 1907, wealthy socialite Alfred Musgrave, the inspiration for Sir Arthur Conan Doyle's Sherlock Holmes story 'The Adventure of the Musgrave Ritual'. In 1984, St Mary's was purchased by author and composer Peter Thorogood who, in collaboration with designer and landscape gardener Roger Linton, embarked upon an extensive programme of restoration. The 5 acres (2ha) of gardens are divided into distinct areas featuring topiary, terracing, a Jubilee rose garden and a secret Victorian garden. Tel: 01903 816205.

Shoreham Airport — 1/2 mile (0.8km) west of Shoreham-by-Sea. The world's oldest continually operational airport, Shoreham was established in 1930 and its Art Deco-style terminal building, now Grade II* listed, was opened in 1936. During World War II international operators such as Sabena, KLM and Imperial Airways used Shoreham instead of Croydon Airport. Recently renamed Brighton City Airport, it now operates scheduled flights to the Channel Islands. It is also host to numerous flying clubs and schools, as well as an annual airshow. Tel: 01273 467374/5.

Sport

football — **Crawley Town** were founded in 1896, reaching the Southern League in 1963 and the Nationwide Conference in 2005. Nicknamed The Red Devils, their home ground since 1997 has been the Broadfield Stadium, Brighton Road, Crawley. They were managed by former Chelsea star John Hollins in the 2005–06 season. Tel: 01293 410000.

horse racing — **Fontwell Park**, Fontwell. Founded in 1924 and several times voted the best small racecourse in southeast England, Fontwell holds National Hunt racing on a left-handed steeplechase course and a unique figure-of-eight course 1 mile (1.6km) in length. Tel. 01243 543335.

Goodwood, Chichester. Racing at Goodwood began in 1802. In late July or early August the course is home to Glorious Goodwood, part of the summer 'Season' since 1906. The Sussex Stand, opened in 1990, received a commendation for its design from the Royal Fine Arts Commission. The Flat racing course is an undulating right-handed loop with a 6 furlong (1.2km) straight of which 5 furlongs (1km) are downhill. Major races include the Stewards' Cup and Sussex Stakes. Tel. 01243 755022.

Stansted Park — 2 miles (3km) north of Westbourne, 8 miles (13km) northwest of Chichester. Set in landscaped parkland that features one of England's longest beech avenues, the 17th century Caroline revival house was rebuilt as a fine Edwardian country mansion after a serious fire in 1903. Its collections include paintings by Joshua Reynolds. The 1700 acres (690ha) of parkland include the Bessborough Arboretum, while the walled gardens feature restored Victorian glasshouses and the 'Garden in Mind', designed on Surrealist principles by landscape gardener Ivan Hicks. The house's postal address of Rowland Castle is in Hampshire but the park straddles the counties and Stansted Park itself is administered by the Funtington ward of Chichester, West Sussex. Tel: 023 9241 2265.

Standen — 1 1/2 miles (2.5km) south of East Grinstead. An Arts and Crafts house built 1891–4, set on a hillside with fine views to the south and designed by Philip Webb, a friend of William Morris, for London solicitor James Beale. The light-filled interiors are plainly decorated, combining panelling with wallpapers and fabrics designed by Morris & Co., and represent one of the best surviving examples of the company's domestic work. There is a 12 acre (5ha) garden, also in the Arts and Crafts style, with bluebell woods in the surrounding estate. The property is owned by the National Trust. Tel: 01342 323029.

Uppark — 1 mile (1.6km) south of South Harting, 9 miles (15km) northwest of Chichester. A Wren style house on the top of the South Downs enjoying panoramic views to the sea. Built in 1690 to designs by William Talman, the house burnt down in a massive fire in 1989 but the Georgian interior has since been comprehensively restored by an army of craftspeople using authentic techniques. Highlights of the interior include a 'Grand Tour' collection of paintings, furniture and ceramics, and an 18th century doll's house with original contents. The Victorian servants' quarters can also be seen, restored to the period when H G Wells's mother was housekeeper. Designed by Humphry Repton, the garden has been restored in the 19th century 'picturesque' style. The property is owned by the National Trust. Tel: 01730 825857.

Wakehurst Place 4 miles (6km) north of Haywards Heath. Situated in the High Weald, the 500 acre (200ha) gardens, surrounding an Elizabethan mansion, feature a wide variety of landscapes from temperate woodlands to bog gardens and formal walled gardens. Four National Collections are featured: hypericums, skimmias, birches and southern beeches. Also on the site is the Millennium Seed Bank, opened in 2000 with the aim of preserving from extinction 24,000 plant species from around the world. The gardens are owned by the National Trust and managed by the Royal Botanic Gardens, Kew. Tel: 01444 894000.

Weald & Downland Open Air Museum Singleton, 7 miles (11km) north of Chichester. Almost 50 buildings from around the southeast of England dating from between the 13th and the 19th century have been dismantled and re-erected in this downland site to create an archive of vernacular architecture. Mostly rescued from dereliction, they include timber-framed houses, a Victorian schoolroom, various workshops and a mill. Some are surrounded by recreated period gardens and there are farm animals and crafts. The Downland Gridshell, completed in 2002, is an innovative timber building constructed to house the museum's workshops and supporting collections. Tel. 01243 811348.

West Dean Gardens West Dean, 5 miles (8km) north of Chichester. Surrounding West Dean House, a flint-faced mansion designed by James Wyatt and built 1804–30, and extended after 1891 by William James, the gardens feature a walled kitchen garden containing a fine range of Victorian glasshouses and an Edwardian pergola 300ft (91.5m) long; the surrounding parkland includes St Roche's Arboretum. In 1964 Edward James, eccentric owner of the estate and patron of Surrealist artists such as Salvador Dalí and René Magritte, set up a foundation for the teaching of the arts. The college established in his former home on his death now provides education in a wide range of arts and crafts. Tel. 01243 828210.

Wiston House 1½ miles (2.5km) west of Steyning. Built by Sir Thomas Sherley in the late 16th century, the house was reduced in size and remodelled in Gothic revival style in the 1740s by Sir Charles Goring, and was again redesigned in the 1830s. The Elizabethan great hall with its hammer-beam roof still remains. During World War II it served as the headquarters of the Canadian forces before D-Day. Although still owned by the Goring family, it has been leased since 1951 by Wilton Park, an organisation established by Sir Winston Churchill in 1946 as a forum to promote democracy and enable international dialogue. The house is set in 5000 acres (2000ha) of parkland containing the estate church. Tel: 01903 815020.

Some famous people born in West Sussex

Armitage, Thomas Rhodes (founder of the RNIB) (1824–90)	Tilgate
Burgess, Melvin (children's author) (1954–)	Ifield
Butt, Clara (contralto) (1872–1936)	Southwick
Cobden, Richard (political reformer) (1804–65)	Midhurst
Elphick, Michael (actor) (1946–2002)	Chichester
Fitzgerald, Tara (actress) (1967–)	Cuckfield
Geeson, Judy (actress) (1948–)	Arundel
Hamilton, Patrick (novelist and playwright) (1904–62)	Hassocks
Hegarty, Antony (singer and songwriter) (1971–)	Chichester
Innes, Hammond (author and adventurer) (1913–98)	Horsham
Johnson, Katie (actress) (1878–1957)	Pyecombe
Lambert, Gavin (screenwriter and biographer) (1924–2005)	East Grinstead
Massey, Anna (actress) (1937–)	Thakeham
Minter, Alan (boxer) (1951–)	Crawley
Otway, Thomas (playwright) (1652–85)	Milland
Roddick, Anita (founder of The Body Shop) (1942–2007)	Littlehampton
Sayer, Leo (singer and songwriter) (1948–)	Shoreham
Scofield, (David) Paul (actor) (1922–2008)	Hurstpierpoint
Shelley, Percy Bysshe (Romantic poet) (1792–1822)	Warnham
Streatfeild, Noel (novelist) (1895–1986)	Amberley

Tyne and Wear

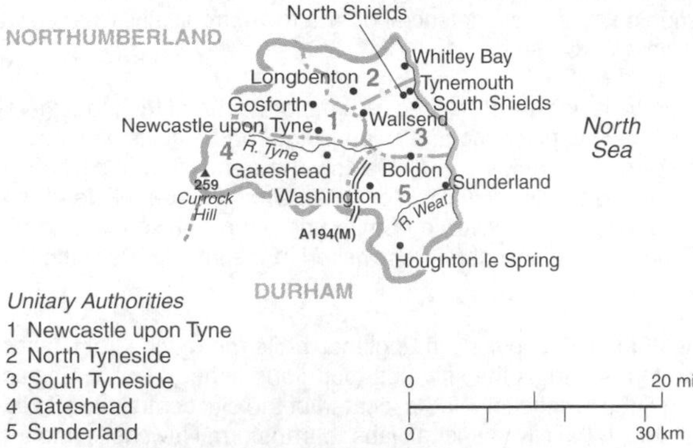
NORTHUMBERLAND
North Shields
Whitley Bay
Longbenton 2
Tynemouth
Gosforth
South Shields
Newcastle upon Tyne 1
Wallsend
North Sea
4 R. Tyne
3
Gateshead
Boldon
Sunderland
259
Currock Hill
Washington 5
R. Wear
A194(M)
Houghton le Spring
DURHAM
Unitary Authorities
1 Newcastle upon Tyne
2 North Tyneside
3 South Tyneside
4 Gateshead
5 Sunderland
0
20 miles
0
30 km

A metropolitan county in the northeast of England situated around the mouths of the rivers Tyne and Wear, bordered to the north and northwest by Northumberland and to the south and southwest by County Durham. Its eastern coast lies on the North Sea. Tyne and Wear was created by the Local Government Act 1972. Sunderland, Gateshead and South Tyneside (all formerly in County Durham) were incorporated into Tyne and Wear along with Newcastle and North Tyneside, previously in Northumberland. The new county was one of the smallest yet most densely populated in the country. In 1986 the metropolitan council was abolished although Tyne and Wear still exists as a legal entity and a ceremonial county. The region is now divided into the metropolitan boroughs (unitary authorities) of South Tyneside, North Tyneside, City of Newcastle upon Tyne, Gateshead and City of Sunderland.

Although the county council was abolished in 1986, several joint bodies remain to run certain services across the area on a county-wide basis, most notably the Tyne and Wear Passenger Transport Authority, which co-ordinates transport policy. Other such bodies include the Tyne and Wear Museums and Archives Service and the Tyne and Wear Fire and Rescue Service. In addition Northumbria Police, created in 1974, serves the whole of Northumberland and Tyne and Wear.

Tyne and Wear is the location of one of the most important religious foundations in English history. The twin monasteries of St Peter in Wearmouth and St Paul in Jarrow, founded by Benedict Biscop in AD 674 and 681, played a crucial part in restoring English intellectual life after the Dark Ages, especially through the writings of the Venerable Bede, who spent his life in the Wearmouth-Jarrow monasteries.

Newcastle upon Tyne is one of two cities in the county. Situated on the north bank of the River Tyne, before boundary changes it was the county town of Northumberland. The Latin term Novocastrian is sometimes applied to residents of Newcastle (a Latin term which can equally be applied to residents of any place called Newcastle, though the term is usually only used for ex-pupils of the city's Royal Grammar School) although people from Newcastle and surrounding areas are more commonly referred to as Geordies. The first settlement in what is now Newcastle was at Benwell. Known at the time as Pons Aelius, it was founded by the Roman emperor Hadrian in the 2nd century AD. The population at this period was estimated at 2000. Hadrian's Wall is still visible in parts of Newcastle, particularly along the West Road. (The course of the 'Roman Wall' can also be traced eastwards to Segedunum Roman fort in Wallsend – the wall's end.)

After the Roman withdrawal from Britain, Newcastle became part of the powerful Anglo-Saxon kingdom of Northumbria, and was known throughout this period as Monkchester. After a series of conflicts with the Danes and the devastation north of the River Tyne inflicted by Odo after the 1080 rebellion against the Normans, Monkchester was all but destroyed. Because of its strategic position, Robert Curthose, son of William I, erected a wooden castle there in 1080 and the town was thereafter known as Novum Castellum or New Castle.

Before the Civil War Charles I bestowed on Newcastle coal-trading rights for the east of England. This monopoly helped the town prosper, but it impacted adversely on the growth of near neighbours

Gateshead and Sunderland, causing a North of Tyne/South of Tyne and a Tyne–Wear rivalry that still exists. Newcastle grew as a royal stronghold through this decision, supporting the king and becoming a barracks for the Royalist army. In 1644 the city was stormed by Cromwell's Scots allies, based in pro-Parliament Sunderland. The grateful king bestowed the motto *Fortiter Defendit Triumphans* ('Triumphing by a brave defence') on the town. Ironically, Charles was imprisoned in Newcastle by the Scots in 1646–7.

During the 19th century Newcastle developed as a major centre of the Industrial Revolution, especially in the fields of heavy engineering and shipbuilding, and it achieved city status in 1882. The development of the city in the 1960s and 1970s saw the demolition of part of Graingertown as a prelude to the modernist rebuilding initiatives of T Dan Smith, leader of Newcastle City Council. A corruption scandal was uncovered involving Smith and John Poulson, a property developer, and both were jailed. Echoes of the scandal were revisited in the late 1990s in the BBC TV series *Our Friends in the North*.

The city itself is the 20th most populous in England, while the much larger Tyneside conurbation, of which Newcastle forms part, is the fifth most populous conurbation in England. The UK's first Biotechnology Village, the 'Centre for Life', is located in the city centre close to the Central Station and marks the first step in the city council's plans to transform Newcastle into a science city.

Sunderland is a city and port in the City of Sunderland metropolitan borough. Its name is thought to be Anglo-Saxon in origin (*Soender-land* = 'parted-land'), probably a reference to the valley carved by the River Wear that runs through the heart of the city. Sunderland was also known as 'Sunderland-near-the-Sea'. There were three original settlements on the site of modern-day Sunderland. On the north side of the river, Monkwearmouth was settled in AD 674 when Benedict Biscop founded St Peter's monastery in Wearmouth. Opposite the monastery on the south bank, Bishopwearmouth was founded in 930. A small fishing village called Sunderland, located toward the mouth of the river (modern-day Hendon), was granted a charter in 1179. Over the centuries, Sunderland grew as a port, trading coal and salt. Ships were first built on the river in the 14th century.

The bitter rivalry created by Charles I's award to Newcastle of the east of England coal-trading rights, stunting Sunderland's economic growth and causing hardship to the local citizens, led to growing anti-Royalist feeling in the town. The split became evident during the Civil War when Sunderland took the side of the Parliamentarians, and provided a landing point and barracks for anti-Royalist mercenaries from Scotland. In 1644, armies from Sunderland-aided Scotland and Newcastle clashed at the Battle of Boldon Hill in Boldon, South Tyneside, roughly halfway between the Tyne and the Wear. The battle was eventually won by the Scottish forces from Sunderland, and Newcastle was besieged and eventually captured. After the Restoration a number of royal charters continued to restrict Sunderland's growth as a trade centre. The towns were on the opposite sides of the political divide again during the Jacobite Rebellion in 1745, when Newcastle once again supported the king and Sunderland the rebels.

Following the Industrial Revolution, heavy manufacturing, particularly shipbuilding on both rivers, began to boom. In a reverse of the coal trading rights issue which had blighted Sunderland during the Commonwealth, the town was given preferred status over the ports on the Tyne. Sunderland now grew rapidly, taking in many workers from Scotland and Ireland. By the 19th century, the port of Sunderland had grown to absorb Bishopwearmouth and Monkwearmouth and by World War II, Sunderland was the biggest shipbuilding town in the world. Until the early 1980s, people from Sunderland were sometimes loosely included under the Geordie banner; however, the evolution of the term 'Mackem', originating in the shipyards, along with the mainly football-based rivalry between Newcastle and Sunderland, has ensured that the latter are no longer included under that definition. Today people born in Sunderland are called either Mackems or Wearsiders.

The rivalry between the two centres was given added impetus by the local government reorganisation of 1974, under which Sunderland residents began paying taxes to a county council based in Newcastle. A series of council decisions, such as the development of the Tyne and Wear Metro, which reached Sunderland only in 2002, left them feeling that they were being forced to contribute towards developments that benefited Newcastle but not Sunderland. Fortunately, today the rivalry between the two great cities is largely confined to the football field, and Sunderland finally matched its rival when it was awarded city status in 1992 as part of the celebrations marking the 40th anniversary of Queen Elizabeth II's accession to the throne.

Tyne and Wear	**Population**			**Area**	
Districts	*male*	*female*	*total*	*sq miles*	*sq km*
Gateshead	92,408	98,743	191,151	55	142
Newcastle upon Tyne	125,473	134,063	259,536	44	113
North Tyneside	91,707	99,952	191,659	32	82
South Tyneside	74,073	78,712	152,785	25	64
Sunderland	136,625	144,182	280,807	53	137
Total	520,286	555,652	1,075,938	209	538

Local Attractions and Information

Administrative headquarters: **Gateshead:** Civic Centre, Regent Street, Gateshead NE8 1HH. Tel: 0191 433 3000.
Newcastle upon Tyne: City Council, Civic Centre, Barras Bridge, Newcastle upon Tyne NE99 1RD. Tel: 0191 232 8520.
North Tyneside: Town Hall, Wallsend NE28 7RR. Tel: 0191 200 5000.
South Tyneside: Town Hall and Civic Offices, Westoe Road, South Shields NE33 2RL. Tel: 01914 277000.
Sunderland: Civic Centre, Burdon Road, Sunderland SR2 7DN. Tel: 0191 520 5555,

Angel of the North: 2 miles (3km) south of Gateshead. A modern steel sculpture of an angel, created by Antony Gormley and standing 65ft (20m) tall, with wings spanning 176ft (54m). It is located on a hill overlooking the A1 and A167 roads into Tyneside and the East Coast Main Line railway. Work began on the project in 1994, the cost, in excess of £1m, being largely provided by the National Lottery. The sculpture itself was created offsite in three parts – the body weighing 110 tons (100 tonnes) and the two wings each weighing 55 tons (50 tonnes) – and brought to its site by road from its construction site in Hartlepool, County Durham. It was finally completed on 16 February 1998. It is sometimes referred to as 'The Gateshead Flasher'.

Arbeia: Baring Street, South Shields. A reconstructed Roman fort situated on Lawe Top, overlooking the River Tyne. It was first excavated in the 1870s and all modern building on the site was cleared in the 1970s. Founded c.AD 120, it later became the maritime supply fort for Hadrian's Wall; it was occupied until the Romans left Britain in the early 5th century and contains the only permanent stone-built granaries found to date in Britain. Its name means 'fort of the Arab troops', referring to the fact that part of its garrison at one time was a squadron of Syrian boatmen from the Tigris. There is evidence that a squadron of Spanish cavalry, the 1st Asturian, was stationed here. Arbeia is now managed by Tyne and Wear Museums.

BALTIC Centre for Contemporary Art: South Shore Road, Gateshead. One of the biggest contemporary art galleries in the world. This major new arts centre on the south bank of the River Tyne close to the Gateshead Millennium Bridge was opened in 2002 in a redundant 1950s flour mill, converted at a cost of £46 million to designs by Dominic Williams of Ellis Williams Architects, winners of an architectural competition in the mid 1990s. BALTIC has no permanent collection but hosts a changing programme of exhibitions and other activities. Tel: 0191 478 1810.

Battles: See separate table for details of the Battles of Boldon Hill and Newburn Ford.

Bede's World: Church Bank, Jarrow. Housing the Age of Bede exhibition, housed in a purpose-built exhibition hall designed in a homage to Roman and early medieval architectural styles and opened by Queen Elizabeth II in 2000. Exhibits include finds from the 7th century St Paul's monastery, the layout of which is marked out on a site still visible. Tel: 0191 489 2146.

Benwell Roman Temple: Broomridge Avenue, Benwell, Newcastle upon Tyne. The remains of a small temple, dedicated to the native god Antenociticus, which stood in the *vicus* or civilian settlement outside Benwell Roman fort. Nearby is the sole remaining stone-built causeway across Hadrian's Wall. The site is managed by English Heritage. Tel: 0191 232 5325.

Bessie Surtees House: Sandhill, Newcastle upon Tyne. An amalgamation of two merchants' houses – Surtees House and Milbank House – on Newcastle's quayside, built in the 16th and 17th centuries and fine examples of Jacobean domestic architecture with impressive plasterwork and wood panelling. Surtees House is best known as the scene of the elopement of Bessie Surtees and John Scott, who later became Lord Chancellor. There is an exhibition detailing the history of the buildings, which are also home to the North East regional branch of English Heritage. Tel: 0191 269 1200.

Black Gate: See Newcastle Castle

Blackfriars: Friars Street, Newcastle upon Tyne. A restored Dominican friary founded in 1239 by local merchant Sir Peter Scott. After its dissolution in 1536 the friary buildings housed the headquarters of the city's craft guilds and almshouses for the destitute until the 19th century. Restored in the 1980s, the buildings now house craft workshops and a restaurant, as well as an exhibition detailing the history of Newcastle. The site is close to the most intact section of the old town walls.

Bowes Railway: Springwell Village, Gateshead. The world's only preserved operational standard-gauge rope-hauled railway system. The earliest section was designed by George Stephenson and opened on 17 January 1826, making it one of the world's first modern railways. Originally built to transport coal from pits in northwest Durham to boats on the River Tyne at Jarrow, it was 15 miles (24km) long when completed in 1855. Each end was worked by locomotives, the 6 mile (10km) middle section consisting of rope-worked inclines with very steep gradients. At its peak, the railway handled over 1 million tons of coal per year; it remained virtually intact until 1968 when most of the line was closed. The original 1826 section between the Black Fell bank head and Springwell bank head – comprising Blackham's Hill West and East inclines, operated by a stationary haulage engine – was acquired for preservation in 1976 by Tyne and Wear County Council. The whole railway, including the buildings, machinery and rolling stock, is now a Scheduled Ancient Monument and is managed by the Bowes Railway Company. Tel: 0191 232 5325.

Bridges

The earliest bridge across the River Tyne, Pons Aelius, was built on a site near the present Tyne Bridge by the Romans C.AD 122. Today six bridges span the Tyne between the centres of Newcastle upon Tyne on the northern bank and Gateshead in the south. From east to west these are:

Gateshead Millennium Bridge, opened to the public on 17 September 2001. Designed by architects Wilkinson Eyre and costing £22 million, it was lifted into place in one piece by the *Asian Hercules II*, one of the world's largest floating cranes. A hydraulic mechanism enables the bridge to tilt on its side, allowing boats and ships underneath. With a height of 165ft (50m) and a width of 414ft (126m), it weighs 850 tons. Its construction won Wilkinson Eyre the 2002 Royal Institute of British Architects (RIBA) Stirling Prize.

Tyne Bridge, a compression arch suspended-deck bridge built 1925–8 by engineering firm Mott, Hay & Anderson (who later designed the Forth Road Bridge) to a design based on that of Sydney Harbour Bridge in Australia. Begun in 1923 and officially opened on 10 October 1928 by George V, it has a span of 530ft (162m) and stands 194ft (59m) above high water. A stone bridge built in 1270 was destroyed in the great flood of 1771 and was replaced in 1781. Due to increased shipping activity, it was removed in 1866 for construction of the present Swing Bridge, which opened in 1876.

Swing Bridge, designed and paid for by William Armstrong to enable larger ships to move upstream to his Elswick engineering works, and built 1873–6. The Swing Bridge operates hydraulically; its 281ft (85.7m) cantilevered span is able to rotate through 360 degrees on a central axis, allowing vessels to pass on either side of it. The Swing Bridge stands on the site of the Old Tyne Bridges of 1270 and 1781.

High Level Bridge, a road and railway bridge designed by Robert Stephenson and built 1847–9, the first major wrought-iron tied arch or bow-string girder bridge ever constructed. It spans a distance of 1337ft (407.5m), including 512ft (156m) of water; its six river spans are 125ft (38m) long sit on masonry piers up to 131ft (40m) high. There are also four land spans on each side, of 36ft 3in (11m). The single-carriageway road and pedestrian walkways occupy the lower deck, 85ft (26m) above the high water mark, and the railway the upper deck a further 27ft (8.2m) above. After restoration in 2005–8 it carries southbound traffic only. Tel: 01904 389876.

Queen Elizabeth II Bridge, a railway bridge carrying the Tyne and Wear Metro over the River Tyne. The line runs through a tunnel on each side of the river and emerges into daylight only to cross the bridge. In April 2007 artist Nayan Kulkarni installed a huge artwork, *Nocturne*, on the bridge. This entails the bridge being painted two distinct tones of blue, while at night 143 LED lighting units create an ever-changing pattern of colours based on photographs submitted by members of the public.

King Edward VII Bridge, a railway bridge designed and engineered by Charles A Harrison, chief civil engineer of the North Eastern Railway, and built by the Cleveland Bridge & Engineering Company. Consisting of four lattice steel spans resting on concrete piers, its total length is 1150ft (350.5m) and it stands 112ft (34m) above high water mark. Trains entering Newcastle Central station had previously used the High Level Bridge, which necessitated reversing to leave the station in the same direction they had entered. The construction of the King Edward VII Bridge provided four more tracks, thus forming a loop through the station and enabling trains to enter or leave from either side. The bridge was opened on 10 July 1906 by Edward VII and Queen Alexandra.

The River Wear is crossed by two major bridges in central Sunderland:

Wear Bridge, a compression arch suspended-deck bridge of similar design to the Tyne Bridge in Newcastle, and the final bridge over the River Wear before it meets the North Sea. The first bridge on the site opened in 1796 and at 240ft (73m) was at the time the longest single-span cast iron bridge in the world; a toll for traffic and pedestrians was abolished in 1846. It was reconstructed in the 19th century by Robert Stephenson and reopened in 1959. The current bridge, the third on the site, was built around the existing structure and completed in 1929.

Queen Alexandra Bridge, a road and pedestrian bridge linking the Deptford and Southwick areas of Sunderland. The steel truss bridge was designed by Charles A Harrison (a nephew of Robert Stephenson's assistant). It was built by Sir William Arrol 1907–09 and opened by Queen Alexandra on 10 June 1909.

Cathedral Church of St Nicholas

See Newcastle Cathedral

Centre for Life

Times Square, Newcastle upon Tyne. A unique science village aiming to increase interest and engagement in science as well as supporting scientific research. It offers an annual programme of exhibitions, lectures and workshops. Scientists based at The Centre for Life are the first in Europe – and only the second in the world – to have been awarded a licence for stem cell research on human embryos, enabling work on new treatments for conditions including diabetes, Alzheimer's disease and Parkinson's disease. Tel: 0191 243 8210.

Church of St Thomas the Martyr

Haymarket, Newcastle upon Tyne. One of the city's most prominent landmarks. Completed in 1830 in Gothic style, the church was an Anglican re-foundation of a medieval chapel supposedly established by one of the assassins of Thomas Becket. Close to the City Hall and to Newcastle and Northumbria Universities, it acts as semi-official church to these institutions.

Discovery Museum — Blandford Square, Newcastle upon Tyne. A science and local history museum whose exhibits include *Turbinia*, the 111ft (34m) long ship built by Charles Algernon Parsons in 1984 to test the use of steam turbines to power ships, and examples of early light bulbs, invented on Tyneside by Joseph Swan. It also houses the regimental museum of the 15/19th King's Royal Hussars and the Northumberland Hussars. Tel: 0191 232 6789.

'F' Pit Museum — Albany Way, Washington, Sunderland. One of England's oldest pits, opened in 1777. The engine house was built in 1926. The pit closed in 1968 and the engine house, with its winding gear and Victorian steam engine, opened as a museum in 1976. Tel: 0191 269 1221.

Freemasons Hall — Queen Street East, Sunderland. A Grade I listed building dating from c.1785, one of the oldest purpose-built Masonic meeting places in the world. The hall contains a virtually unaltered ornate Lodge Room with elaborate thrones from 1735. There is also a cellar in its original condition and the last remaining example of a Donaldson organ, specially constructed for the building in 1785. Managed by English Heritage. Tel: 0191 522 0115.

Geordie — The familiar term used to describe a person from the Tyneside region, in particular the city of Newcastle and the adjacent areas, or the dialect of English spoken by such people. Outside the region, the term is used to describe anyone from the Northeast. When referring to people, as opposed to the dialect, the traditional definition of a Geordie is 'someone born within sight of the River Tyne', which traditionally meant Gateshead or part of Newcastle (a Cockney is similarly defined as someone born within hearing distance of the Bow bells). As the Cockney definition has been taken to mean within three miles of the church of St Mary-le-Bow on Cheapside, the Geordie definition has been loosely taken to mean any location on Tyneside, and is often defined even more loosely to include former areas of County Durham on the south bank of the Tyne, including Ryton, Blaydon, Hebburn, Jarrow and South Shields as well as other parts of Newcastle like Wallsend. There are numerous theories as to how the term came about, but all accept that it derives from a familiar diminutive form of the name George. In recent times 'Geordie' has also been used to refer to supporters of Newcastle United football club. See also Mackem.

Gibside — 1/2 mile (0.8km) east of Rowlands Gill, 5 miles (8km) southwest of Gateshead. A 400 acre (160ha) landscaped forest garden with dramatically staged romantic ruins, located alongside the River Derwent and created in the 18th century by coal baron George Bowes. The estate was the ancestral home of the Queen Mother's family, the Bowes-Lyons, Earls of Strathmore. Architectural features include the Jacobean hall, the Banqueting House (a Landmark Trust property), the monument known as the Column of Liberty, the Orangery – which contains an exhibition about Mary Eleanor Bowes, the 'Unhappy Countess', with whose marriage the Bowes and Lyon families were united at great personal cost to herself – and the Palladian chapel. Within the gardens are lakes and a great avenue of Turkey oaks. Gibside has been designated a Site of Special Scientific Interest. Now owned by the National Trust. Tel: 01207 542255/541820.

Grainger Market — Grainger Street, Newcastle upon Tyne. A covered market constructed in 1835 as part of the 19th century redevelopment of the city to replace markets on the site of Grey Street. It is home to the world's smallest branch of Marks & Spencer – the Penny Bazaar, opened in 1895 and the last of the store's original market stalls still in operation.

Great North Museum — Great North Road, Jesmond, Newcastle upon Tyne. Located on the campus of Newcastle University, the former Hancock Museum – named after local naturalist John Hancock – reopened in 2009 after refurbishment and now houses both the museum's natural history collections and Egyptian and Greek objects previously held at Newcastle's Museum of Antiquities.

Grey's Monument — Grey Street, Newcastle upon Tyne. A monument erected in 1838 to acclaim Charles, 2nd Earl Grey for the passing of the Great Reform Act of 1832. The statue of Lord Grey stands atop a 135ft (41m) high column.

Hadrian's Wall — See Cumbria

Hancock Museum — See Great North Museum

Highest point — Currock Hill at 851ft (259m) on the border of Tyne and Wear and Northumberland, just west of Blaydon.

Holy Jesus Hospital — City Road, Newcastle upon Tyne. One of only two surviving 17th century brick buildings in Newcastle upon Tyne, incorporating the remains of a 14th century church wall and window from the Augustinian friary that once occupied the site. Owned by Newcastle City Council, it is the base for the National Trust's Inner City Project, which began in 1987 in the city's east end and provides access to the countryside for people living in inner-city areas. Tel: 0191 255 7610.

Hylton Castle — Craigavon Road, Sunderland. Originally built by Henry Hilton in the 11th century, and reconstructed in stone as a fortified gatehouse-style manor house in the late 14th century by Sir William Hilton, who also added a nearby chapel. Baron John Hilton incorporated the structure in an Italianate mansion in the 18th century, adding two crenellated wings; these were demolished a century later by William Briggs, leaving the building as it is today. Hylton Castle is also the name of a large social housing estate to the west of the castle, from which it derives its name. The castle is rumoured to be haunted by the Cauld Lad of Hylton, a stable boy killed in a fit of anger by Robert Hilton in the 16th century.

Interesting facts — In 2007 **North Benwell** had the highest rate of property price increases ever seen in Britain. In 1999, ten large, but run-down and abandoned, homes on Hampstead Road were put on the market for 50p each. The area was on the unsavoury side at the time, but with a deal sweetened by a £26,000 grant, young families were moved in and the area cleaned up. Eight years later, the homes were all valued at over £145,000 – a 290,000 per cent increase! **Sid James** suffered a heart attack at the Sunderland Empire Theatre during a performance on the opening night of *The Mating Season* on 26 April 1976 and died on the way to hospital. Later it was rumoured that his ghost was in the dressing room he occupied on the night of his death; after one experience during a performance there, the comedian Les Dawson refused to play the venue again. The spirits of Vesta Tilley, a leading male impersonator of the day, and Molly Moselle, a stage manager for Ivor Novello's *The Dancing Years* in 1949, are also said to haunt the theatre's front-of-house areas. **Carrying coals to Newcastle** (or 'selling coal in Newcastle') is a term used to describe a foolhardy or pointless action, as the city was traditionally a hub of the British coalmining industry. However, there is always an exception to the rule and **'Lord' Timothy Dexter** (1748–1806) was that exception. Born in Malden, Massachusetts, Dexter was an eccentric businessman prone to taking punts on unlikely business ventures, and one such was selling coal to Newcastle. This should have been a certain failure, but his ships happened to arrive during a miners' strike when potential customers were desperate for coal; Dexter made a huge profit, hence his nickname 'Lucky' Dexter. **The Great North Run** is the world's biggest half marathon; it takes place every September/October, starting in Newcastle and finishing on The Leas in South Shields. **The Blaydon Race** is another local athletic event which has become almost as popular as the Great North Run; the 5.7 mile (9.2km) race from Newcastle to Blaydon is steeped in local tradition. It takes place on 9 June every year and starts off with the singing of 'The Blaydon Races', the words of the song providing the basis for the race. The race itself was the inspiration of Dr James Dewar of Blaydon Harriers, who organised the first 24 races, starting in 1981. In the early years, the race attracted around 250 entries, but by 2004 a record 4000 people took part with more than 600 hopefuls having to be rejected. **The Great Fire of Newcastle and Gateshead** began on Friday 6 October 1854, causing an explosion and substantial damage to property in the two towns. At half past midnight on that fateful night the local mill was discovered to be on fire. The fire spread quickly to neighbouring buildings, one of which stored thousands of tons of sulphur, nitrate of soda, and other combustibles. The intense heat caused the sulphur to ignite, melt and stream in a burning blue liquidised state from the windows. The resultant explosion could be heard 20 miles away and devastated the town and the townspeople, killing 53 and injuring hundreds.

Islands
There are several tiny island groups/rock formations in Tyne and Wear, all of which are situated in the North Sea (Tyne Sea Area). There are three in South Tyneside: **Marsden Rock** (see separate entry), **Parsons Rocks** (GR: NZ409599) and **Whitburn Steel** (GR: NZ412609); two in Sunderland: **Roker Rocks** (GR: NZ410591) and **South Rocks** (GR: NZ415578); and one, **St Mary's Island** (aka Bait Island), off the coast of Whitley Bay (see separate entry).

Jarrow
A town on the River Tyne, part of the South Tyneside district of Tyne and Wear and made up of the wards of Bede, Monkton and Primrose, plus part of Boldon Colliery and Fellgate & Hedworth. The Monastery of St Paul in Jarrow, part of the twin foundation Monkwearmouth-Jarrow Priory, was once the home of the Venerable Bede (673–735), whose most notable works include *The Ecclesiastical History of the English People* and the translation of the Gospel of John into Old English. At the time of its foundation, it was reputed to have been the only centre of learning in Europe north of Rome. Excavations in the later 20th century have confirmed Bede's description of the richness of the monastery, discovering coloured window-glass, stone carving and imported pottery. On 5 October 1936, 207 men, known as the Jarrow Marchers, walked from Jarrow to lobby Parliament in London. Known as the Jarrow Crusade (a term used on banners carried by the marchers) or Jarrow March, and carried out to find jobs to support Jarrow men and their families, it was also a bid for respect and recognition both for the people of Jarrow and for others in a similar situation all over the country. The marchers were entirely dependent on public goodwill for resources; wherever they stopped for the night, the local people found them shelter and provided them with food. Their route, with overnight stops, was divided into 22 legs covering a total of $280\frac{1}{2}$ miles (451km). When the marchers arrived in London on 31 October, a petition of 12,000 signatures was handed into Parliament by Ellen Wilkinson, Labour MP for Jarrow. Prime Minister Stanley Baldwin refused to see any of the marchers' representatives. The march achieved little at the time; only the outbreak of World War II three years later finally brought sufficient work to Jarrow to relieve the poverty. The last surviving participant in the march, Cornelius 'Con' Whalen, died on 14 September 2003, aged 93.

Jesmond Dene
Jesmond Dene Road, Newcastle upon Tyne. A park first laid out by William George Armstrong and his wife during the 1860s in a narrow, steep-sided valley (the word 'dene' meaning a valley in the Northumbrian dialect) through which flows the Ouse Burn. The design is intended to reflect a rural setting, with woodland, crags, waterfalls and pools. It is now owned by Newcastle City Council.

Laing Art Gallery
New Bridge Street, Newcastle upon Tyne. Opened in 1904, the gallery's collections include oil paintings, watercolours, glass and ceramics (including the locally produced Maling pottery), and it also exhibits modern and contemporary works. Outside is a public art installation, the *Blue Carpet*, which uses recycled materials to recreate the sensation of a carpet being laid over the paving slabs. Tel: 0191 232 7734.

Lambton Worm, The
See County Durham

Leazes Park
Richardson Road, Newcastle upon Tyne. The city's oldest park, situated to the west of the city centre next to St James' Park and the Royal Victoria Infirmary and opened in 1873. It contains a lake created on the course of the Lort Burn. Leazes Park is separated from the area of the city known as Spital Tongues by Castle Leazes, an area of common land similar to the Town Moor.

Mackem
Sometimes spelt 'Makem', 'Maccam' or 'Mak'em'. A person from Sunderland. The term came into common use in the 1990s, possibly stemming from either shipbuilding or the football rivalry between Sunderland and Newcastle United.

Marsden Rock
Marsden, $1\frac{1}{2}$ miles (2.5km) southeast of South Shields. A 100ft (30.5m) sea stack of magnesium oxide and limestone which lies 100yds (91m) off the coast of Marsden Bay. The once world-famous rock formation regularly featured on postcards and photographs. In 1803 a flight of steps was constructed up the side of the rock, and in 1903 several choirs climbed onto it to perform a

choral service. In 1911 a large section of the rock collapsed into the sea, leaving an arch similar to Durdle Door in Dorset; after the arch itself collapsed in 1996, splitting the rock into two separate stacks, the smaller stack was declared unsafe in 1997 and was demolished in the interests of public safety. The rock is still home to seabird colonies, with thousands of pairs of kittiwakes, fulmars, gulls and cormorants. It is owned by the National Trust.

MetroCentre — Located in Gateshead. The largest shopping centre in both the UK and the European Union. Opened in 1986 on a site previously occupied by Dunston power station, it has 1.78 million sq ft (165,000 sq m) of shopping space and 330 stores. Owned by Capital Shopping Centres plc. Tel: 0191 493 0219/460 2199.

Mitre, The — Benwell Lane, Benwell, Newcastle upon Tyne. The site of a 12th century hall, a 16th century tower house and a Georgian mansion designed by James Paine, it was home to the Shafto family until the 1770s when it was sold by Robert Shafto. The present building was designed by Tyneside architect John Dobson in 1831 and has since fulfilled a number of different functions. The residence of the Bishops of Newcastle 1880–1939, it became a fire station during World War II and a training centre for the National Coal Board in 1947. By the 1970s the building had become the Mitre pub, and went on to achieve national fame in 1989 as the Byker Grove youth club in the BBC children's TV series, *Byker Grove.*

Monkwearmouth Station Museum — North Bridge Street, Monkwearmouth. Monkwearmouth's former railway station, closed in 1968 but featuring a restored Edwardian booking hall. Tyne and Wear Metro and mainline trains still pass through the station, stopping at St Peter's station a few hundred yards to the south. It is part of the Tyne and Wear Museums group. Tel: 0191 567 7075.

Newcastle Castle — Castle Garth, Newcastle upon Tyne. The last remnant of William I's New Castle upon Tyne, from which the modern city takes its name. Located on the site of the Roman fort of Pons Aelius, later occupied by a cemetery belonging to the Anglo-Saxon settlement of Monkchester, the original motte and bailey castle was begun by Robert Curthose, son of William I. The keep, now Grade I listed and a Scheduled Ancient Monument, was designed by Maurice the Engineer for Henry II, 1172–8. The Black Gate was added 1247–50, forming an additional barbican. Having fallen into ruin by the 16th century, the castle was refortified during the Civil War, after which it served as a prison. It was leased in the 1880s to the Society of Antiquaries of Newcastle upon Tyne, one of the world's oldest antiquarian societies, who extensively restored it 1883–5 and have held regular meetings there ever since. The castle is currently owned by Newcastle City Council and managed by the Society of Antiquaries. Tel: 0191 232 7938.

Newcastle Cathedral — St Nicholas Churchyard, Newcastle upon Tyne. The seat of the Bishop of Newcastle and the mother church of the Diocese of Newcastle, the most northerly diocese of the Church of England, which reaches from the River Tyne north to Berwick-upon-Tweed and west to Alston in Cumbria. Dedicated to St Nicholas, the patron saint of sailors and boats, the cathedral was originally a parish church. The first building on the site, dating to 1091, was destroyed in a fire in 1216; rebuilt in 1359, it became a cathedral in 1882 when the diocese was created by Queen Victoria. The cathedral is notable for its unusual lantern spire, constructed in 1448 and for hundreds of years a navigation point for ships using the Tyne. Standing 196ft (60m) high, the tower contains 12 bells: the tenor bell weighs almost 2 tons and there are three 15th century bells, one of which, St Nicholas, is rung for daily services. St Margaret's Chapel contains the only known fragment of medieval stained glass in the cathedral, a roundel of the Madonna and Child. Much of the original glass was broken during the Civil War and most now dates from the 18th century onwards. The oldest of the cathedral's memorials is a 13th century effigy of an unknown knight, probably a member of the household of Edward I; another celebrates Admiral Lord Collingwood, a hero of the Battle of Trafalgar who was baptised and married in the cathedral. The Thornton Brass, a memorial to Roger Thornton, a merchant and three times mayor of Newcastle, is a particularly good example of a Flemish brass and dates from 1441. Tel: 0191 232 1939.

Newcastle Central Station — Neville Street, Newcastle upon Tyne. The city's principal railway station, opened in 1850 and now Grade I listed. It was designed by John Dobson for the North Eastern Railway company and constructed in collaboration with Robert Stephenson (also responsible for the High Level Bridge), 1845–50. The opening ceremony, attended by Queen Victoria, took place on 29 August 1850. The building has a classical style frontage, and its train shed has a distinctive roof with three curved, arched spans. A portico designed by Thomas Prosser was added to the entrance in 1863, and the train shed was extended in the 1890s with a new span designed by William Bell. An underground station for Tyne and Wear Metro trains was constructed during the late 1970s and opened in 1981.

Newcastle Town Wall — Constructed during the 13th century to repel Scottish invaders, Newcastle upon Tyne's defensive wall was 2 miles (3km) long, at least 7ft (2m) thick and up to 25ft (8m) high. It had six major gateways and 17 towers as well as several smaller turrets and postern gates. The walls protected the town for 500 years, but by the mid 18th century they had fallen into disrepair, and large portions were demolished during the next century as the city expanded. The largest remaining portion of the walls can be seen in Back Stowell Street.

North Shields — Known locally as Shields, a town on the north bank of the River Tyne, in the metropolitan borough of North Tyneside, 8 miles (13km) east of Newcastle upon Tyne. Its name derives from Middle English *schele* meaning 'temporary sheds or huts (used by fishermen)'; the area is still synonymous with fishing and other seafaring trades.

North Tyneside Steam Railway — See Stephenson Railway Museum

Path Head Mill — Summerhill, Blaydon. An 18th century watermill in the grounds of the former Stella Hall estate. The site has been undergoing restoration by the Vale Mill Trust since 1994–5 and now features demonstrations of renewable energy. Tel: 0191 414 6288.

Penshaw Monument — 2 miles (3km) southeast of Washington. A folly built in 1844 on Penshaw (locally pronounced Pensh-uh) Hill, formerly in County Durham and now part of Tyne and Wear. Dominating the skyline above Sunderland, it was built as a half-sized imitation of the Temple of Hephaestus in Athens; designed by John and Benjamin Green, it is dedicated to John George Lambton, 1st Earl of Durham and the first governor of Canada. The foundation stone was laid by the 2nd Earl of Zetland on 28 August 1844. The monument was given to the National Trust by the 5th Earl of Durham in 1939. Penshaw Hill, which is also the site of an Iron Age hill fort, and the nearby Worm Hill are closely associated with one of the northeast of England's best-known folk tales, the Legend of the Lambton Worm (see County Durham).

Rivers — **Tyne** see Northumberland

Wear see County Durham

Segedunum Roman Fort, Baths and Museum — Buddle Street, Wallsend. A Roman fort situated at the eastern end of Hadrian's Wall beside the River Tyne. Dating to c.AD 122, it was in use as a garrison for 300 years. The site includes the excavated remains of the original fort, as well as a reconstructed Roman bath based on the baths at Chesters Roman fort (see County Durham) and a reconstruction of what the whole wall might have looked like when new. The museum contains items discovered during the site's excavation. A portion of the original wall is visible across the street from the museum. Tel: 0191 236 9347.

Seven Stories — Lime Street, Newcastle upon Tyne. The only centre in the UK devoted entirely to children's literature. Based in the Ouseburn Valley, close to the city's newly regenerated quayside, the centre was opened in 2005 and takes its name from the theory that there are only seven basic plots in literature, and the fact that the renovated Victorian mill in which it is housed has seven levels. It aims to create and maintain a national corpus of literature aimed at children and has a growing collection of original artwork and manuscripts. Jacqueline Wilson, Terry Jones, Philip Pullman and Quentin Blake are among some of the centre's most distinguished patrons. Tel: 0845 271 0777.

Souter Lighthouse — 2 miles (3km) southeast of South Shields. Opened in 1871 and actually located at Lizard Point, to the north of Souter Point, Souter Lighthouse was the first to use alternating electric current, the most advanced lighthouse technology of its day. The engine room, light tower and keeper's living quarters are all on view. Said to be haunted by a former keeper, the lighthouse has been featured on Living TV's *Most Haunted.* It is managed by the National Trust. Tel: 0191 529 3161.

Sport

general — **Gateshead International Stadium**, primarily an athletics track, is also home to Gateshead Thunder rugby league club (who refer to it as 'Thunderdome') and Gateshead FC, and has also held a number of international rugby league matches. On 11 June 2006, spectators at the Norwich Union British Grand Prix witnessed the equalling of the men's 100m world record of 9.77sec by Asafa Powell.

football — **Newcastle United** were founded in 1892 from the former Stanley cricket club, entering the Football League the following year as Newcastle United after adopting the name Newcastle East End for a short time. Nicknamed The Magpies after their traditional black and white stripes, their home ground is St James' Park, first used by the club in 1892 after the unification of Newcastle East End and Newcastle West End, although football had been played there since 1880. The club's supporters refer to themselves as the 'Toon Army' ('toon' being the pronunciation of 'town' in Geordie dialect). Tel: 0191 201 8400.

Sunderland were formed in 1879 by Glaswegian schoolteacher James Allan as Sunderland and District Teachers Association Football Club. They became Sunderland AFC in 1881 and joined the Football League in 1890, replacing Stoke City. Nicknamed The Black Cats (also previously The Rokerites), the club's traditional strip is red and white striped shirts and black shorts. Their home ground is the Stadium of Light, to which they moved in 1997 after 99 years at Roker Park. Sunderland's traditional local rivals are Newcastle United. Tel: 0871 911 1200.

St Mary's Cathedral — Clayton Street West, Newcastle upon Tyne. The Roman Catholic cathedral is the seat of the Diocese of Hexham and Newcastle, established in 1850 with Bishop William Hogarth as its first bishop. Designed by Augustus Welby Pugin and built 1842–4 in Gothic Revival style, it is now Grade I listed. Tel: 0191 232 6953.

St Mary's Island — Also known as Bait Island. A small sandstone island near the seaside resort of Whitley Bay, connected to the coast at low tide by a rocky causeway. Its main feature is St Mary's Lighthouse. GR: NZ352754.

Stephenson Railway Museum — Middle Engine Lane, North Shields. The museum opened in 1986 on the site of a former Tyne and Wear Metro test track to commemorate local railway pioneers George and Robert Stephenson, and to provide a permanent home for the Tyne and Wear Museums' rail transport collections. George Stephenson lived locally 1802–23, during which time Robert, his son, was born in 1803. The locomotive *Billy*, the predecessor of George Stephenson's *Rocket*, is one of several steam engines housed at the museum. It is also the northern terminus of the North Tyneside Steam Railway, a standard gauge heritage railway run by the North Tyneside Steam Railway Association and operating for 2 miles (3km) from the museum to Rising Sun underbridge, near Percy Main metro station. Tel: 0191 200 7146.

Sunderland Minster — High Street West, Sunderland. Formerly known as St Michael's Church serving the parish of Bishopwearmouth, the Minster Church of St Michael and All Angels (commonly known as Sunderland Minster) was renamed on 11 January 1998 in recognition of Sunderland's attainment of city status. The first parish was founded c.AD 940, with an original stone church being built shortly afterwards; evidence of this building came to light in a 1930s excavation during which Saxon masonry was discovered. Due to colliery subsidence, the church was substantially rebuilt in the early 20th century. Tel: 0191 565 4066.

Sunderland Museum and Winter Gardens Burdon Road, Sunderland. Established in 1852, the museum was the first in England outside London to be municipally funded. In 1876 it moved to a larger building featuring a Winter Garden based on the Crystal Palace. The Winter Garden was demolished after sustaining bomb damage during World War II, to be replaced with a 1960s extension, until in 2001 a lottery-funded refurbishment of the museum created a new Winter Garden containing 2000 species of exotic plants. The museum's varied exhibits include a rare fossil gliding reptile – discovered in nearby Eppleton quarry and at 250 million years old the oldest known vertebrate capable of gliding flight – the world's largest collection of local Sunderland lustreware pottery, the remains of a walrus brought back from Siberia in the 1880s, and the first Nissan car to be made in Sunderland. Tel: 0191 553 2323.

Sunderland Symphony Orchestra A primarily amateur orchestra managed by the City of Sunderland Millennium Orchestral Society (CoSMOS), founded to mark the turn of the millennium, and based at Holy Trinity Church in Sunderland's East End. The orchestra gave its first performance in February 2000, and performed its first full symphony – Dvořák's Symphony No. 9 (the 'New World Symphony') – on 7 April 2001.

Town Moor, The An area of common land in Newcastle upon Tyne covering an area of 1000 acres (400ha), larger than Hyde Park and Hampstead Heath combined, stretching from the city centre and Spital Tongues in the south to Kenton to the west, Gosforth to the north and Jesmond to the east. Freemen of the city still have the right of herbage, which permits them to graze cattle on the moor. The Moor is divided into two major sections: the Town Moor is the major part, while the section beyond the A189 road is known as Nuns Moor.

Tyne Tunnel 7 miles (11km) east of Newcastle upon Tyne. A two-lane toll vehicular tunnel connecting Jarrow on the south side of the River Tyne with Howdon on the north via the A19 road. Completed in 1967, the tunnel is 5500ft (1680m) long; it is in fact one of three Tyne Tunnels, along with pedestrian and cyclists' tunnels opened in 1951.

Tynemouth Castle Pier Road, Tynemouth. The fortified ruins of a Benedictine priory located on a headland between the River Tyne and the North Sea and overlooking Tynemouth Pier. The priory was founded c.1090 by Robert de Mowbray on the site of a 7th century Saxon monastery where early kings of Northumbria such as Oswin were buried, and where a Norman motte and bailey castle may also have stood. The monastery received a licence to crenellate in 1296, when a curtain wall and towers were added. After its dissolution in 1539 the whole site became a royal castle under the guardianship of the 8th Earl of Northumberland, and in 1564 it was the birthplace of Henry Percy, the 9th Earl. There are substantial remains of the priory structure, as well as the castle gatehouse and walls which are 3200 feet (975m) long. During World War II the castle was used as a coastal defence unit; more recently it has hosted the modern buildings of HM Coastguard. It is now managed by English Heritage.

Washington Old Hall The Avenue, Washington. The 17th century stone house, incorporating parts of an earlier medieval building, is the ancestral home of George Washington, first president of the United States. In the 12th century William de Hertburne, Washington's ancestor, assumed tenancy of the estate of Wessyngton from the Bishop of Durham for an annual charge of £4, changing his name soon afterwards to William de Wessyngton (later Washington). The Washingtons retained the estate until the 1500s when they moved south to Sulgrave Manor (see Northamptonshire). As a result of their historic connection, in 2006 Washington DC and Sunderland announced a 'friendship agreement' seeking to strengthen their cultural and economic ties. Outside the house is a Jacobean-style garden. Now owned by the National Trust. Tel: 0191 416 6879.

Wills Building Coast Road, Newcastle upon Tyne. A well-known local landmark built in Art Deco style in the 1940s as a cigarette factory for W D & H O Wills. It was converted to residential apartments in 1997 by George Wimpey.

WWT Washington 1 mile (1.6km) east of Washington. A Wildfowl and Wetlands Trust reserve on the River Wear, established in 1975. Covering 103 acres (41ha), its wildlife includes a large nesting colony of grey herons, as well as more exotic wetland birds such as Chilean flamingos. Tel: 0191 416 5454.

Some famous people born in Tyne and Wear

Atkinson, Rowan (comedy actor) (1955–)	Newcastle upon Tyne
Beardsley, Peter (footballer) (1961–)	Newcastle upon Tyne
Bolam, James (actor) (1938–)	Sunderland
Brent-Dyer, Elinor (novelist) (1894–1969)	South Shields
Burdon, Eric (singer) (1941–)	Newcastle upon Tyne
Collingwood, Cuthbert (admiral) (1748–1810)	Newcastle upon Tyne
Cookson, Catherine (born Kate McMullen) (author) (1906–98)	South Shields
Cram, Steve (athlete) (1960–)	Gateshead
Donnelly, Declan (television presenter) (1975–)	Newcastle upon Tyne
Ferry, Brian (musician) (1945–)	Washington
Gascoigne, Paul (footballer) (1967–)	Gateshead
Havelock, Henry (British Army General) (1961–)	Bishopwearmouth
Herriot, James (veterinary surgeon and writer) (1916–95)	Sunderland
Higgins, Jack (born Harry Patterson) (novelist) (1929–)	Newcastle upon Tyne
Idle, Eric (actor and writer) (1943–)	South Shields
Leybourne, George (music hall artist) (1842–84)	Newcastle upon Tyne
Marvin, Hank (guitarist) (1941–)	Newcastle upon Tyne
McPartlin, Anthony 'Ant' (television presenter) (1975–)	Newcastle upon Tyne
Nail, Jimmy (actor and singer) (1954–)	Newcastle upon Tyne
Plater, Alan (playwright) (1935–)	Jarrow
Robson, Flora (actress) (1902–84)	South Shields
Scott, Ridley (film director) (1937–)	South Shields
Shearer, Alan (footballer) (1970–)	Newcastle upon Tyne
Stewart, Mary (novelist) (1916–)	Sunderland
Sting (born Gordon Sumner) (musician) (1951–)	Wallsend

WARWICKSHIRE

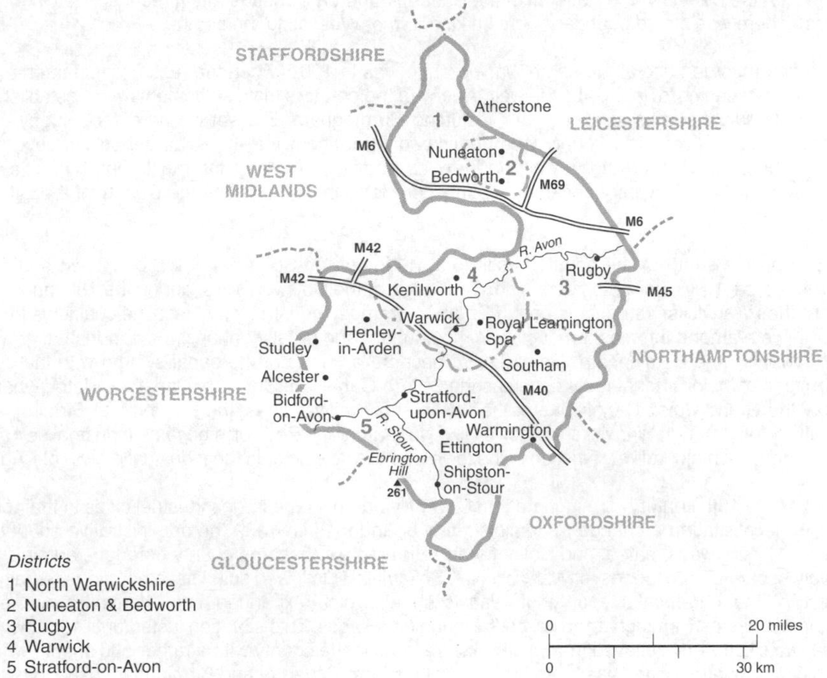
STAFFORDSHIRE
LEICESTERSHIRE
WEST MIDLANDS
NORTHAMPTONSHIRE
WORCESTERSHIRE
OXFORDSHIRE
GLOUCESTERSHIRE
Atherstone
Nuneaton
Bedworth
M6
M69
M42
M45
M40
R. Avon
Rugby
Kenilworth
Warwick
Royal Leamington Spa
Henley-in-Arden
Studley
Southam
Alcester
Bidford-on-Avon
Stratford-upon-Avon
R. Stour
Warmington
Ettington
Ebrington Hill
261
Shipston-on-Stour
1
2
3
4
5
Districts
1 North Warwickshire
2 Nuneaton & Bedworth
3 Rugby
4 Warwick
5 Stratford-on-Avon
0
20 miles
0
30 km

Warwickshire is a landlocked non-metropolitan county in central England. It is bordered by the West Midlands to the northwest, Staffordshire to the northwest and north, Leicestershire to the northeast, Northamptonshire to the east, Oxfordshire to the southeast, Gloucestershire to the southwest and Worcestershire to the west. The southernmost tip of Derbyshire barely touches the northernmost tip of Warwickshire. The county has no cities; Warwick is the county town.

Areas historically part of Warwickshire include Coventry, Solihull and most of Birmingham. These became part of the West Midlands metropolitan county following local government reorganisation in 1974 and since 1986 have effectively been unitary authorities, although remaining legally part of the West Midlands. Some organisations, such as Warwickshire County Cricket Club, which is based in Edgbaston, in Birmingham, still observe the historic county boundaries. Coventry, in the centre of the Warwickshire area, still has strong ties with the county: Coventry and Warwickshire are sometimes treated as a single area and share a single NHS trust and ambulance service as well as other institutions. The town of Tamworth was historically divided between Warwickshire and Staffordshire, but since 1888 has been fully in Staffordshire. In 1931, Warwickshire gained the town of Shipston-on-Stour from Worcestershire and several villages, including Long Marston and Welford-on-Avon, from Gloucestershire.

The Warwickshire area has been inhabited since prehistoric times. Remains of Iron Age hill forts, barrows and stone tools have been found along the Avon valley. For the first few decades after the Roman occupation in AD 43, the area was at the frontier of Roman rule. Watling Street and Fosse Way were constructed and the area was heavily fortified. Later on, Ryknild Street was constructed through the area, passing through what is now Birmingham. In time some of these military settlements grew into civilian towns, notably Tripontium (Cave's Inn near Rugby) and Manduessedum (Mancetter near Atherstone). There is evidence of extensive industry in the region during the Roman period. The area between Manduessedum in the north of the county and what is now Nuneaton had a substantial pottery industry; the remains of up to 30 kilns have been found in this area.

After the Romans left Britain in the early 5th century, the Warwickshire area was settled by Anglo-Saxon tribes. By the 8th and 9th century, the area had become part of the kingdom of Mercia. In the late 9th century the Mercian kingdom declined and, in 874 large parts of it to the east of Warwickshire were ceded to Viking invaders by King Alfred's Treaty of Wedmore with the Danish leader Guthrum. Watling Street, on the northeastern edge of Warwickshire, became the boundary between the Danelaw (the kingdom of the Danes) to the east and the much reduced Mercia to the west. There was also a boundary with the kingdom of Wessex to the south.

The first recorded use of the name Warwickshire was in 1001, when the region was named after Warwick (meaning 'dwellings by the weir'). Many of the county's main settlements were established in the Middle Ages as market towns, including Birmingham, Bedworth, Nuneaton, Rugby and Stratford-upon-Avon. The county was dominated throughout the medieval period by Coventry, which became a centre of the wool and textiles trades and one of the most important cities in England. In 1451 Coventry became a county corporate in its own right: the County of the City of Coventry.

Although the south of the county is still rural (Shipston-on-Stour being the only town south of Stratford-on-Avon), bordering on the northern edge of the Cotswold Hills, during the 18th and 19th centuries Warwickshire became one of Britain's foremost industrial counties. The coalfields in the north were among the most productive in the country, and greatly enhanced the industrial growth of Coventry and Birmingham. Warwickshire became a centre of the canal system with the construction of major arterial routes such as the Oxford Canal, the Coventry Canal and, later, what is now the Grand Union Canal. One of the first intercity railway lines, the London and Birmingham Railway, ran through Warwickshire. Towns like Nuneaton and Bedworth became industrialised and the siting of a major railway junction in the town was the key factor in the industrial growth of Rugby.

By the late 19th century Birmingham and Coventry had become large industrial cities in their own right, necessitating a change in administrative boundaries. In 1889 the administrative county of Warwickshire was created, and Coventry and Birmingham became county boroughs administratively separate from the rest of Warwickshire. Solihull later followed suit. These boroughs remained part of the ceremonial county of Warwickshire, which expanded into Worcestershire and Staffordshire as Birmingham annexed surrounding villages. This situation lasted until 1974, when the two cities were removed from Warwickshire leaving the county with a rather odd shape, which looks as if a large chunk has been bitten out of it where Coventry and Birmingham used to be.

Warwickshire		**Population**		**Area**	
Districts	*male*	*female*	*total*	*sq miles*	*sq km*
North Warwickshire	30,457	31,403	61,860	110	284
Nuneaton & Bedworth	58,519	60,613	119,132	30	79
Rugby	43,351	44,102	87,453	136	351
Stratford-on-Avon	53,975	57,509	111,484	378	978
Warwick	61,965	63,966	125,931	109	283
Total	248,267	257,593	505,860	763	1975

Local attractions and information

Administrative headquarters
Shire Hall, Warwick CV34 4RA. Tel: 01926 410410.

Alvecote Priory
Alvecote, 3 miles (5km) east of Tamworth. The ruins of a Benedictine priory on the Warwickshire/Staffordshire border, founded in 1159 by William Burdett as a dependency of Great Malvern Priory and dissolved in 1536. Very little remains of the priory except a high wall on one side, and the main entrance arch which still stands 20ft (6m) high. A house built from the stone of the old Benedictine priory is also a ruin. The 3 acre (1.2ha) site is located on a bend of the Coventry Canal.

Anne Hathaway's Cottage
Cottage Lane, Shottery, 1 mile (1.6km) west of Stratford-upon-Avon. The pre-marital home of William Shakespeare's wife, Anne. The cottage belonged to the prosperous Hathaway family and is in fact a substantial Elizabethan farmhouse of 12 rooms, known in Shakespeare's day as Newlands Farm. Externally the building with its low thatched roof, timbered walls and lattice windows has changed very little since Anne Hathaway's time. Parts of the structure are earlier than the 15th century, while many 16th century fireplaces remain in situ and the remains of the original great hall are still clearly visible. Beside its original open hearth fireplace is an old wooden settle upon which Shakespeare is said to have courted Anne. The bedroom upstairs contains an Elizabethan wooden bedstead, possibly the bed in which Anne was born. The cottage remained in the Hathaway family until 1892, when it was bought and restored to its 16th century appearance by the Shakespeare Birthplace Trust. Further restoration took place after the cottage was severely damaged by fire in 1969. The cottage once had over 90 acres (37ha) of land; it still has its own old-fashioned English garden, with adjoining orchard. The site also includes the Shakespeare Tree

	Garden, created in 1988; planted with trees mentioned in Shakespeare's plays, it also contains a series of sculptures inspired by his work. Tel: 01789 204016.
Arbury Hall	2 miles (3km) southwest of Nuneaton. An Elizabethan country house built on the site of a 12th century Augustinian priory. The home of the Newdegate family for over 400 years, it was transformed in the 18th century by Sir Roger Newdegate into a fine example of Gothic Revival architecture – it is sometimes referred to as the Gothic Gem of the Midlands. The house contains fine collections of antique furniture, pictures, glass and china, and is surrounded by landscaped gardens laid out in the 18th century with wooded walks and lakes. George Eliot was born on the estate in 1819 and the house features in her novel *Scenes from Clerical Life*. Tel: 0247 638 2804.
Ashby-de-la-Zouch Canal	See Canals
Astley Castle	Astley, 3 miles (5km) southwest of Nuneaton. Built as a fortified manor house during the reign of Edward I, with a licence to crenellate granted in 1266. Rebuilt in the 16th century by the Grey family, it was home to Lady Jane Grey, who was beheaded in 1554 after being queen for only nine days. Her father, the Duke of Suffolk, was also executed and the house was dismantled. It was rebuilt in the 17th century and restored as a country house in the 19th, and later became a hotel; after a fire in 1978 it is no longer open to the public. Astley Castle featured in George Eliot's novel *Mr Gilfil's Love Story* as Knebley Abbey.
Astley Church	Astley, 3 miles (5km) southwest of Nuneaton. The Collegiate Church of St Mary was built in 1343 and extensively reconstructed in the 17th century. The 14th century oak choir stalls still remain. George Eliot's parents were married in the church which, like Astley Castle, featured in her novel *Mr Gilfil's Love Story*, in the guise of Knebley Church.
Baddesley Clinton	5 miles (8km) west of Kenilworth. A moated manor house constructed as a mixture of stone and half-timbering, and probably established in the 13th century. In 1438, John Brome, under-treasurer of England, bought the manor. It then passed to his son, Nicholas, who is thought to have built the east range, which now contains the main entrance. Nicholas was also responsible for the rebuilding of the nearby church of St Michael's, carried out as penance for killing the parish priest, reputedly in the house itself. When Nicholas Brome died in 1517, the house passed to his daughter, who married Sir Edmond Ferrers. Henry Ferrers (1549–1633), known as 'the Antiquary', made many additions, and began a tradition of incorporating in many of the public rooms stained glass bearing the family's coat of arms. Other features include three priest holes, used to hide persecuted Jesuit priests in the 1590s, and a 19th century Catholic chapel. The house remained in the ownership of the Ferrers family until 1940 when it was purchased by Thomas Walker, a relative who then changed his name to Ferrers; his son sold the estate to the National Trust in 1980. The house has extensive gardens and ponds, with many of the farm buildings dating to the 18th century. Tel: 01564 783294.
Baginton Castle	Baginton, 3 miles (5km) south of Coventry. A 13th century fortified manor house above the River Sowe, founded by the de Derlye family. In the 14th century a tower house and ditch were added by Sir William Bagot. Only the foundations of the tower now remain, heavily overgrown, with vaulted chambers in the basement, a spiral stair turret and a rectangular garderobe turret.
Battles	See separate table for the battles of Edgehill and Mancetter.
Beaudesert Castle	Henley-in-Arden, 8 miles (13km) west of Warwick. Norman motte and bailey castle rebuilt in stone in the 13th century and in ruins by the 16th. The motte and ditch are still visible.
Blyth Hall	1/2 mile (0.8km) northeast of Coleshill. Built c.1625 by antiquary and county historian Sir William Dugdale, Garter King of Arms, with a red-brick east front added in the 18th century, the house contains a Tudor fireplace and fine staircases. Still lived in by the Dugdale family, it is not open to the public.
Brandon Castle	1/4 mile (0.4km) northwest of Wolston, 5 miles (8km) west of Rugby. A 12th century earthwork motte and bailey castle founded by Geoffrey de Clinton. A keep and a large outer enclosure were added in the 13th century by the de Verdon family, supporters of the king during the baronial wars. It is believed to have been attacked and slighted in 1265 by troops from the baronial garrison of Kenilworth Castle. Only some earthworks and the foundations of the keep are still visible.
Brinklow Castle	Brinklow, 5 miles (8km) northwest of Rugby. Norman earthwork motte and bailey castle founded by Robert de Mowbray. It was probably abandoned by the 13th century, but substantial earthworks still remain: the large and impressive motte, 40ft (12m) high, is encased by a wide ditch with a counterscarp bank, while a high rampart with a wide ditch surrounds the bailey.
Burton Dassett Hills	10 miles (16km) southeast of Leamington Spa. A group of ironstone hills rising to 666ft (203m) above the village of Burton Dassett. There are still substantial remains of the ironstone quarries which were once located here, and of the small industrial railway which served the quarries until the 1920s. A prominent beacon tower stands on one of the hills. Outside the 12th century All Saints Church in Burton Dassett is a holy well which still provides water. Tel: 01827 872660.
Canal Blacksmith's Shop	1/4 mile (0.4km) east of Hartshill, 2 miles (3km) northeast of Nuneaton. Situated next to the Coventry Canal, the former blacksmith's workshop, located in a building more than 200 years old, was an important part of the canal maintenance yard until 1948. On display in the restored building are the anvils, tools and other equipment required to produce various metal parts needed to maintain the operation of the canal. One of the blacksmith's duties was to maintain and wind the yard's fine tower clock; this local landmark has been fully restored. Tel: 01283 790236.
Canals	Canals in Warwickshire include the **Grand Union Canal**, which runs through Leamington and Warwick (see also West Midlands); the **Oxford Canal**, which runs from near Coventry and then eastwards around Rugby, and then through the rural south of the county towards Oxford; the **Coventry Canal** (see West Midlands); the **Stratford-upon-Avon Canal** which runs from the

Grand Union west of Warwick to Stratford; and the **Ashby-de-la-Zouch Canal**, which passes briefly through Warwickshire from a junction with the Coventry Canal at Bedworth.

Charlecote Park — Charlecote, 3½ miles (5.5km) east of Stratford-upon-Avon. A 16th century country house set in an ancient deer park beside the River Avon. The land has been owned by the Lucy family since 1247. The park was built in 1558 by Sir Thomas Lucy, and Elizabeth I stayed in what is now the drawing room. Successive generations of the Lucy family modified Charlecote Park over the centuries, but in 1823 George Hammond Lucy inherited the estate and set about recreating the house in its original Elizabethan form. The Fairfax baronets inherited the property in the mid 19th century, afterwards changing their family name to Lucy to reflect the traditions of Charlecote. The great hall features a barrel-vaulted ceiling made of plaster painted to look like timber, while other rooms have richly coloured wallpaper, decorated plaster ceilings and wood panelling. There are numerous items of furniture and works of art, including a contemporary painting of Elizabeth I. The original two-storey Elizabethan gateway remains unaltered. The park, landscaped by Capabiity Brown, covers 188 acres (75ha). The property has been owned by the National Trust since 1946. Tel: 01789 470277.

Church of Our Lady, The — 1½ miles (2.5km) west of Atherstone. Originally the gate chapel of Merevale Abbey, the church dates to 1240 is and the only Cistercian gate chapel in the UK still used throughout the year. It contains an important Jesse stained glass window of 1340 and a rare 1777 organ by Johannes Snetzler. The ruins of the Cistercian abbey (founded in 1148 by Robert de Ferrers, Earl of Derby) have been incorporated into farm buildings and can be seen to the east of the churchyard.

Churchover Castle — 1 mile (1.6km) south of Churchover, 3 miles (5km) north of Rugby. An 11th century earthwork motte, founded by the Waure family. The motte is still visible, surrounded by the remains of its wet ditch.

Clopton Bridge — Stratford-upon-Avon. A 14 arch bridge built c.1490 and financed by local merchant Hugh Clopton, later to become Lord Mayor of London.

Collegiate Church of St Mary — Church Street, Warwick. A parish church with a 12th century crypt and a medieval chancel. It contains a 15th century chantry, built to house the tomb of Richard Beauchamp, Earl of Warwick. This chapel also houses the tomb of Robert Dudley, Earl of Leicester, favourite of Elizabeth I. Tel: 01926 403940.

Compton Verney House — 7 miles (11km) east of Stratford-upon-Avon. A country house designed by Robert Adam in the 1760s, and set in 120 acres (48.5ha) of parkland landscaped by Capability Brown. Having been owned by the Verney family for almost 500 years the house was sold in the 1920s and subsequently fell into disrepair; it was bought in 1993 by Littlewoods millionaire Sir Peter Moores and restored as a gallery capable of hosting international exhibitions. The Grade I listed house is now run by Compton Verney House Trust. Tel: 01926 645500.

Compton Wynyates — 5 miles (8km) east of Shipston-on-Stour. A red-brick Tudor house with castellations and turrets, built around a central courtyard. The estate has been owned by the Compton family, later the Earls of Northampton, since the early 13th century, although for many years they lived at Castle Ashby (see Northamptonshire); the house has thus retained much of its original structure. The name Compton meant 'a deep hollow in a hill' and the house is still sometimes known as 'Compton-in-the-Hole'.

Coughton Court — 1½ miles (2.5km) north of Alcester. Coughton (pronounced 'Coat-un') Court has been the home of the Throckmorton family since 1409. The building is constructed around a Tudor gatehouse dating to c.1530, with courtyard buildings featuring Elizabethan half-timbering. The family were staunch Catholics and had close connections to those involved in the Gunpowder Plot in 1605: the interiors feature a priest hole in the tower. Backing onto the lake, the walled garden contains over 100 varieties of roses, and a display of plants including 'hot and cold' herbaceous borders. The site includes a bog garden and riverside walk. Tel: 01789 400777.

Coventry Airport — Baginton, 9 miles (15km) west of Rugby. Located on the Warwickshire/West Midlands border just south of Coventry. Opened as a civic airport in 1936 by Coventry City Council, the airport became a fighter station during World War II as RAF Baginton. Having returned to civilian use, flights to the Channel Islands began in the 1960s and charter flights to Europe in the 1980s. The airport was a base for scheduled flights operated by Thomsonfly 2004–08. See also Midland Air Museum.

Coventry Railway Centre — Rowley Road, Baginton. Owned and operated by the Suburban Electric Railway Association, and home to their sizeable collection of preserved electrical multiple units, the most diverse and historically significant such collection in the UK. The centre is not currently open to the public.

Draycote Water — 1 mile (1.6km) southwest of Dunchurch, 4 miles (6km) southwest of Rugby. A reservoir owned by Severn Trent Water and named after the hamlet of Draycote to its west. Created in the 1960s to supply drinking water to Rugby, the reservoir is the largest in Warwickshire, covering more than 600 acres (240ha) and holding up to 5000 million gallons (22,730 megalitres) of water. It is renowned as a site for birdwatching and has a bird hide, with a feeding station sponsored by the West Midland Bird Club. Severn Trent Water also manage the adjacent 20 acre (8ha) country park.

Farnborough Hall — 14 miles (23km) southeast of Stratford-upon-Avon. This honey-coloured house, built in the 1680s, has been the home of the Holbech family for more than 300 years. Palladian-style façades and richly decorated plasterwork were added in the 18th century, and both house and garden have remained largely unaltered since. The landscape garden, dating from the 1740s, is ornamented with temples and featuring a series of pools, a broad terrace walk and an obelisk. Farnborough Hall is owned by the National Trust but occupied and administered by the Holbech family. Tel: 01295 690002.

Guy's Cliffe House — 1 mile (1.6km) north of Warwick. A ruined country house beside the River Avon, the site of which has been occupied since Saxon times. Edward II's favourite Piers Gaveston was apprehended here by the Earl of Warwick and other nobles before being beheaded at nearby Blacklow Hill, but the most famous legend concerning the site is that of Guy of Warwick. Having returned from his adventures, the legendary 10th century founder of Warwick Castle and killer of the Dun Cow retired to live out his days in a cave by the river, which still survives by the Chapel of St Mary Magdalene. His wife, Felice of Warwick, remained ignorant of his unannounced presence. Just before Guy died, he revealed his true identity to Felice who, overcome by grief, threw herself from the cliff where her husband had lived for so many years. It is said that her ghost still haunts the site. A hermitage was founded on the site, and monks inhabited the cave dwellings until the 15th century. After the Dissolution of the Monasteries the site passed into private hands. The present Grade II* listed house dates from 1751 and was started by Samuel Greatheed. In 1946 it was sold with the intention of converting it into a hotel, but the plans never materialised and the house fell into disrepair. It was purchased by Aldwyn Parker in 1955 and the chapel, which contains a large statue depicting Guy of Warwick, was leased to the Freemasons; the chapel is still used for Masonic ceremonies. Fire seriously damaged the building in 1992 during the filming of *The Adventures of Sherlock Holmes*. Another famous resident was actress Sarah Siddons, who stayed here much later as a guest of Bertie Greatheed. The house is not open to the public.

Hall's Croft — Old Town, Stratford-upon-Avon. A 16th century house with Jacobean additions. Named after Dr John Hall, who married Shakespeare's daughter Susanna, the house contains furniture and paintings as well as an exhibition about medicine in Shakespeare's time, with reference to remedies and potions mentioned in the plays. Outside is a large garden with a 200 year old mulberry tree and herbal bed. Tel: 01789 204016.

Hartshill Castle — Hartshill, 3 miles (5km) west of Nuneaton. Founded in the 12th century by Hugh de Hardreshull as an earthwork motte and bailey fortress. In 1330, John de Hardreshull rebuilt the castle in stone, enclosing the bailey with a curtain wall pierced by cross-shaped loopholes. The circular motte stands to the northwest. In the 16th century, Michael and Edmund Parker founded a castellated timber-framed manor house in the northeast corner of the bailey; much of the house has collapsed but the ruins can be seen in woods below the centre of Hartshill. The village itself was the birthplace in 1563 of poet Michael Drayton, who is buried in Westminster Abbey.

Harvard House — High Street, Stratford-upon-Avon. An ornate Elizabethan town house built in 1596 by Alderman Thomas Rogers. It was the childhood home of his daughter Katherine, mother of John Harvard, the founder of Harvard University, and was presented to the university in 1910 by Chicago millionaire Edward Morris. It is also home to the nationally important Neish Pewter Collection, which includes pieces ranging from the Roman period to the 19th century. The house is managed by the Shakespeare Birthplace Trust on behalf of Harvard University. Tel: 01789 204016.

Hatton Locks — Canal Lane, Hatton, 3 miles (5km) west of Warwick. A flight of 21 locks, known as the 'Stairway to Heaven', at Hatton on the Grand Union Canal.

Henley-in-Arden Heritage Centre — High Street, Henley-in-Arden. Located in Joseph Hardy House, dating to c.1345 and the town's earliest recorded house, the centre has local history exhibits including a model of the Norman castle which once stood on the Mount. Other topics include the history of the ancient market cross, town criers, and a chronicle of the origins of the local ice cream. The town has 12th and 15th century churches and a guildhall.

Heritage Motor Centre — 1 mile (1.6km) northwest of, Gaydon, 9 miles (15km) southeast of Warwick. Located on the site of the former RAF Gaydon, the centre has one of the world's most extensive collections of historic cars. Tel: 01926 645042.

Highest point — Ebrington Hill on the edge of the Cotswold Hills at 856ft (261m), on the Warwickshire/Gloucestershire border in the southwest of the county. GR: SP187426.

Hill Close Gardens — Friars Street, Warwick. A Grade II* listed series of Victorian pleasure gardens on the edge of Warwick town centre where the prosperous tradesmen of Warwick are said once to have taken their recreation. Surrounded by high hedges and decorated with summerhouses (four of which are now Grade II listed), the recently restored site includes abundant old varieties of fruit tree, vegetables and colourful borders. Tel: 01926 493216.

Holy Trinity Church — Old Town, Stratford-upon-Avon. The Collegiate Church of Holy Trinity, dating from 1210, is the site of the baptism and burial of William Shakespeare. Other features include a 14th century sanctuary knocker in the church's porch, misericords in the chancel with religious, secular and mythical carvings, and large stained glass windows at the church's east and west ends, depicting English and biblical saints. Shakespeare's body is thought to be buried 20ft (6m) deep to prevent its theft. Tel: 01789 266316.

Interesting Facts — **Rugby** is the birthplace of the jet engine. In April 1937 Frank Whittle built the world's first prototype jet engine at the British Thomson-Houston works in Rugby; between 1936 and 1941 he based himself at Brownsover Hall on the outskirts of the town, where he designed and developed early prototype engines. In the 19th century the town became famous for its railway junction; once hugely important, it was the setting for Charles Dickens's story 'Mugby Junction'. Rugby is also famous for the invention of rugby football. **Benjamin Satchwell**, one of the founding fathers of Leamington Spa, lived in a cottage in the old town to the south of the River Leam. The village's first postmaster and later a shoemaker, in 1777 he helped set up the Foundation of Hospitality, a savings scheme which helped the poorer people of the village obtain medical attention. It was however on 14 January 1784 that Satchwell made the discovery for which he is remembered. Until that date there was only one known spring in Leamington, located on land belonging to the 4th Earl of Aylesford who refused to sell the water (which was used for bathing and medicinal purposes), instead allowing people to have it for free. However in 1784 Satchwell and his friend William Abbotts found a second spring, and used its supposed medicinal qualities to make money from the leisured classes. After Satchwell and Abbotts' spring was found, several wells were bored and drew water. Leamington quickly grew into on the most fashionable spa resorts of the 19th century, a process which turned it from a sleepy village to a thriving town. Later in his life Satchwell founded the Leamington Spa Charity to help the poor of the town gain free access to spas. Also well known as a writer and performer of poetry, he died aged 77, and is buried in Leamington's parish church, All Saints. **The siege of Kenilworth** in 1266 was the longest siege ever to occur in England. It began in earnest at Kenilworth in May. Inside the castle were over a thousand supporters of the baronial movement that had seen its leader, Simon de Montfort, killed at the battle of Evesham in August 1265. Outside was the feudal host of England as summoned by Henry III, along with his elder son, Edward, and Edmund, who had been attempting to contain the garrison since the autumn before. By 14 December, the leaders of the garrison such as Henry de Hastings, out of supplies and suffering from sickness, accepted the Dictum of Kenilworth and received safe conduct from the king.

Kenilworth Castle

Castle Green, Kenilworth. The largest castle ruin in England. Founded c.1130 as a motte and bailey by Geoffrey de Clinton, the castle was rebuilt in red sandstone 1170–80 with a keep and curtain wall. Having been granted in 1244 to Simon de Montfort, it became a refuge for de Montfort's baronial supporters after he was killed at the Battle of Evesham in 1265 and the following year endured a six-month siege by the forces of Henry III. In 1327, Edward II was imprisoned here before being removed to Berkeley Castle where he was killed. John of Gaunt built a great hall in the late 14th century, before in 1563 the castle was given to Robert Dudley, Earl of Leicester by Elizabeth I, who was a regular visitor. It later became the property of the Earls of Clarendon. The castle was once surrounded by a great lake, the scene of extravagant water pageants staged to entertain Elizabeth. The site also includes a recreated Elizabethan garden. Now owned by English Heritage. Tel: 01926 852078.

Kingbury Water Park

Kingsbury, 7 miles (11km) west of Atherstone. A country park opened in 1975 on the site of former gravel workings in the Tame valley. Its 15 lakes, situated in over 600 acres (240ha) of parkland, are a renowned site for birdlife. The park is owned and managed by Warwickshire County Council, with an information centre and bird hide maintained by the West Midland Bird Club.

Kinwarton Dovecote

½ mile (0.8km) northeast of Alcester. A circular 14th century stone dovecote notable for its 'potence', a pivoted ladder which provides access to the nesting boxes. The building still houses doves today. Now owned by the National Trust. Tel: 01743 708100.

Ladywalk Reserve

Whiteacre Heath, 3 miles (5km) northeast of Coleshill. A nature reserve on the site of the former Ham's Hall power station next to the River Tame. Owned by Powergen, it is managed by the West Midland Bird Club. The reserve is best known for its over-wintering great bitterns.

Leamington Spa

A prosperous former spa town in central Warwickshire, officially known as Royal Leamington Spa. Originally a small village, named Leamington Priors after the River Leam which flows through the town and from its status as part of the estate of Kenilworth Priory, after the discovery of saline springs by Benjamin Satchwell (see Interesting Facts) in 1784 it rapidly grew into a major resort. The 'Royal' prefix was granted in 1838 by Queen Victoria, who had visited in 1830 before her coronation. There are numerous fine Georgian and Regency buildings; the Royal Pump Rooms, opened in 1814, are now occupied by a cultural complex including the town's museum and art gallery. See also Midland Oak.

Lord Leycester Hospital

High Street, Warwick. A group of late 14th century timber-framed buildings that once housed the Warwick guilds. In 1571 Elizabeth I's favourite Robert Dudley, Earl of Leicester, converted the buildings of the dissolved guilds into a retreat for old soldiers, a purpose they still serve today. The Brethren, as the inhabitants are known, attend weekday services in the 12th century chantry chapel over the town's Norman West Gate, which adjoins their home, and still wear the traditional uniform of blue gowns and flat Tudor hats on ceremonial occasions. The museum of the Queen's Own Hussars in the Chaplain's Hall covers the history of the 7th Queen's Own Hussars and the 3rd King's Own Hussars. A new knot garden was created in the courtyard to celebrate the millennium. Tel: 01926 491422.

Lunt Fort

Baginton, 9 miles (15km) west of Rugby. A reconstructed Roman fort dating to c.AD 60 and discovered after large quantities of Roman pottery were unearthed in the 1930s. Excavations in the 1960s discovered a sequence of Roman military camps on the site, the last established c.AD 260. The fort is notable for the *gyrus*, a large circular ring used for training horses and believed to be unique in Britain. In the early 1970s several of the buildings were reconstructed on their original foundations, including a granary that now houses the Museum of the Roman Army. Tel: 024 7630 3567.

Mancetter Roman Site

1 mile (1.6km) southeast of Atherstone. The village of Mancetter, now a suburb of Atherstone, is the site of the significant Roman fortress of Manduessedum on Watling Street, dating to AD 50–70 and possibly home to the XIV Roman legion, and of an associated civilian settlement. It is thought that Boudicca's final defeat by Roman forces took place outside the fort in the Anker Valley. Excavations by Atherstone Archaeological and Historical Society have also revealed what are believed to be Saxon skeletons.

Market Hall Museum

Market Place, Warwick. Housed in a 17th century market hall, one of the few buildings in central Warwick to survive the fire that swept through the town in 1694. Displays on geology, biology and archaeology illustrate the natural and historical heritage of the county. Notable exhibits include the famous Sheldon Tapestry Map of Warwickshire (one of four, also depicting Worcestershire, Oxfordshire and Gloucestershire), dating from the 1580s, displays on local biodiversity, and an observation beehive. Tel: 0870 442 2000. See also St John's House.

Mary Arden's House and Shakespeare

Wilmcote, 3 miles (5km) northwest of Stratford-upon-Avon. A brick and timber farmhouse formerly named Glebe Farm, and the home of William Shakespeare's mother before she married John

Countryside Museum — Shakespeare and moved to Stratford. For many years Mary Arden's House was identified with a large thatched, timber-framed farmhouse nearby; it has now been ascertained that this house was in fact owned by the Palmer family and it has been renamed Palmer's Farm. The farmhouse has displays relating to life and work on the land, while the grounds are occupied by the Shakespeare Countryside Museum and feature a working blacksmith, falconers and livestock. The garden in front of the house is planted in typical country fashion with fruit trees, vegetables, herbs and traditional flowers and shrubs. Tel: 01789 204016.

Maxstoke Castle — 1½ miles (2.5km) north of Maxstoke, 2 miles (3km) east of Coleshill. A 14th century rectangular moated castle with octagonal towers at each corner, built by William de Clinton, Earl of Huntingdon. Although the original wooden bridge and drawbridge have been replaced by a stone bridge, the gatehouse, crenellated curtain walls and corner towers still remain. The castle was bought by Sir Thomas Dilke in 1599 and held by Parliamentary forces during the Civil War. The Fetherston-Dilke family still live in the castle today, and it is not open to the public.

Merevale Abbey — See Church of Our Lady

Merevale Hall — ½ mile (0.8km) west of Atherstone. Standing on top of a hill overlooking Atherstone, the Grade II* listed Gothic hall with embattled towers and walls was built in the 1840s by architect Edward Blore for the Dugdale family. The house's treasures include the diaries and books of local historian Sir William Dugdale (1605–86), Garter King of Arms. The hall is still owned by the Dugdale family and is not open to the public

Middleton Hall — 1 mile (1.6km) east of Middleton, 7 miles (11km) west of Atherstone. Located on the Warwickshire/Staffordshire border, the hall dates from c.1300, with a complex of later additions including a 16th century great hall in which Elizabeth I was entertained and an 18th century Georgian wing. In the 17th century the hall was the home of Francis Willoughby, founder member of the Royal Society, whose interest in natural history was inspired and encouraged by John Ray, one of Britain's greatest naturalists. After Willoughby's death, Ray continued to live at the hall. Tudor explorer Sir Hugh Willoughby, and Cassandra, 1st Duchess of Chandos, were born here. The house also has links with Lady Jane Grey and Jane Austen. The grounds feature a lakeside walk, two walled gardens and a restored smithy. Tel: 01827 283095.

Midland Air Museum — Coventry Airport, Baginton. The museum's exhibits include an Avro Vulcan bomber and more than 30 other historic aircraft, both civil and military. There are also aero engines and a wide range of memorabilia and artefacts. Of particular note is the museum's collection of material relating to Sir Frank Whittle, the Coventry-born engineer who designed the jet engine. The museum houses a heritage centre dedicated to his memory. Tel: 02476 301033.

Midland Oak — An oak tree on the boundary between Leamington Spa and the suburb of Lillington, to the northeast of the town centre. According to a nearby plaque the tree marks the very centre of England, though a number of other locations in the Midlands, including Meriden and Copston Magna, make the same claim. The original tree survived until the mid 20th century, when it was replaced with one grown from an acorn produced by the original. This replacement was itself replaced by another tree, again from an acorn found nearby in the 1990s.

Nash's House — Chapel Street, Stratford-upon-Avon. A 16th century half-timbered house owned by Thomas Nash, first husband of Shakespeare's granddaughter, Elizabeth. In addition to its exceptional collection of Elizabethan furniture and tapestries, Nash's House also has displays on the history of Stratford. Outside in the grounds of New Place (see separate entry) are a recreated knot garden and Great Garden. Tel: 01789 204016.

New Place — Chapel Street, Stratford-upon-Avon. William Shakespeare's final place of residence in Stratford-upon-Avon during his retirement, the house was built by Hugh Clopton in 1483. Shakespeare bought New Place in 1597 for £60 but settled here only in 1610, remaining until his death in 1616. The house was the second largest in Stratford, and the only one at the time to be built of brick. After Shakespeare's death in 1616 it passed to his daughter Susanna Hall, and then to his granddaughter, Elizabeth Hall. Elizabeth married Thomas Nash, who owned the house next door; after her death, New Place was returned to the Clopton family who had originally built the house, and was opened to the public. In 1759, however, the next owner, Rev. Francis Gastrell, became tired of the constant stream of visitors, and is said to have destroyed a mulberry tree in the garden reputedly planted by Shakespeare himself before eventually demolishing the house. The foundations of New Place can still be seen, and are accessible through the museum that occupies Nash's House next door.

Nuneaton — The largest town in Warwickshire, located 13 miles (21km) northwest of Rugby. It is most famous for its associations with 19th century author George Eliot, who was born on a farm on the Arbury estate just outside Nuneaton in 1819 and lived in the town for much of her early life. Nuneaton is referred to as 'Milby' in her novel *Scenes of Clerical Life* (1858). Due largely to its munitions factories, the town suffered heavy bombing during World War II. The heaviest raid took place on 17 May 1941, when 100 people were killed, 380 houses were destroyed, and over 10,000 damaged. On 1 April 1974, Nuneaton's council was merged with that of nearby Bedworth to form the borough of Nuneaton and Bedworth.

Nuneaton Museum and Art Gallery — Coton Road, Nuneaton. Located in Riversley Park, the museum features a gallery dedicated to George Eliot as well as displays on local history. A variety of art works are displayed, including touring exhibitions. Tel: 024 7635 0720.

Offchurch Bury — 2 miles (3km) east of Leamington Spa. Originally built in the 16th century with substantial 17th century addtions, most of the current house dates from the 19th century. It is not open to the public.

Old Market Hall — High Street, Coleshill. The site of the original hall, built in 1750, was Church Hill. Having in the past been used at various times as a magistrates' court, a weekly market and a Victorian reading room, the building was moved just under $^1/_4$ mile (0.4km) to its present site in 1850 and served as the town hall until a dedicated civic centre was built in 1926. The refurbished building was opened by the Duke of Gloucester in May 1999. Today it houses a heritage centre and exhibition area as well as a large function hall. The large restored town stocks outside, reputedly last used in 1863, are unique in the county as they also combine a pillory and whipping post.

Old Quaker Meeting House — Ettington, 6 miles (10km) southeast of Stratford-upon-Avon. The Old Quaker Meeting House, at 23ft (7m) x 18ft (5.5m) one of Britain's smallest, was built in 1684 and has been in continuous use ever since. Originally thatched, it now has a slate roof. The simple room is constructed of local blue lias stone with elm roof timbers which, like the windows and their catches, may be older than the building itself. The walls are lined with rush matting, a 19th century addition refurbished in 1986. The small garden was originally a Quaker burial ground. Tel: 01789 765690.

Packington Hall — 9 miles (15km) southwest of Nuneaton. The home of the Earls of Aylesford, built in 1693 in Italian Renaissance style with interior design by Joseph Bonomi, and extended in the 1770s. It is situated in a 300 acre (120ha) deer park laid out by Capability Brown (whose plans, dating to 1751 are kept in the house) and now containing fisheries and a golf course. The Church of Great Packington in the park, built for the Earl in 1789, contains an organ dating to 1750 designed by Handel and thought to have been played by the composer himself. The house and grounds are not open to the public.

Polesworth Abbey and St Editha Church — Polesworth, 10 miles (16km) northwest of Nuneaton. A Benedictine nunnery located on the north bank of the River Anker and thought to have been founded in the 9th century by St Modwena and King Egbert. The first abbess was Edgytha (Egbert's daughter, sanctified as St Editha). The ruins of the abbey cloister and the two-storey medieval gateway are still visible. The nave of the abbey church, which later became the parish church of St Editha, dates to the 12th century. Tel: 01827 892340.

Pooley Fields Heritage Centre — Polesworth, 10 miles (16km) northwest of Nuneaton. Set in Pooley Country Park on the Coventry Canal, and located on the site of the former Pooley Hall Colliery, the centre is dedicated to the history of the local mining industry which began operating c.1846, and to sustainable energy generation as well as rainwater reuse and conservation. The colliery was the first coal mine in England to install pithead baths, and the first to generate its own electricity from surplus steam used to drive the winding gear. Tel: 01827 897438.

Queen's Own Hussars Museum — See Lord Leycester Hospital

Ragley Hall — 2 miles (3km) south of Alcester, 8 miles (13km) west of Stratford-upon-Avon. The family home of the Marchioness and Marquess of Hertford, designed in Palladian style by Robert Hooke in 1680 and belatedly completed in the mid 1700s by architect James Gibbs. A grand portico was added by James Wyatt in 1780. The house contains paintings, ceramics and antique furniture. The 400 acre (160ha) grounds, landscaped by Capability Brown, are the site of the Jerwood Sculpture Park, opened in July 2004. Works on display include winners of the Jerwood Sculpture Prize for emerging artists, as well as works by Michael Ayrton, Dame Elisabeth Frink and Antony Gormley. During both world wars Ragley Hall served as a hospital. Tel: 01789 762090.

Rivers — The **Arrow** rises north of Redditch in Worcestershire and heads south to become a major tributary of the River Avon. The river flows through Arrow Valley Park in Redditch, to Studley, and then to the back of Coughton Court where it crosses a minor road as a ford. It then flows through the small market town of Alcester and is joined by the River Alne. The river continues south through the village of Arrow, near Ragley Hall, and then through the small village of Wixford. It joins the Avon at Marriage Hill, near Salford Priors, close to the Warwickshire/Worcestershire border.

The **Avon** flows through or adjoins the counties of Leicestershire, Northamptonshire, Warwickshire, Worcestershire and Gloucestershire. It rises northwest of Naseby on the Northants/Leicestershire border, and flows roughly southwest, not far north of the Cotswold Edge and through the Vale of Evesham, passing through the towns and villages of Welford, Rugby, Wolston, Leamington Spa, Warwick, Stratford-upon-Avon, Welford-on-Avon, Bidford-on-Avon, Evesham and Pershore, before joining the River Severn at Tewkesbury. It is navigable from just north of Stratford. Also called the Warwickshire Avon or Upper Avon, its total length is 96 miles (154km). Avon is an Anglicisation of *afon*, the Welsh word for 'river'. The Avon's tributaries include the Rivers Leam, Stour, Sowe, Dene, Arrow, Swift, Alne, Isonbourn, Sherbourne and Swilgate as well as many minor streams and brooks.

The **Itchen** is a small river, 12 miles (19km) long, which flows generally north through east Warwickshire. It rises in a broad valley to the northeast of the ironstone Burton Dassett Hills on the Warwickshire/Northamptonshire border. The infant river is fed by several small brooks and skirts the village of Bishop's Itchington (to which it gives its name) before passing below the London–Birmingham railway; $1^1/_2$ miles (2.5km) north of Bishop's Itchington, it passes under Deppers Bridge, which gives its name to the neighbouring hamlet. It then flows west of the town of Southam and through Stoneythorpe Park before passing the hamlet of Bascote. A mile north of Bascote, the Grand Union Canal crosses the Itchen valley on a $^1/_2$ mile (0.8km) embankment and is carried over the river on an aqueduct. The river reaches the large village of Long Itchington, afterwards swinging to the west and turning north to Marton, where it flows into the River Leam.

The **Leam** rises near the village of Hellidon in Northamptonshire on the north side of a range of low ironstone hills which form the watershed between the systems feeding the rivers Thames and Severn. Its source below Hellidon Hill is less than 1 mile (1.6km) from the source of the River Cherwell, a tributary of the Thames. Several brooks are tributaries of the Leam, including the Rains Brook which joins it near Kites Hardwick and the River Itchen which joins near Marton. After

Offchurch, the Leam enters the outskirts of Leamington Spa beside the Grand Union Canal, which has followed the river at various points from Braunston. After passing an open area of grass and woodland called Newbold Comyn, the river widens dramatically into Jephson Gardens, Leamington's main municipal park, at a weir spanned by an ornate Victorian iron footbridge. Passing the Georgian Pump Rooms in the centre of Leamington, the Leam flows a further 2 miles (3km), joining the Avon midway between Warwick and Leamington.

The **Sowe** is a tributary of the River Avon, and flows into it just south of Stoneleigh. The Sowe's route takes it through the eastern suburbs of Coventry and near the village of Baginton. The Sowe Valley Footpath runs alongside the river for $8^1/_2$ miles (13.5km) from Hawkesbury Junction Conservation Area to Stonebridge Meadows Local Nature Reserve. It also runs through Wyken Slough Local Nature Reserve, Wyken Croft Nature Park and Stoke Floods Local Nature Reserve.

The **Stour** is a tributary of the Avon; with its source in Traitors Ford, it joins the Avon at Clifford Chambers in Stratford-upon-Avon.

Tame see West Midlands

Rollright Stones — See Oxfordshire

Royal Regiment of Fusiliers Museum — St John's House, Warwick. Located in St John's House, the museum tells the story of the 6th Foot (Royal Warwickshire Regiment) from its raising in 1674 to the present day. A variety of uniforms, weapons, equipment, medals, pictures, documents and curios are on display. Tel: 01926 491653.

Royal Shakespeare Theatre — Waterside, Stratford-upon-Avon. Located beside the River Avon and dedicated to William Shakespeare, the theatre opened in 1933 with a proscenium-arch stage and a capacity of almost 1500. Originally called the Shakespeare Memorial Theatre, it was renamed in 1961 and is now managed by the Royal Shakespeare Company. The Grade II listed building closed in 2007 for major redevelopment, and is due to reopen in 2010 as a 1000 seat auditorium with a U-shaped stage surrounded on three sides by the audience. The theatre's numerous Art Deco features include the staircase and corridors at either side of the auditorium.

Rugby School — Lawrence Sheriff Street, Rugby. One of the oldest public schools in England and among the country's top co-educational schools, founded in 1567 with a bequest from Lawrence Sheriff, who made his fortune supplying groceries to Elizabeth I. Rugby's most famous headmaster, appointed in 1828, was Dr Thomas Arnold. He carried out many reforms to the school curriculum and administration and was immortalised in Thomas Hughes' book *Tom Brown's School Days*. The school was one of the original nine public schools defined by the Public Schools Act of 1868. Today Rugby School has both day and boarding pupils, the latter in the majority. Girls were admitted to the sixth form from 1975 and the school became fully co-educational in 1995. The game of rugby owes its name to the school; the legend of William Webb Ellis and the origin of the game are commemorated by a plaque. Notable Old Rugbeians include poet Rupert Brooke, authors Lewis Carroll and Salman Rushdie, former Prime Minister Neville Chamberlain, actor Robert Hardy and Indian musician Adnan Sami. Tel: 01788 556227.

St John's House Museum — St John's, Warwick. A Jacobean house dating from c.1620, which since 1961 has housed the museum's social history collections. Its exhibits include displays relating to costume, domestic life and school life. The museum of the Royal Warwickshire Regiment is situated on the first floor. Tel: 01926 412827.

St Nicholas' Church — High Street, Kenilworth. A 13th century parish church in Perpendicular style with Tudor alterations, built in the local red sandstone and located beside the Norman and medieval ruins of St Mary's Abbey, over which a large part of its graveyard now lies. The substantial tower and the north and south aisles were added in the 14th century. Raised galleries were erected in both of the nave aisles in the middle of the 18th century to accommodate the large congregations of the time. In 1888, a 'pig' of lead in the shape of a ship was unearthed in the ruins of the abbey. During the Dissolution, when the lead from the abbey roof was being stripped away, it seems that this valuable piece of royal property was hidden from the king's superintendents but subsequently forgotten. It now sits in the chancel beside the altar rail, where Henry VIII's seal can be seen. Famous visitors include Henry III who is likely to have lodged in the royal priory during the siege of Kenilworth Castle in 1266. Elizabeth I attended communion at St Nicholas' Church three times in 1575 during an extended stay at the castle. The church still owns and uses a silver chalice from which she was given communion. James I also visited Kenilworth in 1617, and there are records in the parish archives of the great west doorway of St Nicholas' being unsealed for his ceremonial entry. Finally, Charles I came to Kenilworth in 1642 and 1644. Tel: 01926 857509.

Shakespeare, William — Warwickshire's most famous son, the playwright, poet and actor, known the world over for his dramatic legacy, was traditionally born on St George's Day, 23 April 1564, in Stratford-upon-Avon, although there are no records to confirm this. The son of John Shakespeare, a successful glover and alderman from Snitterfield, and of Mary Arden, a daughter of the gentry, William is assumed to have been born at the family house on Henley Street, the third child and eldest boy of eight children, of whom only three brothers and a sister survived infancy. It is recorded that he was christened on 26 April 1564 at Holy Trinity Church, Stratford-upon-Avon. At the age of 18 he married Anne Hathaway, a farmer's daughter from Shottery, near Stratford, on 28 November 1582; she was 26 and pregnant. They had three children: Susanna, born in 1582, and twins Hamnet and Judith, born in 1585. Susanna married Dr John Hall and Judith married Thomas Quiney. Shakespeare's line ended in 1670 with the death of Elizabeth, Susanna's daughter. Shakespeare is generally credited with having penned 37 plays, but this figure could arguably be 36 or 38, depending on the treatment given to the final two works, *Henry VIII* and *The Two Noble Kinsmen*. These plays are thought to be collaborations between Shakespeare and John Fletcher, although only *Henry VIII* appears in the First Folio of 1623. Therefore the question 'Which was the last play Shakespeare wrote?' needs to be phrased very precisely in order to be answered without qualification. The last play wholly credited to Shakespeare is *The Tempest*; the last play cited in the First Folio would be *Henry VIII*; and the last play Shakespeare wrote ignoring these two provisos was *The Two Noble Kinsmen*. There are also doubts as to the chronological order of the plays. There is evidence to suggest, for instance, that his first play was probably not *Henry VI Part I*, but *Henry VI Part 2*. Shakespeare died in Stratford-upon-Avon on 23 April 1616. He therefore, traditionally, died on his birthday, aged 52. There are no names on his gravestone, which bears these words: 'Good friend, for Jesus' sake forbear,/To dig the dust enclosed here./Blest be the man that spares these stones,/And curst be he that moves my bones.' Shakespeare's family erected a monument in Holy Trinity Church, Stratford, in 1623.

Shakespeare's Birthplace — Henley Street, Stratford-upon-Avon. William Shakespeare is thought to have been born here in 1564, and the house offers an insight into the Tudor world and life as it was when Shakespeare was a child. The Shakespeare Exhibition includes an introduction to his life and background, while outside is a recreated period garden. Tel: 01789 204016.

Sport

cricket — **Warwickshire County Cricket Club** was formed in 1864, representing the historic county of Warwickshire although now based in the West Midlands. Its limited overs team is called the Warwickshire Bears. Warwickshire have had many great English players, including Bob Barber, Dennis Amiss, M J K Smith, Tom Cartwright and Eric Hollies; the most famous however is possibly all-rounder Frank (F R) Foster, a dashing batsman and left arm paceman. Just 25 when war ended his career in 1914, with 6548 runs and 718 wickets, two 'doubles' of 1000 runs and 100 wickets in a season, a then county record score of 305 not out in 1914 and leadership of Warwickshire's first title-winning side in 1911, he had won a reputation which remains unchallenged. The county's home ground is The County Ground, Edgbaston, Birmingham (sometimes called Edgbaston Stadium), which also stages Test matches and one-day internationals. The ground's most recognisable feature is the Thwaite Memorial Scoreboard at the City End. Tel: 0870 062 1902.

horse racing — **Stratford-upon-Avon** racecourse, Luddington Road, Stratford-upon-Avon, is a left-handed triangular course of $1^1/_4$ miles (2km), holding National Hunt racing. Tel: 01789 267949.

Warwick racecourse, Hampton Street, Warwick, is a left-handed oval course of $1^3/_4$ miles (2.8km) round holding both National Hunt and Flat racing. Feature races include the Tote Classic Chase over jumps and Eternal Listed Stakes on the Flat. Tel: 01926 491553.

Stoneleigh Abbey — 2 miles (3km) east of Kenilworth. Established in 1154 by a group of Cistercian monks. After its dissolution, the estate was the home of the Leigh family from 1561 until the late 20th century. Many famous people have connections with the abbey: Charles I was entertained here when the gates of Coventry were closed against him; Jane Austen stayed at the abbey and gives descriptions of its grand interiors and gardens in two of her novels; and the bed and bathroom used by Queen Victoria during her 1858 visit with Prince Albert can be seen. Other features of the house include nine state rooms, a chapel and a medieval gatehouse, while the River Avon runs through the surrounding parkland. The property is managed by English Heritage. Tel: 01926 858535.

Swan Theatre — Waterside, Stratford-upon-Avon. A theatre belonging to the Royal Shakespeare Company. Built onto the side of the larger Royal Shakespeare Theatre, it occupies a Victorian Gothic structure formerly housing the Shakespeare Memorial Theatre that preceded the RST. Designed as a modernised Elizabethan theatre, the Swan's thrust stage and a circular auditorium echo the structure of Elizabethan theatres, although unlike 16th century theatres the Swan is indoors, has comfortable seating and features modern lighting and sound technology. Opened in 1986, it was originally intended as a space for the performance of Elizabethan drama, but it has subsequently been used for many other types of theatre including the works of Chekhov, Ibsen and Tennessee Williams.

Tithe Barn — Polesworth, 5 miles (8km) northwest of Atherstone. A Grade II listed barn, dating back to at least 1655 and used for the collection of tithes until 1836. It underwent major restoration in the 1990s and is now used as a community resource centre. Tel: 01827 892480.

Twycross Zoo — $^1/_2$ mile (0.8km) south of Norton-juxta-Twycross, 6 miles (10km) north of Atherstone. Opened in 1963 on a site in Leicestershire and initially a comparatively modest collection, Twycross has grown into one of the major British zoos. Set in 50 acres (20ha) of parkland, the zoo is home to around 1000 animals, most of which are endangered species. Its world famous primate collection ranges from tiny pygmy marmosets to the impressive silverback western lowland gorillas. Twycross is the only UK zoo to house humans' so-called closest relative, the bonobo. Tel: 01827 880250.

University of Warwick — See West Midlands

Upton House — 11 miles (18km) southeast of Stratford-upon-Avon. Upton House was built in 1695 of mellow local stone for London merchant Sir Rushout Cullen. It was purchased in 1927 by Walter Samuel, 2nd Viscount Bearsted, chairman of Shell 1921–46 and son of the company's founder, who in the following years completely remodelled and updated the interiors. The house contains his collection of Old Master paintings, including works by Hogarth, Stubbs, Romney, Canaletto, Brueghel and El Greco. Other items on display include Brussels tapestries, Sèvres porcelain, Chelsea and Derby figures and 18th century furniture. There is also an exhibition of paintings and posters commissioned by Shell during Viscount Bearsted's chairmanship; also Lady Bearsted's restored Art Deco bathroom. The grounds feature an orchard, herbaceous borders, a kitchen garden, ornamental pools and a 1930s water garden, together with the National Collection of asters. The property is owned by the National Trust. Tel: 01295 670266.

Warwick Castle — Castle Hill, Warwick. The original Norman motte and bailey castle overlooking the River Avon was founded by William I in 1068 on the site of an earlier fortification erected by the daughter of King

Alfred in 914; the remains of this ancient fortification can still be seen on Ethelfleda's Mound at the southern end of the castle's courtyard. The castle is traditionally associated with the earldom of Warwick, one of the oldest in England, having been created after the Norman Conquest when William I appointed Henry de Newburgh Earl of Warwick. A shell keep added in the 12th century was rebuilt in the 14th century by Thomas Beauchamp. Unfinished additions by Richard III in the 15th century were repaired in the 17th by Sir Fulke Greville, who converted the castle as a dwelling but was murdered by one of his servants before he could move in. His son Robert, Lord Brooke held the castle for Parliament during the Civil War. The castle is now owned by Tussaud's, and its many features include a mill and engine house demonstrating how electricity was created to light the castle in 1900. Tel: 0870 442 2000.

Webb Ellis Rugby Football Museum St Matthew's Street, Rugby. Housed in the building where shoe and boot maker James Gilbert made the first rugby ball in 1842, the museum is packed with rugby memorabilia. Traditional handmade rugby balls are still made on site. Tel: 01788 567777.

Wellesbourne Watermill $^1/_2$ mile (0.8km) southeast of Wellesbourne, 5 miles (8km) east of Stratford-upon-Avon. An historic watermill on the River Dene with machinery driven by one of the country's largest wooden waterwheels. Not currently open to the public but there is a beautiful working mill nearby at Hampton Lucy, a stone's throw from Charlecote Park (see separate entry)

Some famous people born in Warwickshire

Anderson, Ethel (Australian poet) (1883–1958)	Leamington Spa
Brett, Jeremy (actor) (1933–95)	Berkswell
Brooke, Rupert (poet) (1887–1915)	Rugby
Burbage, James (actor) (1531–97)	Stratford-upon-Avon
Crowley, Aleister (occultist) (1875–1947)	Leamington Spa
Drayton, Michael (poet) (1563–1631)	Hartshill
Eliot, George (Mary Anne Evans) (author) (1819–80)	Arbury
Flint, James (novelist) (1968–)	Stratford-upon-Avon
Hathaway, Anne (wife of Shakespeare) (1556–1623)	Shottery
Kendal, Felicity (actress) (1946–)	Olton
Landor, Walter Savage (poet) (1775–1864)	Warwick
Macaulay, Rose (novelist) (1881–1958)	Rugby
Morrison, James (singer) (1984–)	Rugby
Neville, Anne (queen consort) (1456–85)	Warwick
Painting, Norman (actor) (1924–)	Leamington Spa
Shakespeare, William (playwright) (1564–1616)	Stratford-upon-Avon
Simpson, Robert (composer) (1921–97)	Leamington Spa
Tabor, June (folk singer) (1947–)	Warwick
Turpin, Randolph (boxer) (1928–66)	Leamington Spa
Williams, Steve (rower) (1976–)	Leamington Spa

West Midlands

STAFFORDSHIRE
SHROPSHIRE
WORCESTERSHIRE
WARWICKSHIRE
M6 (Toll)
Brownhills
1
M6 (Toll)
Wolverhampton
M6
Walsall
2
Sutton Coldfield
M42
4
Dudley
Turners Hill
271
West Bromwich
3
Stourbridge
Birmingham
M6
7
Halesowen
5
Solihull
6
Coventry
M5
M42
0
20 miles
0
30 km

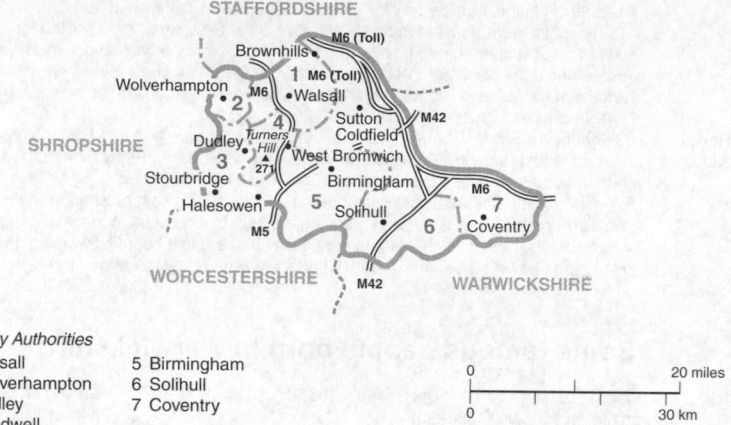

Unitary Authorities
1 Walsall
2 Wolverhampton
3 Dudley
4 Sandwell
5 Birmingham
6 Solihull
7 Coventry

A metropolitan county in western central England, formed on 1 April 1974 under the Local Government Act 1972. It contains three major cities, Birmingham, Coventry and Wolverhampton, plus four other metropolitan boroughs, Dudley, Walsall, Sandwell and Solihull, all of which are unitary authorities. Other large settlements in the county include Sutton Coldfield and West Bromwich, and it incorporates the industrial region known as the Black Country.

The West Midlands no longer has a county council, as the former West Midlands County Council was abolished in 1986, although the county remains in legal existence. It is sometimes described as the 'West Midlands metropolitan area' or the 'West Midlands conurbation' to distinguish it from the much larger West Midlands region. The latter is an official region of England covering the western half of the Midlands, with the large conurbation surrounding Birmingham at its centre; it also encompasses the predominantly rural shire counties of Herefordshire, Shropshire, Staffordshire, Warwickshire and Worcestershire. Unofficially the West Midlands region also spreads as far as Cheshire, Gloucestershire and Oxfordshire, but these are not part of the official region. For the purposes of this section references to the West Midlands are to the metropolitan county.

Birmingham has grown from a tiny Anglo-Saxon farming village into a major industrial and commercial city. In the 12th century it was granted a charter to hold a market, which in time became known as the Bull Ring. By the 16th century, Birmingham's access to supplies of iron ore and coal meant that metalworking industries became established. In the 17th century Birmingham became an important manufacturing town with a reputation for producing small arms. Birmingham manufacturers supplied Oliver Cromwell's forces with much of their weaponry during the Civil War. Arms manufacture became a staple trade and was concentrated in the area known as the Gun Quarter.

During the Industrial Revolution, Birmingham grew rapidly into a major industrial centre. Unlike many other English industrial cities such as Manchester, its industry was based on small workshops rather than large factories or mills. It soon forged a reputation as a powerhouse of the Industrial Revolution, becoming known as 'the workshop of the world' or the 'city of a thousand trades'. Between the 1760s and the 1820s, an extensive network of canals were constructed across Birmingham and the Black Country to transport raw materials and finished goods; Birmingham is often described as having more miles of canals than Venice. Railways arrived in Birmingham in 1837, with the opening of the Grand Junction Railway and later the London & Birmingham Railway. New Street Station was opened as a joint station in 1854; this was soon followed by the Great Western Railway's Snow Hill station. During the Victorian era, Birmingham's population grew to such an extent that it became the second largest population centre in England, and the third in Britain after Glasgow and London. By the late 19th century it had also become the centre of jewellery manufacture in Britain, based in the city's Jewellery Quarter.

Birmingham's importance led to it being granted city status in 1889. The city built its own university in 1900; the University of Birmingham became the first of Britain's redbrick universities. Birmingham was originally part of Warwickshire; however, with the city's expansion in the late 19th and early

20th century, it absorbed parts of Worcestershire to the south and Staffordshire to the west. The city swallowed up Sutton Coldfield in 1974, and at the same time became part of the new West Midlands county. Having suffered heavy bomb damage during World War II during the Birmingham Blitz, the city centre was extensively redeveloped during the 1950s and 1960s, with many concrete office buildings, ring roads and now much-derided pedestrian subways. Birmingham has successfully made the transition from an industrial centre to a tourism and services economy in the 21st century. People from Birmingham are known as 'Brummies', a term derived from the city's nickname of Brum. This comes in turn from the city's dialect name, Brummagem, which is derived from an earlier name of the city, *Bromwicham*.

Coventry is traditionally thought to have been established in 1043 with the founding of a Benedictine abbey by Leofric, Earl of Mercia, and his wife Lady Godiva. Current evidence suggests that this abbey was probably in existence by 1022, therefore Leofric and Godiva most likely endowed it c.1043. In time, a market was established at the abbey gates and the settlement expanded. By the 14th century Coventry had become an important centre of the cloth trade, and throughout the Middle Ages was one of the largest and most important cities in England. It was granted city status in 1345, and later became a county in its own right. The phrase 'sent to Coventry' is believed to have originated in the hostile attitudes of the city's people towards Royalist prisoners held in Coventry during the Civil War.

In the late 19th century Coventry became a major centre of bicycle manufacture, the industry being pioneered by Rover. By the early 20th century this had evolved into motor manufacture, and Coventry became a major centre of the British motor industry. The city suffered severe bomb damage during World War II, most notoriously from a massive German air raid (the 'Coventry Blitz') on 14 November 1940 which destroyed most of the historic city centre and the cathedral. Aside from London and Plymouth, Coventry suffered more damage than any other British city during the Luftwaffe attacks, with huge firestorms devastating most of the city centre. The city was targeted due to its high concentration of armaments, munitions and engine plants. The majority of Coventry's historic buildings were too badly damaged to be saved following the raids, and in the postwar years the city was largely rebuilt under the direction of the Gibson Plan, gaining a new pedestrianised shopping precinct (the first of its kind in Europe on such a scale) and the much-celebrated new St Michael's Cathedral in 1962. Coventry's motor industry boomed during the 1950s and 1960s, but during the 1970s the British motor industry underwent general decline and Coventry suffered badly as a result. By the early 1980s Coventry had one of the highest unemployment rates in the country, although the city has recovered in recent years through the development of newer industries.

Wolverhampton was formerly part of the county of Staffordshire but was granted city status on 18 December 2000, making it the first 'Millennium City'. The city is commonly recognised as being named after Lady Wulfruna, who traditionally founded the town in 985, its name coming from the Anglo-Saxon meaning 'Wulfrun's principal enclosure or farm'. By the 13th century Wolverhampton had grown to become a thriving market town, famous for its part in the woollen trade – a fact indicated by the inclusion of a woolpack on the city's coat of arms, and by the many small streets, especially in the city centre, called 'Fold' (for example, Blossom's Fold, Farmers Fold, Townwell Fold and Victoria Fold), as well as Woolpack Street.

From the 16th century onwards, Wolverhampton became home to a number of metal industries including lock and key making and iron and brass working. In 1512, Sir Stephen Jenyns, a former Lord Mayor of London, who was born in the city, founded Wolverhampton Grammar School, one of the oldest active schools in Britain. In January 1606, two farmers, Thomas Smart and John Holyhead of Rowley Regis, were hanged in High Green, now Queen Square, for sheltering some of the Gunpowder Plotters who had fled to the Midlands. The pair played no part in the original plot but nevertheless suffered the traitor's death of hanging, drawing and quartering on butcher's blocks set up in the square a few days before the execution of Guy Fawkes and several other plotters in London.

In the 19th century the area to the southeast of the city became known as the Black Country, supposedly because of the heavy industrial pollution which covered the area in black soot, although Wolverhampton itself is beyond Black Country boundaries for the most part. In Victorian times, Wolverhampton grew wealthy mainly due to the huge amount of industry that grew up as a result of the abundance of coal and iron deposits in the area. The remains of this wealth can be seen in local houses such as Wightwick Manor and The Mount (both built for the Mander family, prominent varnish and paint manufacturers), and Tettenhall Towers. Many other houses of similar stature were built only to be demolished in the 1960s and 1970s. Wolverhampton High Level station (the current main rail station) opened in 1852, but the original station was demolished in 1965 and then rebuilt.

Wolverhampton Low Level station opened on the Great Western Railway in 1855. Wolverhampton was one of the few towns to operate surface contact trams and the only town to use the Lorain Surface Contact System. Trolleybuses appeared in 1923 and in 1930 for a brief period, Wolverhampton's was the world's largest trolleybus system. The last trolleybus ran in 1967, just as the railway line was converted to electric operation. In the 19th century the city saw much immigration from Wales and Ireland; in the 20th and 21st centuries immigrants have come from places further afield, such as the Caribbean, South Asia, Africa and eastern Europe.

West Midlands	Population			Area	
Districts	*male*	*female*	*total*	*sq miles*	*sq km*
Birmingham Unitary Authority	473,266	503,821	977,087	103	268
Coventry Unitary Authority	149,115	151,733	300,848	38	99
Dudley Unitary Authority	149,714	155,441	305,155	38	98
Sandwell Unitary Authority	136,497	146,407	282,904	33	86
Solihull Unitary Authority	96,683	102,834	199,517	69	178
Walsall Unitary Authority	123,189	130,310	253,499	40	104
Wolverhampton Unitary Authority	115,858	120,724	236,582	27	69
Total	1,244,322	1,311,270	2,555,592	348	902

Local Attractions and Information

Administrative headquarters — **Birmingham:** Council House Extension, Margaret Street, Birmingham B3 3BU. Tel: 0121 303 1111.
Coventry: Council House, Earl Street, Coventry CV1 5RR. Tel: 024 7683 3333.
Dudley: Council House, Priory Road, Dudley DY1 1HF. Tel: 01384 812345.
Sandwell: Sandwell Council House, Oldbury, West Midlands B69 3DE. Tel: 0121 569 2200.
Solihull: PO Box 20, Council House, Solihull, West Midlands B91 3QU. Tel: 0121 704 6000.
Walsall: Civic Centre, Walsall, WS1 1TP. Tel: 01922 650000.
Wolverhampton: Civic Centre, St Peter's Square, Wolverhampton WV1 1SH. Tel: 01902 556556.

Baskerville House — Centenary Square, Birmingham. Previously called the Civic Centre. A former council building designed by architect T Cecil Howitt and built in 1938. It was the only completed component of a planned civic campus, designed by Howitt and which would have covered all of Centenary Square and the Convention Centre, also taking in Rupert Savage's Masonic Hall (built 1926–7) and Birmingham Municipal Bank (also designed by Howitt and built 1931–3) on Broad Street. The building was renovated 2003–07 to provide office space and a health club. Baskerville House was built on the site of Easy Hill, the home of printer John Baskerville, after whom the Baskerville typeface is named. The sculpture *Industry and Genius* (1990), depicting the typeface and created by David Patten, stands in Centenary Square.

Berry Hall Farm — Ravenshaw Lane, Solihull. A 15th century moated half-timbered property originally named Berry Hall. It was renamed Berry Hall Farm by Joseph Gillott, owner of the Berry Hall estate, when he built himself an opulent new home on the estate of the original hall in the 1870s, but became more popularly known as 'Old Berry Hall'. The new house, known as 'New Berry Hall', was demolished in the 1980s.

Bingley Hall — Broad Street, Birmingham. The first purpose-built exhibition hall in Great Britain, designed by architect J A Chatwin and constructed in 1850 by Messrs Branson and Gwyther on the site of Bingley House. Construction, using steel columns surplus to the construction of Euston railway station, took just six weeks and cost £6000. It was built in Roman Doric style in red and blue bricks (the Staffordshire blue bricks being diverted from building the Oxford Street viaduct). Covering $1^1/_4$ acres internally, it measured 224ft x 221ft, used 11,700 feet of 21 inch glass, and had ten entrance doors. Among the first events held in the new hall were the second Birmingham annual cattle show and poultry show (the first had been held in December 1849 in a temporary hall on the corner of Lower Essex Street and Kent Street). It was also the venue of the Birmingham Dog Show, chrysanthemum shows, circus, boxing, cinema and, in its later days, for popular music concerts. It had a competition cycle track. It was also used as a huge meeting space: a two-hour speech by Gladstone in November 1888, following Joseph Chamberlain's split from the Liberal Party over Irish Home Rule, was recorded by the journal *Political World* on an Edison phonograph shipped from New York – the first political speech recorded. The hall was demolished after being damaged by fire in 1983, its purpose having been superseded by the National Exhibition Centre (NEC) just outside the city. The International Convention Centre and Symphony Hall now stand in its place.

Birmingham & Midland Motor Omnibus Trust — See Worcestershire

Birmingham Botanical Gardens and Glasshouses — Westbourne Road, Edgbaston, Birmingham. Designed by garden planner, horticultural journalist and publisher J C Loudon, the 15 acre (6ha) gardens opened to subscribers in 1832. The central Main Lawn is edged with ornamental trees, and there are tropical and subtropical glasshouses. The red-brick Cottage manifests a medley of architectural styles and provides a natural setting for a collection of old favourite plants reminiscent of 19th century cottage gardens. Tel: 0121 454 1860.

Birmingham Central Mosque Belgrave Middleway, Highgate, Birmingham. One of the largest Muslim centres in Europe. Run by the Birmingham Mosque Trust, it is the second purpose-built mosque in the UK, and was the largest mosque in Western Europe when opened in 1975. A golden dome was added to the top of the minaret in 1981. The mosque is open to people of all religious affiliations, men and women; its main prayer halls hold 3500–4000 people during a Friday service and over 20,000 worshippers walk through the mosque's doors during Eid services. Tel: 0121 440 5355.

Birmingham International Airport $5^1/_2$ miles (9km) southeast of Birmingham. Located in the borough of Solihull, Birmingham (BHX) is the sixth busiest airport in the UK after London Heathrow, London Gatwick, Manchester, London Stansted and London Luton. Opened in 1939 as a civil airfield, it served as an RAF station during World War II. Tel: 0870 733 5511.

Birmingham Orthodox Cathedral Arthur Place, Summer Hill Terrace, Birmingham. A Greek Orthodox cathedral dedicated to the Dormition of the Mother of God and St Andrew. Designed in 1873 by J A Chatwin, it was formerly a Catholic church.

Bishop Asbury Cottage Newton Road, Great Barr, West Bromwich. The boyhood home of Francis Asbury (1745–1816), the first American Methodist bishop. Now a museum, the 18th century cottage is furnished in period style, with memorabilia and information relating to Asbury's life in West Bromwich and Great Barr in England and, from 1771, in the United States. There are also displays on the rise of Methodism in the surrounding Black Country, and on John Wesley's life and visits to the local area. Tel: 0121 553 0759.

Black Country A loosely defined area to the north and west of Birmingham, and south and east of Wolverhampton. The whole of Wolverhampton is included by some and none at all by others, but Birmingham is definitely not part of the area. The usual 21st century definition is the four metropolitan boroughs of Dudley, Sandwell, Walsall and the City of Wolverhampton. The town of Dudley is sometimes referred to as being the Black Country's (unofficial) capital. The Black Country now lies wholly within the West Midlands, but was formerly divided between the counties of Staffordshire and Worcestershire. Curiously, the ancient parish (and pre-1965 municipal borough) of Dudley was once a detached part of Worcestershire within Staffordshire and is still considered by some to be within Worcestershire. Even more strangely, until 1845 much of the parish of Halesowen, including Oldbury and Warley Salop (but not Cradley or Warley Wigorn), was a detached part of Shropshire. The area is often said to have gained its name because of pollution produced by the iron and coal industries in the 18th and 19th centuries, which covered the area in black soot. However, historians have suggested that the name has an earlier origin, arising from outcrops of coal that scarred the heathland which formerly covered the area, and from the area's black soil, caused by the presence of the coal seam just below the surface. Now that there is little heavy industry in the region, the Black Country is more typified by its traditional dialect with its many archaic traits of Early Modern and even Middle English. 'Thee', 'thy' and 'thou' are still in use. 'Ow b'ist', meaning 'How beist thou?' is a common greeting, the typical answer being 'Bay too bah', meaning 'I bayn't be too bad'.

Black Country Living Museum Tipton Road, Dudley. An open air museum occupying a 26 acre (10.5ha) park near Dudley Castle, and first opened in 1976. Electric trams and trolleybuses transport visitors from the entrance in a recreated factory to the village area with 30 buildings situated by the canal basin. Coal mine displays include underground workings, colliery surface buildings and a replica of Newcomen's 1712 steam engine. In all, 42 separate displays have either been re-erected or built to old plans. Tel: 0121 557 9643.

Blakesley Hall Blakesley Road, Yardley, Birmingham. A Grade II listed black and white timber-framed farmhouse built in 1590 by Richard Smalbroke and one of the oldest buildings in Birmingham. In 1935, after centuries of use as a private home, it became a museum dedicated to the history of the medieval manors which comprise the city. The hall was seriously damaged by a bomb in November 1941 and did not open again until 1957. After research in the 1970s it was restored to an authentic period appearance. It was last renovated in 2002. An adjacent barn (also Grade II listed) to the east of the hall has also been renovated and is used as an exhibition hall by a group of photographers. A branch of Birmingham Museums and Art Gallery, it is owned and operated by Birmingham City Council. Tel: 0121 464 2193.

Bull Ring, The The famous Birmingham market began in 1154 when local landowner Peter de Birmingham obtained a royal charter. Initially a cattle and food market, it is shown as a cornmarket on a map produced by Westley in 1731 with other markets located nearby on the High Street. This market was moved to the Corn Exchange on Carrs Lane in 1848. The Bull Ring developed into the main retail market area for Birmingham as the town grew into a modern industrial city. It has twice been developed as a shopping centre: first in the 1960s and again in 2003. The new indoor shopping centre, opened on 4 September 2003, features a dramatic landmark building clad in 15,000 shiny aluminium discs and housing a branch of Selfridges department store. It has won eight awards including the 2004 RIBA Award for Architecture. The site is located on the edge of the sandstone city ridge which results in the steep gradient towards Digbeth.

Caludon Castle Caludon Park, Wyken, Coventry. A 12th century fortified manor house founded by Ranulf Blundeville, Earl of Chester. In 1305, John de Segrave was granted a licence to crenellate by Edward I. The large rectangular platform, encased by a wet ditch, now supports the north wall of a first-floor hall, with majestic windows, built by John Mowbray in the mid 14th century above a low undercroft. The castle was abandoned after the Civil War.

Castle Bromwich Aerodrome Castle Bromwich, Solihull. A famous early airfield created on the former Castle Bromwich playing fields, which became the Castle Bromwich private aerodrome. Alfred P Maxwell flew the first

	aeroplane in the Birmingham area in September 1909. In 1911 Bentfield C Hucks flew a Blériot monoplane and gave passenger flights. The Midland Aero Club established itself and a hangar was built for storage of the planes. The aerodrome became a stopping place during early air races. In 1914 the War Office requisitioned it for use by the Royal Flying Corps. In 1934 the Air Ministry stated that Castle Bromwich could not be used for civil purposes indefinitely, and a new airport – the present Birmingham International Airport – was built at Elmdon, just outside the Birmingham city boundary. In 1937 more hangars and a squadron headquarters were built for the Royal Air Force. In 1939 it was extended further to become a fighter station. The airfield was also used for experimental purposes, including the 'Harrow', an early twin-engined heavy bomber.
Castle Bromwich Garden	Chester Road, Castle Bromwich, Solihull. A notable 18th century garden surrounding Castle Bromwich Hall, built 1557–85 by Sir Edward Devereux, the first MP for Tamworth. Sir Orlando Bridgeman bought the property in 1657 for his son, Sir John Bridgeman, who enlarged the house and developed the garden in the late 17th century advised by his cousin, Captain William Winde. The gardens were designed as a formal arrangement of self-contained areas and terraces, separated by walls, hedges or changes in level. On Sir John's death in 1710 his son, Sir John Bridgeman II, continued to extend the gardens westwards until they reached their present size of 10 acres (4ha). He also improved the hall. The walled baroque gardens are now Grade II* listed. The 19th century Holly Maze is a mirror image of the maze at Hampton Court Palace, designed by George London and Henry Wise.
Chamberlain Memorial	Chamberlain Square, Birmingham. Erected in 1880 to commemorate the mayoralty of Joseph Chamberlain (1836–1914), Birmingham businessman, councillor, MP, and the father of Sir Austen Chamberlain and future Prime Minister Neville Chamberlain.
Chinese Pagoda	Inner Ring Road, Birmingham. Located in the centre of the Holloway Circus roundabout, the stone carving of a Chinese pagoda, created in Fujian, China, was donated to the city by local firm Wing Yip. It forms a landmark for the nearby Chinese Quarter of the city.
Coombe Abbey	Brinklow Road, Binley, Coventry. Founded as a monastery in the 12th century. Following the Dissolution of the Monasteries in the 16th century, it became royal property. Elizabeth of Bohemia, the daughter of James I was educated there in the early 17th century. In 1682, the West Wing was added by architect Captain William Winde. He also designed Buckingham House, which later became Buckingham Palace, and the resemblance is notable. In 1771, Capability Brown redesigned the gardens. The abbey was bought by Coventry City Council in 1964 and opened to the public. The grounds remain a popular nature reserve and country park although the Grade I listed abbey itself is now a hotel. Tel: 02476 450450.
Coventry Airport	See Warwickshire
Coventry Canal	Begun by James Brindley and built 1768–89, the Coventry Canal runs for 38 miles (65km) from Coventry via Bedworth, Nuneaton, Atherstone, Polesworth and Tamworth to its junction with the Trent & Mersey Canal just north of Lichfield, Staffordshire.
Coventry Castle	Broadgate, Coventry. Built in the 11th century by Ranulf Meschines, Earl of Chester, originally as a priory. The castle was taken during the 12th century civil war by Robert Marmion and converted into a fortress. It was dismantled by King Stephen c.1147 but repaired during the reign of Henry II. The site of the castle is now occupied by the Cathedral Lanes shopping centre, although a surviving fragment now forms part of St Mary's Guildhall and is known as Caesar's Tower.
Coventry Cathedral	Priory Street, Coventry. Also known as St Michael's Cathedral, the seat of the Bishop and Diocese of Coventry. The city has had three cathedrals. The first was St Mary's, a monastic building, only a few ruins of which remain; the second was St Michael's, a Church of England church later designated a cathedral, the ruined shell of which remains after its bombing during World War II. The third is the new St Michael's Cathedral, built after the destruction of the former and a celebration of 20th century architecture. The design, by Basil Spence, was chosen as the result of a competition held in 1950. The foundation stone was laid by Queen Elizabeth II on 23 March 1956. It was consecrated on 25 May 1962, and Benjamin Britten's *War Requiem*, composed for the occasion, was premiered in the new cathedral on 30 May to mark the occasion. The unconventional spire (known as a flèche) was lowered onto the flat roof by helicopter. The interior is notable for a large tapestry of Christ, designed by Graham Sutherland, and for the baptistry window designed by John Piper, a stained glass window of abstract design occupying the full height of one wall and made up from 195 elemental panes of startlingly bright primary colours. Also of note is the Great West Window, known as the Screen of Saints and Angels, engraved by John Hutton.
Coventry Railway Centre	See Warwickshire
Coventry Transport Museum	Hales Street, Coventry. Formerly known as the Museum of British Road Transport, the museum houses the most extensive collection of British-made road transport in the world. There are more than 240 cars and commercial vehicles, 100 motorcycles and 200 bicycles, but perhaps the most notable exhibits are Thrust2 and ThrustSSC, the British jet cars which broke the land speed record in 1983 and 1997. Tel: 024 7623 4270.
Dudley	The largest town in the Black Country and the second largest in the UK, located south of Wolverhampton. The town centre is traditionally part of an exclave of Worcestershire entirely surrounded by Staffordshire. The town's main football team, Dudley Town FC, has never progressed beyond the Southern Premier League. See also Black Country Living Museum, Dudley Castle, Dudley Zoo
Dudley Castle	Castle Hill, Dudley. Norman motte and bailey castle founded c.1070 by William Fitzansculf. Destroyed by Henry II in 1175 after Roger de Mowbray rebelled against him, it was rebuilt in 1270

by John de Somery and extended early in the 14th century by John de Sutton, who was forced to hand it to Hugh Despenser in 1324. Besieged during the Civil War in 1644 and slighted in 1646, the castle was devastated by fire in 1750. The grounds, featuring an extensive wooded ridge which runs north from the castle, are now home to Dudley Zoo.

Dudley Zoo — Located within the grounds of Dudley Castle. Opened in 1937 by the Dudley Zoological Society, founded in 1935, there are 12 listed buildings, seven Grade II and five Grade II*, erected in 1937 by Berthold Lubetkin's Tecton firm. The site was expanded in 2008 to include an Eden Project-style dome creating a tropical environment. Tel 01384 215313.

Edgbaston Cricket Ground — See Warwickshire: Sport

Erdington Abbey — Sutton Road, Edgbaston, Birmingham. A Grade II listed Roman Catholic parish church in the Archdiocese of Birmingham, served by the Redemptorist order and dedicated to Saints Thomas and Edmund of Canterbury. Designed in Gothic Revival style by Augustus Pugin, architect of other notable Roman Catholic buildings in Birmingham such as St Chad's and Oscott College, the church was built 1848–50 by Charles Hansom (brother of Joseph Hansom, inventor of the Hansom cab) with a steeple 117ft (36m) high. In 1876 Father Haigh handed over the church, parish and 4 acre (1.6ha) estate to Benedictine monks from Beuron in Germany, exiled for their faith from their own country during the *Kulturkampf*, the anti-Catholic and anti-clerical movement headed by Bismarck. After establishing an abbey on land next to the church, the predominantly German monks were later displaced a second time during World War I. The parish came under the control of the Redemptorists in 1922.

Fort Dunlop — Erdington, Birmingham. The common name of the original tyre warehouse and head office of Dunlop Tyres. Established in 1917 and a Grade A locally listed building, it has been refurbished as office and retail space by design partnership Urban Splash, reopening in 2006.

Fox Hollies Hall — Fox Hollies Park, Acocks Green, Birmingham. A manor house belonging to the Walker family. The Italianate hall was built in 1869 to replace nearby Hyron Hall, and was commissioned by retired merchant Zaccheus Walker III. His father, industrialist Zaccheus Walker II, was almost killed in the French Revolution but escaped through his friendship with Robespierre. The only surviving parts of the hall are the pillars to the main gate. Three tower blocks were built at the rear of the site in 1965, and the site of the hall itself is a public park.

Grand Union Canal — A canal system extending for 137 miles (220km) with 166 locks, linking Birmingham and London. It was formed in 1929 by the amalgamation of several earlier canals, including the Warwick & Birmingham Canal, Warwick & Napton Canal (both opened in 1799), and the Grand Junction Canal from Braunston, Northamptonshire, to the River Thames at Brentford in London (fully opened in 1805). The 66 mile (107km) Leicester branch leaves the main canal at Braunston and links with the River Trent near Kegworth, and there are several smaller branches.

Great Barr Hall — Great Barr, Walsall. Home from the 17th century to the Scott family and greatly extended until 1777 when it was lavishly rebuilt by Joseph Scott. During the 1780s the hall was leased by Samuel Galton and was a venue for meetings of the Lunar Society; it was said to be the society's favourite meeting place. The 'Moonstones', eight stone memorials to members of the society erected in 1998, are sited at the nearby Asda supermarket. Two of the extant lodge houses are believed to be by Sir George Gilbert Scott (no relation to the hall's owners). The Grade II* listed hall is owned by the Manor Building Preservation Trust, but is currently in a very poor state of repair.

Great Western Arcade — Colmore Row, Birmingham. A covered Grade II listed Victorian shopping arcade in central Birmingham between Colmore Row and Temple Row. Designed by W H Ward of Stone, Staffordshire, it was built 1875–6 over the Great Western Railway line cutting – roofed over in 1874 – at Birmingham Snow Hill station. Tel: 0121 236 5417.

Green Men of Birmingham — Green Men (more recently known as foliate heads) are carved stone human heads usually with prolific vegetation growing from their faces and used as architectural decoration since the Middle Ages. Over 100 Green Men occur in Birmingham, largely as a revival by Victorian sculptors of the medieval motif. The most recent Green Man to be built in the city was commissioned in 2002 for the refurbished Custard Factory. The work of sculptor Tawny Gray (Toin Adams), it is a huge structure made from vegetation and stone and standing next to a large water feature.

Grimshaw Hall — 1/2 mile (0.8km) north of Knowle, 10 miles (16km) southeast of Birmingham. A half-timbered Elizabethan manor house built c.1560, home to the Grimshaw family 1620–c.1765. The Grade I listed house has a main hall block between two cross-wings with a fine two-storeyed porch in the centre, completing the E plan often favoured at that period. Queen Mary visited Grimshaw Hall in 1927.

Highbury — Yew Tree Road, Moseley, Birmingham. Also known as Highbury Hall, the house was commissioned by Joseph Chamberlain as his Birmingham residence in 1878, two years after he became MP for the city. The architect was John Henry Chamberlain (no relation), who incorporated much terracotta decoration. Joseph Chamberlain lived in Highbury from 1880 until his death in 1914. During World War I the house was used as a hospital annexe and home for disabled soldiers. It was given to trustees in 1919 by Chamberlain's elder son, passing to the Corporation of Birmingham in 1932 when it was used as a home for elderly women. In 1984 it was restored by Birmingham City Council and is now used as a conference centre and occasional restaurant. The Grade II* listed hall overlooks Highbury Park, a public park.

Highest point — Turners Hill at 886ft (271m), located on the border of Dudley and Rowley Regis in the Borough of Sandwell.

Himley Hall — Himley, 3 miles (5km) west of Dudley. Originally a moated manor house, standing beside the medieval church and which for more than 400 years served as a secondary home to the Lords of

Dudley and their knights. Its occupants included Dud Dudley, whose 17th century experiments in smelting iron ore with coal were carried out nearby. In 1645, Charles I encamped in the grounds on his way to defeat at the Battle of Naseby during the Civil War. The present building dates from the 18th century when John Ward demolished the medieval manor, replacing it with a Palladian-style mansion. The village of Himley was relocated at the same time, and the church rebuilt on its present site in 1764. The 180 acres (73ha) of grounds were designed by Capability Brown and include a great lake, fed by a series of waterfalls from a higher chain of smaller pools. The hall remained in the Ward family until the 20th century; in 1934 the Duke and Duchess of Kent honeymooned at the house, while Edward VIII spent the last weekend before his abdication here. The property was sold to the National Coal Board for £45,000 after World War II, but a fire gutted the south wing during its conversion. This part of the house was rebuilt, but unfortunately not in keeping with its former appearance. In 1966 it was purchased jointly by Dudley and Wolverhampton County Borough Councils and the park was opened as a public leisure area. In 1988 Dudley bought Wolverhampton's share.

Interesting facts — **The Little Dry Dock** at Windmill End, Netherton, near Dudley, is a public house with a difference. Originally built as a barge-station, it has a complete narrowboat inside which substitutes as the bar. Another interesting public house is **Somerset House** in Stourbridge, a fairly innocuous West Midlands local, except for the fact that it is possible to park a full pint unsupported on its walls. The phenomenon has been probed by scientists who arrived at the conclusion that the wallpaper glue was responsible. Regular punters are convinced the walls have magical qualities and others believe the pub to be haunted. **England's first automatic traffic lights** were situated in Princes Square, Wolverhampton, on 5 November 1927. The installation was made by J Boot, chief engineer for the Siemens & General Electric Railway Signal Co., and consisted of an aluminium signal-box, suspended above the centre of the roadway from cables, with red, green and amber lights facing in four directions. It remained in use until 1968. The modern traffic lights at this location have traditional striped poles in commemoration. The **Birmingham Six** – Hugh Callaghan, Patrick Hill, Gerard Hunter, Richard McIlkenny, William Power and John Walker – were sentenced to life imprisonment in 1975 in an infamous miscarriage of justice for two pub bombings in Birmingham. On 21 November 1974 bombs exploded in two crowded pubs, killing 21 people (10 at the Mulberry Bush and 11 at the Tavern in the Town) and injuring 182. A third device, outside a bank on Hagley Road, failed to detonate. The convictions of the six men were overturned by the Court of Appeal on 14 March 1991 largely on the basis that minute traces of nitroglycerine found on their bodies could have come from innocuous sources such as soap. The judge at the appeal famously declared of the police witnesses at the original trial, 'They must have lied.' The Birmingham bombings were attributed to the Provisional IRA. In 2001, a decade after their release, the six men were awarded compensation ranging from £840,000 to £1.2m. A **yam yam** is a colloquial name for a person from the Black Country, the name deriving from 'you am' e.g 'yam coming with me ay ya?' Yam yams are quite proud of their friendly rivalry with Birmingham folk.

Joseph Chamberlain Memorial Clock Tower — Located in the centre of Chancellor's Court at the University of Birmingham. Nicknamed 'Old Joe' or 'Big Joe', it stands 330ft (100m) tall and was built to commemorate Joseph Chamberlain, the first chancellor of the university. It is visible for many miles around the campus, and has become synonymous with the university itself. Constructed 1900–08, it was the tallest building in Birmingham until 1969 when it was superseded by the BT Tower in the Jewellery Quarter, which is 500ft (152m) tall. It is still one of the 50 tallest buildings in the UK. The minute hand is 10ft 6in (3.2m) long, the hour hand is 2ft (0.6m) across, the pendulum is 15ft (4.5m) long and the hour bells weigh 6 tonnes.

Jury's Inn — Broad Street, Birmingham. A concrete and steel building constructed in Brutalist style as part of the city's 1960s redevelopment. One of the tallest buildings on Broad Street at 200ft (60m), it forms a prominent part of the city skyline when viewed from the south.

Lunar Society — A discussion club of prominent industrialists, natural philosophers and intellectuals who met regularly in Birmingham 1765–1813. At first called the Lunar Circle, 'Lunar Society' became the formal name by 1775. The society's name came from its members' practice of scheduling their meetings at the time of the full moon. Since there was no street lighting, the extra light made the journey home easier and safer. They cheerfully referred to themselves as 'lunaticks', a pun on lunatics. Venues included Erasmus Darwin's home in Lichfield, Matthew Boulton's home, Soho House, and Great Barr Hall. Among the society's influential members were Matthew Boulton, Erasmus Darwin, Samuel Galton Jr, James Keir, Joseph Priestley, Josiah Wedgwood, James Watt, John Whitehurst and William Withering. Among memorials to the society and its members are the Moonstones (see Great Barr Hall), a statue of Watt in Chamberlain Square, the *Wattelisk* in Dalton Street, and a statue of Boulton, Watt and Murdoch (1956) by William Bloye in Broad Street.

Millennium Point — Curzon Street, Birmingham. A complex situated in the developing Eastside of Birmingham city centre. A Millennium Commission project, it was opened by Queen Elizabeth II on 2 July 2002. The building is home to Birmingham Thinktank Science Museum, the Technology Innovation Centre (part of the University of Central England), the University of the First Age, the Young People's Parliament, an Imax cinema, and commercial leisure, retail and office space around a public mall known as the Hub. The building is constructed as a massive box-like creation with a rotund offshoot which glows in various colours at night.

M6 Toll — Britain's first toll motorway, partially opened (to local traffic only) on 9 December 2003 and fully opened on 14 December the same year. It extends north and west for 27 miles (43km) between Coleshill, Warwickshire, and Cheslyn Hay, Staffordshire. Passing to the east and north of

Birmingham and Walsall in addition to the current M6, it was designed to alleviate congestion at the latter's busiest point near Wolverhampton between the M54 and M5 motorways.

National Exhibition Centre — 7 miles (11km) east of Birmingham. The seventh largest exhibition centre in Europe, adjacent to Birmingham International Airport and Birmingham International railway station. Its 20 interconnected halls are set in 628 acres (300ha). The 11,000 capacity NEC Arena, the largest multi-purpose arena in the UK when opened in the mid 1980s, is also part of the complex and hosts large music concerts.

National Indoor Arena — King Edward's Road, Birmingham. Opened in 1991, the National Indoor Arena (NIA) hosts a range of events including sport and concerts and seats 4000–13,000. When built, it was the largest indoor arena in the UK until the MEN Arena (see Greater Manchester) opened four years later.

National Westminster House — Colmore Row, Birmingham. Also known as 103 Colmore Row and once owned by NatWest. It was designed by John Madin in Brutalist style; built 1973–6, it stands 263ft (80m) high. The brown and dark green colour scheme, very similar to that of the McLaren Building, also in Birmingham, forms a prominent part of the city skyline. It is now owned by British Land, who plan to demolish it and replace it with a new skyscraper.

New Hall Manor — Walmley, 8 miles (13km) northeast of Birmingham. Thought to be one of the oldest inhabited moated houses in Britain, dating from the 13th century when the Earl of Warwick built a hunting lodge on the site. The present building with its great hall dates largely from the 16th century. The buildings served briefly as a school from 1885 until Lt Col. Wilkinson converted it to residential use in 1903. In 1923 it was acquired by Alfred Owen of Rubery Owen and remained the Owen family home until the 1970s, before being converted to a hotel in 1988.

Old Crown, The — High Street, Deritend, Birmingham. A black and white timber-framed building, thought to be one of the oldest secular buildings in Birmingham. Now a pub, it is Grade II* listed and claims to date to c.1368, although almost all of the present building dates from the early 16th century.

Orion Building, The — Navigation Street, Birmingham. A 295ft (90m) tall high-rise residential building completed in 2007. Construction of the tower began in 2004; the original façades of the buildings which made way for it have been incorporated into the design of its lower levels. The tower has 28 floors and five basement floors and houses the city's first penthouse, located at the top of the tower.

Pebble Mill — Located in Pebble Mill Road and once a prominent landmark in the Edgbaston area, the BBC production centre at Pebble Mill was opened by Princess Anne on 10 November 1971. Construction of the studios began in 1967, and the seven-storey site contained offices, television studios, radio studios, two canteens, a post office and a garden. The views from the roof overlooked Cannon Hill Park as well as Birmingham's city centre. The world's longest-running radio soap, *The Archers*, was produced at Pebble Mill, as were talk show *Pebble Mill at One*, television drama *Doctors* and *Midlands Today*. The studios were demolished in 2005.

Perrott's Folly — Waterworks Road, Edgbaston, Birmingham. Also known as The Monument or The Observatory. The 96ft (29m) tall tower was built in 1758 and is now Grade II* listed. It has been suggested that the building, along with the nearby tower of Edgbaston Waterworks, was the inspiration for the Two Towers in J R R Tolkien's *The Lord of the Rings*.

Prisons — **Birmingham**, Winson Green Road, Birmingham, popularly known as Winson Green, was built in 1849 and now holds male Category B and C prisoners, both convicted and on remand. Operational capacity: 1450. Tel: 0121 345 2500.

YOI Brinsford, 4 miles (6km) north of Wolverhampton, opened in 1991 on a site adjacent to Featherstone prison. Operational capacity: 569. Tel: 01902 533450.

Featherstone, 4 miles (6km) north of Wolverhampton, is an adult male Category C training prison built on former Ministry of Defence land and opened in 1976. Operational capacity: 687. Tel: 01902 703000.

Red House Cone — High Street, Wordsley, Stourbridge. A 100ft (30.5m) high conical brick structure, built c.1790 and used for the production of glass. In use by the Stuart Crystal firm until 1936, it is the best preserved of only four such structures in the UK and hosts various exhibits related to the production of glass. The site is managed by Dudley Council. Tel: 01384 812750.

Red House Park — Newton Road, Great Barr, Walsall. A public park within which is a country house built in 1841 for Robert Wellbeloved Scott, Liberal MP for Walsall, and once part of his 27 acre (11ha) estate. The Grade II listed house was formerly used as a convalescent home, but is now owned by Sandwell Metropolitan Borough Council and leased to the British Trust for Conservation Volunteers. The park contains an obelisk in memory of Princess Charlotte, daughter of George IV and Caroline of Brunswick, who died in childbirth aged 21.

Rivers — The **Blythe** is fed by the River Cole and is a tributary of the River Tame. All three rivers meet beside the West Midland Bird Club's Ladywalk reserve. The **Cole** rises between Wythall, Weatheroak, Inkford and Portway, south of Birmingham. After flowing through Birmingham, it passes Coleshill, to which it gives its name. It joins the River Blythe, of which it is a tributary, near Ladywalk, shortly before the Blythe meets the Tame. The Cole drives Sarehole Mill in the south of Birmingham.

The **Rea** is a small river which passes through Birmingham. Its name derives from a root found in many Indo-European languages and means 'to run' or 'to flow'. The river drops about 225ft (69m) in its first mile, but then assumes a gentle slope. It frequently bursts its banks after heavy rain. The Rea is now culverted for much of its course through Birmingham, during which it passes through Cannon Hill Park. Wychall Reservoir, near the river at Cotteridge, was built in the early 1800s by the Worcester Canal Company after mill owners claimed that water was being taken from the river to fill the canal and reducing the working effectiveness of their mills.

The **Tame** flows from the Black Country, through north Birmingham, past Tamworth (which takes its name from the river), and into the River Trent near Alrewas. The name derives from Celtic and is usually thought to mean 'dark' or 'slow moving', although the precise meaning is uncertain. The river is susceptible to spectacular flooding at the village of Hopwas between Tamworth and Lichfield during periods of heavy autumnal rain, attested by the Anglo-Saxon meaning of the village's name: *hop*, nook of land, *was*, watery. There is also a substantial bend in the course of the river between Hopwas and Elford, giving rise to the name of the area of Tamhorn. The river is non-navigable. However, clean-up operations on a notoriously polluted stretch of the river in the Witton area of Birmingham have allowed aquatic wildfowl such as ducks and swans to settle there.

St Augustine's Church — Lyttelton Road, Edgbaston, Birmingham. The Church of St Augustine of Hippo is one of the very few Anglican churches dedicated to St Augustine. Designed in 1868 by J A Chatwin, who added a spire, the tallest in Birmingham at 185ft (56.5m), in 1876, it has a striking painted chancel ceiling and stained glass by Hardman & Co. The wealth of stone carving inside includes work by John Roddis and the Bromsgrove Guild. A spacious narthex, designed by Philip Chatwin, was added in 1968 to mark the church's centenary year. The Grade II* listed church has a notable choral tradition, being the first Anglican church in Birmingham to have a surpliced choir; past Masters of Music have included Alfred Gaul and Sir William Henry Harris. Composer Herbert Howells wrote his *St Augustine's Service* for the choir in 1967.

St Chad's Cathedral — St Chad's Queensway, Birmingham. The seat of the Roman Catholic Province of Birmingham. Dedicated to St Chad of Mercia, it was the first Roman Catholic cathedral to be built in England after the Reformation and is one of only three minor basilicas in England (the others being Downside Abbey and Corpus Christi Priory). The Grade II* listed cathedral was built to a neo-Gothic design by Augustus Pugin, at the behest of Bishop Thomas Walsh, the local apostolic vicar. It was consecrated on 21 June 1841, named a cathedral in 1850 by Pope Pius IX, and declared a minor basilica in 1941 by Pope Pius XII. The first Bishop of Birmingham was William Bernard Ullathorne OSB, whose remains are entombed beneath St Chad's. The cathedral survived bombing in November 1940 although subject to a direct hit: a bomb fell through the roof and bounced from the floor into some central heating pipes, at which point it exploded. Water escaping from the damaged pipes extinguished the subsequent fire.

St Martin's Church — Bull Ring, Birmingham. The parish church of Birmingham, familiarly known as 'The Cathedral of the Bull Ring'. The first church was probably Norman, but was rebuilt in the 13th century. Most of the existing structure dates from the late 19th century, though inside are effigies of the de Berminghams, once lords of the manor, whose home was nearby. There are windows by Burne-Jones and William Morris. The exterior was cleaned and refurbished in 2003, in conjunction with the redevelopment of the adjacent Bull Ring area.

St Paul's Church — St Paul's Square, Birmingham. A Grade I listed church located in a Georgian square in Birmingham's Jewellery Quarter. Designed by Roger Eykyn of Wolverhampton and started in 1777, it was built on land given by Charles Colmore from his Newhall estate and consecrated in 1779. It is a rectangular in shape, similar in appearance to St Martin in the Fields, London. The spire was added in 1823 by Francis Goodwin. The church has excellent acoustics and has long been a concert venue. The organ came from the town hall in 1838. The east window has an important 1791 stained glass window designed by Benjamin West and made by Francis Eginton, showing the Conversion of St Paul. Unusually it consists of two layers of glass, each painted on the inside. St Paul's Square was an elegant and desirable location in the mid 19th century. At the end of the century the square was swallowed by workshops and factories, with the façades of some buildings being pulled down to make shop fronts or factory entrances. Much restoration was done in the 1970s and many of the buildings are now Grade II listed.

St Philip's Cathedral — Colmore Row, Birmingham. An Anglican cathedral designed in Baroque style by architect Thomas Archer and completed in 1715 as a parish church. Enlarged in the late 19th century by J A Chatwin, it gained cathedral status in 1905, when the Diocese of Birmingham was created. The first bishop was Charles Gore, Bishop of Worcester, a statue of whom is located at the entrance. Built of brick and faced with stone, it has stained glass windows by Sir Edward Burne-Jones; these were saved from exposure to bomb damage during World War II by the Birmingham Civic Society, who had them removed and later reinstalled. The third smallest cathedral in England after Derby and Chelmsford, it is now Grade I listed; six monuments in the churchyard also have listed status. There is a memorial in the grounds to the victims of the Birmingham pub bombings.

Sandwell Valley Country Park — 2 miles (3km) east of West Bromwich. Over 2000 acres (800ha) of woodland and parkland in the valley of the River Tame between Birmingham and West Bromwich. Managed by Sandwell Metropolitan Borough Council, it is adjacent to RSPB Sandwell Valley nature reserve.

Sarehole Mill — Cole Bank Road, Hall Green, Birmingham. A watermill on the River Cole, built in 1765 and used both for grinding corn and for metal rolling and blade production. It now houses a museum. The mill and its surroundings are said to have been one of the inspirations for The Shire in J R R Tolkien's *The Lord of the Rings.* Tel: 0121 777 6612.

Selly Manor — Oak Tree Lane, Bournville, Birmingham. A medieval manor house with Tudor additions, Selly Manor is one of Birmingham's oldest buildings. It once stood in Bournbrook Road, but in the early 20th century was to be demolished after many years of decay and neglect to make way for redevelopment. In 1907, George Cadbury decided it was worth saving and arranged for the building to be taken down piece by piece, transported to its current location and reassembled. Restoration commenced in 1912 and the house was opened to the public in 1917; it was subsequently handed over to the Bournville Village Trust. Tel: 0121 472 0199.

Soho House — Soho Avenue, Handsworth, Birmingham. The home of engineer Matthew Boulton (1728–1809) from 1766 until his death. It now houses a museum opened in 1995 and celebrating his life, his partnership with James Watt and his membership of the Lunar Society. Having acquired the lease of the five year old Soho Mill in 1761, afterwards developing it into the Soho Manufactory, Boulton expanded the cottage next to it into Soho House and moved in when the Manufactory was completed in 1766. Soho House was refurbished in neoclassical style 1796–9 to designs by James and Samuel Wyatt, at which time it was clad in sheets of slate painted to give the appearance of large stone blocks. The Soho Manufactory was demolished in 1863. Before the house became a museum, it had several uses, most recently as a residential hostel for police officers. Tel: 0121 554 9122.

Solihull — A large town located 9 miles (15km) southeast of Birmingham city centre. The headquarters of the larger Metropolitan Borough of Solihull, it is commonly regarded as one of the most prosperous towns in the UK. Residents of Solihull and those born in the town are referred to as Silhillians. The town's motto is *Urbs in Rure* ('town in the country').

Spaghetti Junction — One of Birmingham's most famous – and notorious – landmarks. Otherwise known as Junction 6 of the M6, it is officially recorded as Gravelly Hill Interchange, but the title is rarely used. Its colloquial name more closely captures the appearance of the junction, where three motorways meet and tangle with a host of major and minor roads leading into and out of Birmingham. About 2 miles (3km) long from end to end, Spaghetti Junction is raised up to 80ft (24m) above the ground on concrete pillars. It was constructed and opened in the early 1970s, along with the section of the M6 to which it is joined.

Sport

athletics — **Birchfield Harriers** were founded in 1877 and are based at the Alexander Stadium, Birmingham. Tel: 0121 344 4858.

Tipton Harriers, Wednesbury Oak Road, Tipton, were created in September 1910, when the Tipton branch of Birchfield Harriers became an independent club. Tipton's first golden age was dominated on the track by Jack Holden, an outstanding athlete whose career lasted 26 years (1925–51), unique in British athletics history. In international competition 1929–50, in events ranging from middle distances, through cross-country to the marathon in his later years, he held world records and won at least 75 major championships from County to Empire and European levels. Only an Olympic medal eluded him. In 1950, at the age of 43, Holden won an Empire and Commonwealth title in New Zealand and a European title in Brussels. Tel: 0121 502 5534.

football — **Aston Villa** were formed in March 1874 and were founder members of the Football League in 1888. Seven times winners of both the League Championship and the FA Cup, they also won the European Cup in 1982. Their closest rivals are Birmingham City, games between the two clubs being known as the 'Second City Derby'. Villa also enjoy local rivalries with Coventry City, West Bromwich Albion and Wolverhampton Wanderers. Nicknamed The Villans, their home ground is Villa Park, Aston, Birmingham. Their colours are claret and blue shirts and white shorts. Tel: 0871 423 8101.

Birmingham City were founded in 1875 and joined the Football League in 1892. Originally known as Small Heath Alliance, followed by Small Heath in 1888, they became Birmingham FC in 1905 and Birmingham City FC in 1945. Nicknamed The Blues, their home ground is St Andrews Stadium, Bordesley Green, Birmingham. Their colours are blue shirts and white shorts. Tel: 0844 557 1875.

Coventry City were founded in 1883 by the employees of cycle manufacturer Singers (from which the club took its name). In 1898 the club was renamed Coventry City just prior to a move to new playing fields on the site of Highfield Road, their home ground for the next 106 years. Coventry were first nicknamed The Bantams in December 1908; the name was suggested by the local newspaper, which noted that they were one of the few clubs without a nickname and felt this an apt choice for the lightweights of the Southern League. The suggestion proved popular with the press and supporters; the nickname remained until the summer of 1962, when the club revived the sky blue kit worn by its players in the early 20th century and manager Jimmy Hill re-christened them The Sky Blues. Promoted to Division One for the first time in 1967, the club spent an unbroken 34 years in the top flight until relegated in 2001, also winning the FA Cup in 1987. The club's home ground since 2005 has been The Ricoh Arena, Foleshill, Coventry. Tel: 0844 873 1883.

Walsall were formed in 1888 by the amalgamation of Walsall Town and Walsall Swifts and were admitted to the Football League in 1892 as founder members of the new Second Division. Their colours are red shirts and white shorts. Nicknamed The Saddlers, they moved into their current home ground, The Bescot Stadium, in 1990, having played since 1896 at nearby Fellows Park. The stadium is also host to England under-21 international matches and England women's international matches. Tel: 0871 221 0442.

West Bromwich Albion were founded in 1878 as West Bromwich Strollers. The club was one of the 12 founding members of the Football League in 1888. League champions in 1920, they have also won the FA Cup five times, most recently in 1968. Nicknamed The Baggies or less commonly The Throstles, their home ground since 1900 has been The Hawthorns. The club's home strip is blue and white striped shirts and white shorts. Tel: 0871 211 1100.

Wolverhampton Wanderers were formed in 1877 as St Lukes FC. Founder members of the Football League in 1888, they were League champions in 1954, 1958 and 1959 and FA Cup winners in 1893, 1908, 1949 and 1960. Their traditional colours are old gold and black. Nicknamed (The) Wolves, their home ground since 1889 has been Molineux, Whitmore Reans, Wolverhampton (the ground was built on a park named after 18th century merchant Benjamin Molineux, who once had a house on the site). On 24 June 2003, Molineux became Wolverhampton's biggest live concert venue, with Bon Jovi performing in front of 34,000 people. Tel: 0871 222 2220.

golf — **The Belfry**, Wishaw, Sutton Coldfield. A prestigious golf club owned by Irish billionaire Sean Quinn, who acquired the course in 2005, and operated by the De Vere hotel and leisure company. The club has three courses: the Brabazon Course is the main tournament course, the others being the PGA National Course and the Derby Course. The headquarters of the Professional Golfers' Association are located nearby. The Belfry hosted the Ryder Cup in 1985, 1989, 1993 and 2002, and has staged many European Tour events. Tel: 0870 900 0066.

greyhound racing — **Monmore Green**, Sutherland Avenue, Monmore Green, Wolverhampton. 419m track. Tel: 01902 452648.

Perry Barr, Aldridge Road, Perry Barr, Birmingham. 434m track. Tel: 0870 840 7411.

horse racing — **Wolverhampton** racecourse, Dunstall Park, Goresbrook Road, Wolverhampton, is a left-handed all-weather circuit of just under 1 mile (1.6km) round, with turf track for National Hunt racing on the outside of the all-weather course. Tel: 01902 421421.

ice hockey — **Coventry Blaze** ice hockey team originated as Solihull Blaze. In 2000–01, in order to attract a new and larger fan-base, the Blaze moved to the 3000 capacity Coventry Skydome, afterwards becoming one of the more successful British National League teams. They won the league and playoff double in 2002–03, completing the playoffs unbeaten.

speedway — **Coventry Bees** are based at Brandon Stadium, Rugby Road, Brandon, Coventry. Consistently among England's top teams, the Bees' won the British Elite League Speedway Championship in 2005, their sixth such success. Club colours are of course yellow and black.

Sutton Coldfield — A town to the northeast of Birmingham, now within the City of Birmingham metropolitan borough, but until 1974 a municipal borough in its own right and part of Warwickshire, enjoying the title of 'Royal Town'. In 1528 a charter of Henry VIII, secured by Bishop John Vesey, gave the town the right to be known for ever as 'The Royal Town of Sutton Coldfield' and to be governed by a warden and society. This unreformed corporation survived until 1885, when it was replaced by a municipal borough. Although the title 'Royal Town' was still used, the municipality created in 1885 was not itself a royal borough. The formal mayoral chains of office are now on display in Birmingham Council House.

Tipton Three — Between 2002 and 2004 Tipton residents Shafiq Rasul, Ruhal Ahmed and Asif Iqbal were inmates of Guantánamo Bay, although they were released without charge. They are popularly known as the 'Tipton Three'. The film *The Road to Guantánamo* (2006), directed by Michael Winterbottom and released in 2006, claims to be a historically accurate representation of their torture and imprisonment.

Universities — **Aston University** developed from the Birmingham Municipal Technical School, founded in 1895 and later renamed Birmingham College of Technology. Known as one of the 'plate-glass' universities, it received its university charter in 1966. With around 9500 students, it focuses on science, technology and business and occupies a campus in central Birmingham. Former students include comedian Jasper Carrott. Tel: 0121 204 3000.

Birmingham City University was established in 1992, when the former City of Birmingham Polytechnic received its charter as the University of Central England. It adopted its present name in 2007. Its main campus is at Perry Barr, Birmingham, with various sites in other parts of the city. The university has around 24,000 students. Tel: 0121 331 5000.

The **University of Birmingham** was founded in 1900 as a successor to Mason Science College. Birmingham was the first of the so-called 'redbrick' universities to receive its charter, although Liverpool University was founded earlier (see Merseyside). A major research-led institution and a member of the Russell Group, Birmingham currently has over 18,000 undergraduate and over 11,000 postgraduate students. The main campus is in Edgbaston, with another at Selly Oak in the south of Birmingham, formerly the site of the Selly Oak Colleges which were integrated with the university in 1999. Former students include former chief of staff of the British Army Gen. Sir Mike Jackson, comedian Victoria Wood, singer Simon Le Bon, zoologist Desmond Morris and broadcaster Chris Tarrant. Tel: 0121 414 3344. See also Joseph Chamberlain Memorial Clock Tower.

The **University of Warwick** was established in 1965 and is situated on a campus 3 miles (5km) southwest of Coventry. Regarded in the 1960s and 1970s as politically radical, Warwick was one of the first UK universities to develop close links with the business community, and has been successful in the commercialisation of research. The only university to be a member of both the Russell Group and the 1994 Group, it is highly ranked as a research institution. Warwick Arts Centre on the university campus is the second largest arts centre in the UK after the Barbican Centre in London. Former students include MP David Davis, broadcasters Jennie Bond, Timmy Mallett and Simon Mayo, comedian Frank Skinner and musician Sting. Tel: 024 7652 3523.

The **University of Wolverhampton** developed from Wolverhampton and Staffordshire Technical College, built in 1931 in the grounds of the deanery of St Peter's Collegiate Church, and merged with a local art college to form Wolverhampton Polytechnic in 1969. After mergers with other teacher training institutions in the 1980s, the establishment gained university status in 1992 and now has over 23,000 students. Its main campus is at Wulfruna Street, Wolverhampton; it also has sites in Walsall, Telford in Shropshire, and Burton on Trent in Staffordshire. Tel: 01902 321000.

West Bromwich — Situated 5 miles (8km) northwest of Birmingham, and part of the Black Country, West Bromwich is the largest town within the borough of Sandwell with a population of 136,940 (2001). The motto on the town's coat of arms is *Labor Omnia Vincit* ('Work Conquers All'). Local industries include engineering and chemicals.

Wightwick Manor — Wightwick Bank, 3 miles (5km) west of Wolverhampton. The Arts and Crafts style Victorian manor house of Wightwick (pronounced locally as 'Wittick') Manor was built by the Mander family, successful 19th century industrialists, and designed by Edward Ould of Liverpool. Construction took place in two phases; the first was completed in 1887 and the house was extended with the Great Parlour wing in 1893. The house is a notable example of the influence of William Morris, with original Morris wallpapers and fabrics, De Morgan tiles, Kempe glass and Pre-Raphaelite works of art. An attractive 17 acre (7ha) garden reflects the style and character of the house. The house was presented to the National Trust by Sir Geoffrey Mander under the Country Houses Scheme in 1937. Descendants of the family retain a flat in the manor. Tel: 01902 761400.

Wolverhampton Art Gallery — Lichfield Street, Wolverhampton. Opened in May 1884, the Grade II* listed building was designed by Birmingham architect Julius Chatwin, funded and constructed by Philip Horsman and built on land provided by the council. The gallery is faced in Bath stone and has six impressive red granite columns at the main entrance. The 16 characters on the frieze represent the Arts, including sculpture, painting, architecture, pottery, glassblowing and wrought-iron work. The gallery's holdings include not only Georgian and Victorian paintings but a substantial Pop Art collection. Tel: 01902 552055.

Some famous people born in the West Midlands

Balcon, Michael (film producer) (1896–1977)	Birmingham
Burne-Jones, Edward (artist) (1833–98)	Birmingham
Carrott, Jasper (comedian and actor) (1945–)	Birmingham
Cartland, Barbara (novelist) (1901–2000)	Birmingham
Chamberlain, (Arthur) Neville (politician) (1869–1940)	Birmingham
Edwards, Duncan (footballer) (1936–58)	Dudley
Galton, Francis (anthropologist) (1822–1911)	Birmingham
Hancock, Tony (comedian) (1924–68)	Birmingham
Henry, Lenny (entertainer) (1958–)	Dudley
Holder, Neville 'Noddy' (singer and actor) (1946–)	Walsall
Ifield, Frank (singer) (1937–)	Coventry
Jerome, Jerome K (author) (1859–1927)	Walsall
Larkin, Philip (poet and novelist) (1922–85)	Coventry
Newbolt, Henry (author and poet) (1862–1938)	Bilston
Owen, Clive (actor) (1964–)	Coventry
Powell, Enoch (politician) (1912–98)	Birmingham
Rohmer, Sax (novelist) (1883–1959)	Birmingham
Terry, Ellen (actress) (1847–1928)	Coventry
Walters, Julie (actress) (1950–)	Smethwick
Whittle, Frank (inventor of the jet engine) (1907–96)	Coventry

WILTSHIRE

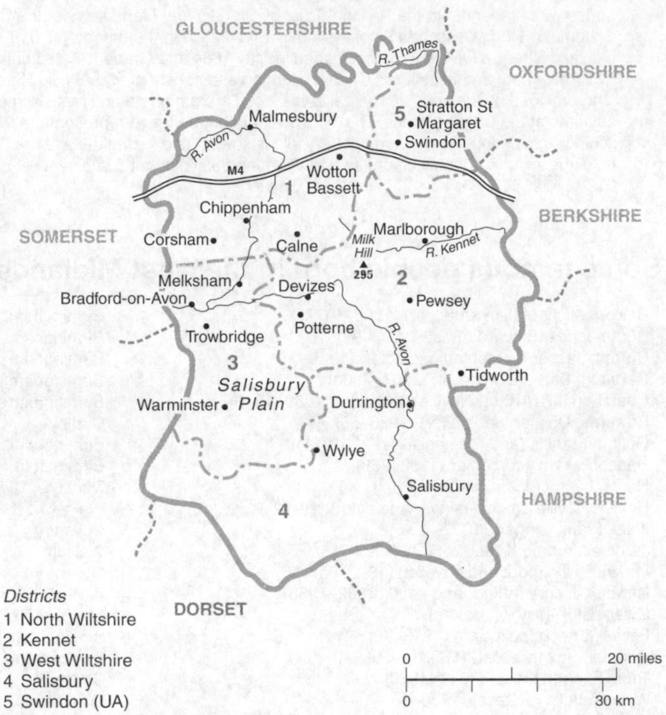

GLOUCESTERSHIRE
R. Thames
OXFORDSHIRE
Malmesbury
R. Avon
5
Stratton St Margaret
Swindon
M4
Wotton Bassett
1
Chippenham
BERKSHIRE
SOMERSET
Corsham
Calne
Marlborough
Milk Hill
R. Kennet
295
2
Melksham
Devizes
Bradford-on-Avon
Pewsey
Trowbridge
Potterne
R. Avon
3
Salisbury Plain
Tidworth
Warminster
Durrington
Wylye
Salisbury
HAMPSHIRE
4
Districts
1 North Wiltshire
2 Kennet
3 West Wiltshire
4 Salisbury
5 Swindon (UA)
DORSET
0
20 miles
0
30 km

Wiltshire is a large landlocked county in the south of England, bordered by the six counties of Hampshire to the east and southeast, Dorset to the south, Somerset to the west, Gloucestershire to the north, Oxfordshire to the northeast and Berkshire to the east. It also contains the unitary authority of Swindon. Known as 'the gateway to the West Country', Wiltshire comprises the districts of Kennet, West Wiltshire, North Wiltshire, Salisbury and the Borough of Swindon. Swindon was part of the Wiltshire local authority until receiving unitary authority status on 1 April 1998 and has 29 per cent of the county's population. The other main population centres are Salisbury and the West Wiltshire towns. The county town is Trowbridge, situated in the west of the county; the third largest town in Wiltshire after Salisbury and Chippenham, it is the administrative centre of both Wiltshire County Council and West Wiltshire District Council. The rest of the county is sparsely populated, with Salisbury Plain in the south/centre comprising over a quarter of the land area.

Although I have listed the four districts that have served the county since 1974, from 1 April 2009 they have been abolished, as has the county council, to form a single unitary authority of Wiltshire; the geographical county now consisting of two unitary authorities.

Wiltshire is mostly rural, and about two-thirds lies on chalk, giving it a high chalk downland landscape. Salisbury Plain is the largest area of chalk, a 300 sq mile (777 sq km) expanse of semi-wilderness covering much of southern Wiltshire, and used mainly for arable agriculture and by the Army as training ranges. The plain has been inhabited since the prehistoric era, as indicated by the location on the plain of Stonehenge and its associated ritual lansdcape; today it is sparsely populated but includes the towns of Durrington and Amesbury. The village of Imber was requisitioned by the Army during World War II and its inhabitants forcibly relocated; they have never since been allowed to return. As well as Salisbury Plain the chalk runs northeast into Berkshire in the Marlborough Downs ridge, and southwest into Dorset as Cranborne Chase. The Marlborough Downs are part of the North Wessex Downs Area of Outstanding Natural Beauty, covering 668 square miles (1730 sq km).

Between the areas of chalk and limestone downland are clay valleys and vales. The largest of these vales is the Avon Vale. The Avon cuts diagonally through the north of the county, flowing through

Bradford-on-Avon and into Bath and Bristol. The Vale of Pewsey has been cut through the chalk into greensand and Oxford clay in the centre of the county. In the southwest is the Vale of Wardour. The southeast of the county lies on the sandy soils of the New Forest.

Wiltshire is particularly well known for its pre-Roman archaeology. The Mesolithic, Neolithic and Bronze Age people who occupied southern Britain built settlements on the county's hills and downland over a period of more than 5000 years. Stonehenge and Avebury are perhaps the most famous Neolithic sites in the UK.

The county, first referred to as *Wiltunscir* in the 9th century, is named after the former county town of Wilton (itself named for the River Wylye, one of eight rivers that drain the county). Wiltshire's wealth in the early modern era was based on wool, the woollen industry being based largely in small industrial towns in west and north Wiltshire such as Bradford-on-Avon, Corsham, Melksham, Westbury, Trowbridge and Calne. The last of these later became famous for the Harris bacon curing factory, closed in 1983.

Wiltshire's more recent economic prosperity has been closely tied to its communication links. The opening of the Kennet & Avon Canal in the early 19th century was followed from the 1840s by that of the Great Western Railway (GWR), nicknamed 'God's Wonderful Railway'. The opening of the GWR railway works in Swindon led to its rapid growth from a very small market town to by far the largest town in the county. As the railways declined, other industries such as aircraft, car manufacturing and various electronics enterprises moved into the Swindon area during and after World War II. The opening of the M4 in 1970 further stimulated growth, particularly in the north of the county. In the west and south there has long been a significant military presence associated with the army training grounds on Salisbury Plain, where the Ministry of Defence owns around 147 sq miles (380 sq km) of land. While numbers of troops may have declined in recent years, this presence is still strongly evident, and is visible in numerous insignia carved into the chalk hillsides by troops stationed in the county, especially during World War I.

As well as a high number of ancient monuments, Wiltshire's varied history is reflected by many more recent buildings and houses of historic interest, such as Salisbury Cathedral, Longleat and Bowood House.

Wiltshire	**Population**			**Area**	
Districts	*male*	*female*	*total*	*sq miles*	*sq km*
Kennet	37,550	37,288	74,838	373	967
North Wiltshire	62,027	63,345	125,372	296	768
Salisbury	56,120	58,493	114,613	388	1004
West Wiltshire	57,696	60,454	118,150	199	516
Swindon Unitary Authority	89,560	90,491	180,051	89	230
Total	302,953	310,071	613,024	1345	3485

Local attractions and Information

Administrative headquarters
: **Swindon:** Civic Offices, Euclid Street, Swindon SN1 2JH. Tel: 0300 456 0100.
Wiltshire: County Hall, Bythesea Road, Trowbridge BA14 8JN. Tel: 01225 713000.

Alexander Keiller Museum
: Avebury, 5 miles (8km) west of Marlborough. Housed in a 17th century thatched barn, the museum was founded in the 1930s by archaeologist Alexander Keiller (1889–1955), heir to the Keiller marmalade business in Dundee, to house finds from his excavations on Windmill Hill, the Avenue and Avebury. It now serves as an interpretative centre for the archaeology of Avebury and the surrounding area. Tel: 01672 539250.

ANZAC Badge
: 1/2 mile (0.8km) east of Codford St Mary, 7 miles (11km) southeast of Warminster. A depiction of the rising sun emblem of the Australian and New Zealand Army Corps, carved into the chalk hill by Australian soldiers stationed at Codford Camp during World War I. It is visible from the A36 road.

Arn Hill Nature Reserve
: 1/2 mile (0.8km) north of Warminster. Standing at 694ft (211m), Arn Hill is one of the many hills fringing Salisbury Plain. The chalkland flora, including orchids, attracts many insects and butterflies, while the woods are a haven for birds. The site, including a former lime-kiln (now in ruins) and rising above the old-fashioned sheep walks of Kidnapper's Hole, was donated to the town by the Marquess of Bath in 1920. Managed by the Wiltshire Wildlife Trust.

Arundells
: Cathedral Close, Salisbury. The home of Prime Minister Sir Edward Heath (1916–2005) for the last 20 years of his life. Originally a medieval canonry in the 13th century, much of the current house's appearance is due to John Wyndham who lived here 1718–50. The name derives from James Everard Arundel, son of the 6th Lord Arundel of Wardour, who married Wyndham's

daughter and was given Arundells as a wedding present. It briefly housed the Godolphin School and, until 1844, a boys' boarding school. The house was opened as a museum in 2008, and Sir Edward's collections of musical and sailing memorabilia, Oriental and European ceramics, paintings (mainly by British artists, including two painted and given to Sir Edward by Sir Winston Churchill), original political cartoons, bronzes and photographs are all on display within. The house is surrounded by a beautiful 2 acre (0.8ha) walled garden stretching down to the River Avon. Tel: 01722 326546.

Ashcombe House — 2 miles (3km) south of Berwick St John, 14 miles (23km) southwest of Salisbury. Also known as Ashcombe Park. A Georgian manor house set in 1134 acres (459ha) of land on Cranborne Chase. It was originally part of a much larger structure dating from c.1740, much of which was pulled down at the beginning of the 19th century. The house was rented and restored in the 1930s and 1940s by photographer Cecil Beaton, who detailed its restoration in his book *Ashcombe: The Story of a Fifteen-Year Lease*. During this period the house was visited by prominent artists and photographers including Salvador Dalí, who used the house as the backdrop for one of his paintings. Madonna and Guy Ritchie owned the Grade II listed house between 2001 and October 2008, when the title passed to Ritchie as part of their divorce settlement.

Athelstan Museum — Cross Hayes, Malmesbury. A local history museum housed in Malmesbury's town hall. Exhibits include coins minted in the town, costume, lace-making, an early fire engine, an early tricycle and collections of early drawings of the town by Thomas Girtin, Thomas Hearne and Luke Sullivan. There is also a collection of photographs of Malmesbury and its branch railway. Tel: 01666 829258.

Atwell-Wilson Motor Museum — Stockley Road, Calne. Museum housing a large collection of vintage cars, lorries, motorcycles, mopeds and bicycles, as well as archive material such as vehicle manuals, and a collection of motor memorabilia. Tel: 01249 813119.

Avebury Manor and Garden — Avebury, 5 miles (8km) west of Marlborough. An early 16th century manor house with Queen Anne alterations, surrounded by an Edwardian garden regularly visited by Vita Sackville-West. Now owned by the National Trust. Tel: 01672 539250.

Avebury Stone Circles — Avebury, 5 miles (8km) west of Marlborough. The village of Avebury is the site of one of the largest Neolithic monuments in Britain – a large henge enclosed by the remains of a major stone circle. The site comprises an external bank henge 0.9 miles (1.4km) in circumference and enclosing $28\frac{1}{2}$ acres (11.5ha). Within this area is an outer circle originally consisting of 98 sarsen standing stones and two inner rings. Construction took place over a period c.2800–2400 BC. Over time, many stones were damaged or buried and others were broken up and used for building work. Some of the stones were re-erected by Alexander Keiller (see Alexander Keiller Museum), who was responsible for excavating and improving knowledge of the site in the inter-war years. Being more accessible than Stonehenge, Avebury is now used for festivals and pagan rituals around the summer solstice. The site is owned by English Heritage and managed by the National Trust.

Avon Valley Path — A long-distance footpath running for 34 miles (55km) from Salisbury Cathedral to Christchurch Priory in Dorset, passing through the towns of Ringwood, Fordingbridge and Downton.

Battles — See separate table for details of the battles of Chippenham, Edington, Ellendun, Mons Badonicus, Roundway Down and Wilton.

Beckhampton Avenue — $\frac{1}{2}$ mile (0.8km) southwest of Avebury. A curving late Neolithic or early Bronze Age avenue of stones that once ran southwest from Avebury towards the Longstones at Beckhampton. Only one stone, known as Eve, remains standing, but the parallel rows of holes which once held the stones were revealed by excavations in 2000.

Bentley Wood — 2 miles (3km) northeast of East Grimstead, 6 miles (10km) east of Salisbury. Bentley Wood and the adjacent Blackmoor Copse together form one of the largest contiguous areas of woodland in Wiltshire. The site is very important for a number of butterfly species, including purple emperor, white admiral and pearl-bordered fritillary.

Bowood House — 4 miles (6km) southeast of Chippenham. Originally built c.1725, the house was extended by architect Henry Keene for the 1st Earl of Shelburne, who contracted Robert Adam to decorate some of the rooms and add an orangery. Adam also built a mausoleum for the 1st Earl. In the 1770s the two parts of the house (the 'Big House' and the 'Little House') were joined together by the construction of an enormous drawing room. The 'Big House' was demolished in 1955. The Bowood Laboratory, in the main house, is where Joseph Priestley, tutor to the 1st Marquess of Lansdowne's sons, discovered oxygen in 1774. The surrounding park, one of many in Wiltshire designed by Capability Brown, covers over 2000 acres (800ha) and includes an arboretum, pinetum, Doric temple, cascade and hermit's cave. The estate also includes a championship standard golf course.

Box Tunnel — Box, 6 miles (10km) southwest of Chippenham. A railway tunnel through Box Hill, built by Isambard Kingdom Brunel for the Great Western Railway and completed in 1841. At the time it was the longest railway tunnel in the world at 1 mile 4356ft (2937m) long; some early travellers were so worried about using it that they left the train before it entered the tunnel and re-embarked on the other side. The tunnel's western portal, designed in classical style, can be seen from the A4.

Bradford-on-Avon — A market town in West Wiltshire which developed in the 18th and 19th centuries as a centre for the textile industry, primarily wool. Situated on the River Avon, the town grew up around a ford on the river, across which a bridge was first built in the 12th century. A wider bridge was built in 1610 and retains two of its original 13th century arches. Other buildings of note include the Saxon church of St Laurence, dating from C.AD 700, and Holy Trinity church, dating from the late 12th century.

Bradford-on-Avon Museum — Bridge Street, Bradford-on-Avon. Situated on the first floor of the town library, the museum is dedicated to Bradford-on-Avon's natural and human heritage. Its main exhibit is an old pharmacy shop, rebuilt in detail after 120 years of service. Tel: 01225 863280.

Bradford-on-Avon Tithe Barn Barton Farm, Bradford-on-Avon. A large timber and stone barn built in the early 14th century as part of the medieval farmstead belonging to Shaftesbury Abbey. Its function was to store the produce of the farm, and of the farms of the manor. King Ethelred gave the Manor of Bradford, including the monastery founded by St Aldhelm, to the Abbess of Shaftesbury in 1001. A packhorse bridge over the River Avon close by also dates to the same period. The barn is now owned and maintained by English Heritage. Tel: 0117 975 0700.

Bratton Castle See Hill Forts

Broadleas Gardens 1 mile (1.6km) south of Devizes. A beautifully maintained 10 acre (4ha) garden. The steeply sloping, sheltered sides of the Dell, descending far down a valley, are densely planted with rhododendrons, magnolias, camellias, azaleas and hydrangeas, as well as underplantings of spring bulbs, hostas, erythoniums and other woodland plants. Closer to the house are herbaceous borders, a rose garden and splendid conifers. Tel: 01380 722035.

Brokerswood Country Park Brokerswood, 4 miles (6km) southwest of Trowbridge. An 80 acre (32ha) country park created from a fragment of the ancient Selwood Forest. It includes the Woodland Heritage Museum and a narrow gauge railway.

Bulford Kiwi 1½ miles (2.5km) east of Bulford, 2½ miles (4km) east of Amesbury. Located on Beacon Hill, above Bulford Camp. Cut in 1918 by New Zealand troops stationed in the area, the carving of a kiwi is 420ft (128m) long and covers 1½ acres (0.6ha).

Caen Hill Locks 1½ miles (2.5km) west of Devizes. A flight of locks on the Kennet & Avon Canal ascending Caen Hill and built 1801–10 by engineer John Rennie. The main flight of 16 locks forms part of a longer series of 29; rising a total of 237ft (72m) in 2 miles (3km), they form one of the steepest such flights in the world. Queen Elizabeth II officially reopened the locks in 1990 after major renovation.

Castle Combe Circuit 4 miles (6km) northwest of Chippenham. A motor racing circuit opened in 1950 on the decommissioned Castle Combe airfield. The village itself was built on the site of an Iron Age hill fort occupied by the Romans due to its proximity to The Fosse Way. The Normans built the now destroyed castle that gives the village its name. Castle Combe has been called 'the prettiest village in England' and has frequently served as a film location, most famously for *Doctor Dolittle*, filmed in and around the village in 1966. Tel: 01249 782417.

Chippenham Founded over 1000 years ago, Chippenham was the base from which Alfred the Great pursued his fight against the invading Danes. In the Middle Ages corn mills made way for the prosperous wool trade and famous cheese market. The town flourished on the Bristol–London stagecoach route and with the coming of the Great Western Railway. Around the Market Place are the 16th century Buttercross, magnificent St Andrew's Church, St Mary Street and the 15th century Yelde Hall – the old town hall, which features an interactive history of the building and access to the original council chamber. On tour with Gene Vincent in early 1960, rock 'n' roll star Eddie Cochran was killed in the town on an overnight journey to London after playing in Bristol, when the Ford Consul taxi in which he was travelling crashed into a lamp post at Rowden Hill.

Clarendon Palace 2½ miles (4km) east of Salisbury. Established as a royal hunting lodge c.1130 and enlarged into a major royal residence by Henry II and III, the palace was the scene of the declaration of the Constitutions of Clarendon, an assertion of relations between church and state which was to provoke the quarrel between Henry II and Thomas Becket. The palace fell into disuse during the late 16th century. Recent excavation of the site, which now lies within Clarendon Park, has revealed that it once covered almost 5 acres (2ha), although little now remains above ground except a fragment of wall which was once part of the great hall.

Clarendon Way A 24 mile (39km) footpath from Salisbury Cathedral to Winchester Cathedral in Hampshire. The path passes through the Clarendon estate and close to the 12th century ruins of Clarendon Palace.

Coate Water Country Park 2 miles (3km) southeast of Swindon. The park takes its name from its main feature, a reservoir originally constructed in the early 1920s to provide water for the Wilts & Berks Canal. Following the arrival of the Great Western Railway in the 1840s the canal fell into decline, and the reservoir and 80 acres (32ha) of land was sold to Swindon Council in 1914. The reservoir was used for water sports until 1958, when swimming was stopped after a polio scare; the 1936 Art Deco diving board remains as a reminder of its past use. The birthplace of Richard Jefferies, now a museum, is nearby.

Corsham Located 4 miles (6km) southwest of Chippenham and once one of the West Wiltshire wool towns, in the 18th century Corsham's principal industry became quarrying, with underground mining of Bath stone extending to the south and west of the town. The town was one of the inspirations for Charles Dickens's novel *The Pickwick Papers*: the name Pickwick is likely to have come from that of a nearby farm, Pickwick Lodge Farm.

Corsham Computer Centre Hudswell, Corsham. A massive underground government installation near RAF Corsham and RAF Rudloe Manor. Built in the 1980s, the centre developed from World War II and Cold War installations that were built into the former underground stone quarries. The exact size and nature of this and similar installations in the area are still partially unknown for state security reasons.

Corsham Court Church Street, Corsham. A country house and estate on the eastern edge of Corsham. Owned by the royal family for many generations, the estate's residents included Henry VIII's wives Catherine of Aragon and Catherine Parr. The existing house, originally built in 1582, was developed by Capability Brown in the 1760s and by John Nash in the early 19th century. The interior includes furnishings by Robert Adam and Thomas Chippendale, as well as many Old Master paintings. Tel: 01249 701610.

Cotswold Hills See Gloucestershire

Cotswold Water Park 4 miles (6km) northwest of Cricklade, 9 miles (15km) northwest of Swindon. An area of over 140 lakes covering 40 sq miles (104 sq km), created from former sand and gravel quarries in the catchment area of the upper Thames and now restored both for wildlife and for recreational activities. The western part of the park is located on the rivers Thames and Churn, near the villages of South Cerney and Ashton Keynes; the eastern part is on the River Coln between Fairford and Lechlade. The central area, still used for gravel extraction, is also gradually being restored as wetland. Tel: 01793 752413.

Courts Garden, The Holt, 2 miles (3km) east of Bradford-on-Avon. An 7 acre (2.8ha) Arts and Crafts style garden created in the 1920s around an 18th century Bath stone house (not open to the public). The lush green lawns, shrubbery and water gardens are a fine example of the English garden style. Now owned by the National Trust. Tel: 01225 782875.

Cranborne Chase A 379 sq mile (982 sq km) chalk plateau extending across parts of Dorset, Hampshire and Wiltshire, and a designated Area of Outstanding Natural Beauty. Part of the English Chalk Formation, it lies between Salisbury Plain and the West Wiltshire Downs in the north, the Dorset Downs in the southwest and the South Downs to the southeast. The highest point is Win Green, Wiltshire, at 910ft (277m).

Cricklade The only Wiltshire town on the River Thames, which regularly bursts its banks and floods fields outside the town. Cricklade was a Roman settlement and the Roman road Ermine Street passes nearby. The later walled Saxon town was built by Alfred the Great as a defence against the Danes and was important enough to produce its own coins. The wide High Street has a remarkable range of buildings, including the 13th century St Sampson's church, St Mary's church, originally founded before the Norman Conquest, and the Robert Jenner School of 1652. Cricklade Museum includes material relating to the Roman occupation, the Saxon borough and 'rotten borough' elections. The Thames Path National Trail passes through the town on its way to London.

Crofton Pumping Station 1 mile (1.6km) south of Great Bedwyn. Built to supply the summit pound of the Kennet & Avon Canal with water, the original steam-powered pumping station contains one of the oldest operational Watt style beam engines in the world, dating from 1812 and restored by the Kennet & Avon Canal Trust in the late 1960s. Tel: 01672 870300.

Devizes A market town southwest of Marlborough. It was formerly an important sheep and cloth market, and the town centre and many Georgian buildings date from this prosperous period. The town later became an inland port on the Kennet & Avon Canal, and the canal museum can be found in the town. Other notable features include the old and new town halls, the Corn Exchange and St John's parish church. Devizes hosts an annual jazz festival.

Devizes Castle Castle Grounds, Devizes. Founded 1080 as a motte and bailey castle by Osmund, Bishop of Salisbury. The stone castle, built c.1120 by Roger, Bishop of Salisbury, was later used as a prison by Henry II and Henry III. Occupied by Royalist forces during the Civil war, it was taken by Parliamentary troops in 1645 and slighted in 1648. The castellated house that stands on the site today was built in the 19th century.

Downton Moot Downton, 6 miles (10km) south of Salisbury. The remains of a Norman motte and bailey castle covering nearly 10 acres (4ha), and built in 1138 by Henry of Blois, Bishop of Winchester and grandson of William I. A Scheduled Ancient Monument, the earthworks were later incorporated into the garden of 18th century Moot House.

Edington Priory Church Edington, 4½ miles (7km) southeast of Trowbridge. A church with striking battlements, built 1352–61 by William of Edington, Bishop of Winchester. Edington Priory, founded by William as a college for priests, was later occupied by Augustinian canons.

Erlestoke Prison Erlestoke, 6 miles (10km) southwest of Devizes. Wiltshire's only prison. Built in the former grounds of Georgian mansion Erlestoke House, converted after a major fire in 1950 and now housing adult male prisoners. Operational capacity: 470. Tel: 01380 814250.

Fonthill Abbey 1 mile (1.6km) southeast of Fonthill Bishop, 8 miles (13km) southeast of Warminster. Also known as 'Beckford's Folly'. A large Gothic-style house built 1795–1813 by James Wyatt for William Beckford (1760–1844). A wealthy eccentric and author of the Gothic novel *Vathek*, Beckford built a 6 mile (10km) wall around his estate and attempted to build his own Gothic cathedral. The 300ft (91.5m) high central tower collapsed three times, and most of the building was later demolished.

Fovant Badges 8 miles (13km) west of Salisbury. A series of military badges carved into the chalk hillside by locally stationed troops during World War I. Visible from the A30 road, they include badges of the Australian Imperial Force, the Royal Corps of Signals, the Royal Wiltshire Yeomanry and the Wiltshire Regiment.

Great Chalfield Manor Great Chalfield, 2 miles (3km) west of Melksham. An early Tudor moated manor house built c.1480 by Thomas Tropnell and altered substantially in the 1830s. The interior features a 40ft (12m) long great hall, while outside is an Arts and Crafts style garden created in the early 20th century. Within the grounds is the parish church of All Saints, a feature of which is the unusual 'bellcote', a stone belfry built onto the roof. Now owned by the National Trust. Tel: 01225 782239.

Hamptworth Lodge Landford, 11 miles (18km) southeast of Salisbury. Set in woodlands on the edge of the New Forest, the house was built in the early 20th century as a recreation of a Jacobean manor house dating to c.1620. The Grade II* listed house contains 17th century furniture and a collection of clocks. Tel: 01794 390215.

Hartham Park 1 mile (1.6km) north of Corsham. A Georgian house built 1790–5 by James Wyatt, surrounded by a 300 acre (120ha) estate including a rare stické tennis (an indoor game halfway between rackets and tennis) court. Since 1997 the house has been converted into office space.

Hawthorn 1 mile (1.6km) southwest of Corsham. Also known as TURNSTILE. A nuclear bunker complex built 120ft (36.5m) below RAF Rudloe Manor between the 1940s and 1960s. Until the early 1990s it contained the Central Government War Headquarters, the government's emergency command centre, finally decommissioned only in 2004. The 35 acre (14ha) complex, which has its own railway line linking to the London–Bristol main line near Box Tunnel, was offered for sale in the late 1990s.

Hazelbury Manor — Box, 2 miles (3km) southwest of Corsham. A Grade I listed manor house (not open to the public) dating in part from the 14th century. The 186 acres (74ha) of grounds include 8 acres (3ha) of Grade II listed formal landscaped gardens laid out in the 1920s. Tel: 01225 722987.

Heale House and Gardens — Middle Woodford, 4 miles (6km) southwest of Amesbury. Originally built by Sir William Greene in 1553 as a wedding present for his daughter and son-in-law. Charles II hid here for six nights while waiting for a ship to arrive at Shoreham, Sussex. Having been largely destroyed by fire in 1835, the whole house except the surviving southwest wing was rebuilt in the 1890s by Hon. Louis Greville, great-uncle of the present owner. The 8 acre (3ha) garden provides a variety of surprise and interest among the overflowing arrangements of flowers and shrubs. The northeast corner, based on plans drawn up for Greville by Harold Peto in 1910, was planted with formal herbaceous plants and a tunnel of figs. There is a water garden with bridge and genuine Japanese tea house. The house is not open to the public. Tel: 01722 782504.

Highest point — Milk Hill, above Alton Priors in the Vale of Pewsey, on the edge of Salisbury Plain, at 968ft (295m). GR: SU104643. Tan Hill, $1^1/_4$ miles (2km) west of Milk Hill and north of the village of Allington, is the second highest point at 965ft (294m). To the north side of the hill is a section of the Wansdyke, an earth rampart which runs east–west for 14 miles (23km) through central Wiltshire. Tan Hill formerly had a white horse.

Highworth — A town 6 miles (10km) northeast of Swindon and part of Swindon Unitary Authority. In the 1974 local government reorganisation, councillors from Highworth Rural Council objected to becoming part of the Borough of Swindon, with the result that the new council, which included Swindon and Highworth, was called the Borough of Thamesdown. This caused much confusion until it was renamed the Borough of Swindon in 1997, after a long-running campaign by Eric Beint, a former Swindon resident living in Burnley, Lancashire.

Hill forts — There are a number of Iron Age hill forts in Wiltshire. The following are among the most significant:

Barbury Castle, 5 miles (8km) south of Swindon, is situated on Barbury Hill and thought to have been first occupied c.500 BC. The fort itself, with its double earth rampart, covers 12 acres (5ha). The ancient Ridgeway path runs through the edge of the site, which has been designated a country park since 1971; there are also a number of round barrows in the surrounding area. A point-to-point course was opened below the castle in 1992, replacing an earlier track returned to farmland in 1962. Tel: 01793 490150.

Battlesbury Hill, $1^1/_4$ miles (2km) east of Warminster, is an impressive hill fort with double ramparts and a ditch on its southwest side, and a triple rampart on the less steep west side. The ramparts follow the kidney-shaped contours of the hill, enclosing nearly 25 acres (10ha).

Bratton Castle, $1^1/_2$ miles (2.5km) east of Westbury, also known as Bratton Camp and located above Westbury White Horse (see White Horses), is a bivallate hill fort with massive fortifications whose two circuits of ditch and bank enclose a pentagonal area of $23^1/_2$ acres (9.3ha), encompassing a Neolithic burial mound. The site is managed by English Heritage.

Cley Hill, 2 miles (3km) west of Warminster, is an isolated chalk hill 804ft (245m) high, topped by a bivallate Iron Age hill fort covering 17 acres (7ha) and two Bronze Age bowl barrows. Cley Hill was formerly owned by the Marquis of Bath, who donated it to the National Trust in the 1950s.

Liddington Castle, 4 miles (6km) southeast of Swindon, is a late Bronze Age and early Iron Age hill fort located on Liddington Hill at 909ft (277m) and clearly visible from the M4 motorway. Thought to date from the 7th century BC, it has been suggested as a possible site for the Battle of Mons Badonicus (see Battles).

Old Sarum see separate entry

Other hill forts in the Warminster area include Scratchbury, White Sheet and Yarnbury.

Iford Manor — Westwood, $1^1/_2$ miles (2.5km) south of Bradford-on-Avon. A Tudor manor house with classical façade located on a steep slope above the River Frome. Today it is most notable as the home from 1898 of garden designer Harold Peto. The Grade I listed Peto Garden, situated by a medieval bridge crossing the River Frome, is an Italianate garden terraced on a steep hillside, leading to a hanging beechwood above the manor house. Tel: 01225 863146.

Interesting facts — **The Pagoda Palace** is the largest Chinese restaurant in the UK. Located in Swindon, it opened in the early 1990s as The Chinese Experience. It overlooks Peatmoor Lagoon and a small island with a miniature pagoda on it. The **Dyson vacuum cleaner** was manufactured in Malmesbury before being transferred to Malaysia. The company's headquarters and research facilities remain in Malmesbury, employing over 1000 people. **Swindon** is the setting for *The Curious Incident of the Dog in the Night-Time*, a novel written by Mark Haddon which won the Whitbread Book of the Year prize in 2003. The book is set in 1998, written in the first-person narrative of Christopher Boone, a 15 year old boy living in Swindon. The town is also the setting for the 'Thursday Next' novels by Jasper Fforde, and is mentioned in Robert Goddard's novels *Into the Blue, Out of the Sun* and *Never Go Back*. **Moonrakers** is the colloquial name for people from Wiltshire. According to legend, local people once hid smuggled goods from the customs officers in a pond. While trying to retrieve them at night, they were caught by the officers, and explained their actions by pointing to the moon's reflection and saying they were trying to rake in a cheese. The excise men, thinking they were simple, laughed at them and went on their way. **Oasis** is a Manchester band but Liam Gallagher took the name from an Inspiral Carpets tour poster on the wall of his and Noel's bedroom. One of the venues listed was the Oasis Leisure Centre in Swindon. **Bremilham Church**, on a farm at Foxley-cum-Bremilham near Malmesbury, measures just 13ft (4m) by 11ft 10in (3.6m). Its single pew has space for four people and there is standing room for six more. The church is listed in the *Guinness Book of Records* as the smallest church in service in Britain.

Ian Fleming, author of the James Bond books, lived at Warneford, Sevenhampton, from 1960 until his death in 1966, and is buried in St James's Church. The **Magic Roundabout** is a notorious multi-mini traffic roundabout located next to Swindon Town's County Ground. Comprising five small roundabouts around a larger central roundabout, it sends traffic clockwise around the outside and anticlockwise around the inside. Opened in 1972, it was originally called County Islands, but was renamed the 'Magic Roundabout' to reflect its local nickname. **Crop circles** have been appearing in Wiltshire since the late 1980s. The most elaborate examples have been seen in the Marlborough Downs and Pewsey Vale area of north Wiltshire. Thought by some to have been caused by UFOs, a number of local people have since claimed to make the circles using a simple stick, rope and wooden board apparatus. Dutch physiologist **Dr Jan Ingenhousz** (1730–99), pioneer of vaccination and discoverer of photosynthesis, worked at Bowood House near Calne and has a memorial in St Mary's church in the town.

Kennet & Avon Canal — Built 1794–1810, the Kennet & Avon canal runs for 57 miles (91km) linking the River Avon at Bath to the River Thames at Reading, and once allowed full navigation from Bristol to London via the 87 miles (140km) of the Kennet & Avon navigation. During World War II the canal formed part of the Kennet & Avon stop line, part of the three-stranded GHQ line, a defensive line meant to stop enemy troops advancing on the industrial heartlands of the Midlands. A number of pillboxes located along the line of the canal can still be seen. A cycle path follows the route of the canal from Reading to Bath. The Kennet & Avon Canal Museum is at the Canal Centre in Devizes. See also Caen Hill

King Alfred's Tower — See Somerset

King's House — See Salisbury and South Wiltshire Museum

Lackham Country Park — 2 miles (3km) south of Chippenham. A 210 acre (85ha) estate now attached to Wiltshire College. Within the park is the Wiltshire Museum of Agriculture and Rural Life, while the extensive gardens include a walled garden, a woodland walk and an animal park.

Lacock — A village 3 miles (5km) south of Chippenham. Owned mainly by the National Trust, it has many stone and half-timbered houses as well as a 14th century tithe barn, a medieval church and a 15th century inn. The village has been used as a film and television location for period productions such as *Pride and Prejudice* (1995), *Emma* (1996) and *Moll Flanders* (1996).

Lacock Abbey — Lacock, 3 miles (5km) south of Chippenham. Founded in 1232 by Lady Eda, Countess of Salisbury. Following its dissolution it was converted into a country house from 1539. Some features of the original abbey survive, including the medieval cloisters, sacristy, chapter house and monastic rooms. It includes the Fox Talbot Museum, commemorating William Fox Talbot, photographic pioneer and inventor of the negative/positive process, who lived at Lacock Abbey for 50 years and whose descendants gave the abbey and village to the National Trust in 1944. The film *Harry Potter and the Chamber of Secrets* (2002) was partially shot on location at the abbey. Tel: 01249 730459.

Larmer Tree Gardens — Tollard Royal, 15 miles (24km) southwest of Salisbury. Located in Cranborne Chase on the Wiltshire/Dorset border, the 11 acre (4.5ha) pleasure gardens were designed in 1880 by General Augustus Pitt-Rivers and contain a collection of buildings including a Roman temple, open-air theatre and Nepalese rooms. Tel: 01725 516228.

Lawn, The — Drove Road, Swindon. An 86 acre (35ha) park situated to the east of Swindon's Old Town. The Lawn was home to the Goddard family from 1563 until 1927, when the last lord of the manor, Fitzroy Goddard, died. The 18th century house was demolished in 1952 having fallen into disrepair after housing American troops during World War II. The park includes the remains of Holy Rood Church, Swindon's original parish church, first mentioned in documents dating from 1154 and now a Scheduled Ancient Monument.

Little Clarendon — Dinton, 8 miles (13km) west of Salisbury. A Tudor house altered in the 17th century and with a 20th century Catholic chapel. The three principal rooms on the ground floor are furnished with vernacular oak furniture. Tel: 01985 843600.

Littlecote House — 5 miles (8km) east of Marlborough. A Grade I listed 16th century manor house and gardens close to the River Kennet and the Berkshire border. In the grounds are the remains of a Roman villa probably dating to the 4th century AD, including a virtually complete mosaic floor showing Orpheus surrounded by female representations of the four seasons. The house is now a hotel.

Lockeridge Dene — Lockeridge, 2 miles (3km) southwest of Marlborough. A field containing numerous gigantic sarsen stones, one of the sites from which the stones used to build Avebury were mined.

Longleat — 4 miles (6km) southeast of Warminster. The first stately home in Britain opened to the public (the first visitors were admitted in 1949), Longleat is set in over 900 acres (360ha) of parkland landscaped by Capability Brown in 1757. It has been the home of the Thynne family since the Elizabethan house was completed in 1580. The estate is currently occupied by the 7th Marquess of Bath, famous for his 'wifelets' and wall paintings, the latter of which can be viewed in the house alongside a multitude of family heirlooms. The grounds feature a large safari park, home to many species of animal including lions, sealions, gorillas and monkeys. The park's numerous attractions include the Shear Water Lakes, designed and constructed in 1791 by famous canal builder Francis, Duke of Bridgwater, and what is claimed to be the world's longest hedge maze. Tel: 01985 844400.

Ludgershall Castle — Ludgershall, 12 miles (19km) southeast of Marlborough. The remains of an 11th century Norman castle with an unfinished keep added in the mid 12th century. The castle was later used as a hunting lodge by Henry VIII. Now in the care of English Heritage, as are the remains of a medieval cross situated in the village centre.

Lydiard House and Park — Lydiard Tregoze, 3 miles (5km) west of Swindon. A 260 acre (104ha) country park on the western outskirts of Swindon. Originally a medieval deer park, the country estate is the former home of the

St John family, the Viscounts Bolingbroke. Lydiard House was originally built in the 16th century and remodelled in Palladian style in the 18th century. By the 1930s the estate was run down, and was used by the US Army during World War II before being purchased by Swindon Council in 1943. The council painstakingly traced and purchased many of the house's former contents (a process which continues to this day) before opening it to the public in 1955. The house now contains period furniture, a family picture collection, painted glass window, and the 'Blue Closet' room, devoted to 18th century society artist Lady Diana Spencer. The south chapel of St Mary's Church, located within the estate, contains several memorials to the St John family, including the Golden Cavalier – a life-size effigy of Royalist supporter Edward St John, who died at the 2nd Battle of Newbury. Bullet holes, allegedly from Civil War executions, are still visible on the outside of the church. The 18th century landscape features are undergoing restoration with the help of a £3m grant from the Heritage Lottery Fund; the lake was reopened in June 2006. Tel: 01793 770401.

Malmesbury England's oldest borough. Set on a hill circled by the River Avon, Malmesbury is called the 'Queen of Hilltop Towns'. The skyline is dominated by the imposing Norman abbey. The monastery, founded in the 7th century by St Aldhelm, became a centre of pilgrimage and learning and in the 10th century Athelstan, first king of a united England, made Malmesbury his capital. The town flourished between the 15th and 17th centuries as a weaving centre and became known for its fine silk and lace.

Malmesbury Abbey Holloway, Malmesbury. A Benedictine monastery founded c.676 by St Aldhelm. The existing abbey church was largely completed by 1180, although the 431ft (131m) tall spire and tower – taller than that of Salisbury Cathedral – collapsed c.1500 and the west tower less than 100 years later, leaving the current building half its original size. After the abbey's dissolution in 1539 the church became a parish church, a role it still fulfils today. In 1010 a monk named Eilmer made a set of artificial wings and 'flew' from the abbey, gliding for 200 yards before landing and breaking his legs, blaming the lack of a tail for the short flight. The abbey is set within 5 acres (2ha) of gardens. The Grade I listed Abbey House, dating from the 13th century (there is evidence of a substantial home on the site a century before), is thought to have been the abbot's residence.

Marlborough A market town 10 miles (16km) south of Swindon in the Kennet valley. Situated close to Savernake Forest and the Marlborough Downs, Marlborough is mentioned in Domesday Book, and received its town charter in 1204. Once located on the main road between London and the West Country, the town was an important staging post in the 18th century, although its importance declined as it was largely bypassed by the railways and now finds itself several miles south of the M4. Marlborough's world-famous High Street is reputedly one of the widest streets in Britain. It has a church at each end: 15th century St Peter's to the west and the church of St Mary's to the east. Marlborough College, close to the town centre, is one of England's most highly regarded public schools and was founded in 1843.

Marlborough Castle Marlborough. Norman motte and bailey castle founded c.1100 by Roger, Bishop of Salisbury, and extended by Henry II. The shell keep was added by King John and further enlarged by Henry III. Now located in the grounds of Marlborough College, the motte still stands 50ft (15m) high.

Marlborough College Bath Road, Marlborough. Founded in 1843 as a boarding school for educating the sons of clergy, the school was first established in an early 18th century mansion built by the 6th Duke of Somerset and more recently leased as a coaching inn. The first English public school to admit girls to its sixth form, in 1968, Marlborough became fully co-educational in 1989. Former pupils include singer Chris De Burgh, cricket writer Christopher Martin-Jenkins, scientist Sir Peter Medawar and poet John Betjeman.

Maud Heath's Causeway A $4^1/_2$ mile (7km) pathway between Bremhill and Chippenham, named after 15th century widow Maud Heath, who left funds for the maintenance of a causeway for farmers to take their produce to market through the frequently flooded valley of the River Avon. A 19th century pillar crowned by a statue of Maud Heath marks the start of the pathway.

Medieval Hall, The Cathedral Close, Salisbury. A 13th century hall with impressive timber-framed roof, built c.1274 as the deanery of Salisbury Cathedral and occupied until the 1920s.

Melksham Having developed in the Anglo-Saxon period at a ford across the River Avon, from the 14th century Melksham established itself as a weaving town, white broad cloth being the chief product. After the decline of the cloth trade in the 18th century and following the discovery of saline and chalybeate springs, the town attempted to develop in the early 19th century as a spa rivalling nearby Bath. Sadly, the attempt failed, but some Regency buildings from the period remain.

Merchant's House, The High Street, Marlborough. A 17th century house with well-preserved original painted wall decorations and panelled chamber, completed in 1656. Tel: 01672 511491.

Mere Castle Mere, 8 miles (13km) south of Warminster. Built in 1253 by the 1st Duke of Cornwall on a hill to the northwest of the village thought to have been artificially steepened for defensive purposes. The castle had fallen into disrepair by the 15th century and none of its fabric now remains.

Mere Museum Barton Lane, Mere, 8 miles (13km) south of Warminster. Based in Mere public library, the museum's collection of local history includes an extensive photographic archive. Tel: 01747 860908.

Mompesson House Cathedral Close, Salisbury. An 18th century house built for Salisbury MP Thomas Mompesson in 1701, and including many original features and period furniture. It was used as Mrs Jennings's London home in the film *Sense and Sensibility* (1995). The house has been in the ownership of the National Trust since 1952. Tel: 01722 335659.

National Monuments Record Office Kemble Drive, Swindon. The public archive of English Heritage, located on the former Swindon Railway Works site. There is a public search room where a huge collection of photographs and historic resources can be viewed. Tel: 01793 414600.

National Trust, The Kemble Drive, Swindon. The National Trust moved its head office to Swindon in 2005, and occupies a building constructed on the site of the former Swindon Railway Works and designed as a model of brownfield renewal. It is named Heelis after Beatrix Potter (whose married name was Mrs Heelis), one of Trust's most important benefactors.

Newhouse Redlynch, 6 miles (10km) southeast of Salisbury. A Grade I listed brick Jacobean house built c.1619 with two Georgian wings and set in extensive grounds. Home to the Eyre family since 1633, the house became linked to Admiral Lord Nelson in 1817 when Harriet Eyre married George Matcham, Nelson's nephew. Various items connected with Nelson are on display, including a wooden cot in which he slept as a child and various items of tableware marked HN or N. Tel: 01244 572037/01725 510055.

New Wardour Castle See Old Wardour Castle

Norrington Manor $\frac{1}{2}$ mile (0.8km) northwest of Alvediston, 11 miles (18km) southwest of Salisbury. The house is thought to have been built by John Gawen, who purchased the property in 1377, and some remnants of the 14th century building still survive. The Gawens are claimed by some to have been one of England's oldest families, being descended from King Arthur's knight Sir Gawain. The estate was bought in 1658 by the Wyndhams, who initiated some rebuilding. Tel: 01722 780367.

Old Sarum $1\frac{1}{2}$ miles (2.5km) north of Salisbury. The site of the earliest settlement of Salisbury, with evidence of human habitation as early as 3000 BC. The Iron Age hill fort is oval in shape and measures 1300ft (396m) by 1200ft (366m), consisting of a single circuit of bank and ditch with an entrance at the eastern end. The site was occupied by the Romans and the Normans, who built a motte and bailey castle and cathedral inside its ramparts. The castle occupied a bull's-eye position in the centre of the earthworks and was mainly built by Roger, Bishop of Salisbury. In the early 13th century the site was largely abandoned as the new Salisbury Cathedral and city were built, and now contains only the ruins of the castle, cathedral and Bishop's Palace. Old Sarum was a parliamentary 'rotten borough' until the Reform Act of 1832. William Pitt the Elder became MP for Old Sarum in 1735, and a commemorative plaque can be seen in nearby Hudson's Fields, at the supposed site of his election. Now owned by English Heritage.

Old Wardour Castle 2 miles (3m) southwest of Tisbury, 13 miles (21km) southwest of Salisbury. A ruined hexagonal tower house built in 1393 by Lord Lovell and reconstructed by Robert Smythson for Sir Matthew Arundell in the late 16th century. The castle was badly damaged by two sieges in the Civil War. In that of 1643, Lady Arundell and a small force held off the large Parliamentary force for a week. The castle was featured on the cover of Sting's album *Ten Summoners' Tales*, and served as a location for the Hollywood blockbuster *Robin Hood, Prince of Thieves* (1991). Old Wardour Castle is now owned by English Heritage. New Wardour Castle, built 1769–76, was sold by the family after the death of the last Lord Arundell – a prisoner of war in the notorious Colditz Castle during World War II – and became a private school. In recent years, the building has been turned into luxury apartments.

Peto Garden See Iford Manor

Pewsey A village in the Vale of Pewsey, 6 miles (10km) south of Marlborough. It was once owned by Alfred the Great, a statue of whom can be found in the village. There are numerous timbered houses and thatched cottages, while Pewsey Wharf lies on the Kennet & Avon Canal. The Pewsey Heritage Centre in the High Street is housed in a foundry building dating from 1870 and containing a collection of old machine tools.

Philipps House and Dinton Park Dinton, 8 miles (13km) west of Salisbury. A Greek Revival house designed by Sir Jeffrey Wyattville for the Wyndham family in 1816, surrounded by landscaped parkland. Now owned by the National Trust. Tel: 01722 716663.

Porton Down Porton, 4 miles (6km) northeast of Salisbury. Officially titled the Defence Science and Technology Laboratory. A government facility for military research, including chemical, biological, radiological and nuclear (CBRN) defence. The complex is operated by the Ministry of Defence's Defence Science and Technology Laboratory.

RAF Boscombe Down $\frac{1}{2}$ mile (0.8km) southeast of Amesbury. An aircraft testing site established in 1939 and formerly operated by the Aircraft and Armament Evaluation Establishment. It has been the site of many significant developments in British aviation, including the first flights of the BAC TSR2 and the English Electric P1, the forerunner of the Lighting. Now operated by Qinetiq, it is also the home of the Empire Test Pilots School and of Tornado and Harrier maintenance units.

Richard Jefferies Museum Coate, 2 miles (3km) southeast of Swindon. A small museum dedicated to Richard Jefferies (1848–87), celebrated writer on the English countryside, and located in the farmhouse near Coate Water where he was born. Jefferies's classic children's book *Bevis* was set around Coate Water. The museum contains manuscripts, first editions and personal items and also commemorates the work of Alfred Williams (1877–1930), the Swindon railwayman, scholar and poet known as the 'Hammerman Poet'.

Ridgeway, The An ancient trackway often described as Britain's oldest road. It runs for 85 miles (137km) from Overton Hill near Avebury to Ivinghoe Beacon near Tring in Hertfordshire, via Berkshire, Oxfordshire and Buckinghamshire. In Wiltshire it runs north and east from Avebury, passing close to Barbury Castle, Liddington Castle and between Fox Hill and Charlbury Hill. Archaeological evidence indicates that the track has been used for over 5000 years. In recent times there have been concerns that the Ridgeway has been damaged by motorcycles and off-road vehicles, and these vehicles were banned from a 22 mile (35km) stretch designated a restricted byway in May 2006.

Rivers **Avon, South** see Hampshire

Avon, North The more northerly Avon rises near Chipping Sodbury in Gloucestershire, flowing east and then south through Luckington, Sherston, Malmesbury, Chippenham, Melksham and

Bradford-on-Avon, before leaving Wiltshire and joining the Severn estuary at Avonmouth. Aka the Bristol Avon, its total length is 75 miles (121km).

The **Bourne** is a tributary of the River Avon. Its source is near Burbage and it flows south through the villages of Collingbourne Kingston, Collingbourne Ducis, Tidworth, Porton, Winterbourne Gunner, Winterbourne Dauntsey, Winterbourne Earls and Laverstock before joining the Avon near Salisbury.

The **Cole** is a tributary of the River Thames which flows through Wiltshire and Oxfordshire, where it partially forms the border.

The **Ebble** is one of five rivers flowing through Salisbury, and joins the River Avon southwest of the city.

The **Kennet** is a tributary of the River Thames. Its lower reaches are navigable to river craft and are known as the Kennet Navigation, which, together with the Avon Navigation, the Kennet & Avon Canal and the Thames, links the cities of London and Bristol. The main source is Swallowhead Spring near Avebury. The river flows through Marlborough, Hungerford and Newbury before flowing into the Thames at Reading.

The **Marden**, a small tributary of the River Avon, flows from the hills surrounding Calne and meets the Avon 1 mile (1.6km) upstream of Chippenham.

Stour see Dorset

The **Wylye** is a tributary of the River Avon. It rises southwest of Warminster, flowing east to form the Wylye Valley. It meets the River Nadder at Wilton, and eventually drains to the sea via the River Avon. Both Wilton and, indirectly, Wiltshire, are named after the river.

Salisbury — Originally located at the Iron Age hill fort of Old Sarum (see separate entry), modern Salisbury has its roots in the town initially called 'New Sarum' and dating to c.1217 when the Bishop of Salisbury moved his ecclesiastical seat from Old Sarum to land further south. The site of the now world-famous cathedral was consecrated in 1219 and the town received its charter in 1226. The Edwin Young Collection of 19th and 20th century paintings, and the John Creasey Museum and Creasey Collection of Contemporary Art, are housed in Salisbury Library and Galleries.

Salisbury and South Wiltshire Museum — Cathedral Close, Salisbury. Located in the Grade I listed building known as The King's House since James I stayed here on a visit to the city. Home of the Stonehenge Gallery and of a nationally important collection of archaeological items, the museum's exhibits include the Monkton Deverill gold torc, dating to the Bronze Age, the Anglo-Saxon Warminster Jewel and the Pitt-Rivers collection, consisting of various archaeological items excavated by General Augustus Pitt-Rivers. There are displays on early man, the Romans and Saxons, and the history of Old Sarum and Salisbury (with the renowned Giant and Hob Nob). The large collection of pictures includes watercolours by J M W Turner. Tel: 01722 332151.

Salisbury Cathedral — Cathedral Close, Salisbury. Dedicated to the Blessed Virgin Mary and founded in 1220 by Richard Poore to replace a previous foundation at Old Sarum, the Gothic style building took 38 years to complete after the bishopric was moved from Old Sarum to Salisbury. The tower and spire – the latter both the tallest in the UK, and the tallest surviving pre-1400 spire in the world, at 404ft (123m) – were completed by 1320. Salisbury has the largest cloister in England, and holds one of the four surviving original copies of the Magna Carta. The cathedral organ was built in 1877 by 'Father' Henry Willis. The cathedral clock, dating from at least 1386, is probably the oldest working clock in existence. The clock has no face because all clocks of that date rang the hours on a bell. It was originally located in a bell tower that was demolished in 1792. Tel: 01722 555120.

Sanctuary, The — 1½ miles (2.5km) southeast of Avebury, 4½ miles (7km) west of Marlborough. A prehistoric site on Overton Hill, originally thought to have been linked to Avebury by the West Kennet Avenue. There is some debate as to the nature of the site; excavation has indicated that it originally consisted of a series of circles of wooden posts, erected c.3000 BC possibly as part of a roofed building although they may have formed a free-standing monument. A stone circle 130ft in diameter was erected c.2400 BC. The Sanctuary was first described as a standing stone circle by John Aubrey in 1648, but appears to have been destroyed in the early 18th century. All that is visible today is a series of concentric circles of concrete blocks and pillars which now mark the position of excavated stone and post holes.

Sarum College — Cathedral Close, Salisbury. An ecumenical Christian institution established in 1995 and occupying the buildings which formerly housed Salisbury and Wells Theological College. The main college buildings were designed by Sir Christopher Wren in 1677; a residential wing and chapel were added by William Butterfield in 1878 and 1881.

Sarum Way — A 32 mile (51km) footpath which follows a complete circle around Salisbury. It follows parts of the Monarch's Way, Clarendon Way and Avon Valley Path.

Savernake Forest — ½ mile (0.8km) southeast of Marlborough. Covering 4500 acres (1800ha), Savernake is the largest privately owned forest in Britain. Over 1000 years old, being named as *Safernoc* in a Saxon charter from King Athelstan in AD 934, it is leased by the Forestry Commission from the owners, the Trustees of Savernake Estate and the Earl of Cardigan.

Sheldon Manor — 1½ miles (2.5km) west of Chippenham. Dating from 1282 and said to be Wiltshire's oldest inhabited manor house, it was originally located in the village of Sheldon, abandoned in the medieval period following a plague. The gardens feature old-fashioned roses, ancient yews and a mulberry tree. Tel: 01249 653120.

Silbury Hill — ¾ mile (1.2km) southwest of Avebury, 6 miles (10km) west of Marlborough. A prehistoric man-made hill, thought to be over 4500 years old and the tallest such mound in Europe. Silbury Hill covers 5 acres (2ha), is 550ft (166m) in diameter, almost perfectly round and stands 130ft (40m) high; its flat summit is 100ft (30.5m) wide. A number of excavations have been made to investigate the hill's purpose: a shaft was dug from top to bottom in 1776 and a tunnel to the centre in 1849, while a BBC televised dig took place in 1968–70. Its exact purpose remains unknown, although legend has it that it is the burial place of King Sil, sitting on a golden horse. People were formerly allowed to climb the hill, but this is now banned by English Heritage, following the collapse of the 1776 shaft in 2000 leaving a large hole on the summit. Work to stabilise the structure was completed in 2008.

Sport

football — **Swindon Town** were formed in 1881 (some sources put the date as 1879). Founder members of the Southern League in 1894, which they won in 1911 and 1914 (they also reached the FA Cup semi-finals in 1910 and 1912), Swindon joined the Football League Third Division South in 1920. In 1969 they won the League Cup at Wembley, beating Arsenal 3–1. They rose from the Fourth Division to the Premiership 1986–93 under managers Lou Macari, Ossie Ardiles and Glenn Hoddle, but only lasted one season in the top flight, conceding 100 goals in the season. Nicknamed The Robins after their traditional colours of red and white, their home ground is the County Ground, Swindon. Tel: 0871 423 6433.

horse racing — **Salisbury Racecourse**, Netherhampton, situated on chalk downland to the southwest of Salisbury, is one of England's oldest racecourses. The Flat racing course with a 7 furlong (1.8km) uphill run-in holds the Totesport Sovereign Stakes in August. Tel: 01722 326461.

ice hockey — **Swindon Wildcats** play in the English Premier Ice Hockey League. Originally formed in 1986 as the Wildcats, they have since been known as Swindon IceLords (1996–7), Swindon Chill (1998–2000), Swindon Phoenix (2000–01) and Swindon Lynx (2001–04). They are based at the Link Centre, Swindon.

Steam – Museum of the Great Western Railway — Kemble Drive, Swindon. Housed in a Grade II listed building, part of the former Swindon Railway Works, the museum tells the story of the Great Western Railway. The atmosphere of the Swindon works is recreated using sounds, real objects, world famous locomotives and a reconstructed station platform. Tel: 01793 466646.

Stonehenge — 2 miles (3km) west of Amesbury, 8 miles (13km) north of Salisbury. One of the most famous prehistoric sites in the world, the Neolithic and Bronze Age megalithic monument is composed of earthworks surrounding a circular setting of large standing stones. The earliest phase of the monument, dating to c.3100 BC, is a circular earth bank and ditch 284ft (86.5m) in diameter. The stones have been dated to 2500–2000 BC; the 82 bluestones which originally constituted the inner circle were brought from Wales c.2150 BC, while the outer circle of massive sarsen stones (weighing up to 50 tonnes), probably carried from the Marlborough Downs, was erected c. 2000 BC. After 1500 BC the bluestones were rearranged as seen today. Stonehenge and its surroundings were designated a UNESCO World Heritage Site in 1986 in combination with the henge monument at Avebury, and the site is also a Scheduled Ancient Monument. Stonehenge itself is owned and managed by English Heritage while the surrounding downland is owned by the National Trust. The site is currently reached from the car park through a tunnel under the A30, and the stone circle cannot be entered or touched. A number of plans to improve the setting, including putting the A30 into a 3 mile (5km) tunnel under the site, have so far failed to come to fruition. Tel: 01980 624715.

Stonehenge Historic Landscape — Formerly known as Stonehenge Down. A National Trust property covering more than 8 sq miles (21 sq km) around Stonehenge and including nearly 400 ancient monuments, including the earthwork known as the Cursus, Woodhenge and Durrington Walls. The estate also includes the Nile Clumps near Amesbury, large copses of trees planted by the 6th Marquess of Queensbury after the Battle of Trafalgar in memeory of Lord Nelson and said to represent the positions of ships at the Battle of the Nile. Tel: 01980 624715.

Stourhead — Stourton, 8 miles (13km) southwest of Warminster. A 2650 acre (1072ha) estate located at the source of the River Stour, including a Palladian mansion and the village of Stourton itself, as well as one of the finest landscape gardens in England. The house, one of the first in the country to be built in Palladian style, was designed by Colen Campbell and built 1720–2 for banker Henry Hoare. Inspired by his Grand Tour of Europe, the gardens were designed by Henry Hoare II and laid out 1741–80 around a large lake created by damming the Stour. They include surprise vistas, Gothic ruins and a number of temples, including the Temple of Apollo, the Temple of Flora and the Pantheon (or Temple of Hercules). The property has been owned by the National Trust since 1946. Tel: 01747 841152.

Stourton House Flower Garden — Stourton, 8 miles (13km) southwest of Warminster. A 19th century house with 4 acres (1.6ha) of informal gardens developed since the 1960s and including a woodland garden, a winter garden, a secret garden, a lily pond and a herbaceous garden. It contains 270 varieties of hydrangeas, and is regularly featured on BBC TV's *Gardeners' World*. Tel: 01747 840417.

Swindon — Growing from an original settlement referred to as *Suindune*, thought to mean either Pig's Hill or Sweyn's Hill, the town developed with the construction of the Wilts & Berks Canal (see separate entry) in 1810 and the Wiltshire Canal in 1819, and more significantly after 1840 when it was chosen to house the Great Western Railway works. The works remained the principal employer for over 100 years, but after World War II Swindon's transport links and geographical position led to the development of light industries such as electronics, as firms such as Plessey moved to Swindon. Swindon was designated an 'Expanded' (or overspill) town under the Town Development Act 1952, and this led to the movement of large numbers of people from London in the 1950s and 1960s. The town also has a large Polish and Italian population partly due to World War II refugee camps and prisoner-of-war camps in the area. Industry has continued to expand over the last 20 years, with firms such as Intel, Motorola, Honda and BMW employing large workforces, leading to practically full employment at times. In popular culture Swindon has been mentioned in such diverse contexts as Sherlock Holmes, *Monty Python's Flying Circus, The Office* and the lyrics of Spinal Tap, usually being portrayed as a sleepy place populated by uneducated people. In fact it is the home of the British quiz champions and a rich vein of expert knowledge can be found in the town.

Swindon & Cricklade Railway A heritage railway operating between Blunsdon and Blades Knoll on $^3/_4$ mile (1.2km) of the former Midland & South Western Junction Railway line between Swindon and Cricklade, opened in 1881 and closed in 1937. It began operations in the late 1970s and is one of the few British heritage railways to undertake complete reconstruction without an inheritance of track and buildings from British Rail. Tel: 01793 771615.

Swindon Museum and Art Gallery Bath Road, Swindon. Situated in Apsley House, an early 19th century house in the Old Town, the museum has displays of local prehistory, geology, archaeology and social history. Exhibits include finds from a Roman villa excavated in north Swindon and a stuffed crocodile nicknamed Georgina. The Swindon Collection of 20th Century British Art, including works by Howard Hodgkin, L S Lowry, Henry Moore, Ben Nicholson and Graham Sutherland, is one of the most significant in England. Tel: 01793 466556.

Swindon Railway Village A village built in the 'New Town' area of Swindon, near the railway works, by the Great Western Railway to house its workers. It included a hospital, schools, swimming baths and the Mechanics' Institute, which contained a library and theatre. Swindon was used as an example of a company town by J K Galbraith in his book *The Age of Uncertainty* (1977). Much of the village still exists, and the Railway Village Museum recreates a railway worker's home.

Swindon Railway Works Built by the Great Western Railway in 1841 under Isambard Kingdom Brunel's chief engineer, Daniel Gooch. For various technical reasons, Swindon was chosen as the most suitable site for the works; according to one oft-repeated myth, Brunel and Gooch were surveying a vale north of Swindon Hill when Brunel either threw a stone or dropped a sandwich and declared the spot to be the location of the works. The site was soon manufacturing one locomotive a week, and a carriage works was opened in 1878. The works grew until, at the turn of the 20th century, it employed an estimated three-quarters of Swindon's entire workforce; shortly before World War II it still employed 14,000 people. The main locomotive fabrication workshop, the A Shop, was at $11^1/_2$ acres (4.5ha) one of the largest covered areas in the world. British Railways' first diesel-hydraulic main line locomotive was built in 1957 and the last steam locomotive, BR Standard Class 9F 92220 *Evening Star*, in 1960. Building of new locomotives ended at Swindon in 1962, although locomotive repairs and carriage and wagon work continued until the closure of the works in 1986. The site has since been redeveloped to house the headquarters of organisations such as the National Trust.

Trafalgar Park $^1/_2$ mile (0.8km) east of Charlton All Saints, 5 miles (8km) southeast of Salisbury. A country house built for Sir Peter Vandeput in 1733 by London architect John James and later associated with the family of Admiral Lord Nelson. Originally called Standlynch House, it was purchased in 1814 to provide a home for Nelson's family, and was renamed Trafalgar House. Having changed hands many times in the intervening period, it is currently undergoing restoration. Tel: 01722 711334.

Trowbridge The county town of Wiltshire, located on the River Biss. A settlement on the site is mentioned in Domesday Book; the name is possibly derived from Anglo-Saxon *treow-brycg* ('tree' + 'bridge', referring either to a bridge by a tree or a bridge constructed from trees). One of five small industrial towns in West Wiltshire based on the woollen industry from the Middle Ages until the 19th century, it is now the third largest town in Wiltshire after Salisbury and Chippenham, and is the administrative centre of both Wiltshire County Council and West Wiltshire District Council.

Trowbridge Castle Fore Street, Trowbridge. Probably fortified c.1139 by Humphrey de Bohun, husband of Matilda during the reign of King Stephen. The castle fell into ruin shortly afterwards. Parts of the motte and ditch have been uncovered during excavations, but no definite fabric of the castle is now visible. It is believed to lie under Home Mills in the Shires shopping centre, now housing Trowbridge Museum; Fore Street traces its outer boundary.

Trowbridge Museum The Shires, Trowbridge. Located in Home Mills, the town's last working woollen mill until it closed in 1982, the museum tells the story of wool production in Trowbridge. Other displays include a reconstruction of the medieval castle and an audio-visual display on the history of the town. Tel: 01225 751339.

Wardrobe, The Cathedral Close, Salisbury. A house dating from 1254 and once a residence of one of the canons of Salisbury Cathedral. It was later owned by the Bishop of Salisbury, for whom it probably served as a storehouse – hence its name. Much altered in the 18th and 19th centuries, the building now houses the Salisbury museum of the Royal Gloucestershire, Berkshire and Wiltshire Regiment. Tel: 01722 419419.

Warminster Warminster lies to the southwest of Salisbury Plain, at the head of the Wylye Valley. It has traditionally had close links with the military and is still considered an important military centre. During the Civil War the town is thought to have changed hands between Royalist and Parliamentary supporters at least four times. During World War I thousands of soldiers from Australia, New Zealand and Canada were encamped around Warminster prior to the invasion of France. There are ANZAC cemeteries in Sutton Veny and Codford (where the victims of a flu epidemic rest) and an annual ANZAC Day service is held on the Sunday nearest to 25 April. American troops were billeted in the town during World War II, and film star James Cagney and boxer Joe Louis were among the celebrities who came to entertain them. More recently, the area around Warminster has becomes famous for UFO sightings.

Warminster Dewey Museum Three Horseshoes Mall, Warminster. Based in Warminster Library, the museum's exhibits cover the history of the area from the Iron Age to the present and include the Victor Manley collection of fossils and other geological finds. Tel: 01985 218548.

Wessex Ridgeway A long-distance footpath running for 136 miles (219km) from Marlborough to Lyme Regis in Dorset via the edge of Salisbury Plain and Cranbourne Chase. Opened in 1994, it is one of four long-distance footpaths which, in combination, run from Lyme Regis to Hunstanton in Norfolk and are referred to as the Greater Ridgeway.

West Kennet Long Barrow 1¼ miles (2km) south of Avebury, 5 miles (8km) west of Marlborough. A Neolithic tomb situated on a prominent chalk ridge near Silbury Hill. Recorded by John Aubrey in the 17th century and by William Stukeley in the 18th, it was first excavated in 1859 by John Thurham. Construction began c.3500 BC and the tomb was in use until c.2200 BC, when it was sealed with large sarsen stones. Classified as a chambered long barrow, it has two pairs of opposing transept chambers and a single terminal chamber used for burial. The stone burial chambers are located at the far end of one of the longest barrows in Britain at 330ft (100m). The entrance consists of a concave forecourt with a façade made from the large slabs of sarsen stones placed to seal entry.

Westbury Situated at the western edge of Salisbury Plain, Westbury is one of west Wiltshire's wool towns. The 15th century All Saints Church, built mainly in Perpendicular style, has a rare oblong crossing tower.

Westonbirt Arboretum 11 miles (18km) northwest of Chippenham. One of the largest and most varied arboreta in the UK, with over 3000 species and 15,500 individual trees and shrubs in an area of 600 acres (240ha). Established in 1829 by Robert Holford and extended by his son George, it has been managed since 1956 by the Forestry Commission. It suffered significant damage in the great storm of October 1987, but has largely recovered over the past 20 years.

Westwood Manor Westwood, 2 miles (3km) southwest of Bradford on Avon. A 15th century stone manor house with Jacobean alterations. There are collections of furniture, needlework and musical instruments. The property has been owned by the National Trust since 1960. Tel: 01225 863374.

White horses Thirteen white horses are known to have existed in Wiltshire, of which eight are still visible. The following are among the most noteworthy:

Broad Town White Horse, ½ mile (0.8km) east of Broad Town, 5 miles (8km) southwest of Swindon. Said to have been cut in 1864 by William Simmonds of Littleton Farm, on whose land it stood, the horse had remained invisible since being covered during World War II. In 1992 it was cleaned and rechalked by a group of local enthusiasts.

Devizes White Horse, 2 miles (3km) northeast of Devizes. Facing east towards the Vale of Pewsey, the horse was cut on Roundway Hill in 1999 to mark the millennium.

Marlborough (Preshute) White Horse, ¼ mile (0.4km) south of Marlborough. Located above Marlborough College and the River Kennet, the horse was cut in 1804 by pupils of a boys' school in Marlborough.

Pewsey White Horse, 1½ miles (2.5km) southeast of Pewsey. Commissioned by Pewsey town council for celebrations to commemorate the coronation of George VI in 1937, and designed by George Maples. The Pewsey horse, 66ft (20m) long and 45ft (14m) high, replaced a late 18th century horse which had become obliterated. It is best seen from the A345 just south of Pewsey.

Westbury White Horse, 2 miles (3km) east of Westbury, 5 miles (8km) southeast of Trowbridge. Located below Bratton Castle (see separate entry) on Bratton Down, on the western edge of Salisbury Plain, the present Westbury White Horse was originally cut in 1778. It is located on the site of an even older white horse, probably 17th century in origin, that commemorated the defeat of the Danes by King Alfred at Ethandun in AD 878.

There are also white horses at Alton Barnes, Cherhill and Hackpen Hill.

Wilton Once nominally the county town of Wiltshire, Wilton was the capital of *Wiltunscire*, a region of the ancient kingdom of Wessex. A place of some significance before the Norman Conquest – Wilton Abbey was founded in 771 and a decisive battle against the Danes was fought here by King Alfred in 871 – it remained the county's administrative centre until the 11th century. However, it was overtaken economically by Salisbury in the early Middle Ages and has remained in its shadow ever since. The abbey was surrendered to Henry VIII in 1539 during the Dissolution of the Monasteries, and in 1541 much of the estate was granted to the Earl of Pembroke. From 1741, when two French weavers were brought in by Lord Pembroke to teach the locals new techniques, Wilton became famous for its carpets. The Wilton Royal Carpet Factory operated until 1995, when it finally closed after a takeover.

Wilton House Wilton, 3 miles (5km) west of Salisbury. Home for 450 years to the Earls of Pembroke, since Henry VIII granted to William Herbert (later the 1st Earl) the estate of the dissolved Benedictine monastery at Wilton in 1542. A Tudor house was built shortly afterwards, and in the 1630s the 4th Earl commissioned Inigo Jones to remodel the house in Palladian style. The splendid state rooms created by Jones include the magnificent Double Cube room (so called because its dimensions form a perfect double cube with 30ft/9m sides), which houses a world famous collection of Van Dyck paintings. There are also paintings by Rembrandt, Brueghel and Reynolds, and Greek, Roman and 17th century sculpture. The extensive grounds are bordered by the rivers Nadder and Wylye; features include the Palladian Bridge, built in 1737 by the 9th Earl, and the Millennium Water Feature, designed by sculptor William Pye. The surrounding open parkland is laid out in the style of Capability Brown. The house is now home to William Herbert, 18th Earl of Pembroke and 15th Earl of Montgomery. Tel: 01722 746714.

Wilton Windmill ½ mile (0.8km) east of Wilton, 6 miles (10km) southeast of Marlborough. A five-floor brick tower mill located on a chalk ridge above the village of Wilton. It was built in 1821 after the River Bedwyn, which had previously powered several water mills in the area, was canalised during the construction of the Kennet & Avon Canal, and was in use until the 1920s. In 1971 it was purchased by Wiltshire County Council and leased to the Wiltshire Historic Buildings Trust, who restored it to working condition.

Wilts & Berks Canal The Wilts & Berks Canal links the Kennet and Avon Canal at Semington, near Melksham, to the River Thames at Abingdon, with a branch to the Thames and Severn Canal at Cricklade. The canal was cut 1796–1810 and was 52 miles (84km) long, with branches to Chippenham, Calne, Wantage and Longcot. The North Wilts Canal, connecting Swindon with the Thames and Severn Canal at Cricklade was opened in 1819, and later merged with the Wilts & Berks Canal. The canal operated for more than a century before being abandoned by Act of Parliament in 1914. In 1977 the Wilts & Berks Canal Trust was formed to preserve and restore the canal where possible.

Wiltshire Heritage Museum, Gallery and Library Long Street, Devizes. Owned by the Wiltshire Archaeological and Natural History Society (founded in 1853), the museum traces the history of Wiltshire and its people from earliest times to the present day. The library contains a comprehensive collection of printed and manuscript material relating to Wiltshire. Tel: 01380 727369.

Woodhenge $1\frac{1}{4}$ miles (2km) northwest of Amesbury. A Neolithic or early Bronze Age henge and timber circle monument dating to c.2300–2000 BC and consisting of six concentric rings of timber posts – now marked by concrete stumps – surrounded by a ditch with a bank on the outside. Located 2 miles (3km) northeast of Stonehenge, with which it is roughly contemporary, it was first identified in 1922 after an aerial survey by Alexander Keiller and O G S Crawford.

Wroughton Science Museum $\frac{1}{2}$ mile (0.8km) south of Wroughton, 4 miles (6km) southwest of Swindon. The large object storage facility for the National Collections of the Science Museum. Located on a former World War II airfield, the collections are stored in five hangars each covering over 1 acre (0.4ha). Among the items held here are airliners, agricultural machinery, cars and lorries, and the Wood press, part of Fleet Street's last operational printing press. In 2007 Wroughton was one of six projects shortlisted for a potential £50m lottery grant under the National Lottery's Living Landmarks: People's Millions initiative to open the site to the public as the National Museum of Science and Industry Collections Centre. Tel: 01793 846200.

Some famous people born in Wiltshire

Aylmer, Sir Felix (actor) (1889–1979)	Corsham
Blunt, James (singer) (1974–)	Tidworth
Channon, Mick (footballer and racehorse trainer) (1948–)	Orcheston
Crawford, Michael (actor) (1942–)	Salisbury
Dors, Diana (actress) (1931–84)	Swindon
Fiennes, Joseph (actor) (1970–)	Salisbury
Francome, John (jockey) (1952–)	Swindon
Grigson, Sophie (cookery writer) (1959–)	Swindon
Hayward, Justin (musician) (1946–)	Swindon
Hobbes, Thomas (philosopher) (1588-1679)	Westport
Hempleman-Adams, David (explorer) (1956–)	Swindon
Howell, David (golfer) (1975–)	Swindon
Lamarr, Mark (comedian and TV presenter) (1967–)	Swindon
Morley, Robert (actor) (1908–92)	Semley
Morris, Desmond (zoologist and TV presenter) (1928–)	Purton
Pitman, Isaac (shorthand inventor) (1813–97)	Trowbridge
Talbot, William Fox (photographer) (1800–77)	Lacock
Wren, Christopher (architect) (1632–1723)	East Knoyle

Worcestershire

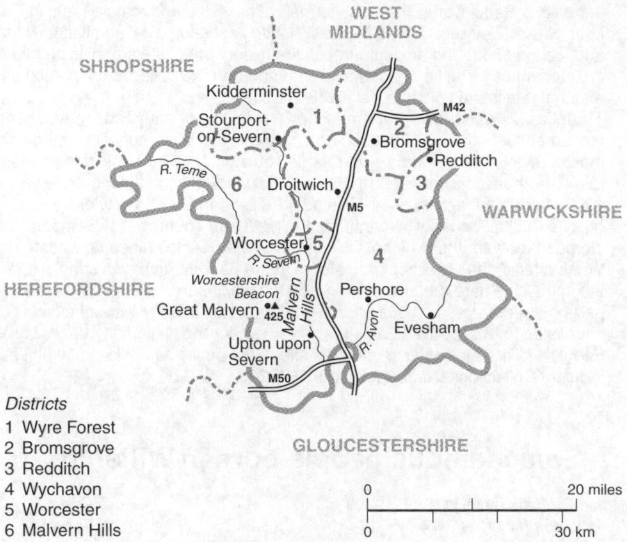
WEST MIDLANDS
SHROPSHIRE
Kidderminster
Stourport-on-Severn
Bromsgrove
Redditch
M42
R. Teme
Droitwich
M5
WARWICKSHIRE
Worcester
R. Severn
HEREFORDSHIRE
Worcestershire Beacon
425
Great Malvern
Malvern Hills
Pershore
Evesham
R. Avon
Upton upon Severn
M50
GLOUCESTERSHIRE
1
2
3
4
5
6
0
20 miles
30 km
Districts
1 Wyre Forest
2 Bromsgrove
3 Redditch
4 Wychavon
5 Worcester
6 Malvern Hills

Worcestershire is located in the West Midlands region of central England. The county borders Herefordshire to the west, Shropshire to the northwest, West Midlands to the northeast, Warwickshire to the east and Gloucestershire to the south. The southernmost tip of Staffordshire has a short boundary with the mid-northern border of Worcestershire between Shropshire and West Midlands. To the west, the county is bordered by the Malvern Hills, beneath which is situated the former spa town of Malvern. The western side of the hills is in the county of Herefordshire. From 1974 to 1998 Worcestershire was administered as part of the county of Hereford and Worcester. Prior to 1974 some areas now part of West Midlands metropolitan county, such as Dudley, Halesowen and Stourbridge, used to be part of northern Worcestershire. Before then, some areas, such as Yardley, had been made part of Birmingham (and hence Warwickshire). The post-1998 county therefore does not correspond exactly to the pre-1974 boundaries. The two major rivers flowing through the county are the Severn and the Avon.

The county is largely rural. The main upland, the Malvern Hills on the county's southwestern border with Herefordshire, are a range of igneous and metamorphic rocks more than 600 million years old. The southeast of the county, around the Vale of Evesham, is traditionally an area of fruit and hop production – the county's products include the Worcester Pearmain apple and the Pershore plum – although numbers of orchards have declined markedly since World War II. The northeast of the county, which once included parts of the Black Country, became heavily industrialised during the Industrial Revolution.

The city of **Worcester**, situated on the River Severn, is also the county town and was founded by the Romans soon after the conquest of Britain in AD 43. The area was originally given the name Vertis, which became Vigornia c.AD 50. By the late 2nd century there was an iron industry in the town. When the last Roman soldiers left Britain in the early 5th century Worcester was deserted. However, by the mid 7th century the Saxons had started a new settlement by a ford in the Severn. The old Roman settlement or *castra* gave its name to the new Saxon town; Vigornia evolved variously into Wirecestrescira, Weorgoran (meaning 'people of the winding river'), Weogorancaster and eventually into Worcester.

In 680 Worcester was given a bishop and a cathedral, after which it grew rapidly. Probably because it had been equipped with defences at the time of the Roman occupation, in the late 9th century the town became part of the network of fortified settlements, called burghs, established across his kingdom by Alfred the Great. In 1041 the county was ravaged by the forces of Danish king Harthacnut after the people of Worcester murdered a tax collector sent to the town; it soon recovered, however, and continued to prosper.

By the time of the Domesday Book in 1086, Worcester was a town with a population of 2000. The Normans had built a wooden castle (which was rebuilt in stone in the 12th century) and the area around grew as the weekly market became popular. Fire devastated Worcester in 1202, prompting the construction of a stone wall around the town to both contain and keep out fire (and of course as a defensive measure).

When King John died in 1216 he was buried in Worcester Cathedral. From 1218 Worcester held an annual fair. The main industries were woollen cloth making and the leather industry. Worcester was also an inland port. The main import was wine, the main export wool. Timber and iron were also brought to Worcester by water from the Forest of Dean.

In 1227 Worcester received its charter, after which the townspeople were allowed to elect two bailiffs to run the town. In the 12th and 13th centuries there was a Jewish community in Worcester but all Jews were forced to leave England in 1290. Like all towns, Worcester was devastated by the Black Death of 1348–9 which may have killed half the population. However recovery was swift and by the late Middle Ages the population was 4000, double that at the time of the Domesday Book.

In the 16th century the wool trade was still the lifeblood of the town but in the 17th century it began to decline. Nevertheless Worcester continued to grow, despite a further severe outbreak of plague in 1637. The town staunchly supported Charles I during the Civil War and was occupied by both sides for a time before the Royalists ultimately surrendered in 1646. The future Charles II, having persuaded the Scots to try and restore him to the throne, came to Worcester in 1651 but his forces were crushed by Oliver Cromwell's army and he was lucky to escape. The fighting disrupted trade and left Worcester impoverished, but the town again recovered, and continued to grow rapidly in the 18th century: a Guildhall was built in 1723, an infirmary in 1746, and a new bridge over the Severn in 1781.

By the end of the 18th century, however, the wool trade was dead. In 1751, Dr John Wall tried to revive local industry by founding a porcelain works; this became the Royal Worcester Porcelain Works in 1778, while other industries included the manufacture of carpets, vinegar, and bricks and tiles. Glove making had by now become the main industry – the first glover in Worcester had been recorded in the 13th century and by the 18th century the industry was booming – but in 1826 import duties on foreign gloves were removed, with disastrous results for the industry.

In the 19th century Worcester became an industrial town. Iron foundries were opened and engineering flourished. The famous Worcester sauce was first made in the town in 1837, and in the same year its boundaries were extended. The Worcester & Birmingham Canal opened in 1815 and the railway reached the town in 1850. Like other such towns, conditions for the poor in Worcester deteriorated with the town's industrialisation. An outbreak of cholera in 1832 killed 79 people, another in 1849 killed 49. Conditions only improved later in the century, when the water supply was improved and extended to all the citizens. Worcester gained its first electricity supply in 1894. During the 20th century Worcester's major industries were sauce making, printing and light engineering; service industries and tourism have become more important in recent years as manufacturing has declined.

Worcestershire	**Population**			**Area**	
Districts	*male*	*female*	*total*	*sq miles*	*sq km*
Bromsgrove	43,141	44,696	87,837	84	217
Malvern Hills	35,042	37,130	72,172	223	577
Redditch	38,828	39,979	78,807	21	54
Worcester	45,486	47,867	93,353	13	33
Wychavon	55,727	57,230	112,957	256	665
Wyre Forest	47,663	49,318	96,981	75	195
Total	265,887	276,220	542,107	672	1741

Local Attractions and information

Abberley Hall — Great Witley, 9 miles (15km) northwest of Worcester. A Grade II* listed Italianate house built 1846–9 by J P St Aubyn, set in Grade II listed gardens. The house has been occupied since 1916 by Abberley Hall School, now a co-educational school for pupils aged 2–13. Abberley Hall Clock Tower is a Victorian folly built c.1883–4 by St Aubyn in a mixture of 13th and 14th century Gothic styles. Standing 161ft (49m) tall, it can be seen from six counties. Tel: 01299 896275.

Abberton Hall — Abberton, 7 miles (11km) northwest of Evesham. A small country house dating to the early 17th century, although much altered in the 1800s. At the core of the two-storey house, faced with modern brick, lies a timber-framed house built by the Sheldon family, former owners of the estate. A loggia in the garden features murals added in 1937 by artist and former owner Benjamin Gibbon. Tel: 01905 723438.

Administrative headquarters — County Hall, Spetchley Road, Worcester WR5 2NP. Tel: 01905 763763.

All Saints — Wilden, 1 mile (1.6km) east of Stourport-on-Severn. Built in 1880 by Alfred Baldwin, father of Prime Minister Stanley Baldwin, for the workforce of Wilden Ironworks. The exquisite windows, originally made of plain glass, were replaced 1902–14 with designs by Edward Burne-Jones, Baldwin's brother-in-law. Tel: 01299 878224.

Almonry Heritage Centre — Abbey Gate, Evesham. A Grade II* listed 14th century house, once occupied by the almoner (the brother responsible for providing material assistance to the poor) of the Abbey of St Ecgwin and now containing 12 rooms of exhibits from 2000 years of Evesham's history. The site includes a garden. Tel: 01386 446944.

Alvechurch — A large village in the district of Bromsgrove, situated in the valley of the River Arrow. Alvechurch means 'the church of the Lady Aelfgiva', who was thought to have been a relative of King Athelstan; Offa gave the land forming the parish to the local church in the late 8th century. In the 13th century it had a weekly market and an annual fair. From the 19th to the mid 20th century there was a brick factory in the hamlet of Withybed on the edge of the village. Other local industries included nail and needle making. The church of St Laurence, dating to 1239, is situated on high ground, and is possibly built on the site of an earlier Mercian church. Much of the church was rebuilt by William Butterfield 1858–61; it contains a 1348-pipe organ, while the tower has a peal of eight bells.

Areley Kings — A village on the River Severn, 1 mile (1.6km) south of Stourport-on-Severn. Situated in the Wyre Forest, from early times the manor of Areley Kings was part of the manor of Martley; the rector of Martley still has the right to appoint the rector at Areley Kings. The manor of Areley originated in a fishery at 'Ernel' which, with the land belonging to it, was granted by the Empress Matilda to Bordesley Abbey on its foundation in 1136, and retained until its dissolution. Prince Rupert of the Rhine is rumoured to have slept a night at Areley House during the Civil War.

Arley Arboretum — Upper Arley, 5 miles (8km) northwest of Kidderminster. Among the oldest arboreta in Britain, and home to one of the best tree collections in the county. Planned c.1800 by Earl Mountnorris, it is now managed by the R D Turner Charitable Trust, established in 1971 by industrialist Roger Turner, a former owner of the estate. Tel: 01299 861368.

Avoncroft Museum of Historic Buildings — Stoke Heath, 2 miles (3km) south of Bromsgrove. An open-air industrial and architectural museum opened in 1967 to provide a location for the reconstruction of a 15th century timber-framed house in Bromsgrove, dismantled to prevent its destruction. Its buildings, which include a fully functioning windmill and a 1940s prefab, have all been rescued from their original sites and restored. The national collection of telephone kiosks – the largest collection of its kind in Britain – is also held here. Tel: 01527 831363.

Barnt Green House — Barnt Green, 4 miles (6km) northeast of Bromsgrove. Built in 1651 and extensively refurbished in Tudor style in the early 19th century. The house was bought by Archer Windsor, 6th Earl of Plymouth, in 1811 from the previous occupants, the Yates family, and became a residence of the Earls of Plymouth. Queen Victoria is reputed to have spent the night here. The building is currently occupied by a gastropub.

Battles — See separate table for details of the three major battles in Worcestershire: Evesham, Powick Bridge and Worcester.

Bevere Island — 5 miles (8km) north of Worcester. The second largest island on the River Severn, which divides into two channels at this point: the western channel has a lock for boats, while to the east the river flows over a fearsome weir. A small cast-iron arched bridge, built in 1844, connects the island to the eastern bank. GR: SO837594.

Bewdley Museum — Load Street, Bewdley. Housed in a historic 18th century butchers' shambles beneath the town hall, the museum explores the growth of the town, the lives of its people and the crafts of the surrounding Wyre Forest area. Displays include artefacts, archive photographs and the work of basket makers, charcoal burners, pewterers, brass founders and wheelwrights. There is a wartime allotment garden, fire fighting display and original lock-up cells. The site also includes a herb garden with wildlife pond. Tel: 01299 403573.

Bordesley Abbey — Needle Mill Lane, Riverside, Redditch. A Cistercian abbey founded c.1138 by Waleran de Beaumont. Although not exceptionally rich, it occupied a site comparable in size with the great abbeys of Fountains and Rievaulx in Yorkshire; it also held political control of the ancient township of Tardebigge until its dissolution in 1538. The ruins are the subject of a longstanding archaeological investigation by the University of Reading's Bordesley Abbey Project. Tel: 01527 62509.

Bredon Barn — Bredon, 8 miles (13km) southwest of Evesham. A large 14th century threshing barn constructed of local Cotswold stone and notable for its dramatic aisled interior and unusual stone chimney cowling. Now owned by the National Trust. Tel: 01985 843600.

Bredon Hill — $1\frac{1}{2}$ miles (2.5km) northeast of Bredon's Norton, 6 miles (10km) southwest of Evesham. A hill above the Vale of Evesham and within the Cotswolds Area of Outstanding Natural Beauty. The remains of an Iron Age hill fort (also known as Kemerton Camp) are located on top of the hill, as well as Roman earthworks and a number of ancient standing stones, including one called the Banbury Stone after the Anglo-Saxon name for the fort, *Baintesburh*. A pair of stones below the summit are known as the King and Queen stones; according to local legend, passing between these stones will bring healing. The small stone tower known as Parsons' Folly was built in the

18th century as a summerhouse for Mr Parsons of Kemerton. The hill's 981ft (299m) natural height may have contributed to the final height of the tower, whose top now reaches 1000ft (305m) (the similar tower on Leith Hill in Surrey increases the overall height from 965ft/294m to 1029ft/313.5m). Since the 1980s the tower has been used as a mobile phone base station. Bredon Hill is the birthplace of Fred Archer (1915–99), whose many books describe life on the local farms and in the villages in the first half of the 20th century. The hill is also immortalised in A E Housman's poem cycle *A Shropshire Lad*. The name 'Bredon Hill' is unusual in that it combines the name for 'hill' in three different languages. In addition to 'hill', the *bre* element is of Celtic origin, and *don* is Old English.

British Camp See Herefordshire Beacon, Herefordshire

Broadway Tower 1 mile (1.6km) southeast of Broadway, 6 miles (10km) southeast of Evesham. A folly situated on the ancient beacon hill of Broadway Hill, 1024ft (312m) above sea level on one of the highest points of the Cotswolds. On a clear day, 13 counties can be seen from the top of the tower. Designed by James Wyatt to resemble a mock castle, and built for Lady Coventry in 1797, the tower itself stands 55ft (17m) high. Over the years, the tower was home to the printing press of Sir Thomas Phillips, and served as a country retreat for artists including William Morris; it now contains examples of Morris's designs and an exhibition on the tower's history.

Burford House and Garden Centre Burford, $^1/_2$ mile (0.8km) west of Tenbury Wells. Surrounding Georgian Burford House, the 7 acres (2.8ha) of lawn and borders beside the River Teme were designed in 1952 by John Treasure. The gardens now contain the National Collection of clematis, as well as 2000 other plant species. Tel: 01584 810777.

Butts, The The Butts, Worcester. An area on the western side of Worcester town centre, 100m from the east bank of the Severn. Currently a council depot and public car park, the vast open space known as The Butts was, as its name suggests, used for archery practice in the Middle Ages. Part of it was also occupied by tenters (frames for stretching and drying cloth after fulling or dyeing – the hooks by which the cloth was hung were called tenterhooks). Over 1000 years earlier it had been a busy part of the Roman town, and the course of a Roman road is still just visible as a slightly parched, lighter line in the grass whose roots cannot penetrate the buried iron-slag surface. An almost intact Roman well, the first complete Roman structure to be unearthed in the town, was discovered in 2003 by Worcester archaeologist Mike Napthan on the site of some Victorian stables. Such was its state of preservation that it initially appeared to be medieval, but debris found inside the well dated it to the time of the Roman occupation. Much of the material showed signs of burning, suggesting perhaps that Roman Worcester came to a sudden and dramatic end. Further archaeological investigation is being carried out prior to the building of a new library and history centre on the site.

Chateau Impney 1$^1/_4$ miles (2km) northeast of Droitwich Spa. A 19th century house in the style of a Louis XIII French chateau set in 155 acres (62.5ha) of parkland. It was built in 1875 for industrialist John Corbett, who made his fortune from salt production. Corbett's wife, Hannah Eliza O'Meara, was of mixed French/Irish descent; he built the house to satisfy her nostalgia for Paris. Ironically, she never lived here, preferring one of Corbett's properties in Towyn, North Wales. Ralph Edwards purchased the house in 1945 and restored and developed it as a hotel. Tel: 01905 774411.

Church of the Sacred Heart and St Catherine of Alexandria Worcester Road, Droitwich Spa. A Catholic church designed in the style of the basilicas at Ravenna in Italy by Frank Barry Peacock and built 1919–21. It is notable for its spectacular mosaics, designed by Gabriel Pippet and installed by Maurice Josey and Fred Oates. Tel: 01905 773258.

Churchill Forge Mill Churchill, 4 miles (6km) east of Kidderminster. A water-powered forge which until the early 1970s produced metal tools such as spades, shovels and ladles. The last surviving forge of its type in England, it has been restored and is now maintained and operated by the Churchill Forge Trust. Tel: 01562 700476.

Clent Hills 6 miles (10km) northeast of Kidderminster. A range of low hills close to Stourbridge and Halesowen (both in the West Midlands) and consisting of, in order from highest to lowest: Walton Hill, Clent Hill, Wychbury Hill, Calcot Hill, and Adams Hill. Walton Hill rises to 1037ft (316m) and offers views to the Malvern Hills, across Shropshire to The Wrekin and the Clee Hills and down the Severn valley. Once part of a Mercian forest, Clent appears in Domesday Book as Klinter, a name which may be derived from the Scandinavian word for a cliff, *klint*. There are the remains of a multivallate Iron Age fort on Wychbury Hill. Local historians have claimed that a battle between Britons and Romans was fought on Clent Heath. Several classically inspired architectural works from the late 1700s can be found on the hills, most of them in the private grounds of Hagley Hall. The Clent Hills are also well known for their role in the legend of St Kenelm, who was murdered on a hunting trip on the northeastern slopes of Clent Hill in AD 821. The Church of St Kenelm in the parish of Romsley marks the site of the murder. One source of the River Stour is within the grounds of the church. Clent Hill and Walton Hill are separated by a valley known as St Kenelm's Pass. On the other side of the valley is Romsley Hill, the valley banks of which are covered by Great Farley Wood. Beyond Romsley Hill are a number of lower hills (Windmill, Chapman's and Waseley) which join the Clent Hills to the Lickey Hills in a single continuous chain. The summits of the two largest hills, Clent Hill and Walton Hill, are now the property of the National Trust, which owns 437 acres (177ha) of woodland (both deciduous and coniferous) and heathland, important for wildlife including fallow deer and common buzzard, plus visiting ring ouzel and common crossbill.

Croome Park $^1/_2$ mile (0.8km) east of High Green, 7 miles (11km) southeast of Worcester. Capability Brown's first complete landcape garden, designed for the 6th Earl of Coventry in 1751 and establishing a style of garden design that was adopted universally over the next 50 years. Surrounding the

Palladian-style house of Croome Court, also designed by Brown with Robert Adam, the gardens include lakes, shrubberies, open parkland, bridges and a grotto, as well as numerous park buildings and other structures mostly by Adam and James Wyatt. Also in the grounds is the last surviving World War II RAF hospital in England. The property is owned by the National Trust, under whom the gardens have been restored since 1996. Tel: 01905 371006.

Droitwich Spa A town in northern Worcestershire on the River Salwarpe. Droitwich stands on huge salt deposits, the natural Droitwich brine containing $2^1/_2$ lb (1.1kg) of salt per gallon – ten times stronger than sea water and matched only by the Dead Sea! In the 19th century, Droitwich became famous as a spa town. Unlike other such towns, the medicinal benefits were not derived from drinking the spa water, but from the muscular relief derived by swimming and floating in the concentrated salt solution. The town's original brine baths, first opened in 1830, have long since closed, but a new brine bath (part of Droitwich Spa private hospital) is open to the public for relaxation and hydrotherapy. The salt industry was developed in the 19th century by John Corbett, who built nearby Chateau Impney (see separate entry).

Droitwich Spa Lido Worcester Road, Droitwich Spa. The Art Deco style lido, a large open-air swimming pool filled with diluted brine from beneath the town, was opened in 1935. The salt in the water was strong enough to keep the pool clean without the need for chemicals such as chlorine. When the lido opened, it was marketed as the 'seaside come to Droitwich Spa', and the unusually large pool, 132ft (40m) by 66ft (20m), was heated to the same temperature as the Mediterranean Sea. During World War II it was closed and the offices used by the military. Having been reopened after the war, it was closed again in the late 1990s but public pressure ensured its reopening in 2007.

Droitwich Transmitting Station $^1/_4$ mile (0.4km) north of Wychbold, 3 miles (5km) northeast of Droitwich Spa. A large BBC long and medium wave transmitter established in 1934. The transmission frequency was 200 kHz until 1989 and is now 198 kHz. The Radio 4 long wave from Droitwich is by far the strongest in the UK, covering most of England and Wales, although with supplementary medium-wave transmitters in London, Scotland, Wales and Northern Ireland. The BBC had wanted to drop Radio 4 on long wave, but was forced to rethink after widespread criticism from listeners. Radio 4 LW transmits the *Daily Service* at 9.45am and *Test Match Special* in the summer. The station is owned and operated by National Grid Wireless.

Elgar Birthplace Museum Crown East Lane, Lower Broadheath, Worcester. Dedicated to the life and music, development and inspirations, family and friends of Sir Edward Elgar, one of England's great composers, whose works include the *Pomp and Circumstance* marches, *Salut d'Amour,* 'Nimrod' and the other *Enigma Variations.* The country cottage where Elgar was born on 2 June 1857 is set in the heart of the Worcestershire countryside, with views towards the Malvern Hills. Following her father's wishes, Elgar's daughter Carice set up a museum here after his death in 1934. Exhibits include Elgar's desk, laid out as it was when he was composing, his music scores and manuscripts, concert programmes, letters, photographs, books and his gramophone. The £20 note issued 1999–2007 bears a portrait of Elgar on its reverse. Tel: 01905 333224.

Fleece Inn, The Bretforton, 4 miles (6km) east of Evesham. A half-timbered building over 600 years old. It has been a pub since 1848 and is now owned by the National Trust. The inn was extensively damaged by fire on 27 February 2004 but reopened, with a new roof and improved facilities, on 18 June 2005. Now run as a museum, the Pewter Room is particularly noteworthy and houses a world famous collection of pewter reputedly abandoned by Oliver Cromwell. Tel: 01386 831173.

Forge Mill Needle Museum Needle Mill Lane, Riverside, Redditch. A historic museum celebrating Redditch's industrial heritage as the world centre for the manufacture of needles in the Victorian era. Opened in 1983 by Queen Elizabeth II. Tel: 01905 763888.

Great Malvern Priory Church Street, Great Malvern. The parish church of St Mary and St Michael was once the church of the Benedictine priory of St Mary, founded c.1085 after Wulfstan, Bishop of Worcester, encouraged a hermit named Aldwyn to found a monastery in what was then the wilderness of Malvern Chase. The priory was built for 30 monks on land belonging to Westminster Abbey. After its dissolution, the locals bought the building for £20 in 1541 to replace their decaying parish church. The building is a combination of Norman and Perpendicular Gothic architecture with 15th century English stained glass, medieval floor and wall tiles, and some unusual carvings. Tel: 01684 561020.

Greyfriars, The Friar Street, Worcester. A timber-framed merchant's house built in 1480 and rescued from demolition in the 1930s. The textiles and furnishings on display in the panelled interior include a restored 17th century Mortlake tapestry. An archway leads to a walled garden. Now owned by the National Trust. Tel: 01905 23571.

Hagley Hall Hagley, 6 miles (10km) northeast of Kidderminster. Located on the edge of the Clent Hills, the Palladian style house was designed by Sanderson Miller and built 1756–60 for George Lyttelton, 1st Baron Lyttelton (1709–73), secretary to Frederick, Prince of Wales, poet and man of letters and briefly Chancellor of the Exchequer. The park landscape was created 1747–58 – before his father's death in 1751, Lyttelton had begun to landscape the grounds in the new 'picturesque' style – and contains various follies and monuments including Wychbury Obelisk on Wychbury Hill, built in 1758 and visible for many miles, a Temple of Theseus, other small Greek and Roman temples, a full-size ruined castle, and the 'Four Stones' on the summit of Clent Hill. These were designed by Lord Camelford, Thomas Pitt of Encombe, Henry Keene, James 'Athenian' Stuart, and Sanderson Miller. The house contains fine rococo plasterwork by Francesco Vassali, a unique collection of 18th century Chippendale furniture and family portraits, including works by Van Dyck, Reynolds and Lely. It is set in 350 acres (140ha) of landscaped deer park. Today the hall is the family home of Lady Cobham (née Lucy Clayton), widow of the the late Viscount Cobham and the first British woman to sail single-handed and non-stop around the world. Tel: 01562 882408.

Hanbury Hall — 1¼ miles (2km) west of Hanbury, 3 miles (5km) east of Droitwich Spa. A William and Mary style country house built by William Rudhall in 1701 for wealthy lawyer Thomas Vernon. On the staircase and in the dining room are murals by renowned history painter Sir James Thornhill. A tercentenary exhibition in the long gallery is dedicated to the house's architectural and social history. The grounds contain an orangery, ice house, pavilion and a restored 18th century formal garden, and are surrounded by nearly 400 acres (160ha) of parkland. Now owned by the National Trust. Tel: 01527 821214.

Hanley Castle — Hanley Castle, 4 miles (6km) southeast of Great Malvern. Built by King John in the early 13th century, the castle at Hanley stood to the south of the village in the southeast corner of the parish, about ½ mile (0.8km) from the right bank of the Severn. Mere Brook, which drains the southern part of the parish, once provided the water for the castle moat. King John stayed here in July 1209 and November 1213. In 1211–12 assizes were held at the castle. It was given by Henry III to Gilbert de Clare and was later surrendered by Hugh le Despenser to Edward II. During the rebellion against the Despensers the castle was attacked and damaged. The castle and manor were surrendered to the Crown in 1487 and the castle fell into decay in the early 16th century. W S Symonds wrote a historical romance entitled *Hanley Castle* in 1885.

Hartlebury Castle — Hartlebury, 3 miles (5km) south of Kidderminster. The manor of Hartlebury belonged to the bishops of Worcester from before the Norman Conquest; the castle was built in the mid 13th century as a fortified manor house and the bishops' principal residence. The walls were demolished after the castle was besieged during the Civil War. It is still the residence of the Bishop of Worcester, although two-thirds of the Grade I listed building is leased out to Worcestershire County Council as the County Museum. Tel: 01299 251890.

Harvington Hall — Harvington, 3 miles (5km) southeast of Kidderminster. A medieval and Elizabethan moated manor house originally built in the 14th century and enlarged in the 1580s by recusant Catholic Humphrey Pakington. There are still seven priest holes in existence in the hall, including four built by Nicholas Owen, the master of the craft. A range of rare Elizabethan wall paintings can also be seen. The property contains four chapels (two in the hall and two in the grounds), three of which are still used for services. A small herb garden, planted and managed by the Hereford and Worcester Gardens Trust, is laid out with the initials of the three families who lived in the hall: the Pakingtons, the Yates and the Throckmortons. Tel: 01562 777846.

Hawford Dovecote — Hawford, 3 miles (5km) north of Worcester. A square half-timbered dovecote dating from the 16th century, the remnant of a former monastic grange. Now owned by the National Trust. Tel: 01743 708100.

Hewell Grange — Tardebigge, 3 miles (5km) northwest of Redditch. The current Jacobean style building was completed in 1894 for Lord Windsor, 1st Earl of Plymouth. The land was originally part of the estate of Bordesley Abbey, and was given to Thomas Windsor Hickman after the abbey's dissolution. The estate remained a seat of the Windsor family until it was sold to the state in the 20th century. Several ruins dotted about the estate suggest that the Windsors built a succession of grand houses over the 400 years in which they owned the property. The Grade II listed house (the gardens are also listed) was used 1946–91 as a Borstal, after which it became HMP Hewell Grange. Tel: 01527 552000. See also Prisons

Highest point — Worcestershire Beacon (see separate entry) at 1395ft (425m), also the highest point of the Malvern Hills. GR: SO768452.

Huntingdon Hall — Crown Gate, Worcester. Today Worcestershire's premier live music venue, the Countess of Huntingdon's Hall was built as a chapel in 1773 by Selina, Countess of Huntingdon, founder of the Calvinist/Methodist group known as the Countess of Huntingdon's Connexion. The chapel prospered until the second half of the 20th century when congregations declined. The last service was held here in 1976. Tel: 01905 611427.

Interesting facts — Mention the word **Shambles** and the historic street in York will probably spring to mind, but Worcester has a street of the same name with the same historical background – a place where butchers slaughtered and sold their meat. Unlike the more famous York street which has kept most of its medieval mystery, the Worcester street has been widened and modernised into the kind of pedestrianised high street seen in many old towns. ***Berrow's Worcester Journal*** lays claim to being the oldest newspaper in the world. Launched in 1690 as the *Worcester Postman*, it was published regularly from 1709 under its new name. The *Daily Courant*, first published in 1702, is often cited as the first regular daily newspaper as the *Postman* was at first produced only occasionally. The **Honeybee Inn,** Doverdale, Droitwich Spa, is Britain's only honey farm pub. Honey is produced on the premises, as it has been for at least 900 years. A plethora of honey-making memorabilia from centuries past adorns this huge and delightfully appointed pub. Honeycomb ale is always available, in addition to a menu offering dishes made with all types of honey. **Lisa Lyttelton, Dowager Viscountess Cobham** (born in Lisa Clayton in 1958), is the first British woman to sail single-handed and non-stop around the world. On 17 September 1994, Lisa set out in her 38ft foot yacht, the *Spirit of Birmingham*, returning on 29 June 1995 after 285 days at sea. Lisa survived the 31,000 mile journey despite capsizing seven times. She married the 11th Viscount Cobham, the owner of Hagley Hall in Worcestershire, on 1 August 1997. He died in 2006. **Geoffrey W A Dummer** (1909–2002) was a radar engineer working at the Telecommunications Research Establishment in Malvern in the 1940s. His work with colleagues at the Ministry of Defence research establishment led him to the belief that it would be possible to fabricate multiple circuit elements on and into a substance like silicon. In 1952 he presented his work at a conference in Washington DC, six years before Jack Kilby of Texas Instruments was awarded a patent for essentially the same idea. Unfortunately Dummer's work could find little funding in Britain and the plug was pulled on his ideas in 1957. So, although the invention of the microchip is usually credited either to Kilby (who received the Nobel Prize for Physics in 2000 for his invention of the integrated circuit) or to Bob Noyce, a Californian scientist who came up with the idea at about the same time as Kilby, in fact the first person to conceptualise the integrated circuit was Geoffrey Dummer MBE. Worcestershire and England cricketer and footballer **Reginald Erskine 'Tip' Foster** (born 16 April 1878 in Malvern, died 13 May 1914 in London) was the only man to captain England at both sports. Educated at Malvern College and Oxford University, he had six other brothers, Basil, Henry, Maurice, Neville, Geoffrey and Wilfrid, all of whom also played cricket for Worcestershire. The remarkable Tip Foster also holds the world record for the highest score on Test debut, 287 for England v. Australia in 1903–04. **Hannah Snell** was born at 25 Friar Street, Worcester, on St George's Day, 23 April 1723. In 1743 she married a Dutch seaman, James Summs, who soon disappeared when he found she was pregnant. After the birth and subsequent death of their child, she determined to track him down. Borrowing a suit of clothes from her brother-in-law, she travelled first to London and then to Coventry where she was pressed, under her husband's name, into General Guise's Regiment of Foot. The Scottish Rising was in full swing. Incognito, Hannah marched with her regiment to Carlisle where she incurred the wrath of her sergeant and was ordered to receive 600 lashes, an excessively harsh sentence even at the time for one considered a mere boy. She received 500 and miraculously still managed to conceal her sex. Hannah next journeyed south to Portsmouth, where she enlisted in Fraser's Regiment of Marines, presumably hoping to travel abroad where she assumed her seafaring husband would be. Hannah was appointed assistant-steward and cook to the officers' mess on the sloop *Swallow*, and sailed to the East Indies on attachment to Admiral Boscawen's fleet. In August 1748 her unit was sent on an expedition to capture the French colony of Pondicherry in India. Later she fought also in the battle in Devicotta in June 1749. She was wounded 11 times to the legs and once to the groin. She either managed to treat her groin wound without revealing her sex or she may have used the services of a sympathetic Indian nurse. She served as an ordinary seaman on two ships, gaining the nickname of 'Molly' because of the smoothness of her face. While in Lisbon, Hannah finally heard news of her husband, but, unfortunately, it transpired that he had been executed in Genoa. Her efforts to find him having proved in vain, when the man-o'-war *Eltham* paid off at Gravesend in 1750, Hannah finished with her tour of duty, and with her disguise. She revealed her sex to her shipmates on 2 June and also sold her story to London publisher Robert Walker, who published her account, *The Female Soldier*, in two different editions. Hannah became a celebrity and performed an act on stage as a soldier singing military ballads – dressed as a man of course. She remarried twice and lived a happy life, but unfortunately premature senility set in and she died at Bedlam Hospital on 8 February 1792. The village of **Pinvin**, a few miles to the north of Pershore, whose name is thought to come from Old English 'Penda's fen' after the Mercian king Penda, was the location of the 1973 TV play *Penda's Fen* by David Rudkin. There are two hamlets called **Nineveh** in England, and both are in the north of Worcestershire. The more northerly is 1$^1/_4$ miles (2km) southeast of Cleobury Mortimer, less than a mile from the River Rea; the other is 2 miles (3km) southeast of Tenbury Wells. A woman's body was discovered inside a wych elm tree in a wood on Wychbury Hill on the Hagley Hall estate during World War II. The victim was never identified, but the find gave rise to a notorious piece of 1940s graffiti, **'Who put Bella in the wych elm?'**, more recently the title of a play and a musical, and of an album by Coventry band The Pristines.

Islands
Bevere Island (see separate entry) is connected to the mainland via a bridge. There are also three unnamed tiny islets in the three lakes of the Hawford Bridge Fishery.

Kidderminster
A town on the River Stour long associated with the carpet industry. William Brinton began manufacturing textiles in nearby Chaddesley in 1783 and the first Brintons factory in Kidderminster opened in 1820. The industry soon became extremely important to the local economy – the local newspaper is still named the *Kidderminster Shuttle* after the shuttles used on the carpet looms. Although it has declined in recent years, the industry is still a significant employer in the area and Brintons is still the town's biggest employer. Kidderminster has also been the home since 1900 of Victoria Carpets plc, manufacturers of high quality carpets. The town centre has undergone substantial redevelopment in recent years, with the development of Weaver's Wharf as a commercial retail area including Grade II listed Slingfield Mill, which has been converted into a retail outlet. The Staffordshire & Worcestershire Canal flows through Kidderminster town centre. See also Wyre Forest

King Charles I School
Comberton Road, Kidderminster. A voluntary-controlled state school given its charter in 1636 by Charles I and the only school in England to bear his name, although the foundation was established 70 years earlier by Thomas Blount, lord of the manor of Kidderminster. The original premises, Woodfield House (a Georgian house built in 1785) and the Hall (built c.1848) are now listed buildings. The present school was formed in 1977 by the amalgamation of King Charles I School and Kidderminster High School for Girls (founded in 1868) with Queen Elizabeth I Grammar School, Hartlebury; the school's site was the home of the High School for Girls from 1912. Tel: 01562 512880.

King's School, Worcester
College Green, Worcester. An independent school founded by Henry VIII in 1541. It occupies a site by Worcester Cathedral and the River Severn. King's Worcester is made up of three different schools, King's Hawford (ages 2–11), King's St Albans (ages 7–11) and King's Worcester (ages 11–18). Girls were first admitted to the sixth form in 1971 and the school became fully coeducational in 1991. Boarding ceased from September 1999. Former pupils include actor Rik Mayall, racing driver Derek Bell, broadcaster Chris Tarrant, Stephen Cleobury, Director of Music at King's College, Cambridge, and world champion rower Zac Purchase.

Kingsford Forest Park	1 mile (1.6km) west of Kingsford, 3 miles (5km) north of Kidderminster. A area of woodland and heathland on the Worcestershire/Staffordshire border to the south of Kinver Edge (see Staffordshire) punctuated by outcrops of red sandstone. The park is home to a variety of wildlife, particularly birds. Tel: 01562 710025.
Kinver Edge	See Staffordshire
Leigh Court Barn	Leigh, 4½ miles (7km) west of Worcester. The largest cruck-framed structure in the UK, built in 1344 for Pershore Abbey. Managed by English Heritage. Tel: 0121 625 6820.
Lickey Grange	Lickey, 4 miles (6km) northeast of Bromsgrove. A Victorian house and estate once owned by renowned automobile designer Herbert Austin (1866–1941), founder of the Austin motor company, who lived here for 31 years. Austin is buried in the graveyard of Lickey Church. After its sale the 100 acre (40ha) estate became a residential school for the blind, and was recently redeveloped for private housing.
Lickey Hills	4 miles (6km) northeast of Bromsgrove. A range of low hills situated on the Worcestershire/West Midlands border, covering an area of 524 acres (222ha). The hills are covered by a mosaic of mixed deciduous woodland, conifer plantations and heathland, and are rich in a variety of wildlife. Part of them form the Lickey Hills Country Park of 525 acres (200ha) belonging to Birmingham City Council and a golf club. The land was given to the City of Birmingham in the 19th century by the Cadbury family, though the hills fall outside the city boundary. The three hilltops geographically comprising the Lickeys – Rednal Hill, Bilberry Hill and Cofton Hill – are the summits of the Lickey Ridge, a formation of hard quartzite. In the hills is an obelisk commemorating the 6th Earl of Plymouth (d.1833), erected to acknowledge his work in forming the volunteer regiment of cavalry known as the Worcestershire Yeomanry. Tel: 0121 447 7106.
Little Malvern Court	Little Malvern, 4 miles (6km) south of Great Malvern. The former prior's hall of Little Malvern Priory. The 15th century house, with oak-framed roof, contains collections of 18th and 19th century needlework and religious vestments and has been home to the Berington family by descent since the Dissolution of the Monasteries. The house is surrounded by 10 acres (4ha) of former monastic grounds, landscaped in the early 1980s with a wide variety of spring bulbs, old-fashioned roses, shrubs and trees. Tel: 01684 892988.
Little Malvern Priory	Little Malvern, 4 miles (6km) south of Great Malvern. A Benedictine monastery founded c.1171 and dissolved in 1537. Little remains of the 12th century St Giles' church, which was rebuilt 1480–82; the building now comprises a medieval chancel and crossing tower, with a modern west porch on the site of the east bays of the nave. The transepts and the two chapels flanking the choir are in ruins. The prior's hall is now Little Malvern Court.
Madresfield Court	Madresfield, 1½ miles (2.5km) east of Great Malvern. The ancestral home of the Lygon family, the house was built in 1593 to replace a 15th century building and was remodelled in the 1800s in Elizabethan revival style with a moat and enlarged to about 100 rooms, as well as an Arts and Crafts style chapel designed by Philip Charles Chadwick. Evelyn Waugh was a frequent guest and was said to have modelled the Flyte family in his novel *Brideshead Revisited* after the Lygons. Madresfield Court is also the name of a variety of apple, first cultivated at the house.
Malvern Hills	See Herefordshire
Malvern Museum	Abbey Road, Great Malvern. Located in the gatehouse, dating to c.1480, of the town's former Benedictine priory, the museum has exhibits relating to local geology, medieval Malvern, the use of Malvern water as a health cure, composer Edward Elgar, the Morgan and Santler car manufacturers and the development of radar. Tel: 01684 567811.
Mamble	7½ miles (12km) west of Stourport-on-Severn. Notable buildings include the 13th century sandstone church of St John the Baptist and the 17th century Sun and Slipper Inn. Roman remains have been found in the area, and at the time of the Domesday Book the settlement was known as Mamele. Although agriculture was always a major industry for the inhabitants of Mamble, coal mining was also important from the 14th century onwards, and the last local pit, at Hunthouse to the southeast of the village, closed only in 1972. In the 1790s the Leominster Canal was opened in the area, allowing coal to be carried to Tenbury Wells and Herefordshire, but the coming of the railways made the canal unprofitable and it was closed in 1859. Poet John Drinkwater wrote a poem about the village, called simply 'Mamble'.
Middle Littleton Tithe Barn	Middle Littleton, 4 miles (6km) northeast of Evesham. A Grade I listed tithe barn thought to have been built in 1376 by Abbot John Ombersley of Evesham, although radiocarbon dating has given a construction date of 1250. One of the largest such structures in England, 138ft (42m) long and 32ft (10m) wide, and built of blue lias limestone, it has a double tie-beam truss supporting its interior roofing construction – a rare feature for a tithe barn. Owned by the National Trust. Tel: 01905 371006.
Monarch's Way	A 615 mile (990km) long-distance footpath that approximates the escape route taken by Charles II in 1651 after his defeat at the Battle of Worcester. Starting at Worcester, it runs north to Boscobel in Staffordshire and then south to Stratford-upon-Avon in Warwickshire, making its way through Gloucestershire to Bristol. It passes through Somerset and Dorset to Charmouth, and then roughly east through Wiltshire and Hampshire before terminating at Shoreham-by-Sea in West Sussex.
Pershore Abbey	Church Street, Pershore. The abbey was founded in the 7th century by St Oswald, Bishop of Worcester, and came under the Benedictine rule in the late 10th century. It was originally dedicated to St Mary the Virgin, St Peter and St Paul, and later to St Mary and St Eadburga. The abbey was dissolved in 1539 and its church, which still contains parts of the 12th century Norman abbey church, became Pershore's parish church. Tel: 01386 552071.
Prisons	**Hewell Grange** was opened in 1946 as a Borstal and held young offenders until 1991. It is now a Category D open prison catering for non-violent adult male prisoners. The former Hewell Grange

estate (see separate entry) also contains Brockhill Young Offenders and Remand Institution with about 150 places, and Blakenhurst Prison with about 1000 places for Category B inmates (e.g. violent crimes, sexual offences). Tel: 01527 552000.

Long Lartin, South Littleton, 3 miles (5km east) of Evesham, opened as a Category C prison in 1971. Operational capacity: 458. Tel: 01386 835100.

Rivers

Arrow, **Avon** see Warwickshire

The **Piddle Brook** is a tributary of the River Avon. Two villages, North Piddle and Wyre Piddle, lie along its course before it joins the Avon near Pershore. A small brewery 1 mile (1.6km) away named itself after the nearby brook, its sole product being Piddle Beer.

The **Salwarpe** rises near Bromsgrove. It passes Stoke Prior, Upton Warren, Wychbold, Droitwich (where the Droitwich Canal starts to run alongside it). After Droitwich, it meets the River Severn, near Hawford.

Severn see Powys

The **Stour**, a tributary of the River Severn, rises in the north of Worcestershire in the Clent Hills, near St Kenelm's Church. It flows north into the adjacent West Midlands at Halesowen, and then west through Cradley Heath and Stourbridge. It is joined by the Smeslow Brook at Prestwood before winding southwards to Kinver and flowing back into Worcestershire. It then passes through Wolverley, Kidderminster and Wilden to join the River Severn at Stourport. The Staffordshire and Worcestershire Canal runs beside the Stour as far as Prestwood and then follows the Smestow Brook. Its length is 25 miles (40km).

Teme see Shropshire

Rosedene

Victoria Road, Dodford, $1\frac{1}{2}$ miles (2.5km) northwest of Bromsgrove. A cottage first occupied in 1849 and built as part of the Chartist Land Plan, which aimed to resettle former industrial workers on the land. Largely unaltered, it shows the conditions in which early participants in the scheme lived. Period features include a dairy, working range, water pump and earth closet. The vegetable garden and orchard have been recently restored. Owned by the National Trust. Tel: 01527 821214.

Royal Worcester

Severn Street, Worcester. A fine China and porcelain manufacturer founded in Worcester in 1751. The factory was established beside the River Severn by a group of local businessmen, with the guidance of physician Dr John Wall. The Worcester factory received a royal warrant in 1789, and still manufactures by appointment to Queen Elizabeth II. Its museum houses the world's largest collection of Worcester porcelain with collections dating back to 1751. Tel: 01905 746000.

Severn End

$\frac{1}{2}$ mile (0.8km) northeast of Hanley Castle, 3 miles (5km) southeast of Great Malvern. A timber-framed house situated on a slight elevation close to the western bank of the Severn, originally built by Richard Lechmere in the late 15th century and altered in the 16th century. Considerable additions were made 1656–73 by Sir Nicholas Lechmere, who also began the gardens and landscape park, with features including a garden pavilion, pigeon house, malt house, formal parterres and tree-lined avenues. The building was almost completely destroyed by fire in 1896, but was rebuilt in the following year, nearly all the original features being reproduced. While retaining all the atmosphere of an Elizabethan and Jacobean mansion, the house is therefore largely a modern structure.

Severn Valley Railway

See Shropshire

St Michael's Church

Abberley, $4\frac{1}{2}$ miles (7km) southwest of Stourport-on-Severn. A 12th century Norman church, the walls and roof of which collapsed in the 19th century under the weight of a spire added in the 1300s. The walls of the tower and nave still stand 4ft (1.2m) high; the 12th century chancel and south chapel, dating to c.1260, were repaired in 1908 and are still used for services. Tel: 01299 896392.

Sport

cricket

Worcestershire County Cricket Club was formed on 4 March 1865 at the Star Hotel in Worcester and entered the County Championship in 1899. Its limited overs team is Worcestershire Royals, although unofficially the county is known by some fans as 'the Pears'. Worcestershire first won the County Championship in 1964, repeating the success the following year. Famous players include Basil D'Oliveira, who made his debut for the county in 1964, and Graeme Hick, scorer of 136 first-class centuries. The club's home ground since 1899 has been New Road, Worcester, owned until 1976 by the Dean and Chapter of Worcester Cathedral. The ground is often flooded in winter by the nearby River Severn; severe flooding in June 2007 forced the club to complete its programme at a variety of grounds including Kidderminster. See also Interesting Facts. Tel: 01905 748474.

football

Kidderminster Harriers were formed in 1886 from an athletics and rugby union club. Having won the Vauxhall Conference in 1994, the club were controversially refused promotion to the Football League due to safety regulations for stadiums imposed after the Bradford City fire disaster. The club finally reached the Football League in 2000 but were relegated to the Nationwide Conference after five seasons. Their home ground is Aggborough Stadium, Kidderminster. The ground was the first in England to host a floodlit FA Cup match, when on 14 September 1955 Harriers played Brierley Hill Alliance in a preliminary round replay, which Harriers won 4–2.

horse racing

Worcester Racecourse, Pitchcroft, Worcester, is a left-handed circuit of 1 mile 5 furlongs (2.8km) holding exclusively National Hunt racing. Tel: 01905 25364.

Staffordshire & Worcestershire Canal

The canal runs for 46 miles (74km) through Worcestershire and Staffordshire from the River Severn at Stourport to the Trent & Mersey Canal at Great Haywood. Built 1766–71 and opened in 1772, it was engineered by James Brindley as part of his Grand Cross plan for waterways connecting Hull, Liverpool and Bristol. In 1959 the canal was due to be closed, but it was saved through the efforts of the Staffordshire and Worcestershire Canal Society. The canal forms part of the Stourport Ring, a popular leisure cruising circuit.

Tardebigge Locks $2^{1}/_{2}$ miles (4km) southeast of Bromsgrove. The longest flight of canal locks in the UK, the flight of 30 locks raise the Birmingham and Worcester Canal 220ft (67m) over the Lickey Ridge.

Tenbury Museum Cross Street, Tenbury Wells. Housed in the former Goff's Free School, the museum holds a collection of items relating to local and social history, including copies of the *Tenbury Advertiser* newspaper dating back to 1871. Tel: 01299 832143.

Three Choirs Festival See Herefordshire

Transport Museum, The Chapel Lane, Wythall, 5 miles (8km) north of Redditch. Run by the Birmingham and Midland Motor Omnibus Trust, the museum has two halls displaying a collection of preserved buses, coaches and other commercial vehicles. Exhibits include buses operated by the Midland Red company and Birmingham City Transport vehicles, as well as a notable collection of battery-powered electric vehicles such as milk floats. Tel: 01564 826471.

Tudor House Friar Street, Worcester. A timber-framed building built c.1550 by a wealthy Worcester citizen on 13th century foundations opposite the town's Franciscan friary. For many years the building was divided into separate dwellings and was a home and workshop for weavers, cloth makers, tailors, a baker and a painter. For almost 200 years part of the building was used as a brewing house and an inn. In the early 20th century it was bought by the Cadbury family and became a confectioner's and tea room, and was known as the Tudor Coffee House. In 1921 it was purchased by Worcester Corporation for use as a school clinic. During World War II, the building was used as an Air Raid Warden's Post and Billeting Office. Tudor House was opened as a branch of Worcester City Museums in 1971 and until 2003 was home to the Museum of Local Life. Today, it houses a heritage centre with exhibits on Tudor life as well as Worcester's industrial and commercial heritage.

University of Worcester Formerly known as University College Worcester, and before that as Worcester College of Higher Education, the University of Worcester was awarded university status in September 2005. With traditional strengths in education, nursing, sports science and health it is the only university in Herefordshire and Worcestershire, and one of the smallest in England with around 8000 students. In 2005 the institution announced plans for a 'superlibrary' in the heart of Worcester, creating a combined university and public library – the first of its kind in the UK. It is currenly based at the St John's campus; construction of a second campus on the site of the old Worcester Royal Infirmary in Castle Street began in 2007. Tel: 01905 855141.

Walker Hall Market Square, Evesham. A 16th century timber-framed building with adjoining Norman gateway. In the late 19th century the floor was removed and it became an open hall. In 1999 it was repaired and refitted to form offices and a retail unit. Tel: 01386 446623.

West Midland Safari and Leisure Park 2 miles (3km) west of Kidderminster. Opened in 1973 in the grounds of Spring Grove House, landscaped by Capability Brown in the 1780s and currently being restored to their 18th century splendour. The park's many species of animals include the only four white lions in the UK and the largest herd of hippopotamus in Europe, as well as leopard and Cape buffalo, all housed in a series of reserves. The house itself was built in 1775 for industrialist Samuel Skey, and is undergoing restoration after a major fire in 2006. The Severn Valley Railway runs parallel to the park at one point between the stations of Kidderminster and Bewdley. Tel: 01299 402114.

Wichenford Dovecote Wichenford, 5 miles (8km) northwest of Worcester. A 17th century half-timbered black-and-white dovecote in a scenic riverside location. Now owned by the National Trust. Tel: 01743 708100.

Witley Court 1 mile (1.6km) southeast of Great Witley, 8 miles (13km) northwest of Worcester. Formerly one of the great houses of the Midlands, today Witley Court stands as a ruin. The original Jacobean manor house was extended by Thomas Foley in 1655 on the site of a former manor house. Two large porticoes designed by John Nash were added by the 3rd Lord Foley in the early 1800s, and in 1846 the house was remodelled in Italianiate style for industrialist William Humble Ward, later 1st Earl of Dudley. The existing landscape garden was redesigned by William Nesfield in the 1850s with formal parterres and spectacular fountains. In 1735 the 1st Lord Foley constructed a new parish church to the west of the courtyard; this church was given a remarkable baroque interior in 1747 when James Gibbs was commissioned to incorporate paintings and furnishings acquired at the auction of the contents of Cannons House, the Middlesex home of the Duke of Chandos. The church still remains in impressive condition. Following a disastrous fire in 1937 the Witley estate, including its gardens, fell into decline. Since its acquisition of the site in 1984 English Heritage has carried out restoration of the west wing of the house and has also restored the south garden. Restoration of William Nesfield's east parterre is also under way. Tel: 01299 896636.

Wood Norton 2 miles (3km) northwest of Evesham. Set in its own grounds, Wood Norton Hall looks over the Vale of Evesham to the nearby Cotswold Hills. The Victorian house was the last home in England of the Duc d'Orléans, claimant to the throne of France. It later became a private school until, with war impending, the BBC bought the site in April 1939 in order to establish a base outside major urban centres. Temporary buildings were erected in the grounds to provide an emergency broadcasting centre. A dozen studios were built, and by 1940 Wood Norton was one of the largest broadcasting centres in Europe with an average output of 1300 programmes a week. After World War II Wood Norton became the BBC's engineering training centre. Purpose-built facilities in the grounds are still used for technical training. The Grade II listed house is now a hotel. Tel: 01386 425780.

Worcester Castle Severn Street, Worcester. Norman motte and bailey castle founded c.1069 by Urse d'Abitot. Burned down in 1113, it was rebuilt in stone in the 12th century and besieged, though not captured, by King Stephen. In use as a prison by 1263, it eventually fell into ruin. The motte was levelled in 1830 and the King's School now occupies the site.

Worcester Cathedral College Yard, Worcester. Situated above the eastern bank of the River Severn, the Cathedral Church of Christ and the Blessed Virgin Mary was established in 680 with Bosel, a monk from

Whitby, as its bishop. A Benedictine foundation with an abbey church was established by Oswald in the 10th century. Nothing now remains of the earlier buildings on the site, but the existing cathedral was begun c.1084 by Bishop Wulfstan and the present crypt dates from this period. Building continued over the next 200 years and the tower was completed in 1374. After the priory's dissolution the church was re-established in 1540 as a cathedral of secular clergy. It underwent major restoration by Sir George Gilbert Scott and A E Perkins in the 1860s; both men are buried at the cathedral. Monuments in the cathedral include the tomb of King John, located in the chancel, and Prince Arthur's Chantry, a memorial to the young prince Arthur Tudor, Henry VIII's elder brother, who is buried here; the cathedral was spared destruction during the Reformation thanks to the presence of the chantry. An image of the cathedral's west face is featured on the reverse of the 1999–2007 issue of the Bank of England £20 note, accompanying the portrait of composer Edward Elgar; the first performance of Elgar's *Enigma Variations* took place at the cathedral during the 1899 Three Choirs Festival. Tel: 01905 28854.

Worcester City Art Gallery and Museum Foregate Street, Worcester. Housed in a Victorian building, the museum's displays include a 20th century chemist's shop and the Worcestershire Soldier galleries, dedicated to the Worcestershire Regiment and the Worcestershire Yeomanry Cavalry. Tel: 01905 25371.

Worcester Guildhall High Street, Worcester. Begun in 1721, the Guildhall replaced an earlier building occupying the same site and was designed by local stonemason Thomas White, a pupil of Christopher Wren. The Queen Anne style building contained the administrative centre for Worcester as well as Worcestershire's civil and assize courts, and is still occupied by Worcestershire City Council. The Guildhall has an Italianate assembly room with an extensive collection of portraits. It is possible to visit the cells. Tel: 01905 723471.

Worcestershire Beacon A hill whose summit at 1395ft (425m) is the highest point of the Malvern Hills (see Herefordshire) on the Herefordshire/Worcestershire border, though Worcestershire Beacon itself lies entirely within Worcestershire. A viewfinder or toposcope on the summit was erected in 1897 to celebrate Queen Victoria's Diamond Jubilee. There are extensive views to The Wrekin, past Birmingham to Cannock Chase, over much of Herefordshire and Gloucestershire, the Welsh borders, the Shropshire Hills and across the valleys of the Severn and Avon to the Cotswolds. The hill was once used as a signalling beacon, a purpose it still fulfils on special occasions; on the millennium night of 31 December 1999 it became one of a national network of hilltop beacons when a large fire was lit for a public celebration.

Worcestershire County Museum Housed in Hartlebury Castle near Kidderminster (see separate entry), the museum narrates the history of the county through a collection of objects and photographs. There are collections of horse-drawn vehicles – including six gypsy caravans – costume and archaeology. Tel: 01299 250416.

Worcestershire Sauce Also known as Worcester sauce. A widely used fermented liquid condiment currently made with vinegar, molasses, corn syrup, water, chilli peppers, soy sauce, pepper, tamarinds, anchovies, onions, shallots, cloves, asafoetida and garlic. A flavouring used in many dishes, both cooked and uncooked, and particularly with beef, it is also an important ingredient in Caesar salad and in a Bloody Mary. John Wheeley Lea and William Henry Perrins, dispensing chemists from Broad Street, Worcester, first sold the sauce in 1838. Lea & Perrins also supplies it in concentrate form to be bottled abroad.

Wyre Forest A large semi-natural woodland on the Worcestershire/Shropshire border, one of the largest remaining ancient woodlands in Britain. The forest covers an area of 6509 acres (2634ha) and is noted for its variety of wildlife. The Dowles Brook flows through the heart of the forest, and the A456 road runs through its southern edge. Wildlife species include fallow deer, while birds include hawfinch, dipper, common crossbill, pied flycatcher and long-eared owl. A branch of the Severn Valley Railway known as the Tenbury Line once ran through the Wyre Forest. It left the main line north of Bewdley and crossed the River Severn at Dowles Bridge, the piers of which still remain. The main track survives in the form of a walking route through the forest. Although much of the ancient Wyre Forest no longer exists, it still extends from east of the A442 at Shatterford, north of Kidderminster in the east, almost to Cleobury Mortimer in the west and from Upper Arley in the north to Areley Kings, near Stourport in the south. The Forestry Commission looks after around half of today's forest. Around two-thirds has been designated as a Site of Special Scientific Interest, while a further fifth is listed as a National Nature Reserve. Wyre Forest is also a local government district, covering the towns of Kidderminster, Stourport-on-Severn and Bewdley and with a council based in Stourport-on-Severn. The district was formed under the Local Government Act 1972 as a merger of Bewdley and Kidderminster municipal boroughs, Stourport-on-Severn Urban District Council and Kidderminster Rural District Council. The district takes its name from the forest, despite the fact that much of the woodland lies outside the district's boundaries.

Some famous people born in Worcestershire

Baldwin, Stanley (politician) (1867–1947)	Bewdley
Ball, Michael (singer and actor) (1962–)	Bromsgrove
Baskerville, John (printer) (1706–75)	Wolverley
Bloomer, Steve (footballer) (1874–1938)	Cradley
Dance, Charles (actor) (1946–)	Redditch
Elgar, Edward (composer) (1857–1934)	Lower Broadheath
Fawcett, Ruth (author) (1961–)	Malvern
Foster, Harry (cricketer) (1873–1950)	Malvern
Foster, Reginald 'Tip' Erskine (cricketer and footballer) (1878–1914)	Malvern
Foster, Wilfred (cricketer) (1874–1958)	Malvern
Fowler, Henry (engineer) (1870–1938)	Evesham
Habington, William (poet) (1605–54)	Worcester
Hamer, Robert (film director) (1911–63)	Kidderminster
Housman, Alfred Edward 'A E' (poet) (1859–1936	Bromsgrove
Housman, Laurence (playwright) (1865–1959)	Bromsgrove
Jameson, Susan (actress) (1944–)	Barnt Green
Leader, Benjamin Williams (artist) (1833–1923)	Worcester
Little, Dorothy Round (tennis player) (1908–82)	Kidderminster
Mansell, Nigel (racing driver) (1953–)	Upton-on-Severn
Morgan, Peter (sports car manufacturer) (1919–2003)	Malvern
Nash, Walter (prime minister of New Zealand) (1882–1968)	Kidderminster
Norris, Tony (ornithologist) (1917–)	Cradley
Pennethorne, James (architect) (1801–71)	Worcester
Scott, Sheila (aviatrix) (1927–88)	Worcester
Snell, Hannah (soldier) (1723–92)	Worcester
Somervile, William (poet) (1675–1742)	Edstone
Stainforth, Martin (artist) (1866–1957)	Martley
Tilley, Vesta (male impersonator) (1864–1952)	Worcester
Weldon, Fay (novelist) (1931–)	Aldechurch
Wilding, Michael (author) (1942–)	Worcester
Williams, Mark (actor) (1959–)	Bromsgrove
Wood, Ellen (author) (1814–87)	Worcester
Yarranton, Andrew (engineer) (1619–1684)	Astley

YORKSHIRE

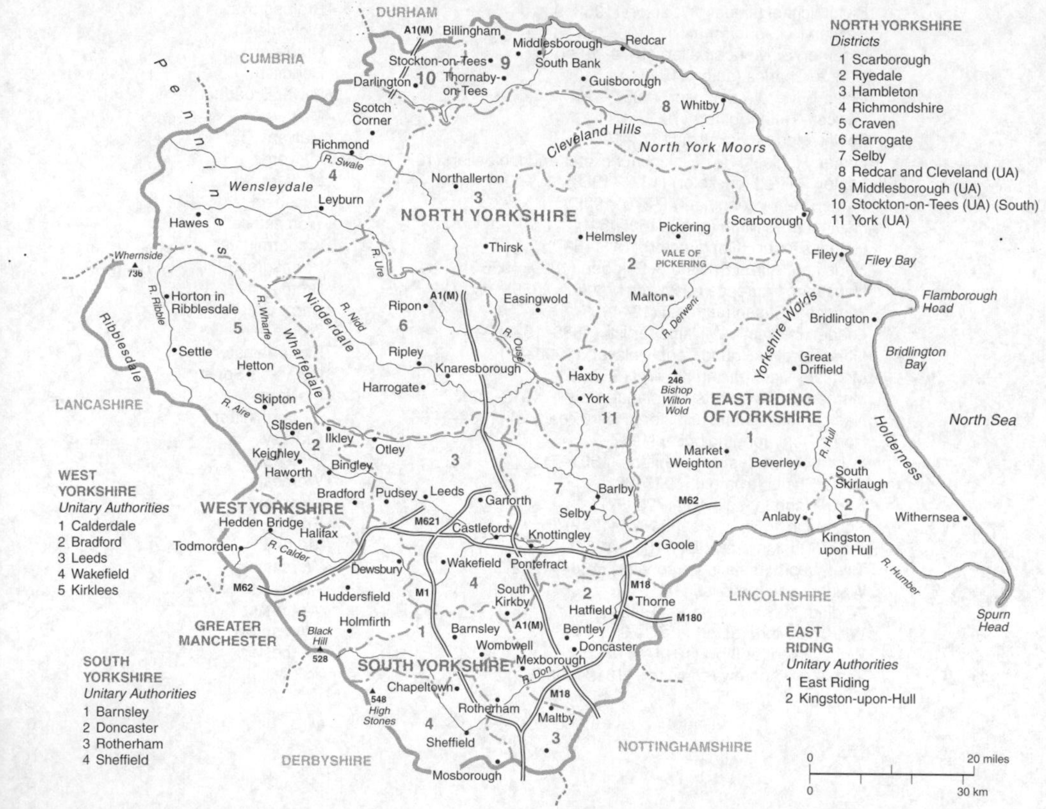
DURHAM
CUMBRIA
Pennines
A1(M)
Billingham
Middlesborough
Redcar
Stockton-on-Tees
9
South Bank
Darlington
10
Thornaby-on-Tees
Guisborough
Scotch Corner
8
Whitby
Cleveland Hills
North York Moors
Richmond
R. Swale
4
Wensleydale
Northallerton
3
Leyburn
NORTH YORKSHIRE
Hawes
Pickering
Scarborough
Helmsley
Thirsk
R. Ure
Whernside
736
VALE OF PICKERING
2
Filey
Filey Bay
A1(M)
Easingwold
Malton
Flamborough Head
Horton in Ribblesdale
R. Ribble
R. Wharfe
Nidderdale
R. Nidd
Ripon
R. Ouse
R. Derwent
Yorkshire Wolds
Bridlington
Ribblesdale
5
6
Settle
Wharfedale
Ripley
Great Driffield
Bridlington Bay
Hetton
Knaresborough
Haxby
246
Bishop Wilton Wold
Harrogate
York
EAST RIDING OF YORKSHIRE
LANCASHIRE
Skipton
11
R. Aire
Holderness
North Sea
Silsden
R. Hull
Ilkley
2
Otley
1
Keighley
Market Weighton
Beverley
WEST YORKSHIRE
Unitary Authorities
1 Calderdale
2 Bradford
3 Leeds
4 Wakefield
5 Kirklees
Haworth
Bingley
3
South Skirlaugh
Bradford
Pudsey
Leeds
7
Barlby
WEST YORKSHIRE
Garforth
M62
Selby
2
Anlaby
Withernsea
Hedden Bridge
Halifax
M621
Castleford
Knottingley
Goole
Kingston upon Hull
Todmorden
R. Calder
1
Dewsbury
Wakefield
Pontefract
R. Humber
M62
4
M1
South Kirkby
2
M18
Thorne
LINCOLNSHIRE
Huddersfield
Hatfield
M180
Spurn Head
GREATER MANCHESTER
5
Holmfirth
Black Hill
528
1
Barnsley
A1(M)
Bentley
EAST RIDING
Unitary Authorities
1 East Riding
2 Kingston-upon-Hull
Wombwell
Doncaster
SOUTH YORKSHIRE
Mexborough
R. Don
SOUTH YORKSHIRE
Unitary Authorities
1 Barnsley
2 Doncaster
3 Rotherham
4 Sheffield
Chapeltown
548
High Stones
M18
Rotherham
Maltby
4
Sheffield
3
NOTTINGHAMSHIRE
DERBYSHIRE
Mosborough
0
20 miles
0
30 km
NORTH YORKSHIRE
Districts
1 Scarborough
2 Ryedale
3 Hambleton
4 Richmondshire
5 Craven
6 Harrogate
7 Selby
8 Redcar and Cleveland (UA)
9 Middlesborough (UA)
10 Stockton-on-Tees (UA) (South)
11 York (UA)

Bordered by Durham to its north, Cumbria to its northwest, Lancashire to its west, Greater Manchester to its southwest and Derbyshire, Nottinghamshire and Lincolnshire to its south, the geographical county of Yorkshire is by far the largest in England, covering 5743 square miles (14,873 sq km) of vastly varying landscapes. There are two National Parks largely within its borders. The county is dotted with castles and fine country houses, as well as more major battlefield sites than any other English county. The businessmen who grew rich on the proceeds of the Industrial Revolution also left their mark, both with their country seats and the many impressive 19th century municipal buildings in the towns and cities.

The symbol of Yorkshire is the White Rose. Believed to have been first adopted in the 14th century by Edmund, 1st Duke of York, a son of Edward III, as a representation of the Virgin Mary, it was later taken up by his grandson, Richard, Duke of York, becoming the symbol of the House of York during the Wars of the Roses. Its popular use to represent the county gradually spread from that period. However, there is little sign of its official use before the 20th century.

Traditionally the county was divided into three Ridings (from Norse for 'a third') – East (with Beverley as its county town), West (county town Wakefield) and North (county town Northallerton). Under local government reorganisation in 1974 the East Riding was abolished, part of it being absorbed into North Yorkshire and the rest replaced by Humberside, which also included part of Lincolnshire. Parts of the West Riding were moved into North Yorkshire and South Yorkshire was established. Cleveland was created from part of the North Riding around Teesside, and parts of the North and West Ridings on the western side of the Pennines were taken into Lancashire and Cumbria.

Further reorganisation in 2002 established a number of unitary authorities to replace the administration of West and South Yorkshire, although these still exist as ceremonial counties. The East Riding was reinstated, although Kingston upon Hull is now a separate unitary authority. The city of York became a unitary authority independent of North Yorkshire, while the unitary authorities of Middlesbrough, Redcar & Cleveland and the southern half of Stockton-on-Tees were reunited within the county's ceremonial boundaries.

For the purposes of this book the county has been divided into four, reflecting the administrative reorganisations of 1974 and 2002 while also representing the traditional divisions of the county and the distinct character of the four regions. The parliamentary constituency of Brigg & Goole is one anomaly of the reorganisations; almost uniquely in the UK it straddles administrative boundaries, Goole being in the East Riding of Yorkshire and Brigg in Lincolnshire.

Traces of human occupation in upland Yorkshire date back to Mesolithic times. The Romans established a military base at Eboracum (modern York) in the 1st century AD. Linked to London by Ermine Street, this grew into the administrative and military capital of northern Roman Britain. Meanwhile the Celtic kingdom of Elmet, in the area around modern-day Leeds, survived well into the Anglo-Saxon period before eventually succumbing and being absorbed into the early Anglian kingdom of Deira. This and the more northerly kingdom of Bernicia eventually merged into Northumbria, which covered the entire north of the country from Edinburgh as far south as Hallamshire, the area round present-day Sheffield.

Edwin of Northumbria was converted to Christianity in 627 and in 664 Whitby was the venue for the famous Synod which established the Roman form of Christianity in England. The region was subject to Viking raids from the 7th century and Northumbria was captured by Vikings in 867. The southern half of Northumbria became part of the Danelaw as the kingdom of Jorvik. From this time date most of the characteristic place and personal names associated with the county.

After the Norman Conquest the region again came under the control of the monarchy. William I brutally put down a number of rebellions and much of the county was laid waste. During the Middle Ages the county, being far from London, was ruled as a succession of semi-independent earldoms. It was controlled by a number of major baronial families, among them the Percys and Nevilles (the Dukes of York actually held relatively little land within the county). From this period date many of the castles to be found throughout the county. Between 1484 and 1641 Yorkshire was governed by the Council of the North, a gathering of barons established by Richard III.

The Wars of the Roses began as a dispute over the succession to the throne. They were initiated when Richard, Duke of York, a descendant of Edward III's second son, challenged the right to rule of Henry VI, descended from Edward's third son. During the ensuing conflict several battles took place in the county, that at Towton in 1461 being one of the bloodiest in English history. Yorkshire remained fiercely independent, however, and in 1536 occurred the Pilgrimage of Grace, a revolt against Henry VIII's Dissolution of the Monasteries led by the lawyer Robert Aske.

Most of the nobility in Yorkshire had retained Catholic sympathies and during the Civil War the county was loyal to the king. Charles I had his base at York for some time. The city was besieged in April 1644 and the Parliamentary forces won the ensuing battle of Marston Moor.

Yorkshire's economic prosperity dates roughly to the 12th century. The foundation of several abbeys with grants of land from William I's successors established a landowning base for the church. They developed a successful trade in wool from sheep grazed on their considerable land holdings. The associated cottage industries of spinning and weaving grew out of this, and with the development of new forms of power from water and steam larger mills were established on the rivers Aire and Calder by the 18th century. The discovery of ironstone near Sheffield and by the Tees meant that another natural resource was available to be exploited (Sheffield was already a major centre of cutlery manufacture). Meanwhile seams of coal were discovered in the south of the county, making power a cheap and readily available resource. The opening up of several rivers for trade meant that the products could easily be exported, and transport was further improved by the coming of the canals in the late 1700s and the railways in the mid 19th century.

With the massive growth of industry, immigrants flooded into Yorkshire during the 19th century. Many of these were originally from Ireland, although thousands also came in search of employment from rural England. A large Jewish community later grew up in Leeds. In the 1950s immigrants began to arrive in the larger towns and cities from the Caribbean, while a second wave of immigrants came from the Indian subcontinent seeking work in the textile industries of Leeds and Bradford. The two cities now have large and vibrant communities with South Asian roots.

With the growth of industry and the availability of cheap labour abroad, many of Yorkshire's heavy industries found it increasingly hard to compete after World War II. The closure of the mines in the

1980s and 1990s impoverished many smaller communities, especially those in South Yorkshire. The larger cities have however reinvented themselves since the 1990s as financial and commercial centres, and have built on the success of their universities to once again become vibrant, forward-looking communities.

The East Riding can be divided roughly into two geographically distinct areas. The Yorkshire Wolds are a range of chalk hills rising to 807ft (246m), arcing from the Humber estuary to meet the sea at Flamborough and Bridlington, where they form high cliffs. The flat plain of Holderness to the east is now fertile agricultural land but was largely marshland until it was drained in medieval times. Its coast suffers more from erosion than any other in Europe, as illustrated by the constantly shifting peninsula of Spurn Head.

South Yorkshire stretches from the Pennines of the Peak District National Park in the west to the marshland of the sources of the Humber in the east. The Pennines here consist of the famous rough sandstone known as millstone grit from its use in flour milling and for grindstones. In between are the coal measures and the towns and cities built on coal mining and manufacturing: Sheffield, Rotherham, Barnsley and Doncaster. Sheffield famously built its prosperity on steel, while the other towns developed through coal mining and have suffered since the coal industry was disbanded in the 1980s. Across the River Don from Sheffield is Rotherham, a town which lies at the heart of the old coal mining district of South Yorkshire. Its main historical feature is the 15th century church associated with Thomas Scot (aka Thomas Rotherham), Chancellor of England and Archbishop of York. Barnsley, to the north of Sheffield, is mentioned in Domesday Book and the church in nearby Darfield contains a monument to the 189 men and boys who died in the Ludhill Colliery disaster of 1857. The valleys of the Dearne and Don provide a contrastingly gentle rural landscape rich in flora and fauna.

West Yorkshire, also bounded by the bleak peat moorland of the Pennines in the west, contains much of the county's industrial base. The cities of Bradford and Leeds developed initially through the wool trade, which with the invention of new power sources developed into milling. Located near the ancient Celtic kingdom of Elmet, Leeds (*Leodis*) is one of the few Celtic-derived place names found in England. The rivers flowing from the Pennines into deep valleys provided power for the mills, while the coal found in the south did the rest. West Yorkshire became a major centre for textile manufacture and the opening of the Leeds & Liverpool Canal enabled further success. Many of the towns in the south of the county grew as a result either of the textile industry (e.g. Halifax) or coal mining. Now cities such as Leeds have reinvented themselves as international business and finance centres. West Yorkshire is also one of the heartlands of rugby league. The breakaway Northern Union was initiated in Huddersfield in 1895 after disputes over payments to players in Bradford and Leeds.

North Yorkshire is vast and largely rural. Remnants of the county's often turbulent history are scattered around in the form of Roman roads and medieval castles. The central lowland strip of the county is known as the Vale of York and consists mostly of rich agricultural land, stretching to the west where the moorland of the Yorkshire Dales begins. The Dales themselves consist of limestone capped by the famous millstone grit. The whole area, riddled with potholes carved by underground rivers through the water-soluble limestone, is a mecca for cavers. Mineral mining, once a major industry, is now largely a thing of the past, but limestone quarrying still takes place on a large scale. The main dales, from south to north, are Wharfedale (cut by the River Wharfe), Nidderdale (Nidd), Wensleydale (Ure) and Swaledale (Swale), while the minor dales include Coverdale, Arkengarthdale and Littondale. Ribblesdale is on the western side of the Dales, the River Ribble flowing westwards.

The Vale of York is bounded to the northeast by the gentle Howardian Hills and the bleak heather upland of the North York Moors. On the east coast are located seaside resorts such as Scarborough and the picturesque Robin Hood's Bay, while Whitby is both a resort and an important port. To the north are the highest sea cliffs in England where the North York Moors abruptly meet the North Sea. Northwards again the moors fall towards the River Tees and the industrial centre of Middlesbrough.

Many English counties have nicknames for people from that county, such as a Calf from Essex and a Yellowbelly from Lincolnshire; the traditional nickname for a person from Yorkshire is a Tyke. Originally a term of abuse given by Yorkshire people to Londoners, because they thought their speech made them sound like yapping mongrel dogs (tykes), Londoners turned this around and used the term to describe Yorkshire folk.

Among Yorkshire's unique traditions is the long sword dance, a traditional dance not found elsewhere in England. It is related to the rapper sword dance of Northumbria, but the character is fundamentally different as it uses rigid metal or wooden swords, rather than the flexible spring steel rappers used by its northern relation. Yorkshire even has its own name for the endangered ladybird, calling it a Cushcow Lady!

East Riding of Yorkshire	**Population**			**Area**	
Unitary Authorities	*male*	*female*	*total*	*sq miles*	*sq km*
East Riding of Yorkshire	153,049	161,064	314,113	930	2,408
Kingston upon Hull	119,131	124,458	243,589	28	71
Total	272,180	285,522	557,702	958	2479

North Yorkshire*	**Population**			**Area**	
Districts	*male*	*female*	*total*	*sq miles*	*sq km*
Craven	25,791	27,829	53,620	455	1177
Hambleton	41,470	42,641	84,111	506	1311
Harrogate	73,183	78,153	151,336	505	1308
Richmondshire	24,268	22,742	47,010	509	1319
Ryedale	25,167	25,705	50,872	582	1507
Scarborough	50,374	55,869	106,243	315	817
Selby	37,424	39,044	76,468	231	599
Middlesbrough Unitary Authority	64,694	70,161	134,855	21	54
Redcar & Cleveland Unitary Authority	67,095	72,037	139,132	95	245
Stockton-on-Tees Unitary Authority (South)	45,447	47,394	92,841	40	102
York Unitary Authority	87,137	93,957	181,094	105	272
Total	542,050	575,532	1,117,582	3364	8711

*see Durham for North Stockton population statistics

South Yorkshire	**Population**			**Area**	
Unitary Authorities	*male*	*female*	*total*	*sq miles*	*sq km*
Barnsley	106,096	111,967	218,063	127	329
Doncaster	140,114	146,752	286,866	219	568
Rotherham	120,691	127,484	248,175	111	287
Sheffield	250,630	262,604	513,234	142	368
Total	617,531	648,807	1,266,338	599	1552

West Yorkshire	**Population**			**Area**	
Unitary Authorities	*male*	*female*	*total*	*sq miles*	*sq km*
Bradford	225,133	242,532	467,665	141	366
Calderdale	93,013	99,392	192,405	141	364
Kirklees	188,832	199,735	388,567	158	409
Leeds	345,754	369,648	715,402	213	552
Wakefield	153,210	161,962	315,172	131	339
Total	1,005,942	1,073,269	2,079,211	784	2030

Local Attractions and Information: East Riding of Yorkshire

Administrative headquarters — **East Riding of Yorkshire**: County Hall, Beverley HU17 9BA. Tel 01942 393939.
Kingston upon Hull: Guildhall, Alfred Gelder Street, Kingston upon Hull HU1 2AA. Tel. 01482 300300.

Bayle Museum — Bayle Gate, Old Town, Bridlington. The old gatehouse to Bridlington Priory, dating to the 12th century. Now Grade I listed, it is home to collections relating to the history of Bridlington. Tel: 01262 674353.

Beverley — The county town of East Yorkshire grew up around its monastery after John of Beverley, a former Bishop of York buried here, was canonised in 1037. A market town whose prosperity, manifested in its impressive minster, was due to the wool trade, in the 14th century it was the 11th richest town in England, although it has never been so wealthy since and today is largely a dormitory town for Hull.

Beverley Minster — Minster Yard, Beverley. Perhaps the finest non-cathedral church in England. Dedicated to St John and St Martin, the church was begun in 1220 on the site of a previous Norman church and completed in 1425. It is notable for displaying all the main styles of English Gothic architecture: the east end and transepts are in Early English style, the nave is in Decorated style and the west towers in Perpendicular. Tel: 01482 868540.

Burton Agnes Hall	5 miles (8km) southwest of Bridlington. An Elizabethan hall with original wood carving and plasterwork. Items on display include the owners' collection of Impressionist and contemporary artworks. Situated in the grounds is Burton Agnes Manor House, a rare example of a 12th century Norman fortified hall; its original structure is now encased in a 17th century brick building designed as the hall's laundry. Tel: 01262 490324.
Burton Constable Hall	9 miles (15km) northeast of Kingston upon Hull. An Elizabethan mansion, home to the Constable family for over 400 years and set in a 300 acre (120ha) park landscaped by Capability Brown. Items on display include an 18th century 'cabinet of curiosities' consisting of a wide range of scientific specimens collected by William Constable (1721–91). Tel: 01964 562400.
The Deep	Citadel Way, Kingston upon Hull. An award-winning aquarium created as the city's Millennium Project and opened in 2002. Features include the deepest viewing tunnel in Europe. Tel: 01482 381000.
Ferens Art Gallery	Queen Victoria Square, Hull. Opened in 1927 and named after industrialist Thomas Ferens, one of the city's leading benefactors. The gallery stages touring exhibitions alongside permanent collections whose holdings range from Frans Hals and Canaletto to contemporary works. Tel: 01482 613902.
Flamborough Head	5 miles (8km) northeast of Bridlington. Designated an area of Heritage Coast, this rugged chalk headland juts out 6 miles (10km) into the North Sea, rising to over 400ft (122m) at Bempton Cliffs. A beacon light tower dating from 1674 is the only remaining example in England, while the lighthouse dates from 1806.
Goole Museum and Art Gallery	Carlisle Street, Goole. The museum's collections focus on local history, especially the town's marine connections, and include models of ships and marine paintings, with a large collection by local artist Reuben Chapell. Tel: 01405 768963.
Highest point	Bishop Wilton Wold, 5 miles (8km) north of the town of Pocklington, at 807ft (246m).
Hornsea Museum	Burns Farm, Newbegin, Hornsea. Award-winning museum of local life, located in a house believed to have been occupied by the Burn family 1645–1945. There is a special collection and display of items from the Hornsea Pottery. Tel: 01964 533443.
Howden Minster	Market Place, Howden, Goole. Formally known as the Collegiate Church of St Peter and St Paul, the church was begun in 1228. One of the largest churches in East Yorkshire, its tower dates from 1390 and is 135ft (41m) high. Dissolved in 1548 by Henry VIII, it was neglected for 400 years before being reconsecrated in 1932. The chapter house, now ruined, is in the style of that at York Minster, though much smaller. The east end of the church is also now in ruins. Tel: 01430 430332.
Hull & East Riding Museum	High Street, Kingston upon Hull. Contains exhibits relating to the history of East Yorkshire, from the only dinosaur bones found in the county and a wide range of prehistoric artefacts to an Iron Age logboat and a Roman bath house. Tel: 01482 613902.
Hull University	Founded as University College Hull in 1927, the University of Hull received its charter in 1954. Its main campus is on Cottingham Road, Hull. It merged with University College Scarborough in 2000, giving it a second campus in the seaside town. It took over the University of Lincoln's next-door campus in 2003, an area which houses the newly founded Hull York Medical School. Student numbers are around 16,000. Poet Philip Larkin was librarian of the Brynmor Jones Library 1955–85. Former students include politicians Roy Hattersley and John Prescott and film director Anthony Minghella. Tel. 01482 346311.
Humber Bridge	A single-span suspension bridge crossing the Humber from Hessle in the north to Barton-on-Humber in the south, and reducing the road distance between Hull and Grimsby by nearly 50 miles (80km). Opened on 24 June 1981, it was at the time the longest such bridge in the world, with a centre span of 4626ft (1410m) and a total length of 7283ft (2220m), and is still the fourth longest. The bridge carries a dual carriageway with a lower-level footpath on both sides; it is designed to tolerate constant motion and bends more than 10ft (3m) in winds of 80mph (130km/h). The two towers, 508ft (155m) in height, each consist of a pair of hollow vertical concrete columns, tapering from 20ft (6m) square at the base to 15ft (4.5m) by 15ft 6in (4.75m) at the top. Although both vertical, the towers are not parallel, being 1.4 in (36mm) further apart at the top than the bottom as a result of the curvature of the earth. The north tower is on the bank, and has foundations down to 26ft (8m). The south tower is in the water, and descends to 118ft (36m) as a result of the estuary's shifting sandbanks. There is sufficient wire in the suspension cables to circle the Earth nearly twice. A toll bridge, it is used by 100,000 vehicles a week. Tel: 01482 647161.
Humber Forts	See Lincolnshire
Interesting facts	The **first lighthouse** to be built in Britain was at Spurn Point in 1427. The present black and white lighthouse was completed in 1895 but ceased operating in October 1986. The **Station Hotel** in Pickering has a gravestone in its ceiling. Discovered during renovations in 1961, it apparently belonged to a lady named Elizabeth who is said to haunt the establishment to this day!
Islands	There are two islands in the North Sea off Spurn Head: **Bull Sand Fort**, a hexagonal concrete fort which stands 50ft (15m) above sea level on a sandbank in the middle of the Humber Estuary (GR: TA370093); and **Stony Binks** (GR: TA400105).
Kingston upon Hull	Usually known simply as Hull and by far the largest centre of population in the East Riding. Formed in the 13th century on the site of the village of Wyke, located at the point where the River Hull joins the Humber, Hull by the 16th century was the largest port in England apart from London. It became extremely prosperous through trade in the following centuries but suffered in the 1970s from the decline of the fishing industry. It is unique in the country for having its own independent telephone company, Kingston Communications. Hull's Holy Trinity Church is the largest parish church in England.
Lower Derwent Valley	5 miles (8km) north of Goole. A National Nature Reserve of 1150 acres (467ha) consisting of flood meadows, pasture and woodland, stretching between the villages of Sutton upon Derwent

and Wressle. It provides a habitat for breeding wildfowl and waders as well as wintering birds, while flora includes many rare wetland species. There are several species of bat, including the brown long-eared bat.

Maister House — High Street, Kingston upon Hull. An 18th century merchant's house demonstrating the wealth of Hull in its heyday, including an ornate plasterwork staircase behind a plain exterior.

Prisons — **Everthorpe**, 9 miles (15km) southwest of Beverley, opened in 1958 as a Borstal. Since 1991 it has been a Category C training prison. Operational capacity: 689. Tel: 01430 426500.

Hull, Hedon Road, Kingston upon Hull, opened in 1870 for both men and women prisoners. It became a Borstal in 1950 and a maximum security prison in 1969, but was closed after a major riot in 1976. It later reopened as a local prison and remand centre. Operational capacity: 1044. Tel: 01482 282200.

The Wolds, Everthorpe, opened in 1992 as a remand prison and now holds Category C male prisoners. Operational capacity: 320. Tel: 01430 428000.

RAF Holmpton Underground Bunker — 2 miles (3km) south of Withernsea. An emergency headquarters of RAF Support Command, established in the 1980s and located 100ft (30.5m) underground. Now an experimental electronic warfare command centre, RAF Holmpton was opened in 1953 as an early warning radar station and from the 1970s undertook training of radar technicans. Access to the Command Bunker was first permitted in 2004. Tel: 01964 630208.

Rivers — The eastern branch of the **Hull** rises at the village of Kilham, while the Driffield Navigation Canal utilises part of the western branch, which has its source in the Yorkshire Wolds. From the junction it flows 20 miles (32km) south to join the Humber at Hull, where Hull Marina is located.

Humber see Lincolnshire

RSPB Bempton Cliffs — 1 mile (1.6km) northeast of Bempton, 4 miles (6km) northeast of Bridlington. RSPB reserve encompassing the highest sea cliffs in England, standing at over 330ft (100m) and providing a nesting habitat for over 200,000 gannets, puffins, razorbills and guillemots. Tel: 01262 851179.

RSPB Blacktoft Sands — 1/2 mile (0.8km) north of Ousefleet, 6 miles (10km) east of Goole. RSPB reserve located on the southern bank of the Humber. It contains England's largest intertidal reedbed, attracting reed and sedge warblers and avocets. Tel: 01405 704665.

Rudston Monolith — Rudston, 5 miles (8km) west of Bridlington. Located in the churchyard of All Saints Church. The tallest standing stone in Britain at nearly 26ft (8m) high, and weighing an estimated 40 tons.

Sewerby Hall and Gardens — Church Lane, Sewerby, 1 1/2 miles (2.5km) northeast of Bridlington. A Georgian house with a 19th century orangery and containing the Museum of East Yorkshire, whose exhibits include a collection of artefacts relating to pioneer aviator Amy Johnson. The house is set in 50 acres (20ha) of walled gardens and parkland. Tel: 01262 673769.

Skipsea Castle — Skipsea, 7 1/2 miles (12km) south of Bridlington. A Norman motte and bailey castle founded c.1086 and therefore one of the first to be built in Yorkshire. It was destroyed in 1221 by order of Henry III and only earthworks, including the impressive motte, remain today.

Sledmere House — Sledmere, 7 miles (11km) northwest of Driffield. Home since the mid 18th century of the Sykes family, Hull merchants and entrepreneurs, the house was built in the 1750s and enlarged to its present form by Sir Christopher Sykes c.1790. It suffered a major fire in 1911 but has since been restored as it was in its Georgian heyday. The drawing room and the impressive library feature splendid plasterwork by Joseph Rose. An elaborate monument nearby, erected in 1865 and 120ft (37m) high, commemorates agriculturalist and horse racing enthusiast Sir Tatton Sykes, 4th Baronet. Tel: 01377 236637.

Sport

football — **Hull City** were founded in 1904 and elected to the Football League the following year. Their highest-ever League finish had been third in Division Two in 1909–10, until they reached the Premier League via the play-offs in 2007–08. Nicknamed the Tigers, they played at Boothferry Park from 1946; their home ground since 2002 has been Kingston Communications Stadium, Walton Street, Hull. Tel. 0870 837 0003.

greyhound racing — **Boulevard Stadium**, Airlie Street, Hull. 387m track. Tel. 01482 213551.

horse racing — **Beverley** racecourse, York Road, Beverley. A right-handed oval Flat racing course of 1 mile 3 furlongs (2.2km). Tel. 01482 867488.

rugby league — **Hull FC** were formed in 1865 and were founder members of the Northern Rugby Union in 1895. They merged with Gateshead in 1999 when, after the formation of the Super League, they were known as Hull Sharks. Nicknamed The Black and Whites, the club played at the Boulevard 1895–2002 and now share the KC Stadium with Hull City. Traditionally Hull FC's support is drawn from western Hull while Hull Kingston Rovers' supporters come from the east. Tel: 01482 327200.

Hull Kingston Rovers were formed in 1882. They were the first club to win the Rugby League Championship and Premiership double in 1984. Nicknamed the Robins, their home ground is Craven Park, Preston Road, Hull. Tel: 01482 374648.

Spurn — 10 miles (16km) southeast of Withernsea. A narrow, curved sand spit on the northern bank of the Humber Estuary, formed by material washed down the coast and constantly being elongated, narrowed and re-formed by the currents to form an ever-shifting landscape. The Spurn National Nature Reserve of 730 acres (296ha) includes sandy beaches on the east with saltmarsh and mudflats on the west which are visited in spring and autumn by large numbers of migrating birds.

Wassand Hall — Seaton, 2 miles (3km) west of Hornsea. Regency house surrounded by gardens and parkland. Exhibits include 18th and 19th century portraits. Tel: 01964 534488.

Wilberforce House — High Street, Hull. The birthplace of William Wilberforce, designed in the 16th century in Artisan Mannerist style and influenced by Dutch and French styles, now connected to the adjoining Georgian houses. There are displays relating to the abolition of slavery as well as collections of 17th century and Victorian artefacts. Tel: 01482 613902.

Wressle Castle	Wressle, 5 miles (8km) northwest of Goole. The only remaining medieval castle in the East Riding, founded c.1380 by Sir Thomas Percy, brother of the Earl of Northumberland. Sir Thomas became a great favourite of Richard II but was executed for siding with his brother against the king at the Battle of Shrewsbury in 1403. The castle was later restored to the Percys and developed into a handsome quadrangular building with four corner towers and a fifth above the gatehouse. Garrisoned by Parliament during the Civil War, it was slighted as a precaution in 1648 leaving only one of the four ranges and two of the corner towers. These remained occupied until 1796 when a fire gutted the interior. A small part of the gatehouse also remains.

Some famous people born in East Riding of Yorkshire

Carmichael, Ian (actor) (1920–)	Kingston upon Hull
Courtenay, Tom (actor) (1937–)	Kingston upon Hull
Empson, William (literary critic) (1906–84)	Howden
Fisher, John (Catholic martyr) (1469–1535)	Beverley
Johnson, Amy (aviator) (1903–41)	Kingston upon Hull
Marvell, Andrew (poet) (1621–78)	Winestead-in-Holderness
Rank, J Arthur (film producer) (1888–1972)	Kingston upon Hull
Rix, Brian (actor) (1924–)	Cottingham
Smith, Stevie (poet) (1902–71)	Kingston upon Hull
Wilberforce, William (slavery abolitionist) (1759–1833)	Kingston upon Hull

Local Attractions and Information: North Yorkshire

Administrative headquarters	**Middlesbrough**: PO Box 99A, Town Hall, Middlesbrough TS1 2QQ. Tel: 01642 245432. **North Yorkshire**: County Hall, Northallerton DL7 8AD. Tel: 01609 780780. **Redcar & Cleveland**: Town Hall, Fabian Rd, South Bank TS6 9AR. Tel: 08456 126126. **Stockton-on-Tees**: PO Box 11, Church Rd, Stockton-on Tees TS18 1LD. Tel: 01642 393939. **York**: Guildhall, York YO1 9QN. Tel: 01904 613161.
Aldborough Roman Site	Aldborough, 10 miles (16km) northeast of Harrogate. The Roman town of Isurium Brigantum (Aldborough) has its origins in the late 1st century when the occupying Romans moved north to the modern counties of Yorkshire and Lancashire, then the territory of the Brigantes, the largest Iron Age tribe in Britain. In AD 71 the Roman governor of Britain, Petillius Cerialis, launched an assault into the region from a new Roman fort at York. Once the ancient tribe had been subjugated, Aldborough was established as an administrative centre in the early 2nd century. The settlement covered 55 acres (22ha); among the finds are two mosaic pavements dating to the 2nd or 3rd century. The site is managed by English Heritage. Tel: 01423 322768.
Ampleforth Abbey	12 miles (19km) east of Thirsk. Situated on the edge on the North Yorkshire Moors National Park, this Benedictine monastery runs the famous Ampleforth College, traditionally a boys' school although girls were admitted for the first time in 2001. The monastery was founded in 1802 by a group of Benedictine monks fleeing from the revolution in France, where they had gone after Henry VIII's Dissolution of the Monasteries in 1538. The school was expanded in the 20th century.
Aske Hall	1½ miles (2.5km) north of Richmond. A Georgian country house built round a 13th century pele tower, and containing an impressive collection of 18th century furniture, paintings and porcelain. In the grounds are a stable block designed by John Carr of York in 1765 and converted into a chapel with Italianate decor in the 19th century, a Gothic-style folly built by Daniel Garrett c.1745 and a coach house with carriage, as well as a walled garden, a terraced garden and a serpentine lake with Roman-style temple. The hall and estate, with parkland attributed to Capability Brown, are currently owned by the Marquess of Zetland. Tel: 01748 822000.
Aysgarth Falls	See Waterfalls
Beningbrough Hall & Gardens	1 mile (1.6km) northwest of Beningbrough, 7 miles (11km) northwest of York. An impressive Georgian mansion, built in 1716 for John Bourchier and featuring a fine Baroque interior. Over 100 pictures from the collection of the National Portrait Gallery are on display, while other highlights of the interior are the cantilevered staircase, fine wood carving and a Victorian laundry. The walled garden has recently been restored. Now owned by the National Trust. Tel: 01904 470666.
Bolton Abbey	5 miles (8km) northeast of Skipton. The 30,000 acres (12100ha) of Bolton Abbey Estate in Upper Wharfedale are owned by the Duke and Duchess of Devonshire. Features include the ruins of 12th century Augustinian Bolton Priory, 15th century Barden Tower – the residence of Henry Clifford – and Strid Wood, the largest remnant of acidic woodland in Yorkshire and a Site of Special Scientific Interest. The Strid itself is a narrow channel in the River Wharfe less than 6ft (1.8m) wide but several feet deep through which the river flows at great speed, tempting to cross but extremely dangerous.
Bolton Castle	Castle Bolton, 5 miles (8km) west of Leyburn. Located in Wensleydale, the quadrangular castle was built by Lord Richard le Scrope in the late 14th century and is today one of the best preserved such buildings in the county. Despite the impressive looking towers its function was as much to provide comfort as protection, although Mary, Queen of Scots was imprisoned here 1568–9 and the castle, held by Royalists during the Civil War, was besieged like many others

in Yorkshire by Parliamentary troops, being taken in 1645. The corner tower collapsed in a storm of 1761. The Wensleydale Folk Museum is housed in the Great Chamber. Tel: 01969 623981.

Braithwaite Hall East Witton, 3 miles (5km) southeast of Leyburn. A 17th century stone-built farmhouse with original fireplaces, panelling and oak staircase. Owned by the National Trust. Tel: 01969 640287.

Bridestones Moor 7 miles (11km) northeast of Pickering. An area of moorland at the head of Stain Dale on the edge of Dalby Forest, on the southern slopes of the North York Moors, and featuring a number of unusually weathered sandstone pillars. The area, owned by the National Trust, also encompasses ancient woodland dating back to the end of the last Ice Age.

Brimham Rocks 3 miles (5km) east of Pateley Bridge, 8 miles (13km) northwest of Harrogate. Enclosed in an area of moorland almost 100ft (300m) above sea level overlooking Nidderdale, this range of weirdly shaped outcrops of millstone grit covers an area of 50 acres (20ha). The weathered rock formations have been given names such as the Dancing Bear, Idol Rock, the Sphinx, the Anvil, the Turtle and the Druid's Desk.

Brockfield Hall 4$^1/_2$ miles (7km) east of York. A fine late Georgian house designed by Peter Atkinson, whose father had been assistant to John Carr of York, for Benjamin Agar. Begun in 1804, its outstanding feature is an oval entrance hall with a cantilevered stone staircase. It is the family home of Mr and Mrs Simon Wood; Mrs Wood is the daughter of the late Lord Martin Fitzalan Howard, brother of the 17th Duke of Norfolk. Tel: 01904 489362.

Broughton Hall Broughton, 3 miles (5km) west of Skipton. A Grade I listed house built in 1597 by Stephen Tempest, who had 18 children and needed space to accommodate them. Substantially altered in the 1800s, the house is surrounded by 19th century Italianate gardens and a 3000 acre (1200ha) estate encompassing the village of Broughton. Still the private home of the family, the hall is often used as a film and TV location. Recent productions include *Wuthering Heights* (1992), *The Tenant of Wildfell Hall* (1996) and *Dalziel and Pascoe*. Tel: 01756 799608.

Byland Abbey Byland, 1 mile (1.6km) northeast of Coxwold, 7 miles (11km) southeast of Thirsk. Located in the Hambleton Hills, the impressive remains of the cathedral-sized church dominate the ruins of one of Yorkshire's largest Cistercian monasteries. The west front displays a mixture of Romanesque and Gothic styles and the rose window, only part of which still survives, is likely to have been the model for that of York Minster. Tel: 01347 868614.

Castle Howard 13 miles (21km) northeast of York. An 18th century Baroque palace designed by Sir John Vanbrugh in 1699 for the Howard family, who have lived here continuously ever since. Built originally with the help of Nicholas Hawksmoor, the house was completed only in 1811, more than 100 years later, when the interior of the Palladian wing added in the 1750s was finally decorated. There are fine collections of paintings and china, while the chapel contains a painted screen by William Morris. Renowned ever since its use as a location for the filming of *Brideshead Revisited* (1981). Tel: 01653 648333.

Castle Museum, York Museum Street, York. Housed in two 18th century prison buildings, this unique museum of social history contains life-size recreations of a Victorian shopping street and a street in Edwardian York. Some of the original prison cells themselves can also be seen, including the one in which Dick Turpin was held in the days before his execution. Tel: 01904 687687.

Clifford's Tower Tower Street, York. A 13th century keep built on the larger of William I's motte and bailey castles in the city. It was the scene in 1190 of the mass suicide of the city's Jews who had sought refuge here after being attacked by a mob; offered the choice between being baptised as Christians or being killed, they chose to take their own lives. It takes its name from Lord Robert Clifford, who was hanged in chains from the tower in 1322. Now owned by English Heritage. Tel: 01904 646940. See also York Castle

Constable Burton Hall Gardens 3 miles (5km) east of Leyburn. The grounds of an 18th century house designed by John Carr, and featuring woodland as well as a stream wetland garden. Tel: 01677 450428.

Devil's Arrows $^1/_4$ mile (0.4km) west of Boroughbridge, 5 miles (8km) southeast of Ripon. (Grid Ref: SE 391665). Three aligned standing stones, the tallest 22ft (7m) high, the tops of which have been weathered by rainfall into fluted, pointed shapes. Dating to c.2000 BC, it is believed that they were once part of a row with at least one or two additional stones. Apart from the Rudston Monolith in East Yorkshire, they are the tallest standing stones in the UK.

Duncombe Park $^1/_2$ mile (0.8km) southwest of Helmsley. Located in the valley of the River Rye, the Baroque mansion was originally completed in 1713 and was first rebuilt in the same style after a fire in 1879. The house became a school after World War I but since 1986 has been restored by the Fevershams, direct descendants of Charles Duncombe, 1st Baron Feversham, who bought the Helmsley estate in 1689. The grounds cover 450 acres (182ha), including a 35 acre (14ha) landscape garden with temples. Part of the estate has been designated a National Nature Reserve; the 255 acre (103ha) site includes many ancient trees with bluebells and wild garlic in spring, while otters can be found in the river. Tel: 01439 770213.

Easby Abbey 1 mile (1.6km) southeast of Richmond (Grid Ref: NZ 185003). The remains of the 12th century abbey of St Agatha, established by the constable of Richmond Castle as a foundation of Premonstratensian 'white' canons and set beside the River Swale. The nearby parish church, also dedicated to St Agatha, is still active and features wall paintings dating from the 13th century. Now owned by English Heritage.

Fairfax House Castlegate, York. One of the finest 18th century town houses in England, and home of the famous Noel Terry collection of furniture. Tel: 01904 655543.

Forge Valley Woods 3 miles (5km) southeast of Scarborough. A National Nature Reserve of 156 acres (63ha) covering the Derwent river valley's steep eastern and western slopes and including mixed deciduous woodland ranging from alder and willow in the valley bottom to ash and wych elm, with oak, rowan and holly on the upper slopes. The woods were once coppiced to provide charcoal for the forge that operated here.

Fountains Abbey — 3 miles (5km) southwest of Ripon. (Grid Ref: SE 271683). The spectacular ruins of the 12th century Cistercian abbey, founded in 1132, are enhanced by the Georgian water garden of Studley Royal, first developed by John Aislabie and extended to include the abbey by his son William from 1742. The entire property was designated a UNESCO World Heritage Site in 1986. The monastic watermill, the finest of its type that survives, is 800 years old. Fountains Hall, also part of the site, was built at the end of the 16th century, partly with stone from the abbey ruins. Owned by the National Trust. Tel: 01765 608888.

Gaping Gill — See Waterfalls

Goddards Garden — Tadcaster Road, York. The gardens of the former home of famous York chocolate maker Noel Goddard Terry. Designed in 1927 by George Dillistone, they feature terraces, a rockery and ponds in a combination of formal and informal layouts. The house is now occupied by the Yorkshire offices of the National Trust. Tel: 01904 702021.

Hambleton Hills — A range of low hills on the southwestern edge of the North York Moors. Their highest point is Black Hambleton above Nether Silton at 1310ft (399m) (GR: SE481945).

Hardraw Force — See Waterfalls

Harlow Carr — See RHS Harlow Carr

Helmsley Castle — Helmsley, 10 miles (16km) east of Thirsk. Norman castle built originally by Walter l'Espec c.1120, but largely restructured as an enclosure castle by the de Roos family 1186–1227. The castle's outstanding features include the keep-like east tower that dominates the town. After being developed into an Elizabethan mansion the castle was besieged by Parliamentarians during the Civil War, falling after three months. Bought for £95,000 in 1689 by Sir Charles Duncombe, owner of Duncombe Park, it is now owned by English Heritage. Tel: 01439 770442.

Heritage railways — **Derwent Valley Light Railway**, located at the Yorkshire Museum of Farming, at Murton, to the east of York, operates on 1/2 mile (0.8km) of the former branch line between Layerthorpe and Cliff Common near Selby.

Embsay & Bolton Abbey Steam Railway, based at Bolton Abbey Station, Skipton, runs for 2 miles (3km) between Embsay and Bolton Abbey on the former Midland Railway branch line between Skipton and Ilkley. Embsay station dates from 1888. Trains operated include both diesel and steam locomotives. Tel. 01756 710614.

North Yorkshire Moors Railway, based at Pickering Station, Park Street, Pickering, is England's second longest heritage railway. It runs for 18 miles (29km) from Pickering to Grosmont via Levisham, Newton Dale and Goathland, with services sometimes extended all the way to the original terminus at Whitby. Mostly operated with steam locomotives though with some diesel, it has gained ever greater popularity since being featured in the Harry Potter films. Tel 01751 472508.

Wensleydale Railway operates between Leeming Bar and Redmire via Bedale, Finghall and Leyburn on part of the Northallerton–Garsdale line, reopened in 2003 after being used by the Ministry of Defence for several years for transporting tanks to Catterick Garrison. Tel. 01677 425805.

Highest point — Whernside at 2414ft (736m). GR: SD738814.

Hovingham Hall — 8 miles (13km) northwest of Malton. A Palladian house built 1750–70 by Thomas Worsley to his own design and unique in being entered through the Riding School. Cricket has been played in front of the house since at least 1858, when a 22-strong Hovingham team took on an All England team – and lost. Today the pitch is used by the village team. The fourth Sir William Worsley captained Yorkshire in 1928 and 1929 and was president of Yorkshire County Cricket Club for many years; during his tenure many of the county's most distinguished players, Herbert Sutcliffe, Len Hutton, Freddie Trueman and Geoff Boycott among them, appeared at Hovingham. Tel: 01653 628771.

Interesting facts — The **Tan Hill Inn**, Keld, is Britain's highest public house. The old stone pub lies 1732ft (528m) above sea level on the Pennine Way where North Yorkshire borders County Durham. Another famous local hostelry is the **Saltersgate Inn**, Pickering. The pub dates back to the 16th century and the fire in its cast-iron range is said to have remained burning constantly for more than 200 years. Local legend has it that should the fire ever be extinguished the devil will plague the locality. The **Manor of Northstead** was once a collection of fields and farms in the parish of Scalby in the North Riding of Yorkshire. By 1600 the manor house had fallen into disrepair and was occupied only by a shepherd. The area of the manor is now part of the Barrowcliff area of the town of Scarborough. The position of Crown Steward and Bailiff of the Manor of Northstead is now used as a procedural device to allow resignation from the House of Commons. Most references say that it was first used in this way on 20 March 1844 to allow Sir George Rose, Member for Christchurch, to resign his seat in Parliament, but the official book containing appointments to the Stewardship (lodged in the Public Record Office under reference E 197/1) indicates that Patrick Chalmers, MP for Montrose Burghs, was appointed to this office on 6 April 1842. The writ for the election of a replacement was moved as if Chalmers had been appointed to the Chiltern Hundreds (see Buckinghamshire). **St Margaret Clitherow** (1556–86), a saint and martyr of the Roman Catholic Church, is sometimes called 'the Pearl of York'. A butcher's wife who lived in the Shambles, she was brought up in the Reformed religion, to which her husband also conformed (they were married in 1571). In 1574, however, she was reconciled to the Catholic Church and allowed her house to be used for the shelter of priests and as lodging for a Catholic schoolteacher for her own children and those of neighbours. She kept this up for 12 years, during which time she was arrested on several occasions and spent a total of three years in prison. Eventually her house was searched, and, under threat, one of the pupils revealed where the Mass vestments were hidden. She refused to plead at her trial, saying she wished to spare the jury's conscience; as a penalty she was pressed naked beneath a heavy stone and left for three days without proper food or drink. The sentence was not fully applied, but she was crushed to death under a weight at the Tollbooth on the Ouse Bridge in York on the feast of the Annunciation in 1586. Her husband never returned to the Catholic faith, but one daughter became a nun, at Louvain in the Low Countries. Margaret was canonised in 1970 by Pope Paul VI.

Islands — See separate entry

Jervaulx Abbey — $4^1/_2$ miles (7km) southeast of Leyburn. The remains of a Cistercian abbey originally founded in 1145 at Fors in Wensleydale, but moved ten years later to this site a few miles away beside the River Ure. The privately maintained site is supported by English Heritage. Tel: 01677 460226.

Jorvik Viking Centre — Coppergate, York. In the 1970s archaeologists found preserved in the wet soil near the River Ouse substantial remains of the Viking city of York, known as Jorvik, including buildings standing 7ft (2m) high and thousands of everyday artefacts. After excavation was complete, an innovative reconstruction of Viking York was opened on the site in 1984, in which it is possible to travel back in time and experience the sights and sounds, even the smells of the Viking city. Tel: 01904 643211.

Kiplin Hall — $2^1/_2$ miles (4km) east of Catterick, 6 miles (10km) northwest of Northallerton. Built in the early 1620s as a hunting lodge by George Calvert, Secretary of State to James I. In 1722, Christopher Crowe bought the red-brick house from his stepson Charles Calvert, 5th Lord Baltimore, adding a service wing to the north of the hall and installing a fine central staircase, fashionable Georgian fireplaces and plasterwork. In 1820, Lord and Lady Tyrconnel (Sarah Crowe and her husband John Delaval Carpenter) added a wing to the south containing a Gothic-style drawing room. When Admiral Walter Talbot inherited Kiplin from his cousin, he changed this room into the Jacobean-style library of today and made improvements to the service wing and grounds. The crest above the front door is that of the Carpenter family, with their motto, *Per acuta belli* ('by the stratagems of war') – probably a reference to their naval background. In the 1970s, some of the service wing was demolished and the north tower restored. Tel: 01748 818178.

Kirkham Priory — 5 miles (8km) southwest of Malton. Founded by Walter l'Espec in the 1120s, this ruined Augustinian priory stands beside the River Derwent. Its gatehouse bears heraldic symbols of the Roos family of Helmsley Castle and there are extensive remains of the gatehouse and a 13th century washroom, although little else of substance is visible. The site was used in World War II during preparations for the D-Day landings. Tel: 01653 618768.

Knaresborough Castle — Castle Yard, Knaresborough. A 12th century Norman castle built by Eustace FitzJohn and improved by Edward II and Edward III 1307–50. Owned by John of Gaunt from 1327, it was taken by Parliamentary troops in 1644 and slighted in 1648, but the ruins still stand high on a cliff overlooking the River Nidd. The Elizabethan courthouse now houses a museum and the castle grounds have been turned into a park. Tel: 01423 556188.

Maiden Castle — $1^1/_2$ miles (2.5km) southwest of Reeth, 9 miles (15km) west of Richmond. One of the most unusual forts in the British Isles, located on the north-facing slope of Harker Hill in Swaledale. The slightly odd but otherwise ordinary Iron Age hill fort has a unique stone entrance corridor, originally 20–25ft (6–8m) wide and lined with an unusual dry stone wall, completely parallel, 361ft (110m) long and tapered to a very low height. The wall of the corridor has largely collapsed but in places the original walling still remains. The site has been described as a defended settlement rather than a hill fort.

Malham Tarn — 5 miles (8km) east of Settle, 11 miles (18km) northwest of Skipton. A range of remarkable features can be found in the limestone landscape to the north of Malham village. Malham Tarn itself is England's highest freshwater lake, while below one of the numerous limestone pavements and the Tarn is Malham Cove, a limestone cliff 260ft (80m) high and 980ft (300m) wide cut by a waterfall after the Ice Age. The gorge of Gordale Scar, over 100ft (30.5m) deep, was formed at the same period. The area around Malham Tarn is a designated National Nature Reserve covering 338 acres (137ha) and including six surrounding farms; nearby New House Farm, southwest of Bordley and $2^1/_2$ miles (4km) east of Malham, is another National Nature Reserve. The 63 acre (26ha) small working farm is owned by the National Trust and includes rare unimproved hay meadows, a haven for many scarce plant species and part of only 1500 acres (600ha) of such habitat remaining in the UK. The meadows have been managed traditionally for at least 90 years.

Markenfield Hall — 2 miles (3km) south of Ripon. A spectacular medieval house, built mainly in 1310 and completely surrounded by a moat. Owned since 1761 by the Grantley family, it remains remarkably little altered since its construction, and is the most complete medium-sized 14th century country house still surviving in England. Tel: 01765 603411.

Marmion Tower — West Tanfield, 5 miles (8km) northwest of Ripon. Located beside the River Ure. The 15th century gatehouse of the Marmion family's riverside manor house, which itself no longer exists, has a beautiful oriel window.

Middleham Castle — Middleham, $1^1/_2$ miles (2.5km) south of Leyburn. Founded c.1190 by Robert fitz Ralph. The Neville family developed the 12th century keep, its walls 12ft (3.5m) thick, into a fortified palace by the mid 15th century. It was the childhood home of Richard III and later his favourite residence. The keep still stands 66ft (20m) high. Now owned by English Heritage.

Middlesbrough — Traditionally located in North Yorkshire until the creation of Cleveland in 1974, Middlesbrough is now a unitary authority, once again included within the ceremonial boundaries of North Yorkshire. A tiny village until the mid 19th century, it grew massively after the discovery of ironstone nearby in 1850 and the subsequent establishment of an iron foundry in the village; its population was 90,000 by 1890 and 130,000 by 1930. As well as iron, the town was a port for coal transport and became a centre of industrial innovation. The traditional dialect of Middlesbrough folk is curiously called Smoggish.

Middlesbrough Cathedral Dalby Way, Coulby Newham, Middlesbrough. A Roman Catholic cathedral dedicated to St Mary. The building's original architect, Frank Swainston, died just after outline plans had been agreed; his assistant Peter Fenton developed the detailed drawings and designed the cathedral furnishings. The foundation stone was blessed on 3 November 1985 by the Rt Rev. Augustine Harris, Bishop of Middlesbrough.

Mother Shipton's Cave Prophecy Lodge, High Bridge, Knaresborough. Supposedly the dwelling place of Elizabethan prophetess Ursula Shipton. Nearby is the Petrifying Well, a cave containing a preserving well – any item placed in the water is quickly coated in calcite dissolving out of the supersaturated water. Tel: 01423 864600.

Moulton Hall $^{1}/_{4}$ mile (0.4km) south of Moulton, 4 miles (6km) east of Richmond. A stone manor house dating from 1650 with a fine carved wood staircase. Owned by the National Trust. Tel: 01325 377227.

Mount Grace Priory 5 miles (8km) northeast of Northallerton (Grid Ref: SE 449985). The 14th century ruins of England's most important Carthusian foundation, with individual cells for monks who lived in hermit-like isolation, feature reconstructions in order to bring to life the monastic existence. Tel: 01609 883494.

National Centre for Early Music Walmgate, York. Housed in St Margaret's Church and home of the internationally renowned York Early Music Festival and the Beverley and East Riding Early Music Festival, the centre also attracts some of the world's finest artists in the fields of jazz, folk and world music. Tel: 01904 632220.

National Railway Museum Leeman Road, York. Established on its present site in 1975, the museum contains over 100 locomotives and 200 other items of rolling stock as well as thousands of other items relating to the history and development of railways. Highlights of the collection include *Puffing Billy*, one of the first ever locomotives, *Mallard*, the world's fastest steam locomotive, the *Flying Scotsman*, and numerous royal carriages and saloons. Tel: 01904 621261.

Newburgh Priory $^{1}/_{2}$ mile (0.8km) southeast of Coxwold, 8 miles (13km) southeast of Thirsk. An Augustinian priory on the edge of the North Yorkshire Moors National Park founded on land granted by William I to Robert de Mowbray in 1145, and established by his son Roger. In 1541, after its dissolution, Henry VIII sold Newburgh for £1062 to one of his chaplains, Anthony de Bellasis, who with his brother Richard was responsible for the dissolution of Newburgh and eight other monasteries in the north. Anthony's nephew William converted the priory into a Tudor mansion; except for alterations and building work carried out 1720–60, the house today is little changed since the Tudor period. Tel: 01347 868435.

Newby Hall 3 miles (5km) southeast of Ripon. Built in the 1690s by Sir Christopher Wren's assistant John Etty and enlarged by John Carr of York. The graceful interior with its fine mouldings is largely the work of Robert Adam, who was commissioned to carry out alterations in the 1760s by William Weddell, an ancestor of the Compton family who still live in the house today. The Regency Dining Room was added in the early 19th century by Weddell's cousin, the 3rd Lord Grantham (later the first president of RIBA, the Royal Institution of British Architects). The magnificent gardens hold the National Collection of cornus (dogwoods). Tel: 01423 322583.

North York Moors National Park At 554 sq miles (1436 sq km), one of the largest expanses of heather moorland in the UK. It was designated a National Park in 1952. The highest point is Round Hill on Urra Moor (GR: NZ594015) at 1489ft (454m). On the east the high moors end abruptly at some of the highest sea cliffs in England, reaching 690ft (210m) above sea level near Boulby.

Norton Conyers 4 miles (6km) north of Ripon. Built in the 14th century and much enlarged since, the house is the original of Thornfield Hall in *Jane Eyre*, the character of the mad Mrs Rochester being inspired by a family legend that a madwoman was kept hidden in the house's attics. A blocked staircase matching the novel's description was discovered in 2004. The surrounding parkland features an 18th century walled garden. Tel: 01765 640333.

Nunnington Hall 4 miles (6km) southeast of Helmsley. This 17th century manor house built in honey-coloured stone and set on the banks of the River Rye was once home to Henry VIII's doctor. The house contains a collection of miniature rooms furnished to reflect various historical periods. There is an organic walled garden featuring an orchard of traditional fruit varieties. Owned by the National Trust. Tel: 01439 748283.

Ormesby Hall Church Lane, Ormesby, 2 miles (3km) southeast of Middlesbrough. Palladian mansion and gardens dating from the mid 18th century. Inside is fine plasterwork and woodcarving. The Georgian stable block houses the horses of the Cleveland Mounted Police, while the old wing contains an exhibition of model railways. The estate has been home to the Pennyman family for over 300 years. Now owned by the National Trust. Tel: 01642 324188.

Parcevall Hall Gardens Skyreholme, 7$^{1}/_{2}$ miles (12km) northeast of Skipton. The only RHS and English Heritage registered gardens open to the public in the Yorkshire Dales National Park, the 16 acres (6.5ha) of formal and woodland gardens lie on a steep hillside commanding impressive views of Simons Seat and Wharfedale. The gardens were laid out by the late Sir William Milner from 1927, and are planted with specimen trees and shrubs collected from Western China and the Himalayas. Tel: 01756 720311.

Pickering Castle Castlegate, Pickering. An earthwork Norman castle fortified in stone in the 13th and 14th centuries. The castle passed to the Duchy of Lancaster in 1326 and was ruined by 1651. Now owned by English Heritage. Tel: 01751 474989.

Piercebridge Roman Bridge Piercebridge, 9 miles (15km) northeast of Richmond. The remains of a bridge which once carried a Roman road across the River Tees to Piercebridge Roman fort. In a field near the river can be seen the masonry blocks that formed the piers of the wooden bridge. The site is managed by English Heritage.

Plumpton Rocks — 3 miles (5km) southeast of Harrogate. A Grade II* listed landscape garden laid out in the 1750s, and covering more than 30 acres (12ha) including lake, woodland walk and millstone grit rock formations. Tel: 01289 386360.

Prisons — **Askham Grange**, Askham Richard, 4 miles (6km) southwest of York, was opened in 1947 as Britain's first women's open prison. Operational capacity: 128. Tel: 01904 772000.

Full Sutton, 9 miles (15km) east of York, is a maximum security Category A and B prison for adult males opened in 1987. Operational capacity: 608. Tel: 01759 475100.

Kirklevington Grange, Yarm, was opened in 1992 as a resettlement prison. Operational capacity: 283. Tel: 01642 792600.

YOI Northallerton, East Road, Northallerton, was opened in 1783 as the North Riding of Yorkshire's house of correction and is the oldest purpose-built prison in Britain still in operation. After spells as a military prison, a training prison and a remand centre it has been a Young Offender Institution since 2002. Operational capacity: 252. Tel: 01609 785100.

RHS Harlow Carr — Crag Lane, Harrogate. Formerly owned by the Northern Horticultural Society until its merger with the Royal Horticultural Society in 2001, the garden covers 58 acres (23ha) of the former Forest of Knaresborough. The area, with its sulphur springs, became a spa resort in the 1840s and was laid out with gardens 20 years later. Conditions are varied but the acidic soil and northerly longitude present special challenges, making it a unique testing ground for growing plants in these conditions. Woodland, arboretum, kitchen garden and herbaceous borders. Tel: 01423 565418.

Richmond Castle — Riverside Road, Richmond. Situated on a rocky promontory high above the River Swale, the keep towers over the market town of Richmond. The Norman triangular enclosure castle was founded in 1071 by Alan the Red, Count of Ponthièvre, with a late 11th century stone hall known as Scolland's Hall after an official of the castle. The 100ft (30.5m) high keep was added by Conan, Duke of Brittany, c.1150–70. The battlements were repaired in the 18th century. Now owned by English Heritage. Tel: 01748 822493.

Rievaulx Abbey — Rievaulx, 2½ miles (4km) northwest of Helmsley, 10 miles (16km) east of Thirsk. Founded by St Bernard of Clairvaux in 1132 near the River Rye on land donated by Walter l'Espec of Helmsley Castle, the first northern Cistercian abbey grew to become one of the most prosperous in England. In 1220 its church was rebuilt to house the remains of the renowned abbot Aelred, and much of this 'presbytery' remains intact. Tel: 01439 798228.

Rievaulx Terrace & Temples — 2½ miles (4km) northwest of Helmsley. A landscaped garden created by Thomas Duncombe III, consisting of a ½ mile (0.8km) grass terrace featuring two 18th century temples, overlooking Rievaulx Abbey. The Ionic Temple has a painted ceiling depicting mythological scenes and was intended for use as a banqueting house; the pavement of the Doric or Tuscan Temple came from Rievaulx Abbey. Now owned by the National Trust. Tel: 01439 748283.

Ripley Castle — Ripley, 4 miles (6km) north of Harrogate. A fortified manor house with one defendable tower, home for nearly 700 years to the Ingilby family. The gatehouse, dating from 1450, bears musket holes from where it was attacked by Parliamentary forces during the Civil War. The fortified tower itself was completed in 1555 while the manor house was built in the 1780s. The grounds feature hothouses, a walled garden, lakes and waterfalls. Tel: 01423 770152.

Ripon Cathedral — Minster Road, Ripon. Founded by St Wilfred in AD 672, the cathedral is the fourth building to stand on the site. The current building was begun in the 12th century as a minster church; the Early English west front was added in 1220, its towers originally topped with wooden spires. It was consecrated as a cathedral only in 1836 with the creation of the Diocese of Ripon, the first new diocese to be established since the Reformation. Tel: 01765 602609.

Rivers — The **Bain** rises in Semerwater and flows for 2 miles (3km). This tributary of the River Ure, which it joins at Bainbridge in Upper Wensleydale, is the shortest river in England. The **Derwent** rises on the North York Moors near Scarborough, flowing southwest and then south for 57 miles (92km) to meet the Ouse at Barmby, east of Selby.

The **Esk** rises on Westerdale Moor on the northern side of the North York Moors, flowing north and then for 30 miles (48km) through Esk Dale and on to meet the North Sea at Whitby.

The **Nidd** rises in the Yorkshire Dales, flowing south through Nidderdale and then east through Knaresborough before joining the Ouse.

The **Ouse** flows southeast from its source at the confluence of the Swale and Ouse Gill Beck for its 57 miles (92km) through York and Selby before meeting the Aire, then eastward to the Humber estuary.

The **Swale** rises in the Yorkshire Dales above Richmond, flowing roughly east before meeting the Ure at Myton-on-Swale near Boroughbridge. The Swale is the fastest flowing river in England and is prone to flash flooding.

Tees see County Durham

The **Ure** rises in the Pennines, flowing through Wensleydale before meeting first the Swale at Myton-on-Swale and then Ouse Gill Beck near Boroughbridge, at which point it becomes known as the Ouse. At Aysgarth it passes over a series of falls 1 mile (1.6km) in length.

Roseberry Topping — 1 mile (1.6km) northeast of Great Ayton, 17 miles (27km) northeast of Northallerton. An unusually shaped hill, like a miniature version of the Matterhorn in Switzerland, that offers unrestricted 360 degree views from its 1050ft (320m) summit as far as Teesside and the Yorkshire Dales. Owned by the National Trust.

Scampston Hall — Scampston, 4 miles (6km) northeast of Malton. Built in the 1690s but substantially remodelled in Regency style in 1801 by Thomas Leverton, and still a family home. The house is surrounded by 420 acres (170ha) of wooded parkland laid out to designs by Capability Brown. A 4½ acre (1.8ha) contemporary walled garden designed by renowned garden architect Piet Oudolf was opened in 2004. Tel: 01944 759111.

Scarborough Castle — Castle Road, Scarborough. Norman castle founded c.1136 by William of Aumale on a headland overlooking the North Sea, once the site of an Iron Age settlement and a Roman signal station. The keep was built by Henry II, who also added the curtain wall and barbican c.1240. In 1312 Edward II established his favourite Piers Gaveston in the castle for protection against his baronial enemies, but Gaveston was forced to surrender after a short siege and was subsequently executed. The castle was seized by Thomas Stafford in 1557 in a short-lived attempt to raise opposition to Mary I. Held by Sir Hugh Cholmley for the king from 1642, it was besieged and captured by Parliamentary forces in 1645 under massive bombardment by cannon. Its garrison later changed sides and declared for the king, but the castle was retaken by Parliament in 1648. George Fox was imprisoned here in 1665. The castle was shelled by German battleships in 1914 and was a secret listening post during World War II. The ruined keep, once 90ft (27.5m) tall, still stands today. Now owned by English Heritage. Tel: 01723 372451.

Scoska Wood — A 25 acre (10ha) National Nature Reserve consisting of of ash woodland and pasture in Littondale between the villages of Litton and Arncliffe, and featuring limestone scars on its upper slopes.

Shambles, The — Mentioned in Domesday Book, The Shambles is York's oldest street. A bustling centrepiece of the historic city, its 15th century buildings lean towards the middle of the cobbled street, their roofs almost touching. The York Shambles was historically a street of butchers' shops and houses; records state that as late as 1872 there were 26 butchers on the street. Its name originates from Middle English *shamel*, a booth or bench, believed to be a reference to the wide shelves below the shop windows from which meat was served, and which by association came to refer to a place where meat was sold. It was also a place where livestock was slaughtered; the pavements on either side of the street are raised in order to create a channel through which the butchers would wash away their waste, and offal and blood would gush down the street twice weekly. A house halfway along The Shambles has been turned into a shrine to St Margaret Clitherow (see Interesting Facts), wife of butcher John Clitherow, although it is believed that she actually lived further down the street.

Shandy Hall — Coxwold, 7 miles (11km) southeast of Thirsk. Built as a timber-framed open hall in the 15th century, the house was enlarged by author Laurence Sterne in the 1700s. It was here in 1760–7 that Sterne wrote *Tristram Shandy* and *A Sentimental Journey*. Tel: 01347 868465.

Sion Hill Hall — Kirby Wiske, 4 miles (6km) northwest of Thirsk. A neo-Georgian house designed in 1912 by renowned York architect Walter H Brierley, known as 'the Lutyens of the North'. The house contains the H W Mawer collection of antique furniture, porcelain, paintings and clocks, all in superb room settings. Tel: 01845 587206.

Skipton Castle — High Street, Skipton. One of the best preserved medieval castles in England, standing on a rock outcrop with a sheer drop behind to the Eller Beck. The original castle, built in 1090, was heavily refortified in the early 14th century by Robert Clifford. Having withstood a three-year siege during the Civil War before surrendering in 1645, it was unroofed on the orders of Oliver Cromwell but repaired by Lady Anne Clifford ten years later, on the condition that it should not be capable of housing cannon. The living quarters and kitchens as well as the defensive towers and gateways remain largely intact. Tel: 01756 792442.

Spofforth Castle — Spofforth, 4 miles (6km) southeast of Harrogate. The ruins of a 14th and 15th century manor house owned by the powerful Percy family, and fortified after Henry de Percy received licence to crenellate in 1308.

Sport

football — **Middlesbrough** were formed in 1876 and turned professional in 1899 when they were elected to the Football League. Promoted to Division One for the first time only in 1974, they won their first major trophy, the League Cup, in 2004. Nicknamed Boro, the club's colours are red and white and their home ground is the Riverside Stadium, Middlesbrough. Tel: 01325 722002.

York City were formed in 1922 and elected to the Football League in 1929; the highlight of their history is an FA Cup semi-final in 1955. The club lost their League status for the first time in 2005 after prolonged financial difficulties. Nicknamed The Minstermen their colours are red and white and their home ground is Bootham Crescent (currently known as KitKat Crescent), York. Tel: 0870 777 1922.

horse racing — **Catterick**, Catterick Bridge, Richmond. 9f (1.8km) Flat course; National Hunt course of 1¼ miles (2km). Tel: 01748 811478.

Ripon, Boroughbridge Road, Ripon. Flat racing only. Right-handed circuit of 1½ miles (2.5km). Tel: 01765 602156.

Thirsk, Station Road, Thirsk. Flat racing on left-handed oval course of 1¼ miles (2km). Tel: 01845 522276.

York, Knavesmire Road, York. The course is known as 'The Knavesmire'. Flat racing on left-handed track of 2 miles (3km). Tel: 01904 620911.

rugby league — **York City Knights** were founded in 1868 as York FC and joined the Northern Union in 1898, becoming members of the Rugby Football League in 1901. Renamed York Wasps in 1996 and adopting their current name in 2003, they play at Roland Court, Huntington Road. Their colours are white, navy blue and light blue. Tel: 01904 758234.

Stanwick Iron Age Fortifications — ¼ mile (0.4km) east of Forcett, 6 miles (10km) north of Richmond. A section of the fortifications of the main trading centre of the Brigantes, the most powerful tribe in pre-Roman Britain. One of the largest Iron Age settlements in Britain, it originally enclosed an area of 766 acres (310ha) and over 4 miles (6km) in length. The site was occupied from c.400 BC but was massively expanded c.AD 40; it was abandoned some time after the Romans arrived in the area in AD 69–70, when the Brigantes moved south to Aldborough.

Steeton Hall Gateway — 1¼ miles (2km) west of South Milford, 4 miles (6km) northeast of Castleford. The well-preserved gatehouse of Steeton Hall, a 14th century manor house most of whose existing fabric consists of

17th and 19th century additions. Dating to c.1360, the Grade I listed gatehouse is owned by English Heritage.

Stockeld Park — 2 miles (3km) west of Wetherby. The house was built 1758–63 by James Paine for William Middleton, a member of a Roman Catholic family who had owned the manor since 1318. In 1893 the property was purchased by Robert John Foster, owner of the Black Dyke Mills in Bradford, and he commissioned the architect Detmar Blow to make extensive alterations. Stockeld Park is set in gardens with lawns, large herbaceous and shrub borders, fringed by woodland and surrounded by 100 acres (40ha) of beautiful parkland. Tel: 01937 586101.

Sutton Park — Sutton-on-the-Forest, 8 miles (13km) north of York. An early Georgian house built in the 1760s by Thomas Atkinson. Its simple exterior hides an interior featuring ornate Rococo plasterwork and its collections of paintings and furniture have been augmented by those of the Sheffield family, who bought the house in 1963. Tel: 01347 810249.

Thornborough Henges — $^1/_2$ mile (0.8km) southwest of Thornborough, 5 miles (8km) northwest of Ripon. A unique alignment of three earth structures situated on a plateau above the River Ure. Each is around 790ft (240m) in diameter and consists of a high earth bank with entrances. The henges are much overgrown and inaccessible to the public on privately owned land, but form an essential part of a 'sacred landscape' similar to those surrounding Stonehenge and Avebury and dating to c.3500 BC. Recent research suggests they may be a physical representation of the arrangement of stars in Orion's belt.

Three Peaks, The — Located to the north of Settle, the three distinctive flat-topped hills of Ingleborough (2373ft/723m), Whernside (2414ft/736m) and Pen-y-Ghent (2273ft/693m) are the main feature of the western part of the Yorkshire Dales National Park. Consisting of millstone grit over a base of limestone, they are riddled with potholes and caves as well as being a target for hillwalkers and fell runners. Ingleborough National Nature Reserve covers 2500 acres (1010ha) of open moorland and includes some of the finest limestone pavements in the country.

Treasurer's House — Minster Yard, York. Built over a Roman road – the ghosts of a Roman legion are still reputed to march through its cellars – this deceptively opulent 17th century house once housed the treasurers of York Minster. Now owned by the National Trust. Tel: 01904 624247.

University of York — Heslington, York. Founded in 1963 and known as one of the 'plate-glass' universities of the 1960s, York is organised into eight colleges: Derwent (opened 1965), Langwith (1965), Alcuin (1969), Vanbrugh (1968), Goodricke (1968), Wentworth (1972), James (1990), Halifax (2002). The main campus is at Heslington, to the east of the city, but the university occupies various buildings in the city centre: King's Manor, once the abbot's house of St Mary's Abbey, is home to the world-renowned Centre for Medieval Studies. Originally based at Heslington Hall, in 1964 the university moved to its campus, built in the grounds of the hall. The prefabricated, mostly concrete buildings, designed by Andrew Derbyshire, are arranged around a large lake and feature the half-octagonal Central Hall. Student numbers are around 13,000. The university's academic reputation has been built on its departments of technology, history and English and it is a member of the 1994 Group. The main campus is to be extended into the area known as Heslington East. Former students include child psychologist Tanya Byron, former BBC director-general Greg Dyke, comedian Harry Enfield, politician Harriet Harman and author and screenwriter Anthony Horowitz. Tel: 01904 430000.

Waterfalls — The following are three of the most famous waterfalls in North Yorkshire:

Aysgarth Falls, located near the village of Aysgarth in Wensleydale. The falls are formed where the River Ure tumbles through a wooded valley over a triple flight of limestone steps. Though the drop from top to bottom is only 98ft (30m), the broken falls extend for almost 1 mile (1.6km) in length. They are featured in the film *Robin Hood, Prince of Thieves* (1991).

Gaping Gill on Ingleborough Hill, one of the deepest potholes in the Yorkshire Dales. The 321ft (98m) deep pothole descends in two stages. A small recess known as Birkbeck's Ledge is found just over halfway down before the shaft breaks into the roof of England's largest natural underground chamber. Under normal weather conditions, Fell Beck falls from the surface to the floor of the main chamber, making GG (as it is referred to by cavers) England's highest **permanent** waterfall (there may be higher temporary waterfalls, for example on Lake District crags during bad weather). The water disappears into the boulder-strewn floor and appears only intermittently in the further reaches of the cave system; it resurges from Ingleborough Cave, which is electrically lit for guided tours. In flood conditions the main chamber becomes an awesome natural spectacle, being filled with lashing spray driven by gale force blasts – and is sometimes therefore known as the 'Hall of the Winds'. The cave system between Gaping Gill and Ingleborough Cave is over 12 miles (19km) long but can only be explored by experienced cavers. Gaping Gill was first descended by Frenchman Edouard Martel by rope ladder in 1895; modern cavers abseil down a slender nylon rope and 'prussik' back up using a pair of clamps and a harness.

Hardraw Force, located within the grounds of the Green Dragon Inn, lays claim to being England's highest unbroken waterfall. Its single drop from Hardraw Beck is more than 98ft (30m) over a rocky overhang (although it is claimed that Scale Force in Cumbria has a single drop of 120ft/36.5m, this drop is not technically a waterfall but a cataract, i.e. it maintains contact with the ground beneath it for much of the drop).

Wharram Percy — $^1/_2$ mile (0.8km) south of Wharram le Street, 6 miles (10km) southeast of Malton. The most renowned and closely studied deserted medieval village in England. The ruins of the church can still be seen above ground, as can the outlines of numerous houses. The village's heyday between the 12th and 14th centuries was followed by rapid decline and it was abandoned c.1500. The site is managed by English Heritage.

Wheeldale Roman Road 2 miles (3km) southwest of Goathland, 10 miles (16km) southwest of Whitby. The hardcore foundations and drainage system of a Roman road, still clearly visible and extending for 1 mile (1.6km) across moorland above Wheeldale Beck.

Whitby Abbey 1/4 mile (0.4km) east of Whitby. The ruins of the 13th century church of St Hilda's abbey stand on the cliffs overlooking the seaside town of Whitby. The first abbey was a Benedictine foundation established in AD 657 by the formidable St Hilda, a Northumbrian princess whose Saxon name Hild means 'battle'. Famously the venue for the Synod of Whitby in 664, the epoch-making international meeting between Celtic and Roman clerics at which Britain opted to follow the authority of the Roman church, it is also known as the home of the first recognised English poet, Caedmon. Having been abandoned in 867 after being sacked by Vikings, it was refounded in 1078 by William de Percy; recent archaeological research indicates that it was also a busy settlement. After its dissolution the fabric of the church survived because it provided a vital landmark for seafarers, although some of the stone was used by the Cholmley family to build a mansion later incorporated into nearby Abbey House. The site is maintained by English Heritage. Tel: 01947 603568.

York Founded in AD 71 when the Romans established a military base at the junction of the rivers Foss and Ouse, Eboracum ('place of the yew trees') grew to become the military and administrative capital of northern Roman Britain. It was linked to London by Ermine Street. Remains of the legionary site have been found under the Minster, and there are traces of Roman occupation still to be seen including parts of the city walls and a masonry column 31ft (10m) high dating to c.AD 70. Saxon York, known as Eoferwic, became capital of Northumbria. After the coming of Christianity, in 627 the first minster was built in York, which became a centre of religious learning under Alcuin. The city was taken by the Vikings in 867, becoming capital of the kingdom of Jorvik until the Vikings were expelled in 954. Many remains from this period have been excavated and can be seen at Jorvik Viking Museum. After the Norman Conquest, York became William I's northern capital and two castles were built; the keep of one of these, now known as Clifford's Tower, still survives. The city soon came to share in Yorkshire's medieval prosperity as illustrated by the building of the magnificent Minster and over 40 other churches in this period, while the influence of the Archbishop of York grew to rival that of Canterbury. Most of the city walls, which survive in an almost complete circuit, date from the 12th to the 14th century. With the decline of the monasteries York's fortunes suffered in the 16th century. Early in the Civil War, Charles I had his base at York at King's Manor. Fairfax's forces besieged the city in April 1644, and it was relieved by Charles's cousin Prince Rupert before the battle of Marston Moor. During the Georgian era the city enjoyed another period of prosperity and growth, and it was further transformed by the arrival of the railway in 1839. Its location halfway between London and Edinburgh made it a natural centre for railway traffic. The station with its remarkable curving layout was built in 1877. The coming of the railway also enabled the growth of industry, and the city became famous for chocolate making after the establishment of Rowntree's Cocoa Works and Terry's Confectionery Works. The influence of Quaker families such as the Rowntrees was manifested with the founding of two Quaker schools, Bootham and the Mount, as well as the village of New Earswick and the mental hospital known as The Retreat. Nestlé Rowntree still has its headquarters in York, although Terry's and the carriage works have closed. Today the city's main earnings are from service industries and tourism, it being a place where 2000 years of history are still visible in the buildings and artefacts.

York Castle Baile Hill, York. Norman motte and bailey castle founded by William I 1068–9. The castle was destroyed almost immediately but rebuilt in stone by Henry III in the mid 13th century. It was repaired during the Civil War. The remaining keep is now known as Clifford's Tower (see separate entry).

York Minster Deangate, York. The successor of a Norman minster built in 1080, York Minster (officially the Cathedral and Metropolitian Church of St Peter in York) was constructed in the new Gothic style between 1220 and 1482. it is the largest Gothic church in England, 524ft (160m) long and 249ft (76m) wide,. The west towers are 184ft (56m) high and the central lantern tower 234ft (71m). The transepts and chapter house were built in the 13th century with the nave and west front following in the 14th. The great east window of 1405 is the largest expanse of medieval glass surviving in England. The famous rose window, dating from the 16th century, was restored after a major fire caused when the minster was struck by lightning in 1984 – a judgement, many rather unjustly believed, on the appointment of the 'liberal' Rev. David Jenkins as Bishop of Durham. Tel. 01904 557216.

York Mystery Plays The most complete surviving cycle of English mystery plays, with 48 episodes telling the story of the Old and New Testaments from Creation to the Last Judgement. Each episode of the cycle was originally staged on wagons, pulled from one site to the next, by one of the city guilds (or 'mysteries'). They date from between the 13th and 16th centuries. Revived as part of the Festival of Britain in 1951, the York Mystery Plays have been performed annually in the city ever since.

Yorkshire Dales National Park Designated in 1954, the area of 680 sq miles (1762 sq km) consists largely of upland pasture, with the higher ground consisting of heather moorland. The high land is divided by a series of glacial valleys. The area covered by the National Park includes Swaledale, Wensleydale, Upper Wharfedale, the Three Peaks and Malham Tarn.

Some famous people born in North Yorkshire

Auden, Wystan Hugh 'W H' (poet) (1907–73)	York
Barry, John (composer) (1933–)	York
Clough, Brian (football manager) (1935–2004)	Middlesbrough
Cook, James (explorer) (1728–79)	Marton
Fawkes, Guy (Catholic martyr) (1570–1606)	York
Flaxman, John (sculptor) (1755–1826)	York
Hill, Susan (author) (1942–)	Scarborough
Howerd, Frankie (comedian) (1917–92)	York
Laughton, Charles (actor) (1899–1962)	Scarborough
Leighton, Frederic (artist) (1830–96)	Scarborough
Rea, Chris (musician) (1951–)	Middlesbrough
Rees, Martin (Astronomer Royal) (1942–)	York
Sitwell, Edith (poet) (1887–1964)	Scarborough
Sutcliffe, Herbert (cricketer) (1894–1978)	Harrogate
Tennant, Smithson (chemist) (1761–1815)	Selby
Wycliffe, John (Bible translator) (c.1329–84)	Hipswell

Islands of North Yorkshire

(Sea Area: North Sea)

Island name	Nearest landmark	General information
Betty Muffett Rocks	Scarborough	GR: TA039901
Bias Scar	Cowbar	GR: NZ768191
Black Nab	Whitby	GR: NZ925108
Calf Allen Rocks	Cayton	GR: TA846076
Castle Rocks	Gristhorpe Cliff	GR: TA091840
Casty Rocks	Gristhorpe Cliff	GR: TA096838
Cat Nab	Bempton	GR: TA213734
Coatham Rocks	Redcar	GR: NZ600260
Cowling Scar	Robin Hood's Bay	GR: NZ957047
Crab Rocks	Bempton	GR: TA200741
East Flashes	Redcar	GR: NZ615253
Flashes, The	Redcar	GR: NZ615255
High Scar	Scarborough	GR: TA064859
High Stone	Redcar	GR: NZ611256
Hill Stones	Runswick Bank Top	GR: NZ826159
Hummersea Scar	Hummersea Beach	GR: NZ725203
Hundales, The	Cloughton	GR: TA027948
Karl Stones	Cayton	GR: TA070845
Lingrow Knock	Runswick Bank Top	GR: NZ810173
Lintycock Stone	Rock Cliff	GR: NZ748202
Long Nab	Cloughton	GR: TA031941
Longhorn Wyke Rock	Burniston	GR: TA032921
Low Balk	Robin Hood's Bay	GR: NZ955033
Mascus	Scarborough	GR: TA039905
Miller's Nab	Robin Hood's Bay	GR: NZ970026
Old Horse	Gristhorpe Cliff	GR: TA101836
Old Horse Rocks	Gristhorpe Cliff	GR: TA100834
Old Nab	Runswick Bank Top	GR: NZ793187
Perilous Rocks	Scarborough	GR: TA062862
Redcar Rocks	Redcar	GR: NZ615254
Salt Scar	Redcar	GR: NZ262613
Saltburn Scar	Saltburn	GR: NZ680210
Saltwick Nab	Whitby	GR: NZ915113
Scalby Ness Rocks	Scarborough	GR: TA039910
Tinkler's Stone	Robin Hood's Bay	GR: NZ959035
West Scar	Redcar	GR: NZ603259
White Nab	Scarborough	GR: TA059865

Local Attractions and Information: South Yorkshire

Abbeydale Industrial Hamlet	Abbeydale Road South, Sheffield. A museum providing an authentic experience of 18th century industry. At the site are waterwheels, tilt hammers, grinding hulls and a unique crucible steel furnace, the only one of its kind operating today. Tel: 0114 236 7731.
Administrative headquarters	**Barnsley**: Town Hall, Barnsley S70 2TA. Tel: 01226 770770. **Doncaster**: 2 Priory Place, Doncaster DN1 1NB. Tel: 01302 734444. **Rotherham**: Civic Building, Walker Place, Rotherham S65 1UF. Tel: 01709 382121. **Sheffield**: Town Hall, Sheffield S1 2HH. Tel: 0114 272 6444.
Aeroventure	Dakota Way, Doncaster Leisure Park, Doncaster. Formerly South Yorkshire Aircraft Museum, now situated on the former RAF Doncaster airfield. Collections of British military aircraft, helicopters and commercial light aircraft are displayed in a 1940 aircraft hangar. The site also includes other historic aircraft buildings, while numerous aircraft are undergoing restoration. Tel: 01302 761616.
Airports	**Robin Hood Airport** (DSA), First Avenue, Doncaster. Built on the site of the former RAF Finningley, which closed in 1996, the site was reopened as a commercial airport serving South Yorkshire on 28 April 2005. A legacy of its usage by long-range bombers, the single runway at just under 2 miles (2891m) long is second only to Manchester in the north of England and makes it suitable for long haul traffic. The airport attracted 1 million passengers in its first year of operation and offered long haul flights from the beginning of 2007. Tel: 0871 220 2210. **Sheffield City Airport** (SZE), Europa Link, Sheffield. Opened in 1997, 4 miles (6km) east of the centre of Sheffield, its small size has limited the number and range of flights it can offer. It currently operates as a general aviation centre and heliport. Tel: 0114 201 1998.
Barnsley Town Hall	Church Street, Barnsley. The town hall of the Metropolitan Borough of Barnsley was constructed in 1932 with a façade of Portland stone. The central tower is 145ft (44m) tall and remains one of the borough's most recognisable landmarks. Outside stands the Barnsley cenotaph.
Beauchief Abbey	Abbey Lane, Sheffield. One of Sheffield's few remaining medieval buildings. Established in 1175 as a Premonstratensian foundation and dedicated to St Mary and the newly canonised St Thomas Becket, only the tower remains of the original abbey buildings. The abbey and nearby 17th century Beauchief Hall have long been the source of ghostly sightings. It is said that the Catholic monks who inhabited the abbey before the Reformation built a tunnel extending from the abbey to a local graveyard, enabling the monks to escape hunting parties sent out by Henry VIII. Today the remains lie within Beauchief golf course. Tel: 0114 221 1900.
Brodsworth Hall	Brodsworth, 4½ miles (7km) northwest of Doncaster. Italianate Victorian country house built in the 1860s for the Thellusson family, whose interests in yachting and horse racing are reflected in the house's collections. The house was continuously occupied by the family until the late 1980s and its original interiors, largely intact, have been conserved without extensive restoration to retain their patina of age. The surrounding gardens have been restored to their original design, with features fashionable in the 1860s such as a fern dell, woodland garden and statue walks. Now owned by English Heritage. Tel: 01302 722598.
Cannon Hall Museum	Bark House Lane, Cawthorne, 4 miles (6km) west of Barnsley. The former home of the Spencer-Stanhope family became a museum in 1957 and holds collections of furniture, paintings and glassware displayed in period settings, along with the Regimental Museum of the 13th/18th Hussars. There is a walled garden with peaches, nectarines and over 40 varieties of pear, while the house is surrounded by 70 acres (28ha) of parkland. Tel: 01226 790270.
Cawthorne Victoria Jubilee Museum	Taylor Hill, Cawthorne, 4 miles (6km) west of Barnsley. Founded in 1884 by the Rev. C T Pratt, vicar of Cawthorne, the museum is a typical Victorian hotch-potch with original collections of butterflies and moths, birds and eggs, fossils, stuffed animals, domestic bygones, wartime relics, old school books and memorabilia. Tel: 01226 790545.
Clifton Park Museum	Clifton Lane, Rotherham. An 18th century mansion housing a collection of Rockingham porcelain, as well as furniture and glassware. Tel: 01709 336633.
Conisbrough Castle	Conisbrough, 4½ miles (7km) southwest of Doncaster. Norman motte and bailey castle founded by William de Warenne c.1070 on a site identified with an Anglo-Saxon *burh* or fortified settlement. It was rebuilt c.1180 by Hamelin, Earl of Surrey, half-brother of Henry II; the stunning white cylindrical tower keep, constructed of magnesium limestone, is the oldest circular keep in England. The site was an inspiration for Walter Scott when writing *Ivanhoe*. Now owned by English Heritage. Tel: 01709 863329.
Cooper Gallery	Church Street, Barnsley. Founded in 1912 by Samuel Cooper, the son of a local linen manufacturer. The collection of art from the 17th to 20th centuries, which includes 18th and 19th century French and Italian paintings and 17th century Dutch works as well as work by J M W Turner, Henry Moore and Edward Lear, is formed largely from donations by Cooper and three other local benefactors. Tel: 01226 790270.
Cusworth Hall Museum of South Yorkshire Life	Cusworth Lane, Doncaster. Housed in a Georgian mansion, the museum illustrates all aspects of local life in the last 250 years. Collections include costume, kitchen equipment, agricultural and craft tools. Tel: 01302 782342.
Doncaster Museum and Art Gallery	Chequer Road, Doncaster. The gallery was established in 1909 and the museum moved to its present building in 1964. Collections include archaeology, regional natural history, geology, local history, ceramics, fine art, paintings and sculpture, costumes, militaria and special exhibitions. It also houses the King's Own Yorkshire Light Infantry Regimental Gallery, opened in 1987, and the collection of the King's Own Yorkshire Light Infantry which includes uniforms, medals and equipment. Tel. 01302 734293.
Elsecar Heritage Centre	Wath Road, Elsecar, 4½ miles (7km) southeast of Barnsley. Located on the site of the former Fitzwilliam Ironworks, the centre's exhibits include a Victorian classroom and the only Newcomen

beam engine in the world still in its original position, used from 1795 to pump water from the nearby colliery. The Elsecar Steam Railway starts here. Tel: 01226 740203.

Elsecar Steam Railway — A heritage railway operating on the former Elsecar branch of the South Yorkshire Railway, which opened in 1850 to serve local industries and closed only in 1984. A number of steam locomotives now run on 1 mile (1.6km) of track from Rockingham Station at Elsecar to the Hemingfield Basin on the Dearne & Dove Canal. Tel: 01226 746746.

Fire Police Museum — Old Fire Station, West Bar, Sheffield. Collections of fire engines, firefighting equipment and memorabilia housed in a previously derelict Victorian fire and police station. The building includes a fire-watching tower, possibly now unique in England. Tel: 0114 249 1999.

Hallam FM Arena — Boughton Lane, Sheffield. The city's main concert venue. The 12,500 capacity stadium was opened as the Sheffield Arena in 1991 and has since hosted an impressive array of concerts, musicals, opera, ice shows and sporting fixtures. The Arena is also home to the Sheffield Steelers (ice hockey) and Sheffield Sharks (basketball) teams. Tel: 0114 256 5656.

Highest point — High Stones at 1798ft (548m), lying on the Howden Moors on the northern boundary of the Peak District National Park.

Hillsborough Disaster — One of the worst disasters in British sporting history occurred on 15 April 1989 at Hillsborough Stadium, the 40,000-seat home of Sheffield Wednesday, before the FA Cup semi-final between Liverpool and Nottingham Forest. At the time, high steel fencing had been fitted between the spectators and the pitch at most stadiums, in response to the hooliganism which had plagued the sport for years. Before kick-off there was a considerable build-up of fans in a small area outside the turnstiles at the Leppings Lane End of the 19th century stadium. A bottleneck developed with more fans arriving than were able to enter. With an estimated 5000 fans trying to get through the turnstiles and the situation becoming increasingly dangerous, the police decided to open a set of exit gates which did not have turnstiles. As a result fans poured through a narrow tunnel at the rear of the terrace and into the already overcrowded central two pens, causing a severe crush at the front where people were pressed against the fencing and unable to escape onto the pitch. Ninety-six Liverpool fans were ultimately crushed to death.

Humberhead Peatlands — Thorne, 10 miles (16km) northeast of Doncaster. A 7134 acre (2887ha) National Nature Reserve on two sites consisting of parts of Thorne, Goole, Crowle and Hatfield Moors. These remains of ancient wetlands form the largest area of lowland raised bog in the UK and have also been declared a Special Area of Conservation. Peat was cut here from the 18th century and extracted on an industrial scale until the late 20th century. Many of the peat cuttings have now been restored to wetland; the reserve also contains areas of fen, scrub, woodland and grassland, and supports 4500 invertebrate species as well as a wide range of birds. It contains the most northerly colony of nightingales in England.

Interesting facts — Harry Brearley invented the **first true stainless steel** in a Sheffield laboratory. The Sheffield-born metallurgist melted the first batch on 13 August 1913. It contained 12.8 per cent chromium, which prevented rusting and revolutionised the steel industry, particularly the manufacture of cutlery which had previously had to be washed before use as corrosion built up. In September 2006, **Nick Matthew** became only the second English winner of the British Open squash title since 1939. **Sheffield FC**, founded in 1857, is the oldest football club in the world and is still going strong. The club currently play home matches at the Bright Finance Stadium, Dronfield, in the Northern Counties East League. Sheffield FC participate in the oldest local football derby in the world (known as the 'Sheffield' or 'Rules' derby) against arch-rivals Hallam FC. **The White Swan** pub in Frenchgate, Doncaster, can make punters feel quite inadequate as the 5ft (1.5m) high bar is the tallest in Britain.

Kelham Island Museum — Alma Street, Sheffield. The museum stands on a 900 year old man-made island and features displays and demonstrations relating to the manufacturing history of Sheffield, including a Bessemer converter, one of only three now in existence and once a vital part of the steel-making process. The giant River Don Steam Engine, built to power an armour-plate rolling mill, is run twice a day. Tel: 0114 272 2106.

Meadowhall Shopping Centre — 3 miles (5km) northeast of Sheffield. The sixth largest shopping centre in the UK. Opened in 1990 on the site of a derelict steelworks, the centre covers an area of over 1.5 million sq ft (139,000 sq m). For specialist shoppers, there is an area of boutiques called 'The Lanes'. With over 280 stores, Meadowhall attracts 30 million visitors annually.

Millennium Gallery — Arundel Gate, Sheffield. Located next to the Winter Garden (see separate entry), the gallery offers a variety of permanent and changing exhibitions with visiting exhibitions drawn from national museum collections. There are also collections of Sheffield metalwork and the Ruskin Gallery containing artefacts collected by John Ruskin. Tel: 0114 278 2600.

Monk Bretton Priory — Abbey Lane, Lundwood, Barnsley. Founded as a Cluniac monastery in 1154 by Adam fitz Swain, the ruins are nowadays surrounded by a housing estate. The 15th century gatehouse still stands, as does the prior's house which was later used as a dwelling. The site is managed by English Heritage and a local trust.

Prisons — **Doncaster**, Marshgate, Doncaster. A private prison opened in 1994. Operational capacity: 1145. Tel: 01302 760870.

Lindholme, Hatfield Woodhouse, was opened on former Ministry of Defence land in 1985. The site includes a Category C prison and Immigrant Removal Centre. Operational capacity: 990. Tel: 01302 524700.

Moorland, Bawtry Road, Hatfield Woodhouse, houses young offenders and Category C adult male prisoners. The site also includes an open prison. Operational capacity: 791. Tel: 01405 746500.

Rivers — The **Dearne** rises in West Yorkshire, flowing east for 20 miles (32km) through Denby Dale, Barnsley and Wath upon Dearne to meet the Don at Conisbrough. Its main tributary is the Dove.

The **Don** rises high in the Pennines, flowing east for 70 miles (112km) through the Don Valley and through Sheffield, Rotherham, Doncaster and Staniforth, joining the River Ouse at Goole.

The **Rother** rises near Clay Cross in Derbyshire and flows north as far as Rotherham (which takes its name from the river) where it meets the Don.

The **Sheaf** rises in Totley, a southwestern suburb of Sheffield, and flows through the city to join the Don at Lady's Bridge.

Roche Abbey — 1 mile (1.6km) south of Maltby, 7 miles (11km) southeast of Rotherham. The ground plan of this ruined Cistercian abbey, built c.1170 in the wooded valley of Maltby Beck, is one of the most complete in England. The eastern end of the church still stands, a fine example of the then new Gothic style. The site is managed by English Heritage.

Rother Valley Country Park — 1/2 mile (0.8km) north of Killamarsh, 7 miles (11km) southeast of Sheffield. Created on a former opencast coal mine and opened in 1983, this vast site covering 750 acres (300ha) is a mecca for birdwatchers and watersport enthusiasts. Tel: 0114 247 1452.

RSPB Old Moor — Brampton, 5 miles (8km) southeast of Barnsley. A 250 acre (101ha) wetland reserve created on former coal mining works in the Dearne Valley. The marshlands, wetlands and grassland are home to golden plovers, lapwings and tree sparrows as well as many species of waders and wildfowl. Tel: 01226 751593.

Sheffield — Although its origins are Anglo-Saxon, Sheffield has been known since the 14th century for the production of knives and by 1600 was the main centre in England for their manufacture. The invention of new methods of steel production during the Industrial Revolution led to the city's period of greatest prosperity as a centre of steel making and cutlery manufacture. Post-war competition from abroad led to the loss of much production but the city is still a major producer of steel. Despite Sheffield's relative decline, the district of Hallam is the most prosperous per head in the UK outside London. The city's population of 513,000 (2001 census) includes 45,000 students. With its 2 million trees, 150 woodland spaces and 50 public parks it is Europe's greenest city, with 61 per cent of the area officially designated 'green space'. In 2005 Sheffield won the 'Entente Florale' competition which confirms its status as the greenest on the continent. Built on seven hills and at the confluence of five rivers, recent research has also shown it to be the most geographically diverse in England. It remains the only city in South Yorkshire.

Sheffield Anglican Cathedral — Church Street, Sheffield. Dedicated to St Peter and St Paul, there has been a church on the site since Saxon times. William de Lovetot built the original church in 1101 and stones from the Norman church, with their dogtooth pattern, can be seen set into the east wall of the sanctuary. In 1430 a new church in Perpendicular style was built with seven altars, a central tower and spire and a splendid hammerbeam roof. This part of the church is one of the oldest buildings in Sheffield still in regular use. In 1520 a family chapel with a burial vault beneath was built for George, 4th Earl of Shrewsbury; the Shrewsbury Chapel houses magnificent Tudor memorials to the 4th and 6th Earls. The 6th Earl of Shrewsbury was the guardian of Mary, Queen of Scots during her imprisonment in Sheffield, 1570–84. In 1914 the church was granted cathedral status with the formation of the new Diocese of Sheffield. At the end of World War I, plans were made to enlarge the building. Under architect Charles Nicholson the axis of the church was to be turned through 90 degrees, a second tower and spire constructed and a new chancel and sanctuary built on the north side, while the nave was to be enlarged on the south side. During the 1930s all the work on the north side was completed, including the Chapel of the Holy Spirit, the Crypt Chapel of All Saints, the Chapel of St George, the Chapter House, the Song School and offices. The Chapel of St Katharine was rededicated and the Shrewsbury Chapel restored. In the early 1960s a narthex entrance was built, leading to an extended west end with a lantern tower, designed by Arthur Bailey. The enlarged cathedral was reconsecrated in 1966.

Sheffield Hallam University — With its roots in the Sheffield School of Design, dating to 1843, the former Sheffield City Polytechnic was awarded university status in 1992. Based on two sites in Sheffield, it now has around 30,000 students. Former students include animator Nick Park. Tel: 0114 225 5555.

Sheffield Roman Catholic Cathedral — Fargate, Sheffield. Built on the site of a house formerly belonging to the Duke of Norfolk and where a Catholic chapel had stood since shortly after Catholic emancipation. Dedicated to St Marie, a new church was designed by leading local architect Matthew Hadfield in 1846 based on a 14th century church at Heckington, Lincolnshire. Expensively decorated with the aid of donations including gifts from from the Duke of Norfolk and his mother, the church was completed in 1850 and opened on 11 September. St Marie's became a cathedral on 30 May 1980 with the creation of the new diocese of Hallam.

Shepherd Wheel — Hangingwater Road, Sheffield. Located in Whiteley Woods in southwest Sheffield. A working knife-grinding workshop on the River Porter powered by a waterwheel dating to the 16th century. See also Abbeydale Industrial Hamlet

Sport

general — **Ponds Forge International Sports Centre** in Sheffield hosts various high-level sports competitions, particularly boxing and international bowls. David Walliams trained at the centre in preparation for his 21 mile (32km) swim across the English Channel in aid of Sport Relief in 2006. The **World Snooker Championship** has been held at the Crucible Theatre in Sheffield since 1977. **Don Valley Stadium** was originally built to host the World Student Games of 1991. The 50,000 seat stadium is the largest purpose-built athletics venue in England and holds pop concerts as well as major sporting events. Tel: 0114 223 3600. The **English Institute of Sport** (see Greater Manchester: Sport) has its regional base at Coleridge Road, Sheffield. Tel: 0114 223 5600.

football — **Barnsley** were formed in 1887 and elected to the Football League in 1898. Despite being in the lower reaches of the Second Division they won the FA Cup after a replay against West Bromwich Albion in 1912. They reached the Premier League for the first time in 1997 but were relegated after one season. Nicknamed The Tykes, their home ground is Oakwell Stadium, Barnsley. Their colours are red and white. Tel: 01226 211211.

Doncaster Rovers were formed in 1879 and first elected to the Football League in 1901. Disbanded during World War I, they reformed in 1920 and rejoined the League in 1923. After 75 years in the lower divisions they lost their Football League status in 1998 but regained it five years later. Nicknamed The Rovers, their colours are red and white. After playing for 84 years at the Earth Stadium, Belle Vue; they moved in January 2007 to the Keepmoat Stadium, a new leisure complex. Tel: 01302 764664.

Rotherham United were formed in 1870 as Thornhill United and made their League debut in 1893. Having changed their name to Rotherham County in 1905, they turned professional and re-entered the League in 1919, merging with Rotherham Town in 1925 to become Rotherham United. They lost to Aston Villa in the first ever League Cup final in 1961. Nicknamed the Merry Millers, their home ground is Millmoor, Millmoor Lane, Rotherham. The club colours are red and white. Tel. 01709 512434.

Sheffield United were formed in 1889. Members of the Football League since 1892, they won the League championship in 1898 and the FA Cup in 1899, 1902, 1915 and 1925. They spent two years in the Premier League, 1992–94, regaining Premiership status for one season in 2005–06. Nicknamed The Blades after the Sheffield cutlery industry, their traditional colours are red and white stripes and their home ground is Bramall Lane, Sheffield, which they shared until 1973 with Yorkshire County Cricket Club. Bramall Lane is the oldest stadium in the world to have continuously hosted football, having been in use since 1889. Tel: 0870 787 1960.

Sheffield Wednesday were formed in 1867 as The Wednesday, an offshoot of a cricket club whose members used to take Wednesday afternoons off to play. The club name was officially changed to Sheffield Wednsday only in 1929, though there is evidence that it was in use in the 1880s. Joining the Football League in 1892, Wednesday won the League championship in 1903, 1904, 1919 and 1920, the FA Cup in 1896, 1907 and 1935 and the League Cup in 1991. Nicknamed The Owls (the name derives from the location of their stadium), they play at Hillsborough, Owlerton, Sheffield. The traditional club colours are blue and white stripes. Tel: 0870 999 1867.

greyhound racing — **Doncaster:** Meadow Court Stadium, Station Road, Stainforth. 430m track. Tel. 01302 351639.

Sheffield: Owlerton Stadium, Penistone Road, Sheffield. 434m track. Tel. 0114 234 3074.

horse racing — **Doncaster** racecourse, Leger Way, Doncaster. Left-handed pear-shaped circuit of about 2 miles (3km) holding Flat and National Hunt racing. The St Leger, the oldest of the five British Classic races, is run at the course each September. Tel: 01302 320066.

rugby league — **Doncaster** were founded in 1951 and reformed in 1994 as Doncaster Dragons after liquidation. They were renamed the Lakers in 2005 after their new home, the Lakeside Community Centre (now itself renamed the Keepmoat Stadium). Since 2007 they have once again been known simply as Doncaster (nickname The Dons) and have reverted to their traditional colours of blue and gold. Tel: 01302 765888.

Sheffield Eagles were founded in 1984 and play at Don Valley Stadium, Worksop Road, Sheffield. Winners of the Challenge Cup in 1998, their colours are red and yellow. Tel: 0114 261 0326.

Tickhill Castle — Tickhill, 6 miles (10km) south of Doncaster. Late 11th century Norman motte and bailey castle founded by Roger de Busli and later given to Robert de Belleme. An 11-sided tower was built on the motte c.1178–80 by Henry II. It was granted to John of Gaunt in 1372 and is still owned by the Duchy of Lancaster. After Civil War slighting, the Hansby family built a large 17th century house, which may incorporate parts of the old hall.

University of Sheffield — One of the original 'red-brick' universities, gaining its royal charter in 1905, the former University College of Sheffield has grown rapidly since the 1950s. Student numbers now stand at over 25,000. It occupies a cluster of buildings 1 mile (1.6km) to the west of Sheffield city centre, with other sites also mainly in the west of the city. Its Arts Tower, completed in 1965, is the tallest student building in England at 255ft (78m) and also the tallest in the city. Academic specialities include archaeology, engineering and music. Sheffield is a member of the Russell Group of research-led universities. Former students include authors Joanne Harris and Hilary Mantel, comedian Eddie Izzard, newsreader Carol Barnes, astronaut Helen Sharman and David Davies, chief executive of the Football Association. Tel: 0114 222 2000.

Wentworth Castle and Gardens — 3 miles (5km) southwest of Barnsley. Originally named Stainborough Hall, the house was built in the 1670s for Sir Gervase Cutler. The estate was bought in 1708 by Thomas Wentworth, who added a Baroque east wing 1710–20; the Palladian style south and west wings were added in the 1760s for William Wentworth. The 600 acre (250ha) estate featured in the BBC series *Restoration*. Home to the National Collections of rhododendrons, camellias and magnolias, the gardens, laid out in the 18th century and the only Grade I listed landscape in South Yorkshire, have recently been restored. Tel: 01226 731269.

Wentworth Woodhouse — Wentworth, 4 miles (6km) northwest of Rotherham, Begun in Baroque style in 1725, this vast country house has the longest façade of any building in England at 606ft (185m). The house was once the home of Charles Watson-Wentworth, Britain's 11th Prime Minister. The grounds feature various monuments and follies including the 115ft (35m) high Keppel's Column, deisgned by John Carr. The house is not open to the public.

Weston Park Museum — Western Bank, Sheffield. Located close to the University of Sheffield, the museum has been at the heart of Sheffield's cultural life since 1875. Weston Park contains the city's main art, archaeology, social and natural history collections. Recently refurbished, the museum's interactive exhibits provide a detailed history of Sheffield life from the earliest settlers through to the Industrial

	Revolution and 20th century steel production, and also enable visitors to explore the wildlife, weather and landscape of the region including prehistoric creatures, plants, rocks and minerals. Tel: 0114 278 2600.
Winter Garden, Sheffield	Surrey Street, Sheffield. An award-winning building opened by Queen Elizabeth II in 2003. Located in in the heart of the city, it features one of the UK's biggest temperate glasshouses, 230ft (70m) long and 70ft (21m) high and large enough to contain 5000 domestic greenhouses. Its nautical style and vast wooden beams encompass over 2000 plants. The design includes a Building Management System which ensures temperatures are kept constant all year round. Tel: 0114 221 1900.
Worsbrough Country Park	2 miles (3km) south of Barnsley. 200 acres (80ha) of parkland containing a fishing reservoir and Wigfield open farm. The park is also the location of Worsbrough Mill Museum, a working flour mill and industrial museum housed in a building dating from 1625.
Wortley Hall	5 miles (8km) southwest of Barnsley. The ancestral home of the Earls of Wharncliffe, the early 19th century hall is surrounded by 11 acres (4.5ha) of formal Italianate gardens and by 15 acres (6ha) of informal pleasure grounds with many fine trees, including 500 year old beeches and oaks. Owned by the Labour, Co-Operative & Trade Union Movement. Tel: 0114 288 2100.

Some famous people born in South Yorkshire

Baker, Janet (opera singer) 1933–)	Hatfield
Banks, Gordon (goalkeeper) (1937–)	Sheffield
Bean, Sean (actor) (1959–)	Sheffield
Blunkett, David (politician) (1947–)	Sheffield
Bradbury, Malcolm (novelist) (1932–2000)	Sheffield
Byatt A S (author) (1936–)	Sheffield
Cocker, Joe (singer) (1944–)	Sheffield
Drabble, Margaret (author) (1939–)	Sheffield
Garrett, Lesley (opera singer) (1955–)	Doncaster
Hawthorn, Mike (racing driver) (1929–59)	Mexborough
Keegan, Kevin (footballer) (1951–)	Doncaster
Palin, Michael (actor) (1943–)	Sheffield
Parkinson, Michael (broadcaster) (1935–)	Barnsley
Rigg, Diana (actress) (1938–)	Doncaster
Trueman, Fred (fast bowler) (1931–2006)	Stainton

Local Attractions and Information: West Yorkshire

Administrative headquarters	**Bradford:** City Hall, Centenary Square, Bradford BD1 1HY. Tel. 01274 4321111. **Calderdale:** Town Hall, Crossley Street, Halifax HX1 1UJ. Tel. 01422 357257. **Kirklees:** Civic Centre 3, Market Street, Huddersfield HD1 1WG. Tel. 01484 221000. **Leeds:** Civic Hall, Calverley Street, Leeds LS1 1UR. Tel. 0113 234 8080. **Wakefield:** Town Hall, Wood Street, Wakefield WF1 2HQ. Tel. 01924 306090.
Aire & Calder Navigation	A canal running for 33 miles (53km) beside the course of the River Aire between Leeds and Goole in East Yorkshire, with a branch along the River Calder between Castleford and Wakefield. Construction began in 1704 and further improvements were made throughout the 19th and 20th centuries. It is still used by commercial traffic, although now mostly a leisure waterway.
Airedale	The valley of the River Aire stretches from the river's source in the Yorkshire Dales of North Yorkshire, down past Bradford, through Leeds and Wakefield and on to join the Humber. The Airedale terrier originated from this area. Sometimes called the 'King of Terriers' because it is the largest of the terrier breeds, the breed has also been called the Waterside Terrier, because it was bred originally to hunt otters in and around Airedale.
Bagshaw Museum	Wilton Park, Batley. Housed in a Victorian Gothic mansion once belonging to mill owner George Sheard, the museum was founded in 1911 by Walter Bagshaw. There are galleries dedicated to life and death in Ancient Egypt, the tropical rainforest, the history of the seaside, and real and imaginary animals from around the world. Tel: 01924 326155.
Bankfield Museum	Akroyd Park, Halifax. Founded in 1887 and housed in an Italianate mansion formerly owned by mill owner Edward Akroyd, the museum holds an internationally important collection of textiles. The building also houses the museum of the Duke of Wellington's Regiment. Tel: 01422 354823.
Battles	See separate table for details of the battles of Adwalton Moor, Bramham Moor, Seacroft Moor, Wakefield and Winwaed.
Bolling Hall	Bowling Hall Road, Bradford. Dating from before the 16th century and the family home of local landowners the Bollings and the Tempests for over 500 years, the house was a Royalist stronghold during the Civil War. Today the rooms are furnished in keeping with a range of historical periods. Items on display include a bed made by Thomas Chippendale for Harewood House. Tel: 01274 723057.
Bradford Cathedral	Church Bank, Bradford. An Anglican cathedral dedicated to St Peter and begun in the mid 15th century on the site of a previous church burnt in a Scottish raid in 1327. The nave was completed in 1458 and the west tower in 1508. It became a cathedral in 1919 with the founding of the

	Diocese of Bradford. Substantial rebuilding took place in the 1950s to designs by Sir Edward Maufe, and the cathedral's new east end was dedicated in 1963.
Bramham Park	1 mile (1.6km) southwest of Bramham, 8 miles (13km) northeast of Leeds. Built in 1698 by Robert Benson, 1st Lord Bingley, MP for York, the house was possibly designed by Benson himself and exhibits Palladian and Baroque influences absorbed on his Grand Tour. It is set in 150 acres (60ha) of grounds, including 66 acres (26.5ha) of formal 18th century gardens in French style influenced by Versailles. Almost unique in England, these consist of a landscape of geometric avenues, water gardens, monuments and temples. The mansion was burnt down in 1828 and restored to the original design only in the early 1900s; today it is still occupied by Benson's descendants, the Lane Fox family. Tel: 01937 846000.
Brontë Birthplace	Market Street, Thornton, 4 miles (6km) west of Bradford. The three Brontë sisters, Charlotte, Emily and Anne, along with their brother Branwell, were all born in this former parsonage when their father was curate 1815–20. Tel 01274 830849.
Bronte Parsonage Museum	Church Street, Haworth. Built 1778–9, the parsonage was the home of the Brontë sisters and their father Patrick, 1820–61. It is now displayed as closely as possible in appearance to how it was when the sisters lived here. Tel: 01535 642323.
Cartwright Hall Art Gallery	Lister Park, Bradford. Bradford's civic art gallery holds permanent collections mainly of 19th and 20th century British art. There are also collections of contemporary prints and South Asian art and craft. The purpose-built gallery, imitating a Baroque country house in style though opened only in 1904, is surrounded by parkland. Tel. 01274 751212.
City Varieties	Swan Street, Leeds. A Grade II* listed music hall built in 1865 by Charles Thornton as an entertainment room of the White Swan Inn, With its layout of a long rectangular space, with boxes at the sides supported on cast-iron columns, it is one of the few music halls in England to survive largely unaltered. It was the home of BBC Television's recreation of traditional music hall, *The Good Old Days*, from 1953–83, and still hosts a wide-ranging programme of music, theatre and light entertainment. It seats 531. Tel. 0113 243 0808.
Cliffe Castle	Spring Gardens Lane, Keighley. Originally belonging to Victorian textile manufacturer H I Butterfield, the house is now a large museum with a wide variety of exhibits including minerals, local rocks and fossils (including a 2m long fossil newt!), mounted birds and animals, original furnished rooms with chandeliers, William Morris stained glass, old dolls, toys and domestic items. There is also a programme of temporary exhibitions. Tel: 01535 618231.
Colour Museum	Providence Street, Bradford. Run by the Society of Dyers and Colourists, the museum explores the history and technology of the use of colour since ancient Egyptian times. Tel. 01274 390955.
East Riddlesden Hall	1 mile (1.6km) northeast of Keighley. An atmospheric mid 17th century manor house built by James Murgatroyd. The ruined Starkie wing (built in 1692 by Edmund Starkie) provides a fine backdrop to the mature garden. The house was used as a film location for *Wuthering Heights* (1992). Now owned by the National Trust. Tel: 01535 607075.
Hardcastle Crags	1½ miles (2.5km) north of Hebden Bridge. These stacks of millstone grit are only one feature of a beautiful wooded Pennine valley sometimes called Little Switzerland and notable for the large anthills of the hairy wood ant. Hebden Water flows through the valley. Gibson Mill, a former 19th century cotton mill, now runs entirely on sustainable energy generated from a mixture of sources including hydroelectric turbines, solar panels and wood from the surrounding woodlands. The 400 acre (160ha) estate is owned by the National Trust.
Harewood House	6 miles (10km) north of Leeds. The home of the Earl of Harewood, a fine country house originally in Palladian style completed in 1772, designed by John Carr and with interiors by Robert Adam, with 19th century alterations by Charles Barry. Thomas Chippendale designed all the original furniture, most notably the ornate state bed and a collection of mirrors which were put into store in the mid 19th century and only rediscovered in the 1980s. Below stairs, the kitchens contain an impressive collection of copperware. The extensive grounds were landscaped by Capability Brown. Tel: 0113 218 1010.
Heritage railways	**Keighley & Worth Valley Railway**, Haworth Station, Keighley. Opened in 1968 to operate steam trains over a steep 5 mile (8km) climb on the former British Rail line between Keighley and Oxenhope. It is perhaps most famous as the location of the film *The Railway Children* (1970). The Vintage Carriages Trust Museum next to the Keighley terminus holds a collection of rolling stock kept in working order, providing a valuable resource for film makers. Tel: 01535 645214. **Kirklees Light Railway**, Park Mill Way, Clayton West, Huddersfield. A narrow-gauge light railway operating steam trains for 8 miles (13km) on an old branch line through the South Pennines between Clayton West (on the A636) and Shelley stations, passing through a ¼ mile (0.4km) tunnel on the way. Tel: 01484 865727. **Middleton Railway,** Moor Road, Leeds. Located 2 miles (3km) south of Leeds city centre. Established by Act of Parliament in 1758 to carry coal from Middleton to Leeds, the Middleton Railway can claim to be the oldest in the world. A range of diesel and steam locomotives now runs over 1 mile (1.6km) of standard gauge track between Hunslet and Middleton. Tel. 0113 271 0320.
Highest point	Black Hill on the West Yorkshire/Derbyshire border at 1732ft (528m). GR: SE078046.
Ilkley Moor	The highest part of Rombalds Moor, the moorland between Ilkley and Keighley, rising to 1319ft (402m) above sea level. The moor has an abundance of prehistoric cup and ring marked stones, and is famous as the inspiration for the Yorkshire county anthem 'On Ilkla Moor Baht'at'. In July 2006 a major fire on the moor destroyed over 500 acres (200ha) of heather moorland.
Interesting facts	The Dunhill family are generally credited with first making the sweets known as **Pontefract** (or **Pomfret** – the Norman name of Pontefract) **cakes** as confectionery from 1760. Each liquorice-based disc is imprinted with an image of a castle; although this is often taken to represent Pontefract Castle, it may equally be because the cakes were first made at the Old Castle Inn, then

run by Richard Dunhill. **Harry Ramsden's**, the worldwide fish and chip shop empire which owns or franchises more than 170 outlets internationally, was started by Harry Ramsden in 1928 in a wooden shed in Guiseley, 6 miles (10km) north of Bradford. **Lucy Tate**'s appointment to the bench in Pontefract in September 2006 made her Britain's youngest magistrate at the age of 19. **Pudsey**, the teddy bear logo of the BBC's Children in Need, created by designer Joanna Ball, was named after Ball's home town of Pudsey in West Yorkshire. **Andy Bolton** (1970–), from Armley in Leeds, lays claim to being the strongest man in the world. Although Phil Pfister from America won the official title in 2006, Andy amazed fellow strongmen across the world by deadlifting – raising to waist level – an incredible 1003lb (455kg) during a competition in New York in December 2006, the first man in history to successfully attempt a 1000lb deadlift. Twenty-five stone Andy delivers heavy tools for Banner Power Tools, Leeds, by day, and much of his spare time is spent at Bodies Gym in Mabgate, Leeds. It has been suggested that the nursery rhyme **'Here We Go Round the Mulberry Bush'** originated at Wakefield Prison as a song sung by prisoners while they exercised around a mulberry bush in the yard. **Huddersfield Ben** is acknowledged to be the foundation sire of the Yorkshire terrier breed of dog. He was born in 1865 in the town of Huddersfield, Kirklees, and won numerous shows before being run over on 23 September 1871. The long-haired terrier is known for its distinctive blue and tan coat. Yorkies can be very small, usually weighing not more than 7lb (3.2kg) with a height of no more than six or seven inches (15–18cm).

Kirkstall Abbey — Kirkstall Road, Leeds. Located on the northern bank of the River Aire, the remains of the Cistercian abbey, founded in 1152 by monks from Fountains Abbey in North Yorkshire, are the most complete of their type in England. Those of the church are particularly impressive, notably the cloisters and chapter house. The Grade I listed remains are now set within a public park. Tel: 0113 230 5492.

Ledston Hall — Ledston, 2 miles (3km) north of Castleford. Built 1653–71 for East India merchant Sir John Lewis and incorporating part of a 13th century chapel built by the monks of Pontefract Priory. There are traces of 17th century formal gardens and pleasure grounds, and of landscaping by Charles Bridgeman dating to 1716, in the surrounding parkland. Tel: 01423 523423.

Leeds & Bradford International Airport — (LBA) Yeadon, 6 miles (10km) northwest of Leeds. Opened in 1931 as Yeadon Aerodrome and offering scheduled flights within the UK since 1935. Peacetime operations recommenced in 1947 and the airport has since grown steadily. Flights are operated to many UK and European destinations as well as the Caribbean and Mexico. The airline Jet2.com is based at the airport. Tel: 0113 250 9696.

Leeds & Liverpool Canal — The longest canal in the UK, extending for 127 miles (204km) from the Aire & Calder Navigation in Leeds to Stanley Dock in Liverpool. Begun in 1770, it was built piecemeal over the next 46 years and finally completed in 1816. There are a total of 91 locks, often grouped in staircases, the most notable being Five Rise Locks at Bingley, opened in 1774. It was used commercially until 1964 and the last movements of coal took place as recently as 1972.

Leeds Cathedral — Great George Street, Leeds. The Roman Catholic cathedral of the Diocese of Leeds, dedicated to St Anne. The city's original Roman Catholic cathedral, established in 1878, was demolished c.1900. The current neo-Gothic building was designed by architect John Henry Eastwood and completed in 1904. Tel: 0113 245 4545.

Leeds City Art Gallery — The Headrow, Leeds. Opened in 1888, the gallery's collections range from early 19th century to contemporary art, specialising in English watercolours and Pre-Raphaelite painting, while the collections of 20th century British art and modern sculpture are the largest in the UK outside London. Tel: 0113 247 8248.

Leeds International Piano Competition — Established in 1963 by Fanny Waterman and Marion Harewood, and held every three years. It is open to professional pianists under the age of 30. The semi-finals (solo piano) and finals (piano concertos) are held in Leeds Town Hall.

Leeds Metropolitan University — Civic Quarter, Leeds. The former Leeds Polytechnic, created in 1970 from Leeds College of Technology, Leeds College of Art, Leeds College of Commerce and Yorkshire College of Education, was awarded its university charter in 1992. There are currently more than 39,000 students following degree-level and further education courses in sport, health science. business and commerce, architecture, cultural studies, law, technology and social science. The main campus near the centre of Leeds is supplemented by Beckett Park in the north of the city and at Hornbeam Park in Harrogate, while the New Technology Institute is in south Leeds. Former students include sculptors Henry Moore and Barbara Hepworth, singer Marc Almond and rugby union player Austin Healey. Tel: 0113 283 2600.

Leeds Pottery — Established in Hunslet in 1770 by brothers John and Joshua Green. The pottery became particularly known for its cream-coloured earthenware, or creamware, often characterised by pierced work (patterns with holes right through the thickness of the china). The original Leeds Pottery went bankrupt in 1820. Until 1878 the old moulds continued to be used by others, although with less skill; from 1888 more skilful reproductions of the early models were produced.

Longley Old Hall — Longley, 1 mile (1.6km) southeast of Huddersfield. A mid 14th or early 15th century house owned by the Ramsden family, lords of the manors of Almondbury and Huddersfield, from 1540 until the late 20th century. The earliest documentary evidence for its date is an Inquisition record of 1574, but an entry in William Ramsden's Commonplace Book of 1544 refers to purchasing timber to repair his 'house at Longley'. Colonel Sir John Ramsden, Sheriff of Yorkshire and owner of the hall during the Civil War, died defending Newark for the king during the great siege of 1646. Tel: 01484 430852.

Lotherton Hall and Gardens — Aberford, 7 miles (11km) east of Leeds. Late Victorian country house redesigned by its owner Richard Oliver Gascoigne in the 19th century and by his grandson Frederick from 1893. After his death in 1937 the estates passed to his son and daughter-in-law, Sir Alvary and Lady Gascoigne, who retired here in 1953 after an active diplomatic career. In 1968 they presented the hall to the City of Leeds, together with its park, garden and art collections. These have since been augmented by items brought from Temple Newsam House and Leeds City Art Gallery, and by objects bought specially for the house since it opened as a museum in 1969. Tel: 0113 281 3259.

Marsden Moor Estate — An area of Pennine moorland around the village of Marsden to the west of Huddersfield, covering 5685 acres (2429ha) and forming the northern tip of the Peak District National Park. It is a designated Site of Special Scientific Interest providing a nesting habitat for large numbers of moorland birds. Since 1955 the estate has been owned by the National Trust.

National Coal Mining Museum — Overton, 5 miles (8km) southwest of Wakefield. Situated on a 17 acre (7ha) site surrounding the former Caphouse Colliery and Hope Pit, and featuring exhibits relating to the history of coal mining worldwide. It is possible to travel 150 yards underground into the former mine workings. Tel: 01924 848806.

National Media Museum — Little Horton Lane, Bradford. Formerly the National Museum of Photography, Film & Television. Part of the National Museum of Science and Industry and sited in Bradford in recognition of the city's place in the history of UK cinema, since 1983 this has regularly been the most visited museum in the UK outside London. Items in the collection include the world's earliest television footage. The cinema collection focuses particularly on items from the UK film industry, and the photography collection includes the entire contents of the Kodak Museum, donated in 1984. There is an IMAX cinema and the only Cinerama cinema in the world still open to the public. Tel: 0870 701 2000.

Nostell Priory — Wragby, 5 miles (8km) southeast of Wakefield. Built by James Paine in 1733 on the site of the 12th century priory of St Oswald, the most notable features of the house are rooms designed by Robert Adam and an original collection of Chippendale furniture supplied for the house in the 1760s. Other items of interest are an 18th century doll's house with original fittings and a 1717 longcase clock with wooden movement made by John Harrison. The house is surrounded by 300 acres (120ha) of parkland. The property is now owned by the National Trust; the library of over 4000 books is one of the finest held by the Trust. Tel: 01924 863892.

Oakwell Hall Country Park — Birstall, 2 miles (3km) north of Dewsbury. 16th century manor house surrounded by 100 acres (40ha) of parkland. The model for 'Fieldhead' in Charlotte Bronte's novel *Shirley*, the house is displayed as it was in the late 17th century when it was the home of the Batt family. Tel: 01924 326240.

Piece Hall — Westgate, Halifax. Opened in 1779 as a place for handloom weavers to sell cloth, and consisting of a large open courtyard 300ft (91.5m) by 273ft (85m), enclosed by a rectangle of colonnaded walkways 330ft (100m) long and 273ft (85m) wide, off which open 300 rooms. By the mid 19th century it was already being used as a market and venue for open-air events. Now Grade I listed, the structure was restored in the 1970s and houses an art gallery and shops, as well as being home to regular markets. Tel: 01422 358087.

Pontefract Castle — Castle Garth, Pontefract. Norman motte and bailey castle founded 1069 by Ilbert de Lacy, improved by Thomas, Earl of Lancaster. The remains of this 11th century castle barely reveal its notorious history. During the 14th century it was held by John of Gaunt, and Richard II was imprisoned here before his death. The castle was ruined in 1644 during the Civil War when, as a Royalist stronghold, it was besieged by Parliamentarians. Tel: 01977 723440.

Prisons — **Leeds**, Stanningley Road, Leeds (familiarly known as Armley prison), opened in 1847 and a place of execution until 1860. It is now a Category B local prison. Operational capacity: 1004. Tel: 0113 203 2600.

New Hall, Flockton, Wakefield, is a women's prison and Young Offenders Institution. Opened as a pioneering men's open prison in 1933, it became a detention centre for young offenders in 1961 and a women's prison in 1987. Operation capacity: 446. Tel: 01924 823000.

Wakefield, Love Lane, Wakefield, dates to 1594 when a house of correction was built in the town on a site near Westgate. The current building was opened in 1847 and is now a Category A high security prison, largely holding sex offenders. Operational capacity: 751. Tel: 01924 246000.

Wealstun, Thorp Arch, Wetherby, was created in 1995 from the amalgamation of Thorp Arch and Rudgate prisons. It now houses Category C and D prisoners in a combined closed and open unit. Operational capacity: 677. Tel: 01937 444400.

YOI Wetherby, York Road, Wetherby. A former naval base opened in 1958 as a Borstal. Operational capacity: 360. Tel: 01937 544200.

Rivers — The **Aire** rises at Aire Head near Malham in North Yorkshire, flowing through Gargrave and Skipton before reaching West Yorkshire at Kildwick. It then flows through Keighley, Bingley, Saltaire and Leeds and east back into North Yorkshire at Knottingley. It finally joins the Ouse at Airmyn north of Goole.

The **Calder** is 45 miles (72km) long, rising in the Pennines northwest of Todmorden and flowing through Hebden Bridge, Mytholmroyd, Sowerby Bridge, Elland, Mirfield, Dewsbury and Wakefield before joining the Aire at Castleford. It is linked to the Aire via the Aire & Calder Navigation, a canal system largely built in the late 18th century.

The **Wharfe** has its source at Langstrothdale Chase in the Yorkshire Dales and flows southeast for 60 miles (97km) through Kettlewell, Bolton Abbey in Upper Wharfedale and then through Ilkley, Otley and Tadcaster. It joins the Ouse north of Selby.

Royal Armouries Museum — Armouries Drive, Leeds. Opened in 1996 to house the national collection of arms and armour, previously kept in the Tower of London. The five galleries are themed with exhibits on war, tournament, self-defence, hunting and oriental arms. Tel: 0870 034 4344.

Saltaire — $^1/_2$ mile (0.8km) west of Shipley, 4 miles (6km) northwest of Bradford. A model village located beside the River Aire, founded in 1853 by industrialist Sir Titus Salt to provide his mill workers with improved living conditions. The former Salts Mill has been converted into the 1853 Gallery, which contains a significant collection of the works of Bradford-born artist David Hockney. The village was declared a UNESCO World Heritage Site in 2001.

Sandal Castle — Sandal, 1½ miles (2.5km) southeast of Wakefield. Norman motte and bailey castle founded by William de Warenne c.1157 on a site overlooking the River Calder. Hamelin de Plantagenet began rebuilding the castle in stone c.1180, and it was further strengthened during the 13th century. The castle features in Shakespeare's *Henry VI Part 3*. Besieged in 1645 and slighted in 1646 during the Civil War, the remains of the entire castle were left uncovered after excavation. The motte, with foundations of a circular keep, and many of the associated earthworks remain intact and clearly visible.

Shibden Hall — Lister's Road, Halifax. Half-timbered manor house built c.1420 and set in 90 acres (37ha) of parkland. Shibden was the home of the Lister family for over 300 years, political activist and traveller Anne Lister, with her partner Ann Walker, being the most famous residents. Tel: 01422 352246.

Shipley Glen Tramway — Prod Lane, Baildon, 3 miles (5km) northwest of Bradford. The oldest working cable tramway in Britain, built in 1895 and originally powered by gas before being converted to electricity in 1928. The wooded valley of Shipley Glen has been a tourist attraction since the Victorian era. Tel: 01274 589010.

Sport

cricket — **Yorkshire County Cricket Club** was founded in 1863 and has produced many of the finest cricketers in the game's history, including George Hirst, Wilfred Rhodes, Herbert Sutcliffe, Len Hutton, Fred Trueman and Geoffrey Boycott. The club's policy of selecting players born within the county's traditional boundaries was abandoned only in 1992, since when overseas players have included Sachin Tendulkar and Darren Lehmann. Yorkshire won their first County Championship in 1867 and have won the title 33 times, more than any other county. They also won the Gillette Cup in 1965 and 1969 and the C&G Trophy in 2002. The club's home ground since 1881 has been Headingley Cricket Ground (now known as Headingley Carnegie), Leeds, although Bramall Lane in Sheffield was also a regular ground until 1973 and Park Avenue in Bradford until 1982; currently Scarborough is the only out-ground. The one-day side is known as Yorkshire Phoenix. Tel. 0870 429 6774.

football — **Bradford City** were formed in 1903 from the former Manningham rugby union club, joining the Football League the same year. Promoted to the First Division in 1908 and winners of the FA Cup in 1911, they spent 77 years in the lower divisions before again reaching the Premier League in 1999, and were relegated after only two seasons. Nicknamed The Bantams, their club colours are claret and amber and their home ground is the Bradford & Bingley Stadium, Valley Parade, Bradford. In 1985 the ground was the scene of a major fire in which 56 people died. Tel. 0870 822 0000.

Huddersfield Town were formed in 1908 and elected to the Football League in 1910. They won the FA Cup in 1922 and the League championship in 1924, 1925 and 1926 under manager Herbert Chapman, who went on to lead Arsenal to similar success. The club's home since 1994 has been the McAlpine (now the Galpharm) Stadium. Nicknamed The Terriers, their colours are blue and white stripes. Tel: 0870 444 4677.

Leeds United were founded in 1919 from the former Leeds City FC and elected to the Football League in 1920. They oscillated between the top two divisions until the 1960s when Don Revie was appointed manager and the club entered its most successful period, winning the League championship in 1969 and 1974, the FA Cup in 1972, the League Cup in 1968 and the European Fairs Cup in 1968 and 1971, as well as being runners-up in all the major competitions. A later period of success was crowned with the Premier League title in 1992 but after financial problems the club was relegated in 2004. Traditionally Leeds played in yellow and blue but Revie changed their kit to all white in emulation of Real Madrid. Nicknamed The Whites (an older nickname is the Peacocks), their home ground is Elland Road, Leeds. Tel: 0113 226 6055.

greyhound racing — **Kinsley Greyhound Stadium**, Wakefield Road, Kinsley, Pontefract. 385m track. Tel: 01977 610946.

horse racing — **Pontefract**, Park Lane, Pontefract. Left-handed Flat racing circuit of 2 miles (3km). Tel: 01977 781307.

Wetherby, York Road, Wetherby. Left-handed oval National Hunt course of 1 mile 4 furlongs (2.5km). Tel: 01937 582035.

rugby league — **Batley Bulldogs** were founded in 1880 as Batley FC. Founder members of the Northern Rugby Union in 1895, they won the Challenge Cup in 1897, 1899 and 1901. They play at Heritage Road, Mount Pleasant, Batley. Tel. 01924 470062.

Bradford Bulls were formed in 1907 as Bradford Northern and are one of the most successful clubs in modern rugby league. One of only two clubs to win the Super League four times, they also have three other Championship titles and six Challenge Cup successes. Their colours are amber, red, black and white and they play at Odsal Stadium, Bradford. Tel. 01274 733899.

Castleford Tigers were formed in 1926. Four times winners of the Challenge Cup, with one Championship, they play in black and orange at Wheldon Road, Castleford. Tel. 01977 552674.

Dewsbury Rams were founded in 1898 and won the Challenge Cup in 1912 and 1943. Their colours are red, amber and black and they play at Owl Lane, Dewsbury.. Tel: 01924 465489.

Featherstone Rovers were founded in 1902 and play at Post Office Road, Featherstone. Tel: 01977 602723.

Halifax were formed in 1873. Founder members of the Northern Rugby Union in 1895, they have four Championships and five Challenge Cups to their credit. The club colours are blue and white and they play at the Shay Stadium, Halifax. Tel: 01422 342792.

Huddersfield Giants were formed in 1866. Founder members of the Northern Rugby Union in 1895, they were one of the great teams in rugby league before World War I, with seven Championships and six Challenge Cup successes. They now share the Galpharm Stadium with Huddersfield Town FC.

Hunslet Hawks were formed in 1893 and were founder members of the Northern Rugby Union in 1895. Winners of the Challenge Cup in 1908 and 1934 and runners-up in 1965, their club colours are white, myrtle and flame. Hunslet play at South Leeds Stadium, Middleton Grove, Leeds. Tel. 0113 271 2730.

Keighley Cougars were founded in 1900 and play in red, green blue and white.

Leeds Rhinos were formed in 1895 and have won the Championship or Super League (1961, 1969, 1972 and 2004), and the Challenge Cup 11 times. They play in blue and amber. Their home ground is the Headingley Carnegie Stadium, Leeds, which they share with Leeds Tykes RUFC. Tel: 0845 070 0881.

Wakefield Trinity Wildcats were founded in 1873 as Wakefield Trinity by members of Holy Trinity Church, and were founder members of the Northern Rugby Union in 1895. They won the Championship in 1967 and 1968, and also have five Challenge Cup successes. They play in white, red and blue at Belle Vue, Doncaster Road, Wakefield. Tel: 01924 211611.

rugby union — **Leeds Carnegie**, formerly known as Leeds Tykes, were formed in 1991 from the merger of the Headingley and Roundhay clubs. Winners of the Powergen Cup in 2005, they share Headingley Carnegie Stadium with Leeds Rhinos. The club colours are blue, white and yellow. Tel. 0113 278 6181.

Stoodley Pike — 2$^1/_2$ miles (4km) east of Todmorden. A hill on Langfield Moor above Calderdale, on which stands a 100ft (30.5m) high monument erected in 1854 (replacing a previous one built in 1814) to commemorate the defeat of Napoleon at the Battle of Leipzig.

Temple Newsam Estate — 4 miles (6km) east of Leeds. This impressive Tudor and Jacobean mansion surrounded by 1500 acres (600ha) of parkland was the birthplace of Lord Darnley, husband of Mary, Queen of Scots. The 30 rooms open to the public have been restored since the 1980s and display both the collections of the Ingram family who lived here for 300 years, and the city's collections of decorative art. The grounds contain a home farm with the world's largest rare breeds collection. Tel: 0113 264 7321.

University of Bradford — Richmond Road, Bradford. The main campus is located in the west of the city centre. Established in 1966 when the Bradford Institute of Technology, whose origins were in the Mechanics Institute founded in 1832, received its charter. In 1996 Bradford and Airedale College of Health merged with the university, providing it with a School of Health Studies. Courses focus on science and technology, while its Peace Studies degree is one of only a few of its kind in the world and internationally renowned. The university has around 13,000 students. Former students include journalist John Pienaar and poet John Hegley. Tel: 01274 232323.

University of Leeds — Woodhouse Lane, Leeds. One of the original 'red-brick' universities, Leeds received its royal charter in 1904, being formed by a merger between Yorkshire College, the Leeds School of Medicine and the Leeds branch of Victoria University. The Brotherton Library, opened in 1936, still has an original Art Deco interior. In 1997 the university opened a new business school in the former buildings of Leeds Grammar School, built in 1857. Leeds has over 33,000 students and offers one of the widest ranges of undergraduate courses in the UK. The main campus is located on a 98 acre (40ha) site to the north of the city centre, with a smaller site in Wakefield. Leeds is a member of the Russell Group of research-led universities. Former students include politicians Clare Short and Jack Straw, cartoonist Steve Bell and broadcaster Gavin Esler. Tel: 0113 243 1751.

Wakefield Castle — Thornes Park, Wakefield. A 12th century earthwork motte and bailey fortress founded by William de Warenne. Built during the civil war in the reign of King Stephen, the adulterine castle was probably abandoned unfinished. The eroded motte is partly encased by a ditch and the two northeastern baileys lie in-line as they drop down the hill. Encasing the baileys are traces of outer ditches but the earthworks have been mutilated by landscaping.

Wakefield Cathedral — Northgate, Wakefield. The medieval parish church of All Saints was built in the 14th century on the site of a Saxon church. The architecture of the present nave and the main part of the choir is basically late 15th century Perpendicular but there has been a stone church here since Norman times and some of the earlier fabric is still evident. The spire, at 247ft (75m) the tallest in Yorkshire and the fourth highest in England after those at Salisbury, Louth and Coventry, was built in the 15th century to replace the central tower which collapsed in the 14th century. In the 19th century the church was improved and restored by Sir George Gilbert Scott and J T Micklewaite before being elevated to the status of a cathedral in 1888 with the creation of the Diocese of Wakefield. Further work was carried out 1897–1905; the new east end, in memory of Bishop Walsham Howe, the first Bishop of Wakefield, was designed by J L Pearson at the turn of the 20th century, the work being executed by F L Pearson following his father's death. The building was consecrated in 1905. Most of the stained glass windows were created by Charles Eamer Kempe and include work from all periods of his long career, from the mid 19th to the early 20th century. The rood above the screen was designed by Sir Ninian Comper; another feature is the memorial to Bishop Walsham Howe. Tel: 01924 373923.

Yorkshire Ripper — A nickname given by the press to Bingley-born Peter Sutcliffe, who between 1975 and 1980 murdered 13 women in the north of England. Many of his victims were prostitutes and were invariably struck over the head with a ball-pein hammer before being stabbed and mutilated. Sutcliffe was eventually caught during a routine check when he was found in a car with a prostitute. Having asked the police if he could relieve himself, unknown to them at the time he hid his murder weapons behind an oil storage tank. When the police ran a routine check on his car, they found it had false number plates. Sutcliffe was arrested and while in custody was found to be on the list of possible suspects. Sutcliffe, now nicknamed the Yorkshire Ripper, made a full confession and on 22 May 1981 was sentenced to life imprisonment. He began his sentence at Parkhurst but after being attacked was transferred to Broadmoor high security psychiatric hospital, where he resides today.

Yorkshire Sculpture Park — West Bretton, $4^1/_2$ miles (7km) southwest of Wakefield. The 500 acres (200ha) of 18th century gardens and parkland attached to the Palladian house of Bretton Hall (occupied until 2007 by a college) contain a wide range of modern and contemporary sculpture by British artists such as Henry Moore, Barbara Hepworth and Elisabeth Frink, as well as international work. Tel: 01924 830302.

Some famous people born in West Yorkshire

Asquith, H H (British Prime Minister) (1852–1928)	Morley
Austin, Alfred (poet) (1835–1913)	Headingley
Bennett, Alan (writer) (1934–)	Leeds
Boycott, Geoffrey (cricketer) (1940–)	Wakefield
Bradford, Barbara Taylor (author) (1933–)	Leeds
Brontë sisters: Anne (1820–49), Charlotte (1816–55), Emily (1818–48) (novelists)	Thornton
Chippendale, Thomas (furniture maker) (c.1718–79)	Otley
Delius, Frederick (composer) (1862–1934)	Bradford
Fairfax, Thomas (Civil War general) (1612–71)	Denton
Harrison, John (clock maker) (1693–1776)	Foulby
Hepworth, Barbara (sculptor) (1903–75)	Wakefield
Hockney, David (artist) (1937–)	Bradford
Hoyle, Fred (astrophysicist) (1915–2001)	Bingley
Hughes, Ted (poet) (1930–98)	Mytholmroyd
Hutton, Len (cricketer) (1916–90)	Pudsey
Moore, Henry (sculptor) (1898–1986)	Castleford
Priestley, J(ohn) B(oynton) (writer) (1894–1984)	Bradford
Priestley, Joseph (chemist) (1733–1804)	Birstall
Ransome, Arthur (author and journalist) (1884–1967)	Leeds
Wilson, Harold (Prime Minister) (1916–95)	Huddersfield

SCOTLAND

Scotland is bordered by England to the south, the North Sea to the east, the Atlantic Ocean to the north and west, and the Irish Sea to the southwest. The strait that separates the Atlantic Ocean and Irish Sea between Scotland and Northern Ireland is called the North Channel. The three main island groups are the Orkneys, situated off the northern coast of mainland Scotland; the Hebrides, off the west coast and sometimes called the Western Isles; and the Shetlands, situated to the north-east of the Orkneys and therefore the most northerly and easterly island group.

In 1603 James VI, king of Scotland, inherited the throne of England, and became also King James I of England. With the exception of a short period under the Protectorate, Scotland remained a separate state until the Scots Parliament and the Parliament of England enacted the twin Acts of Union, which created the Kingdom of Great Britain on 1 May 1707. The continued independence of Scots Law, the Scottish education system, and the Church of Scotland have ensured the continuation of Scottish culture and Scottish national identity since the Union.

Following a referendum on devolution proposals in 1997, Scotland elected its first home parliament on the 6 May 1999, serving for a four-year period. The Scottish Parliament is not however sovereign and the British Parliament in Westminster retains the ability to amend, change, broaden or abolish the devolved government system at will.

The Scottish motto is *In my defens God me defend*, as appearing on the Royal coat of arms, however *Nemo me impune lacessit* (No one provokes me with impunity), the motto of the Order of the Thistle, as appearing on the Royal coat of arms of the United Kingdom used in Scotland, is often cited as the unofficial motto.

There is no official Scottish anthem, although 'Flower of Scotland' is played before every game of the Scottish national football and rugby union teams and 'Scotland the Brave' is played during the medal ceremonies of the Commonwealth Games. This is more an act of expediency, though, as 'Flower of Scotland' relies on its rousing lyrics to be effective and there are inevitably more Scottish fans at national sports competitions.

The flag of Scotland, known as the Saltire, is a white diagonal cross on a blue background (saltire argent in a field azure). The cross represents the crucifixion of Saint Andrew, the patron saint of Scotland, feast day 30 November. Legend states that the relics of the disciple of Jesus Christ were brought under supernatural guidance from Constantinople to the place where the modern town of St Andrews stands today.

The history and geography of Scotland is described within the overviews of the 12 regions into which I have divided the country. Scottish mountains over 3000ft (914m) high are known as 'Munros' after mountaineer Sir Hugh Munro, who first catalogued all such peaks in 1891. There are now reckoned to be 284 Munros. The country has numerous examples of the prehistoric circular stone defensive towers known as brochs, and later fortifications include substantial numbers of castles. Many of the latter in Scotland were laid out on what is known as a 'Z-plan'; this entailed placing two smaller towers at opposing corners of a main rectangular central tower, allowing all the approaches to the castle's walls to be defended. Included in each region is a list of woodlands established by the Woodland Trust as part of the 'Woods on your Doorstep' (Woyd) project to provide community woodland amenities.

Scotland lies between 60° 51' 30" and 54° 38' N. latitude and between 1° 45'32" and 6° 14' W. longitude. The northernmost point of Scotland, and indeed the United Kingdom, is on Out Stack in the Shetlands. The most northern point of mainland Scotland is Dunnet Head and the most western point Corrachadh Mòr on the Ardnamurchan Peninsula, both in the Highlands. Vatersay island is the most westerly point of Scotland and also the United Kingdom depending on how the tiny uninhabited island of Rockall is perceived (dominion is currently disputed). The easternmost point of Scotland is Bound Skerry in the Shetlands and the most eastern mainland point is Keith Inch, forming part of Peterhead Harbour in Aberdeenshire. The Mull of Galloway, some 20 miles south of Stranraer, in Wigtownshire is Scotland's most southerly point.

The population and area figures listed below include the 32 existing unitary authorities split into these 12 regions. A reconciliation to the 2001 Census is included at the back of the book.

Scotland population summaries

(See 2001 Census Reconciliation)

Scotland	Population			Area	
	male	*female*	*total*	*sq miles*	*sq km*
Scottish Borders	51,361	55,403	106,764	1827	4732
Central	134,444	145,036	279,480	1020	2643
Dumfries and Galloway	71,303	76,462	147,765	2481	6426
Fife	167,628	181,801	349,429	512	1325
Grampian	259,735	266,201	525,936	3373	8737
Highland	102,297	106,617	208,914	9907	25,659
Lothian	373,045	405,322	778,367	666	1724
Orkney Islands	9497	9748	19,245	382	990
Shetland Islands	11,071	10,917	21,988	566	1466
Strathclyde	1,052,261	1,156,348	2,208,609	5261	13,624
Tayside	186,770	202,242	389,012	2906	7528
Western Isles	13,082	13,420	26,502	1186	3071
Total	2,432,494	2,629,517	5,062,011	30,087	77,925

SCOTTISH BORDERS

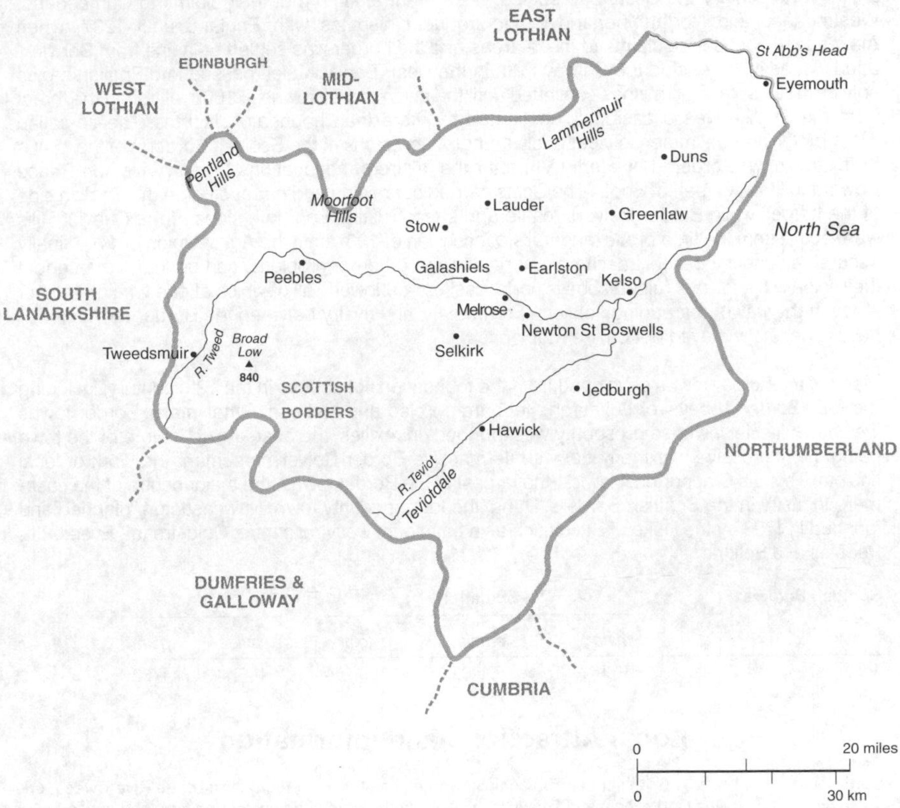
EAST LOTHIAN
St Abb's Head
Eyemouth
EDINBURGH
WEST LOTHIAN
MID-LOTHIAN
Lammermuir Hills
Pentland Hills
Duns
Moorfoot Hills
Lauder
Greenlaw
Stow
North Sea
Peebles
Galashiels
Earlston
Kelso
SOUTH LANARKSHIRE
Melrose
Newton St Boswells
Broad Low
840
Tweedsmuir
R. Tweed
Selkirk
SCOTTISH BORDERS
Jedburgh
Hawick
NORTHUMBERLAND
R. Teviot
Teviotdale
DUMFRIES & GALLOWAY
CUMBRIA
0
20 miles
0
30 km

Usually called simply 'The Borders' or 'The Borderland', the region is one of 32 local government unitary council areas of Scotland. It borders Dumfries and Galloway to the southwest, South Lanarkshire, in Strathclyde, to the west, West Lothian in the northwest, City of Edinburgh, East Lothian and Midlothian to the north, and the English counties of Northumberland to the east and Cumbria to the south. Its northeast shores are washed by the North Sea above Berwick. Borders incorporates all of the former counties of Berwickshire, Peeblesshire, Roxburghshire and Selkirkshire, together with some of Midlothian. Traditionally, however, Borders has a wider meaning, referring to all the burghs adjoining the English border. Covering 1800 square miles (4700 sq km), the Scottish Borders stretches from the rolling hills and moorland in the south, west and north, through gentler valleys to the rich agricultural plains of the east, and on to the rocky Berwickshire coastline with its secluded coves and picturesque fishing villages. Through the centre runs the River Tweed, fed by its many tributaries and providing some of the best fishing in Scotland. The people of the Scottish Borders are very proud of their heritage and often see themselves as 'Borderers' first and foremost. In keeping with this the area has its own dialect and language.

The administrative centre of the region is Newtown St Boswells. Situated on the Bowden Burn above its confluence with the River Tweed, 3 miles (5km) southeast of Melrose, the town developed as an important railway junction and market centre close to St Boswells Green. Although the railway is long gone, Newtown St Boswells thrives as an administrative centre. From 1975 to 1996, it was the centre of Ettrick and Lauderdale District and of Borders Region. It is now home to the headquarters of the Scottish Borders Council.

The history of the Scottish Borders is characterised, like that of so many coterminous nations, by successive territorial and border disputes. The area was occupied by the Romans C.AD 80, Hadrian's Wall being built 40 years later to mark the northern extent of Roman Britain. After the Roman withdrawal the area was fought over for more than 400 years by Pictish tribes, Scots and

Anglo-Saxons, although the eastern part of it formed part of the Anglian kingdom of Bernicia, which extended as far north as the River Forth in Lothian.

By the 11th century the Scots had settled much of the country but their claims to Cumberland, Westmorland and Northumberland led to frequent disputes with England until 1237, when Alexander II abandoned claims to these areas and the border was settled on a line from Berwick-upon-Tweed in the east to the Solway Firth in the west (Berwick itself passed into English hands only in 1482). Border skirmishes continued until the union of the crowns in 1603, although the threat from the English was occasionally instigated by more than boundary disputes. The so-called 'Rough Wooing' (the immensely destructive English invasions of the Scottish Borders) of the 1540s for example, was ordered by Henry VIII after the failure of negotiations to marry his son Prince Edward to Mary, Queen of Scots. The Scots carried out raiding and marauding on the English side of the border, while Border Reivers (cattle and sheep rustlers) on both sides of the Cheviot Hills were active from the time of Alexander II's concession of 1237 until the Act of Union of 1707 finally secured an uneasy peace. Lasting memorials to these border problems can be found throughout the region in the form of ruined abbeys, forts, castles and towers, all of which at one time or another stood in the way of marauding soldiers. Fortunately, any rivalry between the Border towns nowadays is generally played out on the rugby pitch.

Many of the Border towns developed from the foundations of abbeys in the 12th century, including the four 'Border Abbeys' of Dryburgh, Jedburgh, Kelso and Melrose. Other major Border towns include Galashiels, whose prosperity was founded on textiles, the best-known feature of the town being the impressive war memorial with its massive Border Reiver horseman, the work of local sculptor Thomas Clapperton; Hawick, the largest of the Border towns, the major centre of the cashmere industry in the Scottish Borders; Duns, the former county town; Newcastleton, planned and founded in 1793 by the Duke of Buccleuch as a handloom weaving centre; Coldstream, Eyemouth, Peebles and Selkirk.

Scottish Borders	**Population**			**Area**	
	male	*female*	*total*	*sq miles*	*sq km*
Total	51,361	55,403	106,764	1827	4732

Local Attractions and Information

Abbotsford House	1 mile (1.6km) south of Galashiels. Formerly a 100 acre (40ha) farm by the River Tweed, originally called Cartleyhole and known locally as Clarty Hole (muddy hole), the farm and house are now a museum to Sir Walter Scott, who bought the property in 1811 and renamed it Abbotsford. Eventually he owned 1400 acres (570ha), building a new house which was completed in 1824. After Scott died in 1832, the house was occupied by his descendants until the death of Dame Jean Maxwell Scott in 2004. In addition to housing his large collection of rare books, it is also home to Stuart memorabilia such as a lock of Bonnie Prince Charlie's hair and Rob Roy's gun. Tel: 01896 752043.
Administrative headquarters	Newton St Boswells, Melrose TD6 0SA. Tel: 01835 824000.
Ayton Castle	Ayton, 2 miles (3km) southwest of Eyemouth. A red sandstone castle built by the Mitchell-Innes family in the late 1840s on the site of a previous castle destroyed by fire in 1834. The multi-turreted and towered structure is a private home. The house is surrounded by an estate of 3000 acres (1200ha) with views of the Eye Valley. Tel: 01897 81212.
Battles	See separate table for the Battle of Philiphaugh.
Bowhill House and Country Park	Bowhill, 3 miles (5km) west of Selkirk. The home of the Duke of Buccleuch and Queensberry, originally built in 1690 and significantly extended and remodelled 1812–31. It houses an art collection including paintings by Canaletto, Van Dyke, Raeburn, Reynolds and Gainsborough. Other items on display include French furniture, tapestries and Sevres and Meissen porcelain. Memorabilia includes the shirt worn to his execution by the Duke of Monmouth in 1685, proof editions of works by Sir Walter Scott and letters and gifts from Queen Victoria. The grounds cover almost 1500 acres (600ha) and were landscaped by William Sawry Gilpin. Tel: 01750 22204.
Broughton Gallery	Broughton, 4 miles (6km) east of Biggar. A gallery of contemporary arts and crafts focusing on Scottish artists and housed on the ground floor of Broughton Place, a tower house designed by Sir Basil Spence in the 1930s. Tel: 01899 830234.
John Buchan Centre	Old Free Kirk, Broughton, 4 miles (6km) southeast of Biggar. Dedicated to the life and works of novelist John Buchan (1875–1940), whose mother was born in Broughton. Buchan's best-known works are probably *The Thirty-Nine Steps* (1915) and *Greenmantle* (1916); in addition to his literary career he was also a politician and statesman, created 1st Baron Tweedsmuir in 1935 and serving as Governor-General of Canada 1935–40. Tel: 01899 221050.
Cessford Castle	5 miles (8km) northeast of Jedburgh. Situated outside the village of Cessford alongside St Cuthbert's Way are the ruins of a substantial L-shaped fortified tower with walls up to 14ft (4.2m)

thick in places. Built in 1450 by Andrew Ker, it was subject to a number of attacks from England including a successful siege by the Earl of Surrey in 1523. It was abandoned after being damaged by repeated attacks in 1544–5 during Henry VIII's 'Rough Wooing'. The castle remains in the hands of the Ker family, the present owner being the Duke of Roxburghe. The ruins are not accessible to the public.

Cheviot Hills See Northumberland

Robert Clapperton Daylight Photographic Studio Scotts Place, Selkirk. A photographic studio set up by Robert D Clapperton in 1867 and which continued in business under three generations of the Clapperton family until the 1980s. It is now preserved as a working museum, with a collection of negatives and photographic artefacts. Tel: 01750 20523.

Jim Clark Room Newtown Street, Duns, 13 miles (21km) north of Kelso. A celebration of the life and career of racing driver Jim Clark (1936–68). Displays include trophies, photographs and racing memorabilia. Although Clark was born in Fife, his family moved to Duns in 1942. Formula One world champion in 1963 and 1965, achieving 33 pole positions and winning 25 of his 72 Grands Prix as well as winning the Indianapolis 500 in 1965, Clark was killed on 7 April 1968 when his Lotus 48 crashed into trees during a Formula Two race at the Hockenheimring, Germany. He is buried in Chirnside, Berwickshire where the Jim Clark Rally is held each summer on closed roads. Tel: 01361 883960.

Coldstream Museum Market Square, Coldstream. A local history museum also featuring exhibits on the Coldstream Guards, the oldest serving regular regiment in the British Army. The regiment can trace its origin to the formation on 13 August 1650 of Monck's Regiment of Foot by Oliver Cromwell as part of the New Model Army. A month later it took part in the Battle of Dunbar. On 1 January 1660 Monck assembled his troops at Coldstream and marched to London, where he aided the restoration of Charles II. On 14 February 1661 the regiment became part of the Royal Household Troops as the Lord General's Regiment of Foot Guards. (The other regiment of the Household Division which can trace its lineage back to the New Model Army is the Blues and Royals.) Although officially the second senior regiment of Household Troops, the regiment adopted the motto *Nulli Secundus* (second to none) and does not readily accept its designation as 'The Second Guards'. On Monck's death in 1670 the regiment adopted the name the Coldstream Regiment of Foot Guards, gaining its first battle honour at Tangier in 1680, and fought at the Battle of Sedgemoor in 1685. Further battle honours were gained at Namur (1695), Gibraltar (1704–05), Oudenarde (1708) and Malplaquet (1709). During the War of the Austrian Succession the regiment fought at the battles of Dettingen (1743) and Fontenoy (1745) and campaigned under Prince Ferdinand of Brunswick during the Seven Years War. Among many actions during the Napoleonic Wars, the regiment fought in Egypt in 1801 and on the Peninsula under Wellington, 1809–15, before forming part of the 2nd Guards Brigade which defended Hougoumont during the Battle of Waterloo (1815). In 1831 the regiment adopted the bearskin cap previously worn by grenadier regiments, with a red plume on the right side to distinguish it from the other regiments. During the Crimean War it took part in the battles of Alma (1854), Inkerman (1854) and Sevastopol (1855), adopting the name the Coldstream Guards in 1855. Honours in the second half of the 19th century include the battles of Tel-el-Kebir (1882) and Modder River (1899). At the outbreak of World War I the regiment was sent to France as part of the British Expeditionary Force (BEF) and fought in engagements including Aisne (1914), Ypres (1914, 1917), The Somme (1916, 1918) and Cambrai (1917, 1918). From 22 November 1918 the men of the Guards Brigade were given the title 'guardsman' rather than 'private'. At the outbreak of World War II the regiment once more formed part of the BEF in France, also taking part in all the major campaigns in Western Europe and North Africa including Dunkirk (1940), Sidi Barrani (1940), Tobruk (1941, 1942), Tunis (1943), Salerno (1943) and Rhineland (1945). Postwar actions include peacekeeping duties in Palestine (1946–8), Kenya (1959–62), Aden (1964), Northern Ireland and Bosnia (1993–4). The regiment saw battalions deployed during the First Gulf War (1990–1) and in Iraq (2005). The various regiments of Foot Guards can be recognised by the grouping of buttons on the tunic. Coldstream buttons are arranged in pairs. Tel: 01890 882630. The official Guards Museum is at Wellington Barracks, Birdcage Walk, London, tel: 020 7414 3428.

Dawyck Botanic Gardens 6 miles (10km) southwest of Peebles. An arboretum established in the mid 17th century by the Veitch family, and which throughout its history has received seeds collected by seed hunters from around the world including David Douglas and Ernest 'Chinese' Wilson. Subsequently owned by the Naesmith family, 1690–1897, and the Balfour family, the gardens were donated to the Royal Botanic Garden Edinburgh by Alistair Balfour in 1978. Features include an azalea terrace, a beech walk planted in the 1790s, and a rhododendron walk. There is a wood of native Scots pine, grown from seeds collected in the Forest of Mar during the 1840s. A special feature is the Dawyck Beech, grown from a seedling found on the estate and now standing more than 100ft (30m) high, taller than 25 'champion' specimen trees. The garden is split by the Scrape Burn. Tel: 01721 760254.

Drumlanrig's Tower Tower Knowe, Hawick. An L-shaped 16th century tower house, later the home of Anne, Duchess of Monmouth and Buccleuch before being incorporated within Hawick's Tower Hotel. The hotel closed in 1981 and the restored tower is now a visitor centre with exhibits tracing the history of the tower and of Hawick. Tel: 01450 377615.

Duns Castle Duns, 13 miles (21km) north of Kelso. Originally a pele tower built c.1320 and the seat of the Hay family since 1696, the castle was transformed into a much larger building in Gothic revival style, 1818–22. Tel: 01361 883211.

Duns Law 1/2 mile (0.8km) north of Duns, 13 miles (21km) north of Kelso. An Iron Age hill fort with defensive banks, the site of the earliest settlement of Duns. It was used as a fortified camp by the Covenanter army during the Bishops' Wars of 1639 and 1640.

Dryburgh Abbey St Boswells, 3 miles (5km) southeast of Melrose. One of the four Border Abbeys, Dryburgh stands on a loop of the River Tweed. Work began on the abbey in 1150 and it was consecrated the church of St Mary of Dryburgh in 1152 by Premonstratensian monks from Alnwick Abbey in Northumberland, probably on the site of a much earlier church. Like the other Border Abbeys it suffered serious depredations from marauding English armies and was finally destroyed in the 1540s. The remains of the chapter house, cloister and warming house are well preserved, while the north transept of the abbey church is also partially standing and the two chapels in this area came to be used as burial chambers for local notables. Both Sir Walter Scott and Field Marshal Douglas Haig, whose families had close connections with the abbey and the area, are buried here. In the landscaped grounds stands an obelisk erected to the abbey's founder Hugh de Moreville by the 11th Earl of Buchan, who acquired the ruins in the 1780s and was responsible for laying out the gardens and maintaining the remains of the abbey in good repair. Tel: 01835 822381.

Edin's Hall Broch 4 miles (6km) north of Duns, 13 miles (21km) west of Eyemouth. Aka Edinshall. A rare example in southern Scotland of a broch (prehistoric circular stone tower). It is 55ft (17m) in interior diameter with walls 16ft (5m) thick, some of which still stand 7ft (2.1m) high. It is located at one end of an earlier Iron Age hill fort and probably dates from c.AD 100.

Eildon Hills 1 mile (1.6km) south of Melrose. The three conical volcanic peaks of Eildon Hill North (1325ft/404m), Eildon Mid Hill (1384ft/422m) and Eildon Hill Wester (1217ft/371m), overlooking the Tweed Valley, were a favourite spot of Sir Walter Scott. The remains of an Iron Age hill fort are situated on the summit of Eildon Hill North, which was also the site of a Roman signal station. See also Scott's View, Trimontium Roman Fort.

Ettrick Forest A large area of moorland south of Peebles and southwest of Selkirk, once a royal forest and now used largely for grazing sheep. Poet James Hogg, 'The Ettrick Shepherd', was born in Selkirk.

Eyemouth Museum Market Place, Eyemouth. Opened in 1981 in Eyemouth Old Parish Church (Auld Kirk), which dates from 1812. Exhibits cover the history of Eyemouth and particularly the working lives of its people, including millers, fishermen and farmers. On display is a tapestry made by local women to commemorate the Great East Coast Fishing Disaster of 1881. On 'Black Friday' 14 October 1881, 189 local fishermen, including 129 from Eyemouth, lost their lives in the waters just outside Eyemouth harbour when a storm wrecked the fishing fleet. Tel: 01890 750678.

Ferniehirst Castle 1 mile (1.6km) south of Jedburgh. The ancestral home of the Ker family, the first stone castle was built on the site in the 1470s. It changed hands between the Scots and the English several times in the 16th century before being almost demolished by James VI in 1593. Rebuilt as a T-shaped castle in 1598, it was occupied until the late 18th century before falling into decay. Having been leased to the Scottish Youth Hostel Association, 1934–84, it was then bought by Peter Kerr, 12th Marquess of Lothian, who restored it and opened it to the public in 1986. The family are predominantly left-handed and the castle has a 'left-handed staircase'. It is also reputedly haunted by a 'Green Lady'. Tel: 01835 862201.

Floors Castle 1/2 mile (0.8km) west of Kelso. Standing on the northern bank of the River Tweed, the house was designed by William Adam in the 1720s for John Ker, 1st Duke of Roxburghe and remodelled in the late 1830s by William Playfair, who adorned it with turrets and pinnacles. There are collections of art, including paintings by Raeburn and Gainsborough, and of porcelain. The surrounding parkland and woodland contains a holly tree marking the spot where James II of Scotland was killed by an exploding cannon in 1460 while taking part in the siege of Roxburgh Castle. The largest inhabited castle in Scotland, it remains the seat of the Dukes of Roxburghe. Tel: 01573 223333.

Glentress Forest See Tweed Valley Forest Park

Greenknowe Tower Gordon, 8 miles (13km) northeast of Melrose. Aka Greenknowe Castle. A four-storey L-plan tower house built in 1581, the exterior of which is almost intact. Abandoned in the 1850s, it has been maintained by Historic Scotland since 1937.

Halliwell's House Museum and Robson Gallery Market Place, Selkirk. Museum charting the history of the town of Selkirk and in particular the building's former use as an ironmonger's shop. The Robson Gallery houses a regular programme of temporary exhibitions. Tel: 01750 20096.

Harmony Garden St Mary's Road, Melrose. Located opposite Melrose Abbey, the part walled garden is laid to lawn with herbaceous and mixed borders as well as a productive vegetable garden and orchard. It is named after the plantation in Jamaica owned by original owner Robert Waugh. The adjoining Georgian town house, built in 1807, is not open to the public. Maintained by the National Trust for Scotland since 1996. Tel: 08444 932257.

Hawick Museum and Scott Art Gallery Wilton Lodge Park, Hawick. A museum covering the natural and social history of the Hawick region and in particular the knitwear and hosiery industries with which the area is closely associated. The Scott Art Gallery, opened in 1975, houses a collection of 19th and 20th century Scottish paintings as well as regular temporary exhibitions. In addition there are rooms dedicated to the lives and careers of Hawick-born motorcyclists Jimmy Guthrie (1897–1937) and Steve Hislop (1962–2003), as well as statues to both Guthrie and Hislop in the surrounding park. Guthrie gained experience on motorbikes as a despatch rider during World War I and began racing after the war. Having won six Isle of Man TT titles, also breaking the one-hour world speed record in 1935, he was killed in a crash while leading the German Grand Prix at the Sachsenring on 8 August 1937. His funeral in Hawick was attended by thousands of mourners and the bronze statue in his memory was erected in 1939. Steve 'Hizzy' Hislop was twice winner of three Manx TTs in the same year (equalling the record of Mike Hailwood and Joey Dunlop). British 250cc champion in 1990 and British Superbike champion in 1995 and 2002, he was killed in a helicopter crash near Hawick on 29 July 2003. Tel: 01450 373457.

Hermitage Castle 11 miles (18km) south of Hawick. An H-shaped fortress on the banks of Hermitage Water, once the key to the control of Liddesdale. A favourite of Sir Walter Scott, it has a sinister atmosphere and its history is full of legends of murder and treachery. The original wooden structure, probably a motte and bailey construction, was built c.1244, possibly by Sir Nicholas de Soulis. Sir Nicholas's grandson William (known as Bad Lord Soulis) was reputedly a wicked man and a practitioner of the black arts. According to legend the locals complained to Robert the Bruce of his evil doings; the king responded brusquely: 'Boil him if you must but let me hear no more of him,' whereupon they captured him and boiled him in a cauldron on the nearby Nine Stane Rig. However, historical record suggests that William died while held captive at Dumbarton. The castle exchanged hands between the Scots and English many times before it was rebuilt in stone in the 1350s. Having undergone further expansion and fortification until the 16th century, it fell into disuse after the union of England and Scotland and was only saved from complete ruin by the 5th Earl of Buccleuch in the early 1800s. It was taken into state care in 1930.

Highest point Broad Law at 2756ft (840m), 8 miles (13km) northeast of the source of the River Tweed. (GR: NT146235.)

Hirsel Country Park ½ mile (0.8km) northwest of Coldstream. Part of the 3000 acre (1200ha) Hirsel estate, belonging to the Earls of Home, the park contains the 18th century Hirsel Lake and Dundock Wood, a rhododendron and azalea wood created in 1881. There is also a museum of local rural life. Hirsel House, built 1702–14, is not open to the public. Tel: 01890 882834.

Hume Castle Hume, 5 miles (8km) north of Kelso. A 13th century castle located on a prominent outcrop and used as the basis for an 18th century folly. A stronghold of the Hume family, it fell to the English after the Battle of Pinkiecleugh in 1547 before being retaken. It was finally abandoned after falling to a Cromwellian army in 1650. In the 1790s the Earl of Marchmont built a folly on the ruins, consisting of a single wall with a serrated edge. The site was used as a lookout post during World War II.

Interesting facts The Bannock is a traditional Scottish dish of oatmeal, soda and salt akin to bread and usually served with butter, honey or jam. The **Selkirk Bannock**, however, is more of a fruit cake, containing sultanas or seedless white raisins. It was first produced by a baker in Selkirk and was initially only made for festive occasions such as Christmas. Another traditional food of the Scottish Borders is **Berwick Cockles**. Confusingly this is not a savoury dish but an aerated crumbly mint sweet that melts in the mouth. **Rugby sevens** was initially conceived by Ned Haig, a butcher from Melrose, as a fundraising event for his local club in 1883. **Monteviot** in Jedburgh, Roxburghshire, has long been the home of the Ancram family. Pride of place on its walls for 375 years was a portrait of John Donne; painted by an anonymous artist in 1595, it has been described as the most remarkable portrait of any English poet. On his death in 1631, Donne bequeathed the picture to his close friend, Robert Kerr, the 1st Marquess and a forebear of the Ancrams. Michael Ancram, the former Conservative minister and foreign affairs spokesman and now the 13th Marquess of Lothian, was forced to put the painting up for sale to help to meet an inheritance tax bill following the death of his father, the 12th Marquess, one of Scotland's main landowners, in 2004. Following a mass of individual donations the National Portrait Gallery snapped up the painting in May 2006 and put it on display to prevent it being lost to the nation.

Islands There are five islands in the Scottish Borders, all in the North Sea off the coast between Eyemouth and St Abb's Head: **Buss Craig** (GR: NT947650); **East Carr** (GR: NT963618); **Ebb Carrs** (GR: NT924671); **West Carr** (GR: NT963617); **The Wuddy** (GR: NT920682).

Jedburgh Abbey Abbey Bridge End, Jedburgh. One of the four Border Abbeys, its ruins stand on the banks of the Jed Water, probably on the site of an earlier church. Established as a priory in 1138 by David I, it became an abbey for Augustinian monks in 1147. In 1285 Alexander III married Yolande de Dreux (Drew) at the abbey. Its position close to the border with England made it vulnerable during the fighting between the two countries and it was attacked many times during the 15th century, although always repaired. However, an attack by the Earl of Surrey in 1523 and further damage wrought in the 1540s proved decisive. The abbey fell into disrepair and was abandoned in the second half of the 16th century. The reduced site was used as a parish church until the structure was felt to be unsafe and a new church was built. Placed in state care in 1913, it is now maintained by Historic Scotland. Tel: 01835 863925.

Jedburgh Castle Castlegate, Jedburgh. Motte and bailey castle founded in the 12th century by David I and destroyed c.1410 by Regent Albany in order to prevent the English from gaining control of it. The site is now occupied by the 19th century prison.

Jedburgh Castle Jail Castlegate, Jedburgh. A museum of local history housed in a former Howard Reform jail, built in 1823 on the site of Jedburgh Castle, with exhibits recreating the daily lives of the prisoners and staff. Tel: 01835 864750.

Kailzie Gardens 2½ miles (4km) southeast of Peebles. Located on an estate dating to at least the 17th century, the present garden, designed by Angela Lady Buchan-Hepburn, was begun in 1962, after a Georgian house on the site was demolished. The walled garden, dating to 1811, is laid to lawn with herbaceous borders and many climbing plants; other gardens include a wild garden, a laburnum walk and a rose garden. The stands of mature trees, including a larch planted in 1725, have been underplanted with snowdrops, daffodils and bluebells to provide a succession of spring colour. Tel: 01721 720007.

Kelso Abbey Bridge Street, Kelso. The oldest of the four Border Abbeys as well as the largest and richest, Kelso Abbey was founded by David I for an order of Tironensian monks from Selkirk. Building was begun in 1128 but was not dedicated to the Blessed Virgin and St John until 1243. James III was crowned in the abbey in 1460. Badly damaged during the 'Rough Wooing', it was finally destroyed in 1545 and the stones were used to provide local building materials. A parish church stood on the site from 1649 until 1771. Now in the care of Historic Scotland.

Lammermuir Hills 15 miles (24km) north of Melrose. A range of rolling hills forming the border between the Scottish Borders and East Lothian regions. The name means 'Lamb's Moor' and the hills' highest point is Meikle Says Law at 1755ft (535m). The hills are crossed by the Southern Upland Way and there are many long-established hill tracks between the settlements, including the 'Herring Road' from Dunbar to Lauder. The Whiteadder Reservoir, Watch Water Reservoir and Hop's Reservoir are all in the region. The hills are the setting for Donizetti's opera *Lucia di Lammermoor* (1835).

Liddesdale Heritage Centre Museum South Hermitage Street, Newcastleton, 16 miles (26km) south of Hawick. Housed in the Old Townfoot Kirk, the local history museum has a collection of railway memorabilia and a tapestry commemorating the village's bicentenary in 1993. Tel: 01387 375283.

Manderston 1 mile (1.6km) east of Duns. Originally built in the 1790s, the house was completely redesigned in the late 19th century in Adam Revival style by architect John Kinross for Sir James 'Lucky Jim' Millar. The elaborate decoration, including a staircase with a silver balustrade, extends to the servants' quarters and even to the barrel-vaulted stables and the marble panelled dairy. Owned today by Adrian, 4th Baron Palmer, a descendant of Sir James Millar, it was used as the setting for the 2002 Channel 4 series *The Edwardian Country House*. Other features include a museum of Huntley & Palmer's biscuit tins. Much of the garden landscaping, including the man-made lake, dates from the original Georgian estate but Kinross laid out four formal terrace gardens. Tel: 01361 883450.

Marchidun Castle See Roxburgh Castle

Mary Queen of Scots' House Queen Street, Jedburgh. Interpretative centre focusing on the life of Mary, Queen of Scots, located in a 16th century house in which she stayed for a few weeks in October 1566. She fell ill during this visit after a hurried trip to see the Earl of Bothwell, who was himself bedridden by wounds. On display is a copy of her death mask. The house became a museum in 1987, on the 400th anniversary of her death. Tel: 01835 863331.

Mellerstain House 7 miles (11km) northeast of Melrose. A Georgian house built 1725–70 close to the site of an earlier house called Whiteside, made over to an earlier George Baillie by Charles I in 1642 and demolished in 1725 to make way for the new building. The architect commissioned by the owner, George Baillie of Jerviswood, at the beginning of the project was William Adam and two wings of the house were completed before the work was interrupted. In 1770 Baillie's grandson, also named George, engaged William's son Robert to complete the task and join the two wings in a style which was up to date but in keeping with the earlier work. The interior ornamentation retains many of Robert Adam's designs and is notable for its decorated plasterwork and ceilings. There are paintings by Van Dyck and Gainsborough and portraits of members of the Baillie family. The house stands in 200 acres (80ha) of grounds. Tel: 01573 410225.

Melrose Abbey Abbey Street, Melrose. One of the four Border Abbeys, Melrose was founded by David I in 1136 close to the site of a 6th century monastery dedicated to St Aidan and known as Old Melrose (or Mailros Abbey). The king invited an order of Cistercian monks from Rievaulx in North Yorkshire to establish the abbey and it was dedicated in 1146. Alexander II was buried at Melrose in 1249. Like all the Border Abbeys, Melrose regularly came under attack; the invading Edward I assaulted it in 1296 and after further destruction wrought by Edward II in 1322 the abbey was rebuilt with the help of Robert the Bruce. Burned down by Richard II's forces in 1385, it was rebuilt over the following 100 years but faced final ruination during the 'Rough Wooing' of the 1540s. Part of the abbey church was used as Melrose's parish church, 1610–1810. Substantial ruins of the 14th and 15th century abbey buildings still remain and the Commendator's House houses a museum exhibiting finds from the site. There is a tradition that the embalmed heart of Robert the Bruce was buried at Melrose; this received possible confirmation when, during an archaeological dig in 1996, a lead container was unearthed from beneath the floor of the chapter house. It was found to contain a smaller cone-shaped casket with a plaque inscribed 'The enclosed leaden casket containing a heart was found beneath Chapter House floor, March 1921, by His Majesty's Office of Works'. The casket was reburied on 22 June 1998.

Mertoun Gardens 2 miles (3km) northeast of St Boswells, 5 miles (8km) southeast of Melrose. A 26 acre (10.5ha) garden beside the River Tweed, established in the late 17th century at the time Old Mertoun House was built. The gardens include an arboretum, walled kitchen garden, herbaceous borders and a beehive-shaped dovecote dating from 1576. The present house, dating to 1703, is not open to the public. Tel: 01835 823236.

Monteviot House 4 miles (6km) south of Kelso. Located beside the River Teviot and the seat for 300 years of the Marquesses of Lothian, the house originated as a Georgian lodge built by the 1st Earl. It was expanded in the 1830s with the addition of a Jacobean wing designed by Edward Blore, although the planned rebuilding was never completed. Its garden, designed by Percy Cane in the 1930s, includes a water garden, herb garden, arboretum, rose garden and herbaceous borders. Tel: 01835 830380.

Moorfoot Hills A range of grassy hills running northeast from Peebles and straddling the boundary of the Borders and Lothian regions. Their highest point is Windlestraw Law at 2162ft (659m).

National Nature Reserves **Cragbank Wood**, 7 miles (11km) southeast of Hawick, is an area of ancient ash, elm and hazel woodland covering 23 acres (9ha). It was designated a National Nature Reserve in 1985.

St Abb's Head, 26 miles (42km) northeast of Kelso, is home to large colonies of guillemots, kittiwakes and razorbills plus other breeding seabirds such as fulmars, puffins and gulls. It was declared an NNR in 1983; offshore is a voluntary marine nature reserve. Maintained by the National Trust for Scotland.

Whitlaw Mosses, 2 miles (3km) east of Selkirk, consists of four separate sites of moss carpets and sedge fen established in 1992.

Neidpath Castle	1 mile (1.6km) west of Peebles. A four-storey L-plan tower house in a loop of the River Tweed. Originally called Jedderfield, it was built by the Hay family in the 14th century on the site of a castle belonging to their relatives the Frasers. The castle sustained damage during the Civil War and was substantially altered in the late 17th century. A small museum contains local artefacts, while a pit dungeon can also be seen. Tel: 01721 720333.
Old Gala House and Scott Gallery	Scott Crescent, Galashiels. Museum and art gallery housed in a tower house built by the Pringle family in 1457 and subsequently incorporated within a larger house of 1583. There are exhibits covering the history of the house and Galashiels. A painted ceiling in one of the rooms dates from 1635. Tel: 01750 20096.
Paxton House	4 miles (6km) west of Berwick-upon-Tweed. A Palladian country house set beside the River Tweed and built by John and James Adam in 1758 for Patrick Home. Its collection of Chippendale furniture is the largest in Scotland and there are also examples of Regency Scottish furniture by William Trotter of Edinburgh. More than 70 paintings from the National Galleries of Scotland are on display in the Regency Picture Gallery, added in 1811; the collection focuses on British art 1760–1840 and contains works by Raeburn and Wilkie. The surrounding 80 acres (32ha) of gardens, parkland and woodland – with a colony of red squirrels – contain a fishing museum located in a restored Victorian boathouse. Tel: 01289 386291.
Peniel Heugh and Waterloo Monument	4 miles (6km) north of Jedburgh. The hilltop site of a pre-Norman settlement guarding the nearby Dere Street Roman road. The Waterloo Monument, built on the hilltop 1817–24 to commemorate the battle, stands 150ft (46m) high and is not accessible to the public.
Priorwood Garden	Abbey Street, Melrose. Located close to Melrose Abbey, the partially walled garden features plants grown especially to be dried for flower arranging. More than 700 varieties of annuals and herbaceous plants are grown. The drying process is carried out in purpose-built workshops and various drying techniques such as hang drying, sand drying and pressing can be viewed. There is also an orchard laid out to illustrate the history of apple cultivation. Next to the Harmony Garden. Maintained by the National Trust for Scotland since 1974. Tel: 01896 822493.
Rivers	The **Teviot** rises in the western foothills of Comb Hill on the border of Dumfries and Galloway. It flows northeast through Teviotdale and past Teviothead, Hawick and Roxburgh before joining the River Tweed southwest of Kelso. The Teviot is more noted for its trout than its salmon. The **Tweed** is the principal river of the Scottish Borders and, at 96 miles (154km), the fourth longest river in Scotland. It rises at Tweed's Well, 6 miles (10km) north of Moffat, close to the boundary of the Scottish Borders with Dumfries and Galloway, flowing northeast to Peebles and east through Galashiels and Melrose before taking a northeasterly direction through Kelso and Coldstream and finally reaching the North Sea at Berwick-upon-Tweed. For a distance it forms the boundary between England and Scotland. Its catchment is the second largest in Scotland at 1840 sq miles (4843 sq km) and its main tributaries are the Lyne, Gala, Ettrick and Leader Waters, together with the River Teviot. The Tweed is internationally renowned for its salmon fishing.
Robert Smail's Printing Works	High Street, Innerleithen. A restored and working printshop from the early 20th century. Robert Smail's printing works was in operation from 1847 to 1985. Features include an office, composing room, press room, paper store and the waterwheel which originally powered the equipment. The archive of photographs and the weekly newspapers published from 1893 to 1916 cover some of the history of Innerleithen. Maintained by the National Trust for Scotland since 1986. Tel: 01896 830206.
Roxburgh Castle	$^1/_2$ mile (0.8km) west of Kelso. Roxburgh Castle, then known as Marchidun, is first recorded as the residence of the Earl of Northumberland in 1107. Renamed by David I, it became a residence for Scottish kings over the next 200 years. A massive fortress with four towers and at least one church within its walls, it proved strategically important during the Wars of Independence: it was captured by Edward I in 1296 and changed hands frequently thereafter until its destruction by the Scots in 1460 (its recapture in 1313 by Sir James, the 'Black Douglas', is recounted in John Barbour's epic poem *The Bruce*). It was later held by the English, who built a timber fort on the site; this too was destroyed in 1550. Only a few fragments of the stonework and some earthworks from the fort now remain.
St Abb's Head Lighthouse	26 miles (42km) northeast of Kelso. Designed by David and Thomas Stevenson and completed in 1862 following the wreck of the *Martello* in 1857. The lighthouse stands 30ft (9m) high on the 300ft (91m) cliffs of the St Abb's Head promontory (see National Nature Reserves) and was automated in 1993.
St Ronan's Well Interpretive Centre	Wells Brae, Innerleithen, 5 miles (8km) southeast of Peebles. Exhibition charting the history of the former spa, built in 1828. Originally called Doo's Well, its name was changed after Sir Walter Scott published his novel *St Ronan's Well* in 1823. Tel: 01721 724820.
Sir Walter Scott's Courtroom	Market Square, Selkirk. A museum covering the life of Sir Walter Scott, housed in the building where he held office as Sheriff of Selkirk, 1804–32. There are also displays about poet James Hogg ('The Ettrick Shepherd') and explorer Mungo Park, both of whom were Scott's contemporaries. Tel: 01750 20096.
Scott's View	3 miles (5km) east of Melrose. One of Sir Walter Scott's favourite views, located on the side of Bemersyde Hill above Dryburgh Castle and providing a panorama of the Eildon Hills to the southwest. It is said that the horse taking his hearse to Melrose Abbey stopped at the spot, as it had each day when Scott was alive.
Smailholm Tower	1 mile (1.6km) southwest of Smailholm, 6 miles (10km) west of Kelso. Located on a prominent outcrop of rock, the well-preserved 15th century four-storey rectangular tower with garret was built by the Pringle family. It was well known to Sir Walter Scott, who had relatives living nearby; there is an exhibition of costume dolls and tapestries relating to Scott's collection of ballads, *Minstrelsy of the Scottish Border*. Maintained by Historic Scotland. Tel: 01573 460365.

Sport

horse racing — **Kelso** racecourse, originally based at Caverton Edge from 1734 and transferred to Blakelaw in 1818, was relocated to its present site within a mile of Kelso at Berrymoss four years later. The first meeting was held on 24 September 1822. The 1 mile 3 furlong (2.2km) course, holding National Hunt racing, has been voted 'Britain's Friendliest Racecourse'. Tel: 01573 224767.

rugby union — Rugby is a popular sport in the Scottish Borders and the Border League, formed in 1901 was the first rugby union league to be established in the world. The major teams in the area are:

Border Reivers RFC, formed as Scottish Borders Rugby in 1999 to compete in the Heineken Cup. They were merged with Edinburgh in 2001 as Border Reivers but resurrected as The Borders in 2002 playing in the Celtic League, and became the Border Reivers once more for the 2005–06 season. The team was disbanded at the end of the 2006/2007 season.

Hawick RFC, formed in 1873, play in the BT Premiership and the Border League. Their home ground is Mansfield Park, Hawick.

Melrose RFC, formed in 1877, play in the BT Premiership and the Border League and they hosted the first ever seven-a-side rugby tournament in 1883. Their home ground is Greenyards.

The other teams in the Border League are Berwick, Duns, Gala, Jed-Forest, Kelso, Langholm, Peebles and Selkirk.

Thirlestane Castle — Lauder, 7$^1/_2$ miles (12km) north of Galashiels. Considered one of the seven 'Great Houses of Scotland', the ancient seat of the Earls of Lauderdale originated as a strongpoint built in the 13th century on the banks of the Leader Water, a tributary of the River Tweed. The castle was rebuilt as a tower house by the Maitland family in 1590 and extensively remodelled in the 1670s by John Maitland, the 1st and only Duke of Lauderdale, and again in the 1840s. Features include an oak-panelled entrance hall with a scale model of the castle, the room where Bonnie Prince Charlie slept in 1745, a nursery with a collection of toys dating back as far as the Georgian period and the kitchens and laundries which served the household. A substantial restoration programme has been carried out since the 1970s. Tel: 01578 722430.

Three Hills Roman Heritage Centre — The Ormiston, Market Square, Melrose. A museum opened in 1991 and housing the Trimontium Exhibition, which covers the Border region during the Roman period. Exhibits include artefacts, photographs, drawings, models and maps, as well as replica Roman armour and a reconstructed blacksmith's shop. Tel: 01896 822651/822463.

Traquair House — 1/2 mile (0.8km) south of Innerleithen, 10 miles (16km) west of Galashiels. Scotland's oldest continuously inhabited house, dating to 1107 when it was built as a royal hunting lodge beside the River Tweed. One of a network of pele towers built along the Tweed in an attempt to stabilise the border with England, it has been owned by the Stewart (Stuart) family since the 15th century. The original three-storey tower was extended in the late 16th century and incorporated into an early 17th century mansion built by John Stuart, 1st Earl of Traquair, which was transformed into more or less the current house by the end of that century. In 1566 Mary, Queen of Scots, together with her husband Lord Darnley and their baby son, the future James VI, stayed at Traquair; their bed and the baby's wooden cradle can still be seen in the King's Room, while a museum features memorabilia of Mary. Other rooms include the High Drawing Room, the library and the secret Priest's Room; the Stuarts of Traquair were Catholic at a time when the religion had to be practised in secret, remaining staunch supporters of the Jacobite cause following the fall of James II, and the 4th Earl was imprisoned in Edinburgh Castle for his Jacobite sympathies. The Stuarts also played a part in the Jacobite risings of 1715 and 1745. The 5th Earl installed the Bear Gates, through which Bonnie Prince Charlie departed following his visit during the 1745 rebellion. Legend has it that the gates will never be opened until a Stuart king is crowned in London. The earldom became dormant on the death of the 8th Earl and the house passed to the nearest cousin, Henry Constable Maxwell. The 100 acres (40ha) of grounds include areas of woodland possibly dating to the time when the hunting lodge was located within Ettrick Forest; features include a yew tree circle, walled garden and the Traquair Maze which was planted in 1981. The Traquair House brewery was founded in 1965, although a domestic brewery produced beer for the house during the 18th century. Tel: 01896 830323.

Trimontium Roman Fort — Newstead, $^1/_2$ mile (0.8km) east of Melrose. Roman fort located beneath the three Eildon Hills (hence the name Trimontium). The fort is mentioned in early sources including Ptolemy's *Geographia* (c.AD 150). There were in fact at least two forts on the site, and possibly as many as eight. The first, built during the period of Gnaeus Julius Agricola's campaigns in Scotland (AD 80–85), was subsequently extended but abandoned c.AD 105. During the Antonine period, probably c.AD 140, the site was reoccupied and used to house a cavalry squadron whose main task would have been to secure communications along Dere Street, the Roman road from York to the Antonine Wall. This unit may have been the auxiliary cavalry squadron, Augusta Vocontiorum, who hailed from Spain and the South of France. The fort was also occupied at some point by the 20th Legion 'Valeria Victrix' (Valiant and Victorious). The fort was finally abandoned c.185 although it may have been used briefly during the invasion of Scotland by the emperor Septimius Severus in 208–210. The site is marked by a 10ft (3m) high granite altar, erected in 1928 and unveiled by Dr James Curle, who carried out archaeological excavations on the site 1905–10; it is inscribed with these words: 'Here once stood the fort of Trimontium, built by the troops of Agricola in the 1st century AD, abandoned at least twice by the Romans, and ultimately lost by them after fully one hundred years of frontier warfare'.

Tweed Valley Forest Park — The main woodland corridor between Peebles and Selkirk, consisting of several separate forested areas, seven of which are on the River Tweed. Forests in the park include: **Caberston**, a conifer forest with broadleaved planting at the Pim and including an Iron Age settlement; **Cademuir**, mixed woodland on Cademuir Hill; **Cardrona**, a mixed conifer wood; **Craik**, a large conifer forest with a Roman drove road running through it; **Elibank & Traquair**, a large conifer forest in the Tweed Valley, split by the Bold Burn; **Glentress Forest**, a conifer forest created in the 1920s; **Newcastleton**, a large mixed forest in Liddesdale and on the border with England beside the Kershope Burn; **Swinnie**, close to Jedburgh, mainly conifer but with some broadleaf planting; **Thornielee**, a small wood with a variety of walks; **Yair**, aka Lindinney Wood, beside the River Tweed.

Tweedale Museum and Gallery — High Street, Peebles. Housed in the Chambers Institution, a building donated to the people of Peebles in 1859 by publisher Dr W Chambers, a collector of casts of famous statues from antiquity. Although most of these are now lost, the museum still contains a full scale plaster cast of the Parthenon Frieze and a copy of the *Triumph of Alexander*, originally cast in 1812 to honour Napoleon. There are also local history exhibits and an art gallery. Tel: 01721 724820.

Woods on your Doorstep — **Catwalk Wood**, aka Den Wood (10 acres/4ha), West Linton, on the banks of the Lyne Water. Mixed broadleaved woodland including lime, sycamore, oak, ash and birch and some conifers including Scots pine and Norway spruce; **Fairbairn Copse** (2$^1/_2$ acres/1ha), on a coastal cliff in the village of Cove. The area is covered with shrubs such as osier, hawthorn, blackthorn and elder. A designated Site of Special Scientific Interest; **Jacob's Well** (2$^1/_2$ acres/1ha), on the north bank of the River Tweed in Coldstream. Broadleaf woodland, mainly ash with some sycamore and laburnum. The site has also been colonised by giant hogweed; **Plora Wood** (50 acres/20ha), near Innerleithen, semi-natural oak woodland bounded to the west by the Armour Burn. Other species include sycamore, beech, larch and spruce. The site's history as a woodland goes back as far as the 12th century. A designated Site of Special Scientific Interest; **St Ronan's Wood** (67 acres/27ha), on the slopes of Caerlee Hill on the outskirts of Innerleithen. Mainly broadleaved planting with some conifers. Species include mature ash, sessile oak, beech and sycamore plus new plantings of rowan, silver birch and hazel. There is an Iron Age hill fort on the summit of Caerlee.

Some famous people born in Scottish Borders

Alexander III (monarch) (1241–86)	Roxburgh
Blyth, Chay (yachtsman) (1940–)	Hawick
Brewster, David (scientist) (1781–1868)	Jedburgh
Duns Scotus (philosopher) (c.1266–1308)	Duns
Guthrie, Jimmy (motorcycle racer) (1897–1937)	Hawick
Hislop, Steve (motorcycle racer) (1962–2003)	Hawick
Hogg, James (poet) (1770–1835)	Ettrick Forest
Park, Mungo (explorer) (1771–1806)	Foulshiels
Renwick, Jim (rugby player) (1952–)	Hawick
Thomson, James (poet) (1700–48)	Ednam

Central

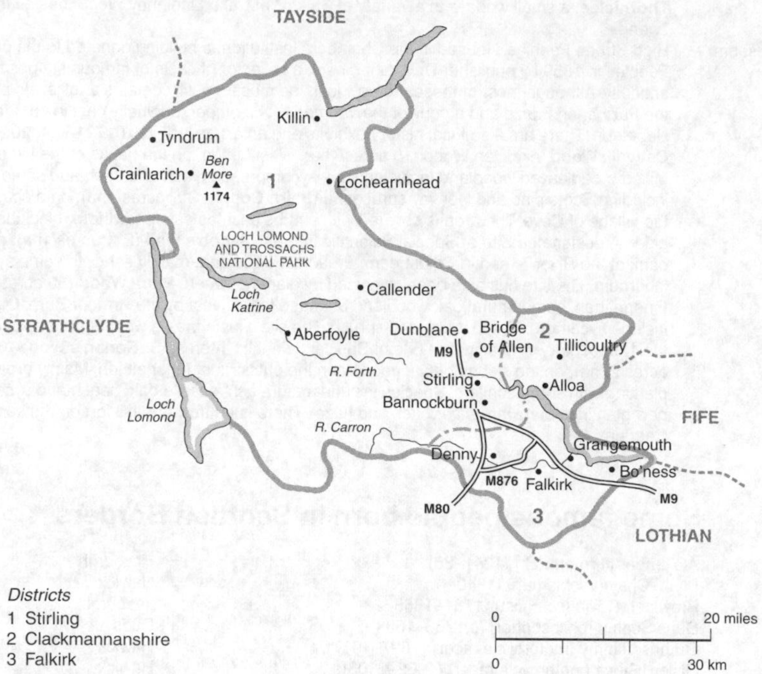
TAYSIDE
Killin
Tyndrum
Crainlarich
Ben More
1174
1
Lochearnhead
LOCH LOMOND AND TROSSACHS NATIONAL PARK
Callender
Loch Katrine
STRATHCLYDE
Aberfoyle
Dunblane
Bridge of Allen
2
Tillicoultry
M9
R. Forth
Stirling
Alloa
Bannockburn
Loch Lomond
FIFE
R. Carron
Grangemouth
Denny
Bo'ness
M876
Falkirk
M9
M80
3
LOTHIAN
Districts
1 Stirling
2 Clackmannanshire
3 Falkirk
0
20 miles
0
30 km

The Central region of Scotland could be described as the country's 'waist'. Covering three districts – Clackmanannshire, Falkirk and Stirling – it is bordered by Fife and the Lothians in the southeast, Strathclyde in the south and west, and Tayside in the north and northeast.

Clackmannanshire is known as the 'Wee County' and is Scotland's smallest county, with an area of only 55 square miles (142 sq km) covering a lowland plain between the River Forth and the Ochil Hills. Since 1822 its administrative centre has been Alloa, the brewing capital of Scotland, which replaced Clackmannan. The economy of the county was based on agriculture and coal mining, while the burns falling from the Ochil Hills provided water power to drive textile and papermills in the so-called 'Hillfoot' villages of Blairlogie, Menstrie, Alva, Tillicoultry, Dollar and Muckhart.

The coastal area of **Falkirk** was settled originally in the Late Palaeolithic and Mesolithic. Later arrivals include the Romans, who built the Antonine Wall in the early 2nd century with its eastern end at Kinneil. Falkirk's name seems to derive from an early church on the site which had a speckled ('faw') appearance, hence Fawkirk became the settlement of Falkirk. In 1298 it was the scene of one of the many battles fought in the region. Its early prosperity revolved around the Livingston family, who built Callendar House in the 14th century. Situated on the River Carron in a central position and benefiting from deposits of raw materials such as coal and iron ore, Falkirk and its neighbouring port of Grangemouth on the Forth grew into industrial centres and communications hubs. Industrial growth was sparked by the opening of the Carron Ironworks in 1759 and the Forth & Union Canal in the 1770s. The Falkirk area was also the site for major cattle markets for Scotland (known as the Falkirk Trysts). Eventually the town expanded to incorporate surrounding industrial villages such as Bonnybridge and Camelon. Despite the decline of more traditional industries during the 20th century, the town has embraced newer technologies and the growth in the service sector. Manufacturing now accounts for 20 per cent of local industries while services have risen to 60 per cent. The area is crossed by the M9 and M876 motorways. The disused canal has been restored and the Falkirk Wheel has become a major tourist attraction. Grangemouth developed during the 20th century into a centre of the petrochemical industry. Larbert and Stenhousemuir, twin villages north of Falkirk, grew into industrial towns with the opening of the Carron Ironworks and the coming of the railways.

The bridge at **Stirling** was built at the lowest crossing point of the River Forth and became the gateway to Perthshire and the Highlands, especially before the Carse of Forth – the flood plain of the River Forth west of Grangemouth – was drained. As a result, for centuries Stirlingshire became a strategic battleground, major battles being fought at Bannockburn, Falkirk and Stirling. North of Stirling is the area known as the Trossachs, often described as the Highlands in miniature, with its mountains, lochs and forests. The economy is largely based on services plus some manufacturing. The town of Stirling grew around the crossing of the River Forth and was thus a strategic location both militarily and in terms of communication. Its main feature is, of course, Stirling Castle. Stirling was awarded city status in 2002.

Central	**Population**			**Area**	
Districts	*male*	*female*	*total*	*sq miles*	*sq km*
Clackmannanshire	23,234	24,843	48,077	61	159
Falkirk	70,016	75,175	145,191	115	297
Stirling	41,194	45,018	86,212	844	2187
Total	134,444	145,036	279,480	1020	2643

Local Attractions and Information

Administrative headquarters — **Clackmannanshire**: Council Headquarters, Greenfield, Alloa FK10 2AD. Tel: 01259 450000.
Falkirk: Municipal Buildings, Falkirk FK1 5RS. Tel: 01324 506070.
Stirling: Old Viewforth, Stirling FK8 2ET. Tel: 01786 443322.

Alloa Tower — Alloa Park, Alloa. Originally a massive 15th century tower house built on the site of an earlier 14th century property; a house was added to the tower after 1710 as its role became residential rather than defensive but this was destroyed in a fire in 1800. The tower was a family seat of the Earls of Mar; according to one legend, the baby James VI died at Alloa during a visit by his mother Mary, Queen of Scots and was substituted by the Earl's baby son. There is a collection of family portraits by artists including David Allan, Henry Raeburn and Godfrey Kneller. Features include an Italianate staircase, pit dungeon and internal well. The property has been managed by the National Trust for Scotland since 1996, when it underwent extensive restoration. Tel: 01259 211701.

Almond Castle — Whitecross, 2 miles (3km) west of Linlithgow. The ruins of an L-plan tower house probably built in the 15th century with 16th century additions. Owned by the Livingston family from 1542 until they were forced to forfeit their lands in 1716, it was abandoned by the end of the 18th century. Originally known as Haining Castle, it stands within the grounds of a former cement factory.

Antonine Wall — Extending for 37 miles (60km) east–west from Bo'Ness on the Firth of Forth to Old Kilpatrick on the Firth of Clyde, the wall was built by Quintus Lollius Urbicus, Roman governor of Britain AD 139–142, following a successful campaign to reoccupy southern Scotland during the reign of Emperor Antoninus Pius (after whom the wall is named). Built of turf on a 15ft (4.5m) wide stone base, it stood a maximum of 12ft (3.5m) high with a wooden breastwork on the top and was fronted by a ditch averaging 40ft (12m) wide by 10ft (3m) deep. The turf rampart was two-thirds as thick as Hadrian's Wall (see Cumbria), saving both time and materials. An 18ft (5.5m) wide road along the southern side of the wall, known as the 'military way', enabled rapid troop movements and communication between the forts along the wall. There were 19 forts built into the wall, approximately 2 miles (3km) apart, all of which faced north. The original plan was for six primary forts: Carriden, Mumrills, Castlecary, Bar Hill, Balmuildy and Old Kilpatrick, plus fortlets at approximately every Roman mile. However, the fortlets were abandoned early in the construction and 13 secondary forts inserted. In general the forts were smaller than those on Hadrian's Wall, covering on average 3 acres (1.2ha). While the Antonine Wall was garrisoned the gates in the milecastles of Hadrian's Wall were removed and the *vallum* (ditch) was slighted. The Antonine wall was abandoned for a short time by AD 150 but was reoccupied by 160. It was abandoned again in 164 and the Romans withdrew to Hadrian's Wall. There was a temporary repair and reoccupation of the wall during the campaigns of the Emperor Septimius Severus in 208 (as a result some ancient sources refer to it as the Severan Wall) but it was finally abandoned shortly afterwards. It is sometimes known locally as Graham's Dyke, after a legendary Scot who supposedly drove the Romans from Scotland.

Argyll's Lodging — Castle Wynd, Stirling. A 17th century townhouse on the approaches to Stirling Castle, converted from a 16th century tower house. The house is grouped round three sides of an irregular courtyard and has turrets with conical roofs. The original house was built by Sir William Alexander, founder of Nova Scotia, passing to the Argyll family on his death in 1640. It has been used as a military hospital and youth hostel and underwent extensive restoration in the 1990s. The principal rooms are the hall, drawing room and bedchamber. The most important surviving town house of its period in Scotland, it is managed by Historic Scotland. Tel: 01786 431319.

Arthur's O'On — A Roman temple which stood by the River Carron near the Carron Ironworks. The circular building, 28ft (8.5m) in diameter with a corbelled dome, was probably built during the period when the Antonine Wall was occupied. Its beehive shape led to its popular name of Arthur's O'on (Oven). It was demolished by the Laird of Stenhouse in 1743 and the site is now a housing estate.

Bannockburn Heritage Centre Glasgow Road, Stirling. A heritage centre opened in 1987 overlooking the 14th century battlefield of Bannockburn, near what is considered to be Robert the Bruce's command post. A rotunda with a statue of Robert the Bruce by Pilkington Jackson was unveiled by Queen Elizabeth II in June 1964. There is also a diorama of the Battle of Stirling Bridge. The site of the battle was presented to the National Trust for Scotland in 1932. Tel: 01786 812664.

Battles See separate table for details of the battles of Bannockburn, Falkirk (I) and (II), Sauchieburn, Sheriffmuir and Stirling Bridge.

Bo'Ness Motor Museum Bridgeness Road, Bo'ness. A privately run museum opened in 2004 which houses more than 20 vehicles including some with links to TV and film. Cars include the Lotus Esprit used in the film *The Spy Who Loved Me* (1977) and the Jaguar XJ6 driven by Samuel L Jackson in *The 51st State* (2001). There is also a collection of car memorabilia and film props and posters. Tel: 01506 828138.

Breadalbane Folklore Centre Killin, 18 miles (29km) north of Callander. Overlooking the Falls of Dochart and housed in the restored St Fillan's mill with a working waterwheel, the centre describes the histories of clans including the MacGregors, MacLarens, MacNabs and Campbells, also exploring local myths and legends. Tel: 01567 820254.

Bridge of Allan A spa town on the Allan Water. The stone bridge over the Allan was built in 1520 and the settlement grew around it. The University of Stirling on the former Airthrey Estate is on its outskirts.

Broomhall Castle Long Row, Menstrie, 4 miles (6km) northeast of Stirling. Built in 1874 for James Johnstone on the slopes of the Ochil Hills, the house became a boys' school in the 1930s but was burned down in 1942. It was restored in the 1980s and is now a hotel. Tel: 01259 763360.

Callendar House Callendar Park, Falkirk. Originally built by William Livingston in the 14th century as a tower house and much altered since, especially in the mid 17th century and in the 1870s. It remained in the hands of the Livingston family until the 1740s. Mary, Queen of Scots spent part of her early life at the house as William Livingston was one of her guardians. The house was visited by Bonnie Prince Charlie in 1746, and the Livingstons were eventually to lose their lands because of their support for the Jacobite cause. The estate was bought by copper merchant William Forbes in 1783. It has been restored as a heritage centre with exhibitions about the growth of Falkirk during the Industrial Revolution and the story of Callendar House. The surrounding park contains a bird sanctuary, a doocot (dovecot) and a mausoleum. Callendar Woods are a mixture of mature oak coppice with pine, larch and spruce. The grounds also contain remains of the Antonine Wall. Tel: 01324 503770.

Cambuskenneth Abbey Cambuskenneth, 1 mile (1.6km) east of Stirling. Originally known as the Abbey of St Mary of Stirling, and established in the 1140s by David I as a foundation for Augustinian monks, a daughter house of the church of St Nicholas, Arrouaise. Built in a loop of the River Forth, the abbey was the burial place of James III in 1488 after the Battle of Sauchieburn; he was buried next to his wife Margaret of Denmark, who had predeceased him in 1486. The abbey was slighted during the Reformation and used as a source of building material. The bell-tower was restored in the 1860s and the remains of the other buildings were preserved. The site is in the care of Historic Scotland.

Carron Ironworks 2 miles (3km) north of Falkirk. An ironworks founded in 1759 and linked by canal to the River Carron. By the early 19th century it was the largest smelting works in Europe. The factory's early output included the short-barrelled lightweight naval canon known as a carronade. The company also cast the parts for James Watt's 1765 steam engine and ammunition invented by Henry Shrapnel. The Carron Company, which had provided an early boost to the growth of Falkirk, became insolvent in 1982; part of the site is now occupied by smaller manufacturers.

Castle Campbell $1^1/_2$ miles (2.5km) north of Dollar, 11 miles (18km) northeast of Stirling. Standing on Gloom Hill between the Burn of Care and the Burn of Sorrow, the castle was known as Castle Gloom or Castle Doom until 1489 when it became a stronghold of the Campbell Earls of Argyll. It was founded in the 15th as a tower house but new ranges of buildings were added in the 16th and 17th centuries. Mary, Queen of Scots stayed here in 1563 during the wedding of the 5th Earl of Argyll's sister. After being sacked in 1654 by Scots unhappy with the Campbells' support of Oliver Cromwell, the castle was abandoned by the clan, who moved to Argyll's Lodging in Stirling (see separate entry). The tower remains in a reasonable state of preservation and the ruins of the later buildings are visible. The site is managed by Historic Scotland. Tel: 01259 742408.

Charlotte Dundas Generally regarded as the world's first practical steamboat, and built at Grangemouth in 1802 by John Allan to a design by William Symington, chief engineer of the Carron Company (see Carron Ironworks). Her maiden voyage took place in Glasgow on 4 January 1803. A further trial, involving towing two barges for 18 miles (29km) on the Forth & Clyde Canal, took place on 28 March 1803. After the canal company refused to take the project further, claiming that the wash from the paddle would damage the canal banks, *Charlotte Dundas* was left in a passing bay at Bainsford and broken up in 1861. The building of a replica was begun in the 1980s and the model was berthed at Falkirk Wheel (see separate entry) until 2006.

Churches **Balquhidder Old Kirk**, Balquhidder, 9 miles (15km) southeast of Crianlarich. The third church to be built on this site, dating from 1855. The original 13th century building, located to the south of the present church, was replaced by a second church built over it in 1631 and beside which stands the grave of Rob Roy MacGregor, who died in 1734.

Bridge of Allan Parish Church, Keir Street, Bridge of Allan. Formerly known as St Andrew's Church and Holy Trinity Church, and now known simply as the Parish Church. The church opened in 1858 and was extended in the late 19th century. Its internal fittings, including the pulpit, organ screen and communion table, were designed in 1904 by Charles Rennie Mackintosh, formerly an apprentice in the firm of John Honeyman, an elder of the church's congregation. Tel: 01786 834155.

Church of the Holy Rude, St John Street, Stirling. Aka Greyfriars Parish Church. Originally founded in the 12th century by David I, the church suffered depredations from marauding armies and a fire in 1405 and the present building probably dates from 1414. The 20 minute coronation of the infant James VI took place in the church on 29 July 1567 in a ceremony conducted by John Knox; thus it claims to be the only active church in the UK, apart from Westminster Abbey, to have held a coronation. Tel: 01786 475275.

Falkirk Old Parish Church, Manse Place, Falkirk. Dedicated to St Modan. The earliest stone church on the site dates from 11th century and was built on the site of an even earlier foundation. Its speckled (or *faw*) appearance may have given rise to the name of the accompanying settlement (Fawkirk becoming Falkirk). The present church developed from a 15th century structure, with a bell tower added in the 1730s; it was much altered in the early 19th century and extended in 1892.

Clackmannan Stone — Main Street, Clackmannan. Aka King Robert's Stone. A standing stone 12ft (3.5m) high, known as the 'Clack' or Stone of Mannan and associated both with the pagan sea-god Man(n)au and with Robert the Bruce. It was housed in Clackmannan Tower until being placed on a plinth in its present location in 1833.

Clackmannan Tolbooth — Main Street, Clackmannan. Built c.1592 as the county gaol and courthouse, a role it fulfilled until the late 18th century. The existing remains are mainly of the west gable and bell tower.

Clackmannan Tower — King's Seat Hill, Clackmannan. Originally a 14th century tower house built by the Bruce family, possibly on the site of a royal hunting lodge, and extended on an L-plan in the 15th century. A mansion house attached in the late 16th century was abandoned and demolished by the early 19th century. The tower has been maintained by Historic Scotland since the 1950s, when extensive repairs were carried out to counter subsidence. It is now undergoing restoration.

Clan McNab Burial Ground — An enclosure on the island of Innis Bhuide in the River Dochart where the clan chiefs of the McNabs were buried in the 17th and 18th centuries.

Cunninghame Graham Memorial — Gartmore, 17 miles (27km) west of Stirling. A cairn to the memory of R B Cunninghame Graham (1852–1936), radical politician, author and, along with Keir Hardie, co-founder of the Scottish Independence Association. He was born Robert Bontine in Perthshire, the son of Major William Bontine of the Scots Greys. Erected near the family home at Castlehill, Dumbarton in 1937, the memorial was moved to Gartmore in 1981 in recognition of Graham's status as the last Laird of Gartmore.

Craigend Castle — Mugdock, 19 miles (31km) southwest of Stirling. Now located within Mugdock Country Park, the now ruined mansion was built in 1815 for James Smith to a Regency Gothic design by Alexander Ramsay. The estate was sold to Sir Andrew Buchanan in 1851 and leased to the Outrams in the early 20th century. In 1949–54 the site was occupied by Craigend Zoo. One particular attraction was Charlie the elephant; after the zoo's closure, Charlie was sold to Billy Butlin and lived out the rest of his life at the Ayr and Filey holiday camps. The Pere David's deer sometimes seen around Loch Lomond are believed to be descended from escapees from the zoo. The stables were converted into the Mugdock Country Park visitor centre.

Denny Muir Bow — An oak hunting bow, probably for ceremonial use, found in 1889 during the construction of a reservoir above the River Carron, 1½ miles (2.5km) west of Denny. Originally misidentified as a paddle, it has been radiocarbon dated to 1300 BC.

Dollar Academy — Dollar, 11 miles (18km) northeast of Stirling. A co-educational day and boarding school for pupils aged 5–18, founded in 1818 with a bequest from merchant and seafarer John McNabb. It is the oldest boarding school in Scotland and the oldest co-educational school in Britain. The school is set in at the foot of the Ochil Hills; its original building, designed by William Henry Playfair in Greek Revival style, was severely damaged in a fire in 1961 but was reopened in 1966. Former pupils include BBC journalist Alan Johnston and scientist Sir James Dewar. Tel: 01259 742511.

Dollar Glen — ½ mile (0.8km) north of Dollar, 11 miles (18km) northeast of Stirling. A wooded glen cutting deeply into the Ochil Hills on the approaches to Castle Campbell (see separate entry). A designated Site of Special Scientific Interest, it is managed by the National Trust for Scotland.

Dollar Museum — High Street, Dollar. A local history museum opened in 1988, charting the history of the village from the Bronze Age to the present day and housed in a 19th century woollen mill. Collections include a substantial photographic archive. Tel: 01259 742895.

Doune Castle — Doune, 7 miles (11km) northwest of Stirling. A late 14th century L-plan castle with courtyard, located on the River Teith and built by Robert Stewart, Duke of Albany. During the 15th century it was used as a royal hunting lodge; since the 16th century it has been owned by the Earls of Moray. It was defended by supporters of Mary, Queen of Scots in the 1560s. The castle was renovated in the 1880s. The main features are the gatehouse, the timber-panelled Lord's Hall with musicians' gallery and the kitchen. The castle and village are described in Sir Walter Scott's *Waverley* but the castle is now perhaps best known as a location for the film *Monty Python and the Holy Grail* (1975) where it served as, among other places, Camelot, Swamp Castle and Castle Anthrax. The castle is maintained by Historic Scotland. Tel: 01786 841742.

Dunblane — A royal burgh at a crossing of the Allan Water, founded in the early 7th century around a religious site established by St Blane. The cathedral was built from the 12th century onwards. Although the town declined after the Reformation it was reinvigorated by the arrival of the railways in the 1840s, becoming a popular commuter town. The Darn Walk links Dunblane with Bridge of Allan along the river. The town was the scene on 13 March 1996 of a shocking massacre, when a gunman killed 16 children and their teacher at Dunblane Primary School.

Dunblane Cathedral The Cross, Dunblane. Dedicated to St Blane and St Laurence and located on the site of a possible 7th century Celtic Christian foundation, the church was originally established in the 12th century and part of the tower remains from that period. The main building dates from the 13th century when it was rebuilt by Bishop Clement. After the Reformation the cathedral fell into disrepair and it was only possible to hold services in the choir. The nave was restored in the late 19th century under the guidance of Robert Rowand Anderson and the choir was restored in 1914 by Robert Lorimer. There is a memorial to the 16 pupils and their teacher of Dunblane Primary School, murdered on 13 March 1996. The cathedral is maintained by Historic Scotland.

Dunblane Museum The Cross, Dunblane. A local history museum opened in 1943 and housed in the former Dean of the Cathedral's house, built in 1624. It was originally known as the Dunblane Cathedral Museum. Exhibits include a collection of communion tokens from all parts of the world. Of more local interest are the photographic archive and a Bronze Age coal necklace found in a nearby quarry. There is also a collection of genealogical records.

Dunmore Pineapple 1/2 mile (0.8km) northwest of Airth, 6 miles (10km) southeast of Stirling. A 53ft (16m) high folly built in 1761 in Dunmore Park walled garden with a spectacular cupola in the shape of a pineapple. It was probably intended as a garden retreat. It is believed pineapples were grown in hothouses on the Dunmore estate. The 16 acres (6.5ha) of gardens also include a pond and orchard. Both the Pineapple and the gardens have been maintained by the National Trust for Scotland since 1974. The property is leased to the Landmark Trust. Tel: 01324 831137.

Falkirk Steeple High Street, Falkirk. A 140ft (43m) high steeple designed by David Hamilton and built 1813–14 on the site of two earlier steeples after the previous steeple became unsafe and was demolished in 1803. Once used as the Falkirk tolbooth, in 1927 the tower was struck by lightning and the top 30– 40ft (9–12m) was dislodged. Later repaired, the steeple now serves as an information point.

Falkirk Tartan A hoard of more than 1900 Roman silver coins hidden in an earthenware vessel found on 9 August 1933 in Bell's Meadow, Falkirk. They were covered in a woollen cloth with a pattern of checks in dark and light brown, regarded by some as the earliest example of a tartan so far identified and known as the 'Falkirk Tartan'. The vast majority of the coins were denarii and dated from c.83 BC to AD 230; it is believed they were hidden c.240. The coins and the tartan are kept in the National Museum of Scotland in Edinburgh.

Falkirk Wheel Lime Road, Falkirk. The world's first rotating boat lift. Opened in 2002 by Queen Elizabeth II, it forms a link between the Forth and Clyde and Union Canals as part of the Millennium Link canal restoration project. It replaced a ladder of 11 locks between the two canals constructed in 1822. The wheel can carry at least eight boats at a time, a single trip taking about 15 minutes. The wheel is 115ft (35m) high with two gondolas or caissons, each of which holds 300 tonnes of water and/or boat. Tel: 0870 050 0208.

Flanders Moss 2 miles (3km) southwest of Thornhill, 11 miles (18km) west of Stirling. Situated in the Carse of Stirling, the name given to the flood plain of the River Forth west of Stirling, Flanders Moss consists of the largest intact raised bog remaining in Britain, a vestige of the Forth Valley boglands that once stretched from Aberfoyle to Stirling. A National Nature Reserve, its main component is sphagnum moss which over the course of thousands of years has formed a dome of peat covered with a surface of plantlife. The bog was greatly reduced by peat cutting and 'improving' during the 18th and 19th centuries. Wildlife includes mountain hares and over-wintering geese.

Forth & Clyde Canal Connecting the Forth at Grangemouth with Bowling on the Clyde, a distance of 35 miles (56km), the canal opened in 1790 after 22 years of construction. It has 39 locks and rises to a height of 156ft (47.5m) above sea level, with a branch to Port Dundas through central Glasgow. The canal was bought by Caledonian Railway in 1867 and is now owned by British Waterways. It was closed on 1 January 1963. The Forth & Clyde Canal Society was formed in 1980 with the aim of regenerating the canal, and it was reopened by HRH Charles, Prince of Wales, in 2001 after undergoing major restoration as part of the Millennium Link project, a major attraction being the Falkirk Wheel.

Gartmorn Dam Country Park and Nature Reserve 2 miles (3km) northeast of Alloa. A 215 acre (87ha) country park containing the 167 acre (67.5ha) reservoir of Gartmore Dam, originally constructed by the Earl of Mar in 1713 to help power pumps in the local mining operations. The reservoir is a popular fishing venue, while part of the park is a Site of Special Scientific Interest.

Glengoyne Distillery 1 mile (1.6km) south of Dumgoyne, 18 miles (29km) southwest of Stirling. A distillery which has been producing single malt Scotch whisky since it was established by George Connell in 1833. One of the original warehouses is still in use. The distillery's water source comes from nearby Dumgoyne Hill (1401ft/427m). Its site lies on the notional line that divides the Highlands from the Lowlands. Tel: 01360 550254.

Grangemouth Originally known as Sealock and then Grangeburnmouth, Grangemouth benefited from the opening of the Forth & Clyde Canal in the late 18th century and became the major port at the head of the Forth estuary. The docks were improved in the 1830s and Junction Dock was added in the middle of the century, during which time the port became a focus for imports of timber from Scandinavia and North America. Settlement in the port's hinterland gradually expanded further east. The Grange Dock was opened in 1906 and Scottish Dyes in 1919, while the establishment of the first oil refinery in 1924 began a process which has seen Grangemouth become a centre for the petrochemical industry. Other industries include engineering, textile manufacture and information technology.

Grangemouth Museum Bo'ness Road, Grangemouth. Located within the town's Victoria Library, the museum charts the story of Grangemouth from its origins as a planned community at the east end of the Forth and

Clyde Canal through to its present position as a centre for the petrochemical industry. Displays include the story of the *Charlotte Dundas* steamboat. Tel: 01324 504699.

Hamilton Toy Collection — Main Street, Callander. A huge collection of toys from all eras displayed in a series of rooms including the Soldier Room, Sci-Fi Room, Teddy Bear and Dolls Room, Edwardian Nursery and Boys' and Girls' Shops. Tel: 01877 330004.

Harviestoun Estate — 1 mile (1.6km) east of Tillicoultry. Located at the foot of the Ochil Hills, Harviestoun Castle was built by Craufurd Tait in 1804 based on an existing 18th century house. It was here in August 1787 that Robert Burns met Charlotte Hamilton, the niece of the owner, whom he described as the 'loveliest flower on the banks of the Devon'. It was also the childhood home of Edinburgh-born Archbishop of Canterbury Archibald Tait (1811–82). The castle was gutted in 1965 and demolished in 1970.

Highest point — Ben More, near Crianlarich, at 3852ft (1174m), the highest of the so-called Crianlarich Hills southeast of the village. (GR: NN432244.) There is no higher land in the British Isles south of Ben More.

Hillfoots Villages — Villages and small towns which lie at the foot of the Ochil Hills: Alva, Blairlogie, Dollar, Menstrie, Muckhart and Tillicoultry.

Inchmahome Priory — The substantial ruins of a 13th century Augustinian priory on Inchmahome, an island in the Lake of Menteith (see separate entry). Founded in 1238 by Walter Comyn, Earl of Menteith, it was briefly a refuge for the infant Mary, Queen of Scots following the Scottish defeat by the English at the Battle of Pinkiecleugh on 10 September 1547. The priory and its lands passed into secular hands after the Reformation and became ruinous. Now in the care of Historic Scotland.

Interesting facts — The **Lake of Menteith** is the subject of one of the most often cited quiz questions, 'How many lakes are there in Scotland?' The answer is of course one, as all the others are called lochs. There is no apparent reason for this anomaly as lochs and lakes are the same thing! **Callander** was used as the fictional town of Tannochbrae in the filming of the popular 1960s TV series *Dr Finlay's Casebook*.

Islands — The following islands are all in the Stirling area of Central Scotland apart from the two in the River Forth, which are in the Clackmannanshire area. Lake of Menteith: **Dog Isle** (GR: NN567003), **Inchmahome** (GR: NN574005), **Inchtalla**, site of a ruined castle of the Earls of Monteith (GR: NN572004); Loch Ard: **Eilean Gorm** (GR: NN457015); Loch Katrine: **Black Island** (GR: NN403118), **Ellen's Isle** (GR: NN488082); Loch Lomond: **Bucinch**, aka The Island of Goats (GR: NS389919), **Ceardach**, the smallest island in the loch, just 32ft (10m) long at its widest (GR: NS391919), **Clairinsh**, aka The Flat Island (GR: NS412899), **Ellanderroch**, aka Island of Oak (GR: NS395905), **Inchcailloch**, aka The Island Of The Nun – for more than 500 years mainlanders would row across the loch for Sunday worship on the island (GR: NS410902), **Inchcruin**, aka The Round Island, although it is not in the least round (GR: NS388911), **Inchfad** (GR: NS400909), **Keppinch**, aka The Kitchen; The Ross Islands (GR: NS364951), River Dochart: **Innes Buidhe**, aka Inchbuie; River Forth: **Inch Island** (GR: NS870918), **Tullibody Inch** (GR: NS862923).

Jupiter Urban Wildlife Centre — Wood Street, Grangemouth. A 10 acre (4ha) wildlife centre created in an industrial estate in Grangemouth and managed by the Scottish Wildlife Trust. Features include gardens demonstrating the creation of wildlife habitats in domestic gardens. There are areas of wetland, woodland and meadow. Tel: 01324 494974.

Kincardine Bridge — A bridge over the Firth of Forth connecting Kincardine-on-Forth in Fife with the Falkirk bank. Built 1932–6 to a design by Donald Watson, it has a swinging central section to allow the passage of shipping to Alloa which was in use until 1988. A second bridge over the Forth at the same location, designed to relieve traffic congestion in Clackmannanshire, Falkirk and Fife and allow for the renovation of the existing bridge, was approved in 2002. Construction on what is to be called the Clackmannanshire Bridge began in June 2006.

Lake of Menteith — 6 miles (10km) southwest of Callander. The only large natural body of water in Scotland referred to as a lake as opposed to a loch. Covering 700 acres (283ha), there are three islands in the lake as well as a number of artificial crannogs. Because it is not particularly deep, the lake occasionally freezes over; if the ice reaches a thickness of 10ft (3m) then a curling tournament called the Bonspiel is held, an event which last occurred in 1979. The lake is a designated Site of Special Scientific Interest.

Loch Ard — A 600 acre (243ha) loch in Loch Ard Forest, part of the Queen Elizabeth Forest Park. The River Forth flows from the loch. On the south shore are the remains of a castle built by Murdoch Stewart, Duke of Albany, Regent of Scotland (c.1362–1425).

Loch Katrine — 12 miles (19km) west of Callander. A freshwater loch 8 miles (13km) long and 0.6 mile (1km) wide, and covering an area of 3059 acres (1238ha). Since 1859 it has been a primary source of water for Glasgow and as a result oil-fired ships are not allowed on the loch. Currently, the wood-burning steamship SS *Sir Walter Scott* and the bio-fuel powered *Ellens Isle* provide tourist trips on the lake. There are two islands in the loch.

Loch Lomond and Trossachs National Park — One of only two National Parks in Scotland, covering 720 sq miles (1865 sq km). Opened by the Princess Royal on 24 July 2002, it was Scotland's first National Park. It encompasses areas including Ben Lomond, Loch Lomond, the Trossachs, Breadalbane and the Argyll Forest, also taking in the Queen Elizabeth Forest Park and the Argyll Forest Park; habitats include lochs, rivers, forests, glens and mountains (including 20 Munros and 20 Corbetts).

Loup of Fintry — 2 miles (3km) east of Fintry, 10 miles (16km) southwest of Stirling. A series of waterfalls on Endrick Water including the 94ft (28.5m) high Loup of Fintry.

Menstrie Castle — Castle Street, Menstrie, 4 miles (6km) northeast of Stirling. A 16th century tower house which was the birthplace of Sir William Alexander, 1st Earl of Stirling (1567–1640), an early coloniser of Nova

Scotia. The castle was converted into housing in the 1960s. There is a commemoration room to the Baronets of Nova Scotia. Managed by the National Trust for Scotland.

Menzies' Castle — See Plane Tower and Manor House

Midland Valley — A geological rift valley bounded on the north by the Highland Boundary Fault and to the south by the Southern Upland Fault. Largely made up of sedimentary rocks containing coal, ironstones, limestone and oil shales, it formed the basis for much of Scotland's industrialisation. It also includes much of the country's prime agricultural land. The combination of these advantages enabled the growth of the cities of Dundee, Edinburgh and Glasgow; as a result, 80 per cent of Scotland's population live within the area encompassed by the Midland Valley.

Moirlanich Longhouse — 1 mile (1.6km) northwest of Killin, 13 miles (21km) northeast of Crianlarich. A preserved cruck-frame cottage owned by the Robertson family and dating to the mid 19th century. Both the family and their livestock would have lived under one roof in the building. Abandoned in the 1960s, the longhouse retains many of its original features including the box beds. There is a display on the history of the building and a collection of clothes. Maintained by the National Trust for Scotland since 1992.

Mugdock Castle — $^3/_4$ mile (1.2km) west of Mugdock, 19 miles (31km) southwest of Stirling. The ruins of a 14th century courtyard castle on a narrow plateau. The home of the Graham family, the castle was enlarged in the 15th century by the erection of another curtain wall enclosing a larger courtyard area. In the late 19th century a mansion and outbuildings were built in the courtyard by J Guthrie Smith; these new buildings were destroyed by a fire in the 1960s. The castle now falls within Mugdock Country Park, opened in 1996 and covering 750 acres (300ha) around the ruins of Mugdock and Craigend Castles, also including Mugdock Loch.

Murdoch's Castle — See Loch Ard

National Wallace Monument — Causewayhead, $1^1/_2$ miles (2.5km) north of Stirling. A 220ft (67m) tower on the summit of Abbey Craig, built to commemorate William Wallace. Designed by J T Rochead, it was completed in 1869 in Victorian Gothic style. There are four rooms, while 246 internal steps lead up to a viewing platform with spectacular views of the countryside. Exhibits in the monument include Wallace's broadsword and a presentation of the story of his life and death, while the Hall of Heroes commemorates Scots who achieved great things in science, industry, education and the arts. These include Robert the Bruce, Robert Burns, Thomas Carlyle, William Ewart Gladstone, John Knox, David Livingstone, Sir Walter Scott, Adam Smith and James Watt. A statue of William Wallace erected in 1997 in the car park adjacent to the monument controversially bore a resemblance to the Australian actor Mel Gibson, who portrayed Wallace in the film *Braveheart*! Tel: 01786 472140.

Ochil Hills — A range of hills located to the north of the Firth of Forth and stretching from Dunblane and Bridge of Allan east into Fife. They were formed by the Ochil Fault. The highest point is Ben Cleuch at 2365ft (721m) (GR: NN902006). Other peaks include Ben Buck at 2228ft (679m), Andrew Gannel Hill at 2198ft (670m) and Kings Seat at 2126ft (648m). The Hillfoot villages were once home to many textile mills utilising the water power generated by the run-off from the hills.

Ochil Hills Woodland Park — 1 mile (1.6km) northeast of Alva, 6 miles (10km) northeast of Stirling. An area of predominantly broadleaved woodland covering the former grounds of Alva House.

Pathfoot Concourse Gallery — Pathfoot Road, Stirling. A gallery on the campus of the University of Stirling which houses the majority of its art collection. The collection, which was begun in 1967, has more than 300 works and in addition to contemporary Scottish art there are sculptures including Barbara Hepworth's *Archaen.* The collection includes gifts of works from the Scottish Arts Council and by colourist John Duncan Fergusson which were presented by his widow. The Pathfoot Building was designed by John Richards (1931–2003).

Plane Tower and Manor House — 1 mile (1.6km) east of Plean, 5 miles (8km) southeast of Stirling. Aka Plean Castle, Menzies Castle. A 15th century rectangular tower house with courtyard and manor house added in the 16th century by the Sommerville family. The buildings fell into disrepair in the 17th century but the tower was restored and remodelled in the early 20th century by Sir David Menzies. Abandoned again by the 1930s, the tower and manor house were restored in the 1990s and are now used as a family home and holiday accommodation. They are set in 4 acres (1.5ha) of grounds.

Plean Castle — See Plane Tower and Manor House

Plean Country Park — $^1/_2$ mile (0.8km) west of Plean, 5 miles (8km) northwest of Falkirk. A country park covering 200 acres (80ha) of the former Plean Estate. The park contains the ruins of Plean House, built in the 18th century and severely damaged by fire in the 1970s; there are indications of the area's past as a centre of coal mining in the spoil heaps, now reclaimed by nature.

Prisons — **Cornton Vale**, Stirling. Scotland's only all-women's prison, opened in 1975. Operational capacity: 230.

Glenochil, Tullibody, Clackmannan. Category B and C prison. Operational capacity: 430.

YOI Polmont, Reddingmuirhead, 3 miles (5km) southeast of Falkirk. The only centre in Scotland holding exclusively convicted young offenders. Operational capacity: 650. Tel: 01324 711558.

Queen Elizabeth Forest Park — Forest park covering 78 sq miles (200 sq km) split between four areas – East Loch Lomond Woodland, Strathyre Forest, Achray Forest and Loch Ard Forest – and encompassing habitats including mountain, moorland, forest, rivers and lochs. It was designated a forest park in 1953 to mark the coronation of Queen Elizabeth II. The East Loch Lomond Woodland is traversed by the West Highland Way. Strathyre Forest is a V-shaped wooded glen. Achray Forest covers the Duke's Pass and also includes the Blackwater Marshes. Loch Ard Forest (or the Great Forest of Loch Ard) lies between Aberfoyle and Loch Lomond and encloses not only Loch Ard but also Loch Chon and several lochans. It is also crossed by the Duchray Water and the Kelty Water.

Regimental Museum of the Argyll & Sutherland Highlanders
Housed in the King's Old Building of Stirling Castle, at one time the headquarters of the Argyll & Sutherland Highlanders. Exhibits include uniforms, medals, weapons and, in the dining room, silver, paintings and porcelain collected over 200 years. The regiment was formed on 1 July 1881 by the amalgamation of the 91st (Princess Louise's Argyllshire) Regiment and the 93rd (Sutherland Highlanders) Regiment. The 91st Argyllshire Highlanders were formed on 9 July 1794 as the 98th (renumbered in 1798). During the 1790s the regiment served in South Africa before returning to defensive duties in England and Ireland early in the Napoleonic Wars. It then served in the Peninsular War, first under Sir John Moore (1808) and later under the Duke of Wellington (1812–14). In 1881 it became the 1st Battalion, Princess Louise's Argyll & Sutherland Highlanders. The 93rd Sutherland Highlanders was raised in April 1799. It recaptured Cape Town in 1805 and remained in South Africa until 1814, afterwards taking part in the Battle of New Orleans in 1815. During the Crimean War the regiment routed a Russian cavalry charge at Balaklava on 24 October 1854 and earned itself the nickname of 'The Thin Red Line'. Thereafter it served in India during and after the mutiny of 1857–8. In 1881 it became the 2nd Battalion, Princess Louise's Argyll & Sutherland Highlanders; its motto, *Sans Peur, Ne Obliviscaris* (French/Latin 'Without fear, do not forget'), combined those of the 91st and 93rd. During World War I the regiment served on the Western Front, gaining 65 battle honours. During World War II the 1st Battalion served in North Africa and Italy, while the 2nd Battalion fought in the Far East until the fall of Singapore. A reconstituted 2nd Battalion took part in the D-Day campaign and the subsequent push to Germany. After World War II the regiment served or undertook peacekeeping duties in regions including Palestine, Korea, Suez, Borneo, Aden, Northern Ireland, Bosnia and Iraq. On 28 March 2006 the 1st Battalion The Argyll & Sutherland Highlanders was renamed The Argyll & Sutherland Highlanders, 5th Battalion The Royal Regiment of Scotland. Tel: 01786 475165.

Rivers
Carron rises in the Campsie Fells and flows eastward into Carron Valley Reservoir and out maintaining its easterly course via Carron Bridge and Denny, then between Larbert and Falkirk, before flowing into the Firth of Forth near Grangemouth; its total length being 20 miles (32km).
Forth rises at Loch Ard (see separate entry) and flows eastward through Aberfoyle, where it joins with Duchray and Kelty Water, and then into Stirling, where it receives the rivers Allan and Teith. The river then flows southeast to Kincardine Bridge where it opens up to become the Firth of Forth. The river runs for 29 miles (47km) from Loch Ard to Kincardine. The firth stretches for another 48 miles (77km) to the Isle of May, with a constriction at North and South Queensferry, spanned by the Forth Bridge (see entry in Fife).

Rough Castle Fort
2 miles (3km) west of Falkirk. The best preserved of the Roman forts along the Antonine Wall. Covering only 1 acre (0.4ha), it was excavated in the early 20th century, in the 1930s and again in the 1950s. The wall itself and accompanying ditch are well preserved along what was the north front of the fort. Excavations have identified a headquarters building, a granary and another stone building, possibly the officers' quarters, within the fort, and a bath-house in the annexe. Some of the troops stationed at the fort were from the cohort VI Nerviorum (6th Cohort of Nervii), an infantry unit recruited in Belgium.

Sauchie Tower
$^1/_2$ mile (0.8km) north of Alloa. The original four-storey tower house was built 1430–40 by Sir James Schaw who married into the Annand family, owners of the Sauchie estate. A mansion, known as Old Sauchie House, was built next to the tower c.1631. The tower was damaged by fire in the 1750s and the house was demolished in the 1930s. The tower is being restored by the Clackmannanshire Heritage Trust.

Sport:

general
The **Scottish Institute of Sport**, Airthrey Road, Stirling, established in 1998, focuses on the development of high performance sport in Scotland. A purpose built facility was opened in Stirling in May 2002. The core sports covered are athletics, badminton, curling, football, golf, hockey, judo, rugby (including rugby sevens) and swimming. Six additional Area Institutes cover Central Scotland, East of Scotland, Grampian, Highland, Tayside and Fife, and West of Scotland. The Central Scotland Institute of Sport is based at the University of Stirling Sports Centre. Tel: 01786 460100.

football
Alloa Athletic were founded in 1878 as Clackmannan County and joined the league in 1883 as Alloa Athletic. Alloa won the Scottish 2nd Division in 1922 and the Scottish 3rd Division in 1998. Nicknamed The Wasps after their traditional gold and black hooped shirts, their home ground is Recreation Park. Tel: 01259 722695.

East Stirlingshire were founded in 1881 as Bainsford Britannia. They won the Scottish 2nd Division in 1932. In 1964–65 the club merged with Clydebank Juniors to create ES Clydebank, and played at Kilbowie Park in Clydebank. After a court case the club reverted to its previous name and ground after only one season. East Stirlingshire was Sir Alex Ferguson's first club as a manager for three months in 1974. Journalist Jeff Connor wrote the book *Pointless: A Season with Britain's Worst Football Team* about his time with East Stirlingshire during the 2004–05 season. Nicknamed The Shire, their traditional colours are black and white hoops; their home ground is Firs Park, Falkirk. Tel: 01324 623583.

Falkirk were founded in 1876. They won the old Scottish 2nd Division in 1936, 1970 and 1975, the new 2nd Division in 1980 and the new Scottish 1st Division in 1991, 1994, 2003 and 2005. Nicknamed The Bairns, their home ground since 2004–05 has been Falkirk Stadium, having previously been based at Brockville Park. Their traditional colours are navy blue and white. Tel: 01324 624121.

Stenhousemuir were founded in 1884. Nicknamed The Warriors, their traditional colours are maroon and white; their home ground is Ochilview Park. Tel: 01324 562992.

Stirling Albion were founded in 1945, replacing Stirling's previous team King's Park. They won the Scottish 2nd Division in 1977, 1991 and 1996. Nicknamed The Binos, The Beanos or The Yo-Yos, their traditional colours are red and white. Their home ground is Forthbank Stadium; they previously played at Annfield 1945–92, where they installed the first artificial pitch in Scotland in 1987.

SS *Sir Walter Scott* — A pleasure steamer built at Dumbarton and launched on Lake Katrine in 1899. The only screw-driven steamer still in regular passenger service in Scotland, it is used on Lake Katrine because it minimises the pollution risk to Glasgow's water supply.

Stirling Castle — Castle Wynd, Stirling. Known as the Key to Scotland, this substantial castle on a promontory with steep cliffs on three sides guards a crossing point on the River Forth. The approach to the castle from the south is the most heavily fortified. The site was fortified some time in the first millennium, although much of the present castle dates from the 15th and 16th century. In 1124 Alexander I died at the castle and by 1174 it was in the hands of the English as part of the release terms for the captive William I. The castle was returned to the Scots in 1189 and William died here in 1214. In 1296 it was captured by the English again but over the next two years it was retaken by the Scots after the Battle of Stirling Bridge, abandoned to the English after the Battle of Falkirk and taken once again by the Scots following a successful siege by Robert the Bruce. During its lifetime the castle has been attacked at least 16 times; during one siege by Edward I he is reported to have employed 'Warwolf', the largest trebuchet (stone-throwing machine) ever built. An English army was attempting to relieve an English garrison holding the castle when it was defeated at the Battle of Bannockburn. Robert the Bruce proceeded to slight the castle defences to avoid its use by the English again but they were later rebuilt. The earliest surviving part of the castle, the north gate, was built in 1380. Stirling Castle was the birthplace of James III in 1451. The King's House (now known as the King's Old Building), the Chapel Royal, the great hall and the forework were built by James IV 1496–1503. The coronation of the infant James V took place at the castle in 1513 and in 1537 he began the building the palace behind the forework. His daughter Mary, Queen of Scots was crowned in the Chapel Royal in 1543, and the chapel was rebuilt in 1594. Even with updated defences known as the French Spur, put in place by Mary of Guise in the second half of the 16th century, the castle was besieged and badly damaged by a Cromwellian army under General Monck in 1650. The castle became solely a military base and was strengthened against the threat of the Jacobites during the reign of Queen Anne, easily withstanding a siege in early 1746. Reconstruction was carried out in the 19th century, during which time it housed army barracks. The army left the castle in 1964 and major restoration work was then carried out. Work on the Chapel Royal was completed in 1996 and the great hall was reopened by Queen Elizabeth II on 30 November 1999. The regimental museum of the Argyll and Sutherland Highlanders is now located in the King's Old Building. The castle is in the care of Historic Scotland. Tel: 01786 450000.

Stirling Old Town Jail — St John Street, Stirling. Originally built as the town jail in the 1840s by Thomas Brown, the jail served as Scotland's only military prison, 1888–1935. Abandoned until the 1990s, it has been restored as a living museum with a guided tour and living history presentations. Tel: 01786 450050.

Stirling Smith Art Gallery and Museum — Dumbarton Road, Stirling. A gallery and museum focusing on Scottish history and founded in 1874 following a bequest by artist Thomas Stuart Smith (c.1815–69). The building was designed by John Lessels and is located in the King's Park. The main exhibition traces the town's history through displays including fine art, archaeology, costumes, numismatics, weapons and memorabilia. Many of the paintings, drawings, etchings and sculptures are from Smith's own collection. Memorabilia include reputedly the world's oldest dated curling stone (c.1511). There is also a toy collection including a doll's house. Tel: 01786 471917.

Strathallan Games — Highland Games held annually on the first Sunday in August at Bridge of Allan, 3 miles (5km) north of Stirling. The games were founded in the mid 19th century by Major J A Henderson and have been held every year since 1863, with the exception of the war years. Sporting events include athletics, heavyweight competitions (including tossing the caber and throwing the 56lb weight over the bar), wrestling, tug-of-war and cycling. Other contests include highland dancing and pipe band competitions.

Torwood Castle — $^1/_2$ mile (0.8km) southwest of Torwood, 3 miles (5km) northwest of Falkirk. Ruins of an L-plan tower house built c.1566 by a Roman road on the outskirts of Tor Wood, and once the home of the Clan Forrester. The tower was formerly enclosed by a courtyard and a range of buildings.

University of Stirling — One of the 'plate-glass' universities of the 1960s, established in 1967 on a purpose-built campus on the former estate of Airthrey Castle surrounding Airthrey Loch. The MacRobert Arts Centre contains a theatre and cinema and there is also the Pathfoot Concourse Gallery in the Pathfoot Building. With around 9000 students, the university has four faculties: Arts, Human Sciences, Management, and Natural Sciences, and In addition to the main campus in Stirling, there are campuses in Inverness, Highland and Stornoway, Western Isles, specialising in nursing and midwifery. The university campus is also home to the Scottish Institute of Sport and its Central Scotland Area Institute. Former students include author Iain Banks, poet Jackie Kay and politician John Reid. Tel: 01786 473171.

Waterfalls — Notable waterfalls in the Central region include: **Falls of Bracklinn**, 1 mile (1.6km) northeast of Callander on the Keltie Water; **Falls of Dochart**, Killin, 9 miles (15km) southwest of Crianlarich on the River Dochart. The falls and village were used as a film location in *The Thirty-Nine Steps* (1959) and *Casino Royale* (1967); **Falls of Falloch**, 4 miles (6km) southwest of Crianlarich on the River Falloch, which flows into Loch Lomond. The deep pool under the highest waterfall is known as Rob Roy's Bathtub.

Woods on Your Doorstep	**Geordie's Wood** (605 acres/245ha), Muckhart, acquired in 2004 with 200,000 local native trees to be introduced to provide a link with Glen Quey and Glen Sherup; **Milton** (1922 acres/778ha), Milton by Callander; **Puidreag Plantation** (2½ acres/1ha), Balquhidder, a small site bounded by the River Balvag to the south. A mixture of native broadleaved woodland planted in 1988 and 2001 plus open grassland. Species include alder, ash, aspen, birch, oak and willow; **Wood Hill Wood** (196 acres/79ha), Alva, on the southern slope of the Ochil Hills. The woodland is dense at the bottom of the slope and becomes sparser towards the hill tops. The main species are ash, beech, larch, oak and sycamore. There is also a plantation of sitka spruce. Part of the site has silver and cobalt mines abandoned in the late 18th century and is fenced off for safety reasons.

Some famous people born in the Central region

Bremner, Billy (footballer) (1942–97)	Stirling
Carson, Willie (jockey) (1942–)	Stirling
Finlayson, James (actor) (1887–1953)	Larbert
Hansen, Alan (footballer) (1955–)	Sauchie
Henry, Robert (historian) (1718–90)	St Ninians
Mitchell, George (musician) (1917–2002)	Stirling
Murray, Andy (tennis player) (1987–)	Dunblane
Stuart, Henry Frederick (Prince of Wales) (1594–1612)	Stirling Castle
Thomson, Alexander 'Greek' (architect) (1817–75)	Balfron
Walker, James (engineer) (1781–1862)	Falkirk

Dumfries and Galloway

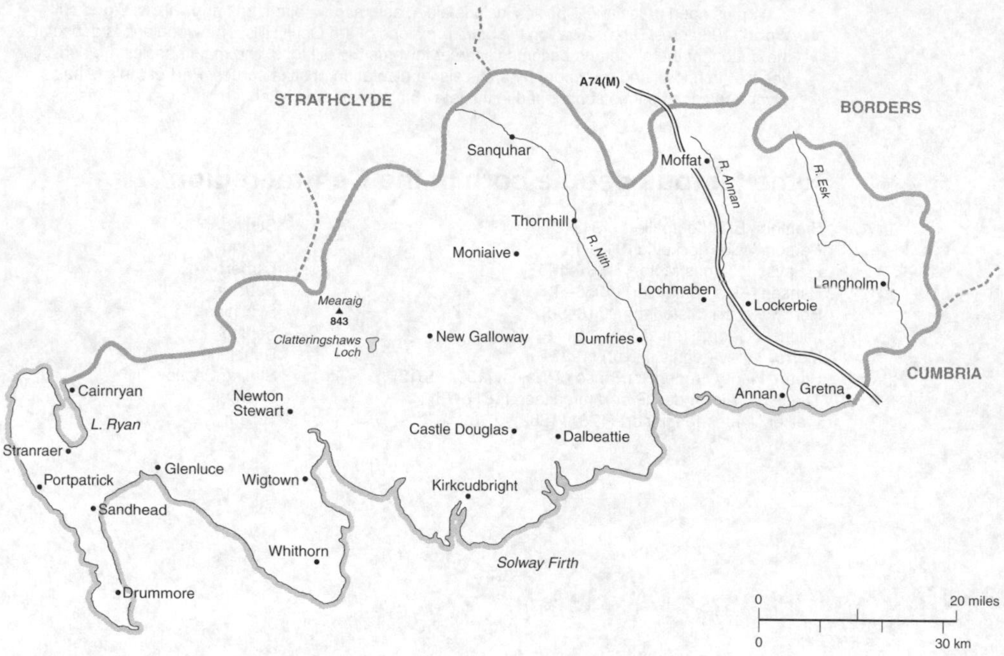
STRATHCLYDE
A74(M)
BORDERS
Sanquhar
Moffat
R. Annan
R. Esk
Thornhill
R. Nith
Moniaive
Lochmaben
Langholm
Lockerbie
Mearaig
843
Clatteringshaws
Loch
New Galloway
Dumfries
CUMBRIA
Cairnryan
Newton
Stewart
Annan
Gretna
L. Ryan
Castle Douglas
Dalbeattie
Stranraer
Glenluce
Portpatrick
Wigtown
Kirkcudbright
Sandhead
Whithorn
Solway Firth
Drummore
0
20 miles
0
30 km

Dumfries and Galloway is one of 32 unitary council areas in Scotland. It is bordered by the Strathclyde regions of South Ayrshire, East Ayrshire and South Lanarkshire to the north, Scottish Borders to the east, and the English county of Cumbria to the southeast. It lies to the north of the Solway Firth and east of the Irish Sea. The region covers the traditional counties of Wigtownshire (west), Kirkcudbrightshire (centre) and Dumfriesshire (east). As a pair Kirkcudbrightshire and Wigtownshire are referred to as Galloway. In 1975 it became a two-tier region with the districts Annandale & Eskdale, Nithsdale, Stewartry and Wigtown. These districts were abolished in 1996, and so Dumfries and Galloway became a unitary authority. Principal towns include Dumfries, Gretna, Castle Douglas, Kirkcudbright and Stranraer.

The term 'Dumfries and Galloway' has been used since the 19th century. Kirkcudbrightshire was at one time known as the Stewartry of Kirkcudbright, the term 'stewartry' applying to any area of Crown property in Scotland administered by a steward rather than a sheriff. The Stewartry of Kirkcudbright was annexed to the Crown in 1455 by James II in his bid to break the power of the Douglas Lords of Galloway.

The Dumfries and Galloway Constabulary is the smallest police force in the United Kingdom. From 21 December 1988, when the wreckage of Pan Am Flight 103 landed on the town of Lockerbie as a result of a terrorist bomb exploding on board, it presided over Britain's largest criminal inquiry. There were 270 victims, 259 on the plane and 11 on the ground in Lockerbie.

Dumfries and Galloway	**Population**			**Area**	
	male	*female*	*total*	*sq miles*	*sq km*
Total	71,303	76,462	147,765	2481	6426

Local Attractions and Information

Administrative headquarters	Council Offices, English Street, Dumfries DG1 2DD. Tel: 01387 260000.
Ardwell Gardens	Ardwell, 10 miles (16km) south of Stranraer. A blend of formal and informal gardens surrounding an 18th century house (not open to the public) above Luce Bay. including a walled garden and woodland and pondside walk. Planting includes azaleas and rhododendrons. Tel: 01776 860227.
Auchen Castle	Beattock, $1^{1}/_{2}$ miles (2.5km) south of Moffat. Founded in the 13th century and slighted by Robert the Bruce, Auchen was rebuilt in the 14th century as a quadrangular castle. The present building, dating from 1849 and built by General Johnstone near the castle ruins, today operates as a hotel. Tel: 01683 300407.
Beattock Summit	8 miles (13km) northwest of Moffat. The high point of the West Coast Main Line railway, at 1030ft (314m).
Bladnoch Distillery	Bladnoch, 1 mile (1.6km) southwest of Wigtown. Scotland's most southerly distillery, situated on the River Bladnoch. Founded in 1817 by farmers T & A McClelland, and enlarged by the family in the 1870s, the distillery was closed in 1938. After World War II it was reopened and passed through several owners before being closed again in 1993. Production was restarted in 2000. Tel: 01988 402605.
Broughton House	High Street, Kirkcudbright. An 18th century town house, the residence of Scottish artist E A (Edward Atkinson) Hornel from 1901 until his death in 1933. Although Hornel was born in Australia in 1864, his family were from Kirkcudbright and they returned to the town shortly after his birth. Hornel was one of the 'Glasgow Boys' and the gallery at Broughton contains many of his later works. The library (originally the drawing room) holds the world's fourth largest collection of Robert Burns literature. The house has been maintained by the National Trust for Scotland since 1997 and reopened in 2005 after a two-year conservation project costing £2m. Tel: 01557 330437.
Bruce's Stone	9 miles (15km) north of Newton Stewart. A large granite stone beside Loch Trool, against which Robert the Bruce is said to have rested after defeating a small English force in a skirmish in the early summer of 1307. Maintained by the National Trust for Scotland since 1932.
Robert Burns Centre	Mill Road, Dumfries. Opened in 1986 and part of the Burns Heritage Trail. Housed in an 18th century watermill on the west bank of the River Nith, the centre presents the story of Robert Burns and his life in southwest Scotland. Burns lived in Dumfries from 1791 until his death in 1796. The exhibition includes some of Burns' manuscripts and belongings as well as a scale model of Dumfries in the 1790s. Tel: 01387 264808.
Burns House	Burns Street, Dumfries. Robert Burns and his family moved into this three-bedroom house in 1793, and Burns died here on 21 July 1796, aged 37. His desk and chair can be seen in the study, which also contains original manuscripts. As was his usual practice, Burns scratched his name in the study window (there are at least 14 known other pieces of glass autographed by Burns). Memorabilia include Jean Armour's spectacles and bible and Burns' walking stick. Tel: 01387 255297.
Caerlaverock Castle	7 miles (11km) southeast of Dumfries. Located close to the mouth of the River Nith on the Solway Firth. Moated castle with twin-towered gatehouse built to a triangular plan c.1280. A stronghold of the Maxwell (de Maccuswell) family, it was besieged and captured by Edward I in 1300 and slighted by Robert the Bruce in 1312. It was substantially rebuilt over the following century. Robert Maxwell, 1st Earl of Nithsdale, built a range of domestic lodgings known as the Nithsdale Lodging inside the castle in the 1630s. However, the castle was captured and severely damaged by a Covenanter army in 1640 and has been left unrepaired ever since. In state care since 1946, it is now maintained by Historic Scotland. Features include a siege warfare exhibition, and a nature trail which leads to the foundations of an earlier castle built c.1220. Tel: 01387 770244.
Caerlaverock National Nature Reserve	8 miles (13km) southeast of Dumfries. An expanse of mudflats and saltmarsh (locally called merse) on the Solway Firth which attracts waders such as oystercatchers and curlew. From late September to March it is a haven for thousands of geese, including 20,000 barnacle geese, plus whooper swans and pintail ducks. Also home to rare natterjack toads which live at the margin of the merse. The reserve was established in 1957. Tel: 01387 770275.
Caerlaverock WWT	8 miles (13km) southeast of Dumfries. A 1400 acre (570ha) Wildfowl and Wetlands Trust reserve, part of the Caerlaverock National Nature Reserve. Tel: 01387 770200.
Cardoness Castle	1 mile (1.6km) southwest of Gatehouse of Fleet. A well-preserved six-storey tower house on a promontory overlooking the Water of Fleet, built by the McCullochs in the late 15th century but abandoned after the execution for murder of Sir Godfrey McCulloch in 1697. In state care since 1927 and now maintained by Historic Scotland. Tel: 01557 814427.
Carlyle's Birthplace	The Arched House, Ecclefechan, 6 miles (10km) southeast of Lockerbie. Social historian Thomas Carlyle was born here on 4 December 1795, in a house built, probably in 1791, by his father and uncle, who were both stonemasons. Carlyle left Ecclefechan at the age of 14 to walk to Edinburgh to study arts and mathematics. The house contains a collection of personal belongings including his hat, walking stick and tobacco cutter. Carlyle died on 5 February 1881 in London and is buried beside his parents in Ecclefechan. The house has been maintained by the National Trust for Scotland since 1936. Tel: 01576 300666.
Castle Douglas	Located on the shore of Carlingwark Loch, the settlement was once known as Causewayend and later Carlingwark before being rebuilt as a planned town by Sir William Douglas of Gelston in the 1790s. It developed into a major market town thanks to the industries introduced by Douglas and the arrival of the railways in the 1850s. Now the home of Michelin starred restaurants and with easy access to a wide range of local produce – 'Fish from the sea, beef from the hills', as the town's motto boldly proclaims – Castle Douglas has become a centre for food and drink, hence its adoption in 2002 of the title 'Castle Douglas Food Town'.

Castle Kennedy Gardens

3 miles (5km) east of Stranraer. A 75 acre (30ha) garden set around Lochinch Castle and the ruins of Castle Kennedy between the White Loch and the Black Loch. Lochinch Castle was built in 1867 to replace Castle Kennedy, which was burnt down in 1716. The gardens were landscaped in the 18th century and extended in the 19th century. There is a walled garden, pinetum, a 2 acre (0.8ha) lily pond and a garden walk between the two lochs. Specimen trees include a monkey puzzle and embothriums (Chilean fire bush). There are spectacular displays of rhododendrons and azaleas in spring. Tel: 01776 702024.

Castle of St John

Charlotte Street, Stranraer. Also known as Stranraer Castle. A tower house built c.1510 by Ninian Adair. It served as the town jail 1815–1907 and was opened to the public in 1990.

Chapelcross Nuclear Power Station

2½ miles (4km) northeast of Annan. The oldest nuclear power station in Scotland and the original sister plant to Calder Hall in Cumbria. Built on the site of the former RAF Annan, it operated from 1959 until June 2004. There were four Magnox reactors, one of which suffered a partial meltdown in 1967, and there was a further incident in 2001 when radioactive fuel rods fell down a shaft. The plant was also used to produce weapons-grade plutonium until 1979.

Corsewall Lighthouse

3 miles (5km) northwest of Kirkcolm, 9 miles (15km) northwest of Stranraer. A lighthouse situated at Corsewall Point, overlooking the North Channel of the Irish Sea at the entrance to Loch Ryan, and standing 111ft (34m) high. Built in 1817 to a design by Robert Stevenson, it was automated in 1994. The former lighthouse keeper's accommodation has been converted into a luxury hotel. Tel: 01776 853220.

Creetown Gem Rock Museum

Chain Road, Creetown, 6 miles (10km) southeast of Newton Stewart. A collection of gemstones, crystals, minerals and fossils opened in 1980. Exhibits include the 'Maverick' gold nugget and a fossilised egg. There is a Crystal Cave where minerals are displayed in a more natural setting plus fluorescent lighting. The Professor's Study is a Victorian themed room. Tel: 01671 820357.

Creetown Heritage Museum

St John Street, Creetown, 6 miles (10km) southeast of Newton Stewart. A museum charting the history of Creetown and the surrounding area from its origins as a small fishing village, through its prosperity in the 19th century as a source of silver-grey granite, to its use as a location for the film *The Wicker Man* (1973). Tel: 01671 820471.

Crichton Estate

1 mile (1.6km) south of Dumfries. Parkland and gardens covering 85 acres (34ha) originally owned by Elizabeth Crichton (1779–1862) and her husband Dr James Crichton, who died in 1823. Having unsuccessfully attempted to fulfil her late husband's wish to establish a university in Dumfries, in 1839 Mrs Crichton instead founded the **Crichton Royal Hospital**, a renowned psychiatric hospital. The hospital grounds were opened to the public in 1940. In 1995 Dumfries & Galloway Council purchased the Crichton estate and in 1996 set up the Crichton Foundation. Maxwell House, the Rutherford McCowan Building, Browne House and Dudgeon on the estate now form the Crichton Campus of the University of the West of Scotland.

Cruggleton Castle

3 miles (5km) northeast of Whithorn, 14 miles (21km) southeast of Newton Stewart. The ruins of a motte and bailey castle founded in the 12th century and reinforced in stone the following century. Located on a coastal promontory, the castle was once the residence of the Lords of Galloway, but only a single arched vault now remains.

David Coulthard Museum

Burn Brae, Twynholm, 2 miles (3km) northwest of Kirkcudbright. A museum dedicated to Formula One driver David Coulthard and located in his home town. Begun by his father and opened in 1999, it includes memorabilia covering Coulthard's career from go-karts to Formula One.

Devil's Porridge

Buttermills Road, Eastriggs, 3 miles (5km) east of Annan. An exhibition about the secret munitions factory built in Gretna (known simply as HM Factory Gretna) in 1915 to boost arms production during World War I. 'Devil's porridge' was Sir Arthur Conan Doyle description of the hand-mixed explosive paste mixture of nitro-glycerine and nitro-cotton used in bullets and shells. There are also exhibits about the Quintinshill rail disaster of 1915, the Gallipoli campaign and evacuation from Glasgow to Dumfries during World War II. Tel: 01461 40460.

Drumlanrig Castle

2½ miles (3.5km) northwest of Thornhill, 16 miles (26km) northwest of Dumfries. Home of the Duke of Buccleuch and Queensferry, the pink sandstone castle was built by William Douglas 1679–91 on the site of a 14th century castle owned by the 'Black' Douglas family. It was visited by Bonnie Prince Charlie during his retreat from Derby in 1745. Built around a courtyard with a circular tower in each corner, it houses Jacobite relics (such as Bonnie Prince Charlie's camp kettle) and art treasures including works by Holbein, Rembrandt, Gainsborough and Leonardo da Vinci, whose *Madonna of the Yarnwinder* was stolen from the castle in 2003. The extensive gardens include the Great North Avenue of lime trees, first planted at the end of the 17th century. Other features include parterres, a pinetum, woodland garden, a 'wilderness', a long terrace walk and planting in intricate and emblematic designs. There is also a water feature known as The Cascade. In the woodlands around the castle are a red oak planted by astronaut Neil Armstrong in 1972, the first Douglas fir to be planted in Scotland and the 300 year old Drumlanrig Sycamore, one of Scotland's top 100 heritage trees. Tel: 01848 330248.

Dumfries

The 'capital' of Dumfries and Galloway, given its royal charter in 1186 and for the first 50 years of its foundation at the forefront of the Scottish Borders until the consolidation of Galloway in 1234. A royal castle, which no longer exists, was built in the 13th century on the site of the present Castledykes Park, and before becoming King of Scots, Robert the Bruce slew the Red Comyn (John III Comyn, Lord of Badenoch) in the town in 1306. His uncertainty about the efficacy of his stabbing caused one of his followers, Roger de Kirkpatrick, to utter famously 'I mak siccar' (I'll make certain) and finish the Comyn off. Although Dumfries has a long history of being a rural backwater, the arrival of the railways made it less remote and it became a middle-class retreat in the 20th century.

Dumfries and Galloway Aviation Museum

2 miles (3km) northeast of Dumfries. An exhibition of aircraft and memorabilia at the former RAF Dumfries (now the Heathhall Industrial Estate), based in and around the airfield's restored

control tower. Aircraft on display include a De Havilland Vampire T11, North American F100D, Lockheed T33A, Hawker Hunter F4, and a Saab A35A Draken. A Spitfire P7540 which crashed into Loch Doon on 25 October 1941 while on a training flight is in the process of restoration. There is also a collection dedicated to the Parachute Regiment and Airborne Forces. Tel: 01387 251623.

Dumfries Museum and Camera Obscura — Rotchell Road, Dumfries. A museum tracing the history of Dumfries and Galloway, housed in an 18th century windmill above Dumfries known as The Observatory. Established in 1836 and one of the oldest museums in Britain, its collections feature items relating to the archaeology, geology and natural history of the area, plus artefacts relating to Robert Burns and domestic life in Victorian times and during World Wars I and II. A camera obscura housed in the top of the windmill gives panoramic views over Dumfries. Tel: 01387 253374.

Dumfries Prison — Terregles Street, Dumfries. A local prison holding remand and convicted male prisoners from the Dumfries and Galloway courts. Tel: 01387 261218.

Dundrennan Abbey — Dundrennan, 4 miles (6km) southeast of Kirkcudbright. Ruins of a Cistercian abbey founded in 1142 by Fergus, Lord of Galloway and David I as a daughter house of the monastery of Rievaulx. It is famous as the last place that Mary, Queen of Scots stayed before her final departure from Scotland on 15 May 1568. By this time the abbey was in serious decline and was being maintained by a commendator, Edward Maxwell, rather than an abbot; in 1587 the abbey and its lands passed to the Crown, and in 1621 it was annexed to the Chapel Royal, Stirling. In the following years much of the abbey's stone was robbed as material for local buildings, including Kirkcudbright Old Courthouse in 1642. What remained was taken into state care in 1842; the existing remains now include the north and south walls of the choir, parts of the north and south transepts, the piers of the central tower and the doorway of the chapterhouse.

Dunskey Garden — Portpatrick, 6 miles (10km) southwest of Stranraer. The restored 18th century walled garden of Dunskey House, built in 1706 and enlarged in the 1830s. The estate's 19th century greenhouses have also been restored and house a selection of exotic plants, shrubs and fruit. Tel: 01776 810211.

Ellisland Farm — Auldgirth, 7 miles (11km) northwest of Dumfries. An 170 acre (69ha) farm on the River Nith. Robert Burns lived and worked on the farm with his wife and son 1788–91 before becoming an excise officer in Dumfries. During his time here he wrote many of his most famous works, including 'The Wounded Hare', 'Sweet Afton', 'Auld Lang Syne' and 'Tam O'Shanter', doing much of his writing in a small cottage known as The Hermitage. The farm is now a museum and houses a number of the family's possessions. Tel: 01387 740426.

Galloway Forest Park — The largest forest park in Scotland, covering 297 sq miles (770 sq km) and extending into South Ayrshire. The various areas encompassed by the park include **Bennan Wood** beside Loch Ken; **Castlemaddy Wood**, a conifer woodland with the Polmaddy Burn running through it; **Glen Trool**, containing the highest peak in the south of Scotland, Merrick at 2766ft (843m), as well as Lochs Enoch, Neldricken and Trool; **Kirroughtree**, a mixed broadleaved and conifer woodland near Bruntis Loch; **Cally Wood**, a mixed broadleaved and conifer woodland near the village of Gatehouse of Fleet; **Clatteringshaws**, by Clatteringshaws Loch reservoir in the Galloway Forest; Barhill, a mixed broadleaved and conifer woodland near Kirkcudbright; and **Carrick**, a woodland near Straiton. Murray's Monument was erected in 1835 in memory of Alexander Murray, a local shepherd boy who became professor of Oriental languages at Edinburgh University.

Galloway House Gardens — Garlieston, 12 miles (19km) southeast of Newton Stewart. Gardens overlooking the beach at Rigg or Cruggleton Bay and surrounding a private house built in the 1740s. Incorporating woodland and walled gardens, features include a specimen handkerchief tree, a pond and a collection of rhododendrons. Rigg Bay was used in World War II to test the construction of the prefabricated 'Mulberry Harbour' prior to its use during the D-Day landings, and a section of superstructure remains in situ. Tel: 01988 600680.

Galloway Hydroelectric Power Scheme — New Galloway, 13 miles (21km) northwest of Castle Douglas. Drawing water from the rivers Ken, Dee and Doon through reservoirs at Loch Doon, Kendoon, Carsfad, Clatteringshaws and Tongland, the network of dams and hydroelectric power stations was built 1932–6. The stations were designed by Sir Alexander Gibb. The Galloway Hydros Visitor Centre, located at Tongland Power Station, the largest in the scheme, tells the story of the construction of the scheme and the operation of the power station.

Galloway Wildlife Conservation Park — 1 mile (1.6km) northeast of Kirkcudbright. A conservation breeding centre set in the 27 acre (11ha) mixed woodland of Lochfergue Plantation, and home to a collection of 150 animals in natural enclosures, including lemurs, wallabies, meerkats and red pandas. Endangered species include anoa, a breed of small wild cattle. Tel: 01557 331645.

Gilnockie Castle — Hollows, 1½ miles (2.5km) north of Canonbie, 7½ miles (12km) northeast of Gretna. Located on the north side of Gilnockie Bridge, the castle was possibly founded by Turgot de Rossedal 1124–53 and destroyed in 1523 by the English.

Gilnockie Tower — Hollows, 1½ miles (2.5km) north of Canonbie, 7½ miles (12km) northeast of Gretna. A four-storey oblong tower house built in the 16th century, possibly as part of the defences for Gilnockie Castle, and believed to have been the home of Johnnie Armstrong, an infamous reiver hanged alongside 50 of his family by James V in 1530. The house was restored in 1980 and bought by Clan Armstrong in 1992. Inside the entrance is a stone slab known as the 'Dead Stone', beneath which it is said that many notable Armstrongs lie buried. The practice of burying the dead at the entrance to the tower was common in the Borders. The building now houses the Clan Armstrong Centre and Museum. Tel: 013873 71876.

Glenluce Abbey — 1 mile (1.6km) west of Glenluce, 7½ miles (12km) east of Stranraer. Cistercian monastery overlooking Luce Bay and founded in 1190 by Roland, Lord of Galloway as a daughter house of Dundredan Abbey. The abbey ceased to function after the Reformation. Remains include the chapter house and south transept. Some of the structure was restored in the 1900s. In state care since 1933, it is now maintained by Historic Scotland.

Glenwhan Gardens — Dunragit, 6 miles (10km) southeast of Stranraer. A 12 acre (5ha) garden overlooking Luce Bay, established and developed by the Knott family since 1979 in the grounds of Glenwhan House. The wetland garden features two lochans planted with water lilies and bordered by willows. The dry garden has a collection of rhododendrons. Tel: 01581 400222.

Gracefield Arts Centre — Edinburgh Road, Dumfries. A Victorian villa opened as an art gallery in 1951 and housing a collection of more than 450 works by major 19th and 20th century artists including E A Hornel, Jessie King and Alan Davey. There is a sculpture garden in the grounds. Tel: 01387 262084.

Gretna — A small town close to the English/Scottish border which has been home to runaway marriages since 1753, when Lord Hardwicke's Marriage Act was passed in England. This stated that if both parties to a marriage were not at least 21 years old, then consent to the marriage had to be given by the parents. As the Act did not apply in Scotland, where it was possible for a couple to marry simply by declaring themselves before witnesses to be man and wife, this led to many elopers fleeing England and making for the first Scottish village they came to, which happened to be Gretna. Many locals set themselves up as priests, the most famous being the blacksmith. His forge became the focal point for the marriage trade. Gretna remains a popular venue for legal wedding ceremonies. The area was also the scene of the worst railway accident in British railway history when, on 22 May 1915, at Quintinshill, a crash involving a troop train and three other trains resulted in the loss of 227 lives.

Grey Mare's Tail — 9 miles (15km) northeast of Moffat. Located in Galloway Forest Park, the 200ft (60m) high 'hanging valley' waterfall was mentioned by Sir Walter Scott in his poem *Marmion.* The waterfall is formed by the outlet of Loch Skeen falling into Moffat Water. The 2278 acre (922ha) Grey Mare's Tail Nature Reserve has been maintained by the National Trust for Scotland since 1962.

Highest point — Mearaig (or Merrick) is the highest mountain in the Southern Uplands at 2766ft (843m).

Interesting facts — **Galloway** is the name given to a hardy breed of black, hornless beef cattle native to the region. The tiny village of **Eskdalemuir,** 12 miles (19km) northeast of Lockerbie, is the surprising home of a traditional **Buddhist temple**. The Samye Ling Monastery and Tibetan Centre was established in 1967 and was the first and largest of its kind in the West. **Wigtown** was selected as **Scotland's National Booktown** in 1997. The small town of just over 1000 people has 19 book businesses. **Port Logan** was made famous in the BBC Scotland drama *Two Thousand Acres of Sky* as the fictional island of Ronansay. **Wanlockhead** is a village nestling in the Lowther Hills, which form part of the Southern Uplands. It is Scotland's highest village at 1531ft (467m). (GR: NS871129.)

Islands — See separate entry

John Paul Jones Museum — $1^1/_2$ miles (2.5km) southeast of Kirkbean, 11 miles (18km) south of Dumfries. Located on the Arbigland estate, the cottage is the birthplace of the American hero sometimes called the 'Father of the American Navy'. Born John Paul on 6 July 1747, he became a sailor in Whitehaven, Cumbria at the age of 13 and by 21 had become a captain, at which time he was arrested in Kircudbright for killing a shipmate but acquitted. While in the West Indies he killed a man during a mutiny and fled to Virginia, where he took the name John Paul Jones. Commissioned as 1st lieutenant in the Continental Navy during the American War of Independence, he achieved fame during raids on the British and Irish coasts, including Whitehaven and Kirkcudbright. It was during a fight between his vessel, the *Bonhomme Richard,* and HMS *Serapis* off Flamborough Head that he uttered, when asked if he wished to surrender, the oft-quoted 'I have not yet begun to fight.' After the war he lived mainly in Paris but in 1788–9 he was a rear-admiral in the Russian navy. He died in Paris on 18 July 1792. In 1905 his newly rediscovered body was reburied with great ceremony at Annapolis Naval Academy. Opened as a museum in 1993 at the instigation of Admiral Wright of the United States Navy and Admiral Henderson of the Royal Navy, the two-roomed cottage is furnished as it might have been in the 1700s, with a room built by Lt Pinckham USN in the 1830s when he was sent to find Jones' birthplace.

Kirkcudbright — A town on the estuary of the River Dee, originally known as Kilcudbrit, derived from the Gaelic *Cii Cudbert* (Chapel of Cuthbert). The town has a long association with the Glasgow art movement, which started when a colony of artists, including the Glasgow Boys and the Scottish Colourists, based themselves in the area over a 30-year period from 1880 to 1910. Kirkcudbright became known as 'the artists' town'. *The Five Red Herrings*, a Dorothy L Sayers detective story featuring Lord Peter Wimsey, is set among the artistic community of Kirkcudbright and the cult movie *The Wicker Man* (1973) was filmed predominantly in the town and surrounding area.

Logan Botanic Garden — 1 mile (1.6km) north of Port Logan, 11 miles (18km) south of Stranraer. An exotic garden overlooking the Mull of Logan and benefiting from the warming effect of the Gulf Stream. Many of the species grown are from the southern hemisphere and include nearly 40 species of eucalyptus. Established in 1869 and presented to the nation in 1969, the $3^1/_2$ acre (1.5ha) walled garden includes a collection of half-hardy perennials plus rare and unusual trees, shrubs and climbers from all over the world. The $12^1/_2$ acre (5ha) woodland garden is partly planted as an Australian woodland and also includes planting more commonly found in Chile. Other features include a peat garden and a gunnera bog. Managed by the Royal Botanic Garden Edinburgh. Tel: 01776 860231.

Logan Fish Pond Marine Life Centre — Port Logan, 13 miles (21km) south of Stranraer. Built by Andrew McDouall in 1800 from a natural blow hole as a place to store live sea fish and used as a fish larder. There is also a restored Victorian bathing hut nearby plus a cave aquarium. Tel: 01776 860300.

MacLellan's Castle — Castle Street, Kirkcudbright. An L-shaped tower house built in 1582 by Thomas MacLellan, Provost of Kircudbright, on the site of the Greyfriars convent, abandoned by 1569. It was itself abandoned in 1742 and the roof was removed. In state care since 1912, it is now maintained by Historic Scotland.

Moffat Museum — Church Gate, Moffat. A museum housed in Moffat's old bakehouse with exhibits spanning the history of the town, a popular spa during the 18th and 19th centuries when the sulphurous waters of Moffat Spa were believed to have healing properties. Tel: 01683 220868.

Mull of Galloway — 4 miles (6km) southeast of Drummore, 20 miles (32km) southeast of Stranraer. Scotland's most southerly point and a nature reserve. A visitor centre is housed in the buildings used by the workmen who built the Mull of Galloway lighthouse. The cliffs are home to thousands of breeding birds, including razorbills, guillemots and puffins. The lighthouse, completed in 1830 to a design by Robert Stevenson, is a white round tower 85ft (26m) high with 114 steps to the top. On 8 June 1944, during foggy weather, a Bristol Beaufighter aircraft crashed into its stores building. The lighthouse was demanned in 1988 and is now remotely monitored. Tel: 01776 840539.

Museum of Lead Mining — Wanlockhead, 19 miles (31km) southwest of Biggar. A museum located in a former mining village and dedicated to the lives of those who worked the lead mines in the Lowther Hills from the 18th to the 20th century. Exhibits include equipment and machinery. Other features of the museum and surrounding area are a guided tour of the Lochnell Mine, restored miners' cottages and the miners' library. Tel: 01659 74387.

National Nature Reserves — There are four National Nature Reserves in Dumfries and Galloway: **Caerlaverock** (19042 acres/7706ha) (see separate entry); **Cairnsmore of Fleet** (4749 acres/1922ha), an area of granite heather uplnad supporting species such as peregrine falcon; **Silver Flowe** (472 acres/191ha), an area of upland bog (or 'flowe') supporting a wide variety of wetland species; **Kirkconnell Flow** (351 acres/142ha), a lowland raised bog.

New Abbey Corn Mill — New Abbey, 6 miles (10km) south of Dumfries. A fully restored and working 18th century watermill, presented to the nation in 1977 and now maintained by Historic Scotland. Tel: 01387 850260.

Newton Stewart Museum — York Road, Newton Stewart. Museum with exhibits relating to the area's natural and social history. More than 95 per cent of the items on display have been donated or lent by local people.

Old Bridge House Museum — Mill Road, Dumfries. A museum of social history opened in 1959 and housed in the oldest domestic building in Dumfries, built in 1660 into the structure of 15th century Devorgilla's Bridge over the River Nith. There are period room settings including a Victorian kitchen, nursery and bedroom, and an early dentist's surgery. Tel: 01387 256904.

Rhins of Galloway — A hammerhead peninsula to the west of Stranraer almost cut off from the rest of the country by Luce Bay and Loch Ryan. Stretching more than 25 miles (40km) north–south, its southern tip is the Mull of Galloway, the southernmost point of Scotland.

Rivers — The **Annan** rises 5 miles north of Moffat and flows south between Lochmaben and Lockerbie to the town of Annan before discharging into the Solway Firth, a total length of 35 miles (56km).

The **Bladnoch** is a spate river that rises out of Loch Maberry and weaves its way southeast through forestry and farmland to the top of The Machars peninsula, entering Wigtown Bay at Wigtown itself. Its total length is 12 miles (19km).

The **Cree** flows from north of Loch Moan in Galloway in a southerly direction to the town of Newton Stewart and into Wigtown Bay, a total length of 12 miles (19km).

The **Esk** rises in the mountains to the east of Moffat and flows southeast through Eskdale to Langholm. The river then flows south alongside the A7 and into England to Longtown before merging with the River Lyne and entering the Solway Firth near the mouth of the River Eden, northwest of Carlisle.

The **Nith** rises west of New Cumnock and flows east alongside the A76 through Sanquhar before taking a more southerly course through Thornhill (still following the A76) to Dumfries, emptying into the Solway Firth. Its total length is 45 miles (72km). An excellent salmon and trout river, its main tributaries – the Cairn, Cample, Shinnel, Scaur and Crawick – are also good fishing rivers and spawning grounds.

RSPB Mersehead — 6 miles (10km) southeast of Dalbeattie. An RSPB reserve on the Solway coast with a variety of habitats including wet meadows, saltmarsh and mudflats. Bird species include barnacle geese, lapwing, pintail, reed warbler and skylark, and in autumn migrating greenshank, sandpiper and godwit. Other wildlife includes otters, badgers and roe deer. Tel: 01387 780579.

Ruthwell Cross — ½ mile (0.8km) north of Ruthwell, 9 miles (15km) southeast of Dumfries. An 8th century Anglo-Saxon preaching cross now located within Ruthwell Church. Standing 18ft (5m) high, it depicts events in the lives of Jesus and St John the Evangelist; there are vine-fruit carvings and a runic inscription generally accepted as part of the text of the famous Anglo-Saxon poem *The Dream of the Rood*.

St Michael's Churchyard — St Michael's Street, Dumfries. The burial place of Robert Burns. Originally buried in the northeast corner of the churchyard, on 19 September 1815 his body was transferred to a large Greek-style mausoleum erected in the southeast corner and paid for by public subscription. Also transferred at the same time were the remains of two of Burns' sons: Maxwell, who died in 1799 (aged 2 years 9 months) and Francis Wallace who died in 1803 (aged 14). The mausoleum was not completed until 1817. Burns' wife Jean was also buried in the mausoleum in 1834. It was restored 1995–6 and is cared for by Dumfries and Galloway Museums.

Sanquhar Tolbooth Museum — Hugh Street, Sanquhar. Local history museum opened in 1975 and housed in the tolbooth built in 1735 by William Arden. Refurbished 1987–90. Exhibits include the cells, and the story of the mines and miners of Sanquhar. There are also displays of the distinctive black and white three-ply knitting style known as Sanquhar Knitting. Tel: 01659 50186.

Savings Bank Museum — Ruthwell, 9 miles (15km) southeast of Dumfries. On 10 May 1810 Dr Henry Duncan (1774–1846), minister of Ruthwell Parish Church and also an amateur geologist, publisher, philanthropist and social reformer, opened the world's first commercial savings bank in Ruthwell. He collected a minimum of sixpence from each subscriber and deposited the sum with the Linen Bank in Dumfries at 5 per cent interest. The members of the scheme received 4 per cent interest and the surplus was sufficient to provide a charitable fund, the money from which he used to build a new school in Ruthwell. The original Ruthwell Parish Bank, built in the 18th century, now houses the Savings Bank Museum which has a collection of savings boxes, coins and bank notes from all over the world. As an antiquarian Dr Duncan restored the 8th century Ruthwell Cross (see separate entry); he also discovered the first fossilised set of quadruped footprints. Towards the end of his life he became Moderator of the General Assembly of the Church of Scotland and was one of the founding ministers of the Free Church of Scotland following the Disruption of 1843. Tel: 01387 870640.

Shambellie House Museum of Costume — New Abbey, 6 miles (10km) south of Dumfries. A Victorian house with a series of period rooms displaying the costume and accessory collection. Rooms include the dining room (dressed as in summer 1895), drawing room (May 1945), library (31 December 1952), bedroom (bridal scene, summer 1939), playroom (August 1913), bathroom (November 1905) and sitting room (summer 1882). Tel: 01387 850375.

Sport: football — **Gretna** were founded in 1946 and originally played in the English leagues, reaching the Northern Premier League 1st Division. During the 1990s, they also became the first club from Scotland to appear in the FA Cup proper since Glasgow Rangers in 1887. In 2002 they were elected to the Scottish Football League and won successive promotions to reach the Scottish Premier League in 2007. They were also runners-up in the Scottish FA Cup in 2006, but were dissolved in 2008 after losing the financial backing of their chairman, Brooks Mileson. Nicknamed The Black and Whites from the colour of their traditional hooped shirts, their home ground was Raydale Park, Gretna. A new club, Gretna FC 2008, was formed by supporters in 2008.

Queen of the South were founded in 1919. Winners of the Scottish 2nd Division in 1951 and 2002, they reached the Scottish FA Cup semi-finals in 1949–50 and were beaten finalists in 2008. Nicknamed The Doonhamers, their colours are blue and white; their home ground is Palmerston Park, Dumfries. Tel: 01387 254853.

Stranraer were founded in 1870. Winners of the Scottish 2nd Division in 1994 and 1998, they reached the Scottish FA Cup quarter-finals in 2002–03. Nicknamed The Blues or The Clayholers, their colours are blue and white; their home ground is Stair Park.

Stewartry Museum — St Mary Street, Kirkcudbright. Opened in 1881 as the county museum and moved into a purpose-built museum in 1893. Collections trace the social and natural history of the eastern half of Galloway, known as 'The Stewartry' (also known as Kirkcudbrightshire). There is a local and family history information service. Tel: 01557 331643.

Stranraer — A town on the shores of Loch Ryan, on the northern side of the isthmus joining the Rhins of Galloway to the mainland. Its name comes from the Scottish Gaelic *An t-Sròn Reamhar*, meaning literally 'The Fat Nose'. Best known as a ferry port connecting Scotland with Belfast and Larne in Northern Ireland, it became a burgh of barony in 1596 and a royal burgh in 1617. Its surrounding area saw significant activity during World War II, as it became a focus for anti U-boat work. Flying boats operated from Stranraer in an effort to secure the waters of the North Channel and the southwest coast of Scotland, areas through which almost all Britain's shipping imports passed en route to the Clyde or the Mersey. Winston Churchill departed from Stranraer in a Boeing flying boat on the night of 25 June 1942, when making his second visit of the war to the USA.

Stranraer Castle — See Castle of St John

Stranraer Museum — George Street, Stranraer. Established as a county museum as part of Stranraer Library in 1939 and housed since 1984 in Stranraer's Old Town Hall, built in 1776. The collections cover the local history and archaeology of Wigtownshire. There is an exhibition about polar explorers Sir John Ross (1777–1856) and Sir James Clark Ross (1800–62) as well as a collection of 3D Victorian photographs. Tel: 01776 705088.

Sweetheart Abbey — New Abbey, 6 miles (10km) south of Dumfries. Originally called New Abbey to distinguish it from its mother house at nearby Dundrennan Abbey, this Cistercian monastery was founded in 1273 by Devorgilla, Lady of Galloway, in memory of her husband John Balliol. She carried his embalmed heart in a silver and ivory casket at all times and it was buried alongside her in the abbey at her death in 1289; the abbey gained its new name (L. *Dulce Cor*) at this time, while the surrounding settlement retained the name New Abbey. The abbey was abandoned towards the end of the 16th century after the Reformation and the buildings robbed for their stonework. In state care since 1928 and now maintained by Historic Scotland.

Threave Castle — 1 mile (1.6km) west of Castle Douglas. A five-storey rectangular tower house built c.1369 by Archibald 'The Grim' Douglas on an island in the River Dee. A stronghold of the Douglas family, it was besieged by James II for three months in 1455 before being taken. The castle remained in royal hands until being transferred to the Maxwell family. It was abandoned in 1640 when it was slighted by Covenanters after another three-month siege. Taken into state care in 1913 and now maintained by Historic Scotland.

Threave Garden and Estate — 1 mile (1.6km) south of Castle Douglas. A 65 acre (26ha) garden created by students of the National Trust for Scotland School of Practical Gardening. There are displays of 200 different daffodil varieties during the spring, as well as a rock garden, rose garden and walled garden. Threave House was built in 1872 and opened to the public in 2002, with interiors restored to their 1930s appearance. The surrounding estate covers nearly 1250 acres (500ha) and is a Special Protection Area designated for its wildfowl habitat. Owned by the National Trust for Scotland. Tel: 01556 502575.

Tolbooth Arts Centre — High Street, Kirkcudbright. Opened in 1993 in Kirkcudbright's 17th century tolbooth, which once held John Paul Jones in one of its cells. It now houses works by local artists and contemporary Scottish artists including E A Hornel, Jessie M King, S J Peploe and Charles Oppenheimer. Tel: 01557 331556.

University of the West of Scotland	See Strathclyde
Whithorn Priory	Main Street, Whithorn. Whithorn is the earliest site of continuous Christian worship in Scotland. A chapel built by St Ninian in AD 397 was the first Christian settlement north of Hadrian's Wall, while the Northumbrians built a church on the site c.730 before being evicted from the area by Viking settlers. The bishopric of Whithorn was re-established in 1128 and Whithorn became a priory of the Premonstratensian order (White Canons) in 1177. Whithorn subsequently became a centre of pilgrimage until it fell into decline following the Reformation. The remains include the 12th century crypt. The priory museum houses a collection of carved stones found in the area including the Monreith Cross, a sandstone cross dating to AD 800–1100. Tel: 01988 500508.
Woods on Your Doorstep	**Aldouran Glen** (aka Glen of the Otter) (32 acres/13ha), northwest of Stranraer between the villages of Leswalt and Lochnaw, contains a tributary of the Sole Burn. A mixture of ancient semi-natural woodland and long established woodland of plantation origin, mainly broadleaved and including sycamore, beech, ash and elm. Bluebell wood in May. The wood also contains Kemp's Grave, the remaining earthworks of an Iron Age hill fort; **Drumlea** ($^3/_4$ acre/0.3ha), Waterbeck. Mixed broadleaves including sycamore, beech, ash and oak, partly bounded by beech hedges.

Some famous people born in Dumfries and Galloway

Carlyle, Thomas (essayist) (1795–1881)	Ecclefechan
Coulthard, David (racing driver) (1971–)	Twynholm
Gillies, William (politician) (1865–1932)	Galloway
Jones, John Paul (naval officer) (1747–92)	Kirkbean
Laurie, John (actor) (1897–1980)	Dumfries
MacMillan, Kirkpatrick (inventor) (1812–78)	Keir
MacDiarmid, Hugh (poet) (1892–1978)	Langholm
Mirrlees, James (economist) (1936–)	Minnigaff
Ross, John (Arctic explorer) (1777–1856)	Inch
Telford, Thomas (engineer) (1757–1834)	Westerkirk

Islands of Dumfries and Galloway

(Shipping areas IS = Irish Sea; M = Malin)

Island name	Area	Nearest landmark	General information	Shipping area
Altar Stone	Solway Firth	Annan	GR: NY218639	IS
Ardwall Island	Wigtown Bay	Gatehouse of Fleet	One of the Islands of Fleet. GR: NX572492	IS
Barlocco Island	Wigtown Bay	Gatehouse of Fleet	One of the Islands of Fleet. GR: NX579482	IS
Big Scare	Luce Bay	Mull of Galloway	One of the Scares group of islets. GR: NX259332	M IS
Black Craigs	Irish Sea	Southerness Point	GR: NX985551	IS
Brewing Scar	Solway Firth	Annan	GR: NY123636	
Burned Isle	Loch Ken	Parton	GR: NX656728	M
Caspin	Firth of Clyde	Milleur Point	GR: NX003732	M
Craig Laggan	North Channel	Dounan Bay	GR: NW959692	IS
Craig Roan	Irish Sea	Castlehill Point	GR: NX860521	IS
Fox Craig	Irish Sea	Kirkcudbright	GR: NX655432	IS
Frenchman's Rock	Kirkcudbright Bay	Kirkcudbright	GR: NX660464	IS
Garvellan Rocks	Wigtown Bay	Gatehouse of Fleet	GR: NX556513	IS
Green Isle	Loch Ken	Parton	GR: NX663727	
Hestan Isle	Irish Sea	Balcary Point	GR: NX838502	IS
Hestan Rack	Irish Sea	Balcary Point	GR: NX838507	IS
Horse Isles	Rough Firth	Almorness Point	GR: NX841517	IS
Horse Mark	Wigtown Bay	Gatehouse of Fleet	GR: NX560504	IS
Howgarth Scar	Solway Firth	Annan	GR: NY135642	IS
Kennan's Isle	River Dee	Tongland	GR: NX703552	
Kid Islands	Mochrum Loch	Door of May	GR: NX298524	
Little Ross	Kirkcudbright Bay	Kirkcudbright	GR: NX659433	IS
Little Scares	Luce Bay	Mull of Galloway	One of the Scares group of islets. GR: NX263345	M
Lodge Island	River Dee	Castle Douglas	GR: NX734610	
Long Island	Mochrum Loch	Door of May	GR: NX300526	
Lot's Wife	Irish Sea	Mereshead	GR: NX910557	IS
Murray's Isles	Wigtown Bay	Gatehouse of Fleet	One of the Islands of Fleet. GR: NX561501	IS

Island name	Area	Nearest landmark	General information	Shipping area
Oust Rock	Firth of Clyde	Corsewall Point	GR: NW970717	M
Powfoot Scar	Solway Firth	Annan	GR: NY144651	IS
Rob's Craig	Irish Sea	Kirkcudbright	GR: NX708435	IS
Rock McGibbon	Loch Ryan	Stranraer	GR: NX082635	M
Rough Island	Rough Firth	Almorness Point	Area: 0.03 sq miles (0.07 sq km). GR: NX843532	IS IS
Rough Scar	Solway Firth	Annan	GR: NY103632	
Round Island	Mochrum Loch	Door of May	GR: NX300528	
Rowan Island	Mochrum Loch	Door of May	GR: NX300529	
Scar Island	Mochrum Loch	Door of Drumwait	GR: NX302537	
Spring Stones	Rough Firth	Almorness Point	GR: NX845528	IS
St Mary's Isle	Kirkcudbright Bay	Kirkcudbright	GR: NX673490	IS
Sugarloaf	Kirkcudbright Bay	Kirkcudbright	GR: NX659439	IS
Threave Island	River Dee	Castle Douglas	GR: NX739623	
Three Brethren	Wigtown Bay	Gatehouse of Fleet	One of the Islands of Fleet. GR: NX581481	IS

FIFE

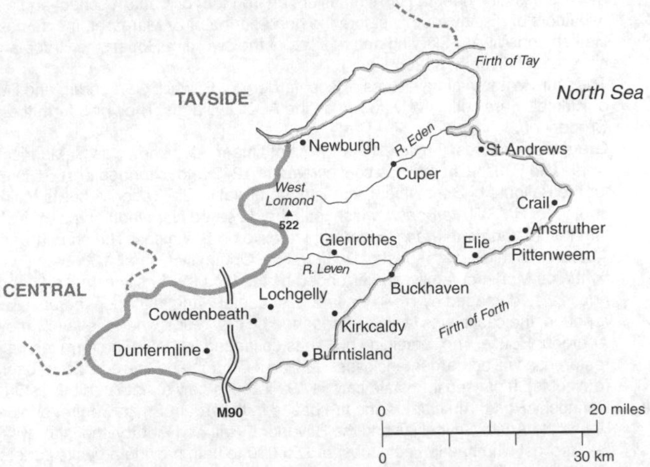
Firth of Tay
North Sea
TAYSIDE
Newburgh
R. Eden
St Andrews
Cuper
West Lomond
522
Crail
Anstruther
Glenrothes
Elie
Pittenweem
R. Leven
CENTRAL
Lochgelly
Buckhaven
Cowdenbeath
Kirkcaldy
Firth of Forth
Dunfermline
Burntisland
M90
0
20 miles
0
30 km

Fife is bounded by the Firth of Tay to the north and the Firth of Forth to the south. It has land borders with Perth & Kinross (on Tayside in the northwest) and Clackmannanshire (in Central) in the southwest. Its main rivers are the River Eden and the River Leven and its major body of water is Loch Leven, although this is dealt with under Tayside as its nearest town, Kinross, is in the Tayside area. From 1975 to 1996 Fife was a local government region divided into three districts – Dunfermline, Kirkcaldy and North East Fife. Since 1996 the functions of the district councils have been exercised by the unitary Fife Council. Major towns include Charlestown, Culross, Dunfermline, Glenrothes, Kirkcaldy and St Andrews.

Historically the coast of Fife was first colonised during the Neolithic period. It was originally one of the Pictish kingdoms, known as Fib or Fibh (after one of the seven sons of the warrior king Cruithne). Within Scotland it is still commonly known as the 'Kingdom of Fife' or the 'Wee Kingdom'. There are numerous examples of decorated Pictish stones and crosses found in Fife. In the medieval period, until the Reformation, St Andrews was a centre for religion, royal patronage and education.

The west of Fife is an industrial area, while the east is more rural and the economy is based around agriculture and fishing. The region's early economy was heavily based on seaborne trade and fishing and expanded during the Industrial Revolution with the discovery of coal and lime deposits. The coal industry is estimated to have been producing more than 15,000 tons per year during the 17th century. Much of this was used in local industries: pottery, glass, salt pans and limestone kilns. There was also a thriving export trade to Scandinavia and northern Europe, the coal ships returning with ballast such as the red pantiles which are still a feature of the roofs in many of Fife's coastal towns.

Other important industries were textiles and paper. Thanks to the country's higher levels of literacy, most paper mills in Scotland made fine white paper as opposed to the brown grades manufactured south of the Border. During the 19th century paper mills in Fife used imported raw material such as esparto grass; as a result, many mills were set up near the coast to benefit from trade. Since the late 20th century, alongside these traditional industries there has been a great growth in technology in the region, particularly electronics production.

Fife	**Population**			**Area**	
	male	*female*	*total*	*sq miles*	*sq km*
	167,628	181,801	349,429	512	1325

Local Attractions and Information

Abbot House Heritage Centre Maygate, Dunfermline. Opened in 1995 and housed in the restored oldest house in Dunfermline, the pink-walled Abbot House which survived the great fire of 1624. In addition to being an abbot's home it has also been a laird's mansion, an iron foundry, an art school and a doctor's surgery. The two floors of display rooms feature the head-shrine of St Margaret, the stories of Lady Anne Halkett and William Skirving and replicas of the sword of Robert the Bruce and the 'poison chalice'. Tel: 01383 733266.

ABCD villages The four former mining villages of Auchterderran, Bowhill, Cardenden and Dundonald to the west of Kirkcaldy are collectively known as the ABCD villages. They now form the parish of Cardenden.

Abdie Church Grange of Lindores, 8 miles (13km) west of Cupar. Also known as St Magridin Parish Church. Abdie Old Parish Church was consecrated in 1242 and extended in 1661 to provide a burial place for the Balfours of Denmylne. There is a memorial to Sir Frederick Lewis Maitland (1777–1839), captain of HMS *Bellerophon*, which took the defeated Napoleon on board in 1815 and transferred him to the *Northumberland* for carriage to exile on St Helena. The church was abandoned in 1827.

Aberdour Castle Aberdour, 5 miles (8km) east of Dunfermline. Originally a small 12th century tower house owned by the de Mortimer family, and extended by the Douglas family in the 16th and 17th centuries. The house was damaged by fire in the late 17th century and, although the east range of buildings was repaired, the castle was largely abandoned by the 1790s when the family moved to nearby Aberdour House. The remaining buildings collapsed in 1844. The terraced gardens are being restored; a walled garden encloses St Fillan's Church and there is also a beehive-shaped doocot (dovecote). It passed into state care in 1924 and is now maintained by Historic Scotland.

Adam Smith Theatre Bennochy Road, Kirkcaldy. A theatre based in the Adam Smith Centre, originally built 1884–9 to house the Adam Smith Hall and the Beveridge Hall and Library; the latter was named after the late provost who had left a bequest of £50,000 to help provide a public park (see Beveridge Park) and a library. The interior was remodelled in the 1970s to provide an auditorium for theatre and conferences. Tel: 01592 412929.

Administrative headquarters Fife House, North Street, Glenrothes KY7 5LT. Tel: 01592 414141.

Andrew Carnegie Birthplace Museum Moodie Street, Dunfermline. A museum dedicated to steel baron and philanthropist Andrew Carnegie, born the son of a weaver in the cottage in 1835. The cottage was bought by Louise Carnegie for her husband on his 60th birthday. Carnegie, sometimes called the 'Star-Spangled Scotchman', paid a visit to the cottage in 1909 and after his death in 1919 a memorial hall was built next door; the museum was opened in 1928. Tel: 01383 724302.

Balbirnie Park $^{1}/_{2}$ mile (0.8km) northwest of Markinch, 2 miles (3km) northeast of Glenrothes. Parkland and woodland covering 416 acres (168ha) and surrounding Balbirnie House, built in 1777. The land is divided between an 18-hole golf course and the public park. There is a collection of exotic trees plus a rhododendron collection. The house is now a hotel.

Balmerino Abbey Balmerino, 11 miles (18km) northwest of St Andrews. Ruins of a Cistercian monastery overlooking the Firth of Tay, founded c.1227 by Alexander II and his mother Queen Ermengarde. It was dedicated to the Virgin and to St Edward the Confessor and its mother house was Melrose Abbey. Ermengarde was buried at Balmerino in the 1230s. The abbey was burned by the English in 1547 and further damaged during the Reformation in the 1550s. By 1603 the abbey was abandoned and the lands were granted to Sir James Elphinstone, 1st Lord Balmerino. Much of the structure was stripped to provide building material; the main structures still standing are the walls and vaulting of the sacristy and chapter house plus parts of the north transept of the abbey church. The grounds contain one of the oldest Spanish chestnut trees in Britain, believed to be as much as 500 years old. Maintained by the National Trust for Scotland since 1936.

Battles See separate table for details of the Battle of Inverkeithing.

Beveridge Park Abbotshall Road, Kirkcaldy. A public park covering 104 acres (42ha), bequeathed to the people of Kirkcaldy by Provost Michael Beveridge in the 1890s and established on an area called Robbie's Park, where Raith Rovers played home matches 1883–91. Tel: 01592 412690.

Bishop's Bridge Ceres, 2 miles (3km) southeast of Cupar. A 17th century packhorse bridge across the Ceres Burn, so called because on 3 May 1679 James Sharp, Archbishop of St Andrews, paused by it shortly before being assassinated by a group of Covenanters at nearby Magus Muir. The bridge was restored in the 1960s.

Blairadam Forest 1 mile (1.6km) west of Kelty, 5 miles (8km) northeast of Dunfermline. A woodland originally planted by architect Sir William Adam in the 1730s as part of his Blairadam House estate. Harvested during World War I, it was afterwards replanted, mainly with conifers, as a commercial forest by the Forestry Commission.

British Golf Museum Bruce Embankment, St Andrews. A museum celebrating the story of British golf and laid out chronologically in a series of galleries. Tel: 01334 460046.

Buckhaven Museum College Street, Buckhaven, 6 miles (10km) northeast of Kirkcaldy. A small local museum dedicated to the lives of local people in the fishing and coal mining industries. Displays include a 1920s kitchen and locally made stained glass windows. Tel: 01592 412860.

Burntisland Edwardian Fair Museum High Street, Burntisland. A local history museum focusing on the lives of the local people during the Edwardian period and in particular on the annual fairground. Tel: 01592 412860.

Cambo Estate Gardens Kingsbarns, 6 miles (10km) southeast of St Andrews. The 1200 acre (485ha) estate has been home to the Erskine family since 1688. The original house on the site, based on a 13th century tower dwelling with substantial later additions, was destroyed by fire in 1878 and replaced by a mansion house built in 1881. The gardens, through which the Cambo Burn runs, were opened to the public in the 1990s and comprise a woodland garden with fine displays of snowdrops in early spring and a Victorian walled garden. Tel: 01333 450054.

Ceres Bannockburn Monument Ceres, 7 miles (11km) southwest of St Andrews. A monument to the men of Ceres who fought at the Battle of Bannockburn, erected by the people of the village on 21 June 1914, the 600th anniversary of the battle. The town also holds the annual Ceres Highland Games.

Charlestown A planned village created in the 1750s by Charles Bruce, 5th Earl of Elgin, who not only named it after himself but also laid out the cottages in terraces to form the initials 'CE' (Charles Elgin). The estate had rich deposits of coal and limestone and the village was built to house the miners, quarriers and their families. The village grew into an industrial centre with 14 limekilns, a harbour and a railway connection with Dunfermline. At its peak the town produced 30 per cent of all the building lime used throughout the UK. Iron-working and ship-building also flourished for a time and then ship-breaking, including some of the German High Seas Fleet after World War I. The limekilns were closed in 1956. The town now houses the Scottish Lime Centre.

Collessie Stone Collessie, 6 miles (10km) west of Cupar. A Bronze Age standing stone 9ft (2.7km) high, with Pictish carvings of a naked figure with a shield on the southeast face and a horseshoe on the adjoining southwest face.

Craigtoun Country Park 2 miles (3km) southwest of St Andrews. Originally the landscaped grounds of Mount Melville House, established as a country park in 1947. Covering 41 acres (16.5ha), its features include a Dutch Village and an Italian garden, both part of the gardens' original design. Tel: 01334 473666.

Crail Museum and Heritage Centre Marketgate South, Crail. A local history museum with dedicated rooms exploring the town's links with the local World War I and II airfield, the Royal Naval Air Squadron HMS *Jackdaw* (1939–47), HMS *Bruce* (1947–9) and the Joint Services School for Linguists (1956–60); the history of the burgh and its kirk since the 12th century; the story of the Crail Golfing Society, founded in 1786; and the area's farming and fishing heritage. Tel: 01333 450869.

Cullaloe Wildlife Reserve $1\frac{1}{2}$ miles (2.5km) north of Aberdour. A wildlife reserve and Site of Special Scientific Interest consisting of mixed woodland, pools and a small loch. The loch was originally a reservoir which supplied water to Burntisland; a sister reservoir was drained in 1986 when the pair were no longer required. The reserve supports colonies of two rare plants: mudwort and water sedge. The woods contain the ruins of the settlement of Cottown and two follies known as the Tower and the Temple.

Culross A royal burgh, and according to one legend the site of the birth of St Mungo, who was born on the beach here in AD 518 after his pregnant mother had been set adrift in a coracle. An abbey was founded in 1217, possibly because of the legend. The village also benefited from the discovery of coal deposits in the area. Mining was begun by monks from the abbey and in 1575 the Moat Pit was sunk from an artificial island in the River Forth. The pit was kept drained by a horse-driven bucket and chain pumping system devised by Sir George Bruce. Bruce used his wealth to build Culross Palace. Two shafts were sunk to improve ventilation and ships could load directly from the island in the river. In addition to being a port Culross was also the biggest producer of salt in Scotland during the 17th century. Unfortunately the pit was destroyed by a flood in 1625 and the town's prosperity dipped dramatically. Under the auspices of the National Trust for Scotland, much of the royal burgh is now preserved as it was in the 16th and 17th centuries.

Culross Abbey Culross, 7 miles (11km) west of Dunfermline. A Cistercian monastery founded in 1217 by Malcolm, Earl of Fife. A daughter house of Kinloss Abbey, it was possibly built on the site of an earlier foundation dedicated to St Mungo (aka St Kentigern), who was born at Culross in 518. The western half of the abbey was abandoned in the late 15th century and the rest was vacated following the Reformation in the second half of the 16th century. The abbey was secularised in 1589; the east choir of the church was converted into a parish church in 1633 and is still in use today. Since 1624 the north transept has housed the tomb of Sir George Bruce of Carnock with effigies of him, his wife and eight children. The abbey was altered in 1823 and restored in 1905. The ruins are now maintained by Historic Scotland.

Culross Palace Culross, 7 miles (11km) west of Dunfermline. Sometimes called 'the Colonel's Close' or 'The Great Lodging', and built by merchant George Bruce 1597–1611. Bruce used many materials garnered through his trading interests including Baltic pine, Dutch floor tiles and Dutch glass. The house features collections of 17th and 18th century furniture and Staffordshire and Scottish pottery. The garden has been restored in 17th century style to include planting patterns and plants. It is maintained by the National Trust for Scotland. Tel: 01383 880359.

Culross Town House Originally the town's 17th century tolbooth, which acted as both the town gaol and the courthouse. Used as the Burgh Town House from the early 19th century until 1975, it has since been maintained by the National Trust for Scotland.

Dogton Stone 4 miles (6km) northwest of Kirkcaldy. A weathered and mutilated 9th century free-standing cross nearly 5ft (1.5m) high in a field on Dogton Farm.

Dunfermline A royal burgh and the historic capital of Scotland. In the 11th century the town was the seat of Malcolm III Canmore and his wife St Margaret, and his tower can be seen on the burgh coat of arms. An industrial centre for Fife, it gained prosperity initially from the weaving of damask and latterly from other industries such as brewing, rope-making and soap-making. It was endowed with a library, park and baths by probably its best-known son, industrialist and philanthropist Andrew Carnegie.

Dunfermline Abbey St Margaret Street, Dunfermline. A Benedictine abbey founded in 1128 by David I, overlying the foundations of the Church of the Holy Trinity, founded by Queen Margaret c.1070. It is the site of the graves of the Scottish kings Edgar (d.1107), Alexander I (d.1124), David I (d.1153), Malcolm IV (d.1165) and Alexander III (d.1286). The abbey was severely damaged by an English army in 1303 and only the church was spared. The original abbey church, consecrated in 1150, consisted of a nave, a tower with spire and north and south transepts. The choir became a shrine to St Margaret. After its rebuilding, its benefactor, Robert the Bruce, was buried in the church. The abbey came to an end as a religious community after it was sacked by a mob in 1560 during the Reformation. The church quickly fell into disrepair, but the nave was repaired, serving for many years as the parish church until a new building was completed in 1821; the new abbey church, the nave of which incorporated that of the old church, held its first service on 30 September of that year. The remains of Robert the Bruce, uncovered during the building of the new church in 1819, were reinterred beneath the pulpit. The ruins, including the old church and gatehouse, are maintained by Historic Scotland.

Dunfermline Carnegie Library Abbot Street, Dunfermline. The first of more than 2500 public libraries around the world – each with 'Let there be light' inscribed above its entrance – financed by Dunfermline-born industrialist and philanthropist Andrew Carnegie. The memorial stone was laid on 27 July 1881 by his mother, Margaret, and the library was opened by Lord Rosebery on 25 August 1883. Tel: 01383 312600.

Dunfermline High School St Leonards Place, Dunfermline. A comprehensive school which can trace its history back to the foundation in the 1120s of Dunfermline Abbey, which had provision for a monastic grammar school. Dunfermline Grammar School was established in 1468 and the education of pupils from the abbey was merged following the Reformation in the late 16th century. The school was destroyed in the great fire of 1624 but was rebuilt on the same site. It became Dunfermline High School in 1877. The school moved to a new location in 1886 and to its current site in 1939. Tel: 01383 312460.

Dunfermline Palace St Margaret Street, Dunfermline. Occupying the site of Dunfermline Abbey's 14th century guest house, in the late 16th or early 17th century the building was raised in height, substantially altered and transformed into a royal palace by William Schaw to be the main residence of James VI's wife, Anne of Denmark. Their son Charles I was born in the palace on 19 November 1600, the last monarch to be born in Scotland. It was last used as a royal residence by Charles II in 1651. The only substantial structure which remains today is the south wall. Maintained by Historic Scotland.

Falkland Palace and Garden Falkland, 4 miles (6km) north of Glenrothes. Built 1530–41 as a Scottish royal residence on the site of an older castle belonging to the Earls of Fife. After the royal court moved to London in 1603 the palace was used less frequently and passed into the care of a non-resident keeper; as a result it fell into disrepair by the end of the 17th century. In 1887 the 3rd Marquess of Bute acquired the keepership and began restoration work. Notable rooms include the King's Bedchamber, the Queen's Room, the chapel royal and the keeper's apartments in the gatehouse. The 3 acre (1.2ha) garden was remodelled by designer Percy Cane after World War II, when it had been turned into an allotment; it is mainly laid with herbaceous borders, with a herb garden and orchard. Another feature is Britain's oldest real tennis court, built in 1539, plus an exhibition. Maintained and restored by the National Trust for Scotland as deputy keeper since 1952. Tel: 01337 857397.

Fife Coastal Path A long-distance footpath covering more than 70 miles (113km) along the coast from the Forth Bridge to the Tay Bridge via Aberdour, Kinghorn, Dysart, Wemyss, Leven Links, Elie, Pittenweem, Crail, St Andrews and Newport-on-Tay.

Fife Folk Museum High Street, Ceres, 7 miles (11km) southwest of St Andrews. A local history museum celebrating everyday rural life in Fife, opened in 1968 in the restored Weigh House (Tolbooth) and adjoining weavers' cottages and extended into a building opposite in 1985. The Weigh House was built in 1673; in addition to the dual function of gaol and courthouse, it was also where local farmers' grain rents were weighed. The museum explores local crafts and portrays the lives of local craftsmen and their families. Exhibits include a selection of weighing machines and grain measures as well as everyday items owned or used by local people, as well as a large collection of lace, patchwork and samplers. Tel: 01334 828180.

Forth Bridge 9 miles (15km) west of Edinburgh. A rail bridge carrying the two tracks of the North British Railway $1\frac{1}{2}$ miles (2.5km) over the Firth of Forth between South Queensferry and North Queensferry. Standing 150ft (46m) above high tide, the bridge has three double-armed cantilevered towers each 340ft (104m) high, one of which stands on the tiny island of Inchgarvie. It was commissioned by the Midland, Great Northern, North Eastern, and North British Railway Companies, designed by Sir John Fowler and Sir Benjamin Baker and constructed by Sir William Arrol at a cost of almost £3m. Edward, Prince of Wales, hammered home the final golden rivet – which was inscribed to that effect – when the bridge was opened on 4 March 1890. During the seven years of construction 55,000 tonnes of steel were used, 194,000 tonnes of stones and concrete, 21,000 tonnes of cement and almost 8,000,000 rivets; 5000 people worked on the bridge and there were 57 deaths. Traditionally 55 people worked endlessly painting and repainting the bridge with red lead paint, working from east to west and then continuously back from west to east. Nowadays the anti-corrosive paint materials used ensure the need for only a vicennial coating, although a team of seven abseiling maintenance workers brave the elements daily. The Category A listed bridge now carries the East Coast main line.

Forth Road Bridge A suspension bridge situated just west of the Forth Bridge, spanning the Firth of Forth and carrying the A90 road, plus two cycle paths and two footpaths, between Fife and Edinburgh. The Forth Road Bridge replaced a ferry service which had operated for more than 700 years. Work began in autumn 1958 and the bridge was opened on 4 September 1964 by Queen Elizabeth II and the Duke of Edinburgh. Over 4 million vehicles crossed the bridge in the first year; now over 23 million vehicles use it each year, making it one of the busiest estuarial crossings in the UK. The total length of the bridge is 8241ft (2512m); the main span is 3300ft (1006m) and it has two side spans each of 1338ft (408m) each, a north viaduct of 827ft (252m) and a south viaduct of 1440ft (438m). The bridge was designed by Mott Hay & Anderson and Sir Freeman Fox & Partners.

Construction was carried out by the ACD group, a consortium of the three largest construction firms in Britain at the time: Sir William Arrol & Company, The Cleveland Bridge & Engineering Company and Dorman Long (Bridge & Engineering). Seven men lost their lives during construction and a memorial plaque dedicated to these men was erected at the Administration Offices of the Joint Board. In April 2002 the Forth Estuary Transport Authority took over responsibility for maintaining and operating the bridge, which is now Category A listed.

Glenrothes
A new town established in 1948, and now the headquarters of Fife Council. Initially based on coal-mining and the paper industry, it has latterly seen a growth in its electronics industry as more traditional industries have declined.

Highest point
West Lomond in the Lomond Hills at 1713ft (522m). (GR: NO197066.)

Hill of Tarvit Mansion House and Garden
2 miles (3km) south of Cupar. An Edwardian mansion house designed by architect Sir Robert Lorimer in 1906 and surrounded by 500 acres (200ha) of grounds. Built for Dundee industrialist F B Sharp on the site of 17th century Wemyss Hall, it was designed to complement Sharp's collections of decorative and fine art objects including Chinese porcelain, French, Chippendale and vernacular furniture, and paintings by Dutch masters and Scots such as Raeburn and Ramsay. The house also has a range of early 20th century labour-saving devices. The formal gardens, including a walled garden and a hilltop viewpoint across the Fife countryside, were also designed by Lorimer. Maintained by the National Trust for Scotland since 1949. Tel: 01334 653127.

Inchcolm Abbey
Located on the island of Inchcolm (G. = Isle of St Columba) in the Firth of Forth. Also known as St Colm's Abbey and 'The Iona of the East'. Originally an Augustinian priory, established in 1123 by Alexander I and raised to abbey status by David I in 1235, the abbey and its lands were secularised in 1609 having been largely abandoned after the Reformation. A medieval inscription carved above the abbey's entrance reads: '*Stet domus haec donec fluctus formica marinos ebibat, et totum testudo permabulet orbem*' ('May this house stand until an ant drains the flowing sea, and a tortoise walks around the whole world'). The ruins are maintained by Historic Scotland.

Inchkeith Castle
Located on the island of Inchkeith. The ruins of a castle built for Mary, Queen of Scots in 1564. It served as a prison until replaced by a lighthouse in 1808.

Interesting facts
Dunfermline-born writer **Iain Menzies Banks** writes science fiction under the name Iain M Banks but drops the 'M' when writing literary fiction.

Islands
See separate table

Isle of May
Also known locally as May Isle. An island at the entrance to the Firth of Forth. St Adrian was murdered by Norsemen here c.870. It is a National Nature Reserve and a Special Protection Area, important for its colonies of breeding seabirds, such as puffins, guillemots and razorbills, and also home to the fourth largest breeding group of grey seals in the UK. A remote controlled camera on the island beams live pictures to the Scottish Seabird Centre in North Berwick. The 80ft (24m) high square lighthouse on the island was built in 1816 by engineer Robert Stevenson (the original lighthouse, built in 1635, was the first in Scotland). The lighthouse buildings also included accommodation for the keepers' families and visitors. It became fully automatic in 1989. Managed by Scottish Natural Heritage. Area: 0.17 sq miles (0.45 sq km). (GR: NT655995.)

Jim Baxter Statue
Hill O' Beath, 1 mile (1.6km) southwest of Cowdenbeath. A one-and-a-half times life size bronze statue of footballer Jim Baxter, erected in his home town. Born on 29 September 1939 and known as 'Slim Jim', Baxter was a midfielder who played for Raith Rovers, Rangers, Sunderland and Nottingham Forest. He won the Scottish League Championship in 1961, 1963 and 1964, the Scottish FA Cup in 1962, 1963 and 1964 and the Scottish League Cup in 1960, 1961, 1963 and 1964, all with Rangers, and gained 34 international caps for Scotland. A broken leg in 1964 diminished his skills but he is perhaps best remembered for the performances which bamboozled England at Wembley in 1963 and 1967. A true wayward genius, his heavy drinking led to two liver transplants in 1994; he is quoted as saying that he burnt his 'candle at both ends and in the middle'. He died from cancer in Glasgow on 14 April 2001.

Jimmy Shand Statue
Upper Greens, Newburgh Road, Auchtermuchty. A statue to Scottish band leader and master of the button key accordion Sir Jimmy Shand, erected in his adopted town. Shand was born in East Wemyss and knighted in 1998. The statue bears a plaque with the inscription, 'Sir Jimmy Shand, MBE MA. Born 28th January 1908, died 23rd December 2000. Happy to meet, sorry to part, happy to meet again.'

John McDouall Stuart Museum
Rectory Lane, Dysart, Kirkcaldy. A museum dedicated to the life of Dysart-born explorer John McDouall Stuart (1815–66) and located in the house in which he was born. In 1862 Stuart became the first European explorer to successfully walk the length of Australia from south to north; the museum describes his journeys, the Australian wilderness and the life of the Aborigines. Orphaned in his teens, Stuart emigrated to Australia in 1838. After working as a surveyor he made his first major expedition in 1858 and made five further journeys between then and 1862. On 22 April 1860, on his fourth expedition, he reached a high point which he considered to be the centre of the continent, naming it Mount Sturt in honour of Captain Charles Sturt, under whom he had begun his career as an explorer. Later known as Mount Stuart, it is no longer regarded as the true centre of Australia. In October 1861 his sixth and final expedition left Adelaide, arriving at Chambers Bay near modern Darwin on 24 July 1862. The house is maintained by the National Trust for Scotland. Tel: 01592 412860.

Kellie Castle and Garden
3 miles (5km) northwest of Anstruther. An early 16th century tower house with later additions to give it an E-plan, although the earliest part of the property may date to 1360. Owned by the Oliphaunt family before passing to the Earls of Mar and Kellie in 1621, it was abandoned and fell into disrepair in the early 19th century but was restored in 1878 by Professor James Lorimer. The

rooms have plaster ceilings and painted panelling. There are also period rooms including a Victorian nursery and kitchen, a collection of furniture designed by architect Sir Robert Lorimer (1864–1929), and works of art by other members of the Lorimer family. Sir Robert was noted for his restoration of and alterations to old Scottish houses and castles and his promotion of the Arts and Crafts style in Scotland (see Hill of Tarvit for example); Hew Lorimer (1907–93) was a sculptor and John Henry Lorimer (1856–1936) a painter. The gardens are ornamented in Arts and Crafts style and include a walled garden and a kitchen garden. The property has been maintained by the National Trust for Scotland since 1970. Tel: 01333 720271.

Kirkcaldy A royal burgh and the largest town in Fife. A port on the north bank of the Firth of Forth, it became prosperous in the 19th century through the linen industry, the manufacture of linoleum and iron-making. The town's Links Market, held since 1304, is Europe's longest street market. The town centre was designated a conservation area in 1980.

Kirkcaldy Museum and Art Gallery War Memorial Gardens, Kirkcaldy. Opened in 1925, the museum houses a collection of 18th to 20th century Scottish paintings including works by William McTaggart, S J Peploe and the 'Glasgow Boys'. There is also an exhibition charting the natural, social and economic history of the area. Tel: 01592 412860.

Laing Museum High Street, Newburgh, 9 miles (15km) west of Cupar. A museum charting the social and economic history of Newburgh. It is named after local banker and antiquarian Alexander Laing (1808–92), around whose collections and library the museum was based. Tel: 01337 840223.

Lindores Abbey Newburgh, 9 miles (15km) west of Cupar. A Benedictine foundation established in 1178. Sacked in 1543 and again by supporters of John Knox in 1559, little of the fabric remains above ground although the ground plan is still visible.

Lochore Meadows Country Park 1 mile (1.6km) south of Ballingry, 7 miles (11km) northeast of Dunfermline. A 1200 acre (485ha) country park surrounding the 260 acre (105ha) Loch Ore. The ruins of Lochore Castle stand on the edge of the loch although it was originally surrounded by water. There are three tiny islands in Loch Ore: Moss Island, Tod Island and Whaup Island. Tel: 01592 414300.

Lomond Hills Regional Park Founded as the Fife Regional Park in 1981 and renamed Lomond Hills Regional Park in 2003. It covers 25 sq miles (65 sq km) in West Central Fife. The two highest peaks in the Lomond Hills are West Lomond at 1713ft (522m), also the highest point in Fife, and East Lomond at 1391ft (424m).

Malcolm Canmore's Tower Pittencrieff Park, Dunfermline. The ruins of a tower house probably built in the 11th century by Malcom III Canmore. The tower is represented in the burgh arms of Dunfermline. It was destroyed during an English invasion in the early 14th century.

Martyrs Monument The Scores, St Andrews. A monument commemorating Protestant reformers Paul Craw (executed 1433), Patrick Hamilton (1528), Henry Forest (1533) George Wishart (1546) and Walter Myln (1558), who were martyred during the Reformation.

Methil Heritage Centre High Street, Lower Methil. A local history museum located in the village's Old Post Office Building and focusing on Methil's history as a port and centre of Fife's coal-mining industry. Tel: 01333 422100.

Newark Castle Newark, 1/2 mile (0.8km) west of St Monans. A clifftop castle probably founded by Sir Alan Durward in the 13th century and referred to as Newark of St Monans in 1545, when lands belonging to the prior of Pittenweem were transferred to Sir James Sandilands of Cruivie. In 1649 the castle was sold to David Leslie, who added another storey and Baroque style gables, although only a fragment of these decorations is still visible. There were outbuildings from the same period, and some earlier, in the courtyard. The crumbling remains include vaults and walls built on the cliff face.

Pittencrieff House Museum Pittencrieff Park, Dunfermline. A local history museum located in a 17th century house with displays exploring the history of Dunfermline. Tel: 01383 313838.

Pittencrieff Park Pittencrieff Street, Dunfermline. The former grounds of Pittencrieff House, bought by Andrew Carnegie in 1902 and given in trust to the people of Dunfermline. It is said that as a child Carnegie had been forbidden to play in the grounds by the Lairds of Pittencrieff. The park covers 76 acres (31ha) near the centre of the town near the abbey ruins. One of its entrances is through the Louise Carnegie Gates, erected in 1929 and named after Andrew Carnegie's wife. Features include a statue of Carnegie, the Pittencrieff House Museum, the remains of Malcolm Canmore's Tower (see separate entries) and landscaped gardens. The park is known locally as 'The Glen'; the Glen Pavilion seats 600 and is used for concerts, exhibitions and private functions. The Glass Hall conservatory, built in 1973 on the site of the old conservatories for Pittencrieff House, houses collections of exotic plants and flowers. Tel: 01383 739272.

RAF Leuchars Leuchars, 4 miles (6km) northwest of St Andrews. Established during World War I, the base became a Naval Fleet Training School in the immediate post-war period. Renamed RAF Leuchars in March 1920, it was an operational station during World War II. On 4 September 1939 a Hudson of 224 Squadron based at Leuchars became the first British aircraft to engage the enemy in World War II when it attacked a Dornier 18 over the North Sea. For most of the war, planes from Leuchars patrolled the important sea lanes around the Scottish coast. In 1950 the base passed from Coastal Command to Fighter Command. RAF Leuchars continues to be an important base in policing UK airspace and is also the base for the Leuchars Mountain Rescue Team. The annual RAF Leuchars Airshow takes place in September and includes a day-long flying programme and ground-based exhibits and displays.

Ravenscraig Castle Ravenscraig Park, Kirkcaldy. A coastal artillery fortress founded in 1460 by James II and located on a headland above the sea on the eastern edge of Kirkcaldy. The castle looks west over industrial development and the remains of its tower are echoed by nearby residential tower blocks built in the 1960s. Now maintained by Historic Scotland.

Rivers — The **Eden** is formed by the confluence of the Carmore and Beattie burns in the Lomond Hills. It flows into the North Sea 2 miles (3km) north of St Andrews and its estuary forms the Eden Estuary Local Nature Reserve, an important overwintering site for wildfowl and waders. Its total length is 30 miles (48km).

The **Leven** flows for 16 miles (26km) from Loch Leven into the Firth of Forth at Leven. It was formerly a source of water power for paper and textile mills.

St Andrews — A royal burgh on the east coast of Fife by the Eden Mouth. Possibly a originating as a Pictish stronghold called Cennrigmonaid or Kilrymont, it was renamed after St Andrew, whose relics were believed to have been brought here by St Rule or Regulus. It was an early centre of Christian worship, the church of St Mary of the Crag built by the Culdees being superseded in turn by St Rule's Church and then St Andrews Cathedral. St Andrews Castle was the residence of the (Arch)Bishop of St Andrews, but both the cathedral and castle fell into disrepair following the Reformation. In more recent times St Andrews has become known as the 'Home of Golf', being the home of six links courses and the Royal and Ancient Golf Club (R & A). It is also home to the University of St Andrews. Sir Hugh Lyon Playfair (1786–1861) helped arrest a decline in the fortunes of the town during his term as Provost and the paved streets and improved sanitation resulted in St Andrews becoming popular as a holiday resort.

St Andrews Botanic Gardens — Canongate, St Andrews. An 18 acre (7ha) botanic garden established in 1960 to replace the original Botanic Garden, founded by the University of St Andrews in 1889 in the precincts of St Mary's College. Planted with more than 8000 species of ferns, herbaceous plants, shrubs and trees, it features a water garden with waterfalls, a rock garden, a heath garden and a peat garden. Two borders are planted to highlight the diverse flora of China and Chile, while the glasshouses are segregated into three temperature zones enabling a wide variety of plants to be grown. Tel: 01334 476452.

St Andrews Castle — The Scores, St Andrews. Enclosing five square towers, the castle was originally built c.1400 by Bishop Walter Trail on the clifftop site of an earlier 12th century fortification which had changed hands on numerous occasions before being slighted by Andrew Moray in 1337 to avoid its use by English invaders. The main residence of the bishops and archbishops of St Andrews, it was the focal point of the Church in medieval Scotland. It was also used as a prison; an 'oubliette' called the Bottle Dungeon, a 22ft (6.5m) bottle-shaped pit below the Sea Tower into which prisoners could be lowered and forgotten, can still be seen. The arrival of gunpowder necessitated the building of two circular gun towers in the 1520s on the landward side of the castle. The castle was captured in 1546 by local Protestant supporters of George Wishart, a preacher executed by Cardinal Archbishop David Beaton. Wishart's friends took the castle by stealth, murdering Beaton and withstanding a siege by forces under the Earl of Arran until bombardment by a French fleet reduced the castle to ruins in July 1547. John Knox, who had entered the castle during the siege, was captured and sent to the French galleys for 18 months. During the siege a countermine was dug by the defenders against a tunnel being constructed towards the castle by the besiegers. The castle was rebuilt by Archbishop John Hamilton and passed into the hands of the Earl of Dunbar in 1606. After a brief return to the ownership of the church it fell into decline after the fall of James II of England. The remains of the castle include the tunnel and countermine as well as the Bottle Dungeon.

St Andrews Cathedral — Abbey Street, St Andrews. The ruins of what was once Scotland's largest cathedral, completed in the mid 12th century near the sites of the earlier churches St Mary on the Crag and St Rule's Church, and consecrated in 1318 in the presence of Robert the Bruce. St Rule's Tower, virtually all that remains of the earlier church, stands 108ft (33m) high. As befitted a major pilgrimage centre, the cathedral once stood 391ft (119m) long and 168ft (51m) wide, but the west end collapsed during a storm in 1270 and the cathedral was damaged by fire in 1378, after which the end of the south transept fell in a storm of 1409. On all these occasions it was repaired and rebuilt; however, on 11 June 1559 a mob incited by a sermon delivered in St Andrews parish church by John Knox ransacked the cathedral and carried off all the statuary and fittings. The friars were expelled and the cathedral never recovered from the desecration, slowly falling into disrepair. As with many religious houses destroyed during the Reformation the structure became a source of local building material. A collection of stonework from all phases of the cathedral's history, including an 8th century piece known as St Andrews Sarcophagus, is now housed in the visitor centre. The graveyard is the resting place of many prominent local people including golfer Tom Morris. The ruins and grounds are maintained by Historic Scotland.

St Andrews Museum — Kinburn Park, Doubledykes Road, St Andrews. A local history museum opened in 1991 and housed in Kinburn Castle, built in 1855. Tel: 01334 412690.

St Andrews Preservation Trust Museum and Gardens — North Street, St Andrews. A local history museum in a 17th century house once occupied by fishermen. The St Andrews Preservation Trust was founded in 1937 with the aim of preserving the buildings, character and history of St. Andrews for future generations. The museum features recreations of old St Andrews shops, including a grocer's and a chemist's. There are also collections of fine art, furniture and photographs. Behind the house is a secluded period garden. Tel: 01334 477629.

St Margaret's Cave — Chalmers Street, Dunfermline. A cave on the Tower Burn used, according to tradition, by St Margaret, queen of Scotland, for her private devotions from 1057 until her death in 1093. Margaret was born in Hungary c.1045, the daughter of Edward Atheling, exiled son of Edmund Ironside and grandson of Ethelred the Unready. The family were brought back to England in 1057 by Edward the Confessor, possibly as a means of securing the succession, but Edward Atheling died shortly afterwards. Her brother Edgar was briefly proposed as king of England following the death of Harold II at the Battle of Hastings in 1066 but he was forced to submit to William I. He once again went into exile but on the voyage the ship carrying him and his family was forced to land in Scotland. Here Margaret met and married the widowed Malcolm III Canmore in 1070. A prime mover in establishing the ascendancy of the Roman Church over the Celtic Church in Scotland (she also established the ferry service across the Forth Estuary – hence Queensferry), she died in 1093 and was buried in Dunfermline Abbey Church. Canonised in 1251, she is now a patron saint of Scotland with a feast day on 16 November. In the 1960s the council decided to fill in the glen where the cave was and build a car park. As the result of a public campaign it was agreed to build a tunnel beneath the car park to allow access to the cave; there are 86 steps down to the cave, which was reopened in 1993.

St Monans Windmill — $^1/_2$ mile (0.8km) east of St Monans, 8 miles (13km) south of St Andrews. Situated on the coast near the fishing village of St Monans, the windmill was used for nearly 200 years to pump water into the nearby salt pans. It fell into disuse in 1823 when salt-panning became uneconomic because of imported rocksalt from England. The windmill includes a display about the industry and is also a lookout point.

Scotland's Secret Bunker — Troywood, 3 miles (5km) north of Anstruther. An underground nuclear command bunker constructed in the 1970s to house 300 people. Constructed at the end of World War II as a radar station and upgraded during the 1950s to become part of the Cold War ROTOR early warning system, it was opened to the public in 1995. There are 24,000 sq ft (2230 sq m) of accommodation on two levels, 100ft (91.5m) underground. The complex is entered through an apparently normal farmhouse which has been reinforced with concrete and steel girders to act as a guardhouse. The first level includes dormitories, a BBC broadcasting studio and the canteen; on the second floor are RAF, central government and nuclear operations rooms. Tel: 01333 310301.

Scotstarvit Tower — $^1/_2$ mile (0.8km) northwest of Craigrothie, 2 miles (3km) south of Cupar. A well-preserved five storey (plus garret) L-plan tower house probably built in the 15th century with later additions and changes. In the early 17th century it was owned by Sir John Scot (1585–1670), author of *The Staggering State of Scots Statesmen*.

Scottish Fisheries Museum — Harbourhead, Anstruther. A museum opened in 1969, dedicated to the history of fishing in Scotland and exploring themes such as primitive fishing, the days of sail and steam, whaling, the herring boom and the future of the industry. It is housed in two buildings – a merchant house built in 1724 and the 16th century abbot's lodging. There are more than 15 full-size vessels on display including *The Reaper* and *Zulu*, the former a fully restored 70ft (21m) long herring drifter built in 1901, as well as a restored wheel-house, a boatbuilder's drawing office, fisherman's house and fishmonger's shop. Tel: 01333 310628.

Scottish Vintage Bus Museum — Lathalmond, $^3/_4$ mile (1.2km) north of Bowershall, 4 miles (6km) north of Dunfermline. A museum run by volunteers with more than 150 buses and other vehicles displayed on a 45 acre (18ha) site. Originally established in 1986 in Whitburn, it moved to its present location in 1995. Tel: 01383 623380.

sport

football — **Cowdenbeath** were formed in 1882 with the merger of Cowdenbeath Rangers and Cowdenbeath Thistle. They are winners of the Scottish League 2nd Division in 1914, 1915 and 1939, and of the 3rd Division in 2006. Nicknamed The Blue Brazil, Cowden or The Miners, their colours are blue and white; their home ground is Central Park. Tel: 01383 610166.

Dunfermline Athletic were founded in 1885 and are winners of the Scottish League 1st Division in 1989 and 1996, the 2nd Division in 1926 and 1986 and the Scottish Cup in 1961 and 1968. Nicknameed The Pars, their colours are black and white stripes; their home ground is East End Park, Halbeath Road. Tel: 01383 724295.

East Fife were founded in 1903, and are winners of the Scottish 3rd Division in 2008 and the Scottish Cup in 1938. Nicknamed The Fifers, their traditional colours are black and gold stripes; their home ground is First 2 Finance Bayview Stadium, Methil. Tel: 01333 426323.

Raith Rovers were founded in 1883 and named after the site of the Battle of Raith, which took place to the west of Kirkcaldy in AD 596. They are winners of the Scottish League 1st Division in 1993 and 1995, the 2nd Division in 1908, 1910, 1938, 1949 and 2003 and the Scottish League Cup in 1995. In the 1937–38 season they scored a British league record of 142 goals in just 34 matches. Nicknamed The Rovers, their colours are navy blue and white; their home ground is Stark's Park, Pratt Street, Kirkcaldy. Tel: 01592 263514.

golf — The **Royal & Ancient Golf Club of St Andrews** was founded on 14 May 1754 by 22 gentlemen as the Society of St Andrews Golfers. Initially its members played for a Silver Club each year on the St Andrews Links and from 1806 for a Gold Medal (superseded in 1837 by the Royal Medal) at the autumn meeting. A Silver Cross became the prize at a spring meeting from 1836. When William IV became the club's patron in 1834, its name was changed to The Royal & Ancient Golf Club of St Andrews (R & A). A clubhouse was built behind the first tee of the St Andrews Links Old Course in 1853. The club organised a Grand National Tournament 1857–9 and in 1872 became jointly responsible for running the Open Championship, the first of which had been organised by Prestwick Golf Club in 1860. The club set up its Rules of Golf Committee in 1897 to establish a uniform code for golf played in Britain. The club was responsible both for maintaining the Old Course and for building the New Course in 1895; the courses are now run by the St Andrews Links Trust. The R & A organises 11 championships and international matches: the Open Championship (since 1920), Amateur Championship (since 1919), Boys' Amateur Championship, Boys' Home Internationals, Seniors' Open Amateur Championship, British Mid-Amateur Championship, Senior British Open Championship, Walker Cup, Junior Open Championships, St Andrews Trophy and the Jacques Leglise Trophy. The role of the club as governing authority for golf everywhere except the United States and Mexico was handed over to a group of companies called The R & A in 2004 and the Royal & Ancient Golf Club reverted to its original purpose as a private golf club with a membership of 2400. The Rules of Golf have been issued jointly by the R & A and the United States Golf Association (USGA) since 1952. The R & A also helps in formulating technical specifications for golfing equipment. Tel: 01334 460046.

There are six public courses on **St Andrews Links**. The Old Course, on which so many Open Championships have been played, is known as 'The Home of Golf'. In 1764 it consisted of 22 holes, 11 out and 11 back; golfers played to the same hole both ways, except for the 11th and 22nd. It was decided that the first four holes were too short and should be made into two instead of four, thus reducing the number of holes in a round from 22 to 18; this became the standard for a round of golf. After a period in which the links were almost lost to rabbit farmers they were bought by James Cheape to be kept for golfing. Double greens were established in 1856–7 to overcome the problem of golfers on their outward half meeting golfers coming back playing the same hole. On the double greens a white flag marks the outward hole and a red flag marks the inward hole. The course evolved rather than being designed but Daw Anderson (1850s), Old Tom Morris (1860s–1900) and Dr Alister Mackenzie (1930s) all contributed to its look and feel. Probably its most famous hole is the 17th, known as the Road Hole and featuring a hard surfaced road and the Road Bunker. The Open Championship was first held on the Old Course in 1873, the winner being local man Tom Kidd. There have been 26 further Open Championships held at St Andrews (winners, GB unless stated): 1876 (Bob Martin), 1879 (Jamie Anderson), 1882 (Bob Ferguson), 1885 (Bob Martin), 1888 (Jack Burns), 1891 (Hugh Kirkaldy), 1895 (John Taylor), 1900 (John Taylor), 1905 (James Braid), 1910 (James Braid), 1921 (Jock Hutchison, USA), 1927 (Bobby Jones, USA), 1933 (Densmore Shute, USA), 1939 (Dick Burton), 1946 (Sam Snead, USA), 1955 (Peter Thomson, Australia), 1957 (Bobby Locke, South Africa), 1960 (Kel Nagle, Australia), 1964 (Tony Lema, USA), 1970 (Jack Nicklaus, USA), 1978 (Jack Nicklaus, USA), 1984 (Seve Ballesteros, Spain), 1990 (Nick Faldo), 1995 (John Daly, USA), 2000 (Tiger Woods, USA), 2005 (Tiger Woods, USA). The New Course, opened in April 1895 in response to the increasing demand for golf, was designed by B Blyth and laid out by Old Tom Morris. The Jubilee Course was opened in 1897 to celebrate Queen Victoria's Diamond Jubilee. Initially a 12 hole course, it was extended to 18 holes in 1905. It was redesigned to championship standard by Donald Steel and opened by Curtis Strange in 1989. The Eden Course was designed by Harry Colt and opened in 1914, and was remodelled by Donald Steel in 1989. The Strathtyrum Course takes its name from the estate from which the land for it was purchased. It was designed by Donald Steel and opened on 1 July 1993. The 9 hole Balgove Course, designed with children and beginners in mind, was opened in 1972 and remodelled by Donald Steel in 1993. The Links were acquired by St Andrews Town Council in 1894 following the passing of the first Links Act by Parliament, which safeguarded public access. When local government reform ended the town council, St Andrews Links Trust was created by another Act of Parliament to continue running the Links as public golf courses. There are two clubhouses, the Links Clubhouse by the Old, New and Jubilee Courses and the Eden Clubhouse for golfers on the Eden, Strathtyrum and Balgove Courses. Tel: 01334 466666.

motor racing — **Knockhill Circuit**, 5 miles (8km) northwest of Dunfermline. Scotland's national motorsport centre, hosting superbike, stock car, touring car and hot rod events. The 1.3 mile (2.1km) motor racing circuit was built by farmer Tom Kinnaird on his own land and opened in 1974. After a plan to expand the circuit failed to come to fruition it was eventually bought by Derek Butcher in 1983. Tel: 01383 723337.

Tay Road Bridge — Spanning the Firth of Tay from Newport-on-Tay in Fife to Dundee, the 1.4 mile (2.25km) long bridge with 42 concrete spans was designed by William A Fairhurst and built 1962–6. Tolls were charged until 2008.

Tentsmuir Forest — 6 miles (10km) north of St Andrews. A mature commercial Forestry Commission forest, largely of Scots and Corsican pine originally planted in the 1920s on moorland and covering 3700 acres (1500ha) on the coast of Fife. Home to natterer's, pipistrelle and brown long-eared bat, it is one of the forests used by the British Siberian Husky Racing Association for its races. It is next to Tentsmuir Point National Nature Reserve.

Tentsmuir National Nature Reserve — 7 miles (11km) north of St Andrews. A National Nature Reserve on the northeast coast of Fife made up of dunes and heathland, and extending west into Tentsmuir Forest. Its three sites – Tentsmuir Point, Tayport Heath and Morton Lochs – cover 1330 acres (539ha) and also encompass the Tayport-Tentsmuir and Morton Lochs Sites of Special Scientific Interest. The reserve supports significant populations of eider, bar-tailed godwit, goosander, long-tailed duck and pink-footed goose. At low tide a finger of sand known as Abertay Sands, stretching east from Tentsmuir Point, is populated by common and grey seals. The dunes were also marked by a line of large concrete blocks erected during World War II as defence against possible enemy tank landings. As part of the site's environmental management, a small herd of Highland cattle are allowed to graze the area between the forest and the dunes to ensure that the encroachment of the woodland is kept at bay.

Townhill Country Park — Townhill, 1 mile (1.6km) north of Dunfermline. Comprising Town Loch and Townhill Wood, the park is located on the site of a former industrial centre; there are the remains of a brickworks, while the water of the loch once powered flax and flour mills. It is the location of the Scottish National Water Ski Centre, a purpose-built national training centre opened in 1992. Tel: 01383 725596.

University of St Andrews — Founded in 1413, St Andrews is the oldest university in Scotland. Its three original colleges were St Salvator's (founded in 1450), St Leonard's (1511) and St Mary's (1538); St Salvator's and St

Leonard's were merged to form United College in 1747. University College Dundee, specialising in medical and applied science, was united with St Andrews 1897–1954, before becoming the University of Dundee in 1967. Today St Andrews has around 8500 students and is a member of the 1994 Group of smaller research-led universities. The university holds collections of fine art, silver, academic dress and furniture, as well as collections specific to the physical sciences and chemistry including historic scientific instruments. The Bell Pettigrew Museum of natural history is housed in the School of Biology. Former students include poet William Dunbar, theologian John Knox, and more recently novelist Fay Weldon, TV presenter Hazel Irvine, Alex Salmond, leader of the Scottish National Party, and cyclist Chris Hoy. Tel: 01334 476161.

Wemyss Caves — East Wemyss, 5 miles (8km) northeast of Kirkcaldy. A series of caves in the sandstone cliffs at Wemyss, some of which are marked with carvings and symbols mainly from the Pictish period (c.AD 400–900) and similar to those found on cross-slabs. The caves include Court Cave, Glass Cave, Doo (Dovecot) Cave, Sliding Cave, Jonathan's Cave, Well Cave, Michael Cave and Gasworks Cave.

Woods on your Doorstep — **Dura Den Wood** (5 acres/2ha), between Kemback and Pitscottie in a deep valley cut by the Ceres Burn. Mainly broadleaved woodland of oak, ash and elm with some Scots pine and European larch. Animal species include roe deer, otter and pipistrelle 55kHz bat ('soprano' pipistrelle); **Formonthills** (292 acres/118ha), north of Glenrothes. Mixed broadleaved woodland with a few stands of conifers; **Inzievar Wood** (30 acres/12ha), south of the village of Oakley. Mature broadleaved woodland of oak, beech, birch and sycamore, the northern part consisting of a more recent conifer plantation; **Keils Den** (44 acres/18ha), near Lower Largo. Mainly ash woodland surrounding the Keil Burn, with small numbers of birch, rowan, oak and willow; **Largo Serpentine** (2½ acres/1ha), between Upper and Lower Largo. Small mixed broadleaved woodland beside the Largo Burn. Planting is a relatively recent mixture of native shrubs such as hawthorn, hazel and elder and trees such as ash and sycamore. The Serpentine Walk, running north–south through the site, may be associated with the designed landscape of the 18th century Largo House estate. The inspiration for Robinson Crusoe, Alexander Selkirk, was born in Lower Largo and part of the wood, known as the Selkirk Ground, at one time belonged to his family.

Some famous people born in Fife

Adam, Robert (architect) (1728–92)	Kirkcaldy
Banks, Iain Menzies (writer) (1954–)	Dunfermline
Baxter, Jim (footballer) (1939–2001)	Hill o'Beath
Carnegie, Andrew (philanthropist) (1835–1919)	Dunfermline
Charles I (king of England) (1600–49)	Dunfermline Palace
Clark, Jim (racing driver) (1936–68)	Kilmany
David II (monarch) (1324–71)	Dunfermline Palace
Dewar, James (scientist) (1842–1923)	Kincardine-on-Forth
James I of Scotland (monarch) (1394–1437)	Dunfermline Palace
Lawson, Robert (architect) (1833–1902)	Newburgh
MacMillan, Kenneth (choreographer) (1929–92)	Dunfermline
Morris, Tom Jr (1851–75), Sr (1821–1908) (golfers)	St Andrews
Rankin, Ian (author) (1960–)	Cardenden
Selkirk, Alexander (castaway) (1676–1721)	Lower Largo
Shand, Jimmy (musician) (1908–2000)	East Wemyss
Shearer, Moira (actress) (1926–2006)	Dunfermline
Smith, Adam (economist) (1723–90)	Kirkcaldy
Steel, David (politician) (1938–)	Kirkcaldy
Vettriano, Jack (artist) (1951–)	Methil
Wilson, Jocky (darts player) (1951–)	Kirkcaldy

Islands of Fife

Name	Location	Information
Birnie Craig	Firth of Forth	GR: NO548022
Black Rocks	Firth of Forth	GR: NT248855
Cambo Brigs	St Andrews Bay	GR: NO605125
Car Craig	Firth of Forth	GR: NT199831
Carr Brigs	Firth of Forth	GR: NO645115
Common Rocks	Firth of Forth	GR: NT211852
Craigdimas	Firth of Forth	GR: NT192840
East Vows	Firth of Forth	GR: NT284889
East Vows	Firth of Forth	GR: NT482990
Haystack	Firth of Forth	GR: NT178825
Hummel Rocks	Firth of Forth	GR: NT274868
Inchcape	North Sea	Aka Bell Rock. GR: NO770267

Name	Location	Information
Inchcolm	Firth of Forth	Formerly known as Aemonia or Emona. GR: NT188825
Inchkeith	Firth of Forth	Heavily fortified virtually continuously since the battle of Pinkie Cleugh in 1547. GR: NT295825
Iron Craig	Firth of Forth	GR: NT292822
Isle of May	Firth of Forth	See separate entry
Long Craig	Firth of Forth	GR: NT172828
Long Craig	Firth of Forth	GR: NT283898)
Long Craig	Firth of Forth	GR: NT298820
Maiden Hair Rock	Firth of Forth	Named in honour of St Tenew who gave birth to Kentigern, later known as St Mungo, patron saint of Glasgow. GR: NT660987
Meadulse	Firth of Forth	GR: NT190831
Moss Island	Loch Ore	GR: NT165961
Mugdrum Island	River Tay	(G. = Hogback Island) Sometimes claimed by Perth & Kinross. GR: NO225190
Oxcars	Firth of Forth	GR: NT205818
Preston Island	River Forth	GR: NT008853
Seal Carr	Firth of Forth	GR: NT289828
Swallow Craig	Firth of Forth	GR: NT192827
Tod Island	Loch Ore	GR: NT165961
Tullybothy Craigs	Firth of Forth	GR: NO639107
West Ness	Firth of Forth	GR: NO612069
West Vows	Firth of Forth	GR: NT285884
West Vows	Firth of Forth	GR: NT475990
Whaup Island	Loch Ore	GR: NT165961

GRAMPIAN

Lossiemouth
Burghead
Portknockie
Moray Firth
Fraserburgh
Elgin
Buckie
Portsoy
Banff
Macduff
Forres
R. Lossie
Turriff
New Deer
Peterhead
R. Spey
Dufftown
Huntly
1
Ellon
Oldmeldrum
Newburgh
2
HIGHLAND
Inverurie
North Sea
R. Don
3
Aberdeen
Ben MacDui
1309
R. Dee
Aboyne
Ballater
Banchory
Braemar
Stonehaven
Fettercairn
TAYSIDE
Districts
1 Moray
2 Aberdeenshire
3 Aberdeen
0
20 miles
0
30 km

The region of Grampian consists of three unitary authorities – Aberdeen City, Aberdeenshire and Moray. It is bounded on the north and east by the Moray Firth and the North Sea respectively, on the south by Tayside and on the west by Highland, and in particular the Grampian mountains. The major rivers are the Rivers Dee, Don and Spey. The area has several distinct districts including Royal Deeside, the Whisky Country of Speyside, and the coastal fringe.

Aberdeen City includes the conurbation of Aberdeen, also known as the 'Granite City'. Scotland's third largest city, it lies mainly between the Rivers Don and Dee. Aberdeen (*Obar Dheathain* in Scots Gaelic) grew from two settlements. The first, on the Don, probably dates from the 7th or 8th century; sometimes known as Aberdon, it later became 'Old Aberdeen' (or Old Town). This settlement was burnt by Danes in the 10th century. 'New Aberdeen' was founded by David I on the northern bank of the Dee in the 12th century. Developing from the amalgamation of the two settlements, the town quickly expanded through its position as a port but, along with many other Scottish settlements, intermittently suffered severe damage from both English and Scottish armies from the early 14th century until the mid 17th century. Aberdeen also suffered twice from plague, once in 1350 (during the 'Black Death') and again in 1647 when up to a quarter of the population are reported to have died. Shipbuilding and the fishing industry led Aberdeen's expansion and economic growth. Other industries which thrived for a shorter time were whaling, textiles, brewing and distilling.

In the early 19th century the passing of the 'Aberdeen New Streets Act' saw the sweeping away of organic development and the laying out of George Street, King Street and Union Street (named for the Act of Union with England). Around these new streets grew up the 'Granite City' of buildings designed by local architects Archibald Simpson (1790–1847) and John Smith (1781–1852). Inland communications with the rest of Scotland were improved by first a canal and then, in the mid 19th century, by the arrival of the railways. Oddly it was only in 1891 that the two burghs of Aberdeen – Old and New – were legally united and the city was incorporated. The recent economic history of Aberdeen has been dominated by the growth of the North Sea oil industry, which has led to it being known as the 'oil capital of Europe'. The scenic town of Dyce, northwest of Aberdeen and best known as the location of the city's airport, also falls within the boundaries of the unitary authority of Aberdeen City.

Aberdeenshire does not include Aberdeen City; however, Aberdeenshire Council has its headquarters in Aberdeen, and is the only Scottish council whose headquarters are based outside the council area. Aberdeenshire borders Angus and Perth & Kinross to the south, and Highland and Moray to the west. The council was established in April 1996, following the abolition of the Scottish Regions. The major employment in the region is in the service industries and there has been some immigration into the area as a result of the oil industry. Ballater, a royal burgh on the River Dee, developed as a spa town in the 18th and 19th centuries, its spring waters having been said to cure 'the King's evil' or scrofula. It was once known as the 'Lourdes of Deeside'. It was also the birthplace of Renaissance man Patrick Geddes (1854–1932), a biologist, botanist and pioneer of town planning. Banff, a coastal town and royal burgh since the 12th century, was once a commercial port but now a leisure facility. Braemar, a village in Upper Deeside, is famous for the Braemar Gathering, held on the first Saturday of September each year. It also has the highest golf course in the UK. Fraserburgh, a major whitefish and shellfish commercial port founded in the 16th century, is the site of Scotland's first lighthouse. Inverurie is a market town on the Rivers Ury and Don. Pennan is where much of the film *Local Hero* was shot (although not the beach scenes). Peterhead, Europe's busiest fishing port, is Aberdeenshire's largest town. Stonehaven, formerly the county town of Kincardineshire, is a coastal resort with an open air Olympic size swimming pool.

Moray lies in the northeast of the county, with coastline on the Moray Firth, and borders the council areas of Aberdeenshire and Highland. Towns in Moray include Buckie, a coastal burgh which was once a thriving port, still has some food processing facilities. Elgin is a royal burgh, the administrative centre and major town of Moray. It developed on the River Lossie and had a cathedral from the 13th century until the Reformation. Like the rest of the region it depends on oil, fishing and tourism for its prosperity. Garmouth is a coastal village where Charles II landed in 1650 and signed the Solemn League and Covenant.

Grampian	**Population**			**Area**	
Districts	*male*	*female*	*total*	*sq miles*	*sq km*
Aberdeen City	103,818	108,307	212,125	72	186
Aberdeenshire	112,470	114,401	226,871	2437	6313
Moray	43,447	43,493	86,940	864	2238
Total	259,735	266,201	525,936	3373	8737

Local Attractions and Information

Aberdeen Art Gallery: Schoolhill, Aberdeen. Opened in 1885 in a neoclassical building designed by Alexander Marshall McKenzie. Collections include contemporary crafts, modern fine art, ceramics, glass, silver, furniture and costume. There are paintings by Sir John Lavery and Sir James Guthrie, both 'Glasgow Boys'; other artists represented include Francis Bacon, William Dyce, Damien Hirst, David Hockney, Theodore Rousseau, Claude Monet, Pierre-Auguste Renoir and Dante Gabriel Rossetti. Tel: 01224 523700.

Aberdeen Harbour: The principal commercial port in northern Scotland and an international port for cargo and container traffic. The north pier, built partly by John Smeaton 1775–81 and partly by Thomas Telford 1810–15, extends nearly 3000ft (900m) into the North Sea. A 29 acre (11.5ha) wet dock with 6000ft (1800m) of quay was completed in 1848 and called Victoria Dock in honour of the queen's visit to the city in that year. Adjoining it is the Upper Dock. A 1050ft (320m) long concrete breakwater was constructed on the south side of the stream as a protection against southeasterly gales. A lighthouse was built in 1833 on Girdleness, the southern point of the bay. Thirty-two people were drowned in the harbour on 5 April 1876, in the River Dee Ferry Boat Disaster. The harbour serves Northlink Ferries, which sail to Kirkwall and the Shetland Islands. Aberdeen Harbour was the first public limited company in the UK.

Aberdeen Maritime Museum: Shiprow, Aberdeen. Relating the story of Aberdeen's centuries-long connection with shipbuilding, the fishing industry and latterly North Sea oil, the museum is housed in buildings overlooking the harbour and incorporates Provost Ross's House. The revamped museum was opened in 1997 and includes interactive exhibits as well as models of drilling rigs and seagoing vessels. There are more than 150 paintings of maritime subjects. Tel: 01224 337700.

Aberdeenshire Canal	Built 1796–1805 under the guidance of engineer John Rennie, the canal ran for 18 miles (29km) with 17 locks between Aberdeen and Inverurie (Port Elphinstone). It was not a great commercial success; bought by the Great North of Scotland Railway Company in 1845, it was closed in 1854.
Aberdeenshire Farming Museum	Mintlaw, 9 miles (15km) west of Peterhead. Agricultural museum situated in Aden Country Park, and incorporating the North East of Scotland Agricultural Heritage Centre and Hareshowe Working Farm. The 20 acre (8ha) farm retains its 1950s character and was relocated stone by stone from its original site 9 miles (15km) away in 1991. Other buildings include a restored semicircular steading which houses the heritage centre. Tel: 01771 624590.
Aboyne Castle	Aboyne, 11 miles (18km) west of Banchory, 26 miles (42km) west of Aberdeen. Located in Royal Deeside and built in the mid 13th century, the castle was handed over to Edward I in 1291 and garrisoned by English troops. From c.1388 the castle and lands were owned by the family of the Marquis of Huntly.
Aden Country Park	1 mile (1.6km) west of Mintlaw, 9 miles (15km) west of Peterhead. A 230 acre (93ha) country park owned by the Russell family until 1937 (GR: NJ983478). Other features include a small lake and a 'lower garden' next to the River Ugie. See also Aberdeenshire Farming Museum.
Administrative headquarters	**Aberdeen City**: Town House, Broad Street, Aberdeen AB10 1LP. Tel: 01224 522000. **Aberdeenshire**: Woodhill House, Westburn Road, Aberdeen AB16 5GB. Tel: 01224 665032. **Moray**: Council Offices, High Street, Elgin IV30 1BX. Tel: 01343 534451.
Airport	**Aberdeen Dyce Airport** (ABZ), 5 miles (8km) northwest of Aberdeen. Opened in 1934, it was an RAF base during World War II before returning to commercial operations in 1947. In addition to fixed-wing operations the airport handles a substantial amount of helicopter traffic as a result of the North Sea oil industry. Tel: 0870 040 0006.
Alford Haughton Country Park	Alford, 12 miles (19km) southwest of Inverurie. Covering 100 acres (40ha), with woodland and riverside habitats together with wildflower meadow and landscaped grassland.
Alford Heritage Centre	Alford, 12 miles (19km) southwest of Inverurie. A heritage centre dedicated to rural life and housed in the village's old Auction Mart. Themed displays include the village shop, the shoemaker's, the schoolroom and the farmhouse kitchen. There are also collections of farm implements and equipment. The life of poet Charles Murray (1864–1941) is also documented and his birthday celebrated each September. Tel: 01975 562906.
Alford Valley Railway	A 2ft (610mm) narrow gauge railway operating between Alford and Haughton Park on part of the former Alford Valley Railway, opened in 1859 and running from Alford to Kintore, where it connected to the Great North of Scotland Railway. After the line closed in 1966, between 1979 and 1984 volunteers laid narrow gauge track between Murray Park, Haughton Park Station and Alford Station (the Murray Park line has since closed). Alford Valley Railway Museum is housed in the rebuilt Alford station: exhibits include a recreated ticket office and waiting room, and scale models of steam trains. Tel: 01975 562811.
Arbuthnot Museum	St Peter Street, Peterhead, A local history museum dedicated to Peterhead's maritime history. Exhibits include models of fishing boats, Inuit artefacts and Arctic natural history. There is also a photographic archive and a large coin collection. The museum was founded by Adam Arbuthnot (1773–1850), whose collections of natural history, antiquities and coins were bequeathed to Peterhead town council. Previously located in Union Street (1851–61), Broad Street (1861–74) and Chapel Street (1874–93), its purpose-built present home was designed by Duncan McMillan; the foundation stone was laid by Mrs Andrew Carnegie on 8 August 1891. Tel: 01779 477778.
Archaeolink Prehistory Park	Oyne, 6 miles (10km) northwest of Inverurie. An award-winning living history park which covers more than 10,000 years of local history from the Mesolithic period to the arrival of the Roman army. Reconstructions include a Mesolithic encampment, a recumbent stone circle, a Class I henge monument, a Bronze Age smith's workshop, a working Iron Age farmstead and a Roman army marching camp. There is also an indoor exhibition centre exploring technology, agriculture, the changing environment and early beliefs. The 40 acre (16ha) site lies at the foot of Bennachie, a possible site of the battle of Mons Graupius fought between the Picts and the Romans in AD 84. Tel: 01464 851500.
Auchindoun Castle	2 miles (3km) southeast of Dufftown. The ruins of an L-plan tower house by the River Fiddich, built in the 15th century by Robert Cochrane on the site of a possible Iron Age hill fort. Later occupied by the Ogilvies and Gordons among others, it was damaged by the Mackintoshes in 1591 but restored. By the 1720s it had fallen into disrepair and was being used for local building material. Now in the care of Historic Scotland.
Balfluig Castle	1 mile (1.6km) southeast of Alford, Aberdeenshire. An L-plan tower built by the Forbes family in 1556. Abandoned in 1753, it was restored in the 1960s.
Ballindalloch Castle	1/2 mile (0.8km) northwest of Bridge of Avon, 17 miles (27km) south of Elgin. A Z-plan tower house built in 1546 on the River Avon in the Spey Valley by the Macpherson-Grant family, who still live here. It was extended during the 18th and 19th centuries with the addition of wings and a courtyard. Known as 'The Pearl of the North', the castle houses a collection of 17th century Spanish paintings; notable rooms include the hall, the drawing room, the library with more than 25,000 volumes, Lady Macpherson-Grant's room, the nursery and the dining room which is said to be haunted by a ghost known as the Green Lady. In the grounds there is a walled garden, a 17th century dovecote and a rock garden, laid out in 1937. The estate includes a 1110 acre (450ha) forest, a golf course and a farm with a herd of Aberdeen Angus cattle, a breed developed at Ballindalloch in the 1860s. Tel: 01807 500205.
Balmoral Castle	Crathie, 7 miles (11km) west of Ballater. A private royal residence on Deeside designed by William Smith of Aberdeen under the supervision of Prince Albert, and built 1853–6 on an estate previously owned by the Duke of Fife and purchased by Queen Victoria in 1852. The original 16th century tower house close by was demolished on completion of the new castle. The ballroom

features fine collections of paintings, porcelain and silverware , while the grounds include a formal garden covering 3 acres (1.2ha), a kitchen garden and a water garden. The estate covers more than 77 sq miles (200 sq km) of mountains, lochs, forests and farming land. The royal family attend Sunday morning service at the parish church of Crathie when in residence at Balmoral. Tel: 01339 742534.

Balquhain Castle — 2½ miles (4km) northwest of Inverurie. The ruins of a 15th century tower house belonging to the Leslie family, which was destroyed in 1526 and rebuilt in 1530. Mary, Queen of Scots spent the night here before the Battle of Corrichie in 1562. The property was extended with a hall and further outbuildings in the late 16th century to form a courtyard. The Leslie family moved out in 1710; the castle was burnt down in 1746, probably by the Duke of Cumberland, and abandoned. Only the east wall of the tower remains standing. A memorial to the fallen of the Battle of Harlaw stands on the other side of the River Urie, 1½ miles (2.5km) to the east.

Balquhain Circle — 2 miles (3km) northwest of Inverurie. The remains of a recumbent stone circle of probably 12 stones, of which only three remain standing. A white quartz outlier stands 10ft (3m) tall; the other stones are a mixture of granite and local stone.

Balvenie Castle — ¼ mile (0.4km) north of Dufftown. Also known as Mortlach. The ruins of a 12th century castle on the River Fiddich originally owned by the Comyns. After their defeat by Robert the Bruce it passed in the early 15th century to the Black Douglasses, who in turn were eliminated by James II, and subsequently to the 4th Earl of Atholl, who remodelled the castle. It was abandoned by the early 18th century. Now in the care of Historic Scotland.

Banchory Museum — Bridge Street, Banchory. A local history museum largely dedicated to the life of the 'Strathspey King', musician and composer J Scott Skinner. There are also collections of royal commemorative ware and 19th century tartan, and exhibits on the area's natural history. Tel: 01771 622906.

Banff Museum — High Street, Banff. One of Scotland's oldest museums, founded in 1828. On display is a copy of the Deskford Carnyx, an Iron Age war trumpet found on the shores of the Moray Firth in 1816, plus exhibits of local natural history, Banff silver, astronomical instruments and arms and armour. Tel: 01771 622906.

Bass of Inverurie — ½ mile (0.8km) south of Inverurie. A 52ft (16m) high mound that once formed the motte of a castle founded c.1180 by David, Earl of Huntingdon. The motte now stands in the middle of a cemetery. Early settlements on Corsman and Dilly Hills and Maiden Castle on the slopes of Bennachie, protected from wild beasts, gave way to a palisaded settlement around the Bass, the medieval Castle Yards, site of the earliest church. Pictish missionaries from the late 7th century preached and converted inhabitants, inscribing crosses or names of early saints in ogham on carved stones. The original dimensions of the ditch were revealed during grave-digging. During excavations in the 19th century the remains of an oaken gangway were discovered. Worked flints have been found round the base of the motte and also a cushion macehead and an adze. Pieces of a 14th century face mask jug were found in the ditch during gravedigging.

Battles — See separate table for details of the battles of Aberdeen, Alford, Bridge of Dee, Corrichie, Culblean, Glenlivet, Harlaw, Inverurie, Lumphanan, Mondynes, Mons Graupius, Mortlach and Torfnes.

Bennachie — 5 miles (8km) west of Inverurie. A mountain whose name means 'hill of the beast'; its nine 'tops' include Oxen Craig at 1732ft (528m), Mither Tap (1699ft, 518m), Watch Craig (1617ft, 493m) and Hermit Seat (1568ft, 478m). It is claimed to be the site of the Battle of Mons Graupius, fought in AD 84 between the Picts and the Romans. According to Roman historian Tacitus in his account of the battle, Pictish leader Calgacus rallied his men by saying famously of the Romans that 'they create a desolation and call it peace.' His stirring words were to no avail and the Romans ground out an inevitable victory. The surrounding forest, mainly of Scots pine, provides a habitat for wildlife including red squirrel and great spotted woodpecker.

Biblical Garden — King Street, Elgin. Opened in August 1996, the secluded 3 acre (1.2ha) walled garden is located in Cooper Park next to Elgin Cathedral. In its beds can be found all 110 plants mentioned in the Bible, each being labelled with the appropriate biblical reference. The walkway through the garden is laid out in the form of a Celtic cross and life-size sculptures throughout the garden depict the Parables, including the Good Shepherd and the Prodigal Son. There is also a sculpture of Samson and the baby Moses can be found among the reeds surrounding the garden's small water feature. Other areas depict Mount Sinai and the cave of the resurrection and there is a floral representation of the rainbow which appeared after Noah's flood.

Blackdog Burn — A stream which rises on the Red Moss and runs for 4 miles (6km) into the North Sea. For its final 1½ miles (2.5km) it forms the boundary between the Aberdeenshire and Aberdeen City council areas.

Blairfindy Castle — Glenlivet, 21 miles (32km) south of Elgin. The ruins of a 16th century L-plan tower beside the River Livet, built as a hunting lodge by John Gordon, Earl of Huntly. It is not accessible to the public.

Book of Deer — An illuminated 10th century manuscript possibly produced at Deer Abbey (see separate entry), although some believe it is Irish in origin. It contains the first six chapters of the Gospel of Matthew, a part of the fifth chapter of Mark and the entire Gospel of John. There is also a part of an Office for the Visitation of the Sick and the Apostles' Creed. These texts are in Latin from the Vulgate but unusually there are other texts in Old Irish and Scottish Gaelic, including charters and details of landholdings. It has been held in Cambridge University Library since 1715.

Bow Fiddle Rock — Portknockie, 17 miles (27km) east of Elgin. A much-photographed quartzite rock formation off the coast of Portknockie, standing 50ft (15m) out of the water and eroded by wave action so that one part resembles the bow of a fiddle.

Braemar Castle — ½ mile (0.8km) north of Braemar. A privately owned L-plan five-storey turreted house built in 1628 by the Earl of Mar. It was attacked and damaged by fire in 1689 but was eventually repaired, refortified and garrisoned by government troops after the Jacobite rising of 1745–6. A star-shaped curtain wall was added in the 18th century. Once its military purpose had ended it was turned into a family home by the Laird of Invercauld. Tel: 01339 741219.

Braemar Highland Gathering — Highland Games held annually in Braemar on the first Saturday of September since 1832 and first attended by royalty when Queen Victoria visited in 1848. Queen Elizabeth II is now the games' patron. Events include pipe and drum competitions, Highland dancing, caber-tossing, shot putting, hammer throwing, sprinting and tug-of-war.

Brander Museum — The Square, Huntly. A local history museum with exhibits including archaeological finds and arms and armour. There is also a display dedicated to Huntly-born author and poet George MacDonald.

Brandsbutt Stone Circle — Inverurie. The outline of a stone circle now lying within a housing estate. In the 19th century at least four stones remained, two still in their original position, although the rest had been removed and either destroyed or used in local buildings. Excavations in 1983 revealed eight stone holes. Nearby stands a 5th century Pictish sculptured stone; 3ft 6in high by 4ft 2in wide and 3ft thick, it was broken up at some point and subsequently reconstructed. It is decorated with a crescent and V-rod over a serpent and Z-rod with an ogham inscription on the left.

Bridges — The **Bridge of Dee** is a seven-arched ashlar bridge carrying the A90 (South Anderson Road) over the River Dee in Aberdeen. Built in the 1520s following a bequest by Bishop William Elphinstone, it was restored 1718–21 and widened in 1841. The bridge was the site of a skirmish on 18–19 June 1639 between Covenanters under James Graham, Earl of Montrose and Royalist forces commanded by James Gordon, Viscount Aboyne. The Covenanters claimed the bridge after an artillery bombardment brought down the gatehouse turret defended by the Royalists.

The **Bridge of Don** is a seven-span dressed stone bridge carrying the A92 (King Street) across the River Don in Aberdeen. Built 1827–39 by Thomas Telford and John Smith, it was widened in the late 1950s retaining its original design and dressed masonry.

The **Brig o' Balgownie**, one of the original bridges across the River Don in Aberdeen, is possibly the oldest original bridge in Scotland. The single-span ashlar Gothic style bridge was built c.1290–c.1320, possibly by Robert the Bruce. It was substantially rebuilt in the early 17th century and buttressed in the later 19th century. The only route into Aberdeen from the north until 1827, it is now only open to foot and bicycle traffic.

Craigellachie Bridge, Craigellachie, 11 miles (18km) southeast of Elgin, is the oldest surviving iron bridge in Scotland. The single-span cast iron bridge over the River Spey was built by Thomas Telford 1812–15. The iron was cast at Plas Kynaston Ironworks in Denbighshire. Restored in 1964, it carried the A941 until 1972.

Brodie Castle — Brodie, 6 miles (10km) east of Nairn. A Z-plan castle built by the Brodie family in the 16th century on the coast of the Moray Firth on the site of earlier properties. Burnt by Lord Lewis Gordon in 1645, it was restored and extended during the 17th and 19th centuries and now contains collections of furniture, porcelain and fine art plus a library of more than 6000 titles. The 175 acres (71ha) of grounds feature a considerable daffodil collection. The castle has been in the care of the National Trust for Scotland since 1980 when it was donated by the Brodie family. See also Rodney's Stone.

Buckie Drifter Maritime Heritage Centre — Freuchny Road, Buckie. A maritime museum opened in 1994 and dedicated to the history of the local fishing industry and lifeboat services of Buckie and the Moray Firth. Tel: 01542 834646.

Burghead Bull Carvings — Six surviving symbol stones with carvings of bulls from more than 20 found during the destruction of Burghead Promontory Fort (see separate entry) due to the expansion of Burghead in the 19th century. Probably carved in the 6th or 7th century, they are: **Burghead 1**, a stone with a carving of a bull, found in the Burghead Well and presented to the National Museum of Antiquities of Scotland in 1891; **Burghead 2**, a bull with head damaged by the workman who discovered it in 1862, now in the care of Moray Museums Service; **Burghead 3**, a complete carving of a bull held at Elgin Museum; **Burghead 4**, a bull with damaged body found in 1867 and in the care of Moray Museums Service; **Burghead 5**, found in 1809 and in the care of the British Museum; **Burghead 6**, a bull with damaged body uncovered in 1854 and held at Elgin Museum.

Burghead Promontory Fort — Burghead, 5 miles (8km) northwest of Elgin. A Pictish hill fort built on a promontory in the Moray Firth. It covered 8 acres (3ha) with three ramparts and ditches across the headland. It was occupied c.450–c.850, when it was destroyed by fire. Much of the vitrified remains were destroyed in the 19th century with the expansion of the village and harbour of Burghead and the building of a coastguard watch tower. The nearby rock-cut well, uncovered in 1809, was possibly used to supply the fort with fresh water.

Cairngorms National Park — See Highlands

Cambus o' May Forest — 2 miles (3km) northeast of Ballater. A mixed conifer and birch woodland within the Cairgorms National Park on Upper Deeside.

Camus's Stone — 1 mile (1.6km) southeast of Hopeman, 4 miles (6km) northwest of Elgin. A standing stone of quartzose micaceous schist supposedly erected to commemorate the victory in 1010 of Malcolm II over the Danes, whose leader Camus was killed. It stands 5ft 9in (1.75m) tall and 5ft 3in (1.6m) wide and bears cup and ring markings.

Candle Stane — 2½ miles (4km) northwest of Ellon. A 10ft 2in (3.1m) tall standing stone, part of a recumbent stone circle of originally eight stones.

Carnegie Inverurie Museum — The Square, Inverurie. A local history museum with exhibits including archaological finds and items highlighting the history of the area from ancient times to the present day.

Castle Fraser — 1½ miles (2.5km) northeast of Sauchen, 6 miles (10km) southwest of Inverurie. Also known as Muchal-In-Mar. Originally a 16th century L-plan tower house, developed into a Z-plan castle with courtyard in 1636 by Michael Fraser. Notable rooms include the great hall and the Victorian kitchen. The gardens in the 350 acre (140ha) estate include an artificial lake. The remains of a stone circle and a pair of standing stones also stand on or near the estate. The castle and part of the grounds were given to the National Trust for Scotland in 1976 and a further 314 acres (127ha) of surrounding land was purchased in 1993. Tel: 01330 833463.

Castlegate Well — Castlegate, Aberdeen. Also known as the Mannie Well. A sculptured well-head dating from c.1708 and built by William Lindsay, the overseer of Aberdeen's water supply. It has since been sited in two other locations before being erected in its current position in 1972.

Churches — **Crathie Kirk**, Crathie, 6 miles (10km) west of Ballater, is the small church where the royal family worship when resident at Balmoral. It was built in 1893 close to the original 13th century church, the remains of which can still be seen, and on the site of an earlier church dating to 1804. The south transept is reserved for royal use. Queen Victoria's loyal ghillie John Brown is buried in the churchyard.

Cullen Old Kirk, Cullen, 6 miles (10km) east of Buckie, was in existence in 1236 and was originally dedicated to St Mary the Virgin. A new aisle was added in 1539 and in 1543 the church was raised to collegiate status; a college was established with a provost, six prebendaries and two choir boys. The church was extended in cruciform shape in the 18th century. The chancel contains the elaborate tomb of Sir Alexander Ogilvie (d. 1554), a patron of the church. The church is still in use for weekly services.

Kineff Parish Church, Kinneff, 5 miles (8km) southwest of Stonehaven, was built c.1242 and dedicated to St Anthony. The Scottish Crown Jewels (the Honours of Scotland – the crown, sceptre and sword of state) were hidden here 1651–60 after being smuggled out of Dunnottar Castle during a siege by Cromwellian forces. The church was in disrepair by the beginning of the 18th century and parts of the earlier building were incorporated in the rebuilt church of 1738. The church had to be extensively repaired in the 1870s and was further restored in the 1960s. It is no longer used for regular worship and now houses an exhibition related to the Crown Jewels.

Kinkell Church, 1½ miles (2.5km) southeast of Inverurie. The remains of a 16th century church by the River Don, possibly designed by Alexander Galloway, parson of Kinkell and architect of the Bridge of Dee. It contains a memorial to Gilbert de Greenlaw, killed at the Battle of Harlaw in 1411. The roof was removed c.1771.

Kirk of St Nicholas, Union Street, Aberdeen. Originally built in the 12th century, although substantially rebuilt between the mid 18th and mid 19th century. After the Reformation it was divided into the Auld Kirk and the New Kirk. The Auld Kirk was replaced by the West Church in the 1750s. The spire of the East Kirk was replaced having been destroyed by fire in 1874; in the 1950s the 37 bells installed in the new steeple were in turn replaced by a carillon of 48 bells, the largest in Britain. Today the church is a member both of the Church of Scotland and the United Reformed Church. Tel: 01224 643494.

Corgarff Castle — ¼ mile (0.4km) south of Cock Bridge, 25 miles (40km) southwest of Huntly. 16th century tower house situated above the River Don. Originally a hunting lodge belonging to the Earl of Mar, it was deliberately burnt by Captain Ker in 1571 on the orders of Adam Gordon; more than 20 of its occupants died, mainly women and children, and including Mistress Forbes, the laird's wife. It was occupied by the Earl of Montrose in 1645; a century later, having been burned down twice more in the interim, it was converted into a barracks for a garrison of government troops, who occupied it until 1831. It passed into state care in 1961 and was restored over the following decade. Now maintained by Historic Scotland.

Coxton Tower — 2 miles (3km) southeast of Elgin. Four-storey 17th century tower house built by the Innes family in a style reminiscent of the 15th century. The tower was sold to William Duff in the late 17th century and was last occupied in the mid 19th century. It was partially restored in the 1930s.

Craig Castle — 2 miles (3km) southwest of Rhynie, 10 miles (16km) southwest of Huntly. 16th century L-plan tower house on the Burn of Craig, probably built by the same mason who worked on the castles at Towie Barclay, Delgatie and Gight. A castellated house and gateway were added to the tower in the 1720s and wings were added in 1832 and 1908.

Craigievar Castle — 4 miles (6km) southwest of Alford. Bought from the Mortimer family during its construction, this L-plan tower house was completed in 1626 by William Forbes, known as 'Danzig Willie' because his wealth had been accrued through trading in timber in the Baltic. It was restored and extended by John Smith of Aberdeen in the 1820s. The castle was presented to the National Trust for Scotland in 1963 and further surrounding land and woodland were purchased in 1978 and 2004. Tel: 01339 883635.

Craigston Castle — Fintry, 3 miles (5km) northeast of Turriff. A U-plan tower house built by John Urquhart in the early 17th century. The gardens were originally laid out by William Adam in 1733.

Crathes Castle — 2 miles (3km) northeast of Banchory. 16th century L-plan tower house on the River Dee built by the Burnett family, with a wing added at a later date. The interior has wooden painted ceilings together with a long gallery and a Muses Room dedicated to the performing arts. There are eight themed gardens with a surrounding wall and yew hedges planted in 1702. The castle was given to the National Trust for Scotland in 1951. Tel: 01330 844525.

Crathie Promontory Fort — 2 miles (3km) east of Cullen, 8 miles (13km) east of Buckie. The rampart and ditch of a promontory fort, located across the headland at Crathie Point.

Cullerlie Stone Circle — 3 miles (5km) east of Echt, 10 miles (16km) west of Aberdeen. Also known as the Standing Stones of Echt. Bronze Age stone circle 36ft (11m) in diameter and consisting of eight stones. Excavations in the 1930s uncovered seven small cairns within the circle.

Cullykhan — ½ mile (0.8km) northwest of Pennan, 9 miles (15km) west of Fraserburgh. An Iron Age promontory fort with a stone and timber laced earth rampart across the headland of Castle Point.

Occupation seems to have begun during the 7th century BC. At some point the fort was burnt, causing vitrification, but it was subsequently rebuilt. Excavations have also revealed evidence of a substantial gate tower together with traces of metalworking. During the 13th century a castle was built on the site by the Troup family and in the 18th century there was an artillery defence battery here.

Culsh Earth House 1$^1/_2$ miles (2.5km) east of Tarland, 10 miles (16km) northeast of Ballater. Well-preserved souterrain (tunnel) or Iron Age earth house measuring 47ft (14.5m) long, 6ft (1.8m) wide and 5ft 6in (1.6m) high. It curves to the northeast and has roofing slabs by the entrance and over its chambers. It would primarily have been used as a communal food store. Maintained by Historic Scotland.

Deer Abbey 2 miles (3km) west of Mintlaw, 10 miles (16km) west of Peterhead. A Cistercian foundation established in 1219 by William Comyn, Earl of Buchan. Following the Reformation the abbey and its lands were secularised and by the end of the 16th century the buildings were beginning to be dismantled. After repairs in 1809 what remained was virtually destroyed in 1854 by Admiral Ferguson, who wanted the stone to build a mausoleum. Some parts of the abbot's house, refectory and kitchen are still visible. Maintained by Historic Scotland.

Deer's Den Roman Camp Kintore, 4 miles (6km) southeast of Inverurie. The site of a Roman marching camp and also of Neolithic and Bronze Age settlements. The Roman camp covered 110 acres (44 acres) when it was first identified in the 19th century. Possibly built during the campaign which culminated in the Battle of Mons Graupius, it was certainly occupied in AD 120. Further excavations were carried out in the late 1990s and early 2000s during the construction of the A96 Kintore bypass and a housing development.

Delgatie Castle 2 miles (3km) east of Turriff. A 16th century four-storey tower house beside the Burn of Colp, built by the Hay family possibly on the site of an earlier fortification and probably designed by the same builder who constructed the castles at Craig, Gight, and Towie Barclay. It was visited by Mary, Queen of Scots after the Battle of Corrichie in 1562. Remodelled in the 18th and 19th centuries with the addition of wings, it was restored during the second half of the 20th century and retains some 16th century painted ceilings; there is a staircase within the thickness of its walls. Maintained by Historic Scotland.

Distilleries **Aberlour** was founded in 1879 by James Fleming (1830–95), replacing an earlier distillery established in 1826, and rebuilt after a fire in 1898. Fleming's family motto 'Let the Deed Show' is displayed on every bottle of Aberlour whisky. The main water source are the springs of Ben Rinnes and the distillery was built on St Drostan's Well. Tel: 01340 871204.

Balvenie, Dufftown, was established in the converted Balvenie New House in 1892 by William Grant, whose family still run the distillery. It stands next to its sister distillery of Glenfiddich. Some of the grain comes from the family farm and the water source is the Robbie Dubh. The distillery has the last active traditional malt floor in use in the Scottish Highlands. Tel: 01340 820373.

Benriach, Longmorn, 3 miles (5km) southeast of Elgin, was established in 1898 by John Duff next to its sister distillery Longmorn, but closed in 1900 when it was decided to keep Longmorn open instead. The malting floors were kept working to produce malt for the distillery next door and in 1965 the Benriach Distillery was restored, refurbished and reopened to meet the increased demand for malt whisky for blending. It was again closed 2002–04, after which new owners recommenced production. The distillery uses local spring water. Tel: 01542 783400.

Benromach, Invererne Road, Forres, Morayshire, founded in 1898 by Duncan MacCallum and F W Brickman, is the smallest working distillery in Speyside. Almost immediately hit by a severe downturn in the whisky market, it did not begin production until 1912. Production remained intermittent until the late 1930s. It was closed again 1983–98 when, refurbished and re-equipped, it was reopened by HRH Prince of Wales on 15 October. The Malt Whisky Centre, charting the story of malt whisky and the whisky producing regions of Scotland, was opened in 1999. The water source is Chapeltown springs. Tel: 01309 675968.

Cardhu, Knockando, Aberlour. Founded by John and Helen Cumming in 1824 but moved to its current site in 1884. It became part of John Walker & Sons Ltd in 1893. The water sources are the springs on Mannoch Hill or the Lyne Burn.

Cragganmore, Ballindalloch, is a Speyside distillery founded by John Smith in 1869 in the grounds of Ballindalloch Estate It was rebuilt in 1902. The water source is the Craggan Burn.

Craigellachie Craigellachie, Aberlour. Speyside distillery opened in 1891 by Peter Mackie and Alexander Edward. Control was acquired by Mackie & Co (Distillers) Ltd in 1916 and it was rebuilt in 1965. The malt is used in White Horse brands. The water source is the spring on Little Conval Hill. Tel: 01340 872970.

Dallas Dhu Historic Distillery, Forres. Speyside distillery originally established in 1899, closed in 1983 and reopened as an industrial museum in 1989. Maintained by Historic Scotland.

Fettercairn, Laurencekirk, was established in 1824, making it one of the oldest licensed malt whisky distilleries in Scotland. It was rebuilt in 1887 after a serious fire and was closed 1926–39. The water sources are springs running from the Cairngorms. Tel: 01561 340244.

Glen Grant, Rothes. Founded by John and James Grant in 1840. The malt produced here is also a component of Chivas Regal. Glen Grant is particularly popular in Italy. The water source is Glen Grant Burn. Tel: 01542 783318.

Glen Moray, Elgin. Speyside distillery established in 1897 when a brewery was converted during the whisky boom of that period. Closed 1910–20, it was then purchased and reopened by Macdonald & Muir. The water source is the River Lossie. Tel: 01343 542577.

Glendronach, Forgue. Speyside distillery founded in 1826. It was purchased by Charles Grant in 1920 and sold to Teacher in 1960. As well as its own bottlings, the malt is used in Teacher's Highland Cream. The water source is a spring simply known as 'The Source'. Tel: 01466 730202.

Glenfarclas, Ballindalloch. Speyside distillery established in 1836 by Robert Hay. It was purchased by John Grant in 1865 and refurbished in the late 1890s. The water sources are the springs on Ben Rinnes. Tel: 01807 500245.

Glenfiddich Dufftown. Speyside distillery founded in 1886 by William Grant & Sons. It began to market its single malt in 1963. The water source is the Robbie Dhu Springs. Tel: 01340 820373.

Glenlivet, Ballindalloch. Speyside distillery founded in 1824 by George Smith. The only distillery allowed to call its whisky 'The Glenlivet'. The company was acquired by Seagram in 1977. The water source is Josie's Well. Tel: 01542 783220.

Royal Lochnagar, Crathie, Ballater. The original distillery, built on this site in 1826, was joined by a second in 1845. It received the royal warrant in 1848. The first distillery was closed in 1860 and the 'new' distillery rebuilt in 1963. The water source is the springs from Lochnagar. Tel: 01339 742273.

Strathisla, Keith. A small distillery originally established as the Milltown Distillery in 1786, making it possibly the oldest working distillery in Scotland. The name was changed to Strathisla in 1870 but it had to be rebuilt following a fire in 1876. The malt is used in Chivas Regal. The water source is the Fons Bulliens Well. Tel: 01542 783042.

Drum Castle — Drumoak, 2 miles (3km) west of Peterculter, 10 miles (16km) southwest of Aberdeen. Standing on a ridge above the River Dee, the castle was the home of the Irvine family from the early 14th century until the 1970s. A mansion was added to the original tower house in 1619 and the castle was subsequently occupied by Covenanters at least twice (1639 and 1644). During the second occupation the castle was stripped of its fixtures and fittings and any portable treasure. The 14th and 17th Lairds of Drum supported the Jacobite risings of 1715 and 1745 respectively. The 18th Laird, who was over 90 when he died in the 1840s, remodelled the mansion, added the walled garden and landscaped the estate. Further modifications were carried out in the 1870s. Rooms include the drawing room, dining room and the library which contain family portraits by artists such as Raeburn. Outside, the walled garden houses 400 varieties of roses in the Garden of Historic Roses, opened in 1991. There is also a pond garden and an arboretum. The estate includes the ancient oak woodland known as the Old Wood of Drum, a designated Site of Special Scientific Interest. The castle was bequeathed to the National Trust for Scotland in 1976.

Drumin Castle — Drumin, 20 miles (32km) southwest of Keith. A 14th century tower house by the confluence of the Rivers Avon and Livet on the Glenlivet Estate. Possibly built by Alexander Stewart (1342–1406), the notorious 'Wolf of Badenoch', it was occupied only briefly, being finally abandoned in the early 18th century and used as a store in the 19th century. Only two walls, which were 9ft (2.8m) thick at the base and were stabilised in the 1990s, remain standing.

Druminnor Castle — 1$\frac{1}{2}$ miles (2.5km) southeast of Rhynie, 9 miles (15km) south of Huntly. 16th century L-plan tower house which was home to the Forbes family of Aberdeenshire. The castle was slighted in 1571 but restored within a few years. The tower was demolished in 1800; a mansion built in its stead was subsequently demolished in the 1960s.

Duff House — $\frac{1}{2}$ mile (0.8km) southeast of Banff. A Georgian house located beside the River Deveron and built 1735–40 to a design by William Adam for William Duff, later Earl Fife, although he never lived here. In the early 20th century the house was used as a hotel and then a sanatorium. During World War II it became a hospital and POW camp. Restored between the 1960s and 1990s, it was opened as a country house gallery in 1995 and is operated by a partnership of Historic Scotland, the National Galleries of Scotland and Aberdeenshire Council. The collections include fine art and furniture; the Dunimarle Library holds more than 4000 volumes. Tel: 01261 818181.

Dufftown Games — A programme of Highland games inaugurated in 1892 and held in Dufftown on the last Saturday of July each year. Events include massed pipe bands, Highland dancing, tug of war, heavy events, track events and the 5 Tops Hill Race.

Duffus Castle — 3 miles (5km) northwest of Elgin. Founded in the 12th century by Freskin de Moravia as a timber and earth motte and bailey; the ditch around the original motte enclosed an area of 8 acres (3ha) and would have stood beside Loch Spynie, once much larger but now drained. Held by supporters of Edward I, the timber castle was burnt down in 1297. A square tower house was built on the motte c.1350 and a range of domestic buildings added in the 15th century. There is evidence that the motte was unable to fully support the new heavier structure, which was finally abandoned in the mid 17th century after sustaining damage in the Civil War. Maintained by Historic Scotland.

Duke of Gordon's Monument — Lady Hill, Elgin. An 80ft (24m) high column erected in 1839 in honour of soldier and politician George Gordon, 5th Duke of Gordon (1770–1836). The duke's statue was placed on top of the column in 1855.

Dunnideer Castle — 1 mile (1.6km) west of Insch, 11 miles (18km) northwest of Inverurie. The remains of a 13th century tower house built on the top of a conical hill standing at 879ft (268m), also the site of an incomplete Iron Age trivallate fort and vitrified inner workings. Traditionally built by Gregory the Great in 890 although first mentioned only in 1260, it is probably the earliest remaining tower house in mainland Scotland.

Dunnottar Castle — 1$\frac{1}{2}$ miles (2.5km) southeast of Stonehaven. Extensive remains of a much enlarged 14th century L-plan castle on a coastal promontory. The site was probably also the location of earlier fortifications, including a Pictish fort besieged in 681 and finally destroyed by the Vikings in the 10th century. A wooden castle probably stood on the site in the 13th century and William Wallace incinerated an English garrison in the castle church in 1297. The stone-built castle was begun in the 14th century. In addition to visits in the 1560s by Mary, Queen of Scots, her descendant Charles II stayed here in 1650 while claiming the Scottish crown; a year later the Honours of Scotland (the Scottish Crown Jewels) were hidden here during a siege by Cromwellian forces and spirited away to safety before the castle was taken. In 1685, 167 Covenanter prisoners were confined for some weeks in a small vault known as the 'Whig's Vault' where nine died. The castle was extended in the late 16th or early 17th century but was abandoned in 1716 and unroofed. The remaining buildings include gatehouse, barracks, a chapel, and stables. Partially restored in the 1920s, the castle was used for as a location for Franco Zeffirelli's film *Hamlet* (1990).

Duthie Park and Winter Gardens — Polmuir Road, Aberdeen. Located beside the River Dee, Duthie Park covers 44 acres (18ha) and was opened on 27 September 1883. It was created from a gift by Lady Elizabeth Crombie Duthie. A striking feature is the Rose Mountain, featuring 120,000 roses. Opened in 1899, and rebuilt and extended after being severely damaged by a storm in 1969, the Winter Gardens now form one of the largest indoor gardens in Europe. There are substantial collections of bromeliads, cacti and succulents, as well as a Japanese garden. Tel: 01224 583155.

Dyce — A town on the River Don 6 miles (10km) northwest of Aberdeen city, and best known as the location of the city's airport. From the mid 1970s, the town grew in size largely due to the oil industry and the associated economic expansion; the main headquarters of BP were built here for easy access to the airport. The railway station, closed for some years, was reopened in September 1984 to serve the airport. Dyce won Britain in Bloom in 2004.

Easter Aquhorthies Stone Circle — 2 miles (3km) west of Inverurie. A stone circle dating to c.2500 BC, 65ft (20m) in diameter and consisting of 11 standing stones and a recumbent stone. The outer stones, mostly of porphyry although one is of jasper, stand up to 6ft (1.8m) high. Two larger granite monoliths stand at right angles to the recumbent stone, which is 12ft 6in (3.7m) in length. The site is unexcavated. Maintained by Historic Scotland.

Elgin Castle — Lady Hill, Elgin. A 13th century castle which once stood on Lady Hill, now the site of the Duke of Gordon's Monument. It was probably built on the motte of an 11th century fortification and was abandoned by the 15th century. Today only some fragmentary remains of masonry are still visible.

Elgin Cathedral — King Street, Elgin. Dedicated to the Holy Trinity and originally built in the early 13th century, the cathedral was rebuilt and enlarged in the 14th century. Unfortunately the new building, one of the largest in Scotland, was then burnt down by Alexander Stewart, the 'Wolf of Badenoch', in 1390. The cathedral was rebuilt over the next 200 years, including an octagonal chapter house almost unique in Scotland, but was abandoned after 1560 following the Reformation, and fell into disrepair; by 1637 it was unroofed and the central tower had collapsed. The substantial ruins of the three-towered cathedral were stabilised in the 19th century; the chapter house with its elaborate vaulting stands almost intact. The site is maintained by Historic Scotland.

Elgin Marbles — Also known as the Parthenon Marbles. A large collection of marble sculptures removed from the Parthenon in Athens and nearby monuments and brought to Britain in 1806 by Thomas Bruce, 7th Earl of Elgin, ambassador to the Ottoman Empire 1799–1803. The sculptures were deposited in the British Museum, London in 1816, and in 1936 were placed in the purpose-built Duveen Gallery. The Elgin Marbles include some of the statuary from the pediments, the metope panels depicting battles between the Lapiths and the Centaurs, and the Parthenon Frieze which decorated the horizontal course set above the temple's interior architrave. They represent more than half of the surviving sculptural decoration of the Parthenon – 247ft (75m) from the original 524ft (160m) of frieze, 15 of the 92 metopes and 17 partial figures from the pediments, as well as other pieces of architecture – wax casts being produced from the remaining ones. Elgin's acquisitions also included objects from other buildings on the Athenian Acropolis: the Erechtheion, reduced to ruin during the Greek War of Independence (1821–33), the Propylaia and the Temple of Athena Nike. There was criticism of Elgin as soon as the marbles were shipped to Britain, and this is maintained today. Lord Byron in his poem *Childe Harold's Pilgrimage* strongly objected to their removal from Greece: 'Dull is the eye that will not weep to see/Thy walls defaced, thy mouldering shrines removed/By British hands, which it had best behoved/To guard those relics ne'er to be restored./Curst be the hour when from their isle they roved,/And once again thy hapless bosom gored,/And snatch'd thy shrinking gods to northern climes abhorred!'

Elgin Museum — High Street, Elgin. A local history museum opened in a purpose-built Italianate building in 1842 and tracing the history of Elgin and region. Collections include fossils, Pictish stones, a Roman coin hoard, natural history subjects and a set of miniatures of the Parthenon Frieze (see Elgin Marbles). The museum also holds an archive of correspondence to one of its founders, geologist and palaeontologist Rev. George Gordon, and writings by Charles Darwin and Thomas Henry Huxley (known as 'Darwin's Bulldog'). Tel: 01343 543675.

Esslemont Castle — 2 miles (3km) west of Ellon. Ruins of what was originally a 15th century L-plan tower house built by the Marshal family. After sustaining fire damage in 1493, it was demolished and replaced in the late 16th century by a Renaissance style residential tower house. The property passed through the hands of the Cheynes and the Earls of Errol; bought by the Gordon family in 1728, it was abandoned by Robert Gordon in 1769.

Façade, The — Union Street, Aberdeen. A colonnade of 12 granite Doric columns designed by John Smith in 1829 and separating Union Street from the Kirk of St Nicholas.

Falconer Museum — Tolbooth Street, Forres. Local history museum founded in 1871 following bequests by merchant Alexander Falconer (1797–1856) and his brother Hugh (1808–65), a leading Victorian geologist and naturalist. The museum's collections trace the economic and social history of Forres. Run by Moray Council since 1992, the museum underwent major refurbishment in 2006–07. Tel: 01309 673701.

Fasque — 1½ miles (2.5km) north of Fettercairn, 15 miles (24km) southwest of Stonehaven. Also known as Fasque House. A castellated Georgian sandstone mansion completed in 1809 on the site of a smaller 1750s house designed by Robert Adam. Purchased by Sir John Gladstone (1764–1851) in 1829, it was often visited by his son, Prime Minister William Ewart Gladstone (1809–98). The house was owned by the Gladstone family until 2007. Tel: 01561 340202.

Fetteresso Castle 2 miles (3km) west of Stonehaven. A 16th century L-plan tower built by the Earls of Marischal and described as a palace by Bishop Leslie in 1578. Partly burned by the Earl of Montrose in 1645, it was restored in the 1670s by the Duff family. The castle was remodelled in 1808 incorporating some of the original building, which had fallen into disrepair. By the mid 20th century the house had again become unoccupied but it has since been restored and turned into private apartments.

Fetternear House 1 mile (1.6km) northwest of Kemnay, 5 miles (8km) southwest of Inverurie. Owned by the Bishops of Aberdeen, Fetternear has been leased to the Barons of Balquhain since the 16th century. A collegiate church was established at Fetternear in 1109 and the imposing structure known as the House of Aquahorties, formerly a seminary and located to the north of Fetternear, was part of this religious complex. While Fetternear became the chief residence of the Balquhain Leslies, it never lost its identity as Fetternear House. An accidental fire destroyed the house in the early 1920s when a maid unwittingly put hot ashes from a fireplace into a wooden bucket, which she left standing, in or near the kitchen. During the night the coals ignited and the resulting fire raged through the palace. Innumerable valuable family possessions, including those pertaining to Mary, Queen of Scots, were lost; the silver service was reduced to globs of metal. The old Chapel was sold for reconstruction at another location. However there is today a small chapel and rectory on the property serving the local Roman Catholic parish. The house and grounds are now undergoing archaeological investigation.

Findhorn Village Heritage Centre Findhorn, 4 miles (6m) north of Forres. Housed in two former fishing huts, one laid out as a fisherman's bothy and the other with exhibits illustrating the local wildlife and the history of the village.

Findlater Castle 1½ miles (2.5km) east of Cullen, 12 miles (19km) northeast of Keith. Ruins of an extensive fortification sited in a dramatic position on a promontory stretching into the North Sea and dating from c.1250, although rebuilt in the 14th or 15th century. The only landward approach was across a narrow isthmus with ditch and rampart broken by two entrances. The castle survived a siege by Mary, Queen of Scots in 1562 but its then owner Sir John Gordon was executed after the Battle of Corrichie. It was abandoned by 1600 and in disrepair by the mid 17th century. Much of the site has been claimed by the sea; although some walls and the remains of buildings still stand, they are precariously situated above sheer cliffs.

Forvie National Nature Reserve 4 miles (6km) southeast of Ellon. Nature reserve around the estuary of the River Ythan, and encompassing covering various coastal habitats including sand dunes, coastal heath, saltmarsh and sea cliffs. Although much of the area was once farmed, the encroaching dunes now form one of the largest such systems in Britain. Evidence of several settlements have been uncovered from the shifting sand dating from the Bronze Age to the medieval period, including the remains of a 12th century kirk. The reserve supports the largest colony of breeding eider ducks in Britain, as well as four breeding species of tern – Arctic, common, little and sandwich. The site is carpeted in flowering plants in August. Tel: 01358 751330.

Fraserburgh Heritage Centre Quarry Road, Fraserburgh. Housed in a former barrel-making factory and foundry on Kinnaird Head. It traces the economic and social history of Fraserburgh, which was founded by Lord Saltoun in 1592. There are also exhibits relating to locally born industrialist and trader with Japan Thomas Blake Glover (1838–1911) and 1970s fashion designer Bill Gibb (1944–88).

Fyvie Castle 1 mile (1.6km) north of Fyvie, 7 miles (11km) southeast of Turriff. A 14th century L-plan tower house on the site of an earlier fortification beside the River Ythan. It has five towers, each named for the family in residence when it was built: Preston, Meldrum, Seton, Gordon and Leith. The towers forming the original 'L' are the Preston Tower and the later Meldrum Tower. A gatehouse was added in the late 16th century, when internal modifications were also carried out by Sir Alexander Seton. A further tower, the Gordon Tower, was erected in 1777. The house has collections of fine art (including many paintings by Sir Henry Raeburn), furniture, arms and armour, as well as an impressive wheel (spiral) staircase. Fyvie also has its share of ghosts and apparitions. Outside is a walled garden, while the grounds, situated beside the Loch of Fyvie, were landscaped in the 19th century. The castle and grounds were bought by the National Trust for Scotland in 1984. Tel: 01651 891266.

Gight Castle 4 miles (6km) east of Fyvie, 10 miles (16km) southest of Turriff. Remains of a 16th century L-plan tower house on the River Ythan. Probably built by the same mason who worked on the castles at Towie Barclay, Delgatie and Craig, it was home to the Gordon family; the last 'Laird' was Lady Catherine Gordon, wife of Captain John 'Mad Jack' Byron and mother of poet Lord Byron. The house was apparently sold in 1787 to pay off the captain's gambling debts, and was abandoned after the new owner, Lord Haddo, eldest son of the 3rd Earl of Aberdeen, was killed in a riding accident in 1791.

Glen Tanar National Nature Reserve 3 miles (5km) southwest of Aboyne. National Nature Reserve covering 16.1 sq miles (41.8 sq km) with habitats including the remains of a Caledonian pine forest, moorland and bog. Wildlife includes the Scottish crossbill, capercaillie and red squirrel.

Glenbuchat Castle 5 miles (8km) southwest of Kildrummy, 17 miles (17km) southwest of Huntly. Also known as Glenbucket Castle. The ruins of a Z-plan residential castle built in 1590 by John Gordon for his wife, standing at 951ft (290m) overlooking the River Don and the Water of Buchat. The castle was sold to the Duff family in 1738 (possibly because of the Gordons' Jacobite sympathies) at which time it had already begun to fall into disrepair. It was unroofed in the 19th century. A motto above the main doorway, dating to the castle's construction reads 'Nothing on Earth remains bot Faime' ('nothing lasts without good repute'). The castle has been in the care of Historic Scotland since 1946.

Glover House Balgownie Road, Bridge of Don. An early home of industrialist Thomas Blake Glover, who helped create the modern Japanese shipbuilding industry and founded the Kirin Beer Company. The house has been restored, partly thanks to a grant from Mitsubishi, and tells the story of this remarkable man who helped transform the politics and economics of 19th century Japan. His house in Nagasaki, built in 1863, is the oldest standing Western-style house in Japan, having survived the 1945 atom bomb. His birthplace in Fraserburgh was not so lucky, having been destroyed by the Luftwaffe during World War II.

Gordon Highlanders Regimental Museum — Viewfield Road, Aberdeen. Housed in St Lukes, which once belonged to painter Sir George Reid, and opened in 1997, the museum includes interactive displays and maps, real-life experiences and personal testimonies, audio-visual presentations, full-scale replicas plus uniforms, medals, arms and equipment and colours. It stands in a 5 acre (2ha) garden and features a Garden of Contemplation and walled garden. The regiment was originally raised by the 4th Duke of Gordon in 1794 as the 100th Regiment of Foot, consisting of recruits from Aberdeenshire, Banffshire and Kincardineshire and particularly from the Gordon Estates. In 1798 it was redesignated the 92nd Regiment of Foot. The regiment saw action during the French Revolutionary Wars in Holland and Egypt, during the Peninsular War at Corunna and Vittoria, and at Waterloo where the Gordon Highlanders seized hold of the stirrups of the Scots Greys in a remarkable charge. Later in the 19th century the regiment engaged in Britain's many colonial wars in Afghanistan, India, Sudan and South Africa. In 1881 the 75th (Stirlingshire) Regiment was amalgamated with the Gordon Highlanders: the 75th became the 1st Battalion Gordon Highlanders, the 92nd Regiment formed the 2nd Battalion, and the Royal Aberdeenshire Militia the 3rd, with a depot fixed at Aberdeen. At the outbreak of World War I the 1st Battalion was part of the British Expeditionary Force in France and the 2nd Battalion fought at the first battle of Ypres. Other actions in World War I included Neuve Chapelle, Loos, Somme (1916, 1918), Delville Wood, Arras, Vimy, Menin Road, St Quentin and the Hindenburg Line. During World War II the regiment formed part of the British Expeditionary Force in France in 1940 until the evacuation from Dunkirk; elements of the regiment also served in the Far East and were present at the fall of Singapore in February 1942. Other actions in World War II included northwest Europe (1940, 1944–5), El Alamein, Sicily (1943) and Burma. Post-war operations involving the Gordon Highlanders include Borneo, Northern Ireland, the first Gulf War and Bosnia. In 1994 the regiment was amalgamated with the Seaforth Highlanders and the Camerons to form The Highlanders (Seaforth, Gordons and Camerons). The soldiers of the Gordon Highlanders were awarded 19 Victoria Crosses and the regiment's battle honours include Egmont-op-Zee, Corunna, Fuentes d'Onor, Vittoria, Waterloo, Delhi (1857), Lucknow, Kabul (1879), Kandahar (1880), Tel-el-Kebir, Defence of Ladysmith, Mons, Le Cateau, Ypres (1914, 1915, 1917), Neuve Chapelle, Loos, Somme (1916, 1918), Vimy (1917), Passchendaele, Cambrai (1917, 1918), Dunkirk (1940), Rhineland, El Alamein, Anzio and Rome. Tel: 01224 311200.

Grampian Transport Museum — Alford, Aberdeenshire. Opened in 1983 and featuring virtually every form of transport from bicycles to cars to trucks to buses to trains. The collection includes several local vehicles including the steam-powered tricycle known as the Craigievar Express (built in 1895), the 1914 Sentinel steam waggon, the Albion fire engine and the Cruden Bay tram. Tel: 019755 62292.

Grassic Gibbon Centre — Arbuthnott, 7½ miles (12km) southwest of Stonehaven. Opened in 1992 to celebrate the life and works of Arbuthnott-raised author Lewis Grassic Gibbon (1901–35), born James Leslie Mitchell, whose works include *The Thirteenth Disciple* (1931), the *Scots Quair* trilogy (1932–4) and *Spartacus* (1933). It has an exhibition of his writings and possessions. Gibbon is also interred in Arbuthnott. Tel: 01561 361668.

Haddo House — 1½ miles (2.5km) north of Tarves, 5 miles (8km) northwest of Ellon, Aberdeenshire. A Palladian style mansion built for the Gordon family in 1732 to a design by William Adam and refurbished in the 1880s. The house has a collection of fine art including many family portraits. Outside there is a terrace garden, spring and summer bedding and a lime tree walk leading to Haddo Country Park, established in 1979 and covering 180 acres (73ha). It has woodland, grassland and a lake with 1 mile (1.6km) long central drive from Haddo House to the deer park. The house and gardens were opened to the public by the National Trust for Scotland in 1979. Tel: 01651 851440.

Hallforest Castle — 1 mile (1.6km) west of Kintore, 4 miles (6km) south of Inverurie. One of the earliest existing towers in Scotland, the early 14th century keep in the ancient forest of Kintore was possibly built as a hunting lodge by Robert the Bruce. It was subsequently presented to the Keith family. The walls stand 60ft (18m) high and are 7ft (2m) thick. It was abandoned around the time of the Civil War but is still in private hands.

Highest point — Ben MacD(h)ui in the Cairngorm mountain range at 4296ft (1309m). (GR: NN989989.) It lies on the Aberdeenshire/Moray border and is the second highest mountain in Great Britain. A creature known as Am Fear Liath Mòr (G. = Big Grey Man), also known as the Big Grey Man of Ben MacDhui or simply the Greyman, is said to haunt the mountain's summit and passes. Described by some as an extremely tall figure covered with short hair, it has also been experienced by climbers as an unseen but disquieting presence.

Huntly Castle — ½ mile (0.8km) north of Huntly. The original fortification on this site between the River Deveron and the River Bogie was a 12th century motte and bailey known as the Peel of Strathbogie which was used by Robert the Bruce during the struggle with England. In the early 15th century this was replaced by an L-plan tower house built by Alexander Seton, Lord Gordon, which in turn was burnt down by the Earl of Moray in 1452. The replacement fortification, built a short distance away in 1460, became known as Huntly Castle in 1506. It was remodelled on a grander scale in the mid 16th century by the 4th Earl of Huntly, but was ransacked in the aftermath of his defeat and death at the Battle of Corrichie in 1562. The castle was further damaged during a siege by James VI in 1594 before it was once again rebuilt by the 1st Marquis of Huntly 1600–06; a giant frieze, dated 1602, on the south front commemorates the Marquis ('GEORGE GORDOVN FIRST MARQVIS

OF HUNTLIE') and his wife ('HENRIETTE STEVART MARQVESSE OF HVNTLIE'). The castle suffered more depredations during the Civil War when it was occupied by Covenanters. After surviving a siege by Jacobites in 1746, it fell into disrepair and was used as a source for local building material. It passed into state care in 1923 and is maintained by Historic Scotland.

Interesting facts — Although the unitary authorities of Aberdeen City, Aberdeenshire and Moray have conveniently been banded together to form the traditional Grampian region for the purposes of this book, care must be taken when using the word '**Grampians**' as nowadays it is more suggestive of the mountain range which straddles the Grampian and Highland region. For instance, Ben MacDhui, the highest mountain in Grampian, is part of the Cairngorm Mountains in the larger Grampian range and as such is only the second-highest mountain in the 'Grampians' behind Ben Nevis, situated in the Highlands. **Dr Alexander Garden** was born in January 1730 in Birse, Aberdeenshire. He emigrated to America to practise medicine in South Carolina, where his father, the Rev. Alexander Garden, had gone to minister to a congregation in Charleston. The younger Garden arrived in April 1752 and started work in Prince William Parish. In his spare time he collected and studied flora and fauna and corresponded frequently with Swedish botanist Carolus Linnaeus, who named the flowering plant gardenia after him. **Ramsay MacDonald** was Labour Prime Minister in 1924 and again 1929–35. Recent letters discovered at the National Archives in Kew reveal that following the death of his wife, Margaret, from blood poisoning in 1911, he engaged in a 15-year relationship with Lady Margaret Sackville, youngest child of the 7th Earl de la Warr. The collection of love letters, of which there are about 150, were kept in the home of Lady Margaret's bank manager in Cheltenham after her death in 1963 before being handed to the Historic Manuscript Collection. **Johnston Gardens** in Aberdeen is a small park covering only 2.5 acres (1ha) but named Britain's best public park in 2002. Featuring a waterfall, ponds, rockeries and a rustic bridge, its displays of alpines and spring bulbs have helped the city win the Britain in Bloom title no less than nine times in a row. The late comedian **Mike Reid** (1940–2007) became Baron of Troup in May 2007 after winning the vote of the local community of Gardenstown, near Banff.

Islands — The 37 named islands in the Grampian region (all in the Cromarty Shipping Area) are as follows. Islands in the Moray Firth: **Arthur's Point** (GR: NJ405651); **Boar's Head Rock** (GR: NJ289679); **Bow Fiddle Rock** (GR: NJ495688); **Collie Rocks** (GR: NJ705652); **Covesea Skerries** (GR: NJ197719); **Craigan Roan** (GR: NJ395645); **Craigenroan** (GR: NJ445675); **East Muck** (GR: NJ435670); **Halliman Skerries** (GR: NJ213722); **Little Skerries** (GR: NJ221712); **Ooze Rocks** (GR: NJ230716); **Skerrie** (GR: NJ111693); **West Muck** (GR: NJ424665). Islands in the North Sea: **Ararat** (GR: NO795665); **Blackdog Rock** (GR: NJ965137); **Brighead Bush** (GR: NO836715); **Couts Rocks** (GR: NO823700); **Craiglethy** (GR: NO880813); **Criagmaroinn** (GR: NO935959); **Dunbuy** (GR: NK110372); **Dunnicaer** (GR: NO884846); **Forley Craig** (GR: NO873779); **Hare Craig** (GR: NK123401); **Kirkton Head** (GR: NK120505); **Long Meg** (GR: NO896895); **Maut Craig** (GR: NK097590); **May Craig** (GR: NO938967); **Meikle Mackie** (GR: NK136427); **Red Man** (GR: NO895888); **Scotstown Head** (GR: NK120519); **The Hassy** (GR: NK103586); **The Ron** (GR: NK111579); **The Skares** (GR: NK090331); **The Skellies** (GR: NK108583); **The Skerry** (GR: NK140432); **The Veshels** (GR: NK073320). There is one island in Peterhead Bay: **Keith Inch** (GR: NK140460), part of the docks at Peterhead.

James Dun's House — Schoolhill, Aberdeen. A restored two-storey Georgian house built in 1769 and once the home of James Dun, rector of Aberdeen Grammar School. Formerly housing a museum, it is currently occupied by a café and hairdressing salon.

James McGrigor Monument — Duthie Park, Aberdeen. A 70ft (21m) high granite obelisk in memory of military surgeon James McGrigor (1771–1851). It originally stood in the grounds of Marischal College, of which he was lord rector, but was relocated to its present site in the 1890s.

Keith & Dufftown Railway — Also known as the Whisky Line. A heritage railway operating for 11 miles (18km) through forest and farmland from Keith Town station to Dufftown via Drummuir. The original line opened in the 1850s and became part of the Great North of Scotland Railway in 1866. Closed in 1995, it was reopened by volunteers in 2001. Tel: 01340 821181.

Kildrummy Castle and Garden — Kildrummy, 14 miles (23km) southwest of Huntly. The ruins of a 13th century castle built by Gilbert de Moray. In plan it resembles the shape of a shield with six round towers. The castle was captured in 1296 by the English, who may have built some of the structure, and it was captured by the English again in 1306 after being betrayed by the castle's blacksmith, who reportedly received his reward in molten gold which was poured down his throat. A further siege was thwarted by Lady Bruce in 1335 but the castle later fell to David II. It was then held by the Crown, the Elphinstone family – who added a tower house in the 16th century – and the Erskine family. The last occupant, John Erskine, Earl of Mar, used the castle as the centre of preparations for the Jacobite rising of 1715. After the failure of this uprising the castle was forfeited and abandoned. Once known as 'the Queen of Highland castles' it is now in the care of Historic Scotland. The extensive gardens include four ponds laid out below the ruins.

Kindrochit Castle — Braemar, 14 miles (23km) southwest of Ballater. Ruins of a royal castle on the Cluny Water originally dating to the 11th century. It was probably built in wood by Malcolm III and was used by Robert II as a hunting lodge in the late 14th century. In 1390 it was given to Malcolm Drummond, who added a tower house. The castle was abandoned by the 17th century.

King's College Chapel — High Street, Old Town, Aberdeen. Dating from 1500, the oldest part of the University of Aberdeen. A collegiate church founded by William Elphinstone, Bishop of Aberdeen (1431–1514) and originally dedicated to the Virgin Mary, the chapel survives alongside the Ivy Tower and the Cromwell Tower, built in 1658. Internally the chapel retains its original ceiling and some furnishings including the choir stalls, while the windows date from the 19th and 20th centuries.

Kinloss Abbey Kinloss, $1^1/_2$ miles (2.5km) northeast of Forres. Located near Findhorn Bay, the Cistercian abbey, dedicated to St Mary, was established c.1150 by David I with the help of monks from Melrose Abbey. It was itself the mother house of foundations at Culross (in 1217) and New Deir (in 1219). The abbey was damaged by fire in 1269 and rebuilt on a grander scale; a spired bell tower was erected at the end of the 15th century. In the late 14th century it was investigated by Rome after reports of scandalous behaviour by the abbot and monks, and there was further scandal in 1492 when the abbot, William Butler, killed a man in the cloister. The abbey was severely damaged by a flood in 1528. The 23rd abbot, Robert Reid, appointed in 1531, inspired a revival, employing an artist and gardener to help in the rebuilding. Employed as a diplomat by James V to negotiate a peace agreement with England and in the arrangement of royal marriages, he was made Bishop of Orkney in 1541. His nephew Walter Reid, a supporter of the Reformation, was the last abbot of Kinloss and acquired the abbey's lands after its secularisation, gradually selling them off. The abbey fell into disrepair after the Reformation, the bell tower collapsing in the 1570s. Much of the stone was used in local buildings and to build the Cromwellian fort at Inverness.

Kinnaird Castle Kinnaird Head, Fraserburgh. A tower house built on Kinnaird Head on the Buchan Coast in 1570 by Alexander Fraser, and converted into a lighthouse in 1787. Only the central tower of the original castle remains.

Kinnaird Head Lighthouse Kinnaird Head, Fraserburgh. Originally built by engineer Thomas Smith on the corner of a tower of Kinnaird Head Castle, the lighthouse began operating in 1787. Alterations were made in the 1820s when a new lantern was installed and accommodation for the lighthouse keepers was constructed. A new automatic light was established in 1991, when the original lighthouse became the Museum of Scottish Lighthouses. It houses a collection of artefacts related to Scottish lighthouses including lenses and equipment. There is a gallery celebrating the Stevenson family of lighthouse engineers. Tel: 01346 511022.

Kintore Town House The Square, Kintore, 4 miles (6km) southeast of Inverurie. A substantial two-storey building with striking curved stairs, built 1737–47 at the expense of the Earl of Kintore. It originally housed a council room, school room and town gaol, as well as providing storage for rents paid in kind by agricultural tenants.

Lang Stane o'Craigearn Craigearn, 5 miles (8km) southwest of Inverurie. One of the tallest standing stones in Aberdeenshire, a granite monolith 11ft 6in (3.4m) high and 9ft (2.7m) wide.

Leith Hall and Garden $^1/_2$ mile (0.8km) north of Kennethmont, 6 miles (10km) south of Huntly. Originally a 17th century rectangular tower house, the home of the Leith family from c.1650 until 1945 is set in a 286 acre (116ha) estate with a 6 acre (2.5ha) garden. The mansion and courtyard were added during the late 18th and early 19th century, the final addition being the west wing in 1868. There is an exhibition recounting the Leith family's military experiences and including memorabilia dating from 1745–1945. The house is said to be haunted by John Leith, who was murdered in 1763. The garden includes herbaceous borders and a rock garden, while the estate has ponds, 18th century stables and an ice house. The house, gardens and the family's collections of furniture and fine art were given to the National Trust for Scotland in 1945. Tel: 01464 831216.

Leslie Castle Leslie, 12 miles (19km) west of Inverurie. Founded after a baronial granted to Bartholf or his son Malcolm, the original motte and bailey castle was replaced in the 14th century by a stone castle consisting of a square tower, rising the whole height of the castle with turreted towers connected to the main tower. The barony remained in the possession of the Leslie family till 1620 when George Leslie, 8th Baron of That Ilk, mortgaged it to John Forbes of Enzean. William Forbes, John's son, who succeeded his father in the barony to became the first Forbes of Leslie, rebuilt the castle in 1651 as appears in an inscription on one of the interior walls, dated 17th June 1651 and he placed the Forbes coat of arms over the entrance to the castle, with the inscription 'Haec Corp. Sydera mentem'. The barony was sold soon afterwards; Leslie Castle was inhabited until the early 19th century but was then allowed to fall into disrepair. The moat was filled and the fine gardens and ornamental trees cut down. The castle has been recently restored.

Loanhead Stone Circle $^1/_2$ mile (0.8km) north of Daviot, $4^1/_2$ miles (7km) north of Inverurie. A recumbent stone circle dating to the 3rd millennium BC, with two concentric circles of stones surrounding a low cairn with kerb. The outer circle of ten stones has an internal diameter of 64ft (19.5m), the inner ring has a diameter of 54ft (16.5m). The site is maintained by Historic Scotland.

Maggie's Hoosie Inverallochy, 3 miles (5km) east of Fraserburgh. A preserved early 19th century fisherman's two-bedroom cottage. The home of Maggie Duthie (1867–1950), it fell into disrepair after her death but was later renovated and restored to its appearance in the late 19th century, featuring appropriate and, in some cases original, furnishings.

Maiden Castle 6 miles (10km) northwest of Inverurie. A small Iron Age hill fort with a stone wall and earth rampart and ditch. It stands in beech woodland at one end of the Maiden Causeway on the slopes of Bennachie, with Mither Tap (see separate entry) at the other end.

Mar Lodge Estate An estate in the Cairngorms National Park to the west of Braemar and centred on Mar Lodge, built in 1895 by the Duke of Fife to look like a German hunting lodge. Covering 113 sq miles (293 sq km), the landscape includes (with the exception of Ben Nevis, the highest) four of the five highest mountains in the UK: Ben Macdui, 4295ft (1309m), Braeriach, 4252ft (1296m), Cairn Toul, 4236ft (1291m) and Sgor an Lochain Uaine, 4127ft (1258m). The estate, largely consisting of forest, hills and moorland, was purchased by the National Trust for Scotland in 1995. Tel: 013397 41433.

Marischal College and Museum Broad Street, Aberdeen. Founded in 1593 by George Keith, Earl Marischal of Scotland, on the site of a Franciscan friary, the college was united with King's College in 1860 to form the University of Aberdeen. It now serves as the university's city-centre site and is used for ceremonies and the home of the museum. The massive granite edifice with a frontage of more than 400ft and 80ft (24m) high, is reputedly the second largest granite building in the world (after the Escorial Palace in Spain). The college was rebuilt in the 1830s and 1840s to a design by Archibald Simpson and was extended 1895–1906 by Alexander Marshall Mackenzie. The museum, founded in 1786, features collections of ancient Egyptian and Classical antiquities, Scottish prehistory and numismatics. Tel: 01224 274301.

Midmar Kirk — 15 miles (24km) west of Aberdeen. A recumbent stone circle in the graveyard of Midmar church, 55ft (17m) in diameter and originally consisting of five stones, a recumbent stone and two flankers. The recumbent stone is 14ft 9in (4.5m) in length and its matching shaped flankers are 8ft (2.5m) tall. The graveyard was landscaped around the circle in 1914, possibly removing traces of a central cairn.

Mill of Benholm — Benholm, 11 miles (18km) southwest of Stonehaven. A restored water-powered meal mill located on a site possibly occupied by a mill since the 13th century. It was bought by Kincardine & Deeside District Council in 1982, on the death of the last miller. Tel: 01561 361969.

Mither Tap — 5 miles (8km) northwest of Inverurie. An Iron Age hill fort located on a tor on the edge of Bennachie Forest at an elevation of 1699ft (518m). The outline of the fort is marked by two stone walls in varying states of collapse. A track known as the Maiden Causeway leads from this fort to another small Iron Age fort nearby known as Maiden Castle (see separate entry). One theory is that this was the scene of the battle of Mons Graupius in AD 84.

Moray Motor Museum — Bridge Street, Bishopmill, Elgin. A collection of vintage motorcycles and cars housed in converted mill buildings. Tel: 01343 544933.

Mortlach Castle — See Balvenie Castle

Mounthooly Doo'cot — 1 mile (1.6km) southwest of Rosehearty, 4 miles (6km) west of Fraserburgh. A 'folly' dovecot in the form of a 12ft (3.5m) square two-storey battlemented octagonal tower. Located on a hilltop, the structure was built in 1800 and forms a notable landmark for fishermen.

Muchalls Castle — 1/2 mile (0.8km) west of Muchalls, 4 miles (6km) northeast of Stonehaven. An L-plan castle overlooking the North Sea, built in the 13th century as a double-groined tower house and expanded into a four-storey courtyard castle by the Burnetts of Leys in 1619. In 1638 a seminal Covenanter gathering took place here prior to the Civil War. The plasterwork ceilings of the principal drawing rooms are among the finest in Scotland.

Muir of Dinnet Nature Reserve — 4 miles (6km) northeast of Ballater. A National Nature Reserve covering 5651 acres (2287ha), located at the southwest corner of the low-lying area on the eastern edge of the Grampians known as the Howe of Cromar. Habitats include heath, fen, bog, loch and birch and pine woodland. The area includes Loch Kinord and Loch Davan.

Museum of Scottish Lighthouses — See Kinnaird Head Lighthouse

Music Hall — Union Street, Aberdeen. The Aberdeen Music Hall was formed from the Assembly Rooms, designed by Archibald Simpson and opened in 1822, and the Concert Hall, added to the north end in 1859 to a design by James Matthews. The two buildings came to be known simply as the Music Hall. The concert hall features a suite of murals painted c.1900 by local artist Robert Douglas Strachan (1875–1950). The building underwent major renovation in the 1980s.

Nelson Tower — Grant Park, Forres. A tower erected on Cluny Hill as a memorial to Admiral Lord Horatio Nelson. The foundation stone was laid on 26 August 1806, less than a year after Nelson's death at Trafalgar on 21 October 1805, and the tower was opened on the seventh anniversary of the battle in 1812. Octagonal in shape, it stands 80ft (24m) high, with an internal spiral staircase of 96 steps to a viewing gallery. Paid for by public subscription and designed by Charles Stewart, the tower has panels commemorating Nelson's victories at Aboukir Bay (1798), Copenhagen (1801) and Trafalgar (1805).

Northfield Farm Museum — New Pitsligo, Fraserburgh. A museum with a collection of historic farming equipment including tractors. Tel: 01771 653504.

Old Royal Station — Station Square, Ballater. The former terminus of the Deeside Railway, used by the royal family and their visitors (including Czar Nicholas II) when they were resident at Balmoral. Closed in 1966, it was restored and reopened in 2001 as a museum and exhibition, including tableaux depicting the arrival of Queen Victoria in 1869 and taking tea in the waiting room in 1900. Tel: 013397 55306.

Peel of Lumphanan — 1/2 mile (0.8km) southwest of Lumphanan, 23 miles (37km) west of Aberdeen. The remains of a 12th century motte and bailey castle built by the Durward family. The motte, which measures 150ft (46m) by 120ft (36.5m), stood 30ft (9m) high and was surrounded by a moat and bank. It may be here that Edward I received the submission of Sir John de Malvill in 1296. During the 15th century a rectangular manor house known as Halton House stood on top of the motte.

Peterhead Maritime Heritage Centre — The Lido, South Road, Peterhead. A museum exploring the influence of the whaling, fishing and oil industries on the port of Peterhead, the largest white fish landing port in Europe.

Picardy Symbol Stone — A 7th century Pictish symbol stone known as the Picardy Stone. It stands 6ft 6in (2m) tall and is incised with a double disc and Z-rod, a serpent and Z-rod, and a mirror symbol.

Pitcaple Castle — Pitcaple, 4 miles (6km) northwest of Inverurie. 15th century Z-plan castle situated beside the River Urie, on the north side of the hill 2 miles (3km) from the Castle of Balquhain. Sir William Leslie of Balquhain resigned the lands of Pethapil (Pitcaple) in favour of his son David on the occasion of David's marriage to Euphemia Lindsay on 5 March 1457. The castle was in the possession of the Leslie family for 300 years, passing to the Lumsdens through the marriage of Janet Leslie, sister of Sir James Leslie, 10th Baron of Pitcaple, to John Lumsden, Professor of Divinity in the University and King's College Aberdeen. Their two daughters, who inherited the castle in 1757, sold it to a relative, Henry Lumsden, a solicitor in Aberdeen, whose descendant, Christopher Burges-Lumsden, still lives with his family in the castle today. When James IV visited the castle in

1511, his host was David Leslie, 3rd Baron of Pitcaple; the room in which James slept is now known as the King's Room. In July 1650, having sailed from Holland and landed at Garmouth on the River Spey on his journey south, Charles II sent word to Lt Col. John Leslie, 7th Baron, that he and his entourage would dine at Pitcaple; Leslie therefore had to hurriedly purchase more provisions to feed the visitors. When Charles crossed the River Urie, he remarked on how the land reminded him of England; the farm has been called 'England' ever since.

Pitmedden House and Garden — Pitmedden, 4 miles (6km) southwest of Ellon. Also known as the Great Garden. A recreation of the formal 17th century parterre walled garden of Pitmedden House. The house was demolished after a major fire in 1807 and rebuilt in 1853. Restoration of the garden, designed in 1675 by Sir Alexander Seton, began in the 1950s and now features over 5 miles (8km) of box hedging, planted in patterns forming six parterres with 40,000 plants. There are also extensive herbaceous borders plus herb and wildlife gardens. The Great Garden was given to the National Trust for Scotland in 1952; the surrounding 100 acre (40ha) estate is adjacent to the Museum of Farming Life, donated to the Trust in 1978 and housing a collection of agricultural and domestic artefacts. Tel: 01651 842352.

Pitsligo Castle — Rosehearty, 4 miles (6km) west of Fraserburgh. The ruins of a 15th century tower house built by the Fraser family on the coast near the fishing village of Rosehearty. It eventually became the home of the Forbes of Pitsligo and during the late 16th century a mansion and courtyard were added to the tower. Its last occupant, Alexander Forbes, a staunch supporter of the 1745 Jacobite rising, was forced to go into hiding after the failure of the rebellion at the Battle of Culloden, and the castle was forfeited and abandoned. Some restoration work was carried out in the 1980s.

Pluscarden Abbey — Barnhill, 5 miles (8km) southwest of Elgin. The only medieval monastery in Britain still inhabited by monks and used for its original purpose. Dedicated to the Blessed Mary, St John the Baptist and St Andrew, Pluscarden Priory was founded c.1230 by the Valliscaulians and Alexander II. Probably burnt during the Wolf of Badenoch's raid on Elgin in 1390, it became a Benedictine foundation in 1454 when it united with Urquhart Priory. It was secularised following the Reformation and, passing through the ownership of several families including the Setons, the Mackenzies of Kintail and Tarbat, the Sinclairs, Earls of Caithness, the Grants of Grant, the Duffs of Braco, the Earls of Fife. The buildings had fallen into disrepair but some of the property was restored in the late 19th century, notably by the 3rd Marquess of Bute. In 1943 the priory was given by the Marquess's son to Benedictine monks from Prinknash Abbey, Gloucestershire, who took up residence in 1948. The buildings have since been considerably restored and the transepts reroofed. Pluscarden became an abbey in 1974.

Prisons — **Aberdeen**, Grampian Place, Aberdeen. Also known as Craiginches. Built in 1881 and the site of the last execution in Scotland, when Henry John Burnett was hanged in 1963 for the murder of merchant seaman Thomas Guyan. Now housing remand and adult male convicted prisoners. Operational capacity: 155. Tel: 01224 238300.

Peterhead, South Road, Peterhead. Built in 1888, the prison now has a specialist unit for treatment of sex offenders. In 2008 plans were announced to close Aberdeen and Peterhead prisons and build a new prison on the Peterhead site, to be called HMP Grampian.

Provost Ross' House — Shiprow, Aberdeen. Built in 1593 by Andrew Jamieson and occupied in 1702 by Provost John Ross. Restored by the National Trust for Scotland in the 1950s, it was for a time the home of the Aberdeen Maritime Museum.

Provost Skene's House — Guestrow, Aberdeen. One of the oldest town houses in Aberdeen, dating from 1545 and now housing a museum. The rooms retain period settings with appropriate décor and furnishings, plus items relating to local history including a Regency parlour and an Edwardian nursery. There is also a collection of costumes. Tel: 01224 641086.

RAF Lossiemouth — Lossiemouth, 5 miles (8km) north of Elgin. Opened in May 1939 as a training school but handed over to Bomber Command during World War II, when it was used by the squadron of Lancasters which sank the German battleship *Tirpitz* in November 1944 at Tromso, Norway. The base became HMS *Fulmar* in 1946, concentrating on Fleet Air Arm operations. Since 1972 it has reverted to RAF Lossiemouth and operations include search and rescue, early warning and maritime strike/attack. It is the home of 12, 14 and 617 (The Dambusters) Squadrons and is one of the RAF's main bases in Britain.

Ramsar sites — There are seven RAMSAR sites in Grampian: Cairngorm Lochs, Loch of Skene, Loch of Strathbeg, Loch Spynie, Moray & Nairn Coast, Muir of Dinnet, Ythan Estuary & Meikle Loch.

Rivers — The **Dee** rises in the Cairngorms on the plateau of Braeriach above Braemar and flows east for 87 miles (140km), entering the North Sea at Aberdeen. There are falls at the Chest of Dee and the Linn of Dee. Tributaries include Lui Water, Quoich Water, Feugh Water, Gairn Burn, Clunie Water and Callater Burn. The river can be divided into three sections: Upper Dee – Mar Lodge to Aboyne Bridge; Middle Dee – Aboyne Bridge to Banchory; Lower Dee – Banchory to Aberdeen. The river is especially well known for its salmon fishing, and also supports sea trout and brown trout. The 17 mile (27km) stretch between Braemar and Ballater has become known as Royal Deeside, as Balmoral Castle is a popular holiday retreat of the royal family. See also Royal Deeside.

The **Don** rises in the Grampians, flows east and enters the North Sea at Aberdeen, a distance of 78 miles (126km). Its tributaries include Conrie Water, Ernan Water, Water of Buchat, Leochel Burn and the River Urie. It is a good river for salmon fishing and also supports sea trout and brown trout.

The **Lossie** is 31 miles (50km) long and flows north and northeast through Moray, passing through Elgin to join the sea at Lossiemouth. Its main tributaries are the Leanoch Burn and the Back Burn. Close to Lossiemouth it is joined by the Innes Canal and Spynie Canal, features associated with the drainage of the area.

The **Spey**, at 107 miles (171km) the second longest river in Scotland, rises at Loch Spey in the Corrieyairack Forest, flowing east and northeast to enter the Moray Firth at Spey Bay. A good river for salmon and trout fishing, it is also notable for the many whisky distilleries along its length. Its tributaries include the Truim, Calder, Feshie, Nethy, Dulnain, Avon, Livet, Aberlour, Rinnes and Fiddich.

Robert Gordon University — Schoolhill, Aberdeen. The beginnings of Robert Gordon University date to 1750 and the establishment of Robert Gordon's Hospital following a bequest by a wealthy Aberdeen merchant to found a residential school for educating boys. In 1881 this became a co-educational day school with evening education for adults and the name was changed to Robert Gordon's College. In 1903 Robert Gordon's Technical College was born; in 1965 this was renamed Robert Gordon's Institute of Technology (RGIT) and in 1991 the Robert Gordon Institute of Technology. University status was awarded in 1992. With around 13,000 students, the university has three faculties: Design and Technology, Health and Social Care, and the Aberdeen Business School. There are two campuses, at Garthdee and Schoolhill. Norman Foster designed buildings at Garthdee to house the Aberdeen Business School and the Faculty of Health and Social Care, and there is also a new sports centre. Tel: 01224 262000.

Rodney's Stone — 4 miles (6km) west of Forres. A Pictish Class II upright cross-slab discovered in 1781. Now located in the grounds of Brodie Castle, it stands 6ft 4in (1.9m) high; a cross is inscribed on its west face and fish monsters, an elephant, double disc and Z-rod on the east side. It also bears an ogham inscription. There is some confusion as to how it gained its name, which derives either from that of the gravedigger, named Rotteny, who found it, or from the victory of Admiral Rodney at the Battle of the Saints in April 1782.

Rothes Castle — Rothes, 9 miles (15km) southeast of Elgin. A 13th century castle built by Peter de Pollock on a hill above the village of Rothes. The castle was visited by Edward I in 1296. By the end of the 14th century it had passed into the hands of the Leslie family, later Earls of Rothes. The castle was abandoned in the 17th century and is believed to have been slighted by locals to prevent it being used as a stronghold by brigands. The ruins were used for building materials for the village of Rothes during the 19th century and today only part of one curtain wall remains standing.

Royal Deeside — The name given to an area in the valley of the River Dee including Braemar, Ballater and Balmoral Castle, the summer residence of the royal family. See also River Dee.

RSPB Fowlsheugh — Crawton, 4 miles (6km) south of Stonehaven. An RSPB reserve and Site of Special Scientific Interest of 25 acres (10ha) with 230ft (70m) sandstone cliffs supporting large colonies of breeding birds, in particular kittiwakes and guillemots. Tel: 01346 532017.

St Andrew's Cathedral — King Street, Aberdeen. The cathedral of the Diocese of Aberdeen and Orkney in the Scottish Episcopal Church. Built in 1816 to a neo-Perpendicular design by Aberdeen-born Archibald Simpson, one of the first major projects for this leading architect of Aberdeen's 'granite city'. The cathedral has strong connections with the United States and it was in Aberdeen in 1784 that Samuel Seabury of Connecticut was consecrated Bishop for America, the first Anglican bishop outside the British Isles. The cathedral was extended in the 1880s and refurbished in the 1930s, when the ceilings of the north and south aisles were decorated with the crests of the American States. A porch was added in 1911.

St Cyrus Nature Reserve — St Cyrus, 16 miles (26km) southwest of Stonehaven. A coastal National Nature Reserve of sand dunes, beach, grassland and cliff, providing a habitat for a variety of butterfly and moth species and also for a wide number of breeding birds such as tern and fulmar. Tel: 01674 830736.

St Machar's Cathedral — The Chanonry, Old Aberdeen. A church is reputed to have been founded on this site on a bend of the River Don by St Machar. This early church was replaced in the late 12th century and succeeded by ever grander edifices in the following two centuries. The cathedral was officially founded in 1424. The south transept and nave was the work of Bishop Gavin Dunbar in the 1520s; the striking oak carved ceiling of the nave is flat and has 48 shields carved in three rows, each row representing in turn the kings of Europe, the Pope and clerics of Scotland, and the king of Scotland and his nobles. Around the ceiling is a frieze listing the bishops of Aberdeen until the Reformation and the monarchs of Scotland from Malcolm II to Mary, Queen of Scots.

Scottish Tartans Museum — Mid Street, Keith. Opened in 2000 and has displays of 700 different tartans. Exhibits include an 18th century pattern book and a 23ft (7m) long kilt belonging to the Duke of Sussex. Displays show the variations in tartan from period to period.

Slain's Castle — Cruden Bay, Aberdeenshire, 6 miles (10km) southwest of Peterhead. Located on a site overlooking the North Sea, the castle was constructed around an existing tower house in 1597 by the 9th Earl of Erroll. Significant rebuilding has since been carried out, most recently in 1837. Altered in 1664 when a corridor was inserted within the courtyard, it was rebuilt in 1836 and faced with granite. At one time it had three extensive gardens. After more than 300 years of occupation by the Errolls, the castle was sold in 1916 and subsequently fell into disrepair. It was bought by shipping magnate Sir John Ellerman, who in turn gave it up in 1925; its roof was removed to avoid paying taxes and it is now a ruin.

sport: general — **Glenshee Ski Centre**, Cairnwell, Braemar, Aberdeenshire. Located in the Cairnwell Pass where skiing has been popular since the 1930s. The ski centre is the largest in the UK, with 21 lifts and 36 runs over four mountains and three valleys covering 2000 acres (800ha). Tel: 013397 41320.

football — **Aberdeen** were founded in 1903 by the merger of three Aberdeen clubs: Aberdeen, Victoria United and Orion. Having joined the Scottish Football League in 1904, they successfully applied to join the Scottish First Division for the 1905–06 season and have remained in the top flight of Scottish football ever since, a feat only matched by Celtic and Rangers. They are winners of the Scottish League championship in 1955, 1980, 1984 and 1985, the Scottish Cup in 1947, 1970, 1982, 1983, 1984, 1986 and 1990 and the Scottish League Cup in 1956, 1977, 1986, 1990 and

1996. In addition they won the European Cup Winners' Cup in 1983 and the European Super Cup in 1984. They adopted their red and white colours in 1939. Nicknamed The Dons or The Sheep, their home ground is Pittodrie Stadium (Pittodrie means 'hill of dung'). Tel: 01224 650434.

Elgin City were founded in 1893 by the merger of Elgin Rovers and Vale of Lossie. They played in the Highland League until they were granted Scottish Football League status in 2000. Nicknamed City or The Black and Whites, their colours are black and white stripes; their home ground is Borough Briggs. Tel: 01343 551114.

Peterhead were founded in 1890 and played in the Aberdeenshire League and Highland League until they were granted Scottish Football League status in 2000. Nicknamed The Blue Toon after their traditional blue strip, their home ground is Balmoor Stadium. Tel: 01779 478256.

Spynie Palace

$1\frac{1}{2}$ miles (2.5km) north of Elgin. The remains of the palace of the Bishops of Moray, located above Loch Spynie which at the time was a sea loch, providing access to the sea. It was established on the site of the short-lived Cathedral of Moray, built in the early 13th century, but remained the bishops' residence until 1686, long after the cathedral had been replaced by the one at Elgin. Most of the existing ruins relate to 14th century rebuilding following the destruction of the palace by Alexander Stewart, the 'Wolf of Badenoch', but the site also includes a substantial six-storey 15th century tower house, started by Bishop David Stewart in 1461 and known as David's Tower. After the palace ceased to be an episcopal residence the building fell into disrepair. The site passed into state care in 1973 and is maintained by Historic Scotland.

Statues in Aberdeen

Adjacent to Union Terrace Gardens stands a colossal bronze statue of William Wallace by W G Stevenson; also near the gardens are a bronze statue of Robert Burns and seated figure of Prince Albert by Charles Marochetti. In front of Robert Gordon's College is the bronze statue of General Gordon by T S Burnett. At the head of Queen's Road stands a bronze statue of **Queen Victoria**, erected in 1893 by the royal tradesmen of the city. Near the Cross stands the granite statue of **George Gordon**, 5th Duke of Gordon. In Duthie Park is a 70ft (21m) high obelisk of Peterhead granite to the memory of **Sir James McGrigor** (1778–1851), military surgeon and director-general of the Army Medical Department, and three times elected lord rector of Marischal College. Originally erected in the square of the college, the obelisk was moved to Duthis Park in the 1890s when the college was extended. In the grounds of Aberdeen Grammar School is a statue commemorating **Lord Byron**.

Sueno's Stone

Forres. Also known as the Forres Pillar. The largest surviving Pictish symbol stone in Scotland, standing 23ft (7m) high and dating to the 9th century. On one side is a ringed Celtic cross and on the other is a detailed battle scene with cavalry, infantry and decapitated bodies and heads. It is now protected from the elements by a reinforced glass case.

Tap o' Noth

$1\frac{1}{2}$ miles (2.5km) northwest of Rhynie, 7 miles (11km) southwest of Huntly. A walled Iron Age hill fort, the second highest in Scotland, on the conical summit of 1848ft (563m) Tap o' Noth. There is a single wall, constructed of stone vitrified apparently by intense heat, on the crest, with traces of a second wall further down the hill. The fort seems to have been rectangular, measuring 330ft (100m) by 100ft (30.5m).

Tolbooth Museum

Castle Street, Aberdeen. A museum housed in Aberdeen's former courthouse and prison, built 1616–29. The history of the dispensing of justice in Aberdeen is explored via interactive exhibits and reconstructions. Of particular interest are the cells where over 50 Jacobite prisoners were held after the Battle of Culloden in 1746. Tel: 01224 621167.

Tolquhon Castle

$1\frac{1}{4}$ mile (2km) northwest of Pitmedden, 7 miles (11km) west of Ellon. The remains of a late 14th or early 15th century tower house, originally known as the Preston Tower and extended into a courtyard and mansion 1584–9 by William Forbes, 7th Laird of Tolquhon. It was sold to the Earl of Aberdeen in 1716 and fell into disrepair. Now in the care of Historic Scotland.

Tomintoul Museum

The Square, Tomintoul, Moray, 27 miles (43km) south of Elgin. Local history museum housed in a former bakehouse and based on a collection of artefacts assembled to celebrate Tomintoul's bicentenary in 1976. The museum features a reconstructed farm kitchen and displays on the social, economic and natural history of the area. Tel: 01309 673701.

Tomnaverie

3 miles (5km) northwest of Aboyne. A recumbent stone circle on the crest of a hill consisting of six stones (five erect, one fallen), a recumbent stone and two fallen flankers. The circle is 56ft (17m) in diameter with an inner ring of kerb stones surrounding a cairn. Several stones were re-erected after excavations were carried out in the late 1990s. It stands next to a disused quarry.

Tor Castle

Dallas, 6 miles (10km) southeast of Forres. Also known as the Castle of Dallas. The remains of a mid 15th century castle, abandoned in the mid 17th century.

Towie Barclay Castle

4 miles (6km) south of Turriff, 26 miles (42km) west of Peterhead. A 16th century L-plan tower house, once the clan seat of the Barclays and probably built by the same mason who constructed the castles at Craig, Delgatie and Gight. On 10 May 1639, during the First Bishops' War, a skirmish between Royalists trying to gain Towie Barclay from Covenanters led to the death of David Prat, who is therefore considered by some to be the first fatality of the civil wars which followed. It was restored in the 1970s and 1980s and is not open to the public.

Tugnet Ice House

Tugnet, Spey Bay, 9 miles (15km) northeast of Elgin. Located near the mouth of the River Spey, the industrial-sized ice house was built in 1830 to serve the salmon fishing industry. It has three turf-covered vaulted bays with a single entrance. Ice was collected in winter from special ponds cut between the nearby salmon station (now a wildlife centre) and the shore; the ice was broken up and used to fill the chambers of the ice house. The ice house was last used for its original purpose in 1968 and is now owned by the Whale and Dolphin Conservation Society. Tel: 01249 449500.

University of Aberdeen

The UK's fifth oldest university, founded in 1495 as King's College by William Elphinstone, Bishop of Aberdeen. It was united with the post-Reformation Marischal College in 1860 to form the University of Aberdeen. Arts and divinity were taught at King's College, while law and medicine were studied at Marischal. Women students were admitted to all faculties in 1892. The university is divided into three colleges: Arts and Social Sciences, Life Sciences and Medicine, and Physical Sciences; its main campus is still based around King's College in Aberdeen's Old Town. Its motto is 'The fear of the Lord is the beginning of wisdom'. Former students include MP Alastair Darling, broadcasters Nicky Campbell and James Naughtie and newsreader Sandy Gall. Tel: 01224 272000.

Woods on Your Doorstep — **Den Wood** (47 acres/19ha), Oldmeldrum, a woodland of mixed native species including beech and birch.

Zoology Museum — Tillydrone Avenue, Aberdeen. Part of the University of Aberdeen and located in the university's Zoology Building, the museum is responsible for the university's collections of zoological specimens. These include the skins of 12 North American birds presented by artist Edward Audubon, an egg of the extinct great auk and skeletons of great apes.

Some famous people born in the Grampian region

Calder, Alexander Milne (sculptor) (1846–1923)	Aberdeen
Davidson, Robert (inventor) (1804–94)	Aberdeen
Dyce, William (artist) (1806–64)	Aberdeen
Garden, Mary (singer) (1874–1967)	Aberdeen
Gibb, Bill (fashion designer) (1943–88)	Fraserburgh
Gibbs, James (architect) (1682–1754)	Aberdeen
Glennie, Evelyn (percussionist) (1965–)	Aberdeen
Law, Denis (footballer) (1940–)	Aberdeen
Lawrie, Paul (golfer) (1969–)	Aberdeen
Lennox, Annie (singer) (1954–)	Aberdeen
MacDonald, James Ramsay (politician) (1866–1937)	Lossiemouth
Ogilvie, John (saint) (1579–1615)	Keith
Simpson, Robert (retailer) (1834–97)	Strathspey
Wilson, George Washington (photographer) (1823–93)	Aberdeen
Yeats, Ron (footballer) (1937–)	Aberdeen

Highland

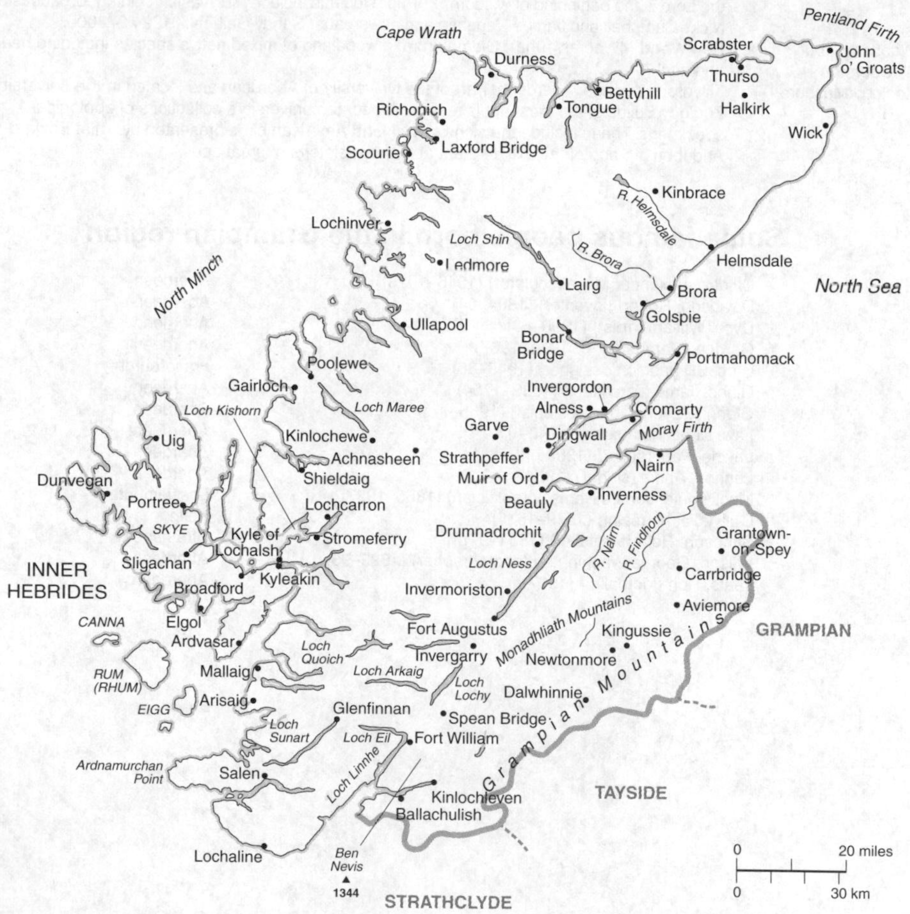
Pentland Firth
Cape Wrath
Durness
Scrabster
John o' Groats
Thurso
Bettyhill
Tongue
Halkirk
Richonich
Wick
Laxford Bridge
Scourie
Kinbrace
R. Helmsdale
Lochinver
Loch Shin
R. Brora
Helmsdale
Ledmore
North Minch
Lairg
Brora
North Sea
Golspie
Ullapool
Bonar Bridge
Portmahomack
Poolewe
Gairloch
Invergordon
Loch Kishorn
Loch Maree
Alness
Cromarty
Garve
Moray Firth
Uig
Kinlochewe
Dingwall
Achnasheen
Strathpeffer
Nairn
Dunvegan
Shieldaig
Muir of Ord
Inverness
Portree
Beauly
Lochcarron
SKYE
Kyle of Lochalsh
Stromeferry
Drumnadrochit
Grantown-on-Spey
Sligachan
R. Nairn
R. Findhorn
INNER HEBRIDES
Loch Ness
Carrbridge
Kyleakin
Broadford
Invermoriston
Aviemore
Monadhliath Mountains
CANNA
Elgol
Fort Augustus
Kingussie
GRAMPIAN
Ardvasar
Loch Quoich
Invergarry
Newtonmore
RUM (RHUM)
Mallaig
Loch Arkaig
Loch Lochy
Dalwhinnie
Grampian Mountains
EIGG
Arisaig
Glenfinnan
Spean Bridge
Loch Sunart
Loch Eil
Fort William
Ardnamurchan Point
Salen
Loch Linnhe
Kinlochleven
TAYSIDE
Ballachulish
Lochaline
Ben Nevis
1344
0
20 miles
0
30 km
STRATHCLYDE

The Highland Council area (G. *Sgìre Comhairle na Gàidhealtachd*) is situated in the Scottish Highlands. It borders Grampian to the east, Tayside to the southeast and Strathclyde to the south. It is the largest local government area in the UK. Its unitary borders of Moray, Aberdeenshire, Perth & Kinross, and Argyll & Bute, as well as Angus and Stirling, also have areas of the Scottish Highlands within their administrative boundaries. The Highland area covers most of the mainland and inner-Hebridean parts of the former counties of Inverness-shire and Ross & Cromarty, all of Sutherland, Caithness and Nairnshire, and small parts of Argyll and Moray. Towns and villages of note include Aviemore, Avoch – a village overlooking Avoch Bay and the Moray Firth on the south side of the Black Isle, and founded according to one legend by survivors of the Spanish Armada of 1588 – Dingwall, Invergordon, Inverness, Nairn, Plockton, Thurso and Wick.

The Scottish Highlands are, as the name suggests, a mountainous region lying to the north and west of the Highland Boundary Fault which runs southwest–northeast from Arran to Stonehaven. The divide between the Highlanders and Lowlanders is manifested in various ways other than geographically, not least in that Gaelic and 'Highland English' is still spoken in the Highlands while the Lallans dialect much used by Robert Burns is almost extinct, despite the efforts of Hugh MacDiarmid to revive it in the mid 20th century. A historical antipathy towards the English might appear to be more prevalent among Highlanders than in southern Scotland, which also adds to the divide. The administrative headquarters of Highland is in Inverness. The region has virtually all the habitats common to the British Isles in one area – coast, forest, mountain, valley, river, loch, grassland and moorland. It is therefore a very popular tourist destination for walkers, climbers and winter sports enthusiasts. The modern Highlands retains an economy based on agriculture, aquaculture and fishing with other industries including tourism and distilling.

The history of the Highlands is dominated by the clan system. A clan is basically a very extended family, arising from one progenitor and owing allegiance to a single clan chief. The clans of the Highlands have various origins including Scots, Irish, Pictish and Norse, and these were later joined by English, Norman and Flemish warlords and adventurers who cut out their own little 'kingdoms'. They gained strength from the disorder over the Scottish monarchy in the 11th and 12th centuries and the following wars of Scottish independence. As recently as the 17th century clans were involved in long-running feuds with neighbours over territorial and financial claims which, if not resolved in court, would end in violence and bloodshed. The last major 'clan' battle in the Highlands was fought at Mulroy in the Braes of Lochaber by a combined force of MacDonalds and Camerons against the Macintoshes on 4 August 1688. The clans also provided mercenaries who fought in Ireland and worked for Lowland lairds. Another favourite practice was raiding a neighbour for cattle, sheep and anything else transportable (commonly known as reiving). By the 17th century the Highlanders were as likely to be raiding in the lowlands as among their fellow highlanders.

During the 17th century Civil War some clans supported the Royalists, some were Covenanters, and others remained neutral. In general the clans supported James II and VII against William of Orange, and the Highlands became the jumping-off point for the subsequent Jacobite uprisings. The result was that following the crushing defeat at Culloden in 1746 the region felt the full weight of government control and repression, which included an attempt to suppress the distinctive Highland culture and clan system. The Heritable Jurisdictions Act removed the feudal authority of the clan chieftains. The Dress Act of 1746 was part of a wider Act of Proscription and specified that, from 1 August 1747, 'no man or boy within that part of Britain called Scotland, other than such as shall be employed as Officers and Soldiers in His Majesty's Forces, shall, on any pretext whatever, wear or put on the clothes commonly called Highland clothes . . . and if any such person shall presume . . . to wear or put on the aforesaid garment or any part of them, every such person so offending . . . shall be liable to be transported to any of His Majesty's plantations beyond the seas, there to remain for the space of seven years.' After the repeal of the Act in 1782, there followed a movement which romanticised the Highland way of life and in part led to Highland garb becoming the national dress of Scotland.

The late 18th century saw the beginning of the Highland Clearances, whereby the clansmen were forced off their land as landlords sought to increase their income by 'improving' their land. This mainly involved removing subsistence crofters from the land, either by force or encouragement, and replacing them with sheep and cattle. Many were moved to the coast to live by fishing or kelp harvesting. Others moved to the growing urban centres in the Lowlands or emigrated to Australia, Canada or the United States.

In Knoydart, Ross, Skye, Tiree, and most notably in the vast tracts of land in Sutherland owned by Elizabeth, Countess of Sutherland, the clearances were particularly noted for the violence used. Lord MacDonald alone cleared most of North Uist and Skye or sold out to the infamous John Gordon of Cluny. The situation was further exacerbated by the potato famine of the mid 19th century. An Act of Parliament in 1886 finally gave crofters security of tenure. Even today, generations after the last Highlanders set sail aboard wooden sailing ships at Ullapool and other ports on the west coast, never again to see the mountains and glens of home, the arguments still rage.

Highland	**Population**			**Area**	
	male	*female*	*total*	*sq miles*	*sq km*
Total	102,297	106,617	208,914	9907	25,659

Local Attractions and Information

Abernethy Forest and Loch Garten: 24 miles (39km) southeast of Inverness. Located within the Cairngorms National Park. The largest native Caledonian pinewood in Britain, which also has an expanse of northern bog. Part of the forest around Loch Garten is an RSPB reserve. Wildlife includes dragonflies, capercaillie, goldeneye, crossbill and osprey. In fact Loch Garten was the first place that the osprey settled on its return to Britain.

Abriachan Gardens: 1 mile (1.6km) southeast of Abriachan, 8 miles (13km) southwest of Inverness. A combination of woodland and landscaped gardens overlooking Loch Ness and adjacent to the Abriachan Wood Community Woodland. The gardens feature collections of primulas, auriculas and perennial geraniums. Tel: 01463 861232.

Administrative headquarters Council Offices, Glenurquhart Road, Inverness IV3 5NX. Tel: 01463 702000.

Airports **Inverness** (INV), Dalcross, 8 miles (13km) northeast of Inverness. Opened as a commercial airport in 1947 after use by the RAF in World War II and owned by Highlands & Islands Airports Ltd. Scheduled flights are operated to numerous UK destinations. Tel: 01667 464000.

Wick (WIC), 1 mile (1.6km) north of Wick. Opened in 1933 as a grass landing strip used by Highland Airways, the airfield became an RAF Coastal Command base during World War II before reverting to civilian use. Operated by Highlands & Islands Airports Ltd with flights to Aberdeen, Edinburgh and Kirkwall. Tel: 01955 602215.

Aluminium Story Visitor Centre Kinlochleven, 9 miles (15km) southeast of Fort William. A visitor centre near the site of the former British Aluminium Company smelter. In addition to housing a local library and information point it also has an audio-visual presentation charting the arrival of heavy industry in the 1900s. Aluminium was produced from 1909 until 2000 when the smelting plant closed. The plant was powered from a hydroelectric generation scheme on the Blackwater Reservoir on Rannoch Moor. Kinlochleven was very much a company town, having grown substantially when the plant arrived, and the visitor centre also explains how the aluminium was produced and the story of some of the local workers. Tel: 01855 831663.

An Teallach 7½ miles (12km) southwest of Ullapool. A mountain in Wester Ross whose two peaks both rate as Munros: Sgurr Fiona (G. = White Peak) at 3474ft (1060m) (GR: NH064837) and Bidein a Ghlas Thuill (G. = Pinnacle of the Green Hollow) at 3484ft (1062m) (GR: NH069844).

Applecross Heritage Centre Applecross, 11 miles (18km) nothwest of Kyle of Lochalsh. Also known as the Clachan Heritage Centre. Located in a restored building next to Clachan Church, the site of the foundation of St Maelrubha's monastery in AD 673, the centre explores the history of Applecross. There is also genealogical information and a photographic archive.

Ardnamurchan Point 4½ miles (7km) northwest of Kilchoan, 36 miles (58km) northwest of Oban. Often cited as the most westerly point in mainland Britain. A 118ft (36m) tall lighthouse was built in 1849 by Alan Stevenson; a large red foghorn, no longer in use, stands on a viewing platform beneath the lighthouse. The light was automated in 1988. A visitor centre in the former head keeper's house, part of which is kept much as it might have been when the keeper was in residence, contains an exhibition on 'The Science of Lighthouses'.

Ardtornish Castle 14 miles (23km) northwest of Oban. The ruins of a castle standing at the end of Ardtornish Point overlooking the Sound of Mull and at the mouth of Loch Aline, within the Ardtornish Estate. Possibly dating from the late 13th century, it was a seat of the Clan Donald, Lords of the Isles. It was here on 13 February 1461 that the Treaty of Westminster-Ardtornish was signed between the Lord of the Isles and the Earl of Ross, by which it was proposed that Edward IV of England and the Earl of Douglas divide Scotland between them. The castle was abandoned by the end of the 17th century, although some crude restoration was attempted 1910–15.

Ardvreck Castle 1½ miles (2.5km) northwest of Inchnadamph, 20 miles (32km) northeast of Ullapool. Ruins of a rectangular three-storey tower house on the shore of Loch Assynt, built in the late 16th century. It was the stronghold of the MacLeods of Assynt. James Graham, Marquis of Montrose was held here having been captured following his defeat at the Battle of Carbisdale in 1650 and prior to being executed in Edinburgh. The castle was abandoned following a siege in 1672 by the MacKenzies, who took some of the stones to build their own Calda House – now also a ruin – nearby.

Ariundle Oakwood 2 miles (3km) northeast of Strontian, 18 miles (29km) southwest of Fort William. A National Nature Reserve consisting of a surviving fragment of ancient oakwood with a wide variety of mosses, ferns and liverworts. The main species is sessile oak and other native trees include alder, brich, hazel, rowan and willow. Wildlife includes more than 200 species of moth plus the northern emerald dragonfly and chequered skipper butterfly. On the woodland floor at various times of year can be found wood sorrel, wood anemone, primrose and bluebell. Managed by Scottish Natural Heritage.

Armadale Castle Armadale, 12 miles (19km) south of Broadford, Skye. Built c.1790 and formerly home to the MacDonalds. The estate was bought in 1971 by the Clan Donald Land Trust which set about restoring the castle and grounds. The Museum of the Isles, opened in 2002, has six galleries of permanent exhibitions charting the history of the isle from its first settlement, plus a seventh gallery which has a new exhibition each year. The castle also houses the Clan Donald Library with more than 7000 books and wide-ranging genealogy resources. The gardens cover 40 acres (16ha) of lawn and woodland. Tel: 01471 844305.

Attadale Gardens Attadale, 2 miles (3km) southwest of Strathcarron. Located above Loch Carron, the 20 acre (8ha) gardens are notable for their spring display of rhododendrons. Other features include water gardens, a Japanese garden and a Himalayan grotto. The Attadale estate, covering 30,000 acres (12,000ha), includes two Munros: Lurg Mhor at 3235ft (986m) and Bidein a'Choire Sheasgaich at 3100ft (945m). Tel: 01520 722217.

Auchgourish Botanic Garden Boat of Garten, 23 miles (37km) southeast of Inverness. The most northerly botanic garden in the British Isles. Opened in 2001, the 10 acre (4ha) gardens include pools and waterfalls, a winter garden, a Japanese garden, a St Andrews garden and a North American rockery. Tel: 01479 831464.

Auchindoune Gardens A Tibetan garden by the Cawdor Burn near the dower house of Cawdor Castle. It was planted after botanist plant collector Frank Kingdom-Ward and Jack Cawdor, 5th Earl of Cawdor, explored the Tsangpo Gorges in Tibet, trying, and failing, to locate the Tsangpo waterfall in 1924. However, the specimens they brought back were planted at Auchindoune on the slopes above the burn. The garden was restored in the mid 1980s. There is also a kitchen garden and arboretum.

Aviemore	An important railway junction in the 19th century which grew substantially after the Cairn Gorm Ski Area was created in the early 1960s. The Aviemore Centre was opened in 1964 with new hotels, indoor sports facilities and a dry ski slope. In the 21st century Aviemore has undergone something of a regeneration to update its rather dated 1960s feel. Enhancements include the Osprey Arena, a leisure arena with swimming pool and a luxury shopping complex.
Ballone Castle	28 miles (45km) northeast of Dingwall. Also known as Tarbat Castle and Castlehaven. Late 16th century Z-plan castle on the coast overlooking the Moray Firth. Abandoned by the mid 18th century, by the 1970s it was reduced to two storeys but in the mid 1990s it was bought by architect Lachlan Stewart and his wife Annie and restored as a private home. The castle is not open to the public.
Balmacara Estate and Lochalsh Woodland Garden	A 6300 acre (2550ha) crofting estate on the Lochalsh peninsula in Wester Ross. Traditional crofting is carried out at Dumbuie and Duirinish. The village of Plockton on the estate is an Outstanding Conservation Area. Lochalsh Woodland Garden on the north shore of Loch Alsh has stands of Scots pine, oak and beech. The estate has been owned by the National Trust for Scotland since 1946. Tel: 01599 566325.
Balnain House	Huntly Street, Inverness. Merchant's house built by the River Ness in 1726, used as a hospital by Government forces after the Battle of Culloden in 1746. The Highland base of the Ordnance Survey in 1880s, it was restored in the 1960s and occupied 1993–2001 by a heritage music centre known as the Home of Highland Music. Tel: 01463 715757.
Barrogill Castle	See Castle of Mey
Battles	See separate table for details of the battles of Auldearn, Carbisdale, Culloden, Glenshiel, and Inverlochy (I) and (II).
Beaufort Castle	3 miles (5km) southwest of Beauly, 11 miles (18km) southwest of Inverness. A Scottish baronial style mansion built in 1885 by the Frasers of Lovat on the banks of the River Beauly. It occcupies the site of a fortress (known as Castle Downie or Dounie) possibly dating from the 11th century, which was severely damaged by a Cromwellian army and razed to the ground after Culloden. The castle is privately owned.
Beauly Centre, The	High Street, Beauly. Opened in November 2002 by the Rt Hon Charles Kennedy MP, the centre is run by the Beauly Firth and Glens Trust and housed in the village's former Catholic primary school. It has a kilt maker, Clan Fraser exhibition and a reconstruction of a village store from the 1920s. Tel: 01463 783444.
Beauly Priory	The Square, Beauly. The ruins of a Valliscaulian priory next to a loop of the River Beauly, founded in the early 13th century by the Bisset family. Later extended by the Frasers of Lovat, the priory was transferred to the Cistercian order in the early 16th century but fell into disrepair following the Reformation. As with its sister house Kinloss Abbey, its stones are believed to have been used to build the Cromwellian fort at Inverness. It passed into state care in 1913 and is maintained by Historic Scotland.
Beinn Eighe National Nature Reserve	Located in the Torridon Mountains on the west coast of Scotland, Britain's first National Nature Reserve was established in 1951. Lying between Loch Maree and Glen Torridon, its habitats include mountains, ancient pinewood and lochs. It was extended in 1962 and 1973 and now covers 18.5 sq miles (48 sq km); the highest peak is Ruadh-Stac Mor at 3314ft (1010m). Wildlife includes golden eagle, Scottish crossbills, pine marten, golden ring dragonflies and the northern eggar moth. There is a Scottish Natural Heritage field station at Anancaun. Tel: 01445 760254.
Ben Nevis	3½ miles (5.5km) southeast of Fort William. At 4406ft (1344m) the highest mountain both in the Grampians and in Great Britain. The 'Ben', as it is fondly known locally, sits majestically at the head of Loch Linnhe, its presence dominating the landscape from all corners of Fort William and parts of Lochaber. The first recorded ascent was made on 17 August 1771 by Edinburgh botanist James Robertson, who was in the region to collect botanical specimens.
Ben Wyvis National Nature Reserve	9 miles (15km) northwest of Dingwall. National Nature Reserve on the ridge of the mountain Ben Wyvis, the highest point of which is Glas Leathad Mòr (G. = 'great green broad slope') at 3432ft (1046m). Around 1 mile (1.6km) of the ridge is covered with fragile woolly hair moss. Wildlife includes pine marten, red grouse and ptarmigan.
Bernera Barracks	¼ mile (0.4km) north of Glenelg. The substantial ruins of a large barracks, built 1719–23 and one of four constructed across the Highlands (Kiliwhimin Barracks, Ruthven Barracks and Inversnaid being the others) following the Jacobite rebellions of 1715 and 1719. The Bernera Barracks, with a garrison of 200 troops, was designed to guard the Skye crossing and thereby act as a deterrent for the local population. Garrisoned until 1797, by which time it had begun to fall into disrepair, it was used as a poor house in the early 19th century.
Blackwater Reservoir	4 miles (6km) east of Kinlochleven, 12 miles (19km) southeast of Fort William. Constructed 1905–09 to supply water to a hydroelectric scheme, power from which was used to run an aluminium smelter in Kinlochleven and is now used to power one at Fort William. The Blackwater Dam, 3000ft (914m) long and 90ft (27.5m) high, was built by 3000 navvies without the use of machinery.
Bright Water Visitor Centre	Kyleakin, Skye. This centre provides information about the island of Eilean Ban (G. = White Island), including the wildlife, the history and the lighthouse. There are interactive displays and a selection of arts and crafts on display. It also celebrates the life of naturalist and author Gavin Maxwell (1914–69), who wrote *A Ring of Bright Water*. He lived from January 1968 to September 1969 in the Eilean Ban cottages, previously occupied by the lighthouse keepers and their families. The cottages now house a museum dedicated to Maxwell and his life and works. Tel: 01599 530040.
Broath Doocot	Auldearn, 2 miles (3km) southeast of Nairn. 17th century dovecot on the site of a motte. A plan of the Battle of Auldearn of 1645 is on display. The dovecot was given to the National Trust for Scotland in 1947.

Brochel Castle 6 miles (10km) north of Clachan, Raasay. Built by the MacSwans in the 15th century. The last inhabitant, Iain Garbh, died in 1671. The ruined remains, once three storeys high, sit on a pinnacle of sheer volcanic rock.

Brochs Among the many brochs (prehistoric circular stone defensive towers) of which there is evidence in the region, the following are among the most notable:

Dunbeath, 19 miles (31km) southwest of Wick. Excavated in the 1860s, the remains were consolidated in 1990 in order to make the structure safe for the general public and to prevent further tree damage to the remains.

Nybster, 7½ miles (12km) north of Wick. Also known as Mervyn Tower. Located on a rocky headland excavated in the 1890s by Sir Francis Tress Barry. The headland was isolated from the mainland by a ditch and there may have been a pre-broch promontory fort on the site from the 1st century BC. The broch had an internal diameter of 23ft (7m) and the walls were 14ft (4.2m) thick. There is a modern monument to Sir Francis Tress Barry nearby.

Ousdale, 4 miles (6km) northeast of Helmsdale. A well-preserved broch dating from the 2nd or 3rd century BC and excavated in 1891. The internal diameter was 24ft (7.3m) with walls up to 14ft (4.2m) thick.

Yarrows, 5 miles (8km) southwest of Wick. The remains of a broch 30ft (9m) in diameter and 15ft (4.5m) high, located on a promontory in the Loch of Yarrows excavated 1866–7 by J Anderson. It was at some point surrounded by dwellings and five skeletons were unearthed from the excavated mound. A wide ditch divided the promontory from the mainland.

Brora Heritage Centre Coal Pit Road, Brora, Sutherland. Charts the history of the village of Brora from earliest times to the present day. Exhibits include artefacts from the local coal and wool industries. Tel: 01408 622024.

Buaile Oscar 8 miles (13km) south of Thurso. (G. = Oscar's Fold). An Iron Age hill fort on the summit of Beinn Freiceadain (G. = Watch Hill). The fort was enclosed by a single wall 12–15ft (3.5–4.5m) thick and encompasses a chambered cairn.

Bucholie Castle 4½ miles (7km) south of John O'Groats. Located on the Ness of Freswick, a promontory divided from the mainland by a trench, the existing ruins are from a 15th century tower built by the Mowat family, and which passed to the Sinclair family in the 1660s. This possibly occupies the site of a broch built in the 12th century, possibly by a Norse pirate named Svein Asleifarson, and known as Lambaborg (a name mentioned in the *Orkneyinga Saga*), although there is some dispute as to whether the two fortifications are one and the same.

Cairngorm Reindeer Centre Glenmore, 5 miles (8km) southeast of Aviemore. Reindeer were reintroduced into Scotland in 1952 by Swedish herder Mikel Utsi at this site near Aviemore. The herd numbers around 130, many of which roam freely over the slopes of the Cairngorms and Glenmore Forest Park. Some reindeer are also paddocked near the centre.

Cairngorms National Park The Cairngorms National Park, opened on 1 September 2003, covers 1467 sq miles (3800 sq km) encompassing a wide variety of habitats including forest, mountain, glen, river and loch. It includes four of the five highest mountains in Scotland (see Grampian: Mar Lodge Estate). Wildlife includes pine marten, wildcats, Scottish crossbill, golden eagle, osprey, capercaillie and freshwater pearl mussel. It is also the home to 16,000 people living in towns and villages such as Aviemore, Braemar, Kingussie and Newtonmore.

Caisteal Bharraich 0.6 miles (1km) west of Tongue, 33 miles (53km) west of Thurso. Also known as Castle Varrich. The ruins of a tower house on a promontory overlooking the Kyle of Tongue. Its date is unknown but it was possibly a 16th century rebuilding of a much earlier tower.

Calda House 1½ miles (2.5km) northwest of Inchnadamph, 20 miles (32km) north of Ullapool. Also known as the White House. The ruins of a house built by the 3rd Earl of Seaforth in 1726 on the shores of Loch Assynt to replace the nearby Ardvreck Castle. Occupied for only a short time, it was destroyed by fire in 1737. What little remains is in an unsafe condition.

Caledonian Canal Following a 60 mile (100km) route from Inverness to Corpach, the Caledonian Canal provided a long hoped-for route between eastern and western Scotland, allowing mariners to avoid the long and often hazardous route round the west of Scotland and through the Pentland Firth. Originally designed by Thomas Telford, construction of the canal was begun in 1803 and it was fully opened in 1822. Ironically, by the time it was finally complete, steam ships could make the passage around Scotland much more easily than the sailing ships in whose era it was designed. Nonetheless, until the arrival of the railway the quickest way from Inverness to Glasgow was by steamer via the Caledonian and Crinan Canals, probably calling at Oban en route. A second phase of construction in the 1840s upgraded the canal to enable it to take larger traffic. It passes through the natural freshwater Loch Lochy, Loch Olch and Loch Ness, and only 22 miles (35km) are within man-made canal banks. There are 29 locks (including a ladder of eight locks known as Neptune's Staircase) and ten swing bridges. The history of the canal is charted at the Caledonian Canal Heritage Centre alongside the locks at Fort Augustus. Tel: 01320 366493.

Cape Wrath The most northwesterly point on mainland Great Britain. Although the area is known for its rough seas the name actually derives from the Norse for 'turning point', as it was in this area that the Vikings would set their course for home. Cape Wrath Lighthouse stands 66ft (20m) high and 400ft (122m) above sea level. It was designed by Robert Stevenson and established in 1828. There are 81 steps to the top of the tower. The lighthouse was converted to automatic status on 31 March 1998.

Carbisdale Castle ½ mile (0.8km) north of Culrain, 15 miles (24km) northwest of Tain. Built in the early 20th century for the Dowager Duchess of Sutherland. It was bought in 1933 by the Christian Salvesen shipping company and used as a refuge during World War II by Haakon VII of Norway after his country was occupied. In 1945 the castle was bequeathed to the Scottish Youth Hostels Association and established as a youth hostel. It is noted for its ghosts, including a phantom piper, a lady in white and a victim from the nearby Battle of Carbisdale; the nursery has been subject to so many strange occurrences that it is known as the 'Spook Room'. Tel: 0870 004 1109.

Castle Girnigoe — 2 miles (3km) north of Wick. The ruins of a 15th century L-plan promontory castle built by the Sinclair family. The neck of the promontory on which it stands is crossed by two ditches to provide further defence. It was replaced by Castle Sinclair, which was built in its outer ward.

Castle Gunn — 7½ miles (12km) southwest of Wick. Also known as Clyth Castle. The meagre ruins of a small tower on the coast which was a stronghold of the Clan Gunn. Possibly established by Snaekoll Gunni in the 13th century, it was abandoned shortly afterwards.

Castle Mestag — ½ mile (0.8km) west of Uppertown, Stroma. A ruined castle situated on a stack 20ft (6m) from the cliffs on the southwest of the island and possibly built by Vikings in the 12th century.

Castle of Brough — ½ mile (0.8km) north of Brough, 8 miles (13km) northeast of Thurso. Also known as the Castle of Braigh. The meagre and much robbed ruins of a castle built on a narrow promontory at the base of Dunnet Head. Its date of origin is unknown, but it is believed to be related to similar castles such as the Castle of Old Wick, which dates from the 12th century. The neck of the promontory was cut across by a flat-bottomed ditch 12ft (3.5m) deep and 40ft (12m) wide.

Castle of Mey — 12 miles (19km) northeast of Thurso. Also known at one time as Barrogill Castle. A 16th century Z-plan castle built by George Sinclair in 1567 and altered in the early 19th century for the Sinclair family to designs by William Burn. The 2000 acre (800ha) estate was bought by the Queen Mother in 1952, at which time the castle was restored. The celebrated gardens are surrounded by the 12ft (3.5m) high Great Wall of Mey, which protects them from the severe winds. The estate is also home to a prize-winning herd of Aberdeen Angus cattle and the Longoe flock of North Country Cheviot sheep. Tel: 01847 851473.

Castle of Old Wick — 1 mile (1.6km) southeast of Wick. The ruins of a 12th century rectangular keep on a promontory south of Wick Bay. Built during the Norwegian rule over Caithness, during its lifetime it was the property of the Cheynes, the Sutherlands, the Oliphants, the Sinclairs, Lord Glenorchy and the Dunbars. The 30ft (9m) wide moat, which can be crossed by a drawbridge, is known as Lord Oliphant's Leap. The castle was abandoned by the 18th century. The site is maintained by Historic Scotland.

Castle Roy — 0.6 miles (1km) north of Nethy Bridge, 4 miles (6km) south of Grantown-on-Spey. The ruins of one of the oldest unmodified castles in Scotland, located on a hill above the Spey Valley and built in 1226 by a son of the Earl of Mar. Its original design, a square tower with curtain wall 7ft (2.1m) thick and 25ft (8m) high, remains largely unchanged. The walls enclose an area of 80ft (24m) by 53ft (16m) with one entrance.

Castle Sinclair — 2 miles (3km) north of Wick. Built in 1606 as a replacement for Castle Girnigoe and situated in the earlier castle's outer ward. Constructed with an eye more for style than defence, it was abandoned after an attack in 1679.

Castle Stuart — 5 miles (8km) northeast of Inverness. Tower house constructed by the Stuarts in 1621 on the site of the ancient home of the Earls of Moray and Stuarts. Abandoned for 300 years, it has recently been restored.

Castle Tioram — 3 miles (5km) west of Ardmolich, 15 miles (24km) southwest of Glenfinnan. Located on the island of Eilean Tioram (aka Dry Island) in Loch Moidart, the castle was a stronghold of the MacDonalds of Calnranald from the 13th century. It was burned down in 1715 by Jacobites led by its former owner, who captured a Government garrison stationed here in an effort to prevent its future use by Government forces. The castle was purchased in 1997 by businessman Lex Brown who wishes to restore the castle as a private residence and clan museum. Although planning consent was received from Highland Council, Scheduled Monument Consent was refused by Historic Scotland. Public access is restricted because of the instability of the building.

Castlehaven — See Ballone Castle

Cawdor Big Wood — 1 mile (1.6km) south of Cawdor, 4 miles (6km) south of Nairn. The remains of an ancient woodland (with planting from the 18th century onwards) close to Cawdor Castle, covering 755 acres (305ha). It contains over 130 species of tree and shrub, including oak, aspen, beech, birch and Scots pine. Wildlife includes capercaillie, herons and crossbills plus red and roe deer.

Cawdor Castle — Cawdor, 4 miles (6km) south of Nairn. A late 14th century or early 15th century tower house built on the Ailt Dearg, and greatly extended in the 17th century in Scottish vernacular style as residential needs overtook concerns of defence. It was built near the site of an earlier fortification which was possibly home to the Thanes of Cawdor (as mentioned in Shakespeare's *Macbeth*). The story goes that the then Thane of Cawdor decided, after a dream, to build a new castle where his donkey decided to rest for the night. As it lay down under a holly tree (the remains of which can be found in the lower levels of the tower), he built the keep around it. It has been radiocarbon dated at 1372. The castle is still the home of the Dowager Countess Cawdor. Rooms include the Thorn Tree Room, the Tapestry Room, the old kitchen, the drawing room, the Pink Room, the Yellow Room and dressing room. The extensive gardens comprise a walled garden dating from the early 17th century, later the kitchen garden and remodelled in the 1980s to create a holly maze and paradise garden; the flower garden, laid out in the early 18th century and developed into herbaceous borders, originally giving late summer and autumn colour when the family was in residence and with a flowering period now extended to begin in the spring; and the wild garden, planted in the 1960s between the castle and the Cawdor Burn, an informal garden created among old woodland and the Cawdor Big Wood. Tel: 01667 404401.

Claish Moss — 5 miles (8km) northwest of Strontian, 23 miles (37km) southwest of Fort William. National Nature Reserve located between the southwest shore of Loch Shiel and Ben Resipol and comprised of a raised bog covered with many varieties of moss, including large clumps of woolly hair moss. Its domes of peat reach a depth of 12ft (3.5m). The moss is particularly notable for its populations of azure hawker and northern emerald dragonfly, and also for wading birds such as greenshank, dunlin and curlew. Covering 1405 acres (568ha) It is also a designated Ramsar site.

Clan Donald Visitor Centre See Armadale Castle

Clan Gunn Heritage Centre Latheron, 15 miles (24km) southwest of Wick. Opened in 1985 and housed in the old parish church, built in 1734, the centre charts the history of one of the oldest clans in Scotland, which has Norse origins. The centre also holds the clan archives.

Clan MacPherson Museum Main Street, Newtonmore, 29 miles (47km) south of Inverness. Dedicated to the Clan MacPherson. Exhibits include the Black Chanter, the Green Banner, Jamie MacPherson's fiddle and the sword of old Cluny. Tel: 01540 673332.

Clan Sinclair Centre 3 miles (5km) north of Wick. Established in 1998 at the former lighthouse keepers' cottages at Noss Head, built by Alan Stevenson in 1849. It provides resources for those studying the history and genealogy of the Clan Sinclair.

Clo Mor Cliffs 7 miles (11km) northwest of Durness. The highest sea cliffs on the British mainland, rising to 920ft (280m).

Clyth Castle See Castle Gunn

Corrieshalloch Gorge National Nature Reserve 11 miles (18km) southeast of Ullapool. A gorge more than $1^1/_2$ miles (2.5km) long and 200ft (60m) deep, cut by the River Droma. Designated a National Nature Reserve in 1967, it is managed by the National Trust for Scotland. The 50ft (15m) plunge of the Falls of Measach can be viewed from a suspension bridge built over the gorge in 1874.

Craigellachie 1 mile (1.6km) south of Aviemore. National Nature Reserve of mature birch woodland on the lower slopes of the Hill of Craigellachie. A nesting site for peregrine falcons, the reserve also has a reservoir, Loch Pulladern and part of Loch Dubh within its boundaries.

Creag Meagaidh 18 miles (29km) southwest of Newtonmore. National Nature Reserve established in 1986 on the north shore of Loch Laggan and encompassing lochs, woodlands and mountains, including the 3701ft (1128m) summit of Creag Meagaidh itself. Wildlife includes hare and ptarmigan. Tel: 01528 544265.

Cromarty Courthouse Museum Church Street, Cromarty. A resource for historians and genealogists housed in the old courthouse and jail which was built in the early 1780s. It retains its 1844 courtroom furnishings on the first floor and there are cells and an exercise yard on the ground floor. Tel: 01381 600418.

Cromarty East Church Cromarty, 16 miles (26km) northeast of Dingwall. A post-Reformation parish church built in 1593 on the site of earlier religious foundations and extended into a T-shape in the 18th century. It was closed for regular worship in the 1990s but continues to be used for community events, weddings and funerals. The church was featured in the BBC's *Restoration Village* in 2006 because of its poor state of repair.

Cromwell's Fort Cromwell Road, Inverness. The remains of a short-lived fort (or citadel) by Inverness harbour, known locally as The Sconce and built 1653–8 by Oliver Cromwell. According to tradition the materials used in its construction were taken from the monasteries of Beauly and Kinross, as well as several other religious sites. The fort was pentagonal in shape, comprising earth ramparts and stone bastions with a moat on four sides and the River Ness on the fifth. It was demolished at the request of the Highland Chiefs to the newly restored Charles II in 1662; excavations have revealed that some of the stone from the fort was reused again to build a quay in the 19th century. A clock tower on the site probably dates from the 18th century.

Cuillin Hills A range of peaks in central Skye, divided by Glen Sligachan into two parts known as the Black Cuillin and the Red Cuillin. The jagged Black Cuillin to the west are composed largely of bare, rough, dark-coloured basalt and gabbro. Although relatively small in area, they provide some of the most severe mountain conditions in the British Isles. The granite hills of the Red Cuillin in the east are more rounded, with vegetation on many of their slopes. The highest point is Sgurr Alasdair in the Black Cuillin at 3258ft (993m).

Culloden Moor 4 miles (6km) east of Inverness. The site of the Battle of Culloden (also known as Drummossie Moor), the last major battle on British soil, fought on 16 April 1746 between 6754 clansmen led by Charles Edward Stuart and 8151 Government troops, including many Scots, commanded by the Duke of Cumberland. Bonnie Prince Charlie (also known as the Young Pretender) had landed at Eriskay and raised his standard at Glenfinnan on 19 August 1745 in an attempt to wrest the British throne from George II and present it to his father James (known as the Old Pretender and the son of the deposed James II). Despite the failure of a supporting fleet from France to reach British shores, the prince set out on what, initially, was a very successful campaign. His army of mainly Highlanders caught the Government forces in Scotland off guard and succeeded in capturing Perth and then Edinburgh following a victory at Prestonpans (21 September 1745). However, the invasion of England, while causing panic in London, had not so far led to a general revolt against George II; it stalled at Derby on 4 December 1745 and the Highland army began its fateful retreat back to Scotland. They won a skirmish at Clifton on 18 December 1745 (the last battle to take place on English soil) and turned back an army attempting to relieve Stirling Castle at Falkirk on 17 January 1746. By February the Jacobites had established a base at Inverness. They left it on 15 April and assembled on treeless, flat Culloden Moor, a site much better suited to the weapons and tactics of their opponents. After a night march to catch the enemy unawares in Nairn proved a tiring and dispiriting failure, the battle took little more than an hour to reach its climax. Government artillery fire goaded the Jacobites into charging. They reached one end of the Government line but were repulsed after fierce fighting and the rest of the charge failed to engage the enemy hand-to hand. Losses amounted to around 2000 Jacobites and just over 300 Government soldiers. In the aftermath, Jacobite supporters were executed, imprisoned or transported and reprisals were taken against Highlanders in general. Bonnie Prince Charlie left the field and eventually escaped back to France. In England, Prince William Augustus, Duke of Cumberland (1721–65), George II's younger son, had the garden flower Sweet William named for him. In Scotland, however, where he is forever remembered as 'Butcher Cumberland', they chose to 'honour' him by giving the name 'Stinking Billy' to the common ragwort, a weed with an unpleasant smell and poisonous to horses and cows. A memorial cairn stands at the place of the most intense fighting, although roads were built and forestry planted across the battlefield itself in the 19th century. More recently attempts at restoring it to the conditions and habitats prevailing in 1746 have been made by the National Trust for Scotland, which was presented with or purchased parts of the battlefield between 1937 and 1998. Leanach Cottage, which stands on the battlefield, has been restored and contains a living history presentation. Tel: 01463 790607.

Dingwall

A burgh at the head of the Cromarty Firth, formerly the administrative centre of Ross and Cromarty. At one time it was a port but it is now an inland market town.

Distilleries

Ben Nevis, Lochy Bridge, near Fort William. Founded in 1825 at the foot of Ben Nevis by 'Long John' Macdonald. Purchased by Joseph Hobbs in 1955 and by Nikka (Japan) in 1989. The water source is the Allt a'Mhuilinn (the Mill Burn). Tel: 01397 700200.

Clynelish, Brora, Sutherland. Founded in 1819 by the Marquis of Stafford as the Brora Distillery and replaced in 1967 by a new distillery. The water source is the Clynemilton Burn. Tel: 01408 621444.

Dalwhinnie, Inverness-shire. Built in 1898 and originally known as the Strathspey Distillery. Its malts are a major component of Buchanan blends. The source of water is the Allt an t'Sluic Burn. Tel: 01528 522240.

Glenmorangie, Morangie, $1\frac{1}{2}$ miles (2.5km) northwest of Tain. Licensed for William Mathieson in 1843 in a converted brewery and rebuilt in the 1880s. Glenmorangie is the best-selling malt whisky in Scotland and the distillery was the first in the country to use steam to heat the stills. It mainly uses ex-bourbon oak casks during maturation rather than the more widely used ex-sherry casks. The distillery only ever employs 16 men. The water source is the Tarlogie Springs. Tel: 01862 892043.

Talisker, Carbost, Skye. Built by the MacAskill brothers in 1830, expanded in 1900 and reconstructed after a fire in 1960. The water source is a burn on Cnoc nan Speireag. Tel: 01478 640314.

Dornoch Cathedral

Dornoch, 5 miles (8km) north of Tain. A cathedral church dedicated to the Conception of the Blessed Virgin Mary and founded by Gilbert de Moravia, Bishop of Caithness (later St Gilbert of Dornoch) in the 13th century. Burnt down by the MacKays of Strathnaver in 1570, it was partially restored in the 17th century for use as a parish church. It was further restored in the 19th century and some of the medieval stonework was revealed in 1924. In December 2000 it was the scene of the christening of Rocco Richie, the son of Madonna and Guy Richie.

Dounreay Nuclear Power Station

$7\frac{1}{2}$ miles (12km) west of Thurso, Caithness. Opened in 1955 as a testing station for fast-breeder reactor technology. The first commercial reactor began operation in 1959 and a second in 1974. Power generation ended in 1994 and the site is due to be decommissioned by 2025. Tel: 01847 802572.

Dunbeath Heritage Centre

Dunbeath, 18 miles (29km) southwest of Wick. A local history museum housed in the village's Old School, and dedicated to the social, natural and economic history of Caithness.

Dunnet Head

$7\frac{1}{2}$ miles (12km) northeast of Thurso. The most northerly point of mainland Britain. Standing almost 300ft (91.5m) above sea level, a lighthouse was established in 1831 by Robert Stevenson. It is 66ft (20m) high with 51 internal steps, and was automated in 1989.

Dunrobin Castle

1 mile (1.6km) northeast of Golspie, 13 miles (21km) northeast of Tain. The seat of the Earls and Dukes of Sutherland, located on the Sutherland coast and originally a tower house possibly dating to the 13th century and extended with a further tower and courtyard in the 17th century. It was remodelled by Sir Charles Barry in the 1840s in the style of a French chateau. The largest house in the Northern Highlands, it has no less than 189 rooms. Damaged by fire in 1915 but restored in the 1920s, it was used as a military hospital during World War I and as a boys' school in the 1960s and 1970s. It is now again a private house, and owned by the Sutherland Trust. There are collections of fine art, furniture and family memorabilia, as well as a museum in the summer house. Tel: 01408 633177.

Dunscaith Castle

$\frac{1}{2}$ mile west of Tokavaig, $7\frac{1}{2}$ miles (12km) southwest of Broadford, Skye. Aka Dun Sgathaich (G. = the Dun of the Shadow). The ruins of a 13th century castle built on the site of an earlier vitrified fort and standing on a 40ft (12m) high promontory overlooking Loch Eishort. The approach from the mainland was defended by a ditch 20ft (6m) wide and 15ft (4.5m) deep. According to legend it was the home of the Queen of Skye, who taught the art of war to the Irish hero Cuchulainn. The seat of the MacDonalds of Skye in the 15th century, it was last occupied in 1570.

Dunskeath Castle

$1\frac{1}{2}$ miles (2.5km) northeast of Cromarty, 17 miles (27km) northeast of Dingwall. A 12th century motte castle located at the mouth of the Cromarty Firth. The visible remains are mostly earthworks.

Duntulm Castle

Duntulm, 19 miles (31km) north of Portree, Skye. The ruins of a 15th century tower located on a promontory 50ft (15m) above sea level. It possibly stood on the site of a Pictish or Norse promontory fort known as David's Fort. The landward side was protected by a ditch. Formerly the seat of the MacDonalds of Sleat, who enlarged the castle in the 17th century, it was abandoned by 1732 and many of the stones used to build Monkstadt House.

Dunvegan Castle

1 mile (1.6km) north of Dunvegan, Skye. A late 14th century tower located on a promontory overlooking Loch Dunvegan. The ancestral home of the Clan MacLeod, it is built on the site of earlier fortifications possibly dating to the 9th century. The tower was built by Alasdair Crotach and

the castle was extended with a 'Fairy Tower' in the early 16th century; more living quarters were added in the 17th and 18th centuries. The various elements of the castle, built over such a long period, were unified by a remodelling carried out in the 1840s. There was no landward approach to the castle before 1748, all visitors having to enter through the sea gate. The castle houses fine art, furniture, arms and armour, and Clan MacLeod memorabilia including the Fairy Flag, said to bring success to the clan chief who unfurls it in times of need. The castle gardens include a formal garden and woodland area. Tel: 01470 521206.

The Eaglestone Strathpeffer, 5 miles (8km) west of Dingwall. Aka Clach an Tiompain (G. = Sounding Stone). A Pictish symbol stone dating to c.AD 600 now located on a hill just above the town, and depicting an inscribed horseshoe above an eagle.

Eas a'Chual Aluinn 4 miles (6km) northeast of Inchnadamph, 19 miles (31km) northeast of Ullapool. The highest waterfall in Britain, with a plunge of more than 650ft (200m).

Edderton Old Church 3/4 mile (1.2km) southeast of Edderton, 4 miles (6km) northwest of Tain. Aka Edderton Free Church. Built c.1745 on the site of an earlier church. In the churchyard stands a Pictish cross-slab, on the west face of which is an incised Celtic cross and on the east face a Latin cross plus a horseman; there are two incised horsemen partly visible above ground level. In 1992 trees were planted around the church, the initial letters of the Gaelic name for each species spelling out the name EADAR DUN – *Eubh* (aspen), *An Fhalm* (elm), *Darach* (oak), *An Fhalm*, *Ruis* (elder), *Darach*, *Ur* (yew), *Nuim* (ash).

Eigg One of the Small Isles of the Inner Hebrides. The beach at Camus Sgiotaig on the northwest coast is renowned for its 'singing sands', caused by the effect of the weather on the white quartz. Area: 11.46 sq miles (29.67 sq km). Population: 67. (GR: NM470865.)

Eilean Donan Castle 1/4 mile (0.4km) south of Dornie, 7 1/2 miles (12km) east of Kyle of Localsh. The former stronghold of the Mackenzies of Kintail, located on an island in Loch Duich and dating from the 13th century. The MacRae family became constables of the castle in the early 16th century. Having been destroyed by fire from three English men-of-war in 1719 when occupied by a Spanish force after the failure of the Jacobite cause at the Battle of Glenshiel, it had virtually disappeared by 1900. However, it was rebuilt for John MacRae-Gilstrap 1912–32 following closely the original design. A bridge to the island was also built. Features include rooms such as the billeting room and banqueting hall, as well as an exhibition on the history of the castle. Tel 01599 555202.

Falls of Glomach 7 miles (11km) northeast of Shiel Bridge, 16 miles (26km) east of Kyle of Lochalsh. One of the highest waterfalls in Britain, plunging 370ft (113m) to the Elchaig Glen. The falls were given to the National Trust for Scotland in 1941, along with 2200 acres (890ha) of surrounding land.

Far North Line A rural railway located wholly within the Highland region, built in the 1860s and which winds its way through spectacular scenery of hill, glen, river and coast. The stations are: Inverness, Beauly, Muir of Ord, Dingwall, Alness, Invergordon, Hill of Fearn, Tain, Ardgay, Culrain, Invershin Halt, Lairg, Rogart, Golspie, Dunrobin, Brora, Helmsdale, Kildonan, Kinbrace, Forsinard, Altnabreac, Scotscalder, Georgemas Junction (the most northerly junction in Britain), Thurso and Wick. The journey between Culrain and Invershin Halt is the shortest distance between two stations on a main line.

Fearn Abbey Fearn, 5 miles (8km) southeast of Tain. A Premonstratensian abbey originally founded at Edderton in the 1220s but transferred to its present location c.1238. Known as 'The Lamp of the North', it was rebuilt during the 14th century. Following the Reformation part of it was used as a parish church until the roof collapsed on the congregation in 1742, killing between 30 and 50 worshippers. A temporary church was erected nearby but in 1772 part of the abbey was rebuilt and again used as a parish church.

Five Sisters of Kintail 14 miles (23km) southeast of Kyle of Lochlash. A mountain range at the head of Loch Duich in Glen Shiel. According to legend the five peaks are the legendary daughters of the king of Kintail, who waited in vain for five Irish brothers to come as promised and take them as brides. Their beauty was preserved by the Grey Magician of Coire Dhunnaid and thus they still wait. They are Sgurr Moraich, 2874ft (876m), Sgurr nan Saighead, 3048ft (929m), Sgurr Fhuaran, 3504ft (1068m), Sgurr na Carnach, 3287ft (1002m) and Sgurr na Ciste Duibhe, 3369ft (1027m).

Floral Hall Bught Lane, Inverness. A set of glasshouses with climatic control opened in 1993 and located in Bught Park by the River Ness. A wide variety of exotic plants grow in a sub-tropical environment and there is a grotto with a pool and waterfall. There are also vivaria with exotic insects and reptiles, a separate cactus house and, outside, several demonstration gardens including a water garden and a Japanese garden. Tel: 01463 713553.

Foinaven and Arkle Foinaven, standing at 2299ft (914m) and Arkle at 2582ft (787m) are adjacent peaks in northwest Sutherland. They are also the names of two steeplechasers, both originally owned by Anne, Duchess of Westminster. Foinavon (note the slightly different spelling), by Vulgan out of Ecilace, was the shock winner of the 1967 Aintree Grand National at odds of 100-1 after a pile-up at the 23rd fence (since known as the Foinavon Fence). In contrast Arkle, a bay gelding foaled 1957 by Archive out of Bright Cherry, is considered by many as the greatest steeplechaser of all time, winning 27 out of his 35 starts including the Cheltenham Gold Cup three times (1964, 1965, 1966), the Irish Grand National (1964), the King George VI Chase (1965), the Hennesey Gold Cup (1964, 1965) and the Whitbread Gold Cup (1965). The Duchess of Westminster had an estate in the area, hence the naming.

Fort Augustus 30 miles (48km) southwest of Inverness. Named for the Duke of Cumberland and built 1729–42 at the southern end of Loch Ness to replace the nearby Kiliwhimin Barracks. It also incorporated a governor's headquarters. Captured and slighted by the Jacobites in 1745, it was rebuilt shortly afterwards but was eventually incorporated into St Benedict's Abbey in the 1890s. The surrounding village is now known by the name Fort Augustus.

Fort George 10 miles (16km) northeast of Inverness. A massive artillery fort and barracks covering 42 acres (17ha) on Ardersier Point, a flat-topped promontory on the Moray Firth. It was designed and built in the 1750s by royal military engineer William Skinner to replace the castle at Inverness, destroyed by the Jacobite army in 1746. Completed in the late 1760s, it has been garrisoned continuously ever since but has never been attacked and its design is therefore virtually unchanged since 1769. Despite still serving as a barracks, parts are open to the public and part of one of the barrack blocks is used by Historic Scotland to provide living history reconstructions. The fort also houses the Regimental Museum of the Queen's Own Highlanders (see separate entry).

Fort William Fort Fort William. The first fort, also known as the Garrison of Inverlochy, was built beside the River Ness by General Monck in 1654; the basic turf and timber structure fell into disuse after the Restoration. A new fort, built in 1690 by General Mackay, was named Fort William, and the modern settlement of Fort William grew around this fort. Remodelled in 1746 after a Jacobite siege, it was abandoned in 1854; the land was eventually bought by the West Highland Railway Co., who used some of the buildings until the mid 20th century when they were demolished.

Fortrose Cathedral High Street, Fortrose. The ruins of a 13th century cathedral dedicated to St Peter and St Boniface, built by Bishop Robert in what was then the bishopric of Ross and extended during the 14th and 15th centuries. Following the Reformation the cathedral fell into disrepair; although partially restored and used as a parish church, much of the stone is believed to have been removed by Cromwell for the building of his fort at Inverness and by locals for village houses. Portions of the south aisle of the nave and chapter house survive. The upper storey of the chapter house was rebuilt in the 19th century as the council chamber and magistrates' court. The site was taken into state care in 1851; the ruins are now maintained by Histoic Scotland and are surrounded by parkland.

Foulis Castle 4 miles (6km) northeast of Dingwall. Foulis (pronounced Fowls) Castle is an 18th century neoclassical mansion built by the Munro family, and incorporating part of an earlier Munro castle possibly dating to the 14th century and destroyed by Jacobites in 1746. The grounds also contain an 11th century motte.

Frank Bruce Sculpture Collection Feshiebridge, 6 miles (10km) southwest of Aviemore. A collection of 12 large sculptures by Scottish artist Frank Bruce, displayed in a walled garden in Inshriach Forest and previously exhibited at the Colleonard Sculpture Garden, Banff.

Freswick House $^{3}/_{4}$ mile (1.2km) southeast of Freswick, $3^{1}/_{2}$ miles (5.5km) south of John O'Groats. A 17th century tower house overlooking Freswick Bay, built by the Mowat family and enlarged by William Sinclair. Latterly known as Freswick Castle, it was restored in the 1970s and is now home of the Wayfarer Trust arts charity.

Glasdrum Wood 13 miles (21km) northeast of Oban. National Nature Reserve designated in 1977 and covering 418 acres (169ha) of ancient woodland on the slopes of Ben Churalain by the shores of Loch Creran. Tree species include oak, ash, birch and hazel; wildlife includes over 20 species of butterfly, of which the rarest is the chequered skipper.

Glen Roy 13 miles (21km) northeast of Fort William. National Nature Reserve designated in 1970 and featuring the 'Parallel Roads' of Glen Roy, the remnants of the shorelines of a series of ice-dammed freshwater glacial lakes formed c.10,500 BC during the Loch Lomond Readvance and located on the 350m, 325m and 260m contour levels. Similar 'roads' occur in nearby Glen Gloy and Glen Spean. Wildlife in the reserve includes golden eagle and red deer.

Glencoe 11 miles (18km) south of Fort William. A steep-sided glen which was the site of the infamous Glencoe Massacre of 13 February 1692. Glen Coe was the home of the MacDonalds, a clan with a reputation as cattle thieves who had a long-standing feud with their neighbours, the Campbells, in Loch Awe and Glen Lyon. Following the 1689 uprising in support of James II, William III offered pardon to any clan swearing an oath of allegiance to him by 1 January 1692. Owing to a mistake, the chief of Clan MacDonald failed to take the oath until a few days after the deadline. Although some other clans had not even attempted to take the oath, the Secretary of State for Scotland decided to set an example by singling the Glen Coe MacDonalds out for punishment: not only were they locally unpopular, their home was relatively easy to attack. A company of Government troops led by Robert Campbell of Glen Lyon were billeted with the MacDonalds on 1 February. At a prearranged signal, they attacked the MacDonalds at 5am on 13 February. The 130 troops (including 12 Campbells) killed 38 MacDonalds and more died from exposure over the next few days. Although seen by many as part of the long-running Campbell/MacDonald rivalry, the massacre was in reality more to do with the Government attempt to suppress the Highlands. The glen itself is dominated by Bidean Nam Bean at 3766ft (1148m), below which is the hidden valley of Allt Coire Gabhail where the MacDonalds kept both their cattle and those stolen from neighbouring clans. The National Trust for Scotland purchased 12,800 cres (5180ha) of the area 1935–7. A new visitor centre opened in 2002 and caused some small controversy at the time when its first manager had the surname Campbell. Tel: 01855 811307.

Glencripesdale 6 miles (10km) west of Strontian, 29 miles (47km) southwest of Fort William. National Nature Reserve on the south shore of Loch Sunart and including native woodland, heath and bog. The woodland, in a cool and damp situation by the loch, is particularly noted for its mix of bryophytes (mosses and liverworts). Wildlife includes otters and sea eagles.

Glenfinnan Monument Glenfinnan, 14 miles (23km) northwest of Fort William. A monument to those who fell during the Jacobite Rebellion of 1745–6, erected in 1815 on the spot where Prince Charles Edward Stuart raised the standard on 19 August 1745. Commissioned by Alexander Macdonald of Glenaladale, it was designed by James Gillespie Graham. The stone column, surmounted by a figure of a kilted Highlander, contains an internal staircase leading to a viewing platform. It was given to the National Trust for Scotland in 1938. Tel: 01397 722250.

Glenmore Forest Park — A forest park created in 1948, covering $13^1/_2$ sq miles (35 sq km) and including the remnants of the ancient Caledonian pine forest. It also surrounds Loch Morlich.

Groam House Museum — High Street, Rosemarkie, 12 miles (19km) east of Dingwall. A museum exploring the local Pictish culture, with a collection based on the Pictish symbol stones found in and around the local churchyard. Its other major collection is dedicated to Scrabster-born artist George Bain (1881–1968), who spearheaded the revival in Celtic art. Tel: 01381 620961.

Highest point — See Ben Nevis

Highland Folk Museum — A living history museum on two sites within the Cairngorms National Park. The Kingussie site opened in 1944 and includes Pitmain Lodge with two exhibition rooms plus a farm museum with a collection of agricultural tools and machinery. In addition there are three recreated buildings: a clack mill, a smokehouse and a traditional Western Isles blackhouse, complete with peat fire. The Newtonmore site was acquired in 1980 and opened in 1995. It covers an area of 80 acres (32ha) and includes a reconstructed township from the 1700s, a working farm steading from the 1930s and a further range of reconstructed buildings such as Leanarch church, Knockbain School, Macpherson's tailor's shop, Ardverikie Estate sawmill and the Newtonmore Curling Club hut. Tel: 01540 661307.

Highland Museum of Childhood — Strathpeffer. An independent museum housed in the old Strathpeffer railway station, built in 1885. The main collection is the Angela Kellie collection of 272 dolls, the majority collected by the museum's founder. Other displays include dolls' houses and furniture, and toys and games from the Victorian period onward. Childhood in the Highlands is portrayed via items such as school equipment, photographs and oral testimony. Tel: 01997 421031.

Highland Wildlife Park — 7 miles (11km) northeast of Newtonmore. Opened in 1972 and managed by the Royal Zoological Society of Scotland. Covering 260 acres (105ha), it specialises in animals which live or have lived in the past in the wilds of Scotland, including wolves, boar, bison, deer and pine marten. Tel: 01540 651270.

Inchnadamph National Nature Reserve — $1^1/_2$ miles (2.5km) southeast of Inchnadamph, 18 miles (29km) northeast of Ullapool. A National Nature Reserve with a network of limestone caves and tunnels at its heart. These are the Allt nan Uamh caves (also known as the 'Bone Caves') at the base of Creag nan Uamh, where in 1889 archaeologists first uncovered what is now believed to be evidence of human burials dating to the Neolithic period. Finds included bones of mammals (including polar bear and northern lynx – the only example found in Scotland), birds (including barnacle goose, eider duck, golden plover, puffin and red grouse), fish and frogs, as well as two sets of human remains. There is no other evidence of permanent human habitation; the caves appear to have been mainly used by animals. There are four 'bone caves': Reindeer Cave, Badger Cave, Bear Cave and Bone Cave. Reindeer Cave and Bone Cave are connected by a narrow tunnel.

Interesting facts — Hugh MacLeod, the current 30th Chief of the MacLeods, succeeded his father John to the title in 2007. Living at **Dunvegan Castle**, he continues a family lineage first started by Leod, the first MacLeod chief, c.1200. With 800 years of continuous occupation, the castle has deservedly earned the title 'oldest inhabited building in Scotland'. **Eilean Donan Castle**, situated on the island of the same name in Loch Duich, is Scotland's most photographed castle. Built c.1220 by Alexander II, it was held by Jacobites in 1719 and bombarded by an English warship, lying in ruins until restored in 1932. **Ardnamurchan Point** is regarded as the westernmost point, **Dunnet Head** the most northerly point (Easter Head is the actual most northerly point of the headland) and **Cape Wrath** the most northwesterly point of mainland Great Britain. **The Old Forge**, Inverie, Knoydart, Mallaig, Inverness-shire, is the most remote pub on mainland Britain. **Bob Dylan** is said to have purchased Aultmore House, an Edwardian property near Nethybridge in Inverness-shire. Dylan is known to be a fan of Scotland and his track 'Highlands', from 1997's *Time Out Of Mind* album, includes the refrain 'My heart's in the Highlands'. He also accepted an honorary doctorate in music from the University of St Andrews in 2004. The property, bought in January 2007, was previously available to rent for £3000 a night, and lies within the boundaries of the Cairngorms National Park. The lyrics to 'Highlands' continue: 'Well, my heart's in the Highlands at the break of day, Over the hills and far away, There's a way to get there, and I'll figure it out somehow.' It seems he has! **John Lennon** was another famous musical legend who loved the Highlands. The ex-Beatle developed a love of the remote hills and glens of Scotland during family holidays and between the ages of nine and 14 he stayed every summer in a croft in the village of Durness in Sutherland. He described his love for the area in the song 'In My Life' and returned to Durness with Yoko and his children in 1969. The **MV *Cromarty Rose***, operating between Cromarty and Nigg, is the smallest car ferry in the UK. It can carry up to 50 passengers and two cars. **Alasdair Ranaldson MacDonell** of Glengarry (1771–1828) invented the famous boat-shaped Glengarry cap without a peak, made of thick-milled woollen material with a toorie or bobble on top and ribbons hanging down behind. MacDonell became the 15th chief of Clan MacDonell of Glengarry in 1788, shortly afterwards designing the bonnet as part of the clan's uniform; it later became a familiar part of the uniform of many Scottish regiments of the British Army. Made famous by Sherlock Holmes, the **Inverness cape** is a water-repellent garment designed to protect kilt-wearers from the traditional inclement weather of the Highlands. The Isle of Skye gives its name to the rare **Skye terrier**, Greyfriars Bobby being the most famous member of the breed. **Ebenezer Place**, Wick, is credited as being the world's shortest street in the *Guinness Book of Records* at 6ft 9in (2.06m). Its single address, 1 Ebenezer Place, was constructed as a hotel in 1883. It was officially declared a street in 1887.

Inverewe Garden — 1 mile (1.6km) northeast of Poolewe, 20 miles (32km) southwest of Ullapool. Sub-tropical gardens with many exotic plants, located on a peninsula on the shore of Loch Ewe. Created by Osgood Hanbury Mackenzie between 1862 and his death in 1922, they benefit from the warm currents of the North Atlantic Drift. Areas include a formal walled garden, a pond garden and rock garden, while gardens named 'America' and 'Japan' feature plants originating in those countries. The Inverewe Estate covers 2100 acres (850ha) and was given to the National Trust for Scotland in 1953. Tel: 01445 781200.

Invergarry Castle 21 miles (34km) northeast of Fort William. A ruined L-plan five storey tower house located on a sheer rock (the Rock of the Raven) above the shores of Loch Oich. Built by the MacDonnell family in the 17th century, it was damaged by General Monck in 1654. Having been restored, it suffered further depredations during the Jacobite uprisings of 1715 and 1745, which finally saw its abandonment. It stands in the grounds of Glengarry Castle Hotel, housed in the former Invergarry House, built in the 1860s.

Invergordon A planned 18th century town laid out by the Gordon family. Its harbour was built in the 1820s and by 1913 the town was a strategic Royal Navy base. In December 1915 HMS *Natal* exploded with the loss of 400 lives. A naval mutiny took place here on 15 and 16 September 1931 after the Navy proposed a 10 per cent pay reduction and a new pay scale for ratings which, for some, amounted to a 25 per cent cut. The unfair pay cut was rescinded and the industrial action called off. After the mutiny some of the organisers were jailed and 200 sailors from the Atlantic Fleet (which was shortly afterwards renamed the Home Fleet) were discharged. The naval base was closed in 1956. Invergordon is now a centre for the maintenance of oil rigs.

Inverlochy Castle 1/2 mile (0.8km) north of Fort William. The substantial ruins of a late 13th century castle built by John Comyn and strategically placed beside the River Lochy. It has a simple square layout with a round tower at each corner, the northwest tower being known as Comyn's Tower. The three sides not fronted by the river were protected by a wide ditch and outer bank. The castle fell into disrepair after the Comyns were overthrown in the early 14th century. Re-garrisoned and repaired by the Earl of Huntly in the early 16th century, it was superseded by the building of Fort William in the 1650s. Inverlochy was the site of battles in 1431 and 1645. Nearby is another building known as Inverlochy Castle, a Victorian mansion which is now a luxury hotel. The ruined castle is sometimes known as Old Inverlochy Castle to avoid confusion.

Inverness Located at the mouth of the River Ness on the Moray Firth, Inverness is the administrative headquarters of the Highlands Council. It was granted city status in December 2000 and is the self-styled 'Capital of the Highlands'. Originally a Pictish stronghold, it was created a royal burgh by William the Lion (1143–1214). It is the site of the only UK Cabinet meeting to be held outside London, an emergency meeting called on 7 September 1921 to discuss the Anglo-Irish Treaty. The Prime Minister, Lloyd George, was holidaying in Inverness at the time.

Inverness Castle Castlehill, Inverness. Located on William Burn by the River Ness and founded either by Malcolm Canmore in the 11th century or by David I c.1141, the original wooden castle was succeeded by several later fortifications. The castle at Inverness was sacked several times, including by Robert the Bruce and supporters of Mary, Queen of Scots. It survived a siege in 1645 but was damaged when occupied by Royalists in 1649. Improved during the late 1720s, when it may have been known as Fort George, this fortification was razed to the ground in 1746 by the Jacobites using explosive charges, and its defensive role was superseded when Fort George was built at Ardersier. The present red sandstone castle, built 1834–6, is now home to the town's courts and council offices, and is depicted on the Royal Bank of Scotland £50 note. The only remnant of the old castle is a well in the courtyard of the present building.

Inverness Cathedral Ardross Street, Inverness. Dedicated to St Andrew. Designed by local architect Alexander Ross in Gothic Revival style and completed in 1869, its twin towers were intended to be topped by spires before funds ran out. A cathedral of the Scottish Episcopal Church, it is the seat of the Bishop of Moray, Ross & Caithness. Tel: 01463 233535.

Inverness Museum and Art Gallery Castle Wynd, Inverness. A museum dedicated to the military, economic, natural and social history of Inverness and its surrounding area. There are displays of Jacobite memorabilia, traditional Highland silverware, costumes, weaponry and musical instruments. The museum also houses the Inverness Museum Records Centre which holds data on local wildlife. The museum underwent a major refurbishment in 2006. Tel: 01463 237114.

Islands There are almost 600 islands (offshore and inshore) in the Highland region. See separate table.

Jacobite Steam Service One of the most scenic lines in Scotland, run by West Coast Railways and operating for 42 miles (68km) between Fort William and Mallaig via Corpach, Glenfinnan, Lochailort, Beasdale, Arisaig and Morar. The company's GWR 'Hall' Class 4-6-0 No. 5972 *Olton Hall*, built in Swindon in 1937, appeared in the Harry Potter films with a new livery as the Hogwarts Express. It can be seen in one film crossing the 21 arch Glenfinnan Viaduct on the Fort William–Mallaig line.

James of the Glens Memorial South Ballachulish, 10 miles (16km) southwest of Fort William. A memorial to James Stewart of Acharn, known as James of the Glens, located on the spot at Cnap Chaolis Mhic Pharaig where he was unjustly hanged in 1757 for the murder of Colin Campbell five years earlier. The tale is told in Robert Louis Stevenson's *Catriona*.

John Lennon Memorial Durness, 44 miles (70km) northeast of Ullapool. A memorial garden to the memory of the former Beatle created in the village where he spent many holidays during his childhood. It features three standing stones on which are engraved lyrics from the Beatles song 'In My Life'.

John O'Groats A village located 874 miles (1406km) from Land's End, and popularly regarded as the northernmost point of the British mainland. The place people start from when they walk the length of Britain, it is named after Dutchman Jan de Groot, who was granted a ferry franchise here by James IV in 1496.

Kerrachar Gardens 9 miles (15km) northwest of Inchnadamph, A remote 2.5 acre (1ha) garden established in 1995 on a derelict croft beside Loch a Chairn Bhain and only accessible by boat from Kylesku. Tel: 01571 833288.

Kessock Bridge — A cable-stayed road bridge crossing the Inverness Firth, linking Inverness with North Kessock and built 1976–82. It replaced a long-standing ferry service and carries the A9 trunk road.

Kiliwhimin Barracks — Fort Augustus, 27 miles (45km) northeast of Fort William. Also known as Kilwhimen/Kilcumein Barracks. Built in 1718 during the same phase of military building which saw the construction of Ruthven Barracks and the military road. It was soon superseded by Fort Augustus, having proved to be situated too far from the water at Loch Ness. In 1745 Kiliwhimin was used by the Jacobites as a base for bombarding and destroying the newer barracks. The south wall of the barracks stands to the rear of the Lovat Arms Hotel, Fort Augustus.

Kilravock Castle — 2 miles (3km) west of Cawdor, $7^1/_2$ miles (12km) northeast of Inverness. A 15th century tower house by the River Nairn extended in the 17th century and an ancestral home of Clan Rose. The castle and its immediate environs, including 40 acres (16ha) of grounds, are now owned by the Kilravock Castle Christian Trust.

Kinloch Castle — Kinloch, Rum. A mansion completed in 1901 for businessman and racehorse owner Sir George Bullough overlooking Loch Scresort. Built from red sandstone sourced from Annan in Dumfries-shire, it had its own electricity supply powered by a hydroelectric scheme in Coire Dubh, as well as an internal telephone system and central heating. When the island became a nature reserve in 1957 it was stipulated that the castle should be 'maintained as far as may be practicable' but by the 1990s it had fallen into disrepair. The castle is in the care of Scottish Natural Heritage and was featured in the first series of BBC TV's *Restoration* (2003).

Kinlochaline Castle — Ardtornish, 15 miles (24km) northwest of Oban. A restored 15th century tower house overlooking the head of Loch Aline, built by Clan Macinnes and remodelled during the next two centuries. It was once known as the Castle of Butter, because, as the story goes, the original builders were paid in butter by the lady of the house. Having suffered from attacks in 1644, 1650 and 1679, it was abandoned in the late 17th century. After it was 'unsympathetically' restored in the 1890s, in the late 1990s a private project to reconstruct the castle was undertaken under the guidance of Historic Scotland. It is now a private residence.

Kintail and Morvich — An estate of 18,362 acres (7431ha) encompassing the Falls of Glomach and the Five Sisters of Kintail. The land was purchased by the National Trust for Scotland in 1944. Tel: 01599 511231.

Knockan Crag National Nature Reserve — 13 miles (21km) north of Ullapool. A world-renowned region for the study of the formation of landscape. The unique rock formations of the Moine Thrust helped reveal the forces at work in creating the landscape, indicating that rocks could be moved sideways in thrusts with the result that older rocks can lie above much younger rocks. The site features a number of contemporary rock art sculptures. Managed by Scottish Natural Heritage. See also North West Highlands Geopark.

Kyle of Lochalsh Line — A branch railway line operated by Scotrail through spectacular countryside between Dingwall and Kyle of Lochals via Garve, Lochluichart, Achanalt, Achnasheen, Achnashellach, Strathcarron, Attadale, Stromeferry, Duncraig Halt, Plockton and Duirinish. At Dingwall it links with the Far North Line. Opened in 1870, it was extended to Kyle of Lochalsh in 1895. Although uneconomic due to the sparse population of the region, it has been repeatedly saved from closure, even when its ferry connection at Kyle was discontinued in the 1970s.

Laidhay Croft Museum — 1 mile (1.6km) northeast of Dunbeath, 17 miles (27km) southwest of Wick. A museum housed in a traditional thatched croft longhouse with dwelling, byre and stable, furnished and equipped as it might have been in the early 20th century. There is also a detached barn. Tel: 01593 731244.

Loch an Eilein Castle — 3 miles (5km) south of Aviemore. Aka Lochaneilean Castle. The ruins of a 15th century castle on an island in Loch an Eilein. Little is known of its history; it was in the hands of the Grant family by the mid 16th century, and may have been attacked by Jacobites in the rising of 1690 and then used to hold prisoners.

Loch a' Mhuilinn — 12 miles (19km) northwest of Inchnadamph. A National Nature Reserve featuring Britain's most northerly remnant of native oak woodland, as well as areas of seashore and bog. Apart from oak, which have a stunted appearance because of the westerly gales in the region, the woodland also includes birch, hazel and rowan. The woods and moorland suffered considerably during the early 19th century when much of the moor was burnt and trees felled to improve the pasture for sheep farming. Wildlife includes otter and pine marten, while ten species of dragonflies have been recorded on the reserve.

Loch Fleet — 3 miles (5km) southwest of Golspie, 9 miles (15km) north of Tain. A National Nature Reserve designated in 1998 and covering more than 2500 acres (1000ha), encompassing a sheltered estuary and including habitats such as woodland, mudflats, sand dunes and coastal heath. It was at one time a wide bay but the prevailing tides caused a narrowing of its mouth by shingle banks. On its northwestern boundary is The Mound, a causeway built by Thomas Telford in 1816. Wildlife includes otter and seal, eider, oystercatcher and tern.

Loch Morar — 3 miles (5km) southeast of Mallaig. Like Loch Ness, a Scottish loch which has seen more than its fair share of sightings of a monster from the deep – this one being nicknamed Morag. One such encounter was in 1969 when two fishermen claimed that their boat had been rammed by a creature up to 30ft (9m) long, with three undulations and a snakelike head. Loch Morar is deeper than Loch Ness, having a maximum depth of 1000ft (305m), and is the deepest freshwater lake in the British Isles. It has six islands: An t-Eilean Meadhoin, Brinacory Island, Eilean a' Phidhir, Eilean Allmha, Eilean Ban, Eilean nam Breac.

Loch Ness — Possibly the most famous of Scotland's lochs. With a length of 23 miles (37km) and a maximum depth of 754ft (230m), it is the largest by volume, the second largest by surface area (after Loch Lomond) and the second deepest (after Loch Morar) in Scotland. Of course it is best known for sightings of the Loch Ness Monster (aka Nessie).

Loch Ness Monster — Drumnadrochit, 15 miles (24km) southwest of Inverness. A centre celebrating the story of the

Exhibition Centre — Loch Ness monster and documenting the evidence for and against its existence, including eyewitness accounts, artefacts, photographs and films. First recorded in an encounter with St Columba in the 6th century, the monster appeared sporadically throughout the following centuries until making a much bigger splash in the 20th century. The first photograph purporting to be of the monster was published by the *Daily Mail* in 1933 and showed a long neck coming out of the depths. In 1951 a three-humped version was snapped. Many attempts have been made to find the monster, some highly scientific and some more frivolous, such as the building of a papier maché 'female' Nessie to tempt a male one out! In addition the centre explores the wider picture of Loch Ness itself and the surrounding area, including its geology and history. Tel: 01456 450342.

Lochindorb Castle — 6 miles (10km) northwest of Grantown-on-Spey, 19 miles (31km) southwest of Inverness. The substantial ruins of a 13th century castle on an island in Lochindorb. Originally a stronghold of the Comyns, it was captured by the English kings Edward I and Edward II before becoming one of the lairs of Alexander Stewart, the 'Wolf of Badenoch', in the late 14th century. The castle was held by Archibald Douglas, Earl of Moray in the 1450s; after his defeat and death at the Battle of Arkinholm in February 1455, James II ordered it to be slighted.

Macleod's Tables — 4 miles (6km) southwest of Dunvegan, Skye. The two flat-topped basalt hills of Healabhal Bheag (1601ft/488m) and Healabhal More (1538ft/469m), located on the Duirinish peninsula in the northwest of Skye.

Mallaig Heritage Centre — Station Road, Mallaig, Inverness-shire. An interpretative centre, museum and archive opened in 1994 and dedicated to the area around Mallaig and Lochaber. Tel: 01687 462085.

Maryck Memories of Childhood Museum — Unapool, 24 miles (39km) north of Ullapool, Sutherland. A museum housing a collection of dolls, dolls' houses, teddy bears and toys dating from the late Victorian period to the present day. Tel: 01971 502341.

Hugh Miller's Cottage and Miller House — Church Street, Cromarty. The birthplace in 1698 of Hugh Miller (1802–56), a man of many attributes and accomplishments who began his working life as a stonemason but became a largely self-taught scientist, specialising in geology. Miller took a great deal of interest in local folklore, collecting more than 300 tales and legends, and was at the centre of the religious controversy which resulted in the founding of the Free Church of Scotland in 1843. He was also editor of *The Witness* newspaper. The cottage is presented as a mariner's cottage and the garden is full of native plants. Nearby Miller House, a Georgian villa built in 1797 by Miller's father, is now a museum, opened in 2004 and celebrating Miller's life and works. Exhibits include his collection of fossils. The cottage and house were given to the National Trust for Scotland in 1938. Tel: 01381 600245.

Mingary Castle — 1 mile (1.6km) southeast of Kilchoan. The substantial ruins of a 13th century castle situated on a promontory on the Ardnamurchan peninsula. The seat of the Maclains of Ardnamurchan, a branch of the Clan Donald, it was remodelled during the late 16th century and further modifications were carried out over the next 200 hundred years. Access from the landward side was defended by a 24ft wide ditch. Having changed hands more than once it came into the hands of the Campbells and was garrisoned by Government troops during the 1745 Jacobite rising. It fell into disrepair in the 19th century.

Monadhliath Mountains — A range of mountains to the west of the Cairngorm range and marking the border between the Inverness district and that of Badenoch and Strathspey, running northeast–southwest and reaching a height of 3100ft (945m) at Carn Dearg, 16 miles (26km) south of Inverness.

Moniack Castle — 7 miles (11km) west of Inverness. An early 17th century L-plan tower built by the Frasers of Lovat, now converted into a winery. Tel: 01463 831283.

Monkstadt House — 4 miles (6km) north of Uig, 16 miles (26km) northwest of Portree, Skye. The ruins of a house built 1732–41 for Sir Alexander MacDonald of Sleat to replace Duntulm Castle, stones from which were used in its construction. Itself abandoned by the MacDonalds when they moved to Armadale in the late 18th century, it was subsequently occupied by tacksmen. The house's main claim to fame is that the fugitive Bonnie Prince Charlie and Flora MacDonald landed nearby in June 1746, after which Flora sought the aid of Sir Alexander's wife Margaret at Monkstadt. Food was taken to the prince, in disguise as an Irish washerwoman named Betty Burke, as he hid in a nearby cave.

Moray Firth — An inlet of the North Sea forming a triangular shape with its apex at the mouth of the Beauly Firth, north of Inverness. It extends north beyond the mouths of the Cromarty Firth and Dornoch Firth to Duncansby Head, in the Highland region, and east along the Moray and Aberdeenshire coast to Fraserburgh in Grampian. The Inner Moray Firth, which includes the Inverness Firth between Inverness and Fort George, stretches as far as Helmsdale to the north and Buckie to the east and receive the waters of the rivers Spey, Lossie, Findhorn and Nairn. The Outer Moray Firth beyond includes Smith Bank and the Beatrice Oilfield. Bounded on two sides by over 500 miles (800km) of coastline, the Moray Firth features diverse coastal landscapes, an abundance of wildlife and an economy based on tourism, fishing and the oil industry.

Muckrach Castle — 1 mile (1.6km) west of Dulnain Bridge, 4 miles (6km) southwest of Grantown-on-Spey. A late 16th century castle beside the River Dulnain built by the Grant family. A ruin by the 19th century and a roofless shell by the 1960s, it was fully restored during the 1980s and now contains holiday accommodation.

Nairn — A royal burgh and seaside resort lying on the Moray Firth. Originally known as North Nairnville, it is now nicknamed the 'Brighton of Scotland' and 'Sunny Nairn' as it claims to have more hours of sunshine than any other Scottish town.

Nigg Cross Slab, The — Nigg, 7 miles (11km) south of Tain. A sculpted Pictish rectangular cross slab found in Nigg churchyard. Now repaired, it stands 7ft 3in (2.2m) high by 3ft 5in (1.1m) wide within the church. On one side is an ornamentally decorated cross with the story of St Paul and St Anthony and the raven who brought them bread in the desert; on the other is a hunting scene, an eagle and an elephant, plus King David playing his harp to a lion and a lamb. A further fragment of the stone was recovered from a nearby stream in 1998.

North West Highlands Geopark Scotland's first geopark, including the geologically significant Moine Thrust. The wide range of rocks in the region, including Durness limestone, Torridonian sandstone, the Moine Rocks, Cambrian quartzite and Lewisian gneiss, draw geologists from around the world. Part of the European Geopark Network, it is endorsed by UNESCO. At its heart is Knockan Crag National Nature Reserve (see separate entry).

Noss Head Lighthouse 3 miles (5km) northeast of Wick. Established in 1849 and built by Alan Stevenson. The tower is 59ft (18m) high and has 76 internal steps. It was automated in 1987.

Old Man of Storr, The 6 miles (10km) north of Portree, Skye. The most prominent of a group of basalt pinnacles on the Trotternish peninsula, 160ft (49m) high and part of the rocky hill known as The Storr.

Pentland Firth A strait separating the Orkney Islands from Caithness in the north of Highland. The name is presumed to be a corruption of 'Pettland's Firth', meaning the fjord of Pictland, and is not related to the Pentland Hills near Edinburgh. On the Caithness side it extends from Dunnet Head in the west to Duncansby Head in the east, and on the Orkney side from Tor Ness on Hoy in the west to Old Head on South Ronaldsay in the east.

Plockton A planned village on the shore of Loch Carron, designed by Thomas Telford. It was used as the village of Lochdubh for the BBC TV series *Hamish Macbeth*.

Quiraing, The 17 miles (27km) north of Portree, Skye. (O.N. = Crooked Enclosure.) Part of spectacular landslip above the east coast of the Trotternish peninsula in northeastern Skye. It features a number of picturesque rock formations including the Needle (a pinnacle 121ft/37m high), the Table (a flat area of grassy land), and the Prison (a natural rock enclosure).

Regimental Museum of the Queen's Own Highlanders Fort George, Ardersier. Collections include uniforms, weaponry, medals, pipes and colours. The Queen's Own Highlanders originate in several Highland regiments established in the late 18th century: the Seaforth Highlanders, the 78th (Highland) Regiment of Foot and the Cameron Highlanders. The Seaforth Highlanders were raised by the Earl of Seaforth in 1778 as the 78th Regiment (Highland) Foot; the regiment was renumbered as the 72nd (Highland) Regiment of Foot in 1786. Its early campaigns were in India, South Africa and Ireland. In 1823 it was renamed the 72nd Regiment of Foot, or The Duke of Albany's Own Highlanders, and the uniform of Royal Stewart trews and highland bonnet was introduced. The regiment saw action at the siege of Sevastopol during the Crimean War and during the 2nd Afghan War (1878–80). In 1881 it was amalgamated with the 78th Highlanders (Highland) Regiment of Foot as the 1st Battalion Seaforth Highlanders (Ross-shire Buffs, The Duke of Albany's). The 78th (Highland) Regiment of Foot was raised in 1793 by Frances Humberstone MacKenzie. In 1795 it was renamed the 78th (Highland) Regiment of Foot, or the Ross-shire Buffs, and it gained a battle honour at Assaye on 23 September 1803 in the 2nd Anglo-Maratha War, in a campaign masterminded by Sir Arthur Wellesley. It took part in the relief of Lucknow during the Indian Mutiny of 1857, winning eight VCs, and served in the 2nd Afghan War (1878–80). In 1881 the regiment was amalgamated with the 72nd Highlanders as the 2nd Battalion Seaforth Highlanders (Ross-shire Buffs). The 1st Battalion took part in the Battle of Omdurman (1898) and the 2nd Battalion served in the 2nd Boer War (1899–1902). During World War I the 2nd Battalion was part of the British Expeditionary Force and was joined in France by the 1st Battalion returning from India in late 1914. The regiment's battle honours included Marne (1914, 1918), Ypres (1915, 1917, 1918), Loos, Somme (1916–18), Arras (1917–18), Vimy (1917) and Cambrai (1917–18), Palestine (1918) and Baghdad. During World War II the regiment's battalions gained battle honours including El Alamein, Middle East (1942), Sicily (1943), Anzio, St Valery, En Caux, Caen, Rhineland, Imphal and Burma (1942–4). The 1st and 2nd Battalions were amalgamated in 1948. In 1961 the regiment was amalgamated with the Queen's Own Cameron Highlanders to form the Queen's Own Highlanders (Seaforth and Camerons). The 79th (Cameronion Volunteers) Regiment of Foot was raised by Alan Cameron in 1793. It served in Egypt in 1801 and was renamed the 79th (Cameron Highlanders) Regiment of Foot in 1804. It saw service in the Peninsular War, including the retreat to Corunna and the battles of Fuentes d'Onor and Salamanca, and took part in the Waterloo campaign, fighting with distinction at both Quatre Bras and Waterloo as part of Picton's Division. During Waterloo it is reported that Piper Kenneth Mackay stepped out from the safety of his square to play 'Cogadh na Sith' (War or Peace) and inspire the men to repel repeated French cavalry attacks. During the Crimean War it fought at Alma and Sevastopol before serving in India 1857–71, helping to relieve Lucknow during the Indian Mutiny. In 1873 the regiment became known as the 79th (Queen's Own Cameron Highlanders) Regiment. In the final years of the 19th century it saw action at the battles of Tel-el-Kebir (1882) and Omdurman (1898) and then served in the 2nd Boer War (1899–1902). The regiment's battle honours in World War I include Marne (1914, 1918), Ypres (1914, 1915, 1917, 1918), Neuve Chapelle, Loos, Somme (1916, 1918), Delville Wood, Arras (1917, 1918) and Macedonia (1915–18). During World War II the regiment saw action in most theatres including France, the Western Desert, Sicily, Italy and Burma. Its battle honours include St Omer-La Bassée, Reichswald, Rhine, Keren, Sidi Barrani, El Alamein, Akarit, Gothic Line, Kohima and Mandalay. The regiment formed from the 1961 amalgamation served in Borneo (1961–4), Belize (1976–7), Northern Ireland (1978–80, 1983–5, 1990–3), the Falklands (1982) and the Gulf (1990–1), also carrying out tours of duty in Germany and Hong Kong. On 17 September 1994 the regiment was combined with the Gordon Highlanders to form the Highlanders (Seaforth, Gordons and Camerons). All private soldiers were known as 'highlander' rather than 'private'. The regiment's motto was 'Cuidich n'Righ' (Aid the King) and the tartans used for the uniform combined aspects of the founding regiments: Gordon (for the kilt), Seaforth Mackenzie (for the trews) and Cameron of Erracht (for the pipers and drummers kilts). On 28 March 2006 the

Highlanders became the Highlanders (4th Battalion, Royal Regiment of Scotland). Tel: 01667 462800.

Rivers
The **Brora** rises to the east of Loch Shin, flowing southeast for 26 miles (42km) through Strath Brora before entering the North Sea at Brora. For almost $4\frac{1}{2}$ miles (7km) of its course it widens to form Loch Brora.

The **Findhorn** rises in the Monadhliath Mountains and runs in a northerly direction for nearly 70 miles (114km), entering the sea at Findhorn Bay just north of Forres. For most of its course it runs parallel with its larger neighbour the Spey in Grampian.

The **Helmsdale** is one of the best salmon rivers in the north of Scotland. It flows from the Strath of Kildonan, the location of the great 1869 gold rush and an area affected by the Highland Clearances. It is a similar length to the Brora and maintains about a 12-mile (19km) distance from it throughout its course.

The **Nairn**, a river to the east of Loch Ness, rises in headstreams on the slopes of Carn Ghriogair in the Monadhliath Mountains and flows northeast through Strathnairn for 38 miles (61km) to empty into the Moray Firth at Nairn.

The **Shin** flows from Loch Shin into the Dornoch Firth and then into the North Sea, a length of 7 miles (11km).

Road to the Isles
A traditional name, celebrated in several songs, for an ancient route crossing Scotland from east to west as far as the Hebrides. It is now applied to the scenic 46 mile (72km) stretch of the A830 from Fort William to Mallaig, passing through Glenfinnan, Lochailort, Arisaig and Morar.

Rosemarkie Stones
A collection of Pictish symbol stones and cross-slabs found in or near Rosemarkie churchyard, 9 miles (15km) northeast of Inverness, in the 18th and 19th centuries. They indicate that an early religious foundation was based in this coastal location. Some are on display in Groam House Museum and others are held at the Royal Museum of Scotland.

Rum
Also known as Rhum, a name given to it by Sir George Bullough, its owner in the early 20th century, to avoid confusion with the drink. One of the Small Isles of the Inner Hebrides (the others are Canna, Eigg and Muck). Kinloch is the 'capital'. The Isle of Rum is a National Nature Reserve designated in 1957; it has also been designated a Biosphere Reserve (1976), a National Scenic Area (1978), a Special Protection Area (1982) and a Site of Special Scientific Interest (1987). It was one of the earliest places in Scotland to be settled, having been colonised during the Mesolithic period. It supports one of the largest breeding populations of Manx shearwater and the white-tailed sea eagle was reintroduced 1975–85. At one time the island had a substantial amount of woodland, most of which was cleared to accommodate flocks of sheep. It is now owned by Scottish Natural Heritage, who have planted more than 1 million native trees and shrubs to create new habitats for the island's wildlife. Tel: 01687 462026. Area: 41.8 sq miles (108.26 sq km). Population: 22. (GR: NM370980.)

Ruthven Barracks
Ruthven, $\frac{1}{2}$ mile (0.8km) southeast of Kingussie, 3 miles (5km) east of Newtonmore. Built beside the River Spey 1718–21 by General Wade on a mound which had been the site of 13th century fortifications, and which in the 14th century was a stronghold of Alexander Stewart, the 'Wolf of Badenoch'. All traces of the earlier castles were removed when the barracks was built. Having survived one Jacobite attempt to take it in 1745, the garrison was overwhelmed in February 1746. On 17 April 1746 a large force of Jacobites rallied here, intending to fight on after the disaster of Culloden the previous day. Informed that the rebellion was over and that it was now a case of every man for himself, they set the barracks alight as a parting gesture of defiance. The ruins mainly comprise the substantial exterior walls.

Shieldaig
An island in Loch Shieldaig, covered with Scots pine planted in the 19th century to provide poles for fishing nets. It was purchased by the National Trust for Scotland in 1970. Area: 0.05 sq miles (0.13 sq km). (GR: NG810542.)

Skibo Castle
5 miles (8km) northwest of Tain, 21 miles (34km) northeast of Dingwall. A stately home located beside the Dornoch Firth, and built 1899–1901 by businessman and philanthropist Andrew Carnegie – who bought the estate in 1895. It was constructed on the site of a bishop's residence dating to the 13th century and of a house built in the 1870s. The house and surrounding 7500 acre (3000ha) estate eventually fell into disrepair; restored and extended, it is now a private residential sporting club. It has also been the host of a number of 'celebrity' weddings, including that of Madonna and Guy Ritchie in December 2000.

Skye
The Isle of Skye is no longer a true island due to the bridge which now connects it to the mainland. Portree is the capital and Sgurr Alasdair (3258ft/993m) is the highest peak. Area: 632.38 sq miles (1637.85 sq km). Population: 9232. (GR: NG388374.)

Skye Bridge
A prestressed concrete cantilever bridge 1640ft (500m long), spanning Loch Alsh and connecting Skye to Kyle of Lochalsh on the mainland. Completed in 1995, it was paid for by a controversial and locally unpopular toll, abolished in December 2004 after the bridge had been purchased by the Scottish Executive. With a central span of 820ft (250m) and two side spans of 410ft (125m), it is supported by two main piers, one of which stands on the island of Eilean Ban.

Smoo Cave
$1\frac{1}{2}$ miles (2.5km) east of Durness. A limestone cave located at the head of a narrow inlet and with an entrance 100ft (30.5m) wide. The Allt Smoo Burn plunges through the roof of the cave, creating a waterfall. Excavations have revealed evidence of human occupation possibly dating back to the Mesolithic period and definitely from the Iron Age.

Soay
An island in the Inner Hebrides. Purchased by author Gavin Maxwell in 1945 for £900, it was the inspiration for his first book *Harpoon at a Venture* (1952). Permitted to issue its own postage stamps. Area: 4.02 sq miles (10.4 sq km). Population: 7. (GR: NG450140.)

Sport: general
The Ice Factor, the National Centre for Ice Climbing and the Mountaineering Council's Regional Centre of Excellence for Rock Climbing, was opened in December 2003 in the converted

aluminium smelter at Kinlochleven, which closed in 1996. It has the biggest indoor ice wall in the world – 50ft (15m high) and with 500 tonnes of packed snow on its face – and the UK's highest articulated rock climbing wall. There are various climbing walls in the main arena aimed at climbers of differing levels of proficiency. The centre also offers courses in other outdoor pursuits. Tel: 01855 831100.

football — **Inverness Caledonian Thistle** were founded in 1994 by the merger of Caledonian FC and Inverness Thistle FC, and were winners of the Scottish League 2nd Division in 2004 and of the 3rd Division in 1997. Their colours are red and blue, combining the blue and white of Caledonian with the red and black of Inverness Thistle. Nicknamed Caley Thistle or Caley Jags, their home ground is Tulloch Caledonian Stadium, East Longman, Inverness. Tel: 01463 222880.

Ross County were founded in 1929. The most northerly League club in Scotland, they joined the Scottish League 3rd Division in 1994, winning the 2nd Division in 2008. Nicknamed The Staggies or The County, their colours are navy blue and white; their home ground is Victoria Park Stadium, Jubilee Road, Dingwall. Tel: 01349 860860.

Steall Falls — 5 miles (8km) southeast of Fort William. A waterfall on the Water of Nevis which plunges 350ft (107m) into the Nevis Gorge.

Strathpeffer Pump Room — The Square, Strathpeffer, 4 miles (6km) west of Dingwall. The restored pump room and gardens in the Victorian spa town of Strathpeffer. Displays and models tell the history of the town at its height as a spa, 1870–1939. Its sulphurous springs were declared the healthiest in Britain in the early 19th century and the pump room was built in 1829. Eventually a railway was built to serve the town as its popularity grew. The station closed in 1951 and now houses the Highland Museum of Childhood. Tel: 01997 421415.

Strathpeffer Spa — Strathpeffer, 4 miles (6km) west of Dingwall. The restored Spa Pavilion was built in 1881 and now serves as an arts venue. Tel: 01997 420124.

Strathspey Steam Railway — A heritage railway based at Aviemore and operating for 10 miles (16km) between Aviemore and Broomhill via Boat of Garten on part of the former Highland Railway line from Aviemore to Forres. The Strathspey Railway opened in 1978. Broomhill station featured as Glenbogle station in the BBC TV drama series *Monarch of the Glen*. Tel: 01479 810725.

Stroma — An island in the Pentland Firth to the north of John O'Groats. At its northern end, off Swilkie Point, is a whirlpool known as 'The Swilkie'; extending from the point in an easterly or westerly direction depending on the tide, it can be particularly violent. In 1958 it was offered as a prize in the US TV show *Bid 'n' Buy*. The island is permitted to issue its own postage stamps. A lighthouse on the island was built in 1896 and automated in 1997. Area: 1.45 sq miles (3.75 sq km). (GR: ND353775.)

Strome Castle — 3 miles (5km) southwest of Lochcarron, 8 miles (13km) northeast of Kyle of Lochalsh. The ruins of a 15th century (possibly earlier) tower house located on a promontory on Loch Carron. A stronghold of the Lords of the Isles before passing to the MacDonalds of Glengarry. It was destroyed after a siege by Kenneth MacKenzie, Lord of Kintail in 1602 and abandoned. It was given to the National Trust for Scotland in 1939.

Tain Through Time — Tower Street, Tain, 19 miles (31km) northeast of Dingwall. A site consisting of three of Tain's historic buildings – a museum, the Collegiate Church of St Duthac (or Duthus) and a visitor centre. The museum opened in 1966 and is housed in the caretaker's cottage for the collegiate church. The displays include a collection of local 18th and 19th century silverware. The church, built in the late 14th century, was a popular pilgrimage destination. Following the Reformation it became the parish church of Tain but fell into disrepair after it was abandoned in 1815. It was restored in the 1870s. The visitor centre is housed in the 17th century schoolhouse. The ground floor gallery is dedicated to James IV, who made regular pilgrimages to the shrine at Tain. The Town Loft has a display telling the story of St Duthus and the building of the church. Tel: 01862 894089.

Tarbat Castle — See Ballone Castle

Thurso — The northernmost town on the British mainland and the most northerly location served by the Britain's rail network. It grew during the 1950s when the Dounreay power station was built nearby.

Tor Castle — Torcastle, 3 miles (5km) northeast of Fort William. Located on the River Lochy and occupied by the Clan Cameron 1528–1650. A previous castle on the site was the 10th century seat of Banquo, reputedly murdered here by Macbeth.

Torridon — A 16,100 acre (6515ha) estate in Wester Ross encompassing spectacular mountain scenery and including the peaks of Liathach (3458ft/1054m) and Beinn Alligin (3232ft/985m). Upper Loch Torridon forms the southwestern boundary of the estate, which has been owned by the National Trust for Scotland since 1967. Tel: 01445 791368.

Tulloch Castle — Tulloch Castle Drive, Dingwall. Possibly dating to the 12th century, the castle belonged to the Bain family until 1762 when it was sold to a relative, Henry Davidson. A tower built by Bain in 1542 was incorporated into the modern structure. Severely damaged by fire in 1850, it was rebuilt and extended in the 1890s, passing to the Vickers family in 1917 and being restored 1918–23. It is said to be haunted by a Green Lady, possibly one of the daughters of Duncan Davidson, the 4th Laird, who was killed falling downstairs in the 19th century after seeing her father with a woman not his wife. Tel: 01349 861325.

Urquhart Castle — 2 miles (3km) east of Drumnadrochit, 14 miles (23km) southwest of Inverness. The ruins of a large castle on Strone Point overlooking Loch Ness. Probably the site of fortifications since the Iron Age, the present castle dates from the 13th century when it belonged to the Durward family. The castle changed hands many times in the 13th and 14th centuries, during the wars between Scotland and England, and in the 15th century was regularly exchanged between the MacDonalds, Lords of the Isles and the Grants. Abandoned by the early 17th century, it was partially slighted following a skirmish between Jacobites and Williamites in 1692 and was

	subsequently used as a source of building stone by the locals. The ruins include the five-storey Grant Tower. Given to the National Trust for Scotland in 2003. Tel: 01456 450551.
West Affric	A stretch of land covering 9049 acres (3662ha) linking the National Trust for Scotland properties of Kintail and Glomach, and a traditional east–west path through the Highlands. The land was purchased by the National Trust for Scotland in 1993 in order to help protect the flora and fauna.
West Highland Museum	Cameron Square, Fort William. An independently run museum opened in 1922 and housed in its present building since 1926. It charts the history of the region from ancient times to the present day, and in particular the period of the Jacobite rebellions, 1689–1746.
Wick	A royal burgh straddling the Wick River estuary on Wick Bay. At one time the administrative centre for Caithness, it was also a major herring fishing port from the late 18th until the early 20th century. It is now a base for offshore supply vessels to the oil industry.
Wick Carnegie Library	Sinclair Terrace, Wick. A library partly funded by philanthropist Andrew Carnegie. It was designed by Thomas Leadbetter and opened in September 1898.
Wick Heritage Museum	Bank Row, Wick. Opened in 1981 as the Wick Heritage Centre, the museum explores the changing fortunes of Wick, Europe's top herring fishing port in the 19th century. A number of rooms are furnished in early 20th century period style. The museum houses an archive of photographs and films. It also holds a large collection of Caithness glass, turned over to the museum when the company, which began in Wick in 1960, closed its local factory in 2005. Probably the company's best known product was the BBC *Mastermind* Trophy. The museum also contains the optical and mechanical workings of Noss Head Lighthouse. Tel: 01955 605393.
Woods on Your Doorstep	**Abriachan Wood** (408 acres/165ha), located in two blocks on the northern shore of Loch Ness and mainly classed as ancient semi-natural woodland. Species include birch, alder, ash, oak and hazel. The Great Glen Way long-distance footpath passes to the north and west of the wood; **Balmacaan** (85 acres/34ha), Lewiston, Drumnadrochit, on the western shore of Loch Ness. Mainly ancient woodland with oak, alder, ash and willow predominating; **Glencharnoch Wood** (37 acres/15ha), Carrbridge, mainly Scots pine with some Norway spruce; **Ledmore & Migdale** (1710 acres/692ha), Spinningdale, Bonar Bridge. Originally part of the Skibo Estate. The topography includes hills, valleys and gorges. Mainly birch, oak and Scots pine; **Uig Wood** (44 acres/18ha) Uig, Skye, located around gorges cut by the Rha and Conon Rivers. Mainly ash, hazel, alder, birch and elm; **Urquhart Bay** (57 acres/23ha), Drumnadrochit, located on the western shore of Loch Ness and at one time part of the Glen Urquhart Estate. Mainly alder, ash and willow.

Some famous people born in the Highlands

Arbuthnot-Lane, William (surgeon) (1856–1943)	Inverness
Brough, Robert (painter) (1872–1905)	Invergordon
Campbell, Colen (architect) (1676–1729)	Nairn
Fraser, Peter (Prime Minister of New Zealand) (1884–1950)	Tain
Kennedy, Charles (politician) (1959–)	Inverness
MacLean, Sorley (poet) (1911–96)	Raasay
MacPherson, James (poet) (1736–96)	Ruthven
Smith, William (Boys' Brigade founder) (1854–1914)	Thurso
Swinburne, James (plastics pioneer) (1858–1958)	Inverness
Whitelaw, William (politician) (1918–99)	Nairn

Islands of Highland

(G. = Gaelic) (Islands in Hebrides area are Inner Hebrides)

Island name	Area	Nearest landmark	General information	Shipping Area
A' Chearc	Sea of the Hebrides	Soay	(G. = The Hen). GR: NG433120	Hebrides
A' Chleit	Atlantic	Faraid Head	(G. = The Reef). GR: NC385702	Fair Isle
A' Chleit	Loch Eriboll	Beinn Ceannabeinne	(G. = The Reef). GR: NC442620	Fair Isle
A' Chleit	The Little Minch	Kirkaig Point	(G. = The Reef). GR: NC030204	Hebrides
A' Ghlas-leac	Inner Sound	Plockton	(G. = The Grey-Green Slab). GR: NG781334	Hebrides
A' Ghoil-sgeir	Atlantic	Sangobeg	(G. = The Stone-Skerry). GR: NC432671	Fair Isle
A' Ghruagach	Sea of the Hebrides	Oigh-Sgeir	(G. = The Brownie). One of the Small Isles Area: 0.19 sq miles (0.49 sq km). GR: NM158962	Hebrides

Island name	Area	Nearest landmark	General information	Shipping Area
Airor Island	Sound of Sleat	Airor	The island lies just off the coast. GR: NG716058	Hebrides
Ais-sgeir	Loch Alsh	Fireach Ard	A bare black rock. GR: NG862262	Hebrides
Am Balg	Atlantic	Rubh' a Bhuachaille	(G. = The Belly). GR: NC185662	Hebrides
Am Bi-bogha Beag	Sea of the Hebrides	Glen Dibidale, Skye	GR: NG195389	Hebrides
Am Bi-bogha Mor	Sea of the Hebrides	Glen Dibidale, Skye	GR: NG190381	Hebrides
Am Bodach	Atlantic	A' Chailleach	(G. = The Old Man). GR: NC250736	Hebrides
Am Bonair	The Minch	Handa Island	GR: NC129486	Hebrides
Am Buachaille	Atlantic	Rubh' a Bhuachaille	(G. = The Herdsman). GR: NC201651	Hebrides
Am Fraoch-eilean	Sound of Arisaig	Torr Mor Ghaoideill	One of the Borrodale Islands. GR: NM674830	Hebrides
Am Fraoch-eilean	Sound of Sleat	Rubh' Arisaig	One of two islands of the same name in the region. GR: NM615855	Hebrides
An Calbha	Eddrachillis Bay	Rubh' a' Mhucard	GR: NC159365	Hebrides
An Camastac	The Little Minch	Dun Gearymore, Skye	GR: NG232655	Hebrides
An Coileach	Sea of the Hebrides	Soay	GR: NG432120	Hebrides
An Corr-eilean	Loch Eriboll	Torr Cruinn	aka Choaric. Contains an ancient disused burial ground. GR: NM841951	Hebrides
An Cruachan	Atlantic	Sangobeg	GR: NC435679	Fair Isle
An Dubh Sgeir	Sea of the Hebrides	Glen Dibidale, Skye	GR: NG190370	Hebrides
An Dubh Sgeir	The Little Minch	Uamh Oir, Skye	GR: NG359747	Hebrides
An Dubh-aird	Inner Sound	Plockton	GR: NG783337	Hebrides
An Dubh-laimhrig	Sea of the Hebrides	Soay	GR: NG474153	Hebrides
An Dubh-sgeir	Sea of the Hebrides	Geodha nan Gobhar,	GR: NG345228	Hebrides
An Dubh-sgeir	Sea of the Hebrides	Soay	GR: NG468140	Hebrides
An Dubh-sgeir	Atlantic	Sangobeg	GR: NC456680	Fair Isle
An Garbh eilean	Sound of Arisaig	Torr Mor Ghaoideill	One of the Borrodale Islands. GR: NM672834	Hebrides
An Garbh-eilean	Atlantic	Cleit Dhubh	(G. = The Rough Island). Aka Garvie Island. GR: NC333735	Fair Isle
An Garbh-eilean	Loch Kishorn	Meall na h-Airde	GR: NG809370	Hebrides
An Glas-eilean	Sound of Arisaig	Smirisary Hill	(G. = The Grey Island). GR: NM635764	Hebrides
An Glas-eilean	Sound of Arisaig	Torr Mor Ghaoideill	One of the Borrodale Islands. GR: NM668825	Hebrides
An Glas-eilean	Sound of Sleat	Triagh Ho	GR: NM648912	Hebrides
An Gobhlach	Inner Sound	Pabay	GR: NG667261	Hebrides
An Innis	Caol Raineach	Eilean Nan Ron	GR: NC632650	Fair Isle
An Ruadh-eilean	Inner Sound	Eilean na Ba	GR: NG698389	Hebrides
An Stac	Moonen Bay	Waterstein Head, Skye	GR: NG145467	Hebrides
An Stac	Atlantic	Loch nan Aigheann	GR: NC527686	Fair Isle
An Steidh	Sea of the Hebrides	Canna	GR: NG215035	Hebrides
An t-Each	Sea of the Hebrides	Canna	GR: NG277066	Hebrides
An t-Eilean Meadhoin	Loch Morar	Torr na Ba	GR: NM703920	
An t-lasgair	The Little Minch	Uamh Oir, Skye	GR: NG359748	Hebrides
An t-Saothair	Gruinard Bay	First Coast	GR: NG919917	Hebrides
Ardtoe Island	Sea of the Hebrides	Kilmory	GR: NM526713	Hebrides
Avon Rock	Sound of Mull	Ardtornish Point	Lies off the coast of Rubha Leth Thorcaill.	Hebrides
Black Islands	Atlantic	Portnacloich Point	GR: NG752293	Hebrides
Bo Crithean	Loch Sunart	Carna	GR: NM614590	Malin
Bogh' a' Churaich	Sound of Eigg	An Corrach, Eigg	GR: NM434853	Hebrides
Bogh' Oitir	Sound of Sleat	Portnaluchaig	GR: NM643891	Hebrides
Bogha an t-Sasunnaich	Atlantic	Rubha na h-Airde Glaise, Skye	GR: NG720265	Hebrides
Bogha Daraich	Sea of the Hebrides	Tarskavaig Point, Skye	GR: NG573105	Hebrides
Bogha Lurcain	Sound of Mull	Lochaline	Lies 100m from Bolorkle Point. GR: NM682441	Hebrides
Bogha Mhic Gill'-losa	Sound of Eigg	Eilean Chasthastail	GR: NM484829	Hebrides
Bogha Mor	The Minch	Handa Island	GR: NC122474	Hebrides
Bogha na Fionn-aird	Sea of the Hebrides	Port Mor, Muck	GR: NM418781	Hebrides
Bogha nam Meann	Atlantic	Oldany Island	GR: NC080339	Hebrides
Bogha Ruadh	Sea of the Hebrides	Port Mor, Muck	GR: NM428785	Hebrides
Bogha Thangaraidh	Bay of Laig	Cleadale, Eigg	GR: NM466895	Hebrides

Island name	Area	Nearest landmark	General information	Shipping Area
Boor Rocks	Loch Ewe	Boor	GR: NG845821	Hebrides
Bottle Island	The Little Minch	Rubha Dubh Ard	GR: NB955020	Hebrides
Boursa Island	Atlantic	Aultivullin	GR: NC808674	Fair Isle
Brinacory Island	Loch Morar	Brinacory	GR: NM756909	
Broad Rock	Loch Sunart	Carna/Risga		Malin
Caisteal an Fhithich	Loch Snizort	Biod a' Choltraiche,	GR: NG263647	Hebrides
Calbha Beag	Eddrachillis Bay	Rubh' a' Mhucard	Calbha Beag (G. = Little Headland). GR: NC155368	Hebrides
Calbha Mor	Eddrachillis Bay	Rubh' a' Mhucard	Calbha Mor (G. = Great Headland). GR: NC165370	Hebrides
Canna	Sea of the Hebrides	Sanday	One of the Small Isles. Joined to the island of Sanday by a bridge. Permitted to issue its own postage stamps. Area: 11.48 sq kms (4.43 sq miles). Population: 6. GR: NG240060	Hebrides
Car an Daimh	Sound of Arisaig	Doire Fhada	GR: NM652833	Hebrides
Carn Deas	The Little Minch	Rubha Dubh Ard	Carn Deas (G. = South Rock). GR: NB965024	Hebrides
Carn Iar	The Little Minch	Rubha Dubh Ard	Uninhabited but produces its own set of postage stamps. GR: NB960025	Hebrides
Carn nan Sgeir	The Little Minch	Rubha Dubh Ard	One of the Summer Isles. GR: NC011018	Hebrides
Carna	Loch Sunart	Glenborrodale	Area: 0.71 sq miles (1.83 sq km). GR: NM620590	Malin
Carrachan	Inner Sound	Eilean Meadhonach	One of the Crowlin Islands.	Hebrides
Ceann Hilligeo	Moray Firth	Lybster	GR: ND259351	Cromarty
Ceann Mor	Sea of the Hebrides	Oigh-sgeir	One of the Small Isles. GR: NM158968	Hebrides
Ceannamhor	Atlantic	Rubh'an Dobhrain	Ceannamhor (G. = Bighead). One of the Badcall Islands. GR: NC140400	Hebrides
Choaric	Loch Eriboll	Torr Cruinn	aka An Corr-eilean.	Hebrides
Clach Bheag na Faraid	Atlantic	Faraid Head	GR: NC396712	Fair Isle
Clach Mhor na Faraid	Atlantic	Faraid Head	GR: NC399712	Fair Isle
Clach nan Ramh	The Minch	Steall a' Ghreip, Skye	GR: NG468730	Hebrides
Clachan Uaine	Sea of the Hebrides	Soay	GR: NG472157	Hebrides
Cleac Dubh	Sound of Raasay	Ben Tianavaig, Skye	GR: NG522417	Hebrides
Cleat Skerry	Loch Vatten	Ardroag, Skye	GR: NG280428	Hebrides
Cleats, The	The Little Minch	Rubha Huish, Skye	GR: NG369798	Hebrides
Cleit an t-Seabhaig	Atlantic	Loch nan Aigheann	GR: NC523688	Fair Isle
Cleit Mhor	Moray Firth	Inver	GR: ND175300	Cromarty
Clett	Loch Dunvegan	Rubha nam Both, Skye	Clett (G. = Low, Concealed Rock). Pop singer Donovan bought the island in 1968 and wrote a song about it, *And Clett Makes Three*. GR: NG225582	Hebrides
Cnoc a' Mhoil Bhain	Atlantic	Oldany Island	GR: NC099347	Hebrides
Coomb Island	Caol Beag	Clashbuie	aka Neave Island (G. *naomha*, 'holy'). GR: NC665645	Fair Isle
Corr Eileanan	Loch Hourn	A' Chiste Dhubh	(G. = Tapering Island). GR: NG864065	Hebrides
Cow Rock	The Minch	Island of Rona	GR: NG629621	Hebrides
Creag an Eilein	Loch Nevis	A' Chruach	GR: NM764980	Hebrides
Creag an Eilein	The Minch	Rubha Beag	GR: NG891978	Hebrides
Creag Mhor	Glenelg Bay	Glenelg	GR: NG807203	Hebrides
Creag Ruadh	Torrisdale Bay	Clachan	GR: NC695630	Fair Isle
Creagan nan	The Anchorage	Tanera Mor	GR: NC000072	Hebrides
Crowlin Islands	Inner Sound	Scalpay		Hebrides
Cul Eilean	Eddrachillis Bay	Culkein Drumbeg	(G. = Island at the Back). GR: NC124337	Hebrides
Dry Island	Loch Moidart	Cul Doirlinn	aka Eilean Tioram. The site of Castle Tioram. Area: 0.03 sq miles (0.07 sq km). GR: NM662724	Malin

Island name	Area	Nearest landmark	General information	Shipping Area
Dubh Sgeir	Sound of Arisaig	Torr Beithe	GR: NM615699	Hebrides
Dubh Sgeir	Sound of Eigg	An Corrach, Eigg	GR: NM451836	Hebrides
Dubh Sgeir	Atlantic	Rubh'an Dobhrain	GR: NC134392	Hebrides
Dubh Sgeir	Atlantic	Droman	GR: NC171591	Hebrides
Dubh Sgeir	Loch Torridon	Ardheslaig	GR: NG774579	Hebrides
Dubh Sgeirean	Atlantic	Cnoc Loch en Roin	GR: NC170543	Hebrides
Dubh Sgeirean	The Minch	Scourie More	GR: NC139441	Hebrides
Dubh Sger	Sea of the Hebrides	Port Mor, Muck	GR: NM425784	Hebrides
Dubh-sgeir Beag	Tongue Bay	Talmine	GR: NC591632	Fair Isle
Dubh-sgeir Mhor	Tongue Bay	Portvasgo	GR: NC599645	Fair Isle
Dustic	Atlantic	Cape Wrath	GR: NC268759	Hebrides
Eag Mhor	Loch Gairloch	Longa Island	GR: NG740775	Hebrides
Eagamol	Sea of the Hebrides	Eilean nan Each	GR: NM389813	Hebrides
Eigg	Sound of Eigg	Rum	See separate entry	Hebrides
Eilean a' Bhreitheimh	Atlantic	Rubh'an Dobhrain	One of the Badcall Islands. GR: NC131397	Hebrides
Eilean a' Bhuic	Caolas a' Mhill Ghairbh	Tanera Mor	(G. = Buck Island). One of the Summer Isles. GR: NB978082	Hebrides
Eilean a' Bhuic	The Minch	Scourie More	(G. = Buck Island). GR: NC138449	Hebrides
Eilean a' Chadh-fi	Loch a' Chadh-fi	Cnoc na Suil Chruthaiche	GR: NC213511	Hebrides
Eilean a' Chait	Loch Carron	Plockton	(G. = Cat Island). GR: NG807347	Hebrides
Eilean a' Chaoil	Tongue Bay	Portvasgo	GR: NC591651	Fair Isle
Eilean a' Chaoil	Upper Loch Torridon	Bad-callda	GR: NG812563	Hebrides
Eilean a' Chaolais	Loch Ailort	Rubha Chaolais	(G. = Kyle Island). GR: NM693801	Hebrides
Eilean a' Char	The Little Minch	Tanera Mor	(G. = Island of Seal Flesh) One of the Summer Isles. GR: NB965087	Hebrides
Eilean a' Choire	Sound of Arisaig	Eilean Shona	(G. = Corrie Isle). GR: NM625739	Hebrides
Eilean a' Chonnaidh	Loch Clash	Kinlochbervie	(G. = Island of the Faggot of Firewood). GR: NC203570	Hebrides
Eilean a' Chuilinn	Loch Sunart	Bunalteachan	GR: NM737621	Malin
Eilean a' Chuilinn	Loch Hourn	Coille Mhialairigh	GR: NG818113	Hebrides
Eilean a' Ghaill	Sound of Arisaig	Cruach Doire 'n Dobhrain	(G. = Stranger's Isle). GR: NM627825	Hebrides
Eilean a' Ghamhna	Loch a' Chairn Bhain	Rientraid	(G. = Island of the Stirks). GR: NC205333	Hebrides
Eilean a' Gharb-lain	Loch Hourn	A' Chiste Dhubh	GR: NG870067	Hebrides
Eilean a' Mhadaidh	Loch Laxford	Foindle	(G. = Isle of the Dog). GR: NC195497	Hebrides
Eilean a' Mhal	Atlantic	Kyle of Lochalsh	Below-water rocks encircle the island. GR: NG749280	Hebrides
Eilean a' Mhuineil	Loch Hourn	Coire an Eich Bhain	GR: NG844067	Hebrides
Eilean a' Mhuirich	Loch Sunart	Ardnastang	GR: NM800609	Malin
Eilean a' Phidhir	Loch Morar	Torr na Ba	GR: NM708920	
Eilean a' Phiobaire	Loch Hourn	Glac nan Sgadan	(G. = The Piper's Island). GR: NG831083	Hebrides
Eilean Aigastan	Sound of Sleat	Inverguseran	GR: NG744083	Hebrides
Eilean Aird nan Gobhar	Churchton Bay	Clachan, Raasay	Lies on a drying reef. GR: NG541362	Hebrides
Eilean Aird nan Uan	Sound of Eigg	Aird nan Uan, Muck	(G. = Island of the Headland of the Lambs). GR: NM393809	Hebrides
Eilean Allmha	Loch Morar	Coille Almha	GR: NM756900	
Eilean an Achaidh	Eddrachillis Bay	Culkein Drumbeg	(G. = Field Island). GR: NC121338	Hebrides
Eilean an Aigeach	The Minch	Tarbet	(G. = Stallion Island). GR: NC153489	Hebrides
Eilean an Eich Bhain	Fionn Loch	Bad Bog	GR: NG932812	
Eilean an Eireannaich	Loch Laxford	Rubh na h-Airde Bige	GR: NC201503	Hebrides
Eilean an Eoin	Sound of Sleat	Ard Ghunel, Skye	GR: NG711121	Hebrides
Eilean an Fheidh	Loch Sunart	Glenborrodale	GR: NM610605	Malin
Eilean an Fheidh	Loch Moidart	Shona Beag	GR: NM672729	Malin
Eilean an Fhraoich	Caol Rona	An Caol, Raasay	(G. = Heather Island). GR: NG612536	Hebrides
Eilean an Inbhire Bhain	Loch Shieldaig	Rhuroin	GR: NG794550	Hebrides
Eilean an Roin Beag	Atlantic	Droman	(G. = Little Seal Island). GR: NC172582	Hebrides

Island name	Area	Nearest landmark	General information	Shipping Area
Eilean an Roin Mor	Atlantic	Droman	(G. = Large Seal Island). GR: NC180587	Hebrides
Eilean an t-Sabhail	Sound of Arisaig	Eilean Shona	GR: NM631731	Hebrides
Eilean an t-Sionnaich	Loch Sunart	Ceol na mara	GR: NM752611	Malin
Eilean an t-Sithein	Loch Laxford	Ardmore Point	(G. = Isle of the Fairy Mound). GR: NC174512	Hebrides
Eilean an t-Snidhe	Sound of Arisaig	Cruach Doire 'n Dobhrain	GR: NM630814	Hebrides
Eilean an t-Sratha	Loch Carron	Ardaneaskan	One of the Strome Islands. GR: NG837348	Hebrides
Eilean an Tuim	Loch Glencoul	Liath Bhad	GR: NC263303	Hebrides
Eilean Ard	Loch Laxford	Ardmore Point	(G. = High Island). GR: NC185503	Hebrides
Eilean Assynt	Loch Assynt	Torr an Eilein	GR: NC195250	
Eilean Balnagowan	Loch Linnhe	Rubha Mor	GR: NM952540	Hebrides
Eilean Ban	Kyle Akin	Kyle of Lochalsh	The island was once owned by naturalist and author Gavin Maxwell and is used as support for the Skye Bridge. GR: NG748271	Hebrides
Eilean Ban	Loch Morar	Rubhar Ban	Area: 0.04 sq miles (0.1 sq km). Population: 2. GR: NM698922	
Eilean Beag	Loch Snizort	Dun Santavaig, Skye	GR: NG363577	Hebrides
Eilean Beag	Inner Sound	Scalpay	(G. = Little Island). One of the Crownlin Islands. Area: 0.01 sq miles (0.03 sq km). GR: NG682358	Hebrides
Eilean Beag	The Anchorage	Tanera Mor	(G. = Little Island). One of the Summer Isles. GR: NB995073	Hebrides
Eilean Buidhe	Loch Ailort	Alisary	GR: NM732793	Hebrides
Eilean Camas Drollaman	Loch Schiel	Rubha na h-Airde	GR: NM763694	
Eilean Ceann Feidh	Loch nan Uamh	The Prince's Cairn	GR: NM720840	Hebrides
Eilean Chathastail	Sound of Eigg	Galmisdale, Eigg	(G. = Castle Island). GR: NM488833	Hebrides
Eilean Chlamail	Loch Hourn	Rubha a' Chaisteil	GR: NG773127	Hebrides
Eilean Choinaid	The Little Minch	Tanera Mor	(G. = Rabbit Island). One of the Summer Isles. GR: NB969087	Hebrides
Eilean Choinnich	Loch Hourn	Carn Mairi	GR: NG872062	Hebrides
Eilean Choraidh	Loch Eriboll	Laid	aka Horse Island. Used as target practice prior to the assault on the *Tirpitz* during World War II. GR: NC421580	Fair Isle
Eilean Chrona	Atlantic	Glac Fhearna	(G. = Faulty Island). GR: NC068338	Hebrides
Eilean Chuaig	Atlantic	Rubha Chuaig	(G. = Twisted Island). GR: NG700597	Hebrides
Eilean Cluimhrig	Atlantic	Rispond	GR: NC462659	Fair Isle
Eilean Coille	Sound of Arisaig	Smirisary Hill	(G. = Wooded Isle). GR: NM639763	Hebrides
Eilean Creagach	Loch Snizort	Biod a' Choltraiche, Skye	One of the Ascrib Islands. GR: NG292652	Hebrides
Eilean Creagach	Tongue Bay	Talmine	GR: NC589631	Fair Isle
Eilean Da Chuain	Sound of Sleat	Camusdarach	GR: NM648917	Hebrides
Eilean Dearg	Sound of Sleat	Torr na h-Innse	(G. = Red Island). GR: NG705010	Hebrides
Eilean Donan	Loch Duich	Dornie	This home of Scotland's most photographed castle is linked to the mainland by a bridge. GR: NG881259	Hebrides
Eilean Dubh	Loch Ailort	Brealach Breac	(G. = Black Island). GR: NM747813	Hebrides
Eilean Dubh	Loch Dunvegan	Colbost, Skye	GR: NG222490	Hebrides
Eilean Dubh	Loch Eishort	Ord, Skye	GR: NG615143	Hebrides
Eilean Dubh	Atlantic	Balnakeil	GR: NC374690	Hebrides
Eilean Dubh	Atlantic	Rubh a' Mhilt Bhain	GR: NC203555	Hebrides
Eilean Dubh	Inner Sound	Plockton	GR: NG792338	Hebrides
Eilean Dubh	Loch Moidart	Meall an Aoil	GR: NM692723	Malin
Eilean Dubh	Loch Schiel	Carn Mhic Labhraich	GR: NM882785	

Island name	Area	Nearest landmark	General information	Shipping Area
Eilean Dubh	The Little Minch	Rubha Dubh Ard	Area: 0.15 sq miles (0.39 sq km). GR: NB973035	Hebrides
Eilean Dubh Dhurinish	Inner Sound	Port-an-eoina	GR: NG775329	Hebrides
Eilean Dubh na Fionndalach Bige	Loch Laxford	Creag na Foinndalach	GR: NC203490	Hebrides
Eilean Dubh na Sroine	Loch Maree	Stattadale	GR: NG910720	
Eilean Dubha	Loch Dughaill	Ardmore Point	GR: NC188519	Hebrides
Eilean Dughaill	Loch Shieldaig	Rhuroin	GR: NG795546	Hebrides
Eilean Eachainn	Loch Maree	Stattadale	GR: NG933718	
Eilean Fada Mor	The Little Minch	Tanera Mor	(G. = Big Long Island). One of the Summer Isles. GR: NB972080	Hebrides
Eilean Fhianain	Loch Schiel	Achnanellan	GR: NM752682	
Filean Fladday	The Minch	Creag an Eoin, Raasay	Flat-topped island joined to Raasay by a drying reef. Area: 0.46 sq mlles (1.2 sq km). GR: NG590510	Hebrides
Eilean Flodigarry	The Minch	Flodigarry, Skye	GR: NG480718	Hebrides
Eilean Fraoch	Fionn Loch	Glac Chaol	GR: NG945805	
Eilean Furadh Mor	The Minch	Meall Glac a' Bheithe	GR: NG799931	Hebrides
Eilean Gaineamhach	Loch Eishort	Boreraig, Skye	GR: NG622157	Hebrides
Eilean Garave	Loch Snizort	Biod a' Choltraiche, Skye	One of the Ascrib Islands. GR: NG300643	Hebrides
Eilean Garbh	The Minch	Farhead Point	(G. = Rough Island). One of the Badcall Islands. GR: NC145405	Hebrides
Eilean Garbh	The Minch	Island of Rona	GR: NG605562	Hebrides
Eilean Giubhais	Sound of Sleat	Sgurr an Eilein Ghubhais	GR: NM730981	Hebrides
Eilean Glas	Loch Dunvegan	Colbost, Skye	(G. = Grey Island). GR: NG215498	Hebrides
Eilean Gobhlach	Loch nan Uamh	The Prince's Cairn	(G. = Forked Island). GR: NM716840	Hebrides
Eilean Grianal	Loch Dunvegan	Uiginish Point, Skye	The sea area around the island is part of The Little Minch. GR: NG228497	Hebrides
Eilean Heast	Loch Eishort	Heaste, Skye	GR: NG648159	Hebrides
Eilean Hoan	Atlantic	Sangobeg	(G. = Haven Island). GR: NC445675	Fair Isle
Eilean Horrisdale	Loch Gairloch	Badachro	Lies in the south side of the loch. GR: NG787744	Hebrides
Eilean Iarmain	Sound of Sleat	Duisdalemore, Skye	Not a true island but part of Isle Ornsay on the southeast of Skye. Area: 0.15 sq miles (0.38 sq km). GR: NG713124	Hebrides
Eilean Ighe	Sound of Sleat	Gortenachullish	GR: NM632880	Hebrides
Eilean Leac na Gainimh	Inner Sound	Rubh' a' Chinn Mhoir, Scalpay	GR: NG597332	Hebrides
Eilean Iosal	Loch Snizort	Biod a' Choltraiche, Skye	(G. = Humble Island). One of the Ascrib Islands. GR: NG288656	Hebrides
Eilean Iosal	Caol Raineach	Eilean Nan Ron	GR: NC631660	Fair Isle
Eilean Maol	Sound of Sleat	Creag-a-Chaim, Skye	GR: NG640032	Hebrides
Eilean Maol	Loch Nevis	Camusrory	GR: NM854952	Hebrides
Eilean Meadhonach	Inner Sound	Scalpay	(G. = Middle Island). One of the Crownlin Islands. Area: 0.2 sq miles (0.5 sq km). GR: NG686345	Hebrides
Eilean Meall a' Chaorainn	Loch Laxford	Creag na Foinndalach	(G. = Island Hillock of the Rowan Tree). GR: NC221485	Hebrides
Eilean Mhic an Fhularaich	Loch Maree	Stattadale	GR: NG937713	
Eilean Mhic Dhomhnuill Dhuibh	Loch Schiel	Seilag	GR: NM820727	
Eilean Mhic Neill	Sound of Arisaig	Cnoc nan Sguab	GR: NM640720	Hebrides
Eilean Mhogh-sgeir	Loch Hourn	Runival	GR: NG910071	Hebrides
Eilean mo Shlinneag	Loch Sunart	Gearr Chreag	GR: NM722624	Malin
Eilean Moineseach	Enard Bay	Rubh' a' Bhrocaire	(G. = Diffident Island). GR: NC064176	Hebrides

Island name	Area	Nearest landmark	General information	Shipping Area
Eilean Mor	Loch Dunvegan	Colbost, Skye	GR: NG226486	Hebrides
Eilean Mor	Loch Snizort	Dun Santavaig, Skye	GR: NG358571	Hebrides
Eilean Mor	Loch Sunart	Camuschoirk	GR: NM758605	Malin
Eilean Mor	Inner Sound	Scalpay	One of the Crownlin Islands. Area: 0.66 sq miles (1.7 sq km). GR: NG695345	Hebrides
Eilean Mor	Sound of Sleat	Sandaig	One of the Sandaig Islands. GR: NG762146	Hebrides
Eilean Mor	The Anchorage	Tanera Mor	One of the Summer Isles. GR: NB997073	Hebrides
Eilean Mor	Enard Bay	Rubh' a' Bhrocaire	GR: NC057173	Hebrides
Eilean Mor	Loch Sionascaig	Inverpolly Forest	GR: NC120140	
Eilean Mor	Loch Torridon	Rubha Glas	GR: NG757583	Hebrides
Eilean Mullagrach	The Little Minch	Isle Ristol	One of the Summer Isles. GR: NB958117	Hebrides
Eilean na Ba	Inner Sound	Toscaig	(G. = Isle of the Cattle). GR: NG695380	Hebrides
Eilean na Ba Mor	Inner Sound	Plockton	(G. = Isle of the Big Cow). GR: NG795342	Hebrides
Eilean na Bearachd	Atlantic	Rubh'an Dobhrain	(G. = Isle of the Pointed Snout). One of the Badcall Islands; the largest of the group. GR: NC148398	Hebrides
Eilean na Beinne	Loch Carron	Rubha Alasdair Ruaidh	GR: NG825356	Hebrides
Eilean na Beitheiche	Sound of Mull	Fiunary	Lies alongside the Fiunary Rocks. GR: NM620461	Hebrides
Eilean na Creadha	Inner Sound	Drumbuie	GR: NG762311	Hebrides
Eilean na Creige Duibhe	Loch Carron	Creag an Duilisg	GR: NG823335	Hebrides
Eilean na Gamhna	Sound of Sleat	Torr na h-Innse	GR: NG708011	Hebrides
Eilean na Glaschoille	Loch Nevis	Rubha Raonuill	GR: NG738000	Hebrides
Eilean na Gualainn	Loch Ailort	Roshven	GR: NM721790	Hebrides
Eilean na h-Acairseid	Sea of the Hebrides	Rubha na h-Acairseid	GR: NM587725	Hebrides
Eilean na h-Acairseid	Sound of Sleat	Mallaig	(G. = Harbour Island). GR: NM672970	Hebrides
Eilean na h-Airde	Sea of the Hebrides	Prince Charles's Cave,	GR: NG522112	Hebrides
Eilean na h-Aiteig	Atlantic	Oldshore Beg	GR: NC193585	Hebrides
Eilean na h-Oitire	Sound of Arisaig	Rubha nan Clach Dearga	GR: NM642752	Hebrides
Eilean na Rainich	Atlantic	Rubh'an Dobhrain	(G. = Island of the Ferns). One of the Badcall Islands. GR: NC142393	Hebrides
Eilean na Rainich	Loch a' Chairn Bhain	Kylestrome	GR: NC231342	Hebrides
Eilean na Saille	Caolas a' Mhill Ghairbh	Tanera Mor	(G. = Island of the Salt). One of the Summer Isles. GR: NB981085	Hebrides
Eilean na Saille	Atlantic	Rubh' a' Cheathraimh Ghairbh	GR: NC177534	Hebrides
Eilean na t-Stratha	Loch Carron	Ardaneaskan	GR: NG834345	Hebrides
Eilean nam Bairneach	Loch Ailort	Roshven	(G. = Isle of the Limpets). GR: NM721792	Hebrides
Eilean nam Ban	Loch Schiel	Dalelra	GR: NM725691	
Eilean nam Breac	Loch Morar	Rubha Garbh	GR: NM708915	
Eilean nam Gillean	Loch Sunart	Ben Laga	GR: NM642601	Malin
Eilean nan Cabar	Loch nan Uamh	Rubh' Aird Mhoir	(G. = Island of the Rafters). One of the Borrodale Islands. GR: NM683835	Hebrides
Eilean nan Clach	Loch Moy	Moy	GR: NH778341	
Eilean nan Each	Sound of Eigg	Aird nan Uan, Muck	(G. = Horse Island). GR: NM394814	Hebrides
Eilean nan Eildean	Loch Sunart	Glenborrodale	GR: NM611582	Malin
Eilean nan Gabhar	Loch Sunart	Tom nan Eildean	Despite being called Goat Island there is not a goat to be seen but there are plenty of basking seals. GR: NM617575	Malin
Eilean nan Gobhar	Loch Ailort	Cooper's Knowe	(G. = Goat Island). GR: NM694793	Hebrides
Eilean nan Gobhar Mor	Inner Sound	Drumbuie	GR: NG764312	Hebrides
Eilean nan Naomh	Inner Sound	Camusterrach	(G. = Island of the Saints). GR: NG701412	Hebrides

Island name	Area	Nearest landmark	General information	Shipping Area
Eilean nan Ron	Caol Raineach	Strathan Skerry	(G. = Seal Island). An SSSI where hundreds of grey seals gather in the autumn to pup. Area: 0.53 sq miles (1.38 sq km). GR: NC640655	Fair Isle
Eilean nan Trom	Loch Ailort	Laggan	GR: NM721797	Hebrides
Eilean nan Uan	Atlantic	Oldany Island	(G. = Lamb Island). GR: NC099350	Hebrides
Eilean Port a' Choit	Loch Laxford	Creag na Foinndalach	(G. = Island of the Small Boat Harbour). GR: NC214481	Hebrides
Eilean Port nam Murrach	Sound of Sleat	Rubh' Arisaig	GR: NM611835	Hebrides
Eilean Rairidh	Eddrachillis Bay	Creag a' Phris	GR: NC165351	Hebrides
Eilean Raonuill	Sound of Arisaig	Farquar's Point	(G. = Ranald's Island). GR: NM629729	Hebrides
Eilean Rarsaidh	Loch Hourn	Coille Mhialairigh	GR: NG812116	Hebrides
Eilean Reamhar	Loch Scavaig	Coire-a Chruidh, Skye	(G. = Fat Island). GR: NG486186	Hebrides
Eilean Riabhach	The Minch	Farhead Point	(G. = Grizzled Island). One of the Badcall Islands. GR: NC148408	Hebrides
Eilean Ruairidh	Sea of the Hebrides	Druim Dubh, Skye	(G. = Rory's Island). GR: NG593124	Hebrides
Eilean Ruairidh Mor	Loch Maree	Stattadale	GR: NG898733	
Eilean Rubha an Ridire	Sound of Mull	Rubha an Ridire	(G. = Island at the Promontory of the Knight). GR: NM725406	Hebrides
Eilean Seamraig	Caol Rona	Rona	(G. = Shamrock Island). GR: NG616537	Hebrides
Eilean Sgorach	Sound of Sleat	Point of Sleat, Skye	(G. = Scallop Island). GR: NM560992	Hebrides
Eilean Shamadalain	Sound of Sleat	Samadalan	GR: NG731066	Hebrides
Eilean Shona	Loch Moidart	Farquar's Point	Leased by J M Barrie in the early 1920s to complete the screenplay for a silent movie version of *Peter Pan* (1924). Area: 2.76 sq miles (7.14 sq km). Population: 9. GR: NM645740	Malin
Eilean Sionnach	Sound of Sleat	Ard Ghunel, Skye	Lies southeast of Ornsay island. GR: NG712122	Hebrides
Eilean Stacan	Inner Sound	Plockton	GR: NG782330	Hebrides
Eilean Subhainn	Loch Maree	Stattadale	GR: NG920722	
Eilean Thuilm	Sound of Rum	Talm, Eigg	GR: NM481913	Hebrides
Eilean Tigh	Caol Rona	Shielings, Raasay	(G. = Home Island). Area: 0.21 sq miles (0.54 sq km). GR: NG603540	Hebrides
Eilean Tioram	Loch Duich	Ardelve	(G. = Drying Island). GR: NG875260	Hebrides
Eilean Tioram	Loch Hourn	Arnisdale	GR: NG838102	Hebrides
Eilean Tioram	Loch Moidart	Cul Doirlinn	See Dry Island	Malin
Eilean Tioram	Loch Nevis	Camusrory	GR: NM861955	Hebrides
Eilean Tioram	Loch Torridon	Red Point	GR: NG736671	Hebrides
Eilean Tioram	Loch Torridon	Fearnmore	GR: NG726609	Hebrides
Eilean Trodday	The Little Minch	Rubha Huish, Skye	(G. = Troll Island). GR: NG440788	Hebrides
Eilean Uaine	Loch Moidart	Cul Doirlinn	GR: NM660717	Malin
Eileanan Dubha	Loch Laxford	Foindle	(G. = Black Islands).	Hebrides
Eileanan Dubha	Kyle Akin	Kyle of Lochalsh	GR: NG767268	Hebrides
Eileanan Loisgte	Kentra Bay	Kentra	GR: NM642693	Hebrides
Eileanan nan Gad	Kentra Bay	Gorteneorn	GR: NM643681	Hebrides
Eileanan Sgurra	Sound of Arisaig	Torr Mor Ghaoideill	(G. = Rocky Islands). Part of the Borrodale Islands. GR: NM674828	Hebrides
Eileannan Comhlach	Loch Schiel	Gaskan	GR: NM802725	
Ewe, Isle of	Loch Ewe	Aultbea	Highest point is Creag Streap, 236ft (72m). Area: 1.44 sq miles (3.74 sq km). Population: 12. GR: NG850880	Hebrides

Island name	Area	Nearest landmark	General information	Shipping Area
Fiunary Rocks	Sound of Mull	Fiunary	Tiny rock stacks off the coast of Eilean na Beitheiche. GR: NM620461	Hebrides
Fladda-chuain	The Little Minch	Rubha Huish, Skye	GR: NG362810	Hebrides
Flod Sgeir	Sound of Eigg	Galmisdale, Eigg	GR: NM490843	Hebrides
Fraoch Eilean	Loch Hourn	Carn Mairi	(G. = Heather Island). GR: NG875063	Hebrides
Fraoch Eilean Mor	Gruinard Bay	Torr Mor	GR: NG949911	Hebrides
Fraoch-eilean	Loch Gairloch	Badachro	GR: NG798738	Hebrides
Fraochlan	Enard Bay	Rubha na Breige	GR: NC051181	Hebrides
Gaeilavore Island	The Little Minch	Rubha Huish, Skye	GR: NG365799	Hebrides
Gairbh Eilein	Loch Dunvegan	Uiginish Point, Skye	The sea area around the island is part of The Little Minch. GR: NG240495	Hebrides
Galta Beag	The Minch	Steall a' Ghreip, Skye	GR: NG464736	Hebrides
Garay Island	Loch Dunvegan	Uiginish Point, Skye	GR: NG228492	Hebrides
Garbh Eilean	Caol Rona	An Caol, Raasay	Connected to Rona by a drying reef. GR: NG618540	Hebrides
Garbh Eilean	Loch Sunart	Rubha an Daimh	GR: NM741620	Malin
Garbh Eilean	Loch a' Chairn Bhain	Kylestrome	Kylesku Bridge built on this island. GR: NC225340	Hebrides
Garbh Eilean	Loch Maree	Stattadale	GR: NG906708	
Garbh Sgeir	Sound of Eigg	Galmisdale, Eigg	GR: NM490839	Hebrides
Garbh Sgeir	Sea of the Hebrides	Oigh-sgeir	(G. = Rough Rock). One of the Small Isles. Area: 0.02 sq miles (0.04 sq km). GR: NM154960	Hebrides
Garbh-eilean	Atlantic	Strathy Point	GR: NC826699	Fair Isle
Garra Islands	Loch Kishorn	Meall na h-Airde	Group of tiny rock islets.	Hebrides
Garvie Island	Loch Kishorn	Meall na h-Airde	See An Garbh-eilean	Hebrides
Gearran Island	The Little Minch	Rubha Huish, Skye	GR: NG368795	Hebrides
Geodha Cul an Fhraochaidh	Atlantic	Sithean na h-Iolaireich	GR: NC244701	Hebrides
Glas Eilean	Loch Sunart	Camuschoirk	(G. = Pale Grey-green Island). GR: NM755603	Malin
Glas Eilean	Loch Alsh	Avernish	GR: NG845252	Hebrides
Glas Eilean	Loch Gairloch	Charlestown	GR: NG793753	Hebrides
Glas Eilean	Loch Hourn	Torr an Tuir	GR: NG786117	Hebrides
Glas Eilean	Sound of Sleat	Torr na h-Innse	GR: NG708003	Hebrides
Glas Eileanan	Sound of Mull	Rubha an Ridire	(G. = Pale Grey-green Islands). On 19 October 1690 the Royal Navy frigate *Dartmouth* was wrecked on one of the two islands after dragging her anchor in Duart Bay (the wreck was discovered in 1973). GR: NM715400	Hebrides
Glas Leac	The Minch	Farhead Point	One of the Badcall Islands. GR: NC137407	Hebrides
Glas Leac	Atlantic	Rubh a' Mhilt Bhain	GR: NC200557	Hebrides
Glas Leac	Loch Inver	Strathan	GR: NC075220	Hebrides
Glas Leac	The Minch	Handa Island	GR: NC139469	Hebrides
Glas Sgeir	Loch Torridon	Kenmore	GR: NG760579	Hebrides
Glas-leac Beag	The Little Minch	Tanera Mor	(G. = Little Green Slab). One of the Summer Isles. Area: 0.04 sq miles (0.11 sq km). GR: NB927050	Hebrides
Glas-leac Mor	The Little Minch	Tanera Mor	(G. = Big Green Slab). One of the Summer Isles. GR: NB952096	Hebrides
Godag	Sound of Eigg	Blar Mor, Muck	GR: NM418818	Hebrides
Great Stack, The	The Minch	Handa Island	aka Stac an t-Seabhaig. GR: NC132488	Hebrides
Green Island	Enard Bay	Rubha Phollaidh	GR: NC057151	Hebrides
Griana-sgeir	The Minch	Eilean Fladday	GR: NG580513	Hebrides
Gruinard Island	Gruinard Bay	Rubha na Moire	Test bombed with anthrax in 1941 and only declared clear of infection in 1990. Area: 0.76 sq miles (1.96 sq km). GR: NG945940	Hebrides

Island name	Area	Nearest landmark	General information	Shipping Area
Gualann Mhor	Loch Ewe	Isle of Ewe	GR: NG862870	Hebrides
Guillamon Island	Inner Sound	Rubh' an Trusaidh, Scalpay	GR: NG639272	Hebrides
Gulnare Rock	Inner Sound	Rubha Doire na y Boceinein, Scalpa	Situated between Longay and Scalpay. One of the Sgeirean Tarsuinn.	Hebrides
Handa	The Minch	Tarbet	SSSI run by the Scottish Wildlife Trust. Area: 1.19 sq miles (3.09 sq km). GR: NC140480	Hebrides
Hanni Geo	Moray Firth	East Clyth	GR: ND308387	Cromarty
Harlosh Island	Loch Bracadale	Harlosh Point, Skye	GR: NG280393	Hebrides
Harlosh Skerry	Loch Bracadale	Harlosh Point, Skye	GR: NG277402	Hebrides
Haslam	Sea of the Hebrides	Canna	GR: NG250047	Hebrides
Holm Island	Sound of Raasay	Holm, Skye	GR: NG525514	Hebrides
Holoman Island	Sound of Raasay	Balachuirn, Raasay	Not strictly an island as it is connected to Raasay Island by a pebble strand. GR: NG549400	Hebrides
Horse Island	Horse Sound	Rubha Dubh Ard	One of the Summer Isles. Treasure from a Spanish Armada ship is said to have been buried here in 1588. Area: 0.20 sq miles (0.53 sq km). GR: NC023045	Hebrides
Horse Island	Loch Eriboll	Laid	See Eilean Choraidh	Fair Isle
Humla	Sea of the Hebrides	Canna	GR: NG198005	Hebrides
Innis Bheag	Dornoch Firth	Dornoch	GR: NH870840	Cromarty
Innis Mhor	Dornoch Firth	Dornoch	GR: NH850861	Cromarty
Iolla Bheag	Horse Sound	Rubha Dubh Ard	One of the Summer Isles. GR: NC039036	Hebrides
Iolla Mhor	Horse Sound	Rubha Dubh Ard	(G. = Big Drying Rock). One of the Summer Isles. GR: NC023036	Hebrides
Isay	Loch Dunvegan	Rubha nam Both, Skye	(O.N. = Porpoise). Area: 0.23 sq miles 90.6 sq km). GR: NG218570	Hebrides
Isle Maree	Loch Maree	Stattadale	GR: NG931723	
Isle Martin	The Minch	Ardmair	Island consists of a single rounded hill 394ft (120m). high. Area: 0.52 sq miles (1.36 sq km). GR: NH093995	Hebrides
Isle Ristol	The Little Minch	Old Dornie	Not usually listed as a Summer Isle but lies amid the group. GR: NB970113	Hebrides
Kishorn Island	Loch Kishorn	Meall na h-Airde	Most northerly of the Garra Islands. GR: NG807377	Hebrides
Knee, The	Pentland Firth	Duncansby Head	GR: ND407728	Fair Isle
Lampay	Loch Dunvegan	Groban na Sgeir, Skye	GR: NG220550	Hebrides
Larach Tigh Mhic Dhomhnuill	Loch Alsh	Avernish	GR: NG852254	Hebrides
Leac nam Faoileann	Sea of the Hebrides	Soay	GR: NG426145	Hebrides
Little Clett	Pentland Firth	Brough	GR: ND221742	Fair Isle
Little Stack	The Minch	Handa Island	Annexed to the north of Handa Island. GR: NC143488	Hebrides
Loch an Eilein Castle	Loch an Eilein	Ord Ban	NH898079	
Loch Mor Isle	Soay Sound	Loch Mor, Soay		Hebrides
Lochindorb Castle	Lochindorb	Craig Tiribeg	See separate entry	
Longa	Loch Gairloch	Big Sand	Highest point is Druim an Eilean at 230ft (70m). Area: 0.49 sq miles (1.26 sq km). GR: NG745776	Hebrides
Longay	Inner Sound	Rubha Doire na Boceinein, Scalpay	An island with steep shores and cliffs. One of the Sgeirean Tarsuinn. Area: 0.19 sq miles (0.5 sq km). GR: NG659310	Hebrides
Lord Macdonald's Table	The Little Minch	Rubha Huish, Skye	GR: NG369795	Hebrides
Luinga Bheag	Sound of Sleat	Rubh' Arisaig	GR: NM610860	Hebrides
Luinga Mhor	Sound of Sleat	Rubh' Arisaig	GR: NM610860	Hebrides

Island name	Area	Nearest landmark	General information	Shipping Area
Macleod's Maidens	Sea of the Hebrides	Idrigill Point, Skye	Three large rock stacks sculpted by the sea. GR: NG242361	Hebrides
Manish Island	Sound of Raasay	Manish Point, Raasay	GR: NG566485	Hebrides
McFarlane's Rock	Sea of the Hebrides	Sgurr Mor, Skye	GR: NG300314	Hebrides
McMillan's Rock	Sound of Raasay	Upper Ollach, Skye	Marked by a lighted buoy.	Hebrides
Meall Beag	Eddrachillis Bay	Rubh'an Dobhrain	(G. = Little Lump). GR: NC125375	Hebrides
Meall Earca	The Minch	Farhead Point	GR: NC134404	Hebrides
Meall Holm	Caol Raineach	Eilean Iosal	aka Meall Thailm. GR: NC629662	Fair Isle
Meall Mor	Eddrachillis Bay	Rubh'an Dobhrain	(G. = Big Lump). GR: NC120379	Hebrides
Meall nan Caorach	The Little Minch	Rubha Dubh Ard	(G. = Sheep Hump). One of the Summer Isles. GR: NC012012	Hebrides
Meall nan Gabhar	Horse Sound	Horse Island	Connected to Horse Island by a reef which dries at low water. One of the Summer Isles. Area: 0.05 sq miles (0.13 sq km). GR: NC022056	Hebrides
Meall Thailm	Caol Raineach	Eilean Iosal	See Meall Holm	Fair Isle
Meallan Odhar	Sound of Sleat	Rubh' Arisaig	GR: NM604840	Hebrides
Men of Mey	Pentland Firth	St John's Point	GR: ND310755	Fair Isle
Mingay	Loch Dunvegan	Rubha nam Both, Skye	The sea area around the island is part of The Little Minch. GR: NG223577	Hebrides
Muck Island	Sound of Eigg	Sanna Point	One of the Small Isles. Area: 2.09 sq miles (5.41 sq km). Population: 30. GR: NM410797	Hebrides
Na Cluasnadh	Atlantic	Oldshore Beg	GR: NC200573	Hebrides
Na Gamhnaichean	Sea of the Hebrides	Soay	GR: NG432122	Hebrides
Na Gamhnaichean	The Minch	Island of Rona	GR: NG631630	Hebrides
Na Glas Leacan	Atlantic	A' Ghoil	GR: NC346720	Fair Isle
Neave Island	Caol Beag	Clashbuie	See Coomb Island	Fair Isle
Oigh-sgeir	Sea of the Hebrides	Rum	(G. = Virgin Rock). Aka Hyskeir. One of the Small Isles. Area: 0.19 sq miles (0.49 sq km). GR: NM158962	Hebrides
Old Man of Stoer	The Little Minch	Point of Stoer	GR: NC018352	Hebrides
Oldany Island	Atlantic	Culkein Drumbeg	Linked to the mainland by a drying channel. GR: NC090345	Hebrides
Ornsay	Sound of Sleat	Duisdalemore, Skye	Not a true island as it is joined to the southeast of Skye. Area: 0.15 sq miles (0.38 sq km). GR: NG713124	Hebrides
Oronsay	Sea of the Hebrides	Ullinish Point, Skye	GR: NG315360	Hebrides
Ox Rock	Atlantic	Rubh'an Dobhrain	One of the Badcall Islands. GR: NC139387	Hebrides
Pabay	Inner Sound	Broadford, Skye	Permitted to issue its own postage stamps as it is uneconomic for the post office to provide a boat. Area: 0.76 sq miles (1.98 sq km). GR: NG675270	Hebrides
Priest	The Little Minch	Tanera Mor	Owned by the RSPB. One of the Summer Isles. Area: 0.47 sq miles (1.22 sq km). GR: NB925022	Hebrides
Raasay	Sound of Raasay	Gedintailor, Skye	Inverarish is the 'capital'. Area: 24.26 sq miles (62.82 sq km). Population: 192. GR: NG566443	Hebrides
Rabbit Islands	Tongue Bay	Talmine	GR: NC605635	Fair Isle
Risga	Loch Sunart	Carna	Lies off the coast of Carna. GR: NM620590	Malin
Riska	Loch Moidart	Shona Beag	GR: NM663729	Malin
Roag Island	Loch Vatten	Ardroag, Skye	GR: NG278426	Hebrides

Island name	Area	Nearest landmark	General information	Shipping Area
Rona	Sound of Raasay	Raasay	aka South Rona to distinguish it from the more northerly island of the same name. Permitted to issue its own postage stamps. Area: 4.04 sq miles (10.47 sq km). Population: 2. GR: NG624580	Hebrides
Rubha Dubh	Sea of the Hebrides	Soay	GR: NG430129	Hebrides
Rubha Dubh nam Fiadh	Loch Quoich	Meall a' Chait	GR: NH056011	
Rubha Mor	Loch Badanloch	Badanloch Forest	GR: NC769346	
Rum	Sound of Rum	Eigg	See separate entry	Hebrides
Samalaman Island	Sound of Arisaig	Samalaman	GR: NM661781	Hebrides
Sandaig Islands	Sound of Sleat	Sandaig	Group of tiny islets joined to the mainland at low water. GR: NG765145	Hebrides
Sanday	Sound of Canna	Canna	Joined to the island of Canna by a bridge. One of the Small Isles. Area: 0.78 sq miles (2.03 sq km). Population: 6. GR: NG280043	Hebrides
Scalp Rock	Loch Snizort	Biod a' Choltraiche, Skye	One of the Ascrib Islands. GR: NG299632	Hebrides
Scalpay	Inner Sound	Creag Strollamus	Mullach na Carn at 1286ft (392m). is the highest peak. Area: 9.65 sq miles (24.99 sq km). Population: 10. GR: NG610300	Hebrides
Seal Rock	Loch Snizort Beag	Knott, Skye	GR: NG379551	Hebrides
Seana Sgeir	Atlantic	Droman	GR: NC177597	Hebrides
Sgarbhag	The Minch	Farhead Point	GR: NC137404	Hebrides
Sgeir a' Bhuic	Loch Eriboll	Rubh' a' Mhuilt	GR: NC471630	Fair Isle
Sgeir a' Bhuic	Loch Ewe	Isle of Ewe	GR: NG837892	Hebrides
Sgeir a' Chaolais	Sound of Arisaig	Ardtoe	GR: NM622700	Hebrides
Sgeir a' Chapuill	Loch Snizort	Biod a' Choltraiche, Skye	One of the Ascrib Islands. GR: NG303648	Hebrides
Sgeir a' Chapuill	Caolas a' Mhill Ghairbh	Tanera Mor	One of the Summer Isles. GR: NC989089	Hebrides
Sgeir a' Chlaidheimh	Eddrachillis Bay	Rubh'an Dobhrain	GR: NC134371	Hebrides
Sgeir a' Choire	Loch Sunart	Carna		Malin
Sgeir a' Chuain	Loch Bracadale	Ose Point, Skye	GR: NG299410	Hebrides
Sgeir a' Chuain	Loch Dunvegan	Rubha nam Both, Skye	The sea area around the island is the Little Minch. GR: NG218583	Hebrides
Sgeir a' Chuain	Loch Snizort	Biod a' Choltraiche, Skye	One of the Ascrib Islands. GR: NG302656	Hebrides
Sgeir a' Ghaill	Loch Nevis	Sgurr an Eilein Ghubhais	GR: NM740979	Hebrides
Sgeir a' Ghair	Atlantic	Rubha na Fearn	GR: NG725615	Hebrides
Sgeir a' Phuirt	Sea of the Hebrides	Sanday	GR: NG285047	Hebrides
Sgeir an Aon Iomairt	The Little Minch	Tanera Mor	One of the Summer Isles. GR: NB965055	Hebrides
Sgeir an Araig	Loch Ewe	Mellon Charles	GR: NG831899	Hebrides
Sgeir an Durdain	Sound of Arisaig	Farquar's Point	GR: NM632728	Hebrides
Sgeir an Eididh	Sound of Arisaig	Ardtoe	GR: NM619712	Hebrides
Sgeir an Fheoir	Loch Carron	Meall na h-Airde	GR: NG811365	Hebrides
Sgeir an Fheoir	Sound of Sleat	Rubh' Arisaig	GR: NM622865	Hebrides
Sgeir an Oir	Tongue Bay	Portvasgo	GR: NC611645	Fair Isle
Sgeir an Roin	Inner Sound	Waterloo, Skye	GR: NG673247	Hebrides
Sgeir an t-Seangain	Loch Sunart	Rubha Aird Earnaich	GR: NM715627	Malin
Sgeir an t-Sruith	Loch Eishort	Boreraig, Skye	GR: NG623153	Hebrides
Sgeir Bheag	Loch Bracadale	Colbost Point, Skye	GR: NG301398	Hebrides
Sgeir Bheag	Sea of the Hebrides	Sgurr Mor, Skye	GR: NG343241	Hebrides
Sgeir Bhuidha	Inner Sound	Port-an-eoina	GR: NG774325	Hebrides
Sgeir Bhuidhe	Inner Sound	Eilean na Ba	GR: NG694377	Hebrides
Sgeir Bhuidhe	Loch Carron	Meall na h-Airde	GR: NG802360	Hebrides
Sgeir Bhuidhe	Loch Carron	Plockton	GR: NG812336	Hebrides
Sgeir Biodaig	Tarskavaig Bay	Rubha Sloc an Eorna, Skye	GR: NG570085	Hebrides
Sgeir Buidhe Bhorlum	Sound of Raasay, The Minch	Island of Rona	GR: NG615606	Hebrides
Sgeir Charrach	Sea of the Hebrides	Rubha Aird Druimnich	GR: NM583733	Hebrides

Island name	Area	Nearest landmark	General information	Shipping Area
Sgeir Chnapach	Holoman Bay	Oskaig Point, Raasay	Lies off the coast of Eilean Aird nan Gobhar. GR: NG541388	Hebrides
Sgeir Dhearg	Inner Sound	Rubha Doire na Boceinein, Scalpay	A reef-fringed islet of the Sgeirean Tarsuinn group. GR: NG638330	Hebrides
Sgeir Dhubh	Loch Sligachan	Peinchorran, Skye	GR: NG527328	Hebrides
Sgeir Dhubh	Sound of Raasay	Upper Ollach, Skye	Lies southwest of McMillan's Rock. GR: NG526362	Hebrides
Sgeir Dhubh	The Minch	Rubha nam Brathairean, Skye		Hebrides
Sgeir Dhubh	Loch Torridon	Arinacrinachd	GR: NG748591	Hebrides
Sgeir Dorcha	Loch Scavaig	The Bad Step, Skye	GR: NG490189	Hebrides
Sgeir Dubh	Inner Sound	Drochaid Lusa, Skye GR: NG693255		Hebrides
Sgeir Dubh	The Little Minch	Glas-leac Mor	One of the Summer Isles. GR: NB962095	Hebrides
Sgeir Dughall	Loch Torridon	Lower Diabaig	GR: NG778604	Hebrides
Sgeir Eskernish	Sound of Eigg	An Corrach, Eigg	GR: NM445843	Hebrides
Sgeir Fhada	Sea of the Hebrides	Beinn Airean, Muck	GR: NM408791	Hebrides
Sgeir Fhada	Tarskavaig Bay	Rubha Sloc an Eorna, Skye	GR: NG571086	Hebrides
Sgeir Fhearchair	Atlantic	Rubha na h-Airde Glaise, Skye	GR: NG701252	Hebrides
Sgeir Ghainmheach	Loch nan Ceall	Torr Mor	GR: NM632868	Hebrides
Sgeir Ghlas	Loch Ailort	Cooper's Knowe	GR: NM691791	Hebrides
Sgeir Ghlas	Sound of Mull	Achadh Fada, Mull	GR: NM623434	Hebrides
Sgeir Ghlas	Loch Torridon	Red Point	GR: NG731669	Hebrides
Sgeir Ghlas	Loch Torridon	Kenmore	GR: NG763576	Hebrides
Sgeir Ghobhlach	Inner Sound	Pabay	Drying rock marked by a beacon. GR: NG666257	Hebrides
Sgeir Ghobhlach	Sea of the Hebrides	Sanna Point	GR: NM437703	Hebrides
Sgeir Gormul	Loch Eishort	Meall Buaile nan Caorach, Skye	GR: NG635154	Hebrides
Sgeir Graidach	The Little Minch	Rubha Huish, Skye		Hebrides
Sgeir Iasgach	The Little Minch	Eilean a' Char	One of the Summer Isles. GR: NB968094	Hebrides
Sgeir Iosal	Loch Laxford	Ardmore Point	GR: NC179508	Hebrides
Sgeir Lang	The Little Minch	Kilmuir, Skye	GR: NG369708	Hebrides
Sgeir Leathan	Atlantic	Sangobeg	GR: NC430667	Fair Isle
Sgeir Maol Mhoraidh	The Minch	Meall Glac a' Bheithe	GR: NG808930	Hebrides
Sgeir Maol Mhoraidh Shuas	The Minch	Meall Glac a' Bheithe	GR: NG814925	Hebrides
Sgeir Mhali	Loch Sunart	Rubha an Daimh	GR: NM743613	Malin
Sgeir Mhic Eachain	Sound of Sleat	Calligarry, Skye	GR: NG627025	Hebrides
Sgeir Mhor	Loch Bracadale	Eabost West, Skye	GR: NG302401	Hebrides
Sgeir Mhor	Loch Slapin	Tobar Ceann, Skye	GR: NG576196	Hebrides
Sgeir Mhor	Sea of the Hebrides	Rubh' an Dunain, Skye	GR: NG393158	Hebrides
Sgeir Mhor	Sound of Raasay	Portree, Skye	GR: NG494433	Hebrides
Sgeir Mhor	Tarskavaig Bay	Rubha Sloc an Eorna, Skye	GR: NG577089	Hebrides
Sgeir Mhor	Sound of Sleat	Morar	GR: NM665932	Hebrides
Sgeir Mhor	The Little Minch	Rubha na Breige	GR: NC063199	Hebrides
Sgeir na Caillich	Loch Alsh	Rubha na Caillich	GR: NG800247	Hebrides
Sgeir na Caorach	The Little Minch	Rubha Maol, Skye	GR: NG227560	Hebrides
Sgeir na Eireann	The Minch	Flodigarry, Skye	GR: NG480723	Hebrides
Sgeir na h-Iolaire	The Minch	Island of Rona		Hebrides
Sgeir na Trian	The Minch	Red Point	GR: NG731650	Hebrides
Sgeir nam Biast	The Little Minch	Rubha Maol, Skye	GR: NG238566	Hebrides
Sgeir nam Feusgan	Caolas a' Mhill Ghairbh	Tanera Mor	(G. = Skerry of the Mussels). One of the Summer Isles. GR: NB977088	Hebrides
Sgeir nam Fiadh	Loch Eishort	Cnoc na Fuarachad, Skye	GR: NG611132	Hebrides
Sgeir nam Maol	The Little Minch	Rubha Huish, Skye	GR: NG395816	Hebrides
Sgeir nam Meann	Sound of Arisaig	Torr Beithe	GR: NM620697	Hebrides
Sgeir nam Mult	The Little Minch	Rubha Dubh Ard	GR: NB960039	Hebrides
Sgeir nan Cuag	Sea of the Hebrides	Oigh-sgeir	(G. = Twisted Skerry). One of the Small Isles. GR: NM160960	Hebrides
Sgeir nan Eilid	Loch nan Uamh	Rubh' Aird Ghamhsgail	GR: NM701841	Hebrides
Sgeir nan Eun	Caol Rona	An Caol, Raasay	GR: NG616535	Hebrides

Island name	Area	Nearest landmark	General information	Shipping Area
Sgeir nan Gall	Atlantic	Oldany Island	GR: NC085357	Hebrides
Sgeir nan Gillean	Loch Linnhe	Rubha na h-Earba	GR: NM909549	Hebrides
Sgeir nan Ron	Loch Teacuis	Carna	GR: NM616577	Malin
Sgeir nan Ruideag	The Little Minch	Uamh Oir, Skye	GR: NG359749	Hebrides
Sgeir nan Sgarbh	Sea of the Hebrides	Canna	GR: NG215060	Hebrides
Sgeir nan Sgarbh	The Little Minch	Rubha Voreven, Skye	GR: NG405746	Hebrides
Sgeir nan Sgarbh	Caolas a' Mhill Ghairbh	Tanera Mor	One of the Summer Isles. GR: NB979088	Hebrides
Sgeir Neill	Loch Sunart	Glenborrodale	GR: NM621605	Malin
Sgeir Philip	Loch nan Ceall	Gortenachullish	GR: NM637868	Hebrides
Sgeir Revan	The Little Minch	Tanera Mor	One of the Summer Isles. GR: NB973058	Hebrides
Sgeir Sgaothaig	Sound of Eigg	An Corrach, Eigg	GR: NM438851	Hebrides
Sgeir Shalac	Caolas Mor	Toscaig	GR: NG702365	Hebrides
Sgeir Shuas	Sound of Raasay, The Minch	Island of Rona	GR: NG624618	Hebrides
Sgeir Stapaig	Inner Sound	Rubha Aosail Sligneach, Scalpay		Hebrides
Sgeir Thraid	Inner Sound	Rubha Doire na y Boceinein, Scalpa	Drying rock marked by a beacon. One of the Sgeirean Tarsuinn. GR: NG629335	Hebrides
Sgeirean an Uisge Ghlais	Inner Sound	Portractoich	GR: NG760306	Hebrides
Sgeirean Buidhe	Loch nan Ceall	Torr Mor	GR: NM640856	Hebrides
Sgeirean Buidhe	Loch Shieldaig	Doire-aonar	GR: NG808531	Hebrides
Sgeirean Dubha Fhiadhach	Sound of Arisaig	Rubh' Aird an Fheidh	GR: NM632760	Hebrides
Sgeirean Glasa	Inverie Bay	Rubha Raonuill	GR: NM742997	Hebrides
Sgeirean Glasa	The Little Minch	Rubha Dubh Ard	GR: NB968023	Hebrides
Sgeirean Glasa	The Minch	Tarbet	GR: NC155492	Hebrides
Sgeirean Goblach	Sound of Sleat	Portnaluchaig	GR: NM640894	Hebrides
Sgeirean Mora	Sea of the Hebrides	Rhubha na Pairce, Rum	GR: NM360917	Hebrides
Sgeirean Mora	Loch Shieldaig	Rhuroin	GR: NG795549	Hebrides
Sgeirean nan Torran	Loch Linnhe	Torran na Mointich	GR: NM931569	Hebrides
Sgeirean Rarsaidh	Loch Hourn	Rarsiadh	GR: NG822115	Hebrides
Sgeirean Shallachain	Loch Linnhe	Crofts of Sallachan	GR: NM978621	Hebrides
Sgeiteadh	Sea of the Hebrides	Geodha nan Gobhar, Skye	GR: NG353228	Hebrides
Shieldaig Island	Loch Shieldaig	Shieldaig	See separate entry	Hebrides
Shona Beag	Loch Moidart	Eilean Shona	GR: NM667735	Malin
Skerry	Pentland Firth	Island of Stroma	GR: ND342759	Fair Isle
Skerry Mor	Moray Firth	Clyth	GR: ND286358	Cromarty
Skye	Sea of the Hebrides	Kyle of Lochalsh	See separate entry	Hebrides
Sleiteil Rocks	Caol Raineach	Sletell	GR: NC630633	Fair Isle
Soay	Soay Sound	Ulfhart Point, Skye	See separate entry	Hebrides
South Ascrib	Loch Snizort	Biod a' Choltraiche, Skye	One of the Ascrib Islands. GR: NG302635	Hebrides
Soyea	Loch Inver	Strathan	(G. = Sheep). GR: NC046220	Hebrides
Spur, The	Dunnet Bay	Murkle	GR: ND170699	Fair Isle
Sron na h-Airde Baine	Inner Sound	Ardban	GR: NG696399	Hebrides
Stac a' Bhothain	Loch Snizort	Cirein Mor, Skye	GR: NG289596	Hebrides
Stac a' Mheadais	Sea of the Hebrides	Ben Scaalan, Skye	GR: NG330254	Hebrides
Stac an t-Seabhaig	The Minch	Handa Island	See The Great Stack	Hebrides
Stac an Tuill	Sea of the Hebrides	Sgurr an Duine, Skye	GR: NG356215	Hebrides
Stac Buidhe	The Minch	Balmacqueen, Skye	GR: NG448746	Hebrides
Stac Dubh	Atlantic	Midfield	GR: NC585655	Fair Isle
Stac Mhic Aonghais	The Little Minch	Tanera Mor	One of the Summer Isles. GR: NB955056	Hebrides
Stac Suisnish	Loch Slapin	Rubha Suisnish, Skye	GR: NG585163	Hebrides
Stacan Gobhlach	The Minch	Balmacqueen, Skye	GR: NG451745	Hebrides
Stachan Geodh Bhrisidh	Puffin Bay	Handa Island	(G. = Stack of the Broken Chasm). GR: NC135488	Hebrides
Stack Aros	Loch Snizort	Gillen, Skye	GR: NG273600	Hebrides
Stack Clo Kearvaig	Atlantic	Kearvaig	GR: NC295737	Fair Isle
Stack of Mid Clyth	Moray Firth	Mid Clyth	GR: ND300373	Cromarty
Stacks of Duncansby	Pentland Firth	Duncansby Head	GR: ND400720	Fair Isle
Stacks, The	Moray Firth	Occumster	GR: ND274354	Cromarty
Stacks, The	Pentland Firth	Brough	GR: ND232742	Fair Isle
Staffin Island	The Minch	Rubha Garbhaig, Skye	GR: NG491692	Hebrides
Stirk Rock	Gruinard Bay	Gruinard Island	GR: NG938952	Hebrides

Island name	Area	Nearest landmark	General information	Shipping Area
Stroma	Pentland Firth	St John's Point	See separate entry	Fair Isle
Strome Island	Loch Carron	Ardaneaskan	GR: NG837348	Hebrides
Sula Skerry	Loch Bracadale	Ullinish, Skye	GR: NG317381	Hebrides
Talmine Island	Tongue Bay	Skinnet	GR: NC591623	Fair Isle
Tanera Beg	The Little Minch	Tanera Mor	Notable for its bank of fine coral sand, rare in the Highlands. Area: 0.25 sq miles (0.66 sq km). GR: NB965075	Hebrides
Tanera Mor	The Little Minch	Rubha Dunan	Largest of the Summer Isles. Permitted to issue its own postage stamps. Area: 1.20 sq miles (3.1 sq km). Population: 5. GR: NB990075	Hebrides
Tarner Island	Loch Bracadale	Colbost Point, Skye	GR: NG299390	Hebrides
Tulm Island	The Little Minch	Ru Meanish, Skye	GR: NG408750	Hebrides
Ulluva	Loch Carron	Creag an Duilisg	GR: NG826338	Hebrides
Wiay	Loch Bracadale	Ulinish Point, Skye	Area: 0.57 sq miles (1.48 sq km). GR: NG295365	Hebrides
Yule Rock	Sound of Mull	Rubha an Ridire	Lies southwest of Glas Eileanan.	Hebrides

Lothian

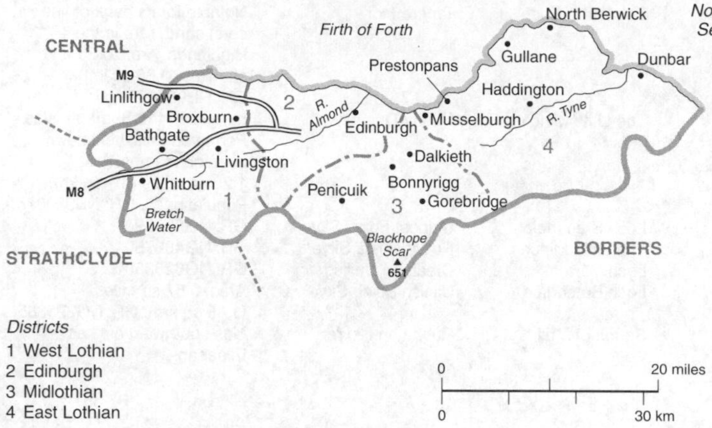

North Berwick
North Sea
Firth of Forth
CENTRAL
Gullane
Prestonpans
Dunbar
M9
Haddington
Linlithgow
2
R. Almond
R. Tyne
Broxburn
Musselburgh
Edinburgh
Bathgate
4
Dalkieth
Livingston
M8
Whitburn
Penicuik
Bonnyrigg
1
3
Gorebridge
Bretch Water
Blackhope Scar
651
BORDERS
STRATHCLYDE
Districts
1 West Lothian
2 Edinburgh
3 Midlothian
4 East Lothian
0
20 miles
0
30 km

Lothian is a former government region encompassing the unitary authorities of City of Edinburgh, East Lothian, Midlothian and West Lothian. Traditionally the region is named after the 6th century Pictish King Loth. It has borders with the Scottish Borders to the south, Falkirk in the Central region to the northwest, and North Lanarkshire and South Lanarkshire in Strathclyde to the southwest. Its northern coast is on the Firth of Forth and its eastern coast on the North Sea. Its main rivers are the Almond, the Esk, the Tyne and the Water of Leith.

East Lothian, once known as Haddingtonshire, has borders with the Scottish Borders region, the City of Edinburgh and Midlothian. To the north and east it is bounded by the Firth of Forth and the North Sea. To the south are the Lammermuir Hills. The main employer is the local council and the region's main industries are farming and tourism. In the past fishing and coal mining were also major employers in the region. The administrative centre is Haddington, while other towns include Dunbar, Musselburgh, North Berwick, Prestonpans and Tranent.

Landlocked **Midlothian** has borders with Scottish Borders, the City of Edinburgh and East Lothian. Its traditional industries such as papermaking, coal mining and heavy engineering have largely disappeared to be replaced by agriculture and service industries including tourism. In the past it was known as Edinburghshire and many towns in the area now serve as satellite towns for the capital. Dalkeith is home to its administrative centre, while other towns include Penicuik, Newtongrange and Roslin. The area has grown in popularity with the recent development of interest in Rosslyn Chapel, believed by many to be connected with the Holy Grail.

West Lothian has borders with City of Edinburgh, Scottish Borders, South Lanarkshire, North Lanarkshire and Falkirk and has an administrative centre at Livingston. It has a short coastline on the Firth of Forth. In the past it was known as Linlithgowshire. The main employing industries in the region are electronics and software development and the older industries of coal mining and oil are now non-existent. Linlithgow Palace was the birthplace of Mary, Queen of Scots. Other main towns are Bathgate, Armadale, Broxburn and Whitburn.

The **City of Edinburgh** unitary authority encompasses Edinburgh itself, the second-largest city in Scotland, as well as the port of Leith. During the Iron Age the area around the Forth River valley was controlled by the Votadini, the tribe encountered by the Romans under Agricola during the 1st century. Din Eidyn (Fort of Eidyn) is the most likely derivation of the name Edinburgh with Castle Rock being an easily defensible position. The area was controlled by the Northumbrians from the 7th century until the early 11th century. A castle was built by Malcolm III Canmore at Edinburgh during the 11th century and Holyrood Abbey was established in 1128 by David I. These, along with a connection to the port of Leith, formed the basis for the growth of the city of Edinburgh. The city became the capital of Scotland in 1437. The Old Town, which grew up around the castle, has retained its medieval street plan and narrow multi-storey housing.

The city's prosperity can be said truly to have begun following the Act of Union in 1707 when Edinburgh became the focus for the Scottish Enlightenment. In order to escape the cramped conditions of the Old Town a competition was held in the 1760s to design a New Town. This was won by James Craig, who laid out new streets including George Street and Princes Street on a grid pattern. The Nor Loch (North Loch) between the Old and New Towns was drained in the 1820s and Princes Gardens were created. The Mound, on which the National Gallery of Scotland and the Royal Scottish Academy Building were built, was formed from the spoil from the new construction. The population of the city rose from 57,195 in 1755 to 160,511 in 1851, by which time it had also become fashionable to take the waters of seaside resorts.

Edinburgh is the home of the devolved Scottish Parliament. The city's economy has never been based around heavy industry but instead is founded on financial services and more recently tourism. The world-renowned Edinburgh International Festival was established in 1947. The Old Town and New Town districts were designated a UNESCO World Heritage Site in 1995. Edinburgh is nicknamed 'Auld Reekie' (Old Smoky) and, more favourably, the 'Athens of the North' (thanks both to the grandeur of its architecture and its reputation as an intellectual centre), and has the reputation of being the most haunted city in Britain.

Lothian	**Population**			**Area**	
Districts	*male*	*female*	*total*	*sq miles*	*sq km*
East Lothian	42,963	47,125	90,088	262	679
Edinburgh City	214,711	233,913	448,624	102	264
Midlothian	38,670	42,271	80,941	137	354
West Lothian	76,701	82,013	158,714	165	427
Total	373,045	405,322	778,367	666	1724

Local Attractions and Information

LOTHIAN

Abercorn Monastery Abercorn, 2 miles (3km) west of South Queensferry. A monastic site close to Abercorn Parish Church. Established c.685 by Northumbrians and believed to be the *Aebbercurnig* mentioned by Bede, it was the seat of Bishop Trumwin, after which it may have been abandoned following the Battle of Nechtansmere but reoccupied during the 8th century.

Aberlady Bay Nature Reserve 4 miles (6km) northwest of Haddington. Assigned as Britain's first Local Nature Reserve in 1952, the reserve covers 1315 acres (532ha) of sand, mudflats, mussel beds and salt marsh bordered by dunes, freshwater marsh and woodland, supporting wildfowl and waders plus 550 different species of plant life. Bird species include lapwing, redshank, roseate tern, pink-footed, barnacle and greylag goose, whooper swans, wigeon, mallard, teal, shoveler, shelduck and goldeneye. The German High Seas Fleet surrendered off Aberlady Bay in 1918, while in the bay are the remains of two XT-Craft midget submarines used for target practice by the RAF in 1946.

Administrative headquarters **East Lothian**: Haddington House, Haddington EH41 4BU. Tel: 01620 826789.
Edinburgh City: City Chambers, High Street, Edinburgh EH1 1YJ. Tel: 0131 200 2000.
Midlothian: Midlothian House, Buccleuch Street, Dalkeith EH22 1DJ. Tel: 0131 270 7500.
West Lothian: West Lothian House, Almondvale Boulevard, Livingston EH54 6QG. Tel: 01506 777000.

Airport **Edinburgh** (EDI), 7 miles (11km) west of Edinburgh. Operated by the British Airports Authority and known at one time as Turnhouse Airport. It was an RAF base until 1947; a passenger terminal was opened in 1954. A new terminal designed by Robert Matthew was opened in 1977 and the airport has three runways. There are flights to numerous destinations in the British Isles, Europe and North America. Tel: 0870 040 0007.

Almond Valley Heritage Centre Millfield, Livingston Village, 1/2 mile (0.8km) southwest of Livingston. A local history museum run by the Almond Valley Heritage Trust which interprets the history and environment of West Lothian. Housed in a restored working watermill and farm buildings set in 20 acres (8ha) by the River Almond, it was named Scottish Museum of the Year in 2002. Tel: 01506 414957.

Almondell and Calderwood Country Park Broxburn, West Lothian. Located in the Almond Valley between Broxburn and East Calder and consisting of the adjoining estates of Almondell (97 acres/39ha) and Calderwood (130 acres/53ha) by the River Almond. In the spring Calderwood features natural bluebell woods, mainly of oak and hazel. Tel: 01506 882254.

Amisfield Park 1 mile (1.6km) east of Haddington. The former estate of notorious libertine Colonel Francis Charteris. Amisfield House, built for Charteris in 1755 by Isaac Ware, was demolished in 1928 but some of the stable block plus an ice-house and temple remain. The estate has been home to Haddington Golf Club since 1865.

Archerfield Estate Dirleton, 6 miles (10km) north of Haddington. The 1000 acre (400ha) estate was named after English archers who camped on the site in 1298. Archerfield House, built in 1733 and formerly the home of the Nisbet family, was used during World War II for a meeting between Churchill and Roosevelt to discuss D-Day. It fell into disrepair in the second half of the 20th century before being renovated as a clubhouse of the private Archerfield Links; the original links course, dating

	to the mid 19th century, was abandoned after the Ministry of Defence took over the estate during World War II. Tel: 01620 850542.
Arniston House	$1^1/_2$ miles (2.5km) southwest of Gorebridge, 9 miles (15km) southeast of Edinburgh. Palladian mansion designed by William Adam for the Dundas family and built 1726–50 on the site of a 16th century tower house. After Adam's death in 1748, the house was completed by his son John. A porch was added in 1872, and parts of the house were gutted and restored in the 1990s. The Dundas family are still in residence; the house has collections of porcelain and paintings of the family by Sir Henry Raeburn. Tel: 01875 830515.
Arthur's Seat	Holyrood Park, Edinburgh. A peak formed from the remains of an extinct volcano, standing 823ft (251m) high and dominating the Edinburgh skyline. The parabola of red cliffs known as Salisbury Crags rises to 150ft (46m) on a spur of Arthur's Seat. Many archaeological finds have been made on its slopes, including Bronze Age axes and a Roman ring, and there is evidence of an Iron Age hill fort and cultivation terraces. In July 1836 schoolboys hunting rabbits came across a small cave concealed in which were 17 tiny (4–6in/10–15cm long) wooden coffins, each containing a clothed wooden doll. Many theories have been proposed as to who made them and placed them on Arthur's Seat, from witchcraft to sailors' good luck charms; a connection has even been suggested with the notorious Burke and Hare body snatchings. Some of the remaining coffins can be seen at the Museum of Scotland in Edinburgh.
Auld Kirk Green	North Berwick, 7 miles (11km) northeast of Haddington. Aka Anchor Green. The oldest surviving part of North Berwick harbour. St Andrew's Church, the Auld Kirk (old church) itself, originally stood on what was an island from at least 1177 until 1656, when the eastern part was damaged by a storm. North Berwick was a ferry point for pilgrims to St Andrews and moulds for pilgrim badges have been found on the site. Following the storm damage, the church was rebuilt in 1659; it was replaced by the present North Berwick Parish Church in 1861. According to legend, in 1590 the 5th Earl of Bothwell stood on Auld Kirk Green in the guise of the Devil and tried to raise a storm to sink the ship carrying James VI and his bride home from Norway, his attempt giving rise to the North Berwick Witch Trials and the outbreak of witch hunts during James VI's reign. Excavations in preparation for the building of the Scottish Seabird Centre in 1999 uncovered several burials near the Auld Kirk, including that of an apparent murder victim. More recent digs have revealed that the church was built on an earlier (possibly 7th century) religious establishment.
Barnbougle Castle	5 miles (8km) northwest of Edinburgh. Overlooking Drum Sands on the Firth of Forth and originally built in the 13th century as a tower house, by the 17th century the property had passed into the hands of the Rosebery family. It was abandoned by the family when they built nearby Dalmeny House in 1817 but in 1881 the 5th Earl of Rosebery (1847–1929), Prime Minister 1894–5, decided to restore it as a retreat. It is now the main Rosebery family residence and a private house.
Barns Ness	3 miles (5km) southeast of Dunbar. A promontory on the North Sea coast of East Lothian with a 121ft (37m) tall lighthouse built in 1901 by David A Stevenson. The lighthouse was automated in 1986 but ceased to operate in October 2005.
Bass Rock	An island 2 miles (3km) off the East Lothian coast east of North Berwick, rising 350ft (107m) out of the water. It supports the largest single gannetry in the world, with at least 40,000 nesting pairs between February and September each year. It is believed that St Baldred lived on the island in the 7th or 8th century; a chapel was built on the site of his cell c.1491 and dedicated in 1542. A castle built on the island in the 16th century by the Launders of Bass, possibly on the site of an earlier fortification, passed to the Crown in 1671 and was used as a prison to house Covenanters until the Glorious Revolution. In 1691 the island was taken over by Jacobite prisoners who held it for four years before being forced to surrender. The fort was partially demolished and in 1706 the island passed to Sir Hew Dalrymple. From then until after World War I the gannet colony regularly suffered from 'harrying', where eggs were taken and young birds killed by local fishermen. The colony can now be studied by remotely controlled cameras at the Scottish Seabird Centre in North Berwick. The uninhabited island is a designated Site of Special Scientific Interest. Bass Rock Lighthouse was built in 1903 by David A Stevenson. The 65ft (20m) white tower stands on a gun platform once belonging to the old fortress and was automated in December 1988. Area: 0.01 sq miles (0.025 sq km). (GR: NT602873.)
Bathgate	An industrial and former mining town in West Lothian developed during the 19th century with the coming of the railway, which benefited the local coal and lime industries. The world's first truly commercial oil refinery was established in the town in the mid 19th century after the discovery by James Young that paraffin could be extracted from the local shale fields.
Battles	See separate table for details of the battles of Dunbar (I) and (II), Pinkiecleugh, Prestonpans, Roslin and Rullion Green.
Belhaven Brewery	Spott Road, Dunbar. An independent brewery founded in 1719 by John Johnstone, the largest regional brewer in Scotland and claimed to be the oldest operating brewery in Britain. It is believed that brewing has been conducted on the site since the 12th century; Belhaven ale was supplied to Dunbar Castle in the 1550s. The brewery was rebuilt after fires in 1814 and 1887. Tel: 01368 862734.
Bennie Museum	Mansefield Street, Bathgate. A local history museum opened in 1989, housed in two adjoining 18th century cottages and dedicated to the life and history of Bathgate. A further building was opened in 1999. Exhibits include examples of Bathgate glass and a photographic archive. There are also displays on locally born Sir James Young Simpson (1811–70), the inventor of chloroform, and James 'Paraffin' Young (1811–83), who refined paraffin from oil shale and established the world's first oil refinery in the town. Tel: 01506 634944.

Birkhill Fireclay Mine $2^1/_2$ miles (4km) southwest of Bo'ness, West Lothian. Set in the wooded Avon Gorge beside Birkhill Station on the Bo'ness & Kinneil Railway. The mine, which operated 1908–80, provided alumina fireclay to line industrial furnaces and was reopened in 1987 as a relic of the area's industrial heritage.

Blackness Castle Blackness, 3 miles (5km) east of Bo'Ness. Standing on a promontory in Blackness Bay on the River Forth, the castle was built by the Crichton family and dates from at least 1449. Originally designed as a tower house (the present central tower) to protect the port of Blackness, further towers (the north and south towers) and gun platforms were added in the 16th and 17th centuries to enhance its defensive capabilities. The resulting castle resembles a ship heading out into the river. The castle was used as a prison for much of its life and held Cardinal David Beaton in the 1540s, Covenanters in the late 17th century and French prisoners of war during the Napoleonic Wars. Having been repaired after suffering damage during a successful siege by Cromwellian forces in 1650, in the 19th century it served as the central ammunition depot for Scotland, at which time a barracks was built for the garrison and more comfortable accommodation for the officers. The castle was abandoned as a military base after World War I and was designated an ancient monument. It is now in the care of Historic Scotland. Tel: 01506 834807.

Blawhorn Moss 4 miles (6km) west of Armadale. A National Nature Reserve mainly consisting of active raised bog, rare in lowland Scotland.

Bo'ness & Kinneil Railway Union Street, Bo'ness. A heritage railway operating for 4 miles (6km) between Bo'ness and Birkhill via Kinneil on the course of the former Slamannan & Borrowstounness Railway. The railway was established in 1979 and Bo'ness Station was opened in 1981, a number of railway buildings from around Scotland being re-erected to form the station and signalling complex. The line reached Kinneil in 1987 and in 1989 was further extended to Birkhill, where it connects with the Edinburgh–Glasgow main line at Manuel. The railway operates steam and diesel locomotives. Display sheds next to Bo'ness Station house the Scottish Railway Exhibition. It is also the headquarters of The Scottish Railway Preservation Society, founded in 1961. Tel: 01506 822298. See also Birkhill Fireclay Mine.

Borthwick Castle 1 mile (1.6km) east of North Middleton, 11 miles (18km) southeast of Edinburgh. A thick-walled, twin-towered castle beside Gorè Water, built c.1430 as a tower house for Lord Borthwick on the site of an earlier fortification known as the Mote of Lochorwart. It was visited by Mary, Queen of Scots and her new husband James Hepburn, Earl of Bothwell in May 1567 in the wake of their controversial marriage, but both she and her husband were forced to flee. Her ghost is said to appear dressed as a page boy, the disguise she used when making her escape. The castle was besieged and captured by Oliver Cromwell in November 1650, and afterwards abandoned. Fully restored by the Borthwick family in the late 19th century, it was converted into a hotel in 1973. Tel: 01875 820514.

Brass Rubbing Centre and Trinity Apse Chalmers Close, Royal Mile, Edinburgh. The restored apse of Trinity College Church, founded c.1460. The church was dismantled in the 1870s to make way for Waverley railway station, after which the apse was rebuilt on its present site. It is now home to the Brass Rubbing Centre, which contains replicas of monumental brasses from all over Scotland. Tel: 0131 556 4364.

Burgh Halls The Cross, Linlithgow. Linlithgow's town hall, built 1668–70 to replace the previous town house after its destruction by Cromwellian troops. The building was damaged by fire and repaired in the 1840s; a clock tower was added in 1858. Tel: 01506 848821.

Cairnpapple Hill 2 miles (3km) northeast of Bathgate. Standing at 1024ft (312m) above sea level and with outstanding views in all directions, Cairnpapple Hill is a significant prehistoric site showing evidence of human activity between 3000 BC and AD 400. Excavation of the site in 1947–8 revealed that the earliest find, a cremation cemetery, was followed by a henge with 24 standing wooden posts (or standing stones). This was replaced c.2000 BC by a cyst cairn extended to cover two cremation urns. Finally there were four inhumation burials dating to the early Christian era. A concrete reconstruction of the cairn was erected in 1949, enabling the graves inside to be viewed. The site is maintained by Historic Scotland.

Caiy Stane Caiystane View, Fairmilehead, Edinburgh. Also known as the Kel Stane or Camus Stone. Located in Edinburgh's southeastern suburbs, the 9ft 3in (2.8m) standing stone, inscribed with cup marks, is said to mark the site of an ancient battle. It has been owned by the National Trust for Scotland since 1936.

Calder House Mid Calder, 2 miles (3km) east of Livingston. An extended L-plan house originally built in the 16th century for the Sandilands family, the Lords Torpichen. Visitors to the house include John Knox in 1556 and Frederic Chopin in 1848. The house remains a private residence of the family.

Calton Hill A hill in east central Edinburgh, rising to 312ft (95m) above sea level. It is the location of a number of monuments and historic buildings including the National Monument, the Nelson Monument, the Royal High School and the Observatory.

Cammo Estate Park $^1/_2$ mile (0.8km) south of Cramond Bridge, 4 miles (6km) west of Edinburgh. A landscape designed 1711–19 by Sir John Clerk (or Clarke) of Penicuik surrounding Cammo House, built in 1693 for John Menzies and possibly the model for the House of Shaws in Robert Louis Stevenson's *Kidnapped*. Although the house itself is now a ruin, some of the trees planted when the park was established are still standing. These older broadleaved parkland trees are mixed with younger conifers. Species include ash, giant redwood and umbrella pine. A large standing stone in the park is known as the Cammo Stone.

Canongate Tollbooth Canongate, Royal Mile, Edinburgh. Built in 1591 as the town courthouse and gaol, the building now houses a museum charting the history of the people of Edinburgh since the 18th century. Tel: 0131 529 4057.

Castlelaw Fort 7 miles (11km) south of Edinburgh. An Iron Age hill fort and settlement on a spur on the slopes of Castlelaw Hill, standing at 1601ft (488m) in the Pentland Hills. Excavations in the 1930s and 1940s revealed evidence of a single trench and timber palisade, expanded to become a multivallate fort – oval in shape with possibly three entrances – in the immediate pre-Roman period, c.AD 78. Some 2nd century Roman finds and a well constructed 3rd century souterrain 70ft (21m) long were also found. The site is in the care of Historic Scotland, but most of Castlelaw Hill is covered by military ranges and is therefore a danger area.

Chesters Hill Fort 2 miles (3km) north of Haddington. An Iron Age hill fort and settlement originally measuring 900ft (274m) by 500ft (152m) externally. A multivallate fort with up to six ramparts, it was nevertheless not built in an easily defensible position, being located below a scarp from which missiles could have been directed into it.

Churches **Abercorn Parish Church**, 2 miles (3km) west of South Queensferry, dedicated to St Serf, was originally built in the 12th century close to Abercorn's 7th century monastic settlement. Reconstructed in 1579 and further altered by the Hope family in the early 1700s, it underwent major refurbishment in 1893. A small museum in the churchyard has fragments of an 8th century cross and Viking hog-back burial stones.

Aberlady Parish Church, 4 miles (6km) northwest of Haddington, was originally built on Aberlady Bay in the 12th century and rebuilt in the 15th century. Extended and refurbished in 1773, the church underwent major restoration in 1886 under the auspices of the Earl of Wemyss.

Bolton Parish Church, 2½ miles (4km) south of Haddington, is a Gothic style church built in 1809; in the churchyard are the graves of Robert Burns' mother Agnes, sister Annabella and brother Gilbert, estates manager to Lord Blantyre.

Easter Pencaitland Church 5 miles (8km) southwest of Haddington, is a late 12th century church extended in the 17th century. The west tower, which may have been built in 1631, is square for most of its height, but at the top becomes octagonal and apparently served as a combined belfry and dovecot.

Greyfriars Tolbooth & Highland Kirk, Greyfriars Place, Edinburgh, is a parish church built on the site of the Grey Friars, a 15th century Franciscan friary. The right to use the area for burials was granted by Mary, Queen of Scots in 1562. The church was built in the early 17th century and in 1638 the National Covenant was signed here; in 1679 1200 Covenanters were imprisoned in the kirkyard following the Battle of Bothwell Brig. An extension was added in 1721 and separate congregations worshipped in the two halves of the church until the dividing wall was removed in 1938. Dwindling numbers of worshippers during the 20th century saw many neighbouring churches close, their congregations uniting at Greyfriars Kirk. The kirkyard is the site of the vigil of Greyfriars Bobby and is also said to be haunted by the spirit of 'Bluidy' George MacKenzie.

St Mary's Church, Haddington, located beside the River Tyne and also known as the 'Lamp of Lothian', is the longest parish church in Scotland at 206ft (62.8m). Begun in 1380, consecrated c.1400 and completed in 1462, it replaced the original 'Lamp of the Lothian', a church founded nearby by the Grey Friars in 1242 and destroyed during Edward III's 'Burnt Candlemas' campaign in February 1356. The new church was itself severely damaged during the Siege of Haddington in 1548–9; only the nave was restored to be used as a parish church, the tower, transepts and choir being left roofless. Major restoration work 1971–3 returned the church to much of its original condition.

St Michael's Church, Kirkgate, Linlithgow, was established in the 12th century on a promontory above Linlithgow Loch. The present building, consecrated in 1242, was used as a storehouse by English troops during an invasion in 1301 and severely damaged by the Linlithgow fire in 1424, the subsequent repairs taking until 1540 to complete. In 1559 all evidence of 'popishness' was removed. Some ill-advised restoration in the early 19th century was rectified in the 1890s and the church was rededicated in 1896.

City Chambers High Street, Edinburgh. A neoclassical building designed by Robert and John Adam and built 1753–61. Originally designed as the city's Royal Exchange, it proved unpopular with Edinburgh merchants and was taken over by the town council in 1811. It was extended during the 19th century; the council chambers are housed in the north range, added in 1903. A statue of *Alexander Taming Bucephalus* (1833) by Sir John Steell stands in the courtyard.

Craigleith An island rising 80ft (24m) out of the Firth of Forth and home to colonies of seabirds including cormorants, guillemot and puffins. The birds are monitored by cameras remotely controlled from the Scottish Seabird Centre in North Berwick. In recent years the colony of puffins has suffered because of the intrusion of the tree mallow, a plant that destroys the burrows in which they nest. (GR: NT553870.)

Craigmillar Castle Craigmillar Castle Road, Edinburgh. A well-preserved castle standing on a rocky hilltop and originally built c.1400 as an L-plan tower house by the Preston family. In 1440 a curtain wall was added to form an inner courtyard; an outer wall was built in 1510 to create an outer courtyard. The castle was damaged during its capture by English forces in 1544 and was subsequently repaired and embellished with a range of residential buildings. Mary, Queen of Scots visited in 1563 when she met with Thomas Randolph, an ambassador from Elizabeth I. During a second visit in 1566 the Earls of Argyll, Huntly and Bothwell are said to have agreed the Craigmillar Bond, by the terms of which Mary's then husband, Henry, Earl of Darnley, was to be disposed of. The Prestons sold the castle to Sir John Gilmour in 1660 and it was abandoned by the Gilmours in the 1700s. Much of the original structure still stands, including a dovecote. Craigmillar Castle Jubilee Park, designated in 2002 and covering 150 acres (60ha) mainly of meadow and woodland, was opened in 1965. A further 150 acres from the estate of Woolmet house were purchased in 2004 and the park was extended towards the New

Edinburgh Royal Infirmary. The castle passed into state care in 1946 and is now in the care of Historic Scotland.

Cramond Roman Fort Cramond, 4 miles (6km) northwest of Edinburgh. A Roman fort at the mouth of the River Almond, covering 5 acres (2ha) and originally constructed c.AD 140. Abandoned c.165, it was reoccupied in the early 3rd century, when it was used as a base for the military campaigns in Scotland led by the emperor Septimus Severus. There was a *vicus* (civil settlement) associated with the fort and possibly a harbour nearby. The site was first excavated 1954–66; buildings uncovered include a bath house and a granary. In late 1996 a sculpture was spotted on the bed of the River Almond near the ferry steps; when this was excavated it was found to be a representation of a crouching lioness, with the head and body of a naked man in her grip and two snakes underneath her belly, which sat on a plinth. Known as the Cramond Lioness, the sculpture dates from the late 2nd or early 3rd century and may be part of a tomb monument for a high-ranking Roman army officer.

Crichton Castle 3/4 mile (1.2km) southwest of Crichton, 2 miles (3km) east of Gorebridge. A ruined castle beside the Tyne Water, originally built by John Crichton as a tower house in the 14th century and extended over the next 200 years. The castle was stormed in the 1440s and captured by James III in 1483 after William Crichton was implicated in a conspiracy against him. The castle and lands were forfeited and eventually came into the possession of Patrick Hepburn, Earl of Bothwell. On the downfall of his son James, husband of Mary, Queen of Scots, the castle passed to James Francis Stuart, who became 5th Earl of Bothwell. He made considerable changes in the late 1580s, adding a new range of rooms in continental style. Notorious for his behaviour – James VI also felt threatened by his position as next in line to the throne – the Earl was forced into exile and died in Italy in 1612; the castle then passed through several owners and fell into ruin. It passed into state care in 1926 and is now managed by Historic Scotland. Tel: 01875 320017.

Cross Well High Street, Linlithgow. Located in front of the Burgh Halls and erected in 1807 as a facsimile of the original Cross Well, built in the 1620s, the well is topped by a sculpture in the shape of a crown. Stones from the original well cover are on display in Annet House, Linlithgow.

Dalhousie Castle 1 1/2 miles (2.5km) southeast of Bonnyrigg, 4 miles (6km) southeast of Edinburgh. Located next to the River Esk and originally built as an L-plan tower house in the 13th century. The Drum Tower and well were added in 1450 and it was further altered and extended in the 17th and 18th centuries. The castle was successfully defended against Henry IV in 1400 and was occupied by Oliver Cromwell in 1648. It was visited by Mary, Queen of Scots in June 1563 and Queen Victoria in 1840. During the 20th century it was occupied by a prep school; it remained uninhabited from the 1950s until 1972 when it was converted into a hotel. In 2000 the storage vaults were converted into an aqueous spa. Tel: 01875 820153.

Dalkeith Palace Dalkeith, 7 miles (11km) southeast of Edinburgh. Aka Dalkeith House. Located beside the River North Esk, the house was begun c.1700 by Ann, daughter of Francis Scott, 2nd Earl of Buccleugh, to a design by James Smith. It incorporated parts of the 15th century L-plan tower house known as Dalkeith Castle and which formed the south wing of the new building. The tower house, a former stronghold of the Douglases of Dalkeith, was used as a hunting lodge by Charles I and attacked and captured by Covenanters in 1639. Purchased by Francis Scott, 2nd Earl of Buccleugh in 1642, it was used by Cromwell and General Monck as a base for the governance of Scotland in 1650. The Dukes of Buccleugh and Queensberry stopped living in Dalkeith Palace c.1914. The house was used as a company headquarters in the 1970s; since 1984 it has been leased to the University of Wisconsin and is known as Wisconsin-in-Scotland (WIS). The surrounding 860 acre (344ha) estate, featuring landscaped lawns and semi-natural woodland as well as remnants of the Caledonian Oak Forest, has been open to the public as a country park since 1975.

Dalmeny House 2 miles (3km) east of South Queensferry, 5 miles (8km) northwest of Edinburgh. A manor house designed by William Wilkins in Tudor Gothic style and built 1814–17 for Archibald, 4th Earl of Rosebery to replace Barnbougle Castle. Today it features two major collections: the Rosebery Collection includes items collected before the move from Barnbougle and those collected by the 5th Earl of Rosebery up to his death in 1929; the Rothschild Collection includes objects, paintings and furniture collected by the Rothschild family during the 19th century and came into the Rosebery family through the marriage of Hannah Rothschild to the 5th Earl of Rosebery in 1878. Both collections feature fine art and furniture. In addition the house has a collection of items relating to Napoleon, a Burns collection and several unusual items including a mechanical dice game from 1737, a Covenanter's execution knife and a scold's bridle. There is an enclosed garden adjacent to the house. Tel: 0131 331 1888.

Dean Gallery Belford Road, Edinburgh. Opened in 1999 as part of the National Galleries of Scotland and housed in a building originally constructed in the 1830s as the Dean Orphan Hospital. The main holding is the Paolozzi Gift, donated to the Scottish National Gallery of Modern Art in 1994 by Leith-born sculptor Sir Eduardo Paolozzi (1924–2005); the gallery includes a reconstruction of Paolozzi's London studio. Other works include 26 drawings and paintings by Dalí, Delvaux, Ernst, Magritte and Picasso bought from the Penrose Collection in 1995, and works bequeathed by Gabrielle Keiller from her collection of Dada and surrealist art. The grounds contain works by sculptors including Antoine Bourdelle, George Rickey and Paolozzi. Tel: 0131 624 6200.

Dirleton Castle Dirleton, 2 miles (3km) west of North Berwick. A 13th century castle standing on an outcrop of rock and built for the de Vaux family on the site of an earlier castle. Held by the English from 1298, it was retaken in 1311 by Robert the Bruce, who promptly slighted it to prevent it being used by the English again. It was rebuilt later in the 14th century by the Haliburton family, to whom it had devolved through marriage, and further extended and modernised by the Ruthvens in the 16th century. Following the Gowrie Conspiracy in 1600 it passed to Thomas Erskine, but was abandoned shortly after being captured and damaged by Cromwellian troops led by General Monck in 1650. The still substantial ruins have been in the care of Historic Scotland since 1923. The formal gardens contain (according to the *Guinness Book of Records*) the longest herbaceous border in the world, as well as a 16th century beehive doocot built for the Ruthven family.

Drem Airfield Drem, 3 miles (5km) north of Haddington. Established in 1916 as West Fenton Aerodrome, when it was used by the Royal Flying Corps during World War I. In 1939 it was designated RAF Drem and became the base for 602 Squadron of Spitfires. A new lighting system developed at Drem to enable safer night landing later became standard at all RAF airfields. In 1945–6 the airfield came under the auspices of the Admiralty and was renamed HMS *Nighthawk*; it was decommissioned shortly after the end of World War II. Part of the airfield is now occupied by a retail park; a small museum dedicated to the airfield was opened in 2003 in the Village Arts and Craft Gallery.

Dunbar Castle Victoria Harbour, Dunbar. The ruins of a substantial 12th century castle located on a promontory overlooking Dunbar harbour. It was built on the site of earlier Pictish fortifications, a strategically important location as Dunbar provided the best landing point on the west coast north of Berwick-upon-Tweed, and therefore saw more than its fair share of action during the medieval wars between England and Scotland. Dunbar was the scene of an English victory in 1296 when the Earl of Surrey defeated John Balliol. Besieged January–June 1338 by the Earl of Salisbury, the castle was successfully defended by a force commanded by Lady 'Black Agnes' Randolph, Countess of Dunbar. As part of an agreement with England it was slighted in 1488 but was soon rebuilt. Mary, Queen of Scots was held here by her husband, the Earl of Bothwell, in 1567. On her abdication the castle was once again slighted, this time by order of the Scottish Parliament. The remains were further damaged when a new entrance to Dunbar harbour was blasted out in 1844. Now located within the John Muir Country Park, the castle is not open to the public because of safety concerns.

Dunbar Town House Museum High Street, Dunbar, East Lothian. A local history museum housed in the former town house or tolbooth, which formerly contained the council offices, courthouse and gaol. It was built c.1593 of red freestone and has a lead-covered spire. The last council meeting was held here in 1975 and the museum opened in 1994. Displays include local archaeology and a photographic archive. Tel: 01368 863734.

Easter Craiglockhart Hill Craiglockhart, Edinburgh. A local nature reserve in the south of Edinburgh, designated in 2005 and covering 37 acres (15ha). The hill stands 519ft (158m) above sea level. Habitats include water, grassland and woodland.

Edinburgh & Glasgow Union Canal More usually known simply as the Union Canal. Running for $31^1/_2$ miles (50km) from Fountainbridge, Edinburgh to Falkirk where it joins the Forth & Clyde Canal, it was a contour canal designed without the need for locks and was built 1818–22, its main purpose being the transportation of coal from the coalfields into Edinburgh. The canal's decline as both a passenger and commercial enterprise began with the arrival of the Glasgow–Edinburgh railway in 1842; although it did not close for commercial use until the 1930s, several sections in Edinburgh were abandoned and filled in. The canal was closed in 1965 but restoration work was begun in the 1990s. New sections were dug and it was rejoined to the Forth & Clyde Canal in 2000 by means of the Falkirk Wheel. It now crosses the Antonine Wall by means of a tunnel. The Linlithgow Canal Centre is located at Manse Road Basin, Linlithgow.

Edinburgh Castle Castlehill, Edinburgh. Britain's second most popular tourist attraction after the Tower of London. A fortification of some kind has probably stood on this hilltop site 260ft (80m) above the city since the Iron Age. The oldest surviving building in the castle and its environs is the 12th century St Margaret's Chapel, dedicated to St Margaret of Scotland who died in Edinburgh on 16 November 1093. The castle was developed as a royal stronghold by David I in the first half of the 12th century but was one of many Scottish castles handed over to Henry II of England in 1174 following the Scottish defeat at the Battle of Alnwick. It was back in Scottish hands from 1186 until its capture by Edward I in 1296. The castle changed hands more than once over the next half-century before David II began a massive rebuilding process in the 1360s. It served as a royal residence for many years until the Stewarts (Stuarts) began to use Holyroodhouse for that purpose instead, but remained the main defence for Edinburgh. After Mary, Queen of Scots fled to England in 1568, some of her supporters were besieged in the castle 1571–3 by the forces of her son James VI, in what is known as the Lang Siege. Oliver Cromwell used the castle as a base for his Scottish campaign in 1650 and in 1689 it was held briefly by Jacobite forces supporting James VII (James II of England). Jacobite rebels failed to take the castle in 1715 and 1745. The castle was repaired and extended with the 'new barracks' in 1799 during the Napoleonic Wars, when it also housed prisoners of war. The gatehouse was rebuilt in 1888 and the great hall was restored in the 1890s. Today the castle houses the Honours of Scotland (the Scottish Crown Jewels), as well as the Scottish National War Museum, the Royal Scots Regimental Museum and the Scottish National War Memorial. It is also host to the annual Edinburgh Military Tattoo, which takes place on the Esplanade. The one o'clock gun is fired each day from the castle. Although now a major tourist attraction, the castle still continues in its role as a military base. Tel: 0131 225 9846.

Edinburgh City Art Centre Market Street, Edinburgh, Lothian. A fine art gallery opened in 1980 in a former newsprint store built in 1899, which later became a fruit warehouse. It contains over 3500 paintings by Scottish artists from the 17th century until the present, including Sir William Gillies (1898–1973), E A Hornel (1864–1933), John Henry Lorimer (1856–1936), Samuel Peploe (1871–1935), Sir Eduardo Paolozzi and Anne Redpath (1895–1965). Tel: 0131 529 3993.

Edinburgh Corn Exchange — Newmarket Road, Edinburgh. Designed by James A Williamson and built in 1909. It was converted into a live music venue in 1999 and is now also a conference and exhibition centre. Tel: 0131 477 3500.

Edinburgh Crystal — The Edinburgh Crystal company was founded in 1867 as the Edinburgh & Leith Flint Glass Company by Alexander Jenkinson. It moved to Penicuik in 1969, before going into administration and being taken over by Waterford Crystal in 2006.

Edinburgh Festival — A world-renowned cultural festival, established as the Edinburgh International Festival in 1947 and taking place over three weeks each August. The programme includes performances of music, drama and dance, which take place at a range of venues including Edinburgh Playhouse, the Festival Theatre, The Hub, the King's Theatre, the Queen's Hall, the Royal Lyceum Theatre and the Usher Hall. The festival has spawned many imitators, while various other festivals and events take place in the city around the same time of the year including the Edinburgh Festival Fringe and the Edinburgh Military Tattoo. The Fringe began in 1947 at the same time as the main Edinburgh Festival when eight theatre groups (six Scottish and two English) arrived at the Festival uninvited. As the main venues were obviously taken they began performing at less familiar places, including pubs, with little or no advance publicity. The Fringe was named by Robert Kemp from the *Evening Standard*, who in 1948 described the performances of groups 'around the fringe of the official Festival'. A central box office was established in 1954 and the Festival Fringe Society was founded in 1958. More than 700 performance companies now take part in the Fringe each year. Tel: 0131 473 2099.

Edinburgh Festival Theatre — Nicolson Street, Edinburgh. Opened as the Empire Palace Theatre on 7 November 1892, and reopened in 1994 as a venue for opera and ballet. Occupying a site previously occupied 1830–90 by a series of performance halls, including the Royal Amphitheatre, the Alhambra Music Hall and Newsome's Circus, the Empire Palace was designed by Frank Matcham for Edward Moss and seated 3000 in plush surroundings. On 9 May 1911 a fire on the stage at the end of a performance by the illusionist The Great Lafayette killed 11 performers and stage hands including the artist himself. He was buried in Piershill Cemetery, Edinburgh, beside his dog Beauty, who had died only a few days before. Legend has it that his double, who 'helped' with the illusions, was mistakenly buried in his place before Lafayette's body was recovered from the debris. All 3000 customers left the theatre unscathed but a ghostly Lafayette is rumoured still to tread the boards. The theatre was reopened within a few months. In 1927 it was re-equipped as a variety theatre and opera house and was used as a major venue for ballet performances from the outset of the Edinburgh Festival in 1947. In 1963 the theatre was closed and used as a bingo hall until 1991. The new Edinburgh Festival Theatre was designed by Colin Ross and its decoration harks back to the 1928 reconstruction. It has a seating capacity of 1915. Tel: 0131 529 6000.

Edinburgh Military Tattoo — An annual display by military bands and display teams which takes place on the esplanade of Edinburgh Castle during the Edinburgh International Festival. The first tattoo took place in 1950. The name is derived from the closing-time cry in the inns in the Low Countries during the 17th and 18th centuries: '*Doe den tap toe*' ('Turn off the taps'). Tel: 0131 225 9661.

Edinburgh Prison — Stenhouse Road, Edinburgh. Aka Saughton Prison. Opened in 1919, a local prison holding adult male and under 21 prisoners on remand or serving sentences of less than four years. Operational capacity: 558. 0131 444 3000.

Edinburgh World Heritage Site — Representing, according to their designation criteria, 'a remarkable blend of two urban phenomena – organic medieval and neo-classical town planning', Edinburgh's Old and New Towns were designated a UNESCO World Heritage Site in December 1995. The site encompasses Edinburgh Castle, the National Gallery of Scotland, John Knox House, The Georgian House, Gladstone's Land, the Palace of Holyroodhouse, National Museums of Scotland, City Chambers, Scott Monument, Royal Scottish Academy, Usher Hall, Scottish Gallery of Modern Art, Greyfriars Church, Scottish Parliament, Canongate Tolbooth, High Kirk of St Giles and the Scottish National Portrait Gallery.

Edinburgh Zoo — Corstorphine Road, Edinburgh. Established by Thomas Gillespie and opened on 22 July 1913 on an 82 acre (33ha) site in the west of the city under the auspices of the Royal Zoological Society of Scotland. Its design was based on that of Hamburg Zoo with large open enclosures rather than cages. The zoo was the first in the UK to feature penguins; it still has the world's largest penguin pool, while the zoo's logo depicts a king penguin. Tel: 0131 334 9171.

Fenton Tower — Kingston, North Berwick. A 16th century tower house built by Patrick Whitelaw c.1550 on the site of an earlier tower and which served as a refuge for James VI when he was facing a rebellion in 1591. The tower was severely damaged by a Cromwellian force in 1650 and remained abandoned until its restoration began in 1998. A luxury hotel since 2002, it served as the location for Archie's Castle in the BBC children's TV series *Balamory*. Tel: 01620 890089.

Fidra — An uninhabited island and RSPB reserve in the Firth of Forth, home to a large colony of puffins. The island was reputedly the inspiration for the layout of Robert Louis Stevenson's *Treasure Island*. The lighthouse was established in 1885 by Thomas Stevenson and automated in 1970. Area: 0.04 sq miles (0.1 sq km). (GR: NT512868.)

Georgian House and Charlotte Square — Charlotte Square, Edinburgh. A town house built in 1706 and designed by Robert Adam. Now furnished to reflect the period when it was built, it has been in the care of the National Trust for Scotland since 1966. Numbers 26–31 Charlotte Square were also bought by the National Trust for Scotland in 1996 and are now the Trust's head offices. Tel: 0131 226 3318.

Gladstone's Land — Lawnmarket, Edinburgh. A typical 17th century 'land' or tenement in Edinburgh's Old Town. Built in 1620, the six-storey merchant's house was owned by Thomas Gledstanes, whose apartments feature a painted ceiling and period furniture. Other parts of the house would have been let to a variety of tenants, while the ground floor has recreations of shop booths. It was purchased by the National Trust for Scotland in 1934 and opened to the public in 1977. Tel: 0131 226 5856.

Glenkinchie Distillery 1 mile (1.6km) south of Pencaitland, 6 miles (10km) southwest of Haddington. A distillery was opened on this site in 1837 by John and George Rate and the Glenkinchie Distillery was established in the 1880s. The water source is the Lammermuir Springs. Tel: 01875 340333.

Greyfriars Bobby Greyfriars Kirkyard, Edinburgh. A statue in memory of Bobby, a Skye terrier who belonged to policeman John Gray. When Gray died of tuberculosis on 15 February 1858 he was buried in Greyfriars Kirkyard and Bobby is said to have kept vigil by his grave for the next 14 years. He was fed by local residents, who also built him a shelter, and the annual dog licence was paid for by the Lord Provost of Edinburgh. Bobby was buried just inside the entrance to the kirkyard and his headstone reads 'Greyfriars Bobby – died 14th January 1872 – aged 16 years – Let his loyalty and devotion be a lesson to us all'. Erected in November 1873, the memorial is a life-size bronze sculpture of Bobby created by William Brodie.

Haddington A town on the River Tyne in East Lothian, established in the 11th century and granted royal burgh status by David I. Its position on the route into central Scotland meant it suffered repeated depredations from marauding armies, including an 18 month siege in 1547–9. Despite this, the town prospered through its connection with the nearby port of Aberlady. It is now the administrative centre for East Lothian Council.

Hailes Castle $1^1/_2$ miles (2.5km) southwest of East Linton, 4 miles (6km) east of Haddington. Built on a rocky bluff overlooking the River Tyne to its north, while to its south the ground rises steadily to the ancient hill fort on the top of Traprain Law, Hailes is one of the oldest surviving stone castles in Scotland, probably built by Hugo de Gourlay in the late 13th century. The Gourlays lost their land in the early 14th century and Sir Adam de Hepburn became the new owner. The Hepburns made extensive alterations to the castle, increasing both its defensive capability and domestic facilities. The castle remained in the ownership of the Hepburns until 1567 when James Hepburn, 4th Earl of Bothwell and 3rd husband of Mary, Queen of Scots, forfeited his lands and fled to Norway. The castle passed first to the Stewarts, then to the Setons and finally, in 1700, to the Dalrymples of Hailes, but was soon abandoned by the Dalrymples in favour of a new mansion.

Hawthornden Castle 1 mile (1.6km) south of Bonnyrigg. A 17th century L-plan house standing above the ruins of a 15th century tower house on a promontory beside the River Esk. Home in the 17th century to poet William Drummond, who built its L-plan additions, it was fully restored in the 1980s.

Heart of Midlothian The nickname of the Edinburgh Tolbooth or Old Tolbooth Prison, originally built in 1386 and demolished in 1817. The tolbooth served as council chambers, courthouse and gaol and featured in Sir Walter Scott's novel *The Heart of Midlothian.* It was usually the final stop before condemned prisoners went to their execution nearby. A heart shape set in cobblestones on the Royal Mile now marks the tolbooth's position; a tradition that to spit in the centre of the heart may bring good luck is believed to derive from criminals' practice of spitting on the tolbooth's door as they passed.

Hermitage of Braid Braid Road, Edinburgh. A local nature reserve designated in 1993 and covering 147 acres (59ha) in the valley of the Braid Burn, in the south of Edinburgh. An area of ancient broadleaved woodland with grassland and gorse scrub, the main tree species include ash, beech, birch, elm, oak, rowan and sycamore. Bird species include owls and woodpeckers. Hermitage House, standing within the reserve and built in 1785, was presented to the City of Edinburgh in 1938; it now serves as a visitor centre for the reserve and is the headquarters of the Edinburgh Ranger Service. There is also an ice house and a large dovecot on the estate.

Heriot-Watt University The eighth oldest higher education institution in the UK. The name commemorates goldsmith George Heriot, a 16th century financier to James VI of Scotland (James I of England), and the great 18th century inventor and engineer James Watt. Originating as the School of Arts of Edinburgh in 1821, and opening its doors to women as early as 1869, Heriot-Watt received its university charter in 1966. The Scottish College of Textiles in Galashiels merged with Heriot-Watt in 1998. The university's Watt Club, founded in 1854, is the oldest alumni association in the UK. Today Heriot-Watt has four campuses: three in Scotland – Edinburgh, the Scottish Borders and Orkney – and one in Dubai, opened in 2006. Former students include author Irvine Welsh and Adam Crozier, chief executive of Royal Mail. Tel: 0131 449 5111.

Highest point Blackhope Scar in the Moorfoot Hills at 2136ft (651m). (GR: NT315483.)

Holyrood House See Palace of Holyroodhouse

Holyrood Park Also known as Queen's Park. A royal park next to the Palace of Holyroodhouse in the heart of Edinburgh, covering 642 acres (260ha) and encompassing Arthur's Seat, Salisbury Crags, Duddingston Loch, St Margaret's Loch and Dunsapie Loch.

Hopetoun House 2 miles (3km) west of South Queensferry, West Lothian. A country house of palatial proportions overlooking the River Forth, built for the Hope family 1699–1707. The house was enlarged to a design by William Adam in 1721 and completed by his sons John and Robert. The public rooms are furnished and decorated in period style with fine art including paintings by Canaletto and Gainsborough. The grounds cover 100 acres (40ha) of parkland and woodland, including a deer park. Part of the house is still lived in by the Hope family. John Adrian Hope (1860–1908), 7th Earl of Hopetoun, created 1st Marques of Linlithgow in 1902, was the first Governor General of Australia. Tel: 0131 331 2451.

Hopetoun Monument 1 mile (1.6km) north of Haddington. A 100ft (30.5m) tall monument in the Garleton Hills, erected in 1824 to commemorate General Sir John Hope, 4th Earl of Hopetoun (1765–1823), a hero of the Battle of Corunna (1808) during the Peninsular War, where he was called upon to take over command after the death of Sir John Moore. The monument bears the following inscription: 'This monument was erected to the memory of the Great and Good John Fourth Earl of Hopetoun by his affectionate and grateful tenantry in East Lothian. MDCCCXXIV'. The 132 steps inside lead to a viewing platform. Sir John Hope was also a governor of the Royal Bank of Scotland, and a statue to him stands in front of Dundas House, the bank's head offices in St Andrew's Square, Edinburgh.

House of the Binns — 4 miles (6km) east of Linlithgow. A house acquired, restored and 'modernised' by butter merchant Thomas Dalyell in 1612 and extended in the 1740s and c.1810. It was here in 1681 that General Tam Dalyell formed the Royal Scots Greys. The rooms are furnished in period style and include family memorabilia and portraits. A ruined round tower nearby was built in 1826 apparently as the result of a wager. The house and the tower have been maintained by the National Trust for Scotland since 1944; the Binns was the first house to be acquired by the Trust under the Country Houses Scheme and is still partly occupied by the Dalyell family. The surrounding parkland has views over the Firth of Forth. Tel: 01506 834255.

Hub, The — Castlehill, Edinburgh. A concert venue opened in 1999 in the former Assembly Hall and Tolbooth Church on the Royal Mile. The foundation stone for the Assembly Hall and offices of the Church of Scotland was laid by Queen Victoria in 1842 and it was completed in 1845. Designed by J Gillespie Graham and Augustus Pugin and originally known as Victoria Hall, the building has the tallest spire in Edinburgh at 240ft (73m). The meeting place of the Scottish General Assembly until 1929, in 1956 it was renamed the Highland Tolbooth St John's Church. After the church closed in 1979, the building was acquired by the Edinburgh International Festival in 1995 and reopened as The Hub by Queen Elizabeth II on 6 July 1999. Tel: 0131 473 2015.

Huntly House Museum — See Museum of Edinburgh

Interesting facts — The **Encyclopaedia Britannica** was first published in Edinburgh in 1768 by a 'Society of Gentlemen in Scotland'. Since 1929 it has been published in Chicago, USA. **George Street** in Edinburgh is the most lucrative street for traffic wardens in Britain with tickets worth £1.3m handed out in 2005–6. **Inchmickery** off the coast of Edinburgh has an interesting story to tell. James IV of Scotland was said to have sent two newborn babies and a dumb nurse to live on this uninhabited island to discover if they would speak the 'original language' of the human race, Hebrew, and after two years announced that the children 'spak extremely guid Ebrew'. **Stuart or Stewart?** There has been much debate over the years on exactly how the family name of so many kings and queens should be spelt. The Stewarts descend from Walter the Steward, one of the Anglo-Norman knights introduced to Scotland by David I. Walter accompanied David I on his return from England to Scotland and was created Steward of Scotland, and was one of the commanders who defeated Somerled of the Isles in 1164. James, the 5th High Steward, initially opposed Robert the Bruce but afterwards secured the family's position, his son Sir Walter Stewart marrying Bruce's daughter Marjorie. On the death of Bruce's only son David II, Robert Stewart – Sir Walter's son and Bruce's grandson – became Robert II. The Stewart royal line was maintained through a series of male heirs until Mary, Queen of Scots, the Stewarts holding the Scottish (and later the English and British) throne from Robert II in 1371 until Queen Anne in 1714. Of course, after the Hanoverian line succeeded to the throne, the Royal Stewart line continued through the uncrowned James VIII and James Francis Edward Stewart, Bonnie Prince Charlie, and Jacobite rebellions continued until final defeat occurred at Culloden in 1746. The 'Stuart' spelling arose because there was no letter 'w' in the French language; Mary, Queen of Scots, in particular, became Mary Stuart following her marriage to the Dauphin of France (later Francis II). The Stewart clan motto is *Virescit vulnere virtus* ('Courage grows strong at a wound'). The Royal Commission on the Ancient and Historical Monuments of Scotland ran a competition ahead of its centenary in 2008 to decide **Scotland's most treasured place**. Lady Victoria Colliery in Newtongrange, Midlothian came out top of the poll of more than 20,000 subscribers, despite its closure in 1981.

Inveresk Lodge Garden — Inveresk, 2 miles (3km) east of Musselburgh, East Lothian. A walled terraced garden surrounding a 17th century lodge (not open to the public). Features include a shrub and rose border, a restored conservatory and aviary. Beside the garden is a woodland area and a pond. Owned by the National Trust for Scotland since 1959. Tel: 0131 665 1855.

Islands — Offshore islands in the Lothian region are mainly in East Lothian and Edinburgh in the Forth Shipping Area. Islands in the Firth of Forth (East Lothian): **Bass Rock** (see separate entry) (GR: NT602874); **Bubbly Bus** (NT528859); **Craigleith** (aka Lamb Island) (NT553870); **Eyebroughy** (NT494864); **Fidra** (see separate entry) (NT512868); **The Gegan** (NT604848); **Hummel Ridges** (NT545860); **Hummel Rocks** (NT469831); **Lamb** (has a dog guarding each side of it which are in fact skerries) (NT535866); **Law Rocks** (NT541862); **The Leithies** (NT572858); **Longskelly Rocks** (NT509863); **North Dog** (NT512871); **Podlie Craig** (NT590856); **The Sisters** (NT557857); **South Dog** (NT512866); **Weaklaw Rocks** (NT500860). Islands in the North Sea: **Beggar's Cap** (NT623836); **Frances Craig** (NT631816); **Hurker** (NT878703); **Long Craigs** (NT669795); **The Reef** (NT755745); **The Rodgers** (NT615846); **Scart Rock** (NT678797). Islands in the Firth of Forth (Edinburgh): **Birnie Rocks** (NT216775); **The Buchans** (NT171792); **Cow & Calves** (NT207811); **Cramond Island** (NT197786); **Eastern Craigs** (NT283771); **Inchmickery** (NT207805); **Little Ox** (NT368739); **Long Craigs** (NT422766); **Mackie Rocks** (NT389748); **Middle Craigs** (NT277776); **Ox Rocks** (NT384745). Islands in the River Forth off Edinburgh: **Beamer Rock** (NT120800); **Inchgarvie** (NT137795); **Long Craig** (NT125803). In addition there are two inshore islands in Linlithgow Loch, West Lothian: **Cormorant Island** (NT005776) and **The Rickle** (NT001775).

John Knox House — High Street, Edinburgh. A late 15th century house in Netherbow, home at some point to James Mosman, goldsmith to Mary, Queen of Scots and in 1572 to Protestant reformer John Knox (1505–72), who is believed to have lived in the house from July 1572 until his death on 24

November. The house was saved from demolition by the Free Church of Scotland in the 1840s and now houses a museum charting the history of the house and its inhabitants. Restored in 2005, it is now linked to the modern home of the Scottish Storytelling Centre. Tel: 0131 556 9579.

John Muir Country Park — 1½ miles (2.5km) west of Dunbar. A country park named after Dunbar-born naturalist John Muir (1838–1914), founder of the United States National Parks. Designated in 1976, it covers 1812 acres (733ha) of the coastline of East Lothian around Belhaven Bay. The various habitats include sand dunes, grassland and woodland. More than 400 species of plant occur in the park, as well as numerous wading birds and waterfowl. Dunbar Castle lies within its boundaries.

John Muir Way — A footpath forming part of the North Sea Coastal Path Project (Nortrail), a project to develop coastal paths and ancient tracks not only in Scotland and England but also in northern European countries including the Netherlands, Denmark, Germany, Norway and Sweden. There are currently two sections of the John Muir Way: the western half runs for 14 miles (23km) from Fisherrow Harbour, Musselburgh to Gullane via Aberlady; the eastern half covers 17½ miles (28km) from East Linton to Dunglass, near Cockburnspath.

King's Theatre — Leven Street, Edinburgh. Opened in 1906 and now the sister theatre to the Festival Theatre. The King's Theatre has a long tradition of specialising in variety theatre and operatic and musical performances, in particular an annual pantomime, and is one of the main venues for the Edinburgh Festival. Refurbished in the 1980s, it seats 1350.

Kinneil House and Museum — 1¼ miles (2km) west of Bo'ness. Originally built as a tower house in the 15th century overlooking the River Forth and remodelled by the Earl of Arran in 1553. It was demolished in 1570 and replaced by an L-plan house which formed the north wing of a much larger house built in the 1660s. The house was in the process of being demolished in the 1930s when a number of 16th and 17th century decorative murals were discovered and instead some of the rooms were restored. Legend has it that the ghost of Lady Alicia Lilbourne haunts the house. Her husband, Cromwellian General Lilbourne, requisitioned the house in 1651 and she is said to have thrown herself from the attic window. The grounds contain the ruins of James Watt's cottage and the boiler of his Newcomen engine. Watt and John Roebuck were attempting to improve the efficiency of the pump used in the Bo'ness coal mine. Kinneil Museum, housed in the former stable block, is an interpretative centre for the estate and also has displays of Roman artefacts connected with the nearby site of a Roman fortlet attached to the Antonine Wall. The house is no longer open to the public.

Kirk of Calder — Mid Calder, 1½ miles (2.5km) southeast of Livingston. Built in 1541 on the site of an earlier (possibly 12th century) structure, and originally dedicated to St Cuthbert and later to St John. Extended in 1863 with the addition of north and south transepts and a belfry added, it was refurbished and restored in the 1990s.

Knock Stone Circle — Knock, 2 miles (3km) north of Bathgate. A modern replica of a stone circle, erected in 1988 in the Bathgate Hills.

Lady Stair House — See Writers' Museum

Lady Victoria Colliery — See Scottish Mining Museum, Interesting Facts

Lauriston Castle — Cramond Road South, Davidson's Mains, Edinburgh. A 16th century L-plan tower house overlooking the Firth of Forth, built by Sir Archibald Napier (father of John Napier, inventor of logarithms) and at one time the home of economist John Law. Extended in the 1820s by Thomas Allen, the castle was left in state care in 1926 and has since been maintained unaltered. It houses a collection of blue john ornaments. The enclosed gardens were landscaped during the 19th century and the croquet lawn is the home of the Edinburgh Croquet Club. A large Japanese garden known as the Edinburgh/Kyoto Friendship Garden was opened in 2002. Tel: 0131 336 2060.

Leith — A port and industrial centre originally known as Inverlet, located on the southern side of the Firth of Forth and now part of the City of Edinburgh unitary authority. Granted to the monks of Holyrood Abbey by David I in 1143, it has always had a close association with Edinburgh and was included in the charter granted to the city in 1329, although that association has not always been one of peace and goodwill. By the charter, although the trade went through Leith, the revenue went to Edinburgh, which was a source of antipathy between the two. As with many towns in the area, Leith suffered from attack by hostile forces – it was burned in 1544 and 1547 and was at the centre of a siege involving supporters and opponents of Mary, Queen of Scots. Leith was also a centre for shipbuilding from 1502 and in the 17th century glass-making and sugar-refining industries began to develop. A dry dock was built in 1720, the harbour was deepened in the 1750s and a wet dock was opened in 1804, all of which contributed to the prosperity of the port in the 19th century. Although both the population of Leith and its MP, Captain William Benn (father of Tony Benn), were strongly opposed, the port was amalgamated with Edinburgh in 1920. During the 20th century shipbuilding in Leith declined, leading to increased unemployment and a drift of population into Edinburgh. However, there was an upturn thanks to the Leith Project, which saw the regeneration of the port area and the arrival of the Royal Yacht *Britannia* at Ocean Terminal. It is now also home to the offices of the Scottish Executive.

Lennoxlove House — 1½ miles (2.5km) south of Haddington. Originally a 14th century L-plan tower house known as Lethington owned by the Maitland family. In 1720 it was bought by the Duchess of Richmond and Lennox for her nephew Lord Blantyre and renamed 'Lennox's Love to Blantyre'; over the years this was contracted to Lennoxlove. The house was refurbished in 1912 and was bought by the 14th Duke of Hamilton in 1946. It houses a collection of portraits and paintings by artists including Van Dyck and Raeburn, originally part of the Hamilton Palace Collection, and memorabilia of Mary, Queen of Scots including her death mask. Also on display are the map and compass used by Adolf Hitler's deputy Rudolf Hess when he flew to Britain in 1941 on a secret mission involving the 14th Duke. Tel: 01620 828604.

Linlithgow A royal burgh situated on Linlithgow Loch in West Lothian, on the road from Edinburgh to Stirling. The site of Linlithgow Palace, the birthplace of Mary, Queen of Scots in 1542, the town was once a centre of tanning, brewing, textiles and papermaking and is now a popular centre for tourism and commuters from Edinburgh.

Linlithgow Palace Linlithgow Peel, Linlithgow. Located on a promontory jutting into Linlithgow Loch, the palace started life as a pele tower built on the site of an earlier manor by English forces under Edward I in the early 14th century to guard the supply route from Edinburgh to Stirling. Abandoned by the English following the Battle of Bannockburn, the castle was slighted by the Scots. The earlier manor was resurrected; rebuilt after being destroyed in a fire of 1424, over the succeeding centuries it was extended into a residence for the Scottish royal family. Both James V (10 April 1512) and Mary, Queen of Scots (8 December 1542) were born here. The palace fell into disrepair and following the union with England its use by monarchs declined; its final 'royal' visitor was Bonnie Prince Charlie, who visited in September 1745. The following year the palace was again burned by troops marching to meet the Young Pretender at Culloden. The ruins were cleared and made safe in the early 19th century; the substantial remains are now maintained by Historic Scotland. The palace grounds now form Linlithgow Park, one of only two royal parks in Scotland, and expanded to incorporate the Peel, the Rose Garden, the North Shore and Fiddler's Croft. The loch is a designated Site of Special Scientific Interest.

Linlithgow Story High Street, Linlithgow. A local history museum housed in Annet House and run by the Linlithgow Heritage Trust. It focuses on local industries including tanning, mining and papermaking, and there are recreations of a pharmacy and a cobbler's; the town's royal connections are also explored. Annet House was built c.1787 as a private residence and became a police station in the 1930s. After World War II it was a library and council offices, becoming a museum in the 1990s. Outside is a long narrow sloping garden divided into four terraces: a sun terrace, a formal garden with ice house, a cottage garden with herbs and vegetables and a high terrace with views across the town and a statue commemorating Mary, Queen of Scots, born in Linlithgow Palace in 1542. Tel: 01506 670677.

Livingston A new town on the River Almond in West Lothian, built in the 1960s around Livingston Village and Livingston Station as an overflow for Glasgow. The main employment providers, originally electronics companies, are now the NHS and the retail sector. The town is home to the Almondvale Shopping Centre and an Asda WalMart which is Europe's largest shop.

Malleny Garden Balerno, 3 miles (5km) southwest of Edinburgh. A 3 acre (1.2ha) walled garden surrounding a 17th century house (not open to the public). Noted for its old roses and herbaceous borders, the garden is dominated by four clipped yews known as the Four Apostles, the only survivors of 12 yews (the Twelve Apostles) planted in the 17th century. The garden is surrounded by woodland and is home to the Scottish National Bonsai Collection, and also contains a doocot (dovecot) with 915 nesting holes. The house and garden were presented to the National Trust for Scotland in 1968. Tel: 0131 449 2283.

Melville Castle 1½ miles (2.5km) northeast of Bonnyrigg. Located beside the River North Esk, the castle was built in 1786 by Lord Melville to a design by James Playfair on the site of an earlier fortification, demolished to make way for it. According to legend a Spanish chestnut in the grounds was planted by Mary, Queen of Scots for her secretary David Rizzio (or the other way around). In the 1980s the castle was sold by the Dundas family; having fallen into disrepair, it was acquired by the Hay Family Trust in 1993 and is now operated as a luxury hotel. The grounds cover 50 acres (20ha) of parkland and woodland. Tel: 0131 654 0088.

Mons Meg An iron cannon measuring 13ft 4in (4.1m) long, forged in Mons in Belgium c.1449 and one of a pair of siege guns given to James II in 1457 by Philip the Good, Duke of Burgundy. It would have fired gun stones weighing 330lb (149.5kg) with a range of 2½ miles (4km). Records show the gun was used at the siege of Norham Castle in 1497 and was last fired in a ceremonial salute for James VII (and II) in 1681, at which point the barrel ruptured. It was removed to the Tower of London in 1754 and returned to Edinburgh Castle on 9 March 1829; it is now displayed in the castel outside St Margaret's Chapel.

Moorfoot Hills See Scottish Borders

Muiravonside Country Park 1½ miles (2.5km) southwest of Linlithgow. A country park covering 170 acres (69ha) on the River Avon, which forms the border of West Lothian and Falkirk. The habitats include woodland and parkland. Tel: 01506 845311.

Museum of Childhood High Street, Edinburgh. The brainchild of local councillor Patrick Murray, this was the first museum of its kind when it opened in 1955. There are five floors of exhibits including toys, games and comics from around the world and from all eras. Tel: 0131 529 4142.

Museum of Edinburgh Canongate, Edinburgh. Aka Huntly House Museum. A museum celebrating the history of Edinburgh, housed in Huntly House, built in the 16th century and extended over the next 200 years. Among its exhibits are the National Covenant, signed in 1638, archaeological artefacts, collections of silver and glass, Edinburgh shop signs, and Greyfriars Bobby's collar and feeding bowl. Tel: 0131 529 4143.

Museum of Flight East Fortune Airfield, 3 miles (5km) northeast of Haddington. A museum housing Britain's largest aviation collection, opened in 1975 and exploring the commercial, scientific and military history of aviation. The four hangars are home to a massive collection of planes ranging from a Wright Brothers' Model A biplane to one of the few Concordes on exhibition anywhere in the world. The military collection includes a Supermarine Spitfire Type 380, an English Electric Lightning, an Avro 504, a replica Sopwith F1 Camel from World War I, a 1940 De Havilland DH82A Tiger Moth, a 1944 Bristol Type 156 Beaufighter, a 1954 Hawker Sea Hawk F2, a 1966 Hawker Siddeley Harrier and a 1968 McDonnell Douglas M98 F4S Phantom II; civil aircraft include a De Havilland Comet, the world's first commercial jet airliner, a De Havilland Dove and Concorde G-BOAA, the first of the British Airways fleet to fly commercially. Other planes on display include Percy Pilcher's Hawk (the oldest heavier-than-air craft in the UK, built in 1896). In addition there are helicopters, microlites, gliders, rockets and missiles including Blue Streak and Polaris. The museum also has collections of instruments, models and clothing. The airship R34 set out on her transatlantic flight from East Fortune Airfield in 1919; some relics from the flight are on display. The museum is part of the Royal Museums of Scotland. Tel: 01620 880308.

Museum of Scotland Chambers Street, Edinburgh. A museum exploring the social, economic and cultural history of Scotland; opened in 1998, it is housed in a new building designed by Gordon Benson, clad in Clashach sandstone from Morayshire and inspired by the brochs, tower houses and tenements which mark Scotland's history from the Iron Age to the Victorian period. The collections and exhibits cover Scottish geology and the lives of the country's first settlers, the history of Scotland until the Act of Union in 1707, the country's emergence into the modern world and in particular the contribution of its people to the Industrial Revolution, and the impact of industrialisation on the social and economic life of Scotland and its people in the 19th and 20th centuries. Tel: 0131 247 4422.

Myreton Motor Museum Aberlady, 4 miles (6km) northwest of Haddington. A privately owned motor museum opened in August 1966. On show are cars, vans, military vehicles and motorcycles dating from as far back as 1899. There is also a large collection of memorabilia including posters and road signs. Models on display include an 1897 Arnold Benz, a 1902 Wolseley, a 1907 De Deon Bouton, a 1919 Model TT Ford and a 1927 Rolls-Royce. Tel: 01875 870288.

Napier University Opened as Napier Technical College in 1964 and named after John Napier, the inventor of logarithms, who was born on the site of the Merchiston campus. Renamed Napier College of Science and Technology in 1966, it has offered degree-level education since 1971. In 1974 it merged with the Sighthill-based Edinburgh College of Commerce to form Napier College of Commerce and Technology, which became a Central Institution in 1985. The college was renamed Napier Polytechnic in 1986 and in the same year acquired the former hydropathic hospital buildings at Craiglockhart. It gained university status in June 1992. In 1994 Napier University acquired its Craighouse campus and in 1996 a new Faculty of Health Studies was formed by the merger of the Scottish Borders College of Nursing and Lothian College of Health Studies. The university has campuses at Merchiston, Craighouse, Craiglockhart and Sighthill, with smaller medical campuses at Canaan Lane's Astley Ainslie Hospital and Comely Bank in Edinburgh, as well as in Melrose and Livingston's St John's Hospital at Howden. Tel: 08452 606040.

National Archives of Scotland Princes Street, Edinburgh. Established in 1993 as a replacement for the Scottish Record Office, the National Archives of Scotland (NAS) is responsible for preserving and making accessible Scotland's archives (those for England and Wales and for Northern Ireland are dealt with by agencies in London and Belfast respectively). In addition to government records it also holds records related to individuals, families, estates, churches and businesses. In 1296 Edward I invaded Scotland and, along with the Stone of Scone, removed the existing archives to London. Those remaining records were not returned to Edinburgh until 1948. In 1650–1 a similar scenario, this time involving Oliver Cromwell, saw more records removed to London; although they were returned at the time of the Restoration, many were lost in the journey to and from England. The archives are now based in General Register House in Princes Street, Western Register House, Charlotte Square and Thomas Thomson House in the west of the city. The foundation stone of General Register House was laid in 1774 but the building, designed by Robert Adam, was not opened until 1789 and was completed by Robert Reid only in the 1820s. Western Register House was built as St George's Church 1811–14 by Robert Reid. It closed as a place of worship in 1961 and opened as a storage building in 1971. Thomas Thomson House, named after a 19th century Deputy Clerk Register who created the basis for the modern record office, was opened in 1995. Tel: 0131 535 1314.

National Flag Heritage Centre Athelstaneford, 2 miles (3km) northeast of Haddington. An interpretation centre funded by the Scottish Flag Trust and dedicated to the story of the Scottish national flag, the saltire. It was opened in 1997 using surplus money raised from the restoration of the nearby Saltire Monument, erected in 1965. Bearing a permanently flying saltire, the inscription on the monument reads: 'Tradition says that near this place in times remote Pictish and Scottish warriors about to defeat an army of Northumbrians, saw against a blue sky a great white cross like Saint Andrew's, and in its image made a banner which became the flag of Scotland', a reference to the 9th century Battle of Athelstaneford. The centre is housed in the Hepburn Doo'cot (dovecot), built in 1583.

National Gallery of Scotland The Mound, Edinburgh. Scotland's greatest collection of fine art, concentrating on Scottish and European sculpture and paintings from the Renaissance to the early 20th century. It was opened in 1859 in a building designed by William Henry Playfair. Artists represented include: Botticelli (*Virgin Adoring the Sleeping Christ Child*), Canova (*The Three Graces*), Gainsborough, Gauguin (*Vision after the Sermon*), Poussin (*Seven Sacraments*), Raeburn (*Reverend Robert Walker Skating on Duddingston Loch*), Rembrandt, Reynolds and Titian. It stands next to the Royal Scottish Academy Building and an underground connection between the two buildings was opened in 2004. Tel: 0131 624 6200.

National War Museum of Scotland Edinburgh Castle, Edinburgh. Formerly known as the Scottish Naval and Military Museum and later the Scottish United Services Museum, this museum dedicated to Scottish military history is located in Edinburgh Castle. Exhibits include weaponry, flags, medals, uniforms and equipment; there are also paintings, ceramics and glass related to Scottish military life. Tel: 0131 247 4413.

Nelson Monument Calton Hill, Edinburgh. A tower designed by Robert Burn and erected in 1816 to commemorate Nelson's victory at the Battle of Trafalgar. Resembling an upturned telescope, and standing 106ft (32m) tall with 143 steps inside leading to a viewing platform, it also served the purpose of a signal tower which could be seen from the port of Leith. In 1852 a time signal was installed at the top of the monument and a large time-ball still drops at 12 noon GMT (1pm in summer) on weekdays to enable ships' captains to set their chronometers accurately. Tel: 01315 562716.

New Scottish Parliament Holyrood, Edinburgh. The devolved Scottish Parliament was created by the Scotland Act 1998 and the first session was officially opened on 1 July 1999 with 129 Members of the Scottish Parliament (MSPs). Prior to the opening of the new Parliament building the Scottish Parliament met at the General Assembly Hall of the Church of Scotland. On other occasions it has met in the Strathclyde Regional Council debating chamber (May 2000), the University of Aberdeen (May 2002) and The Hub (March 2006). The Scottish Parliament building, designed by Catalan architect Enric Miralles, was opened by Queen Elizabeth II on 9 October 2004. Its construction was subject to delays and spiralling costs and it opened three years later than planned, costing an estimated £431m compared to the original £109m (the much quoted original cost of £40m was based on the use of the Royal High School and did not cover a new building).

Newhailes Newhailes Road, Musselburgh. A 17th century Palladian style house with well-preserved rococo interiors, surrounded by an 18th century landscape garden. Originally known as Whitehill when it was built c.1686, the name was changed to Newhailes by Sir David Dalrymple, who bought the property in 1707. The house was extended in the 18th century to a design by William Adam. In the 86 acre (35ha) gardens there are ruined follies, a water garden, a hidden rococo shell grotto and woodland paths. Newhailes was acquired by the National Trust for Scotland in January 1997 and is undergoing a programme of restoration and conservation. Tel: 0131 653 5599.

Newhaven Heritage Centre Pier Place, Newhaven Harbour, Edinburgh. A local history museum opened in 1994 in part of Newhaven's converted fishmarket, and exploring the maritime history of the port. In the Middle Ages Newhaven was a shipyard where the *Great Michael,* the largest ship of its time, was built 1507–11 for James IV's navy; the shipyard declined shortly afterwards and the site eventually developed into a fishing port. Tel: 0131 551 4165.

Niddry Castle Winchburgh, 3 miles (5km) southwest of South Queensferry. A late 15th or early 16th century L-plan tower house on the Niddry Burn, originally a home of the Seton family and known as Niddry Seton. On 2 May 1568 Mary, Queen of Scots was brought here after her escape from Loch Leven Castle. It later fell into disrepair but has been restored as a private residence.

North Berwick Law $^1/_2$ mile (0.8km) south of North Berwick. A conical volcanic hill above North Berwick, rising to 613ft (187m) and topped since 1709 by a succession of whale-jaw arches. The most recent, placed here in 1933, rotted and was removed in 2005, to be replaced by a fibreglass replica in 2008.

Ormiston 11 miles (18km) east of Glasgow. Scotland's first planned village, built in 1735 by John Cockburn of Ormiston and later sold to the Earl of Hopetoun.

Palace of Holyroodhouse Horse Wynd, Edinburgh. A royal residence standing at the eastern end of the Royal Mile. It was established as an Augustinian monastery, with monks from Merton Abbey in Surrey, by David I in 1128. The abbey guesthouse was regularly used by Scottish kings and James II was born there in 1430. At the end of the 15th century James IV built a new palace on the site, and this was extended by his son in the 1530s. Mary, Queen of Scots was twice married at the abbey, and was in residence when her secretary David Rizzio was murdered in her presence on 9 March 1566 in the northern turret room. After James VI became king of England, the royal court was moved to London and the palace was rarely visited, although Charles I was crowned king of Scotland at Holyrood Abbey in 1633. In 1650 the palace was burned during a visit by Oliver Cromwell; although he rebuilt it, the present palace was built by Charles II 1671–9. Briefly the headquarters of Bonnie Prince Charlie in 1745, the palace was used by members of the displaced French royal family after both the French Revolution and the revolution of 1830, and is now used as a residence during state occasions. When there is no royal resident it is open to the public.

Penicuik A burgh in Midlothian on the banks of the River North Esk, developed as a planned village by Sir James Clerk in 1770. The town was a centre for papermaking from the early 18th century until the last mill closed in 2004.

Pentland Hills A range of hills extending for 15 miles (24km) to the southwest of Edinburgh. The highest point is Scald Law at 1899ft (579m); other peaks include Carnethy Hill (1880ft/573m), West Cairn Hill (1843ft/562m), East Cairn Hill (1841ft/561m) and Byrehope Mount (1769ft/536m). The Pentland Hills Regional Park, designated in 1984, covers 39 sq miles (100 sq km) on the northern edge of the Pentland Hills; it encompasses the Glencorse and Loganlea reservoirs, which supply water to Edinburgh, the Midlothian Snowsports Centre, and working farms and military training areas. Tel: 0131 445 3383.

Polkemmet Country Park 1 mile (1.6km) northwest of Whitburn. A 169 acre (68ha) country park located on an estate owned by the Baillie family from 1620 until 1957. The park has been maintained for public use by West Lothian District Council since 1978. There is mature oak, beech and sycamore woodland along the banks of the River Almond. Tel: 01501 743905.

Preston Mill and Phantassie Doocot
$^{1}/_{4}$ mile (0.4km) east of East Linton, 6 miles (10km) east of Haddington. An 18th century watermill on the River Tyne. The mill was in operation until 1959 and the waterwheel and mechanism are still in working order. There is an exhibition on the history of the mill. The nearby doo'cot (dovecot) housed up to 500 birds. The mill was given to the National Trust for Scotland in 1950 and the doocot in 1962. Tel: 01620 860426.

Prestongrange Museum
1 mile (1.6km) southwest of Prestonpans. An industrial heritage museum on the site of the former Prestongrange Colliery, exploring the history of local industries such as coal mining, brick-making and pottery and the workers in those industries. Exhibits include a beam engine and a brick kiln. Tel: 0131 653 2904.

Princes Street Gardens
Princes Street, Edinburgh. Located on the southern side of Princes Street, the West Princes Gardens cover 30 acres (12ha) and the East Princes Gardens 9 acres (3.5ha). Opened in 1876 as a public park, the gardens include the Scott Monument, the Ross Band Stand, the Ross Fountain, the Ross Open Air Theatre, a floral clock and many statues including those of David Livingstone, Thomas Guthrie and Dean Edward Ramsay.

Queensferry Museum
High Street, South Queensferry. A local history museum exploring the story of the people of Queensferry and Dalmeny. Displays cover the ferry and the bridges crossing the Firth of Forth, as well as the tradition of the 'Burry Man', who parades through the town on the second Friday of each August dressed in a costume made from burrs from the burdock plant. There is also a collection of artefacts connected with pharmaceutical retailing, including bottles and dispensing machinery. Tel: 0131 331 5545.

Ravelston Woods
Corstophine, Edinburgh. A local nature reserve of 20 acres (8ha) designated in 2002. The habitat is mainly ancient woodland, the main species including ash, holly and oak. In spring there is an abundance of bluebells.

Rivers
The **Almond** is 28 miles (45km) long, rising at Shotts, North Lanarkshire in Strathclyde and flowing northwesterly into Livingston, West Lothian, before draining into the Firth of Forth at Cramond, just east of Edinburgh.

The **Esk** initially runs as two rivers, the North Esk rising just north of the village of Carlops adjacent to the A702, before flowing northeast through Penicuik, and the South Esk rising at Blackhope Scar and flowing due north towards Dalkeith. The two rivers converge just north of Dalkeith and continue north for 4 miles (6km), discharging into the Firth of Forth at Musselburgh. The North Esk is about 16 miles (26km) long; the South Esk is somewhat shorter due to various name changes as it picks up burns along its length.

The **Tyne** is 30 miles (48km) long, rising in the Moorfoot Hills near Gorebridge and flowing northeast through Haddington before entering the sea at Tyningham, just west of Dunbar.

The **Water of Leith** is 24 miles (39km) long, rising at Millstone Rig in the Pentland Hills and flowing through Edinburgh to reach the Firth of Forth at Leith. The 12 mile (19km) Water of Leith Walkway, running alongside the river from Balerno to Leith, is a designated Urban Wildlife Site. Tel: 0131 455 7367.

Roslin Castle
$^{1}/_{2}$ mile (0.8km) southeast of Roslin, 7$^{1}/_{2}$ miles (12km) southeast of Edinburgh. Originally an early 14th century pele tower built by the St Clair (Sinclair) family in a bend in the River Esk near the site of an earlier fortification. It is also known as Rosslyn Castle (G. *ross* = promontory, *lyn* = pool). Much altered and extended over the following 200 years, it was accidentally damaged by fire in the mid 15th century and was again burnt, this time on purpose, by English forces under the Earl of Hertford in 1544. The castle was severely damaged by English artillery commanded by General Monck in 1650. A house built within the ruins of the castle was attacked in 1688 by a local mob (which also attacked nearby Rosslyn Chapel) to remove evidence of 'popery', but was later repaired. The site abounds with legends, such as that of the 'sleeping lady' who will one day awake and reveal the location of a treasure, and of the 'Hound of Roslin', an enormous English wolfhound killed at the Battle of Roslin in 1303 who still howls for his dead master on dark and stormy nights.

Roslin Glen Country Park
4 miles (6km) northeast of Penicuik. A wooded glen on the River North Esk, featuring semi-natural woodland of ash, beech and oak. It was once the home of a gunpowder factory, and some of the old factory buildings and stores are still standing. The glen is crossed by a network of paths some of which pass Roslin Castle and Wallace's Cave.

Roslin Institute
Roslin, 7 miles (11km) southeast of Edinburgh. A centre for the study of animal genetics established in 1993 where Dr Ian Wilmut and Keith Campbell created Dolly the Sheep, the first mammal to be cloned from an adult cell. Funded by the Biotechnology and Biological Sciences Research Council, it is an associated institution of the University of Edinburgh.

Rosslyn Chapel
$^{1}/_{2}$ mile (0.8km) southeast of Roslin, 7$^{1}/_{2}$ miles (12km) southeast of Edinburgh. Formerly known as St Matthew's Collegiate Church and built c.1446–84 by Sir William St Clair (Sinclair). It stands near Roslin Castle on the River Esk. Only the choir of the original planned cruciform building was completed before Sir William's death and this is covered with a pointed barrel vault divided into bays by cusped transverse arches. The chapel was considered a monument to idolatry during the Reformation and its altars were ordered to be destroyed in 1592 (the St Clairs were a Roman Catholic family). Used as stables by General Monck's troops during their siege of Roslin Castle in 1650 and damaged by an anti-Popery mob in 1688, it was repaired only in 1736 under the supervision of James St Clair. It underwent further restoration in the 1860s and was rededicated in 1862. The apse was added in the early 1880s. After ill-considered restoration in the 1950s the stonework began to suffer and much remedial work was found to be necessary in the late 1990s. Rosslyn Chapel is particularly noted for the elaborate ornamental detail of its stonework, which has provoked various legends. A carving identified as possibly depicting Indian corn, unknown at the time of the building's construction, has led to suggestions that a member of the St Clair

family reached North America before Columbus. Links with the Knights Templar and the Masons are frequently identified and some have speculated that the vaults of the chapel hold artefacts sought after by adventurers throughout the centuries, including the Holy Grail (as heavily featured in Dan Brown's novel *The Da Vinci Code*) and the Ark of the Covenant. Many fervently hold to the equally plausible belief that these antiquities were uncovered by archaeologist Professor Henry Jones Jr in the 1930s.

Royal Botanic Gardens Inverleith Row, Edinburgh. Founded in 1670 adjacent to Holyrood Palace by Dr Robert Sibbald (later first Professor of Medicine at Edinburgh University) and Dr Andrew Balfour as a physic garden to grow medicinal plants. There was a sister garden at Trinity Hospital. In 1763 both collections were moved to Leith Walk and in 1820 they were moved to their current site at Inverleith. The Temperate Palm House, built in 1858, remains the tallest in Britain. An arboretum was planted in 1888. In 1986 Inverleith House became a gallery and exhibition centre for the garden. The various types of garden on display, covering 76 acres (31ha), include a Scottish heath garden, a woodland garden, a rock garden, a winter garden and a Chinese hillside garden, as well as an azalea lawn and an alpine collection. There is also an extensive area of glasshouses. In all 17,000 different species of plant are represented at the garden. Tel: 0131 552 7171.

Royal High School One of the oldest schools in the UK, founded in 1128 at same time as the founding of the Abbey of Holyrood. Housed in various buildings during its history, including Cardinal Beaton's Palace and what is now known as the Old Royal High School building on Calton Hill, it moved to its present home in 1968. It has been a state comprehensive school since 1974. Former pupils include Sir Walter Scott, Alexander Graham Bell, politician Robin Cook and Ronnie Corbett.

Royal Lyceum Theatre Grindlay Street, Edinburgh. Built for actor-managers J B Howard and F W P Wyndham and opened on 10 September 1883, the theatre originally specialised in programmes of drama, musicals and opera. With the coming of cinema it expanded its repertoire to include film shows but by the 1930s was concentrating solely on dramatic productions. It has been one of the main venues for the Edinburgh Festival since its inception in 1947. In 1965 the theatre was sold to the Edinburgh Corporation and used by the newly founded Royal Lyceum Theatre Company.

Royal Mile Probably Edinburgh's best-known tourist area. The succession of streets runs through Edinburgh's Old Town between Edinburgh Castle and the Palace of Holyroodhouse, starting at Castle Esplanade and moving on to Castlehill, Lawmarket, High Street and Canongate before ending at Abbey Strand. Landmarks include the Castle, The Hub, St Giles Cathedral, the Heart of Midlothian, John Knox's House, the Canongate Tolbooth, the Kirk of Canongate and the new Scottish Parliament Building.

Royal Museum of Scotland Chambers Street, Edinburgh. Housed in a building designed by Captain Francis Fowke and built 1861–88, the museum's collection was originally based on that accumulated by Edinburgh University. The galleries are arranged into Natural World, Art & Culture and Science & Industry. Under Natural World are displays including Birds, British Animals, Insects & Molluscs, Rocks & Minerals, Fossils, Skeletons and World in our Hands. The Art & Culture Galleries include displays on Ancient Egypt, Arms & Armour, Art & Industry since 1850, Glass & Ceramics, Jewellery, European Arts up to 1800, Middle Eastern & Asian Cultures, and Decorative Arts and Crafts. The Science & Industry galleries cover subjects including scientific instruments and transport, while an interactive exhibition charts the history of human communication. Tel: 0131 247 4422.

Royal Observatory Edinburgh Blackford Hill, Edinburgh. A Royal Observatory stood on Calton Hill in Edinburgh in the 19th century. Thanks to a gift by the Earl of Crawford which included his collection of astronomical books and instruments, this was replaced in 1896 by a new observatory on Blackford Hill, designed and equipped under the supervision of Ralph Copeland, Astronomer Royal for Scotland. The East Dome has a 36in (914mm) reflector telescope (installed 1930) and the West Dome a 14/24in (356/610mm) Schmidt telescope. In addition to the buildings and telescopes the Observatory also houses the Crawford Collection, the archives of the Royal Observatory Edinburgh (ROE) and a collection of scientific instruments. The Blackford Hill establishment is also home to the United Kingdom Astronomy Technology Centre. Tel: 0131 668 8405.

Royal Scots Regimental Museum A museum dedicated to the Royal Scots Regiment, opened in 1991 and located in Edinburgh Castle. Its displays chart the history of the regiment and include exhibits of medals, equipment and silverware. Raised by Sir John Hepburn in 1633, the Royal Scots are the oldest infantry regiment in the British army and the senior infantry Regiment of the Line. The regiment served in France until 1661 when it was recalled to Britain. It won its first battle honour at Tangier in 1680 and also took part in the defeat of Monmouth's Rebellion at Sedgemoor in 1685. In 1684 it had been given the title 'Royal Regiment of Foot' by Charles II. After serving in the War of the Spanish Succession and gaining battle honours at Blenheim, Ramillies, Oudenarde and Malplaquet, the 1st Battalion fought at Fontenoy in the War of the Austrian Succession while the 2nd Battalion was engaged at Culloden in 1746. The regiment was designated the 1st (Royal) Regiment of Foot in 1751. It saw action in the Napoleonic Wars in theatres as diverse as Egypt, the West Indies and India, while the 3rd Battalion was engaged in the Peninsular War and at the Battle of Waterloo. In 1812, the regiment was retitled the 1st Regiment of Foot (Royal Scots) and in 1816 its strength was cut from four battalions to the pre-1804 status of two. It was engaged in both the Crimean War and the Boer War before its strength was raised to 35 battalions during World War I, when it accrued 79 battle honours and saw action in many campaigns including those on the Western Front, the Dardanelles and Egypt. In 1921, the regiment was renamed The Royal Scots (The Royal Regiment). At the outset of World War II the 1st Battalion served in the BEF sent to France and was overwhelmed in the withdrawal to Dunkirk. The 2nd Battalion was stationed in the Far East and was in Hong Kong when it fell in 1941. A reconstituted 1st Battalion then served in Burma, while a new 2nd Battalion saw action in Italy. Other newly raised battalions took part in the D-Day landings and the liberation of Western Europe. After World War II the 2nd Battalion was disbanded and the regiment served in Korea, Suez, Aden, Northern Ireland and in the first Gulf War. The nickname of the regiment is Pontius Pilate's Bodyguard, given to it thanks to a legend that the Roman legionaries guarding Christ's tomb were actually Scottish born. The origin of the legend seemingly stems from the time of the regiment's formation in France. In an effort to outscore some French troops with whom they were arguing about the regiment's age, the Scots claimed to be descended from the Roman legion whose detachment guarded Jesus' tomb; the French replied that had they (the French) been on guard, Christ's body would not have gone missing. In 2006 the regiment was amalgamated with the King's Own Scottish Borderers to become the 1st Battalion of the Royal Regiment of Scotland. Tel: 0131 310 5016.

Royal Yacht *Britannia* — Ocean Terminal, Leith, Edinburgh. Launched at John Brown's Shipyard in Clydebank on 16 April 1953 and decommissioned at Portsmouth Naval Base on 11 December 1997, the royal yacht is now berthed at the Port of Leith. *Britannia* was the 83rd and possibly last royal yacht. Tel: 0131 555 5566.

St Anthony's Chapel, Well and Cave — Holyrood Park, Edinburgh. Ruins of a 15th century rectangular chapel and hermitage. Traditionally held to have been built to guard the nearby St Anthony's Well, the 'hermitage' adjacent to the chapel was in reality probably used as a storehouse. The well is formed from a natural spring and appears to have been a venerated site since pre-Christian times. St Anthony's Cave, a natural cave between the chapel and the well, is too small ever to have been inhabited.

St Cecilia's Hall Musical Instrument Museum — Niddry Street, Cowgate, Edinburgh. The oldest purpose-built concert hall in Scotland, dating to 1763. Designed by Robert Mylne for the Edinburgh Musical Society, it is now owned by the University of Edinburgh and houses the Raymond Russell and Rodger Mirrey Collections of Early Keyboard Instruments and the Macaulay Collection of Plucked String Instruments. The exhibits include 50 important examples of early keyboard instruments such as harpsichords, virginals, spinets, organs and fortepianos.

St Giles Cathedral — Royal Mile, Edinburgh. Also known as the High Kirk of Edinburgh, and the Church of Scotland parish church for Edinburgh's Old Town. Although probably founded in the 1120s, the church was dedicated to St Giles in 1243. Largely rebuilt after a fire in 1385, it was extended in the following centuries by the addition of around 50 chapels endowed by guilds and merchants. The stone crown was added to the spire c.1500. During the Reformation the church was split into different sections; parts were used for worship, while other areas were used as a school, a police station, a gaol and a store for 'The Maiden', the Edinburgh guillotine. It was also used as a meeting place for the General Assembly of the Church of Scotland, the Town Council and the Parliament. The church underwent major restoration in the 19th century; both the buildings added to its exterior walls and the interior divisions were removed, as were some chapels, to create a larger single space for worship. The church is most notable for its stained glass windows, many of which date from the 1870s restoration. These include the Life of Christ cycle, the Burne-Jones windows, the 20th century north window designed by Douglas Strachan and the great west window designed by Leifur Breidfjord, installed in 1985 and dedicated to Robert Burns. The many memorials include one to Robert Louis Stevenson and another to John Knox, who was minister here in the 1560s. A new chapel built in 1911 for the Order of the Thistle includes a stall for each Knight of the Order and two royal stalls. In 1992 a 4000 pipe organ was installed in the south transept. Although not strictly a cathedral, it was built on such a grand scale that it was considered as one. Tel: 0131 225 9442.

St Mary's Episcopal Cathedral — Palmerston Place, Edinburgh. The foundation stone for this three spire cathedral was laid on 21 May 1874 by the Duke of Buccleuch and Queensberry. The main design, by Sir George Gilbert Scott, won an architectural competition held to find the best design. Scott's design had only one spire but he was 'persuaded' to add two further spires from a losing design by Alexander Ross. The cathedral was consecrated on 29 October 1879.

St Mary's Roman Catholic Cathedral — Broughton Street, Edinburgh. The Cathedral Church of the Archdiocese of St Andrews and Edinburgh. Bishop Hay, Vicar Apostolic for the Lowland District, chose the site in 1801 after his chapel in Blackfriars Wynd was burnt down by a mob; the new site was supposedly in a more sheltered spot, protected by surrounding buildings. Designed by prominent ecclesiastical architect James Gillespie Graham, the Chapel of St Mary's was opened by Bishop Cameron in 1814, the first masses being celebrated in August of that year. A prominent feature of the interior is a painting surmounting the sanctuary arch by Belgian artist Louis Beyart, depicting the Coronation of the Blessed Virgin Mary as Queen of Heaven. The liturgical highlight of the cathedral's life was the visit of Pope John Paul II on 31 May 1982 during his pastoral visit to Scotland; he addressed a large congregation of priests, female and male religious in the cathedral and prayed at the shrine of St Andrew.

Salisbury Crags — See Arthur's Seat

Scott Monument — Princes Street, Edinburgh. A monument to Sir Walter Scott designed by George Kemp and featuring a marble statue of the author sculpted by John Steell. It was officially unveiled on 15 August 1846 and stands 200ft (60m) high and 55ft (17m) square at the base. It was restored in the 1990s. Tel: 0131 529 4068.

Scottish Korean War Memorial — $1^1/_4$ miles (2km) east of Torphichen, 3 miles (5km) south of Linlithgow. Located in Beecraigs Country Park, the memorial is in the form of a small wooden pagoda enclosed by 110 Korean pine trees (one for every ten Britons who died in the conflict) and 1090 birch trees (one for each of the fallen).

Scottish Mining Museum Newtongrange, Midlothian. Opened in 1984 at the Lady Victoria Colliery, which was operational 1894–1981. Exhibits present the history of coal mining and the story of the miners and their families, while there is a recreation of an underground railway and coalface. Equipment on display includes the largest winding engine in Scotland.

Scottish National Gallery of Modern Art Belford Road, Edinburgh. Housed in a neoclassical building designed by William Burn for John Watson's School in 1825–8, the gallery opened in 1960; originally housed in Inverleith House at the Royal Botanic Gardens, it moved to its present location in 1984. The gallery covers the period from the late 19th century and has works by, among others, Francis Bacon, Georges Braque, Lucien Freud, David Hockney, Roy Lichtenstein, Matisse, Mondrian, Picasso and Andy Warhol. Modern Scottish artists such as John Bellany, Christine Borland, Ken Currie, Joan Eardley, William Gillies, Douglas Gordon, Peter Howson, S J Peploe and Robin Philipson are also represented. There is a sculpture garden with works by Henry Moore, Rachel Whiteread and Barbara Hepworth. Also in the grounds is *Landform*, an award-winning earth sculpture by Charles Jencks based on the concept of chaos theory and part sculpture, part garden, part land art. Tel: 0131 624 6200.

Scottish National Portrait Gallery Queen Street, Edinburgh. Opened in 1889, the gallery provides a history of Scotland through a large collection of portraits of its greatest sons and daughters, from monarchs to poets to actors. It is housed in a Gothic revival building designed by Sir Robert Rowand Anderson. Among those featured are Robert Burns, Sean Connery, Alex Ferguson, David Hume, Mary, Queen of Scots, Walter Scott, Jimmy Shand and Bonnie Prince Charlie. There are portraits by such diverse artists as Copley, Gainsborough, Rodin and Van Dyck, as well as Scottish artists including Raeburn and John Bellany. In addition the gallery holds the Scottish National Photography Collection, with more than 27,000 studies starting from the 1840s. Tel: 0131 624 6200.

Scottish National War Memorial Crown Square, Edinburgh Castle. A monument commemorating over 200,000 Scottish casualties in warfare since 1914. Adapted by Sir Robert Lorimer from the castle's Northern Barracks building (originally St Mary's Church), the memorial comprises three elements: the hall of honour, with stained glass windows and depictions of scenes from World War I; the national shrine; and within the shrine a casket containing the Roll of Honour, which lists the name of all the dead. It was opened on 14 July 1927 by the Prince of Wales.

Scottish Railway Exhibition Union Street, Bo'ness. Opened in 1995 by the Scottish Railway Preservation Society in a large display hall built next to Bo'ness Station. The hall was extended in 2002. Exhibits include goods wagons and passenger coaches, while restoration work can be seen being carried out in a demonstration workshop. Tel: 01506 825855.

Scottish Seabird Centre The Harbour, North Berwick. Opened in 2000 in a specially designed building, the centre features displays on Scottish wildlife and live remote control video connections to the seabird colonies on the nearby islands of Fidra, Craigleith and the Bass Rock. Tel: 01620 890202.

Scottish Storytelling Centre High Street, Edinburgh. Established in 1992 'to encourage and support the telling and sharing of stories across all ages and all sectors of society' and housed in the Netherbow Arts Centre, opened in 2006 on the Royal Mile. A tower houses the 1621 Netherbow Bell (the city bell of Edinburgh) and the centre also has a 99-seat theatre, the George Mackay Brown Storytelling Library and a storytelling court. A 'storytelling wall' celebrates famous stories and characters old and new, including such as Tam O'Shanter, Greyfriars Bobby and Inspector Rebus. There is a display dedicated to Robert Louis Stevenson. The original Netherbow Arts Centre opened in 1972 and closed in 2003. The building is linked to John Knox's House. Tel: 0131 556 9579.

Seton Collegiate Church 1 mile (1.6km) east of Cockenzie & Port Seton. Set in woodland, the Collegiate Church of St Mary and the Holy Cross was built in the 15th century by the St Clair family around Seton Parish Church, dedicated in 1242. The existing building served as the nave, the church being extended with a choir and north and south transepts. With the permission of Pope Alexander VI a college of priests was established in 1493 by George, 2nd Lord Seton for the support of a provost, six prebendaries, two singing boys and a clerk. Work on the church was completed by his widow Lady Janet Seton, including repairs made following an attack by English forces in 1544. A tower was also begun, although the proposed spire was never added. After the Reformation the church returned to its original use as a parish church and later it was used only as a family chapel. Over time it suffered depredations from Covenanters and because of the family affiliation to the Jacobite cause. The 13th century part of the building was later demolished, leaving only the foundations on view. Ruins of the priest's accommodation can also be seen surrounding the church. Eventually the building ceased to be used for worship and by the mid 19th century was in use as a burial vault. Restoration was carried out by Lord Wemyss in the 1870s and it passed into state care in 1946. The church is now maintained by Historic Scotland. Tel: 01875 813334.

Signet Library Parliament Square, Edinburgh. Still in use as a working law library, and owned since 1833 by The Society of Writers to Her Majesty's Signet (WS Society), an independent association of Scottish lawyers, the building was designed by Robert Reid and completed in 1822. It comprises the Upper Library – described by George IV as the most beautiful room he had ever seen – the Lower Library and the much later West Wing. The Upper and Lower libraries are linked by a grand staircase. Tel: 0131 225 0651.

Soutra Aisle 2 miles (3km) southeast of Fala, 6 miles (10km) east of Gorebridge. Aka the House of the Holy Trinity at Soutra. Originally an Augustinian hospital and monastic foundation, founded by Malcolm IV in 1164 for lodging travellers and pilgrims making their way along Dere Street. Believed to have been the best endowed hospital in medieval Scotland, it was also designated as a place of sanctuary for fugitives. In the 1460s Stephen Fleming, Master of the Hospital, was accused of misconduct and the hospital's estates were transferred to Trinity College Hospital in Edinburgh. By the early 18th century the site had fallen into ruin and was being used by the Pringle family as a private burial place. Excavations since 1988 have uncovered the remains of a range of domestic buildings including a kitchen, plus fragments of ointment jars containing residues from medicinal plants and herbs such as cloves and opium poppies.

Sport

football

Heart of Midlothian, usually known simply as Hearts, were formed in 1874 and named indirectly via the name of a local dancehall from Sir Walter Scott's novel. They are winners of the Scottish League championship in 1895, 1897, 1958 and 1960, the Scottish 1st Division in 1980 and the Scottish FA Cup in 1891, 1896, 1901, 1906, 1956, 1998 and 2006. Nicknamed The Jam Tarts, their home ground is Tynecastle Stadium, Gorgie Road, Edinburgh. Their traditional colours are maroon and white. Tel: 0871 663 1874.

Hibernian were formed in 1875 and originally represented Edinburgh's Irish-Catholic community, although the club is now more closely associated with its home in Leith. They are winners of the Scottish League championship in 1903, 1948, 1951 and 1952, the Scottish 1st Division in 1981 and 1999, the 2nd Division in 1894, 1895 and 1933, and the Scottish FA Cup in 1887 and 1902; they were also the first British club to appear in a European competition (the European Cup) in the 1955–56 season. Nicknamed Hibs or The Hibees, the club's traditional colours are green and white; their home ground is Easter Road, Albion Place, Edinburgh. Tel: 0131 661 2159.

Livingston were formed in 1995 when the former Meadowbank Thistle, themselves founded in 1974 and based at Meadowbank Stadium, Edinburgh, relocated to Livingston. They are winners of the Scottish 1st Division in 2001, the 2nd Division in 1999 and the 3rd Division in 1996, and also defeated Hibernian to win the Scottish League Cup in 2004. Nicknamed The Livi Lions, their colours are gold and black; their home ground is Almondvale Stadium, Livingston. Tel: 01506 417000.

golf

Muirfield Golf Course, Duncur Road, Muirfield, Gullane, East Lothian. A par 70, 18-hole links course. It is home to the Honourable Company of Edinburgh Golfers (with 400 members), one of the oldest golf clubs in the world, with records going back as far as 1744. The club originally played at Leith Links and then Musselburgh before moving to a new course designed by Tom Morris at Muirfield in 1891. The course has hosted the Open Championship 15 times: 1892 (winner: Harold Hilton), 1896 (Harry Vardon), 1901 (James Braid), 1906 (James Braid), 1912 (Ted Ray), 1929 (Walter Hagen), 1935 (Alf Perry), 1948 (Henry Cotton), 1959 (Gary Player), 1966 (Jack Nicklaus), 1972 (Lee Trevino), 1980 (Tom Watson), 1987 (Nick Faldo), 1992 (Nick Faldo), 2002 (Ernie Els). It has also hosted the Ryder Cup, the Walker Cup and the Curtis Cup. Tel: 01620 842123.

Musselburgh Links, Balcarres Road, Musselburgh, East Lothian. The 9-hole links course, located inside Musselburgh Racecourse, is one of the original venues of the Open Championship and one of the oldest courses in Britain. Mary, Queen of Scots reputedly played golf at Musselburgh in 1567 and there is documentary evidence of play taking place in 1672. Originally there were seven holes, with another added in 1838 and a ninth in 1870. The Honourable Company of Edinburgh Golfers played at Musselburgh 1836–91, when they moved to Muirfield. The course hosted the Open Championship on six occasions: 1874 (winner: Mungo Park), 1877 (Jamie Anderson), 1880 (Bob Ferguson), 1883 (Willie Fernie), 1886 (David Brown), 1889 (Willie Park Jr). Tel: 0131 665 5438.

horse racing

Musselburgh racecourse, Linkfield Road, Musselburgh, East Lothian, is a right-handed track 1 mile 2 furlongs (2km) round and staging both Flat and National Hunt races. Musselburgh was established in 1816 and is also known as Edinburgh Racecourse. The Edwardian grandstand has been refurbished and a new hospitality stand was opened in 1995. Musselburgh Golf Course is in the centre of the course. Tel: 0131 665 2859.

ice hockey

Edinburgh Capitals were founded in 1998. They succeeded the Murrayfield Racers, founded as the Murrayfield Royals in 1952 and who won the British Championship in 1969, 1970, 1971 and 1972, becoming the Edinburgh Racers in the 1990s. They play home games at Murrayfield Ice Rink.

rugby union

Edinburgh Gunners were founded in 1996 and play in the Magners League along with other Scottish rugby clubs Border Reivers and Glasgow Warriors. For a short time they were merged with the Border Reivers as Edinburgh Reivers before becoming Edinburgh Rugby in 2001–02. From 2005–06 the nickname Gunners was officially incorporated into the team's name. They play home games at Murrayfield Stadium.

Murrayfield Stadium, Edinburgh, the home of Scottish rugby union, opened on 21 March 1925. Prior to this the first permanent home for Scottish rugby internationals was at Inverleith. The record attendance of 104,000 was for a match against Wales in March 1975. The stadium was extensively reconstructed and refurbished 1992–5. The stadium is also used for some football matches, hockey games and music concerts. Tel: 0131 346 5000.

Tantallon Castle

2½ miles (4km) east of North Berwick. Located on a sheer cliff top overlooking the Firth of Forth, the castle was built in the 14th century by William, 1st Earl of Douglas. Having become a stronghold of the 'Red Douglas' Earls of Angus, in 1491 it was besieged by James IV and in 1528 it was handed over to his son following a prolonged siege, after which repairs were carried out and defensive improvements were made. These were not enough to prevent a further occupation, this time by English forces, in 1544. Finally, the castle was taken and severely damaged by Cromwellian forces under General Monck in 1651. The ruined curtain wall stands in places as high as 50ft (15m) and some of the towers still stand 80ft (24m) tall. The property passed into state care in 1924 and is maintained by Historic Scotland. Tel: 01620 892727.

Tartan Weaving Mill and Exhibition Castlehill, Edinburgh. A working exhibition of tartan design and weaving housed in the converted Castlehill Reservoir, a 2 million gallon (9.1 million litre) cistern built in 1849 to supply water to Edinburgh New Town. The centre includes a working watermill and a highland dress exhibition. Tel: 0131 226 1555.

Torness Nuclear Power Station $^1/_4$ mile (0.4km) north of Thorntonloch, 5 miles (8km) southeast of Dunbar. Located on a 200 acre (80ha) site on the coastal promontory of Torness Point. Construction began in 1980 and the first of two advanced gas-cooled reactors became operational in 1987. The main construction was completed in 1989 and the station is due to operate until 2023.

Torphichen Preceptory Torphichen, 4 miles (6km) southwest of Linlithgow. The surviving tower and two transepts of a 12th century church, extended in the 14th century. This was the only house in Scotland of the Knights Hospitallers (Knights of St John of Jerusalem), who received the lands of 'Torphigan' from David I in the 1140s. The order was suppressed in Scotland after the Reformation in 1560s and the estate was secularised shortly afterwards when the last preceptor, Sir James Sandilands, bought it and the title of Lord Torphichen. The nave was used as Torpichen Kirk until its demolition in 1756, when it was replaced with a new T-plan church. The transepts and tower were used as a courthouse. The tower was re-roofed in 1947. The property is in the care of Historic Scotland.

Tranent A small town 10 miles (16km) east of Edinburgh. It was the site of the Massacre of Tranent on 29 August 1797, when a proclamation by local miners objecting to the enforced recruitment of militia resulted in the killing and wounding of up to 20 local men, women and children by a recruitment squad.

Traprain Law 4 miles (6km) east of Haddington. Also known in the past as Dumpender Law. An isolated hill 723ft (221m) above sea level with steep sides, which was once the site of one of the largest Iron Age hill forts in Scotland, covering 40 acres (16ha). Possibly the capital of the Votadini tribe, it was occupied intermittently from at least the 10th century BC to the 5th century AD, and was in continuous occupation throughout the Roman period. The Traprain Treasure, a hoard of continental silver plate, was uncovered on the hill on 10 May 1919 and included two coins of the Emperor Honorius. A medieval religious building on the summit was abandoned during the 14th century. Much of the northeast side of the hill was destroyed during 20th century quarrying operations.

Tron Kirk High Street, Edinburgh. A church built by John Mylne 1636–47. Shortened in the 1780s and severely damaged by fire in 1824, it ceased to be a place of worship in 1952 and now houses a visitor centre. During excavations in 1974 the remains of the 16th century Marlin's Wynd, which was demolished to make way for the Kirk, including shops and cellars, were uncovered and can be seen in the centre. In the past it has been the focus of Edinburgh's New Year celebrations.

University of Edinburgh Founded by a royal charter of James VI in 1582. Old College (at the time called New College) was designed by Robert Adam in 1789 and largely completed by W H Playfair by 1827. The dome was added by Robert Rowand Anderson in 1887. Old College now houses the Playfair Library Hall. During the 19th century the university spread into many buildings within the city and still has no central campus, being based in a number of sites. The New College was originally a Free Church college designed by W H Playfair in the 1840s, becoming the home of the Faculty of Divinity in the 1930s. The Chancellor's Building, which is connected to the Edinburgh Royal Infirmary, was opened in August 2002 and houses the Medical School. The university is a member of the Russell Group of research-led universities and today has around 26,000 students. Former students include Prime Minister Gordon Brown, physicist James Clerk Maxwell, authors Ian Rankin and Alexander McCall Smith, broadcaster Kirsty Wark and former MI5 chief Stella Rimington. Tel: 0131 650 1000.

Usher Hall Lothian Road, Edinburgh. The city's principal concert venue, built in 1896 thanks to a gift of £100,000 by philanthropist Andrew Usher (1826–98). A competition held to select the design was won by Stockdale Harrison and Howard H Thomson. The foundation stone was laid in 1911 by George V and Queen Mary and the hall was opened on 16 March 1914. The hall seats 2900 and is a major music venue for the Edinburgh International Festival. It has hosted a diverse range of performers and in 1972 was the venue for the Eurovision Song Contest; today it is the home of the Royal Scottish National Orchestra. A major refurbishment was carried out 1998–2000, and a second phase of refurbishment to include a new wing was begun in 2005. Tel: 0131 228 1155.

Vogrie House $1^1/_2$ miles (2.5km) northeast of Gorebridge, 11 miles (18km) southeast of Edinburgh. Located between the Tyne Water and the Vogrie Burn and built in the 1870s for the Dewar family on the site of an 18th century house. It became a nursing home for the Royal Edinburgh Hospital for Mental and Nervous Disorders in 1924 and was bought by Midlothian Council in the 1960s. It is now the home of the Midlothian Ranger Service. The estate, covering 250 acres (100ha) of landscaped grounds, now forms Vogrie Country Park, opened in 1982.

Wallace's Cave Roslin, 7 miles (11km) southeast of Edinburgh. Aka Hawthornden Castle Cave. An artificial cave in Roslin Glen said to have been a hiding place of Sir William Wallace.

Waverley Railway Station Princes Street, Edinburgh. The main railway station in Edinburgh and the northern terminus of the East Coast Main Line. Opened in 1868 to replace three previous stations operated by separate companies, it stands on the site of a loch drained in the early 19th century. Covering 25 acres (10ha), it is the second largest mainline railway station in the UK after London Waterloo and has 14 platforms.

West Calder Library — Main Street, West Calder, 4 miles (6km) southwest of Livingston. Designed in Art Nouveau style by William Baillie and opened by Lord Rosebery on 20 November 1904. The library was funded by a grant from the Andrew Carnegie Foundation. Tel: 01506 871371.

West Calder Memorial — West Calder, 4 miles (6km) southwest of Livingston. A memorial to 15 men killed on 10 January 1947 in an explosion at the Burngrange oil-shale mine.

West Lothian question — The term used to describe a constitutional situation whereby, under devolution, MPs sitting for Scottish constituencies in Parliament would be able to influence affairs in England while having no similar influence over Scottish matters, because of the existence of a separate Scottish Assembly. It derives from the following question posed by Tam Dalyell, MP for West Lothian, during a 1977 Parliamentary debate on the introduction of devolution: 'If the UK is to remain in being, then there can be no question but that the Scottish Constituencies must continue to be represented at Westminster . . . Yet once the [Scottish] Assembly had come into being, and was legislating for those areas that had not been reserved to the United Kingdom Government, the position of the 71 Scottish Westminster MPs would become awkward and invidious. Their credibility – like those of their counterparts in the Assembly – would be deeply suspect, simply because there would be so many areas of concern to their electors on which they could not pronounce.' It was dubbed the West Lothian Question by Ulster Unionist (and former Conservative) MP Enoch Powell.

Winton House — Pencaitland, 5 miles (8km) southwest of Haddington. The original 15th century tower house was built by the Seton family beside the Tyne Water on the site of a 12th century house. Damaged by English forces led by the Earl of Hertford in 1545 during the 'Rough Wooing', the house was not repaired until 1600, when it was extended to form an L-plan mansion. It was forfeited by the Seton family in 1715 because of their support for the Jacobite cause, but briefly occupied by Bonnie Prince Charlie in 1745 during his attempt to gain the throne. The house and estate were bought by the Hamilton Nisbet family of Pencaitland in 1779 and the house was further extended in 1805. The 464 acre (188ha) grounds were landscaped in the 17th century and again in the 19th. It remains the family home of the Ogilvys. Tel: 01875 340222.

Writers' Museum — Lady Stair's Close, Lawnmarket, Edinburgh. Dedicated to the lives and works of Robert Burns (1759–96), Sir Walter Scott (1771–1832) and Robert Louis Stevenson (1850–94), and housed in 17th century Lady Stair's House. The three-storey house was originally built in 1622 and was then known as Lady Gray's House after its first owner. It acquired its present name after 1719 when it was occupied by her granddaughter Elizabeth, 1st Countess of Stair and widow of John Dalrymple. It was bought in 1895 by Lord Rosebery, who restored it and presented it to the city of Edinburgh in 1907. Exhibits include portraits, manuscripts, furniture and memorabilia relating to the writers, while temporary exhibitions cover other Scottish writers old and new. A courtyard outside the museum is designated a 'Maker's Court' and has quotations from many Scottish poets and authors inscribed in its stonework. Tel: 0131 529 4901.

Woods on your Doorstep — **Beeslack Wood** (32 acres/13ha), Penicuik, located on the River North Esk and with the Loan Burn running through the site. A mainly broadleaved woodland with oak, beech, ash, elm and sycamore; **Bellsquarry Wood** (45 acres/18ha), Livingston, designated a Long Established Woodland of Plantation Origin (LEPO). Mainly birch plus some beech and oak. The Dedridge Burn borders the wood and feeds a pond in the woodland; **Blaeberry Community Wood** (86 acres/35ha), between Whitburn and East Whitburn, is crossed by the Bickerton Burn and the White Burn. A mixture of broadleaf and conifer including beech, larch, Scots pine and sycamore; **Butterdean Wood** (105 acres/42ha), near Tranent. Designated a Long Established Woodland of Plantation Origin (LEPO) dating to the late 18th or early 19th century. In the 1960s many broadleaves were felled and replaced with conifers including Scots pine, sitka and Norway spruce and Douglas fir; **Cousland Woods** (23 acres/9ha), west of Livingston, consists of seven separate woodland blocks screening and separating residential and industrial areas, each block including conifers such as larch, Scots pine, Sitka spruce and broadleaves such as alder, beech, birch, oak and sycamore; **Currie Wood** (52 acres/21ha), in Borthwick Glen and crossed by the Middleton South Burn, is a mixed broadleaf woodland with 40 per cent conifer planting dating from the 1960s. Species include alder, ash, birch, oak, rowan, Norway spruce and Douglas fir; **Deans Wood** (32 acres/13ha), northwest Livingston, consists of six woodland blocks originally forming part of Derchmont Law Park and providing noise barriers, shelter, screening and separation of the road system, residential and industrial areas. Species include conifers such as Scots pine and broadleaves such as beech and sycamore; **Dedridge Wood** (10 acres/4ha), south of Livingston, a small wood consisting of three separate blocks providing shelter and screening and separation for residential developments. Species include Scots pine, Noway maple, oak and sycamore; **East Woods** (30 acres/12ha), Livingston, consists of three separate blocks providing shelter, screening and separation for residential and office developments. They are remnants of 19th century estate plantations with oak, beech, sycamore and Scots pine; **Eliburn Woods** (20 acres/8ha), northwest Livingston. Seven blocks providing noise barriers, shelter, screening and separation of the road system for residential areas. Dominated by stands of Scots pine with some larch; **Foulshiels** (70 acres/28ha), on the site of reclaimed mineworkings at Stoneyburn and mainly planted in the 1980s. Species include birch, willow and rowan plus conifers such as lodgepole pine. The mine was closed in the late 1950s and capped in the 1960s; **Hermand Beech Wood** (8 acres/3ha), near West Calder. Designated as Long Established Woodland of Plantation Origin (LEPO) and originally planted in the late 18th century. Its name is somewhat misleading as few original beech trees remain; these have been replaced with birch, sycamore, alder, ash and horse chestnut; **Kirkton Woods** (15 acres/6ha), west Livingston. Four blocks providing screening and separation for industrial areas. Species include ash, Scots pine, larch, beech and sycamore; **Knightsridge Woods** (32 acres/13ha), northeast Livingston. Species include beech, birch, oak and Scots pine. The woods provide screening and separation for residential areas; **Ladywell Woods** (20 acres/8ha) in the Ladywell West district of Livingston. Four blocks providing screening and separation for residential areas. Designated as Long Established Woodlands of Plantation Origin (LEPO), the plantations consist of mixed broadleaves and Scots pine; **Murieston Woods** (8 acres/3ha), south Livingston. Two blocks providing noise barriers, shelter, screening and separation for residential and industrial areas. Mainly Scots pine plus broadleaves such as ash, beech, oak and Norway maple; **North Wood** (86 acres/35ha), north of Livingston between the town and the village of Dechmont. Designated as an Area of Great Landscape Value. Main species include alder, ash, sessile oak, Scots pine, Sitka spruce and sycamore. There is a pond in the wood; **Pressmennan Wood** (212 acres/86ha), Stenton, near Dunbar. Mixed conifer and broadleaves including European larch, Douglas fir, ash and sessile oak. Bennet's Burn runs through part of the wood. According to legend, timber from Pressmennan was used in the building of the warship *The Great Michael* at Leith in the 15th century; **Railway Wood** (15 acres/6ha), northeast of Livingston. A single block of woodland providing separation and screening between industrial areas and major transport routes. Main species include single stands of beech, larch, sessile oak, Sitka spruce, sycamore and Scots pine; **Seton Dean** ($2^1/_2$ acres/1ha), a small strip of woodland between Longniddry and Port Seton. Many mature trees were destroyed by Dutch elm disease and the site is dominated by a few widely spaced mature trees of ash, sycamore, yew and lime plus mixed scrub. Wild garlic dominates the ground flora and there are patches of bluebells in spring; **Wilderness** (45 acres/18ha), on the southwest edge of Livingston, a diverse plantation woodland of mixed broadleaves and conifers including sessile oak, downy birch, Douglas fir, Scots pine and lodgepole pine.

Yester Castle

$1^1/_2$ miles (2.5km) southeast of Gifford, 4 miles (6km) southeast of Haddington. Built in 1297 by Hugo de Gifford, the so-called 'Wizard of Yester', on the grounds of an earlier motte and bailey castle. Beneath is the sizeable Goblin Ha', where Gifford is said to have made magic. This name is echoed in a small hotel in the village of Gifford and the goblins were immortalised in Sir Walter Scott's *Marmion.* The castle passed to the Hay family through marriage in the 14th century, but was abandoned after the Hays moved to a more comfortable new home on the site of the present Yester House. Today the remains of the castle are located on the margins of the Yester Estate, owned by Italian composer Gian Carlo Menotti.

Some famous people born in Lothian

Alexander II (king of Scotland) (1198–1249)	Haddington
Armour, Tommy (golfer) (1894–1968)	Edinburgh
Balfour, Arthur (politician) (1848–1930)	Whittingehame
Bell, Alexander Graham (inventor) (1847–1922)	Edinburgh
Blair, Tony (politician) (1953–)	Edinburgh
Boswell, James (writer) (1740–95)	Edinburgh
Buchanan, Ken (boxer) (1945–)	Edinburgh
Calder, Finlay (rugby player) (1957–)	Haddington
Conan Doyle, Arthur (author) (1859–1930)	Edinburgh
Connery, Sean (actor) (1930–)	Edinburgh
Grahame, Kenneth (writer) (1859–1932)	Edinburgh
Greig, John (footballer) (1942–)	Edinburgh
Haig, Douglas (soldier) (1861–1928)	Edinburgh
Hamilton-Gordon, George (politician) (1784–1860)	Edinburgh
Hastings, (Andrew) Gavin (rugby player) (1962–)	Edinburgh
Hoy, Chris (cyclist) (1976–)	Edinburgh
Hume, David (philosopher and economist) (1711–76)	Edinburgh
Irvine, Andy (rugby player) (1951–)	Edinburgh
James II (king of Scotland) (1430–60)	Edinburgh
James V (king of Scotland) (1512–42)	Linlithgow
James VI (of Scotland), I (of England and Ireland) (1566–1625)	Edinburgh
Knox, John (founder of Presbyterianism) (c.1510–72)	Haddington
Lauder, Harry (entertainer) (1870–1950)	Edinburgh
Mackay, Dave (footballer) (1934–)	Edinburgh
Mary, Queen of Scots (Mary I of Scotland, Mary Stuart) (1542–87)	Linlithgow
Maxwell, James Clerk (physicist) (1831–79)	Edinburgh
Napier, John (inventor of logarithms) (1550–1617)	Edinburgh
Paolozzi, Eduardo (sculptor) (1924–2005)	Leith
Raeburn, Henry (portrait painter) (1756–1823)	Edinburgh
Rutherford, Daniel (scientist) (1749–1819)	Edinburgh
Scott, Walter (novelist and poet) (1771–1832)	Edinburgh
Sim, Alastair (actor) (1900–76)	Edinburgh
Smiles, Samuel (author) (1812–1904)	Haddington
Spark, Muriel (Muriel Camberg) (author) (1918–2006)	Edinburgh
Stevenson, Robert Louis (novelist and poet) (1850–94)	Edinburgh
Tait, Archibald Campbell (archbishop) (1811–82)	Edinburgh
Tennant, David (actor) (1971–)	Bathgate
Wells, Allan Wipper (athlete) (1952–)	Edinburgh
Welsh, Irvine (author) (1958–)	Leith

Orkney Islands

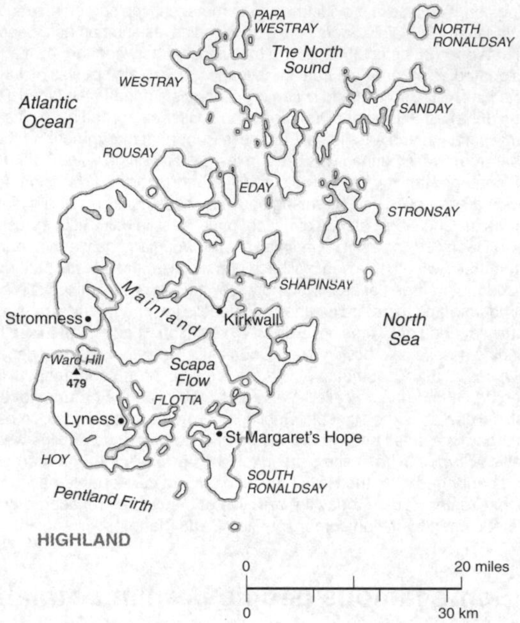

PAPA WESTRAY
NORTH RONALDSAY
The North Sound
WESTRAY
Atlantic Ocean
SANDAY
ROUSAY
EDAY
STRONSAY
SHAPINSAY
Mainland
Stromness
Kirkwall
North Sea
Ward Hill
479
Scapa Flow
FLOTTA
Lyness
St Margaret's Hope
HOY
SOUTH RONALDSAY
Pentland Firth
HIGHLAND
0
20 miles
0
30 km

The Orkney Islands (or Orkney) lie off the northern tip of Scotland where the North Sea and the Atlantic Ocean meet in the Pentland Firth. The islands were fashioned by glacial erosion of the underlying sandstone, limestone and igneous rocks into low, undulating hills; the strong westerly winds accounting for the general scarcity of trees.

The main island is Mainland (the Scottish mainland is known as Scotland to Orcadians) and the other populated islands are Auskerry, Burray, Eday, Egilsay, Flotta, Gairsay, Graemsay, Hoy, North Ronaldsay, Papa Stronsay, Papa Westray, Rousay, Sanday, Shapinsay, South Ronaldsay, Stronsay, Westray and Wyre. The 'capital' is Kirkwall on Mainland. In total there are more than 150 islands and named rocks and stacks in Orkney.

There is archaeological evidence that the Orkney Islands were settled c.3800 BC. It is likely that Mesolithic hunter-gatherers were present before this date, although they left no trace. During the Neolithic era the islands proved to be rich and fertile land for farming and the people have left behind settlements such as Skara Brae, chambered cairns such as Maes Howe and ceremonial places such as the Stones of Stenness. The 'Heart of Neolithic Orkney', which includes many of these sites, has been designated a UNESCO World Heritage Site. An earlier period of climate change saw a drop in temperatures and increase in rainfall in the area. This probably led to a fall in population but at the same time to an increase in the protection of the surviving workable land by means of defensive Iron Age sites such as brochs. The islands had trading connections with the mainland and in c.320 BC were possibly visited by the Greek explorer Pytheas, who is later quoted by Pliny as writing: 'There are 40 Orcades separated by moderate distances'. The survival of sherds of Roman pottery indicates that either the Orcadians were trading directly with Roman merchants or were trading with people who were. There is some speculation that the Roman general Agricola visited and 'subdued' the islands in AD 84.

By the 4th century the Orkneys were part of the Pictish kingdom which controlled northern Scotland but by the 9th century they had been displaced by Norse settlers. There is continuing debate concerning whether the Vikings slaughtered the Picts they found on the Orkneys, peacefully integrated with them or in fact found very few people actually living there when they arrived. During the 6th century some of the islands became the homes of priests (Papa) as Christianity arrived in the Orkneys. A history of the Norse earls of Orkney is recorded in the *Orkneyinga Saga*, although some of the narrative is perhaps not historically accurate on all points. The first earl was

Sigurd the Mighty (c.874–90) and subsequent earls included Einar Rognvaldsson (c.894–c.936), Thorfinn Einarsson the Skull-Splitter (c.936–c.963), Thorfinn Sigurdsson the Mighty (1019–c.1065), Magnus Erlendsson, St Magnus (c.1105–15) and Rognvald Kolsson, St Rognvald (1136–58). The last Norse earl was Jon Haraldsson, who died in 1231. The earldom passed to the son of the Earl of Angus and then to the Sinclairs, but the earldom still owed allegiance to the Norwegian crown (and later the Danish crown). In 1468 the impoverished Christian I, king of Denmark, Norway and Sweden, gave Orkney to the Scottish crown as part of a marriage agreement with James III of Scotland, who was to marry his daughter Margaret of Denmark. After the earldom was annexed to the Scottish crown in 1472, the influence of Norse culture gradually declined and the islands became more 'Scottish' in character. The variant of the Norse language spoken in the Orkney Islands was called Norn and its last speakers died in the early 19th century.

During the 20th century the islands played a significant part in both world wars as the deep-water anchorage of Scapa Flow was used by the Royal Navy as a base to monitor and intercept German warships heading for the North Atlantic. After the Armistice in 1918 the German High Seas Fleet was transferred in its entirety to Scapa Flow, where its crews scuttled all the ships.

The main industries in Orkney are farming, in particular beef farming, the oil terminal at Flotta, and tourism, which is the biggest sector of the local economy. Of agricultural land use more than 90 per cent is devoted to pasture, with a further 7 per cent given over to the growing of barley. Because the oil-related development has been confined largely to Flotta there has been relatively little impact on the other island communities. The amount of crude oil shipments through the Flotta oil terminal showed a 63 per cent decline in the 10 years between 1994 and 2004. The fishing industry no longer contributes significantly to the local economy. Manufacturing industry in Orkney is on a small scale and apart from food products and distilling is based on arts and craft goods such as textiles, jewellery and pottery. The main employers in the islands are Orkney Islands Council and Orkney Health Board (NHS), who between them employ almost one third of the working population of the islands. A further 25 per cent work in distribution, hotels and restaurants. Only 7 per cent of the population work in agriculture and fishing. One of the most recent significant population trends has been the decline in population on Orkney's smaller islands.

Orkney Islands	**Population**			**Area**	
	male	*female*	*total*	*sq miles*	*sq km*
Total	9497	9748	19,245	382	990

Local Attractions and Information

Administrative headquarters — Council Offices, School Place, Kirkwall, KW15 1NY. Tel: 01856 873535.

Airport — **Kirkwall Airport** (KOI) was established as RAF Grimsetter during World War II and became a civilian airport in 1948. Now operated by Highland and Islands Airports Ltd, it runs scheduled services to Aberdeen, Edinburgh, Glasgow, Inverness, Sumburgh (Shetland) and Orkney Inter-Island. There are inter-island services to the small island airstrips on Eday, Sanday, North Ronaldsay, Stronsay, Westray and Papa Westray. The flight from Westray to Papa Westray is, at less than two minutes, the shortest scheduled air service in the world. Tel: 01856 872421.

Balfour Castle — Balfour, Shapinsay. A Scottish Baronial style castle built 1847–8 by David Bryce for David Balfour. It is designed as a 'calendar house' with seven turrets, 12 exterior doors, 52 rooms and 365 panes of glass, The public rooms include a long gallery off which are a furnished dining room, drawing room and library complete with secret passage. The last Balfour died in 1960 and the house and estate were bought by Captain Tadeusz Zawadski, a Polish cavalry officer and his family. Now operated as a farm and hotel, it is claimed to be the world's most northerly castle hotel. The 70 acres (28ha) of grounds include a walled kitchen garden amid woodland. Tel: 01856 711282.

Barnhouse Settlement — 3 miles (5km) southwest of Finstown, Mainland. A large late Neolithic settlement situated on the northeast tip of the Stenness promontory overlooking the Loch of Harray. Close to the Stones of Stenness and contemporary with Skara Brae, it was discovered in 1984, although much of the site had been destroyed by ploughing. Subsequent excavations revealed at least 15 stone-built houses of the same basic internal layout as those of an earlier stage at Skara Brae, although they were rounder and without roofed passageways, indicating that they were not encased in a midden but free-standing. There were also two larger houses, the use of which is not clear but may be connected with the Stones of Stenness. Large amounts of grooved ware pottery were discovered, along with stone axes, skail knives, a mace head and a worked Arran pitchstone. The site is maintained by Historic Scotland.

Barnhouse Stone — 4 miles (6km) southwest of Finstown, Mainland. A monolith located to the southeast of the Stones of Stenness and apparently aligned with the entrance passage of Maes Howe. Standing 10ft 6in (3.2m) high, it is wider at the top than at the base, tapering from 6ft (1.8m) to 3ft 8in (1.1m).

Bishop's Palace — Palace Road, Kirkwall, Mainland. Built in the mid 12th century for Bishop William the Old (1102–68) close to St Magnus Cathedral, with a layout based on royal Norwegian palaces of the period. King Haakon IV of Norway died here on 15 December 1263 following his defeat at the

Battle of Largs. The palace went into a period of decline before being restored in the 1540s by Bishop Robert Reid, who added a round tower known locally as the Moosie Tower. The palace passed into the possession of Earl Robert Stewart in 1568; his grandson, also named Robert, was besieged here in 1614 after seizing the palace – along with the Earl's Palace and Kirkwall Castle – in support of his father Patrick, who had been imprisoned for treason in 1610. The rebellion ended with the capture and execution of both Robert and his father. The shell of the main building and the Moosie Tower are still visible. Now in the care of Historic Scotland.

Broch of Gurness — 8 miles (13km) north of Finstown, Mainland. Aka Knowe of Gurness, Knowe of Aikerness. Located on the Point of Helia overlooking Eynhallow Sound opposite Rousay and built c.200 BC, the structure was once 26ft (8m) high (about 12ft/3.5m still stand) and 63ft (19m) in diameter, with walls 14ft (4.2m) thick. Surrounded by a rampart and three ditches, it was built in three phases with a sprawl of houses radiating from the central tower. There was an entrance causeway on the eastern side of the settlement. It had been abandoned by the early 2nd century; although there is evidence of Pictish occupation in the nearby 'Shamrock House' and a Viking burial on the mound, the area was only sporadically inhabited afterwards. The site was first excavated in 1929 after accidentally being found by Orkney poet Robert Rendall.

Brough of Birsay — 11 miles (18km) northwest of Finstown, Mainland. A tidal island connected to the mainland by a concrete causeway with remains of Pictish and Norse settlements and a 12th century Romanesque church. The Picts lived on the island in the 7th and 8th centuries until supplanted by the Vikings, who overbuilt their settlement. The site is in the care of Historic Scotland. A 36ft (11m) high unmanned lighthouse was built on the island in 1925.

Carrick House — ½ mile (0.8km) west of Calfsound, Eday. A 17th century house overlooking the Calf of Eday, built in 1633 by John Stewart, Earl of Carrick. The notorious pirate John Gow (1698–1725), born in Wick but known as 'The Orkney Pirate', was captured and held prisoner here in 1725 before being taken to his trial and execution in London. Tel: 01857 622260.

Churchill Barriers — Four permanent barriers linking the chain of islands from Mainland in the north to South Ronaldsay in the south, constructed by order of Winston Churchill to safeguard the fleet anchored in Scapa Flow following the sinking of HMS *Royal Oak* by U-47 on 14 October 1939. Work began in May 1940 using mainly Italian prisoners of war as labourers and the barriers were completed on 12 May 1945, four days after the end of the war in Europe. The total length of the four causeways is 9150ft (2788m). Barrier No. 1 connects Mainland with Lamb Holm, No. 2 connects Lamb Holm with Glimps Holm, No. 3 connects Glimps Holm with Burray and No. 4 connects Burray with South Ronaldsay; they carry the A961 road.

Corrigall Farm Museum — Harray. A working farm museum recreating a 19th century Orcadian farmstead and including traditional livestock, a weaver's loom plus a barn with a grain-drying kiln. Tel: 01856 771411.

Cobbie Row's Castle — Wyre. Aka Cubbie Roo's Castle. Probably one of the earliest stone castles to survive in Scotland, consisting of a small rectangular tower surrounded by an outer wall. The *Orkneyinga Saga* tells how, c.1145, Norse chieftain Kolbein Hruga – Cobbie Row is a corrupted form of his name – built a stone castle (*steinkastala*), 24ft (7.5m) square and enclosed within a deep stone-faced ditch, on the island. According to the *Hakonar Saga* it was besieged in 1231. The ruined 12th century chapel of St Mary is nearby. Now maintained by Historic Scotland.

Comet Stone — 3½ miles (5.5km) northeast of Stromness, Mainland. A monolith standing 5ft 9in (1.7m) high to the southeast of the Ring of Brodgar. There are the stumps of two further standing stones nearby.

Covenanters Memorial — 10 miles (16km) east of Kirkwall, Mainland. Located near Mull Head and erected in 1888 to mark the site where 200 Covenanters captured following the Battle of Bothwell Brig drowned after their ship went aground in December 1697. The prisoners were being transported to the West Indies to be sold as slaves when the ship, the *Crown of London*, was hit by a storm. The captain had ordered them locked in the hold to prevent their escape, as this would have meant he would forfeit their price. The act of one member of the crew in opening a hatch enabled around 50 of the 250 on board to escape with their lives.

Cubbie Roo's Castle — See Cobbie Row's Castle.

Earl's Bu — 6 miles (10km) southeast of Stromness, Mainland. Aka the Bu of Orphir. Located overlooking Orphir Bay. The foundation courses of what may be the 'Earl's Bu', a drinking-hall mentioned in 1136 in the *Orkneyinga Saga*, according to which Earl Harald died here in 1127 and Sveinn Brestrope was murdered here in 1136. A souterrain or underground tunnel and a horizontal watermill have also been identified on the site.

Earl's Palace — Palace Road, Kirkwall, Mainland. Ruins of a 17th century U-plan building located close to St Magnus Cathedral and built in 1607 in French Renaissance style by Patrick Stewart, 2nd Earl of Orkney, as a replacement for the adjacent Bishop's Palace. Besieged during his son Robert's rebellion of 1614 (see Bishop's Palace), the Earl's Palace passed into the possession of the Bishop of Orkney but fell into ruin in the 18th century. Now in the care of Historic Scotland.

Heart of Neolithic Orkney — An area of Mainland designated a UNESCO World Heritage Site in 1999 and including major sites such as Maes Howe, the Ring of Brodgar and the Stones of Stenness as well as less well-known sites such as the Watch Stone, the Barnhouse Stone and the Barnhouse Settlement. It also protects the many unexcavated burial, ceremonial and settlement sites in the area. According to its citation, 'The group constitutes a major prehistoric cultural landscape which gives a graphic depiction of life in this remote archipelago in the far north of Scotland some 5000 years ago . . . the monuments of Orkney, dating back to 3000–2000 BC, are outstanding testimony to the cultural achievements of the Neolithic peoples of northern Europe.'

Highest point — Ward Hill on Hoy at 1571ft (479m). GR: HY229022.

Highland Park Distillery — ¾ mile (1.2km) south of Kirkwall, Mainland. Described as the most northerly Scotch whisky distillery in the world. It was established by Magnus Eunson in 1798 on High Park above Kirkwall and was run as an illicit business until it was legalised in 1826. The water for the distillery comes from an underground spring called Cattie Maggie and the peat used in the drying process comes from Hobbister Moor. Tel: 01856 873107.

Interesting facts — Although born in Salford, **Sir Peter Maxwell Davies** (b. 8 September 1934), Master of the Queen's Music, moved to the Orkney Islands in 1971, initially to Hoy and later to Sanday. Kirkwall hosts the **St Magnus Festival**, an arts festival founded by Davies in 1977 and during which he frequently premieres new works (often played by the local school orchestra). His light orchestral work *An Orkney Wedding, with Sunrise* (featuring the bagpipes) was inspired by the islands. Between the 16th and 18th centuries the island of Mainland was sometimes referred to as Pomona, after the Roman goddess of Fruit and Plenty. It is believed George Buchanan, a Scottish scholar of Latin, mistranslated a passage by the Roman author Solinus referring to Thule rather than Mainland.

Islands — See separate table.

Italian Chapel — Lamb Holm. A wonderfully decorated chapel created from a Nissen hut in the former World War II Camp 60, constructed to house Italian prisoners of war building the Churchill Barriers. The prisoners were allocated two huts, one to be used as a school and the other as a chapel. Much of the decoration was done by Domenico Chiocchetti, who produced a copy of Barabina's *Madonna of the Olives* taken from a picture he carried in his wallet as well as a statue of St George and the Dragon made from barbed wire and cement. The hut was lined with plasterboard and decorated. The altar and fittings were made of concrete and another prisoner named Palumbo created a wrought-iron rood screen. The exterior of the hut was embellished with a concrete façade. Chiocchetti stayed on after the rest of the prisoners were released in order to complete work on the chapel. A Chapel Preservation Committee was established in 1958 and the chapel is now one of Orkney's best-loved attractions. Chiocchetti returned and restored the paintwork in 1960, also giving the chapel 14 wooden Stations of the Cross in 1964.

Kirbuster Farm Museum — Birsay. A working farm museum with a central peat hearth homestead and a mixture of period-furnished 16th and 18th century farmhouses. The grounds include a Victorian garden and there are collections of farm equipment in the outbuildings. Tel: 01856 771268.

Kirkwall Castle — Kirkwall, Mainland. Built in 1383 by Earl Henry St Clair and severely damaged during Robert Stewart's rebellion in 1614 (see Bishop's Palace). It was eventually demolished in 1865. No trace of the castle is visible today apart from a commemorative plaque on a building in Castle Street.

Kirkwall Cathedral — See St Magnus Cathedral.

Knap of Howar — Papa Westray. A well-preserved Neolithic farmstead overlooking Papa Sound and occupied 3700–2800 BC, probably the oldest standing stone houses in northwest Europe. The site was excavated in the 1930s and 1970s: the buildings consist of two oblong interconnected dry-stone buildings facing the sea but probably lying inland when they were built, and overlying an earlier kitchen midden. The interiors are furnished with stone furniture including fireplaces, partition screens, beds and storage shelves. Organic remains indicate that the occupants raised cattle, sheep and pigs and grew wheat and barley, while fish and shellfish were also a staple element of their diet. Sherds of Unstan ware pottery have also been found. Knap of Howar means 'mound of mounds'.

Lyness Visitor Centre — Lyness, Hoy. Aka Scapa Flow Visitor Centre. An interpretive centre housed in the former oil pumping station of Lyness exploring the role of the Royal Navy based at Scapa Flow during both world wars; it was a naval base, HMS *Prosperine*, during World War II. Collections include military equipment, vehicles and weaponry. Exhibits include artefacts from HMS *Hampshire* (sunk in 1916) and the German High Seas Fleet (scuttled in 1919); there is also a large photographic collection. Tel: 01856 791300.

Maes Howe — 5 miles (8km) northeast of Stromness, Mainland. A spectacular chambered tomb overlooking the Loch of Harray and dating to c.2800–2300 BC. It was built on a levelled circular platform, encircled by a low bank composed of earth scraped up from a shallow ditch on its inner side. The mound is more than 115ft (35m) in diameter and 23ft (7m) high. A 4ft 6in (1.4m) high passage through the mound leads to a large square chamber with three smaller chambers leading off it. Buttresses in each corner of the chamber help support the weight of the corbelled roof. There are several 12th century runic inscriptions and carvings, suggesting that the tomb was reused and its external appearance improved for the burial of a Viking chieftain. According to the *Orkneyinga Saga*, Viking crusaders sheltered in the tomb c.1153 after breaking in through the roof. The tomb was opened in 1861 but only a portion of a human skull was found, making accurate interpretation of the site very difficult. Now in the care of Historic Scotland.

RSPB Marwick Head — 10 miles (16km) north of Stromness, Mainland. An RSPB reserve encompassing one of Orkney's three biggest seabird colonies. The cliffs of the red sandstone headland provide an internationally important nesting site for guillemots and kittiwakes.

Mid Howe Broch — 2 miles (3km) southwest of Wasbister, Rousay. Iron Age broch standing between the unexcavated North Howe broch and the badly eroded South Howe broch overlooking Eynhallow Sound, and surrounded by a group of other buildings. The remains of the 15ft (4.5m) thick walls stand 14ft (4.2m) high and the broch's interior diameter was 30ft (9m). The site was excavated 1930–3; artefacts found include bronze jewellery, a fragment of a Roman *patera* (a broad, shallow dish) and Roman potsherds which would indicate trading links with mainland Britain. Midhowe chambered cairn is nearby. The site is in the care of Historic Scotland.

Midhowe Chambered Cairn — 2 miles (3km) southwest of Wasbister, Rousay. Located a few hundred yards from Mid Howe Broch, the cairn dates to 3500 BC and measures 107ft (32.5m) long and 43ft (13m) wide. The chamber is divided by pairs of upright slabs into 12 compartments, some of which have stone benches. The outer face of the cairn has a 'herringbone' pattern in the stonework. The site was excavated in the 1930s and found to contain the remains of 25 people. Now in the care of Historic Scotland.

Mull Head Nature Reserve A local nature reserve covering 200 acres (80ha) of coastal grassland, heath and sea cliffs with a large population of seabirds.

Noltland Castle 1/2 mile (0.8km) west of Pierowall, Westray. Extended four-storey Z-plan castle overlooking the Bay of Pierowall, begun by Bishop Thomas Tulloch in the mid 15th century and completed only in 1560 by Gilbert Balfour, Master of the Household to Mary, Queen of Scots. The lower floors were designed for defence and are pierced by 71 gunloops. After Balfour was forced to flee Orkney in 1572 because of his support for Mary, the castle fell into the hands of Robert Stewart, 1st Earl of Orkney. Over the next 30 years its ownership yo-yoed between the Balfours and the Earls of Orkney until the Balfours sold it to Sir John Arnot in 1606. The castle was subject to many alterations and changing plans by its various owners, including a grand spiral staircase in the southwest tower, and was still unfinished when it began to fall into decline in the 17th century.

Old Man of Hoy 2 miles (3km) west of Rackwick, Hoy. A 137m (450ft) tall sandstone sea stack standing on a basalt base just off the coast of Hoy. It has been popular with climbers since it was the subject of a televised climb in 1966 by Chris Bonington, Tom Patey and Rusty Baillie.

Orkney Fossil and Vintage Centre Viewforth, Burray. A museum opened in 1993 and housing two separate collections put together by the Firth family: a social history collection with exhibits highlighting the everyday lives of Orcadians, including photographs, furniture, china and tools; and a collection of fossils and minerals originally found in the Cruaday Quarry in Sandwick (now a designated Site of Special Scientific Interest) and later expanded to include finds from around the world. Tel: 01856 731255.

Orkney Museum Broad Street, Kirkwall, Mainland. Housed in Tankerness House opposite St Magnus Cathedral, built in 1574 and owned by the Baikies of Tankerness from 1641 until 1951. The museum charts the history of the Orkneys. Separate galleries cover the story of the Orkneys in the Neolithic, Bronze Age and Iron Age and during the occupations by Picts and Norsemen. Other displays include 'Life and Death in Viking Orkney' and 'Medieval Orkney'. Exhibits include a Pictish Burrian symbol stone, Viking grave goods, St Magnus's reliquary and a variety of craft and trade items. The museum features a drawing room and library furnished in late 18th century style. Behind the house is a secluded walled garden. Tel: 01856 873191.

Orkney Wireless Museum Kiln Corner, Kirkwall, Mainland. A privately run museum specialising in Orkney wartime and domestic radio memorabilia, based on the collection of James MacDonald and opened in its present position in 1997. Tel: 01856 873191.

Orkneyinga Viking Saga Centre Earl's Bu, Orphir, Mainland. An interpretive centre exploring Viking Orkney as described in the 12th century *Orkneyinga Saga*. Situated by Earl's Bu and St Nicholas' Church.

Pentland Firth See Highland.

Pier Arts Centre Ferry Road, Stromness, Mainland. Opened in 1979 and housing a collection of 20th century British art and temporary displays of contemporary art from around the world. Exhibits include works by Barbara Hepworth and Ben Nicholson. The centre was originally housed in two separate listed buildings by Stromness Pier, linked into a single complex 2005–7. Tel: 01856 850209.

Quoyness Chambered Cairn Sanday. A chambered cairn located on the Elsness peninsula and of a similar type and date to Maes Howe. It has a rectangular chamber with six cells enclosed within an ovoid cairn and accessed by a low entrance passage. During its initial excavation in the 19th century, the bones from at least ten adults and five children were removed from the cairn.

Ring of Brodgar 5 miles (8km) northeast of Stromness, Mainland. Aka the Ring of Brogar. A Class II henge monument believed to have been built 2500–2000 BC and located on a strip of land between the Loch of Stenness and the Loch of Harray. Consisting of a stone circle 340ft (104m) in diameter and bounded by a ditch 30ft (9m) wide and 6ft (1.8m) deep, in terms of area enclosed it is the third largest ring in Britain (behind Avebury in Wiltshire and Stanton Drew in Somerset). There were once at least 40 stones and possibly as many as 60, of which 27 remain upright. The stones vary in height from 7ft (2.1m) to 15ft (4.5m). The site was taken into state care in 1906 and is maintained by Historic Scotland.

Rousay Heritage Centre Pierhead, Rousay. Aka Trumland Visitor Centre. A small visitor centre attached to the ferry waiting room and charting the story of the island, including the rich archaeology which led to Rousay being christened 'the Egypt of the north'. Tel: 01856 821374.

St Magnus' Cathedral Broad Street, Kirkwall, Mainland. Britain's most northerly cathedral, founded by Earl Rognvald in 1137 and dedicated to his kinsman St Magnus, executed at Egilsay in 1116. Owned by the city of Kirkwall rather than the church, having been granted by James III in 1468, it is built in Romanesque style from locally quarried yellow and red sandstone; because it took more than 300 years for the building to be completed, there are also elements of later architectural styles such as Gothic. Unlike the other major buildings in Kirkwall, it survived Robert Stewart's 1614 rebellion intact. It has undergone virtually continuous restoration and renovation since the early 20th century. The cathedral houses what are believed to be the bones of St Magnus and Earl Rognvald, both sets of which were discovered at different times interred in holes in separate columns in the cathedral. Unusually, the cathedral has a dungeon or oubliette known for reasons which are now obscure as Marwick's Hole. It was originally entered from the Hall of Justice but once this entrance was blocked a new one was opened in the cathedral.

St Nicholas' Church Orphir, 7 miles (11km) southeast of Stromness, Mainland. The remains of Scotland's only medieval round church, built in Romanesque style 1090–1136 and unique in Scotland in having been modelled on the Church of the Holy Sepulchre in Jerusalem. Mentioned in the *Orkneyinga Saga*, it is believed to have been built by Earl Håkon of Orkney on his return from pilgrimage to Jerusalem as a penance for ordering the murder of St Magnus. The church was destroyed in 1757 to provide building material for a new parish church nearby, which was in turn demolished in 1953. The site is close to the Orkneyinga Viking Saga Centre and Earl's Bu.

Shapinsay Heritage Centre Balfour, Shapinsay. Housed in the old blacksmith's shop, with displays exploring the island's history. Tel: 01856 711258.

Skaill House — 7 miles (11km) north of Stromness, Mainland. A much extended house located between the Loch of Skaill and the Bay of Skaill, close to Skara Brae, and originally built by Bishop George Graham in the 1620s on the site of an earlier hall. Major alterations were made in the 1950s. Features include the drawing room and Bishop Graham's bedroom, while Captain Cook's dinner service and paintings by Stanley Cursiter are among the items on display. Numerous haunting episodes have been reported in the house. It is now the home of the Laird of Breckness, while the public areas are managed by Historic Scotland. Tel: 01856 841501.

Skara Brae — 7 miles (11km) north of Stromness, Mainland. A Neolithic/Early Bronze Age settlement dating to c.3200–c.2200 BC. Uncovered by a storm in 1850, having been buried under centuries of blown sand, it was initially excavated by William Watt of Skaill but the dig was abandoned in 1868 after four houses had been uncovered. After another storm damaged the site in 1925, further structures were revealed during work to build a protective seawall around the site. Excavations by Gordon Childe carried out 1928–30 revealed a cluster of eight dry-stone huts connected by covered alleys, all contained within a heap of midden material covering 387 sq ft (36 sq m). Each house shares the same basic layout, being a large square room with a central hearth, a bed on either side and a shelved dresser on the wall opposite the doorway. It has been estimated that there was a population of between 50 and 100 at any one time. There were perhaps two or three phases of occupation, all of similar nature. Although it now stands close to the shore of the Bay of Skaill, when it was occupied the settlement would have been some way inland. There is a recreation of a Skara Brae type house at the site, which is maintained by Historic Scotland.

Stones of Stenness — 4 miles (6km) northeast of Stromness, Mainland. A Class II henge monument dating to c.3100 BC. It originally consisted of a series of standing stones set in an ellipse around the upper margin of a flat-topped mound 144ft (44m) in diameter, around which was a circular bank with an external diameter of 234ft (71m). The bank and ditch have been obliterated by cultivation. Excavations have revealed that there were probably 12 monoliths in the circle, of which four remain. The stones are up to 16ft (5m) high; at least one was deliberately destroyed in the 19th century. After visiting the site in 1814, Walter Scott suggested that the central stone slab had once been an altar or dolmen; a reconstruction of such an altar was erected in 1907 but damaged in 1972. The nearby Watch Stone and Barnhouse Stone are thought to have some connection with the henge. The site was taken into state care in 1906.

Stromness Museum — Alfred Street, Stromness, Mainland. A museum dedicated to the maritime and natural history of Stromness, housed in a building dating to 1858 and which originally served as both the museum and the town hall. There are exhibits relating to the fishing industry, the scuttling of the German High Seas Fleet and Orkney-born Arctic explorer John Rae; the museum also holds the original collections of the Orkney Natural History Society (founded in 1837), including bird specimens, eggs and fossils. Tel: 01856 850025.

Stronsay Fish Mart — Whitehall Village, Stronsay. A museum near the ferry terminal depicting life on the island during and after the herring boom, which lasted from the late 19th century until just before World War II. Tel: 01857 616386.

Tomb of the Eagles — 7 miles (11km) south of St Margaret's Hope, South Ronaldsay. Aka Isbister Chambered Cairn. A chambered cairn on the edge of a sheer cliff discovered in 1958, dating to c.3000 BC and named after the remains of white-tailed eagles found inside. Excavated in 1976, it also contained the bones of more than 300 people, together with three stone axes, a mace head and a polished stone knife.

Tormiston Mill — Stenness, 3½ miles (5.5km) northeast of Stromness, Mainland. A late 19th century watermill with original machinery, now serving as an interpretive centre for Maes Howe. Tel: 01856 761606.

Watch Stone — 4 miles (6km) northeast of Stromness, Mainland. A monolith located on the Brodgar causeway, northwest of the Stones of Stenness, and standing 18ft 6in (5.6m) high, 5ft (1.5m) wide and 1ft (0.3m) thick. It was possibly one of a pair of standing stones, as the stump of another was discovered close by.

Westray Heritage Centre — Pierowall, Westray. Opened in 1997 and dedicated to the local and natural history of the island. Tel: 01857 677414.

Wyre Heritage Centre — Wyre. Housed in the old community hall and charting the history of the island from early times to the 21st century, including Cubbie Row and his castle and poet Edwin Muir, who spent part of his childhood on the island; there is also a photographic archive of the places and people of Wyre. Tel: 01856 821211.

Some famous people born in the Orkneys

Baikie, William Balfour (explorer) (1824–64)	Kirkwall
Brunton, Mary (novelist) (1778–1818)	Orkney
Cursiter, Stanley (artist) (1887–1976)	Kirkwall
Erlendsson, Magnus (1st Earl of Orkney, saint) (c.1075–c.1116)	Orkney
Kolsson, Rognvald Kali (Earl of Orkney, saint) (c.1103–1158)	Orkney
Laing, Malcolm (writer) (1762–1818)	Orkney
Laing, Samuel (writer) (1780–1868)	Papdale
Linklater, Magnus (journalist) (1942–)	Orkney
Mackay Brown, George (writer) (1921–96)	Stromness
Muir, Edwin (writer and poet) (1887–1959)	Deerness
Rae, John (explorer) (1813–93)	Orphir

Spence, William (Australian trade unionist) (1846–1926)	Eday
Stout, Cameron (*Big Brother* winner) (1971–)	Stromness
Traill, Thomas Stewart (doctor) (1781–1862)	Kirkwall
Webster, Thomas (geologist) (1773–1844)	Orkney

Islands of Orkney

Island name	Area	Nearest landmark	General information
Altars of Linnay	North Sea	Ancumtoun, North Ronaldsay	Part of the Northern Isles. GR: HY758560
Auskerry	North Sea	Stronsay	The lighthouse at Baa Taing was automated in the 1960s. One of the Northern Isles. Area: 0.21 sq miles (0.55 sq km). Population: 5. GR: HY675163
Bakie Skerry	Westray Firth	Berst Ness, Westray	Part of the Northern Isles. GR: HY443418
Barrel of Butter	Scapa Flow	Cava	GR: HY351009
Bee Skerries	Odin Bay	Cliva, Stronsay	One of the Northern Isles. GR: HY687249
Black Holm	Copinsay Pass	Point of Ayre, Mainland	Connected to Corn Holm by drying reefs. GR: HY595020
Bow Skerries	Atlantic	Brough Head, Mainland	GR: HY238288
Braga	Hoy Sound	Breck Ness, Mainland	GR: HY220090
Broad Shoal	Westray Firth	Point of Huro, Westray	One of the Northern Isles. GR: HY491391
Brough, The	North Sea	Burgh Head, Stronsay	One of the Northern Isles. GR: HY698229
Brough of Birsay	Atlantic	Brough Head, Mainland	Drying island on the northwest of Mainland. GR: HY235285
Burray	Holm Sound	Ayre of Cara, South Ronaldsay	Joined to Mainland by the Churchill Barriers. One of the Southern Isles. Area: 3.89 sq miles (10.07 sq km). Population: 357. GR: ND477962
Calf of Eday	Calf Sound	Furrowend, Eday	One of the Northern Isles. Area: 0.94 sq miles (2.43 sq km). GR: HY582390
Calf of Flotta	Scapa Flow	Roan Head, Flotta	One of the Southern Isles. Almost a drying island as the water across Calf Sound to Flotta is very shallow. GR: ND382968
Cava	Scapa Flow	Holm of Houton, Mainland	One of the Southern Isles. The Calf of Cava lies to the north of the island but is joined to it by a stony ridge. Area: 0.41 sq miles (1.07 sq km). GR: ND328995
Clett of Crura	North Sea	The Brough, South Ronaldsay	One of the Southern Isles. GR: ND462875
Clettack Skerry	Pentland Firth	Muckle Skerry	One of the Pentland Skerries. GR: ND485775
Clumps, The	Westray Firth	Point of Huro, Westray	One of the Northern Isles. GR: HY489388
Copinsay	Copinsay Pass	Point of Ayre, Mainland	Administered by the RSPB since 1972. Area: 0.28 sq miles (0.73 sq km). GR: HY610015
Corn Holm	Copinsay Pass	Point of Ayre, Mainland	Joined to Copinsay by a long rock saddle, Isle Rough, and to Black Holm and Ward Holm by drying reefs. GR: HY598018
Crook, The	Bay of Newark	Tres Ness, Sanday	One of the Northern Isles. GR: HY707385
Cruis Taing	Bay of Newark	Tres Ness, Sanday	One of the Northern Isles. GR: HY713385
Damsay	Bay of Firth	Holm Point, Mainland	(O.N. = Pond Island). GR: HY390138
Dead Wife's Geo	Shapinsay Sound	Newlot, Shapinsay	One of the Northern Isles. GR: HY525148
Ebb of the Riv	The North Sound	Ortie, Sanday	One of the Northern Isles. GR: HY680470
Eday	Eday Sound	Weather Ness, Westray	(O.N. = Isthmus Island). One of the Northern Isles. Area: 10.7 sq miles (27.73 sq km). Population: 121. GR: HY560340
Egilsay	Rousay Sound	Scrimpo, Rousay	St Magnus martyred here 1117. One of the Northern Isles. Area: 2.24 sq miles (5.81 sq km). Population: 37. GR: HY470300
Eynhallow	Eynhallow Sound	Moa Ness, Rousay	Permitted to issue its own postage stamps. One of the Northern Isles. Area: 0.29 sq miles (0.75 sq km). GR: HY360290
Fara	Scapa Flow	Ly Ness, Hoy	One of the Southern Isles. Area: 1.14 sq miles (2.95 sq km). GR: ND328960
Faray	Sound of Faray	Greenan Nev, Eday	One of the Northern Isles. Area: 0.69 sq miles (1.8 sq km). GR: HY530370
Flotta	Scapa Flow	Crockness, Hoy	Base for North Sea oil industry in the Orkneys. One of the Summer Isles. Area: 3.77 sq miles (9.76 sq km). Population: 81. GR: ND359938.
Gairsay	Gairsay Sound	Queenamuckle, Mainland	Permitted to issue its own postage stamps. One of the Northern Isles. Area: 1 sq mile (2.57 sq km). Population: 3. GR: HY443220

Island name	Area	Nearest landmark	General information
Galpo	Mill Bay	Hill of Howness, Stronsay	One of the Northern Isles. GR: HY682261
Galt Skerry	Veantrow Bay	The Galt, Shapinsay	One of the Northern Isles. GR: HY488218
Galtie Rock	North Sea	Greenspot, North Ronaldsay	One of the Northern Isles. GR: HY769539
Garthna Geo	Atlantic	Inga Ness, Mainland	GR: HY217152
Geo of Lincro	Westray Firth	Point of Huro, Westray	Part of the Northern Isles. GR: HY485383
Glimps Holm	Holm Sound	Northtown, Burray	Joined to Burray by Churchill Barrier No 3 and to Lamb Holm by Churchill Barrier No 2. One of the Southern Isles. GR: ND473990
Glimpsholm Skerry	Holm Sound	Burray Haas, Burray	One of the Southern Isles. GR: ND483996
Graemsay	Hoy Sound	Moness, Hoy	Two lighthouses, Hoy High and Hoy Low, stand on the northeast and northwest of the island respectively. One of the Southern Isles. Area: 1.52 sq miles (3.93 sq km). Population: 21. GR: HY260053
Grass Holm	Wide Firth	Banks of Runabout, Shapinsay	One of the Northern Isles. GR: HY465197
Grit Ness	Eynhallow Sound	Knowe of Stenso, Mainland	GR: HY368267
Helliar Holm	The String	Point of Dishan, Shapinsay	One of the Northern Isles. GR: HY483155
Holm of Aikerness	Papa Sound	Aikerness, Westray	One of the Northern Isles. GR: HY470522
Holm of Boray	Gairsay Sound	Ness of Boray, Gairsay	One of the Northern Isles. GR: HY451207
Holm of Elsness	Sanday Sound	Els Ness, Sanday	One of the Northern Isles. GR: HY664373
Holm of Faray	Sound of Faray	The Steeths, Westray	One of the Northern Isles. GR: HY528390
Holm of Grimbister	Bay of Firth	Holm Point, Mainland	GR: HY379135
Holm of Huip	Huip Sound	Point of Comely, Stronsay	One of the Northern Isles. GR: HY629313
Holm of Kirkness	Loch of Harray	Kirk Ness, Mainland	GR: HY291189
Holm of Papa	The North Sound	Surhoose Taing, Papa Westray	One of the Northern Isles. GR: HY507520
Holm of Rendall	Gairsay Sound	Hall of Rendall, Mainland	GR: HY429208
Holm of Scockness	Rousay Sound	Scrimpo, Rousay	(O.N. = Islet of the Crooked Headland). One of the Northern Isles. GR: HY458315
Holms of Spurness	Spurness Sound	Spur Ness, Sanday	One of the Northern Isles. GR: HY605321
Horse of Copinsay	Copinsay Pass	North Nevi, Copinsay	GR: HY621029
Hoy	Atlantic	Stromness, Mainland	One of the Southern Isles. Hoy is the highest of the Orkney Islands, Ward Hill at 1571ft (479m) being the highest peak. The north of the island is an RSPB nature reserve. St John's Head on the northwest coast at 1148ft (350m) is one of the highest sea cliffs in the British Isles with the world-famous rock pinnacle, the Old Man of Hoy (449ft, 137m) to its south. Area: 55.5 sq miles (143.75 sq km). Population: 392. GR: ND258960
Hucklinsower	The North Sound	Ortie, Sanday	One of the Northern Isles. GR: HY680461
Hunda	Scapa Flow	Littlequey, Burray	One of the Southern Isles. GR: ND438967
Ingale Skerry	Ingale Sound	Langa Mae, Stronsay	One of the Northern Isles. GR: HY675200
Inganoust	Bay of Holland	Mells Kirk, Stronsay	One of the Northern Isles. GR: HY654225
Inner Holm	Stromness Harbour	Stromness, Mainland	GR: HY260088
Ire	The North Sound	Whale Point, Sanday	One of the Holms of Ire. GR: HY650460
Itherie Geo	Atlantic	Bring Head, Rousay	One of the Northern Isles. GR: HY369334
Kili Holm	Westray Firth	Weyland, Egilsay	One of the Northern Isles. GR: HY475325
Kirk Rocks	Hoy Sound	Cemy, Mainland	GR: HY233080
Kirk Taing	Holm Sound	Southtown, Burray	One of the Southern Isles. GR: ND492965
Lamb Holm	Holm Sound	West Breckan, Mainland	Joined to Glimps Holm by Churchill Barrier No 2 and to Mainland by Churchill Barrier No 1. One of the Southern Isles. GR: HY485004
Lang Taing	Sty Wick	Conninghole, Sanday	One of the Northern Isles. GR: HY690386
Lashy Skerries	Lashy Sound	Grassy Geos, Calf of Eday	One of the Northern Isles. GR: HY596387
Ling Holm	Loch of Harray	Biggings, Mainland	GR: HY305143
Ling Holms	Loch of Harray	Humasun Point, Mainland	GR: HY290155
Linga Holm	Linga Sound	Links Ness, Stronsay	Owned by the Scottish Wildlife Trust since 1999. One of the Northern Isles. Area: 0.22 sq miles (0.57 sq km). GR: HY615275
Little Galt Skerry	Veantrow Bay	The Galt, Shapinsay	One of the Northern Isles. GR: HY487213

Island name	Area	Nearest landmark	General information
Little Green Holm	Sound of the Green Holms	Axna Geo, Muckle Green Holm	GR: HY525262
Little Linga	Spurness Sound	Links Ness, Stronsay	(O.N. = Heather). One of the Northern Isles. GR: HY608302
Little Skerry	Shapinsay Sound	Yinstay Head, Mainland	GR: HY518113
Little Skerry	Pentland Firth	Muckle Skerry	One of the Pentland Skerries. GR: ND472766
Long Holm	Loch of Harray	Biggings, Mainland	GR: HY308142
Lotheran, The	The North Sound	Whale Point, Sanday	One of the Holms of Ire. GR: HY648467
Louther Skerry	Pentland Firth	Muckle Skerry	One of the Pentland Skerries. GR: ND479772
Lunga Skerries	North Sea	Auskerry	Part of the Northern Isles. GR: HY666168
Lurns of the Sound	North Sea	Point of Sinsoss, North Ronaldsay	Part of the Northern Isles. GR: HY778561
Mainland	Atlantic	Hoy	Mainland is composed of the sedimentary red sandstone typical of all the Orkney Islands. Kirkwall (O.N. *Kirkjuvagr* = Church Bay) is the 'capital' and Mid Hill at 889ft (271m) the highest peak. Following the loss of 833 men aboard HMS *Royal Oak* in 1939, after a German submarine evaded the blockships in the eastern approach to Scapa flow, Winston Churchill ordered barriers to be built between the eastern islands. Area: 194.37 sq miles (503.4 sq km). Population: 15,315. GR: HY335136
Middle Skerry	Burra Sound	Bu Hill, Hoy	One of the Southern Isles. GR: HY241052
Muckle Green Holm	Fall of Warness	War Ness, Eday	One of the Northern Isles. GR: HY525271
Muckle Skerry	Pentland Firth	Duncansby Head	The lighthouse was built in 1794. One of the Pentland Skerries. GR: ND465782
Nevi Skerry	Scapa Flow	Tween the Wicks, Flotta	One of the Southern Isles. GR: ND398958
North Ronaldsay	North Ronaldsay Firth	Toftsness, Sanday	The whole island is enclosed by the Sheep Dyke, a 7ft (2m) high wall. One of the Northern Isles. Area: 3.01 sq miles (7.8 sq km). Population: 70. GR: HY760540
Oessen Skerry	North Sea	Auskerry	One of the Northern Isles. GR: HY668165
Old Man of Hoy	Atlantic	Tuaks of the Boy, Hoy	One of the Southern Isles. GR: HY175009
Outer Holm	Stromness Harbour	Stromness, Mainland	GR: HY260083
Papa Stronsay	Papa Sound	Grice Ness, Stronsay	(O.N. = Priest's Island of Stronsay). One of the Northern Isles. Area: 0.32 sq miles (0.83 sq km). Population: 10. GR: HY665295
Papa Westray	Papa Sound	Spo Ness, Westray	Flight from the airstrip on Westray to that on Papa Westray is the shortest scheduled air flight in the world (on average 2 min but has been completed in 58 sec). One of the Northern Isles. Area: 3.24 sq miles (8.4 sq km). Population: 65. GR: HY490520
Pig Island	Pentland Firth	Barth Head, South Ronaldsay	aka Swona. One of the Southern Isles. Area: 0.36 sq miles (0.92 sq km). GR: ND390845
Pow, The	Bay of Houseby	Housebay, Stronsay	One of the Northern Isles. GR: HY675219
Puldrite Skerry	Wide Firth	Crookness, Mainland	GR: HY437182
Quanterness Skerry	Wide Firth	Quanter Ness, Mainland	GR: HY420149
Red Holm	Sound of Faray	Broad Ebb, Eday	Part of the Northern Isles. GR: HY541398
Riv, The	The North Sound	Ortie, Sanday	One of the Northern Isles. GR: HY681476
Rousay	Westray Firth	Aiker Ness, Mainland	Sometimes dubbed 'Egypt of the North' due to the large number of chambered cairns on the island. One of the Northern Isles. Area: 18.55 sq miles (48.05 sq km). Population: 212. GR: HY406306
Runna Clett	The North Sound	Woo, Sanday	One of the Northern Isles. GR: HY667455
Rusk Holm	Rapness Sound	Fers Ness, Eday	One of the Northern Isles. GR: HY512356
Rysa Little	Rysa Sound	Pegal Head, Hoy	(O.N. = Little Heap of Stones). One of the Southern Isles. GR: ND310976
Salt Ness	Wide Firth	Banks of Runabout, Shapinsay	Part of the Northern Isles. GR: HY475198
Sand Holm	Loch of Harray	Bockan, Mainland	GR: HY293141
Sanday	The North Sound	Greeny Brae, Eday	(O.N. = Sand Island). One of the Northern Isles. Area: 20.49 sq miles (53.06 sq km). Population: 478. GR: HY670420
Savil Less	The North Sound	Ness, Papa Westray	One of the Northern Isles. GR: HY505537
Scair Tack	Otters Wick	Northskaill, Sanday	One of the Northern Isles. GR: HY684445
Scare Gun	Shapinsay Sound	Yinstay Head, Mainland	GR: HY519112
Scarvie Clett	Shapinsay Sound	Newlot, Shapinsay	One of the Northern Isles. GR: HY530153

Island name	Area	Nearest landmark	General information
Seal Skerry	Gairsay Sound	North Aittit, Mainland	GR: HY435204
Seal Skerry	North Sea	Point of Sinsoss, North Ronaldsay	One of the Northern Isles. Overlooked by North Ronaldsway lighthouse, the tallest land-based lighthouse in the British Isles at 108ft (33m). GR: HY781569
Seal Skerry	Westray Firth	Point of Sandybank, Eday	One of the Northern Isles. GR: HY530314
Selki Skerry	Pentland Firth	Swona	GR: ND381840
Shapinsay	Stronsay Firth	Head of Work, Mainland	aka Shapansay. Home to the parents of author Washington Irving. One of the Northern Isles. Area: 10.87 sq miles (28.17 sq km). Population: 300. GR: HY504176
Sheep Skerry	Eynhallow Sound	Eynhallow	One of the Northern Isles. GR: HY361285
Sheep Skerry	Pentland Firth	Melberry, Hoy	One of the Southern Isles. GR: ND263886
Skaill Skerries	North Sea	Tangi, Mainland	GR: HY597064
Skea Skerries	Westray Firth	Berst Ness, Westray	One of the Northern Isles. GR: HY442402
Skerries of Clestrain	Clestrain Sound	Clestrain, Mainland	GR: HY288070
Skerries of Coubister	Bay of Firth	Coubister, Mainland	GR: HY380148
Skerries of Lakequoy	Deer Sound	Whitecleat, Mainland	GR: HY521082
Skerries of Skaigram	Pentland Firth	Liddel, South Ronaldsay	One of the Southern Isles. GR: ND468831
Skerry of Cletts	Clestrain Sound	The Lash, Graemsay	One of the Southern Isles. GR: HY255066
Skerry of Vasa	Wide Firth	Rosecraigie, Shapinsay	One of the Northern Isles. GR: HY468185
Skerry of Wastbist	Westray Firth	Taftend, Westray	One of the Northern Isles. GR: HY483418
Skerry of Yinstay	Shapinsay Sound	Yinstay Head, Mainland	GR: HY515113
Skrowa Skerry	Atlantic	Black Craig, Mainland	GR: HY219109
Smoogro Skerry	Scapa Flow	Smoogro, Mainland	GR: HY365052
Sooth Clett	Pentland Firth	Swona	GR: ND389838
South Ronaldsay	Pentland Firth	Duncansby Head	Joined to Mainland by Churchill Barrier No 4. One of the Southern Isles. Area: 19.2 sq miles (49.73 sq km). Population: 854. GR: ND450870
South Skerry	Shapinsay Sound	Newlot, Shapinsay	One of the Northern Isles. GR: HY528149
South Walls	Scapa Flow	Brims Ness, Hoy	Joined to Hoy by causeway called The Ayre. The lighthouse at Cantick Head was built by David Stevenson in 1858. One of the Southern Isles. GR: ND320900
Stack of Kame	North Sea	Grim Ness, South Ronaldsay	One of the Southern Isles. GR: ND490925
Standard	Atlantic	Ramna Geo, Mainland	GR: HY301303
Stronsay	Stronsay Firth	Ness of Ork, Shapinsay	Whitehall is the 'capital'. One of the Northern Isles. Area: 13.64 sq miles (35.32 sq km). Population: 343. GR: HY657248
Sule Skerry	Atlantic	Brough Head, Mainland	(O.N. = Lone Skerry). Area: 0.07 sq miles (0.19 sq km). GR: HX621245
Sule Stack	Atlantic	Brough Head, Mainland	GR: HX562179
Swarf, The	Spurness Sound	Spur Ness, Sanday	(O.N. = Grit). One of the Northern Isles. GR: HY608328
Swarf, The	Sanday Sound	Els Ness, Sanday	One of the Northern Isles. GR: HY675370
Sweyn Holm	Gairsay Sound	North Head, Gairsay	(O.N. = Servant Islet). GR: HY455228
Switha	Sound of Hoxa	Crowtaing, South Walls	One of the Southern Isles. Area: 0.16 sq miles (0.41 sq km). GR: ND364907
Swona	Pentland Firth	Barth Head, South Ronaldsay	See Pig Island
Tails of the Tarf	Pentland Firth	Swona	One of the Southern Isles. GR: ND380837
Taing of Westove	The North Sound	Woo, Sanday	One of the Northern Isles. GR: HY661458
Taing Skerry	Wide Firth	Banks of Runabout, Shapinsay	One of the Northern Isles. GR: HY459197
Thieves Holm	Bay of Kirkwall	Car Ness, Mainland	GR: HY461149
Ward Holm	Copinsay Pass	Point of Ayre, Mainland	Connected to Corn Holm by drying reefs. GR: HY595014
Wart Holm	Westray Firth	Point of Huro, Westray	One of the Northern Isles. GR: HY484381
Weelie's Taing	The North Sound	Ness, Papa Westray	One of the Northern Isles. GR: HY505535
West Wini Skerry	Pentland Firth	Swona	GR: ND383835
Westray	Westray Firth	Faraclet Head, Rousay	aka The Queen of the North Isles. Area: 18.5 sq miles (47.92 sq km). Population: 563. GR: HY440460
Wyre	Wyre Sound	Point of Avelshay, Rousay	Cubbie Row's Castle is possibly the earliest stone castle to have survived in Scotland. One of the Northern Isles. Area: 1.07 sq miles (2.78 sq km). Population: 18. GR: HY444261
Wyre Skerries	Wyre Sound	Point of Nichol's Croo, Wyre	Part of the Northern Isles. GR: HY414259

SHETLAND ISLANDS

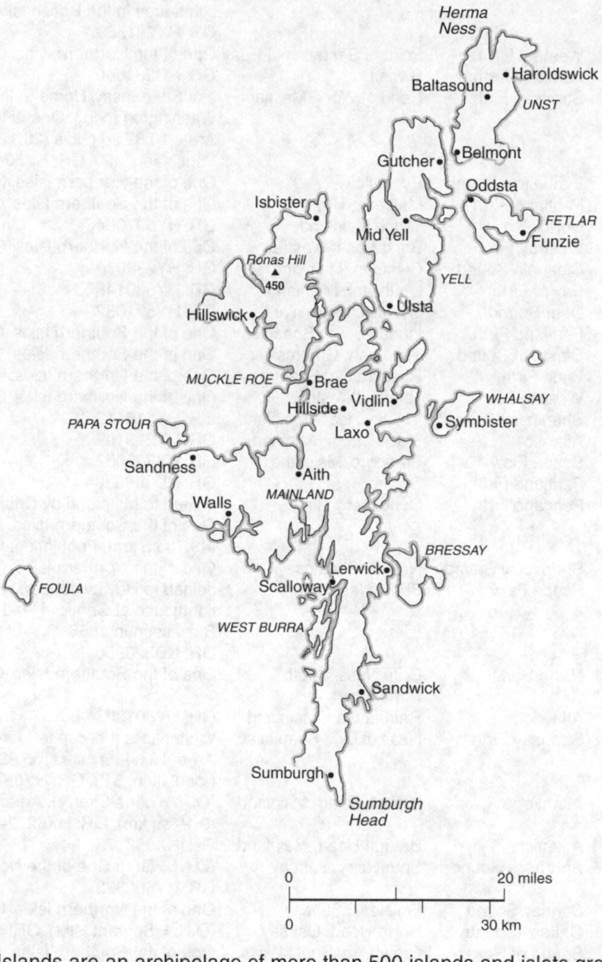
Herma Ness
Haroldswick
Baltasound
UNST
Belmont
Gutcher
Oddsta
FETLAR
Funzie
Isbister
Mid Yell
Ronas Hill
450
YELL
Hillswick
Ulsta
MUCKLE ROE
Brae
WHALSAY
Vidlin
Hillside
Symbister
PAPA STOUR
Laxo
Sandness
Aith
MAINLAND
Walls
BRESSAY
Lerwick
Scalloway
FOULA
WEST BURRA
Sandwick
Sumburgh
Sumburgh Head
0
20 miles
0
30 km

The Shetland Islands are an archipelago of more than 500 islands and islets grouped together as one of the 32 council areas of Scotland. The inhabited islands are, in descending order of population size in 2001: Mainland (Shetland Mainland), Whalsay, Yell, West Burra, Unst, Bressay, Trondra, Muckle Roe, Fair Isle, East Burra, Housay, Foula, Bruray, Papa Stour, Vaila. The main town is Lerwick on Mainland and this also acts as the county town for the whole area. Around 22,000 people live in the Shetlands, mostly in small farming communities; of these, 17,550 live on Shetland Mainland.

Lying along the same latitude as St Petersburg in Russia and Anchorage in Alaska, the Shetland Islands hold most records for the 'northernmost' in the British Isles, including the northernmost settlement, castle and church.

The economy of the islands was traditionally built around crofting and fishing but at present the main income-generating industry is oil and related supporting industries, such as engineering. Aquaculture is a growth industry. Craft industries such as knitting and an increase in tourism are also responsible for keeping the level of employment high. The Shetland Islands have been declared an Environmentally Sensitive Area so that traditional farming and crofting practices which benefit nature can be encouraged.

In terms of environment the Shetland Islands are a mixture of moorland and coastline dominated by high cliffs. They thus provide very attractive nesting habitats for a remarkable number of bird species, including great skua (also known as Bonxie in the Shetlands), Arctic skua, fulmars, puffins (known locally as Tammie Nories), guillemots, razorbills, kittiwakes and gannets (known locally as solan geese). The blanket bog provides a nesting environment for red-throated divers, dunlin and golden plover. The islands are home to three National Nature Reserves and four RSPB reserves. The lack of trees means that many birds use the remains of man-made structures such as brochs for nesting.

The islands were first settled in the Neolithic period and the roundhouses and brochs – circular stone-built defensive towers – of the Iron Age attest to the development of social organisation and building skills during that period. Christianity probably arrived in the 6th century and Norsemen began to settle the islands in the late 8th century. They held sway over the Shetland Islands for more than 500 years, finding them a convenient stopping-off point on voyages to Greenland and Ireland. In 1468 the impoverished Christian I, king of Denmark, Norway and Sweden, pledged the islands (along with the Orkney Islands) to the Scottish Crown as part of a marriage agreement with James III of Scotland, who was to marry his daughter Margaret of Denmark. The earldom was annexed to the Scottish crown on 20 February 1472 following non-payment of the marriage dowry.

During the 16th and 17th centuries the islands developed a close relationship with the Hanseatic League of the Baltic and northern Europe, the main trade being in salted fish. Unfortunately for the islanders this trade effectively came to an end after the Act of Union with England in 1707 and the merchants instead turned their attentions to deriving more profit from the land at the expense of their tenants. Many Shetlanders joined (or were pressed to join) the Royal Navy and, later, the Merchant Navy. Inoculation against smallpox, which had virtually wiped out the populations on some islands, saw an increase in the population which, on the down side, resulted in land shortages. A brief boom in herring fishing was not enough to stave off waves of emigration during the 20th century, but since the 1960s the islands have experienced something of an economic renaissance.

Shetland Islands	**Population**			**Area**	
	male	*female*	*total*	*sq miles*	*sq km*
Total	11,071	10,917	21,988	566	1466

Local Attractions and Information

Administrative headquarters — Town Hall, Lerwick ZE1 0HB. Tel: 01595 693535.

Airports — **Fair Isle Airport** (FIE), Ward Hill, Fair Isle; **Scatsta Airport** (SCS), 24 miles (39km) northwest of Lerwick near the oil terminal at Sullom Voe. Originally an RAF base during World War II. Subsequently abandoned, it was reopened in 1978 to support the oil industry; **Sumburgh Airport** (LSI), 20 miles (32km) south of Lerwick. Flights are available to Aberdeen, Edinburgh, Fair Isle, Glasgow, Inverness, Kirkwall and Wick. An RAF fighter base during World War II, it became Shetland's main airport in 1953; **Tingwall Airport** (LWK), Gott, 6 miles (10km) south of Lerwick. Used for internal flights within Shetland to Fair Isle, Foula, Out Skerries and Papa Stour. Tel: 01595 840306. There are small island landing strips on Foula, Out Skerries, Papa Stour and Unst.

Benie Hoose — 3/4 mile (1.2km) north of Isbister, Whalsay. A Neolithic or Bronze Age homestead excavated in the 1950s. The excavations produced a large number of tools and querns and the structure was originally interpreted as being a priest's house associated with the nearby Stones of Yoxie.

Böd of Gremista Museum — Gremista, 2 miles (3km) north of Lerwick, Mainland. The böd (booth) was built in the 1780s and provided family accommodation, as well as working space and storage for the fishermen above the artificial beach used for fish drying. The birthplace of Arthur Anderson (1792–1868), co-founder of the Peninsular and Oriental Steam Navigation Company (P&O), it was extensively restored in the 1980s and now contains exhibits exploring both the house's place in the local fishing industry and the life of Arthur Anderson. Some of the rooms are furnished as they would have been in Anderson's time. Tel: 01595 694386.

Bressay Lighthouse — Kirkabister Ness, Bressay. A 52ft (16m) high white tower constructed in 1858 by David and Thomas Stevenson and automated in 1989. In 1995 the keepers' cottages were acquired by the Shetland Amenity Trust and have been refurbished as holiday accommodation.

Bressay Sound — The site of battles between Dutch and Spanish fleets in 1640 and Dutch and French fleets in the early 18th century during a fishing war. Dutch fishing boats (known as busses) used the Sound as a gathering point during the herring fishing season, eventually leading to the establishment of Lerwick as a trading point. The fishing and preparation of herring was a major industry for the Dutch – it has been said that Amsterdam was built on herring bones – while the Shetlanders, restricted to smaller non-ocean-going boats than the Dutch busses, which were also protected by men-of-war, were unable to benefit from the bountiful supplies of herring in their local waters.

Bressay Stone Bressay. A sculptured cross-slab 3ft 9in (1.15m) high with inscriptions in ogham script on its narrow sides, believed to have been found near St Mary's Church. The script has not been fully deciphered but appears to refer to a Norse princess. The original is held in the National Museum of Scotland in Edinburgh.

Broch of Burland 4 miles (6km) southwest of Lerwick, Mainland. An Iron Age broch built on a high promontory and protected inland by ditches and walls.

Burgi Geos Fort Yell. The remains of an Iron Age promontory blockhouse fort. A ditch divided the neck of the promontory from inland and was defended by a wall 35ft (10.5m) long and 13in (0.3m) thick. A pathway from the wall to the fort was edged by blocks to prevent people falling over the cliff-side.

Cabin Museum Wirlie, Vidlin. A local history museum built around the personal collection of medals, badges and uniforms of Andy Robertson. Tel: 01806 577243.

Clickimin Broch 1/2 mile (0.8km) southwest of Lerwick, Mainland. An Iron Age broch built in the 1st or 2nd century on the south shore of the Loch of Clickimin. It was located on the site of settlements dating back to the Late Bronze Age (7th century BC) and including a farm and a blockhouse built in the 1st century BC. The broch would have originally stood up to 50ft (15m) high. The defensive elements of the site became less important by the middle of the 1st millennium and it had been abandoned by the time of the arrival of the Vikings in the 9th century. It was excavated by an amateur antiquarian in the 1850s and was subject to a professional dig 100 years later. The site is maintained by Historic Scotland.

Earl Patrick's Castle Scalloway, Mainland. Built with forced labour in 1600 to a medieval design, and abandoned 15 years later when its owner was executed.

El Gran Grifón A 650 ton ship in the Spanish Armada of 1588. A supply ship (hulk) commanded by Juan Gomez de Medina, on 8 August 1588 she ran aground on the Sivars Geo rocks on Fair Isle. The 200 or so Spaniards who survived the wreck were treated well by the locals but with dwindling local supplies they became a burden and began to take food which the islanders needed for the coming winter. They were eventually shipped to Shetland and repatriated to Spain or, according another account, thrown off a cliff by the Fair Isle islanders.

Esha Ness Lighthouse 10 miles (16km) northwest of Sullom, Mainland. A white square tower standing 40ft (12m) high built by David and Charles Stevenson in 1929. The light was automated in 1974 and the keeper's lodgings are now a private house.

Fair Isle An island halfway between the Shetlands and the Orkneys, famous for birds, sweaters and shipwrecks, as well as being a shipping forecast area. Statistics show that prior to the advent of radar there was an average of one wreck every four or five years. In 1954 the island was bought by the National Trust for Scotland from George Waterson, founder of the Fair Isle Lodge and Bird Observatory established overlooking Bu Ness and opened to visitors on 28 August 1948. Fair Isle lies in the flight line of many migrant birds, and 345 species have been recorded on the island. Like Hirta in the Orkneys, Fair Isle has its own sub-species of wren and fieldmouse. Area: 3.15 sq miles (8.15 sq km). Population: 69. GR: HZ210720.

Fetlar Known as 'The Garden of Shetland', Fetlar is popularly thought to be the first island settled by the Norsemen before they colonised the other islands around Scotland. It was substantially cleared by Sir Arthur Nicholson in the 1820s to make way for sheep, after which he used the stone from the deserted crofts to build himself a three-storey house. At some point in antiquity it was divided in two by the dyke known as the Funzie Girt (see separate entry). The northern part of Fetlar is an RSPB reserve. Area: 15.75 sq miles (40.78 sq km). GR: HU620920.

Fetlar Interpretive Centre Beach of Houbie, Fetlar. An award-winning local history museum focusing on local archaeology, folklore and natural history. Exhibits include Norse steatite bowls, sail and rope making tools, a Loder horn used as a fog horn, peat digging and transporting equipment, household items and craftwork. There are interactive computer displays, a large archive of photographs and documents and a searchable genealogical database. There is also a collection relating to Sir William Watson Cheyne who worked with Joseph Lister on the development of antiseptic. Although born on board a ship lying off Hobart, Tasmania, Cheyn is considered to be a native of Fetlar as his parents were from here and he was brought up here. He returned to live in Fetlar at the end of his life. Tel: 01957 733206.

Fort Charlotte Lerwick, Mainland. A roughly pentagonal fort originally built by Robert Milne in 1665 to protect the Sound of Bressay against the Dutch. Badly designed and without a secure water supply, the fort was unmanned when it was burned by the Dutch in 1673 along with the rest of the town. Eventually rebuilt in 1781 and named after George III's wife, it never saw action and was later used as a town jail and court house. It originally overlooked the harbour but due to land reclamation it is now inland. Five gun platforms were exposed during excavations in 1993.

Foula The most westerly of the Shetland Islands and also the most isolated inhabited island in the British Isles, which has led to a few idiosyncrasies over the years. It used Norse udal law until the late 17th century and Norn was still spoken into the 19th century. It is also the only place in the British Isles still using the Julian calendar, in which Christmas Day falls on what is 6 January for everybody else. The sheep on Foula, which are a unique variety, have taken to biting the heads off young birds to supplement their diet. Like Fair Isle, Foula has its own sub-species of fieldmouse. Area: 4.97 sq miles (12.86 sq km). Population: 31. GR: HT960390.

Funzie Girt Fetlar. Aka Finnigirt or Finnigord. The remains of a 3ft (0.9m) wide dyke which in antiquity divided the island into two approximately equal parts. Its builders and true purpose are unknown although according to legend it was built overnight as a result of a disagreement by two landowners.

Gardie House Bressay. A two-storey building erected in 1724 and formerly the Laird's house. It is now home to the Lord Lieutenant of Shetland.

Haltadans	Fetlar. A stone circle with a diameter of 37ft (11.5m) which may have originally been a cairn. Haltadans means 'limping dance', and according to legend the stones are petrified Trows (little people who lived on Fetlar) who danced all through the night and were turned to stone at the rising of the sun. Two larger stones in the centre of the circle are said to be the fiddlers (or the fiddler and his wife) who were playing for them. A similar story is told about the Merry Maidens stone circle at the other end of the British Isles in Cornwall, where the legend is of 19 maidens dancing on a Sunday who were transformed into stones, along with the pipers who had played for them.
Hanseatic Booth	Symbister, Whalsay. A house used by the Hanseatic League during the 17th century boom in sales of Shetland salted fish. In 1696 the Hanseatic merchant booths in the Shetlands were attacked by pirates; this, along with the Act of Union and a salt tax introduced in 1715, effectively brought an end to the trade. Now restored, the house has an exhibition charting the history of the Hanseatic trading links. Poet Hugh MacDiarmid lived in the house 1935–42.
Haroldswick Methodist Church	Haroldswick, Unst. The most northerly church in the British Isles. The present church, designed by Frank Robertson on a Norwegian pattern, was erected in the 1990s to replace the previous building which had been damaged by high winds.
Hermaness National Nature Reserve	3 miles (5km) northwest of Haroldswick, Unst. Located on a rocky headland on the northwest tip of the island and designated in 1955, the reserve is home to more than 100,000 pairs of seabirds of 13 species during the breeding season. Species represented include great skua (also known as Bonxie in the Shetlands), Arctic skua, fulmar, puffin (known locally as Tammie Nories), guillemot, razorbill, kittiwake and gannet (known locally as solan geese). The blanket bog on the reserve is home to red-throated diver, dunlin and golden plover. One particular black-browed albatross visited the reserve virtually every year from 1972 until 1995, and was named Albert – as in albert (ross). He was initially spotted among the gannets on Bass Rock in 1967 before making his first appearance among Unst's gannet colony in 1972. As the black-browed albatross is a rare visitor to Britain and can live up to 60 years, the sighting of an individual in 2005 on Sula Sgeir in the Hebrides raised the possibility that Albert had returned to the Scottish islands after a long gap. While at Hermaness this lone individual – most of his species live in the South Atlantic and he may be the only one in the North Atlantic – nested on the same ledge each year and regularly attracted twitchers from all over the UK. Tel: 01957 711278.
Highest point	Ronas Hill, $2\frac{1}{2}$ miles (4km) west of Fladda on Mainland at 1476ft (450m). GR: HU305835.
Hill of Cruester Standing Stone	$\frac{3}{4}$ mile (1.2km) north of Maryfield, Bressay. A monolith standing 9ft 6in (2.9m) high and tapering from 4ft 6in (1.4m) at the base to 2ft 7in (0.75m) wide at 6ft (1.8m) above the ground. It is sited within the meagre remains of a circular feature.
Hoswick Visitor Centre	Hoswick, 11 miles (18km) south of Lerwick, Mainland. A centre with displays on the local weaving industry (including textile machinery), crofting and fishing. There is also an exhibition of radio equipment and tape recorders. Tel: 01950 431215.
Interesting facts	In 1886 59-year-old **Betty Mouat** set out for Lerwick from Scatness on board the *Columbine*, a 50ft (15m) sailing boat, to try to sell some knitted shawls made by herself and her neighbours. During the voyage Captain Jamieson fell overboard and his crew of two launched a small boat to save him. Unfortunately the skipper had drowned and the rescue boat was unable to regain the *Columbine* in the rough seas. Betty stayed on board alone for eight days as the boat drifted for 300 miles (480km), and was rescued only when it ran aground in Norway on 7 February 1886, afterwards becoming something of a celebrity. Her house is close to the Old Scatness excavations (see separate entry). **Aith**, on Aith Sound on Mainland, is home to the most northerly lifeboat station in Britain. **East** and **West Burra** and **Trondra** are three islands connected to Mainland and to each other by bridges. The main settlement, Hamna Voe on West Burra, began life as a planned settlement in 1850. **Eshaness**, a wild part of the Atlantic coast of Mainland, has views of the stacks Dore Holm – which has a 70ft (21m arch) – and The Drongs, stacks carved by the sea from red sandstone. **The Skerries**, also known as the Out Skerries, are a lightly populated group of islands lying to the east of Shetland. The main islands are Grunay, Bruray and Housay, the last two linked by a bridge. **Sullum Voe**, an inlet between North Mainland and Northmavine, is famous for its oil terminal. **Unst** is home to all that is 'most northerly' in the British Isles.
Islands	See separate table for the 529 islands of Shetland.
Jarlshof Prehistoric and Norse Settlement	Sumburgh, 20 miles (32km) south of Lerwick, Mainland. An important complex of buildings ranging in date from the Bronze Age to the 16th century. In the 19th century the only building visible on the site was the ruined 16th century Old Laird's House, a name translated into Norse as 'Yarlshof' (Jarlshof) by Sir Walter Scott for his book *The Pirate*. This is the name now used for the site. Towards the end of the century a series of storms began to uncover previously hidden structures. In the early 1900s a local archaeologist exposed an Iron Age broch and wheelhouse. After the site was taken into state care, further excavations in the 1930s and late 1940s revealed a continuous pattern of settlement stretching from the Bronze Age, through the Iron Age and Norse occupation and into the medieval period. Occupation of the site began c.1800 BC with a Bronze Age village of roundhouses. These were eventually abandoned and were covered with sand. Further houses were built on the site c.800 BC, along with a smithy. Among the finds relating to this period were a rib-tanged knife, fragments of clay moulds for at least eight socketed axes, seven swords and a socketed axe. During the Iron Age a broch was built c.200 BC. The remains of this structure have been half-destroyed by marine erosion but it was originally 63ft (19m) in diameter. Following the abandonment of the broch, a roundhouse was built and four wheelhouses erected AD 200–600. The arrival of the Norsemen in the 9th century saw the building of longhouses with family accommodation at one end and an animal byre at the other. After four

centuries the Norse settlement had metamorphosed into a medieval farmstead and in the late 16th century the 'Jarlshof' was built nearby. This was abandoned by the late 17th century, bringing nearly 3500 years of almost continuous occupation to an end. The site is now in the care of Historic Scotland.

Johnnie Notions' Bod — Hamnavoe, West Burra. The home of John Williamson (c.1740–c.1796), also known as 'Johnnie Notions', a self-educated Shetlander who invented a means of inoculating local people against smallpox in the 1700s. His former house is now available as holiday accommodation.

Keen of Hamar — 2 miles (3km) southeast of Haroldswick, Unst. A National Nature Reserve established in 1975 and covering 75 acres (30ha) of unusual serpentine rock debris noted for its rare flowering plant-life. A small white-flowered plant, Edmondston's chickweed (*Cerastium nigrescens*), also known as Shetland mouse-ear, is only found on Unst; it is named after Thomas Edmondston of Buness, who discovered it in 1837. Other rare plants include Norwegian sandwort, northern rock-cress, hoary whitlow grass, moss campion and alpine meadow-rue. What little soil there is on the reserve was most likely deposited during the last Ice Age more than 10,000 years ago.

Lerwick — Located on Mainland, the chief town and only burgh in the Shetland Islands, with a population of around 9000 in 2005. It originally developed as a shanty town set up to service, in most ways imaginable, the Dutch herring fishing fleet anchored in Bressay Sound. It was burned down more than once in its early years both by the French and by the men of Scalloway who were threatened by its growth. It replaced Scalloway as capital of the islands in 1708.

Lunna Kirk — 9 miles (15km) southeast of Sullom, Mainland. Possibly the oldest site of Christian worship in the Shetland Islands. Lunna Chapel Knowe lies nearby and was possibly the site of a 12th century monastery. The church was rebuilt in the 1750s after a brief period of abandonment. The interior has a gallery and raised pulpit.

Mavis Grind — 3 miles (5km) southwest of Sullom, Mainland. Mavis Grind means 'gateway of the narrow isthmus' and is the name given to the narrow neck of land only 330ft (100m) wide dividing Sullom Voe from St Magnus Bay. Both the Vikings and more recent fishermen were known to drag their boats across the grind rather than sail to the north of Shetland.

Mousa Broch — Mousa. Well-preserved and remarkably intact Iron Age broch located on a promontory on the uninhabited island. The external diameter was 50ft (15m) at the base, tapering to 43ft (13m) at the top with walls 15ft (4.5m) thick and standing more than 43ft (13m) tall. As is usual with brochs, the stairway is within the hollow wall, which also contains six galleries. At some point during the Pictish period a wheelhouse-type structure was inserted into the fabric of the broch. The site is in the care of Historic Scotland.

Mucklaberry Castle — Vaila. An ancient two-storey watchtower of unknown origin, restored in the 1890s by Yorkshire mill-owner Herbert Anderton (who also owned the island at the time) with additional crenellations and an angle turret.

Muckle Flugga Lighthouse — Muckle Flugga. The most northerly lighthouse in the British Isles, a 66ft (20m) tall white tower built in 1858 by Thomas and David Stevenson to replace a temporary light erected in 1854. Known as North Unst light until 1964, the lighthouse was automated in 1995. The lighthouse's original shore base now contains the visitor centre for the Hermaness National Nature Reserve.

Muness Castle — 3$^{1}/_{2}$ miles (5.5km) east of Belmont, Unst. The most northerly castle in the British Isles, designed by Andrew Crawford and built in 1598 by Laurence Bruce. The three-storey Z-plan castle, 73ft (22m) long and 26ft (8m) broad with two circular towers, one each at the opposing north and south corners, had only a short life, falling into disrepair after being burned by Dunkirk privateers in August 1627. During the early 18th century it was used by the Dutch East India Company to store salvaged cargo but it had been completely abandoned by 1750. Outlines of what may have been formal gardens have been detected in aerial photography. The site is maintained by Historic Scotland.

Noss — An uninhabited island, just across the Noss Sound from Bressay, designated a National Nature Reserve in 1955. The sandstone sea cliffs, up to 590ft (180m) high, have been carved by erosion into ledges perfect for nesting. They attract more than 150,000 breeding seabirds each year including guillemot, gannet, fulmar, kittiwake, razorbill, puffin, great skua or Bonxie and shag. The numerous stacks around the coast of the island include 99ft (30m) high Cradle Holm, home to a colony of great black-backed gulls. Mostly covered by moorland, the reserve also provides a habitat for flowering plants such as blue spring squill, white sea campion and sheep's bit scabious. The island is also a working sheep farm. At Gungstie there is a restored pony pund where in the late 19th century the Marquis of Londonderry bred Shetland ponies for his County Durham coal mines. Area: 1.32 sq miles (3.43 sq km). GR: HU545405.

Old Haa Visitor Centre — Burravoe, Yell. A visitor centre and local history museum housed in 'Da Haa o' Brough' (the Hall of Brough), built in 1672 by fish merchant Robert Tyrie and restored in 1987. The museum features items of local interest and relating to the island's natural history. A memorial to local bird photographer Bobby Tulloch, unveiled in 2005, consists of a sculpture of a life-size kittiwake feeding chicks on a rock ledge nest. Tel: 01957 722339.

Old Scatness Broch — 1 mile (1.6km) northwest of Sumburgh, Mainland. During the construction of a perimeter road at Sumburgh Airport in 1975 part of a broch was exposed in the edge of a green mound about 16ft (5m) high and 263ft (80m) in diameter. Excavations to uncover the broch, begun in 1995, also revealed evidence of settlement on the site from the Bronze Age until the 20th century. The remains of the broch – much of which was destroyed in the building of the road – stand at the centre of the site with several roundhouses around it creating a village. The Iron Age settlement was overlaid by a Pictish occupation level with a typical wheelhouse which may have been reused by Norse settlers. Other layers have produced evidence of a 19th century croft house and a 17th century midden. Reconstructions of some of the buildings found at Old Scatness have been erected nearby, including an Iron Age roundhouse and Pictish wheelhouses.

Out Stack — Aka Oosta. The most northerly island in the British Isles, located 2 miles (3km) north of the island of Unst. In 1849 Lady Jane Franklin, the wife of missing Arctic explorer Sir John Franklin, landed on the island to pray for her spouse. GR: HP612202.

Oxna — It was on Oxna in the late 19th century that James Fullerton found a gold Viking armlet with an internal diameter of 25in (63.5cm) and made of slender gold rods intertwined to give a chain-like appearance. Uninhabited since shortly after World War I.

Papa Stour — (O.N. = Big Island of the Priests.) A small island off Mainland referred to in the earliest Norse manuscript found in the Shetlands, dating back to 1299. Biggings is the 'capital'. When the island's population dipped to only 16 in the 1970s, an advert was placed in *Exchange and Mart* offering free crofts and five sheep to any takers. The resulting boost to the numbers on the island was brief, but in 2001 there was a population of 23 and a one-pupil school. Area: 3.41 sq miles (8.83 sq km). Population: 23. GR: HU165605.

Quendale Water Mill — Quendale, 2 miles (3km) northwest of Sumburgh, Mainland. A restored overshot watermill and dam originally built in 1867 for the Grierson family. A working mill until 1948, grinding the grain produced by local crofters, it now houses exhibits including agricultural tools and machinery, as well as a photographic archive. Tel: 01950 460969.

RSPB Fetlar — Fetlar. An RSPB reserve above the Loch of Funzie, home to 90 per cent of the British population of wading red-necked phalarope. Other species include Arctic skuas, great skuas, red-throated divers and whimbrels.

RSPB Loch of Spiggie — 15 miles (24km) southwest of Lerwick, Mainland. The RSPB reserve on Loch Spiggie is the most important winter wildfowl site in the Shetland Islands, home to birds such as whooper swans and teal.

RSPB Mousa — An RSPB reserve on the island of Mousa. It is home to 6000 pairs of storm petrels as well as other species including Artic tern, Artic skua, black guillemot and ringed plover.

RSPB Sumburgh Head — Sumburgh Head, 1 mile (1.6km) south of Sumburgh, Mainland. An RSPB reserve close to the airport at the southern tip of Mainland with populations of guillemots, puffins, razorbills and fulmars. Rarer visitors to the reserve include brown shrike, White's thrush and lanceolated warbler. Killer whales and dolphins can sometimes be seen in the waters around the Head.

St Mary's Church — Bressay. The ruins of the oldest cruciform church in the Shetlands, located overlooking the Voe of Cullingsburgh. The churchyard has several ornate gravestones and two 8th or 9th century crosses.

St Ninian's Isle Treasure — Described as 'the most important single discovery in Scottish archaeology'. On 4 July 1958, local schoolboy Douglas Coutts was helping out at an archaeological dig at St Ninian's Chapel on St Ninian's Isle when he uncovered a larch box containing 28 items of Pictish silver, covered by a stone on which was incised a Celtic cross. The objects included seven bowls, a hanging-bowl, a spoon and a penannular brooch. It is believed the silver was hidden to protect it from Viking raiders. The hoard is kept at the National Museum, Edinburgh, with replicas held by Lerwick Museum. St Ninian's chapel dates from the 12th century and was built on an earlier establishment.

St Sunniva's Chapel — Balta. The grass-covered remains of a chapel formerly dedicated to the Norse St Sunniva, located on the now uninhabited island of Balta. Possibly the site of a monastic settlement.

Scalloway Castle — Scalloway, 5 miles (8km) west of Lerwick, Mainland. Ruins of an L-plan tower house built in 1600 by Andrew Crawford for Earl Patrick Stewart in what was then the capital of the Shetland Islands. It was still in use after Stewart's fall from grace in 1614 and in 1650 it was used as a barracks by troops supporting Oliver Cromwell. However, the move of the capital to Lerwick in 1708 saw its importance diminish rapidly and it fell into disrepair. The outbuildings were demolished in the 1750s and the stones used for local building work. It has been in the care of Historic Scotland since 1908.

Scalloway Museum — New Street, Scalloway, 5 miles (8km) west of Lerwick, Mainland. A local history museum exploring both the local fishing industry and in particular the story of the 'Shetland Bus', which operated between Scalloway and Norway during World War II. The museum began undergoing enlargement in 2006. Tel: 01595 880783.

Shetland Bus — A boat operation between Scalloway and German-occupied Norway during World War II. Based at Lunna for one season before its move to Scalloway in 1942, missions were originally carried out using small fishing boats which secretly landed agents and equipment in Norway, returning to the Shetlands with refugees. Several boats and more than 30 men were lost due to enemy action and bad weather, and the closing of the service was considered until the US Navy provided three fast motor torpedo boats (MTBs) named *Hirta*, *Hessa* and *Vigra* to replace the fishing boats in November 1943.

Shetland Croft House Museum — Voe, Dunrossness, Mainland. A museum opened in 1971 set in a typical mid 19th century thatched crofthouse restored using traditional methods and materials. The layout of the typical crofthouse was to have two rooms, an inner sleeping room (the 'ben end') and an outer main room (the 'but-end'). The house is interconnected with a byre where the animals were kept, a barn and stables, resulting in parallel thatched buildings. The main elements were brought together to provide a building of strength and comfort for the crofter and his extended family. The house is furnished in typical crofthouse style with furniture and implements made from local materials including driftwood. Nearby is a small watermill. Tel: 01950 460557.

Shetland Museum and Archives — Hays Dock, Lerwick, Mainland. Shetland's most northerly museum, originally opened in 1966 at Hillhead and closed in March 2005 to be replaced by a new museum and archive complex in 2006. There are collections relating to the cultural, economic, natural and social history of the Shetland Islands. Exhibits include works by local and contemporary artists, the archaeology of the Shetlands from the Neolithic to the medieval period, a collection of 20 boats, and a set of Shetland textiles including Fair Isle garments, lace knitting and Shetland 'taatit' rugs.

Shetland ponies	Also known locally as shelts. A very hardy breed probably descended from a cross between the indigenous horses of the islands and horses imported from Scandinavia by Norse settlers. Originally used for transporting and ploughing, during the second half of the 19th century they were used down British coal mines. They are now mainly used as children's ponies. According to the Shetland Pony Stud Book, ponies cannot be more than 42in (106cm) tall and come in a variety of colours including bay, black, brown, chestnut, cream and roan.
Shetland Textile Working Museum	Weisdale. A collection of textiles and woollens from the Shetland Islands, including Fair Isle located at Weisdale Mill (see separate entry). There are illustrations of the different traditional styles and the techniques used to produce them. Exhibitions include a history of Shetland textiles. Tel: 01595 890419.
Stones of Yoxie	$^3/_4$ mile (1.2km) north of Isbister, Whalsay. Aka Pettigarth's Field. A Neolithic or Bronze Age homestead near the Benie Hoose (see separate entry), originally interpreted as a temple when excavated in 1954.
Tangwick Haa Museum	Tangwick, 10 miles (16km) northwest of Sullom, Mainland. Housed in a 17th century haa (laird's house) located in Esha Ness and built for the Cheyne family, the museum was opened in 1988 and is dedicated to the past and present lives of the people of Northmavine. Displays include a furnished dining room, a model of an open fishing boat and a collection of children's toys. There is also a family history corner and a walled garden. Tel: 01806 503389.
Unst Boat Haven	Haroldswick, Unst. A museum dedicated to the maritime history of the Shetland Islands. Exhibits include a collection of 17 boats built between 1860 and 1960, including not only traditional Shetland working craft such as a 19th century sixareen but also a Welsh coracle and a Berhon dinghy as well as tools and equipment, photographs and charts. The museum is housed in a large purpose-built shed and the boats are displayed as if pulled up on a beach. Tel: 01957 711528.
Unst Heritage Centre	Haroldswick, Unst. Dedicated to the economic and social history of the island. Displays include examples of Unst lace knitting and there are recreations of a schoolroom and the interior of a croft. Tel: 01957 711528.
Up-Helly-Aa	An annual fire festival held in Lerwick on the last Tuesday of January and dating in its present form to 1878, although it is often claimed to have much older origins. It involves a procession of more than 800 'guizers' (street performers akin to mummers and other participants in traditional festivals), each carrying burning staves and led by the 'guizer jarl' in a replica Viking ship. The ship is carried to a site where it is burned while the crowd sings 'The Norseman's Home'. There follows a series of parties at which the guizers dance and quench their hunger and thirst. The next day is a public holiday. Preparations for the festival begin each autumn with the construction of the replica galley and the making of the torches in the Galley Shed, St Sunniva Street, Lerwick, where there is also an exhibition with a photographic archive of previous festivals. The name is also applied to several local fire festivals held during the winter in other areas of the Shetland Islands.
Valhalla Brewery	Baltasound, Unst. The most northerly brewery in the British Isles, established in 1997. It produces a range of cask conditioned ales and bottled beers. Tel: 01957 711658.
George Waterston Memorial Centre and Museum	Utra, Fair Isle. A local history museum housed in the Auld Skoll – the former Fair Isle School – and named after George Waterston (1911–80), Scottish Director of the Royal Society for the Protection of Birds, who owned the island from 1947 until selling it to the National Trust for Scotland in 1955. Collections cover the archaeology and the economic, natural and social history of the island.
Weisdale Mill	Weisdale, 10 miles (16km) northwest of Lerwick, Shetland. A large corn mill located beside the Burn of Weisdale at the head of Weisdale Voe and built in 1855. Restored in the 1990s, it now houses the Bonhoga Gallery – opened in 1994 and the most northerly art gallery in the UK – and the Shetland Textile Working Museum. Tel: 01595 830400.

Some famous people born in Shetland

Anderson, Arthur (co-founder of P & O) (1792–1868)	Lerwick
Anderson, Tom 'Muckle Tammie' (fiddler) (1910–91)	Eshaness
Bain, Aly (fiddler) (1946–)	Lerwick
Bairnson, Ian (guitarist and saxophonist) (1953–)	Levenwick
Grierson, Herbert (literary critic) (1866–1960)	Lerwick
Irvine, John (artist) (1805–88)	Lerwick
Lamont, Norman (politician) (1942–)	Lerwick
Mouat, Betty (weaver) (1825–1918)	Levenwick
Stout, Robert (New Zealand Premier) (1844–1930)	Lerwick
Tulloch, Bobby (naturalist) (1929–96)	Yell

Islands of Shetland

Island name	Area	Nearest landmark	General information
Aa Skerry	The Deeps	Aaskerry Taing, Mainland	The headland of Roe Ness is 1/2 mile (0.8km) to the east. GR: HU313428
Aa Skerry	Atlantic	South Havra	A skerry is a reef or rocky island. GR: HU366272
Aa Stack	Atlantic	North Neaps, Yell	GR: HP477045
Aa Stack	Atlantic	Nev of Stuis, Yell	GR: HU457969
Aalie, The	Atlantic	Uyea	Lies off the coast of Uyea island near The Ness, Mainland. GR: HU314927
Aiplin	North Sea	Gletness, Mainland	Tiny island lying just off Shetland Mainland. GR: HU480512
Arva Skerry	Atlantic	Da Logat, Foula	GR: HT953415
Aswick Skerries	North Sea	The Noup, Mainland	GR: HU483526
Atla Holm	Atlantic	Atla Ness, West Burra	GR: HU369365
Ayre of Birrier	Colgrave Sound	Birrier, Yell	GR: HU545883
Bagi Stack	Atlantic	North Neaps, Yell	GR: HP477052
Bak, The	Atlantic	The Nev, Mainland	GR: HU271424
Balta	North Sea	Unst	An early concrete lighthouse was built in 1895 but demolished in 2003 and replaced by a solar-powered light. Area: 0.31 sq miles (0.8 sq km). GR: HP660080
Bark Stack	Yell Sound	Point of Fethaland, Mainland	GR: HU380946
Bars o' Strem Ness	Atlantic	Strem Ness, Foula	GR: HT971415
Big Kiln	Atlantic	Colsay	GR: HU356185
Bigga	Yell Sound	Mio Ness, Mainland	Nature reserve managed by the RSPB. Area: 0.3 sq miles (0.78 sq km). GR: HU445792
Big-nev Geo	Atlantic	Uyea	GR: HU309928
Billia Cletts	Atlantic	Tromba of Griskerry, Mainland	GR: HU365234
Billia Skerry	Yell Sound	Newton, Mainland	GR: HU379857
Billia Skerry	North Sea	Mio Ness, Housay	One of the Out Skerries. GR: HU653682
Black Holm	Atlantic	Mathers Head, Fair Isle	GR: HZ194701
Black Skerry	North Sea	White Wife, Yell	GR: HU530850
Black Skerry	Atlantic	Too Brekk, Mainland	GR: HU319692
Black Skerry	Atlantic	Ness of Westshore, Mainland	GR: HU382384
Black Skerry	Atlantic	Little Havra	GR: HU351267
Black Skerry of Ramnageo	Atlantic	Hill of Meodale, Mainland	GR: HU309701
Black Stane	Atlantic	Face of Neeans, Mainland	GR: HU275602
Blackhead of Breigeo	Atlantic	Villians of Ure, Esha Ness	GR: HU211799
Blobrick	Atlantic	Summons Head, Foula	GR: HT948409
Boinna Skerry	Atlantic	North Ness, Papa Stour	GR: HU186610
Bonibrik	Atlantic	South Ness, Foula	GR: HT965361
Borse Skerry	Atlantic	Virda Field, Papa Stour	GR: HU156626
Bound Skerry	North Sea	Angry Head, Grunay	One of the Out Skerries. GR: HU702718
Braava Skerries	Atlantic	Westing, Unst	GR. HP570075
Braga	North Sea	Urie Lingey	GR: HU595960
Braga	The Deeps	Skelda Ness, Mainland	GR: HU316408
Brei Holm	Atlantic	North House, Papa Stour	GR: HU189604
Breiti Stack	Atlantic	Burrashield, Fair Isle	GR: HZ201725
Bressay	North Sea	Lerwick, Mainland	(O.N. = Crash Island). Maryfield is the 'capital'. Bressay Heritage Centre, next to the ferry pier, features archaeological artefacts found on the island, along with exhibits charting its natural and social history. Area: 12 sq miles (31.06 sq km). Population: 384. GR: HU505410
Brethren	North Sea	Fore Ness, Mainland	GR: HU482471
Brindacks	Atlantic	Virda Pund, Unst	GR: HP571116
Broad Stack	Atlantic	Siggar Ness, Mainland	GR: HU348117
Brother Isle	Yell Sound	Uynarey	Lies between Yell and Shetland mainland. Area: 0.15 sq miles (0.4 sq km). GR: HU425815
Brough Holm	Atlantic	Westing, Unst	GR: HP565058
Brough Skerries	Atlantic	Ness, Mainland	GR: HU216584
Bruddans, The	Atlantic	Sae Breck, Esha Ness	GR: HU201775
Bruray	North Sea	Whalsay	One of the Out Skerries. Linked to Housay by a bridge built in 1957. Area: 0.2 sq miles (0.52 sq km). Population: 26. GR: HU690720

Island name	Area	Nearest landmark	General information
Bruse Holm	Lunning Sound	Dragon Ness, Mainland	aka Brusim. GR: HU520640
Brusim			See Bruse Holm.
Bullia Skerry	Atlantic	Fulga Ness, West Burra	GR: HU358364
Burga Stacks	Atlantic	The Nev, Mainland	GR: HU255441
Burgastoo	Busta Voe	Roesound, Mainland	GR: HU345660
Burland Skerry	Atlantic	Burland, Trondra	GR: HU390367
Burrian	Atlantic	Oxna	GR: HU350365
Burrian, The	Atlantic	Busta, Fair Isle	GR: HZ209697
Burwick Holm	Atlantic	Ness of Burwick, Mainland	GR: HU386402
Calf of Daaey	North Sea	Daaey	GR: HU605953
Calf of Linga	Linga Sound	Saltness, Whalsay	GR: HU531633
Calf of Linga	North Sea	East Linga	Tiny islet off the coast of East Linga. GR: HU619628
Cannon, The	Atlantic	Sae Breck, Esha Ness	GR: HU202778
Castle, The	Yell Sound	Ness of Queyfirth, Mainland	GR: HU370829
Cheynies	Atlantic	Oxna	GR: HU345385
Clapper, The	Atlantic	North Neaps, Yell	GR: HP483066
Cleiver, The	Ronas Voe	Ketligill Head, Mainland	GR: HU280853
Clett	Atlantic	Silwick, Mainland	GR: HU291413
Clett, The	North Sea	Busta Hill, Fetlar	GR: HU641945
Clettnadal	Atlantic	Minn, West Burra	GR: HU357300
Climnie	North Sea	Ling Ness, Mainland	GR: HU502555
Clingra Stack	Atlantic	Herma Ness, Unst	GR: HP599176
Cloki Stack	Atlantic	Fora Ness, Mainland	GR: HU356180
Club, The	Atlantic	Gruney	GR: HU384969
Clubb, The	Atlantic	Papa Stour	One of the Ve Skerries. GR: HU098650
Coar Holm	Atlantic	St Ninian's Isle	GR: HU363203
Colsay	Atlantic	Northern Ness, Mainland	GR: HU360187
Corbie Geo	Atlantic	John's Head, Vementry	GR: HU285614
Corbie Geo	Atlantic	Knowe of Bugarth, Mainland	GR: HU369244
Corbie Geo	Atlantic	Noup Noss, Mainland	GR: HU355170
Coukie Geo	Atlantic	East Ward, Vaila	GR: HU235456
Cradle Holm	North Sea	Feadda Ness, Isle of Noss	aka Holm of Noss. GR: HU55039
Crog Holm	Roe Sound	Roesound, Mainland	GR: HU338662
Croga Skerries	Atlantic	Sneuga, Unst	GR: HP572129
Cudda Stack	North Sea	Lamba Ness, Unst	GR: HP672158
Cunning Holm	South Nesting Bay	Linga Ness, Mainland	GR: HU485552
Da Stab	Atlantic	The Kame, Foula	GR: HT938399
Daaey	North Sea	Fetlar	GR: HU605950
Dore Holm	Atlantic	Utstabi, Esha Ness	(O.N. = Doorway Islet). GR: HU219762
Dorra Stack	Atlantic	Uyea	GR: HU309930
Drid Geo	Atlantic	Villians of Ure, Esha Ness	GR: HU209790
Drongs, The	Atlantic	Pund of Grevasand	GR: HU260755
Duncansclett	West Voe	Houss, East Burra	GR: HU374310
Eagle Stack	Atlantic	North Neaps, Yell	GR: HP487061
East Burra	Clift Sound	West Burra	Notable for its sea caves and Neolithic remains, including a burnt mound. Area: 2.08 sq miles (5.4 sq km). Population: 66. GR: HU38330
East Hoevdi	Atlantic	Soberlie Hill, Foula	GR: HT951413
East Linga	North Sea	Rooier Head, Whalsay	Tiny island with an even tinier calf. GR: HU615624
Easter Land Taing	Yell Sound	Bigga	GR: HU442802
Easter Score Holm	The Deeps	Johnny Sinclair's Nose, Mainland	GR: HU349434
Easter Skerries	North Sea	Mio Ness, Housay	One of the Out Skerries. GR: HU665691
Egilsay	Atlantic	Pund of Mangaster	Area: 0.08 sq miles (0.22 sq km). GR: HU315695
Eric's Ham	Colgrave Sound	Birrier, Yell	GR: HU545879
Ern Stack	Atlantic	Nev of Stuis, Yell	Nesting place of the last recorded sea eagle in the Shetlands. GR: HU453964
Erne's Stack	Atlantic	Deep Dale, Mainland	GR: HU172543
Eswick Holm	North Sea	The Noup, Mainland	GR: HU483529
Fair Isle	Atlantic	Sumburgh Head, Mainland	See separate entry.
Fetlar	North Sea	Yell	See separate entry.
Fidlar Geo	Atlantic	The Hamar, Mainland	GR: HU191493

Island name	Area	Nearest landmark	General information
Fill Geo	Atlantic	Hagdales Ness, Unst	GR: HP577086
Filla	North Sea	Mio Ness, Housay	One of the Out Skerries. GR: HU661686
Fish Holm	Yell Sound	Northness, Mainland	National Nature Reserve. GR: HU476743
Fiska Skerry	South Nesting Bay	Ling Ness, Mainland	GR: HU489558
Flada Cap	North Sea	Hole of Bugars, Bressay	GR: HU517366
Fladda	Atlantic	Gruney	GR: HU375972
Fladda	Atlantic	Ockran Head, Mainland	GR: HU218848
Flae-ass	Atlantic	Gruney	GR: HU378969
Flaes, The	Yell Sound	Burravoe, Mainland	GR: HU373889
Flaeshans, The	Linga Sound	Brough Head, Whalsay	GR: HU538650
Flaeshans of Rumble	North Sea	Rumble	GR: HU606613
Flaeshans of Sandwick	North Sea	Haa Ness, Whalsay	GR: HU533610
Flaeshins, The	North Sea	Urie Ness, Fetlar	GR: HU601944
Flat Lamba Stack	North Sea	Bruray Wart, Bruray	GR: HU694724
Fless, The	Atlantic	Busta, Fair Isle	GR: HZ212699
Fless, The	Atlantic	Dronger, Fair Isle	GR: HZ204741
Flodda Stack	Atlantic	Herma Ness, Unst	GR: HP599175
Flotta	Atlantic	Strom Ness, Mainland	(O.N. = Flat.) GR: HU375463
Fludir, The	North Sea	Urie Lingey	GR: HU594950
Fogla Skerry	Atlantic	Little Virda Field, Papa Stour	GR: HU140612
Fogli Stack	Atlantic	Malcolm's Head, Fair Isle	GR: HZ194707
Fore Holm	Sand Voe	Fota Ness, Mainland	GR: HU351448
Forewick Holm	Sound of Papa	North House, Papa Stour	GR: HU187594
Form Geo	North Sea	Skaw, Unst	GR: HP663170
Foula	Atlantic	West Burra	See separate entry.
Frau Stack	Atlantic	North House, Papa Stour	aka Maiden Stack. GR: HU189606
Fru Stack	North Sea	The Flaach, Mainland	GR: HU502535
Fugla Stack	Atlantic	Minn, West Burra	GR: HU356299
Furra Stacks	North Sea	Woodenbreck, Fetlar	GR: HU664887
Gaada Stack	Atlantic	Ristie, Foula	GR: HT958416
Gaada Stacks	Atlantic	East Ward, Vaila	GR: HU238453
Galti Stack	Atlantic	The Breck, Mainland	GR: HU328924
Galti Stack	Atlantic	Hellia, Mainland	GR: HU259859
Galti Stacks	Atlantic	Wilma Skerry, Papa Stour	GR: HU154598
Gamli Stack	Atlantic	Hevda Hill, Unst	GR: HP581105
Gaut Skerries	Atlantic	Gruney	GR: HU375981
Geo Claver	Atlantic	Haswalls, Fair Isle	GR: HZ215711
Geo of Bodista	North Sea	Aithsetter North, Mainland	GR: HU447305
Geo of Slough	Atlantic	Ireland, Mainland	GR: HU371222
Geo Riva	Atlantic	Hill of Deepdale, Mainland	GR: HU378258
Giltarump	Atlantic	The Nev, Mainland	GR: HU273420
Gloup Holm	Atlantic	North Neaps, Yell	Makes a spectacular backdrop to the Ramna Stacks. GR: HP486063
Gluss Isle	Yell Sound	Ness of Bardister, Mainland	GR: HU372785
Gordi Stack	Atlantic	Ness of Hillswick, Mainland	GR: HU274748
Gorsun Geo	North Sea	Skaw, Unst	GR: HP659170
Grava Skerries	Sound of Papa	Ness of Melby	GR: HU186583
Green Holm	North Sea	Burra Ness, Yell	GR: HU516787
Green Holm	Atlantic	North Ward, Mainland	GR: HU292583
Green Holm	North Sea	Fora Ness, Mainland	GR: HU495474
Green Holm	Atlantic	Ness of Westshore, Mainland	GR: HU382380
Green Isle	Dury Voe	Muckle Head, Mainland	GR: HU483613
Greing, The	Atlantic	Herma Ness, Unst	Part of the Outer Hebrides. GR: HP600181
Greybearded Man	Colgrave Sound	Hascosay	GR: HU558915
Grif Skerry	North Sea	Rooier Head, Whalsay	(O.N. = Deep Sea). GR: HU630624
Griskerry	Atlantic	Tromba of Griskerry, Mainland	GR: HU368229
Gruna	Atlantic	Milder Ness, Vementry	(O.N. = Green Island). GR: HU283599
Gruna Stack	Atlantic	The Crook, Mainland	GR: HU289869
Grunay	North Sea	Housay	One of the Out Skerries. Permitted to issue its own postage stamps. GR: HU695715

Island name	Area	Nearest landmark	General information
Gruney	Atlantic	Point of Fethaland, Mainland	National Nature Reserve. GR: HU382968
Grunka Hellier	Atlantic	Herma Ness, Unst	GR: HP584155
Gungstie	North Sea	Upperton, Mainland	GR: HU415208
Gunnister, Isle of	Atlantic	Nibon, Mainland	GR: HU301738
Haaf Gruney	North Sea	Uyea	Lies $1^1/_4$ miles (2km) southeast of Unst. GR: HU635982
Haerie	North Sea	Moul of Eswick, Mainland	aka Ooter Vooder. GR: HU519554
Haerie	North Sea	Moul of Eswick, Mainland	aka Litla Billan. GR: HU534555
Hagmark Stack	North Sea	Hill of Clibberswick, Unst	GR: HP665127
Hascosay	Colgrave Sound	Yell	(O.N. = Cottager's Island). Area: 1.06 sq miles (2.75 sq km). GR: HU555925
Hawse of Halla	North Sea	Gudna Lee, Fetlar	GR: HU645932
Heag, The	Atlantic	Heill Head, Vementry	GR: HU281600
Heag, The	Heag Sound	Head of Onibery, Mainland	GR: HU249583
Heelors, The	Atlantic	Vaasette, Fair Isle	GR: HZ220710
Helligoblo	Atlantic	Papa Stour	One of the Ve Skerries. GR: HU101654
Hevda	North Sea	Saxa Vord, Unst	GR: HP643175
Hevda Skerries	North Sea	North Hill, Housay	Part of the Out Skerries. GR: HU683729
Hevda Skerry	North Sea	Cletts of Ramnageo, Mainland	GR: HU503542
Hich Holm	Atlantic	St Ninian's Isle	GR: HU356210
Hildasay	The Deeps	Scalloway, Mainland	Permitted to issue its own postage stamps. Area: 0.42 sq miles (1.08 sq km). GR: HU355404
Hirdie Geo	Atlantic	Aesha Head, Papa Stour	GR: HU150606
Hoe Skerry	The Deeps	Ramna Taing, Mainland	GR: HU343426
Hog, The	North Sea	Uyea	GR: HU615975
Hog, The	Ronas Voe	Ketligill Head, Mainland	GR: HU281852
Hog Island	North Sea	Hill of Neap, Mainland	GR: HU510581
Hog of Breigeo	Atlantic	Scat Ness, Mainland	GR: HU387088
Hog of the Holm	Atlantic	Horse Island	GR: HU382075
Hog of the Ness	Atlantic	Ness of Burgi, Mainland	GR: HU385081
Hogg, The	North Sea	Grunay	One of the Out Skerries. GR: HU699714
Hogg of Linga	Atlantic	Hildasay	GR: HU359395
Hogg of Papa	Atlantic	Ness of Westshore, Mainland	GR: HU371379
Hoggs of Hoy	Atlantic	Strom Ness, Mainland	GR: HU372452
Hoggs of Oxna	Atlantic	Oxna	GR: HU348377
Hoiliff	Atlantic	Colsta, Fair Isle	GR: HZ200721
Holm, The	North Sea	Housay	One of the Out Skerries. GR: HU680711
Holm of Beosetter	North Sea	Ness of Beosetter, Bressay	GR: HU490452
Holm of Breibister	Vaila Sound	Burrastow, Mainland	GR: HU226479
Holm of Brough	Atlantic	Migga Ness, Yell	GR: HP541049
Holm of Califf	Dales Voe	South Califf, Mainland	GR: HU451458
Holm of Cruester	Bressay Sound	Lerwick, Mainland	GR: HU477425
Holm of Gruting	Gruting Voe	Ayres of Selivoe, Mainland	GR: HU273479
Holm of Gunnista	North Sea	Sweyn Ness, Bressay	GR: HU500445
Holm of Heogland	North Sea	Point of Burkwell, Unst	GR: HU575991
Holm of Maywick	Atlantic	The Ness, South Havra	GR: HU375263
Holm of Melby	Sound of Papa	Neap of Norby	GR: HU193585
Holm of Noss	North Sea	Feadda Ness, Isle of Noss	See Cradle Holm.
Holm of Sandwick	North Sea	Haa Ness, Whalsay	GR: HU539610
Holm of Setter	Loch of Tingwall	South Setter, Mainland	GR: HU416429
Holm of Skaw	North Sea	Skaw, Unst	GR: HP668170
Holm of Skellister	South Nesting Bay	Ness of Skellister, Mainland	GR: HU478557
Holm of Tressaness	North Sea	Tressa Ness, Fetlar	GR: HU621950
Holm of West Sandwick	Yell Sound	The Brough, Yell	GR: HU435893
Holms of Uyea-sound	Swarbacks Minn	Cow Head, Vementry	GR: HU310610
Holms of Vatsland	Bight of Vatsland	Easter Rova Head, Mainland	GR: HU472458
Hoo Stack	North Sea	The Flaach, Mainland	GR: HU505520
Horn Skerry	North Sea	Grunay	One of the Out Skerries. GR: HU700715
Horns of the Roe	Yell Sound	Knowe of Bugarth, Yell	GR: HU441929

Island name	Area	Nearest landmark	General information
Horse Island	Atlantic	Sumburgh Head, Mainland	GR: HU383073
Houlls Geo	North Sea	Nousta Head, Fetlar	GR: HU669896
Housay	North Sea	Whalsay	Linked to Bruray by a bridge built in 1957. One of the Out Skerries. Area: 0.59 sq miles (1.52 sq km). Population: 50. GR: HU680720
Housensellar	Atlantic	Stane Loro, Mainland	GR: HU382272
Houss Ness	Atlantic	East Burra	GR: HU375300
Hoy	Atlantic	Strom Ness, Mainland	(O.N. = High Island). GR: HU373448
Humla Stack	Atlantic	Herma Ness, Unst	GR: HP599180
Humla Stack	Atlantic	Green Head, Vaila	GR: HU243457
Hund Geo	Atlantic	Little Virda Field, Papa Stour	GR: HU147617
Hunder Holm	Lunning Sound	Dragon Ness, Mainland	aka Unerim. GR: HU514635
Hundi Stack	Atlantic	Kista, Fair Isle	GR: HZ199714
Huney	North Sea	Unst	Linked to Unst at low tide. GR: HP650064
Hunts Holm	North Sea	Mu Ness, Unst	GR: HP639005
Il Holm	North Sea	Busta Hill, Fetlar	GR: HU631945
Inn Geo	Atlantic	Egga Field, Mainland	GR: HU310886
Inner Booth	Atlantic	Point of Fethaland, Mainland	GR: HU377954
Inner Flaess	North Sea	Skaw, Unst	GR: HP669174
Inner Holm of Skaw	North Sea	Sponger Point, Whalsay	GR: HU600675
Inner Score	North Sea	Score Head, Bressay	GR: HU513455
Inner Skerry	Atlantic	Point of the Alter, West Burra	GR: HU361340
Inner Voder	North Sea	Moul of Eswick, Mainland	GR: HU509549
Inns Holm	Atlantic	St Ninian's Isle	GR: HU369201
Isbister Holm	North Sea	Nisthouse, Whalsay	(Isbister – O.N. = East Farm). GR: HU604643
Junk	Atlantic	Strom Ness, Mainland	GR: HU370453
Kame of Flouravoug	Atlantic	Herma Ness, Unst	GR: HP594167
Kame of Riven Noup	Atlantic	Virda, West Burra	GR: HU361311
Kay Holm	Mid Yell Voe	Head of Hevdagarth, Yell	GR: HU528913
Keels, The	Atlantic	Head of Tind, Fair Isle	GR: HZ200694
Ketill Holm	Lunning Sound	Dragon Ness, Mainland	aka Kettlim. GR: HU523642
Kettlim	Lunning Sound	Dragon Ness, Mainland	See Ketill Holm.
Kinglia	Atlantic	Ham, Foula	GR: HT978398
Kirk Holm	Sand Voe	Kirka Ness, Mainland	GR: HU338460
Kirk Skerry	Whiteness Voe	White Ness, Mainland	GR: HU391440
Koda Skerry	Atlantic	North Ness, Papa Stour	GR: HU186621
Lady's Holm	Atlantic	Scat Ness, Mainland	Lies 2 miles (3km) northwest of Sumburgh Head. GR: HU375097
Lamba	Yell Sound	Saberstone, Mainland	(O.N. = Lamb Island). Area: 0.17 sq miles (0.43 sq km). GR: HU390815
Lamba Stack	Atlantic	Wick, Unst	GR: HP558040
Lamba Stack	North Sea	Bruray Wart, Bruray	One of the Out Skerries. GR: HU694723
Landvillas	Atlantic	Noss Hill, Mainland	GR: HU350158
Lang Holm	Atlantic	Kirkaby, Unst	GR: HP562064
Lang Stack	Atlantic	Blouk Field, Mainland	GR: HU173536
Lang Stack	Atlantic	Snarra Ness, Mainland	GR: HU235577
Langa	Atlantic	Point of the Pund, Mainland	(O.N. = Long Island). GR: HU373395
Leera Stack	North Sea	Saxa Vord, Unst	GR: HP626174
Linga	Bluemull Sound	Gutcher, Yell	(O.N. = Heather Isle). Area: 0.17 sq miles (0.45 sq km). GR: HU560985
Linga	Cole Deep	Grobs Ness, Mainland	(O.N. = Heather Isle). Area: 0.27 sq miles (0.7 sq km). GR: HU354639
Linga	Yell Sound	Northness, Mainland	(O.N. = Heather Isle). GR: HU467735
Linga	Vaila Sound	Stapness, Mainland	(O.N. = Heather Isle). GR: HU239479
Linga	Atlantic	Shaabers Head, Mainland	(O.N. = Heather Isle). GR: HU283591
Linga	Atlantic	Hildasay	(O.N. = Heather Isle) GR: HU362396
Linga Skerries	South Nesting Bay	Ling Ness, Mainland	GR: HU493552
Litla Billan	North Sea	Moul of Eswick, Mainland	See Haerie (2).
Litla Stack	Atlantic	Deep Dale, Mainland	GR: HU172547
Little Gruna Stacks	Atlantic	Turls Head, Mainland	GR: HU289865
Little Havra	Atlantic	South Havra	GR: HU352264
Little Holm	Yell Sound	Mainland	GR: HU403862
Little Holm	Cat Firth	Freester, Mainland	GR: HU447530

Island name	Area	Nearest landmark	General information
Little Holm	Atlantic	Scat Ness, Mainland	GR: HU380097
Little Linga	Lunning Sound	Swevers Taing, Mainland	(O.N. = Heather). GR: HU523653
Little Ossa	Atlantic	Ockran Head, Mainland	Smaller rock than Muckle Ossa and lying due south of it. GR: HU220849
Little Roe	Yell Sound	Mio Ness, Mainland	Lies 2 miles (3km) east of Ollaberry on Shetland Mainland's eastern coast. GR: HU403796
Little Skerry	North Sea	Mio Ness, Housay	GR: HU636711
Long Geo	Atlantic	Garths Ness, Mainland	GR: HU363113
Long Guen	North Sea	Mio Ness, Housay	One of the Out Skerries. GR: HU653683
Long Skerry	Atlantic	Face of Neeans, Mainland	GR: HU271597
Long Taing	Yell Sound	Newton, Mainland	GR: HU380854
Longa Skerries	North Sea	Rooier Head, Whalsay	(Longa – O.N. = Long). GR: HU626620
Longa Skerry	Yell Sound	Newton, Mainland	GR: HU378856
Longa Skerry	Yell Sound	Hill of State, Mainland	GR: HU532748
Longa Skerry	Lunning Sound	Swevers Taing, Mainland	GR: HU523657
Longa Skerry	North Sea	Cemy, Mainland	GR: HU437275
Longa Stacks	Atlantic	Tonga, Unst	GR: HP581153
Lu Ness	Atlantic	Biargra, West Burra	GR: HU371352
Lug, The	North Sea	The Noup, Unst	GR: HP637181
Lunga Skerries	The Deeps	Ramna Taing, Mainland	GR: HU346424
Lunna Holm	Yell Sound	Hill of State, Mainland	Lies off the northeastern coastline of the Lunna Ness headland. GR: HU528749
Lyra Skerry	Atlantic	Little Virda Field, Papa Stour	GR: HU143613
Maiden Stack	Atlantic	North House, Papa Stour	See Frau Stack.
Mainland	Atlantic	Sanday, Orkney Islands	Scalloway (O.N. *Scola Voe* = Huts on the Bay), the largest settlement on the Atlantic coast of Shetland, was capital of the islands until 1708. The highest point of Mainland (and the whole of the Shetland Islands) is Ronas Hill at 1476ft (450m). On the last Tuesday in January the Viking fire festival of Up-Helly-Aa is celebrated in the 'capital', Lerwick (O.N. = Mud Creek). Area: 374.51 sq miles (969.97 sq km). Population: 17,550. GR: HU414475
Marra Flaeshins	Lunning Sound	Swevers Taing, Mainland	GR: HU528660
Meokame Skerry	Yell Sound	Claypow, Mainland	GR: HU378871
Merry Holm	Atlantic	Ness of Westshore, Mainland	GR: HU385378
Moo Stack	Atlantic	Hamara Field, Mainland	GR: HU306901
Moo Stack	Atlantic	Villians of Ure, Esha Ness	GR: HU209792
Moo Stack	Atlantic	Wilson's Noup, Mainland	GR: HU299719
Moo Stack	Atlantic	Spoot-hellier, Mainland	GR: HU298406
Mooa	North Sea	Mid Breck, Whalsay	(O.N. = Narrow Isle). GR: HU608650
Mousa	Mousa Sound	The Houll, Mainland	Notable for its broch. The island consists of two pieces of land known as North Isle and South Isle, joined by an isthmus. Area: 0.69 sq miles (1.8 sq km). GR: HU460240
Muckla Billan	North Sea	The Keen, Mainland	aka Peerie Fladdacap. GR: HU549569
Muckla Fladdicap	North Sea	Meo Ness, Whalsay	aka Muckle Fladdacap. GR: HU561583
Muckle Fladdacap			See Muckla Fladdicap.
Muckle Flaes	Atlantic	Keolki Field, Mainland	GR: HU249451
Muckle Flugga	North Sea	Herma Ness, Unst	The lighthouse was built by David Stevenson in 1854, originally to protect ships during the Crimean War. GR: HP607197
Muckle Geo of Hoini	Atlantic	Kista, Fair Isle	GR: HZ198719
Muckle Holm	Yell Sound	Mainland	GR: HU403888
Muckle Ossa	Atlantic	Ockran Head, Mainland	Lies immediately north of Little Ossa. GR: HU220850
Muckle Roe	Atlantic	Busta, Mainland	Linked to Mainland by a bridge on the northeast of the island. Area: 6.68 sq miles (17.3 sq km). Population: 104. GR: HU318647
Muckle Skerry	North Sea	Stour Hevda, Mainland	GR: HU628735
Muckle Skerry of Neapaback	North Sea	Heoga Ness, Yell	GR: HU537786
Munga Skerries	Atlantic	Stany Sneulit, Mainland	GR: HU298876
Munger Skerries	Bressay Sound	Ness of Sound, Mainland	GR: HU472390
Nacka Skerry	North Sea	Skaw Taing, Whalsay	GR: HU612663

Island name	Area	Nearest landmark	General information
Neean Skerry	Atlantic	Face of Neeans, Mainland	GR: HU270598
Nev, The	The Deeps	Roe Ness, Mainland	GR: HU343421
Nibon, Isle of	Atlantic	Nibon, Mainland	GR: HU300730
Niddister, Isle of	Atlantic	Ness of Hillswick, Mainland	GR: HU270753
Nista	North Sea	Mid Breck, Whalsay	(O.N. = Northernmost Isle). GR: HU610654
Nista Skerries	Atlantic	The Breck, Mainland	GR: HU326929
Nort Veedal	Atlantic	Crougar, Foula	GR: HT974404
North Benelip	North Sea	Mio Ness, Housay	One of the Out Skerries. GR: HU665697
North Havra	Atlantic	Binna Ness, Mainland	Lies at the mouth of Weisdale Voe. GR: HU369425
North Holm	South Nesting Bay	Ling Ness, Mainland	GR: HU491551
North Holm of Burravoe	Yell Sound	Burravoe, Mainland	GR: HU382896
North Holms	Atlantic	Virda Pund, Unst	GR: HP570115
North Isle of Gletness	North Sea	Gletness, Mainland	Tiny island lying just off Shetland Mainland. GR: HU477503
North Score Holm	The Deeps	Johnny Sinclair's Nose, Mainland	GR: HU347435
North Skerry	Atlantic	Papa Stour	One of the Ve Skerries. GR: HU102658
Norther Geo	Atlantic	Stany Hill, Yell	GR: HU447952
Noss, Isle of	North Sea	Bressay	See separate entry.
Nouns Geo	Atlantic	Maamy's Hole, Vaila	GR: HU219462
Noup Geo	North Sea	The Noup, Unst	GR: HP633182
Noup of Noss	North Sea	Isle of Noss	GR: HU552398
Oa Stack	Atlantic	The Nizz, Fair Isle	GR: HZ220742
Oe Stack	Atlantic	Isle of Nibon	GR: HU298726
Old Man's Stack	North Sea	The Calf, Grunay	One of the Out Skerries. GR: HU691712
Oosta	North Sea	Herma Ness, Unst	aka Out Stack. See separate entry.
Ooter Vooder	North Sea	Moul of Eswick, Mainland	See Haerie (1).
Ord Skerries	Atlantic	The Ords, Mainland	GR: HU341138
Orfasay	Yell Sound	Ness of Copister, Yell	Lies to the south of Yell. GR: HU492775
Ormal	Atlantic	Papa Stour	One of the Ve Skerries. GR: HU104654
Out Shuna Stack	Atlantic	Uyea	GR: HU306928
Out Stack	North Sea	Herma Ness, Unst	See Oosta.
Outer Booth	Atlantic	Point of Fethaland, Mainland	GR: HU377957
Outer Brough	North Sea	Strandburgh Ness, Fetlar	GR: HU671932
Outer Flaess	North Sea	Skaw, Unst	GR: HP670177
Outer Holm of Skaw	North Sea	Sponger Point, Whalsay	GR: HU604678
Outer Score	North Sea	Score Head, Bressay	GR: HU517458
Outer Skerry	Yell Sound	Newton, Mainland	GR: HU382854
Outer Stack	Atlantic	Gruney	GR: HU377978
Oxna	Atlantic	Scalloway, Mainland	One of the Scalloway Islands. Area: 0.28 sq miles (0.73 sq km). GR: HU350372
Papa	Atlantic	Atla Ness, West Burra	One of the Scalloway Islands. Area: 0.23 sq miles (0.59 sq km). GR: HU365375
Papa Little	Sound of Houbansetter	Selie Ness, Mainland	Lies northwest of Shetland Mainland, south of Muckle Roe. Area: 0.87 sq miles (2.26 sq km). GR: HU340610
Papa Skerry	Atlantic	Ness of Westshore, Mainland	GR: HU372384
Papa Stour	Atlantic	Melby, Mainland	See separate entry.
Peak, The	Atlantic	The Hamar, Mainland	GR: HU205475
Peerie Fladdacap	North Sea	The Keen, Mainland	See Muckla Billan.
Poil, The	Colgrave Sound	Stoat, Yell	GR: HU545871
Quidin, The	Atlantic	North Neaps, Yell	GR: HP483054
Quilse, The	Atlantic	Ness of Hillswick, Mainland	GR: HU283751
Ramna Stacks	Atlantic	Gruney	Designated a Special Protection Area. GR: HU375974
Reaverack	Atlantic	Papa Stour	One of the Ve Skerries. GR: HU100651
Retta Skerries	Atlantic	Oxna	GR: HU348386
Ripack Stack	Atlantic	Siggar Ness, Mainland	GR: HU347117
Rippack Stack	Atlantic	South Ness, Foula	GR: HT968364
Robert Irvine's Skerries	Yell Sound	Ness of Sound, Yell	GR: HU448828
Robert Irvine's Skerry	Atlantic	Uyea	GR: HU314936
Roodrans, The	Ronas Voe	Ketligill Head, Mainland	GR: HU277849
Root Stacks	Burra Firth	Burrafirth, Unst	GR: HP616144
Round Holm	Atlantic	Westing, Unst	GR: HP562060
Ruir Holm	North Sea	Urie Lingey	GR: HU598951

Island name	Area	Nearest landmark	General information
Rumble	North Sea	Guttald, Whalsay	(O.N. = Round Rocks). GR: HU605608
Rumble	Yell Sound	Holm of Copister, Yell	GR: HU485765
Rumblings	Atlantic	Herma Ness, Unst	GR: HP602192
Runk, The	Atlantic	The Neap, Mainland	GR: HU256774
Rurhella	North Sea	Saxa Vord, Unst	GR: HP647172
Rusna Stacks	Atlantic	Mucklure, Mainland	GR: HU210468
Salta Skerry	North Sea	Balta	GR: HP660069
Samphrey	Yell Sound	Holm of Copister, Yell	Situated north of Shetland Mainland and south of Yell. Area: 0.25 sq miles (0.66 sq km). GR: HU468762
Sand Skerry	Yell Sound	Hill of State, Mainland	GR: HU523746
Sanda Little	The Deeps	Roe Ness, Mainland	GR: HU346420
Sanda Stour	The Deeps	Hildasay	(O.N. = Big Sandy Island). GR: HU346415
Sava Skerry	North Sea	Haa Ness, Whalsay	GR: HU535606
Scarfa Skerry	Brei Wick	Hellia, Mainland	GR: HU470398
Scor Berg	Clift Sound	Royl Dale, Mainland	GR: HU387291
Scordar	Atlantic	Gruney	GR: HU374077
Score Holm	Lunning Sound	Swevers Taing, Mainland	aka Skuirm. GR: HU520652
Scraada	Atlantic	Villians of Ure, Esha Ness	GR: HU211797
Scrubba Skerry	Ronas Voe	Heillia, Mainland	GR: HU265840
Segil	Atlantic	Nev of Stuis, Yell	GR: HU457971
Seli Geo	North Sea	White Gate, Bressay	GR: HU520389
Seli Stack	Atlantic	Bonn Knowes, Mainland	GR: HU255462
Setter Holm	Yell Sound	Ness of Setter, Mainland	GR: HU480708
Sheep Rock	Atlantic	Vaasette, Fair Isle	Joined to Fair Isle by a rock stack. GR: HZ222711
Sheepie	Atlantic	Ristie, Foula	GR: HT960417
Ship Stack	North Sea	Valtoes, Unst	GR: HP667132
Short Guen	North Sea	Mio Ness, Housay	One of the Out Skerries. GR: HU657686
Sinna Skerry	Yell Sound	Northness, Mainland	GR: HU472737
Sinna Stack	Atlantic	Hevda Hill, Unst	GR: HP580102
Skate Stack	Atlantic	Sneuga, Unst	GR: HP578118
Skerries of Easter Paill	Atlantic	The Hamar, Mainland	GR: HU199478
Skerries of Fulganess	Atlantic	Fulga Ness, Mainland	GR: HU314911
Skerries of Kellister	Atlantic	Crussa Ness, Yell	GR: HP544034
Skerry, The	Atlantic	Hildasay	GR: HU361399
Skerry, The	Atlantic	Head of Tind, Fair Isle	GR: HZ199691
Skerry of Eshaness	Atlantic	Utstabi, Esha Ness	GR: HU204765
Skerry of Lambaness	Atlantic	Lamba Ness, Papa Stour	GR: HU165625
Skerry of Lunning	Lunning Sound	Lunning Head, Mainland	GR: HU509666
Skerry of Okraquoy	Bay of Okraquoy	Ocraquoy, Mainland	GR: HU442314
Skerry of Scord	Clift Sound	Clift Hills, Mainland	GR: HU394321
Skerry of Stools	Atlantic	Ness, Mainland	GR: HU221582
Skerry Wick	North Sea	The Sulock, Yell	GR: HU539840
Skersund Skerry	Voe of Sound	Ness of Trebister, Mainland	GR: HU461382
Skervie Skerry	Atlantic	Ness of Westshore, Mainland	GR: HU382387
Skuirm	Lunning Sound	Swevers Taing, Mainland	See Score Holm.
Skulla Geo	Colgrave Sound	Hascosay	GR: HU562921
Skult, The	The Deeps	North Score Holm	GR: HU346434
Skurdie Geo	North Sea	East Yell, Yell	GR: HU524850
Sligga Skerry	Yell Sound	Bigga	GR: HU435802
Slithers, The	North Sea	Sumburgh, Mainland	GR: HU409088
Snap	The Deeps	Roe Ness, Mainland	GR: HU323420
Snap, The	North Sea	Funzie Ness, Fetlar	GR: HU658878
Sneckan, The	North Sea	The Flaach, Mainland	GR: HU520528
Sound Gruney	North Sea	Fetlar	Lies 2 miles (3km) northeast of the Burra Ness Headland on Yell. GR: HU580961
South Benelip	North Sea	Mio Ness, Housay	One of the Out Skerries. GR: HU665694
South Floin Geo	Atlantic	Mass John's House, Yell	GR: HU449959
South Havra	Atlantic	Slane Loro, Mainland	One of the Scalloway Islands. Area: 0.23 sq miles (0.59 sq km). GR: HU360268
South Holm of Burravoe	Yell Sound	Burravoe, Mainland	GR: HU379893
South Holms	Atlantic	Hevda Hill, Unst	GR: HP573102
South Isle of Gletness	North Sea	Gletness, Mainland	Lies off the eastern coast of Shetland Mainland. GR: HU472507
Spoose Holm	Atlantic	Oxna	GR: HU350381
St Ninian's Isle	Atlantic	Bigton, Mainland	GR: HU368208
Stab, The	Atlantic	Haa of Stong, Mainland	GR: HU285855
Stack a Mooth	South Mouth	Pilliar, Housay	GR: HU688714

Island name	Area	Nearest landmark	General information
Stack a Pillar	South Mouth	Pilliar, Housay	GR: HU686712
Stack of Birrier	North Sea	Busta Hill, Fetlar	GR: HU638946
Stack of Okraquoy	Bay of Okraquoy	Ocraquoy, Mainland	GR: HU442313
Stack of Otter Geo	North Sea	Point of Tangpool, Mainland	GR: HU409114
Stack of Sandwick	Atlantic	Mid Field, West Burra	GR: HU359325
Stack of Stavgeo	Yell Sound	Skelberry, Mainland	GR: HU378865
Stack of Sumra	Ronas Voe	Heillia, Mainland	GR: HU265838
Stack of the Horse	North Sea	Horse of Burravoe, Yell	GR: HU536811
Stack of Wirrgeo	North Sea	East Linga	GR: HU617623
Stacks	Yell Sound	Knowe of Bugarth, Yell	GR: HU444934
Stacks of Houssness	Atlantic	Houss Ness	GR: HU372286
Stacks of Poindie	Atlantic	Sneuga, Unst	GR: HP579139
Stacks of Scambro	North Sea	Head of Hosta, Fetlar	GR: HU675921
Stacks of Skroo	Atlantic	Saaversteen, Fair Isle	GR: HZ210742
Stacks of Stuis	Atlantic	Nev of Stuis, Yell	GR: HU464975
Stacks of Vatsland	Bight of Vatsland	Kebister Ness, Mainland	GR: HU469461
Stacks of Wirrvie	Atlantic	Wirrvie Brecks, Fair Isle	GR: HZ222734
Stany Hog	North Sea	Hill of Neap, Mainland	GR: HU511580
Stany Holm	North Sea	Woodenbreck, Fetlar	GR: HU665890
Staves Geo	North Sea	Funzie Ness, Fetlar	GR: HU653888
Steggies	Atlantic	Oxna	GR: HU350360
Stenness, Isle of	Atlantic	Utstabi, Esha Ness	GR: HU208768
Stivva	Atlantic	Hill of Meodale, Mainland	GR: HU304702
Stocka	Ronas Voe	Hill of Burriesness, Mainland	GR: HU282832
Stongir Holm	North Sea	Urie Ness, Fetlar	GR: HU598947
Stoura Clett	North Sea	Mana Berg, Bressay	GR: HU519381
Stoura Stack	North Sea	Grunay	One of the Out Skerries. GR: HU689711
Swarbacks Skerry	Swarbacks Minn	Swarbacks Head, Vementry	GR: HU291621
Swart Skerry	Atlantic	Siggar Ness, Mainland	GR: HU356118
Swarta Skerries	North Sea	Rooier Head, Whalsay	(Swarta – O.N. = Black). GR: HU635623
Swarta Skerry	North Sea	Gudna Lee, Fetlar	GR: HU645938
Swarta Skerry	Yell Sound	Catta Ness, Mainland	GR: HU487683
Swarta Skerry	Yell Sound	Stour Hevda, Mainland	GR: HU532736
Swarta Skerry	Lunning Sound	Swevers Taing, Mainland	GR: HU523660
Swarta Skerry	Dury Voe	Muckle Ness, Mainland	GR: HU476618
Swarta Skerry	Atlantic	Nibon, Mainland	GR: HU297731
Swarta Skerry	Atlantic	Wilma Skerry, Papa Stour	GR: HU155593
Swarta Skerry	The Deeps	Ramna Taing, Mainland	GR: HU346430
Swarta Skerry	Atlantic	Noss Hill, Mainland	GR: HU347160
Sweinna Stack	Yell Sound	Knowe of Bugarth, Yell	GR: HU436918
Sweyn Holm	Atlantic	St Ninian's Isle	GR: HU359205
Taing of Loosswick	Atlantic	Herma Ness, Unst	GR: HP601186
Taing Skerry	Atlantic	Little Havra	GR: HU354268
Tainga Skerries	Atlantic	Crokna Vord, Mainland	GR: HU255588
Targies	Atlantic	The Burr, Esha Ness	GR: HU223807
Tinga Skerry	Yell Sound	Brother Isle	GR: HU414808
Tipta Skerry	North Sea	Herma Ness, Unst	GR: HP605194
Tonga Stack	Atlantic	Tonga, Unst	GR: HP579150
Trolla Stack	Yell Sound	Ness of Queyfirth, Mainland	GR: HU372827
Trollsholm	Bod Voe	The Calf, Grunay	GR: HU689715
Trondra	Clift Sound	Easterhoull, Mainland	Joined to Mainland by bridge. Area: 1.05 sq miles (2.71 sq km). Population: 133. GR: HU395370
Trota Stack	North Sea	Nista	GR: HU612656
Turl Stack	Atlantic	Crokna Vord, Mainland	GR: HU261589
Turla	Atlantic	Gruney	GR: HU374975
Unerim	Lunning Sound	Dragon Ness, Mainland	See Hunder Holm.
Ungam	Sullum Voe	Scatsa Ness, Mainland	GR: HU381748
Ungla Skerry	North Sea	Guttald, Whalsay	GR: HU591619
Unst	North Sea	Gutcher, Yell	Britain's most northerly dwelling is at Wick of Skaw on Unst. Baltasound is the 'capital'. Area: 48.48 sq miles (125.57 sq km). Population: 720. GR: HP603082
Ura Stack	North Sea	Hill of Neap, Mainland	GR: HU502577
Urie Lingey	North Sea	Fetlar	Lies $^1/_2$ mile (0.8km) north of Urie Ness. GR: HU597956

Island name	Area	Nearest landmark	General information
Uyea	North Sea	Unst	Home of the 12th century St Olaf's chapel. Area: 0.79 sq miles (2.05 sq km). GR: HU605990
Uyea	Atlantic	The Ness, Mainland	Lies northwest of the Northmavine peninsula of Shetland Mainland. GR: HU315930
Uynarey	Yell Sound	Yell	(O.N. = Venerated Island). GR: HU442810
Vaila	Atlantic	Burrastow, Mainland	(O.N. = Falcon Island). A notable building on the island is the Mucklaberry Castle tower. Area: 1.14 sq miles (2.95 sq km). Population: 2. GR: HU231463
Vaila Holm	Atlantic	Burrastow, Mainland	GR: HU225471
Vedders Geo	North Sea	Baa-neap, Fetlar	GR: HU675912
Vementry	Atlantic	Shaabers Head, Mainland	Largest uninhabited island in the Shetlands. Area: 1.43 sq miles (3.7 sq km). GR: HU298605
Vere, The	North Sea	Ham Ness, Unst	GR: HP647032
Vere, The	Atlantic	Houllnan Ness, Unst	GR: HP558055
Vesta Skerry	Atlantic	Herma Ness, Unst	GR: HP601191
Vongs	North Sea	Mio Ness, Housay	GR: HU639705
Wedder Holm	North Sea	The Hog	GR: HU613976
West Burra	Atlantic	East Burra	Joined to East Burra and Trondra by bridges. Hamna Voe is the 'capital'. Area: 3.05 sq miles (7.9 sq km). Population: 753. GR: HU370330
West Burrafirth, Isle of	Heag Sound	Crokna Vord, Mainland	GR: HU251588
West Head of Papa	Atlantic	Papa	GR: HU359380
West Linga	Linga Sound	Brough Head, Whalsay	Lies between the northeast coast of Shetland Mainland and Whalsay. Area: 0.48 sq miles (1.25 sq km). GR: HU532645
West Moulie Geo	Atlantic	Spoot-hellier, Mainland	GR: HU298405
West Skerry	Atlantic	Point of the Alter, West Burra	GR: HU353337
Wester Land Taing	Yell Sound	Bigga	GR: HU436800
Wester Skerry	North Sea	Red Stane, Mainland	GR: HU430275
Westerhouse, Isle of	Houlma Sound	Pund of Grevasand	GR: HU265759
Wether Holm	Yell Sound	Fora Ness, Mainland	(O.N. = Isle of the Castrated Ram). GR: HU468720
Wether Holm	Linga Sound	Kirk Ness, Whalsay	GR: HU539658
Wether Holm	North Sea	North Hill, Housay	One of the Out Skerries. GR: HU681728
Whal Geo	Atlantic	Burrier Head, Mainland	GR: HU171514
Whale Geo	North Sea	Kegga, Fetlar	GR: HU673920
Whale Geo	Yell Sound	Knowe of Bugarth, Yell	GR: HU441933
Whale Geo	Atlantic	Fora Ness, Mainland	GR: HU357175
Whalsay	North Sea	Stava Ness, Mainland	(O.N. = Whale Island). Symbister is the 'capital'. Area: 8.15 sq miles (21.11 sq km). Population: 1034. GR: HU560640
Whelsiego Stacks	North Sea	Mid Breck, Whalsay	GR: HU592654
Whilkie Stack	Atlantic	North Neaps, Yell	GR: HP483061
Windy Geo	Atlantic	Ness of Hillswick, Mainland	GR: HU273751
Witha Geo	North Sea	Herma Ness, Unst	GR: HP611187
Wurs Stack	North Sea	Herma Ness, Unst	GR: HP616179
Yell	Yell Sound	Fugla Ness, Mainland	The Sands of Breckon, composed of crushed shells, is a notable feature. Area: 83.51 sq miles (216.29 sq km). Population: 957. GR: HU493915

STRATHCLYDE

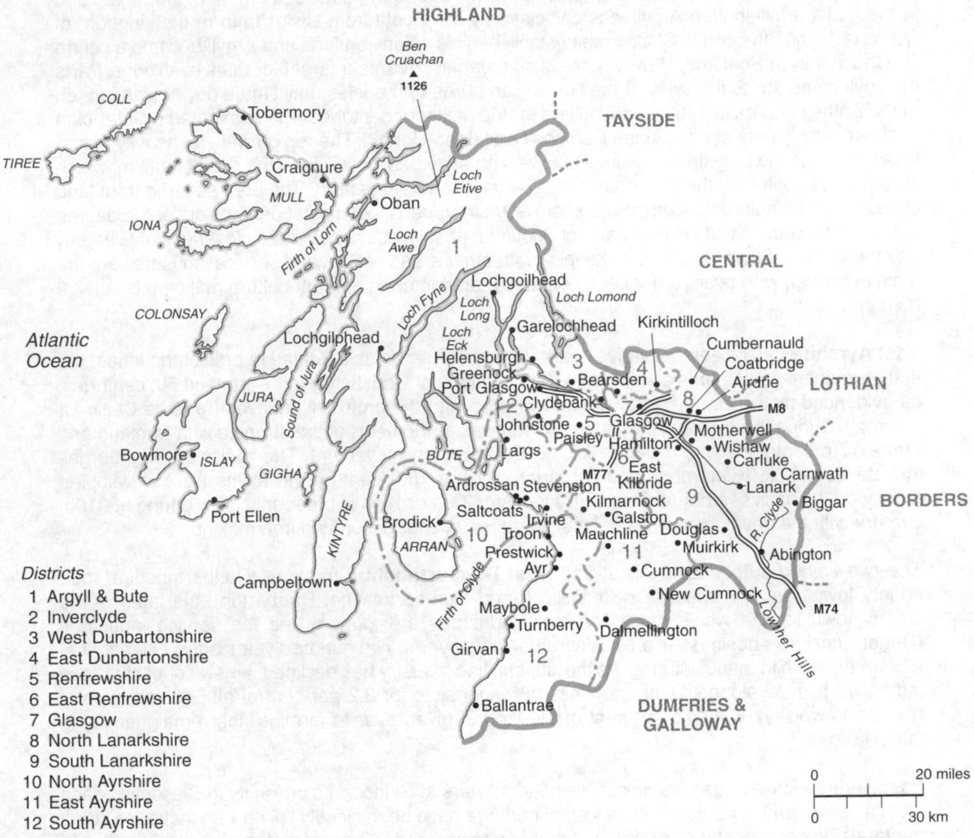
HIGHLAND
Ben Cruachan
1126
TAYSIDE
COLL
Tobermory
TIREE
Craignure
MULL
Oban
Loch Etive
IONA
Loch Awe
Firth of Lorn
1
CENTRAL
Lochgoilhead
Loch Fyne
Loch Long
Loch Lomond
COLONSAY
Loch Eck
Garelochhead
Kirkintilloch
Atlantic Ocean
Lochgilphead
Cumbernauld
Helensburgh
3
4
7
Coatbridge
Greenock
Bearsden
Airdrie
LOTHIAN
Port Glasgow
8
JURA
2
Clydebank
M8
Sound of Jura
Johnstone
5
Glasgow
Motherwell
Paisley
Hamilton
Wishaw
6
Bowmore
ISLAY
BUTE
Largs
East Kilbride
Carluke
GIGHA
M77
Carnwath
Ardrossan
Stevenston
Kilmarnock
9
Lanark
Saltcoats
Galston
Biggar
BORDERS
Port Ellen
Brodick
Irvine
R. Clyde
KINTYRE
10
Troon
Mauchline
Douglas
ARRAN
Muirkirk
Prestwick
11
Abington
Ayr
Cumnock
Districts
1 Argyll & Bute
2 Inverclyde
3 West Dunbartonshire
4 East Dunbartonshire
5 Renfrewshire
6 East Renfrewshire
7 Glasgow
8 North Lanarkshire
9 South Lanarkshire
10 North Ayrshire
11 East Ayrshire
12 South Ayrshire
Campbeltown
New Cumnock
Firth of Clyde
M74
Maybole
Turnberry
Dalmellington
Lowther Hills
Girvan
12
Ballantrae
DUMFRIES & GALLOWAY
0
20 miles
0
30 km

The region of Strathclyde is bordered by Highland to the north, Tayside to the extreme northeast, Central to the north-northeast, Lothian to the east, Borders to the southeast and Dumfries and Galloway to the south.

Historically Strathclyde is one of the kingdoms of Scotland that arose at the end of the Roman occupation.

It extended over the Clyde basin, and adjacent western coastal districts, its capital being at Dumbarton, 'fortress of the Britons', then known as Al(t) Clut (Brythonic: Ystrad Clud), the local name for Dumbarton Rock. Converted to Christianity in the early 6th century, the local Brythonic people, in alliance with the Cumbrians, waged war against the still pagan Anglo-Saxon kingdom of Bernicia (later part of the larger kingdom of Northumbria) and not until AD 756 was an uneasy peace restored through the sheer might of the Northumbrians.

The name Strathclyde first came into common usage after the sack of Dumbarton Rock by a Viking army from Dublin in 870 and there is some evidence that its capital was moved to Govan at this time, possibly as a defiant gesture, as the earliest known Christian site in the area was based there.

In the early 10th century Strathclyde fell under the domain of the Anglo-Saxon kings of England, one of whom, Edmund I, in 945 leased it to Malcolm I, king of Scots, and it eventually became a province of Scotland.

Strathclyde was created a region of western Scotland in 1975 but the regional tier of government was abolished in 1996 and its responsibilities merged with the district councils to create the following unitary authorities:

Argyll & Bute includes many islands such as Bute, Colonsay, Fladda, Iona, Islay, Jura, Mull and Ulva. Including these islands it has more than 3000 miles (4800km) of coastline. The county town was historically at Inveraray but the administrative headquarters has long been at Lochgilphead. The many prehistoric remains in the region bear witness to the early settlement of the region and in the mid 1st millennium Argyll was colonised by the Scotti from Ulster to form the kingdom of Dalriada. In the 6th century St Columba established his colony on Iona and Argyll became a centre for Christianity in Scotland. However, this also meant it became a target for raids by Vikings. Parts of Argyll came under the sway of the Norwegian Lords of the Isles until Norse power was broken at the Battle of Largs in 1263. Local politics for the next four centuries was dominated by inter-clan rivalries, mainly between the clans Campbell and (Mac)Donald. The region was not heavily industrialised during the Industrial Revolution but was an early beneficiary from the rise of tourism, which in turn was boosted by the coming of the railways in the 19th century. The area suffered from land clearances by landlords attempting to 'improve' their property, but did not perhaps suffer the degree of hardship experienced in other parts of Scotland, possibly because of the closeness of Glasgow and the growth of Campbeltown. In keeping with other areas of Scotland service industries are the main employer, with over 70 per cent, whereas manufacturing and agriculture make up barely 10 per cent.

East Ayrshire has its administrative headquarters in Kilmarnock. Settled in prehistoric times, the first permanent settlements developed with the coming of Christianity in the 4th and 5th centuries, as evidenced by the number of towns and villages with the prefix 'kil' (derived from the Celtic for 'church'). During the medieval period the region was at the heart of the struggle with England and in the 17th century it was a centre for the Covenanting movement. The region's many burghs include Cumnock, Kilmarnock and Riccarton. By the 18th century the towns were developing rapidly on the back of a burgeoning textile industry. This economic prosperity grew during the 19th century with the development of coal mining, railway construction and iron making.

The two unitary authorities of **East** and **West Dunbartonshire** make up Dunbartonshire, their county towns being respectively Kirkintilloch and Dumbarton (not Dunbarton); the latter is the county town for the whole area. The main industries are tourism and the service industries (Dunbartonshire's businesses are mainly small employers). Two hundred years ago 47 per cent of all workers were in manufacturing. As the shipbuilding industry has declined, a new set of high-tech industries has developed. Dunbartonshire is responsible for 2.2 per cent of all Scottish exports (excluding whisky). Over 75 per cent of the land is given over to farming, the remainder being largely urban.

East Renfrewshire has its administrative headquarters at Giffnock. Its proximity to Glasgow means that its history and in particular its industrial heritage have been closely linked with that city. During the late 18th century and most of the 19th many towns and villages developed around the textile industries which grew up along the banks of the rivers Cart and Leven. At present 60 per cent of employment in the region is in the service industries.

City of Glasgow, Scotland's largest city, stands on the River Clyde. The area has been settled since the Neolithic period. It is first noted in the 1st century as Cathures, a Roman settlement, and in the 6th century St Kentigern (St Mungo) established a church there on the banks of the Molendinar Burn, a tributary of the Clyde. Glasgow became a burgh in 1175. Glasgow Cathedral was begun in the 1230s, the University of Glasgow was founded in 1451 and by the close of the 15th century the city was a centre for worship and learning. This was checked by the Reformation. The Battle of Langside, which saw the end of Mary, Queen of Scots' power, was fought outside the city in 1568.

Glasgow suffered devastating fires during the 17th century but it was also during this period that the city began to become a trading centre. During the early 18th century the trade in tobacco from North America enriched many Glasgow merchants. After the American War of Independence this trade was curtailed but was replaced by trade in sugar from the West Indies. The dredging of the Clyde in the 1770s opened up the city to further economic expansion. The Industrial Revolution here was mainly based around shipbuilding and heavy industry but other manufacturing industries such as textiles, chemicals and distilling also blossomed. From 1870 until 1914 Glasgow produced around one-fifth of the world's ships and one-quarter of all locomotives. The city hosted two Great Exhibitions, in 1888 and 1901, in celebration of its position as the 'Second City of the Empire'. But it was not to last. The onset of the Great Depression saw a downturn in Glasgow's fortunes, although there was an Empire Exhibition in 1938, and John Brown's Clyde shipyard produced the liners *Queen Mary* and *Queen Elizabeth*. The launch of the *Queen Elizabeth 2* in 1967 proved to be the climax of the Clyde shipbuilding industry. The economic downturn also saw a change in housing patterns. The city's population peaked at 1,128,473 in 1939 and the period after World War II saw the demolition of tenements and the creation of New Towns and peripheral estates.

By the 1980s Glasgow, like many of Britain's cities. was ripe for regeneration. Since then the city has experienced an architectural and cultural renaissance with the opening of such buildings as the Burrell Collection (1983), the Scottish Exhibition and Conference Centre (SECC) (1985), the Royal Concert Hall (1990) and the Glasgow Gallery of Modern Art (GoMA) (1996). The Glasgow's Miles Better campaign (1983) and the Glasgow Garden Festival (1988) promoted the city, which was also designated a European City of Culture (1990), UK City of Architecture and Design (1999) and European Capital of Sport (2003). The regeneration of the waterfront is ongoing.

Inverclyde borders Renfrewshire and North Ayrshire. Its main towns are Greenock, Port Glasgow and Gourock. Historically the area relied for employment on shipbuilding, sugar refining, papermaking, barrel making and wool manufacturing. Today, electronics, financial services and tourism are the most significant industries.

North Ayrshire, with its headquarters at Irvine, includes the Isle of Arran. Its main towns are Ardrossan, Irvine, Largs, Saltcoats and West Kilbride.

North Lanarkshire has its administrative headquarters at Motherwell. Its other major towns are Airdrie, Coatbridge, Cumbernauld and Kilsyth. Once noted for its heavy industry such as coal mining and steel, the region's main employment now falls within the area of services.

The main towns of **Renfrewshire** are Erskine, Houston, Johnstone, Linwood, Paisley – location of the administrative headquarters – and Renfrew. Its most famous son is William Wallace, who was born, possibly in Elderslie, in 1270. As with many areas of Strathclyde, an economy traditionally based on heavy industry has been replaced by one largely based on services. Paisley, on the River Cart, boomed in the 19th century with its shipbuilding, engineering and textile industry, the name 'Paisley' being applied to the Kashmiri pattern of curving shapes on silk and cotton fabric.

South Ayrshire has its administrative headquarters in Ayr. Other major towns are Girvan, Prestwick, Troon and Turnberry. In the mid 19th century manufacturing industry accounted for 40 per cent of employment but by the beginning of the 21st century this had fallen to 15 per cent. In contrast, service employment has risen from 20 per cent to over 60 per cent. Agriculture now represents only 3 per cent compared to 18 per cent in the 1850s. South Ayrshire features three of the most famous golf courses in Britain, Prestwick, Royal Troon and Turnberry having hosted 34 Open Championships between them.

South Lanarkshire borders the southeast of Glasgow, with its administrative headquarters in Hamilton. A largely rural region, its principal towns are East Kilbride, Cambuslang and Rutherglen.

Strathclyde	**Population**			**Area**	
Districts	*male*	*female*	*total*	*sq miles*	*sq km*
Argyll & Bute	44,877	46,429	91,306	2668	6909
East Ayrshire	57,842	62,393	120,235	487	1262
East Dunbartonshire	52,014	56,229	108,243	68	175
East Renfrewshire	42,583	46,728	89,311	67	174
Glasgow City	272,309	305,560	577,869	68	175
Inverclyde	40,098	44,105	84,203	62	160
North Ayrshire	64,238	71,579	135,817	342	885
North Lanarkshire	153,966	167,101	321,067	181	470
Renfrewshire	82,525	90,342	172,867	101	261
South Ayrshire	53,406	58,691	112,097	472	1222
South Lanarkshire	144,206	158,010	302,216	684	1772
West Dunbartonshire	44,197	49,181	93,378	61	159
Total	1,052,261	1,156,348	2,208,609	5261	13,624

Local Attractions and Information

Achadun Castle — 3 miles (5km) southwest of Achnacroish, Lismore. Aka The Bishop's Castle. Located on the west coast of the island overlooking Bernera Island, the 13th century castle was the property of the bishops of Argyll. It was abandoned in the 16th century after Bishop Hamilton built a castle at Saddell and is now a ruin.

Achallader Castle 3 miles (5km) northeast of Bridge of Orchy. The ruins of a late 16th century tower house, built by Sir Duncan Campbell and destroyed by Jacobite forces in 1689.

Achamore Gardens 1 mile (1.6km) south of Ardminish, Gigha. A 50 acre (20ha) garden established 1944–72 by Sir James Horlick surrounding 19th century Achamore House, and featuring internationally recognised collections of rhododendrons, azaleas and camellias, including the Horlick Hybrids, rhododendron varieties bred by Sir James himself.

Administrative headquarters
Argyll and Bute: Kilmory, Lochgilphead, Argyll PA31 8RT. Tel: 01546 602127.
East Ayrshire: London Road Centre, London Road, Kilmarnock KA3 7DG. Tel: 0845 724 0000.
East Dunbartonshire: Tom Johnson House, Civic Way, Kirkintilloch, Glasgow G66 4TJ. Tel: 0141 776 9000.
East Renfrewshire: Council Headquarters, Eastwood Park, Rouken Glen Road, Giffnock, Glasgow G46 6UG. Tel: 0141 621 3000.
Glasgow City: City Chambers, George Square, Glasgow G2 1DU. Tel: 0141 287 2000.
Inverclyde: Municipal Buildings, Greenock PA15 1LY. Tel: 01475 882701.
North Ayrshire: Cunningham House, Irvine KA12 8EE. Tel: 01294 324100.
North Lanarkshire: Civic Centre, Motherwell, ML1 1TW. Tel: 01698 302222.
Renfrewshire: The Robertson Centre, 16 Glasgow Road, Paisley PA1 3QG. Tel: 0141 887 8212.
South Ayrshire: County Buildings, Wellington Square, Ayr KA7 1DR. Tel: 01463 702000.
South Lanarkshire: Almada Street, Hamilton ML3 0AA. Tel: 01698 454444.
West Dunbartonshire: Garshake Road, Dumbarton, G82 3PU. Tel: 01389 737000.

Ailsa Craig Aka The Rock or Paddy's Milestone (the latter because it marks the halfway point on the journey from Belfast to Glasgow). Ailsa Craig (meaning 'Elizabeth's Rock') is an island in the Firth of Clyde rising 1100ft (335m) from the sea. Used as a refuge by Catholics during the Reformation, the island was a source of high quality granite, including that used for curling stones, from the mid 19th to the mid 20th century. It is home to 40,000 breeding pairs of gannet, as well as to guillemots, kittiwakes, puffins and razorbills which have begun to breed again following the eradication of rats from the island, and became an RSPB nature reserve in 2004. The 36ft (11m high) lighthouse was established in 1886 and designed by Thomas and David A Stevenson. Prior to the installation of a wireless telephone in 1935 the lighthouse keepers and quarry workers communicated with the mainland using homing pigeons or by a system of fire signals. There are 37 steps to the top of tower. The lighthouse was automated in 1990. The isand is owned by Cassilis Estates (Marquess of Ailsa). Area: 0.38 sq miles (0.99 sq km). (1.04 sq km). GR: NX019997.

Airports **Glasgow International Airport** (GLA), Paisley, Renfrewshire, opened as Glasgow Airport in 1966 as a replacement for Renfrew Airport. The original buildings were designed by Sir Basil Spence. The site had previously been an RAF and Royal Navy base. Originally the airport only handled UK and European traffic with Prestwick handling transatlantic destinations. The restrictions were removed in the 1980s and the airport was renamed Glasgow International Airport in 1989. It now serves destinations in the UK, Europe, North Africa, North and Central America, Pakistan and the Middle East. Tel: 0870 040 0008.

Prestwick International Airport (PIK), Prestwick, has been the site of an airfield since at least the early 1930s, with passenger facilities by the end of the decade. After World War II Orangefield House, built in the 1690s, was used as a terminal building and control tower. Scottish Aviation Ltd had an aircraft manufacturing facility at the airport which incorporated the relocated Palace of Engineering, built as part of the Empire Exhibition at Bellahouston Park in Glasgow in 1938. Aircraft component manufacture is still carried out at Prestwick. The airport was greatly expanded in the 1960s with a new terminal building and an extension to the runway to accommodate large new jet aircraft. The new terminal building was opened in 1964 and Orangefield House was demolished at this time. Transatlantic flights moved to Glasgow International Airport in the 1990s but Prestwick is now a centre for the expanding budget airlines, with flights to numerous European destinations. The airport has its own railway station. The Prestwick Airshow ran every two years 1967–92. Prestwick Airport is the only piece of UK soil that Elvis Presley ever set foot on, when the US Army transport plane taking him for service in Germany stopped to refuel on 3 March 1960. Tel: 0871 223 0700.

All Saints' Episcopal Church Inveraray, 20 miles (32km) northwest of Helensburgh. A church built in 1886 and notable for its dominant bell tower, which makes it a mecca for bell-ringers: the tower's ten bells are claimed to be the second heaviest peal of ten in the world. The tower is also known as the Duke's Tower after the 10th Duke of Argyll, who supported the building of the church.

Alloway Kirk Alloway, $1^1/_2$ miles (2.5km) south of Ayr. The ruins of a 16th century church dedicated to St Mungo, possibly built on the site of an earlier ecclesiastical structure. The kirkyard was used by Robert Burns as the setting for part of his poem 'Tam O'Shanter'. Burns's father William was buried in the kirkyard.

An Cala Garden Isle of Seil. A 5 acre (2ha) garden established in the 1930s. Surrounded by 15ft (4.5km) high walls to protect it from Atlantic gales, the planting includes roses, abutilons, rhododendrons, hydrangeas, camellias and azaleas. Features include streams and waterfalls.

An Turas Ferry Shelter Tiree. Opened in 2003 and the winner of Best Building in Scotland, the Royal Institution of British Architects Award and the Royal Scottish Academy Gold Medal for Architecture in that year. It has three elements – an open-topped white walled corridor, a black-felted timber bridge and a glass belvedere. It was also short-listed for the 2003 Stirling Prize.

Ardanaiseig Gardens 14 miles (23km) east of Oban. Woodland gardens covering 100 acres (40ha) overlooking Loch

Awe and surrounding Ardanaiseig House, designed by William Burn in 1834 and now a hotel. Originally laid out in the 1830s, the gardens are undergoing restoration after years of neglect. The major feature plants are rhododendrons and azaleas plus exotic trees and shrubs.

Ardchattan Priory and Garden $7^1/_2$ miles (12km) northeast of Oban. The Valliscaulian priory of Ardchattan was founded in the 1230s on the shores of Loch Etive. Expanded during the early 16th century, it was secularised following the Reformation; parts of the priory became a private house, the nucleus of which was formed by the refectory. The gardens are open to the public and feature herbaceous borders, a rockery and a wild garden. The priory remains a private house and the ruins of the chapel are in the care of Historic Scotland.

Ardchonell Castle Aka Innis Chonnel Castle. The ruins of Ardchonnel Castle, probably dating from the 13th century and remodelled in the 15th century, stand on Innis Chonnel, a small island in Loch Awe. The castle was the chief stronghold of the Campbells until the 15th century when they moved to Inveraray, and was a ruin by the early 19th century. The castle is not open to the public.

Ardencaple Castle Helensburgh. A castle on Gare Loch originally dating from the late 12th or early 13th century. Much of the castle was demolished by the Royal Navy in 1957 to provide space for housing. The current ruins of a single square tower probably date from the 16th century.

Ardencraig Gardens Craigmore, 1 mile (1.6km) east of Rothesay. A walled garden originally laid out for Ardencraig House and developed in the late 20th century as a show garden with annual bedding displays. There are also aviaries and fish ponds with exotic species. Tel: 01700 504644.

Ardfad Castle $1^1/_2$ miles north of Balvicar, Seil. The scant remains of a castle built by the MacDougalls of Ardencaple.

Ardgowan Castle $^1/_2$ mile (0.8km) north of Inverkip, 4 miles (6km) southwest of Greenock. Aka Inverkip Castle. A 15th century square three-storey tower house within the Ardgowan Estate. It was abandoned after the completion of Ardgowan House.

Ardgowan House $^1/_2$ mile (0.8km) north of Inverkip, 4 miles (6km) southwest of Greenock. A late 18th century country house within a 400 acre (160ha) estate on the shores of the Firth of Clyde. The parkland was landscaped to a design by Paul Ramsay when the house was built in the 1790s. Tel: 01475 521656.

Ardkinglas Woodland Garden Cairndow, 19 miles (31km) northwest of Helensburgh. Gardens surrounding Ardkinglas House (not open to the public) and overlooking Loch Fyne. There are large collections of rhododendrons and azaleas. A silver fir whose planting dates to 1750, and now with a girth of more than 31ft (9.5m), was selected as one of 50 Great British Trees to celebrate Queen Elizabeth II's Golden Jubilee. There is also a gazebo housing a 'Scriptorium'. Tel: 01499 600261.

Ardmaddy Castle 7 miles (11km) southwest of Oban. A 15th century castle and walled garden overlooking Ardmaddy Bay and Seil Sound. The garden has collections of rhododendrons, azaleas and climbing plants. There is also a water garden, and a daffodil and bluebell wood in spring. Tel: 01852 300353.

Ardrossan Castle Castle Hill, Ardrossan. Courtyard castle standing high above Ardrossan and founded in the late 13th century, with a gatehouse improved in the 15th and 16th century. Important during the Scottish–English wars, the castle was the scene in 1296 of the infamous event known as Wallace's Larder. An English garrison was stationed at the castle, and William Wallace arranged a decoy fire in the village. When the English went down to investigate, Wallace and his followers stormed the castle, slaughtering the entire garrison and throwing the bodies into the dungeon. The garrison's food supplies were thrown in after them, hence Wallace's Larder. Wallace was later captured and executed in London in 1305. The castle was empty during the 17th century and much of the stone structure was robbed by Cromwell's army to build a fort at Ayr. It is said to be haunted by the ghost of Wallace, who wanders the ruins on stormy nights.

Ardtornish Garden 2 miles (3km) northeast of Lochaline, 15 miles (24km) northwest of Oban. A 28 acre (11.5ha) garden located on a hillside overlooking Loch Aline and surrounding Ardtornish House, built in the 1880s. Rhododendrons and azaleas provide spring and early summer colour, with autumn colour supplied by acers, katsura and enkianthus. Tel: 01967 421288.

Arduaine Garden Arduiane, 13 miles (21km) south of Oban. Sheltered garden covering 20 acres (8ha), located on a headland overlooking Asknish Bay and the Sound of Jura and benefiting from the effects of the Gulf Stream. Best known for its collection of rhododendrons, azaleas and magnolias. Begun in the 1890s by James Arthur Campbell, the garden was restored during the 1970s and 1980s by Edmund and Harry Wright, who gave it to the National Trust for Scotland in 1992. Tel: 01852 200366.

Argyll Forest Park The UK's first forest park, covering 60,000 acres (24,280ha) and opened in 1935. Located to the north of Dunoon on the western shore of Loch Long, its wide variety of habitats include mountains, lochs and woodland.

Aros Castle Aros, 7 miles (11km) southeast of Tobermory, Mull. Located on a promontory overlooking a harbour on the Sound of Mull, the castle was probably built in the 13th century by the MacDougalls of Lorn. It comprised a hall and bailey and was defended on the landward side by a bank and ditch. In the possession of the Lords of the Isles in the 14th century, it had become ruinous by the end of the 17th century.

Arran Heritage Museum $^1/_2$ mile (0.8km) northwest of Brodick, Arran. Local history museum opened in 1979 and exploring the archaeology and geology of the Isle of Arran. The museum is housed in a variety of buildings including a farmhouse, cottage, bothy and stable. Exhibits include reconstructions of a smithy and a schoolroom, and there are displays on the seafaring history of the island. The museum also has a genealogical resource section. Tel: 01770 302636.

Ascog Hall Fernery and Garden Ascog, Bute. A baronial-style hall built in 1844 and especially noted for its gardens, designed by Edward La Trobe Bateman (1816–97). The gardens and fernery fell into disrepair after World War

II. The sunken Victorian fernery with a glass roof was restored by new owners in the 1990s with the help of Historic Scotland and the Royal Botanic Garden, Edinburgh; opened to the public in 1997, it now houses over 80 sub-tropical fern species. The 3 acre (1.2ha) gardens have also been restored and replanted, although little of the 19th century planting remained. Tel: 0170 050 4555.

Auchagallon Stone Circle 7 miles (11km) west of Brodick, Arran. Located on the west coast of Arran, a Bronze Age kerbed cairn surrounded by a circle of 15 stones. The circle is 47ft (14.5m) in diameter and the stones range in height from 2ft (0.6m) to 8ft (2.5m). The site is maintained by Historic Scotland.

Auchans Castle $^1/_4$ mile (0.4km) west of Dundonald, 5 miles (8km) west of Kilmarnock. A mansion/castle mostly built c.1644 by Sir William Cochrane of Cowdon and probably incorporating an earlier T-plan tower belonging to the Wallace family. The house was in a state of disrepair by the early 19th century. The ruins now stand in woodlands.

Auchengeich Memorial Moodiesburn, 8 miles (13km) northeast of Glasgow. A memorial on the northern outskirts of Moodiesburn, located on the site of the former pit village of Bridgend and erected in memory of 47 men who lost their lives in the Auchengeich Colliery Disaster on 18 September 1959. Worked by miners living in the village, the colliery fell into decline after the disaster and was closed in 1967.

Auchindrain Township Open Air Museum 5 miles (8km) southwest of Inveraray. The first open-air museum established in Scotland, this conserved highland township includes more than 20 cottages, barns and longhouses, each furnished in period fashion as they might have looked at the end of the 19th century. The village was abandoned in the 1960s. Tel: 01499 500235.

Auld Kirk Kirkintilloch Cowgate, Kirkintilloch. Dedicated to St Mary and built in 1644 to replace a 12th century parish church dedicated to St Ninian. It was itself replaced in the 1910s and since 1961 has housed a museum. Collections include artefacts and photographs relating to local history. Tel: 0141 578 0144.

Ayr Castle Founded in 1197 by William the Lion, probably in stone, but besieged by the English in 1298. Burnt by Robert the Bruce the following year, it was retaken by the English in 1306 and recaptured by Bruce in 1314 before being slighted. It was demolished before 1659 when the town's fort was constructed by Oliver Cromwell and nothing of the structure now remains.

Ayr Cathedral John Street, Ayr. The Roman Catholic Church of the Good Shepherd was opened in 1957 to serve the communities of Whitletts, Dalmilling, Lochside and Braehead in Ayr. A parish church for the first four years of its life, it was consecrated the cathedral of the Diocese of Galloway in 1961, after fire destroyed St Andrew's Cathedral in Dumfries. The cathedral was closed in 2007 and transferred to St Margaret's Cathedral at 27 John Street in Ayr town centre. Tel: 01292 263488.

Bachelors' Club Sandgate Street, Tarbolton, 7 miles (11km) northeast of Ayr. A 17th century thatched house on the first floor of which on 11 November 1780 Robert Burns, his brother and five friends inaugurated a debating society which they called 'The Bachelors' Club'. Burns also took dancing lessons and was initiated as a Freemason in the house. The meeting room where the society convened has been restored and contains Burns memorabilia, also hosting a Burns Night supper each year. The ground floor also contains late 18th century artefacts. The house was purchased by the National Trust for Scotland in 1938. Tel: 01292 541940.

Baird Institute Lugar Street, Cumnock, 15 miles (24km) east of Ayr. A local history museum opened in 1891 and exploring the industrial and social history of the area. There are collections of Mauchline and Cumnock pottery and of mining equipment. There is also a display about Keir Hardie, renowned as the founder of the Labour Party, and who lived much of his life in the town.

Balloch Castle 5 miles (8km) east of Helensburgh. Located at the southern tip of Loch Lomond and built by the Earls of Lennox in 1238. The castle was abandoned in favour of Inchmurrin in the late 14th century and is now little more than a moated mound. A new mansion, originally called Tullichewan Castle but now also referred to as Balloch Castle, was built for businessman John Stirling by John Buchanan of Ardoch in 1808 to a Gothic design by Robert Lugar. The castle is at the heart of the 200 acre (80ha) Balloch Castle Country Park. Tel: 01389 758216.

Balloch Hill 3 miles (5km) southwest of Campbeltown. Located on the summit of Balloch Hill are the remains of two hill forts one inside the other, occupied between the 8th and 1st century BC.

Balloch Old Castle See Balloch Castle

Baltersan Castle 1 mile (1.6km) southwest of Maybole, 9 miles (15km) south of Ayr. The ruins of a 16th century L-plan tower house built by John Kennedy near Crossraguel Abbey. It was abandoned in the mid 18th century, possibly as the result of a fire. It is in private hands.

Bar Hill Roman Fort 1 mile (1.6km) southwest of Kilsyth, 10 miles (16km) northeast of Glasgow. A 2nd century Roman fort on the Antonine Wall. An altar to Silvanus was discovered on the site in 1895 and the fort was first properly excavated 1902–5, when it was found to measure 369ft (112.5m) by 375ft (114m). Buildings identified on the site include a headquarters building, a well, a granary and a bath house. Further excavations were undertaken in the late 1970s and some remains were left uncovered for display. Located to the rear of the Wall, the fort was built and garrisoned by elements of the 2nd and 20th Legions and also by a cohort of Syrian archers, the only ones in Britain, who erected the altar to Silvanus.

Barochan Cross Now located in Paisley Abbey, this free-standing medieval cross once stood near Mill of Barochan. Restored and standing 11ft (3.3m) high, it has interlaced decorations on both faces.

Barguillean's Angus Garden 11/2 miles (2.5km) southwest of Taynuilt, 7 miles (11km) east of Oban. A 9 acre (3.5ha) woodland garden beside Loch Angus. Noted for its collections of rhododendrons and azaleas, the garden was created in 1957 to commemorate journalist and writer Angus Macdonald, killed in Cyprus in the previous year. Tel: 01866 822333.

Barr Castle $^1/_2$ mile (0.8km) southwest of Lochwinnoch, 8 miles (13km) southwest of Paisley. The ruins of an early 16th century castle, originally rectangular in plan and extended in the 17th century to provide larger living quarters.

Barrowlands Market	Stevenson Street, Glasgow. Aka the Barras. The market was founded in the 1920s by Margaret McIver, who had worked on a fruit stall in her youth and owned a fruit shop. She and her husband then bought some land and rented out static barrows to traders. The market was enclosed by the early 1930s; a ballroom opened above the market in 1934 is now a popular music venue. Tel: 0141 552 4601.
Battles	See separate table for details of the battles of Bothwell Bridge, Drumclog, Kilsyth, Langside, Largs and Loudoun Hill.
Beinn a' Bheithir	1 mile (1.6km) south of Ballachulish, 12 miles (19km) south of Fort William. Aka Ben Vair. A horseshoe-shaped ridge which includes the peaks of Sgorr Dhearg, 3359ft (1024m) and Sgorr Dhonuill, 3284ft (1001m).
Bellahouston Park	A 175 acre (71ha) park in Glasgow with formal gardens and parkland, opened to the public in 1896 and extended in 1901 and 1903. The Empire Exhibition of 1938 was held in the park. In 1982 it was the venue for the visit of Pope John Paul II. It is the location of the House for an Art Lover, Bellahouston Leisure Centre, the Palace of Art Sports for Excellence Centre and Glasgow Ski Centre.
Belleisle House	Alloway, 2 miles (3km) south of Ayr. An 18th century mansion built by the Hamilton family and set in a 290 acre (117ha) estate. Purchased in 1926 by Ayr Burgh Council, the estate forms a public park with a golf course designed by James Braid, while the house is now a hotel.
Ben Lomond	3 miles (5km) southeast of Tarbet, A mountain on the eastern shore of Loch Lomond standing at 3196ft (974m) and the most southerly of the Munros. The area was purchased by the National Trust for Scotland in 1994 and forms part of the Ben Lomond National Memorial Park and the Loch Lomond & the Trossachs National Park. Tel: 01360 870224.
Benmore Botanic Garden	Benmore, 5 miles (8km) north of Dunoon. A 120 acre (48ha) woodland garden established in the 1870s and later acquired by the Royal Botanic Garden, Edinburgh, with a wide variety of tree species and more than 250 species of rhododendrons. Features include an avenue of giant sierra redwood trees planted in 1863, a formal garden with herbaceous borders and Puck's Hut, a wooden hut tiled with red cedar and erected in memory of Isaac Bayley Balfour, keeper of the Royal Botanic Garden 1888–1922 and instigator of the garden at Benmore. Recent additions include a glade of plants grown from seeds collected in Bhutan, a Tasmanian ridge and a recreation of a Chilean rainforest. Tel: 01369 706261.
Biggar Gasworks Museum	Gasworks Road, Biggar. Biggar Gasworks was built in the 1830s to provide local street lighting and domestic services by producing gas from coal. It remained in operation until 1973, when coal gas was replaced by North Sea gas. Unlike other small-town gasworks in Scotland, it was preserved and is now a museum with restored plant and machinery. On selected days the boiler is powered up.
Blair House	1 mile (1.6km) southeast of Dalry, 9 miles (15km) northeast of Kilmarnock. A 17th century castle incorporating an earlier L-plan tower, dating to 1105. It has been the home of the Blair/Borthwick family for many centuries.
Blairquhan Castle	1 mile (1.6km) northwest of Straiton, 10 miles (16km) south of Ayr. Tudor-style country house designed by William Burn and built 1821–4 for Sir David Hunter Blair on the site of the Castle of Blairquhan, built by the McWhirters c.1346. The estate covers 2000 acres (800ha) of parkland and woodland. The gardens were designed by John Tweedie (1775–1862) and feature a pinetum (including a giant sequoia), ice house and Regency glass house. Tel: 01655 770239.
Bonawe Iron Furnace	Taynuilt, 9 miles (15km) east of Oban. Aka Lorne Iron Furnace. One of the earliest industrial sites in Scotland, located above Airds Bay on Loch Etive and established in the early 1750s by the Newland Company (founded by Richard and William Ford, James Backhouse and Michael Knot). The furnace was used to smelt ore brought by sea from Cumbria using local charcoal (ore being easier to transport than charcoal). In addition to the ironworks, a settlement grew up around the furnace which included workers' houses, a church and a school. Nearby Bonawe House was built to house the company manager. When the furnace ceased operation in the 1870s the community dispersed and the buildings fell into disrepair. The site is maintained by Historic Scotland.
Bothwell Castle	Uddingston, 7 miles (11km) southeast of Glasgow. Overlooking the River Clyde and founded in the 1270s by the Moravia family, the original castle was built by Walter of Moray. The large circular keep at the western end was captured by Edward I in 1296 before the castle had been completed. Recaptured by the Scots, it fell again to the English within five years. Having surrendered it after the Battle of Bannockburn in 1314 the English returned and retook the castle in 1336. Dismantled by Sir Andrew de Moravia in 1337 and rebuilt by Black Douglas in the 1360s, the castle was abandoned by the end of the 17th century. It passed into state care in 1935 and is maintained by Historic Scotland. Tel: 01698 816894.
Bothwellhaugh Roman Fort and Bath House	Motherwell. A 2nd century fort located on the eastern bank of Strathclyde Loch. It is thought to have been trapezoidal in shape and covered an area of more than 4 acres (1.2ha). The defences were formed by a rampart, a 33ft (10m) wide berm (flat area) and two ditches each 15ft (4.5m) wide and 4ft (1.2m) deep. It was contemporary with the Antonine Wall. A Roman bath house a little to the northwest, on the left bank of the South Calder Water, was discovered in 1973. It was furnished with a cold room, two warm rooms, a hot room and a plunge bath, and was contemporary with the fort and the Antonine Wall. Today the fort and bath house lie within Strathclyde Country Park.
Boturich Castle	2 miles (3km) north of Alexandria. Built in the 1830s by Robert Lugar on the eastern shore of Loch Lomond and incorporating an earlier property. It stands in 140 acres (56ha) of grounds.
Breachacha Castle	4 miles (6km) southwest of Arinagour, Coll. Situated on the southeastern tip of Coll at the head of Loch Breachacha, the castle was built as a four-storey tower house in the 15th century, and

although ruined has recently been restored. Nearby stands Breachacha House, built in 1750 by Hector Maclean.

Brodick Castle $1\frac{1}{4}$ miles (2km) north of Brodick, Arran. A red sandstone 16th century castle at the foot of Goatfell with 19th century additions in the same style, built on the site of earlier fortifications overlooking Brodick Bay. The original castle dated from before 1306, when Robert I Bruce fled here, and may have been the location of a pre-1000 Viking fort. It was levelled in 1455 by the Earl of Ross, rebuilt but destroyed again in 1544 by the Earl of Lennox under orders from Henry VIII. By the late 15th century it had become the seat of the Hamilton family, who made further alterations in the 1580s and 1650s. Parts of the present castle date from the 1580s during the ownership of the 2nd Earl of Arran, formerly guardian and regent of Mary, Queen of Scots. Repaired again in the 1630s and finally rebuilt as a stately home by James Gillespie Graham in the 1840s, the castle now houses collections of fine art, porcelain and furniture. The gardens, also developed in the 1840s, feature a large collection of rhododendrons and include a walled garden, summer house and ice house. The castle and gardens lie within Brodick Country Park. The castle and estate passed to the National Trust for Scotland in 1958. Tel: 01770 302202.

Brodick Country Park Located on the Isle of Arran and stretching from Brodick Bay to the summit of Goatfell (2867ft/874m), the park encompasses Brodick Castle and gardens. Its various habitats include shore, woodland and mountain. The park is in the care of the National Trust for Scotland.

Brunston Castle $\frac{1}{4}$ mile (0.4km) west of Dailly, 14 miles (13km) southwest of Ayr. A 16th century T-plan tower house on the northern bank of the Water of Girvan. The ruins now stand in the middle of a golf course.

Burns House Museum Castle Street, Mauchline, Ayrshire. Opened in 1969 and dedicated to Robert Burns's life and works, the museum is located in the house where Burns and his wife Jean Armour lived after their marriage in the 1780s; they met while Burns was farming at Mossgiel Farm near Mauchline. The museum also features local crafts including Mauchline Box Ware and curling stones.

Burns National Heritage Park Alloway, $1\frac{1}{2}$ miles (2.5km) south of Ayr. Heritage park dedicated to Robert Burns and including Burns's Cottage and the Burns Monument. The cottage, built in 1757, was Burns's birthplace on 25 January 1759. Now restored, it holds a collection of Burns memorabilia including manuscripts and artefacts. The Greek style monument was built in the 1820s with funds raised by public subscription. Tel: 01292 443700.

Burrell Collection Pollokshaws Road, Glasgow. A collection of more than 9000 works of art gifted to Glasgow by ship-owner Sir William Burrell and his wife, Constance, Lady Burrell in 1944. The wide-ranging collection (of which one-third is on display at any one time) includes examples from around the world of fine art, furniture, arms and armour, ceramics, glass, carpets and tapestries, as well as ancient artefacts from Assyria, Mesopotamia, Egypt and the Classical age. The collection is housed in an award-winning building purpose-built within Pollok Country Park and opened in 1983. The fabric of the building incorporates some of the architectural elements of the collection. Tel: 0141 287 2550.

Cadzow Castle $1\frac{1}{4}$ miles (2km) southeast of Hamilton. The substantial ruins of a castle overlooking the Avon Water. Originally the site of an occasional residence of David I and his successors until Robert the Bruce, the current structure dates from the 1530s. It had a large keep with drum towers at the southwest and southeast angles, guarding the landward approaches. Built by Sir James Hamilton of Finnart on behalf of his half-brother, the 2nd Earl of Arran, it had a short working life, being slighted in 1579 by the Earl of Mar and subsequently abandoned. The ruins became a feature of the landscaped grounds of Hamilton Palace and were romanticised during the 19th century to provide picturesque ruins for the Hamilton family and their guests. A concentrated programme of excavation was carried out 2001–3. The ruins are located in the grounds of Chatelherault Country Park and are maintained by Historic Scotland.

Cairnbaan Cup and Ring Marks $\frac{1}{4}$ mile (0.4km) north of Cairbaan, 2 miles (3km) northwest of Lochgilphead. A set of prehistoric carvings on two rock outcrops in open moorland. The markings are conjoined multiple-ringed cups and have been dated to the Bronze Age. The site is in the care of Historic Scotland.

Cambusnethan House $1\frac{1}{2}$ miles (2.5km) southwest of Wishaw. Aka Cambusnethan Priory. Gothic-style house designed by James Gillespie Graham for the Lockhart family and completed in 1820. It replaced a tower house and mansion which had burned down ten years earlier. The house has fallen into considerable disrepair since the death of Sir Muir Sinclair-Lockhart in 1985.

Campbeltown Heritage Centre Witchburn Road, Campbeltown. A local history museum with exhibits focusing on daily life and the fishing industry. There is also a model of the Campbeltown–Machrihanish light railway, opened in 1876 as a colliery railway and extended to carry passengers across the Kintyre peninsula in the early 20th century before its closure in 1931.

Cardross Castle 1 mile (1.6km) northeast of Cardross, 4 miles (6km) northwest of Dumbarton. Located by the River Leven, the castle was reputedly the site of Robert the Bruce's death from leprosy in 1329. No trace of its fabric now remains.

Carfin Lourdes Grotto Newarthill Road, Carfin, 2 miles (3km) northeast of Motherwell. A major site of Catholic pilgrimage in the mid 20th century, the replica of the Lourdes Grotto was built in 1922 following a visit by Canon Thomas Taylor and some parishioners to Lourdes. The grotto also honours the life of St Thérèse of Lisieux. A pilgrimage centre opened in 1996. Tel: 01698 268941.

Carnasserie Castle 1 mile (1.6km) north of Kilmartin, $7\frac{1}{2}$ miles (12km) north of Lochgilphead. The substantial ruins of a 16th century keep and hall built by John Carswell, Bishop of the Isles, on the site of an earlier fortification. Having passed into the ownership of the Campbell family in the 1570s, it was destroyed and abandoned in 1685 after its owner Sir Douglas Campbell joined the Monmouth Rebellion. The ruins are maintained by Historic Scotland.

Carradale Network Heritage Centre — Carradale, 13 miles (21km) northeast of Campbeltown, Argyll. A heritage centre housed in a former school and featuring displays on the local fishing, farming and forestry industries. Tel: 01583 431296.

Cassillis House — 1½ miles (2.5km) southwest of Dalrymple, 5 miles (8km) south of Ayr. A tower house beside the River Doon, originally built in the 15th century by the Kennedy family and remodelled and extended in the 17th and 19th centuries. It is a private residence.

Castle Asgog — 1 mile (1.6km) west of Millhouse, 14 miles (23km) southwest of Dunoon. The ruins of a 15th century castle on the shore of Loch Asgog. A stronghold of the Lamonts of Ascog, it was destroyed by the Marquis of Argyll in 1646.

Castle House Museum — Castle Gardens, Dunoon. A local history museum housed in part of Castle House, built in 1824 by Lord Provost Ewing of Glasgow. Opened in 1998, it explores the development of the Cowal peninsula from prehistoric times to the present day, with exhibits including models of Clyde steamers. The house stands near the meagre ruins of a 12th century castle abandoned by the 17th century, and which appears to have been triangular in plan with round towers at each angle.

Castle Lachlan — 15 miles (24km) northwest of Dunoon. A Queen Anne style house located on the eastern shore of Loch Fyne, built in the late 18th century and remodelled in Scottish baronial style at the end of the 19th. Strachlachlan is still home to the Clan Maclachlan.

Castle Lachlan, Old — 15 miles (24km) northwest of Dunoon. The ruins of a 15th century keep occupied by the Maclachlans until 1746. Standing above Loch Fyne, it was abandoned after being attacked from the sea by a government warship during the Jacobite Rebellion.

Castle of Braidwood — ½ mile (0.8km) southwest of Braidwood, 2 miles (3km) south of Carluke. Aka the Tower of Hallbar. A four-storey 16th century tower house, converted into holiday accommodation during the 1990s.

Castle Semple Collegiate Church — 1 mile (1.6km) northeast of Lochwinnoch, 7 miles (11km) southwest of Paisley. The ruins of an early 16th century church above Castle Semple Loch (originally known as Loch Winnoch). Founded by John, Lord Semple, who later died at the Battle of Flodden, it supported a college of priests. The church is rectangular in plan with a tower at the western end and is still substantial. It was abandoned following the Reformation of the 1560s.

Castle Semple Loch Tower — ½ mile (0.8km) southeast of Lochwinnoch, 8 miles (13km) southwest of Paisley. The ruins of a pele tower built on an island in Castle Semple Loch by the Semple family during the early 16th century. Due to the lowering of the loch's water level, the tower now stands on a spur of land.

Castle Stalker — ½ mile (0.8km) west of Portnacroish, 12 miles (19km) northeast of Oban. Standing on an islet at the mouth of Loch Laich, south of Shuna, the three-storey oblong tower house was built in the early 16th century by Sir John Stewart on the site of an earlier fortification. The inter-clan 'bloody' Battle of Stalc, in which the Stewarts and MacLarens together defeated the MacDougalls, took place opposite the castle in 1468. Having been lost in a wager and then regained, the castle eventually passed to the Campbells and was used to garrison government troops during the Jacobite Rebellion of 1745–6. Abandoned in the 1830s in favour of a new house at Airds, it was purchased by Charles Stewart in 1908 and preserved. The castle was restored and occupied again in the 1970s. It can be seen in the film *Monty Python and the Holy Grail* (1975) as Castle Aaaaarrrrrrggghhh; it also featured in the film *Highlander: Endgame* (2000).

Castle Sween — ¼ mile (0.4km) southwest of Kilbride, 8 miles (13km) southwest of Lochgilphead. One of the earliest stone castles in Scotland, built in the 12th century on Loch Sween by the MacSweens. It was later substantially remodelled by the Earls of Menteith, with the addition of three towers, including MacMillan's Tower. Having passed through the hands of the MacDonalds, Campbells, Stewarts, MacNeills and MacMillans, it was destroyed by Alisdair Macdonald in 1647 and abandoned. The castle passed into state care in 1933 and is maintained by Historic Scotland.

Cathedral of the Isles — College Street, Millport, Great Cumbrae Island. Designed by William Butterfield for George Boyle, 6th Lord Glasgow, the 19th century owner of the island. Dedicated to the Holy Spirit, the church opened in 1851 and was designated Cathedral of the Isles and Pro-Cathedral of Argyll in 1876. The cathedral seats 100 and with a nave 40ft (12m) long by 20ft (6m) wide lays claim to be the smallest cathedral in Europe. It does however have a spire 123ft (37.5m) tall. Attached to the cathedral is a theological college and retreat centre. Extensive restoration was carried out in the 2000s.

Cessnock Castle — 1 mile (1.6km) southeast of Galston, 6 miles (10km) southeast of Kilmarnock. A tower house originally built in the late 13th century and remodelled in the 16th and 17th centuries. It was restored towards the end of the 19th century and is a private residence.

Chatelherault Country Park — 1½ miles (2.5km) southeast of Hamilton. A 500 acre (200ha) country park opened in 1987 and formerly part of the Hamilton Estate. It surrounds a former hunting lodge built 1731–43 by William Adam for the 5th Duke of Hamilton, also Duc de Châtellerault, and once linked by a lime tree avenue with the now demolished Hamilton Palace. The Avon Water gorge and the ruins of Cadzow Castle lie within the park. Tel: 01698 426213.

Citizens' Theatre — Gorbals Street, Glasgow. Originally the Royal Princess's Theatre, built in 1878 and used in its early days for presentations of drama, variety and pantomime. The Citizens' Theatre Company, previously based at the Athenaeum, took the lease of the theatre in 1945 and gave it its present name. Since 1992 the theatre has had three auditoria – the Citizens' Theatre (600 seats), the Circle Studio (120 seats) and the Stalls Studio (60 seats). Tel: 0141 429 0022.

Clachan Bridge — 8 miles (13km) southwest of Oban. Aka the 'Bridge Over the Atlantic'. A single arch stone bridge over the Clachan Sound, connecting Seil Island with the mainland and built in 1792 by Thomas Telford.

Claig Castle — 4 miles (6km) southwest of Craighouse, Jura. Situated on Am Fraoch Eilean, a small island off the south coast of Jura. Built by Somerled in 1154 to defend the Sound of Islay, the castle was a

MacDonald stronghold until the early 17th century, when the clan fell out of favour with the Scottish Crown and it was given to the Campbells. It must have been a formidable building as the remaining walls of the tower are 9ft (2.7m) thick.

Cloch Lighthouse 3 miles (5km) southwest of Gourock. Located on Cloch Point on the Firth of Clyde and built in 1797 by John (or James) Clarkson. The light was installed by Smith and Stevenson. The lighthouse was automated in 1973.

Cloncaird Castle 1$^1/_2$ miles (2.5km) southeast of Kirkmichael, 4 miles (6km) southeast of Maybole. A late 15th or early 16th century tower house by the Girvan Water. Substantially modernised in the early 19th century, including the construction of a new frontage, it was used as a convalescent home in the 1950s and is now in private ownership.

Clyde Muirshiel Regional Park Regional park to the west of Glasgow, designated in 1990, covering 108 sq miles (280 sq km) and incorporating Muirshiel Country Park (created 1970), Castle Semple County Park (created 1971) and a further centre at Cornalees (created 1973).

Clyde Valley Woodlands A 1250 acre (505ha) National Nature Reserve located along the valley of the River Clyde between Lanark and Hamilton and incorporating three separate woodlands: Glenholm Glen, Cartland Craigs and Jock's Gill Wood. Habitats include steep woodland gorges of oak, ash and wych elm.

Clydebuilt Scottish Maritime Museum Kings Inch Road, Glasgow. Located at Braehead, the museum explores the history of shipbuilding and shipping on the Clyde. Also on show is the MV *Kyles*, built in 1863 and the oldest Clyde-built vessel still afloat in the UK. Part of the Scottish Maritime Museum. Tel: 0141 886 1013.

Coats Memorial Church High Street, Paisley. Sometimes known as 'The Baptist Cathedral of Europe', the church was built in 1894 in memory of industrialist, philanthropist and devout Baptist Thomas Coats. Dominated by a 197ft (60m) high crown spire, it was designed in Gothic style by Edinburgh architect Hippolyte Blanc and seats 1000. It also houses the Hill Organ, one of the finest in Europe.

Coats Observatory Oakshaw Street West, Paisley. An observatory built 1891–3 by John Honeyman for Paisley industrialist Thomas Coats, who died shortly after it was opened. It consists of a square tower surmounted by a circular observation drum covered by a copper dome. The original dome was replaced with a new one in 1985. The observatory records both astronomical and daily meteorological data. There are also displays on astronomy, astronautics, seismology and meteorology. Tel: 01418 892013.

Coeffin Castle 1$^1/_2$ miles (2.5km) north of Achnacroish, Lismore. The ruins of a 13th century hall on a promontory on the coast of the Isle of Lismore, probably built by the MacDougalls of Lorn on the site of a Viking fortress and abandoned in the post-medieval period.

Colonsay House Garden Kiloran, 1$^1/_2$ miles (2.5km) north of Scalasaig, Colonsay. The house was built in 1722, possibly on the site of an early Christian chapel (Cill Oran) and well (Tobar Oran). The gardens, covering more than 20 acres (8ha), were originally laid out in the 1930s and feature a notable collection of rhododendrons. In addition to the woodland garden there are formal walled gardens including a lighthouse garden. Tel: 01951 200211.

Colzium House and Estate Kilsyth, 11 miles (18km) northeast of Glasgow. Built in 1783 by the Edmonstone family close to the site of the ruined Colzium Castle, an L-plan tower house built by the Livingston family in the 15th or 16th century and itself replacing a 12th century fortification on a motte. A hall was added to the tower in the mid 16th century and was used as a base by James Graham, Marquis of Montrose, before the Battle of Kilsyth was fought nearby in 1645. The castle was demolished in 1703 and very little remains. Remodelled in the 1860s, the house was bought by the Lennox family in 1930 and presented to the Kilsyth Burgh in 1937. Features of the estate include a walled garden, ice house and curling pond. The estate also hosts the annual Kilsyth International Carnival.

Conal's Castle See Dun Chonnuill Castle.

Corra Castle 1$^1/_2$ miles (2.5km) south of Lanark. The ruins of a 16th century castle perched above the Corra Linn falls on the River Clyde, located within the Falls of Clyde Wildlife Reserve.

Coulthalley Castle 1$^1/_4$ miles (2km) northwest of Carnwath, 6 miles (10km) northeast of Lanark. Founded in the 12th century by the Somerville family and rebuilt c.1375, the castle was altered c.1415 and c.1520 and finally rebuilt after a siege of 1557. It fell into ruin in the 19th century.

Craignethan Castle $^1/_2$ mile (0.8km) west of Crossford, 4$^1/_2$ miles (7km) northwest of Lanark. The substantial remains of a 16th century tower house with 17th century additions, located between the River Nethan and Craignethan Burn. Built by Sir James Hamilton in the 1530s, after his execution for treason in 1540 it eventually passed to his half-brother James Hamilton, 2nd Earl of Arran. The Hamiltons were supporters of Mary, Queen of Scots, which subsequently led to the fall of the castle almost without a fight to the forces of James VI in 1579. The castle's defences were slighted and it was thereafter used only for residential rather than defensive purposes. The most heavily defended part was the western approach, which, rather than steep slopes and a waterway, was protected by a massive rampart and ditch with a caponier – a protected passageway or chamber with firing ports which extended into the ditch, unique in British military architecture. The castle was immortalised by Sir Walter Scott as 'Tillietudlem Castle' in his novel *Old Mortality*. It passed into state care in 1949 and is maintained by Historic Scotland.

Crarae Gardens Crarae, 10 miles (16km) southwest of Inveraray. An informal garden in a glen, established by Lady Campbell in 1912. Featuring more than 400 rhododendrons and azaleas, it also has a wide variety of broadleaf trees including the National Collection of southern beech. The garden was given to the National Trust for Scotland in 2002 following an appeal to save it from closure. Tel: 01546 886614.

Crawford Castle Crawford, 14 miles (23m) south of Lanark. Aka Tower Lindsay. The ruins of a 17th century castle beside the River Clyde. It was built on the site of a 12th century motte, indicating the long-established strategic importance of the location; there is also evidence for both Flavian and

Antonine Roman forts in the immediate area. Abandoned in the late 18th century, its stones were robbed to help build nearby Crawford Castle Farm.

Crawfordjohn Heritage Venture Croft Head, Crawfordjohn, 13 miles (21km) southwest of Biggar. A local history centre housed in the 18th century former Crawfordjohn Church and exploring life in South Lanarkshire with displays on the life of the rural community. Tel: 01864 504206.

Crinan Canal Running for 9 miles (15km) between Ardrishaig on Loch Fyne and Crinan, and built 1794–1801, the canal was designed as a short cut between the west coast and islands and the Clyde Estuary, thus avoiding the south end of the Kintyre Peninsula. Originally designed by John Rennie, it was partly redesigned by Thomas Telford in 1816 and has 15 locks. Upgraded and repaired in the 1930s, the canal is operated by British Waterways and is now mainly used by yachts and pleasure craft.

Crookston Castle Brockburn Road, Pollok, Glasgow. A 15th century rectangular fortification with additional corner towers, built on the ring earthworks of a 12th century castle overlooking Levern Water. A 12th century chapel founded by Sir Robert Croc stood within its walls. Having at one time been the property of Henry, Lord Darnley, the second husband of Mary, Queen of Scots, the castle was probably abandoned in the late 16th century and only one tower still stands at its full height. It was presented to the National Trust for Scotland in 1931 and the site, which affords good views over Glasgow, is maintained by Historic Scotland.

Crossraguel Abbey $1\frac{1}{2}$ miles (2.5km) southwest of Maybole. A 13th century Cluniac (Benedictine) abbey established as a daughter house of one at Paisley. The earliest buildings were probably destroyed during the ongoing conflicts with England and a new church and abbot's house were built in the 14th century. Further changes over the following centuries included the building of a new tower house for the abbot in 1530. The abbey was severely damaged during the Reformation and the remaining monks had probably all died by the 1590s. The gatehouse has been restored and the ruins of the chapter house, abbey church and cloister can be seen.

Croy Hill Roman Fort $\frac{1}{2}$ mile (0.8km) northeast of Croy, 2 miles (3km) northwest of Cumbernauld. A 2nd century Roman fortlet on the Antonine Wall located on Croy Hill and excavated in the 1930s and 1970s. Evidence of a *vicus* (civil settlement) has also been found. The fort measured 270ft (82m) by 240ft (73m), the Antonine Wall forming its northwest defence line, and had gates for the Military Way, which ran behind the Wall. It appears to have been garrisoned at one point by elements of the 6th Legion, normally based at York.

Cruachan Power Station 2 miles (3km) west of Lochawe, $13\frac{1}{2}$ miles (22km) east of Oban. A pumped-storage hydroelectric power station opened in October 1965 and hidden within the 3694ft (1126m) mountain of Ben Cruachan, overlooking Loch Awe. Tel: 01866 822618.

Culzean Castle 4 miles (6km) west of Maybole. Located on the cliffs above Culzean Bay on the Firth of Clyde and originally dating from as early as the 12th century. Sea caves beneath the cliffs once led into the castle. By the 17th century it had been developed into an L-plan tower house but in the 1770s it was completely remodelled and greatly extended by Robert Adam for David, 10th Earl of Cassilis. Work on the castle was finally completed with more improvements in the 1870s. It contains collections of fine art, armour and weapons, and furniture. An apartment at the top of the castle was presented to US General (and future President) Dwight D Eisenhower for his lifetime in 1945 in recognition of his role during World War II, and he stayed here four times. Other important rooms include the armoury, the library, the dining room, the round drawing room, the blue drawing room, the long drawing room and the state bedroom. The surrounding estate, covering more than 550 acres (220ha) and landscaped by Robert Adam, was established in 1969 as Scotland's first country park. Features include the Swan Pond (a flooded 13 acre/5ha water meadow created in the 19th century to provide fishing, with a restored pagoda on its shore), picturesque ruins such as the 'Roman Viaduct', an ice house, deer park, Camellia House and Fountain Court. It incorporates more than 3 miles (5km) of shoreline, as well as cliffs, woodland and parkland. The house was presented to the National Trust for Scotland in 1945. Tel: 0870 118 1945.

Cumbernauld House 1 mile (1.6km) north of Cumbernauld. Built in 1731 to a neoclassical design by William Adam and replacing the earlier Cumbernauld Castle, destroyed by General Monck in 1651. The remains of the older house were converted to stables and burnt down during the Jacobite Rebellion in 1745.

Cumbernauld Museum Allander Walk, Cumbernauld. Local history museum exploring the history of Cumbernauld. Exhibits include dinosaurs and Roman artefacts, the story of the Comyns, and Cumbernauld in the 19th century and during both world wars. Tel: 01236 725664.

Cumbrae Lighthouses Two lighthouses on Little Cumbrae Island. The Old Lighthouse stands on Lighthouse Hill and was built in 1757 by James Ewing with a coal fire light; abandoned in 1792, it was restored in 1956. A new lighthouse on the west of the island replaced the old one in 1793.

Custom House Museum Custom House Quay, Greenock. A museum dedicated to the work of HM Customs and Revenue and exploring the history of customs men and the struggle with smugglers. Tel: 01475 881300.

Dalgarven Mill Museum Dalgarven, 2 miles (3km) north of Kilwinning. A restored 17th century grain mill on the River Garnock, housing the Museum of Ayrshire Country Life and Costume. Opened in 1987 by the Ferguson family, who had run the mill since 1883, the museum is now run by a charitable trust. It features exhibits relating to country life – including farming and domestic memorabilia and reconstructed interiors – as well as the wide-ranging Ferguson Costume Collection of clothes and accessories from the 1770s to the 1980s. Tel: 01294 552448.

Dalmellington Motte Dalmellington, 11 miles (18km) east of Maybole. An Anglo-Norman motte probably dating to the 12th century and originally supporting a wooden castle.

Dalquharran Castle $\frac{1}{2}$ mile (0.8km) north of Dailly, 5 miles (8km) south of Maybole. A late 18th century castle-style country house on the north bank of the Water of Girvan, designed by Robert Adam and built for the Kennedy family. Interior work was completed in the early 19th century. It was extended in the

1880s with the addition of Scottish baronial style wings. After the Kennedys sold the house, it became a youth hostel before World War II, serving as a school for the deaf during the war before reverting to a private residence. Unroofed by its owners in 1967, it is now a shell.

Dalquharran Castle, Old — $^1/_4$ mile (0.4km) northeast of Dailly, 5 miles (8km) south of Maybole. The ruins of a 15th century castle on the Water of Girvan, extended in the 17th century but abandoned once the new Dalquharran Castle was completed in the late 18th century.

David Livingstone Museum — Station Road, Blantyre. A museum housed in Shuttle Row, the birthplace of explorer David Livingstone (1813–73), near the former Blantyre Cotton Mills. It celebrates his life from its beginnings in the local cotton mills to its culmination in his journeys in Africa. Exhibits include equipment used during his explorations and native artefacts. Managed by the National Trust for Scotland since 1999. Tel: 01698 823140.

Dean Castle — Dean Castle Country Park, Kilmarnock. A 14th century tower or keep with later additions including the Place or Palace, added in the 15th century to provide residential rather than purely defensive accommodation. Owned by the Boyd family, it was known as Kilmarnock Castle until the early 18th century. Accidentally burnt down in 1735, it was fully restored during the early 20th century by the 8th Lord Howard de Walden; the keep now houses his collection of arms and armour and tapestries plus a collection of musical instruments. The gatehouse was built in the 1930s to a design compatible with the original buildings. The castle and its collections were presented to Kilmarnock by the 9th Lord Howard de Walden in 1975 along with the Dean and Assloss Estates, established as a country park in 1981.

Denny Ship Model Experiment Tank — Castle Street, Dumbarton. Now part of the Scottish Maritime Museum, the Denny Tank was built in 1882 by shipbuilders William Denny & Brothers and was the first commercial ship model testing tank built in the world. The length of a football pitch, the tank has been restored and is still used for testing ship designs. Tel: 01389 763444.

Dick Institute — Elmbank Avenue, Kilmarnock. Opened in 1901, the institute houses two galleries of fine and contemporary art and three galleries of museum exhibits exploring local history. Tel: 01563 554343.

Distilleries — **Ardbeg**, Port Ellen, Islay. Established by the MacDougalls in 1815. The distillery was closed 1981–97, when it was restored to full working order. The water sources are Loch Arinambeast and Loch Uigidale. Tel: 01496 302244.

Bowmore, Islay. The oldest distillery on Islay, founded in 1779. The water source is the Laggan River.

Bruichladdich, Islay. Built in 1881 by the Harvey brothers. The distillery was closed for much of the 1990s but reopened in 2001 and still has much of its original machinery. Tel: 01496 850221.

Bunnahabhain, 3 miles (5km) north of Port Askaig, Islay. Established in 1881. The water source is the River Margadale. Tel: 01496 840646.

Caol Ila, Port Askaig, Islay. Built in 1846 by Hector Henderson. The distillery was demolished in 1972 and a larger operation was opened in 1974. The water source is Loch Nam Ban. Tel: 01496 302760.

Isle of Arran, Lochranza, Arran. A relatively new distillery opened in 1995. The water source is Loch na Davie. Tel: 01770 830264.

Jura, Craighouse, Jura. The only distillery on Jura, founded in 1810 and rebuilt in 1876, with further rebuilding during the second half of the 20th century. The water source is Loch a Bhaille Mhargaidh. Tel: 01496 820240.

Kilchoman, Bruichladdich, Islay. The newest distillery on Islay, opened in June 2005 and the first new distillery for more than 120 years. The barley for the whisky is grown on the farm where the distillery is sited. Tel: 01496 850011.

Lagavulin, Port Ellen, Islay. Founded in 1837 after two early distilleries were amalgamated. The water source is Solum Lochs. Tel: 01496 302400.

Laphroaig, Port Ellen, Islay. Established in 1815 by Alexander and Donald Johnston. The distillery received a royal warrant from Prince Charles in 1994. The water source is the Kilbride Dam. Tel: 01496 302418.

Oban, founded in 1794 by the Stevenson brothers. The distillery was closed in the late 1960s and the still house was rebuilt. It was reopened in 1972. The water source is the lochs in Ardconnel. Tel: 01631 562110.

Tobermory, Isle of Mull. The only distillery on the Isle of Mull, founded in 1798 by John Sinclair but out of production for considerable periods since then. It was reopened in 1993 by Burn Stewart Ltd. Tel: 01688 302645.

Dreghorn Church — Dreghorn, 1 mile (1.6km) east of Irvine. An unusual parish church built in 1780 in the shape of an octagon. It is nicknamed the 'threepenny church', after the shape of the pre-decimal 'threepenny bit', or the 'put 'n' take', after the shape of the spinner used in a card game of the same name, although neither of these items was actually octagonal.

Drumpellier Country Park — Townhead Road, Coatbridge. A former estate belonging to the Buchanan family, opened as a public park in 1919 and designated a country park in 1984. Covering 500 acres (200ha), it features woodlands, two lochs and the Monklands Canal.

Drumsargard Castle — Hallside, Cambuslang, 7 miles (11km) southeast of Glasgow. A 14th century castle which once stood on a motte. It had long been abandoned by the 18th century and the stones used for local building, although the motte, surrounded by modern housing, is still visible.

Duart Castle — 2 miles (3km) southeast of Craignure, Mull. Standing on the promontory of Duart Point (G. *dubh aird*, 'black promontory'), the original fortifications may date from the 13th century. The Macleans enlarged the castle in the 14th century and built a tower house. A new range of buildings was added and further modifications were made in the 17th century. The castle passed into the hands of the Campbell Earls of Argyll in the 1670s but had fallen into disrepair by the mid 18th century. It was recovered in 1910 by the MacLeans, who carried out a major restoration programme to make the castle habitable once again. Tel: 01680 812309.

Dumbarton Castle — Dumbarton. Located on Dumbarton Rock, a steep promontory of volcanic rock on the River Clyde. Records attest to some form of fortification at this location as early as the 8th century and probably much earlier; it is believed that a 9th century settlement was swept away in a Viking assault. The first recognisable castle was in place by the 13th century, the surviving portcullis arch dating from just after this period. Despite its strong position the castle was taken by siege several times, including in 1489 by James IV, in 1514 by the Earl of Lennox, and in 1545 when it was captured by supporters of the young Mary, Queen of Scots. In 1568 she was heading for the castle, which was still held by her supporters, when her army was intercepted and defeated at the Battle of Langside; the Marians in Dumbarton were eventually overwhelmed in 1571. Having proved so liable to capture, the castle was completely remodelled in the 17th and 18th centuries – although the late 16th century guard house remains in situ – and served as a Government base during successive Jacobite uprisings; the Governor's House (now housing a museum) and King George's Battery were built during this period. The Duke of York's Battery and the French Prison were constructed in the late 18th century, the latter to hold prisoners-of-war during the Napoleonic Wars. Apart from the two world wars, the castle's military function ceased with the withdrawal of its garrison in 1865. Now in the care of Historic Scotland.

Dun Chonnuill Castle — Dun Chonnuill, 15 miles (24km) southwest of Oban. Situated on an island of the same name off the coast of Garbh Eileach in the Garvellach group of islands. The ruined castle (G. = 'Conal's Castle') was built by Maclean of Duart when he was given the island by Robert III in the early 15th century.

Dunadd Fort — 1½ miles (2.5km) north of Cairnbaan, 4 miles (6km) northwest of Lochgilphead. An Iron Age and later fort on a hilltop above the River Add, believed to have been the site of the capital of the Scottish kingdom of Dalriada in the 6th–8th centuries. It stands out sharply above the surrounding floodplain, which formerly consisted largely of the boggy Mòine Mhòr. During its lifetime it seems to have had two enclosures and was occupied until the 9th century. Many of the rocks found within the fort bear carvings, including a boar and a footprint which, it has been surmised, was used during coronation ceremonies. Maintained by Historic Scotland.

Dunans Castle — 12 miles (19km) northwest of Dunoon. An 18th century house on the River Ruel, belonging to the Fletcher family and set in a Victorian designed landscape incorporating Thomas Telford's 1815 Dunans Bridge. It was remodelled in French baronial style in 1864 by architect Andrew Kerr. Severely damaged by fire in 2001, the house is being restored by its current owners.

Dunaskin Heritage Centre — Waterside, 8 miles (13km) east of Maybole. An open air centre located on the 110 acre (44ha) site of the former Dalmellington Iron Company ironworks, which produced iron from 1848 until 1921 and coal and bricks until 1976 and many of whose buildings are preserved as a Scheduled Ancient Monument. Tracing the history of the Doon Valley from the Industrial Revolution until the present day, Exhibits include the Mary Gallagher Experience, a recreation of late 19th century life, a restored ironworker's cottage and industrial machinery. The centre is also the home of the Scottish Industrial Railway Centre. Tel: 01292 531144.

Dundonald Castle — Dundonald, 4 miles (6km) southwest of Kilmarnock. Located on a hill on the western outskirts of Dundonald and founded c.1250 by Walter Stewart. After sustaining damaged during the conflicts with England, part of the original castle, including drum towers, was demolished and incorporated into a large tower built by Robert II (Alexander Stewart's grandson) in the late 14th century. He died here in 1390 and it was a royal residence until the 1480s. The castle was then in the possession of the Cathcarts and the Wallaces before being abandoned by the 17th century. Excavations have revealed that the site was used during the Iron Age and there is also evidence for a 12th century motte which would have supported a timber fortification. The substantial ruins are maintained by Historic Scotland. Tel: 01563 851489.

Dunollie Castle — 1 mile (1.6km) northwest of Oban. The ruins of a 12th century castle on a promontory overlooking Oban Bay and the Firth of Lorn. The present remains date from the 15th and 16th centuries. A seat of the MacDougalls, it was probably abandoned in the 18th century after the failure of the Jacobite Rebellion of 1745.

Dunstaffnage Castle — 3 miles (5km) north of Oban. The impressive ruins of a 13th century castle on a promontory overlooking the entrance to Loch Etive. The site is a strategic location and was probably used as a fort during the 1st millennium; it has been said that the Stone of Destiny was kept here prior to being taken to Scone in the 9th century. Originally a MacDougall stronghold, in the early 14th century it became a possession of the Campbells of Lorn. The castle was burned in 1685 and was garrisoned by Government troops during the 1745 Jacobite Rebellion. Flora MacDonald was temporarily held captive at Dunstaffnage after helping Bonnie Prince Charlie to escape. The castle was occupied until the 19th century and is still in the care of the hereditary Captain of Dunstaffnage.

Dunure Castle — Dunure, 7 miles (11km) southwest of Ayr. The ruins of a castle on the coast above Ayr Bay and the Firth of Clyde and originally built in the 13th century by the Kennedy family. The castle was extended during the 15th and 16th centuries with the addition of more domestic buildings. It is believed to have been slighted in the 1640s and was certainly in a ruinous condition by the end of the 17th century, its structure being further robbed to provide material for local buildings. A 16th century beehive dovecote stands nearby.

Dunyvaig Castle — 2 miles (3km) east of Port Ellen, Islay. Aka Dunyveg Castle, Dun Naomhaig (G. = 'Fort of the Little Ships'). The ruins of an early 16th century castle standing on a rocky knoll on a promontory overlooking Lagavulin Bay, near Lagavulin Distillery on the east coast of the Isle of Islay. An earlier fortification built in the 13th century also stood on the site. It was a stronghold of the MacDonalds until 1494 when it passed to John MacLean under royal custody. During the 16th century it was occupied by the Campbells before reverting to the MacDonalds and again being taken into royal custody because of MacDonald opposition to the Crown. Captured by Angus Oig MacDonald in 1615, it was then recaptured by a Royalist force led by Sir John Campbell and Sir Oliver Lambert. In 1647 it was besieged and captured by a Covenanter force under David Leslie. It is believed to have been demolished in the 1670s.

Dunyveg Castle See Dunyvaig Castle.

Easdale Island Folk Museum Easdale. Local history museum opened in 1980 and housed in a cottage on the island, and particularly dedicated to exploring the daily lives of workers in the local slate quarries during their heyday in the 19th century. Devastated by a sea flood during a storm in 1881, the quarries were finally closed just before World War I. Exhibits include a photographic archive, local artefacts and genealogical records. Tel: 01852 300370.

Eglinton Castle 1 mile (1.6km) southeast of Kilwinning. A late 18th century castle built on the site of a much older property which was demolished in order to make way for it. The house was unroofed in the 1920s and was used for gunnery practice and commando training during World War II. Much of what remained was demolished in 1973. The ruins now stand in Eglinton Country Park, opened in 1986 and covering 1000 acres (400ha) of the former castle estate, with habitats ranging from woodland to wetland and from farmland to formal gardens. The last medieval style tournament held in Britain took place on the estate in 1839.

Fairlie Castle Fairlie, 3 miles (5km) south of Largs. The ruins of a 15th century tower house overlooking Fairlie Roads.

Falls of Clyde Wildlife Reserve 1 mile (1.6km) south of Lanark. Located within the River Clyde gorge, the Falls of Clyde consist of Dundaff Linn (10ft/3m), Corra Linn (92ft/28m) and Bonnington Linn (36ft/11m); they have supplied power either as direct water-driven power or as part of the Lanark Hydro-Electric Scheme. The reserve covers 147 acres (59ha) along the River Clyde gorge. Wildlife includes peregrine falcons, tawny owls, sparrowhawks, kingfishers, badgers, foxes and roe deer. The reserve is owned and managed by the Scottish Wildlife Trust.

Fincharn Castle 10 miles (16km) north of Lochgilphead. The ruins of a 16th century castle located on a promontory in Loch Awe, and built on the site of a hall house possibly dating to the 13th century.

Finlaystone House 2 miles (3km) east of Port Glasgow. Built in the 1740s and incorporating parts of the original keep, Dinniston's Tower, the house is set in a 500 acre (200ha) estate beside the River Clyde. From the 12th century the estate was successively owned by the Dennistouns, the Cunninghams, and the Cunninghame Grahams. The house was bought in 1863 by Sir David Carrick-Buchanan, who sold it to George J Kidston in 1897; extensively remodelled at the end of the 19th century, it is now owned by the MacMillans. The estate includes woodland, formal gardens, mudflats and river, and features the second largest heronry in southwest Scotland. The gardens were originally laid out in the early 20th century and include the so-called 'smelly' garden, featuring a wide range of scented plants. The visitor centre has displays on the natural history of the park and the history of the Clan MacMillan, as well as a collection of dolls from around the world. Finlaystone House is not open to the public. Tel: 01475 540505.

Fossil Grove Victoria Park, Glasgow. A unique site containing 11 fossil tree stumps around 300 million years old, accidentally uncovered in 1887 when the park was being created. The trees are examples of giant clubmoss plants. Tel: 0141 287 2000.

Fraoch Eilean Castle Fraoch Eilean, 15 miles (24km) east of Oban. The ruins of a 13th century castle located on an island in Loch Awe. A stronghold of the MacNaughtons, it was abandoned before the mid 18th century.

Garrion Tower 1 mile (1.6km) east of Larkhall. An L-plan tower house on the River Clyde, dating from the late 15th century and at one time the summer residence of the Bishop of Glasgow.

Geilston Garden Cardross, 4 miles (6km) west of Dumbarton. A walled garden with glasshouses leading to woodland set around Geilston House (not open to the public). The Geilston Burn runs through the woodland. The garden was bequeathed to the National Trust for Scotland in 1989. Tel: 01389 849187.

Gilbertfield Castle 3/4 mile (1.2km) south of Cambuslang. Ruins of an early 17th century L-plan mansion, located on Dechmont Hill and built by Sir John Cunningham. It was later the residence of poet William Hamilton of Gilbertfield (1665–1751).

Gladstone Court Museum Northback Road, Biggar. Museum with reconstructions of various Victorian shops and businesses including a bank, chemist, cobbler, milliner, printer and ironmonger, plus a schoolroom and village library.

Glasgow Botanic Gardens Great Western Road, Glasgow. An acclaimed garden instituted in 1817 and established on its current site beside the River Kelvin in 1842. Covering 28 acres (11.5ha), it features 12 conservatories including the recently restored Kibble Palace, moved from John Kibble's house in Coulport on Loch Long in 1873. The main range of glasshouses contain extensive collections of tropical plants including orchids, begonia and tree ferns. Outside there are formal gardens, a world rose garden, an 'uncommon vegetable' garden, a children's garden, a chronological garden and an arboretum.

Glasgow Caledonian University Cowcaddens Road, Glasgow. Scotland's fourth largest university in terms of student numbers, with around 17,000 students. Though its history dates to 1875, the university was officially formed in 1993 with the merger of Glasgow Polytechnic and The Queen's College, Glasgow. The Saltire Centre is the latest addition to the campus. Tel: 0141 331 3000.

Glasgow Cathedral (St Mary's) Great Western Road, Glasgow. The cathedral of the united Diocese of Glasgow & Galloway in the Scottish Episcopal Church. It was built to replace St Mary's Episcopal Church, Renfield Street, dating from 1825 and which became inadequate during the rapid growth of industrial Glasgow. The new church, located in the expanding western suburbs, was designed by Sir George Gilbert Scott, already working as architect for Glasgow University. One of the city's best Gothic Revival style buildings, with fine craftsmanship including stained glass designed by the studios of Hardman and Clayton & Bell, it was opened for worship in 1871 and consecrated in 1884. Tel: 0141 339 6691.

Glasgow Cathedral (St Mungo's) Cathedral Street, Glasgow. A Church of Scotland cathedral consecrated in 1136 and located on the site of a 6th century monastery founded by St Mungo (aka St Kentigern), whose tomb is in the Lower Church. The cathedral was rebuilt after sustaining fire damage, and was reconsecrated in 1197. It was extended in the early 13th century and further rebuilt later in the century. Towers were added in the 15th century, although two of these were later removed. Following the Reformation the cathedral was divided into two, both the Outer High (1647–1835) and the Lower Church (1596–1801) being used by separate congregations. Between 1801 and the 1850s the Lower Church was used for burials. The post-Reformation alterations were reversed in the later 19th century. The cathedral is 285ft (87m) long by 63ft (19m) wide. Crown property, it is maintained by Historic Scotland.

Glasgow City Chambers George Square, Glasgow. The headquarters of the City of Glasgow Council, located on the east side of George Square. Designed by William Young in Italian Renaissance style, the building was completed in 1888 and opened by Queen Victoria the same year. Tel: 0141 287 4018.

Glasgow City Halls Candleriggs, Glasgow. A complex in the Merchant City area including the Grand Hall and the Old Fruitmarket. The Grand Hall, designed by George Murray and opened in 1841, was used for concerts and assemblies including the first General Assembly of the Free Church of Scotland in 1843. The adjacent Old Fruitmarket, built in 1852, was as its name suggests a market until its closure in 1969. Subsequently it was used to host concerts and festivals. The halls underwent extensive renovations 2002–6 and there are now three main performance spaces. The Grand Hall is the home of the BBC Scottish Symphony Orchestra and seats 1036. The Old Fruitmarket is a flexible space seating 1000–2000 and is used for music concerts of all genres. The Recital Room is used by, among others, the Scottish Chamber Orchestra and seats 100. The City Halls also house the Scottish Music Centre, established to promote all forms of Scottish music.

Glasgow Gallery of Modern Art Royal Exchange Square, Glasgow. Aka GoMA. Opened in 1996 in a neoclassical building dating to 1778 and originally the home of tobacco baron William Cunninghame. Having been subsequently used as a bank, an exchange and a library, it now houses collections of contemporary art by international and Scottish artists. Each of the gallery's four floors is dedicated to one of the four natural elements – earth, air, fire and water. Tel: 0141 229 1996.

The Glasgow Hat Outside the Glasgow Gallery of Modern Art in Royal Exchange Square stands a bronze equestrian statue of the Duke of Wellington, created 1840–4 by sculptor Baron Carlo Marochetti. This might seem hardly worth a mention as there are numerous statues of the Iron Duke dotted around the country. However, during the 1980s a tradition of placing a plastic orange traffic cone at a jaunty angle on the Duke's head began. Each cone was swiftly removed by the authorities, only to be replaced equally swiftly by another. Eventually the cone became tolerated and became a tourist attraction known as 'The Glasgow Hat', regarded as an icon of Glaswegian's irreverent sense of humour. Not to be left out, the Duke's horse (presumably Copenhagen) now also regularly sports a similar titfer. In 2003 Glasgow City Council gave beer company Amstel permission to replace the Glasgow Hat with a Champions League hat in the shape of a football, to commemorate the final of the tournament being played at Hampden Park Stadium.

Glasgow Museums Resource Centre Woodhead Road, South Nitshill Industrial Estate, Glasgow. A purpose-built museum storage and visitor centre housing a wide range of collections which would otherwise be held in storage and inaccessible to the public. The 200,000 objects on display include substantial numbers of works from the Kelvingrove Art Gallery and Museum and the Glasgow Gallery of Modern Art. Tel: 0141 276 9300.

Glasgow Necropolis Castle Street, Glasgow. A Victorian garden cemetery near St Mungo's Cathedral on the hill known as Grey Rock. Laid out on the site of Fir Park, in which a statue of John Knox was erected in 1825, the necropolis was designed to emulate Père Lachaise cemetery in Paris as an 'ornamental cemetery which would embrace economy, security and a picturesque effect'. The first interment took place in September 1832. The entrance gates were designed by David Hamilton and his son James, who also designed the bridge over the Molendinar Burn on the approach to the cemetery; being on the route of funeral processions, this bridge was quickly dubbed the 'Bridge of Sighs'. Some of the 3500 monuments were designed by leading Glaswegian architects including Bryce, Hamilton, Mackintosh and Thompson. The cemetery was non-denominational and there are an estimated 50,000 interments, many in communal graves.

Glasgow Police Musuem St Andrews Square, Glasgow. A museum dedicated to the history of the Glasgow police force and its individual officers from its inception in 1779 until 1975. Exhibits include a photographic archive, uniforms and equipment, and also feature some of the city's more interesting criminal cases. The original force of only eight officers was founded by the Glasgow Merchant and Trades Baillies in 1779; on 30 June 1800 the Glasgow Police Act effectively created Britain's first police force. By 1846 there were more than 350 police officers split between four divisions. In 1900 the force numbered more than 1300 officers and men. The first policewoman was recruited in 1915. In 1975 the City of Glasgow Police, Lanarkshire Constabulary, Renfrew & Bute Constabulary, Dunbartonshire Constabulary, Argyll County Police, Ayrshire Constabulary and a small portion of Stirling & Clackmannan Police, were amalgamated to form Strathclyde Police. The museum also hosts the International Police Exhibition, which illustrates the influence of the Glasgow police on world policing. Tel: 0141 552 1818.

Glasgow Royal Concert Hall Sauchiehall Street, Glasgow. Opened in October 1990 as part of the City of Culture celebrations to replace St Andrews Hall, burned down in 1962. Designed by Sir Leslie Martin, the hall seats up to 2500 in two auditoria and hosts a variety of performances, ranging from the Moscow State Orchestra to the Buena Vista Social Club. Tel: 0141 353 8000.

Glasgow School of Art Renfrew Street, Glasgow. A world-renowned institution for the study and advancement of fine art, design and architecture. The school was founded in 1845; probably its most famous student was Charles Rennie Mackintosh, who designed a new School of Art building in 1896. The Mackintosh Building (also known as 'the Mac') features an extensive collection of designs by Mackintosh and other celebrated alumni. Other campus buildings include the Newbery Tower, Foulis Building, the Richmond Building, the Barnes Building, the Bourdon Building and the Assembly Building. The digital design studio is located within the House for an Art Lover. Tel: 0141 353 4500.

Glasgow Science Centre Pacific Quay, Glasgow. Opened in 2001 and housed in three buildings by the River Clyde, the centre features a multitude of interactive exhibits plus the Scottish Power Planetarium, an IMAX cinema, Science Show Theatre, Climate Change Theatre and the Glasgow Tower. The exhibits are laid out in the Science Mall over three floors. The Glasgow Tower stands 344ft (105m) high and features the 'sky high cabin', capable of turning through 360 degrees from the ground up and offering spectacular views over Glasgow. Tel: 0871 540 1005.

Glasgow Underground The Glasgow underground railway system was opened on 14 December 1896, making it the world's third oldest after London and Budapest. Having been forced to close the same day because of problems and accidents, it was reopened on 21 January 1897. Officially known as 'The Subway', the sytem is also known familiarly as 'The U', 'The Clockwork Orange' or 'The Orange', owing to the fact that the trains originally had an orange livery (now replaced by carmine and white) and the stations were marked by large illuminated orange 'U' for Underground signs. The circular system above and below the River Clyde has remained unexpanded since its inception, it was originally powered by a clutch and cable system before being electrified in the 1930s. There are 15 stations: Govan, Partick, Kelvinhall, Hillhead, Kelvinbridge, St George's Cross, Cowcaddens, Buchanan Street, St Enoch, Bridge Street, West Street, Shields Road, Kinning Park, Cessnock and Ibrox. Now owned and operated by the Strathclyde Partnership for Transport, the system was modernised and the stations refurbished between 21 May 1977 and 16 April 1980.

Glenbarr Abbey Glenbarr, 10½ (17km) miles northwest of Campbelown. An 18th century house now known as Barr House and housing the MacAlister Clan visitor centre. There are also collections of china, toys, jewellery and thimbles. Tel: 01583 421247.

Glengorm Castle 4 miles (6km) northwest of Tobermory, Mull. Built in 1860 and situated on the northern tip of the Isle of Mull, Glengorm Castle overlooks the Atlantic and has views over 60 miles (100km) to the Outer Hebrides and Islands of Skye, Rhum and Canna. It sits at the headland of Glengorm (G. = The Blue Glen), a vast area of coastline, forestry, lochs and hills. Tel: 01688 302321.

Greenan Castle 2 miles (3km) southwest of Ayr. The ruins of an early 17th century tower, standing on cliff tops overlooking Ayr Bay and possibly built by John Kennedy on the site of earlier earthworks which may have been a motte.

Greenbank Garden Flenders Road, Clarkston, Glasgow. A 2½ acre (1ha) walled garden surrounded by woodland and adjacent to 18th century Greenbank House. There are over 3500 named plants, including collections of narcissus and bergenia. The house and land were given to the National Trust for Scotland in 1976. Tel: 0141 616 5126.

Gylen Castle Located at the southern end of Kerrera island. Gylen Castle (G. *caisteal nan geimhlean* = Castle of the Springs) was built in 1587 by chieftain Duncan MacDougall of Dunollie and destroyed in 1647 during the Covenanting Wars by General Leslie's army. Protestant minister John Neave persuaded troops to slaughter every MacDougall defender. At the northern end of the 4 mile (6km) long island stands a monument to David Hutcheson, the first man to start a regular ferry service to the Hebrides. The island's other claim to fame is that Alexander II died in Horseshoe Bay in 1249 while attempting to recover the Hebrides from Haakon IV of Norway.

Hampden Park Letherby Drive, Glasgow. Scotland's national football stadium, although owned by Queen's Park Football Club. The club had owned two previous grounds of the same name before the current one was opened. The first match, against Celtic, was played on 31 October 1903. The stadium was almost immediately adopted for home matches by the Scottish national team, with Scotland beating England 2–1 in 1906. It also became the venue for Scottish FA Cup finals. Queen's Park still owns the stadium, which was largely rebuilt and modernised in the 1990s, but it is leased to the Scottish Football Association and has been operated by Hampden Park Ltd since April 2000. Record attendances include the 149,547 who saw Scotland beat England 3–1 on 17 April 1937. Its current seating capacity is 52,000. In addition to football matches the stadium acts as a concert venue and hosts other sports such as rugby union and American football. Hampden was also home to the Glasgow Tigers speedway team 1969–72.

Hebridean Whale and Dolphin Trust Main Street, Tobermory, Mull. Established in 1994 to study the distribution, behaviour and ecology of whales and dolphins around the Hebrides.

Highest point Ben Cruachan at 3694ft (1126m), the high point of the Cruachan Horseshoe, a ring of mountains surrounding the reservoir of Cruachan Power Station (see separate entry), which is built within the mountain. The horseshoe includes a further Munro, Stob Diamh (3274ft/998m), the Corbett of Beinn a'Bhuiridh (2943ft/897m), and several subsidiary summits.

Hill House Upper Colquhoun Street, Helensburgh. A house overlooking the Clyde Estuary designed in 1902 for publisher Walter Blackie by Charles Rennie Mackintosh, who also designed the garden and the house's furnishings. There is a gallery displaying the works of contemporary artists and designers. The house was donated to the National Trust for Scotland in 1982. Tel: 01436 673900.

Holmwood House — Netherlee Road, Cathcart, Glasgow. A villa designed in 1858 by Alexander 'Greek' Thomson for paper-mill owner James Couper. It is now the base for the Alexander Thomson Society and houses a study centre dedicated to his work. The gardens cover 5 acres (2ha). The house was acquired by the National Trust for Scotland in 1994 and its original decoration is undergoing restoration. Tel: 0141 637 2129.

Holy Island — Situated in Lamlash Bay off the coast of Arran. An island with a continuing spiritual tradition, its earliest association is with 6th century monk St Molaise, whose cave – excavated in the early 20th century and again in the 1990s – contains several runic inscriptions carved by Viking visitors and dating to the 12th and 13th centuries. The island is now home to the Buddhist Centre for World Peace and Health, opened in 2003. Area: 1.02 sq miles (2.64 sq km). Population: 13. GR: NS060300.

House for an Art Lover — Dumbreck Road, Glasgow. A house built in the 1990s in Bellahouston Park to designs submitted by Charles Rennie Mackintosh in 1901 as an entry to a competition run by German design magazine *Deutsche Kunst*. Although the entry was late and therefore disqualified, the designs garnered a special prize. The idea of actually building the house was put forward by engineer Graham Roxburgh; the rooms have been created by contemporary artists and craftsmen using Mackintosh's original design portfolio as a guide. Featured rooms include the dining room, music room and oval room. The Glasgow School of Art Digital Design Studio is also based in the house. Tel: 0141 353 4770.

Hunter House Museum — Maxwellton Road, Calderwood, East Kilbride. A museum dedicated to pioneering medical brothers John and William Hunter and housed in their former home. Exhibits include medical instruments and a lifelike body employed to explain 18th century medical practice. Tel: 01355 261261.

Hunterian Museum and Art Gallery — A museum and art gallery split over three sites within the University of Glasgow – the museum (Main/Gilbert-Scott Building, University Avenue), the art gallery (Hillhead Street) and the zoology museum (Graham Kerr Building) – and originally created around the varied collections of William Hunter, including fine art, coins, manuscripts, plus medical, geological, botanical and zoological items, bequeathed to the university in 1783. Hunter also left a sum of money to build a museum to house the collection. The new museum, designed by William Stark in classical style, was opened in 1807 and is the oldest in Scotland. The art gallery features a recreation of the Mackintosh House, a recreation of interiors from 6 Florentine Terrace, Glasgow, the home of Charles Rennie Mackintosh 1906–14, and including the original furniture designed by Mackintosh himself. The house and furniture were bought by the University of Glasgow in 1946 but the building had to be demolished in 1963. The proportions and sequence of rooms in the gallery closely reflect the layout of the original house. The museum underwent refurbishment in preparation for its bicentenary in 2007. Museum, tel: 0141 330 4221; Art Gallery, tel: 0141 330 5431; Zoology Museum, tel: 0141 330 4772.

Hunterston Castle — 5 miles (8km) south of Largs. A 13th century pele tower located on the North Ayrshire coast. The home of Clan Hunter, it was extended in the 16th and 17th centuries.

Hunterston Power Stations — 5 miles (8km) south of Largs. There are two nuclear power stations at the site: Hunterston A and Hunterston B. Hunterston A is a Magnox reactor, opened in 1964 and closed in 1990. It is currently being decommissioned by the Nuclear Decommissioning Authority. Hunterston B was opened in 1976 and has two advanced gas-cooled reactors. Operated by British Energy Plc, it is due to be decommissioned in 2016.

Hutcheson's Hall — Ingram Street, Glasgow. Designed by David Hamilton and built 1802–05, incorporating statuary from a 17th century hospice built by Thomas and George Hutcheson. The hall was acquired by the National Trust for Scotland in 1982. Tel: 0141 552 8391.

Inchgalbraith Castle — Ruined medieval castle of the Galbraith family, situated on an island of the same name in Loch Lomond.

India of Inchinnan — Inchinnan, 4 miles (6km) north of Paisley. An Art Deco style administration block built in 1930 for the India of Inchinnan tyre company. The adjacent factory, built by India Tyres of Akron, Ohio, was opened in 1927 on a site formerly occupied by an airship construction station on which four airships were built – including the R34, the first flying craft to cross the Atlantic east–west (it also made a return trip) – before its closure in 1922. The tyre factory was bought out by local businessmen Andrew Melville and Walter Naismith in 1929 after the Wall Street Crash, the company itself being bought by Dunlop in 1933 and eventually closed in 1981. The building was restored in 1999 and is now occupied by Graham Technology. A Rolls-Royce factory was opened on the old factory site in 2004.

Innis Chonnel Castle — See Ardchonell Castle.

Interesting facts — **St John's Cathedral, Oban** is unique in being the only cathedral in Britain which is only part built. Work finished when funds were exhausted in August 1910, and by then only the sanctuary, chancel, one transept and one bay of the nave were completed. Several attempts to raise sufficient funds to complete the cathedral have foundered, although local residents raised funds to make the cathedral safe in 1988. Any donations would be gratefully received! The **PS *Waverley***, built in Glasgow in 1947 and now based at Finnieston, near the city centre, is the world`s last sea-going paddleship. Immensely popular with Glaswegians and visitors alike, it travels in the Clyde waters, off the west coast – and even around southern England – during the summer months. The **Clachan Inn**, on a corner of The Square, Drymen, north of Glasgow, carries a sign proclaiming that it was first licensed in 1734, making it the oldest pub in Scotland. Another interesting pub is The **Horseshoe Bar**, Drury Street, Glasgow. It lays claim to being the busiest pub in Scotland and has the longest continuous island bar in Europe at 114ft (34.7m). **Strathclyde** is a fairly amorphous region both geographically and historically but it has a distinct love of castles – in fact it contains more castles than any other area of Britain or Ireland, 100 in total. **Moira Cameron** from Argyll made history in 2007 when she became the first woman to become a Yeoman Warder of the Tower of London. The 42-year-old donned the traditional scarlet and blue livery and took up her duties as a Beefeater after serving 25 years in the army. **Colonsay** experienced its first burglary in living memory in November 2006 when a visiting workman stole £60 from a local pensioner's cottage. The last crime of any nature on the tiny island had been a joyriding incident in 2004. The **Largs Viking Festival** was instituted in 1980 to celebrate the Scottish victory over the Vikings at the Battle of Largs in 1263, which marked the end of the last Viking invasion of Britain. Beginning as a re-enactment of the battle by the local Viking Society, it now lasts a week in early September each year. The much-maligned planning of the **Cumbernauld town centre**, which has twice received the 'Plook on the Plinth' award for Scotland's worst architecture, surprisingly made the short list of the 10 most treasured places in Scotland in a 2007 survey carried out by the Royal Commission on the Ancient and Historical Monuments of Scotland (RCAHMS) to help celebrate its centenary in 2008. The area around the Antonine Shopping Centre has been severely criticised by local residents for its Art Brut décor. The North Lanarkshire town centre eventually came bottom of the top 10.

Inveraray Castle
$^{1}/_{2}$ mile (0.8km) north of Inveraray, 20 miles (32km) north of Dunoon. An 18th century castle overlooking Loch Fyne built on the site of an earlier fortification. The seat of the Dukes of Argyll, it was commissioned by the 3rd Duke and built by the 5th Duke in the 1760s to plans originally drawn up by Sir John Vanbrugh in the 1720s and revised by Roger Morris and William Adam. It was completed in 1789 by Adam's sons John and Robert. Four conical spires were added in the late 19th century after a fire in 1877 destroyed some of the upper rooms. Rooms include the state dining room, the tapestry drawing room, the armoury hall, the saloon, the Victorian room and the MacArthur room; there is also a room devoted to the history of Clan Campbell. Items on display include fine art, tapestries, porcelain, arms and armour, and photographs. The castle is surrounded by 16 acres (6.5ha) of parkland, woodland and gardens. Tel: 01499 302203.

Inveraray Jail
Church Square, Inveraray. A visitor centre and museum housed in the village's old courthouse and prison, closed in the 1930s. The courtroom, old prison and new prison have been restored and the experience of crime, trial and punishment in the 19th century recreated with the aid of mannequins. Tel: 01499 302381.

Inveraray Maritime Experience
The Pier, Inveraray. A maritime museum housed in the three-masted schooner *Arctic Penguin*, one of the last iron sailing ships, built in 1911 and now moored at Inveraray Pier. Exhibits include a celebration of the life of Neil Munro of the *Vital Spark*. Another member of the 'fleet' is the puffer *Eilean Eisdeal*, built in Hull in 1944. Tel: 01499 302213.

Iona Abbey
Iona. A monastery on the site was first established by St Columba in the 6th century, its monks being responsible for producing the Book of Kells and the Chronicle of Ireland. During the 9th century the community was subject to repeated attacks by Viking raiders. The first stone abbey of c.1200 was dedicated to St Columba, with a church dedicated to St Mary. The abbey was damaged during the Reformation and was in ruins by the 17th century. Restoration began in the late 19th century; continued until 1938 by the Iona Cathedral Trust and thereafter by the resident Iona community, it was completed in 1965. The abbey's infirmary now houses a museum with a collection of Christian carved stones, including the restored 9th century Cross of St John the Evangelist. The buildings have been in the care of Historic Scotland since 2002. John Smith, leader of the Labour Party, was buried at Iona in 1994.

Iona Heritage Centre
Iona. Opened in 1990 in the former Church of Scotland manse, the centre charts the secular history of the island.

Iona Nunnery
Iona. The ruins of an early 13th century Augustinian priory dedicated to St Mary or St Oran. It was dissolved in the 16th century following the Reformation. Unlike the nearby abbey it has not been restored, but the ruins are surrounded by a peaceful garden.

Islands
See separate table for a list of the more than 800 islands of Strathclyde, many forming part of the Inner Hebrides. All the islands of Strathclyde are in Argyll & Bute apart from Perch Rock in Dumbarton, and those in the Firth of Clyde and Millport Bay, which belong to Ayrshire.

James Watt College
Finnart Street, Greenock. A further and higher education college opened as the James Watt Memorial College in 1907 and originally funded by Andrew Carnegie. There are four campuses: Finnart, Waterfront, North Ayrshire and Largs. Tel: 01475 724433.

John Hastie Museum
Threestanes Road, Strathaven. A local history museum on the edge of Strathaven Park charting the story of the local community of farmers and weavers from the 17th to the 20th century. The collection was begun by businessman John Hastie and the museum was established by his bequest on his death in 1899. Tel: 01357 521257.

Johnstone Castle
Tower Place, Johnstone. A 16th century fortalice originally belonging to the Cochrane family and known as Easter Cochran. The name was changed when it came into possession of the Houston family in the 1730s. The original tower was castellated and enlarged during the 18th and 19th century, and Frédéric Chopin was a notable house guest in 1848. Most of the mansion had fallen into disrepair by the end of World War II and it was demolished during the 1950s. The remains, including the original tower, are now surrounded by a housing estate also known as Johnstone Castle.

Jura House Walled Garden
Craighouse, Isle of Jura. An organically run garden surrounding Jura House, built by the Campbells in the late 18th century, and sheltered by a 16ft (5m) high stone wall. The plants include an Australasian collection. Tel: 01496 820315.

Kames Castle
2 miles (3km) northwest of Rothesay, Isle of Bute. A majestic tower house overlooking Kames Bay. Built by the Bannatyne family in the 14th century and surrounded by 20 acres (8ha) of beautiful grounds, it is one of the oldest continuously inhabited houses in Scotland.

Keills Chapel and Cross 12 miles (19km) southwest of Lochgilphead. A restored chapel housing a collection of early and late medieval stone slabs including the Keills Cross, dating to the 9th century and carved in Celtic style with interwoven designs. Maintained by Historic Scotland.

Keir Hardie Memorial Glaisnock Street, Cumnock. A bronze bust of North Lanarkshire-born James Keir Hardie, founder of the Labour Party. It stands outside Cumnock Town Hall and was unveiled in 1939.

Kelburn Castle 1½ miles (2.5km) south of Largs. The seat of the Boyle family, Earls of Glasgow, who first erected a fortification on the site overlooking the Firth of Clyde in the 12th century. Originally a late 16th century Z-plan tower to which a mansion was added in the 18th century. The surrounding estate includes Kelburn Glen, with woodland and waterfalls on the Kel Burn. Tel: 01475 568685.

Kelvin Hall Argyle Street, Glasgow. Opened in 1927 as an exhibition centre and hosted a regular circus among other activities. It was converted to its present condition in 1987 and it now houses the Museum of Transport and the International Sports Arena. Tel: 0141 357 2525.

Kelvingrove Art Gallery and Museum Argyle Street, Glasgow. One of the city's most popular attractions, the museum and gallery opened on 2 May 1901 as part of the Glasgow International Exhibition; the building was funded by profits from a previous International Exhibition held in 1888. The design of the red sandstone building has been described as 'Spanish Baroque'. Early exhibits included Old Master paintings collected by Archibald McLellan (1797–1854) and which can still be seen. Artists exhibited include Botticelli, Dalí, Monet, Picasso, Rembrandt and Van Gogh. Other areas covered include natural history, geology, arms and armour, prehistory and ancient Egypt. There is also a restored Spitfire on view. Tel: 0141 276 9599.

Kelvingrove Park Glasgow's first public park, created in the 1850s and designed by Sir Joseph Paxton. It covers 85 acres (34ha) and is split by the River Kelvin. It was the site of International Exhibitions in 1888 and 1901 and of the Scottish National Exhibition in 1911. Monuments in the park include the Stewart Memorial Fountain, dedicated to the memory of Robert Stewart, Lord Provost 1851–4, designed in French Gothic style and erected in 1872; there are also a number of statues, including Joseph Lister and Field Marshal Lord Roberts.

Kempock Stone Kempock Point, Gourock. Known locally as Granny Kempock's Stone. A monolith 6ft (1.8m) high and 2ft (0.6m) wide, and said to resemble a hooded old woman – hence the name. It was used as a landmark for shipping until it became obscured by buildings.

Kerelaw Castle Stevenston, 4 miles (6km) northwest of Irvine. The ruins of a 12th century castle built by the Lockhart family and standing above the town. It was rebuilt in the 15th century but abandoned by the late 18th century.

Kilchurn Castle ½ mile (0.8km) northeast of Lochawe, 17 miles (27km) east of Oban. The ruins of a 15th century castle on a promontory on Loch Awe. A seat of the Campbell family, the original five-storey tower house with walled courtyard was enlarged during the 16th and 17th centuries. Round towers and barrack blocks were added when the castle was substantially remodelled by John Campbell, 1st Earl of Breadalbane, in 1693. It housed garrisons of Government troops during the Jacobite uprisings. In the 1760s the top of one of the towers was apparently dislodged by a lightning strike and within ten years it was completely abandoned and in a state of disrepair. It passed into state care in 1951 and is maintained by Historic Scotland. Access is currently restricted to visitors by boat from Lochawe.

Kildalton Chapel and Crosses 7 miles (11km) northeast of Port Ellen, Islay. The restored ruins of the old Kildalton parish church, which stood on the site of an earlier foundation. In the old graveyard stands a high cross probably dating to the late 8th century, carved from grey-green epidiorite and 9ft (2.7m) high with arms 4ft (1.2m) in width. The shaft and cross-head are carved with spiral and knotwork designs incorporating serpents, birds and lions. There are also scenes of the Virgin and Child with angels, Cain killing Abel, and the sacrifice of Isaac by Abraham. Nearby stands a medieval cross known as The Thief's Cross.

Kildonan Castle Kildonan, 9 miles (15km) south of Brodick, Arran. The ruins of a 13th or 14th century tower house on cliffs overlooking the Sound of Pladda on the southern tip of the Isle of Arran. It was at one time a MacDonald stronghold and eventually passed to the Earls of Arran. The hunting seat of the Scottish kings when Arran was a Crown property, it is now an ivy-clad ruin. Kildonan was named after an Irish monk who lived in the town in the 6th century.

Kilmarnock Castle See Dean Castle.

Kilmartin Castle Kilmartin, 7 miles (11km) north of Lochgilphead. A 16th century Z-plan tower house, thought to have been built c.1580 by Neil Campbell, Rector of Kilmartin and later home to John Carswell, Bishop of the Isles, before he occupied Carnasserie Castle. In ruins for several hundred years, it has recently been restored and is privately owned.

Kilmartin Glen A remarkable historic landscape surrounding the village of Kilmartin, and including cup and ring-marked stones, Neolithic and Bronze Age monuments, and medieval castles. Most notable is a Bronze Age 'linear cemetery' of five cairns stretching for 3 miles (5km). From north to south the cairns are: Glebe Cairn, 100ft (30m) in diameter and 10ft (3m) high, first excavated in 1864, when two burials and a jet necklace were found; Nether Largie North Cairn, containing a stone-lined burial chamber decorated with cup and ring marks and depictions of axe heads. The cairn has been reconstructed and the burial chamber can be entered via a trapdoor; Nether Largie Mid Cairn, 100ft (30m) in diameter, excavated in 1929 but badly damaged by the removal of stones for building; Nether Largie South Cairn, a Neolithic chambered cairn dating to c.3000 BC, originally 130ft (40m) in diameter and 13ft (4m) high but also damaged by the removal of building stone. Its inner chamber is 20ft (6m) long and 7ft (2m) wide; Ri Cruin Cairn, originally 63ft (19m) in diameter, dating to c.2000 BC and also featuring carved axe-head designs. Other monuments include Ballymeanoch stone row, consisting of two lines of four and two (originally three) standing stones, and associated with a cairn; and Temple Wood stone circle, a 40ft (12m) circle of 13 stones dating originally to c.3000 BC, when there may have been 22 stones, and a smaller circle to the north, consisting of a ring of river stones. Kilmartin Church has a notable collection of grave slabs. There is also a museum in Kilmartin House in the village. See also Cairnbaan Cup and Ring Marks, Carnasserie Castle, Dunadd Fort, Kilmartin Castle.

Kilmory Castle	1 mile (1.6km) south of Lochgilphead. A Gothic-style mansion with an octagonal tower, built in the 1830s by John Orde on the site of an earlier 19th century house constructed by the Campbells. The house now contains the headquarters of Argyll & Bute Council. Located beside Loch Gilp, it stands within gardens laid out in the 18th century and extended in the 19th, and noted for their collections of rhododendrons and hardy ferns. Tel: 01546 602127.
Kilmory Knap Chapel	13 miles (21km) southwest of Lochgilphead. A restored chapel roofed with glass in 1934 and housing a number of late medieval sculptured stones and grave slabs. These include the MacMillan Cross, which originally stood in the graveyard and which is inscribed '+hec est crux Alexandri Macmulen', with a crucifixion and sword on one face and a hunting scene on the other. The chapel is in the care of Historic Scotland.
Kilmun Collegiate Church	2 miles (3km) north of Dunoon. The ruins of a collegiate church on the northern shore of Holy Loch, built in the 1440s and dedicated to St Fintan (also known as St Mun or Mund). The main remaining structure is a tower standing 40ft (12m) high. A parish church was built adjacent to the tower in 1841.
Kilwinning Abbey	Main Street, Kilwinning. A Tironensian Benedictine abbey possibly founded by either Hugh or Richard de Morville in the second half of the 12th century. The abbey fell into disrepair following the Reformation; the church was used as a parish church until 1775 and the tower fell in 1814 having been struck by lightning five years earlier. A new parish church was built on part of the site, while a tower built in 1851 now houses a heritage centre dedicated to the history of the abbey and the town of Kilwinning. Now in the care of Historic Scotland.
Kingencleugh Castle	$1^1/_2$ miles (2km) south of Mauchline, 10 miles (16km) northeast of Ayr. The scant remains of a 16th century castle built by the Campbells.
Largs Museum	Kirkgate House, Manse Court, Largs. A local history museum featuring a programme of changing exhibitions as well as a collection of Mauchline Ware. Tel: 01475 687081.
Law Castle	$^1/_4$ mile (0.4km) east of West Kilbride. Aka the Tower of Kilbride. Tower house built in 1468 by Thomas Boyd for his new wife Mary, sister of James III, and recently restored.
Leadhills & Wanlockhead Railway	Leadhills, 17 miles (27km) southwest of Biggar. Britain's highest adhesion railway, reaching 1498ft (456m) above sea level on the Dumfries and Galloway/Lanarkshire border. The 2ft (610mm) narrow gauge railway operates for 0.6 miles (1km) on a line originally built in 1900 by the Caledonian Railway Company to transport refined lead, and closed in the 1930s following the closure of the lead mines. The Leadhills & Wanlockhead Railway Society was formed in 1983 and a limited service began in 1988, a station at Leadhills having been built from scratch. There is a Museum of Lead Mining at Wanlockhead.
Leadhills Miners Library	Main Street, Leadhills, 17 miles (27km) southwest of Biggar. The oldest subscription library in the British Isles, opened in 1741. The original members met once a month to exchange books. Similar reading societies were established nearby at Wanlockhead in 1756 and Westerkirk in 1792. The library was closed in 1965 but was reopened in 1972 thanks to the efforts of the local community.
Lighthouse, The	Mitchell Lane, Glasgow. An architecture and design centre opened in July 1999 in a conversion of Charles Rennie Mackintosh's *Glasgow Herald* newspaper office, built in 1895 and his first major commission. The six-floor centre features exhibitions, a Charles Rennie Mackintosh interpretation centre and a dedicated education floor. Tel: 0141 221 6362.
Linn Botanic Gardens	Cove, $7^1/_2$ miles (12km) west of Helensburgh. A garden developed in the 1970s around a gully of Meikle Burn on land surrounding a 19th century house above the Linn. Tel: 01436 842242.
Loch Doon Castle	14 miles (23km) southeast of Maybole. Late 13th century enclosure castle built by the Earls of Carrick and originally located on an island in Loch Doon; it was rebuilt on the western shore of the loch 1934–5 when the water level was raised to provide hydroelectric power.
Loch Lomond	The largest freshwater loch in the UK, with a surface area of 27.4 sq miles (71 sq km) and a volume of 572 billion gallons (2.6 billion cu m). It is crossed by the Highland fault line and the surrounding terrain changes dramatically from south to north. There are numerous islands in its waters: see separate table.
Loch Lomond & Trossachs National Park	See Central.
Loch Lomond Seaplanes	The only commercial seaplane service in Scotland. Starting in 2004, it is based on Loch Lomond and has planes which can set down on both land and water. The company offers services to such destinations as Loch Linnhe, Loch Earn, Loch Tay, Loch Voil, Loch Fyne, Jura and Islay. A seaplane service from the River Clyde in the heart of Glasgow began in 2007.
Loch Thom	2 miles (3km) southwest of Greenock. A reservoir built in the mid 1820s to supply clean water to Greenock, designed by Robert Thom (1774–1847) and originally known as the Great Reservoir or Little Caspian before being renamed after its designer. The water leaves the reservoir through the Compensation Reservoir and is taken to its destination across the Greenock Cut aqueduct, known as 'The Cut'.
Lochranza Castle	$10^1/_2$ miles (17km) north of Brodick, Arran. Late 13th century L-plan tower which was once a hunting lodge of Scottish kings. It was reconstructed in the 16th century and raised in height. Garrisoned by both James VI and Cromwell, it had fallen into ruin by the 18th century. According to some sources it was the inspiration for Hergé's Tintin adventure *The Black Island*.
Loudoun Castle	$^3/_4$ mile (1.2km) north of Galston, 5 miles (8km) east of Kilmarnock. The ruins of an early 19th

century mansion incorporating elements of much earlier buildings. The earliest fortification possibly dates from the 12th century and a 16th century keep which stood here was damaged during a siege by General Monck. The castle was rebuilt for Flora Mure-Campbell 1804–11, but was destroyed by fire in 1941 and now stands within the grounds of Loudoun Castle Theme Park. In its heyday the castle was known as the 'Windsor of Scotland' and was said to be haunted by three ghosts – the Grey Lady, a phantom piper and a monk.

Low Parks Museum Muir Street, Hamilton. A local history museum housed in a 17th century building which served as a coaching inn (the Hamilton Arms) in the early 19th century. There are exhibits relating to the social history of the area, and in particular telling the story of the now demolished Hamilton Palace. The house was bought by Hamilton Town Council in 1964 and restored in the late 1990s. To the rear is the Regimental Museum of the Cameronians.

Machrie Moor Stone Circles 7 miles (11km) southwest of Brodick, Arran. A group of five Bronze Age stone circles dating to c.1800–1600 BC. Their differing layout and design suggests that they were erected at various periods and there is evidence (including the existence of hut circles to the west) to indicate that the site was occupied during the Neolithic period. **Machrie Moor 1**: a group of 11 (possibly originally 12) stones set in an ellipse. Six of the stones are granite and the other five are sandstone; **Machrie Moor 2**: originally a group of seven or eight standing stones in a circle, of which only three survive intact; **Machrie Moor 3**: originally consisted of nine stones, only one of which remains standing; **Machrie Moor 4**: four rounded boulders forming an ellipse; **Machrie Moor 5**: ten upright stones revealed by excavation in 1978.

Mackintosh House See Hunterian Art Gallery.

Macquarie Mausoleum Gruline, 10 miles (16km) southeast of Tobermory, Mull. The mausoleum of Ulva-born Lachlan Macquarie, the first Governor of New South Wales and known as the 'father of Australia'. Maintained by the National Trust for Scotland on behalf of the National Trust of Australia (New South Wales).

Marymass Festival An annual festival held in Irvine in August, inaugurated by the town's carters in the medieval period and possibly dating to the 12th century. In the 1920s the tradition was established of choosing a Marymass Queen, four ladies-in-waiting (four Marys) and two page boys. In the afternoon there are horse races on the moor followed by the parade with decorated horses and floats. No motorised vehicles are allowed in the parade.

Martyrs' School Parson Street, Glasgow. The first building designed by Charles Rennie Mackintosh, commissioned in 1895 once he had completed his apprenticeship with the firm of Honeyman & Keppie. The school was opened in 1897 for children from the surrounding district of Townhead. Restored in 1999, the building now houses offices for Glasgow Museums staff. Tel: 0141 553 2557.

Mauchline Castle Mauchline, 7 miles (11km) southeast of Kilmarnock. Aka Abbot Hunter's Tower. A 15th century tower house used as a monastic residence by Melrose Abbey. Once the abbey was secularised following the Reformation, the building was remodelled and dwelling houses added. Robert Burns reportedly married Jean Armour here.

Maybole Castle High Street, Maybole. The oldest inhabited house in the town, dating to c.1560, the L-plan turreted tower house was the town house of the Kennedy family, Earls of Cassillis. Having fallen into disrepair by the early 19th century, it was partly demolished to make way for a new road; the remainder was repaired and reoccupied by the Earl and his family. It is now occupied by offices.

McCaig's Tower Battery Hill, Oban. Aka McCaig's Folly. A structure overlooking Oban, resembling the Colosseum in Rome and forming a prominent landmark above the town. Built 1895–1900 by banker and philanthropist John Stuart McCaig (1824–1902) as a monument to his family and as a scheme to keep local stonemasons in employment during the winter months, it was left unfinished at his death, when his family abandoned the project. Its circumference is more than 600ft (183m) and it features 94 pointed arches arranged in two tiers. It was proposed that statues of McCaig family members should be added, but these were never put in place and an envisaged art gallery and museum were also never begun.

McLean Museum and Art Gallery Kelly Street, Greenock. A museum and art gallery originally established in the early 19th century. The museum building was funded by Greenock-born timber merchant James McLean (1802–77) and opened in 1876, shortly before his death in January 1877. The wide-ranging collections cover ancient Egypt, world culture – items collected by ships' captains on the museum's behalf – and natural history. The art gallery has an excellent collection of fine art including paintings, prints and sculptures. There is also a photographic archive. Tel: 01475 715624.

McLellan Galleries Sauchiehall Street, Glasgow. Built in 1856 by Archibald McLellan and purchased by Glasgow City Council on his death. The galleries were severely damaged by fire in the 1980s but were subsequently restored and reopened in 1990 as a state-of-the-art temporary exhibition space. Situated on a busy shopping thoroughfare, the galleries are not permanently in use. Tel: 0141 565 4137.

Mitchell Library North Street, Glasgow. Familiarly known as The Mitchell. Founded in 1877 as a general library for the people of Glasgow, and now reputedly the largest public reference library in Europe, it was established with a bequest from tobacco manufacturer Stephen Mitchell (1789–1874) and eventually moved into a newly designed building in North Street in 1911. An extension building, created from the former St Andrew's Halls, was opened in 1982 to accommodate the library's ever-growing collection. It began a lending library facility in 2005 and there is also a genealogy centre. Tel: 0141 287 2999.

Moat Park Heritage Centre Kirkstyle, Biggar. A local history museum with scale model displays recreating local archaeological sites dating from the Neolithic era, the Bronze and Iron Ages, the Roman and medieval periods and the 17th century. Other exhibits include fine art and photographs. Tel: 01899 221059.

Motherwell Cathedral — Coursington Road, Motherwell. Roman Catholic cathedral founded in 1875 and consecrated in 1900. Dedicated to Our Lady of Good Aid, its outstanding feature is a window depicting the traditional Tree of Jesse, the ancestry of Christ as described in Matthew 2: 5–16. Tel: 01698 258116.

Motoring Heritage Centre — Main Street, Alexandria. Located in the Loch Lomond Outlet Shopping Centre, which is housed in a large Edwardian red sandstone building built in 1905 as the Argyll Motor Works and at that time the largest motor vehicle factory in the world. The centre tells the story of Scotland's motoring history. Cars on display include an Argyll 12.4, an Arrol-Johnston Pearl, a Ford GT40, a Model T Ford, a JP and a Chrysler Sunbeam. Tel: 01389 607862.

Mount Stuart — 3 miles (5km) south of Rothesay, Bute. A 19th century house built on the site of an earlier property built in 1719 and destroyed by fire in 1877. The seat of the Stuarts of Bute, the spectacular Gothic-style mansion was designed by Robert Rowand Anderson for John Crichton-Stuart the 3rd Marquess of Bute. Unfinished during Crichton-Stuart's lifetime, work was completed in the late 20th century and the house was opened to the public in 1995. Notable rooms include the 80ft (24m) high Marble Hall with stained glass windows depicting signs of the zodiac, the Marble Chapel, lined with white Carrara marble, the dining room, featuring elaborate oak carving, the Gallery, with its vaulted ceiling, and the Horoscope Room and Conservatory, the ceiling of which depicts the positions of the planets at the 3rd Marquess's birth in 1847. The house is surrounded by 300 acres (120ha) of grounds including a 19th century 'wee garden' of 5 acres (2ha), a kitchen garden designed in the 1990s and 2000s, pinetums, a lime tree avenue and an 1890s rock garden. There is also a walk replicating the Via Dolorosa using pools and cascades on the Racers Burn. A new visitor centre, opened in 2001, received the 2002 RIBA Award and was shortlisted for the Stirling Prize; a new garden was planted to complement it. Tel: 01700 503877.

Moy Castle — Lochbuie, 10 miles (16km) southwest of Craignure, Isle of Mull. Three-storey tower built above a natural spring in the 15th century by the MacLaines of Lochbuie. The castle is not open to the public.

Mull & West Highland Railway — Craignure, Mull. The only island passenger railway in Scotland, operating for $1^1/_4$ miles (2km) from Craignure to Torosay. The railway was purpose-built in 1984 to provide transport to and from Torosay Castle and Duart Castle for visitors arriving by ferry. Locomotives currently or formerly in use on the service are *Lady of the Isles* (steam), Green Diesel, *Glen Audlyn* (diesel), Waverley 4-4-2 *Atlantic* (steam), Victoria 2-6-2T (steam) and *Frances* (diesel).

Mull Museum — Columba Buildings, Tobermory, Mull. A local history museum charting the history of the Isle of Mull from prehistoric times to the present day. Exhibits include archive photographs and craft implements. Tel. 01688 302493.

Mull of Kintyre Lighthouse — 13 miles (21km) southwest of Campbeltown. Founded in 1788 and one of the first lighthouses to be established by the Northern Lighthouse Board's Commissioners. Built by Thomas Smith, it stands 40ft (12m) high on top of a sheer cliff and around 300ft (90m) above sea level. There are 15 steps to the top of the tower. The lighthouse was automated in 1996 and the former lighthouse keeper's cottage has been converted to holiday accommodation under the auspices of the National Trust for Scotland.

Museum of An Iodhlann — Scarinish, Isle of Tiree. A museum with artefacts relating to the history of the island together with a photographic and genealogical archive. Tel: 01879 220793.

Museum of Islay Life — Port Charlotte, Islay. A local history museum housed in a former church and charting the story of Islay from the Mesolithic period until the 20th century. Exhibits include recreations of the interiors of a croft and a Victorian farmhouse, Edwardian children's toys and medieval carved grave slabs. Tel: 01496 850358.

Museum of Scottish Country Life — Kittochside, East Kilbride, 6 miles (10km) southeast of Glasgow. Opened in 2001 and dedicated to the history of Scottish rural communities and agricultural methods. The 170 acre (69ha) site includes a Georgian farmhouse and a purpose-built exhibition centre. Exhibits include agricultural implements and machinery such as an early reaping machine and combine harvesters. The museum continues the work of the Scottish Agricultural Museum, founded in 1949 at Ingliston near Edinburgh, and is run jointly by the National Museums of Scotland and the National Trust for Scotland. Wester Kittochside farm, a working concern managed using methods and equipment in practice in the 1950s, was given to the National Trust for Scotland in 1992; additional land was purchased in 1997. Tel: 01355 224181.

Museum of Transport — Bunhouse Road, Glasgow. Opened in 1964 in what is now the Tramway Theatre and moved to its current location in the Kelvin Hall in 1987, the museum's collections cover all forms of transport from cycle to ship. Cars include a selection of Scottish-built makes plus the March 701 in which Jackie Stewart won the 1971 Formula One world championship. The Clyde room has models of many famous ships built on the river, including HMS *Hood*, the *Queen Mary* and the *QE2*. Scottish railways and locomotives are well represented; along with a Glasgow tram there is a recreation of Kelvin Street station (including the subway station) in the late 1930s. The museum is due to be relocated to a purpose-built facility beside the River Clyde in 2009. Tel: 0141 287 2720.

New Lanark — A restored cotton mill village located on the eastern bank of the River Clyde and designated a UNESCO World Heritage Site in 2001. The village was founded in 1786 by David Dale around his cotton mill and developed 1800–25 by his son-in-law, social reformer Robert Owen (1771–1858), as an experiment in utopian socialism. The employees and their families were provided with a school and church, good housing and an Institute for the Formation of Character. The mills closed in 1968 and were saved by the New Lanark Conservation Trust in the 1970s. The majority of the residential buildings have been restored and the village has a resident population of around 200. Tel: 01555 661345.

Newark Castle (1) — Port Glasgow. A well-preserved castle overlooking the Firth of Clyde. The original four-storey keep was built by George Maxwell in the 15th century. Additions, including a mansion to provide more family accommodation, were made in the late 16th century. The great hall, with its several winding entrances, has been partially restored. The castle passed into state care in 1909 and is maintained by Historic Scotland.

Newark Castle (2) — Newark, 2 miles (3km) south of Ayr. Aka the New-wark of Bargany. A restored 16th century tower house with 17th and 19th century additions. The castle is in private ownership.

Newmilns Castle — Newmilns, 7 miles (11km) east of Kilmarnock. A 16th century tower built by Hugo Campbell, restored in the 1990s.

North Ayrshire Museum — Manse Street, Saltcoats. Local history museum housed in the former Ardrossan parish church, built in 1744, and dedicated to the archaeology and social and cultural history of North Ayrshire. Exhibits include artefacts, paintings and photographs. Tel: 01294 464174.

Oban Cathedrals — See St Columba Cathedral, St John's Cathedral.

Old Byre Heritage Centre — Dervaig, Mull. A local heritage centre dedicated to the history and wildlife of the Isle of Mull. Displays include a miniature model of Mull through the ages and a very large model of a midge. Tel: 01688 400229.

Paisley Abbey — Abbey Close, Paisley. A Cluniac abbey founded as a priory by Walter Fitzalan in the 1160s at Renfrew with monks from Wenlock in Shropshire. In 1245 it became an abbey dedicated to St Mary, St James, St Mirin and St Milburga. Destroyed by fire in 1307 but immediately rebuilt, it was again accidentally burned in 1498; its tower collapsed in 1553 destroying the transepts and choir. It suffered further damage during the Reformation and was secularised by the end of the 16th century, after which the nave became the parish church but the rest of the structure fell into ruin. Restoration began in the 1860s and a new church was created when the restored transepts and choir were rejoined to the nave in the early 20th century. The restoration programme is continuing, including a new timber ceiling erected in 1981. Tel: 0141 889 7654.

Paisley Cathedral — Incle Street, Paisley. Roman Catholic cathedral built in the 1930s and dedicated to St Mirin, one of the founders of Paisley Abbey.

Paisley Museum and Art Galleries — High Street, Paisley. Scotland's first municipal museum, designed by John Honeyman, funded by Peter Coats and opened in 1871. The museum is renowned for having the finest collection of Paisley shawls in the world; there are also exhibits covering the history of weaving, as well as collections of Scottish fine art and ceramics. Tel: 0141 889 3151.

Palace of Art — Bellahouston Park, Glasgow. Designed by Launcelot Ross from original sketches by Thomas S Tait and the only building retained on site from the 1938 Empire Exhibition. Originally it contained seven galleries and exhibited works by artists such as Jacob Epstein. It has been refurbished and now serves the West of Scotland Area Institute of Sport as a centre for conditioning and cardiovascular training. It also has facilities for club activities such as boxing, judo and weightlifting.

Palacerigg Country Park — Cumbernauld. A 100 acre (40ha) country park created in the mid 1970s when thousands of native species of tree were planted. The Millennium Longhouses were opened in 1998 and are used for demonstrations of woodland and other country crafts.

Peel Park — Kirkintilloch. A public park established in the late 19th century and containing a number of historical features including a medieval pele tower with moat and the site of a Roman fort which stood on the Antonine Wall. It also has an ornate bandstand built in 1905 and a fountain.

Penkill Castle — Penkill, 3 miles (5km) east of Girvan, 16 miles (26km) southwest of Ayr. A 16th century tower with 17th century additions, restored in 1857 by Spencer Boyd, 12th Laird of Penkill. The castle is privately owned.

People's Palace — Glasgow Green, Glasgow. Built in 1898, the People's Palace and Winter Gardens originally included reading and recreation rooms for the people of Glasgow as well as a museum and art gallery. It now houses a social history museum charting the story of the city and its people from the 1750s. The first floor explores Glasgow social life and entertainment, and also has displays on life in the city during the two world wars and about the Glasgow dialect. The second floor features recreations of working people's lives, plus the history of the city as painted by Ken Currie in 1987. Other exhibits range from Billy Connolly's banana boots to trade union banners. The adjacent Winter Gardens glasshouses include exotic plants. Outside is the Doulton Fountain, the largest terracotta fountain in the world. Tel: 0141 271 2962.

Piping Centre — McPhater Street, Cowcaddens, Glasgow. A national centre for bagpiping, housed in Old Cowcaddens Church, built in Italianate style in 1872. The centre was opened in 1996 and offers day and evening classes in piping, including courses leading to a degree in Scottish Music. There is also a museum and interpretation centre, and a reference library. As well as Highland bagpipes the centre also offers tuition in Scottish smallpipes, Uillean pipes, fiddle, accordion and drumming. Tel: 0141 353 0220.

Pollok Country Park — Pollokshaws Road, Glasgow. A country park south of Glasgow created from more than 350 acres (140ha) of the Old Pollok Estate and Pollok House, given to the City of Glasgow in 1966 by the Maxwell family. Divided by the White Cart Water, it has the Burrell Collection and Pollok House within its borders. Features include a walled garden, a wildlife garden and woodland walks.

Pollok House — Pollok Country Park, Glasgow. A neo-Palladian mansion beside the White Cart Water, designed by William Adam and built 1747–52 for Sir John Maxwell. The house was extended in the 1890s and was opened as a museum in 1967; there are collections of fine art, furniture, glass, silverware and ceramics. The paintings, collected by Sir William Stirling Maxwell (1818–78), include works by El Greco, Goya, Murillo and William Blake. The formal walled garden surrounding the house has notable displays of rhododendrons. The Maxwell family owned the house and estate from the 13th century until 1966 when they were presented to the people of Glasgow. The house is managed by the National Trust for Scotland on behalf of Glasgow City Council. Tel: 0141 616 6410.

Portencross Castle Portencross, $1^1/_2$ miles (2.5km) west of West Kilbride. The ruins of a 14th century castle on a promontory in the Firth of Clyde which was owned by the Ross family and later the Boyd family. A new tower was built in the 15th or 16th century. Unroofed by a storm in 1739, it became ruinous. The castle was featured in the BBC television series *Restoration* (2004).

Provand's Lordship Castle Street, Glasgow. The oldest surviving house in Glasgow, built in 1471 by Andrew Muirhead, Bishop of Glasgow, as part of the Hospital of St Nicholas, founded by the bishop for the support of 12 aged poor men. The house has seen a variety of uses since the 15th century including a priest's house, an alehouse and a sweetshop. Restored in post-medieval style, it now contains 17th century furniture from the Burrell Collection and a display about the life of a 16th century priest. Behind the house is the St Nicholas garden, created in 1997 and planted as a medical herb garden with plants used during the hospital's active life in the 15th century. Tel: 0141 552 8819.

Regimental Museum of the Cameronians Muir Street, Hamilton. Housed in the Low Parks Museum and dedicated to Scotland's only rifle regiment, whose origins stem from the arming of Covenanters in the first half of the 17th century. The regiment was formed on 14 May 1689, its name being taken from Richard Cameron, 'The Lion of the Covenant', who was killed at the battle of Airds Moss in 1680. Early in its history the regiment saw action at Dunkeld (1689) and Blenheim (1704). In 1751 the regiment was designated the 26th Regiment of Foot, The Cameronians, and in 1786 became the 26th Cameronian Regiment. During the Napoleonic Wars it took part in the retreat to Corunna (1809). During the 1st Opium War (1st Anglo-Chinese War of 1840–2) the regiment fought conspicuously at the siege of Amoy. In 1881 it was amalgamated with the 90th (Perthshire Light Infantry) to form The Cameronians (Scottish Rifles). The 90th (also known as the 'Perthshire Greybreeks') had been raised in 1794 by Thomas Graham of Balgowan as the 90th Regiment of Foot or Perthshire Volunteers, and saw action during the Napoleonic Wars, the Crimean War, the Indian Mutiny and the Zulu War of 1879. In 1815 the regiment was designated the 90th Perthshire Light Infantry. The Cameronians formed the 1st battalion of the new regiment, the Perthshires becoming the 2nd battalion. As a rifle regiment they adopted the traditional green uniform with black buttons. After seeing action during the 2nd Boer War (1899–1902) the regiment fought in many theatres of World War I including the Western Front and Gallipoli. During World War II its battalions fought as part of the BEF in France in 1939–40, in Burma and Sicily, also taking part in D-Day and the campaign in Northwest Europe. After World War II the 1st battalion was disbanded and the 2nd Battalion was redesignated the 1st. Battle honours include Blenheim, Ramilies, Oudenarde, Malplaquet, Corunna, Sevastopol, Lucknow, Ladysmith, Mons, Marne (1914–18), Neuve Chapelle, Loos, Somme (1916–18), Ypres (1917–18), Hindenburg Line, Gallipoli (1915–16), Northwest Europe (1940, 1944–5), Sicily (1943), Italy (1943–4), Chindits (1944) and Burma (1942, 1944). The Cameronians (Scottish Rifles) was disbanded in 1968. Tel: 01698 328232.

Rivers The **Clyde** is the third longest river in Scotland, rising in the Lowther Hills and running northwest from the Lanarkshire hills to the town of Greenock, falling 2000ft (600m) on its journey downstream; thereafter it turns south and becomes the Firth of Clyde. Its total length to the Firth of Clyde is 98 miles (157km). Its main tributaries in Glasgow are the River Kelvin and the White Cart Water. Glaswegians would claim it to be the country's most important river, as it flows through the most densely populated area of Scotland and has been closely connected with many of the country's industries. The well-known phrase 'Glasgow made the Clyde and the Clyde made Glasgow' reflects the role of the river in more recent centuries. It proved to be a major spur to industrial growth in the region, first providing a power source and later becoming the base for a thriving shipbuilding industry until after World War II. Like many rivers in the UK's industrial cities, the Clyde is being cleaned up and the riverside in Glasgow is now being regenerated.

The **Kelvin** is a non-tidal tributary of the River Clyde which rises in the Kilsyth Hills and reaches the Clyde west of Glasgow city centre. The four-arched Kelvin Aqueduct in Maryhill carries the Forth & Clyde Canal across the river.

Ross of Mull Historical Centre Bunessan, 23 miles (37km) west of Craignure, Mull. Local history centre with exhibits on the geology, wildlife and social history of Mull. There is also a genealogical archive. Tel: 01681 700659.

Rossdhu Castle 5 miles (8km) northeast of Helensburgh. The scant remains of a 16th century tower house built by the Clan Colquhoun and now standing near Loch Lomond Golf Course. It was abandoned c.1770, after which its stones were used for local building.

Rothesay Castle Castlehill Street, Rothesay, Bute. Founded in the 12th century as a wooden keep on a flattened motte. A circular stone curtain wall was built in the early 13th century but the walls were breached by Norwegian forces in 1230 and 1263. To strengthen the defences four towers and a new gatehouse were added in the late 13th century, giving it an unusual ground plan for a Scottish castle. One tower, known as the Pigeon Tower, was converted into a dovecot. Abandoned in the 17th century after being damaged by both Cromwellian troops in the 1650s and by the Duke of Argyll in 1685, the castle fell into disrepair, but during the 19th century successive Marquesses of Bute carried out repairs and reconstruction, including making the great hall usable. The castle passed into state care in 1961 and is maintained by Historic Scotland. Tel: 01700 502691.

Rowallan Castle $2^1/_2$ miles (4km) north of Kilmarnock. A 20th century 'castle' close to a 16th century fortification. The earlier castle (known as Rowallan Old Castle) was built by the Muir family and itself incorporated elements of a 13th century hall house and tower house reputed to have been the birthplace of Elizabeth Muir, mother of Robert II. The castle was abandoned in the late 18th century. The new castle, designed by Sir Robert Lorimer, now stands at the heart of Rowallan Castle Golf Course, designed by Colin Montgomerie.

Royal Scottish Academy of Music and Drama Renfrew Street, Glasgow. The origins of the Royal Scottish Academy of Music and Drama go back to the formation in 1847 of the Glasgow Athenaeum, which offered classes in music and, after 1886, drama. The music department became the Scottish National Academy of Music in 1929 and received royal approval in 1944, becoming the Royal Scottish National Academy of Music. The College of Dramatic Art was established in 1950, and in 1968 the Royal Scottish Academy of Music and Drama was formed as a union of the two academies. The academy has degree-awarding powers. It moved to its present address in 1988, having previously been in Buchanan Street.

Rozelle House and Galleries Rozelle Park, Monument Road, Ayr. A gallery established in Rozelle House, originally built in 1760 to a design by Robert Adam and remodelled by David Bryce in the 19th century. The house was given to the Royal Burgh of Ayr in 1968 and became the council's museum and art gallery. The Maclaurin Galleries were opened in converted stables and servants' quarters in the 1970s. The four galleries hold collections largely consisting of 20th century sculpture, paintings and drawings, and including the Tam O'Shanter collection of paintings by Alexander Goudie (1833–2004). Rozelle House also houses the Ayrshire Yeomanry museum. Tel: 01292 445447.

RSPB Loch Gruinart 15 miles (24km) north of Port Ellen, Islay. RSPB reserve on Loch Gruinart, a sea loch visited in winter by Greenland white-fronted and barnacle geese and later in the year by breeding waders such as snipe and redshank. Tel: 01496 850505.

RSPB Lochwinnoch $^{1}/_{4}$ mile (0.4km) south of Lochwinnoch, 9 miles (15km) southwest of Paisley. An RSPB reserve on Barr Loch, which lies within Clyde Muirshiel Regional Park. It is visited by whooper swans, geese and goldeneyes in winter and provides a habitat for great crested grebe and lapwing in spring. Tel: 01505 842663.

Saddell Abbey Saddell, 8 miles (13km) northeast of Campbeltown. The slight remains of a 12th or 13th century Cistercian abbey overlooking Kilbrannan Sound, founded c.1160 by Somerled. The abbey is believed to have been abandoned during the late 15th century and the buildings were later used to provide material for Saddell Castle. There is a collection of 14th to 16th century burial slabs on the site.

Saddell Castle $^{1}/_{2}$ mile (0.8km) southeast of Saddell, 8 miles (13km) northeast of Campbeltown. A four-storey tower house overlooking Saddell Bay and Kilbrannan Sound, built 1508–12 by the Bishop of Argyll. Some of the stones used in its construction were taken from the ruins of nearby Saddell Abbey. Rebuilt and enlarged over the next 200 years, the castle was abandoned at the end of the 18th century and fell into disrepair. It was bought by the Landmark Trust in 1976 and has been restored as holiday accommodation.

St Columba Cathedral Corran Esplanade, Oban. The Roman Catholic cathedral for the Diocese of Argyll & the Isles, designed by Sir Giles Gilbert Scott and built 1932–59. It replaced a temporary late 19th century building with corrugated-iron cladding and known as the 'Tin Cathedral'.

St John's Cathedral George Street, Oban. The cathedral of the historic United Diocese of Argyll & the Isles, within the Scottish Episcopal Church. The middle zone of the cathedral, designed by David Thomson after the death of his partner Charles Wilson, the original architect, was completed in 1864 and a south aisle added in 1882. In the late 19th century a new church building in Oban was planned by Bishop Chinnery-Haldane, and on his premature death in 1906 the congregation was encouraged to build this new church as his memorial. Work on the new building, designed by James Chalmers of Glasgow as a church of cathedral proportions, began on the existing site, but funds were exhausted by August 1910 befoe construction was incomplete. Two major campaigns to complete the building have been unsuccessful. One, the famous Oban Cathedral Fund Appeal run from Staten Island, New York, and spearheaded by the redoubtable Mary Alice Cisco, foundered in the Wall Street Crash. The other, led by two Highland chiefs from the diocese, Maclean of Duart and Cameron of Lochiel, only raised funds sufficient for Ian G Lindsay in 1968 to improve the existing structure, including the creation of a narthex. In 1988 the structure was stabilised after 80 years of settlement and pressures, not the least being the noise from Concorde's trial flights, which were partly monitored by movement to the cathedral structure, which lay below the flight path.

St Meddan's Church St Meddan's, situated in the Clyde Coast resort of Troon, placed fourth in a 2007 survey of more than 20,000 people to establish Scotland's most treasured landmark. The church, built in 1889, has a tall and stately spire that houses a clock which was originally part of the University of Glasgow's Old College in High Street, Glasgow.

St Mungo Museum of Religious Life and Art Castle Street, Glasgow. Housed in a building which stands on the site of the Bishop's Castle and opened in 1993, the museum is divided into four exhibition spaces: a gallery of religious art, a gallery of religious life, a Scottish gallery and a space for temporary exhibitions. Outside is a Zen garden. Tel: 0141 553 2557.

Scotland Street School Museum Scotland Street, Glasgow. A museum dedicated to the history of education in Scotland, housed in a school designed 1903–6 by Charles Rennie Mackintosh. There are reconstructions of schoolrooms from the Victorian, World War II and 1950s–60s periods. Other exhibits include reminiscences of children who attended the school between 1906 and its closure in 1979. Parts of the school, including the cookery room and drill hall, have been restored to match Mackintosh's designs, and the building reopened as a museum as part of Glasgow's European City of Culture celebrations in 1990. Tel: 0141 287 0500.

Scottish Exhibition and Conference Centre (SECC) Exhibition Way, Finnieston, Glasgow. The largest exhibition, conference and concert centre in the UK. Popularly known as 'the Glasgow Jellyfish' and covering 64 acres (26ha) on the northern bank of the River Clyde on the site of Queen's Dock, it opened in 1985. In 1997 the 3000-seat Clyde Auditorium, designed by Sir Norman Foster, was added to the complex. Because of its shape it has been nicknamed the 'Armadillo'. Hall 3 has a seating capacity of 3000 and Hall 4 can seat

8200. The development of a new 12,500-seat Glasgow Arena on the site is due for completion in 2011. Tel: 0141 248 3000.

Scottish Football Museum Hampden Park Stadium, Glasgow. Established as Scotland's national museum of football by the Scottish Football Association (SFA). Among the more than 2000 artefacts on display are a cap and ticket from the first ever football international, played between Scotland and England at the West of Scotland Cricket Ground, Hamilton Crescent, Peel Street, Partick, Glasgow, on 30 November 1872 (the result was a 0–0 draw). Trophies on display include the SFA Challenge Cup, first contested in 1874, and the Championship of the World Trophy won by Scottish Cup holders Renton in 1888 when they beat English FA Cup holders West Bromwich Albion. The museum also hosts the Hall of Fame, which honours the great Scottish players, managers and officials. Tel: 0141 616 6139.

Scottish Maritime Museum Harbourside, Irvine. Exhibits include the Linthouse Engine Shop where much of the museum's collection is on display, the harbour pontoons, a recreated shipyard worker's tenement flat and the hulk of the tall ship *Carrick* (aka *City of Adelaide*). The museum also includes exhibits of machinery, the former Longhope Lifeboat and smaller boats. It is the largest of the Scottish Maritime Museum's three sites, the others being Clydebuilt at Braehead and the Denny Ship Model Experimental Tank at Dumbarton (see separate entries). Tel: 01294 278283.

Scottish Slate Islands Heritage Trust Centre Ellenabeich, Seil. Opened in 2000 and housed in a former slate quarrier's cottage in the slate mining village of Ellenabeich, the museum explores the social and working lives of slate miners during the height of the industry in the 19th century. There is also information on the local flora, fauna and geology plus a genealogy archive. Tel: 01852 300449.

Sharmanka Kinetic Gallery Osborne Street, Glasgow. A theatre and gallery founded by sculptor-mechanic Eduard Bersudsky and theatre director Tatyana Jakovskaya in St Petersburg in 1989, and based in Glasgow since 1996. *Sharmanka* is the Russian word for a hurdy-gurdy, and the performance consists of hundreds of carved figures and pieces of scrap choreographed to music and synchronised lighting. Tel: 0141 552 7080. In September 2009 the gallery is due to become part of Glasgow's major visual arts resource, Trongate 103. The building has been designed by award-winning architects Elder and Cannon, whose design supports the needs of the arts organisations and their audiences, incorporating two floors of exhibition spaces, and a further four floors of purpose-designed production spaces.

Shuna Castle Situated on the southern tip of the island of Shuna. A domestic tower house 33ft (10m) high, built in the late 16th century by John Stewart, or possibly his son Duncan, and abandoned at the end of the 18th century.

Skerryvore Lighthouse Built by Alan Stevenson 1838–44 on a large rock 11 nautical miles (20km) west-southwest of Tiree. It has ten storeys, stands 138ft (42m) high and is considered to be one of the most graceful of all lighthouse towers. The lighthouse was repaired after being badly damaged by fire in 1954. It was automated in 1994.

Skipness Castle $^1/_4$ mile (0.4km) east of Skipness, 19 miles (31km) south of Lochgilphead. The substantial ruins of a late 13th century castle overlooking the Sound of Bute, built by Suihbne, founder of the Clan MacSween, or his son. The castle was remodelled in the 16th century by the Campbells but appears to have been abandoned by the end of the 17th century. Maintained by Historic Scotland.

Skipness Chapel $^1/_2$ mile (0.8km) east of Skipness, 19 miles (31km) south of Lochgilphead. Aka Kilbrannan Chapel, St Brendan's Chapel. The ruins of a late 13th or early 14th century chapel believed to have been built to replace a chapel incorporated into nearby Skipness Castle. It was abandoned as a place of worship during the 18th century. There are several medieval tombstones on the site.

Sma' Shot Cottages George Place, Paisley. A restored 18th century weaver's cottage with loom shop and living quarters plus a 19th century artisan's house and a garden. Tel: 0141 889 1708.

Sorn Castle Sorn, 11 miles (18km) southeast of Kilmarnock. A baronial style house located beside the River Ayr and incorporating earlier structures including a 14th or 15th century tower house and 16th century extensions. Further additions were made in the late 18th century and the house was remodelled by architect David Bryce in the 1860s.

Souter Johnnie's Cottage Main Road, Kirkoswald, 4 miles (6km) southwest of Maybole. A cottage built in 1785 which was the home of souter (shoemaker) John Davidson and his wife Ann, friends of Robert Burns. Burns depicted Souter Johnnie as Tam's drinking companion in the poem *Tam O'Shanter*, while Tam himself was based on a fellow resident of Kirkoswald, Douglas Graham. The cottage is divided into two living rooms and the shoemaker's workshop and recreated in late 18th century style. A restored alehouse behind the cottage contains statues of Tam O'Shanter, Souter Johnnie, the Innkeeper and the Innkeeper's Wife, carved in the 1830s. The cottage was given to the National Trust for Scotland in 1932. Tel: 01655 760603.

Sport

football **Airdrie United** were formed in 2002 after Airdrieonians went bankrupt and Clydebank FC was relocated to Airdrie. They were winners of the Scottish 2nd Division in 2004. Nicknamed The Diamonds or The Waysiders, their colours are red and white; their home ground is Excelsior Stadium (aka New Broomfield), St Enoch Square, Glasgow. Tel: 0771 023 0775.

Albion Rovers were founded in 1882 and were winners of the Scottish 2nd Division in 1934 and 1989. Nicknamed The Wee Rovers or The Vers, their colours are red and yellow; their home ground is Cliftonhill Stadium, Main Street, Coatbridge. Tel: 01236 606334.

Ayr United were founded in 1910, and were winners of the Scottish 1st Division in 1982 and the 2nd Division in 1912, 1913, 1928, 1937, 1959, 1966, 1988 and 1997. Nicknamed The Honest Men, their colours are black and white; their home ground is Somerset Park, Tryfield Place, Ayr. Tel: 01292 263435.

Celtic were founded in 1888 by members of Glasgow's Irish community and are traditionally identified with the city's Catholic population. They and Rangers form what is known as the city's 'Old Firm'. Unusually, their players did not wear numbers until 1960, and from then until 1995 these were worn only on their shorts. Celtic were the first British club to win the European Cup, beating Inter Milan in Lisbon on 25 May 1967. They have won the Scottish League championship in 1893, 1894, 1896, 1898, 1905, 1906, 1907, 1908, 1909, 1910, 1914, 1915, 1916, 1917, 1919, 1922, 1926, 1936, 1938, 1954, 1966, 1967, 1968, 1969, 1970, 1971, 1972, 1973, 1974, 1977, 1979, 1981, 1982, 1986, 1988, 1998, 2001, 2002, 2004, 2006, 2007 and 2008; the Scottish FA Cup in 1892, 1899, 1900, 1904, 1907, 1908, 1911, 1912, 1914, 1923, 1925, 1927, 1931, 1933, 1937, 1951, 1954, 1965, 1967, 1969, 1971, 1972, 1974, 1975, 1977, 1980, 1985, 1988, 1989, 1995, 2001, 2004, 2005 and 2007; and the Scottish League Cup in 1957, 1958, 1966, 1967, 1968, 1969, 1970, 1975, 1983, 1998, 2000, 2001 and 2006. Nicknamed The Bhoys or The Hoops (the latter after their famous green and white hooped shirts), their home ground is Celtic Park, Glasgow. Tel: 0871 226 1888.

Clyde were founded in 1877, and won the Scottish FA Cup in 1939, 1955 and 1958. Nicknamed The Bully Wee (i.e. 'the good little club'), their colours are black, white and red; their home ground is Broadwood Stadium, Cumbernauld. Tel: 01236 451511.

Dumbarton were founded in 1872 and won the Scottish FA Cup in 1883, the Scottish 1st Division in 1891 and 1892, the 2nd Division (old) in 1911 and 1972, and the 2nd Division (new) in 1992. Nicknamed The Sons, their colours are gold and black; their home ground is Strathclyde Homes Stadium, Castle Road, Dumbarton. Tel: 01389 762569.

Greenock Morton were founded in 1874 and are also known as Morton. They were winners of the Scottish FA Cup in 1922, the Scottish 1st Division in 1978, 1984 and 1987, the 2nd Division (old) in 1950, 1964 and 1967, the 2nd Division (new) in 1995 and 2007, and the 3rd Division in 2003. Nicknamed The Ton, their colours are blue and white; their home ground is Cappielow Park, Sinclair Street, Greenock. Tel: 01475 723571.

Hamilton Academical were founded in 1874 and were winners of the Scottish 1st Division (new) in 1986, 1988 and 2008, the 2nd Division (old) in 1904 and the 3rd Division (new) in 2001. Nicknamed The Accies, their colours are red and white hoops; their home ground is New Douglas Park, Cadzow Avenue, Hamilton. Tel: 01698 368650.

Kilmarnock were founded in 1869 and were winners of the Scottish League championship in 1965, the 2nd Division in 1898 and 1899, and the Scottish FA Cup in 1920, 1929 and 1997. Nicknamed Killie, their home ground is Rugby Park, Kilmarnock. Tel: 01563 545300.

Motherwell were founded in 1886 and were winners of the Scottish League championship in 1932, the Scottish 1st Division (new) in 1982 and 1985, and the 2nd Division (old) in 1954 and 1969. Nicknamed The Well or The Steelmen, their colours are maroon and gold; their home ground is Fir Park, Firpark Street, Motherwell. Tel: 01698 333333.

Partick Thistle were founded in 1876 and were winners of the 1st Division in 1976 and 2002, the 2nd Division (old) in 1897, 1900 and 1971, the 2nd Division (new) in 2001, the Scottish FA Cup in 1921, and the Scottish League Cup in 1972. Nicknamed The Jags, their colours are red, yellow and black; their home ground is Firhill Stadium. Firhill Road, Glasgow. Tel: 0141 579 1971.

Queen's Park were founded in 1867. The oldest surviving football club in Scotland, they are the only amateur club in the Scottish League, with the motto *Ludere causa ludendi* ('to play for the sake of playing'). The club also played in the English League during the late 19th century and were beaten FA Cup finalists in 1884 and 1885. They were winners of the Scottish 2nd Division (old) in 1923, the 2nd Division (new) in 1981, the 3rd Division (new) in 2000, and the Scottish FA Cup in 1874, 1875, 1876, 1880, 1881, 1882, 1884, 1886, 1890 and 1893. Nicknamed The Hoops (after their traditional black and white hooped shirts) or The Spiders, their home ground is Hampden Park, Glasgow.

Rangers were founded in 1873. Scotland's most successful club in terms of trophies and European appearances, they are part of what is known as the 'Old Firm', along with Celtic. Based in the city's west end, they became traditionally identified with Glasgow's Protestant community, although like Celtic they have made strenuous efforts to distance themselves from sectarian rivalry. Winners of the European Cup Winners' Cup in 1972, they have also won the Scottish League championship in 1891, 1899, 1900, 1901, 1902, 1911, 1912, 1913, 1918, 1920, 1921, 1923, 1924, 1925, 1927, 1928, 1929, 1930, 1931, 1933, 1934, 1935, 1937, 1939, 1947, 1949, 1950, 1953, 1956, 1957, 1959, 1961, 1963, 1964, 1975, 1976, 1978, 1987, 1989, 1990, 1991, 1992, 1993, 1994, 1995, 1996, 1997, 1999, 2000, 2003 and 2005; the Scottish FA Cup in 1894, 1897, 1898, 1903, 1928, 1930, 1932, 1934, 1935, 1936, 1948, 1949, 1950, 1953, 1960, 1962, 1963, 1964, 1966, 1973, 1976, 1978, 1979, 1981, 1992, 1993, 1996, 1999, 2000, 2002, 2003; and the Scottish League Cup in 1947, 1949, 1961, 1962, 1964, 1965, 1971, 1976, 1978, 1979, 1982, 1984, 1985, 1987, 1988, 1989, 1991, 1993, 1994, 1997, 1999, 2002, 2003, 2005 and 2008. Nicknamed The Gers or the Teddy Bears, their traditional colours are blue and white; their home ground is Ibrox Stadium, Glasgow.

St Mirren were founded in 1877 and were winners of the Scottish 1st Division in 1977, 2000 and 2006, and the Scottish FA Cup in 1926, 1959 and 1987. Nicknamed The Buddies or The Saints, their colours are black and white stripes. The club moved to a new stadium at Greenhill Road in February 2009 having been based at St Mirren Park, Love Street, Paisley since 1894. Tel: 0141 889 2558.

golf

Prestwick, Links Road, Prestwick. Founded in 1851, the clubhouse was built in 1868. The 18 hole links course has hosted the Open Championship 24 times, including the first 11 championships: 1860 (winner Willie Park Sr), 1861 (Tom Morris Sr), 1862 (Tom Morris Sr), 1863

(Willie Park Sr), 1864 (Tom Morris Sr), 1865 (Andrew Strath), 1866 (Willie Park Sr), 1867 (Tom Morris Sr), 1868 (Tom Morris Jr), 1869 (Tom Morris Jr), 1870 (Tom Morris Jr), 1872 (Tom Morris Jr), 1875 (Willie Park Sr), 1878 (Jamie Anderson), 1881 (Bob Ferguson), 1884 (Jack Simpson), 1887 (Willie Park Jr), 1890 (John Ball Jr), 1893 (William Auchterlonie), 1898 (Harry Vardon), 1903 (Harry Vardon), 1908 (James Braid), 1914 (Harry Vardon), 1925 (Jim Barnes). Tel: 01292 477404.

Royal Troon, Craigend Road, Troon. The Troon Golf Club was established in 1878 and a stone clubhouse built in 1886. The club received the royal accolade in its centenary year of 1978. There are two 18 hole links courses – the Old Course (Championship) and the Portland Course (opened 1895) – and the 9 hole Par 3 Course. The most famous hole on the Old Course is the par 3 8th, known as the 'Postage Stamp'. The Open Championship has been played at Royal Troon on eight occasions: 1923 (winner Arthur Havers), 1950 (Bobby Locke), 1962 (Arnold Palmer), 1973 (Tom Weiskopf), 1982 (Tom Watson), 1989 (Mark Calcavecchia), 1997 (Justin Leonard), 2004 (Todd Hamilton). Tel: 01292 311555.

Turnberry is a championship golf course, now part of the Westin Turnberry Resort. There are three links courses: the original Ailsa Course, the Kintyre Course (Old Arran Course), and the 9 hole Arran Course. The course was laid out in 1903 and Turnberry Hotel opened in 1906. A spa and leisure complex was opened in 1991. Turnberry has hosted four Open Championships on the Ailsa Course: 1977 (winner Tom Watson), 1986 (Greg Norman), 1994 (Nick Price) and 2009.

horse racing — **Ayr Racecourse**, Whitletts Road, Ayr, is a left handed oval track of 1m 4f (2.5km) hosting both Flat and National Hunt racing. Its first official meeting was held in 1777 and it moved to its current location in 1907. It is home to the prestigious Ayr Gold Cup (Flat), first run in 1804, and the Scottish Grand National, transferred from Bogside in 1966. Tel: 0870 850 5666.

Hamilton Park Racecourse, Bothwell Road, Hamilton, opened in its present location in 1926. In 1947 it became the first racecourse in Britain to stage evening racing. The 1m 5f (2.7km) layout is 'buttonhook' in plan with a right-handed loop; the course is known as the 'Goodwood of the North' because of its similarity in layout. Tel: 01698 283806.

rugby union — **Glasgow Warriors** were formed in 1999 as Glasgow Rugby and took the name Glasgow Caledonian after amalgamating with Caledonia Reds in 2001, adopting their present name in 2005. One of Scotland's two professional rugby union teams, they compete in the Celtic League. They share Partick Thistle FC's Firhill Stadium.

Strachur Smiddy — Strachur, 16 miles (26km) northwest of Dunoon. The village blacksmith's shop, which operated between 1791 and the mid 1950s, now restored and housing a museum. Exhibits include the smith's implements and photographs. Tel: 01369 860565.

Summerlee Museum of Scottish Industrial Life — Heritage Way, Coatbridge. A 22 acre (9ha) open air industrial heritage centre, located on the recently excavated site of Summerlee Iron Works. Founded in 1836, the works closed in 1930 and were demolished in 1939. An exhibition hall houses period room reconstructions as well as vintage cars, a 'Green Goddess' fire engine and working equipment; there are also reconstructions of miners' cottages from the 19th and 20th centuries. A recreated adit mine can be accessed through a sloping mineshaft, and there is a working electric tramway. A reopened section of the Monkland Canal runs through the park. Tel: 01236 638460.

Tall Ship at Glasgow Harbour — Stobcross Road, Glasgow. An open air museum whose centrepiece is the restored three-masted barque *Glenlee*, moored at Yorkhill Quay. Built on the Clyde at Port Glasgow in 1896, it was used as a training ship by the Spanish navy 1922–81, after which it fell into disrepair and sank before being raised and bought at auction in 1992 by Glasgow Maritime Museum. It was restored and opened as a tourist attraction in 1999. Tel: 0141 222 2513.

Tenement House — Buccleuch Street, Garnethill, Glasgow. A typical middle-class Glasgow tenement house built in 1892 and owned 1911–65 by Miss Toward, a shorthand typist. It has been restored to its early 20th century appearance and retains many of its original fixtures and fittings, including gas lighting and bed recesses. The house was purchased by the National Trust for Scotland in 1982. Tel: 0141 333 0183.

Terringzean Castle — ½ mile (0.8km) west of Cumnock. The ruins of a 15th century castle overlooking the River Lugar and once the property of the Crawford family, who had gained it at the expense of Thomas Boyd.

Theatre Royal, Glasgow — Hope Street, Glasgow. The home of Scottish Opera, also presenting Scottish Ballet. The original theatre opened in 1867 but suffered from two fires, reopening in 1895. Tel: 0141 332 9000.

Torosay Castle — 1 mile (1.6km) south of Craignure, Mull. A 19th century mansion overlooking Duart Bay. The baronial style castle was designed by David Bryce in 1856 and the 12 acres (5ha) of gardens by Sir Robert Lorimer in 1899. Rooms of note include the dining room, the library, the children's nursery and drawing room. Tel: 01680 812421.

The Tramway — Albert Drive, Glasgow. A contemporary visual and performing arts venue based in the former Coplawhill tramshed. Built in 1893, this served as the tram terminus and depot until the tram system was discontinued in the 1960s, when it became the base for the Glasgow Museum of Transport. The museum relocated to Kelvin Hall in 1986 and the building was in danger of being demolished before it was transformed into The Tramway in 1988. It promotes and presents exhibitions by contemporary Scottish and international artists, in both visual and performing spheres with both exhibition and theatre spaces. Tel: 0141 422 2023.

Tron Theatre — Trongate, Glasgow. Opened on 10 May 1981 in what was at one time the city's mercantile area. The theatre was built in the 1790s to a design by James and Robert Adam.

Trongate 103 — See Sharmanka Kinetic Gallery.

Turnberry Castle — 1 mile (1.6km) north of Turnberry, 13 miles (21km) south of Ayr. The scant remains of a 12th or 13th century castle on a promontory. It appears to have had a partially circular keep and was the property at one time of the father of Robert the Bruce. It was certainly the childhood home, and might well have been Robert I's birthplace on 21 March 1274. It is now the site of Turnberry Lighthouse – a 80ft (24m) high white tower with 76 internal steps, designed by David and Thomas Stevenson, which began operating in 1873 and was automated in 1986 – and stands close to the 17th hole of Turnberry golf course.

University of Glasgow Founded in 1451, when James II of Scotland persuaded Pope Nicholas V to grant a bull authorising Bishop Turnbull of Glasgow to set up a university. Thus, 40 years after the creation of St Andrew's University, Scotland, like England, could boast two universities. Modelled on the University of Bologna, Glasgow has remained a university in the great European tradition. Initially based at Glasgow Cathedral, in 1460 it moved to the High Street, which remained its home for 400 years until the encroaching overcrowding and squalor of factories and railways – ironically, fruits of the industrial expansion it had helped to shape – forced the university to move to its present site in what was then suburban Gilmorehill, a location it has occupied since 1870. With almost 16,000 undergraduate and 4000 postgraduate students, it is one of the country's largest universities. Most of its 100 departments are still located on the Gilmorehill campus; centred on Sir George Gilbert Scott's neo-Gothic main building (its spire, added by his son John Oldrid Scott, is a landmark across the city), the campus has more listed buildings than any other and reflects a vast range of architectural styles. Pearce Lodge and the Lion and Unicorn Staircase are relics of the old university, moved stone by stone to the new site. The circular Reading Room dates from the 1930s while the Library, Boyd Orr and Adam Smith Buildings reflect post-war fashions in public building design. The new Wolfson Medical School Building was opened in 2003. The University Veterinary School is located 3 miles (5km) away at the Garscube Campus, also home to the new outdoor sports facilities. The University's Crichton Campus, located on the outskirts of Dumfries in southwest Scotland, is operated jointly with the University of the West of Scotland. Glasow is a member of the Russell Group of research-led universities. Among the university's many famous former students are politicians Henry Campbell-Bannerman, Charles Kennedy, Vincent Cable and John Smith, author of *The Golden Bough* Sir James Frazer, journalist Andrew Neil, and authors William Boyd and Alasdair Gray. Tel: 0141 330 5511.

University of the West of Scotland Formed in 2007 by the merger of the University of Paisley (founded in 1897 to offer vocational courses and began offering degree studies in the early 1900s gaining university status in 1992; in 1998 it entered partnership with the University of Glasgow to create Crichton University Campus in Dumfries) and Bell College of Technology, Hamilton (founded in 1972). The university's seven academic schools, offering a wide range of largely vocational courses – Business, Computing, Education, Engineering & Science, Health, Nursing & Midwifery, Media, Language & Music and Social Sciences – are based on four campuses in Ayr, Hamilton, Paisley and Dumfries. Tel: 0141 848 3000.

University of Strathclyde Richmond Street, Glasgow. Founded in 1796 when John Anderson, Professor of Natural Philosophy at Glasgow University, left in his will instructions for 'a place of useful learning', open to everyone, regardless of gender or class. The resulting college was established in High Street, Glasgow before moving to George Street, and developed rapidly throughout the 19th century. In the late 1950s and early 60s it merged with the Scottish College of Commerce, the enlarged Royal College receiving its royal charter in 1964 as the University of Strathclyde. In 1993 the university merged with Jordanhill College of Education, for many years Scotland's premier teacher training college. Today, Strathclyde is the third largest university in Scotland, with 67 buildings over 500 acres (200ha) of land and teaching over 20,000 students in five faculties: Arts & Social Sciences, Education, Engineering, Science and Strathclyde Business School. Including distance learning, short courses, continuing professional development and evening courses, Strathclyde has over 50,000 students annually, making it the UK's largest provider of postgraduate and professional education. Tel: 0141 552 4400.

Vennel Gallery Glasgow Vennel, Irvine. A gallery presenting contemporary arts and crafts, housed in a restored 18th century cottage where Robert Burns worked as a flax heckler (a process of drawing the flax stems through a large comb to remove impurities). The heckling shop can still be seen. Tel: 01294 275059.

Victoria Park Victoria Park Drive North, Glasgow. A 50 acre (20ha) park opened in July 1887 and named for Queen Victoria's Golden Jubilee in 1886. In addition to landscaped lawns and floral displays the park also features an arboretum, a pond, curling rinks, miniature lamp post clock, and the Fossil Grove (see separate entry).

Wallace Memorial Stoddard Square, Elderslie, Johnstone. A monument erected on the traditional site of the birthplace of William Wallace, and bearing bronze panels displaying episodes from his life. Although no structure contemporary with Wallace remains, excavations have revealed that a 13th or 14th century moated house once stood on the site.

Weaver's Cottage The Cross, Kilbarchan, 4 miles (6km) west of Paisley. Kilbarchan boasted a thriving weaving industry from the 17th to the 19th century, eventually focusing on producing tartans. The weaver's cottage, built in 1723 was given to the National Trust for Scotland in 1954 and is still used to present weaving demonstrations. Tel: 01505 705588.

West Kilbride Museum Arthur Street, West Kilbride. Local history museum housed in the village hall and dedicated to the social and working history of the people of West Kilbride. Exhibits include examples of weaving and other crafts.

Willow Tea Rooms Sauchiehall Street and Buchanan Street, Glasgow. Two tea rooms designed by Charles Rennie Mackintosh and originally owned by Kate Cranston, the daughter of a tea merchant and promoter of the temperance movement. Mackintosh designed the murals for the Buchanan Street tearooms – which were designed by George Washington Brown – in 1896. He then designed the furniture for tea rooms in Argyle Street, also designing the White Dining Room in Ms Cranston's Ingram Street establishment, before designing in their entirety the tea rooms in Sauchiehall Street, which opened in October 1903 and came to be known as the Willow Tea Rooms. The premises included a ladies' tea room on the ground floor, a 'room de luxe' for ladies on the first floor and men's smoking and billiards rooms on the second floor. Mrs Cranston sold the tea rooms after the death of her husband in 1917, the room de luxe becoming part of Daly's department store until the 1980s. The Willow Tea Rooms were extensively restored and reopened in 1983 with the first floor room de luxe and tea gallery. A further tea room opened in 1997 in Buchanan Street, next to the site of the original Cranston Buchanan Tea Rooms, features recreations of Mackintosh's original designs.

Woods on Your Doorstep

Crinan Woods, Crinan (86 acres/35ha), covers two hills near the village of Crinan. A mixture of ancient woodland and more recent planting, species include oak, birch and ash; **Whinny Hill Wood**, Boturich (252 acres/102ha), covering two hills to the south of Loch Lomond. Mature conifer woodlands, formerly part of the Boturich Estate.

Some famous people born in Strathclyde

Arrol, William (engineer) (1839–1913)	Houston
Baird, John Logie (inventor) (1888–1946)	Helensburgh
Baxter, Stanley (comedian) (1926–)	Glasgow
Bone, Muirhead (artist) (1876–1953)	Glasgow
Buchanan, Walter 'Jack' (entertainer) (1891–1957)	Helensburgh
Burns, Robert (poet) (1759–96)	Alloway
Busby, Matt (football manager) (1909–94)	Bellshill
Campbell-Bannerman, Henry (Liberal politician) (1836–1908)	Glasgow
Carlyle, Robert (actor) (1961–)	Glasgow
Coltrane, Robbie (actor) (1950–)	Glasgow
Connolly, Billy (comedian and actor) (1942–)	Glasgow
Cook, Robin Finlayson (politician) (1946–2005)	Bellshill
Cook, Steph (athlete) (1972–)	Irvine
Dalglish, Kenny (footballer) (1951–)	Glasgow
Docherty, Tommy (footballer) (1928–)	Glasgow
Donegan, 'Lonnie' (pioneer of skiffle music) (1931–2002)	Glasgow
Duffy, Carol Ann (poet and playwright) (1955–)	Glasgow
Ferguson, Alex (football manager) (1941–)	Glasgow
Fisher, Andrew (Prime Minister of Australia) (1862–1928)	Crosshouse
Fleming, Alexander (scientist) (1881–1955)	Lochfield
Forsyth, Bill (film director) (1946–)	Glasgow
Henderson, Arthur (politician and Nobel Laureate) (1863–1935)	Glasgow
Higgins, John (snooker player) (1975–)	Wishaw
Keir Hardie, James (politician) (1856–1915)	Newhouse
Kerr, Deborah (actress) (1921–2007)	Glasgow
Kidd, William (pirate) (c.1645–1701)	Greenock
Knopfler, Mark (musician) (1949–)	Glasgow
Livingstone, David (explorer) (1813–73)	Blantyre
Lynch, Benny (flyweight boxer) (1913–46)	Glasgow
Macdonald, John A (first Prime Minister of Canada (1815–96)	Glasgow
Macintosh, Charles (chemist and inventor) (1766–1843)	Glasgow
Mackintosh, Charles Rennie (architect and artist) (1868–1928)	Glasgow
MacLean, Alistair (author) (1922–87)	Glasgow
McAlpine, Robert (industrialist 'concrete Bob') (1847–1934)	Newarthill
McCallum, David (actor) (1933–)	Glasgow
McCoist, Ally (footballer) (1962–)	Bellshill
McGowan, Walter (flyweight boxer) (1942–)	Hamilton
Montgomerie, Colin (golfer) (1963–)	Glasgow
Murray, Charles 'Chic' (comedian) (1919–85)	Greenock
Pinkerton, Allan (detective) (1819–84)	Glasgow
Ramsay, William (chemist) (1852–1916)	Glasgow
Reid, George (Prime Minister of Australia) (1845–1918)	Johnstone
Robert I, the Bruce (Scottish monarch) (1274–1329)	Turnberry
Shankly, Bill (footballer) (1913–81)	Glenbuck
Stein, Jock (footballer) (1922–85)	Burnbank
Stewart, Andy (entertainer) (1933–93)	Glasgow
Stewart, Jackie (racing driver) (1939–)	Milton
Watt, James (inventor) (1736–1819)	Greenock
Watt, Jim (lightweight boxer) (1948–)	Glasgow
Wilson, Richard (actor) (1936–)	Greenock

Islands of Strathclyde

(IH) denotes Inner Hebridean Island
(shipping area = Malin)

Island name	Area	Nearest landmark	General information
A' Chairidhe (IH)	Atlantic	Calgary Point, Coll	(G. = The Weir or Fish Pound). . GR: NM115541
A' Chleit (IH)	Atlantic	Aird a Chrainn, Mull	(G. = The Reef). GR: NM415182
A' Chleit (IH)	Atlantic	Heanish, Tiree	(G. = The Reef). GR: NM038427
A' Chuli (IH)	Firth of Lorn	Garbh Eileach	(G. = The Retreat). St Brendan is reputed to have been buried here. One of the Garvellachs group. GR: NM655112
Abbot's Isles (IH)	Loch Etive	Achnacloich	A small group of tiny islets. GR: NM952343
Aber Isle	Loch Lomond	Gartochraggan	aka The Island at the Mouth of the River Endrick. GR: NS420889
Ailsa Craig	Firth of Clyde	Girvan	See separate entry.
Aird Mor (IH)	Atlantic	Barrapol, Tiree	(G. = Great Promontory). GR: NL935421
Airne na Sgeire (IH)	Atlantic	Rubha Ban, Coll	GR: NM220544
Allens, The	Millport Bay	Millport, Great Cumbrae	The two islands of The Allens (N. = Islands) are also known as The Eileans.
Am Brican (IH)	Sound of Mull	Rubha Mor, Mull	GR: NM597450
Am Buachaille (IH)	Atlantic	Staffa	(G. = The Herdsman). GR: NM325351
Am Fraoch Eilean (IH)	Atlantic	Ardfin, Jura	(G. = The Heather Isle).The ruins of Claig Castle can be found on the island. GR: NR471627
Am Plodan (IH)	Atlantic	Traigh Bhan, Islay	GR: NR348436
An Calbh (IH)	Atlantic	Gometra	One of the Treshnish Isles. GR: NM270408
An Carraigean (IH)	Loch Scridain	Traigh nam Beach, Mull	GR: NM461251
An Cleireach (IH)	Atlantic	Miodar, Tiree	GR: NM072500
An Cleiteadh (IH)	Seil Sound	Luing, Seil, Torsa	
An Coire (IH)	Atlantic	Rhinns Point	GR: NR162510
An Doirlinn (IH)	Atlantic	Coul Point, Islay	GR: NR189640
An Dubh Sgeir (IH)	Atlantic	Colonsay	GR: NR328915
An Dubh-sgeir (IH)	Sound of Gigha	Cnoc nan Gobhar, Gigha	GR: NR665557
An Dunan (IH)	Sound of Jura	Ardfernal, Jura	GR: NR564711
An Fhearsaid (IH)	Loch na Keal	Inch Kenneth	GR: NM445361
An Ganradh (IH)	Atlantic	Traigh Bhan, Islay	GR: NR346435
An Glas-eilean (IH)	Sea of the Hebrides	Rubha Sgor-innis, Coll	GR: NM278642
An Gra' dar (IH)	Atlantic	Rubh' an Fhaing, Tiree	GR: NM009489
An Lanach (IH)	Atlantic	Middleton, Tiree	GR: NL935430
An Oitir	Loch Fyne	Minard Castle	GR: NR982948
An Sgonnag (IH)	Atlantic	Ceann Caol, Texa	
An Snoig (IH)	Atlantic	Middleton, Tiree	GR: NL935434
An t-Sail (IH)	Atlantic	Oronsay	GR: NR338862
An t-Sron (IH)	Atlantic	Middleton, Tiree	GR: NL934426
An Tudan (IH)	Atlantic	Lunga	GR: NM694088
Ardmore Islands (IH)	Atlantic	Cnoc an Doire Leathain, Islay	GR: NR468492
Arran, Isle of	Firth of Clyde	Carradale	Once owned by the heirs of the Duchess of Montrose. Area: 165 sq miles (428 sq km). Population: 5058. GR: NR956359
Bac Beag (IH)	Atlantic	Gometra	aka Dutchman's Cap. One of the Treshnish Isles. GR: NM239378
Bac Mor (IH)	Atlantic	Gometra	One of the Treshnish Isles. GR: NM243387
Bacastair (IH)	Atlantic	Oronsay	GR: NR332889
Bach Island (IH)	Firth of Lorn	Rubha na Feundain, Kerrera	(G. = Windward Island). GR: NM778268
Balkenna Isle	Firth of Clyde	Turnberry	GR: NS198044
Balvica (IH)	Seil Sound	Rubha nan Ron, Seil	GR: NM774170
Barmore Island	Loch Fyne	Barr Hill	Peninsula included by virtue of its name. GR: NR870715
Belach Rocks (IH)	Atlantic	Ardnave Point, Islay	GR: NR313778
Bell Rock	Firth of Clyde	Troon	Formerly known as Inchcape (G. = Island Stumbling Block). Robert Stevenson built the famous lighthouse in 1811 which helped to prevent ships colliding with the tiny island. GR: NS339248
Bell Stane	Firth of Clyde	Seamill	GR: NS190478

Island name	Area	Nearest landmark	General information
Belnahua (IH)	Firth of Lorn	Rubha Bhuidhe, Luing	In 1936 a Latvian vessel, *Helena Faulbaums*, sank off the coast with the loss of 16 lives. One of the Slate Islands. GR: NM714128
Bernera	Loch Linnhe	Lismore	GR: NM795394
Big Stirk (IH)	Atlantic	Auliston Point	Lies north of the entrance to Loch Sunart. GR: NM535578
Biod nan Sgarbh (IH)	Atlantic	Sgairail, Islay	GR: NR355762
Black Islands	Loch Awe	Cladich	GR: NN098241
Black Rock (IH)	Loch Crinan	Crinan	GR: NR789948
Black Rocks	Firth of Clyde	Troon	GR: NS323291
Blackburn Rocks	Firth of Clyde	Ayr	GR: NS322210
Boating Stone	Firth of Clyde	Ailsa Craig	GR: NS017003
Bogha Bhuilg (IH)	Sound of Mull	Rubha nam Feannag	GR: NM559527
Bogha Crom (IH)	Atlantic	Balnahard, Mull	GR: NM444343
Bogha Dearg (IH)	Atlantic	Rubha Fasachd, Coll	GR: NM171521
Bogha Garbh-aird (IH)	Firth of Lorn	Rubha Garbh-aird	GR: NM867365
Bogha Ghuthalum (IH)	Atlantic	Rubha Port Bhiosd, Tiree	GR: NL960497
Bogha Leathan (IH)	Atlantic	Balnahard, Mull	GR: NM441347
Bogha Mor (IH)	Atlantic	Bogh' an Sgulain, Mull	Situated in the approach to Loch Tuath. GR: NM409245
Bogha Mor (IH)	Atlantic	Hynish, Tiree	GR: NL982387
Bogha Mor (IH)	Sea of the Hebrides	Garbh-aird Mor, Coll	GR: NM262653
Bogha Ruadh (IH)	Atlantic	Gometra	One of the Treshnish Isles. GR: NM299428
Bogha Sgiobagair (IH)	Atlantic	Carrastaoin, Tiree	GR: NL935488
Boghachan Mora (IH)	Atlantic	Traigh Nostaig, Islay	GR: NR269740
Boghachan Ruadha (IH)	Atlantic	Balnahard, Mull	GR: NM442341
Brest Rocks	Firth of Clyde	Turnberry	GR: NS192050
Brither Rocks	Firth of Clyde	West Kilbride	GR: NS197470
Broad Islands	Firth of Clyde	Little Cumbrae	GR: NS153518
Broad Rock	Firth of Clyde	Ardrossan	GR: NS218428
Brosdale Island (IH)	Atlantic	Rubha na h-Acairseid, Jura	GR: NR499623
Burnt Islands	Kyles of Bute	Buttock Point, Bute	Three islands: Eilean Mor, Eilean Fraoch, Eilean Buidhe. GR: NS017752
Bute	Firth of Clyde	Strone Point	Principal owner is former GP driver Johnny Dumfries, 7th Marquess of Bute, although Sir Richard Attenborough owns 1480 acres (600ha) at Rudhabodach. The island is known as 'Scotland's Madeira'. Rothesay is its only town. Area: 46.98 sq miles (121.68 sq km). Population: 7228. GR: NS060660
Cairn na Burgh Beag (IH)	Atlantic	Gometra	One of the Treshnish Isles. GR: NM309449
Cairn na Burgh More (IH)	Atlantic	Gometra	One of the Treshnish Isles. GR: NM305448
Cairns of Coll (IH)	Sea of the Hebrides	Garbh-aird Mor, Coll	GR: NM288665
Calve Island (IH)	Sound of Mull	Tobermory, Mull	Permitted to issue its own postage stamps. Area: 0.28 sq miles (0.72 sq km). GR: NM523545
Cam Sgeir (IH)	Atlantic	Texa	GR: NR389428
Cam Sgeir (IH)	Atlantic	Ardbeg, Islay	GR: NR426447
Cams Rock (IH)	Lynn of Lorn	Lismore	GR: NM835375
Cara (IH)	Sound of Gigha	Slocan Leim, Gigha	Uninhabited since the 1940s. The Brownie of Cara is said to be the ghost of a Macdonald murdered by a Campbell. Area: 0.25 sq miles (0.66 sq km). GR: NR640440
Carmichael's Rocks (IH)	Atlantic	Ardbeg, Islay	GR: NR421447
Carragh an t-Sruith (IH)	Sound of Islay	Inver Cott, Jura	GR: NR438718
Carraig an Daimh (IH)	Atlantic	Lagandorain, Iona	GR: NM275257
Carraig an Daimh (IH)	Sound of Jura	Island of Danna	(G. = Isle Connected to the Rock). One of the MacCormaig Isles. GR: NR662789
Carraig an Ratha (IH)	Atlantic	McArthur's Head, Islay	GR: NR461588
Carraig Bhan (IH)	Atlantic	Creag Loisgte, Islay	GR: NR259727
Carraig Bun Aibhne (IH)	Atlantic	Stremnishmore, Islay	GR: NR314404
Carraig Dhubh (IH)	Loch Indaal	Blackrock, Islay	GR: NR304626
Carraig Fhada (IH)	Atlantic	Traigh Bhan, Islay	GR: NR349443
Carraig Mhicheil (IH)	Firth of Lorn	Rubh'a'Bhearnaig, Kerrera	GR: NM846312
Carraig Mhor (IH)	Atlantic	Cnoc Mor, Mull	GR: NM369179
Carraig Mhor (IH)	Atlantic	Ardmore Point, Islay	GR: NR473513
Carraig Mhor (IH)	Atlantic	Dun nan Gall, Islay	GR: NR468559

Island name	Area	Nearest landmark	General information
Carraig na h-Acairseid (IH)	Sound of Jura	Point of Knap	GR: NR697735
Carraigean (IH)	Atlantic	Colonsay	GR: NR329899
Carsaig Island (IH)	Sound of Jura	Carsaig	Possibly the last Scottish home of the chough. GR: NR731891
Carsamull (IH)	Gott Bay	Ruaig, Tiree	GR: NM069468
Castle Craigs	Firth of Clyde	Ardrossan	GR: NS227416
Castle Island	Firth of Clyde	Little Cumbrae	Almost touching Little Cumbrae's east coast. GR: NS152513
Castle Stalker (IH)	Loch Laich	The Knap	An island fortress used by James IV as a hunting lodge, it fell into ruin but has now been restored. GR: NM921473
Cath Sgeir (IH)	Sound of Gigha	Achamore, Gigha	GR: NR618474
Ceann a' Chlachain (IH)	Loch Indaal	Rubha an t-Saile, Islay	GR: NR283586
Ceann Caol (IH)	Atlantic	Texa	GR: NR385434
Ceann Garbh (IH)	Sound of Islay	Rubha na h-Acairseid, Jura	GR: NR497620
Ceann Mor (IH)	Atlantic	Vaul, Tiree	GR: NM058493
Ceann nan Sgeirean (IH)	Atlantic	Cnoc an Doire Leathain, Islay	One of the Ardmore Islands. GR: NR456473
Ceann Riobha (IH)	Atlantic	Oronsay	GR: NR360859
Clach, The	Millport Bay	Millport, Great Cumbrae	(G. = Stone). GR: NS158540
Clach Gharbh	Loch Fyne	Carrick	GR: NR924875
Clach na Gile (IH)	Atlantic	Sliabh Aird na Sgitheich, Jura	GR: NR469787
Cleit a' Ghlaisrig (IH)	North Channel	Bruthach Mor, Islay	GR: NR275412
Cleit Ruaig (IH)	Atlantic	Ruaig, Tiree	GR: NM079458
Cleiteadh Buidhe	Firth of Clyde	Kilmory, Isle of Arran	GR: NR959203
Cnap a' Chailbhe (IH)	Sound of Mull	Tobermory, Mull	GR: NM527539
Coire Cara (IH)	Sound of Gigha	Cara	GR: NR637449
Coire Sgeir (IH)	Atlantic	Sanna Point	GR: NM434696
Coiresa (IH)	Atlantic	Sron an Droma	GR: NM746004
Coll (IH)	Atlantic	Tiree	Ben Hogh at 341ft (104m) is the island's highest hill. Area: 29.82 sq miles (77.23 sq km). Population: 164. GR: NM200570
Colonsay (IH)	Atlantic	Rubh' a' Mhail, Islay	The island is leased to the RSPB. Around the coast eider are so common that they are known locally as 'Colonsay duck'. The 'capital' of Colonsay is Scalasaig. Area: 16.74 sq miles (43.36 sq km). Population: 108. GR: NR375940
Conslum (IH)	Atlantic	Carrastaoin, Tiree	GR: NL935471
Corr Eilean (IH)	Sound of Gigha	Gigalum Island	(G. = Tapering Island). GR: NR645455
Corr Eilean (IH)	Sound of Jura	Kilmory	One of the MacCormaig Isles. GR: NR678758
Corr Sgeir (IH)	Atlantic	Ard Imersay, Islay	GR: NR432457
Cour Island	Kilbrannan Sound	Cour	GR: NR826476
Craro (IH)	Sound of Gigha	Ardlamey, Gigha	GR: NR627478
Creachasdal Beag (IH)	Atlantic	Mullach nan Gall, Tiree	GR: NM105484
Creachasdal Mor (IH)	Atlantic	Mullach nan Gall, Tiree	GR: NM105482
Creag (IH)	Lynn of Lorn	Lismore	GR: NM835370
Creagan a' Chaolais Bhain (IH)	Caolas Ban	Calgary Point, Coll	GR: NM110520
Creagan Dubha	Loch Lomond	Luss	GR: NS369929
Creaglan	Loch Gilp	Castleton	GR: NR874844
Creinch	Loch Lomond	Ross Priory	aka The Island of Trees. GR: NS393888
Cubaig (IH)	Atlantic	Oronsay	GR: NR329865
Cuilean Rock (IH)	Loch Linnhe	Lismore	GR: NM884476
Cul Sgathain (IH)	Hynish Bay	Hynish, Tiree	GR: NL987396
Culbhaie (IH)	Atlantic	Gemmil	GR: NM780055
Davaar	Campbeltown Loch	Macringan's Point	Permitted to issue its own postage stamps. Davaar is only an island at high water. Area: 0.2 sq miles (0.52 sq km). Population: 2. GR: NR759203
Dearg Sgeir (IH)	Atlantic	Sron an Droma	(G. = Red Rock). GR: NM745014
Dearg Sgeir (IH)	Loch Linnhe	Eriska	GR: NM899437
Dearg Sgeir (IH)	Sound of Gigha	Slocan Leim, Gigha	GR: NR628459
Dearg Sgeir	Sound of Mull	Rubha Mor, Mull	The cargo ship *Rondo* was in collision with the island in 1935, wrecking the ship and demolishing the original lighthouse. The most northern rock of Eileanan Glasa. GR: NM595452
Dearg Sgeir)IH)	Atlantic	Torr Mor Chonairst, Mull	One of the Torran Rocks. Where David Balfour is shipwrecked in *Kidnapped*. GR: NM294156

Island name	Area	Nearest landmark	General information
Diar Sgeir (IH)	Sound of Luing	Bardrishaig, Luing	GR: NM730116
Don Cruit (IH)	Atlantic	Lunga	One of the Treshnish Isles. GR: NM276421
Dubh Eilean (IH)	Atlantic	Oronsay	GR: NR340886
Dubh Sgeir (IH)	Atlantic	Erraid, Mull	GR: NM279189
Dubh Sgeir (IH)	Firth of Lorn	Seil	GR: NM740205
Dubh Sgeir (IH)	Firth of Lorn	Kerrera	GR: NM765252
Dubh Sgeir (IH)	Firth of Lorn	Rubha Lagain Aillidh, Seill	GR: NM740695
Dubh Sgeir (IH)	Loch Linnhe	Lismore	GR: NM859451
Dubh Sgeir (IH)	Sound of Gigha	Achamore, Gigha	GR: NR625470
Dubh Sgeir (IH)	Sound of Jura	Island of Danna	GR: NR663788
Dubh Sgeir (IH)	Sound of Jura	Kilmory	GR: NR661748
Dubh Sgeir (IH)	Sound of Luing	Rubha Bhuidhe, Luing	GR: NM727120
Dubh Sgeir (IH)	Atlantic	Druim an Aoineidh, Iona	GR: NM250218
Dubh Sgeir (IH)	Atlantic	Soa Island	GR: NM244195
Dubh Sgeir Mhor (IH)	Atlantic	Mackinnon's Cave, Mull	GR: NM435325
Dubh-fheith (IH)	Firth of Lorn	Dun Chonnuill	GR: NM702150
Dun an Garbh-Sroine (IH)	Atlantic	Garraron	GR: NM796088
Dun Chonnuill (IH)	Firth of Lorn	Garbh Eileach	(G. = Conal's Castle). One of the Garvellachs. GR: NM680126
Duncuan Island	Loch Gilp	Ardrishaig	GR: NR861850
Dutchman's Cap (IH)	Atlantic	Gometra	See Bac Beag.
Each Donn (IH)	Firth of Lorn	Seil	GR: NM788211
Eag na Maoile (IH)	Sea of the Hebrides	Garbh-aird Mor, Coll	(G. = Cleft Bare Rock). GR: NM276655
Easdale (IH)	Firth of Lorn	Easdale, Seill	(*Eas* G. = Waterfall; *Dal(e)* O.N. = Valley). Aka Ellenabeich (G. = Island of the Birches). The most densely populated island of Scotland; permitted to issue its own postage stamps. One of the Slate Islands. Area: 0.09 sq miles (0.24 sq km). Population: 58. GR: NM737172
Eich Donna (IH)	Atlantic	An Crap	GR: NM791098
Eileach an Naoimh (IH)	Firth of Lorn	A' Chuli	Owned by Lord Richard Sandys (the family of Lord Duncan Sandys, the former minister of state. Burial place of St Eithne, mother of St Columba. One of the Garvellachs. Area: 0.22 sq miles (0.56 sq km). GR: NM640100
Eilean (inner)	Millport Bay	Millport, Great Cumbrae	(G. = Island). The two islands of The Eileans are also known as The Allens (N. = Islands). GR: NS165546
Eilean (outer)	Millport Bay	Millport, Great Cumbrae	The two islands of The Eileans are also known as The Allens. GR: NS165544
Eilean a' Bhealaich (IH)	Sound of Luing	Lunga	GR: NM715071
Eilean a' Bhorra (IH)	Atlantic	Cnoc na h' iolaire, Jura	GR: NR636863
Eilean a' Bhuic (IH)	Sound of Alva	Ulva, Mull	(G. = Buck Island).
Eilean a' Bhuic	Loch Fyne	Glenan	GR: NR913704
Eilean a' Chaolais (IH)	Loch Tuath	Ardalum House, Ulva	(G. = Kyle Island). GR: NM440400
Eilean a' Chapuill (IH)	Sound of Jura	Kilmory	GR: NR695748
Eilean a' Chladaich (IH)	Atlantic	Colonsay	(G. = Shore Isle). GR: NR338922
Eilean a' Choire (IH)	Loch Tuath	Baligortan, Ulva	GR: NM385420
Eilean a' Chomhraidh	Loch Awe	Ardanaiseig	(G. = Meeting-place Island). GR: NN095248
Eilean a' Chomhraidh	Loch Leven	Alltan Mhic Aoidh	GR: NN087593
Eilean a' Chomhraig	Loch Fyne	Cnoc Glas	GR: NR887675
Eilean a' Chrabhaiche (IH)	Loch Buie	Coill a Chaiginn, Mull	GR: NM594242
Eilean a' Chuil (IH)	Sound of Gigha	Gallochoille, Gigha	GR: NR654483
Eilean a' Chuirn (IH)	Atlantic	Cnoc an Doire Leathain, Islay	(G. = Heap-of-Stones Island). One of the Ardmore Islands. GR: NR471489
Eilean a' Mhadaidh (IH)	Firth of Lorn	Gorsten, Mull	GR: NM752320
Eilean Amalaig (IH)	Loch Spelve	Rubha na Faing	GR: NM708299
Eilean an Aodaich (IH)	Atlantic	Hynish, Tiree	GR: NL976384
Eilean an Duilisg (IH)	Atlantic	Torr Mor, Mull	GR: NM388249
Eilean an Duin (IH)	Atlantic	Craobh Haven	(G. = Island of the Fort). GR: NM792080
Eilean an Easbuig (IH)	West Loch Tarbert	Cnoc Rubh a' Choire, Jura	GR: NR550811
Eilean an Eoin (IH)	Atlantic	Oronsay	(G. = Bird Isle). GR: NR365865
Eilean an Fheoir (IH)	Loch Scridain	Killunaig, Mull	GR: NM490261
Eilean an Fhuarain (IH)	Atlantic	Sorne Point, Mull	GR: NM428580
Eilean an Loin (IH)	Atlantic	Uamh nam Fear, Texa	GR: NR393432
Eilean an Righ (IH)	Atlantic	Rubha na Traighe Baine, Ulva	(G. = Royal Island). GR: NM399381
Eilean an Rubha (IH)	Atlantic	Lussa Point, Jura	GR: NR642864

Island name	Area	Nearest landmark	General information
Eilean an Ruisg (IH)	Loch Feochan	Carn Breagach	(G. = Bare Island). GR: NM845235
Eilean an Stalcair	Loch Tulla	Black Mount	GR: NN291425
Eilean an Tannais-sgeir (IH)	Atlantic	Coul Point, Islay	GR: NR188639
Eilean an Treogh (IH)	Atlantic	Ruaig, Tiree	GR: NM078460
Eilean an t-Sagairt	Loch Awe	Creag an Taghain	GR: NN073222
Eilean an t-Sluic (IH)	Atlantic	Ard Imersay, Islay	GR: NR434461
Eilean Annraidh (IH)	Atlantic	Lagandorain, Iona	GR: NM297265
Eilean Aoghainn	Loch Fyne	Minard Castle	GR: NR985945
Eilean Ard (IH)	Atlantic	Staon Bheinn, Jura	GR: NR559820
Eilean Ardgaddan	Loch Fyne	Rubha Beag	GR: NR913799
Eilean Arsa (IH)	Atlantic	Craobh Haven	(G. = Ancient Island). GR: NM786073
Eilean Ascaoinneach (IH)	Atlantic	Ben Feall, Coll	GR: NM130548
Eilean Ban (IH)	Atlantic	Rubha na Traighe Baine, Ulva	GR: NM392377
Eilean Ban (IH)	Loch na Lathaich	Rubh' nam Buthan, Mull	(G. = Pale Island). GR: NM372228
Eilean Ban (IH)	Sound of Mull	Mon, Mull	GR: NM733360
Eilean Ban-leac (IH)	Sound of Insh	Insh Island	GR: NM732194
Eilean Beag (IH)	Atlantic	Bagh Gleann nam Muc, Jura	GR: NM683010
Eilean Beag (IH)	Atlantic	Traigh Nostaig, Islay	GR: NR278748
Eilean Beag (IH)	Firth of Lorn	Ledaig Point	GR: NM889351
Eilean Beith	Loch Awe	Achlian	GR: NN109254
Eilean Bhoramuil (IH)	Atlantic	Calgary Point, Coll	GR: NM115505
Eilean Bhride (IH)	Atlantic	Cnoc an Doire Leathain, Islay	(G. = Bridget's Island). One of the Ardmore Islands. GR: NR460479
Eilean Bhride (IH)	Sound of Jura	Rubha Bhride, Jura	One of the Small Isles. GR: NR554698
Eilean Buidhe	Kyles of Bute	Buttock Point, Bute	(G. = Yellow Island). The island has the remains of a vitrified fort on it. One of the Burnt Islands. GR: NS018750
Eilean Buidhe (IH)	Atlantic	Craobh Haven	GR: NM797081
Eilean Buidhe (IH)	Firth of Lorn	Seil	GR: NM779201
Eilean Buidhe	Loch Fyne	Black Harbour	GR: NR905719
Eilean Buidhe	Loch Fyne	Lub na Faochaige	GR: NR917693
Eilean Buidhe Mor (IH)	Atlantic	Doire Dhonh, Jura	GR: NR661891
Eilean Cam (IH)	Atlantic	Cladville, Islay	GR: NR164543
Eilean Carrach (IH)	Atlantic	Point of Arnamurchan	GR: NM425680
Eilean Carrach	Kilbrannan Sound	Carradale	GR: NR821387
Eilean Carrach (IH)	Sound of Iona	Druim Dhughail, Iona	GR: NM278225
Eilean Ceann na Creige (IH)	West Loch Tarbert	Kennacraig	GR: NR819626
Eilean Chalba (IH)	Atlantic	Lagandorain, Iona	GR: NM280262
Eilean Chalmain (IH)	Atlantic	Torr Mor Chonairst, Mull	GR: NM307175
Eilean Choinneich	Loch Leven	Alltan Mhic Aoidh	aka Kenneth's Isle. GR: NN070592
Eilean Clach nan Uamhannan (IH)	Sound of Jura	Rubha Cruitiridh	GR: NR715611
Eilean Coltair (IH)	Loch Melfort	Druim an Fhaillich	GR: NM801128
Eilean Craobhach (IH)	Atlantic	Cnoc an Doire Leathain, Islay	(G. = Tree-covered Island). One of the Ardmore Islands. GR: NR468492
Eilean Creagach (IH)	Atlantic	An Cnap	(G. = Craggy Island). GR: NM785090
Eilean da Ghallagain (IH)	West Loch Tarbert	Rubha na h-Earba	GR: NR835659
Eilean da Mheinn (IH)	Loch Crinan	Crinan	GR: NR781945
Eilean Dearg	Loch Riddon	Port an Eilein	GR: NS008771
Eilean Deargannan	Loch Lomond	Luss	Name derives from G. *Deargan* = 'a heather-coloured dye'. GR: NS378908
Eilean Didil (IH)	Atlantic	Culbuirg, Iona	GR: NM262242
Eilean Dioghlum (IH)	Loch Tuath	Gometra	GR: NM350420
Eilean Diomhain (IH)	Sound of Jura	Craighouse, Jura	(G. = Idle Island). One of the Small Isles. GR: NR548685
Eilean Dubh (IH)	Atlantic	Colonsay	(G. = Black Island). GR: NR349937
Eilean Dubh (IH)	Atlantic	Staffa	GR: NM323359
Eilean Dubh (IH)	Atlantic	Colonsay	GR: NM421012
Eilean Dubh (IH)	Atlantic	Erraid, Mull	GR: NM287197
Eilean Dubh (IH)	Atlantic	Torr Mor Chonairst, Mull	GR: NM305184
Eilean Dubh (IH)	Atlantic	Beinn Ceann a Mhara, Tiree	GR: NL935412
Eilean Dubh (IH)	Loch Craignish	Duine	GR: NM792020
Eilean Dubh (IH)	Loch Frisa	Tom nam Fitheach, Mull	GR: NM479490
Eilean Dubh (IH)	Loch Linnhe	Lismore	GR: NM874420
Eilean Dubh (IH)	Lynn of Lorn	Lismore	GR: NM840381
Eilean Dubh (IH)	Sound of Jura	Tayvallich	GR: NR720873
Eilean Dubh	Loch Riddon	Binnein Mor	GR: NS006757

Island name	Area	Nearest landmark	General information
Eilean Dubh Beag (IH)	Firth of Lorn	Eilean Dubh Mor	GR: NM695112
Eilean Dubh Cruinn (IH)	Atlantic	Balmeanach, Mull	(G. = Round Black Island). GR: NM441332
Eilean Dubh Mor (IH)	Firth of Lorn	Rubha Fiola, Lunga	Area: 0.25 sq miles (0.65 sq km). GR: NM695105
Eilean Duin (IH)	Firth of Lorn	Seil	(G. = Fort Island). GR: NM779212
Eilean Eoghainn (IH)	West Loch Tarbert	Rhu Point	GR: NR824637
Eilean Fada (IH)	Loch Caolisport	Rubha Garbh	GR: NR752759
Eilean Feoir (IH)	Loch na Keal	Rubha Aird nan Eisirein, Mull	GR: NM531389
Eilean Frachlan (IH)	Atlantic	Gunna	GR: NM100516
Eilean Fraoch	Kyles of Bute	Buttock Point, Bute	(G. = Heather Island). One of the Burnt Islands. GR: NS018750
Eilean Fraoch (IH)	Sound of Jura	Barbreack	GR: NR713861
Eilean Gainimh (IH)	Loch Linnhe	Lismore	(G. = Island of Fine Sand). GR: NM891474
Eilean Gamhna (IH)	Atlantic	An Cnap	(G. = Farrow Cow Island). GR: NM782109
Eilean Garbh (IH)	Loch Tuath	Ardalum House, Ulva	(G. = Rough Island). GR: NM440400
Eilean Ghamhna (IH)	Sound of Jura	Kilmory	(G. = Island of the Farrow Cow). One of the MacCormaig Isles. GR: NR680759
Eilean Ghaoideamal (IH)	Caolas Mor	Oronsay	(G. = The Blemished Isle). GR: NR370872
Eilean Ghomain (IH)	Sound of Iona	Erraid, Mull	GR: NM290205
Eilean Ghreasamuill (IH)	Atlantic	Kilkenneth, Tiree	GR: NL932442
Eilean Ghreasamuill (IH)	Atlantic	Miodar, Tiree	GR: NM087497
Eilean Glas (IH)	Loch Crinan	Crinan	(G. = Grey Island). GR: NR799947
Eilean Glas (IH)	Loch Linnhe	Lismore	GR: NM899477
Eilean Grianain	Kilbrannan Sound	Kirnashie Hill	GR: NR813420
Eilean Halum (IH)	Atlantic	Calgary Point, Coll	GR: NM111535
Eilean Imersay (IH)	Atlantic	Ard Imersay, Islay	GR: NR429461
Eilean Inshaig (IH)	Loch Craignish	Ardfern	GR: NM812045
Eilean Iomallach (IH)	Atlantic	Port-na-Luing, Coll	GR: NM156509
Eilean Iosal (IH)	Atlantic	Lunga	(G. = Humble Island). GR: NM707098
Eilean Leathan (IH)	Atlantic	Colonsay	(G. = Broad Island). GR: NR328906
Eilean Leim (IH)	Sound of Gigha	Slocan Leim, Gigha	GR: NR633455
Eilean Liath (IH)	Atlantic	Gometra	GR: NM349407
Eilean Liath (IH)	Atlantic	Mullach nan Gall, Tiree	GR: NM098481
Eilean Liath (IH)	Atlantic	Cnoc Choisprig, Islay	GR: NR186596
Eilean Liath (IH)	Atlantic	Ardtalla, Islay	GR: NR470545
Eilean Liath (IH)	Loch na Keal	Aird Deag, Mull	GR: NM471390
Eilean Liath (IH)	Sound of Gigha	Gallochoille, Gigha	GR: NR656473
Eilean Loain (IH)	Loch Sween	Ashfield	(G. = Pack-of-Hounds Island). GR: NR754855
Eilean Loch Oscair (IH)	Loch Linnhe	Lismore	GR: NM862455
Eilean Loisgte (IH)	Sound of Luing	Bardrishaig, Luing	The lobster pond between Eilean Loisgte and Fraoch Islean is one of the largest in Scotland. GR: NM735117
Eilean Macaskin (IH)	Loch Craignish	Creag a Bhanan	Area: 0.2 sq miles (0.5 sq km). GR: NR786995
Eilean Maol Mhartuin (IH)	Atlantic	Druim an Aoineidh, Iona	GR: NM258226
Eilean Maol Mor (IH)	Atlantic	Cnoc Shoirbidh, Coll	GR: NM190530
Eilean Math-ghamhna	Loch Fyne	Barr nan Damh	GR: NS035986
Eilean Meall na Suiridhe (IH)	Atlantic	Colonsay	GR: NR401992
Eilean Mhartan (IH)	Loch Sween	Kilmichael of Inverlussa	GR: NR773863
Eilean Mhic Chiarain (IH)	Sound of Luing	Dubh Leathad, Luing	GR: NM730111
Eilean Mhic Chrion (IH)	Loch Craignish	Barfad	(G. = MacNiven's Island). GR: NM805035
Eilean Mhic Mhaolmhoire (IH)	Atlantic	Cnoc an Doire Leathain, Islay	One of the Ardmore Islands. GR: NR452483
Eilean Mhugaig (IH)	Atlantic	Oronsay	GR: NR355899
Eilean Mor	Kyles of Bute	Buttock Point, Bute	(G. = Big Island). One of the Burnt Islands. GR: NS018750
Eilean Mor (IH)	Atlantic	Glentrosdale, Jura	GR: NM675010
Eilean Mor (IH)	Atlantic	Traigh Gheal, Mull	GR: NM342168
Eilean Mor (IH)	Atlantic	West Hynish, Tiree	GR: NL959389
Eilean Mor (IH)	Atlantic	Sliabh Bhrothain, Islay	GR: NR210698
Eilean Mor (IH)	Firth of Lorn	Ledaig Point	GR: NM888348
Eilean Mor (IH)	Gulf of Corryvreckan	Uamh Breacain, Jura	GR: NM675010
Eilean Mor (IH)	Loch Buie	Lochbuie, Mull	GR: NM610243
Eilean Mor (IH)	Loch Finlaggan, Islay	Keills, Islay	Island seat of the Lord of the Isles. One of two islands in Loch Finlaggan, the other being Eilean na Comhairle. GR: NR389681
Eilean Mor (IH)	Sea of the Hebrides	Garbh-aird Mor, Coll	GR: NM280650

Island name	Area	Nearest landmark	General information
Eilean Mor (IH)	Sound of Iona	Druim Dhughail, Iona	GR: NM280228
Eilean Mor (IH)	Sound of Jura	Kilmory	Owned by the National Trust for Scotland. One of the MacCormaig Isles. GR: NR667753
Eilean Mor	Loch Fyne	Castleton	GR: NR883838
Eilean Munde	Loch Leven	Alltan Mhic Aoidh	Burial place of the Macdonalds of Glencoe. GR: NN085592
Eilean Musdile (IH)	Lynn of Lorn	Lismore	GR: NM780353
Eilean Musimul (IH)	Atlantic	Druim an Aoineidh, Iona	GR: NM258216
Eilean na Beithe	Loch Fyne	Lub na Faochaige	GR: NR921700
Eilean na Beithe (IH)	Sound of Mull	Tobermory, Mull	GR: NM518550
Eilean na Bilearach (IH)	Atlantic	Colonsay	(G. = Sea-grass Isle). GR: NR334914
Eilean na Cille (IH)	Sound of Jura	Craignish Point	(G. = Chapel Island). GR: NR750970
Eilean na Cloiche	Lynn of Lorn	Lismore	(G. = Island of the Stone). GR: NM838382
Eilean na Comhairle (IH)	Loch Finlaggan, Islay	Keills, Islay	(G. = Council Island). Eilean na Comhairle (pronounced 'coa-oorloo') is one of two islands in Loch Finlaggan, the other being Eilean Mor. GR: NR388680
Eilean na Creiche (IH)	Atlantic	Rubha na Traighe Baine, Ulva	GR: NM390380
Eilean na h-Acairseid (IH)	Atlantic	Rubha na h-Acairseid	GR: NM586725
Eilean na h-Airde (IH)	Sound of Gigha	Tarbert, Gigha	GR: NR645523
Eilean na h-Aoirinn (IH)	Atlantic	Tarbert, Jura	GR: NR622831
Eilean na h-Aon Chaorach (IH)	Atlantic	Druim an Aoineidh, Iona	GR: NM260210
Eilean na h-Eairne (IH)	Sound of Jura	Craignish Point	GR: NR748962
Eilean na h-Uamha (IH)	Atlantic	Caisteal Mor, Ulva	(G. = Cave Island). GR: NM402379
Eilean na h-Uamhaidh (IH)	Loch Caolisport	Rubha Garbh	GR: NR750765
Eilean na h-Uilinn (IH)	Sound of Gigha	Gigalum Island	GR: NR646462
Eilean na Liathanaich (IH)	Loch na Lathaich	Rubh' nam Buthan, Mull	A group of tiny rocky islets lying north of the west entrance to the loch.
Eilean na Nighinn (IH)	Caolas an Eilean	Ceann Caol, Texa	GR: NR386436
Eilean na Nighinn (IH)	Loch Craignish	Duine	Part of Eilean Dubh at low water. GR: NM797025
Eilean na Seamair (IH)	Atlantic	Torr Mor Chonairst, Mull	GR: NM311173
Eilean nam Ban (IH)	Atlantic	Colonsay	(G. = Women's Isle). GR: NR350948
Eilean nam Ban (IH)	Sound of Iona	Fionnphort, Mull	GR: NM301245
Eilean nam Beathach (IH)	Firth of Lorn	Seil	(G. = Isle of the Beasts). GR: NM783208
Eilean nam Bo (IH)	Sound of Iona	Fidden, Mull	GR: NM293215
Eilean nam Caorach (IH)	Loch Scridain	Traigh nam Beach, Mull	GR: NM466245
Eilean nam Freumha (IH)	Firth of Lorn	Seil	(G. = Isle of the Roots). GR: NM777204
Eilean nam Maidean (IH)	Atlantic	Gunna	GR: NM105519
Eilean nam Meann (IH)	Loch Linnhe	Lismore	(G. = Kid Island). GR: NM875456
Eilean nam Meann	Loch Awe	Portinnisherrich	GR: NM974117
Eilean nam Muc (IH)	Atlantic	Meall nam Muc, Coll	(G. = Isle of the Pigs). GR: NM244573
Eilean nam Muc (IH)	Atlantic	Erraid, Mull	GR: NM282192
Eilean nam Muc (IH)	Loch Caolisport	Cuil Rubha	GR: NR728743
Eilean nan Caorach (IH)	Atlantic	Port Ellen, Islay	(G. = Sheep Island). GR: NR367444
Eilean nan Caorach (IH)	Loch Linnhe	Lismore	GR: NM901468
Eilean nan Ceann (IH)	Sound of Luing	Lunga	GR: NM715094
Eilean nan Coinean (IH)	Sound of Jura	Barbreack	(G. = Rabbit Island). GR: NR712862
Eilean nan Coinean (IH)	Sound of Jura	Scodaig	GR: NR778968
Eilean nan Coinein (IH)	Sound of Jura	Craighouse, Jura	One of the Small Isles. GR: NR545685
Eilean nan Gabhar (IH)	Loch Craignish	Old Poltalloch	(G. = Goat Island). GR: NM791003
Eilean nan Gabhar (IH)	Sound of Mull	Bunavullin	GR: NM558535
Eilean nan Gabhar (IH)	Sound of Jura	Craighouse, Jura	One of the Small Isles. GR: NR539675
Eilean nan Gamhna (IH)	Gunna Sound	Gunna	(G. = Island of the Stirks – a stirk is a year-old calf).
Eilean nan Gamhna (IH)	Firth of Lorn	Sidhean Riabhach, Kerrera	GR: NM819303
Eilean nan Gamhna (IH)	Lynn of Lorn	Lismore	GR: NM831381
Eilean nan Gobhar (IH)	Atlantic	Heanish, Tiree	GR: NM039432
Eilean nan Gobhar (IH)	Atlantic	Rhinns Point	GR: NR183512
Eilean nan Laogh (IH)	Loch Craignish	Eilean Macaskin	One of the MacCormaig Isles. GR: NR780986
Eilean nan Leac (IH)	Sound of Jura	Kilmory	(G. = Island of the Grave). One of the MacCormaig Isles. GR: NR690755
Eilean nan Ron (IH)	Atlantic	Oronsay	(G. = Seal Island). A nature reserve. GR: NR333868
Eilean nan Seachd Seisrichean (IH)	Atlantic	Druim Reidh-dhalach	GR: NM424640

Island name	Area	Nearest landmark	General information
Eilean nan Slat (IH)	Atlantic	Culbuirg, Iona	GR: NM262240
Eilean nan Uan (IH)	Atlantic	Oronsay	GR: NR340883
Eilean nan Uan (IH)	Loch Gorm	Aird Reamhar, Islay	Loch Gorm is a freshwater loch on Islay. GR: NR223657
Eilean nan Uan (IH)	Sea of the Hebrides	A Chroic, Coll	GR: NM233635
Eilean nan Uan (IH)	Sound of Jura	Island of Danna	GR: NR685778
Eilean Naomhachd (IH)	Sound of Jura	Point of Knap	GR: NR694732
Eilean Nostaig (IH)	Atlantic	Traigh Nostaig, Islay	GR: NR273736
Eilean Odhar (IH)	Atlantic	Ben Feall, Coll	GR: NM129551
Eilean Olmsa (IH)	Atlantic	Colonsay	GR: NR412961
Eilean Ona (IH)	Atlantic	Drum Beag	GR: NM762021
Eilean Orasaig (IH)	Firth of Lorn	Ardmore, Kerrera	GR: NM794265
Eilean Ornsay (IH)	Atlantic	Arinagour, Coll	GR: NM225554
Eilean Port a' Bhata (IH)	Atlantic	Caisteal Beag, Ulva	GR: NM419378
Eilean Puirt Leithe (IH)	Sound of Jura	Kilmory	GR: NR697757
Eilean Rainich (IH)	Loch Tuath	Normann's Ruh	GR: NM413442
Eilean Ramsay (IH)	Loch Linnhe	Lismore	GR: NM881460
Eilean Reilean (IH)	Atlantic	Cragaig, Ulva	GR: NM405388
Eilean Riabhach (IH)	Lynn of Lorn	Fionn Ard	GR: NM871390
Eilean Righ (IH)	Loch Craignish	Old Poltalloch	Area: 0.33 sq miles (0.86 sq km). GR: NM801015
Eilean Tomulam (IH)	Atlantic	Port-na-Luing, Coll	GR: NM146519
Eilean Tornal (IH)	Balvicar Bay	Balvicar	GR: NM775170
Eilean Traighe (IH)	Sound of Jura	Rubha Riabhag	GR: NR688805
Eilean Traighe (IH)	Sound of Jura	Tayvallich	GR: NR723875
Eilean Traighe (IH)	West Loch Tarbert	Leac Dhubh Earrainn	GR: NR745578
Eilean Traighte (IH)	Loch Craignish	Craigdhu	GR: NM818051
Eilean Treadhrach (IH)	Atlantic	Oronsay	GR: NR380888
Eilean Treunaig (IH)	Atlantic	Oronsay	GR: NR344868
Eilean Trianach (IH)	Sound of Mull	Duart Point, Mull	GR: NM736352
Eilean Uamh Ghuaidhre (IH)	Loch Buie	Cnoc a' Chronain, Mull	GR: NM613230
Eilean Uillne (IH)	Atlantic	Cnoc na Staing	GR: NM545565
Eileanan Bana (IH)	Sound of Mull	Rubha Mor, Mull	GR: NM585435
Eileanan Glasa (IH)	Sound of Mull	Rubha Mor, Mull	(G. = Grey-green Islands). Group of steep grassy rocks. GR: NM595450
Eileanan Gleann Righ (IH)	Atlantic	Meall Righ Beag, Jura	(G. = Islands of the Royal Glen). GR: NR513821
Eileanan Mora (IH)	North Channel	An Gleann, Islay	GR: NR271435
Eileanan na h-Aornan (IH)	Atlantic	Carnan, Coll	GR: NM257593
Eileans, The	Millport Bay	Millport, Great Cumbrae	The two islands of The Eileans are also known as The Allens (N. = Islands).
Ellenabeich (IH)	Firth of Lorn	Easdale, Seil	See Easdale
En Buidhe (IH)	Firth of Lorn	Seil	
En Liath (IH)	Sound of Iona	Fionnphort, Mull	GR: NM297247
Eorsa (IH)	Loch na Keal	Rubha Mor, Mull	Lies in mid-channel of the loch. Area: 0.47 sq miles (1.22 sq km). GR: NM484379
Erisgeir (IH)	Atlantic	Stac Glas Bun an Uisge, Mull	Lies 2 miles (3km) off the coast between Loch Scridain and Loch na Keal. GR: NM381324
Eriska (IH)	Loch Creran	South Shian	(G. = Water Nymph). GR: NM903428
Erraid (IH)	Sound of Iona	Knockvologan, Mull	Robert Louis Stevenson wrote *Kidnapped* here; in the book David Balfour is washed ashore on the island. Area: 0.88 sq miles (2.29 sq km). Population: 8. GR: NM300200
Eun Eilean (IH)	Sound of Gigha	Achamore, Gigha	(G. = Bird Island). GR: NR633476
Fadamull (IH)	Atlantic	Salum, Tiree	GR: NM069496
Fairy Isles (IH)	Loch Sween	Eilean Loain	GR: NS753857
Findlay's Rock (IH)	Atlantic	Lagandorain, Iona	GR: NM285264
Fiola an Droma (IH)	Atlantic	Lunga	(G. = Drum-shaped Tidal). GR: NM708095
Fiola Meadhonach (IH)	Sound of Luing	Lunga	(G. = Middle Tidal). GR: NM710098
Fladda (IH)	Sound of Luing	Rubha Bhuidhe, Luing	(O.N. = Flat Island). One of the Slate Islands of the Inner Hebrides. GR: NM720123
Fladda (IH)	Atlantic	Gometra	One of the Treshnish Isles. GR: NM299438
Frank Lockwood's Island (IH)	Firth of Lorn	Rubha nam Fear, Mull	GR: NM628196
Fraoch Eilean (IH)	Sound of Luing	Bardrishaig, Luing	(G. = Heather Island). The lobster pond between Fraoch Islean and Eilean Loisgte is one of the largest in Scotland. GR: NM735117

Island name	Area	Nearest landmark	General information
Fraoch Eilean	Loch Awe	Achlian	GR: NN109252
Fraoch Eilean	Loch Lomond	Luss	GR: NS367927
Frenchman's Rocks (IH)	Atlantic	Rubha na Faing, Islay	GR: NR153540
Frith Sgeirean (IH)	Atlantic	Oronsay	GR: NR345879
Funaich Mhor (IH)	Sound of Luing	Dubh Leathad, Luing	GR: NM727109
Gamhna Gigha (IH)	Sound of Gigha	Rubh' a' Chairn Bhain, Gigha	GR: NR688547
Gamhnach Mhor (IH)	Atlantic	Aoineadh a Mhaide Ghil, Mull	(G. = Big Cow). GR: NM546206
Gantocks, The	Firth of Clyde	Dunoon	GR: NS179759
Garbh Eileach (IH)	Firth of Lorn	Lunga	One of the Garvellachs. Area: 0.55 sq mile (1.42 sq km). GR: NM670120
Garbh Eilean (IH)	Atlantic	Rubha na Traighe Baine, Ulva	Separated from Little Colonsay by a deep-water channel. GR: NM389375
Garbh Eilean (IH)	Atlantic	Cnoc Mor, Mull	GR: NM410185
Garbh Reisa (IH)	Sound of Jura	Craignish Point	(G. = The Rough One in the Tidal Race). GR: NR755980
Garbh-sgeir Mhor (IH)	Atlantic	Cnoc an Doire Leathain, Islay	GR: NR448477
Geasgill Beag (IH)	Atlantic	Dun Bhioramuill, Ulva	GR: NM430372
Geasgill Mor (IH)	Atlantic	Dun Bhioramuill, Ulva	GR: NM432371
Gigalum Island (IH)	Sound of Gigha	Slocan Leim, Gigha	GR: NR647458
Gigalum Rocks (IH)	Sound of Gigha	Gigalum Island	GR: NR651462
Gigha (IH)	Sound of Gigha	Rhunahaorine Point	Bought by the islanders in 2001. Former owners include Sir James Horlick (d. 1972), of well-known beverage fame, who purchased the island in 1944 and built Achamore, one of the finest gardens in Scotland. Ardminish is the chief town. Area: 5.28 sq miles (13.68 sq km). Population: 110. GR: NR645495
Glas Eilean (IH)	Atlantic	Colonsay	(G. = Pale Grey-green Island). GR: NR335905
Glas Eilean (IH)	Atlantic	Mucraidh, Jura	GR: NR449650
Glas Eilean (IH)	Atlantic	Kilchoan	GR: NM483629
Glas Eilean (IH)	Atlantic	Soa Island	GR: NM239195
Glas Eilean (IH)	Loch Linnhe	Eriska	GR: NM893433
Glas Eilean (IH)	Sound of Jura	Point of Knap	GR: NR695727
Glas Eilean (IH)	Sound of Luing	Bardrishaig, Luing	GR: NM733118
Glas Eilean	Loch Fyne	Achnaba	GR: NR912858
Glasson Rock	Firth of Clyde	Maidens	GR: NS219099
Glunimore Island	Sound of Sanda	Sanda Island	GR: NR742050
Gometra (IH)	Loch Tuath	Ulva	A drying channel separates Gometra from Ulva. Area: 0.04 sq mile (0.11 sq km). Population: 5. GR: NM360410
Great Cumbrae	Firth of Clyde	Largs	Millport is the 'capital'. Area: 4.46 sq miles (11.55 sq km). Population: 1434. GR: NS170570
Greave (IH)	Atlantic	Druim an Aoineidh, Iona	GR: NM240201
Guirasdeal (IH)	Atlantic	Lunga	GR: NM692078
Gunna (IH)	Atlantic	Calgary Point, Coll	Area: 0.27 sq miles (0.69 sq km). GR: NM100515
Half Tide Rock	Firth of Clyde	Lady Isle	GR: NS278295
Hamilton Isle	Firth of Clyde	Clauchlands Point, Isle of Arran	GR: NS058328
Heads of Ayr	Firth of Clyde	Ayr	GR: NS285188
Heather Island (IH)	Sound of Kerrera	Mount Pleasant, Kerrera	GR: NM840295
Henderson's Rock (IH)	Firth of Lorn	Barr Mor, Seill	GR: NM749160
Henrietta Reef	Sound of Sanda	Sheep Island	GR: NR736058
Holy Island	Firth of Clyde	Lamlash, Isle of Arran	See separate entry.
Horse Isle	Firth of Clyde	Ardrossan	Five species of gull nest on this island. GR: NS212428
Horse Isle Shelves	Firth of Clyde	Ardrossan	GR: NS212423
Hough Skerries (IH)	Atlantic	Carrastaoin, Tiree	A group of tiny islets off the coast of Tiree. GR: NL920480
Inch Kenneth (IH)	Loch na Keal	Creag Nmhor, Mull	Named after Kenneth, abbot of Achabo, Ireland, who possibly saved St Columba from drowning through the power of prayer. Area: 0.21 sq miles (0.55 sq km). GR: NM438355
Inchconnachan	Loch Lomond	Luss	aka The Colquhoun's Island. Wallabies were introduced to this island by Lady Arran Colquhoun and can still be seen on occasion. GR: NS374915

Island name	Area	Nearest landmark	General information
Inchgalbraith	Loch Lomond	Luss	aka 'The Island of the Galbraiths'. GR: NS369903
Inchlonaig	Loch Lomond	Luss	aka 'The Island of Yew Trees'. GR: NS380935
Inchmarnock	Sound of Bute	St Ninian's Point	aka The Calf of Bute. Permitted to issue its own postage stamps. The island is divided into three farms: Northpark, Midpark and Southpark. Area: 0.98 sq miles (2.53 sq km). GR: NS020598
Inchmoan	Loch Lomond	Luss	aka 'The Island of Peat'. GR: NS378908
Inchmurrin	Loch Lomond	Knockour	aka 'The Island of St Mirren'. The largest of the islands of Loch Lomond. GR: NS380870
Inchtavannach	Loch Lomond	Luss	aka 'The Monk's Island'. It is thought that St Kessog was killed here. Area: 0.2 sq miles (0.52 sq km). Population: 3. GR: NS366913
Inishail	Loch Awe	Ardanaiseig	GR: NN100245
Inistrynich	Loch Awe	Millside	GR: NN107236
Inn Island (IH)	Loch Linnhe	Lismore	GR: NM900462
Inner Nebbock	Firth of Clyde	Saltcoats	GR: NS245409
Innis Chonain	Loch Awe	Monadh Driseig	Area: 3.02 sq miles (7.83 sq km). Population: 1. GR: NN108258
Innis Chonnell	Loch Awe	Portinnisherrich	Site of the ruined Ardchonell Castle, once a stronghold of the Campbell family. GR: NM978119
Innis Sea-ramhach	Loch Awe	Portinnisherrich	GR: NM972111
Innis Stiuire	Loch Awe	Kilmaha	GR: NM943081
Insh Island (IH)	Firth of Lorn	Rubha Lagain Aillidh, Seill	aka Sheep Island. GR: NM730195
Inveruglas Isle	Loch Lomond	Inveruglas	aka 'The Isle at the Mouth of the Black Stream'. GR: NN323096
Iomallach (IH)	Atlantic	Ardbeg, Islay	GR: NR433443
Iona (IH)	Atlantic	Fionnphort, Mull	St Columba died on the island in 597. Permitted to issue its own postage stamps. Area: 3.3 sq miles (8.55 sq km). Population: 125. GR: NM275240
Iseanach Mor (IH)	Atlantic	Ardbeg, Islay	GR: NR422455
Island I Vow	Loch Lomond	Ceann Mor	aka 'The Island Of The Cow'. The northernmost Island of Loch Lomond. GR: NN331127
Island of Danna	Sound of Jura	Kilbride	Area: 1.22 sq miles (3.15 sq km). Population: 5. GR: NR695785
Island Ross	Kilbrannan Sound	Kildonald Point, Kintyre	GR: NR785273
Islay (IH)	Atlantic	Jura	Best known for its eight whisky distilleries: Ardbeg, Bowmore, Bruichladdich, Bunnahabhain, Caol Ila, Lagavullin, Laphroaig and Port Ellen (now only producing maltings for the other distilleries). Bowmore is the 'capital'. Area: 237.44 sq miles (614.97 sq km). Population: 3,457. GR: NR329652
Jura (IH)	Sound of Jura	Point of Knap	Stag shooting season commences in mid-August so it can be dangerous for strangers to walk around unheralded (a large community of adders adds to the fun!). Craighouse Distillery was built on the island in 1963. Area: 141.09 sq miles (365.43 sq km). Population: 188.
Kenneth's Isle	Loch Leven	Alltan Mhic Aoidh	aka Eilean Choinneich. GR: NN070592
Kerrera (IH)	Firth of Lorn	Oban	Area: 4.69 sq miles (12.14 sq km). Population: 42. GR: NM810285
Kilbride Island	Loch Fyne	Barr Mor	GR: NS005968
Kilchurn Castle	Loch Awe	Stronmilchan	GR: NN133277
Lady Isle	Firth of Clyde	Troon	Colonies of common, sandwich and arctic tern nest on the island. GR: NS275293
Lady's Rock (IH)	Firth of Lorn	Lismore	Elizabeth, wife of Lachlan Cattanach, was marooned here by her husband in 1497 before being rescued by her brother. GR: NM772343
Lainne Sgeir (IH)	Calgary Bay	Cnoc a' Chaisteil, Mull	GR: NM361503
Lair Bhan (IH)	Atlantic	Shuna	GR: NM765065
Lappock Rock	Firth of Clyde	Irvine	GR: NS301349
Leac Bhuidhe (IH)	Atlantic	Traigh Nostaig, Islay	GR: NR280740
Leac Chogaidh (IH)	Atlantic	Ben Feall, Coll	GR: NM142551
Leac nan Geadh (IH)	Atlantic	Oronsay	GR: NR365883
Leth Sgeir (IH)	Atlantic	Barbreack	GR: NR708857

Island name	Area	Nearest landmark	General information
Leth Sgeir (IH)	Sound of Jura	Carsaig	GR: NR735896
Leuach, The	Millport Bay	Millport, Great Cumbrae	(G. = Calf). GR: NS161542
Liath Eilean (IH)	Loch Caolisport	Point of Knap	(G. = Grey Island). GR: NR712725
Liath Eilean (IH)	Sound of Jura	Island of Danna	One of the MacCormaig Isles. GR: NR685783
Liath Eilean	Loch Fyne	Silver Craigs	GR: NR889838
Liath Sgeir (IH)	Atlantic	Craobh Haven	GR: NM788068
Liath Sgeir (IH)	Firth of Lorn	Eilean Dubh Mor	GR: NM695100
Liath Sgeir (IH)	Loch Linnhe	Lismore	GR: NM780371
Liath Sgeir (IH)	Sound of Jura	Leum Beathaig, Jura	GR: NR525645
Liath-sgeir Bheag (IH)	Sound of Jura	Berian Ardifuir	GR: NR779982
Liath-sgeir Mhor (IH)	Sound of Jura	Berian Ardifuir	GR: NR778979
Librig Bheag (IH)	Atlantic	Rubha Nead a' Gheoidh, Tiree	GR: NM098475
Librig Mhor (IH)	Atlantic	Rubha Nead a' Gheoidh, Tiree	GR: NM098473
Liever Island	Loch Awe	Rubhar Mhic Chaisein	GR: NM894049
Limpet Craig	Firth of Clyde	West Kilbride	GR: NS200463
Lismore (IH)	Loch Linnhe	Port Appin	Area: 8.66 sq miles (22.44 sq km). Population: 146. GR: NM840410
Little Ailsa	Firth of Clyde	Ailsa Craig	GR: NX015993
Little Colonsay (IH)	Atlantic	Ulva	Separated from Garbh Eilean by a deep-water channel. Area 0.34 sq miles (0.88 sq km). GR: NM378368
Little Crags	Firth of Clyde	Troon	GR: NS324294
Little Cumbrae	Firth of Clyde	West Kilbride	The island is maintained as a nature reserve and has a 13 bedroom Victorian mansion, six cottages, two lighthouses and a 13th century keep. Area: 1.21 sq miles (3.13 sq km). GR: NS145515
Little Stirk (IH)	Atlantic	Auliston Point	Lies north of the entrance to Loch Sunart. GR: NM534575
Livingston's Rocks (IH)	Atlantic	Aird Mor, Mull	GR: NM319170
Lon na Dubh-sgeir (IH)	Atlantic	West Hynish, Tiree	GR: NL957392
Long Rue	Firth of Clyde	Ayr	GR: NS298191
Luing (IH)	Sound of Luing	Cuan, Seill	The island has a large lobster-fishing centre. One of the Slate Islands. Area: 5.56 sq miles (14.4 sq km). Population: 212. GR: NM745100
Lunga (IH)	Sound of Luing	Cobblers of Lorn, Luing	Area: 1 sq mile (2.59 sq km). Population: 7. GR: NM705085
Lunga (IH)	Atlantic	Gometra	Largest of the Treshnish Isles. Area: 0.31 sq miles (0.81 sq km). GR: NM277417
MacQuarrie's Rock (IH)	Atlantic	Dun Bhioramuill, Ulva	Lies 1 mile (1.6km) east-northeast of Geasgill. GR: NM450378
Maiden Island (IH)	Firth of Lorn	Rubh'a'Bhearnaig, Kerrera	Name derives from the propensity of chieftains to use the island as a refuge for their womenfolk in time of war. GR: NM848319
Maisgeir (IH)	Loch Tuath	Gometra	(O.N. = Seagull Skerry). GR: NM349394
Maol an Domhnaich (IH)	Loch na Keal	Creag Nmhor, Mull	GR: NM443367
Maol Eilean (IH)	Gulf of Corryvreckan	An Cruachan, Jura	GR: NM701012
McPhail's Anvil (IH)	Atlantic	Torr Mor Chonairst, Mull	One of the Torran Rocks. GR: NM267135
Meall an Arbhair (IH)	Atlantic	Colonsay	GR: NR390907
Meall Donn (IH)	Port a'Mhuilinn	Kilbride, Seill	GR: NM749165
Meikle Craigs	Firth of Clyde	Troon	GR: NS325287
Mhic Coinnich (IH)	Atlantic	Portnahaven, Islay	GR: NR161522
Mon (IH)	Atlantic	Rubha an Aird, Mull	GR: NM402543
Mor-mheall (IH)	Atlantic	Rubha Port Bhiosd, Tiree	GR: NL969491
Mull (IH)	Firth of Lorn	Lochaline	Ben More on Mull at 3169ft (966m) is the only Munro in the Scottish Islands as, although Skye is included in my list and has 22 Munros, it no longer qualifies as a true island because it is linked to the mainland by a bridge. Christianity was introduced to the island after St Columba's arrival in AD 563. Tobermory (G. Tobar Mhoire = Mary's Well) is the 'capital'. Area: 344.06 sq miles (891.11 sq km). Population: 2667. GR: NM563361
Na Cuiltean (IH)	Sound of Jura	Leum Beathaig, Jura	GR: NR549645
Na Dubh-sgeireagan (IH)	Sound of Gigha	Cnoc nan Gobhar, Gigha	GR: NR665555
Na h-Iseanan (IH)	Hynish Bay	Baugh, Tiree	GR: NM014435

Island name	Area	Nearest landmark	General information
Na Liathanaich (IH)	Atlantic	Carraig Ghilliondrais, Mull	GR: NM360250
Na Maoil Mhora (IH)	Atlantic	Rubha nam Maol Mora, Mull	GR: NM336164
Na Minn (IH)	Atlantic	Aird Dubh, Mull	GR: NM382181
Na Sgeirean Mora (IH)	Atlantic	Rubh' an Fhaing, Tiree	GR: NM008485
Na Torrain (IH)	Atlantic	Torr Mor Chonairst, Mull	Largest islet of the Torran Rocks. GR: NM267140
Nave (IH)	Atlantic	Ardnave Point, Islay	GR: NR290760
New Rocks (IH)	Sound of Mull	Calve Island	Rock stack north of Calve Island.
Oitic nam Bo (IH)	Loch Gruinart	Bunpan-uillt, Islay	GR: NR290695
Oitir Mor	Sound of Sanda	Macharioch, Kintyre	GR: NR744091
Ormsa (IH)	Sound of Luing	Rubha Fiola, Lunga	GR: NM711118
Oronsay (IH)	Atlantic	Colonsay	Separated from Colonsay by 'The Strand' which can be walked across when the tide is out. Area: 2.23 sq miles (5.76 sq km). Population: 5. GR: NR355885
Orsay (IH)	Atlantic	Portnahaven, Islay	The site of the world's first commercial wave-energy electricity generator. GR: NR164515
Outer Nebbock	Firth of Clyde	Saltcoats	GR: NS241410
Outram (IH)	Atlantic	Cnoc an Doire Leathain, Islay	One of the Ardmore Islands. GR: NR466483
Pan Rocks	Firth of Clyde	Troon	GR: NS320314
Paterson's Rock	Sound of Sanda	Sanda Island	GR: NR751045
Perch Rock	Firth of Clyde	Rosneath Point	GR: NS278809
Pladda (IH)	Sound of Jura	Craighouse, Jura	One of the Small Isles. GR: NR541689
Pladda	Firth of Clyde	Kildonan, Isle of Arran	Known for the seals which inhabit its shores. Area: 0.04 sq miles (0.11 sq km). GR: NS028193
Pladda (IH)	Lynn of Lorn	Lismore	GR: NM838371
Plaide Mhor (IH)	Atlantic	Colonsay	GR: NR345923
Poll na Sgeire Ruaidhe (IH)	Loch na Keal	Creag Nmhor, Mull	GR: NM443356
Post Rocks (IH)	Atlantic	Port a'Chotain, Islay	GR: NR401800
Rankin's Rocks (IH)	Atlantic	Erraid, Mull	GR: NM288188
Red Rocks (IH)	Atlantic	Auliston Point	Lies north of the entrance to Loch Sunart. GR: NM530591
Reidh Eilean (IH)	Atlantic	Carraig an Daimh, Iona	(G. = Levelled Island). GR: NM244262
Reisa an t-Sruith (IH)	Sound of Jura	Aird of Kinuachdrachd, Jura	(G. = The Tidal Race Island in the Current). GR: NR735993
Reisa Mhic Phaidean (IH)	Atlantic	Sron an Droma	(G. = McFadyen's Island in the Tidal Race). GR: NM750010
Roc Dearg	Loch Fyne	Furnace	GR: NN037003
Ross Islands	Loch Lomond	Ross Promontory	Three islets off the Ross Promontory. GR: NS364951
Ruadh Sgeir (IH)	Atlantic	Rubha nam Maol Mora, Mull	GR: NM309149
Ruadh Sgeir (IH)	Sound of Jura	Bogh a'Chuirn, Jura	GR: NR722927
Rubh' a' Bhogha Mhoir (IH)	Atlantic	Little Colonsay	GR: NM372376
Rubh' Aird Luing (IH)	Sound of Luing	Aird Luing, Luing	GR: NM743053
Rubha Fiola (IH)	Sound of Luing	Lunga	(G. = Tidal Headland). The owner runs the island as an adventure centre. GR: NM712105
Rubha Mor (IH)	Firth of Lorn	Garbh Eileach	One of the Garvellachs.
Samalan Island (IH)	Loch na Keal	Creag Nmhor, Mull	GR: NM452365
Sanda Island	Sound of Sanda	Southend, Kintyre	Permitted to issue its own postage stamps. The island is known locally as 'Spoon Island'. Area: 0.54 sq miles (1.39 sq km). Population: 1. GR: NR725045
Scarba (IH)	Firth of Lorn	Luing	Owned by Lord Richard Sandys, a member of the family of former minister of state Lord Duncan-Sandys. Area: 5.69 sq miles (14.74 sq km). GR: NM700045
Scarisdale Rocks (IH)	Loch na Keal	Scarisdale Point, Mull	GR: NM521386
Scart Rock	Firth of Clyde	Ardrossan	GR: NS213447
Scart Rock	Firth of Clyde	Lady Isle	GR: NS278297
Scart Rocks	Sound of Sanda	Sheep Island	GR: NR737053
Scott Rock (IH)	Loch na Lathaich	Rubh' nam Buthan, Mull	Lies in the middle of the loch entrance.
Scoul Eilean (IH)	Atlantic	Degnish Point	GR: NM769112
Seal Rock	Kilbrannan Sound	Peninver, Kintyre	GR: NR770255
Seal Rock	Firth of Clyde	Troon	GR: NS319299

Island name	Area	Nearest landmark	General information
Seil (IH)	Firth of Lorn	Clachan	One of the Slate Islands. Joined to the mainland by the Clachan Bridge. Area: 5.42 sq miles (14.05 sq km). Population: 560. GR: NM760170
Sgaigein (IH)	Atlantic	Little Colonsay	Tiny islet off the northeast coast of Little Colonsay. GR: NM383372
Sgat Beag	Loch Fyne	Cnoc Mor	GR: NR942665
Sgat Mor	Loch Fyne	Eilean Aoidhe	GR: NR930666
Sgavoch Rock	Firth of Clyde	Ballantrae	GR: NX072810
Sgeir a' Bhuntata (IH)	Caolas an Eilean	Cara	GR: NR638451
Sgeir a' Caolas (IH)	Sound of Gigha	Gallochoille, Gigha	GR: NR670475
Sgeir a' Chaisteil (IH)	Atlantic	Lunga	One of the Treshnish Isles. GR: NM279429
Sgeir a' Charraigein (IH)	Loch na Keal	Aird Deag, Mull	GR: NM457389
Sgeir a' Cheirde (IH)	Loch na Keal	Samalan Island	
Sgeir a' Chiaidheimh Beag (IH)	Atlantic	Mackinnon's Cave, Mull	GR: NM427328
Sgeir a' Chiaidheimh Mor (IH)	Atlantic	Mackinnon's Cave, Mull	GR: NM420326
Sgeir a' Chlachain (IH)	Atlantic	Ardbeg, Islay	GR: NR431455
Sgeir a' Chleirich (IH)	Seil Sound	Degnish Point	GR: NM772123
Sgeir a' Choire (IH)	Atlantic	Ceann Garbh, Texa	GR: NR400438
Sgeir a' Gheoidh (IH)	Firth of Lorn	Eilean Dubh Mor	GR: NM701111
Sgeir a' Phuirt (IH)	Firth of Lorn	Garbh Eileach	GR: NM670118
Sgeir an Eirionnaich (IH)	Atlantic	Gometra	One of the Treshnish Isles. GR: NM285433
Sgeir an Eitich (IH)	Firth of Lorn	Ganavan	GR: NM853326
Sgeir an Fheidh (IH)	Atlantic	Na h-Ursainnan, Jura	GR: NR503839
Sgeir an Fheoir (IH)	Atlantic	Gometra	One of the Treshnish Isles. GR: NM292428
Sgeir an Fhiodh (IH)	Sound of Jura	Kilberry, Kintyre	GR: NR708678
Sgeir an Oir (IH)	Atlantic	Druim an Aoineidh, Iona	GR: NM259206
Sgeir an Roin (IH)	Sound of Gigha	Cruachan	GR: NR687451
Sgeir an Tairbh (IH)	Atlantic	Rubha Port Bhiosd, Tiree	GR: NL966488
Sgeir Beul na h-Uamhaidh (IH)	Sound of Insh	Insh Island	GR: NM737196
Sgeir Bharrach (IH)	Atlantic	Vaul, Tiree	GR: NM046494
Sgeir Bheag (IH)	Sound of Gigha	Ardminish Point, Gigha	GR: NR666505
Sgeir Bheathaig	Kilbrannan Sound	Oragaig	GR: NR851539
Sgeir Bhiorach (IH)	Atlantic	Colonsay	GR: NR321904
Sgeir Bhioramuill (IH)	Loch na Keal	Dun Bhioramuill, Ulva	GR: NM441381
Sgeir Bhuidhe (IH)	Firth of Lorn	Seil	GR: NM779208
Sgeir Bhuidhe (IH)	Firth of Lorn	Rubha Bhuidhe, Luing	GR: NM735125
Sgeir Bhuidhe (IH)	Loch na Keal	Samalan Island	
Sgeir Bhuidhe (IH)	Loch na Keal	Eorsa	
Sgeir Bhuidhe	Kilbrannan Sound	Ravensbay	GR: NR839519
Sgeir Blar nan Each (IH)	Atlantic	Gometra	One of the Treshnish Isles. GR: NM243383
Sgeir Blath-shuileach (IH)	Sound of Gigha	Rubh'an Stearnail, Gigha	GR: NR669515
Sgeir Buidell (IH)	Caolas an Eilean	Cara	GR: NR637445
Sgeir Bun an Locha (IH)	Sound of Jura	Island of Danna	GR: NR695770
Sgeir Caillich (IH)	Loch Creran	Balure	GR: NM912423
Sgeir Chaol (IH)	Sound of Gigha	A'Chleit	GR: NR681422
Sgeir Charrach (IH)	Atlantic	Rubha Aird Druimnich	GR: NM583732
Sgeir Chorrach Mhor (IH)	Atlantic	Rubha Liath, Tiree	GR: NM089463
Sgeir Chreagag (IH)	Atlantic	Shuna	GR: NN775092
Sgeir Criaraidh (IH)	Shuna Sound	Luing	GR: NM758108
Sgeir Cul an Rubha (IH)	Sound of Jura	Rubh' a'Chamais	GR: NR600784
Sgeir Dhearg (IH)	Atlantic	Rubha an Aird, Mull	GR: NM408548
Sgeir Dhoirbh (IH)	Atlantic	Torr Mor Chonairst, Mull	One of the Torran Rocks. GR: NM284113
Sgeir Dhonn (IH)	Firth of Lorn	Rubh'Ard an Duine, Kerrera	GR: NM829309
Sgeir Dhonncha (IH)	Sound of Jura	Island of Danna	GR: NR687770
Sgeir Dhubh (IH)	Atlantic	Rubha na Traighe Baine, Ulva	GR: NM387381
Sgeir Dhubh (IH)	Loch Craignish	Rubha Dubh nan Cuileann	GR: NM813039
Sgeir Dhubh Bheag (IH)	Atlantic	Caisteal Mor, Ulva	GR: NM399376
Sgeir Dubh (IH)	Gunna Sound	Gunna	GR: NM098506
Sgeir Dubh (IH)	Loch Feochan	Minard Point	GR: NM819229
Sgeir Dubhail (IH)	Loch Tuath	Rubha nan Gall, Ulva	Drying rock stack which is a hazard to shipping. GR: NM428417
Sgeir Fhada (IH)	Atlantic	Port Ellen, Islay	GR: NR360445
Sgeir Fharspaig (IH)	Atlantic	Port-na-Luing, Coll	GR: NM148513
Sgeir Fhiacail (IH)	Sound of Gigha	Cnoc nan Gobhar, Gigha	GR: NR665548

Island name	Area	Nearest landmark	General information
Sgeir Ghlas (IH)	Sound of Mull	Faoileann Ghlas, Mull	GR: NM622434
Sgeir Ghobhlach (IH)	Atlantic	Sanna Point	GR: NM436701
Sgeir Ghobhlach (IH)	Atlantic	Torr Mor Chonairst, Mull	One of the Torran Rocks. GR: NM278128
Sgeir Gigalum (IH)	Sound of Gigha	Gigalum Island	GR: NR658461
Sgeir Lag Choan (IH)	Loch Etive	Lag Choan	GR: NN030339
Sgeir Laith (IH)	Firth of Lorn	Seil	GR: NM781212
Sgeir Leathan (IH)	Atlantic	Colonsay	GR: NR325904
Sgeir Leathan (IH)	Atlantic	Rubha Dubh, Mull	GR: NM406241
Sgeir Leathan (IH)	Atlantic	Rubha Nead a' Gheoidh, Tiree	GR: NM091467
Sgeir Leathan (IH)	Firth of Lorn	Portfield, Mull	GR: NM721263
Sgeir Leathan (IH)	Loch na Keal	Creag Nmhor, Mull	GR: NM440362
Sgeir Leathann (IH)	Atlantic	Colonsay	GR: NM412005
Sgeir Leathann (IH)	Atlantic	Oronsay	GR: NR362862
Sgeir Leathann	Loch Fyne	Barmore Island	GR: NR872717
Sgeir Leth a' Chuain (IH)	Firth of Lorn	A' Chuli	One of the Garvellachs. NM650108
Sgeir Liath (IH)	Atlantic	Ardtalla, Islay	GR: NR471549
Sgeir Liath (IH)	Lynn of Lorn	Tralee	GR: NM875398
Sgeir Maldaig (IH)	Loch na Keal	Cnocan Buidhe, Mull	GR: NM513400
Sgeir Mhaola Cinn	Loch Fyne	Barmore Island	GR: NR871721
Sgeir Mhic an Altair (IH)	Sound of Luing	Barr a' Bhealaich	GR: NM715075
Sgeir Mhic Chomhain (IH)	Sound of Mull	Java, Mull	GR: NM708391
Sgeir Mhogalach (IH)	Firth of Lorn	Eilean Dubh Mor	
Sgeir Mhor (IH)	Atlantic	Druim nan Cliabh, Jura	GR: NR654982
Sgeir Mhor (IH)	Atlantic	Quinish Point, Mull	GR: NM397564
Sgeir Mhor (IH)	Atlantic	Rubha Port Bhiosd, Tiree	GR: NL966489
Sgeir Mhor (IH)	Loch Scridain	Killunaig, Mull	GR: NM489259
Sgeir Mhor (IH)	Loch Scridain	Tiroran, Mull	GR: NM481274
Sgeir Mhor (IH)	North Channel	Muasdale	GR: NR674399
Sgeir Mhor (IH)	Sound of Gigha	Ardminish Point, Gigha	GR: NR665503
Sgeir Mhor a'Bhrein-phuirt (IH)	Atlantic	Na h-Ursainnan, Jura	GR: NR504841
Sgeir Mor (IH)	Sound of Mull	Glenmorven Cott	GR: NM566513
Sgeir na Caillich (IH)	Atlantic	Torr Mor Chonairst, Mull	GR: NM293179
Sgeir na Caillich (IH)	Loch Melfort	Druim an Fhaillich	GR: NM808125
Sgeir na Cille (IH)	Loch Tuath	Kilninian	GR: NM392451
Sgeir na Cusha (IH)	Sound of Luing	Dubh Leathad, Luing	GR: NM727107
Sgeir na Dubhaidh	Loch Fyne	Barmore Island	GR: NR871712
Sgeir na Fainne (IH)	Atlantic	Vaul, Tiree	GR: NM058497
Sgeir na Faoilinn (IH)	Atlantic	Stac Glas Bun an Uisge, Mull	GR: NM419310
Sgeir na Faoilinn (IH)	Loch Spelve	Fellonmore, Mull	GR: NM685279
Sgeir na h-Aireig (IH)	Firth of Lorn	Cuan Point, Luing	GR: NM743143
Sgeir na h-Iolaire (IH)	Atlantic	Gometra	One of the Treshnish Isles. GR: NM289439
Sgeir na Laimhrige Moire (IH)	Loch na Keal	Creag Nmhor, Mull	(G. = The Rock of Mary's Landing Place). GR: NM444364
Sgeir na Luib (IH)	West Loch Tarbert	Rubh'a'Bharr Ruaidh	GR: NR773590
Sgeir na Maoile (IH)	Sound of Jura	Craignish Point	GR: NR745975
Sgeir na Mine (IH)	Atlantic	Guirasdeal	GR: NM692081
Sgeir na Nighinn (IH)	Atlantic	Ardnave Point, Islay	GR: NR299744
Sgeir na Skeineadh (IH)	Loch Tuath	Rubha Bhrisdeadh-ramh, Ulva	GR: NM371390
Sgeir nam Ban (IH)	Atlantic	Cnoc an Doire Leathain, Islay	GR: NR469498
Sgeir nam Faoileann (IH)	Atlantic	Sron an Droma	GR: NM752015
Sgeir nam Faoileann (IH)	Firth of Lorn	Barr Mor, Seill	GR: NM749154
Sgeir nam Figheadair (IH)	Sound of Luing	Aird Luing, Luing	GR: NM746052
Sgeir nam Marag (IH)	Firth of Lorn	A' Chuli	One of the Garvellachs. GR: NM654107
Sgeir nan Damh (IH)	Loch na Keal	Inch Kenneth	GR: NM444354
Sgeir nan Eun (IH)	Atlantic	Rubh' a' Mhile	GR: NM510631
Sgeir nan Gabhar (IH)	Atlantic	Scarba	GR: NM686058
Sgeir nan Gabhar (IH)	Sound of Luing	Rubha Fiola, Lunga	GR: NM713110
Sgeir nan Gael (IH)	Lynn of Lorn	Lismore	GR: NM779349
Sgeir nan Garbhanach (IH)	Atlantic	Calgary Point, Coll	GR: NM122501
Sgeir nan Gobhar (IH)	Sound of Mull	Java, Mull	GR: NM709393
Sgeir nan Leac (IH)	Loch na Keal	Dun Bhioramuill, Ulva	GR: NM442381
Sgeir nan Ordag (IH)	Atlantic	Lunga	GR: NM702095
Sgeir nan Ron (IH)	Loch Tuath	Torr an Aird	GR: NM428428
Sgeir nan Saidhean (IH)	Atlantic	Eilean Dubh Beag	GR: NM702116
Sgeir nan Sgarbh (IH)	Atlantic	Traigh Nostaig, Islay	GR: NR282747

Island name	Area	Nearest landmark	General information
Sgeir nan Sgarbh (IH)	Sound of Jura	Kilberry, Kintyre	GR: NR708677
Sgeir nan Sian (IH)	Atlantic	Camas an Staca, Jura	GR: NR466638
Sgeir nan Sligean (IH)	Laggan Bay	Knockangle Point, Islay	GR: NR319500
Sgeir nan Taod (IH)	Atlantic	Eilean Dubh Beag	GR: NM692111
Sgeir nan Tom (IH)	Loch Linnhe	Lismore	GR: NM888478
Sgeir Nuadh (IH)	Sound of Gigha	Rubh'an Stearnail, Gigha	GR: NR674509
Sgeir Phlocach (IH)	Atlantic	Port Ellen, Islay	GR: NR364443
Sgeir Phlocach (IH)	Sound of Jura	Creag nan Sgarbh, Jura	GR: NR521634
Sgeir Poll nan Corran (IH)	Sound of Luing	Lunga	GR: NM712080
Sgeir Port a' Ghuail	Loch Fyne	Rubha Bhadan	GR: NR874700
Sgeir Ruadh (IH)	Loch Tuath	Ardalum House, Ulva	GR: NM434410
Sgeir Ruadh (IH)	Sound of Iona	Druim Dhughail, Iona	GR: NM276223
Sgeir Ruadh (IH)	Sound of Mull	Mon, Mull	GR: NM732362
Sgeir Sgorach (IH)	Loch na Keal	Aird Deag, Mull	GR: NM470389
Sgeir Sgoraig (IH)	Lynn of Lorn	Lismore	GR: NM810369
Sgeir Shealg (IH)	Atlantic	Carrastaoin, Tiree	GR: NL929488
Sgeir Thraghaidh (IH)	Caolas an Eilean	Islay	
Sgeir Traighe (IH)	Atlantic	Sgriob na Caillich, Jura	GR: NR453769
Sgeir Uilleim (IH)	Atlantic	Rubha Nead a' Gheoidh, Tiree	GR: NM093465
Sgeir-dhubh an Amomaidh (IH)	Sound of Jura	Point of Knap	GR: NR695724
Sgeirean a' Mhaoil (IH)	Sound of Luing	Scarba	GR: NM720049
Sgeirean an Loin (IH)	Atlantic	Uamh nam Fear, Texa	GR: NR394432
Sgeirean an Roin (IH)	Gott Bay	Gott, Tiree	GR: NM058461
Sgeirean Beaga (IH)	Atlantic	Rubha an Aird, Mull	GR: NM395552
Sgeirean Buidhe (IH)	North Channel	Beinn Mhor, Islay	GR: NR282405
Sgeirean Buidhe (IH)	Sound of Jura	Craighouse, Jura	GR: NR528676
Sgeirean Buidhe Ghil (IH)	North Channel	Dun an Fhithich, Islay	GR: NR271441
Sgeirean Dearga (IH)	Caolas an Eilean	Texa	GR: NR391445
Sgeirean Dubh (IH)	Atlantic	Portnahaven, Islay	GR: NR159526
Sgeirean Dubha (IH)	Sound of Kerrera	Rubha'an Fheurain	GR: NM815263
Sgeirean Dubha (IH)	Firth of Lorn	Eileach an Naoimh	One of the Garvellachs. GR: NM642095
Sgeirean Fada (IH)	Atlantic	Oronsay	GR: NR342900
Sgeirean Giusaich (IH)	Atlantic	Gometra	One of the Treshnish Isles. GR: NM288428
Sgeirean Leathann (IH)	Atlantic	Traigh Nostaig, Islay	GR: NR281751
Sgeirean Mor (IH)	Atlantic	Rubha Dubh, Mull	GR: NM408242
Sgeirean Mor (IH)	Atlantic	Gometra	One of the Treshnish Isles. GR: NM288419
Sgeirean na Giusaich (IH)	Atlantic	Gometra	One of the Treshnish Isles.
Sgeirean nan Cuiseag (IH)	Atlantic	Port-na-Luing, Coll	GR: NM156518
Sgeirean Poll a' Chaca (IH)	Atlantic	Ceann Caol, Texa	GR: NR388432
Sgeirean Traghaidh (IH)	Atlantic	Carn Mor, Islay	GR: NR194657
Sgeireig a' Bhogadain (IH)	Atlantic	Rubh' Ardalanish, Mull	GR: NM359161
Sgiath Mhor (IH)	Sound of Mull	Salen, Mull	GR: NM570440
Sgiath Ruadh (IH)	Sound of Mull	Glenaros Cott, Mull	GR: NM565445
Sgor Cainnteach (IH)	Sound of Gigha	Rhunahaorine Point	GR: NR694509
Shearwater Rock	Sound of Bute	Inchmarnock	GR: NS028580
Sheep Island	Sound of Sanda	Sanda Island	Area: 0.01 sq miles (0.03 sq km). GR: NR733055
Shian Island (IH)	Atlantic	Shian Bay, Jura	GR: NR528882
Shuna (IH)	Shuna Sound	Toberonochy, Luing	Owned by Christopher Gully, who inherited the island from his father Edward Gully, 5th Viscount Selby. One of the Slate Islands. Area: 1.69 sq miles (4.38 sq km). Population: 1. GR: NM765080
Shuna (IH)	Loch Linnhe	The Knap	Area: 0.6 sq miles (1.55 sq km). GR: NM915490
Skerryvore (IH)	Atlantic	Tiree	GR: NL842264
Skervuile Lighthouse (IH)	Sound of Jura	Rubh'an Leim	GR: NR604712
Sligneach Beag (IH)	Atlantic	Rubha Aird Shlignich	GR: NM553601
Sligneach Mor (IH)	Atlantic	Rubha Aird Shlignich	GR: NM561601
Smerby Rocks	Kilbrannan Sound	Lower Smerby, Kintyre	GR: NR764231
Soa (IH)	Atlantic	Port-na-Luing, Coll	GR: NM156512
Soa (IH)	Atlantic	Druim an Aoineidh, Iona	(O.N. = Sheep Island).
Soa (IH)	Gott Bay	Ruaig, Tiree	GR: NM070460
Soa Island (IH)	Atlantic	Erraid, Mull	GR: NM242192
Soy Gunna	Caolas Ban	Gunna	GR: NM106520
Spoig, The	Millport Bay	Millport, Great Cumbrae	(G. = Ham-shaped Rock). GR: NS161542
Sron an Fhraoich (IH)	Atlantic	Beinn Ceann a Mhara, Tiree	GR: NL931407
St Nicholas Rock	Firth of Clyde	Ayr	GR: NS328226

Island name	Area	Nearest landmark	General information
Stac a' Bhodaich (IH)	Atlantic	Gott, Tiree	GR: NM043460
Stac an Aoineidh (IH)	Atlantic	Druim an Aoineidh, Iona	GR: NM251227
Stac Liath (IH)	Atlantic	Culbuirg, Iona	GR: NM261239
Stac Mhic Mhurchaidh (IH)	Atlantic	Carraig an Daimh, Iona	The larger of two steep islets lying $2^1/_2$ miles (4km) northwest of Iona (Reidh Eilean being the smaller island). GR: NM241261
Staffa (IH)	Atlantic	Gometra	Site of Fingal's Cave (Sir Joseph Banks named the cave after legendary Irish hero Fionn McCool). Permitted to issue its own postage stamps. Area: 0.13 sq miles (0.33 sq km). GR: NM325355
Stinking Rocks	Firth of Clyde	Troon	GR: NS323335
Suil Ghorm (IH)	Sea of the Hebrides	Garbh-aird Mor, Coll	(G. = Blue Eye). GR: NM281658
Tarbet Isle	Loch Lomond	Cruach Tairbeirt	aka 'The Island of the Drag Boat'. GR: NN329054
Tarr Sgeir (IH)	Atlantic	Texa	GR: NR388421
Taynish Island (IH)	Loch Sween	Old Ulva	GR: NR728827
Texa (IH)	Atlantic	Rubh' a'Chuirn, Islay	Ceann Garbh is the highest point at 157ft (48m). The island was inhabited until the early 19th century. Area: 0.19 sq miles (0.48 sq km). GR: NR392436
Thorn Isle	Kilbrannan Sound	Peninver, Kintyre	GR: NR771259
Tighchoie (IH)	Atlantic	Gometra	One of the Treshnish Isles. GR: NM282435
Tiree (IH)	Atlantic	Coll	Area: 31.62 sq miles (81.91 sq km). Population: 770. GR: NM000450
Torr an t-Saothaid (IH)	Atlantic	Torr Mor Chonairst, Mull	One of the Torran Rocks. GR: NM278140
Torran Sgoitte (IH)	Atlantic	Torr Mor Chonairst, Mull	One of the Torran Rocks. GR: NM279129
Torrinch	Loch Lomond	Craigie Fort	aka 'The Tower Island'. GR: NS402893
Torsa (IH)	Seil Sound	Ardinamir, Luing	(O.N. = Thor's Island). One of the Slate Islands. Area: 0.39 sq miles (1 sq km). GR: NM762130
Torsa (IH)	Seil Sound	Cuan, Seill	One of the Slate Islands. GR: NM760130
Torsa Beag (IH)	Seil Sound	Torsa	(O.N. *Torsa* = Thor's Island; G. *Beag* = Little). GR: NM756128
Tra na h-Uil	Sound of Bute	Inchmarnock	GR: NS013599
Traigh Bail'-a-mhuilinn (IH)	Atlantic	Rubha na Bo Maoile, Tiree	GR: NL955480
Traigh Bhan (IH)	Atlantic	Rubha na Traighe Baine, Ulva	GR: NM391384
Traigh Mor (IH)	Sound of Iona	Druim Dhughail, Iona	GR: NM281228
Traigh Uamha Seilbhe (IH)	Atlantic	Oronsay	GR: NR360875
Trail	Firth of Clyde	Little Cumbrae	GR: NS153512
Trealbhan (IH)	Loch Tuath	Rubha na Diollaide	GR: NM386387
Ulva (IH)	Loch Tuath	Oskamull, Mull	(O.N. = Wolf Island). General Lachlan MacQuarie (1761–1824), the 'father of Australia', was born on the island. Area: 7.29 sq miles (18.88 sq km). Population: 16. GR: NM410400
Ulva Islands (IH)	Loch Sween	Old Ulva	GR: NR720822
Wallace's Isle	Loch Lomond	Inveruglas	aka 'The Island of Someone Called Wallace'. GR: NN321091
Wee Rocks (IH)	Sound of Gigha	Gigalum Island	GR: NR658460
West Reef (IH)	Atlantic	Torr Mor Chonairst, Mull	One of the Torran Rocks. GR: NM240139
Whilk Isle	Firth of Clyde	Lendalfoot	GR: NX114892
White's Rock (IH)	Atlantic	Rubh' Ardalanish, Mull	GR: NM355163
Wright's Island	Firth of Clyde	Dipple	GR: NS196022
Yellow Crags	Firth of Clyde	Ardrossan	GR: NS220435
Yellow Rock	Kilbrannan Sound	Peninver, Kintyre	GR: NR762245

TAYSIDE

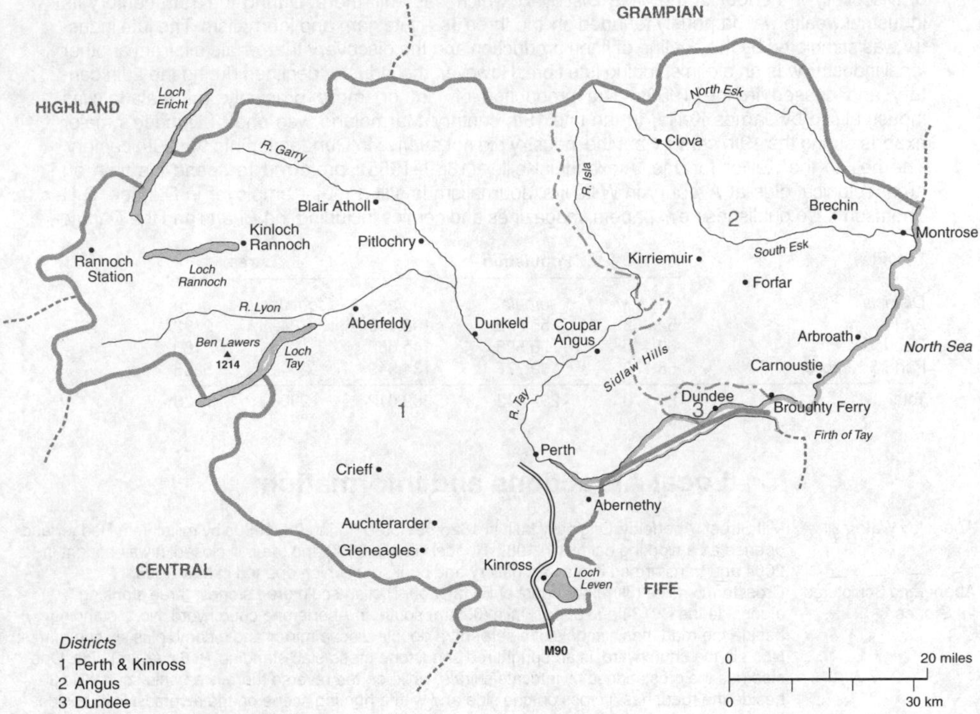
GRAMPIAN
HIGHLAND
Loch Ericht
North Esk
Clova
R. Garry
R. Isla
Blair Atholl
Brechin
2
Kinloch Rannoch
Montrose
Pitlochry
Rannoch Station
Loch Rannoch
South Esk
Kirriemuir
Forfar
R. Lyon
Aberfeldy
Dunkeld
Coupar Angus
Arbroath
North Sea
Ben Lawers
1214
Loch Tay
Sidlaw Hills
Carnoustie
Dundee
3
Broughty Ferry
1
R. Tay
Firth of Tay
Perth
Crieff
Abernethy
Auchterarder
Gleneagles
Kinross
CENTRAL
Loch Leven
FIFE
M90
Districts
1 Perth & Kinross
2 Angus
3 Dundee
0
20 miles
0
30 km

Tayside is bordered by Grampian to the northeast, Highland to the northwest, Strathclyde on its western extremity, Central on the southwest and Fife on the southeast. The North Sea washes its eastern shores. From 1975 to 1996 Tayside was a local government region divided into three districts – Perth & Kinross, Angus, and the City of Dundee. Since 1996 the districts have been stand-alone unitary authorities but are included here under their old region heading. Although the three council areas have their own administrative headquarters, Tayside continues to have a joint police service, fire service, and electoral, valuation and health boards. Tayside has a rich maritime history, the port records of Dundee being some of the oldest in Europe, and Arbroath building an industry exporting barrels of herring to Königsberg (now Kaliningrad) on the Baltic Sea.

Perth & Kinross is one of 32 unitary council areas in Scotland. It shares borders with the Aberdeenshire, Angus, City of Dundee, Fife, Clackmannanshire, Stirling, Argyll & Bute and Highland council areas. Perthshire and Kinross-shire had a joint county council from 1929 until 1975. The area was created a single district in 1975, in the Tayside region, under the Local Government (Scotland) Act 1973, and reconstituted as a unitary authority (with a minor boundary adjustment) in 1996, by the Local Government (Scotland) Act 1994. A good gauge of how rural the area is can be seen in the fact that its area is ninety times that of Dundee and yet its population is smaller. Principal towns include Dunkeld and Perth.

Angus shares borders with Aberdeenshire, Perth & Kinross and the City of Dundee. Historically a county (known officially by its anglicised title of Forfarshire until 1928), in 1975 it became a district of the Tayside region. The former county had borders with Kincardineshire to the northeast, Aberdeenshire to the north and Perthshire to the west. To the south, it faced Fife across the Firth of Tay. Main industries include agriculture and fishing. Major towns in the Tayside area include Arbroath, Brechin, Forfar and Montrose. Angus is largely a rural area, particularly in the north and west where the Braes (hills) of Angus, emanating from the Strathmore Valley, form the south-eastern edge of the Grampian Mountains in the southern area of the Cairngorms National Park. The Ardler, Shee, Isla, Prosen, South Esk and North Esk rivers cut down through the braes forming deep glens (valleys), the most famous being the so-called Five Glens of Angus, i.e., from west to east Glens, Isla, Prosen, Clova, Lethnot and Esk

Dundee (Dun Dèagh = Fort on the Tay), a unitary authority and royal burgh on the Firth of Tay, is Scotland's fourth largest city. and celebrated its 800th anniversary in 1991. It was founded as a Pictish settlement and granted its royal charter by William the Lion in 1191. It is known as 'The City of Discovery' in honour of the RRS *Discovery* which was built there. During the 19th century its industrial wealth was famously founded on 'the three Js' – jute, jam and journalism. The jute industry was stimulated by the decline of linen production and the discovery that whale oil, from another local industry, was an aid in spinning jute fibre. However, the industry declined during the 20th century and ceased in the 1960s. The production of jam or, more precisely, marmalade was industrialised by James Keiller in the late 18th century. Marmalade was one of Dundee's major exports during the 19th century but the industry did not survive in Dundee far into the 20th century. The heir to the Keiller fortune, Alexander Keiller (1889–1955), preferred to spend his time on archaeological digs at Avebury in Wiltshire. Journalism is still a major employer in Dundee. D C Thomson & Co publishes newspapers, magazines and comics including the *Beano* and the *Dandy*.

Tayside	**Population**			**Area**	
Districts	*male*	*female*	*total*	*sq miles*	*sq km*
Angus	52,458	55,942	108,400	842	2182
Dundee	69,140	76,523	145,663	23	60
Perth & Kinross	65,172	69,777	134,949	2041	5286
Total	186,770	202,242	389,012	2906	7528

Local Attractions and Information

Aberfeldy Watermill — Mill Street, Aberfeldy. Originally built in 1825, restored during the 1980s by miller Tom Rodger and opened as a working oat mill in 1987. Rodger died in 2002 and the mill closed. It was bought in 2004 and transformed into an art gallery and bookshop which opened in May 2005.

Aberlemno Sculptured Stones — Crosston, 5 miles (8km) northeast of Forfar. Four Pictish sculptured stones, three standing alongside the B9134 and one $^1/_4$ mile (0.4km) south, in Aberlemno churchyard. No.1, standing beside the road, has symbols of a serpent, a double disc, a mirror and a comb plus six cup marks; No.2, in the churchyard, is an upright red sandstone cross-slab standing 7ft 6in (2.3m) high. One side has the cross edged by intricate spirals, while on the reverse there is a battle scene; No.3, beside the road, has a cross on one side and with a hunting scene on the reverse; No.4, beside the road, is much weathered but with traces of a crescent.

Abernethy Round Tower — Abernethy, 8 miles (13km) southeast of Perth. An 11th century Irish-style round tower, one of only two in Scotland (the other is at Brechin), standing more than 70ft (21m) high. There is a Pictish symbol stone at the foot of the tower. Maintained by Historic Scotland.

Aberuchill Castle — 1$^1/_2$ miles (2.5km) southwest of Comrie, 22 miles (35.5km) west of Perth. A 16th century castle built by the Campbell family and extended during the 19th century. Restored following a fire during the 20th century, the castle and 3300 acre (1330ha) estate overlooking Loch Earn was sold for £6m in 2005.

Administrative headquarters — **Angus**: County Buildings, Market Street, Forfar DD8 1BX. Tel: 01307 461460.
Dundee: 21 City Square, Dundee DD1 3BY. Tel: 01382 434000.
Perth & Kinross: 2 High Street, Perth PH1 5PH. Tel: 01738 475000.

Airlie Castle — 3 miles (5km) northeast of Alyth, 10 miles (16km) west of Forfar. A pink sandstone castle standing at the junction of the Melgam Water and the River Isla and bought in 1432 by its present owners, the Ogilvie family. The castle was burnt during the Bishops' Wars of the early 1640s and the estate was confiscated by George II after the Jacobite Rebellion of 1745–6. When the Ogilvies returned from exile in the 1790s, the castle was restored and extended into a country house; the gardens were landscaped at the same time. The Airlie Estate spans Glen Gova, Glen Moy and part of Glen Prosen.

Airlie Monument — 4 miles (6km) north of Kirriemuir. A memorial on 1287ft (387m) Tulloch Hill, erected in 1901 in honour of David Ogilvy, 9th Earl of Airlie (1856–1900), killed in South Africa at the Battle of Diamond Hill during the Boer War. It is similar in design to Balmashanner War Memorial (see separate entry).

Airport — **Dundee Airport** (DND), Riverside Drive, Dundee. Opened in 1963 and operated since 2007 by Highlands and Islands Airports Ltd. Served by services from Dublin and London (City). The terminal building was opened in 1997. Tel: 01382 662200.

Albert Institute and McManus Galleries — Albert Square, Dundee. Built in 1867 by Sir George Gilbert Scott to a Victorian Gothic architectural design which he had originally submitted for the town hall in Hamburg, the Albert Institute was founded as a memorial to Prince Albert and became a library in the 1870s. It was extended with the building of the Victoria Art Galleries in 1887. The building was renamed the McManus Galleries and Museum in the 1980s in commemoration of Lord Provost Maurice McManus, at which time the library was moved to new facilities and the whole building became a museum and gallery. The building was extensively restored and refurbished 2005–8. Tel: 01382 432084.

Alyth Church — Bamff Road, Alyth. Designed by Thomas Hamilton and completed in 1839 close to the site of a 6th century foundation by St Molaug. The ruined arches of a 12th century stone church stand in

Alyth High Street. A Pictish cross-slab found in 1887 and now standing in the vestibule of the church has a cross on the face and a double-disc and damaged Z-rod symbol on the reverse.

Alyth Museum Commercial Street, Alyth. Local history museum focusing on domestic and agricultural life in and around Alyth. Tel: 01738 632488.

Angus Folk Museum Kirkwynd, Glamis, 5 miles (8km) southwest of Forfar. Folk museum housed in six 18th century cottáges donated by the Earl of Strathmore and Kinghorne in 1957. Originally brought together by Jean, Lady Maitland, the collection provides an insight into local rural life and includes a 'Life on the Land' exhibition based around a reconstructed farm courtyard. There are stables and hearse house with the 'Glenisla' horse-drawn hearse, while the cottages house a range of domestic artefacts. Maintained by the National Trust for Scotland since 1974. Tel: 01307 840288.

Arbirlot Manse Stone Arbirlot, 2 miles (3km) west of Arbroath. A sculptured stone probably dating from the 12th century discovered in the foundations of Arbirlot Church in 1831. It stands 5ft 6in (1.6m) high with small crosses inscribed at the top and bottom and is now situated in the garden of the manse. Tel: 01241 434479.

Arbroath The largest town of Angus. A royal burgh and fishing port originally known as Aberbrothock, it lies on the North Sea coast, around 12 miles (19km) northeast of Dundee and 51 miles (82km) south of Aberdeen. It is famous for the Arbroath Declaration of 1320 (see Arbroath Abbey) and the smoked haddock delicacy known as the Arbroath Smokie.

Arbroath Abbey Abbey Street, Arbroath. A Tironensian abbey founded in 1178 by William I (the Lion) and dedicated to St Thomas of Canterbury. William was buried at Arbroath in December 1214. The abbey holds a significant place in Scottish history as the site where the Declaration of Arbroath was supposedly written on 6 April 1320, although it is now thought that, rather than being put together by a meeting of nobles at Arbroath (à la Runnymede), the document was drafted at Newbattle Abbey and finalised and sealed at Arbroath by Abbot Bernard, Chancellor of Scotland. Addressed to Pope John XXII at Avignon, the Declaration set out to confirm Scotland's status as an independent, sovereign state. It was one of three such letters sent to the Pope, the other two being from Robert the Bruce and from four Scottish bishops. Robert had been excommunicated in 1306 for his part in the murder of his rival John Comyn in front of the high altar of Greyfriars Kirk, Dumfries; the Pope did not remove the excommunication until 1329, the year of Bruce's death, but he did promote talks between England and Scotland which eventually resulted in an uneasy peace. Like most British abbeys, Arbroath fell into decline following the Reformation in the mid 16th century. Many of its buildings were used as a source of building materials, while the lady chapel was used as a parish church; conservation of the ruins began in 1815. The Arbroath Abbey Pageant Society holds a commemorative event each year on 6 April – the date been officially recognised as Tartan Day in the United States since 1998 – and periodically produces a full-scale pageant at the abbey, the next being due in 2010. A modern visitor centre opened in 2001 has a scale-model of the abbey plus a computer-generated 'fly-through' reconstruction of the church as it was when complete. The site is maintained by Historic Scotland.

Arbroath Art Gallery Hill Terrace, Arbroath. Housed above Arbroath Public Library. The collection includes local paintings plus two by Peter Breughel the Younger. Tel: 01241 875598.

Arbroath Signal Tower Museum Ladyloan, Arbroath. Local history museum housed in Regency buildings on Arbroath harbour front dating from 1813. Until 1955 the buildings were the shore station for the Bell Rock Lighthouse and the home of the lighthouse keepers' families. The museum is dedicated to the natural, social and industrial history of Arbroath and in particular the lives of the fishermen of the area, 'Arbroath Smokies' and the story of the building of the lighthouse. Exhibits include the lighthouse lens and bell, civic treasures and memorabilia; there are recreations of a 1950s classroom and a lighthouse parlour, as well as a reconstruction of Auchmithie fishing village as it might have looked in the 1890s. The museum underwent extensive renovation and refurbishment in the 2000s. Tel: 01241 875598.

Ardoch Roman Camp Braco, 7½ miles (12km) south of Crieff. The earthworks of two Roman forts and several marching camps, possibly correlating with the Alauna fortifications mentioned in Ptolemy's *Geographia* and part of a line of forts established on the northern frontier of Roman Britain before the building of Hadrian's Wall. The original and larger fort was built c.AD 80, during the Flavian period around the time of Agricola's campaigns. Later abandoned, it was reoccupied c.140 during the Antonine period, when it was surrounded by an unusually complex multi-ditch defensive system more reminiscent of an Iron Age hill fort. The marching camps would have been constructed while campaigning was in progress and may have been used by the labour forces building the forts.

Ascreavie Gardens 4 miles (6km) northwest of Kirriemuir. A 50 acre (20ha) landscaped garden developed 1950–78 by plant collector George Sherriff and his wife Betty around an early 19th century house. Plants developed at Ascreavie include the blush pink and white climbing rose 'Betty Sherriff', the primula 'Soup Plate' and several poppy varieties including *Meconopsis ascreavie*.

Ashintully Castle 2 miles (3km) northeast of Kirkmichael, Perthshire, 10½ miles (17km) east of Pitlochry. A 16th century castle built as a fortified tower house by the Spalding family. The castle is reputed to have numerous ghosts, its most famous being a figure dressed in green known as 'Green Jean', thought to be the spirit of a young woman murdered by her uncle. It is said that her footsteps can still be heard as she walks the castle in sadness. In some tales she was murdered in a green dress, and then stuffed unceremoniously up the chimney by a servant. She is also said to wander the family burial ground. Green Ladies are common ghosts in Scottish castles; a surprising number are called Jean or Jeanie, suggesting a supplanted tradition.

Atholl Country Life Museum Blair Atholl, 7 miles (11km) northwest of Pitlochry. Museum exploring the social history and life of the local community, in particular farming and road and rail communication. Displays include recreated rooms such as the old kitchen, the school, the kirk and the post office.

Atholl Memorial Fountain Dunkeld, 12 miles (19km) northwest of Perth. A memorial to George Augustus Frederick John, 6th Duke of Atholl, who introduced a piped water supply to Dunkeld. Built in 1866 to a design by C S Robertson and funded by public subscription, it was erected on the site of Dunkeld Market Cross. Maintained by the National Trust for Scotland.

Auchterarder Heritage High Street, Auchterarder. A small local history exhibition. Tel: 01764 663450.

Balgay Park Glamis Road, Dundee. A public park in the west of Dundee comprising a hill on top of which stands a cemetery and The Mills Observatory. Opened in 1871 by the Earl of Dalhousie, the park was intended to improve the health of local mill workers.

Balhousie Castle Hay Street, Perth. A 16th century L-plan tower house restored and greatly extended by the Hay family in the 1860s. It became a convent between the wars and since 1962 it has housed the Black Watch Regimental HQ and the Regimental Museum. The museum spans three storeys within the castle, one wing of which serves as offices for the regiment's officers.

Balmashanner War Memorial 1/2 mile (0.8km) southeast of Forfar. A tower located on Balmashanner Hill and known locally as Boammie. Built 1920–1 to a design by architect Thomas R Soutar and commemorating those fallen in World War I, it stands 55ft (17m) high and has 86 steps inside although it is very rarely open to the public.

Barrack Street Museum Barrack Street, Dundee. A natural history museum exploring Scottish wildlife. Exhibits include the skeleton of the Tay Whale, a humpback whale that swam up the River Tay in 1883. Tel: 01382 432067.

Barry Links 8 miles (13km) east of Dundee. An area of sand dunes and machair behind Buddon Ness, between Monifieth and Carnoustie, and a designated Site of Special Scientific Interest and Special Area of Conservation covering 1970 acres (790ha). A military training area and a rifle range occupy part of the dunes, while on the northeastern side is Carnoustie golf course.

Barry Mill Barry, 1 mile (1.6km) west of Carnoustie. A working watermill producing animal fodders built in 1814 and located on a site in use for milling since 1539. The mill produced oatmeal until the 1970s and closed in 1982. It has been maintained by the National Trust for Scotland since 1988. Tel: 01241 856761.

Battles See separate table for details of the battles of Dunkeld, Dunsinane Hill, Dupplin Moor, Killiecrankie, Methven, Nechtanesmere and Tippermuir.

Beatrix Potter Exhibition and Garden Station Road, Birnam, 1 mile (1.6km) southeast of Dunkeld, 12 miles (19km) northwest of Perth. An exhibition housed in the Birnam Arts & Conference Centre. Beatrix Potter spent many of her childhood summers in Birnam and the area greatly encouraged her interest in flora and fauna. Later, while staying at Eastwood, Dunkeld, on 4 September 1893 she wrote a 'picture letter' to Noel Moore which later became *The Tale of Peter Rabbit*. She used many of the people she met in Dunkeld as the basis for her characters. Footpaths in the garden lead to Mr Tod and Mrs Tiggywinkle's houses. Tel: 01350 727674.

Bell Rock Lighthouse The world's oldest surviving sea-washed lighthouse. Situated in the North Sea on Bell Rock (aka Inchcape Rock), 12 miles (19km) off the coast from Arbroath, it was established on 1 February 1811 having been built by Robert Stevenson 1807–10 following the loss of HMS *York* in 1804. The lighthouse stands 118ft (36m) tall and has 96 steps. It used the first revolving light with red and white reflectors in Scotland, and worked in tandem with the Arbroath Signal Tower. During World War II it was strafed by aircraft and a bomb was dropped at its base, but no serious damage was caused. It was also struck by a helicopter attempting to deliver supplies on 14 December 1955, resulting in the loss of the helicopter and crew. The lighthouse was automated in 1998.

Ben Lawers At 3984ft (1214m) Ben Lawers (G. = 'hill of the loud stream') is the highest point in Perth & Kinross. The Ben Lawers National Nature Reserve was designated in 1975 and is managed by the National Trust for Scotland. The slopes of the mountain support a collection of arctic-alpine plants. In 1878 a cairn was built on the summit in an attempt to raise its height above 4000ft (1219m) but it quickly collapsed.

Birks of Aberfeldy 1/2 mile (0.8km) south of Aberfeldy, 8 miles (13km) southwest of Pitlochry. The steep-sided wooded glen of the Moness Burn, containing birch (birk), oak and beech woodland below the Falls of Moness. The name derives from a song by Robert Burns; a plaque marks the spot where he supposedly sat in 1787 to compose the work.

Birnam Oak Birnam, 1 mile (1.6km) southeast of Dunkeld, 12 miles (19km) northwest of Perth. Believed to be the sole surviving tree from Birnam Wood, famous from Shakespeare's *Macbeth* ('Fear not, till Birnam wood do come to Dunsinane'). A sessile oak, standing beside the River Tay, it has a girth of 18ft (5.5m) and its spreading lower limbs are supported by crutches. One of the trees highlighted in 'The Big Tree Country' campaign, which also includes the Fortingall Yew (see separate entry).

Black Watch Memorial Located at the spot of the first muster of the Black Watch near Wade's Bridge on the bank of the River Tay at Aberfeldy in early 1740. It is in the form of a soldier in the first Black Watch service uniform looking down over the city. Upon its unveiling in 1877 it was the subject of a poem by William McGonagall which begins: 'Ye Sons of Mars, it gives me great content,/To think there has been erected a handsome monument,/In memory of the Black Watch, which is magnificent to see,/Where they first were embodied at Aberfeldy.'

Black Watch Regimental Museum Hay Street, Perth. Housed in Balhousie Castle, the museum is laid out chronologically in seven rooms with displays of artefacts illustrating the history of the regiment plus a collection of pictures. Exhibits include regimental colours, equipment, bagpipes and sporting trophies. The regiment was originally raised as six independent companies in 1725. The name derives from their task of keeping peace and order in the Highlands, or 'watching', together with the dark colour of the tartan they wore. In 1739 the six companies were embodied as a Regiment of the Line and in early 1740 paraded for the first time on the banks of the River Tay at Aberfeldy. They were designated the 42nd (Royal Highland) Regiment of Foot. The regiment's first action was at the Battle of Fontenoy in 1745 and it then saw service in the Americas. In 1795 it adopted the Red Hackle in its bonnets. During the Napoleonic Wars the regiment fought in Egypt and the Peninsula, including the retreat to Corunna. In 1815 the 42nd fought hard at Quatre Bras in the prelude to the Battle of Waterloo. It formed part of the Highland Brigade during the Crimean War and helped to quell the Indian Mutiny. In 1881 the 42nd and 73rd (Perthshire) Foot formed the 1st and 2nd Battalions of The Black Watch (Royal Highlanders). The regiment saw action in Africa at Tel-el-Kebir in 1882 and at Magersfontein during the Boer War. During World War I the regiment's various battalions gained battle honours including Ypres (1914), Somme (1916, 1918), Passchendaele (1917), Hindenburg Line (1918), Macedonia (1915–18) and Mesopotamia (1915–17). During World War II battalions of the Black Watch fought in most theatres including North Africa, Sicily and Italy, in northern Europe and in Burma. Post World War II actions include The Hook (1952) during the Korean War and peacekeeping roles in Northern Ireland and the Balkans. The regiment is now known as The Black Watch (3rd Battalion, Royal Regiment of Scotland). Its motto is *Nemo me impune lacessit* ('No one touches me with impunity').

Blair Castle $^1/_2$ mile (0.8km) northwest of Blair Atholl, 7 miles (11km) northwest of Pitlochry. The seat of the dukes and earls of Atholl. The oldest and highest part of the castle is Cumming's Tower, which dates from 1269. An extension was added in 1530. The 2nd Duke of Atholl employed architect James Winter to remodel the medieval castle into a Georgian mansion in the 1740s. Blair Castle was the last castle in Britain to endure a siege, when it was besieged by Lord George Murray in 1746. Further changes were made in the second half of the 19th century including the installation of modern facilities. There are 30 rooms with collections of paintings and furniture plus displays of arms and armour, porcelain and family and Jacobite memorabilia. The exhibits cover not just the lives of the dukes and earls but also the staff of the castle and estate. The rooms include the entrance hall with arms from Culloden, Earl John's room with arms from Killiecrankie, the drawing room with a marble chimney piece, the tapestry room which contains the Mortlake Tapestries and the ballroom and dining room. The estate covers more than 145,000 acres (58,700ha) with a 2500 acre (100ha) landscaped garden. The Banvie Burn runs through Diana's Grove (named after the Roman goddess), laid out by the 2nd Duke of Atholl in 1737. The ruins of St Bride's Kirk hold the burial vault of Viscount Dundee (John Graham of Claverhouse, known as Bonnie Dundee), who was killed at the Battle of Killiecrankie in 1689. The 9 acre (3.5ha) walled Hercules Garden, also established by the 2nd Duke, features a large statue of Hercules and has now been restored. The castle is the HQ of the Atholl Highlanders, the only legal private army in Britain. Founded as the 77th Regiment of Foot by the 4th Duke in 1777 only to disband four years later, it was reformed by the 6th Duke in 1839 and was given regimental status by Queen Victoria after it acted as her bodyguard during her visit to the castle in 1844. It is a purely ceremonial regiment with a force of 125 men, including two pipe bands. Tel: 01796 481207.

Bolfracks Garden Bolfracks, Aberfeldy. A 4 acre (1.6ha) woodland garden on a hillside overlooking the Tay valley, originally created in the 18th century by the Menzies and redesigned in the 1970s. There is a walled garden plus a rose garden, while the Burn Garden is a less formal wooded area. The burial ground, which contains the tombs of two members of the Menzies family and their wives, is planted with a wide range of specimen trees. There are also ten 18th century German gnomes. Tel: 01887 820344.

Branklyn Gardens Dundee Road, Perth. Garden on the River Tay begun in 1922 by John and Dorothy Renton with seeds collected by plant hunters such as George Forrest, Frank Ludlow and Major George Sherriff. There is a rock garden and plants include rhododendrons, alpines, and in particular the blue Himalayan poppy. Branklyn holds National Collections of Cassiope and Lilium (Mylnefield lilies). Managed by the National Trust for Scotland since 1967, following the deaths of Mr and Mrs Renton. Tel: 01738 625535.

Brechin A royal burgh in Angus, famous for its cathedral. Traditionally Brechin has been considered a city because of its status as the seat of a pre-Reformation Roman Catholic diocese (which continues today as an episcopal seat of the Episcopal Church of Scotland), although the burgh lacks a city charter.

Brechin Bridge Known locally as the 'Auld Brig'. Crossing the River South Esk in Brechin on the site of previous structures dating to at least the 13th century, it is one of the oldest stone bridges in Scotland and dates to the mid 17th century.

Brechin Castle Ladeside Road, Brechin. The seat of the Earls of Dalhousie and located above the River South Esk, the castle was founded in the 13th century. Edward I received the submission of John Balliol here on 10 July 1296. Seven years later Sir Thomas Maule was killed at the end of a three-week siege. The castle was in royal hands until Patrick Maule, 1st Earl of Panmure, bought the estate from the Earl of Mar in 1643. Alexander Edward, the 4th Earl, carried out major rebuilding before being exiled in the aftermath of the Jacobite Rebellion of 1715. The castle descended through marriage to the Earls of Dalhousie. The garden was also originally landscaped by the 4th Earl of Panmure and includes woodland and parkland covering 40 acres (16ha) as well as a 13 acre (5ha) walled garden. The surrounding Dalhousie Estate includes a 65 acre (26ha) country park. Tel: 01356 624566.

Brechin Cathedral Church Street, Brechin. Dedicated to the Triune God. Founded as a monastery by David I c.1150 on the site of an earlier Celtic foundation and later altered to serve as a post-Reformation parish church. An 11th century Irish-style round tower is built into the cathedral's fabric; one of only two such towers on the Scottish mainland (the other being at Abernethy) and originally free-standing, it is 87ft (26.5m) high with a projecting base, and tapers upwards to a conical roof added in the

14th century. It is built of large sandstone blocks with internal string-courses which indicate division into seven storeys, with a large window facing each of the cardinal points at the top. Having suffered considerable neglect in the 17th and 18th centuries, major alterations were made to the cathedral in 1806 when the north and south transepts were removed and new and wider aisles built on each side of the nave. The outer walls were extended to a height which enabled the nave to be covered with a single span roof. Further changes in the early 20th century restored the church more to its medieval proportions. There are beautiful stained glass windows by Edward Burne-Jones and 20th century Scottish artists. The Mary Stone and other early Christian monuments can also be seen. Tel: 01356 629360.

Brechin Round Tower See Brechin Cathedral

Brechin Town House Museum High Street, Brechin. A local history museum housed in the old town house, which replaced the town's tolbooth in 1790 and had a shop, courtroom and prison on the ground floor and a meeting chamber on the first floor. First housed in the Mechanics' Institute before relocating to Brechin Library in 1976, and opened in 2003 in its present location, the collection includes artefacts, photographs and memorabilia covering the social and economic history of Brechin. Exibits include the Brechin Town Drum, formerly used at civic events, and a Bronze Age jet necklace. Tel: 01356 625536.

Broughty Castle Broughty Ferry, 4 miles (6km) east of Dundee. Located on a rocky promontory at the mouth of the Tay and built by Lord Gray in 1496 on the site of an earlier fortification. Surrendered to the English in 1547 following the Battle of Pinkie, the castle was recaptured in 1550, and was taken for Parliament by General Monck during the Civil War. The castle fell into disrepair during the 17th and 18th centuries and was acquired by the Edinburgh & Northern Railway Company in 1846. Fears of invasion triggered by the Crimean War led to the castle being bought by the War Office; the area was refortified and the castle was rebuilt to a design by Robert Anderson including nine gun emplacements, a new west wing and a courtyard. In the 1880s the castle accommodated the Tay Division Submarine Miners, whose job it was to lay a minefield across the Tay in an emergency. The castle remained in military use until 1932 and was also used during World War II as a defence post. It is now in the care of Historic Scotland; the tower has housed a museum since 1969.

Broughty Ferry The name probably derives from 'Bruach Tatha' (Taybank). A suburb on the eastern edge of Dundee, once home to the city's jute barons and known as the 'richest square mile in Europe'.

Broughty Ferry Castle Museum Housed in the tower of Broughty Castle and dedicated to the area's social and economic history. Exhibits include arms and armour, seashore life and memorabilia of the former Dundee whaling industry.

Caird Hall City Square, Dundee. A large hall fronting one side of City Square and intended to form the centrepiece of Dundee's early 20th century city plan, which was never completed. Designed as both a city hall and a concert hall, it was built 1914–22 thanks to a donation of £100,000 by Sir James Key Caird (1837–1914) of the Ashton Jute Works; a colonnade of ten Doric columns was added to the frontage after a donation of a further £75,000 by Caird's sister Mrs Emma Grace Marryat. She also funded the Marryat Hall which is attached to the west of the main hall. Following major refurbishment the hall is now a multi-function venue offering moveable seating for up to 2150 people but which can also be used for exhibitions. Tel: 01382 434451.

Caledonian Railway (Brechin) Park Road, Brechin. A private railway operating for 4 miles (6km) between the restored Brechin and Bridge of Dun on a branch line which was formerly part of the Aberdeen Railway and later the Caledonian Railway. The original Caledonian Railway (familiarly known as the 'Caley') was founded in the 1840s and initially ran trains from Carlisle to Glasgow, Edinburgh and Greenhill near Falkirk, later acquiring other lines to provide services to towns and cities including Aberdeen, Dundee, Forfar, Perth, Stirling, Oban, Ardrossan and Peebles. All passenger train services from Brechin ceased on 4 August 1952 and the Strathmore line, the West Coast route through Bridge of Dun, was closed on 4 September 1967. The Caledonian Railway (Brechin) was opened in 1993 by members of the Brechin Railway Preservation Society formed in 1979. The railway has a fleet of nine steam engines and ten diesel locomotives. There is a museum at Brechin Station. Tel: 01356 622992.

Camperdown Country Park Coupar Angus Road, Dundee. The largest park in the city of Dundee, covering 395 acres (160ha) and including Templeton Woods, Clatto Reservoir, Camperdown House and Camperdown Golf Club. Camperdown Wildlife Centre, a small zoo run by Dundee City Council Parks Department and located within a walled garden in the park, is home to more than 50 species of animals, birds and reptiles including European brown bears, lynx, wolves and pine marten. The park was officially opened to the public in 1946. Tel: 01382 431818.

Camperdown House 3 miles (5km) west of Dundee. A house completed in 1828 on his Lundie Estate for the 1st Earl of Camperdown, Robert Dundes Haldane-Duncan, son of Admiral Adam Duncan (1731–1804), victor over the Dutch on 11 October 1797 at the naval Battle of Camperdown (known to the Dutch as Kamperduin). Now standing within Camperdown Park, the neoclassical house was designed by William Burn and constructed from lemon-white sandstone on a site close to the family's previous home, Lundie House, which was demolished after the completion of Camperdown House. The house and estate were purchased by Dundee Corporation in 1946. Reopened in the summer of 2003 after restoration and refurbishment, the ground floor houses exhibits relating to Dundee's maritime history, Admiral Duncan and the Battle of Camperdown. In 1800 Duncan planted a sycamore tree now known as the 'Admiral's Tree' on the lawn near the south elevation of what would become Camperdown House. The bicentenary of the battle was marked in Dundee on 11 October 1997 and a privately funded statue of Admiral Duncan was erected next to his birthplace in Dundee. The club house of Camperdown golf club is also situated within Camperdown House.

Castle Menzies	1 mile (1.6km) northwest of Aberfeldy, 8 miles (13km) southwest of Pitlochry. A 16th century castle visited by Bonnie Prince Charlie in 1746 before the Battle of Culloden. The room he slept in is furnished in period style. The castle has been restored by the Menzies Clan Society. The gardens consist of a series of three terraced walled gardens. Tel: 01887 820982.
Caterthuns, The	5 miles (8km) northwest of Brechin. The twin Iron Age hill forts of Brown Caterthun and White Caterthun (*cathair* means a circular stone fort). Brown Caterthun is a multivallate and multi-period hill fort dating from 3000–500 BC with six lines of defence around the flat summit of a 912ft (287m) high hill. The outer rings are built of heather and turf while the innermost is a stone wall, now ruined. Including the ramparts, the site extends to 20 acres (8ha). The ramparts are split by multiple entrances, a design interpreted as indicating a social function for the site; the thick stone wall suggests that this was eventually abandoned in favour of defence. It may have been abandoned completely in favour of the nearby White Caterthun, an oval enclosure about 500ft (150m) long by 200ft (60m) wide on a 978ft (298m) high hill, and surrounded by two thick walls of white stone, in contrast to the turf walls of its twin – hence its name. The walls appear to have been very thick, perhaps up to 20ft (6m) and 40ft (12m) in width. Both sites are maintained by Historic Scotland.
Claypotts Castle	Castle Gardens, Broughty Ferry, 4 miles (6km) east of Dundee. A three-storey Z-plan and fortified house with circular wings, built 1569–88 by John Strachan. The castle and estate were sold to Sir William Graham of Ballunie in 1601 and to Sir William Graham of Claverhouse in 1616. After the death of John Graham of Claverhouse ('Bonnie Dundee') at the Battle of Killiecrankie in 1689, the castle passed into the hands of the Crown. The estate was granted to James, 2nd Marquis of Douglas, eventually passing by marriage into the Home family. It was taken into state care in 1926 and is maintained by Historic Scotland. Claypotts Castle is not open to the public.
Clova Castle	1/2 mile (0.8km) northwest of Clova, 16 miles (26km) northwest of Forfar. Remains of a 16th century tower house overlooking the River South Esk in Glen Clova, and once belonging to the Ogilvy family.
Cluny House Gardens	Cluny House, Aberfeldy. A Himalayan/North American woodland garden planted by Bobby and Betty Masterton from 1950. Plants include giant Himalayan lilies and blue poppies beneath acers, rowans and birches. Tel: 01887 820795.
Corrie Fee	5 miles (8km) northwest of Clova, 20 miles (32km) northwest of Forfar. National Nature Reserve covering 405 acres (164ha) of a glacial corrie within the Cairngorms National Park. One of the most important sites in Britain for mountain flora and arctic alpines, species include purple coltsfoot, the fern alpine woodsia and yellow oxytropis. Corrie Sharroch, within the reserve, has the largest area of mountain (montane) willow scrub in Britain. Carved by glaciers during the Ice Age, the Fee Burn now meanders through the floor of the corrie. The reserve is within the Caernlochan Site of Special Scientific Interest, Special Area of Conservation and Special Protection Area and the Deeside and Lochnagar National Scenic Area. Managed by Scottish Natural Heritage in partnership with Angus Glens Ranger Service.
Cortachy Castle	Cortachy, 7 miles (11km) northwest of Forfar. A 15th century courtyard castle overlooking the River South Esk, built by Sir Walter Ogilvie on the site of an earlier fortification. Having been damaged by Parliamentarian forces during the Civil War because of Ogilvie's Royalist sympathies, the castle and surrounding estate were forfeited following the Jacobite Rebellion of 1745–6 and did not return to the family until the 1770s. The house was much altered and extended during the 19th century.
Cox's Stack	Lochee, Dundee. A 282ft (86m) tall decorated campanile-style factory chimney designed by James Maclaren in 1865. A relic of the Camperdown Works, established in 1864 and once the largest jute factory in the world, it now stands in the middle of a modern housing development in a suburb of Dundee.
Craigower	1 1/2 miles (2.5km) northwest of Pitlochry. (G. = Goat's Crag.) A rocky outcrop above the confluence of the rivers Tummel and Garry, rising to 1335ft (407m). Managed by the National Trust for Scotland.
Cultybraggan Camp	1 mile (1.6km) south of Dalginross, 5 miles (8km) southwest of Crieff. The most complete prisoner-of-war camp still remaining in the UK, built in 1939 to house German prisoners of war during World War II and officially known as No 21, War Working Camp. It held many senior German troops, and Rudolf Hess was held here for a night en route to England after crash-landing in Scotland. Later used as an army training camp, it is now derelict.
Discovery Point	Discovery Quay, Dundee. Home to Robert Falcon Scott's famous polar exploration ship RRS *Discovery* and also to a museum dedicated to her history, as well as to Captain Scott and other Antarctic explorers. Built by the Dundee Shipbuilders' Company for the Royal Geographical Society and launched on 21 March 1901, *Discovery* took part in Scott's National Antarctic Expedition (1901–4) where she was frozen in the ice at Hut Point, Ross Island, 28 March 1902–16 February 1904. *Discovery* was owned by the Hudson Bay Company, 1905–15. During and immediately after World War I she ran merchant voyages, including missions to the White Russians in 1919. She became a Royal Research Ship in the 1920s, taking part in the Discovery Oceanographic Expedition (1925–7) around the Falkland Islands and the British, Australian and New Zealand Antarctic Research Expedition (1929–31) in the South Seas. In 1936 *Discovery* was given to the Boy Scouts' Association as a training ship for sea scouts and as a memorial to Captain Scott. From 1955 until 1979 she was used by the Royal Navy Auxiliary Reserve as a drill ship, but was open to the public at weekends. She was transferred to the Maritime Trust on 2 April 1979 and berthed in St Katharine's Dock near the Tower of London, where she was restored to her 1925 condition. In 1986 she was transferred to her home port of Dundee and moored at Discovery Point where she underwent further restoration. Ownership was passed to the Dundee

Heritage Trust in 1996. Tel: 01382 201245.

Distilleries **Blair Athol**, Perth Road, Pitlochry. One of the oldest working distilleries in Scotland, established in 1798 by John Stewart and Robert Robertson. The water source is the Allt Dour Burn.

Edradour, 1 mile (1.6km) east of Pitlochry. Established in 1825 and the smallest distillery in Scotland. An original 'farm' distillery using traditional equipment including the smallest legal stills permissible, it is situated next to the Edradour Burn. Only 12 casks of single Highland malt whisky are produced each week. Tel: 01796 472095.

Tullibardine, Blackford, 16 miles (26km) southwest of Perth. In medieval times Blackford was noted for the quality of its beer, and in 1488 James IV purchased beer from the brewery in celebration of his coronation. The brewery closed in the early 20th century and was reopened as a distillery in 1949 by William Delme Evans. In production until 1994, it was then mothballed by its then owners, Whyte & Mackay, but was reopened in 2003 under private ownership and now operates as a working distillery. Tel: 01764 682252.

Drummond Castle and Gardens 2 miles (3km) southwest of Crieff. Originally a tower house built c.1490 by John, 1st Lord Drummond, the castle was rebuilt after being badly damaged by Cromwell's forces in 1653 and a mansion house added in the late 17th century. The estate was forfeited after the 1745 Jacobite Rebellion when the Drummonds supported Bonnie Prince Charlie. Restored and largely remodelled by the 1st Earl of Ancaster in 1890, the castle is now famous for its Italianate parterre gardens, originally laid out in 1630 by John Drummond, 2nd Earl of Perth, and redesigned in the 1840s. The John Mylne obelisk sundial, erected in 1630, has a number of faces giving the time in various world capitals. Queen Victoria planted two beech trees to commemorate a visit in 1842. Tel: 01764 681433.

Dundee Law A hill in central Dundee formed from the basalt plug of an extinct volcano and once the site of an Iron Age hill fort. It is the highest point in the city of Dundee at 571ft (174m).

Dunkeld A town in Perth & Kinross, possibly founded in 820. It was largely destroyed during the Battle of Dunkeld in 1689 and rebuilt in the 18th century. Many of the buildings have been restored by the National Trust for Scotland.

Dunkeld Cathedral Cathedral Street, Dunkeld, 13 miles (21km) northwest of Perth. An early centre of Christianity in Scotland, dedicated to St Columba and at one time housing his relics for safe keeping from Viking raids. King Kenneth Mac Alpin built a church in Dunkeld c.848, intending that Dunkeld (the See of Alba) should be the primary centre of the church in eastern Scotland, although this was subsequently transferred to St Andrews. Several Pictish cross-slabs have been found on the site including one known as the Apostles' Stone, decorated on all four faces and which had been in use as a gatepost at the entrance to the churchyard. The back of the stone is carved with panels of figures and heads; the two central rows contain six standing figures (some bearded), giving rise to the stone's name. The building of the cathedral beside the River Tay was begun in the 13th century and the choir was completed in the 14th century; the west tower, the south porch and the chapter house were added 1450–75. The building was deliberately damaged when the see was declared void at the time of the Reformation in the mid 16th century, although the choir was later partly re-roofed to serve as the parish church before both the town and the church suffered further destruction during the Battle of Dunkeld in 1689. As a result the cathedral is now a building of two distinct halves: its east end is the parish church while its west end, apart from the restored bell tower and chapter house, is a roofless ruin. Exhibits in the Chapter House Museum include the tombstone of 18th century fiddler Neil (Niel) Gow, who inspired many of Robert Burns's most famous songs. Now in the care of Historic Scotland. Tel: 01350 727249.

Dunsinane Hill 1 mile (1.6km) east of Kirkton of Collace, 8 miles (13km) northeast of Perth. Dunsinane Hill rises to 1017ft (310m) and is famous from Shakespeare as the place where Macbeth meets his end. In fact he survived the battle fought here in 1054, only to lose his life at the Battle of Lumphannan near Aberdeen in 1057.

Eassie Church Slab 8 miles (13km) west of Forfar. A red sandstone Pictish cross-slab found in the bed of a stream near Eassie Old Church and now kept inside the church, where it was taken in 1850. Rectangular in shape but slightly pointed at the top and standing 6ft 8in (2m) high, it is sculptured in relief on both faces. On the front is a cross plus two angels, a man hunting with a hound and a stag; on the back are a Pictish beast (which may be an elephant), double-disc and Z-rod symbols, four human figures, three of them in procession, and a pot with a tree growing in it. The site is maintained by Historic Scotland.

Edzell Castle and Garden 1 mile (1.6km) west of Edzell, 5 miles (8km) north of Brechin. A ruined early 16th century L-plan tower house built by the Lindsay family on the site of a 12th century motte and bailey. The oldest part is incorrectly known as Stirlings' Tower as it was built after the property had passed from the Stirlings to the Lindsays in 1358. An unfinished mansion was added in the late 16th century. Like many Scottish castles, it was visited by the much travelled Mary, Queen of Scots, who stopped here on 23 and 24 August 1562 before a meeting of the Privy Council in the castle's great hall. Her son James VI also visited in 1580 and 1589. The estate was bought by the Earl of Panmure in 1715 but his Jacobite sympathies meant that he was forced to forfeit his property and the buildings eventually fell into disrepair. The castle's much praised walled garden, with its carvings and decorated walls and gaps for nesting and flower boxes, designed probably 1604–10 by Sir David Lindsay, Lord Edzell, was recreated in the 1930s when the estate passed into state care. The garden also contains the remains of a summer house, bath house and well. Managed by Historic Scotland. Tel: 01356 648631.

Elcho Castle $4\frac{1}{2}$ miles (7km) southeast of Perth. A 16th century Z-plan tower house beside the Tay built by the Wemyss family. David, Lord Elcho, fought for the Jacobites at Culloden and fled to France; by 1780, the castle was abandoned and had fallen into ruin. It was reroofed in 1830 by the 8th Earl of

Wemyss. The castle passed into state care in 1929 and is managed by Historic Scotland.

Ell Shop — The Cross, Dunkeld. An 18th century building so called because it has an iron ell-stick – formerly used to measure cloth and other commodities in the adjacent marketplace – attached to one corner. Managed by the National Trust for Scotland, it is one of several buildings in Dunkeld restored by the Trust. Tel: 01350 727460.

Explorers: Scottish Plant Hunters' Garden — Port na Craig, Pitlochry. A 6½ acre (2.6ha) garden established alongside Pitlochry Festival Theatre, conceived and built in conjunction with the Royal Botanic Garden Edinburgh and celebrating the Scottish plant collectors and botanists who contributed so much to establishing the flora seen in present-day British gardens. It is laid out as a series of gardens illustrating the collections of a selection of 18 Scottish plant hunters. These include: **David Douglas** (1799–1834), born in Scone and the first European to climb the northern Rocky Mountains. He collected throughout North America and his plants include the Douglas fir, lupins, phlox, penstemon, sunflowers, clarkia and Californian poppy. He was killed in Hawaii in 1834 by a wild bull after falling into a pit; **James Drummond** (1786–1863), born in Hawthorden in Midlothian and who spent much of his life exploring in the South Seas. He died in Perth, Australia; **George Forrest** (1873–1932), born in Falkirk, who went on expeditions to China and the Himalayas, bringing back 10,000 plants including rhododendron, azaleas and primulas; **William Forsyth** (1737–1804), born at Old Meldrum, Aberdeenshire, not strictly a 'plant hunter' but responsible for starting an international seed and plant exchange, and best remembered now for the family of plants known as forsythia; **Robert Fortune** (1812–80), born in Edrom in the Scottish Borders, who made five journeys to Japan and China and brought back tea seeds which were then introduced into India; **John Fraser** (1750–1811), born near Tomnacloich, Inverness, who travelled widely in North America and was 'botanical collector' for Tsar Paul I of Russia; **David Lyall** (1817–95), born in Auchenblae, Aberdeenshire, naval surgeon on the Antarctic expeditions of Sir James Ross and who also collected in North America; **Francis Masson** (1741–1805), born in Aberdeen, appointed as Kew's first plant hunter and who travelled with Captain Cook to Capetown before collecting in Canada; **Archibald Menzies** (1754–1842), born at Weem in Perthshire and another ship's surgeon, who travelled widely in the South Seas and North America; **George Sherriff** (1898–1967), born in Larbert and who served in the army in India, partnering fellow collector Frank Ludlow on expeditions in the Himalayas and returning with many plants including *Primula sherriffae*, *Meconopsis sherriffii* and *Rhododendron sheriffii*; and **Thomas Thomson** (1817–78), born in Glasgow, who served as a surgeon with the East India Company and collected widely in Afghanistan, Kashmir and Tibet before publishing the first volume of *Flora Indica* in 1855. Other features of the garden include the David Douglas Pavilion, constructed from Douglas fir, larch and oak with a balcony in the form of the bow of a ship, and the George Forrest Pavilion constructed from renewable, home-grown timbers. Tel: 01796 484600.

Fergusson Gallery — Marshall Place, Perth. Opened in 1992 in a former waterworks built in 1832, the gallery is devoted to the life and work of Leith-born 'colourist' painter John Duncan Fergusson (1874–1961). It houses the largest collection of his work in existence, including paintings, drawings and sculptures. Tel: 01738 441944.

Forfar — A royal burgh and market town, once the county capital of the former county of Angus and now its administrative headquarters. It has been the seat of a sheriff from the 12th century and several Scottish kings of the House of Canmore stayed in the royal castle.

Fortingall Yew — Fortingall, 14 miles (23km) southwest of Pitlochry. Possibly the oldest living organism in Europe, the Fortingall Yew (*Taxus baccata*) stands in the corner of Fortingall churchyard and is estimated to be somewhere between 3000 and 9000 years old. There are various local legends attached to the yew; according to one, Pontius Pilate was born in Fortingall, the son of a Roman ambassador and the local chief's daughter, and played under the yew as a child; another claims that the tree stands at the geographical centre of Scotland. The yew suffered heavily from vandalism in the 19th century and is now protected by railings. Cuttings have been planted in other sacred sites such as Glastonbury Abbey.

HMS *Unicorn* — Victoria Dock, Dundee. A 46 gun frigate built at Chatham Royal Docks and launched on 30 March 1824. Constructed during a time of relative peace, she was largely 'laid up' and protected, and as a result has the best preserved and least altered old wooden hull in the world. She became a drill ship for the Royal Naval Reserve at Dundee from November 1873, and she has remained berthed in the city ever since. As part of the Royal Naval Reserve, she was used during both world wars as the Area HQ of the Senior Naval Officer, Dundee. Faced with being scrapped in the 1960s, the frigate was saved by the Unicorn Preservation Society. Tel: 01382 200900.

Glamis Castle — 1 mile (1.6km) nouth of Glamis, 5 miles (8km) southwest of Forfar. The family seat of the Earls of Strathmore and Kinghorne, the house has its origins in the late 14th century but the main tower was built c.1435 for Sir John Lyon. It was extended in the 17th and 18th centuries. King Malcolm II died at the royal hunting lodge at Glamis on 25 November 1034, possibly from battle wounds. Shakespeare incorrectly gives the title Thane of Glamis to Macbeth. James V claimed the castle in the late 1530s and held his court here, and it was visited by Mary, Queen of Scots in 1562. After the 5th Earl had been killed at the Battle of Sheriffmuir aged only 19 on 13 November 1715, during the Jacobite Rebellion, his younger brother, now the 6th Earl, entertained James Francis Edward Stuart (the Old Pretender) at Glamis during his short-lived visit to Scotland in 1716. The castle is renowned for various tales of hauntings and apparitions including the 'Grey Lady' and Lord Crawford, who lost his soul in a game of cards with the Devil. It was the childhood home of Queen Elizabeth the Queen Mother, youngest daughter of the 14th Earl, and was also the birthplace of Princess Margaret in 1930. The castle has been open to the public since the 1950s. The landscaped gardens contain an Italian garden and a pinetum. Glamis is depicted on £10 notes issued by the Royal Bank of Scotland. Tel: 01307 840393.

Glen Lyon — The longest and one of the grandest glens in the Western Highlands, extending west for 35 miles (56km) from Fortingall to near Tyndrum. It derives its name from the River Lyon, which finds its way from its origin on the southeast side of Ben-a-Chastle, and is often a placid stream, but sometimes during a winter spate a raging torrent, expanding midway in its course into Loch Lyon, and flowing thence until it becomes a tributary of the Tay, near Taymouth Castle, its entire length being nearly 40 miles.

Glendoick Gardens — 1/2 mile (0.8km) north of Glendoick, 7 miles (11km) east of Perth. A garden surrounding the early Georgian Glendoick House, based on plants collected by the Cox family in the Himalayas with collections of rhododendrons, azaleas and meconopsis. There is a woodland garden, a peat garden and a test bed with new hybrids. Tel: 01738 860205.

Glenesk Folk Museum — 1 mile (1.6km) southeast of Tarfside, 14 miles (23km) northwest of Brechin. Opened in 1955 and housed since 2007 in a new purpose-built gallery next to The Retreat, a typical glen shooting lodge built in the 1840s. A series of appropriately furnished rooms, including a smiddy, a kitchen, a parlour and a music room, reflect life in the glens. There is also a collection of genealogical material including local census returns and parish registers. The museum is run by the people of Glenesk. Tel: 01356 670254.

Guthrie Castle — Guthrie, 8 miles (13km) east of Forfar. A three-storey tower house built by Sir David Guthrie in 1468, and connected in 1848 to a nearby house built by the Guthries in 1760. The gardens cover 156 acres (63ha) and include a horseshoe-shaped walled garden, a wild garden and a 9 hole golf course. Another feature is a 160 year old yew hedge in the shape of a Celtic cross.

Highest point — See Ben Lawers.

House of Dun — 3 miles (5km) west of Montrose. A Georgian mansion overlooking the Montrose Basin, designed by William Adam and completed in 1730. The rooms have fine examples of elaborate plasterwork together with collections of period furniture and porcelain. There is a model theatre. The estate was owned by the Erskine family from the 14th century until 1980 and is associated with Lady Augusta (FitzClarence) Kennedy-Erskine, daughter of William IV, and the actress Mrs Jordan. The 909 acre (368ha) estate is located next to the Montrose Basin Local Nature Reserve and includes Lady Augusta's walk, laid out in the 19th century. Maintained by the National Trust for Scotland since 1980. Tel 01674 810264.

House of Memories — High Street, Monifieth. A local history museum with pictures, memorabilia and recorded facts pertaining to Monifieth's social and industrial past.

Howff Burial Ground — Meadowside, Dundee. Dundee's oldest established cemetery. Formerly the orchard of a Franciscan friary until its destruction in 1548, the land became a burial ground in 1564, after it was given to the town by Mary, Queen of Scots. For 300 years until its closure in the mid 19th century, the Howff was the chief burial ground for the area.

Huntingtower Castle — 1 mile (1.6km) west of Perth. Aka The House of Ruthven. Originally two separate late 15th and early 16th century tower houses, the eastern tower having been built first and the L-plan western tower some years later. The two were originally connected by a wooden bridge. The 10ft (3m) gap between the two towers is known as 'The Maiden's Leap' after a legend that a Ruthven daughter (possibly Dorothea, daughter of the 1st Earl of Gowrie) leapt it to avoid being found by her mother in her lover's bedroom. The gap was bridged by walls in the 1600s. The castle was visited by Mary, Queen of Scots and Lord Darnley in 1565 and Mary's son James VI was held prisoner here in 1582 during what is known as the Ruthven Raid. As a result of this and further plots against the monarch, the Ruthven name was proscribed and the name of the castle changed to Huntingtower. The castle was eventually transferred to the Murray family but was abandoned in the second half of the 18th century. The hall of the eastern tower has a decorated wooden ceiling. The castle is said to be haunted by Lady Greensleeves, a tall young woman in a green silk dress who is sometimes linked to the leaping young lady mentioned above. Her appearance is said to be an ill omen and a forewarning of disaster. Now maintained by Historic Scotland.

Inch parks — The North Inch and the South Inch are two separate areas of parkland close to the centre of Perth. The North Inch has views over the River Tay and was the site of the so-called Battle of the Clans on 28 September 1396 between the MacKays and the Chattans.

Innerpeffray Castle — 3 miles (5km) southeast of Crieff. A tower house built for John Drummond in the 15th century and heightened for James Drummond in 1610. Innerpeffray Library (see separate entry) was built in its grounds in 1762.

Innerpeffray Library — 3 miles (5km) southeast of Crieff. The oldest free lending library in Scotland, founded by David Drummond, 3rd Lord Madertie, c.1680 when he made his family books available to the public. The present building was completed in 1762 under the patronage of Robert Hay Drummond, Archbishop of York. The stock of books was increased by contributions from the Hay Drummond family but the public lending facility was ended in 1968. The collection includes 3000 titles printed between 1502 and 1799 and contains many rare works, as well as a further 1400 volumes printed after 1799. There is a continuous record of all borrowings made from 1747 to 1968.

Interesting facts — **Dundee cake** is a rich fruit cake decorated on top with split almonds. The name first appears in print in the late 19th century but did not have any exclusive link with Dundee.

Invermark Castle — 16 miles (26km) northwest of Brechin. A tower house at the end of Glenesk close to Loch Lee, built in the 1520s by the Lindsay family and based around an earlier keep. In 1607 the castle was used as a refuge by David Lindsay, who was on the run after murdering Lord Spynie in Edinburgh. By the early 19th century the castle was in a poor state of repair and the building was robbed to provide material for nearby Lochlee parish church. Maintained by Historic Scotland, but not open to interior viewing for safety reasons.

Islands — There are 11 islands in Tayside. The two in Angus are: **The Brithers**, off the North Sea coast near

Carnoustie (GR: NO594358), and **Rossie Island** (aka Inchbraoch) in the Montrose Basin (GR: NO710568). The eight in Perth & Kinross are: **Alice's Bower**, one of three tiny islets off Castle Island (GR: NO134019); **Castle Island**, the site of Loch Leven Castle where Mary, Queen of Scots was imprisoned 1567–8 (GR: NO139017); **Eilean nam Faoileag** in Loch Rannoch (GR: NN531577); **Moncrieffe Island** (aka Friarton), situated in the River Tay (GR: NO123222); **Reed Bower**, one of three tiny islets off Castle Island (GR: NO139014); **Roy's Folly**, one of three tiny islets off Castle Island; **Scart Island** (GR: NO135025); and **St Serf's Island**, largest island of Loch Leven (GR: NO160004). There is also **Fowler's Island** in the River Tay in Dundee (GR: NO411300).

J M Barrie's Birthplace — Brechin Road, Kirriemuir. The weaver's cottage where the creator of Peter Pan was born in May 1860. It is thought that the character of Wendy was inspired by his mother Margaret and Peter Pan by his brother David, who died aged 13 and therefore never grew up. The communal bath house nearby may have been the original 'Wendy House' and was certainly used as a makeshift theatre. The upper floors of the house are furnished as in Barrie's youth. A museum in the house next door celebrates Barrie's life and works. Maintained by the National Trust for Scotland since 1937. A statue of Peter Pan stands in the centre of Kirriemuir. Tel: 01575 572646.

Kenmore Hotel — The Square, Kenmore. Reputedly the oldest hotel in Scotland, built in 1752 on the site of an earlier inn.

Kerr's Miniature Railway — The 'wee railway' is the oldest small-gauge ($10^1/_4$in/260mm) railway in Scotland, opened on Arbroath seafront on 22 June 1935. It runs for 400 yards (0.4m) alongside the Dundee–Aberdeen mainline during the summer months. Planned and built by Matthew Kerr as a commercial venture, it carried more than 60,000 people in 1955 but went into decline as British holidaymakers sought out warmer climes and, like mainline railways, its steam trains were replaced by a battery-electric 'diesel' train. On his father's retirement in 1977, Matthew Jr took the railway over as a non-profit-making venture. The railway now has six miniature locomotives (two steam, including *Big Bertha*, which had been sold in 1960), a miniature bus and a fire engine. Matthew Kerr Jr died on 17 April 2006 and the railway has since been operated by his wife Jill.

Kinnoull Hill Woodland Park — A country park opened in 1991 to the east of Perth, covering 755 acres (305ha) and encompassing five hills – Corsiehill, Deuchny Hill, Barnhill, Binn Hill and Kinnoull Hill – which provide outstanding views of Perth and the surrounding countryside. The woodland is approximately 50 per cent broadleaves including oak, ash, beech and rowan, the other half being conifers such as spruce, Scots pine and larch. It encompasses the ancient coronation road used by the kings of Scotland travelling from Scone Palace to Falkland Palace. There is an Iron Age hill fort on Deuchny Hill and the top of Kinnoull Hill is dominated by a folly of a ruined castle. An arboretum which stood on Deuchny Hill is undergoing restoration. The park is managed by Perth and Kinross Council and the Forestry Commission Scotland.

Kinross House Gardens — Kinross, 13 miles (21km) south of Perth. Gardens on the shores of Loch Leven surrounding Kinross House created 1679–85 in the contemporary Franco-Dutch style, with terraces, parterres and orchards. It is believed that 100,000 trees had been planted on the estate by 1700; a chestnut tree still standing in the garden is thought to be one of 300 grown from seed brought from Paris. The house was unoccupied from 1819 until 1902 when Sir Basil Montgomery took up residence and re-reconstructed the gardens. One striking feature is the Fish Gate in the park walls, which depicts a basket containing, it is said, the seven varieties of fish that could be caught in the loch at that time. Kinross House was built in 1685, after the gardens were completed, by Sir William Bruce, surveyor and architect to Charles II and also responsible for rebuilding Holyrood House in Edinburgh. The house and estate were purchased by merchant George Graham in 1777 and passed by marriage to the Montgomery family, who preferred living at Stobo Castle in Peeblesshire. The house is not open to the public.

Kirriemuir Aviation Museum — Bellies Brae, Kirriemuir. A museum built around the private collection of American-born Richard Moss, who served in the RAF for ten years, and including uniforms, medals, insignia, model aircraft, photographs and equipment. Tel: 01575 573233.

Kirriemuir Camera Obscura — Kirrie Hill, Kirriemuir. One of only three camera obscura in Scotland. Located in a cricket pavilion overlooking the town and the valley of Strathmore, it was donated, along with the pavilion, by J M Barrie in 1930. Managed by the National Trust for Scotland since 1999.

Kirriemuir Gateway to the Glens Museum — High Street, Kirriemuir. Opened in 2001 in the restored Kirriemuir Town House, dating from 1604. Exhibits cover the culture, environment and history of Kirriemuir and the Western Angus Glens. There are also displays on famous sons and daughters of the town, including author J M Barrie, author Violet Jacob and rock singer Bon Scott. Exhibits include the Kirriemuir 'Weavers' Banner', an anti-Corn Law banner dating from c.1836, and several Pictish stones. The museum was named Scottish Museum of the Year in 2001. Tel: 01575 575479.

Lawers Village — 18 miles (29km) southwest of Pitlochry. Burial place of the Lady of Lawers, a 17th century soothsayer and prophetess.

Lindertis Estate — The family estate near Kirriemuir of Sir Hugh Munro (1856–1919), the first person to list methodically all the separate mountains above 3000ft (914m) in Scotland, which are now called 'Munros'. He published his tables in 1891. Munro was a founder member of the Scottish Mountaineering Club (1889) and served as its president 1894–7.

Linn of Tummel — 2 miles (3km) northwest of Pitlochry. The meeting point of the River Tummel and the River Garry, forming a fast moving pool at the entrance to Loch Faskally. An obelisk commemorates a visit by Queen Victoria in 1844. Owned by the National Trust for Scotland.

Little Houses, The — Brightly coloured houses in Dunkeld built in the 18th century. These are private houses restored as part of the Little Houses Improvement Scheme (LHIS) of the National Trust for Scotland.

Loch Earn — 25 miles (40km) west of Perth. The $6^1/_2$ mile (10.5km) long Loch Earn lies within the Loch Lomond & Trossachs National Park. The River Earn issues from its eastern end. It is unusual in having its own 'tidal system', caused by a persistent prevailing wind blowing along the loch and applying stress to the water surface.

Loch Leven — $^{1}/_{2}$ mile (0.8km) east of Kinross, 13 miles (21km) south of Perth. The largest loch in lowland Scotland, covering 3500 acres (1400ha) and one of the most important sites for waterfowl in Britain. It was designated a National Nature Reserve in 1964 and has the largest concentrations of inland breeding ducks in Europe. Bird species include tufted duck, lapwing, oystercatcher, widgeon, greylag geese, pink-footed geese, mute swans and whooper swans. St Serf's Island holds 90 per cent of the loch's wildlife. In addition to being an NNR, parts of the loch are also a designated Ramsar site, Site of Special Scientific Interest and Special Protection Area.

Loch Leven Castle — $^{1}/_{2}$ mile (0.8km) east of Kinross, 13 miles (21km) south of Perth. Located on an island towards the western end of Loch Leven and originally built in the 13th century, possibly by an invading English army. It changed hands many times over the next century before being extended by David II. Two circular towers were added in the early 15th century, by which time the Douglas family had been made castellans. The castle served as a state prison many times but its most famous prisoner was Mary, Queen of Scots. She had previously visited the castle in 1563 and 1565 but was held against her will 17 June 1567–2 May 1568 on the third floor of the castle's Glassin Tower, before being moved to the solar storey of the Main Tower, and was forced to abdicate in favour of her infant son on 24 July 1567. During her stay on the island she miscarried twins. She escaped with the help of Sir William Douglas's son Willie. The castle and estate was bought in the 1670s by Sir William Bruce who then built Kinross House on the shore of the loch, which was reduced to a picturesque ruin. The water level in the loch was lowered by over 3ft (0.9m) in the 1830s; as a result, the island on which the castle stands quadrupled in size and the water no longer lapped against its walls as it would have done during its heyday. The castle is in the care of Historic Scotland.

Loch of the Lowes — 1 mile (1.6km) northeast of Dunkeld, 10 miles (16km) northwest of Perth. A 242 acre (98ha) wildlife reserve managed by the Scottish Wildlife Trust and most notable as a site for nesting ospreys. Other wildlife include fallow and roe deer and red squirrels.

Loch Tay — 7 miles (11km) southwest of Aberfeldy, 13 miles (21km) southwest of Pitlochry. At 14 miles (23km) long, the sixth largest loch in Scotland by area. The loch is fed by the rivers Dochart (local name for the Tay) and Lochay at its head. It is the site of at least 18 of the early Iron Age loch dwellings known as crannogs; an example has been reconstructed by the Scottish Trust for Underwater Archaeology on the south side of the loch at the Scottish Crannog Centre (see separate entry). Tel: 01887 830583.

Lunan Lochs — Five lochs on the Lunan Burn between Dunkeld and Blairgowrie: Loch of Craiglush, Loch of Lowes, Loch of Butterstone, Loch of Clunie and Loch of Dromellie/Marlee Loch. All five are designated Sites of Special Scientific Interest populated by bird species include osprey, greylag geese, Slavonian grebe, little grebe and great crested grebe, and mammals such as otter, red squirrel, pine marten and pipistrelle bat.

Meffan Museum and Art Gallery — West High Street, Forfar. 'The Meffan' was built in 1898 with a bequest from the daughter of Provost Meffan. Originally Forfar's library and museum, the building now houses an art gallery and museum. There are two galleries devoted to the works of contemporary Scottish artists. Another gallery explores the archaeology, social history and economic development of the town; exhibits include a collection of Pictish stone, a display about the area in the 11th century, a recreation of a cobbled street with a clockmaker's, weaver's, baker's, shoemaker's and sweet shop, and a depiction of the execution of a witch during the witch hunts of the 1660s. Tel: 01307 464123.

Meggernie Castle — $1^{1}/_{2}$ miles (2.5km) west of Bridge of Balgie, 24 miles (39km) southwest of Pitlochry. A 16th century tower house situated in the heart of Perth & Kinross, and the principal historic centre of the beautiful valley of Glen Lyon. Located on the site of a previous fortification built by the Clan MacGregor, the exact date of its original construction has not been ascertained, but it is named in a charter of 4 March 1603 as the chief house of the baron of Glen Lyon and was probably built c.1585.

Meigle Sculptured Stone Museum — Dundee Road, Meigle, 11 miles (18km) southwest of Forfar. A museum in Meigle kirkyard housing more than 30 sculptured stones discovered in the immediate area. Liberal Prime Minister Sir Henry Campbell Bannerman (1836–1908) is buried in Meigle alongside his wife. The museum is operated by Historic Scotland. Tel: 01828 640612.

Meikleour Beech Hedge — $^{1}/_{2}$ mile (0.8km) south of Meikleour, 10 miles (16km) northeast of Perth. The tallest hedge in the world, consisting of a wall of beech trees 1739ft (530m) long and standing an average 98ft (30m) high. The trees were planted in 1745 by Jean Mercer and her husband Robert Murray Nairne of nearby Meikleour House. According to legend, the hedge was planted by labourers who were to die shortly afterwards at the Battle of Culloden; the hedge is an abiding living monument to their sacrifice.

Methven Castle — A mid to late 17th century five-storey tower house built on the site of an earlier fortification. It was in this earlier property that Margaret Tudor, elder sister of Henry VIII, wife of James IV and mother of James V died in 1541. Her third husband was Henry Stewart, Lord Methven. The castle has been restored and is not open to the public.

Mills Observatory — Glamis Road, Balgay Park, Dundee. Located on Balgay Hill and opened on 28 October 1935. The only full-time public observatory in Britain, its main telescope is a 10in (254mm) Cooke refractor made in York in 1871. There are exhibits of equipment, photographs and models and a small planetarium. Tel: 01382 435967

Monikie Country Park — Panmure Road, Monikie, Broughty Ferry. A country park opened in August 1981 surrounding three ponds, formerly reservoirs dating from 1847–53. They stopped supplying water to Dundee in 1981 and are now an important nesting site for great crested grebe. The landscape includes parkland (known as the Old Park) and woodland, home to red squirrel and stoat. Tel: 01382 370202.

Montrose
A royal burgh and the most northerly of the Angus coastal towns. It was a major trading port in the past and has benefited in recent years from the oil and gas industry. It overlooks the Montrose Basin tidal lagoon. The town boasts the widest high street in Scotland.

Montrose Air Station Heritage Centre
Waldron Road, Montrose. Museum housed at and telling the story of the former RAF Montrose, the first operational air station in Britain, opened in February 1913 and used in both world wars. Exhibits include a Bristol Sycamore HR14, a De Havilland 115 Vampire T11 and a Hawker Sea Hawk FGA6. Run by the Montrose Aerodrome Heritage Society and Montrose Air Station Heritage Trust. Tel: 01674 678222.

Montrose Basin
1 mile (1.6km) west of Montrose. Part of the estuary of the South Esk forming a tidal basin near the town of Montrose. The area attracts over 50,000 migratory birds each year and 2530 acres (1024ha) of the basin is a Local Nature Reserve run by the Scottish Wildlife Trust. Bird species include pink-footed goose, eider, mute swan, redshank, shelduck, knot, oystercatcher and reed bunting.

Montrose Museum and Art Gallery
Panmure Place, Montrose. A local history museum opened in 1842 in a neoclassical building designed to house the collections of the Montrose Natural History & Antiquarian Society. The collections cover areas such as social, industrial and natural history and fine art and natural sciences. Exhibits include Pictish stones, Montrose silver and Dryleys pottery. The art gallery has exhibitions of paintings and sculptures by local artists such as William Lamb and Edward Baird. Tel: 01674 673232.

Newton Castle
Newton Street, Blairgowrie. A 14th or 15th century Z-plan castle built by the Drummond family and later owned by the Grahams before being purchased in 1787 by Col. Allan MacPherson. It has remained the seat of the Clan MacPherson ever since. The castle is said to be haunted by a Green Lady, a common apparition and folklore motif in many Scottish castles and fortified homes. There are a number of stories to explain her origin; one story suggests that she is the phantom of Lady Jean Drummond, who unwisely fell in love with one of the Blairs of Ardblair – with whom the Drummond family were often feuding. Inevitably their love was abandoned due to a violent and bloody feud, and she drowned herself in one of the nearby lochs. Another story suggests that a lady at the castle wished to gain the affections of a certain man, and went to the local wise woman for magical advice. She was informed that she would have to wear green – the colour of the fairies – and spend a long night waiting at the Corbie Stane (a nearby standing stone). Unfortunately she died before her affections could be gratified, and she now haunts the castle in grief wearing the green dress she wore in her quest for love. The apparition is thought to be strongest at Halloween; it was during the night of Halloween that her gravestone was said to turn around three times.

Perth
Known as 'The Fair City', Perth is a royal burgh on the River Tay established near the site of the Roman fort of Bertha. At one time the city was known as St John's Town (hence the name of the football team, St Johnstone). It was granted burgh status in 1125 by King David I. Formerly the county town of Perthshire, it is now the administrative centre of Perth & Kinross.

Perth Cathedral
See St Ninian's Cathedral.

Perth Museum and Art Gallery
George Street, Perth. Opened in 1824 in a neoclassical building designed by David Morison for the purpose of housing the collections of the city's Literary & Antiquarian Society. Collections cover archaeology, photography and social and natural history. Tel: 01738 632488.

Pictavia
$1^1/_2$ miles (2.5km) west of Brechin. Opened in 1999 at Brechin Castle Centre, Pictavia explores the story of the tribes known as the Picti (Picts) who ruled the region which developed into modern Scotland in the 1st millennium. Exhibits include replicas and original artefacts such as carved standing stones. The Tower of Sound features reconstructions of musical instruments taken from designs on the stones; music has been recorded using these replicas. Tel: 01356 626241.

Pitmuies Gardens and Grounds
Guthrie, 6 miles (10km) northwest of Arbroath. Two semi-formal walled gardens adjoining a Georgian house. The 25 acre (10ha) gardens feature mass spring planting and long herbaceous borders with roses and delphiniums. In addition there is an alpine meadow of wild flowers, a woodland garden and woodland and riverside walks. Tel: 01241 828245.

Queen's View
5 miles (8km) west of Pitlochry. A spectacular and much photographed panorama of loch and mountain scenery over Loch Tummel towards Glencoe. It is named after either Mary, Queen of Scots or Queen Victoria, or indeed both.

Queen's Well, The
20 miles (32km) northwest of Brechin. A crown-shaped monument at the head of Glenesk built in 1861 over a natural spring from which Queen Victoria drank while on the way to Balmoral.

Rannoch Moor
33 miles (53km) west of Pitlochry. A plateau rising to 1260ft (384m) and consisting of more than $18^3/_4$ sq miles (48.5 sq km) of lochs, lochans and peat bogs. Although it is crossed by the A82, the West Highland Way and the West Highland Railway, it is regarded as one of the last truly wild places in Scotland.

Rivers
As with the river system of the same name in Lothian, the **Esk** has two distinct channels. The South Esk rises in the wilderness area of Glen Doll in the southern Grampians on the border between Angus and Aberdeenshire. The river plots a southeast course through Glen Clova and into the wide valley of Strathmore, before meandering eastwards past Brechin and entering Montrose Basin through which it flows outwards to the North Sea by a narrow channel between Montrose and Ferryden. The total length of the river is approximately 49 miles (79 km). The North Esk is formed in the southern Grampians by the meeting of the Water of Mark and the Water of Lee, some 10 miles east of the source of the South Esk. It flows southeast through Glen Esk, and then east some 4 miles (7km) north of Brechin before entering the North Sea 3 miles (5km) north of Montrose. Its length is approximately 29 miles (47km). The **Garry** emerges at the north end of Loch Garry and flows southeast for 22 miles (35km), adjacent to the A9, through Glen Garry before joining the

Tummel 2 miles (3 km) northeast of Pitlochry. The **Isla** rises about 2 miles (3km) west of the source of the South Esk and flows south through the Strathmore Valley and then southwest to join the Tay about 3 miles (5km) west of Coupar Angus. Its length is approximately 46 miles (74km). The **Lyon** (see entry for Glen Lyon). The **Tay** rises on the slopes of Ben Lui in the southern Grampians, close to the intersection of the A82 and A85, in the northwest area of the Loch Lomond and the Trossachs National Park, on the border of Strathclyde and Central. The river is known locally as the Connonish until it flows southeasterly through Strath Fillan when it becomes the Fillan. As it enters Loch Lubhair, near Crianlarich, it becomes the Dochart. It then takes a northeasterly course into Loch Tay at Killin and after exiting at the northeast of the loch at Kenmore the Tay maintains a northeasterly route through Aberfeldy and then loops south, adjacent to the A9, through Dunkeld and Perth before discharging into the Firth of Tay and ultimately the North Sea. At 120 miles (192km) in length it is the longest river in Scotland. It is widely known as one of the best salmon rivers in Europe. The **Tummel** emerges from Loch Rannoch at Kinloch Rannoch and initially flows in an easterly direction and is joined by the Garry just north of Pitlochry. The Tummel then flows southeastward to merge with the River Tay a mile (2 km) to the south of Ballinluig.

RSPB Loch of Kinnordy — 2 miles (3km) west of Kirriemuir. An RSPB nature reserve covering 218 acres (88ha) and providing a habitat for birds such as black-necked grebes and black-headed gulls.

RSPB Vane Farm — 4 miles (6km) southeast of Kinross. An RSPB reserve overlooking Loch Leven and part of the Loch Leven National Nature Reserve. Bird species include lapwing, pink-footed goose, oystercatcher, shoveler duck, greylag goose, osprey, redshank and whooper swan. Habitats include birch woodland and heather moorland. Tel: 01577 862355.

St Andrew's Cathedral — Nethergate, Dundee. A Gothic style church built in 1836, the oldest Catholic church in the city of Dundee. The architect was George Mathewson, a native Dundonian. The church is 108ft (33m) long and 55ft (17m) wide, with gallery accommodation for about 1200 people. It became a cathedral in 1923. Tel: 01382 225228.

St Ninian's Cathedral — North Methven Street, Perth. The seat of the Episcopal Bishop of St Andrews, Dunkeld & Dunblane, built 1849–90. Tel: 01738 632053.

St Orland's Stone — 4 miles (6m) west of Forfar. Aka Cossans or Cossins Stone. An early Christian sculpted stone standing 7ft 9in (2.4m) high, with carvings of figure scenes – mounted hunters, men in a boat and two animals – and symbols including the crescent and V-rod, double disc and Z-rod. On the other side is a weathered cross. Maintained by Historic Scotland.

St Paul's Episcopal Cathedral — High Street, Dundee. The seat of the Episcopal Bishop of Brechin, built 1853–5 to a decorated Gothic design by Sir George Gilbert Scott on the site of a medieval castle. It was dedicated on 1 November 1865 and raised to cathedral status in 1905. Tel: 01382 224486.

St Vigean's Church — St Vigeans, 1 mile (1.6km) north of Arbroath. St Vigean is the latinised form of St Fechin of Fohbar, an Irish saint who died in 664. The church was consecrated in 1242 and reconsecrated in 1485 after alterations to its layout. It was restored in 1871. Many early Christian sculptured stones have been found at the site.

Scone Palace — 2 miles (3km) north of Perth. The family home of the Earls of Mansfield, overlooking the River Tay. The location is of ancient importance and was the site of a 6th century church. An Augustinian abbey was founded on the site by Alexander I in 1114 and the abbot's house became the palace where Scottish kings lodged for their coronations. The abbey was destroyed in 1559 by a mob incited by preacher John Knox. The palace was also damaged and was later incorporated into a new building by Sir David Murray, Lord Scone, in 1618. Major restoration and expansion was carried out in 1802, resulting in the Gothic-style building designed by William Atkinson which can be seen today. It houses collections of furniture, paintings, ivory and porcelain plus heirlooms belonging to James VI and his mother, Mary, Queen of Scots. Some of the Earl's large collection of orchids are on display in the state rooms. The grounds feature the Moot Hill (also known as the Hill of Credulity), the ancient crowning place of the kings of Scots from Kenneth Mac Alpin until 1 January 1651 when Charles II was the last monarch to be crowned here. Located immediately in front of the palace, it has a small Presbyterian chapel. A replica of the Stone of Scone sits in front of the chapel. The grounds also include a pinetum dating from 1848 and featuring a Douglas fir raised from the original seed sent from America in 1826. This specimen ranks among Britain's 50 most notable trees. The maze was grown from more than 2000 beech trees planted in the shape of the five-pointed Murray Star, part of the family's heraldic crest. Old Scone village was dismantled in 1805 to permit an enlarged parkland around the newly built palace. Tel: 01738 552300. See also Stone of Scone.

Scottish Crannog Centre — 1/4 mile (0.4km) southwest of Kenmore, 13 miles (21km) southwest of Pitlochry. Located beside Loch Tay and dedicated to the study of crannogs, artificial islands some of which date back more than 4000 years, constructed as defensible mounds and linked to the shore by either a stone causeway or a timber gangway. The exhibition centre features Iron Age artefacts and a full-size reconstruction of a 2600 year old crannog built by the Scottish Trust for Underwater Archaeology. Tel: 01887 830583.

Sport

football — **Arbroath**, founded in 1878, are forever famous for their 36–0 win over Bon Accord FC in the Scottish Cup in 1885, with Jocky Petrie scoring a record 13 goals. Nicknamed The Red Lichties due to the red light that used to guide fishing boats back from the North Sea to the harbour, their colours are maroon and white; their home ground is Gayfield Park, Arbroath. Tel: 01241 872157.

Brechin City were founded in 1906. They were winners of the Scottish 2nd Division in 1983, 1990, 2003 and 2005 and of the 3rd Division in 2002. Nicknamed The City, their colours are red and white; their home ground is Glebe Park, Trinity Road, Brechin. Tel: 01356 622856.

Dundee were founded in 1893. They were winners of the old Scottish League 1st Division in 1962, the new 1st Division in 1979, 1992 and 1998 and the old 2nd Division in 1947, also winning the Scottish Cup in 1910 and the Scottish League Cup in 1952, 1953 and 1974. Nicknamed The Dark Blues (after their traditional colours) or The Dees, their home ground is Dens Park Stadium, Sandeman Street, Dundee. Tel: 01382 889966.

Dundee United were founded in 1909 as Dundee Hibernian by members of the city's Irish community, adopting their present name in 1923. Winners of the Scottish Premier Division in 1983, the 1st Division in 1996 and the old 2nd Division in 1925 and 1929, they also won the Scottish Cup in 1994 and the Scottish League Cup in 1980 and 1981. They were runners-up in the UEFA Cup in 1987. Variously nicknamed The Terrors, The Arabs and The Tangerines – the latter after their orange and black strip (previously they played first in green and white and later in black and white), adopted in the 1960s – their home ground is Tannadice Park, Tannadice Street, Dundee. The two Dundee clubs, with grounds less than 100m apart, are claimed to be the closest neighbours in world football. Tel: 01382 833166.

Forfar Athletic were founded in 1885 and were winners of the Scottish 2nd Division in 1984 and the 3rd Division in 1995. Nicknamed The Loons (local dialect for 'young men', reflecting their origins as the 2nd XI of Angus Athletic), their colours are light and dark blue and white; their home ground is Station Park, Carseview Road, Forfar. Tel: 01307 463576.

Montrose were founded in 1879 and won the Scottish 2nd Division in 1985. Their colours are blue and white; their home ground is Links Park Stadium, Wellington Street, Montrose. Tel: 01674 673200.

St Johnstone, based in Perth, were founded in 1885. They are the only club with a 'J' in its name in the whole of the English and Scottish football leagues. They won the Scottish 1st Division in 1983, 1990 and 1997 and the 2nd Division in 1924, 1960 and 1963. Nicknamed The Saints or Saintees, their colours are blue and white; their home ground is McDiarmid Park, Crieff Road, Perth. Tel: 01738 459090.

golf

Carnoustie Golf Course is a public links course founded in 1850 and originally designed by Alan Robertson of St Andrews. In the 1870s it was extended to 18 holes by Old Tom Morris. In 1926 the Championship course was redesigned by James Braid. Prior to the 1937 Open Championship the final three holes were redesigned by James Wright to provide one of the toughest finishes in golf, including the Barry Burn which proved to be Jean Van de Velde's downfall in the 1999 Open. There are three links courses: the Championship Course, the Burnside Course and the Buddon Course. Open Championships staged at Carnoustie: 1931 (winner, Tommy Armour), 1937 (Henry Cotton), 1953 (Ben Hogan), 1968 (Gary Player), 1975 (Tom Watson), 1999 (Paul Lawrie) and 2007 (Padraig Harrington). Tel: 01241 853789.

Gleneagles Hotel & Golf Course, 2 miles (3km) southwest of Auchterarder, opened in 1924, although the courses were already in use while the hotel was being completed. There are four courses: the **King's Course**, designed by James Braid, opened in 1919. The holes have names such as 'Het Girdle' (Hot Pan) (5th hole) and 'Warslin' Lea' (Wrestling Ground) (17th hole); the **Queen's Course** was designed by James Braid. The 1st hole is called the 'Trystin' Tree' (Lover's Meeting Tree); the **PGA Centenary Course** was designed by Jack Nicklaus and will be the venue for the 2014 Ryder Cup. Using the back tees it measures 7088 yards, making it the longest inland course in Scotland; the **Wee Course** is based on an original 9 hole course from 1928. Tel: 01764 694469.

horse racing

Perth Racecourse, Scone Palace Park, Perth. Located in the grounds of Scone Palace, beside the River Tay. Horse racing began at North Inch in the early 17th century but the first official races were in the 1790s. The move to Scone Palace Park took place in 1908. The 1m 2f (2km) course stages National Hunt racing. Tel: 01738 551597.

ice hockey

Dundee Tigers, founded in 1987 and known in the late 1980s as Tayside Tigers, were Scottish National League champions in 2001. Previous incarnations include the original Dundee Tigers, formed in 1938 and Scottish League champions 1939, 1940 and 1948; and the Dundee Rockets, Northern League champions 1973 and 1982, British champions 1982, 1983 and 1984, Scottish National League Champions 1982, Premier winners 1984 and Scottish Cup winners 1986 and 1987. **Dundee Stars** were formed in 2001. Dundee Stars and Dundee Tigers both play at the Dundee Ice Arena, part of the Camperdown Leisure Complex.

Stone of Scone

Aka the Stone of Destiny or the Coronation Stone. A rectangular slab of reddish-grey sandstone traditionally believed to have been the stone which Jacob took for a pillow (Genesis 28:11), although several other versions of its legend prevail. What is certain is that the stone found its way to Scotland and since the time of Kenneth Mac Alpin, the first King of Scots, in around 847, Scottish monarchs were seated upon the stone during their coronation ceremony. At this time the stone was situated at Scone, a few miles north of Perth, but in 1296 it was seized by Edward I as spoils of war and taken to Westminster Abbey where it was installed as the centrepiece of the Coronation Chair. All subsequent British sovereigns except Queen Mary II have been crowned on this stone. On Christmas Eve 1950, a group of four Scottish students (Ian Hamilton, Gavin Vernon, Kay Matheson and Alan Stuart) from Glasgow University stole the stone in a fit of nationalistic fervour and accidentally broke it in two. It was eventually repaired and found its way to the altar of Arbroath Abbey on 11 April 1951 and was returned to Westminster Abbey shortly after. In 1996 the stone was returned to Scotland and now sits in Edinburgh Castle where it remains although arrangements have been made for its return to London for future coronation ceremonies. The dimensions of the stone are approximately 26 inches (660mm) by 16 inches (407mm) by 10.5 inches (267mm) in size and it weighs approximately 336 pounds (153kg). See also Scone Palace.

Tay Rail Bridge A double track railway bridge $2^1/_4$ miles (3.6km) long spanning the Firth of Tay between Dundee and Newport-on-Tay. Opened on 13 July 1887, it replaced the original single-track bridge which was opened by Queen Victoria on 1 June 1878, the central section of which ('High Girders') collapsed during a storm on 23 December 1879 while carrying a train, with the loss of 75 lives. An official inquiry found that the bridge was 'badly designed, badly built and badly maintained'. The disaster was famously the subject of a poem by William McGonagall.

Taymouth Castle 1 mile (1.6km) northeast of Kenmore, 12 miles (19km) southwest of Pitlochry. Located at the mouth of Loch Tay and built in the early 19th century incorporating some of the 16th century Balloch Castle, the castle was the seat of the Campbells of Breadalbane until 1921. Prior to World War II it was operated as a hotel and the deer park was developed into a golf course. It is now in private ownership.

Tealing Dovecot and Earth House Tealing, $4^1/_2$ miles (7km) north of Dundee. A stone dovecot probably dating from the 17th century; it incorporates a date-stone of 1595, but this is believed to have come from an earlier building. Close by is an Iron Age souterrain (underground passage), discovered in 1871 and now in the care of Historic Scotland.

Tealing Parish Church Tealing, $4^1/_2$ miles (7km) north of Dundee. Built in 1806 on the site of a 7th century church founded by St Boniface and dedicated to St Peter. A medieval sacrament house which also stood on the site was demolished prior to the building of the present church. Various symbol-stones were discovered on the site, some of which are now displayed in the Dundee Museum.

University of Dundee Established in 1881 as University College Dundee to promote 'the education of persons of both sexes and the study of Science, Literature and the Fine Arts'. It became part of the University of St Andrews in 1897. The University of Dundee came into being on 1 August 1967 and now has around 16,000 students, mostly based on a campus in central Dundee, with additional sites at Ninewells to the west of the city and Kirkcaldy in Fife. Former students include author Kate Atkinson, BBC journalist Alan Johnston and newsreader John Suchet. Tel: 01382 383000.

University of Dundee Botanic Gardens Riverside Drive, Dundee. Opened in 1971 and covering 22 acres (9ha) close to the River Tay. There are two greenhouses for tropical and exotic plants plus two outside pools and one indoor pool. The garden features a collection of native British plants, established according to their different habitats from montane (above the tree line) to coastal and linked by a burn. There are also exotic plants from Australasia, North America, Asia and the Mediterranean. Tel: 01382 647190.

Verdant Works West Henderson's Wynd, Dundee. A museum housed in a restored 19th century jute mill, and charting the story of the jute industry from its beginnings in India through to the story of the industry in Dundee and the social history of those who worked in the mills. The Verdant Works opened in 1833 as a flax mill before switching to processing jute. It was bought in the 1850s by John Ewan, a manufacturer of canvas, sacking and bagging. Ewan retired in 1880, and from 1893 until the 1960s the works were owned by china and waste merchants Alexander Thomson & Sons. Dundee Heritage Trust bought the works in 1991 and opened the museum in 1996. Exhibits include original working machinery. Tel: 01382 225282.

Wade's Bridge A five-span bridge across the River Tay in Aberfeldy designed by William Adam to the order of Lt General George Wade. The first stone was laid by Wade himself on 23 April 1733; the bridge opened to traffic at the end of October 1733 and was formally opened on 8 August 1735. It was an integral part of Wade's 1000 mile (1600km) network of military roads.

William Lamb Memorial Studio Market Street, Montrose. The studio of sculptor William Lamb until his death in 1951, when the studio and its contents were given to Montrose Town Council. Opened in 1955, the building contains a permanent exhibition of Lamb's work, including portrait heads of Princesses Elizabeth and Margaret Rose and of the Duchess of York dating from 1932. Tel: 01674 673232.

Wishart Arch Cowgate, Dundee. Aka Cowgate or East Port. A gateway and surrounding remnant of Dundee's 16th century city walls. Probably built c.1590, although Protestant reformer George Wishart (1513–46) is said to have preached from the gate in 1544.

Woods on Your Doorstep **Backmuir Wood** (121 acres/49ha), east of the Carse of Gowrie near the village of Muirhead. Classified as a Long Established Woodland of Plantation Origin (LEPO). Mixed broadleaved and conifer planting; **Boat Brae** (5 acres/2ha), on the edge of Dunkeld, on the north side of the River Tay in the River Tay National Scenic Area. On a severe slope, Boat Brae is an ancient woodland covered by mature high forest, composed predominantly of oak. Other species include ash, sycamore, beech and Scots pine and larch. There is some regeneration at the western end of the wood – one patch of pole-stage ash and occasional stems of young ash, beech and holly; **Brighty Wood** (12 acres/5ha), north of Dundee. Classified as a LEPO. Mixed broadleaved and conifer planting; **Glen Quey** (946 acres/383ha) and **Glen Sherup** (1495 acres/605ha) form the Glen Devon property covering 3047 acres (1233ha) and also including Geordie's Wood, a project to establish a new native woodland which will link to adjacent conifer woodlands in order to create an area of continuous but varied forest; **Huntly Wood** (32 acres/13ha) in the Carse of Gowrie north of the village of Longforgan, a long-established woodland of plantation origin including both mixed broadleaved and conifer plantings; **Kilmagad Wood** (67 acres/27ha) on Bishops Hill overlooking the village of Scotlandwell and the Loch Leven catchment. Mature mixed broadleaves, with conifers on the upper slopes; **Moncreiffe Hill** (324 acres/131ha) (GR: NO138197), classified as a LEPO, with a wide range of species including ash, sycamore, larch, Scots pine and sitka spruce; **Portmoak Moss** (106 acres/43ha), close to the village of Scotlandwell and consisting of mature conifer plantation woodland and an open area of raised bog. The main species are sitka spruce and Scots pine.

Some famous people born in Tayside

Barrie, James Matthew (author) (1860–1937)	Kirriemuir
Bell, Patrick (inventor of the reaping machine) (1799–1869)	Auchterhouse
Brown, Bill (footballer) (1931–2004)	Arbroath
Duncan, Adam (admiral) (1731–1804)	Lundie
Ewing, James Alfred (physicist) (1855–1935)	Dundee
Fyffe, Will (music hall artist) (1885–1947)	Dundee
Johnstone, Derek (footballer) (1953–)	Dundee
Lamb, William (sculptor) (1893–1951)	Montrose
Lorimer, Peter (footballer) (1946–)	Dundee
Lyell, Charles (geologist) (1797–1875)	Kinnordy
MacAulay, Fred (comedian) (1956–)	Perth
Marra, Michael 'Atlas' (musician) (1952–)	Dundee
McAlpine, Hamish (footballer) (1948–)	Kilspindie
McGregor, Ewan (actor) (1971–)	Crieff
McKenzie, Alexander (Canadian prime minister) (1822–92)	Logierait
Newall, Robert Stirling (astronomer) (1812–89)	Dundee
Nichol, John Pringle (astronomer) (1804–59)	Brechin
Playfair, John (geologist) (1748–1819)	Benvie
Watson-Watt, Robert (inventor of radar) (1892–1973)	Brechin
Windsor, Margaret (princess) (1930–2002)	Glamis

Western Isles/Outer Hebrides

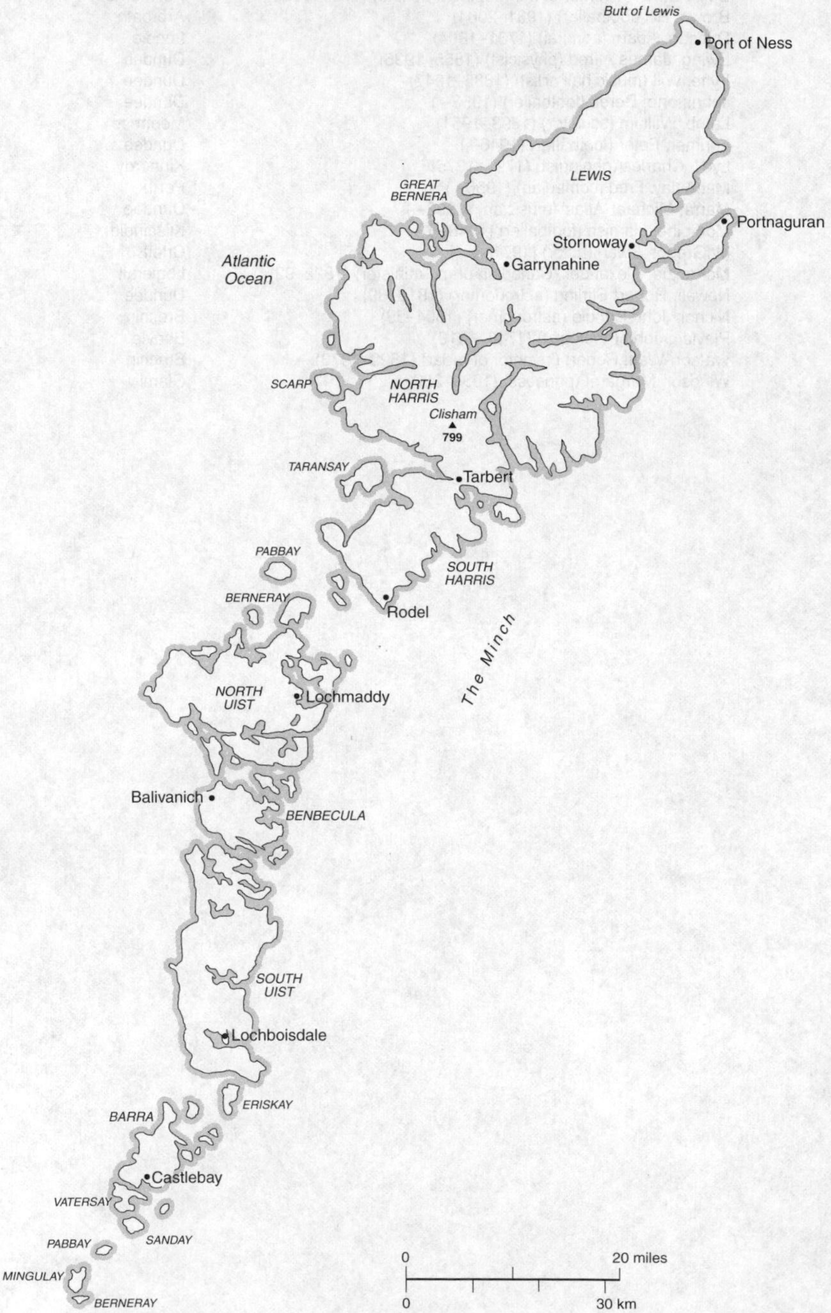
Butt of Lewis
Port of Ness
LEWIS
GREAT BERNERA
Portnaguran
Stornoway
Garrynahine
Atlantic Ocean
SCARP
NORTH HARRIS
Clisham
799
TARANSAY
Tarbert
PABBAY
SOUTH HARRIS
BERNERAY
Rodel
The Minch
NORTH UIST
Lochmaddy
Balivanich
BENBECULA
SOUTH UIST
Lochboisdale
ERISKAY
BARRA
Castlebay
VATERSAY
SANDAY
PABBAY
MINGULAY
BERNERAY
0
20 miles
0
30 km

Officially known as Na h-Eileanan Siar but also known as the Outer Hebrides, the Western Isles or the Long Island, this island chain off the northwest coast of Scotland stretches 130 miles (209km) from the Butt of Lewis in the north to Barra Head in the south. They are separated from the Scottish mainland in the north and from the Inner Hebrides in the south by the treacherous stretch of water known as the Minch. The populated islands are Baleshare, Barra, Benbecula, Berneray, Eriskay, Flodda, Great Bernera, Grimsay, Lewis and Harris, North Uist, Scalpay, South Uist and Vatersay.

Unlike most of the rest of Scotland, where similar councils were not established until 1996, the Western Isles have been a unitary council area since 1975. Since then the islands have formed one of the 32 unitary council areas which now cover the whole of Scotland. The Western Isles council is officially known by its Gaelic name Comhairle nan Eilean Siar, known locally simply as 'the Comhairle' or 'a Chomhairle', having changed its name under the Local Government (Gaelic Names) (Scotland) Act 1997. The council has its base in Stornoway on Lewis, a fishing port and the only burgh in the Western Isles.

The Hebrides are first mentioned by Pliny, who called them the Hebudes, and Ptolemy who placed the Eboudai islands above Ireland. They had been settled during the Neolithic period, during which time the forest which dominated the inland on Lewis and Harris (the largest offshore island of mainland Britain and Ireland) was cut down for fuel and to clear land for farming. Many of the islands have monuments dating from the Neolithic through to the Iron Age such as the Callanish Stones, Dun Carloway and Cladh Hallan.

Norsemen settled in Lewis and Harris in the 9th century and their control of the Hebrides was formalised in 1098 when Edgar of Scotland signed the islands over to Magnus III of Norway. The Outer Hebrides came under the control of the King of Mann and the Isles. As a result of the 1266 Treaty of Perth the Outer Hebrides were yielded to the kingdom of Scotland.

Power in the islands, much as on the mainland of Scotland, devolved upon a few families or clans. The Clan MacNeil controlled Barra, the MacDonalds were overlords in The Uists and Benbecula, the Macleods were in control of Harris. Meanwhile Lewis, once the influence of the Macleods had diminished, was divided between three clans, the Morisons, the MacAulays and the MacKenzies. These surnames still predominate in many of these islands. Power struggles between the various clans would dominate the history of the Western Isles for many centuries and these, together with economic change, were responsible in part for the emigrations and population declines which marked the 19th and 20th centuries. In 1772 more than 200 Catholics from South Uist, Arisaig and Moydart were forced to emigrate to Prince Edward Island, Canada, by MacDonald of Boisdale. In the 1820s kelp traders emigrated to Cape Breton, and they were followed by crofters as the growth in sheep farming saw many villages cleared. In the middle of the 19th century, along with those islanders who moved to mainland Scotland in search of employment, many families were 'encouraged' or assisted to leave the islands for Australia and Canada. Towards the end of the century families from Harris were heading for the Falkland Islands and those from Lewis were leaving for Patagonia, both enticed by the sheep farming in those regions. After World War I a renewal of emigration began, this time to all parts of the world, especially by young Hebrideans in search of employment. In the 19th century Sir James Matheson had used his fortune to try to improve the wealth of the people of Lewis; in the 1920s Lord Leverhulme had plans to develop the economic strength of the islands by improving the infrastructure and streamlining the vertical integration of the fishing industry from catching the fish through to retail distribution. Unfortunately neither of them managed to see their schemes through to any sort of success.

The decline of the clan system and the social organisation attached to it saw a shift in land use, land tenure and employment. Land was parcelled out in plots too small to be self-sufficient, especially as the best land had been allocated to the new sheep farms. These plots were laid out together in specific areas, particularly in relation to the developing road system, and leased to crofters. This resulted in the settlement patterns still prevalent in the Western Isles today. The house and any agricultural buildings and infrastructure on the croft were to be provided by the crofter himself. Because the landowner had full control of his land and its use the crofts, and indeed townships, could be moved or cleared at any time if a landowner felt that the land could be used in a more profitable manner. This system, together with problems such as the potato blight, eventually led to social unrest and the so-called Crofters' War in the 1880s. The Crofters Act (1886) gave crofters security of tenure, a fair rent and the right to pass their crofts on through their family. However, it did not guarantee the release of more land to provide the greater number of crofts needed for the island population. A Crofters Commission was set up in 1955 and this has the job of overseeing legislation concerning crofting and further developing crofting as an agricultural system and way of life. Since 1976 it has been possible for a crofter to acquire title to his croft, thus becoming an owner-occupier.

The main industries in the Western Isles are the traditional ones of weaving, fishing and crofting with many areas totally self-sufficient. Lewis is the centre of Harris tweed production, with an output of more than 4 million yards of cloth per year. Tourism has begun to play a greater part in the economies of the local communities and the exporting of whisky and locally produced merchandise has also increased.

The archipelago is home to some flora and fauna unique to the British Isles and the isolation of some of the islands has meant the evolution of breeds of birds and animals which differ from their mainland equivalents. The islands are also important nesting sites for seabirds and home to colonies of grey seals. Almost half of all Scottish machair – a low-lying fertile coastal plain rich in plant species and one of the most scarce habitat types in Europe – occurs in the Outer Hebrides, and the Hebridean machair is one of the last UK strongholds of the corncrake.

Comhairlenan Eilean Siar

(Council of the Western Isles)

Western Isles/Outer Hebrides	Population			Area	
	male	*female*	*total*	*sq miles*	*sq km*
Total	13,082	13,420	26,502	1186	3071

Local Attractions and Information

Administrative headquarters	Council Offices, Sandwick Road, Stornoway, HS1 2BW. Tel: 01851 703773.
Airports	**Barra Traigh Mhor** (Cockle Strand): beach landing strip with landings dependent on the tide. Flights to Benbecula and Glasgow. **Benbecula**: a military airport with a dual civilian role. Flights to Barra, Glasgow and Stornaway. Address: Balivanich, Isle of Benbecula. **Stornaway**: on Lewis. A military airport with a dual civilian role. Flights to Aberdeen, Benbecula, Edinburgh, Glasgow and Inverness.
Amazon's House	Gleann Mor, Hirta. The remains of a beehive house possibly dating from the Iron Age.
Amhuinnsuidhe Castle	9 miles (15km) northwest of Tarbert, Harris. The most westerly castle in Scotland, Amhuinnsuidhe (G. = River Seat) was designed in Scottish baronial style by David Bryce and built for the Earl of Dunmore in 1868 beside stepped falls where the waters of Loch Leosaid tumble over smooth rock slabs and into the sea. It was here that J M Barrie wrote *Mary Rose* in 1912.
Arnol Blackhouse Museum	Arnol, 11 miles (18km) northwest of Stornoway, Lewis. Located in a crofting village and split between four buildings: an interpretive centre, a blackhouse, a 'whitehouse' and the excavated ruin of an older blackhouse, furnished in early 20th century style and including a burning peat fire. A blackhouse was a long, narrow windowless building with unmortared stone walls, the gaps being filled with peat or earth. The roof was turfed and then thatched but was without a chimney; the smoke from the peat fire in the central hearth filtered out through the thatch. There was also a byre for the family's animals at one end. The 'whitehouse' is furnished as it would have been in the 1950s and represents a type of building introduced in the late 19th and early 20th century, splitting the keeping of animals from the human habitation and eventually replacing the blackhouse. In fact blackhouses were only named as such after the introduction of the more modern 'whitehouses'. The original Arnol village (Old Arnol) was nearer the sea and the blackhouses on the museum site are of more modern construction, probably having been built from the mid 19th century onwards. The museum is run by Historic Scotland. Tel: 01851 710395.
Barpa Langass	6 miles (10km) southwest of Lochmaddy, North Uist. A chambered cairn 14ft (4.2m) high and 80ft (24m) in diameter, located on the slopes of Ben Langass. A passage leads into an oval chamber 13ft (4m) long by 6ft (1.8m) wide, capped with three large lintel stones. The central chamber is constructed from seven large orthostats (upright stones). Excavations in 1911 found evidence of burnt burials and pottery sherds.
Barra	Thought to be named after the 6th century St Barr (G. Finbar = St Barr). Owned by the MacNeil family, reputedly descended from Niall of the Nine Hostages, the island has been a MacNeil possession since at least the 15th century except for a period from 1838 to 1937. In 1838 the then MacNeil chief sold the island to a Colonel Gordon, who proceeded to clear the island of its crofters and despatch them to Canada and the United States. This policy was continued by the next owners; it was only in 1937 that the present chief's father, an American architect, bought much of the island back for the family. He then restored the family home at Kisimul Castle in the bay opposite the main town of Castlebay. The island has a beach airstrip (see Airports). Area: 23.85 sq miles 61.73 (sq km). Population: 1078. GR: NF680010.

Barra Madonna and Child 1 mile (1.6km) northeast of Castlebay, Barra. A white Carrara marble statue of the Madonna and child on the slopes of Ben Heaval (Sheabhal).

Berneray The only inhabited island in the Sound of Harris; the presence of stone circles and other signs date its habitation to the Bronze Age. It was also the birthplace of the 'Cape Breton Giant' Angus MacAskill (1825–63) who grew to 7ft 9in (2.36m) in height. Area: 4.08 sq miles (10.56 sq km). Population: 136. GR: NF913820.

Big Garden, The Cille Bhrìghde, South Uist. Aka An Gàrradh Mòr (G. = The Big Garden). A garden originally established in the 1740s to serve Boisdale House, the ruins of which stand a few yards away. The wall of An Gàrradh Mòr stands 10–13ft (3–4m) high around a restored garden and house now home to the Bridge family, who are developing it as an organic, self-sufficient kitchen garden. It was in this garden that potatoes were first grown in the Outer Hebrides. Tel: 01878 700828.

Blue Men of the Minch, The The legendary inhabitants of The Minch. These blue-skinned sea creatures in human shape can lure sailors to their doom and conjure storms at will, but can be beaten by making sure you get the last word in a contest of rhymes and riddles with their chieftain.

Borve Castle 4 miles (6km) south of Balivanich, Benbecula. The ruin of a three-storey 14th century hall house, probably the castle of Vynvawle granted in a royal charter to Ranald, son of John of Islay, in 1372.

Bosta Iron Age House 20 miles (32km) west of Stornoway, Lewis. Remains of a Norse and Pictish settlement revealed on Bostadh (Bosta) Beach by a storm in January 1993 and excavated in 1996. Five Iron Age Pictish figure-of-eight houses (also known as 'jelly baby' houses because of their shape) and their associated middens were found beneath the Norse layers. The settlement was probably occupied AD 400–800. Designed to be subterranean, the houses had one entrance and circular central area and at least one annexe leading from this. The house walls were 3ft (1m) thick and still stood to their full height. After the dig the excavation site was largely backfilled to preserve the remains against the elements, although two houses were protected by the construction of sea defences. A reconstruction of one of the houses, funded by Comunn Eachdraidh Bhearnaraidh (Bernera Historical Society) was erected nearby in 1998. Although no vestiges of the original roof remained, archaeologists carrying out the experiment decided on a single thatched roof to cover the figure-of-eight wall line.

Bridge to Nowhere A bridge on the B895 on Lewis outside Tolsta which was intended to be part of a route up the east coast of the island to connect Stornaway with Port Ness. Unfortunately, the road peters out at the bridge. The road was the brainchild of Lord Leverhulme who was interested in developing the islands. His plans had the full support of the local community and work on the Tolsta/Ness road began in 1920. However, a combination of poor economic conditions and administrative obstacles led to Leverhulme abandoning the plan.

Butt of Lewis Lighthouse 21 miles (32km) northeast of Stornoway, Lewis. A red brick tower standing 121ft (37m) high, designed by David and Thomas Stevenson and established in 1862 at the northernmost point of the Isle of Lewis. It was automated in 1998. At one time the Butt of Lewis was regarded as the windiest place in the UK.

Callanish Stones 14 miles (23km) west of Stornoway, Lewis. A group of ancient monuments including a series of stone circles and standing stones and known collectively as the Callanish (or Calanais) Stones. **Callanish I**: the best known of the monuments, also known as Cnoc An Tursa (Hill of Sorrow) and dated to 2200–1800 BC. An arrangement of 50 stones with a circle of 13 stones between 8ft (2.5m) and 13ft (4m) high at its heart, itself surrounding a 16ft (5m) tall standing stone. The circle is 40ft (12m) in diameter and the stones are Lewis gneiss possibly quarried from the west side of the ridge Na Dromannan. An avenue of stones extends north from the circle with single rows emanating from the other cardinal points of the compass around the circle. Inside the circle, the remains of a chambered cairn incorporate the central pillar within the line of its kerb on the west and two of the circle's stones on the east. It is probably a later addition to the site. There is a second cairn, now not visible above ground level, at the northeast arc of the circle. When first uncovered in the mid 19th century the stones and cairn were encased in a layer of peat more than 5ft (1.5m) deep. **Callanish II**: also known as Cnoc Ceann a'Gharaidh (Hill at the End of the Wall). A stone circle, actually an ellipse measuring 70ft (21m) by 62ft (19m) consisting originally of nine or ten stones, of which five are still standing. The tallest stone is almost 11ft (3.3m) high. There is a cairn built eccentrically inside the circle. **Callanish III**: also known as Cnoc Filibhir Bheag (Little Hill of Filibhir). A stone circle consisting of 20 stones forming a double ring, of which 12 are still standing, eight on the outer circle and four on the inner. The diameter of the outer circle is 53ft (16m) and that of the inner 28ft (8.5m). The maximum height of the stones in the outer circle is 5ft 10in (1.7m) and in the inner 7ft (2.1m). **Callinish IV**: also known as Ceann Hulavig (Head of Hula Bay). A circle of five stones with a diameter of 33ft (10m) around the remains of a cairn. The tallest stone is 9ft (2.7m) high and the distances between the stones suggest there may originally have been more. **Callanish V**: a double row of stones. **Callanish VI**: also known as Cul a' Chleit. Two megaliths on the summit of Cul a' Chleit, the larger of the two standing 5ft 6in (1.6m) high. There has been a suggestion that they are the remains of a circle. **Callanish VIII**: also known as Tursachan. A semicircular arrangement of four stones on the slope of a hill overlooking Loch Barraglom on Great Bernera. The tallest stone stands 9ft (2.7m) high. **Callanish X**: also known as Na Dromannan. This is possibly a collapsed stone circle where, because the ground was bedrock, the stones were erected and kept upright by packing boulders around their base. The result was that eventually they all collapsed. The site is on the ridge of a hill overlooking Callanish I. It is also considered to be the area from which the stones for some of the other nearby monuments could have been quarried; some have queried whether the circle was ever erected or whether the stones found here were being prepared for other monuments. A visitor centre on the hillside south of Calanish I and run by Urras nan Tursachan (The Standing Stones Trust) was opened in 1995. The stones are in the care of Historic Scotland.

Cladh Hallan 1 mile (1.6km) west of Daliburgh, South Uist. An archaeological site on the west coast occupied c.1000–400 BC, and the only place in the UK where prehistoric mummies have been found. The site is under the island's machair grassland, first settled during the Neolithic period but particularly settled by farming communities in the Bronze Age and Iron Age. Excavation of the site began in 1989 and a terrace of up to seven roundhouses was discovered, indicating continuous settlement in the area from the early Bronze Age to the early Iron Age, with houses being built upon the remains of previous dwellings. In 2003 archaeologists discovered two bodies buried under the floor of one of the houses alongside the body of an entire sheep. One was a male who died c.1600 BC, the other a female who died c.1300 BC; both bodies had remained unburied until 1000 BC when the settlement was constructed on the site of an earlier one. It was later discovered that the male was an amalgam of three separate bodies: the head and neck was from one man, the jaw from a second and the rest of the body from a third; each had died perhaps hundreds of years apart. Examination indicated that the bodies had been submerged in a peat bog for up to 18 months before being retrieved, and had perhaps been set up in a 'mummy house' as a ritual practice. The excavation of the remainder of the settlement revealed further unusual practices in addition to the discovery of the two mummies. Under the floors of other houses were the interments of a teenage girl and a baby (possibly also mummified) and in one house the skeletons of two dogs. There was also a great quantity of pottery which appeared to have been deliberately smashed. The excavations also discovered that the farmers were dairy herders, having found traces of cow's milk in the bottom of some of the pots.

Dualchas Barra Heritage and Cultural Centre Castlebay, Barra. A heritage centre opened in 1996. Exhibits include a vast range of photographs and documents relating to the history of the island. There is also a restored thatched cottage (The Thatched House) housing a collection of local artefacts, including furniture and items from the 19th and 20th centuries. Tel: 01871 810413.

Dun Carloway 16 miles (26km) northwest of Stornoway, Lewis. The best-preserved Iron Age broch in the Western Isles, located on a site overlooking East Loch Roag and with an external diameter of 47ft (14.5m) and an outer wall between 10ft (3m) and 12ft (3.5m) thick. Part of the outer wall still stands 22ft (6.5m) high, although it may originally have been as high as 43ft (13m). Maintained by Historic Scotland.

Dun Eistean A small flat-topped island just off the northwest coast of Lewis, and separated from it by a ravine. It was once the ancestral home of the Clan Morrison. There are the ruins of a wall along the cliff facing Lewis and also the remains of several buildings and possibly a broch.

Eilean Glas Lighthouse Located on the Eilean Glas peninsula, Scalpay. One of the earliest lighthouses in the Hebrides and indeed in Scotland. Originally established in 1789 by engineer Thomas Smith, it was replaced in 1824 by a 100ft (30m) high tower built by Robert Stevenson, Smith's stepson. It was automated in 1987.

Eriskay An island located between South Uist and Barra, and linked to South Uist by a causeway opened in 2001. On 23 July 1745 Bonnie Prince Charlie stepped ashore here at the start of the Jacobite Rebellion of 1745–6. On 5 February 1941 the steamship *The Politician* carrying 264,000 bottles of whisky was wrecked in the Sound of Eriskay. Subsequent events were made famous in the book *Whisky Galore!* by Sir Compton Mackenzie and the later film of the same name. The island is also renowned for the Eriskay Jersey (made without a seam). The 'capital' is Haun. Area: 2.91 sq miles (7.54 sq km). Population: 133. GR: NF795105.

Eye Church 4 miles (6km) east of Stornoway, Lewis. Aka the Chapel of Ui (or Eye), St Columba's Church. Located on the Eye Peninsula. A medieval (14th–16th century) church built on the site of the cell of St Catan. The church was the burial ground of the MacLeods of Lewis. Nearby is a memorial cairn set up to commemorate the riots of 1888 in support of land reform.

Flannan Lighthouse Mystery In December 1900 the lighthouse on Eilean Mor, 15 miles (24km) west of the Isle of Lewis, was at the centre of a mystery which still baffles to this day. The lighthouse was erected in 1899 by engineers David and Charles Stevenson. Following a report that the light had not been seen for some days, the supply vessel *Hesperus* was sent on 26 December 1900 to ascertain the situation. On board was lighthouse keeper Joseph Moore, who was returning from shore leave to replace one of the three men in situ, principal keeper James Ducat, first assistant keeper Thomas Marshall and occasional keeper Donald MacArthur, who was himself deputising for a sick member of the roster. When he entered the lighthouse Moore noted that the entrance door had been closed, the kitchen table was laid for a meal and two of the three sets of boots and oilskins were missing. Recorded on a slate was the fact that the light had been extinguished on the morning of 15 December, but that was the final entry. The last entry in the log, dated 12 December, was written by Marshall and read: 'Gale N by NW. Sea lashed to fury. Never seen such a storm. Waves very high. Tearing at lighthouse . . . wind steady. Stormbound. Cannot go out. Ship passing sounded fog horn. Could see lights of cabins. Ducat quiet. Donald McArthur crying.' On the slate was written: '13 December: Storm continued throughout night . . . Marshall, Ducat and McArthur prayed. 15 December: Storm ended, sea calm. God is over all.' The clocks were all stopped. There was no sign of any of the keepers. A subsequent board of inquiry discounted foul play for lack of evidence and arrived at a verdict of death by misadventure, concluding that the three men must have been washed away by a monstrous wave. This verdict has been disputed ever since and the mystery has been compared to that of the *Marie Celeste*. Among the unsolved questions are, why would a ship be sounding its fog horn during a gale and why were the keepers crying and praying. Suggested explanations include the possibility of a row in which two were killed and the murderer committed suicide. One fact in favour of the verdict, however, is that the iron railings round the crane platform, which stood 70ft (21m) above sea level, were displaced and twisted, a lifebuoy 100ft (30m) above the waves had been ripped off its moorings and a 20cwt (1016kg) block of stone had been dislodged from its position. This would seem to indicate a massive wave had hit the lighthouse at some point. The mystery was the inspiration for composer Peter Maxwell Davies's opera *The Lighthouse*; the events are also commemorated in Wilfrid Wilson Gibson's ballad 'Flannan Isle'.

Gearrannan Blackhouse Village — Carloway, Isle of Lewis. A group of nine traditional late 19th century crofting houses, abandoned in 1974 and restored by the Garenin Trust (G. Urras nan Gearrannan) 1989–2001. One house was restored using traditional techniques to its near-original appearance and is used as a museum. Other houses serve as an interpretive centre, craft shop and holiday accommodation. There is also a youth hostel on the site. Tel: 01851 643416.

Highest point — Clisham on Harris at 2621ft (799m). GR: NB155073.

Hirta — One of the islands of the St Kilda group. Inhabited from the Bronze Age, it developed independently of most outside interference, the islanders being largely self-sufficient. The arrival of tourists as early as 1834 and the appearance of the Rev. John Mackay led to the gradual decline of the island's society; his insistence on daily attendance at church left little time for the islanders to cultivate the crops on which they were dependent. Population growth was also curtailed by severe infant mortality caused by tetanus, which claimed up to 80 per cent of newborn babies. It was later discovered that this was caused by the use of fulmar oil during delivery. The island was evacuated on 29 August 1930, after which a military base was established in 1957. The island has unique wildlife such as the St Kilda wren and a long-tailed fieldmouse; there is also a breed of mouflon sheep introduced from Soay. Now owned by the National Trust for Scotland. Permitted to issue its own postage stamps. Area: 2.45 sq miles (6.33 sq km). GR: NF090995.

Howmore — A village on South Uist which has the remains of several medieval chapels and a 19th century white-harled parish church. The village also has a collection of thatched cottages.

Interesting facts — The archipelago of **St Kilda** is collectively known as 'the islands at the edge of the world' as they are so remote from the mainland. Rather confusingly perhaps, Hirta Island is also known as St Kilda and this island is the home of the most remote pub in the British Isles. Lying 50 miles (80km) out in the Atlantic, the **Puff Inn** is only accessible for three months of the year by boat, although at other times it is possible to charter a helicopter from Benbecula.

Islands — See separate table for the 772 islands of the Outer Hebrides.

Kildonan Museum — Kildonan, Lochboisdale, South Uist. A local history museum opened in 1998, exploring the story of the people of South Uist and featuring a recreated croft. Exhibits include the 16th or 17th century Clan Ranald Stone, a sandstone slab found in the ancient Howmore church and bearing the Clanranald arms. Stolen from its site in Howmore in 1990, it was recovered in London in 1995 and returned to Uist in 1999. Tel: 01878 710343.

Kisimul Castle — Castlebay, Barra. A 15th century castle and stronghold of the Clan MacNeil on a rocky island in the middle of Castle Bay. Kisimul (G. *Chiosmuil* = 'the rock in the bay') may have been fortified from the 11th century. The original three-storey square tower house was extended and a curtain wall raised. To be able to withstand sieges, the castle had two artesian wells to provide fresh water and a fish trap in a catchment basin. It was largely rebuilt after being largely destroyed in a fire in 1795, but was abandoned in 1838 when the island was sold. It was also damaged by fire and much of the stonework was robbed for use in other buildings. It was bought in 1937 by American architect and clan chief Robert MacNeil, who restored the castle over the next 30 years as a family home. The castle has been managed by Historic Scotland since 2000, MacNeil having leased the building to them for £1 and a bottle of Talisker whisky each year!

Lewis Chessmen — The remains of 78 chess pieces from eight separate sets, discovered by a crofter in 1831 in an underground chamber on the Isle of Lewis. Believed to date from the 12th century, the chessmen are made from walrus ivory and depict various figures such as church dignitaries and Norse warriors of the period. Sixty-seven of the pieces are in the British Museum, and the other 11 are in the National Museum in Edinburgh.

Lewis Loom Centre — Bayhead Street, Stornoway, Lewis. Housed in the Old Grainstore, and exploring the history and techniques involved in producing Harris tweed. Tel: 01851 703117.

Lews Castle — 1/4 mile (0.4km) west of Stornoway, Lewis. A mock-Tudor castle overlooking Stornoway, built in 1849 by Charles Wilson for Sir James Matheson on the site of a previous MacKenzie family property (1796–1878). Matheson bought Lews in 1844 for £190,000. The house was subsequently bought by Lord Leverhulme who gave it to the people of Lewis. It served as a naval hospital during World War II and was used as an educational facility 1953–88, when it was left empty due to structural problems. The extensive grounds feature over 100 species of tree plus a Woodland Centre. The grounds are also home to Lews Castle College.

Loch Druidibeg Nature Reserve — South Uist. A coastal National Nature Reserve covering 4144 acres (1677ha) and including beaches, machair and heather moorland. It was designated an NNR in 1958 (extended in 1962) and has also been designated a Ramsar site (1976), Special Protection Area (1982) and Site of Special Scientific Interest (1987). The coastal areas are important breeding sites for wading birds such as dunlin, redshank, lapwing and ringed plover and the loch is an important breeding site for greylag geese. Corncrakes can also be heard but rarely seen on the reserve's hayfields.

Minch, The — A body of water off the northwest coast of Scotland. The North Minch divides the north of the Outer Hebrides from the mainland, while the Little Minch separates the Isle of Skye from North Uist and South Harris.

Monach Islands — Aka Heisgeir. A group of eight islands 4 miles (6km) west of North Uist, notable for their beaches, consisting of crushed sea shells, and machair which contains more than 200 species of flowering plants and grasses. The islands were abandoned in 1943 and became a National Nature Reserve in 1966, supporting large numbers of seabirds including black guillemot, fulmar and cormorant. There is also a large colony of grey seals every autumn. Local shepherds still tend sheep on the islands.

Monach Lighthouse — Shillay, Monach Islands. Established in 1864 and designed by David and Thomas Stevenson, the red-brick tower stands 135ft (41m) high. Two lighthouse keepers were drowned in 1936 when rowing back to the island after collecting their mail from the nearby island of Ceann Iar. The light was decommissioned in 1948 and a new, smaller lighthouse established in 1997.

Museum Nan Eilean — Francis Street, Stornoway, Lewis. Opened in 1984 in the town hall before moving to its present home in 1995, the museum holds collections of artefacts, photographs, prints and paintings illustrating the archaeology, social, domestic and economic history of the Western Isles. Exhibits include the Galson Enamel Mount, possibly a Norse horse harness decoration, and an Iron Age pot or craggan from Galson. Tel: 01851 709266.

Ness Heritage Centre — Habost, Ness, Lewis. A local history museum built around the work and collections of the Comunn Eachdraidh Nis (G. = Ness Historical Society). Originally based at Lionel Old School, it moved to its present home in 1992. Exhibits include artefacts relating to the cultural, social, domestic, agricultural and maritime history of the community with particular reference to the way of life of crofters. Recollections by local volunteers have been collected via audio and video recordings and have been enriched by a photographic archive to provide a substantial local history resource. Tel: 01851 8100377.

Ormiclate Castle — South Uist. Built 1701–8 by a French architect but burned down in 1715 during a raucous Jacobite party, the castle was the residence of the Clanranald chiefs before its untimely demise.

Ramsar sites — There are four Ramsar sites (wetlands of international importance) in the Western Isles: Lewis Peatlands (145.573 acres/58,984ha), Loch An Duin (6477 acres/2621ha), North Uist Machair and Islands (11626 acres/4705ha), South Uist Machair and Lochs (12,402 acres/5019ha).

Rona and Sula Sgeir National Nature Reserve — Rona lies 45 miles (72km) out to sea and a further 12 miles (19km) to the southwest lies Sula Sgeir. Sula Sgeir has never been inhabited and Rona was abandoned in 1844, having first been settled by St Ronan. They were designated a National Nature Reseve in 1956 due to their importance as a breeding ground for guillemot, puffin, kittiwake and fulmar. Leach's and storm petrels nest in abandoned buildings and there are more than 1000 pairs of black-backed gulls. There are usually 10,000 pairs of gannet on Sula Sgeir and a licensed harvest of 2000 fledglings (called 'gugas') by men from Ness takes place annually. There is a colony of grey seal all year round which expands during the autumn breeding season.

RSPB Balranald — 13 miles (21km) west of Lochmaddy, North Uist. RSPB reserve established in 1966 on the west coast of North Uist. Habitats include sand dunes, rocky foreshore, grassland, marshes and lochs, and in particular machair, home to rare carpet flowers such as Irish lady's tresses, orchids and yellow rattle. The machair of Balranald is home to a population of around 40 corncrakes, as well as twite, dunlin, corn bunting and ringed plover. In addition the reserve is a haven for waders and seabirds. Apart from birdlife, two colonies of the rare collete bee, only found in the Hebrides – a 'mining' bee that burrows underground to store its honey and favours sandy banks and dunes, covered in herb-rich meadows – have been discovered on the reserve.

Rueval Madonna and Child — South Uist. Aka Our Lady of the Isles. A 30ft (9m) high granite statue of the Madonna and Child, erected in 1957 on the slopes of Rueval. It was commissioned by Father John Morrison, sculpted by Hew Lorimer (1907–93) and paid for by contributions from the people of the island.

St Clement's Church — 3 miles (5km) southeast of Leverburgh, Harris. Aka Tur Chliamainn, the Church of Rodel. Probably built c.1520 by Alexander MacLeod on the site of an earlier, possibly 13th century, foundation. It fell into disrepair in the 1560s, after the Reformation, but was restored by Captain Alexander MacLeod in 1784. Unfortunately it was burned down only three years later and had to be rebuilt again. It was abandoned by 1840 and restored yet again in 1873 by the Countess of Dunmore. During its early history it was the preferred burial place of the MacLeods; the richly carved tomb of the church's founder, Alexander MacLeod, in the south wall of the nave bears the inscription: 'This tomb was prepared by Lord Alexander, son of William MacLeod, Lord of Dunvegan, in the year of our lord 1528.' The church has a tower at its west end, the outside of which is adorned with carvings including in the south wall a sheela-na-gig (shiel na gig) comprising a nude female nursing a child and in a crouching attitude. Sheela-na-gigs are sexually explicit carvings and it is not clear why they should be found in churches and other buildings, especially following the Reformation. The church is in the care of Historic Scotland.

St Kilda — A group of islands 41 miles (66km) west of Benbecula. Hirta, the main island, has been settled since at least the Bronze Age and was occupied from the late 17th century by a small community of farming tenants. After suffering food shortages and illness in the late 19th and early 20th century, the last 36 members of the dwindling population were evacuated in 1930. In the following year the islands were bought by the Marquess of Bute as a bird reserve; they were passed on in 1957 to the National Trust for Scotland, who in turn leased them to the Nature Conservancy (a predecessor body of Scottish Natural Heritage) as a National Nature Reserve. The islands were designated a Site of Special Scientific Interest in 1986 and in the same year received the accolade of becoming Scotland's first UNESCO World Heritage Site. In 2004 this designation was extended to include the surrounding marine environment, and in 2005 St Kilda was awarded Dual World Heritage Status for its natural and cultural significance. Hirta has the highest sea cliffs in the British Isles, Conchair at 1415ft (430m), and the highest sea stack, Stac na Armin at 627ft (191m). St Kilda is Europe's most important seabird colony and one of the major seabird breeding stations in the North Atlantic, with more than 1 million birds including the largest colony of gannets in the world on Boreray and the adjacent stacks, with 60,000 pairs. The colonies of fulmars and puffins average 62,000 pairs and 140,000 pairs respectively. In addition the islands support a

	breed of sheep which originated in the Neolithic period and unique sub-species of wren and field-mouse. GR: NF090995.
St Ronan's Chapel	North Rona. Possibly the oldest unaltered Christian building in Britain. It began life in the 7th or 8th century as a corbelled oratory and was extended in the 13th century. A number of carved simple cruciform stones of local hornblende gneiss are preserved in the chapel.
Scalpay Bridge	5 miles (8km) southeast of Tarbert, Harris. A 984ft (300m) long bridge linking Scalpay with Harris. It was officially opened by Prime Minister Tony Blair in 1998, but the first cars were led across the bridge the previous December by the island's oldest resident, 103 year old Mrs Kirsty Morrison.
Scarp	A small island off the west coast of Harris, uninhabited since 1971. It is best remembered for a failed experimental rocket postal service in July 1934, devised by German rocket enthusiast Gerhard Zucher. The rocket sending letters to Harris exploded but that from Harris to Scarp worked. However, the project was abandoned. On his return to Germany Zucher was accused of selling rocket technology to the British and imprisoned for 15 months. Area: 4.03 sq miles (10.45 sq km). GR: NA970150.
Scolpaig Tower	10 miles (16km) northwest of Lochmaddy, North Uist. A folly built by Alexander MacLeod in 1830 on an islet in Loch Scolpaig, and now used by birds as a nesting site.
Seallam Visitor Centre	An Taobh Tuath (Northton), Harris. A visitor centre and family history research resource opened in July 2000. In addition to genealogy resource materials (census returns, civil registration, etc.) there is a collection of oral traditions, including songs and stories, gathered by local history groups. There are permanent and temporary exhibits on the people and the landscape of the Western Isles. Tel: 01859 520258.
Seana-Chaisteal	Situated on the island of Pabbay, the ruined castle of Seana-Chaisteal (G. = Ancient Castle) was once the site of the old MacLeod castle or dun. Today, only a few fragments of the walls remain amid a pointed sandy hillock on the east coast of the island.
Shiant Isles	(G. *shiant* = 'enchanted'.) A group of 11 islands including the larger Garbh Eilean, Eilean an Tigh and Eilean Mhuire. They were bought for £500 at auction in 1925 by writer Sir Compton MacKenzie, who sometimes stayed here in a shepherd's cottage during the summer months. Now owned by the Nicholson family, they are the migratory home to thousands of puffins and many other seabirds; there is also a colony of black rats (*Rattus rattus*) on the islands which are rare in Britain (perhaps luckily, as they are the 'plague rat').
Soay	Like Hirta part of the St Kilda group, the island is home to a species of horned sheep (*Ovis aries*) first brought to the British Isles during the Neolithic period. They were confined to Soay until 1930 when some were taken to Hirta to form a new flock. The islanders used to pluck the wool from the sheep to make tweed. Area: 0.38 sq miles (0.99 sq km). GR: NA065015.
Stornaway Trust Woodland Centre	Stornoway, Lewis. An interpretive centre run by the Stornoway Trust in the grounds of Lews Castle. The 600 acre (240ha) grounds were planted from 1847 with a mixture of exotic and native tree species, providing a woodland habitat unique in the Western Isles. Native species include alder, ash, beech, birch, lime, oak, pine, sycamore and willow; exotics include noble fir, monkey puzzle, Lawson's, Hinoki, Sawara and Monterey cypress, Japanese red and black pine, western hemlock, sugar maple and Irish yew. Tel: 01851 706916.
Taigh Chearsabhagh Museum and Arts Centre	Lochmaddy, North Uist. A museum and arts centre housed in a building dating to 1741 and believed to be the first slate-roofed building on the island. During its lifetime the building has also been an inn, a post office and a workshop before opening as a museum in 1995. Collections cover the economic and social history of North Uist and include an extensive archive of photographs. Tel: 01876 500293.
Tiumpan Head Lighthouse	10 miles (16km) northeast of Stornoway, Lewis. A lighthouse established in 1900 on Tiumpan Head, built by David and Charles Stevenson and standing 180ft (55m) tall. It was automated in 1985.
Uig Heritage Centre	Uig, 25 miles (40km) west of Stornoway, Lewis. A local history centre with displays of artefacts and photographs. Tel: 01851 672456.
Uists, The	A group of islands the best known of which are North Uist, South Uist, Benbecula and Grimsay. Unlike most of the Western Isles the island of South Uist (and also Barra) has a largely Catholic population. It was from Rossinish on Benbecula (or 'Mountain of the Ford') that in 1746 Bonnie Prince Charlie went 'over the sea to Skye' disguised as a woman called Betty Burke. The main settlement on Benbecula is Balivanich (G. = Settlement of the Monks). The causeway to South Uist was built in 1983 and that to North Uist in 1960.
Weaver's Castle	Eilean Leathan. A ruined castle on the largest of the Stack Islands. The castle was the base for a notorious MacNeil pirate and wreck-plunderer.

Some famous people born in the Western Isles

Kennedy, Calum (singer) (1928–2006)	Stornaway
MacAskill, Angus (giant strongman) (1825–63)	Berneray
MacDonald, Flora (heroine) (1722–90)	Milton, South Uist
MacKenzie, Alexander (explorer) (1764–1820)	Stornaway
Mackenzie, Colin (surveyor) (1754–1821)	Stornaway
McCormack, Alyth (singer and actress) (1970–)	Sandwick, Lewis
McPhee, Catherine-Ann (singer) (1959–)	Barra
Matheson, Hans (actor) (1975–)	Stornoway
Smith, Ian (novelist and poet) (1928–98)	Lewis
Stewart, Donald (politician) (1920–92)	Stornoway

Islands of Na h-Eileanan Siar (Outer Hebrides)

Island name	Area	Nearest landmark	General information
A' Chearc	Atlantic	Gob na Creige, Lewis	(G. = The Hen). GR: NB496288
Aird Gheiltinis	An Oitir Mhor	Aird Mhor, Barra	Lies off the larger island of Orasaigh. GR: NF715043
Aird Orasaigh	Loch an Stroim	Geisiadar, Lewis	The only island in the loch. GR: NB130314
Aird Reamhar	Loch nan Geireann	Cnoc Mhic Eoghainn, North Uist	(G. = Fat Promontory). GR: NF842730
Am Plastair	Atlantic	Soay	GR: NA059020
An Ceotham	Caolas Monach	Calla Geodha, Benbecula	GR: NF777558
An Corran	Atlantic	Boreray	GR: NF858803
An Dubh-sgeir a Deas	The Little Minch	Wiay	GR: NF871445
An Glais-eilean Meadhonach	Loch nam Madadh (aka Loch Maddy)	Rubha an Fhigheadair, North Uist	GR: NF940687
An Laogh	An Oitir Mhor	Meall an Laoig, Gighay	Miniature stack at the northern tip of Gighay. GR: NF770055
An Laogh	Sea of the Hebrides	Maol Domhnaich (aka Muldoanich)	GR: NL692944
An Laogh	Loch a Siar	Soaidh Mor	GR: NB066045
An Stac	Sound of Barra	Leac na Banaraich, Eriskay	GR: NF786070
An t-Sail	Atlantic	Boreray	GR: NA153060
Archie Rock	Sound of Fuday	Fuday	GR: NF735000
Arnamul	Atlantic	Mingulay	GR: NL545825
Bail Uachdraich	Beul an Toim	Baleshare, North Uist	GR: NF813607
Bailshare	Caolas Monach	North Uist	aka Baile Sear. Its sister island Baile-iar was destroyed by a 16th century tsunami. Area: 3.92 sq miles (10.15 sq km). Population: 49. GR: NF790610
Barnacle Rock	Atlantic	Mingulay	aka Creag a' Bharnaich. GR: NL573849
Barra	Atlantic	Leac na Banaraich, Eriskay	aka Barraigh. See separate entry
Bearnaraigh Beag	Loch Rog an Ear	Great Bernera	aka Little Bernera. Permitted to issue its own postage stamps. Area: 0.53 sq miles (1.38 sq km). GR: NB143410
Bearnaraigh Mor	Loch Rog an Ear	Iarsiadar, Lewis	aka Great Bernera. Connected to Lewis by a bridge built in 1953. Permitted to issue its own postage stamps. Area: 8.65 sq miles (22.4 sq km). Population: 233. GR: NB155375
Bearasay	Pol Gainmhich	Great Bernera	aka Bearasaigh. GR: NB121426
Bearran	Loch Uisgebhagh (aka Loch Uiskevagh)	Meanais, Benbecula	GR: NF865511
Benbecula	Atlantic	North Uist	aka Beinn na Faoghia. Situated between the traditionally Protestant North Uist and Catholic South Uist. Balivanich is the chief town. Area: 31.8 sq miles (82.35 sq km). Population: 1219. GR: NF810520
Berneray	Sound of Berneray	Mingulay	aka Bearnaraigh. SSSI owned by the National Trust for Scotland. Sron an Duin at Barra Head is the most southerly point of the Outer Hebrides. Area: 0.79 sq miles (2.04 sq km). GR: NL560800
Berneray	Sound of Harris	Rubh a' Charnair Mhoir	aka Bearnaraigh. See separate entry
Bhacasaigh	Sound of Harris	Tobha Beag, North Uist	aka Vaccasay. GR: NF977746
Bhacsaigh	Caolas Phabaigh (aka Sound of Pabbay)	Cnip, Lewis	aka Vacsay. Area: 0.16 sq miles (0.41 sq km). GR: NB115370
Bhaiteam	Sound of Harris	Rubha Mhanais, Bernaray	GR: NF939805
Bhalaigh	Sound of Harris	Renish Point, Harris	GR: NG051825
Bhalaigh	Atlantic	Calarnais, North Uist	aka Vallay. GR: NF780765
Bharanais	Loch Baghasdail	Aird Buidhe, South Uist	GR: NF772191
Bhatam	Sound of Harris	Grodhaigh (aka Groay)	GR: NG005797
Bhatarsaidh	The Minch	Crosbost, Lewis	One of the Barkin Isles. GR: NB409237
Bhorogaigh	Caolas Honach	Baleshare, North Uist	GR: NF782641
Bhotarsaigh	Sound of Harris	Sromaigh	aka Votersay. GR: NF949761
Big Shillay	Loch Sgiopoirt	Loch Sgioport, South Uist	aka Siolaigh Mor. GR: NF844384

Island name	Area	Nearest landmark	General information
Bioreilean	Caolas Honach	Cladach Chireboist, North Uist	GR: NF761651
Bioruaslum	Atlantic	Vatersay	GR: NL608963
Bird Rock	Sloc na Sealbhaig	Sotan, Bernaray	GR: NL552798
Bo' annan Beaga	The Little Minch	Rubha Cam nan Gall, Wiay	GR: NF883479
Bo Bheanachan	Caolas Theilisigh (aka Sound of Hellisay)	Flodaigh	GR: NF756025
Bo' Carrach	The Little Minch	Rubha Cam nan Gall, Wiay	GR: NF884477
Bodach	Sound of Shianti	Rubha Bhrolluim, Harris	One of the Shiant Islands (aka Eileanan Mora). GR: NG400982
Bogh' a' Mheadhon La	Atlantic	Rona	GR: HW806317
Bogh an Fheidh	The Little Minch	Ronay	GR: NF911566
Bogha Bhad Ghlais	Loch Rog	Fuaidh Mor	GR: NB125355
Bogha Bhealt	Caolas na Sgeire Leithe	Pabaigh Mor	GR: NB108377
Bogha Corr	Atlantic	Butt of Lewis, Lewis	GR: HW613312
Bogha Dubh	An Caolas	Pabaigh Mor	GR: NB105387
Bogha Mairi	Atlantic	Boreray	GR: NF850823
Bogha nan Sgeirean Mora	An Oitir Mhor	Rubh' a' Mhorbhuile, Hellisay	GR: NF740050
Bogha Ruadh	Loch Sealg	Rubha Buidhe, Lewis	GR: NB369106
Bogha Thearbaso	Caolas Phabaigh (aka Sound of Pabbay)	Bhacsaigh (aka Vacsay)	GR: NB111369
Boghannan Lisgear	Atlantic	Rona	GR: HW811338
Boreray	Atlantic	St Kilda	aka Boraraigh. Owned by the National Trust for Scotland. The island requires ideal tidal and weather conditions to access. Area: 0.30 sq miles (0.77 sq km). GR: NA154050
Boreray	Atlantic	Aird a' Mhorain, North Uist	aka Boraraigh. Area: 0.76 sq miles (1.98 sq km). GR: NF850812
Bradastac	Atlantic	St Kilda	GR: NA096006
Braigh nan Stacannan	Caolas Champaigh	Bearnaraigh Beag (aka Little Bernera)	GR: NB135411
Braighe Beag	Atlantic	Butt of Lewis, Lewis	GR: NB529657
Braighe Mor	Atlantic	Coig Peighinnean, Lewis	GR: NB538651
Bratanish Mor	Loch Rog	Calanais, Lewis	aka Bratanais Mor. GR: NB207330
Broad Rocks	Sea of the Hebrides	Stulaigh (aka Stuley)	GR: NF829242
Brona Cleit	Atlantic	Gallan Head, Lewis	(G. = Sad Sunk Rock). One of Na h-Eileanan Flannach (aka The Flannan Isles). GR: NA688464
Buaile Mhor	Loch Griomssiadar	Ranais, Lewis	GR: NB400252
Caigionn	Beul an Toim	Aird nan Struban, North Uist	GR: NF830578
Caiream	Loch Ghreosabhaigh	Rubha Chliuthairt, Harris	GR: NG162910
Caisteal Bheagram	Loch an Eilein	Dreumasdal, South Uist	GR: NF761371
Calavay	The Little Minch	Rarainis, Benbecula	aka Calabhagh. GR: NF863549
Calbhaigh	Loch Baghasdail	Beinn Bheag, South Uist	GR: NF819180
Calbhalgh	Loch Aineort	Taobh a' Tuath, South Uist	GR: NF773285
Calvay	Caolas Eiriosgaigh	Roisinis, Eriskay	aka Calbhaigh. Site of the wreck of the 12,000 ton steamship *The Politician* in 1941 which was the inspiration for *Whisky Galore!* GR: NF810128
Campay	Caolas Champaigh	Aird Laimisadair, Lewis	aka Campaigh. GR: NB141426
Caolaigh	Sound of Harris	Killegray	GR: NF977818
Carais	An Oitir Mhor	Meall Mor, Hellisay	GR: NF765038
Carminish Islands	Atlantic	Leverburgh, Harris	aka Eilean Chairminis. GR: NG017853
Catuam	Atlantic	Beinn Mhor, North Uist	GR: NF910748
Causamul	Atlantic	Aird an Runair, North Uist	GR: NF660706
Ceabhagh	Loch Rog an Ear	Ribha Arspaig, Lewis	aka Keava. GR: NB198350
Cealasaigh	Caolas Champaigh	Bearnaraigh Beag (aka Little Bernera)	GR: NB145418
Ceallasaigh Beag	Loch nam Madadh (aka Loch Maddy)	Bac-a-stoc, North Uist	aka Keallasay Beg. GR: NF918713

WESTERN ISLES

Island name	Area	Nearest landmark	General information
Ceallasaigh Mor	Loch nam Madadh (aka Loch Maddy)	Bac-a-stoc, North Uist	aka Keallasay More. GR: NF910724
Ceann a' Gharaidh	Atlantic	Smeircleit, South Uist	GR: NF735153
Ceann Aird Ghrein	Atlantic	Aird Ghrein, Barra	GR: NF646049
Ceann Ear	Caolas Shiolaigh (aka Sound of Shillay)	Baleshare, North Uist	(G. = East Head). One of the Monach Islands, aka Heisker (O.N. = Bright Skerry). Permitted to issue its own postage stamps. Area: 0.89 sq miles (2.31 sq km). GR: NF640620
Ceann Iar	Caolas Shiolaigh (aka Sound of Shillay)	Baleshare, North Uist	(G. = West Head). One of the Monach Islands, aka Heisker (O.N. = Bright Skerry). Area: 0.52 sq miles (1.34 sq km). GR: NF610625
Ceann nan Leac	Atlantic	Borgh, Barra	GR: NF648008
Ceann Traigh na Croise	Atlantic	Cille Bhrighde, South Uist	GR: NF742144
Cearstaigh	Atlantic	Scarp	aka Kearstay. GR: NA964171
Ceileagraigh	Atlantic	Leverburgh, Lewis	(G. = Graveyard). Aka Killegray. GR: NF980835
Clach Mhor Sheamsgeir	Sound of Harris	Rubha na h-Aibhne Duibhe, North Uist	GR: NF935778
Cladach Dhiobadail	Atlantic	Aird Dhiobadail, Lewis	GR: NB555543
Cleit a' Ghlinne Mhoir	Sea of the Hebrides	Glean n' Mor, South Uist	GR: NF824254
Cleit an Iasgaich	Basin of Vaccasay	Bhacasaigh	GR: NF980750
Cleit Charmaig	Bagh nam Faoilean	Fodragaigh	GR: NF854453
Cleit Mhor	Bagh nam Faoilean	Carnan-aird-Fuidhaigh, Benbecula	GR: NF858466
Cleit Ruadh	Atlantic	Boreray	GR: ND173000
Cleit Steiseigh	Bagh nam Faoilean	Wiay	GR: NF846448
Cleite	Caolas Phabaigh (aka Sound of Pabbay)	Sandray	GR: NL647899
Cleite Loisgte	Sound of Harris	Aird Thormaid, North Uist	GR: NF979765
Cleite nan Luch	Sound of Harris	Sursaigh	GR: NF954757
Cliasay Beg	Loch nam Madadh (aka Loch Maddy)	Taigh Sponais, North Uist	aka Cliasaigh Beag. GR: NF928705
Cliasay More	Loch nam Madadh (aka Loch Maddy)	Taigh Sponais, North Uist	aka Cliasaigh Mor. GR: NF930702
Cliatasay	Loch Rog	Geisiadar, Lewis	aka Cliatasaigh. GR: NB130332
Cnap Ruigh Dubh	Loch nam Madadh (aka Loch Maddy)	Taigh Sponais, North Uist	GR: NF929693
Coddem Island	Atlantic	Killegray	aka Eilean Chodam. GR: NF990845
Colla	An Oitir Mhor	Meall Mor, Hellisay	GR: NF765041
Colla	Caolas Theilisigh (aka Sound of Hellisay)	Fuidheigh	(G. = Hazel). GR: NF745030
Collam	Loch Uisgebhagh (aka Loch Uiskevagh)	Lidiostrom, Benbecula	GR: NF845508
Coppay	Atlantic	Toe Head, Harris	aka Copaigh (G. = Cup-shaped Island). GR: NF932938
Cordail Mor	Sound of Barra	Mullach Neacall, Fuday	(G. = Big Tapering Valley). GR: NF743081
Corran Ban	Atlantic	Fiaraidh	GR: NF709104
Corr-eileanan	The Little Minch	Caolas Liursaigh, South Uist	GR: NF862409
Crago	Sound of Harris	Lingeigh	GR: NG016785
Craigeam	Atlantic	Aird Laimisadair, Lewis	GR: NB168432
Craobhagun	Loch Mhic Phail	Cnoc Mor Thormaid, North Uist	GR: NF931757
Craraigh-Mhor	Bagh nam Faoilean	Griomasaigh, Benbecula	GR: NF840454
Creag a' Bharnaich	Atlantic	Mingulay	See Barnacle Rock.
Creag an Tuill	The Little Minch	Thernatraigh	GR: NF992735
Creag Bheag	Atlantic	Bideinean, Harris	GR: NF984883
Creag Dhail	Atlantic	Cobha Sgeir, Lewis	GR: NB472634
Creag Mhor	Sound of Barra	Leac na Banaraich, Eriskay	GR: NF785071
Creag Mhor Bhatasgeir	Loch a Tuath	Bac, Lewis	GR: NB492398
Creag na Sealladh	Sound of Harris	Aird Thormaid, North Uist	GR: NF990759
Creag na Staid	Sound of Harris	Aird Thormaid, North Uist	GR: NF989753

Island name	Area	Nearest landmark	General information
Creagan Sheadair	Caolas Shandraigh (aka Sound of Sandray)	Sandray	aka Sheader Rocks. GR: NL628915
Crois an t-sleuchd	Beul an Toim	An Tom, Benbecula	GR: NF803573
Cruitear	Caolas Champaigh	Bearnaraigh Beag (aka Little Bernera)	GR: NB158409
Cuidhnis	Atlantic	Pabbay	aka Quinish. GR: NF880862
Cul Champaigh	Pol Gainmhich	Aird Laimisadair, Lewis	GR: NB142430
Curachan	Sea of the Hebrides	Rubha Bhruairnis, Barra	GR: NL747994
Dearc na Sgeir	Atlantic	Gallan Head, Lewis	One of Na h-Eileanan Flannach (the Flannan Isles). GR: NA730470
Deasker	Atlantic	Aird an Runair, North Uist	aka Deasgeir (G. = South Skerry). GR: NF645667
Dioraigh	Bagh nam Faoilean	Sanndabhaig, South Uist	GR: NF831434
Drowning Rock	Sound of Harris	Aird Ma-Ruibhe, Bernaray	GR: NF917790
Dubh Sgeir	Atlantic	Leverburgh, Harris	GR: NG001855
Dubh Sgeir	Atlantic	Islibhig, Lewis	GR: NA983283
Dubh Sgeir	Atlantic	Aird Laimisadair, Lewis	GR: NB173440
Dubh Sgeir Lachdunn	Atlantic	Islibhig, Lewis	GR: NA981278
Dubh-sgeir a' Deas	The Little Minch	Wiay	GR: NF877474
Dubh-sgeir a' Tuath	The Little Minch	Wiay	GR: NF877447
Dubh-sgeir Bheag	Sea of the Hebrides	Caolas Stulaigh (aka Stuley Sound), South Uist	GR: NF838234
Dubh-sgeir Mhor	Sea of the Hebrides	Caolas Stulaigh (aka Stuley Sound), South Uist	GR: NF840235
Duibh-eilean	The Little Minch	Ronaigh Beag, Ronnay	GR: NF914579
Duisgeir	Loch a Siar	Aird an Tolmachain, Harris	GR: NB081042
Duisgeir	Loch a Siar	Aird Chathanais, Harris	GR: NB111031
Duisker	Atlantic	Scarp	aka Duisgeir (G. Dubh Sgeir = Black Skerry). GR: NA961186
Dun	Atlantic	St Kilda	GR: NF104976
Dun Corr Mor	Braigh Mor	Rubha Phlocrapoil, Harris	GR: NG193944
Dun Eistean	The Minch	Coig Peighinnean, Lewis	GR: NB535650
Dun Mhic Laitheann	Seolaid na h-Eala	Grodaigh	GR: NF978732
Dun Ragbaill	Loch Druidibeg	Meall Thucrabhat	GR: NF778371
Dun-arn	Sound of Harris	Renish Point, Harris	aka Dun-aarin. GR: NG026805
Ealean Baile Bharcais	Atlantic	Rubha nan Caorach, North Uist	GR: NF727757
Easaigh	Atlantic	Leverburgh, Harris	(G. = John's Isle). Aka Ensay. Area: 0.72 sq miles (1.86 sq km). GR: NF980860
Eilean a' Bhlair	The Minch	Eilean Chaluim Chille	GR: NB380220
Eilean a' Bhogha	The Little Minch	Caltanais, South Uist	GR: NF850417
Eilean a' Ceud	Bagh Shintinis	Gighay	(G. = Hundred Island). GR: NF765044
Eilean a' Chaise	The Minch	Pabaillarach, Lewis	GR: NB537311
Eilean a' Chrotaich	Atlantic	Gob Grutha, Lewis	GR: NB516290
Eilean a' Ghamhna	An Oitir Mhor	Beinn a' Charnain, Hellisay	(G. = Island of the Stirks – a stirk is a year-old calf). GR: NF757048
Eilean a' Gheoidh	Loch An Tairbeairt (Tarbert)	Aird Dhirecleit, Harris	GR: NG168981
Eilean a' Gheoidh	Atlantic	Leac na Banaraich, Eriskay	Linked to Eileanan Dubha by drying reefs. One of the Stack Islands (aka Na Stachan Dubha). GR: NF791079
Eilean a' Ghiorr	Beul an Toim	Cladach Chairinis, North Uist	GR: NF849585
Eilean a' Ghobha	The Little Minch	Beinn an t-Sagairt, Ronay	(G. = Island of the Blacksmith). GR: NF879570
Eilean a' Ghobha	Atlantic	Gallan Head, Lewis	One of Na h-Eileanan Flannach (the Flannan Isles). GR: NA692464
Eilean a' Ghuail	Loch An Tairbeairt (Tarbert)	Aird Dhirecleit, Harris	GR: NG163988
Eilean a' Mhadaidh	Bagh nam Faoilean	Sanndabhaig, South Uist	(G. = Isle of the Dog). GR: NF849430
Eilean a' Mhail	Sea of the Hebrides	Earsairidh, Barra	GR: NL710999
Eilean Aird Meithinis	Loch Rog	Uigen, Lewis	GR: NB095339
Eilean an Dunain	Atlantic	Bernaray	GR: NF895800

WESTERN ISLES

Island name	Area	Nearest landmark	General information
Eilean an Fhraoich Miatha	The Little Minch	Caolas Liursaigh, South Uist	GR: NF858411
Eilean an Sguirr	Sea of the Hebrides	Rubha Roiseal, South Uist	GR: NF869340
Eilean an Tigh	Sound of Shianti	Rubha Bhrolluim, Harris	aka Eilean an Taighe. One of the Shiant Islands (aka Eileanan Mora). GR: NG420970
Eilean an Tighe	Loch Ceann Hulabhig	Linsiadar, Lewis	GR: NB221310
Eilean Ard an Eoin	Bagh nam Faoilean	Ard-an-eoin, Benbecula	GR: NF816466
Eilean Arderanish	Loch An Tairbeairt (Tarbert)	Aird Mhiabhaig, Harris	aka Eilean Aird Rainis. GR: NG170869
Eilean Bhacam	Sound of Harris	Killegray	aka Vacam. GR: NF991822
Eilean Arnoil	Atlantic	Arnol, Lewis	GR: NB301497
Eilean Bagh Mhic Rois	Loch Baghasdail	Rubha Bhuailt, South Uist	One of the Eileanan Iasgaich (G. = Fish Islands). GR: NF785184
Eilean Baile Gearraidh	The Little Minch	Roisinis, Benbecula	GR: NF873523
Eilean Beag a' Bhaigh	The Little Minch	Aird a' Bhaigh, Harris	(G. = Little Island at the Bay). GR: NB259013
Eilean Bhacasaigh	Loch Rog an Ear	Great Bernera	GR: NB188362
Eilean Bhalaig	Loch nam Madadh (aka Loch Maddy)	Cam-ard-Mor, North Uist	GR: NF920672
Eilean Bheirean	Atlantic	Sniseabhal, South Uist	GR: NF728349
Eilean Bhinndealaim	Loch Charlabhaigh	Cleibesgeir, Lewis	GR: NB176417
Eilean Bholuim	Sea of the Hebrides	Rubha Bholuim, South Uist	GR: NF830282
Eilean Buidhe	Loch nan Eun	Bogach Loch nan Eun, North Uist	GR: NF845675
Eilean Cearstaigh	Loch Rog	Calanais, Lewis	aka Eilean Kearstay. Area: 0.3 sq miles (0.77 sq km). GR: NB198335
Eilean Chairminis	Atlantic	Leverburgh, Harris	See Carminish Islands.
Eilean Chalaibrigh	The Minch	Eilean Chaluim Chille	GR: NB384224
Eilean Chaluim Chille	Loch Eireasort	Crobeag, Lewis	(G. = Island of Columba's Church). GR: NB385215
Eilean Cheois	Loch Eireasort	Glib Cheois, Lewis	GR: NB367211
Eilean Chircebost	Caolas Honach	Cladach Chireboist, North Uist	aka Kirkibost. GR: NF755650
Eilean Chuidhtinis	Loch Fionnsabhagh	Aird Caol, Harris	aka Eilean Quidnish. GR: NG095861
Eilean Cuithe nam Fiadh	Bagh nam Faoilean	Lochdar, South Uist	GR: NF783472
Eilean Dallaig	Atlantic	Eolaigearraidh, Barra	GR: NF694080
Eilean Domhnuill	Loch Oileabhat	Druim Dearcag, North Uist	Crannog built 5000 years ago. GR: NF747753
Eilean Dubh	Loch Ceann Dibig	Aird Dhirecleit, Harris	(G. = Black Island). GR: NG166981
Eilean Dubh	Sound of Harris	Bhacasaigh	GR: NF972745
Eilean Dubh	Loch Ghreosabhaigh	Rubha Chliuthairt, Harris	GR: NG160903
Eilean Dubh	Loch An Tairbeairt (Tarbert)	Sgeotasaigh (aka Scotasay)	GR: NG190966
Eilean Dubh a' Bhaigh	The Little Minch	Aird a' Bhaigh, Harris	(G. = Black Island at the Bay). GR: NB260009
Eilean Dubh Chollaim	Loch Chollaim	Rubha Chliuthairt, Harris	GR: NG157911
Eilean Dubh Mor	Loch Scadabhagh	Lainis, North Uist	GR: NF855683
Eilean Dubh na Muice	The Little Minch	Rubha Liasain, Benbecula	GR: NF882492
Eilean Eallan	Loch Aineort	Mullach a Ghlinn mhoir, South Uist	GR: NF804262
Eilean Fada	Loch Obasaraigh	Burabhal, North Uist	GR: NF893618
Eilean Fhionnsbhaigh	The Little Minch	Sron Ghaoithe, Harris	GR: NG090857
Eilean Fir Chrothair	Caolas Champaigh	Bearnaraigh Beag (aka Little Bernera)	(G. = Isle of the Shepherd). GR: NB139419
Eilean Fuam	Sound of Harris	Aird Ma-Ruibhe, Bernaray	GR: NF917795
Eilean Glas	Loch nan Geireann	Aird Reamhar, North Uist	(G. = Grey Island). GR: NF845725
Eilean Glas	The Minch	Beinn Mhor, Lewis	GR: NB423240
Eilean Glas	Loch Baghasdail	Ceann a Deas Loch Baghasdail, South Uist	GR: NF790178
Eilean Glas na h-Acarsaid Fhalaich	The Little Minch	Aird a' Bhaigh, Harris	GR: NB270010
Eilean Hasgeir	Atlantic	Rubha Ghriminis, North Uist	See Haskeir Island.
Eilean Kearstay	Loch Rog	Calanais, Lewis	See Eilean Cearstaigh.
Eilean Iasgaich Beag	Loch Baghasdail	Rubha Bhuailt, South Uist	One of the Eileanan Iasgaich (G. = Fish Islands). GR: NF785188

Island name	Area	Nearest landmark	General information
Eilean Iasgaich Meadhonach	Loch Baghasdail	Rubha Bhuailt, South Uist	One of the Eileanan Iasgaich (G. = Fish Islands). GR: NF782185
Eilean Iasgaich Mor	Loch Baghasdail	Rubha Bhuailt, South Uist	One of the Eileanan Iasgaich (G. = Fish Islands). Area: 0.2 sq miles (0.5 sq km). GR: NF790185
Eilean Leasait	Loch Stocinis	Eilean Stocinis (aka Stockinish)	GR: NG133899
Eilean Leathan	The Little Minch	Roisinis, Benbecula	Linked to Calavay by a long tidal strand. GR: NF879541
Eilean Leathan	Atlantic	Leac na Banaraich, Eriskay	Largest of the Stack Islands (Na Stachan Dubha). GR: NF786072
Eilean Leathann	Beul an Toim	Cladach Chairinis, North Uist	GR: NF840589
Eilean Leathann	Loch Obasaraigh	Burabhal, North Uist	GR: NF900619
Eilean Leireabhagh	Loch nam Madadh (aka Loch Maddy)	Lochmaddy, North Uist	GR: NF914679
Eilean Lingreabhagh	Lingreabagh	Lingreabagh, Harris	aka Lingarabay Island. GR: NG065843
Eilean Lochdrach	Beul an Toim	Aird nan Struban, North Uist	GR: NF828584
Eilean Lubhard	Caolas Tuath (aka North Channel)	Rubha Buidhe, Lewis	aka Eilean Liubhaird. Area: 0.48 sq miles (1.25 sq km). GR: NB383100
Eilean Mharaig	Loch Seaforth (aka Shiphoirt)	Maraig, Harris	aka Maaruig. GR: NB207061
Eilean Mhanais	Loch Gheocrab	Aird Mhanais, Harris	GR: NG116886
Eilean Mhealasta	Atlantic	Aird Ghriamanais, Harris	aka Mealista Island. Area: 0.48 sq miles (1.24 sq km). GR: NA980215
Eilean Mhiabhag	Loch Liurbost	Liurbost, Lewis	GR: NB373246
Eilean Mhiathlas	An Caolas Fuideach (aka Sound of Fuday)	Saltainis, Barra	GR: NF714086
Eilean Mhic Caoilte	Beul an Toim	An Tom, Benbecula	GR: NF818570
Eilean Mhic Fhionnlaidh	Braigh Mor	Rubha Phlocrapoil, Harris	GR: NG190933
Eilean Mhidhinis	Loch Midhinis	Blathaisbhal, North Uist	GR: NF905709
Eilean Mhorain	Atlantic	Aird a' Mhorain, North Uist	GR: NF838798
Eilean Mhuire	Sound of Shianti	Rubha Bhrolluim, Harris	(G. = Virgin Mary's Island). One of the Shiant Islands (aka Eileanan Mora). GR: NG431985
Eilean Molach	Atlantic	Aird Mor Mangurstadh, Lewis	GR: NA995323
Eilean Mor	Loch Baghasdail	Ceann a Deas Loch Baghasdail, South Uist	GR: NF772184
Eilean Mor	Beul an Toim	Baleshare, North Uist	GR: NF808610
Eilean Mor	Beul an Toim	Aird nan Struban, North Uist	GR: NF842565
Eilean Mor	Loch Obasaraigh	Burabhal, North Uist	GR: NF893622
Eilean Mor	Caolas Honach	Cladach Chireboist, North Uist	GR: NF765651
Eilean Mor	Loch Rog an Ear	Great Bernera	GR: NB173380
Eilean Mor	Loch Langabhat	Roineabhal, Lewis	GR: NB218220
Eilean Mor	Atlantic	Gallan Head, Lewis	One of Na h-Eileanan Flannach (the Flannan Isles). Permitted to issue its own postage stamps. Area: 0.07 sq miles (0.18 sq km). GR: NA725468
Eilean Mor a' Bhaigh	The Little Minch	Aird a' Bhaigh, Harris	(G. = Big Island at the Bay). GR: NB263003
Eilean Mor Phabail	The Minch	Rubh' Dubh, Lewis	GR: NB531300
Eilean na Cartach	Bagh Shintinis	Carais, Hellisay	GR: NF762039
Eilean na Ceardaich	Sound of Harris	Killegray	(G. = The Tinker's Island). GR: NF991820
Eilean na Cille	Bagh nam Faoilean	Griomasaigh, Benbecula	(G. = Chapel Island). GR: NF846460
Eilean na Cloiche	The Little Minch	Ronay	(G. = Island of the Stone). GR: NF906549
Eilean na Cloiche	Sound of Harris	Aird Ma-Ruibhe, Bernaray	GR: NF919791
Eilean na Fheidh	The Little Minch	Ronaigh Beag, Ronnay	GR: NF909562
Eilean na Gearrabreac	Braigh Mor	Rubha Phlocrapoil, Harris	(G. = Guillemot Island). GR: NG190929
Eilean na h-Airigh	Beul an Toim	Aird nan Struban, North Uist	GR: NF838572
Eilean na Moil Moire	Atlantic	Scarp	GR: NA972136
Eilean na Praise	Loch An Tairbeairt (Tarbert)	Scalpay	(G. = Pot Island). GR: NG205969
Eilean na Sgaite	Braigh Mor	Rubha Phlocrapoil, Harris	(G. = Skate Island). GR: NG192929

Island name	Area	Nearest landmark	General information
Eilean na Slettich	Sound of Harris	Sursaigh	GR: NF959758
Eilean nam Bridianach	Atlantic	Leverburgh, Harris	GR: NG019847
Eilean nam Feannag	Loch Rog	Aird Toranais, Lewis	GR: NB144334
Eilean nam Feannag	Loch Baghasdail	Rubha Bhuailt, South Uist	One of the Eileanan Iasgaich (Fish Islands). GR: NF786189
Eilean nam Mult	Loch Euphort	Sponais, North Uist	(G. = Island of the Castrated Rams). GR: NF882636
Eilean nan Carnan	Beul an Toim	Baleshare, North Uist	GR: NF805615
Eilean nan Daoine Beaga	Atlantic	Roinn a' Roidh, Lewis	(G. = Isle of the Little People). Aka Luchruban or Pygmy Island. GR: NB508661
Eilean nan Each	The Little Minch	Meanais, Benbecula	GR: NF873517
Eilean nan Eun	The Little Minch	Eilean Stocinis (aka Stockinish)	GR: NG134895
Eilean nan Gamhna	Bagh nam Faoilean	Griomasaigh, Benbecula	GR: NF834460
Eilean nan Gamhna	Sea of the Hebrides	Mullach a Ghlinn mhoir, South Uist	GR: NF821260
Eilean nan Gearr	The Little Minch	Liernis, North Uist	(G. = Isle of the Hares). GR: NF891584
Eilean nan Imireachean	Loch Baghasdail	Ceann a Deas Loch Baghasdail, South Uist	(G. = Island of the Processions). GR: NF777185
Eilean nan Uan	Atlantic	Stornaway, Lewis	GR: NB460305
Eilean Orasaidh	The Minch	Cromor, Lewis	GR: NB412214
Eilean Orasaigh	Loch Ceann Hulabhig	Linsiadar, Lewis	GR: NB218320
Eilean Orasaigh	Loch Liurbost	Liurbost, Lewis	GR: NB368254
Eilean Orasaigh	The Minch	Crosbost, Lewis	One of the Barkin Isles. GR: NB402240
Eilean Ornais	Sea of the Hebrides	Ornais, South Uist	aka Ornish. GR: NF857386
Eilean Quidnish	Loch Fionnsabhagh	Aird Caol, Harris	See Eilean Chuidhtinis.
Eilean Raineach	Loch An Tairbeairt (Tarbert)	Sgeotasaigh	GR: NG191971
Eilean Reinis	Sound of Harris	Renish Point, Harris	aka Renish. GR: NG042815
Eilean Reinigeadail	Loch Trolamaraig	Reinigeadal, Harris	aka Rhenigidale. GR: NB229011
Eilean Rosaidh	The Minch	Cromor, Lewis	GR: NB420209
Eilean Scarista	Loch Rog	Beinn Scarastaigh, Lewis	aka Eilean Scarastaigh. GR: NB195327
Eilean Sheumais	Caolas Theilisigh (aka Sound of Hellisay)	Fuidheigh	GR: NF740029
Eilean Shiphoirt	Loch Seaforth (aka Shiphoirt)	Mhulaidh, Harris	aka Seaforth. Area: 1.05 sq miles (2.73 sq km). GR: NB210105
Eilean Smuaisibhig	Loch Claidh	Tathas Mhor, Harris	GR: NB271039
Eilean Stocinis	The Little Minch	Cliuthar, Harris	aka Stockinish Island. GR: NG138900
Eilean Teinis	Loch Rog	Rubha Sheotharaid, Lewis	GR: NB119351
Eilean Thinngartsaigh	Loch Claidh	Tathas Bheag, Harris	GR: NB279021
Eilean Thoraidh	The Minch	Cromor, Lewis	GR: NB422200
Eilean Thuilm	Atlantic	Stornaway, Lewis	GR: NB450303
Eilean Tighe	Atlantic	Gallan Head, Lewis	(G. = House Island). One of Na h-Eileanan Flannach (the Flannan Isles). GR: NA730464
Eilean Trosdam	Loch Ceann Hulabhig	Linsiadar, Lewis	GR: NB213321
Eilean Trostain	Atlantic	Aird an Runair, North Uist	GR: NF692716
Eilean Vanish	Sea of the Hebrides	Maol Domhnaich (aka Muldoanich)	GR: NL686931
Eileana Dubha	Sound of Harris	Tobha Beag, North Uist	GR: NF971736
Eileanan a' Ghille-bheid	Loch An Tairbeairt (Tarbert)	Aird Mhiabhaig, Harris	GR: NG176961
Eileanan Airde	Beul an Toim	An Tom, Benbecula	GR: NF815575
Eileanan Chearabhaigh	Loch a' Laip	Rairnis, Benbecula	aka Keiravagh Islands. GR: NF870478
Eileanan Direcleit	Loch An Tairbeairt (Tarbert)	Aird Dhirecleit, Harris	GR: NG165986
Eileanan Dubha	Bagh a Tuath	Bruairnis, Barra	GR: NF728028
Eileanan Dubha	Sound of Barra	Leac na Banaraich, Eriskay	(G. = Black Islands). Linked to Eilean a' Gheoidh by drying reefs. Part of the Stack Islands (Na Stachan Dubha). GR: NF788078
Eileanan Glasa	Beul an Toim	Gramasdail, Benbecula	(G. = Grey-green Islands). GR: NF825565
Eileanan Iasgaich	Loch Baghasdail	Rubha Bhuailt, South Uist	aka the Fish Islands. Group of three islands, Eilean Iasgaich Beag, Eilean Iasgaich Meadhonach and Eilean Iasgaich Mor (the largest of the group).
Eileanan na Yacht	Sound of Harris	Tobha Beag, North Uist	aka Righe nam Ban. GR: NF969741
Eileanan Stafa	Bagh nam Faoilean	Griomasaigh, Benbecula	GR: NF825464

Island name	Area	Nearest landmark	General information
Eimisgeir	Loch Ceann Hulabhig	Coire an Fhuarain, Lewis	GR: NB224316
Eire	Sound of Harris	Grodhaigh (aka Groay)	GR: NF998798
En Dubh nan Uan	The Little Minch	Ronay	GR: NF895577
Ensay	Atlantic	Leverburgh, Harris	See Easaigh
Eriskay	Sound of Barra	Taobh a' Chaolais, South Uist	aka Eiriosgaigh. See separate entry.
Eughlam	Loch Rog an Ear	Great Bernera	GR: NB160397
Eunaigh Beag	Caolas Fuaigh	Great Bernera	aka Eunay Beag. GR: NB138358
Eunaigh Meadhonach	Caolas Fuaigh	Great Bernera	aka Eunay Meadhonach. GR: NB137359
Eunaigh Mor	Caolas Fuaigh	Great Bernera	aka Eunay Mor. GR: NB135360
Faithoire	Loch nam Madadh (aka Loch Maddy)	Cam-ard-Mor, North Uist	aka Faihore. GR: NF931680
Ferramas	Loch nam Madadh (aka Loch Maddy)	Taigh Sponais, North Uist	aka Fearamas. GR: NF931700
Fiaray	Atlantic	Gob Sgurabhal, Barra	aka Fiaraidh. Area: 0.16 sq miles (0.41 sq km). GR: NF702104
Fish Islands, The	Loch Baghasdail	Rubha Bhuailt, South Uist	See Eileanan Iasgaich.
Fladaigh	Atlantic	Scarp	aka Fladday. GR: NA995152
Flannan Isles, The	Atlantic	Gallan Head, Lewis	aka Na h-Eileanan Flannach. Group of islets off the coast of Lewis. GR: NA725452
Fleisgeir	Pol Gainmhich	Great Bernera	GR: NB123419
Floday	Loch Rog	Uigen, Lewis	aka Flodaigh. GR: NB105333
Floday	Pol Gainmhich	Great Bernera	aka Flodaigh. GR: NB122414
Flodda	The Little Minch	Benbecula	aka Flodaigh. Area: 0.56 sq miles (1.45 sq km). Population: 11. GR: NF845552
Flodday	Loch nam Madadh (aka Loch Maddy)	Lochmaddy, North Uist	aka Flodaigh. GR: NF941696
Flodday	Atlantic	Sandray	aka Flodaigh. GR: NL611922
Flodday	Caolas Theilisigh (aka Sound of Hellisay)	Bruairnis, Barra	aka Flodaigh. Area: 0.15 sq miles (0.4 sq km). GR: NF752022
Floddaybeg	The Little Minch	Ronaigh Beag, Ronnay	aka Flodaigh Beg. GR: NF918580
Floddaymore	The Little Minch	Ronaigh Beag, Ronnay	aka Flodaigh Mor. Area: 0.22 sq miles (0.58 sq km). GR: NF913572
Fodragaigh	Bagh nam Faoilean	Griomasaigh, Benbecula	GR: NF844457
Fuam	Sound of Harris	Bhacasaigh	Full name of island is Fuam an Aon Fhoid (G. = Far Out Isle of the One Peat). GR: NF980741
Fuam an Tolla	Loch An Tairbeairt (Tarbert)	Scalpay	GR: NG208962
Fuam na h-Ola	Sound of Harris	Aird Thormaid, North Uist	GR: NF978758
Fuday	Sound of Barra	Saltainis, Barra	aka Fuideigh. Area: 0.9 sq miles (2.32 sq km). GR: NF735085
Fuiay	Bagh a Tuath	Bruairnis, Barra	aka Fuidheigh. Area: 0.32 sq miles (0.84 sq km). GR: NF740025
Fuidhaigh	The Little Minch	Benbecula	aka Wiay. Area: 1.45 sq miles (3.75 sq km). GR: NF870460
Fuidhaigh Beag	The Little Minch	Roisinis, Benbecula	GR: NF866525
Gairbh-eilean	Beul an Toim	Cladach Chairinis, North Uist	GR: NF847588
Gaisgeir	Sound of Harris	Aird Thormaid, North Uist	GR: NF969762
Gaisgeir	Caolas Champaigh	Bearnaraigh Beag (aka Little Bernera)	GR: NB152410
Gaisgeir Beag	Atlantic	Scarp	GR: NA888108
Galeac	Atlantic	Leac na Banaraich, Eriskay	GR: NF796074
Gallan Beag	Atlantic	Gallan Head, Lewis	GR: NB037382
Galta Beag	Sound of Shianti	Rubha Bhrolluim, Harris	One of the Shiant Islands (aka Eileanan Mora). GR: NG401982
Galta Mor	Sound of Shianti	Rubha Bhrolluim, Harris	One of the Shiant Islands (aka Eileanan Mora). GR: NG390983
Garbh Eilean	Loch Rog	Geisiadar, Lewis	(G. = Rough Island). GR: NB128321
Garbh Eilean	Loch Eireasort	Glib Cheois, Lewis	GR: NB362211
Garbh Eilean	Sound of Shianti	Rubha Bhrolluim, Harris	One of the Shiant Islands (aka Eileanan Mora). Area: 0.55 sq mile (1.43 sq km). GR: NG415985
Garbh Eilean Mor	Bagh Clann-Neil	Ceallan, Grimsay	(G. = Big Rough Island). GR: NF885555

Island name	Area	Nearest landmark	General information
Garbh Lingay	Caolas Theilisigh (aka Sound of Hellisay)	Rubh' a' Mhorbhuile, Hellisay	aka Garbh Lingeigh (G. = Rough Heather). GR: NF741032
Garbh Lingeigh	Caolas Theilisigh (aka Sound of Hellisay)	Rubh' a' Mhorbhuile, Hellisay	aka Garbh Lingay. GR: NF741032
Gasaigh	Loch Baghasdail	Loch Baghasdail, South Uist	GR: NF800189
Gasay	Bagh nam Faoilean	Sanndabhaig, South Uist	aka Gasaidh. GR: NF840431
Gasker	Atlantic	Scarp	aka Gaisgeir. GR: NA875115
Gealldruig Bheag	Atlantic	Rona	GR: HW820317
Gealldruig Mhor	Atlantic	Rona	GR: HW819314
Gealtaire Beag	Atlantic	Gallan Head, Lewis	One of Na h-Eileanan Flannach (the Flannan Isles). GR: NA737465
Gealtaire Mor	Atlantic	Gallan Head, Lewis	One of Na h-Eileanan Flannach (the Flannan Isles). GR: NA743466
Gearum Beag	Atlantic	Rubha Liath, Mingulay	GR: NL551813
Gearum Mor	Atlantic	Rubha Liath, Mingulay	GR: NL549812
Geile Sgeir	Caolas Phabaigh (aka Sound of Pabbay)	Rubha Sheotharaid, Lewis	GR: NB121360
Geiriscleit	Atlantic	Traigh Bhalaigh, North Uist	GR: NF769754
Geo na Ba Glaise	Atlantic	St Kilda	GR: NF083989
Geodha Biatha Mo	Atlantic	Butt of Lewis, Lewis	GR: HW619306
Geodha Caol	Atlantic	Loch Nasabhaig, Lewis	GR: NC244701
Geodha Garbh	Atlantic	Rubha Aird a' Mhuile, South Uist	GR: NF706299
Geodha Mor	Atlantic	Rubha Aird a' Mhuile, South Uist	GR: NF710300
Geodha Nasabhaig	Atlantic	Loch Nasabhaig, Lewis	GR: NB034366
Gighay	An Oitir Mhor	Aird Mhor, Barra	Mullach a' Charnain (G. = Cairn Summit) is the highest peak at 312ft (95m). Area: 0.37 sq mile (0.96 sq km). GR: NF767045
Gilsay	Sound of Harris	Renish Point, Harris	aka Gilsaigh. GR: NG020800
Glas Eilean	Atlantic	Aird Mor Mangurstadh, Lewis	(G. = Pale Grey-green Island). GR: NB014337
Glas Eilean	Loch Rog	Tacleit, Great Bernera	GR: NB138338
Glas Eilean Mor	Loch nam Madadh (aka Loch Maddy)	Rubha nam Pleac, North Uist	(G. = Big Pale Grey-green Island). GR: NF947681
Glas Sgeir	Loch Seaforth (aka Shiphoirt)	Torscaram, Harris	GR: NB225039
Glas Sgeir	The Minch	Cromor, Lewis	GR: NB425205
Glas Sgeir	Loch Fhleoideabhaigh	Fhleoideabhaigh, Harris	GR: NG104884
Glas Sgeir	Loch Ghreosabhaigh	Rubha Chliuthairt, Harris	GR: NG162913
Glas-eilean Beag	Sea of the Hebrides	Caolas Stulaigh (aka Stuley Sound), South Uist	(G. = Little Green Island). GR: NF822237
Glas-eilean Beag	Caolas Honach	Baleshare, North Uist	GR: NF788639
Glas-eilean Mor	Atlantic	Eliogar, South Uist	(G. = Big Green Island). GR: NF838230
Glas-eilean Mor	Sea of the Hebrides	Caolas Stulaigh (aka Stuley Sound), South Uist	GR: NF838230
Glas-eilean na Creige	The Little Minch	Rubha Shanndabhaig, South Uist	GR: NF847421
Glas-eileanan	The Little Minch	Caolas Liursaigh, South Uist	GR: NF865415
Glas-sgeir	Caolas Shodhaigh	Bearragan, Harris	GR: NB051070
Gloraig a' Chaimbeulaich	Braigh Mor	Rubha Phlocrapoil, Harris	GR: NG190943
Gloraig Dhubh	Braigh Mor	Rubha Phlocrapoil, Harris	GR: NG184949
Gloraig Huisnis	Atlantic	Rubha Bhogha-sgeir, Harris	GR: NA989099
Gloraig Iosal	Braigh Mor	Rubha Phlocrapoil, Harris	GR: NG189948
Gloraig Tharasaigh	Atlantic	Rubha Bhogha-sgeir, Harris	GR: NA970060

Island name	Area	Nearest landmark	General information
Gob na h-Airde Bige	Atlantic	Aird Sheag, Harris	GR: NB017185
Gob Thais	Loch a Tuath	Bac, Lewis	GR: NB491404
Gousam	Loch Rog	Uigen, Lewis	GR: NB109339
Gousman	Sound of Harris	Grodhaigh (aka Groay)	GR: NF990790
Gradaire Leathann	Caolas Champaigh	Great Bernera	GR: NB141366
Gralisgeir	Atlantic	Butt of Lewis, Lewis	GR: HW618298
Greanamul	An Oitir Mhor	Rubh' a' Mhorbhuile, Hellisay	(O.N. = Green Hump). GR: NF735056
Greanamul	Caolas Phabaigh (aka Sound of Pabbay)	Lingeigh (aka Lingay)	GR: NL620898
Greanamul	The Little Minch	Meanais, Benbecula	GR: NF894519
Greanamul Deas	The Little Minch	Rairnis, Benbecula	(G. = South Greanamul). GR: NF885487
Greanem	Grey Horse Channel	Hermetray	(O.N.= Green Holm).
Great Bernera	Loch Rog an Ear	Iarsiadar, Lewis	See Bearnaraigh Mor.
Greineam	Sound of Harris	Rubha na h-Aibhne Duibhe, North Uist	GR: NF922778
Greineam	Sound of Harris	Thernatraigh	GR: NF995749
Greineam	Caolas Champaigh	Great Bernera	GR: NB130389
Greineim	Atlantic	Mealasta, Lewis	GR: NA980245
Greinem	Loch An Tairbeairt (Tarbert)	Scalpay	aka Greineam. GR: NG215942
Greinem	Loch An Tairbeairt (Tarbert)	Scalpay	aka Greineim. GR: NG245956
Greine-Sgeir	Atlantic	Rubha Glas, Harris	GR: NB010157
Grey Rock	Sea of the Hebrides	Flodaigh	GR: NF755019
Grimsay	The Little Minch	Benbecula	aka Griomasaigh. Linked to North Uist and Benbecula by a causeway opened in 1961. Area: 4.88 sq miles (12.63 sq km). Population: 220. GR: NF860565
Groatay	Sound of Harris	Tobha Beag, North Uist	aka Grodaigh. GR: NF980732
Groay	Sound of Harris	Renish Point, Harris	aka Grodhaigh. GR: NG002792
Gruagach	Atlantic	Fiaraidh	GR: NF697101
Gualan	Bagh nam Faoilean	Lochdar, South Uist	GR: NF775480
Gumersam Beag	Sound of Harris	Renish Point, Harris	GR: NG021811
Gumersam Mhor	Sound of Harris	Renish Point, Harris	GR: NG019814
Gunamul	Atlantic	Mingulay	Annexed to Mingulay. GR: NL547824
Hairsgeir	An Caolas	Great Bernera	GR: NB110409
Hairsgeir Beag	Atlantic	Mealasta, Lewis	GR: NA971231
Hairsgeir Mor	Atlantic	Mealasta, Lewis	GR: NA975232
Hamarsay	Loch An Tairbeairt (Tarbert)	Scalpay	aka Thamarasaigh. GR: NG210947
Hamatan	Atlantic	St Kilda	GR: NF109970
Hamersay	Loch nam Madadh (aka Loch Maddy)	Lochmaddy, North Uist	aka Thamarasaigh. GR: NF932687
Harsgeir	Atlantic	Rona	GR: HW801320
Harsgeir Beag	Atlantic	Mealista (aka Eilean Mhealasta)	GR: NA980200
Harsgeir Mor	Atlantic	Mealista (aka Eilean Mhealasta)	GR: NA980200
Hartamul	Atlantic	Ronais, Eriskay	aka Thairteamul. GR: NF833114
Hasgeir Eagach	Atlantic	Rubha Ghrlmlnls, North Uist	(O.N. = Wild or Deep-Sea Skerry). GR: NF595809
Haskeir Island	Atlantic	Rubha Ghriminis, North Uist	aka Eilean Hasgeir. GR: NF615820
Hasselwood Rock	Atlantic	Rubha Mhanais	Lies close to Rockall.
Haunaray	The Little Minch	Ronay/North Uist	GR: NF911560
Heastam Sromaigh	Loch Amhlasaraigh	Tobha Beag, North Uist	GR: NF941745
Heilem	Sea of the Hebrides	Rubha Bhruairnis, Barra	GR: NL747994
Heisker	Caolas Shiolaigh (aka Sound of Shillay)	Baleshare, North Uist	(O.N. = Bright Skerry). Aka Monach Islands. Group of islands in the Outer Hebrides uninhabited since 1942 and designated a National Nature Reserve for their grey seal population; permission to land is required from Scottish Natural Heritage.
Heisker	Sound of Harris	Killegray	aka Theisgeir. GR: NG008803
Hellisay	An Oitir Mhor	Aird Mhor, Barra	aka Theiliseigh. Area: 0.55 sq miles (1.42 sq km). GR: NF755041

Island name	Area	Nearest landmark	General information
Hermetray	Sound of Harris	Tobha Beag, North Uist	aka Thernatraigh. Area: 0.28 sq miles (0.72 sq km). GR: NF988740
Hestam	Atlantic	Stolie Shieling, North Uist	GR: NF911744
Hestem	Sound of Harris	Killegray	aka Theisteam. GR: NF990827
Hirta	Atlantic	Rubha Ghriminis, North Uist	aka Hiort or St Kilda, although that is properly the name of the archipelago rather than the island. See separate entry.
Holaisgeir	Atlantic	Aird an Runair, North Uist	GR: NF695691
Hornish Rocks	An Caolas Fuideach (aka Sound of Fuday)	Mullach Neacall, Fuday	GR: NF735216
Huanaraigh	The Little Minch	Ronaigh Beag, Ronnay	GR: NF908578
Hulmatray	Sound of Harris	Bhacasaigh	aka Thulmatraigh. GR: NF982750
Hulmetray	Basin of Vaccasay	Bhacasaigh	GR: NF987500
Inner Heisker	Caolas Mhiughlaigh (aka Sound of Mingulay)	Pabbay	aka Theisgeir a-staigh. GR: NL585868
Iola Sgeir	Caolas Phabaigh (aka Sound of Pabbay)	Pabaigh Mor	GR: NB096376
Iosaigh	Loch a Siar	Tothan Cartach, Harris	GR: NB105024
Irishman Rock	Caolas Theilisigh (aka Sound of Hellisay)	Flodday (aka Flodaigh)	GR: NF756020
Isay	West Loch Tarbert	Soay Mor	(O.N. = Porpoise).
Kealasay	Caolas Champaigh	Bearnaraigh Beag (aka Little Bernera)	See Cealasaigh.
Keallasay Beg	Loch nam Madadh (aka Loch Maddy)	Bac-a-stoc, North Uist	See Ceallasaigh Beag.
Keallasay More	Loch nam Madadh (aka Loch Maddy)	Bac-a-stoc, North Uist	See Ceallasaigh Mor.
Kearstay	Atlantic	Scarp	See Cearstaigh.
Keava	Loch Rog an Ear	Ribha Arspaig, Lewis	See Ceabhagh.
Keiravagh Islands	Loch a' Laip	Rairnis, Benbecula	See Eileanan Chearabhaigh.
Killegray	Atlantic	Leverburgh, Harris	See Ceileagraigh.
Kirkibost	Caolas Honach	Cladach Chireboist, North Uist	See Eilean Chircebost.
Lada Sgeir	Loch a Tuath	Drochaid Ghriais, Lewis	GR: NB503406
Lamalum	Caolas Theilisigh (aka Sound of Hellisay)	Aird Mhidhinis, Barra	GR: NF729033
Lamh a' Sgeir Bheag	Atlantic	Gallan Head, Lewis	One of Na h-Eileanan Flannach (aka the Flannan Isles). GR: NA728467
Lamh a' Sgeir Mhor	Atlantic	Gallan Head, Lewis	One of Na h-Eileanan Flannach (aka the Flannan Isles). GR: NA727466
Langa Sgeir	Atlantic	Killegray	GR: NG000842
Langa Sgeir Mhor	Loch a Tuath	Mealabost, Lewis	GR: NB479327
Langay	Sound of Harris	Renish Point, Harris	aka Langaigh. GR: NG013817
Leac Mhor Fianuis	Atlantic	Rona	One of the Western Isles. GR: HW815332
Leac Nighe	Sound of Shianti	Eilean an Taighe	One of the Shiant Islands (aka Eileanan Mora). GR: NG418969
Leibhinis	Atlantic	St Kilda	GR: NF133966
Leumadair Mor	Atlantic	Eilean Mhealasta	GR: NA980223
Lewis and Harris	The Minch	Rubha Hunish, Skye	Often considered as distinct islands, but south Lewis and north Harris are only separated by a 6 mile (10km) range of hills and are now connected by road, although maintaining their different Gaelic dialects. Harris tweed, known locally as Clo Mor (G. = Big Cloth), originated in Harris but the centre of production is now in Lewis. The 'capital' of Lewis is Stornoway. It is the most northerly island of the Outer Hebrides. Area: 838.56 sq miles (2171.86 sq km). Population: 19,918. GR: NB212175
Liacam	Caolas Phabaigh (aka Sound of Pabbay)	Bhacsaigh (aka Vacsay)	GR: NB119371
Lianamul	Atlantic	Mingulay	Annexed to Mingulay. GR: NL549837
Lingarabay Island	Lingreabagh	Lingreabhagh, Harris	See Eilean Lingreabhagh.

Island name	Area	Nearest landmark	General information
Lingay	Caolas Phabaigh (aka Sound of Pabbay)	Sandray	aka Lingeigh (G. = Heather). GR: NL603897
Lingay	Atlantic	Sudhanais, North Uist	aka Lingeigh. GR: NF870785
Lingay	Sound of Harris	Renish Point, Harris	aka Lingeigh. GR: NG014790
Lingay	Sound of Barra	Hornais, Barra	aka Lingeigh. GR: NF753115
Lingay	Bagh nam Faoilean	Fodragaigh	aka Lingeigh. GR: NF855450
Lingay-fhada	Caolas Theilisigh (aka Sound of Hellisay)	Aird Mhidhinis, Barra	aka Lingeigh-Fhada (G. = Long Heather). GR: NF731037
Linngeam	Loch Rog	Aird Toranais, Lewis	GR: NB141333
Liongaim	Atlantic	Rubha Loisgte, Harris	aka Liongam. GR: NA998198
Lisgeir Mhor	Atlantic	Rona	aka Lisgear Mhor. GR: HW813338
Lith Sgeir	Atlantic	Butt of Lewis, Lewis	GR: NB519669
Little Bernera	Loch Rog an Ear	Great Bernera	See Bearnaraigh Beag.
Little Shillay	Atlantic	Siolaigh (aka Shillay)	aka Siolaigh Bheag. GR: NF875907
Liursaigh Dubh	The Little Minch	Caolas Liursaigh, South Uist	GR: NF863404
Liursaigh Glas	The Little Minch	Caolas Liursaigh, South Uist	GR: NF868402
Loba Sgeir	Atlantic	Rona	GR: HW802319
Luchruban	Atlantic	Roinn a' Roidh, Lewis	See Eilean nan Daoine Beaga.
Maaruig	Loch Seaforth (aka Shiphoirt)	Maraig, Harris	See Eilean Mharaig.
MacQueen's Rock	Loch An Tairbeairt (Tarbert)	Scalpay	GR: NG204971
Madadh Beag	Loch nam Madadh (aka Loch Maddy)	Rubha an Fhigheadair, North Uist	(G. = Little Dog). GR: NF957688
Madadh Gruamach	Loch nam Madadh (aka Loch Maddy)	Rubha nam Pleac, North Uist	(G. = Surly Dog). GR: NF952667
Madadh Mor	Loch nam Madadh (aka Loch Maddy)	Rubha nam Pleac, North Uist	(G. = Great Dog). GR: NF955673
Magaskel	Atlantic	Taranasay	aka Magasgeir. GR: NA987002
Maithidh Glas	The Little Minch	Uisgeabhaigh, Benbecula	GR: NF885498
Maithidh Riabhach	The Little Minch	Uisgeabhaigh, Benbecula	(G. = Grizzled Seagull Island). Aka Maaey Riabhach. GR: NF880502
Maragaidh Beag	Loch Uisgebhagh (aka Loch Uiskevagh)	Roisinis, Benbecula	(G. = Little Pudding). Aka Maragay Beag. GR: NF887527
Maragaidh Mor	Loch Uisgebhagh (aka Loch Uiskevagh)	Roisinis, Benbecula	(G. = Big Pudding). Aka Maragay Mor. GR: NF890525
Mas Sgeir	An Caolas	Pabaigh Beag	GR: NB098391
Mas Sgeir	Pol Gainmhich	Aird Laimisadair, Lewis	GR: NB141440
Mas Sgeir	Atlantic	Butt of Lewis, Lewis	GR: NB519667
Masgeir	Caolas Honach	Cnoc an Torrain, North Uist	GR: NF716673
Mealista Island	Atlantic	Aird Ghriamanais, Harris	See Eilean Mhealasta.
Mealla Bru	Atlantic	Beinn Mhor, North Uist	GR: NF907748
Mile-sgeir	Sound of Harris	Killegray	GR: NG013830
Mina Stac	Atlantic	St Kilda	GR: NA104008
Mingulay	Atlantic	Pabbay	aka Miughlaigh. Uninhabited since 1912. Owned by National Trust for Scotland. The islands south of Barra and Vatersay were formerly known as the Bishop's Isles, Mingulay being the largest. Area: 2.47 sq miles (6.4 sq km). GR: NL560830
Mol Mor	Loch Rog	Fuaidh Mor	GR: NB132352
Mol na Cuile	Loch Sealg	Orasaigh, Lewis	GR: NB367115
Mol nan Stop	Loch a Siar	Aird Grodanais, Harris	GR: NB070015
Mol Tiacanais	Atlantic	Mealasta, Lewis	GR: NA989241
Monach Islands	Caolas Shiolaigh (aka Sound of Shillay)	Baleshare, North Uist	See Heisker.
Muldoanich	Sea of the Hebrides	Sandray	aka Maol Domhnaich (G. = Sunday Rock). Area: 0.3 sq miles (0.78 sq km). GR: NL689938
Na Gilleacha' Ruadha	Atlantic	Mingulay	aka The Red Boy. GR: NL566851
Na h-Eileanan	The Minch	Crosbost, Lewis	GR: NB399239
Na h-Eileanan Flannach	Atlantic	Gallan Head, Lewis	See Flannan Isles.
Narstay	Sound of Harris	Aird Thormaid, North Uist	aka Narstaigh. GR: NF977770

Island name	Area	Nearest landmark	General information
Nicholson's Leap	The Little Minch	Rubha Bhilidh, South Uist	GR: NF864332
North Uist	The Little Minch	Rubha Hunish, Skye	aka Uibhist a Tuath. Eavel at 1138ft (347m) is the highest point. Lochmaddy is the 'capital'. Area: 133.07 sq miles (344.64 sq km). Population: 1271. GR: NF799708
Obe Rocks	Atlantic	Scarp	GR: NA946157
Odarum	Caolas Shiolaigh (aka Sound of Shillay)	Baleshare, North Uist	One of the Monach Islands. GR: NF593630
Oitir Bheag	Bagh nam Faoilean	Ard-an-eoin, Benbecula	GR: NF817472
Oitir Mhor	Caolas Bhearnaraigh	Rubha na h-Iulain, North Uist	GR: NF895791
Old Woman's Rock	An Caolas Fuideach (aka Sound of Fuday)	Mullach Neacall, Fuday	GR: NF735230
Opsay	Sound of Harris	Aird Thormaid, North Uist	aka Opasaigh. GR: NF982760
Or Eilean	Sound of Harris	Sromaigh	GR: NF950752
Or Eilean	Loch An Tairbeairt (Tarbert)	Scalpay	GR: NG218949
Orasaigh	Sea of the Hebrides	Earsairidh, Barra	GR: NL706993
Orasaigh	Loch Uisgebhagh (aka Loch Uiskevagh)	Scaraileod, Benbecula	GR: NF849511
Orasaigh	The Little Minch	Meanais, Benbecula	GR: NF865521
Orasaigh	Atlantic	Greinetobht, North Uist	GR: NF845760
Orasaigh	Loch Euphort	Langais, North Uist	GR: NF835641
Orasaigh	Loch Amhlasaraigh	Cnoc Mor an t-Sagairt, North Uist	GR: NF943736
Orasaigh	Sound of Harris	Tobha Beag, North Uist	GR: NF965736
Orasaigh Uisgeabhaigh	The Little Minch	Uisgeabhaigh, Benbecula	GR: NF867507
Orassaigh	Atlantic	An Leth Meadhanach, South Uist	GR: NF727172
Orassaigh	Bagh nam Faoilean	Loch a' Charnain, South Uist	GR: NF822436
Ornish	Sea of the Hebrides	Ornais, South Uist	See Eilean Ornais.
Oronsay	Atlantic	Loch nan Geireann, North Uist	aka Orasaigh.
Orosay	Calaos Orasaigh	Beinn Eolaigearraidh, Barra	aka Orasaigh. GR: NF715062
Orosay	Caolas Bhatarsaigh	Beinn Orasaigh, Vatersay	aka Orasaigh. GR: NL641971
Ostem	Atlantic	Scarp	aka Oisteim. GR: NA961171
Outer Heisker	Caolas Mhiughlaigh (aka Sound of Mingulay)	Pabbay	aka Theisgeir a-mulgh. GR: NL573867
Pabaigh	Loch Baghasdail	Ceann a Tuath Loch Baghasdail, South Uist	(G. = Hermit; O.N. = Priest). GR: NF778198
Pabay Beag	An Caolas	Pabaigh Mor	aka Pabaigh Beag (G. = Little Priest; O.N. = Little Hermit). Area: 3.17 sq miles (8.2 sq km). GR: NB100389
Pabay Mor	An Caolas	Bhaltos, Lewis	aka Pabaigh Mor (G. = Great Hermit; O.N. = Great Priest). Area: 0.39 sq miles (1.01 sq km). GR: NB101380
Pabbay	Caolas Phabaigh (aka Sound of Pabbay)	Sandray	aka Pabaigh. Every able-bodied man on the island was lost in a storm on 1 May 1897. Owned by the National Trust for Scotland. Area: 0.97 sq miles (2.5 sq km). GR: NL602875
Pabbay	Caolas Phabaigh (aka Sound of Pabbay)	Bernaray	aka Pabaigh (G. = Hermit; O.N. = Priest). Area: 3.17 sq miles (8.2 sq km). GR: NF890880
Quinish	Atlantic	Pabbay	See Cuidhnis.
Racaisgeirean	Sound of Harris	Aird Thormaid, North Uist	GR: NF968770
Raiream	South Harbour Scalpay	Scalpay	GR: NG215956
Raisgeir	Caolas Shiolaigh (aka Sound of Shillay)	Baleshare, North Uist	One of the Monach Islands. GR: NF595618
Rangas	Sound of Harris	Cnoc Mor Thormaid, North Uist	GR: NF938763

Island name	Area	Nearest landmark	General information
Reagam	The Little Minch	Wiay	GR: NF868448
Red Boy, The	Atlantic	Mingulay	See Na Gilleacha' Ruadha.
Renish	Sound of Harris	Renish Point, Harris	See Eilean Reinis.
Rhenigidale	Loch Trolamaraig	Reinigeadal, Harris	See Eilean Reinigeadail.
Righe nam Ban	Sound of Harris	Tobha Beag, North Uist	See Eileanan na Yacht.
Riobhag Mhor	Loch Euphort	Clachan Bhiurabhal, North Uist	GR: NF908633
Riobhagan Midhinis	Loch Midhinis	Blathaisbhal, North Uist	GR: NF911709
Riosaidh	The Minch	Crosbost, Lewis	One of the Barkin Isles. GR: NB395235
Risgay	Loch Aineort	Rubha na h-Eighich, South Uist	aka Riosgaidh. GR: NF797282
Roaiream	Atlantic	Gallan Head, Lewis	One of Na h-Eileanan Flannach (the Flannan Isles). GR: NA691468
Rockall	Atlantic	Rubha Mhanais	The most isolated islet in the British Isles. Located 57º 36' N, 13º 41' W and lying 230 miles (370km) west of Manish Point, North Uist, Scotland. The islet is 70ft (21m) high and 80ft (24m) by 100ft (30.5m) wide. Officially annexed by Britain in September 1955 when a landing was made by helicopter from the navy vessel HMS *Vidal*, it became part of the United Kingdom in February 1972 when the Isle of Rockall Act was passed in the UK Parliament.
Rona	Atlantic	Butt of Lewis, Lewis	aka Ronaidh. One of the Western Isles. Traditionally St Ronan departed Lewis to live as a hermit on the island, although it is not clear whether it took its name from him or from *hrauney* (O.N. = Rough Island). Area: 0.42 sq miles (1.09 sq km). GR: HW810325
Ronay	The Little Minch	Grimsay	aka Ronaigh. Area: 2.17 sq miles (5.63 sq km). GR: NF895560
Rosinish	Caolas Phabaigh (aka Sound of Pabbay)	Pabbay	aka Roisinis. A drying island joined to the east coast of Pabbay. GR: NL616871
Rossay	Loch An Tairbeairt (Tarbert)	Scalpay	aka Rosaigh. GR: NG203952
Rubha Niosaim	Atlantic	Bernaray	GR: NL577799
Rubha Raghnaill	Caolas Honach	Rubha Mor, North Uist	GR: NF719663
Ruigh Liath	Loch nam Madadh (aka Loch Maddy)	Cam-ard-Mor, North Uist	GR: NF928679
Rusgaidh	Loch Amhlasaraigh	Tobha Beag, North Uist	GR: NF945741
Sagay Beg	Atlantic	Aird an t-Sruith, Harris	aka Saghaigh Beag. GR: NF995869
Sagay More	Atlantic	Aird an t-Sruith, Harris	aka Saghaigh Mhor. GR: NF999868
Sandray	Caolas Shandraigh (aka Sound of Sandray)	Vatersay	aka Sanndraigh. Area: 1.49 sq miles (3.85 sq km). GR: NL640915
Sarstay	Sound of Harris	Aird Thormaid, North Uist	aka Sarstaigh. GR: NF973759
Scalpay	Loch An Tairbeairt (Tarbert)	Carnach, Harris	aka Scalpaigh. Area: 2.71 sq miles (7.02 sq km). Population: 322. GR: NG230960
Scaracleit	The Little Minch	Wiay	GR: NF885464
Scaravay	Sound of Harris	Renish Point, Harris	aka Sgarabhaigh. GR: NG010780
Scarp	Atlantic	Huisnis, Harris	See separate entry.
Scotasay	Loch An Tairbeairt (Tarbert)	Aird Mheadhonach, Harris	aka Sgeotasaigh. Area: 0.19 sq miles (0.49 sq km). GR: NG185972
Scrot Mor	Caolas Shiolaigh (aka Sound of Shillay)	Baleshare, North Uist	One of the Monach Islands. GR: NF630603
Seaforth	Loch Seaforth (aka Shiphoirt)	Mhulaidh, Harris	See Eilean Shiphoirt.
Seana Chnoc	Pol Gainmhich	Great Bernera	GR: NB118433
Seana-chaisteal	The Little Minch	Wiay	GR: NF866449
Seildeim	Caolas Champaigh	Bearnaraigh Beag (aka Little Bernera)	GR: NB152408
Seumas Cleite	The Minch	Crosbost, Lewis	One of the Barkin Islands. GR: NB410234
Sgarbh Sgeir	Atlantic	Gabhsann bho Thuarth, Lewis	GR: NB447601
Sgarbhstac	Atlantic	Boreray	(G. = Cormorant Stack). GR: NA153044
Sgeir a' Bhuallt	Caolas Tharasaigh (aka Sound of Taransay)	Taranasay	GR: NG031989

Island name	Area	Nearest landmark	General information
Sgeir a' Chail	Sound of Harris	Aird Thormaid, North Uist	GR: NF967793
Sgeir a' Chais	An Caolas	Pabaigh Mor	GR: NB102387
Sgeir a' Chaise	Caolas Shodhaigh	Cliasmol, Harris	GR: NB075058
Sgeir a' Chlogaid	Caolas Shandraigh (aka Sound of Sandray)	Eorasdail, Vatersay	GR: NL650938
Sgeir a' Choin	Bagh nam Faoilean	Sanndabhaig, South Uist	GR: NF845438
Sgeir a' Chuan	Sound of Harris	Narstaigh	GR: NF983774
Sgeir a' Mhill	Atlantic	Rubha Mealabhaig, South Uist	GR: NF835127
Sgeir a Mhoil Mhoir	Camas Bostdh	Bearnaraigh Beag (aka Little Bernera)	GR: NB136409
Sgeir a' Mhurain	Caolas Champaigh	Bearnaraigh Beag (aka Little Bernera)	GR: NB149413
Sgeir an Daimh	The Little Minch	Leac Eascadail, Harris	GR: NG243988
Sgeir an Fheidh	Calaos Eiriosgaigh	Taobh a' Chaolais, South Uist	GR: NF788133
Sgeir an Fheidh	Atlantic	Triuirebheinn, South Uist	GR: NF832216
Sgeir an Leum Mhoir	Braigh Mor	Rubha Phlocrapoil, Harris	GR: NG193939
Sgeir an Rubha Mhoir	Caolas Honach	Rubha Mor, North Uist	GR: NF720661
Sgeir Bocaig	Caolas na Sgeire Leithe	Bhacsaigh (aka Vacsay)	GR: NB111374
Sgeir Chaise	Loch Baghasdail	Ceann a Deas Loch Baghasdail, South Uist	GR: NF789181
Sgeir Cheothaim	Caolas Monach	Calla Geodha, Benbecula	GR: NF774566
Sgeir Chrionain	Atlantic	Skate Point, Bernaray	GR: NL547805
Sgeir Chruaidh	Sound of Harris	Killegray	GR: NF990805
Sgeir Cnoc Easgann	Loch Fhleoideabhaigh	Fhleoideabhaigh, Harris	GR: NG101878
Sgeir Coillt	Atlantic	Dail bho Dheas, Lewis	GR: NB484628
Sgeir Cul an Rudha	Atlantic	Dun	GR: NF104971
Sgeir Dhearg	Pol Gainmhich	Aird Laimisadair, Lewis	GR: NB147436
Sgeir Dhomhnaill	Atlantic	Killegray	GR: NF995841
Sgeir Dhomhnuill	Atlantic	St Kilda	GR: NA105002
Sgeir Dhubh Mhor	Loch Rog	Fuaidh Mor	GR: NB128365
Sgeir Dreumasdail	Atlantic	Dreumasdal, South Uist	GR: NF747374
Sgeir Dubh	Atlantic	Ensay (aka Easaigh)	GR: NF960855
Sgeir Dubh Mor	Atlantic	Calarnais, North Uist	GR: NF753770
Sgeir Eoghainn	Atlantic	Breanais, Lewis	GR: NA981255
Sgeir Fail	Caolas Phabaigh (aka Sound of Pabbay)	Bhacsaigh (aka Vacsay)	GR: NB116377
Sgeir Fhadabhig	Sound of Harris	Killegray	GR: NF980823
Sgeir Fhiabhaig Tarras	Atlantic	Cradhlastadh, Lewis	GR: NB028351
Sgeir Fhiaclach Beag	Sea of the Hebrides	Rubha Bhruairnis, Barra	GR: NL732994
Sgeir Fhiaclach Mhor	Sea of the Hebrides	Rubha Bhruairnis, Barra	GR: NL737998
Sgeir Flod	Caolas na Sgeire Leithe	Bhacsaigh (aka Vacsay)	GR: NB114374
Sgeir Fraoich	Caolas a Tuath	Eilean Liubhaird	GR: NB380106
Sgeir Gallan	Atlantic	Gallan Head, Lewis	GR: NB049398
Sgeir Gheideim Fhlich	Camas Bostdh	Bearnaraigh Beag (aka Little Bernera)	GR: NB135417
Sgeir Ghlas	Loch Eireasort	Tabost, Lewis	GR: NB323200
Sgeir Ghlas	Loch An Tairbeairt (Tarbert)	Sgeotasaigh (aka Scotasay)	(G. = Pale Grey-green Skerry). GR: NG182970
Sgeir Ghlas	Caolas a Tuath	Eilean Liubhaird	GR: NB378107
Sgeir Ghlas	An Caolas	Pabaigh Beag	GR: NB100387
Sgeir Ghlas Bheag	Atlantic	Breanais, Lewis	GR: NA980260
Sgeir Ghlas na Roinne	Atlantic	Eilean Mhealasta	(G. = Grey Rock of the Seals). GR: NA982208
Sgeir Ghobhlach	Atlantic	Mealasta, Lewis	GR: NA981241
Sgeir Ghobhlach	Braigh Mor	Rubha Phlocrapoil, Harris	GR: NG189935
Sgeir in-ao	The Little Minch	Scalpay	GR: NG292919
Sgeir Leathann	Loch a Tuath	Drochaid Ghriais, Lewis	GR: NB502410
Sgeir Leum	Loch Sealg	Orasaigh, Lewis	GR: NB365108
Sgeir Liath	Atlantic	Allathasdal, Barra	GR: NF651032
Sgeir Liath	Caolas Bhatarsaigh	Rubha Glas, Barra	GR: NL649971
Sgeir Liath	Atlantic	Taranasay	GR: NB008018
Sgeir Liath	Caolas Honach	Hanglam, North Uist	GR: NF703683

Island name	Area	Nearest landmark	General information
Sgeir Liath	Atlantic	Mealasta, Lewis	GR: NA982237
Sgeir Liath	Atlantic	Aird Mheadhonach, Lewis	GR: NB017330
Sgeir Liath	Caolas na Sgeire Leithe	Pabaigh Mor	GR: NB107373
Sgeir Liath	Loch Rog	Fuaidh Mor	GR: NB133355
Sgeir Lithinis	Caolas Phabaigh (aka Sound of Pabbay)	Sandray	aka Sgeir Leehinish. GR: NL653900
Sgeir Mac Righ Lochlainn	Atlantic	Soay	GR: NA059008
Sgeir Mhic a' Ghobha	Sound of Shianti	Rubha Bhrolluim, Harris	One of the Shiant Islands (aka Eileanan Mora). GR: NG389983
Sgeir Mhic Tamain	The Little Minch	Rubha Shanndabhaig, South Uist	GR: NF853429
Sgeir Mhinig a' Mhuigh	Caolas Phabaigh (aka Sound of Pabbay)	Pabaigh Mor	GR: NB095383
Sgeir Mhinig a' Stigh	Caolas Phabaigh (aka Sound of Pabbay)	Pabaigh Mor	GR: NB095380
Sgeir Mhir Coma	Atlantic	Aird an t-Sruith, Harris	GR: NG004863
Sgeir Mhor	An Oitir Mhor	Beinn Bhaslain, Barra	GR: NF710048
Sgeir Mhor	Atlantic	Bernaray	GR: NL577796
Sgeir Mhor	Caolas Tharasaigh (aka Sound of Taransay)	Taranasay	GR: NG040998
Sgeir Mhor	Atlantic	Aird Bheag Bhragair, Lewis	GR: NB280501
Sgeir Mhor Bhalamais	The Little Minch	Gob Rubha Bhalamuis Bhig	GR: NB298006
Sgeir Mhuran	Atlantic	Ensay (aka Easaigh)	aka Sgeir Vuran. GR: NF964850
Sgeir Mianais	Sound of Shianti	Eilean an Taighe	One of the Shiant Islands (aka Eileanan Mora). GR: NG419961
Sgeir Mol Srupair	The Minch	Marbhig, Lewis	GR: NB420193
Sgeir na Cille	Caolas na Sgeire Leithe	Pabaigh Mor	GR: NB106377
Sgeir na Galla	An Caolas	Great Bernera	GR: NB111416
Sgeir na Geodha Ruaidhe	Camas Leire Geodha	Eilean Mhealasta	GR: NA973218
Sgeir na h-Adaig	Loch Rog	Fuaidh Mor	GR: NB137348
Sgeir na h-Aon Chaorach	Caolas Phabaigh (aka Sound of Pabbay)	Bhacsaigh (aka Vacsay)	(G. = Lone Sheep Rock). GR: NB116376
Sgeir na h-Aon Chaorach	Caolas na Sgeire Leithe	Pabaigh Mor	GR: NB107378
Sgeir na h-Aon Chaorach	Caolas Champaigh	Bearnaraigh Beag (aka Little Bernera)	GR: NB149417
Sgeir na h-Aon Chaorach	Atlantic	Rubha Thol, Lewis	GR: NB177409
Sgeir na h-Eigheach	The Little Minch	Gob Rubha Bhalamuis Bhig	GR: NB289004
Sgeir na Muice	Sea of the Hebrides	Creag Mhor, Vatersay	GR: NL671951
Sgeir na Muice	Sound of Harris	Renish Point, Harris	GR: NG038827
Sgeir na Parlamaid	Sound of Harris	Aird Thormaid, North Uist	GR: NF964765
Sgeir na Ruideag	Sound of Shianti	Eilean Mhuire	One of the Shiant Islands (aka Eileanan Mora). GR: NG431981
Sgeir na Snathaid	Caolas Honach	Rubha Mor, North Uist	GR: NF715662
Sgeir nan Caorach	Loch Sealg	Eilean Liubhaird	GR: NB371100
Sgeir nan Cliabh	Loch Rog an Ear	Aird Laimisadair, Lewis	GR: NB198355
Sgeir nan Each	Loch Eireasort	Cabharstadh, Lewis	GR: NB375208
Sgeir nan Sgarbh	Caolas a Tuath	Eilean Liubhaird/Lewis	
Sgeir nan Sgarbh	Atlantic	St Kilda	GR: NF112993
Sgeir nan Sgarbh	The Little Minch	Gob Rubha Bhalamuis Bhig	GR: NB303008
Sgeir nan Soaoidhean	Pol Gainmhich	Great Bernera	GR: NB120419
Sgeir nan Uibhein	Atlantic	Mingulay	GR: NL577850
Sgeir Oireabhal	Atlantic	Caisteal Odair, North Uist	GR: NF735770
Sgeir Riabhach	Loch Stocinis	Eilean Stocinis (aka Stockinish)	GR: NG132907

Island name	Area	Nearest landmark	General information
Sgeir Righinn	Atlantic	Gallan Head, Lewis	(G. = Princess Skerry). One of Na h-Eileanan Flannach (the Flannan Isles). GR: NA725451
Sgeir Ruadh	Loch Rog	Fuaidh Mor	GR: NB135350
Sgeir Sgianailt	Loch Rog an Ear	Aird na Moine, Lewis	GR: NB201367
Sgeir Sheilibhig	Atlantic	Cradhlastadh, Lewis	GR: NB024341
Sgeir Sine	Sound of Harris	Aird Thormaid, North Uist	GR: NF975789
Sgeir Tanais	The Minch	Marbhig, Lewis	GR: NB420191
Sgeir Tarcall	Loch a Siar	Beinn Dhubh, Harris	GR: NB082018
Sgeir Thal	The Little Minch	Rubha Briodog, Harris	GR: NB242011
Sgeir Toman	Atlantic	Gallan Head, Lewis	One of Na h-Eileanan Flannach (the Flannan Isles). GR: NA725452
Sgeir Uaine a' Bhain Bhig	Atlantic	Eilean Mhealasta	GR: NA973213
Sgeir Urgha	Loch An Tairbeairt (Tarbert)	Carragraich, Harris	GR: NG182987
Sgeir Vuran	Atlantic	Ensay (aka Easaigh)	aka Sgeir Mhuran. GR: NF964850
Sgeirean a' Bhaigh	Sound of Shianti	Garbh Eilean	One of the Shiant Islands (aka Eileanan Mora). GR: NG415989
Sgeirean an Arbhair	The Minch	Crosbost, Lewis	One of the Barkin Isles. GR: NB409241
Sgeirean Fiaclach	Sea of the Hebrides	Maol Domhnaich (aka Muldoanich)	GR: NL678945
Sgeirean Mas a' Mhill	Caolas Shandraigh (aka Sound of Sandray)	Am Meall, Vatersay	GR: NL658943
Sgeirean Thigaborra	Loch Barraglom	Tobhtara, Great Bernera	GR: NB181340
Sgeirean Thindealan	Loch Barraglom	Lundal, Lewis	GR: NB185334
Sgeirisleum	Bagh a Tuath	Bruairnis, Barra	GR: NF741029
Sgor na Lice Moire	Atlantic	Rona	GR: HW815333
Sheader Rocks	Caolas Shandraigh (aka Sound of Sandray)	Sandray	See Creagan Sheadair.
Sheileam	Sea of the Hebrides	Rubha Bhruairnis, Barra	GR: NF736006
Shelter Rock	Caolas Bhearnaraigh	Leac a' Langaich, Bernaray	GR: NL562806
Shiaram Beag	Caolas Phabaigh (aka Sound of Pabbay)	Cnip, Lewis	aka Siaram Beag. GR: NB104369
Shiaram Mor	Caolas Phabaigh (aka Sound of Pabbay)	Cnip, Lewis	aka Siaram Mor. GR: NB103367
Shillay	Atlantic	Pabbay	aka Siolaigh (G. = Seal). Area: 0.18 sq miles (0.47 sq km). GR: NF880912
Shillay	Caolas Shiolaigh (aka Sound of Shillay)	Baleshare, North Uist	One of the Monach Islands. GR: NF593628
Shivinish	Caolas Shiolaigh (aka Sound of Shillay)	Baleshare, North Uist	aka Shibhinis. One of the Monach Islands. Area: 0.11 sq miles (0.28 sq km). GR: NF628620
Siaram Bostadh	Caolas Champaigh	Great Bernera	GR: NB132407
Siolaigh	Atlantic	Pabbay	(G. = Seal). See Shillay.
Siolaigh Bheag	Atlantic	Siolaigh (aka Shillay)	See Little Shillay.
Siolaigh Mor	Loch Sgiopoirt	Loch Sgiopoirt, South Uist	See Big Shillay.
Siusaigh	Bagh nam Faoilean	Griomasaigh, Benbecula	GR: NF827468
Sleicham	Atlantic	Ensay (aka Easaigh)	GR: NF994850
Slugan	Caolas Honach	Baleshare, North Uist	GR: NF768635
Snagaras	Caolas Theilisigh (aka Sound of Hellisay)	Bruairnis, Barra	GR: NF753028
Snuasimul	Sea of the Hebrides	Creag Mhor, Vatersay	GR: NL669953
Soay	Atlantic	St Kilda	aka Soaigh. See separate entry.
Soay Beag	Caolas Shaoidh	Aird Thurnais, Harris	aka Soaigh Beag. GR: NB055059
Soay Mor	Caolas Shaoidh	Aird Thurnais, Harris	aka Soaigh Mor. Area: 0.17 sq miles (0.45 sq km). GR: NB062050
Soay Stac	Atlantic	St Kilda	aka Stac Shoaigh. GR: NA073013
Solon Beag	Atlantic	Mingulay	GR: NL577848
Solon Mor	Atlantic	Mingulay	GR: NL577840
Soray	Atlantic	Gallan Head, Lewis	aka Soraidh (G. = Eastward Isle). One of Na h-Eileanan Flannach (the Flannan Isles). GR: NA725454

Island name	Area	Nearest landmark	General information
South Uist	Sea of the Hebrides	Rubha Hunish, Skye	aka Uibhist a Deas. Beinn Mhor at 2034ft (620m) is the highest point. Flora MacDonald was born on South Uist. Area: 123.92 sq miles (320.94 sq km). Population: 1818. GR: NF799344
Spleadhairs	Sound of Harris	Aird Thormaid, North Uist	GR: NF955776
Sromaigh	Beul an Toim	Baleshare, North Uist	GR: NF800581
Sromaigh	Loch Mhic Phail	Aird Innis, North Uist	GR: NF938747
Stac a' Chaorainn	Loch An Tairbeairt (Tarbert)	Sgeotasaigh (aka Scotasay)	(G. = Stack of the Rowan Tree). GR: NG194970
Stac an Armin	Atlantic	Boreray	(O.N. = Stack of the Warrior). The highest monolith in the British Isles at 643ft (196m). Also the site of the death of the last great auk in July 1840, beaten to death by two St Kildans. GR: NA151063
Stac an Tuill	Pol Gainmhich	Great Bernera	GR: NB122422
Stac Biorach	Atlantic	St Kilda	GR: NA073014
Stac Dona	Atlantic	Soay	GR: NA070010
Stac Lee	Atlantic	Boreray	(O.N. = Sheltered Stack). GR: NA141049
Stac nam Baig	Pol Gainmhich	Great Bernera	GR: NB115434
Stac nam Faolieag	Loch Stocinis	Eilean Stocinis	GR: NG137894
Stac Thabhaidh	The Minch	Beinn Mhor, Lewis	One of the Barkin Isles. GR: NB421225
Staca Leathann	Atlantic	Islibhig, Lewis	GR: NA981282
Stacanan Neideaclibh	Atlantic	Gallan Head, Lewis	GR: NB057383
Stangraidh	The Minch	Cromor, Lewis	GR: NB410220
Stangram	Atlantic	Traigh Bhalaigh, North Uist	GR: NF778751
Steisaigh	Loch Euphort	Loch Euphort, North Uist	GR: NF851648
Steisay	Bagh nam Faoilean	Wiay	aka Steiseigh. GR: NF852444
Stiolamair	Loch An Tairbeairt (Tarbert)	Scalpay	aka Stilamair. GR: NG219945
Stiughay	Loch An Tairbeairt (Tarbert)	Scalpay	aka Stiughaigh. GR: NG201963
Stiughay na Leum	Loch An Tairbeairt (Tarbert)	Scalpay	aka Stiughaigh na Leum. GR: NG201960
Stockay	Caolas Monach	Baleshare, North Uist	aka Stocaidh. One of the Monach Islands. GR: NF660630
Stockinish Island	The Little Minch	Cliuthar, Harris	See Eilean Stocinis.
Stromaigh	Caolas Honach	Cladach Chireboist, North Uist	GR: NF768656
Stromay	Atlantic	Bideinean, Harris	aka Sromaigh. GR: NF988886
Stuley	Sea of the Hebrides	Caolas Stulaigh (aka Stuley Sound), South Uist	aka Stulaigh. Area: 0.17 sq miles (0.45 sq km).GR: NF830234
Suam	Atlantic	Leverburgh, Harris	aka Suem. GR: NF999859
Sula Sgeir	Atlantic	Butt of Lewis, Lewis	(O.N. = Gannet Skerry). GR: HW620305
Sunam	Atlantic	Leverburgh, Harris	GR: NG010857
Sunamul	Beul an Toim	An Tom, Benbecula	GR: NF803570
Sursay	Sound of Harris	Bhotarsaig	aka Sursaigh. GR: NF958760
Tabhaidh Bheag	The Minch	Beinn Mhor, Lewis	One of the Barkin Isles. GR: NB418229
Tabhaidh Mhor	The Minch	Beinn Mhor, Lewis	One of the Barkin Isles. GR: NB422228
Tahay	Sound of Harris	Tobha Beag, North Uist	aka Taghaigh. Area: 0.2 sq miles (0.53 sq km). GR: NF962750
Taigh Iamain	Bagh nam Faoilean	Sanndabhaig, South Uist	GR: NF839437
Taitealach	Atlantic	Leverburgh, Harris	GR: NG017851
Tamna	Pol Gainmhich	Great Bernera	GR: NB122411
Tanaraidh	The Minch	Eilean Chaluim Chille	GR: NB396222
Tannaraidh	The Minch	Crosbost, Lewis	One of the Barkin Isles. GR: NB402235
Taransay	Caolas Tharasaigh (aka Sound of Taransay)	Aird Niosaboist, Harris	aka Tarasaigh. Uninhabited from 1942 – except for brief occupation by a family in the 1960s and 1970s – until 2000 when it was the location of the BBC series *Castaway 2000*. Permitted to issue its own postage stamps. Area: 5.7 sq miles (14.75 sq km). GR: NB020010
Tathanais	Bagh nam Faoilean	Sanndabhaig, South Uist	GR: NF836446
Thairteamul	Atlantic	Ronais, Eriskay	See Hartamul.
Thalta Sgeir	Caolas Champaigh	Cealasaigh	GR: NB143421

Island name	Area	Nearest landmark	General information
Thamarasaigh	Loch An Tairbeairt (Tarbert)	Scalpay	See Hamarsay.
Thamarasaigh	Loch nam Madadh (aka Loch Maddy)	Lochmaddy, North Uist	See Hamersay.
Thamna Sgeir	Atlantic	Butt of Lewis, Lewis	GR: HW623307
Theisteam	Sound of Harris	Killegray	See Hestem.
Theistearmuil	Bagh nam Faoilean	Creag Ghoraidh, Benbecula	GR: NF790485
Theiliseigh	An Oitir Mhor	Aird Mhor, Barra	See Hellisay.
Theisgeir	Sound of Harris	Killegray	See Heisker.
Theisgeir a-staigh	Caolas Mhiughlaigh (aka Sound of Mingulay)	Pabbay	See Inner Heisker.
Theisgeir a-mulgh	Caolas Mhiughlaigh (aka Sound of Mingulay)	Pabbay	See Outer Heisker.
Thernatraigh	Sound of Harris	Tobha Beag, South Uist	See Hermetray.
Thuisgeirean	Caolas Monach	Baleshare, North Uist	GR: NF572645
Thula Geddha	Atlantic	Caisteal Odair, North Uist	GR: NF742767
Thulmatraigh	Sound of Harris	Bhacasaigh	See Hulmatray.
Tolm	Atlantic	Cradhlastadh, Lewis	GR: NB034335
Tom	Atlantic	Carnais, Lewis	GR: NB029331
Torogaigh	Atlantic	Traigh Bhalaigh, North Uist	GR: NF779748
Torogay	Sound of Harris	Aird Ma-Ruibhe, Bernaray	aka Torogaigh. GR: NF920788
Traillisker	An Caolas Fuideach (aka Sound of Fuday)	Mullach Neacall, Fuday	aka Traillisgeir. GR: NF725089
Trathasam	Caolas Phabaigh (aka Sound of Pabbay)	Bhacsaigh (aka Vacsay)	GR: NB113366
Treanay	Loch Euphort	Ceithinis, North Uist	aka Treanaigh. GR: NF891638
Triallabreac	Bagh nam Faoilean	Carnan-aird-Fuidhaigh, Benbecula	GR: NF850462
Triallabreac Mor	Beul an Toim	Gramasdail, Benbecula	GR: NF812568
Triasamol	Atlantic	Cradhlastadh, Lewis	GR: NB032337
Trolaisgeir	Atlantic	Gleann, South Uist	GR: NF722275
Trollaman	Sound of Harris	Tobha Beag, North Uist	GR: NF961745
Uibhist a Deas	Sea of the Hebrides	Rubha Hunish, Skye	See South Uist.
Uibhist a Tuath	The Little Minch	Rubha Hunish, Skye	See North Uist.
Uineasan	Sea of the Hebrides	Creag Mhor, Vatersay	GR: NL665956
Vacam	Sound of Harris	Killegray	See Eilean Bhacam.
Vaccasay	Sound of Harris	Tobha Beag, North Uist	See Bhacasaigh.
Vacsay	Caolas Phabaigh (aka Sound of Pabbay)	Cnip, Lewis	See Bhacsaigh.
Vallay	Atlantic	Calarnais, North Uist	See Bhalaigh.
Vatersay	Atlantic	Beinn Tangabhal, Barra	Linked to Barra by a causeway completed in 1990. Prior to this cattle being taken to market had to swim across the Sound of Vatersay; after a prize bull, Bertie, drowned in the attempt in 1986, the resultant outcry led to the building of the causeway. Area: 3.68 sq miles (9.53 sq km). Population: 94. GR: NL630960
Votersay	Sound of Harris	Sromaigh	See Bhotarsaigh.
Votersay	Sound of Harris	Bhotarsaig	GR: NF957500
Vuia Beag	Loch Rog	Gob Sgrithir, Lewis	aka Fuaigh Beag. GR: NB122335
Vuia Mor	Loch Rog	Great Bernera	aka Fuaigh Mor. Area: 0.32 sq miles (0.84 sq km). GR: NB130350
Wiay	The Little Minch	Benbecula	See Fuidhaigh.

WALES

The Principality of Wales is bounded by England to the east, the Bristol Channel to the south and the Irish Sea to the west and north. The strait between Dyfed and Wexford in Ireland is known as St George's Channel and the inlet of the Irish Sea bordering Gwynedd and Dyfed is Cardigan Bay.

The death of Llywelyn the Last in 1282 led to the annexation of Wales by Edward I of England. Edward's ring of impressive stone castles assisted the domination of Wales, and he eventually crowned his conquest by giving the title Prince of Wales to his son and heir in 1301. The Statute of Rhuddlan of 1284 divided parts of Wales into the counties of Anglesey, Merioneth, Caernarvon, Denbighshire and Flintshire, which were created out of the remnants of Llywelyn's kingdom of Gwynedd. The statute also introduced the English common law system. Owain Glyndwr led a rebellion in the early 15th century and kept control of Wales for a few years before the English crown reasserted its authority. The Statute remained in effect until Henry VIII's Laws in Wales Act of 1536, which fully incorporated Wales into England.

In the 20th century, Wales saw a revival of its national status. Plaid Cymru was formed in 1925, seeking greater autonomy from the rest of the United Kingdom. In 1955, the term England and Wales became common for describing the area to which English Law applied, and Cardiff was proclaimed as capital. Plaid Cymru won its first seat at Westminster in 1966 and devolution became an item on the political agenda. A referendum on devolution in 1979 resulted in a 'no' vote, but a second referendum in 1997 resulted in a 'yes' vote by a narrow margin and led to the Welsh Assembly being established in Cardiff. The National Assembly for Wales (Cynulliad Cenedlaethol Cymru) was formed in 1999, with powers to amend primary legislation from the UK Parliament. These powers were widened by the Government of Wales Act 2006, which took effect after the 2007 Welsh Assembly election. Since 1984 the conservation of the built heritage of Wales has been the responsibility of CADW: Welsh Historic Monuments. Cadw (to keep) is the Welsh equivalent of English Heritage, Historic Scotland, Northern Ireland Environment and Ireland's Office of Public Works.

The Welsh motto is *Cymru am byth* (Wales for ever) and the national anthem is 'Hen Wlad Fy Nhadau' (Land of My Fathers). Approximately 20 per cent of the population are Welsh speakers although English is predominantly the first language.

St David (c.500–89) is the patron saint of Wales and unlike the patron saints of the other countries of Britain and Ireland, St David was a native of the country he represents. St David's Day is celebrated on 1 March, the day of his death. Although the Flag of David (gold cross on a black field) is a popular Welsh ceremonial flag, the official national flag of Wales is the Red Dragon (Y Ddraig Goch), consisting of a horizontal bicolour of white over green charged with a red dragon passant.

Wales lies between 53° 26' 4" and 51° 22' 3" N. latitude and between 2° 45' and 5° 20' W. longitude. The northernmost point of Wales is Middle Mouse Island, off Anglesey, and the most southerly point is Flat Holm, Cardiff. The most westerly point is in Grassholm, Pembrokeshire, and the easternmost point of Wales is Lady Park Wood, near Monmouth.

The history and geography of Wales is described within the overviews of the eight regions into which I have divided the country and requires no further explanation here. The population and area figures listed below include the 22 existing unitary authorities, split into the eight traditional counties. A reconciliation to the 2001 Census is included at the back of the book.

Wales population summaries

(See 2001 Census Reconciliation)

	Population			Area	
	male	*female*	*total*	*sq miles*	*sq km*
Clwyd	232,321	247,410	479,731	1122	2905
Dyfed	174,750	187,164	361,914	2230	5775
Gwent	267,789	284,639	552,428	599	1551
Gwynedd	88,377	95,295	183,672	1254	3246
Mid Glamorgan	201,892	214,680	416,572	304	786
Powys	62,493	63,861	126,354	2000	5181
South Glamorgan	203,117	221,528	424,645	182	470
West Glamorgan	173,043	184,726	357,769	316	819
Total	1,403,782	1,499,303	2,903,085	8007	20,733

Clwyd

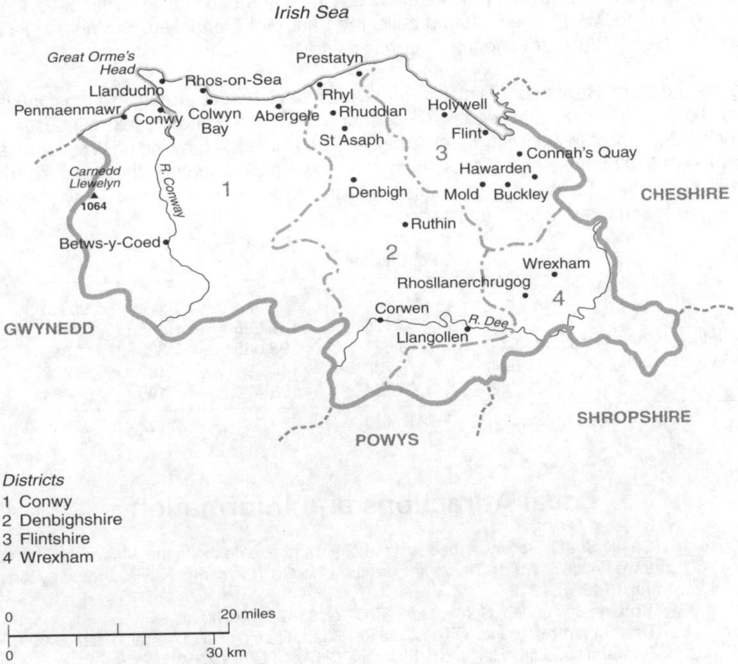
Irish Sea
Great Orme's Head
Llandudno
Rhos-on-Sea
Penmaenmawr
Conwy
Colwyn Bay
Abergele
Prestatyn
Rhyl
Rhuddlan
St Asaph
Holywell
Flint
Connah's Quay
Hawarden
Mold
Buckley
Denbigh
Ruthin
Carnedd Llewelyn
1064
R. Conway
Betws-y-Coed
Wrexham
Rhosllanerchrugog
Corwen
R. Dee
Llangollen
1
2
3
4
CHESHIRE
GWYNEDD
SHROPSHIRE
POWYS
Districts
1 Conwy
2 Denbighshire
3 Flintshire
4 Wrexham
0
20 miles
0
30 km

Clwyd, encompassing the unitary authorities of Flintshire, Wrexham County Borough, Denbighshire and Conwy, is bordered to the west by Gwynedd, to the south by Powys, to the southeast and east by the English counties of Shropshire and Cheshire, and to the north by the Irish Sea. Its main geographical features are part of the Snowdonia National Park (which is mostly in Gwynedd), the rivers Clwyd, Conwy and Dee and the Clwydian Range, a chain of hills in the northeast of the region. The north coast has fine stretches of beach at Penmaenmawr, Prestatyn, Llandudno and Rhos on Sea. Major towns in the region include Llangollen (famous for its International Eisteddfod), Conwy and Wrexham.

Clwyd was formed in 1974 under the Local Government Act 1972 as a merger of the administrative county of Flintshire and a large part of Denbighshire, along with Edeyrnion Rural District from Merionethshire. It was divided into six districts: Alyn & Deeside, Colwyn, Delyn, Glyndwr, Rhuddlan and Wrexham. In 1996 it was split into the unitary authorities of Flintshire, Wrexham County Borough, Denbighshire, and parts of Conwy (the remainder being part of Gwynedd) and Powys. In 2003, the remainder of Conwy was incorporated into Clwyd. The postal addresses of much of Conwy rather confusingly remain as Gwynedd but are administered separately and distinctly.

The area has been settled since at least the Neolithic period. Settlement during the Bronze Age and Iron Age is evidenced by the discovery of Brymbo Man near Wrexham in 1958, the existence of copper mines on the Great Orme above Llandudno and the presence of many hill forts in the Clwydian Range. The Ordovices, who occupied Gwynedd and the south of Clwyd, were defeated c.AD 70 by the Roman forces, led by Agricola, and never recovered their previous strength. Flintshire and Denbighshire were the homelands of the Deceangli, who appear to have been more cooperative with the Romans than their neighbours. Christianity was introduced into the area in the 4th and 5th centuries. The region remained largely independent from England during the Saxon period, although this did not prevent the Welsh princes from involving themselves in Anglo-Saxon politics. In 1055 Gruffydd ap Llewelyn gave aid to outlawed Earl Aelfgar in trying to regain the latter's earldom and attacked and burnt Hereford. Gruffydd's palace at Rhuddlan was in turn destroyed in 1062 and he was killed while on the run from Harold Godwinson's army a year later. Following the Norman conquest of England the independence of the Welsh and their princes was gradually eroded. An attack on Hawarden Castle by Dafydd ap Gruffydd in 1282 led to a country-wide uprising against the English; in response Edward I invaded North Wales, set up a ring of strong castles and named his newborn son Edward, Prince of Wales.

Several of the traditional 'Seven Wonders of Wales', as delineated in a late 18th or early 19th century rhyme, are in Clwyd – the Gresford bells, the bridge at Llangollen, St Winefride's Well, the steeple of St Giles', Wrexham and the Overton yew trees.

During the Industrial Revolution, Flintshire and Denbighshire were among the most industrialised regions of the country with coal deposits, copper and zinc mining and the textile industry driven by the abundant supply of fast-flowing water. Other industries include brewing (in Wrexham), steel and brick making. Most of these enterprises suffered during the 20th century; the major manufacturing industries still in the area include aerospace, steel and paper making. The majority of employment is now in the agricultural, tourism and services sectors.

Clwyd	**Population**			**Area**	
	male	*female*	*total*	*sq miles*	*sq km*
Conwy	52,161	57,435	109,596	435	1126
Denbighshire	44,544	48,521	93,065	323	837
Flintshire	72,894	75,700	148,594	169	438
Wrexham	62,722	65,754	128,476	195	504
Total	232,321	247,410	479,731	1122	2905

Local Attractions and Information

Aberconwy House
Castle Street, Conwy. A medieval merchant's house dating to the 14th century, possibly the oldest town house in Wales. The rooms are furnished in 15th century style. Owned by the National Trust. Tel: 01492 592246.

Administrative headquarters
Conwy: Bodlondeb, Conwy LL32 8DU. Tel: 01492 574000.
Denbighshire: Council Offices, Station Road, Ruthin LL15 1AT. Tel: 01824 706000.
Flintshire: County Hall, Mold, Flintshire CH7 6NB. Tel: 01352 752121.
Wrexham: The Guildhall, Wrexham LL11 1WF. Tel: 01978 292000.

Basingwerk Abbey
1 mile (1.6km) northeast of Holywell. The remains of a prosperous Cistercian abbey founded in the 12th century as a daughter house of the abbey at Savigny in Normandy. Its English connections meant that it avoided suffering overmuch during the English conquest of the north of Wales. The abbey was abandoned following its dissolution in the 1530s.

Bersham Colliery Mining Museum
Bersham, 2 miles (3km) southwest of Wrexham. A small mining museum on the Bersham industrial estate, based on the headgear and winding gear of Shaft No. 2 of Bersham Colliery. Located in the Denbighshire coalfield, the colliery's first shaft was sunk in 1868, and Bersham was the last working colliery in the coalfield before it was closed down in 1986. It is now in the care of Wrexham County Borough Council and Bersham Colliery Trust.

Bersham Ironworks
Bersham, 2 miles (3km) southwest of Wrexham. Bersham Ironworks was opened during the Civil War but expanded rapidly during the Industrial Revolution under the ownership of the Wilkinson family. John Wilkinson invented a process, driven by Watt steam engines, capable of accurately boring cannon and cylinders from solid cast metal, and Bersham cannon were sold worldwide. However, the ironworks closed in 1812 shortly after Wilkinson's death. The site was excavated 1987–91. Surviving buildings include the cannon foundry, a boring mill, and the excavated remains of a wooden railway and a furnace. An industrial heritage centre on the site is housed in the former Bersham School, open 1874–1961, and explores the area's industrial history, including the coal mine, ironworks and paper mills.

Bodelwyddan Castle
Bodelwyddan, 4 miles (6km) south of Rhyl. A Gothic style castle built 1830–52 for Sir John Hay Williams on the site of an earlier manor house owned by the Williams family since the late 17th century. During World War I it was used as a recuperation hospital. The house was then taken over by Lowther College, a private girls' school, which was based here until 1982, and about which there is an exhibition. Much of the original Victorian layout and décor was restored during the 1980s; the Grade II* listed building now houses not only collections from the National Portrait Gallery but also furniture from the Victoria & Albert Museum and sculpture from the Royal Academy of Arts. The 260 acres (105ha) of grounds include formal gardens and woodland, as well as a series of practice trenches dug during World War I by recruits at nearby Kimmel Park Training Camp. Other features include a maze. Tel: 01745 584060.

Bodnant Garden
1 mile (1.6km) northeast of Tal-y-Cafn, 4 miles (6km) southeast of Colwyn Bay. A world-famous garden begun in 1875 by the Aberconway family and covering 80 acres (32ha) above the River Conwy. Plant collections include rhododendrons, azaleas, magnolias, camellias, clematis and hydrangeas; specimen trees include Californian redwood, Oregon Douglas fir and dawn redwood. The upper garden features Italianate terraces, herbaceous borders, rose gardens and formal lawns, while the lower garden includes a wild garden and woodland valley with a stream. Owned by the National Trust since 1949. Tel: 01492 650460.

Britain's Smallest House Quayside, Conwy. A tiny 'one up, one down' house built in the gap between two terraces. Although it only measures 6ft (1.8m) wide and 10ft (3m) high, its last occupant is said to have been 6ft 3in (1.9m) tall fisherman Robert Jones. Dating to the 16th century, it was left unoccupied in May 1900 after being condemned because of its lack of toilet facilities. Tel: 01492 593429.

Brymbo Man In August 1958 the capstone of a burial chamber was uncovered 1ft (0.3m) below the surface by workmen digging a pipe-laying trench in Brymbo, 3 miles (5km) northwest of Wrexham. Excavation revealed a stone cist under the capstone containing part of the skeleton of a man, accompanied by a small pot and a flint knife; these items allowed the burial to be dated to the early Bronze Age, c.1600 BC. It is estimated that Brymbo Man, as the buried figure became known, was 5ft 8in (1.73m) tall and around 35 years old when he died; a reconstruction of his face, based on the surviving portions of the skull, is displayed in Wrexham Museum.

Bryn Eisteddfod 1/2 mile (0.8km) northeast of Llansanfraid Glan Conwy, 2 miles (3km) east of Conwy. A series of period gardens above the River Conwy, including an 18th century formal garden, a 19th century kitchen garden and a 1920s arboretum.

Caer Drewyn 1 mile (1.6km) northwest of Carrog, 7 1/2 miles (12km) west of Llangollen. An Iron Age hill fort overlooking the River Dee, with evidence of occupation during the medieval period. Unlike many such forts, there are the remains of stone walls in addition to the usual multivallate ditch and bank construction.

Caergwrle Castle Caergwrle, 5 miles (8km) northwest of Wrexham. The remains of a castle built by Dafydd ap Gruffydd c.1278 on land given to him by Edward I. Dafydd used it as a base for his attack on an English garrison, leading to an invasion by Edward I in 1282. Probably unfinished, it fell into ruin after being slighted to prevent its use by the English.

Castell Dinas Bran 1 mile (1.6km) northeast of Llangollen. The scant remains of a castle located on a levelled hilltop and built on the site of an Iron Age hill fort and an earlier fortification. Built by Gruffydd II ap Madog in the 1260s, it fell to English forces in 1277 and was burned down, finally being abandoned in 1283. It has been suggested as a possible resting place for the Holy Grail.

Chirk Castle Chirk, 8 miles (13km) south of Wrexham. Originally completed in 1310 by Roger Mortimer on the site of an earlier motte and bailey castle founded in the mid 12th century. The interior was later remodelled several times. Occupied during its early history by Sir William Stanley and later by Robert Dudley, Earl of Leicester, until 1588, it was bought in 1595 by the Myddleton family, who have remained in residence ever since. It sustained damage during the Civil War but was restored and extended; the state rooms were redesigned by Joseph Turner in the 1770s. The 18th century parklands, designed by William Emes, feature the thatched Hawk House plus woodland walks and a lime tree avenue. Offa's Dyke also runs through the park. The property has been maintained by the National Trust since 1981. Tel: 01691 777701.

Clwydian Range A chain of hills rising to the east of the Vale of Clwyd and running for 22 miles (35km) northwest of Llangollen. The area covers 62 sq miles (160 sq km) and is a designated Area of Outstanding Natural Beauty. Its highest point is Moel Famau at 1817ft (554m). See also Moel Famau Country Park.

Coleshill Castle 1 mile (1.6km) west of Flint. Aka Hen Blas. The remains of an earthwork which may have supported a fortified manor house in the 13th century.

Conwy Castle Rose Hill Street, Conwy. The substantial, impressive and well-preserved ruins of one of Edward I's ring of castles in North Wales. Built 1283–92 on a rock outcrop, it was designed by the king's military architect, Master James of St George, with two wards each bounded by four towers. The castle survived a siege by Madog ap Llywelyn in 1295 but in 1403 fell by deception to the forces of Owain Glyndwr. Described as 'utterlie decayed' in 1609, the castle was sold to Lord Conway in 1627. Having been refortified by the Archbishop of York during the Civil War, it was taken by Major-General Mytton in 1646; eventually abandoned after 1655, it was left to fall into disrepair. Although now ruined, the castle retains its medieval town walls. It now forms part of a UNESCO World Heritage Site along with Edward I's castles at Beaumaris, Caernarfon and Harlech (see Gwynedd). Now owned by CADW.

Conwy RSPB 1/2 mile (0.8km) south of Llandudno Junction. RSPB reserve located on the eastern bank of the Conwy Estuary and created in 1995 on the former construction site of the Conwy Tunnel. Consisting of two large pools surrounded by mudflats, saltmarsh, reedbeds, scrub and marshland, the reserve provides a habitat for a wide range of bird species including black-tailed godwit, lapwing, reed warbler, shelduck, skylark and water rail. Tel: 01492 584091.

Conwy Suspension Bridge Built by Thomas Telford and completed in 1826 to replace the ferry crossing of the Conwy Estuary. It stands next to the castle and mirrors some of its architectural features. The tollhouse on the bridge has been restored and is furnished in period style. The bridge and tollhouse are in the care of the National Trust. Tel: 01492 573282.

Deganwy Castle Deganwy, 1 mile (1.6km) south of Llandudno. The scant remains of a 13th century castle built by Llywelyn the Great on a hilltop overlooking Conwy Sands. Excavations in the 1960s revealed evidence of Roman occupation and an 11th century Norman fortification. The castle was slighted by the Welsh in 1241 to prevent it falling into English hands. Partially rebuilt by the English under Henry III in the 1250s, it was captured and abandoned by Llywelyn ap Gruffydd in 1263.

Denbigh Castle Castle Hill, Denbigh. The ruins of a castle built by Master James of St George for Henry de Lacy on a hilltop in 1282 on the site of an earlier Welsh fortification. The settlement of Denbigh was enclosed by town walls at the same time. The castle had an unusual triple polygonal towered gatehouse. Construction was disrupted by an attack in 1294 and was not completed until the early 14th century. The castle survived sieges in the 15th century and was garrisoned during the Civil War by Royalist troops before being captured after a long siege. After this it fell into decay. Now maintained by CADW.

Dolwyddelan Castle $^{3}/_{4}$ mile (1.2km) west of Dolwyddelan, 5 miles (8km) southwest of Betws-y-Coed. The ruins of a castle located on a rocky ridge and originally founded c.1170 by Iorwerth Trwyndwn. Completed in the early 13th century, it had two towers linked by a curtain wall. It has been mooted as the birthplace of Llewelyn ap Iorwerth (Llewelyn the Great), although given the dates he is more likely to have been born at nearby Tomen Castell, of which no trace remains. Dolwyddelan Castle was captured by Edward I in 1283, but was abandoned in favour of more coastal defences. The castle was reoccupied briefly in the 15th century. Having fallen into disrepair, it was partially restored by Lord Willoughby de Eresby in the 1840s.

Dyserth Castle $^{1}/_{2}$ mile (0.8km) north of Dyserth, 2 miles (3km) south of Prestatyn. The site of a 13th century English castle built in the 1240s by Henry III and abandoned in the 1260s, having been destroyed by Llywelyn ap Gruffydd (Llywelyn the Last) in 1263. The ruined walls were demolished during quarrying in the 19th century, and only banks and ditches now remain.

Eisteddfod Festival of literature, music and performance, possibly dating to 1176 (see entry for Cardigan Castle in Dyfed). The prizes awarded to professional Welsh Bards were a miniature silver chair to the successful poet, a silver crwth to the winning fiddler, a silver tongue to the best singer, and a tiny silver harp to the best harpist. Eisteddfods (derived from the Welsh word *eistedd*, meaning 'to sit') were subsequently held at Carmarthen in 1451 and Caerwys in 1568 and were revived at Corwen by Thomas Jones in 1789. The public were allowed in to this event for the first time and this proved very successful. The first *Gorsedd* (enthronement of the Great Bard) was held at Primrose Hill, London, in 1792 and in 1858 John Williams ab Ithel held a 'National' Eisteddfod complete with Gorsedd in Llangollen. The first true National Eisteddfod organised by the National Eisteddfod Council was held in Denbigh in 1860. The National Eisteddfod of Wales is held annually over eight days in the first week of August, venues usually alternating between North and South Wales. The International Eisteddfod, inaugurated in 1947, is held annually in Llangollen in July.

Eliseg's Pillar $^{1}/_{2}$ mile (0.8km) north of Pentrefelin, 2 miles (3km) north of Llangollen. The shaft of a Celtic cross commemorating Eliseg, the last king of Powys, located near Valle Crucis Abbey (see separate entry). The remainder of the cross is believed to have been destroyed during the Civil War. The original inscription naming Eliseg can no longer be seen. The cross was re-erected in 1779 and is now protected by railings.

Erddig Castle 1 mile (1.6km) southwest of Wrexham. The site of a motte and bailey castle, possibly dating to the 12th century, on the Afon Clywedog.

Erddig Hall 1 mile (1.6km) southwest of Wrexham. A mansion built 1684–7 to a design by Thomas Webb, enlarged in the 1720s with the addition of north and south wings and remodelled in the late 18th century by Philip Yorke. The state rooms include collections of period furniture and fittings plus family portraits. Outbuildings include the kitchen, laundry, stables and smithy. Most rooms have no electric lighting. The surrounding parkland includes a walled garden with yew walk, and features the National Collection of ivies. The house has been in the care of the National Trust since 1973. Tel: 01978 355314.

Ewloe Castle $^{1}/_{2}$ mile (0.8km) northwest of Ewloe, 1 mile (1.6km) southeast of Connah's Quay. The remains of a 13th century Welsh-built castle standing on a motte. It was founded in 1146 by Owain Gwynedd as a wooden fort and rebuilt in stone in 1210 by Llywelyn the Great. Curtain walls and a circular tower were added c.1257, probably by Llywelyn ap Gruffydd. The site, which is very ruinous, is maintained by CADW.

Flint Castle Castle Dyke Street, Flint. The remains of a 13th century English castle located on the Dee Estuary, giving it access from the sea. It was built 1277–84 for Edward I by his military architect Master James of St George, the town of Flint being laid out at the same time. The castle had round towers at three corners and a square keep at the fourth. It survived sieges during the Welsh revolts of 1282 and 1294. Richard II was surrendered to supporters of Henry Bolingbroke (the future Henry IV) here in 1399 after his return from a campaign in Ireland. The castle was slighted during the Civil War in 1647. The outer bailey was later used to house the county jail from the 18th century until the 1960s. Now maintained by CADW.

Gop Cairn $^{1}/_{4}$ mile (0.4km) northwest of Trelawnyd, 2 miles (3km) southwest of Prestatyn. The biggest prehistoric monument in Wales, a massive oval-shaped cairn constructed of piled limestone blocks, dating to c.3000 BC; measuring 300ft (91.5m) by 240ft (73m), it stands 40ft (12m) high. Also known as Cop y Goleuni or 'Mount of Lights', it was used as a beacon during the 17th century. The mound was investigated in the 1880s but nothing was discovered in the interior. Caves nearby were used as a Neolithic burial place.

Great Orme Copper Mines Great Orme, Llandudno. A system of Bronze Age copper mines uncovered in 1987 and still being explored and excavated. The scale of operations is believed to cover 6 acres (2.5ha) and go as deep as 200ft (60m); the mines were still being worked in the 19th century. Artefacts excavated include bone tools and hammer stones.The tunnels and the Bronze Age Cavern can be explored, while the visitor centre has exhibits of tools plus a model of a Bronze Age village. Tel: 01492 870447.

Great Orme 1 mile (1.6km) north of Llandudno. A limestone headland jutting out into the sea and rising to 681ft (207m). The cliffs are a haven for breeding seabirds; the grassland has several rare species of plant and is also home to the rare silver studded blue butterfly, and to a herd of Kashmir mountain goats descending from a pair presented to Llandudno by Queen Victoria. The Summit Complex hotel was once owned by world champion boxer Randolph Turpin. See also Great Orme Tramway.

Great Orme Tramway Church Walks, Llandudno. A funicular railway opened in July 1902 and running from Victoria Station in Llandudno up to Halfway Station, which houses an exhibition, and then on to Summit

Station on the Great Orme promontory. It is the only cable-hauled tramway still operating on British public roads; the restored original tramcars – each named after a saint – carry a maximum of 48 passengers. Tel: 01492 879306.

Greenfield Valley Country Park — Greenfield, Holywell. A 70 acre (28ha) country park and outdoor museum along the Holywell Stream between Holywell and the River Dee estuary. The area was at the heart of the Industrial Revolution in North Wales with cotton mills and copper and brass foundries. In addition to ancient monuments already located within the park, such as St Winefride's Holy Well and Basingwerk Abbey, several buildings have been relocated to the site, reconstructed and furnished, including 16th century and 19th century farmhouses and the local Spring Gardens School. The site also includes a farm museum, as well as a museum celebrating the life of naturalist Thomas Pennant.

Gresford Church — The Green, Gresford, 2 miles (3km) northeast of Wrexham. All Saints Church dates originally from the 13th century, but most of the present church was built in Perpendicular style in the 15th century. The church is much admired for its architecture; the tower, containing a peal of eight bells, is regarded as one of the traditional 'Seven Wonders of Wales'. The existence of the bells was first recorded in the late 18th century with at least two dating to the 1620s. The present bells were cast 1775–1875.

Gwrych Castle — 1 mile (1.6km) west of Abergele. A large 19th century replica of a 13th century castle with 19 battlemented towers, built in 1819 by industrialist Lloyd Hesketh Bamford-Hesketh, supposedly on the site of earlier fortifications. It passed through many owners and uses after being sold by the family after World War II and has fallen into disrepair following the failure of plans to turn it into a hotel. It has a reputation for being extensively haunted by, among others, a Red Lady and a White Lady.

Gwydir Castle — Llanrwst, 3 miles (5km) north of Betws-y-Coed. Originally built by Howell Coetmore, who commanded the longbowmen at Poitiers, the house was rebuilt by the Wynne family after the Wars of the Roses. It was further remodelled in the late 16th century and by Sir Charles Barry in the 1820s. The original panelling of the dining room, sold to the Metropolitan Museum, New York, was recovered in 1996 and the room has since been restored to its 1640s condition. The castle has a reputation for being haunted, especially by a lady in the north wing. Tel: 01492 641687.

Haulfre Gardens — Cwlach Road, Llandudno. Public gardens opened in 1929 and stretching between the North Shore of Llandudno and the Great Orme. Affording panoramic views, they represent the remains of a terraced garden on steep site laid out in the 1870s by industrial chemist and plantsman Henry Pochin.

Hawarden House — $^1/_2$ mile (0.8km) east of Hawarden, 9 miles (15km) north of Wrexham. Built in 1752 and at one time the home of Prime Minister William Ewart Gladstone. Situated in Hawarden Park, the house is still in the ownership of the Gladstone family.

Hawarden Old Castle — Hawarden, 9 miles (15km) north of Wrexham. The ruins of a late 13th castle built on the site of an earlier motte and possibly an Iron Age hill fort. The attack on and capture of Hawarden by Dafydd ap Gruffydd in 1282 sparked the invasion of Wales by Edward I and ended in Daffydd's death. Partially demolished in the 1660s, the castle is now located within the grounds of Hawarden Park.

Highest point — Carnedd Llewelyn in Snowdonia at 3491ft (1064m). GR: SH683644.

H M Stanley Exhibition — Hall Square, Denbigh. Housed in Denbigh Library and opened in 2003, the exhibition celebrates the life of Denbigh-born journalist and explorer Henry Morton Stanley (born John Rowlands) (1841–1904). Exhibits include memorabilia such as his Welsh Bible and a model of his hand.

Holt Castle — 5 miles (8km) northeast of Wrexham. The remains of a red sandstone castle on the England/Wales border built by John de Warren 1282–1311, also known as Chastellion or Castrum Leonis from the lion sculpture above its gateway. It was partly demolished in the 1670s to provide building material for Eaton Hall.

Home Front Experience — New Street, Llandudno. A museum celebrating the lives of those who fought World War II from their homes. There are recreated period rooms and shop as well as exhibits on air raids, rationing and Digging for Victory. Tel: 01492 871032.

Interesting facts — **Bangor-on-Dee** is famed for being the only racecourse in Britain without a grandstand. The racecourse is often referred to as simply Bangor, but legend tells of many a green jockey travelling in error to Bangor City in Gwynedd and on at least one occasion Bangor in County Down, Northern Ireland. The **Sportsman's Arms** in Conwy is the highest pub in Wales; in winter people come from all over the British Isles to compete in their husky dog teams in dog-sled trials. **Alice Liddell** (1852–1934), who provided the inspiration for Lewis Carroll's Alice in Wonderland stories, spent her summer holidays at Llandudno in a house built there by her father 1861–72. Wrexham-born **John Godfrey Parry-Thomas** broke the Land Speed Record on 27 April 1926 at Pendine Sands (a 7-mile-long beach on the shores of Carmarthen Bay). His car, *Babs*, powered by a huge 27-litre Liberty V-12 aero-engine, attained a speed of 170mph. John became the first driver to be killed in pursuit of the land speed record when he crashed at Pendine Sands in March 1927 while trying to regain his record that had been broken just weeks earlier by Malcolm Campbell on the same beach.

Sir Henry Jones Museum — Y Cwm, Llangernyw, Abergele. Opened in 1934 and housed in the childhood home of philosopher and educationalist Sir Henry Jones (1852–1922). It celebrates his life and works, also providing a picture of rural life in this part of Wales. Jones started life working with his father as a shoemaker in the house before gaining a scholarship and eventually becoming Professor of Moral Philosophy at Glasgow University. Exhibits include costumes, books and shoemaking equipment. Tel: 01492 575571/01745 860661.

Jubilee Tower — See Moel Famau Country Park.

Llandudno Museum — Gloddaeth Street, Llandudno. Opened in 1927 in Rapallo House, the home of collector Francis Edouard Chardon, gifted in his will along with its contents for the benefit of the people of

Llandudno. The museum moved to Chardon House in the 1980s and houses exhibits including many local artefacts dating from the Palaeolithic to the present day. Tel: 01492 876517.

Llandudno Pier Designed by Charles Henry Driver and built by James Brunlees. Opened in 1878, it is regarded as the finest surviving Victorian pier in Britain. The pier is 2300ft (701m) in length with a 45 degree turn a third of the way along.

Llangar Church 1 mile (1.6km) southwest of Corwen, 10 miles (16km) southwest of Llangollen. Situated overlooking the confluence of the rivers Dee and Alwen, All Saints Church originally dates at least to the 13th century and possibly earlier. It has a 12th century font, extensive medieval wall paintings, a minstrel's gallery and an 18th century triple-decker pulpit. Rug Chapel (see separate entry) is close by.

Llangollen Bridge One of the 'Seven Wonders of Wales'. Spanning the River Dee and originally built c.1346, traditionally by John Trefor, Bishop of Asaph, it had four arched spans; a fifth was added in 1863 to accommodate a railway line. The bridge was widened in 1873 and 1968.

Llangollen Canal Originally part of the Ellesmere Canal and then the Shropshire Union Canal, the Llangollen Canal runs for 41 miles (66km), linking Llangollen in Denbighshire with Nantwich in south Cheshire, via Ellesmere in northwest Shropshire. The Pontcysyllte Aqueduct carries the canal across the Dee Valley. Designed and built by Thomas Telford beginning in 1793, the canal is regarded as his first major civil engineering work. Renamed due to the increasing popularity of pleasure boats, in an effort to attract more visitors, it is now one of Britain's most popular canals with holidaymakers.

Llangollen Motor Museum Pentrefelin, Llangollen. A museum featuring more than 30 vehicles dating from the 1920s to the 1970s. Models include a 1962 Triumph TR4 and a Model 'T' Ford, as well as a selection of classic British motorcycles. There is a recreation of a 1950s garage. Tel: 01978 860324.

Llangollen Steam Railway A heritage railway running for 7½ miles (12km) alongside the River Dee and through the Berwyn Tunnel from Llangollen to Carrog. The original commercial line was opened in 1865 and closed in 1965; the first train on the reconstructed line ran on 26 July 1981 between Llangollen and Ffordd Junction. The track was extended in stages to Berwyn (1985), Glyndyfrdwy (1992) and Carrog (1996); there are plans to extend the line to Corwen and perhaps to the national rail network at Ruabon. The railway operates both steam and diesel locomotives.

Llyn Brenig Reservoir 7 miles (11km) southwest of Denbigh. Located on the Denbigh Moors beside the Clocaenog Forest, the Llyn Brenig Reservoir covers 920 acres (373ha) and was opened in December 1976. Tel: 01490 420463.

Loggerheads Country Park 2 miles (3km) southwest of Mold. An 80 acre (32ha) country park along the River Alyn within the Clwydian Range, and featuring many traces of the area's industrial heritage, which included lead mines and water mills.

Maenan Abbey 3 miles (5km) north of Llanwrst, 7 miles (11km) north of Betws-y-Coed. A 12th Cistercian abbey founded by monks from Aberconwy and largely demolished after its dissolution to provide building materials for royal buildings in Caernarfon. The excavated remains now lie beneath the car park and gardens of a hotel of the same name.

Minera Lead Mines Minera, 4 miles (6km) west of Wrexham. The mineral deposits at Minera have been mined since at least the early medieval period and possibly since Roman times. The mines were a source of lead, zinc and silver; demand peaked in the 1860s, but a slump in the price of lead saw the mines closed in 1914. The remaining spoil heaps were a source of pollution and in the 1980s it was decided to clear them. As a result, the site was excavated in the early 1990s and the mine workings stabilised. Two shafts – Taylor's Shaft and Meadow Shaft – were uncovered; the latter has since been recreated as a heritage site. Tel: 01978 261529.

Moel Arthur 3 miles (5km) southwest of Nannerch, 5 miles (8km) west of Mold. A hilltop standing 1498ft (456m) above sea level and crowned by an Iron Age multivallate hill fort.

Moel Famau Country Park One of the largest country parks in Wales, with more than 2000 acres (800ha) of heathland and forest. The highest point in the park (and also in Flintshire), Moel Famau at 1817ft (554m), is marked by the remains of the Jubilee Tower – an Egyptian-style tower built in 1810 to commemorate the golden jubilee of George III, only its base now stands after it was damaged by a storm in 1862. Offa's Dyke National Trail runs through the park.

Mold Castle Bailey Hill, Mold. The site of a 12th century motte and bailey castle believed to have been built by Robert de Montalt. It is now the site of a bowling green.

Nant Mill ½ mile (0.8km) south of Coedpoeth, 4 miles (6km) west of Wrexham. A former corn mill in woodland beside the River Clywedog. It now houses a visitor centre with displays about the history and environment of the area.

Oriel Mostyn Gallery Vaughan Street, Llandudno. Wales's leading gallery for contemporary modern and fine art. Mostyn Art Gallery was originally established in 1901 by Lady Augusta Mostyn to show the work of the Gwynedd Ladies Art Society. However, it closed during World War I and was not reopened until 1979. The Grade II listed building is undergoing a programme of expansion and is due to reopen fully in 2009. Tel: 01492 879201.

Overton Yews Overton-on-Dee, 6 miles (10km) southeast of Wrexham. One of the traditional 'Seven Wonders of Wales', 21 ancient yew trees in the churchyard of St Mary's Church. The oldest is believed to date from the 12th century.

Pantasaph Friary Pantasaph, 3 miles (5km) west of Holywell. A Franciscan friary which welcomes those interested in exploring the Catholic faith. The grounds feature a landscaped garden representing the Stations of the Cross. Nearby St David's Church, built 1849–52, houses the bones of the early Christian martyr St Primitivus.

Penrhos Engine House Brymbo, 3 miles (5km) northwest of Wrexham. The oldest surviving colliery engine house in Wales, built by John Wilkinson to house an engine to pump water from his coal mine on the site.

Once the engine was no longer in use the house was used for a variety of purposes before being finally abandoned in the 1950s. It was made safe in the late 1990s and opened to the public in 2001. Close by are the remains of the Wilkinson-built Brymbo Bottle Chimney, which was used to condense fumes from the lead smelting works.

Penycloddiau — 3 miles (5km) southwest of Nannerch, 6 miles (10km) northwest of Mold. The site of a large multivallate Iron Age hill fort on a ridge in the Clwydian Range.

Plas Mawr — High Street, Conwy. Possibly the best preserved Elizabethan town house in Britain. It was built 1576–85 by courtier and merchant Robert Wynn and has a gatehouse, stepped gables and a lookout tower. The interior is largely unaltered and features include original 16th century fireplaces, panelling, friezes and plaster ceilings. At one point it was used as as school before being restored by the Royal Cambrian Academy in the late 19th century. Tel: 01492 580167.

Prestatyn Castle — Prestatyn Road, Prestatyn. 12th century English stone motte and bailey castle built by Robert Banastre in 1157 and destroyed by Owain ap Gruffydd in 1167. Only traces of the motte now remain.

Rhuddlan Castle — Rhuddlan, 2 miles (3km) south of Rhyl. The substantial ruins of a 13th century castle on the River Clwyd. It stands near the former site of a palace of Gruffydd ap Llywelyn, burned by Harold Godwinson (later Harold II) after Gruffydd's defeat in 1063. After the Norman Conquest a motte and bailey castle was erected by Robert of Rhuddlan on the site in 1073; the motte, known as Twthill, stands to the south of the ruins of Edward I's new castle, designed by Master James of St George and built 1277–82 after Edward's successful campaign in 1277, following which he accepted the submission of Llywelyn ap Gruffydd at Rhuddlan. The castle has a diamond-shaped inner ward, an outer ward and two twin-towered gatehouses, while the partial canalisation of the River Clwyd provided water-borne access to the defences. The Statute of Rhuddlan, issued from the castle on 3 March 1284, divided Llywelyn's kingdom into Anglesey, Merioneth and Caernarvon and introduced the English common law system; it remained in effect until Henry VIII's Laws in Wales Act in 1536. The castle withstood sieges in 1294 and 1400 and was eventually made indefensible following its fall when in Royalist hands during the Civil War.

Rivers — The **Conwy** rises on the Migneint Moor and flows north for 27 miles (43km), discharging in Conwy Bay at Conwy.

The **Dee** rises in Snowdonia National Park and initially flows via Lake Bala and then across North Wales, northeast to Corwen and eastward past Llangollen, travelling north again to Chester, reaching the Irish Sea at the Dee Estuary at Flint. Its total distance is 70 miles (114km).

Royal Cambrian Academy — Crown Lane, Conwy. Established in 1882 and devoted to the visual arts in Wales. Its Academicians include many of Wales's most popular and respected artists. The gallery holds nine exhibitions each year and also hosts lectures, workshops and demonstrations. The academy was housed in Plas Mawr (see separate entry) from 1885 until 1994, when a purpose-built gallery was constructed nearby. Tel: 01492 593413.

Rug Chapel — 1 mile (1.6km) west of Corwen, 10 miles (16km) west of Llangollen. A little-altered private chapel built in 1637 which features an original carved and painted hammer-beam roof. An original wooden chandelier hangs from the central truss. The rood screen pews are richly carved while one wall features a painting of the recumbent figure of Death. The exterior of the chapel was restored in the 1850s but the interior was largely untouched. All Saints Church, Llangar (see separate entry) is close by.

Ruthin Castle — Castle Street, Ruthin. A red sandstone castle built in 1277 and extended by military architect Master James of St George for Reginald de Grey at the end of the 13th century. The 13th century castle was largely demolished following a siege in 1646. The remains were incorporated in a new house built in the 1820s and extended in the mid 19th century, and which is now a hotel.

Ruthin Gaol — Clwyd Street, Ruthin. A museum of crime and punishment in North Wales housed in Ruthin Gaol, which has stood on the site since the 17th century. The gaol closed in 1916 after many changes and additions had been made to the original House of Correction. Exhibits include the condemned man's cell, padded cell, the treadmill and work activities. Tel: 01824 708281.

St Asaph Cathedral — High Street, St Asaph. Reputedly the smallest ancient cathedral in Britain. Built near the site of St Kentigern's 6th century church, the original cathedral was begun perhaps as early as 1143 but was accidentally burnt down in 1282. St Asaph was St Kentigern's successor. The present building was begun in 1284 using a variety of stone including limestone and yellow and red-purple sandstone and completed by 1392. The rebuilding was, at least for a period, under the supervision of Master Henry of Ellerton. It was damaged by attack during the revolt of Owain Glyndwr but immediately repaired. Major restoration was carried out in the late 18th and 19th centuries by Gilbert Scott. The cathedral contains the earliest Welsh translation of the Bible and a 16th century ivory statue of the 'Spanish Madonna'.

St Deiniol's Library — Church Lane, Hawarden. Founded by William Ewart Gladstone and based on his vast collection of books. It is unusual in being a residential library, offering accommodation plus conference rooms; it was opened in 1902, the residential wing first being used in 1906. An exhibition about its founder, who lived at nearby Hawarden Castle, features displays of memorabilia and documents relating to Gladstone's life and career.

St Giles' Church — Church Street, Wrexham. One of the finest parish churches in Wales, built in the late 15th and early 16th century in Perpendicular style and featuring a wall painting of Judgement Day over the chancel arch. The church tower is one of the traditional 'Seven Wonders of Wales' and has a peal of ten bells. The church was restored during the 19th century. The tomb of Elihu Yale, the benefactor of Yale University, lies in the churchyard and the Royal Welch Fusiliers have a chapel within the church.

St Margaret's Church	Bodelwyddan, 4 miles (6km) south of Rhyl. Aka the Marble Church. Erected 1856–60 by Lady Willoughby de Broke in memory of her husband. The church has a 200ft (60m) spire but the main features are internal, including pillars and shafts of Anglesey marble and red Belgian marble.
St Trillo's Chapel	Marine Drive, Rhos-on-Sea, $1\frac{1}{2}$ miles (2.5km) west of Colwyn Bay. One of the smallest chapels in Britain, with room to seat only six people. It stands above a spring whose waters reputedly have healing powers. First mentioned in a 13th century taxation survey, although the current structure probably dates from the 16th century, the chapel was restored in the 19th century when it was whitewashed to serve as a landmark for shipping.
St Winefride's Well	Greenfield Street, Holywell. Believed to be the oldest continuously operating pilgrimage site in Britain, and also one of the 'Seven Wonders of Wales'. Legend has it that St Winefride's Well erupted at the spot where, in the 7th century, the saint's assailant Caradog cut off her head. She was subsequently restored to life through the power of prayer, after which the well immediately became a place of pilgrimage and healing. The chapel above the well was built in the late 15th or early 16th century, possibly on the instruction of Lady Margaret Beaufort. The well chamber with a central basin is still accessible by arrangement to pilgrims who wish to bathe. The saint was buried in Gwytherin, where she was abbess, but her bones were removed to Shrewsbury Abbey in the 12th century.
Sport	
football	**Airbus UK** were formed in 1946 and named after the company (and have therefore also been called Vickers-Armstrong, de Havilands, Hawker Siddeley, British Aerospace and BAe Systems). The club was promoted to the League of Wales in 2004. Nicknamed The Wingmakers or The Planemakers, their home ground is The Airfield, Broughton.
	Connah's Quay Nomads were founded as Connah's Quay Juniors in 1947 and adopted their current name in 1951. They were founder members of the League of Wales in 1992. Their home ground is Deeside Stadium, although in 2006–7 they shared Flint Town United's ground at Cae-y-Castell, Marsh Lane, Flint.
	Newi Cefn Druids were founded in 1992 from the amalgamation of Cefn Albion FC and Druids United FC, and promoted to the League of Wales in 1999. Their home ground is Plaskynaston Lane, Cefn Mawr, Wrexham.
	Rhyl were founded in 1883. Promoted to the League of Wales in 1994, they are winners of the Welsh Premiership in 2004 and the Welsh Cup in 1952, 1953, 2004 and 2006. Nicknamed The Lilywhites, their home ground is Belle Vue, Grange Road, Rhyl.
	Wrexham were founded in 1872 and played in the English Football League from their election in 1921 until they were relegated to the Conference in 2008. Nicknamed The Red Dragons or The Robins, their home ground is the Racecourse Ground, Mold Road, Wrexham.
horse racing	**Bangor-on-Dee** racecourse, Bangor-on-Dee, Wrexham, is a left-handed course of 1m 4f (2.5km), established in 1859 and staging National Hunt racing. Tel: 01978 780323.
The Stiwt	Broad Street, Rhosllanerchrugog, 4 miles (6km) southwest of Wrexham. A theatre and Welsh cultural centre housed in the former Miners' Institute, built in 1926 to provide a variety of social functions for the local mining community including a cinema, theatre and ballroom. The Institute closed in 1977 but was saved from demolition thanks to a community effort, and was reopened as The Stiwt in 1990. It now hosts a wide variety of events including drama, music, pantomime and dance.
Theatr Colwyn	Abergele Road, Colwyn Bay. Theatre and cinema originally built as a public hall in the 19th century. It hosted music hall acts before becoming a cinema (as the Rialto and later the New Rialto), and became the Prince of Wales Theatre in the late 1950s. Today it offers a wide variety of entertainment including drama, music, pantomime and films.
Trefriw Woollen Mill	Trefriw, 4 miles (6km) north of Betws-y-Coed. A mill on the River Crafnant, producing Welsh double weave (tapestry), bedspreads (carthenni) and tweeds. Originally built in the 18th century as a 'pandy' or fulling mill, it has been in the hands of the Williams family since 1859. Tel: 01492 640462.
Twthill Castle	See Rhuddlan Castle.
Tŷ Mawr Wybrnant	$1\frac{1}{2}$ miles (2.5km) northwest of Penmachno, 3 miles (5km) southwest of Betws-y-Coed. A 16th century two-storey house, the birthplace of Bishop William Morgan (1545–1604), the first translator of the whole Bible into Welsh. The house has been restored to its early appearance and features a collection of Bibles. Maintained by the National Trust since 1951. Tel: 01690 760213.
Valle Crucis Abbey	$1\frac{1}{2}$ miles (2.5km) north of Llangollen. The remains of an early 13th century Cistercian abbey. It was restored after a fire in the 1230s, repaired after damage later in the century and extended during the 15th century. Part of the abbey was turned into a house after the Dissolution and this was occupied until 1654. The name, meaning 'vale of the cross', derives from the nearby Pillar of Eliseg (see separate entry).
Victoria Pier	The Promenade, Colwyn Bay. Designed by Maynall and Littlewood and opened in June 1900. Originally 316ft (96m) long, the pier was extended to 750ft (229m) in 1903 and was from the outset illuminated by electric lighting at night. During its life two pavilions and a theatre on the pier have been destroyed by fire; the current pavilion was built in 1933. The pier's fortunes declined in the 1970s and 1980s along with those of many British holiday resorts; it was threatened with demolition, and was closed to the public in 1991. Although reopened in 1995, its long-term future is still in doubt.
Welsh Mountain Zoo	1 mile (1.6km) west of Colwyn Bay. Founded by naturalist Robert Jackson and opened on 18 May 1963 in Flagstaff Gardens, a former Victorian pleasure garden. Substantially redeveloped in the 1980s, the zoo features more than 60 varieties of mammals, birds and reptiles, including Andean condors, Bactrian camels, bearded dragon, Californian sealions, Chilean flamingos, chimpanzee, European brown bears, golden eagles, Humboldt penguins, Mississippi alligators, Przewalski wild

	horses, red pandas, royal python and Sumatran tigers. In November 2008 it was designated the National Zoo of Wales. Tel: 01492 532938.
Wepre Park	Wepre Drive, Connah's Quay. A country park covering 160 acres (65ha) of open spaces and ancient woodland. Heritage features include Ewloe Castle and the remains of the formal garden of Wepre Old Hall (built in 1788 by Edward Jones, who made his fortune when deposits of lead were discovered on his land, and demolished in 1960).
Wrexham County Borough Museum	Regent Street, Wrexham. A local history museum housed in the former Royal Denbighshire Militia barracks, which later became the Wrexham magistrates' court and police station. It has a wide range of exhibits from the Bronze Age up to the present day, and is also home to the Welsh Football Collection.
Wrexham Roman Catholic Cathedral	Regent Street, Wrexham. Dedicated to Our Lady of Sorrows and built in 1857 in Gothic Revival style to a design by Edward Welby Pugin. The cathedral is the main church of the Diocese of Wrexham, which encompasses the whole of North Wales.

Some famous people born in Clwyd

Apperley, Charles James (sports writer, aka Nimrod) (1777–1843)	Wrexham
Dalton, Timothy (actor) (1946–)	Colwyn Bay
Elis, Islwyn Ffowc (author) (1924–2004)	Wrexham
Parry-Thomas, John Godfrey (land speed record holder) (1884–1927)	Wrexham
Pownall, Leon (actor) (1943–2006)	Wrexham
Prescott, John (politician) (1938–)	Prestatyn
Pryce, Jonathan (actor) (1947–)	Holywell
Rush, Ian (footballer) (1961–)	St Asaph
Savage, Robbie (footballer) (1974–)	Wrexham
Southall, Neville (goalkeeper) (1958–)	Llandudno
Stanley, Henry Morton (explorer and journalist) (1841–1904)	Denbigh
Yates, Paula (presenter) (1959–2000)	Colwyn Bay

Dyfed

GWYNEDD
Aberystwyth
R. Rheidol
Devil's Bridge
Cardigan Bay
1
Aberaeron
New Quay
R. Teifi
Tregaron
POWYS
Aberporth
Lampeter
Cardigan
Newcastle Emlyn
St George's Channel
Pumsaint
Newport
Fishguard
Llandovery
3
2
W. Cleddau
R. Towy
St David's
RAMSEY ISLAND
Llandissilio
R. Taf
Llandeilo
Black Mountain
Fan Foel
781
Haverfordwest
E. Cleddau
St Clears
Carmarthen
Broad Haven
Narberth
Ammanford
SKOMER
Milford Haven
Kidwelly (Cydwelli)
R. Loughor
SKOKHOLM
Saundersfoot
Pembroke Dock
Pembroke
Tenby
Llanelli
M4
CALDAY
WEST GLAMORGAN
Districts
1 Ceredigion
2 Pembrokeshire
3 Carmarthenshire
0
20 miles
0
30 km

Dyfed is a preserved county which covers the administrative counties of Ceredigion (Cardiganshire), Carmarthenshire and Pembrokeshire. It is bordered to the west by St George's Channel, to the south by the Bristol Channel and to the northwest by Cardigan Bay. Its main land border to the east is with Powys although it has short borders at its northern tip with Gwynedd and at its southeastern tip with West Glamorgan. The main geographical features include the long coastline with many sandy beaches, the Cambrian Mountains (which stretch through the heart of Wales from the Brecon Beacons in the south to Snowdonia in the north and are also known here as the Mid Wales uplands of Pumlumon (Plynlimon), Elenydd and Mynydd Mallaen), the Preseli Hills and their numerous rivers, including the Towy, the longest wholly in Wales. The region includes the Pembrokeshire Coast National Park. St David's is the UK's smallest city. The most important industries are agriculture, fishing and tourism, although in the past textiles, lead-mining, whaling and the dockyards were also significant industries.

The area, including the offshore islands, has been settled at least since Palaeolithic times and is dotted with evidence of settlement and ritual with many standing stones, stone circles, burial chambers, cairns and hill forts. The Preseli Hills were the source of the bluestones used at Stonehenge. By pre-Roman times what is known as Dyfed was settled by the Celtic tribes of the Demetae in the west and southwest and the Ordovices in the north and east. The Ordovices strongly resisted the Roman invasion and helped Caractacus in his guerrilla war against the Romans. The Demetae did not resist the invasion, one result of which is the lack of Roman fortifications in the area compared with the part previously controlled by the Ordovices. The Romans explored the region extensively in search of gold and silver deposits.

The kingdoms of Dyfed and Ceredigion were formed after the Roman withdrawal, a period which saw an invasion by the Irish and the arrival of Christianity. St David was born in Pembrokeshire (birth dates range from AD 462 to 512) and established a monastery which is now the site of St David's Cathedral. The coast of Dyfed was subjected to repeated raids and devastation by Viking raiders until the late 11th century. In the 9th century Dyfed was joined with Gwynedd by Cadell ap Rhodri, who established its capital at Dinefwr, and in the early 10th century it was united with the South Wales kingdom of Seisyllwg by Hywel Dda to form the kingdom of Deheubarth. The Dinefwr dynasty ruled Deheubarth until the conquest by the English in the late 13th century.

The Normans had already made their presence felt soon after the invasion of England in 1066. Pembrokeshire in particular became a royal lordship, hence the string of castles in the area; southern Pembrokeshire was known as 'Little England beyond Wales'. Along with English settlers many Flemish immigrants also arrived, encouraged to come to England by Henry I who soon decided to 'plant' many of them to Rhos in south Pembrokeshire. The Flemish helped to build the protective line of castles and earthworks known as the Landsker Line. Gilbert de Clare was created 1st Earl of Pembroke in 1138. Pembrokeshire was fought over many times during the struggle for Welsh independence and was also a stronghold during the Wars of the Roses for the Twdwr (Tudor) family, later to rule England. On 22 February 1797 a French force of 1400 men led by the Irish-American Colonel William Tate landed at Strumble Head, but soon surrendered to a force of Pembroke yeomanry and locals. This is regarded as the last invasion of mainland Britain.

Economic depression in the region in the early 19th century led to the unusual 'Rebecca Riots' of 1839–44; groups of men dressed in women's clothes destroyed toll gates in protest against the high tolls which had to be paid on the local turnpike roads, which they had to use in order to transport their goods. The region provided raw materials for the Industrial Revolution but did not move towards manufacturing, remaining a predominantly agricultural economy. During the late 20th century the county became increasingly dependent on tourism, thanks to its popular seaside resorts and the designation of the Pembrokeshire Coast National Park.

Dyfed		**Population**		**Area**	
	male	*female*	*total*	*sq miles*	*sq km*
Carmarthenshire	83,171	89,671	172,842	915	2371
Ceredigion	36,546	38,395	74,941	693	1794
Pembrokeshire	55,033	59,098	114,131	622	1610
Totals	174,750	187,164	361,914	2230	5775

Local Attractions and Information

Aberdeunant — 3 miles (5km) southeast of Talley, 6 miles (10km) southwest of Llandovery. An example of a small traditional Carmarthenshire farmhouse. The property is administered by the National Trust and maintained by a resident tenant. Tel: 01558 650177.

Aberglasney House and Gardens — Llangathen, 3 miles (5km) west of Llandeilo. A house with its origins in the late 16th and early 17th centuries and said to have been rebuilt by Bishop Anthony Rudd (c.1548–1614). It was remodelled in the early 18th century by the Dyer family and a huge Ionic portico was added to the front elevation by Thomas Phillips, who bought the house in 1801. When the Phillips line died out the estate was broken up and the house and gardens fell into disrepair. However, in 1995 the house and garden were purchased by the Aberglasney Restoration Trust, which has set about restoring the lost gardens to their late 16th and early 17th century Jacobean-style layout. The most distinctive feature is the yew tunnel; the garden also boasts a cloister garden with parapet walkway, a pool garden and a stream garden. There is a remnant of native woodland by the stream, plus a lower and upper walled garden and the unusual Ninfarium (named after a garden created amid ruins south of Rome at Ninfa), established in 2005 within the ruinous central rooms and courtyard of the mansion. The rooms have been covered by a glass atrium to create an environment suitable for sub-tropical plants. Tel: 01558 668998.

Aberystwyth Arts Centre — Penglais Campus, Aberystwyth. The largest arts centre in Wales, presenting a wide variety of performances and visual arts presentations. Opened in 1970, it underwent major refurbishment in 2000. It features a 900 seat Great Hall, the 300 seat Theatr y Werin and an exhibition gallery. In addition there is a 125 seat studio theatre, a 120 seat cinema, plus dance studios and workshop

	spaces. The Arts Centre is a department of the University of Wales Aberystwyth and is located on the university's campus.
Aberystwyth Camera Obscura	Constitution Hill, Aberystwyth. Claimed to be the largest camera obscura in the world. The first camera obscura in the town was built in 1880 on the promenade before being relocated on Constitution Hill to provide a better view. This had been dismantled by the 1920s but a replacement was erected in 1985. It has a 14in (356mm) lens and provides a sweeping panorama covering 1000 sq miles (2590 sq km) of sea and shore including Snowdonia.
Aberystwyth Castle	New Promenade, Aberystwyth. Founded by Gilbert de Clare in 1110 on a promontory overlooking Cardigan Bay, the original castle was replaced by a larger castle built 1277–89 by Edward I, under the aegis of Edmund Crouchback and Master Giles of St George. It was constructed to a diamond-shaped concentric plan with round towers and twin-towered gatehouses; the inner ward contained a great hall. Damaged during a Welsh attack in 1292 but quickly restored and completed, it changed hands three times during Owain Glyndwr's uprising in the early 15th century and began to fall into disrepair as its strategic importance diminished. There is evidence that a mint was established by Thomas Bushell in the castle hall in 1637. The castle was held by Royalists during the Civil War but was slighted at the war's end and its stones were probably used for local building projects. The ruins stand within a small public park.
Aberystwyth Cliff Railway	Cliff Terrace, Aberystwyth. The longest cliff railway in Britain at 778ft (237m). It originally used a water balance sytem but is now powered by electricity. The railway opened in 1896 to ferry tourists to the summit of Constitution Hill (the site of 'Luna Park'), which had gardens, a bandstand, a ballroom and, until the 1920s, the town's first camera obscura. See also Aberystwyth Camera Obscura.
Aberystwyth Library	See National Library of Wales.
Administrative headquarters	**Carmarthenshire**: County Hall, Carmarthen, Carmarthenshire SA31 1JP. Tel: 01267 234567. **Ceredigion**: Town Hall, Aberystwyth, Ceredigion SY23 2EB. Tel: 01970 617911. **Pembrokeshire**: County Hall, Haverfordwest SA61 1TP. Tel: 01437 764551.
Battles	Four battles have been fought in Dyfed: Crug Mawr, Cymerau, Fishguard and Mynydd Carn. See separate table for details; see also Maes Gwenllian.
Blaenporth Castle	Blaenporth, 5 miles (8km) northeast of Cardigan. Aka Ralph's Castle, Castell Gwithian. A 12th century Norman motte and bailey castle destroyed by the Welsh in 1215.
Caldey Abbey	Caldey Island. Founded as a Benedictine abbey built in 1910 in Italianate style. It was sold to the Cistercian Order in 1926, when the Benedictine monks moved to Prinknash Abbey in Gloucestershire, and has been occupied by a Cistercian Trappist community since 1929.
Caldey Island	Located 2 miles (3km) south of Tenby across the Caldey Sound, Caldey has been settled since prehistory but has been a haven for religious orders since at least the 6th century. The Benedictines built a priory in the 12th century and the island was bought by Anglican Benedictines in 1906. The post office was purpose-built in 1913, shortly after the completion of the abbey, and houses a small museum charting the island's archaeology and history. The island is $1\frac{1}{4}$ miles (2km) long and less than $\frac{3}{4}$ mile (1km) wide and has a population of approximately 50 people. GR: SS140965. See also Caldey Abbey, Caldey Lighthouse.
Caldey Lighthouse	The lighthouse on Caldey Island was built in 1829. A round tower standing 56ft (17m) high, it was automated in 1929 and was the last Trinity House lighthouse to be powered by gas, eventually being converted to electricity in 1997.
Caldey Priory	The ruins of a priory originally founded in the 12th century by monks from the Benedictine order at St Dogmael's in North Pembrokeshire. Altered and extended over the following centuries, it fell into disrepair after its dissolution and was eventually partly incorporated into a farmhouse. The priory church, dedicated to St Illtyd, is still in use as a parish church.
Capel Dyddgen	$\frac{1}{2}$ mile (0.8km) southwest of Crwbin, 5 miles (8km) southeast of Carmarthen. The ruins of a small 13th century church. Most of the stonework has disappeared, but the tower still stands almost to its full height.
Cardigan Castle	Castle Street, Cardigan. Norman castle standing above the River Teifi and founded c.1093 by the de Clare family. In the 1130s it fell into the possession of Rhys ap Gruffydd, who began to rebuild it in stone and in 1176 held a gathering of bards, poets and musicians that is regarded by many as the foundation of the Welsh National Eisteddfod. After his death in 1197 the castle changed hands many times and was destroyed by Llywelyn the Great in 1231, after which it was completely remodelled in the 1240s. Like many Welsh castles, it was slighted by Parliamentary forces at the end of the Civil War in the 17th century. The substantial ruins include curtain walls and the remains of three semicircular towers, the largest of which was incorporated into Castle Green House, a Georgian house built within the keep in 1808 by John Bowen. At the same time as the house was built it seems that much of the castle's then existing fabric was destroyed in a garden landscaping scheme. The house and castle were in private hands but have been bought by Ceredigion Council, who have instigated a restoration project.
Cardigan Guildhall	Priory Street, Cardigan. An L-shaped Ruskinian Gothic style building erected 1858–60 by R J Withers. The front has a ground-floor level with five stone arches and the second floor has five arched windows. A four-faced clock tower was added in 1892. The multi-arched crypt now houses Cardigan Indoor Market. In front stands a captured Russian field gun from the Crimean War, commemorating the Charge of the Light Brigade led by the 7th Earl of Cardigan on 25 October 1854.
Cardigan Heritage Centre	Teifi Wharf, Castle Street, Cardigan. A local history centre housed in a Grade II listed building beside the River Teifi and charting the history of Cardigan from pre-Norman times to the present day. The centre is managed by Cardigan's historic society. Tel: 01239 614404.
Carew Castle	Carew, 5 miles (8km) northwest of Tenby. The ruins of a substantial castle beside the Carew River,

built in the early 12th century by Gerald de Windsor (later de Carew) on the site of earlier fortifications dating to the Iron Age. Part of a tower erected at the period still stands as part of the castle's east range. It was reconstructed in the late 13th century by Sir Nicholas Carew with the addition of curtain walls and two large drum towers. The castle was bought in the late 15th century by Rhys ap Thomas, who modernised and extended it in Tudor style. On the execution of his grandson in 1531 the castle became Crown property; it was leased in 1558 to Sir John Perrot, who removed some of its redundant defensive features and added more domestic accommodation in grand Elizabethan style. The castle was bought back by the Carew family in the early 17th century and remains in their hands today. It was the scene of fierce fighting during the Civil War, at the end of which it was slighted by Parliamentary forces and the south range demolished. The Carews returned to live here after the Restoration but abandoned it in the 1680s. The castle is now leased by the Pembrokeshire Coast National Park Authority, who have instigated an extensive programme of restoration. It is a designated Site of Special Scientific Interest due to its bat population and several locally or regionally rare species of plants. Carew Tidal Mill is nearby.

Carew Tidal Mill — $^1/_2$ mile (0.8km) west of Carew, $5^1/_2$ miles (9km) northwest of Tenby. Aka Carew French Mill. The only complete tide mill still surviving in Wales; although the current building dates to the early 19th century its origins are much earlier and probably date to at least the early 16th century. It stands at the edge of a dam across the Carew River which created a mill pond for Carew Castle. The mill's commercial working life ended in 1937 and it was derelict until renovated from the 1970s. The site is owned by Pembrokeshire Coast National Park Authority.

Carmarthen Castle — Castle Hill, Carmarthen. Founded in the early 12th century by Henry I as a motte and bailey castle on a site above the River Twyi and rebuilt in stone from c.1180. Captured and damaged by Llywelyn the Great in 1215, the castle survived a three-month siege by Richard Marshall, Earl of Pembroke, Rhys Gryg, Maelgwn Fyhan, and Owain ap Gruffydd in 1233. It was further attacked and sacked, along with the town, during Owain Glyndwr's uprising in the early 15th century. The castle was used as the county jail from the 18th century. The substantial remains are obscured by modern buildings but include a shell keep, a gatehouse, a section of curtain wall and two towers.

Carmarthenshire County Museum — Abergwili, 2 miles (3km) east of Carmarthen. A local history museum housed in the former palace of the Bishops of St David's, where the New Testament was first translated into Welsh in 1567. The museum charts the history of the area, including its industry and education, and contains collections of Welsh pottery and furniture, costume and farming equipment, as well as fine art and archaeological artefacts. There are also recreations of a Victorian schoolroom, a clogmaker's workshop and a 1940s kitchen and living room. The Bishop's Chapel is an integral part of the museum and the Bishop's Library holds part of the Carmarthenshire Antiquarian Society's collection of books and journals. Tel: 01267 228696.

Carn Goch — 4 miles (6km) northeast of Llandeilo. Aka Garn Goch. The site of two neighbouring Iron Age hill forts, Gaer Fach and Gaer Fawr. Gaer Fach, the smaller of the two, measures 550ft (166m) by 370ft (113m); a track leads to Gaer Fawr, which has stone walls surrounding an area measuring 2230ft (680m) by a maximum of 620ft (189m).

Carreg Cennen Castle — 3 miles (5km) southeast of Llandeilo. The substantial remains of a late 13th century castle built by John Giffard on a prominent hilltop above Afon Ciennen, a site of fortifications dating to at least the Roman period and probably earlier. The castle's various owners included Hugh Despenser and John of Gaunt. It survived an attack by Owain Glyndwr in 1403 but was slighted by Yorkists during the Wars of the Roses in 1462, although some effort at restoration was made during the 19th century. The ruins include curtain walls and a gatehouse, while a flight of steps in one corner of the inner ward leads down to a cave in the bedrock under the castle, the use of which is unclear. The castle is located within the Brecon Beacons National Park and is maintained by CADW.

Castell Allt Craig-Arth — See Dinerth Castle.

Castell Gwallter — Llandre, 4 miles (6km) northeast of Aberystwyth. Norman motte and bailey castle founded c.1110 and destroyed in 1135. The flat-topped motte stands 15ft (4.5m) tall and has a ditch and counterscarp.

Castell Gwithian — See Blaenporth Castle.

Castell Henllys — 1 miles (1.6km) east of Felindre Farthog, 5 miles (8km) southwest of Cardigan. An Iron Age inland promontory fort beside the River Duad, bounded on three sides by the river and by a double rampart and ditch on the land side. It was occupied until the beginning of the 1st millennium AD, although there is some evidence of reoccupation in the late/post-Roman period. The site is now used to conduct experimental archaeology with the reconstruction of thatched Iron Age buildings on their original foundations. The Old Roundhouse, constructed in the 1980s, is the longest-standing recreated Iron Age roundhouse in Britain. There are also herds of livestock which would have existed during the Iron Age. Tel: 01239 891319.

Castell Pen-yr-Allt — 1 mile (1.6km) west of Bridell, 3 miles (5km) southwest of Cardigan. Banked and ditched earthworks measuring 170ft (52m) by 130ft (40m) which may have supported a medieval castle. A mound in its centre may represent the remains of a circular tower.

Castell Tan-y-Castell — Rhydyfelin, 1 mile (1.6km) south of Aberystwyth. Aka Old Aberystwyth Castle. The site of Aberystwyth's first castle, built in 1110 by Gilbert de Clare to the south of the River Ystwyth. It was unsuccessfully attacked by Gruffydd ap Rhys in 1116 and eventually fell in 1136 to the Welsh, who occupied it until the 1140s. The remains of the ringwork can still be seen.

Castell Trefilan — Trefilan, 5 miles (8km) northwest of Lampeter. An 18ft (5m) high motte encircled by a moat, possibly the site of a 12th century castle.

Castle Hill Memorial	Castle Hill, Tenby. The Welsh national memorial to Prince Albert, erected in 1864–5.
Castle Pill	1 mile (1.6km) northeast of Milford Haven. The scant remains of a possibly medieval castle which may have been used as a Civil War strongpoint.
Cilgerran Castle	Cilgerran, 2 miles (3km) south of Cardigan. The ruins of a 13th century castle perched above a deep river gorge in the Teifi valley. Occupying the site of an earlier Norman enclosure castle founded c.1110 by Gerald of Windsor, the castle was possibly Welsh built but changed hands several times. The main stone construction, including two round towers, was probably the work of the Marshall family. The castle was already in ruins by the mid 14th century but some repair work was carried out in the 1380s when a further tower was added. In its later state this picturesque ruin was a popular subject for artists. Now maintained by CADW. Tel: 01239 615007.
Ceredigion Museum and Art Gallery	Terrace Road, Aberystwyth. A large local history museum housed in the Coliseum, a restored Edwardian theatre built 1904–5. Converted into a cinema in 1932 and closed in 1977, the Coliseum reopened in 1982 as a museum for the county of Ceredigion. Its wide variety of exhibits include over 50,000 individual items reflecting life in Ceredigion, particularly from the Victorian period onwards. Some of the areas covered are animals, crafts, dairy, fabric, farming, food, furniture, transport and work. Tel: 01970 633088.
Colby Woodland Garden	Amroth, 5 miles (8km) northeast of Tenby. An 8 acre (3ha) walled and woodland garden surrounding a 19th century house (not open to the public). There are notable collections of rhododendrons and azaleas and the woods have displays of daffodils and bluebells in spring. The walled garden features a Gothic style gazebo. The property is in the care of the National Trust. Tel: 01834 811885.
Cresswell Castle	$^1/_2$ mile (0.8km) north of Cresswell Quay, 4 miles (6km) northeast of Pembroke. The scant ruins of a 13th century castle founded by Haverfordwest Priory beside the River Cresswell.
Devil's Bridge	10 miles (16km) east of Aberystwyth. A village which is the site of three vertically stacked bridges crossing a woodland gorge cut by the River Mynach. The first (and lowest) bridge is traditionally said to have been built by the monks of Strata Florida (although another tradition appoints the Knights Templar to the task); the second bridge was built above this one, while the third is a 20th century construction. The river plunges 300ft (91m) to meet the River Rheidol in a series of waterfalls below the bridge. The story by which the Devil's Bridge gets its name involves an old woman, a lost cow and a dog and the outwitting of Old Nick.
Din Weilir	1 mile (1.6km) north of Llanegwad, 7 miles (11km) northeast of Carmarthen. The earthworks of a motte and bailey standing above the River Cothi.
Dinefwr Castle	$1^1/_2$ miles (2.5km) west of Llandeilo. Aka Dynevor Castle. A Welsh-built late 12th century and early 13th century castle above the River Towy; it was probably at first the site of a stronghold of Rhys ap Gruffydd, the stone castle being built by his son. The castle was remodelled by Edward I and extended during its occupied life, changing hands many times; it was damaged during Welsh attacks against its then owner Hugh Despenser and later during Owain Glyndwr's early 15th century uprising. The castle was abandoned in favour of nearby Newton House, built in 1660, and damaged by fire in the 18th century. The modern castle was constructed in 1856 but the ruins of the original castle still stand, including a circular keep, two towers and a curtain wall. It stands within Dinefwr Park, an 18th century landscaped park with a herd of more than 100 fallow deer and a small herd of Dinefwr White Park Cattle. Owned by the National Trust. Tel: 01558 824512.
Dinerth Castle	$1^1/_4$ miles (2km) southwest of Pennant, 14 miles (23km) southwest of Aberystwyth. Aka Castell Allt Craig-Arth. An earthwork castle on a steep-sided promontory above the confluence of the rivers Arth and Erthig. The motte stands 24ft (7.5m) high and 100ft (30.5m) in diameter and is surrounded by double ramparts and ditches. There is also an adjacent 18ft (5m) high motte. Possibly built in the early 12th century, it was abandoned in the first decade of the 13th century.
Dolaucothi Gold Mines	1 mile (1.6km) east of Pumsaint, 7 miles (11km) northwest of Llandovery. A gold-mining complex established by the Romans and located within the 2500 acre (1000ha) Dolaucothi Estate. The mines were reopened in the 19th century and worked until 1938. The underground workings can be explored, while above ground is an exhibition on the history of gold and gold mining, a collection of 1930s mining machinery and the chance to try gold panning. Owned by the National Trust since 1941. Tel: 01558 650177.
Dryslwyn Castle	$4^1/_2$ miles (7km) west of Llandeilo. The ruins of a 13th century Welsh-built castle on a hilltop above the River Towy. It stands not far from the ruins of Dinefwr Castle and may have a similar building date. Surrendered to the English in 1271, it remained in the hands of the then owner, Rhys ap Mareddud, who began a campaign against the English in 1287 which resulted in a three-week siege of the castle. Rhys escaped but was later captured and executed. Like its neighbour, Dinefwr Castle, Dryslwyn was damaged during Welsh attacks against its then unpopular owner Hugh Despenser. In 1403 it was handed over to Owain Glyndwr who used it as a base for his uprising. After the rebellion failed the English burned and dismantled the castle to prevent it being used in such a manner again. The ruins include some curtain walling, part of a gatehouse, a round tower and the keep.
Dylan Thomas Boathouse	Dylan's Walk, Laugharne. The home beside the Taf Estuary of Dylan Thomas and his family, 1949–53. During his time here Thomas wrote many poems, as well as his radio play *Under Milk Wood.* The house is furnished in period style, including some Thomas family furniture; there are also audio and visual presentations including recordings of Thomas reading his own poems. Thomas also lived in Laugharne 1938–40, using it – as affirmed by his widow Caitlin – as the basis for Llareggub in *Under Milk Wood.* The 'Writing Shed', the former wooden garage where Thomas worked, has been restored largely as it was in his time. The Boathouse remained the Thomas family home after Dylan's death in 1953 until it was sold in 1973, and was opened as a memorial in 1975. Thomas is buried in St Martin's Churchyard, Laugharne; Caitlin, who died in 1994, is buried beside him. Tel: 01994 427420.

Gateholm Island	A small half-tidal islet west of Marloes, connected to the mainland by a causeway that is exposed at low tide. It was the site of a settlement which appears from archaeological evidence, including hut circles and a round barrow, to have been occupied from the late Roman to the early medieval period. It is also possibly the site of a medieval castle. GR: SM770072.
Gelli Aur Country Park	2 miles (3km) southwest of Llandeilo. The Gelli Aur (Golden Grove) covers 60 acres (24ha) of parkland and woodland surrounding a house (not open to the public) built in the 1820s and designed in Tudor/Scottish baronial style by Sir Jeffry Wyatville for the Cawdor family. Features include a 20 acre (8ha) deer park with a small herd of fallow deer, an arboretum with giant redwoods and Monterey pines plus terraced gardens. Tel: 01558 668885.
Gwaun Valley	3 miles (5km) southeast of Fishguard. A steep-sided valley formed by Ice Age glacial action and the River Gwaun, which rises in the Preseli Hills. The residents of the valley celebrate New Year on 13 January each year (known as Hen Galan) because they still support the Julian Calendar, which was abandoned by the rest of Britain in favour of the Gregorian Calendar in 1752.
Gwili Railway	Bronwydd Arms, 2 miles (3km) northeast of Carmarthen. A standard-gauge heritage railway operating from Bronwydd Arms to Danycoed Halt alongside the River Gwili on part of the former Great Western Railway branch line from Carmarthen to Aberystwyth, which finally closed in 1964. The preserved railway, which opened in March 1978, runs both steam and diesel locomotives. Tel: 01267 230666.
Haverfordwest Castle	Castle Back, Haverfordwest. Originally established c.1120 by Gilbert de Clare as a Norman stone fortress, although the surviving ruins date from later 13th and 14th century constructions founded by William de Valence. The castle successfully resisted all attempts by the Welsh to capture it, although the town was burned down on several occasions. Parts were demolished after the Civil War by order of Oliver Cromwell in 1648 but the castle was already in a ruinous condition by that time. Part of the castle was converted into a county prison in 1779 and in 1820 a new prison building was built in the grounds; this now houses the Pembrokeshire Record Office.
Haverfordwest Town Museum	Castle Street, Haverfordwest. Local history museum located in Castle House and dedicated to the civic, social and industrial life of the people of Haverfordwest. Displays include mayoral robes and regalia, retail and industrial equipment, a model of Haverfordwest Castle, medieval woodcarvings, photographs and fine art. Tel: 01437 763087.
Highest point	Fan Foel, part of the Black Mountain range in the Brecon Beacons at 2562ft (781m). GR: SN821223.
Hywel Dda Gardens	St Mary Street, Whitland, 13 miles (21km) west of Carmarthen. A garden and heritage centre celebrating the life and works of Hywel Dda (Hywel the Good) (c.880–950), who ruled most of Wales and codified Welsh laws. Extracts from the laws are carved on slate slabs in the centre's garden. The garden is divided into six small gardens, each representing a separate division of the Law (Society and Status, Crime and Tort, Women, Contract, Court and King, Property) and each has a particular tree, reflecting the symbolic meaning of trees to Celtic people. The interpretive centre contains an exhibition about Hywel and the Law as well as descriptive artwork in glass, brick, ceramics and steel. It is said to be the only garden in Europe dedicated to the law. Tel: 01994 240867.
Interesting facts	**Fishguard**'s ancient Royal Oak pub saw the signing of the surrender following the last invasion of Britain in 1797. The whole story is told by the Fishguard Tapestry, created for the 200th anniversary of the invasion as a deliberate echo of the Bayeux Tapestry, and on display in a hall near the town centre. A French force of 1400 troops in four warships landed at Carregwastad Head (or possibly Llanwnda) near Fishguard, their aim being to start an uprising against the English and march to Bristol and London. Many of the French troops were conscripted prisoners and discipline and morale were low. The invasion soon lost momentum when the convicts discovered the locals' supply of whisky and was concluded with little harm – other than a few fatalities and some looting – on either side. The surrender took place on 25 February and the local heroine of the invasion was Jemima Nicholas, who with her pitchfork single-handedly rounded up 12 reportedly tipsy invaders. A shipwreck supposedly belonging to the invasion fleet was found in 2003 and lies off Strumble Head. Fishguard is also famous for its regular ferry service to Rosslare in Ireland, although Fishguard Harbour is not in Fishguard itself but about a mile away at Goodwick. Fishguard is also the terminus of the A40 London–Fishguard trunk road. Nearby in **Maenclochog** is a stone circle over 70ft (21m) in diameter. The **Tafarn Sinc Preseli** pub and restaurant in Rosebush, a traditional Welsh village in the heart of the Preseli Hills, offers a warm Welsh welcome. Constructed in 1876 when the railway ran from Rosebush to Clunderwen, the inn was originally a thriving hotel but was closed by the brewery in 1992 and subsequently bought by the local residents. It is now something of a tourist attraction, being situated on the reconditioned railway halt and platform. **Aberystwyth** pedestrians had an unexpected windfall in June 2006 when a man showered what is thought to be thousands of pounds into the air at a pedestrian crossing before driving away in his BMW. The man was heard to shout 'Who wants free money?' seconds before hurling the cash into the air in Alexandra Road. The incident caused chaos as drivers and pedestrians, some on their hands and knees, picked up the money. Dyfed-Powys Police said a 40-year-old man was later arrested for driving offences in nearby Aberaeron!
Islands	There are more than 160 islands off the coast of Dyfed. See separate table.
Kidwelly Castle	Castle Road, Kidwelly. The substantial and impressive remains of a 13th century castle built above the town of Kidwelly on the River Gwendraeth. The original Norman castle, founded c.1106 by Roger, Bishop of Salisbury, was burnt by the Welsh in 1215. It was replaced by a stone enclosure castle, built in the 1270s by Payn de Chatworth and substantially remodelled in the late 13th century by the Chatworth family on the concentric pattern typical of Edward I's castles. In the 14th century the castle was in the possession of the Duchy of Lancaster and John of Gaunt built

	the great gatehouse. It withstood an attack by Owain Glyndwr in 1403 but by the early 17th century had long been abandoned. The ruins include the semicircular outer ward with three corner towers still standing, and the square inner ward with four towers.
Kidwelly Industrial Museum	1 mile (1.6km) northeast of Kidwelly. Housed in the former Kidwelly Tinplate Works, which operated 1737–1941. The museum not only covers the story of the tinplate industry but also coal mining, brick manufacture and industrial transport. Among the relics rescued from the tinplate works are a water-powered mill and the steam engine which powered the cold rolls. At the north end of the site, the headframe and winding engine from Morlais Colliery have been re-erected. Tel: 01554 891078.
Lamphey Bishop's Palace	1/4 mile (0.4km) northeast of Lamphey, 2 miles (3km) east of Pembroke. The substantial ruins of a former palace occupied by the bishops of St David's. The earliest structures date from the 13th century; much of the palace was built for Bishop Henry de Gower in the first half of the 14th century but additions were made until the 16th century. Tel: 01646 672224.
Laugharne Castle	Laugharne, 9 miles (15km) southwest of Carmarthen. The ruins of a 13th century Welsh castle at the mouth of the River Taf, built by the de Brian family on the site of an earlier timber ringwork fortification burned down in 1215. The stone castle withstood all attempts to capture it and, once the prime need for defence had passed, at the end of the 16th century its tenant Sir John Perrot converted it into a Tudor mansion. The house and castle were severely damaged by cannon fire during the Civil War and then slighted and abandoned to fall into ruins. The grounds were landscaped in the 18th century and the ruins made safe; restoration work was carried out in the 1930s. Dylan Thomas wrote *Portrait of the Artist as a Young Dog* in the gazebo in the castle garden.
Llandovery Castle	Castle Street, Llandovery. The ruins of a Norman motte and bailey castle founded in the early 12th century by Robert Fitzpons. Built on a motte on the River Bran, it was captured by the Welsh in 1116 and changed hands several times until again becoming an English possession at the end of the 13th century. It was slighted by Cromwell and later burned down in 1532.
Llandovery Heritage Centre	Kings Road, Llandovery. Heritage centre with displays about the town and about outlaw Twm Sion Cati (aka Thomas Jones, 1530–1609) and hymn writer William Williams Pantycelyn (1717–91). Tel: 01550 720693.
Llanerchaeron	2 miles (3km) southeast of Aberaeron. An 18th century gentry house beside the River Aeron, designed and built by John Nash. Much of the house is unaltered from its original layout including a service courtyard with dairy, laundry, brewery and salting house. The grounds include two walled gardens and parkland. There is also a working organic farm with Welsh black cattle, Welsh pigs and Llanwenog sheep. The house and estate were bequeathed to the National Trust in 1989. Tel: 01545 570200.
Llanio Roman Fort	2 1/2 miles (4km) northwest of Llandewi Brefi, 8 miles (13km) northeast of Lampeter. Aka Bremia. The site of a Roman fort, covering 5 acres (2ha) and believed to have been occupied AD 75–120. The defences consisted of a wide ditch backed by an 18ft (5m) rampart. A military bath house associated with the fort has also been discovered.
Llansteffan Castle	Llansteffan, 7 miles (11km) southwest of Carmarthen. A 12th century stone castle built on the site of a possible Iron Age settlement beside the Towy estuary. The original wooden castle, built in 1112, was burned in 1146 by the Welsh, who then also captured a rebuilt timber replacement; the stone castle was erected by the English after the Welsh were driven out in the 1150s. It was briefly in the hands of the Welsh again in 1189 before being granted by Henry II to William de Camville and his family, who kept it until the 14th century despite Welsh efforts to displace them. In the late 15th century Jasper Tudor received the castle from his nephew Henry VII but it was allowed to fall into disrepair. The ruins include the three-storey square inner gate and a gatehouse with a pair of D-plan flanking towers. The castle is in the care of CADW.
Llawhaden Castle	Llawhaden, 7 miles (11km) east of Haverfordwest. The ruins of a 13th century castle built on the site of an earlier earth and timber fortification, established by the bishops of St David's Cathedral and destroyed by the Welsh in 1193. The new stone castle, also built by the bishops, included a circular keep and a curtain wall, plus two round, two octagonal and two square towers. The castle was abandoned and the stonework robbed following the Dissolution. The ruins include fragments of the 14th century great hall, two octagonal towers, one square tower, and the façade of the three-storey twin-towered gatehouse.
Llywernog Silver and Lead Mine Museum	1 1/4 miles (2km) west of Ponterwyd, 9 miles (15km) east of Aberystwyth. Heritage mine on the site of the Poole's Minework, first worked in the 1740s. It was at its height in the early 19th century when 60 miners were employed, and was leased to Cornish miners 1824–34. However, the lode became less productive and extraction more problematical as the workings went deeper, involving constant pumping out of water, and the mines were virtually closed by 1910. The mining museum was opened in 1973 and the mines restored for exploration by visitors. Other features include a panning shed, working waterwheels and antique mining equipment. Tel: 01970 890620.
Maes Gwenllian	1/4 mile (0.4km) north of Mynyddygarreg, 1 1/2 miles (2.5km) northeast of Kidwelly. A field said to be the site of a battle fought in 1136 between Gwenllian, wife of Gruffydd ap Rhys, and Maurice de Londres, the Norman lord of Kidwelly. Gwenllian's forces were marching against Kidwelly Castle but were slaughtered and Gwenllian and her son Morgan were killed. Another son, Maelgwyn, was captured. Gwenllian and Morgan are said to be buried in the field.
Manorbier Castle	Manorbier, 4 1/2 miles (7km) west of Tenby. Late 11th century Norman enclosure castle overlooking Manorbier Bay, founded by Otto de Barri and considerably modified and strengthened in the 12th century. The castle is noted for being the birthplace of the scholar Giraldus Cambrensis (aka Gerald de Barri or Gerald of Wales) (c.1146–c.1223); it was Gerald's opinion – possibly biased – that 'In all the broad lands of Wales, Manorbier is the most pleasant place by far'. The castle saw

very little action during its lifetime. During the 19th century it was renovated by its tenant, J R Cobb, who built a house within the walls. The ruins include the great hall and chapel. The castle is located within Pembrokeshire National Park.

Manorowen Walled Garden Manorowen, 1$^1/_2$ miles (2.5km) west of Fishguard. A restored 18th century garden of 1$^1/_2$ acres (0.6ha) with summerhouse. Tel: 01348 872168.

Merlin's Hill 3 miles (5km) northeast of Carmarthen. The site of a large Iron Age hill fort, located on a flat-topped hill and measuring 980ft (299m) by 600ft (183m). Merlin is traditionally said to have been imprisoned in a cave on the hill.

Milford Haven Museum The Docks, Milford Haven. Local history museum housed in the Old Customs House and telling the story of the town's whaling, fishing and oil industries. Tel: 01646 694496.

Millennium Coastal Park A 13$^1/_2$ mile (22km) stretch of former industrial land on the Burry Estuary to the west of Llanelli, reclaimed and restored as parkland overlooking the Gower peninsula. The Millennium Coastal Path runs through the park, which also encompasses Pembrey Country Park and the National Wetland Centre of Wales at Penclacwydd. Tel: 01554 777744.

Nanteos Mansion 1$^1/_2$ miles (2.5km) east of Rhydyfelin, 2$^1/_2$ miles (4km) southeast of Aberystwyth. Georgian mansion built 1739–57 by the Powell family. It is now a country hotel and restaurant. Tel: 01970 624363.

Nant y Coy Mill Arts 1 mile (1.6km) north of Treffgarne, 6 miles (10km) north of Haverfordwest. Located in Treffgarne Gorge and reputedly the site of a mill since the 14th century. The current mill, rebuilt in 1844, remained in use as a corn mill until the 1970s and has now been converted into an art gallery. Tel: 01437 741671.

Narberth Castle Narberth, 8 miles (13km) north of Tenby. The ruins of a single-ward rectangular stone castle with corner towers, sited on a steep-sided knoll and probably dating to the 13th century. Internal viewing of the ruins is not permitted for safety reasons.

National Botanic Garden of Wales 1 mile (1.6km) south of Llanarthne, 7 miles (11km) east of Carmarthen. A garden opened in July 2000 to celebrate the millennium and created on the former Middleton Estate, established in the early 17th century. The estate was bought in 1789 by William Paxton, who created the water park from which the garden's network of lakes and streams are derived. The estate fell into decline during the early 20th century and the mansion at its heart burned down in 1931; restoration of the grounds for public use began in 1978. The garden now boasts an extraordinarily wide range of plants and facilities: the great glasshouse features plants from around the world which are suitable for a Mediterranean climate; the double-walled garden, built in the 18th century, explains the evolution of flowering plants; while the apothecaries' garden highlights medicinal herbs. There are collections of hazel, cistus and sorbus and the garden is also collecting the seeds of, and propagating, some of Wales's rarest plants. Other features include the broadwalk with its long herbaceous border, a Japanese garden and a bog garden. Tel: 01558 667148.

National Library of Wales Located next to the University of Wales campus in Aberystwyth, the National Library of Wales has enjoyed the right to collect, free of charge, a copy of every printed work published in Britain and Ireland since 1911. The library has books, newspapers, magazines, documents and maps plus audio and video recordings and photographs. Its treasures include the first three Welsh books to be printed, in 1546 and 1547, William Morgan's first Welsh translation of the complete Bible in 1588, the Black Book of Carmarthen (the earliest surviving manuscript entirely in Welsh), the Book of Taliesin, and the Hengwrt manuscript of the works of Geoffrey Chaucer. Tel: 01970 632800.

National Wetlands Centre Wales 2 miles (3km) southeast of Lllanelli. Wildfowl and Wetlands Trust centre covering more than 550 acres (220ha) of Burry Inlet, which is also a Ramsar site. It features a wide variety of wetland habitats including lakes, pools, lagoons and reedbeds which are home to a diversity of wildlife. The centre is also an important site for wetland conservation. Tel: 01554 741087.

National Wool Museum Drefach-Felindre, 3 miles (5km) east of Newcastle Emlyn. A museum housed in the former Cambrian Mills and dedicated to the nationally important woollen industry. The site also includes a commercial woollen mill. Tel: 01559 370929.

Nevern Castle Nevern, 7 miles (11km) northeast of Fishguard. The site of a motte with a possibly round tower on its summit, located on a promontory on precipitous crags above the River Gamman and the River Nevern. The castle may date from the late 12th or early 13th century and was occupied only for a short period.

Newcastle Emlyn Castle Newcastle Emlyn, 8 miles (13km) southeast of Cardigan. The ruins of an early 13th century castle on the River Teifi, possibly one of the few Welsh-built stone castles. It fell into English hands in the late 13th century. In disrepair in the 15th century but then repaired, it took its final bow during the Civil War when, while in the hands of a Royalist force, a Parliamentary siege attempt was driven off. However, at the end of the war the castle was blown up and slighted. The best-preserved part of the ruins is the twin-towered gatehouse to the inner ward, which stands 25ft (8m) high.

Newport Castle Newport, 6 miles (10km) northeast of Fishguard. The remains of a 13th century castle, including a gateway and two towers which were incorporated into a house in 1859. The house is privately owned and is not open to the public.

Parc Howard Museum and Art Gallery Felinfoel Road, Llanelli. Local history museum housed in a mansion built by the Buckley family in 1885. It has a renowned collection of Llanelli pottery (1839–1921), plus fine art and exhibits related to the history of the town. Tel: 01554 772029.

Paxton's Tower 1 mile (1.6km) southeast of Llanarthne, 8 miles (13km) east of Carmarthen. Aka Nelson's Tower. A three-sided tower with a turret at each angle, built 1808–15 by Sir William Paxton to commemorate the victory at the Battle of Trafalgar (hence its alternative name). Incorporating a banqueting room, it stands on a hill above the Tywi valley, the Dinefwr Estate and the National Botanic Garden Wales. Maintained by the National Trust.

Pembroke Castle Westgate Hill, Pembroke. The birthplace of Henry VII, founded by Arnulf de Montgomery in 1093 as a motte and bailey castle, and located at the junction of the Pembroke river with Monkton Pill. The stone castle was built by William Marshal, Earl of Pembroke (1146–1219) and his sons, in particular Gilbert Marshal; the inner bailey was constructed in the 1190s and an outer bailey in the first half of the 12th century. The castle's most noteworthy feature is the large 80ft (24m) high cylindrical keep with its stone dome. In the 13th century it passed to the Valence family and eventually became a royal property, after which it was let out to tenants. It was given to Jasper Tudor (Tewdwr) (c.1431–95), the son of Henry V's widow Catherine de Valois and her second husband Owen Tewdwr, and thus the half-brother of Henry VI. He was twice created Earl of Pembroke: first by Henry VI, 1452–61 and later by his nephew Henry VII, 1485–95. In January 1457 Margaret Beaufort, the wife of Jasper's brother Edmund, was staying for safety at Pembroke Castle after her husband's death two months earlier while a captive of Yorkists at Carmarthen Castle; she gave birth at the castle to Henry Tudor, the future Henry VII, on 28 January. The life of the castle was relatively peaceful, although it survived a siege by Royalists during the Civil War only to fall after a seven-week siege by Oliver Cromwell in 1648 after its occupants changed sides. The castle was then slighted by Parliamentary forces and fell into complete disrepair until the 1880s, when it was rescued and partially restored by J R Cobb. The restoration was continued by Major-General Sir Ivor Phillips, who acquired the ruins in 1928 and returned the towers and walls to something approaching their original appearance. The castle is now owned by a private charitable trust.

Pembroke Dock Gun Tower Front Street, Pembroke Dock. Local history museum housed in a former gun tower (a Cambridge Tower, sometimes incorrectly referred to as a Martello tower) in Pembroke Dock, built in the late 1840s. The museum opened in 2001 and tells the story of the dockyard, ship building and the town's military history.

Pembrokeshire Coast National Park Britain's only truly coastal National Park, designated in 1952 and covering 240 sq miles (620 sq km) along Wales's southwest coast. Habitats include beaches, cliffs, woodland, hills and estuaries. The park encompasses Caldey Island, the Daugleddau estuary, St Bride's Bay and the Preseli Hills, as well as most of the Pembrokeshire Coast Path. Heritage features include Castell Henllys Iron Age fort and Carew Castle and Tidal Mill. Tel: 0845 345 7275.

Pembrokeshire Coast Path A National Trail established in 1970 and running along the Welsh coast for 180 miles (290km) from Poppit Sands, near St Dogmaels, to Amroth, via Newport, Goodwick, Trefin, Whitesands, Solva, Little Haven, Dale, Neyland, Angle, Bosherston and Manorbier. It is almost entirely contained within the Pembrokeshire Coast National Park.

Pembrokeshire Motor Museum Simpson Cross, Keeston. A museum with more than 40 exhibits including a 1906 Rover, an MG L-type and an E-type Jaguar series II. The museum also has a large collection of model cars. Tel: 01437 710950.

Pen Dinas Hill Fort 1/4 mile (0.4km) south of Aberystwyth. Large Iron Age hill fort standing high above Aberystwyth. Excavations during the 1930s revealed at least four phases of development; the original univallate enclosure grew to eventually enclose both summits of the coastal hill and involved elaborate defences and a series of gateways. The total area enclosed is 10 acres (4ha). It was occupied from c.300 BC into the Romano-British period.

Pendine Museum of Speed Pendine, 13 miles (21km) southwest of Carmarthen. A museum celebrating the use of the 7 mile (11km) stretch of Pendine Sands for land speed attempts and motor and motorcycle racing. Its star exhibit every summer is *Babs*, the car used by racing driver J G Parry-Thomas in his land speed world record attempts. In 1924 Parry-Thomas purchased a Higham Special from the estate of the late Count Zborowski. Powered by a 27-litre Liberty aero engine, the car was of an unusual design with an exposed chain to connect the engine to the right-hand drive wheel, and was christened *Babs* by Parry-Thomas. In April 1926 Parry-Thomas took the world land speed record to 172.331mph (277.339km/h) on Pendine Sands, only to see the record increased to more than 174mph (280km/h) by Malcolm Campbell at Pendine on 4 February 1927. Parry-Thomas returned to Pendine on 3 March 1927 to make another attempt. It is not known for certain what happened but during the first run the car turned over and Parry-Thomas is believed to have been almost decapitated by the exposed drive chain. In the immediate aftermath of the accident the car was simply buried where it lay in the sand. Parry-Thomas was buried near Brooklands in Surrey. In 1969 *Babs* was disinterred and eventually restored to working order by Owen Wyn-Owen. Other record-breaking and high-speed vehicles can be seen at various times during the year. Tel: 01994 453488.

Pentre Ifan Burial Chamber 7 miles (11km) southwest of Cardigan. Once known as Arthur's Quoit. A spectacular Neolithic stone-chambered tomb dating to c.3500 BC. Its capstone weighs 16 tonnes, is more than 16ft (5m) long and is held up by three 8ft (2.5m) high uprights. It would originally have been covered by earth or boulders within a mound up to 120ft (36.5m) long.

Penlan-Uchaf Farm Gardens 5 miles (8km) east of Fishguard. A 3 acre (1.2ha) garden in the Gwaun Valley overlooking the Preseli Hills. Features include a sweet pea pergola, a spring bulb display and a sensory area for the blind and disabled. Tel: 01348 881388.

Picton Castle and Gardens 4 miles (6km) southeast of Haverfordwest. Located near the confluence of the East and West Cleddau rivers. Founded in the 13th century by Sir John Wogan, Justiciary of Ireland, as a fortified manor house with several towers, the enclosure castle was built near a Norman motte and bailey castle founded c.1090 by William de Picton. It passed to the Dwnn family and in the 15th century to the Philipps, who still own the castle, having added an impressive Georgian wing in the 1790s and restored it as a modern residence. The interior was remodelled in the early 18th century and despite being refenestrated the building retains a medieval appearance. The castle is surrounded by 40 acres (16ha) of walled and woodland gardens; the walled garden features a comprehensively planted herb garden and there is a recently planted maze, while the woodland garden features a collection of rhododendrons and azaleas. The gardens were first landscaped in the 18th century and retain some of their original layout and planting. Tel: 01437 751326.

Picton Point Fort — 4 miles (6km) southeast of Haverfordwest. The site of a possibly Iron Age fort built at the confluence of the East and West Cleddau rivers near Picton Castle.

Preseli Hills — A range of hills in the north of Pembrokeshire within the Pembrokeshire Coast National Park. The highest point is Foel Cwmcerwyn at 1759ft (536m). Stone from the Preseli Hills was used to build Stonehenge (the 'bluestones') and the hills themselves are dotted with prehistoric structures including burial chambers and cairns.

Ralph's Castle — See Blaenporth Castle.

Rivers — The **Cleddau,** consisting of the Eastern and Western Cleddau rivers, which unite to form the Daugleddau estuary, near Milford Haven, at the heart of the Pembrokeshire Coast National Park. The Eastern Cleddau rises in the foothills of Mynydd Preseli (the Preseli Hills northern extension of the National Park) at Blaencleddau and flows southwest to reach the northeastern tip of the estuary at Robeston Wathen. The Western Cleddau has two sources just southwest of Fishguard. The sources soon meet to flow through Wolf's Castle, where it enters the spectacular 90m-deep Treffgarne Gorge, cutting through the hard volcanic rocks of Treffgarne Mountain. It then continues south to join the estuary at Haverfordwest. The Western Cleddau at approximately 25 miles (40km) is slightly longer than the Eastern at 20 miles (32km). The **Loughor** rises on the southeastern outskirts of Black Mountain (see Powys) just north of Ammanford. It flows in a southwesterly direction past Ammanford and divides Hendy in Carmarthenshire from Pontarddulais in Swansea. The river discharges into Carmarthen Bay at its estuary near the town of Loughor where it separates the south coast of Carmarthenshire from the north coast of the Gower peninsula. Its length is approximately 15 miles (24km). The **Rheidol** rises in the headwaters of the Nant y Moch reservoir, 12 miles northwest of Aberystwyth. It initially flows south through the village of Ponterwyd before joining the River Mynach at the bottom of the falls at Devil's Bridge. The river then flows due west adjacent to the Vale of Rheidol Railway before discharging into Cardigan Bay at Aberystwyth where it shares the harbour with the River Ystwyth; its total length approximately 20 miles (32km). The **Tâf** (not to be confused with the more famous Taff) rises in the eastern extremity of the Preseli Hills, at Crymmych, 8 miles south of Cardigan. It flows for 30 miles (48km) in a southeasterly direction into Carmarthen Bay, sharing an estuary with the Towy. The **Teifi** has its source in Llyn Teifi, one of several lakes known collectively as Teifi Pools, approximately 15 miles southeast of Aberystwyth. The river flows in a generally southwesterly direction, initially past Strata Florida Abbey and then Pontrhydfendigaid before travelling through the great raised mire of Gors Goch Glan Teifi (the Tregaron Bog). The Teifi moves on through Llanddewi Brefi, Lampeter, Llanybydder, Llandysul, Newcastle Emlyn, Cenarth (where salmon can be seen climbing the artificial ladder up the falls), Llechryd and finally discharging into the bay at Cardigan. The river's length is approximately 56 miles (90km) and forms the border with Carmarthenshire and Pembrokeshire for some of its length. The **Towy** (Afon Tywi) rises 8 miles southeast of Tregaron, near the slopes of Dibyn Dhu in the Cambrian Mountains. Eight miles south of its source is the Llyn Brianne Reservoir, and in 1972 the river was dammed here to preserve drinking water during dry periods. From this point the river has a continuous run to Llandovery before veering southwest to Llandello and then west into Abergwili, where it is joined by its main tributary, the Afon Gwili. Finally the river flows through Carmarthen and into Carmarthen Bay in a combined estuary with the River Tâf. From its continuous flow at Rhandirmwyn (the southern point of Llyn Brianne) it travels 65 miles (104km) and is the longest river wholly in Wales.

Roch Castle — Roch, 6 miles (10km) northwest of Haverfordwest. A restored D-shaped tower first built in the 13th century by the de Rupe family on a rocky outcrop. It was occupied until the Civil War when, under the ownership of the Walter family, it was besieged and taken by Parliamentary forces. During the 20th century it was restored and renovated and more living accommodation added. It is located within the Pembrokeshire Coastal National Park.

St Anne's Head Lighthouse — 6 miles (10km) southwest of Milford Haven. There have been warning lights on St Anne's Head, the headland at the approach to Milford Haven, since the 17th century, and the first lighthouses proper were built in 1714 by local landowner Joseph Allen. The current lighthouse, which stands 42ft (13m) high, was erected in 1841; it was converted to mains electricity in 1958 and was automated in 1998.

St David's Bishop's Palace — Quickwell Hill, St David's. The ruins of a palace used by the bishops of St David's and originally built in the 12th century close to the cathedral. Begun 1280–96 by Bishop Thomas Bek, the later main period of construction by Bishop Henry de Gower 1328–47 included the building of the great hall. Following the Reformation the bishops took up residence at Abergwili and most of the palace was left to fall into disrepair. The ruins are in the care of CADW.

St David's Cathedral — The Pebbles, St David's. Dedicated to St David and St Andrew, the cathedral dominates Britain's smallest city. It stands on the site where St David founded a monastery in AD 589. The monastery and earlier church suffered severe depredations from Viking attacks. The construction of the present cathedral was begun in 1181 by Bishop Peter de Leia and Geraldus de Barri, who were excused service during the Third Crusade if they carried out the work. The main construction was completed by the 1220s when the collapsed 'new tower' was rebuilt. Further alterations and additions were made over the next 300 years. The cathedral suffered damage from an earthquake in the mid 13th century, during the Reformation when its relics were removed, and from Parliamentary troops in 1648. The west front was restored by John Nash in 1793 but was granted a more sympathetic restoration by Sir Gilbert Scott, 1862–77. The nave is the oldest surviving part of the cathedral. Tel: 01437 720691.

St Dogmaels Abbey — St Dogmaels, 1 mile (1.6km) west of Cardigan. The ruins of a Benedictine abbey established in the early 12th century beside the River Teifi by monks from Tiron in France. The abbey was extended in the 13th century and further remodelled in the 14th and 16th centuries. After an outbreak of plague in the mid 14th century it was reduced to only four monks, but recovered a little before being dissolved in 1536. After the Dissolution the abbey church continued in use by the parish until a new parish church was built in the early 18th century. The main ruins include the infirmary, the north transept and the north nave wall of the abbey church. Now in the care of CADW.

St Govan's Chapel — 5 miles (8km) south of Pembroke. Built in the 13th century in a rocky gorge on St Govan's Point, the most southerly point on the Pembrokeshire coast. A simple chapel with only a single chamber measuring 18ft (5m) by 12ft (3.5m), it stands on the site of the purported hermitage of St Govan, where the saint miraculously escaped from pirates when a rock opened for him to hide in. It later became a place of pilgrimage noted for its miraculous cure of lameness and eye diseases. The chapel can only be reached by a set of steps which it is said cannot be counted (I counted 74!). Nearby is St Govan's holy well.

St Lawrence's Gumfreston — Gumfreston, 1 mile (1.6km) west of Tenby. A small 12th century church with the faded fragments of a wall painting of 'Christ of the Trades' on the north wall.

Scolton Manor — Spittal, 4½ miles (7km) north of Haverfordwest. A 19th century two-storey neoclassical manor house built for the Higgons family and standing amid 60 acres (24ha) of grounds including parkland and woodland. The house was bought by Pembrokeshire County Council in 1972. It now houses the Pembrokeshire County Museum, which features exhibits tracing the county's social, economic, natural and industrial history. The exhibition hall also has a signal box and a locomotive. Tel: 01437 731457.

Sheep Island Fort — 6 miles (10km) northwest of Pembroke. The site of a promontory fort located on Castle Bay promontory and Sheep Island. The period of occupancy is not clear but may extend into the medieval period.

Skokholm Island Lighthouse — Located on the southwest point of Skokholm Island. Established in 1916 and standing 59ft (18m) high, the lighthouse was automated in 1983.

Smalls Lighthouse — Erected in 1861 on the site of an earlier lighthouse on a rock 20 miles (32km) west of St David's Head. The current lighthouse stands 138ft (42m) high and was designed by James Walker. The original lighthouse, built in the 1770s, an unusual structure erected on pillars to allow the passage of the seas beneath it, was the scene of one of the more macabre episodes in the history of lighthouse-keeping. The two keepers on Smalls in 1800 were Messrs Howell and Griffin, a pair not noted for being on the best of terms. Unfortunately, Howell died on duty (whether by accident or natural causes is not clear) and Griffin, fearing that he might be accused of causing the death, decided to keep the body in a makeshift coffin which he slung outside to await the arrival of his relief team. The coffin was disturbed during a storm and Howell's decomposing body was left hanging outside the window, seemingly taunting poor Griffin. The relief ship was delayed by the storms and its crew arrived to find one keeper dead and the other alive, but white-haired and quite out of his mind. From that point onwards lighthouse-keeping teams consisted of three members.

South Bishop Lighthouse — Located on South Bishop (aka Em-sger), a rock 5 miles (8km) west of St David's Head. Designed by James Walker and established in 1839, the lighthouse stands 37ft (11.5m) high; it was converted to electric operation in 1959 and automated in 1983.

Sport

football

Aberystwyth Town were founded in 1884 and were founder members of the League of Wales in 1992. They won the Welsh Cup in 1900. Their home ground is Park Avenue, Maesgogerddan, Aberystwyth.

Carmarthen Town were founded in 1948. Nicknamed The Old Gold or The Town, their home ground is Richmond Park, Priory Street, Carmarthen.

Haverfordwest County were founded in 1899 as Haverfordwest FC and have also been known as Haverfordwest Town. They were founder members of the League of Wales in 1992. Their home ground is Bridge Meadow Stadium, New Bridge Meadow, Haverfordwest.

Llanelli were founded in 1896 and were founder members of the League of Wales in 1992. Nicknamed The Reds, their home ground is Stebonheath Park, Llanelli. The club is owned by Catherine Zeta-Jones's uncle Robert Jones.

rugby union

Llanelli RFC, founded in 1872, were one of the leading club sides in Wales, beating Australian national teams in 1967 and 1992 and a New Zealand team in 1972. In 2003 the club rebranded as part of Llanelli Scarlets, although Llanelli RFC continued to play in the Welsh Premier Division and Welsh Cup. They were winners of the Welsh Premier Division in 1993, 1999 and 2002, and of the Welsh Cup in 1973, 1974, 1975, 1976, 1985, 1988, 1991, 1992, 1993, 1998, 2000, 2003, 2005. Nicknamed The Scarlets, their home ground from 1879 until 2008 was Stradey Park, Llanelli.

Scarlets RFC were founded in 2003 as Llanelli Scarlets, a professional regional team playing in the Celtic League, which they won in 2004. Represented by Llanelli RFC, Carmarthen RFC, Llandovery RFC and Narberth RFC, the club officially represents the whole of West and North Wales. Their home ground until 2008 was Stradey Park, and they have also played several games at the Racecourse Ground in Wrexham; their new home ground, Parc y Scarlets (Scarlets Park), Pemberton, opened in November 2008.

Stackpole Estate — 4 miles (6km) south of Pembroke. An estate of over 2000 acres (800ha) of coastal land which once surrounded Stackpole Court, formerly owned by the Cawdor family and demolished in 1963. Now situated within the Pembrokeshire Coast National Park, the estate is a designated National Nature Reserve with habitats including beach, cliff, lakes and woodland. It has been managed since 1976 by the National Trust in partnership with the Countryside Council for Wales. Tel: 01646 661359.

Strata Florida Abbey Strata Florida, 14 miles (23km) southeast of Aberystwyth. The substantial ruins of a Cistercian abbey founded in 1164 beside the Afon Fflur (hence its name, Ystrad Fflur) and moved to this nearby location in 1184. It was a daughter house of the Cistercian abbey at Whitland. Most of the ruins date from the main building period of the 13th century. As a Welsh house it suffered depredations throughout its early life because of the continual conflict with England. It is believed that the annals known as the Chronicle of the Princes may have been transcribed at the abbey and it appears that many local princes were buried here. The abbey was abandoned following the Dissolution. The ruins are maintained by CADW.

Strumble Head Lighthouse 5 miles (8km) northwest of Fishguard. Located on Ynys Meicel (St Michael's), a rocky island off Strumble Head at the northwest corner of Pencaer and connected to the mainland by a narrow bridge. Standing 55ft (17m) high and established in 1908, the lighthouse was electrified in 1965 and automated in 1980.

Talley Abbey Talley, 16 miles (26km) northeast of Carmarthen. The ruins of a Premonstratensian abbey founded in the late 12th century by white canons from St John at Amiens. The abbey suffered from lack of funds and the depredations of the wars between Wales and England but survived until the Dissolution. The abbey church was used as a parish church until 1772. The main feature of the ruins is the 85ft (26m) wall of the crossing tower.

Teifi Valley Railway A narrow gauge heritage railway operating for 2 miles (3km) between Henllan and Riverside on part of the former standard gauge line between Carmarthen and Newcastle Emlyn, closed in 1973. The service uses both steam and diesel locomotives. Tel: 01559 371077.

Tenby Castle Castle Hill, Tenby. The ruins of a Norman castle located on a headland above Tenby, founded after 1153. Sacked by the Welsh in 1187 and 1260, it was rebuilt in the late 13th century and saw action during the Civil War, when a unit of Royalist rebels held out for ten weeks before being starved out. Tenby Museum and Art Gallery is housed in what must have been a medieval domestic building attached to the castle. Tenby is also noted for its surviving circuit of medieval (probably 13th century) town walls; one gate and seven towers from the original layout survive. The castle now stands within a public park; the main surviving structure is a tower which commands outstanding views of the area, while there are fragmentary remains of the castle walls on the cliffs.

Tenby Merchant's House Quay Hill, Tenby. A three-floor 15th century house furnished in period style and featuring a Tudor herb garden. Maintained by the National Trust since 1937. Tel: 01834 842279.

Tenby Museum and Art Gallery Castle Hill, Tenby. Housed in one of the former domestic buildings of medieval Tenby Castle. It has five galleries: the Wilfred Harrison Gallery was opened in 1972 and houses the museum's permanent art collection, including works by locally born Augustus John; the New Art Gallery was opened in 1995 and houses temporary exhibitions; the Lower Gallery has local history and archaeology exhibits dating from the Precambrian Age to the Romano-British period; the Maritime Gallery explores the influence of the sea on the fortunes of the town and in particular the history of the lifeboat service; and the Story of Tenby narrates the history of the town from the Anglo-Saxon period to the present day. Tel: 01834 842809.

Trinity College, Carmarthen College Road, Carmarthen. Founded in 1848 as an Anglican college and became a constituent member of the federal University of Wales in 2005. It is mainly a teacher training college but also offers courses in Advertising and Tourism, English, History and Theology. Tel: 01267 676767.

University of Wales Aberystwyth King Street, Aberystwyth. Established in 1872 as University College Wales; in 1894 it became a founder member of the University of Wales. The world's first Department of International Politics was founded at Aberystwyth in 1919. The main campus of the university is now on Penglais Hill where 13 of the 18 departments are located, and the university's administration is housed in the original building, known as Old College. The Institute of Rural Sciences and the Department of Information Studies are on the Llanbadarn campus. Tel: 01970 623111.

University of Wales Lampeter College Street, Lampeter. Founded in 1822 as St David's College and opened in 1827. It became St David's University College and part of the University of Wales in 1971, changing its title to the University of Wales, Lampeter in 1996. Located on a small rural campus with only around 1000 students and originally specialising in theology and religious studies, it now offers a range of arts courses. Tel: 01570 422351.

Upton Castle Gardens $1^1/_4$ miles (2km) northeast of Cosheston, 2 miles (3km) northeast of Pembroke. A 35 acre (14ha) garden of parkland and woodland located above the Carew River and surrounding the much altered 13th century Upton Castle. In addition to a collection of camellias and rhododendrons there is also a rose garden and herbaceous borders. The castle is not open to the public. Tel: 01646 651782.

Vale of Rheidol Railway A narrow gauge (1ft $1^3/_4$in/349mm) heritage railway operating for $11^3/_4$ miles (19km) from Aberystwyth to Devil's Bridge via Llanbadarn, Glanrafon, Capel Bangor, Nantyronen, Aberffrwd, Rheidol Falls and Rhiwfron. The original commercial service opened in 1902 to serve the lead mines in the Rheidol Valley. It was the last steam line to be operated as part of the nationalised British Railways network and was privatised in 1989. Tel: 01970 625819.

Walwyn's Castle Walwyn's Castle, 3 miles (5km) northwest of Milford Haven. A complex rampart and ditch earthwork probably dating from the Iron Age and which may have later supported a castle.

Whitland Abbey 1 mile (1.6km) north of Whitland, 13 miles (21km) west of Carmarthen. A Cistercian abbey founded in 1140 at Trefgarn near Haverfordwest as a daughter house of St Bernard's Abbey at Clairvaux, and relocated to Whitland in 1151. Possibly the earliest Cistercian abbey in Wales, it was itself the mother house of Cwmhir (1143), Strata Florida (1164) and Strata Marcella (1170). The abbey was under the patronage of a succession of Welsh princes and was relatively prosperous. It was also a supporter of Welsh independence from England and, as such, suffered the consequences both materially and financially during the conflict with Edward I. The abbey

	went into decline and was closed at the time of the Dissolution. The ruins are meagre but the outline of the buildings is marked out.
Wiston Castle	Wiston, 4$^1/_2$ miles (7km) northeast of Haverfordwest. The remains of a motte and bailey castle with a stone shell keep, probably built in the 12th century and reported destroyed in 1220. The motte stands 40ft (12m) high and is 60ft (18m) in diameter at its summit.
Ystrad Meurig Castle	Ysrad Meurig, 10$^1/_2$ miles (17km) southeast of Aberystwyth. Motte and bailey castle founded c.1110 by Gilbert de Clare. The remains include earthworks and traces of a rectangular keep. The castle had a relatively short lifespan of about 100 years.

Some famous people born in Dyfed

Bale, Christian (actor) (1974–)	Haverfordwest
Bennett, Hywel (actor) (1944–)	Garnant
Bennett, Phil (rugby player) (1948–)	Felinfoel
David (saint) (c.500–589)	Pembrokeshire
Griffiths, Terry (snooker player) (1947–)	Llanelli
Ifans, Rhys (actor) (1968–)	Haverfordwest
John, Augustus (artist) (1878–1961)	Tenby
John, Barry (rugby union player) (1945–)	Cefneithin
John, Gwen (artist) (1876–1939)	Haverfordwest
Recorde, Robert (mathematician) (c.1510–1558)	Tenby
Roberts, Rachel (actress) (1927–80)	Llanelli
Swann, Donald Ibrahim (musician) (1923–94)	Llanelli
Tudor, Henry (Henry VII, king of England) (1457–1509)	Pembroke

Islands of Dyfed

Island name	Area	Nearest landmark	General information	Shipping Area
Ceredigion				
Birds Rock	Cardigan Bay	New Quay	GR: SN376602	Irish Sea
Cardigan Island	Cardigan Bay	Cardigan	aka Ynys Aberteifi. GR: SN160515	Irish Sea
Carreg Ifan	Cardigan Bay	Llangranog	GR: SN313549	Irish Sea
Carreg Lydan	Cardigan Bay	Cardigan	GR: SN162514	Irish Sea
Carreg Ti-pw	Cardigan Bay	Llanrhystud	GR: SN535708	Irish Sea
Carreg y Nodwydd	Cardigan Bay	Llangranog	GR: SN298536	Irish Sea
Carreg y ty	Cardigan Bay	Llangranog	GR: SN301538	Irish Sea
Cormorant Rock	Cardigan Bay	Aberystwyth	aka Craig y Fulfran. GR: SN583830	Irish Sea
Craig y Fulfran	Cardigan Bay	Aberystwyth	See Cormorant Rock.	Irish Sea
Traeth y Coubal	Cardigan Bay	New Quay	GR: SN371593	Irish Sea
Ynys Aberteifi	Cardigan Bay	Cardigan	See Cardigan Island.	Irish Sea
Ynys-Lochtyn	Cardigan Bay	Llangranog	GR: SN314555	Irish Sea
Pembrokeshire				
Aber Hywel	Fishguard Bay	Dinas Cross	(W. = Eminent Estuary). GR: SM989386	Irish Sea
Abereiddy Tower	St George's Channel	Abereiddy	GR: SM795315	Irish Sea
Anvil, The	Broad Sound	Martin's Haven	GR: SM754088	Lundy
Bancyn-ffald	St George's Channel	Ramsey Island	GR: SM693228	Irish Sea
Bench, The	Broad Sound	Martin's Haven	GR: SM755082	Lundy
Bitches, The	Ramsey Sound	Ramsey Island	GR: SM709237	Irish Sea
Black Rock	St Bride's Bay	Solva	GR: SM 801235	Lundy
Black Scar	St Bride's Bay	Solva	Small reef inhabited only by seals. GR: SM792225	Lundy
Black Stones	Broad Sound	Midland Isle	GR: SM746084	Lundy
Brimstone Rock	Atlantic	Linney Head	GR: SR881968	Lundy
Bull Rock	Milford Haven	Little Castle Head	GR: SM857065	Lundy
Caldey Island	Atlantic	Caldey Island	aka Ynys Pyr. See separate entry.	Lundy
Careg Yspar	St George's Channel	Witches Cauldron	GR: SN099448	Irish Sea
Careg-y-fran	Fishguard Bay	Dinas Head	GR: SM999404	Irish Sea
Carreg Bica	St George's Channel	Traeth Cell-Howel	GR: SN091441	Irish Sea
Carreg Bwch-du	St George's Channel	Penbwchdy	GR: SM875374	Irish Sea
Carreg Coffin	Fishguard Bay	Fishguard	GR: SM963378	Irish Sea
Carreg Dandy	St George's Channel	Porth Dwgan	GR: SM882355	Irish Sea
Carreg Ddu	St George's Channel	Strumble Head	GR: SM883387	Irish Sea

Island name	Area	Nearest landmark	General information	Shipping Area
Carreg Dilys	St Bride's Bay	Solva	GR: SM807237	Lundy
Carreg Fran	St Bride's Bay	St David's Head	GR: SM731229	Lundy
Carreg Gefeilog	St George's Channel	Point St John	GR: SM720263	Irish Sea
Carreg Gerwynau	St George's Channel	Strumble Head	GR: SM888383	Irish Sea
Carreg Golchfa	St George's Channel	Aber Bach	GR: SM883352	Irish Sea
Carreg Gwylan	St George's Channel	Ynys Barry	GR: SM797322	Irish Sea
Carreg Gwylan	St George's Channel	Ramsey Island	GR: SM692235	Irish Sea
Carreg Gwylan-fach	St George's Channel	Castell Coch	GR: SM773305	Irish Sea
Carreg Gybi	St George's Channel	Strumble Head	GR: SM904414	Irish Sea
Carreg Herefio	St George's Channel	Porth Coch	GR: SM881361	Irish Sea
Carreg John Evan	Newport Bay	Dinas Head	GR: SN017405	Irish Sea
Carreg Lion	St George's Channel	Cemaes Head	GR: SN121489	Irish Sea
Carreg Onnen	St George's Channel	Strumble Head	GR: SM888412	Irish Sea
Carreg Pen-las	Fishguard Bay	Aber Bach	GR: SM995389	Irish Sea
Carreg Rhoson	St George's Channel	Ramsey Island	One of the Bishops and Clerks group. GR: SM670255	Irish Sea
Carreg Tomas	Fishguard Bay	Fishguard	GR: SM965379	Irish Sea
Carreg y Barcud	St Bride's Bay	Trelerw	GR: SM770240	Lundy
Carreg y Wrach	St George's Channel	Strumble Head	GR: SM895414	Irish Sea
Carreg yr Esgob	St Bride's Bay	St David's Head	GR: SM728230	Lundy
Carregedrywy	St George's Channel	Morfa Head	GR: SN045419	Irish Sea
Cat Rock	Newport Bay	Parog	GR: SN041399	Irish Sea
Cerrig Duon	Fishguard Bay	Dinas Head	GR: SM996393	Irish Sea
Cerrig Gwylan	St George's Channel	Abereiddy	Twin stacks. Cerrig is the plural of Carrig (rock).	Irish Sea
Church Rock	Atlantic	St Govan's Head	GR: SR983938	Lundy
Cow and Calf	Fishguard Bay	Fishguard	Group of tiny scars, with a wall all around the largest one. GR: SM955395	Irish Sea
Crab Rocks	Broad Sound	Skokholm Island	GR: SM740046	Lundy
Crab Stones	St George's Channel	Midland Isle	GR: SM750092	Irish Sea
Cribog	St George's Channel	Ramsey Island	One of the Bishops and Clerks group. GR: SM666237	Irish Sea
Crow Rock	Atlantic	Linney Head	GR: SM886948	Lundy
Daufraich	St George's Channel	Ramsey Island	One of the Bishops and Clerks group. GR: SM661236	Irish Sea
Elegug Stacks	Atlantic	Flimston Bay	GR: SR927945	Lundy
Garland Stone	St George's Channel	Skomer Island	GR: SM721104	Irish Sea
Gateholm Island	Broad Sound	Marloes	See separate entry.	Lundy
Gateholm Stack	Broad Sound	Marloes	Rock stack off the coast of Gateholm Island. GR: SM773075	Lundy
Grassholme	St George's Channel	Skomer Island	Favourite haunt of divers as the marine life is rich. The island itself has a seal colony and gannets hover and swoop endlessly. Around the coast porpoises are common. Area: 0.03 sq mile (0.08 sq km). GR: SM598083	Irish Sea
Gray Rocks	Milford Haven	Great Castle Head	GR: SM087059	Lundy
Green Scar	St Bride's Bay	Solva	A scar is another name for a skerry (rock outcrop). GR: SM795226	Lundy
Gwahan	St George's Channel	St David's Head	GR: SM706260	Irish Sea
Haccesh	St Bride's Bay	Upper Solva	GR: SM789239	Lundy
Half Tide Rock	St Bride's Bay	St David's Head	GR: SM741228	Lundy
Halfway Rock	St Bride's Bay	Warey Haven	GR: SM808119	Lundy
Hanging Tar	Atlantic	Linney Head	GR: SR882967	Lundy
Haroldston Chins	St Bride's Bay	Druidston	GR: SM859162	Lundy
Howney Stone	St Bride's Bay	Broadmoor	GR: SM820129	Lundy
Howney Stone	St Bride's Bay	Marloes	GR: SM776092	Lundy
Limpet Rocks	Broad Sound	Martin's Haven	GR: SM755086	Lundy
Llech Ganol	St George's Channel	Trwyncastell	GR: SM778313	Irish Sea
Llech Isaf	St George's Channel	Trwyncastell	GR: SM769313	Irish Sea
Llech Uchaf	St George's Channel	Ynys Barry	GR: SM788322	Irish Sea
Llechau-isaf	St George's Channel	Ramsey Island	GR: SM680239	Irish Sea
Llechau-uchaf	St George's Channel	Ramsey Island	GR: SM682245	Irish Sea
Lowrey's Rock	Milford Haven	Milford Haven	GR: SM842029	Lundy
Maen Bachau	Ramsey Sound	St David's Head	GR: SM723245	Irish Sea
Maen Cam	St George's Channel	Point St John	GR: SM722262	Irish Sea

Island name	Area	Nearest landmark	General information	Shipping Area
Maen Daufraich	St George's Channel	Ramsey Island	One of the Bishops and Clerks group. GR: SM661239	Irish Sea
Maen Porth-llong	St George's Channel	St David's Head	GR: SM732286	Irish Sea
Maen Rhoson	St George's Channel	Ramsey Island	One of the Bishops and Clerks group. GR: SM665258	Irish Sea
March Bach	St George's Channel	Strumble Head	GR: SM882400	Irish Sea
March Mawr	St George's Channel	Strumble Head	GR: SM880397	Irish Sea
Mare, The	St Bride's Bay	Solva	GR: SM799226	Lundy
Meini Duon	St George's Channel	Ramsey Island	GR: SM696216	Irish Sea
Mew Stone	Broad Sound	Skomer Island	GR: SM726083	Lundy
Middleholm	St George's Channel	Skomer Island	aka Midland Isle. GR: SM747090	Irish Sea
Midland Isle	St George's Channel	Skomer Island	See Middleholm.	Irish Sea
Moelyn	St George's Channel	Ramsey Island	One of the Bishops and Clerks group. GR: SM669239	Irish Sea
Monkstone	Carmarthen Bay	Saundersfoot	GR: SN150032	Lundy
Needle Rock	Newport Bay	Dinas Head	Depths of up to 50ft (15m). Favoured island for divers. GR: SN015409	Irish Sea
Needle Rock	Fishguard Bay	Penrhyn	GR: SM975380	Irish Sea
North Bishop	St George's Channel	St David's Head	GR: SM670280	Irish Sea
Ogof Cadno	St George's Channel	Traeth Cell-Howel	GR: SN091440	Irish Sea
Ogof Goch	St George's Channel	Moylgrove	GR: SN095445	Irish Sea
Pains Rock	St George's Channel	Skomer Island	GR: SM717102	Irish Sea
Pen Brush	St George's Channel	Strumble Head	GR: SM880397	Irish Sea
Pen Sidan	Fishguard Bay	Dinas Head	GR: SM998405	Irish Sea
Pen-cw	Fishguard Bay	Fishguard	GR: SM955394	Irish Sea
Penpleidiau	St Bride's Bay	St David's Head	GR: SM762238	Lundy
Pen-y-Holt Stack	Atlantic	Linney Head	GR: SR896953	Lundy
Pig Stone	St George's Channel	Skomer Island	GR: SM712092	Irish Sea
Pig y Barcut	St George's Channel	Penrhyn Ffynnon-las	GR: SM753291	Irish Sea
Pont yr Eilun	St George's Channel	Ramsey Island	One of two islets southeast of Ramsey Island (the other being Ynys Eilun). GR: SM709219	Irish Sea
Raggle Rocks	Broad Sound	Marloes	GR: SM776076	Lundy
Rainy Rock	Broad Sound	Marloes	GR: SM763079	Lundy
Ramsey Island	St George's Channel	St David's Head	Owned by the RSPB, the island also has the most important grey seal breeding colony in southern Britain. Area: 1.02 sq miles (2.63 sq km). GR: SM705240	Irish Sea
Rat Island	Milford Haven	Milford Haven	GR: SM840027	Lundy
Reef Solva	St Bride's Bay	Solva	Lies southwest of Green Scar.	Lundy
Rye Rocks	St George's Channel	Skomer Island	GR: SM738096	Irish Sea
St Catherine's Island	Carmarthen Bay	Tenby	Linked to Tenby by a beach at low tide. Area: 0.01 sq miles (0.03 sq km). GR: SN139003	Lundy
St Elvis Rock	St Bride's Bay	Solva	GR: SM802236	Lundy
St Margaret's Island	Caldey Sound	Caldey Island	Name derives from a chapel that once stood on the island. GR: SS120793	Lundy
Scalds Rocks	St Bride's Bay	Druidston	GR: SM862172	Lundy
Segar Rock	St Bride's Bay	The Cradle	GR: SM790236	Lundy
Shag Rock	St Bride's Bay	Broad Haven	GR: SM858142	Lundy
Shag Rock	Broad Sound	Skomer Island	GR: SM736088	Lundy
Sheep Island	Milford Haven	Milford Haven	Tiny islet strewn with large boulders. GR: SM843016	Lundy
Shoe Rock	Ramsey Sound	Pen Dal-aderyn	GR: SM715232	Irish Sea
Sker Rock	Carmarthen Bay	Tenby	GR: SN141002	Lundy
Skokholm	Broad Sound	St Ann's Head	R M Lockley, a pioneering ornithologist especially famous for his work on puffins and shearwaters, leased Skokholm in 1927 and wrote many books featuring the island. Area: 0.41 sq miles (1.05 sq km). GR: SM735050	Lundy

Island name	Area	Nearest landmark	General information	Shipping Area
Skomer	St George's Channel	Wooltack Point	Best known for its huge bird population, stone circle and standing stone. Area: 1.13 sq miles (2.92 sq km). GR: SM715090	Irish Sea
Sledges, The	St George's Channel	Abereiddy	Group of large rocks off Abereiddi Beach.	Irish Sea
Smalls, The	St George's Channel	Skomer Island	GR: SM047089	Irish Sea
South Bishop	St George's Channel	St David's Head	GR: SM651225	Irish Sea
Stacan Barcutan	St George's Channel	Aber-pwll	GR: SM781308	Irish Sea
Stacen y Brenhin	St Bride's Bay	Dinas Fach	GR: SM822230	Lundy
Stack, The	Broad Sound	Skokholm Island	GR: SM745055	Lundy
Stack Rock	Milford Haven	South Hook Point	GR: SM865049	Lundy
Stack Rocks	St Bride's Bay	Howney Stone	GR: SM810132	Lundy
Star Rock	Atlantic	St Govan's Head	GR: SR979938	Lundy
Table, The	St George's Channel	Skomer Island	GR: SM712096	Irish Sea
Table Rock	Carmarthen Bay	Tenby	GR: SN138016	Lundy
Thorn Island	Milford Haven	Milford Haven	GR: SM845039	Lundy
Thorn Rock	St George's Channel	Skomer Island	GR: SM740089	Irish Sea
Traeth Rock	St George's Channel	Abereiddy	Traeth means beach or strand.	Irish Sea
Tri Maen-trai	St George's Channel	Strumble Head	GR: SM880390	Irish Sea
Trwynmynacdy	St George's Channel	Ramsey Island	GR: SM699226	Irish Sea
Tusker Rock	St George's Channel	Wooltack Point	GR: SM753094	Irish Sea
Ynys Bery	St George's Channel	Ramsey Island	SS *Graffoe* (a 2996 ton steamship bound from Glasgow to Buenos Aires with coal) struck Ramsey Island and sank at the northern end of Ynys Bery in 1903. GR: SM702220	Irish Sea
Ynys Cantwr	St George's Channel	Ramsey Island	Small tidal island south of Ramsey Island, its highest point being 180ft (55m). GR: SM705223	Irish Sea
Ynys Ddu	St George's Channel	Strumble Head	GR: SM886388	Irish Sea
Ynys Deullyn	St George's Channel	Abercastle	GR: SM845342	Irish Sea
Ynys Dinas	Ramsey Sound	St David's Head	GR: SM722252	Irish Sea
Ynys Dol-rhedyn	Newport Bay	Dinas Head	GR: SN021397	Irish Sea
Ynys Eilun	St George's Channel	Ramsey Island	One of two islets southeast of Ramsey Island (the other being Pont yr Eilun). GR: SM706219	Irish Sea
Ynys Gwair	St George's Channel	Castell Coch	GR: SM775305	Irish Sea
Ynys Gwelltog	St George's Channel	Ramsey Island	(Welsh = Grassy Island). GR: SM704224	Irish Sea
Ynys Hwrddod	Ramsey Sound	Ramsey Island	GR: SM706236	Irish Sea
Ynys Meicel	St George's Channel	Strumble Head	GR: SM893413	Irish Sea
Ynys Melyn	St George's Channel	Strumble Head	GR: SM885386	Irish Sea
Ynys Onnen	St George's Channel	Strumble Head	GR: SM890412	Irish Sea
Ynys Pyr	Atlantic	Caldey Island	See Caldey Island.	Lundy
Ynys y Castell	St George's Channel	Abercastle	GR: SM852339	Irish Sea
Ynys y Ddinas	St George's Channel	Strumble Head	GR: SM887387	Irish Sea
Ynys-fach	St George's Channel	Porthgain	GR: SM823327	Irish Sea
Carmarthenshire				
Carreg-ddu	River Loughor	Llanelli	GR: SS520971	Lundy
Carreg-fach	River Loughor	Llanelli	GR: SS510971	Lundy

GWENT

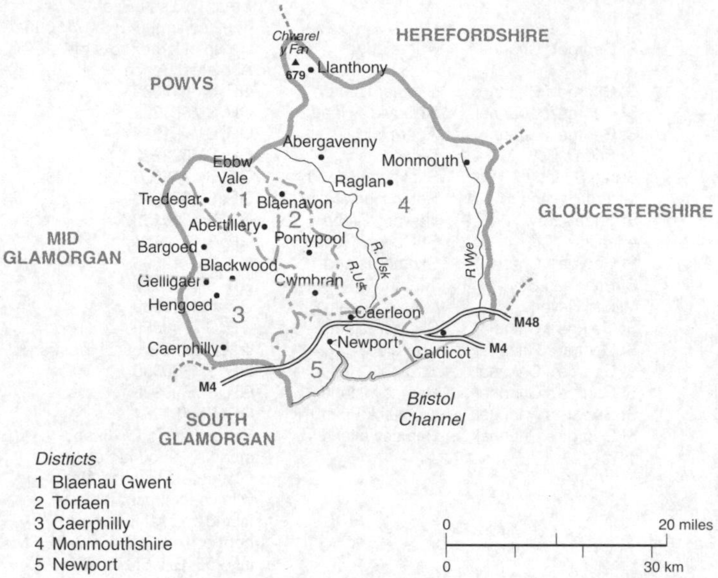
HEREFORDSHIRE
POWYS
Llanthony
679
Abergavenny
Monmouth
Ebbw Vale
Raglan
Tredegar
1
Blaenavon
4
2
GLOUCESTERSHIRE
Abertillery
MID GLAMORGAN
Bargoed
Pontypool
R. Usk
R Wye
Blackwood
Gelligaer
Cwmbran
Hengoed
3
Caerleon
M48
Caerphilly
Newport
Caldicot
M4
5
M4
Bristol Channel
SOUTH GLAMORGAN
0
20 miles
0
30 km

Districts
1 Blaenau Gwent
2 Torfaen
3 Caerphilly
4 Monmouthshire
5 Newport

Gwent is a preserved county which covers the unitary authorities of Blaenau Gwent, Caerphilly, Monmouthshire, Newport and Torfaen. It is bordered to the east and northeast by the English counties of Gloucestershire and Herefordshire, to the northwest by Powys, to the south by the Severn Estuary and the Bristol Channel, to the west by Mid Glamorgan and to the southwest by South Glamorgan. Newport, one of only five cities in Wales, is the third largest city after Cardiff and Swansea. It is the cultural capital and largest urban area of the traditional county of Monmouthshire and is governed by the unitary Newport City Council.

The area of Gwent has been settled since at least the Mesolithic period and in the Iron Age was occupied by the Silures. Shortly after their arrival the Romans established a major fortress at Caerleon to guard the crossing of the Usk where the Silures themselves had established a major hill fort. This later became Newport. Caerleon was also the Roman base for the control of South Wales in general and along with Chester and York was one of the three legionary fortresses in England and Wales. The smaller kingdom of Gwent, sandwiched between the rivers Wye and Usk and the Severn Estuary, was formed after the withdrawal of the Romans in the early 5th century and had its capital at Caer Gwent. It survived until the Norman invasion of the 11th century, its rulers including Athrwys ap Meurig, who is sometimes identified with King Arthur – an analogy drawn because Athrwys resisted a Saxon invasion and also had a 'court' at Caerleon, or the old Iron Age fort nearby.

The kingdom was overrun in the 1090s by the Normans, who built a series of massive castles in the area, including those at Chepstow, Caerphilly and Newport. The Normans also partitioned the area into the lordships of Abergavenny, Monmouth, Striguil (Chepstow) and Usk and these remained the basic units of administration until the Laws in Wales Act 1535 established the county of Monmouthshire. Even today there is some debate as to the 'Welshness' of Monmouthshire.

The economy of the rest of the region remained strictly rural and agricultural until the Industrial Revolution, when rich veins of iron ore and coal were discovered and new settlements quickly developed around the ironworks erected in the west of the region at Dowlais (1759), Merthyr Tydfil (1765), Tredegar (1778), Blaenavon (1789), Ebbw Vale (1790), Nant-y-glo (1791), Pontypool (1796), Rhymney (1800) and Aberdare (1802). Meanwhile in the east Chepstow developed into a flourishing market town and port, although its role declined in the 19th century as the iron, steel and coal industries sent their exports through Cardiff, Newport and Swansea.

The prosperity of the region throughout the 19th and 20th centuries was decided by the vicissitudes of the markets. The iron industry was in sharp decline by the early 20th century and the steel and coal industries suffered during the inter-war period, becoming surplus to the requirements of the market economy in the 1980s and 1990s. Steel manufacture at the Corus works near Newport ceased in 2001.

As in many towns and cities around the UK, regeneration throughout the region has begun in the 1990s and 2000s. Gwent's economy is now based on light manufacturing, services and tourism. European Union funding has been used throughout the area either to remove the relics of the industrial past or to transform them into heritage sites or recreational facilities. More than three-quarters of businesses are now in the service sector.

Newport (Casnewydd), standing on the banks of the River Usk, was a major port during the medieval period, having replaced Caerleon, hence the name (New Port). The town was the scene of a mass demonstration in support of the Chartist Movement on 3 November 1839, when 7000 men from Blackwood, Ebbw Vale, Nant-y-glo and Pontypool marched on the town, led by John Frost. An armed confrontation ensued at the Westgate Hotel during which 20 people were killed and a further 50 injured. Frost was arrested and stood trial for high treason. His original sentence of death by being hanged, drawn and quartered was commuted to transportation for life to Australia. He was granted a pardon in 1854 on condition that he never return to Britain, but even this condition was rescinded in 1856 and he returned to Britain where he remained until his death in 1877. John Frost Square, in the centre of Newport, is named in his honour. In recent years the Riverfront Arts Centre has been developed and improvements have been made to Newport's retail sector and transport infrastructure. The city has also benefited from the relocation of the headquarters of the Office for National Statistics and the Patent Office.

Gwent	**Population**			**Area**	
	male	*female*	*total*	*sq miles*	*sq km*
Blaenau Gwent	33,969	36,095	70,064	42	109
Caerphilly	82,594	86,925	169,519	107	277
Monmouthshire	41,448	43,437	84,885	328	849
Newport	65,764	71,247	137,011	73	190
Torfaen	44,014	46,935	90,949	49	126
Total	267,789	284,639	552,428	599	1551

Local Attractions and Information

Abergavenny Castle — Castle Street, Abergavenny. Norman motte and bailey castle beside the River Usk, founded by Hamelin of Ballon c.1090. Captured by the Welsh c.1172 but recaptured by the English three years later, on Christmas Day 1175 the castle witnessed the 'Abergavenny Massacre' when William de Braose murdered his guest and long-standing Welsh rival Seisyll ap Dyfnwal, along with the Welshman's family. The timber castle and hall were destroyed in the 1230s and replaced by a stone keep. The castle was strengthened in the 13th and 14th centuries. It was badly damaged during the Civil War after Charles I ordered its destruction in 1645 and was afterwards slighted. A house was built on the original motte in the 19th century as a hunting lodge for the Marquess of Abergavenny, and this now houses Abergavenny Museum. The grounds and some of the ruins were also 'landscaped' in the 19th century. Nearby is the site of Gobannium Roman fort.

Abergavenny Museum — Castle Street, Abergavenny. Local history museum opened in 1959 and housed in a 19th century hunting lodge built within the ruins of Abergavenny Castle. It focuses on the town's economic and social history, with exhibits ranging from the beginnings of the town during the Roman period through to the Agricultural and Industrial Revolution and Welsh culture. A recreated saddler's shop dating from c.1910–30 displays a collection relating to this important 19th and earlier 20th century occupation, and there are also recreations of a late Victorian farmhouse kitchen and a well-known local grocery shop of the 1940s. The museum also has a photographic archive. Tel: 01873 854282.

Abertillery and District Museum — Market Street, Abertillery. Local history museum housed on the ground floor of the Metropole Conference and Cultural Centre, and charting the history of the town and its surrounding area from the Bronze Age to the present with particular reference to the coal industry. Most of the exhibits relate to the communities of the lower Ebbw Fach valley: Abertillery, Cwmtillery, Blaenau Gwent, Six Bells, Aberbeeg, Llanhilleth, Brynithel and Swffryd. Tel: 01495 211140.

Administrative headquarters — **Blaenau Gwent**: Municipal Offices, Civic Centre, Ebbw Vale NP23 6XB. Tel: 01495 350555.
Caerphilly: Nelson Road, Tredomen, Hengoed, Ystrad Mynach CF83 7WF. Tel: 01443 815588.
Monmouthshire: County Hall, Cwmbran NP44 2XH. Tel: 01633 644644.
Newport: Civic Centre, Newport, South Wales NP20 4UR. Tel: 01633 656656.
Torfaen: Civic Centre, Pontypool, Torfaen NP4 6YB. Tel: 01495 762200.

Allt-yr-yn	1 mile (1.6km) west of Newport. A nature reserve consisting of ancient woodland, $2^1/_2$ acres (1ha) of meadows and five ponds.
Bedwellty House and Park	Morgan Street, Tredegar. The Grade II listed house was built in 1818 by Samuel Homfrey, the ironmaster at Tredegar Iron Company, and contains memorabilia relating to the history of Tredegar and its residents. Bedwellty House was presented, along with 26 acres (10.5ha) of surrounding parkland, to the people of Tredegar by the Morgan family in 1901. The park's features include an ice house, grotto, arboretum and an octagonal iron bandstand, built in 1912 at the expense of Bedwellty Park Athletic Club.
Big Pit, The	Blaenavon, 4 miles (6km) southwest of Abergavenny. A working museum with underground access, operated under the auspices of the National Museums and Galleries of Wales as the National Mining Museum of Wales and part of the Blaenavon World Heritage Site. The commercial pit was operated by the Blaenavon Iron & Coal Company and the shaft was first sunk in 1860, being deepened to 293ft (89m) in the late 1870s. The pit gained its name from the dimensions of the oval shaft, at the time of its construction the only shaft in the country wide enough to wind up two trams of coal side by side. Operated by the National Coal Board from 1947 until its closure on 2 February 1980, the mine was reopened as a museum in 1983 and the site was redeveloped in 2003. There is a guided underground tour, beginning with a 300ft (90m) descent down the mineshaft by pit cage; the various colliery buildings include the pithead baths, the fan house, blacksmith's forge, stables and winding engine house. Tel: 01495 790311.
Blaenavon Community Heritage & Cordell Museum	Lion Street, Blaenavon, 4 miles (6km) southwest of Abergavenny. Local history museum exploring the economic and social history of the town from the beginning of the Industrial Revolution to the present day, opened in 2002 and housed in the former Blaenavon Town Hall. Many of its exhibits, including industrial artefacts, furniture, coins and militaria, have been contributed by the local community. A room is dedicated to the life and works of writer Alexander Cordell (the pen name of George Alexander Graber, 1914–97), who lived for much of his life in Abergavenny. Many of his works, including *Rape of the Fair Country* (1959), *The Hosts of Rebecca* (1960), *Song of the Earth* (1969), *The Fire People* (1972) and *This Proud and Savage Land* (1985), revolve around the story of South Wales during the early Industrial Revolution and in particular the Chartist movement and the rise of trade unionism. Exhibits include his desk and typewriter. The museum also holds extensive local genealogical resources and a photographic archive. Tel: 01495 790991.
Blaenavon Ironworks	North Street, Blaenavon, 4 miles (6km) southwest of Abergavenny. Possibly the best-preserved example of an 18th century ironworks in western Europe. Blaenavon Ironworks was opened in 1789, with three furnaces, by a consortium including the Hill family. The plant was sold to the Blaenavon Iron & Coal Company in 1836. A new furnace was added in 1861 but economic decline and competition saw the ironworks cease production by the early 1900s. A feature of the site is the restored water balance tower, which was used to lift iron and raw materials in trams between the furnace tops and the yard area below. There are scale models, working models and restored workers' cottages on Stack Square and Engine Row. Blaenavon Ironworks has been in state care since 1975. A Scheduled Ancient Monument, the ironworks is being restored by CADW and lies at the centre of the Blaenavon World Heritage Site. Tel: 01495 792615.
Blaenavon Workmen's Hall	High Street, Blaenavon. A conference centre housed in a miners' institute built in 1894 and opened in January 1895 as a social meeting place, with rooms for reading, recreation and billiards, plus a library and a large hall capable of seating over 1600 people. It was built through contributions from iron and coal workers. A cinema was added in the 1920s. However, after World War II local interest in the hall declined and in 1980 the library was moved out of the premises. The hall was refurbished in the early 1990s and officially reopened for its centenary year on 7 January 1995. Today it has a 300 seat auditorium and a 90 seat cinema or lecture theatre. It is located within the Blaenavon World Heritage Site. Tel: 01495 792661.
Blaenavon World Heritage Site	The town of Blaenavon on the Llwyd River, at the centre of the Industrial Revolution in South Wales from the mid 18th century, was designated a UNESCO World Heritage Site in November 2000. Since the decline of the iron and coal industries in the region, the area has been regenerated in order to highlight the significance of the part played by the people and resources of South Wales in spurring and sustaining Britain's early industrial growth. Blaenavon originally grew around the ironworks established in 1789 and the coal-mining and steel-making industries which followed during the 19th century. There are several Scheduled Ancient Monuments within the Blaenavon Industrial Landscape, including Iron Bridge Blaenavon, Blaenavon Ironworks, Hill's Tramroad, the Engine Pit, Blaenavon and Garn-Ddyrys Ironworks. See also The Big Pit Blaenavon Ironworks, Pontypool & Blaenavon Railway.
Blaina Heritage Centre	High Street, Blaina, 7 miles (11km) southwest of Abergavenny. A volunteer-run local history museum opened in January 2007 and telling the story of the town and its surrounding district using artefacts collected by the Blaina Heritage Action Group. The centre features displays about the social and industrial history of the area including the coal and iron industries, religion, education and sport. The main exhibit is a fully furnished reconstruction of a Victorian Welsh kitchen. The centre is also a resource for local and family historians.
Brynmawr Museum	Market Street, Brynmawr. A volunteer-run local history museum opened in June 2003. Exhibits include examples of Brynmawr furniture, only made at the Brynmawr Furniture Factory. The museum also has works by world-renowned local artists Mac Adams and Andrew Vicari.
Bulwarks Camp	Alpha Road, Chepstow. The site of a multivallate fort resting on steep natural slopes beside the River Wye. From excavations it appears that it was occupied during the Iron Age and into the Romano-British period. The fort was used as a prisoner-of-war camp during World War II. The site is managed by CADW.

Burrium Usk, 7 miles (11km) northeast of Cwmbran. The site of a short-lived Roman legionary fortress around which grew the settlement of Usk. Although the fort was only occupied AD 54–69, the civil settlement outside it continued to thrive into the 4th century.

Caerleon Roman Fort Caerleon, 2 miles (3km) north of Newport. The site of the Roman legionary fortress at Isca, built c.AD 75 as a base for Legio II Augusta beside the River Usk. The name Isca derives from the Latinised version of Usk and Caerleon was also known as Isca Silures. Much evidence of the fortress remains on the ground, including an amphitheatre, the remains of the fortress wall, barrack buildings, headquarters buildings and the fortress baths. One of three legionary fortresses in Britain (the others being at Chester and York), the fort was the main base from which the Romans controlled the tribes of South Wales, including the Silures who had built the nearby Iron Age hill fort. The extensive settlement which developed around the fort remained even after the fort's abandonment in the late 3rd century. In the post-Roman period the fort has been long linked with the legend of King Arthur and was cited by Geoffrey of Monmouth as the place where Arthur held court – possibly because of the circular remains of the amphitheatre. The nearby hill fort on Lodge Wood Hill has also been proposed as a possible contender for Camelot. The site is maintained by CADW.

Caerleon Castle Caerleon, 2 miles (3km) north of Newport. An 11th century Welsh motte and bailey castle to which a great tower was added 1158–73. The early timber castle was probably rebuilt in stone when the site was taken by the English in the 13th century. At its greatest extent the castle on the summit of the motte had at least one tower (part of which survives) plus a twin-towered gate house. Little now remains apart from the motte.

Caerphilly Castle Castle Street, Caerphilly. The extensive and impressive ruins of a 13th century moated castle on a 30 acre (21ha) site in the centre of Caerphilly, originally built 1268–70 by Gilbert de Clare, Earl of Gloucester. The largest medieval castle in Wales and the second largest in Britain after Windsor Castle, it was besieged by Llywelyn ap Gruffudd in 1271 when nearly complete; after its destruction it was rebuilt immediately to a concentric plan with rectangular inner and middle wards surrounded by water and more outer defences, and completed in 1280. Attacked, again unsuccessfully, in 1316 by Llywelyn Bren, it passed to Hugh Despenser the younger through marriage; it was besieged by Queen Isabella when pursuing Edward II and later captured by Owain Glyndwr. The relatively peaceful existence which prevailed in the area during the 15th century led to the castle's virtual abandonment by the century's end. Possibly slighted at the end of the Civil War, the castle was partially restored by successive Marquises of Bute in the 19th century and the outer main gatehouse was reconstructed in the 20th century. The castle's lakes were reflooded in the 1950s. One of the features that makes the castle so recognisable is the 'leaning tower' – the southeast tower, which leans at a steeper angle than the Leaning Tower of Pisa. Now owned by CADW.

Caerwent 4½ miles (7km) southwest of Chepstow. The modern village of Caerwent is the site of the Roman town known as Venta Silurum, founded in AD 75 and the *civitas* (centre of administration) of the Silures in southeast Wales. Excavations have revealed town walls, shops, a temple, a possible amphitheatre and the remains of the forum. The *venta* in its name also indicates that it was a market town. This is another place in Gwent which has been suggested as a possible site for King Arthur's Camelot.

Caldicot Castle Church Road, Caldicot. Norman motte and bailey castle founded by Walter fitz Roger in the early 12th century and developed by Humphrey de Bohun, Earl of Hereford, later in the century. In 1376 the castle passed to Thomas Woodstock, Duke of Gloucester, third son of Edward III, who commissioned new building work including the Woodstock Tower in 1381 and the gatehouse in 1385. The castle became a Crown possession when Woodstock was kidnapped and murdered on the order of his nephew Richard II in 1391, although the Earls of Buckingham later owned Caldicot for a period. The castle was considerably repaired in the late 19th century and is now surrounded by the 55 acre (22ha) Caldicot Castle Country Park. Tel: 01291 420241.

Chepstow Castle Bridge Street, Chepstow. The substantial ruins of a massive castle on cliffs above the River Wye. Begun by William fitzOsbern, Earl of Hereford, in 1067, within a few months of the Norman invasion, at the southern end of the border between England and Wales and commanding an important crossing of the Wye, it is regarded as the oldest surviving stone castle in the UK. Unlike many other castles in the area it appears to have been mainly of stone construction from the outset, the great hall/keep (great tower) being the oldest surviving secular stone building in Britain. Stones from the ruins of the Roman town of Caerwent are believed to have been used in the construction. Further defences were added in the early 13th century by William Marshal and his sons and by Roger Bigod, Earl of Norfolk, in the late 13th century. It was extended by building on a series of terraces above the river with towers connected by curtain walls. The castle was held by Royalist forces during the Civil War and was besieged and captured in 1645 and 1648. It was used as a prison during the second half of the 17th century before being abandoned and allowed to become a 'picturesque' ruin. Marten's Tower was where Henry Marten was imprisoned after the Restoration. The castle is now in the care of CADW.

Chepstow Museum Bridge Street, Chepstow. Local history museum housed in a late 18th century merchant's house and featuring exhibits about past Chepstow industries such as the wine trade, salmon fishing and shipbuilding. There is also a photographic archive and a fine art collection. Tel: 01291 625981.

Croes Robert Wood 1 mile (1.6km) south of Cwmcarvan, 5 miles (8km) southwest of Monmouth. Nature reserve covering 35 acres (14ha) of traditionally coppiced ancient deciduous woodland in the Wye Valley, designated a Site of Special Scientific Interest in 1981. It has a wide diversity of woodland plants together with uncommon butterflies such as the white-letter hairstreak, silver-washed fritillary and white admiral, plus the endangered dormouse.

Dan-y-Graig	$^1/_2$ mile (0.8km) southwest of Risca. Small local nature reserve covering 5 acres (2ha) of a steep hillside above Risca in the valley of the River Ebbw. It has young woodland, grassland and a pond.
Drenewydd Museum	Lower Row, Butetown, Rhymney. Local history museum housed in two cottages, one of which has been restored to its appearance in the 1870s and portrays family life at the period. Outside the museum is a recreated Victorian organic garden.
Fourteen Locks	High Cross, 1$^1/_2$ miles (2.5km) west of Newport. Fourteen deep locks on the Monmouthshire & Brecon Canal, grouped in pairs and built c.1800 by Thomas Dadford Jr. The locks raise the canal level by 160ft (49m) in 800 yards (730m). Only the top lock has water as the remainder are being restored. Tel: 01633 894802.
Gaer Hill Fort	Gaer Park Avenue, Newport. Aka the Gollars, Tredegar Fort. The site of a multiple enclosure hill fort overlooking the Ebbw River. In the 17th century it was incorporated into an ornamental landscaping scheme by the Morgans of nearby Tredegar House.
Gobannium Roman Fort	Abergavenny. The Roman fort of Gobannium was occupied from the late 1st until the 2nd century. Its site is located beside the River Usk in Abergavenny, which developed from the settlement that grew up around the fort.
Griffithstown Railway Museum	Griffithstown, Pontypool. Housed in a restored former Great Western Railway goods shed. There is a large collection of railway memorabilia, including many items from local stations. Tel: 01495 762908.
Grosmont Castle	Grosmont, 10 miles (16km) northwest of Monmouth. Located by the River Monnow and founded in the 12th century as a timber fortification. Along with White Castle and Skenfrith Castle, it is one of the 'Three Castles' (or castles of the Trilateral) built in the Monnow Valley between Hereford and South Wales. In the late 12th century the timber castle was replaced and a great hall built in stone. Hubert de Burgh, Earl of Kent greatly increased its defences in the 1220s, while Prince Edmund, Earl of Lancaster and son of Henry III, made further changes in the late 13th century, adding more accommodation and a new keep. Having been abandoned by the mid 16th century, the castle passed into state care in 1923 and is now maintained by CADW.
Highest point	Chwarel y Fan in the Black Mountains northwest of Llanthony at 2228ft (679m). GR: SO259292.
Hill's Tramroad	A primitive railway built by Thomas Hill in 1812 and connecting the Blaenavon Ironworks with the Abergavenny Canal. It also enabled ore and limestone from the north at Pwll-Du and Tyla to be conveyed to the ironworks and later connected the blast furnaces at Blaenavon to the wrought-iron forge opened at Garn-Ddyrys in 1817. The 1$^1/_2$ mile (2.5km) long tunnel under the mountain at Pwll-Du was the longest ever constructed for a horse-operated railway in Britain. It is located within the Blaenavon World Heritage Site.
Interesting facts	**Rhys Davies** from Tredegar was hired by a group of American businessmen in 1833 to build an ironworks in Richmond, Virginia, which later became known as the Tredegar Iron Works and Belle Isle Iron Works. **Caerphilly cheese** is a hard cheese that originates in the area around the town; although it was not originally made in Caerphilly, it was sold at market there, hence taking the town's name. A light-coloured (almost white) crumbly cheese made from cow's milk, generally with a fat content of around 48 per cent, it has a mild taste, but perhaps its most noticeable feature is its saltiness. It is said that the cheese was developed over time to provide coal miners with a convenient way of replenishing salt lost through hard work underground, and so became a staple of their diet. The **Skirrid Mountain Inn**, located in Llanvihangel, Crucorney, near Abergavenny, is Wales's oldest inn. It has stood since at least the turn of the 12th century, as in 1100 one Jamie Crowther was hanged from a beam in the bar for stealing sheep. Apart from being a coaching inn, it also used to be a courthouse and was the scene of many hangings.
Islands	There are four named islands in Gwent, all in the Severn Estuary (Sea Area: Lundy) near Portskewett, and all under the auspices of the former county of Monmouthshire: **Black Rock** (GR: ST515881), **Charston Rock** (GR: ST519881), **Gruggy** (GR: ST509865) and **Lady Bench** (GR: ST514875).
Kymin, The	1 mile (1.6km) east of Monmouth. Two Georgian buildings surrounded by 9 acres (3.5ha) of woodlands on a hilltop overlooking Monmouth and the Wye Valley and with views over ten of Wales's 'old' counties. The Kymin Roundhouse is a two-storey round banqueting house built in 1794 to serve as a refuge for gentlemanly lunch parties in case of inclement weather. The Naval Temple opened in 1801 and was visited by Horatio Nelson in 1802. Both buildings were donated to the National Trust by the people of Monmouth in 1902. Tel: 01600 719241.
Llancaiach Fawr Manor	$^1/_2$ mile (0.8km) north of Nelson, 1 mile (1.6km) east of Treharris. A three-storey Tudor manor house which has been restored as a living history museum set in 1645, with guided tours provided by the 'servants' of the owner, Colonel Prichard. Tel: 01443 412248.
Llanmelin Wood Hill Fort	1$^1/_2$ miles (2.5km) northwest of Caerwent, 4 miles (6km) west of Chepstow. A large oval multivallate Iron Age hill fort measuring 450ft (137m) by 330ft (100m), possibly occupied by the Silures and dating to c.150 BC. It was probably abandoned C.AD 75, at the time of the Roman invasion. The site is managed by CADW.
Llantarnam Abbey	Llantarnam, 1 mile (1.6km) southeast of Cwmbran. A convent of the Sisters of St Joseph of Annecy, housed since 1946 in a 16th century mansion remodelled in Elizabethan Revival style in the 19th century. The building occupies the site of a 12th century Cistercian abbey, a daughter house of Strata Florida purchased in 1553 by William Morgan after its dissolution and adapted as a family home.
Llanthony Priory	Llanthony, 8 miles (13km) north of Abergavenny. The ruins of a late 12th century Augustinian priory above the River Honddu. Originally founded in the early 12th century, it was abandoned in 1135 due to a Welsh rising; the canons were forced to found a new priory outside Gloucester

called Llanthony Secunda, returning to the original site in the late 12th century to rebuild the priory. The priory was abandoned after the Dissolution; part of the south transept and the crossing tower remain and the prior's house has been incorporated into a hotel, the undercroft being the hotel's cellar bar. The nearby parish church may originally have been the priory's infirmary.

Llantilio Castle — See White Castle.

Llanyrafon Mill — Llanyrafon Way, Cwmbrân. A triple-stoned corn mill located on a site occupied by mills since at least the early 17th century. It was worked until 1951, after which it fell into disrepair and was damaged by a fire in the 1970s. Having been made stable and weatherproof in the 1980s, it is being restored to working order by the Friends of Llanyrafon Mill. Inside is a display of agricultural and milling artefacts.

Lodge Hill Fort — 1 mile (1.6km) northwest of Caerleon. A large multivallate Iron Age hill fort above Caerleon, covering 7 acres (2.8ha). Established c.600–300 BC, it was probably abandoned while the Isca Roman fortress was occupied but seems to have been reoccupied for a time in the post-Roman period.

Magor Marsh — 6 miles (10km) east of Newport. A nature reserve in the last remnant of traditionally managed fenland in the Gwent levels. Featuring a wet rush pasture and two hay meadows maintained using traditional methods, it is a designated Site of Special Scientific Interest. The drainage ditches (reens) which managed the fenland date from the 14th century.

Monmouth Castle — Castle Hill, Monmouth. The scant remains of an 11th century castle beside the River Monnow, begun by William fitzOsbern in 1070 at about the same time as Chepstow Castle. The castle was extended by Prince Edmund, Earl of Lancaster, who built a hall to hold courts. The great tower was the probable birthplace of the future Henry V in September 1387. The castle was partially demolished during the Civil War, including the large keep. The Great Castle House, built in 1673 on the site of the demolished keep, became the headquarters of the Royal Monmouthshire Royal Engineers (Militia) in 1875. The ruins of the 12th century great tower and hall are all that survive today.

National Roman Legion Museum — High Street, Caerleon. Part of the National Museum Wales housing artefacts found at the site of Isca Roman fortress and the surrounding area. There is also a full-size reconstruction of a legionary's living quarters. The nearby Roman Baths Museum, run by CADW, recreates the baths using modern technology. Tel: 01633 423134 (Legionary Museum); 01633 422518 (Baths Museum).

Nelson Museum — Priory Street, Monmouth. Although Horatio Nelson has little directly to do with Monmouth, the Nelson Museum and Local History Centre has a collection of Nelson material and memorabilia bequeathed by Lady Llangattock, who lived nearby at The Hendre, and including ceramics, silver, glass, models and weapons. In addition the museum charts the history of Monmouth and celebrates the lives of local resident Charles Stuart Rolls and of Henry V, who was born in the town.

Newport Castle — Old Green Interchange, Newport. The ruins of the 14th century castle which gave Newport its original name (Casnewydd or New Castle). The castle was probably built by either Hugh d'Audele or by his son Ralph. The defences were strengthened by Humphrey Stafford, 1st Duke of Buckingham, in the early 15th century but it was probably abandoned soon after the execution of the 3rd Duke in 1521. It retains a central tower plus two octagonal towers marking its limits to the north and south. The castle has been conserved since the 1930s but the western half of the site was destroyed by road-building in the 1970s.

Newport Cathedral — See St Woolos Cathedral.

Newport Medieval Ship — The remains of a 15th century clinker-built ship measuring over 80ft (24m) long and 25ft (8m) in the beam, were found in 2002 while the site for the Newport Riverfront Theatre and Arts Centre was being prepared. The mud of the banks of the River Usk had preserved the ship's timbers and the dating was confirmed by tree-ring analysis. The main timbers were oak, while the keel was made of beech. Some of the artefacts found, particularly coins, were of Portuguese origin, indicating that this armed merchantman traded with the Iberian peninsula. During the excavation the ship was nicknamed the *Isca*. The lifting process took 13 weeks and the last timber was raised in November 2002. The stern of the ship was not excavated. Some of the objects lifted during the excavation have been on display at Newport Museum and Art Gallery. The ship's timbers are currently conserved in a Newport warehouse; it is planned to display them in a basement beneath the ground-floor gallery and main foyer of the Riverfront Theatre and Arts Centre, close to where the ship was found.

Newport Museum and Art Gallery — John Frost Square, Newport. The museum traces the history of Newport, with particular emphasis on Roman Caerwent and the Chartist movement; the art gallery's collections include paintings by Sir Stanley Spencer and L S Lowry, as well as ceramics including Wemyss ware and a collection of 300 teapots. Tel: 01633 414701.

Newport Transporter Bridge — Mendalgief Road, Newport. Regarded by many as the most recognisable symbol of Newport, the transporter bridge across the River Usk was designed by French engineer Ferdinand Arnodin and R H Haynes and opened on 12 September 1906. It was built because the river banks at this point are low and a conventional bridge would need very long approaches to enable it to reach a height whereby ships could pass beneath it. The bridge consists of two towers supporting a main boom, on which a trolley operated by continuous cable transports a gondola. The height of the towers is 242ft (74m); the boom supporting the gondola is at a height of 177ft (54m). The bridge has a span of 594ft (181m) and a total length of 645ft (197m); the gondola is 33ft (10m) long and 40ft (12m) wide and travels at 10ft (3m) per second. The bridge was closed in 1985 due to wear and tear and did not reopen until 1995 after substantial refurbishment. The Grade I listed bridge is owned and operated by Newport Council. Tel: 01633 250322.

Newport Wetlands	2 1/2 miles (4km) south of Newport. Formerly known as Gwent Levels Wetlands Reserve. The 1080 acre (438ha) nature reserve, located at the mouth of the River Usk between Uskmouth and Goldcliff, was created in mitigation for the loss of the mudflats of Cardiff Bay and opened in March 2000; the site formerly consisted of storage lagoons for pulverised fuel ash from the neighbouring Uskmouth Power Station, and some poorly improved nearby land. Its reedbeds now attract a wide variety of waterfowl and wetland birds including wigeon, shoveler, teal, shelduck and pintail. Other birds include avocet, bittern, Cetti's warbler, lapwing, little egret, oystercatcher and redshank, while 50,000 starlings use the reedbeds to roost in winter. The wetlands are artificially drained by ditches known as reens which originally date back to ancient times.
Old Mill, The	Gelligroes, 1 mile (1.6km) southwest of Pontllanfraith. A 17th century grain mill now housing a radio museum and candle-making workshop. Formerly the home of amateur wireless enthusiast Arthur (Artie) Moore, who picked up the distress signal broadcast by the *Titanic* as she foundered in 1912. Tel: 01495 222322.
Old Station, The	Tintern. A former Victorian railway station on the Wye Valley Railway, closed in 1964 and now housing a café and tourist information centre.
Parc Bryn Bach	Merthyr Road, 1/2 mile (0.8km) northwest of Tredegar. Country park covering 400 acres (160ha) of a previously derelict former coal-mining landscape. The habitats include parkland and woodland plus a 36 acre (14.5ha) lake. Tel: 01495 711816.
Parc Coetir Bargod	1/4 mile (0.4km) east of Bargoed. Country park of 188 acres (75ha) created from the land of three former collieries outside Caerphilly on the Rhymney River. Once the site of Europe's highest coal tip, it can be entered through any one of 11 sculpted gateways and there are sculptures throughout the park.
Parc Cwm Darran	2 miles (3km) west of New Tredegar. A park in the Darran Valley, created on the site of the former Ogilvie Colliery. It has parklands, woodlands and a lake and contains the Cwmllwydrew Meadows Local Nature Reserve. Tel: 01443 875557.
Parc Penallta	1 mile (1.6km) west of Hengoed, 2 miles (3km) south of Bargoed. Country park created in the late 1990s on 445 acres (180ha) of derelict land around the former Penallta Colliery, which closed in 1992.
Pen-y-fan Pond	1 mile (1.6km) west of Llanhilleth. One of the few remaining canal feeder reservoirs in Wales, constructed in 1797 to supply a branch of the Brecon & Monmouthshire Canal. It is now the centre of a country park.
Penhow Castle	Penhow, 7 miles (11km) northeast of Newport. Supposedly the oldest inhabited castle in Wales, built in the 12th century as a tower house by Roger de St Maur (Seymour) and much extended over the next few centuries; a manor house built in the 16th century was remodelled in the late 17th century. It was a tenanted farm from the 18th century until the 1960s; restored in the 1970s, it is now a private residence.
Pontypool & Blaenavon Railway	Broad Street, Blaenavon. A standard gauge heritage railway established in 1981 and operating on a short section of the former Blaenavon & Brynmawr Branch of the London & North Western Railway (LNWR), opened in the 1860s from Pontypool to Brynmawr. The line northwards is the steepest standard gauge preserved passenger-carrying line in Britain, the Whistle Halt terminus being the highest station in England and Wales. The passenger operation was closed in 1941 and freight traffic ceased in 1954, although the section from Blaenavon to Pontypool was used to transport coal until the Big Pit closed in 1980. The first services on the heritage railway ran in 1983. Tel: 01495 792263.
Raglan Castle	1/4 mile (0.4km) north of Raglan, 6 miles (10km) southwest of Monmouth. The ruins of a large 15th century moated manor house built by Sir William ap Thomas on the site of an earlier Norman motte and bailey castle founded c.1070 by the Bloet family. Built for residential purposes rather than defence, it was greatly extended by Sir William's son William Herbert, Lord Raglan, and was thereafter described as palatial. The building was dominated by a hexagonal tower built from yellow sandstone and known as the 'Yellow Tower of Gwent'; other parts of the house were built in red sandstone. It suffered a severe onslaught by Parliamentary forces under Sir Thomas Fairfax during the Civil War; having been taken from the Earl of Worcester after a ten-week siege, it was slighted in 1646. Now owned by CADW.
Rivers	**Usk** see Powys. The **Wye** rises within 2 miles (3km) of the Severn's source on the slopes of Plynlimon in northern Powys and flows for 130 miles (209km), close to or on the border between England and Wales, to Chepstow where it enters the Bristol Channel at the Severn Estuary. It is the fifth longest river in the UK and passes through many beauty spots and towns including Rhayader, Builth Wells, Hay-on-Wye, Hereford, Ross-on-Wye, Symonds Yat, Monmouth and Tintern. The whole river is a designated Special Site of Scientific Interest. It is in the main unpolluted and is a popular river for salmon fishing and canoeing. For its final 16 miles (26km) it forms the England/Wales border.
Royal Monmouthshire Regimental Museum	Housed within Monmouth Castle. The museum of the Royal Monmouthshire Royal Engineers, the only present-day regiment to have survived from the Militia, is housed in a 19th century barrack wing attached to Great Castle House within the ruins of Monmouth Castle. The regiment was mustered in 1537 by Posse Comitatus and became the Monmouthshire Militia in 1539. It went through several name changes and amalgamations with other units before becoming the Royal Monmouthshire Light Infantry (31st Foot) in 1853. In 1877 the regiment accepted an invitation to transfer into a Special Reserve section of the Royal Engineers and its members were able to serve overseas for the first time as the Royal Monmouthshire Engineers Militia. The regiment became known as the Royal Monmouthshire Royal Engineers in 1896. Having served in the Boer War building bridges and railways, in World War I it served on the Western Front, in Italy, Gallipoli and the Middle East and in World War II in France until the evacuation from Dunkirk, afterwards

assisting with the D-Day landings and the war in northern Europe. In 1953 the regiment was transferred to the Territorial Army. The regiment is unique in having a double 'Royal' in its title: one 'Royal' has been inherited from the militia, and one is owed to the Royal Engineers. Tel: 01600 772175.

St Illtyd's Church
$^{3}/_{4}$ mile (1.2km) north of Llanhilleth, 1$^{1}/_{2}$ miles (2.5km) south of Abertillery. Originally built by monks from the Cistercian abbey at Llantarnam, possibly in the 13th century. Although much restored, it is the oldest building in the area and was originally dedicated to St Heledd (Hyledd), hence the place name Llanhilleth. Tel: 01495 355972.

St Mary's Priory Church
Monk Street, Abergavenny. One of the finest parish churches in Wales, sometimes called the 'Westminster Abbey of South Wales'. Originally the conventual church of St Mary's Priory (Benedictine), founded in the early 12th century, the present structure, cruciform in design with a central tower, dates to at least the 14th century. Following the Dissolution in the 16th century it became a parish church. It was much altered internally and externally during the 19th century. One of the church's treasures is a wooden statue of Jesse carved in the 15th century from a single block of oak. Tel: 01873 853168.

St Woolos Cathedral
Stow Hill, Newport. Aka Newport Cathedral. A 13th century church built on the possible site of a 5th century chapel traditionally founded by St Woolos (Gwynllyw). The structure was extended in Gothic style in the 15th century; established in 1949 as the cathedral of the Diocese of Monmouth in the Church in Wales, it was enlarged again in the early 1960s.

Silent Valley Reserve
$^{1}/_{2}$ mile (0.8km) east of Ebbw Vale. A nature reserve mainly consisting of beech and alder woodland, the highest and most westerly of its type in Britain. The beechwood was designated a Site of Special Scientific Interest in 1984.

Sirhowy Ironworks
Grahams Yard, Dukestown Road, Sirhowy, Tredegar. The Sirhowy Ironworks was erected in 1750 by a man named Kettle from Shropshire. The remains of the ironworks' first coal-fired furnace, opened in 1778, have been conserved and restored. Tel: 01495 355972.

Skenfrith Castle
Skenfrith, 5 miles (8km) northwest of Monmouth. Located by the River Monnow and founded in the early 12th century by William fitzOsbern, probably as a timber motte and bailey castle. Along with White Castle and Grosmont Castle it is one of the 'Three Castles' (or castles of the Trilateral) built in the Monnow Valley between Hereford and South Wales. The timber castle was replaced by a stone structure built 1219–32 by Hubert de Burgh. Its plan is rectangular, with a round tower at each corner and a further round tower (keep) on the southwestern frontage. The castle was the property of the Duchy of Lancaster until 1825 but had been abandoned by the mid 16th century and is now a ruin. Skenfrith Castle was given to the National Trust in 1936 and is now in the guardianship of CADW.

sport

football
Cwmbran Town were founded in 1951. They were founder members of the League of Wales in 1992 and won the title in 1993. Nicknamed The Crows, their home ground is Cwmbran Stadium, Henllys Way, Cwmbran.

Newport County were founded in 1912 and reformed in 1989. From 1920–88 they competed in the English Football League, reaching the quarter-finals of the European Cup Winners' Cup in 1980–81 while in Football League Division 3. They were winners of Division 3 South 1939 and of the Welsh Cup 1980.They went out of business in 1989 but reformed in the same year and were elected to the Hellenic League, reaching the Southern League Premier Division (now Conference South) in 1995. Nicknamed The Exiles or The Ironsides, their home ground is Newport Stadium.

golf
Celtic Manor Resort, 2 miles (3km) northeast of Newport, is a 1400 acre (560ha) facility with three golf courses – the Roman Road championship course where the Welsh Open was held in 2005 and 2006, the Montgomerie which opened in 2007 and the Ryder Cup championship course, which also opened in 2007 and will host the tournament in 2010. Tel: 01633 413000.

horse racing
Chepstow racecourse, opened in 1926, stages Flat and National Hunt racing on a 1m 7f (3km) circuit. The highlight is the annual Welsh Grand National which transferred from the defunct Caerleon course in 1948. In 1933 Gordon Richards created a record when winning 11 consecutive races at Chepstow over two days. Tel: 01291 622260.

rugby union
Newport RFC were founded in 1874. In 1912 they were the first club side to beat the touring South Africans. They beat Australia in 1957, New Zealand in 1963, South Africa in 1969 and Tonga in 1974. Honours: Welsh club champions 1951, 1956, 1962 and 1969. Welsh Cup winners 1977 and 2001. Their home ground was Rodney Parade, Newport. They were superseded in 2003 by the regional team **Newport Gwent Dragons** (founded as Gwent Dragons), who officially represent southeast Wales in the Celtic League and who drew their original teams largely from the Newport RFC and Ebbw Vale RFC sides. Their home ground is also Rodney Parade.

Tintern Abbey
Tintern Parva, 4 miles (6km) north of Chepstow. The substantial and atmospheric ruins of a Cistercian foundation beside the River Wye. The abbey was founded in the 1130s by Walter de Clare with monks from a daughter house of Cîteaux, L'Aumone, in the diocese of Blois in France. Tintern was a relatively prosperous foundation in its early years and itself later founded daughter houses at Kingswood in Gloucester and Tintern Parva. The abbey was remodelled in the 13th century and the great abbey church, much of which still stands, was built 1269–1301. The abbey was dissolved and surrendered to secular authorities in September 1536; afterwards it was stripped of its treasures and its roof and the site was overtaken by the surrounding nature. The picturesque ruins inspired William Wordsworth's poem 'Lines Composed a Few Miles Above Tintern Abbey' (1798) and paintings by J M W Turner. The site is now managed by CADW.

Tredegar House
Newport. A 17th century mansion built 1664–72 by Sir William Morgan and surrounded by a 90 acre (36ha) park. Built around a quadrangle incorporating an earlier 15th or 16th century hall in the southwest wing, the house was occupied by the Morgan family (Lords Tredegar) until the early

	1950s when it became a Catholic girls' school. In 1974 the house and grounds were purchased by Newport Borough Council. Outside are woodland walks and a lake. Tel: 01633 815880.
Trellech Standing Stones	Trellech, 8 miles (13km) north of Chepstow. Aka Harold's Stones. Three large monoliths dating from the late Neolithic or Early Bronze Age.
University of Wales Newport	Founded in 1975 as Gwent College of Higher Education. The college became an affiliated institution of the University of Wales in 1992 and a university college in 1996. There are four schools: Art, Media & Design, Business, Education & Health, and Social Sciences. Tel: 01633 430088.
Usk Castle	Usk, 6 miles (10km) northeast of Cwmbran. The ruins of a substantial 12th century castle built by the de Clare family standing on a spur overlooking Usk. The original Norman motte and bailey castle was captured by the Welsh at least twice 1120–80. A stone gatehouse or keep was constructed in the late 12th century and both William Marshal and Gilbert de Clare strengthened the castle in the 13th century, a period when the round towers and the curtain wall around the inner ward were built. Of particular interest is the four-storey garrison tower. The outer bailey was later also protected by walls and a gatehouse. The castle was largely abandoned by the 17th century although Castle House was built at the original entrance to the outer bailey in the 1680s.
Usk Rural Life Museum	New Market Street, Usk. Housed in a traditional malt barn and its adjoining buildings, the museum celebrates life in rural Monmouthshire between 1850 and the end of World War II. The displays of agricultural equipment are arranged by season and there is also a collection of scale-model horse-drawn farm vehicles. The museum has recreations of a farmhouse kitchen, laundry and dairy.
Valley Inheritance Museum	Park Buildings, Pontypool. Local history museum housed in a former Georgian stable block beside Pontypool Park, charting the history of the Torfaen Valley and also holding local and family history resources. Tel: 01495 752036.
White Castle	1 mile (1.6km) southeast of Llanvetherine, 5 miles (8km) northeast of Abergavenny. Aka Llantilio Castle, but called White Castle after it was at some point given whitewash rendering. Founded by Pain fitzJohn as a timber fortification with two earthworks in a pear-shaped plan with an outer bailey known as the 'hornwork', it seems probable that a stone keep was built in the 1180s. Along with Grosmont Castle and Skenfrith Castle, it is one of the 'Three Castles' (or castles of the Trilateral) built in the Monnow Valley between Hereford and South Wales. Its defences were improved by Gilbert Talbot in the mid 13th century with the addition of a twin-towered gatehouse. Abandoned by the mid 16th century, it passed into state care in 1922 and is now maintained by CADW.
Winding House, The	White Rose Way, New Tredegar. A two-storey winding house with its original steam winding engine built in 1891 for Elliot Colliery, which operated 1883–1967. The winding house has now been restored as a museum telling the story of the colliery and the local coal industry, and underwent major redevelopment in 2007. Tel: 01443 822666.
Ysgyryd Fawr	2 miles (3km) northeast of Abergavenny. Aka Skirrid Fawr or Sacred Hill. A mountain in the Black Mountains, 1594ft (486m) high and with an Iron Age hill fort and a medieval chapel on its summit. Ysgyryd Fawr has belonged to the National Trust since 1939.

Some famous people born in Gwent

Banks, Jeff (fashion designer) (1943–)	Ebbw Vale
Bevan, Aneurin (politician) (1897–1960)	Tredegar
Cooper, Tommy (comedian) (1922–84)	Caerphilly
Davies, William Henry (poet) (1871–1940)	Newport
Greenaway, Peter (film director) (1942–)	Newport
Henry V (king of England) (1387–1422)	Monmouth
Hocking, Gary (motorcycle racer) (1937–62)	Caerleon
Kinnock, Neil (politician) (1942–)	Tredegar
Reardon, Ray (snooker player) (1932–)	Tredegar
Russell, Bertrand (philosopher) (1872–1970)	Trellech
Thomas, Leslie (writer) (1931–)	Newport
Watkins, David (rugby player) (1942–)	Blaina
Weston, Simon (soldier and broadcaster) (1961–)	Caerphilly
White, Ethel Lina (writer) (1876–1944)	Abergavenny
Williams, Mark (snooker player) (1975–)	Cwm

GWYNEDD

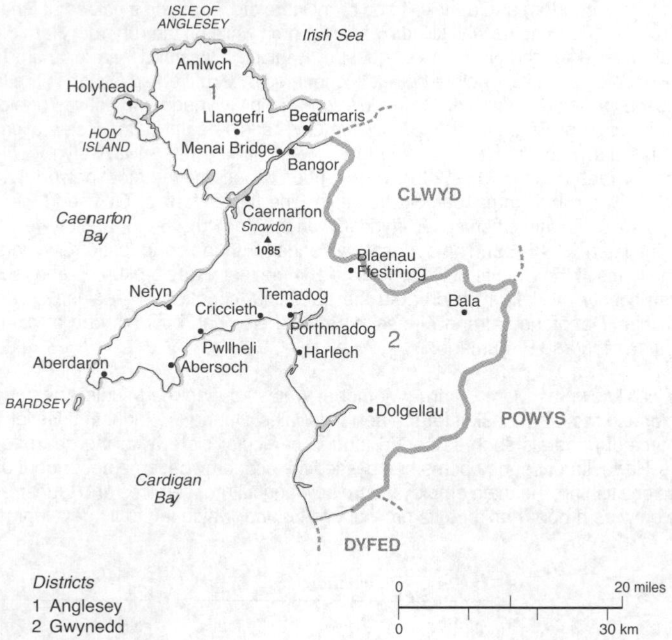

ISLE OF ANGLESEY
Irish Sea
Amlwch
Holyhead
1
Llangefri
Beaumaris
HOLY ISLAND
Menai Bridge
Bangor
CLWYD
Caenarfon Bay
Caernarfon
Snowdon
1085
Blaenau Ffestiniog
Bala
Nefyn
Tremadog
Criccieth
Porthmadog
2
Pwllheli
Harlech
Aberdaron
Abersoch
BARDSEY
Dolgellau
POWYS
Cardigan Bay
DYFED
Districts
1 Anglesey
2 Gwynedd
0
20 miles
0
30 km

Gwynedd encompasses the unitary authorities of Gwynedd and the Isle of Anglesey. It is bordered to the east by Clwyd, to the south by Dyfed, to the southeast by Powys and to the north and west by the Irish Sea, the inlet shared by Gwynedd and Dyfed being Cardigan Bay. Its main geographical features are the Snowdonia National Park and the coast with its excellent beaches. The mountains of Snowdonia are classed as one of the traditional 'Seven Wonders of Wales'. Bangor is its only city and one of only five in the whole of Wales. The major attractions are the castles, seaside resorts, industrial heritage and narrow gauge railways.

Anglesey (Ynys Môn) is an island separated from the mainland by the Menai Strait. It is connected to the mainland by two bridges, the original Menai Suspension Bridge and the Britannia Bridge. Holy Island is off the west coast of Anglesey and connected to it by causeways. The main towns on Anglesey are Beaumaris, Menai Bridge and Holyhead. It is also where the village with the longest place name in Britain is located – Llanfairpwllgwyngyllgogerychwyrndrobwllllantysiliogogogoch. The name, when translated into English, means 'The church of St Mary in a hollow of white hazel near a rapid whirlpool and near St Tysilio's church by the red cave' and is actually a 19th century invention to attract tourists (it works). In practice it is abbreviated to Llanfairpwll or Llanfair PG.

The region was settled during the Mesolithic period, as evidenced by the existence of numerous stone circles and burial chambers, and by the Llyn Cerrig Bach hoard. It was occupied by the Ordovices and Gangani (the latter on the Llŷn Peninsula) during the Iron Age but they were virtually wiped out by the Roman forces led by Agricola c.AD 70. Earlier, in AD 60, the Roman general Suetonius Paulinus attacked Anglesey and destroyed the Druidic cult based there which had been fomenting resistance to the Roman advance across Britain. The Romans then occupied Anglesey and left a garrison to resist attacks from Ireland. During the period from the end of the Romano-British era until the effective end of Welsh independence at the end of the 13th century, Gwynedd was one of the principalities of Wales. It traditionally covered the northwest of Wales including the Isle of Anglesey. Its founder is said to have been Cunedda Wledig ap Edern (Cunedda the Imperator) (ruled c.450–c.460), who threw out Irish invaders who had settled in Anglesey. Early rulers include Cadwallon ap Cadfan (c.625–634), Cadfael the Battle-Shirker (634–c.655), Cadwaladr the Blessed (c.655–c.682), Rhodri the Bald and Grey (c.720–c.754), Rhodri the Great

(844–878) and Anarawd ap Rhodri (878–916), who established the Aberffraw dynasty. During this period Gwynedd and Anglesey suffered repeated attack from Irish and Viking raiders.

In 1055 Gruffydd ap Llywelyn, king of Gwynedd, gave aid to outlawed Earl Aelfgar in an attempt to regain the latter's earldom and attacked and burnt Hereford. Gruffydd's palace at Rhuddlan was in turn destroyed in 1062 and he was killed by his own men while on the run from Harold Godwinson's army a year later. After the Norman conquest of England, Gwynedd was for a time ruled by the Norman, Robert of Rhuddlan, before being reconquered by Gruffydd ap Cynan in the late 11th century. The kingdom was extended by Gruffydd's son Owain Gwynedd and he was one of the leaders of a failed invasion of England in 1165. Owain Gwynedd's death in 1170 saw a power struggle between his sons which reduced Gwynedd's power until the rise of Llywelyn Fawr ap Iorwerth (Llywelyn the Great) (ruled 1195–1240), who went on to become the most powerful ruler in Wales. The kingdom was ruled from Aber Garth Celyn. The final rulers of Gwynedd were Dafydd ap Llywelyn (1240–6), Owain Goch ap Gruffydd (Owen the Red) (1246–55) and Llywelyn ap Gruffydd (Llywelyn the Last) (1246–82). The dynasty was ended with the conquest of Gwynedd by Edward I. Under the terms of the Statute of Rhuddlan in 1284 the realm was broken up and reorganised into the English county model which created the traditional counties of Anglesey, Carnarvonshire, Merionethshire, Denbighshire and Flintshire. Edward also had built his ring of castles including Conwy, Caernarfon and Beaumaris.

Anglesey was known as Mam Cymru ('Mother of Wales') during the Middle Ages because its fertile fields formed the breadbasket for the north of Wales. During the Industrial Revolution the area was a source of minerals such as copper and in particular slate, with the quarries being major employers. However, once the booms had passed the economy became dependent once again on agriculture and fishing; the main employers are now agriculture, services and tourism. Holyhead on Anglesey grew as a port thanks to its proximity to Ireland, which led to its development as a ferry terminal.

Gwynedd	**Population**			**Area**	
	male	*female*	*total*	*sq miles*	*sq km*
Gwynedd	56,029	60,814	116,843	979	2535
Isle of Anglesey	32,348	34,481	66,829	275	711
Total	88,377	95,295	183,672	1254	3246

Local Attractions and Information

Aberdyfi Castle	1/4 mile (0.4km) west of Glandyfi, 4 1/2 miles (7km) southwest of Machynlleth. 12th century castle beside the River Dovey, built by Lord Rhys.
Abergwyngregyn Castle	Abergwyngregyn, 4 miles (6km) east of Bangor. Aka Pen-y-Mwd. A flat-topped motte near Pen-y-Bryn which supported a wooden fortification in the 11th century. There may have been a later stone fortification near the site; Gwenllian, daughter of Eleanor de Montfort, was reportedly born here in 1282.
Administrative headquarters	**Gwynedd**: Council Offices, Caernarfon, Gwynedd LL55 1SH. Tel: 01286 672255. **Isle of Anglesey**: Council Offices, Llangefni, Anglesey LL77 7TW. Tel: 01248 750057.
Amlwch Industrial Heritage	Amlwch, 14 miles (23km) northeast of Holyhead, Anglesey. The town of Amlwch grew up around the industry and services generated by the Parys Mountain copper workings. The industrial and social history of the area is charted in a heritage centre opened in the watch house in 1999 and moved to the nearby renovated sail loft in 2000, and covering not just copper mining but also the harbour, shipbuilding, smelting and chemicals. Tel: 01407 832255.
Anglesey, Isle of	aka Ynys Mon. The largest island in England and Wales. It is connected to the mainland by two bridges, the original Menai Suspension Bridge (carrying the A5), built by Thomas Telford in 1826 as a road link, and the newer, twice reconstructed Britannia Bridge, carrying the A55 and the North Wales Coast Railway line. The highest point on the Isle of Anglesey is Holyhead Mountain at 722ft (220m) (GR: SH218829). Area: 274.52 sq miles (711 sq km). Population: 66,829. GR: SH369808.
Anglesey Sea Zoo	Brynsiencyn, 5 miles (8km) southwest of Menai Bridge, Anglesey. Wales's largest marine aquarium, opened in 1983. It features recreations of a variety of local marine and shore habitats and is closely involved in seahorse conservation. The zoo is the home of the Anglesey Sea Salt Company. Tel: 01248 430411.
Bala Lake	13 miles (21km) northeast of Dolgellau. Aka Llyn Tegid. The largest natural body of water in Wales, at 4 miles (6km) long and a maximum 1 mile (1.6km) wide. Its level is now automatically controlled as part of the River Dee Regulation System. The lake has its resident 'monster' in the shape of 'Teggie'. Bala Lake has stocks of perch, pike and trout plus gwyniad, a form of herring unique to the lake.

Bala Lake Railway A 2ft (610mm) narrow gauge railway operating for $4^1/_2$ miles (7km) alongside Bala Lake from Llanuwchllyn to Bala (Penybont) via Llangower, on part of the route of a former standard gauge main line service which operated from 1868 until 1965. The company runs both steam and diesel engines. Tel: 01678 540666.

Bangor Cathedral Cathedral Close, Bangor. Founded in the 12th century on the site of a 6th century monastic foundation, and dedicated to St Deiniol. Damaged by King John in 1211, the cathedral also suffered during the wars between the Welsh princes and Edward I in the 1280s and again during Owain Glyndwr's early 15th century uprising. Glyndwr is buried under the high altar. The cathedral underwent extensive rebuilding in the 16th century and was partially restored by George Gilbert Scott, 1868–80. A central tower with a pyramidical cap was raised in 1966.

Barclodiad y Gawres Burial Chamber 9 miles (15km) southeast of Holyhead, Anglesey. Aka the Giantess's Apronful. A Neolithic chambered tomb on a promontory on the west coast of Anglesey, possibly dating to c.2400 BC. Laid out with three chambers off a central corridor spine, the tomb features six slabs decorated with a mixture of chevrons, lozenges, cupmarks and spirals. It was reconstructed after excavation in the 1930s.

Bardsey Island Aka Ynys Enlli. Located 2 miles (3km) off the tip of the Llŷn Peninsula, the island is the site of a monastery founded by Saint Cadfan in the 6th century, and of the Bardsey Bird and Field Observatory (founded in 1953). Its highest point is Mynydd Enlli at 413ft (167m). The island was bought by the Bardsey Island Trust in 1979 and is managed by the Trust in conjunction with the Countryside Council for Wales and CADW; it is a designated National Nature Reserve, Site of Special Scientific Interest, Special Protection Area and Area of Outstanding Natural Beauty. Bardsey is home to nationally important numbers of breeding red-billed chough and Manx shearwater. In 2003 a Manx shearwater was caught that had been ringed as an adult in 1957, making the bird at least 51 years old and thus the oldest known living wild bird. Other seabird species include kittiwake, storm petrel, razorbill and guillemot, while the island is also an important site for migrant birds as it lies on the Irish seaboard migration route; there is also a significant population of grey seals. Much of Bardsey is given over to agriculture; a 'new' variety of apple discovered on the island in 2000, and known as the Bardsey Island apple, is believed to be a survivor of ones grown by the abbey monks in the 13th century. The 100ft (30m) tall square-towered lighthouse was established in 1821 and automated in 1987. Area: 0.7 sq miles (1.82 sq km). GR: SH120215.

Barmouth RNLI Museum The Promenade, Barmouth, Gwynedd. Dedicated to the story of the Barmouth lifeboat and its crews. Exhibits include memorabilia, models and photographs.

Barmouth Sailors' Institute Quayside, Barmouth. The story of maritime Barmouth told using text, maps and illustrations. The institute was established in 1890 by Canon Edward Hughes, rector of Barmouth. There is a reading room and the original billiard room is still in use.

Beaumaris Castle Castle Street, Beaumaris, Anglesey. The largest and last castle built by Edward I in Wales. Designed by the king's chief military architect, Master James of St George, and purportedly constructed on the 'beautiful marsh' (*beau marais*) – hence the name – it was begun in concentric style with no central keep and surrounded by an 18ft (5m) moat in 1295–6; the moat was connected to a tidal dock, enabling the castle to be supplied by sea. The main building work was not completed until the 1330s, when a barbican was added. Despite its formidable appearance with six massive inner towers, the castle was never completed according to the original plans and saw very little action during its lifetime. It nevertheless remains one of the best examples of the art of medieval castle building. Beaumaris was surrendered without a fight to Major-General Mytton during the Civil War in 1646. Now owned by CADW, it is part of a UNESCO World Heritage Site along with Edward I's other castles at Conwy, Caernarfon and Harlech.

Beaumaris Courthouse Castle Street, Beaumaris, Anglesey. An early 17th century courthouse, now open to the public and featuring its original dock. Tel: 01248 811691/724444.

Beaumaris Gaol Steeple Lane, Beaumaris, Anglesey. Designed in 1829 by architect Joseph Aloysius Hansom (1803–82), inventor of the Hansom cab. It features a working treadmill, a gibbet and a condemned cell.

Breakwater Country Park 1 mile (1.6km) northwest of Holyhead. A park created since 1988 on the site of the quarry (closed in 1976) which supplied stones for the Holyhead breakwater. Covering 106 acres (43ha), it encompasses a variety of habitats including shoreline, parkland and lake, while an open air Industrial Trail Centre charts the history of the quarry and the breakwater; related artefacts and quarry equipment are on display.

Britannia Bridge A tube and box-girder railway bridge over the Menai Strait, built 1846–50 by William Fairbairn and Robert Stephenson. Damaged by an accidental fire in 1970, it was reconstructed with the addition of a road on an upper deck above the railway which opened in 1980. Now supported by arches, the bridge carries the A55 expressway. Sculptures of four lions, carved by John Thomas, guard the original bridge.

Bryn Celli Ddu 3 miles (5km) southwest of Menai Bridge, Anglesey. Neolithic passage grave beneath a large cairn, probably built c.3500 BC and partially restored in the 1930s. The passage is 27ft (8m) in length and leads to a polygonal burial chamber covered by two capstones. The chamber contains a replica of a free-standing pillar, the function of which is unknown (the original pillar is now kept at the National Museum of Wales in Cardiff). The site was plundered in 1699; excavations in the late 1920s revealed that there had originally been a henge and stone circle on the site.

Caer Gybi Roman Fort Stanley Street, Holyhead, Anglesey. The remains of a small 4th century Roman fort, possibly a base used by the Classis Britannia, the Roman navy based in Britain, to protect the coast against incursions by Irish and Saxon raiders. Measuring 220ft (67m) by 144ft (44m), it is rectangular in shape with walls 5ft (1.5m) thick on three sides and the fourth side facing the sea. There were

	also round angle turrets at three corners. St Cybi's Church (see separate entry) now stands within the area enclosed by the fort.
Caer y Twr	2 miles (3km) west of Holyhead, Anglesey. An Iron Age hill fort on the summit of Holyhead Mountain. The fort covered 18 acres (7ha) and used the natural defensive properties of the site with the addition of a stone rampart. The Romans built what appears to be a watchtower on the highest point. The site is managed by CADW.
Caernarfon Castle	Castle Ditch, Caernarfon. A formidable castle situated on the Menai Strait at the mouth of the River Seiont. Built between 1283 and the 1330s by Edward I, its grandeur acted as a symbol of English power in Wales. Constructed to a polygonal plan, it has 13 polygonal towers including the Eagle Tower, Queen's Tower, Chamberlain Tower and Black Tower, plus two gatehouses. Built in the aftermath of the English invasion, on the site of an Anglo-Norman motte erected in 1093 by Earl Hugh of Chester but destroyed by the Welsh in 1115, the first phase of construction was designed by the king's chief military architect, Master James of St George, and is thought to be an attempt to recreate the style of the defences of Constantinople. Building was interrupted by a successful attack by Madog ap Llywelyn in 1294. It saw little action during its history, although it withstood sieges by Owain Glyndwr in the early 15th century and surrendered to Parliamentary forces led by Major-General Mytton in 1646. It was restored during the 19th century. The first English Prince of Wales (the future Edward II) was born in Caernarfon in 1284, and the castle was the site of the ceremonial investitures as Prince of Wales of the future Edward VIII in 1911 and of Prince Charles in 1969. The castle also houses the Regimental Museum of the Royal Welch Fusiliers. Along with Edward I's castles at Beaumaris, Conwy and Harlech, it is part of a UNESCO World Heritage Site. Now owned by CADW.
Caernarfon Maritime Museum	Victoria Dock, Caernarfon. A museum charting the maritime and industrial history of the port of Caernarfon. Exhibits include artefacts, models, maps and photographs.
Capel Lligwy	1 mile (1.6km) west of Moelfre, 9 miles 15km) northwest of Menai Bridge, Anglesey. The ruins of a 12th century chapel overlooking Lligwy Bay. The chapel was rebuilt in the 14th century but little is known of its history.
Captain Skinner's Monument	Holyhead, Anglesey. A monument erected to American-born sea captain John MacGregor Skinner (1760–1832), who died when he was washed overboard from his ship the *Escape* in heavy seas on 13 October 1832. After losing an arm during the American War of Independence Skinner worked for the Post Office Shipping Service between Holyhead and Dublin for more than 30 years. The statue was erected in his honour by the people of Holyhead and bears the inscription, 'This monument was erected by his numerous friends to the memory of John Macgregor Skinner, R.N., and for 33 years captain of one of the post office packets on this station, in testimony of his virtues, and their affectionate remembrance of him in his public capacity. He was distinguished for zeal, intrepidity and fidelity. In private life he was a model of unvarying friendship, disinterested kindness and unbounded charity. MDCCCXXXII.'
Carreglwyd	Llanfaethlu, 5 miles (8km) northeast of Holyhead, Anglesey. Wooded gardens surrounding a 17th century house and featuring an ornamental lake and a walled garden. Tel: 01407 730208.
Castell Aberlleiniog	$^{1}/_{4}$ miles (0.4km) east of Llangoed, 6 miles (10km) northeast of Menai Bridge, Anglesey. A late 11th century motte and bailey beside the River Lleiniog (hence the name), believed to have been raised by Hugh of Avranches, Earl of Chester. During the Civil War the motte supported a stone 17th century fortlet, now in ruins.
Castell Bryn Gwyn	$^{3}/_{4}$ mile (1.2km) west of Brynsiencyn, 7 miles (11km) southwest of Menai Bridge, Anglesey. An oval enclosure 200ft (60m) in diameter on level ground with defences similar to those of a hill fort. When excavated in the late 1950s, it revealed an apparent history of occupation from the Iron Age to the Roman period. The first settlement was defined by a stone bank with a ditch and berm (flat area of land); the succeeding settlement, enclosed by a stone-revetted bank and ditch, was followed by another remodelling of the defences with a timber-revetted bank and a V-shaped ditch.
Castell Carndochan	2 mile (3km) west of Llanuwchlyn, 5 miles (8km) southwest of Bala. The ruins of a 13th century castle on a steep craggy summit, with D-shaped towers to the south and north surrounding an earlier rectangular keep.
Castell Cynfal	1$^{1}/_{4}$ miles (2km) northeast of Tywyn, 9 miles (15km) west of Machynlleth. Aka Bryn-y-Castell. A motte and circular ditch probably dating to the mid 12th century. It may have been a Welsh rather than a Norman fortification.
Castell-y-Bere	$^{1}/_{2}$ mile (0.8km) southwest of Llanfihangel-y-Pennant, 7 miles (11km) northwest of Machynlleth. An enclosure castle located along a flat-topped high ridge, and founded c.1221 by Llywelyn the Great. It was roughly rectangular in plan with D-shaped towers, a rectangular keep and a curtain wall. The castle was captured by an English force in April 1283 and restored 1286–90. After a failed attempt to recapture it by Madog ap Llywelyn in 1294 it was slighted and abandoned. It is now in the care of CADW.
Castles and Town Walls of King Edward in Gwynedd	The castles and military complexes built by Edward I at Beaumaris, Caernarfon, Conwy (see Clwyd) and Harlech were designated a UNESCO World Heritage Site in 1986.
Criccieth Castle	Castle Street, Criccieth. An early 13th century castle on a headland above Tremadog Bay. Built by Llywelyn the Great and originally known as the Castle of the Welsh Princes, it was extended by Llywelyn ap Gruffudd. In 1239 Dafydd ap Llywelyn imprisoned his half-brother Gruffudd and Gruffudd's son Owain in the castle, hence the name Criccieth (Mound of the Captives). The castle was captured by English forces in 1283 and subsequently remodelled by Edward I and his son Edward II. It has a twin-towered gatehouse, a rectangular tower known as the Engine Tower and a possible keep known as the Montfort Tower. It is uncertain during which of the phases of construction these fortifications were built, although the Leyburn Tower was certainly added by

Edward I. After falling to the English it withstood a siege by Madog ap Llywelyn in 1294. The castle was severely damaged by fire and abandoned in 1404 after a successful siege by Owain Glyndwr. Very little of the interior structure now remains. The castle is in the care of CADW. Tel: 01766 522227.

Cymer Abbey $1\frac{1}{4}$ miles (2km) north of Dolgellau. The ruins of a Cistercian abbey beside the River Mawddach. Founded in 1198 by Maredudd ap Cynan, the house fell into decline after the English invasion at the end of the 14th century. A silver gilt chalice and paten were discovered nearby in the 19th century and it is believed that these might have been deliberately hidden at the time of the Dissolution of the Monasteries in the 1530s. The main surviving ruin is that of the abbey church.

Deudraeth Castle Portmeirion, $1\frac{1}{2}$ miles (2.5km) southeast of Porthmadog. A Victorian mansion built in the 1850s for David Williams, great-uncle of Sir Clough Williams-Ellis, and which later became part of the estate of Portmeirion. It opened as a hotel in 2001. The original Castell Deudraeth was probably built by the Welsh in the 12th century. Its last remnants were demolished c.1850. Tel: 0870 418 8189.

Dic Evans' sculpture Moelfre, Anglesey. A 7ft (2.1m) high bronze sculpture of lifeboatman Richard 'Dic' Evans (1905–2001), who served on the Moelfre lifeboat for 50 years and was coxswain 1954–70. During his service he was awarded two RNLI gold medals and an MBE. The sculpture was created by Samantha Holland and is dedicated to all lifeboatmen and especially those who have lost their lives in carrying out their duties. It was unveiled by HRH the Prince of Wales in November 2004.

Din Lligwy 1 mile (1.6km) west of Moelfre, 9 miles (15km) northwest of Menai Bridge, Anglesey. A 4th century settlement with the remains of two round and seven rectangular huts with a circuit wall. There is evidence of both domestic and industrial activity.

Dinas Emrys $1\frac{1}{4}$ miles (2km) northeast of Beddgelert, 11 miles (18km) southeast of Caernarfon. A site on the summit of a volcanic outcrop in the Gwynant valley, originally the site of an Iron Age hill fort and occupied intermittently until the 12th century. It has traditionally been linked with Ambrosius (Emrys Wledig) and Merlin.

Dolbadarn Castle $\frac{1}{2}$ mile (0.8km) east of Llanberis. The ruins of a castle strategically placed above the causeway between the lakes Llyn Padarn and Llyn Peris. Built by Llywelyn the Great in the early 13th century, the only substantial structure remaining is the 40ft (12m) high round tower which is also 40ft (12m) in diameter and has walls 8ft (2.5m) thick. Captured by English forces in 1282, it was partially dismantled by Edward I in 1284 and abandoned soon after. Now in the care of CADW.

Eglwys-y-Bedd Holyhead, Anglesey. Aka St Cybi's Chantry. The nave of a 14th century chapel located within the walls of Caer Gybi (see separate entry) and converted into Holyhead's first school in 1748. The ruins of the chancel were demolished in 1810 to clear a path to St Cybi's Church. The name means 'church of the grave' and according to tradition it marks the grave of an Irish chieftain called Seregri.

Electric Mountain Llanberis. The familiar name for Dinorwig Power Station, a hydroelectric scheme located within Elidir Mountain in Europe's largest man-made cave. Tel: 01286 870636.

Ffestiniog Railway One of Wales's top tourist attractions, the 1ft $11\frac{1}{2}$in (590mm) gauge track runs for $13\frac{1}{2}$ miles (22km) from the harbour at Porthmadog to the slate mining town of Blaenau Ffestiniog, via Minffordd, Penrhyn, Tan-y-Bwlch, Dduallt and Tanygrisiau. The narrow gauge railway was originally built to transport slate from quarries in the mountains around Blaenau Ffestiniog to the port at Porthmadog. Opened in 1836, the line was closed in 1946 following the severe decline of the slate industry but was reopened in 1955 by enthusiasts and volunteers. The railway uses both steam and diesel engines.

Gelert's Grave Beddgelert, 11 miles (18km) southeast of Caernarfon. The reputed burial place of Llywelyn the Great's faithful and possibly legendary dog Gelert. According to the well-known story, the Welsh prince left his dog to guard his baby son while he himself went hunting. On his return he found his son missing and the dog covered in blood. He immediately killed Gelert but then found his son alive beside the body of the wolf which his loyal hound had killed. He buried the dog with great ceremony on the spot, and the village of Beddgelert (Gelert's Grave) grew around it.

Harlech Castle Castle Square, Harlech. The substantial ruins of one of Edward I's ring of fortresses in North Wales. The castle was constructed 1283–9 and further extended in the 1320s. It is concentric in plan with an inner and an outer ward, both bounded by four round corner towers connected by a curtain wall. There is also a large gatehouse; it was formerly possible to resupply the castle from the sea during a siege by means of the 'way from the sea', but the sea has since receded and the castle is now landlocked. The first phase of the building was designed by the king's chief military architect, Master James of St George. The castle survived an attack by Madog ap Llywelyn in 1294 when defended by 37 men but fell to the more determined Owain Glyndwr in 1404 when defended by 40 men, subsequently becoming Owain's headquarters. Recaptured by Prince Henry (the future Henry V) in 1408, it was subjected to another long siege when a Lancastrian garrison was captured by Yorkist forces during the Wars of the Roses in 1468; this last siege is said to have inspired the song 'Men of Harlech'. In 1647 it was also the final Royalist fortress to fall at the end of the Civil War, and was then slighted by the Parliamentarian forces. The outer wall is now ruinous. Along with Edward I's other castles at Beaumaris, Caernarfon and Conwy, it is a designated UNESCO World Heritage Site. The castle is now in the care of CADW.

Highest point The highest point in Gwynedd, and indeed the whole of Wales, is Mount Snowdon at 3560ft (1085m). GR: SH609543.

Holyhead Maritime Museum Newry Beach, Holyhead, Anglesey. A museum housed in a 19th century lifeboat house and charting the maritime history of Holyhead. Exhibits include memorabilia, figureheads, medals and photographs. Tel: 01407 769745.

Holy Island	aka Ynys Cybi. Connected to the Isle of Anglesey by causeways carrying the A5/A55 road and the railway. The 'capital' is the port of Holyhead, from which passenger ferries travel to Dun Laoghaire and Dublin, Ireland, and freight ferries also travel to Dublin.
Interesting facts	**Bangor** is one of the smallest cities in the UK. Its population of around 14,000 includes approximately 9000 students of the University of Wales. The city is often confused with Bangor-on-Dee, near Wrexham. Bangor does have two small rivers within its boundaries: the Adda is a largely culverted watercourse which only appears above ground at its western extremities near to the Faenol estate, while the Cegin enters Port Penrhyn at the eastern edge of the city. The city has at least two other claims to fame: it has possibly the longest high street in Wales and, in 1967, the Beatles came to Bangor (staying at Neuadd Reichel) for their first encounter with Maharishi Mahesh Yogi, a visit during which they learned of the death of their manager Brian Epstein. **Portmeirion** is an Italianate resort village on the coast of Snowdonia. Created by architect Clough Williams-Ellis, it has become a major tourist site, not so much because of its magnificent architecture and design but because it was featured as 'The Village' in the cult television series *The Prisoner* (1967).
Islands	See separate table.
Llanberis Lake Railway	A narrow gauge (2ft/610mm) heritage railway running for $2\frac{1}{2}$ miles (4km) from Llanberis along the shore of Padarn Lake, passing the Welsh Slate Museum and Dolbadarn Castle, to Gilfach Ddu station in Padarn Country Park. It was opened in 1971 and uses the trackbed of the Padarn Railway which operated from the 1820s, closing in 1961. The railway uses three steam engines (*Elidir*, *Thomas Bach* and *Dolbadarn*) and one diesel engine (*Topsy*). Tel: 01286 870549.
Llechwedd Slate Caverns	$\frac{1}{2}$ mile (0.8km) north of Blaenau Ffestiniog. A working slate mine also offering trips underground to experience the life of Victorian slate miners. There are exhibitions and restored mine buildings on the surface. Tel: 01766 830306.
Lligwy Burial Chamber	1 mile (1.6km) west of Moelfre, 9 miles 15km) northwest of Menai Bridge, Anglesey. A Neolithic burial chamber dating to the end of the 3rd millennium BC. Originally buried under an earth mound, access to the central chamber was through a small passage. It has a massive capstone measuring 18ft (5.5m) by 15ft (4.5m) and weighing 25 tons. Excavations carried out in 1909 uncovered the remains of 25–30 people.
Lloyd George Museum	Llanystumdwy, 1 mile (1.6km) west of Criccieth. The childhood home of Prime Minister Lloyd George (1863–1945). The house has been restored to its possible appearance during his boyhood; exhibts include memorabilia and a recreation of a Victorian schoolroom. The cottage garden has also been restored. Tel: 01766 522071.
Llyn Cerrig Bach Hoard	A hoard of Iron Age artefacts found in the lake of Llyn Cerrig Bach on Anglesey in 1943, while RAF personnel were clearing a lake for the building of a new runway on the nearby RAF Valley airfield. The artefacts included swords, spears and many chariot wheels dating from the 2nd century BC to the 1st century AD, although their immersion seems to end around the time of the conquest of Anglesey by Suetonius Paulinus in AD 60. The hoard probably originated from the Celtic ritual of making offerings in water.
Llys Rhosyr	Newborough, 9 miles (15km) southwest of Menai Bridge, Anglesey. The site of a 13th century royal court (*llys*), preserved under a layer of sand until it was uncovered in the 1990s. It was used as a stopping-off point for the court during the regular royal progresses of the Welsh kings and princes. During these stops they would collect rents and sit in judgement of local disputes. The plan of the buildings uncovered include a timber hall with accompanying stone buildings. There is an audio-visual presentation about the site at the Prichard Jones Institute in Newborough. Tel: 01248 440608.
Marquess of Anglesey's Column	Llanfairpwll, Anglesey. A monument erected in 1817 on the site of an Iron Age hill fort near Llanfairpwllgwyngyllgogerychwyrndrobwllllantysiliogogogoch to commemorate the allied victory at the Battle of Waterloo on 18 June 1815. On top of the column stands a statue of Henry William Paget, Earl of Uxbridge, 1st Marquess of Anglesey, second in command at Waterloo, where he lost his leg. The statue was erected in 1860. There are 115 steps to the top of the column.
Melin Llynnon Mill	Llanddeusant, 6 miles (10km) northeast of Holyhead, Anglesey. The only working windmill in Wales, built in the 1770s and operational until 1918 when it was damaged by a storm. It was bought by Anglesey Borough Council, restored and opened in 1986 as a fully working mill. Tel: 01407 730797.
Menai Suspension Bridge	Suspension bridge over the Menai Strait designed by Thomas Telford. Begun in 1819 and opened in 1826, it was designed to have sufficient clear space under the span to allow the passage of tall sailing ships. The road surface was repaired in 1839 and the wooden deck was replaced by one made of steel in 1893. The original iron suspension chains were replaced in the late 1930s. The bridge now carries the A5.
Moelfre Seawatch Centre	Moelfre, Anglesey. A visitor centre charting the maritime history of this area of Anglesey. The main exhibit is a modern lifeboat and there is information on the life of the lifeboat crews. Tel: 01248 410277.
Museum of Childhood Memories	Castle Street, Beaumaris, Anglesey. An award-winning museum exploring childhood experiences from the Victorian period to the present. Each room has a different theme: art gallery, clockwork tin-plate toys, doll houses, entertainment, nursery furniture and push-along toys, pottery and glass, rocking horses and cycles, teddy bears, and money boxes. It opened in Menai Bridge in 1973 and moved to its current location in 1985. Tel: 01248 712498.
National Slate Museum	$\frac{1}{4}$ mile (0.4km) east of Llanberis. Part of National Museum Wales and located in the Victorian workshops on Elidir mountain, near the Dinorwig quarry. It tells the story of the Welsh slate industry which thrived during the Industrial Revolution. Features include a working waterwheel, practical demonstrations and a tour of the workshops, foundry and forge. Other restored buildings

on the site include the engineer's house, the barracks, the cabin, the sawing sheds and the pattern loft. A row of four restored quarrymen's houses have been furnished to reflect different periods in the history of the quarry: 1860 when it was at its height, 1901 at the time of the Penrhyn Strike and 1969 when the quarry closed (the fourth has interactive displays). The 'incline' used to transport the slates down the mountain to the trains for transportation to port has also been restored to working order. Tel: 01286 870630.

Nelson Memorial Llanfairpwll, Anglesey. A memorial to Horatio Nelson erected overlooking the Menai Strait below Plas Llanfair in 1873. Created by amateur sculptor Admiral Lord Clarence Paget, it bears the inscriptions 'Nelson' and 'Fell at Trafalgar 1805. England expects that every man will do his duty'.

Padarn Lake Country Park An 800 acre (320ha) park to the east of Llanberis and including the glacial lake of Llyn Padarn and Coed Allt Wen, a rare sessile oak woodland. A local nature reserve, it is also a designated Site of Special Scientific Interest. The park also contains the Welsh Slate Museum, the Llanberis Lake Railway and the Quarry Hospital Musuem.

Parc Glynllifon Llandwrog, 5 miles (8km) south of Caernarfon. A country park covering 60 acres (24ha) in part of the former estate of Lord Newborough. The former seat of the family has been an agricultural college since 1954, while the park opened to the public in 1989. The Grade I listed formal gardens are full of follies (including the Mill and the Hermitage), streams and fountains; there is also an arboretum with over 50 different species of tree. The park also features a Welsh arts gallery and the grounds are dotted with contemporary sculpture sites celebrating Welsh literature; there is an open air theatre on the man-made Yew Tree Island.

Parys Mountain Copper Mines 2 miles (3km) south of Amlwch, Anglesey. Mynydd Parys (Parys Mountain) was at one time the most productive copper mine in the world. Although mining has been carried out on the site since perhaps as early as the Bronze Age, the remains on view date largely from the 18th century onwards when the mines were at the height of production. In addition to two opencast mines (Parys and Mona), there is a pumping windmill, Cornish beam engine and shaft winch which served the many underground workings. There is no public access to the mines but there is a footpath around the top of the mountain. An exhibition of artefacts recovered from the mine can be seen at the Sail Loft in Amlwch.

Penmon Church & Dovecote Penmon, 2½ miles (4km) northeast of Beaumaris, Anglesey. The ruins of a 13th century Augustinian priory built on the site of a 6th century monastery established by St Seiriol. It was abandoned following the Dissolution and the ruins now mainly comprise a refectory and a dormitory. The priory church, which continued in use as the parish church, houses two 10th century Celtic crosses. Nearby is a large 17th century dovecote with a vaulted stone roof crowned with an open cupola.

Penrhyn Castle 1 mile (1.6km) east of Bangor. Large neo-Norman castle built 1820–45 by Thomas Hopper for the Pennant family, with an interior also decorated and furnished in 'Norman' style. The castle has a collection of fine art and also features oddities such as a 1 ton slate bed made for Queen Victoria. The servants' quarters and Victorian kitchen have been restored to their condition in 1894, when the Prince of Wales paid a visit to the castle. There is also a doll collection and an industrial railway museum plus a model railway museum. The 45 acre (18ha) gardens afford fine views of Snowdonia and feature parkland, a terrace and a walled kitchen garden. Maintained by the National Trust since 1951. Tel: 01248 353084.

Plas Brondanw ½ mile (0.8km) northeast of Garreg, 4 miles (6km) northeast of Porthmadog. A beautifully landscaped Italianate garden of 2 acres (0.8ha), originally created by architect Sir Clough Williams-Ellis (1883–1978) in the 1920s and 1930s at his family home. The garden is divided into a series of 'rooms' by yew hedging and Italian cypress, and is studded with topiary and sculpture. The house originally dated to the 16th century and was given to Williams-Ellis by his father in 1908, and has been restored after suffering severe fire damage in 1951. The garden is also 4 miles (6km) northeast of Williams-Ellis's most famous creation, Portmerion. Tel: 01766 770000.

Plas Newydd 1½ miles (2.5km) southwest of Llanfairpwyll, Anglesey. The mansion home of the Marquess of Anglesey, located beside the Menai Strait and built in the 18th century to a design by James Wyatt. The house has an exhibition of the works of painter Rex Whistler (1905–44) including his largest work, a 58ft (17.5m) panorama with romantic allusions, commissioned by the 6th Marquess of Anglesey. The military collection includes the first articulated wooden leg ever manufactured; it belonged to the 1st Marquess, who lost a leg during the Battle of Waterloo, where he was a senior commander. The gardens overlook the Menai Strait and include a large rhododendron garden and an Australasian arboretum. The house and gardens have been maintained by the National Trust since 1976. Tel: 01248 714795.

Plas Tan-y-Bwlch Maentwrog, 5 miles (8km) northeast of Porthmadog. Informal gardens surrounding a 19th century house in the Snowdonia National Park which is now used as a centre for residential courses. The garden features formal terraces, a water garden and a pond plus semi-wild areas to encourage local wildlife.

Plas yn Rhiw 1 mile (1.6km) northeast of Rhiw, 9 miles (15km) southwest of Pwllheli. Small 16th century manor house with Georgian additions. The plantsman's garden, which affords views over Porth Neigwl (Hell's Mouth Bay), has been formally laid out with beds outlined by box hedges and grass paths. A nearby woodland has spectacular displays of snowdrops and bluebells in late winter and spring. The house and garden have been maintained by the National Trust since 1952. Tel: 01758 780219.

Porthmadog Maritime Museum The Harbour, Porthmadog. A museum celebrating the story of the local topsail schooners, housed in a former slate shed on Porthmadog wharf. Other exhibits include models, equipment and paintings.

Portmeirion 1½ miles (2.5km) southeast of Porthmadog. The coastal village of Portmeirion was created 1925–75 by architect Clough Williams-Ellis, and was designed, he explained, to show that 'the development of a naturally beautiful site need not lead to its defilement'. The original site, known as Aber Iâ, was a long-abandoned wilderness which Williams-Ellis bought for £5000. He renamed it the Port of Merioneth, which thus became Portmeirion. The layout of the village and the main buildings were erected during the first stage of construction, 1925–39, largely in Arts and Crafts style. The second stage, 1954–76, ensured the details of the design were 'filled in', and displays Palladian influences. Several of the buildings were rescued from other sites.

Quaker Heritage Centre — Tŷ Meirion, Sgwar Eldon Square, Dolgellau. A centre charting the history of the Quaker community in Dolgellau from the 17th to the 19th century. Tel: 01341 424680.

Quarry Hospital Museum — Gilfach Ddu, Llanberis. Housed in the former Dinorwig Quarry Hospital, purpose built in 1860 solely to serve workers in the nearby slate quarry, the museum features a restored ward, operating theatre and mortuary. Exhibits include medical equipment and an original X-ray machine. Between 1822 and 1969 362 men were killed in the quarries, mostly in rockfalls. Perhaps the most famous doctor resident in the hospital was Dr Robert Herbert Mills-Roberts. A respected surgeon who once created functioning metal arms for an amputee, he was also an accomplished amateur footballer who won eight full caps for Wales 1885–92 and played in goal for Aberystwyth and Preston North End. While with Preston he featured in the FA Cup finals of 1888 and 1889, and was on the winning side in the latter.

Regimental Museum of the Royal Welch Fusiliers — Housed within the Queen's Tower and Chamberlain Tower of Caernarfon Castle, the museum contains displays of uniforms, weaponry and memorabilia laid out in a series of tableaux. The Royal Welch Fusiliers is Wales's oldest infantry regiment, having been formed as Lord Herbert's Regiment of Foot at Ludlow on 16 March 1689, during the war against the Jacobites. Pressed quickly into the fray, it saw action at the Battle of the Boyne in 1690. From 1702 it became the Welch Regiment of Fusiliers. Awarded the royal accolade following its sterling service during the War of the Spanish Succession, it was designated the 23rd Regiment of Foot in 1751. During the Napoleonic Wars the regiment fought in Egypt, the Peninsula and also at the climactic Battle of Waterloo. During the 19th century the regiment took part in action at Alba in the Crimean War, at Lucknow during the Indian Mutiny and at the siege of Peking legations in 1900. In 1881 it was renamed the Royal Welsh Fusiliers but in 1921 the ancient spelling 'Welch', which the regiment had unofficially continued to use, was officially restored. Elements of the regiment fought in virtually every theatre of conflict during both world wars. Its numerous honours include Namur (1695), Blenheim, Ramillies, Oudenarde, Malplaquet, Dettingen, Minden, Corunna, Martinique (1809), Albuhera, Badajoz, Salamanca, Vittoria, Pyrenees, Nivelle, Orthes, Toulouse, Peninsula, Waterloo, Alma, Inkerman, Sevastopol, Lucknow, Ashantee (1873–4), Burma (1885–7), Relief of Ladysmith, South Africa (1899–1902), Pekin (1900), Mons, Le Cateau, Marne (1914), Ypres (1914, 1917, 1918), Somme (1916, 1918), Passchendaele, Cambrai (1917, 1918), Hindenburg Line, Vittorio Veneto, Doiran (1917, 1918), Suvla, Gallipoli (1915–16), Egypt (1915–17), Baghdad, Mesopotamia (1916–18), Caen, Falaise, Lower Maas, Rhineland, Reichswald, Northwest Europe (1940, 1944–5), Madagascar, Middle East (1942), Donbaik, North Arakan, Kohima, Mandalay, Ava and Burma (1943–5). On 1 March 2006 the regiment formed the new 1st Battalion The Royal Welsh Regiment (The Royal Welch Fusiliers). The Royal Regiment of Wales forms the 2nd Battalion. Tel: 01286 673362.

RSPB South Stack Cliffs — 2 miles (3km) west of Holyhead, Anglesey. An RSPB reserve encompassing the clifftop nesting sites of seabirds including puffins, fulmars, guillemots and razorbills. The reserve is also home to chough and peregrine falcon. The visitor centre is housed in Ellin's Tower, a castellated tower built by archaeologist and Anglesey MP William Owen Stanley (1802–84), and named after his wife. Tel: 01407 764973.

St Cybi's Church — Stanley Street, Holyhead, Anglesey. Located within the ruins of Caer Gybi Roman fort (see separate entry). The original church was built in the 6th century by St Cybi, a cousin of St David. The earliest part of the current structure dates from the 13th century but additions were made over many centuries including a 17th century tower. The interior was defaced by Cromwellian troops during the Civil War.

St Mary's Abbey — Bardsey Island. The ruins of an early 13th century Cistercian or Augustinian foundation abandoned following the Dissolution. The abbey tower is a major landmark on the island.

Segontium Roman Fort — Llanbeblig Road, Caernarfon. The site of a Roman auxiliary fort established in the 1st century and probably abandoned in the 4th century. The fort covered an area 2100ft (640m) by 1800ft (549m) and would have served as a barracks for 1000 troops. Its later task was to defend the coast from Irish raiders. Excavations were carried out in the 1920s and the 1970s. A museum opened in 1924 tells the story of the conquest and occupation of Wales, also exhibiting some of the finds excavated from the site. Maintained by CADW.

Snowdon Mountain Railway — A single track rack and pinion railway running for more than 4 miles (6km) from Llanberis to the top of Snowdon, via stations at Waterfall (closed), Hebron (non-alighting), Halfway (non-alighting), Rocky Valley Halt (where trains terminate in bad weather) and Clogwyn. It has operated since 1896 and reaches within 66ft (21m) of the summit. It has a gauge of 2ft 7½in (800mm) and an average gradient of 1 in 7.86. A single journey takes about one hour. The company runs four steam engines, three of which have operated since the beginning of the railway. There are also four more modern diesel locomotives and three diesel electric railcars. Tel: 0870 458 0033.

Snowdonia National Park — Britain's third largest National Park (after the Cairngorms and Lake District), covering 823 sq miles (2132 sq km) and designated in 1951. It is not a 'wild' National Park and has more than 26,000 people living and working within its boundaries. It contains a wide variety of habitats including 37 miles (60km) of coastline, 370 sq miles (960 sq km) of moorland, 139 sq miles (360 sq km) woodland, more than 90 mountains over 2000ft (600m) and more than 100 lakes more than 1 acre (0.4ha) in size. The park includes a World Biosphere Site and a Ramsar site plus Special Areas of

Conservation, Special Protection Areas and Sites of Special Scientific Interest. In particular, of course, Snowdonia is notable for its mountain scenery which includes the following peaks over 3000ft (900m): Snowdon (Yr Wyddfa), 3560ft (1085m); Crib-y-Ddysgl, 3495ft (1085m); Carnedd Llywelyn, 3490ft (1064m); Carnedd Dafydd 3424ft (1044m); Y Glyder Fawr, 3279ft (999m); Y Glyder Fach, 3262ft (994m); Pen yr Ole Wen, 3210ft (978m); Foel Grach, 3202ft (976m); Yr Elen, 3156ft (962m); Y Garn, 3107ft (947m); Foel Fras, 3091ft (942m); Garnedd Uchaf, 3037ft (926m); Elidir Fawr, 3029ft (923m); Crib Goch, 3027ft (922m); and Tryfan, 3002ft (915m). The area around Blaenau Ffestiniog is not part of the designated National Park. Tel: 01766 770274.

South Stack — Aka Ynys Lawd. An island located off Holy Island on the edge of Anglesey and famous for its 91ft (28m) lighthouse, designed by David Alexander. The lighthouse was established in 1809 and designed to allow safe passage for ships on the treacherous Dublin–Holyhead–Liverpool sea route; the mail light is visible to passing vessels for 28 miles (45km). The lighthouse was electrified in 1938 and automated in 1984. A footbridge joining the rock on which it stands to the 'mainland' of Holy Island was completed in 1997, replacing an earlier bridge which had become unusable. GR: SH202823.

Sport

football — **Bangor City** were founded in 1876 as Bangor FC and were winners of the League of Wales in 1994 and 1995, and the Welsh Cup in 1889, 1896, 1962, 1998, 2000. Their home ground is The Stadium, Farrar Road, Bangor, Gwynedd.

Caernarfon Town were founded in 1876 as Caernarvon Athletic, and were formerly named Caernarvon Ironopolis and Caernarvon United before emerging as Caernarfon Town in 1937. From 1980–95 the team played in English non-league football and the FA Cup before joining the League of Wales. Nicknamed the Canaries, their home ground is The Oval, Marcus Street, Caernarfon.

Porthmadog were founded in 1884. Nicknamed Port, their home ground is Y Traeth Stadium, Porthmadog.

Stone Science — Bryn Eglwys, Llanddyfnan, 3 miles (5km) northeast of Llangefni, Anglesey. A museum of geology and archaeology with dioramas depicting the evolving ages of the earth. Exhibits include fossils, jewellery, minerals and crystals. Tel: 01248 450310.

Swtan Cottage — Church Bay (Porth Swtan), Rhydwyn, 4 miles (6km) northeast of Holyhead, Anglesey. A heritage museum housed in a thatched crofting longhouse, last occupied in the 1970s and restored using traditional skills. It is furnished to reflect its possible appearance in the late 19th and early 20th centuries. Local history displays and exhibits chart the history of the cottage, its inhabitants and the surrounding area. Swtan is owned by a trust and managed by the local community.

Sygun Copper Mine — 1 mile (1.6km) east of Beddgelert, 6 miles (10km) north of Porthmadog. A former copper mine in Snowdonia which was at its height in the 18th and 19th centuries. Closed in 1903, it was reopened to the public in 1986. The surrounding countryside was transformed into a walled Chinese city by production designer John Box for the film *The Inn of the Sixth Happiness* (1958). The Red Dragon Heritage Centre features the story of the mythical fight between the red dragon and the white dragon on Dinas Emrys, which had been undermining King Vortigern's castle until discovered by Merlin. Tel: 01766 890595.

Tacla Taid — 3/4 mile (1.2km) northeast of Newborough, 7 miles (11km) southwest of Llanfairpwll, Anglesey. The Anglesey Transport and Agriculture Museum, featuring a private collection of cars including a Morris Eight, Ford Zodiac Mk III, Hillman Minx, Humber Super Snipe, Jaguar S-Type, Austin Big Seven and a Vauxhall 12hp, as well as lorries, motorcycles and tractors. Tel: 01248 440344.

Talhenbont Hall — 3 miles (5km) west of Criccieth. A Grade II listed house built in 1607 and situated within more than 70 acres (28ha) of ancient woodland beside the River Dwyfach.

Talyllyn Railway — A popular narrow gauge (2ft 3in/686mm) heritage railway operating for 7 1/4 miles (11.5km) from Tywyn on the Cardigan Bay coast to Nant Gwernol, via Tywyn Pendre, Rhydyronen, Brynglas, Dolgoch and Abergynolwyn. There are also several halts, of which Cynfal Halt has the smallest railway platform in Britain. The line was originally opened in 1865 to transport slate from the Bryn Eglwys quarries near Abergynolwyn and also carried passengers. Slate traffic ceased in 1946 and the line was closed in October 1950, but was quickly reopened by the Talyllyn Railway Preservation Society in 1951. The line has six steam locomotives for passenger trains and four diesel locomotives for haulage work. A new station building and museum were opened at Tywyn Wharf by Prince Charles and the Duchess of Cornwall in 2005. The line was used by the Rev W Awdry of *Thomas the Tank Engine* fame in his writing about Skarloey Railway. Tel: 01654 710472.

Tre'r Ceiri — 1 mile (1.6km) west of Llanaelhaearn, 6 miles (10km) north of Pwllheli. A stone-ramparted hill fort on the summit of one of the peaks of Yr Eifl (1591ft/485m) on the Llŷn Peninsula. Occupied during the Romano-British period (AD 150–400), it measures 1000ft (305m) by 350ft (107m), with five gateways, and encloses around 150 hut circles.

Tŷ Isaf — Beddgelert, 6 miles (10km) north of Porthmadog. This 17th century cottage is the oldest house in Beddgelert. Now housing a 'plot to plate' exhibition on local produce and how diets have changed since the 19th century, it has been maintained by the National Trust since 1985. Tel: 01766 510129.

University of Wales, Bangor — Founded as the University College of North Wales in October 1884 with 58 students and 10 staff. Initially housed in an old coaching inn called the Penrhyn Arms, it became one of the three original constituent colleges of the University of Wales in 1893. A purpose-built main building was erected in 1911 and the Science Department moved into its own building in 1926. Formerly known as the University College of North Wales (UCNW) and University College, Bangor (UCB), it was designated the University of Wales, Bangor in 1997. It now has more than 9000 students, 20 departments and over 600 teaching staff. Tel: 01248 351151.

Waterloo Bridge	A cast-iron bridge spanning the River Conwy $^1/_2$ mile (0.8km) east of Betws-y-Coed, and carrying the A5 road. It was designed by Thomas Telford and construction began in 1815, the year of the Battle of Waterloo.
Welsh Highland Railway	A narrow gauge (1ft $11^1/_2$in/597mm) heritage railway operating in two sections for 13 miles (21km) from Caernarfon to Rhyd Ddu via Bontnewydd, Dinas, Waunfawr, Plas-y-Nant, Snowdon Ranger, Beddgelert Forest, Beddgelert, Pont Croesor, Pen-y-Mount and Porthmadog Harbour, and for 1 mile (1.6km) between Pen-y-Mount and Porthmadog. The line originally ran from Dinas near Caernarfon to Porthmadog, with a branch line to Bryngwyn and the slate quarries at Moel Tryfan, and was in commercial operation from 1922 until 1936. In 1980 a short service was opened from Porthmadog (WHR) to Pen-y-Mount. A section between Caernarfon and Dinas was opened in 1997 and further sections between Dinas and Waunfawr and from Waunfawr to Rhyd Ddu followed up to 2003. It is planned to join the sections in the late 2000s.

Some famous people born in Gwynedd

Adams, Tony (actor) (1940–)	Anglesey
Deacon, Richard (Turner Prize-winner) (1949–)	Bangor
French, Dawn (comedian) (1957–)	Holyhead
Griffith, Hugh (actor) (1912–80)	Marian Glas
Jones, Aled (singer and broadcaster) (1970–)	Bangor
Lawrence, Thomas Edward (soldier) (1888–1935)	Tremadog
Lloyd George, Megan (politician) (1902–66)	Criccieth
Timothy, Christopher (actor) (1940–)	Bala
Williams, Johnny (boxer) (1926–2007)	Barmouth
Williams, Kyffin (artist) (1918–2006)	Llangefni

Islands of Gwynedd and Anglesey

(shipping area = Irish Sea)

Island name	Area	Nearest landmark	General information
Gwynedd			
Bardsey Island	Bardsey Sound	Aberdaron	See separate entry.
Caer Arianrhod	Caernarfon Bay	Penygroes	GR: SH424547
Carreg Chwisten	Cardigan Bay	Llanfaelrhys	GR: SH195258
Carreg Ddu	Bardsey Sound	Aberdaron	GR: SH149239
Carreg Ddu	Caernarfon Bay	Morfa Nefyn	GR: SH279421
Carreg Gybi	Cardigan Bay	Aberdaron	GR: SH190253
Carreg y Defaid	Cardigan Bay	Llanbedrog	GR: SH345324
Carreg y Trai	Cardigan Bay	St Tudwal's Island East	GR: SH349256
Carreg yr Honwy	Bardsey Sound	Bardsey Island	GR: SH109213
Carreg yr Imbill	Cardigan Bay	Pwllheli	GR: SH389344
Cei Ballast	Tremadog Bay	Pothmadog	GR: SH570379
Cerrig y Barcdy	Cardigan Bay	Penrhyn	GR: SH440359
Cerrig-y-Gorllwyn	Barmouth Bay	Barmouth	GR: SH623148
Gored Beuno	Caernarfon Bay	Clynnog-fawr	GR: SH412509
Llech Lydan	Caernarfon Bay	Llithfaen	GR: SH332435
Maen Bugail	Bardsey Sound	Bardsey Island	GR: SH119232
Maen Gwenonwy	Cardigan Bay	Llanfaelrhys	GR: SH201259
Maen Lau	Bardsey Sound	Bardsey Island	GR: SH113223
Maen Mellt	St George's Channel	Penrhyn Mawr	GR: SH163317
Mochras	Tremadog Bay	Llanbedr	aka Shell Island. GR: SH555265
St Tudwal's Island East	Cardigan Bay	Abersoch	aka Ynys Tudwal. Believed to be the original hermitage of St Tudwal. GR: SH342259
St Tudwal's Island West	Cardigan Bay	Abersoch	Sister island of St Tudwal's Island East. GR: SH335252
Shell Island	Tremadog Bay	Llanbedr	See Mochras.
Trwyn Carreg y-Tir	Hell's Mouth	Mynydd Cilan	GR: SH287241
Ynys Enlli	Bardsey Sound	Aberdaron	See Bardsey Island.
Ynys Gifftan	Tremadog Bay	Pothmadog	GR: SH601370
Ynys Gwylan-Bach	Cardigan Bay	Aberdaron	GR: SH182243
Ynys Gwylan-Fawr	Cardigan Bay	Aberdaron	GR: SH184245
Ynys Piod	Aberdaron Bay	Aberdaron	GR: SH165257
Ynys Tudwal	Cardigan Bay	Abersoch	See St Tudwal's Island East.

Island name	Area	Nearest landmark	General information
Anglesey			
Anglesey, Isle of	Irish Sea	Isle of Anglesey	See separate entry.
Braich Goch	Caernarfon Bay	Rhosneigr	GR: SH314723
Braich par Wr	Caernarfon Bay	Rhosneigr	GR: SH316723
Braich yr Oreedd	Caernarfon Bay	Rhosneigr	GR: SH315727
Britannia Rock	Menai Straits	Pont Britannia	GR: SH542710
Capel Island	Caernarfon Bay	Rhosneigr	GR: SH312732
Carreglydan	Caernarfon Bay	Bryn Du	GR: SH322719
Carreg-y-Fran	Holyhead Bay	Llanfaethlu	GR: SH289872
Carreg-y-Trai	Caernarfon Bay	Braich-lwyd	GR: SH337671
Caseg Malltraeth	Caernarfon Bay	Pen-y-Parc	GR: SH370647
Cerig Brith	Irish Sea	Cemlyn Bay	GR: SH341938
Cerrig y Gwyr	Holyhead Bay	Holyhead	GR: SH274824
Cerrig-y-Brain	Caernarfon Bay	Rhosneigr	GR: SH312728
Cerrig-y-Gwyr	Caernarfon Bay	Rhosneigr	GR: SH301731
Church Island	Menai Straits	Menai Bridge	GR: SH552717
Cow and Calf	Caernarfon Bay	Rhosneigr	GR: SH303732
Craif yr Irwch	Irish Sea	Cemlyn Bay	GR: SH325939
Craig Dafydd	Holyhead Bay	Llanfaethlu	GR: SH284853
Creigiau	Holyhead Bay	Llanfaethlu	GR: SH288866
Creigiau Cliperau	Holyhead Bay	Penrhyn	GR: SH289850
Creigiau'r Odyn	Caernarfon Bay	Rhosneigr	GR: SH313728
Cribbin Rock	Menai Straits	Menai Bridge	GR: SH544711
East Mouse	Irish Sea	Amlwch	aka Ynys Amlwch. GR: SH445942
Ellin's Twr	Caernarfon Bay	Goferydd	GR: SH206818
Garreg Allan	Irish Sea	Dulas	GR: SH505901
Graig-ddu	Irish Sea	Amlwch	GR: SH441938
Half Tide Rock	Menai Straits	Menai Bridge	GR: SH558716
Harry Furlough's Rocks	Irish Sea	Cemlyn Bay	GR: SH332943
Holy Island	Irish Sea	Isle of Anglesey	See separate entry.
Maen Mawr	Caernarfon Bay	Rhosneigr	GR: SH312724
Maen Piscar	Caernarfon Bay	Rhoscolyn	GR: SH244761
Maen y Bugael	Irish Sea	Carmel Head	aka West Mouse. GR: SH303943
Maen yr Esgyll	Caernarfon Bay	Rhoscolyn	GR: SH257753
Maen-y-fran	Caernarfon Bay	Rhoscolyn	GR: SH258751
Main y Sais	Caernarfon Bay	Rhoscolyn	GR: SH259750
Middle Mouse	Irish Sea	Llanbadrig	aka Ynys Badrig. GR: SH382959
Nimrod Rocks	Holyhead Bay	Holyhead	GR: SH264822
North Stack	Caernarfon Bay	Holyhead Mountain	GR: SH213839
Pen-las Rock	Caernarfon Bay	Abraham's Bosom	GR: SH208816
Penrhyn Mawr	Caernarfon Bay	Abraham's Bosom	GR: SH209797
Perch Rock	Irish Sea	Isle of Anglesey	GR: SH645814
Priestholm	Irish Sea	Isle of Anglesey	aka Puffin Island. GR: SH651821
Puffin Island	Irish Sea	Isle of Anglesey	See Priestholm
Rhoscolyn Beacon	Caernarfon Bay	Rhoscolyn	GR: SH262741
Skerries, The	Irish Sea	Carmel Head	aka Ynysoedd y Moelrhoniaid. Area 0.07 sq miles (0.17 sq km). GR: SH268949
South Stack	Caernarfon Bay	Holy Island	aka Ynys Lawd. See separate entry.
Swelly Rock	Menai Straits	Menai Bridge	GR: SH549713
Trwyn Ffynnon-y-Sais	Caernarfon Bay	Newborough	GR: SH388632
West Mouse	Irish Sea	Carmel Head	See Maen y Bugael.
Ynys Amlwch	Irish Sea	Amlwch	See East Mouse.
Ynys Arw	Irish Sea	Carmel Head	One of the Skerries group. GR: SH266947
Ynys Badrig	Irish Sea	Llanbadrig	See Middle Mouse.
Ynys Benlas	Menai Straits	Menai Bridge	One of the Swellies group. GR: SH549715
Ynys Castell	Menai Straits	Menai Bridge	GR: SH564727
Ynys Cybi	Irish Sea	Isle of Anglesey	See Holy Island
Ynys Dulas	Irish Sea	Dulas	GR: SH501902
Ynys Faelog	Menai Straits	Menai Bridge	GR: SH560722
Ynys Feirig	Caernarfon Bay	Rhosneigr	GR: SH303735
Ynys Gaint	Menai Straits	Menai Bridge	GR: SH562725
Ynys Gorod Goch	Menai Straits	Menai Bridge	GR: SH544713
Ynys Groes	Caernarfon Bay	Rhosneigr	GR: SH312728
Ynys Gybi	Caernarfon Bay	Rhoscolyn	GR: SH272745
Ynys Lawd	Caernarfon Bay	Holy Island	See South Stack.
Ynys Llanddwyn	Caernarfon Bay	Newborough	GR: SH389628
Ynys Moelfre	Irish Sea	Moelfre	GR: SH519869

Island name	Area	Nearest landmark	General information
Ynys Mon	Irish Sea	Isle of Anglesey	See Isle of Anglesey.
Ynys Peibio	Holyhead Bay	Holyhead	GR: SH261823
Ynys Syth	Caernarfon Bay	Bryn Du	GR: SH329715
Ynys Tobig	Menai Straits	Menai Bridge	GR: SH561724
Ynys Traws	Caernarfon Bay	Rhoscolyn	GR: SH272746
Ynys Welltog	Menai Straits	Menai Bridge	One of the Swellies group. GR: SH549717
Ynys y Big	Menai Straits	Menai Bridge	GR: SH565729
Ynys y Carcharorion	Irish Sea	Dulas	GR: SH491898
Ynys y Fydlyn	Holyhead Bay	Carmel Head	GR: SH290918
Ynysoedd Gwylanod	Caernarfon Bay	Rhoscolyn	GR: SH265743
Ynysoedd y Moelrhoniaid	Irish Sea	Carmel Head	See The Skerries.
Ynys-y-Cranc	Caernarfon Bay	Newborough	GR: SH385621

Mid Glamorgan

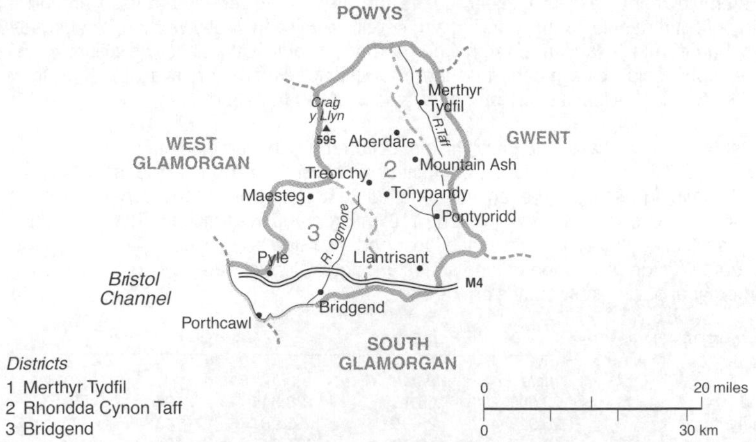
POWYS
WEST GLAMORGAN
GWENT
SOUTH GLAMORGAN
Bristol Channel
1
2
3
Merthyr Tydfil
Crag y Llyn
595
Aberdare
R. Taff
Mountain Ash
Treorchy
Tonypandy
Maesteg
Pontypridd
R. Ogmore
Pyle
Llantrisant
M4
Bridgend
Porthcawl
Districts
1 Merthyr Tydfil
2 Rhondda Cynon Taff
3 Bridgend
0
20 miles
0
30 km

Mid Glamorgan consists of the unitary authorities of Bridgend, Merthyr Tydfil and Rhondda Cynon Taff. It is bordered to the east by Gwent, to the north by Powys, to the south by South Glamorgan and to the west by West Glamorgan. Its southwest coast lies on the Bristol Channel. The area is probably better known as the Welsh Valleys as this properly describes the main geographical features. Although the Welsh Valleys stretch from Pontypool in the east to Neath in the West, the great tract of upland, cut through by deep, high-sided valleys, is concentrated in the Mid-Glamorgan area. For a time in the first quarter of the last century the Valleys produced a third of the world's coal. Since the decline of the coal industry, however, much of this landscape has been reclaimed and the Valleys have had to reinvent themselves, with walking trails through gritty industrial landscapes and wild hilltops that are now country parks and nature reserves.

The area has been settled since at least the Bronze Age. In the Iron Age it was occupied by the Silures, and evidence of this occupation can be found both at defended hill forts such as Y Bwlwarcau and lowland settlements such as Blaenrhondda. After the Roman invasion the area was relatively peaceful, but the resistance offered to the encroaching Anglo-Saxons following the departure of the Romans in the early 5th century inspired numerous legends, some linked with the story of King Arthur. The arrival of Christianity also gave rise to the legend of the martyr Tydfil, the daughter of a local chieftain who was killed by Saxons in the late 5th century. The church built in her memory was the foundation of Merthyr Tydfil.

With the invasion of the Normans in the 11th century came the construction of castles along the Welsh Marches on the border between Wales and England. There was also conflict between the new arrivals and the local Welsh chieftains. The three castles of Ogmore, Coity and Newcastle formed a defensive triangle and a fortified church was built at Ewenny Priory. The main Norman families were the de Turbervilles and the de Londres.

The area was steadfastly rural and no major changes occurred until the end of the 17th century with the coming of the Industrial Revolution. The first coal mines were opened north of Bridgend and with them followed the ironworks opened by John Bedford in the 1750s at Dowlais, Penydarren and Cyfarthfa. The effect on the local economy and population was staggering – for example, the village of Merthyr Tydfil became a major industrial centre with a population of 8000 in 1801, rising to more than 50,000 by 1861. At the time Merthyr was described as a 'Vision of Hell'. The demand for iron was fuelled and helped by the expansion of railways throughout the world. However, these massive increases in economic and social activity came at a great social cost and tensions between employer and worker sometimes spilled over into conflict, especially at times of a downturn in markets, as in the Merthyr Riot of June 1831. This was the first time workers are recorded as marching behind a red flag, and one of the leaders, Richard Lewis (also known as Dic Penderyn), who was hanged for wounding a soldier, is regarded by many as a martyr. The area was also renowned for its support of the Chartist movement.

The wealth and prosperity of the region was completely linked with the market for iron, steel and coal and as these industries met with increased competition from overseas the local economy suffered greatly, particularly during the inter-war period. After World War II the decline in the traditional industries continued and the iron-making industry and coal mining were gone by the 1980s. Mass unemployment was experienced before the area could regenerate itself around a mixed economy of light manufacturing, retailing and service provision. Many workers are forced to commute to Cardiff and Swansea for both work and social activities, since the failure of the Celtic Warriors rugby union club means that there is little top-level sport available. Fortunately, the Millennium Stadium is just a short journey by car or public transport.

One of the worst civil disasters in British history occurred on the morning of Friday 21 October 1966 when Merthyr Vale colliery tip no. 7, containing half a million tonnes of coal waste, slid down towards the mining village of Aberfan and engulfed 20 houses, a farm and Pantglas Junior School. The result was the loss of 144 lives including 116 children and five teachers. The landslide occurred after two days of continual heavy rain had loosened the huge heap of coal slag, which was, moreover, situated on top of an underground spring. Pantglas School was later completely demolished and a memorial garden now stands on the site.

Mid Glamorgan	**Population**			**Area**	
	male	*female*	*total*	*sq miles*	*sq km*
Bridgend	62,506	66,139	128,645	97	251
Merthyr Tydfil	26,929	29,052	55,981	43	111
Rhondda Cynon Taff	112,457	119,489	231,946	164	424
Total	201,892	214,680	416,572	304	786

Local Attractions and Information

Administrative headquarters	**Bridgend**: Civic Offices, Angel Street, Bridgend CF31 4WB. Tel: 01656 643643. **Merthyr Tydfil**: Civic Centre, Castle Street, Merthyr Tydfil CF47 8AN. Tel: 01685 725000. **Rhondda Cynon Taff**: The Pavilions, Cambrian Park, Clydach Vale, Cardiff CF40 2XX. Tel: 01443 424000.
Bedford Park	Cefn Cribwr, 3 miles (5km) northwest of Bridgend. A 40 acre (16ha) park surrounding the remains of the former Cefn Cribwr Ironworks, established in 1770 by John Bedford of Birmingham who also founded a forge and brickworks nearby. A Scheduled Ancient Monument, it includes remains of a blast furnace, casthouse and beehive coke ovens. The working life of the ironworks was relatively short, as they closed in the 1830s. Habitats include parkland, woodland and meadows.
Blaenrhondda	1½ miles (2.5km) north of Blaenrhondda, 3 miles (5km) southwest of Hirwaun. An undefended Iron Age settlement covering an area 300ft (91.5m) by 90ft (27.5m). It contained several Iron Age roundhouses, the low walls of which can still be seen.
Bryngarw House	½ mile (0.8km) north of Brynmenyn, 3 miles (5km) north of Bridgend. Probably originating as a farmhouse and dating to at least the 18th century, the Tudor-style house was renovated and enlarged in the 1830s by Morgan Traherne. By the 1960s it was owned by the council and was used as accommodation and offices; restored in the 1980s, it has been developed as a conference and banqueting centre. Bryngarw Country Park, created in 1983, covers 113 acres (46ha) of surrounding parkland, woodland, formal gardens (originally laid out in 1910 by Captain O P Traherne) and water features. Planting includes specimen trees and shrubs, including Japanese maples, magnolias and rhododendrons. Tel: 01656 729009.
Y Bwlwarcau	2 miles (3km) southwest of Maesteg. A large Iron Age hill fort on the slopes of Mynydd Margam. It consists of a concentric series of enclosures defined by a bank, ditch and counterscarp.
Cambrian Wheel, The	Clydach Vale, 2 miles (3km) west of Tonypandy. A replica of a pit wheel together with a memorial plaque erected on the site of the Cambrian Colliery, which operated 1870–1966. The colliery suffered two tragic accidents: an explosion on the evening of 10 March 1905 cost the lives of 33 men and another on 18 May 1965 caused the deaths of 31 men. A memorial garden was opened in 1992.
Candleston Castle	Merthyr Mawr, 2 miles (3km) southwest of Bridgend. The ivy-covered ruins of a 14th century fortified manor house on the edge of the sand dunes of Merthyr Mawr Warren. It was later used as a farmhouse but was abandoned by the 19th century. Reputedly haunted, it is linked with the lost village of Treganllaw (The Town of a Hundred Hands) which is said to lie underneath the shifting sands.
Cefn Coed Viaduct	Cefn Coed y Cymmer, 1½ miles (2.5km) northwest of Merthyr Tydfil. Built in 1866 to carry the Brecon & Merthyr Railway across the River Taff. It is 725ft (221m) long, 122ft (37m) high and has 15 spans. The line was closed in the 1960s and the viaduct now carries a public footpath.
Cefn Cribwr Ironworks	See Bedford Park.
Clydach Vale Country Park	1½ miles (2.5km) west of Tonypandy. Country park covering 279 acres (113ha) and established on land reclaimed from the former Cambrian Colliery, which operated 1870–1966.

Coity Castle	Coity, 1 mile (1.6km) east of Bridgend. A 12th century stone castle built by Payn de Turberville on the site of an earlier wooden fortification. Much of the castle seems to have been remodelled in the 14th century, and it was abandoned in the late 17th century. The ruins consist mainly of a square keep and curtain walls. The site is managed by CADW.
Cwmaman Institute	Alice Place, Cwmaman, 2 miles (3km) south of Aberdare. Opened in 2001 on the site of the village's Miners' Institute. The original building, which opened in 1892, was funded by a scheme whereby a halfpenny in each pound was deducted weekly from the wages of workmen at the local colliery. This was a normal method of raising funds for the building of miners' institutes throughout South Wales, although the amount deducted could vary. The building provided a 700 seat public hall, reading rooms and a billiards room. With the demise of the coal industry after the 1960s the old building became difficult to maintain and the decision was taken to rebuild. The institute caters for conferences, weddings, the arts and live entertainment and also acts as a community centre. Tel: 01685 887100.
Cyfarthfa Castle Museum and Art Gallery	Brecon Road, Merthyr Tydfil. A castellated mansion designed by Richard Lugar and built in 1825 for William Crawshay, owner of the Cyfarthfa Ironworks, and his family. It was converted into a school and a museum in 1910. The museum's collections cover fine art, ceramics, textiles and artefacts from classical antiquity, as well as chronicling the social and industrial history of the area. The basement galleries, refurbished in the 1990s, are dedicated to the history of Merthyr Tydfil, from its Celtic origins through the Agricultural Revolution and into the Industrial Revolution. There are displays about the four major ironworks of Cyfarthfa, Dowlais, Penydarren and Plymouth, plus the story of Richard Trevithick's steam locomotive, built at the Penydarren Ironworks in 1804. The gallery also explores the sometimes turbulent development of the labour movement in the area. Tel: 01685 723112.
Cynon Valley Museum	Depot Road, Gadlys, Aberdare. Building complex opened in 2001 on the site of the 19th century Gadlys Ironworks and including a museum, an art gallery and a temporary exhibition gallery. The museum charts the social history of the Cynon Valley from 1800 to the present day, while the art gallery presents national and international contemporary art and design. Tel: 01685 886729.
Dare Valley Country Park	Trecynon, 1 mile (1.6km) west of Aberdare. Country park established on 500 acres (200ha) of what was previously a derelict colliery. Tel: 01685 874672.
Dipping Bridge, The	Merthyr Mawr, 2 miles (3km) south of Bridgend. A 15th or 16th century bridge spanning the River Ogmore. There are holes in its parapets through which farmers pushed their sheep to dip or wash them.
Glamorganshire Canal	Built 1790–8 in order to transport iron from Merthyr Tydfil to the port at Cardiff via Pontypridd and Nantgarw. The canal had 50 locks over its 25 mile (40km) course. Only partial traces still remain to be seen.
Gorsedd Stones, The	Druids Close, Treorchy. A Bardic stone circle erected in 1928 to mark the holding of the National Eisteddfod in the town that year.
Highest point	Craig y Llyn at 1952ft (595m). GR: SN909031.
Interesting facts	**Kenfig**, near Porthcawl, was once a thriving walled town but by the 1600s, sand had swamped it to such a degree that only a handful of people lived there. The Welsh lord Iestyn ap Cwrgan had been the owner of the land but he was defeated by the Norman conqueror Robert Fitzhamon, Earl of Gloucester, who built a motte and bailey which was later converted into a stone shell keep around which the medieval town grew. Kenfig was a town of some importance as by charter it could levy its own taxes and make its own by-laws. The town had a high street, and a guildhall of which the townspeople were so proud that long-term prisoners were permitted to enter its cells only through a side entrance. It even had a hospital. Throughout the 12th and 13th centuries the town suffered badly from raids by the disinherited Welsh Lords of Afon. It was burned down so often that the inhabitants built a stockade around the perimeter, only to have it struck by lightning and burned down again. It was attacked by both Llywelyn ap Gruffudd and later by Owain Glyndwr, who destroyed it. Having been rebuilt, the town was once again attacked, but this time the enemy was not man but the ever-changing sands. From the 13th century onwards it was gradually engulfed until today only the ruinous stump of the castle keep is still visible. The Prince of Wales Inn, dating from 1605, was built as a town hall to replace the one lost beneath the sands and remarkably is still standing. The only other building of note that overcame the sand is the ancient church of St Mary Magdalen (or Mawdlam); at least 750 years old, it first appeared in historic records in 1255. Merthyr-born industrialist **John Hughes** sailed to the Ukraine in 1869 with eight shiploads of equipment and around a hundred specialist ironworkers and miners, mostly from South Wales, to build a metallurgical plant and rail-producing factory. Hughes gave his name to the town which grew around his plant, Hughesovka (Yuzovka). The town, known as Donetsk since 1961, remains one of the largest metallurgical centres in the former Soviet Union.
James James and Evan James Memorial	Ynysangharad Park, Pontypridd. A memorial to Evan James (1809–78) and his son James (1833–1902), who between them composed 'Land of My Fathers', the Welsh national anthem. It is said that Evan James wrote the words in January 1856 to accompany a tune composed by his harpist son. The song came to prominence at the National Eisteddfod held at Bangor in 1874.
Kenfig Castle	1 mile (1.6km) west of Pyle. The scant remains of a castle built in the 1120s by Robert, Earl of Gloucester. Although a borough was established around Kenfig (Cynfigg), the castle was eventually abandoned to the elements and the sands of Kenfig Burrows.
Kenfig Dunes	1 mile (1.6km) west of Pyle. A National Nature Reserve and Site of Special Scientific Interest consisting of an extensive system of sand dunes covering 1500 acres (600ha). It provides a habitat for rare plants such as the fen orchid. Tel: 01656 743386.

MID GLAMORGAN

Llangynwyd Castle — 1/2 mile (0.8km) west of Llangynwyd, 1 1/2 miles (2.5km) south of Maesteg. Norman motte and bailey castle burnt down in the 1250s. It was replaced by a stone castle but this too was destroyed in the late 13th century. The motte, surrounded by a deep ditch, is still visible but little masonry remains.

Llantrisant Castle — Yr Allt, Llantrisant. A 12th century Norman castle rebuilt in stone c.1250 by Richard de Clare. Possibly destroyed by Owain Glyndwr, it had fallen into disrepair by the 16th century. The ruins consist of a fragment of a tower plus some curtain wall.

Llyn Fawr Hoard — A metalwork hoard dating to the Late Bronze Age and Early Iron Age, discovered at the lake of Llyn Fawr, 2 miles (3km) southwest of Hirwaun, when it was partially drained 1911–13 in order to construct a new reservoir. The items recovered include two bronze cauldrons, bronze axes and sickles, bronze horse harness gear and part of a rare decorated iron sword with bone handle. An iron sickle represents the earliest evidence for native ironwork in the British Isles, dating to c.600 BC. The various items were probably thrown into the lake as part of the ritual practice of offering such items to the goddess of water.

Merthyr Mawr Warren — 2 miles (3km) east of Porthcawl. An extensive sand dune system outside the village of Merthyr Mawr. It is claimed that they hold the highest single sand dune in Europe, known locally as the 'big dipper'. Scenes from the film *Lawrence of Arabia* (1962) were filmed at the dunes.

Miner's Family Statue — Llwynypia, 1 mile (1.6km) north of Tonypandy. A statue of a miner, his wife and child unveiled in 1993 on the site of the Cambrian Colliery, which was the centre of the Tonypandy Riots of 1910–11.

Model House Craft & Design Centre — Bull Ring, Llantrisant. A centre providing studio space for up to 14 craft tenants, opened in May 1989. It is housed in the town's former workhouse, built in 1784, and which later served as a pub, a grocer's shop and finally a glove manufacturer. Tel: 01443 237758.

Morlais Castle — 2 miles (3km) north of Merthyr Tydfil. Ruins of a 13th century castle built 1286–90 by Gilbert de Clare on the site of an Iron Age hill fort. Its active life was very short as it seems to have been destroyed by Madog ap Llywelyn in 1294 before its completion. Although there are few remains at ground level, the plan of the castle can be seen from the air. It was oval in shape with five circular towers and surrounded by a rock-cut ditch. The main feature is the undercroft, revealed by excavations in the 1840s, which has a central pillar with 12 vaulted rib supports.

Museum of Law and Order — Ystrad Road, Pentre, Rhondda. A museum featuring the 1902 magistrates' court from Ton Pentre Police Station along with displays on national and international law and order. There is a particular emphasis on the effects of drugs on the everyday life of the Rhondda. Viewing is currently by appointment only. Tel: 01443 441600.

Nantgarw China Works Museum — Tyla Gwyn, Nantgarw, 4 miles (6km) southeast of Pontypridd. Located in Nantgarw House, a mid 18th century farmhouse on the site of the famous Nantgarw porcelain factory, opened in the 1810s beside the Glamorganshire Canal by Worcester potter William Billingsley. The Billingsley porcelain factory was eventually replaced by a pottery run by the Pardoe family which produced clay pipes and earthenware pottery. The site includes some of the pipeworks and a reconstructed bottle kiln. There are exhibits of porcelain and displays telling the story of William Billingsley. Tel: 01443 841703.

Newcastle Castle — Newcastle Hill, Bridgend. The remains of a courtyard castle built beside the River Ogmore in the early 12th century and refortified in the 1180s by Henry II. It was abandoned in the 16th century. The main feature is a complete decorated Norman doorway which still stands within the ring of curtain walls and two mural towers.

Old Bridge, The — Bridge Street, Pontypridd. A graceful single-arched bridge across the River Taff, built by William Edwards in 1756 and, at 144ft (44m), believed to be the largest single-arched bridge then known. Designed to ensure that the span was stable, it unfortunately proved to be too steep for most wheeled traffic and a new three-arched bridge was built next to it in 1857. The Old Bridge was repaired and restored in 1997.

Our Lady of Penrhys — Penrhys, 2 miles (3km) north of Tonypandy. A statue of the Virgin Mary located on a hillside above the village of Penrhys. The story is that the original statue, which was said to be 'indescribably beautiful', was discovered in the 13th century by monks from Llantarnam Abbey who were working in fields near the abbey's grange at Penrhys. They erected a chapel and shrine to house the statue and this soon became a place of pilgrimage. In 1538 it was secretly removed, taken to Thomas Cromwell in London and publicly burned on 26 September that year. The replacement statue, erected in 1953, is carved from Portland stone and designed to resemble the original as it is described in contemporary sources. Another replica, carved from oak, can be found at Our Lady of Penrhys Church in Ferndale.

Parc & Dare Theatre — Station Road, Treorchy. Housed in a building begun in 1903 as a working men's institute and funded by subscription from the local colliery workers. The main hall was added in 1913. Its 900 seat auditorium serves as both a theatre and a cinema. It is the home of the famous Treorchy Male Choir, the Parc & Dare band and Rhondda Cynon Taff Community Arts. Tel: 01443 773112.

Parc Slip — 1 mile (1.6km) west of Tondu, 2 miles (3km) northwest of Bridgend. Nature reserve created on the site of a former colliery. Covering 305 acres (123ha), it features a variety of habitats including woodlands, wetlands and meadows. Tel: 01656 724100.

Parry's Cottage — Chapel Row, Georgetown, Merthyr Tydfil. A restored ironworker's cottage, built in the 1820s for workers employed at the Cyfarthfa Ironworks. The birthplace of composer Joseph Parry (1841–1903), whose best-known works are the song 'Myfanwy' and the hymn tune 'Aberystwyth', it now houses a museum celebrating his life and works and also has a section on the industrial history of Merthyr Tydfil.

Penydarren Fort — Penydarren Park, Merthyr Tydfil. The site of a Roman auxiliary fort, occupied until c.AD 140 and now located beneath Merthyr Tydfil FC's football ground. Remnants of the associated bath house and stone floors are visible in the nearby Tregenna Hotel.

Pontsarn Viaduct — 2 miles (3km) north of Merthyr Tydfil. Built in 1866 to carry the Brecon & Merthyr Railway across the Taff Fechan. The viaduct is 455ft (139m) long and 92ft (28m) high, and has seven spans.

Pontypridd Museum — Bridge Street, Pontypridd. A museum dedicated to the industrial, social and cultural history of Pontypridd and housed in a converted Welsh Baptist chapel, built in 1861 and closed in 1983. Exhibits include a panoramic painting depicting Pontypridd in the mid 19th century. Tel: 01443 490748.

Rhondda Heritage Park — Trehafod, 1 mile (1.6km) west of Pontypridd. A heritage park located within the former Lewis Merthyr Colliery, which operated from 1850 until 1983. Opened in 1989, it explores the history of the local mining industry and the lives of mine workers and their families. Cage rides are available to the bottom of the pit, where the underground roadways and coalface can be seen. Other features include a museum and an art gallery, while the visitor centre includes a recreated 1950s village street with three period shops and a cottage. The centre also has a large mural and exhibition depicting the Tynewydd mining disaster of 1877, in which five men died and five others were trapped underground for several days. Tel: 01443 682036.

Rivers — The **Ewenny** is a tributary of the Ogmore and flows northeast of Bridgend, past the village of Pencoed before entering the River Ogmore estuary just below Ogmore Castle. The **Ogmore** (Afon Ogwr) rises near the cemetery mountain, north of Treorchy, and flows in a southerly direction for 18 miles (29km) from Ogmore Vale and Pentre, past Bridgend and Ogmore, before discharging into the Bristol Channel between Ogmore-by-Sea and the Merthyr Mawr sand dunes. The **Rhondda** has two branches. The Large Rhondda (Rhondda Fawr) and the Little Rhondda (Rhondda Fach). The Rhondda Fawr rises northwest of Treherbert, just north of Blaenrhondda, and runs down the Rhondda Valley (Cwm Rhondda) to its confluence with the River Taff at Pontypridd, passing Treorchy, Tonypandy and Porth, before joining the River Taff at Pontypridd. The Rhondda Fach also has its source on the hills above Blaenrhondda, but flows through Maerdy, Ferndale and Tylorstown, before joing its sister tributary at Porth. Both branches run for approximately 10 miles (16km) before converging as one for the final 4 miles (7km) from Porth to Pontypridd. The **Taff** – see South Glamorgan.

Royal Mint — Ynysmaerdy, 1 mile (1.6km) northwest of Llantrisant. The Royal Mint was originally established in the Tower of London and by 1279 occupied secure quarters within the Tower. In 1812 it was transferred to a new building on nearby Tower Hill, which remained its home until the 1960s when new facilities were required. Between 1968 and 1975 production was progressively transferred from Tower Hill to a new 38 acre (15ha) site near Llantrisant. The Royal Mint Museum was established in 1816 by the Master of the Mint, William Wellesley Pole, in order to guarantee 'a regular Deposit in the Office of His Majesty's Mint, of a Proof Impression of every Coin and of every Medal which, from this time forth, shall be struck at the Royal Mint'. It also benefited from the donation of the coin collections of Sir Joseph Banks and his late sister, Sarah Sophia Banks. The museum now comprises a collection of 100,000 coins and medals along with minting machinery, dies and designs. Rare British coins on display include the 1933 penny, the 'Una and the Lion' £5 gold coin of 1839, depicting Queen Victoria as Una ('Truth') protected by a lion, and the proposed coins of Edward VIII. There are also exhibits about various Masters of the Mint including Sir Isaac Newton, Sir John Herschel and Thomas Graham.

Sker House — 2 miles (3km) northwest of Porthcawl. A 16th century mansion built around what was originally a grange belonging to Neath Abbey. Restored in the late 20th century, it is privately owned.

South Wales Police Museum — Cowbridge Road, Bridgend. A museum holding one of the largest collections of police memorabilia outside London, with exhibits including truncheons, cutlasses, handcuffs, whistles and uniforms. There are virtual recreations of an Edwardian charge room and a prisoner in his cell, while a Second World War Diorama shows a scene from the Blitz. The first organised police authority in South Wales was the Glamorgan Constabulary, established in 1841. It was divided into four districts: Ogmore, Newbridge, Merthyr and Swansea. The South Wales Constabulary was formed in 1969 from the police forces of Glamorgan, Cardiff, Merthyr Tydfil and Swansea. Today South Wales Police covers the areas of Bridgend, Cardiff, Merthyr Tydfil, Neath Port Talbot, Rhondda Cynon Taff, Swansea and Vale of Glamorgan. Tel: 01656 303207.

Sport

football — **Merthyr Tydfil** were formed in 1945 after the closure of Merthyr Town FC. They compete in English non-league football, having joined the Southern League in 1946 after one season in the Welsh League. Nicknamed the Martyrs (after St Tydfil), their home ground is Penydarren Park.

rugby union — **Celtic Warriors** were formed in 2003 as a regional team playing in the Celtic League, but lasted only one season. Intended to represent the Glamorganshire Valleys, it was created from the Pontypridd RFC and Bridgend RFC Welsh Premier League clubs, and was originally to be known as the Valley Ravens to reflect its club origins. After various difficulties, including a decision to play all home matches at Bridgend's Brewery Field rather than a shared arrangement with Pontypridd's Sardis Road ground, the club was liquidated in the summer of 2004.

Ynysangharad Park — Bridge Street, Pontypridd. A public park first laid out in the 1920s as a memorial to the fallen in World War I. It was once the home of Pontypridd RFC, while Glamorgan CCC played occasional County Championship matches and one-day games on the cricket square between 1926 and 1996.

Some famous people born in Mid Glamorgan

Ashley, Laura (fashion designer) (1925–85)	Merthyr Tydfil
Baker, Stanley (actor) (1928–76)	Ferndale
Burrows, Stuart (operatic tenor) (1933–)	Cilfynydd
Davies, Lynn (athlete) (1942–)	Nant-y-moel
Davies, Richard (actor) (1926–)	Merthyr Tydfil
Emanuel, David (fashion designer) (1952–)	Bridgend
Evans, Geraint (singer) (1922–)	Cilfynydd
Gibbs, Scott (rugby player) (1971–)	Bridgend
Henson, Gavin (rugby player) (1982–)	Bridgend
Hughes, John (industrialist) (1815–89)	Merthyr Tydfil
James, Evan (poet) (1809–78)	Pontypridd
Jenkins, Neil (rugby player) (1971–)	Church Village
Jones, Ruth (actress) (1966–)	Bridgend
Jones, Tom (singer) (1940–)	Pontypridd
Owen, Johnny (bantamweight boxer) (1956–80)	Merthyr Tydfil
Parry, Joseph (composer) (1841–1903)	Merthyr Tydfil
Welsh, Freddie (lightweight boxer) (1886–1927)	Pontypridd
Wilde, Jimmy (flyweight boxer) (1892–1969)	Merthyr Tydfil
Winstone, Howard (featherweight boxer) (1939–2000)	Merthyr Tydfil
Whitehouse, Paul (comedian) (1958–)	Stanleytown

Powys

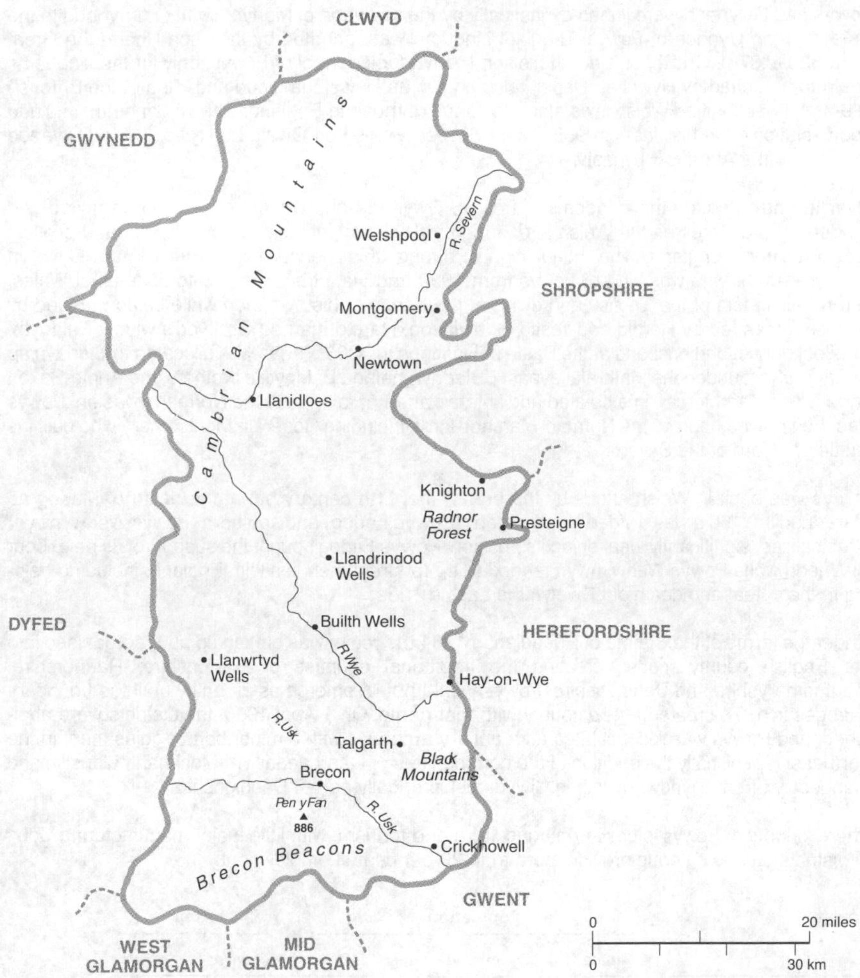
CLWYD
GWYNEDD
Cambrian Mountains
R. Severn
Welshpool
Montgomery
SHROPSHIRE
Newtown
Llanidloes
Knighton
Radnor Forest
Presteigne
Llandrindod Wells
Builth Wells
DYFED
HEREFORDSHIRE
Llanwrtyd Wells
R. Wye
Hay-on-Wye
R. Usk
Talgarth
Black Mountains
Brecon
Pen y Fan
886
R. Usk
Crickhowell
Brecon Beacons
GWENT
WEST GLAMORGAN
MID GLAMORGAN
0
20 miles
0
30 km

Powys is the largest local authority in Wales by area and covers the administrative counties of Montgomeryshire and Radnorshire, and parts of Brecknockshire and Denbighshire. It is bordered to the northwest by the preserved county of Gwynedd, to the north by Clwyd, to the west by Dyfed, to the south by West and Mid Glamorgan, to the southeast by Gwent, and to the east by the English counties of Shropshire and Herefordshire. The only landlocked preserved Welsh county, its main geographical feature is the mountainous area of the Brecon Beacons National Park; the major rivers of the Severn, Usk and Wye also pass through it. Hay-on-Wye, the intersection of the Welsh and English section of the river, is famous for its bookshops and literary festival.

During the Iron Age the area was settled by the Silures in the south and the Ordovices in the north. Both these tribes provided stiff resistance to the Roman invasion and helped Caractacus in his guerilla war against them. They were eventually subdued in the second half of the 1st century. After the departure of the Romans in the early 5th century the kingdom of Powys emerged as a powerful state with its early capital possibly at Caer Guircon (Roman Viroconium Cornoviorum), now Wroxeter in Shropshire, England. There followed centuries of struggle with the English in warding off encroachments by neighbouring Mercia and the then powerful Northumbria. Eventually disagreements over precise borders were settled by the building first of Wat's (or Watt's) Dyke, which has not been conclusively dated but may be late 7th century, and then Offa's Dyke in the late 8th century.

Powys and Gwynedd were joined dynastically by the marriage of Merfyn Frych of Gwynedd to the sister of King Cyngen of Powys. The joint kingdom was inherited by their son Rhodri the Great (c.AD 820–c.878). On Rhodri's death his son Merfyn took control of Powys, only for the kingdoms again to be united by Hywel ap Cadell (also known as Hywel the Good and 'King of the Britons') in 942. Hywel codified Welsh laws along the lines of those in England, with whom he maintained good relations. On his death in 950 Powys passed to his son Owain ap Hywel, while Gwynedd reverted to the Aberffraw dynasty.

Over the next century the kingdoms of Powys, Gwynedd and Deheubarth would be united and divided several times as the Welsh lords fought off military incursions from Vikings and political pressure from England. The major figure during this period was Gruffydd ap Llywelyn (c.1000–1063), who was king of Powys from 1039 and went on eventually to unite all of Wales, before falling foul of the English and dying at the hands of his own men while being pursued by English forces led by Harold and Tostig Godwinson. Harold married Gruffydd's widow Ealdgyth, who lost her second husband at the Battle of Hastings in 1066. Powys was allocated to Bleddyn ap Cynfyn, who founded the Mathrafal dynasty. Bleddyn helped Ealdgyth's brothers, the Anglo-Saxon earls Edwin and Morcar, in a belated and ill-fated attempt to oppose the Norman invasion. Powys was then preyed upon by the Norman 'Marcher' lords including Roger de Montgomery who built his castle on a ford of the Severn.

Powys was back in Welsh hands by the end of the 11th century but at the death of Madog ap Maredudd in 1160 it was divided into northern (Powys Fadog) and southern (Powys Wenwynwyn) principalities, significantly weakening its position. Powys Fadog sought the support of its neighbour Gwynedd while Powys Wenwynwyn tended to try to strengthen ties with England, including helping in the defeat and death of Llywelyn the Last in 1282.

Under the terms of the Statute of Rhuddlan in 1284 the realm was broken up and reorganised into the English county model, creating the traditional counties of Breconshire, Radnorshire, Montgomeryshire and Denbighshire. Powys would not re-emerge as an entity until the boundary changes in 1974 created a new county with that name. On 1 April 1996, the districts were abolished, and Powys was reconstituted as a unitary authority, with a minor border adjustment in the northeast (specifically the addition of the communities of Llanrhaeadr-ym-Mochnant, Llansilin and Llangedwyn from Glyndwr district in Clwyd, all historically part of Denbighshire).

The economy of Powys is based on agriculture and tourism, with little major manufacturing. Jobs in distribution and catering provide more than 20 per cent of employment.

Powys	**Population**			**Area**	
	male	*female*	*total*	*sq miles*	*sq km*
Total	62,493	63,861	126,354	2000	5181

Local Attractions and Information

Abbey Cwmhir — 6 miles (10km) north of Llandrindod Wells. The remains of a 12th century Cistercian abbey by the Clywedog River. Traditionally the burial place of Llywelyn ap Gruffudd after his death near Builth in 1282, at one point it was a large foundation supporting 60 monks, but its fortunes waned after it sustained damage during Owain Glyndwr's uprising in the early 15th century. It was abandoned after the Dissolution although the buildings were fought over during the Civil War.

Administrative headquarters — County Hall, Llandrindod Wells LD1 5LG. Tel: 01597 826000.

Agen Allwedd — 12 miles (19km) southeast of Brecon. An extensive cave system on the Llangattock Escarpment. The 23 miles (37km) of caves contain the longest single section of traversable streamway in the country.

Andrew Logan Museum of Sculpture — Aqueduct Road, Berriew, Welshpool. Dedicated to the works of artist Andrew Logan, born in Oxford in 1945. Opened in 1991 in converted squash courts, the museum contains many of Logan's sculptures, mirrored portraits, costumes and jewellery, plus personal commissions left to the museum. Logan, who originated a regular alternative Miss World contest (involving both women and men) in the 1970s, has an individualistic and eccentric style with the aim of showing that 'art does not have to be pretentious but can be fun'. Tel: 01686 640689.

Battles See separate table for the battles of Cefn Carnedd, Maes Madog, Montgomery, Orewin Bridge and Pilleth.

Beacon Ring 2½ miles (4km) southeast of Welshpool. The site of an Iron Age hill fort standing 1338ft (408m) above sea level. Measuring 630ft (192m) by 430ft (131m), its outline is delineated by a single bank, berm and ditch.

Black Mountains A range of hills in the east of the Brecon Beacons National Park. Peaks include Waun Fach (2661ft/811m), Pen y Gadair Fawr (2661ft/811m), Pen Allt Mawr (2362ft/720m), Pen Rhos Dirion (2339ft/713m), Pen Cerrig Calch (2300ft/701m), Iwmpa (2264ft/690m), Chwarel y Fan (2228ft/679m), Mynydd Llysiau (2175ft/663m), Pen Twyn Mawr (2159ft/658m), Pen Twyn Glas (2119ft/646m) and Mynydd Troed (2000ft/609m).

Brecknock Museum Captain's Walk, Brecon. Museum and art gallery established in 1928. Exhibits cover local history, including an the early medieval crannog (artificial island) in Llangorse Lake with its associated log boat or dugout canoe; there are also recreations of the Victorian assize court as it might have been in the 1830s and of Breconshire rural life. The art gallery hosts temporary exhibitions, usually of works by local or Welsh artists. Tel: 01874 624121.

Brecon A town located beneath the Brecon Beacons at the confluence of the rivers Usk and Honddhu. To the northwest are the remains of Pen-y-crug, an Iron Age hill fort, and 2 miles (3km) to the west lies Brecon Gaer Roman Fort. Brecon was a Roman crossroads and some Roman roads remain visible on the Beacons even today. After the Roman evacuation in the early 5th century, the local ruler is said to have sent his daughter to Ireland in search of a husband. Many of her retinue of guards died on the journey, but she eventually found her Irish prince and their son, Brychan, was sent to Wales to grow up at the court of his grandfather. It is from the name Brychan that the old country name, Brysheiniog, and later Brecon was derived. One of Brychan's daughters, Tudful, was killed by barbarians, and gives her name to the settlement of Merthyr Tydfil (*merthyr* being Welsh for martyr), 20 miles (32km) to the south.

Brecon Beacons A range of peaks south of Brecon which gained their name from the practice of lighting beacon fires on the summits to warn of English invasion. The highest peak is Pen y Fan at 2907ft (886m); other notable peaks include Corn Du (2864ft/873m), Cribyn (2608ft/795m) and Fan y Bîg (2359ft/719m). These summits form a long ridge, known as the 'Beacons Horseshoe', around the head of the Taf Fechan river.

Brecon Beacons National Park Established in 1957 and covering 519 square miles (1344 sq km), from Llandeilo in the west (in Dyfed) to Hay-on-Wye in the east. The park's wide variety of habitats is dominated by moorland and mountain ranges, with the Black Mountains in the east and (rather confusingly) the Black Mountain in the west. The Great Forest (Fforest Fawr) range was designated a Geopark by UNESCO in 2005. Other features include the glacial lakes Llyn y Fan Fach and Llyn y Fan Fawr and the rivers which descend from the hills. The park is notable for its waterfalls, including the 88ft (27m) Henrhyd Waterfall, one of the highest in Britain. Tel: 01874 623366.

Brecon Castle Castle Square, Brecon. Norman castle founded in 1090 by Bernard de Neufmarche, extended and fortified in stone in the 12th century and unsuccessfully besieged by the Welsh in 1216, 1233 and 1404. Evidence has been found of the manufacture of flint tools on the site, dating back 4–5000 years. The hall block, dating from 1300, is now part of a hotel which occupies the site.

Brecon Cathedral Cathedral Close, Brecon. Formerly the Benedictine priory of St John the Evangelist, built in the 13th and 14th centuries on the site of an earlier church. The priory was dissolved by Henry VIII but the church continued to serve as Brecon's parish church, becoming the cathedral of the Church of Wales Diocese of Swansea and Brecon in 1923. Tel: 01874 623857.

Brecon Gaer Roman Fort 2 miles (3km) northwest of Brecon. Aka Y Gaer. The site of a round-angled rectangular Roman auxiliary fort north of the River Usk, excavated in the 1920s by Sir Mortimer Wheeler. A bath house and *mansio* (an official stopping place on a Roman road used by those on official business) plus a *vicus* (civilian settlement) were found outside the northern gate. The stone fort, measuring 650ft (200m) by 500ft (150m), was built in the late 2nd century on the site of a 1st century fort. Its buildings were those associated with a standard Roman fort, including a headquarters building, barracks, granary, a second bath house, stables and smithy. The first regiment in occupation probably came from northwest Spain.

Brecon Mountain Railway A narrow gauge (2ft/610mm) heritage railway operating for 3½ miles (5.5km) through the Brecon Beacons National Park from Pant to Dolygaer, via Pontsticill and alongside the Taf Fechan Reservoir. It was opened in June 1980 on the route of a standard gauge commercial service which operated 1859–1964. Tel: 01685 722988.

Bronllys Castle 7 miles (11km) northeast of Brecon. Norman motte and bailey castle founded in the 12th century, with a cylindrical tower added c.1176 after a fire. In 1384, the castle was granted to the de Bohun heiress, Mary, and her husband, Henry, Earl of Derby, son of John of Gaunt. The Duke of Gloucester, who had married the other de Bohun heiress, Eleanor, also claimed hereditary rights to the castle; however, in 1399, after the Earl of Derby was crowned Henry IV, all property held by the de Bohuns reverted to the monarchy. Despite another claim to its lordship by Anne Stafford, daughter of Eleanor de Bohun, the castle remained a royal property. Roger Vaughan of Tretower held it as the monarch's custodian for much of the 15th century, until it finally passed in 1478 to Henry, Duke of Buckingham, an heir of the Staffords. Though the Duke was executed in 1483 for his support of Henry Tudor (Henry VII), his estates passed to his heir, Edward. The new Duke did not actually gain possession until 1509, and the castle remained his property for only 12 years, reverting to the Crown for the last time in 1521 after Buckingham's ill-conceived rebellion and execution. By that date, however, Bronllys was already 'beyond repair', having suffered 100 years of neglect. Even though the castle remained in the royal inventory, it never again saw military action and continued to decay until the state took over its care in 1962. It is now manitained by CADW.

Builth Castle Castle Road, Builth Wells. Late 11th century motte and bailey castle founded by Philip de Braose. Destroyed by Llywelyn ap Gruffydd in 1260, Ii was rebuilt in stone under direction of Master James of St George as one of the great castles erected in the 1280s by Edward I to control Wales. Having survived a siege by Owain Glyndwr during the uprising of the early 15th century, it was demolished in the late 16th century and the stones used as building material for the expanding town of Builth Wells. The extensive earthworks are still visible.

Burfa Hill Fort 3 miles (5km) southwest of Presteigne, 15 miles (24km) east of Llandrindod Wells. A large multivallate Iron Age hill fort on the England/Wales border, measuring 1900ft (579m) by 600ft (183m).

Capel Maelog Llandrindod Wells. The foundations of an 11th century chapel with semicircular apses added at each end, probably in the late 12th century. The stones to build the church are believed to have been brought from the long abandoned Roman fort of Castell Collen.

Capel-y-ffin 13 miles (21km) east of Brecon. A small Welsh Baptist church built in 1762 on the site of an earlier building, and featuring a crooked belfry and a medieval font.

Castell Collen Roman Fort 1 mile (1.6km) north of Llandrindod Wells. The site of a round-angled rectangular Roman auxiliary fort on the River Ithon. Its outline, measuring 510ft (155m) by 360ft (110m), is defined by stone revetted banks and a ditch. The original fort was built by Julius Frontinus c.AD 70 during a campaign to subdue the local tribe; it was rebuilt and improved by the Legio II Augusta in the 2nd century, the new smaller layout including two semicircular stone towers. The fort was abandoned with withdrawal of the Roman army in the early 5th century. The site was first excavated in 1911 and more extensively 1954–6.

Castell Dinas 1/2 mile (0.8km) east of Pen-y-genfordd, 8 miles (13km) east of Brecon. The site of both an Iron Age hill fort and a ruined late 12th century castle, the latter probably abandoned in the early 15th century.

Centre for Alternative Technology 2 miles (3km) north of Machynlleth. Europe's leading eco-centre, founded in 1973 on the site of the disused Llwyngwern slate quarry. The centre features working examples of environmentally responsible buildings, energy conservation, and organic growing and composting methods. In particular there are new displays on Energy, Recycling and The Home. Other features include a 180ft (55m) water-cliff railway and tropical organic gardens. Tel: 01654 705950.

Clive Museum Welshpool, Powys. Housed in part of the old ballroom of Powis Castle, and opened in 1987 by Countess Mountbatten of Burma. Exhibits include textiles, armour, bronzes, jade, ivory and furniture; many of these are items brought back from India by Sir Robert Clive (Clive of India) (1725–74), whose son Edward married into the Herbert family, owners of the castle. Tel: 01938 551929.

Corris Railway Corris, 4 miles (6km) north of Machynlleth. A narrow gauge (2ft 3in/686mm) heritage railway operating for 1 mile (1.6km) between Corris and Maespoeth on part of a former commercial line btween Machynlleth and Aberllefenni. Opened in 1859 to transport slate, the railway operated a regular passenger service from the 1880s until the 1930s; after slate traffic also declined, the line was closed in 1948. Although the track had been dismantled and rolling stock disposed of to the Talyllyn Railway, a museum was opened in 1970 in a stable block at the former Corris Station by the Corris Railway Society; a passenger service was resumed in 2002 and the railway was officially reopened in June 2003. There are plans are to extend to the line Tan-y-Coed. Steam locomotives were reintroduced in 2005. Tel: 01654 761303.

Craig-y-Nos Castle 1 1/4 miles (2m) north of Pen-y-Cae, 15 miles (24km) southwest of Brecon. An early Victorian country house set in parkland alongside the River Tawe in the Upper Swansea Valley. Built in 1840 by Captain Rice Davies Powell, it was purchased in 1878 by opera singer Adelina Patti who wished to develop it into her own private estate. After her second marriage, to Ernesto Nicolini, she embarked on a major development of the site, adding the north and south wings, clock tower, conservatory, winter garden and theatre, all incorporating the latest technologies of the day. The Spanish Ambassador and Baron Julius Reuter (founder of Reuter's news agency) officiated at the opening of her private theatre (modelled on the Theatre Royal in Drury Lane, London) on 12 July 1891. Still used today for operatic performances, this offers one of the few remaining examples of fully functional, mechanically operated, Victorian backstage theatre equipment. The glass winter garden, with its soaring roof, tropical plants and exotic birds, was her great delight and in 1918, the year before her death, she presented it to the City of Swansea. Swansea had already made Adelina its first 'free-woman' and they re-erected her winter garden close to City Hall, naming it the Patti Pavilion (see West Glamorgan). One of her original pair of crane fountains – made in the local ironworks at Ystradgynlais, owned by a Mr Crane, who manufactured decorative ironware featuring his favourite bird and namesake – can still be seen in the castle grounds. The castle itself is now a hotel while the 40 acres (16ha) of landscaped grounds are open to the public as Craig-y-Nos Country Park, within the Brecon Beacons National Park.

Criggion Radio Masts 7 miles (11km) northeast of Welshpool. Built in 1942, for 60 years the radio masts at Criggion were a part of the scenery of the Shropshire/Wales border until their demolition in 2003. During World War II the set of three masts and three towers were used for communications between the Admiralty and Royal Navy ships. When the war ended their role continued as a signal relay station for the Navy's nuclear submarines in the Cold War, as well as for overseas telephone communications. The station used VLF (Very Low Frequency) signals, which allowed the Admiralty to contact a ship anywhere in the world. Aerials were strung between three towers and the peak of the Breidden Hills (the station stood in the shadow of Rodney's Pillar, a monument erected in 1782 on the summit of the hill). The station was operated by the GPO and later British Telecom, although workers at the station apparently had no idea of the content of the messages they were sending; the 300 acre (120ha) site was top secret, and its role as an MoD station has never been officially confirmed.

Crug Hywel — $1^1/_4$ miles (2km) north of Crickhowell. An Iron Age hill fort on a spur near the summit of Table Mountain (1480ft/451m) in the Black Mountains, covering an area of 500ft (150m) by 200ft (60m) enclosed by bivallate ramparts.

Dolforwyn Castle — $^1/_2$ mile (0.8km) west of Abermule, 4 miles (6km) northeast of Newtown. Built in 1270 by Llywelyn ap Gruffydd on a ridge overlooking the Severn Valley. Its building increased tension between the Welsh prince and Edward I and its active life was comparatively short. It was captured by Roger Mortimer in 1277 and had become ruinous by the end of the 14th century. The ruins are in the care of CADW.

Elan Valley Reservoirs — 4 miles (6km) west of Rhyader. A series of reservoirs created in the early 20th century to supply clean water to the Birmingham area using the rivers Elan and Claerwen. The first phase, the Elan Valley dams, were opened in July 1904; the second phase, Claerwen, was begun in 1946 and completed in 1952. The reservoirs are Claerwen (650 acres/263ha), Craig Goch (218 acres/88ha), Pen-y-Gareg (124 acres/50ha), Careg-ddu and Caban Coch (500 acres/202ha). During World War II the Elan Valley, and in particular the Nant-y-Gro dam, was used by Barnes Wallis to test the use of bouncing bombs against the Ruhr dams. There is a scale model of the reservoir network, in the form of ornamental ponds, in Cannon Hill Park in Birmingham.

Fforest Fawr — Part of the Brecon Beacons National Park, the Fforest Fawr Geopark was established in October 2005 by UNESCO in recognition of the area's geological significance. The landscape of Fforest Fawr (the Great Forest) was shaped by the last Ice Age and contains evidence of ancient seas, caves and waterfalls within the range of mountains between the Black Mountain and the central Brecon Beacons. The Geopark includes the whole of the western half of the National Park.

Ffridd Faldwyn — $^1/_2$ mile (0.8km) northwest of Montgomery, 7 miles (11km) northeast of Newtown. A multivallate Iron Age hill fort near Montgomery Castle measuring 1650ft (500m) by 830ft (253m). It developed in four phases from a simple 3 acre (1.2ha) enclosure on the summit of the hill.

Glansevern Hall Gardens — Berriew, Welshpool. A 20 acre (8ha) garden originally laid out in the early 19th century around Glansevern Hall beside the River Severn. Features include formal lawns, island flower beds, a walled garden, orangery and a rock garden with a 'spooky grotto'. There is also a collection of unusual trees beside the lake and the garden is dotted with unusual sculptures. Tel: 01686 640644.

Glyndwr's Way National Trail — A 135 mile (217km) long-distance footpath established in 2000 and running from Knighton to Welshpool via Llanidloes and Machynlleth. It is named after Owain Glyndwr.

Hay-on-Wye Castle — Castle Lane, Hay-on-Wye. Norman motte and bailey castle founded in the early 12th century by William Revell. The castle was destroyed by King John; its replacement, built on a different site, was destroyed by Owain Glyndwr.

Hen Domen Castle — $1^1/_4$ miles (2km) northwest of Montgomery, $7^1/_2$ miles (12km) northeast of Newtown. Often referred to as the first Montgomery Castle. The Norman motte and bailey castle, built in the 1070s by Roger de Montgomery, Earl of Shrewsbury, and commanding a ford on the River Severn, was occupied until the 1220s when Montgomery Castle, located to the south, was built in stone to replace it.

Highest point — Pen-y-Fan at 2907ft (886m), the highest mountain not only in Powys and the Brecon Beacons National Park, but in the whole of South Wales. GR: SO012215.

Howell Harris Museum — Trefeca, 6 miles (10km) east of Brecon. A museum in the Coleg Trefeca (a lay training centre owned by the Presbyterian Church of Wales), dedicated to Howell Harris (1714–73), a founder of Welsh Methodism. Harris converted to Methodism in 1735 while listening to a sermon by the Rev. Pryce Davies and in 1752 founded a religious community at his home at Trefeca, known as Teulu Trefeca (The Trefeca family) and with himself as 'father'. Twenty thousand people are said to have attended his funeral at Talgarth. The museum has a collection of 32 religious books, a photographic archive, plus artefacts and furniture from Harris's period at the college. Tel: 01874 711423.

Hyssington Castle — Hyssington, 13 miles (21km) east of Newtown. Aka the Castle of Sned or Snead. The remains of a motte and bailey castle probably dating from the 13th century. Traces of the bailey are still visible but there is no longer any evidence of building above ground.

Interesting facts — The **Red Lion** in Llanafan-fawr, Builth Wells, is the oldest pub in Powys (and probably in Wales) and dates back to at least 1189. It has retained much of its original structure but now offers superb food, ale and atmosphere. It also hosts the **World Tippit Championships** each autumn. The game is played using a small coin (the Tippit). Two teams of three face each other across a table and toss the coin for who goes first. The winning team put their hands under the table and move the coin unseen between the three pairs of hands. When ready the centre player knocks three times on the underside of the table and all three pairs of clenched fists (one containing the coin) are placed on the table. The opposing team, who can confer, must then find the coin in the following manner. The person who is trying to find the Tippit can give only two kinds of order, and in each case must touch the hand in question: 'Take your left/right hand away,' whereupon the person named opens the hand mentioned and if the coin is not there puts the hand by their side; or, if they think they can guess where the Tippit is, 'Tippit in your left/right,' in which case the fist mentioned has to be opened to reveal the Tippit – or not! If the Tippit is revealed after a 'Take away . . .' order, the team hiding the Tippit wins the round; they score one point and get to hide the Tippit among themselves again. If the 'Tippit in . . .' order is given and the Tippit is *not* in the fist mentioned, the searcher has lost; the team with the Tippit score a point and get to hide it again – once they have revealed who had it all along. If the Tippit is revealed following a 'Tippit in . . .' order, the team searching for the Tippit wins the coin. They score no points but get the opportunity to hide the coin. Games are usually played until one team reaches a score of 11. **Bog-snorkelling** is another world championship that takes place in Powys. Every August bank holiday, people flock to the Neuadd Arms Hotel in Llanwrtyd Wells to take part in the bog-snorkelling race. The bog, up on the mountain above the hotel, has a 200ft (60m) long trench cut into it. Competitors must swim two lengths face down, using only a snorkel for breathing, through the murky water. Entrants must bring their own snorkel and flippers. The fastest time so far is 2 minutes 11 seconds. Tel: 01591 610236 to sign up! Brecon-born **Frances Hoggan** was the first woman in Britain to receive a Doctor of Medicine degree, in 1870, and also the first woman doctor to be registered in Wales. Another local heroine was **Gwenllian Morgan** (born in Defynnog). Gwenllian was not only the first woman town councillor in Wales, in 1907, but also became the first woman mayor in 1912.

Judges' Lodgings — Broad Street, Presteigne. A living museum in the Judges' Lodgings, Court and Shire Hall, built in 1829 when Presteigne was the county town and seat of legal affairs for the county of Radnorshire. In later years the building had a variety of other uses but continued to be used for assizes until 1970. The apartments, along with the gas-lit servants' quarters and 1830s courtroom, were restored in 1997, and furnished with original pieces and items loaned by the Museum of Welsh Life; visitors are now able to lie on the beds, read the judge's books and even pump water in the kitchen. The house also features a local history exhibition and the Presteigne Museum collection. Tel: 01544 260650.

Leighton Hall — 2 miles (3km) southeast of Welshpool. A Grade I listed Gothic-style house with corner turrets and an octagonal tower, built 1850–6 for John Naylor. The hall is not open to the public.

Llanafan-fawr Castle — Llanafan-fawr, 8 miles (13km) southwest of Llandrindod Wells. A modest ringwork surrounded by a double ditch, and lying west of the village church. The earthwork and mound is one of several ancient sites found in this tiniest and most beautiful of mid-Wales villages; possibly dating to the Norman period, there is no documentation of its early history but archaeological evidence suggests that it has its origin in the Iron Age. A yew tree in the churchyard has been dated to an age of between 2200 and 2300 years.

Llangorse Lake — 6 miles (10km) southeast of Brecon. Aka Lake Syfaddan. Llangorse Lake, located within the Brecon Beacons National Park, covers 378 acres (153ha) with a circumference of 5 miles (8km). An early medieval crannog (man-made island) measuring 140ft (43m) by 95ft (29m) lies off the northern shore and in 1925 a well-preserved 9th century dugout canoe (now in Brecon Museum) was found in the lake, its date being consistent with the occupation of the crannog. The lake contains a number of fish species including roach, perch, pike, carp and eel, and is also an important site for overwintering waterfowl; the reed beds provide excellent habitat for reed warbler, reed bunting and starlings.

Llanidloes Museum — Great Oak Street, Llanidloes. A museum of local history and industry established in 1930, originally located in the former Market Hall and housed since 1995 on the ground floor of the town hall. It is divided into themed galleries, dedicated to the history of Llanidloes from the 18th century and to local wildlife; there is also a recreated Victorian parlour and kitchen with appropriate furniture and fittings. Tel: 01686 413777.

Minerva Arts Centre — High Street, Llanidloes. Established by the Quilt Association to house the Welsh Heritage Collection of antique Welsh quilts. Consisting of several hundred quilts with dates ranging from 1760–1930, the collection includes examples of most styles and techniques specific to Welsh quilts. Each year the Quilt Association hosts a summer exhibition featuring examples from the collection as well as quilts from other collections. Tel: 01686 413467.

Monmouthshire & Brecon Canal — A scenic canal route combining the Monmouthshire Canal from Newport to Pontymoile and the Brecon & Abergavenny Canal from Pontymoile to Brecon, a total length of 35 miles (56km), almost all of it within the Brecon Beacons National Park. The canals amalgamated in 1865; commercial traffic ceased in 1933 and a restored section of the canal from Pontypool to Brecon was opened in October 1970. Towns on the canal include Brecon, Talybont-on-Usk, Llangynidr, Crickhowell, Abergavenny, Pontypool, Cwmbran and Newport.

Montgomery Canal — Aka the Montgomeryshire Canal. Begun in the 1790s and built over many decades from the 1790s onwards by several different companies, the canal runs for 38 miles (61km) from Frankton Junction on the Llangollen Canal in Shropshire to Newtown, via Welshpool. It was abandoned in the 1940s, and only a 7 mile (11km) northern section near Frankton Junction and a 17 mile (27km) central section around Welshpool are now navigable.

Montgomery Castle — Castlewalk, Montgomery. Enclosure castle located on a promontory above Montgomery, begun in 1223 by Baldwin de Boller and mostly constructed in the 13th century to replace the nearby Hen Domen Castle. The castle survived attacks by Llywelyn ap Iorwerth in 1228 and 1231, and by Dafydd ap Llywelyn in 1245. It was strengthened during the 1280s following the successful English campaigns in Wales but had become less strategically important by the mid 14th century. The castle was demolished in 1649 after having been used by Royalist supporters during the Civil War. See also Hen Domen Castle.

Mortimer Trail — A 30 mile (48km) walking trail from Ludlow in Shropshire to Kington. There are also five looped walks connected to the trail at Lingen, Shobdon, Titley, Wigmore and Yarpole. It is named after the Mortimer family, prominent Marcher lords.

Museum of Mechanical Magic — Llanbrynmair, 9 miles (15km) east of Machynlleth. A museum featuring a collection of mechanical models and automata. Tel: 01650 521635.

Museum of Modern Art Wales — Heol Penrallt, Machynlleth. Museum of Modern Art Wales (MOMA Wales) is housed alongside the Tabernacle, a former Wesleyan chapel, and hosts the Tabernacle Collection, including works by Augustus John, Percy Wyndham Lewis and Stanley Spencer and modern Welsh art, plus a range of temporary exhibitions. Tel: 01654 703355.

National Cycle Collection Temple Street, Llandrindod Wells. A museum charting the history of the bicycle. Exhibits include a replica hobby horse and boneshakers, tandems and tricycles; there are also sections dedicated to road, touring, off-road, and folding bikes, as well as memorabilia, accessories, photographs and posters, a recreation of a 1920s street with a garage and bicycle shop, and displays about British cycling legends such as Tommy Simpson and Beryl Burton. Tel: 01597 825531.

National Showcaves Centre for Wales Dan-yr-Ogof, 14 miles (23km) southwest of Brecon. Three limestone caves at the source of the Afon Llynfell in the south of the Brecon Beacons National Park: the Dan-yr-Ogof Showcave, the Cathedral Showcave and the Bone Cave. The Dan-yr-Ogof Showcave, part of a cave system extending for more than 10 miles (16km), features not only stalactites and stalagmites but also helectites, which grow out sideways. The Cathedral Showcave includes a great domed cave with two waterfalls highlighted by dramatic lighting and music. The Bone Cave (also called Ogof-yr-Esgyrn) is so named because of the existence of evidence of human habitation such as hearths, animal remains and the skeletal remains of at least 40 human individuals. The caves were first discovered in 1912 and were opened to the public in 1939.

New Radnor Castle New Radnor, 10 miles (16km) east of Llandrindod Wells. The site of a 13th century castle built by Edward Mortimer on the site of earlier fortifications probably founded by Philip de Braose c.1095. Captured by Owain Glyndwr during his uprising in 1402 and left to fall into disrepair, it was finally demolished by Parliamentary forces during the Civil War. Only earthworks now survive.

Newtown Textile Museum Commercial Street, Newtown. Opened in 1967 and housed in an early 19th century weaving shop consisting of a three-storey row of cottages. The families would have lived on the ground floor and worked on the upper two floors, which run the full length of the row. The museum charts the early 19th century rise of the textile industry in Newtown and its decline in the early 20th century. Tel: 01686 622024.

Offa's Dyke A massive linear earth bank and ditch running for 176 miles (283km), virtually the entire length of the England/Wales border. Built to discourage raids from the Welsh kingdom of Powys, traditionally its construction has been attributed to Offa, ruler of the English kingdom of Mercia AD 757–96. It is a testament to Offa's control that a workforce could be mustered and directed to produce the structure. Offa's intention was to provide Mercia with a well-defined boundary from Prestatyn to Chepstow, and natural barriers were utilised where practicable; where it was not, an earth embankment was built which in places still stands a maximum of 65ft (20m) wide and 8ft (2.5m) high, the maximum height from the bottom of the ditch to the bank top being 20ft (6m). Gaps in the Dyke have been variously ascribed to the existence of natural defensive features, the erection of a timber palisade which left no archaeological trace or that the Dyke only covered a 64 mile (103km) central section of the border rather than reaching from sea to sea. Unlike Hadrian's Wall, Offa is an earth structure, and it was never garrisoned, its purpose being to denote rather than defend the frontier. In places it lies side by side with the earlier Wat(t)'s Dyke, which is up to 23ft (7m) to the east of Offa's Dyke; Wat(t)'s Dyke places Oswestry in Wales, while Offa's Dyke locates it in England. Wat(t)'s Dyke furthermore marked the boundary of the lowlands, while parts of Offa's Dyke are located as much as 1300ft (400m) above sea level.

Offa's Dyke Path A 177 mile (283km) long-distance footpath from Sedbury Cliffs on the Severn Estuary near Chepstow to the North Wales resort of Prestatyn on Liverpool Bay. Opened in 1971, it is one of Britain's premier National Trails and draws visitors from throughout the world. Towns on or near the trail include Monmouth, Hay-on-Wye, Kington, Knighton, Presteigne, Montgomery, Welshpool, Oswestry, Chirk and Llangollen. Straddling the Wales/England border, for 70 miles (114km) it follows the course of the 8th century Offa's Dyke earthwork; notably, it is the only National Trail to follow a man-made feature. The dyke crosses a variety of different landscapes, including the Black Mountains, the Shropshire Hills, the Eglwyseg mountains near Llangollen, and the Clwydian Hills. The halfway point is marked by the Offa's Dyke Centre in Knighton. Tel: 01547 528753.

Old Bell Museum Arthur Street, Montgomery. A local history museum run by the Montgomery Civic Society and housed in a 16th century inn. Its 11 rooms chart the social and economic history of the town, including scale models of medieval and Norman castles.

Old Market Hall Great Oak Street, Llanidloes. A two-storey timber-framed building with five bays and an open ground floor, built 1612–22 and which at one time would have been used for market booths. The only timber-framed market hall to survive in Wales, it now houses a permanent display about the history, construction, use and future of timber-framing or half-timbering. There are also sections about tree-ring dating and the destruction and restoration of timbered buildings. Part of the building has been restored to its 17th century appearance. Tel: 01686 412388.

Pen y Crug $1^1/_4$ miles (2km) northwest of Brecon. A large oval multivallate Iron Age hill fort measuring 560ft (171m) by 450ft (137m) internally.

Pen y Gaer Roman Fort $1^1/_4$ miles (2km) northwest of Tretower. The site of a Roman auxiliary fort on a knoll. Measuring 420ft (128m) by 300ft (91.5m) and covering more than $2^1/_2$ acres (1ha), it was probably constructed and occupied c.AD 80–130.

Pistyll Rhaeadr $3^1/_2$ miles (5.5km) northwest of Llanrhaeadr-ym-Mochnant, 17 miles (27km) northwest of Welshpool. Magnificent waterfall in a mystical piece of land, held in high esteem by Welsh Druids and nature-lovers generally. It is one of the traditional 'Seven Wonders of Wales'. After the initial drop of 240ft (73m) the waterfall descends in two further stages, the second of approximately 27ft (8m) and the third about 50ft (15m). The main drop is sheer and not navigable by raft and therefore is undoubtedly the highest/tallest true waterfall in Wales and England.

Plynlimon The highest point of the Cambrian Mountains, the Plynlimon massif borders North Powys and Ceredigion in Dyfed. The highest point is Pen Pumlumon Fawr at 2467ft (752m); its other important peaks are Y Garn (2486ft/752m) and Pen Pumlumon Arwystli (2385ft/727m). Five rivers have their source at Plynlimon: the Severn, the Wye, the Dulas, the Llyfnant and the Rheidol, the last of which meets the Afon Mynach in a 300ft (90m) plunge at the Devil's Bridge chasm. Plynlimon is corrupted from the Welsh *pumlumon*, 'Five Peaks'.

Powis Castle 1 mile (1.6km) southwest of Welshpool. The seat of the Earls of Powys, the Herbert family. The core of the castle was built on a ridge above the Severn Valley in the 13th century by Gruffydd, Baron de la Pole, but was destroyed in the 1270s by Llywelyn the Last. The present structure is the result of considerable remodelling by the Herberts after their purchase of the castle in 1587 and which continued into the mid 19th century. The house was captured by Parliamentarian forces under Sir Thomas Myddelton in 1644 and subsequently restored. The house now contains the Clive Museum: Edward Clive, Sir Robert Clive's son, married Lady Henrietta Herbert in 1784, thus uniting the Powis and Clive estates. The garden below the castle was laid out in Italian and French styles in the 18th and 19th centuries and features an orangery, terraces and original statues, while the remains of two mottes and baileys, one named Ladies' Mount and the other Domen Castell, testify to the strategic importance of the area in the early Norman period. Certainly the area was at the heart of the powor of the princes of Powys. The castle has been maintained by the National Trust since 1952. Tel: 01938 551929.

Powysland Museum Canal Wharf, Welshpool. Local history museum opened in 1874 by a group of friends each with a collection of artefacts. In the 1980s the museum was moved from its original site to a restored warehouse on the Montgomery Canal, reopening in 1990. The museum charts the history of the people of Montgomeryshire; exhibits include agricultural equipment and a collection related to the development of the canal, as well as galleries dedicated to archaeology and social history. There is also a map and photography archive. Tel: 01938 554656.

Radnor Forest An upland area to the northwest of New Radnor, formerly a royal hunting forest and now including a 4500 acre (1800ha) mixed woodland of spruce plantations and broadleaves. Its highest point is Rhos Fawr at 2165ft (660m).

Radnorshire Museum Temple Street, Llandrindod Wells. A local history museum detailing the story of Radnorshire and in particular of the spa town of Llandrindod Wells. Exhibits include artefacts from the Roman fort at Castell Collen and a sheela-na-gig (a carving of a naked woman displaying an exaggerated vulva more usually found in Ireland). There is also a preserved 12th century oak log boat found in the River Ithon. The Victorian era of the spa town is celebrated with costumes, ceramics and memorabilia. The museum also has an exhibition devoted to the life of Victorian diarist Rev. Francis Kilvert. There is also a photographic archive. Tel: 01597 824513

Rivers The **Severn** is the longest river in Britain at 220 miles (352km). It rises in the Cambrian Mountains at an altitude of 2001ft (610m) on Plynlimon, 8 miles (13km) northwest of Llangurig, in northern Powys. The river flows east to Llanidloes and then northeast through Newtown and Welshpool before leaving Wales at the northeastern tip of Powys and flowing east through Shropshire to begin its trek through three English counties. After reaching Shrewsbury the river then flows southeast below Telford and into its second English county town, Worcester, before again taking a more southerly course to its third, Gloucester, where it becomes the Bristol Channel at its estuary, eventually discharging into the Irish Sea and the Atlantic Ocean. The river is sometimes known as Afon Hafren by Welsh speakers. The two bridges of the Severn crossing carrying roads (opened in 1966 and 1996) link Wales with the southwestern counties of England and are among the most important in Britain.

The **Usk** rises on the Black Mountain and flows generally east through the Brecon Beacons National Park and southeast through the towns of Brecon, Crickhowell, Abergavenny and Usk, entering the Bristol Channel at Newport. Its total length is 57 miles (91km).

Wye – see Gwent.

Robert Owen Museum The Cross, Broad Street, Newtown. A museum devoted to the life of Newtown-born Robert Owen (1771–1858), social reformer, early socialist and inspirer of the Co-operative movement. The museum is housed on the ground floor of the town council building, completed in 1902 with part of the cost subscribed by the Co-operative movement. Exhibits include portraits, prints and busts of Owen plus memorabilia including letters, pamphlets and his bureau. Owen is buried in the churchyard of St Mary's Church in Newtown. Tel: 01686 626345.

St Mary of the Salutation Church Church Street, Welshpool. A parish church dating to the mid 13th century, but much altered since including major restorations in the 1770s and late 1860s. The church contains the tomb of the 3rd Earl of Powis and several memorials to the Herbert family of Powis Castle. There is also a stone which may have originated from the 12th century Cistercian abbey of Strata Marcella, which stood outside Welshpool but is now only visible in outline from aerial photographs (GR: SJ251104).

St Nicholas Church Churchstoke, 10 miles (16km) northeast of Newtown. A 13th century church largely rebuilt in the second half of the 19th century when its original square tower was reduced in height. The tower bears marks from musket shots from an incident during the Civil War when Royalist troops took refuge in the church and were besieged by Parliamentarians, eventually being smoked out. The tower's timber-framed belfry and pyramidal slate roof were added in 1815 when the tower was shortened. Originally dedicated to St Mary, it was rededicated to St Nicholas in 1881 after the rebuilding.

Sgwd Henrhyd 1/4 mile (0.4km) north of Coelbren, 15 miles (24km) southwest of Brecon. The highest waterfall in South Wales, with a drop of 90ft (27.5m). Located in the Nant Llech river valley, within the Brecon Beacons National Park.

Simon's Castle
1 mile (1.6km) east of Churchstoke, 11 miles (18km) east of Newtown. The remains of a motte and bailey probably dating to the 12th or early 13th century.

South Wales Borderers Museum
The Barracks, Brecon. Featuring the Zulu War Room, which tells the story of the regiment during the Anglo-Zulu War of 1879, the museum's exhibits also include a gun collection tracing the evolution of soldiers' weapons from the 18th century to the present day. Other exhibits include medals (including 16 replica VCs). The regiment was formed in 1689 as Sir Edward Dering's Regiment of Foot and saw action during the War of the Spanish Succession. In 1751 it was designated the 24th Regiment of Foot and fought in North America during the American War of Independence. As a result of army reforms in 1782 which attempted to allocate infantry regiments to specific recruiting areas, it was redesignated the 24th (2nd Warwickshire) Regiment of Foot. Service during the Napoleonic Wars, mainly in Egypt and the Peninsula, was followed by action in the Gurkha War (1814) and Second Sikh War (1846). The regiment's most famous engagements took place during the Zulu War of 1879: it fought gallantly but unsuccessfully at the Battle of Isandhlwana on 22 January 1879, where 540 of its men died and only six escaped. On the following day a small garrison which had remained at the missionary post of Rorke's Drift was subjected to a concerted attack by a band of Zulus which outnumbered it by more than 20 to 1. The garrison held out for 24 hours before the Zulu army withdrew. Nine VCs were awarded to members of the regiment for these actions. On 1 July 1881 the regiment was renamed the South Wales Borderers; the 2nd Battalion then served in Burma and during the Second Boer War. During World War I the 1st Battalion was part of the original British Expeditionary Force (BEF) and the 2nd Battalion was stationed on the Western Front from 1916. Other battalions saw action in the Dardanelles. In World War II the regiment saw action in Northwest Europe, Africa and the Middle East. During the post-war period its members were posted to such places as Palestine and Malaya. On 11 June 1969 it was amalgamated with the Welch Regiment to form the Royal Regiment of Wales (24th/41st Foot), and on 1 March 2006 it formed the new 2nd Battalion The Royal Welsh Regiment (the Royal Welch Fusiliers forms the 1st Battalion). The museum also contains artefacts related to the Monmouthshire Regiment, formed in 1908 from the three volunteer battalions of the South Wales Borderers recruited in Monmouthshire and the territorial element of the regiment, but which disappeared in the Territorial Army reforms of 1967. Regimental honours include Blenheim, Ramillies, Oudenarde, Peninsula, South Africa (1877–9), Burma (1885–7), South Africa (1900–02), Mons, Marne (1914), Ypres (1914, 1917, 1918), Somme (1916, 1918), Menin Road, Passchendaele, Cambrai (1917, 1918), Hindenburg Line, Gallipoli (1915–16), Norway (1940), Normandy Landing, Arnhem (1945), Northwest Europe (1944–5), North Africa (1942) and Burma (1944–5). Tel: 01874 613310.

Spaceguard Centre
Llanshay Lane, Knighton. A working astronomical observatory located at the former Powys County Observatory. The centre is mainly concerned with Near Earth Objects (NEOs), i.e. asteroids and comets, and the potential threat they pose to the Earth. There is a small planetarium and a working model of the solar system. Tel: 01547 520247.

Sport
football
Caersws were formed in 1887 as Caersws Amateurs. They were founder members of the League of Wales in 1992. Nicknamed The Bluebirds, their home ground is the Recreation Ground, Caersws.

The New Saints have had two earlier incarnations, as Llansantffraid, formed in 1959, and Oswestry Town, formed in 1860. Llansantffraid were promoted to the League of Wales in 1993 and won the Welsh Cup in 1996; changing their name to Total Network Solutions Llansantffraid FC in accordance with an agreement with new sponsors, they became Total Network Solutions FC in 1997. The club merged with nearby Oswestry Town in 2003. After Total Network Solutions were taken over by BT in 2006 the club changed its name once again to The New Saints FC. They won the League of Wales in 2000, 2005 and 2006, and the Welsh Cup in 1996 and 2005. Nicknamed The Saints, their home ground is the Recreation Ground, Treflan, Llansantffraid.

Newtown were founded in 1875 as Newtown White Stars. Their home ground is Latham Park, Newtown.

Welshpool Town were founded in 1878. Promoted to the League of Wales in 1997, they were relegated a year later but returned to the top flight in 2002. Their home ground is Maes y Dre Recreation Ground, Howells Drive, Welshpool.

Tretower Castle
Tretower, 10 miles (16km) southeast of Brecon. Norman motte and bailey castle founded by the Picard family and rebuilt in stone in the mid 12th century. The L-plan stone castle was extended with the construction of a great circular tower in the first half of the 13th century. It was replaced as a residence by nearby Tretower Court during the first half of the 14th century although it probably retained its defensive function in times of unrest. The tower still stands almost to its full height among substantial remains of the walls.

Tretower Court
Tretower, 10 miles (16km) southeast of Brecon. A medieval country house begun in the early 14th century, eventually supplanting nearby Tretower Castle as a residence as the need for defensive capabilities receded. Arranged in four ranges of two-storey buildings around a central courtyard and largely completed by the end of the 15th century, the house has been altered over the centuries but retains much of its medieval fabric.

Welshpool & Llanfair Light Railway
A narrow gauge (2ft 6in/762mm) heritage railway operating for $8^1/_2$ miles (14km) through the Banwy valley between Welshpool and Llanfair Caereinion. It runs on part of a former narrow gauge commercial line opened in 1903 and operated by Cambrian Railways and later by the Great Western Railway; passenger traffic ceased in 1931 and the line was completely closed in 1956. The narrow gauge railway opened in April 1963 and the terminus at Raven Square on the

	outskirts of Welshpool in 1981. The service uses both steam and diesel locomotives. Tel: 01938 810441.
W H Smith Museum	High Street, Newtown. A museum dedicated to the story of stationers W H Smith & Son, housed in a former branch which had remained largely unaltered since its opening in 1927. Tel: 01686 626280.
Wye Valley Walk	A long-distance footpath running for 136 miles (219km) from Chepstow to Plynlimon in Powys, via Tintern, Monmouth, Ross-on-Wye, How Caple, Hereford, Bredwardine, Hay-on-Wye, Erwood, Builth Wells, Newbridge, Llanwrthwl, Rhayader and Llangurig.
Y Breiddin	1/2 mile (0.8km) south of Criggion, 7 miles (11km) northeast of Welshpool. A large ramparted Iron Age hill fort covering 70 acres (28ha) and occupied from the 7th century BC until the 4th century AD. Some of the site has been damaged by quarrying and forestry. Y Breiddin has been suggested as a possible site of the battle in AD 50 between Caractacus and the Roman general Ostorius Scapula.

Some famous people born in Powys

Davies, David (coal magnate) (1818–90)	Llandinam
Dawkins, William Boyd (geologist) (1837–1929)	Welshpool
Everest, George (surveyor) (1790–1866)	Crickhowell
Frere, Henry Bartle (colonial governor) (1815–84)	Clydach
Hoggan, Francis (pioneering doctor) (1843–1927)	Brecon
Herbert, George (poet) (1593–1633)	Montgomery
Mills, Phil (rally driver) (1963–)	Trefeglwys
Owen, Robert (industrialist) (1771–1858)	Newtown
Pryce-Jones, Pryce (businessman) (1834–1920)	Newtown
Robinson, Carl (footballer) (1976–)	Llandrindod Wells
Siddons, Sarah (actress) (1755–1831)	Brecon
Williams, Iolo (TV presenter) (1962–)	Builth Wells

South Glamorgan

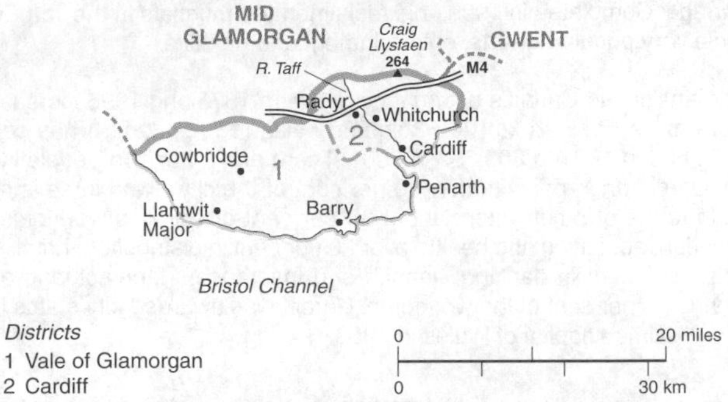

MID GLAMORGAN
Craig Llysfaen
264
GWENT
M4
R. Taff
Radyr
Whitchurch
2
Cardiff
Cowbridge
1
Penarth
Llantwit Major
Barry
Bristol Channel
Districts
1 Vale of Glamorgan
2 Cardiff
0
20 miles
0
30 km

South Glamorgan consists of the unitary authorities of Cardiff and the Vale of Glamorgan. It is bordered to the south by the Bristol Channel, to the north by Mid Glamorgan and shares a short border in the northeast with Gwent. The main river is the Taff and the main geographic feature is that part of the Glamorgan Heritage Coast between Llantwit Major and Aberthaw, which showcases some beautiful low cliffs and dramatic coastal scenery. Its major conurbation is the city of Cardiff which is the capital of Wales and its largest city.

South Glamorgan has been settled since at least Neolithic times. During the Iron Age it was occupied by the Silures, who met the Roman invasion of the 1st century with some resistance. Around AD 55 the Roman governor Aulus Didius Gallus established a fort where Cardiff Castle now stands. Following the withdrawal of Roman troops in the early 5th century the area was part of the kingdom of Morgannwg, traditionally founded by Morgan (hence Glamorgan). Morgannwg was generally subordinate to Gwent and along with that kingdom suffered from the first incursions by the invading Norman lords in the 11th century. The remains of the Roman fort on the Taff was used as the basis for a Norman castle and, later, a Welsh castle was built nearby which became known as Castell Coch (the Red Castle). Other Norman castles built in the area at this time as a result of continual clashes between the Normans and the Welsh include Fonmon, St Donat's and Ogmore.

The history of South Glamorgan is inextricably entwined with that of the city of **Cardiff**. The derivation of the name Cardiff (Caerdydd) is a matter of some dispute. The first half clearly derives from the word *caer* (fort); the 'Diff' (*dydd*) has been claimed both as a corruption of (the river) Taff and of the name of Aulus Didius Gallus, the *caer* of Didius thus becoming Cardiff. A cathedral at Llandaff was built in the 12th century, while the village established around the castle grew slowly into a town, and was granted its first royal charter in 1581. A long-established port, it changed little until the growth of iron smelting in Merthyr Tydfil created a need to reach the coast quickly and at low cost. The problem was solved by the building in 1790–8 of the Glamorganshire Canal, which connected Merthyr Tydfil with the Taff Estuary. Cardiff's population in 1801 was under 2000, small when compared to Merthyr Tydfil and Swansea which both had populations of more than 5000. The canal was eventually replaced by the Taff Vale Railway after the 1840s and the industrialisation of the area was further boosted by the demand for coal from the South Wales coalfields.

The docks were in much need of expansion because of the increasing iron and coal trade and a number of new docks were constructed from the 1830s onwards, including the Bute West Dock (1839), the Bute East Dock (1855), Roath Basin (1874), Roath Dock (1887) and the Queen Alexandra Dock (1907). The River Taff was diverted in 1853 to reduce the threat of flooding and the reclaimed riverbed would later become the site of Cardiff Arms Park. The growth of the docks and their hinterland brought to Cardiff a cosmopolitan population of sailors and immigrant dock workers, especially in the bay area which came to be known as 'Tiger Bay'.

By the 1880s Cardiff was the world's largest coal handling port with a population of 82,761. Exports of coal through the port peaked in 1913 and from that point the trade declined, virtually ceasing by the 1960s. Over the following decades heavy industry and coal mining went into even sharper decline. Bute West Dock was closed in 1964 and Bute East Dock in 1970. However, like so many UK cities, Cardiff has been undergoing major regeneration since the mid 1990s. This has been mainly based around the Cardiff Bay area, which was artificially created by the construction of the Cardiff Bay Barrage. Completed in 1999, this reclaimed the mudflats in the Taff Estuary. The area has now become very popular for arts, entertainment and nightlife.

Seven major expansions to Cardiff's boundaries between 1875 and 1996 increased its area from around 3 square miles (7.75 sq km) to 53 square miles (137 sq km). It has seen a population increase from 26,630 in 1851 to 305,353 in 2001. There are 1.4 million people living within a 45-minute drive of Cardiff and approximately 40 per cent of the city's workforce is made up of daily in-commuters. In terms of employment about 30 per cent of Cardiff's workforce is employed in public administration, education and health, over 20 per cent in distribution, hotels and restaurants ,and a further 20 per cent in banking, finance and insurance. Manufacturing and construction account for around 10 per cent of the workforce. Cardiff was awarded city status by Edward VII in 1905 and was proclaimed capital of Wales in 1955

South Glamorgan	**Population**			**Area**	
	male	*female*	*total*	*sq miles*	*sq km*
Cardiff	145,761	159,592	305,353	54	139
Vale of Glamorgan	57,356	61,936	119,292	128	331
Total	203,117	221,528	424,645	182	470

Local Attractions and Information

Administrative headquarters	**Cardiff**: County Hall, Atlantic Wharf, Cardiff CF10 4UW. Tel: 029 208 7208. **Vale of Glamorgan**: Civic Offices, Holton Road, Barry CF63 4RU. Tel: 01446 700111.
Airport	**Cardiff International Airport** (CWL) is the only airport in Wales offering scheduled flights. It was originally established as a training base for Royal Air Force Spitfire pilots during World War II. Commercial flights began between Cardiff and Dublin in 1952. The extension of the runway in 1986 enabled the airport to expand. Further refurbishment and modernisation was carried out in 2006. The airport now serves a number of destinations in Europe, North and Central America. Tel: 01446 711111.
Barry Castle	Barry Town. The ruins of a 13th century defensible manor house built by the de Barry family on the site of an earlier Norman ringwork on a hill outside Barry. It was improved in the 14th century with the addition of a gatehouse and hall. Derelict by the first half of the 16th century, the remains of the gatehouse and attached walls have been landscaped and made safe; the remains are now surrounded by housing.
Barry Island	Aka Ynys Barri. A peninsula and formerly an island until the 1880s, when it was linked to the mainland as the docks were developed. Barry is now known for its beach and for Barry Island Pleasure Park. The island used to house a Butlin's holiday camp, which was used as a location for the Doctor Who serial *Delta and the Bannermen*, as the 'Shangri-La' holiday camp. The site has been redeveloped for housing, but was once again used for location shooting in the 2005 Doctor Who episodes 'The Empty Child' and 'The Doctor Dances', standing in for a bomb site in 1941 London.
Barry Island Railway	Formerly the Vale of Glamorgan Railway. A heritage railway based at Barry Island Railway Station, and operating steam and diesel services for 2 miles (3km) on two branch lines to Hood Road, Woodham Halt and Plymouth Road, where there are an engine shed and museum displays. Tel: 01446 748816.
Battles	See separate table for details of the Battle of St Fagans in 1648.
Beaupre Castle	$1^1/_2$ miles (2.5km) southeast of Cowbridge. Aka Old Beaupre. The substantial remains of a 16th century mansion built by Sir Rice Mansel incorporating an earlier 14th century house, and completed by William and Richard Bassett. The buildings stand around an inner courtyard and the ruins include a three-storey gatehouse, a Tudor storeyed porch and a curtain wall.
Bute Park	Western Avenue, Cardiff. Large park in the middle of Cardiff beside the River Taff and flanked by Pontcanna Fields and Sophia Gardens. The park was designed by Andrew Pettigrew but the grounds were originally landscaped by Capability Brown, with later changes made by the 3rd Marquis of Bute. It was presented to Cardiff Council in 1947. The Blackwell Fields in the north of the park are recreation grounds and there is an arboretum with a variety of specimen trees. Tel: 029 2022 7281.
Butetown Community and Arts Centre	Dock Chambers, Bute Street, Cardiff Bay, Cardiff. Local community museum exploring the lives of the people of the Cardiff Bay area, once better known as Tiger Bay. It holds a large photographic archive plus audiotaped oral recollections from Butetown's older residents and former residents. It is also a wide-ranging family history resource. Tel: 029 2025 6757.
Caerau hill fort	Caerau, 4 miles (6km) west of Cardiff. The site of a bivallate Iron Age hill fort covering 12 acres (5ha).

Cardiff Castle Castle Street, Cardiff. One of Wales's top tourist attractions. It was built on the site of a Roman fort originally constructed in the 3rd century although the site had been temporarily occupied in the 1st century during the early stages of the Roman invasion. The curtain walls stand on the Roman foundations. The original wooden Norman keep, built c.1080 by Robert Fitzhamon on a distinct motte, was replaced in the 12th century by a stone keep erected by Robert the Consul, the illegitimate son of Henry I. The gatehouse and Black Tower were built by Gilbert de Clare in the 13th century and further additions such as the Octagon Tower were made in the 15th and 16th centuries. A wholesale restoration of the castle was undertaken by the Bute family from the late 18th century. The grounds were landscaped by Capability Brown and Henry Holland, and the castle was later given a Gothic remodelling and the lodgings provided with themed interiors by designer William Burges for the 3rd Marquess of Bute. Allegedly the richest man in the world, the 3rd Marquess gave testimony to his wealth in several of the rooms (notably the Arab Room, Lord Bute's Bedroom and The Bachelor Bedroom) with emeralds, rubies and sapphires in abundance on walls, ceilings and windows. Several towers were built, including the Clock Tower, the walls were restored and a new library and banqueting hall were built on the site of the old medieval Hall. Perhaps the greatest room is the Summer Smoking Room with its magnificent décor and aestheticism. A hidden gem is the roof garden inspired by the Marquess's travels to the Middle East and Rome. The castle was given to the City of Cardiff in 1947.

Cardiff Bay A regeneration area created by the construction of the Cardiff Bay Barrage, built as part of the project to reverse the decline of Cardiff's docklands during the second half of the 20th century. Completed in 1999 to create a 500 acre (200ha) freshwater lake from the impounded Taff and Ely rivers, the barrage measures 3630ft (1106m) and has eliminated the effect of the tide. As was the case with many British cities, the decline of Cardiff's non-container-based ship-borne trade led to the inevitable abandonment of warehousing, docks and wharves. The Cardiff Bay Development Corporation was created in 1987 to stimulate the redevelopment of this run-down area and was wound up in 2000 having attracted investment to regenerate the bay with offices, housing, leisure facilities and retail outlets. The site includes the visitor centre (the 'Tube'), Goleulong 2000 Lightship, the Norwegian Church Arts Centre, the Pierhead building, Techniquest, the land train, the Atlantic Wharf Leisure Village and the Wales Millennium Centre.

Cardiff Bay Visitor Centre Pier Head, Cardiff Bay. Opened in 1991 and innovatively designed by Will Alsop to resemble a giant telescope, which has led to it being known as 'The Tube' by locals. Tel: 029 2046 3833.

Cardiff City Hall Cathays Park, Cardiff. Built in Baroque style of Portland stone, 1901–04. The interior features a council chamber in Italian High Renaissance style, grand stained glass window, reception hall with paired Siena marble columns and a Grand Assembly Hall with vaulted ceiling. The marble-paved hall on the first floor landing is decorated with 11 marble statues of famous figures from Welsh history, each the work of a different contemporary British artist. The figures depicted are: Bishop William Morgan, Boudicca, Dafydd ap Gwilym, Gerald of Wales, Henry VII, Hywel Dda, Llywelyn the Last, Owain Glyndŵr, Saint David, Sir Thomas Picton, William Williams. Originally there were only intended to be ten but as those chosen were all men, the memorial to Boudicca was added. The building is dominated by a 194ft (59m) high clock tower and a dome surmounted by a Welsh dragon. Tel: 029 2087 1727.

Cardiff International Arena Mary Ann Street, Cardiff. Aka the CIA. A multi-purpose venue opened in 1993 hosting a wide variety of events including concerts, conferences, sporting events and exhibitions. It has a 48,440 sq ft (4500 sq m) main arena plus suites, meeting rooms and flexible spaces. Tel: 029 2022 4488.

Cardiff Metropolitan Cathedral of St David Charles Street, Cardiff. Built in 1887 and designated a cathedral and the seat of the Roman Catholic Archbishop of Cardiff in 1916. Like Llandaff Cathedral it was seriously damaged by bombing during World War II and spent the next 15 or more years being restored.

Cardiff University Established by royal charter in 1883 as the University College of South Wales and Monmouthshire. In 1972, the college was renamed University College, Cardiff and in 1988 it merged with the University of Wales Institute of Science and Technology to become the University of Wales College, Cardiff. It adopted the title of the University of Wales, Cardiff in 1996 and its current name in 2004, when it merged with the University of Wales College of Medicine and separated from the collegiate University of Wales. Cardiff is a member of the Russell Group of research-led universities. Its main building stands in Cardiff's Civic Centre and it is structured in 28 academic schools within two colleges, catering for around 30,000 students – the College of Humanities and Sciences, and the Wales College of Medicine, Biology, Life and Health Sciences. Former students include BBC newsreader Huw Edwards, composer Alun Hoddinott and broadcaster Sian Lloyd. Tel: 029 2087 4000.

Castell Coch Castle Hill, Tongwynlais, Cardiff. Mainly a 19th century construction based on the plan of a 13th century castle which formerly stood on the site. The original castle was built in the early to mid 13th century by the de Clare family but is believed to have been abandoned in the 14th century. The site was excavated and cleared in 1871 and in 1874 the construction of a new castle was begun by the 3rd Earl of Bute with architect William Burges; the pair were also responsible for the restoration of Cardiff Castle. It was constructed of local red-stained limestone, hence the name Castell Coch ('Red Castle'). Its three conically roofed cylindrical towers of unequal height give it a somewhat fairytale appearance. The interiors, designed in the 1880s, follow similar 'fantasy' themes to those of Cardiff Castle. Intended as a holiday lodge but rarely used, it is now in the care of Cardiff Council and maintained by CADW.

Cathays Park The focus of Cardiff's civic centre, consisting of three formal garden areas containing statuary: Alexandra Gardens, Gorsedd Gardens and Friary Gardens. Buildings surrounding the park include the National Assembly Building, the Temple of Peace and Health, Glamorgan County

	Hall, Law Courts, Cardiff City Hall, the National Museum of Wales and the University College of South Wales. The land was acquired from 1898 by Cardiff Council from the 3rd Marquis of Bute, who made a condition of its sale that it was to be used for civic, cultural and educational purposes.
Coal Exchange, The	Mount Stuart Square, Cardiff Bay, Cardiff. An arts, entertainment, functions and broadcasting venue housed in the former coal trading exchange, designed by Edwin Seward & Thomas and built 1883–6. The large central coal and shipping hall was rebuilt in 1911. The world's first recorded £1m business deal was reputedly struck in the Coal Exchange in 1907. It has recently hosted ceremonies such as the Welsh BAFTAs and the Welsh Rock, Pop and Dance Awards. Closed for redevelopment in late 2007, its future is currently uncertain. Tel: 029 2049 4917.
Cosmeston Country Park	Penarth. Country park covering 250 acres (100ha) and created from a former limestone quarry, closed in 1970, of which 113 acres (46ha) has been designated a Site of Special Scientific Interest. The park has a wide range of habitats including lakes, reedbeds, woodlands and meadows. Tel: 029 2070 1678.
Cosmeston Medieval Village	Lavernock Road, Penarth. Recreated 14th century village on the site of the abandoned village of Cosmeston, uncovered by excavation in the 1980s. It is a living history experience with costumed villagers acting as guides and demonstrating work practices and crafts. Tel: 029 2070 9141.
Cowbridge Physic Garden	Church Street, Cowbridge. A physic garden created on the site of Cowbridge Old Hall, with a variety of species of medicinal plants and divided into parterres with specific beds for each type of plant. Tel: 08457 484950.
Dinas Powys Castle	Dinas Powys, 4 miles (6km) southwest of Cardiff. The scant ruins of an early 12th century castle on the site of an earlier bank and ditch earthwork dating to c.AD 500. The Norman castle was a timber palisade set into a stone revetted bank. There are also the ivy-covered ruins of a stone keep.
Dunraven Hill Fort	6 miles (10km) northwest of Llantwit Major. An Iron Age promontory fort on a headland above Dunraven Bay. The headland was cut off from the interior by ramparts and ditches.
Dyffryn Gardens	Dyffryn, 3 miles (5km) north of Barry. A formal garden first laid out by Thomas Mawson in 1904 and now being restored to its original condition. The Grade I listed gardens, arranged in a series of rooms separated by clipped yew hedges, include water features, walled gardens, an arboretum, a collection of rhododendrons and herbaceous borders. Tel: 029 2059 3328.
Ewenny Priory	6 miles (10km) northwest of Llantwit Major. Benedictine priory founded in 1141 by Maurice de Londres. It was built as a fortified church with towers and a curtain wall – much of which still remains – enclosing 5 acres (2ha). After its dissolution the monastic portion of the building became private property and the nave of the priory was used as the parish church. The eastern or monastic end, divided from the nave by a wall, contains the tombs of the de Londres family and is now in the guardianship of CADW.
Ffotogallery	Plymouth Road, Penarth. A changing exhibition of photography-based artwork established in 2003 and housed in the Turner House Gallery, built in 1888. Tel: 029 2070 8870.
Flat Holm	Aka Ynys Echni. An uninhabited island 5 miles (8km) from Cardiff in the Bristol Channel. A local nature reserve and Site of Special Scientific Interest, its main claim to fame is that on 13 May 1897 Guglielmo Marconi, assisted by George Kemp, a Cardiff Post Office engineer, transmitted the first wireless signals over water from Lavernock (near Penarth) to Flat Holm. The message, sent in Morse code, was 'ARE YOU READY'. The island is also the site of several artillery batteries, an infectious diseases hospital and a lighthouse. The Flat Holm Battery is a series of four gun emplacements built in the 1860s: Well Battery, Farmhouse Battery, Castle Rock Battery, and Lighthouse Battery and Fort. They were abandoned in the 1900s but the island was an important and active anti-aircraft installation during World War II. The Flat Holm Isolation Hospital was built in 1896. An annual service is held to bless the island. The island is situated north of Steep Holm, which falls within the boundary of North Somerset unitary authority. Area: 0.08 sq miles (0.2 sq km). GR: ST220648.
Flat Holm Lighthouse	The first lighthouse on Flat Holm was in operation from 1737. The tower was rebuilt in 1820 and a new lantern fitted in 1866, raising the height to 99ft (30m). Automated in 1988, the lighthouse was converted to solar power in 1997.
Fonmon Castle	Rhoose, 3 miles (5km) west of Barry Town. This still-occupied castle stands on the site of earlier fortifications dating to the 12th century. The first stone keep was built c.1200, probably within a timber palisade. The castle was extended and rebuilt in the 13th century by the St John family, who added a curtain wall as well as square and round towers. A north wing was built in the 16th century, and in the 1650s the castle was sold by the St Johns to Colonel Philip Jones, whose successors still own it today. Internal improvements and external embellishments were put in place in the late 17th century, at which time the four-storey rectangular Watch Tower was probably added. The castle is surrounded by formal gardens and woodland. The castle is a licensed venue for weddings. Tel: 01446 710206.
Glamorganshire Canal	See Mid Glamorgan.
Highest point	Craig Llysfaen at 866ft (264m). GR: ST189850.
Holy Trinity Church	Marcross, 3 miles (5km) west of Llantwit Major. A parish church founded in the 12th century, with a 14th century tower. Features include a 12th century font and a leper window.
Interesting facts	**Wales Millennium Centre**, in Cardiff Bay, played host to a world record on 3 November 2006. The world record gathering of the most people with the same surname – Jones – was hosted in its Donald Gordon Theatre, with 1224 Joneses in attendance. **The Captain's Wife** public house, in Swanbridge, overlooks Sully Island; because the tide comes in to the island twice as fast as it goes out, visitors who walk across the causeway often get stranded. Rumour has it that the locals have an uncanny propensity to maroon themselves. **Anna Kashfi** appeared in a number of films,

although the Cardiff-born actress, of Irish descent, was never a leading lady. Her sultry Mediterranean looks typecast her in Asian and Mexican roles and Marlon Brando is said to have married her in 1957, mistakenly believing her to be of Asian Indian descent!

Islands — There are 10 named islands in South Glamorgan, all in the Bristol Channel (in the Lundy Sea Area). There are five in the Cardiff Area: **Bendrick Rock** (GR: ST132667), **Flat Holm** (see separate entry), **Monkstone** (GR: ST235690), **Sully Island** (see separate entry) and **The Wolves** (GR: ST205656); and five in the Vale of Glamorgan: **Barry Island** (see separate entry), **Black Rocks** (GR: SS845769), **Ffynnon-wen Rocks** (GR: SS793789), **Gwely'r Misgl** (GR: SS782805) and **Tusker Rock** (see separate entry).

Llanblethian Castle — Llanblethian, 1/2 mile (0.8km) southwest of Cardiff. The ruins of an early 14th century castle mainly consisting of the twin-towered gatehouse and an earlier keep.

Llandaff Cathedral — Cathedral Green, Llandaff, Cardiff. Dedicated to St Peter and St Paul and founded in the early 12th century, the cathedral is also dedicated to the three Welsh saints Dyfrig, Teilo and Euddogwy, who established a monastic foundation on the site beside the River Taff in the 6th century. The cathedral was built 1120–33, further work taking place from 1190 until the 1220s. The chapter house was added 1244–65 and the lady chapel 1266–87. The Jasper Tower was built by Jasper Tudor in the late 15th century. Following the Dissolution the income derived from pilgrimages to the tomb of St Teilo disappeared and the upkeep of the cathedral was abandoned. During this time only the lady chapel was in use. In 1734 work was begun on an attempt to restore parts of the cathedral in a new style, designed by John Wood of Bath and known as the 'Italian Temple'; however, this was never completed. A more traditional restoration was carried out in the 19th century and the southwest tower and spire were completed in 1869. The cathedral was severely damaged by a German bomb on 2 January 1941 and underwent repair and restoration until 1960. Tel: 029 2056 1545.

Nash Point Lighthouses — 1 mile (1.6km) west of St Donat's, 3 miles (5km) southwest of Llantwit Major. Originally two lighthouse towers 1000ft (305m) apart, built in 1832 to a design by James Walker. The east tower, which still operates, is 122ft (37m) high; it was electrified in 1968 and automated in 1998. The west tower, 67ft (20.5m) high, has no light.

National Museum Cardiff — Cathays Park, Cardiff. Museum and art gallery located in Cardiff's Civic Centre. The building was designed in Classical style by Dunbar Smith & Brewer and begun before World War I, but completed only in 1932 with the addition of the east wing and lecture theatre, by which time it had already been open to the public for five years. A double flight of granite steps leads up to the main entrance of bronze doors under a portico of Doric columns. The museum holds a significant collection of fine art, including a notable collection of Impressionist art and works by prominent Welsh artists, as well as 20th century art including works by Jacob Epstein, Eric Gill, Stanley Spencer, L S Lowry and Oskar Kokoschka. There are also collections of silverware and ceramics, as well as exhibits relating to the evolution, archaeology, numismatics, natural history, environment and geology of Wales. Tel: 029 2039 7951.

Norwegian Church Cultural Centre — Pier Head, Cardiff. An arts centre housed in the former Scandinavian Lutheran Church and Mission, built and consecrated in 1868 for the benefit of Norwegian sailors visiting Cardiff. A gallery and bell-tower were added in 1885. Author Roald Dahl, born of Norwegian parents in Cardiff, was christened in the Norwegian Church in 1916. With the decline of the coal trade and the number of Norwegian ships visiting the need for the mission declined and, although the local congregation and other Lutheran organisations funded its continued use, it was eventually deconsecrated in 1974. The church fell into disrepair but to avoid its complete demolition to make way for a new road it was dismantled and re-erected in its new location in the late 1980s. Tel: 029 2049 3331.

Ogmore Castle — Ogmore, 7 miles (11km) northwest of Cowbridge. Located beside the Ewenny River and founded c.1110 by William de Londres as an earth and timber castle, but quickly rebuilt in stone including a large keep. Extended in the 13th century, after a relatively uneventful existence the castle was abandoned in the 16th century, although the court house within the castle was used until the early 19th century. The extensive ruins, including those of the keep, can still be explored today and are in the care of CADW.

Old Brewery Quarter — St Mary's Street, Cardiff. An award-winning leisure and retail regeneration development on the site of the former Brains Old Brewery, dating from 1713 and acquired by Brains in 1882. The brewery was closed in 1999 and the development of the site includes offices, apartments, leisure and retail outlets integrating the brewery's original vaults and old clocktower.

Penarth Pier — The Esplanade, Penarth. Built in 1894 and opened in 1895. It is 650ft (200m) long and 50ft (15m) wide at the landing stage end. The middle of the pier is built on cast-iron piles with wooden decking whereas the landward and landing stage end have concrete piles. A wooden pavilion at its seaward end was severely damaged in 1931 by a fire which destroyed much of the pier. Having been rebuilt, in 1947 the pier suffered further damage when struck by the 7000 ton *Port Royal Park*. Further repairs took place and the pier continued in use. Restored during the 1990s, it was formally reopened in May 1998 and is still a landing stage for paddle steamers. Tel: 029 2070 8849.

Penmark Castle — Penmark, 3 miles (5km) west of Barry. The scant ruins of a 13th century castle beside the River Waycock, built on the site of an early 12th century timber castle.

Plas Llanmihangel — Llanmihangel, 1 1/2 miles (2.5km) southwest of Cowbridge. A 16th century manor house restored in the 19th century. Grade I listed, it is a rare example of a complete Elizabethan building in Glamorgan. Tel: 01446 774610.

Point, The — Mount Stuart Square, Cardiff Bay, Cardiff. A live music venue housed in the converted former St Stephen's Church in Butetown, built in 1894 as the chapel of St Mary's and consecrated in 1912 as St Stephen's. The church was deconsecrated in 1992 and used as a community centre and a theatre before major restoration in 2003 saw it emerge as a venue for performances by local, national and international bands. Tel: 029 2046 0873.

Porthkerry Country Park — 1/2 mile (0.8km) west of Barry Town. A country park established on parkland originally landscaped by the Romilly family in the 1840s, and which passed into the ownership of the local council in the 1920s. Among its features is a viaduct built in 1900 by the Vale of Glamorgan Railway Company. The park has a range of habitats including woodlands, beach and open parkland.

River Taff — The Taff rises in the Brecon Beacons as the Taff Fechan (Little Taff) and Taff Fawr (Big Taff). These join to form the Taff north of Merthyr Tydfil. The river continues its 38 mile (61km) journey south through Merthyr, Pontypridd and Cardiff to reach the Bristol Channel at Cardiff Bay, where it has been barraged. The river was extremely polluted during the Industrial Revolution and well into the 20th century, but with the decline of heavy industry and coal mining, the quality of its water has improved greatly.

Roath Park — Lake Road West, Roath, Cardiff. A 130 acre (53ha) park laid out by William Harpur and planted by William Pettigrew. It was opened in 1894 on boggy land donated by the Marquis of Bute in 1887. The main feature is a 30 acre (12ha) lake with four islands, formed by the damming of the Nant Fawr stream and now designated a Conservation Area for its waterfowl and habitat. The park is also noted for its floral dicplays and specimen trees. In addition there is a Victorian glasshouse with exotic plants. Tel: 029 2022 7281.

Royal Welsh College of Music & Drama — Cathays Park, Cardiff. Established in 1949 as Cardiff College of Music and a constituent college of the University of Wales. Located in purpose-built accommodation in the grounds of Cardiff Castle, it gained its royal designation at Queen Elizabeth II's Golden Jubilee in 2002. The college offers undergraduate degrees in acting, music, stage management and theatre design, presenting over 300 public performances each year.

St David's Hall — The Hayes, Cardiff. The national concert hall and conference centre of Wales, built in 1982 and opened in February 1983. The concert hall auditorium has a seating capacity of 1500 and presents a range of entertainment including comedy and all genres of music. It is home to the Welsh Proms and also hosts the bi-annual BBC Cardiff Singer of the World competition. The BBC National Orchestra and Chorus of Wales is the orchestra-in-residence. Tel: 029 2087 8444.

St Donat's Castle — St Donats, 11 miles (18km) west of Barry Town. Standing on the coast above St Donat's Bay, the castle was originally built in the 12th century and has been occupied ever since. The current castle, built in the early 14th century by the Stradling family, is concentric in plan with inner and outer curtain walls. It had been neglected for some time when it was bought in the 1860s by a descendant of the family who began to restore it. The interior was partially remodelled in the 1920s and 1930s after it was bought by newspaper baron William Randolph Hearst. Since 1960 the castle has been occupied by Atlantic College, an international school. The former tithe barn has been converted into an arts centre. Tel: 01446 799100.

St Fagans Castle — St Fagans, Cardiff. The centrepiece of St Fagan's National History Museum, an Elizabethan mansion above the River Ely probably built by Nicholas Herbert c.1596. It stands within the ruined curtain walls of an earlier fortification, built in the 13th century on the site of a late 11th century Norman ringwork founded by Peter le Sore. The interior of the house was altered in the 17th and 19th centuries and now features items of furniture chosen by the National History Museum to represent various historical periods.

St Fagans National History Museum — St Fagans, Cardiff. An open air museum located in the grounds of St Fagans Castle and part of National Museum Wales. Covering 100 acres (40ha), it was opened in 1948 as the Welsh Folk Museum and chronicles developments in Welsh industrial and rural life and culture. In addition to the two castle buildings, it features 40 historic buildings dismantled and re-erected on the site and selected to represent the architecture of Wales. These include a Celtic village, a Nonconformist chapel, St Teilo's medieval church, a school house, a tollbooth, a workmen's institute and workmen's cottages. There are also collections covering costumes, agricultural equipment, transport and music and culture. Tel: 029 2057 3500.

St Illtud's Church — Church Street, Llantwit Major. A 12th century church restored during the 14th and 15th centuries, with further restoration in the 19th and 20th centuries. It is divided into an 'Eastern' and 'Western' church, the latter housing a collection of early Christian memorial stones including the Houelt Cross and the Samson Cross. The church was described by John Wesley as 'the most beautiful as well as the most spacious church in Wales'.

St Lythans Chambered Tomb — 1/2 mile (0.8km) northeast of Dyffryn, 2 miles (3km) northwest of Barry Town. Neolithic chambered tomb with no covering mound and thus known as a portal dolmen. Its three uprights hold up a large capstone measuring 14ft (4.2m) by 10ft (3m) to a height of 6ft (1.8m).

Senedd Building — Cardiff Bay, Cardiff. The assembly building of the National Assembly for Wales, designed by Richard Rogers and opened by Queen Elizabeth II on 1 March 2006. The building has three levels including an observation area allowing overhead views through glass windows to the debating chamber below. The Senedd Building was constructed mostly using Welsh materials and labour and has been designed to have minimal impact on the environment; it has a design life of at least 100 years. The National Assembly visitor centre next door is housed in the historic Pierhead Building, built in 1897 for the Bute Dock Company. Tel: 029 2089 8200.

Sport

general — The **Millennium Stadium**, St Mary's Street, Cardiff, was built on the site of the National Stadium, which stood in Cardiff Arms Park. Opened in 1999, it has a seating capacity of 74,500 and is fitted with a retractable roof. It was originally built to be ready in time for the Rugby Union World Cup; the first game played saw Wales defeat South Africa in a friendly. In addition to home rugby internationals, the stadium has hosted Celtic League and Heineken Cup rugby matches. The

Welsh national football team also play the majority of their home internationals at the Millennium Stadium. Because of the prolonged delay in the construction of the new Wembley Stadium, the Cardiff venue hosted the FA Cup and League Cup finals 2001–6, as well as Football League play-off finals and the FA Community Shield. Its permanent tenants are Welsh Rugby Union and the Football Association of Wales. The **National Indoor Athletics Centre** opened in 2000 and is part of the sports facilities of the University of Wales Institute Cardiff. **Sophia Gardens**, Cathedral Road, Cardiff, takes its name from Sophia, wife of the 2nd Marquis of Bute, whose family owned the land beside the River Taff on which the recreation grounds were laid out in the 19th century. It has been the home of Glamorgan County Cricket Club since 1967. Sophia Gardens is also home of the **Welsh Institute of Sport**, opened in 1972 with a remit to provide facilities to help develop excellence in Welsh sport. Tel: 0845 045 0902.

cricket — **Glamorgan County Cricket Club** was founded in Cardiff in July 1888, joining the County Championship in 1921. They were winners of the County Championship in 1948, 1969 and 1997. The limited overs team is called the Glamorgan Dragons. Most of the club's home fixtures are played at the SWALEC Stadium (known until its redevelopment in 2008 as Sophia Gardens), Cardiff, although matches also take place at St Helen's in Swansea, Abergavenny, Colwyn Bay, Ebbw Vale and Cresselly. From 1921–66 the club played at Cardiff Arms Park. Tel: 0871 282 3401.

football — **Barry Town** were founded in 1912 as Barry AFC, becoming Barry Town FC in 1923. They were winners of the League of Wales in 1996, 1997, 1998, 1999, 2001, 2002 and 2003, and of the Welsh Cup in 1955, 1994, 1997, 2001, 2002 and 2003. Nicknamed The Dragons or The Linnets, their home ground is Jenner Park, Barry Road, Barry.

Cardiff City were founded in 1899 as Riverside FC, becoming Cardiff City FC in 1908. They play in the English Football League and are, to date, the only non-English side to have won the FA Cup, beating Arsenal 1–0 in 1927. Also winners of the FA Charity Shield in 1927, they were champions of Division 3 (South) in 1947 and of Division 3 in 1993. Nicknamed The Bluebirds, their home ground is Ninian Park, Sloper Road, Cardiff. Tel: 029 2022 1001.

rugby union — **Cardiff Arms Park** was the home of Cardiff Blues regional rugby union club, and the Welsh national rugby stadium 1968–97, when it was demolished and replaced by the neighbouring Millennium Stadium and the new Cardiff Rugby Ground. Although the name is usually given to the rugby stadium, Cardiff Arms Park is actually the name of the complex in which the two stadiums are located and originally consisted of land behind the Cardiff Arms Hotel. In addition to rugby, Glamorgan County Cricket Club played first-class cricket here 1921–66.

Cardiff Blues were formed in 2003 as a regional rugby union team playing in the Celtic League and were in effect a rebranded version of Cardiff RFC. Their home ground is Cardiff Arms Park, Westgate Street, Cardiff, although they have also used the neighbouring Millennium Stadium for some matches. Tel: 029 2030 2000.

Sully Island — An island in the Bristol Channel, off Barry. The rate of tidal rise and fall in the area is the second highest in the world (only that of the Bay of Fundy, Nova Scotia, is greater). A causeway connects the island to the mainland at low tide and many people have been swept to their deaths while trying to leave the island as the tide rises. GR: ST168670.

Temple of Peace — Cathays Park, Cardiff. The Temple of Peace and Health is the HQ of the Welsh Centre for International Affairs, whose aims are to raise awareness of global issues in Wales, campaign to promote world peace, human rights and international understanding, and provide a key point of contact in Wales for international bodies and institutions. The building was begun in 1937 and opened on 23 November 1938 but was not completed until 1946. It was dedicated to the memory those who lost their lives as a result of World War I and houses the Welsh National Book of Remembrance. Originally occupied by the League of Nations Union Welsh National Council and the King Edward VII National Memorial Association, it now houses the Velindre Health Trust in addition to the Welsh Centre for International Affairs. Tel: 029 2022 8549.

Tinkinswood Chambered Tomb — 1 mile (1.6km) north of Dyffryn, 4 miles (6km) north of Barry Town. Neolithic chambered tomb inside a mound measuring 130ft (40m) long by 60ft (18m) wide. The cairn is wedge-shaped with a rectangular stone chamber and is topped by a huge capstone measuring 24ft (7.5m) by 15ft (4.5m) and weighing 40 tons. Excavations in 1914 revealed the skeletal remains of more than 40 individuals. Shards of pottery dating from the Neolithic to the Roman period were also found within the tomb.

Tusker Rock — Located in the Bristol Channel, near Ogmore-by-Sea, and fully visible only at low tide, the rock was formerly a notorious hazard for ships. On 23 April 1947 the *Santampa* was wrecked on the rock, leading to the loss of 39 officers and hands, plus eight crew of the Mumbles lifeboat while attempting a rescue. GR: SS842742.

University of Wales Institute Cardiff — Western Avenue, Cardiff. Founded in 1996 and part of the federated University of Wales. It has its roots in South Glamorgan Institute of Higher Education, created in 1976 from the merger of four further education colleges. It has five academic schools: Cardiff School of Health Sciences (based at the Llandaff Campus), Cardiff School of Art & Design (Howard Gardens), Cardiff School of Management (Colchester Avenue), Cardiff School of Education and Cardiff School of Sport (both Cyncoed). Tel: 029 2041 6070.

Vale of Glamorgan Railway — See Barry Island Railway.

Wales Millennium Centre — Bute Place, Cardiff. A performing arts centre located in the Cardiff Bay waterfront and opened in November 2004. It has a distinctive design with slate-clad walls and a bronzed dome. Two lines of verse, written by Welsh poet Gwyneth Lewis, are inscribed above the entrance and lit from within: the Welsh line reads 'Creu Gwir fel gwydr o ffwrnais awen' ('Creating truth like glass from the furnace of inspiration'); the English is 'In these stones, horizons sing'. The centre has two theatres, the 1900 seat Donald Gordon and the 250 seat Weston Studio and is home to a number of arts companies. Tel: 029 2063 6400.

Welch Regiment Museum

Housed in the Black and Barbican Towers of Cardiff Castle and tracing the history of the 41st and 69th Regiments of Foot from 1719 until 1969, when the Welch Regiment amalgamated with others to form the Royal Regiment of Wales (which became the Royal Welsh in 2006). The Welch Regiment was created at the time of the 1881 Cardwell army reforms and united two regular regiments: the 41st (The Welsh) Regiment of Foot (which became the 1st Battalion) and the 69th (South Lincolnshire) Regiment of Foot (which formed the 2nd Battalion). The 41st Foot was formed in 1719 of Out Pensioners from the Royal Hospital Chelsea and was titled Sir Edmund Fielding's Regiment of Invalids; it was originally only destined for garrison duties. In 1753 it was renamed the 41st Regiment of Foot (or Invalids) and in 1773 was redesignated as a marching regiment. It joined the line in 1787 and dropped 'Invalids' from the name. The regiment saw action in the West Indies during the early years of the Napoleonic Wars and was in Canada 1799–1815, seeing action during the Anglo-American War of 1812–14. In the early to mid 19th century the 41st was in India, Burma and Afghanistan before serving in the Crimea at the battles of Alma and Inkerman. The 69th Foot was originally raised as the 2nd Battalion of the 24th Regiment of Foot in 1756, becoming the 69th Foot in April 1758. Its men served as marines with the Royal Navy for much of the rest of the 18th century, taking part in the Battle of the Saints (1782), St Vincent (1792), the Corsica Expedition and the 'Glorious First of June' (both 1794). In the first half of the 19th century they served in India and later in Burma and Canada. A 2nd Battalion was in existence 1803–16 and fought at the Battle of Waterloo. The Welch Regiment was formed in 1881 and served in South Africa in the 1880s and during the Boer War. During World War I it served on the Western Front and in Salonika and Gallipoli; during World War II the regiment saw action in North Africa, Sicily and Italy. It served as part of the Commonwealth Division during the Korean War. Honours include Detroit, Queenstown, Miami, Niagara, Waterloo, Alma, Inkerman, Sevastopol, South Africa (1899–1902), Marne (1914), Ypres (1914, 1915, 1917), Loos, Somme (1916, 1918), Messines (1917, 1918), Menin Road, Passchendaele, Cambrai (1917, 1918), St Quentin, Bapaume (1918), France and Flanders (1914–18), Macedonia (1915–18), Suvla, Gallipoli (1915), Egypt (1915–17), Palestine (1917–18), Mesopotamia (1916–18), Falaise, Lower Maas, Reichswald, Northwest Europe (1944–5), North Africa (1940–2), Sicily (1943), Italy (1943–5), Crete, Burma (1944–5) and Korea (1951–2). The museum also commemorates the history of the Glamorgan militia, and the auxiliary land forces of South Wales (1757–1969), including the Infantry and Rifle Volunteers and Yeomanry Cavalry. Tel: 029 2022 9367.

Some famous people born in Cardiff

Barrett, Michael (Shakin' Stevens) (singer) (1948–)
Bassey, Shirley Veronica (singer) (1937–)
Brockington, Leonard (businessman) (1888–1966)
Church, Charlotte (singer) (1986–)
Dahl, Roald (writer) (1916–90)
Davies, Len (footballer) (1899–1945)
Edmunds, Dave (musician) (1944–)
Erskine, Joe (heavyweight boxer) (1934–90)
Follett, Ken (novelist) (1949–)
Giggs, Ryan (footballer) (1973–)
Grey-Thompson, Tanni (athlete) (1969–)
Humphrys, (Desmond) John (presenter) (1943–)
Jackson, Colin (athlete) (1967–)
Matthews, Cerys (singer) (1969–)
Morgan, Henry (pirate) (1635–88)
Morgan, (Hywel) Rhodri (politician) (1939–)
Nation, Terry (screenwriter and novelist) (1930–97)
Novello, Ivor (composer) (1893–1951)
O'Shea, Tessie (entertainer) (1913–95)
Rees, Angharad Mary (actress) (1949–)
Rhys Jones, Griffith (actor and comedian) (1953–)
Rubens, Bernice (writer) (1928–2004)
Thomas, R(onald) S(tuart) (poet) (1913–2000)
Toshack, John (footballer) (1949–)
Wingfield, Peter (actor) (1962–)

West Glamorgan

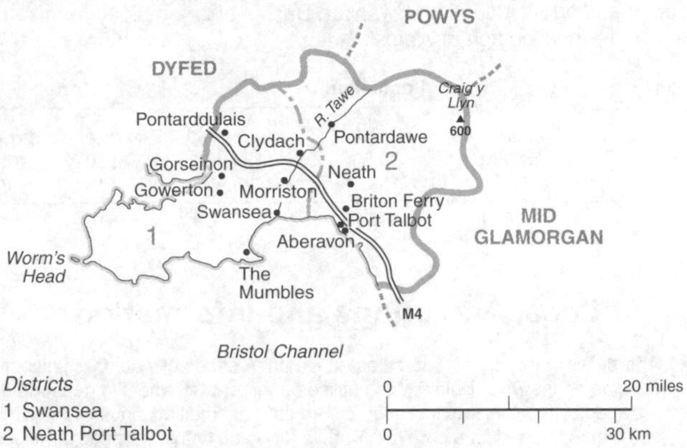
POWYS
DYFED
MID GLAMORGAN
R. Tawe
Craig'y Llyn
600
Pontarddulais
Clydach
Pontardawe
Gorseinon
Gowerton
Morriston
Neath
Swansea
Briton Ferry
Port Talbot
Aberavon
1
2
Worm's Head
The Mumbles
M4
Bristol Channel
Districts
1 Swansea
2 Neath Port Talbot
0
20 miles
0
30 km

West Glamorgan consists of the unitary authorities of Swansea and Neath Port Talbot. It is bordered to the south by the Bristol Channel, to the west and northwest by Dyfed, to the north by Powys and to the east by Mid Glamorgan. The main rivers are the Tawe, which drains into Swansea Bay, and the Loughor, which forms the boundary with Dyfed. The main geographic features are the Lliw Uplands and the Gower Peninsula.

The 70 square miles (180 km^2) of the Gower Peninsula was the first area in the United Kingdom to be designated as an Area of Outstanding Natural Beauty in 1956. Its history, however, dates back much further and it is in fact among the earliest settled regions in Wales, as evidenced by the discovery of the 'Red Lady of Paviland' (actually a male) who has been dated to the Upper Paleolithic period. The Gower has many structures dating to the Bronze and Iron Ages, including chambered tombs such as Arthur's Stone and promontory forts such as the Knave and the Bulwark. During the Iron Age the region was settled by the Demetae. Although little is known of this Celtic tribe, they do not appear to have resisted the Roman invasion in the same way that their neighbours the Silures and the Ordovices did. As a result there are fewer Roman settlements in this area than in the rest of South Wales, although an auxiliary fort was established at the mouth of the Tawe.

West Glamorgan was part of the kingdom of Deheubarth and after the Norman invasion Gower became a Marcher lordship. The economy of the area was wholly agricultural until the 16th century when local resources such as coal and limestone began to be exploited. It was at this time that the port of Swansea began to expand. The 18th century also saw the establishment of the copper smelting industry around the port, which eventually led to Swansea being known as 'Copperopolis'. The downturn in the importance of heavy industry during the 20th century caused severe problems for the region. The economy is now predominantly service-based.

Swansea (Abertawe, 'mouth of the Tawe') is the second largest city in Wales. The settlement grew up around the Old Castle built in the early 12th century by Henry de Beaumont, Earl of Warwick, and its successor, the New Castle, built by William de Braose, Lord of Gower, at the end of the 13th century. The local economy was predominantly based on agriculture until the late 18th century, when the combination of the local coalfields, a navigable river and the proximity to the copper-ore mines of Devon and Cornwall saw a drastic change in the port and its hinterland. Swansea became a hub for the Industrial Revolution in South Wales. During the 19th century it was a centre for tin-plate production, copper smelting and the production of Swansea porcelain. The growth of Swansea was boosted first by the development of the canal network and later by the growth of the railways. The North Dock was built in the 1850s and four further docks were added in the late 19th and early 20th centuries. Rapid urban growth occurred with the influx of labourers to man the docks and heavy industries. With the decline in Swansea's industrial base during the 20th century, particularly since World War II, the local economy has become more dependent on the service sector and public administration. Government departments and agencies such as the Driver and Vehicle Licensing Agency were purposely relocated in order to boost local employment opportunities. Swansea was granted city status in 1969. The 1990s and early 21st century have seen a regeneration of the city with the development of the SA1 Waterfront. In addition to being a commercial centre, Swansea, standing as it does on Swansea Bay, is also a holiday resort which in the 19th century was known as 'the Brighton of Wales'.

South Glamorgan	**Population**			**Area**	
	male	*female*	*total*	*sq miles*	*sq km*
Neath Port Talbot	64,968	69,500	134,468	170	441
Swansea	108,075	115,226	223,301	146	378
Total	173,043	184,726	357,769	316	819

Local Attractions and Information

Aberdulais Falls	Aberdulais, 2 miles (3km) northeast of Neath. A series of waterfalls powering a hydroelectric scheme on the River Dulais which utilises a large waterwheel to generate electricity. The power provided by the falls was first used by the copper smelting industry in the 16th century. It was subsequently used for a corn mill, ironworking and tin-plate works. Some remains of the tin works, which ceased production in 1939, can still be seen. Now owned by the National Trust. Tel: 01639 636674.
Administrative headquarters	**Neath Port Talbot**: Civic Centre, Port Talbot SA13 1PJ. Tel: 01639 763333. **Swansea**: County Hall, Oystermouth Road, Swansea SA1 3SN. Tel: 01792 636000.
Afan Forest Park	Cynonville, 6 miles (10km) northeast of Port Talbot. A 27,000 acre (11,000ha) forest park jointly run by the Forestry Commission and Neath Port Talbot County Borough Council. It houses the South Wales Miners' Museum (see separate entry) and the Theatr Tymaen open air amphitheatre. Tel: 01639 850564.
Arthur's Stone	1 mile (1.6km) northeast of Reynoldston, Gower. Aka Maen Ceti. A chambered tomb consisting of 12 upright stones crowned with an enormous capstone. According to ancient Welsh sources the raising of the capstone was one of 'the three mighty achievements of the Isle of Britain' (the others being Silbury Hill and Stonehenge). The stone, which measures 13ft (4m) by 10ft (3m) by 7ft (2.1m), is a natural boulder which has suffered human and frost damage.
Bishop's Wood Nature Reserve	Caswell Bay Road, Caswell, Swansea. A nature reserve covering 46 acres (18.5ha) of limestone woodland, some of which is ancient woodland. It was designated a Local Nature Reserve in 1975, a Site of Special Scientific Interest in 2003 and Special Area of Conservation in 2004. The visitor centre is a timber-framed roundhouse. It was awarded a Green Flag (an award recognising the value of green spaces for communities) in 2005 and 2006. Tel: 01792 361703.
Botanical Garden at Singleton Park	Gower Road, Sketty, Swansea. Based in the old walled garden of Singleton Park, the garden is renowned for its collection of rhododendrons and also holds the National Collection of pelargoniums. There are also large glasshouses with a selection of plants from different environments around the world. The Botanics in Bloom festival is held every August. Tel: 01792 298637.
Brangwyn Hall and Guildhall	St Helen's Road, Swansea. Swansea's civic centre and the seat of local government, the Guildhall was opened in October 1934. The Art Deco style building of white Portland stone houses the Brangwyn Hall, a performance and conference venue also staging events at the Swansea Festival, and seating a maximum of 1000. The main features are the Brangwyn Hall panels, also known as the British Empire Panels and originally painted in the 1920s by Sir Frank Brangwyn (1867–1956) for the Royal Gallery of the House of Lords. Unfortunately the panels were rejected as 'too colourful' and eventually found their home in the newly built Guildhall. The Guildhall complex also includes the George Hall, which seats 200, and the smaller Kent Room. Tel: 01792 635432.
Brynmill Park	Brynmill Lane, Sketty, Swansea. A Grade II listed Victorian park opened in 1872 and at one time housing a mini-zoo with animal and bird cages. Restoration of the park began in 2007 and a new discovery centre was opened in June 2008. Tel: 01792 280210.
Bulwark, The	½ mile (0.8km) southeast of Llanmadoc, Gower. Located on Llanmadoc Hill, one of the highest points on the Gower peninsula. An oval Iron Age hill fort defended by a complex of banks and ditches.
Cefn Coed Colliery Museum	1 mile (1.6km) southwest of Crynant, 4 miles (6km) northeast of Neath. A museum telling the story of Cefn Coed Colliery, once the deepest anthracite coal mine in the world. The first shaft was sunk in 1921 and the pit closed in 1968. The museum includes an underground gallery and the story of the pit and its miners is told in words and photographs. The remaining colliery buildings include the steel lattice headframes of Nos. 1 & 2 shafts, the south shaft winding engine house, the pumphouse, the boilerhouse and chimney. The museum also houses a unique gas tram, which ran in Neath until 1920. Tel: 01639 750556.
Cil Ifor Top	½ mile (0.8km) east of Llanrhidian, Gower. A multivallate Iron Age promontory fort measuring 1000ft (305m) by 350ft (107m).
Clyne Gardens	Mill Lane, Blackpill, 2 miles (3km) southwest of Swansea. A 50 acre (20ha) garden established by Admiral Algernon Walker-Heneage-Vivian between the 1920s and his death in 1952. The admiral,

who sponsored plant collecting expeditions overseas, incorporated a bog garden, bluebell wood and wild flower meadow amid beautiful scenic lawns. The gardens hold National Collections of pieris, enkianthus and rhododendrons. Features also include a Japanese bridge, the Admiral's Tower and a gazebo. Tel: 01792 401737.

Craig-y-Nos Castle — See Powys.

Cross Keys Inn — Mary Street, Swansea. The oldest building in Swansea. It incorporates the remains of the Hospital of the Blessed St David, built in 1332 by Henry Gower, Bishop of St David's, to provide sustenance for old or infirm priests.

Cwmdonkin Park — Park Drive, Uplands, Swansea. A 13 acre (5ha) Victorian park opened in 1874, notable for the inspiration it gave to poet Dylan Thomas, who was born nearby. In the poem 'Should Lanterns Shine' he wrote 'The ball I threw while playing in the park has not yet reached the ground'. Memorials to Thomas in the park include the triangular Dylan Thomas Shelter and an engraved memorial stone erected in 1963. Tel: 01792 280210.

Dylan Thomas Centre — Somerset Place, Swansea. A centre dedicated to the life and works of Swansea-born poet Dylan Thomas and featuring a permanent exhibition based on the Jeff Towns collection, acquired by Swansea Council in 1999. The many audio and visual displays recount episodes of Thomas's life as well as readings of his poems, together with paintings and sculptures of Thomas and his family. The centre's facilities include a 118 seat theatre; it is also home to the Ty Llen literature programme, which organises annual literary events including the Dylan Thomas Festival during October and November. Tel: 01792 463980.

Egypt Centre — Singleton Park, Swansea. Opened in 1998 as a wing of the Taliesin Arts Centre on the campus of Swansea University, and housing the largest collection of Egyptian antiquities in Wales. Based on the collection of pharmacist Sir Henry Wellcome (1853–1936), amassed in the late 19th and early 20th centuries and consisting of more than 4000 items, it includes artefacts such as busts, weapons, jewellery and coffins, as well as an Egyptian mathematics exhibition. Tel: 01792 295960.

Glynn Vivian Art Gallery — Alexandra Road, Swansea. Opened in a purpose-built gallery in July 1911. It was founded by Richard Glynn Vivian (1835–1910) who donated his art collection to the people of Swansea and funded the building of the gallery. Unfortunately, he died a year before the building was completed. The gallery contains both traditional and modern works, by artists and sculptors such as Barbara Hepworth, Gwen and Augustus John, Claude Monet, Lucien Pissarro and Ceri Richards as well as some Old Masters. There is also a collection of ceramics, including Swansea china. Tel: 01792 516900.

Gnoll Country Park — 1/2 mile (0.8km) east of Neath. A 200 acre (80ha) park on the edge of Neath, based around an 18th century landscaped garden designed for the now demolished Gnoll House. The house and garden were created for the Mackworth family, local industrialists who owned the estate in the 1700s. The landscape was partly designed by Thomas Greening and features both formal and informal elements, including a formal cascade restored in the 1990s. The park encompasses the disused 19th century Mosshouse Reservoir and is located beneath the viewpoint of Cefn Morfudd. Tel: 01639 635808.

Gower Heritage Centre — Parkmill, 7 miles (11km) southwest of Swansea. Housed in an operational water-powered corn mill dating to the 12th century which ceased grinding corn in the 1960s. The mill closed in 1983 and was reopened in 1990 as a centre for countryside crafts including pottery, glassware and a woollen mill. Other features include a wheelwright's shop, miller's cottage and an outdoor agricultural museum. Tel: 01792 371206.

Hardings Down — 3/4 mile (1.2km) southeast of Llangennith, Gower. A hill which is the site of one large and two smaller Iron Age hill forts. The large fort, enclosed by a bank and ditch, is located on the summit, with the other forts close by on the lower slopes. It is not clear why this layout was adopted rather than having one large fort.

High Pennard hill fort — 2 miles (3km) south of Bishopston, Gower. A multivallate promontory fort on Pwlldu Head overlooking the Bristol Channel. Excavations have uncovered evidence of its occupation in the 1st and 2nd centuries AD.

Highest point — Craig y Llyn at 1970ft (600m). GR: SN906031.

Interesting facts — **Swansea Jack**, a black retriever born c.1930, is the only dog to be awarded two bronze medals (the canine VC) by the National Canine Defence League. Having rescued a 12 year old boy from the River Tawe In June 1931, he went on to rescue perhaps as many as 27 people from the river before his death in 1937. A memorial to Swansea Jack stands on the promenade near St Helen's Cricket Ground, while the Swansea Jack Award was created in 2006 'to honour anyone the Lord Mayor feels has made an exceptional effort and shown great bravery for others connected with the city'. Port Talbot-born Millicent Lilian **'Peg' Entwistle** was a good enough actress to have inspired the great Bette Davis to take up the profession; however, she was prone to depression and self-doubt and on Friday 16 September 1932 she took her life by jumping from the 'H' of the Hollywood sign (which then read 'Hollywoodland'), shortly after filming her appearance in the RKO film *Thirteen Women*. Swansea-born **Pete Ham** had an equally tragic death. The *Badfinger* member who co-wrote the much-covered multi-million selling 'Without You', hanged himself in 1975 following bitter disputes over royalty arrangements. Ironically, his former *Badfinger* bandmate Tom Evans, who wrote the chorus of 'Without You', 'I can't live, if living is without you ...' and never fully came to terms with the death of his friend, also committed suicide, in 1983, by hanging himself from a willow tree.

Islands — There are five islands in West Glamorgan, all within the Swansea administrative area and in the Lundy Sea Area. **Burry Holms** is in Carmarthen Bay, near Rhossili Beach (GR: SS397926), while there are four islands in the Bristol Channel: **Middle Head** (GR: SS632872), **Mumbles Head** (GR:

SS635871), **Rothers Sker** (GR: SS611869) all close to Mumbles Head, and **Worm's Head** (named after the Norse for 'dragon'), near Rhossili Beach (GR: SS385877).

Ivy Tower — 1 mile (1.6km) northeast of Neath. A late 18th century castellated folly located on the Gnoll Estate and built by architect John Johnson for the Mackworth family. A prominent landmark, it is 30ft (9m) in diameter. There is no public access.

Knave Promontory Fort, The — $1^1/_4$ miles (2km) southeast of Rhossili, 14 miles (23km) southwest of Swansea. A bivallate promontory fort, one of a series of such forts built along this stretch of coastline during the Iron Age. There is evidence of occupation 50 BC–AD 50.

Leucarum Roman Fort — Loughor, 6 miles (10km) northwest of Swansea. The site of a Roman fort covering 5 acres (2ha) established by Legio II Augusta c.AD 75 to guard communication routes along a Roman road. It was abandoned c.120 but reoccupied in the second half of the 3rd century. Loughor Castle and a church were later built over parts of the site.

Lliw Reservoirs — 3 miles (5km) northwest of Clydach. A pair of reservoirs built in the 19th century to improve the supply of water to Swansea. The Lower Reservoir was constructed 1862–72; the Upper Reservoir was created in the 1880s when it was discovered that the Lower Reservoir suffered from structural problems which restricted supply.

Loughor Castle — Loughor, 6 miles (10km) northwest of Swansea. The ruins of a 13th century castle built in a strategic position on the corner of the site of Leucarum Roman Fort to guard a river crossing beside the River Loughor as it passes through narrows into the Loughor Estuary. The original Norman ringwork castle was founded in the early 12th century and destroyed in the 1150s; the stone castle was first raised by John de Braose in the early 13th century on the top of the 12th century earthworks. The ruins of a two-storey square tower inserted into the existing curtain walls in the late 13th century can still be seen. The ruins now stand close to the A484 road. The site is maintained by CADW.

Margam Abbey — 1 mile (1.6km) southeast of Margam, 4 miles (6km) southeast of Port Talbot. The remains of a Cistercian abbey dedicated to St Mary and founded c.1147 by Robert of Gloucester, probably on the site of an earlier foundation. A prosperous foundation, it had vast estates generating income during the 12th and 13th centuries, although it attracted unwanted attention during the conflicts between England and Wales. The abbey was dissolved in 1536 but the restored nave of the abbey church now serves as a parish church.

Margam Castle — $1^1/_4$ miles (2km) southeast of Margam, 4 miles (6km) southeast of Port Talbot. Gothic style mansion built 1830–40 by Thomas Hopper for Christopher Rice Mansel Talbot. An octagonal tower with attached stair turret rises two storeys above the main house. The house was in a state of disrepair when it was acquired by the county council in 1974. The interior is currently undergoing restoration after being extensively damaged by fire in 1977; the north wing is used as a residential centre for educational purposes and the Great Hallway is on display to the public during the summer. The surrounding 800 acre (320ha) grounds now form Margam Country Park, the features of which include a fuchsia collection and an 18th century orangery fronted by a terrace and three fountains. The 275ft (84m) long orangery was restored in the 1970s. The park has a herd of more than 300 deer, predominantly fallow deer but also including red and Père David's deer. Tel: 01639 881635.

Margam Stones Museum — 1 mile (1.6km) southeast of Margam, 4 miles (6km) southeast of Port Talbot. A museum featuring collections of early Christian sculpture and inscribed stones and crosses from across Wales. The collection includes the Wheel Cross of Conbelin, a highly decorated 10th century wheel-headed cross. The museum is in the care of CADW. Tel: 02920 500200.

Marina Towers Observatory — The Marina, Swansea. Aka the Tower of the Ecliptic. Designed by Robin Campbell in 1989 and equipped with a 20in (508mm) Shafer-Maksutov catadioptic telescope. There is an observation platform and a model of the solar system. The building is topped by a figurehead representing Charles Darwin. Tel: 01639 773783.

Mumbles Lighthouse — 3 miles (5km) south of Swansea. Built in 1794 on Mumbles Head, the outer of two islands. The tower stands 56ft (17m) high and unusually has two tiers, because initially two open coal-fire lights were displayed. A defence battery was built around the southern side of the lighthouse in 1860. The lighthouse was automated in 1934 and converted to solar-powered operation in 1995. The lighthouse is accessible by foot at certain states of the tide.

Mumbles Pier — Mumbles, 3 miles (5km) south of Swansea. Built in 1898, the 800ft (244m) long pier has a fully functioning lifeboat station and slipway. Tel: 01792 365204.

Mumbles Train, The — Linking Mumbles and Swansea, the first passenger railway service in the world, having begun operation on 25 March 1807. Construction of what was formally known as the Swansea & Mumbles Railway began in 1804 and by the spring of 1806, the first horse-drawn goods train was operational. Steam was introduced in 1878 and the line was electrified in 1929. The railway was closed in 1960.

Mynydd-y-castell — $1^1/_2$ miles (2.5km) southeast of Margam, 4 miles (6km) southeast of Port Talbot. The site of an Iron Age hill fort with a bank and ditch enclosing an area of 7 acres (2.8ha).

National Waterfront Museum — Oystermouth Road, Maritime Quarter, Swansea. Opened in 2005 and housed in a building combining an early 20th century dockside warehouse and a suite of new exhibition galleries. The museum is dedicated to Wales's industrial and maritime heritage and the country's contribution to the UK's economy and society, including the role of individual Welsh men and women. A waterfront terrace overlooks a collection of historic ships. Tel: 01792 638950.

Neath — The town of Neath (Castell Nedd), located on the River Neath, originated in the Roman period when the Nidum auxiliary fort was established in AD 75. The town expanded during the Industrial Revolution with the growth of the iron, steel and tin-plate industries. It was also a market and communication centre for the region. Its economy is now based on services and tourism.

Neath Abbey — Monastery Road, Neath. Originally established in 1130 by Richard de Granville as a daughter house of Savigny in Normandy, and absorbed by the Cistercian order in 1147. The foundation was a prosperous one, which caused some friction with the equally well-endowed Margam Abbey, and like that establishment Neath suffered damage during the conflicts between England and Wales. The abbey was dissolved in 1539, after which some of the buildings were used for secular purposes: the cloisters were converted into a mansion. In the following centuries a copper-smelting works and an iron foundry were established in or near the ruins, which include much of the east and west range, the church and the dormitory undercroft. Excavation of the site was carried out in the 20th century. The site is in the care of CADW.

Neath & Tennant Canal — Constructed 1791–5 to link Neath with Abernant. Mainly used for transporting coal, the canal thrived until competition from the Vale of Neath Railway in the 1850s saw the trade dwindle. The canal was eventually closed in 1934. The Tennant Canal was built 1821–4 and joins the Neath Canal at Aberdulais Basin. Only 2 miles (3km) of the canal are now open and navigable.

Neath Castle — Castle Street, Neath. A 13th century castle beside the River Neath, built on the site of an earlier earthwork. Damaged during the conflict between the English barons and the Despensers, who held the castle, it was rebuilt with the addition of a towered gatehouse, the ruins of which can still be seen.

Neath Museum and Art Gallery — Orchard Street, Neath. A local history museum housed in Grade II listed Gwyn Hall, built in 1887. There are two galleries, one featuring archaeological and natural history exhibits and the other containing paintings and temporary exhibitions. Periods covered in detail include Roman, medieval and Victorian Neath. Tel: 01639 645726.

Nidum Roman Fort — Roman Way, Neath. The site of a Roman auxiliary fort occupied intermittently AD 75–320, around which grew the settlement of Neath. Now surrounded by a housing estate, a small section of the stone gatehouse is still visible.

1940s Swansea Bay — Baldwins Crescent, Crymlyn Burrows, Swansea. A museum recreating the Home Front in Swansea Bay during World War II when the port was subjected to bomber raids. Displays include an RAF operations room and an air raid shelter, as well as a reconstructed Swansea street with houses, shops, a pub and the railway station. Tel: 01792 458864.

Norwegian Church — Langdon Road, Swansea. The Norwegian Mission Church was originally erected c.1900 at Newport Docks but was moved to Swansea in 1910. The building had a seamen's mission at its west end and a Gothic-style church at the other. It has been restored and moved to yet another site overlooking the Prince of Wales Dock on Swansea waterfront, next to two other historic dockland buildings, the J Shed and the Ice Factory, and is currently occupied by an art and craft gallery.

Oxwich Castle — Oxwich, 10 miles (16km) southwest of Swansea. Located on a headland overlooking Oxwich Bay on the Gower Peninsula, the ruins of a 16th century fortified manor house built by Sir Rice Mansel incorporate the fabric of the late medieval Oxwich Castle. Built in the 1520s, the house was extended by Sir Rice's son Edward to include a multi-storied range and a six-storey southeast tower. The Mansels moved out in the 1630s and the house was abandoned and left to fall into disrepair, although the south range was adapted for use as a farmhouse. The building has been in the care of CADW since 1949.

Oystermouth Castle — Castle Road, Mumbles, 3 miles (5km) southwest of Swansea. Located on a hill above Swansea Bay, the original Norman timber and earthwork fortification was built c.1100. Destroyed in 1215, it was replaced later in the 13th century by William de Braose with a central keep, gatehouse and curtain walls and became the residence of the Lords of Gower. It was attacked and damaged at least twice by Welsh armies. A chapel was built in the early 14th century but the castle was probably abandoned by the middle of the century and was in ruins by the 16th century. The castle is reputedly haunted by a White Lady.

Pant-y-Sais Fen — 2 miles (3km) east of Swansea. Nature reserve covering 44 acres (18ha) of fenland beside the Tennant Canal towpath. It is a designated Site of Special Scientific Interest. Tel: 01639 763333.

Patti Pavilion — Victoria Park, Gorse Lane, Swansea. Built in 1891 in the grounds of Craig-y-Nos Castle (see Powys) by its then owner, opera singer Adelina Patti, and originally forming a Winter Garden pavilion. Patti donated the pavilion to the people of Swansea in 1918, the year before her death, and it was dismantled and re-erected in Victoria Park in 1920. It has since been used for many activities including rock concerts and as an examination hall, and has recently been refurbished to create a multi-functional space for concerts, conferences and weddings. Tel: 01792 477710.

Paviland Cave — $1\frac{1}{2}$ miles (2.5km) southeast of Rhossili, 14 miles (23km) southwest of Swansea. The site on the south coast of the Gower peninsula of the discovery in the 1823 of an adult male skeleton (originally considered to be female and therefore still referred to as the 'Red Lady of Paviland'), covered in red ochre and ceremonially buried with ivory ornaments and perforated sea shells. Recent excavations and radiocarbon dating indicates that the human presence in the cave dates back 50,000 years, with the skeletal remains dated to 24,000 BC. Although now on the coast, at the time of the burial the cave would have been 70 miles (113km) inland. The skeleton is currently housed at the Oxford University Natural History Museum.

Pennard Castle — $\frac{1}{2}$ mile (0.8km) northwest of Southgate, Gower. The ruins of a small castle probably built in the 13th century beside the valley of the Pennard Pill and above Three Cliffs Bay. Some of the curtain wall remains to almost its full height and there are traces of the gatehouse and towers. It had definitely been abandoned by the end of the 14th century and left to fall into disrepair.

Penlle'r Castell — 5 miles (8km) north of Clydach. The scant remains of a 13th century castle standing on Swansea's highest point, 1227ft (374m) above sea level. There is a substantial earthwork but little masonry remains.

Penrice House — $^1/_2$ mile (0.8km) northeast of Penrice, Gower. Built in the 1770s by Thomas Mansel Talbot and designed by Anthony Keck, with gardens landscaped by William Emes. The house was restored in the 1960s, the Georgian and Victorian sections being demolished to return it to its original layout. Tel: 01792 391212.

Penrice Old Castle — $^1/_2$ mile (0.8km) northeast of Penrice, Gower. The substantial ruins of a 13th century castle standing on an 11th century motte on a headland by the Penrice Dingle. The curtain walls follow the contours of the headland. The castle was occupied by the Penrice family and then the Mansel family until the mid 15th century when they moved to Oxwich Castle. The defences were probably slighted after the Civil War and the castle was in ruins by the 18th century. The ivy-clad ruins, including the keep and gatehouse, stand on private land and are not accessible to the public.

Plantasia — Parc Tawe, Swansea. A hothouse garden divided into three climate zones: tropical, arid and humid. The Tropical Zone recreates a tropical rainforest and includes such plants as the spotted dumb cane and the paw paw. The Arid Zone has a desert environment and plants here include the Cowboy Cactus, aloe vera and a century plant, which blooms every 100 years. The Humid Zone features a butterfly house with a variety of species. Tel: 01792 474555.

Port Talbot — Originally a small market town on Swansea Bay, Port Talbot (Aberafan, Porth Talbot) grew along with the general industrialisation of the region during the Industrial Revolution. By the 20th century the town's economy was built around the Port Talbot steelworks; having suffered a decline during the 1970s and 1980s, along with many other places in South Wales the town is undergoing a programme of regeneration.

Pump House, The — Pump House Quay, Maritime Quarter, Swansea. A hydraulic-power pump house with a tall tower, built in 1900 on Swansea quayside to supply power for the new swing bridge and locks. The building was no longer in use after 1971 and was allowed to fall into disrepair. It was refurbished during the 1980s and became a leisure facility. After further extensive refurbishment in 2004 it now houses a public house and restaurant. Tel: 01792 651080.

River Tawe — Rises below Moel Feity in the Old Red Sandstone hills of the western Brecon Beacons and flows mainly southwesterly for approximately 28 miles (45km) before discharging into Swansea Bay just south of Swansea.

Sail Bridge — A pedestrian/cycle bridge over the River Tawe in Swansea, linking Swansea Marina with the SA1 Waterside Development. It was designed by William Eyre and opened in June 2003. The bridge is 465ft (142m) long; its deck is supported by cables strung from a 140ft (43m) high mast, making the structure resemble the sail of a yacht.

South Wales Miners' Museum — Cynonville, Port Talbot. Located in the visitor centre of Afan Forest Park, this award-winning museum opened in 1976. The entrance passageway resembles a mine tunnel, leading to two rooms with exhibits of early mining equipment plus photographs. Items such as lamps are displayed in chronological order, highlighting developments in technology and safety. There is also a recreation of the life of the children who worked down the mines. Outside the museum are four further exhibits: a blacksmith's shop with forge, an engine house, a lamproom and a sheave wheel. Tel: 01639 850564.

Sport

general — **The Gnoll**, Neath, is a rugby and cricket ground built on part of the former Gnoll Estate. After the land was sold in the early 19th century, the playing of ball games was permitted in the grounds near Gnoll House. A cricket field was established and Neath Cricket Club was founded in 1848. Matches staged in the 1860s included a Glamorganshire XI against a Carmarthenshire side and a Cadoxton XII (one of the many names of Neath CC over the years) and United South of England side featuring W G Grace (who bagged a pair). When Neath RFC was formed in 1871 the playing field was divided, cricket being played in the north and east and rugby in the south and west, and a grandstand was built to join the pavilion. In 1934 Glamorgan played Essex in the first first-class cricket fixture played at The Gnoll and at least one County Championship match was played virtually each year thereafter until the early 1970s. However, the ground was prone to poor drainage; after a series of matches were affected, the ground was dropped from Glamorgan's fixture list. First-class cricket returned in 1985 with a game against the touring Australians but the ground was dropped again in 1995, the last game being played between Glamorgan and Young Australia in July that year. The indoor cricket school built by Glamorgan CCC at the ground in 1954 is still in use; the Gnoll rugby ground continues to be used by Neath RFC. The **Liberty Stadium**, Landore, Swansea, a £27m 20,000-seater stadium opened in July 2005, is the home of Ospreys RFC and Swansea City AFC. It was built on the site of the Morfa Athletics Stadium. Tel: 08712 223224. **St Helen's Rugby and Cricket Ground**, Brynmill, Swansea, was established in 1873 on a reclaimed sandbank and is named after the nearby St Helen's convent. A new cricket pavilion was built and a rugby grandstand erected along the Mumbles Road in the 1920s; the ground is still used by both Glamorgan CCC and Swansea RFC and has staged international cricket, rugby union and rugby league. Its capacity is 4500. The cricket pitch was used by Glamorgan before they joined the County Championship in 1921 and is still used for Championship games. The last one-day international was staged between Pakistan and Sri Lanka during the 1983 World Cup. St Helen's is famous as the venue where in 1968 Garfield Sobers, playing for Nottinghamshire, smashed six sixes off one over from Glamorgan's Malcolm Nash, the first time the feat had been achieved in first-class cricket. The ground is the home of Swansea RFC (the All Whites) and also staged rugby international matches between 1882 and 1954. The **Wales National Pool**, Sketty Lane, Swansea, is the only 50m pool in Wales and is built to Fédération Internationale de Natation (FINA) standards. Tel: 01792 513513.

cricket	**Glamorgan County Cricket Club** see South Glamorgan.
football	**Port Talbot Town** were founded in 1901 as Port Talbot Athletic and renamed to mark the club's centenary in 2001. The club was promoted into the League of Wales in 2000. Nicknamed The Steelmen, their home ground is the Remax Stadium, Victoria Road, Port Talbot. **Swansea City** were founded in 1912 as Swansea Town, changing their name in 1971 when Swansea was awarded city status. Founder members of the English Football League 3rd Division (South) in 1920, they were winners of the division in 1925 and 1949 and of the 3rd Division in 2000, also reaching sixth place in the 1st Division in 1982. Nicknamed The Swans, their traditional colours are black and white. Their home ground until 2005 was the Vetch Field, after which they moved to the Liberty Stadium. Tel: 01792 616600.
rugby union	**Ospreys** were formed in 2003 and play in the Celtic League, of which they were winners in 2005. A regional team initially created as a partnership between the area's two most successful clubs – Neath RFC and Swansea RFC – they were formerly known as Neath-Swansea Ospreys but became simply Ospreys at the start of the 2005–6 season. In their first two seasons, the Ospreys played home games at Swansea's St Helen's ground and Neath's The Gnoll ground; in 2005 they moved to the new Liberty Stadium, which they share with Swansea City FC. Tel: 08712 223224.
Swansea Bay Barrage	The UK's first tidal barrage across a river, built across the mouth of the River Tawe in 1992 in order to create Swansea Marina. The barrage structure includes a boat lock, spillway, fish pass and generator turbine. The turbine serves a dual use, acting as a power generator for the National Grid as well as being used to pump water back into the Tawe river system.
Swansea Bay Foreshore	A promenade running southwest around Swansea Bay from the city of Swansea to the village of Mumbles. The many leisure facilities along its length include Blackpill Lido, Singleton Park and Southend Gardens.
Swansea Castle	Castle Street, Swansea. Norman motte and bailey castle founded by Henry Beaumont on a hilltop below which the River Tawe once flowed. Severely damaged by fire in 1116 and possibly destroyed by the Welsh in 1217, the original earth and timber castle was replaced 1221–84 by a stone castle (also known as the 'New Castle'), the ruins of which cover almost 5 acres (2ha) in the centre of Swansea. Part of the castle was remodelled during the 14th century. In the 18th century it served as a debtors' prison and blacksmith's premises.
Swansea Cathedral	Convent Street, Greenhill, Swansea. A Roman Catholic cathedral dedicated to St Joseph and completed in 1888 to a design by Peter Paul Pugin. It has been the seat of the Bishop of Menevia since 1987, when it gained cathedral status. The total length of the church is 146ft (44.5m) and the height to the apex of the roof is 60ft (18m). The chancel is divided from the nave by a stone arch rising to a height of 43ft (13m), on the jambs of which are niches containing figures of St Patrick and St Benedict. Music-playing angels are carved into the spandrels of the arches and the arch-braced roof is supported on long wall-posts. The five-sided chancel has stained glass by Harding over the high altar. Tel: 01792 652683.
Swansea Market	Market Hall, Oxford Street, Swansea. The largest indoor market in Wales with over 100 stalls, specialising in traditional Welsh fare.
Swansea Museum	Victoria Road, Maritime Quarter, Swansea. The oldest surviving museum in Wales, opened in 1841. Its six galleries house exhibits not only from Swansea and Wales but from all parts of the world, including an Egyptian mummy. There is also a recreation of a traditional Welsh kitchen. The building is undergoing a programme of restoration which began in the 1990s when Swansea City Council took over the running of the museum. Tel: 01792 653763.
Swansea University	Singleton Park, Swansea. Established in 1920 as University College, Swansea and later redesignated the University of Wales, Swansea, adopting its present title in 2007 when it became an independent institution. It has around 15,000 students. The university's academic departments are organised into ten schools: Art, Business & Economics, Environment & Society, Health Science, Engineering, Humanities, Human Science, Medicine, Law and Physical Sciences. Former students include Nicky Wire and Richey Edwards of the band Manic Street Preachers, and politician Sylvia Heal. Tel: 01792 205678.
Sweyne's Howes	$1^1/_4$ miles (2km) north of Rhossili, Gower. A two-part chambered tomb with a northern and southern cairn.
Trafalgar Bridge	A pedestrian/cycle bridge spanning the River Tawe in Swansea and opened on 21 October 2005, the 200th anniversary of the Battle of Trafalgar. It has a fixed span of 260ft (79m) and an opening span of 36ft (11m). The fixed span was brought in by sea in one piece on the largest floating crane barge in the UK.
Tramshed, The	Dylan Thomas Square, Swansea. A museum featuring memorabilia from Swansea's street trams and the Mumbles tram. These include a double-decker tram, a reconstruction of the horse-drawn Mumbles tram of 1804, the front part of a 1960s Mumbles tram and a model of Swansea Bay Station.
Victoria Gardens	Victoria Gardens, Neath. Created in 1897 to celebrate Queen Victoria's Diamond Jubilee. Features include Howel Gwyn's Statue, a Spanish Civil War Memorial, the Gorsedd stone circle (used in bardic ceremonies during the National Eisteddfods of 1918, 1934 and 1994) and an ornate bandstand.
Weobley Castle	$1^1/_2$ miles (2.5km) west of Llanrhidian, 9 miles (15km) west of Swansea. The substantial remains of a fortified manor house built by the de la Beres in the early 14th century. Abandoned in the 16th century, it now stands on the edge of Llanrhidian Marsh. An exhibition within the castle tells the story of Weobley and the locality. Tel: 02920 500200.

Some famous people born in West Glamorgan

Allchurch, Ivor (footballer) (1929–97)	Swansea
Austin, Jimmy (baseball player) (1879–1965)	Swansea
Boyce, Max (comedian and singer) (1945–)	Glynneath
Brydon, Rob (comedian) (1965–)	Swansea
Burton, Richard (actor) (1925–84)	Pontrhydyfen
Charles, (William) John (footballer) (1931–2004)	Swansea
Croft, Robert Damien Bale (cricketer) (1970–)	Swansea
Dalton, (Edward) Hugh (politician) (1887–1962)	Neath
Davies, (Thomas) Mervyn (rugby player) (1946–)	Swansea
Emmanuel, Ivor (singer) (1927–)	Margam
Entwistle, Peg (actress) (1908–32)	Port Talbot
Evans, Edgar (explorer) (1876–1912)	Rhossili
Ham, Peter (singer) (1947–75)	Swansea
Heseltine, Michael Ray Dibdin (politician) (1933–)	Swansea
Hislop, Ian (journalist and broadcaster) (1960–)	Swansea
Hopkins, Anthony (actor) (1937–)	Margam
Howard, Michael (politician) (1941–)	Gorseinon
Howe, Geoffrey (politician) (1926–)	Port Talbot
Jenkins, Clive (trade union leader) (1926–99)	Port Talbot
Jenkins, Katherine (mezzo-soprano) (1980–)	Neath
Jones, Cliff (footballer) (1935–)	Swansea
Jones, Colin (boxer) (1959–)	Gorseinon
Lewis, Tony (cricketer) (1938–)	Swansea
Maccarinelli, Enzo (boxer) (1980–)	Swansea
Milland, Ray (actor) (1907–86)	Neath
Nash, Richard 'Beau' (dandy) (1674–1762)	Swansea
Secombe, Harry (comedian) (1921–2001)	Swansea
Thomas, Dylan Marlais (poet) (1914–53)	Swansea
Tyler, Bonnie (singer) (1951–)	Skewen
Vaughan-Thomas, Wynford (broadcaster) (1908–87)	Swansea
Williams, Rowan (archbishop) (1950–)	Swansea
Zeta-Jones, Catherine (actress) (1969–)	Swansea

Northern Ireland

Northern Ireland is divided into 26 administrative units, called Districts, which were created in 1973. Each District has an elected council which looks after local aspects of government. There are five settlements with city status: Armagh, Belfast, Derry, Lisburn and Newry. Historically, Northern Ireland was divided into six counties – Fermanagh, Antrim, Tyrone, Londonderry, Armagh and Down (FAT LAD being a useful, if politically incorrect, mnemonic). Although these counties no longer have any administrative function they are still very much in use when referring to areas and are the divisions used to subdivide the country for the purposes of this book. Other names in use for Northern Ireland by the various communities are 'The Six Counties', 'The North' – although Malin Head, the most northerly point in Ireland, is in County Donegal – or 'The Province' or 'Ulster'. These last two are also not strictly correct, as the historic Province of Ulster consisted of the six counties of Northern Ireland plus Cavan, Donegal and Monaghan.

At the heart of Northern Ireland is Lough Neagh, the largest lake in the United Kingdom. Five of the counties have an inland border on the lough, the exception being County Fermanagh. Other major inland loughs are Lough Beg, Upper and Lower Lough Erne and Lough Melvin. Lough Neagh drains north to the Atlantic by means of the Lower River Bann and Lough Erne drains westward to the Atlantic Ocean by the lower River Erne. The other major rivers in the area are the Upper River Bann, River Blackwater, River Bush, River Foyle and River Lagan; each of these has many tributaries, which helped to contribute to the development of water-powered mill-based industry at the beginning of the Industrial Revolution. The River Bann system as a whole is the longest river of Northern Ireland at 76 miles (121km). Strangford Lough, Carlingford Lough, Belfast Lough and Larne Lough are all sea loughs. The region has two mountain ranges, the Mournes and the Sperrins, plus other areas of hill country along the Antrim coast, in Down, Fermanagh, South Tyrone and around Belfast. The highest point in the country is Slieve Donard in the Mournes, at 2788ft (850m).

The economy is closely linked to the rest of the United Kingdom with farming a more important sector than in the other UK regions. Agriculture is largely grass-based, with livestock production dominating. In arable farming the main crops are potatoes, barley and wheat. The leading manufacturing industries are machinery manufacturing, food processing, textiles and electronics. There has been a shift away from the traditional industries such as shipbuilding towards aerospace and engineering. The service industry accounts for the majority of employment and output of the Northern Ireland economy.

For a fuller introduction to Northern Ireland please see that for the Republic of Ireland which begins on page 1017.

Northern Ireland population summary

See 2001 Census reconciliation

	Population			Area	
	male	*female*	*total*	*sq miles*	*sq km*
Antrim	328,749	355,625	684,374	1250	3238
Armagh	109,771	112,221	221,992	753	1951
(London)Derry	114,552	119,031	233,583	784	2032
Down	156,576	164,699	321,275	634	1642
Fermanagh	28,818	28,709	57,527	724	1876
Tyrone	82,983	83,533	166,516	1312	3398
Total	821,449	863,818	1,685,267	5457	14,137

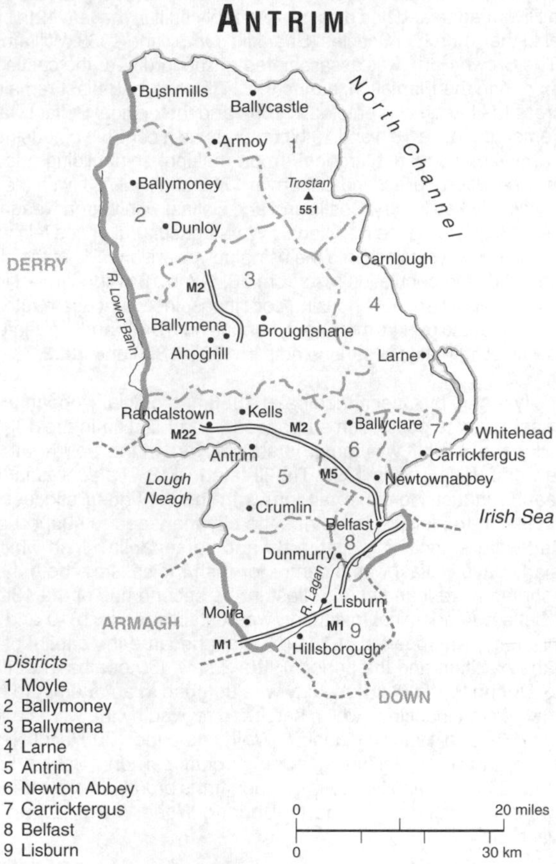
ANTRIM
North Channel
Bushmills
Ballycastle
Armoy
1
Ballymoney
Trostan
551
2
Dunloy
DERRY
R. Lower Bann
Carnlough
M2
3
4
Ballymena
Broughshane
Ahoghill
Larne
Randalstown
Kells
M22
M2
Ballyclare
7
Whitehead
6
Carrickfergus
Antrim
Lough Neagh
5
M5
Newtownabbey
Crumlin
Irish Sea
Belfast
8
Dunmurry
R. Lagan
Lisburn
Moira
ARMAGH
M1
9
M1
Hillsborough
DOWN
Districts
1 Moyle
2 Ballymoney
3 Ballymena
4 Larne
5 Antrim
6 Newton Abbey
7 Carrickfergus
8 Belfast
9 Lisburn
0
20 miles
0
30 km

ANTRIM

County Antrim is bordered on the east and northeast by the North Channel. The River Lagan forms the county's border with County Down to the south and the Lower Bann with County Derry to the west. Lough Neagh forms part of the border to the southwest and the Craigavon district of County Armagh completes the southwest border. The county is administered by nine local unitary authorities.

Lisburn City Council administers 30 electoral wards, however several of these (i.e. Drumbo, Dromara, Ballymacbrennan, Moira and Hillsborough) are geographically located in County Down. Several other Lisburn wards, such as Blaris, Hillhall, Lambeg and Maze, are located partly in County Down. The actual population of Lisburn District is therefore 71,465 as at the 2001 census and the total population of County Antrim is actually 37,229 less then given overleaf i.e. 647,145.

The region has been settled since Neolithic times, when the presence of the rock porcellanite near Cushendall and on Rathlin Island saw the establishment of Stone Age axe factories and extensive trading. During the Iron Age the county was settled by the Dal Riata (called Scotti by the Romans) and the Dál n-Araidhe.

Antrim was conquered by the Normans in the 12th century and became part of the Earldom of Ulster. The county was not officially part of the Plantation of Ulster but MacDonnell, Earl of Antrim, was confirmed in the ownership of a large area of the county, stretching from north of Carrickfergus to Dunluce. English landowners, including Sir Arthur Chichester, acquired estates in the northern part of Clandeboye, an area around Belfast in both County Antrim and County Down, previously held by the O'Neills. The arrival of Scottish and English planters during the 17th century together with a later influx of Huguenot refugees, led to the encouragement of flax cultivation and the development of local linen industries in many of the towns and villages in the county.

Belfast's motto is 'Pro Tanto Quid Retribuamus' (In return for so much, what shall we give back). The name Belfast originates from *Béal Feirste* (G. = the Mouth of the Farset). The settlement is recorded as the Chapel at the Ford in 1306. The original village stood on a ford on the River Farset where it meets the River Lagan and had a castle (probably built in the late 12th century), a church, a mill and a chapel to the Church of Sancles (Shankill). On 6 June 1333, William de Burgo, Earl of Ulster (known as The Brown Earl), was assassinated at 'the ford near the castle'. Although settled by Scots and Manx during the Plantation, during the 17th century Belfast remained a small town. The first bridge across the Lagan was erected in 1682 and the original Belfast Castle burned down in 1708. The town emerged in the 18th and 19th centuries as a centre for industries such as linen – stimulated by the arrival of Huguenot families – rope-making, shipbuilding and engineering. The Newry Canal opened between Belfast and Lisburn in 1763 and by 1793, with the completion of the Lagan Canal, the system linked Newry, Coalisland and Belfast with Lough Neagh. The White Linen Hall was built in the 1780s. During the Napoleonic Wars agricultural prices fell, which helped drive local workers out of the countryside and into the rising power-driven mills of the city. With the arrival of the railway in the 1830s the population rose from 70,447 in 1841 to 174,412 in 1871. The down sides of the rising population were poor housing conditions, the worst death rate in the UK, including a major typhus outbreak during the Great Famine in 1847, and an increase in sectarian violence, which saw its culmination in serious riots in 1864, 1876 and 1882.

Belfast was given city status by Queen Victoria in 1888 and officially became, albeit briefly, the largest city in Ireland when its population surpassed that of Dublin in the 1891 Census. By the end of the 1890s Harland & Wolff was the greatest shipyard in the world, with the *Oceanic*, the largest ship in the world, launched in 1899. The ill-fated RMS *Titanic* was launched in 1911. A flourishing engineering industry grew in tandem with the continued success of the linen and shipbuilding industries. In the leisure industries the city managed to support successful manufacturers of aerated waters (including ginger ale and sarsaparilla), Irish whiskey and tobacco (Gallaher). In its early days Belfast was a centre for Irish radicalism – both the Irish Volunteers and the United Irishmen were founded in Belfast in the second half of the 18th century. In education, the Royal Belfast Academical Institution was established in 1810 and Queen's College (later Queen's University) was opened in 1849. Belfast became the capital of Northern Ireland in 1921 following the partition and the period 1920–2 saw 450 deaths in Belfast as a result of sectarian violence. During World War II the city was bombed in an attempt to disrupt the important shipbuilding and aircraft industries which had been revived by the war economy following the depression of the 1920s and 1930s. Harland & Wolff launched 170 Royal Navy and merchant ships between 1939 and 1945, including three aircraft carriers. Shorts built 1200 Stirling bombers and 125 Sunderland flying boats, while linen firms produced two million flax fabric parachutes. Belfast was also strategically important during World War II as a deep-water port in Ireland with a naval base.

During The Troubles more than 1500 conflict-related deaths were recorded in Belfast, with a further 207 in the rest of County Antrim after 1969. The decline in manufacturing industries, including shipbuilding, affected the local economy but the 1990s and 2000s have seen the beginning of a major regeneration of the city, particularly along its waterfront, Laganside, Custom House Square, Victoria Square and the 'Titanic Quarter' on Queen's Island.

Lisburn (*Lis-na-garvoch* or Lisnagarvey = Fort of the Gamblers) was settled during the Plantation by Sir Fulke Conway. Subject to devastating fires in 1641 and 1707 (thus giving rise to its motto, *Ex Igne Resurgam* – 'I will arise out of the fire'), the town became the centre of the linen industry after the arrival of Huguenots fleeing persecution in France. Louis Crommelin, appointed overseer of Royal Linen Manufacture in 1698, set up a factory in the town, where fellow Huguenots had already begun linen manufacture. Large-scale production began in the second half of the 18th century and the town became a communication hub, connected to the rest of Ireland by canal, coach and finally, in 1839, by rail. Lisburn became a city in 2002.

Antrim	**Population**			**Area**	
Districts	*male*	*female*	*total*	*sq miles*	*sq km*
Antrim	24,242	24,124	48,366	223	577
Ballymena	28,571	30,039	58,610	244	632
Ballymoney	13,323	13,571	26,894	161	418
Belfast	129,778	147,613	277,391	44	115
Carrickfergus	18,239	19,420	37,659	32	82
Larne	15,125	15,707	30,832	130	336
Lisburn	52,979	55,715	108,694	173	447
Moyle	7,831	8,102	15,933	185	480
Newtonabbey	38,661	41,334	79,995	58	151
Total	328,749	355,625	684,374	1250	3238

Local Attractions and Information

Administrative headquarters
Antrim: The Steeple, Antrim BT41 1BJ. Tel: 028 9446 3113.
Ballymena: Ardeevin, 80 Galgorm Road, Ballymena BT42 1AA. Tel: 028 2566 0300.
Ballymoney: Riada House, 14 Charles Street, Ballymoney BT53 6DZ. Tel: 028 2766 2280.
Belfast: City Hall, Belfast BT1 5GS. Tel: 028 9032 0202.
Carrickfergus: Town Hall, Joymount, Carrickfergus BT38 7DL. Tel: 028 9335 1604.
Larne: Victoria Road, Larne BT40 1RU. Tel: 028 2827 2313.
Lisburn: The Island Civic Centre, Lisburn BT27 4RL. Tel: 028 9250 9250.
Moyle: Sheskburn House, 7 Mary Street, Ballycastle BT54 6QH. Tel: 028 2076 2225.
Newtonabbey: Mossley Mills, Carnmoney Road North, Newtonabbey BT36 5NL. Tel: 028 9034 0000.

Airports
The George Best Belfast City Airport (BHD), Belfast. Opened in 1938 as Belfast Harbour Airport, becoming RAF Belfast during World War II, it opened as a commercial operation in June 1983 and was renamed in honour of footballer George Best in May 2006. The single runway serves an average of 2 million passengers per year. Tel: 028 9093 9093.
Belfast International Airport (BFS), Belfast, began life as Aldergrove in 1917 when it was established as a Royal Flying Corps training site. A regular civil air service was begun in 1933 between Aldergrove and Glasgow. A service to London was begun in 1934 from the nearby airfield at Nutts Corner. Both Aldergrove and Nutts Corner were RAF Coastal Command bases during World War II. Nutts Corner was Northern Ireland's main civil airport, 1946–September 1963, when operations were moved to Aldergrove because the runways at Nutts Corner were unsuitable for larger commercial aircraft and weather conditions were more variable. Nutts Corner was the site of the largest air disaster in Northern Irish history when, in 1953, a BEA Vickers Viscount crashed after striking landing lights and a building; 27 people were killed. With two runways and opffering scheduled flights to Britain, Europe and North America, the airport serves on average 4 million passengers per year. Tel: 028 9448 4848.

Albert Memorial Clock
Queen's Square, Belfast. Designed by W J Barre in 1865 and completed by 1870, the tower stands 113ft (34m) high and incorporates a statue of Prince Albert. Having been built on marshy land reclaimed from the River Farset, it has developed a lean of 4ft (1.2m) from the vertical. Restoration work was carried out in the early 2000s with the hope of curtailing further listing.

Antrim
A market town on the banks of Six Mile Water and the administrative centre for Antrim Borough Council. An early monastic settlement here was followed by a 12th century Norman motte. There are many historic buildings, especially in and around High Street; the courthouse sits at the end of the street, near the Barbican Gate, the old gateway to Antrim Castle. There are also hidden gems such as a 19th century smithy (now a shop) on Bridge Street with a distinctive horseshoe entrance. Mill Row alongside the river was home to a paper mill, brewery and corn mill, and to linen manufacture between 1864 and 2000.

Antrim Castle Gardens
Randalstown Road, Antrim. Located within the old demesne of Antrim Castle, the grounds were laid out as water gardens in the late 17th century. There are formal canals lined with clipped lime and hornbeam hedges, as well as yew hedges reaching as high as 20ft (6m). The layout also includes a cascade, a round pond, a parterre and an ancient motte with a spiral yew path. Built by Sir John Clotworthy in 1662 on the site of earlier fortifications, little of Antrim Castle survived after it was gutted by fire during a ball on 28 October 1922. The 'White Lady', the ghost of Miss Ethel Gilligan of Westmeath, a young woman killed in the fire, is said to haunt the gardens. The former stable block now houses Clotworthy Arts Centre. The Deer Park Bridge crosses the Six Mile Water River nearby.

Antrim Round Tower
Steeple Road, Antrim. Aka The Steeple. Built c.10th century, the tower is 92ft (28m) high with a conical cap and remains in good condition, although all trace of the monastic settlement of which it was a part has disappeared. Nearby is the Witch's Stone, a bullaun stone (a large rock where a basin or bullaun has been carved out) with two hollows said to have been made by a witch's knee and elbow when she jumped from the tower in a fit of pique.

Arthur Cottage
Culleybackey, 3 miles (5km) northwest of Ballymena. The restored ancestral home of Chester Alan Arthur, 21st President of the United States. Arthur's father, William, was born in the open straw-thatched cottage on 5 December 1797. He emigrated along with his parents before 1820 and they settled in Vermont. Arthur himself was born in Fairfield, Vermont in 1830 and was US President 1881–5. Tel: 028 2588 0781.

Ballance House
Lisburn Road, Glenavy. A house on the site where John Ballance (1839–93), a future Prime Minister of New Zealand, was born. The current house, which is still on land owned by the Ballance family, was built in the 1840s, replacing the cottage in which John was born. It contains a farmhouse museum, while the parlour is furnished in 1850s period style. Ballance emigrated to New Zealand in 1863, setting up the *Evening Herald* newspaper in Wanganui and entering Parliament in 1875. Prime Minister 1891–3, he was nicknamed 'The Rainmaker' and was noted for his promotion of women's suffrage, progressive taxation and trying to solve Maori land problems. He was also the first Prime Minister of New Zealand to die in office. Now restored, the house is administered by the Ulster New Zealand Trust. Tel: 028 9264 8492.

Ballealy Cottage
Staffordshire Road, Randalstown. A replica of the ranger's lodge in Windsor Forest, built in 1835 for the deer-keeper of Shane's Castle, and restored as holiday accommodation by the Irish Landmark Trust.

Ballinderry Moravian Church
Lower Ballinderry, 8 miles (13km) west of Lisburn. Built by preacher John Cennick and opened on Christmas Day 1751, the original building was renovated in 1821 but was accidentally destroyed

	by fire on Easter Sunday 1835. The present church and adjoining house were erected in late 1835.
Ballycastle Forest	2 miles (3km) south of Ballycastle. Located on the southern slopes of Knocklayd and first planted in 1931.
Ballycastle Museum	Castle Street, Ballycastle. Housed in the 18th century courthouse, the museum's exhibits include the Glentaisie banner from the inaugural Feis na nGleann (1904) and cover the folk and social history of the Glens. Tel: 028 2076 2942.
Ballymena	(G. 'An Baile Meanach' = Middle Townland). A market town built on land given to the Adair family by Charles I in 1626. It hosts an annual agricultural show.
Ballymoney	(G. 'Baile Monaidh' = Townland of the Moor). A Plantation town destroyed during the 1641 Rebellion and subsequently rebuilt. It has hosted the annual Ballymena Drama Festival since 1934. The town's motto is 'Goodwill to all people'.
Ballypatrick Forest	4 miles (6km) southeast of Ballycastle. Mixed conifer forest with pockets of broadleaved species covering more than 2500 acres (1000ha).
Battles	See separate table for details of the Battle of Antrim.
Belfast Botanic Gardens	College Park, Botanic Avenue, Belfast. Established in 1828 by the Belfast Botanic and Horticultural Society on a 28 acre (11.5ha) site purchased by the Belfast Corporation in 1895 and opened as a public park. The cast iron conservatory known as the Palm House was begun in 1839 to a design by Charles Lanyon and built by engineer Richard Turner. A dome was added in 1852. The Tropical Ravine House, known as 'The Glen', was designed by Charles McKimm and opened in 1889. There are many tropical plants including cycads, palms, coffee, sugar, banana, papyrus, bromeliads and a pool with an Amazonian giant water-lily. The Palm House underwent major renovations 1975–83. Outside the glasshouse are a large rose garden, herbaceous borders and rare oak trees, as well as a bandstand.
Belfast Castle	Cave Hill, Antrim Road, Belfast. The original Belfast castle was built by the Normans in the late 12th century. This was superseded in 1611 by a stone and timber castle which was the home of the Chichester family until it burned down in 1708. In 1868–70 a new Scottish baronial style castle was built on the slopes of Cave Hill by George Hamilton Chichester, 3rd Marquess of Donegall, to a design by John Lanyon. The castle and 200 acre (80ha) estate was presented to the City of Belfast in 1934. After World War II the castle became a popular venue for wedding receptions. It was closed 1978–88 for major refurbishment and remains a popular function and conference venue; it also houses the visitor centre for Cave Hill Country Park, with exhibits exploring the story of the people of Cave Hill and the area's wildlife, geology and environment. Tel: 028 9077 6925.
Belfast City Hall	Donegall Square, Belfast. Built of Portland stone 1898–1906 on the site of the former White Linen Hall, the building was designed by Alfred Brumwell Thomas. It has a central dome crowned by a lantern, with towers at each of its four corners. Internal features include a marble lined entrance hall and a marble grand staircase. In addition to the council chamber there is a great hall and a banqueting hall. The great hall was destroyed in an air raid in May 1941 but rebuilt with the original stained glass windows, which had been removed for safe keeping on the outbreak of hostilities. The grounds feature a statue of Queen Victoria and a statue commemorating the sinking of the *Titanic*.
Belfast Custom House	Custom House Square, Belfast. A two-storey Italianate building constructed 1854–7 to a design by Charles Lanyon and W H Lynn. It is decorated with figures of Neptune, Mercury, Britannia, Manufacture, Peace, Commerce and Industry, and originally housed Northern Ireland's Post Office, Civil Service and Internal Revenue Service. Author Anthony Trollope worked here in the late 1850s.
Custom House Square	Custom House Square in Belfast was built on land reclaimed from the River Farset, which runs underground along the edge of the square. For many years it was Belfast's equivalent of London's Speaker's Corner, with orators lining the steps of the Custom House which dominates the square. *The Speaker*, a bronze life-sized statue, and *The Hecklers*, large copper-based lights along the edge of the square, have been put up as part of a restoration and refurbishment project. Belfast's first and oldest drinking fountain for horses, the Calder Fountain, has also been returned to its original position in the square. Today the square's main use is as an outdoor events space.
Belfast Zoological Gardens	Antrim Road, Belfast. Covering 60 acres (24ha), the zoo houses more than 150 species of rare or endangered animals. Opened on 28 March 1934 as Bellevue Zoo, part of Bellevue Pleasure Gardens, established at Cavehill by the Belfast City Tramways in 1913, the zoo suffered during World War II. Having been taken over by Belfast City Council Parks Committee in 1962, the site was expanded and improved, the cramped cages being replaced by natural landscaping with an escarpment and paddocks. The new Belfast Zoological Gardens were opened in 1978. In addition to the normal collection of zoo animals – elephants, big cats, primates and penguins – the zoo also boasts rarer breeds such as the Mhorr gazelle, fossa and Verreaux's Sifaka lemurs. Tel: 028 9077 6277.
Belvoir Park Forest	Belvoir Drive, Belfast. Located in South Belfast on the banks of the River Lagan and opened in 1961 on the former Belvoir estate. The estate includes a Norman motte. The original house was built during the 1740s, when the estate was enclosed, and an ice house was later built into the side of the motte. The house stood empty by the early 1920s, after which it was used as a naval armaments depot during World War II and then a building materials store. The estate was bought by the Northern Ireland Housing Executive (as it is now) in 1955 and in 1960 150 acres (60ha) were leased by the Forest Service. The main house was demolished at around this time; the remaining estate buildings now house the Northern Ireland headquarters of the Royal Society for the Protection of Birds. A new species of tree was found in the forest: Robinson Gold (*x cupressocyparis leylandii*) is named after the Belvoir Forest Service supervisor who spotted a

seedling growing among weeds in 1962. The tree appears on the coat of arms of Castlereagh Borough Council. Tel: 028 9049 1264.

Benvarden House and Garden
Dervock, 4 miles (6km) northeast of Ballymoney. Mid 18th century house by the River Bush in a 17th century demesne. The house and estate have been owned since 1798 by the Montgomery family, who extended the house in 1805; it has since been restored following fire damage in the 1940s. The family built an iron bridge across the River Bush in 1878. The gardens include a 17th century walled garden with rose garden and box and lavender parterre, a productive kitchen garden with hothouses and a woodland pond fed by a burn. Tel: 028 2074 1331.

Bittle's Bar
Victoria Street, Belfast. Bar in a wedge-shaped building reminiscent of New York's Flatiron Building, designed by Thomas Jackson & Son in 1868. Previously known as the Shakespeare, it retains an intimate atmosphere.

Bonamargy Friary
$^{1}/_{2}$ mile (0.8km) southeast of Ballycastle. The remains of a Franciscan friary founded near the coast c.1500 by Rory McQuillan. After its dissolution in 1537 the monastery survived to serve a number of functions but in 1584 it was burned down during an attack by Irish and Scots on English troops quartered there. It was repaired and reoccupied by missionary friars during the early 17th century before finally being abandoned. The buildings were partially restored by the Belfast Natural History and Philosophical Society in 1931 and were placed in state care in 1933. The remains include the gatehouse, church, refectory and dormitory. The graveyard includes burials of sailors from both world wars.

Brookhall Historical Farm
Horse Park, Ballinderry Road, Magheragall, Lisburn. Rare breeds farm and farm museum. The main farmhouse (not open to the public) was burned down during the uprising of 1641 but rebuilt during the 18th century. Cattle include Limousin and Highland. The farm museum has a collection of early 20th century farm implements and machinery. Tel: 028 9262 1712.

Broughshane
(G. Bruach Sheáin = Shane's Dwelling). A market town in the Ballymena District Council area. Known as 'the garden village of Ulster', it is noted for its floral displays and is a multiple Britain in Bloom award-winning village.

Carnfunnock Country Park
Coast Road, Larne. A country park overlooking the sea and covering 473 acres (191ha). Carnfunnock House was built in 1947 on the site of Cairncastle Lodge. The house and estate were purchased by Larne Borough Council in 1957 and Carnfunnock Country Park was opened in 1990. The name derives from *Carn Feanog* (Carn of the Hooded Crow). The park features a hornbeam maze in the shape of Northern Ireland, a Norman motte, an ice house and three lime kilns. The walled garden encloses a series of separate gardens: water garden, rock garden, heather garden, flower garden, scented garden and butterfly garden. Of particular note is the Time Garden, which is divided into four sections of a clock, each three-hour period representing a season of the year (12 o'clock–3 o'clock is spring, etc.) with the planting mirroring the season. The garden also features several sundials, including a sunclock or human sundial. Tel: 028 2827 0541.

Carrick-a-Rede
4 miles (6km) northwest of Ballycastle. A rock island connected to the cliffs by a rope bridge. Carrick-a-Rede (or Carrickarede or Carraig-a-Rade) means 'rock in the road'. The 2ft (0.6m) wide rope bridge was originally used by salmon fishermen to bring home their catch from the sea and spans a chasm 80ft (24m) deep and 60ft (18m) wide. Maintained by the National Trust since 1967, the original single handrail has been replaced, first by a double handrail and, since 2000, by a caged bridge.

Carrickfergus
(G. 'Carraig Fhearghais' = The Rock of Fergus). Possibly Northern Ireland's oldest town, established on the coast around a castle built by John de Courcy in 1180. The castle was surrendered to Edward Bruce in 1316 after a year-long siege and the town also suffered depredations in 1386, 1402 and at the end of the 16th century. During the Plantation the town was repopulated with Scots and English under the guidance of Arthur Chichester. William III landed at Carrickfergus on 14 June 1690 to begin his campaign in Ireland which culminated in the Battle of the Boyne. During the 18th and 19th centuries the town was an important centre for the textile industry.

Carrickfergus Castle
Marine Highway, Carrickfergus. Spectacular castle overlooking Belfast Lough, originally built by John de Courcy in the 1170s and greatly expanded and embellished over the succeeding centuries. It was captured by King John in 1210 and besieged by Edward Bruce in 1315. The castle was again at the centre of conflict during the Civil War and during the Jacobite Rebellion of 1689–90, when it was captured by the Williamites under General Schomberg. It was also briefly seized by the French in 1760 in a raid during the Seven Years' War. After being used as a prison during the Napoleonic Wars it continued to be used by the army until 1928, when it was transferred into state care. It was used as an air-raid shelter during World War II. Tel: 028 9335 1273.

Carrickfergus Museum
Antrim Street, Carrickfergus. A museum dedicated to the history of Carrickfergus. Tel: 028 9335 8049.

Causeway School Museum
Priestland Road, Bushmills. Designed by Clough Williams-Ellis and operated as a National School 1915–62. Exhibits include furniture, equipment and fixtures, toys and books. The previous schoolhouse, built in the mid 19th century, has also been restored. Tel: 028 2073 1777.

Cave Hill Country Park
Cave Hill stands at the end of the Antrim Plateau and, at 1182ft (360m) above sea level, dominates the northern Belfast skyline. The country park covers 750 acres (300ha) and incorporates the Belfast Castle, Hazlewood, Bellevue and Wallace Estates. Originally known as Ben Madigan, the hill has been occupied since prehistoric times and there are five man-made caves which would have acted as temporary refuges. McArt's Fort, named for either the mythical Cormac MacArirt or for the real Art O'Neill, stands on the highest point, which is known as Napoleon's Nose. The profile of Cave Hill is said to have inspired Jonathan Swift to create the giants of Brobdingnag in *Gulliver's Travels*, as from some angles the hill can look like a sleeping giant.

Colin Glen Forest Park Dunmurry, Belfast. Located in a wooded glen on the Colin River in West Belfast and covering 200 acres (80ha). The Colin Glen Trust was established in 1989 to help reclaim the environment of the glen, which had been damaged by the local brick-making industry and land-filling. The upper glen is owned and maintained by the National Trust. Tel: 028 9061 4115.

Conway Mill Conway Street, Belfast. Local economic regeneration project on the site of the Falls Flax Spinning Company (originally established in the 1840s as James Kennedy & Son Flax Spinners) in the Falls Road. One of the earliest mechanical flax spinning mills in Belfast, it closed in 1972. The site and derelict buildings were purchased by the Pound Loney Social Club, which was forced to relocate in 1981 during the redevelopment of the Divis Flats area. The building is listed and owned by the Conway Street Preservation Trust. In addition the Conway Community Enterprises Project works to conserve and regenerate the site and promote and stimulate local enterprises, of which there are more than 40 on site. Tel: 028 9024 7276.

Cranfield Church Cranfield, 6 miles (10km) west of Antrim. Ruins of a 13th century church and shrine to St Olcan, located on Churchtown Point on the shore of Lough Neagh. The nearby holy well produces spring water and amber coloured crystals with supposed powers of healing and protection from drowning.

Crown Liquor Saloon Great Victoria Street, Belfast. A restored Victorian public house, complete with gas lighting. Built in 1826, it was originally known as the Railway Tavern. In 1885 the then owner, Patrick Flanagan, clad the exterior with faience and tiles, while the interior was given an elaborate baroque-style overhaul, possibly with the help of Italian craftsmen working on the newly emancipated Catholic churches in Belfast. The Crown has ten booths known as snugs or boxes, designed for clientele who preferred to drink relatively unseen. They are equipped with original fittings such as metal match-striking plates and a bell system to alert staff that service is required. Maintained by the National Trust since 1978, the pub was restored in 1981. Tel: 028 9027 9901.

Curfew Tower Mill Street, Cushendall. Aka Turnly's Tower. The five-storey tower was built c.1820 by Francis Turnly, possibly as the town jail but equally likely as a folly. It has a single room on each floor (from ground level: dungeon with kitchen extension, bathroom, living room, bedroom, bedroom). Turnly gave instructions that the tower be permanently guarded. The first 'guard', Dan McBride, was armed with a musket, bayonet, two pistols and a 13ft (4m) pike. McBride was succeeded by the one-legged Mr Stewart and finally by Bob Hume. The tower was restored 1992–3 and now offers accommodation for artists.

Divis and Black Mountain 3 miles (5km) west of Belfast. Opened by the National Trust in June 2005 after being acquired from the Ministry of Defence. Divis stands at 1562ft (476m) and the Black Mountain is 1275ft (388m) high. Out of bounds for 30 years while they were being used as a communications centre, they stand as a backdrop to Belfast. The area covers 1500 acres (600ha) of heathland and blanket bog with viewpoints of Lough Neagh and the Mournes. On a clear day the views can take in the Isle of Man and the coast of Scotland. In 1825 surveyor Thomas Drummond (1797–1840) set up his Drummond Limelight on Divis Mountain. The light could be seen more than 60 miles (96km) away in County Donegal, and was used in preparing the Ordnance Survey of Ireland.

Joey Dunlop Memorial Garden Castle Street, Ballymoney. Memorial garden established in the home town of motorcycle racer Joey Dunlop. Born William Joseph Dunlop on 25 February 1952, he began racing at the age of 18. Having won the Jubilee Manx TT in 1977 on a Yamaha and the Classic TT in 1980, he broke Mike Hailwood's record of 14 Manx TT wins in 1992 and eventually took his tally to 26 TT wins, including five TT Formula 1 world titles (1982–6). Awarded the MBE in 1986 and the OBE in 1995, he was killed while taking part in a 125cc race outside Talinnn in Estonia on 2 July 2000. The garden features a statue of Dunlop riding a Honda VTR SP1. There is also a Joey Dunlop Leisure Centre in Ballymoney.

Dunluce Castle 2 miles (3km) west of Bushmills, 10 miles (16km) northwest of Ballymoney. The remains of a castle built, possibly built during the 14th century, on a headland jutting from the north Antrim coast. There are no records until the 16th century, when it was a stronghold of the MacQuillans and later the MacDonnells. Damaged during an attack by Sir John Perrott in 1584, it was repaired and extended by Sorley Boy and James MacDonnell. Randal McDonnell, grandson of Sorley Boy and 2nd Earl of Antrim, built a manor house within the walls for his wife Katherine Manners. The castle was besieged during the 1641 uprising, during which the nearby village was burned down. The 2nd Earl was arrested in 1642, at which time the castle was ransacked. It fell into disrepair after finally being abandoned by the MacDonnells as a residence from the late 17th century. The ruins of St Cuthbert's Church stand close to the castle. The castle remained in the hands of the Earls of Antrim until 1928 when it passed into state care.

Dunseverick Castle 9 miles (15km) northwest of Ballycastle. The O'Cahan family held the castle from c.1000–c.1320, regaining it in the mid 1500s. The last family member to possess the castle was Giolla Dubh Ó Catháin, who left it in 1657 to settle in the Craig/Lisbellanagroagh area; it was then ruined by Cromwellian troops in 1657. Dunseverick Castle and the peninsula on which it stands were given to the National Trust in 1962 by local farmer Jack McCurdy. The Causeway Cliff Path also runs past on its way to Dunseverick Harbour to the east and to the Giant's Causeway to the west.

Feis na nGleann The Festival of the Glens, founded in Glenariff in 1904 under the inspiration of folklorist and historian F J Biggar. Held in June, it includes competitions in language, music and dance, athletics and hurling.

Fernhill House Glencairn Road, Glencairn Park, Belfast. Built 1861–4 by Belfast butter merchant John Smith, Fernhill eventually became one of three houses on the 100 acre (40ha) Glencairn Estate, owned by the Cunningham family (the others were Glencairn and Glendivis). The stables at Fernhill House once housed the surprise winner of the 1928 Grand National, Tipperary Tim. The 100-1 outsider was subsequently bought by the Cunningham family as a hunter. Fernhill now houses the

People's Museum, established by the Glencairn People's Project in 1966. A neighbourhood museum with exhibits covering the social, industrial and labour history of the Shankhill district, it includes a recreation of a 1930s 'wee kitchen house', and also covers the Home Rule crisis – the estate was used by the Ulster Volunteer Force before World War I – and the history of the area during both world wars. The building also has a resident ghost. Tel: 028 9071 5599.

First Presbyterian Church — Rosemary Street, Belfast. The oldest surviving place of worship in Belfast, built 1781–3 to a design by Roger Mulholland.

Flame! The Gasworks Museum of Ireland — Irish Quarter West, Carrickfergus. The only surviving coal-gas manufacturing plant in Ireland. Gas production took place 1855–1965 and the facility was closed in 1987. Restored and managed by the Carrickfergus Gasworks Preservation Society, the museum houses a variety of gas-related appliances and exhibits. Tel: 028 9336 9575.

Forests — **Ballyboley Forest**, first planted in 1957, contains the Killylane reservoir which supplies Larne, Ballymena and Ballyclare. The Ulster Way threads through the forest; **Portglenone Forest** is an ancient broadleaved woodland beside the River Bann; **Randalstown Forest**, on the shore of Lough Neagh, was previously the deer park of Shane's Castle Estate. It was turned into a commercial forest (1934–40) covering 425 acres (172ha). The forest also encloses a nature reserve; **Tardree Forest**, covering 336 acres (136ha) and encompassing two hills – Tardree and Carnearny – is a mixed conifer state forest planted in 1929.

Giant's Causeway — 3 miles (5km) northeast of Bushmills, 11 miles (18km) northwest of Ballycastle. Northern Ireland's only UNESCO World Heritage Site, designated in 1986, and also a National Nature Reserve since 1987. Located on the north Antrim coast, it consists of 40,000 polygonal columns of layered basalt extending from the foot of the cliffs into the sea. 'Discovered' by the Bishop of Derry in 1692, according to legend the causeway was laid by Finn MacCool, either as a means to bring his wife Oonagh from Staffa or to let his rival, the Scottish giant Benandonner who could not swim, reach him in Ireland. More prosaically, the causeway was formed 62–65 million years ago during a long period of volcanic activity. The pattern of the causeway stones was formed as a result of rock crystallisation under conditions of accelerated cooling when the molten lava came into contact with the sea. The same formations can be seen on the island of Staffa, off the coast of Scotland. The Giant's Causeway & Bushmills Railway runs to the Old Bushmills Distillery. A tram service was in operation 1883–1949. The Giant's Causeway is the most popular tourist attraction in Northern Ireland, although Samuel Johnson wrote, rather unfairly, it was 'worth seeing, but not worth going to see'. Maintained by the National Trust since 1962. Tel: 028 2073 1855.

Giant's Ring — 2 miles (3km) southeast of Dunmurry. A late Neolithic or Early Bronze Age henge monument, 590ft (180m) in diameter and rising to 13ft (4m), enclosed by a bank and inner ditch, with a megalithic tomb east of its centre. The presence of a ditch inside the wall and ramp delineating the ring indicates that it was not intended as a defensive structure. The tomb inside the ring is a small passage grave. Excavations and accidental finds indicate that the area surrounding the ring was used for burials during the Late Neolithic and Bronze Age. Pottery finds indicate that the site was in use for several hundred years. A stone-lined chamber containing at least five cremations and five burials was discovered by a local farmer to the northwest of the ring in 1855. Nearby, palisaded enclosures (known as Ballynahatty 5 and Ballynahatty 6) were excavated during the 1990s. These were possibly part of a burial complex involving excarnation (exposure of the corpse to the elements and animals) followed by burial of the bones in 'family' tombs. The whole area appears to have had considerable spiritual significance during this period. During the 19th and 20th centuries horse races and ploughing contests were held within the ring.

Glenariff Forest Park — 5 miles (8km) southwest of Cushendall. Located in the Glens of Antrim and incorporating Parkmore Forest, the park covers 2928 acres (1185ha), including 2225 acres (900ha) of forest. Two rivers, the Inver and Glenariff, run through the forest, while other features include the Ess-na-Laragh waterfall.

Glenarm Castle — Glenarm, 9 miles (15km) northwest of Larne. The original castle was built in the 13th century by John Bissett on the banks of the Glenarm River, which runs into Glenarm Bay to the north. The Bissett chieftains were known as MacEoin of the Glens; the last was killed fighting against the O'Donnells in 1522. The present house was built 1750–6 by the 5th Earl of Antrim and was remodelled in the 1820s. It was damaged by fire in 1929, apparently caused by a fire lit by a servant to warm a featherless parrot, and again in 1965. The 1317 acre (533ha) estate, which includes a working farm, has played host to the World Championship Highland Games. Tel: 028 2884 1203.

Glens of Antrim — A series of nine valleys in the northeast of Antrim, running from the Antrim Mountains to the coast. The nine glens are: **Glenaan** (Blue Glen or Glen of the Proverb), **Glenariff** (Glen of the Plough or Queen of the Glens), **Glenarm** (Glen of the Army), **Glenballyeamon** (Glen of Edwardstown), **Glencloy** (Glen of the Stone Ditches), **Glencorp** (Glen of the Dead), **Glendun** (Brown Glen or Glen of the Dun River), **Glenshesk** (Glen of the Sedges) and **Glentaisie** (Glen of Princess Taisie).

Grand Opera House — Great Victoria Street, Belfast. Opened on 23 December 1895 as a general entertainment venue featuring opera, drama and pantomime. Over the next 80 years it saw the rise and fall of variety as the backbone of live entertainment. By the early 1960s the building was in decline and was mostly used as a cinema, but after a successful campaign to have it listed, it was restored as a venue for musicals, concerts, ballet, pantomime and drama. During 2005 and 2006 an extension was added to improve both front-of-house and back-of-house facilities. Luciano Pavarotti made his UK debut on the stage of the Opera House in *Madame Butterfly* in 1963. Tel: 028 9024 1919.

Grovelands — Stockman's Lane, Belfast. Landscaped gardens located inside the 48 acre (19ha) Musgrave Park, close to Belfast city centre. The series of ornamental gardens, covering 7 acres (2.8ha), feature

	Art Deco entrance gates, lawns, rock gardens, conifers and heathers, plus seasonal bedding and herbaceous borders. Tel: 028 9032 0202.
Harland & Wolff	A Belfast shipbuilding company formed in 1861 by Edward James Harland (1831–95) and Hamburg-born Gustav Wilhelm Wolff (1834–1913). Harland had bought the small shipyard on Queen's Island, in which he was employed as general manager, from Robert Hickson in 1858. Following Harland's death, William James Pirrie was chairman of the company until his death in 1924. During this period the company built RMS *Titanic* and her sister ships RMS *Olympic* and HMHS *Britannic* (the Olympic Class liners became known respectively as 'The Beloved', 'The Damned' and 'The Forgotten'). These were three of over 70 ships constructed for the White Star Line. The shipyard has built many types of ships continuously since then; its main business today is ship repair and conversion work, ship design and bridge building. Harland & Wolff also owns the world's largest dry dock, located in Belfast. See also Queen's Island, Titanic Quarter.
Highest point	Trostan in the Antrim Hills at 1807ft (551m).
HMS *Caroline*	Alexandra Wharf, Queen's Road, Queen's Island, Belfast. A light cruiser built by Cammell Laird and launched from Birkenhead in 1914. The second oldest commissioned warship in the Royal Navy and probably the only surviving combatant from the Battle of Jutland, she serves as the HQ for the Ulster Division Royal Naval Reserve, a role she has taken since 1924. Not open to the public. Tel: 028 9073 9880.
Interesting facts	**Antrim** (*Antroim* in Irish) means 'a single house or solitary place', referring to an early monastery north of the town. The ***Belfast Newsletter***, an Irish newspaper that began publication in Belfast in 1737 and is still going strong, has good claim to be the oldest continually published English-language newspaper. Published thrice weekly during the 18th century, in issues of four pages each, during its time the *Newsletter* was seldom equalled in the breadth and quality of its coverage of local and international events. On 23 August 1776 the paper claimed the first world exclusive when it published the first copy of the American Declaration of Independence seen outside America. **The world's first hydroelectric tramway** opened in 1883 and initially ran from Portrush to Bushmills, but in 1887 was extended to the Giant's Causeway. The project was pioneered by Colonel William Traill (1844–1933) of Ballyclough, Bushmills. Although the line closed in 1949 the stretch between Giant's Causeway and Bushmills was reopened in 2001 using steam and diesel locomotion. **Lillian Bland** was the granddaughter of a Dean of Belfast. As a young woman she wore trousers, smoked cigarettes and tinkered with car engines. She was also a successful press photographer and sports journalist. Louis Blériot's cross-Channel flight of 1909 inspired her to build her own biplane glider, the *Mayfly*, which successfully left the ground on Carnmoney Hill, with four Royal Irish Constabulary constables hanging on to the wings. This 1910 flight made Lillian the first woman in the world to design, build and fly an aeroplane. The flight, which covered approximately a quarter of a mile, was all the more remarkable as the eccentric aviatrix fed the engine whiskey during the flight via her aunt's old ear trumpet. **St Gobbans**, the smallest church in Ireland at 12ft (3.5m) by 6ft 6in (2m), is found in Portbraddan. The church is often visited as part of the 11 mile (18km) **Portballintrae to Ballintoy walk.** From Portballintrae, the clifftop path leads to the Giant's Causeway, continues west past ruined Dunseverick Castle, into Portbraddan and onward to Whitepark Bay, which has a long beach with 'singing sands' – the grains squeak underfoot. Past the islets of Carricknaford, it reaches Ballintoy harbour and the Carrick-a-Rede rope bridge. **Kilroot**, near Carrickfergus, is probably best known for its power station, owned by AES Corporation (the only remaining coal-fired power station in Northern Ireland, providing about one-third of the country's electricity); it also boasts the only salt mine in Ireland. Belfast-born poet **William Drennan** was the first person to refer in print to Ireland as 'the emerald isle' in his poem of 1795, 'When Erin First Rose'.
Islands	There are 20 islands in Lough Neagh. See separate table for details of those within County Antrim.
Andrew Jackson Centre	Boneybefore, Carrickfergus. A restored 18th century thatched cottage close to the home of the parents of the 7th President of the United States, Andrew Jackson (1767–1845). In the grounds is a museum dedicated to the 1st Battalion of the US Rangers, a unit first activated in Carrickfergus in 1942.
Lagan Lookout Centre	Donegall Quay, Belfast. Opened in 1994 to provide an interpretive centre for the Lagan Weir and to chart the history of the city of Belfast and the regeneration of the Laganside area. It features a 6ft 6in (2m) model of the *Titanic* and the story of its maiden voyage. The Lagan Weir was completed in 1994 to control water levels. Tel: 028 9031 5444.
Lagan Meadows	Knightsbridge Park, South Belfast. Pastures, meadows and wetland covering 120 acres (48ha) next to the River Lagan and part of the Lagan Valley Regional Park. Owned by Belfast City Council and managed by the Ulster Wildlife Trust as a nature reserve. Tel: 028 9027 0348.
Lagan Valley Regional Park	A large and diverse country park established in 1967 covering 1600ha, stretching from the Stranmillis in Belfast to the Union Locks in Lisburn and with 11 miles (18km) of the River Lagan running through it. Straddling the Belfast, Castlereagh and Lisburn Council areas, it consists of open countryside (such as Minnowburn Beeches), parks (Sir Thomas and Lady Dixon Park and the Barnett Demesne), nature reserves (Lagan Meadows) and heritage sites (Giant's Ring). Tel: 028 9049 1922.
Larne	(G. *Latharna* = Lands of Lathar). A passenger and freight ferry port for the short sea passage to Troon and Cairnryan in Scotland. There is also a service to Fleetwood in England. Naval activity is recorded from ancient times, but it was only in the 18th century that Larne became an important port both for freight (in particular coal) and emigration. A monument in the town commemorates the *Friends Goodwill*, the first emigrant ship to sail from Larne in May 1717. The development of the port as a ferry terminal was boosted in the second half of the 19th century by the building of a

rail link, and a passenger and mail route to Stranraer was established. Much of the success was due to James Chaine, the son of a linen merchant who bought the harbour in 1866 and set about improving its facilities and communications links. A quay named after Chaine was opened in 1978, while a monument to him in the shape of an Irish round tower stands at the harbour entrance. The port was also a pick-up point for transatlantic crossings from Glasgow to New York. The first dedicated roll-on/roll-off (RoRo) ramps in the UK were installed at Larne and Stranraer in 1938. On 31 January 1953 the MV *Princess Victoria* sank during a gale while en route from Stranraer to Larne, with the loss of 133 lives including 27 inhabitants of Larne. Larne is the major RoRo port in Ireland, with four RoRo berths.

Larne Museum Victoria Road, Larne. A local history museum with exhibits including a country kitchen and a blacksmith's forge. Tel: 028 2827 9482.

Layd Old Church 1 mile (1.6km) northeast of Cushendall. Franciscan foundation and a burial place of the MacDonnells located above Port Obe. It served as a parish church from 1306 until the late 18th century.

Leslie Hill Open Farm Macfin Road, Ballymoney. The largest open farm in Northern Ireland, owned and run by the Leslie family for more than 200 years. The present house and farm buildings were built in 1760, examples of the early buildings including the bell barn, the byre, the potato house and the pay house. The buildings house exhibits of farm machinery, carriages and carts plus written records charting the economic and social history of the farm and its contribution to the local area. It is still a working farm with sheep and poultry. In addition there is a walled garden and a deer park. The farm is described in Arthur Young's 1780 book *A Tour in Ireland 1776–1779*. Tel: 028 2766 6803.

Linen Hall Library Donegall Square North, Belfast. The oldest library in Belfast, established as the Belfast Reading Society in 1788 and located from 1802 in the White Linen Hall. Its proper name is the Belfast Library and Society for Promoting Knowledge, but it is still known by the name of its first home. Much of the 19th century was spent in arguments with Queen's College and whether fiction should be allowed on the library shelves before the library was moved to its present home in 1892. At this time efforts were made to acquire a wide-ranging collection of early Belfast and Ulster publications. By the early 1980s the library was in decline and proposals were presented to close it and move the collections to Queen's University. After a successful campaign to save it, the library now focuses on its general collections and its specialist Irish and Local Studies Collection and Northern Ireland Political Collection. Other reference material held includes a theatre and performing arts archive, a genealogy and heraldry collection and a Burns and Burnsiana collection. An exceptional resource for anyone with interest in Irish studies, the library was restored and extended during the 1990s. Tel: 028 9032 1707.

Lisburn Castle Gardens Castle Street, Lisburn. Located on the site of Lisburn Castle, built by Sir Fulke Conway in 1622 and destroyed by fire in 1707. Only the castle gateway remains. Given to Lisburn Town Council by Sir John Murray Scott in 1901, the park is part of Lisburn's regenerated Historic Quarter and underwent restoration in 2007. It features a Crimean War cannon and the Wallace Memorial, erected in 1892 in tribute to Sir Richard Wallace. Wallace was in Paris during its siege in the France-Prussian War of 1870–1. During the siege he erected 50 drinking fountains to provide clean drinking water for the people of Paris, a number of which still remain today. Five more fountains were presented to Lisburn; only two of these remain, one of them located in the Castle Gardens.

Lisburn Museum Market Square, Lisburn. Housed in the 17th century Market House, which was remodelled in 1888 as the Assembly Rooms, Lisburn Museum was founded in 1979 and expanded with the opening of the Irish Linen Centre in 1994. Exhibits cover the archaeology, social history, art and industry of the Lagan Valley with particular reference to the Irish linen industry. There is also a weaving workshop with hand looms. Tel: 028 9266 3377.

Lissanoure Castle Loughguile, 8 miles (13km) east of Ballymoney. Originally built c.1300, athough little is known about the estate until it passed into the hands of George Macartney in 1733. Macartney's grandson, also named George, was ambassador to China. On 5 October 1847, during preparations for a ball, gunpowder stored during the 1798 rebellion was accidentally ignited and the main body of the castle was destroyed by a massive explosion. Lady Macartney was killed in the blast. The semicircular coach house survived and has been converted into a restaurant. Tel: 028 2764 1132.

Lough Neagh See County Armagh

Loughareema 5 miles (8km) southeast of Ballycastle. (G. *Loch an Rith Amach*). Aka The Vanishing Lake. Located near Ballypatrick Forest on the road to Cushendall. It is so named because one day the level of water in the lake can stand at a depth of as much as 25ft (8m), while within days it can be dry as a bone. It is currently thought that the fluctuating level is due to the seepage of water through porous gravels until it aligns with the local water table. A roadway through the area is reputed to have seen many mishaps, including the occasion on 30 September 1898 when Colonel Jack McNeill, his driver, coach and two horses, disappeared into the depths of the lough while trying to cross it by the road when it was in flood. A ghostly coach can sometimes be seen crossing the lough in the middle of the night. The road is now walled on both sides for safety.

Malone House and Barnett Demesne Malone Road, Belfast. A park set around a restored house built in 1825 by the Legge family. The house was located on the site of the ruins of a fort built by the Hill family which had been destroyed in the 1641 uprising. After passing through several hands, the house was bought in 1921 by Belfast corn merchant and racehorse breeder William Barnett (1868–1946), who bred Trigo, winner of the Epsom Derby in 1929. The house and grounds were bequeathed to the citizens of Belfast on Barnett's death and the park was opened in 1951. The gardens were landscaped in the 1830s and now lie in the heart of the Lagan Valley Regional Park. The park has an extensive collection of daffodils. There is also an arboretum and 11 acres (4.5ha) of meadows, containing more than 70 species of wild flowers. Tel: 028 9068 1246. Close by are Clement Wilson Park and Mary Peters Athletics Track.

McHugh's Bar — Queens Square, Belfast. The oldest surviving building in Belfast, originally located in the Town Dock, which was demolished when the River Farset was covered over. Built 1711–25 as a dwelling house, it was quickly converted into a pub. Tel: 028 9050 9999.

Minnowburn Beeches — An area of woodland in the Lagan Valley. The Minnowburn, a tiny tributary of the River Lagan, joins with the Lagan close to Shaw's Bridge on the southern outskirts of Belfast. Maintained by the National Trust.

Moira Railway Station — Station Road, Moira. The oldest surviving building from the Ulster Railway. Designed by John Goodwin, it is painted in the colour scheme of the Great Northern Railway. It was taken into state care in 1991.

Mossley Mill — Newtownabbey. A former bleaching mill, flax scutching mill and calico cotton printing factory which became a flax spinning factory under Edmund Grimshaw in 1834. Both dry spinning, which produces a coarse yarn, and wet spinning for finer yarn were carried out at the mill. The mill was bought by the Campbell family in 1859; John Campbell improved workers' conditions while expanding the mill and the attached workers' village. Facilities at the mill eventually included a sports field, reading room and cinema. The mill was closed in 1995 and bought by Newtownabbey Borough Council; the buildings were converted to become the Council civic centre, which was opened in 2000. Tel: 028 9034 0000.

Moyle — Moyle district council covers the North Antrim coast and includes the towns of Armoy, Ballycastle, Bushmills, Cushendall, Cushendun and Waterfoot. The smallest local authority in Northern Ireland, it includes the Giant's Causeway, the Glens of Antrim and Rathlin Island.

Nature reserves — **Belshaw's Quarry**, a basalt quarry abandoned in 1950 and now colonised by wildlife; **Breen Oakwood**, a fragment of ancient oakwood underpinned with rowan, holly, hawthorn and hazel; **Giant's Causeway** – see separate entry; **Portrush**, geological formations of fossil-bearing sedimentary shale; **Randalstown Forest and Farr's Bay**, adjacent reserves on the shore of Lough Neagh. Dry and wet woodland with birdwatching facilities; **Rea's Wood**, wet woodland on the shore of Lough Neagh; **Slieveanorra**, four areas of peat bog in different stages of formation on the slopes of Slieveanorra Mountain; **Straidkilly**, mixed woodland on Straidkilly Point giving views of Glenarm, a bluebell wood in spring.

Newtownabbey — Formed by Act of Parliament as a new town in 1958 from the villages of Carnmoney, Glengormley, Jordanstown, Monkstown and Whiteabbey, Whitehouse and Whitewell. Its original motto was *Septem in Uno Resurgent* (Seven shall arise as one). Newtownabbey District Council was formed in 1973 from the original seven villages plus Ballyclare, Ballynure, Doagh and Straid, thus necessitating a change of motto to *Multi in Uno Resurgent* (Many shall arise as one).

The Northern Whig — Bridge Street, Belfast. Built as a commercial hotel and gentlemen's club to a design by John McCutcheon. The foundation stone was laid on St Patrick's Day 1819 and completed by 1822. It was used as offices for the *Northern Whig* newspaper 1922–63. The building was almost destroyed during the Blitz in 1941. After being used as offices from 1963 until 1997, it was completely refurbished and transformed into a bar and restaurant also called The Northern Whig. Tel: 028 9050 9888.

Old Bushmills Distillery — Distillery Road, Bushmills. The oldest operating licensed whiskey distillery in the world and the only one in Northern Ireland. In 1608 Sir Thomas Phillips was granted a license to distill whiskey in Antrim by James I and Bushmills distillery became an officially registered company in 1784. The diaspora since the beginning of mass Irish emigration during the 19th century has resulted in a burgeoning export market for Irish whiskey, which suffered a downturn only during Prohibition in the United States. Located 2 miles (3km) from the Giant's Causeway, the distillery draws its water from St Columb's Rill, a tributary of the River Bush. Malt distilling, blending, maturation and bottling all take place on site. The distillery was improved and extended following a fire in 1885. The company was owned by Irish Distillers Group (now part of the Pernod Ricard Group) from 1972 until August 2005, when it became part of Diageo plc. Tel: 028 2073 1521.

Ormeau Park — Ormeau Road, Belfast. Belfast's oldest public park, opened on 15 April 1871. It is located in the south of the city next to the River Lagan on the site of Ormeau demesne, formerly owned by the Marquis of Donegall. Ormeau House, left derelict in the 1850s, was demolished and the land leased to Belfast Corporation in 1869. The design of the park was the result of a competition won by young designer Timothy Hervey. The park originally reached down to the river but there is now a road along the embankment. Tel: 028 9024 6609.

Ossian's Grave — 2 miles (3km) west of Cushendall. Neolithic court tomb on a hillside above Glendun and Glenaan. It has a semicircular forecourt with a two-chambered gallery. According to legend, Ossian (Oisin), the poet and warrior, son of Fionn Mac Cumhaill (Fingal), is buried here.

Patterson's Spade Mill — Antrim Road, Templepatrick. The last working water-driven spade mill in Ireland. Founded in 1919 on a site previously occupied by a corn mill, a paper mill and a linen beetling mill, it closed as a commercial spade-producing venture in 1990. An exhibition explains the traditional process and the history and culture of the spade. Maintained by the National Trust since 1991. Tel: 028 9443 3619.

People's Park — Doury Road, Ballymena. A 12 acre (5ha) park donated to Ballymena by the Adair family in 1870 and landscaped in 1908. The central features are an artificial lake and adjacent pavilion.

Pogue's Entry Historical Cottage — Church Street, Antrim. Former home of preacher and author Dr Alexander Irvine (born in Antrim on 19 January 1863, died in Los Angeles on 15 March 1941). Having emigrated to the United States in 1889, Irvine graduated in theology from Yale University in 1903, becoming a missionary in the Bowery district of New York as minister at the Fifth Avenue Church of the Ascension. He also wrote many books, including *My Lady of the Chimney Corner*, a memoir of his mother which also evoked rural life in Ulster during the Famine; the cottage is also known as 'Chimney Corner'. Tel: 028 9442 8000.

Police Museum

Knock Road, Belfast. Housed in the Brooklyn HQ and established in 1983 to preserve the history of the Irish police force. Exhibits include uniforms and equipment covering nearly 200 years of organised policing in Ireland. There is also an archive of documents, photographs and personnel records. The Peace Preservation Force was introduced in 1814 by Sir Robert Peel, Chief Secretary in Ireland 1812–18, to combat the general lawlessness caused by such bands as the Defenders and the Peep o'Day Boys, in addition to illegal distilling. On becoming Home Secretary Peel pushed through the Constabulary Act. The Irish Constabulary Act in 1822 saw the formation of the Irish Constabulary Police, the UK's first organised police force. A further Act in 1836 centralised control of the force under a single inspector-general in Dublin and renamed the force the Constabulary of Ireland. The first code of regulations was issued in 1837. Recruiting was on a non-sectarian basis and recruits served their duties in counties where they had no familial connections. On 29 July 1848 a greatly outnumbered force of police managed to quash a putative rising by William Smith O'Brien and Young Ireland in Ballingarry, County Tipperary (derogatively known as the 'battle for widow McCormack's cabbage patch'). The force became the Royal Irish Constabulary in 1867, the first 'Royal' police force in the British Empire, in recognition of its loyalty and effectiveness in quelling the Fenian Rising that year. The RIC wore a dark green uniform with silver buttons and insignia including a badge of the harp and crown of the Most Illustrious Order of St Patrick. The number of constables at the end of the 19th century was 11,000, housed in 1600 barracks. Under a rigid code of conduct, constables were prohibited from entering a pub socially and prospective spouses were vetted. The RIC bore the brunt of attacks during the Partition struggle and the period saw many resignations from the force, which in turn contributed to the raising in Britain of the Black-and-Tans, the Auxiliaries and the Ulster Special Constabulary (divided into three divisions known as the A, B and C Specials according to pay and conditions) in November 1920. During the conflict over Partition the RIC lost 418 men killed, or 1 in 20 of its strength at that time. In January 1922 the RIC was disbanded. In the Irish Republic the force became the Civic Guard (later known as Garda Siochana). The RIC staged its final parade in Dublin on 4 April 1922, the 100th anniversary of the founding of the Constabulary. The Royal Ulster Constabulary came into being on 1 June 1922. Its HQ became Atlantic Buildings, Waring Street, Belfast and the uniform was virtually unchanged from that of the RIC. Its remit covered not only law enforcement but what would now be called anti-terrorism duties. A traffic branch was formed on 1 January 1930 and the first women police recruits were enrolled on 15 November 1943. The traditional high-necked jacket was phased out in 1958. The IRA's 'short campaign' of 1956–62 saw seven RUC deaths. The HQ was moved to Knock in Belfast in 1962. With the onset of the Troubles the police came under considerable pressure and, following an October 1969 report by Lord Hunt, the RUC underwent a complete restructuring in an attempt to modernise it and bring it more into line with police organisation in the rest of the UK. Rank and promotion structures were aligned with those of other British forces. The Ulster Special Constabulary (the B Specials) was disbanded and the RUC Reserve became an auxiliary police force. All military-style duties were transferred to the Ulster Defence Force. A Police Authority was created to represent the entire community. Between 1969 and 1994 195 RUC and 101 RUC Reserve members lost their lives; RUC officers received 16 George Medals and 103 Queen's Gallantry Medals. A Policing Review under the terms of the Belfast Agreement was carried out by the Patten Commission. As a result the RUC became the Police Service of Northern Ireland (PSNI) on 4 November 2001. The PSNI badge features the saltire of St Patrick and six symbols representing shared traditions: a crown, a harp, a shamrock, scales of justice, a torch and a laurel leaf. Tel: 028 9065 0222.

Prisons

Crumlin Road, a former prison (derelict since 1996) in north Belfast where Republican and Loyalist suspects facing terrorist charges were held on remand. Crumlin Road also held top security prisoners; an underground tunnel connected it with one of Belfast's main courts.

Hydebank Wood, Hospital Road, Belfast. A Young Offenders' Centre opened in 1979 and housing young adult male prisoners. Operational capacity: 306. Tel: 028 9025 3666.

Maghaberry, Lisburn. A high security prison opened in 1987 and housing adult male offenders. Operational capacity: 745. Tel: 028 9261 1888.

Maze (known locally as the H Blocks, Long Kesh or the Maze), a disused prison sited at the former RAF station at Long Kesh, near Lisburn. The name 'Maze' is taken from the nearby village of the same name. The prison housed mainly political prisoners and was the focus of much controversy. It became notorious as the scene of the 'blanket protest', part of a dispute involving Provisional IRA and Irish National Liberation Army prisoners. Republican prisoners' status as political prisoners had begun to be phased out in 1975. Among other things, this meant that they would now be required to wear prison uniforms like ordinary convicts. The men refused to accept that they were ordinary criminals and refused to wear the prison uniform; instead, they modified prison blankets and wore those instead. The blanket protest was combined with the 'dirty protest' (in which prisoners accused wardens of beating them during 'slopping out' and retaliated by urinating on the floors and smearing the walls with faeces). Both protests were eventually abandoned after the 1981 Irish Hunger Strike, which witnessed the death of newly elected MP Bobby Sands. Two days later, the incoming Northern Ireland Secretary, James Prior, announced that from then on all paramilitary prisoners would be allowed to wear their own clothes. The prison was closed in 2000.

Queen's Island

A 17 acre (7ha) island on the east side of the River Lagan, created in 1849 from the spoil dredged to make the Victoria Channel, which enabled larger ships to enter the River Lagan irrespective of tidal conditions. Originally named Dargan's Island, it was renamed Queen's Island on the occasion of the royal family's visit to Belfast the same year. In 1851 the first ships were built at Queen's Island after Kirwan McCune moved their yard there. See also Harland & Wolff, Titanic Quarter.

Queen's University — Established as a non-denominational college in 1845 and opened as one of three Queen's Colleges in Ireland (the others being Cork and Galway) with 195 students in 1849. Many of its early staff and students had transferred from the Royal Belfast Academical Institution, which had been established in 1810 and which closed its collegiate department in October 1849 when Queen's opened. In 1908 the three Queen's Colleges were dissolved and replaced by the Queen's University of Belfast and the National University of Ireland. Full rights for women students were granted in the 1880s and a charter of 1908 guaranteed women equal eligibility to hold office and also made provision for a student on the Senate, the university's governing body. The university has more than 23,000 postgraduate and undergraduate students and has three faculties: Arts, Humanities & Social Sciences, Medicine, Health & Life Sciences, and Engineering and Physical Sciences. Teacher training is covered by St Mary's University College and Stranmillis University College. The first college building was designed by Sir Charles Lanyon; the university now has facilities at the Royal Victoria and City Hospitals and the Marine Biology Station at Portaferry. The campus also boasts the Queen's Film Theatre, the Naughton Gallery and the Seamus Heaney Centre for Poetry. Former students include poets Seamus Heaney and Paul Muldoon, actors Simon Callow and Liam Neeson, and film critic Alexander Walker. Tel: 028 9024 5133.

Ramsar Sites — **Garry Bog** (155ha), lowland raised bog; **Garron Plateau** (4650ha), large area of blanket bog; **Larne Lough** (398ha), lough supporting internationally important numbers of light-bellied brent geese; **Belfast Lough** (432ha), intertidal sea lough supporting internationally important numbers of redshank.

Randalstown — A town established around an iron works on the River Maine in the first half of the 17th century. Originally called *An Dun Mor* (The Great Fort) and then Mullynierin (Iron Mills), it was renamed in 1666 after Randal MacDonnell, 2nd Earl and 1st Marquis of Antrim. Textile manufacture began in the early 19th century. The town benefited from being a coach stop and later a railway halt. The Old Bleach Linen Company factory was opened in 1864 and remained a major employer until its closure in 1980. The town was the first in Ireland to be lit by electricity generated by turbines; one of the original turbines now forms the base of a sculpture which, together with artefacts from the Old Bleach Linen factory, reflects Randalstown's industrial heritage.

Rathlin Island — Located 6 miles (10km) off Ballycastle on the north Antrim coast. A Special Protection Area and Special Area of Conservation, the island supports internationally important breeding numbers of migratory species including razorbill, guillemot and kittiwake. Geologically composed of a foundation of Ulster white limestone topped by layers of basalt. Inhabited since the Mesolithic period, it has a rich history. During the Neolithic it appears to have been a trading centre for stone tools and over the next centuries it was home to the Firbolgs, Tuatha De Danann, Celts and Scoti. The first church was built on Rathlin in 580 and the island was subject to Viking raids. During the Norman invasion of Ireland the island changed hands many times between John de Courcy, King John and Hugh de Lacy until it came under control of the Bisset and McDonnell families. Bruce's Cave is purportedly the place where Robert the Bruce gained encouragement from the trials of a spider in 1306 (one of at least three places to make this claim). The island was also litigated over between Scotland and Ireland, and found to be Irish because there were no snakes (St Patrick is said to have banished all snakes from Ireland in the 5th century). It saw conflict during the 16th and 17th century, its inhabitants being massacred in 1557, 1575 and 1642. The island's later history is of relative peace interspersed with the occasional shipwreck, such as the torpedoing of HMS *Drake* by German U-boat *U79* on 2 October 1917. The ship was able to enter Church Bay on Rathlin before sinking. There are three lighthouses on the island: East (built 1856), West (built 1917) and Rue Point (built 1921). Three wind turbines, known as the Children of Lir after the legendary children who were turned into swans by their wicked stepmother, have been erected to provide electricity generation. There is an RSPB reserve located on Rathlin Island, near West Lighthouse in the Kebble National Nature Reserve, and home to a large colony of seabirds including fulmars, guillemots, kittiwakes and puffins. Tel: 028 2076 3948. Area: 12.91 sq miles (33.44 sq km). Population: 100.

Rivers — The **Lower Bann** see entry in County Derry. The **Lagan** rises on Slieve Croob mountain in County Down and runs for 40 miles (64km) to Belfast Lough. The river forms the border between County Antrim and County Down. Its maximum width is 360ft (110m) below McConnell Piers. It is at its narrowest at 98ft (30m) between Cutters Wharf and Stranmillis Weir. The Lagan is fully tidal from Belfast Lough to the Lagan Weir, which was completed in 1994 to control the level of water upstream as far as Stranmillis Weir.

Robinson & Cleaver's — Donegall Square North, Belfast. Robinson & Cleaver's Royal Irish Linen Warehouse was designed by Young and Mackenzie and built 1886–8. The building is adorned with the carved heads of 50 of the department store's patrons, including Queen Victoria, Prince Albert, the Kaiser and the Maharajah of Cooch Behar. The interior was notable for the staircase, made from Australian jarrah wood. It closed in 1970s and the building now houses shops and offices.

Royal Belfast Academical Institution — College Square East, Belfast. The RBAI (also known simply as Inst.) was established in 1810 to replace William Bruce's Belfast Academy and opened in a building designed by John Soane on 1 February 1814. Originally both a school and a college, the collegiate department was closed in 1849 when Queen's College opened. Tel: 028 9024 0461.

Royal Irish Regiment Museum — St Patrick's Barracks, Ballymena. The museum includes exhibits covering the regiment's history from 1689, when the Inniskilling Regiment was raised (see County Fermanagh: Royal Inniskilling Fusiliers). On 1 July 1968 the Royal Inniskilling Fusiliers, Royal Ulster Rifles and Royal Irish

Fusiliers became the Royal Irish Rangers, which in turn amalgamated with the Ulster Defence Regiment on 1 July 1992 to become the Royal Irish Regiment. The regiment has a chapel in Belfast St Anne's Cathedral. Tel: 028 2566 1383.

Royal Ulster Rifles Museum Waring Street, Belfast. Located behind the Northern Ireland War Memorial Building, the museum is dedicated to the history of the Royal Ulster Rifles and the Royal Irish Rifles from their foundation in 1793 as the 83rd and 86th Regiments of Foot. The regiments saw action in the West Indies, Egypt, South Africa, the Peninsula and India during the Napoleonic Wars, also serving with distinction during the Indian Mutiny of 1857. In 1881 they were formed into the Royal Irish Rifles. Service during the Boer War was followed by World War I, when the regiment was present on the Western Front throughout the conflict and also sent battalions to Gallipoli, Macedonia and Palestine. In 1921 the regiment's name was changed to the Royal Ulster Rifles (RUR). The London Irish Rifles joined the RUR in 1937. During World War II battalions of the regiment saw action at Dunkirk, in Africa, Sicily, Italy and Austria, also taking part in D-Day and the drive through France, Belgium and Holland into Germany. After World War II the regiment saw service in Palestine, Korea, Cyprus and Borneo. On 1 July 1968 the Royal Inniskilling Fusiliers, Royal Ulster Rifles and Royal Irish Fusiliers became the Royal Irish Rangers,and were in turn amalgamated with the Ulster Defence Regiment on 1 July 1992 to become the Royal Irish Regiment. Its motto is *Quis Separabit* (Who will separate us?). Tel: 028 9023 2086.

St Anne's Cathedral Donegall Street, Belfast. A Church of Ireland cathedral built in Hiberno-Romanesque style on the site of St Anne's Church (itself founded in 1776 and demolished in 1903). It was constructed in stages; although the foundation stone was laid in 1899, the north transept was not completed until 1981. It contains the largest Celtic cross in Ireland.

St Catherine's Parish Church Killead, 3 miles (5km) northeast of Crumlin. Located inside the Aldergrove RAF base. Built in 1712 and altered in 1885 in Gothic Revival style with a William Morris stained glass window, the church was restored 2003–04.

St George's Market May Street, Belfast. Constructed 1890–5 to a design by J C Bretland. Originally a market for fruit, butter, eggs and poultry, it is the only surviving original market building in Belfast. After going into decline along with the rest of Belfast's market district, the building was restored and reopened in 1999 as a covered market and retail space.

St Peter's Cathedral St Peter's Square, Belfast. Catholic cathedral built 1860–6 in Gothic Revival style to a design by Fr Jeremiah McAuley. The land for the building was donated by bakery magnate Bernard 'Barney' Hughes (1808–78). The distinctive twin spires were added in 1885. It was officially dedicated as the cathedral church of Down and Connor in 1988.

Samson and Goliath Twin shipbuilding gantry cranes built by Krupp on behalf of Harland & Wolff Shipbuilders. Situated at Queen's Island, they dominate the Belfast skyline. Goliath, completed in 1969, stands 315ft (96m) high; Samson was completed in 1974 and is 348ft (106m) high. Each has a lifting capacity of 840 tonnes. Scheduled as historic monuments since 2003, the cranes stand over the largest dry dock in the world, now located next to the Titanic Quarter.

Shanes Castle Randalstown Road, Antrim. Aka the Castle of Edenduffcarrick (G. Éadan Duibh Charraige = Hill of the Black Rock). Ruins of a 17th century tower house within an 18th century castle on the shore of Lough Neagh. The original castle was built by Shane O'Neill and the estate is the family seat of the O'Neills of Clanaboy. The castle was destroyed by fire in 1816 although a camellia house and long terrace remain standing. The present house was built in 1958. The woodland at Shane's Castle includes oak, beech, ash, sycamore and Scots pine plus specimen trees from the former park, much of which west of the River Main is now in Randalstown Forest.

Sinclair Seamen's Presbyterian Church Corporation Square, Belfast. Dedicated to seafarers and built 1856–7 in the Sailortown area of Belfast to a design by Charles Lanyon, W H Lynn and John Lanyon. The church has an unusual 'L' shape with a prominent campanile and was erected in memory of merchant John Sinclair. It is bedecked with naval memorabilia: the pulpit is shaped like a ship's prow, the baptismal font is a binnacle (compass house), the collection boxes are shaped as lifeboats and the organ has port and starboard lights. A bell from HMS *Hood* is rung at the start of each service The stained glass windows also have a nautical theme.

Sir Thomas and Lady Dixon Park Upper Malone Road, Belfast. Rolling parkland of 130 acres (53ha) south of Belfast. A series of circular themed rose gardens feature a total of 25,000 bushes; in the Historic Rose Garden the species are laid out along a spiral path in the chronological order of their introduction into cultivation, while the Heritage Rose Garden emphasises Northern Ireland's contribution to rose breeding. In addition to a walled garden there is an area with 100 camellia varieties as part of the International Camellia Trials, and a Japanese garden which has the six qualities believed to create a perfect garden: abundant water, antiquity, artifice, broad views, seclusion and spaciousness. Tel: 028 9027 0466.

Sport

football **Ballymena United** were founded in 1928 and won the Irish League 1st Division in 1997. Nicknamed The Sky Blues, they play at Ballymena Showgrounds.

Cliftonville were founded in 1879. They are winners of the Irish League championship in 1906, 1910 and 1998, and the Irish Cup in 1883, 1888, 1900, 1901, 1907, 1909 and 1979. Nicknamed The Reds, their home ground is The Solitude, Belfast.

Glentoran were founded in 1882. They are winners of the Irish League championship in 1894, 1897, 1905, 1912, 1913, 1921, 1925, 1931, 1951, 1953, 1964, 1967, 1968, 1970, 1972, 1977, 1981, 1988, 1992, 1999 and 2003, of the Irish Premier League in 2005, and of the Irish Cup in 1914, 1917, 1921, 1932, 1933, 1935, 1951, 1966, 1973, 1983, 1985, 1986, 1987, 1988, 1990, 1996, 1998, 2000, 2001 and 2004. Nicknamed The Glens, their home ground is The Oval Grounds, Mersey Street, Belfast.

Larne were founded in 1890. Nicknamed The Harbour Rats, their home ground is Inver Park, Inver Road, Larne.

Linfield were founded in 1886. They are winners of the Irish League championship in 1891, 1892, 1893, 1895, 1898, 1902, 1904, 1907, 1908, 1909, 1911, 1914, 1922, 1923, 1930, 1932, 1934, 1935, 1949, 1950, 1954, 1955, 1956, 1959, 1961, 1962, 1966, 1969, 1971, 1975, 1978, 1979, 1980, 1982, 1983, 1984, 1985, 1986, 1987, 1989, 1993, 1994, 2000 and 2001, of the Irish Premier League in 2004, 2006, 2007 and 2008, and of the Irish Cup in 1891, 1892, 1893, 1895, 1898, 1899, 1902, 1904, 1912, 1913, 1915, 1916, 1919, 1922, 1923, 1930, 1932, 1934, 1936, 1939, 1942, 1945, 1946, 1948, 1950, 1953, 1960, 1962, 1963, 1970, 1978, 1980, 1982, 1994, 1995 and 2002. Nicknamed The Blues, their home ground is Windsor Park, Donegall Avenue, Belfast.

Lisburn Distillery were founded in 1880. They are winners of the Irish League championship in 1896, 1899, 1901, 1903, 1906 and 1963, and of the Irish Cup in 1884, 1885, 1886, 1889, 1894, 1896, 1903, 1905, 1910, 1925, 1956 and 1971. Nicknamed The Whites, their home ground is New Grosvenor Stadium, Larne.

horse racing

Down Royal Racecourse, Maze, Lisburn. The Down Royal Corporation of Horsebreeders was created by royal charter in 1685 and moved from Downpatrick to Down Royal in the early 1700s. The square right-handed track, almost 2 miles (3km) in circumference, has a downhill run into the straight with a slight uphill finish to the post. Tel: 028 9262 1256.

ice hockey

Belfast Giants, founded in 2000, are winners of the Superleague in 2002, the Superleague play-offs in 2003, the British Cross-League in 2005 and the Elite League in 2006. They play at the Odyssey Arena, Belfast.

rugby union

The **Irish Rugby Football Union Ulster Branch** (known as Ulster Rugby) was founded in 1879 and is responsible for the Ulster team which plays at Ravenhill, Belfast. The team won the Heineken Cup in 1999, the Celtic Cup in 2004 and the Celtic League in 2006.

Stormont Estate

Area of government grounds and buildings in the Stormont suburb of east Belfast. The main buildings include Stormont Castle (castle in name only and erstwhile residence of the Prime Minister of Northern Ireland and now the main meeting place of the Northern Ireland Executive), the Parliament Buildings (the seat of the Northern Ireland Assembly, usually referred to as Stormont), and the Castle Buildings (headquarters for Office of the First Minister and Deputy First Minister and the Department of Health, Social Services and Public Safety).

Titanic Quarter

A waterfront development of residential, business, light industrial and leisure facilities on part of the former Harland & Wolff shipyard on Queen's Island, Belfast. It includes the Northern Ireland Science Park, as well as heritage sites such as the former Harland & Wolff HQ Building, the Alexandra Graving Dock, the Thompson Graving Dock (including the Pump House), the Hamilton Graving Dock and the RMS *Titanic* and *Olympic* slipways.

Ulster Hall

Bedford Street, Belfast. Built in 1862 to a design by W J Barre and now a venue for sporting events, classical and pop concerts and religious services. Purchased by Belfast City Council in 1902, it houses the Mulholland Grand Organ and is home to the Group Theatre. Tel: 028 9032 3900.

Ulster Museum

Botanic Gardens, Belfast. Opened in 1929 as the Belfast Museum and Art Gallery. It became the Ulster Museum as a national museum serving the whole of Northern Ireland in the 1960s, and reopened after major redevelopment in 2009. The museum charts the heritage and natural history of Ulster. It is part of the National Museums and Galleries of Northern Ireland, which also includes the Ulster Folk and Transport Museum, the Ulster-American Folk Park and the interactive discovery centre W5. Tel: 028 9038 3000.

War Memorial Building

Waring Street, Belfast. The Northern Ireland War Memorial, commemorating the dead of both world wars. The building fund was launched in 1947 and the building was opened in 1963. An exhibition highlighting the part played by the people of Northern Ireland during World War II, including the role of women and the contribution of local industry to the war effort, is housed on the ground floor. Tel: 028 9032 0392.

The White House

Whitehouse Park, Newtownabbey. Fortified house overlooking Belfast Lough built in the early 16th century and given to Captain Brunker by Elizabeth I in 1574. Originally painted with a limestone wash (hence the name), it was initially four or five storeys in height, with round towers on the corners of the frontage and a third in the centre of the rear. William III met with General Schomberg here in 1690 having sailed into Belfast Lough and landed at Carrickfergus. After falling into decline the White House was used for stabling until 1923 when it became a Gospel Hall. In the late 1990s it was purchased on behalf of the Abbey Historical Society. Tel: 028 9080 1690.

Whitehead Excursion Station

Castleview Road, Whitehead, 5 miles (8km) northwest of Carrickfergus. Opened in 1907 as an overflow platform for excursions from Belfast, since 1966 the station has been the HQ of the Railway Preservation Society of Ireland. The site includes a carriage shed and a locomotive workshop. There is a large collection of Irish standard gauge steam locomotives and coaches, including the last steam locomotive built for an Irish railway, No. 27 *Lough Erne*.

Whitepark Bay

7 miles (11km) northwest of Ballycastel. A north-facing sandy bay on the Atlantic, lying between Port Braddan and Dundriff. In Neolithic times it was home to some of Ireland's earliest settlers; the limestone cliffs which form a backdrop to the bay were a rich source of flint. There are a number of dolmen burial chambers in the area. The bay is a designated Area of Special Scientific Interest notable for its flora and fauna such as the frog orchid, pyramidal orchid, fragrant orchid and bee orchid. Butterfly species include the dark green fritillary. Many birds such as ringed plover, oystercatcher and eider use the bay for nesting. Also in the area is St Gobhan's Church in Port Braddan, reputedly Ireland's smallest church at just 10ft (3m) by 6ft (1.8m). Owned by the National Trust.

Woods on Your Doorstep

Carnmoney Hill (168 acres/68ha), above Newtownabbey, mainly mixed ashwoods and hedgerow; **Clements Wood** (10 acres/4ha), Ballygowan Road, Larne. Named for the first owners of the land in the 1800s and located between the River Inver and the disused railway. Planting includes 3000 native trees, mainly oak; **Dorothy's Wood** ($2^1/_2$ acres/1ha), Kilcorig. Named for Dorothy Balmer, whose husband donated the land. Planted with 1800 trees including alder, oak, wild cherry, aspen, silver birch and rowan; **The Drum** (20 acres/8ha), Cargan. On the slopes of Slievenanee Mountain. Planted with oak, ash, rowan, birch and alder; **Ecos Wood** (18 acres/7ha), part of the Ecos Millennium Environment Centre, Ballymena. The trees were grown from seeds collected within a 15 mile (24km) radius of the centre; **Galgorm Wood** ($7^1/_2$ acres/3ha), a restored mature woodland in the Fernaghy House demesne. A millrace and sluice which originally fed a linen mill on the site have been restored along with an artificial lake created at the end of 1800s. The site also has an early Christian rath. Planting includes mixed native broadleaved trees such as oak, willow, alder and birch; **Keel Wood** (18acres/7ha), Ballymena. Divided by the River Braid. Planting includes alder and birch; **Ligoniel Wood** (1.3 acres/0.5ha), North Belfast. Small area with a planting of 1800 native trees including rowan, aspen, elder, oak and ash; **Little Acorn Wood** ($7^1/_2$ acres/3ha), Broughshane, located beside the River Braid. Planting includes pedunculate oak, red oak, copper beech, alder, white willow, Scots pine, crab apple; **Mill Dam Wood** (5 acres/2ha), Upper Springfield, Belfast. On the site of the former Springfield Dyeing Works where the Old Rock Dam fed the millrace. Planted with mixed broadleaves plus willow, alder and birch; **Monkstown Wood** (23 acres/9ha), Newtownabbey. By the Three Mile Water on the site of a water mill. Mixture of mature woodland by the river and oak, ash, rowan and wild cherry; **Oakfield Glen** (23 acres/9ha), Carrickfergus. Planting includes 12,000 native trees and a selection of exotic species such as redwood, deodar, stone pine and cypress; **Old Warren Woodland** (5 acres/2ha), Lisburn. By the River Lagan and the Lagan Towpath. Existing woodland extended by planting of native broadleaves and willow, birch and alder; **Seaview Wood** (4 acres/1.5ha), Seacourt, Larne, with views of the Irish Sea. Planted with a mixture of broadleaves and native pines; **Seymour Hill** (25 acres/10ha), Dunmurry. By the River Lagan. Open ground and existing trees have been augmented by planting of oak, ash, rowan, birch and cherry; **Silver Eel Wood** (4 acres/1.5ha), Toome. Wet woodland by the Toome Canal and Lough Neagh. Named for the eels which run from the lough. Planted with native tree species; **Throne Wood** (14 acres/5.5ha), North Belfast. Named for *Antron* (the nose), a rock called Napoleon's Nose on Cavehill. A mature wood of beech, elm and lime in a suburban area just below Belfast Zoo.

Some famous people born in County Antrim

Adams, Gerry (politician) (1948–)	Belfast
Adrain, Robert (scientist) (1775–1843)	Carrickfergus
Ballance, John (Premier of New Zealand 1891-93) (1839–93)	Mallusk
Banks, Tony (Baron Stratford) (politician) (1943–2006)	Belfast
Bell, John Stewart (physicist) (1928–90)	Belfast
Best, George (footballer) (1946–2005)	Belfast
Blanchflower, (Robert) Danny (footballer) (1926–93)	Belfast
Blanchflower, Jackie (footballer) (1933–98)	Belfast
Bland, Lillian (aviation pioneer) (1877–1972)	Carnmoney
Boyd, Stephen (actor) (1931–77)	Glengormley
Branagh, Kenneth (actor) (1960–)	Belfast
Burns, Gordon (television presenter) (1942–)	Belfast
Carroll, Ronnie (singer, born Ronald Cleghorn) (1934–)	Belfast
Carson, Frank (comedian) (1926–)	Belfast
Corrigan, Mairead (Nobel Laureate – Peace) (1944–)	Belfast
Craig, James (first PM of Northern Ireland, 1921–40) (1871–1940)	Belfast
Daly, Fred (golfer) (1911–90)	Portrush
Dougan, (Alexander) Derek (footballer) (1938–)	Belfast
Drennan, William (poet) (1754–1820)	Belfast
Dunlop, Joey (motorcycle racer) (1952–2000)	Ballymoney
Dunwoody, Richard (jockey) (1964–)	Belfast
Eaton, Timothy (Canadian retailer) (1834–1907)	Ballymena
Ferguson, Samuel (poet) (1810–86)	Belfast
Galway, James (musician) (1939–)	Belfast
Gibson, Mike (rugby player) (1942–)	Belfast
Herzog, Chaim (President of Israel, 1983-93) (1918–97)	Belfast
Higgins, Alex (snooker player) (1949–)	Belfast
Lavery, John (painter) (1856–1941)	Belfast
Lewis, (Clive Staples) C S (author) (1898–1963)	Belfast
McAleese, Mary (2nd female President of Ireland) (1951–)	Belfast
McArthur, Kenneth (Olympic marathon winner of 1912) (1881–1960)	Dervock
McBride, Willie John (rugby player) (1940–)	Toomebridge
McCoy, Tony (jockey) (1974–)	Moneyglass
Moore, Brian (author) (1921–99)	Belfast
Morrison, George 'Van' (musician) (1945–)	Belfast

Murray, Ruby (singer) (1935–96)	Belfast
Neeson, Liam (actor) (1952–)	Ballymena
Rodgers, Clodagh (singer) (1947–)	Ballymena
Thomson, William (1st Baron Kelvin) (scientist) (1824–1907)	Belfast
Williams, Betty (Nobel Laureate – Peace) (1943–)	Belfast

Islands of Antrim

Island name	Area	Nearest landmark	General information
Blind Rock	Portballintrae Harbour	Bushfoot Strand	Can be a hazard to ships entering the harbour.
Carrickarede Island	Atlantic	Ballintoy	aka Carrick-a-Rede. Connected to the mainland by a rope bridge during the summer. Owned by the National Trust.
Castle Island	Atlantic	Ramore Head	One of the Skerries.
Cormorant Rock	Lough Neagh	Flat Point	Named after the seabirds that frequent the rock.
Duck Island	Lough Neagh	Sandybay Point	Ownod by the National Trust.
East Maiden	North Channel	Ballygalley	Most easterly part of all Ireland. One of The Maidens (aka Hulin Rocks).
Hulin Rocks	North Channel	Ballygalley	aka The Maidens
Islandmagee	n/a	n/a	Peninsula between the towns of Larne and Carrickfergus.
Kettlebottom Island	Lough Neagh	Antrim	
Long Rock	Lough Neagh	Flat Point	Lies close to Cormorant Rock.
Maidens, The	North Channel	Ballygalley	See Hulin Rocks
Muck Island	North Channel	Portmuck	Owned by the National Trust. Three small rock stacks lie off the north end of the island.
Queen's Island	River Lagan	Belfast	See separate entry
Rams Island	Lough Neagh	Sandybay Point	Owned by the National Trust.
Rathlin Island	Atlantic	Ballycastle	See separate entry
Sheep Island	Atlantic	Ballintoy	Owned by the National Trust since 1967. Area: 0.02 sq miles (0.04 sq km).
Skady Tower	Lough Neagh	Flat Point	Lies close to Cormorant Rock.
Skerries, The	Atlantic	Ramore Head	Group of small rocky basalt islands.
Storks, The	Atlantic	Dunluce Castle	Rocks lying $1^1/_4$ miles (2 km) ESE of The Skerries and 0.6 miles (1 km) NNW of Dunluce Castle. They are marked by a tall unlit red beacon.
Three Islands, The	Lough Neagh	Ballynaleney	
Tolans Flat	Lough Neagh	Tolans Point	
West Maiden	North Channel	Ballygalley	The North Tower Lighthouse and its attendant three-storey cut-stone buildings dominate the island. One of the Maidens (aka Hulin Rocks).

ARMAGH

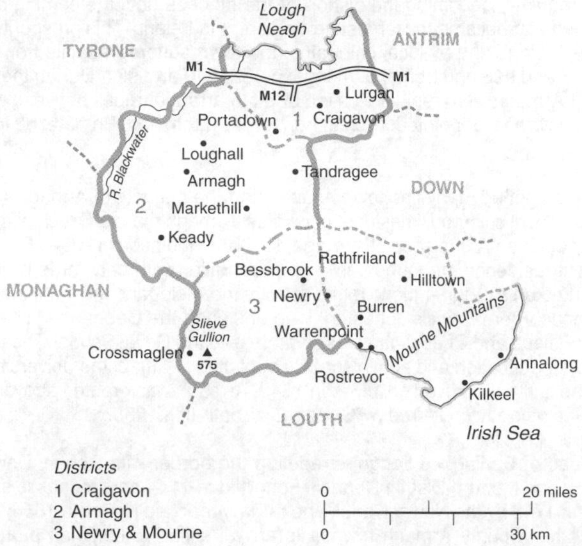

Lough Neagh
TYRONE
ANTRIM
M1
M1
M12
Lurgan
Portadown
1
Craigavon
R. Blackwater
Loughall
Armagh
Tandragee
DOWN
2
Markethill
Keady
Rathfriland
Bessbrook
Hilltown
MONAGHAN
Newry
3
Burren
Mourne Mountains
Slieve Gullion
Warrenpoint
Crossmaglen
575
Annalong
Rostrevor
Kilkeel
LOUTH
Irish Sea
Districts
1 Craigavon
2 Armagh
3 Newry & Mourne
0
20 miles
0
30 km

County Armagh is bordered by County Down to the east, County Antrim to the northeast, Lough Neagh to the north, County Tyrone to the northwest, County Monaghan to the west and County Louth to the south (the latter two counties in the Republic). The county contains the cities of Armagh and Newry.

Newry and Mourne District Council administers the towns and villages around the Mourne Mountains located geographically in County Down. Therefore the population figures given overleaf should be reduced by approximately 18,390 and added to County Down to accommodate Warrenpoint, Rostrevor, Burren and Kilbroney, Kilkeel and Annalong; all wards of Newry and Mourne.

Armagh is known as 'The Orchard County'; it is said that St Patrick planted an apple tree at Ceangoba, east of Armagh City. William of Orange was also said to have quenched his thirst with local cider at the Battle of the Boyne and sent his cider maker to Portadown to secure supplies for the army. Those brought over in the Plantation were also encouraged to plant and protect orchards. The vast majority, perhaps as much as 90 per cent, of the apples grown in Armagh's orchards are Bramley Seedlings. These were introduced in 1884 by a Mr Nicholson of Crangill, who brought over 60 trees from England. More than 4000 acres (1600ha) of County Armagh are covered in apple trees. Annual production in Northern Ireland of Bramley apples amounts to 30–40,000 tonnes, providing about 500 full-time and 1000 part-time jobs. About 97 per cent of the production is sold outside Northern Ireland.

The other industry which historically flourished in County Armagh was linen production. Armagh was part of the 'linen triangle' between the 17th and 19th century and the industry was greatly boosted by the local production of flax, the landscape providing many streams to supply water power to the increasingly mechanised industry. The railway line from Belfast to Armagh via Lurgan and Portadown was completed in 1848, driven by the need of Armagh linen producers to export their goods via the port of Belfast, although rail services to Armagh ceased in 1957. As a border county, Armagh was termed 'Bandit Country' during the Troubles, particularly the area of the salient that juts into the Irish Republic around Crossmaglen, where there was a large, and sometimes unwelcome, contingent of British troops at this time. As many as 476 'conflict-related' deaths have been recorded in the county since 1969.

Armagh City, often referred to as the City of Saints and Scholars, has long held the reputation of being the spiritual capital of Ireland. It is home to the Primate of All Ireland for both the Church of Ireland (Anglican) and Roman Catholic denominations. It takes its name from the goddess Macha, and translates as 'Macha's Height' (*Árd Macha*); its origins are intrinsically linked with St Patrick, who built a stone church here in AD 445. The surrounding area is also rich in pre-Christian archaeology, such as Navan Fort, showing that it has always had a spiritual significance. The monastery established around St Patrick's church in the 6th century became a centre for learning and influence, the abbot regularly becoming the bishop of the diocese until the coming of the Normans. The town flourished and became the largest urban centre in Ireland. This prosperity tempted incursions both by the Vikings and by local chieftains: the town suffered attacks from the Airgialla of Fermanagh in 793 and 996 and from the Vikings in 832, 840 and 921. During the early 11th century the abbots of Armagh were regularly called upon to arrange truces between warring factions. In 1132 St Malachy was appointed Archbishop of Armagh and Primate of Ireland by Pope Innocent II.

During the Georgian period many fine town houses and the majority of Armagh's public buildings were built using the local coloured limestone, known as 'Armagh marble'. Much of this building work was promoted by the then Archbishop of Armagh, Richard Robinson (1709–94). Having made the city his permanent residence, he found it in a poor condition with only three buildings with slate roofs, and embarked on a programme to make the city more elegant and industrious. His principal architect was Armagh-born Francis Johnston, who designed the Georgian Mall, the Courthouse, the Archbishop's Palace and Chapel, the Observatory and the Royal School. The town once again became a centre for education and administration but failed to attract the university that Robinson had hoped for. The first train arrived on 1 March 1848. Armagh was granted a royal charter in 1994 and city status was officially conferred by Queen Elizabeth II in 1995.

Newry, at the head of Carlingford Lough, straddling the border with County Down, is the headquarters of Newry and Mourne District Council. Founded in 1144 as a monastic site, it was linked to Lough Neagh in 1742 by the Newry Canal. The railway reached Newry in 1856, although in contrast to several other County Armagh towns, its arrival stifled rather than promoted economic progress during the later 19th century. Newry was granted city status in 2002.

Armagh	**Population**			**Area**	
Districts	*male*	*female*	*total*	*sq miles*	*sq km*
Armagh	26,923	27,340	54,263	259	671
Craigavon	39,753	40,918	80,671	146	378
Newry & Mourne	43,095	43,963	87,058	348	902
Total	109,771	112,221	221,992	753	1951

Local Attractions and Information

Administrative headquarters	**Armagh**: Council Offices, The Palace Demesne, Armagh BT60 4EL. Tel: 028 3752 9600. **Craigavon**: Civic Centre, Lakeview Road, Craigavon BT64 1AL. Tel: 028 3831 2400. **Newry and Mourne**: District Council Offices, Monaghan Row, Newry BT35 8DJ. Tel: 028 3031 3037.
Ardress House	Ardress, 6 miles (10km) west of Portadown. A farmhouse built in 1660 and greatly extended and redesigned both internally and externally, including a new façade, in the late 18th century. The grounds feature a walled apple orchard and formal rose garden plus woodland, while the surrounding 100 acre (40ha) estate includes a working farmyard with a blacksmith's, a piggery and a collection of farm implements. Maintained by the National Trust since 1959. Tel: 028 8778 4753.
Argory, The	2$^1/_2$ miles (4km) northeast of Moy, 6 miles (10km) southeast of Dungannon. Two-storey 19th century house and garden by the River Blackwater. The house was built c.1820 and has been left largely unaltered in terms of facilities: there is no electric light, and it still contains the accumulated contents left by the McGeough Bond family. There is a working cabinet barrel organ built by James Bishop of London in the early 1820s. Outside is a stableyard with coach house and other related buildings. There are two formal gardens – a rose garden and the Pleasure Ground, which has two stone houses with Chinese-style windows and yew arbours. The estate covers more than 300 acres (120ha). Maintained by the National Trust since 1979 and opened in 1981. Tel: 028 8778 4753.
Argory Mosses	2$^1/_2$ miles (4km) northeast of Moy, 6 miles (10km) southeast of Dungannon. A nature reserve on the Argory Estate consisting of two areas: the High Moss covers 25 acres (10ha) of raised bog, while the Low Moss (17 acres/7ha) is largely birch scrub. Owned by the National Trust and managed since 1982 by Ulster Wildlife Trust.
Armagh County Museum	The Mall East, Armagh. The oldest county museum in Northern Ireland, opened in 1937 and housed in a former school building dating from 1834 which previously housed the Armagh Natural History & Philosophical Society collection. Its wide range of collections cover the county's history from prehistoric times to the present day and include costume, local crafts, natural history, military history and the railways. There is also a collection of Irish art. Tel: 028 3752 3070.

Armagh Courthouse The Mall, Armagh. A neoclassical building designed by Francis Johnston and constructed in 1809 from the local limestone, known as 'Armagh marble'.

Armagh Friary Friary Road, Armagh. A Franciscan friary founded by Archbishop Patrick O'Scanail in 1263. After its dissolution in 1542, the buildings suffered at the hands of the O'Neills and were plundered by local builders. The remains consist mainly of the west gable of the 13th century church; at 163ft (49.5m) long, this was the longest friary church in Ireland. Tel: 028 3885 1102.

Armagh Gaol Gaol Square, The Mall, Armagh. Designed by Francis Cooley and William Murray as a new approach to prison planning, the main block was built in 1780 and a front block added in 1819. It was originally split into three prisons: one for women, one for debtors and one for felons. The jail was used for public executions until the 1860s, after which executions took place within the gaol, the last taking place in 1904. The gaol was closed in 1986 and the proposed restoration of the building was one of Northern Ireland's entries in the BBC series *Restoration* in 2004.

Armagh Observatory College Hill, Armagh. Modern observatory and astronomical research institute housed in a building designed by Francis Johnston and constructed 1789–91 under the auspices of Archbishop Richard Robinson. The dome, and the round tower which supports it, dominate the front of the building. The grounds feature the Armagh Astropark – a themed walkway presenting a scale model of the universe. The solar system is laid out so that visitors can compare the sizes of the planets and the distances between them; the Hyper Cube shows how only 28 cubes, each one 10 times the size of the one inside immediately inside it, would be sufficient to enclose the universe; and the Hill of Infinity extends the scale model into the far reaches of the universe. Other features include the Stone Calendar – an example of how a prehistoric stone circle could be used to map out a calendar – and the Lindsay Sundial. John Thomas Romney Robinson (1792–1882), the third director of the observatory, is best known as the inventor (in 1846) of the cup-anemometer for registering the velocity of the wind, a device still used all over the world. Tel: 028 3752 2928.

Armagh Planetarium College Hill, Armagh. The only planetarium in Ireland, opened to the public in May 1968 and expanded in 1974 to include the Lindsay Hall of Astronomy, named after the seventh director of the Armagh Observatory (whose idea the Planetarium was) and in 1995 the Eartharium. A 16in reflecting telescope is available for use by the public. Tel: 028 3752 3689.

Armagh Public Library Abbey Street, Armagh. Founded in 1771 by Archbishop Richard Robinson as part of a project to establish a university and built to a design by Thomas Cooley. The core of the collection is the Archbishop's personal library and his collection of engravings. There is also a collection of antiques belonging to Archbishop Beresford. The library holds a first edition of Jonathan Swift's *Gulliver's Travels* with handwritten annotations by the author. Tel: 028 3752 3142.

Armagh Railway Disaster On Wednesday 12 June 1889 the Armagh Methodist Church Sunday School excursion, destined for Warrenpoint, County Down, left Armagh station at 10.15am with 13 coaches and 1200 passengers, many more than anticipated. It soon reached a steep incline which, due to the volume of passengers, the engine was unable to manage. It was decided to split the train, take four carriages on to Hamiltownsbawn and then return for the rest. Unfortunately the methods used to restrain the carriages on the gradient, a hand brake and stone wedges, were ineffective; the remaining nine carriages rolled downhill and collided with the 10.35am passenger train from Newry, resulting in 88 fatalities. The Armagh accident remains Ireland's worst railway disaster.

Ballydougan Pottery Gilford, 6 miles (10km) south of Craigavon. Located in Bloomvale House, a restored thatched house built by a Huguenot family and dating from 1785. The house was originally owned by a linen merchant, where the work of out-weavers was finished off and despatched. Established at Bloomvale House since 1996, the pottery produces hand-thrown functional and decorative ware. Tel: 028 3834 2201.

Battles The **Battle of the Diamond** took place on 21 September 1795 outside the small village of Loughgall. Following the repeal of penal laws restricting Catholic access to landed property in 1778 and 1782, Catholic competition with Protestants for leases intensified, driving up prices and provoking Protestant resentment. Then in 1793 the Catholic Relief Act enfranchised 40-shilling freeholders in the counties, thus increasing the political value of Catholic tenants to landlords. In addition, Catholics began to enter the linen weaving trade, depressing Protestant wage rates. From the 1780s onwards the Protestant Peep O'Day boys (so called from their practice of attacking Catholic homes at dawn – the 'peep of day' – and wrecking their linen weaving machinery) began attacking Catholic homes, disarming Catholics of any weapons they were holding. The Defenders were formed in response to these attacks, but rapidly began making their own raids on Protestant households. The skirmish known as the Battle of the Diamond lasted 15 minutes and was centred on Daniel Winter's public house, located at the Diamond crossroads. Winter's pub was burnt to the ground by the attacking Defenders, who had targeted it as a gathering house of the local Protestant militia. Around 30 Catholic Defenders, but no Peep O'Day Boys, were killed in the fight. Hundreds of Catholic homes and at least one church were burned down in the aftermath. After the battle Daniel Winter, James Wilson and James Sloan formed the Orange Order at Sloane's Bar in Loughgall, to protect Protestant property. This was the catalyst for the formation of the Orange Order and 'Dan Winter's House' became known as the Birthplace of Orangeism.

See separate table for details of the battles of Moyry Pass and Yellow Ford.

Bessbrook A model village founded in 1845 by Quaker linen manufacturer John Grubb Nicholson. After the original mill, run by the Richardson family from 1802, burned to the ground in 1839, Nicholson acquired the property and set about providing a 'temperate' environment for his workers. The town was laid out with streets and squares surrounding the mill. As a social experiment it is similar to the model of the better-known Bournville founded by the Cadbury family near

Birmingham, England; however, it predates this development by more than 30 years. It is likely that the model on which it was based was the industrial village at Portlaw, County Waterford, founded in 1825 by the Quaker Malcolmson family. Among the principles on which the village was based was a philosophy of 'Three Ps'; although the workers were provided with schools, shops, dispensary, bank and churches, there were to be no public houses, no pawn shops and no police. The first two still apply to the town, the police having arrived in the 1890s. In the 1880s the Bessbrook Spinning Company also built a tramway to the outskirts of Newry for the conveyance of raw materials, finished goods and workers to and from the company's various mills. The Bessbrook Institute was built in 1886 to a design by William Watson as a community centre for their workers and was recently restored. During the Troubles the mill was converted into a British army base, with the result that the town became a target for terrorism. On 5 January 1976, ten workers from Bessbrook were ambushed and shot dead while travelling by minibus to Glennane.

Brownlow House — Windsor Avenue, Lurgan. Aka Lurgan Castle. An Elizabethan style mansion designed by Edinburgh architect W H Playfair for Charles Brownlow – who was raised to the peerage as Lord Lurgan in 1839 for services to the Whig Party – and built c.1833–40. Its tower and forest of chimneys present an impressive skyline, easily recognisable from most parts of the town and the surrounding countryside. Together with the elegant wrought-iron entrance gates, it is listed by the Department of the Environment (NI) as being of special architectural historical interest. The house became the headquarters of the Imperial Grand Black Chapter of the British Commonwealth in 1925. The Cushnie Room of the Imperial Grand Black Chapter was named in memory of Alexander H Cushnie MBE, JP, a Lurgan man who held the position of Imperial Grand Registrar 1936–78, and houses the flags of those dominions where the Black Institution has members. The house is now the largest Orange Hall in the world; the grounds have been turned into a public park.

Cardinal O Fiaich Heritage Centre — Cullyhanna, 12 miles (19km) southwest of Newry. Established in memory of Cardinal Tomas O Fiaich (1923–90), Archbishop of Armagh 1977–90, who was born near Cullyhanna. He was raised to cardinal in 1979, the year Pope John Paul II visited Ireland. The centre is housed on the site of a church which served as the Cullyhanna National School 1894–1972. There are audio-visual displays and memorabilia relating to Cardinal O Fiaich, as well as a research library with important collections on Irish history and language. The centre also covers the history of the local area, including models, maps, photographs and recordings of local poems and songs.

Coney Island — The only inhabited island in Lough Neagh, with a resident caretaker living in a Victorian cottage built in 1895. Located 1 mile (1.6km) offshore, it can be visited by boat by arrangement. Features include heavy oak, beech and horse chestnut woodland, a 13th century Norman motte and a 16th century stone tower used as a store by the O'Neills. Excavations during the early 1960s uncovered evidence of occupation since the Neolithic period and at one time the island was connected to the mainland by a causeway known as St Patrick's Road. St Patrick's Stone on the island is said to be where the saint rested while on retreat. Extensive habitat for both woodland birds and waterfowl plus colonies of bats. New York's Coney Island is named after the island. Owned by the National Trust since 1984, the island is maintained by Craigavon Borough Council. Area: 0.014 sq miles (0.036 sq km). Population: 1.

Craigavon — Located so as to create a single conurbation linking Lurgan and Portadown, Craigavon was designated a new town in 1965 and named for James Craig, Northern Ireland's first Prime Minister. Problems with the town's large-scale housing developments were not helped by the onset of the Troubles, while economic difficulties occurred when the Goodyear fan-belt plant, opened in 1967 in the Silverwood Industrial Estate and which at one time employed more than 1800 workers, closed on 25 July 1983. However, Craigavon has since benefited from new housing developments and the presence of the Rushmere Centre (previously Craigavon Shopping Centre) at its heart.

Craigmore Viaduct — 1 mile (1.6km) east of Bessbrook. The 18 arch viaduct, spanning about 400 metres, is Ireland's highest railway bridge at 126ft (38.5m) at its centre, although the outer arches are 66ft (20m) high. Opened in 1852, it is still used by the Belfast–Dublin line.

Crossmaglen — A large village close to the border with the Republic of Ireland, laid out around a very large central square.

Dan Winter's House — Derryloughan Road, The Diamond, Loughgall. House and land still owned by descendants of the Winter family, and which was the site of the Battle of Diamond (see Battles) on 21 September 1795. Restored in 2000, it contains relics from the battle plus everyday items from the period.

Derrymore House — Bessbrook, 2 miles (3km) northwest of Newry. A thatched cottage designed and built c.1776 by Isaac Corry, Chancellor of the Irish Parliament, who represented Newry in the Irish House of Commons. Set in parkland landscaped by John Sutherland (1745–1826). The Treaty Room, in which it is believed the details of the Act of Union were drafted in 1801, is open to the public. Owned by the Richardson family 1859–1952, it has been maintained by the National Trust since 1953. Tel: 028 8778 4753.

Dorsey, The — $1^{1}/_{4}$ miles (2km) northeast of Cullyhanna, 9 miles (15km) west of Newry. The Dorsey (G. *Na Doirse* = The Gateways.) is an Iron Age linear earthwork extending for $2^{1}/_{2}$ miles (4km) and believed to have formed a frontier to the kingdom based at Navan Fort. It may have later been incorporated into the so-called Black Pig's Dyke. As with other barriers such as Hadrian's Wall, its main purpose may have been to restrict and control access to the area rather than primarily acting as a defensive measure.

Gosford Forest Park — Markethill, 6 miles (10km) southeast of Armagh. The former estate of Gosford Demesne, acquired by the Department of Agriculture in 1958. The forest park covers 600 acres (240ha) and in 1986 became the first designated conservation forest in Northern Ireland. Featuring a heritage poultry and rare animal breeds collection, deer park and walled garden, the park also includes Gosford Castle, designed in Norman revivalist style by Thomas Hopper and built 1819–39 for Archibald Acheson, 2nd Earl of Gosford. It replaced a previous castle which was destroyed by fire in 1805. Author Anthony Powell, who was stationed here during World War II, based Castlemallock in his novel sequence *A Dance to the Music of Time* on Gosford. The arboretum, established in the 1820s, contains two specimens of Armands Pine – one is the British Isles girth champion and the other is the height champion. There are also specimens of noble fir, Weymouth pine and Prince Albert yew. Jonathan Swift was a visitor to the earlier house and Dean Swift's Chair is a sheltered spot near ornamental ponds where he is supposed to have sat. Tel: 028 3755 1277.

Haughey's Fort 2¼ miles (3.5km) west of Armagh. A trivallate hill fort located 0.6 miles (1km) west of Navan Fort and occupied 1100–900 BC. Its inner ditch encloses an area 500ft (150m) in diameter.

Highest point Slieve Gullion (G. *Sliabh gCullinn* = Cullinn's Mountain), part of the Ring of Gullion, at 1886ft (575m). A passage tomb and a Bronze Age burial cairn are located on the summit.

Interesting Facts **Armagh** is the ecclesiastical capital of Ireland and the seat of Roman Catholic and Protestant archbishops, both of whom are entitled to call themselves Primate of All Ireland. Lurgan-born critic, poet and painter **George William Russell** was an Anglo-Irish supporter of the Nationalist movement in Ireland. He used the pseudonym AE, or more properly, Æ. This derived from the Latin word *Æ'onl*, signifying the lifelong quest of man, subsequently shortened. **Lurgan** was also famous for holding the first settled meeting of the Society of Friends (Quakers) in 1654. **Charles Davis Lucas**, a 20-year-old mate in the Royal Navy, was the first recipient of the Victoria Cross. On 21 June 1854 in the Baltic, HMS *Hecla*, with two other ships, was bombarding Bomarsund, a fort in the Åland Islands off Finland. The fire was returned from the shore, and at the height of the action a live shell landed on *Hecla*'s upper deck with its fuse still hissing. All hands were ordered to fling themselves flat on the deck, but Lucas hurled the shell into the sea, where it exploded with a tremendous roar before hitting the water. Thanks to Lucas's action no one was killed or seriously wounded. He later achieved the rank of rear-admiral. Armagh-born **William McCrum** was not a footballer of note but revolutionised the game in 1890 when, as a member of the Football Association, he proposed the idea of the penalty kick in order to stop defenders fouling an attacking player in order to stop a goal. William's proposal was approved as number 13 in the Laws of the Game, on 2 June 1891, at the Alexandra Hotel in Glasgow. Another famous Armagh-born pioneer was **George Buchanan Armstrong** (1822–71). While assistant postmaster of Chicago, George proposed to send mail via the railway as a means of faster delivery and in 1864 postmaster general Montgomery Blair implemented this practice. Thus George B. Armstrong is considered the founder of the United States Railway Mail Service.

Islands The following islands are located in the part of Lough Neagh that falls within County Armagh: **Coney Island**, **Coney Island Flat**, **Croaghan Island**, **Derrywarragh Island**, **Oxford Island**, **Padian**, **Phil Roe's Flat**, **Rathlin Island** and **The Shallow Flat**.

Killevy Old Churches 3 miles (5km) southwest of Newry. The site of a 6th century Christian convent founded by St Monenna on the eastern slopes of Slieve Gullion. The remains of two churches built back to back are visible. One is pre-Norman and dates from the 11th century, while the other was used by the Franciscan order from the 15th century until the dissolution in 1542.

Kilnasaggart Stone Edenappa, 1½ miles (2.5km) south of Jonesborough, 8 miles (13km) south of Newy. Standing stone 7ft (2.1m) high with the following inscription on the southeast face: 'IN LOC SO TANIMMARNI TERNOHC MAC CERAN BIC ER CUL PETER APSTEL' (this place, bequeathed to Ternoc, son of Ceran the Little, under the patronage of Peter the Apostle). If this is the same Ternoc whose death is recorded as taking place in AD 714 or 716, the stone can be dated to c.700, making it the oldest datable stone monument in Ireland. The northwest face of the stone is inscribed with encircled crosses.

King's Stables 2¼ miles (3.5km) west of Armagh. Deep artificial pool from the Late Bronze Age, dug c.1150–1000 BC and used for ritual offerings. Possibly connected with the nearby Haughey's Fort (see separate entry), the hollow is 85ft (26m) in diameter, steep sided and with a maximum depth of 13ft (4m). It was excavated in 1975, finds including sword mould fragments, pottery sherds, six sets of antlers and a human skull.

Lough Neagh Bordered by five of the six Northern Irish counties, Lough Neagh is Ireland's largest freshwater lake, fed by six major rivers with the Lower Bann carrying the water to the north coast. It provides 40 per cent of Northern Ireland's drinking water. It covers an area of 148 sq miles (383 sq km) with an average depth of 29.2ft (8.9m). The length of the shoreline is 78 miles (125km). A Ramsar site, Special Protection Area and Area of Special Scientific Interest, the lough is a haven for wildlife, in particular fish and wildfowl. In addition to brown trout it is home to freshwater shrimp, river lamprey, pollan and eel. Internationally important numbers of whooper swans, pochard, tufted duck, scaup and goldeneye all overwinter on the lough. It is also an important summer breeding site for black-headed gulls and great crested grebe. According to legend the lough was formed when Finn McCool scooped up the earth to throw at a Scottish giant. The rocks and soil landed to form the Isle of Man and the hole left behind became Lough Neagh. The lough is the ancestral property of the Earls of Shaftesbury.

Loughgall A village at the heart of Armagh's apple-growing industry. The Orange Order was founded in Loughgall in 1795 following the Battle of the Diamond.

Loughgall Country Park 5 miles (8km) southwest of Portadown. Country park covering 464 acres (188ha) incorporating part of the estate of Loughgall Manor, established after the Plantation by the Cope family. It includes a picturesque hermitage dating to c.1800 and an 18th century walled garden which now holds a collection of rare apple varieties.

Loughnashade — 1 mile (1.6km) west of Armagh. A lake lying northeast of Navan Fort, and probably used in the Bronze Age as a sacred lake into which ritual offerings were thrown. In 1798 men digging drains near the lake discovered four great bronze horns which had probably been deposited in the lake. They were decorated in traditional Celtic style and dated to the 1st century BC. Only one of the horns survives; known as the Loughnashade Trumpet, it is in the National Museum in Dublin. An exact replica was made in 1999 and has been used in the recreation of Bronze Age music.

Lurgan — (G. = Long Ridge). A market town close to the border with County Down, at the southern edge of Lough Neagh. It is strongly connected with the Brownlow family, who were granted 2500 acres (1000ha) of land in the area in 1610 and established a town around their house and bawn. The town was captured and burned during the 1641 Rebellion but recovered relatively quickly. In the late 17th century Lurgan became a prosperous market town and centre for linen manufacture. While the linen industry itself declined from the mid 19th century, the town continued to benefit from other branches of the textile industry.

Moneypenny's Lock and Lockhouse — Horseshoe Lane, Brackagh, Portadown. A restored 18th century house, stable and bothy located at the final (or first, depending on the direction of travel) lock of the Newry Canal before it joins the River Bann and named for the Moneypenny family, lock keepers on the canal for 85 years. Owned by Craigavon Borough Council. Tel: 028 3832 2205.

Moyry Castle — $1^1/_4$ miles (2km) south of Jonesborough, 8 miles (13km) south of Newry. Ruins of a castle built by Lord Mountjoy to guard the Moyry Pass (the Gap of the North) immediately following the battle of September–October 1600. A three-storey tower with rounded corners and gun loops, it stands close to the railway line to Dublin.

Nature reserves — **Annagarriff**, 7 miles (11km) northwest of Portadown. Located within Peatlands Country Park and edged by fens and raised bogs, with Annagarriff Wood, an oak and birch woodland, at its centre. The only Irish site supporting colonies of wood ants; **Brackagh Moss**, 2 miles (3km) southeast of Portadown. Heavily cut raised bog plus alder and willow woodland. Butterflies include marsh fritillary and green hairstreak; **Mullenakill**, located within Peatlands County Park. Raised bog supporting sphagnum moss. Frequented by the rare large heath butterfly.

Navan Fort — $1^1/_2$ miles (2.5km) west of Armagh. One of Northern Ireland's most important archaeological sites. A large circular earthwork in a low hill-top position, it has been identified with Emain Macha, ancient capital of the kings of Ulster. It covers an area of 12 acres (5ha) surrounded by a bank; there is a ditch inside the bank, a configuration which would normally indicate that the site was not used as a defensive structure, where the ditch would be dug outside the bank. Excavations 1961–71 revealed that the site was occupied from the Neolithic period, with structures being erected during the late Bronze Age from c.700 BC. Major changes were made in the Iron Age, c.100 BC, when the site was cleared and a circular wooden structure was erected, 130ft (40m) in diameter, with five concentric rings of 275 posts inside it, and possibly roofed. It has been postulated that this was a temple. This unique structure was burned, possibly on purpose, and the remains covered to form a mound which still exists within the circle. Abandoned as Ulster's capital following the coming of Christianity sometime between AD 331 and the end of the 5th century, it was used as a campsite by Brian Boru in 1005.

Newry Canal — The oldest summit canal in the British Isles, opened in March 1742. The ship canal runs from Newry to Victoria Locks on Carlingford Lough; the inland canal runs from Newry to Portadown, where it joins the River Bann at the Point of Whitecote; the navigation then continues into Lough Neagh. Designed by Thomas Steers, its construction began in 1731 after coal deposits were discovered at Coalisland in County Tyrone. The coal was transported via the canal to Carlingford Lough and on to Dublin, where it replaced coal imported from England. It was also used to transport agricultural products and manufactured goods such as linen, and had a passenger service in rivalry to the mail coach. The inland canal was 18 miles (29km) long, with 14 locks. Having fallen into decline following the construction of the railway line which runs virtually in parallel with it, the canal was abandoned in 1949 and is now jointly owned by the four councils through which it runs. The towpath from Newry to Portadown is open for 20 miles (32km) from Newry Town Hall to the Bann Bridge in Portadown.

Oxford Island — 3 miles (5km) northwest of Lurgan. A National Nature Reserve located on a peninsula at the southeast corner of Lough Neagh, and providing a habitat for a variety of waterfowl including cormorant, goldeneye, grebes, herons, swans and terns.

Palace Demesne — Friary Road, Armagh. The walled demesne of the former Archbishop's house, designed by Cooley and Johnston and built 1770–1825. Formerly the residence of the Church of Ireland Primate and recently restored, the demesne is now home to the offices of Armagh City and District Council.

Palace Stables Heritage Centre — Friary Road, Armagh. Restored Georgian stable block in the Palace Demesne, including the coachman's kitchen, the tack room, the servant's tunnel and an ice house. The Garden of the Senses, opened in 1996, offers sensory experiences to both able-bodied and disabled people; the garden includes two bubbling water sculptures, *Sensory Form* and *Kinetic Flowers*. Tel: 028 3752 9629.

Peatlands Country Park — 6 miles (10km) east of Dungannon. Covering 650 acres (265ha) and established to promote peatland awareness, the site was acquired from the Irish Peat Development Company in 1978 and the park was opened in 1990. The Peatlands Park Railway runs through the park. Habitats include woodland and bog, while flora and fauna include waterfowl, red and grey squirrel, badgers and hares. Tel: 028 3885 1102.

Peatlands Park Railway — A narrow gauge railway transporting up to 70 passengers on a journey of 0.9 miles (1.5km) through Peatlands Park. Built by the Irish Peat Development Company in 1901 and originally used to transport cut turf from the bog to a processing plant at Maghery. It was operated by horse

1901–07; electrified in 1907, it used diesel locomotives from 1954 until the company ceased operations in the mid 1960s. The original diesels used by the company, *The Planet* and *The Schoema*, were restored to working order and have been joined by the specially built *K40*.

Portadown — A town in Craigavon Borough. Its name means 'port of the fortress'.

Richhill Castle — Richhill, 5 miles (8km) northeast of Armagh. Aka Richhill House. House built c.1665 by Major Edward Richardson and originally known as Richardson's Hill. The house's wrought-iron gates, made by the Thornberry brothers from Falmouth in 1745, were moved to Hillsborough Castle in 1936.

Ring of Gullion — A ring of rugged hills surrounding the mountain Slieve Gullion and forming a ring dyke, one of the finest examples of such a geological landform in the British Isles. A designated Area of Outstanding Natural Beauty covering 59 sq miles (153 sq km), it consists largely of grassland and arable land, also including woodlands, particularly in coniferous State forests, heathland, fens and bogs; it also encompasses Cam Lough, a glacial ribbon lake, and the Upper and Lower Cashel Loughs. The area is rich with myths and legends and is known for its ancient sites including the Dorsey (see separate entry). It has also developed its own particular folklore, poetry and language. The area was once known as 'The District of Songs' and 'The District of Poets'.

Rivers — The **Blackwater** rises to the north of Fivemiletown, County Tyrone, and flows east through the county via Clogher and Aughnacloy before taking a southeasterly route along the border with County Monaghan, its most southerly extreme being close to the borders of all three counties. The river now follows a northerly route following the border between Counties Armagh and Tyrone via Moy in Tyrone and Charlemont in Armagh, before discharging into Lough Neagh just west of Derrywarragh Island in the most southwesterly area of the lough. The tiny village of Maghery in Armagh lies between the estuaries of the Blackwater and Bann rivers which are only two miles apart at this point. The total length of the Blackwater is approximately 42 miles (68km).

Royal Irish Fusiliers Museum — Beresford Row, The Mall East, Armagh. Housed in Sovereigns House, a Georgian house built in 1809 and designed by John Quinn and Francis Johnston. The regiment was formed as the 87th Prince of Wales' Irish Regiment of Foot and the 89th Regiment of Foot in 1793. The 87th gained some glory in the Peninsular War with the capture of a French eagle by Sergeant Patrick Masterman at the Battle of Barossa on 5 March 1811. The 87th Foot were known during the campaign for their battle cry *Faugh a Ballagh* ('Clear the way'). The regiment went on to fight in Nepal and in the First Burma War (1825–6), after which it became known as the Prince of Wales' Own Irish Regiment in 1827. The 89th served in Ireland during the 1789 rebellion before fighting in Argentina, Cape Colony, Ceylon and India, and captured Java in 1811; it also fought in Canada, gaining the battle honour 'Niagara'. The 89th became Princess Victoria's Regiment in 1866. The two regiments were merged as the Princess Victoria's Royal Irish Fusiliers in 1881, together with the militia infantry of Counties Armagh, Cavan and Monaghan. The Fusiliers saw action in Egypt, Sudan and during the Boer War. During World War I the regiment fought on the Western Front, at Gallipoli and in the Balkans; during World War II it formed part of the British Expeditionary Force, playing a vital part in securing the evacuation of troops from Dunkirk. The 1st Battalion went on to fight through the campaigns in North Africa, Sicily and Italy. The 2nd Battalion was stationed in Malta, (1939–43), and then fought an unsuccessful defensive action on the island of Leros. On 1 July 1968 the Fusiliers were merged with the Royal Inniskilling Fusiliers and the Royal Ulster Rifles to form the Royal Irish Rangers. Tel: 028 3752 2911.

Royal School Armagh — College Hill, Armagh. Established by royal decree in 1608 and originally believed to be located at Mountnorris. It moved to Abbey Street in Armagh City following the 1641 Rebellion, during which the headmaster John Starkey and his family were murdered. Archbishop Robinson funded a new school building on College Hill in 1774. The school had 36 pupils in 1836, 63 in 1849 and 111 in 1879. After the 1947 Education Act its intake was widened and in 1986 it was amalgamated with Armagh Girls' High School. Famous former pupils include Viscount Castlereagh, Richard Wellesley and Major General Edward Pakenham.

St Malachy — Born Maolmhaodhog Ua Morgair in Armagh in 1094, Malachy was trained by Imhar O'Hagan and ordained in 1119, becoming Bishop of Down and Connor in 1124 and rebuilding the Abbey of Bangor. On the death of Ceallach (St Celsus) in 1129 he was appointed Archbishop of Armagh but did not take up the position until 1132. Satisfied that he had re-established the see and restored Church discipline, Malachy resigned his position in 1138 and made a pilgrimage to Rome in 1139. While in France he visited Bernard of Clairvaux. After he was appointed papal legate to Ireland he took five monks from Clairvaux and returned to Ireland to establish the Abbey of Mellifont in 1142, outside Drogheda, County Louth. This was the first Cistercian foundation in Ireland. St Malachy set out on a second pilgrimage to Rome in 1148, but on arriving at Clairvaux he fell sick, and died in the arms of St Bernard on 2 November. Credited with the gift of prophecy – he made prophecies relating to both Ireland and the papacy – Malachy was canonised by Pope Clement III in 1190. His bones remained in France until 1982, when some were placed in the new altar of St Patrick's Roman Catholic Cathedral in Armagh during a rededication ceremony.

St Patrick's Cathedral (Church of Ireland) — Cathedral Close, Armagh. Built on the site of a stone church founded by St Patrick in AD 445 on Druimsailech (Sallow Ridge). The original church, an oblong building 140ft (43m) long, was the central point of a monastic foundation and school. St Patrick ordained that Armagh should be the pre-eminent church in Ireland. Brian Boru was buried close to the church in 1014 after his death in the Battle of Clontarf. The building has suffered no less than 17 destructions during its lifetime including the depredations of the Vikings, warfare and rebellion, accidents and natural calamities. It was expanded to its present plan in 1268–70 by Archbishop O'Scanlan. Until the Reformation the cathedral held three ancient relics: St Patrick's crosier (*Bachal Isa*, The Staff of Jesus) was taken to Dublin and burned, but the Bell of St Patrick and the Book of Armagh survived, and are kept in the Irish Royal Academy and Trinity College Library respectively. The cathedral was restored and refurbished in Gothic style in 1834 to a design by Lewis Nockalls Cottingham under the auspices of Lord John George Beresford.

St Patrick's Cathedral (Roman Catholic) — Cathedral Road, Armagh. A twin-spired cathedral located on Sandy Hill, where St Patrick is said to have rescued a young deer from hunters. Construction began on 17 March 1840 (St Patrick's Day), but work was suspended in 1848 during the Great Famine as church funds were diverted to relief work. Building recommenced on Easter Monday 1854. As a result of this delay, the bottom half was designed by Thomas Duffy of Newry in English Perpendicular style, while the top half was designed by J J McCarthy of Dublin in French Decorated Gothic style, Duffy having died in 1848. Work on the interior continued into the early 20th century. The cathedral was dedicated in 1873 and consecrated in 1904. Following the 2nd Ecumenical Council of the Vatican (Vatican II), the interior was reordered in the 1980s, resulting in the removal of the original altar and many other elaborate fittings. The cathedral was rededicated on 13 June 1982.

St Patrick's Trian Visitor Complex — English Street, Armagh. Housed in two buildings – the Bank House, built in 1800, and the Presbyterian Meeting House, built in 1722 – and houses three innovative audio-visual exhibits on the history of Armagh. **The Armagh Story**, tracing the history of the city from prehistory, through the coming of Christianity and on to the Georgian buildings of Armagh-born architect Francis Johnston; **Patrick's Testament**, focusing on the early Christian treasure, the *Book of Armagh*, and St Patrick's links with Armagh; and **The Land of Lilliput**, narrating the adventures of Jonathan Swift's creation Lemuel Gulliver. The name derives from the division of Armagh into three districts or 'Trians' (pronounced 'tree-ans'): Trian Mor, Trian Masain and Trian Sassenach, roughly marked by English Street, Irish Street and Scotch Street. Tel: 028 3752 1801.

Slieve Gullion Forest Park — 7 miles (11km) southwest of Newry. A 2500 acre (1000ha), mainly coniferous forest park on the southern slopes of the mountain of Slieve Gullion. There is also a walled garden.

Slieve Gullion Passage Tomb — 5 miles (8km) southwest of Newry. Known locally as Calliagh Berra's House (The Witch of Berra's House). A granite passage tomb on the top of Slieve Gullion mountain, built 2500–2000 BC. It stands 13ft (4m high), with a diameter of 89ft (30m), and was excavated in 1961. There is also a cist cairn close by.

Sport:

general — **Road Bowls** (aka Long Bullets or Road Bullets) is a game now mainly played in County Armagh and County Cork, although a version is also played in Holland. Two contestants throw a 28oz (793.8g) solid iron ball along a course laid out over the twists and turns of country roads, the winner being the one who covers the distance (usually about 2½ miles/4km) in the fewest shots. The sport is very popular and players have an entourage of helpers and guides to help them.

football — **Armagh City** were founded in 1964 and are winners of the Irish League 1st Division in 2005. Nicknamed The Eagles, they play at Holm Park Ardmore, Newry Road, Armagh.

Glenavon were founded in 1889 and are winners of the Irish League championship in 1952, 1957 and 1960, and of the Irish Cup in 1957, 1959, 1961, 1992 and 1997. Nicknamed The Lurgan Blues, their home ground is Mourneview Park, Mourneview Avenue, Lurgan.

Loughgall were founded in 1967 and won the Irish League 1st Division in 2004. Nicknamed The Villagers, their home ground is Lakeview Park.

Newry City were founded in 1923. Originally known as Newry Town, they were renamed when Newry gained city status. They are winners of the Irish League 1st Division in 1998. Their home ground is The Showgrounds, Greenbank Industrial Estate, Newry.

Portadown were founded in 1924. They are winners of the Irish League championship in 1990, 1991, 1996 and 2002, and of the Irish Cup in 1991, 1999 and 2005. Nicknamed The Ports, their home ground is Shamrock Park.

Gaelic football — **Armagh** won the GAA All-Ireland Senior Gaelic Football Championships in 2002.

Woods on Your Doorstep — **Canal Wood** (23 acres/9ha), outside Poyntz Pass between the Newry Canal and the railway line. Planted with mixed wetland species, mainly willow and alder; **Carnbane Wood** (2½ acres/1ha), at Newry beside the Bessbrook River and the Newry canal towpath; **Corcrain Community Woodland** (10 acres/4ha), at Portadown by the River Ballybay. Unimproved grassland and mixed wetland planting; **Cranagh Wood** (8 acres/3ha), a hilltop site outside Armagh. Planted with more than 5000 trees including oak, ash, rowan, wild cherry and crab apple; **Daisy Hill Wood** (8 acres/3ha), overlooking Newry. A plant nursery 1890–1990, with many non-native trees and shrubs as a result of planting by the nursery. Main woodland is mixed native planting; **Markethill Wood** (1 acre/0.4ha), a small wood opposite Gosford Forest Park with mainly mixed deciduous planting. Of the 900 trees planted the main species are oak, ash, wild cherry and beech; **Taghnevan Community Woodland** (15 acres/6ha), between Lurgan and Craigavon, a mixed site including wetland, meadow and a natural pond. The woodland is mainly oak, ash, rowan and birch.

Some famous people born in County Armagh

Aiken, Frank (founding-member of Fianna Fáil) (1898–1983)	Camlough
Hunniford, (Mary Winifred) Gloria (TV and radio presenter) (1940–)	Portadown
Johnston, Francis (architect) (1760–1829)	Armagh
Logan, James (founding father of Pennsylvania) (1674–1751)	Lurgan
Makem, Tommy (musician) (1932–2007)	Darkley
St Malachy (Archbishop of Armagh, 1132-38) (1094–1148)	Armagh
O Fiaich, Tomas (Primate of All Ireland) (1923–90)	Cullyhanna
Paisley, Ian (politician and churchman) (1926–)	Armagh
Palmer, Arthur Hunter (Premier of Queensland, 1870-74) (1819–98)	Armagh
Russell, George William 'Æ' (poet and painter) (1867–1935)	Lurgan

(LONDON)DERRY

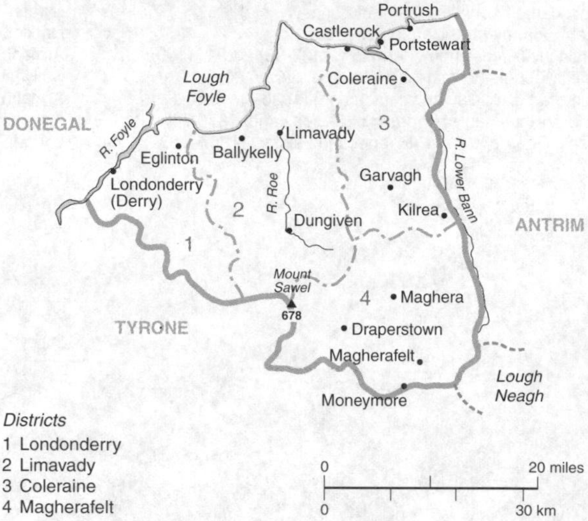
Portrush
Castlerock
Portstewart
Coleraine
Lough Foyle
DONEGAL
R. Foyle
Limavady
3
Eglinton
Ballykelly
R. Lower Bann
Londonderry (Derry)
R. Roe
Garvagh
2
Kilrea
Dungiven
ANTRIM
1
Mount Sawel
678
4
Maghera
TYRONE
Draperstown
Magherafelt
Lough Neagh
Moneymore
Districts
1 Londonderry
2 Limavady
3 Coleraine
4 Magherafelt
0
20 miles
0
30 km

County Derry is bordered by County Antrim to the west and County Tyrone to the south and east. Its northwest border touches County Donegal in the Republic of Ireland and its southeast tip borders Lough Neagh. Its northern shores are washed by the Loch Foyle Estuary and Atlantic Ocean. Administratively, the traditional county contains four of the 26 councils of Northern Ireland, established in 1973: Coleraine, Derry City, Limavady and Magherafelt.

To begin with, the very tricky problem of what to call the county and city. Put plainly, to unionists it is County Londonderry and the City of Londonderry, to nationalists it is County Derry and the City of Derry – although even that is not a hard and fast rule. The name Derry derives from the Gaelic *doire* ('oak grove'), a common appelation in Ireland. The need to distinguish this site from other Derrys resulted in it being called Doire Calgaich and Doire Colmcille (St Columba's Oak Wood); the 'London' was added after the granting by James I of a charter for a settlement by the merchant guilds of London. The nationalist-controlled local authority has officially changed its name from Londonderry County Borough Council to Derry City Council. However, no request has been made to the British Secretary of State for Northern Ireland to change the name of the city itself. One solution offered is to call the city Derry/Londonderry (or Derry stroke Londonderry), which has led to the city being known locally as 'Stroke City'. Another name in common usage is 'The Maiden City', in reference to the fact that the city was not breached during the siege of 1689. Attempts to be even-handed and call the city Derry, and the county County Londonderry, have not been seriously taken up. The parliamentary and Northern Ireland Assembly constituencies covering the city are known as Foyle in an attempt to avoid controversy. In this section Derry will be used for expediency unless the official usage is Londonderry (as in parliamentary constituencies or in the name of a company).

The borough of **Coleraine** stretches along the coast from Castlerock in the west to Portballintrae in the east including Portrush and Portstewart. Inland it encloses the towns and villages of Aghadowey, Kilrea, Garvagh and Macosquin. Its eastern edge is marked by the River Bann, which also flows through the main town of Coleraine itself. The economy is largely rural, although the port at Coleraine is used for the export of scrap metal. What is believed to be the earliest known settlement in Ireland (c.7000 BC) was discovered at Mountsandel in what is now the suburbs of Coleraine. The town was associated with St Patrick in the 5th century and a monastic site was established near where Coleraine Bridge stands. The River Bann itself was used as a highway by the Vikings and the Normans built the first bridge over the river at Coleraine. A centre for Christian teaching in 13th century, the present town was established during the Plantation by the Coleraine-based Honourable the Irish Society in 1610 with 200 timber houses, and the 17th century earthen defences are still visible in places. Coleraine's population in 1659 was 633. Railway links and industrialisation saw the town expand during the 19th and 20th centuries. The New University of Ulster was established at the end of the 1960s.

Derry City, the capital of the geographical county, has a western boundary on County Donegal and the River Foyle. To the south it stretches as far as the Sperrin Mountains. The city, which straddles the Foyle, is Northern Ireland's second largest and one of the finest walled cities in Europe. Evidence of a Neolithic settlement was discovered on the edge of the city in 2000 and this is believed to be the earliest known farming community in Ireland. St Columba founded a monastery in AD 546 on the site of the present-day Long Tower Church. The first cathedral (Tempull Mor) was built in 1164 by the first Bishop of Derry, Flahertach O'Brolchain, but was destroyed by fire in 1567. Other religious buildings included a Cistercian nunnery and a Franciscan friary. A castle was built by the O'Doherty family and defensive fortifications were raised in the mid 16th century, although these failed to prevent the sack of the city by English troops during the O'Neill rebellion. English troops again occupied the city in 1600 and it suffered further at the hands of Cahir O'Doherty, who set it alight in April 1608. In 1613 the Society of the Governor and Assistant, London, of the New Plantation in Ulster within the Realm of Ireland (later known as the Honourable the Irish Society) was granted a charter to oversee the plantation of the area around Derry and fortify the city at an initial cost of £20,000, rising swiftly to £60,000. The area allotted was originally called County Coleraine. The society was formed and the cost shared equally by the 12 great livery companies of London. As a result the lands made available to the Society were divided into 12 portions. Most of the existing buildings were demolished and the early city, now known as Londonderry, was quickly established. The city walls were built 1614–19, along with over 200 stone houses, a town hall and the Bishop's House. St Columb's Cathedral was built 1628–33; the city survived a siege during the rebellion of 1641 and a further siege in 1649. The population in 1659 was 1052 but suffered a serious fire in 1668. The main export during this period was salted salmon.

The Great Siege (1688–9) was the next significant chapter in the city's history. During James II's attempt to defeat the supporters of William of Orange in Ireland the city, spurred on by the actions of 13 apprentice boys, closed its gates against the Earl of Antrim on 7 December 1688. James II arrived outside its walls on 18 April 1689 and a 105 day siege and blockade ensued. On 28 July government supply ships, led by *Mountjoy*, broke the defensive boom across the River Foyle and resupplied the city. The siege was broken and the Jacobites had departed by 1 August 1689.

The Market House was built in 1692. During the 18th century the city continued to develop as a port within the walled city with the establishment of Shipquay Street and Bishop Street. Long Tower Church was built 1784–6. An era of expansion was triggered by the building of Bishop's Bridge over the Foyle in 1789–91 by the then Bishop of Derry, Frederick Augustus Hervey, with substantial building activity during the early Victorian period. During the 1840s two railway lines were built from Derry: the Londonderry & Coleraine Railway and the Londonderry & Enniskillen Railway. The Londonderry & Lough Swilly Railway was opened in 1863. A further line from Derry to Strabane was opened in 1900. However, after World War II all the lines were closed down and the only line now operating is between Derry (Waterside) and Belfast. The steel Carlisle Bridge was erected in 1863 (demolished in 1933). Over 20 years in the building, St Eugene's Cathedral was completed in 1873.

The city's economy centred on the manufacture of the world famous 'Celtic' style cotton shirt, begun by William Scott in the 1830s. The factory run by Messrs Tillie and Henderson in Foyle Road is mentioned by Karl Marx in *Das Kapital* and by 1902 more than 30 factories and many more outwork stations employed 18,000 people, the vast majority of them women. During the Great Famine the county's population fell from 222,174 in 1841 to 192,000 in 1851, but in fact the county fared better than most of the rest of Ireland. At the same time the port became a mecca for emigrants to North America, bolstering the city's population.

Alongside the shirt-making industry the economy was based on distilling, fisheries and shipbuilding. In 1882 Charles Bigger established the Foyle Shipyard in Pennyburn and the *Foyle* and the *Victoria* were completed by 1887. This yard closed in 1892 but shipbuilding was recommenced in 1899 by the Londonderry Shipbuilding & Engineering Company, and after expansion and transfer to Swan Hunter in 1912 more than 2000 men were employed. However, the Derry shipyard was closed after the launch of the *New York News* in 1922. Derry served as a major naval base during World War II and was the object of a single German air raid in April 1941, during which 13 people were killed. It was the chosen point for the surrender of 70 German U-Boats on 14 May 1945. Craigavon Bridge replaced Carlisle Bridge in 1934 and Foyle Bridge was erected in 1984.

Rioting, fighting and a shooting war between the Irish Republican Army (IRA), the Ulster Volunteer Force (UVF) and the army had occurred during April–June 1920, resulting in 40 deaths. On 5 October 1968 the second civil rights march to take place in Northern Ireland began in the Waterside district and was met with violence by the Royal Ulster Constabulary (RUC). The failure of Stormont to make sufficient reforms contributed to the start of what would eventually be known as the Troubles. Escalating violence during and after the Apprentice Boys' march on 12 August 1969, which became known as the Battle of Bogside (12–15 August 1969), led to the arrival of British troops in Northern Ireland. The neighbourhood known as the Bogside was allowed to remain a 'no-go' area (August 1969–March 1972). A march in Derry organised by the Northern Ireland Civil Rights Association (NICRA) against the policy of internment ended with the shooting dead of 13 civilians by British troops on 30 January 1972. This became known as Bloody Sunday. In the following March the Northern Ireland government at Stormont was suspended and power transferred to Westminster. The no-go areas were dismantled. As many as 227 'conflict-related' deaths have been recorded in Derry City and a further 121 in County Derry since 1969.

Derry City is split by the River Foyle, and the building of the first bridge in 1790 eventually led to the development of the east bank. The part of the city on the west bank of the Foyle is known as Cityside and that on the east bank as Waterside. According to the 2001 census, 88 per cent of the population of Cityside and 45 per cent of the population of Waterside is Catholic. Areas of Derry City include Ballymagroaty (or 'Ballymac' as it is known locally), a recent housing development; Bogside, built, as the name suggests, just outside the walled city on boggy land beside the Foyle; Brandywell, adjacent to Bogside on the west bank of the river and home to Derry FC; Creggan, which also sits next to Bogside, towards the border with Donegal, and was originally a 1940s housing estate; Culmore, which sits on the border with Donegal; Drumahoe, a village on the outskirts of the city on the River Faughan; Galliagh, a large estate built during the 1970s on the Cityside; Kilfennan, a large integrated estate in the Waterside; Rosemount, on the west bank and one of the oldest residential areas outside the city walls; Shantallow, a large 1960s housing estate in the Cityside; Strathfoyle, on the eastern bank of Lough Foyle and the location of the port; and the Fountain, one of the few Protestant areas in the Cityside. The borough of Derry includes City of Derry Airport and the nearby village of Eglinton, founded by the Grocers' Company in 1825.

The borough of **Limavady** falls largely within the River Roe and Lower Bann valleys with the sea to the north and Lough Foyle to the west. The first record of settlement is of St Columba presiding over a convention on Mullagh Hill in the area in AD 572. Limavady town is a Plantation settlement beside the River Roe established in 1612 after James I granted the district to Sir Thomas Philips. In its early days it had an association with the linen industry but did not expand to more than a market town. The name Limavady (*Leim an Mhadaidh* = 'The Leap of the Dog') derives from the occasion when a faithful hound belonging to an O'Cahan chieftain jumped a gorge on the River Roe near O'Cahan's Castle in order to save his master from an enemy attack. Other towns in the borough include Dungiven.

The borough of **Magherafelt** stretches from Lough Neagh in the east to the Sperrin Mountains in the west. Magherafelt's origins date back to the 15th century but the present town is based on the layout of the Plantation settlement, centred on a diamond. Other towns and villages in the borough include Castledawson, Draperstown and Maghera, the latter the seat of a bishopric in the 12th and 13th centuries.

(London) Derry	**Population**			**Area**	
Districts	*male*	*female*	*total*	*sq miles*	*sq km*
Coleraine	26,877	29,438	56,315	188	486
Derry	51,137	53,929	105,066	149	387
Limavady	16,497	15,925	32,422	226	586
Magherafelt	20,041	19,739	39,780	221	573
Total	114,552	119,031	233,583	784	2032

Local Attractions and Information

Administrative headquarters — **Coleraine**: Cloonavin, 66 Portstewart Road, Coleraine BT52 1EY. Tel: 028 7034 7034.
Derry: Council Offices, 98 Strand Road, Derry BT48 7NN. Tel: 028 7136 5151.
Limavady: 7 Connell Street, Limavady BT49 0EA. Tel: 028 7772 2226.
Magherafelt: 50 Ballyronan Road, Magherafelt BT45 6EN. Tel: 028 7939 7979.

Airport — **City of Derry Airport** (LDY), Airport Road, Eglinton. The original airport was a Fleet Air Arm base named HMS *Gannet* used to provide convoy cover during World War II. It remained a military base until the 1950s when much of it was returned to local landowners. Eglinton Flying Club used the remaining airfield and during the 1960s a commercial service to Glasgow was operated by Emerald Airways. A decision to expand the airport, then named Eglinton, to include commercial services was taken by Derry City Council in 1978. Loganair began a scheduled service to Glasgow in 1979 and 10 years later British Airways introduced a service to Manchester. After a sizeable investment programme 1989–93 a new terminal was opened in 1994 and the airport was renamed City of Derry Airport. With scheduled flights to London, Glasgow, Manchester, Birmingham, Dublin, Liverpool and Nottingham East Midlands, it has an estimated 250,000 passengers per year. Tel: 028 7181 0784.

Amelia Earhart Centre — Ballyarnet Country Park, Derry. A cottage containing an exhibition about Amelia Earhart, the first woman to fly the Atlantic solo. Earhart unexpectedly landed in a field at Ballyarnet on 21 May 1932, having in fact been heading for Paris. She disappeared over the Pacific Ocean in 1937 while attempting to circumnavigate the globe. Tel: 028 7135 4040.

Apprentice Boys Memorial Hall — Society Street, Derry. Designed by John Guy Ferguson and built in 1877, with an extension added in 1937. Locally known as 'the Mem', it now houses a museum of local items including the original locks for the city gates.

Ashbrook — Derry. A 17th century demesne beside the River Faughan with a house (not open to the public) built in 1686. The grounds feature mature trees with a glenside walk.

Ballaun Stone — 3 miles (5km) south of Coleraine. Located near the graveyard in which stands the Camus High Cross (see separate entry). The stone has a hollow which holds water (which is said never to dry out) and is believed to have been used as a font. Another such stone can be found at Banagher Old Church; they were more properly originally used as mortar stones for pounding food.

Ballybriest Court Tomb — 2½ miles (4km) south of Draperstown. Dual-chambered court tomb. It has been badly disturbed but the forecourt and galleries are visible. Burnt bone and pottery sherds were uncovered during an excavation in 1937. The remains of a wedge tomb dating to before 2000 BC and a stone circle are nearby.

Banagher Glen — 2½ miles (4km) southwest of Dungiven. A nature reserve, Special Area of Conservation and Area of Special Scientific Interest consisting largely of broadleaved deciduous woodland covering (232 acres/94ha) and including Banagher Lake. The largest block of semi-natural woodland in Northern Ireland, it is also an example of a calcifuge oak woodland. The woodland was subject to clearance in the 1770s and has been largely undisturbed since. Birdlife includes peregrine falcon and redstart. Tel: 028 7776 0304.

Banagher Old Church — 2 miles (3km) southwest of Dungiven. Ruin of a 12th century church whose foundation has been ascribed to both St Patrick and St Muiredagh O'Heney. An inscription on the west door reads: 'this church was built in ye year of God 474', but this was probably carved in the 1730s, long after the church had become a ruin. A chronicle states that in 1121 'the King of Ciannacht was killed by his own kinsmen in the centre of the cemetery in Bennchar'. In the churchyard is a ballaun stone. To the southeast of the church stands a mortuary house, resembling a miniature church and possibly holding the remains of St Muiredagh O'Heney. The sand from under the tomb is said to be lucky for members of the O'Heney family.

Battles — See Siege of Derry

Bellaghy Bawn — Castle Street, Bellaghy. A restored two-storey fortified Plantation house built in 1618 by the London Vintners' Company. Opened to the public in 1996, it now features exhibitions relating to local history and to Nobel Prize-winning poet Seamus Heaney, born in Bellaghy in 1939. It also holds the Seamus Heaney Archive, a collection of audio-visual material about the poet and his works. Tel: 028 7938 6812.

Bishop's Road — A scenic route over Benenvenagh Mountain from Downhill to Limavady, built by the Earl Bishop of Derry and passing Mussenden Temple, leading to Gortmore Viewing Point. The annual Eagle's Rock Hill Climb follows the route.

Bovevagh Church — Bovevagh, 5 miles (8km) south of Limavady. An early monastic site on a promontory on the Bovevagh River with a record of a church prior to 1100. Bovevagh (Both Maeve) means the church of Maeve. The church was in ruins by 1622 but was refurbished and in use until the early 19th century. There is a mortuary house (possibly 12th century) similar to that at Banagher, with a hand hole enabling pilgrims to touch the remains or relics of the occupant.

Brackfield Bawn — Brackfield, 6 miles (10km) southeast of Derry. Remains of a two-storey bawn built in the early 17th century by Sir Edward Doddington of the London Skinners' Company. It was abandoned by 1700 but the ruins are substantial.

Bridewell Jail — Church Street, Magherafelt. The former courthouse and jail, now housing a tourist information centre and new library (opened in 2002). Tel: 028 7963 1510.

Broighter Gold, The — A collection of gold ornaments unearthed by ploughman Tom Nicholl in 1896 and named after the area near Limavady in which they were found. Dating to the 1st century BC, the items included necklaces, torcs and a miniature boat complete with oars, mast and rudder. They were sold to the British Museum for only £600 but eventually returned to Ireland following a court case. The gold can now be seen at the National Museum in Dublin.

Camus High Cross	3 miles (5km) south of Coleraine. The only high cross in Derry. Located in a roadside graveyard, the red sandstone cross is carved with biblical scenes such as the Adoration of the Magi and the Marriage Feast of Cana.
Castledawson	A village on the River Moyola, founded in 1710 by Joshua Dawson, Chief Secretary for Ireland.
Causeway Museum Service	Provides museum services within the Coleraine, Ballymoney, Moyle and Limavady local authorities. The **Coleraine Museum collection** traces the history of the town through personalities, art, settlement and civic and commercial history. Particular emphasis is placed on the Bann River as a means of communication, trade and resources. The collection is made available through Coleraine Town Hall. The **Ballymoney Museum collection** features artifacts from the Mesolithic, Neolithic and Bronze Ages and also specialises in the important local history of road racing. Currently not on exhibition. The **Ballycastle Museum collection** is displayed seasonally in the Old Courthouse and Market House in Ballycastle and features Irish arts and crafts. The **Limavady Museum collection** features local industrial heritage and is housed at the Roe Valley Country Park.
Claragh Heritage Centre	Moneydig Road, Kilrea. A private museum dedicated to the history of rural life and set in a $3\frac{1}{2}$ acre (1.4ha) garden. Tel: 028 2954 0370.
Creggan Country Park	Derry. Based around the Glenowen Fisheries Workers' Co-operative, opened in 1992 and expanded by 2002 into a fishing, watersports and outdoor activity centre. The site consists of three former reservoirs built in the 19th century. Tel: 028 7136 3133.
Derry City Walls	The only remaining complete city walls in Ireland. About 1 mile (1.6km) in circumference, the walls were built 1613–18 by the Honourable the Irish Society to protect Plantation settlers. Constructed by Peter Benson to a design by Sir Edward Doddington of Dungiven, the wall includes four original gates – Bishop's Gate, Shipquay Gate, Ferryquay Gate and Butcher's Gate – plus some of the original bastions, and provides a walkway around the old inner city. Three further gates were added later: New Gate (1789), Castle Gate (1803) and Magazine Gate (1865). Tel: 028 7126 7284.
Derry Guildhall	Guildhall Square, Shipquay Place, Derry. Originally built in neo-Gothic style in 1887 as the administrative centre for the Londonderry corporation and named in honour of the London guilds. The building was destroyed by fire on Easter Sunday 1908 and subsequently rebuilt. Standing on ground reclaimed from the River Foyle, it has the largest clock tower in Ireland and a set of impressive stained-glass windows illustrating the history of the city. It now houses the council chamber and mayor's office for Derry City Council, also hosting orchestral concerts, organ recitals, dancing championships and the annual feiseanna. It seats 400. Tel: 028 7137 7335.
Derry Harbour Museum	Harbour Square, Derry. Dedicated to the maritime history of Derry and housed in the former Londonderry Port and Harbour Commission building, designed in 1882 by John Kennedy. It contains a 30ft (9m) replica of the curragh in which St Columba sailed to Iona in AD 563. Tel: 028 7137 7331.
Derry Work House Museum	Glendermott Road, Derry. Located in an original workhouse building on the Waterside designed by George Wilkinson in 1840. Closed on the advent of the NHS, it then served as Waterside Hospital. Exhibits depict the effects of the Great Famine and the subsequent Victorian poverty; there is also an exhibition on the Battle of the Atlantic and its impact on the city. Tel: 028 7137 7331.
Downhill Castle and Mussenden Temple	1 mile (1.6km) west of Castlerock, 5 miles (8km) west of Coleraine. Ruins of an 18th century palace built on a headland by Frederick Augustus Hervey, Earl Bishop of Derry. Mussenden Temple was built in honour of Hervey's cousin Mrs Frideswide Mussenden, who died at the age of 22. The domed rotunda, built on a clifftop in 1783 as a summer library, was inspired by the Tivoli Temple of Vesta outside Rome and now houses a display depicting Hervey's life. Other buildings include a mausoleum, while at Bishop's Gate Lodge there is a modern ornamental garden. The extensive garden includes a glen walk, woodlands and two artificial lakes. There is also a stand of giant sitka spruce. Maintained by the National Trust since 1949. Tel: 028 7084 8728.
Draperstown	Known locally as Ballinascreen. A village in the Sperrin Mountains which has a market house built in 1839 for the Drapers' Company.
Dungiven	A small town located beside the River Roe beneath Benbradagh mountain. The former seat of the O'Cahan Clan, it developed around the castle and church, expanding towards the bank of the Roe.
Dungiven Castle	Main Street, Dungiven. Victorian neo-Gothic castle overlooking the River Roe, built 1820–39 by the Ogilby family, agents for the Skinners Company. Located on the site of a Plantation era bawn and a late 17th century fortification, possibly known as Lady Cooke's Castle, the building has been substantially restored and is now used as a hostel and activity centre. Tel: 028 7774 2428.
Dungiven Priory and O'Cahan's Tomb	Glenshane Road, Dungiven. The site of a Celtic monastery established by St Naechtain, and of an early church built c.AD 680 overlooking the River Roe. This was replaced after 1100 by an Augustinian priory dedicated to St Mary and which became a centre for teaching. There is a ruined 13th century chancel and also a tomb traditionally ascribed to Cooey-na-Gall (Terror of the Stranger), an O'Cahan chieftain who died between 1385 and 1390. The tomb features a reclining figure of a soldier and, below this, six niches each with a figure of a gallowglass (Scottish soldier).
Ebrington Barracks	Limavady Road, Londonderry. A self-contained barracks built inside Derry city walls in 1841 and extended to the south and east during the next century. It housed mainly locally recruited regiments until after World War I, when English and Scottish regiments were posted to the city. These were replaced by a territorial unit from Wales at the outbreak of World War II. In 1942 the barracks were transferred to the Royal Navy, which was to spearhead the defence of North Atlantic convoys from Derry. Ebrington was also a base for the development of anti-submarine devices such as sonar and the Squid mortar system. It remained a naval base after World War II,

being renamed HMS *Sea Eagle* in 1947, and continued to fulfil this function until the late 1950s. Reverting to full army use with the onset of the Troubles in the early 1970s, its parade ground doubled as a helicopter pad and it was attacked several times by the IRA. The closure of the barracks was announced in January 2002, after which ownership was transferred to the Office of the First and Deputy First Minister.

Errigal Old Church — 2 miles (3km) southwest of Garvagh, 9 miles (15km) southeast of Limavady. Small church founded by St Columba and possibly built by Errigal c.AD 560. Destroyed by Viking raiders in the 9th century, it was rebuilt but finally destroyed following the 1641 rebellion. Found near the church was Onan's (Adamnan's) Rock, which has imprints of the feet of St Adamnan.

Ervey Wood Country Park — 5½ miles (9km) southeast of Derry. A country park covering 50 acres (20ha) and including Ervey Wood and Tamnymore Wood, which are separated by the Crunkin Burn. Probably at its best during spring, with a woodland carpet of bluebell, wood sorrel and primrose. Animal species include red squirrel, and buzzards are also to be seen. Part of the Ervey Wood ASSI, it is maintained by the Environment and Heritage Service. Tel: 028 7772 2074.

Flowerfield Arts Centre — Coleraine Road, Portstewart. Opened in 1980 in a restored Victorian house built in 1855 and rescued from dereliction by Coleraine Borough Council. Recently refurbished, it provides classes and workshops in a wide variety of artistic disciplines. Tel: 028 7083 1400.

Forests — In addition to country parks and nature reserves, the county is studded with many forests, including: **Altbritain Forest**, in the Sperrins near Draperstown; **Ballykelly Forest**, west of Ballykelly, designated the first state forest in the north of Ireland in 1910; **Castleroe Forest**, 1½ miles (2.5km) south of Coleraine; **Garvagh Forest**, northwest of Garvagh on the Agivey River; **Glenshane Forest**, on the southern side of Glenshane Pass. The Ulster Path passes through the forest; **Gortnamoyagh Forest**, east of Dungiven behind Benbradagh Mountain; **Loughermore Forest**, southwest of Ballykelly on the southern slopes of Loughermore Mountain; **Mountsandel Forest**, 52 acres (21ha) of mature mixed woodland on the River Bann; **Portglenone Forest** 65 acres (26ha) of ancient woodland by the River Bann on the Derry/Antrim border; **Somerset Forest**, mature mixed woodland on the outskirts of Coleraine; **Springwell Forest**, on the A37 Coleraine–Limavady Road.

Freemasons Hall — Bishop Street, Derry. Built by Bishop Barnard in 1753 on the site of the original house of the Bishop of Londonderry and extended by the Earl Bishop to become known as the Bishop's Palace. Used as a barracks in 1798 before being returned to the bishopric, it was home 1867–96 of Mrs Cecil Frances Alexander, wife of Bishop Alexander, who wrote 'All Things Bright and Beautiful' and 'There is a Green Hill Far Away'. Sold to the masonic order in 1945, it has been used by the Freemasons since 1946.

Garvagh — A town founded as a 'private plantation' on the banks of the Argivey River in the 17th century by George Canning, an agent for the Ironmongers' Company of London. The land had originally been owned by Manus O'Cahan, who lost it after the 1641 rebellion. The Cannings kept the freehold until selling up in 1920 and returning to England.

Garvagh Museum and Heritage Centre — Main Street, Garvagh. Museum exhibiting over 2000 local artefacts including Neolithic implements and domestic Victoriana. Features include a memorial to Denis Hempson, the blind harper. There is also a blacksmith's shop with a display of agricultural machinery. Tel: 028 2955 8216.

Guy Wilson Daffodil Garden — Portstewart Road, Coleraine. The world's largest collection of daffodil varieties (more than 800), mainly Irish bred and set in a planned landscape beside the River Bann on the campus of the University of Ulster in Coleraine. Begun in 1872, it is a memorial to Northern Ireland's leading daffodil breeder, Guy Livingstone Wilson (1885–1962) from Broughshane, Co. Antrim, who specialised in white-trumpeted and reverse bicolour daffodils and developed varieties such as 'Driven Snow', 'Ava', 'Chinese White', 'Spellbinder', 'Knowehead' and 'Preamble'. The first bulbs were planted in 1971 and the garden was opened to the public in 1974. Tel: 028 7032 4431.

Hezlett House — 5 miles (8km) northwest of Coleraine. A thatched former rectory built in the 17th century with a cruck-truss roof construction. It now houses a small museum of farm implements. Maintained by the National Trust. Tel: 028 7084 8728.

Highest point — Mount Sawel in the Sperrin Mountains at 2224ft (678m).

Interesting facts — Derry is famous for its **murals**, usually painted on the sides of houses. They are linked to their geographical location and the make-up of the surrounding community. Among the most notable are Free Derry Corner, at the junction of Fahan Street and Rossville Street and marking the entry into the Bogside, a Catholic enclave to the west of the Derry city walls; this was originally painted by John Casey in 1969 with the words 'You are now Entering Free Derry'. In 1972, Free Derry Corner was the scene of 'Bloody Sunday', when 13 people were killed in one of the most infamous incidents of the modern Troubles. Another area with notable murals is the Fountain, where the wall and kerb paintings reflect the area's strong Unionist identity and include a mural of the Battle of the Boyne. The ***Great Northern***, the biggest screw-propelled ship in the world at that time, was launched from Derry shipyard in 1842. It was built by William Coppin (1805–95), who is buried in St Augustine's Church in Derry. **Magilligan Strand**, running for more than 6 miles (10km) between the mouth of Lough Foyle and Portstewart, is the longest beach in Ireland. **Roaring Meg** is a cannon situated on the Double Bastion at the southwest corner of the walls of Derry. The cannon got its name from the tumultuous noise it made when fired during the Siege of Derry in 1688–9. **Shipquay Street**, within the walls of Derry, is the steepest commercial street in Britain or Ireland. The **Mitred Earl** is the popular nickname of Frederick Augustus Hervey, Bishop of Derry and 4th Earl of Bristol. In 1775 the eccentric cleric built himself a vast palace at Downhill, near Portstewart, and promptly filled it with books and paintings. The Mitred Earl initiated a great sporting event on the sands of Downhill. The steeplechase competitors were all clergymen and the prize was a benefice or a curacy! **Lough Foyle** is the only place in the world where north is south, and south is north, i.e. the north side of the lough is in Donegal in Southern Ireland while the south side is in Derry, Northern Ireland.

Kilrea A small market town in the southeast of Coleraine Borough west of the River Bann, developed by the Mercers' Company of London at the time of the Plantation. It has a typical Plantation layout with a long main street and a 'diamond' at the centre. An ancient 'fairy thorn' (hawthorn) stands protected near Kilrea's ancient church, and the town is home to an annual summer Fairy Thorn Festival.

King's Fort Drumsurn, 5 miles (8km) southeast of Limavady. Well preserved early Christian rath.

Londonderry Air: origin of In 1851 Jane Ross, who lived at 51 Main Street, Limavady, was listening to a blind fiddler, traditionally said to be Jimmy McCurry (1830–1910), playing outside the Burns & Laird Shipping Office. A collector of traditional tunes, she transcribed the melody he was playing. This melody may have been originally composed by yet another blind harper, Rory Dall O'Cahan (according to legend he was helped by fairies), in the early 17th century. Possibly a variation of *Aislean an Oigfear* ('The Young Man's Vision'), the tune was carried on through harpers such as blind Denis O'Hampsey and eventually to McCurry. Ross later passed the melody to collector and music publisher George Petrie. It was published by Petrie in his collection *Ancient Music of Ireland* (1855) and given the title 'Londonderry Air'. Various attempts were made to write lyrics for the melody, but it was only in 1910 that Somerset lawyer Fred Weatherly adapted some lyrics he had already written and 'Danny Boy' was born. A statue of Jane Ross stands on Catherine Street, Limavady, and she is buried at Christ Church Dromachose Parish Church, Limavady. Jimmy McCurry is buried in Ballykelly. Incidentally, Dennis Hempson (aka Denis O'Hampsey) was born in Garvagh in 1695 and died in Magilligan on 5 November 1807, thus living in three centuries. A most accomplished harper despite having lost his sight as a result of smallpox at the age of three, his harp, presented to him in 1713, is in the Guinness Museum in Dublin.

Lough Beg 6 miles (10km) northeast of Magherafelt. The lough is 2780 acres (1125ha) in area and on average 6ft 6in (2m) in depth; it lies to the north of Lough Neagh at the start of the Lower Bann River, of which it is essentially a widening. It is a designated Ramsar site, Area of Special Scientific Interest, Special Protection Area and National Nature Reserve, with Church Island as its focal point. Migrating birds include black-tailed godwit, green sandpiper, wood sandpiper and greenshank. Rare plants include pennyroyal and Irish lady's tresses orchid. Fish include salmon, bream, roach and pike. An area of wet grassland on the west shore is known as the Strand.

Lough Foyle An estuary bordering both Northern Ireland and the Irish Republic, and fed by the rivers Foyle, Faughan and Roe. It covers 69.1 sq miles (179 sq km) and has an average depth of 16ft (5m). Areas of the lough are designated a Ramsar site, Area of Special Scientific Interest, Special Protection Area and National Nature Reserve. Fisheries include salmon fishing and mussel dredging. An important site for migrating birds, Lough Foyle attracts flocks of whooper swan and light-bellied brent goose as well as red-breasted merganser and eider, and provides a habitat for waders including bar-tailed godwit and golden plover. An RSPB nature reserve stretches from Longfield Point to border the Roe Estuary National Nature Reserve.

Lough Foyle Base Line The Ordnance Survey base line for Ireland was established in 1824 on the shore of Lough Foyle under the guidance of Major General Thomas F Colby. The site was chosen because it was close enough to be connected with the Scottish triangulation. The north base tower is at Ballymulholland and the south base tower at the rear of the Kings Lane Estate at Ballykelly. There is a third base tower at Mineary, while a fourth has been lost to the sea. The length of the base was 41,640.8873ft (12,692.142m).

Macosquin A village to the south of Coleraine. Originally a 6th century monastic settlement and the site of a 12th century Cistercian abbey, it subsequently developed as a Plantation village.

Maghera Old Church Church Street, Maghera. A 10th century church with a finely decorated 12th century west door, located on the site of a 6th century monastery founded by St Lurach. It was in use as a parish church until the 19th century. The sculpture of the crucifixion above the doorway is one of the earliest in Ireland.

Magilligan Martello Tower 12½ miles (20km) northwest of Coleraine. Located in the nature reserve off Magilligan Point. It is one of a series of towers built around the coast of the British Isles during the Napoleonic Wars but the only one in Northern Ireland, its twin at Greencastle being in County Donegal in the Irish Republic. With walls 9ft (2.7m) thick and with a 24 pound cannon, the tower was built c.1812 to guard the entrance to Lough Foyle; it would have been manned by one officer and between five and 27 artillerymen. Tel: 028 7776 3982.

Millennium Forum, The Newmarket Street, Derry. Ireland's largest purpose-built theatre, opened in 2001 and with an auditorium seating 1100. Tel: 028 7126 4455.

Moneymore A small town originally established by the Drapers' Company and containing two market houses built in 1819 and 1839. Although it lies within County Londonderry, it is administered by Cookstown District Council in County Tyrone.

Moneymore Model Village High Street, Moneymore. A historically accurate scale model of Moneymore in the Plantation period including cottages, manor house, bawn and church. The layout is derived from Raven's map of 1622. Tel: 028 8674 8910.

Motto The motto of County Derry is *Vita Victoria Veritas* (Life, Victory, Truth); the motto of Derry City is 'No Surrender'.

Mountsandel Fort 1 mile (1.6km) southeast of Coleraine. Remains of an early hunter-gatherer settlement next to the River Bann in Mountsandel Forest. Dating to c.7000 BC, it is the oldest known settlement in Ireland.

Museum of Free Derry Glenfada Park, Derry. Housed in the Bloody Sunday Centre, established in renovated flats at the southern end of Glenfada Park and opened in the summer of 2006. Exhibits illustrate the struggle for civil rights, including the Battle of the Bogside, Free Derry (taken to cover the Bogside, Brandywell, Bishop Street and Foyle Road areas) and Bloody Sunday. Tel: 028 7136 0880.

Mussenden Temple — See Downhill Castle and Mussenden Temple

Nature Reserves — **Altikeeragh**, 445 acres (180ha) of peatland including blanket bog. Vegetation includes mosses, heather, deergrass, crowberry, bog asphodel and common cottongrass; **Ballymaclary,** an area of dune slack in which the moss *Rhytidium rugosom* makes its only appearance in Ireland and also home to the rare marsh helleborine. Completely within an MOD danger zone and therefore not accessible to the public; **Ballynahone Bog**, 242 acres (98ha) of the southern portion of the raised bog of Ballynahone Bog. One of the largest remaining areas of uncut lowland raised bog in Northern Ireland. Also a Ramsar site covering 600 acres (243ha). Birdlife includes curlew, snipe and hen harrier; **Binevenagh**, includes Binevenagh Mountain and the man-made Binevenagh Lake. Basalt crags above flat coastal plain. Plants rare in Northern Ireland, such as moss campion and purple saxifrage, are found on the cliff faces. Birdlife includes buzzards, peregrine falcon, fulmars and kittiwakes; **Magilligan Point**, the tip of a large area of shifting sand dunes. Vegetation includes bird's-foot trefoil and pyramidal orchids. Birdlife includes great northern diver, red-throated diver and sanderling; **Roe Estuary**, an area of mud flats harbouring vast quantities of seashore animals such as lugworms and periwinkles which also attract waders and waterfowl. See also Benagher Glen, Lough Beg.

Ness Wood Country Park — 7 miles (11km) southeast of Derry. Covers 124 acres (50ha) of mixed woodland, originally part of the extensive oak woodland which once covered the area and gives its name to all the sites called 'Derry' (*doire*). Some of the oak was cleared during the Plantation by the Grocers' Company, who then introduced larch, beech and sycamore. Since then native species such as birch, rowan, ash, hazel and elm have been added to the mix. The park contains the 30ft (9m) Ness Fall, Ulster's highest waterfall, on the Burntollet River. Tel: 028 7772 2074.

Phoenix Peace Fountain — Anderson Park, Coleraine. Dedicated on 4 July 2002, the fountain is a gift from the communities of the United States to those of Northern Ireland. Some of the metal used in its construction was recovered from the melting down of US firearms used in violent crimes. Its six-sided base represents the six counties, while 26 granite pillars represent the councils of Northern Ireland and a phoenix, flame and nest, represent Northern Ireland rising from the ashes of its past. Anderson Park is named after Hugh Anderson JP, who donated £3000 to provide the park in 1876. It is currently undergoing a modernisation project.

Plantation of Ulster Visitor Centre — High Street, Draperstown. Audio-visual presentation and interactive displays covering the period of the Flight of the Earls and The Plantation, including the life of Hugh O'Neill. Tel: 028 7962 7800.

Port of Derry — The UK's most westerly port. Its sheltered deep-water harbour is accessible at all times and can handle ships up to 30,000 tonnes. Main exports are potatoes and animal feeds; main imports grains, animal feeds and fuel oils.

Portrush — A thriving seaside resort close to the County Antrim border which developed from a fishing village after the arrival of the railways in 1855.

Portstewart — A seaside resort named after Lieutenant Stewart, who obtained a lease for the area. It was developed under the influence of local landlord John Cromie but, because he was resistant to the influence of a railway connection, it developed as a genteel equivalent of its near neighbour Portrush. Its west-facing promenade looks out across the 2 miles (3km) Portstewart Strand to Inishowen. In recent years it has developed a large student and second-home owner population.

Prehen House — Prehen Park, Derry. Prehen means 'Place of the Crows'. An early Georgian house designed by Michael Priestley and built c.1740. The original owners of the estate were the Elvins and the Tompkins; it became the home of the Knox family after Honoria Tompkins married Andrew Knox in 1738. Knox's daughter, Mary Ann, was tricked into marrying the wastrel John MacNaughten in 1761 and when her family attempted to spirit her away to Dublin she was murdered by MacNaughten during an ambush. He was captured and sentenced to death, but the rope broke on the first attempt to hang him. Although successfully hanged at the second attempt, he was afterwards given the epithet 'Half Hanged MacNaughten'. Tel: 028 7134 2829.

Rivers — The **Burn Dennet** rises south of Plumbridge and enters the River Foyle near Cloghcor in County Tyrone.

The **Foyle** forms the border between County Tyrone and County Donegal above Strabane, entering County Derry near Magheramason before flowing into Lough Foyle.

The **Faughan** rises in the northern Sperrins near Park and runs into Lough Foyle, 6 miles (10km) north of Derry.

The **Lower Bann** marks the border between County Derry and County Antrim and reaches the sea at Portstewart, running from Lough Neagh and forming Lough Beg. Tributaries include the Agivey and the Clady.

The **Moyola** runs into Lough Neagh.

The **Roe** rises south of Dungiven and enters Lough Foyle above Limavady.

Roe Valley Country Park — 1 mile (1.6km) south of Limavady. Runs either side of the River Roe, culminating in Carrick Rocks. It encompasses the site of the old town of Limavady and an O'Cahan castle, as well as ruined water mills which were used in linen production. The park is also the site of Ulster's first domestic hydroelectric power station, opened in 1896; the building, which still houses all its original machinery, is now the Power House Museum. There is a countryside museum and visitor centre. The park is home to over 60 species of bird. Tel: 028 7772 2074.

Rough Fort, The — 1 mile (1.6km) west of Limavady. Fine example of a prehistoric ring fort about 1 acre (0.4ha) in area. Maintained by the National Trust.

St Columb's Cathedral — London Street, Derry. Built inside the Derry city walls in 1633 and thus the oldest surviving building in the city. Built in the style known as 'Planters' Gothic', it was the first cathedral constructed in the British Isles after the Reformation. A spire was added in 1776 but had to be taken down after it showed signs of falling; it was re-erected in 1822. The interior of the cathedral was refurbished in 1861. A chancel was added in 1887 and a chapterhouse in 1910. The chapterhouse has on display the keys used to lock the city gates against the Jacobites in 1688–9. Stained glass windows also depict episodes from the Siege of Derry. A stone in the porch bears the following saying: 'If stones could speake then London's prayse should sound who built this church and cittie from the grounde.' Tel: 028 7126 7313.

St Eugene's Cathedral — Creggan Road, Derry. Built 1851–73 of Newry sandstone with a spire added in 1902. The catholic diocese of Derry covers County Derry, the Inishowen peninsula and parts of Counties Donegal and Tyrone. Each October St Eugene's and St Columb's take part in the Two Cathedrals Festival, in which the combined chorus is joined by international musicians and singers.

St Patrick's Church — Brook Street, Coleraine. Located in the centre of Coleraine on site of an earlier church founded by St Patrick in the 5th century, close to the town's 17th century defences.

Sampson's Tower — Farlow Road, Limavady. A fortified rubble and sandstone tower located near the Rough Fort (see separate entry), and built by public subscription in memory of Arthur Sampson, an agent of the London Fishmongers' Company.

Siege of Derry — Richard Talbot, 1st Earl of Tyrconnell, acting as James II's viceroy in Ireland, was anxious to ensure that all strong points in the country were held by garrisons completely loyal to the Roman Catholic cause. By November 1688, only the walled city of Londonderry still had a Protestant garrison and so the Earl of Antrim was ordered to replace it with a more reliable force. Alexander MacDonnell, 3rd Earl of Antrim, despite his age of 76, keenly responded to this command but wasted valuable time searching for men who were 6ft tall or more. An army of around 1200 men, mostly 'Redshanks' (Highlanders) set out on the week William of Orange landed in England. When the army arrived on 7 December 1688 the city gates were closed against them and the siege began; according to tradition the gates were closed and the city thus saved by 13 apprentice boys. For many months the city suffered appalling conditions as cannonballs and mortar-bombs rained down, and famine and disease took their toll. Having been deposed by William, James fled to France, where Louis XIV gave him support to regain his crown, and on 12 March 1689 he landed in Kinsale, Ireland, with 6000 French soldiers. He took Dublin and with a Jacobite army of Catholics, Protestant Royalists and French marched north, joining the siege on 18 April and summoning the city to surrender. The king was rebuffed and actually fired at by some of the more determined defenders. The governor of the city, Lt-Col. Robert Lundy, who favoured an accommodation with James, fled under the cover of darkness. The people took up arms under the direction of Major Henry Baker and Captain Adam Murray, who organised the famous defence in conjunction with the Rev. George Walker under the refrain 'No Surrender'. British warships arrived off Londonderry on 11 June but refused to risk shore guns until, ordered by Marshal Frederic Schomberg, a relief ship, the *Mountjoy*, sailed up the Foyle and broke the barricading boom which had been stretched across the river, thus relieving the siege on 28 July 1689. The city had endured 105 days of siege, during which 4000 people died. The siege is commemorated annually by the Apprentice Boys of Derry, who stage the week-long Maiden City Festival; this culminates in a parade around the walls of the city by local members, followed by a parade of the city by the full Association.

Sport: general — The **FIM World Motocross Championship GP of Ireland** was held at Ballykelly Motocross Park in 2006.

football — **Derry City** were founded in 1928 and won the Irish League championship in 1965. Having left the Irish Football League (which covers Northern Ireland) in 1973 because of safety issues, they joined the League of Ireland (which covers the Republic of Ireland) in 1985, winning the treble of Premier Division championship, FAI Cup and League Cup in 1989. They won another league title in 1997, the FAI Cup again in 1995 and 2002 and the League Cup in 1991, 1992, 1994, 2000 and 2005. Their home ground is Brandywell Stadium.

The Irish Football League clubs in Derry are:

Coleraine, formed in 1927, winners of the Irish League championship in 1974 and of the Irish Cup in 1965, 1972, 1975, 1977 and 2003. Their home ground is The Showgrounds, Ballycastle Road, Coleraine.

Institute, formed in 1905. Their home ground is YMCA Grounds, Glenshane Road, Drumahoe

Limavady United, formed in 1884. Their home ground is The Showgrounds, Rathmore Road, Limavady.

Gaelic football — **Derry** won the All-Ireland Senior Football Championships in 1993.

Springhill — Springhill Road, Moneymore, 5 miles (8km) southwest of Magherafelt. A 17th century Plantation house, sometimes called the 'prettiest house in Ulster' and now housing a costume exhibition. It is reputedly haunted by a lady called Olivia. In the garden straight avenues lead to the house and to a folly tower behind it. A series of walled gardens, including a herb garden and a perennial garden, have been created on the site of former outbuildings. There is also a shell-lined grotto with a weeping ash and a mountain ash lined walk. Maintained by the National Trust, to whom it was willed in 1957. Tel: 028 8674 8210.

Tirkane Sweathouse — 3 miles (5km) northwest of Maghera. One of the few remaining examples of an Irish sweathouse (a type of sauna) constructed during the 18th or 19th century, although dating is difficult. Like most such structures, the Tirkane sweathouse is in a secluded area. Built of stone, covered with turfs, and with a chimney hole and a small entrance, these structures may have been used as a means to a 'sweating cure' for certain ailments, although the precise reason for their existence is unknown.

Tower Museum — Union Hall Place, Derry. A museum dedicated to the history of the city of Derry from prehistoric times. Exhibits include artefacts recovered from the large Spanish ship *La Trinidad Valencera*, which sank in Kinnegoe Bay in 1588 during a storm while trying to return to Spain after the failure of the Spanish Armada. The wreck was discovered by the City of Derry Sub-Aqua Club in 1971 and is now housed in the O'Doherty Tower, erected in 1986 close to the site of a castle built by the O'Doherty family in the 16th century. Tel: 028 7137 2411.

University of Ulster — Formed in 1984 by the amalgamation of the New University of Ulster (Coleraine), Ulster Polytechnic (Jordanstown), Magee College (Derry) and the Art College (Belfast). In 2003, the Northern Ireland Hotel and Catering College was also integrated, becoming the Portrush site of the Coleraine campus. The university's two campuses in County Derry are at Magee and Coleraine. The main building of the Magee Campus, Northland Road, Derry, was designed by A P Gibbon of Dublin and overlooks the Foyle. Tel: 028 7137 1371. The Coleraine Campus, Cromore Road, Coleraine, is the university's administrative HQ and site of the Millennium Arboretum. There are two halls, the Octagon (500 seats) and the Diamond (1200 seat) used for recitals and concerts; the Riverside Theatre, opened in 1976, is the third largest professional theatre in Northern Ireland. Former students include comedian Omid Djalili, and writer and former Middle East hostage Brian Keenan.

Some famous people born in County Derry

Beatty, William (surgeon aboard *The Victory*) (1773–1842)	Derry
Burke, James (science historian and TV presenter) (1936–)	Derry
Burton, Amanda (actress) (1956–)	Ballougry
Cary, Joyce Arthur (novelist) (1888–1957)	Derry
Chichester-Clark, James (5th Prime Minister of Northern Ireland) (1923–2002)	Castledawson
Coyle, Nadine (singer) (1985–)	Derry
Doherty, Peter (footballer) (1913–90)	Magherafelt
Farquhar, George (dramatist) (1678–1707)	Derry
Gregg, Harry (footballer) (1932–)	Tobermore
Heaney, Seamus (poet) (1939–)	Castledawson
Hume, John (politician) (1937–)	Derry
Locke, Josef (singer) (1917–99)	Derry
Massey, William (Prime Minister of New Zealand) (1856–1925)	Limavady
McGuinness, Martin (politician) (1950–)	Derry
O'Neill, Martin (footballer and manager) (1952–)	Kilrea

Down

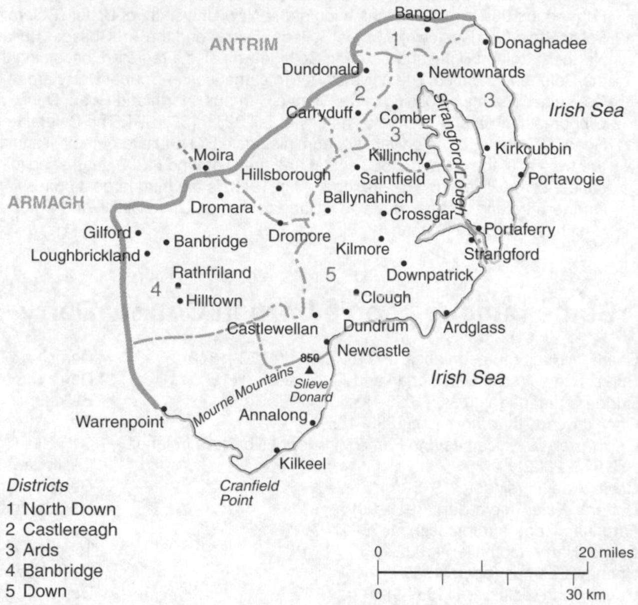

Bangor
Donaghadee
ANTRIM
Dundonald
Newtownards
Irish Sea
Carryduff
Comber
Strangford Lough
Killinchy
Kirkcubbin
Moira
Hillsborough
Saintfield
Portavogie
Ballynahinch
ARMAGH
Dromara
Crossgar
Gilford
Banbridge
Dromore
Portaferry
Loughbrickland
Kilmore
Strangford
Rathfriland
Downpatrick
Hilltown
Clough
Castlewellan
Dundrum
Ardglass
Newcastle
850
Mourne Mountains
Slieve Donard
Irish Sea
Warrenpoint
Annalong
Kilkeel
Cranfield Point
Districts
1 North Down
2 Castlereagh
3 Ards
4 Banbridge
5 Down
0
20 miles
0
30 km

County Down is bounded on the east by the Irish Sea and has western and northern borders with County Armagh and County Antrim; its northwesterly extremity is on Lough Neagh. It includes both Northern Ireland's southernmost point, Cranfield Point, and its easternmost point, Burr Point.

It is an anomaly of the Northern Ireland boundaries that Lisburn City Council has several areas administered in Antrim but located in County Down (see Antrim introduction). Similarly Newry and Mourne District Council in County Armagh administers several areas situated in County Down (see Armagh introduction). The population shown opposite should in actuality be 376,894 to accommodate these anomalies and give a true reflection.

The main geographical features of the county are the Mourne Mountains, the peninsulas of Ards and Lecale and Strangford and Carlingford Loughs. The county is split into five administrative districts: Ards Borough Council, Banbridge District Council, Castlereagh Borough Council, Down District Council and North Down Borough Council. County Down also incorporates the eastern half of Belfast, which traditionally includes the main industrial activities such as shipbuilding and aircraft construction. Early manufacturing in the county concentrated on the linen industry, given impetus by an influx of Huguenot refugees at the end of the 17th century. In addition to agriculture the long coastline of County Down provided a thriving fishing industry centred on the port of Kilkeel.

The areas around Carlingford and Strangford Loughs were colonised during the Neolithic period because of their rich resources of fish and fowl. Early in the historical period the area was occupied by the Dal Fiatach and Cruthin tribes and an early leader was Niall of the Nine Hostages. St Patrick carried out the majority of his missionary work in County Down and County Armagh, having landed on the shores of Strangford Lough in AD 432. A Viking fleet was defeated on Strangford Lough in 926. A small Norman force of 22 knights and 300 infantry invaded County Antrim and East Down in 1177 and captured Down(patrick); the ensuing Battle of Downpatrick resulted in the defeat of the Dal Fiatach under Rory MacDonleavy. The Normans then followed their normal practice of subjugating the local populace by building a series of motte and bailey castles at such places as Dundrum, Dromore and Clough. However, John de Courcy and his wife Affreca, as was also the custom of the time, founded a number of monasteries in Down, chief among them the Benedictine monastery on Cathedral Hill in Down and the Cistercian Inch Abbey.

The Battle of Drumderg on 12 May 1260 resulted in a Norman victory during which the Irish leader Brian O'Neill was killed. During the Plantation of Ulster Conn O'Neill, Hugh Montgomery and James Hamilton were all granted substantial portions of County Down and restored much of the land wasted during the Nine Years' War of 1594–1603. County Down rose in rebellion in 1798 and there were actions and skirmishes at Saintfield, Newtownards and Portaferry. The United Irishmen, led by Henry Munro, a Lisburn tailor, were defeated by government forces at the Battle of Ballynahinch, fought on 12–13 June 1798. The Great Famine took its toll on the county – census records show that between 1841 and 1851 the population declined by almost 44,000.

During the second half of the 19th century towns such as Dundonald and Holywood benefited from their proximity to Belfast, although ports such as Portaferry and Donaghadee suffered from competition from Belfast and Larne. The Belfast & County Down Railway (BCDR) was opened in 1848. The main line ran from Belfast to Newcastle, with branches to Ardglass, Ballynahinch and Donaghadee. It incorporated the Downpatrick, Dundrum & Newcastle Railway in 1881 and the Belfast, Holywood & Bangor Railway in 1884. The BCDR was absorbed into the Ulster Transport Authority in 1948.

During the Troubles as many as 243 'conflict-related' deaths have been recorded in the county since 1969. Close to Narrow Water at Warrenpoint 18 British soldiers were killed on 27 August 1979 by two IRA bombs detonated from within the Irish Republic.

The city of **Newry**, at the head of Carlingford Lough, straddles the border with County Armagh (see Armagh for details). Major towns in County Down include Banbridge, Bangor, Downpatrick, Dundonald and Newtownards. Other towns and villages include Ardglass (*Ard Ghlas*) – a fishing port on the Lecale Peninsula – Ballynahinch, Donaghadee, Helen's Bay, Hillsborough – named for the Hill family and the site of a notable courthouse and fort as well as a castle – Holywood, Katesbridge, Kilkeel, Millisle, Newcastle, Portaferry and Spa.

Down	**Population**			**Area**	
Districts	*male*	*female*	*total*	*sq miles*	*sq km*
Ards	35,759	37,485	73,244	145	376
Banbridge	20,705	20,687	41,392	175	453
Castlereagh	31,669	34,819	66,488	33	85
Down	31,622	32,206	63,828	250	647
North Down	36,821	39,502	76,323	31	81
Total	156,576	164,699	321,275	634	1642

Attractions and General Information

Administrative headquarters
Ards: 2 Church Street, Newtownards BT23 4AP. Tel: 028 9182 4000.
Banbridge: Downshire Road, Banbridge BT32 3JY. Tel: 028 4066 0600.
Castlereagh: 1 Bradford Court, Upper Galwally, Castlereagh BT8 6RB. Tel: 028 9049 4500.
Down: 24 Strangford Road, Downpatrick BT30 6SR. Tel: 028 4461 0800.
North Down: Town Hall, The Castle, Bangor BT20 4BT. Tel: 028 9127 0371.

Admiral Leslie Hall
Millisle Road, Donaghadee. Built in 1872 and founded the same year as Admiral Leslie's Free School by the legacy of his widow, Martha Leslie and dedicated to the memory of her late husband, the Rear-Admiral Samuel Leslie. It is now a Baptist church.

Annalong Corn Mill
Marine Park, Annalong. Restored water-powered corn mill overlooking the harbour and using water channelled from the Annalong River. Originally constructed in 1830, it ceased working commercially during the 1960s. The visitor centre has an exhibition on windmills and water power.

Audley's Castle
Strangford, 7 miles (11km) northeast of Downpatrick. A three-storey 15th century tower house and bawn in the grounds of the Castle Ward estate, near Strangford Lough. It is named after John Audley, who owned the tower in the 16th century.

Ballycopeland Windmill
1 mile (1.6km) west of Millisle. The only working windmill in Ireland. A tower mill with a mobile cap, it was probably built in the late 18th century, and was run 1845–1915 by the McGilton family who sold it to the state in 1935 after it had fallen out of use. It was restored to working order in 1978. The miller's house, kiln house and grain stores have also been restored and contain a visitor centre and exhibitions.

Ballynahinch
A market town founded by Sir George Rawdon in the 1630s and the site of a battle in 1798. Connected to the railway in 1858.

Ballynahinch Market House
The Square, Ballynahinch. Built by John Rawdon, 1st Earl of Moira, 1792–5 and damaged during the Battle of Ballynahinch in 1798. The estate, including the town square, was sold in 1800 to the Ker family, who restored the Market House and installed a town clock in 1841. The town square was leased from the Ker Estate in 1998 by Down District Council and the Ballynahinch Regeneration Committee was made responsible for the maintenance of the Market House. In 2002 the building was restored to its original 1795 appearance, minus the clock.

Ballydugan Mill	Drumcullen Road, Ballydugan, Downpatrick. Originally a water-powered flour mill built in 1792 but afterwards steam power was added. Eight storeys high, it produced flour, bran and starch. Poor economic conditions forced its closure by 1857 and thereafter it fell into ruin. In 1987 a restoration project was begun by Noel Killen; the mill now serves as a hotel and restaurant. There is also an exhibition about its mill's history and the restoration. Tel: 028 4461 3654.
Ballynoe Stone Circle	$2^1/_2$ miles (4km) south of Downpatrick. A stone circle 115ft (35m) in diameter consisting of 50 uprights varying from 2ft (0.6m) to 6ft (1.8m) in height. It was excavated during the 1930s, when a burial mound within the circle was found to contain several cremations.
Banbridge	Named for the first bridge over the Upper Bann River, which was built in 1712, the town of Banbridge was a centre for the linen and flax industry. The main street is built on a hill but has an underpass (The Cut), constructed in 1834 to enable an easier run for the stagecoach service. There is a memorial to Francis Crozier, resplendent with four polar bears, who died while on the expedition with Sir John Franklin in the attempt to find the Northwest Passage.
Bangor	Bangor (Beannchar) is an affluent seaside resort on the northern coast of the county and Belfast Lough. One of Ulster's earliest towns, having been founded in the 6th century around a monastic settlement, it was developed during the Plantation period by Sir James Hamilton, who built the Custom House and Tower. Further expansion took place with the development of the cotton industry in the first half of the 19th century; the town became a popular seaside destination when the railway from Belfast arrived in 1865.
Battles	See separate table for details of the battles of Ballynahinch, Downpatrick and Drumderg.
Bronte Homeland Interpretive Centre	Ballyroney, 3 miles (5km) northeast of Rathfriland, 8 miles (13km) southeast of Banbridge. Housed in Drumballyroney Church and Schoolhouse, where Patrick Bronte (born Patrick Brunty in Emdale in 1777), the father of Charlotte, Branwell, Emily and Anne, first preached and taught. Nearby are Bronte's mother's house (Alice McClory's Cottage), his birthplace cottage in Emdale and another school at Glascar where he also taught in the 1790s.
Carlingford Lough	A lough forming part of the western border of County Down and more than 2500 acres (1000ha) in area. Internationally important numbers of wildfowl and waders overwinter here, including pale-bellied brent geese, great crested grebe, shelduck, redshank and oystercatcher. Carlingford Lough is also important for terns, especially breeding roseate terns, with 4.3 per cent of the European Community population.
Castle Espie	Ballydrain Road, Comber. A former quarry, now a Wildfowl and Wetlands Trust centre opened in 1990 and providing a habitat for species including light-bellied brent geese, white-faced whistling ducks and whooper swans. Tel: 028 9187 4146.
Castle Ward	Strangford, 7 miles (11km) northeast of Downpatrick. A house built in the 1760s by Bernard Ward, 1st Viscount Bangor and his wife Anne overlooking Strangford Lough. Because they could not agree on the style, the front façade is classical in style and the rear façade Gothic. The different styles also run through the interior of the house. One of the most popular interior exhibits is the Squirrels' Boxing Match, a tableau of stuffed squirrels dressed in bloomers and wearing boxing gloves, competing in a well-choreographed boxing match. The house stands in a 750 acre (300ha) estate with walled landscaped grounds and woodland. An early 18th century canal, 1739ft (530m) long, called the Temple Water, flows past the ruins of Audley's Castle and Lady Anne's Temple (built 1755–60). A 40 acre (16ha) garden includes yew terraces, a small arboretum, a sunken garden and a rock garden. The estate also features the Strangford Lough Wildlife Centre, a farm and the Victorian Past Times centre. Maintained by the National Trust since 1953. Tel: 028 4488 1204.
Castlewellan Forest Park	Main Street, Castlewellan. Originally an estate of the Annesley family; the castle was built by William Richard Annesley, 4th Earl Annesley, in 1856 inside an 18th century walled demesne. Sold to the Department of Agriculture in 1967, the estate became a forest park in 1969. It covers 1100 acres (450ha) and contains the 1 mile (1.6km) long, 100 acre (40ha) Castlewellan Lake. The Annesley Garden and National Arboretum is a walled garden first built in 1740, and planted since 1850 with specimens of trees and shrubs from all over the world including Chilean eucryphias, Japanese maples, Australian athrotaxis and American sorrel. In particular it hosts 18 of the oldest living trees in the British Isles as well as many trees with record heights for the British Isles. The parkland includes stands of beech, ash and oak plus commercial plantings of sitka spruce. Tel: 028 4377 8664. See also Peace Maze.
Churches	**St Andrew's Parish Church**, Carricknaveagh Road, Boardmills. Located in Killaney Parish (Church of Ireland) and built 1865–7 on land donated by the Marquis of Downshire. The architects were Welland and Gillespie. Consecrated on Thursday 19 April 1867 in the name of St John the Evangelist and known as such until c.1904, it later became known as St Andrew's. **Holy Trinity Parish Church**, Ballylesson Road, Drumbo. Located in Drumbo Parish and built on a new site in Ballylesson townland to a design by Charles Lilly at a cost of £1251. Consecrated in 1791, the church was enlarged in 1863, with a new roof added in 1874. Extra lighting was installed in 1981 and the church underwent remedial and restoration work in 2004–5. **St John the Evangelist**, Castlewellan Road, Hilltown. Neoclassical Catholic church built 1844–50 to a design by Patrick Byrne.
Clough Castle	Clough, $5^1/_2$ miles (9km) southwest of Downpatrick. Motte and bailey castle erected during the reign of King John. A 15th century stone tower, which replaced the original wooden structure, stands atop a 25ft (8m) motte. There was a crescent shaped bailey to the south of the mound. Its location suggests it may have been a outlier for Dundrum Castle.
Cockle Row Cottages	Groomsport, 2 miles (3km) northeast of Bangor. A row of refurbished fishermen's cottages, restored externally and internally to their possible appearance in 1910 and opened in 1997. The row includes a heritage cottage, an out-centre of the North Down Heritage Centre, and a tourist information centre. Tel: 028 9145 8882.

Crawfordsburn Country Park	Helen's Bay, $2\frac{1}{2}$ miles (4km) west of Bangor. Country park located on the shore of Belfast Lough and encompassing beaches, woodland, a waterfall and Grey Point Fort. Tel: 028 9185 3621.
Delamont Country Park	Killyleagh, 5 miles (8km) northeast of Downpatrick. Country park on the shore of Strangford Lough and including both woodland and parkland. The Strangford Stone, Ireland's tallest standing stone at 33ft (10m) high, lies within the park, which also contains a rath and a heronry.
Donaghadee	Aka The Dee. Donaghadee (*Domhnach Daoi*) is a fishing port on the Ards peninsula with lighthouse and lifeboat station. An early harbour was built by royal warrant of 1616 and a new harbour was built in 1821. Today it is a growing commuter town and seaside resort.
Down Cathedral	Cathedral Hill, The Mall, English Street, Downpatrick. Cathedral Church of the Holy and Undivided Trinity (Church of Ireland). The hilltop site has ancient ecclesiastical connections. St Patrick died in Down and his grave is marked in the cathedral graveyard. The first recorded abbot of Down was Scannlan, who died in 753. The monastery was raided by Vikings many times and a round tower and stone church on the site were damaged by lightning in 1016. The church was repaired and enlarged by St Malachy. Norman adventurer John de Courcy arrived in 1177, expelled Malachy's Augustinian monks and established a Benedictine foundation. The cathedral was rebuilt in 1321 after further destruction and suffered again during the Bruce Wars, before being laid waste in 1541 during the Dissolution of the Monasteries. The cathedral lay in ruins for the next 250 years before the present building was begun in 1790. Consecrated in 1818, it retained the basic form of earlier churches on the site. The tower was completed in 1829. Extensive renovations were carried out 1986–7.
Down County Museum	The Mall, English Street, Downpatrick. Housed in the former Down County Gaol, built 1789–96 and in use 1796–1830. Afterwards it served as a cholera hospital, private house, infantry barracks (1859–1901, and during the two world wars), and after 1945 had a variety of uses before it was transformed into a museum from 1980. The first public gallery opened in 1984. Some of the gaol cells and courtyards have been restored. There are collections relating to the story of St Patrick, the history of the county, the Normans in Down and the history of the gaol and its inmates; exhibits include early Christian artefacts, costumes, tools and everyday items. Tel: 028 4461 5218.
Downpatrick	Originally called Down (Dun) after the hill fort that once stood on the site, the town became Downpatrick (Dun Padraig) in 1609 when a charter of James I to the cathedral insisted it be rededicated to the Trinity rather than St Patrick. The name Patrick was added to the town's name so that the connection with the saint should not be lost. Restored under the influence of the Southwell family during the early 18th century, Downpatrick was a port until 1745 when a tidal barrage was built across the River Quoile. It has an English Street, an Irish Street and a Scotch Street, which meet at Town Hall Corner.
Downpatrick & County Down Railway	Market Street, Downpatrick. The only Irish standard gauge (5ft 3in/1.6m) heritage railway in Northern Ireland. Founded in 1985, the railway operates over 1 mile (1.6km) of restored Belfast & County Down Railway track from Downpatrick to Newcastle, passing the burial mound of Magnus Barefoot. The ultimate aim is to extend the line as far as Ballyduggan Halt. There is also a line from Downpatrick to Inch Abbey across the River Quoile. The railway runs one steam locomotive and five diesel locomotives. The original station building, by then serving as an Ulsterbus depot, was demolished in the 1970s to make way for a supermarket. This was demolished in turn and replaced by a nearby 19th century gasworks manager's house, moved brick by brick from its original site because it was in a dangerous condition; this now serves as the station and houses part of the working museum. Tel: 028 4461 5779.
Dromantine House	Glen Road, Newry. Neoclassical house built by Arthur Innes in 1808 on land originally owned by the Magennis family. Extended in the 1860s by his son, Arthur Charles Innes, the house was bought in 1926 by its present owners, the Society of African Missions, who ran it as a seminary until 1974 and opened it as a retreat centre in 1975. Renovation was completed in 2001. Tel: 028 3082 1224.
Dunbarton House	Gilford, 4 miles (6km) northwest of Banbridge. Located opposite Gilford Mills and built in 1840 overlooking Gilford by the Dunbar McMaster family, who owned the town's important linen mills. The house was used as a hospital during both world wars.
Dundonald	Now a suburb of East Belfast and the site of the Ulster Hospital, the original village was established around a Norman motte. Recorded as a borough in 1333, it remained relatively undisturbed even after the coming of the railways. Dundonald International Ice Bowl is the only Olympic sized ice rink in Ireland.
Dundrum Castle	Dundrum, 3 miles (5km) northeast of Newcastle. Early medieval ruined castle located on a hilltop site dominating the surrounding countryside and overlooking Dundrum Bay. The site was occupied in the pre-Norman period and was chosen by John de Courcy in 1177 as the site for a coastal castle. Originally known as the Castle of Rath, it became known as Dundrum Castle from the 16th century. The castle was in possession of Hugh de Lacy in 1205 and captured by King John in 1210. After another brief spell under de Lacy's stewardship it returned to royal possession in 1234. Held by the Gaelic chiefs the Magennises of Mourne in the 16th century before being relinquished to Lord Mountjoy in 1601, it suffered during the 1641 Rebellion and was slighted by Cromwellian forces in 1652. From 1636 it was owned by the Blundell family, who despite such depredations built an L-shaped mansion house (now in ruins) in the lower ward. From the Blundells it passed into the hands of the 2nd Marquess of Downshire in the early 19th century, and into state care in 1954.
Exploris Aquarium	The Rope Walk, Castle Street, Portaferry. The Northern Ireland Aquarium, located on the shore of Strangford Lough. Opened in 1987 before being extended and reopened in 1994 as Exploris (Exploration of the Irish Sea). The aquarium has sections for Strangford Lough, the coastal zone

and on out into deep water. The facility also has a purpose-built sanctuary to help sick or abandoned seals. Tel: 028 4272 8062.

Forests — **Ballymoyer Forest** (45 acres/18ha), coniferous woodland on National Trust land; **Ballysallagh Forest** (406 acres/164ha), mixed woodland on the Craigantlet Hills; **Donard Forest** (702 acres/284ha), at the foot of the Mournes on the Glen River, planted with Scots and Corsican pine in 1927; **Drumkeeragh Forest** (500acres/200ha), on the lower slopes of Slieve Croob. Commercial forest planted with sitka and Norway spruce, Scots, Corsican and lodgepole pine, larch and cedar; **Fathom Forest** (350acres/140ha), on the Newry to Dundalk road.

Greencastle — 4 miles (6km) southwest of Kilkeel. Ruins of a castle built by Hugh de Lacy, probably in the 1230s. A rectangular castle with D-shaped towers at each corner, it commands the mouth of Carlingford Lough. It changed hands more than once before becoming the residence of Richard de Burgh (Burgo), the 'Red Earl' of Ulster, whose daughter married Robert the Bruce. Sacked by Edward Bruce in 1316, it was captured and damaged by Irish attacks in 1343 and 1375. It was owned by the Earls of Kildare and the Bagnals before finally being destroyed by Parliamentarian forces in 1652.

Grey Abbey — Greyabbey, 6 miles (10km) southeast of Newtownards. Ruins of a Cistercian foundation on the shore of Strangford Lough established in 1193 by Affreca, wife of John de Courcy and daughter of Godred, king of the Isle of Man. The Gothic style abbey was known as *Iugum Dei* (Yoke of God). The grounds include a re-creation of a monastic physic garden, with a selection of varieties of medicinal plants and herbs. The ruins are now surrounded by the 18th century parkland of nearby Rosemount House.

Grey Point Fort — Located within Crawfordsburn Country Park on the shore of Strangford Lough. The only restored coastal battery of its type in the UK, it features a 6in (152mm) coastal defence gun previously located at Spike Island in Cork harbour, the two original guns having been sold for scrap in 1957.

Helen's Bay — An affluent seaside resort named after Lady Helen Selina Dufferin (1807–67), mother of Lord Dufferin and granddaughter of playwright Richard Brinsley Sheridan. It originated as a planned village, which developed with the advent of the railway when builders of houses within a mile of the new station were offered free travel for a period on the Belfast & County Down Railway.

Helen's Tower — 3 miles (5km) south of Bangor. Standing on a wooded hilltop on the Clandeboye Estate, the monument was built in the 1850s by Lord Dufferin and dedicated to the memory of his mother, Lady Helen Selina Dufferin (see Helen's Bay). Lady Helen wrote the poem *The Lament of the Irish Emigrant*. A full-scale replica of Helen's Tower called the Ulster Memorial Tower stands in Thiepval Cemetery in northern France. The tower is dedicated to the officers and men of the 36th (Ulster) Division and 'the sons of Ulster in other forces' who fell during World War I. In particular it stands in tribute to the 5500 Ulstermen who fell dead or wounded on 1 July 1916 during the opening salvos of the Battle of the Somme. It was unveiled on 19 November 1921 by Field-Marshal Sir Henry Wilson and rededicated on 1 July 1981 by Princess Alice.

Highest point — Slieve Donard at 2707ft (850m), also the highest point in Northern Ireland. Located in the Mourne Mountains close to the sea $2^1/_2$ miles (4km) south of Newcastle, it is named after St Donard, a follower of St Patrick.

Hillsborough Castle — Main Street, Hillsborough. Country house built for Wills Hill, 1st Marquis of Downshire and Earl of Hillsborough and completed in 1797, four years after his death. Its design by R F Brettingham incorporated an earlier house. The south front was extended in the 1830s following the closure of a public road which had run alongside the house. The house was bought from the Wills family by the British government in 1922 to be the official residence of the Governor of Northern Ireland. It has been the residence of the Secretary of State for Northern Ireland since 1973 and is the official residence of the royal family when they visit Northern Ireland. The Anglo-Irish Agreement was signed in the Throne Room of Hillsborough Castle in 1985. The extensive grounds include parkland and forest planting, along with Europe's largest rhododendron bush.

Hillsborough Court House — The Square, Hillsborough. Originally built as the Market House in 1760 by Wills Hill, 1st Marquis of Downshire and Earl of Hillsborough. A south wing was added in 1810 to provide a market hall, a function it still fulfils. At the same time a new north wing housed a courthouse. It is now home to a Tourist Information Centre and an exhibition showing the development of justice in Ireland.

Hillsborough Fort — The Square, Hillsborough. Artillery fort built by Peter Hill in 1630 on the site of a Magennis stronghold and strengthened by Arthur Hill in 1650. Located in the grounds of Hillsborough Castle, the fort was given to the people of Northern Ireland in 1959.

Holywood — A seaside resort named after a wood adjoining an early Christian church and developed after the opening of the railway in 1848. It holds a annual Jazz and Blues Festival.

Inch Abbey — $^3/_4$ mile (1.2km) west of Downpatrick. The ruins of a Cistercian abbey beside the River Quoile. As the area is marshy the building actually stands on an island (Inis Cumhscraigh), as indicated by its name. A church established on the site prior to 800 suffered more than once from predation by the Vikings. The abbey, established by John de Courcy in 1180, remained a distinctly English rather than Irish foundation, with strong ties with its mother house of Furness in Lancashire. At its dissolution in 1541 the monastery's lands passed to the Perceval Maxwell family, who retained them until they were transferred into state care in 1910.

Interesting facts — **Amanda McKittrick Ros** (1860–1939) was a novelist born in Drumaness, Co Down. Nick Page, author of *In Search of the World's Worst Writers,* rated Ros the worst of the worst. Her novels provided the entertainment at gatherings of the Inklings, the group of Oxford dons including C S Lewis and J R R Tolkien who met from the 1930s to the 1950s. They competed to see who could read her work aloud for longest before starting to laugh. Her novel *Delina Delaney* begins: 'Have you ever visited that portion of Erin's plot that offers its sympathetic soil for the minute survey and scrutinous examination of those in political power, whose decision has wisely been the means before now of converting the stern and prejudiced, and reaching the hand of slight aid to share its strength in augmenting its agricultural richness?' **Benjamin Franklin** stayed at Hillsborough in October 1771 as a guest of Wills Hill, 1st Marquess of Downshire. Hill and Franklin, the American Colonial Envoy, met to try and reach an amicable solution to the problems between Britain and her American colonies. Unfortunately the two men loathed each other on sight; on his return to America, Franklin told the anxious colonists that there was no alternative to revolution, and in 1776 they issued the Declaration of Independence. George III always blamed Wills Hill for the loss of the American colonies. **The first Irishman to fly**, Harry Ferguson (1884–1960), did so at Hillsborough on 31 December 1909. The so-called 'Mad Mechanic', born on the family farm at Growell, 3 miles (5km) from Hillsborough, made Ireland's first powered flight in a self-built monoplane, flying 390ft (119m) at an altitude of 12ft (3.7m) above Hillsborough Park. Ferguson later built the lightweight tractors affectionately known as 'Fergies'. Comber-born **Thomas Andrews Jr** was the man responsible for overseeing the design of the *Titanic* and went down with the ship when it struck an iceberg on 15 April 1912. **Burr Point**, 1 mile (1.6km) south of the village of Ballyhalbert on the Ards Peninsula, is the most easterly point of mainland Ireland. **St Patrick's Church** in Newry, dating from 1578, was the first church to be built for the Protestant faith in Ireland. **Grace Neill's Bar** in Donaghadee, on the Ards Peninsula, was built in 1611, making it the oldest public house in Ireland. The **Eagle Wing Festival** is held annually in Groomsport in July to celebrate Ireland's links with America. Is is named after the *Eagle Wing*, an emigration ship which took 140 Presbyterians to the New World in 1636. Killyleagh-born Hans Sloane, president of the Royal College of Physicians, is best remembered for bequeathing his collection to the British nation which became the foundation of the British Museum, however in the late 1600s he visited Jamaica, tried the chocolate and considered it 'nauseous', but found it became more palatable when mixed with milk. When he returned to England, he brought the recipe with him, thus becoming the inventor of drinking chocolate.

Islands
There are 150 islands in Strangford Lough, 14 islands in Carlingford Lough and ten offshore islands in the Irish Sea, totalling 174. See separate table.

Jordan's Castle
Ardglass, 6 miles (10km) southeast of Downpatrick. A 15th century three-storey tower house, one of a series of such houses in the town which helped to protect the harbour. It was possibly named for Simon Jordan, who withstood a siege here during the Tyrone Rebellion in the late 16th century. Restored by antiquarian Francis Bigger after 1911, it passed into state care in 1926. Other tower houses in Ardglass are Margaret's Castle and Choud Castle.

Katesbridge
A village named after Kate McKay, who lodged the workmen who built the bridge over the Upper Bann River.

Kilclief Castle
Kilclief, $2\frac{1}{2}$ miles (4km) south of Strangford. Early tower house beside Strangford Lough, built 1413–41 for John Sely, Bishop of Down. It is said that he lived here with his married mistress, Lettice Whalley Savage.

Kilkeel
The fishing port of Kilkeel (*Cill Chaoil*) is known as the capital of the Kingdom of Mourne.

Killyleagh Castle
Killyleagh, $5\frac{1}{2}$ miles (9km) northeast of Downpatrick. Norman castle built by John De Courcy in 1180, the only castle built by the knight still inhabited today. The castle dominates the attractive little port on Strangford Lough. Sir Hans Sloane, who gave the world drinking chocolate and the British Museum, was born in Killyleagh.

Kilwarlin Moravian Chruch
Kilwarlin Road, Hillsborough. Built in 1835 by the Rev. Basil Patras Zula on the site of a former Moravian Church of Ireland building, established by John Cennick in 1755. Zula was a Greek who in his youth had fought against the Turks at Missolonghi. In memory of his homeland he landscaped the grounds of the church in the form of the Battle of Thermopylae.

Kirkistown Castle
Kirkistown, 12 miles (19km) northeast of Downpatrick. Three-storey tower house and bawn built in 1622 by Roland Savage of Ballygalet and remodelled in 1800 in Gothic Revival style by Colonel Johnston. It was opened to the public in 2001.

Mahee Castle
7 miles (11km) southeast of Newtownards. Aka Nendrum Castle. Tower house standing on Mahee Island and built in 1572 by a Captain Browne.

Mahee Island
Located in Strangford Lough, Mahee Island boasts an early Celtic monastery (see Nendrum); monks were believed to have occupied the area from the 5th to the 10th century. Between Mahee and Island Taggart are dozens of tiny islands, known as the 'basket of eggs'. See also Mahee Castle.

Millisle
A popular seaside resort on the Ards Peninsula. During World War II it was a destination of the Kindertransport, which helped Jewish children escape from mainland Europe; the Millisle Refugee Farm was open 1938–48.

Mount Stewart
Portaferry Road, Newtownards. A Neoclassical house surrounded by the best known garden in Northern Ireland, created by Edith, Lady Londonderry (1879–1959) in the 1920s. The main house was enlarged in 1840 and contains *Hambletonian*, a painting by George Stubbs of a famous racehorse with connections to the family, considered to be one of the finest paintings in Ireland. Also on display are 22 chairs used at the Congress of Vienna in 1815. The land, originally known as Mount Pleasant, was purchased in 1744 by Alexander Stewart, whose son Robert became 1st Marquess of Londonderry in 1816. The garden was named European Garden of Inspiration in 2003 and contains plants and planting schemes evoking regions throughout the world. Its features include Spanish and Italian gardens, a sunken English garden and a shamrock garden. Trees include oaks, Japanese maples and eucalyptus. The grounds feature a 5 acre (2ha) lake and the Temple of the Winds, a private dining house built 1782–5. Maintained by the National Trust since 1976. Tel: 028 4278 8387.

Mourne Mountains
An iconic area of Ireland and an Area of Outstanding National Beauty covering more than 220 sq miles (570 sq km) of moorland, woodland and coast to the northeast of Carlingford Lough. There

are 12 peaks, the highest being Slieve Donard (2707ft/850m), also the highest in Northern Ireland. The range is composed of hard granite, much prized by the building industry.

Movilla Abbey
Movilla Road, Newtownards. Ruins of a 12th century Augustinian abbey founded by St Malachy on the site of a 6th century foundation by St Finian. In 561 St Columba (Colmcille), a pupil of St Finian at Movilla, made a secret copy of the manuscript, 'St Martin's Gospel'. On discovering this, St Finian demanded that the book be kept in the library at Movilla. The disagreement resulted in the bloody 'Battle of the Books' at Cuildrevne, County Sligo. A synod held at Teltown decided that, as a penance for the loss of life, Columba should be exiled from Ireland; he subsequently settled on Iona. The ruins of a 13th century church on the site contain Anglo-Norman decorated trapezoidal coffin lids. Evidence of industrial activity connected to the abbey was unearthed during excavations during the early 1980s.

Murlough National Nature Reserve
3 miles (5km) northeast of Newcastle. A coastal system of sand dunes, woodland and heath, owned by the National Trust and covering 697 acres (282ha). The Trust has introduced Dexter cattle and Exmoor ponies to the area, while wild mammals include badger and stoat. Bird species include willow warblers, whitethroats and redwing; the nearby estuary has Brent geese, redshank, greenshank and shelduck. It is also home to numerous butterfly species. Tel: 028 9751 2365.

Nendrum
A monastic site on Mahee Island in Strangford Lough, possibly founded by St Mochaoi (Machaoi) during the 5th century; there is archaeological evidence of occupation from 639. The monastery was subject to Viking raids and the abbot of Nendrum was killed in 976. A short-lived Benedictine house was established on the island in 1177 by John de Courcy. Excavation of the site in 1922–4 revealed three concentric walled enclosures. In addition to a round tower, the buildings included a guesthouse, bronze-smith's hut, school and abbot's house. An iron bell was also found.

Newcastle
Newcastle (*An Caislean Nua*) is a seaside resort located on the site of a Magennis stronghold at the base of Slieve Donard, at the point where the Shimna River flows into the Irish Sea. It expanded greatly after the railway line from Belfast reached it in 1869.

Newry Canal
The oldest summit canal in Britain and Ireland, opened in 1741. Linking Lough Neagh with Newry, a series of six locks takes the canal from the river Bann at Portadown up to the summit at Poyntzpass, 82ft (25m) above sea level, from where nine other locks descend into Newry. The towpath is part of the Ulster Way.

Newry and Mourne Museum
Bank Parade, Newry. Opened in1986. Collections cover all periods from prehistory to modern times and concentrates on the development of the local area. Also a repository for an archive of photographs and documents relating to the economic and social development of Newry and Mourne. Tel: 028 3026 6839.

Newtownards
Aka Ards. A market town at the head of Strangford Lough, now a commuter town for Belfast. The New Town of the Ardes or the New Town of Blathewyc was established by the Normans under John de Courcy and recorded as a borough in 1333. Re-established by Hugh Montgomery in 1605, it prospered following the connection to the railway.

Newtownards Priory
Court Street, Newtownards. Dominican priory believed to have been founded by the Savage family in 1244. Enlarged during the 14th century, it was abandoned at the time of the Dissolution of the Monasteries in 1541 and subsequently burned. It was partially rebuilt by Hugh, Viscount Montgomery at the time of the Plantation.

North Down Heritage Centre
Castle Park Avenue, Bangor. Town Hall, The Castle. Exhibition of the history of Bangor from prehistory to the 1950s. Exhibits include Bronze Age swords and a model of the now demolished Bangor Abbey. Tel: 028 9127 1200.

Old Narrow Water Castle
Warrenpoint. Three-storey tower house and bawn built c.1560 overlooking Carlingford Lough and the River Newry near the site of a Norman motte. The tower is high with 6ft (1.8m) thick walls. The tower changed hands many times and was held by the Magennis during the late 16th century. Under State Care since 1956. It was close to Narrow Water that 18 British soldiers were killed on 27 August 1979 by two IRA bombs detonated from within the Irish Republic.

Peace Maze
Located in Castlewellan Forest Park (see separate entry), the maze covers 2.7 acres (1.1ha) and is the largest hedge maze in the world, with a total hedge length of more than 2 miles (3km). Planted with 6000 yew trees to a design by Beverley Lear incorporating ideas submitted in a competition open to schoolchildren, the maze, which has an overall pattern resembling the human brain, is designed with choices at various points to represent the path and decisions needed to be taken to achieve peace in Northern Ireland following the Good Friday Agreement. The hedges are cut 5ft (1.5m high) to encourage communication and co-operation between visitors.

Portaferry
A village standing on The Narrows at the entrance to Strangford Lough. It hosts an annual regatta of the classic Irish sailing ships known as Galway Hookers.

Portaferry Visitor and Information Centre
Castle Street, Portaferry. Housed a restored stable block of Portaferry Castle, a 16th century tower house overlooking the harbour, the visitor centre focuses on the heritage and environment of Portaferry and Strangford Lough. Tel: 028 4272 9882.

Raholp Church
2 miles (3km) east of Saul. Ruins of a church linked with St Tassach, who administered the last rites to St Patrick on 17 March 461. It was restored in 1915 by J F Bigger and again in 1989.

Redburn Country Park
1$^1/_4$ miles (2km) south of Holywood. Located on an escarpment above Belfast Lough, the estate was originally owned by the Dunville family, who owned the Dunville Whiskey Company in Belfast. It features beech woodland with a bluebell carpet each spring. As part of the Woodland Trust Trafalgar Woods Project, the 'Dreadnought Wood' was planted in 2005, one of 33 new woods planted across the UK each named after one of Nelson's Trafalgar fleet. HMS *Dreadnought* was manned mainly by Irish officers and seamen. Tel: 028 9127 5787.

Rivers
The **Annacloy** rises in the Dromara Hills and flows into Strangford Lough via Kilmore, Annacloy and Downpatrick. The river is known as the Quoile from Annacloy down through Downpatrick to the Barrage where it flows into the lough. The **Lagan** – see County Antrim.

Rostrevor Forest	1 mile (1.6km) northeast of Rostrevor. (G. *Ros Treabhair* = 'Trevor's Wood'.) Forest of 4200 acres (1700ha) planted with over 2500 acres (1000ha) of sitka spruce, Douglas fir and pine from 1931. The Cloghmore Stone, a 40 tonne granite boulder, is a local landmark in the forest, which lies on the southwestern side of the Mourne Mountains and overlooks Carlingford Lough.
Rowallene Gardens	Saintfield, Ballynahinch. Developed by Hugh Armitage Moore in the early 20th century. Covering 52 acres (21ha), the main features are the spring garden with massed open field displays of rhododendrons and azaleas, the rock garden and the walled garden. The garden also hosts the National Collection of penstemons. Maintained by the National Trust since 1956. Tel: 028 9751 0131.
St Patrick	St Patrick is inextricably linked with County Down and County Armagh. He was born, possibly named Succat (or Sochet), C.AD 389 in Britain of Romano-British parentage. His birthplace is uncertain, suggestions ranging from Gloucestershire to South Wales to Strathclyde. At 16 years old he was captured during a raid by King Niall of the Nine Hostages and enslaved in County Antrim. After six years he escaped and returned to Britain before being summoned back to Ireland as a missionary in a vision of the angel Victor. Having studied and become a bishop he returned to Ireland in 432, now known as Patricius. He landed at the mouth of the River Slaney on Strangford Lough and set up a church in a barn at Saul given to him by the local chieftain Dichu. Although he travelled extensively throughout Ireland, Ulster remained his base. He died on 17 March 461, receiving the last sacrament from Bishop Tassach at his church at Raholp. Like his birthplace, the site of his burial is subject to dispute. He may have been buried at either Saul or Downpatrick, where a stone was set up in 1900 next to the cathedral. He recorded an outline of his missionary work and his life in his *Confession* and *Letter to the Soldiers of Coroticus*. The main sites in County Down associated with St Patrick are Saul, Downpatrick, Struell Wells and Raholp. St Patrick's Day, celebrated on the anniversary of his death, became a public holiday in Ireland in 1903 by Act of Parliament. It is also a public holiday on the Caribbean Island of Montserrat, where many Irishmen were transported during the 17th century.
St Patrick Centre	Lower Market Street, Downpatrick. An exhibition opened in 2001 which explores the story and legacy of St Patrick and other early Christian missionaries in Europe. Tel: 028 4461 9000.
St Patrick's Church	Saul Road, Saul, Downpatrick. A replica of an early Christian church built in 1933 overlooking Strangford Lough. Located on the site of St Patrick's first church and close to his possible burial place, it was built to commemorate the 1500th anniversary of his arrival in Ireland in 432. Designed by Henry Seaver, the plan of the church is based on that of the Church of St Finghin at Clonmacnoise. Tel: 028 4461 3101.
Scarva Visitor Centre	Main Street, Scarva. Exhibits tracing the story of the Newry Canal and the local linen industry. Tel: 028 3883 2163.
Scrabo Country Park	1¼ miles (2km) southwest of Newtownards. A country park consisting of woodlands and disused quarries, the result of the mining of Scrabo stone, plus a prehistoric hill fort.
Scrabo Tower	Scrabo Road, Newtownards. Located in Scrabo Country Park on Scrabo Hill at the head of Strangford Lough, and overlooking Newtownards. Designed by Sir Charles Lanyon and built in 1857 at a cost of £3010 as a memorial to Charles William Stewart, 3rd Marquis of Londonderry (1778–1854), the tower stands 135ft (41m) high; inside there are 122 steps to a viewing level. Constructed from sandstone and basalt, the memorial was raised partly because of the kindness Stewart showed to the local population during the potato famine. Stewart was the brother of Viscount Castlereagh, 2nd Marquis of Londonderry (1729–1822).
Seaforde Garden	Seaforde, Downpatrick. A 17th century demesne containing an early 19th century house. Seaforde garden is a 5 acre (2ha) walled garden within the estate; its centrepiece is a hornbeam maze planted in 1975. In addition to a commercial tree and shrub nursery there is a Butterfly House and 'Pheasantry' with specimen trees and shrubs. The garden holds the National Collection of Eucryphias. There is also a Mogul Tower from which the garden can be viewed. Tel: 028 4481 1225.
Silent Valley Mountain Park	A 200 acre (80ha) site of moorland and woodland in the Mourne Mountains encompassing the Silent Valley and Ben Crom Reservoirs. The area is enclosed by the Mourne Wall, an 8ft (2.5m) high, 22 mile (35.5km) long wall built 1904–22.
Sketrick Castle	Sketrick Island, Strangford Lough. A four-storey tower house first mentioned in 1470. A subterranean passage discovered during excavations in 1957 helped provide fresh water. The building was severely damaged in a storm in 1896.
Somme Heritage Centre	Bangor Road, Newtownards. Reconstructed trenches from the Battle of the Somme highlighting Ireland's contribution to World War I, and commemorating the 36th (Ulster) and 16th (Irish) Divisions at the Somme and the 10th (Irish) Division at Gallipoli and in the Near East. Maintained by the Somme Association. Tel: 028 9182 3202.
Spa	As its name suggests, this village near Ballynahinch was developed as a health resort during the Regency period at the beginning of the 19th century. Following a brief expansion after the arrival of the railways, the health tourist industry gradually declined.
Sport	
football	**Ards** were founded in 1902 and are winners of the Irish League championship in 1958, the Irish League 1st Division in 2001, the Irish Cup in 1927, 1952, 1969 and 1974, and the League Cup in 1995. Nicknamed The Red and Blues, their home ground (which they share with Bangor FC) is Clandeboye Park, Portaferry Road, Newtownards. **Newry City**, founded in 1923 and originally known as Newry Town, were renamed when Newry gained city status in 2002. They are winners of the Irish League 1st Division in 1998. Their home ground is The Showgrounds, Greenbank Industrial Estate, Newry.

Gaelic football	**Down** won the All-Ireland Senior Gaelic Football Championships in 1960, 1961, 1968, 1991 and 1994.
horse racing	**Downpatrick** Racecourse, Lismore Road, Bishopscourt, Downpatrick. Right-handed, 1m 3f (2.2km) circuit with a short straight to the winning post. Tel: 028 4461 2054.
Strangford Lough	A shallow sea lough to the south of Newtownards, covering more than 57.8 sq miles (149.7 sq km) and a designated Marine Nature Reserve, Ramsar Site, Special Protection Area, Special Conservation Area and Area of Special Scientific Interest. Encompassing a wide variety of marine and intertidal habitats, it supports over 2000 marine species plus a multitude of wetland plants and animal species, including marine sponges, sea urchins, eelgrass, common seal, grey seal and otter. The five-year winter peak for overwintering waterfowl was more than 70,000 between 1992–3 and 1996–7. Bird species include bar-tailed godwit, curlew, dunlin, greylag goose, oystercatcher and shelduck. There are more than 150 islands in the lough and other features include The Narrows, where sea water enters the lough through a narrow entrance and The Dorn, a silled lagoon.
Struell Wells	$1^1/_4$ miles (2km) east of Downpatrick. Four healing wells located in a rocky valley and said to have been blessed by St Patrick. There are two main wells in covered buildings: the Eye Well is said to cure eye complaints and the Drinking Well to cure stomach ailments. The wells are fed by an underground stream which also supplies a nearby Victorian bath house, split into a men's and a women's bath house. There is also a ruined church on the site, which was a major pilgrimage centre from the 16th to the 19th century.
Tollymore Forest Park	2 miles (3km) west of Newcastle. Northern Ireland's first forest park, designated in 1955 and covering 500 acres (200ha) at the foot of the Mourne Mountains. The Shimna River flows through the park, which has several stone follies and bridges, reflecting the eccentricities of then owner Lord Clanbrassil and his friend, garden designer Thomas Wright (1711–86). There is an avenue of Himalayan cedars as well as exotic species such as monkey puzzle and giant redwoods, plus an arboretum with cork oak and strawberry tree. The arboretum also has the oldest tree in any Irish arboretum – the spruce *Picea abies* 'Clanbrassiliana', believed to have been planted in 1750. Oak from Tollymore was the preferred source for the wood used on White Star liners, including the *Titanic*.
Ulster Folk and Transport Museum	Cultra, Holywood. Formed by the merging of the Ulster Folk Museum, which opened in 1961, and the Belfast Transport Museum, the museum includes an outdoor collection of buildings taken from all parts of Northern Ireland and laid out on a 175 acre (71ha) site as a town known in the early 20th century as Ballycultra. The buildings include Ballinderry House (originally in Ballinderry), Ballyverdaugh National School, Bairds Printshop (Coleraine), Drumcree Catholic Church, Christ Church Church of Ireland (Kilmore), Corner Shop (Carrickfergus), Market and Court House (Cushendall), McCuskers Pub (Armagh), Northern Bank (Portglenone), Parochial Hall (Portaferry), Post Office (Antrim), Presbyterian Meeting House (Omagh), RIC Barracks (Antrim), Temperance Hall (Carrickfergus) and The Old Rectory (Toomebridge). The museum is the repository for Northern Ireland's photographic, TV and radio archives. The Transport Museum contains collections related to Northern Ireland's railways and road transport. There is also a Titanic Exhibition and a Flight X2 Exhibition. Tel: 028 9042 8428.
Ulster TT	The Ulster TT motor race was run on a $13^1/_2$ mile (22km) circular road circuit from Dundonald via Newtownards and Comber. It first took place in 1928 and was won by Kaye Don in a Lea Francis. In 1929 the race was won by Rudi Caracciola in a Mercedes-Benz SS and in 1930 the great Tazio Nuvolari won for Alfa Romeo. Nuvolari won again in 1933, this time in an MG K3 Magnette. In 1934 the specifications were changed in a move towards more normal road cars. Unfortunately in 1936, Jack Chambers in a Riley lost control at Regent Street, Newtownards and crashed into the crowd, killing eight spectators and injuring 40 others, 18 seriously. The race was never run again.
Ulster Wildlife Centre	Killyleagh Road, Crossgar. Large conservatory opened by Sir David Attenborough in 1992 and containing exotic fauna and vines. The 1 acre (0.4 acre) site also includes a reconstruction of Irish habitats such as meadowland, woodland and bogland. It is part of the Tobar Mhuire Estate Passionist Monastery. Tel: 028 4483 0282.
Woods on Your Doorstep	**Ballymaganlis Wood** ($2^1/_2$ acres/1ha), on the outskirts of Dromore. More than 2000 trees planted in 2000, including rowan, hazel, ash and pedunculate oak. Known locally as 'the ski slope'; **Carrowood** (1.3 acres/0.5ha), in Carrowdore village. Planted with native shrubs and trees; **Corrog Wood** (12 acres/5ha), north of Portaferry. Planting of native mixed woodland. A statue of a dryad in the wood is known locally as 'the frump in the stump'; **Cypress Park** ($2^1/_2$ acres/1ha), south of Donaghadee. Species include oak, ash, alder and scots pine; **Belvoir Wood** (15 acres/6ha), on the southern edge of Belfast. Planting to extend a development by the Friends of Belvoir. Includes paths, ponds and a wildflower meadow; **Glasswater** (15 acres/6ha), at Crossgar close to the Glasswater River. Plantings of oak, ash, willow and alder; **Kilcooley Wood** (12 acres/5ha), in southwest Bangor. Planted with oak, willow, alder and birch; **Nut Wood** ($9^1/_2$ acres/4ha), on the edge of Delamont Country Park. Planted with oak, willow, alder and birch. Includes a live willow sculpture of a hazel leaf; **Pond Wood and Compass Hill** ($2^1/_2$ acres/ha), northwest of Strangford village. Mixed broadleaf and conifer planting. The Lecale Way passes through the wood; **Windmill Hill Wood** (8 acres/3ha), Ballynahinch, close to the site of the denouement of the battle of 1789. Planted with native species, mainly oak; **Woodland View** (10 acres/4ha), on the edge of Newtownards with views of Strangford Lough and Scrabo Tower. Planted with native broadleaves; **The Woodland Walkway** ($2^1/_2$ acres/1ha), near Knock in East Belfast. Planted with a mixture of native species and Swedish hornbeam.

Some famous people born in County Down

Andrews, Thomas (shipbuilder) (1873–1912)	Comber
Clanny, William Reid (inventor of the Clanny Safety Lamp) (1770–1850)	Bangor
Faulkner, Brian (politician) (1921–77)	Helen's Bay
Hutcheson, Francis (philosopher) (1694–1746)	Saintfield
Irvine, Eddie (racing driver) (1965–)	Newtownards
Kielty, Patrick (television presenter) (1971–)	Dundrum
Macoun, John (Canadian naturalist) (1831–1920)	Magheralin
Martin, Sir James (inventor of the airplane ejector seat) (1893–1981)	Crossgar
McLarnin, Jimmy Archibald (welterweight boxer) (1907–2004)	Hillsborough
O'Neill, Sean (Gaelic footballer) (1940–)	Newry
Opik, Lembit (politician) (1965–)	Bangor
Pantridge, Frank (inventor of the portable defibrillator) (1916–2004)	Hillsborough
Salmon, Zöe (television presenter) (1980–)	Bangor
Sloane, Hans (physician and collector) (1660–1753)	Killyleagh
Yeats, John Butler (artist) (1839–1922)	Tullylish

Islands of Down

Island name	Area	Nearest landmark	General information
Angus Rock	Strangford Lough	Ballyquintin Point	Although it has a lighthouse, the tiny islet is almost covered at high water.
Ballyhenry Island	Strangford Lough	Portaferry	Owned by the National Trust.
Ballywallon Island	Strangford Lough	Ballywallon	
Big Bow Meel Island	Irish Sea	Ards Peninsular	aka Plough Rock. Ireland's most easterly point.
Bird Island	Strangford Lough	Black Nab	
Black Island	Strangford Lough	Ringcreevy	One of three Black Islands in the lough.
Black Island	Strangford Lough	Danes Point	One of three Black Islands in the lough.
Black Island	Strangford Lough	Tullycarnan	One of three Black Islands in the lough.
Black Islands	Strangford Lough	Bankmore Hill	Tiny rock stack.
Blockhouse Island	Carlingford Lough	Cranfield Point	Between County Down in Northern Ireland and County Louth in the Republic. Owned by the National Trust.
Boretree Island East	Strangford Lough	Temple Hill	One of the two Boretree Islands.
Boretree Island West	Strangford Lough	Temple Hill	One of the two Boretree Islands.
Bradock Island	Strangford Lough	Whiterock	
Brown Rock	Strangford Lough	Danes Point	
Bryalle, The	Irish Sea	Ballyhalbert	aka Burial Island.
Bullock Pladdies	Strangford Lough	Ballgarvan	
Bullock Rock	Strangford Lough	Ballgarvan	
Burial Island	Irish Sea	Ballyhalbert	See The Bryalle.
Butterlump Stone	Strangford Lough	Eden Vale	
Calf Island	Strangford Lough	Sketrick Island	
Calf Rock	Strangford Lough	Paddy's Point	
Carriganean	Carlingford Lough	Seafield	G. = Rock of the Bird.
Carrigaroan	Carlingford Lough	Seafield	Lies next to Carriganean.
Castle Island	Strangford Lough	Drumildoo Point	One of three Castle Islands in the lough.
Castle Island	Strangford Lough	Danes Point	One of three Castle Islands in the lough.
Castle Island	Strangford Lough	Ringmore Hill	One of three Castle Islands in the lough.
Chanderies	Strangford Lough	Temple Hill	
Chapel Island	Strangford Lough	Greyabbey	One of two Chapel Islands in the lough.
Chapel Island	Strangford Lough	Templecormick	One of two Chapel Islands in the lough.
Charleys Rock	Carlingford Lough	Cranfield Point	The lough has a history of shipwrecks.
Cloghy Rocks	Strangford Lough	Cloghy	
Cockle Rock	Strangford Lough	Paddy's Point	
Conly Island	Strangford Lough	Pea Island Point	aka Hulin Rocks.
Copeland Island	Irish Sea	Donaghadee	Largest of the three Copeland Islands. See also John's Island, Mew Island.
Craigaveagh	Strangford Lough	Whiterock	
Cross Island	Strangford Lough	Reagh Island	aka Hulin Rocks.
Darragh Island	Strangford Lough	Drumildoo Point	
Dead Man's Island	Carlingford Lough	Duggans Point	So named as it is thought that anyone who drowns in the lough will be washed up here.
Dickey's Rocks	Carlingford Lough	Seafield	Named after a local family.
Dickson's Island	Strangford Lough	Strangford	
Dodd's Island	Strangford Lough	Shrigley	
Downey's Pladdy	Strangford Lough	Mahee Island	
Downey's Rock	Strangford Lough	Mahee Island	
Drummond Island	Strangford Lough	Pea Island Point	

DOWN

Island name	Area	Nearest landmark	General information
Duck Rock	Strangford Lough	Reagh Island	
Dullisk Rock	Strangford Lough	Kircubbin	
Dunnyneill Islands	Strangford Lough	Killyleagh	
Dunsy Island	Strangford Lough	Drumildoo Point	
Dunsy Rock	Strangford Lough	Drumildoo Point	
Eel Rock	Strangford Lough	Nuns Quarter	
Feehary Island	Strangford Lough	Pea Island Point	
Flat Rock, The	Strangford Lough	Greyabbey	
Gabbock Island	Strangford Lough	Hawks Hill	
Gannaway Rock	Carlingford Lough	Warren Point	Popular for dinghy racing.
Garter Rock	Strangford Lough	Ballyquintin Point	
Gibbs Island	Strangford Lough	Scaddy	One of few tree-lined islands in the lough.
Gilpin Rock	Irish Sea	Killard Point	Tiny rock lying just off the coast.
Gores Island	Strangford Lough	Ringbane	
Gowland Rock	Strangford Lough	Strangford	
Great Minnis's Island	Strangford Lough	Pea Island Point	
Green Island	Carlingford Lough	Duggans Point	Owned by the National Trust.
Green Island	Strangford Lough	Pea Island Point	One of two Green Islands in the lough.
Green Island	Strangford Lough	Nickey's Point	One of two Green Islands in the lough.
Gull Island	Strangford Lough	Temple Hill	
Gull Rock	Strangford Lough	Mahee Island	
Guns Island	Irish Sea	Ballyhornan	Southeast is a mass of nesting seabirds.
Halftide Rock	Strangford Lough	Mahee Island	
Hare Island	Strangford Lough	Greyabbey	One of two Hare Islands in the Lough.
Hare Island	Strangford Lough	Scaddy	One of two Hare Islands in the Lough.
Hen Island	Strangford Lough	Whiterock	
Horse Island	Strangford Lough	Drum Hill	One of two Horse Islands in the Lough.
Horse Island	Strangford Lough	Gransha	One of two Horse Islands in the Lough.
Hulin Rocks	Strangford Lough	Pea Island Point	aka Conly Island.
Hulin Rocks	Strangford Lough	Reagh Island	aka Cross Island.
Inishanier Island	Strangford Lough	Whiterock	
Inisharoan Island	Strangford Lough	Whiterock	
Island Taggart	Strangford Lough	Shrigley	One of the largest islands in the lough. It supports two small farms belonging to the National Trust.
Islandacorr	Strangford Lough	Bankmore Hill	
Islandmore	Strangford Lough	Warren Point	
Isle O'Valla	Strangford Lough	Strangford	
Jackdaw Island	Strangford Lough	Templecormick	An important nesting site for terns.
Jane's Rock	Strangford Lough	Greyabbey	One of two Jane's Rocks in the lough.
Jane's Rock	Strangford Lough	Islandmore	One of two Jane's Rocks in the lough.
John's Island	Irish Sea	Donaghadee	aka Lighthouse Island. One of the three Copeland Islands. Owned by the National Trust.
Launches Little	Strangford Lough	Walshestown	
Launches Long	Strangford Lough	Walshestown	
Lighthouse Island	Irish Sea	Donaghadee	See John's Island
Limestone Pladdies	Strangford Lough	Ringburr Point	
Limestone Rock	Strangford Lough	Ringburr Point	
Lindens Lump	Carlingford Lough	Duggans Point	One of several islets in the lough.
Little Minnis's Island	Strangford Lough	Pea Island Point	
Long Island	Carlingford Lough	Lisgarron Point	One of several islets in the lough.
Long Island	Strangford Lough	Drum Hill	One of two Long Islands in the lough.
Long Island	Strangford Lough	Ardkeen	One of two Long Islands in the lough.
Long Rock	Strangford Lough	Killyleagh	
Long Sheelah	Strangford Lough	Islandmore	
Long Skart Rock	Strangford Lough	Kircubbin	
Lythe Rock	Strangford Lough	Mahee Island	
Maggy's Rock	Carlingford Lough	Killowen Point	One of several islets in the lough.
Mahee Island	Strangford Lough	Cadew Point	See separate entry
McCammon Pladdy	Strangford Lough	Nuns Quarter	
McCulley's Rock	Strangford Lough	Ballyewry	
McKaigs Rocks	Strangford Lough	Castle Espie	
Mew Island	Irish Sea	Donaghadee	One of the three Copeland Islands. Owned by the Commissioners of Irish Lights, it has a number of small associated islands, all linked, on its southwest side.
Michael's Rock	Strangford Lough	Kircubbin	
Mid Island	Strangford Lough	Greyabbey	
Mid Island	Strangford Lough	Gransha Point	
Mill Rock	Carlingford Lough	Ballygowan	One of several islets in the lough.

Island name	Area	Nearest landmark	General information
Needo	Strangford Lough	Lisbane	
Newton Rock	Strangford Lough	Nuns Quarter	
North Boretree Rock	Strangford Lough	Temple Hill	One of the Boretree Islands.
North Buckey Rock	Strangford Lough	Rowreagh Point	
North Rock	Strangford Lough	Castle Espie	
Ogilby Island	Strangford Lough	Ringcreevy	
Oilean na Coille	Strangford Lough	Cadew Point	aka Wood Island.
Old Man's Head	Strangford Lough	Ballywallon	
Parton Island	Strangford Lough	Drumildoo Point	
Pawle Island	Strangford Lough	Warren Point	
Peggy's Island	Strangford Lough	Patterson's Hill	
Phersons Island	Strangford Lough	Ardkeen	
Pig Island	Strangford Lough	Cunningburn	
Pladdy Lug	Strangford Lough	Ballyquintin Point	
Plough Rock	Irish Sea	Ards Peninsula	See Big Bow Meel Island
Portnamana	Irish Sea	Ballyhornan	Tiny islet lying off the coast.
Ragheries, The	Strangford Lough	Hawks Hill	
Rainey Island	Strangford Lough	Sketrick Island	The tide runs at up to five knots.
Rat Island	Strangford Lough	Moore's Point	
Reagh Island	Strangford Lough	Paddy's Point	
Reid's Rock	Strangford Lough	Greyabbey	
Rig Pladdy	Strangford Lough	Mahee Island	
Roe Island	Strangford Lough	Pea Island Point	
Rolly Island	Strangford Lough	Paddy's Point	
Rough Island	Strangford Lough	Ringcreevy	
Round Island	Strangford Lough	Ballywallon	
Round Skart Rock	Strangford Lough	Kircubbin	
St Patrick's Rock	Irish Sea	Killard Point	Named after the patron saint of Ireland.
Salt	Strangford Lough	Moore's Point	Owned by the National Trust.
Sand Rock	Strangford Lough	Rowreagh Point	
Scartock Rock	Strangford Lough	Nuns Quarter	
Scotchman, The	Strangford Lough	Scaddy	
Scotchman's Rock	Strangford Lough	Strangford	
Selk Rock	Strangford Lough	Hawks Hill	One of three Selk Rocks in the lough.
Selk Rock	Strangford Lough	Killyleagh	One of three Selk Rocks in the lough.
Selk Rock	Strangford Lough	Ballyhenry Island	One of three Selk Rocks in the lough.
Shamrock Island	Strangford Lough	Conly Island	
Shark Island	Strangford Lough	Walshestown	
Sheelah's Island	Strangford Lough	Ballygarvan	
Shones Island	Strangford Lough	Ringbane	
Simmy Island	Strangford Lough	Danes Point	
Skate Rock	Strangford Lough	Killyleagh	
Sketrick Island	Strangford Lough	Whiterock	
Skullmartin	Irish Sea	Ballywalter	Rocky islet deemed a hazard to shipping.
Slave Rock	Strangford Lough	Gransha Point	
Soldiers Point	Carlingford Lough	Cranfield	One of several islets in the lough.
South Boretree Rock	Strangford Lough	Temple Hill	One of the Boretree Islands.
South Buckey Rock	Strangford Lough	Rowreagh Point	
South Dougherty Rock	Strangford Lough	Nuns Quarter	
South Island	Strangford Lough	Greyabbey	
South Rock	Strangford Lough	Castle Espie	One of two South Rocks in the lough.
South Rock	Strangford Lough	Little Minnis's Island	One of two South Rocks in the lough.
South Sheelah's Island	Strangford Lough	Nuns Quarter	
Strife Rock	Strangford Lough	Warren Point	
Swan Island	Strangford Lough	Strangford	
Thompsons Island	Carlingford Lough	Lisgarron Point	One of several islets in the lough.
Town Rock	Strangford Lough	Killyleagh	Site of St Patrick's first conversion.
Trasnagh Island	Strangford Lough	Whiterock	
Turley Rock	Strangford Lough	Temple Hill	
Walter Rocks, The	Strangford Lough	Portaferry	
Washington Rock	Strangford Lough	Kircubbin	
Wee Wife	Strangford Lough	Moore's Point	
West Boretree Rock	Strangford Lough	Temple Hill	One of the Boretree Islands.
West Dougherty Rock	Strangford Lough	Nuns Quarter	
West Rock	Strangford Lough	Castle Espie	One of two West Rocks in the lough.
West Rock	Strangford Lough	Little Minnis's Island	One of two West Rocks in the lough.
Whitebank Pladdy	Strangford Lough	Kircubbin	
Woman's Rock	Strangford Lough	Black Nab	
Wood Island	Strangford Lough	Cadew Point	aka Oilean na Coille.
Yellow Rocks	Strangford Lough	Lisbane	
Youran	Strangford Lough	Lisbane	

FERMANAGH

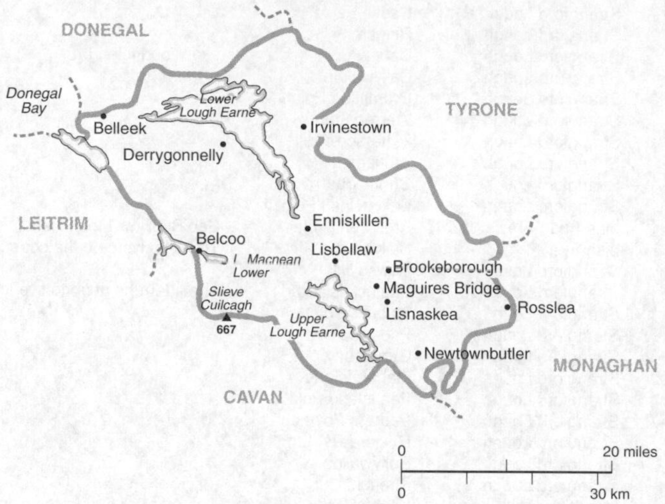
DONEGAL
Donegal Bay
Lower Lough Earne
Belleek
Irvinestown
TYRONE
Derrygonnelly
LEITRIM
Enniskillen
Belcoo
L. Macnean Lower
Lisbellaw
Brookeborough
Maguires Bridge
Slieve Cuilcagh
667
Lisnaskea
Rosslea
Upper Lough Earne
Newtownbutler
MONAGHAN
CAVAN
0
20 miles
0
30 km

Fermanagh borders only one Northern Ireland county, Tyrone, to the northeast. Its other four coterminous borders are Republic counties, i.e. Monaghan to the southeast, Cavan to the south and southwest, Leitrim to the west, and Donegal to the northwest. It is the only one of the six counties of Northern Ireland that does not have a border on Lough Neagh. Its other geographical distinction is in being the most westerly county of Northern Ireland, indeed, the area to the west of Belleek is the most westerly inhabited part of the United Kingdom.

The local government structure in Fermanagh was the first to be organised and pre-dates the setting up of the other 25 local councils of Northern Ireland in 1973. The borders of the district are very similar to those of the traditional County Fermanagh, containing all of that county plus a small section of County Tyrone in the Dromore and Kilskeery road areas. Fermanagh District Council can be said to be a unique local authority in as much as it covers at least one entire traditional county.

Fermanagh (*Fir Meanach*, the men of Meanach) is often referred to as Northern Ireland's Lake District, 20 per cent of the county being covered with water. The outstanding feature of the county is Lough Erne, the two halves of which (Upper and Lower) virtually bisect it. The lakes are linked to the Shannon waterway system via the Shannon–Erne Waterway Canal. Over 70 per cent of the population live in rural areas and Fermanagh's economy has been firmly rooted in agriculture for its entire existence. The population density is 78 people per sq mile (31 per sq km) against the average figure for Northern Ireland of 293 per sq mile (117 per sq km). Unusually, the county's population has consistently shrunk since the 19th century. In 1841 the figure was 156,841, in 1901 65,430; by 2001 it had shrunk further to 57,527.

It is believed that the first people began to arrive in Fermanagh around 6500 years ago. The only relics of these hunter-gatherers so far discovered are seven stone axes and a double-pointed pick, found on Cushrush Island. These hunters were followed about 500 years later by Stone Age farmers who began to clear the pine forest. They have left behind examples of court tombs and portal tombs. Along with hill forts there is evidence of Bronze Age lake dwellings (crannogs) on Lough Macnean and stone circles such as that at Drumskinny. Bronze Age jewellery such as gold lunulae (crescent-shaped necklaces) have been found in bogs north of Enniskillen. The arrival of the Celts c.300 BC heralded the Iron Age, during which period the giant earthwork named Black Pig's Dyke was constructed, the remains of which can be found on the Fermanagh/ Leitrim border.

Christianity came to Fermanagh in the 6th and 7th centuries AD. Monastic settlements on the islands of Lough Erne provided safe ports of call on the waterway from Donegal Bay to central Ireland. Thriving communities developed with cattle farming the main form of agriculture. The

Vikings raided down the waterways, attacking the monastery at Devenish in 837. However, they made no attempt at settling in Fermanagh, although they overwintered at Belleek in 942. The Airghialla Tuath are recorded as dominant in Fermanagh between the 9th and 12th century, having evicted the indigenous tribes the Fir Manach and the Cineal Eanna. The Airghialla leaders called themselves kings of Fermanagh. In 1211 the Normans, led by Bishop John de Grey and Gilbert de Costello, arrived and built a motte and bailey castle near Belleek. A year later it was destroyed by the O'Neills and a similar attempt at establishing a strongpoint in the 1250s was similarly dealt with.

From c.1300 the dominant clan in Fermanagh were the Maguires. From a stronghold at Knockninny they established a seat at Lisnaskea known as Sciath Gabhra. The early chieftains include Thomas the Great, (1395–1430), Thomas the Younger, (1430–71) and Eamonn, (1471–84). Thomas the Younger's brother Ross was Bishop of Clogher 1447–83. Another brother, Phillip, established a junior branch of the clan and further developed the stronghold at Enniskillen which had been established by Thomas the Great's brother, Hugh the Hospitable. Throughout the 16th century the lords of Fermanagh had to contend with the power struggle between the O'Neills and the O'Donnells, with the Maguires sometimes shifting loyalties and sometimes acting as arbitrators. In 1585 Cuchonnacht II surrendered Fermanagh to Elizabeth I. It was then returned to him in perpetuity on condition that the English presence was recognised and accepted.

Cuchonnacht died in 1589 and was succeeded by the last official Maguire chieftain, Hugh (1589–1600). In 1592 he provided a haven for his fugitive cousin Red Hugh O'Donnell, expelled the English sheriff and invaded Connacht. This was the prelude to the Nine Years' War (1594–1603). Enniskillen was besieged and captured by the English in February 1594 and recaptured after the Battle of the Ford of the Biscuits. Hugh Maguire led his forces alongside Hugh O'Neill and Hugh Roe O'Donnell at the Irish victory at the Battle of Yellow Ford in Armagh (1598). He was killed in single combat with Sir Warham St Leger in January 1600 while raiding in Cork. The lordship of Fermanagh was split between the branches of Conor Roe (senior branch 1600–25) and Cuchonnacht the Younger (junior branch 1600–07). Eventually Cuchonnacht decided to leave Ireland and, after collecting a ship in France, was instrumental in organising the 'Flight of the Earls' in 1607. He died in Genoa.

Fermanagh was then subject to the Plantation; the senior Maguires were allocated the barony of Magherasteffany, the junior Maguires were given Tempo and Tullyweel in the barony of Tirkennedy, and the rest of Fermanagh was divided between English and Scottish undertakers and servitors. Planter families included Archdale, Atkinson, Balfour, Blennerhasset, Cole and Hume. The Plantation was not uniformly successful and a rebellion in 1641 saw all the planter castles besieged, only Enniskillen holding out. Conor Maguire, 2nd Lord Enniskillen, led a failed expedition against Dublin (he was captured and eventually executed in 1644) and his brother Rory led the uprising in Fermanagh. The rebellion expanded into the Irish Confederate War/The Eleven Years' War (1641–53) and at one point the Ulster forces were commanded by Heber MacMahon, Bishop of Clogher, until defeat at Scarriffholis and betrayal by Brian Maguire of Tempo (who had kept out of the conflict) ended with his execution in 1650. When the rebels' land was confiscated, only Maguire of Tempo kept his property. During the first Jacobite Rising (1689–91) Fermanagh was invaded by Jacobite forces. Enniskillen once again survived a siege and a battle at Newtownbutler saw the Jacobite army destroyed.

Along with the rest of Ireland, Fermanagh was severely affected by the Great Famine caused by the potato blight of 1845–7. During the period between the census of 1841 and that of 1851 the county's population declined by 25.8 per cent. As a result of this and the repeal of the Corn Laws, the agricultural economy became more dependent on raising livestock than on arable farming. During the 19th century transport links with the county were also strengthened with the Shannon–Erne Waterway link to Dublin and the building of the Great Northern Railway. Branch lines from Enniskillen connected with Clones and Londonderry. The Sligo, Leitrim & Northern Counties railway connected with the Great Northern at Enniskillen and the Clogher Valley Railway connected with it at Maguiresbridge. The Clogher Valley Railway closed on New Year's Day 1942, and there have been no rail services in Fermanagh since 30 September 1957.

Fermanagh played an interesting role in the partition of Ireland which followed the crisis over Home Rule and the formation of the Ulster Volunteer Force and the Irish Volunteers (later Irish Republican Army). When partition was mooted in 1914 Fermanagh's population was equally divided between Catholics and Protestants. An attempt to solve the issue of whether the county (along with Tyrone) would become part of the Union at a conference at Buckingham Palace in 1914 ended in failure. At the 1918 British general election, South Fermanagh was won by Sinn Fein and North Fermanagh by the Unionists. Fermanagh was included as one of the six counties of Ulster under the provisions of the Government of Ireland Act (December 1920). On 15 December 1921 Fermanagh County Council pledged its allegiance to Dail Eireann, the Irish Parliament, before being dissolved on 23 December 1921. Fermanagh (and Cavan) was actually represented in the 1921 Dail Eireann by Sean Milroy (but not at the first Dail of 1919 or at any subsequent sittings). It was believed by many that under the conditions of Article 12 of the Anglo-Irish Treaty, providing for the establishment of a boundary commission to determine the frontier 'in accordance with the wishes of the inhabitants', Fermanagh would be excluded from Northern Ireland. However, in the end only minor changes were made to those specified under the Government of Ireland Act 1920.

On 1 January 1957 one of the infamous incidents of the IRA's Border Campaign occurred in Fermanagh. An attack on the police station in Brookeborough resulted in the death of two members of the IRA, Fergus O'Hanlon and Sean South. As a border county, Fermanagh also suffered during the Troubles after 1969. As many as 112 'conflict-related' deaths have been recorded in the county since 1969. The worst atrocity occurred on 8 November 1987 when a time-bomb planted by the IRA exploded during the Remembrance Day ceremony in Enniskillen, killing 11 people and injuring a further 63.

Enniskillen is the county town of Fermanagh. Other towns and villages include Ballinamallard, Belleek (*Beal Leice* = Mouth of the Flagstone) – straddling the Fermanagh/Donegal border and home of the world famous Belleek Pottery, Brookeborough – named after Sir Henry Brooke who was granted the village in 1666, Garrison, Irvinestown, Lisnaskea and Newtonbutler, scene of a Williamite victory over a superior Jacobite force in 1689.

Fermanagh	**Population**			**Area**	
	male	*female*	*total*	*sq miles*	*sq km*
	28,818	28,709	57,527	724	1876

Local Attractions and Information

Administrative headquarters	Town Hall, Enniskillen, BT74 7BA. Tel: 028 6632 5050.
Aghalurcher Church	Lisnaskea, 12 miles (19km) southeast of Enniskillen. Founded by St Ronan in the 7th century and the burial place of many Maguire chieftains. The ruins consist mainly of a side chapel with a square headed window.
Aghanaglack Dual Court Tomb	11 miles (18km) west of Enniskillen. Aka the Giant's Grave. Located in a clearing in Ballintempo Forest. Two burial galleries, each with two chambers sharing a common back stone and with semi-circular forecourts at each end. When excavated it was found to contain both Neolithic and Bronze Age finds.
Battles	See separate table for details of the battles of Ford of the Biscuits and Newtonbutler.
Belle Isle Castle Estate	Lisbellaw, $4^1/_2$ miles (7km) southeast of Enniskillen. A planned 17th century landscape. The original 17th century house, much enlarged over the centuries, is situated on an island in Upper Lough Erne. The estate covers 470 acres (190ha) in an area spread over eight islands. Under the ownership of the Duke of Abercorn, the main house and outbuildings have been converted to provide luxury visitor accommodation. Tel: 028 6638 7231.
Belleek Pottery	Belleek, 20 miles (32km) northwest of Enniskillen. An internationally renowned pottery works which since 1858 has produced Belleek Fine Parian China, a translucent porcelain, following the discovery of feldspar clay at nearby Castle Caldwell. Its speciality is lattice-patterned baskets. Originally constructed on Rose Isle in the River Erne, the building also houses a museum and showroom. On display is the 71cm (28in) high International Centre Piece, which won a gold medal at the 1900 Paris Exhibition. Tel: 028 6865 8501.
Boa Island	A long, narrow island in the north of Lower Lough Erne linked to the mainland by bridges to the east and west. In the graveyard at Caldragh on the island can be seen two pre-Christian stone statues. The figure known as Janus is 2ft 4in (0.7m) high, double-faced with crossed arms; the east side is male and the west side female. The smaller figure was brought over from nearby Lusty More island and is known as the Lusty Man, although its actual gender is not clear.
Castle Archdale Country Park	10 miles (6km) northwest of Enniskillen. A former estate covering more than 230 acres (93ha) along the shore of Lower Lough Erne, with access to White Island. It was established in 1615 by John Archdale, a Plantation undertaker from Suffolk, who built a house destroyed by Rory Maguire in 1641. Only the courtyard buildings remain of Archdale Manor House, which was built in 1778. An exhibition in the visitor centre highlights the period during World War II when RAF Catalina flying boats were stationed on Lough Erne and took part in the Battle of the Atlantic. There are also exhibitions of farm equipment and a history of the Archdale family. Tel: 028 6862 1588.
Castle Balfour	Main Street, Lisnaskea. A Scottish-style strong house built 1616–25 by Sir Charles Balfour, a Plantation undertaker from Fifeshire, on the site of a Maguire stronghold. Continuously occupied until damaged by fire in 1803, it was sold to the 1st Earl of Erne in 1821. The castle ruins are in

state care. A stone from the castle inscribed with a verse from Ovid can be seen in Lisnaskea's Corn Market. Tel: 028 9054 3037.

Castle Caldwell Forest
4 miles (6km) east of Belleek. Early 17th century demesne located at the western end of Lower Lough Erne, with the ruins of a house built in 1612. The estate was owned by John Caldwell Bloomfield, founder of the nearby Belleek Pottery. A state forest since 1913, it serves as a breeding ground for the common scoter duck. Tel: 028 6634 3032.

Castle Coole
1½ miles (2.5km) southeast of Enniskillen. A fine Neoclassical house designed by James Wyatt and built 1790–8 by Armar Lowry-Corry, 1st Earl Belmore, at a cost of £90,000. The house contains lavish Regency rooms with original decor and furniture. There is also a state bedroom designed in 1821 for George IV, who never actually slept here. Other buildings include a dairy and an ice house. The gardens were landscaped c.1780 by W King, with extensive woodlands laid out by James Frazer during the 1840s; an oak avenue and canal remain from an earlier garden. The lake has a colony of greylag geese. Maintained by the National Trust since 1951. Tel: 028 6632 2690.

Castle Hume
See Ely Lodge

Cethlin's Island
aka Inis Ceathleann. Large natural island between Lower and Upper Lough Erne with numerous adjoints to the mainland and usually thought of as synonymous with the traditional area of Enniskillen.

Churches (Enniskillen)
Enniskillen's first bishop was St Macartin (or Macartan) who lived c.AD 500.

Enniskillen Methodist Church, Darling Street, Enniskillen, designed by William J Barre of Belfast and built 1865–7, features a balcony installed in 1883 and apparently bowed in order to accommodate the crinolines then in fashion.

Enniskillen Presbyterian Church, East Bridge Street, Enniskillen, was built after 1882 and opened in 1897 at a cost of £2000 with an adjoining manse. **St Marcartin's Church of Ireland Cathedral**, Church Street, Enniskillen, was designed by Thomas Elliot and completed in 1842, adjacent to an earlier church of 1620. The cathedral tower houses a bell cast from a cannon used at the Battle of the Boyne. In 1923 it was promoted to cathedral status within the diocese of Clogher. It houses the Royal Inniskilling Regimental Chapel.

St Michael's Roman Catholic Church, Darling Street, Enniskillen, is a tall, thin church standing near the Anglican cathedral, designed by John O'Neill in French Gothic revival style and built 1870–5. It replaced an older church where worship took place 1803–67. The nave has 13 bays of French Gothic windows.

Colebrooke
Colebrooke Park, Brookeborough, 9 miles (15km) east of Enniskillen. House beside the Colebrooke River, built 1820–5 by William Farrell for Sir Henry Brooke. The name derives from the 17th century marriage of Thomas Brooke to Catherine Cole. Colebrooke was the home of Sir Basil Brooke, 5th Baronet and 1st Viscount Brookeborough, Prime Minister of Northern Ireland 1943–63. The house was left empty 1973–80 because of the cost of upkeep and maintenance while the family lived in the dower house, Ashbrooke, built in 1830. A walled garden contains a cast-iron framed glasshouse built 1834–7 by Richard Turner. The estate covered at least 28,000 acres (11,000ha) during the mid 19th century but is now about 1000 acres (400ha). Since 1980 the house has been transformed into a centre for shooting and fishing; in addition to being a family home the manor and estate provides guest accommodation and is also a location for corporate functions. Tel: 028 8953 1402.

Cole's Monument
See Forthill Park

Crom Castle
4 miles (6km) southwest of Newtownbutler, 15 miles (24km) southeast of Enniskillen. The ruins of Old Crom Castle, built in 1611 by Michael Balfour. It resisted two Jacobite sieges but was severely damaged by a fire in 1764 and never rebuilt. The castle gardens are noted for an ancient pair of yew trees which have been named among the 50 greatest British trees. The present house (not open to the public), known as Crom Castle, was begun in 1831; the surrounding parkland was designed by William Sawrey Gilpin in 1838. The estate now forms one of Ireland's most important nature conservation areas, a wooded lough shore and island demesne covering more than 1000 acres and containing many rare species. The castle is privately owned; the estate is maintained by the National Trust. Tel: 028 6773 8118.

Cuilcagh Mountain Park
12 miles (19km) southwest of Enniskillen. A 650 acre (265ha) conservation area for blanket peat bog, designated in 2001 as Northern Ireland's first European Geopark (endorsed by UNESCO in 2002). Tel: 028 6634 8855.

Devenish Island
1½ miles (2.5km) north of Enniskillen. L-shaped island of 70 acres (28ha) in Lower Loch Erne. A 6th century monastery on the island, believed to have been founded by St Molaise, was raided by Vikings in 837 and burned in 1157. It is also the site of a 100ft (30m) high 12th century round tower and a ruined 15th century Augustinian priory, the Abbey Church of St Mary. The Augustinian and Culdee communities on the island ceased in 1603. Tel: 028 6682 1588.

Drumskinny Stone Circle
8 miles (13km) north of Irvinestown. Kerbed cairn and stone circle, 43ft (13m) in diameter and possibly dating to the Bronze Age in the 2nd millennium BC. Originally the circle had 39 stones, of which seven have been lost and replaced with stones marked MOF (Ministry of Finance).

Ely Lodge
4 miles (6km) northwest of Enniskillen. Located on a promontory in Lough Erne and developed from the former stable block of Castle Hume, enlarged into a house after the castle was blown up by the Ely family for uncertain reasons in 1870. Castle Hume itself was built c.1730 by Richard Cassels for Sir Gustavus Hume, High Sheriff of Co. Fermanagh, before passing to the 1st Earl of Ely. The Ely Estate is now the home of Castle Hume Golf Course; there is also extensive woodland covering 620 acres (250ha). Tel: 028 6632 7076.

Enniskillen
Enniskillen (*Inis Ceithleann*, the Island of Kathleen) sits on Cethlin's island between Upper and Lower Lough Erne, which has been a hub for trade and movement since prehistoric times. It is

named after the legendary Ceithleann of the Crooked Tooth, the warrior wife of the pirate Balor (Balor of the Evil Eye, Balor of the South Blows or Balor of the Great Blows), who sought refuge on the island while fleeing from the king of the Tuatha de Danaan after defeat in battle, and was formerly the site of a stronghold of the junior branch of the Maguire clan. Situated in the baronies of Tyrkennedy and Magheraboy, the area was surveyed in 1609 and the town was established by charter of James I in 1612. The first provost was Captain William Cole, who rebuilt the castle and laid out the town. Its population in the early 1630s was around 180. Having survived a siege during the 1641 rebellion and supported Parliament during the Civil War, in 1689 the town raised two regiments to fight for William III against James II and, under the governorship of Gustavus Hamilton, survived another siege. In 1705 a fire destroyed 80 houses. Beggar Street (later Henry Street) was established by refugees from the French invasion in 1798; the town expanded outside the island in the early 19th century and became a garrison town, the castle serving as a barracks. Building in the 19th century reflected increased prosperity and by 1841 there were more than 800 houses. During the Great Famine, the population of Enniskillen rose to 8000 due to the influx of rural workers seeking work and relief in the Poor House. The arrival of the railway contributed to the growth of the town and its eventual further spread into suburbs. The town is built around a long and narrow main street which changes its name five times over its length. Notable buildings in Enniskillen include the castle, Cole's Monument, the Buttermarket and Ardhowen Theatre. The population in 2001 was 13,585.

Enniskillen Castle — Castle Barracks, Enniskillen. Originally a stronghold of the Maguire chieftains of Fermanagh, the first castle was built in the early 15th century (first mention 1439) by Hugh 'the Hospitable' Maguire, and became the principal Maguire seat in 1484. During the Nine Years' War Enniskillen Castle changed hands many times. At one point the English holding the castle were forced to surrender through starvation following the Battle of the Ford of the Biscuits. Following their ultimate defeat at Kinsale in 1601 the Maguires severely damaged their own castle to prevent its use by the English. Captain William Cole, appointed the first Constable of the Royal Fort at Enniskillen after the Plantation in 1607, and who established the Plantation town, repaired the Maguire stronghold, adding the twin-turreted watergate and doubling the height of the curtain wall. He also built a house for himself nearby. Later additions include a two-storey barrack block to accommodate the resident cavalry regiment. The Cole family stayed in residence until a fire in 1710, after which they moved to Portora Castle and ultimately to Florence Court. Tel: 028 6632 5000.

Fermanagh County Museum — Castle Barracks, Enniskillen. A local history museum housed in Enniskillen Castle. Dioramas cover the natural habitats, flora and fauna and the lives of Fermanagh's people from the Stone Age until the 20th century. There are also exhibits on the history of lace-making and the history of Belleek pottery. Tel: 028 6632 5000.

Florence Court — 8 miles (13km) southwest of Enniskillen. An important house built by the Earls of Enniskillen. The original house was built by John Cole, father of the 1st Earl of Enniskillen, and named after his wife. The present mid 18th century house with later additions is notable for its rococo plasterwork and fine Irish furniture. Outside are a water-powered sawmill and ice house. The walled garden has only three walls, the fourth side being left open to allow frost to drain out. The estate is home of the Irish yew (*Taxus baccata fastigiata*), also known as the Florence Court yew; the original tree was discovered c.1760 and can still be seen in Cottage Wood. Maintained by the National Trust, to which it was given in 1953, the main building has been restored following a damaging fire in 1955. Adjoining the property is Florence Court Forest Park, which sits on the northeast shoulder of Cuilcagh mountain and covers an area of 3000 acres (1200ha). Tel: 028 6634 8249.

Forthill Park and Cole's Monument — Belmore Street, Enniskillen. Hilltop park on the site of a 17th century fort, and containing Cole's Monument, built in 1857 to commemorate General Galbraith Lowry-Cole GCB, Colonel of the 27th (Inniskilling) Regiment of Foot, who commanded the 4th Division during the Peninsular War. There are 108 steps to the top. Tel: 028 6632 5050.

Garrison — A village located at the eastern end of Lough Melvin and a mecca for anglers. It is named after a barracks erected by William III after the Battle of Aughrim.

Highest point — Slieve Cuilcagh in the Cuilcagh Mountains at 2188ft (667m). The mountain borders the counties of Fermanagh and Cavan. Other peaks include Tiltinbane, Belmore, Slieve Rushen, Knockninny and Tappagham.

Inishmacsaint — (G. *Inis-maige-samh* = The Island of the Sorrel Plain). A 66 acre (26ha) island in Lower Lough Erne near Ross Point. Monastic site founded by St Ninniad in the 6th century. A church on the island served as parish church between the 13th and 16th century.

Inish Rath — An island in Upper Lough Erne 300 yards from the mainland. A house on the island, built 1856–60 by Henry Cavendish Butler, has been the home of the Krishna Spiritual Community since 1984.

Interesting facts — The **Rev. James Macdonald**, from the village of Ballinamallard (*Beal Atha na Mallacht*, Mouth of the Ford of the Curses), north of Enniskillen, had four famous daughters. Two of them married painters Sir Edward Burne-Jones and Sir Edward Poynter, another became the mother of Nobel Prize-winning author Rudyard Kipling and a fourth became the mother of British Prime Minister Stanley Baldwin. **The only diamond ever found in Ireland** was discovered in the early 19th century in the Colebrook river at Brookeborough, east of Enniskillen. **Michael Barrett**, the last man to be publicly hanged in Britain and Ireland, was born near Kesh in Fermanagh. He was hanged outside Newgate Prison in London on 26 May 1868, for his part in an attempt to rescue two convicted Fenians, Burke and Casey, from Clerkenwell Prison. A young boy was badly injured in an explosion during the failed mission.

Irvinestown — A small town to the east of Lower Lough Erne. Originally named Lowtherstown by Sir Gerald Lowther in 1618 and renamed when ownership moved to the Irvine family, it boasts a wide main

	street typical of Plantation towns. It also hosts the Lady of the Lake Festival, beginning on the first Friday following 12 July and lasting for 10 days.
Islands	There are 106 named islands in Lower Lough Erne and 43 in Upper Lough Erne. See separate table. Only the islands on the Fermanagh side of Lough Macnean Upper (5), Lough Macnean Lower (2), Lough Melvin (3) and the River Erne (3) are listed.
Lisgoole Abbey	$2^1/_2$ miles (4km) south of Enniskillen. An early 19th century house beside Upper Lough Erne, built on the site of the Augustinian priory of St Aid, formally known as the Abbey Church of St Peter, St Paul and St Mary, Lisgoole. Established as an Augustinian community c.1145–1583, the abbey housed a Franciscan community 1583–98 and 1616–1811.
Lisnaskea	Lisnaskea (*Lios na Sceithe* = the Fort of the Shield) is County Fermanagh's second town. It was once a seat of the Maguire clan.
Lough Navar Forest Park	5 miles (8km) northwest of Derrygonnelly. Rising to the top of the Magho cliffs and giving excellent views over Lower Loch Erne and the Sperrin Mountains. Tel: 028 6634 3032.
Marble Arch Caves	9 miles (15km) southwest of Enniskillen. An extensive cave system in the foothills of the Cuilcagh Mountains, first explored in 1895 by Frenchman Edouard Martel and naturalist Lyster Jameson, and opened to the public in 1985. Large deposits of calcite have left behind some spectacular cave formations, in particular cascades. The system gets its name from the polished limestone arch over the river, which was thought to be marble. Tel: 028 6634 8855.
Monea Castle	Blaney, 6 miles (10km) northwest of Enniskillen. The best preserved of the Plantation castles, the castle and bawn were built by the Rev. Malcolm Hamilton (later Archbishop of Cashel) 1616–19. The castle survived an attack in 1641 but was abandoned after a fire in 1750. Now in state care. Tel: 028 6632 3110.
Motto	The (unofficial) local motto of Fermanagh is 'once fished never forgotten'.
Necarne Castle	Irvinestown, 8 miles (13km) north of Enniskillen. Formerly known as Castle Irvine. Originally settled as part of the Plantations in 1610, the castle was remodelled in Gothic Revival style and is now occupied by the Enniskillen College of Agriculture. The outbuildings have been converted to provide a home for the Necarne Castle Equestrian School, which hosts an international three-day event, a dressage festival and stallion parades. The estate covers 400 acres (160ha) of parkland and woodland. Tel: 028 6634 4832.
Noon's Hole	3 miles (5km) northwest of Boho. Located in the limestone hills west of Enniskillen, Noon's Hole is the deepest pothole in Ireland at 250ft (76m) deep. It gets its name from an infamous murder. Dominic Noon arrived in the area from Co. Roscommon and earned his living as a highwayman. He was a member of the Ribbonmen, an illegal secret organisation formed to defend Catholic farmers from the Orangemen. When group member John Maguire was arrested, suspicion fell on Noon as an informer and he was subsequently lured up into the hills one night and bludgeoned to death, his body being thrown down the pothole.
Pettigoe Plateau	4 miles (6km) northeast of Belleek. A large expanse of blanket bog on the border with the Republic. A designated Ramsar site, Special Area of Conservation and Special Protection Area, it supports nationally important numbers of breeding golden plover and, occasionally, wintering Greenland white-fronted goose. Other important breeding birds include hen harrier, merlin, dunlin, common tern, lapwing, curlew and snipe.
Portora Castle	1 mile (1.6km) northwest of Enniskillen. House and bawn built 1612–15 by Captain William Cole, overlooking the narrow exit of the River Erne into Lower Lough Erne. It was leased by Cole to James Spottiswood, the Lord Bishop of Clogher before once again becoming a Cole family residence. The grounds house Portora Royal School; the castle's ruinous state is attributed to the efforts of some unruly schoolboys to blow it up and dig under the foundations.
Portora Royal School	Derrygonnelly Road, Enniskillen. Aka Enniskillen Royal School. Founded by a decree of James I issued in 1608 and originally established at Ballybalfour in 1618 before moving to Enniskillen c.1661. The present building dates from 1777. Sometimes referred to as the 'Eton of Ireland' and a boarding school for most of its existence, it became a day school in 1993. Former pupils include Oscar Wilde, Samuel Beckett, singer Neil Hannon and politician Harry West. The school hymn, 'Abide with Me', was written by another former pupil, Henry Francis Lyte. Tel: 028 6632 2658.
Rivers	Rivers in Fermanagh include the Arney, Ballinamallard, Ballycassidy, Bannagh, Cladagh, Colebrooke, Erne (Upper and Lower), Finn, Garvary, Hollybrook, Kesh, Roogagh, Sillees, Swanlinbar, Tempo, Termon and Woodford.
Roslea Manor and Heritage Centre	Monaghan Road, Roslea. Restored school building with a reconstructed early 20th century classroom. Other exhibitions include spademaking and Roslea lace. Provides a genealogical searching service. Tel: 028 6775 1750.
Royal Inniskilling Dragoons	Originally known as Sir Albert Cunningham's Regiment of Dragoons and formed by the amalgamation of various regiments raised in 1688 at Enniskillen to fight for the Williamite cause. Having fought at the Boyne, other early battle honours include Dettingen (1743). At the Battle of Waterloo the 6th Inniskilling Dragoons formed part of the Union Brigade (along with the Royals and the Scots Greys) which charged up to the French gun line before they were in turn overwhelmed by French cavalry. Opposite and facing Apsley House in London is a bronze statue of Wellington riding Copenhagen; a Grenadier, a Royal Highlander, a Royal Welch Fusilier and an Inniskilling Dragoon guard Wellington. The regiment took part in the charge of the Heavy Brigade at Balaklava (1854) and saw service in India and South Africa. In 1922, the 5th Dragoon Guards (Princess Charlotte of Wales's) and the Inniskilling (6th Dragoons) amalgamated to form the 5th/6th Dragoons. In 1927 the regiment was redesignated the 5th Inniskilling Dragoon Guards and in 1935 it became the 5th Royal Inniskilling Dragoon Guards. In 1938 the regiment was mechanised and initially equipped with the 4.5 ton two-man Mk 2 light tank. 20th century battle honours include Ypres (1914), the Somme (1916, 1918), Cambrai

(1917, 1918), Dunkirk (1940), the Normandy landings (1944) and The Hook (1952). Known as 'The Skins'. On 1 August 1992 the regiment was amalgamated with the 4th/7th Royal Dragoon Guards to form the Royal Dragoon Guards, whose motto is *Vestigia nulla retrorsum* (We do not retreat). One of the Dragoons' most famous sons is Laurence Edward Grace Oates, who sacrificed his life on 17 March 1912 in an attempt to save his comrades on Scott's Antarctic expedition. Each year on the Sunday nearest to 17 March, the Inniskilling Dragoons hold a memorial service in St Mary the Virgin Church at Gestingthorpe, Essex, where Oates was born and raised.

Royal Inniskilling Fusiliers
The regiment has its origin in troops raised in 1688 to combat an attack by the Jacobite forces of James II; they were incorporated into the army of William III in 1689 as the Inniskilling Regiment. Early actions include the Battles of the Boyne and Culloden. The regiment became known as the 27th Inniskillings in 1751. Having fought in North America and the West Indies during the Seven Years War, the American Revolutionary War and the early stages of the Napoleonic Wars, its exploits during the Peninsular War gained it battle honours such as Badajoz, Salamanca and Vittoria. The only Irish Regiment of foot at Waterloo, it held an important crossroads under heavy bombardment, 450 out of 700 men dying in the squares where they stood while repelling French cavalry charges. The Duke of Wellington said the men 'saved the centre of my line at Waterloo'. After service in India and helping to suppress the Mutiny, the 27th became the 1st Battalion Royal Inniskilling Fusiliers and a second battalion was also formed. The 1st Battalion saw service during the Boer War, helping to relieve Ladysmith, and took part in the Gallipoli landings during World War I. The 1st Battalion fought in Burma during World War II while the 2nd Battalion saw action in France, North Africa and Italy. The regiment was awarded the Freedom of Enniskillen in 1952 and later in the 1950s also received the Freedom of Nairobi after the Mau Mau unrest. On 1 July 1968 the Royal Inniskilling Fusiliers, Royal Ulster Rifles and Royal Irish Fusiliers became the Royal Irish Rangers, which in turn amalgamated with the Ulster Defence Regiment on 1 July 1992 to become the Royal Irish Regiment. Motto: *Nec Aspera Terrent* (By difficulties undaunted).

Royal Inniskilling Fusiliers Museum
Housed in Enniskillen Castle, the collection traces the history of the regiment from 1689 to its amalgamation in 1968, including weapons, uniforms, medals and other regimental memorabilia. Tel: 028 6632 3142.

Sheelin Lace Museum
Bellanaleck, 4 miles (6km) south of Enniskillen. Exhibits include antique Irish lace dating from 1850–1900, including wedding dresses, baby dresses, bonnets and parasols, and examples of all types of Irish lace: Youghal needle lace, Inishmacsaint needle lace, crochet, Limerick and Carrickmoss lace. Tel: 028 6634 8052.

Tempo Manor
Tempo, 12 miles (19km) northeast of Enniskillen. Aka Tempo Dessell. Once a seat of the Maguire chieftains. Former owners include 'Wicked Colonel' Hugh Maguire who in the mid 18th century incarcerated his wife, the beautiful Elizabeth, Lady Cathcart – married for the fourth time – here for many years in order to force her to hand over to him the title deeds of her English property. This story and the park are said to be the inspiration for Maria Edgeworth's novel *Castle Rackrent*. The River Tempo runs through the 300 acre (120ha) estate. The present manor house, built 1862–7 by Sir James Emerson Tennent, is owned by the Langham family and provides facilities for corporate events. Tel: 028 8954 1953.

Tully Castle
10 miles (16km) northwest of Enniskillen. The ruins of a plantation house and bawn built in 1613 by Sir John Hume of Berwickshire on the west shore of Lower Lough Erne, captured and burned, together with 75 occupants, by the Maguires on Christmas Day 1641. An early 17th century Renaissance style formal garden has been recreated within the bawn. Maintained by the Department of the Environment. Tel: 028 9054 3037.

Vintage Cycle Museum
Main Street, Brookeborough. Exhibition of over 100 cycles, plus toys and household memorabilia. Tel: 028 8953 1206.

White Island
One of the best known islands on Lower Lough Erne. About 74 acres (30ha) in area, it is notable for the remains of a 12th century church with a fine Romanesque doorway, the only such example in Northern Ireland. There are also figures carved in stone, dating to at least the 9th century, set into the north wall of the church. Originally the site of a monastery.

Some famous people born in Fermanagh

Adrian, Max (actor) (1903–73)	Enniskillen
Armstrong, John (US Congressman and general) (1717–95)	Brookeborough
Brooke, Basil, 1st Viscount Brookeborough (politician) (1888–1973)	Brookeborough
Burkitt, Denis (surgeon) (1911–93)	Enniskillen
Dunbar, Adrian (actor) (1958–)	Enniskillen
Gamble, James (founder of Proctor & Gamble) (1803–91)	Enniskillen
Gamble, William (US Civil War officer) (1818–66)	Lisnarick
Kerr, Bobby (Olympic gold medal winner for Canada) (1882–1963)	Enniskillen
Lawson, Charles (actor) (1959–)	Enniskillen
McIvor, Basil (politician) (1928–2004)	Pettigo
McMenamin, Ciarán (actor) (1975–)	Enniskillen
Plunket, William, 1st Baron Plunket (politician) (1764–1854)	Enniskillen

Islands of Fermanagh

Lower Lough Erne

	Nearest landmark
Bess Island	Tully Point
Bingham's Rock	Bigwood
Black Rock	Camplany
Bloomfield's Rocks	Rossmore
Boa Island (See separate entry)	Clonelly
Buck Island	Rossergole
Captain's Island	Rossmore
Car Island	Quarry Point
Cleenishgarve Island	Gubbaree Point
Cleenishmeen Island	Gubbaree Point
Coghran's Island	Bigwood
Creefin	Gubbaree Point
Crevinishaughy Island	Rossbeg Point
Cruninish Island	Boa Island
Curley's Rock	Camplany
Davy's Island (Inish More)	Rossbeg Point
Deerahan Island	Gubbaree Point
Devenish Island (See separate entry)	Derryargon
Duck Island	Camplany
Eagle Island	Gubnagole Point
Ely Island	Ely Lodge Forest
Estea Island	Muckros Point
Ferny Island	Slawin
Ferny Island	Quarry Point
Fod Island	Muckros Point
Gaffer Island	Lignameetoge Point
Gall Island	Carrickreagh Point
Gay Island	Gubbaree Point
Goat Island	Rossigh
Gravel Ridge	Gubbaree Point
Gravelly Island	Gubnagole Point
Great Ridge Island	Gubbaree Point
Gull Rock	Lignameetoge Point
Halfpenny Rock	Ely Island
Hare Island	Muckros Point
Hay Island	Blackrock Point
Heron Island	Tully Point
Hill's Island	Drumcrow West
Horse Island	Camplany
Horse Island	Blackrock Point
Humphrey's Island	Derryinch
Inis Maige Samh (Inishmacsaint)	Point Ross
Inish Beg (Tom's Island)	Rossbeg Point
Inish Conra	Rossigh
Inish Dacharne	Rossfad
Inish Davar	Rossinnan Point
Inish Divaan	Gublusk Point
Inish Doney	Ross Point
Inish Fovar	Lodge Point
Inish Free	Gublusk Point
Inish Garve	Rossinnan Point
Inish Lougher	Lodge Point
Inish More (Davy's Island)	Rossbeg Point
Inishmacsaint (See separate entry)	Point Ross

	Nearest landmark
Inishmakill (The island is a nature reserve).	Rossmore Point
Inishmeely	Boa Island
Inishturk	Boa Island
Isle Namanfin	Lignameetoge Point
Kerney Island	Lignameetoge Point
Kinnausy	Gubbaree Point
Lamb Island	Carrickreagh Point
Loftus Island	Bigwood
Long Island	Srahenny Point
Long Rock	Lowery
Long Rock	Boa Island
Lusty Beg Island	Clonelly
Lusty More Island	Clonelly
Macart Island	Muckros Point
Magurk's Island	Coagh
Montgomery Rocks	Lignameetoge Point
Muckinish	Slawin
Ned's Island	Rossmore
Old Man's Hat	Gublusk Point
Owl Island	Rossigh
Paris Island Big	Gublusk Point
Paris Island Little	Ely Island
Physicberry Island	Muckros Point
Piper's Cairn	Muckros Wood
Purgatory Island	Boa Island
Pushen Island	Carrickreagh Point
Rabbit Island	Kesh
Rabbit Island	Tully Point
Rocky Island	Tully Point
Rosscor Island	Lowerbybane
Rossharbour Island	Tullyfad
Rough Island	Rossmore
Rush Island	Muckros Point
Sallow Island	Boa Island
Sally Islands	Rossinnan Point
Sam's Island	Rossergole
Scallan's Rock	Kesh
Scattered Rocks	Camplany
Screegan Island	Boa Island
Smith's Rock	Rossogie Point Outer
Spike, The	Gubbaree Point
Stallion Cowes	Gubbaree Point
Stony Islands	Rossmore
Strongbow Island	Gubbaree Point
Swallow Island	Tawnaghgorm Hill
Teefin Island	Gubbaree Point
Teige's Rock	Rossogie Point Outer
Tom's Island (Inish Beg)	Rossbeg Point
Trasna	Quarry Point
Troublesome Rocks	Gubbaree Point
Water Horse	Camplany
White Cairn	Drumcrow West
White Island (See separate entry)	Aghinver
White Island	Rossbeg Point
White Island	Quarry Point

Upper Lough Erne

	Nearest landmark
Aghinsh	Tiraroe
Belle Isle	Enniskillen
Bleanish Island	Killard
Bockan Island	Corratistune
Bunnahola Island	Enniskillen
Carrickmacrourk Island	Enniskillen
Cleenish Island	Enniskillen
Creagawaddy Island	Curragh
Creaghamanone Island	Inishroost
Creaghanarourke Island	Inishcollan
Creagnarouk Island	Corraslough Point
Crehan Island	Dernish Island
Deal Island	Inishroost
Dernish Island	Cornakill
Doocharn	Corraslee Point
Edergole Island	Cornaleck
Friar's Island	Inishcollan
Galoon Island (Noted for its ghoulishly carved gravestones).	Enniskillen
Geddagh Island	Curragh
Inish Rath (See separate entry)	Derryad
Inishcorkish	Curragh
Inishcreagh	Enniskillen
Inishcrevan	Corradovar
Inisherk	Crom Castle
Inishfausy	Inishroost
Inishfendra	Gubb
Inishkeen (Site of St Fergus's cemetery and Lisgole Abbey).	Enniskillen
Inishleague	Inishroost
Inishlirroo	Corraslee Point
Inishlught	Corradovar
Inishmore	Enniskillen
Inishore	Curragh
Inishturk	Tiraroe
Killygowan Island	Enniskillen
Knock Island	Enniskillen
Mountjoy Island	Inishroost
Naan Island	Cornaleck
Rabbit Island	Inishcollan
Shave Island	Corraslough Point
Staff Island	Corraslough Point
Tonregee Island	Corraslough Point
Trannish	Corratistune
Trasna	Dresternan

Lough Macnean Lower

	Nearest landmark
Cushrush	Cushrusheen
Inishee	Mullaghbane

Lough Macnean Upper

	Nearest landmark
Buck Islands (Garrow Islands)	Killyphort
Garrow Islands (Buck Islands)	Killyphort
Inishkeen	Killyphort
Inishteige	Killyphort
Kilrooscagh	Rushin
Rosscorkey Island	Rushin

Lough Melvin

	Nearest landmark
Bilberry Island	Garvros
Gorminish	Garvros
Sally Island	Garvros

River Erne

	Nearest landmark
Castle Island	Enniskillen
Cethlin's Island (Inis Ceithleann – see separate entry)	Enniskillen
Cherry Island	Enniskillen
Inis Ceithleann (Cethlin's Island)	Enniskillen

TYRONE

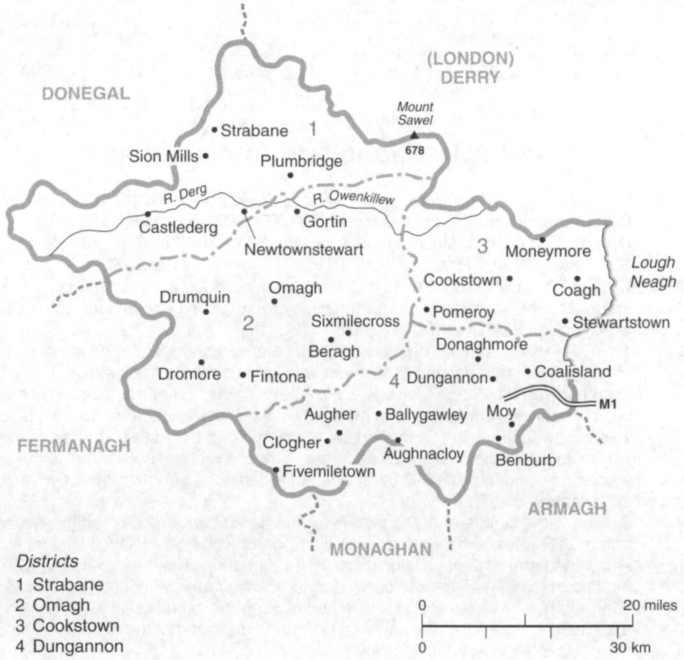

DONEGAL
(LONDON) DERRY
Mount Sawel
678
Strabane
1
Sion Mills
Plumbridge
R. Derg
R. Owenkillew
Castlederg
Gortin
Newtownstewart
3
Moneymore
Lough Neagh
Cookstown
Coagh
Drumquin
Omagh
Pomeroy
Sixmilecross
Stewartstown
2
Beragh
Donaghmore
Dromore
Fintona
4
Dungannon
Coalisland
M1
Augher
Ballygawley
Moy
FERMANAGH
Clogher
Aughnacloy
Benburb
Fivemiletown
ARMAGH
MONAGHAN
Districts
1 Strabane
2 Omagh
3 Cookstown
4 Dungannon
0
20 miles
0
30 km

County Tyrone borders Armagh to the southeast, Fermanagh to the southwest and Londonderry to the northeast. The county also borders Lough Neagh to the east. Its borders with the Republic of Ireland are County Monaghan to the south and County Donegal to the northwest. Tyrone is divided into four administrative districts: Cookstown District Council, Dungannon & South Tyrone Borough Council, Omagh District Council and Strabane District Council. Omagh is the largest town and has been the county town since 1769.

The name Tyrone derives from *Tir Eoghain*, or the territory of Eoghan (Owen), a son of Niall of the Nine Hostages. The largest county in Northern Ireland, County Tyrone has a diverse landscape from gently rolling drumlins in the south to the Sperrin Mountains in the north. The county was from an early period a popular region for settlement, as the many Neolithic, Bronze Age and Iron Age remains testify. The area was also the seat of the first bishopric in Ireland, established in the 5th century in Clogher. Tyrone was developed along with the rest of Ulster during the Plantation, and became a centre of industry and trade with the discovery of large deposits of coal at Brackaville (later known as Coalisland) during the 1720s and the subsequent building of canals to transport it to Dublin. Although the county did not suffer as badly as some during the Great Famine of the 1840s and 1850s, its population fell from 312,956 in 1841 to 238,500 in 1861.

Tyrone was included as one of the six counties of Northern Ireland under the provisions of the Government of Ireland Act (December 1920) and this was confirmed by the subsequent Border Commission. As a border county Tyrone also suffered more than most during the Troubles after 1969. East Tyrone was part of the 'murder triangle' where terrorist murders were frequent. As many as 339 'conflict-related' deaths have been recorded in the county since 1969, the worst atrocity being the death of 29 people in August 1998 as the result of a bomb planted by the Real IRA.

The borough of **Cookstown** is bordered on the east by Lough Neagh. It is mostly in County Tyrone but also partly in County Derry, Moneymore for instance being just over the boundary.

Tyrone	Population			Area	
Districts	*male*	*female*	*total*	*sq miles*	*sq km*
Cookstown	16,188	16,393	32,581	240	622
Dungannon	23,624	24,111	47,735	303	784
Omagh	24,038	23,914	47,952	436	1130
Strabane	19,133	19,115	38,248	333	862
Total	82,983	83,533	166,516	1312	3398

Local Attractions and Information

Administrative headquarters	**Cookstown**: Council Offices, 12 Burn Road, Cookstown BT80 8DT. Tel: 028 8676 2205. **Dungannon**: Council Offices, Dungannon, BT71 6DT. Tel: 028 8772 5311. **Omagh**: The Grange, Mountjoy Road, Omagh BT79 3BL. Tel: 028 8224 5321. **Strabane**: 47 Derry Road, Strabane BT82 8DY. Tel: 028 7138 2204.
An Creagan Visitor Centre	Creggan, 11 miles (18km) west of Cookstown. Housed in a semicircular building modelled on the nearby stone cairns, the centre features displays covering the archaeology, culture and natural history of the local area. Tel: 028 8076 1112.
Ardboe Cross and Abbey	10 miles (16km) east of Cookstown. A 10th century cross situated on a rocky height on the shore of Lough Neagh. A national monument, it is believed to be the first high cross of Ulster. Standing 18ft 6in (5.5m) high and 3ft 6in (1.1m) wide, it features 22 panels depicting various biblical scenes. Ardboe (Ard Bo) means 'hill of the cow'; according to local legend, the cross was built with the help of a magic cow which stepped out of the lough and provided the workmen with a plentiful supply of cream, milk and butter. There are also the remains of a monastery founded c.AD 590 by St Colman Muchaidhe and destroyed by fire in 1166, and a 16th century church.
Ballywholan Tombs	3 miles (5km) southeast of Clogher. Two chambered tombs located on the Tyrone/Monaghan border at Ballywholan (pronounced Ballyhullion or Ballyhollan). One is a portal tomb in a cairn known as Patrick's Cairn (Campatrick); 86ft (26m) long, it was excavated in 1897. The other is a dual court tomb – two back-to-back court tombs in the same mound – known as Cat's Cairn (Carnagat). It has a semicircular forecourt leading to a burial gallery with two chambers, and was excavated in the 1890s. The name comes from a legend that the tomb was home to a clutter of fairy cats. Both tombs date to c.3000 BC.
Baronscourt House and Estate	Newtownstewart, 9 miles (15km) northwest of Omagh. Home of the Dukes of Abercorn since 1612, the present house dates from 1779. The grounds were landscaped by Broomfield and Hudson during the 18th century. The estate encompasses Lough Catherine, Lough Fanny and Lough Mary, while the parkland features an award-winning managed herd of wild Japanese sika deer. Also part of the estate is Newtownstewart Golf Club, established after Hurricane Debbie destroyed over 100 acres (40ha) of woodland in 1961. Tel: 028 8166 1683.
Battles	See separate table for details of the Battle of Benburb.
Beaghmore Stone Circles	10 miles (16km) west of Cookstown. Beaghmore means 'moor of the birches'. Seven early Bronze Age stone circles made up of no less than 1269 stones in three paired circles and a single circle, built on the site of a Neolithic field system. The stones are quite small, the tallest being 4ft (1.2m) in height; there are also stone rows and cairns associated with each circle. Discovered in the 1930s, the site was excavated in 1945 and again in 1965. There are a dozen small cairns, all kerbed with small borders, and most of which were found to contain cremations. It is suggested that the circles and alignment functioned as a lunar observatory.
Benburb	A village on the River Blackwater south of Dungannon. Its parish church was built in 1618, and it was the site of a battle on 5 June 1646 during the Irish Confederate War/Eleven Years' War (1641–53). It is now home to the Servite Priory of Our Lady of Benburb (see Benburb Castle).
Benburb Castle	Main Street, Benburb. Aka Wingfield's Castle. Plantation castle built by Sir Richard Wingfield (later Viscount Powerscourt) above the River Blackwater on the site of a 16th century O'Neill stronghold. The west keep has been restored. The castle now stands in the grounds of a Servite priory, originally built within the walls of the Plantation bawn as a manor house by James Bruce in 1887. Used as a military hospital during World War II, it was purchased on behalf of the Servite Fathers in 1947 and used as a training seminary until 1967. The student accommodation was released for wider community use during the 1990s and the priory has installed innovative and environmentally friendly renewable energy technologies. Tel: 028 3754 8241.
Benburb Valley Heritage Centre	Milltown Road, Benburb. Collection of industrial machinery dating from 1850–1950, including an 1899 Victor Coates & Co. steam engine, housed in a former linen weaving mill located between the Ulster Canal and the River Blackwater. Also featured is a scale model of the Battle of Benburb. Tel: 028 3754 9752.
Benburb Valley Park	Main Street, Benburb. A woodland park covering 90 acres (37ha) surrounding a limestone gorge carved by the River Blackwater. Tel: 028 3754 8241.
Bog Museum	Dunganon Road, Coalisland. An exhibition of artefacts extracted from the Irish boglands. Exhibits include an indoor bog, bones and antlers of the great Irish elk, as well as bog oak sculptures and turf products. Tel: 028 8774 9041.
Caledon	A Plantation town with a wide main street on the River Blackwater, on the border with Armagh. Originally known as Kinnaird (or Kennard) or Aghaloo, it was developed by James Alexander (1st

	Earl of Caledon) and his descendants. Caledon was designated a Conservation Area in 1984.
Caledon Mansion	$7^{1}/_{2}$ miles (12km) west of Armagh. Standing above the River Blackwater on the site of at least three previous houses, the current house was designed by Thomas Cooley in 1779 and enlarged by John Nash 1806–10 at a cost of £17,000 to include domed wings. The 2402 acre (972ha) estate features a folly built by Lord Orrery in 1747 from the knuckle bones of cattle; there are also a lake and deer park, pinetum and monkey-puzzle avenue. The estate was home to the US 23rd Infantry Regiment 1942–4.
Carleton's Cottage	Springtown, 1 mile (1.6km) south of Augher, 2 miles (3km) east of Clogher. The childhood home of Victorian novelist William Carleton (1794–1869), described by W B Yeats as 'the greatest novelist of Ireland'. His works include *Traits and Stories of the Irish Peasantry* (vol 1 1829, vol 2 1833), *Fardorougha the Miser* (1939), *The Black Prophet* (1847) and *The Squanders of Castle Squander* (1852). His autobiography was unfinished at his death. An annual William Carleton Summer School, one of Ireland's most significant literary festivals, has been held since 1992 to celebrated his life and writings, and takes place in the first week of August in the Clogher Valley. Tel: 028 8776 7259.
Castle Caulfield	3 miles (5km) west of Dungannon. Mansion, now in ruins, built by Sir Toby Caulfield in 1619 on the site of an O'Donnelly stronghold, after which Ballydonnelly was renamed Castlecaulfield. The structure include murder holes and gun loops. Burned during the rebellion of 1641, it was rebuilt and reoccupied by the Caulfield family until 1660.
Castlecaulfield	A town located on the River Torrent. Originally known as Ballydonnelly, it was renamed after Sir Toby Caulfield, who built the town in 1619.
Castlederg	Aka Castlesessiagh. A Plantation town with ruined castle and bawn built 1609–22 by Sir John Davies. Excavations in 1991 revealed that the bawn occupied the site of an earlier O'Donnell stronghold. The bawn was rendered unfit for occupation by an attack of Sir Phelim O'Neill. The visitor centre features local heritage exhibits, including a model of the Alamo in remembrance of Davy Crockett, whose ancestors came from Castlederg. It hosts an annual Apple Fair in October. Tel: 028 8167 8727.
Castlesessiagh	See Castlederg
Churches	**St Luran's Church (Derryloran Parish Church)** Church Street, Cookstown. A Church of Ireland parish church designed by John Nash and built in 1822 at a cost of £2769. Quickly extended to account for the growing population of Cookstown, the church was substantially rebuilt 1859–61 to a design by Joseph Welland, with only Nash's tower, spire and first part of the nave remaining. Major restoration was completed in early 2000 at a cost of more than £500,000. **St Macartan's Cathedral (Clogher Cathedral)**, Main Street, Clogher. Designed by James Martin and built by Bishop John Stearne in 1744. **St Mary's & St Joseph's Church**, Brackaville Road, Coalisland, a Georgian Gothic style Catholic church built in 1857 and refurbished in 1996. **Church of the Sacred Heart**, Brook Street, Omagh. Designed by prolific Gothic revivalist architect William Hague (1836–99). Building started in 1893 and the church was consecrated in 1899.
Clogher	A town located between the rivers Blackwater and Fury. It was the seat of the first bishopric in Ireland, established in the 5th century.
Coach and Carriage Museum	Blessingbourne, Fivemiletown. Museum with collection of 15 coaches dating from 1790–1910, including the 1825 London–Oxford stagecoach. Tel: 028 8952 1188.
Coalisland	A town developed at the terminus of the Coalisland Canal, built 1733–87 to transport coal from the largest coalfield in Northern Ireland to Dublin. During the 19th century Coalisland became a trans-shipment centre for goods such as sand, bricks and agricultural goods with an accompanying infrastructure of warehouses and mills. Competition from rail and road eventually forced the closure of the canal in 1954. The town is still a centre for brick-making.
Cookstown	Built on land owned by the O'Mellans until the Plantation, when the land was transferred to the Archbishop of Armagh. Leases were granted to an English lawyer, Dr Allen Cooke, who established Cooke's Town as a market town in 1628. When the area was fought over during the 1641 rebellion Cookstown was burned and left as a small community of only a few houses. In 1734 the largest local landowner, William Stewart, built a new town to the south of the original settlement with a wide main street. The town benefited from the expansion of the linen industry and agriculture. It remains a thriving market town, boasting the longest main street in Ireland at more than 1 mile (1.6km) long and 135ft (41m) wide. It also features the Burnavon Arts and Cultural Centre.
Cookstown Old Station	Molesworth Street, Cookstown. Restored Great Northern Railway station, now converted into a local heritage and railway museum. Tel: 028 8676 6727.
Copney Stone Circles	9 miles (15km) northeast of Omagh. An important Bronze Age stone circle complex located on the slope of Copney Hill to the southwest of Creggan Wood, and consisting of nine circles with west-southwest–east-northeast alignment. Recorded in 1979 and surveyed in 1981, the site was partially excavated in 1994–5.
Cornmill Heritage Centre	Lineside, Dungannon Road, Coalisland. Aka Coalisland Heritage Centre. Housed in the restored Stewart's Mill, originally built in 1907 and closed in 1978. The building was renovated in 1990 and now hosts an exhibition and interpretative display recounting the history of Coalisland's industrial development over 400 years. Tel: 028 8774 8532.
Coyle's Cottage	2 miles (3km) east of Coagh, Cookstown. The only remaining example of a mid 18th century eel fisherman's cottage on the western shore of Lough Neagh. Built from mud and with lough-shore reed used for the thatch, it was restored and opened to the public in 1993. Maintained by the Muintirevlin Historical Society. Tel: 028 8673 7564.

Cregganconroe Court Grave — 2 miles (3km) south of Creggan. Aka Creggan Connroe. Neolithic chambered grave located close to Cam Lough and built 3000–2000 BC. A rectangular cairn measuring 60ft (18m) long by 40ft (12m) wide, it consists of a two-segment burial gallery opening onto a forecourt at the eastern end. Not yet excavated.

Creggandevesky Court Tomb — 3 miles (5km) northwest of Pomeroy. Creggandevesky means 'the rock of the black water'. Well preserved court tomb overlooking Lough Mallon. Constructed c.3500 BC, it is 50ft (15m) long, 40ft (12m) wide and 7ft (2.1m) high. Excavated 1979–82, it was found to contain three burial chambers containing the remains of 21 people, along with pottery, a stone beaded necklace and flint tools.

Donaghmore Heritage Centre — Pomeroy Road, Donaghmore. Housed in a converted National School building dating from 1885. Displays include photographs, maps and documents focusing on local interests and heritage. Tel: 028 8772 4187.

Drum Manor Forest Park — 4 miles (6km) west of Cookstown. An 18th century demesne of 92 acres (37ha), located immediately south of the Sperrin Mountains and west of Lough Neagh. It features a manor house built in 1876, a walled butterfly garden, Japanese garden, arboretum and two artificial lakes. Acquired by the Forest Service in 1964 from Mr Archibald Close, it was opened to the public as a forest park in 1970. Tel: 028 8676 2774.

Dunemana — Aka Dunnamanagh (Fort of the Monks), Dunemana. A market town located on the Burn Dennet, on the County Tyrone/County Derry border, and built by Sir John Drummond at the time of the Plantation.

Dunemana Castle — See Earl's Gift Castle

Dungannon — Dungannon (Ceannan's Fort) was strategically built on a hill in the southeast of County Tyrone. It was once a seat of the O'Neills, Hugh O'Neill being made Baron of Dungannon in 1568. The first Bible in Irish was produced in Dungannon in 1567. The town was captured by Sir Phelim O'Neill during the 1641 rebellion but recaptured in 1642. Industrial expansion was dependent on the linen industry and the railways, and the town suffered with the decline of those industries. Now revived largely by the services sector, Dungannon is the commercial, administrative and financial centre for the surrounding borough.

Dungannon Park and Lake — Moy Road, Dungannon. Formerly the private demesne of the Ranfurly family, the park covers 70 acres (28ha) and includes a 12 acre (5ha) lake created by Viscount Northland in the 1790s. Previously known as Northland Park (1790–1826), Ranfurly Park (1826–1933) and Dungannon Park Farm, (1933–89), it was purchased by Dungannon & South Tyrone Borough Council in 1987 and opened to the public in 1989. Tel: 028 8772 7327.

Dyan Corn Mill — Dyan, 3 miles (5km) north of Caledon. Complex of buildings erected in 1829 on the Earl of Caledon's estate including a cornmill and two mill houses. There is a working water wheel in the restored watercourse.

Earl's Gift Castle — Dunemana, 7 miles (11km) northeast of Strabane. Aka Dunemana Castle. The remains of a castle begun in 1629 by Sir John Hamilton but never completed. It was apparently being built as a gift for Sir John's French fiancee, but she was drowned in a shipwreck off Dover and the castle was left unfinished. The rear part was brought down by Hurricane Debbie in 1961.

Erganagh House — Glen Park Road, Omagh. Substantial two storey stone-built Georgian rectory, rebuilt in 1836. It housed the American 82nd Airborne Division in 1943. Tel: 028 8225 2852.

Favour Royal — 4 miles (6km) east of Augher, 14 miles (21km) southwest of Dungannon. 17th century demesne on the border with County Monaghan in the River Blackwater valley. Supposedly named for a grant of land made by Charles I to Sir James Erskine in 1630, it features an artificial lake, wild flower meadow and deer lawn, surrounding a private house built in 1824. Part of the estate was bought by the Northern Ireland Forest Service to plant a Milliennium Forest.

Forests and woodlands — **Fardross Forest**, near Fivemiletown. Parkland and forest planting of sitka spruce, lodgepole pine and Norway spruce in the Clogher Valley, surrounding a private house. It was the scene of a UFO sighting in August 2004; **Favour Royal Forest**, 790 acres (320ha) of woodland between Augher and Aughnacloy, designated a People's Millennium Forest and opened in October 2001. Adjacent to the Derrygorry People's Millennium Forest in County Monaghan and connected to it by a Millennium Bridge, these woodlands have been created to increase the number of native trees in Ireland, with planting of 40,000 oak, ash and Scots pine; **Knockmany Forest**, 3 miles (5km) west of Clogher. Forest of conifers (including compartments of sitka spruce and Douglas fir), hardwoods and mixed planting. Home to a fallow deer herd. Site of Knockmany Passge Tomb; **Lough Bradan Forest,** 1 mile (1.6km) south of Drumquin, 12 miles (19km) west of Omagh, a coniferous forest with herd of Sika deer. Excellent bird watching area. **Pomeroy Forest**, a mixture of old estate woodland planted 1780–1830 and composed of mixed deciduous woodland plus colonising Scots pine. The original house, dating to 1780, has now been demolished; **Seskinore Forest**, Fintona, Omagh, a 19th century demesne around the former Seskinore Lodge with some trees dating to 1833. Now with managed forest planting; Sitka and Norway spruce dominate but there are also mixed broadleaves including oak, beech and ash. A small Japanese sika deer herd was culled by the NI Forest Service in 2006.

Goles Stone Row — 1¼ miles (2km) west of Draperstown. Aka Goles Alignment. A Neolithic monument consisting of 11 standing stones located on a site overlooking the confluence of the Glenelly and Goles rivers, and arranged in a straight line aligned north-south over 52ft (16m). The tallest stone is 6ft 6in (2m) in height and all the stones are of local sandstone or schist. It was excavated and restored in 1994, when two orthostats were discovered in addition to the nine then on view. The monument is believed to be part of a lunar ritual site. Tel: 028 7138 2204.

Gortin Glen Forest Park — 7 miles (11km) north of Omagh. A 3790 acre (1534ha) forest park opened in 1967 and featuring an enclosure for sika deer. Tel: 028 8167 0666.

Grant Ancestral Home — Dergenagh, 13 miles (21km) west of Dungannon. The restored home of John Simpson, maternal great-grandfather of Ulysses S Grant (1822–85), 18th President of the United States and Union commander-in-chief during the American Civil War. Simpson was born at Dergenagh in 1738 and emigrated to the US in 1760. (Grant's paternal antecedents came to the US from Dorset in 1630.) The cottage was purchased for the public in the 1970s and now includes a Civil War exhibition and collection of farm implements. In the grounds are a butterfly garden and wildlife pond. Tel: 028 8555 7133.

Gray's Printing Press Museum — Main Street, Strabane. Museum established to celebrate Strabane's 19th century status as a centre for publishing in Ireland. The town is also associated with John Dunlap, printer of the American Declaration of Independence. Born in Strabane in 1747, Dunlap emigrated to America in his teens and joined his uncle's printing business in Philadelphia, founding the *Pennsylvania Packet*, America's first daily paper, in 1784. Exhibits include a collection of printing presses. Maintained by the National Trust since 1966, with a section administered by Strabane District Council covering canals, railways and a photographic exhibition of the history of Strabane. Tel: 028 7188 0055.

Harry Avery's Castle — 1 mile (1.6km) southwest of Newtownstewart. Ruins of an O'Neill stronghold apparently built by Henry Aimbreidh O'Neill (Harry Avery O'Neill), who died in 1392. A rare example of a medieval Irish pre-Plantation structure, the rectangular castle is fronted by two D-shaped towers which are still in situ.

Highest point — Mount Sawel in the Sperrin Mountains at 2224ft (678m).

Interesting facts — **Irish Coffee** was invented in 1942 by Joe Sheridan, born in Bridgetown, Castlederg. While working as a chef at Foynes flying-boat seaport, Sheridan realised that passengers on the 18 hour transatlantic flight would be cold and tired and in need of a hot restorative drink, and developed what quickly became known as Irish Coffee. Ingredients: 1 measure Irish whiskey; 1 measure black coffee; 2 teaspoons sugar; 2 teaspoons fresh whipping cream. Recipe: heat the glass with boiling water. Add coffee, whiskey and sugar. Float cream on surface of coffee by resting the bowl of a spoon on the surface and pouring the cream into it, slowly lifting the spoon as the cream builds up. Do not stir. Best drunk by sipping the coffee through the cream. The **Fintona Horse Tramway** operated for 104 years (1853–1957) and consisted of a tramcar, always pulled by a horse called Dick, which took passengers transferring from Fintona Station to Fintona Junction Station on the main Omagh–Enniskillen railway line. The tram was introduced in 1883 and was divided into first class and second class in the lower deck and third class on the exposed upper deck. The journey took 10 minutes on the downhill route and 15 minutes on the way back up hill, up to seven times a day. It is estimated that the tram covered 125,000 miles in its entire service history; it is now kept at the Belfast Transport Museum. The Fintona branch, together with the entire Great Northern Railway, closed on 30 September 1957. Cookstown-born **Mary Mallon** (1869–1938) was the first person in the United States to be identified as a healthy carrier of typhoid fever. 'Typhoid Mary' as she became known, infected at least 47 people, three of whom died from the disease. Her notoriety is in part due to her non-acceptance of culpability of her part in spreading the disease, and her refusal to cease working as a cook. She was forcibly quarantined twice by public health authorities and died in quarantine. She was still infectious on the day she died: an autopsy found evidence of live typhoid bacteria in her gallbladder. Another Tyrone-born killer, of the more premeditated variety, was **William Burke (1792–1829).** Burke was hanged in Edinburgh in 1829 after his partner in crime William Hare gave evidence of his complicity in the murder of 17 people between 1827and 1828, the corpses being sold to the Edinburgh Medical College for dissection. Altmore-born **James Shields** (1810–79) emigrated to America in 1826**,** and has the distinction of being the only person in United States history to serve as a US Senator for three different states: Illinois (1849–55), Minnesota (1858–9) and Missouri (1879).

Irish World Family History Centre — Dungannon Road, Coalisland. Holds genealogical databases covering Tyrone and Fermanagh including parish records, tithe books and 1901 census. Part of the Irish Family History Foundation, which co-ordinates a network of government-approved genealogical research centres in Northern Ireland and the Irish Republic. Tel: 028 8774 6065.

Islands — The islands in Lough Neagh which lie within County Tyrone are **Blackers Rock** (a marshy islet thought to be a breeding ground for the hairy dragonfly), **Scaddy Island** and **Taylor's Rock. Island McHugh** in Lough Catherine is on the Baronscourt Estate. A crannog occupied from Neolithic times until the late 16th century, it is believed to have the longest history of any known habitation site in Western Europe. It is also recognised as being the earliest artificial island discovered in the British Isles. The ruins of a medieval castle still stand on the island.

Killymoon Castle — Killymoon Road, Cookstown. Located by the Killymoon and Ballinderry Rivers, the original house was built in 1671 by James Stewart. Destroyed by fire in 1801, it was rebuilt by William Stewart to a design by John Nash at a cost of £80,000. The adjacent parkland is now occupied by Killymoon Golf Club. Tel: 028 8676 3514.

Kinturk Cultural Centre — Ardboe, 10 miles (16km) east of Cookstown. Exhibition and interpretative display of the history of the Lough Neagh fishing and eel industry, including displays of boats and equipment. Tel: 028 8673 6512.

Knockmany Passage Tomb — 12 miles (19km) southeast of Omagh. Aka Annia's (Anya's) Cove, probably a corruption of Grania's Cave. A decorated passage tomb on the summit of Knockmany Hill in Knockmany Forest with a view of the Clogher Valley. The upright stones are decorated with devices such as lozenges, triangles and concentric circles. It is now located inside a reconstructed earth mound erected to protect the tomb.

Lough Ash Wedge Tomb — 2 miles (3km) north of Plumbridge, $8^{1}/_{2}$ miles (13.5km) east of Strabane. Wedge-shaped stone tomb dating to 4000–4500 BC. It has a west-facing double portal with single burial chamber and a single remaining capstone. On excavation it was found to contain at least three cremations.

Lough Fea	6 miles (10km) northwest of Cookstown. Natural freshwater lough covering 365 acres (147ha), located in the Sperrin Mountains close to the border with County Derry. It was opened as a source of water for mid-Ulster in 1965.
Loughry Manor	1¼ miles (2km) south of Cookstown. Demesne granted to the Lindesay family in 1611 during the Plantation. The present house dates from 1800. Jonathan Swift was a close friend of the Lindesay family and is reputed to have written *Gulliver's Travels* while a guest at Loughry Manor; the estate includes Swift's Summer House, which overlooks the Killymoon River. The estate is now home to the Loughry campus of the College of Agriculture, Food & Rural Enterprise, established on the site in 1908 as the Ulster Dairy School.
Magherakeel Monastic Site	Killeter, 4½ miles (7km) southwest of Castlederg. Magherakeel means 'the plain of the church'. Located near St Patrick's Well on the pilgrim's trail to Lough Derg, the site consists of the remains of a 6th century monastic foundation including the ruin of St Caireall's church. The church was restored in 1693 but again fell into disuse.
Millennium Sculpture	Lifford Road, Strabane. Sculpted by Maurice Harron and officially titled *Let the Dance Begin*, this impressive sculpture consists of five stainless steel figures, each 13ft (4m) high and representing a fiddler, flautist, drummer and two dancers. It stands on the site of an old border checkpoint. One of the dancers and the fiddler are on the Lifford side, the other dancer and the fife player are on the Strabane side; they are linked by the drummer. The idea of harmony is linked with Irish tradition of song and dance. Tel: 028 7138 2204.
Mountjoy Castle	Magheralamfield, 3 miles (5km) southeast of Stewartstown. Ruined fort overlooking Lough Neagh, built by Lord Mountjoy in 1602 during the O'Neill rebellion. It was captured by the Irish during the 1641 rebellion and subsequently slighted by the English. Legend has it there is a tunnel from the castle to Bellville House, ¼ mile (0.4km) away. Tel: 028 9023 5000.
Moy Iron Gates	Moy, 5 miles (8km) southeast of Dungannon. An elaborate set of wrought-iron gates, originally the entrance gates to Roxborough Castle, a chateau-style mansion burned down by Republicans in 1922. The are believed to be the work of Dublin iron founder Richard Turner, who constructed the Palm House in Kew Gardens.
Mullaghmore House	Old Mountfield Road, Omagh. A Grade B+ listed Georgian house on a 4 acre (1.2ha) site. Restored by the owners and opened to the public in 2004, its features include stained glass windows and period library and drawing room. It was the birthplace of Sir John Gorman and actor Sam Neill. Tel: 028 8224 2314.
Newtownstewart	A town located at the confluence of the rivers Strule and Owenkillew, and overlooked by hills called Bessy Bell and Mary Gray. Named after Sir William Stewart, it hosts the Northern Ireland Carriage Driving Championships (at Baronscourt).
Newtownstewart Castle	Main Street, Newtownstewart. Aka Stewart Castle. A three-storey Plantation house with crow-stepped gables built in 1619 by Sir Robert Newcomen. A lack of defensive works contributed to its burning in the 1641 rebellion. Subsequently rebuilt, it was largely demolished in 1689 on the orders of James II after he slept here on the retreat from the failed siege of Derry. Only the south gable now remains in situ. It is also the site of the significant discovery of an intact Bronze Age double cist grave and capstone.
Ogilby's Castle	Dunemana, 7 miles (11km) northeast of Strabane. Aka Altnacree or Altinaghree Castle. Ruins of a Victorian mansion on the outskirts of Dunemana, built in 1860 of Irish cut stone.
Omagh	The largest town in County Tyrone, Omagh stands at the confluence of the Camowen and Drumragh rivers and is often subject to inundation. Founded in 1610 during the Plantation, it was burned during the Jacobite war of 1689. It was served by rail between 1852 and 1965. At 3.10pm on Saturday 15 August 1998, an explosion caused by a 500lb car bomb planted by the Real IRA killed 29 people. Omagh Community House, created by a coalition of community and voluntary groups based in the Omagh area, is built on the site of the bombing. There is also a memorial garden in the grounds of County Hall.
Omagh Court House	High Street, Omagh. One of the town's most prominent buildings, the imposing classical structure was built by John Hargrave of Cork in two phases between 1814 and 1863 on the site of Omagh Gaol. A listed building, it is supposedly haunted. Tel: 028 8224 2056.
Parkanaur	4 miles (6km) west of Dungannon. Built in 1802 and extended by Thomas Duff in 1815 in Tudor Revival style to include a great hall and a minstrel's gallery. Part of the house is now occupied by Parkanaur College, a residential college committed to promoting the vocational education and personal development of people with learning difficulties and disabilities. Tel: 028 8776 1272.
Parkanaur Forest Park	4 miles (6km) west of Dungannon. Mixed conifer and broadleaf woodland, formerly part of the Burgess Estate. The gardens are particularly attractive in springtime, while the park is home to a herd of white fallow deer. Tel: 028 8775 9311.
Peatlands Country Park and Railway	See entry in Armagh
Plumbridge	A town located in the Glenelly Valley astride the Glenelly River. According to legend the town gets its name from the bridge over the river, which was built without the use of a plumb line. It is the centre of five crossroads.
Rivers	The **Upper Ballinderry** rises in the Sperrin Mountains and flows east into Lough Neagh 4 miles (6km) east of Coagh and 3 miles (5km) south of Ballyronan. It is one of the few rivers in Northern Ireland to retain a significant population of the rare freshwater pearl mussel; other species include otter, kingfisher and brook lamprey. One of the best trout rivers in Ulster. Other species include salmon and dollaghan. The **Blackwater** see entry in Armagh. The **Derg** flows from Lough Derg in Donegal in a northeast direction to Castlederg and then east to Newtownstewart. It then continues eastwards as the Owenkillew. The **Drumragh** is formed just north of Fintona, where Quiggery Water and Ballynahatty Water meet. The river then flows north to Omagh. The **Owenkillew** rises

in Davagh Forest in the Sperrin Mountains and flows westward into the Lough Foyle system, meeting the Strule at Newtownstewart. It supports the largest population (10,000 individuals) in Northern Ireland of the freshwater pearl mussel in a 2$^1/_2$ mile (4km) stretch of its upper reaches; other species include atlantic salmon, brown trout, brook lamprey, otter, dipper and kingfisher. Woodland along its banks is old sessile oak wood. The **Strule** is formed by the Camowen and Drumragh rivers, as they meet at Omagh, and flows north to Newtownstewart.

Roughan Castle — Roughan Road, Newmills. Ruins of a three-storey compact castle built in 1618 by Andrew Stewart. Consisting of a central square tower surrounded by round towers at each corner, it was slighted on the orders of Parliament after being held by Sir Phelim O'Neill during the Confederacy. It is now located in the grounds of Roughan House residential nursing home.

Royal School, Dungannon — Ranfurly Road, Dungannon. Established at Mountjoy in 1614 before moving to Dungannon in 1636. The first headmaster died from exposure, having been driven from his home during the 1641 rebellion. The school moved to its present site in 1789, and amalgamated with Dungannon High School for Girls in 1986. It is known by former pupils as 'The Old Grey Mother'.

St Patrick's Chair and Well — 4 miles (6km) east of Clogher, 13 miles (21km) southwest of Dungannon. Located in Altadaven Wood, part of Favour Royal Forest, the chair is a 6ft 6in (2m) high block of stone sitting on another block. The well is an open chamber with a bullaun stone above – another bullaun which is said never to run dry.

St Patrick's Well — Killeter, 4$^1/_2$ miles (7km) southwest of Castlederg. The well is located on the old pilgrim trail to Lough Derg. St Patrick is said to have slaked his thirst here after spending Lent on an island in Lough Derg. According to legend, water from the well will ease toothache.

Silverbrook Mills — Dunemana, 7 miles (11km) northeast of Strabane. A working water powered corn, flax and saw mill on the River Dennet. Tel: 028 7139 7097/7137 7888.

Sion Mills — Established by the Herdman family as a model village centred on their linen business at Herdman's Mill on the River Mourne, south of Strabane. The mill was founded in 1835 and expanded until 1855. The village became known as Sion Mills when it became part of the railway network. The Herdmans provided housing, schooling, recreational facilities (although no pub until 1896) and churches for all their workers in a religiously integrated community. Many of the buildings were designed by English architect William Unsworth, who had married a Herdman, and who also designed the original Shakespeare Memorial Theatre at Stratford-upon-Avon. The village was sold to its occupants during the 1960s; the mill was closed in 1989 and is now overseen by the Sion Mills Buildings Preservation Trust. Sion Mills was also the site of a famous sporting upset when Ireland beat the West Indies at cricket on 2 July 1969. Sion Mills was featured in BBC2's *Restoration* series.

Slieve Beagh — 18 miles (29km) south of Omagh. One of the largest areas of intact blanket bog in Northern Ireland. A designated Special Area of Conservation, Special Protection Area and Ramsar site, it also features numerous lakes.

Sperrin Mountains — A mountain range in a 20 mile (32km) arc straddling the County Tyrone/County Derry border. High rainfall has resulted in the development of extensive peatland and blanket bog, together with lakes and forests in the river valleys such as Glenelly Valley. Mount Sawel is the highest point at 2224ft (678m), while Mullaclogher and Mullaghaneany both exceed 2000ft (608m). The Sperrins Area of Outstanding Natural Beauty covers 390 sq miles (1010 sq km). The area is rich in archaeology. The Central Sperrins Way begins and ends near the village of Plumbridge.

Sport

football — **Dungannon Swifts**, founded in 1949, are winners of the Irish League 1st Division in 2003. Their home ground is Stangmore Park, Dungannon.

Gaelic football — **Tyrone GAA** were winners of the All-Ireland Senior Football Championship in 2003 and 2005, having been runners-up in 1986 and 1995. They won the National Football League in 2002 and 2003. The team captain in 2003 was Cormac McAnallen, a history teacher from Benburb born in 1980. Named Young Footballer of the Year in 2001, he died suddenly from a viral infection of the heart on 2 March 2004; the Cormac McAnallen Cup, contested between Ireland and Australia under International Rules, is named in his honour.

motorcycling — Road races include the **Cookstown 100** and the **Bush Road Races**, Dungannon.

Strabane — Strabane (*An Srath Ban* = The Fair Holm) was established by the 1st Earl of Abercorn in 1611 on the River Mourne, on the border with County Donegal. It was captured by the Irish in the 1641 rebellion before being recaptured after a few days and was later burned during the Jacobite Rebellion of 1688–9. Strabane eventually developed into a market town and commercial centre for the area due to its position. It was a major staging post for coaching services, was connected to the River Foyle by the Strabane Canal and then was a mainline station on the Great Northern Railway. In addition to the agricultural sector, the town benefited from the growth of the linen industry. The town's motto is *Concordia Crescit* (Let Goodwill Increase).

Tullaghoge Fort — 2$^1/_2$ miles (4km) southeast of Cookstown. Aka Tullyhogue Fort (Hill of the Young Warriors). A Celtic ring-fort earthworks, an ancient sanctuary which became a stronghold of the O'Hagans who performed the coronations of the O'Neill kings. Hugh O'Neill was the last to be enthroned on the Leac na Ri (Stone of the Kings) in the coronation chair in 1593, although Sir Phelim O'Neill took part in a ceremony during the rebellion of 1641. The chair was probably destroyed by Mountjoy in 1602, although legend has it that it still survives.

Ulster American Folk Park — 3 miles (5km) north of Omagh. Outdoor museum mainly dedicated to the mass emigrations of the 18th and 19th centuries. Established in 1976, it is based around the story of the Mellon family who emigrated from Camphill, County Tyrone to Pittsburgh, Pennsylvania. The park is laid out with areas covering both the Old World and the New World. The park's original and replica buildings include the Matthew T Mellon Visitor Centre, a single-room cabin, blacksmith's forge, weaver's

	cottage, Presbyterian meeting house, Mellon Homestead, Campbell House, Tullyallen Mass House, Hughes House, Castletown National Schoolhouse, Mountjoy Post Office. There are also reconstructions of a 19th century Ulster street, a dockside gallery with a full-size replica of the emigrant sailing ship *Brig Union*, a 19th century American street, Samuel Fulton Stone House, log cabin, Pennsylvania log barn, smoke house, Pennsylvania log farmhouse and Western Pennsylvania log house. There is also an Emigrants Exhibition and a Centre for Migration Studies. Tel: 028 8224 3292.
Ulster History Park	Cullion, 3 miles (5km) north of Omagh. A 35 acre (14ha) open air museum near Gortin Glen Forest Park which chronicles the development of the region from 8000 BC to the Plantation, providing examples of dwellings and monuments typical of the area. The 14 full-scale replicas are set out chronologically, including a Mesolithic camp, a rath, a crannog, a monastic settlement (including a 89ft/27m round tower) and a motte and bailey castle. There is also a dolmen, a wedge tomb and a stone circle. Tel: 028 8164 8188.
Wellbrook Beetling Mill	Wellbrook Road, Corkhill, Cookstown. Water-powered 18th century linen hammer mill set in a glen alongside the Ballinderry River. Beetling is hammering the cloth to produce a sheen. Maintained by the National Trust since 1968. Tel: 028 8674 8210.
Wilson Ancestral Home	Dergalt, 2 miles (3km) southeast of Strabane. Aka The White House. A whitewashed, thatched traditional one-room wide cottage, formerly the home of Judge James Wilson, grandfather of Woodrow Wilson, 28th President of the United States and winner of the Nobel Peace Prize. James Wilson emigrated in 1807. The house is furnished with original family heirlooms, while the Wilsons still run the adjacent farm. Tel: 028 8224 3292.
Wingfield's Castle	See Benburb Castle
Woods on Your Doorstep	**The Burn Walk** (*Bealach an tSruthain*) ($2^1/_2$ acres/1ha), by Pattens Glen and Cavanlee River, Drumrallagh, Strabane, planted with 1925 trees of native species; **Cabin Wood** (18 acres/7ha), beside the Killymoon and Ballinderry rivers and bordering the Killymoon Estate in Cookstown. Species include oak, birch, ash, alder, willow and aspen; **Cullion Community Woodland** ($2^1/_2$ acres/1ha), Gortin, Omagh, adjacent to the Ulster History Park and linked to Gortin Glen Forest Park. Native tree trail with an example of one of each of the native tress in Ireland planted along the path; **Gortgonis Wood** (5 acres/2ha), beside the Coalisland Canal in Coalisland. More than 4400 trees planted in 2001. Species include oak, ash, birch and rowan; **Lettervad Wood** ($6^1/_2$ acres/2.5ha), between a greyhound stadium and housing estate in Dungannon. Main species oak and rowan.

Some famous people born in Tyrone

Bates, David (physicist) (1916–94)	Omagh
Carleton, William (novelist) (1794–1869)	Clogher
Clarke, Darren (golfer) (1968–)	Dungannon
Devlin McAliskey, Bernadette (politician) (1947–)	Cookstown
Dunlap, John (printer) (1747–1812)	Strabane
Friel, Brian (playwright) (1929–)	Omagh
Hughes, Aaron (footballer) (1979–)	Cookstown
Kennedy, Jimmy (songwriter) (1902–84)	Omagh
McAnallen, Cormac (Gaelic footballer) (1980–2004)	Dungannon
Neill, Sam (New Zealand actor) (1947–)	Omagh
O'Nolan, Brian (humourist – as Flann O'Brien) (1911–66)	Strabane
Taylor, Dennis (snooker player) (1949–)	Coalisland

Ireland

Ireland has been settled since at least Neolithic times, as indicated by the appearance of pottery, polished stone tools, rectangular wooden houses and communal megalithic tombs, some of which are huge stone monuments like the passage graves of Newgrange, Knowth and Dowth (all in County Meath). In the regions later known as Leinster and Munster individual adult males were buried in small stone structures, called cists, under earthen mounds and were accompanied by distinctive decorated pottery. This culture apparently prospered, and the island became more densely populated. Towards the end of the Neolithic period new types of monuments developed, such as circular embanked enclosures and timber, stone and post and pit circles. There was early industry such as the stone-axe factories near Cushendall and on Rathlin Island. During the Bronze Age and early Iron Age there was a flourishing of art, which is attested to by archaeological finds and buildings such as Navan Fort and the Dorsey. This period is described in the story cycle known as the Ulster Cycle, a set of mythical tales which includes the *Táin Bó Cúailnge* ('The driving-off of cows of Cooley', also known as the Cattle Raid of Cooley or the Táin).

The spread of the Roman Empire encouraged the migration of Celtic tribes, some of which settled in Ireland. The Romans referred to Ireland as Hibernia although it was never formally a part of the Roman Empire. There is some evidence however that the Attacotti of south Leinster may have served in the Roman military in the mid to late 4th century. The island was divided into 'fifths' (Old Irish *cóiceda*, Modern Irish *cúige*) at this time. The divisions were Ulaid (Ulster) in the north, Cóiced Ol nEchmacht (Connacht) in the west, Mumha or Mhumhain (Munster) in the south, and Laighin (Leinster) in the east. They all surrounded the central kingdom of Míde (whose name has survived in the modern counties Meath and Westmeath). Each of the outer four-fifths had its own king, with the High King of Ireland ruling over them from Tara in Míde. In historical times Míde disappeared as a province.

The four remaining fifths contained large numbers of *tuatha* or sub-kingdoms, constantly shifting as old dynasties died and new ones formed. Within these kingdoms a rich culture flourished. The area known as the over-kingdom of the Ulaidh was colonised and fought over between the indigenous population – possibly the Cruthin or Pritani (after which Britain is named) – and various Gaelic tribes or clans, resulting in the formation of the kingdoms of Dal Fiatach, Dal Riata and Dal nAraide. A dominant tribe were the Uí Neill, descended from perhaps the earliest historical figure for the region, the High King of Ireland Niall Noígiallach (Niall of the Nine Hostages). Niall lived at the turn of the 5th century but his story is also shrouded in myth. An energetic man in many ways, with genetic research revealing that 1 in 12 Irish people may be descended from him, his death in AD 405 or later (up to 455) is always placed outside Ireland (in the English Channel, in France on the banks of the River Loire, in the Alps or in Scotland) and he was constantly raiding the failing Roman Empire. Indeed, on one of his raids on Britain he captured a young man named Succat, who would later become St Patrick.

After spending six years sheep-herding in Antrim, Succat (or Sochet) escaped and, having studied and become a bishop, returned to Ireland in 432, now known as Patricius. According to Prosper of Aquitaine, a contemporary chronicler, Palladius was sent to Ireland by the Pope in 431 as 'first Bishop to the Irish believing in Christ', which demonstrates that there were already Christians living in Ireland. Palladius seems to have worked purely as bishop to Irish Christians in the Leinster and Meath kingdoms, while Patrick worked first and foremost as a missionary to the pagan Irish, converting in the more remote kingdoms located in Ulster and Connacht. The fact remains though that if this chronicler is accurate, Palladius may have pre-dated Patrick. Whatever the truth of the foundation of Christianity in Ireland, the resulting establishment of monastic centres, including the largest pre-Norman urban centre at Armagh, increased trade and prosperity but also led to incursions by both the Vikings and local chieftains. The first English involvement in Ireland took place in this period when, in the summer of AD 684, an English expeditionary force sent by Northumbrian King Ecgfrith invaded Ireland. The English forces seized a number of captives and booty, but apparently did not stay in Ireland for long. It is from the period between the 4th and 8th centuries that the bulk of inscriptions in the Old Irish script known as Ogham, many of them names on gravestones, are believed to date.

The first recorded Viking raid in Irish history occurred in 795 when Vikings from Norway looted the island of Lambay, located off the Dublin coast. Early Viking raids were generally swift and small in scale. These early raids interrupted the golden age of Christian Irish culture and marked the beginning of 200 years of intermittent warfare, with waves of Viking raiders plundering monasteries and towns throughout Ireland. The Viking invasions resulted in the building of round towers, many of which still exist, as refuges on the monastic sites that survived. This internal warfare seriously weakened the country economically and militarily, eventually rendering it vulnerable to invasion by the Norman rulers of England.

In the south, power was exercised by the heads of a few regional dynasties vying against each other for supremacy over the whole island. One of these, the king of Leinster, Diarmait Mac Murchada (anglicised as Diarmuid MacMorrough), was forcibly exiled from his kingdom by the new High King, Ruaidri mac Tairrdelbach Ua Conchobair. Fleeing to Aquitaine, Diarmait obtained permission from Henry II to use Norman forces to regain his kingdom. The first Norman knight landed in Ireland in 1167, followed by the main forces of Normans, Welsh and Flemings at Bannow Bay in Wexford in 1169. With their superior military technology and organisation, they made rapid inroads against the Irish and Hiberno-Norse. As in England and Wales, the conquest was consolidated by the building of a series of castles, at first of the motte and bailey type but later substantial structures like that at Carrickfergus. Within a short time Leinster was regained, while Waterford and Dublin were under the control of Diarmait, who named his son-in-law, Richard de Clare, heir to his kingdom. This caused consternation to Henry II, who feared the establishment of a rival Norman state in Ireland. Accordingly, he resolved to establish his authority. With the authority of the papal bull *Laudabiliter* from Pope Hadrian IV, Henry landed with a large fleet at Waterford in 1171 and promptly awarded his Irish territories to his younger son John with the title *Dominus Hiberniae* ('Lord of Ireland'). When John unexpectedly succeeded his brother as King John, the 'Lordship of Ireland' fell directly under the English Crown.

In 1177 a small Anglo-Norman force of 22 knights and 300 foot soldiers under John de Courcy was able to carve out the Earldom of Ulster in the east of the province. The Earldom consisted of five bailiwicks: Antrim, Ards, Blathewic, Carrickfergus and Lecale (later five counties: Antrim, Blathewic, Carrickfergus, Down and Twescard), each under control of a seneschal or sheriff. Ruling Anglo-Norman families included de Burgo (Earls of Ulster, who later became the Burkes), de Mandeville, FitzWarin, Savage, Bisset and de Logan.

The invasion of Ireland by Edward Bruce in 1315 forced the Anglo-Normans to withdraw to the area around Dublin known as the Pale and there was a resurgence of Gaelic power in Ulster, which became known to the English as 'The Great Irishry'. The dominant families during this period were the O'Neills and the O'Donnells. The majority of Irish tower houses were constructed during the 14th and 15th centuries, with the last dating from the early 17th century. They were originally built for defence but later structures show signs of less functional architectural features. Larger tower houses, which were more usually for defensive purposes, would have an accompanying bawn or courtyard. The keep or principal tower would usually be quadrangular or circular with three or four storeys. Tower houses are generally located by a river, lake or coastal area, and are frequently decorated with a sheela-na-gig (a symbolic pagan nude carved on one of the stones, possibly to ward off evil spirits – the origins of these images are obscure, often being attributed to a pre-Christian fertility cult although there are few remaining examples from before the 12th century).

The Hundred Years War and the Wars of the Roses distracted the English from vigorously pursuing any claims over Ireland and it was not until the 16th century that the conflict was renewed. In 1541 Henry VIII declared himself king of Ireland (as opposed to his previous title of Lord of Ireland) and his daughter Elizabeth I made a concerted attempt to impose her will on all Ireland. The first such scheme – the Plantation of Laois and Offaly in 1556 – was born during the reign of her sister, Mary. The O'Moore and O'Connor clans which occupied the area had traditionally raided the English-ruled Pale around Dublin. The Lord Deputy of Ireland, the Earl of Sussex, ordered them to be dispossessed and replaced with an English settlement. He also renamed the counties as King's County and Queen's County respectively. However, the plantation was not a great success. The O'Moores and O'Connors retreated to the hills and bogs and fought a local war against the settlement for much of the following 40 years. The result was a series of clashes first with Shane O'Neill, Sorley Boy MacDonnell, and finally with Hugh O'Neill, Earl of Tyrone in Tyrone's Rebellion, also known as the Nine Years' War (1593–1603).

The Munster Plantation of the 1580s was the first mass plantation in Ireland. It was instituted as punishment for the Desmond Rebellions, when the Geraldine Earl of Desmond had rebelled against English interference in Munster. The Desmond dynasty was annihilated in the aftermath of the 2nd Desmond Rebellion (1579–83) and their estates were confiscated. This gave the English authorities the opportunity to settle the province with colonists from England and Wales, who, it was hoped, would be a bulwark against further rebellions. In 1584, the Surveyor General of Ireland, Sir Valentine Browne, and a commission surveyed Munster, to allocate confiscated lands to English undertakers (wealthy colonists who 'undertook' to import tenants from England to work their new lands). The undertakers were also supposed to build new towns and provide for the defence of planted districts from attack. The core of the estates established by the new landowners (and of those still retained by the surviving Catholic gentry), set aside for their own use and enjoyment and often in succeeding centuries landscaped as gardens, were known as 'demesnes', a term still used in Ireland today.

As well as the former Geraldine estates (spread through the modern counties Limerick, Cork, Kerry and Tipperary) the survey took in the lands belonging to other families and clans that had supported the rebellions in southwest Cork and Kerry. The Munster Plantation was supposed to produce compact defensible settlements, but in fact the English settlers were spread in pockets across the province, wherever land had been confiscated. Initially the undertakers were given detachments of English soldiers to protect them, but these were abolished in the 1590s. As a result, when the Nine Years' War reached Munster in 1598, most of the settlers were chased off their lands without a fight. They took refuge in the province's walled towns or fled back to England. However, when the rebellion was put down in 1601–03, the Plantation was reconstituted by the Governor of Munster, George Carew.

The power of the Earls was further diminished under James I and the Lord Deputy of Ireland, Arthur Chichester, with the result that the Earls of Tyrone and Tyrconnell sailed from Lough Swilly on 4 September 1607 (the Flight of the Earls). Their lands, which included the counties of Londonderry, Tyrone, Armagh, Donegal and Fermanagh, were escheated (confiscated) and almost immediately used to provide land for the Plantation of Ulster. The land was divided into great, middle and small proportions (2000, 1500 and 1000 acres), each of which was to be passed on favourable terms to one of the following classes – undertakers (English, Manx or Lowland Scots as principal landlords), servitors (ex-army officers and Crown officials), 'deserving natives' (only on land set aside for the servitors), college land (land in County Donegal given to Trinity College, Dublin) and 12 London companies (Clothworkers, Drapers, Fishmongers, Goldsmiths, Grocers, Haberdashers, Ironmongers, Mercers, Salters, Skinners, Tailors and Vintners). The undertakers were expected to settle 24 British males per 1000 acres of lands granted and the native Irish population was to be expelled. An undertaker with 2000 acres was expected to build a castle and those with less had to build a stone bawn. In order to forestall attempts by the Earls to reclaim their land, originally all the building and settlement had to be completed within three years, although this proved to be wildly optimistic. Early take-up was slow. However, serious economic problems in Scotland meant a major increase in the numbers of Scots coming to Ireland, especially during the 1630s.

The 17th century was perhaps the bloodiest in Ireland's history. Two periods of civil war (1641–53 and 1689–91) caused huge loss of life and resulted in the final dispossession of the Irish Catholic landowning class and their subordination under the Penal Laws. In the mid 17th century, Ireland was convulsed by 11 years of warfare, beginning with the rebellion of 1641, when Irish Catholics rebelled against English and Protestant domination, in the process massacring thousands of Protestant settlers. The Catholic gentry briefly ruled the country as Confederate Ireland (1642–9) against the background of the Wars of the Three Kingdoms until Oliver Cromwell reconquered Ireland in 1649–53 on behalf of the English Commonwealth. Cromwell's conquest was the most brutal phase of a brutal war; his treatment of the defenders of Drogheda and Wexford still haunts the Irish folk memory. By the close of the war, up to a third of Ireland's pre-war population was dead or in exile. As punishment for the rebellion of 1641, almost all lands owned by Irish Catholics were confiscated and given to British settlers. Several hundred remaining native landowners were transplanted to Connacht. The establishment of the Commonwealth by Cromwell saw a further reduction in Catholic landownership in Ulster.

The restoration of Charles II to the throne of England in 1660 raised the hopes of Catholics, both Old English and Irish, in Ireland. Charles was acutely conscious of the need to retain the loyalty of his Protestant subjects in Ireland so his concessions to the Catholics were not as sweeping as they would have wished, but many of the newer Protestant settlers in Ireland regarded any concessions to the Catholic majority with disfavour. The atrocities committed by Catholic forces during the 1641 rebellion were fresh in the Protestant memory and Catholics, by virtue of their loyalty to the Pope, were regarded as potential traitors to the English government.

The accession of the Catholic James II as king of England in 1685 served to heighten the fears of Protestants in both England and Ireland. When a son was born to James's wife in 1688, the prospect of a Catholic dynasty ruling England proved to be too much for the Protestant ascendancy in England and William of Orange, the ruler of Holland, and his wife Mary, the daughter of James, were invited to become the rulers of England. James II fled to France to seek help from his French allies. The wealthier Irish Catholics backed James to try to reverse the remaining Penal Laws and land confiscations, whereas Protestants supported William to preserve their property in the country. After initial successes in Ulster during the Williamite Wars the Jacobites were repulsed at the Siege of Derry. In June 1690 William landed at Carrickfergus and marched through Belfast and Lisburn to fight the Battle of the Boyne, where James's outnumbered forces were defeated. Jacobite resistance was finally ended after the Battle of Aughrim in July 1691. (Drumcree Church, to the north of Portadown in County Armagh, has become noted for the Orange Order service held annually on the Sunday before 12 July to commemorate the Protestant victory. The service, or more precisely the Orangemen's march both to and from the service, has been the catalyst for sectarian unrest between the Protestant marchers and the Catholic residents of the area.)

The century after the end of the Williamite Wars was relatively peaceful and saw the rise of the linen industry following an influx of Huguenot refugees. The country's prosperity during the 18th century owed much to its improved political stability. However, this stability disguised undercurrents of dissension and dissatisfaction, due largely to resentment at the concentration of all political power and most economic power in the hands of the minority Ascendancy class. The late 18th century witnessed an increase in political and economic restrictions on both the Catholic and Presbyterian communities, together with unrest connected with the rapid changes taking place in agriculture and industry. This gave rise to various groups and societies, one of which, the Society of United Irishmen, was formed in October 1791 in Belfast. They carried out an abortive rising in 1798 with violent clashes in County Antrim and County Down; an accompanying French invasion (which led to 1798 being nicknamed the 'Year of the French') was defeated at the Battle of Ballinamuck in September. This eruption of underlying discontent and disaffection brought havoc and carnage to those parts of Ireland most affected by the outbreak.

The Kingdom of Ireland became part of the United Kingdom of Great Britain under the terms of the Act of Union of 1800 (which came into force on 1 January 1801). The 19th century saw a rise in industrial activity through the success of the linen industry and the growth of shipbuilding in Belfast. The region's trading and manufacturing facilities also benefited from the development of an integrated transport system, initially from canals and roads – the Antrim Coast Road was completed in 1838 – and then from the railway.

Then, however, came the Great Famine of 1845–9. In 1841 Ireland supported a population of 8,175,124. Approximately 3 million of these depended almost entirely on potatoes, supplemented with milk, for their subsistence. A general failure of the potato harvest would obviously spell disaster for huge numbers of people. Reports of an outbreak of potato blight began to circulate in the autumn of 1845. By the winter of 1845–6 it was clear that more than half of the crop was unusable and widespread hardship was felt among the rural and urban poor. The enormous scale of the problem overwhelmed all the efforts at amelioration, while the laissez-faire economic doctrine dominant at the time, which viewed government interference in the economy as an inherently bad thing, hampered government relief measures throughout the period of the Famine. The winter of 1846–7, 'Black 47' in folklore, was the worst in living memory. The potato harvest of 1847 was good but only a small crop of potatoes had been sown. In desperation, many of the poor had eaten the seed potatoes. In 1848 the crop failed again.

By 1850, the worst of the famine was over, but its effects would be felt for generations and one of its worst legacies was the poisoning of the atmosphere between Ireland and England. Emigrants who fled to the USA would carry with them the memory of ships laden with food leaving the country while thousands died of starvation and disease. The reality was more complex, but the myth of 'perfidious Albion' among Irish-Americans ensured a ready audience for those Irish political leaders who sought to 'break the connection with England' by whatever means. Between 1845 and 1851 the population of Ireland decreased by approximately 2 million. Historians and demographers estimate that a million died during the period and another million emigrated. The northeast region, which was to become Northern Ireland, was perhaps the least affected, being less dependent on the potato crop.

The hardening of attitudes over Home Rule dominated the end of the 19th century and the period before World War I. As tensions increased armed 'volunteer armies' arose, the Unionists forming the Ulster Volunteer Force (UVF) and the Nationalists the Irish Volunteers. The 3rd Home Rule Bill was enacted, receiving royal assent on 18 September 1914; it established 'an Irish Parliament of HM the King and two houses, namely, the Irish Senate and the Irish House of Commons'. However, the Act was suspended for one year or for the duration of the war, whichever was the longer. In January 1919, after the December 1918 general elections, 73 of Ireland's 106 MPs elected were

Sinn Féin members who refused to take their seats in the British House of Commons. Instead, they set up an extra-legal Irish parliament called Dáil Éireann. This Dáil in January 1919 issued a Unilateral Declaration of Independence and proclaimed an Irish Republic. Against a background of increasing violence, eventually Ireland was partitioned under the provisions of the Government of Ireland Act (1920), the parliamentary counties of Antrim, Armagh, Down, Fermanagh, Londonderry and Tyrone, and the parliamentary boroughs of Belfast and Londonderry becoming Northern Ireland.

Armed conflict in Northern Ireland between the Irish Republican Army, the UVF and the Ulster Special Constabulary virtually ended with the outbreak of the Irish Civil War in June 1922. The war was precipitated when 26 of the counties of Ireland seceded from the United Kingdom of Great Britain and Ireland (the remaining six counties remained within the UK as Northern Ireland). After the bitterly fought War of Independence, representatives of the British government and the Irish rebels had negotiated the Anglo-Irish Treaty in 1921 under which the British agreed to the establishment of an independent Irish state, thereby creating the Irish Free State (I. *Saorstát Éireann*) with dominion status. The Dáil Éireann narrowly ratified the treaty.

The Irish Civil War (28 June 1922–24 May 1923) was a conflict between supporters and opponents of the Anglo-Irish Treaty. Anti-treaty forces, led by Éamon de Valera, objected to the fact that acceptance of the treaty abolished the Irish Republic of 1919 to which they had sworn loyalty, arguing in the face of public support for the settlement that the 'people have no right to do wrong'. They objected most to the fact that the state would remain part of what was then the British Commonwealth and that Teachtaí Dála (members of the Dáil Éireann) would have to swear an oath of fidelity to George V and his successors. Pro-Treaty forces, led by Michael Collins, argued that the treaty gave 'not the ultimate freedom that all nations aspire to and develop, but the freedom to achieve it'. Other opponents of the treaty objected to the fact that the six counties of Northern Ireland would not be included in the Free State. The Civil War cost the lives of more than had died in the War of Independence that preceded it and left Irish society deeply divided. Its influence in Irish politics remains evident today

The Irish Civil War delayed until 1924 the activating of Article 12 of the treaty, which provided for the setting up of a boundary commission to determine the frontier 'in accordance with the wishes of the inhabitants, so far as may be compatible with economic and geographic conditions, the boundaries between Northern Ireland and the rest of Ireland'. However, in the end only minor changes were made to those specified under the 1920 Government of Ireland Act. The first Northern Ireland Parliament was opened by George V in Belfast City Hall on 22 June 1921. Between 1921 and 1932 sessions were held in the Presbyterian Church's Assembly's College before the final move to Stormont. Sir James Craig (1st Viscount Craigavon) was Prime Minister from 7 June 1921 until his death on 24 November 1940. The parliament was bicameral, with a 52 seat House of Commons and an indirectly elected Senate of 26 seats. Between 1921 and 1929 elections to the House of Commons were by single transferable vote (STV) but this was changed to first past the post from 1929 onwards (although STV was retained for the four university seats which were abolished in 1969). The Ireland Act (1949) guaranteed that Northern Ireland would not cease to be part of the UK without the consent of a majority of its citizens (a guarantee reaffirmed by the Northern Ireland Act 1998).

On 29 December 1937, a new constitution, the Constitution of Ireland, came into force. It replaced the Irish Free State by a new state called simply 'Ireland'. Though this state's constitutional structures provided for a President of Ireland instead of a king, it was not yet technically a republic; the principal key role possessed by a head of state, that of symbolically representing the state internationally, remained vested, in statute law, in the king as an organ. On 21 December 1948, the Republic of Ireland Act declared a republic, with the functions previously given to the Governor-General acting on the behalf of the king given instead to the President of Ireland. The Irish state had remained a member of the British Commonwealth after independence until the declaration of a republic on 18 April 1949. Under Commonwealth rules declaration of a republic automatically terminated membership of the association; since a reapplication for membership was not made, Ireland consequently ceased to be a member.

After the country had been stabilised politically following the Civil War, Ireland endured decades of comparative economic stagnation. Protected behind tariff barriers, the Irish economy relied to a great extent on its home market. The standard of living was poor by European standards and emigration was one of the great scourges of Irish life. During the inter-war period Northern Ireland suffered from the world-wide economic depression and had the highest unemployment rate and highest infant mortality rate in the United Kingdom. At the outbreak of World War II Northern Ireland was largely unprepared for the conflict. On 7 April 1941 an air raid targeting the shipyards and industrial areas of Belfast caused some damage and was followed on 15 April 1941 by a much more devastating raid which cost the lives of more than 900 people. Lone bombers also attacked Derry, Newtownards and Bangor. Aid in the form of volunteer firemen and fire tenders was requested from and supplied by the neutral Irish Republic. During the rest of the war and especially after the entry of the United States, the region became an important base for the protection of allied convoys in the North Atlantic, including a Catalina flying boat station on Lough Erne. Northern Ireland also served as a base for troops preparing for the invasion of Europe.

On 11 December 1956 the IRA launched a new military campaign in Northern Ireland, Operation Harvest (1956–62), which became commonly known as the 'Border Campaign'. Despite this, the post-war period was relatively peaceful in terms of community relations, but by the mid 1970s there were demands for reform of a system which discriminated against the Catholic community. Reforms put in place by Prime Minister Terence O'Neill were not felt to be sufficient and the Northern Ireland Civil Rights Association (NICRA) was formed in Belfast on 29 January 1967. Among its demands was an end to discrimination in government employment and in the awarding of local authority housing, plus an end to the gerrymandering of local electoral districts, which helped to ensure Unionist control over local government even in towns with Nationalist majorities. The first civil rights march in Northern Ireland was held on 24 August 1968 between Coalisland and Dungannon.

Escalating violence during and after the Apprentice Boys' march in Derry on 12 August 1969, which became known as the Battle of Bogside (12–15 August 1969), led to the arrival of British troops in Northern Ireland. Between August 1969 and March 1972 the Bogside was allowed to stand as a 'no-go' area. A march in Derry organised by NICRA against the policy of internment ended with the shooting dead of 13 civilians by British troops on 30 January 1972. This became known as Bloody Sunday and 1972 became the most violent year of what were referred to as 'the Troubles', with over 450 'conflict-related' deaths recorded in Northern Ireland that year. More than 3500 'conflict-related' deaths were recorded between 1969 and 2001.

The Northern Ireland Parliament was prorogued on 30 March 1972 and direct rule from Westminster was imposed. A power-sharing executive took office in January 1974 as a result of the Sunningdale Agreement of 9 December 1973, which also proposed an elected 78 member Northern Ireland Assembly and a cross-border Council of Ireland. However, the executive was short-lived as Unionist opposition, Provisional IRA violence and a general strike organised by anti-Agreement Unionists and called by the loyalist Ulster Workers' Council forced its collapse on 28 May 1974. A Northern Ireland Assembly was established at Stormont in 1982 as a scrutinising body for the Secretary of State for Northern Ireland. It was dissolved on 23 June 1986.

The Anglo-Irish Agreement was signed on 15 November 1985 by British Prime Minister Margaret Thatcher and the Irish Taoiseach, Garret FitzGerald. In it the Irish government agreed to recognise the legitimacy of Northern Ireland in return for being involved in matters related to Northern Ireland's nationalist minority. The agreement also set up an intergovernmental conference based at Maryfield near Stormont, headed by the British Secretary of State for Northern Ireland and the Irish Foreign Minister and staffed by civil servants from both countries. The agreement was bitterly received by the Unionist community and not seen as a solution by the Nationalist minority. Nevertheless it set the British and Irish governments on the road to the Downing Street Declaration and the Belfast Agreement. Although violence continued, including the horrendous bombing in Enniskillen in 1987 and the Shankill Road bombing and Greysteel killings in October 1993, there were more moves towards finding political solutions to the crisis, including talks between the Social Democratic and Labour Party (SDLP) and Sinn Féin and between the Secretaries of State for Northern Ireland, Peter Brooke and Sir Patrick Mayhew, and the various Northern Irish political parties, including the Ulster Unionist Party (UUP), the SDLP, the Democratic Unionist Party (DUP), and the Alliance Party of Northern Ireland (APNI). These became known as the Brooke/Mayhew talks.

The Joint Declaration for Peace (also known as the Downing Street Declaration) was proclaimed on 15 December 1993 by Prime Minister John Major and Taoiseach Albert Reynolds with the stated aim 'to foster agreement and reconciliation, leading to a new political framework founded on consent and encompassing arrangements within Northern Ireland, for the whole island, and between these islands'. It offered parties linked with paramilitary organisations the opportunity to take part in a settlement, so long as they abandoned violence. After receiving 'clarification' about the meaning of the declaration, the Provisional IRA announced a ceasefire on 31 August 1994, followed by the Combined Loyalist Military Command on 13 October 1994. The IRA ceasefire ended on 9 February 1996 when a bomb exploded at South Quay, Docklands, London, but was eventually reinstated on 20 July 1997. On 10 June 1996 multi-party negotiations under the chairmanship of ex-US

Senator George Mitchell began at Stormont (with some talks also taking place at Lancaster House, London) which eventually led to the Belfast Agreement.

The Belfast Agreement of 10 April 1998 (also known as the Good Friday Agreement or the Stormont Agreement), the provisions of which were endorsed by referenda in Northern Ireland and the Irish Republic on 22 May 1998, included: the establishment of a Northern Ireland Assembly with devolved legislative powers; the creation of a 'power-sharing' Northern Ireland Executive; the conditional early release within two years of paramilitary prisoners belonging to organisations observing a ceasefire; a two year target for decommissioning of paramilitary weapons; police reform; and the establishment of the Northern Ireland Human Rights Commission. The new Northern Ireland Assembly was first elected on 25 June 1998. It was suspended from 11 February 2000 until 30 May 2000, 11 August 2001 and 22 September 2001 (both for 24 hours) and again from 14 October 2002 until 7 May 2007 after Unionists walked out of the power-sharing executive after Sinn Féin's offices at Stormont were raided by the police investigating alleged intelligence gathering on behalf of the IRA. The previous suspensions were caused by a lack of progress on the decommissioning issue. Despite the suspension, elections to the 108 seat Assembly were held on 26 November 2003, although they had been delayed for six months by the Secretary of State for Northern Ireland. The Northern Ireland Executive was formed on 2 December 1999 with executive positions for 11 departments, including the Office of First and Deputy First Minister, shared between parties supporting the agreement on the basis of their electoral performance. The Assembly elects the First Minister and Executive.

The political rapprochement was not immediately accompanied by an end to violence and at 15.10 on Saturday 15 August 1998 an explosion caused by a 500lb car bomb planted by the Real IRA killed 29 people in Omagh, County Tyrone. However, the IRA carried out a series of decommissioning exercises of their weaponry and ordered an end to its armed campaign in July 2005.

The ending of the Troubles has enabled Northern Ireland to begin a regeneration process with, in particular, major building and rebuilding projects in Belfast and Derry and the enhancement of the region's infrastructure.

Prime Ministers of Northern Ireland: Sir James Craig (7 June 1921–24 November 1940 (death); John Millar Andrews (27 November 1940–1 May 1943); Sir Basil Brooke (1 May 1943–26 March 1963); Terence O'Neill (25 March 1963–1 May 1969); James Chichester-Clark (1 May 1969–23 March 1971); Brian Faulkner (23 March 1971–30 March 1972).

Secretaries of State for Northern Ireland: William Whitelaw (24 March 1972–2 December 1973); Francis Pym (2 December 1973–4 March 1974); Merlyn Rees (5 March 1974–10 September 1976); Roy Mason (10 September 1976–4 May 1979); Humphrey Atkins (5 May 1979–14 September 1981); James Prior (14 September 1981–11 September 1984); Douglas Hurd (11 September 1984–3 September 1985); Tom King (3 September 1985–24 July 1989); Peter Brooke (24 July 1989–10 April 1992); Sir Patrick Mayhew (10 April 1992–2 May 1997); Mo Mowlam (3 May 1997–11 October 1999); Peter Mandelson (11 October 1999–24 January 2001); John Reid (25 January 2001–24 October 2002); Paul Murphy (24 October 2002–6 May 2005); Peter Hain (6 May 2005–27 June 2007); Shaun Woodward (27 June 2007–).

First Minister of Northern Ireland: David Trimble (1 July 1998–1 July 2001); Reg Empey (acting) (1 July 2001–1 November 2001); David Trimble (1 November 2001–14 October 2002); Ian Paisley (8 May 2007–5 June 2008); Peter Robinson (5 June 2008–).

According to the 2001 census, 53.1 per cent of the Northern Irish population was Protestant and 43.8 per cent Roman Catholic. In contrast, the population of the Republic of Ireland is 88 per cent Roman Catholic.

The **Republic of Ireland** is divided into 26 counties. Technically, there are now 29 administrative counties as local government units have been restructured, with the now-abolished County Dublin (as per EU directive) distributed between three new county councils in the 1990s and County Tipperary having been administratively two separate counties since the 1890s. However, the traditional counties remain very much established in the minds and hearts of the Irish people, to the extent that the directive has been largely ignored except in name only. There are five cities of the Republic – Dublin, Cork, Limerick, Galway and Waterford – all administered separately from the remainder of their respective counties. Five boroughs – Clonmel, Drogheda, Kilkenny, Sligo and Wexford – have a level of autonomy within their respective counties. Until the 1980s the Catholic Church had great influence in Irish society but this was undermined by a series of scandals which contributed to an increased secularisation of the state. Since 1992 the state has become less socially conservative. Liberalisation has been championed by figures like Mary Robinson, a radical feminist senator who became President of Ireland, and David Norris, who led the Campaign for Homosexual Law Reform.

The Republic of Ireland joined the United Nations in 1955 and the European Community (now the European Union) in 1973. The President of Ireland, who serves as head of state, is elected for a seven-year term and can be re-elected only once. The president is largely a figurehead but can still carry out certain constitutional powers and functions, aided by the Council of State, an advisory body. The Taoiseach (prime minister), is appointed by the President on the nomination of parliament. The Taoiseach is normally the leader of the political party which wins the most seats in the national elections. It has become normal in the Republic for coalitions to form a government, and there has not been a single-party government since the period of 1987–9.

The bicameral parliament, the Oireachtas, consists of a Senate, Seanad Éireann, and a lower house, Dáil Éireann. The Seanad is composed of 60 members; 11 nominated by the Taoiseach, 6 elected by two universities, and 43 elected by public representatives from panels of candidates established on a vocational basis. The Dáil has 166 members, Teachtaí Dála, elected to represent multi-seat constituencies under the system of proportional representation by means of the Single Transferable Vote. Under the constitution, parliamentary elections must be held at least every seven years, though a lower limit may be set by statute law. The current statutory maximum term is every five years.

Gripped by poverty and emigration for most of its existence, the state became one of the fastest growing economies in the world by the 1990s, a phenomenon known as the Celtic Tiger. By the early 2000s, the Republic had become the second richest (in terms of GDP per capita, adjusted for purchasing power parity) member of the European Union, had moved from being a net recipient of EU funds to a net contributor and from a position of net emigration to one of net immigration. In 2005, its per capita GDP (adjusted for purchasing power parity) became the second highest in the world (behind Switzerland) with 10 per cent of the population born abroad.

In 2006 it was announced that the Republic of Ireland would be referred to at European Union meetings from 2007 as Éire-Ireland. This followed from the adoption of Irish as a working language of the European Union as of 1 January 2007; it would be illogical for the Republic to request that Irish should be an official language, but not use it in its name as a member state. The President of Ireland (Irish: Uachtarán na hÉireann) is the head of state of the Republic of Ireland. The President is usually directly elected by the people for seven years, and can be elected for a maximum of two terms. The presidency is largely a ceremonial office, but the President does exercise certain limited powers at his/her absolute discretion. The office was established by the Constitution of Ireland in 1937. The President's official residence is Áras an Uachtaráin in Dublin. The current office-holder is President Mary McAleese.

The national anthem played at state events in Northern Ireland is 'God Save the Queen'; however, the Londonderry Air, also known as the tune of 'Danny Boy', is played at sporting events where it is necessary to distinguish the country from potentially competing home nations. The Ulster Banner (a red cross with a red hand, a six pointed star, and a crown; both the hand and the cross on a white background) is used on such occasions although both the anthem and flag are unofficial. The national anthem of the Republic is 'Amhrán na bhFiann' (The Soldier's Song) and its flag is a vertical tricolour of green, white and orange.

The local history and geography of Ireland is described within the overviews of the 32 traditional counties into which I have divided the country and requires no further explanation here. Included in each Northern Ireland county is a list of woodlands established by the Woodland Trust as part of the 'Woods on your Doorstep' (Woyd) project to provide community woodland amenities. The population and area figures listed below include the 26 existing unitary authorities of Northern Ireland split into the six traditional counties and the 26 de facto counties of the Republic. A reconciliation to the 2001 Census (2002 for the Republic) is included at the back of the book.

Ireland population summaries

See 2001 and 2002 Census reconciliation

	Population			Area	
	male	*female*	*total*	*sq miles*	*sq km*
Antrim	328,749	355,625	684,374	1250	3238
Armagh	109,771	112,221	221,992	753	1951
(London)Derry	114,552	119,031	233,583	784	2032
Down	156,576	164,699	321,275	634	1642
Fermanagh	28,818	28,709	57,527	724	1876
Tyrone	82,983	83,533	166,516	1312	3398
Northern Ireland total	821,449	863,818	1,685,267	5457	14,137
Carlow	23,403	22,611	46,014	347	898
Cavan	29,015	27,531	56,546	746	1932
Clare	52,063	51,214	103,277	1329	3442
Cork	222,317	225,512	447,829	2899	7508
Donegal	69,016	68,559	137,575	1876	4860
Dublin	544,075	578,746	1,122,821	355	921
Galway	104,367	104,710	209,077	2375	6151
Kerry	66,572	65,955	132,527	1828	4735
Kildare	82,735	81,209	163,944	654	1694
Kilkenny	40,540	39,799	80,339	800	2072
Laois	30,131	28,643	58,774	664	1719
Leitrim	13,324	12,475	25,799	613	1589
Limerick	87,631	87,673	175,304	1066	2760
Longford	15,794	15,274	31,068	421	1091
Louth	50,489	51,332	101,821	321	832
Mayo	59,149	58,297	117,446	2158	5588
Meath	67,733	66,272	134,005	901	2335
Monaghan	26,806	25,787	52,593	500	1296
Offaly	32,185	31,478	63,663	768	1990
Roscommon	27,583	26,191	53,774	984	2548
Sligo	28,771	29,429	58,200	709	1837
Tipperary	70,863	69,268	140,131	1662	4304
Waterford	50,672	50,874	101,546	718	1859
Westmeath	35,960	35,898	71,858	705	1825
Wexford	58,170	58,426	116,596	913	2365
Wicklow	56,800	57,876	114,676	785	2033
Republic of Ireland total	1,946,164	1,971,039	3,917,203	27,097	70,184

Carlow

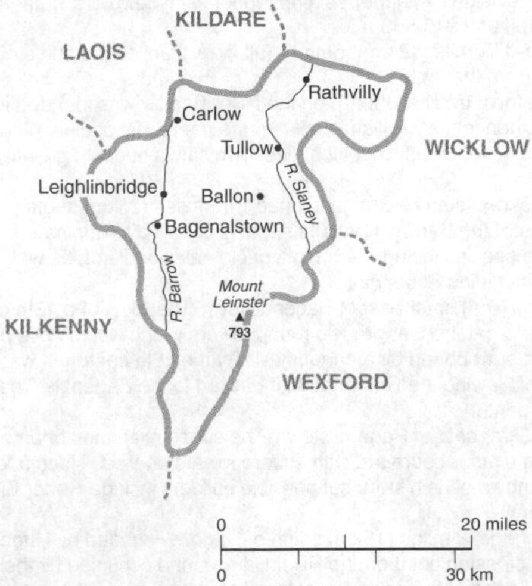
KILDARE
LAOIS
Rathvilly
Carlow
Tullow
WICKLOW
R. Slaney
Leighlinbridge
Ballon
Bagenalstown
R. Barrow
Mount Leinster
793
KILKENNY
WEXFORD
0
20 miles
0
30 km

County Carlow (*Contae Cheatharlach*, 'four-part lake' or the 'four lakes') is part of the province of Leinster in the southeast of the Republic of Ireland. Its main geographic features are the Blackstairs Mountains, the Killeshin Hills and the rivers Barrow and Slaney. A landlocked county, it is bordered by five other counties: Kildare to the north, Wicklow to the northeast, Wexford to the east, Kilkenny to the southwest and west and Laois to the northwest. The economy is largely based on agriculture, with industry confined to factories owned by a few large firms.

C A R L O W

County Carlow has been settled since at least the Mesolithic period and numerous examples of tombs and standing stones dot the county's landscape. Early Christian settlements were established at St Mullins, Glonmore and Old Leighlin. Before the arrival of the Anglo-Normans Carlow was part of the Gaelic kingdom of Uí Cinnseallaigh. Along with County Wexford, County Carlow was at the heart of the fighting during the 1798 uprising by the United Irishmen.

Carlow is the largest town and the county's administrative headquarters. Other towns and villages of note include Bagenalstown, Ballon, a village under the Blackstairs and Wicklow Mountains which was first settled in the Bronze Age, Clonegal, a twin village with the Watch at the terminal of the Wicklow Way, and located at the confluence of the Slaney and Derry Rivers, Leighlinbridge, Rathvilly, St Mullins and Tullow.

Carlow	**Population**			**Area**	
Districts	*male*	*female*	*total*	*sq miles*	*sq km*
Baltinglass	1889	1744	3633	52	135
Carlow Rural Area	13,963	13,221	27,184	253	654
Carlow Town	6490	6728	13,218	3	7
Idrone Rural Area	1061	918	1979	39	102
Total	23,403	22,611	46,014	347	898

Local Attractions and Information

Administrative headquarters — County Offices, Athy Road, Carlow. Tel: 059 917 0300.

Altamont Gardens — $4^1/_2$ miles (7km) south of Tullow, 9 miles (15km) southeast of Carlow. Located on a 100 acre (40ha) estate centred on Altamont House, which was extended and improved in the 18th and 19th centuries. Developed since the 1920s by the Watson family, the gardens include a formal garden, a wild garden and the Ice Age Glen with oak grove by the River Slaney. There is also an artificial lake created in the 19th century, an arboretum and a riverside walk. The principal plant collections include conifers, broadleaves (including acer), shrubs (in particular rhododendrons and roses), herbaceous perennials and bulbs (including galanthus and narcissus). Tel: 050 359444.

Ardattin Cottage Museum — Ballynow, Ardattin, 3 miles (5km) southeast of Carlow. A museum run by Frankie and Jimmy Quinlan, opened in 1994 in a restored cottage. It houses a collection of artefacts such as vintage radios, televisions, telephones, gramophones, typewriters, cameras, sewing machines, toys and games. Tel: 059 915 5639.

Ardristan Standing Stone — Ardristan, 1¹/₄ miles (2km) south of Tullow. A granite standing stone 9ft (2.7m) tall with six vertical grooves from the top.

Bagenalstown — Bagenalstown (Muine Bheag) on the River Barrow was founded in the 18th century by Walter Bagenal, hence the English version of the name. His original plan of producing a town based on Versailles never came to fruition. The town saw a boost to growth with the arrival of the railways in the 1840s.

Bahana Forest — 3 miles (5km) south of Graiguemanagh, 16 miles (26km) south of Carlow. An ancient woodland on the banks of the Barrow River; its name is believed to originate from *beith* (Irish for 'birch'). The main tree species include remnants of old oak woodland, as well as beech, birch and a range of conifers including Scots pine.

Ballyloughan Castle — 2¹/₂ miles (4km) southeast of Bagenalstown. The ruins of a 13th century castle. The remains consist of a gatehouse with two round towers which would have provided an entrance to a large courtyard surrounded by a curtain wall. By the 16th century it was a stronghold of the Kavanagh clan and following the Reformation it passed to the Bagenals. The castle had been abandoned by the 18th century.

Ballymoon Castle — 2 miles (3km) east of Bagenalstown. The substantial ruins of an early 14th century castle enclosing a large courtyard with square towers on three sides and a gatehouse on the fourth. Little is known of its history but possible builders include Roger Bigod, Earl of Norfolk, or the Carew family.

Black Castle — Leighlinbridge, 8 miles (13km) south of Carlow. Founded by Hugh de Lacy in 1181 to defend a strategic crossing point on the River Barrow, and occupied by the Norman John de Claville. It was replaced in the 16th century by a castle built by Sir Edward Bellingham which fell to Cromwellian troops in 1650.

Borris House — Borris, 7 miles (11km) south of Bagenalstown. The home of the MacMurrough Kavanagh family, located in the Barrow valley on an estate of more than 600 acres (240ha) bordering the river. The house was built in 1731 by Morgan Kavanagh, probably on the site of an earlier fortification defending the river. Tel: 059 977 1884.

Brownshill Dolmen — 2 miles (3km) east of Carlow. A megalithic tomb with a granite capstone said to be the heaviest in Europe, weighing in at 100 tonnes. The capstone rests on three uprights each 5ft 10in (1.77m) high. It dates to c. 2500 BC.

Carlow Castle — Castle Hill, Carlow. The substantial ruins of an early 13th castle probably built by William de Marshal on the eastern bank of the River Barrow on the site of an earlier earth and timber structure. It was successfully attacked in 1494, 1642 and 1650. The castle was partially destroyed in 1814 when Dr Middleton, a local physician, blew it up while trying to remodel it into an asylum. Only one wall and two towers of the original four-towered keep now remain.

Carlow Cathedral — College Street, Carlow. Occupying the site of an earlier chapel, Carlow's Catholic Cathedral of the Assumption was built 1828–33 to a Gothic design by Thomas Cobden. Its tower and lantern were partly modelled on the Belfry Tower in Bruges. A statue to Bishop James Doyle, who inspired the building of the cathedral, was erected in 1839.

Carlow College — College Street, Carlow. Aka St Patrick's College. Founded in 1793 as a lay college by Bishops Daniel Delaney and James Keefe, from then until 1892 it served as a college of the humanities and a seminary; from 1892 until 1989 it was mainly a seminary for the education of priests. The National Centre for Contemporary Art and the George Bernard Shaw Theatre for the Performing Arts, opened in 2009, is located on the college campus. Tel: 059 915 3200.

Carlow County Museum — Founded in 1973 by the Carlow Historical & Archaeological Society, the museum was originally housed in the old Academy School before transferring to the Town Hall in 1979. A new site on College Street is under development but the museum was closed in 2002.

Carlow Courthouse — Dublin Street, Carlow. An imposing Greek Revival neoclassical building designed by William Vitruvius Morrison in 1830. It has eight Ionic columns above a flight of steps and is based on Greek temple design. A Russian cannon, captured during the Crimean War, stands at the top of the steps. The basement contains cells for the prisoners. According to a local story, inspired probably because of its grandeur, it was meant to be built in Cork but was accidentally built in Carlow. The courthouse underwent major restoration during the 1990s.

Carlow Military Museum — Athy Road, Carlow. A museum opened in 1996 at the headquarters of the Carlow Reserve Defence Force (*Forsa Cosanta Aitiuil*, FCA) and relocated to St Dympna's Hospital Church in 2001. Displays include uniforms of the Irish defence forces and explore their role in the UN peacekeeping forces in the Congo, Lebanon and Somalia. There is also a reconstruction of a World War I trench and audio-visual presentations on the Irish War of Independence and the Civil War. An exhibition in the museum celebrates the life of Captain Myles Keogh (1840–76), one of a band of Irish mercenaries who fought overseas and were therefore referred to as Wild Geese. Leighlinbridge-born Keogh left Ireland in his teens and joined the Papal Army, in which he fought with distinction and was awarded the Medaglia de Pro Petri Sede and the Cross of the Order of St Gregory by Pope Pius IX. In 1862 he sailed from Italy to the USA to join the Union Army during the American Civil War and saw action at the Battles of Brandy Station and Gettysburg in 1863. After the war he joined the regular army and on 25 June 1876 he was in command of Company I of the 7th Cavalry at the Battle of the Little Bighorn. He was killed, along with all of George Armstrong Custer's command that day, but his was the only body not mutilated; his horse Comanche was the sole US survivor of the battle. According to some Native American accounts of the battle, Keogh may have been the last trooper to fall, still clutching the reins of his wounded horse. Comanche became a living memorial to those who fell on the Montana battlefield and he was never ridden or worked again.

Carlow
Lying at the confluence of the rivers Barrow and Burrin, the town grew up around the 12th century castle which defended the strategic river crossing. Carlow's economy received a boost in 1926 when the Irish Sugar Manufacturing Company was established (it closed in 2005). More recently, thanks to its rail links, the town has developed into a satellite of Dublin. There is also a large student population based at Carlow College and the Institute of Technology.

Churches
The **Adelaide Memorial Church of Christ the Redeemer**, Myshall, 7 miles (11km) east of Bagenalstown, built in 1912 in Gothic style for John Duguid. A miniature version of Salisbury Cathedral, it was built to commemorate Duguid's wife Adelaide and daughter Constance, who were killed in a hunting accident. The Duguid family, including John himself, are buried within the church. The design of the marble floor in the chancel was taken from St Mark's in Venice.

St Fiaac's, Clonegal, 8 miles (13km) southeast of Tullow, a Church of Ireland church built overlooking Clonegal in 1819 on the site of a dun and an earlier church. It was designed by John Bowden in Gothic style with a tower. The boundaries of the churchyard are delineated by the steep sides of the dun.

St Lazerians, Ballinkillen, 4 miles (6km) southeast of Bagenalstown, a Catholic church built in 1793 in with a T-plan design. It was extended in the 1820s, re-roofed in early 20th century and modernised in the late 1970s.

St Mary's, Castle Street, Carlow, a Church of Ireland church built in 1727 to which a tower and spire designed by Thomas Cobden were added in 1834. It was located on the site of an earlier church which had fallen into disrepair.

The **White Church**, Killoughternane, 7 miles (11km) southeast of Bagenalstown, the ruin of a 5th century church.

Cloch An Phoill
Aghade, $2\frac{1}{4}$ miles (3.5km) south of Tullow. Aka Aghade Holed Stone. A pillar stone with a hole pierced through it. It was possibly originally part of a megalithic tomb. The hole is 1ft (0.3m) in diameter; for many centuries it was believed that if a sick infant was passed through the hole, then it would be cured.

Clonegal Castle
See Huntington Castle

Clonmore Castle
Clonmore, 9 miles (15km) east of Carlow. The ruins of a late 13th century square plan castle, subsequently remodelled. It was captured by Cromwellian forces in 1650.

Cranavane Well
$1\frac{1}{4}$ miles (2km) west of Kildavin, 8 miles (13km) south of Tullow. A holy well believed to have been a Druidic site in pre-Christian times. Until the 1870s an annual gathering in honour of the Virgin Mary took place at the well on the Sunday nearest to 3 May. The well was restored in the late 1990s.

Croppies Grave
Chapel Street, Carlow. A monument erected above the mass grave of 640 United Irishmen – known as Croppies because of their hairstyle – who were killed in the 1798 Rebellion. The spot was also marked by the planting of three trees (two of which still stand) by the mother of three of the dead.

Duckett's Grove
5 miles (8km) east of Carlow. The ruins of a country house built c.1745 by the Duckett family on their 5000 acre (2000ha) estate. Extensively remodelled in castellated Gothic style in the 1820s to a design by Thomas A Cobden, it was further extended in the 1840s and 1850s with the addition of more towers and turrets as well as an elaborate gateway. The Duckett family had left by 1915 and during the 1920s it was used as a training base by the IRA. It was partially destroyed by fire in April 1933. The house and the adjoining walled garden and lawns were acquired by Carlow County Council in 2005 for use as a public park.

Dunleckney Manor
1 mile (1.6km) northeast of Bagenalstown. A country house built for the Bagenal family in the 17th century and remodelled c.1845 in Tudor Revival style to a design by Daniel Robertson. Tel: 059 972 1932.

'Follow Me Up to Carlow'
An Irish folk song which celebrates the victory of the Irish under Feagh MacHugh O'Byrne over an English army commanded by Arthur Grey, Lord de Wilton at Glenmalure, Co. Wicklow. The battle was fought on 25 August 1580 during Desmond's Rebellion.

George Bernard Shaw Theatre and Visual Arts Centre
Situated in the grounds of Carlow College, the magnificent glass building, designed by English architect Terry Pawson, opened in September 2009 and holds a 353-seat main auditorium plus four viewing galleries with 3500 square feet of floor space. Tel: 059 917 9242.

Graiguecullen Bridge
A five-arch bridge spanning the River Barrow in Carlow, built in 1569 and widened in 1815.

Haroldstown Dolmen
4 miles (6km) northeast of Tullow. A portal dolmen with two capstones, one 12ft (3.5m) long and the other 9ft (2.7m) long. The capstones were supported by ten uprights in order to create a large chamber. The tomb was used as a home in the 19th century.

Hermitage Gardens
Hanover Road, Carlow. A $1\frac{1}{2}$ acre (0.6ha) walled garden with several separate areas each with a different planting and colour scheme.

Highest point
Mount Leinster at 2602ft (793m). Bordering Co. Wexford, it is also that county's highest point.

Hillview Museum
Corries, 4 miles (6km) southeast of Bagenalstown. A museum housing a collection of agricultural and household machinery and equipment. Tel: 059 972 1795.

Huntington Castle and Gardens
Clonegal, 8 miles (13km) southeast of Tullow. Aka Clonegal Castle. Located on the site of an earlier fortification, itself built on the site of a priory, the castle has been the home of the Durdin-Robertson family since the original tower house was built c.1625 by the 1st Lord Esmonde. It was extended and remodelled in the 1880s. The current owner, artist and writer Olivia Robertson, is a

co-founder of the Fellowship of Isis, which was founded at Huntington Castle at the Vernal Equinox of 1976. There is a Temple of Isis in the basement of the house. The house stands in 50 acres (20ha) of gardens and parkland beside the rivers Slaney and Derry. It is reputed to have a variety of ghosts including Ailish O'Flaherty, who waits in vain for the return of her husband and son from war. The Office of Contemporary Art, a gallery in the castle's gate lodge, specialises in contemporary works on paper.

Interesting facts — Carlow-born Rev. Samuel Haughton invented the '**Haughton Drop**' in 1866. This was a relatively humane way of hanging someone by way of ensuring that the drop would be of such a nature that the victim was unlikely to be left dangling in a state of agony. Haughton calculated that a person weighing 10 stone (63.5kg) would need to fall 15ft (4.6m) to achieve a clean snap of the neck and instant death. The Haughton Drop was eventually adopted throughout Europe at public hangings. **John Tyndall**, born in Garrison House, Leighlinbridge, was the first scientist to be called a physicist. He was the first man to recognise the 'greenhouse effect' of carbon dioxide and also the first to accurately measure atmospheric pollution. Tyndall was a prolific inventor and some of his more famous offerings include the modern foghorn, the fireman's respirator, the light pipe (which directly led to the invention of fibre optic cables) and a form of food sterilisation called Tyndallisation. For good measure, Tyndall was the first man to climb the Weisshorn, a 14,780ft (4505m) mountain in Switzerland. Unfortunately the great man suffered a tragic end to his life when his wife administered an overdose of a narcotic in the belief it was for indigestion. **Arthur MacMurrough Kavanagh** of the famous Carlow family of Kavanaghs was born in the 19th century. He had neither arms nor legs but overcame his disabilities to such effect that he became an MP and Privy Councillor; he also painted, wrote, rode and hunted. Kavanagh also had a great sense of humour. On a trip to Abbeylix one day he exclaimed to a friend that 'It's an extraordinary thing – I haven't been here for five years and yet the station-master recognised me!' **William Dargan** was known as 'The Father of Irish Railways' as he was the engineer responsible for the building of the first railway in Ireland, from Dublin to Dun Laoghaire in 1833. **The last Irish wolf** was killed in 1786, by John Watson of Ballydarton, Leighlinbridge, a master of foxhounds. The deed was performed at Baltinglass, just across the border in Co. Wicklow. Ireland's **first polo club**, the All-Ireland Polo Club, was founded in 1872 by Horace Rochfort of Clogrenane. The village of **Rathvilly**, located on the east bank of the River Barrow on the border with Kildare and Wicklow, has won the award for Ireland's Tidiest Village three times. **Tullow** is known as 'Granite town' because of its granite approach roads. It was the ancestral home of the Wolseley family, including the inventor Frederick York Wolseley who gave his name to the Wolseley car.

Islands — Although Carlow is landlocked it does have one or two islands. **Aughnabinna Island** is situated in the River Barrow south of Milford and the **Orchard Islands** (or Islands of Orchard) lie just south of Aughnabinna, towards Rathvinden Lock.

Kevin Barry Monument — Rathvilly, 8 miles (13km) northeast of Carlow. A monument to Kevin Barry (1902–20), a student hanged in Mountjoy Prison for his part in an ambush of British soldiers during the Irish War of Independence. Although born in Dublin, he was brought up in Rathvilly.

Leighlinbridge — A village on the River Barrow, based around a 12th century Norman castle and an early priory.

Leighlinbridge Motte — Leighlinbridge, $2^1/_2$ miles (4km) north of Bagenalstown. A motte located at the confluence of the rivers Barrow and Madlin and fortified by the Normans in the 12th century. It is possibly the site of Dinn Righ, the residence of the ancient kings of Leinster.

Liberty Tree — Hanover Street, Carlow. A memorial in the shape of a tree to the dead of the 1798 Rising of the United Irishmen. It was designed by internationally renowned artist John Behan. Born in Dublin, Behan's works include the sculpture *Arrival*, located on the United Nations Plaza in New York.

Milford Mills — 5 miles (8km) south of Carlow. A mill complex on both sides of the River Barrow, originally built in 1790 by the Alexander family. Among other uses, the buildings on the east bank of the river (Strong Stream Mill) served as a flour mill and the mill on the west bank eventually became a tannery. From 1891 the east mill was used as a hydroelectricity generating station and Carlow became the first town in the UK whose lighting system was fully supplied from its own local electricity. After a gap, the mill has supplied some power to the national grid since the early 1990s.

Millennium Garden, The — Leighlinbridge. A community garden consisting of seven separate gardens, each with a different theme symbolising aspects of life from birth to death.

Oak Park — 1 mile (1.6km) north of Carlow. A public forest park opened in 2006. Composed predominantly of mixed broadleaved woodland, the park is located on the former Oak Park Estate, originally owned by the Cooke family and later the home to the Bruen family until 1960 when it was acquired by the Land Commission.

Old Leighlin Cathedral — See St Lazerians Cathedral

Rathgall Hll Fort — Shillelagh Road, Carlow. A late Bronze Age hill fort used into the Iron Age and again in the post-medieval period. Excavations have revealed that it was a centre for metal working, in particular for producing weaponry. Tel: 059 913 1324.

Rathvilly Motte — Rathvilly, 8 miles (13km) northeast of Carlow. A large motte standing 16ft (5m) high and possibly built to protect the crossroads next to which it is located.

Rivers — The **Barrow** is the second longest river in Ireland. It rises in the Slieve Bloom mountains in Co. Laois just south of Clonaslee, flowing through Portarlington, Monasterevin, Athy, Carlow, Leighlinbridge, Muinebheag, Graiguenamanagh and New Ross before joining the River Suir at Cheelpoint. The Barrow, the Nore and the Suir all rise in the Slieve Bloom mountains and are known as the 'three sisters'. It is navigable (the Barrow Navigation) for 43 miles (69km) between Athy and St Mullins; a canal runs parallel to shallower sections of the river. South of St Mullins the Barrow becomes tidal. It has a total length of 119 miles (191km) and flows into the Irish Sea at Dunmore East.

The **Slaney** rises in the Glen of Imaal near Lugnaquilla in the Wicklow Mountains. It passes through Baltinglass, Rathvilly, Tullow, Bunclody, Enniscorthy, Ferrycarrig and reaches the sea at Wexford, the estuary forming Wexford Harbour. Its total length is 73 miles (117km). A popular salmon fishing river, its tributaries include the Derreen, Derry, Douglas, Clody, Bann and Sow rivers.

St Lazerians Cathedral — Old Leighlin, 4 miles (6km) northwest of Bagenalstown. Aka Old Leighlin Cathedral. This 13th century cathedral replaced a 7th century monastery founded by St Gobban. It was the scene in AD 630 of a synod to decide the correct formula for the dating of Easter each year. This monastery was destroyed by fire in the 11th century and the present stone building was begun in the late 12th century. It was extended in the 16th century. It was renovated and re-roofed during the 19th century. St Lazerian (also known as Molaise), was the founder of the See of Leighlin and its first bishop.

St Mullins — A village on the River Barrow which grew up around the site of a 7th century monastery founded by St Moling. The fact that the river is tidal up to St Mullins meant that it was subject to raiding by the Vikings and the Normans, and the monastery was ransacked by Vikings in the 10th century. The complex of religious buildings includes the ruins of a medieval abbey and a church built in 1811; there is also a Norman motte and a stump of a round tower. The lock system for the Barrow Navigation begins here.

Shean Garden — Shean, 1/2 mile (0.8km) east of Garryhill, 5 miles (8km) east of Bagenalstown. A 1 acre (0.4ha) garden surrounding a farmhouse with a variety of rare plants and trees. Tel: 050 357652.

Statue of Father John Murphy — Market Square, Tullow. Statue commemorating Father John Murphy, parish priest of Boulavogue, Co. Wexford, at the beginning of the 1798 rebellion in that county. After first attempting to calm the situation, he eventually became a leader of the insurgents. Initial victories were followed by defeat at Vinegar Hill. He was arrested while on the run and executed in Tullow Market Square on 2 July 1798.

Tobinstown Garden — 4 miles (6km) northeast of Tullow. A 0.5 acre (0.2ha) garden around the Georgian farmhouse of Tobinstown House, laid to lawn with herbaceous borders and shrubs. Tel: 059 915 1233.

Triple Bullaun Stone — Clonmore, 7 miles (11km) northeast of Tullow. An ancient stone with three hollows in its surface which may have been used to grind materials.

Tullow Museum — Bridge Street, Tullow. A local history museum housed in a former Methodist church built c.1850. Exhibits include the vestments of Father John Murphy, who was executed in Tullow Market Square in 1798 for his part in the uprising. Tel: 059 915 1286.

Weavers' Cottages — Clonegal, 8 miles (13km) southeast of Tullow. A row of restored weavers' cottages built in the late 17th century by Alexander Durdan. They are now used for spinning demonstrations during the day and for traditional evenings of story telling, music and dance.

Wicklow Way — See Wicklow. Carlow is home to two more of Ireland's key national walking routes, the South Leinster Way and the Barrow Way.

Some famous people born in County Carlow

Burke, Lisa (television weather forecaster) (1977–)	Carlow
Butler, Pierce (soldier and American statesman) (1744–1822)	Carlow
Dargan, William (engineer) (1799–1867)	Carlow
Donoghue, Denis (literary critic) (1928–)	Tullow
Haughton, Samuel (scientist) (1821–97)	Carlow
Kavanagh, Richie (entertainer) (1949–)	Bagenalstown
Keogh, Myles (soldier) (1840–76)	Leighlinbridge
Moran, Cardinal Patrick (Australia's first cardinal) (1830–1911)	Leighlinbridge
Thomas, Kathryn (television presenter) (1979–)	Carlow
Tyndall, John (scientist) (1820–93)	Leighlinbridge

Cavan

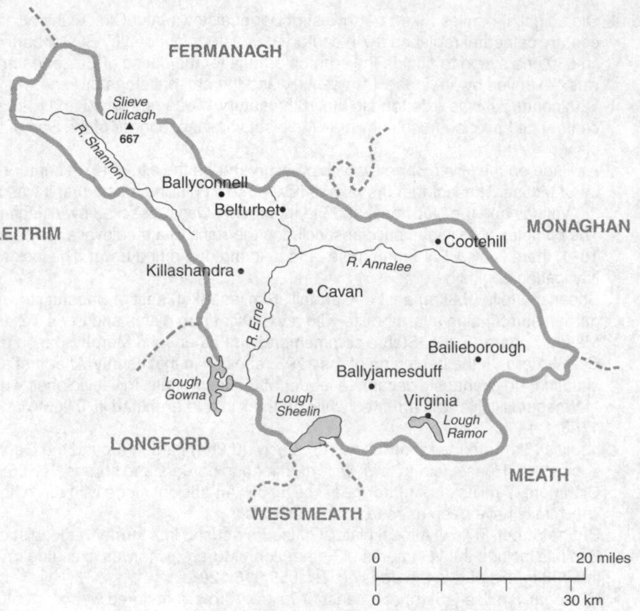
FERMANAGH
Slieve Cuilcagh
667
R. Shannon
Ballyconnell
Belturbet
LEITRIM
MONAGHAN
Cootehill
R. Annalee
Killashandra
Cavan
R. Erne
Bailieborough
Ballyjamesduff
Lough Gowna
Lough Sheelin
Virginia
Lough Ramor
LONGFORD
MEATH
WESTMEATH
0
20 miles
0
30 km

Cavan lies in the northeast of the Republic of Ireland, and is its smallest county. One of three counties situated in the province of Ulster without being part of Northern Ireland, Cavan borders Monaghan to the east, Meath to the southeast, Longford to the southwest and Leitrim to the west and northwest. To the north it also borders County Fermanagh in Northern Ireland. The most northerly tip of Westmeath shares a short border with the southern tip of Cavan.

Originally part of the ancient kingdom of Breifne, this inland Ulster county contains the towns of Cavan, Bailieborough, Virginia, Belturbet, Ballyjamesduff, Cootehill and Kingscourt. This part of Breifne was ruled by the O'Reillys, whose base was the town of Cavan. Other families associated with the county are McBrady, O'Mulleady, McGowan (often anglicised as Smith), O'Farrelly, McKiernan, O'Curry, O'Clery and McIlduff. Due both to the skill of their cavalry and also to the difficulty of the Cavan terrain, with its forests, bogs and lakes, the O'Reillys retained control over the county for several centuries after the arrival of the Normans in Ireland in 1169.

Elizabeth I of England created the new county of Cavan in 1584, its boundaries being set by her administrators and then divided into baronies. Bitter struggles ensued over the next 25 years but following the defeat of the rebels, lands were parcelled out to 'adventurers' from England. Between 1641 and 1649 Catholics, led by O'Reilly, joined the Catholic confederacy in rebellion against the English but their uprising was cruelly defeated by Cromwell and confiscated land in Cavan was again gifted to English soldiers and others.

Cavan is a very popular holiday destination; the proliferation of rivers, streams and lakes provide excellent opportunities for boating, cruising, fishing and swimming. It is said that Cavan has 365 lakes – one for each day of the year. The Shannon–Erne Waterway links the two rivers, which spring from the barren Cuilcagh Mountains in Cavan's northwest. The mystical source of the Shannon, known as the 'Shannon Pot', is a few miles north of Dowra, on the Cavan Way.

The county town is Cavan, situated towards the north of the county. The name Cavan means 'the hollow' in Irish, and the town sits in a pleasant district of low green hills (drumlins, formed by glaciation). It is the only medieval town in Ireland founded by the Irish themselves, and its narrow streets still follow the pattern set down seven centuries ago. Cavan is home to the popular Cavan Crystal brand of hand-cut glass.

If there are not quite 365 lakes in Cavan there are certainly 18 electoral areas, most of them with fewer than 1000 inhabitants. Cavan also has a number of famous natives, but perhaps the two best known are John Patrick Wilson (1923–2007), a former Fianna Fáil politician and Tánaiste (deputy prime minister of Ireland), and Paddy Smith (1901–82), who holds the distinction of being the longest-serving member of Dáil Éireann (serving for 53 years and 11 months).

Cavan	**Population**			**Area**	
Districts	*male*	*female*	*total*	*sq miles*	*sq km*
Bailieborough	5334	5076	10,410	112	291
Bawnboy	2034	1817	3851	97	251
Castlerahan	3357	3066	6423	69	179
Cavan rural area	14,841	14,235	29,076	368	953
Cavan Town	1697	1841	3538	1	2
Enniskillen	656	532	1188	65	167
Mullaghoran	1096	964	2060	34	89
Total	29,015	27,531	56,546	746	1932

Local Attractions and Information

Administrative headquarters — Courthouse, Farnham Street, Cavan. Tel: 049 433 1799.

Bailieborough — A town in the east of the county. Of particular interest is the Catholic church with unusual stations of the cross by George Collie. A 17th century vaulted castle, with a bawn 90ft (27.5m) square and two flanking towers, was demolished in 1923.

Ballyconnell — Small village in the north of the county. Above the village rises Slieve Russell at 1331ft (406m). A bawn 100ft (30.5m) square and 12ft (3.5m) high, with two flanking towers and a strong castle, three storeys high, the whole occupying a site well adapted for the defence of the surrounding county, was built by Captain Culme and Walter Talbot in the early 17th century but was destroyed by fire in 1764.

Ballyjamesduff — A medium sized town in the south of the county, to the north of loughs Sheelin and Ramor. It was immortalised in Percy French's song 'Come back Paddy Reilly to Ballyjamesduff'.

Ballymagauran Castle — 3 miles (5km) south of Bawnboy. A two-storey tower built by the Magauran family in the late 16th century. Only the base of the castle now survives.

Bellamont House — Cootehill, $12^{1}/_{2}$ miles (20km) northeast of Cavan. A Palladian style house (not open to the public) designed by Edward Lovett Pearce and built in 1725.

Belturbet — A small market town in the north of the county. It lies on the east bank of the River Erne, midway between Lough Oughter and Upper Lough Erne. According to tradition, the town is named after Conal Cearnach, a 1st century hero of the Red Branch Knights. A small castle built in the 16th century by Hugh Connallach O'Reilly has long since been demolished.

Belturbet Station — Railway Road, Belturbet. A railway museum housed in the restored former Great Northern Railway station, built in 1885. Tel: 049 952 2074.

Cabra Castle — Kingscourt, 7 miles (11km) east of Bailieborough. The current Cabra Castle was built in 1808 by the Pratt family and stands near the ruins of Old Cabra Castle (formerly known as Cormey Castle), which was slighted during the English Civil War. The new castle now houses a 22 bedroom hotel. Tel: 042 966 7030.

Carraig Craft Visitor Centre — Mountnugent, 13 miles (21km) southeast of Cavan. Basketry museum with an exhibition of traditional baskets in rod, rush and straw. Tel: 049 40179.

Carrickacroy Dolmen — 1 mile (1.6km) northeast of Kilnaleck, 4 miles (6km) west of Ballyjamesduff. The remains of a portal tomb dating to c. 2000 BC.

Castle-Gearroid — See Muff Castle

Castle of Clanchye — See Muff Castle

Castle Saunderson and St Felim — 4 miles (6km) northeast of Belturbet. The remains of a house beside the River Finn, originally built in 1573 and remodelled in Scottish baronial style in the 19th century. The seat of the Saunderson family until 1977, it suffered a damaging fire in 1990. The house is surrounded by a 103 acre (41ha) estate.

Cathedral of St Patrick — Farnham Street, Cavan. Built 1938–42, one of the last of the huge Roman Catholic cathedrals built in Ireland from the 1850s onwards. Unlike most Irish cathedrals, it is neoclassical in style with a single spire rising to 230ft (70m). The portico consists of a tympanum supported by four massive columns of Portland stone with Corinthian caps. The tympanum figures of Christ, St Patrick and St Felim were executed by Dublin sculptor Edward Smith. See also Kilmore Cathedral.

Cavan County Museum — Virginia Road, Ballyjamesduff. Local history museum established in 1996 and housed in a building designed by William Hague. Its aim is to provide an insight into the heritage of Cavan from ancient times to the present day. Exhibits include the three-faced Corleck Head, dating to the 2nd century BC, the 18th century Silver Mace of the Borough of Cavan, the 1000 year old Lough Errol Log Boat, and the 4000 year old Killycluggin Stone. Tel: 049 854 4070.

Churches — The **Church of the Immaculate Conception**, Kingscourt, 7 miles (11km) east of Bailiborough. Built in Gothic style 1869–72. There are four stained glass windows by artist Eve Hone, three depicting the Annunciation, Crucifixion and Resurrection and the fourth commemorating the miracle of the Sun of Fatima.

Killinagh Church, $^{1}/_{2}$ mile (0.8km) west of Blacklion, 23 miles (37km) northwest of Belturbet, the ruins of a 12th century church built on the site of a 6th century monastic site founded by St Laigneach.

Milltown Parish Church, 3 miles (5km) southwest of Belturbet, A Catholic church designed by prominent Cavan architect William Hague Jr and opened in 1868.

Moybolgue Church, 4 miles (6km) south of Bailieborough, the ruins of a 15th century church.

Clough Oughter Castle
$4^{1}/_{2}$ miles (7km) west of Cavan and 5 miles (8km) east of Killeshandra. 13th century circular castle on an island in Lough Oughter, probably built by William Gorm de Lacy. The castle stands 18 metres high and has a diameter of $15^{1}/_{2}$ metres. A seat of the clan O'Reilly until its capture by Sir Richard Wingfield in 1607, it was retaken by the O'Reillys during the 1641 Rebellion and it was here that Eoghan Roe O'Neill was training his forces when he died in 1649. The castle was abandoned after falling to a siege by Cromwellian forces in 1653.

Cohaw Court Cairn
2 miles (3km) east of Cootehill, 13 miles (21km) northeast of Cavan. A Neolithic double cairn arranged as two single-court tombs built back to back. It was excavated in 1949 but no human remains were found.

Cootehill
A small town in the northeast of the county near the border with Monaghan. It gets its name from the marriage of Thomas Coote, a colonel in the Cromwellian forces, and Frances Hill. The town has an annual angling festival in September and an annual arts festival each October.

Cormey Castle
See Cabra Castle

Corravahan House
$^{1}/_{2}$ mile (0.8km) west of Drung, 6 miles (10km) northeast of Cavan. A Georgian style house built in the 1840s. Tel: 087 977 2224.

Crover Castle
1 mile (1.6km) west of Mountnugent, $4^{1}/_{2}$ miles (7km) southwest of Ballyjamesduff. Standing on the shore of Lough Sheelin, Crover Castle was reputedly built by Thomas O'Reilly in the late 14th century. In the later Middle Ages the lough was seen as the border between the Irish and the English.

Dowra
A small village to the east of the county; part of the settlement actually lies in Leitrim. The village overlooks Lough Allen. It is the first village on the River Shannon on its journey south to Limerick and the sea.

Drumlane Abbey
$^{1}/_{2}$ mile (0.8km) south of Milltown, 6 miles (10km) northwest of Cavan. The ruins of a monastic site located between loughs Drumlane and Derrybrick, and including a 6th century tower and a 13th/14th century church. The church contains some late medieval carvings. Tel: 049 433 1942.

Dun Na Ri Forest Park
Kingscourt, 7 miles (11km) east of Bailieborough. A 565 acre (228ha) forest park located along the banks of the River Cabra and consisting largely of Norway spruce and oak plantations. Part of the former Cabra Estate, once owned by the Pratt family, it encompasses a gorge. Tel: 049 433 1942.

Fair of Muff
An annual horse fair held in the village of Muff, west of Kingscourt, each 12 August and originating in the 17th century.

Garrett's Castle
See Muff Castle

Gartnanoul Court Tomb
1 mile (1.6km) east of Killeshandra, 7 miles (11km) west of Cavan. Neolithic dual court tomb located in Killykeen Forest Park and incorporating two tombs back to back with, unusually, a 32ft (10m) gap between them.

Highest point
Slieve Cuilcagh at 2188ft (667m) in the Cuilcagh Mountains, source of the Shannon.

Interesting facts
Cavan in Ontario, Canada, is named after the Irish county. The original settlers were Protestants who emigrated from Ireland in the early 19th century, many of them associated with the Orange Order. **Bishop William Bedell** (1571–1642), who first translated the Bible into Irish, is buried in the graveyard next to Kilmore Cathedral. It was at **Cuilcagh House**, which once stood 4 miles (6km) west of the town of Virginia, that Dean Jonathan Swift would visit his friend the Rev. Thomas Sheridan (1687–1738), father of actor Thomas Sheridan (1719–88) and grandfather of playwright Richard Brinsley Sheridan (1751–1816). Swift wrote *Gulliver's Travels* here and based his giant Brobdingnagians on a local man called Mr Doughty.

Islands
Named islands in Co. Cavan include **Port Island** near Leck, the solitary island in the Cavan area of Lough Macnean Upper; **St Mogues Island** in Templeport Lough (see separate entry); **Trinity Island** (see separate entry) and **Turbet Island**.

Killeshandra Festival of the Lakes
Annual June celebrations held in Killeshandra, near Lough Oughter, and centred around angling, music, dancing and many other activities.

Killykeen Forest Park
7 miles (11km) west of Cavan. A 600 acre (240ha) forest park largely of Norway and Sitka spruce, located on the eastern shore of Lough Oughter.

Kilmore Castle
3 miles (5km) southwest of Cavan. Walter de Lacy constructed the castle in 1211 as part of a chain to control and contain the north for the Normans. Cathal O'Reilly dismantled the fort in 1224, although it was later rebuilt. An excellent example of a motte and bailey still remains today.

Kilmore Cathedral
3 miles (5km) southwest of Cavan. The site of the original cathedral of the Diocese of Kilmore, situated in the present parish of Kilmore. Some time in the 6th century St Felim established a church here. Rebuilt as a cathedral in the mid 15th century, it was confiscated during the Reformation. The present Cathedral of St Feithlimidh (Felim) was built in Early Decorated or Middle Pointed style in 1860 to a design by William Slater. It incorporates a 12th/13th century doorway which is believed to have originally been part of the nearby priory at Trinity Island in Lough Oughter. Other parts of an earlier cathedral were also incorporated into the new structure and its surrounding buildings, including the parish hall. Adjacent to the cathedral grounds is an Anglo-Norman motte and bailey.

Kingscourt	A town in the extreme east of the county, close to the border with Meath, and which hosts an international band festival every July.
Lakeview Gardens	$1^{1}/_{4}$ miles (2km) west of Mullagh, 7 miles (11km) south of Bailieborough. A sloping garden surrounding Lakeview House and overlooking Mullagh Lake. Established in the 1930s on an estate established in the 17th century, the garden was restored in the 1990s. Tel: 00 353 (0)46 924 2480.
Lifeforce Watermill	Mill Rock, Cavan. A restored working flour mill on the Kennypottle River, powered by a water turbine built in 1846. Tel: 049 436 2722.
Lough Gowna	12 miles (19km) southwest of Cavan. Located on the border of Co. Cavan and Co. Longford, the lakes are the source of the River Erne and cover 1800 acres (730ha).
Lough Oughter	5 miles (8km) west of Cavan. One of the finest coarse fishing lakes in Ireland. Covering 3618 acres (1464ha) and part of the Lough Erne system, it is linked to Upper Lough Erne (see Fermanagh) by the River Erne. It is also the site of numerous crannogs. See also Clough Oughter Castle.
Magh Slécht	9 miles (15km) southwest of Belturbet. A plain covering an area of 3 sq miles (8 sq km), located to the south of Templeport Lough. It is notable as the site of a large number (more than 80) of ancient monuments, including stone circles, tombs, barrows, standing stones and crannogs.
Maguire's Chair	Altachullion, 4 miles (6km) east of Glangevlin, 14 miles (23km) northwest of Belturbet. A large rock so named because it was supposedly the site where members of the Maguire clan were inaugurated in medieval times.
Maudabawn Cultural Centre	Maudabawn, 4 miles (6km) southeast of Cootehill, 13 miles (21km) northeast of Cavan. The centre has information about the landscape and history of the area from ancient times to the present day. Tel: 049 555 9504.
Muff Castle	Enniskeen, $^{1}/_{2}$ mile (0.8km) south of Kingscourt. Aka Castle-Gearroid, Garrett's Castle, Castle of Clanchye. Built in 1608 with a grant given to Garrett Fleming.
Relagh Beg	4 miles (6km) south of Bailieborough. An early 13th century Norman motte near the old church of Moybolgue.
Rivers	The **Annalee** rises in Co. Monaghan and flows into the Erne at Urney. The **Erne** rises on the southern slopes of Slieve Glah (319m) in Co. Cavan and flows through Lough Gowna in Co. Longford, Lough Oughter in Co. Cavan, Belturbet and into Upper Lough Erne, Co. Fermanagh, Northern Ireland. Sheltered by the Cuilcagh Mountains, where the River Shannon rises, the river empties into Lower Lough Erne en route to Donegal Bay and the Atlantic Ocean. **Shannon** see Clare
St Kilians Heritage Centre	Mullagh, $7^{1}/_{2}$ miles (12km) south of Bailieborough. A centre celebrating the life, martyrdom and canonisation of St Kilian, who was born in Mullagh in 640. There is also an exhibition about the development of writing in Ireland between the 4th and 7th century. Tel: 046 924 2433.
St Mogues Island	A small island in Templeport Lough, $1^{1}/_{4}$ miles (2km) south of Bawnboy. On St Patrick's Day 1943, Pilot Officer Richard Kukura and his navigator/wireless operator Tommy Hulme (an Englishman from Marple Bridge, near Stockport) were test flying the new Bristol Beaufighter aircraft when the entry hatch cover flew open and everything was sucked out of the plane. After they were eventually forced to bale out over the west of Ireland (one of them near Kinawley and the other near Corlough), the plane crashed into Templeport Lough next to St Mogues Island.
Shannon Pot	3 miles (5km) north of Glangevlin, 21 miles (33km) northwest of Belturbet. (I. *Lag na Sionna* = Hollow of the Shannon). A turlough (low-lying area of limestone) on the slopes of Cuilcagh Mountain. An aquifer-fed naturally fluctuating pool, it is the source of the River Shannon. Located 344ft (105m) above sea level, it forms a natural well that collects the waters of several small streams running off the mountainside.
Sport	
Gaelic football	**Cavan** were winners of the All-Ireland Senior Football Championship in 1933, 1935, 1947, 1948 and 1952.
Swanlinbar	A small village in the west of the county beside the Ulster Walkway and River Cladagh. The area was once famous for the healing properties of its many spas and natural springs.
Tonymore Castle	2 miles (3km) southwest of Cavan. A well-preserved 16th century castle featuring a 'murder hole', used to throw missiles or boiling water on any unwelcome visitors.
Trinity Island	3 miles (5km) southeast of Killeshandra. A private island of 150 acres (70ha) on Lough Oughter, covered largely by woodland and the location of one of the oldest religious sites in Cavan. The abbey was built 750 years ago by the monks of the Premonstratensian Order. Most of the surviving remains date from the Middle Ages when it was a popular destination for pilgrims.
Virginia	A town in the south of the county, located on the northern side of Lough Ramor. The annual Virginia Street Fair, held during the summer, is a reconstruction of Virginia's original 'Fairday'.
Wesleyan Chapel, Arts, Cultural and Tourism Centre	Adelaide Row, Bailieborough. A multi-purpose centre for education in all disciplines of the arts, housed in a restored and converted former Wesleyan chapel built in 1833. Tel: 00 353 042 966 6666.

Some famous people born in County Cavan

Brook, Charlotte (writer) (1740–93)	Rantavan
Daly, Marcus (American businessman) (1841–1900)	Ballyjamesduff
Kilian, Saint (apostle of Franconia) (640–689)	Mullagh
McKenna, Thomas Patrick 'T. P.' (actor) (1929–)	Mullagh
McKiernan, Catherina (athlete) (1969–)	Cornafean
O'Reilly, J J (Gaelic footballer) (1919–52)	Killeshandra
Reavy, Ed (songwriter and fiddler) (1897–1988)	Barnagrove
Sadlier née Madden, Mary Anne (author) (1820–1903)	Cootehill
Saunderson, Edward James (politician) (1837–1906)	Castlesaunderson
Sheehy-Skeffington, Francis (suffragist) (1878–1916)	Bailieborough

CLARE

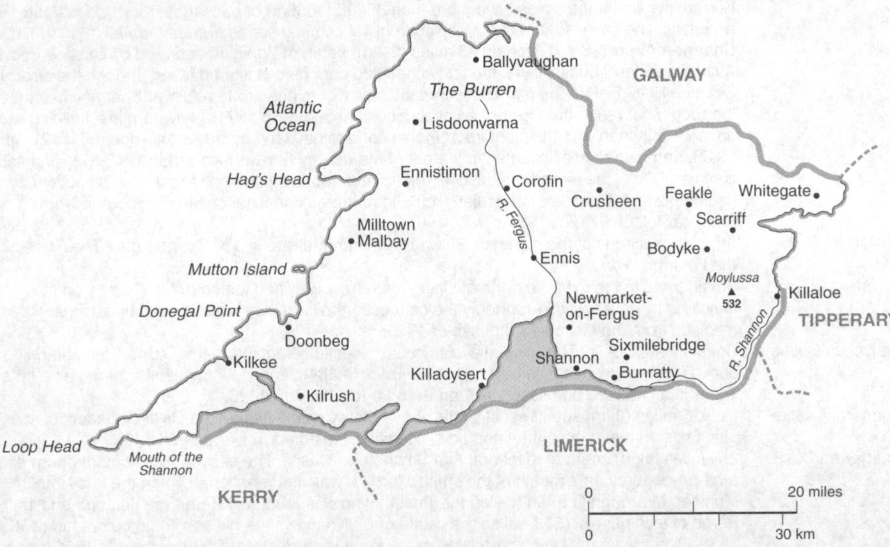

Ballyvaughan
The Burren
GALWAY
Atlantic Ocean
Lisdoonvarna
Hag's Head
Ennistimon
Corofin
Crusheen
Feakle
Whitegate
Scarriff
R. Fergus
Milltown Malbay
Bodyke
Ennis
Mutton Island
Moylussa
532
Killaloe
Newmarket-on-Fergus
Donegal Point
TIPPERARY
Doonbeg
R. Shannon
Sixmilebridge
Shannon
Kilkee
Killadysert
Bunratty
Kilrush
Loop Head
Mouth of the Shannon
LIMERICK
KERRY
0
20 miles
0
30 km

Clare is part of the province of Munster. It lies in the west of Ireland and borders Galway to the northeast, Tipperary to the east and Limerick to the southeast. Its southern coastline faces Kerry and Limerick across the Shannon Estuary. To its west is the Atlantic Ocean. The county's main geographical features are the extensive limestone plateau of the Burren, the Cliffs of Moher and the River Shannon.

There are 33 electoral areas in Clare, with fewer than 1000 inhabitants. The county town is Ennis, situated in the centre of the county; other major towns are Kilrush, Killaloe, Lahinch, Newmarket-on-Fergus, Shannon and Sixmilebridge. Clare is an idyllic mix of town and country. Ennis is a thriving town only a short journey from most parts of Clare; although many of the dairy farms are sadly now closed, green areas are still to be found in abundance. Clare is sometimes called the 'banner county', which may refer to a tradition of carrying banners at political meetings and public occasions.

County Clare has a strong history of traditional music, both professional and amateur, and many local pubs have itinerant musicians. The county has many traditional music festivals; one of the best known is the Willie Clancy Summer School, held every July in the town of Miltown Malbay.

Perhaps Clare's best-known native is Brian Boru, High King of Ireland 1002–14. Other notables include Michael Cusack, founder of the Gaelic Athletic Association; John Holland, inventor of the submarine; Patrick Hillery, former President of Ireland; best-selling author Edna O'Brien; rugby player Keith Wood; and Kieren Fallon, multi-Classic-winning former champion jockey.

Clare		**Population**		**Area**	
Districts	*male*	*female*	*total*	*sq miles*	*sq km*
Ballyvaughan	1255	1367	2622	112	290
Corofin	1630	1472	3102	96	248
Ennis rural area	13,247	12,796	26,043	188	487
Ennis Town	9018	9812	18,830	7	17
Ennistimon	4830	4652	9482	154	400
Killadysert	2168	2025	4193	130	336
Kilrush rural area	5437	4907	10,344	240	624
Kilrush Town	1330	1369	2699	2	6
Meelick	6877	6671	13,548	110	285
Scarriff	3284	3316	6600	153	395
Tulla	2987	2827	5814	137	354
Total	52,063	51,214	103,277	1329	3442

Local Attractions and Information

Administrative headquarters	New Road, Ennis. Tel: 065 682 1616.
Aillwee Caves	2$^1/_2$ miles (4km) south of Ballyvaughan, 18 miles (29km) northwest of Ennis. Located on the Burren, the limestone caves have more than 3500ft (1050m) of passages, rock bridges and waterfalls. The caves featured in an episode of TV comedy series *Father Ted*. Tel: 065 707 7036.
Airport	**Shannon** Airport (SNN), located 15 miles (24km) south of Ennis, is operated by Dublin Airport Authority. Established in 1942, the first scheduled commercial flight passed through the airport in October 1945. Before the mid 1960s transatlantic flights needed to refuel at Shannon because they could not reach their European destinations non-stop. In 1971 a new terminal building was opened. Shannon was the first airport in the world to have a duty-free shop (opened on 21 April 1947), and Irish coffee, invented in the bar of the nearby Foynes Seaport in 1943, was first sold commercially in the airport bar, also in 1947. The airport is also used for military stopovers by foreign powers. There are scheduled flights to numerous destinations in Europe and North America. Tel: 061 712000.
Aran Islands	A group of islands at the mouth of Galway Bay, immortalised in J M Synge's play *The Playboy of the Western World*.
Aughinish	Small island in the extreme north of Clare, in Galway Bay, and joined to Co. Galway on the mainland by causeway. Purportedly the connection to Co. Clare was severed by a tsunami resulting from the Lisbon earthquake of 1755.
Ballinalacken Castle	Coast Road, Doolin. The ruins of a 15th century castle belonging to the O'Brien clan, standing above a more recent castle built by Lord O'Brien in 1840. The 'new' castle is now run as a hotel. There is a fine view across to the Aran Islands. Tel: 065 707 4025.
Ballyhannon Castle	Quin, 5 miles (8km) southeast of Ennis. A five-storey castle beside the River Shannon, built as a pele tower in the 15th century and now extensively restored. Tel: 065 682 5640.
Ballynagowan Castle	2$^1/_2$ miles (4km) south of Kilfenora. Aka Smithstown Castle. The castle takes its name from *beal-atha-an-ghobhan* (the mouth of the smith's ford). It was first mentioned when the last king of Munster, Murrough O'Brien (called the Tanist), who was created 1st Earl of Thomond and 1st Baron of Inchiquin in 1543, willed the castle of Ballynagowan to his son Teige before his death in 1551. Over the years it accommodated many famous characters of Irish history. In 1600 legendary Irish rebel 'Red' Hugh O'Donnell (see Donegal) and his men rested here during his attack on North Clare, spreading ruin everywhere when seeking revenge on the Earl of Thomond for having made alliance with the English. In 1649 a Cromwellian army under Edmund Ludlow swept into North Clare, attacking the castle with cannons. In 1650 Conor O'Brien of Lemeneagh inherited the castle; soon afterwards, however, he was fatally wounded in a skirmish with troops commanded by Ludlow at Inchicronan in 1651. With him had fought his wife Maire Rua O'Brien ('The Red Mary'), named after her long red hair, one of the best-known characters in Irish tradition. She had lived in the castle as a young woman and her name has been kept alive by the ferocity and cruelty attributed to her. According to legend, in order to save her children's heritage after Conor's death she married several English generals who were mysteriously killed one after the other, while she ended her bloody career entombed in a hollow tree. In 1652 almost all habitable castles in Clare, including Smithstown, were occupied by Cromwellian garrisons under military rule. Over the following decades Ballynagowan Castle was the seat of army generals, the High Sheriff of Co. Clare and the Viscounts Powerscourt, among Ireland's most powerful aristocratic families, who had their main residence in Dublin. The castle was last inhabited in the mid 19th century and until its recent restoration served as a meeting point for couples, songs and poems about it finding their way into local pubs. Today it is a popular hotel complex.
Ballyportry Castle	1$^1/_4$ miles (2km) northeast of Corrofin, 8 miles (13km) northwest of Ennis. A 500 year old Gaelic tower house with fine views across the landscape of the Burren. It stands 90ft (27.5m) high and has been sympathetically restored as holiday accommodation.
Ballyvaughan	Located on the southern shore of Galway Bay in the old parish of Drumcreehy, the village takes its name from *Baile ua Bheachain* (O'Beahan's or O'Vaughan's residence). For a while Ballyvaughan was the official capital of northwest Clare, with its own workhouse, coastguard station and police barracks. In the early 19th century the Quays established Ballyvaughan as a fishing village. Three of the old piers lying north and northeast of Dr O'Dea's Clareville House were built by the inhabitants of the village. At high tide they are virtually unusable as they are generally covered by several feet of water. This factor probably led the Fishery Board to erect a new quay in 1829. As the roads improved and the piers deteriorated Ballyvaughan lost its importance as a fishing port. Today the piers are used mainly for pleasure craft and for charters to Galway or the islands. Ballyvaughan is sometimes referred to as the Gateway to the Burren.
Ballyvaughan Castle	The old castle of Ballyvaughan stood on the very edge of the harbour. It was always an O'Loughlin stronghold, except for a short time during the 16th century when it was held by the O'Briens. Apparently, in 1540 a stolen cow was found here, resulting in heavy penalties being paid by the O'Loughlins. The fines included cattle, goats and sheep, as well as the loss of the town. In 1569 the village was taken by Sir Henry Sydney's forces but somehow the O'Loughlins survived within their old territories. By 1840 the castle was a ruin but its foundations can still be seen today.
Battles	See separate table for details of the Battle of Dysert O'Dea.
Beal Boru	1 mile (1.6km) north of Killaloe. The site of a large ring fort beside the River Shannon which has been identified as the seat of Brian Boru, High King of Ireland from 1002 until his death at the Battle of Clontarf in 1014. It is sometimes called Brian Boru's Fort. This strategic position had been settled since Neolithic times and the Normans later attempted to set up defences here.

Biddy Early Brewery — Inagh, 8 miles (13km) northwest of Ennis. Ireland's first pub brewery, started in 1995 by industrial chemist Dr Peadar Garvey using traditional methods and using only natural ingredients with no artificial additives. Tel: 065 683 6742.

Bishop's Island — (I. *Oileán-an-Easpoig-gortaigh* = The Island of the Hungry (or Starving) Bishop). A barren, precipitous rock with perpendicular or overhanging cliffs 250ft (76m) high. Access is difficult and only to be effected by a skilful climber in calm weather. Sheltered from south and southwest swells, the terrain consists of large boulders and gullies. There are also the ruins of a beehive-shaped house 115ft (35m) in circumference. Area: 0.001 sq mile (0.0025 sq km).

Bridgetown — A small village near the town of O'Brien's-Bridge, 4 miles (6km) southwest of Killaloe. Fairs are held in June and November. My mother was born in the village and I have many happy childhood memories of my grandfather's farm and the surrounding countryside. The farms are long closed now but the fishing on the Shannon remains second to none.

Bunratty Castle — Bunratty, 3 miles (5km) east of Shannon. The most complete and authentically restored and furnished castle in Ireland. The present castle was built in 1425 by the MacNamara family but by 1475 it was a stronghold of the O'Briens. However, the site had a long history before this castle was erected. In 970 the Vikings had established a trading post here and in 1250 a wooden castle was built by Robert De Muscegros. This was later replaced with a stone structure by Thomas de Clare, but this castle was also destroyed by an Irish force in 1318. During the 14th century the castle was restored, only to be destroyed once again. The 15th century castle stayed in the hands of the O'Briens until they were dispossessed by Parliamentary forces during the Civil War. During the early 19th century the castle fell into disrepair. It was bought by Lord Gort in the 20th century and fully restored. Opened to the public in 1960, it now forms part of Bunratty Folk Park.

Bunratty Folk Park — Bunratty, 3 miles (5km) east of Shannon. An open air museum with a collection of buildings representing rural and urban life in 19th century Ireland, most of which have been reconstructed on site. The wide variety of houses includes ten types of farmhouse from different regions (including Loop Head, Shannon, Golden Vale and Byre). Other buildings, many forming a village street, include a schoolhouse, church, pub, shops, and watermill. Major houses include Hazelbrook House and Bunratty House, the latter built by the Studdarts, the last owners of Bunratty Castle before its restoration, and standing on its original site. The gardens, including a Regency walled garden, were restored in the late 1990s.

Burren Centre, The — Kilfenora, 14 miles (23km) northwest of Ennis. Visitor centre exploring the archaeology, geology and natural history of the Burren. Tel: 065 708 8030.

Burren, The — A unique karst region in the north of the county covering 97 sq miles (250 sq km). The name comes from Irish *boireann*, 'a rocky place', and it was formed by the combination of glacial activity and the solution of limestone by water, the latter process known scientifically as 'karstification'. Thanks to the unusual micro-habitats created by the rock formations, the area has a wide variety of flora, many of which would not usually grow together in the same vicinity, such as spring gentian, bloody cranesbill and heathers. It contains cave systems (including Pollinagollum, the longest cave in Ireland at 10 miles/16km), ancient hill forts and standing stones. Carron, in the heart of the Burren, is the home of Ireland's first perfumery.

Burren National Park — Established in 1991 as Ireland's fifth National Park. It covers 2840 acres (1150ha) on the southeastern edge of the Burren. Habitats include limestone pavement and grassland, hazel scrub, deciduous woodland, lakes, turloughs, springs and fen.

Cahercommaun Stone Fort — Carron, 6 miles (10km) southeast of Ballyvaughan. A stone ring fort on the edge of a steep valley in the Burren which flourished in the 9th and 10th centuries. Excavations carried out during the 1930s found a number of spindle whorls, suggesting that wool production formed a large part of the economy. It is estimated that the fort would have supported a community of around 40 people.

Caherconnell Stone Fort — Carron, 6 miles (10km) southeast of Ballyvaughan. Circular stone fort in the Burren measuring 140ft (43m) in diameter. It was built from large stone blocks; the walls are 12ft (3.5m) thick and a maximum of 14ft (4.2m) high. It would have been the home to a farming community of up to 30 people and would have provided excellent protection against raiding parties and wild animals. Although it was originally built c. AD 400, because of its build quality and state of preservation, there is evidence that it was sporadically occupied until the 17th century. The best preserved of the Burren stone forts, it houses a visitor centre with information about the Burren, its people and the other monuments in the area. Tel: 065 708 9999.

Cahermacnaughten Stone Fort — A stone ring fort with a diameter of 100ft (30.5m). Occupied until the 16th century, it was the home of the Ó'Duibhdábhoireann Law School, which maintained the tradition of the Brehon legal system in the region and to which is attributed the compilation of the Egerton 88, an important ancient Irish legal manuscript compiled 1564–9.

Cahermore Stone Fort — $2^1/_2$ miles (4km) south of Ballyvaughan, 18 miles (29km) northwest of Ennis. A stone ring fort located in the Burren close to the Ailwee Caves. Although not so well preserved as neighbouring stone forts, its doorway has been reconstructed.

Canon Island — Aka Innisneganangh, Inis na Canánach. An island situated in the Shannon Estuary at the confluence of the rivers Shannon and Fergus. Located in the parish of Kildysart, it was anciently called Elanagranoch. An Augustinian abbey (now ruined) was founded here in the 12th century by Donal Mor O'Brien (Donald O'Brien), king of Limerick. The island is in the shape of a figure-of-eight, being very narrow at its central point.

Carrigaholt Tower House — 9 miles (15km) southwest of Kilrush. The remains of a five-storey tower house on the Shannon Estuary. Built in the late 15th century by the McMahons, in the 17th century it was the home of the Clare Dragoons under the command of Daniel O'Brien, son of the Earl of Thomond. Excavations in 2003 revealed the remains of a manor house which once adjoined the castle tower.

Clare Heritage Centre	Church Street, Corofin. Housed in the former St Catherine's Church, dating to 1718, the centre focuses on the story of western Ireland 1800–60, covering topics such as land tenure, the famine and emigration. Tel: 065 683 7955.
Clare Museum	Arthur's Row, Ennis. Local history museum charting the story of Clare from prehistoric times to the present day. Tel: 065 682 3382.
Cliffs of Moher	21 miles (33km) northwest of Ennis. A range of sea cliffs on the western edge of the Burren and rising to a maximum of 700ft (213m) above the Atlantic. They are home to many thousands of birds including colonies of puffins, guillemots and shags. The cliffs are the most popular tourist attraction in the west of Ireland and the views are amazing, but it is invariably breezy to say the least on the cliff tops.
Corcomroe Cistercian Abbey	1 mile (1.6km) northeast of Bealaclugga, 4 miles (6km) northeast of Ballyvaughan. Aka the Abbey of Burren. The ruins of the Cistercian abbey of Sancta Maria de Petra Fertilis (St Mary of the Fertile Rock), founded in the late 12th century by Donal Mor O'Brien.
Crab Island	Tiny rocky island notable for its reef break, beloved of surfers. The island is near Doolin Pier.
Craggaunowen The Living Past	3 miles (5km) east of Quin, 8 miles (13km) southeast of Ennis. A living history park covering 50 acres (20ha) and interpreting Ireland's prehistoric and early Christian eras. Features include recreations of a hunters' cooking site, a crannog (lake house), a 4th/5th century farmer's house, a souterrain, a ring fort and an Iron Age 'roadway' or wooden track. The 'Brendan Boat', built in 1976 by Tim Severin and which sailed from Ireland to Greenland in an attempt to re-enact the 6th century voyage of St Brendan, a candidate for the discoverer of America, is also on display; 16th century Craggaunowen Castle is located in the grounds. Tel: 061 36 0788.
Cratloe Castle	Cratloe, 5 miles (8km) east of Shannon. Aka Cratloemoyle Castle. The ruins of a 16th century castle with a five-storey square tower.
Cratloe Keel Castle	Cratloe, 5 miles (8km) east of Shannon. The remains of a 16th century tower house which was occupied until the 1950s when it was damaged by a fire. It is sometimes known as Punch's Tower after the family which owned it from the early 18th century until its demise.
Cratloe Woods House	Cratloe, 5 miles (8km) southeast of Shannon. Dating to the late 17th or early 18th century, Cratloe Woods House is said to be the only surviving Irish longhouse still lived in as a home. In fact it is a mansion dating to c. 1730 and once known as Cratloe Hall, the design of which strongly resembles that of a traditional medieval longhouse. Still standing on the estate are Garrannon Oak Woods, which provided the timber for the hammerbeam roof of Westminster Hall in London in 1399, and also for what is now the royal palace in Amsterdam. The principal rooms have collections of furniture, curiosities and family portraits. Tel: 061 32 7028.
Daniel O'Connell Column	O'Connell Square, Ennis. A Doric column erected on the site of the old courthouse where Daniel O'Connell was declared MP for Clare in 1828.
Doolin Cave, The	Doolin, 18 miles (29km) northwest of Ennis. A cave on the western edge of the Burren, discovered in 1952 and home to the Great Stalactite, measuring over 20ft (6m) and purportedly the longest stalactite in the northern hemisphere.
Doonagore Castle	1/2 mile (0.8km) southwest of Doolin. A restored 14th or 15th century tower house on the coast above the town of Doolin. It is said that 170 Spanish sailors were executed at Doonagore in 1588 after their ship was wrecked while returning to Spain as part of the failed Armada. The castle is not open to the public.
Dough Castle	Lahinch, 2 1/2 miles (4km) southwest of Ennistymon. The ruin of a tower house founded by the O'Connors in 1306 and enlarged in the 1670s. Only one wall now remains standing.
Dromoland Castle	1 mile (1.6km) north of Newmarket-on-Fergus, 6 miles (10km) southeast of Ennis. Built by Sir Edward O'Brien 1822–35, the current building stands on the site of a 15th or 16th century tower house. Designed in Gothic Revival style by the Pain brothers, the castle is now run as a luxury hotel. Tel: 061 368144.
Dungaire Castle	1 mile (1.6km) east of Kinvara, 9 miles (15km) northeast of Ballynahinch. Located in a beautiful spot to one side of the harbour, the castle was converted and lived in by a well known hunting lady before being taken over by Shannon Development.
Dysert O'Dea Castle and Archaeological Centre	3 miles (5km) south of Corofin. Dysert O'Dea tower house was built by Diarmuid O'Dea in 1480. The Battle of Dysert O'Dea had been fought near this site in 1318. The castle was damaged by Cromwellian forces in 1651 but was later repaired. In 1986 it was opened to the public as an archaeology centre; there are over 20 field monuments within a 4 mile (6km) radius of the castle, including St Tola's 12th century high cross and a Romanesque doorway at Dysert Church. Tel: 065 683 7401.
East Clare Heritage Centre	Tuamgraney, 19 miles (31km) east of Ennis. Opened in 1991 in the former St Cronan's church, dating to the 10th century. It was formed by a voluntary group who also carry out heritage projects such as the restoration of a famine graveyard in the village. Tel: 061 921351.
Ennis	A market town on the River Fergus, the county town of Clare and the largest town in the county. Ennis dates to 1240 when the O'Brien clan helped to establish the Franciscan order here. Ennis is sometimes referred to as 'The Big E'.
Ennis Cathedral	O'Connell Street, Ennis. The Cathedral of St Peter and St Paul was mainly built 1828–42 to a design by Dominick Madden, who also designed the cathedrals in Ballina and Tuam, and was consecrated in 1843. The tower and spire were added in 1874, and renovation and additional work was carried out in the 1890s. Further changes were made in the 1970s before the church was dedicated as a cathedral in 1990.
Ennis Friary	Abbey Street, Ennis. The ruins of a Franciscan friary founded in the 13th century and famous for its numerous sculptures dating from the 15th and 16th centuries including a figure of St Francis, the McMahon tomb, a Virgin and Child and the Ecce Homo. Tel: 061 29100.
Feenish Island	Aka Fynish. An island located southwest of Deenish Island at the confluence of the rivers Fergus

	and Shannon. According to Archdall, it was anciently called Inis-fidhe or Cluan-fidhe, and was the seat of a nunnery over which St Bridget presided in the 5th century: the ruins of the old church still exist. St Senán also founded a church on Feenish Island at around the same time, but no trace of it remains.
Gleninagh Castle	3 miles (5km) northwest of Ballyvaughan. The remains of a four-storey L-plan tower house on the shore of Galway Bay towards Black Head. The castle was built for the O'Loughlins (O'Lochlainns), who were still resident in the 1840s. The well preserved ruins are home to breeding chough. Nearby is the Pinnacle Well, a stone-built Gothic well-house where fairy foxgloves grow. The castle is not open to the public.
Gregan's Castle	3½ miles (5.5km) south of Ballyvaughan. Built in 1750 by the Martyns, who had married into the O'Loughlin family and were granted the Gregan Estate in 1656. There are a myriad botanical, archaeological and cultural treasures in the vicinity of the castle, which is now a luxury hotel.
Highest Point	Moylussa, in the Slieve Bearnagh range at 1745ft (532m), located northwest of Killaloe.
Holy Island	Aka Inis Cealtra, Inishcaltra. Site of numerous churches. St Camin founded the first monastery here c. AD 520.
Innismacnaughten	Island in the parish of Kilconry, on the eastern shore of the River Fergus.
Interesting facts	**Daniel O'Connell**, **MP**, returned for the Clare electoral area, was known as 'The Liberator' for his winning of Catholic Emancipation in 1829. **Bicycles are for hire** from the launderette in Ballyvaughan at about 13 Euros per day. Clare is a great place for a cycling holiday – visitors will find unexpected treasures wherever they go and a host of quaint and friendly cafés. **The North Clare Agricultural Show** takes place on a Saturday at the end of July in Corofin. Show jumping and displays of turf, hens, eggs and cakes are just some of the delights. There is also judging of cattle, ponies and dogs, plus a display of veteran agricultural machines. **Muhammad Ali**'s great-grandfather, Abe Grady, was from Ennis. In the 1860s Grady emigrated to Kentucky, where he married a freed black slave. Clare is the location of the story of the **Colleen Bawn**. In the autumn of 1819, at Moneypoint, Kilrush, the body of Ellen Hanley was washed ashore six weeks after her marriage. Now known through story, drama and opera as the Colleen Bawn (Irish for 'beautiful fair-haired girl'), Ellen was not quite 16 years of age; she had been murdered at the insistence of her husband, John Scanlan. There is some uncertainty about where the marriage took place but it may have been in the Old Church at Kilrush. Shortly afterwards, Scanlan tired of his young bride, and with his servant, Stephan Sullivan, her murder was planned. Using Scanlan's boat and armed with a gun, Sullivan took Ellen for a trip on the river, but he lost his nerve just as he was about to commit the awful deed, and returned with her to Glin. Scanlan plied Sullivan with more whiskey and convinced Ellen to resume the boat trip. In mid-stream Sullivan murdered her with a musket. He removed her garments and ring, which he kept in the boat. She was tied with a rope which was attached to a stone and the remains were dumped in the Shannon. Six weeks later the body was washed ashore at Moneypoint. This appalling crime created feelings of horror and pity among all classes. Scanlan was captured and although defended by the famous lawyer Daniel O'Connell, he was found guilty and sentenced to death. Taken from jail on 16 March 1820, he was hanged at Gallows Green, on the Clare side of the Shannon. Sullivan was found shortly afterwards and his trial took place four months after that of Scanlan. Tried at Limerick, he too was found guilty and sentenced to death. On the gallows he confessed his guilt, admitting that his master had been the proposer and he himself the agent of the murder. Ellen Hanley is buried in Burrane cemetery, between Kildysart and Kilrush. The late Mrs Reeves, of Bessborough House, which is situated near the graveyard, erected a Celtic cross at the head of the grave. It bore the following inscription: 'Here lies the Colleen Bawn, Murdered on the Shannon, July 14th 1819. R.I.P.' There is no longer any trace of this cross; it was chipped away, bit by bit, by souvenir hunters. A novel based on the story, *The Collegians* (1829) by Gerald Griffin, was the inspiration for Anglo-Irish dramatist Dion Boucicault's 1860 play *The Colleen Bawn*; this in turn became the opera *The Lady of Killarney* (1862) by Sir Julius Benedict. **Kilfenora Cathedral** is the smallest cathedral diocese in Ireland; however, due to an ecclesiastical anomaly, its bishop is none other than the Pope.
Islands	See separate table
Kilfenora Cathedral	Kilfenora, 14 miles (23km) northwest of Ennis. Dedicated to St Fachtna and dating from the late 12th century, the cathedral is partially in ruins, although the western portion is still used for worship. The cathedral is noted for its three high crosses.
Killaloe	A town perhaps best known as the traditional birthplace of Brian Boru, Ireland's heroic High King (1002–14), who routed the Vikings from Ireland. Brian's palace was actually at the green mound of Kincora, about 1 mile (1.6km) outside Killaloe. The town is also famous as the location of St Flannan's cathedral and for the air 'Killaloe', a popular march among the Irish regiments of the British Army. The tune was written c.1887 by 41-year-old Irish composer Robert Martin for the London musical *Miss Esmeralda*, and was sung by a Mr E J Lohnen. The lyrics relate the sorry story of a French teacher attempting to make himself understood to a difficult Killaloe class who totally misunderstood his French, and as a consequence beat him up. The song, with its original melody in 2/4 time, was popularised in military circles by a cousin of Lt Charles Martin, who served with the 88th. He composed a new set of lyrics, in 6/8 time, celebrating his regiment's fame. 'Killaloe' was adopted by the Royal Irish Regiment on its formation on 1 July 1992.
Killone Abbey	3 miles (5km) south of Ennis. Located in the grounds of Newall House on the bank of Lake Killone. The ruins of an Augustinian convent, dedicated to St John and founded c.1190 by Donal Mor O'Brien.
Kilmacreehy Church	1 mile (1.6km) northwest of Lahinch. A 12th century church built on the site of a 6th century school founded by St Macreiche.

Kilnaboy	Aka Kilinaboy. Kilnaboy (meaning 'Church of the Daughters of Baoth') is a small village on the southern edge of the Burren, near Corofin, on the northern extremity of Lough Inchiquin. There are substantial remains of a castle, said to be the birthplace of Colonel Thomas Blood (see London: Interesting Facts), and an 11th or 12th century church.
Kilrush Heritage Centre	Market House, Kilrush. A local heritage centre telling the story of Kilrush from its foundation in the 18th century. Tel: 065 905 1577.
Knappogue Castle	Quin, 5 miles (8km) southeast of Ennis. Tower house built in 1467 by Sean MacNamara; from the late 16th century was the seat of the MacNamara Clan. It was confiscated by Cromwellian forces at the end of the 1650s only to be returned to the MacNamaras after the Restoration. The castle was restored and extended in the 19th century but fell into disrepair in the 1920s. It was again restored in the 1960s by a new owner and was purchased by Shannon Development in 1996. The grounds include a newly restored 19th century walled garden. Tel: 061 368103.
Lahinch	A village on the shore of Liscannor Bay. The name means 'half island' in Irish.
Lemanagh Castle	3 miles (5km) east of Kilfenora, 8 miles (13km) south of Ballyvaughan. Aka Maire Rua's Castle. The ruin of an O'Brien stronghold in the Burren. Lemanagh was the principal castle of the O'Briens and stands at a meeting of two of the main routes through the Burren. Built in the late 15th century, originally as a five-storey tower house, it was later enlarged with the addition of a four-storey mansion. It fell into ruin at the end of the 18th century. It was connected with Maire Rua. The stair tower is similar to Ballyportry. There are the remains of extensive walled gardens and a racetrack.
Liscannor	Fishing village located at the end of Liscannor Bay. It is the birthplace of John Philip Holland, inventor of the submarine.
Lisdoonvarna	A spa town and holiday resort on the edge of the Burren, famous for its annual music festivals.
Loop Head	20 miles (32km) southwest of Kilrush. The most southerly and southwesterly point of the county, overlooking the Shannon estuary and the Atlantic Ocean.
Lough Derg	See Tipperary
Maire Rua's Castle	See Lemanagh Castle
Mooghaun Hill Fort	1 mile (1.6km) north of Newmarket-on-Fergus, 6 miles (10km) southeast of Ennis. Located in the grounds of Dromoland Castle, Mooghaun (Moghane) is thought to be the largest hill fort in Ireland. Built 1260–930 BC, it is situated on a low hillock in a gently undulating agricultural landscape dotted with small lakes. It sits 263ft (80m) above sea level, and with an area of 27 acres (12ha) it dominates the surrounding landscape. A trivallate fort with three circular ramparts, it was the site of the Great Clare Gold Find of 1854 when workmen unearthed a stone box full of gold ornaments, the largest collection of such objects ever found in Europe.
Newmarket-on-Fergus	A town located between the estuaries of the rivers Shannon and Fergus. Formerly known as Tradaree, it was renamed by Lord Inchiquin after the horse-racing centre in England.
Newtown Castle	$1\frac{1}{2}$ miles (2.5km) southwest of Ballyvaughan. A restored 16th century tower house built by the O'Briens and later owned by the O'Loughlins. It is now used as an exhibition centre for the adjacent Burren Art College.
O'Brien's Tower	3 miles (5km) west of Liscannor, 20 miles (32km) west of Ennis. A tall tower built by Cornelius O'Brien in 1835 as an observation point for tourists visiting the Cliffs of Moher.
O'Briensbridge	5 miles (8km) southwest of Killaloe. A village on the River Shannon. The first bridge across the Shannon at this point was built in 1506 by Turlough O'Brien, 1st Earl of Thomond, and his brother, the Bishop of Killaloe.
Poulawack Cairn	$\frac{1}{2}$ mile (0.8km) southeast of Caherconnell, 6 miles (10km) south of Ballyvaughan. A hilltop cairn in the Burren dating to 2000–3000 BC. Excavations in 1934 revealed the bones of 16 individuals, who were buried over a period of 1000 years.
Poulnabrone Dolmen	1 mile (1.6km) northeast of Caherconnell, 5 miles (8km) south of Ballyvaughan. A spectacular portal dolmen in the Burren. Dating to c. 2500 BC, it has two uprights plus a thin capstone. The burial chamber was excavated in the 1980s and the remains of up to 33 individuals were exposed. The name means 'The hole of the sorrows'.
Quin Abbey	Quin, 5 miles (8km) southeast of Ennis. The ruins of a Franciscan friary built 1402–33 by Sioda Cam Macnamara on the site of an earlier monastery. Various earlier buildings, including a 13th century church, a Norman castle and another church, built by the Macnamaras in the 1350s using parts of the castle structure, have also been located on the site.
Rivers	The **Aille** rises on Sliabh Elva in the Burren, flowing through Lisdoonvara and Doolin before reaching the sea below the Cliffs of Moher. The **Fergus** rises in The Burren (see separate entry) in north Clare, and flows southwards through the village of Corofin and the town of Ennis to join the tidal waters of the Shannon Estuary at Newmarket-on-Fergus. It is approximately 26 miles (42km) long to Lough Fergus (approx 7km east of Ennistymon) although it disappears into a swallow hole at Cahermacon for approx 1km, and then opens up to share an estuary with the Shannon. The **Shannon** is the longest river in Ireland at 240 miles (384km). With its source in the Tiltinbane Mountains in the Cuilcagh range in Co. Cavan, it flows through Leitrim and the boundaries of Roscommon, Longford, Westmeath, Offaly, Galway, Tipperary, Clare and Limerick before entering the Atlantic Ocean at Loop Head in Clare. It is linked to the River Erne by the Shannon–Erne Waterway.
Scattery Island Centre	Merchants Quay, Kilrush. An interpretive centre detailing the story of Scattery Island and its flora and fauna, and in particular the 6th century monastery with the remains of its round tower. Tel: 065 905 2139.
St Flannan's Cathedral	Abbey Street, Killaloe. Located beside the Shannon and dating from the early 13th century, the present cathedral replaced a 12th century church built by Donal Mor O'Brien which was destroyed in

	1185. The height of the central tower was raised in the 1790s and again in 1900. In the churchyard is a delightful 12th century oratory with a Romanesque doorway. Inside the cathedral is Thorgrim's Stone, the shaft of a Viking cross carved over 1000 years ago. It is one of only a few examples in the world of a bilingual stone with inscriptions in both Irish Ogham and Scandinavian runes.
Shannon	After Ennis the largest town in the county. It officially became a town in 1982. Shannon was planned after being built on reclaimed land.
Sleeping Stone Cow	5 miles (8km) south of Ballyvaughan. A peculiar rock formation close to Caherconnell Stone Fort (see separate entry).
Smithstown Castle	See Ballynagowan Castle
Spanish Point	19 miles (31km) west of Ennis. The central point of the county's west coast, located between Mal Bay and Liscannor Bay. It is so named because the *San Marcos*, a ship of the Spanish Armada, was wrecked off Mutton Island and the headland above Quilty in 1588. The 6th President of Ireland, Sir Patrick Hillery, was born here.
Tau Cross, The	Roughan, 1 mile (1.6km) northwest of Kilnaboy, $2^1/_2$ miles (4km) northwest of Corofin. A primitive cross, carved with two heads, perhaps a local version of Iron Age work found in France, and originally located set in a wall on Roughan Hill. The original is now on display at the heritage centre in Corofin; a replica now stands near the site where the cross was discovered.
Tomb of McMahon	Aka the Royal Tomb. Located at Ennis Friary, it bears carvings representing the Passion of Christ.
Tuamgraney Church	Tuamgraney, 19 miles (31km) east of Ennis. Possibly the oldest Irish church still in use, founded by St Cronan and dating to before AD 969.
Vandeleur Walled Gardens	1 mile (1.6km) southeast of Kilrush. Once the garden of Kilrush House, home to the Vandeleur landlords. Located within Vandeleur Demesne in 420 acres (170ha) of woodland, it was restored beginning in the late 1990s. The Vandeleur Glasshouse was rebuilt in 2005. Tel: 065 905 1760.
West Clare Railway	Moyasta, 3 miles (5km) northwest of Kilrush. A heritage railway based at the restored Moyasta Junction station house and seeking to restore 3 miles (5km) of the former 3ft (0.9m) narrow gauge West Clare Railway, which ran between Ennis, Kilrush and Kilkee from 1887 to 1961. Tel: 065 905 1284.

Some famous people born in County Clare

Clancy, Willie (musician) (1918–73)	Miltown Malbay
Cusack, Michael (founder of GAA) (1847–1906)	Carron
Fallon, Kieren (jockey) (1965–)	Crusheen
FitzGerald, Davy (hurling player) (1971–)	Sixmilebridge
Hillery, Patrick (6th Taoiseach of Ireland) (1923–2008)	Miltown Malbay
Holland, John Philip (inventor) (1840–1914)	Liscannor
Lohan, Brian (hurling player) (1971–)	Shannon
Loughnane, Ger (hurling player) (1953–)	Feakle
Lynam, Des (broadcaster) (1942–)	Ennis
Merriman, Brian (poet) (1749–1805)	Ennistymon
Mulready, William (painter) (1786–1863)	Ennis
O'Brien, Edna (writer) (1930–)	Tuamgraney
O'Connell, Maura (singer and actress) (1958–)	Ennis
O'Loghlen, Michael (politician) (1789–1842)	Ennis
Russell, Micho (musician) (1915–94)	Doolin
Smyth, Jimmy (hurling player) (1931–)	Ennis
Wood, Keith (rugby player) (1972–)	Killaloe

Islands of County Clare

(shipping area = Shannon)

Island name	Area	Nearest landmark	General information
An Branan Mor	Galway Bay	Doolin	aka Branaunmore
Aughinish	Galway Bay	Burren	See separate entry
Battle Island	River Shannon	Limerick	aka Inniscathay, Oileán an Comhrúath
Beeves Rock	Shannon-Fergus	Killadysert	Lies south of the Wide Rocks.
Bergers Island	Shannon-Fergus	Shannon	Tiny islet off the east coast of Inishloe.
Big Trummera	Shannon Estuary	Killadysert	Lies south of Little Trummera.
Big Venture	Shannon-Fergus	Shannon	Lies off the southeast coast of Deenish.
Bishop's Island	Atlantic	Kilkee	See separate entry
Black Rock	Atlantic	Loop Head	Tiny rock stack just north of Loop Head.
Blackthorn Island	Shannon-Fergus	Shannon	Tiny islet off the northeast coast of Inishloe. There is another island of the same name nearby; southwest of Tina Island.
Branaunmore	Galway Bay	Doolin	aka An Branan Mor
Breac Inis	Shannon-Fergus	Kilmaleery	aka Breckinish
Breckinish	Shannon-Fergus	Kilmaleery	aka Breac Inis. Lies in the northeast area of the estuary.

Island name	Area	Nearest landmark	General information
Bush Island	River Shannon	Cratloe	aka Oileán na Shgeach
Canon Island	Shannon-Fergus	Killadysert	See separate entry
Carrignanagh	Shannon-Fergus	Killadysert	Tiny islet off the west coast of Doon Island.
Coney Island	Shannon-Fergus	Shannon	aka Inis Cuinínidhe, Rabbit's Island. The next island east of Deer Island.
Coonagh Islands	Shannon-Fergus	Kilmaleery	Group of tiny islets south of Breckinish
Corcory Island	Shannon-Fergus	Killadysert	aka Cork Rock.
Cork Rock	Shannon-Fergus	Killadysert	aka Corcory Island. Lies due south of The Needles.
Cow Island	Shannon-Fergus	Ennis	Smaller western neighbour of Horse Island
Crab Island	Galway Bay	Doolin Pier	See separate entry
Croan Rock	Atlantic	Loop Head	Tiny rock located between Kilkee and Loop Head.
Deenish Island	Shannon-Fergus	Shannon	aka Dynish. Sometimes known as the Island of Sorrow. Lies south of the Coonaghs.
Deer Island	Shannon-Fergus	Ballynacally	aka Innismore/Inishmore. Lies south of Horse Island. It is the largest island in the estuary. Population: 1.
Doon Island	Shannon-Fergus	Killadysert	Tiny islet off the southwest coast of Inishmacowney.
Dynish	Shannon-Fergus	Shannon	See Deenish Island
Feenish Island	Shannon-Fergus	Shannon	aka Fynish. See separate entry
Fynish	Shannon-Fergus	Shannon	See Feenish Island
Gull Island	Atlantic	Loop Head	Lies south of Croan Rock.
Herring Rock	Shannon Estuary	Killadysert	Lies southwest of Beeves Rock.
Hoadway Rock	Shannon-Fergus	Shannon	Lies south of Rat Island, east of Coney.
Hog Island	Shannon Estuary	Kilrush	Smaller neighbour of Scattery Island.
Holy Island	Lough Derg	Mountshannon	aka Inishcaltra, Inis Cealtra. See separate entry
Horse Island	Shannon-Fergus	Ennis	Lies in the northwest area of the estuary.
Horse Rock	Shannon-Fergus	Shannon	Lies southeast of Tina Island.
Illaunaroan	River Shannon	Shannon	aka Oileán an Rón
Illaunatoo	River Shannon	Shannon	aka Oileán an Samhadh, Sorrell Island
Illaunban	River Shannon	Shannon	aka Oileán Bán, White Island
Illaunbeg	Shannon-Fergus	Killadysert	Smaller islet southwest of Shore Island.
Illaunloo	Galway Bay	Scanlon's Island	Tiny rocky islet situated in South Galway Bay.
Illaunmore	Lough Derg	Whitegate	One of two islands in the lough.
Illaunyregan	River Shannon	Shannon	aka Oileán ua Riagán, O'Regan's Island
Inchalughoge	River Shannon	Shannon	aka Inis an Luchóg
Inchbeg	River Shannon	Shannon	aka Inis Beag
Inchicronan	River Shannon	Shannon	aka Inis ui Crónain, St Cronan's Island
Inchiquin	River Shannon	Shannon	aka Inis ui Chúinn, O'Quinn's Island
Inis an Luchóg	River Shannon	Shannon	aka Inchalughoge
Inis Beag	River Shannon	Shannon	aka Inchbeg
Inis Cealtra	Lough Derg	Mountshannon	See Holy Island
Inis Cuinínidhe	Shannon-Fergus	Shannon	See Coney Island
Inis Da Drom	Shannon-Fergus	Killadysert	aka Inishdadroum
Inis Muire	Shannon Estuary	Killadysert	(I. = The Blessed Virgin Mary's Island). Aka Inishmurry. Lies southwest of Canon Island.
Inis na Canánach	River Shannon	Killadysert	See Canon Island
Inis ui Chúinn	River Shannon	Shannon	aka Inchiquin, O'Quinn's Island
Inis ui Crónain	River Shannon	Shannon	aka Inchicronan, St Cronan's Island
Inish Cathach	Shannon Estuary	Kilrush	(I. = Dragon Island). Aka Scattery Island. Lies north of Carrig Island of Kerry.
Inishcaltra	Lough Derg	Mountshannon	aka Holy Island, Inis Cealtra
Inishcorker	River Shannon	Killadysert	Latitude: 52° 40' 05", longitude: 9° 05' 21"
Inishdadroum	Shannon-Fergus	Killadysert	aka Inis da Drom. Tiny islet southwest of Coney.
Inishloe	Shannon-Fergus	Killadysert	aka Inishluaidhe. Lies to the east of Canon Island.
Inishluaidhe	Shannon-Fergus	Killadysert	aka Inishloe.
Inishmacowney	Shannon-Fergus	Killadysert	Larger island south of Shore Island. There was once a castle belonging in 1580 to Teige MacConor O'Brien, ancestor of the Ballycorick family of that name.
Inishmore	Shannon-Fergus	Ballynacally	See Deer Island
Inishmurry	Shannon Estuary	Killadysert	See Inis Muire
Inishoul	Shannon-Fergus	Killadysert	aka O'Grady's Island. Tiny islet northwest of Inishtubrid

Island name	Area	Nearest landmark	General information
Inishtubrid	Shannon-Fergus	Killadysert	Lies west of Canon Island, its name possibly derives from Tobar, a well.
Inniscathay	River Shannon	Limerick	See Battle Island
Innismacnaughten	River Shannon	Bunratty	Lies at the confluence of the rivers Fergus and Shannon.
Innismore	Shannon-Fergus	Ballynacally	See Deer Island
Innisneganangh	River Shannon	Killadysert	See Canon Island
Islandcosgry	River Shannon	Shannon	aka O'Cosgary's Island
Islandgar	River Shannon	Shannon	aka Oileán Gár
Islandmacnevin	River Shannon	Shannon	aka Oileán Mhic Nemhín
Islandmagrath	River Shannon	Shannon	Aka Magrath's Island, Oileán Magraith
Islandmore	River Shannon	Shannon	aka Oileán Mór
Kinatevdilla	Atlantic	Clare Island	Tiny islet off Clare Island.
Ladder Rock	Shannon Estuary	Kilrush	Lies at the mouth of the river near Loop Head.
Little Trummera	Shannon Estuary	Killadysert	Tiny islet southwest of Herring Rock.
Little Venture	Shannon-Fergus	Shannon	Small islet off the north coast of Big Venture.
Magrath's Island	River Shannon	Shannon	See Islandmagrath
Mattle Island	Atlantic	Emlagh Point	Lies south of Mutton Island.
Moylaun's Rock	Shannon Estuary	Shannon	Lies northeast of Horse Rock.
Mutton Island	Atlantic	Emlagh Point	aka Oileán Caorach. Most northerly island of Clare.
Mweelaun Island	Atlantic	Clare Island	Tiny island lying off Clare Island.
Needles, The	Shannon-Fergus	Killadysert	Group of rocks south of Inishloe and west of Sand Island.
O'Cosgary's Island	River Shannon	Shannon	aka Islandcosgry
O'Grady's Island	Shannon-Fergus	Killadysert	aka Inishoul
Oileán an Comhrúath	River Shannon	Limerick	See Battle Island
Oileán-an-Easpoig-gortaigh	Atlantic	Kilkee	See Bishop's Island
Oileán an Rón	River Shannon	Shannon	(I. = The Seal's Island). Aka Illaunaroan
Oileán an Samhadh	River Shannon	Shannon	See Illaunatoo
Oileán Bán	River Shannon	Shannon	See Illaunban
Oileán Caedh	River Shannon	Shannon	aka Quay Island
Oilean Caorach	Atlantic	Emlagh Point	aka Mutton Island
Oileán Dubhach	River Shannon	Shannon	aka Sod Island
Oileán Gár	River Shannon	Shannon	aka Islandgar
Oileán Magraith	River Shannon	Shannon	See Islandmagrath
Oileán Mhic Nemhín	River Shannon	Shannon	aka Islandmacnevin
Oileán Mór	River Shannon	Shannon	(I. = Great Island). Aka Islandmore
Óileán na Náomh	River Shannon	Shannon	aka Saints Island
Oileán na Shgeach	River Shannon	Cratloe	aka Bush Island
Oileán ua Riagán	River Shannon	Shannon	aka Illaunyregan, O'Regan's Island
O'Quinn's Island	River Shannon	Shannon	aka Inis ui Chúinn, Inchiquin
O'Regan's Island	River Shannon	Shannon	aka Oileán ua Riagán, Illaunyregan
Priest Rock	Shannon-Fergus	Shannon	The rock, off the west coast of Feenish, is a hazard to shipping.
Quay Island	River Shannon	Shannon	See Oileán Caedh
Rat Island	Shannon-Fergus	Shannon	Tiny islet northeast of Coney Island.
Rabbit's Island	Shannon-Fergus	Shannon	See Coney Island
St Cronan's Island	River Shannon	Shannon	aka Inis ui Cronain, Inchicronan
Saints Island	River Shannon	Shannon	aka Óileán na Náomh
Sand Island	Shannon-Fergus	Killadysert	Lies south of Inishloe.
Scanlon's Island	Ballyvaughan Bay	Ballyvaughan	Accessible from the mainland at low water.
Scattery Island	Shannon Estuary	Kilrush	See Inish Cathach
Seal Rock	Shannon Estuary	Limerick	Tiny rock southeast of Big Trummera.
Shore Island	Shannon-Fergus	Killadysert	Tiny round islet south of Deer Island.
Sod Island	River Shannon	Shannon	aka Oileán Dubhach
Sorrell Island	River Shannon	Shannon	aka Oileán an Samhadh, Illaunatoo
Sturamus Rock	Shannon Estuary	Killadysert	Lies northeast of Foynes Island (administered by County Limerick).
Tarbert Island	Shannon	Kilkerin Point	The island contains a battery built towards the end of the Napoleonic Wars to guard the estuary against a French invasion.
Tina Island	Shannon-Fergus	Shannon	Tiny islet south of Blackthorn, east of Bergers.
Trummer Island	Shannon-Fergus	Killadysert	Tiny islet lying midway between the southern tips of Deer and Coney Islands.
White Island	River Shannon	Shannon	aka Oileán Bán, Illaunban
Wide Rocks	Shannon-Fergus	Killadysert	Group of rocks south of Sand Island.

Cork

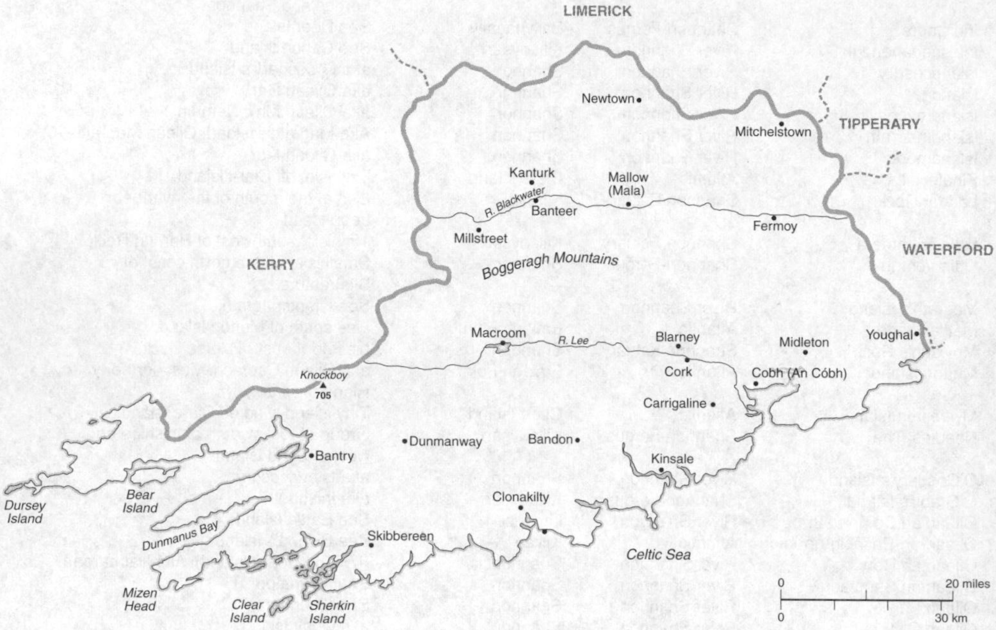
LIMERICK
TIPPERARY
WATERFORD
KERRY
Newtown
Mitchelstown
Kanturk
Mallow (Mala)
R. Blackwater
Banteer
Fermoy
Millstreet
Boggeragh Mountains
Macroom
R. Lee
Blarney
Midleton
Youghal
Cork
Cobh (An Cóbh)
Knockboy 705
Carrigaline
Dunmanway
Bandon
Bantry
Kinsale
Clonakilty
Dursey Island
Bear Island
Dunmanus Bay
Skibbereen
Celtic Sea
Mizen Head
Clear Island
Sherkin Island
0 20 miles
0 30 km

County Cork is Ireland's most southerly county. It is bordered by Kerry to the west, Limerick to the north, Waterford to the northeast, and it has a short border with Tipperary on its most northeasterly point. To the south lies the Celtic Sea. The largest of the modern counties of the Republic of Ireland, Cork is part of the province of Munster. It is nicknamed 'The Rebel County', as a result of the support of the townsmen of Cork for Perkin Warbeck (a pretender to the English throne) in 1491, although in more recent times the name has referred to the prominent role Cork played in the Irish War of Independence (1919–21) and its position as an anti-treaty stronghold during the Irish Civil War (1922–3).

There are 81 electoral areas in Cork, many of them with just a few thousand inhabitants. The major towns are Carrigaline, Cobh, Mallow, Youghal and Bandon, all having populations greater than 5000. There are Gaeltacht (Irish-speaking) areas on Cape Clear Island and around Ballyvourney to the south of the Derrynasagart Mountains.

Cork has a number of contenders for the most famous son or daughter. There are a number of sporting heroes: Sam Maguire, Vincent O'Brien, Sonia O'Sullivan, Dennis Irwin and Roy Keane to name but a few. The arts are represented too with William Trevor, Cillian Murphy and Danny La Rue, but perhaps the most well known is the 'Big Fella' Michael Collins, killed on the road from Brandon to Cork in 1922.

The county town of Cork is **Cork City**, the second largest city (after Dublin) in the Republic of Ireland. It stands on the River Lee, and was granted its charter in 1185. The name 'Cork' derives from the Irish *Corcach Mór Mumhan* (the great marsh of Munster) and refers to the fact that the centre of the city is built on islands, surrounded by the River Lee, which were marshy and prone to flooding. The waterways between the islands were built over to form some of the main streets of present-day Cork. Traditionally, St Finbarre or Bairre has been credited with the foundation c. AD 682 of the monastery of Cork, the earliest human settlement in the city for which there is irrefutable evidence. The immigrant Vikings and the monastic community coexisted peacefully in the main; indeed the Vikings' seafaring and trading abilities were a boon to the monastery, which they provided with wine, salt and other commodities. In 914 there was a massive raid on Cork and Munster from Scandinavia and members of this raiding party possibly expropriated the existing Viking community.

By the 12th century the descendants of the original settlers had intermarried with the native Irish and had become known as the Ostmen or Eastmen. They had established Cork as an important trading centre and its importance was enhanced with the coming to power in the 12th century of the MacCarthys of Desmond, who established Cork as their capital. The MacCarthys built a residence and fortress near Cork. In Latin this fortress was called *vetus castellarum*; an exact translation of the Irish *sean dún* (old fort), this may be identified with the present-day Shandon area of Cork. The Ostmen acknowledged the overlordship of the MacCarthy kings but retained some form of autonomy. It is known that the Ostmen built a fortification on the south island in the Lee and it is thought that this may have served as a template for the wall of Cork, which was built during the Norman era. The last known leader of Ostman Cork, Gilbert mac Turgar, was killed in a sea battle near Youghal in 1173. In 1171, many of the provincial kings had taken an oath of fealty to Henry II of England, including Dermot MacCarthy, King of Munster and overlord of Ostman Cork. At the Council of Oxford in 1177, Henry II granted the kingdom of Cork to Robert FitzStephen and Milo de Cogan, but he reserved the city of Cork for himself. An army led by FitzStephen and de Cogan arrived at Cork the same year and took the city. The Ostmen had their property confiscated and they were expelled from the city by the Normans, thus beginning the Norman era of the history of Cork.

Prince John, Lord of Ireland, visited Ireland in 1185 and sometime around that date granted a charter which made Cork a corporate town with powers of local government. The Normans constructed a wall on the south island of the Lee in 1182, possibly based on the former Ostman defensive structure. Over time this wall was extended and the entire medieval city centre became one of the great walled towns of Ireland. During the 13th and 14th centuries Cork was regarded as the principal port of southwest Ireland. Its main imports would have been wine, cloth and spices, the principal exports wool, grain, beef and other agricultural produce from the surrounding countryside. The prosperity of the city suffered a devastating blow with the arrival of the Black Death in 1349. In the 15th century the governance of Cork continued to be dominated by an oligarchy of wealthy merchant families who made their money mainly from the importation of goods, including grain, and the export of hides, furs and timber. Among the most prominent of these families were the Galweys, the Roches, the Tirrys, the Goulds and the Skiddys. in the late 15th century, Cork was visited by Perkin Warbeck, pretender to the throne of England, who was supported by the Mayor of Cork, John Walters. Walters was later executed for supporting Warbeck.

The 16th century was remarkably turbulent, marked by the Desmond Rebellion, the impact of the Reformation on Ireland and the beginning of the Elizabethan wars. By the end of the century, the size of the town's population was estimated to be about 800. The charter of 1608, while it created the County of the City of Cork which covered a much larger area than the old medieval walled city and adjoining suburbs, also retained for the Crown the right to poundage, tonnage and customs in the port of Cork. This was a severe financial blow to the city's merchants. The period from 1641 to 1649 was another turbulent period in Ireland; matters came to a head in 1644, following the 1641 rebellion. In that year it was discovered that some of the leading citizens of Cork had been conspiring with Lord Muskerry, a military commander loyal to the Catholic Confederacy. On learning of this Lord Inchiquin took extreme action. On 26 June 1644 he decreed the expulsion of the Irish and Catholic population of Cork from the city. The power of the Catholic merchant families which had dominated the civic life of Cork for centuries, was broken. The forces of the Catholic Confederacy struggled against the English forces, which were themselves in the prelude to the English Civil War. The city's dispossessed merchants of the city were briefly reinstated in 1648 when English forces in Cork declared for the Royalist side. Their reinstatement was short-lived; they were expelled again in 1649 on the arrival of Cromwell.

After the defeat of the Royalists in the English Civil War, Cromwell was free to turn his attention to Ireland, which he quickly and brutally subdued. Cork City was under military governance 1644–56 when Cromwell granted a new municipal charter to the city's Protestants. The municipal government was to remain firmly in Protestant hands until the reform of the Corporation in the mid 19th century, apart from a brief period during the reign of James II when the Old English regained control of the city.

When James II landed at Kinsale in 1689, hoping to use Ireland as a base from which to regain his crown from William of Orange, the Catholics of Cork unsurprisingly rallied to the Jacobite cause. A Williamite army, under the control of the Duke of Marlborough, was dispatched to Cork to regain the city for William and Mary. On 28 September 1690, this army attacked from both sides of the river, supported by artillery and by warships which had sailed up the river and joined in the bombardment. The Duke of Grafton was mortally wounded in this attack and his memory is commemorated in the name of Grafton Street in Cork. Recognising that the situation was hopeless,

MacElligott, after some haggling, agreed to hand over Elizabeth Fort immediately and to surrender the city on the following day. Marlborough agreed to treat the garrison as prisoners of war and to show clemency to the inhabitants of the city. The siege of Cork was over. Its walls, which had stood for centuries, were exposed as powerless against the new weapons of war.

The turbulence of the 1640s and 1650s had set back Cork's economic development. The city began to recover in the period from 1660 to 1700 and the 18th century witnessed a major expansion in its economy. Salted beef, pork and butter were exported to the West Indies and were used to provide the British navy. The unrivalled ability of Cork Harbour to shelter the biggest fleets assembled during the American War of Independence and later during the Napoleonic Wars was a major factor in the expansion of the provisions trade. Cork Butter Market, with its strict and rigorously enforced system of quality control, was world famous and became the largest of its kind in the world for its time. The textile industries also flourished during this period. The demand for linen for sailcloth helped the growth of the Douglas sailcloth factory, which by 1726 was the biggest such factory in Europe. The woollen and cotton industries were very important, O'Mahony's woollen mills in Blarney and Sadleir's cotton mills in Glasheen being particularly prominent. The tanning, brewing and distilling industries flourished in the late 1700s. The Beamish & Crawford brewery, established in 1792, became the biggest of its kind in Ireland and is still a major employer in Cork. The late 18th century also saw the construction of bridges linking the centre of the city to the suburbs. The first St Patrick's Bridge, Parliament Bridge and Clarke's Bridge all date from this period. The North and South Gate Bridges had been rebuilt in the 1710–15 period. The South Gate Bridge has one of the oldest surviving three-centred arches in Ireland.

The prosperity of Cork and Ireland during the 18th century owed much to the country's improved political stability. However, the eruption of the underlying discontent and disaffection in the 1798 rebellion brought havoc and carnage to many parts of Ireland. While Cork City was relatively untouched by the rebellion itself, the United Irishmen had been active in the city for some time, and the military authorities took severe action against those found guilty of being members. Many were transported and many shot by firing squads in a field on the western edges of the city through which the Western Road now runs. The National Monument on Grand Parade commemorates some of those who suffered in the aftermath of 1798.

As the effects of the Great Famine became evident, the Cork Relief Committee was set up in March 1846 and with government support organised the distribution of maize (known as Indian meal) to the poor, also starting schemes of public works to enable those employed to earn enough to buy food from the food depots. The maize was not given to the poor; it had to be paid for. The winter of 1846–7, 'Black 47' in folklore, was the worst in living memory. The rural poor fleeing from starvation and evictions poured into the city. The workhouse and the city hospitals were full, and starving beggars died on the streets. The city's cemeteries couldn't cope with the numbers to be buried and a new cemetery was opened at Carr's Hill outside the city. Often, the mass graves contained so many coffins that those interred near the tops of the graves were insufficiently covered with earth allowing the foetid odour of decaying corpses to escape. Even the carts transporting the coffins to Carr's Hill gave off such an odour that it was proposed to convey the corpses to the cemetery using large balloons. By 1849 the very worst of the Famine was over and deaths from starvation began to decrease. However, accompanying diseases such as typhus, yellow fever, dysentery, bacillary dysentery (known at the time as 'the bloody flux') and other diseases claimed the lives of thousands. Paradoxically, the population of Cork increased during the harrowing years of the Famine due to the influx of the rural poor fleeing from the devastated countryside.

Architecturally, Cork is very much a city of the 19th century. The majority of the buildings on the principal streets and many of the churches and public buildings date from that period. A small number of architects contributed enormously to the city's architecture during the century. The Pain brothers, James and George R, designed a number of public buildings in the first half of the century, as did the Deane brothers, Kearns and Sir Thomas. In the second half of the century Sir John Benson was very influential and notable contributions were made by William Burges, designer of St Fin Barre's Cathedral, and E W Pugin, who designed St Peter and St Paul's Church. Among the works of G R Pain are the interior of St Mary's and St Anne's Cathedral (extensively refurbished in recent times), St Patrick's Church and Holy Trinity Church. With J Pain he also designed the old County Gaol (now part of UCC) and the County and City Courthouse (another building which has undergone major refurbishment). Sir Thomas Deane designed the Commercial Buildings (now the Imperial Hotel) and the Queen's College that later became UCC. Kearns Deane designed St Mary's Church on Pope's Quay and the Cork Savings Bank on Lapp's Quay. Sir John Benson left his mark on Cork with his designs for St Patrick's Bridge, the Athenaeum (later the old Opera House), the English Market, St Vincent's Church and others.

In the early 20th century Cork was profoundly affected by events of international and national importance. Ironically the century began very auspiciously with the Cork International Exhibition of 1902–03. In the years preceding World War I political life in Ireland centred on the struggle to achieve Home Rule. On 28 September 1918 Asquith's Home Rule became law with the support of the Irish Parliamentary Party led by John Redmond. Its provisions were immediately suspended for the duration of the war. World War I, as it came to be known, was expected to be over in a matter of months. Redmond, William O'Brien and other nationalist leaders called for support for the war; the more radical wing of the nationalist movement opposed it. This difference in attitude led to a split in the Irish Volunteer movement in Cork as in the rest of the country. Support for the war was widespread in Cork. Many men volunteered for the army and organisations were set up to support the troops, the wounded and the families of those in the armed forces. For a time divisions between nationalists and unionists appeared to be forgotten. The German invasion of Catholic Belgium outraged Irish Catholic opinion and anti-German sentiment was common among the population, fuelled by reports of German atrocities.

Cork tasted the horrors of World War I when the *Lusitania* was sunk off the Old Head of Kinsale on 8 May 1915. The treatment of the leaders of the 1916 Rising and the attempt to introduce conscription to Ireland in 1918 caused widespread outrage. Members of the Cork City Corps of the Irish Volunteers occupied St Francis Hall on Sheares Street during the 1916 Rising but no actual violence occurred in the city, thanks partly to the efforts of Bishop Daniel Cohalan and Lord Mayor Thomas C Butterfield. The feeling that Britain would renege on the promise of Home Rule and the withdrawal of the Irish Parliamentary Party from Westminster were among the factors that led to the victory of Sinn Féin in the general election of 1918. The divisions between nationalists and unionists were to the fore again as Ireland slid seemingly inexorably towards the War of Independence. During World War I over 2000 Corkmen were killed, 1100 of them from Cork City alone.

During the War of Independence Cork was one of the major centres of resistance to British rule. Many of the most famous figures during that war came from Cork. Perhaps the three best-remembered episodes from the period are the deaths of Lord Mayor Tomás MacCurtain, Lord Mayor Terence MacSwiney and the burning of Cork City. In one of the worst atrocities, British forces deliberately set fire to several blocks of buildings along the east and south sides of St Patrick's Street during the night of Saturday, 11 December 1920, and the following Sunday morning. The City Hall and the Carnegie Library were also completely destroyed by fire. The Auxiliaries and Black & Tans were allegedly taking revenge for an earlier attack on British troops.

Tomás MacCurtain took an active role in the war. Originally from Ballyknockane in County Cork, he became involved with the Gaelic League, the Irish Republican Brotherhood and the Irish Volunteers. He was in command of the latter in Cork during the 1916 Rising in Dublin. Although no violence took place in Cork during the Rising, MacCurtain was subsequently arrested and imprisoned. Following Sinn Féin's victory in the local elections of January 1920 he was elected Lord Mayor of Cork on 31 January 1920, the first Republican to hold the office. His term as Lord Mayor was brutally cut short. In the early hours of 20 March 1920, members of the Royal Irish Constabulary (RIC) burst into his house and shot him dead before ransacking the house. The murder outraged public opinion and brought near universal condemnation. Cork went into mourning for its murdered first citizen. A massive crowd attended his funeral. At the coroner's inquest into the killing the jury passed a verdict of wilful murder against Lloyd George and certain inspectors of the RIC. One of the named inspectors, Oswald Swanzy, was shot dead in Lisburn on 22 August 1920.

On MacCurtain's death Terence MacSwiney was elected Lord Mayor. Like MacCurtain, he had been a member of the Irish Volunteers and an enthusiast for the Irish language. He had also been imprisoned following the Easter Rising. A talented writer, he wrote a drama entitled *The Revolutionist*, several volumes of poetry and a political tract entitled *The Principles of Freedom*. As well as being Lord Mayor of Cork he was Commandant of the First Cork Brigade of the IRA. On 12 August 1920 he was arrested for possession of seditious documents and of a cipher key to coded messages used by the RIC. He was tried by court martial on 16 August 1920 and sentenced to two years' imprisonment. After his arrest he immediately went on hunger strike. He was imprisoned in Brixton Prison, where his continuing hunger strike attracted worldwide attention. He died on 25 October 1920 and his body was brought home for burial. He lies beside MacCurtain in the Republican plot in St Finbarr's Cemetery in Cork. His funeral on 1 November 1920 attracted huge crowds.

During the early days of the Irish Civil War the anti-treaty IRA controlled Cork City. It took over the *Cork Examiner* and used it to promote its side in the conflict. The newly formed Free State army landed at Passage West on 9 August 1922, surprising the Republicans who were expecting an attack by land. The Free State forces encountered stiff resistance from the Republicans near Rochestown and Douglas during what later came to be known as the Battle of Douglas. Within days the much better equipped army of the Free State had driven the IRA from the city.

After the country had been stabilised politically following the Civil War, Ireland endured decades of comparative economic stagnation. Boatloads of emigrants boarded the *Innisfallen* at Penrose Quay. So many Corkmen emigrated to work in the Ford factory in Dagenham that it became known as 'Little Cork'. Many of the Dagenham emigrants returned home every year for their holidays. With their more fashionable clothes and the slight traces of English accents they became known, affectionately as 'The Dagenham Yanks'. The most important employers in Cork during this period included Ford, Dunlop, Sunbeam Wolsey, Irish Steel and Verolme Cork Dockyards.

After World War II, while government grants and loans were offered to firms to remedy these defects, among which was the lack of cooperation between firms operating in the same industries, not enough Cork firms availed themselves of the opportunities. The closures of Ford and Dunlop in the early 1980s were hammer blows to the city's economic wellbeing. While Cork had enjoyed economic prosperity in the 1960s and early 1970s, the city was economically devastated during the late 1970s and 1980s with the indigenous industries unable to compete with foreign enterprises which had freer access to the Irish market since Ireland had joined the EEC (now the EU). Thousands of young Cork people were forced to emigrate in search of work while unemployment rose to levels not experienced since the early 1950s.

Cork's economy, along with that of Ireland itself, began to recover in the late 1980s and record-breaking rates of economic growth were achieved in the 1990s, the era of the so-called 'Celtic Tiger'. The transformation of the city from its run-down condition in the 1980s has been remarkable. New hi-tech industries were set up in the city and its surrounding hinterland. Some of the giants of the electronic, computer and pharmaceutical industries established factories in the area. Unemployment levels fell dramatically. New shopping centres were opened both in the city centre and the outlying suburbs. The construction industry boomed with the demand for new houses far exceeding the supply. The communications and transport infrastructures of the city were improved enormously. Cork began to take on a continental air with young, fashionably dressed people sipping coffee and beer inside and outside an increasing number of stylish new restaurants. Nowhere was the transformation more complete than in the Huguenot Quarter around French Church Street, Paul Street and Carey's Lane. In the late 1970s these streets had become dingy and shabby; now they are among the busiest and liveliest in the city.

Cork	**Population**			**Area**	
Districts	*male*	*female*	*total*	*sq miles*	*sq km*
Bandon	9143	8820	17,963	160	414
Bantry	4330	4354	8684	168	434
Castletown	2198	1994	4192	116	301
Clonakilty rural area	5074	4885	9959	126	327
Clonakilty Town	1627	1805	3432	2	5
Cobh	3372	3395	6767	1	2
Cork City	59,263	63,799	123,062	15	40
Cork rural area	52,106	52,835	104,941	258	667
Dunmanway	3999	3672	7671	162	421
Fermoy rural area	7778	7487	15,265	231	599
Fermoy Town	1092	1178	2270	1	1
Kanturk	7899	7608	15,507	290	752
Kinsale rural area	8491	8582	17,073	126	327
Kinsale Town	1137	1120	2257	0	1
Macroom rural area	7028	6647	13,675	276	714
Macroom Town	1377	1459	2836	4	11
Mallow rural area	9897	9757	19,654	262	678
Mallow Town	3394	3697	7091	3	6
Midleton rural area	10,674	10,459	21,133	172	447
Midleton Town	1821	1977	3798	1	2
Millstreet	3236	2999	6235	117	303
Mitchelstown	3807	3682	7489	76	196
Skibbereen rural area	5554	5302	10,856	181	470
Skibbereen Town	945	1055	2000	2	4
Skull	2044	1965	4009	90	233
Youghal rural area	1961	1846	3807	57	148
Youghal Town	3070	3133	6203	2	5
Total	222,317	225,512	447,829	2899	7508

Local Attractions and Information

Administrative headquarters	Co. Hall, Cork. Tel: 021 427 6891.
Adrigole	Small coastal village on the Beara Peninsula, overlooked by Hungry Hill. It gave its name to a novel by Daphne Du Maurier about local 19th century copper barons the Puxleys (called the Brodericks in the book). Adrigole is where the global ban on CFCs originated, after scientist Sir James Lovelock was sitting in the garden of his holiday home in the summer of 1968 pondering the thick smog that hung over the village. Using a device he had previously invented, Lovelock discovered not only that the smog was indeed industrial pollution, but that it contained a high concentration of CFCs. The first in a worldwide network of stations monitoring atmospheric pollution was established at Adrigole shortly afterwards.
Aghadoe Castle	2 miles (3km) northwest of Killarney. Ruined castle notable for its sheela-na-gig.
Airport	**Cork International Airport** (ORK), located in Ballygarvan to the south of Cork City, is operated by Dublin Airport Authority. The airport was opened in October 1961 and a new terminal building was opened in August 2006. There are scheduled flights to numerous destinations in Great Britain and Europe. 021 431 3131.
Allihies	One of the westernmost settlements in Cork, located near the tip of the Beara Peninsula. In the 19th century it experienced a great influx of Cornish people, brought over to mine the rich veins of copper discovered nearby in 1812.
Annes Grove Gardens	Castletownroche, 9 miles (15km) east of Mallow. A wild garden beside the River Awbeg originally laid out in the early 18th century. It covers 30 acres (12ha) and includes a walled garden, a water garden, a Robinsonian garden in a glen and a riverside garden. The woodlands and riverside walks include rare trees and shrubs plus collections of rhododendrons, magnolias, hoherias and eucryphias. Tel: Tel: 022 26145.
Ardgroom Stone Circle	1 mile (1.6km) east of Ardgroom, 6 miles (10km) north of Castletown Bearhaven. Aka Canfea Stone Circle. An incomplete circle of nine stones ranging in height from 4ft 4in (1.3m) to 6ft 6in (2m).
Ardnagashel House	3 miles (5km) northwest of Bantry. An 18th century house on the shore of Bantry Bay. The surrounding estate features the remains of a plantsman's garden and arboretum established in the early 1800s by Arthur Hutchins, brother of Ellen Hutchins, Ireland's first female botanist.
Ashbourne House and Gardens	Glounthaune, 6 miles (10km) east of Cork. A 6 acre (2.5ha) garden originally laid out in the early 20th century by Richard Henrik Beamish. It features a bog garden and an Irish yew walk with New Zealand cabbage trees interplanted between the yews. There is also an arboretum. The garden was designed under the influence of William Robinson (1838–1935), the Irish gardener and journalist whose ideas about 'wild gardens' spurred the English cottage garden movement, an outgrowth of the Arts and Crafts movement. He advocated planting wild flowers to create a natural look and reacted against formal High Victorian gardening, created using tropical plants grown in greenhouses. Tel: 021 435 3319.
Ballinacarriga Castle	Dunmanway, 15 miles (24km) northeast of Bantry. The ruins of a four-storey tower house probably date to the early 16th century. The top floor was once used as a church and has windows decorated with scriptural subjects, including the Crucifixion. The remains of a bawn and a round tower stand nearby. Tel: 021 427 3251.
Ballincollig Castle	Ballincollig, 5 miles (8km) west of Cork. The ruins of a castle built in the 14th century by the Barrett family. It fell into ruin following the Williamite War of 1689.
Ballingeary	(I. *Béal Atha an Ghaorthaidh*). A Gaeltacht village in the Shehy Mountains, situated on the River Lee and its associated lakes.
Ballybeg Priory	$^{1}/_{2}$ mile (0.8km) south of Buttevant, 5$^{1}/_{2}$ miles (9km) north of Mallow. The ruins of an Augustinian priory founded in the 1230s by Philip de Barry. The remains include the base of the church tower and a nearby two-storey round tower, the lower storey of which forms a dovecot or pigeon house with 300 roosts. Tel: 021 425 5100.
Ballydehob	(I. *Béal an dá Chab* = The Ford at the Mouth of Two Rivers). Small village near a 12-arch viaduct last used by West Cork Rail.
Ballyvourney	(I. *Baile Mhuirne*). A village west of Macroom and part of the Gaeltacht area. Sean O Riada is buried in the graveyard.
Baltimore	Small historic south coast fishing port and yachting centre. In 1631 the village was remarkably attacked by Algerian pirates and more than 100 of its residents were carried off into slavery.
Baltimore Beacon	Baltimore, 6 miles (10km) southwest of Skibbereen. Aka 'Lot's Wife'. A white, bottle-shaped structure overlooking the harbour. It was built by the English after the 1798 rebellion as an early warning beacon and a lighthouse.
Baltimore Castle	Baltimore, 6 miles (10km) southwest of Skibbereen. The ruin of a castle overlooking the harbour. It was historically held by the O'Driscolls, one of the most important clans in West Cork, who controlled fishing in the area and were able to levy dues on all the fishing fleets.
Bandon	The largest town in West Cork. Established by the great Earl of Cork, Richard Boyle, it lies south of the river from Cork, and is sometimes called the 'Gateway to West Cork'. It was on the road from Bandon to Cork that Michael Collins was killed in 1922.
Banteer	A small town in the north of the county. Historically it is associated with the last battle, in 1651, of the Irish Confederate Wars, which took place nearby.
Bantry House and Gardens	$^{1}/_{2}$ mile (0.8km) southwest of Bantry. An 18th century house with collections of tapestries, furniture and art treasures mainly collected by Richard White, 2nd Earl of Bantry. The gardens were also originally laid out by the 2nd Earl and consist of seven terraces including the Hundred Steps, a monumental staircase built of local stone, set amid azaleas and rhododendron. Having fallen into neglect, the gardens have been gradually restored since 1997. In the grounds is the French

Armada Exhibition, which tells the story of the ill-fated expedition led by Wolfe Tone which arrived in Bantry Bay in 1796. The exhibition has a 1:6 scale model of the frigate *Surveillante*, plus a life-sized statue of Wolfe Tone in his cabin. The house was opened to the public in 1946. Tel: 027 50047.

Barleycove A small coastal village with pronounced sand dunes, produced as a result of the tidal wave that swept Europe after the earthquake in Lisbon in 1755.

Barryscourt Castle Carrigtwohill, 4 miles (6km) west of Midleton. The present tower house dates from the 16th century and was the seat of the Barry family. It is surrounded by a largely intact bawn wall and corner towers. The castle has been restored; the main hall and great hall feature an exhibition dedicated to the arts in Ireland from the Norman invasion to the Plantation. Tel: 021 488 2218.

Battles Four battles have been fought in Cork: Kinsale, Knocknaclashy, Knocknanuss and Liscarroll. See separate table for details; see also separate entries for the Battle of Kinsale and the Siege of Dunboy.

Béal na Blath (I. = Mouth of the Flowers). 7 miles (11km) northwest of Bandon. A small village where Irish commander Michael Collins was killed in 1922, when returning from Bandon to Cork.

Bealick Mill Heritage Centre Macroom. A heritage and exhibition centre housed in a former corn mill built in the early 19th century. The water wheel and mill machinery are in working order. Tel: 026 42811.

Beamish & Crawford South Main Street, Cork. The Beamish & Crawford brewery was founded in 1792 by William Beamish and William Crawford, who purchased an existing brewery on a site that had been used for brewing for at least 100 years. In the early 19th century it was the largest brewery in Ireland, until overtaken by Guinness. In 1962 it was purchased by Canadian brewing firm Carling-O'Keefe Ltd, who embarked on a modernisation programme. In 1987, Elders IXL purchased Canadian Breweries (incorporating Carling-O'Keefe); in 1995 the brewery was sold to Scottish & Newcastle. In addition to their own produce, they brew and distribute a number of internationally known brands of beer. Beamish stout is Beamish & Crawford's flagship product. Beamish is similar to two other popular Irish stouts: Guinness and Murphy's. Beamish Red is a sweetish red ale, made to resemble Smithwick's or Murphy's Irish Red, but brewed solely for the export market, being particularly popular in France.

Beara Peninsula A rugged peninsula in southwest Cork, the southernmost of the main peninsulas (Dingle, Iveragh and Beara) in the southwest of Ireland. It is dotted with stone circles, megalithic monuments, Martello towers, Ogham stones, and spectacular coastline and scenery. The Beara Way, a long-distance coastal walking trail which follows the perimeter of the peninsula from Kenmare in Kerry to Glengarriff via Dursey, is 125 miles (201km) long. Half in Kerry and half in Cork, the Ring of Beara links the towns of Glengarriff in Cork with Kenmare in Kerry.

Beenalaght Bween, 7 miles (11km) southwest of Mallow. An alignment of six standing stones.

Blarney Castle Blarney, 5 miles (8km) northwest of Cork. The ruins of a 15th century castle built by Cormac Laidir MacCarthy. The main remains are the large rectangular keep and corner tower. The castle is famous for the 'Blarney Stone', high up on the battlements, the kissing of which is said to bestow the gift of eloquence on the kisser. Legend has it that (after Francis Sylvester Mahony) 'There is a stone that whoever kisses, Oh! he never misses to grow eloquent. 'Tis he may clamber to a lady's chamber, Or become a member of parliament.' In the mid 18th century James St John Jefferyes built a four-storey house on to the castle; this was burned down early in the 19th century and not rebuilt. The nearby Rock Close area has the remains of a dolmen. Tel: 021 438 5252.

Blarney Stone See Blarney Castle

Bohonagh Stone Circle $1\frac{1}{2}$ miles (2.5km) northeast of Rosscarbery, $5\frac{1}{2}$ miles (9km) southwest of Clonakilty. A recumbent stone circle now comprising nine of its original 13 stones. The portal stones stand 8ft (2.5m) high, among the tallest of any stone circle in Ireland.

Bridgetown Priory Castletownroche, 8 miles (13km) northeast of Mallow. The ruins of an early 13th century Augustinian priory founded by Alexander FitzHugh Roche. It fell into decline following the suppression of the monasteries in the 16th century. The main remains are some domestic buildings and a covered passage beside the cloister.

Buttevant A small village in the north of the county. The first ever steeplechase, from the steeple of Buttevant Protestant Church to that of Doneraile, $4\frac{1}{2}$ miles (7km) away, took place here in 1752. The town's Cahirmee Horse Fair is where, according to legend, Napoleon's horse, *Marengo*, was bought.

Buttevant Friary Buttevant, 6 miles (10km) north of Mallow. The ruins of a Franciscan friary founded in 1251 by David Oge Barry and dedicated to St Thomas a Becket. Following its dissolution the friary became the property of the Barry family. The friars stayed in residence until the end of the 18th century.

Cahervagliar Fort Coppeen, $7\frac{1}{2}$ miles (12km) south of Macroom. A bivallate ring fort 115ft (35m) in diameter, dating to c. AD 1000 and believed to have been a chief residence of the Laoighaire clan.

Call of the Sea North Road, Castletown Bearhaven. Local history centre dedicated to the naval and mining history of the Beara Peninsula.

Canfea Stone Circle See Ardgroom Stone Circle

Cape Clear Aka Clear Island, Oilean Chleire. A Gaeltacht area and the southernmost inhabited part of the Republic of Ireland, with a population of around 129. To the southwest stands Ireland's most southerly point, Fastnet Rock. It is also the largest island in Roaringwater Bay, although its eastern and southeastern shores are usually considered Atlantic waters. A bird observatory was established on the island in 1959.

Cape Clear Heritage Centre Cape Clear Island, Skibbereen. Local history centre housed in a converted restored schoolhouse and showcases the economic, social and natural history of the island. Tel: 028 39119.

Carrigaline The main population centre in the Cork Harbour area. It is a bustling satellite town and convenient stopping-off point for both the airport and ferry port. The name means 'rock of lions' in Irish. Famous for its pottery, but its main attraction is the ruined castle situated on a high limestone bluff 1 mile (1.6km) from the centre

Castle Hyde Fermoy, 19 miles (31km) northeast of Cork. Aka Castlehyde. A fine Georgian house located on the River Blackwater and built in 1801 for the Hyde family. It is an historic place: Republican leader Michael Collins used to meet his lover here, Winston Churchill and Fred Astaire visited, and it was once the home of the first Irish President, Douglas Hyde. It is currently owned by dancer Michael Flatley.

Castlelyons Friary Castlelyons, 4 miles (6km) southeast of Fermoy. The ruins of a Dominican friary founded in 1307 by John de Barry. The remains now visible probably date to the 15th century.

Castlemartyr A small town near Midleton in the east of the county. It received its charter in 1675 and is noted for its Carmelite monastery, and for the gardens laid out in the early 19th century by the 4th Earl of Shannon.

Castletown Bearhaven Aka Castletownbere. A busy fishing port on the the Beara Way route. It is the largest whitefish port in Ireland. The Siege of Dunboy took place here in 1602, and it is also the home of the famous McCarthy's Bar, as written about by the late Pete McCarthy in the book of the same name.

Castletownshend A quaint village which provided inspiration for writers Somerville and Ross. The main street is a steep hill, which leads down past the castle to the waterfront. Local attractions include two sycamore trees growing in the roundabout in the centre of the village, St Barrahane's Church and Somerville and Ross Graves. The ancient castle, the walls of which are still visible near the mouth of the harbour, was built by the O'Driscolls, and subsequently belonged to the family of Touchet, of which George Touchet, Lord Audley, who had been governor of Utrecht, and was wounded at Kinsale in 1602 was created Earl of Castlehaven, in 1616.

Cathedral of St Mary and St Anne Roman Street, Cork. The cathedral was dedicated in 1808 and underwent a complete renovation in the 1990s. It is the mother church of the Dioceses of Cork and Ross and is known locally as the North Cathedral or North Chapel. Tel: 021 430 4325.

Charles Fort Summercove, $1^1/_4$ miles (2km) southeast of Kinsale. A huge star-shaped fort with five bastions, designed by William Robinson. Built c.1680, it was garrisoned until 1922. Of the five bastions, two are to seaward (the Devil's and the Charles') and three to landward (the North, the Flagstaff and the Cockpit). During the Williamite War it was surrendered to William III's forces in 1690 after a 13 day siege. Tel: 021 477 2263.

Church of St Anne Shandon Church Street, Cork. Built of red sandstone and limestone in 1722 on the site of earlier foundations, including a medieval church destroyed during the Williamite War. Tel: 021 450 5906.

Clonakilty A small town in the central south of Cork. Known as 'the beach centre of West Cork', it is perhaps best remembered as the birthplace of Michael Collins. A statue of Collins can be found in the town. The town itself was designed in 1641 by the 1st Earl of Cork. Today, Clonakilty is famous for its black puddings.

Cloyne Round Tower Cloyne, 4 miles (6km) southeast of Midleton. The tower stands 100ft (30.5m) high and is a relic of the monastic foundation at Cloyne. It suffered damage by lightning strike in the late 1740s and has been altered since.

Cobh Cobh (pronounced 'cove') is a large estuary town east of Cork. It was formerly called Queenstown (after a visit by Victoria in 1849), and from here many Irish people left for the New World after the Great Famine of the 1840s. It was also from here that the *Titanic* sailed on its fateful journey.

Cobh Heritage Centre Lower Road, Cobh. Local history centre housed in the restored Victorian railway station and telling the story of Cobh from its founding to the present day. Family history resources and a genealogy workshop are also available. Tel: 021 481 3591.

Conna Castle Conna, 8 miles (13km) southeast of Fermoy. Tower house perched on a rock overlooking the Bride River. The residence of Sir Thomas Fitzgerald until his death in 1599, it was later granted to Richard Boyle. Today it is the venue for an annual rock concert, held every June.

Coolclough Church Millstreet, 11 miles (18km) northwest of Macroom. A Gothic style church built in 1833 and designed by local sculptor Charles O'Connell.

Cork City Gaol & Radio Museum Experience Convent Avenue, Sunday's Well, Cork. Housed in the former Cork City Gaol which opened in 1824. It was remodelled in 1870 and was an all-female prison from 1878 until 1922. It closed in 1923 and was allowed to fall into disrepair apart from the top floor of the Governor's House which was used as a radio broadcasting station by Radio Éireann from 1927 until the 1950s. It was restored and opened as a visitor attraction in 1993. Visitors can see what it was like to be incarcerated together with waxworks, furnished cells and sound effects. The former broadcasting room houses the Radio Museum Experience. Tel: 021 430 5022.

Cork Vision Centre North Main Street, Cork. The centre's presentations explore Cork's evolution and development and include a collection of architectural stones. Tel: 021 427 9925.

Courtmacsherry A small village midway between the old head of Kinsale and the Seven Heads on the rugged West Cork coast. It was formerly the summer home of the Earl of Shannon.

Crookhaven A picturesque village with a large sheltered harbour. There are many Bronze Age field monuments in the surrounding hills. Historically it was the last port of call for ships going to and from America. The village also has a scientific claim to fame in that it was here that Marconi attempted to send his first radio message across the Atlantic. The lighthouse is also an attraction.

Desmond Castle Cork Street, Kinsale. Originally built as a custom house in the early 16th century by Maurice Bacach Fitzgerald, 9th Earl of Desmond. It was captured by the Spanish during their occupation of Kinsale in 1601. During the American War of Independence it was used as a prison to house captured American sailors. In 1747, 54 French prisoners were killed in a fire and the castle is locally known as 'The French Prison'. It was declared a National Monument in 1938. Today it houses a wine museum which explores Ireland's wine links with Europe and the wider world. Tel: 021 477 4855.

Desmond Rebellion An uprising against English rule in 1579, led by the Fitzgerald Earl of Desmond and joined by the MacAuliffes under the leadership of their aged chieftain, Malachy. A month later the frail Malachy, further weakened by the rigours of the campaign, died. In January 1580, English forces were joined by the Earl of Ormond, a member of the Butler family, traditional enemies of the Fitzgeralds, in a campaign of vengeance against the Earl of Desmond and his supporters. Clanawley, the land of the MacAuliffes, was not spared, and a terrible war of extermination took place. Men, women and children, including the old and weak and babes in arms, were put to the sword. Those who could sought refuge in the mountains or in the bogs and woods. Homes were burned to the ground, crops destroyed and cattle were driven off to feed the Queen's armies. In 1583 MacDonagh, MacAuliffe, O'Keeffe and O'Callaghan paid their respects to the Earl of Ormond and gave pledges of good behaviour. The Desmond Rebellion ended in 1583 with the treacherous murder of the Earl, by which time Clanawley had been entirely laid waste.

Doneraile Wildlife Park — Turnpike Road, Doneraile. Established on 410 acres (166ha) of parkland landscaped in the 18th century. Features include woodland, water features and a number of deer herds. Tel: 022 24244.

Drishane Castle — Millstreet, 11 miles (18km) northwest of Macroom. Built by the McCarthy clan 1436–50, the castle is situated on a limestone rock on the southern bank of the River Finnow. A prominent and important feature is the tower, commanding a beautiful view of the chain of mountains which, commencing with Claragh, run 19 miles (31km) in an uninterrupted line to Killarney. The Sisters of Infant Jesus operated a very successful boarding school for girls from 1909 until its closure in 1992.

Dromagh Castle — 13 miles (21km) west of Mallow. An O'Keeffe castle boasting impressive ruins with four circular towers 50ft (15m) high guarding a square court. The O'Keeffes, having been driven westwards from Fermoy, also established fortified homes at Ahane, Ballymaquirk and Cullen. In 1651 Lord Muskery marched out of Dromagh Castle for the famous Battle of Knocknaclasy where the last hope for the Confederate Irish was quenched. It is now in the possession of the O'Leary family.

Dunboy, Siege of — The Siege of Dunboy took place in the aftermath of the Battle of Kinsale, from 5 to 18 June 1602. The stone tower house of Dunboy Castle was a stronghold of Donal Cam O'Sullivan Beare, a Gaelic clan leader and the 'Chief of Dunboy'. O'Sullivan was part of a confederation of Gaelic leaders who had rebelled against Elizabeth I of England. After the defeat at Kinsale O'Sullivan resolved to continue the fight and rallied his forces at Dunboy. Taking possession of his castle, which was garrisoned by a small force of Spanish troops, he kept all of their arms, ordnance and munitions, and immediately strengthened the castle in readiness for the inevitable assault. He left a force of 143 of his best men to defend the castle in his absence under the charge of Captain Richard MacGeoghegan and Friar Domenic Collins. The Crown sent a 5000 strong army under the command of Sir George Carew, Lord President of Munster, to suppress the resistance. But before the siege got under way, O'Sullivan himself and most of his forces had already marched to another of his fortresses, Ardea Castle, on the northern coast of the Beara Peninsula, in order to secure money and supplies that had just arrived by ship from Spain. Carew began the siege with a fierce artillery bombardment by land and sea. One of O'Sullivan's cousins, Owen O'Sullivan of Carrignass, who had allied himself with Carew, then informed Carew of a weak point in the castle walls at a stairwell. Carew directed his bombardment to that point, and the walls were eventually breached. By the tenth day of the assault, the castle had been reduced to ruins, and final defeat seemed certain. MacGeoghegan sent a messenger to Carew requesting a surrender, and Carew responded by hanging the messenger in sight of the defenders. Certain of their fate, some swam to nearby Dursey Island, where they were murdered or captured in the water; the remaining defenders repelled another assault and sealed themselves in the cellar of the castle. During the siege, Crown forces raided nearby Dursey Island, where O'Sullivan families resided. Men were burned in the church, and women and children were thrown from the cliff. The assault continued relentlessly until on the 11th day the castle cellar was finally overrun amid desperate hand-to-hand fighting. MacGeoghegan was hacked to pieces by Captain Power as he attempted to ignite the powder stores and blow up the cellar. All but three of those captured during the siege were hanged in the market square in nearby Castletown Bearhaven. Friar Domenic Collins was interrogated by Carew, who demanded he renounce his faith for propaganda purposes prior to execution. The other two were hanged on failing to give information, and Fr Collins was taken to Youghal where he was hanged, having held firm under torture. After Dunboy fell, O'Sullivan went on a campaign of guerrilla warfare around West Cork, taking at least six castles. Faced with overwhelming odds and starvation, he set out on a tough march to join his allies in the north of Ireland, with 1000 men, women and children in his train ('O'Sullivan's March'). O'Sullivan's people were besieged by enemies and the elements throughout the long journey. On their arrival at the refuge of O'Rourke's castle in Leitrim, only 35 remained, many having died in battles or from exposure and hunger. Others had settled along the route, where their descendants are known to this date as 'the Beres'. In Leitrim, O'Sullivan sought to join with other northern chiefs to fight the English and organised a force to this end, but resistance ended when the Earl of Tyrone successfully sued for peace and swore an oath of loyalty to the Crown. O'Sullivan declined this option and sought exile in Spain, where he was later murdered.

Dunboy Castle — 1 mile (1.6km) southwest of Castletown Bearhaven. A seat of the O'Sullivan family, built to control and defend the harbour of Bearhaven. See Battles.

Dundanion Castle — Blackrock, Cork (I. = The Strong Fortress). Located on a large rock overlooking the Marina in Cork Harbour. The Irish name indicates that a fort, probably belonging to the O'Mahony family, stood on the rock, perhaps before AD 800. The castle appears to have been built in the 16th century by the Galways, an influential family in the life of the city at that time. It is clearly marked as 'Galwaies castle' in a map of the city of 1585. William Penn, the Quaker, sailed from Dundanion on his first voyage to America in 1682 on his way to found the state of Pennsylvania. Dundanion Castle is the only true castle remaining within the city area. Dundanion Castle was taken over by the Board of Works in the 1980s.

Dursey Island	An island off the southwestern tip of the county, home to many colonies of nesting birds and a variety of ancient stones. It is joined to the mainland by cable car at Dursey Sound. Population: 6.
Fastnet Rock	Aka Carraig Aonair (I. = 'Lonely Rock'). The southernmost point of Ireland. It has the nickname 'Ireland's Teardrop'. The lighthouse is the highest in Ireland. The Fastnet race is considered one of the classic offshore yachting races. It takes place every two years over a course of 608 miles (970km); competitors begin off Cowes, sailing to the Fastnet Rock, which they round, and then back to Plymouth via the south side of the Isles of Scilly. The prize is known as the Fastnet Challenge Cup. The first Fastnet race, with seven entries, was won by *Jolie Brise* in 1925. The race was part of the Admiral's Cup racing series from 1957 to 1999. Storms during the 1979 race resulted in the deaths of 17 competitors. The race drew further attention from outside the sport in 1985 when the maxi-yacht *Drum* capsized after her experimental keel sheared off. Pop star Simon Le Bon, co-owner and crew member of *Drum*, was trapped under the hull with five other crew members for 20 minutes, until being rescued by the Royal Navy.
Fermoy	A large town located towards the east of the county in the centre of the lush Blackwater Valley. It developed around a Cistercian abbey founded in 1170.
Fota House	Fota Island, 6 miles (10km) east of Cork. A large Regency house dating from the mid 1820s and incorporating an earlier hunting lodge. The house was previously briefly opened to the public in 1893 and was restored 1999–2001. The Fota Arboretum and Gardens cover 27 acres (11ha); in addition to a selection of rare specimen trees, other features are an ornamental pond, a restored Victorian orangery, fernery and walled pleasure gardens. Tel: 021 481 5543.
Fountainstown House	Fountainstown, south of Cork. An 18th century stately home.
Garinish Island	Aka Ilnacullin (Island of Holly). An island covering 37 acres (15ha) near Glengarriff, noted for its Italian garden (designed by Harold Peto) and its Martello tower.
Glanworth Castle	Glanworth, 5 miles (8km) northwest of Fermoy. A Norman castle located on a cliff of rock alongside the River Funcheon and built in 1197. Within the bawn are the remains of a square gate tower. Excavation uncovered a sheela-na-gig in one of the vaulted ground floor chambers. The village of Glanworth has a 12-arch 15th century bridge.
Gougane Barra National Forest Park	Ireland's first National Forest Park, opened in 1966. It covers 350 acres (140ha), the main tree species being lodgepole pine, Sitka spruce and Japanese larch, many of which were first planted in 1938.
Highest point	Knockboy (I. *An Cnoc Bui* = Yellow/Golden Hill) in the Shehy Mountains at 2321ft (705m), located on the border with Kerry.
Hungry Hill	$5^1/_2$ miles (9km) northeast of Castletown Bearhaven. Located above Adrigole, on the Beara Peninsula, at 2250ft (686m), the hill is the highest point of the Caha Mountains.
Inniscara Lake	7 miles (11km) west of Cork. Created in 1956 on the River Lee by the construction of two hydroelectric generating stations, one in Carrigadrohid and the other at Inniscarra Lake. The lake covers 1310 acres (530ha) and is noted for its fishing, particularly bream.
Innishannon	A picturesque village immortalised by Alice Taylor in books such as *To School Through the Fields*. I understand her family still tends the local market and post office. A Monterey cypress tree growing in the village is said to have the widest girth (39ft/12m) of any tree in Ireland.
Interesting facts	The **Cork Butter Market** opened in 1770 and continued trading for 150 years. It brought great wealth to Cork. The gates of the market opened at 6am every weekday morning. From then on all the nearby streets were busy with horse-drawn carts bringing butter to the market or carrying it away to the local factories and waiting steamers on the quays. The salted butter was brought to the market in wooden caskets called firkins. All butter firkins were made of oak, sycamore or good hardwood. The very best casks in the country were Cork-made ones, and these were compulsory for butter going to tropical parts of the world. Butter was brought by cart from West Cork and Kerry along routes known as butter-roads. After the closure of the Butter Exchange the building housed a hat factory. Derelict for a long period after being devastated by fire, today the circular building has been restored as an arts and performance centre. It is now known as the Firkin Crane Building. Cork Harbour lays claim to being the second largest natural harbour in the world (Port Jackson, Sydney, being the largest). Despite extensive investigations with Cork Co. Council I have been unable to gauge exact dimensions of either coastline or acreage of water to compare it with Poole Harbour in Dorset, which makes a similar claim. I can only say for certain that Cork Harbour is the largest harbour in Ireland and Poole is the largest in England. The town of **Cobh**, located on Great Island (aka Oilean Mor an Barraigh), was the last port of call for the ill-fated *Titanic* which sank after hitting an iceberg on Sunday 14 April 1912. Ironically, the ship dropped off nine passengers but picked up a huge shipment of ice! **RMS *Lusitania*** is also part of Co. Cork history. When the ship was sunk by German submarine U-20 on 7 May 1915 the rescue efforts were coordinated out of Kinsale. A statue in Kinsale harbour commemorates this night. **Robert Emmet** was an Irish nationalist rebel leader who led an abortive rebellion against British rule in 1803. Following a failed attempt to seize Dublin Castle, the rising degenerated into confusion and general rioting and Emmet fled into hiding but was captured on 25 August near Harold's Cross, having endangered his life by moving his hiding place from Rathfarnham, Co. Dublin, so that he could be near his sweetheart, Sarah Curran. He was tried for treason on 19 September; the Crown repaired the weaknesses in its case by secretly buying the assistance of Emmet's defence attorney, Leonard Macnally, for £200 and a pension. On 20 September Emmet was executed by hanging and beheading in Dublin. His remains were then secretly buried. After he had been sentenced Emmet delivered a speech (the so-called Speech from the Dock), which is especially remembered for its closing sentences and secured his posthumous fame among the pantheon of Irish Republican martyrs: 'Let no man write my epitaph; for as no man who knows my motives dares now vindicate them, let not prejudice or ignorance asperse them. When my country takes

	her place among the nations of the earth then and not till then, let my epitaph be written.' The 38th **Eurovision Song Contest** was held in Cork (at Millstreet) in 1993 and was won by Niamh Kavanagh with 'In Your Eyes'. The small village of **Ballinspittle**, close to Kinsale, became notorious in the mid 1980s when locals claimed to have witnessed a statue of the Blessed Virgin Mary moving of its own accord. Another small village, **Ballinascarthy**, between Bandon and Clonakilty, is the birthplace of the father of motor car pioneer Henry Ford.
Islands	See separate table
James Fort	$^{1}/_{2}$ mile (0.8km) southeast of Kinsale. The ruins of a fort built in 1602 on a promontory on the west side of Kinsale Harbour. It lies across the estuary from Charles Fort.
Jameson Heritage Centre	Distillery Walk, Midleton. Housed in the Old Midleton Distillery, the home of Jameson Irish whiskey. The restored industrial complex includes an operational water wheel and the largest pot still in the world. Tel: 021 461 3594.
Kanturk Castle	Kanturk, 11 miles (18km) northwest of Mallow. Built c.1601 by Dermod MacOwen MacDonagh but never completed. The large four-storey rectangular house with four large square corner flankers is noted for its many well-preserved fireplaces.
Kilcolman Castle	8 miles (13km) north of Mallow, 2$^{1}/_{2}$ miles (4km) northeast of Buttevant. The residence in Ireland of Sir Edmund Spenser, who served as secretary to Sir Arthur Grey, Lord Deputy of Ireland, from 1580 until the end of his life in 1599. Here Spenser worked on his great epic, *The Faerie Queene* (Sir Walter Raleigh visited Kilcolman in the late 1580s and reports that Spenser was composing the poem at the time, but he also is known to have worked on it at Lismore Castle Gardens across the border in Co. Waterford). Parts of this great epic poem, particularly Book V, 'Justice', can be seen as allegorical depictions of the need for a sterner rule of Ireland by the English. Spenser's prose work *A View of the Present State of Ireland* (written in the early 1590s), was a clear call for a militant conquest of Ireland. Spenser's castle was destroyed and he was driven back to England during the Irish revolts in the 1590s; only a small shell remains, in the midst of a farmer's field and a bird sanctuary.
Kilmichael Ambush	A major turning point in the battle for Irish independence. It took place on 28 November 1920, 36 Irish Republican Army volunteers killed 17 auxiliaries of the Royal Irish Constabulary on a road near the village of Kilmichael, south of Macroom. The incident resulted in massive British reprisals including the burning of the city of Cork.
Kinsale	A picturesque resort on the southwest coast of Ireland. Situated to the west of Oysterhaven at the mouth of the Bandon River, the town was the scene of an historic battle. In the 17th and 18th centuries Kinsale was an important English naval base. The town is steeped in nautical history: in 1703, the 90 tonne *Cinque Ports* sailed from the port with Alexander Selkirk on board. The town is widely regarded as the gourmet capital of the south; the Kinsale Gourmet Festival is held every October.
Kinsale, Battle of	In September 1601 a Spanish force of 5300 men, with some artillery, landed at Kinsale. Spanish help had been eagerly awaited for some time, and they were quickly joined by Hugh O'Neill and Red Hugh O'Donnell. On his way south O'Donnell passed through Clanawley. There is a tradition that the MacAuliffes took part in the battle. Although there is no documentary evidence, knowing the history of the clan and judging by subsequent events, it seems likely that they would not have missed this chance to strike another blow at English tyranny. On Christmas Eve 1601 the Irish army deployed itself on open ground where it was no match for the English cavalry and in a short time the battle was lost. The Spanish quickly sought terms.
Knocknakilla	6 miles (10km) northwest of Macroom. A complex of megalithic monuments on the slopes of Musherabeg mountain and including a recumbent stone circle, a standing stone 5ft 6in (1.6m) tall, a cairn and a dolmen.
Leap	A small village whose main claim to fame is in the sphere of horse racing. Its Central Track is used for trotting and sulkey racing.
Lios-na-gCon Ringfort	Darrara, 2 miles (3km) east of Clonakilty. A 10th century defended farmstead, restored on the basis of excavations carried out 1987–9. Reconstructions include a souterrain (underground chamber) and a thatched central round house. The site is within the grounds of Clonakilty Agricultural College. Tel: 087 785 2238.
Liscarroll Castle	Liscarroll, 10$^{1}/_{2}$ miles (17km) northeast of Mallow. Built c.1280 and said to be the third largest 13th century castle in Ireland. A very large keep and four towers survive.
Lisselan House	Lisselan, 2$^{1}/_{2}$ miles (4km) northeast of Clonakilty. A French chateau style house designed by Lewis Vulliamy and built 1851–3 for William Bence-Jones. The surrounding 30 acre (12ha) garden was laid out in Robinsonian style in the 1850s to enhance the natural features of the Argideen valley. Features include a rockery, rhododendron garden, water garden, azalea garden, shrubbery and fuchsia garden. Tel: 023 33249.
Lough Hyne	4 miles (6km) southwest of Skibbereen. Said to be Europe's largest seawater lake. It has a depth of up to 360ft (110m) and is rich in marine fauna.
Macroom Castle	Castle Street, Macroom. An early 13th century castle possibly occupied by the Carew family and later by the McCarthys. It was also once the property of Admiral Sir William Penn, father of the founder of Pennsylvania. All that remains of the castle is the gateway or castle arch in the centre of the town.
Mallow Castle	Bridewell Lane, Mallow. A mansion built in 1689 by the Jephson family beside the River Blackwater. It replaced a late 16th century house and bawn built by Sir Tomas Norreys on the site of an earlier Desmond fortress, and which was abandoned shortly after its capture in 1645 by Lord Castelhaven. The ruins of both earlier castles are still visible.
Midleton	A large town in the southeast corner of the county. Midleton derives its name from *Mainistir na Corann*, 'the abbey of the Coir'. Its main association is with whiskey, and according to some tales

	Midleton is where whiskey production began in Ireland. The town is home to the largest distillery in Ireland, which began life as a woollen mill in 1796 but was converted to a whiskey distillery in 1820 by the Murphy Brothers. See also Jameson Heritage Centre
Millstreet Country Park	11 miles (18km) northwest of Macroom. A country park with 500 acres (200ha) of lakes, waterfalls, streams, wetlands.
Mizen Head Peninsula	The most southerly peninsula in the southwest of Ireland. An area of rugged beauty. Mizen Head itself is Ireland's most southwesterly point; the Fastnet Rock Lighthouse can be seen in the distance.
Model Village	A small village 10 miles (16km) west of Cork, also known as Dripsey.
Muskerry	One of the county's two Gaeltacht areas (Cape Clear being the other), where Irish is spoken as the main language.
Myrtle Grove	William Street, Youghal. This Elizabethan mansion was the home of Sir Walter Raleigh when he was Mayor of Youghal and tradition has it that here he smoked the first cigarette. Perhaps more certainly, the first potatoes in Ireland were planted in the gardens of Myrtle Grove in 1585.
National Michael Collins Memorial Statue	Clonakilty. A monument to the 'Big Fella', unveiled by Liam Neeson on the 80th anniversary of Collins' death on 22 August 2002.
North Cathedral	See Cathedral of St Mary and St Anne
Rath Luirc	A town near the border with Limerick and formerly known as Charleville, after Charles II. It is historically associated with the milk and cheese industry and is the current home of Golden Vale Co-operative Creameries, one of the largest milk processing and cheese-making concerns in Ireland.
Ring of Beara	See Beara Peninsula
Ringaskiddy	A small fishing village southeast of Cork City. The Martello tower built in 1804 can still be visited.
Rivers	The **Blackwater**, sometimes called the Munster Blackwater, rises 4 miles (6km) from Ballydesmond on the slopes of Knockanefune mountain in the Mullaghareirk Mountain Range on the border of Cork and Kerry, and flows east through Mallow and Fermoy before entering Co. Waterford where it flows through Lismore, before turning south at Cappoquin, and finally draining into the sea at Youghal Harbour. Its total length is 104 miles (167km). Some of the tributaries that feed this river provide good fishing for brown trout, although the Blackwater itself is renowned as an excellent salmon water with an international reputation for good fishing. The River Bride, which joins the Blackwater south of Cappoquin, holds stocks of sea trout in its lower reaches. The **Lee** (An Laoi) is a sandstone river which rises in the Shehy Mountains, near Gouganbarra on the western border of Co. Cork, and flows eastwards through Macroom and Cork City, where it splits in two for a short distance and empties into the Celtic Sea at Cork Harbour on the south coast. Its total length is approximately 56 miles (90km). A hydro-electric scheme was built on the river in 1956, just west of Cork City, and this dammed off part of the river now contains the Carrigadrohid and Inniscarra reservoirs. The Lee and its tributaries, the Sullance and Laney, drain a catchment area of some 484 square miles.
Rosscarbery	A small picturesque town on the Celtic Sea overlooking a sandy inlet of the rugged West Cork coastline. It grew up around a monastery established by St Fachtna in the late 6th century.
Royal Cork Yacht Club	Crosshaven, 9 miles (15km) southeast of Cork. Reputedly the oldest yacht club in the world, established in 1720 by William O'Brien as the Water Club of the Harbour of Cork.
Royal Gunpowder Mills	Ballincollig, 4 miles (6km) west of Cork. An industrial complex covering 130 acres (53ha) along the bank of the River Lee. Established in 1794 by Charles Henry Leslie, the mills were bought by the British Board of Ordnance during the Napoleonic Wars and continued to produce gunpowder until 1903. The visitor centre closed in 2002 but the Regional Park is open to the public and many of ruins associated with the gunpowder manufacture can be seen.
St Brendan the Navigator	St Brendan of Clonfert (c. AD 484–c. 578), called 'the Navigator' or 'the Voyager', was born near Tralee. According to Irish lore he was the first person to discover America. A statue to him can be found at Bantry.
St Coleman's Cathedral	Cloyne, 4 miles (6km) southeast of Midleton. A Church of Ireland parish church in the Diocese of Cork, Cloyne and Ross.
St Colman's Cathedral	Cathedral Place, Cobh. A Roman Catholic cathedral built 1868–1915 in Gothic Revival style by E W Pugin and George Ashlin. In 1916 a carillon of 47 bells was installed, the largest bell being 200ft (60m) above the ground and weighing $3^1/_2$ tons. The cathedral has been undergoing restoration since the early 1990s.
St Fachtna's Cathedral	Rosscarbery, 7 miles (11km) southwest of Clonakilty. The present cathedral was built in 1612, replacing a 12th century church which stood on the site of a 6th century monastic foundation. It was restored following the 1641 rebellion, while further restoration work took place in the late 19th century.
St Fin Barre's Cathedral	Bishop Street, Cork. A three-spired cathedral located at the centre of Cork and named after the city's patron saint. The present cathedral was built 1862–79 to a Gothic Revival design by William Burges, and was consecrated in 1870. It is adorned with more than 1200 sculptures. There have been at least two previous cathedral buildings on the site: the medieval church was damaged during the Williamite Wars and a smaller building was incorporated into the remaining structure in 1735. These buildings were demolished to make way for the present cathedral. Tel: 021 496 3387.
Shanagarry	A small village that was home to the founder of Pennsylvania, William Penn. Today it is perhaps best known as the location of Darina Allen's Ballymaloe cookery school and gardens and Ballymaloe House.
Shandon Steeple	Church Street, Cork. Located on the city's north side, the most famous landmark in the city. Shandon (Sean Dun) means 'old fort'. The steeple is 170ft (52m) high with walls 7ft (2.1m) thick.

The present 'pepper pot' shaped tower was built in 1722, using sandstone from the old Shandon Castle and the limestone from the Franciscan abbey which was located on the North Mall. The limestone faces limestone country to the south and west, while the northern and eastern sides face sandstone country. A local rhyme says: 'Parti-coloured like its people, Red and white stands Shandon Steeple.' At the steeple's highest point is a weather vane in the form of a fish. Almost 13ft (4m) long and gilded, it is commonly known among Cork people as 'the goldy fish'. A fish was chosen because of the importance, at the time, of the salmon industry on the River Lee. Within the tower are housed the famous Bells of Shandon. They were cast in Gloucester, England, in 1750 and first rang out over the city on 7 December 1752. The bells weigh over 6 tons. Also within the tower is the famous clock, known as the 'Four Faced Liar' because the minute hands on the east and west faces gain on their companions on the north and south faces, although complete agreement is reached again on the hour. The clock was a gift to the Lord Mayor and Corporation in 1847 and is still maintained by them. It weighs $2^1/_2$ tons and the dials are almost 16ft (5m) in diameter. Inscribed on the clock are the following words of wisdom: 'Passengers measure your time; For time is the measure of your being.'

Sheep's Head — A rugged peninsula to the south of Bantry Bay. The Sheep's Head Way is a noted walking route of 55 miles (88km) around the majestic peninsula.

Sherkin Island — Aka Inis Earcain. Located northeast of Clear Island, off the southwest coast of Cork. The second-largest island in Roaringwater Bay, it features the ruins of a Franciscan friary, founded in c.1460 by the O'Driscoll family for the Franciscan Friars of Strict Observance, as well as a 13th century O'Driscoll castle and an Iron Age fort. Population: 129.

Skibbereen Heritage Centre — Upper Bridge Street, Skibbereen. Housed in the restored former Gasworks Building. There are two main exhibitions, one exploring the Great Famine Exhibition and the other explaining the unique nature of Lough Hyne, a salt water marine lake which was Ireland's first Marine Nature Reserve. Tel: 028 40900.

Sport

football — **Cobh Ramblers** were founded in 1922 and were winners of the FAI League of Ireland 1st Division in 2007. The first team of Roy Keane, their home ground is St Colman's Park, Cobh.

Cork City were founded in 1984, although a previous team with the same name existed in the 1930s. They are winners of the League of Ireland in 1993 and 2005. Their home ground is Turner's Cross, Cork.

Gaelic football — **Cork** were winners of the GAA All-Ireland Senior Football Championship in 1892, 1911, 1945, 1973, 1989 and 1990.

horse racing — **Cork Racecourse**, Mallow, was founded in 1924 as Mallow Racecourse, and was renamed in 1997. The right-handed track of $1^1/_2$ miles (2.5km) stages both National Hunt and Flat racing. Tel: 00353 022 50207/50210.

hurling — Cork were winners of the GAA All-Ireland Senior Hurling Championship in 1890, 1892, 1893, 1894, 1902, 1903, 1919, 1926, 1928, 1929, 1931, 1941, 1942, 1943, 1944, 1946, 1952, 1953, 1954, 1966, 1970, 1976, 1977, 1978, 1984, 1986, 1990, 1999, 2004 and 2005.

rugby union — **Munster Rugby** were founded in 1879 and represent the Munster division of the Irish Rugby Football Union. They are 22 times winners of the Irish Inter-Provincial Championship and winners of the Heineken Cup in 2006 and 2008. They play at Musgrave Park, Cork, and Thomond Park, Limerick.

Stags of Toe Head — Three very conspicuous rocks lying 4 miles (6km) from the entrance of Castlehaven harbour in the Celtic Sea. The broad promontory of Toe Head is less than 1 mile (1.6km) away.

Templebryan Stone Circle — $1^1/_4$ miles (2km) north of Clonakilty. The circle originally consisted of nine stones, of which four upright stones and one fallen stone remain.

Timoleague Friary — Timoleague, $5^1/_2$ miles (9km) northeast of Clonakilty. The ruins of a Franciscan friary founded in 1240 by the MacCarthys.

Tynte's Castle — North Main Street, Youghal. A 15th century urban tower house built by the Walsh family and owned in the late 16th century by English soldier and administrator Robert Tynte.

Union Hall — A small fishing village close to Castletownshend. It still has a holy well dedicated to St Brigid which is an annual place of pilgrimage in February. The village was used as a location for the film *War of the Buttons* (1994).

West Cork Heritage Centre — North Main Street, Bandon. Housed in Christ Church, built in 1610 and reputedly the first church built in Ireland for Protestant worship. It was deconsecrated in 1973 and now has an exhibition charting the history of Bandon with recreations of an old shop, schoolhouse, forge and kitchens. Tel: 023 41677.

West Cork Regional Museum — Western Road, Clonakilty. A local history museum housed in a former Methodist school, and has exhibitions relating to the political history of the area from 1800 with particular reference to Michael Collins and Tom Barry. There are also displays about the postal service and the GAA. Tel: 023 33115.

Whiddy Island — Located off Bantry Bay. The small permanent population are mainly farmers and fishermen. An anchor from the French Armada force of December 1796 was discovered off the northeast point of the island in 1980. Whiddy is the main petroleum terminus for Ireland. Population: 29.

Wolfe Tone Square — Bantry. Named after Theobald Wolfe Tone (1763–98), a leading figure in the United Irishmen. Captured while on board a French ship in Lough Swilly (see Donegal) on 12 October 1798, he took his own life following an illness after being sentenced to death for his part in the 1798 Rebellion. A statue of Tone stands in the square.

Some famous people born in County Cork

Allen, Denis 'Dinny' (Gaelic footballer) (1952–)	Cork
Ashlin, George (architect) (1837–1921)	Little Island
Barry, James (painter) (1741–1806)	Cork
Cantwell, Noel (footballer) (1932–2005)	Cork
Collins, Michael (soldier and politician) (1890–1922)	Clonakilty
Cunningham, Ger (hurling player) (1961–)	Cork
Doyle, Jack (actor, boxer and singer) (1913–78)	Cobh
Driscoll, Patricia (actress) (1927–)	Cork
Elmore, Alfred (painter) (1815–81)	Cork
Ireland, Stephen (footballer) (1986–)	Cobh
Irwin, Denis (footballer) (1965–)	Cork
Keane, Roy (footballer) (1971–)	Mayfield
Kingston, Mary (TV presenter) (1970–)	Inchdoney
La Rue, Danny (entertainer born Daniel Patrick Carroll) (1927–)	Cork
Lynch, Jack (4th Taoiseach of Ireland) (1917–99)	Cork
Lynch, Joe (actor) (1925–2001)	Mallow
Maclise, Daniel (painter) (1806–70)	Cork
Magnier, John (racehorse breeder) (1948–)	Fermoy
Maguire, Sam (Gaelic footballer) (1879–1927)	Dunmanway
Mahony, Francis Sylvester (writer 'Father Prout') (1804–66)	Cork
Mulhare, Edward (actor) (1923–97)	Carrigaline
Murphy, Cillian (actor) (1976–)	Douglas
O'Brien, Vincent (racehorse trainer) (1917–)	Churchtown
O'Callaghan, Pat (athlete) (1906–91)	Kanturk
O'Connor, Frank (author as Michael O'Donovan) (1903–66)	Cork
O'Farrell, Frank (football manager) (1927–)	Cork
Ó'Riada, Seán (composer born John Reidy) (1931–71)	Cork
O'Sullivan, Sonia (athlete) (1969–)	Cobh
Scott, Patrick (artist) (1921–)	Killbrittain
Trevor, William (author) (1928–)	Mitchelstown

Islands of County Cork

(shipping area = Fastnet)

Island name	**Area**	**Nearest landmark**	**General information**
Adam's Island	Glandore Harbour	Glandore	Craft entering Glandore Harbour obey the saying 'avoid Adam, hug Eve', referring to the deeper waters surrounding neighbouring Eve's Island.
Aghillaun	Roaringwater Bay	Skibbereen	A tiny islet off the northeast coast of Spanish Island.
An tOilean Mor	Bantry Bay	Castletown Bearhaven	aka Bear Island, Mor or Bere Island. Rerrin is the 'capital'. There are two Martello towers on the island. Population: 207.
Ballycotton Island	Ballycotton Bay	Ballycotton	Known locally as Outer Island.
Bark Island	Glengariff Harbour	Glengariff	Small lumpy island full of rhododendron and fern.
Bear Island	Bantry Bay	Castletown Bearhaven	See An tOilean Mor
Bere Island	Bantry Bay	Castletown Bearhaven	See An tOilean Mor
Bridaun Beg	Coulagh Bay	Inishfarnard	Lies between Bridaun Mor and Inishfarnard.
Bridaun Mor	Coulagh Bay	Inishfarnard	Usually referred to simply as Bridaun.
Bull Rock, The	Atlantic	Dursey Head	Appears as a pyramid with a lighthouse on top from the direction of Dursey.
Bullock Island	Lough Hyne	Barloge	Lough Hyne is the only inland sea lake in Europe.
Cable Island	Youghal Bay	Knockadoon Head	aka Capel Island. Owned by the Marquess of Thomond.
Calf Island East	Roaringwater Bay	Skibbereen	One of the three Calves Islands.
Calf Island Middle	Roaringwater Bay	Skibbereen	Largest of the Calves Islands.
Calf Island West	Roaringwater Bay	Skibbereen	Smallest of the Calves Islands.
Calf, The	Atlantic	Dursey Head	There is a red iron pillar on the Calf, the stub of a lighthouse destroyed in 1881.
Cape Clear	Roaringwater Bay	Baltimore	aka Clear Island, Oileán Chléire
Capel Island	Youghal Bay	Knockadoon Head	See Cable Island
Carbery Island	Dunmanus Bay	Dunmanus	Largest of the islands in Dunmanus Bay.
Carraig Aonair	Atlantic	Baltimore	(I. = Lonely Rock). See Fastnet Rock
Carrogoona Rocks	Roaringwater Bay	Skibbereen	Lies off Sherkin Island.

Island name	Area	Nearest landmark	General information
Carthy's Islands	Roaringwater Bay	Skibbereen	aka The Carthys. Scattered group of four tiny islets sometimes referred to by compass point designations. North Island was formerly grazed by sheep.
Castle Island	Lough Hyne	Barloge	Site of ruins of O'Driscoll's Castle.
Castle Island	Roaringwater Bay	Coosheen Point	Situated due west of Horse Island, the island holds the ruins of an O'Mahony castle.
Catalogues, The	Roaringwater Bay	Skibbereen	Group of five small islands.
Chapel Island	Bantry Bay	Bantry	Owned by the Duke of Devonshire.
Clear Island	Roaringwater Bay	Baltimore	See Cape Clear
Clonard Rock	Youghal Bay	Clonard	Lies just off the coast and accessible at low tide.
Cold Island	Dunmanus Bay	Dunmanus	The remotest and smallest of the group of islands in Dunmanus Bay.
Coney Island	Roaringwater Bay	Coosheen Point	Small ungrazed privately owned island with a refurbished holiday home.
Cow, The	Atlantic	Dursey Head	The island lies midway between Dursey Head and The Bull Rock.
Dinish Island	Bantry Bay	Castletown Bearhaven	Joined to mainland by a bridge.
Dursey Island	Atlantic	Garinish Point	See separate entry
Eve's Island	Glandore Harbour	Glandore	See Adam's Island
Eyeries Island	Coulagh Bay	Ardacluggin Point	Coulagh Bay is known locally after this island.
Fastnet Rock	Atlantic	Baltimore	aka Carraig Aonair. See separate entry
Fota Island	Cork Harbour	Carrigtohill	aka Foaty. Joined by bridge to Carrigtohill and Great Island. It is host to Ireland's only wildlife park. Population: 188.
Furze Island	Dunmanus Bay	Dunmanus	Almost as large as Carbery Island.
Garanboy Island	Glengariff Harbour	Glengariff	See Murphy's Island
Garinish Island	Bantry Bay	Bantry	See separate entry
Garinish Island	Garinish Bay	Garinish Point	One of two islands of the same name in County Cork.
Garvillaun	Glengariff Harbour	Glengariff	Sister island of Ship Island, lying to its southeast.
Globe Rocks	Roaringwater Bay	Skibbereen	Lies close to Sherkin Island.
Goat Island (Great)	Roaringwater Bay	Coosheen Point	Twin island of Little Goat Island (Beg)
Goat Island (Little)	Roaringwater Bay	Coosheen Point	Twin island of Great Goat Island (Mor)
Great Island	Cork Harbour	Cork	aka Oilean Mor an Barraigh
Gull Rock	Atlantic	The Bull Rock	Tiny rock lying just off The Bull Rock.
Hare Island	Roaringwater Bay	Skibbereen	aka Heir, Inis Ainghin. Famous for the cuisine of its restaurant, Island Cottage. Population: 27.
Hare Island	Roaringwater Bay	Skibbereen	aka Inishodriscol. Population: 27.
Haulbowline	Cork Harbour	Cork	There is a Martello tower on the island, which is joined to the mainland on its southern side by a road bridge from Paddy Blocks to Rocky Island near Ringaskiddy. Population: 75.
Hawlbowling	Cork Harbour	Cork	Site of one of the 16 military stations of Cork.
Heifer, The	Atlantic	The Calf	Half the size of its neighbour The Calf.
Heir	Roaringwater Bay	Skibbereen	See Hare Island
High Island	Celtic Sea	Myross	Lies southeast of its smaller neighbour, Low Island.
Hog Island	Bantry Bay	Bantry	Owned by the Duke of Devonshire.
Holy Island	River Lee	Gougane Barra	Linked to the shore by a causeway.
Horse Island	Roaringwater Bay	Skibbereen	Lies due east of Castle Island. Population: 3.
Horse Island	Bantry Bay	Bantry	Owned by the Duke of Devonshire.
Horse Island	Celtic Sea	Castletownsend	Lies south of Castlehaven harbour.
Horse Island	Dunmanus Bay	Dunmanus	One of four islands of the same name in County Cork.
Illanabeg	Atlantic	Garinish Point	Joined to Dursey Island at low water.
Illaunameania	Coulagh Bay	Ardacluggin Point	Coulagh Bay is also known as Eyeries Bay.
Illauninagh East	River Lee	Ballingeary	aka Oilean Eidhneach Thoir
Illauninagh West	River Lee	Ballingeary	aka Oilean Eidhneach Thiar
Ilnacullin	Bantry Bay	Bantry	See Garinish (The Near Island).
Inchydoney	Clonakilty Bay	Clonakilty	Population: 134.
Inis Ainghin	Roaringwater Bay	Skibbereen	See Hare Island
Inis Earcain	Roaringwater Bay	Baltimore	See Sherkin Island
Inis Fada	Roaringwater Bay	Coosheen Point	See Long Island
Inishbeg	Baltimore Harbour	Skibbereen	Population: 13.

Island name	Area	Nearest landmark	General information
Inishfarnard	Coulagh Bay	Kilcatherine Point	Formerly inhabited; the abandoned houses remain.
Inishleigh	Roaringwater Bay	Skibbereen	The island is grazed by cattle which cross over from the mainland at low tide.
Inishodriscol	Roaringwater Bay	Skibbereen	See Hare Island
Jeremy Island	Roaringwater Bay	Skibbereen	Rocky islet with traces of purple moor-grass.
Kedge Island	Celtic Sea	Baltimore	Rocky islet 2 miles (3km) east of the southern entrance to Baltimore Harbour.
Long Island	Roaringwater Bay	Coosheen Point	aka Inis Fada. Third largest island in the bay (Sherkin and Cape Clear are larger). Population: 12.
Long Island	Garinish Bay	Garinish Point	One of two islands of the same name in County Cork.
Lousy Rocks	Roaringwater Bay	Skibbereen	Tiny rock stacks off Sherkin Island.
Low Island	Celtic Sea	Myross	Lies just northwest of its larger neighbour, High Island.
Mannin	Roaringwater Bay	Skibbereen	Grazed by sheep and rising to just 65ft (20m).
Mannin Beg	Roaringwater Bay	Skibbereen	Small satellite islet of Mannin.
Minane Island	Bantry Bay	Castletown Bearhaven	Situated 0.6 miles (1km) east of Dinish Island.
Murphy's Island	Glengariff Harbour	Glengariff	aka Garanboy Island. Owned by actress Maureen O'Hara.
Oileán Chléire	Roaringwater Bay	Baltimore	See Cape Clear
Oilean Eidhneach Thiar	River Lee	Ballingeary	aka Illauninagh West
Oilean Eidhneach Thoir	River Lee	Ballingeary	aka Illauninagh East
Oilean Mor an Barraigh	Cork Harbour	Cork	aka Great Island
Outer Island	Ballycotton Bay	Ballycotton	aka Ballycotton Island
Quarantine Island	Roaringwater Bay	Skibbereen	There is a small saltmarsh on the eastern side of the island.
Rabbit Island	Celtic Sea	Myross	The island is inhabited by wild horses, burros, chough and linnet. Otters have been seen on the west side and also at the Stack of Beans on the east side.
Ringarogy	Baltimore Harbour	Skibbereen	aka Rinn Ghearroige. Population: 88.
Rinn Ghearroige	Baltimore Harbour	Skibbereen	See Ringarogy
Rocky	Cork Harbour	Cork	Site of one of the 16 military stations of Cork.
Sandy Cove Island	Kinsale Harbour	Kinsale	The island is grazed only by goats.
Sandy Island	Roaringwater Bay	Skibbereen	Despite its name there is no sand on the heathy grassland of the island.
Sherkin Island	Roaringwater Bay	Baltimore	See separate entry
Skeam East	Roaringwater Bay	Skibbereen	Twin island of Skeam West.
Skeam West	Roaringwater Bay	Skibbereen	Twin island of Skeam East.
Small Island	Ballycotton Bay	Ballycotton	Known locally as Inner Island. One of the Ballycotton Islands.
Sovereign Rocks	Celtic Sea	Kinsale	The rocks lie off Sandy Cove Island.
Spanish Island	Roaringwater Bay	Skibbereen	Aghillaun Pool is a mangrove swamp on the east of the island.
Spike Island	Cork Harbour	Cork	Site of one of the 16 military stations of Cork. Population: 61. A bridge to the mainland is planned.
Stags	Celtic Sea	Toe Head	See separate entry
Whiddy Island	Bantry Bay	Bantry	See separate entry

DONEGAL

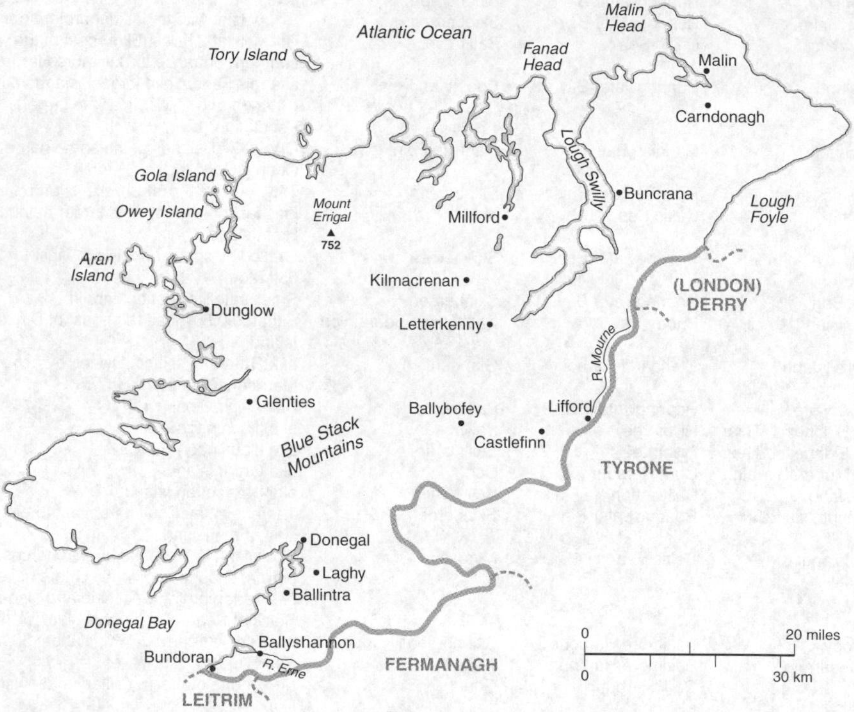

Atlantic Ocean
Tory Island
Malin Head
Fanad Head
Malin
Carndonagh
Lough Swilly
Gola Island
Owey Island
Mount Errigal
752
Millford
Buncrana
Lough Foyle
Aran Island
Kilmacrenan
(LONDON) DERRY
Dunglow
Letterkenny
R. Mourne
Glenties
Ballybofey
Lifford
Blue Stack Mountains
Castlefinn
TYRONE
Donegal
Laghy
Ballintra
Donegal Bay
Ballyshannon
Bundoran
R. Erne
FERMANAGH
LEITRIM
0
20 miles
0
30 km

County Donegal is the most northerly county of the Republic of Ireland. Part of the province of Ulster, it was one of the three counties in the province not incorporated in Northern Ireland under the provisions of the Government of Ireland Act (1920). It is bounded to the west and north by the Atlantic Ocean and shares a 6 mile (10km) border with County Leitrim in its extreme south and a combined 87 mile (140km) border with the Northern Ireland counties of Derry, Tyrone and Fermanagh. Possibly because of this it has a distinct sense of separateness from the Republic of Ireland. Donegal has a large Gaeltacht area – an area where the Irish language is officially the major language spoken. The area includes Arranmore, Gweedore, Glencolmcille and Tory Island.

Physically the centre of the county is dominated by the Derryveagh Mountains and the Bluestack Mountains, which form the Hills of Donegal. The county's major rivers are the Erne and the Foyle, which forms the boundary with County Derry. It includes the peninsulas of Inishowen and Fanad.

County Donegal was settled from at least 3500 BC and many Bronze Age circles and tombs are evident in the countryside. The county's early recorded history was dominated by the Ui Neill and its three branches the Cenel Conaill, Cenel Eogain and Cenel Enna, dynasties founded by sons of Niall of the Nine Hostages. The major part of modern Donegal was held by the Cenel Conaill, the leading family or clan being the O'Donnells. Indeed, the county was known for many centuries as Tir Conaill (the land of Conall). The Cenel Conaill remained rivals of the O'Neills, who retained some presence in the county. Colmcille (St Columba), born at Gartan in AD 521, was a member of the Cenel Conaill.

County Donegal was subject to invasion and settlement by both the Vikings and the Normans but Tir Conaill was effectively ruled by the O'Donnell clan from the early 13th century until the beginning of the 17th. Eventually, faced with the strength of Anglo-Norman ambitions, the O'Donnells and the O'Neills combined forces and rose in rebellion, only to be defeated at Kinsale in 1601. The end of the Gaelic order was marked by the 'Flight of the Earls' (Hugh O'Neill, 2nd Earl of Tyrone, and Rory O'Donnell, 1st Earl of Tyrconnell) from Rathmullan in September 1607. As with the rest of

Ulster, the county was subject to the Plantation, at which time Tir Conaill (Tyrconnell) was renamed County Donegal.

The Plantation saw the division of the county into areas settled by Scots, English and Irish natives. New families such as the Brookes, Murrays, Conollys and Cunninghams rose to prominence as landlords. Donegal was affected by the Great Famine and the population dropped by more than 40,000 in the decade following 1841, but the consequences were mitigated by the long coastline which encouraged an increase in fishing activity. However, emigration saw the population fall from 237,395 in 1861 to 173,722 in 1901.

The county's economy is largely dependent on agriculture but Donegal is Ireland's most important sea fishing county. The tourism sector also provides employment and income. The county's administrative headquarters are in Lifford and its largest town is Letterkenny. Other notable towns and villages include Ardara, Ballybofey, a market town on the south bank of the River Finn opposite Stranorlar, which stands on the north bank in the Finn Valley, Ballyshannon, Buncrana, Bundoran, Burtonport, Donegal Town, Glenties, Greencastle, a fishing port at the entrance to Lough Foyle and the location of the National Fisheries College, Killybegs, a prosperous fishing port on the north side of Donegal Bay which hosts an annual sea angling festival each July, and Rathmullan.

County Donegal's favourite sons and daughters include guitarist Rory Gallagher, singers Enya and Daniel O'Donnell, and Irish international goalkeepers Packie Bonner and Shay Given.

Donegal	**Population**			**Area**	
Districts	*male*	*female*	*total*	*sq miles*	*sq km*
Ballyshannon	2965	3002	5967	64	165
Buncrana	1688	1732	3420	2	4
Bundoran	806	872	1678	1	4
Donegal	5904	5779	11,683	248	642
Dunfanaghy	5663	5472	11,135	198	512
Glenties	9415	9110	18,525	414	1076
Inishowen	14,309	14,099	28,408	341	884
Letterkenny rural area	7387	7424	14,811	157	406
Letterkenny Town	3692	4273	7965	2	5
Millford	6047	5730	11,777	175	454
Stranorlar	11,140	11,066	22,206	274	708
Total	69,016	68,559	137,575	1876	4860

Local Attractions and Information

Administrative headquarters	County House, Lifford, Co. Donegal. Tel: 074 917 2222.
Airport	**Donegal Airport** (CFN), Carrickfinn, Kincasslagh, Letterkenny. Originally a grass landing strip until the 1980s. Flights operate to Dublin and Glasgow Prestwick. Tel: 074 954 8284.
An tSean Bheairic	Main Street, Falcarragh. A visitor resource centre in the market town of Falcarragh celebrating the language, culture and heritage of the region. It is housed in what was originally built in 1890 as the Falcarragh Police Barracks. There is a permanent exhibition in the barracks, which became a Garda station in 1920. Tel: 074 918 0888.
Aranmore	(I. *Árainn Mhór*). Aka Aran Island. An island off the Donegal coast which was first settled in the Iron Age. One of the Rosses group, it is the second largest island off Ireland. Population (2002): 543.
Ardara Heritage Centre	Ardara, 14 miles (23km) northwest of Donegal. Celebrates the history of Donegal tweed from the 19th century. Exhibits include models, photographs and artefacts. The town hosts an annual weavers' fair. Tel: 075 41704.
Ardnamona Gardens	4 miles (6km) northeast of Donegal. Located beside Lough Eske. Ardnamona means 'height of the bog' and this garden was a wilderness prior to the building of Ardnamona House in the 1830s. The pinetum was planted at the same time and rhododendrons in the 1890s. Having been allowed to return to wilderness from the mid 1950s until new owners began a programme of restoration and conservation in 1990, the garden was designated a National Heritage Garden in 1991. Tel: 074 972 2650.
Ards Forest Park	3 miles (5km) southeast of Dunfanaghy, 25km) northwest of Letterkenny. A forest park covering 1200 acres (480ha) on the shores of Sheephaven Bay, and encompassing saltmarsh, fenland and a beach as well as four ring forts and a holy well. The main broadleaf species are sessile oak, ash, birch and rowan and the conifers include Sitka spruce, Scots pine and Corsican pine.
Ballymagroarty Heritage Centre	6 miles (10km) south of Donegal. Celebrates the history of Ballymagroarty monastery, founded by St Patrick in the 5th century and reconsecrated by St Columba in 540. Tel: 074 973 4966.

Ballyshannon	A town on the River Erne, often claimed to be the oldest town in Ireland. It hosts an annual folk and traditional music festival.
Ballyshannon Falls	1/2 mile (0.8km) east of Ballyshannon. The Cathleen Falls (aka Assaroe Falls) on the River Erne were in existence prior to the building of a dam in the 1950s in order to power a hydroelectric station. Assaroe Lake, which covers 1100 acres (445ha), was also created by the scheme.
Battles	See separate table for details of the Battles of Farsetmore and Scarrifholis (or Letterkenny).
Beltany Stone Circle	1 1/4 miles (2km) south of Raphoe, 8 miles (13km) southeast of Letterkenny. Sometimes known as the 'Stonehenge of Donegal', this megalithic monument stands on Tops Hill. The circle is 145ft (44m) in diameter with 64 stones remaining out of possibly as many as 80. The stones have an average height of 6ft (1.8m). There is a tumulus inside the circle. The monument was left in poor condition following poorly carried out excavation in the early 20th century.
Bocan Stone Circle	1 mile (1.6km) south of Culdaff, 16 miles (26km) northeast of Buncrana. A stone circle with seven stones in situ out of the original 12. Excavations in 1816 revealed graves and burial pots within the circle.
Bonny Glen Lough Wood	2 miles (3km) southwest of Narin, 16 miles (26km) northwest of Donegal. A mixed broadleaf and conifer wood beside Bonny Glen Lough. The main tree species include birch, hazel, larch, oak and lodgepole pine.
Buncrana	A town on the Inishowen Peninsula, standing on the River Crana on the eastern shore of Lough Swilly. The second largest town in Co. Donegal, it has hosted an annual music festival since 1992.
Buncrana Castle	Buncrana. The ruins of an early 17th century castle by the River Crana. It is believed that it was to Buncrana Castle that Wolfe Tone was taken after his capture in 1798. It stands next to O'Doherty's Keep. Tone was captured aboard the French warship *Hoche* after a fierce fight against an English fleet off Lough Swilly. From Buncrana Castle he was taken to Dublin where he was sentenced to hang but slit his throat before execution could be carried out.
Bundoran	A seaside resort on Donegal Bay, formed from villages on either side of the River Bradog when the railway arrived in the 1860s. At one time known as the 'Brighton of Ireland', it hosted the European Surfing Championships in 1997.
Burt Castle	1 1/2 miles (2.5km) north of Newtown Cunningham, 10 miles (16km) northeast of Letterkenny. The ruin of a 16th century castle located on private land on a hill beside the Derry–Letterkenny road. In 1588 it was garrisoned against a landing by the Spanish Armada, and in the early 1600s it was in the hands of Henry Dowcra and then the O'Doherty family. After they were dispossessed following the rebellion of 1608 it passed to the Chichesters. Garrisoned by English troops at least until the end of the 17th century, it was abandoned and in disrepair by the early 19th century.
Burtonport	The port for the ferry to Arranmore. It was the site of a landing by French forces under Irishman James Napper Tandy (1740–1803) on 16 September. Their stay was cut short after they heard of the failure of General Humbert's expedition.
Cairn Visitor Centre	Drumaweir, Greencastle. Opened in 1999, the centre explores the history of this area of Ireland from ancient times to the present day. The peoples covered include the Celts and the Vikings, and the stories of the Plantation and the Famine are also told. Tel: 074 938 1104.
Carrickabraghey Castle	Doagh Island, Inishowen. The ruins of a pre-17th century coastal castle possibly built by Phelemy Brasleigh O'Doherty. It was abandoned in the 1650s. Tel: 074 936 2600.
Cavanacor House	2 miles (3km) west of Lifford. Early 17th century house, the birthplace in 1634 of Magdalene Tasker. Magdalene grew up to marry another native of Donegal, Robert Pollock, after which they emigrated to America and shortened their name to Polk. In 1845 their great-great-great-grandson James Knox Polk became the 11th President of the United States. The Cavanacor Gallery, opened in 1999 in the grounds, has regular exhibitions of established and promising artists both from Ireland and from around the world.
Colmcille Heritage Centre	1/2 mile (0.8km) northwest of Church Hill. Located on the shore of Lough Gartan, the centre celebrates the life of St Columba (Colmcille), who is said to have been born in Gartan c. AD 521. Tel: 074 913 7306.
Corveen Castle	See Lough Eske Castle
Creeslough Church	Creeslough, 13 1/2 miles (22km) northwest of Letterkenny. The Catholic Church of St Michael the Archangel was opened in August 1971. Its striking design by Liam McCormick mirrors the outline of nearby Muckish Mountain. It replaced the Doe Chapel, built in 1784, and closed the day the new church opened.
Doagh Island Visitor Centre	Doagh Island, Inishowen. An outdoor museum and visitor centre telling the story of the effects of the Great Famine and land clearances on the people of Inishowen. Exhibits include a recreated famine village, wake house, hedge school, mass rock and eviction scene. Tel: 074 937 8078.
Doe Castle	2 miles (3km) northeast of Creeslough, 13 1/2 miles (22km) northwest of Letterkenny. A 16th century four-storey tower house standing on a promontory in Sheephaven Bay. Protected on three sides by steep cliffs and on the landward side by a moat, it was the seat of the MacSuibhe (MacSweeney) family. In 1606 it was granted to Sir Basil Brooke and was occupied for a short time by Sir Cahir O'Doherty during the rebellion of 1608. Captured by Cromwellian forces in 1650, after the Restoration the castle was garrisoned by English troops before returning to the MacSweeneys for a short time during the Williamite Wars. It was restored in the late 18th century and occupied until the early 20th century, after which it fell into disrepair. Taken into state care in 1922, it was renovated in the 2000s.
Donagh Cross	Carndonagh, 11 miles (18km) northeast of Buncrana. Aka St Patrick's Cross, Carndonagh Cross. Standing outside Donagh Church and dating from the 7th century, the stone cross was carved with a combination of Celtic and Christian design, although it has suffered from the effects of erosion. It is one of the earliest Christian crosses found outside mainland Europe.
Donegal Abbey	Quay Street, Donegal. The ruins of a Franciscan abbey located beside the River Eske and

founded by Nuala O'Donnell, the wife of Red Hugh O'Donnell. The friary fell into disrepair after the Reformation. See also Four Martyrs Memorial

Donegal Ancestry Centre The Quay, Ramelton, 6 miles (10km) northeast of Letterkenny. The official family history research centre for Co. Donegal. An exhibition charts the geography and history of the area. Tel: 074 915 1266.

Donegal Castle Castle Street, Donegal. A 15th century castle built by the O'Donnell family beside the River Eske. Hugh O'Donnell burnt the castle to the ground in 1607 rather than leave it for the English. Subsequently rebuilt and remodelled by Sir Basil Brooke, it had fallen into disrepair by the 18th century and passed into state care in 1898. It has recently been restored.

Donegal County Museum High Road, Letterkenny. Opened in 1987 and housed in the former Letterkenny Workhouse. Exhibits cover all aspects of the history of Donegal from ancient times to the present day. Tel: 074 912 4613.

Donegal Railway Heritage Centre Tyrconnell Street, Donegal Town. The headquarters of County Donegal Railway Restoration, opened in 1995 and housed in the restored old station house. The centre has a working model railway, static models, railway artefacts, photographs, and a steam train driving simulator. Restoration of County Donegal Railway rolling stock, including Class 5 steam locomotive *Drumboe*, is carried out on site. Tel: 074 972 2655.

Donegal Town Located on the site of a settlement at the mouth of Donegal Bay possibly founded by Vikings and which later became the seat of the O'Donnell family. Following the Flight of the Earls the modern town was laid out by the Brooke family in the early 17th century. The market square, known as The Diamond, was laid out by Sir Basil Brooke and is located at the convergence of the Killybegs, Ballyshannon and Ballybofey roads.

Donegals See Interesting facts

Drumboe Castle $^1/_4$ mile (0.4km) north of Ballybofey. The ruins of a 16th century castle by the River Finn demolished to make the car park for Drumboe Wood. On 14 March 1923 four Republican soldiers (Timothy O'Sullivan, Charles Daly, John Larkin and Daniel Enright) were executed by Free State forces near the woods beside Drumboe Castle.

Drumboe Woods $^1/_4$ mile (0.4km) north of Ballybofey. A mixed broadleaf and conifer wood covering 55 acres (22ha) beside the River Finn. Species include ash, beech, oak, hazel, and Sitka and Norway spruce. There is a bluebell display in spring.

Fintown Railway Fintown, 16 miles (26km) southwest of Letterkenny. A heritage railway operating for 3 miles (5km) along the shore of Lough Finn on part of the former County Donegal Railway, closed in 1959. The Comhlacht Traenach na Gaeltachta Lair (Central Train Society) narrow gauge railway was reopened in 1995 with 2$^1/_4$ miles (3.5km) of track from Fintown Station relaid by volunteers. The opening day was 3 June 1995, 100 years after the original track was opened. The rolling stock is a Simplex 102T locomotive and three Belgium tramcars. It is planned ultimately to extend the line to Glenties. 074 954 6280.

Flight of the Earls Heritage Centre Rathmullan, 11 miles (18km) northeast of Letterkenny. A heritage centre charting the story of the Flight of the Earls (Hugh O'Neill, 2nd Earl of Tyrone, and Rory O'Donnell, 1st Earl of Tyrconnell) from Rathmullan in September 1607. No one knows why the earls left in such haste for Spain leaving behind their worldly goods. In fact they only reached France before eventually ending their days in Rome. The centre is housed in the Battery, a restored Martello tower originally built in 1812 to thwart a possible French invasion. Tel: 074 915 8131.

Fort Dunree Military Museum 5$^1/_2$ miles (9km) northwest of Buncrana. Opened in 1986 and housed in a fort originally erected on the west side of the Inishowen Peninsula after the capture of Wolfe Tone in 1798 in order to deter further French attempts at invasion through Lough Swilly. Enlarged and modernised in the late 19th century, it was handed over to the Irish government in 1938. The museum charts and recreates the history of the fort. Artefacts are housed in the fort's underground bunkers. Tel: 074 936 1817.

Four Masters Memorial The Diamond, Donegal. A 25ft (8m) high memorial erected in 1937 and dedicated to Michael O'Clery, Peregrine O'Clery, Fearfasa O'Mulconry and Peregrine O'Duigenan, known as the Four Masters. They transcribed the *Annals of the Kingdom of Ireland* or the *Annals of the Four Masters*, compiled in Irish 1632–6 at the Franciscan monastery in Donegal Town. The annals chronologically record the history of Ireland between c. AD 550 and 1616, giving the dates of important events and births and deaths of significant people, both religious and secular. Manuscript copies of the *Annals* are kept in Trinity College Dublin, the Royal Irish Academy and University College Dublin.

Franciscan Friary Centre of Peace and Reconciliation Rossnowlagh, 7 miles (11km) southwest of Donegal. A Franciscan friary overlooking Donegal Bay which opened in the 1950s. The friary and its gardens, which include a plantation of 12,000 trees, seeks to promote peace and reconciliation between people of all faiths. The friary also houses the Donegal Historical Museum, which opened in 1954. Tel: 071 985 1342.

Glebe House and Gallery 1 mile (1.6km) northwest of Church Hill, 8 miles (13km) northwest of Letterkenny. A Regency house set in 10 acres (4ha) of woodland gardens on the shore of Lough Gartan. The gallery features works by 20th century Irish and international artists including Kokoschka, Picasso and Jack Butler Yeats. It is based around the collection of English portrait and landscape painter (Arthur) Derek Hill (1916–2000). Tel: 074 913 7071.

Glenevin Waterfall 1$^1/_4$ miles (2km) west of Clonmany, 9 miles (15km) north of Buncrana. A waterfall situated in the Glenevin Valley and falling 30ft (9m) into a pool known as Pohl-an-eas (the Ferment Pool).

Glenveagh Castle 4$^1/_2$ miles (7km) northwest of Church Hill, 15 miles (24km) northwest of Letterkenny. A Scottish baronial style country house built in the 1870s by George Adair and now the centrepiece of Glenveagh National Park. The gardens cover 10 acres (4ha) and are particularly noteworthy. They include a pleasure garden joined to a walled garden by the Belgian Walk, so called because it was laid down in 1915 by convalescing Belgian soldiers. Other features include an Italian garden, a Swiss Walk and a View Garden. The house was purchased in 1937 by Henry P McIlhenny (1910–86), philanthropist, socialite and chairman of the Philadelphia Art Museum. Andy Warhol once described him as 'the only person in Philadelphia with glamour' and during his ownership of Glenveagh Castle he was noted for entertaining the likes of Greta Garbo, Clark Gable and Charlie Chaplin on the estate. McIlhenny gifted the castle and gardens to the Irish nation in the 1980s.

Glenveagh National Park — 11 miles (18km) northwest of Letterkenny. Located in the Derryveagh Mountains and covering more than 64 sq miles (165 sq km) with habitats including mountain, glen, forest and lake. It was created from the estate of John Adair, who cleared the land of tenants on the 1860s. The Glenveagh Estate was purchased by the state in 1975 and the park was opened in 1986. It encompasses the peaks of Errigal and Slieve Snacht, oak and birch forest and also Lough Veagh. The park has the largest herd of red deer in Ireland and golden eagles were reintroduced in 2000. Glenveagh Castle stands at the heart of the park.

Greencastle — Greencastle, 19 miles (31km) northeast of Buncrana. The meagre ruins of an early 14th century Norman tower house on the bank of Lough Foyle. It was possibly built by Richard de Burgo. There is also a Martello tower beside the ruin.

Greencastle Fort — Greencastle, 19 miles (31km) northeast of Buncrana. A Martello tower built c.1800 to defend the entrance to Lough Foyle against attack during the wars with France. It has a sister tower across the lough at Magilligan in Co. Derry. The tower has been converted into a restaurant.

Grianan of Aileach — 13 miles (21km) northeast of Letterkenny. An impressive circular stone fort (cashel) built in the 6th century on the site of an Iron Age bank and ditch defensive system. It stands at the entrance to the Inishowen Peninsula. The fort has a diameter of 70ft (21m); the walls, 15ft (4.5m) high and 12ft (3.5m) thick, contain chambers and stairways. It was the seat of the Uí Néill family and was said to have been destroyed by Murtogh O'Brien, king of Munster, in the early 12th century. It was reconstructed in the 1870s by Dr Bernard.

Highest point — Mount Errigal at 2467ft (752m), the tallest peak of the Derryveagh Mountains.

Horn Head — A peninsula on Sheephaven Bay, designated a Special Area of Conservation and with a wide range of habitats. The cliffs reach a maximum height of 680ft (207m) and there is also a dune system, machair, and a lake (Port Lough). The cliffs support breeding colonies of seabirds including razorbill, guillemot, kittiwake and fulmar.

Inishowen — The largest peninsula in Ireland, with Lough Swilly to its west and Lough Foyle on its east. In its earliest history it was a separate political entity from Tir Conaill (Tyrconnell).

Inishowen Lighthouse — 5 miles (8km) northeast of Greencastle, 22 miles (3km) northeast of Buncrana. A lighthouse established on the west point of Inishowen in 1837. A sister lighthouse at the east point was built at the same time. In 1871, in order to distinguish it from the east light, the height of the west lighthouse was raised by 25ft (8m) by building an iron superstructure on top of the original stone base. The east light was discontinued in 1961; the west light was automated in 1979.

Inishowen Maritime Museum — Greencastle, 19 miles (31km) northeast of Buncrana. A museum and planetarium housed in the old coastguard station near the Lough Foyle ferry landing. It features exhibits on the Malin Head Radio Station, the Drontheim boat (a fishing boat design whose name is a corruption of the Norwegian port of Trondheim), sea captains, 19th century rocket carts, the Irish Navy, the wreck of *La Trinidad Valencera*, the war in the Atlantic and emigration from Ireland. The Inishowen Maritime Memorial outside the museum was unveiled in 1997 and commemorates those from the area who have lost their lives at sea.

Interesting facts — **Donegals** are high quality hand-woven rugs and carpets. The company which produces them was established in 1898 by Alexander Morton, who opened a factory in the village of Killybegs. The factory closed in 1987, but was reopened in 1999 after the villagers of Killybegs petitioned the Irish government to save it. It is now the only place in the British Isles where hand-knotted carpets are still made. **Malin to Mizen** is Ireland's equivalent of Land's End to John O'Groats. From Malin in Donegal to Mizen in Co. Cork is 289 miles (466km) as the crow flies, although a straight line path is impossible, passing as it does over the sea. The most frequent route between Ireland's most southerly and northerly points covers a distance in excess of 400 miles (640km). **Ramelton**, a small port on Lough Swilly, is home to Ireland's oldest Presbyterian church, built in 1680. On **Friday 13** June 2003 a boat full of contestants for the RTE reality television show *Cabin Fever* hit the rocks off Tory Island and sank, causing a lengthy postponement of filming. Fortunately there were no fatalities. **Glenties**, a town at the meeting of two glens from the Bluestack Mountains, is a five times winner of Ireland's 'Tidy Towns' competition. Killygordan-born newspaper publisher **Hugh McLaughlin** (1918-2006) also had a flair for inventiveness, his most famous example is the water hog, originally designed to remove water from cricket pitches and putting greens but now used at other sporting venues such as Gaelic football stadiums where it has proved very successful.

Ionad Cois Locha — Dunlewey, 16 miles (26km) west of Letterkenny. A visitor centre and farm museum on the shore of Dunlewey Lough including a preserved weaver's cottage.

Iosas Centre — Derryvane, 2 miles (3km) southwest of Muff, 7 miles (11km) southeast of Buncrana. A visitor centre with an attached Celtic Prayer Garden depicting the lives of Ireland's early saints. A foundation of the Columba Community established by Fr Neal Carlin in 1981, the garden has representations of the Cross of Patrick, the Boat of Brendan, the Island of Columba and the Oratory of Canice. The garden covers 8 acres (3ha) and is intended as a place for peace and reflection. Tel: 074 938 4866.

Isaac Butt Heritage Centre — Cloghanbeg, 11 miles (18km) southwest of Letterkenny. Dedicated to Isaac Butt, founder in 1874 of the Home Rule League, subsequently known as the Irish Parliamentary Party, and to Dr Nancy

	McGlinchey. It opened in 1998 and is housed in the old Brockagh National School in Cloghan, built in the 1920s. Butt also founded the *Dublin University Magazine.* There are exhibitions on his life and on the educational system in Glenfin. Other exhibits include agricultural tools and equipment. Tel: 074 913 3108.
Islands	See separate table
Kilclooney Dolmen	Kilclooney, 4 miles (6km) north of Ardara. A striking example of a portal tomb with 6ft (1.8m) tall erect stones supporting a capstone 13ft (4m) long by 20ft (6m) wide. A smaller collapsed dolmen close by may have been enclosed within the same cairn.
Killaghtee Art Gallery and Model Heritage Museum	Dunkineely, 10 miles (16km) west of Donegal. Opened in 1995 and housed in Killaghtee House, the gallery displays the work of the owner, Robin Atkinson. The museum depicts the archaeology of the area in model form. Tel: 073 37453.
Knockalla Fort	6 miles (10km) northwest of Rathmullan. A Martello tower and fort overlooking Lough Swilly, built in 1810 during the Napoleonic Wars. It was restored during the 1960s and 1970s and is not open to the public.
Letterkenny	The town of Letterkenny, situated on the River Swilly, is the biggest in Co. Donegal and also boasts the longest main street in Ireland. The Letterkenny Festival is held annually in August.
Letterkenny Institute of Technology	Port Road, Letterkenny. A third level institution serving Donegal and the northwest of Ireland. It awards Higher Certificates, bachelors' degrees and honours degrees in Business, Computing, Design, Engineering, Nursing and Science.
Lifford	Situated on the River Foyle, Lifford is the county town of Donegal and the seat of Donegal County Council. The Lifford Bridge connects it to Strabane in Co. Tyrone in Northern Ireland on the opposite bank of the Foyle.
Lifford Old Courthouse	The Diamond, Lifford. Built 1746–50 to a design by Mick Priestley and now a museum and visitor centre. Exhibitions explore the history of the courthouse and the famous trials which took place here. The courthouse basement houses models of infamous local criminals. A separate county gaol was opened in 1793 but the courthouse continued to hold trials until 1938, after which it was allowed to fall into disrepair. At the end of the 1980s a community-led effort saw its restoration and it reopened as the visitor centre in 1994. Tel: 074 914 1733.
Lough Derg	9 miles (15km) southeast of Donegal. A lake 2200 acres (890ha) in area. The numerous islands on the lough include Station Island (see separate entry), a major place of pilgrimage. There is another, larger Lough Derg in Co. Clare.
Lough Eske	Lough Eske covers 900 acres (365ha) at the foot of the Blue Stack Mountains and is the source of the River Eske. There are several small islands in the lough, one of which was reportedly used by the O'Donnell family to hold prisoners. Fish species in the lough include brown and sea trout.
Lough Eske Castle	3 miles (5km) northeast of Donegal. Aka Corveen Castle. A large Elizabethan style mansion on the shore of Lough Eske, built by the Brooke family in 1861 on the site of earlier mansion. The two-storey house has a four-storey square tower. The earlier mansion had an acrobatic figure, similar to that in the Nun's Chapel, Clonmacnoise, etched into the walls of its coach house. Severely damaged by fire in 1939, it was restored in 2007 as a luxury hotel.
Lough Foyle	A sea lough bordering Co. Donegal and Co. Derry in Northern Ireland. Its area is 69 sq miles (179 sq km), with an average depth of 16ft (5m). It is fed by the Rivers Foyle, Faughan and Roe. Fishing in the lough includes salmon fishing and mussel dredging. It is an important site for migrating birds, attracting flocks of whooper swan and light-bellied brent goose. There is an RSPB nature reserve extending from Longfield Point to border the Roe Estuary National Nature Reserve. Other water fowl include red-breasted merganser and eider; waders include bar-tailed godwit and golden plover.
Lough Swilly	A long sea lough 25 miles (40km) in length. To its east is the Inishowen Peninsula and to the west lies the Fanad Peninsula. It is fed by the rivers Swilly, Lennan and Crana. Part of the lough is a Special Area of Conservation; an important site for waterfowl in autumn and winter with species including curlew, dunlin, mallard, oystercatcher, redshank, shelduck and wigeon, it also supports a population of otter plus common and grey seals. There is also a growing aquaculture industry including the farming of Pacific oysters, blue mussels and Atlantic salmon. Historically Lough Swilly has featured in several important episodes of Irish history including the Flight of the Earls in 1607 and the defeat of a French fleet in 1798. The lough was used by the Royal Navy in World War I and was one of the Treaty Ports agreed in the Anglo-Irish Treaty. There are many wrecks in or near the lough, the most famous probably being that of *Laurentic*, a White Star liner built at the Harland & Wolff shipyard in Belfast and launched in 1908. She sank after striking two submerged mines off the entrance to the lough on 25 January 1917 with the loss of 354 lives. The fact that she was carrying 32 tonnes (3200 bars) of gold, of which 22 tonnes were still unrecovered after a seven year operation by the Royal Navy, means that she remains a mecca for divers. Her other claim to fame is that in July 1910 she was used by Scotland Yard to outpace another liner, the *Montrose*, carrying Dr Crippen across the Atlantic. Crippen was arrested on his arrival in Montreal.
Malin Head	17 miles (27km) north of Buncrana. The most northerly point in Ireland. A tower standing on Banba's Crown, and built in the early 20th century as a Lloyds Signal Station, later housed the Malin Head Wireless Station. The promontory gives its name to the surrounding Sea Area, as used in shipping forecasts.
Malin to Mizen	See Interesting facts
Mary from Dungloe International Festival	Dungloe, 25 miles (40km) west of Letterkenny. An annual festival established in 1968 and inspired by the traditional ballad 'Mary from Dungloe'. Held over ten days, the main features of the festival are street music, concerts and sporting competitions. The festival culminates with the selection of

the 'Mary' for the year. Irish communities from around the world are invited to select a candidate to represent them in the competition.

Napoleonic Anchor Donegal. An anchor retrieved from Donegal harbour after it was cut away by the sailors of the French ship *Romaine*, which had arrived in the hope of supporting the 1798 Rebellion. On finding that the uprising had failed and being menaced by English forces, the anchor chain was cut and the ship beat a hasty retreat. The anchor is on display on the quayside.

Neds Point Fort $^{1}/_{2}$ mile (0.8km) northwest of Buncrana, 16 miles (26km) northeast of Letterkenny. A battery built in 1799 to defend Lough Erne from French fleets during the Napoleonic Wars. It was remodelled in 1897.

New Lake Dunfanaghy, 18 miles (29km) northwest of Letterkenny. A freshwater lake formed in the early 20th century when a tidal inlet was blocked by blown sand dunes. Managed as a wildfowl sanctuary, it is also designated a Special Protection Area and supports nationally important wintering populations of Greenland white-fronted goose and barnacle goose.

Newmills Complex Churchill Road, Letterkenny. A mill complex on the River Swilly, including a corn mill and a flax mill. Some of the buildings date from the 17th century. The mills were in use until the 1980s and were taken into state care in 1986. Tel: 074 912 5115.

O'Doherty's Keep Buncrana, 16 miles (26km) northeast of Letterkenny. The ruins of a tower house in Swan Park beside the River Crana and Buncrana Castle. Built by the O'Doherty family in 1602 on the foundations of a Norman keep, in 1608 it was seized following the death of Sir Cahir O'Doherty during the rebellion of that year. It was the home of the Vaughan family until the early 18th century.

Oakfield Park Raphoe, 7$^{1}/_{2}$ miles (12km) southeast of Letterkenny. A private house surrounded by 100 acres (40ha) of formal gardens, parkland and woodland. The house (not open to the public) was built in 1739 as the Deanery for Raphoe Cathedral and remained so until 1869. The gardens have been undergoing restoration since the late 1990s. Features include a walled pleasure garden, a new man-made lake with 'castle' folly, a garden railway, parterre and boardwalk. There has been a major programme of tree planting including 45,000 saplings of native Irish species. Tel: 074 917 3068.

Old Lough Eske Castle 3 miles (5km) northeast of Donegal. The scant remains of a castle built by the O'Donnells beside Lough Eske.

Owencarrow Viaduct Creeslough, 13 miles (21km) northwest of Letterkenny. A railway viaduct crossing the River Owencarrow and which once carried the Letterkenny & Burtonport Extension Railway of the Londonderry & Lough Swilly Railway. On 31 January 1925 a combined goods and passenger train from Derry was crossing the viaduct during a gale when it was hit by a gust of wind so strong that it blew one carriage off the viaduct and left others hanging. Four passengers of the 36 on the train were killed and more were injured. The line was closed in 1941.

Polestar Port Bridge Roundabout, Letterkenny. A sculpture by Derry artist Locky Morris, made from 104 timber poles and unveiled in 2006.

Raphoe Bishop's Palace Raphoe, 7$^{1}/_{2}$ miles (12km) southeast of Letterkenny. The substantial ruins of a 17th century episcopal palace built by John Leslie, Bishop of Raphoe. It was unsuccessfully besieged in 1641 and later by Cromwellian forces. The building was severely damaged by fire in the 1830s.

Rathmullan A seaside resort on Lough Swilly. It was from here that in 1607 the Earls took flight and in 1798 Wolfe Tone was captured.

Rathmullan Abbey Rathmullan, 13 miles (21km) northeast of Letterkenny. Ruins of a 16th century Carmelite friary on the shore of Lough Swilly. It was built by Ruaidhrí, son of Maol Mhuire, and his wife Máire, daughter of Ó Máille (Eoghan), and completed in 1516. Ruaidhrí also built Rathmullan Castle, the beach fortress of the MacSweeneys. Although the castle has long since vanished, the abbey still stands. In the early 17th century it was converted into a bishops' palace by Andrew Knox.

Rathmullan Castle See Rathmullan Abbey

Red Hugh O'Donnell Son of Hugh McManus O'Donnell and Lord of Tyrconnell, Red Hugh O'Donnell (1572–1602) was a leader of the revolt against English rule known as the Nine Years' War. In 1587, in order to bring Donegal into subjection, Sir John Perrot, Lord Deputy of Ireland, bribed a sea captain, appropriately named Skipper, to take 50 soldiers on board his ship and sail to Rathmullan with a cargo of white wine, pretending they came from Spain. Young Hugh, then only 15 years of age, was staying at Rathmullan Castle with the MacSweeneys, and he innocently went on board with a few friends (including Daniel MacSweeney and Hugh O'Gallagher) to sample the wine. Suddenly the British soldiers appeared and clapped them in irons, whereupon the ship set sail. They were to spend six years living in terrible conditions at Dublin Castle, mostly on food they had to beg for through the prison bars. Inghean Dubh, Red Hugh's mother, was harbouring 25 survivors of the Spanish Armada, and she offered them in exchange for her son. The offer was accepted and the Spaniards were marched to Dublin to make the exchange. When the British took charge of the Spaniards, they beheaded them on the spot and refused to honour the agreement. On Christmas night 1591 Red Hugh escaped with Henry and Art O'Neill, sons of Shane O'Neill. They made for Glenmalur, Co. Wicklow, in bitter winter weather to seek refuge with Fiach MacHugh O'Byrne. Art O'Neill died from exposure on the way, but Red Hugh survived and later made his way to his father's castle at Ballyshannon. Here physicians amputated his two great toes due to frostbite. Hugh's treatment in prison had filled him with a hatred of the British, who were to pay dearly in lives for their cruelty. In May 1592 he was inaugurated as chief of the O'Donnells (Lord of Tyrconnell), and before long seized Sligo and overran Connacht. He joined forces with Hugh O'Neill and others and shared in the victory of the Yellow Ford in August 1598, when the English, under Bagenal, suffered a heavy defeat. The Irish cause prospered for the following two years. After the recall of the Earl of Essex towards the end of 1599 and the arrival of Lord Mountjoy in February 1600, Irish fortunes waned. They had long expected aid from

Spain, and in September 1601 a Spanish fleet entered Kinsale, Co. Cork, with 3400 troops under Don Juan del Águila. O'Neill and O'Donnell at once marched south, while Mountjoy laid siege to the Spaniards in Kinsale. This was effectively the last action of the so-called Nine Years' War and Red Hugh fled to Spain, where he died in 1602. The Treaty of Mellifont in 1603 officially brought the war to its end.

Rivers — The **Erne** rises on Slieve Glah in Co. Cavan and runs for 75 miles (121km) into Donegal Bay, passing through Lough Gowna and Upper and Lower Lough Erne. It is linked to the River Shannon by the Shannon–Erne Waterway, which was reopened in 1994.

Salthill Gardens — Mountcharles, 3 miles (5km) west of Donegal. A contemporary walled garden developed since 1985. Tel: 074 973 5387.

Slieve League — 9 miles (15km) west of Killybegs. A spectacular sea cliff rising over 984ft (300m) above sea level which can be reached by the coastal path known as 'One Man's Path'. These are among the highest sea cliffs in Europe, second only to those on Achill Island.

St Aengus Church — Burt, 13 miles (21km) northeast of Letterkenny. A distinctive and award-winning church designed by Donegal architect Liam McCormick and built in the 1960s. Its design was inspired by the Grianán of Aileach cashell. It is therefore circular in plan with a sweeping copper roof. The church won a millennium poll as Building of the Century.

St Connell's Church — Glenties, 11 miles (18km) northwest of Donegal. A distinctive modern church consecrated in 1974 and designed by renowned church architect Liam McCormick. Its long, sweeping roofline mirrors the local mountains.

St Connell's Museum & Heritage Centre — Mill Road, Donegal. Local history museum with exhibits on the economic and social history of the region from ancient times to the modern day, including the effect of the Great Famine of the 19th century. There are room reconstructions and collections of photographs and memorabilia. Tel: 074 955 1277.

St Eunan's Cathedral — Cathedral Road, Letterkenny. The only cathedral in Co. Donegal, located on a site overlooking the town of Letterkenny. Built in the 1890s in Gothic style with a 212ft (64m) high spire, it opened for worship in 1901.

Sport

general — Located on Lough Erne, the **National Watersports Centre**, Belleek Road, Ballyshannon, offers organised watersports plus courses from trained instructors. Activities include archery, canoeing, kayaking, orienteering, raft building, sailing, surfing and windsurfing. Tel: 071 982 2922.

football — **Finn Harps** were founded in 1954 and joined the Football League of Ireland in 1969. They were winners of the League of Ireland 1st Division in 2004 and the FIA Cup in 1974. Their home ground is Finn Park, Navenney Street, Ballybofey.

Gaelic football — **Donegal** were winners of the All-Ireland Senior Football Championship in 1992.

Station Island — Aka St Patrick's Purgatory. An island on Lough Derg, said to have been where St Patrick once lived in a cave and fasted. The island has been a site of pilgrimage since medieval times. The island is a popular place of pilgrimage between 1 June and 15 August. The cave in the centre of the island was once thought to be the entrance to the underworld, but was filled in and replaced by a chapel in 1790. In 1925 the foundation stone was laid for St Patrick's Basilica, designed in Hiberno-Romanesque style by W A Scott. It is octagonal in plan with a copper clad dome. There is a column known as St Patrick's Cross and an icon of Our Lady of Perpetual Succour. Opposite the basilica is a labyrinth. A statue entitled *Patrick the Pilgrim* was unveiled in 2002 and stands on the lakeshore.

Temple of Deen — 1 mile (1.6km) south of Culdaff, 5 miles (8km) northeast of Carndonagh. A megalithic monument near Bocan Stone Circle. Twenty stones make up what was probably originally a forecourt tomb.

Tory Island — Aka Toraigh. An island 7 miles (11km) off the coast of Donegal. There is an artist community and an annual music festival. One of the artists, Patsaí Dan Mac Ruairí, holds the position of *Rí Thoraí* (King of Tory); this title has no formal power, but is chosen by consensus of the islanders to represent the community. On 22 September 1884 the British frigate HMS *Wasp*, sent to collect taxes, was shipwrecked near the lighthouse, 52 of the 58 on board losing their lives. In the 1970s the Irish government planned to relocate the islanders to council houses in order to use the island as an artillery firing range, but the islanders refused to be moved. Population (2002): 133.

Water Wheels, The — Rossnowlagh Road, Ballyshannon. A set of mills on the Erne Estuary, originally operated by the Cistercian foundation of the Abbey Assaroe. In 1989 they were acquired by the Abbey Mill Restoration Trust and restored. The ruins of the 12th century abbey stand nearby. Tel: 071 985 1580.

Workhouse, The — Dunfanaghy, 18 miles (29km) northwest of Letterkenny. Built 1843–4 to a design by George Wilkinson to accommodate 300 people, the workhouse officially opened in 1845. It had an entrance block, a main block plus a fever hospital. After the workhouse closed down the main block and hospital were demolished, but in 1994 the entrance block was restored and became a museum which now tells the story of 'wee Hannah', an inmate of the workhouse from the 1830s. Tel: 074 913 6540.

Some famous people born in County Donegal

Allingham, William (poet and man of letters) (1824–89)	Ballyshannon
Anderson, Ian (president of Isle of Man Council) (1925–2005)	Rathmullan
Bonner, Patrick 'Packie' (footballer) (1960–)	Cloughglass
Brennan, Máire (singer) (1952–)	Gweedore
Coughlan, Mary (politician) (1965–)	Donegal
Egan, Felim (painter) (1952–)	Donegal
Gallagher, (Liam) Rory (musician) (1948–95)	Ballyshannon
Given, Séamus 'Shay' (footballer) (1976–)	Lifford
Harte, Mickey Joe (singer) (1973–)	Lifford
McAnally, Ray (actor) (1926–89)	Buncrana
McGuinness, Frank (playwright) (1953–)	Buncrana
Ní Bhraonáin, Eithne (Enya) (singer) (1961–)	Gweedore
Ó Maonaigh, Proinsias (Francie Mooney) (fiddler)(1922–2006)	Gweedore
O'Donnell, Daniel (singer) (1961–)	kincasslagh
St Columba (saint) (521–597)	Gartan

Islands of Donegal

(shipping area = Malin)

Island name	Area	Nearest landmark	General information
Allagh Island	Atlantic	Derrybeg	aka Oilean Eala
An Chruit	Atlantic	Kincaslough	aka Cruit Island. Part of the Rosses group. Population: 61.
An Dun Ramhar	Atlantic	Annagary	aka Doonrower Island
An tIochtar	Atlantic	Burtonpoint	aka Eighter Island
An tOilean Leathan	Atlantic	Burtonpoint	aka Lahan Island. A beautiful stone cottage with blue-painted doors and windows adorns this island. Area 0.33 sq miles (0.85 sq km).
An Tor Glas	Atlantic	Gola Island	aka Torglass Island
An Tor Mor	Atlantic	Port Hill	aka Tormore Island
Anna Island	Atlantic	Burtonpoint	aka Inis Anna
Arainn Mhor	Atlantic	Burtonpoint	See separate entry for Aranmore
Aran Island	Atlantic	Burtonpoint	See separate entry for Aranmore
Aranmore	Atlantic	Burtonpoint	See separate entry
Bo Island	Atlantic	Derrybeg	Almost joined to Inishinny.
Calf Island	Atlantic	Derrybeg	This island is the mooring place of Aran's modern lifeboat.
Carriff Island	Atlantic	Burtonpoint	Area: 0.01 sq miles (0.03 sq km).
Connellagh Rocks	Donegal Bay	St John's Point	Popular with snorkellers.
Cruit Island	Atlantic	Kincaslough	See An Chruit
Doagh Island	Atlantic	Inishowen	Connected to Inishowen peninsula, Ballyliffin by road.
Doonrower Island	Atlantic	Annagary	aka An Dun Ramhar
Duck Island	Atlantic	Burtonpoint	aka Oilean Lachan
Eadarinis	Atlantic	Burtonpoint	aka Edernish
Eadarinis Fraoigh	Atlantic	Burtonpoint	aka Edernishfree Island. Lies southeast of An tOilean Leathan.
Eagle's Nest Island	Donegal Bay	Burtonpoint	Tiny islet in Donegal Bay.
Edernish	Atlantic	Burtonpoint	aka Eadarinis
Edernishfree Island	Atlantic	Burtonpoint	See Eadarinis Fraoigh
Eighter Island	Atlantic	Burtonpoint	aka An tIochtar
Friars Island	Lough Derg	Pettigo	Inshore island.
Gabhla	Atlantic	Derrybeg	aka Gola Island. Population: 5.
Gabla Island	Atlantic	Derrybeg	aka Inishinny
Garvan Isles	Atlantic	Malin Head	aka Na Garbh Oilean (Islands of the Rough Sea). See separate entries
Glashedy Island	Atlantic	Malin Head	Lies 2 miles (3km) west of the mouth of Trawbreaga Bay.
Go Island	Atlantic	Derrybeg	aka Oilean Ghabba
Gola Island	Atlantic	Derrybeg	See Gabhla
Green Isle	Atlantic	Malin Head	One of the three Garvan Isles.
Gull Island	Atlantic	Loughros Point	Only separated from the main Slievetooey cliffs at high spring tides.
Illanaran Island	Atlantic	Derrybeg	aka Oilean Arann. Population: 13.
Illancarragh Island	Atlantic	Derrybeg	Almost joined to Inishinny and Bo Islands.
Illancrone	Atlantic	Dunglow	aka Oilean Crona. Population: 6.

Island name	Area	Nearest landmark	General information
Illion Crone	Atlantic	Termon	aka Termon Island. Lies $^{1}/_{2}$ mile (0.8km) west of Termon.
Inch Island	Lough Swilly	Burnfoot	aka Inis Island. Now attached to the mainland. Population: 439.
Inis Anna	Atlantic	Burtonpoint	aka Anna Island. Area: 0.0077 sq miles (0.02 sq km).
Inis Beag	Atlantic	Bloody Foreland	aka Inishbeg
Inis Bo Finne	Atlantic	Bloody Foreland	aka Inishbofin. Population: 16.
Inis Caorach	Atlantic	Burtonpoint	aka Inishkeeragh
Inis Cu	Atlantic	Burtonpoint	aka Inishcoo
Inis Ean	Dunglow Bay	Dunglow	aka Inisheane
Inis Fraoigh	Atlantic	Bunbeg	aka Inishfree Lower
Inis Fraoigh	Dunglow Bay	Dunglow	aka Inishfree Upper
Inis Island	Lough Swilly	Burnfoot	See Inch Island
Inis Meain	Atlantic	Derrybeg	aka Inishmeane
Inis Mhic an Doirn	Atlantic	Burtonpoint	aka Inishmacadurn, Rutland Island
Inis Mil	Atlantic	Burtonpoint	aka Inisnmeal
Inis Oileantraigh	Atlantic	Kincaslough	aka Inishillintry
Inis Oirthir	Atlantic	Derrybeg	aka Inishsirrer
Inis Saille	Dunglow Bay	Dunglow	aka Inishal
Inishal	Dunglow Bay	Dunglow	aka Inis Saille
Inishbarnog	Loughros More Bay	Loughros Point	Lies 0.6 miles (1km) south of Dawros Head.
Inishbeg	Atlantic	Bloody Foreland	aka Inis Beag
Inishbofin	Atlantic	Bloody Foreland	aka Inis Bo Finne. Population: 16.
Inishcoo	Atlantic	Burtonpoint	aka Inis Cu
Inishdooey	Atlantic	Bloody Foreland	aka Oilean Duiche
Inishduff	Donegal Bay	Muckros Head	aka Shalwy Island
Inisheane	Dunglow Bay	Dunglow	aka Inis Ean
Inishfree Lower	Atlantic	Bunbeg	aka Inis Fraoigh
Inishfree Upper	Dunglow Bay	Dunglow	aka Inis Fraoigh. One of The Rosses group. Population: 7.
Inishillintry	Atlantic	Kincaslough	aka Inis Oileantraigh
Inishinny	Atlantic	Derrybeg	aka Gabla Island. Almost joined to Bo Island.
Inishkeel	Gweebarra Bay	Dunmore Head	Almost joined to the mainland at its southeast extremity.
Inishkeeragh	Atlantic	Burtonpoint	aka Inis Caorach
Inishmacadurn	Atlantic	Burtonpoint	aka Rutland Island, Inis Mhic an Doirn. Part of the Rosses group. Area: 3.12 sq miles (8.08 sq km).
Inishmeal	Atlantic	Burtonpoint	aka Inis Mil
Inishmeane	Atlantic	Derrybeg	aka Inis Meain
Inishsirrer	Atlantic	Derrybeg	aka Inis Oirthir
Inishtrahull	Atlantic	Malin Head	The most northerly of Ireland's true islands and indeed the most northerly point of Ireland.
Iompainn	Atlantic	Derrybeg	aka Umfin Island. Flat grassy islet.
Island Reagh	Atlantic	Melmore Head	In recent years has been surrounded by a barbed wire fence.
Island Roy	Mulroy Bay	Fanad/Rosgoill Peninsulas	aka Oilean an Bhraighe. Population: 7.
Isle of O'Donnell	Lough Eske	Donegal Town	Inshore island
Lahan Island	Atlantic	Burtonpoint	See An tOilean Leathan
Middle Isle	Atlantic	Malin Head	One of the three Garvan Isles.
Na Garbh Oilean	Atlantic	Malin Head	aka Garvan Isles. See separate entries.
Oilean an Bhraighe	Mulroy Bay	Fanad/Rosgoill Peninsulas	(I. = Prisoner's Island). See Island Roy
Oilean Arann	Atlantic	Derrybeg	See Illanaran Island
Oilean Crona	Atlantic	Dunglow	See Illancrone
Oilean Duiche	Atlantic	Bloody Foreland	aka Inishdooey
Oilean Eala	Atlantic	Derrybeg	aka Allagh Island
Oilean Ghabba	Atlantic	Derrybeg	aka Go Island
Oilean Lachan	Atlantic	Burtonpoint	aka Duck Island
Óileán na Náomh	Lough Derg	Pettigo	aka Saints Island. The sanctuary lands on the island were known in the Middle Ages as Termon Dabheoc (from the 6th century St Dabheoc who presided over the retreat).
Owey Island	Atlantic	Kincaslough	aka Uaigh. Area: 3 sq miles (7.8 sq km).
Rathlin O'Birne Island	Atlantic	Malin Beg	aka Reachlainn Ui Bhirn
Reachlainn Ui Bhirn	Atlantic	Malin Beg	aka Rathlin O'Birne Island
Rinn Raithni	Atlantic	Burtonpoint	aka Rinrainy Island
Rinrainy Island	Atlantic	Burtonpoint	aka Rinn Raithni. Area: 0.19 sq miles (0.5 sq km).

Island name	Area	Nearest landmark	General information
Roaninish	Gweebarra Bay	Dunmore Head	Has a sheltered sandy beach on its east side.
Rutland Island	Atlantic	Burtonpoint	aka Inishmacadurn, Inis Mhic an Doirn. One of the Rosses group.
St Patrick's Purgatory	Lough Derg	Pettigo	See Station Island
Saints Island	Lough Derg	Pettigo	See Oilean na Naomh
Shalwy Island	Donegal Bay	Muckros Head	aka Inishduff
Stag Rocks, The	Atlantic	Kincaslough	Rock stack lying off the coast in Donegal Bay.
Station Island	Lough Derg	Pettigo	aka St Patrick's Purgatory. See separate entry
Termon Island	Atlantic	Termon	See Illion Crone
Tor Beg	Atlantic	Malin Head	The smaller of two islands just off the headland. The most northerly possible landing in Ireland, save Rockall.
Tor More	Atlantic	Malin Head	The larger of two islands just off the headland.
Tor na gColpach	Atlantic	Gola Island	aka Tornagolpagh Island
Toraigh	Atlantic	Bloody Foreland	aka Tory Island
Toralaydan	Atlantic	Port Hill	At low water it is possible to walk to the mainland.
Torglass Island	Atlantic	Gola Island	aka An Tor Glas
Tormore Island	Atlantic	Port Hill	aka An Tor Mor
Tornagolpagh Island	Atlantic	Gola Island	aka Tor na gColpach
Tory Island	Atlantic	Bloody Foreland	See separate entry
Uaigh	Atlantic	Kincaslough	See Owey Island
Umfin Island	Atlantic	Derrybeg	aka Iompainn. Flat grassy islet.
White Isle	Atlantic	Malin Head	One of the three Garvan Isles.

Dublin

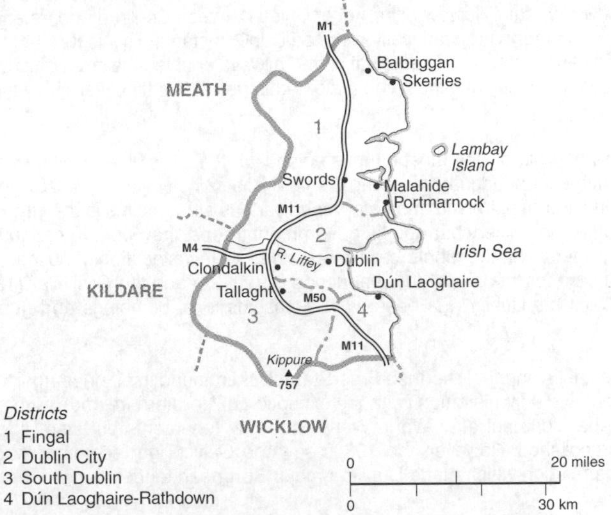
M1
Balbriggan
Skerries
MEATH
1
Lambay Island
Swords
Malahide
Portmarnock
M11
2
M4
R. Liffey
Dublin
Irish Sea
Clondalkin
KILDARE
Dún Laoghaire
Tallaght
M50
4
3
M11
Kippure
757
Districts
1 Fingal
2 Dublin City
3 South Dublin
4 Dún Laoghaire-Rathdown
WICKLOW
0
20 miles
0
30 km

Dublin (*Dubh Linn* = Black Pool) is part of the province of Leinster. It lies in the east of Ireland and has borders with Meath to the northwest, Wicklow to the south and Kildare to the southwest, with its eastern coast on the Irish Sea. The city of Dublin is the capital and the largest city of the Republic of Ireland.

At this point perhaps I should attempt to clear the murky waters regarding the status of County Dublin. Section 9 Part 1(a) of the Local Government (Dublin) Act 1993 stated that as of 1 January 1994 'the county shall cease to exist'. At that time, and in response to a European Council report highlighting Ireland as the most centralised country in the European Union, it was decided that a single County Dublin was unmanageable and undemocratic from a local government perspective. The county was formally abolished and replaced with Dún Laoghaire-Rathdown, Fingal and South Dublin. County Dublin is now defined in legislation as the 'Dublin Region', although for the purposes of this book I have adhered to the traditional name as it remains a de facto county, and indeed after talking at great length with each individual council of Dublin it is clear to me that this ruling was meant purely as a method of dividing the county administratively. Each of the three new 'counties' and Dublin City Council exist to serve their areas, but all have told me they feel this is done within the wider network of County Dublin. Therefore the only concession I have made to this change of status is to include the four county council addresses in the Attractions section.

The city of **Dublin** was officially founded by Vikings in AD 988 (it celebrated its 1000 years of existence in 1988) although a settlement probably existed on the site of the present city by the 2nd century. By the 10th century there were two settlements on the Liffey, one Viking (Dyflin, 'black pool') and one Irish (Ath Cliath, 'ford of hurdles'). In 988 the Norse king Glun Iarainn recognised Mael Seachlainn II Mor, the High King of Ireland. The arrival of the Anglo-Normans saw a build-up of English power and the settlement of English and Welsh immigrants in the area which would eventually evolve into what became known as 'The Pale' – a region centred on Dublin which was fortified against the revitalised native Irish. The area was administered and controlled by the Fitzgeralds until they were ousted by a force sent by Henry VIII in order to restore some semblance of English control. Although blessed with two cathedrals, the city only really began to grow during the 16th and 17th centuries. During the troubles of the 1640s the Catholic population of Dublin was expelled or driven out, first by the influx of Protestants fleeing unrest in other parts of the country and then by the arrival of Oliver Cromwell and his army. Dublin became the capital of the kingdom of Ireland with the administration and Parliament based in Dublin Castle.

A major building programme in the 18th century resulted in the demolition of medieval dwellings and the creation of wide streets such as Sackville Street (now called O'Connell Street) and Dame Street, along with squares such as Rutland Square (now called Parnell Square), Mountjoy Square and Merrion Square. The only areas to retain the medieval street pattern were Temple Bar and the area around Grafton Street. The attraction of Dublin and the beginnings of an agricultural revolution saw rural migration to the city which swung the balance of population to a Catholic majority by the end of the 18th century. However, the Act of Union between England and Ireland in 1800 abolished the Irish Parliament and drastically reduced Dublin's status. This is turn led to an economic decline in the city and hinterland. The arrival of the railways enabled the creation of suburbs in such places as Ballsbridge and Rathmines. The major industries at this time were brewing, distilling and transport.

The Easter Rising, probably the most famous episode in the city's history, occurred in April 1916. Rebel forces, with their headquarters at the General Post Office in O'Connell Street, declared the creation of an independent Ireland and established various strongpoints in the city. Subjected to an intense and tightening artillery barrage by government troops, they were forced to surrender after a week. Initially unpopular, the rebels' cause was aided by the execution of 16 leaders and proved to be a springboard for the War of Independence (1919–21) and the Civil War (1922–3). During both of these conflicts Dublin was beset with assassinations, bombings and gun battles in the streets.

With the final establishment of the Irish Free State, Dublin found itself once again at the heart of Irish government and administration (with the exception of Northern Ireland). Much of the city was subjected to redevelopment after World War II; not only tenements but also much of Georgian Dublin were demolished. However, the 1990s saw the Celtic Tiger economic boom and a programme of regeneration which made Dublin a major European tourist city.

Dublin has so many famous natives that it would be difficult to pick any one representative. If one had to choose an area where Dublin is overly blessed it would be the arts, in particular authors, poets and playwrights. Just a few of the luminaries include Oscar Wilde, George Bernard Shaw, Bram Stoker, Christy Brown, Brendan Behan, James Joyce, Samuel Beckett, W B Yeats, Richard Brinsley Sheridan, Sean O'Casey and Maeve Binchy.

Dublin	**Population**			**Area**	
Districts	*male*	*female*	*total*	*sq miles*	*sq km*
Dublin City North	140,257	150,264	290,521	29	75
Dublin City South	97,556	107,704	205,260	17	43
Dún Laoghaire-Rathdown	91,337	100,455	191,792	49	127
Fingal	97,409	99,004	196,413	175	453
South Dublin	117,516	121,319	238,835	86	223
Total	544,075	578,746	1,122,821	355	921

Local Attractions and Information

Abbey Theatre — Lower Abbey Street, Dublin. The world-renowned Abbey Theatre was founded in 1904 as the Irish National Theatre Company by William Butler Yeats and Lady Augusta Gregory. It was originally housed in the refitted Mechanics' Institute on Marlborough Street but this was badly damaged by fire on the night of 17–18 July 1952. The theatre reopened in a purpose-built theatre on Abbey Street on 18 July 1966. The theatre has a policy of promoting and developing new Irish plays and acts as a guardian of the Irish dramatic repertoire. There are two stages: the Abbey – the main auditorium, with a seating capacity of 628 – and the Peacock, situated under the Abbey foyer, with a seating capacity of 157 and dedicated primarily to the presentation of new plays. Tel: 01 878 7222.

Administrative headquarters — **Dublin**: Civic Offices, Wood Quay, Dublin. Tel: 01 222 2222.

Dún Laoghaire-Rathdown: County Hall, Marine Road, Dún Laoghaire, Co. Dublin. Tel: 01 205 4700.

Fingal: County Hall, Swords, Fingal, Co. Dublin. Tel: 0 890 5000.

South Dublin: County Hall, Tallaght, Dublin. Tel: 01 414 9000.

Airport — **Dublin Airport** (DUB). Originally named Collinstown Airport and located on a former World War I British air base. The inaugural flight took place in 1940 and the terminal building, designed by Desmond FitzGerald, brother of former Taoiseach Garret FitzGerald, was opened in 1941. A new terminal was opened in 1972 and a second terminal is due for completion in 2010. The airport is the headqarters of Aer Lingus, Ireland's national airline, and of leading budget airline Ryanair. Flights operate to destinations in Britain, Europe, the Middle East and North America as well as within Ireland; the airport handled over 23 million passengers in 2007. Tel: 01 814 1111.

Aras an Uachtarain Phoenix Park, Dublin. The official residence of the President of Ireland. The original house was built in 1751 by Nathaniel Clements (the park ranger) and in 1782 it was acquired to become the residence of the Viceroy of Ireland (the Viceregal Lodge). The east wing was added in 1849 for the state visit of Queen Victoria and the west wing was extended in 1911 for the visit of George V. After the creation of the Irish Free State in 1922 the house became the residence of the Governor-General until 1932, and the official residence of the President of Ireland in 1938.

Ark Children's Centre, The Eustace Street, Temple Bar, Dublin. Europe's first custom-designed cultural centre for children. It contains a gallery, workshops and a 150 seat theatre.The building was designed by Shane O'Toole and Michael Kelly on the site of the former Presbyterian Meeting House, dating to 1728. Tel: 016 707788.

Ashtown Castle Phoenix Park, Dublin. Tower house hidden within the house of the Papal Nuncio in Phoenix Park and not 'discovered' until that building was demolished in the 1980s. It is of indeterminate date but may be as old as the 15th century. It now forms part of the Phoenix Park Visitor Centre.

Baggotrath Castle A castle formerly located in Dublin where Upper Bagot Street now stands. Built in the early 1300s by the Bagot family, after whom the castle and the streets that now surround the site are named, it was occupied in 1379 by William Fitzwilliam, and in 1403 by Sir Edward Perrers. When his widow died in 1441, the castle was taken by an executor of her will. It was seized back for the Fitzwilliam and Perrers families by their daughter's husband William Fitzwilliam in 1442 and was the family seat until Sir Thomas Fitzwilliam moved to Merrion Castle c.1550. Baggotrath Castle was wrecked in 1649 in the time of the Royalist 1st Viscount Fitzwilliam; abandoned, it fell into ruin in the early 1700s. The ruins were finally demolished in the early 19th century as the area around the Grand Canal was developed. See also Battles: Rathmines.

Baily's Lighthouse Howth Head, 8 miles (13km) east of Dublin. A cottage lighthouse built on the site in 1667 was replaced in 1790 by a short-lived tower designed by Thomas Rogers. This was replaced in turn by the current 42ft (13m) high structure, designed by George Halpin Sr. Since 1983 it has been the mainland base for helicopter operations to the Kish Bank and Rockabill lighthouses. It was automated in 1997.

Balbriggan Martello Tower Balbriggan, 19 miles (31km) northeast of Dublin. A Martello tower built c.1805.

Baldongan Castle Skerries, 17 miles (27km) northeast of Dublin. The ruin of a Knights Templar castle built in the 13th century. Having passed through various owners, including the de Birmingham and Barnwell families, it was damaged by Parliamentary forces in the 1640s and abandoned.

Baldoyle Estuary Nature Reserve 6 miles (10km) northeast of Dublin. A nature reserve covering 502 acres (203ha) of a tidal bay and of international importance for brent geese.

Bank of Ireland Arts Centre Foster Place, Dublin. A performing and visual arts venue and interactive museum, in a building that once housed the Irish Parliament; built 1729–39, it is believed to be the first purpose-built Parliament House in the world. It was converted to a bank in 1803 after the Parliament was persuaded to vote itself out of existence through the Act of Union in August 1800. The centre offers live performances including drama, recitals and readings, as well as exhibitions; the museum charts the role of the Bank of Ireland (founded in 1783) in the Irish economy through 200 years of history. As at Westminster the Parliament consisted of two houses, the House of Commons and the House of Lords. The Commons is now the banking hall while the Lords remains intact. The Daniel O'Connell Room celebrates the life of the politician known as 'The Liberator'. Tel: 01 661 5933.

Battles Five battles have been fought in Dublin: Clontarf, Dublin (I), Dublin (II), Glen Mama and Rathmines. See separate table for details. See also Easter Rising.

Bloomsday A day named after 38-year-old advertising agent Leopold Bloom, the central character in James Joyce's novel *Ulysses*. The events of the novel take place on 16 June 1904 and devotees of the book recreate its events in Dublin on 16 June each year.

Brazen Head Bridge Street, Dublin. Dublin's oldest pub, built in 1754. It is mentioned in *Ulysses* by Corley incorrectly as 'The Brazen Head over in Winetavern Street'.

Bridges The following bridges, from west to east, cross the River Liffey in Dublin:

Sean Heuston Bridge, an iron bridge opened in 1828 and originally named King's Bridge after George IV. Renamed Sarsfield Bridge in 1923, it was renamed again in 1941, this time for Sean Heuston, one of the executed leaders of the 1916 Easter Rising. It was restored in 2003.

Frank Sherwin Bridge, opened in 1982 to relieve traffic on the narrower Rory O'More Bridge, and named after Dublin politician Frank Sherwin.

Rory O'More Bridge, an iron bridge erected in 1859, when it was named the Queen Victoria Bridge. It was renamed in 1939 for Rory O'More, one of the ringleaders of a plot to capture Dublin in October 1641. It stands on the site of a 17th century wooden bridge known as Barrack Bridge, which became known as Bloody Bridge after several ferrymen were killed trying to destroy it.

James Joyce Bridge, designed by Spanish architect Santiago Calatrava and opened on 16 June 2003 (Bloomsday). Named for Dublin author James Joyce, it joins the South Quays to Blackhall Place.

Mellows Bridge, aka **Queen Maeve Bridge**. The oldest standing bridge spanning the Liffey, built 1764–8. It was originally known as Queen's Bridge after the wife of George III, but was later renamed after the legendary Queen Maeve of Connacht who invaded Ulster.

Father Mathew Bridge, opened in 1818 and originally named after the Earl of Whitworth.

Known 1923–38 as Dublin Bridge, it was then renamed again for temperance campaigner Father Theobald Mathew (the 'Apostle of Temperance'). It stands at or near the site of several earlier bridges, including until 1674 the only bridge across the Liffey in Dublin.

O'Donovan Rossa Bridge, built 1813–16 and originally known as Richmond Bridge. It was renamed in 1923 after Jeremiah O'Donovan Rossa (1831–1915), a leading Republican.

Grattan Bridge, linking Capel Street to Parliament Street and sometimes known as the Capel Street Bridge. A remodelled version of the 17th century Essex Bridge, it was reopened in 1874 and named for Henry Grattan MP (1746–1820). It has had cosmetic additions in the 2000s.

Millennium Bridge, designed by Howley Harrington and opened in 2000. One of three footbridges over the river, the others being Ha'penny Bridge and Sean O'Casey Bridge, it joins Eustace Street in Temple Bar to the North Quays.

Ha'penny Bridge, originally the Wellington Bridge and now officially the Liffey Bridge. Dublin's oldest pedestrian crossing over the River Liffey, it was named the Ha'penny Bridge from the toll paid to cross the river until 1919. The bridge was the only pedestrian bridge on the Liffey until the Millennium Bridge was opened in 2000. It underwent major restoration 2001–03.

O'Connell Bridge, designed by James Gandon and built 1794–8. The bridge was originally named after Lord Carlisle but was renamed after Daniel O'Connell when it was widened in the 1880s.

Butt Bridge, opened in 1932 to replace a previous swing bridge of the same name, built in 1879. It is named after Home Rule campaigner Isaac Butt.

Loopline Bridge, a railway bridge built in 1891.

Talbot Memorial Bridge, opened in 1978. Linking Custom House Quay and City Quay, it is named after Dublin temperance campaigner Matt Talbot.

Sean O'Casey Bridge, a pedestrian bridge linking Custom House Quay with City Quay. Designed by Cyril O'Neill, who won an international competition organised by the Dublin Docklands Development Authority (DDDA) in 2002, it was opened in July 2005. It is named after playwright Sean O'Casey (1880–1964) who lived in the North Wall area of Dublin. The bridge is in two sections which swing through 90 degrees to allow boats to pass through.

Broom Bridge — A small bridge across the Royal Canal in Dublin. Inscribed on a plaque is the mathematical formula that defines quaternions, as it was on this site that mathematician William Rowan Hamilton (1805–65) came upon the formula in a flash of genius and scratched it into the stone of the bridge.

Bull Island — aka North Bull Island. An island in Dublin Bay 3 miles (5km) long and $^1/_2$ mile (0.8km) wide. It is connected to the shore by an ancient wooden bridge at its southwest end, and by a causeway midway along the island, built in 1962. There is a low lying sandy beach in the northern part of Dublin Bay and the island is covered with dune grassland. Bull Island Nature Reserve, covering 3548 acres (1436ha), is of international scientific importance for brent geese. The island is popular for walking and bird watching. Area: 1.54 sq miles (4 sq km). Population: 17.

Casino, The — Marino, Dublin. Although sometimes described as a folly, the Casino (Italian = 'small house') is an architecturally important building designed and built between 1755 and the 1770s by William Chambers for Lord Charlemont as a garden pavilion at his Marino Estate. It was taken into state care in 1930 and has since been restored.

Castleknock Castle — Castleknock, 6 miles (10km) northwest of Dublin. The ruin of a castle located in the grounds of Castleknock College. Possibly built by the Tyrrell family in the 12th century, it was slighted following the wars in the 1640s.

Chapelizod — A village whose rather odd name is derived from 'Seipeil Izod', or the Chapel of Isolde. The daughter of the 6th century Irish King Aengus, Isolde had a legendary romance with Tristan which is immortalised in Wagner's opera *Tristan und Isolde.* The village is traditionally said to be her burial place.

Chester Beatty Library — Dublin Castle, Dublin. A library and gallery located in the gardens of Dublin Castle and containing a world-renowned collection of manuscripts, prints, icons, miniature paintings, early printed books and objets d'art originating from around the world. The permanent collections are divided between 'Sacred Traditions' and 'Artistic Traditions'. The former consists of sacred texts and illuminated manuscripts from the great religions and belief systems, including biblical papyri and a collection of Qur'an manuscripts; the latter includes a collection of rare printed books as well as decorative arts from East Asia. It was voted European Museum of the Year in 2002. Tel: 01 407 0750.

Christ Church Cathedral — Christ Church Place, Dublin. Formally titled the Cathedral Church of the Holy Trinity in Dublin, the cathedral stands on the site of a church established after the Viking settlement in 1038 by Donat (Dunan), first Bishop of Dublin, and the Viking king Sitriuc. It was begun by Strongbow and his fellow Norman invaders in the early 1170s and was completed in 1240. The crypt is 175ft (53.5m) long and stretches under both the nave and choir. In 1486 Lambert Simnel, pretender to the English throne, was 'crowned' here as Edward VI. Following the Dissolution the Augustinian priory of the Holy Trinity was suppressed and the last prior became the first dean of Christ Church. The roof of the nave collapsed in 1562 and temporary repairs were carried out; these were still in place in the 1870s when extensive restorations and renovations were carried out by George Edward Street. The north nave wall continues to incline by 18in (46cm) and is known as the 'leaning wall of Dublin'. On 13 April 1742 the cathedral choir sang at the world premiere of Handel's *Messiah.* Until the 1700s houses were built up against the cathedral on all sides; these were cleared by Street, allowing it to be viewed unhindered. The roof and stonework were restored in the 1980s. The crypt has been restored and houses an exhibition including the plate given to the cathedral by William III in 1697 as a thanksgiving for his victory at the Battle of the Boyne.

Churches — **Baldongan Church**, Skerries, 17 miles (27km) northeast of Dublin. The remains of a church adjoining Baldongan Castle and possibly built in the 15th century.

Killiney Church, 9 miles (15km) southeast of Dublin. The ruin of an 11th or 12th century church which stood on the site of a 7th century monastic foundation.

St Augustine and St John, Thomas Street, Dublin. Designed by E W Pugin and built by G C Ashlin in the 1880s. It has the tallest spire in Dublin at 231ft (70.5m).

St Audeon's, High Street, Dublin. One of the oldest existing churches in Dublin, dating to the late 12th century. The three bells in its tower date to the 15th century and are reputed to be the oldest in Ireland. The Guild Chapel of St Anne has been reroofed and houses an exhibition on the importance of St Audeon's in the life of medieval Dublin.

St Laurence's, Chapelizod, Dublin. A small church built in 1832 and incorporating a 14th century tower.

St Mary's, Howth, 8 miles (13km) northeast of Dublin. The ruin of a late 14th century church overlooking Howth harbour. It stands on the site of two earlier churches.

St Michael's, Christchurch Place, Dublin. The tower of a 12th century church incorporated with the Christ Church Synod Hall by G E Street.

St Michan's, Church Street, Dublin. Built in the 1680s on the site of a late 11th century Viking church established to serve the Viking community that was expelled from the walled city. The church also has an organ on which Handel is said to have played while composing the *Messiah*. The vaults hold several mummified bodies, including those of some of the leaders of the 1798 rebellion.

St Werburgh's, Werburgh Street, Dublin. The original St Werburgh's was built in the late 12th century. Burned down in 1301 and subsequently rebuilt, it was said to be ruinous by the early 18th century and was rebuilt 1716–19 to a design by Thomas Burgh. The church was again burned down on the night of 6–7 November 1754, leaving only the tower and walls standing. It was rebuilt and services resumed in 1759. The spire is said to have been removed in the 1830s because it overlooked Dublin Castle and could have been used as a vantage point by attackers.

Clondalkin Library — Clondalkin, 6 miles (10km) southwest of Dublin. A library built in 1912 to an Arts and Crafts design by T J Byrne. It has a mixture of stone, brickwork and render, with horizontal glazing.

Clondalkin Round Tower — Clondalkin, 6 miles (10km) southwest of Dublin. A well-preserved 8th century round tower; 84ft (25.5m) high, it stands on the site of a 6th century monastic foundation of St Cronan.

Clontarf Castle — Castle Avenue, Clontarf, Dublin. The original castle was built in 1172 but was demolished as unsafe in 1835. The current castle dates to 1837. Used as a cabaret venue 1972–97, it has since been refurbished and is now a hotel. Tel: 01 833 2321.

Custom House — Custom House Quay, Dublin. Designed by James Gandon, the Custom House is considered to be one of Dublin's finest Georgian buildings. Built 1781–91, it has four individual classical monumental façades linked by corner pavilions. Among its features are sculpted keystones symbolising the 13 principal rivers of Ireland. The building was reduced to a shell by a five-day long conflagration started by the IRA in 1921 during the Irish Civil War. It was subsequently reconstructed and has been more sympathetically restored since the 1980s with the addition of a new Portland stone cornice, fitted to replace the limestone one fitted after the fire. A visitor centre located under the restored Dome contains some of the few interior features which survived the 1921 fire. Tel: 01 888 2538.

Dalkey Castle and Heritage Centre — Castle Street, Dalkey. An award-winning heritage centre incorporating a 15th century tower house and 10th century graveyard. Tel: 01 285 8366.

Donnybrook Fair — The Donnybrook Horse Fair was held from the 13th century until 1855, when it was banned because of its riotousness (so much so that Donnybrook became synonymous with a brawl).

Drimnagh Castle — Long Mile Road, Drimnagh, Dublin. A 13th century castle believed to have been continuously occupied until 1954. It is surrounded by a flooded moat which is stocked with fish. A major restoration project was undertaken in 2000 and many of the castle's original interior and exterior features including the 17th century gardens have been restored. Tel: 01 450 2530.

Dublin Castle — Castle Street, Dublin. Built 1204–30 on the orders of King John, the castle stands on the site of earlier fortifications including a Viking fort. It has served many functions over its lifetime including official residence, state prison, seat of Parliament, law court, barracks and treasury. Restored and remodelled in the 16th century, it became the seat of English government and administration for all of Ireland. Much of the castle was damaged by a fire on 7 April 1684, including the blowing up of sections to prevent the fire's spread to the Powder Tower and archives held in the Bermingham Tower. It was rebuilt in the late 17th and early 18th centuries, although its governmental functions declined with the passing of the 1800 Act of Union. The Viceroy's residence was moved to Phoenix Park in the 19th century although 'court' was still held at the castle. After the signing of the Anglo-Irish Treaty, the castle was handed over to the new Irish government on 16 January 1922. Since restored, it now hosts European Union presidencies, heads of state, and leaders of business, industry and government. Rooms open to the public include the state apartments and the undercroft as well as the grounds and house. See also Chester Beatty Library, Garda (Police) Museum.

Dublin City Gallery The Hugh Lane — Parnell Square North, Dublin. A gallery of modern art and the municipal gallery for the city of Dublin. It is housed in Charlemont House, designed by William Chambers and built in the 1760s, and which was the General Register and Census Office for Ireland before becoming the Municipal Gallery for Modern Art. The original collection, donated by the gallery's founder, Sir Hugh Lane, included works by Manet, Monet, Renoir and Degas and has been augmented with works by national and international contemporary artists. The gallery holds the largest public collection of

20th century Irish art and has recently acquired the entire contents of Francis Bacon's Reece Mews studio. Tel: 01 225550.

Dublin City University Innovative university situated on an 85 acre (34ha) campus 3 miles (5km) north of the River Liffey in the city centre. DCU was initially set up to fulfil the national requirement for a highly trained workforce with skills in the areas of business, science and electronics, computer technology, communications and languages and as an agent for change in its local community. The college opened in 1980 and was awarded university status in 1989. DCU was the first university in Ireland to introduce work placement as part of its degree programmes; it also offered the country's first interdisciplinary degree programmes. Many DCU students study at universities in Spain, France, Germany and Austria as part of their degree programmes under Erasmus exchange agreements. Tel: 01 700 5566.

Dublin Spire O'Connell Street, Dublin. A public artwork chosen through a competition to stand on the site of Nelson's pillar, which had been blown up in 1966. Designed by Ian Ritchie Architects, it was erected December 2002–January 2003. It is 393ft (120m) high, 10ft (3m) wide at the base and tapers to a 6in (15cm) wide beacon at the top. The top section is perforated and lit by small LEDs.

Dublin Writers Museum Parnell Square, Dublin. Opened in 1991 to house a history and celebration of literary Dublin. Jonathan Swift, Richard Brinsley Sheridan, George Bernard Shaw, Oscar Wilde, W B Yeats, James Joyce and Samuel Beckett are among the many writers presented through their books, letters, portraits and personal items. Tel: 01 872 2077.

Dublin Zoo The largest zoo in Ireland, covering 30 acres (12ha) of Phoenix Park and housing more than 200 species of animals and tropical birds. It was founded in 1830 with animals supplied by London Zoo. Like many zoos around the world, Dublin Zoo had become run down and cramped by the 1980s but increased investment has expanded the space and facilities for the animals. The famous MGM lion was reputedly bred at the zoo.

Dublin City Hall Dame Street, Dublin. Designed by Thomas Cooley as a Royal Exchange, although he died before its completion; much of the building was designed by James Gandon and it was completed in 1779. Acquired by the City Corporation in 1852, the building now houses an exhibition telling the story of the city from its foundation.

Dublinia St Michael's Hill, Christchurch, Dublin. Heritage centre and museum which charts the history of Dublin from its origins as a Viking settlement through to the mid 16th century. It is housed in the former Synod Hall and St Michael's Church, which is linked to Christ Church Cathedral.

Dún Laoghaire Dún Laoghaire (pronounced 'Dunleary') is a suburban seaside town and ferry port, situated $7^1/_2$ miles (12km) south of Dublin city centre, and is the administrative centre of the county of Dún Laoghaire-Rathdown. The town was officially renamed Kingstown in 1821 in honour of a visit by George IV, but reverted to its ancient Irish name in 1921, a year before Irish independence. The name derives from its founder, Laoghaire, a 5th century High King of Ireland, who chose the site as a sea base from which to carry out raids on Britain and France (the Irish word *dún* means 'fort'). King Laoghaire is famous for having allowed St Patrick to travel the country and preach Christianity. Dún Laoghaire has a ferry connection to Holyhead in Anglesey, Wales. The Dublin–Dún Laoghaire railway, constructed in 1837, was the first railway built in Ireland. The harbour has an East and West Pier; a lighthouse is located at the end of the East Pier. Other features of the town include the National Maritime Museum of Ireland, a Martello tower in nearby Sandycove known as the James Joyce Tower, and the Queen Victoria Fountain, known locally as the Birdcage. Erected in 1900, to a standardised design by Glasgow manufacturers Walter McFarland & Co, to commemorate the visit to Ireland of Queen Victoria, it was seriously damaged in the 1980s, but has been recently restored.

Dundrum Castle Dundrum, Dublin. The ruin of a 13th century castle, rebuilt in the 16th century by the Fitzgerald family and abandoned in the 19th century.

Dunsink Observatory Dunsink Lane, Castleknock, Dublin. Built 1783–5, the observatory now houses the Astronomy department of the School of Cosmic Physics in the Dublin Institute for Advanced Studies. Dublin-born Sir William Rowan Hamilton, the discoverer of quaternion mathematics, was its director during the late 1820s. Tel: 018 387911.

Dunsoghly Castle St Margaret's, 6 miles (10km) northwest of Dublin. A 15th century four-storey tower house built by the Plunkett family and still retaining its medieval trussed roof. It was occupied by the Plunketts until the late 19th century.

Easter Rising, The A Republican uprising which took place in Dublin during Easter week, 1916. From 24 to 29 April 1916 Irish rebels led by Patrick Pearse and James Connolly occupied selected buildings in positions surrounding Dublin Castle, Pearse reading the Proclamation of Independence from the General Post Office at 12.30 on 24 April 1916. British government forces under Sir John Maxwell and W H M Lowe gradually tightened a cordon around the rebels and forced their surrender on Saturday 29 April. While popular sympathy was initially with the government, the subsequent executions of the leaders, including Pearse and Connolly, eventually led to the insurgents becoming the inspiration for the future formation of the Irish Republic.

Famine Memorial Custom House Quay, Dublin. A monument designed by Dublin sculptor Rowan Gillespie and presented to the City of Dublin in 1997. It consists of a number of emaciated figures, placed as if walking towards an emigration ship.

GAA Museum Croke Park Stadium, Dublin. The Gaelic Athletic Association (GAA) Museum was opened in 1998 and is housed under the Cusack Stand in Croke Park Stadium. It celebrates the GAA's contribution to Irish sporting, cultural and social life since its foundation in 1884. Exhibits include the medal collections of famous Gaelic football and hurling players, trophies (the Sam Maguire Cup and Liam MacCarthy Cup), and more than 40 audio-visual presentations about famous players and historic matches. There is also an exhibition covering the events of 21 November 1921 (Bloody Sunday). Tel: 018 192323.

Gaiety Theatre — South King Street, Dublin. The Gaiety was opened in 1871 and continues to present drama, musicals, music and dance. Tel: 016 795622.

Gate Theatre — Cavendish Row, Parnell Square, Dublin. The renowned Gate Theatre was established as a theatre in 1928 by Hilton Edwards and Micheál MacLiammóir to produce avant garde theatre. Housed in the Supper Rooms of the former Rotunda Hospital, built in the 1740s, it showcases Irish writing, acting and theatrical talent. Tel: 087 44045.

General Post Office — O'Connell Street, Dublin. Built 1814–18 to a design by Francis Johnston. Its main feature is its Doric portico, above which are three statues representing Fidelity, Hibernia and Mercury. The building has a special place in the history of Dublin as the focal point of the 1916 Easter Rising (see separate entry); having proclaimed independence, the rebels remained inside for almost a week before they were eventually forced out by shelling. The building was seriously damaged by the siege and retains some evidence of it. A statue of mythical Irish hero Cúchulainn and a plaque inside the building commemorate the Rising and there are plans to turn it into a monument to the events of 1916.

Griffeen Valley Park — Lucan, 8 miles (13km) west of Dublin. A linear park located along the Griffeen River, a tributary of the Liffey. St John's Bridge, which crosses the river between Old Esker and Arthur Griffith Park, dates to at least the 18th century and has been claimed to be the oldest bridge in Ireland.

Guinness Brewery — St James's Gate, Dublin. The Guinness Brewery was established by Arthur Guinness at a disused brewery in 1759, and was extended in 1790 with the building of Vathouses 1 and 2. Guinness West Indies Porter was first brewed in 1801 (the name porter derived from the popularity of the ale among porters at London markets such as Borough and Billingsgate). The famous Guinness beer label was introduced in 1862 and the harp became a registered trademark in 1876. The storehouse, built in 1904 to house the fermentation process, closed in 1988 and was reopened as a visitor centre in 2000. Tel: 01 408 4800.

Highest point — Kippure at 2484ft (757m). The granite mountain straddles the Co. Dublin and Co. Wicklow borders; at its summit is a television and radio transmitter mast.

Howth Abbey — Howth, 8 miles (13km) east of Dublin. The ruin of a 13th century church founded by the Archbishop of Dublin on the site of an earlier foundation overlooking Howth Harbour. Most of the remains date to the 15th century.

Howth Castle — Howth, 8 miles (13km) east of Dublin. A 14th century tower house overlooking Dublin Bay, much enlarged over the centuries and restyled in 1909 by Sir Edwin Lutyens for Julian Gaisford-St Lawrence. The grounds house the National Transport Museum of Ireland and are also noted for a collection of rhododendrons. A popular legend about the castle concerns an incident that apparently occurred in 1576. During a trip from Dublin, the pirate Grace O'Malley (see Mayo) attempted to pay a courtesy visit to the 8th Baron Howth. However, she was informed that the family was at dinner and the castle gates were closed against her. In retaliation, she abducted the grandson and heir, the 10th Baron. He was eventually released when a promise was given to keep the gates open to unexpected visitors, and to set an extra place at every meal. At Howth Castle today, this agreement is still honoured by the Baron's descendants.

Interesting facts — **The Honourable Arthur Wesley** (his family legally changed their surname to Wellesley in March 1798) was probably born at Mornington House, his family's Dublin residence during the social season, although it is possible that he was born at his family seat, Dangan Castle, near Trim, Co. Meath. What is certain is that he was commissioned an ensign in the British Army, rose to prominence in the Napoleonic Wars, and eventually reached the rank of field marshal. After a highly successful military career he was created 1st Duke of Wellington in 1813, a title still held by his descendants. Wellington twice served as Tory Prime Minister of the UK and was one of the leading figures in the House of Lords until his retirement in 1846. **Portmarnock Beach** was the starting point for two aviation firsts. On 23 June 1930 Australian aviator Charles Kingsford Smith and his crew took off in the *Southern Cross* on the first westbound transatlantic flight (to Newfoundland, Canada). The first solo westbound transatlantic flight also began from Portmarnock Beach on 18 August 1932 when Jim Mollison, a British pilot and husband of aviatrix Amy Johnson, took a de Havilland Puss Moth from Portmarnock to Pennfield, New Brunswick, also in Canada. **Ireland's only nudist beach** is situated at Forty Foot Leap, beneath the James Joyce Martello Tower at Sandycove, Dún Laoghaire. The ill-fated champion racehorse **Killiney** was named after the seaside town. Fred Winter trained the horse to win the Royal & SunAlliance Chase at Cheltenham in 1973, the shortest-priced winner ever apart from the even greater Arkle. Killiney was destined for greatness but was tragically killed in a racecourse accident before he could fulfil his destiny.

Irish Museum of Modern Art — Military Road, Kilmainham, Dublin. Housed in the former Royal Hospital Kilmainham, designed by William Robinson in the late 17th century as a home for invalided soldiers. Its design is based on Les Invalides in Paris; the interiors were largely destroyed when it was converted into an art gallery. The permanent collection of the Irish Museum of Modern Art concentrates principally on the works of living artists but includes works produced since the 1940s. It includes works by Gilbert and George, Damien Hirst, Peter Doig and Marina Abramovic. Tel: 016 129900.

Irish Photography Centre — Meeting House Square, Temple Bar, Dublin. The Irish Photography Centre contains three main elements – the Dublin Institute of Photography, the Gallery of Photography, and the National Photographic Archive. The latter, opened in 1998, hosts the photographic collection of the National Library of Ireland, including more than half a million photographs both historical and contemporary. Tel: 016 030374.

Islands	See separate table
James Joyce Tower and Museum	Sandycove, 8 miles (13km) southeast of Dublin. A Martello tower where Joyce spent six nights in 1904, when it was owned by his university friend Oliver St John Gogarty. The tower is described by Joyce in the opening pages of *Ulysses*. Its appearance in 1904 has been recreated and it now houses literary memorabilia associated with Joyce. Tel: 01 280 9265.
Killiney Hill Park	Killiney, 9 miles (15km) southeast of Dublin. Opened in 1887 to commemorate Queen Victoria's Golden Jubilee. There are magnificent views of Killiney and Dublin Bay. The highest point in the park is the obelisk at 558ft (170m).
Kilmainham Gaol	Inchicore Road, Kilmainham, Dublin. Built in the 1790s, over the years Kilmainham housed many famous prisoners including leaders of Irish rebellions. The leaders of the 1916 Easter Rising were held and executed here, and the last prisoner held before the gaol was closed in 1924 was Éamon de Valera. The gaol has been recently restored and now houses an exhibition on the political and penal history of the prison and its restoration. Tel: 01 453 5984.
Kilmashogue Wedge Tomb	7 miles (11km) south of Dublin. A tomb located on Kilmashogue Mountain overlooking Dublin Bay, and probably dating to c. 2000 BC. A little to the east is a standing stone.
Lady's Well	Blanchardstown, 7 miles (11km) northwest of Dublin. An ancient shrine with a ruined 14th century church nearby.
Lambay	(O.N. = Lamb Island). Also Reachrainn. Although the Romans never reached the Irish mainland they did reach the island of Lambay, trading with it and calling it Limnios. In AD 795 the first ever raid by the Vikings on Ireland took place here. Part of Co. Dublin – Fingal. Population: 6.
Leinster House	Kildare Street and Merrion Street, Dublin. Designed by Richard Cassels in 1745 for the Fitzgerald family (Earls of Kildare and Leinster). Occupied by the Royal Dublin Society from 1815 until 1925, when it was bought by the Irish government, it now hosts both houses of the Irish Parliament – the Dáil Éireann and the Senate. The latter is located in the bow-fronted library, while the Dáil Éireann sits in a former lecture theatre built by the Royal Dublin Society.
Lusk Round Tower	Lusk, 13 miles (21km) northeast of Dublin. An early Christian round tower which originally stood within a monastery founded by St Macculin in the 6th century. The tower stands 90ft (27.5m) high and its conical cap is still in place. It is now attached to a square tower house, probably dating to the 16th century.
Luttrellstown Castle	Clonsilla, 7 miles (11km) northwest of Dublin. A 15th century castle built by the Luttrell family and later owned by bookseller and MP Luke White, father of the 1st Baron Annaly. Established in 1983 as a hotel and golf complex (it staged the Guardian Irish Open in 1997), it came into prominence in July 1999, when David Beckham and Victoria Adams married here.
Malahide Castle	Malahide, 8 miles (13km) northeast of Dublin. The seat of the Talbot family from 1185 until 1976, with a short gap in the 1640s. One of the more poignant legends concerns the morning of the Battle of the Boyne in 1690, when 14 members of the family breakfasted together, never to return, as all were dead by nightfall. The castle houses Tara's Palace, a doll's house made in 1980. Tel: 018 462184.
Molly Malone Statue	Grafton Street, Dublin. Created by Jeanne Rynhart and erected in 1987 to commemorate the legendary street seller, subject of a famous song. Located opposite Trinity College, the statue is known colloquially as 'The Tart With The Cart', 'The Dish With The Fish' or 'The Trollop With The Scallops'. The semi-historical/legendary figure supposedly died of cholera.
Mountjoy Prison	Phibsboro, Dublin. A closed medium security prison designed by military engineer Joshua Jebb and opened in 1850. Mountjoy was originally intended as the first stop for men sentenced to transportation; they would spend a period here in separate confinement and then be transferred to Spike Island, where they would be transported to Van Diemen's Land (Tasmania). Some Irish leaders were held here during the Anglo-Irish War and Irish Civil War. Kevin Barry was among those executed at the prison. On 31 October 1973 it was the scene of a spectacular escape by helicopter by three Provisional IRA prisoners, including Seamus Twomey. A new 150 acre site has been acquired at a cost of 30m at Thornton Hall, Co. Dublin, on which a replacement for Mountjoy is to be constructed. The new facility will accommodate 1200 convicts. Tel: 01 806 2800.
National Botanic Gardens	Glasnevin, Dublin. Founded in 1795 by the Royal Dublin Society and covering a total area of 48 acres (19.5ha), part of which is the natural flood plain of the River Tolka. The Curvilinear House was opened in 1849 and restored for the Gardens' bicentenary; the Palm House was opened in 1883. A new visitor centre was opened in 2000. Tel: 018 040300.
National College of Art and Design	Thomas Street, Dublin. Established in 1971, the National College of Art and Design has a long list of antecedents including the Dublin Metropolitan School of Art. Tel: 016 364200.
National Concert Hall	Earlsfort Terrace, Dublin. Situated close to St Stephen's Green, the building was designed by Rudolph Maximilian Butler and was built in the Coburg Gardens, which staged the Dublin International Exhibition of 1865. It was converted into the central building of University College Dublin (UCD) at the foundation of the National University of Ireland in 1908. When UCD relocated to a new campus at Belfield in the 1960s, the building was again converted and was opened as the National Concert Hall by President Patrick Hillery on 9 September 1981. It is regarded as one of Europe's premier centres for the performance of live music, including orchestral, choral, contemporary and traditional works. Tel: 014 170000.
National Gallery of Ireland	Merrion Square West and Clare Street, Dublin. The National Gallery of Ireland was opened in 1864. Its collection spans Irish and European master paintings from the 14th to the 20th century, including works from Italian, French, British and Dutch schools. Irish painters represented include Jack B Yeats, William Orpen, Nathaniel Hone and Louis le Brocquy; European masters include Caravaggio, David, El Greco, Fra Angelico, Gainsborough, Goya, Mantegna, Poussin, Raeburn, Titian, Velázquez, Vermeer and Zurbarán. More modern works include Monet, Picasso and

Pissarro. The Millennium Wing, designed by Benson and Forsyth, was added as an extension in 2000. Tel: 016 615133.

National Library of Ireland — Kildare Street, Dublin. A research library with several reading rooms, housed in a neoclassical building designed by Thomas N Deane and his son Thomas M Deane after a competition held in 1885. It opened in 1890 and has a mission to 'collect, preserve and make available books, manuscripts and illustrative material of Irish interest'. It presents a programme of exhibitions and has a large collection of W B Yeats manuscripts. Tel: 016 030200.

National Maritime Museum of Ireland — Haigh Terrace, Dún Laoghaire. Opened in 1978 and housed in the former Mariners' Church, built in 1837 for seafarers and which remained open until 1971. The main exhibit is the 'Bantry Boat' from a French frigate, captured during the failed French invasion of 1796 after it landed on Bere Island.

National Museum of Ireland, Archaeology and History — Kildare Street, Dublin. One of three sites of the National Museum of Ireland in Dublin. It opened in 1890 and is housed in a building designed by Thomas N Deane and Thomas M Deane as part of the same scheme as the National Library. It has more than two million artefacts distributed between many exceptional collections celebrating Ireland's history from prehistory to the late medieval period. These include galleries on Viking Ireland and medieval Ireland and in particular those covering the late prehistoric (Bronze Age and Iron Age) and early Christian periods. Exhibits include the Ardagh Chalice, the Broighter Hoard, the Derrynaflan Hoard, the Tara Brooch and the Tully Lough Cross. Tel: 016 777444.

National Museum of Ireland, Decorative Arts and History — Benburb Street, Dublin. One of three sites of the National Museum of Ireland in Dublin. It is housed in the Calvary Square ranges of Collins Barracks, built in 1701 to the designs of Thomas Burgh (1670–1730). Apart from the Royal Hospital at Kilmainham (now the Irish Museum of Modern Art), this is the earliest public building still in existence in Dublin. Originally known simply as The Barracks, it became the 'Royal Barracks' in the 19th century but was named for Michael Collins in 1922 when it was handed over to the troops of the Free State army. Assigned to the National Museum of Ireland in 1994, the building was opened after restoration as the Museum of Decorative Arts and History in 1997. This division of the museum covers the economic, social, industrial, political and military history of Ireland from the late medieval period onwards. The many collections cover such areas as weaponry, furniture, coins, costume, silver, ceramics and glassware. Notable exhibits include the Fonthill Vase, the William Smith O'Brien Gold Cup and the Eileen Gray chrome table. Collins Barracks is also the museum's administrative headquarters. Tel: 016 777444.

National Museum of Ireland, Natural History — Merrion Street, Dublin. One of three sites of the National Museum of Ireland in Dublin. The oldest part of the museum, it is housed in a purpose-built neoclassical style building designed by architect Frederick Clarendon and erected in 1856–7. The oldest purpose-built museum building in Ireland, it retains its original 'Victorian cabinet' style of presentation. The ground floor is given over to native fauna including the skeletons of two Irish elks; the upper gallery has three levels set around an atrium and includes animals, birds and insects from across the globe. The museum is known colloquially as the 'Dead Zoo'. Tel: 016 777444.

National Photographic Archive — See Irish Photography Centre

National Print Museum of Ireland — Haddington Road, Dublin. Opened in 1996 and housed in the Garrison Chapel of Beggars Bush Barracks, the museum is home to a unique collection of implements, artefacts and machines (some working) from all sectors of the printing industry in Ireland. Tel: 01 660 3770.

National Transport Museum of Ireland — Howth, 8 miles (13km) northeast of Dublin. Opened in June 1986 in the Heritage Depot in the grounds of Howth Castle. There are collections of passenger transport, commercial vehicles, military vehicles, emergency vehicles and utility transport, the oldest items dating from 1883 and the newest from 1984. Tel: 018 320427.

Old Jameson Distillery — Bow Street, Smithfield, Dublin. The Jameson Distillery was founded by John Jameson in 1780. Tel: 018 072355.

Olympia Theatre — Dame Street, Dublin. Opened in 1879 as music hall. The theatre was remodelled in 1897 and restored in the 1980s. Tel: 016 793323.

O_2, The — North Wall Quay, Dublin. Formerly known as the Point. A large entertainment venue housed in a former train depot built in 1878 as a rail terminus for the Midland & Great Western Railway. It was converted and opened in 1988 with a maximum capacity of 8500. It was the venue of the Eurovision Song Contest in 1994, 1995 and 1997 and is known as the place where *Riverdance* was performed for the first time as a Song Contest interval act (1994). It was closed for remodelling and renovation in 2007, reopening with an increased capacity in 2008. Tel: 081 871 9391.

Pearse Museum — Grange Road, Rathfarnham, Dublin. A museum dedicated to the memory of Patrick Pearse, executed for his part in the 1916 Easter Rising. Located in St Enda's Park, it is housed in the Hermitage, which was at one time occupied by Pearse's experimental school. Tel: 014 934208.

Phoenix Monument — A monument in Phoenix Park. Erected by Lord Chesterfield in 1747, it consists of a Corinthian column topped by a statue of a phoenix rising from the ashes.

Phoenix Park — Located to the west of Dublin city centre and extending for 1760 acres (712ha), Phoenix Park is reputed to be the largest municipal park within a city's limits in the world. The name is derived from Irish *fionn uisce*, 'clear water'. It is where the Phoenix Park Murders took place in 1882. The park is home to the official residence of the President as well as Dublin Zoo, a herd of wild fallow deer, and many other points of interest.

Phoenix Park Murders — The assassination of the Chief Secretary for Ireland, Lord Frederick Cavendish, and the Permanent Under Secretary, Thomas Henry Burke, on the evening of 6 May 1882 while they were walking to the Viceregal Lodge in Phoenix Park from Dublin Castle.

Point, The
See O_2, The

Rathfarnham Castle
Rathfarnham Road, Rathfarnham, Dublin. Possibly dating to the late 16th century, the castle was built by the Loftus family on the site of an earlier Anglo-Norman castle. It changed hands several times during the Civil War of the 1640s but eventually remained in the hands of the Loftuses. Remodelled as a Georgian mansion in the late 18th century, it was owned by the Jesuit Order 1913–85. It passed into state care in 1987 and is subject to ongoing restoration. Tel: 014 939462. See also Cork: Interesting facts for details of Rathfarnham's involvement in Emmet's Rising.

Rivers
The **Liffey** (I. *An Life*) rises near Kippure, a mountain straddling the Co. Dublin/Co. Wicklow border, and flows for 50 miles (80km) through Wicklow, Kildare and Dublin before entering the Irish Sea in Dublin Bay. Towns along the river include Ballymore Eustace, Newbridge, Caragh, Leixlip and Lucan.

Rogerstown Estuary Nature Reserve
$1^{1}/_{4}$ miles (2km) west of Portraine, $4^{1}/_{2}$ miles (7km) northeast of Swords. A site of international importance for brent geese covering 482 acres (195ha) of a tidal bay in the north of Co. Dublin.

Royal Dublin Society
Merrion Road, Ballsbridge, Dublin. A society founded in 1731 to promote and develop agriculture, arts, industry, and science in Ireland. Its premises are a centre for exhibitions, concerts, shows and other cultural events. Tel: 016 680866.

St Patrick's Cathedral
St Patrick's Close, Dublin. The National Cathedral and Collegiate Church of St Patrick was originally built between the 1190s and 1270. It was located on the site of a wooden church raised beside a well where, according to tradition, St Patrick baptised several converts. It became a Protestant cathedral following the Reformation. Jonathan Swift, author of *Gulliver's Travels*, was dean of the cathedral 1713–45 and is buried here. The spire was added in 1769. The cathedral was 'restored' and rebuilt in the 1860s, funded by Sir Benjamin Lee Guinness. St Patrick's is regarded as the national cathedral for the whole of Ireland.

Skerries Mills
Skerries, 17 miles (27km) northeast of Dublin. Two windmills and a watermill located in Skerries Town Park. The windmills are both tower mills, one with five sails and one with four. Tel: 084 95208.

Sport

general
Croke Park, Dublin, is home to the Gaelic Athletic Association (GAA). In use since 1884, it was purchased by the GAA in 1913 and renamed after the GAA's first patron, Archbishop Croke of Cashel. The Railway End was constructed from the rubble left in Sackville Street (now O'Connell Street) after the 1916 Easter Rising (it has since been renamed Hill 16). This was followed by the Hogan Stand (1924), Cusack Stand (1937), the Canal End (1949) and the Nally Stand (1952). The stadium was redeveloped in the 1990s; with the completion of the final phase in 2004, it now holds a maximum of 82,300. Until 2007 the use of Croke Park for 'games with interests in conflict with the interests of the GAA' was prohibited under Rule 42 of the GAA constitution. This in effect banned Croke Park from being used for rugby union and association football (games seen as having British roots). However, mainly because of the redevelopment of Lansdowne Road, this rule was temporarily relaxed after a vote at the 2005 GAA Annual Congress and the first international soccer and rugby matches were played at Croke Park in 2007. It also houses the GAA Museum. The darkest episode in the stadium's history occurred on 21 November 1921, when 12 members of a crowd attending a Gaelic football match between Dublin and Tipperary were killed by the indiscriminate shooting of British auxiliary police in retaliation for the assassination of at least a dozen British Intelligence officers earlier in the day. Tipperary captain Michael Hogan was also shot dead. Tel: 01 819 2300.

Lansdowne Road Stadium, Lansdowne Road, Dublin, is used mostly for rugby and association football internationals and cup finals, as well as concerts. It was opened in 1872 thanks to the efforts of Henry Wallace Doveton Dunlop (1844–1930), organiser of the first All-Ireland Athletics Championships. The first international rugby match was played against England on 11 March 1978 and the first international football match was played between Ireland and England on St Patrick's Day 1900. No football matches were played at Lansdowne Road between 1926 and 1968. The stadium has recently been redeveloped to increase the seating capacity to 50,000, all seated. Tel: 016 440066.

football
Bohemian FC, usually known as Bohemians, were founded in 1890 and are one of only two clubs to have been part of the League of Ireland since its inception, They were winners of the League of Ireland in 1924, 1928, 1930, 1934, 1936, 1975, 1978, 2001, 2003 and 2008, and of the FAI Cup in 1928, 1935, 1970, 1976, 1992, 2001 and 2008. Their home ground is Dalymount Park, Phibsborough, Dublin.

St Patrick's Athletic were founded in 1929. They were winners of the League of Ireland in 1952, 1955, 1956, 1990, 1996, 1998 and 1999, and of the FAI Cup in 1959 and 1961. Their home ground is Richmond Park, Inchicore, Dublin.

Shamrock Rovers, founded in 1901, are historically Ireland's most successful club. They were winners of the League of Ireland in 1923, 1925, 1927, 1932, 1938, 1939, 1954, 1957, 1959, 1964, 1984, 1985, 1986, 1987 and 1994, and of the FAI Cup in 1925, 1929, 1930, 1931, 1932, 1933, 1936, 1940, 1944, 1945, 1948, 1955, 1956, 1962, 1964, 1965, 1966, 1967, 1968, 1969, 1978, 1985, 1986 and 1987. In 2009 they moved to a new ground at Tallaght Park, Dublin.

Shelbourne were founded in 1895 and, like Bohemians, have been part of the League of Ireland since its inception. They were winners of the League of Ireland in 1926, 1929, 1931, 1944, 1947, 1953, 1962, 1992, 2000, 2002, 2003, 2004 and 2006, and of the FAI Cup in 1906, 1911 and 1920. Their home ground is Tolka Park, Drumcondra.

University College Dublin, the university's football team, was founded in 1895 and joined the League of Ireland in 1979. They were winners of the League of Ireland 1st Division in 1995 and of the FAI Cup in 1984. Their home ground is the UCD Bowl, Belfield, Dublin.

Gaelic football — **Dublin** were winners of the All-Ireland Senior Football Championship in 1891, 1892, 1894, 1897, 1898, 1899, 1901, 1902, 1906, 1907, 1908, 1921, 1922, 1923, 1942, 1958, 1963, 1974, 1976, 1977, 1983 and 1995.

horse racing — **Leopardstown** Racecourse, Foxrock, Dublin, holds both Flat and National Hunt racing on a left-handed track of 1 mile 6 furlongs (2.8km) with a run-in of 2$^3/_4$ furlongs (0.5km) and an uphill finish. It stages some of the most prestigious races in Ireland including the Irish Champion Stakes, the Irish Champion Hurdle and the Hennessy Cognac Gold Cup. Tel: 012 893607.

hurling — **Dublin** were winners of the All-Ireland Senior Hurling Championship in 1889, 1917, 1920, 1924, 1927 and 1938.

rugby union — **Leinster Rugby** was formed in 1895 as one of the divisions of the Irish Rugby Football Union. They were winners of the Celtic League/Magners League in 2002 and 2008, and of 22 Irish Inter-Provincial championships. Their home grounds are Donnybrook and the RDS Showgrounds, Dublin.

Swords Castle — Swords, 8 miles (13km) north of Dublin. This National Monument is the extensive ruin of a castle built in the early 13th century as a residence of the Archbishops of Dublin. The area enclosed by its bawn covers 1$^1/_2$ acres (0.6ha). The Archbishops stopped using the castle in the 1320s and it was in ruins by the late 16th century.

Swords Museum — Swords, 8 miles (13km) north of Dublin. A local history museum housed in the town's Carnegie Library.

Swords Round Tower — Swords, 8 miles (13km) north of Dublin. An 85ft (26m) high round tower with evidence of restoration.

Tailors' Hall — High Street, Dublin. The only one of the old medieval guild halls that still exists in Dublin. It dates to 1706 and was the meeting place of the Guild of Merchant Tailors until 1841. The building is now the headquarters of An Taisce, the National Trust for Ireland.

Temple Bar — An area of Dublin City bounded on the north by the River Liffey, to the east by the old Houses of Parliament, to the west by Fishamble Street and to the south by Dame Street. Since the 1990s it has been developed as Dublin's cultural quarter, with many galleries, archives and exhibition spaces and a lively nightlife.

Trinity College Dublin — College Green, Dublin. Founded in 1592 and the only constituent college of the University of Dublin. The college provides academic programmes and academic staff, while the university confers degrees. The college has five faculties: Arts & Humanities, Social & Human Sciences, Engineering & Systems Sciences, Health Sciences, and Natural Sciences. Trinity College Library is a legal deposit library, which means it is legally entitled to a copy of every book published in Great Britain and Ireland. Its most famous holding is the Book of Kells, a Celtic illustrated manuscript produced c.800. The annual Trinity Ball, which marks the beginning of Trinity Week in May, is reputedly the largest private music party in Europe. Tel: 01 896 1000.

Tully's Castle — Clondalkin, 6 miles (10km) west of Dublin. The ruin of a (possibly) 15th century tower house. It is traditionally said to be haunted by one Betty O'Tullach searching for her dead lover.

University College Dublin — The origins of University College Dublin (UCD) date back to the Catholic University of Ireland, founded in the mid 19th century by Paul Cullen and John Henry Newman. In 1881, under the Royal Universities Act, the university was renamed University College Dublin. Among the professors during this phase of UCD's history was poet Gerard Manley Hopkins and among its most famous pupils was writer James Joyce. In 1908, UCD was granted its own charter and was incorporated as a constituent college of the National University of Ireland. Under the Universities Act, 1997, UCD was established as an autonomous university within the National University of Ireland framework. The main campus is situated at Belfield, a 132ha site 2$^1/_2$ miles (4km) south of the city centre. It is an attractively landscaped complex of modern architectural buildings, accommodating most of the university colleges and schools as well as its student residences and numerous leisure and sporting facilities. Other university buildings include Earlsfort Terrace, adjacent to St Stephen's Green in the city centre. The UCD Smurfit School of Business is located at the Blackrock campus, and the School of Agriculture, Food Science & Veterinary Medicine runs a research farm in Lyons Estate, Co. Kildare. Former students include authors Maeve Binchy and Roddy Doyle, actors Gabriel Byrne and Cyril Cusack, and comedians Dermot Morgan and Dara O Briain. Tel: 01 716 7777.

University of Dublin — See Trinity College Dublin

Wall of Fame — Temple Lane, Temple Bar, Dublin. A tribute to some of Ireland's favourite musical heroes, celebrated in a permanent outdoor photographic exhibition.

War Memorial Gardens — South Circular Road, Islandbridge, Dublin. Designed by Sir Edwin Lutyens and dedicated to the memory of 49,400 Irish soldiers who died in World War I. A number of granite pergolas or 'bookrooms' contain the names of all the soldiers.

Wellington Monument — Phoenix Park, Dublin. An obelisk commemorating the victories of the Duke of Wellington. Designed by Robert Smirke, it stands 205ft (62.5m) high; although begun in 1817 it was not completed until 1861 through lack of funds.

Some famous people born in County Dublin

Ahern, Bertie (Taoiseach of Ireland) (1951–)	Drumcondra
Allen, Dave (comedian) (1936–2005)	Firhouse
Andrews, Eamonn (TV presenter) (1922–87)	Dublin
Bacon, Francis (painter) (1909–92)	Dublin
Balfe, Michael William (composer) (1808–70)	Dublin
Barnardo, Thomas (philanthropist) (1845–1905)	Dublin
Beckett, Samuel (playwright and poet) (1906–89)	Foxrock
Behan, Brendan (playwright and poet) (1923–64)	Dublin
Binchy, Maeve (author) (1940–)	Dalkey
Brady, Liam (footballer) (1956–)	Dublin
Brown, Christy (author) (1932– 81)	Crumlin
Burke, Edmund (political theorist) (1729–97)	Dublin
Byrne, Gay (TV presenter) (1934–)	Dublin
Coghlan, Eamonn (athlete) (1952–)	Drimnagh
Collins, Steve (boxer) (1964–)	Cabra
Cosgrave, Liam (Taoiseach of Ireland) (1920–)	Dublin
Cosgrave, W T (President of the Irish Free State) (1880–1965)	Dublin
Costello, John (Taoiseach of Ireland) (1891–1976)	Dublin
Doherty, Ken (snooker player) (1969–)	Dublin
Doyle, Roddy (author) (1958–)	Dublin
Farrell, Colin (actor) (1976–)	Castleknock
Field, John (composer) (1782–1837)	Dublin
FitzGerald, Barry (actor) (1888–1961)	Dublin
FitzGerald, Garret (Taoiseach of Ireland) (1926–)	Dublin
Gambon, Michael (actor) (1940–)	Dublin
Geldof, Bob (singer) (1951–)	Dún Laoghaire
Griffith, Arthur (politician) (1872–1922)	Dublin
Harrington, Pádraig (golfer) (1971–)	Ballyroan
Herbert, Victor (composer) (1859–1924)	Dublin
Joyce, James (author) (1882–1941)	Rathgar
Keane, Robbie (footballer) (1980–)	Tallaght
Keating, Ronan (singer) (1977–)	Dublin
Kinsella, Thomas (poet) (1928–)	Inchicore
Le Fanu, Sheridan (author) (1814–73)	Dublin
Lemass, Seán (Taoiseach of Ireland) (1899–1971)	Dublin
Murdoch, Iris (writer) (1919–1999)	Dublin
O'Casey, Sean (dramatist) (1880–1964)	Dublin
O'Connor, Sinéad (singer) (1966–)	Dublin
O'Hara, Maureen (actress) (1920–)	Ranelagh
O'Kelly, Sean Thomas (President of Ireland) (1882–1966)	Dublin
O'Shea, Milo (actor) (1926–)	Dublin
Pollen, Daniel (New Zealand Prime Minister) (1813–96)	Ringsend
Roche, Stephen (cyclist) (1959–)	Dundrum
Shaw, George Bernard (writer) (1856–1950)	Dublin
Sheridan, Richard Brinsley (playwright) (1751–1816)	Dublin
Steele, Richard (co-founder of the *Spectator*) (1672–1729)	Dublin
Stoker, Bram (author) (1847–1912)	Fairview
Swift, Jonathan (author) (1667–1745)	Dublin
Synge, John Millington (playwright) (1871–1909)	Rathfarnham
Wellesley, Arthur (soldier and statesman) (1769–1852)	Dublin
Wilde, Oscar (playwright) (1854–1900)	Dublin
Yeats, William Butler (poet and dramatist) (1865–1939)	Sandymount

Islands of County Dublin

(shipping area = Irish Sea)

Island name	Area	Nearest landmark	General information
Bill, The	Irish Sea	Skerries	Smaller of the two twin islands of Rockabill. At low water it is possible to walk across to Lighthouse Island.
Bull Island	Dublin Bay	Dublin	See separate entry
Church Island	Irish Sea	Skerries	aka Colt Island
Colt Island	Irish Sea	Skerries	aka Church Island
Dalkey Island	Killiney Bay	Dalkey	Small grassy island just offshore from Dalkey, close to Dún Laoghaire. There is evidence of habitation as far back as 4000 BC, but there is now no indigenous population. There is a Martello tower and fort on the island.

Island name	Area	Nearest landmark	General information
Inis Mac Neasain	Irish Sea	Howth	See Ireland's Eye
Ireland's Eye	Irish Sea	Howth	aka Inis Mac Neasain. Now a bird sanctuary. There are the ruins of an old chapel, the successor of one built in the 7th century, and a Martello tower.
Lambay	Irish Sea	Portraine	See separate entry
Lighthouse Island	Irish Sea	Skerries	Part of the Rockabill islets. Designated a Special Protection Area in 1988. The lighthouse, first constructed in 1860, was rebuilt in 1900 and automated in April 1989.
Maiden Rock	Dalkey Sound	Dalkey	Lies just off the coast of Dalkey Island.
Muglins, The	Killiney Bay	Dalkey	Close neighbour of Dalkey Island.
North Bull Island	Dublin Bay	Dublin	See Bull Island
Reachrainn	Irish Sea	Portraine	See Lambay
St Patrick's Island	Irish Sea	Skerries	There is the ruin of an early Christian church and monastery dating to the Viking era. A synod held on the island in 1148 was attended by 15 bishops and 200 priests.
Shenick Island	Irish Sea	Skerries	The island is dominated by a Martello tower at its northern end. The passage between the island and the mainland virtually dries out at low water.

Galway

Inishark
Inishbofin
MAYO
Omey
Clifden
Benbaun
727
Connemara
Atlantic Ocean
Cashel
Oughterard
Lough Corrib
Iar Connaught
Croaghnakeela
Tuam
R. Clare
ROSCOMMON
Mountbellew Bridge
Monivea
Ballinasloe
Galway
Athenry
Oranmore
Gorumna Island
Galway Bay
R. Shannon
OFFALY
Loughrea
Kinvarra
Gort
Slieveaughty Mountains
Portumna
TIPPERARY
CLARE
0
20 miles
0
30 km

Galway is part of the province of Connacht. It lies in the west of Ireland and is the second largest county, after County Cork. It is bordered by Mayo to the northwest, Roscommon to the northeast, Offaly to the east, Tipperary to the southeast and Clare to the south. Its western coastline lies on the Atlantic Ocean. County Galway is home to Lough Corrib (the largest lake in the Republic of Ireland), the Na Beanna Beola (Twelve Bens) mountain range, Na Sleibhte Mham Toirc (the Maum Turk mountains), and the low mountains of Sliabh Echtghe (Slieve Aughty). The major towns are Athenry, Ballinasloe, Clifden, Tuam, Loughrea and Galway, the county town.

Galway City takes its name from the Gaillimh River (River Corrib) that formed the western boundary of the earliest settlement, which was called Dun Bhun na Gaillimhe ('fort at the bottom of the Gaillimh'). The word Gaillimh means 'stony' as in 'stony river'. The Galway urban area is the sixth largest in the whole of Ireland (after Dublin, Belfast, Cork, Limerick and Derry). Galway is unique among Irish cities because of the strength of its Irish language, music, song and dancing traditions – it is often referred to as the 'Bilingual Capital of Ireland'. The city is well known for its 'Irishness', mainly due to the fact that it has on its doorstep the Galway Gaeltacht (Irish-speaking area). The language is visible on the city streets, with bilingual signage on display on shops and road signs, and can be heard by locals around the city. Irish theatre, TV production and Irish music are an integral part of Galway City life, with both An Taibhdhearc, the National Irish Language Theatre, and TG4 headquarters in Galway.

Galway has a number of candidates for its best-known native. For the sportsman there are Grand National winning jockey Graham Lee or golfer Christy O'Connor Jr, while the arts are represented by two figures from the turn of the 20th century: Nora Barnacle, muse of James Joyce, and Lady Augusta Gregory, who with W B Yeats co-founded the Irish Literary Theatre and the Abbey Theatre.

Galway	Population			Area	
Districts	*male*	*female*	*total*	*sq miles*	*sq km*
Ballinasloe rural area	4228	3941	8169	190	492
Ballinasloe Town	3017	2967	5984	7	17
Clifden	4668	4369	9037	305	791
Galway City	31,015	34,817	65,832	20	51
Galway rural area	16,289	15,612	31,901	305	791
Glennamaddy	2870	2676	5546	130	336
Gort	5151	4877	10,028	168	434
Loughrea	9862	9747	19,609	312	808
Mount Bellew	4102	3673	7775	160	414
Oughterard	5984	5616	11,600	315	817
Portumna	3140	2942	6082	131	339
Tuam	14,041	13,473	27,514	333	861
Total	104,367	104,710	209,077	2375	6151

Local Attractions and Information

Administrative headquarters	County Hall, Prospect Hill, Galway. Tel: 091 509000.
Airport	**Galway Airport** (GWY), Carnmore, 5 miles (8km) northeast of Galway. Opened in 1987 and owned by Corrib Airports Ltd. Aer Arann operates flights to Dublin as well as to various destinations in the UK, with limited services to Europe. Tel: 091 755569.
Annaghdown Castle	8 miles (13km) north of Galway. The well-preserved ruin of a five-storey tower house beside Lough Corrib. It is believed to have been built in the 15th century by the Archbishop of Tuam.
Annaghkeen Castle	$4^1/_2$ miles (7km) southwest of Headford, 13 miles (21km) northwest of Galway. The ruin of a tower house on the shore of Lough Corrib, possibly dating to c.1240.
Anthony Raftery Statue	Craughwell, 5 miles (8km) south of Athenry. A sculpture of the last of the great Gaelic bards, created by Donal O'Murhcadha.
Ardamullivan Castle	5 miles (8km) west of Gort. The well preserved ruin of a five-storey tower house probably dating to the 16th century.
Arkin's Castle	Inishmore. A Cromwellian fort garrisoned in the 17th and 18th centuries.
Athenry Arts and Heritage Centre	The Square, Athenry. Opened in 1999 and housed within the ruins of the 13th century collegiate church. Exhibits include the town's original mace and seal, dating to c.1320. The centre also presents exhibitions of visual arts. Tel: 091 844661.
Athenry Castle	Court Lane, Athenry. Built in 1240 by Meiler de Bermingham and abandoned in the 15th century. The castle was restored during the 1990s and now houses an exhibition and an audio-visual room. Tel: 091 844797.
Athenry Priory	Bridge Street, Athenry. The ruin of a Dominican friary founded in 1241 by Meiler de Bermingham, 2nd Baron of Athenry, who was buried near the high altar in 1252. It was dedicated to St Peter and St Paul. Accidentally burned shortly after its foundation and rebuilt on a larger scale, it escaped the Dissolution as the friars agreed to adopt a secular habit. The buildings were damaged in 1652 by Cromwellian troops, who also expelled the friars. In the mid 18th century a barracks was built within the ruins and troops were housed here until the mid 19th century. The remains are mainly those of the nave and chancel church. The priory is a National Monument in state care.
Athenry Town Gate	North Gate Street, Athenry. The only surviving gate out of the original five town gates of Athenry. Much of the town wall remains.
Aughnanure Castle	2 miles (3km) southeast of Oughterard, 13 miles (21km) northwest of Galway. A well-preserved 16th century six-storey tower house with a double bawn, built by the O'Flaherty family and located on the shore of Lough Corrib. Tel: 091 552214.
Ballinasloe Fair	One of the oldest horse fairs in Europe, dating to the 8th century. It attracts tens of thousands of visitors annually.
Ballindooley Castle	Menlough, 2 miles (3km) north of Galway. A 16th century four-storey tower house built by the Burke family, and recently restored.
Ballykine Castle	1 mile (1.6km) northeast of Clonbur, 20 miles (32km) west of Tuam. Aka Ballykyne Castle. A possibly 16th century structure formerly owned by the O'Kyne family and later part of the Guinness estate.
Ballynahinch Castle	Recess, $12^1/_2$ miles (20km) southeast of Clifden. A mansion situated in one of the most picturesque areas of Connemara, overlooking the Ballynahinch River, and built in 1756 by Robert Martin, father of 'Humanity' Richard Martin (see Interesting facts). The estate is strongly associated with Connemara's clans, notably the O'Flahertys, and was the home in the 16th century of the Pirate Queen of Connacht, Grace O'Malley (see Mayo), who married Donal O'Flaherty in 1546. In 1926 it was bought by Indian cricketer Prince Ranjitsinhji, who owned it until his death in 1933. Today, the castle is a luxury hotel.
Banagher Martello Tower	13 miles (21km) southeast of Ballinasloe. An early 19th century Martello tower located on the west bank of the Shannon, on the Galway/Offaly border, and designed to defend the river against a possible Napoleonic attack. The interior is not accessible.

Battle of Aughrim Interpretative Centre	Aughrim, 7 miles (11km) southwest of Ballinasloe. The centre explains the course of the battle fought on 12 July 1691, along with the background to the conflict and its aftermath. Tel: 090 967 3939.
Battles	Two battles have been fought in Co. Galway: Athenry and Aughrim. See separate table for details.
Brackloon Castle	$1\frac{1}{4}$ miles (2km) southwest of Clonfert, 9 miles (15km) southeast of Ballinasloe. The ruin of a four-storey 15th century tower house once owned by the O'Maddens.
Brigit's Garden	Pollagh, 1 mile (1.6km) east of Roscahill, 10 miles (16km) northwest of Galway. A series of themed gardens reflecting the four Celtic seasonal festivals of Samhain, Imbolc, Beltane and Lughnasa. Tel: 091 550905.
Caherdangan Castle	$\frac{1}{2}$ mile (0.8km) east of Craughwell, 5 miles (8km) south of Athenry. A restored 15th century castle, now a private residence.
Carna	A major lobster fishing area situated at the head of Iorras Aintheach Peninsula. Mweenish Island and Golam Head are close by.
Cathedral of Our Lady Assumed into Heaven and St Nicholas	Gaol Road, Galway. Aka Galway Cathedral. Located on Nun's Island in the River Corrib and built on the site of the city jail, the cathedral was designed by J J Robinson and completed in 1965. Noted for its mixture of styles, which include Romanesque, Renaissance, Byzantine and Spanish, it has a large octagonal dome and a series of contemporary stained glass windows.
Claregalway Abbey	Claregalway, 6 miles (10km) northeast of Galway. The ruin of a Franciscan friary founded in the mid 13th century. The ruins are dominated by a central tower.
Claregalway Castle	Claregalway, 6 miles (10km) northeast of Galway. The ruin of a 15th century five-storey tower house built by the Burke family.
Clifden Castle	Sky Road, Clifden. The ruin of a Gothic Revival style castle built in the mid 18th century by John d'Arcy. Abandoned in the 1840s, it fell into disrepair.
Cloghan Castle	Kilchreest, 4 miles (6km) southwest of Loughrea. Originally built as an outpost fortification in the 13th century, the castle was last inhabited in the 15th century by Hugh de Burgo (Burke), son of Walter de Burgo, Earl of Ulster. For centuries it stood derelict until again acquired by the Burke family in 1973. Comprehensive restoration of the castle as a holiday and wedding venue took place 1974–9, and further restoration 1996–9.
Clonfert Cathedral	Clonfert, 9 miles (15km) southeast of Ballinasloe. A cathedral on the site of a 6th century monastic site founded by St Brendan. The cathedral mainly dates from the 15th century but features a decorated 12th century Romanesque doorway.
Clontuskert Abbey	4 miles (6km) south of Ballinasloe. The ruin of an Augustinian friary founded in the 12th century. The church was burned down in 1413 but rebuilt on a grander scale. The monastery was dissolved in 1540 but the friars returned in the 17th century. Its main feature is its decorated west doorway.
Connemara	A region in the west of Co. Galway towards the Atlantic coast, and featuring an amazing variety of bog, moorland, lake and mountain scenery. Its unofficial capital is at Clifden.
Connemara National Park	Established in 1980, partly from the lands of the former Kylemore Abbey Estate, and consisting of 7400 acres (3000ha) of mountain, bog, grassland and woodland. It includes some of the Twelve Bens or Beanna Beola mountain range. Wildlife includes Connemara ponies. Tel: 095 41054.
Coole Park	2 miles (3km) northwest of Gort. An estate once owned by Lady Augusta Gregory and now part of the Coole-Garryland Nature Reserve, covering 900 acres (364ha) of woodland and lakes. W B Yeats' poem 'The Wild Swans at Coole' was inspired by Coole Park. Of particular interest is the autograph tree, engraved with initials of many of the leading figures of the Irish Literary Revival. The 'Seven Woods Trail' connects the different woods made famous in Yeats' poetry.
Craughwell Statues	Craughwell, $4\frac{1}{2}$ miles (7km) south of Athenry. The village green at Craughwell has statues of Lady Augusta Gregory and the great Gaelic bard Anthony Raftery (c.1784–1835). Both statues were crafted by sculptor Donal O'Murhcadha.
Cromwell's Castle	Inishbofin. A castle remodelled in the early 19th century which was designed to defend Banagher Bridge on the Shannon against a possible Napoleonic attack.
Dartfield Horse Museum	Kilrickle, 5 miles (8km) northeast of Loughrea. A purpose built museum opened in 2000 which celebrates the horse and its contribution to Irish society. Exhibits include artefacts, farm equipment and carriages; there is also an art gallery. The museum is surrounded by 350 acres (140ha) of parkland. Tel: 091 843968.
Deerpark Castle	1 mile (1.6km) southwest of Kilchreest, 5 miles (8km) southwest of Loughrea. The ruin of a 15th century tower house built by the Burke family.
Derrygimlagh Bog	4 miles (6km) south of Clifden. An area of blanket bog which on 15 June 1919 was the landing place of the Vickers Vimy flown from Newfoundland by John Alcock and Arthur Brown. Their pioneering transatlantic flight lasted 16 hours 28 minutes.
Derryhivenny Castle	3 miles (5km) northeast of Portumna. The ruin of a 17th century tower house built by Daniel O'Madden, one of the last such castles to be built in Ireland.
Drumharsna Castle	1 mile (1.6km) southwest of Ardrahan, 13 miles (21km) southeast of Galway. The ruin of a 16th century five-storey tower house built by Shane Ballagh and occupied until 1920.
Dun Aonghasa	Kilmurvey, Inishmore, Aran Islands. A triple-walled stone fort on a promontory believed to have been occupied 1500 BC–AD 1000.
Dunguaire Castle	Kinvara, 10 miles (16km) southeast of Galway. A restored 75ft (23m) high tower house on the shore of Galway Bay, built in 1520 by the Hynes family. Tel: 061 360788.
Eyre Square	A square in Galway City which is now the site of two cannons from the Crimean War and a statue of the Padraic O'Conaire. In 1965, the square was officially renamed Kennedy Memorial Park in honour of US President John F Kennedy, who visited Galway in 1963.
Feartagar Castle	Castlegrove, 5 miles (8km) northwest of Tuam. Aka Jennings' Castle. The well preserved ruin of a 16th century four-storey tower house built by the Burke family. It was abandoned in the mid 17th century.

'Fields of Athenry, The'	A song famous for its associations with Irish rugby. Although seemingly ancient, it was actually composed in 1970 by Pete St John. *By a lonely prison wall* *I heard a sweet voice calling,* *'Danny, they have taken you away.* *For you stole Travelian's corn,* *That your babes might see the morn,* *Now a prison ship lies waiting in the bay.'* *Fair lie the fields of Athenry* *Where once we watched the small freebirds fly.* *Our love grew with the spring,* *We had dreams and songs to sing* *As we wandered through the fields of Athenry.* *By a lonely prison wall* *I heard a young man calling* *'Nothing matters, Jenny, when you're free* *Against the famine and the crown,* *I rebelled, they ran me down,* *Now you must raise our children without me.'* *On the windswept harbour wall,* *She watched the last star rising* *As the prison ship sailed out across the sky* *But she'll watch and hope and pray,* *For her love in Botany Bay* *Whilst she is lonely in the fields of Athenry.* *Whilst she is lonely in the fields of Athenry.*
Fields of Athenry Thatched Heritage Cottage	North Gate Street, Athenry. A recreated traditional Irish cottage with displays of artefacts from the early 20th century. Tel: 091 844113.
Friar's Cut, The	Reputedly the first canal in Ireland, cut in the 12th century to allow boats to pass from Lough Corrib to the sea at Galway.
Galway Cathedral	See Cathedral of Our Lady Assumed into Heaven and St Nicholas
Galway City Museum	Spanish Arch, Galway. A folk museum concentrating on the fishing industry in Galway. Exhibits include a 30ft (9m) Galway Hooker boat. Tel: 091 532460.
Glengowla Mines	2 miles (3km) west of Oughterard, 15 miles (24km) northwest of Galway. A heritage 19th century silver and lead mine, now offering underground tours. The site also contains a museum. Tel: 091 552021.
Highest point	Benbaun at 2385ft (727m), the highest of the Twelve Bens.
Inishbofin	Aka Inis Bo Finne (White Cow Island). Inishbofin, along with Inishlyon and Inishark, lies 5 miles (8km) off the northwest coast of Connemara. In AD 665 St Coleman founded a monastery on the island and there are also the remains of a Cromwellian barracks (see Cromwell's Castle). One of the Outer Islands. Population: 178.
Interesting facts	Irish politician **Colonel Richard Martin**, born in Ballynahinch, was nicknamed the 'Wilberforce of Hacks', and more famously 'Humanity Dick', partly due to his fight for Catholic emancipation but mainly due to his animal rights campaigning. Martin is now most famous for his work against cruelty to animals, especially bear baiting and dog fighting. His actions eventually led to the Ill Treatment of Cattle Bill, which in 1822 became an Act of Parliament and is known as Martin's Act. Martin also tried to spread his ideas in the streets of London, becoming the target of jokes and political cartoons that depicted him with ears of an ass. He also sometimes paid the fines of minor offenders. On 16 June 1824 he was present when the Society for the Prevention of Cruelty to Animals was founded in the London coffee shop Old Slaughter's, although he denied being the founder of the society, gallantly deferring this honour to the Rev. Benjamin Waugh. Renmore-born **Pat Gibson** lays claim to being the cleverest man in Ireland. Pat has the distinction of winning the jackpot on the British version of *Who Wants to Be A Millionaire?* and followed that up by winning the BBC TV programme *Mastermind.* For good measure he subsequently became Brain of Britain to complete a memorable treble. Pat has also been British and World Quiz Champion.
Islands	See separate table. There are over 300 islands in Lough Corrib.
Kilbennan Round Tower	$2^{1}/_{2}$ miles (4km) northwest of Tuam. A possibly 12th century round tower, partly collapsed but still standing 52ft (16m) high. It has a doorway 12ft (3.5m) above ground level.
Kilcolgan Castle	Kilcolgan, 8 miles (13km) southeast of Galway. Standing beside the Kilcolgan River overlooking Galway Bay, the original castle was built in the 11th century and rebuilt in the late 18th century by the St George family. It has recently been refurbished to provide holiday accommodation. Tel: 091 796112.
Kilconnell Abbey	Kilconnell, 7 miles (11km) west of Ballinasloe. The ruin of a Franciscan friary founded in 1353 by William O'Kelly on the site of an earlier monastic foundation.
Kilmacduagh Monastic Site	5 miles (8km) southwest of Gort. The site of a 7th century monastic foundation on which stands a virtually complete round tower and the ruin of a 12th century church, once the cathedral of the Diocese of Kilmacduagh.
Kiltartan Gregory Museum	Kiltartan, 3 miles (5km) north of Gort. A museum housed in the restored former National School, which closed in 1960. The museum opened in 1996 and includes an old Irish classroom, photographs, memorabilia, and genealogy resources. Tel: 091 632346.
Kylemore Abbey	$2^{1}/_{2}$ miles (4km) east of Letterfrack, 7 miles (11km) northeast of Clifden. Originally a neo-Gothic

style castle designed by Samuel Ussher Roberts for Mitchell Henry and built 1867–71. It became an abbey in 1920 when it was purchased by the Benedictine Order. Standing on the edge of a lake, it features a restored neo-Gothic church built in the late 1870s and a restored Victorian walled garden which won the Europa Nostra Award for Gardens in 2000. The castle also houses a convent and a girls' school. Tel: 095 41146.

Lackagh Castle — Lackagh, 1¼ miles southwest of Turloughmore, 10 miles (16km) northeast of Galway. A ruined five-storey tower house beside Lackagh Bridge on the River Clare.

Lackagh Museum and Heritage Park — Lackagh, 1¼ miles southwest of Turloughmore, 10 miles (16km) northeast of Galway. A museum housed in a restored traditional Irish cottage with domestic furniture and agricultural artefacts. Tel: 091 797444.

Lough Corrib — The largest lake in the Republic of Ireland and second largest in both Ireland (after Lough Neagh) and the British Isles, covering 77 sq miles (200 sq km).

Lough Derg — See Tipperary

Lynch's Castle — Shop Street, Galway. An early 16th century tower house which was converted into a bank in the 1960s.

Maum Turk Mountains — A range of mountains to the west of the village of Maum, and part of the Connemara Highlands. Their highest point is Binn Idir an Da Log at 2037ft (703m). The ancient Pilgrim's Path leads to St Patrick's Holy Mountain, the site of a chapel and of the rock known as St Patrick's Bed.

Na Seacht Teampaill — Inishmore, Aran Islands. The 'seven churches' of pilgrimage of which only two now survive: Temple Brecan and Teampall an Phoill. These are the ruins of two stone churches which date to the 12th and 15th century respectively.

Nature reserves — **Bealacooan Bog**, 2 miles (3km) north of Inverin, 17½ miles (28km) west of Galway, covering 3081 acres (1247ha), part of the Connemara Bog complex and an intact example of Atlantic or oceanic blanket bog.

Coole-Garryland see Coole Park

Derryclare, 10 miles (16km) east of Clifden, 47 acres (19ha) of native semi-natural woodland, pond and wet moorland on the shore of Derryclare Lough.

Derrycrag Wood, ½ mile (0.8km) southeast of Woodford, 8 miles (13km) southwest of Portumna, 274 acres (111ha) of largely oak and ash woodland. A remnant, along with Pollnaknockaun and Rossturra Woods, of the once much more extensive forest that covered the area.

Leam West Bog, 2 miles (3km) southeast of Maam Cross, 8 miles (13km) west of Oughterard, one of the largest areas of intact bog in Connemara, covering 922 acres (373ha). One of the few sites containing both lowland and highland bog.

Pollnaknockaun Wood, ½ mile (0.8km) north of Woodford, 11 miles (18km) southeast of Loughrea, 97 acres (39ha) of semi-natural woodland.

Richmond Esker, 2½ miles (4km) northwest of Moylough, 11 miles (18km) east of Tuam, covering 40 acres (16ha) and comprising two of the few esker ridges (gravel ridges created by glaciation) in Ireland which still carry native woodland.

Rossturra Woods, 2 miles (3km) northeast of Woodford, 45 acres (18ha) largely of oak and ash woodland.

Nora Barnacle House Museum — Bowling Green, Galway. Reputedly the smallest museum in Ireland. Formerly the home of Nora Barnacle, wife of author James Joyce, the house was derelict from the 1960s until the late 1980s, when it was purchased and restored to its turn of the century condition before being opened to the public. Exhibits include letters, photographs and memorabilia. Tel: 091 564743.

O'Brien's Castle — Inishere, Aran Islands. The ruin of a 15th century tower house, owned by the O'Briens and later seized by the O'Flahertys.

Oranmore Castle — Oranmore, 5 miles (8km) east of Galway. A tower house built by the Burke family and dating to the 15th or 16th century.

Pallas Castle — 2 miles (3km) southeast of Duniry, 10 miles (16km) southeast of Loughrea. A well-preserved early 16th century five-storey tower house with attached bawn, built by the Burke family.

Portumna Castle — Portumna, 16 miles (26km) southeast of Loughrea. A fortified house built in 1618 by Richard Burke, 4th Earl of Clanrickarde, and gutted by fire in 1826. The surrounding formal gardens include a willow maze and a kitchen garden. There are exhibitions in the castle and the gatehouse. Tel: 090 974 1658.

Portumna Forest Park — 1 mile (1.6km) west of Portumna, 16 miles (26km) southeast of Loughrea. A mainly coniferous forest on the shore of Lough Derg covering 1500 acres (600ha) of an estate formerly belonging to the Clanrickarde family.

Rinville Park — Oranmore, 5 miles (8km) east of Galway. A park created from a 16th century demesne, with views over Galway Bay from Rinville Point and Saleen Point.

Rivers — The **Beagh** flows from Lough Cutra near the village of Gort close to the border with Co. Clare. The **Clare** rises in Ballyhaunis, Co. Mayo, and flows in a southerly direction entering Co. Galway north of Dunmore. The river continues south through Milltown, Tuam, Lackagh and Claregalway before finally entering Lough Corrib north of Galway City, its total length approximately 53 miles (85km). The middle section of the limestone river is artificial (geographically known as a turlough) and is partially dry during hot dry spells. The **Corrib** flows for 4 miles (6km) from Lough Corrib through Galway to Claddagh and into Galway Bay. **The Suck** – see entry in Co. Roscommon.

Roscam Round Tower — 3 mile (5km) southeast of Galway. The 30ft (9m) high stump of a round tower on an early monastic site.

Ross Castle — Rosscahill, 11 miles (18km) northwest of Galway. Aka Ross House. Built in 1590 by Robert Martin and situated within a 120 acre (48ha) estate beside Ross Lake. The grounds include parkland and walled gardens. It was the birthplace of Violet Florence Martin (1862–1915), who under the pen name Martin Ross is best known for writing *Some Experiences of an Irish R.M.* (1899) and *Further Experiences of an Irish R.M.* (1908) along with Edith Somerville (1858–1949). Tel: 091 550183.

Ross Errilly Friary	1 mile (1.6km) northwest of Headford, 11 miles (18km) southwest of Tuam. The extensive ruin of a Franciscan friary founded in 1351 by Sir Raymond Burke.
St Brendan's Cathedral	Barrack Street, Loughrea. The cathedral of the Diocese of Clonfert, designed by William Byrne and built 1897–1902. It is noted for its decorated interior, stained glass windows and carved capitals which tell the story of St Brendan and the diocese. A small museum in the grounds houses the Clonfert Diocesan Museum collection, including chalices and vestments dating from the 15th to the 18th century.
St Nicholas Collegiate Church	Lombard Street, Galway. The largest medieval parish church in Ireland, founded in 1320 and dedicated to St Nicholas of Myra, who in addition to being the patron saint of children is also the patron saint of sailors and fishermen. The church was raised to the status of a collegiate church in 1484. Traditionally Christopher Columbus worshipped here in 1477 and in September 2002, the church was the scene of the first public same-sex marriage in an Irish church.
Spanish Arch, The	A surviving section of the walls of Galway City. It dates from the 16th century and was built to allow ships to come into the harbour and unload their goods.
Sport	
football	**Galway United** were founded as Galway Rovers in 1937, changing their name in 1981. They were winners of the League of Ireland 1st Division in 1993 and the FAI Cup in 1991. Their home ground is Terryland Park, Galway City.
Gaelic football	**Galway** are winners of the All-Ireland Senior Football Championship in 1925, 1934, 1938, 1956, 1964, 1965, 1966, 1998 and 2001.
horse racing	**Galway Racecourse**, Ballybrit. The first official race meeting at Ballybrit was held on 17 August 1869. The course now stages the Galway Plate, one of the most important steeplechases in Ireland. The right handed, almost rectangular course of 1 mile 2 furlongs (2km) has a sharp descent to the turn and an uphill finish of 2 furlongs (0.4km). Tel: 091 753870.
rugby union	**Connacht Rugby** represent the Connacht branch (founded in 1885) of the Irish Rugby Football Union, and compete in the Magners League (formerly the Celtic League). Their home ground is Galway Sportsgrounds, Galway.
Synge House Museum	Inishmaan, Aran Islands. A former holiday home of playwright John Millington Synge (1871–1909). Now restored to its appearance when Synge stayed here, it houses a museum with exhibits including photographs, drawings and letters. Tel: 099 73036.
Teampall Caomhain	Inishere, Aran Islands. The ruin of a church founded in the 10th century by St Caomhain (Kevin).
Thoor Ballylee	4 miles (6km) northeast of Gort. A 16th century tower house with adjacent cottages which were bought by poet W B Yeats in 1916. It fell into disrepair after the family left in 1929 but has been restored and now houses a museum celebrating Yeats' life and times. The title of Yeats' book of poems *The Tower* (1928) is believed to refer to Thoor Ballylee. Tel: 091 631436.
Town Hall Theatre	Courthouse Square, Galway. Originally built in the 1820s as a court house and later used as a town hall. It was converted into a cinema in the 1950s, and opened as a theatre in 1995 after a major refurbishment. It has a 390 seat auditorium. Tel: 091 569777.
Tuam Cathedral	High Street, Tuam. The Cathedral Church of the Assumption of the Blessed Virgin Mary was largely constructed 1827–37, but incorporates a richly decorated 12th century Romanesque chancel arch. The Tuam Market Cross stands within the cathedral.
Tuam Mill Museum	Shop Street, Tuam. A visitor centre and seasonal tourist information office housed in a mill which closed in 1964. Visitors can view the old milling process. Tel: 093 25486.
Tullira Castle	1 mile (1.6km) south of Ardrahan, 5 miles (8km) north of Gort. A 17th century tower house remodelled in the 19th century. The home of playwright, poet and independence activist Edward Martyn, it has associations with W B Yeats and Lady Gregory.
Tyrone House	2 miles (3km) west of Kilcolgan, 7 miles (11km) southeast of Galway. Built in 1779 for the St George family.

Some famous people born in County Galway

Connolly, Joe (hurling player) (1956–)	Castlegar
Connolly, John (hurling player) (1948–)	Connemara
Daly, Dominick (politician) (1798–1868)	Ardfry
Fallon, Padraic (poet) (1905–74)	Athenry
Feeney, Julie (singer) (1978–)	Athenry
Gavin, Frankie (musician) (1956–)	Corrandulla
Gibson, Pat (champion quiz player) (1961–)	Renmore
Harney, Mary (politician) (1953–)	Ballinasloe
Hoogan, Desmond (author) (1950–)	Ballinasloe
Keane, Dolores (singer) (1953–)	Caherlistrane
Lee, Graham (jockey) (1975–)	Galway
Martin, Violet Florence (author) (1862–1915)	Connemara
Murphy, Tom (playwright) (1935–)	Tuam
Noone, Nora Jane (actress) (1984–)	Newcastle
O'Connor, Christy Jnr (golfer) (1948–)	Galway
O'Connor, Christy Snr (golfer) (1924–)	Knocknacarra
O'Flaherty, Liam (writer) (1896–1984)	Inishmore
O'Toole, Peter (actor) (1932–)	Connemara
Pettit, Philip (philosopher) (1945–)	Ballygar
Reddin, Tony (hurling player) (1919–)	Mullagh

Islands of County Galway

(shipping area = Malin)

Island name	Area	Nearest landmark	General information
An Ballasta	Kilkieran Bay	Ardmore Point	Tiny rock off the coast of Finish Island.
An Bheitheach	Kilkieran Bay	Inishtravin	aka Na Beitheacha, Beaghy Island. One of the Gorumna group.
An Bheitheach Thuaidh	Kilkieran Bay	Inishtravin	aka Beaghy Island North. One of the Gorumna group.
An Buachal	Atlantic	Claddaghduff	aka The Boy. One of the Outer Islands group.
An Cnapach	Atlantic	Lettermullan Island	aka Crappagh Island. One of the Gorumna group. Joined to Lettermullan Island by causeway.
An Cro	Kilkieran Bay	Kilkieran	aka Crow Island. One of the Gorumna group.
An Cruach Island	Atlantic	Aughrus Point	(I. = The Stack). Aka An Cruagh Island, Cruagh Island. One of the Outer Islands.
An Cruagh Island	Atlantic	Aughrus Point	See An Cruach Island
An Gearran	Kilkieran Bay	Ardmore Point	Tiny rock off the coast of Finish Island.
An Ros	Atlantic	Lettermore Island	aka Rossroe. Population: 19.
An tAibhnin Mor	Camus Bay	Rosmuck	aka Evneeamor Island
An tOilean Ban	Lough Mask	Clonbur	aka White Island
An tOilean Garbh	Kilkieran Bay	Inishtravin	aka Illaunard Island. One of the Gorumna group.
An tOilean Gorm Theas	Bertraghboy Bay	Cashel	aka Illaungorm South Island
An tOilean Gorm Thuaidh	Bertraghboy Bay	Cashel	aka Illaungorm North Island
An tOilean Iarthach Theas	Atlantic	Lettermore Island	aka Eragh Island. One of the Gorumna group.
An tOilean Iartharach	Kilkieran Bay	Kilkieran	aka Illauneeragh West. One of the Gorumna group.
An t-Oilean Iatharach	Galway Bay	Black Head	aka Rock Island or Earagh Island. The more westerly of the two Brannock Islands and the most westerly of the Aran Islands.
An tOilean Iseal	Atlantic	Claddaghduff	aka Eeshal Island. One of the Inner Islands.
An tOilean Mor	Kilkieran Bay	Turlough	aka Illaunmore, Big Island. One of the Gorumna group. Population: 1.
An tOilean Mor	Lough Mask	Clonbur	aka Big Island
An tOilean O Thuaidh	Kilkieran Bay	Illaunard	aka North Island. One of the Gorumna group.
An tOilean Rua	Atlantic	Lettermore Island	aka Illaunroe, Red Island. One of the Gorumna group.
Annaghvaan	Atlantic	Lettermore Island	One of the Gorumna group. Population: 121.
Arainn	Galway Bay	Black Head	aka Inishmore, Inis Moir. The largest and most westerly of the three main Aran Islands. Area: 17 sq miles (44 sq km). Population: 831.
Aran Islands	Galway Bay	Black Head	The three main islands in the group are Inishmore (Large Island), Inis Meain (Middle Island) and Inis Oirr (Eastern Island). There are also three tiny satellite islands annexed to Inishmore: Straw Island, Rock Island and Brannock Island.
Ard Oilean	Atlantic	Aughrus Point	aka High Island. One of the Outer Islands.
Ard Oilean	Atlantic	Aughrus Point	aka High Island. One of the Outer Islands.
Ardillaun Island	Lough Corrib	Clonbur	aka Ardoilean
Ardoilean	Lough Corrib	Clonbur	aka Ardillaun Island
Avery Island	Atlantic	Mace Head	aka Oilean Aimhreidh
Beaghy Island	Kilkieran Bay	Inishtravin	See An Bheitheach
Beaghy Island North	Kilkieran Bay	Inishtravin	See An Bheitheach Thuaidh
Big Island	Kilkieran Bay	Turlough	See An tOilean Mor (1)
Big Island	Lough Mask	Clonbur	aka An tOilean Mor
Bilberry Island	Lough Corrib	Inchagoill	Lies southeast of Inchagoill.
Bior Beag	Kilkieran Bay	Ardmore Point	aka Birbeg Island. One of the Gorumna group.
Bior Beag	Kilkieran Bay	Ardmore Point	Lies off the coast of Finish Island.
Bior Mor	Kilkieran Bay	Ardmore Point	aka Birmore Island. One of the Gorumna group.
Bior Mor	Kilkieran Bay	Ardmore Point	aka Burr Island. Lies off the coast of Finish Island.
Birbeg Island	Kilkieran Bay	Ardmore Point	aka Bior Beag. One of the Gorumna group.
Birmbeg Island	Kilkieran Bay	Ardmore Point	aka Bior Beag. One of the Gorumna group.
Birmore Island	Kilkieran Bay	Ardmore Point	See Bior Mor (1)
Black Rock	Atlantic	Inishbofin	Tiny islet off the coast of Inishbofin.
Bob's Island	Lough Corrib	Sullivan's Point	The island is good all around for trout for 50 yards offshore and fishes best in a west wind.
Booey Island	Lough Corrib	Clonbur	aka Buai

Island name	Area	Nearest landmark	General information
Booeybeg	Lough Corrib	Clonbur	Tiny sister island of Booey.
Boolard Island	Streamstown Bay	Clifden	Small grass and fern island in the middle of the bay. One of the Inner Islands.
Bouchal Rock	Atlantic	Inishshark	The vertical rock lies 100ft (30m) off the coast of Inishshark.
Boy, The	Atlantic	Claddaghduff	See An Buachal
Brannock Island	Galway Bay	Black Head	aka Oilean Da Bhranog. One of the six Aran Islands; with Rock Island, also constitute the Brannock Islands.
Brickeen Island	Lough Corrib	Rinnerroon Point	Situated in the Rinnerroon Bay area of the lough.
Bronteen Islands	Lough Corrib	Oughterard	Group of three tiny islets in the lough.
Buai	Lough Corrib	Clonbur	aka Booey Island
Burr Island	Kilkieran Bay	Ardmore Point	See Bior Mor (2)
Caislean na Circe	Lough Corrib	Clonbur	The castle (aka Hen's Castle or Castlekirk) that dominates the island was built in a night by a cock and a hen according to legend.
Calf Islands	Atlantic	Slyne Head	One of the Doonloughan group of fragmented grassy mounds grazed by cattle.
Cannaver Island	Lough Corrib	Curraghduff	aka Ceannuir
Carbry Island	Lough Corrib	Annaghcloon Point	The channel between Carbry Island and Malachy's Island is a popular haunt for pike fishing.
Carraig an Iolra	Kilkieran Bay	Ardmore Point	Tiny rock off the coast of Finish Island.
Carraig an Mart	Kilkieran Bay	Ardmore Point	Tiny rock off the coast of Finish Island.
Carraig an tSeoighigh	Kilkieran Bay	Ardmore Point	Tiny rock off the coast of Finish Island.
Carraig Bhaird	Kilkieran Bay	Ardmore Point	Tiny rock off the coast of Finish Island.
Carraig Chonchubhair	Kilkieran Bay	Ardmore Point	Tiny rock off the coast of Finish Island.
Carraig Éamoinn	Kilkieran Bay	Ardmore Point	Tiny rock off the coast of Finish Island.
Carraig na bPortán	Kilkieran Bay	Ardmore Point	Tiny rock off the coast of Finish Island.
Carraig Sheáin Uí Fhéinne	Kilkieran Bay	Ardmore Point	Tiny rock off the coast of Finish Island.
Carrickarone	Atlantic	Slyne Head	One of the Doonloughan group.
Carrickarone	Atlantic	Aughrus Point	Lies off the coast of High Island.
Carrickawhilla	Atlantic	Aughrus Point	Lies off the coast of High Island.
Carricklahan East	Atlantic	Clifden	Lies just off the coast and accessible at low tide.
Carrickmahoy	Atlantic	Inishbofin	Lies 0.6 miles (1km) south of Inishbofin.
Carricknamackon	Atlantic	Lettermullan Island	Tiny islet off the coast of Lettermullan Island.
Carrickrana Rocks	Atlantic	Clifden	One of several rock stacks lying just off the coast.
Castlekirk	Lough Corrib	Inchagoill	An impressive 13th century fortress can be seen on this island.
Ceannuir	Lough Corrib	Curraghduff	aka Cannaver Island
Chapel Island	Atlantic	Slyne Head	aka Oilean an Teampaill
Cladhnach	Atlantic	Rosmuck	aka Clynagh Island
Cleenillaun	Lough Corrib	Clonbur	Notable for its floating jetty.
Clynagh Island	Atlantic	Rosmuck	aka Cladhnach
Conor's Island	Lough Corrib	Dooros	aka Oilean Ui Chonchuir
Crappagh Island	Atlantic	Lettermullan Island	See An Cnapach
Creenillaun	Lough Corrib	Dooros	Extensive shallows run from the Needle Islands to within 300 yards (274m) of Creenillaun.
Creeve Island	Lough Corrib	Creeve Bay	Noted for its salmon fishing.
Croaghnakeela	Atlantic	Mace Head	aka Deer Island, Cruach na Caoile
Croghnut Island	Dooletter Lough	Illaungorm	aka Cruachnait
Crow Island	Kilkieran Bay	Kilkieran	See An Cro
Cruach na Caoile	Atlantic	Mace Head	aka Croaghnakeela, Deer Island
Cruachnait	Dooletter Lough	Illaungorm	aka Croghnut Island
Cruagh Island	Atlantic	Aughrus Point	See An Cruach Island
Crump Island	Atlantic	Rinvyle Point	aka Oilean Da Chruinne. One of the Inner Islands.
Cuddoo Rock	Atlantic	Aughrus Point	Known for its severe breakers.
Curryskahan Island	Lough Corrib	Headford	Trout fishing is popular all along the shores of the island.
Cussafuara Island	Lough Corrib	Oughterard	Annexed to Inishool.
Daighinis	Atlantic	Gorumna Island	aka Dinish Island. One of the Gorumna group.
Damhoilean	Atlantic	Rinvyle Point	aka Davillaun, Ox Island or Stag Island. One of the Outer Islands.
Davillaun	Atlantic	Rinvyle Point	aka Damhoilean, Ox Island or Stag Island. One of the Outer Islands.

Island name	Area	Nearest landmark	General information
Dawsy's Rock	Atlantic	Lettermullan Island	One of the Gorumna group.
Deer Island	Atlantic	Mace Head	aka Croaghnakeela, Cruach na Caoile
Deer Island	Galway Bay	Aughinish	Lies little more than 1 mile (1.6km) north of Aughinish Island, Co. Clare.
Deer Island	Lough Inagh	Bencorr	Tiny islet off the Tawin peninsula.
Devenish Island	Lough Corrib	Birchall Bay	The fishing here is at its best around mid April during duckfly hatches.
Dinish Island	Atlantic	Gorumna Island	aka Daighinis. One of the Gorumna group.
Dog Island	Atlantic	Lettermullan Island	aka Oilean an Mhadra. One of the Gorumna group.
Dog Island	Atlantic	Aughrus Point	One of two islands of the same name in Galway.
Doolick Rock	Atlantic	Mace Head	Joined to the mainland at low water.
Doonguddle	Atlantic	Mace Head	A Spanish trawler, the *Arosa*, was shipwrecked on the island, 3 October 2000. Of the crew of 13, only one was saved; two others were taken off alive but died en route to hospital. Of the ten that drowned, only four bodies were recovered.
Doonpatrick	Atlantic	Mace Head	Latitude: 53° 16' 19"; longitude: 10° 00' 50"
Dubhros Island	Lough Corrib	Fornocht Point	The lough descends to 165ft (50m) deep around this island.
Duck Island	Atlantic	Mweenish Island	aka Oilean Lachan
Duck Island	Atlantic	Slyne Head	aka Oilean Lachan
Eagle Rock	Atlantic	Lettermullan Island	Lies south of Redflag Island.
Earagh Island	Galway Bay	Black Head	See An t-Oilean Iatharach
Earl's Island	River Corrib	Galway City	aka Oilean an Iarla. Situated in the heart of the city with various bridges and walkways to the town centre.
Eddy Island	Galway Bay	Eddy Point	Joined to mainland by coral sandbank.
Eeshal Island	Atlantic	Claddaghduff	aka An tOilean Iseal. One of the Inner Islands.
Eragh Island	Atlantic	Lettermore Island	See An tOilean Iarthach Theas
Evneeamor Island	Camus Bay	Rosmuck	aka An tAibhnin Mor
Ferroonagh West	Atlantic	Aughrus Point	Tiny rock lying just off the coast.
Fiddoun Island	Kinvara Bay	Parkmore	Lies northwest of the entrance to Kinvara Bay.
Finish Island	Kilkieran Bay	Ardmore Point	aka Oilean Finis. One of the Gorumna group. There are numerous rocks off the coast of this island including Carraigreacha Roisín an Bholgáin and Leacracha Mhuintir Churraoin. Others are included in the table.
Finnis Rock	Galway Bay	Black Head	Lies 0.6 mile (1km) from Inishere.
Fish Rock	Atlantic	Lettermullan Island	Lies west of Eagle Rock and southwest of Redflag Island.
Flynn Island	Lough Corrib	Birchall Bay	The fishing here is at its best around mid April during duckfly hatches.
Foal Island	Atlantic	Cloghmore Point	aka Oilean an Bhromaigh.
Foirinis	Atlantic	Lettermullan Island	aka Furnace Island. One of the Gorumna group. Population: 56.
Foorannagh	Lough Corrib	Oughterard	Lies in the centre of Glynn's Bay.
Fox Island	Atlantic	Doonhill	Lies in the waters between Doon Hill and Bunowen.
Fraochoilean	Bertraghboy Bay	Mace Head	(I. = Heather Island). Aka Freaghillaun
Fraochoilean Beag	Atlantic	Lettermullan Island	aka Freaghillaun Beg. One of the Gorumna group.
Fraochoilean Mor	Atlantic	Lettermullan Island	aka Freaghillaunmore. One of the Gorumna group.
Fraochoilean Theas	Ballynakill Harbour	Tully Mountain	aka Freaghillaun South. One of the Inner Islands.
Freaghillaun	Bertraghboy Bay	Mace Head	aka Fraochoilean
Freaghillaun Beg	Atlantic	Lettermullan Island	aka Fraochoilean Beag. One of the Gorumna group.
Freaghillaun South	Ballynakill Harbour	Tully Mountain	aka Fraochoilean Theas. One of the Inner Islands.
Freaghillaunmore	Atlantic	Lettermullan Island	aka Fraochoilean Mor. One of the Gorumna group.
Freheen Island	Lough Corrib	Birchall Bay	The fishing here is at its best around mid April during duckfly hatches.
Friar Island	Atlantic	Aughrus Point	aka Oilean na mBrathar. One of the Outer Islands.
Fuidges Island	Lough Corrib	Birchall Bay	The fishing here is at its best around mid April during duckfly hatches.

Island name	Area	Nearest landmark	General information
Furnace Island	Atlantic	Lettermullan Island	aka Foirinis. One of the Gorumna group. Population: 56.
Galcarrick Island	Lough Corrib	Ballinduff Bay	Huge trout are caught off this island.
Glasoilean	Atlantic	Lettermore Island	Lies in the harbour just off the coast.
Glat Island	Lough Corrib	Birchall Bay	The fishing here is at its best around mid April during duckfly hatches.
Goat Island	Lough Corrib	Birchall Bay	The smaller Kid Island is its appropriately named neighbour.
Golam Island	Atlantic	Lettermullan Island	aka Golam. One of the Gorumna group.
Gorumna Island	Atlantic	Carraroe	aka Oilean Gharumna. Many of the islands in the Gorumna group are connected to the mainland and to each other by a series of causeways and bridges. Population: 1015.
Greeve Islands	Kilkieran Bay	Illaunard	aka Oileain na Craoibhe. Part of the Gorumna group.
Hen Island	Atlantic	Doon Hill	One of the Slyne Head Islands.
High Island	Atlantic	Aughrus Point	aka Ard Oilean. One of the Outer Islands.
Hog Island	Atlantic	Claddaghduff	One of the Inner Islands.
Horse Island	Atlantic	Slyne Head	One of the Slyne Head Islands.
Illaunacloch	Lough Corrib	Inchagoill	Lies southeast of Inchagoill.
Illaunacric	Lough Corrib	Dooros	Trout and salmon in abundance off this island.
Illaunacroghnut Island	Atlantic	Slyne Head	aka Oilean Cruachnaite
Illaunagappul	Kilkieran Bay	Illaunmore	aka Oilean na gCapall. One of the Gorumna group.
Illaunagappul	Kilkieran Bay	Illaunmore	aka Oilean na gCapall. One of the Gorumna group.
Illaunagawna Island	Atlantic	Slyne Head	aka Re Ghamhna
Illaunakirka	Kilkieran Bay	Inishtravin	aka Oilean na Circe. One of the Gorumna group.
Illaunaknick Island	Atlantic	Slyne Head	aka Oilean an Chnoic
Illaunaknock Island	Atlantic	Slyne Head	aka Oilean an Chnoic
Illaunaleana	Atlantic	Slyne Head	One of the Doonloughan group.
Illaunamenara	Atlantic	Slyne Head	aka Oilean na Meannan. One of the Doonloughan group.
Illaunamid	Atlantic	Slyne Head	aka Oilean Imill (Edge/Margin Island). One of the Doonloughan group.
Illaunananima	Atlantic	Gorumna Island	aka Oilean an Anama
Illaunananima	Atlantic	Rinvyle Point	aka Oilean an Anama. One of the Inner Islands.
Illaunaneel Island	Atlantic	Slyne Head	aka Oilean an Aoil
Illaunaranaun	Lough Corrib	Oughterard	Notable only as a fishing area.
Illaunard Island	Kilkieran Bay	Inishtravin	See An tOilean Garbh
Illaunarogghmul	Bertraghboy Bay	Cashel	Tope, ray and dogfish are caught off this island.
Illaunatraghta Island	Atlantic	Slyne Head	aka Oilean na dTrachta
Illaunaveetry Island	Atlantic	Slyne Head	aka Oilean an Bhiatra
Illaunawehichy Island	Atlantic	Slyne Head	aka Oilean na bhFaochacha
Illauncasheen	Casheen Bay	Furnace	aka Illauncosheen, Oilean an Chaisin. One of the Gorumna group.
Illauncosheen	Casheen Bay	Furnace	See Illauncasheen
Illauncurragilka	Atlantic	Mace Head	aka Oilean Chora an Ghiolcaigh
Illaundabreach	Lough Corrib	Kitteen's Bay	Good wet-fly fishing for trout all around this island.
Illaundalaur	Lough Corrib	Inchagoill	Lies southeast of Inchagoill.
Illaundarragh	Atlantic	Mace Head	aka Oilean Darach
Illauneeragh	Kilkieran Bay	Kilkieran	aka Oilean Iarthach. One of the Gorumna group.
Illauneeragh West	Kilkieran Bay	Kilkieran	aka An tOilean Iartharach. One of the Gorumna group.
Illaunfadda	Lough Corrib	Oughterard	Notable only as a fishing area.
Illaungorm North Island	Bertraghboy Bay	Cashel	aka An tOilean Gorm Thuaidh.
Illaungorm South Island	Bertraghboy Bay	Cashel	aka An tOilean Gorm Theas.
Illaungurrag	Atlantic	Lettermore Island	aka Oilean na nGeabhrog. One of the Gorumna group.
Illaunmaan	Kilkieran Bay	Turlough	aka Oilean Meana
Illaunmore	Kilkieran Bay	Turlough	See An tOilean Mor (1)
Illaunnacroagh Beg	Atlantic	Mace Head	aka Oilean na Cruaiche Beg
Illaunnacroagh More	Atlantic	Mace Head	aka Oilean na Cruaiche Mor
Illaunnanownim	Atlantic	Lettermullan Island	aka Oilean an Anama (Island of the Soul) One of the Gorumna group.
Illaunnginga	Atlantic	Mace Head	aka Oilean na Ginge
Illaunree Island	Atlantic	Mace Head	aka Oilean Fhraoigh

Island name	Area	Nearest landmark	General information
Illaunribbeen	Lough Corrib	Clonbur	aka Oilean Roibin
Illaunroe	Atlantic	Lettermore Island	See An tOilean Rua
Illaunrossalough	Atlantic	Mace Head	aka Oilean Ros an Locha
Illaunrush	Atlantic	Mace Head	Lies close to Doolin Rock in Clifden Bay.
Illaunurra	Atlantic	Slyne Head	aka Oilean Ura
Inchacommaun	Kilkieran Bay	Lettermore Island	aka Inis Camain
Inchaghaun	Kilkieran Bay	Lettermore Island	Population: 3.
Inchagoill	Lough Corrib	Dooros	aka Inis an Ghaill (Island of the Foreigner). Largest and regarded as the jewel in the crown of the Lough Corrib islands, with its 5th and 12th century ruins.
Inchamakinna	Atlantic	Lettermore Island	aka Inis Mhic Cionaith. One of the Gorumna group.
Inchiquin	Lough Corrib	Headford	Particularly good trout fishing March, April, May and September.
Inchnagael	Lough Corrib	Inchagoill	
Inis Aillte	Atlantic	Rosmuck	aka Inisheltia.
Inis Airc	Atlantic	Inishbofin	aka Inishshark. One of the Outer Islands.
Inis an Ghaill	Lough Corrib	Dooros	aka Inchagoill.
Inis Bearachain.	Kilkieran Bay	Lettermore Island	aka Inishbarra. One of the Gorumna group.
Inis Bigir	Bertraghboy Bay	Mace Head	aka Inishbigger
Inis Bo Finne	Atlantic	Rinvyle Point	See Inishbofin
Inis Boinne	Lough Corrib	Headford	aka Inishbiana
Inis Camain	Kilkieran Bay	Lettermore Island	aka Inchacommaun
Inis Caorach	Atlantic	Slyne Head	aka Inishkeeragh. One of the Doonloughan group.
Inis Daith Bhui	Lough Corrib	Clonbur	aka Inishdauwee
Inis Duga	Atlantic	Slyne Head	aka Inishdugga. One of the Doonloughan group.
Inis Durois	Lough Corrib	Dooros	aka Inishdoorus
Inis Eirc	Atlantic	Gorumna Island	aka Inisherk. One of the Gorumna group.
Inis Goirt	Atlantic	Inishbofin	(I. = Salty Island). Aka Inishgort. One of the Outer Islands.
Inis Laighean	Atlantic	Inishbofin	aka Inishlyon. One of the Outer Islands.
Inis Leacain	Bertraghboy Bay	Roundstone	aka Inishlackan
Inis Leith	Atlantic	Lettermore Island	aka Inishlay. One of the Gorumna group.
Inis Loiscthe	Atlantic	Lettermore Island	aka Inishlusk. One of the Gorumna group.
Inis Meain	Galway Bay	Black Head	aka Inishmaan. One of the Aran Islands. The location of Dun Connor, one of the finest complete ring forts in existence. Area: 6 sq miles (15 sq km). Population: 187.
Inis Mhic an Trir	Lough Corrib	Castletown	aka Inishmicatreer
Inis Mhic Cionaith	Atlantic	Lettermore Island	aka Inchamakinna. One of the Gorumna group.
Inis Mhionlais	Lough Corrib	Dooros	aka Inishvinlush
Inis Moir	Galway Bay	Black Head	See Arainn
Inis Muscrai	Kilkieran Bay	Ardmore Point	aka Inishmuskerry or Oilean Mhuscrai. One of the Gorumna group.
Inis na nEan	Lough Corrib	Clonbur	aka Inishnanean Island
Inis Ni	Bertraghboy Bay	Roundstone	aka Inishnee. Population: 24.
Inis Oirr	Galway Bay	Black Head	aka Inishere, Inisheer. Smallest of the three Aran Islands. O'Brien's Castle and Old Tower on the hill are the dominant landmarks. St Caomhán is the patron saint. Area: 2.19 sq miles (5.67 sq km). Population: 262.
Inis Scine Beag	Atlantic	Ship Sound	aka Inishskinnybeg. One of the Outer Islands.
Inis Scine Mor	Atlantic	Ship Sound	aka Inishskinnymore. One of the Outer Islands.
Inis Strathair	Atlantic	Carna	aka Inishtroghenmore
Inis Toirc	Atlantic	Claddaghduff	aka Inishturk. One of the Inner Islands.
Inis Toirc	Atlantic	Barnabaun Point	aka Inishturk
Inis Treabhair	Kilkieran Bay	Rosmuck	aka Inishtravin. One of the Gorumna group. Population: 1.
Inis Troighe	Bertraghboy Bay	Mace Head	aka Inishtreh
Inishanboe Island	Lough Corrib	Oughterard	Excellent fishing off northwest to southwest shores.
Inishannagh	Lough Corrib	Dooros	Neighbouring island of Inchagoill (Inis an Ghaill).
Inishbarra	Kilkieran Bay	Lettermore Island	aka Inis Bearachain. One of the Gorumna group.
Inishbiana	Lough Corrib	Headford	aka Inis Boinne
Inishbigger	Bertraghboy Bay	Mace Head	aka Inis Bigir

Island name	Area	Nearest landmark	General information
Inishboanagh	Lough Corrib	Headford	Trout fishing is popular all along the shores of the island.
Inishbofin	Atlantic	Rinvyle Point	See separate entry
Inishbroon	Atlantic	Rinvyle Point	One of the Outer Islands.
Inishcash	Lough Corrib	Oughterard	Good wet-fly fishing all round and there is a duckfly hatch on the eastern shore. The southeast of the island is a noted pike-holding area.
Inishdauwee	Lough Corrib	Clonbur	aka Inis Daith Bhui
Inishdawros	Ballyconneely Bay	Ballyconneely	Ballyconneely Bay is a small inlet of the Atlantic.
Inishdoorus	Lough Corrib	Dooros	aka Inis Durois
Inishdugga	Atlantic	Slyne Head	aka Inis Duga. One of the Doonloughan group.
Inisheer	Galway Bay	Black Head	See Inis Oirr
Inisheltia	Atlantic	Rosmuck	aka Inis Aillte
Inishere	Galway Bay	Black Head	See Inis Oirr
Inisherk	Atlantic	Gorumna Island	aka Inis Eirc. One of the Gorumna group.
Inishgarraun	Lough Corrib	Oughterard	The channel between the island and the mainland is navigable only at high water.
Inishgort	Atlantic	Inishbofin	See Inis Goirt
Inishkannagh	Lough Corrib	Dooros	
Inishkeeragh	Atlantic	Slyne Head	aka Inis Caorach. One of the Doonloughan group.
Inishlackan	Bertraghboy Bay	Roundstone	aka Inis Leacain
Inishlannaun	Lough Corrib	Curraghduff	
Inishlay	Atlantic	Lettermore Island	aka Inis Leith. One of the Gorumna group.
Inishlusk	Atlantic	Lettermore Island	aka Inis Loiscthe. One of the Gorumna group.
Inishlyon	Atlantic	Inishbofin	aka Inis Laighean. One of the Outer Islands.
Inishmaan	Galway Bay	Black Head	See Inis Meain
Inishmicatreer	Lough Corrib	Castletown	aka Inis Mhic an Trir
Inishmore	Galway Bay	Black Head	See Arainn
Inishmuskerry	Kilkieran Bay	Ardmore Point	aka Oilean Mhuscrai or Inis Muscrai. One of the Gorumna group.
Inishnanean Island	Lough Corrib	Clonbur	aka Inis na nEan
Inishnee	Bertraghboy Bay	Roundstone	aka Inis Ni. Population: 24.
Inishool	Lough Corrib	Oughterard	Annexed to Cussafuara island.
Inishrone	Galway Bay	Connemara	Situated at the mouth of Galway Bay.
Inishshanboe	Lough Corrib	Oughterard	
Inishshark	Atlantic	Inishbofin	aka Inis Airc (Sea Monster Island). One of the Outer Islands.
Inishskinny	Atlantic	Inishbofin	Lies off Inishbofin.
Inishskinnybeg	Atlantic	Ship Sound	aka Inis Scine Beag. One of the Outer Islands.
Inishskinnymore	Atlantic	Ship Sound	aka Inis Scine Mor. One of the Outer Islands.
Inishthee	Lough Corrib	Clonbur	aka Inis Tui
Inishtravin	Kilkieran Bay	Rosmuck	aka Inis Treabhair. One of the Gorumna group. Population: 1.
Inishtreh	Bertraghboy Bay	Mace Head	aka Inis Troighe
Inishtroghenmore	Atlantic	Carna	aka Inis Strathair
Inishturk	Atlantic	Barnabaun Point	aka Inis Toirc
Inishturk	Atlantic	Claddaghduff	aka Inis Toirc. One of the Inner Islands.
Inishvinlush	Lough Corrib	Dooros	aka Inis Mhionlais
Island off the Woods	Lough Corrib	Oughterard	
Islaunalaur	Lough Corrib	Inchagoill	Lies southeast of Inchagoill.
Kelly's Island	Lough Corrib	Dooros	aka Oilean Ui Cheallaigh
Kid Island	Lough Corrib	Birchall Bay	The larger Goat Island is its appropriately named neighbour.
Kinelly Islands	Atlantic	Lettermore Island	Tiny islets off Lettermore Island.
Laidhean	Atlantic	Rosmuck	aka Leighorn Island
Lecky Rocks	Atlantic	Rinvyle Point	The rocks lie off the coast near Rinvyle Point.
Lee's Island	Lough Corrib	Headford	Good for trout and an excellent salmon lie.
Leighorn Island	Atlantic	Rosmuck	aka Laidhean
Leitir Meallain	Atlantic	Gorumna Island	aka Lettermullan. One of the Gorumna group. Population: 219.
Leitir Moir	Atlantic	Bealadangan	aka Lettermore. One of the Gorumna group. Population: 497.
Lettermore	Atlantic	Bealadangan	See Leitir Moir
Lettermullan	Atlantic	Gorumna Island	See Leitir Meallain
Loughcarrick Island	Atlantic	Gorumna Island	One of the Gorumna group.
Mainis	Bertraghboy Bay	Knockboy	aka Oilean Mhuighinse, Mweenish. Accessible from the mainland. Population: 146.

Island name	Area	Nearest landmark	General information
Malachy's Island	Lough Corrib	Annaghcloon Point	The channel between Malachy's Island and Carbry Island is a popular haunt for pike fishing, although Malachy's Island itself fishes well for trout all round on the west and southwest shores.
Mason Island	Atlantic	Mace Head	aka Oilean Maisean
Mile Rock	Atlantic	Mace Head	One of a group of rocky islets off Mace Head.
Morgan's Island	Lough Corrib	Inchagoill	Lies southeast of Inchagoill.
Mucklough Island	Lough Corrib	Inchagoill	
Muirbheach	Atlantic	Murvagh	aka Murvagh Island
Mullan an Rón	Kilkieran Bay	Ardmore Point	Tiny rock off the coast of Finish Island.
Mulroney's Island	Kinvara Bay	Parkmore	The north of the island is dominated by a huge oyster shell midden.
Murvagh Island	Atlantic	Murvagh	aka Muirbheach
Mutton Island	Galway Bay	Galway	Joined to the mainland since 2000 by a non-portagable causeway
Mweenish	Bertraghboy Bay	Knockboy	See Mainis
Na Beitheacha	Kilkieran Bay	Inishtravin	See An Bheitheach
Needle Islands	Lough Corrib	Dooros	Excellent trout fishing between Needle Islands and Kelly's Island.
North Island	Kilkieran Bay	Illaunard	aka An tOilean O Thuaidh. One of the Gorumna group.
Oghly Island	Bertraghboy Bay	Roundstone	aka Oilean an Chlai
Oileain na Craoibhe	Kilkieran Bay	Illaunard	aka Greeve Islands. Part of the Gorumna group.
Oilean Aimhreidh	Atlantic	Mace Head	aka Avery Island
Oilean an Anama	Atlantic	Gorumna Island	aka Illaunananima
Oilean an Anama	Atlantic	Rinvyle Point	(I. = Live Island). Aka Illaunananima. One of the Inner Islands.
Oilean an Anama	Atlantic	Lettermullan Island	aka Illaunnanownim. One of the Gorumna group.
Oilean an Aoil	Atlantic	Slyne Head	aka Illaunaneel Island
Oilean an Arbhair	Atlantic	Furnace	One of the Gorumna group.
Oilean an Bhiatra	Atlantic	Slyne Head	aka Illaunaveetry Island
Oilean an Bhromaigh	Atlantic	Cloghmore Point	aka Foal Island
Oilean an Chaisin	Casheen Bay	Furnace	See Illauncasheen
Oilean an Chnoic	Atlantic	Slyne Head	aka Illaunaknock Island
Oilean an Chnoic	Atlantic	Slyne Head	aka Illaunaknick Island
Oilean an Iarla	River Corrib	Galway City	aka Earl's Island. Situated in the heart of the city with various bridges and walkways to the town centre.
Oilean an Mhadra	Atlantic	Lettermullan Island	aka Dog Island. One of the Gorumna group.
Oilean an Phocaide	Atlantic	Gorumna Island	aka Puck Island. One of the Gorumna group.
Oilean an Teampaill	Atlantic	Slyne Head	aka Chapel Island
Oilean Chora an Ghiolcaigh	Atlantic	Mace Head	aka Illauncurragilka
Oilean Cruachnaite	Atlantic	Slyne Head	aka Illaunacroghnut Island
Oilean Da Bhranog	Galway Bay	Black Head	aka Brannock Island. One of the six Aran Islands, which with Rock Island also constitute the Brannock Islands.
Oilean Da Chruinne	Atlantic	Rinvyle Point	aka Crump Island. One of the Inner Islands.
Oilean Darach	Atlantic	Mace Head	aka Illaundarragh
Oilean Fhraoigh	Atlantic	Mace Head	aka Illaunree Island
Oilean Finis	Kilkieran Bay	Ardmore Point	See Finish Island
Oilean Gharumna	Atlantic	Carraroe	See Gorumna Island
Oilean Iarthach	Kilkieran Bay	Kilkieran	aka Illauneeragh. One of the Gorumna group.
Oilean Imill	Atlantic	Slyne Head	(I. = Wood Island). Aka Illaunamid. One of the Doonloughan group.
Oilean Iomai	Atlantic	Aughrus Point	aka Omey Island. Accessible from the mainland. A lake dominates the centre of the island. One of the Inner Islands. Population: 4.
Oilean Lachan	Atlantic	Mweenish Island	aka Duck Island
Oilean Lachan	Atlantic	Slyne Head	aka Duck Island
Oilean Maisean	Atlantic	Mace Head	aka Mason Island
Oilean Meana	Kilkieran Bay	Turlough	aka Illaunmaan
Oilean Mhatha Bhreatnaigh	Inland	Annaghdown/Killeany	aka Walsh's Island. Two tiny townlands in central County Galway (one in Annaghdown and the other in Killeany) included in this list by virtue of their name.
Oilean Mhic Dara	Atlantic	Mace Head	aka St Macdara's Island. Dedicated to the patron saint of Galway hookers (a type of fishing boat!). Those sailing one of these are expected to dip their sails when passing the island.

Island name	Area	Nearest landmark	General information
Oilean Mhuighinse	Bertraghboy Bay	Knockboy	See Mainis
Oilean Mhuscrai	Kilkieran Bay	Ardmore Point	aka Inishmuskerry or Inis Muscrai. One of the Gorumna group.
Oilean Mhuscrai	Kilkieran Bay	Ardmore Point	aka Inishmuskerry. One of the Gorumna group.
Oilean na bhFaochacha	Atlantic	Slyne Head	aka Illaunawehichy Island
Oilean na Bo	Atlantic	Gorumna Island	One of the Gorumna group.
Oilean na Circe	Kilkieran Bay	Inishtravin	aka Illaunakirka. One of the Gorumna group.
Oilean na Cruaiche Beg	Atlantic	Mace Head	aka Illaunnacroagh Beg
Oilean na Cruaiche Mor	Atlantic	Mace Head	aka Illaunnacroagh More
Oilean na dTrachta	Atlantic	Slyne Head	aka Illaunatraghta Island
Oilean na gCapall	Kilkieran Bay	Illaunmore	aka Illaunagappul. One of the Gorumna group.
Oilean na gCoinini	Lough Corrib	Headford	aka Rabbit Island
Oilean na Ginge	Atlantic	Mace Head	aka Illaunnginga
Oilean na mBrathar	Atlantic	Aughrus Point	aka Friar Island. One of the Outer Islands.
Oilean na Meannan	Atlantic	Slyne Head	aka Illaunamenara. One of the Doonloughan group.
Oilean na Muirileach	Atlantic	Slyne Head	aka Strawbeach Island
Oilean na nGeabhrog	Atlantic	Lettermore Island	aka Illaungurrag. One of the Gorumna group.
Oilean Roibin	Lough Corrib	Clonbur	aka Illaunribbeen
Oilean Ros an Locha	Atlantic	Mace Head	aka Illaunrossalough
Oilean Ui Cheallaigh	Lough Corrib	Dooros	aka Kelly's Island
Oilean Ui Chonchuir	Lough Corrib	Dooros	aka Conor's Island
Oilean Ura	Atlantic	Slyne Head	aka Illaunurra
Omey Island	Atlantic	Aughrus Point	See Oilean Iomai
Ox Island	Atlantic	Rinvyle Point	aka Damhoilean, Davillaun or Stag Island. One of the Outer Islands.
Potatoe Island	Lough Corrib	Birchall Bay	The fishing here is at its best around mid April during duckfly hatches.
Puck Island	Atlantic	Gorumna Island	aka Oilean an Phocaide. One of the Gorumna group.
Rabbit Island	Lough Corrib	Headford	aka Oilean na gCoinini
Re Ghamhna	Atlantic	Slyne Head	aka Illaunagawna Island
Red Island	Atlantic	Lettermore Island	See An tOilean Rua
Redflag Island	Atlantic	Lettermullan Island	Lies north of Eagle Rock.
Rock Island	Galway Bay	Black Head	See An t-Oilean Iatharach
Roeillaun	Lough Corrib	Oughterard	aka Rua-Oilean
Roeillaun	Atlantic	Aughrus Point	aka Rua-Oilean
Roeillaunbaun	Lough Corrib	Oughterard	aka Rua-Oilean Ban
Roeillaundoo	Lough Corrib	Oughterard	aka Rua-Oilean Dubh
Roisin an Chalaidh	Mweenish Bay	Carna	aka Rusheennacholla. Population: 3.
Rossroe	Atlantic	Lettermore Island	See An Ros
Rua-Oilean	Atlantic	Aughrus Point	aka Roeillaun
Rua-Oilean	Lough Corrib	Oughterard	aka Roeillaun
Rua-Oilean Ban	Lough Corrib	Oughterard	aka Roeillaunbaun
Rua-Oilean Dubh	Lough Corrib	Oughterard	aka Roeillaundoo
Rusheennacholla	Mweenish Bay	Carna	See Roisin an Chalaidh
St Macdara's Island	Atlantic	Mace Head	See Oilean Mhic Dara
Sandy Island	Lough Corrib	Foorannagh Point	Best fished in a west or east wind.
Scallop Island	Lough Corrib	Dooros	One of the numerous islands in the lough renowned for its fishing.
Sceirde Beag	Atlantic	Mace Head	aka Skerdbeg. A series of tiny rocks lie odd the coast of the island.
Sceirde Mor	Atlantic	Mace Head	aka Skerdmore. A group of tiny rock islets lie off the coast of the horseshoe-shaped island.
Seanavach Islands	Lough Corrib	Seanavach Point	Group of tiny islets.
Sedge Island	Lough Corrib	Headford	Situated in Murray's Bay.
Shanvally Beg	Atlantic	Rinvyle Point	One of the Inner Islands.
Skerdbeg	Atlantic	Mace Head	See Sceirde Beag
Skerdmore	Atlantic	Mace Head	See Sceirde Mor
Smith's Island	Lough Corrib	Oughterard	Popular fly-fishing site.
Snadaun Islands	Lough Corrib	Rinnerroon Point	Group of tiny islets.
Stag Island	Atlantic	Rinvyle Point	aka Damhoilean, Davillaun and Ox Island. One of the Outer Islands.
Stags of Bofin	Atlantic	Inishbofin	Situated off the northwest tip of Inishbofin.
Straw Island	Killeany Bay	Inishmore	One of the minor islets of the Aran Island Group. There is a shingle beach and a lighthouse on the island.
Strawbeach Island	Atlantic	Slyne Head	aka Oilean na Muirileach
Sunfish Rock	Atlantic	Inishbofin	Only visible at low water.
Tairbeart	Atlantic	Claddaghduff	aka Turbot Island. One of the Inner Islands.
Talbot Island	Atlantic	Claddaghduff	One of the Inner Islands.

Island name	Area	Nearest landmark	General information
Tanai Island	Lough Corrib	Headford	Lies southwest of Inchiquin.
Tawin Island	Galway Bay	Galway	The island is accessible by road.
Turbot Island	Atlantic	Claddaghduff	See Tairbeart
Urkaun	Lough Corrib	Oughterard	aka Urkaunmore
Urkaunbeg	Lough Corrib	Oughterard	Smaller sister island of Urkaunmore.
Urkaunmore	Lough Corrib	Oughterard	aka Urkaun
Walsh's Island	Inland	Annaghdown/Killeany	See Oilean Mhatha Bhreatnaigh
Wherune Island	Atlantic	Doon Hill	One of the Slyne Head Islands.
White Goat Island	Lough Corrib	Dooros	Good trout fishing all around the island.
White Island	Lough Mask	Clonbur	aka An tOilean Ban
White Rock	Atlantic	Inishbofin	Lies off the Stags of Bofin.
Wild Bellows Rock	Atlantic	Roundstone	Lies close to Doonguddle Rock.
Wynn's Island	Lough Corrib	Headford	Situated in Murray's Bay.

KERRY

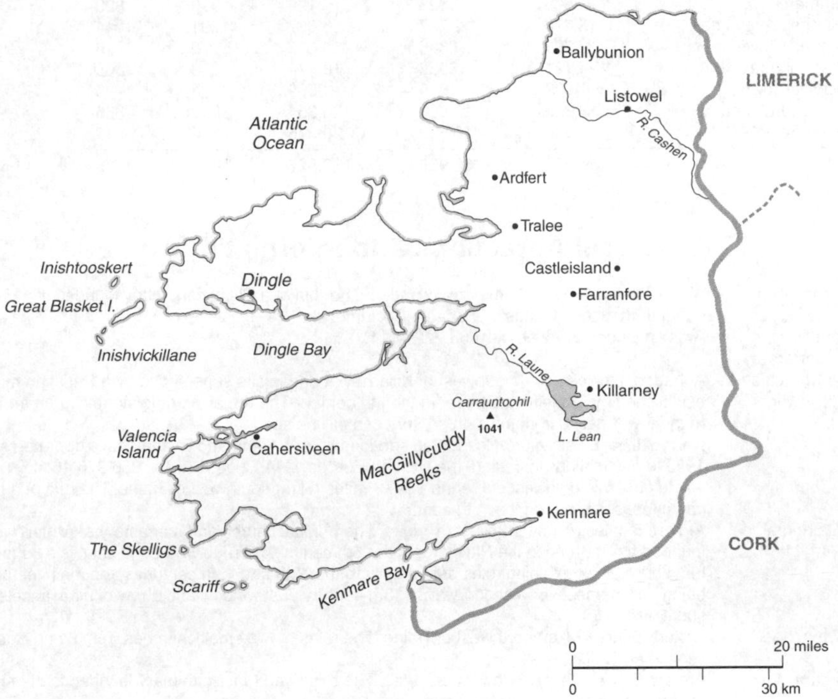
Ballybunion
LIMERICK
Listowel
Atlantic Ocean
R. Cashen
Ardfert
Tralee
Castleisland
Inishtooskert
Dingle
Farranfore
Great Blasket I.
Inishvickillane
Dingle Bay
R. Laune
Killarney
Carrauntoohil
1041
L. Lean
Valencia Island
Cahersiveen
MacGillycuddy Reeks
Kenmare
CORK
The Skelligs
Scariff
Kenmare Bay
0
20 miles
0
30 km

Kerry is part of the province of Munster. It lies in the southwest of the Republic of Ireland and is bordered by Cork to the southeast and Limerick to the northeast. Its western coast lies on the Atlantic Ocean and its northern coast on the River Shannon. The county has two national parks, the Killarney Lakes and Dingle Peninsula. The rivers Feale and Laune and the Roughty River flow through Kerry into the Atlantic. Kerry also encompasses the highest range of mountains in Ireland, the MacGillycuddy Reeks. The west of the Dingle Peninsula is a Gaeltacht (Irish-speaking) area, as is part of the Iveragh Peninsula.

The towns of Tralee (the county town), Killarney and Listowel are administered by their respective town councils and are separate administrative entities from Kerry County Council. However, each town elects representatives to the county council. A rail service from stations at Tralee, Farranfore and Killarney serves Cork and Dublin, via Mallow.

Kerry is known as 'the Kingdom' on account of its independence and disregard for Dublin rule. Its most famous native, Daniel O'Connell, perhaps embodies this spirit. Born in 1775, he campaigned for freedom from English rule and the end of the union between Ireland and Great Britain. To this end he achieved the nickname of 'the Uncrowned King of Ireland'. Kerry is also known for its senior Gaelic football team, the most successful in Ireland, having won the Sam Maguire Cup 34 times; the next nearest team is Dublin with 22 wins.

Kerry	Population			Area	
Districts	*male*	*female*	*total*	*sq miles*	*sq km*
Cahersiveen	4569	4259	8828	316	817
Dingle	4683	4545	9228	198	513
Kenmare	3675	3523	7198	310	803
Killarney rural area	13,370	12,727	26,097	391	1014
Killarney Town	5781	6306	12,087	6	15
Listowel rural area	9721	9053	18,774	258	668
Listowel Town	1699	1890	3589	3	6
Tralee rural area	13,388	12,963	26,351	342	886
Tralee Town	9686	10,689	20,375	5	12
Total	66,572	65,955	132,527	1828	4735

Local Attractions and Information

Abbeydorney Abbey	Abbeydorney, 5 miles (8km) north of Tralee. The ruin of a Cistercian abbey founded in 1154 as a daughter house of Monasteranenagh, Co. Limerick.
Administrative headquarters	Aras an Chontae, Tralee. Tel: 066 712 1111.
Aghadoe Church and Round Tower	Aghadoe, 2 miles (3km) northwest of Killarney. A pagan site superseded by a Christian monastery established by St Finian the Leper in the 7th century. The remains of the stone church and a round tower dating from the 11th century can still be seen.
Airport	**Kerry Airport**, Farranfore. Scheduled services by Aer Arann and Ryanair have operated since 1989 to destinations in Ireland, the UK and Europe. IATA Code KIR, Tel: 066 976 4644.
Annagh Church	1 mile (1.6km) southwest of Blennerville, 3 miles (5km) southwest of Tralee. The ruin of a parish church, possibly built in the 15th century.
Ardfert Cathedral	Ardfert, 5 miles (8km) northwest of Tralee. The original church and monastery at Ardfert were founded by St Brendan the Navigator in the 6th century, close to where the saint is said to have been born. The remaining ruins date mainly to the 12th and 13th centuries, the main features being a Romanesque west doorway, a 13th century east window and a row of nine lancets in the south wall.
Ardfert Churches	Ardfert, 5 miles (8km) northwest of Tralee. The ruins of two small churches: Temple na Hoe and Temple na Griffin.
Ardfert Friary	Ardfert, 5 miles (8km) northwest of Tralee. The ruin of a Franciscan friary founded in the mid 13th century, probably by Thomas Fitzmaurice.
Ashe Memorial Hall	Denny Street, Tralee. Dedicated to the memory of Thomas Ashe, who took part in the Easter Rising of 1916, commanding the Fingal battalion of the Irish Volunteers. He was sentenced to life imprisonment and on 25 September 1917 he died while on hunger strike in Mountjoy Prison. Designed by Thomas J Cullen and completed in 1928, the hall was the administrative headquarters of Kerry County Council until the 1980s. It now houses the 'Kerry the Kingdom' County Museum, which tells the story of Kerry and Ireland over 8000 years. Tel: 066 712 7777.
Ballinskelligs Priory	9 miles (15km) southwest of Cahersiveen. The ruin of an Augustinian priory founded for monks who came to the mainland from Skellig Michael in the 12th or 13th century.
Ballybunion Castle	Ballybunion, 8 miles (13km) northwest of Listowel. The focal point of the village, the castle was erected in the 14th century by the Geraldines. Acquired in 1582 by the Bunyan family, from whom the village derives its name, the castle was lost a year later by William Bunyan for the role he played in the Desmond rebellion. In 1612 the castle and lands were granted to the 16th Lord of Kerry and Lixnaw; in 1783 Richard Hare was in possession of the castle. In 1923 it came under the care of the Office of Public Works, who remain its custodians to this day.
Ballycarbery Castle	2 miles (3km) west of Cahersiveen. The ivy-covered ruin of a 15th century castle built by MacCarty Mor. Parts of the ground floor vaulting still remain.
Ballydavid Tower	7 miles (11km) northwest of Dingle. A watch tower and garrison house located on Ballydavid Head, and built in the early 19th century against the possibility of a French invasion.
Ballyheigue Castle	Ballyheigue, 10 miles (16km) northwest of Tralee. The ruin of a castle built by the Crosbie family in 1812 which overlooks Ballyheigue Castle Golf Course. The castle was burned down by the IRA in 1922 during the War of Independence.
Ballymacaquim Castle	$2^1/_2$ miles (4km) northwest of Abbeydorney, 8 miles (13km) north of Tralee. The ruin of a 15th century tower house built by the Fitzmaurice family.
Ballymalis Castle	$2^1/_2$ miles (4km) northwest of Beaufort, 7 miles (11km) west of Killarney. A partially restored tower house on the River Laune, possibly built in the 16th century by the Ferris or O'Moriarty family and known locally as Ferris Castle.
Basement Museum	Killorglin, 12 miles (19km) west of Killarneey. A museum with a collection of local memorabilia including historic local newspapers. Tel: 066 976 1353.
Battles	See separate table for details of the Battle of Smerwick
Beara Peninsula	See Cork
Beara Way	See Cork
Beenkeragh	The second highest mountain in Ireland and, like the highest (Corrán Tuathail), part of the MacGillycuddy Reeks range. It stands at 3314ft (1010m).

Blasket Islands
A group of uninhabited islands off the western coast of Kerry, a few miles from Dunmore Head. The Blasket Islands are the most westerly not only in Ireland but in continental Europe. The major islands that make up the group are Great Blasket Island, Beginish, Inishnabro, Inishvickillane, Inishtooskert and Tearaght.

Great Blasket Island, aka An Blascaod Mor, is separated from the mainland by Blasket Sound, the currents of which can be lethal when the tide turns. Two ships of the Spanish Armada are among the many to have foolishly sought shelter here. Most have met their fate on the underwater Stromboli Rock, named after HMS *Stromboli*, and the origin of the phrase 'Caught between a rock and a hard place'. Great Blasket was abandoned in 1953. Traditionally its inhabitants would claim that the next parish was in New York; many of their descendants currently live in Springfield, Massachusetts. **Tearaght**, aka An Tiaracht, situated $7\frac{1}{2}$ miles (12km) west of the Dingle Peninsula, is the most westerly of the Blasket Islands and also the most westerly point of Ireland. Despite being 47 acres (19ha) in area and 602ft (183.5m) high, Tearaght is more a large sea rock than an island. Tearaght Island Nature Reserve covers 118 acres (48ha) and supports internationally important colonies of seabirds.

Blennerville Windmill
Blennerville, 2 miles (3km) southwest of Tralee. The largest working windmill in Ireland, built in 1800 by Sir Rowland Blennerhassett on the shores of Tralee Bay but ruinous by 1850. It was restored during the 1980s and reopened in 1990. It is a five-storey tower with an external walkway at first floor level, allowing the miller to adjust the cap to turn the sails into the wind. There is an emigration museum housing the Jeanie Johnston Commemorative Quilt, made to commemorate the emigrant barque *Jeanie Johnston* which made 16 transatlantic trips and never lost a crew member or passenger. Tel: 066 712 1064.

Caherdargan Cashel
Kilmakedar, 5 miles (8km) northwest of Dingle. Aka Caherdorgan Cashel. A circular stone cashel containing the remains of six round houses or beehive huts. It was partially restored in the 20th century.

Cahergal Stone Fort
$1\frac{1}{2}$ miles (2.5km) northwest of Cahersiveen. An 8th or 9th century circular stone fort with 7ft (2.1m) high reconstructed walls. There is a rectangular house within the fort.

Cahersiveen Heritage Centre
Bridge Street, Cahersiveen. Housed in the former barracks of the Royal Irish Constabulary (RIC), which were designed in an 'Asian' style; according to tradition, the barracks were originally designed for India but their blueprints became with those for the Irish barracks.

Lough Carragh
5 miles (8km) southwest of Killorglin. A 4 mile (6km) long expanse of water set among broom and heather-covered hills.

Carrigfoyle Castle
$1\frac{1}{2}$ miles (2.5km) north of Ballylongford, 8 miles (13km) north of Listowel. The ruin of a tower house located beside the Shannon estuary on what was originally an island, and built in 1490 by Conor Liath O'Connor Kerry. It fell to a land and water siege by Sir William Pelham in 1580, after which the combined Irish and Spanish garrison was massacred.

Chorca Dhuibhne Regional Museum
Ballyferriter, 6 miles (10km) northwest of Dingle. Housed in the former Ballyferriter schoolhouse, built in 1875. There is an exhibition interpreting the archaeology of the Dingle Peninsula, and also of the people and events in the area's history. Tel: 066 915 6100.

Conway Castle
Killorglin, 12 miles (19km) northwest of Killarney. Aka Killorglin Castle. The ruin of a 12th century Desmond castle.

Crag Cave
2 miles (3km) north of Castleisland. A limestone cave system discovered in 1983 and opened as a visitor attraction with dramatic sound and lighting effects. Tel: 066 714 1244.

Croppy Boy
Denny Street, Tralee. The nickname of a statue of a pikeman erected to commemorate the 1798 rebellion.

Crotta House
$\frac{1}{2}$ mile (0.8km) north of Kilflynn, 7 miles (11km) northeast of Tralee. The childhood home of Lord Horatio Kitchener (1850–1916), of whom Prime Minister Herbert Asquith is reputed to have said 'He is not a great man but he is a great poster.'

Derrynane House, National Historic Park
1 mile (1.6km) west of Caherdaniel, 13 miles (21km) south of Cahersiveen. The ancestral home of Daniel 'The Liberator' O'Connell, the Irish statesman who played an important role in gaining Catholic Emancipation in 1829. It is surrounded by Derrynane National Historic Park, which covers 300 acres (120ha) of woodland and garden walks dating to the 18th and 19th centuries. Tel: 066 947 5113.

Dingle Peninsula
The most northerly of the four peninsulas that project into the Atlantic Ocean from the southwest corner of the Irish mainland. Dunmore Head, the tip of the Dingle Peninsula, is the most westerly point in mainland Ireland.

Dinis Island
4 miles (6km) southwest of Killarney. The meeting point of the three Killarney lakes, joined to the mainland on one side by Toothache Bridge and on the other by Brickeen Bridge. Dinis Cottage dates back to at least 1810, and has operated as a tea room for 200 years. It is traditional for newlyweds to carve their names and the date in the windows with their wedding rings for good luck, the earliest names being recorded in 1812. See also Meeting of the Waters.

Dun an Oir
$1\frac{1}{2}$ miles (2.5km) north of Ballyferriter, 7 miles (11km) northwest of Dingle. Aka Fort del Oro, The Golden Fort. The site of a promontory fort at the entrance to Smerwick Harbour. In 1580 more than 600 Spanish and Irish soldiers surrendered the fortress after three days' siege, gave themselves up and were then massacred by troops commanded by Lord Grey. A monument commemorating the massacre was erected in 1980.

Dunbeg Fort
Fahan, 6 miles (10km) southwest of Dingle. A small stone fort dating to c. 500 BC and located on a promontory projecting south into Dingle Bay at the base of Mount Eagle. Its multivallate defences consisted of four lines of banks, five ditches and stone-lined entrances.

Dunloe Ogham Stones
$\frac{1}{2}$ mile (0.8km) south of Beaufort, 5 miles (8km) west of Killarney. A group of eight Ogham stones which were removed to their present location in the 19th century. The centre stone came from Kilbonane church, and the other stones formed the roof of a souterrain at Coolmagort.

Dunmore Head	Part of the Dingle Peninsula, this is the most westerly point of Ireland (and therefore also Europe). Garraun Point is the exact location of this most westerly point.
Dunquin Interpretative Centre	Dunquin, 8 miles (13km) west of Dingle. Aka Great Blasket Centre. An interpretative centre opened in 1993 on the tip of the Dingle Peninsula. It celebrates the unique community who once lived on Great Blasket Island and its literature, which is referred to as 'The Blasket Library'. Tel: 066 915 6444.
Eightercua Standing Stones	1 mile (1.6km) south of Waterville, 9 miles (15km) south of Cahersiveen. An alignment of four standing stones ranging in height from 7ft (2.1m) to 10ft (3m) and possibly dating to c.1700 BC.
Famine Cottage	Fahan, 6 miles (10km) southwest of Dingle. An early 19th century mud and stone cottage on the Dingle Peninsula.
Fenit Castle	Fenit, 7 miles (11km) west of Tralee. The ruin of a 15th or 16th century tower built to guard the entrance to Barrow Harbour.
Ferriter's Castle	2 miles (3km) northwest of Ballyferriter, 8 miles (13km) northwest of Dingle. The meagre ruins of a castle built in 1460 by the Ferriter family. The castle was held by soldier-poet Pierce Ferriter, the last chieftain to hold out against Cromwell.
Friar's Island	One night in 1589, friars from nearby Muckross Abbey hid here to avoid religious persecution. Two of their brethren who failed to reach the boat were beheaded for refusing to reveal the whereabouts of the abbey's treasure. The treasure has not been seen since and is allegedly hidden on the island.
Gallarus Castle	5 miles (8km) northwest of Dingle. A restored tower house possibly built by the Fitzgerald family in the 15th century.
Gallarus Oratory	5 miles (8km) northwest of Dingle. An 8th century church built using a dry stone technique in the shape of an inverted boat. It remains weatherproof even after 1200 years.
Garden of Europe	Town Park, Listowel. Created on a former landfill site and opened in 1995, this garden is divided into 12 sections, each representing one of the 12 members of the European Union at the time the project was commenced. It also features Ireland's only Holocaust Memorial.
Garfinny Bridge	2 miles (3km) northeast of Dingle. A restored medieval bridge over the River Garfinagh, the only bridge to be declared a National Monument of Ireland.
Great Skellig	See Skellig Michael
Highest point	Carrauntoohil or Carrantuohill (Corrán Tuathail) in the MacGillycuddy Reeks at 3414ft (1041m), also the highest point in Ireland. The name means 'left-handed sickle' in Irish, a reference to the shape of the mountain.
Innisfallen	aka Inishfallen. The 11th/12th century Augustinian monastery and 7th century ruined abbey (founded by Finian the Leper) on this island gives the lough its name. The first European university after the Dark Ages was once situated here, Brian Boru being its most famous student. Area: 0.03 sq miles (0.085 sq km).
Interesting facts	**Ballybunion** (Baile an Bhunneanaibhgh) is situated in the north of Kerry at the mouth of the River Shannon. Ideally located between two airports – Kerry Airport and Shannon Airport. Ballybunion faces out west to the north Atlantic and across the Shannon estuary to the shores of Co. Clare. The village of Ballybunion was the site of the first transatlantic telephone transmission, made from the Marconi wireless station in 1919 to Louisbourg Cape Breton Nova Scotia by W T Ditcham a Marconi engineer. Ballybunion is home to the Ballybunion golf course, a world-renowned golf links that is ranked in the top ten golf courses in the world. The original golf course is over 100 years old (formerly known as the Cashen course, a name acquired due to its location at the mouth of the Cashen of the Feale River) this original course was designed by Robert Trent Jones. The golf course was visited by US President Bill Clinton in August 1999. **Valentia Island** was the location for one of Europe's first weather-forecasting stations in 1860. The station was set up by Vice-Admiral Robert Fitzroy, erstwhile captain of HMS *Beagle* during Darwin's expedition (1831–6).
Islands	See separate table
Iveragh Peninsula	The largest of the three main peninsulas of southwest Ireland. Cahersiveen is the main town on the peninsula and the MacGillycuddy Reeks mountain range is located to the east.
Jeanie Johnston	A replica of an Irish emigrant sailing ship, built at Blennerville, 2 miles (3km) west of Tralee. The original *Jeanie Johnston*, built in Quebec in 1847, was used as a means of mass emigration during the Great Famine. Unlike many 'coffin ships' of that era, she held a proud reputation, having never lost a single passenger or crew member while making 16 transatlantic trips.
Kenmare Bay	Inlet of the Atlantic Ocean between the Iveragh Peninsula to the north and Beara Peninsula to the south. Sometimes called the Kenmare River, the town of Kenmare is located at the head of the bay and the N70 runs west from there, running adjacent to the Ring of Kerry for much of its route. The bay opens up to the Atlantic at Cod's Head.
Kenmare Heritage Centre	Kenmare, 13 miles (21km) southwest of Killarney. Opened in 1994 and exploring the history of Kenmare and its people – including Margaret Anna Cusack, known as the Nun of Kenmare and founder of the Sisters of St Joseph of Peace, who founded a convent of Poor Clares in Kenmare – and of the Great Famine. It also features an exhibition dedicated to Kenmare Lace. Tel: 064 41233.
Kerry Bog Village Museum	Glenbeigh, 7½ miles (12km) southwest of Killorglin. A museum offering an insight into how people lived and worked in Ireland in the 18th century. Exhibits include an authentic turf cutter's house, stable dwelling and dairy house, and a working blacksmith's forge. Tel: 066 976 9184.
Kerry Poets Monument	Killarney. A statue of the Speir Bhean (the 'Beautiful Woman', a personification of Ireland), sculpted by Seamus Murphy and erected in 1940 to commemorate Kerry's four best-known Gaelic poets: Pierce Ferriter, Aogan O'Rahilly, Geoffrey O'Donoghue and Eoghan Rua O'Sullivan.
Kerry County Museum	Denny Street, Tralee. A museum is housed in Ashe Memorial Hall and celebrating Kerry's history using state of the art techniques. In the Geraldine Experience, visitors can stroll through the

streets of Tralee in 1450 and experience the sights, sounds and smells of the period. The award-winning Antarctica Exhibition tells the story of Annascaul man Tom Crean, who went on three of the most famous expeditions of the early 20th century: *Discovery* (1901–04), *Terra Nova* (1910–13) and *Endurance* (1914–16). Tel: 066 712 7777.

Kerry Way A long-distance path around the Ring of Kerry. At 134 miles (215km) it is the longest signposted walking trail in the Republic of Ireland.

Killagh Priory $^{1}/_{2}$ mile (0.8km) northeast of Milltown, 4 miles (6km) northeast of Killorglin. The ruin of an Augustinian abbey founded in the 13th century by Geoffrey de Marisco. It was suppressed during the Dissolution and damaged by Cromwellian troops.

Killarney Lakes Three lakes to the south of Killarney, known as the Upper Lake, Muckross Lake (Middle Lake) and Lough Leane (Lower Lake), and joined at the 'Meeting of the Waters' (see separate entry). Lough Leane (I. = Lake of Learning).is by far the largest of the three at 8 sq miles (19 sq km), while Muckross Lake (1 sq mile/2.7 sq km) is the deepest with a maximum depth of 75m) (250 feet). The Upper Lake is 0.7 sq miles (1.8 sq km) in area. Both Muckross Lake and Lough Leane lie astride the sandstone/limestone boundary, and the presence of limestone means that both of these lakes are slightly richer in natural nutrients than the Upper Lake. The three lakes hold a large population of brown trout, Arctic char, Killarney shad and an annual run of salmon.

Killarney National Park Ireland's first National Park came into being in 1932 when the Muckross Estate was presented to the nation by Senator Arthur Vincent and his parents-in-law, Mr and Mrs William Bowers Bourn, in memory of his late wife Maud. The park covers 39 sq miles (100 sq km) of mountain, moorland, woodland, waterways, parks and gardens. The mountainous old red sandstone uplands support large areas of blanket bog, and the remoteness and relative inaccessibility of some of these areas aids the continued survival of Ireland's only remaining wild herd of native red deer. The three Lakes of Killarney make up almost a quarter of the park's area, while it also includes the peaks of Mangerton, Torc, Shehy and the Purple Mountains. It was designated a UNESCO Biosphere Reserve in 1981. The Killarney National Park Visitor Centre is located at Muckross House.

Kilmalkedar Monastic Site $^{1}/_{2}$ mile (0.8km) east of Murreagh, 5 miles (8km) northwest of Dingle. The ruin of a 12th century Hiberno-Romanesque church on the possible site of a 7th century foundation of St Maolcethair.

Knockreer House $^{1}/_{4}$ mile (0.4km) west of Killarney. Built in the 1950s to replace a 19th century house built by the Kenmare family and which was destroyed by fire. It is now occupied by the field study centre for Killarney National Park. The surrounding gardens lie on the shore of Lough Leane.

Ladies' View 8 miles (13km) southwest of Killarney. A spectacular panorama of the Ring of Kerry so named after Queen Victoria's ladies-in-waiting, who stopped to look at the scenery from this spot during the Queen's visit to Killarney in 1861.

Lartigue Monorailway, The John B Keane Road, Listowel. A unique railway line designed by French engineer Charles Lartigue which ran for 9 miles (15km) between Listowel and Ballybunion, opening in 1888 and closing in 1924. The engine and carriages ran along a single rail which stood 3ft (0.9m) off the ground and ran through the centre of the train. A 0.6 mile (1km) section of track operating replica trains and carriages was reconstructed in 2003. Tel: 068 24393.

Leacanabuaile Stone Fort 2 miles (3km) northwest of Cahersiveen. A reconstructed stone fort with walls 4ft (1.2m) high and 10ft (3m) thick.

Lislaughtin Friary $^{1}/_{2}$ mile (0.8km) northeast of Ballylongford, 7 miles (11km) northeast of Listowel. The ruin of a Franciscan friary founded in 1478 by John O'Connor Kerry.

Listowel Castle The Square, Listowel. The ruin of a 12th century castle, the last stronghold to fall at the end of the Desmond Rebellion in the late 16th century. A National Monument, it has been restored since 2005.

Loher Stone Fort $2^{1}/_{2}$ miles (4km) south of Waterville, 11 miles (18km) south of Cahersiveen. A restored circular cashel measuring 65ft (20m) in diameter and with walls up to 7ft (2.1m) high.

Lough Leane See Killarney Lakes

MacGillycuddy Reeks (I. = The Black Tops). A mountain range in the southwest of the county that contains the three highest mountain in Ireland, Carrauntoohill (see Highest point), Beenkeragh (3314ft/1010m) and Caher (3284ft/1001m).

Meeting of the Waters The point where the waters of the Upper Lake meet those of the Muckross Lake (Middle Lake) and Lough Leane at the Old Weir Bridge. See also Dinis Island.

Minard Castle 2 miles (3km) southeast of Lispole, 7 miles (11km) southeast of Dingle. The ruin of a 16th century castle probably built by the Fitzgerald family and blown up by a Cromwellian force c.1650. It featured as a location in the film *Ryan's Daughter* (1970).

Mount Brandon Small mountain, part of the Slieve Mish range on the Dingle Peninsula. It is named after St Brendan the Navigator, who climbed to the top to see North America before setting off to discover it on his famous voyage.

Muckross Abbey Muckross, 3 miles (5km) south of Killarney. The well-preserved ruin of a Franciscan friary founded in the 15th century, possibly by Donal McCarthy. It features the only Franciscan-built tower in Ireland. The friary was abandoned in the 1650s after the monks were expelled by Cromwell's troops.

Muckross House and Gardens 4 miles (6km) south of Killarney. Situated within Killarney National Park beside Muckross Lake, Muckross House was built 1839–43 for Colonel Henry Herbert to an Elizabethan Revival design by Scottish architect William Burn. The estate and house were bestowed on the nation in 1932 on the understanding that its peace and tranquillity would never be disturbed by the sound of motor cars. The gardens include a collection of rhododendrons; other features include a sunken garden and a stream garden. In addition an arboretum was established in 1972. The house is now occupied by the Killarney National Park Visitor Centre. Tel: 064 31440.

Muckross Lake See Killarney Lakes

Muckross Pensinula — 3 miles (5km) south of Killarney. A small peninsula separating Lough Leane from Muckross Lake and containing one of the most extensive yew woods in Europe.

Muckross Traditional Farming Project — Three separate working farms located within Killarney National Park and seeking to recreate rural Ireland in the early 20th century, prior to the widespread use of electricity. All work is carried out using traditional methods, while the dwellings are also furnished in the traditional manner and each farm is complete with animals, poultry and horse-drawn farm machinery.

National Museum of Irish Transport — Scotts Gardens, Killarney. A museum with large collections of both four- and two-wheeled transport including what is claimed to be Ireland's oldest bicycle and an 1898 Benz, said to be the very first car to take to Irish roads. The museum includes a 1930s garage with tools, spare parts and oil cans (and a working mechanic). Other vehicles include a 1904 Germain, an Austin Seven from 1930 and an Austin 10 from 1934. Tel: 064 32638.

Nature Reserves — **Castlemaine Harbour**, 14 miles (23km) southwest of Tralee, an internationally important site for overwintering birds at the head of Dingle Bay, covering 2280 acres (923ha).

Cummeragh River Bog, 5 miles (8km) northeast of Waterville, 7 miles (11km) southeast of Cahersiveen, the most southerly intact lowland blanket bog in Ireland, covering 113 acres (46ha).

Derrycunihy Wood, 7 miles (11km) southwest of Killarney, located in the Killarney Valley to the south of the Upper Lake, covering 336 acres (136ha) largely of old native oak woodlands.

Derrymore Island, 5 miles (8km) west of Tralee, a compound spit of land in Tralee Bay composed of a series of pebble beaches and covering 263 acres (106ha).

Great Skellig, covering 57 acres (23ha), an internationally important breeding site for seabird species including Manx shearwaters, storm petrels and puffins. See also Skellig Michael.

Lough Yganavan and Lough Nambrackdarrig, 2 miles (3km) southwest of Killorglin. The freshwater lakes of Lough Nambrackdarrig (10 acres/4ha) and Yganavan (62 acres/25ha) are important breeding sites for the natterjack toad.

Mount Brandon, a blanket bog/heath complex covering 1142 acres (462ha) on the northeast side of the Dingle Peninsula.

Tearaght Island see Blasket Islands

Tralee Bay, 4 miles (6km) west of Tralee, 1866 acres (755ha) of wetland on the north side of the Dingle Peninsula, of international importance for waterfowl, especially overwintering populations of brent geese.

Uragh Wood, 7 miles (11km) southwest of Kenmare, an area of hyper-oceanic, semi-natural oak woodland located on the shore of Lough Inchiquin and covering 214 acres (87ha).

O'Connell Memorial Church — Church Street, Cahersiveen. Designed by George Ashlin in French Gothic style and begun in 1875 to mark the centenary of the town's most celebrated son, Daniel O'Connell. The first Mass was celebrated in 1900. Tel: 064 31633.

Parkavonear Castle — Aghadoe, 2 miles (3km) northwest of Killarney. The ruin of a small 13th century Norman castle, cylindrical in shape and therefore known as 'The Bishop's Chair'.

Puck Fair — A fair held annually in August in Killorglin. There are various legends as to its origin; some involve Cromwell while others the time of Daniel O'Connell, but it may have officially begun with a charter of 1603 allowing a fair to take place in the village. The main events of the festival include a traditional horse fair, the parade and coronation ceremony of King Puck, dancing, singing and fireworks.

Rahinnane Castle — 1 mile (1.6km) northwest of Ventry, 5 miles (8km) west of Dingle. The ruin of a 15th or 16th century tower, built by the Geraldine family on the site of an existing ring fort.

Rattoo Round Tower — ½ mile (0.8km) south of Ballyduff, 8 miles (13km) west of Listowel. A rare complete early 12th century round tower, standing 88ft (27m) high and located near the ruin of a small, possibly 15th century, church. A sheela-na-gig carved on the inside of the north window of the tower is the only such example to be found on a round tower in Ireland.

Riasc Monastic Settlement — Ballyferriter, 6 miles (10km) northwest of Dingle. An excavated monastic site occupied from the 5th to the 12th century, and including the remains of beehive huts and an oratory, enclosed by a stone wall. A stone pillar dating to 1000 BC and carved with both Celtic and Christian symbols stands on the site.

Ring of Kerry — A tourist trail which covers a 106 mile (170km) circular route around the Iveragh Peninsula, starting and ending at Killarney.

Rivers — The **Feale** rises near Rockchapel in the Mullaghareirk Mountains of Co. Cork and flows generally northwestwards through Abbeyfeale and Listowel in Co. Kerry before finally emptying into the mouth of the Shannon at Ballyduff. Its total length is approximately 46 miles (73km). The **Laune** flows from Lough Leane through the town of Killorglin, and empties into the sea, first at Castlemaine harbour beside the River Maine and then out through Dingle Bay and into the Atlantic. Both rivers are among the finest in ireland for salmon and trout fishing. See also Kenmare Bay.

Ronayne's Island — One of eight islands in the Upper Lake. Mr Ronayne was an English gentleman who apparently fought at Waterloo. After the battle he came to Killarney and became a total recluse on the island, travelling into Killarney once a year for provisions and for shot for his gun. He would fire on any boat attempting to approach the island.

'Rose of Tralee' — A 19th century Irish ballad, the words of which are credited to C (or E) Mordaunt Spencer and the music to Charles William Glover, although a story has circulated that the song was actually written by William Pembroke Mulchinock, a wealthy Protestant, out of love for Mary O'Connor, a poor Catholic maid in service to his parents. The annual Rose of Tralee festival (usually in late August) is an international beauty competition which takes its inspiration from the song. Each of the 32 counties in Ireland selects a 'Rose' and there is also a 'Rós Fódhla' representing the Gaeltacht areas. Gay Byrne hosted the competition for 20 years. The competition began in 1959, Alice O'Sullivan (Dublin) being the first winner. The lyrics of the song are as follows:

The pale moon was rising above the green mountains,
The sun was declining beneath the blue sea;
When I strayed with my love by the pure crystal fountain,
That stands in the beautiful Vale of Tralee.
She was lovely and fair as the rose of the summer,
Yet 'twas not her beauty alone that won me;
Oh no, 'twas the truth in her eyes ever dawning,
that made me love Mary, the Rose of Tralee.
The cool shades of evening their mantle were spreading,
And Mary all smiling was listening to me;
The moon through the valley her pale rays was shedding,
When I won the heart of the Rose of Tralee.
Though lovely and fair as the Rose of the summer,
Yet 'twas not her beauty alone that won me;
Oh no, 'twas the truth in her eyes ever dawning,
that made me love Mary, the Rose of Tralee.
In the far fields of India, 'mid war's dreadful thunders,
Her voice was a solace and comfort to me,
But the chill hand of death has now rent us asunder,
I'm lonely tonight for the Rose of Tralee.
She was lovely and fair as the rose of the summer,
Yet 'twas not her beauty alone that won me;
Oh no, 'twas the truth in her eyes ever dawning,
that made me love Mary, the Rose of Tralee.

Ross Castle — $1^1/_4$ miles (2km) southwest of Killarney. A restored late 15th century castle on the shore of Lough Leane, built by the O'Donoghue Ross chieftains. It houses a fine collection of 16th and 17th century oak furniture.

Ross Island — A peninsula at low water, the island lies south of Killarney and juts into Lough Leane at Ross Castle. It was extensively mined during the Iron Age for its copper, mining only ceasing 200 years ago. Because Killarney copper has a high arsenic content, it is easily identified and artefacts made of the metal have been found as far away as Egypt.

St Mary's Cathedral — New Street, Killarney. Dedicated to the Assumption of the Blessed Virgin Mary. The cathedral was designed by Augustus Welby Pugin, whose Gothic design drew on both the ruin of St Brendan's at Ardfert and Salisbury Cathedral for inspiration. The foundation stone was laid in 1842 but building was stopped in 1848 during the Great Famine. Construction resumed in 1853, J J McCarthy replacing Pugin, who had died in 1852, as architect. The cathedral was consecrated in 1855 and a great tower and spire were added in the early 20th century. Tel: 064 31014.

Skellig Experience, The — Valentia Island. A purpose built grass roofed centre beside the Valentia Island bridge exploring the life and work of the early Christian Skellig monks and the Skellig light keepers. Tel: 066 947 6306.

Skellig Michael — aka Great Skellig, Sceilg Mhichil. One of the two Skellig Islands (the other being Little Skellig), and part of the Valentia group, Skellig Michael is only accessible by boat on calm days. The roads and pathways accessing the different parts of the island are breathtaking to behold. Used as a refuge by monks from AD 800 to 1100. A ship of the Spanish Armada sank here in 1588.

Sport

Gaelic football — **Kerry** were winners of the All-Ireland Senior Football Championship in 1903, 1904, 1909, 1913, 1914, 1924, 1926, 1929, 1930, 1931, 1932, 1937, 1939, 1940, 1941, 1946, 1953, 1955, 1959, 1962, 1969, 1970, 1975, 1978, 1979, 1980, 1981, 1984, 1985, 1986, 1997, 2000, 2004, 2006 and 2007.

horse racing — **Killarney** Racecourse, Clonfert, Fossa, Killarney. Racing took place at two venues, 1827–1901, and began at the present course beside the River Flesk in 1936. The racecourse holds both Flat and National Hunt racing on a left-handed oval track of just over 9 furlongs (1.8km) with a run-in of 3 furlongs (0.6km). Tel: 064 31125.

Listowel Racecourse, William Street, Listowel. Racing started at Listowel in 1858. The course stages Flat and National Hunt racing on a left-handed rectangular flat track of 1 mile (1.6km) with a run-in of 2 furlongs (0.4km). Tel: 068 21144.

hurling — **Kerry** were winners of the All-Ireland Senior Hurling championship in 1891.

Staigue Stone Fort — 5 miles (8km) southwest of Sneem, 13 miles (21km) southeast of Cahersiveen. A restored circular stone cashel measuring 100ft (30.5m) in diameter and with walls at a maximum height of 16ft (5m).

Tarbert House — Tarbert, 9 miles (15km) northeast of Listowel. A Queen Anne house built in 1690 for the Leslie family. It is preserved in its original form with furniture and pictures from the 17th century. Tel: 068 36198.

Torc Waterfall — 4 miles (6km) south of Killarney. A waterfall formed where the Owengarriff River cascades through Friar's Glen into Muckross Lake.

Tralee–Blennerville Steam Train — A heritage railway operating regular steam services for 2 miles (3km) between Tralee and Blennerville on part of the former Tralee to Dingle Light Railway, open 1891–1953. Tel: 066 712 1064.

Upper Lake — See Killarney Lakes

Valentia Island — aka Valencia. Europe's westernmost inhabited location. The first transatlantic cable was laid from the island to America in 1857. The island is famous for its slate quarry, which was used for the roof

	and floors of Westminster Abbey; Some years ago, when the abbey underwent restoration, the quarry was reopened to provide similar slate. It has remained open and is now a thriving industry. Knightstown is the 'capital'. Population: 690.
Vintage Wireless Museum	Cherrytree Drive, Listowel. A privately owned museum opened in 1986 to mark 50 years of Irish broadcasting. It has more than 1000 items related to wireless broadcasting including an extensive collection of receivers, and other exhibits such as BBC studio microphones from the 1930s and 1940s. Tel: 068 21652.

Some famous people born in County Kerry

Clifford, Julia (musician) (1914–97)	Lisheen
Crean, Tom (explorer) (1877–1938)	Annascaul
Doyle, Mick (rugby player) (1941–2004)	Castleisland
Keane, John B (playwright) (1928–2002)	Listowel
Kelly, Hugh (playwright) (1739–77)	Killarney
Kennelly, Brendan (poet) (1936–)	Ballylongford
Kennelly, Tadhg (Gaelic and Australian rules footballer) (1981–)	Listowel
Kitchener, Horatio Herbert (soldier) (1850–1916)	Ballylongford
O'Connell, Daniel (politician) (1775–1847)	Cahersiveen
O'Connell, Mick (Gaelic footballer) (1937–)	Valentia Island
O'Dwyer, Mick (Gaelic footballer) (1936–)	Waterville
O'Keefe, Padraig (musician) (1887–1963)	Castleisland
Sayers, Peig (seanachaí – storyteller) (1873–1958)	Dunquin
Spillane, Pat (Gaelic footballer) (1955–)	Templenoe

Islands of County Kerry

(shipping area = Shannon)

Island name	**Area**	**Nearest landmark**	**General information**
Abbey Island	Derrynane Harbour	Lamb's Head	The family graveyard of Daniel O'Connell (The Liberator) is on the island. While his wife is buried here, the man himself is buried in Glasnevin Cemetery in Dublin.
An Blascaod Mor	Atlantic	Slea Head	See separate entry for Blasket Islands
An Tiaracht	Atlantic	Slea Head	aka Tearaght
Arbutus Island	Upper Lake	Ladies View, Killarney	Named after the shrub that proliferates on the island. Arbutus is a Mediterranean plant native to Killarney because of its mild climate. It is the only plant to flower, fruit and leaf at the same time.
Ash Island	Loch Leane	Killarney	Tiny islet which no longer has a trace of mountain ash.
Beginish	Atlantic	Slea Head	(I. *Beag Inis* = Small Island). One of the Blasket Islands.
Beginish	Portmagee Channel	Portmagee	Despite the Gaelic name suggesting a small island, Beginish is in fact quite expansive. It was the birthplace of Gaelic football legend Mick O'Connell, famed for rowing across to the mainland for training. Part of the Valentia group.
Bird Rock	Atlantic	Ballybunion	Lies just south of Pierce's Island
Black Rock	Portmagee Channel	Portmagee	Rocky islet lying just off Short Island. Part of the Valentia group.
Blasket Islands	Atlantic	Slea Head	See separate entry
Brown Island	Lough Leane	Mahoney's Point	Second largest of the islands and rocks in the lake. Located beside Innisfallen island. Accessible from the west only because of extensive sandbanks on the other sides.
Bull Rock	Portmagee Channel	Long Island	Lies off the west tip of Long Island. Part of the Valentia group.
Burned Island	Atlantic	Lamb's Head	Barely detached from Lamb's Head at low water.
Burnt Island	Loch Leane	Dinis Cottage, Killarney	Realistically only accessible by boat. Very remote. Very beautiful. Good area for salmon fishing.
Carrig Island	Shannon Estuary	Ballylongford	Famous for Carrigfoyle Castle, ancestral home of the Kerry O'Connor clan. Destroyed on the orders of Elizabeth I, the castle has been renovated and reopened to the public in 2005. Population: 10.
Cherry Island	Loch Leane	Ross Castle, Killarney	Low-lying. Favourite congregation spot for mute swans.

Island name	Area	Nearest landmark	General information
Church Island	Portmagee Channel	Portmagee	Part of the Valentia group. Lies just east of Beginish Island.
Colleen Bawn Rock	Muckross Lake (Middle Lake)	Muckross House	Famous in song and poem, legend has it that Danny Mann threw The Colleen Bawn (white girl) from the top of the rock when she refused his hand in marriage. Sadly, it is based on the facts surrounding a drowning in the River Shannon in the 19th century. Nice spot for a picnic.
Cow Island	Lough Leane	Lake Hotel, Killarney	Lies next to Rough Island just off the Ross Peninsula. Most of Lough Leane's islands were once grassed during the summer. Cattle would be tied to a boat by rope and pulled out to the islands. Probably got its name this way. Was also mined for copper in the 19th century.
Crow Island	Lough Leane	Killarney	
Crow Rock	Dingle Bay	Reenbeg Point	Popular with scuba divers.
Daniel's Island	Kenmare Bay	Nedanone	
Deenish Island	Atlantic	Lamb's Head	One of the outer islands of the Lamb's Head group.
Derby's Garden	Loch Leane	Killarney	
Devil's Island	Muckross Lake	Killarney	
Dinis Island	Kenmare Bay	Feoramore	One of two islands of the same name in Kerry.
Dinis Island	Muckross Lake, Lough Leane, Upper Lake	Dinis Cottage, Killarney	See separate entry
Doonagaun Island	Atlantic	Rough Point	Mainly grassy islet with a sand southeast coast. One of the Magharee Islands.
Duck Island	Upper Lake	Lord Brandon's Cottage, Killarney	One of eight islands in the lough.
Dunacapple Island	Atlantic	Smerwick Harbour	Tiny island on the east of the harbour.
Eagle Island	Upper Lake	Lord Brandon's Cottage, Killarney	Killarney always had a large population of golden eagles. Unfortunately, the value of their eggs in the 19th century led to a decline in population. The habit of firing cannons at their nesting spots to make them fly for passing tourists probably did not help either. The last eagle died of sexual frustration c.1900.
Edye Rocks	Atlantic	Smerwick Harbour	Latitude: 52° 07' 31" Longitude: -10° 31' 39"
Einaun Island	Kenmare Bay	Sneem	One of the Sneem Harbour Islands.
Elephant Rock	Loch Leane	Lake Hotel, Killarney	
Fir Island	Loch Leane	Lake Hotel, Killarney	Probably derives its name from *fir* (I. = 'man')
Foze Rocks	Atlantic	Slea Head	One of the Blasket Islands
Friar's Island	Loch Leane	Muckross Abbey, Killarney	See separate entry
Garinish	Kenmare Bay	Sneem	Private island. One of the Sneem Harbour Islands. Population: 2.
Great Blasket Island	Atlantic	Slea Head	aka An Blascaod Mor.
Great Samphire Island	Tralee Bay	Fenit	A large bronze sculpture of St Brendan was erected on the rock in 2004.
Great Skellig	Atlantic	Bolus Head	See Skellig Michael
Greenane Island	Kenmare Bay	Kenmare	
Heron Island	Loch Leane	Killarney	
Horse Island	Portmagee Channel	Portmagee	Part of the Valentia group. Lies just northeast of Long Island.
Horse Island	Ballinskelligs Bay	Ballinskelligs	Outermost island of the Lamb's Head group, just east of Ballinskellig's Pier.
Illaunacummig	Atlantic	Lamb's Head	Largest island of the Lamb's Head group.
Illaunanadan	Kenmare Bay	Sneem	Middle of the three outer islands of the Sneem Harbour group (Sherky and Inishkeragh being the other two).
Illaunboe	Atlantic	Rough Point	Almost joined to Illauntannig by a low water reef. One of the Magharee Islands.
Illaunboy	Atlantic	Slea Head	aka Oilean Bui. One of the Blasket Islands.
Illaundrane	Kenmare Bay	Nedanone	
Illaunimmil	Atlantic	Rough Point	High-rocked island with two cave systems. One of the Magharee Islands.
Illaunleagh	Kenmare Bay	Sneem	The most westerly of the Sneem Harbour Islands.
Illaunloughan	Portmagee Channel	Portmagee	It is possible to walk to the mainland at low water. Part of the Valentia group. Contains old monastic ruins. Used for generations as a burial ground for children that had died prior to baptism.

Island name	Area	Nearest landmark	General information
Illaunlurlogh	Atlantic	Rough Point	One of the Magharee Islands.
Illaunnanoon	Atlantic	Rough Point	Rocky islet lying just off Scraggane Pier. One of the Magharee Islands.
Illaunnaweelaun	Atlantic	Lamb's Head	Separated from Lamb's Head by a 165ft (50m) sound.
Illaunsillagh	Atlantic	Lamb's Head	The shingle beach in the middle almost makes it two islands at low water. Part of the Lamb's Head group.
Illaunslea	Kenmare Bay	Sneem	Privately owned island. One of the Sneem Harbour Islands.
Ilauntannig	Atlantic	Rough Point	Largest of the Magharee Islands, aka Oilean an Mhachaire or The Seven Hogs (although there are actually eight islands in the group). A monastic site on Illauntannig was founded by St Senagh. There are also the remains of three beehive huts.
Inis Mhic Aoibhleain	Atlantic	Slea Head	aka Inishvickillane. Most southerly of the Blasket Islands. Possibly the only privately owned island off the coast of Ireland. Owned by former Prime Minister (Taoiseach) Charles Haughey. Well known for its seals and now for its private herd of deer.
Inis Tuaisceart	Atlantic	Slea Head	aka Inishtooskert, Northern Island. One of the Blasket Islands.
Inishfallen	Loch Leane	Killarney	See Innisfallen
Inishkeelaghmore	Kenmare Bay	Sneem	There is a miniature rockclimbers' cliff on the south side of the island. One of the Sneem Harbour Islands.
Inishkeragh	Kenmare Bay	Sneem	One of the three outer islands of the Sneem Harbour Islands (Sherky and Illaunanadan being the other two).
Inishnabro	Atlantic	Slea Head	One of the Blasket Islands. North of the island is dominated by cliffs.
Inishtooskert	Atlantic	Slea Head	aka Inis Tuaisceart
Inishtooskert	Atlantic	Rough Point	Lies northwest of Illaunimmil Island. One of the Magharee Islands.
Inishvickillane	Atlantic	Slea Head	aka Inis Mhic Aoibhleain
Innisfallen	Lough Leane	Killarney	See separate entry
Jackdaw Island	Lough Leane	Killarney	
Juniper Island	Upper Lake	Killarney	One of eight islands in the lough.
Kippin Rock	Atlantic	Ballybunion	North of Pierce's Island.
Lamb Island	Lough Leane	Killarney	
Lambs Island	Portmagee Channel	Portmagee	Lies northeast of Beginish Island. Part of the Valentia group.
Lamb's Island	Atlantic	Lamb's Head	Steep conical islet detached from Lamb's Head by a 165ft (50m) sound.
Lamb's Island	Derrynane Harbour	Lamb's Head	Twin of Abbey Island. Part of the Lamb's Head group.
Lemon Rocks	Atlantic	Bolus Head	Often a stop-off point for kayakers between the Skelligs. Part of the Valentia group.
Little Skellig	Atlantic	Bolus Head	aka Sceilg Bheag. One of the Skellig Islands. Little Skellig Nature Reserve covers 20 acres (8ha). The highly exposed and isolated island off the Iveragh Peninsula is the site of an internationally important colony of gannets.
Long Island	Portmagee Channel	Portmagee	Separated from Short Island by a cliff-lined long narrow channel. Part of the Valentia group.
McCarthy's Island	Upper Lake	Killarney	Named after a powerful Kerry chief. One of eight islands in the lough.
Mouse Island	Loch Leane	Killarney	Tiny tree-covered island. Now known locally as Micky Mouse Island, to the delight of children of all ages.
Moylaun Island	Atlantic	Lamb's Head	Grass-covered rocky islet. Part of the Lamb's Head group.
Mucklaghbeg	Atlantic	Rough Point	Rocky islet 1 mile (1.6km) east of Illauntannig. One of the Magharee Islands.
Oak Island	Upper Lake	Killarney	One of eight islands in the lough.
O'Donoghue's Spyglass	Loch Leane	Killarney	
Oilean Bui	Atlantic	Slea Head	aka Illaunboy. One of the Blasket Islands.
Oilean na nOg	Atlantic	Slea Head	aka Young's Island. Part of the Blasket Islands.
Ormond's Island	Kenmare Bay	Feoramore	

Island name	Area	Nearest landmark	General information
Osprey Rock	Loch Leane	Killarney	
Otter Island	Loch Leane	Killarney	
Pierce's Island	Atlantic	Ballybunion	Lies east of Kerry Head
Prince of Wales Rock	Loch Leane	Killarney	
Puffin Island	Atlantic	Ballynahow	As its name suggests, puffins can be seen in abundance on this island. Part of the Valentia group. Very popular site for scuba diving. Puffin Island Nature Reserve covers 212 acres (86ha) of the island off the Iveragh Peninsula.
Reenafardarrig	Atlantic	Rough Point	Lies northeast of Illauntannig. One of the Magharee Islands.
Ronayne's Island	Upper Lake	Killarney	See separate entry
Ross Island	Loch Leane	Killarney	See separate entry
Rossdohan Island	Kenmare Bay	Sneem	
Rossmore	Kenmare Bay	Feoramore	Population: 7.
Rough Island	Loch Leane	Killarney	Lies next to Cow Island just off the Ross Peninsula.
Scariff Island	Atlantic	Lamb's Head	Part of the Lamb's Head group. It is said that all the children of this island died of the measles.
Sceilg Bheag	Atlantic	Bolus Head	See Little Skellig
Sceilg Mhichil	Atlantic	Bolus Head	See Skellig Michael
Sherky Island	Kenmare Bay	Sneem	The largest of the Sneem Harbour Islands.
Short Island	Portmagee Channel	Portmagee	Separated from Long Island by a cliff-lined long narrow channel. Part of the Valentia group.
Skellig Islands	Atlantic	Bolus Head	Two small, uninhabited steep and rocky islands lying 10 miles (16km) west of Bolus Head on the Ivereagh Peninsula. Part of the Valentia group.
Skellig Michael	Atlantic	Bolus Head	One of the Skellig Islands. See separate entry
Stag Island	Upper Lake	Killarney	One of eight islands in the lough.
Stag Island	Lough Leane	Killarney	
Sunken Island	Muckross Lake	Killarney	
Swallow Island	Lough Leane	Killarney	
Tearaght	Atlantic	Slea Head	See separate entry for Blasket Islands
Two Headed Island	Atlantic	Lamb's Head	Name derives from the midway waist which almost makes it two separate islands.
Valencia	Portmagee Channel	Portmagee	aka Valentia Island
Valentia Island	Portmagee Channel	Portmagee	See separate entry
Washerwoman's Rock	Atlantic	Bolus Head	Lies southeast of Skellig Michael. Part of the Valentia group.
Yew Island	Lough Leane	Killarney	
Young's Island	Atlantic	Slea Head	aka Oilean na nOg. Part of the Blasket Islands.

KILDARE

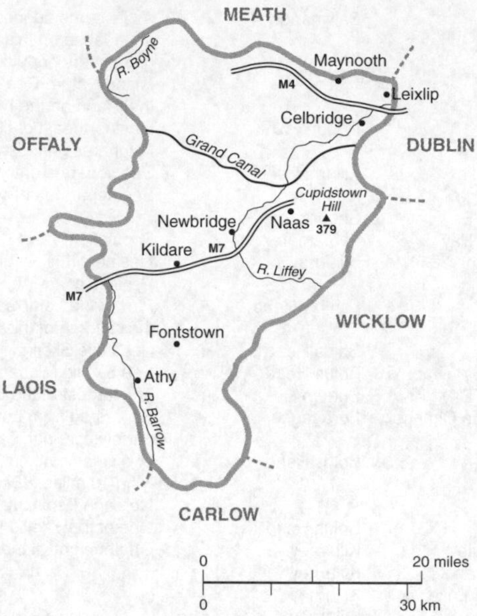
MEATH
R. Boyne
Maynooth
M4
Leixlip
Celbridge
OFFALY
Grand Canal
DUBLIN
Cupidstown Hill
379
Newbridge
Naas
Kildare
M7
R. Liffey
M7
WICKLOW
Fontstown
Athy
LAOIS
R. Barrow
CARLOW
0
20 miles
0
30 km

Kildare is part of the province of Leinster. A landlocked county in the east of the Republic of Ireland, it is bordered by Dublin to the northeast, Meath to the north, Offaly to the northwest, Laois to the west, Carlow to the south and Wicklow to the east. Naas (the county town) and Newbridge (Droichead Nua), Kildare's largest town, are situated in the centre of the county, near the Curragh plain.

Kildare became a shire in 1297 and assumed its present borders in 1832. It is also known as the Shortgrass County. Ireland's flattest county, it contains the greater part of the world's largest peat bog, the Bog of Allen. The county has more miles of canal than any other Irish county.

Kildare has a number of famous natives. Ernest Shackleton, the great polar explorer, was born at Kilkea House near Athy. Jockeys Ruby Walsh and Pat Eddery both hail from Kildare, as did the boxer Jack (Nonpareil) Dempsey (born John Edward Kelly), not to be confused with the equally famous heavyweight boxer who adopted the name of the Kildare man. However, to many, Celbridge-born Arthur Guinness will also be very familiar!

Kildare		**Population**		**Area**	
Districts	*male*	*female*	*total*	*sq miles*	*sq km*
Athy rural area	8353	7954	16,307	200	518
Athy Town	2965	3084	6049	4	9
Celbridge	25,981	25,641	51,622	84	217
Edenderry	4590	4448	9038	108	281
Naas No. 1 rural area	31,596	31,044	62,640	251	650
Naas Town	9250	9038	18,288	7	18
Total	82,735	81,209	163,944	654	1694

Local Attractions and Information

Administrative headquarters	St Mary's, Naas. Tel: 045 873800.
Áras Chill Dara	Devoy Park, Naas. The headquarters of Kildare County Council and Naas Town Council. The building was designed by Heneghan Peng/Arthur Gibney & Partners on the site of the Devoy barracks.
Athy Heritage Centre	Emily Square, Athy. Housed in the restored former town hall, designed in Palladian style by Richard Castle and built in 1740, the centre charts the history of Athy and its people from its origins as an Anglo-Norman town to the present day. There are exhibitions on locally born polar explorer Sir Ernest Shackleton (1874–1922) and the 1903 Gordon Bennett Motor Race which took place over a distance of $327\frac{1}{2}$ miles (527km) with four laps of a circuit passing through Ballyshannon, Kilcullen, Kildare, Monasterevin, Stradbally and Athy, alternating with three laps of a smaller circuit of Kilcullen, Carlow and Athy. Tel: 059 863 3075.
Ballindoolin House and Gardens	Carbury, 5 miles (8km) north of Edenderry. Surrounded by a 250 acre (100ha) demesne, Ballindoolin House was built in 1822 by Humphrey Bor and is remarkably unchanged with its original plasterwork and furnished in period style. The grounds include a walled garden laid out when the house was built and featuring a rockery, rose garden and summer bedding. The gardens were restored in the 1990s. Tel: 046 973 1430.
Ballitore Library and Quaker Museum	Ballitore, 7 miles (11km) east of Athy. A library and museum opened in 1975 and housed in Mary Leadbeater House, the restored Meeting House of the Society of Friends. The museum has artefacts and memorabilia related to the history of Ballitore, which was founded by Quakers in 1685 around wool and flour watermills. Exhibits include costumes, furniture and documents. Tel: 059 862 3344.
Battles	See separate entry for the Battle of Confey and separate table for details of the Battle of Kilrush.
Belan House	Moone, 7 miles (11km) east of Athy. A 17th century house built by the Stratford family on the site of a Fitzgerald castle destroyed in 1641. It was designed by Castle and Bindon and was surrounded by extensive grounds dotted with obelisks and a Greek temple. Unfortunately Benjamin O'Neale Stratford, 4th Earl of Aldborough (c.1746–1833), lost the family fortune by gambling and had to mortgage the house. It was allowed to fall into disrepair and is now a ruin.
Blackhall Castle	1 mile (1.6km) west of Calverstown, 6 miles (10km) southwest of Newbridge. The ruin of a Fitzgerald castle which was the scene of a bloody siege during the persecution of Catholics in the 1640s. Francis Moore, son of Viscount Mellifont, is said to have massacred old men, women and children, and transfixed the infants on their mothers' breasts with his swords and lances. The story goes that having spent a night with some of his officers in the house of a noble lady whose husband was absent, he was treated with splendid hospitality and costly presents; but when the lady followed him to the door to bid him adieu on his departure, he ordered a rope to be thrown around her neck, and hanged her before her own door for nothing more than following the Catholic faith. Villagers and friends laid siege to Moore's castle, but to no avail – they were all butchered mercilessly. A sheela-na-gig once located on the castle wall was removed for safekeeping when part of the structure collapsed in 1999.
Bog of Allen	A large area of lowland peat bog between the rivers Liffey and Shannon. Covering 370 sq miles (958 sq km), it stretches into Co. Laois, Co. Meath, Co. Offaly and Co. Westmeath, but the larger part of it is in Co. Kildare.
Broadlease Stone Circle	$1\frac{1}{4}$ miles (2km) south of Ballymore Eustace, 7 miles (11km) south of Naas. A stone circle measuring 100ft (30.5m) in diameter with 27 stones.
Canal System	There are more than seventy miles of canal channel wholly within Co. Kildare. The **Grand Canal** spans the breadth of central Ireland from the River Liffey in Grand Canal Dock, Dublin, to the Shannon Harbour in Co. Offaly. The canal has several branches in Kildare. At Sallins the Naas/Corbally branch diverts southwards while the main canal continues west, south of the Bog of Allen, passing Caragh, Prosperous and Robertstown, its highest point. At Caragh, the canal passes over the River Liffey at the Leinster Aqueduct. Just west of Robertstown is the busiest junction on the canal with the Old Barrow Line, Milltown Feeder and the entrances to the Athy & Barrow Navigation. The Monasterevin branch lies adjacent to the M7 motorway. The **Royal Canal** lies to the north of the Grand Canal and connects the River Liffey in Dublin to the River Shannon at Cloondara in Co. Longford, via Kildare, Meath and Westmeath. In Kildare the canal's route is adjacent to the River Rye and serves Leixlip, Maynooth and Kilcock.
Carrick Castle	Carrick, $2\frac{1}{2}$ miles (4km) north of Edenderry. Former residence of the Bermingham family in the barony of Carbery. There are scant remains of the castle.
Carton House	1 mile (1.6km) east of Maynooth. Originally built by the Talbot family in the early 17th century before passing into the possession of the Earls of Kildare. The house was remodelled, enlarged and modernised in the early 19th century. Used in the location shooting of the film *Barry Lyndon* (1975), it is now a luxury hotel. Tel: 015 052000.
Castle Rheban	2 miles (3km) north of Athy. The ruin of a castle built by Richard de St Michael. It was fought over continuously during the War of the Confederacy and was in ruins by the end of the 18th century.
Castledermot Friary and High Crosses	8 miles (13km) southeast of Athy. The ruin of a Franciscan friary founded in 1302 with a residential tower house attached to the church. In a nearby churchyard stand two high crosses.
Castletown House	$\frac{1}{2}$ mile (0.8km) northeast of Celbridge. The largest Palladian country house in Ireland. Built in the 1720s for William Conolly (1662–1729), Speaker of the Irish House of Commons, it is the only Irish house designed by Italian Alessandro Galilei (1691–1737) and his friend and fellow architect Edward Lovett Pearce. The house was purchased by Desmond Guinness in 1967 and became the

headquarters of the Irish Georgian Society. It was restored and refurbished before passing into state care in 1994. Tel: 016 288252.

Celbridge Abbey

Clane Road, Celbridge. Built by Bartholomew Van Homrigh, Lord Mayor of Dublin, in 1697. Jonathan Swift was a regular visitor. It was remodelled in the 18th century by the Bishop of Waterford and was for a time the residence of the parliamentarian Henry Grattan. The grounds came into the possession of the St John of God Order in 1952 and were developed by the order as a public amenity from 1988. Tel: 016 275062.

Churches

Kilteel Church, 6 miles (10km) east of Naas, the ruin of a Romanesque church with heads carved on its capitals.

St David's, Naas. Built in 1650 incorporating parts of a 12th century church also dedicated to St David and built by William Fitzmaurice, possibly on the site of an early Irish church dedicated to St Patrick. The tower was erected in the 1780s but was left without a steeple.

St Mary's, Leixlip. The current church dates from the 18th or 19th century but incorporates a 12th century tower which is said to have been the only survivor of an attack by a Bruce army in the 14th century.

St Mary's, Maynooth. Originally built in the 13th century as a private chapel for Maynooth Castle and since incorporated into the outer wall of St Patrick's College. It was renovated in the 1630s but foll into ruin after the conflicts of the 1640s. It was repaired by James, Duke of Leinster, in 1770.

St Michael and All Angels, Millicent, 2 miles (3km) south of Clane. Built in Hiberno-Romanesque style and consecrated in 1883. Both its exterior and interior have examples of work heavily influenced by the Arts and Crafts movement.

St Michael's, Athy. The ruin of a 14th century church possibly built by the St Michael family, hence its dedication.

Confey, Battle of

The Battle of Confey (or Ceannfuait) was fought between Danish and/or Norwegian Vikings and the Irish king of Leinster c. AD 915–917. There is some debate as to the site of the battle but it possibly took place near modern Leixlip, 4½ miles (7km) southeast of Maynooth, although the *New History of Ireland* gives the location as Glynn, near St Mullins in Co. Wexford. The battle took place during a time of increased Viking attacks. The Vikings were victorious and were led by King Sigtrygg Caech (also called Sigtrygg Gael or Sithric the Blind), who was based in Dublin, then an important Viking settlement. The *Annals of the Four Masters* states that the Irish dead included King Augaire mac Ailella (called Ugaire in the translation), but it may be that High King Niall Glundub was in fact leader of the Irish. According to the *Annals*, 600 Leinstermen were killed. Danish settlers founded Leixlip after the battle.

Connolly's Folly

1½ miles (2.5km) north of Celbridge. An obelisk on the border between the Carton and Castletown Estates. Designed by Richard Castle in 1740 for Kathleen Conolly of Castletown, its building provided work for the local labourers. It stands 140ft (43m) high and was restored in the 1960s by Desmond Guinness, whose first wife Mariga is interred under the central arch.

Coolcarrigan House

10 miles (16km) northwest of Naas. A Georgian house built in the 1830s by Robert Mackay Wilson and surrounded by 10 acres (4ha) of gardens and arboretum, noted for their collections of rhododendron, azalea and sorbus. Tel: 045 863527.

Donadea Forest Park

Donadea, 7 miles (11km) southwest of Maynooth. A forest park with mixed woodland and parkland covering 640 acres (260ha) which surrounds the ruin of a medieval castle. A scale replica of the Twin Towers, bearing the names of all the firefighters and police officers who died on 11 September 2001, was erected in the park in 2003 in memory of fireman Sean Tallon, whose father was born in Donadea.

Donnelly's Hollow

1¼ miles (2km) southwest of Newbridge. A natural amphitheatre near The Curragh racecourse where boxer Dan Donnelly defeated his English opponent George Cooper in 1815.

Grand Canal

See Offaly

Grange Castle and Gardens

Located 20 miles (32km) north of Kildare, just off the R401 (Edenderry Road). The 15th century tower house and walled garden has been recently restored by Duchas (The Heritage Service) and Failte Ireland (National Tourism Development Authority). The gardens cover seven acres and include parkland and woodland. Tel: (0) 46 9733316.

Great Connell Abbey

1 mile (1.6km) east of Newbridge. The meagre ruin of an Augustinian priory beside the River Liffey, founded in 1202 by Meiler FitzHenry. It was suppressed in 1541 and much of the stone was used in the 19th century as building material for the cavalry barracks in Newbridge.

Harristown House

2 miles (3km) east of Kilcullen, 6 miles (10km) southwest of Naas. Originally built in the mid 18th century by Whitmore Davis for the La Touche family, and rebuilt in the 1890s after being gutted by fire. It features period furniture and decorations. Tel: 045 483614.

Highest point

Cupidstown Hill at 1245ft (379m).

Interesting facts

Nicholas Callan was born in 1799 at Darver, Co. Louth, but was Professor of Natural Philosophy (now called Physics) at St Patrick's College, Maynooth, from 1826 until his death in 1864. A pioneering scientist in the field of electrical science as well as a Roman Catholic priest, unfortunately his inventions were subsequently attributed to other scientists and his great work is only now starting to gain recognition. Callan invented the induction coil in 1836 and his work on electromagnets in 1836–8 was based on that of William Sturgeon and Joseph Henry. He was slow to claim credit for his invention and it is often attributed instead to Heinrich Ruhmkorff in 1857. Callan also invented the world's first transformer. **Theobald Wolfe Tone** (1763–98), Irish revolutionary and leader of the Society of the United Irishmen, is buried in Bodenstown cemetery. The site of his grave sees annual commemorations in June by various parties of the Irish Republican tradition. These commemorations were begun by members of the Irish Republican Brotherhood in the late 19th century and have continued to the present day. The ballad 'Tone's

Grave', popularly known as 'Bodenstown churchyard', celebrates and commemorates Tone's life. **The largest artificial lake in Ireland**, situated on the Lyons Demesne at Hazelhatch, is owned by Tony Ryan, founder of Ryanair.

Japanese Gardens — Tully, 1 mile (1.6km) southeast of Kildare. The Japanese Gardens at the Irish National Stud were laid out 1906–10 on the estate of Colonel William Hill-Walker by Japanese craftsman Tassa Eida and his son Minoru, after whom the 1909 Epsom Derby winner bred at the farm was named. Designed to symbolise the Life of Man, they are regarded as among the finest Japanese gardens in Europe. Tel: 045 521617.

Jigginstown Castle — 1 mile (1.6km) southwest of Naas. The ruin of a large house built in the 17th century for Thomas Wentworth, Earl of Strafford. It is not clear whether the house was completed following Strafford's execution for treason in 1641.

Kilcullen Round Tower — Kilcullen, 7 miles (11km) southwest of Naas. A round tower standing 40ft (12m) high and possibly once part of a 5th century monastery founded by St Patrick.

Kildare Cathedral — Market Square, Kildare. Originally built in 1223 by Ralph of Bristol on the site of a nunnery founded in the 5th century by St Brigid. It was restored in the 15th century and almost completely rebuilt in the late 19th century. The cathedral houses many treasures, while outside are the remains of the ancient High Cross of Kildare. There is also an accessible 108ft (33m) high round tower in the grounds. Tel: 045 441654.

Kildare Heritage Centre — Market Square, Kildare. Housed in the restored former 18th century Market House, and celebrating the history of the town from the foundation of a nunnery by St Brigid in the 5th century to the present day. Tel: 045 530672.

Kilkea Castle — Kilkea, 5 miles (8km) southeast of Athy. The oldest continuously inhabited castle in Ireland, built in 1180 by Sir Walter de Riddlesford, a young knight who had accompanied the first invasion party of Anglo-Normans in 1170. Notable features include the so-called 'Evil-Eye Stone', a carved stone let into the wall 17ft (5.2m) up on the groin of what was once the Guard Room, and the carving of a monkey on the bracket which supports the projecting chimney, high up towards the top of the so-called Haunted Tower.

Kilteel Castle — Kilteel, 6 miles (10km) east of Naas. The well-preserved ruin of a 15th century tower house, located on the site of a 13th century castle built by Maurice FitzGerald as a preceptory for the Knights Hospitallers of St John of Jerusalem. It was built on the site of an early monastic foundation.

Larchill Gardens — 2 miles (3km) north of Kilcock, 4 miles (6km) northwest of Maynooth. An 18th century ornamental parkland garden ('Ferme Ornée'), restored 1994–9. It features an 8 acre (3ha) lake with an island castle folly as well as nine other follies, including a shell tower. There is a Gothic model farmyard with dovecotes, stables and pigsties, as well as an open air theatre. Tel: 016 287354.

Leixlip Castle — Main Street, Leixlip. Originally built by Adam de Hereford in the 12th century at the confluence of the rivers Rye and Liffey. It was extended in the 14th century and passed in 1485 to the Fitzgerald Earls of Kildare, with whom it remained until the failure of Silken Thomas's rebellion in 1535. It was remodelled in the 18th century to reflect a more domestic use. The castle features fine tapestries and period furniture. The village of Leixlip is the site of the original Guinness Brewery, founded by brothers Arthur and Richard Guinness in 1755. Tel: 016 244430.

Lodge Park Walled Gardens — Straffan, 4½ miles (7km) south of Maynooth. A restored garden adjoining the Palladian style Lodge Park, built in 1773. It is divided into four sections delineated by box-edged paths and clipped yew trees. The garden is located beside the Steam Museum. Tel: 016 288412.

Lullymore Heritage and Discovery Park — Lullymore, 6 miles (10km) southeast of Edenderry. Opened in 1993, the park combines historic exhibits and replica houses. It stands on a small mineral island in the Bog of Allen. Displays include a replica Neolithic farmstead with round huts, the Early Christian Visitor Centre which examines the transition from paganism to Christianity, the story of John Doorly, a United Irishman in the 1798 Rebellion, a Famine commemoration area and an indoor exhibit of a 19th century eviction. There are folklore sites throughout the surrounding woodlands. Tel: 045 870238.

Maynooth Castle — Maynooth. A seat of the Kildare FitzGeralds, the castle was begun in the early 13th century by the family and enlarged by John, 6th Earl of Kildare, in the 1420s. It remained in the hands of the FitzGerald family almost continuously until they abandoned it in 1656. The Earls of Kildare at one point governed Ireland in the name of the king of England and the castle was therefore the centre of political power. However, a rebellion by the 10th Earl, known as Silken Thomas, ended with the castle being captured by an English force under Sir William Skeffington in March 1535 while Thomas was away gathering reinforcements to relieve it. The garrison was put to death in what became known as the 'Maynooth Pardon'. Thomas was later executed in London. By the 17th century the castle was in a state of disrepair and today only the ruined keep and the gatehouse survive. There is an exhibition on the history of the castle and the family in the keep. Tel: 016 286744.

Moone High Cross — Moone, 7 miles (11km) east of Athy. An 8th century high cross reputed to be the second tallest in Ireland, standing 17ft 6in (5.4m) high. It originally stood at a monastic site founded in the 5th or 6th century. The upper part and base of the cross were discovered in the graveyard of the ruined Moone Abbey in 1835 and the middle section was found in 1893. The cross has been repaired and re-erected within the ruined church. The carvings on the cross include the sacrifice of Isaac, Daniel in the lion's den and episodes from the life of Jesus plus intricate Celtic designs.

Mullaghmast — 2 miles (3km) west of Ballitore. A hill dominated by Rath Mor. A National Monument, it is the site of an O'Toole fort and features many earthworks and ring forts.

Oughterard Round Tower — Oughterard, 5 miles (8km) east of Clane, 6 miles (10km) northeast of Naas. The 30ft (9m) tower is all that remains of a 6th century monastic foundation. The doorway is 9ft (2.7m) above ground level. A 16th or 17th century church and the ruin of a tower house are also located nearby.

Peatland World Museum — Lullymore, 8 miles (13km) north of Kildare. Housed in a restored 19th century courtyard and dedicated to explaining the development of bogs, their exploitation and their future importance. Tel: 045 860133.

Pollardstown Fen — 4 miles (6km) northeast of Kildare. The largest remaining spring-fed fen in Ireland, covering 540 acres (220ha) with 322 acres (130ha) designated as a nature reserve.

Punchestown Standing Stone — 3 miles (5km) southeast of Naas. Located next to Punchestown racecourse. A huge granite standing stone standing 19ft (5.7m) high with a further 4ft (1.2m) below ground. It weighs more than 9 tonnes. After it collapsed in 1931, an empty Bronze Age cist was found near the base. It was re-erected in 1934. There are other standing stones at Craddockstown West (13ft/4m high) and Forenaghts Great (16ft/5m high).

Rathcoffey Castle — 3 miles (5km) north of Clane, 8 miles (13km) north of Naas. The ruin of a castle which once belonged to the Wogan family, who were granted the land by King John in 1317. It was largely demolished by Archibald Rowan in the 1780s to provide building material for a new house.

Rivers — The **Barrow** – see Co. Carlow. The **Boyne** – see Co. Meath. The **Liffey** – see Co. Dublin. The **Rye** – Rises north of Kilcock and flows for 12 miles (19km) adjacent to the M4 motorway before joining the Liffey at Leixlip. Its major tributary, the **Lyreen**, flows through Maynooth.

St Fiachra's Garden — Tully, 1 mile (1.6km) southeast of Kildare. Located at the Irish National Stud and dedicated to St Fiachra, the patron saint of gardeners. Created in 1999, the garden was designed by Martin Hallinan. It is set within woodlands, and is aimed to recreate a little of the spirituality of the early Christian monastic movement in Ireland. The entrance is through an underground stone passage and the garden features monastic cells, a waterfall and a sunken oak forest.

St Patrick's College — Kilcock Road, Maynooth. Often referred to as Maynooth College, St Patrick's was founded in 1795 as the National Seminary for Ireland. The building of the college was begun in April 1796 and the site was extended in the 1840s with the construction of St Mary's Square, designed in Gothic style by A W Pugin. The college chapel was designed by J J McCarthy and built 1875–91, a tower and spire being added ten years later. St Patrick's became a Pontifical University in 1896; despite this, in 1910 it became a recognised college of the National University of Ireland. Lay students were first admitted in 1966. In 1997 the National University of Ireland, Maynooth was created and now exists alongside St Patrick's College, which remains a Pontifical University and the National Seminary. The two institutions share the same campus. Tel: 017 083576.

Sport

football — **Kildare County** were formed in 2002. Their home ground is Station Road, Newbridge.

Gaelic football — **Kildare** were winners of the All-Ireland Senior Football championship in 1905, 1919, 1927 and 1928.

golf — The **K Club** Golf and Spa Resort, Straffan, more correctly the Kildare Hotel and Golf Club, was built on the old grounds of Straffan House. It has two 18 hole courses, both designed by Arnold Palmer: the Palmer Course and the Smurfit Course. The K Club hosted the Ryder Cup in 2006, Europe winning by 18½ points to 9½ points. Tel: 016 017300.

horse racing — **The Curragh** is the headquarters of Irish racing, which began here during the 17th century. It became the centre of Irish thoroughbred racing. The Curragh is Ireland's premier Flat racing course, hosting all five classic races in the Irish racing calendar: the Irish 1000 Guineas (first run in 1922); Irish 2000 Guineas (1921); Irish Derby Stakes (1866); Irish Oaks (1895); and Irish St Leger (1915). The track is horseshoe shaped with a circuit of 2 miles (3km), a run-in of 3 furlongs (0.6km) and an uphill finish. Tel: 045 441205.

The **Irish National Stud**, Tully, 1 mile (1.6km) southeast of Kildare, was established as a stud farm in 1900 and has been home to some of Ireland's finest thoroughbreds. In the period 1904–14 seven classic winners were bred at Tully, including the winner of the 2000 Guineas and Epsom Derby in 1909. It was established as the Irish National Stud in 1946. The Irish Horse Museum traces the history of the horse and horse racing in Ireland, with exhibits including the skeleton of legendary steeplechaser Arkle. Tel: 045 521617. See also Japanese Gardens, St Fiachra's Garden.

Naas Racecourse, Tipper Road, Naas, stages both National Hunt and Flat meetings. It is a left-handed oval of 1½ miles (2.5km) with a run-in of 4 furlongs (0.8km) and an uphill finish. Tel: 045 897391.

Punchestown Racecourse, Punchestown, Naas, held its first meeting in 1854. The course is a right-handed oval of 2 miles (3km) with run-in of 3½ furlongs (0.7km). There is also a 3 mile (5km) bank course. Tel: 045 897704.

Steam Museum — Straffan, 4½ miles (7km) south of Maynooth. Housed in the former Medieval Revival Church of St Jude, which once stood in the Inchicore railway works in Dublin. The Power Hall exhibits stationary steam engines from the 1830s, while the Model Hall displays the Richard Guinness Collection of Inventors and early large size prototype railway models. Tel: 016 273155.

Taghadoe Round Tower — 4 miles (6km) southwest of Maynooth. Originally part of a monastic site founded in the 6th century. It stands more than 60ft (18m) high with the door 12ft (3.5m) above ground level.

White's Castle — Leinster Street, Athy. A 15th century castle built by the 8th Earl of Kildare to guard a crossing of the River Barrow.

Wonderful Barn — Leixlip, 4½ miles (7km) southeast of Maynooth. An unusually shaped stone barn, built for Laura Catherine Connolly in 1743, largely to provide labour for the poor of the district. Conical in shape, it rises to seven storeys, with 94 steps winding around the outside. Its purpose is unclear, but it has been suggested that it was intended as a grain store or a dovecote.

Some famous people born in County Kildare

Dempsey, Jack (Nonpareil) (boxer) (1862–95)	Curran
Eddery, Pat (jockey) (1952–)	Newbridge
Goff, Matt (Gaelic footballer) (1901–56)	Leixlip
Guinness, Arthur (brewer) (1725–1803)	Celbridge
Hamilton, Willoughby (tennis player) (1864–1943)	Monasterevin
Hayes, Gabriel (artist) (1909–78)	Monasterevin
Higgins, Aidan (writer) (1927–)	Celbridge
Keane, Molly (writer) (1904–96)	Ballyrankin
Lawless, Emily (writer) (1845–1913)	Ardclough
Lonsdale, Kathleen (scientist) (1903–71)	Newbridge
Moore, Christy (singer) (1945–)	Newbridge
Rice, Damien (singer) (1973–)	Celbridge
Robinson, Robbie (musician) (1965–)	Athy
Shackleton, Ernest (explorer) (1874–1922)	Kilkea
Walsh, Rupert 'Ruby' (jockey) (1979–)	Kill

KILKENNY

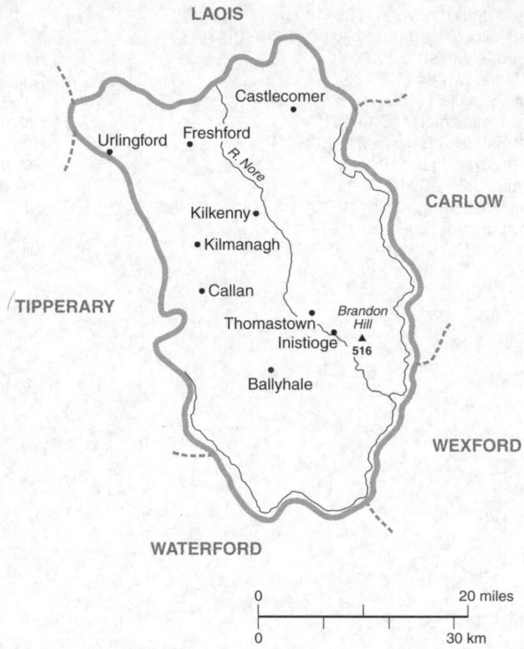
LAOIS
Castlecomer
Urlingford
Freshford
R. Nore
CARLOW
Kilkenny
Kilmanagh
Callan
TIPPERARY
Brandon Hill
Thomastown
Inistioge
516
Ballyhale
WEXFORD
WATERFORD
0
20 miles
0
30 km

Kilkenny is part of the province of Leinster and lies in the south of the Republic of Ireland. The county has borders with Tipperary to the west, Wexford to the southeast, Waterford to the south, Laois to the north and Carlow to the northeast. Kilkenny (the county town) is the only city. The River Nore bisects the county from north to south and the rivers Barrow and Suir (pronounced 'shoor') are natural boundaries to the east and south respectively. The economy of County Kilkenny is based mainly on technology, tourism, craft and design, and food processing.

The area was settled in prehistoric times and the name Kilkenny is derived from the Gaelic *Cill Chainnigh* (Church of Canice). It arises because of the monastic foundation of St Canice in the 6th century near the present site of St Canice's Cathedral in the city of Kilkenny. The county was formerly the kingdom of Osraige, the name being preserved in the bishopric of Ossory. Osraige was a semi-independent state within the kingdom of Leinster. A turning point in the county's history was the banishment of Diarmuid MacMurrough, king of Leinster, for abducting the wife of another chieftain. He appealed to Henry II of England and was allowed to raise troops and supporters from Normans in Wales to help him recover Leinster. He promised Richard Fitzgilbert de Clare, Earl of Pembroke (Strongbow), his daughter in marriage in return for aid and thus established a Norman heir to Leinster. Strongbow invaded in 1169 and took most of the present county under his control with his seat at a crossing of the Nore, which was to become Kilkenny City.

The castle at Kilkenny passed to James Butler, 3rd Earl of Ormond, in 1391 and this powerful family dominated the history of the county for many centuries, continuing to live in Kilkenny until the 1930s. The Anglo-Irish Parliament often met here and in 1367 the Statutes of Kilkenny were enacted. These were 35 acts passed in an effort to halt the 'slide' of Irish based Anglo-Norman families into becoming 'more Irish than the Irish themselves'. They included the statute that 'every Englishman is to use the English language, and be named by an English name, leaving off entirely the manner of naming used by the Irish; and that every Englishman use the English custom, fashion, mode of riding and apparel, according to his estate'. The town of Kilkenny became a city in 1609. During the 1640s a large proportion of Ireland was governed by the Irish Catholic Confederation, also known as the 'Confederation of Kilkenny' because its Supreme Council was based in the city of Kilkenny.

Kilkenny has produced a host of famous hurlers, notably Lory Meagher, but perhaps the county's best-known native is George Berkeley of Thomastown, founder of the philosophical dictum *Esse est percipi* (to be is to be perceived) and after whom Berkeley, California, is named.

Kilkenny	**Population**			**Area**	
Districts	*male*	*female*	*total*	*sq miles*	*sq km*
Callan	3193	3078	6271	97	252
Carrick-on-Suir	1846	1732	3578	51	131
Castlecomer	3964	3892	7856	90	234
Ida	1280	1213	2493	45	117
Kilkenny Borough	4178	4413	8591	1	4
Kilkenny rural area	11,809	11,958	23,767	172	445
Thomastown	6224	5893	12,117	169	437
Urlingford	2177	2034	4211	83	214
Waterford No. 2	5869	5586	11,455	92	238
Total	40,540	39,799	80,339	800	2072

Local Attractions and Information

Administrative headquarters	County Hall, John Street, Kilkenny. Tel: 056 775 2699.
Aghaviller Round Tower	$^1/_2$ mile (0.8km) south of Newmarket, 13 miles (21km) south of Kilkenny. The 30ft (9m) stump of a round tower, located on the site of an early Christian monastery. See also Churches.
Ballylarkin Abbey	1 mile (1.6km) southwest of Freshford, 8$^1/_2$ miles (13.5km) northwest of Kilkenny. An abbey and fortified church built in 1350 by the Shorthall family.
Ballyrafton Wood	5 miles (8km) north of Kilkenny. Native oak woodland beside the River Dinan.
Ballyragget Castle	Ballyragget, 10 miles (16km) northwest of Kilkenny. A 15th century castle with rounded turrets and a bawn, built by the Mountgarret family. It stands on private land and is not open to the public.
Battles	Three battles have been fought in Kilkenny: Clashacrow, Kilkenny and Piltown. See separate table for details.
Black Abbey	Abbey Square, Kilkenny. A Dominican abbey founded in 1225 by William Marshal outside the walls of the city. Suppressed in the 1540s, it was converted into a courthouse, which it remained until the late 17th century. It was restored in the late 18th century but was not used as a place of worship again until the mid 19th century when it became a parish church. Inside is an alabaster statue representing the Holy Trinity. Tel: 056 772 1279.
Brod Tullaroan	Tullaroan, 8 miles (13km) west of Kilkenny. A restored 17th century two-storey thatched homestead which was once the home of famous Kilkenny hurler Lory Meagher. It now houses the Lory Meagher Heritage Centre, a museum celebrating the history of hurling from its beginnings to the establishment of the Gaelic Athletic Association (GAA). Tel: 056 776 9202.
Burnchurch Castle	Burnchurch, 5 miles (8km) southwest of Kilkenny. The ruin of a 15th century six-storey castle built by the Fitzgerald family.
Callan Motte	Callan, 9 miles (15km) southwest of Kilkenny. A 13th century motte measuring 40ft (12m) high by 150ft (46m) wide and which would originally have been surmounted by a wooden fortification. It is believed that Cromwell mounted cannon on the earthwork during the siege of Callan in 1650.
Callan Friary	Callan, 9 miles (15km) southwest of Kilkenny. The ruin of a 15th century Augustinian friary, located on the site of an Augustinian priory founded c.1215 by William Marshal.
Carn Dubh Moat	3 miles (5km) northwest of Castlecomer. Reputedly the burial site of Lughaidh Mac Con in the 2nd century.
Castlecomer Demesne	$^1/_2$ mile (0.8km) northeast of Castlecomer. A 180 acre (73ha) demesne surrounding 17th century Castlecomer House, which was destroyed by fire in the 1960s. The landscape includes artificial caves and lakes connected by cascades. Tel: 056 444 0707.
Castleinch Wood	Callan, 9 miles (15km) southwest of Kilkenny. Aka Coille an Fhaltaigh (Wall's Wood). A People's Millennium Forest consisting largely of semi-mature conifers but also including old oak woodland.
Churches	**Aghaviller Church**, $^1/_2$ mile (0.8km) south of Newmarket, 13 miles (21km) south of Kilkenny. The ruin of a 12th century church dedicated to St Brenainn on the site of an early Christian monastery. **Clonamery Church**, 1$^1/_2$ miles (2.5km) southeast of Instioge, 16 miles (26km) southeast of Kilkenny, the ruin of a small nave and chancel church, probably built on the site of an earlier foundation. **Freshford Church**, The Square, Freshford, An 18th century church on the site of a 7th century foundation of St Lachtain. The present church incorporates a 12th century Romanesque doorway. **Kilfane Church**, 2 miles (3km) north of Thomastown, 8 miles (13km) southeast of Kilkenny. The ruin of a small church, the main feature of which is the larger than life-size effigy (known locally as the 'long man of Kilfane') of a 14th century knight believed to be Thomas Cantwell, who may have either founded or rebuilt the church. The effigy was buried for a time but later recovered. **St Mary's**, Callan, 9 miles (15km) southwest of Kilkenny. The remains of a 15th century church which replaced a 13th century one. The tower of the earlier church still stands. **St Mary's Collegiate Church**, Main Street, Gowran. Built c.1275 on the site of an earlier foundation. A central tower, built in the 14th or 15th century, was incorporated into the parish

church which occupies the former chancel of the original church. The north wall of the nave of the original church survives to full height.

Sheepstown Church, 1 mile (1.6km) west of Knocktopher, 12 miles (19km) south of Kilkenny. The ruin of a 12th century church with a Romanesque doorway.

Clara Castle — $4^1/_2$ miles (7km) east of Kilkenny. A well-preserved 15th century five-storey tower house and bawn, occupied by the Shortall family until the early 20th century. Although unrestored it still has many original features in place, including its oak floors.

Clomantagh Castle — 3 miles (5km) west of Freshford, 10 miles (16km) northwest of Kilkenny. A tower house once occupied by the Shortall family and dating to c.1430, with an attached farmhouse built c.1800. There is a sheela-na-gig high up on the tower wall. The castle is now a small hotel.

Duiske Abbey — Graiguenamanagh, 14 miles (23km) southeast of Kilkenny. Originally founded in 1204 by William Marshal the Elder as a Cistercian monastery (the largest in Ireland). It was suppressed at the time of the Dissolution and fell into disrepair, the tower falling into the nave. In the late 18th and early 19th century the ruins of the chancel, transepts and parts of the nave were reroofed and restored. Further restoration has led to part of the abbey becoming a parish church. The building has now been completely restored.

Dunmore Cave — 4 miles (6km) north of Kilkenny. A system of limestone caves extending for $^1/_4$ mile (0.4km) and noted for their calcite formations. The caves have been in state care since 1940 and are a designated National Monument. Tel: 056 770 7726.

Edmund Rice Heritage Centre — Callan, 9 miles (15km) southwest of Kilkenny. Housed in Westcourt, the restored thatched house where Catholic missionary Edmund Ignatius Rice (1762–1844) was born. Rice was the founder of two orders of religious brothers – the Congregation of Christian Brothers and the Presentation Brothers – and spent most of his life teaching or training teachers for the poor and marginalised in Ireland and in particular Waterford. He was beatified in 1996. The house has six rooms including the bedroom where Rice was born. Tel: 056 7725141.

Foulksrath Castle — Jenkinstown, 7 miles (11km) northwest of Kilkenny. A 15th century tower house now used as a hostel. Tel: 056 776 7674.

Gairdin An Ghorta — Newmarket, 12 miles (19km) south of Kilkenny. A commemorative garden for the victims of the Great Famine. Tel: 056 776 8624.

Gowran Castle — Gowran, 8 miles (13km) east of Kilkenny. The remains of a possibly 14th century tower house which stands to its full height. This may be the Gowran Castle which surrendered to Oliver Cromwell in March 1650. There is no public access.

Grangefertagh Round Tower — $2^1/_4$ miles (3.5km) northeast of Johnstown, 14 miles (23km) northwest of Kilkenny. A round tower standing 100ft (30.5m) high, the only remains of a 6th century monastic site possibly founded by St Ciaran.

Granny Castle — Granagh, $5^1/_2$ miles (9km) southwest of Mullinavat, 23 miles (37km) south of Kilkenny. Aka Granagh Castle. The ruin of a 13th century castle beside the River Suir, originally built by the Le Poer family. It was passed to the Earls of Ormond in the late 14th century and remained in their possession until it was surrendered to Cromwell's troops in 1650. Some restoration was carried out in the 19th century and further work in 1925.

Harristown Dolmen — Harristown, 4 miles (6km) northwest of Mullinavat, 19 miles (31km) south of Kilkenny. Aka the Kilmogue Dolmen and locally as Leac an Scail (Stone of the Warrior). One of the largest dolmens in Ireland, with a capstone resting on two 14ft (4.2m) uprights and a back stone.

Highest point — Brandon Hill, southeast of Thomastown, at 1690ft (516m). On the top is a cairn and stone circle. There are fine views of the Barrow and Nore valleys.

Interesting facts — **Dame Alice le Kyteler** was accused and convicted in 1324 in one of the first cases of witchcraft in Europe. Born in 1280 at Kyteler House on Kieran Street in Kilkenny, Alice was a wealthy and powerful woman. She married four times, all her husbands dying and leaving her their fortunes. After she arranged herself as the beneficiary of the estate of her final husband, John Le Poer, she disinherited his three children. Suspicions were raised and when Le Poer began suffering a mysterious wasting disease resulting in the loss of all his hair, he and the children accused Alice of witchcraft. The story goes that Le Poer and his children went to Alice's seaside home and found the body parts of an unbaptised infant, evil powders, communion wafers imprinted with satanic images, the nails of corpses boiled in the skull of a robber, and candles made of human fat – all and any of which would have implicated her in the practice of the dark arts. The Le Poer family put the terrible items into crates and brought these to the Bishop of Ossory, Richard Ledrede. Alice's powerful enemies insisted that she was a witch, but she had powerful friends as well. The Lord Chancellor of Ireland was her brother-in-law and her son William was a friend of the treasurer. She had enough power that when Bishop Ledrede came to investigate her, she had him imprisoned in the castle. The Dean of St Patrick's Cathedral in Dublin was outraged by this deed, and a power struggle followed. Bishop Ledrede spent 17 days in jail, emerging with a renewed zeal for Alice's prosecution. The result was the conviction of Alice, her son William, and ten others. Alice's maid Petronilla died by burning, after a severe beating. (She had confessed under torture, and had implicated Alice as well.) William was sentenced to hear Mass three times daily for a year, to feed a certain number of the poor, and to reroof St Canice's Cathedral. Alice herself disappeared the night before she was to be executed. Her ultimate fate is obscure: some accounts tell that she went to England, and lived to be an old woman. **James Hoban**, born in Desart, near Callan, was the architect of 1600 Pennsylvania Avenue, Washington DC, USA, better known as the White House, the official home and principal workplace of the President of the United States of America. Hoban based the original structure on Leinster House, Dublin, to which it still bears a striking resemblance, particularly in the north façade. **The Ladies of Llangollen** were two upper-class Kilkenny women whose close relationship scandalised and fascinated their contemporaries.

Lady Eleanor Butler (1739–1829) was considered an over-educated bookworm by her family, who occupied Kilkenny Castle. She spoke French and was educated in a convent in France. Her mother tried to make her join a convent because she was becoming a spinster. The Honourable Sarah Ponsonby (1755–1831) lived with relatives in Woodstock, near Inistioge. They met in 1768, and quickly became friends. Over the years they formulated a plan of a private rural retreat. Rather than face the possibility of being forced into unwanted marriages, they ran away together in April 1778. Their families hunted them down and forcefully tried to make them give up their plans – in vain. They decided to move to England but ended up in Wales and set up home in Plas Newydd ('New Place' – see Gwynedd), near the town of Llangollen in 1780. Nobody knows for certain whether their relationship was sexual but they have become iconic figures for the lesbian community.

Islands — **Fiddown Island** in the River Suir (pronounced 'shoor') is the only island in Kilkenny, although the Fiddown Bridge joins the island to the mainland. See also Nature Reserves: Fiddown Island.

Jenkinstown Wood — 5 miles (8km) north of Kilkenny. Originally part of the Bryan-Bellew Estate. Dublin-born poet Thomas Moore wrote the 'Last Rose of Summer' while staying at Jenkinstown House in 1805. The woodland is mainly ash, beech, oak and Norwegian spruce, but also includes rare species such as a Chinese Necklace poplar.

Jerpoint Abbey — $1^1/_4$ miles (2km) southwest of Thomastown, 11 miles (18km) south of Kilkenny. A ruined Cistercian abbey believed to have been founded in 1160 by Donal MacGillapatrick, king of Ossory. Jerpoint was the mother house for abbeys at Kilcooly and Killenny. The tower was added in the 15th century.

Kells Priory — Kells, $7^1/_2$ miles (12km) south of Kilkenny. The extensive ruins, covering 4 acres (1.6ha), of a fortified Augustinian priory founded by Geoffrey de Marisco in 1193. It was ransacked in 1252 and 1327. Although the abbey was handed over to James, Earl of Ormond, at the time of the Dissolution it continued to function until the 1640s.

Kilfane Glen — Kilfane, 2 miles (3km) north of Thomastown, 8 miles (13km) southeast of Kilkenny. A woodland garden dating from the 1790s which was originally part of the Kilfane House demesne. Features include a 30ft (9m) waterfall, stream and woodland paths. The garden is also dotted with works of art. Tel: 056 772 4558.

Kilkenny — Kilkenny (*Cill Chainnigh*, St Cainneach's church) is the largest population centre in the county. Located in the northwest, on a small hill above the River Nore, it is Ireland's smallest city and was granted its charter in 1609. Many of the buildings are made from the local black polished limestone known as Kilkenny Marble, which gives the city its nickname of the 'Marble City'.

Kilkenny Castle — The Parade, Kilkenny. Originally built in the 13th century by William Marshal on the site of a former Strongbow fortification which had been destroyed. From 1391 until 1935 it was the home of the Butler family, who remodelled it in the 19th century. The castle now houses the Butler Gallery, while one of the towers now serves as a conference centre. The property was given to the nation in 1967 and the castle and grounds are now managed by Duchas, the National Heritage Council. The garden has a long established rose garden, together with 50 acres (20ha) of pleasure grounds overlooking the River Nore.

Kilkenny Cats — The origin of the term 'to fight like a Kilkenny cat' is obscure but refers to anyone who is a dogged and unrelenting fighter. The inhabitants of Co. Kilkenny are often referred to as Kilkenny Cats and it is the nickname of the successful county hurling team.

Kilkenny College — Castlecomer Road, Kilkenny. A co-educational school founded in 1538 as Kilkenny Grammar School by Piers Butler, Earl of Ormonde, and refounded in 1666 as Kilkenny College having been closed during the English Civil War. Notable former students include Jonathan Swift, Bishop Berkeley, and playwrights George Farquhar and William Congreve. Tel: 056 776 1544.

Kilkenny Tholsel — High Street, Kilkenny. The Tholsel (tax hall) was built in 1761 and acted as customs house, court house and municipal offices. The ground floor has a five-bay arcade where markets were held. The forecourt provided a place for street performers to entertain their audience. The roof is topped by a restored three-tier octagonal clock tower which has been recently restored.

Kilmacoliver Hill — $1^1/_2$ miles (2.5km) south of Tullaghought, 17 miles (27km) south of Kilkenny. An 856ft (261m) hill topped by a stone circle of uncertain date.

Kilree Monastic Site — $1^1/_2$ miles (2.5km) south of Kells, 8 miles (13km) south of Kilkenny. The site of a monastery founded by St Brigid of Kildare in the 6th century. The most impressive remains are a 10th century round tower.

Knockroe Passage Tomb — $^1/_2$ mile (0.8km) east of Windgap, 14 miles (23km) southwest of Kilkenny. A passage tomb with 30 decorated stones, excavated in 1990.

Knocktopher Abbey — Knocktopher, 12 miles (19km) south of Kilkenny. The site of a castle and a Carmelite abbey founded in the 13th century. It was the home from 1679 to 1981 of the Langrishe family, who rebuilt the abbey in Gothic style after a fire in 1850. It reputedly has the oldest working chimney in Ireland. Now offering self-catering accommodation. Tel: 056 776 8618.

Lory Meagher Heritage Centre — See Brod Tullaroan

Nature Reserves — **Ballykeeffe**, $1^1/_2$ miles (2.5km) southeast of Kilmanagh, 6 miles (10km) southwest of Kilkenny, 137 acres (55ha) mainly of oak and ash woodland.

Fiddown Island, 22 miles (35km) south of Kilkenny, 156 acres (63ha) of marsh and woodland on an island on the River Suir, consisting largely of willow scrub bordered by reed swamps.

Garryricken, $2^1/_2$ miles (4km) north of Windgap, 3 miles (5km) south of Callan, 70 acres (28ha) mainly of oak and ash woodland.

Kyleadohir, 3 miles (5km) southwest of Callan, 12 miles (19km) southwest of Kilkenny, 146 acres (59ha) mainly of oak and ash woodland.

Nore View Folk Museum	Bennettsbridge, 5 miles (8km) southeast of Kilkenny. A local history museum with more than 10,000 exhibits, as well as displays including a pub, forge, dairy, petrol station and carpenter's workshop. Tel: 056 772 7749.
Rivers	Co. Kilkenny is bordered on the south and southwest by the **Suir** (see Tipperary), and on the southeast by the **Barrow** (see Carlow). The **Nore** (see Tipperary) bisects the county from north to southeast and converges with the Barrow at the point where Kilkenny, Wexford and Carlow meet. Other rivers include the **Arrigle** which flows north and joins the River Nore near Ballyduff; the **Dinin**, a tributary of the Nore in the north of the county, flowing east into Carlow; the **Douske** which flows through Graiguenamanagh; the **Goul** flowing north from the Urlingford area into Co. Laois; the **King's**, a tributary of the Nore in the centre of the county, flowing west into Tipperary; and the **Nuenna** which flows through Freshford.
Rothe House	Parliament Street, Kilkenny. Built in 1594 by merchant John Rothe on the occasion of his marriage, Rothe House is actually a complex of three houses separated by courtyards. The house is now the headquarters of the Kilkenny Archaeological Society, and also contains a heritage centre dedicated to the history of Kilkenny and a family history resource centre. The house includes period furniture and costume galleries. Tel: 056 772 2893.
St Canice's Cathedral	Irishtown, Kilkenny. Church of Ireland cathedral built by Bishop Hugh de Mapilton in early English Gothic style. Begun in the early 13th century but not completed until the 1280s, it was built on the site of an earlier church and is the second longest of Ireland's medieval churches. It was ransacked by Cromwell's army in 1650. The church was extensively restored in the 1860s. A 9th century round tower 100ft high (30.5m) stands beside the cathedral; it may be climbed and has a viewing platform. Tel: 056 776 4971.
St Francis Abbey	Parliament Street, Kilkenny. A Franciscan friary founded in the 1230s by Richard Marshal. The choir was extended in 1321 by Dame Isabella Pairner, when the large seven-light east window was built. It was turned over to secular uses following the Dissolution but the friars eventually returned until the end of the 17th century. The bell tower and chancel are within the grounds of Smithwicks Brewery (the St Francis's Abbey Brewery) and it is not open to the public. The sacristy has been restored as an oratory at the brewery.
St John's Priory	John Street, Kilkenny. The site of an Augustinian priory dedicated to St John and founded in the 13th century. The present church of St John the Evangelist was built on the site in 1908.
St Mary's Cathedral	James's Street, Kilkenny. The Roman Catholic cathedral of the Diocese of Ossory, built in the 1840s to a design by William Deane Butler. The interior was remodelled in line with the Vatican II proposals.
Shee Alms House	Rose Inn Street, Kilkenny. Founded by merchant Sir Richard Shee in 1582 'to accommodate twelve poor persons' and used for this purpose at least until the 1830s. The house was restored in the late 1970s and now houses the city tourist office. There is a scale model of 16th century Kilkenny on the second floor. Tel: 056 775 1500.
Sport	
football	**Kilkenny City** were founded in 1966 and were winners of the League of Ireland 1st Division in 1977. Their home ground is Buckley Park, Kilkenny.
horse racing	**Gowran Park** Racecourse, Mill Road, Gowran (pronounced 'Goran'), opened in 1914 and stages both Flat and National Hunt racing. It is a right-handed oval of $1^1/_2$ miles (2.5km) (National Hunt) and 1m 3 furlongs (Flat) with a run-in of 3 furlongs (0.6km) and an uphill finish. It is well known as a trials course for big Flat and National Hunt races. Gowran Park also features an 18-hole golf course, five holes of which lie within the race track itself. Tel: 056 772 6225.
hurling	**Kilkenny** have won the GAA All-Ireland Senior Hurling championship more often (31 times) than any other county, with successes in 1904, 1905, 1907, 1909, 1911, 1912, 1913, 1922, 1932, 1933, 1935, 1939, 1947, 1957, 1963, 1967, 1969, 1972, 1974, 1975, 1979, 1982, 1983, 1992, 1993, 2000, 2002, 2003, 2006, 2007 and 2008.
Tinnahinch Castle	$^1/_4$ mile (0.4km) south of Graiguenamanagh, 15 miles (24km) southeast of Kilkenny. The ruin of a fortified house built by James Butler in the early 17th century. It was burned down c.1700 and abandoned.
Tory Hill	2 miles (3km) southeast of Mullinavat. A hill 962ft (293m) above sea level, the site of a number of ancient monuments including a double court cairn.
Tullaherin Round Tower	Tullaherin, 7 miles (11km) southeast of Kilkenny. A 75ft (23m) high round tower, dating to the 9th century and the main remnant of an early monastic foundation dedicated to St Kieran (GR: S591478).
Tybroughney Castle	1 mile (1.6km) west of Piltown, 8 miles (13km) southwest of Mullinavat. A well-preserved and occupied castle beside the River Suir, said to have been built by the future King John in 1185.
Woodstock Gardens and Arboretum	1 mile (1.6km) south of Inistioge, 5 miles (8km) southeast of Thomastown. A 50 acre (20ha) garden and arboretum located above the valley of the River Nore. The gardens once surrounded Woodstock House, designed by Francis Bindon and built 1745–7, and which was destroyed by fire in 1922. Originally laid out in the 1800s, they are currently undergoing restoration to their late 19th century condition. Formal avenues and gardens lead into woodland walks; other features include a yew walk, a rose garden and a walled garden. The arboretum has a number of rare Asian and South American trees. Tel: 056 775 8797.

Some famous people born in County Kilkenny

Banim, John (author) (1798–1842)	Kilkenny
Battle, Cormac (radio presenter and musician) (1972–)	Kilkenny
Blunt, Theresa Lennon (writer) (1931–)	Kilkenny
Carey, Denis Joseph 'D J' (hurling player) (1970–)	Gowran
Cody, Brian (hurling player and manager) (1954–)	Sheestown
Fitzpatrick, James 'Cha' (hurling player) (1985–)	Knockmoylan
Garvey, Edmund (painter) (1740–1813)	Kilkenny
Hoban, James (architect) (1762–1831)	Desart
Keher, Eddie (hurling player) (1941–)	Inistioge
Kilroy, Thomas (playwright) (1934–)	Callan
McGarry, James (hurling player) (1971–)	Bennettsbridge
Meagher, Lory (hurling player) (1899–1973)	Tullaroan
Rice, Edmund Ignatius (missionary) (1762–1844)	Callan
Shefflin, Henry (hurling player) (1979–)	Ballyhale
Walsh, Patrick 'Ollie' (hurling player) (1937–96)	Thomastown

Laois

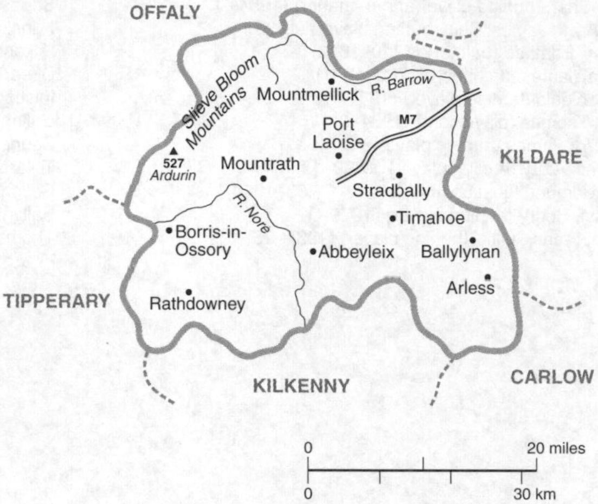
OFFALY
Slieve Bloom Mountains
Mountmellick
R. Barrow
M7
Port Laoise
527
Ardurin
Mountrath
KILDARE
Stradbally
R. Nore
Timahoe
Borris-in-Ossory
Abbeyleix
Ballylynan
Arless
TIPPERARY
Rathdowney
KILKENNY
CARLOW
0
20 miles
0
30 km

Laois (Irish – Laoighis), pronounced 'leash', is part of the province of Leinster. It lies in the centre of Ireland and is bordered by Offaly to the west, northwest and north, Kildare to the northeast, Carlow to the southeast, Kilkenny to the south and Tipperary to the southwest. The landlocked county has the distinction of being the only Irish county bordered by other landlocked counties. Its county town is Portlaoise (Irish – Portlaoighise, formerly called Maryborough). The county's economy is largely based on agriculture although it does have a small industrial base, with industrial parks at Portlaoise and Mountmellick.

Laois was first settled in the Mesolithic period and there are Neolithic burial mounds at Clonaslee and Cuffsborough. During the Bronze and Iron Ages several hill forts were established, including one at Clopook. In the 1st century AD Laois was part of the kingdom of Osraige (Ossory), an independent buffer state between Leinster and Munster. The county was ruled by the Seven Septs of Laois: O'More, O'Lalor, O'Doran, O'Dowling, O'Devoy, O'Kelly and McEvoy. After the coming of Christianity, monastic foundations were established at Aghaboe and Timahoe in the 6th and 7th centuries.

After the Norman invasion stone castles were sited at the Rock of Dunamase and Portarlington and the creation of Norman boroughs. In the 14th century the Normans were forced to give ground in the face of a Gaelic revival under the Dempseys and the O'Mores but by the mid 16th century the English were back, establishing Maryborough (Portlaoise) and the County of Laois or Queen's County in honour of Mary I. The county was successfully 'Planted' in the early 17th century and suffered depredations during Cromwell's war in Ireland. In the second half of the 17th century there was settlement by Huguenots in Portarlington and Quakers in Mountmellick. The county was devastated by the Great Famine and further crop failures later in the century brought to a head a land war between tenants and landlords. The county reverted to being known as County Laois rather than Queen's County in 1922 following the Irish War of Independence.

Perhaps Laois's best-known natives are the poets Cecil Day-Lewis and Pat Boran, programme director of the annual Dublin Writers Festival and editor of the Dedalus Press.

Laois	Population			Area	
Districts	*male*	*female*	*total*	*sq miles*	*sq km*
Abbeyleix	6442	6127	12,569	198	514
Athy	2621	2576	5197	75	194
Mountmellick	17,097	16,166	33,263	276	713
Roscrea	1356	1268	2624	57	148
Slievemargy	2615	2506	5121	58	150
Total	30,131	28,643	58,774	664	1719

Local Attractions and Information

Abbeyleix Carpet Works Abbeyleix, 8 miles (13km) southwest of Portlaoise. The original carpet factory made carpets for the *Titanic*. The factory interior of the 1900s has been recreated in the Abbeyleix Heritage House. Tel: 057 873 1653.

Abbeyleix Heritage House Abbeyleix, 8 miles (13km) southwest of Portlaoise. A local history museum housed in the former North Boys school which charts the history of Abbeyleix and Laois from pre-Christian times to the present day. There is an exhibition about the de Vesci family, who laid out the planned estate town of Abbeyleix. Tel: 057 873 1653.

Abbeyleix House Abbeyleix, 8 miles (13km) southwest of Portlaoise. Built 1733–4 by James Wyatt, and the former home of the de Vesci family, benign landlords of the estate town of Abbeyleix. Tel: 057 873 1961.

Abbey Sense Abbeyleix, 8 miles (13km) southwest of Portlaoise. A sensory garden within the Brigidine convent, created to appeal by the stimulation of the senses: vision, smell, touch, taste and sound. Tel: 057 873 1325.

Administrative headquarters County Hall, Portlaoise. Tel: 050 222044.

Aghaboe Abbey Aghaboe, 7 miles (11km) west of Abbeyleix. The ruin of an abbey originally founded by St Canice in AD 576. It was attacked, burned and rebuilt many times, finally as an Augustinian priory, before the 14th century. In 1382 the monastery buildings were granted by Fingan MacGillipatrick, Lord of Ossory, to the Dominican Order, who built a new abbey in the late 14th century and remained here until the 19th century despite the Dissolution.

Ballaghmore Castle 3 miles (5km) northwest Borris-in-Ossory, 10 miles (16km) southwest of Mountrath. Built in 1480 by MacGillipatrick (aka Fitzpatrick) and partially slighted by Cromwellian forces in 1647. There is a sheela-na-gig in the front wall. A restoration was attempted in the 1830s but the castle was again left to fall into disrepair until it was fully restored by the present owner in the 1990s. It now contains holiday accommodation. 050 521453.

Ballinakill Castle Ballinakill, 3 miles (5km) southeast of Abbeyleix. The ruin of a 17th century castle built by the Dunnes family.

Ballyadams Castle 5 miles (8km) southeast of Stradbally, 11 miles (18km) southeast of Portlaoise. The ruin of a tall five-storey 15th century tower house once owned by the O'Moore family. The castle cannot be approached for safety reasons.

Ballyfin House Ballyfin, 5 miles (8km) west of Portlaoise. A fine neoclassical mansion built by Sir Charles Coote in the 1820s and incorporating a wing of a 17th century building built by the Wesley-Poole family. The house was designed by Richard Morrison, who worked on the project with his son, William Vitruvius. It was later acquired by the Patrician Order, a distinguished Irish teaching brotherhood.

Brittas Wood $\frac{1}{2}$ mile (0.8km) west of Clonaslee, 13 miles (21km) northwest of Portlaoise. A woodland along the Clodagh River consisting largely of Norway spruce planted in the 1940s.

Capponellan Wood 1 mile (1.6km) south of Durrow, 15 miles (24km) southwest of Portlaoise. Woodland at the northern end of Golden Vale and including stands of beech, Scots pine, Norway spruce and Sitka spruce.

Castle Durrow Durrow, $13\frac{1}{2}$ miles (22km) southwest of Portlaoise. A country house beside the River Erkina, built 1712–16 by the Flower family. During the early 1920s it was unoccupied before becoming the home of St Fintan's College and Convent in 1929. It is now a country house hotel. Tel: 057 873 6555.

Clonenagh Cross-inscribed Slabs Clonenagh, $1\frac{1}{4}$ miles (2km) east of Mountrath. Early Christian incised slabs located on the site of a monastery founded by St Fintan in AD 548.

Cullahill Castle Cullahill, 4 miles (6km) southwest of Durrow, 8 miles (13km) southwest of Abbbeyleix. The ruin of a five-storey tower house built by the MacGillipatricks in 1425. It has a sheela-na-gig on its south wall.

Donaghmore Famine Workhouse Museum Donaghmore, 11 miles (18km) southwest of Abbeyleix. A museum housed in the former famine workhouse of Donaghmore and telling the story of the lives of its inmates. The workhouse opened in 1853 and closed in 1886; the dormitories, a kitchen and a waiting hall have been restored. There is also an agricultural museum. Tel: 086 829 6685.

Emo Court House 1 mile (1.6km) northeast of Emo, 7 miles (11km) northeast of Portlaois. A neoclassical mansion designed in 1790 by architect James Gandon for John Dawson, 1st Earl of Portarlington, and completed in the 19th century by the 2nd and 3rd Earls. The gardens were first laid out in the 18th century. During the early 20th century the house was owned by the Jesuits; it was restored in the late 1960s, and the house and gardens were taken into state ownership in 1994. Tel: 057 862 6573.

Gash Gardens	Gash, 1/2 mile (0.8km) south of Castletown, 9 miles (15km) southwest of Portlaoise. A contemporary 4 acre (1.6ha) garden located on the bank of the River Nore and including a rock garden, a heath garden and herbaceous borders in Castletown. Tel: 057 873 2247.
Glenbarrow	4 miles (6km) southeast of Clonaslee, 8 miles (13km) northwest of Portlaoise. An area of mainly native broadleaved woodland alongside the River Barrow in the Slieve Bloom Mountains. There are also natural and artificial waterfalls along the river.
Grattan Lodge Gardens	Vicarstown, 9 miles (15km) east of Portlaoise. A new garden created in the grounds of Victorian Grattan Lodge. Tel: 057 862 5401.
Heywood Gardens	Ballinakill, 3 miles (5km) southeast of Abbeyleix. Designed by Sir Edwin Lutyens and completed in 1912. The gardens may have been landscaped by Gertrude Jekyll and are composed of four elements linked by a terrace that ran along the front of a now demolished house. Other features include herbaceous borders, a formal lawn, parkland and a lake. Tel: 056 21450.
Highest point	Arderin in the Slieve Bloom Mountains at 1729ft (527m).
Interesting facts	**Cecil Day-Lewis** was born at Ballintubbert, near Stradbally. Brought up in London, he rose to become British Poet Laureate 1967–72, and, under the pseudonym of Nicholas Blake, a well-known mystery writer. Day-Lewis's two marriages yielded five children, one of whom is Academy Award-winning actor Daniel Day-Lewis. Among his other children are TV critic and writer Sean Day-Lewis, who wrote a biography of his father, *C Day-Lewis: An English Literary Life*, published in 1980, and journalist Tamasin Day-Lewis. Day-Lewis died on 22 May 1972 in the Hertfordshire home of Kingsley Amis and Elizabeth Jane Howard, where he and his wife were staying. He was a great admirer of Thomas Hardy, and had arranged to be buried as close as possible to the author's grave in Stinsford churchyard. **Baron Arlington**, founder of the town of Portarlington, was a member of Charles II's so-called cabal. The term 'cabal' derives from Kabbalah, the mystical interpretation of the Hebrew scripture, and originally meant either an occult doctrine or a secret. It was introduced into English by the publication of *Cabala*, a curious medley of letters and papers of the reigns of James I and Charles I that appeared in 1654. The term took on its present meaning from a group of Charles II's ministers (Sir Thomas Clifford, Lord Arlington, the Duke of Buckingham, Lord Ashley, and Lord Lauderdale), whose initial letters coincidentally spelled Cabal. They worked in secret and made hugely unpopular decisions, so the acronym is uncannily accurate in its description.
Irish Fly Fishing and Game Shooting Museum	Durrow, 13 miles (21km) southwest of Portlaoise. Opened in 1986 and housed in a restored traditional farmhouse. It has displays of vintage rods, reels, guns, tackle, tools and specimens of birds and fish. One room is dedicated to Garnett's & Keegan's, an Irish firm that supplied fine fishing and hunting equipment worldwide. There are recreations of a gamekeeper's room from the 1800s and a gunsmith's workshop from c.1900.
Killeshin Church	Killeshin, 15 miles (24km) southwest of Abbeyleix. The ruin of a 12th century church with a fine Romanesque west doorway. It was built on the site of a late 5th century monastic foundation. The doorway features stone carvings of heads with intertwining hair, foliage and animal motifs and is a rare survival of the Hiberno-Romanesque style.
Lea Castle	2 miles (3km) east of Portarlington. The ruin of a castle built in 1260 by William de Vesey, probably on the site of an earlier fortification. It changed hands many times and was rebuilt after being burned in 1346. A stronghold of the O'Dempseys 1422–52, it was abandoned after being blown up by Cromwellian besiegers in 1650.
Midlands Prison	Dublin Road, Portlaoise. A medium security prison opened in 2000 and housing adult males. Operational capacity: 469. Tel: 057 867 2110.
Monicknew Woods	5 1/2 miles (9km) northwest of Mountrath, 10 miles (16km) northwest of Portlaoise. Located on a ridge of the Slieve Bloom Mountains, the woods are crossed by the River Glen. The Monicknew Bridge (also known as the Glen Bridge), built in 1840, has the form of a Roman arch. The woodlands are mainly broadleaf with oak, ash, birch and elm plus some Sitka spruce, Japanese larch and lodgepole pine.
Mountmellick Museum	Mountmellick, 5 1/2 miles (9km) north of Portlaoise. A museum exploring the industrial past of Mountmellick and in particular the unique embroidery of the area. The designs were created in 1825 and were inspired by the flora and fauna found on the banks of the River Owenass. The museum opened in 2003 to conserve and display original pieces of Mountmellick Work. A Quaker school was opened in Mountmellick in 1786 and the craft has a long association with the Quakers, who fostered the tradition by teaching and adapting it. Tel: 057 862 4525.
Nature Reserves	**Coolacurragh Wood**, 5 miles (8km) northwest of Durrow, 20 acres (8ha) of wet woodland established as a nature reserve in 1982. **Grantstown Wood and Granston Lough,** 5 miles (8km) northwest of Durrow, 121 acres (49ha) of wet woodland and an infilled lough, established in 1982. **Slieve Bloom Mountains**, an area of mountain blanket bog covering 5680 acres (2300ha) and including the peaks of Arderin, Wolftrap and Carnahinch, established as a National Nature Reserve in 1985. **Timahoe Esker**, 1/2 mile (0.8km) northeast of Timahoe, a rare remaining example in Ireland of an esker ridge (a gravel ridge created by glaciation) still carrying native woodland, covering 32 acres (13ha) and established in 1985.
Poets Cottage	Camross, 5 miles (8km) west of Mountrath. A replica thatched cottage named after Patrick Ryan, a poet who lived in Camross 1750–1825.
Portarlington	Portarlington was founded in 1666, by Sir Henry Bennet, Home Secretary to Charles II and later 1st Earl of Arlington. Portarlington lies on the border of Laois and Offaly, often resulting in light-hearted rivalry between each side of the town, particularly in relation to local and national Gaelic football matches.

Portlaoise	The county town of Co. Laois. Established by Mary I in 1556 as 'the Fort of Maryborough' and renamed in 1922, the town is now a major commercial, retail, and arts centre for the Midlands. It is home to Ireland's maximum-security Portlaoise Prison, which houses the majority of paramilitary prisoners sentenced in the Republic, and to the Midlands Prison. Both establishments are major employers in the town. There are also several hundred employed in the Department of Agriculture a number expected to increase further under planned decentralisation of government departments from Dublin. Thanks to its rail and motorway connections to Dublin, Limerick and Cork, the town also has a growing commuter population.
Portlaoise Prison	Dublin Road, Portlaoise. A maximum security prison built in the 1830s, making it one of the oldest in the Irish prison system. Operational capacity: 210. Tel: 050 221318.
Rivers	Barrow (see Carlow) and Nore (see Tipperary).
Rock of Dunamase	4 miles (6km) east of Portlaoise. A rocky outcrop standing 150ft (46m) above the surrounding countryside and which is the site of both a 9th century dun or fort and an Anglo-Norman castle. Following the Norman invasion the fortified site was passed to Richard 'Strongbow' de Clare, Earl of Pembroke, and was later remodelled in stone by Meyler FitzHenry and/or William Marshal.
Sexton's House	Abbeyleix, 8 miles (13km) southwest of Portlaoise. The restored house of Bill Galbraith, who served as sexton to the Church of Ireland for almost 58 years. The house fell into disrepair after his death in 1981 but has been restored to reflect life in Laois in the early 20th century.
Slieve Bloom Mountains	A range of low mountains on the Laois/Offaly border. Their highest peaks are Arderin (1729ft/527m) and Baunreaghcong (1676ft/511m). The Slieve Bloom Environment Park was established in 1987 to promote the environmental resources of the Slieve Bloom Mountains for recreation and tourism.
Sport	
Gaelic football	**McCann Park**, Portarlington, is the home of the Portarlington GAA club. The Laois inter-county team usually train here. The Colm Maher Memorial Stand was built in the memory of Portarlington footballer Colm Maher, who died on 2 June 1996.
hurling	**Laois** won the All-Ireland Senior Hurling Championship in 1915.
Stradbally Hall	Stradbally, 5 miles (8km) east of Portlaoise.
Stradbally Hall Narrow Gauge Railway	Stradbally, 5 miles (8km) east of Portlaoise. Located in the grounds of Stradbally Hall, this is the oldest established heritage railway in Ireland. It was built between 1969 and 1982. The gauge is 3ft (0.9m) and the passenger trains are usually hauled by a steam locomotive. Tel: 057 862 5160.
Stradbally Steam Museum	Stradbally, 5 miles (8km) east of Portlaoise. A museum with examples of steam engines and farm machinery including a Land Rover fire engine and a Guinness loco engine. The village of Stradbally also stages a steam rally. Tel: 057 864 1878.
Timahoe Round Tower	Timahoe, $4^1/_2$ miles (7km) southeast of Portlaoise. The 96ft (29m) high round tower is almost all that remains on the site of a 7th century monastery founded by St Mochua. It has a double Romanesque doorway 16ft (5m) above ground level and probably dates from the 12th century. After the suppression of the monasteries in the 16th century the church was turned into a castle by the Crosby family, but only a single wall now stands.

Some famous people born in County Laois

Allen, Darina (television personality and chef) (1951–)	Portlaoise
Boran, Pat (poet) (1963–)	Portlaoise
Cosby, William (British governor of New York) (1690–1736)	Stradbally
Day-Lewis, Cecil (poet) (1904–72)	Ballintubbert
Flanagan, Oliver J (politician) (1920–87)	Mountmellick
Hyland, Liam (politician) (1933–)	Ballacolla
Lalor, James Fintan (journalist) (1807–49)	Raheen
Murphy, Tommy (Gaelic footballer) (1921–85)	Graiguecullen
O'Higgins, Kevin (politician) (1892–1927)	Stradbally
Tully, Kivas (architect) (1820–1905)	Garryvacum

LEITRIM

Donegal Bay
DONEGAL
L. Melvin
Truskmore
647
FERMANAGH
Manorhamilton
L. Gill
Dromohair
SLIGO
Dowra
L. Allen
CAVAN
Ballinamore
Drumshanbo
Fenagh
Leitrim
Carrick-on-Shannon
ROSCOMMON
Dromod
LONGFORD
0
20 miles
0
30 km

Leitrim is part of the province of Connacht in the west of the Republic of Ireland. Its Irish name means 'grey ridge'. The county is bordered to the west and southwest by Sligo and Roscommon respectively, to the south by Longford, to the east by Cavan, and to the north by Donegal. It also shares a border with Fermanagh in Northern Ireland to the northeast. Leitrim just qualifies as a coastal county, having only $2^1/_2$ miles (4km) of coastline on the Atlantic. The county is divided by the River Shannon and Lough Allen into North Leitrim and South Leitrim. Geographically it is noted for its lakes and rivers. The Shannon–Erne Waterway weaves its way through the region and it has many loughs including Lough Gill, Lough Allen, Lough Garadice, Lough Glenade, Lough Rynn, Lough MacNean and Lough Melvin.

The area was settled in Neolithic times, as evidenced by the numerous tombs found, while several ring forts attest to settlement during the period between the 4th and 12th centuries, when the county was part of the kingdom of Breifne (Breffni). In the 13th century it was invaded by the Normans, who took the south of the county. The north remained under the control of the O'Rourkes until the 16th century. However, County Leitrim officially came into being in 1583, when John Perrott, the Lord Deputy, marked out its boundaries. Some measure of Plantation was attempted in the early 17th century and, although largely unsuccessful, the market towns of Carrick-on-Shannon, Manorhamilton, Ballinamore and Mohill were founded. The county's poor and boggy soil meant that it had few alternative resources to fall back on when the Great Famine hit in the 1840s. The population fell from 155,000 in 1841 to 112,000 ten years later and this was the beginning of a dramatic rise in emigration, which has lasted ever since, leaving the current population of the county at less than 30,000.

Carrick-on-Shannon is the county town of Leitrim and lies near the border with Roscommon. As is suggested by the name, the town lies on the River Shannon. The town is growing quickly due to the increase in tourism and it is one of the best locations on the Shannon for hiring cruising boats.

Carrick-on-Shannon is also reputed to boast the largest number of pubs per head of population in all of Ireland. One of the pleasures of driving outside Dublin is the lack of traffic lights to halt your progress, but in 2003 the first sets of traffic lights in Leitrim were installed at a pedestrian crossing in Carrick-on-Shannon.

Leitrim	**Population**			**Area**	
Districts	*male*	*female*	*total*	*sq miles*	*sq km*
Ballinamore	1562	1497	3059	68	177
Carrick-on-Shannon	3342	3327	6669	106	274
Kinlough	1022	890	1912	58	149
Manorhamilton	3541	3228	6769	234	608
Mohill	3857	3533	7390	147	381
Total	13,324	12,475	25,799	613	1589

Local Attractions and Information

Administrative headquarters	Governor House, Carrick-on-Shannon. Tel: 071 962 0005.
Ballinamore Museum	Ballinamore, 13 miles (21km) northeast of Carrick-on-Shannon. A collection of household and farm items housed in the town's County Library. Tel: 078 44012.
Breffni Castle	Dromahair, 21 miles (34km) northwest of Carrick-on-Shannon. Breffni Castle was once home to the powerful O'Rourke clan. It was from here in the 12th century that Dearbhorgaill eloped with the king of Leinster, Diarmaid Mac Murchu. This was an act that changed the course of Irish history for ever by precipitating the Anglo-Norman invasion of Ireland.
Cavan & Leitrim Railway	Dromod, 9 miles (15km) southeast of Carrick-on-Shannon. Aka Dromod Steam Railway. A narrow gauge (3ft/0.9m) heritage railway operating for 1/2 mile (0.8km) from Dromod to Clooncolry Crossing on part of the former Cavan & Leitrim Railway, which ran from 1887 until its closure in 1959. It was mainly used to transport coal and there was only limited passenger travel. There is a collection of steam and diesel trains and vintage buses. Tel: 071 963 8599.
Cherry Island	Located in Lough Garadice, east of Ballinamore, the island was formerly known as Hog Island (Inis na dTorc). It was frequented by the United Irishmen in 1798 as a place of refuge from the English army.
Church Island	Located in Lough Garadice, east of Ballinamore. The ancient walls on the island are the ruins of an old house of worship built by Tiegherneach O'Rourke in AD 547.
Cloonmorris Church and Ogham Stone	2 miles (3km) south of Dromod, 11 miles (18km) southeast of Carrick-on-Shannon. The church was built in the early 13th century. In the churchyard stands a stone discovered in 1908, on which is a fading inscription in Ogham script that reads 'Qenuven', probably the name of the person commemorated by the stone.
Corracloona Megalithic Tomb	2 miles (3km) south of Kiltyclogher. Aka Prince Connell's Grave. This court tomb, probably dating to the 2nd millennium BC, is unusual in that the large door slab has a rectangular hole cut through it, presumably to allow subsequent burials to take place.
Costello Chapel	Bridge Street, Carrick-on-Shannon. Tiny Roman Catholic chapel measuring 16ft (5m) long by 12ft (3.5m) wide, reputedly the smallest in Ireland and the second smallest chapel in the world. It was built by merchant Edward Costello in memory of his wife, Mary Josephine Costello, after her death at the age of 47 on 6 October 1877. The chapel was dedicated on 22 April 1879. When Costello himself died on 7 March 1891 he was buried in the chapel beside his wife.
Crane Island	Located in Lough Garadice, east of Ballinamore, the island is said to be linked to the mainland by a subterranean passage that was used by the United Irishmen.
Creevelea Friary	Dromahair, 21 miles (34km) northwest of Carrick-on-Shannon. The ruins of a Franciscan friary beside the River Bonet, founded in 1508 by Owen O'Rourke and his wife Margaret. It had only a short initial existence as a friary before its dissolution, by which time it had already suffered a damaging accidental fire. The friars did not relinquish their hold on the site easily and were in residence off and on until the end of the 17th century, despite being driven away by Cromwellians in the 1640s. In the ruins is a carving of St Francis with the stigmata and another of the saint preaching to the birds. Tel: 071 962 0170.
Drumkeeran Heritage Centre	Drumkeeran, 15 miles (24km) northwest of Carrick-on-Shannon. A small heritage centre housed in a reconstructed Irish cottage and farmyard. Features include a sweathouse, pig sty and thatched cottage. Tel: 071 964 8118.
Fenagh Abbey and Church	Fenagh, 2 1/2 miles (4km) southwest of Ballinamore. The ruins of a medieval church built on the site of a late 6th century monastic foundation of St Caillin, who is said to have turned the local druids to stone. The monastery was renowned for its school of divinity. The ruined church was used for Church of Ireland worship until the present parish church was built in 1798.
Glenade Lough	5 miles (8km) northwest of Manorhamilton. Small lough on the upper reaches of the Bonet River and in a valley between the Arroo and Benbulben mountain ranges. A Special Area of Conservation, it holds stocks of char and perch and supports a population of the rare white-clawed crayfish. The lough has a legend of a monster named the Dobharcu (pronounced 'Dowarcoo'), half water dog and half fish, which emerged from the lake in ancient times to ravage the area. There have been no recent sightings.

Glencar Waterfall	8 miles (13km) northwest of Manorhamilton. A 50ft (15m) high waterfall in Glencar Lough.
Glenview Folk Museum	Aghoo, 2 miles (3km) south of Ballinamore. A private collection of more than 6000 artefacts and memorabilia from pre-famine Ireland. The main exhibits are agricultural machinery and equipment. There is also a street scene with a number of reconstructed shops and a pub. Tel: 00 353 (0) 71 9644 157.
Highest point	Truskmore at 2123ft (647m) on the Co. Sligo border, the highest summit in the Dartry Mountains.
Hog Island	See Cherry Island
Inis na dTorc	See Cherry Island
Interesting facts	Lough Melvin is home to two species of trout that have unique genes and are not found anywhere else in the world. The **gillaroo** (*Salmo stomachicus*) is named from *Giolla Rua* (Irish for 'red fellow'), due to its distinctive colouring of bright buttery golden flanks with bright crimson and vermilion spots. The gillaroo is also characterised by its 'gizzard', which is used to aid the digestion of hard food items such as water snails. According to legend, the fish originated after St Brigid was offered chicken to eat on a Friday (a taboo for Catholics) as she walked through Garrison, in modern Co. Fermanagh. Enraged, she threw the entire bird into the river where it changed into a fish, hence the 'gizzard'. The **sonaghen** (*Salmo nigripinnis*) usually has a light brown or silvery hue with large, distinctive black spots. There are sometimes small, inconspicuous red spots located along its posterior region. Its fins are dark brown or black with elongated pectorals. Sonaghen are found in areas of open, deep water, where they feed on mid-water planktonic organisms.
Islands	There are 11 named islands in Leitrim. Five are in Lough Melvin: **Inisheher**, **Inishkeen**, **Inishmeen**, **Inishtemple** and **Castle Island**; three in Lough Macnean Upper: **Bilberry Island**, **Patrick's Island** and **Trawnish Island**; and three in Lough Garadice: **Cherry Island**, **Church Island** and **Crane Island**. See individual entries for the last three named islands.
Kilahurt Ring Fort	$^{1}/_{2}$ mile (0.8km) west of Carrigallen, 8 miles (13km) southeast of Ballinamore. Aka Killahurk Ring Fort. A well-preserved example of a medieval enclosure fortification.
Kinlough Folk Museum	Kinlough, 11 miles (18km) northwest of Manorhamilton. The museum contains a unique, unaltered old style public bar featuring a long counter with a lift-up hatch. Old bottles adorn the shelves and the kitchen with its open fire, settle bed, and assortment of delph and kitchen utensils conjures up an atmosphere of bygone days when the fire was the heart and engine of the house. The museum also contains a display room featuring newspaper cuttings and farm implements. Tel: 071 916 6296.
Lough Allen	A lake on the River Shannon, located mostly in Co. Leitrim with a smaller portion in Co. Roscommon. At 8 miles (13km) long and 3 miles (5km) wide, it is Leitrim's largest lough.
Lough Gill	See Sligo
Lough Macnean Sculpture Trail	A 40 mile (64km) circular trail around the shores of Upper and Lower Lough Macnean. There are 11 pieces of sculpture by renowned Irish artists.
Lough Rynn Castle	2 miles (3km) south of Mohill, 11 miles (18km) southeast of Carrick-on-Shannon. A Gothic style mansion located beside Loughs Rynn and Errew and built in 1833 by Robert Bermingham, Viscount Clements (1805–39). After his death it became the seat of the Earls of Leitrim and the administrative centre of the Earls' estate, covering more than 140 sq miles (260 sq km) in four counties. Today it has been restored as a luxury hotel. Nick Faldo is also designing a Championship golf course on the estate. Tel: 071 963 2700.
Manorhamilton Castle	Castle Street, Manorhamilton. The ruins of a fortified house built by Sir Frederick Hamilton on the border of Leitrim and Sligo. A two- or three-storey rectangular house enclosed by a rectangular bawn, it was completed by 1636 and survived a siege in 1642, although the Plantation town of Manorhamilton was burned down. The castle's brief lifespan came to an end in 1652 when it was burned down by the Earl of Clanrickard.
Parkes Castle	$^{1}/_{2}$ mile (0.8km) south of Fivemilebourne, 7 miles (11km) southwest of Manorhamilton. A Plantation era fortified manor house located beside Lough Gill, and built in 1610 by Robert Parke on the site of an earlier 15th century O'Rourke tower house, demolished before the Parke house was erected. The three-storey rectangular structure forms part of one side of a five-sided bawn with large rounded turrets at two corners. Abandoned by the end of the 17th century, the manor house has been restored by the Office of Public Works and now features exhibitions and audio-visual presentations. Tel: 071 916 4149.
Rainbow Ballroom of Romance	Glenfarne, 8 miles (13km) east of Manorhamilton. Built by John McGivern in 1934 and named the Rainbow Ballroom after it was renovated in 1952. A major venue for Irish showbands in their heyday from the 1950s to the 1980s. It received its romantic tag after McGivern introduced his 'romantic interlude', during which he sang popular romantic songs, the lights were dimmed and dancing couples were encouraged to get to know each other better. In addition to the dances, the ballroom was also a popular concert venue. As the popularity of showbands declined in the 1990s, so did the use of the ballroom, but this trend has been reversed in recent years by the Glenfarne Development Trust. The ballroom was the subject of a short story by William Trevor, from which a film was made by the BBC in the 1980s.
Rivers	The **Drowes** runs from Lough Melvin to the sea, for most of its course also forming the boundary between Co. Leitrim and Co. Donegal. It is a famous salmon river with the season opening on 1 January, which means it regularly returns the first Irish salmon of the year. Although only $4^{1}/_{2}$ miles (7km) long, the river's catchment area covers 103 sq miles (267 sq km). The **Duff** (or Bunduff) flows for 14 miles (23km) from the Glenade valley to the sea and forms part of the boundary between Co. Leitrim and Co. Sligo. It is a prolific little spate river for salmon.

Rossclogher Castle	$2^1/_2$ miles (4km) southeast of Kinlough, 10 miles (16km) northwest of Manorhamilton. Ruined castle on Castle Island in Lough Melvin.
Shannon–Erne Canal	Built 1845–56 as a navigation and drainage scheme but never completed. The Shannon–Erne Canal was restored and reconstructed in the 1990s as the Shannon–Erne Waterway, extending for 39 miles (63km) and linking the Shannon Navigation to Lower Lough Erne at Enniskillen in Northern Ireland.
Sliabh an Iarainn Visitor Centre	Drumshanbo, $7^1/_2$ miles (12km) north of Carrick-on-Shannon. Visitor centre dedicated to life, transport and industry in the area between Arigna and the Sliabh an Iarainn mountains, including the Cavan & Leitrim Railway, canal, lakes, iron, coal mining and sweathouses. Tel: 071 964 1522.
Tullaghan Stone Cross	Tullaghan, 13 miles (21km) northwest of Manorhamilton. A 9th or 10th century cross rescued from a now lost monastery.

Some famous people born in County Leitrim

Mac Diarmada, Seán (rebel leader) (1883–1916)	Kiltyclogher
McGirl, John Joe (politician) (1921–1988)	Ballinamore
O'Rourke, Colm (Gaelic footballer) (1957–)	Aghavas
Parke, Thomas Heazle (Surgeon-General) (1857–93)	Drumsna
Sheerin, Joe (poet) (1941–)	Leitrim
Williams, Paul (author) (1964–)	Ballinamore

Limerick

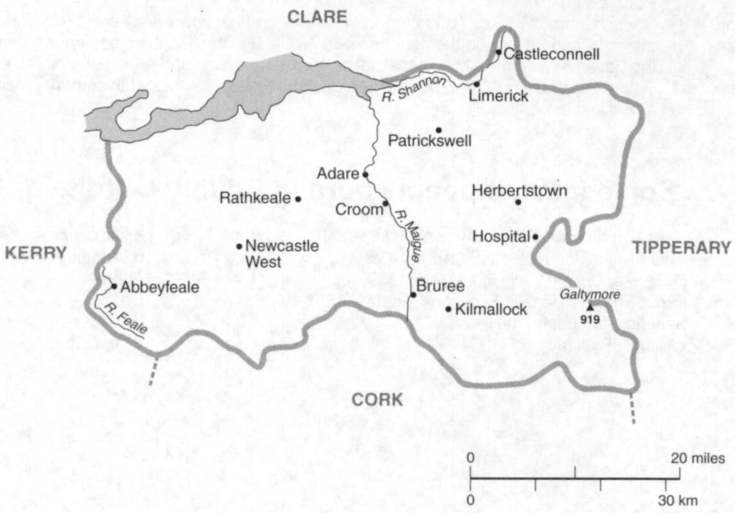
CLARE
Castleconnell
R. Shannon
Limerick
Patrickswell
Adare
Rathkeale
Herbertstown
Croom
R. Maigue
Hospital
KERRY
Newcastle West
TIPPERARY
Abbeyfeale
Bruree
Galtymore
Kilmallock
919
R. Feale
CORK
0
20 miles
0
30 km

Limerick is part of the province of Munster. It lies in the southwest of Ireland and is bordered by Cork to the south, Kerry to the west, Clare to the north across the Shannon and Tipperary to the north and east. The county town is the city of Limerick. The River Shannon flows through the city of Limerick and into the Atlantic Ocean at the north of the county. Limerick County Council is the administrative entity for the county, but the City of Limerick is a distinct administrative region and entity. Below the city, the waterway is known as the Shannon Estuary. Because the estuary is shallow, the county's most important port is several miles west of Limerick city, at Foynes. Newcastle West (An Caisleán Nua Thiar in Irish) is the largest town in County Limerick, excluding Limerick city, and is the major urban centre in west County Limerick.

Christianity came to Limerick in the 5th century, and resulted in the establishment of important monasteries at Ardpatrick, Mungret and Kileedy. From this golden age in Ireland of learning and art (5th–9th century) comes one of Ireland's greatest artefacts, the Ardagh Chalice, a masterpiece of metalwork, which was found in a west Limerick fort in 1868. The town of Limerick was established after the arrival of the Vikings in the 9th century. Following the death of Donal Mór O'Brien, king of Munster in 1194 the invading Normans took control of Limerick, and in 1210, the County of Limerick was formally established.

After the establishment of English colonies in the county by the Tudors in the 16th century, the leading Limerick Normans, the Geraldines, revolted against English rule in 1569. This sparked the savage war in Munster known as the Desmond Rebellions, during which the province was laid waste, and led to the confiscation of the vast estates of the Geraldines. The county was to be further ravaged by war over the next century. After the Irish Rebellion of 1641, Limerick City was taken in a siege by Catholic general Garret Barry in 1642. The county was not fought over for most of the Irish Confederate Wars of 1641–53, being safely behind the front lines of the Catholic Confederate Ireland. However it became a battleground during the Cromwellian conquest of Ireland in 1649–53. The invasion of the forces of Oliver Cromwell in the 1650s included a 12 month siege of the city by Cromwell's New Model Army led by Henry Ireton. The city finally surrendered in October 1651. During the Williamite War (1689–91) the city was to endure two further sieges, one in 1690 and another in 1691. It was during the 1690 siege that the infamous destruction of the Williamite guns at Ballyneety, near Pallasgreen, was carried out by the heroic defender of Limerick, General Patrick Sarsfield. The Catholic Irish, comprising the vast majority of the population, had eagerly supported the Jacobite cause, but the second siege of Limerick resulted in a defeat to the Williamites. Sarsfield managed to force the Williamites to sign the Treaty of Limerick, the terms of which were satisfactory to the Irish. However, the Treaty was subsequently dishonoured by the English and the city became known as the City of the Broken Treaty.

The 18th and 19th centuries saw a long period of persecution against the Catholic majority, many of whom lived in poverty. The Great Famine of the 1840s set in motion mass emigration and a huge decline in Irish as a spoken language in the county. This began to change in the early 20th century, as changes in law from the British government enabled the county's farmers to purchase lands they had previously only held as tenants, paying high rent to absentee landlords. Limerick saw much fighting during the War of Independence of 1919–21, particularly in the east of the county. The subsequent Irish Civil War saw bitter fighting between the newly established Irish Free State soldiers and IRA 'Irregulars', especially in the city. However, Limerick, and indeed all of Ireland, has overcome the lows of the Civil War to become the prosperous place it is today.

Limerick is widely regarded as the Irish home of rugby, and a number of current players were born here. However perhaps the county's best-known natives are J P McManus, Terry Wogan, Dolores O'Riordan and Richard Harris.

The city of **Limerick**, located in the central north of the county on the River Shannon, is the fourth largest in Ireland. There is evidence that a settlement on King's Island existed in the early Christian era; this was sacked in 812 by the Vikings, who established a town on the island in 922. The core Danish town was taken over in the late 12th century by the Anglo-Normans, and re-walled and extended to the north to form medieval Englishtown. Limerick was granted city status by a charter of King John in 1197. Later the Irish borough on the southern side of the Abbey River was walled 1310–1495 as Irishtown. The city was therefore like a figure-of-eight in the medieval period, with Baal's Bridge connecting the two halves. The modern city centre had its origins in the 18th century, and was located to the southwest of the old towns. The new town was planned as a grid with straight lines and square blocks of buildings. Today Englishtown can be entered from the city centre by proceeding along O'Connell Street, Patrick Street, Rutland Street, past the Hunt Museum and across Matthew Bridge over the Abbey River.

Limerick	**Population**			**Area**	
Districts	*male*	*female*	*total*	*sq miles*	*sq km*
Croom	5925	5702	11,627	130	338
Glin	1232	1128	2360	43	111
Kilmallock	7630	7234	14,864	197	509
Limerick City	26,128	27,895	54,023	8	20
Limerick rural area	25,332	25,215	50,547	167	434
Mitchelstown	1619	1430	3049	60	156
Newcastle	10,446	10,164	20,610	225	582
Rathkeale	7030	6768	13,798	180	466
Tipperary	2289	2137	4426	56	144
Total	87,631	87,673	175,304	1066	2760

Local Attractions and Information

Adare Friary	Adare, 10 miles (16km) southwest of Limerick. An Augustinian friary founded in 1316 by John FitzThomas FitzGerald, and also once known as the 'Black' Abbey. Its church is now the St Nicholas Church of Ireland parish church.
Adare Castle	$^{1}/_{4}$ mile (0.4km) northeast of Adare, 10 miles (16km) southwest of Limerick. Aka Desmond Castle. The ruin of a Norman castle beside the River Maigue. It appears to have been occupied between the early 13th century and the late 16th century although by no means continuously. The remains include substantial curtain walls, a gatehouse and a D-shaped tower.
Adare Friary	$^{1}/_{4}$ mile (0.4km) northeast of Adare, 10 miles (16km) southwest of Limerick. The ruin of a Franciscan friary founded in 1464 by Thomas, Earl of Kildare. The remains of the church, cloister, refectory and central tower are still visible. It now stands within Adare Manor Golf Course.
Adare Heritage Centre	Adare, 10 miles (16km) southwest of Limerick. A heritage centre charting the development of Adare and its range of historic buildings. Tel: 061 936255.
Adare Trinitarian Church	Adare, 10 miles (16km) southwest of Limerick. Founded in the 13th or 14th century and now a Roman Catholic church. Much of the present structure dates from the 19th century. It was also known as the 'White' Abbey.
Administrative headquarters	County Hall, Dooradoyle Road, Limerick. Tel: 061 496000.
Ardagh Ring Fort	Ardagh, 3 miles (5km) north of Newcastle West. A ring fort with high earthen banks to the north and south, possibly never completed. It is renowned as the site of the discovery in September 1868 of the Ardagh Chalice, an 8th century chalice 6ft (1.8m) high made of silver, bronze and gold

	(now in the National Museum of Ireland), unearthed by Jimmy Quin and Paddy Flanagan while digging potatoes within the fort.
Ardpatrick Church and Round Tower	Ardpatrick, 5 miles (8km) southeast of Kilmallock. The ruin of an 11th or 12th century church built on an earlier monastic site. Nearby is the stump of a round tower.
Askeaton Castle	Askeaton, 16 miles (26km) southwest of Limerick. The ruin of a late 12th century castle on an island in the River Deel. The major remains are a five-storey high 15th century tower, of which one wall stands to its full height. It was abandoned in the mid 17th century.
Askeaton Friary	Askeaton, 16 miles (26km) southwest of Limerick. A Franciscan friary founded in the early 15th century by Gerald, 4th Earl of Desmond. The main ruin is the long church.
Ballygrennan Castle	$^{1}/_{4}$ mile (0.4km) southeast of Bruff, $5^{1}/_{2}$ miles (9km) northeast of Kilmallock. The ruin of a tower house and bawn.
Ballyhoura Mountains	A range of mountains in the southeast of the county on the border with Co. Cork. The highest peak is Seefin at 1732ft (528m).
Ballynacourty Gardens	Ballysteen, 3 miles (5km) north of Askeaton, 15 miles (24km) west of Limerick. A 4 acre (1.6ha) garden beside the River Shannon which consists of a series of interlinked small gardens including fruit, vegetables and roses. Tel: 061 396409.
Battle	See separate table for details of the Battle of Limerick.
Bishops' Palace	Church Street, King's Island, Limerick. A Palladian style building which formerly housed the Protestant Bishops of Limerick. It has been restored and now houses the Limerick Civic Trust. Tel: 061 313399.
Blossom Gate	Emmet Street, Kilmallock. The only surviving gate of the five which originally stood in the Kilmallock town walls. It stands three storeys high and may date to the 16th century. Its name is a corruption of the original name, Flower Gate. The remains of the town wall extend for $^{1}/_{4}$ mile (0.25km) north from the gate.
Boyce Gardens	Foynes, 9 miles (15km) northwest of Rathkeale. An award winning 1 acre (0.4ha) garden beside the River Shannon. Developed over 20 years by the Boyce family, it is designed for year-round colour and consists of a series of interlinked small gardens with collections of plants from around the world. Individual gardens include a rose garden, vegetable garden, sunken garden and water garden. Tel: 069 65302.
Caherelly Castle	Caherelly, 9 miles (15km) southeast of Limerick. A tower house once famous for its sheela-na-gig, although nothing remains of the building today.
Carrigogunnell Castle	Mungret, 4 miles (6km) southwest of Limerick. The overgrown ruin of a 15th century castle on a rocky outcrop overlooking the River Shannon (GR: R489553). It was destroyed during the siege of Limerick in 1691.
Castle Matrix	$^{1}/_{2}$ mile (0.8km) southwest of Rathkeale. A restored castle built in the mid 15th century by Thomas FitzGerald, 7th Earl of Desmond. It is yet another Irish location said to have inspired Edmund Spenser's *The Faerie Queene*. Tel: 087 792 1702.
Cathedral of St Mary Blessed Virgin	Bridge Street, Limerick. One of two cathedrals in Limerick, founded in 1168 on the site of a palace donated by Donal Mor O'Brien, king of Munster. The palace, parts of which are thought to have been incorporated into the cathedral, was itself built on the site of a Viking meeting house. The cathedral was probably completed in 1194. The Romanesque west door is only used on ceremonial occasions, when the Bishops of Limerick knock and enter as part of the installation ceremony. The cathedral was extended and remodelled in the 15th century. It was used as a stable by Cromwellian troops during the capture of Limerick in 1651, apparently a regular practice by the Protector's army. Of particular note are the 15th century carved oak misericords. Tel: 061 310293.
Celtic Park and Gardens	5 miles (8km) northwest of Adare, 10 miles (16km) southwest of Limerick. A garden featuring a mixture of wild and formal plantings and also including structures from Ireland's ancient past, such as a stone circle and a dolmen. Tel: 061 394243.
Church of St Peter and St Paul	Sheares Street, Kilmallock. A Catholic church built 1879–89 to a design by J J McCarthy which adapted aspects of other Kilmallock religious foundations (for example the Collegiate Church and the Dominican priory – some of the windows in the new church were modelled on those of the ruined priory) in order to stress the continuity of worship in the parish.
Croom Mills	Croom, $4^{1}/_{2}$ miles (7km) southeast of Adare. An award winning heritage centre housed in a watermill on the River Maigue, built in 1782 and restored in the 1990s, and has an audio visual presentation on the history of grain milling in Croom. Tel: 061 397130.
Curraghchase Forest Park	4 miles (6km) northwest of Adare. A forest park established on the former estate of 18th century Curraghchase House, home of poet Aubrey de Vere. The park covers 600 acres (240ha) and includes an arboretum and a lake.
De Valera Museum and Bruree Heritage Centre	Bruree, 4 miles (6km) northwest of Kilmallock. A museum and heritage centre celebrating the life and achievements of Eamonn de Valera (1882–1975). Born in New York but brought to Ireland in 1885 on the death of his father, de Valera was raised by his grandmother Elizabeth Coll in the village of Bruree beside the River Maigue. He was Taoiseach for three terms (1937–48, 1951–4 and 1957–9) and President of Ireland for two terms (1959–73). He was also President of Dáil Éireann (1919–21) and President of the Republic (1921–2). The cottage in which he lived is preserved and the National School he attended also houses a museum. Tel: 063 90900.
Dunnaman Castle	2 miles (3km) west of Croom, $2^{1}/_{2}$ miles (4km) south of Adare. Ruined castle famous for its sheela-na-gig.
Duntryleague Stones	1 mile (1.6km) west of Galbally, 12 miles (19km) east of Kilmallock. A passage tomb on top of Duntryleague Hill (GR: R779284), close to the Tipperary border.
Dysert Oenghusa Church and Round Tower	1 mile (1.6km) west of Croom, 4 miles (6km) southeast of Adare. A 65ft (20m) high round tower and a 16th century church on site of a 9th century monastic foundation possibly established by Oenghus the Culdee.

Fantstown Castle 2$^{1}/_{2}$ miles (4km) east of Kilmallock. A 16th century castle, once home of the Fant and Moloney families but now ruined. It is famous for its sheela-na-gig.

Fenian Monument Sarsfield Avenue, Kilmallock. A Celtic cross erected to mark the centenary year of the 1798 rebellion. It carries the names of the men who fell in an attack on Kilmallock Barracks in 1867.

Foynes Flying Boat Museum Foynes, 9 miles (15km) northwest of Rathkeale. During the late 1930s and 1940s the port of Foynes was the European terminal of a flying boat service over the North Atlantic, which began when the *Yankee Clipper* landed on 9 July 1939. The first non-stop passenger flight from Foynes to New York took 25 hours 40 minutes. In 1945 the service was replaced by one from New York to Shannon. Housed in the former terminal building, originally built in the 1860s as the Monteagle Arms Hotel and which became a college after the closure of the airport, the museum's exhibits include radio equipment, a flight simulator and a full scale model of the B314 flying boat. Irish Coffee was invented in Foynes in 1942 by chef Joe Sheridan, who made it to help warm up passengers newly arrived from New York. Tel: 069 65416.

Georgian House, The Pery Square, Limerick. One of six houses built in the late 1830s and fully restored with all its original architectural features. An exhibition on the history of Limerick, housed in the stables at the rear of the house, is based around the book and film *Angela's Ashes* by Frank McCourt. The house holds the Carrol Collection of military memorabilia. The original garden has also been recreated. Tel: 061 314130.

Glenquin Castle 1 mile (1.6km) northwest of Ballagh, 5 miles (8km) southwest of Newcastle West. A restored 15th century six-storey castle.

Glenstal Abbey 1 mile (1.6km) northeast of Murroe, 10 miles (16km) east of Limerick. Originally a house built for the Barrington family in the 1830s and designed to resemble a Norman castle. It was purchased by the Benedictine Order in 1927 and became an abbey in 1957. Tel: 061 386103.

Glin Castle Glin, 15 miles (24km) west of Rathkeale. Located beside the River Shannon and originally built in the late 17th century. The home of Desmond Fitzgerald, 29th Knight of Glin, it was extended in the early 18th century and remodelled in the 1780s to a design by Davis Ducart and Christopher Colles. The gardens have been extensively restored and include a formal garden, pleasure grounds and a kitchen garden. The house is now also a country house hotel. Tel: 068 34173.

Golden Vale An area of open woodland, hills and pasture in the southwest of the county, near the borders of Limerick, Tipperary and Cork.

Grange Stone Circle $^{1}/_{4}$ mile (0.4km) north of Holycross, 11 miles (18km) south of Limerick. The largest stone circle in Ireland at 150ft (46m) in diameter. Located a little to the west of Lough Gur, it dates to c. 2000 BC and contains 113 stones, the largest of which is 13ft (4m) high.

Highest point Galtymore in the Galtee Mountains at 3015ft (919m). Located on the Limerick/Tipperary border, it is Ireland's sixth highest mountain.

Honey Fitz Theatre Patrickswell, Lough Gur, 12 miles (19km) southeast of Limerick. The Honey Fitz Theatre is housed in the former Lough Gur National School building, which operated 1854–1966. Named for the Mayor of Boston, John Francis Fitzgerald, who was known as 'Honey Fitz', it was reopened and re-named after refurbishment in 1994 by Fitzgerald's granddaughter, Jean Kennedy-Smith, then US Ambassador to Ireland. Tel: 061 385386.

Hospital Church Hospital, 8 miles (13km) northeast of Kilmallock. The roofless ruin of a church founded in 1215 by the Knights Hospitallers and featuring three tombs with the effigies of knights.

Hunt Museum Rutland Street, Limerick. Housed in the former Custom House, designed by Italian Daviso de Arcort (aka Davis Ducart) and built 1765–9. It is the home of an extensive private collection of art and antiquities including works by Picasso, Renoir and Yeats. Tel: 061 312833.

Interesting facts **J P McManus**, known as 'The Sundance Kid', has a fortune estimated to be in excess of 500m, making him one of the richest men in Ireland. **Dolores McNamara**, a mother of six from Garryowen, near Limerick, collected 113m on the Euromillions lottery in August 2005. **Mary Jane Kelly** (1863–88), the fifth and final victim of Jack the Ripper, was born in Limerick. A **limerick** is a poem of five lines, the first, second and fifth of which rhyme as usually (but not always) do the third and fourth. Although there is little doubt the verse form was named after the Irish city, its origin remains obscure, but is thought to have first been referred to in the 19th century.

Islands There are several 'islands' in the River Shannon in Co. Limerick – Bolands Rock is in the estuary where Limerick, Kerry and Clare meet. To its east are the Carrigeen Rocks and then the first island proper Foynes (population: 5), Rincawinaun (off the east coast of Foynes), Curmweela (southwest of Greenish), Greenish Island (east of Foynes, just off the coast near Askeaton), King's Island (see separate entry) and Wallers Island (an islet popular with fishermen). There is also Castle Island in the River Deel (see Askeaton Castle).

John's Castle Sarsfield Avenue, Kilmallock. Although named for King John, this 60ft (18m) high four-storey tower house probably dates to the 15th century. It has been used as an armoury, a hospital and a forge in the past and at some time arches were built through the ground floor to allow a road to pass through.

Kilmallock Collegiate Church Orr Street, Kilmallock. The ruin of Kilmallock Collegiate Church, founded in the 13th century and dedicated to St Peter and St Paul. There is a 56ft (17m) high round tower close to the church and the site may have had an earlier monastic foundation.

Kilmallock Priory $^{1}/_{4}$ mile (0.4km) northeast of Kilmallock. The substantial ruin of a Dominican priory (known locally as an abbey) founded in 1291, possibly by Gilbert Callan. A tower was added in the 15th century.

Kilmallock Museum Sarsfield Avenue, Kilmallock. A local history museum featuring scale models of houses excavated in the area and a model of medieval Kilmallock. Exhibits include agricultural and industrial implements. Tel: 063 91300.

King John's Castle	King's Island, Limerick. A substantial Norman castle built 1200–10 and which became the centre of the original settlement of Limerick. Excavations in the 1990s revealed evidence of a pre-Norman settlement beneath the castle. It is five sided and had four large round towers, of which one was later replaced by a bastion in the early 17th century, plus a gatehouse flanked by D-shaped towers. Features include a reconstruction of a siege mine used during the siege of 1642. In fact it surrendered three times in the 17th century – to the Confederacy in 1642, to Cromwellian forces under Ireton in 1651 and to Williamite forces in 1691. A military barracks was erected within the walls in 1751, some of which still remains. A purpose built visitor centre designed by Murray O'Laoire Architects and located within the walls spans an archaeological dig of the former wall and bastion, the results of which can be viewed in the building's undercroft. One side incorporates the original wall of the castle. Tel: 061 360788.
King's Island	King's Island (*Inis-Sibtonn*) was originally formed by the Shannon and Abbey rivers. The original Viking establishment of Limerick (at a time when it was known as Englishtown), it is the site of two of the city's best-known landmarks, King John's Castle (possibly founded by King John of England c.1200), and St Mary's Cathedral, built in 1168 (the oldest structure in the city, with the exception of certain portions of the cathedral). It is no longer a true island but is the riverfront area of the city.
Knockainy Castle	3 miles (5km) east of Bruff, 14 miles (23km) southeast of Limerick. The overgrown ruin of a tower house which may have been a Desmond castle.
Knockpatrick Gardens	Knockpatrick, 1 mile (1.6km) south of Foynes, 10 miles (16km) north of Newcastle West. A 3 acre (1.2ha) garden overlooking the Shannon Estuary, and featuring an arboretum and collections of rhododendron, camellia, azalea, bamboo and magnolia. Tel: 069 65256.
Limerick City Gallery of Art	Pery Square, Limerick. Founded in 1948 and housed in a gallery addition to the Carnegie Free Library and Museum. As well as collections of paintings (including works by Irish artists from the 18th century), sculpture, and photography and multi-media, it holds the National Collection of Contemporary Drawing. A contemporary exhibition programme features the works of local, national and international artists. Tel: 061 310633.
Limerick City Museum	Castle Lane, Nicholas Street, Limerick. Properly named the Jim Kemmy Municipal Museum, the museum opened in 1916 and had two previous homes before moving into a new granary style building beside King John's Castle in 1999. Limerick Museum won the first Gulbenkian Award in 1992. The collections include local history artefacts dating from the Neolithic through to the present day, as well as a display of Limerick lace. Tel: 061 417826.
Lough Gur Stone Age Centre	10 miles (16km) southeast of Limerick. The area around the shore of Lough Gur has been inhabited continuously since the Neolithic period, and near the lough is a high concentration of ancient monuments including at least two stone circles (see Grange Stone Circle), two castles and several ring forts. The centre, opened in 1980 and housed in a mock Neolithic hut using two excavated houses as its floor plan, narrates the history of the settlement of the area; exhibits include a replica of the Bronze Age Lough Gur Shield, dating to c.700 BC and now on display at the National Museum of Ireland, Dublin. Tel: 061 360788.
Martyrs' Monument	Located behind the Church of St Peter and St Paul, Kilmallock. A monument commemorating three priests (Patrick O'Hely, Conn O'Rourke and Maurice MacEnraghty) martyred during the 16th century.
Monasteranenagh Abbey	Monaster, 2 miles (3km) east of Croom, 10 miles (16km) south of Limerick. The substantial ruin of a Cistercian monastery founded in 1150 by Turlough O'Brien, King of Limerick. Suppressed at the time of the Dissolution, it was abandoned after a battle in 1579 between an English force and an Irish contingent. Some Irish troops hid in the monastery and it was reduced by cannon fire.
National Self-Portrait Collection of Ireland	A growing collection of mainly contemporary self-portraits in a wide variety of media including sculpture. It is housed in a gallery in the University of Limerick. Tel: 061 333644.
Rathkeale Priory	Rathkeale, 16 miles (26km) southwest of Limerick. The ruin of an Augustinian priory founded in the 13th century by Gilbert Harvey.
Rivers	The **Feale**, a tributary of the River Shannon, rises in the mountains of Co. Cork, near Rock Chapel, and flows west for 46 miles (74km) through Co. Limerick to the Atlantic. It is a popular salmon and sea trout river. The **Maigue** rises in the Ballyhoura Mountains in Co. Cork and flows northwards through Croom and Adare to join the Shannon Estuary west of Limerick City. It has three tributaries: the rivers Loobagh, Morning Star and Camoge. The **Mulkear** rises north of Tipperary Town and flows northwest to meet the Shannon at Annacotty Weir. **Shannon** see Co. Clare
Rockstown Castle	1 mile (1.6km) southwest of Stonepark, 7 miles (11km) south of Limerick. The ruin of a tower house standing on a rocky outcrop.
Mullaghareirk Mountains	A mountain range stretching for 20 miles (32km) near the border with Co. Kerry. Their highest point is Baraveha in Kerry at 1480ft (451m).
St John's Cathedral	Cathedral Place, Limerick. One of two cathedrals in Limerick, the Roman Catholic cathedral was designed by Philip Charles Hardwick and built 1856–61. The spire was completed in 1883 and, at 280ft (85m), is one of the three tallest in Ireland (those of St Mary's Cathedral in Killarney and St Macartan's in Monaghan are the same height). Tel: 061 414624.
St Mary's Cathedral	See Cathedral of St Mary Blessed Virgin
Shanagolden Manisternagalliagh-duff Convent	2 miles (3km) east of Shanagolden, 8 miles (13km) north of Newcastle West.The ruin of a Augustinian convent, possibly founded in the 13th century and dedicated to St Catherine, beside the River Camoge.
Shanid Castle	1½ miles (2.5km) southwest of Shanagolden, 7 miles (11km) north of Newcastle West. The ruin of a castle standing on a motte, which probably dates to the early 13th century. Considered to be

one of the first Desmond castles to be built in the area, it has a polygonal tower with walls 11ft (3.3m) thick and which still stands to a height of 30ft (9m). The castle was abandoned after being damaged in the 1640s.

Sport

general — The **University Arena**, opened in 2002 on the campus of the University of Limerick, is Ireland's largest indoor sports facility, housing the Olympic size National 50m Swimming Pool, a 35,500 sq ft (3300 sq m) sports hall, a 60m six-lane indoor sprint track, a 400m eight-lane International Athletics Arena and 40 acres (16ha) of grass pitches. Tel: 061 213555.

football — **Limerick 37** were formed in 2007 after Limerick FC were refused admission to the reorganised League of Ireland, their name being a recollection of the city's first league representation in 1937. Their home ground is Jackman Park, Limerick.

Gaelic football — **Limerick** were winners of the GAA All-Ireland Senior Football Championship in 1887 (the initial year of the competition) and 1896.

horse racing — **Limerick Racecourse**, Greenmount Park, Patrickswell, opened in 2001 and stages both National Hunt and Flat racing. The course is a right-handed circuit of 1 mile 3 furlongs (2.2km) with a wide sweeping turn into the straight and a run-in of $2^1/_2$ furlongs (0.5km). Tel: 061 320000.

hurling — **Limerick** were winners of the GAA All-Ireland Hurling Championship in 1897, 1918, 1921, 1934, 1936, 1940 and 1973.

rugby union — **Munster Rugby** play at Thomond Park, Limerick. See also Cork.

Treaty Stone, The — Thomond Bridge, Limerick. Located near St Munchins Church opposite King John's Castle. A limestone block on which, according to tradition, the Treaty of Limerick was signed on 3 October 1691, marking the surrender of the city to William of Orange. Under the terms of the treaty the rights of the defeated Jacobites were protected. However, the terms were rejected by the English Parliament and harsh anti-Catholic laws were subsequently introduced.

Tullavin Castle — 2 miles (3km) southeast of Croom, 12 miles (19km) southwest of Limerick. Ruined castle famous for its sheela-na-gig.

University Concert Hall — A purpose built concert hall opened in 1993 on the campus of the University of Limerick. It has a 1000 seat auditorium and is the permanent home of the Irish Chamber Orchestra. Tel: 061 331549.

University of Limerick — Established in 1972 as the National Institute for Higher Education, Limerick, becoming a university in 1989. It occupies 200 acres (80ha) of the 600 acre (240ha) National Technological Park alongside the River Shannon. The university has six faculties (or colleges): Kemmy Business School, College of Education, College of Engineering, College of Humanities, College of Informatics & Electronics, and College of Science. The University Arena and the University Concert Hall are located on its campus. Tel: 061 202700.

Some famous people born in County Limerick

Browne, Vincent (broadcaster and journalist) (1944–)	Broadford
Carey, Ciarán (hurling player) (1970–)	Patrickswell
Garstin, Norman (artist) (1847–1926)	Cahirconlish
Harris, Richard (actor) (1930–2002)	Limerick
Hartigan, Pat (hurling player) (1950–)	Drombanna
Hayes, Catherine (opera singer) (1818–61)	Limerick
Hogan, Noel (musician) (1971–)	Limerick
Kenny, Jon (comedian) (1957–)	Hospital
Keyes, Marian (author) (1963–)	Limerick
Armstrong-Jones, Serena (Viscountess Linley) (1970–)	Limerick
Mackey, Mick (hurling player) (1912–82)	Castleconnell
McManus, J P (racehorse owner) (1951–)	Limerick
O'Brien, Kate (writer) (1897–1974)	Limerick
O'Connell, Paul (rugby player) (1979–)	Limerick
O'Riordan, Dolores (singer) (1971–)	Ballybricken
Rehan, Ada (actress) (1859–1916)	Limerick
Rosenstock, Gabriel (poet) (1949–)	Kilfinane
Smith, Constance (actress) (1928–2003)	Limerick
Wallace, David (rugby player) (1976–)	Limerick
Wogan, Terry (broadcaster) (1938–)	Limerick

Longford

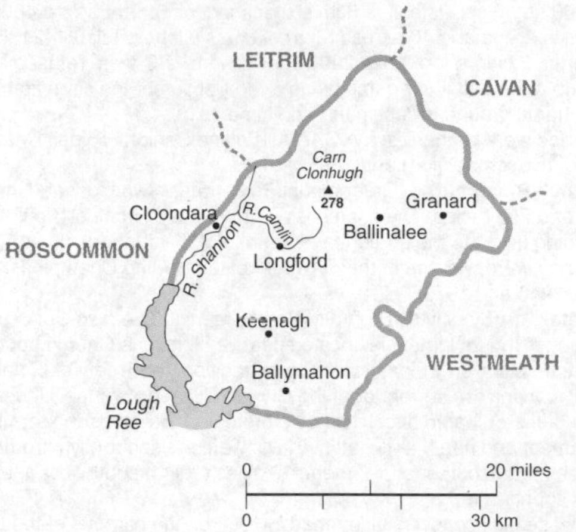
LEITRIM
CAVAN
Carn Clonhugh
278
Granard
Cloondara
Ballinalee
R. Camlin
ROSCOMMON
R. Shannon
Longford
Keenagh
WESTMEATH
Ballymahon
Lough Ree
0
20 miles
0
30 km

Longford is part of the province of Leinster. It lies in the centre of the Republic of Ireland in the Irish Midlands. It is bordered by Roscommon to the west, Leitrim to the northwest, Cavan to the northeast and Westmeath to the east, south and southeast. The county town is Longford and the other major towns are Granard and Ballymahon. The economy is largely based on agriculture.

Longford gets its name from the Long Fort, a stronghold of the O'Farrells, former rulers of the area, and was part of the kingdom of Annaly (Anghaile) or Teffia (Teabhtha). There are many early Christian foundations in County Longford and more were established after the Norman invasion of the 12th century. The Irish resurgence in the 14th century saw the O'Farrells re-establish their control. Although the county officially became a shire in 1586, English control was only established at the conclusion of the Plantation in the 1650s. The county found itself at the centre of the 1798 uprising, the last battle of that rebellion being fought at Ballinamuck.

Most of Longford lies in the basin of the River Shannon, which forms its western boundary, much of it in the form of a large lake, Lough Ree. The northeastern part of the county, however, drains towards the River Erne, and much of Lough Gowna is within the county boundary. Lakeland, bogland, pastureland and wetland typify Longford's generally low-lying landscapes.

Perhaps Longford's best-known native is Oliver Goldsmith, the writer of *She Stoops to Conquer*, *The Deserted Village* and *The Vicar of Wakefield*.

Longford	**Population**			**Area**	
Districts	*male*	*female*	*total*	*sq miles*	*sq km*
Ballymahon	2750	2600	5350	120	310
Granard	3825	3562	7387	126	326
Longford rural area	5929	5571	11,500	172	446
Longford Town	3290	3541	6831	3	9
Total	15,794	15,274	31,068	421	1091

Local Attractions and Information

Abbeyderg Monastery — Abbeyderg, 2 miles (3km) northeast of Kenagh, 7 miles (11km) south of Longford. The ruin of an Augustinian monastery founded in 1206 by Gorman O'Quinn, Lord of Rathcline. It was dedicated to St Peter, also referred to as St Peter De Rablo. The monastery was destroyed by English forces in 1565.

Abbeylara Abbey	Abbeylara, 2 miles (3km) southeast of Granard. The ruin of a Cistercian abbey founded in the early 13th century by Anglo-Norman Richard de Tuit. It was ransacked by the invading troops of Edward Bruce in 1315. The abbey was abandoned following the Dissolution and all that remains is the central tower and some walls. Traditionally there was a church nearby founded by St Patrick in the 5th century. There are also two stone circles in the parish.
Abbeyshrule Abbey	Abbeyshrule, 12 miles (19km) southeast of Longford. The ruin of a Cistercian abbey founded in the 12th century by the O'Farrells. Rebuilt after burning down in 1476, it was abandoned following the suppression of the monasteries in the 16th century. The remains mainly consist of the walls of the abbey church.
Abbeyshrule Air Show	$^1/_2$ mile (0.8km) northeast of Abbeyshrule, 12 miles (19km) southeast of Longford. Ireland's longest running air show, held annually in late July/early August at Abbeyshrule Airfield.
Administrative headquarters	Aras an Chontae, Great Water Street, Longford. Tel: 043 46231.
Aghanoran Lake	A lake and tributary of the River Erne, situated to the east of Lough Gowna. It is renowned for its fishing, especially bream, roach, perch, pike and eels.
Ardagh House	Ardagh, 6 miles (10km) southeast of Longford. The estate on which Ardagh House stands was bought by the Fetherston family in the early 18th century. It remained in the family until it was sold in 1927 to the Sisters of Mercy, who now run it as a School of Domestic Science. The house has a place in literary history after a young Oliver Goldsmith mistook it for an inn and the Fetherstons for landlord and servants. He later turned this incident into the basis for his comedy *She Stoops to Conquer*. The house was damaged by fire in 1922, and only two of its original three storeys survived another fire in 1949.
Ardagh Visitor Centre	Ardagh, 6 miles (10km) southeast of Longford. Housed in a former school built in 1898, the centre's displays and exhibits tell the story of the village from ancient times to the present day. It has both historical interest, through the nearby pre-Christian sites of Bri Leith and the early Christian settlement of St Mel (the ruin of his 5th century 'cathedral' stands near the present Church of Ireland church), and literary connections, which include Oliver Goldsmith, Sir Walter Scott and Maria Edgeworth.
Aughnacliffe Dolmen	Aughnacliffe, 11 miles (18km) northeast of Longford. A portal dolmen with two capstones which rest on a single portal stone.
Ballinamuck Visitor Centre	Ballinamuck, 10 miles (16km) north of Longford. A heritage centre commemorating the Battle of Ballinamuck, which took place during the 1798 rebellion. There is also a 1798 Garden of Remembrance in the village.
Ballyclare Castle	$^1/_4$ mile (0.4km) east of Killashee, $4^1/_2$ miles (7km) southwest of Longford. The ruin of a castle built in 1430 by the O'Farrells.
Ballymacrolly Mill	Granard, 13 miles (21km) northeast of Longford. A mill originally dating to the 11th century.
Battles	See separate table for details of the Battle of Ballinamuck.
Bully's Acre	Ballinalee, 6 miles (10km) northeast of Longford. A graveyard where more than 100 insurgent prisoners were executed and buried during the 1798 Rebellion.
Carrigglas Manor	3 miles (5km) northeast of Longford. A Tudor Gothic style mansion designed by Daniel Robertson and built in 1837 for Thomas Langlois Lefroy, Lord Chief Justice of Ireland, to replace an earlier house. It remains a Lefroy home. Thomas Lefroy was a friend of Jane Austen and is believed by some to be the model for Darcy in *Pride and Prejudice*. The stableyard was designed by James Gandon in 1790. A costume and lace museum contains memorabilia and artefacts. Tel: 043 45165.
Cashel Heritage Centre	Newtowncashel, $7^1/_2$ miles (12km) west of Ballymahon. A local history museum housed in a restored cottage and including displays of agricultural equipment.
Castleforbes	Newtown Forbes, 3 miles (5km) northwest of Longford. The seat of the Earls of Granard, Castleforbes was built in the 19th century incorporating an earlier house built in 1624.
Clondra Abbey	Clondra, 4 miles (6km) west of Longford. The ruin of a late 12th century abbey, possibly built on the site of a 9th century foundation.
Clondra Church	Clondra, 4 miles (6km) west of Longford. Noted for its ancient carved gravestones in Old Irish, reputedly dating to the 5th century.
Clonmore Ring Fort	1 mile (1.6km) north of Killashee, 3 miles (5km) southwest of Longford. A well-preserved double ring fort dating to the immediate pre-Christian period.
Cloonshanagh Manor	Granard, 13 miles (21km) northeast of Longford. Aka Coolamber Manor. A country house built in the 1820s by the Blackhall family. It is now a National Training and Development Centre.
Corbeagh Lake	2 miles (3km) south of Ballinalee, 7 miles (11km) northeast of Longford. Aka Currygrane Lough. A small lake containing two crannogs. Its name means 'Round hill of the birch trees' in Irish.
Corlea Trackway	$^1/_2$ mile (0.8km) southeast of Corlea, 8 miles (13km) south of Longford. An Iron Age wooden trackway which ran for more than $^1/_2$ mile (0.8km) across the Corlea Bog and which dates to 148 BC. The roadway was discovered in 1984 and is the largest of its kind yet discovered in Europe. A 60ft (18m) stretch of preserved road is on permanent display at the visitor centre in a specially designed hall with humidifiers to prevent the wood from deteriorating. Tel: 043 22386.
Culnagore Wood	$1^1/_4$ miles (2km) southwest of Newtowncashel, 6 miles (10km) south of Lanesborough. An ancient hazel woodland covering 90 acres (37ha) along the edge of Lough Ree.
Derrycassan Wood	4 miles (6km) northwest of Granard, 12 miles (19km) northeast of Longford. A woodland beside Lough Gowna which at one time surrounded a now demolished mansion. Some of the foundations of the house and gardens are still visible.
Edgeworthstown House	Edgeworthstown, 8 miles (13km) east of Longford. Originally built in 1672 by Richard Edgeworth, and enlarged and remodelled in the 1780s by inventor Richard Lovell Edgeworth, father of writer

	Maria Edgeworth (1767–1849). Her works include *Castle Rackrent* (1800), *Tales of Fashionable Life* (1809) and *Ormond* (1817). The house and 50 acres (20ha) were donated to the Sisters of Mercy in 1939 and the house is now a nursing home.
Granard Motte	Granard, 13 miles (21km) northeast of Longford. The remains of reputedly the largest motte in Ireland, standing 534ft (163m) high and believed to have been built by Richard de Tuit. There is a statue of St Patrick on its summit.
Gurteen Lake	1/2 mile (0.8km) south of Ballinalee, 7 miles (11km) northeast of Longford. Aka Gorteen Lough. A small 'bog lake' popular with bird watchers and anglers.
Highest point	Carn Clonhugh (aka Cairn Hill) in the northwest of the county, at 916ft (278m). It is the site of a television transmitter broadcasting to much of the Irish Midlands. A local saying, used when referring to someone with exceptionally keen eyesight, is 'He could see a speck on the top of Cairn Hill'.
Inchcleraun Island	Aka Quaker Island, Inis Clothrann. An island on Lough Ree containing the ruins of a 6th century monastery founded by St Ciaran and six churches. The churches include Teampul Mor (Big Church), Temple Diarmuid, the Church of the Dead, the Women's Church and the Belfry Church. The island was subject to frequent attack. It is also, according to one tradition, the island where Queen Maeve was struck down while bathing by a slingshot cast from a mile away on the shore.
Interesting facts	**Edgeworthstown House**, Newtowncashel, was the first house in Ireland to be centrally heated. **Charles Clinton** was born in Newtown Forbes in 1690. In 1722 he married local girl Elizabeth Deniston and they sailed for the New World aboard the *George and Anne*. Four months later they arrived at Cape Cod, Massachusetts, and founded a small colony on the Hudson River, north of New York, which they named Little Britain. In 1739 the Clintons had a son, George, who became the first Governor of New York (he is often referred to as the Father of New York) and vice-president to both Thomas Jefferson and James Madison. **Ardagh** is three-times Supreme Winner of the National Tidy Towns Competition (1989, 1996 and 1999).
Islands	The following islands can be found on Lough Ree: **Hare Island** (there are early monastic ruins on this island), **Inchbolin**, **Inchcleraun** (see separate entry) and **Saints Island** (see separate entry). Lough Gowna is the site of **Inchmore Island**, which also has monastic remains.
Kenagh Clock Tower	Kenagh, 9 miles (15km) south of Longford. A 60ft (18m) high stone monument built in 1878 to commemorate Lawrence Harman King-Harman, the local landlord. It has recently been restored.
Land War Monument, The	Drumlish, 6 miles (10km) north of Longford. A monument designed by John Carthy and Mattie Casey and erected in 1981 to commemorate the people who took part in the Land War of the 1880s.
Longford Museum	Lower Main Street, Longford. A local history museum featuring exhibits such as the antler of a giant elk, the 10th century Aughafad Cross and a gold watch given by Michael Collins to his Granard-born girlfriend, Kitty Kiernan.
Lough Kinale Shrine	An 8th century wooden shrine found in 1986 on the bed of Lough Kinale, 3 miles (5km) east of Granard. Thought to be a casket or shrine for a book, it was in a dismantled state when found, and is being reconstructed and restored by the National Museum in Dublin.
Lough Ree	The second largest lake on the Shannon after Lough Derg and the fifth largest in Ireland, covering 40 1/2 sq miles (105 sq km). It supports a small commercial eel fishery and also has stocks of trout. A large expanse of water known as the Inner Lakes comprises Coosan Lough and Killinure Lough. Parts of the lough lie in Co. Roscommon and Co. Westmeath.
Newtowncashel	A beautiful multi-award-winning village set high on the Longford Hills close to Lough Ree. The approach to the village has an elegant sculpture of four waterbirds (entitled *Home Coming*) by Michael Casey. Further sculptures can be seen in the village centre, some of which are by Michael's son, Kevin; all are made from bogwood.
Oghill Bog	6 miles (10km) northeast of Longford. A 60 acre (24ha) area of regenerating cut-bog near Cairn Hill.
Pigeon House	Kenagh, 9 miles (15km) south of Longford. A restored dovecote, one of only six remaining in Ireland, built in 1808 to provide the Mosstown Estate with eggs and meat.
Richmond Mill	Clondra, 4 miles (6km) west of Longford. An 18th century corn mill which was occupied by a whiskey distillery 1837–43. It closed in the 1950s and has recently been restored.
Rivers	The **Camlin** rises at Abbeylara, near Granard, and forms a natural boundary between north and south Longford, flowing west through Clonbroney, Ballinalee, and Longford Town before joining the Shannon at Cloondara, north of Lough Ree.
Royal Canal	The Royal Canal runs for more than 90 miles (145km) from Dublin to Shannon Harbour in Clondra, Co. Longford, and has 46 locks. The canal was begun in the 1790s and the Longford branch was opened in 1830. It was purchased by the Midland Great Western Railway in 1845, after which passenger and freight traffic began to decline. It was closed to traffic in the 1950s. Restoration projects are being carried out along the canal.
St Brigid's Church	Ardagh, 6 miles (10km) southeast of Longford. Designed in neo-Gothic style by William Hague and completed in 1881.
St John's Church	Edgeworthstown, 8 miles (13km) east of Longford. Maria Edgeworth and Oscar Wilde's sister are buried here.
St Mel's Cathedral	Dublin Street, Longford. The Roman Catholic cathedral of the Diocese of Ardagh and Clonmacnois, built 1840–56 in neoclassical style. The roof is supported by 24 columns made from stone from the Newtowncashel limestone quarries.
St Mel's Diocesan Cathedral Museum	Housed at the rear of St Mel's Cathedral. Exhibits include St Mel's Crozier and the episcopal ring of Bishop O'Higgins. Tel: 043 46465.

Saint's Island	An island on Lough Ree containing the ruin of an Augustinian monastery founded in the 14th century. The Annals of All Saints were compiled here during the 15th century by Augustine McGradion. The monastery was abandoned following its suppression in the 16th century.
Sean Connolly Barracks	Church Street, Longford. Cavalry barracks established in the 19th century on the site of the original castle and market house. They were renamed the Sean Connolly Barracks in 1922.
Sonnagh Fort	1 mile (1.6km) south of Aughnacliffe, 10 miles (16km) northeast of Longford. The largest and best preserved of seven forts encircling Aughnacliffe church.
Sport	
football	**Longford Town** were founded in 1924 and are winners of the FAI Cup in 2003 and 2004. Their home ground is Flancare Park, Longford.

Some famous people born in County Longford

Clinton, Charles (soldier) (1690–1773)	Corbay
Colum, Padraic (poet and dramatist) (1881–1972)	Collumbkille
Cunningham, Larry (country singer) (1938–)	Granard
Dobson, George Edward (zoologist) (1848–95)	Edgeworthstown
Goldsmith, Oliver (writer) (1730–74)	Ballymahon
Kiernan, Kitty (fiancee of Michael Collins) (1892–1945)	Granard
Macken, Eddie (show jumper) (1949–)	Granard
O'Brien, James Bronterre (Chartist) (1805–64)	Granard

Louth

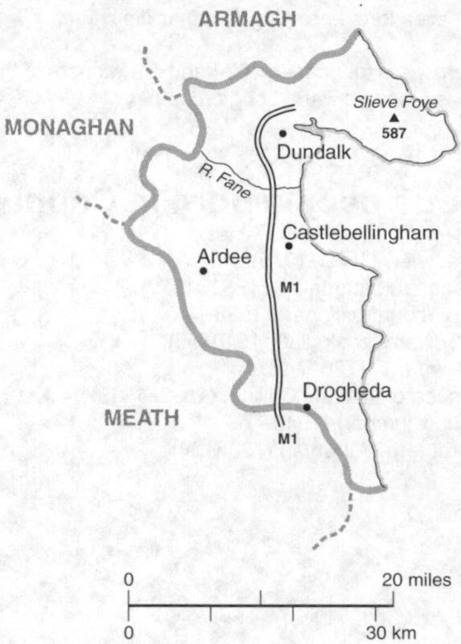
ARMAGH
MONAGHAN
Slieve Foye
587
Dundalk
R. Fane
Castlebellingham
Ardee
M1
Drogheda
MEATH
M1
0
20 miles
0
30 km

Louth is part of the province of Leinster. It lies in the east of the Republic of Ireland and is bordered by Armagh in Northern Ireland to the north, Meath to the south and southwest, and Monaghan to the west. Its most westerly tip is just short of the most easterly tip of County Cavan. The major towns are Ardee, Carlingford, Drogheda and Dundalk. The village of Louth lies in the heart of the county, 5 miles (8km) southwest of Dundalk. The county takes its name from the village, which was once an important town.

Also known as 'the Wee County', County Louth is the smallest county in Ireland. Its position on the border with Northern Ireland, and yet so close to the city of Dublin, gives the county a unique mix of people, heavily influenced by the present political situation in the north although clearly separated from it. Stretching northwards from the River Boyne to Carlingford Lough, Louth consists mainly of countryside and coastline and is a county steeped in myth, legend and history, going back to the pre-historical days of the Táin Bó Cúailnge (Cattle Raid of Cooley).

Louth has a number of famous natives. The Corrs all hail from Dundalk, and Pierce Brosnan was born in Drogheda. The most famous daughter of Louth is undoubtedly St Brigid, patron saint of scholars.

Louth	**Population**			**Area**	
Districts	*male*	*female*	*total*	*sq miles*	*sq km*
Ardee	8189	7866	16,055	105	272
Drogheda	13,818	14,515	28,333	9	23
Dundalk rural area	10,397	10,136	20,533	136	355
Dundalk Town	13,250	14,135	27,385	10	25
Louth	4835	4680	9515	61	157
Total	50,489	51,332	101,821	321	832

Local Attractions and Information

Administrative headquarters — County Offices, Dundalk. Tel: 042 933 5457.

Ardee Castle — Castle Street, Ardee. A 15th century tower house flanked by much more modern buildings. The castle is known locally as the Courthouse and is the largest fortified medieval tower house in

Ireland. The village of Ardee on the River Dee takes its name from the Irish *Ard Fhirdia*, where Cúchulainn fought and killed his friend Ferdia (see Táin Bó Cúailnge).

Ballug Castle — 1 mile (1.6km) south of Grange, 8 miles (13km) east of Dundalk. Ruins of a 15th century tower house located on the Cooley Peninsula and a former stronghold of the Bagnall family. Only the east and south walls remain standing to any great height.

Battles — Two very significant actions have taken place in Co. Louth. See separate entry for the Siege of Drogheda and separate table for details of the Battle of Faughart (also known as the Battle of Dundalk).

Beaulieu House and Garden — $1^1/_4$ miles (2km) southwest of Baltray, $2^1/_2$ miles (4km) northeast of Drogheda. A late 17th century unfortified mansion built by Sir Henry Tichbourne. There are 4 acres (1.6ha) of walled garden including herbaceous borders and a Victorian knot garden. The house is also home to a motor museum of classic cars and memorabilia. Tel: 041 983 8557.

Boyne Viaduct — Drogheda. Built over the River Boyne 1850–55 to carry the main Dublin–Belfast railway. Designed by John MacNeill, it stands 98ft (30m) high and has 15 stone arches.

Carlingford — A village opposite Warrenpoint in Co. Down. It is approximately midway between Dublin and Belfast and sits on the shore of Carlingford Lough, where St Patrick landed in AD 432 at the start of his mission to convert Ireland to Christianity. The village gets its name from the Norse for 'Fjord of Carlinn'. It won the National Tidy Towns award in 1988 and is regarded as the oyster capital of Ireland, holding an annual oyster festival in August.

Carlingford Priory — $^1/_2$ mile (0.8km) south of Carlingford, 9 miles (15km) northeast of Dundalk. The ruin of a 14th century Dominican priory abandoned after the Dissolution of the Monasteries in the 16th century.

Castleroche Castle — Roche, $5^1/_2$ miles (9km) northwest of Dundalk. The impressive ruin of a 13th century keepless castle built on a rocky outcrop by the de Verdun family. It is triangular in plan with high curtain walls around the central courtyard. Inside the courtyard was a three-storey great hall. A separate bailey is divided from the castle by a ditch and protected by a gatehouse.

Castletown Castle — 1 mile (1.6km) northwest of Dundalk. A four-storey tower house built in the late 15th century.

Cooley Distillery — Riverstown, 6 miles (10km) east of Dundalk. An independent Irish-owned distillery founded in 1987 and located on the Cooley Peninsula. The water source is the Sliabh na Gloch River in the Cooley Mountains. Tel: 042 937 6102.

County Museum Dundalk — Jocelyn Street, Dundalk. Local history museum housed in a restored late 18th century warehouse and charting the history of Co. Louth from prehistoric times to the present day. Tel: 042 932 7056.

Cúchulainn's Castle — See Dun Dealgan

Drogheda — The second-largest town in the county. It lies at the southern extremity of the county near the border with Meath. During the summer Drogheda hosts a samba festival.

Dromiskin Monastic Site — Dromiskin, 3 miles (5km) north of Castlebellingham, 6 miles (10km) south of Dundalk. The site of a 6th century monastic foundation probably established by St Lugad (Lughaidh), a disciple of St Patrick. The monastery was ransacked several times between its foundation and the end of the 11th century. The main structure on the site is a 55ft (17m) high round tower which at one time would have been used as a belfry. Its conical roof was restored in the late 19th century. The doorway stands 12ft (3.5m) above ground level. There are also the remnants of a high cross which has been re-erected on a granite base and shaft.

Dun Dealgan — Castletown, 1 mile (1.6km) northwest of Dundalk. Aka Cúchulainn's Castle. A late 12th century Norman circular motte 33ft (10m) high and 140ft (43m) in diameter. On the top is a castellated folly built in 1780 by merchant Patrick Byrne and unsurprisingly known as 'Byrne's Folly'. Dun Dealgan may be the place mentioned in the Táin (see separate entry) as Delga.

Dundalk — The county town and the largest in the county. It lies on the Castletown River at Dundalk Bay. Its charter was granted in 1189. In Dundalk Bay stands a lighthouse, built in 1849, which stands aloft iron legs fixed to the seabed using a screw pile system devised by blind engineer Alexander Mitchell (1780–1868). See also St Patrick's Cathedral.

Dunmahon Castle — $2^1/_2$ miles (4km) east of Knockbridge, 4 miles (6km) southwest of Dundalk. The ruin of a 15th century tower house which was inhabited until the late 17th century.

Glaspistol Castle — $^1/_4$ mile (0.5km) south of Clogherhead, 7 miles (11km) northeast of Drogheda. A 16th century tower house built by the Dowdalls.

Greenmount Motte — 2 miles (3km) south of Castlebellingham, 6 miles (10km) east of Ardee. A substantial Norman motte probably built in the late 12th century on the site of earlier earthworks.

Hatch's Castle — Castle Street, Ardee. A small four-storey tower house which stands within a row of terraced houses. The castle is still inhabited.

Haynestown Castle — 3 miles (5km) west of Blackrock, 5 miles (8km) southwest of Dundalk. The ivy-covered ruin of a three-storey tower house.

Highest point — Slieve Foye on the Cooley Peninsula at 1926ft (587m).

Holy Trinity Heritage Centre — Carlingford, 9 miles (15km) northeast of Dundalk. A local history museum housed in a restored medieval church and charting the history of Carlingford from the Vikings to the present day. Tel: 042 73454.

Interesting facts — **Eliza O'Neill** was the daughter of an actor and stage manager who became one of Ireland's greatest actresses. Her first appearance on the stage was made at the Crow Street theatre in 1811 as the Widow Cheerly in *The Soldier's Daughter*, and after several years in Ireland she came to London and made an immediate success as Juliet at Covent Garden in 1814. For five years she was the favourite of the town in comedy as well as tragedy, but in the latter she particularly excelled, being compared favourably with Sarah Siddons. In 1819 she married William Wrixon Becher, an Irish MP who was created a baronet in 1831. Eliza never returned to the stage.

Faughart is famous for the battle that took place in 1318 but also as the birthplace of **St Brigid**, the secondary patron saint of Ireland, after St Patrick. St Brigid was an abbess and the founder of a number of convents. Her feast day, 1 February, is the traditional first day of spring in Ireland. In 1933 a shrine was dedicated in her home town of Faughart. Brigid is generally regarded as the patron saint of scholars but her benevolent nature has led her to be adopted as patron saint of babies, blacksmiths, illegitimate children, dairy workers, chicken farms, Ireland, midwives, travellers, sailors and nuns!

Kildemock Jumping Church
Millockstown, $1\frac{1}{2}$ miles (2.5km) south of Ardee. The ruin of a 14th century nave and chancel church. It is known as the 'jumping church' because part of the west gable now stands 2ft (0.6m) inside the line of the original wall foundation. The legend has it that the wall moved to ensure that the grave of an excommunicated person remained outside the church walls.

Killincoole Castle
3 miles (5km) southeast of Louth, 6 miles (10km) southwest of Dundalk. The ruin of a four-storey tower house. It stands on private land and is not open to the public.

King John's Castle
Carlingford, 9 miles (15km) northeast of Dundalk. Aka Carlingford Castle. Known as King John's Castle because the monarch is believed to have spent three days here in 1210, the castle's construction probably dates to a few years before this visit. The ruin stands on a rocky outcrop overlooking the harbour of Carlingford within landscaped grounds and includes the remains of a gatehouse, 13th century rectangular hall, and curtain wall. The castle changed hands twice during the conflicts of the 1640s and was used as a hospital by Williamite forces in the 1690s.

Knockabbey Castle and Gardens
Thomastown, 1 mile (1.6km) west of Tallanstown, 5 miles (8km) northwest of Ardee. Knockabbey Castle began life as a late 14th century tower house known as Thomastown Castle. It was extended by its owners in the mid 17th century and was remodelled a century later by new owners the Tenison family. In the 1850s and 1860s Myles O'Reilly had further additions and adornments made in Gothic Revival style. The castle was rebuilt after being burned by the Irish Republican Army in 1923. The extensive gardens were first laid out by the Tenison family in the 1730s and were developed by succeeding owners, thus retaining elements of garden planning over a long period. The 30 acre (12ha) gardens included parkland, ornamental canals, a lake, formal gardens and woodland, and contain a number of specimen trees including possibly the largest tulip tree in Ireland. A Victorian glasshouse has been reconstructed. Tel: 016 778816.

Louth
A village southwest of Dundalk. St Patrick is said to have built the original church here and to have appointed St Mochta as the first Bishop of Louth.

Magdalene Tower
Magdalene Street, Drogheda. The only remains of the Priory of St Mary Magdalene, founded in 1224 by Lucas de Netterville, Archbishop of Armagh. It was formerly the priory's belfry tower and appears to date to the 14th century. It was here that four Irish kings made submission to Richard II in 1394. The church had been abandoned by the early 16th century.

Mayoralty House
North Quay, Drogheda. Designed by Hugh Darley and erected in 1765 to accommodate municipal receptions and other functions. It was here in 1884 that the freedom of the borough was conferred on Charles Stewart Parnell. The building has been in use as commercial premises for many years.

Mellifont Abbey
2 miles (3km) west of Tullyallen, 5 miles (8km) northwest of Drogheda. The ruin of the first Cistercian abbey built in Ireland, founded in 1142 by St Malachy of Armagh with monks from Clairvaux in France. The abbey was rebuilt in stone from 1157 when a national synod was held on the site, although the building work was not completed until the 1220s. The abbey was burned during the 14th century and partially rebuilt. A tower was added in the 15th century. The monastery was dissolved in 1538–9, after which the buildings passed into secular use; Hugh O'Neil surrendered to Lord Mountjoy here in 1603. The abbey's most unusual feature is the 13th century lavabo (communal washing place). Among the exhibits in the visitor centre are fragments of carved masonry. A new Cistercian abbey was founded nearby in 1938.

Millmount Fort
Millmount, Drogheda. A Martello tower located on the top of a 12th century Norman motte providing fine views over the surrounding area. The fort was built in 1810 and is nicknamed the 'Cup and Saucer'. It was damaged during the civil war in 1922 but has since been restored.

Millmount Museum
Millmount, Drogheda. A local history museum housed in the former military barracks, built in 1808. Among its exhibits is a nationally important collection of guild and trade banners. There are also recreations of a kitchen, dairy and laundry, plus an Irish history room charting the major events in the county's history. Tel: 041 983 3897.

Milltown Castle
1 mile (1.6km) northwest of Dromiskin, 5 miles (8km) southwest of Dundalk. The ruin of a four-storey 15th or 16th century tower house.

Mint, The
Carlingford, 9 miles (15km) northeast of Dundalk. As suggested by its name, this small 15th century three-storey tower house is believed to have been used as a mint at one time.

Monasterboice Monastic Site
5 miles (8km) northwest of Drogheda. The remains of a 6th century monastic foundation established by St Buite and featuring the ruins of two churches (known as the South Church and the North Church), a round tower and three sculpted crosses. The monastery seems to have survived several ransackings up to the 12th century. The round tower stands 100ft (30.5m) high beside the North Church and is lacking its conical cap; there is a Romanesque doorway 7ft (2.1m) above ground level. The 9th or 10th century high crosses are: **Muirdeach's Cross** (or the South Cross), standing 17ft (5.2m) high and richly decorated with biblical scenes including Cain slaying Abel, David and Goliath, the Adoration of the Magi and scenes from the Crucifixion; the **Tall Cross** (or the West Cross), the tallest cross in Ireland, standing 21ft (6.4m) high and also carved with numerous biblical scenes; and the **North Cross**, which is more fragmentary. There is also a pillar stone with a medieval sundial.

Proleek Dolmen
Ballymascanlon, $2\frac{1}{2}$ miles (4km) northeast of Dundalk. A portal dolmen dating to c. 3000 BC. The capstone measures 12ft 5in (3.7m) by 10ft 6in (3.2m) and weighs 40 tonnes. It is supported by three uprights standing 8ft (2.5m) high. There are at least two legends surrounding this monolithic structure. One is that a wish will be granted to those who can throw a pebble on to the top of the capstone so that it stays there; another is that anyone who walks three times round the dolmen

will be married within a year. The monument stands in the grounds of the Ballymascanlon Hotel; in the same field is a wedge tomb.

Rathdrummin Ring Fort — 1/2 mile (0.8km) southeast of Grangebellew, 7 miles (11km) north of Drogheda. A circular fortification 170ft (52m) in internal diameter and surrounded by three substantial earthern banks.

Rivers — The **Fane** originates from Lough Ross and flows southeast for 38 miles (61km), entering the Irish Sea at Blackrock, Co. Louth. It holds good stocks of brown trout, salmon and sea trout.

Roodstown Castle — 2 1/2 miles (4km) northeast of Ardee. The well-preserved ruin of a 15th century four-storey tower house standing 50ft (15m) high.

St Brigid's Shrine and Well — Faughart, 2 1/2 miles (4km) north of Dundalk. A shrine to St Brigid, born in the village c. AD 451. Faughart is the site of several early Christian monuments and the ruin of a medieval church.

St Laurence's Gate — Chord Road, Drogheda. One of the town's two remaining gateways, a 13th century barbican standing four storeys and 60ft (18m) high, and flanked by round towers with stone stairways in each tower to the first floor and modern stairs to the second floor. A portion of the town wall stands nearby.

St Mary's Priory — Old Abbey Lane, Drogheda. The remains of a 13th century priory and hospital founded by Ursus de Swemele. It later passed into the ministry of the Augustinians and was surrendered to secular authorities at the time of the Dissolution. The remains include the central belfry tower and a further archway.

St Mochta's House — Louth, 7 miles (11km) southwest of Dundalk. A single-cell church said to have been originally built to be a resting place for the saint, who died in 1534. It stands close by the ruin of a 12th century Augustinian priory.

St Peter's Church — Peter Street, Drogheda. A Church of Ireland church located on the site of a 12th century Norman church dedicated to St Peter. Apparently very large, containing six chapels, it was an important ecclesiastical centre, acting after the 13th century as a pro-cathedral for the Diocese of Armagh. The steeple was burned down by Cromwellian troops during the Siege of Drogheda (see separate entry) in 1649 but was later repaired, partly with funds donated by Cromwell's army. However, the damage seems to have seriously affected the structure of the church and by the early 18th century it is reported as being in ruins. The site was cleared and the present church was built 1747–52. It was damaged by fire in 1999 and has since been completely restored.

St Patrick's Cathedral — Roden Place, Dundalk. A Roman Catholic cathedral designed by Thomas Duff and built 1835–47 on the model of King's College Chapel, Cambridge. Duff died before completion and the interior was completed by J J McCarthy (as was that of Duff's Armagh Cathedral). The tower, added in 1903, was modelled on that of another English church, this time Gloucester Cathedral by G C Ashlin.

St Peter's Church — West Street, Drogheda. A French Gothic style Roman Catholic church built in the late 19th century to a design by O'Neill and Byrne. It incorporates parts of the previous church, built in 1791 as a memorial to Oliver Plunkett, Archbishop of Armagh, who was martyred at Tyburn in London in 1681. The saint's major relics, including his preserved head, are displayed for veneration in the church.

Seatown Tower — Castle Road, Dundalk. Aka Seatown Castle. A tower which was once part of the church of a Franciscan friary, possibly founded in the 13th century by the de Verdun family and abandoned in the 16th century.

Siege of Drogheda — The siege took place in September 1649 during the Irish Confederate War/Eleven Years' War (1641–53). Oliver Cromwell had landed in Dublin on 15 August and, faced with no enemy in the field, immediately began destroying the Royalist fortresses, beginning with Drogheda, whose garrison was commanded by Sir George Aston. On 11 September 1649, after a two-day bombardment, the town fell and on Cromwell's orders 'all men found in arms', including Aston, were killed. Cromwell justified the massacre, in which the casualties numbered far more than the total garrison as 'a righteous judgement of God'.

Sport

football — **Drogheda United** were founded in 1919, merging in 1975 with Drogheda FC (formed in 1962). They are winners of the League of Ireland in 2007 and the FAI Cup in 2005. Their home ground is United Park, Drogheda.

Dundalk were founded in 1903 and are Ireland's second most successful club (after Shamrock Rovers: see Dublin), winning the League of Ireland in 1933, 1963, 1967, 1976, 1979, 1982, 1988, 1991 and 1995, and the FAI Cup in 1942, 1949, 1952, 1958, 1977, 1979, 1981, 1988 and 2002. Their home ground is Oriel Park, Dundalk.

horse racing — **Bellewstown Racecourse**, Palace Street, Drogheda. The first record of races on this course is in 1726. The Flat and National Hunt course is a sharp left-handed oval of 9 furlongs (1.8km) with a run-in of 3 furlongs (0.6km) and an uphill finish. Tel: 041 984 2111.

Dundalk Racecourse, Racecourse Road, Dundalk. Ireland's first all-weather course, opened in 2007, although there has been racing on the site since 1889. It stages Flat racing on a 1 mile 2 furlong (2km) oval course with a 5 furlong (1.1km) run-in. Tel: 042 933 4438.

Stephenstown Pond Nature Park and Agnes Burns Cottage — Knockbridge, 5 miles (8km) southwest of Dundalk. A nature park covering 5 acres (2ha) of woodlands and lake. The restored cottage of Agnes Burns, sister of Scottish poet Robert, and her husband William Galt, stands within the park.

Taaffe's Castle — Carlingford, 9 miles (15km) northeast of Dundalk. A four-storey 16th century tower house named after the Taaffe family, who became Earls of Carlingford in the 1660s.

Táin Bó Cúailnge — The story of the Cattle Raid of Cooley (abbreviated 'the Táin'), the earliest written version of which is recorded in the late 11th century manuscript known as *Lebor na hUidre* (the Book of the Dun Cow), compiled in the monastery at Clonmacnoise (see Offaly). Set in the 1st century AD, it tells

	how the teenage hero Cúchulainn defended the Kingdom of Ulster from Mebd (Maeve), queen of Connacht, climaxing in the single combat between Cúchulainn and his best friend Ferdia.
Termonfeckin Castle	5 miles (8km) northeast of Drogheda. A well-preserved three-storey tower house originally built in the 15th or 16th century. It was reported to have been repaired by a Captain Brabazon in 1641. The second-floor chamber is barrel vaulted.
Tholsel Carlingford	Carlingford, 9 miles (15km) northeast of Dundalk. Originally a town gate, in which capacity it was also used for the collection of tolls and taxes on goods entering the town. It has also been used as a council meeting place and town gaol.
Tholsel Drogheda	West Street, Drogheda. Built in 1770 as the council municipal centre. It is now occupied by the Bank of Ireland Group.
White River Mill	Dunleer, 8 miles (13km) northwest of Drogheda. A working water-powered corn mill dating to the late 17th century. Tel: 041 685 1141.

Some famous people born in County Louth

Brigid of Kildare (saint) (c. 451–525)	Faughart
Byrne, Tommy (racing driver) (1958–)	Drogheda
Corr, Andrea (singer and actress) (1974–)	Dundalk
Corr, Caroline (musician) (1973–)	Dundalk
Corr, Jim (musician) (1964–)	Dundalk
Corr, Sharon (musician) (1970–)	Dundalk
Horgan, Shane (rugby player) (1978–)	Bellewstown
Lenihan, Brian (politician) (1930–95)	Dundalk
Lynch, Evanna (actress) (1991–)	Termonfeckin
Macardle, Dorothy (author) (1889–1958)	Dundalk
McGee, D'Arcy (Canadian statesman and journalist) (1825–68)	Carlingford
O'Neill, Eliza (actress) (1791–1872)	Drogheda
O'Reilly, John Boyle (poet) (1844–90)	Drogheda
Smyth, Des (golfer) (1953–)	Drogheda
Staunton, Steve (footballer) (1969–)	Drogheda

MAYO

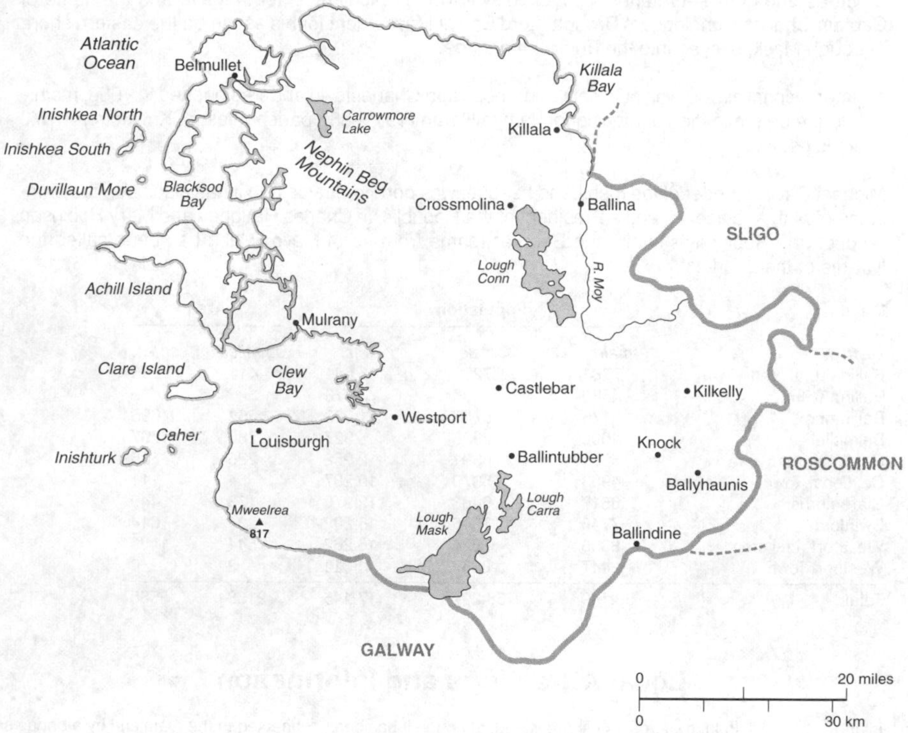
Atlantic Ocean
Belmullet
Inishkea North
Inishkea South
Duvillaun More
Blacksod Bay
Carrowmore Lake
Nephin Beg Mountains
Killala Bay
Killala
Crossmolina
Ballina
SLIGO
Lough Conn
R. Moy
Achill Island
Mulrany
Clare Island
Clew Bay
Castlebar
Kilkelly
Westport
Caher
Louisburgh
Inishturk
Knock
Ballintubber
ROSCOMMON
Ballyhaunis
Mweelrea
817
Lough Carra
Lough Mask
Ballindine
GALWAY
0
20 miles
0
30 km

County Mayo is part of the province of Connacht. It lies in the northwest of the Republic of Ireland and is bordered by Sligo to the northeast, Roscommon to the east and Galway to the south. To the west lies the Atlantic Ocean. There are Gaeltacht (Irish-speaking) areas around Belmullet and on part of Achill Island in the west and around the Partry Mountains in the south.

The area was probably first settled during the Mesolithic period but evidence only exists from the Neolithic onwards. During the early Christian period St Patrick fasted for 40 days and nights on the mountain of Croagh Patrick and several monastic sites such as Balla, Aughagower, Balla, Ballintubber, Cong, Errew, Moyne, Killala and Turlough were founded, as was 'Mayo of the Saxons' from which the county eventually gained its name. The invasion of the Vikings from the 9th century onwards resulted in the building of the many round towers as refuges on the monastic sites that survived.

Mayo has played its part in many of the political upheavals that have visited the Republic of Ireland over the years. The area came under Norman control in 1235 and many famous Mayo families are descended from the invaders (Burke or Bourke, Costello and Walsh being just three). During the 13th and 14th centuries many friaries and abbeys were founded by the mendicant orders in the region. The following centuries were typified by feuds and disputes within and among the families until English power was strengthened in the 1560s. A rebellion by the Burkes in the 1580s was violently suppressed by the Governor of Connacht, Sir Richard Bingham. County Mayo was at the centre of the uprising and French invasion of 1798 with victories by the rebels at Killala, Ballina and Castlebar. The 'Republic of Connacht' was proclaimed at Castlebar, with John Moore from Moore Hall as its president. The rebellion was eventually defeated.

County Mayo was particularly badly hit by the Great Famine, its recorded population dropping from 388,887 in 1841 to 274,499 in 1851. On 21 August 1879 an apparition of the Virgin Mary, St Joseph and St John the Evangelist was witnessed at Knock, which has become a major pilgrimage site. In August 1879 Michael Davitt established the National Land League of Mayo in Castlebar; this shortly became the Irish National Land League, with Charles Stewart Parnell as its president and Davitt as one of its secretaries. The 'Land War' was particularly bitter in Mayo and the name of Captain Charles Cunningham Boycott, Lord Erne's Mayo agent for his estate on the eastern shore of Lough Mask, passed into the English language.

An international airport was built between Knock and Charlestown and was opened in 1986, mainly due to the determination of Monsignor James Horan (1911–86), parish priest of Knock from 1970 until his death.

Michael Davitt, founder of the Irish Land League, was born in Straide and it has also been the birthplace of both a Taoiseach and a President of the Republic, in Charles Haughey and Mary Robinson respectively. Robinson's family, the Bourkes, came from north Mayo, which has been called the 'Cradle of the Bourkes'.

Mayo	**Population**			**Area**	
Districts	*male*	*female*	*total*	*sq miles*	*sq km*
Ballina rural area	7781	7260	15,041	411	1065
Ballina Town	4583	4895	9478	6	15
Ballinrobe	6176	5747	11,923	268	695
Belmullet	4002	3925	7927	285	737
Castlebar rural area	6651	6301	12,952	226	585
Castlebar Town	4908	5379	10,287	4	11
Claremorris	6517	6453	12,970	173	449
Swinford	7746	7546	15,292	237	614
Westport rural area	8338	7924	16,262	544	1409
Westport Town	2447	2867	5314	3	8
Total	59,149	58,297	117,446	2158	5588

Local Attractions and Information

Achill Island — Ireland's largest offshore island, although it has been connected to the mainland by a bridge since 1887. The island is 14 miles (23km) long by 12 miles (19km) wide at its extremities. Its landscape includes cliffs, bogs and the mountain of Slievemore (2022ft/671m). Area: 60 sq miles (155 sq km). Population: 2620.

Aghagower Round Tower — Aghagower, 4 miles (6km) southeast of Westport. A 50ft (15m) high round tower on the site of an early monastic foundation of St Senach. The original doorway stands 7ft (2.1m) above ground level and there is a later entrance at ground level. It is believed that the top of the tower was dislodged by a lightning strike.

Airport — **Ireland West Airport Knock** (NOC). Opened in 1986 following a long campaign by Monsignor James Horan to enable pilgrims to visit the nearby Knock Shrine. The airport was formerly known as Knock International Airport, Connacht Regional Airport and Horan International Airport. Flights operate to destinations in Great Britain, Ireland, Europe and the United States. Tel: 094 936 8100.

Ashford Castle — 1/2 mile (0.8km) south of Cong, 6 miles (10km) southwest of Ballinrobe. Located on the shore of Lough Corrib and originally a de Burgo (Burke) stronghold built in the first half of the 13th century. Having been remodelled during the early 18th century in the style of a French chateau, the castle was bought in 1852 by Sir Benjamin Lee Guinness (1798–1868), grandson of the founder of the brewery, who extended both the building and acreage of the estate. Further rebuilding was carried out by his son. In 1939 it was bought by Noel Huggard, who opened the castle as a luxury hotel. It was restored and refurbished in the 1970s by new owners who added a golf course, and it has been further expanded and improved since. Tel: 094 954 6003.

Aughleam Heritage Centre — Aughleam, 9 miles (15km) southwest of Belmullet, 32 miles (51km) northwest of Westport. Aka Ionad Deirbhle. A local history centre opened on 13 August 1997 by Mary Robinson, then President of Ireland. It celebrates the way of life of the inhabitants of the Mullet Peninsula since ancient times; exhibits include many local artefacts. The building's 10ft (3m) high stained glass window illustrates the story of St Deirbhle, after whom the centre is named. The plan of the building follows that of the traditional type of house found on the Inis Geidh Islands. Tel: 097 85727.

Balla Round Tower — Balla, 8 miles (13km) southeast of Castlebar. The 30ft (9m) stub of a round tower on the site of a 7th century monastic foundation of St Mochua. At one point it was used as a bell tower for a nearby church.

Ballina Dolmen — 1/4 mile (0.4km) southwest of Ballina. Aka Dolmen of the Four Maols, or locally the Table of the Giants. A large kist with a capstone resting on three uprights. It stands close to Ballina railway station.

Ballintubber Abbey 7 miles (11km) south of Castlebar. Aka Tobar Patraic. Located close to the shore of Lough Carra and founded in 1216 by Cathal Crovdearg O'Conor, King of Connacht, near the site of early Patrician church. Ballintubber is unique in Ireland in being a royal abbey in continuous use since its foundation. It was the subject of a C Day-Lewis poem, 'The Abbey that Refused to Die' (1967). Partly burned in 1265 and rebuilt, the abbey was suppressed at the time of the Dissolution but its geographical position made this difficult to enforce. It is believed that Augustinian friars ran the abbey 1603–53, at which point it was again partially burned, this time by Cromwellian troops. Although the domestic quarters and cloisters were destroyed, the church seems to have survived, worship continuing uninterrupted through the following centuries. Concerted restoration began in the second half of the 19th century and in the 1960s the nave was restored and reroofed. The chapter house was restored in the late 990s and a restoration programme continues. In August 2001 then James Bond actor Pierce Brosnan married Keely Shaye Smith at Ballintubber. A visitor centre charts the history of the abbey, also featuring an exhibition tracing the story of farming in the area from Neolithic times and its relation to the seasonal pagan festivals of Imbolc (1 February), Bealtaine (1 May), Lughnasa (1 August) and Samhain (1 November). The abbey is the parish church for the local community. Tel: 094 903 0934.

Ballycroy National Park Established in November 1998 as Ireland's sixth National Park and covering 46 sq miles (118 sq km) in northwest Mayo, encompassing part of the Nephin Beg mountain range and large areas of Atlantic blanket bog. Ireland's western blanket bogs are the most important remaining in Western Europe. The region is drained by the Owenduff River.

Ballyglass Court Tomb $^1/_2$ mile (0.8km) northwest of Ballycastle, 15 miles (24km) northwest of Ballina. A court tomb 75ft (23km) in length with two chambered galleries.

Ballymagibbon Cairn 2 miles (3km) east of Cong, 5$^1/_2$ miles (9km) south of Ballinrobe. A large cairn measuring more than 115ft (35m) in diameter and 60ft (18m) high, and dating to c. 3000 BC.

Barnacahogue Stone Fort 5 miles (8km) southwest of Charlestown. The remains of a walled ring fort 50ft (15m) in diameter and probably dating to the Iron Age. It is now located close to the runway at Knock International Airport.

Battles Three battles were fought in Co. Mayo during the Irish Insurrection (1797–8): Ballina, Castlebar and Killala. See separate table for details.

Belcarra Eviction Cottage Belcarra, 5 miles (8km) southeast of Castlebar. A restored cottage from which the Walshe family were evicted on 2 October 1886. The restoration was carried out 1997–9 as a project of the Belcarra community Co-Op. Tel: 087 909 0046.

Brackloon Wood Knappagh, 3 miles (5km) southwest of Westport. A native oak woodland representing one of the last remaining areas of Atlantic oakwood in Ireland. Conifers planted in the 1960s have been removed in order to restore the wood to its original state.

Burriscarra Churches 2 miles (3km) south of Carrownacon, 11 miles (18km) southeast of Castlebar. The ruins of two churches, one dating to the 15th century and standing on the site of a 13th century Carmelite priory. The other is from the 14th century.

Burrishoole Friary 1$^1/_2$ miles (2.5km) northwest of Newport, 7 miles (11km) northwest of Westport. The ruin of a Dominican friary founded c.1470 by Richard de Burgo of Turlough. All that remains today is the church and the eastern wall of the cloister.

Carrickkildavnet Castle Cloghmore, 18 miles (29km) northwest of Westport. Aka Kildavnet Castle. A four-storey 15th century tower house on Achill Island. It was probably built by the ancestors of the pirate Grace O'Malley.

Carrowkilleen Court Tomb 2 miles (3km) west of Crossmolina, 9 miles (15km) west of Ballina. A cairn 183ft (56m) long and containing three separate court tombs.

Céide Fields 4 miles (6km) northwest of Ballycastle, 18 miles (29km) northwest of Ballina. An area of stone walls, field systems, enclosures, settlements and tombs covering 3700 acres (1500ha) and dating to c. 3500 BC, making them the oldest known field system in the world. The remains, preserved beneath a blanket of peat, were first noted by local schoolteacher Patrick Caulfield in the 1930s. His son Seamus, an archaeologist, established the extreme significance of his father's findings. The location and distribution of the remains were determined by non-destructive methods such as probing with iron rods. An award-winning pyramid shaped visitor centre offering spectacular views over land and sea opened in May 1993, and explores the geology, flora and development of the area as well as the history of the field system. Tel: 096 43325.

Christchurch Castlebar The Mall, Castlebar. A church completed in 1739 and renovated 1800–28. Tel: 098 25127.

Clare Island Located in the entrance of Clew Bay. It has two peaks, Knockaveen (729ft/222m) and Knockmore (1520ft/463m). Its features include the ruins of a 13th century Cistercian abbey and Granuaile Castle by the harbour. Area: 6.33 sq miles (16.4 sq km). Population: 127.

Clew Bay A bay on the west coast of Co. Mayo famous for its many islands, the largest of which is Clare Island.

Clew Bay Heritage Centre The Quay, Westport. A local history museum housed in a 19th century building and tracing the history of Clew Bay and Westport from the prehistoric period to the present day. Displays include a scale model of Westport Town and Quay, the story of Grace O'Malley, and the lives and works of Co. Mayo authors including George Moore and Michael Mullen. The centre also has genealogical research resources. Tel: 098 26852.

Clogher Heritage Complex Clogher, 7 miles (11km) southeast of Castlebar. The complex includes a heritage cottage built in 2003 and opened in July 2004, recreating a typical one-bedroom labourer's cottage with typical furniture and a cottage garden, and Stauntons Forge, a restored working forge closed in 1960 and reopened in 2001. Tel: 094 936 0891.

Cong Village on the extreme southern Mayo/Galway border. Cong gets its name from Irish *cung*, a narrow strip of land, the village itself being a narrow strip of land between Lough Mask and Lough Corrib. See also Cross of Cong.

Cong Abbey — ½ mile (0.8km) south of Cong, 6 miles (10km) southwest of Ballinrobe. The substantial ruin of an Augustinian abbey located in the grounds of Ashford Castle. Founded in the early 12th century by Turlough O'Connor, it stands on the site of a 6th century monastic foundation established by St Feichin which was burned down and then replaced by O'Connor's building. Some carving was added to the capitals in the cloister in the 19th century.

Croagh Patrick — 6 miles (10km) southwest of Westport. Ireland's most holy mountain. It overlooks Clew Bay and is a place of pilgrimage. Probably a meeting place in pre-Christian times – archaeological discoveries made on the summit include evidence of an Iron Age hill fort – it is best known for St Patrick's fast of 40 days and 40 nights in AD 441. A stone oratory dating to between AD 430 and 890 has also been discovered. The annual pilgrimage in St Patrick's honour takes place on the last Sunday in July, known as 'Reek Sunday' after the local name for the mountain. A visitor centre was opened in 2000. Tel: 098 64114.

Cross of Cong — A 12th century gold and silver cross made on behalf of Turlough O'Connor, king of Connacht and High King of Ireland, and believed to have once contained a relic of the True Cross. Made for Tuam Cathedral, Co. Galway, it was later housed in Cong Abbey. It is now held in the National Museum in Dublin.

Doonfeeny Standing Stone — 2 miles (3km) northwest of Ballycastle, 12 miles (19km) northwest of Ballina. A slightly leaning stone measuring 16ft (5m) high and 16in (40cm) wide by 8in (20cm) thick.

Enniscoe Gardens — 2 miles (3km) south of Crossmalina, 5 miles (8km) southwest of Ballina. Part of the estate of the early 18th century Enniscoe House on the shore of Lough Conn, the gardens include a restored 18th century walled garden, an organic vegetable garden and pleasure grounds. Mayo North Heritage Centre was opened on the estate in 1992 by the then President of Ireland, Mary Robinson, and includes a large collection of local farm and household artefacts. There is also a genealogy resource centre. Tel: 096 31809.

Errew Abbey — 4 miles (6km) southeast of Crossmolina. The ruin of an Augustinian abbey founded in the 15th century, although the church dates to the 13th century. A ruined oratory close by known as Templenagalliaghdoo, or 'Church of the Black Nun', may date to the 6th century.

Foxford Woollen Mills Visitor Centre — St Joseph's Place, Foxford. Opened in 1992, the centre tells the story of Mother Agnes Morrogh-Bernard (1842–1932), founder of the mills in 1892. The mill is renowned for its production of high quality tweeds, rugs and blankets. Tel: 094 925 6756.

Granuaile Visitor Centre — Louisburgh, 12 miles (19km) southwest of Westport. A visitor centre telling the story of the seafaring O'Malleys and O'Flahertys, and in particular of 16th century pirate queen Grace O'Malley (Granuaile), who sailed out of Clew Bay. The centre also has an exhibition about the Great Famine. Tel: 098 66341.

Granuaile Castle — Clare Island. The former stronghold of Grace O'Malley (Granuaile), located above the island's harbour. Grace is reputedly buried on the island.

Hennigan's Heritage Centre — Killaser, 2½ miles (4km) north of Swinford. A farm museum overlooking Creagaballa Lough and exploring how the Hennigan family have scraped their living on 10 acres (4ha) of poor soil for nearly 200 years. Tel: 094 925 2505.

Highest point — Mweelrea in the southwest of Co. Mayo at 2680ft (817m).

Inishmaine Abbey — 4 miles (6km) southwest of Ballinrobe. A 13th century Augustinian abbey church on a peninsula on Lough Mask which was originally an island.

Interesting facts — **Grace O'Malley (Irish: Gráinne Ní Mháille)**, the 'Pirate Queen of Mayo' (1530–c.1600), nicknamed Grace the Bald ('Grainne Mhaol' or Granuaile) because of her short hair, was the daughter of the O'Malley chieftain. Having first married Donal O'Flaherty, nicknamed Donal an Chogaidhher or Donal of the Battles, upon his death she married a rival, Richard 'Iron Dick' Burke, who owned Rockfleet Castle. In 1593 she travelled to Greenwich Palace for an audience with Elizabeth I which was carried out entirely in their common language of Latin. O'Malley has a firm place in Irish folklore and although many of the stories are perhaps apocryphal there is no doubt that she was one of the most powerful Irish women of the day and made her reputation as the tough 'Sea Queen of Connaught' by forcibly charging ships for 'safe passage' between Clare Island and Galway. **Knock** is possibly the smallest village in the world to have its own international airport, serving London, New York and many parts of Europe. This was necessitated by the huge influx of tourists visiting the Marian Shrine. The **Musical Bridge Inn** at Bellacorrick, just west of Ballina – named for the adjacent bridge over the Owenmore River – is a famous landmark and popular pub in the region. Since the closure of the local power generating station it has become a natural stopping point for through traffic, tourists and local fisherman. Legend has it that if you roll a pebble along the stone parapet of the bridge a melodic note can be heard.

Islands — In addition to the numerous offshore islands there are 22 islands in Lough Carra and several in Lough Mask. See separate table for details.

Keel East Court Tomb — Achill Island. A court tomb which may hold three chambers.

Killala Round Tower — Killala, 7 miles (11km) northwest of Ballina. An 84ft (25.5m) high round tower with a doorway 11ft (3.3m) above ground level. It stands on the site of an early, possibly 5th century monastic foundation. It was repaired in the first half of the 19th century after being struck by lightning and has an intact cap.

Kiltimagh Town Museum — Aiden Street, Kiltimagh, 12 miles (19km) east of Castlebar. Opened in 1989 in the restored goods store of the town's railway station; the stationmaster's house is now occupied by an art centre. Kiltimagh was the birthplace of Rafteiri, the blind Irish poet. Tel: 094 938 1494.

Knock Folk Museum — Knock, 16 miles (26km) southeast of Castlebar. Opened in May 1987 and featuring a fully furnished thatched cottage built inside the museum. It is divided into sections, each on a different aspect of 19th century rural life in Ireland. There are permanent displays on religion, fishing (an original currach), farming, crafts (blacksmith, carpenter, and shoemaker), education (life-size typical classroom), housing, clothing, sport and transport (pony and trap and penny-farthing bicycle). There is also information about the story of the Knock Apparition of 1879, the development of Knock Shrine and the life of Monsignor James Horan. Tel: 094 938 8100.

Knock Shrine — Knock, 16 miles (26km) southeast of Castlebar. Ireland's main centre of Marian pilgrimage and devotion, established after 15 people witnessed an apparition of the Virgin Mary – accompanied by St Joseph and St John the Evangelist – in August 1879 outside the south gable of the parish church. Two separate Commissions of Enquiry (in 1879 and 1936) found that 'the testimony of the witnesses, taken as a whole, was trustworthy and satisfactory'. In 1979 (the shrine's centenary year) Pope John Paul II said Mass for 450,000 people. The church of Our Lady Queen of Ireland was built 1974–6 and was raised to the status of basilica by the Pope on his visit. Knock International Airport (see separate entry) was opened in 1986 largely to serve the shrine. The main pilgrimage season is from the last Sunday in April to the second Sunday in October.

Loughs — The numerous loughs in Co. Mayo include **Lough Carra**, 8 miles (13km) south of Castlebar, the smallest of the western lakes at 4000 acres (1600ha); **Lough Conn**, 5 miles (8km) west of Ballina, covering 14,000 acres (5660ha) and popular for brown trout fishing; and **Lough Mask**, 12 miles (19km) south of Castlebar, a limestone lough covering 34.4 sq miles (89 sq km), one of the best-known brown trout fisheries in Ireland.

Mayo Abbey — 9 miles (15km) southeast of Castlebar. Aka Mayo of the Saxons. The village of Mayo Abbey is the site of an early Christian 7th century monastic foundation established by St Colman. Because it was founded for Saxon monks the area is still known as 'Mayo of the Saxons'. In 1152 the Synod of Kells named Mayo Abbey the seat of the Diocese of Mayo and this continued until its union with Tuam in 1631. The county of Mayo was named after the town of Mayo in 1570. There is the ruin of the 15th century monastery plus a resource centre with heritage room named after Bishop Patrick O'Healy of Mayo, the first Irish bishop to die for the faith when he was executed in 1579. Tel: 094 936 5735.

Mayo North Heritage Centre — See Enniscoe Gardens

Meelick Round Tower — 4 miles (6km) southwest of Swinford. A 70ft (21m) high round tower dating to c. AD 950 and restored in the late 19th century.

Michael Davitt Museum — Straide, 8 miles (13km) northeast of Castlebar. Opened in 1984 in a restored former church to celebrate the life of Straide-born Michael Davitt (1846–1906), the 'father of the Land League', who was christened in the church in 1846. Davitt was MP for South Mayo and a founding patron of the Gaelic Athletic Association (GAA). The museum has personal memorabilia, documents and photographs plus exhibits relating to the Land League. Davitt is buried in the grounds of Straide Abbey, beside the museum. Tel: 094 903 1022.

Moore Hall — 2 miles (3km) northeast of Partry, 10 miles (16km) southeast of Castlebar. The ruin of a Georgian house located on a promontory on the eastern shore of Lough Carra. It was formerly the home of the Moore family, whose members included John Moore (1763–99), president of the 'Provisional Republic of Connacht' during the French invasion in 1798, and writer George Augustus Moore (1852–1933), whose works include *A Modern Lover* (1883), *Esther Waters* (1894), *The Untilled Field* (1903), *The Lake* (1905) and *Hail and Farewell* (1914). George Henry Moore (1810–70) was a much loved landlord, and it speaks volumes that no deaths or evictions are recorded on the estate during the Great Famine. Moore's ashes are buried on Castle Island (aka Moore's Island) on Lough Carra. The house was deliberately gutted by fire in January 1923.

Moyne Abbey — 2 miles (3km) southeast of Killala, 6 miles (10km) north of Ballina. The ruin of a Franciscan friary founded by the Burke family in the 15th century. The friary was largely abandoned following a destructive raid by Sir Richard Bingham in 1590. However, it is believed that the last friar died as late as 1800.

Murrisk Abbey — Murrisk, 5 miles (8km) southwest of Westport. The ruin of an Augustinian abbey located in the shadow of Croagh Patrick, founded in 1452 by the O'Malley family and abandoned c.1800. The east wall of the church features five surviving trefoil pointed windows surmounted by interconnecting bar tracery.

National Famine Memorial — Murrisk, 5 miles (8km) southwest of Westport. The National Famine Monument near the Croagh Patrick Visitor Centre was unveiled by Mary Robinson, then President of Ireland, on 20 July 1997. It takes the form of a bronze sculpture of a 'coffin ship' designed by John Behan.

National Museum of Ireland: Country Life — Turlough, 4½ miles (7km) northeast of Castlebar. Located in the grounds of Turlough Park, alongside the restored Turlough Park House (see separate entry). A purpose-built branch of the National Museum of Ireland (the other three branches are in Dublin) opened in September 2001 and telling the story of Irish country life 1850–1950 via a wide range of displays, artefacts and interactive screens. In 2002 it received the title of Museum of the Year, awarded jointly by the Gulbenkian Foundation and the Heritage Council of Ireland, in association with the Northern Ireland Museums Council. Tel: 094 903 1773.

Nature Reserves — **Knockmoyle Sheskin**, 4 miles (6km) north of Bellacorick, 16 miles (26km) west of Ballina, an extensive area of lowland blanket bog covering 2960 acres (1198ha).

Oldhead Wood, 2 miles (3km) northeast of Louisburgh, 42 acres (17ha) of semi-natural woodland, mainly oak, birch, rowan and willow, located on a promontory on the southern shore of Clew Bay.

Owenboy, 6 miles (10km) west of Crossmolina, 13 miles (21km) west of Ballina, 981 acres (397ha) of intermediate bog providing a habitat for Greenland white-fronted geese.

Partry House	1 mile (1.6km) south of Partry, 12 miles (19km) south of Castlebar. Located beside Lough Carra and built in 1667 by Arthur Lynch incorporating the remains of Cloonlagheen Castle. The house is surrounded by woodland and parkland. The Lynchs occupied the house continuously until 1991. Tel: 094 954 3004.
Partry Mountains	A range of hills in the south of Co. Mayo, to the west of Lough Carra and Lough Mask. Their highest point is Maumtrasna at 2238ft (682m).
Patrick Peyton CSC Memorial Centre	Attymass, 5 miles (8km) southeast of Ballina. A memorial centre commemorating the life of Fr Patrick Peyton (1909–92), founder of the Family Rosary Crusade. Known as the 'Rosary Priest', Fr Peyton worked to promote the family recitation of the Rosary, stating that 'the family that prays together stays together'. The centre was opened in 1998 and presents Fr Peyton's life story, with a recording of Fr Peyton praying the Rosary. Tel: 096 45374.
Quiet Man Heritage Cottage	Circular Road, Cong. A typical Irish cottage of the 1920s, named for the film *The Quiet Man* (1952), starring John Wayne, Maureen O'Hara, Barry Fitzgerald and Victor McLaglen, and directed by John Ford, and filmed mainly in Cong. The ground floor has been designed as an exact replica of the original set in Hollywood where the interior scenes were shot. The furnishings, artefacts and costumes are reproductions of those seen in the film. The upper floor houses the Cong Archaeological and Historical Exhibition, which charts the history of the area from prehistoric times to the present day. Tel: 092 46089.
Rathfran Friary	2 miles (3km) north of Killala, 9 miles (15km) north of Ballina. The ruin of the Priory of the Holy Cross, a Dominican friary founded in 1274. The friary was burned down by Sir Richard Bingham in 1590 but, as elsewhere, some friars remained in the area until the 18th century.
Rivers	The **Moy** rises in the Ox Mountains, flowing for 62 miles (100km) across Co. Sligo and Co. Mayo before entering the Atlantic at Killala Bay. The river is internationally renowned for its salmon fishing. The famous Ridge Pool, especially known as 'a salmon angler's paradise', is located in the heart of the town of Ballina. The **Owenduff** is a very fine salmon and sea trout river, draining into Tullaghan Bay, a few miles north of Ballycroy.
Rockfleet Castle	3 miles (5km) west of Newport, 8 miles (13km) northwest of Westport. A well-preserved tower house by Clew Bay. Owned by Richard 'Iron Dick' Burke, it passed to his wife, the pirate Grace O'Malley, on his death in 1583.
Rosserk Friary	4 miles (6km) north of Ballina. The well-preserved ruin of a Franciscan friary founded c.1440 and abandoned following an attack by Sir Richard Bingham in the 1590s.
St Attracta's Well	Tample, 2 miles (3km) south of Charlestown. A holy well possibly dating to the 5th century and dedicated to St Attracta, said to have been abbess of a convent established by St Patrick beside Lough Gara. The feast day of the well was 11 August.
Sport	
Gaelic football	**Mayo** were winners of the All-Ireland Senior Football Championship in 1936, 1951 and 1952.
horse racing	**Ballinrobe** Racecourse, Keel Bridge, Ballinrobe. Racing at the current location began in 1921. Ballinrobe stages both Flat and National Hunt racing on a right-handed oval course of 9 furlongs (1.8km) with a run-in of 2½ furlongs (0.5km). Tel: 094 954 1811.
Srahwee Wedge Tomb	½ mile (0.8km) northwest of Cregganbaun, 4 miles (6km) south of Louisburgh. A wedge tomb dating to c. 3000 BC with a large flat capstone resting on 3ft (0.9m) uprights and sealed with a door stone.
Straide Friary	Straide, 8 miles (13km) northeast of Castlebar. The ruin of a Dominican (although originally Franciscan) friary founded in the 13th century. Most of the remains date to the 15th century. It has a finely sculptured 15th century tomb portraying, among others, the Magi, Christ, St Peter and St Paul.
Tochar Phadraig	Aka Patrick's Causeway. A 22 mile (35km) pilgrim road tracing the route of St Patrick from Ballintubber to Croagh Patrick. In fact it predates St Patrick in origin, probably dating to C. AD 350 when it formed the main route to Croagh Patrick from Cruachan, seat of the kings of Connacht (see Roscommon: Rathcrogan Mound); it has recently been revived as a pilgrimage/tourist trail.
Turlough Park House	Turlough, 4½ miles (7km) northeast of Castlebar. Designed for the Fitzgerald family by Thomas Newenham Deane and built in the 1860s. The gardens include a lake and an ornamental freestanding glasshouse The estate includes the Museum of County Life and a round tower. Tel: 094 902 4444.
Turlough Round Tower	Turlough, 4½ miles (7km) northeast of Castlebar. A 75ft (23m) tall round tower of uncertain date with a doorway 13ft (4m) above ground level, located on a monastic site possibly founded by St Patrick. An 18th century church stands next to the tower.
Westport Heritage Centre	James Street, Westport. A local history museum charting the history of the town. Tel: 098 25711.
Westport House	½ mile (0.8km) west of Westport. A largely 18th century house overlooking Clew Bay beside the Carrowbeg River. The home of the Browne family, the core of the house was designed in 1731 by Richard Castle for John Browne, 1st Earl of Altamont, and incorporated parts of an earlier O'Malley castle. The house was enlarged in the 1770s with interiors by James Wyatt. The estate includes restored gardens, a small zoo and amusement park and a collection of farm buildings. Tel: 098 27766.

Some famous people born in County Mayo

Brennan, Louis (inventor) (1852–1932)	Castlebar
Brown, William (father of the Argentine Navy) (1777–1857)	Foxford
Cassidy, Patrick (composer) (1956–)	Claremorris
D'Alton, John (Primate of All Ireland) (1882–1963)	Claremorris
Davitt, Michael (founder of Irish Land league) (1846–1906)	Straide
Delaney, Edward (sculptor) (1930–)	Claremorris
Flanagan, Seán (Gaelic footballer and politician) (1922–93)	Ballyhaunis
Haughey, Charles (Taoiseach of Ireland) (1925–2006)	Castlebar
Higgins, F R (poet) (1896–1941)	Foxford
MacBride, John (Irish rebel) (1865–1916)	Westport
Moore, George (author) (1852–1933)	Ballyglass
Murphy, Richard (poet) (1927–)	Kilmaine
Robinson, Mary (7th President of Ireland) (1944–)	Ballina
Ruane, Martin (wrestler – Giant Haystacks) (1946–98)	Kiltimagh
Walsh, Louis (music industry manager) (1952–)	Kiltimagh

Islands of County Mayo

(shipping area = Malin)

Island name	Area	Nearest landmark	General information
Acaill Bheag	Atlantic	Cloghmore, Achill Island	aka Achillbeg Island. The government ordered the evacuation of the island in 1965, many of its inhabitants now residing on Achill.
Achill Island	Atlantic	Malaranny	See separate entry
Achillbeg Island	Atlantic	Cloghmore, Achill Island	See Acaill Bheag
An Bad Breige	Atlantic	Benwee Head	Small rock to the east of An Teach Beag. Not one of the main five Stags of Broad Haven (Na Stacai), but considered part of the group.
An Glasoilean	Atlantic	Claggan	(I. = The Grey Island). Aka Glassillan
An Teach Beag	Atlantic	Benwee Head	Lies east of Teach Donal O'Cleirigh. One of the Stags of Broad Haven (Na Stacai).
An Teach Mor	Atlantic	Benwee Head	Lies south of Teach Donal O'Cleirigh. One of the Stags of Broad Haven (Na Stacai).
An tOighean	Atlantic	Benwee Head	Lies northwest of Teach Donal O'Cleirigh beyond Carraig na Faola. One of the Stags of Broad Haven (Na Stacai).
An tOilean Ban	Atlantic	Glinsk	aka Illanbaun Island
An tOilean Rua	Lough Carrowmore	Glenturk	(I. = The Red Island). Aka Derreen's Island, Red Island. Special Protection Area that supports a large colony of common gulls.
Annagh Island	Atlantic	Claggan	Largest of the Annagh Islands.
Annagh Islands	Clew Bay	Killadangan	Part of the Clew Bay group.
Ballinchalla	Lough Mask	Ballinrobe	Popular site for trout fishing.
Ballybeg Island	Atlantic	Barnabaun Point	Lies just southwest of Caher Island.
Ballycally Island	Lough Carra	Doon Promontory Fort	
Barranagh Island	Atlantic	Barranagh	aka Oilean Bearanach
Bartragh Island	Killala Bay	Killala	Latitude (DMS): 54° 12' 52" N; longitude (DMS): 9° 9' 53" W
Bartraw	Clew Bay	Curraghmore Point	Part of the Clew Bay group.
Bills Rocks	Atlantic	Dooega Head, Achill Island	Three large grass-covered steep rocky islets.
Bird Island	Lough Carra	Doon Promontory Fort	
Black Rock	Atlantic	Blacksod Point	aka Tor Mor
Bush Island	Lough Carra	Doon Promontory Fort	
Caher Island	Atlantic	Barnabaun Point	The island is the alleged resting place of St Patrick. Archaeological features are the Carved Cross and the brain-like Cursing Stone.
Calf Island	Clew Bay	Kilmeena	Part of the Clew Bay group.
Calliagheron Rock	Atlantic	Clare Island	Part of the Clew Bay group.
Caolaigh	Atlantic	Mullet Peninsula	aka Keely Island. One of the Duvillaun Islands.
Carraig an Mhoilt	Atlantic	Tiraun Point	aka Carrickawilt
Carraig na Faola	Atlantic	Benwee Head	Lies northwest of Teach Donal O'Cleirigh. One of the Stags of Broad Haven (Na Stacai).
Carrick McHugh	Killary Harbour	Mweelrea	Rock lying north of Freehill Island.

Island name	Area	Nearest landmark	General information
Carrickabullog Rocks	Atlantic	Garraun	Lies just off the coast and accessible at low tide.
Carrickawilt	Atlantic	Tiraun Point	aka Carraig an Mhoilt
Carrickgaddy Rocks	Atlantic	Tonakeera Point	Tiny rocks situated beyond Carrickabullog Rocks.
Carrickmoylenacurhoga	Atlantic	Tiraun Point	Most northerly of the three separated islets.
Carricknaweelion	Atlantic	Tiraun Point	Connected to Inishkea North at low tide.
Carrigee	Atlantic	Tiraun Point	The middle of three separated islets (Carrickawilt and Carrickmoylenacurhoga being the other two).
Carrigeenanore	Lough Mask	Toorinakeady	Lies next to Seerilaun and joined to the mainland in an area enclosed by mobile homes.
Carrigeendauv	Lough Mask	Toorinakeady	Lies close to Carrigeenanore and Seerilaun.
Carrigeenglass North	Clew Bay	Kilmeena	Part of the Clew Bay group.
Carrignaglamph	Atlantic	Tonakeera Point	aka Inishdegil Beg
Castle Island	Lough Carra	Doon Promontory Fort	
Church Island	Lough Carra	Doon Promontory Fort	
Clare Island	Atlantic	Roonagh Quay	See separate entry
Clynish	Clew Bay	Kilmeena	Part of the Clew Bay group. Population: 5
Collan Beg	Clew Bay	Kilmeena	Part of the Clew Bay group.
Collan More	Clew Bay	Kilmeena	Part of the Clew Bay group. Population: 3.
Cong	Cong River	Cong	aka Conga. Setting for the film *The Quiet Man* (1951).
Connors Island	Lough Carra	Doon Promontory Fort	
Cow Island	Lough Carra	Doon Promontory Fort	
Creevagh Island	Lough Carra	Doon Promontory Fort	
Creggandillisk	Clew Bay	Curraghmore Point	Part of the Clew Bay group.
Crovinish	Clew Bay	Carraholly	Part of the Clew Bay group.
Dead Island	Lough Mask	Bohawl	Popular for trout fishing.
Deer Island	Lough Carra	Doon Promontory Fort	
Derreen's Island	Lough Carrowmore	Glenturk	See An tOilean Rua
Derrinish	Clew Bay	Kilmeena	Part of the Clew Bay group.
Devenish Island	Lough Mask	Ballinrobe	Popular site for fishermen.
Doonbog Island	Lough Carra	Doon Promontory Fort	
Dorinish	Clew Bay	Curraghmore Point	One of the Clew Bay group. Bought by John Lennon in 1969.
Droim an Chapaill	Atlantic	Mullet Peninsula	aka Drumacappul Island. One of the Duvillaun Islands.
Drumacappul Island	Atlantic	Mullet Peninsula	See Droim an Chapaill
Dubhoilean Beag	Atlantic	Blacksod Point	aka Duvillaun Beg
Dubhoilean Mor	Atlantic	Blacksod Point	aka Duvillaun More
Duvillaun Beg	Atlantic	Blacksod Point	aka Dubhoilean Beag
Duvillaun More	Atlantic	Blacksod Point	aka Dubhoilean Mor
Eagle Island	Atlantic	Doonamo Point	There is a lighthouse on the west of the island.
Erris Head	Atlantic	Erris Head	Notable for its varied birdlife.
Freaghillan	Clew Bay	Kilmeena	Part of the Clew Bay group.
Freaghillan East	Clew Bay	Durrishoole	Part of the Clew Bay group.
Freaghillan West	Clew Bay	Durrishoole	Part of the Clew Bay group.
Freaghillanluggagh	Clew Bay	Durrishoole	Part of the Clew Bay group.
Freaghillaun North	Atlantic	Rinvyle Point	Latitude: 53° 37' 1" N; longitude: 10° 0' 55" W
Freehill Island	Killary Harbour	Mweelrea	Carrick McHugh rock lies off the north coast of the island.
Gaghta Island	Atlantic	Blacksod Point	aka Geachta. One of the Duvillaun Islands.
Geachta	Atlantic	Blacksod Point	See Gaghta Island
Glassillan	Atlantic	Claggan	See An Glasoilean
Gleneary Island	Lough Carra	Doon Promontory Fort	
Govern Island	Killary Harbour	Mweelrea	Lies 0.6 miles (1km) southeast of Freehill Island.
Heath Island	Achill Sound	Achill Island	aka Oilean Fraoigh
Hog Island	Lough Carra	Doon Promontory Fort	
Holy Island	Lough Corrib	Billypark	Wild brown trout are to be caught on the island's shores.
Horse Island	Lough Carra	Doon Promontory Fort	
Illanataggart	Clew Bay	Carraholly	Part of the Clew Bay group.
Illanbaun Island	Atlantic	Glinsk	aka An tOilean Ban
Illanbelfarsad	Atlantic	Glinsk	aka Oilean Bheal Feirste
Illancroagh	Achill Sound	Achill Island	Together with Heath Island guards the entrance to the southeast corner of Achill Sound North.

Island name	Area	Nearest landmark	General information
Illandavuck	Atlantic	Glinsk	aka Oilean Dhabhaic
Illanmaster	Atlantic	Glinsk	aka Oilean Maigheastar
Illanmaw	Clew Bay	Rosturk	Part of the Clew Bay group.
Illannanbraher	Clew Bay	Rosturk	Part of the Clew Bay group.
Illanoona	Atlantic	Glinsk	aka Oilean Una
Illaunamona	Clew Bay	Kilmeena	Part of the Clew Bay group.
Illaunmore	Atlantic	Garraun	The Carrickabullog Rocks lie close to this island.
Inis Caorach	Atlantic	Carrauin Point	aka Inishkeeragh
Inis Ge Theas	Atlantic	Tiraun Point	aka Inishkea South
Inis Ge Thuaidh	Atlantic	Tiraun Point	aka Inishkea North
Inis Gluaire	Atlantic	Carrauin Point	aka Inishglora
Inishbarna	Killary Harbour	Mweelrea	(I. = Island of the Gap)
Inishbee	Clew Bay	Kilmeena	Part of the Clew Bay group.
Inishbiggle	Atlantic	Achill Island	Low marshy island separated from Achill at the north end of Achill Sound by the Bull's Mouth. Population: 39.
Inishbobunnen	Clew Bay	Rosturk	Part of the Clew Bay group.
Inishcarrick	Clew Bay	Rosturk	Part of the Clew Bay group.
Inishcooa	Clew Bay	Rosturk	Part of the Clew Bay group.
Inishcoog	Lough Mask	Ballinrobe	Lough Mask House, the residence of the infamous Captain Boycott, is across the water from the island.
Inishcoragh	Clew Bay	Rosturk	Part of the Clew Bay group.
Inishcottle	Clew Bay	Kilmeena	Part of the Clew Bay group. Population: 4.
Inishdaff	Clew Bay	Kilmeena	Part of the Clew Bay group.
Inishdalla	Atlantic	Barnabaun Point	Lies a little over 1 mile (1.6km) southeast of the inhabited Inishturk.
Inishdaneel	Clew Bay	Durrishoole	Part of the Clew Bay group.
Inishdasky	Clew Bay	Rosturk	Part of the Clew Bay group.
Inishdaugh	Clew Bay	Curraghmore Point	Part of the Clew Bay group.
Inishdegil Beg	Atlantic	Tonakeera Point	aka Carrignaglamph
Inishdegil More	Atlantic	Tonakeera Point	Inhabited until the 1940s.
Inishdurra	Lough Mask	Ballinrobe	One of several islands in the lough.
Inisheeny	Clew Bay	Curraghmore Point	Part of the Clew Bay group.
Inisherkin	Clew Bay	Rosturk	Part of the Clew Bay group.
Inishgalloon	Atlantic	Trawmore, Achill Island	Lies off Achill Island.
Inishgeny	Clew Bay	Curraghmore Point	Part of the Clew Bay group.
Inishglesty	Lough Mask	Ballinrobe	Notable only as a fishing area.
Inishglora	Atlantic	Carrauin Point	aka Inis Gluaire
Inishgort	Clew Bay	Kilmeena	Part of the Clew Bay group. Population: 1.
Inishgowla	Clew Bay	Kilmeena	Part of the Clew Bay group.
Inishgowla	Clew Bay	Rosturk	Part of the Clew Bay group.
Inishgowla South	Clew Bay	Carraholly	Part of the Clew Bay group.
Inishilra	Clew Bay	Rosturk	Part of the Clew Bay group.
Inishimmel	Clew Bay	Curraghmore Point	Part of the Clew Bay group.
Inishkea North	Atlantic	Tiraun Point	aka Inis Ge Thuaidh
Inishkea South	Atlantic	Tiraun Point	aka Inis Ge Theas
Inishkee	Clew Bay	Durrishoole	Part of the Clew Bay group.
Inishkeel	Clew Bay	Rosturk	Part of the Clew Bay group.
Inishkeeragh	Atlantic	Carrauin Point	aka Inis Caorach
Inishkillew	Clew Bay	Kilmeena	Part of the Clew Bay group.
Inishlagan	Clew Bay	Curraghmore Point	Part of the Clew Bay group.
Inishlaughal	Clew Bay	Kilmeena	Part of the Clew Bay group.
Inishleague	Clew Bay	Curraghmore Point	Part of the Clew Bay group.
Inishlim	Clew Bay	Rosturk	Part of the Clew Bay group.
Inishloy	Clew Bay	Kilmeena	Part of the Clew Bay group.
Inishlyre	Clew Bay	Kilmeena	Part of the Clew Bay group. Population: 7.
Inishmaine	Lough Mask	Killour	
Inishnacross	Clew Bay	Rosturk	Part of the Clew Bay group.
Inishnakillew	Clew Bay	Kilmeena	Part of the Clew Bay group. Population: 5.
Inishoght	Lough Mask	Ballinrobe	
Inishoo	Clew Bay	Kilmeena	Part of the Clew Bay group
Inishowel	Lough Mask	Ballinrobe	
Inishowen	Lough Mask	Ballinrobe	
Inishquirk	Clew Bay	Rosturk	Part of the Clew Bay group.
Inishraher	Clew Bay	Old Head	Announced as Maharishi Capital of the Global Country of World Peace in May 2005. Part of the Clew Bay group. Area: 0.05 sq miles (0.12 sq km). Population: 4.
Inishtubrid	Clew Bay	Rosturk	Part of the Clew Bay group.

Island name	Area	Nearest landmark	General information
Inishturk	Clew Bay	Clare Island	The island has had a regular ferry service since 1997. Part of the Clew Bay group. Population: 72.
Inishturk	Clew Bay	Kilmeena	Part of the Clew Bay group.
Inishturlin	Clew Bay	Newport	Part of the Clew Bay group.
Island More	Clew Bay	Kilmeena	Part of the Clew Bay group. Population: 1.
Keely Island	Atlantic	Mullet Peninsula	See Caolaigh
Kid Island	Atlantic	Benwee Head	aka Oilean Mionnan
Kila Island	Lough Carra	Doon Promontory Fort	
Knockycahillaun	Clew Bay	Newport	Part of the Clew Bay group.
Ladys Island	Lough Carra	Doon Promontory Fort	
Lakeview Island	Lough Carra	Doon Promontory Fort	
Leamareha	Atlantic	Blacksod Point	aka Leim an Reithe. One of the Duvillaun Islands.
Leamnahaye Island	Lough Carra	Doon Promontory Fort	
Leim an Reithe	Atlantic	Blacksod Point	See Leamareha
Lusteen Islands	Lough Mask	Knocknamuck	Group of tiny grass-covered islets lying close to the shore of the lough.
Meaning Island	Lough Carra	Doon Promontory Fort	
Moneybeg	Clew Bay	Kilmeena	Part of the Clew Bay group.
Moynish More	Clew Bay	Rosturk	Part of the Clew Bay group.
Muckinish	Clew Bay	Rosturk	Part of the Clew Bay group.
Na Stacai	Atlantic	Benwee Head	aka Stags of Broad Haven. See separate entries for the five Stags.
Oilean Bearanach	Atlantic	Barranagh	aka Barranagh Island
Oilean Bheal Feirste	Atlantic	Glinsk	aka Illanbelfarsad
Oilean Dhabhaic	Atlantic	Glinsk	aka Illandavuck
Oilean Fraoigh	Achill Sound	Achill Island	aka Heath Island
Oilean Maigheastar	Atlantic	Glinsk	aka Illanmaster
Oilean Mionnan	Atlantic	Benwee Head	aka Kid Island
Oilean na Muice	Atlantic	Porturlin	See Pig Island
Orrageon Island	Atlantic	Mullet Peninsula	One of the Duvillaun Islands.
Oilean Una	Atlantic	Glinsk	aka Illanoona
Otter Island	Lough Carra	Doon Promontory Fort	
Pig Island	Atlantic	Porturlin	aka Oilean na Muice. Island named after its porcine appearance viewed from east or west.
Pleasure Island	Lough Carra	Doon Promontory Fort	
Priest Island	Lough Carra	Doon Promontory Fort	
Rabbit Island	Clew Bay	Newport	Part of the Clew Bay group.
Rams Island	Lough Mask	Doon Rock	Popular fishing retreat.
Red Island	Lough Carrowmore	Glenturk	See An tOilean Rua
Roeillan	Atlantic	Achill Island	Tiny islet off Achill Island.
Roeillaun	Clew Bay	Rosturk	Part of the Clew Bay group.
Roisin	Atlantic	Tiraun Point	aka Rusheen Island
Rosbarnagh Island	Clew Bay	Newport	Part of the Clew Bay group.
Roslynagh	Clew Bay	Durrishoole	Part of the Clew Bay group.
Rusheen Island	Atlantic	Tiraun Point	aka Roisin
Saints Island	Lough Mask	Ballinrobe	Popular site for trout fishing.
Seerilaun	Lough Mask	Toorinakeady	Lies next to Carrigeenanore and joined to the mainland in an area enclosed by mobile homes.
Shiraghy Island	Atlantic	Mullet Peninsula	One of the Duvillaun Islands.
Stags of Broad Haven	Atlantic	Benwee Head	aka Na Stacai. See separate entries for the five Stags.
Story Island	Lough Carra	Doon Promontory Fort	
Teach Donal O'Cleirigh	Atlantic	Benwee Head	The central, and highest, of the five Stags of Broad Haven (Na Stacai).
Tor Mor	Atlantic	Blacksod Point	aka Black Rock
Turduvillaun	Atlantic	Mullet Peninsula	One of the Duvillaun Islands.

MEATH

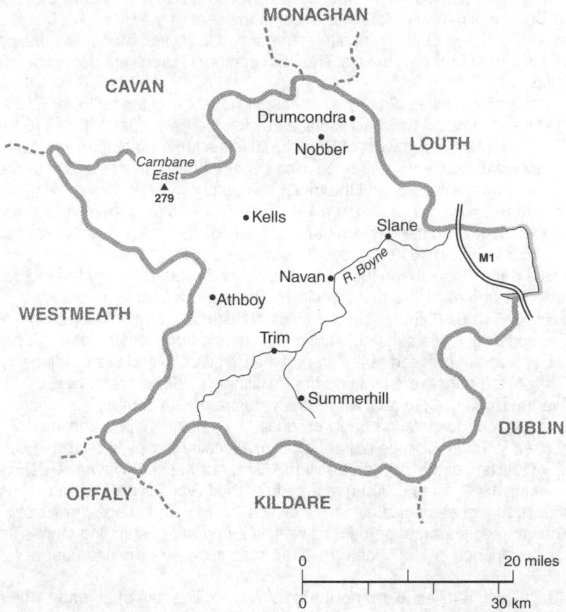
MONAGHAN
CAVAN
Drumcondra
Nobber
LOUTH
Carnbane East
279
Kells
Slane
M1
Navan
R. Boyne
Athboy
WESTMEATH
Trim
Summerhill
DUBLIN
OFFALY
KILDARE
0
20 miles
0
30 km

Meath is part of the province of Leinster and is often called 'the Royal County'. It lies in the east of the Republic of Ireland and is bordered by Louth to the northeast, Monaghan at its most northern tip, Cavan to the northwest, Westmeath to the west, Offaly to the southwest, Kildare to the south and Dublin to the east, with a short stretch of coast on the Irish Sea between Louth and Dublin. The county town is Navan and the other major towns are Kells and Trim.

The area is dotted with Neolithic monuments which are among the most significant in Ireland, if not in Europe. This is particularly true of the passage graves of Dowth, Knowth and Newgrange in the Brú Na Bóinne ('Quarters of the Boyne') UNESCO World Heritage Site. County Meath was probably at its height in terms of influence between the 1st and 12th centuries when the Hill of Tara was the seat of the High King of Ireland and later Trim became the centre of politics and religion in the region.

Meath has a number of candidates for its best-known native; it seems however to have produced a large number of entertainers. The acting Moore brothers were all born in Fordstown Crossroads, while Perrier Award winning comedians Tommy Tiernan and Dylan Moran were both born in Navan. Perhaps the best-known historical figure is Oliver Plunkett, the last Catholic martyr to die in England; it is possible that Arthur Wellesley, 1st Duke of Wellington, was born at his family seat, Dangan Castle, near Trim, although his birthplace is more likely to have been his family's Dublin residence during the social season, Mornington House.

Meath	**Population**			**Area**	
Districts	*male*	*female*	*total*	*sq miles*	*sq km*
Ardee	1493	1427	2920	47	123
Ceannanus Mór (Kells) Town	1227	1295	2522	0	1
Dunshaughlin	17,822	17,416	35,238	167	432
Kells rural area	6466	6017	12,483	161	417
Meath	9616	9423	19,039	86	223
Navan rural area	15,095	14,863	29,958	147	381
Navan Town	1668	1738	3406	1	2
Oldcastle	2006	1811	3817	71	183
Trim rural area	11,611	11,564	23,175	221	572
Trim Town	729	718	1447	0	1
Total	67,733	66,272	134,005	901	2335

Local Attractions and Information

Administrative headquarters	County Hall, Navan. Tel: 046 902 1581.
Ardbraccan Church	Ardbraccan, 2 miles (3km) west of Navan. The site of a 7th century Christian settlement founded by St Breacain, and which later became the seat of the Bishop of Meath. In the 18th century a new church was built on the site of the previous church which was dedicated to St Ultan; the tower of this earlier church survives. The 18th century church was deconsecrated in 1981. Tel: 041 988 0305.
Ashbourne Memorial	Ashbourne, 15 miles (24km) southeast of Navan. Erected by Peter Grant to commemorate a major engagement which took place outside the town during the 1916 Easter Rising.
Athcarne Castle	$2^1/_2$ miles (4km) southwest of Duleek, 10 miles (16km) southeast of Navan. A 16th century four-storey tower house with a ruined 19th century house attached. The former home of the Bathe family, it was occupied until the mid 20th century.
Athlumney Castle	Athlumney, Navan. The ruin of a 15th century four-storey tower house with attached three-storey house, located on the eastern bank of the River Boyne. It was destroyed by the owners, the Maguire family, in 1649 to prevent its use by Oliver Cromwell.
Battles	Three battles have been fought in Meath: the Boyne, probably the most significant battle in Irish history, Dungan's Hill and Julianstown. See separate table for details.
Bective Abbey	Bective, 5 miles (8km) south of Navan. A Cistercian abbey founded in 1147 and dedicated to the Blessed Virgin. The substantial ruin, including a large tower, dates mainly to the 15th century. The abbey was suppressed at the time of the Dissolution and the buildings were put to secular uses. Parts of the ruins were used during the filming of *Braveheart* (1995).
Book of Kells	Aka the Book of Columba. An ornately illustrated 9th century manuscript depicting the stories from the four gospels, probably produced by monks on Iona and later sent to Kells Abbey. It is now housed in Trinity College Library, Dublin; a facsimile copy is on display at Kells Heritage Centre.
Brú na Bóinne	(I. = Quarters of the Boyne). 9 miles (15km) northeast of Navan. A UNESCO World Heritage Site covering 1927 acres (780ha) at a bend of the River Boyne and consisting of a collection of important archaeological sites. It includes the major passage graves of Newgrange, Dowth and Knowth (see separate entries) as well as a number of standing stones and henges. The visitor centre, opened in 1997, features a full-scale replica of the chamber at Newgrange. Tel: 041 988 0300.
Cruicetown Church	Cruicetown, 4 miles (6km) northeast of Navan. The ruin of an early 13th century church with a 17th century high cross.
Donaghmore Round Tower	Donaghmore, 1 mile (1.6km) northeast of Navan. An 85ft (26m) high round tower on the site of an early Christian monastery said to have been founded by St Patrick. The tower was partially restored in the 19th century.
Donore Castle	Donore, 11 miles (18km) northeast of Navan. A three-storey tower house probably built in the 1430s after Henry VI gave a grant of £10 to anyone building a castle of the required dimensions. It was captured by a Cromwellian force in 1650 and the occupants are said to have been butchered.
Dowth Passage Grave	A passage grave within the Brú na Bóinne UNESCO World Heritage Site. A passage grave, as the name might suggest, is where the burial chamber is reached by means of a passage into the tomb. It is believed to be the oldest of the Neolithic tombs in Brú na Bóinne. The mound is surrounded by a kerb of 115 stones and has two tombs facing westwards. The Dowth passage grave is not open to the public.
Dunmoe Castle	3 miles (5km) northeast of Navan. The ruin of a four-storey tower house built beside the River Boyne, probably in the 15th century. It was the home of the D'Arcy family and is believed to have been abandoned after a fire at the end of the 18th century.
Fourknocks	$2^1/_2$ miles (4km) southeast of Ardcath, 15 miles (24km) southeast of Navan. An excavated and preserved passage grave dating to c.1800 BC and featuring notable rock carvings. A concrete roof was erected over it in 1952.
Grove Gardens	Fordstown, 4 miles (6km) south of Kells. A 4 acre (1.6ha) garden featuring a clematis walk and an extensive rose garden.
Hamwood House and Gardens	$^1/_2$ mile (0.8km) southwest of Dunboyne, 19 miles (31km) south of Navan. A Palladian style house built in 1768. The gardens, originally created in the early 1800s, feature a rock garden, herb garden and rose garden. In spring a bluebell wood can be reached down the pine walk. Tel: 018 255210.
Highest point	Carnbane East at 915ft (279m).
Hill of Skreen	7 miles (11km) southeast of Navan. A hill opposite the Hill of Tara across the Gabhra valley. The site of an early Christian monastery said to have held at one time the shrine and relics of St Columba (Columcille), the hill is topped by the ruin of a 14th century nave and chancel church which was abandoned by the Elizabethan period.
Hill of Slane	$^1/_4$ mile (0.4km) north of Slane, 8 miles (13km) northeast of Navan. A hill standing at 519ft (158m), on which in AD 433 St Patrick is said to have lit the Pascal Fire, which symbolised the triumph of Christianity over paganism. The hill now has the ruin of a 16th century Franciscan friary with St Patrick's church, tower and 'college'.
Hill of Tara	6 miles (10km) southeast of Navan. A low ridge 522ft (159m) above sea level which had enormous political and religious significance in the early history of Ireland. From the Neolithic period onwards monuments and earthworks were constructed on the hill, including a passage grave (the Mound of Hostages), a hill fort (Rath na Rioch) and two interlinked ringworks (raths) known as Cormac's House and the Royal Seat. To the south is an enclosure known as Rath Laoghaire and to the north is the Rath of the Synods. Tara was a place of ritual significance and

the place where the High King of Ireland was enthroned (but did not live). A standing stone known as Lia Fáil (Stone of Destiny) may have had a part to play in a coronation ceremony. The Hill of Tara was eventually abandoned in the early 11th century. Tel: 046 902 5903.

Hill of Ward — 1/2 mile (0.8km) east of Athboy, 8 miles (13km) southwest of Navan. An Iron Age hill fort which was once the meeting place for the Celtic festival of Samhain.

Interesting facts — **Pierce Brosnan** was born in St Mary's Hospital, Drogheda, in 1953. Although I have listed his birth in Co. Louth, technically he was born in Co. Meath as the hospital is just within the county boundary. His parents actually lived in Navan, which is where Pierce grew up. **Laytown** holds Europe's only horse race meeting on a beach. The annual meeting plays host to top-class thoroughbreds and the golden sands make for spectacular viewing. Bective-born **John Watson** formulated the official rules of the game of polo in India in the 1870s; his grandfather, also named John Watson, was the man who killed the last wolf in Ireland (see Carlow – Interesting facts).

Kells Heritage Centre — Headfort Place, Kells. Housed in the restored former courthouse, the centre celebrates and interprets the art and culture of monastic Ireland, highlighting the local monastic site and the famous Book of Kells, a facsimile copy of which is on display. Tel: 046 924 7840.

Kells Monastic Site — Cannon Street, Kells. The site of a monastery believed to have been originally founded in the 6th century by St Columba and re-founded in the 9th century by monks from Iona fleeing Viking raids. An Augustinian abbey was established in the 12th century. The site includes an early church, five high crosses and a round tower.

Knowth Passage Tomb — A passage tomb complex located to the west of Newgrange within the Brú na Bóinne UNESCO World Heritage Site. It consists of a large mound covering two passage tombs placed back to back and surrounded by more than 120 kerbstones. Many of these stones, as well as those used in constructing the tomb, are decorated with motifs including circles and spirals. Eighteen smaller tombs surround the large tomb. There is no access to the interior.

Lloyds Tower — 2 miles (3km) west of Kells. A lighthouse-shaped folly 100ft (30.5m) tall which stands in the People's Park near Kells. It was built by the son of the Earl of Bective in his father's memory.

Loughcrew Cairns — 2 miles (3km) southeast of Oldcastle, 9 miles (15km) west of Kells. Aka Slieve na Calliagh (Hills of the Witch). A group of 30 Neolithic passage tombs distributed over three hillsides.

Loughcrew Church — 2 1/2 miles (4km) southeast of Oldcastle, 10 miles (16km) west of Kells. The family church of the Plunketts, located on the Loughcrew Estate. Their four-storey tower house forms the oldest part of the church.

Loughrew House — 2 1/2 miles (4km) southeast of Oldcastle, 10 miles (16km) west of Kells. Originally built in the 17th century by the Napier family and later destroyed by fire. St Oliver Plunkett (1629–81) was born here. The house was replaced by a neoclassical mansion designed by Charles Cockerell and built in 1821, which was itself destroyed by fire in 1964. The surrounding gardens retaining both 17th and 19th century features, and include water gardens, a herb garden, grotto and herbaceous borders.

Moynagh Lough — 1/2 mile (0.8km) southwest of Nobber. A small lough on which is a crannog in use until the early Christian era but with evidence of occupation dating back to the Neolithic period.

Nanny Bridge — A bridge across the River Nanny in Duleek where the final action of the Battle of the Boyne was fought.

Navan — (I. *An Uaimh* = The Cave). The county town and the largest in the county. It stands at the meeting of the Boyne and Blackwater rivers.

Newgrange Passage Tomb — Probably the best known and most spectacular monument within the Brú na Bóinne UNESCO World Heritage Site. It dates to 3200 BC and consists of a mound 280ft (85m) in diameter and 37ft (11.5m) high. Inside the mound an 80ft (24m) long passage leads to the burial chamber, which has a corbelled roof with many decorated stones. The mound is surrounded by nearly 100 kerbstones, some of which are decorated. The entrance has been reconstructed using stones found during excavation. At dawn on the winter solstice a shaft of sunlight enters the burial chamber through an opening over the doorway.

Rathmore Church — Rathmore, 7 miles (11km) west of Navan. The ruin of an early 15th century nave and chancel church probably built by Sir Thomas Plunkett and dedicated to St Lawrence. There are the remains of two towers, one a belfry and the other possibly a residence. A stone with a maze carved into it was found in the church.

Rivers — The **Boyne** rises at Trinity Well in Co. Kildare and runs for 70 miles (112km) through Co. Meath to reach the Irish Sea at Drogheda, Co. Louth.

Robertstown Castle — 3 miles (5km) southwest of Nobber, 11 miles (18km) northwest of Navan. The ruin of a 17th century three-storey tower house.

St John's Friary — Newtown, Trim. The substantial ruin of a friary and hospital of St John the Baptist, established by the crusader order of Crutched Friars in the 13th century.

St Patrick's Cathedral — Lornan Street, Trim. A late 19th century church with a 15th century church tower attached to it. Raised to cathedral status in 1955, it was reroofed in 1992. Tel: 046 943 6698.

St Peter and Paul Cathedral — Newtown, Trim. The substantial ruin of a cathedral founded in the early 13th century by Simon de Rochfort. It is reputed to have been the largest Gothic church in Ireland at that time.

Slane Castle — Slane, 7 miles (11km) northeast of Navan. The seat of the Mountcharles family since 1701. The castle stands beside the River Boyle and was remodelled in the late 18th century by renowned architects James Gandon, James Wyatt and Francis Johnston. The parkland was landscaped by Capability Brown. U2 recorded their album *The Unforgettable Fire* here in 1984. Severely damaged by fire in 1991, the castle reopened in 2001 after an extensive restoration programme, and is now best known for staging regular summer rock concerts by such acts as U2, REM, Oasis, Bruce Springsteen, David Bowie, Bob Dylan, Robbie Williams and the Rolling Stones. Tel: 041 982 4163.

Sonairte – The National Ecology Centre — Laytown, 18 miles (29km) east of Navan. The centre has a 2 acre (0.8ha) organic garden plus exhibitions on wind, rain and solar power, and a number of ecologically constructed buildings. Tel: 041 27572.

Sport

Gaelic football — **Meath** are winners of the All-Ireland Senior Football Championship in 1949, 1954, 1967, 1987, 1988, 1996 and 1999.

horse racing — **Fairyhouse** Racecourse, Ratoath, is a major venue for National Hunt races including the Irish Grand National, which is run every Easter Monday. The first meeting was held in 1848 and the first Irish Grand National was run in 1870 (winner Sir Robert Peel). Subsequent winners include such greats of steeplechasing as Arkle, Flying Bolt and Desert Orchid. Perhaps the most extraordinary winner was in 1929 when Alike came home, ridden by Frank Wise who was missing three fingers and who rode with a wooden leg. The right-handed course 1 mile 6.5 furlongs (2.9km) round has a run-in of 3 furlongs (0.6km) and a slight uphill finish. Tel: 018 256167.

Navan Racecourse, Proudstown, Navan, opened in 1920 and holds primarily National Hunt racing. A left-handed oval of $1\frac{1}{2}$ miles (2.5km), it has a run-in of $3\frac{1}{2}$ furlongs (0.7km) and an uphill finish. Navan also has an 18-hole golf course, nine holes of which are alongside the track and nine within it. Tel: 046 902 1350.

Talbot Castle — Abbey Lane, Trim. Built in 1415 and thought to have incorporated elements of the Augustinian Abbey of St Mary. During the 18th century it was used as a school and Arthur Wellesley, the future Duke of Wellington, was a pupil.

Tara Brooch — An example of early Christian Irish art discovered on the seashore at Laytown in 1850. It is believed to date to the late 7th or early 8th century and has intricate Celtic knotwork decoration, but has no known connection with the Hill of Tara. The brooch is on display at the National Museum of Ireland in Dublin.

Tara Mines — Knockumber, 1 mile (1.6km) west of Navan. Europe's largest lead and zinc mine, currently producing 2.6 million tonnes of ore annually. It was formerly called Tara Mines/Outokumpu Zinc. The ore was first discovered in 1970.

Tremblestown Castle — 3 miles (5km) west of Trim. The ruin of a three-storey tower house which had a mansion attached to it during the 18th century. It was abandoned in the early 19th century and was allowed to fall into disrepair.

Trim Castle — Castle Street, Trim. The largest Anglo-Norman castle in Ireland, built by Hugh de Lacy and his son Walter between 1176 and the 1210s on the site of an earlier wooden fortification. Its most distinctive feature is the massive cruciform keep; its curtain walls, with five D-shaped towers and two gatehouses, enclosed 3 acres. King John visited the castle in 1210 and it was besieged by William Marshal for seven weeks in 1224. It was damaged by Cromwell's troops in 1649 during the Confederate War. Having been used as a location for the film *Braveheart* (1995), the castle reopened to the public in 2000 after an extensive excavation and restoration programme. Tel: 046 943 8619.

Trim Visitor Centre — Castle Street, Trim. An exhibition celebrating the early history of Trim, when the castle, cathedral and abbeys dominated the town. Tel: 046 943 6633.

Yellow Steeple — Navan Gate, Trim. The ruin of a tall tower attached to the Augustinian priory of St Mary and rebuilt after a fire in 1368. It is so named because the stonework takes on a yellow hue at sunset.

Some famous people born in County Meath

Ball nee Birmingham, Margaret (religious martyr) (1515–84)	Skreen
Beaufort, Francis (inventor of the wind scale) (1774–1857)	Navan
Brosnan, Pierce (actor) (1953–)	Navan
Bruton, John (Taoiseach of Ireland) (1947–)	Dunboyne
Carolan, Turlough (harpist) (1670–1738)	Nobber
Connell, Jim (writer of 'The Red Flag') (1852–1929)	Kells
Geraghty, Barry (jockey) (1979–)	Meath
Keenan, Paddy (musician) (1950–)	Trim
Ledwidge, Francis (poet) (1887–1917)	Slane
Moore, Matthew (actor) (1888–1960)	Fordstown Crossroads
Moore, Owen (actor) (1886–1939)	Fordstown Crossroads
Moore, Thomas J (actor) (1883–1955)	Fordstown Crossroads
Moran, Dylan (comedian) (1971–)	Navan
Plunkett, Oliver (Primate of All Ireland) (1629–81)	Loughcrew
Watson, John (drafted the rules of polo) (1856–1908)	Bective

MONAGHAN

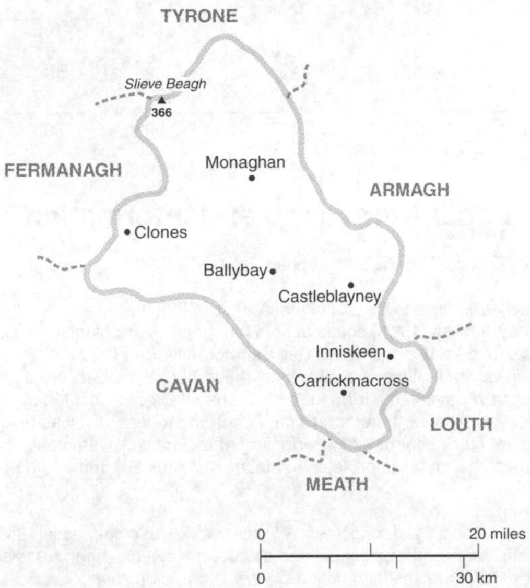
TYRONE
Slieve Beagh
366
FERMANAGH
Monaghan
ARMAGH
Clones
Ballybay
Castleblayney
Inniskeen
Carrickmacross
CAVAN
LOUTH
MEATH
0
20 miles
0
30 km

Monaghan is part of the province of Ulster, one of the three counties within the province which are not part of Northern Ireland. It is bordered by Cavan to the southwest, Louth to the southeast, Fermanagh to the northwest, Tyrone to the north and Armagh to the east. The southernmost tip of Monaghan touches the northernmost tip of Meath. The county town is Monaghan.

Monaghan was part of the ancient kingdom of Airgíalla (Oriel) and was known as the MacMahon country because of the dominance of that powerful clan from the 13th to the 16th century. However, in 1589 it was divided between the MacMahons, other local chieftains and the English Crown. This 'native' plantation was not overturned by the Plantation of Ulster in the early 17th century. The county was severely affected by the Great Famine because it was particularly dependent on the potato. The opening of famine workhouses did little to alleviate the destitution. Lacemaking was introduced at Clones and Carrickmacross as a famine relief scheme, and Monaghan was proclaimed to be 'The Lace County of Ireland'. At the time of the partition of Ireland the county, although part of the province of Ulster, was included in the Irish Free State.

Geographically the area shows a great deal of evidence of glaciation; there are a large number of drumlins which produce the tell-tale 'basket of eggs' landscape. The county's name is from Irish *Muine Cheain*, meaning the 'Land of the Small Hills'. There are several mountains in the county: Mullyash Mountain, Slieve Beagh (on the border with Tyrone and Fermanagh in Northern Ireland) and Coolberrin Hill. There are also a large number of lakes. Rivers in Monaghan include the Fane (in the southeast of the county and along the border with Louth), Glyde (along the Louth and Meath borders), Blackwater (along the border with Tyrone, Northern Ireland) and Dromor (along the border of Cavan, linking Cootehill to Ballybay). The county also has a number of forests, including Rossmore Forest and Dartry Forest.

Monaghan	Population			Area	
Districts	*male*	*female*	*total*	*sq miles*	*sq km*
Carrickmacross rural area	5263	4947	10,210	102	264
Carrickmacross Town	980	984	1964	1	1
Castleblayney rural area	4808	4543	9351	101	261
Castleblayney Town	811	901	1712	1	2
Clones rural area	2782	2653	5435	100	259
Clones Town	842	879	1721	1	2
Monaghan rural area	8590	7893	16,483	192	501
Monaghan Town	2730	2987	5717	2	6
Total	26,806	25,787	52,593	500	1296

Local Attractions and Information

Administrative headquarters	County Offices, The Glen, Monaghan. Tel: 047 30500.
Battles	See separate table for details of the Battle of Clontibret
Billy Fox Memorial Park	Ballybay, 8 miles (13km) southeast of Monaghan. A woodland park established in 1976 and dedicated to assassinated Irish Dáil Senator Billy Fox (1939–74).
Black Pig's Dyke	A massive discontinuous earthwork running from the Down/Armagh border through Monaghan, Cavan and Fermanagh to Donegal Bay. In Co. Monaghan it is known as either the Black Pig's Dyke or the Worm Ditch. According to legend it was ploughed up by the tusks of a giant black boar or by the wriggling of a giant worm. In reality it was built 300 BC–AD 300 to protect the routes into Ulster. In places it stands 20ft (6m) high and 30ft (9m) thick at the base.
Blayney Castle	See Hope Castle
Carrickmacross Famine Workhouse	Shercock Road, Carrickmacross. A former workhouse opened in 1843 with the onset of the Great Famine. Later used as a school and a warehouse, it has been restored and now houses the Farney Resource and Information Centre, a one-stop shop for various local community groups. Tel: 042 966 4540.
Carrickmacross Lace Gallery	Market Square, Carrickmacross. The Carrickmacross lace industry was established in the 1820s and is now carried on by the Carrickmacross Lace Co-operative. The hand-stitched lace was used by the Emmanuels on the late Princess Diana's wedding dress. Tel: 042 966 2506.
Castle Leslie	Glaslough, 5$^1/_2$ miles (9km) northeast of Monaghan. Built by John Leslie MP in the 1870s, incorporating part of an earlier house. It is now run as a luxury hotel. The 400 acre (160ha) estate also has several gate lodges built at various times during the 19th century, including one designed by John Nash. Tel: 047 88109.
Clones High Cross	The Diamond, Clones. A 9th/10th century cross standing in Clones marketplace. It appears to consist of fragments of two different crosses placed together. The cross is decorated on one side with Old Testament scenes including the Fall of Man, the Sacrifice of Isaac and Daniel in the Lions' Den, and on the other side with scenes from the life of Christ.
Clones Lace Guild	Fermanagh Street, Clones. Clones was once the centre of a world-renowned crochet lacemaking industry with 1500 local lacemakers. In the 1850s the women of Clones introduced their own way of producing lace using a crochet hook rather than by more traditional methods, thus enabling them to produce pieces ten times faster – an important consideration when trying to generate income at the time of the Great Famine. The Clones Lace Guild was formed in 1989 to revive the craft, which had begun to disappear since the 1940s. A 'Celebrating Lace' festival was held in 1995 to commemorate the 150th anniversary of the introduction of lacemaking at Clones and Carrickmacross. Tel: 047 51718.
Clones Round Tower	Abbey Street, Clones. A round tower (probably 12th century) standing 75ft (23m) high on the site of a monastery founded by St Tighernach in the 6th century; there is a shrine nearby in the shape of a house.
Donagh Graveyard	$^1/_2$ mile (0.8km) southwest of Glaslough, 5 miles (8km) northeast of Monaghan. The ruin of an early Christian church and a high cross.
Donaghmoyne Manann Castle	2 miles (3km) northeast of Carrickmacross. A tree-covered motte with a causeway and bailey possibly dating to the 12th century, next to the scant remains of a 15th century stone castle.
Highest point	Slieve Beagh at 1200ft (366m), located on the county's northwestern boundary, on the Irish border with Tyrone and Fermanagh.
Hilton Park Garden	3 miles (5km) south of Clones. Hilton Park house was built 1803–18 by the Madden family after their earlier house had been accidentally burned down, and was remodelled in Italian 'palazzo' style in the 1870s to a design by William Hague. The grounds cover 500 acres (200ha) and were first laid out during the early 18th century. The oak wood was planted in 1752, while many specimen trees were introduced to the park by John Madden from the 1860s onward. The house now offers luxury accommodation. Tel: 047 56007.
Hope Castle	$^1/_2$ mile (0.8km) east of Castleblayney. Aka Blayney Castle (from which the nearby Plantation town of Castleblayney gets its name). A Georgian house with 19th century embellishments, located on the shore of Lough Muckno. Sold in 1853 by last Lord Blayney to the Hope family (after whom the Hope Diamond is named – see Surrey – Interesting facts), it later became a convent, after which it

	remained empty for many years. It has now been restored as a hotel. Lough Muckno Leisure Park has been created from part of the Blayney estate.
Iniskeen Round Tower	Iniskeen, 10 miles (16km) southeast of Castleblayney. A 42ft (13m) high round tower on the site of a monastery founded by St Daig in the 6th century. The doorway stands 14ft (4.2m) above ground level.
Interesting facts	**Monaghan** is the birthplace of poet and writer Patrick Kavanagh, who based much of his work in the county. Kavanagh is one of the most significant figures in mid 20th century Irish poetry. The poems 'Stony Grey Soil' and 'Shancoduff' refer to the county. **Castle Leslie** played host to the ill-fated marriage of Sir Paul McCartney to model Heather Mills in 2002. Sir Paul's mother, Mary Mohan, was a native of Tully-Namalroe, near Castleblayney.
Loughs	Loughs in Co. Monaghan include Lough Avaghon, Drumlona Lough, Lough Egish, Lough Emy, Lough Fea, Inner Lough (in Dartry Forest), Lough Major, Lough Muckno and White Lough.
Market House	Market Street, Monaghan. Built in 1792 to a design by Colonel Samuel Hayes and 'Dedicated to the convenience of the inhabitants of Monaghan' by Lieutenant-General Robert Cunningham. It was refurbished as an arts venue and opened in November 2003. Tel: 047 38162.
Monaghan	Monaghan town centre is made up of four interconnecting squares: Market Square (or Street), Church Square, The Diamond and Old Cross Square. The oldest remaining architectural feature in the town is the 17th century Old Cross (which may in fact have been a sundial); originally located in the Diamond, it was moved to its present location in Old Cross Square in 1876 to allow for the construction of the Rossmore Memorial. The most outstanding building is St Macartan's Cathedral.
Monaghan County Museum	Hill Street, Monaghan. Local history museum charting the story of the county from earliest times to the present day. Artefacts include the 14th century Cross of Clogher, as well as uniforms and extensive prehistoric and medieval collections. Tel: 047 82928.
Monaghan Veteran and Vintage Club	Ballinode, 3 miles (5km) northwest of Monaghan. The club's museum illustrates the changes experienced in rural life through increased mechanisation. Exhibits include steam engines and tractors. Tel: 047 57249.
Monaghan Way	A long-distance walking route around Monaghan which takes in most of the county's landscape and heritage. It extends for 40 miles (64km) from Inniskeen to Monaghan Town and there are plans to extend the route.
Patrick Kavanagh Centre	1 mile (1.6km) south of Inniskeen, 11 miles (18km) southeast of Castleblayney. A literary resource centre and folk museum dedicated to poet Patrick Kavanagh, who was born and buried in Inniskeen. The centre has exhibitions on Kavanagh and local history. Displays include 12 specially commissioned paintings illustrating Kavanagh's poem 'The Great Hunger'. The area around Inniskeen is known as Kavanagh Country. Tel: 042 937 8560.
Patrick Kavanagh Silhouette	$^{1}/_{2}$ mile (0.8km) southeast of Carrickmacross. A statue of Patrick Kavanagh sitting on a bench overlooking the Brothers Lake (Lisanisk Lake).
Richard Dawson Monument	1 mile (1.6km) north of Cootehill, 8 mile (13km) southeast of Clones. An obelisk style monument erected by local electors in honour of 18th century MP Richard Dawson, who was returned to five successive Parliaments. He died in 1807.
Rossmore Forest Park	2 miles (3km) south of Monaghan. A park created from part of the former Rossmore Estate. It includes the remains of Rossmore Castle, dating to the early 19th century, and two megalithic tombs.
St Finbarr's Church	Market Street, Carrickmacross. A Church of Ireland church built in the 1770s to replace an earlier church built in 1682.
St Joseph's Church	O'Neill Street, Carrickmacross. A Gothic style church designed by J J McCarthy and completed in 1866. The tower and spire, one of the tallest in Ireland, were built by McCarthy's son C J. It has ten stained glass windows by artist Harry Clarke and complementing Stations of the Cross by Richard King. Tel: 042 966 3200.
St Louis Convent	Castle Street, Carrickmacross. The convent in Carrickmacross stands on the site of a castle built by the Earl of Essex in 1630, when the town was founded. The castle was demolished at the time of the Williamite Wars.
St Louis Convent Heritage Centre	Broad Road, Monaghan. A heritage centre telling the story of the Congregation of the Sisters of St Louis from their foundation in Juilly, France, in 1842. Named for the saintly Louis IX of France, the order's original aim was to educate the children of French nobility. However this evolved into the education of poor children in Europe, South America and Africa. The order came to Monaghan in 1859 and the St Louis Secondary School was founded in 1888. Exhibits include artefacts and memorabilia related to the order's worldwide mission as well as examples of local crafts such as Carrickmacross lace, Clones crochet and Belleek china. Tel: 047 83529.
St Macartan's Cathedral	Dublin Road, Monaghan. Located on a hill overlooking Monaghan and constructed 1861–91 to a Gothic design by J J McCarthy, the 'Irish Pugin'. After McCarthy's death in 1882 the cathedral was completed by William Hague. The spire stands 280ft (85m) high and is a local landmark. Originally the nave was intended to be two bays longer but lack of funds meant that the design was cut back. The interior is dominated by its wooden hammerbeam roof and wonderful rose window; the exterior is decorated with statuary of local saints and bishops carved in Italy of Carrara marble set in stone arcaded niches at the end of the transepts. Over the main doorways are carved panels depicting scenes from the New Testament.
St Macartan's College	A post-primary school for boys located on a hill overlooking Monaghan. It was built 1840–8 to a classical design by Thomas Duff. Tel: 047 81642.
Sport	
football	**Monaghan United** were founded in 1979 and elected to the League of Ireland in 1985. Their home ground is Kingspan Century Park, Monaghan.

Tyrone Guthrie Centre	2 miles (3km) south of Newbliss, 10 miles (16km) southwest of Monaghan. A residential arts centre beside Annaghmakerrig Lough established at the bequest of actor Sir William Tyrone Guthrie (1900–71), whose will stated that 'my said dwelling-house, furniture, pictures and chattels and the income of my residuary estate to be used for the purpose of providing a retreat for artists and other like persons … so as to enable them to do or facilitate them in doing creative work.'
Ulster Canal Stores	Cara Street, Clones. A restored 18th century stone canal warehouse with exhibits of Clones Lace. Tel: 047 52125.

Some famous people born in County Monaghan

Duffy, Sir Charles (member of Young Ireland) (1816–1903)	Monaghan
Gregg, John (inventor of Gregg shorthand) (1867–1948)	Rockcorry
Kavanagh, Patrick (poet) (1904–67)	Inishkeen
McGuigan, Barry (featherweight boxer) (1961–)	Clones
McCabe, Patrick (author) (1955–)	Clones
O'Hanlon, Ardal (comedian and actor) (1965–)	Carrickmacross

Offaly

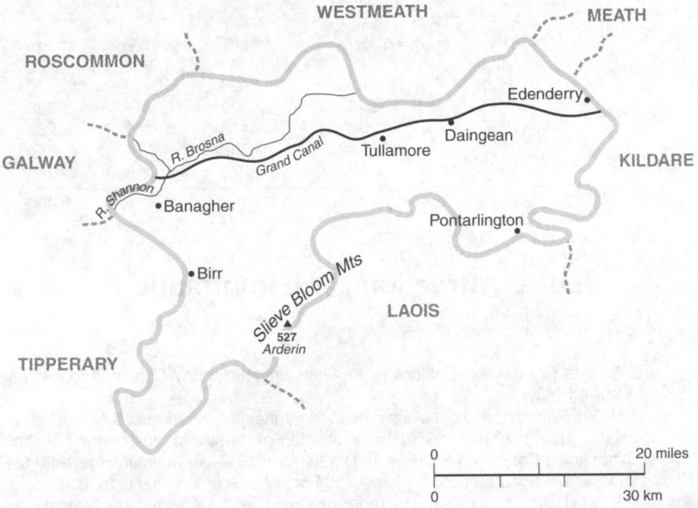
WESTMEATH
MEATH
ROSCOMMON
Edenderry
R. Brosna
Daingean
Tullamore
Grand Canal
GALWAY
KILDARE
R. Shannon
Banagher
Pontarlington
Birr
Slieve Bloom Mts
LAOIS
527
Arderin
TIPPERARY
0
20 miles
0
30 km

Offaly is part of the province of Leinster. It became a county in 1556 and was originally named King's County, after Philip II of Spain. The county town was Daingean until the 19th century but is now Tullamore. It is bordered by Galway to the west, Roscommon to the northwest, Westmeath to the north, Meath to the northeast, Kildare to the east, Laois to the southeast and Tipperary to the south. The main geographical features are the rivers Shannon and Brosna and the Slieve Bloom Mountains. Much of the land in the county is peat bog. The county's economy is mainly based on agriculture (including peat workings), plus a burgeoning tourist industry built around the river cruises and watersports available on the Shannon.

The discovery of a Mesolithic settlement (7000–6500 BC) in the Lough Boora Parklands in the late 1970s proved that Offaly was one of the earliest areas of Ireland to be settled. Evidence for settlement during the Neolithic is scant, with few megalithic tombs identified. The Offaly bogs have given up several 'hoards' (collections of various items of value/coins which have been hidden, sacrificed or lost) including the Dowris Hoard of 26 bronze trumpets/horns, axes, a bronze bucket, bronze cauldron and numerous other artefacts which attest to a thriving Bronze Age society. This was confirmed by the discovery of the site of a late Bronze Age palisaded enclosure containing circular houses at Clonfinlough. An Iron Age 'La Tene' style gold torc (arm or neck bangle) dating to c.100 BC–AD 300 was dug out at Clonmacnoise. This is likely to be an import from Gaul and may have been a votive offering. Evidence of wooden trackways (toghers) has also been found in Offaly.

In the early medieval period the area was on the frontier between the Uí Néill in the north and the Eóganacht in the south and was a crossroads for the provinces of Meath, Leinster, Munster and Connacht. The important ridgeway of the Esker Riada also passed through the region and this combination of circumstances drew the founders of churches and monasteries to settle. Major monastic foundations existed at Birr, Clonmacnoise, Durrow, Gallen, Kinnitty, Lemanaghan and Rahan. The period also saw the production of some of the 'treasures' of Offaly, such as the Book of MacRegol and the shrine of St Manchan. Settlements grew up around these monasteries which themselves developed from wooden structures to stone buildings in the Romanesque style.

The arrival of the Normans in the 12th and 13th century had a temporary impact on Offaly but the Irish kings regained control of their areas from the late 13th century onwards and Norman castles and settlements were largely abandoned. The Plantation of the late 16th and early 17th century saw the building of tower houses and bawns. Industry began with the establishment of glass-making factories by Huguenot settlers. The Agricultural Revolution saw an improvement to some land quality, and rural industries such as milling and brewing began to grow. A major project was the construction of the Grand Canal from Dublin to Shannon Harbour in the late 18th and early 19th centuries, which also saw the growth of the inland ports of Edenderry, Daingean and Tullamore. However, the county's main contribution to the Irish economy was the supply of peat from the extensive bogs. This included supplying peat-fired power stations at Portarlington, Boora and Rhode.

Offaly	**Population**			**Area**	
Districts	*male*	*female*	*total*	*sq miles*	*sq km*
Birr rural area	7866	7579	15,445	280	727
Birr Town	1729	1861	3590	2	6
Edenderry	5176	4944	10,120	127	328
Roscrea	2432	2038	4470	103	267
Tullamore rural area	10,074	9694	19,768	253	654
Tullamore Town	4908	5362	10,270	3	8
Total	32,185	31,478	63,663	768	1990

Local Attractions and Information

Administrative headquarters — Courthouse, Tullamore. Tel: 050 646800.

Ballycowan Castle — 2½ miles (4km) west of Tullamore. The ruin of a four-storey 17th century tower house built by the Herbert family.

Banagher Forts — ¼ mile (0.4km) northwest of Banagher. Banagher is located near a strategically vital crossing point of the River Shannon. The forts include **Fort Falkland**, built by the English c.1624; **Cromwell's Castle**, built c.1654 and modified in 1817; a rare inland **Martello tower** built c.1811; and the five-sided gun battery known as **Fort Eliza**, constructed c.1812.

Birr Castle Demesne — ¾ mile (1.2km) east of Birr. The renowned Birr Castle Demesne, the largest in Ireland, surrounds the Parsons family castle (not open to the public). The Normans established a castle on the site c.1170, although the present building dates to the 1620s and was refurbished in Gothic style in the 1800s. The grounds were first landscaped in the 17th century. The formal gardens were first laid out with box hedges in the early 1700s; still in existence, these are now reputedly the tallest box hedges in the world. A lake was created in the 18th century by the diversion of the River Camcor, while a fountain, waterfall, and winter garden and fernery were added in the 19th century and an arboretum and river garden in the 20th century. The arboretum and woodland has over 1000 different species of trees and shrubs. The grounds also include the Turbine House, powered by the waterfall and which supplied electricity to the castle and town from 1879 to the 1950s, and a wrought-iron suspension bridge built c.1820. Tel: 057 912 0336. See also Birr Great Telescope, Ireland's Historic Science Centre.

Birr Great Telescope — A 72in (180cm) telescope built by the 3rd Earl of Rosse at Birr Castle in the 1840s. It was at that time the largest in the world and remained so for more than 70 years. The Earl had completed the building of a 36in (90cm) telescope in 1839 (the mirror was cast in the castle grounds) and was so encouraged by the results that he began work on the larger telescope (to be nicknamed 'The Leviathan of Parsonstown') almost immediately. The new instrument was first used in February 1845. The mirror weighs 3 tons and the telescope tube is 58ft (17.5m) long. It is mounted between walls 70ft (21m) long and 50ft (15m) high. Using the Great Telescope the 3rd Earl discovered the Whirlpool nebula. After the 4th Earl's death the telescope fell into disrepair and was eventually dismantled; it was restored to full working order 1996–9, together with its mounting. One of the original mirrors is on exhibition in the Science Museum in London. Tel: 057 912 0336.

Birr Theatre and Arts Centre — Oxmantown Mall, Birr. Housed in Oxmantown Hall, built in 1888 to provide a venue for community events and entertainment. It proved a popular home for a variety of activities including dances, concerts and even indoor sport but had fallen into disrepair by the 1980s. With the designation of Birr as a Heritage Town in 1993 the building was purchased by a local group and restored 1999–2000. Tel: 057 912 2911.

Blundell's Castle — ¼ mile (0.4km) south of Edenderry. The ruin of a castle overlooking Edenderry.

Bog of Allen — See Kildare

Cloghan Castle — Cloghan, 5 miles (8km) northeast of Banagher. Located between the rivers Shannon and Little Brosna. Originally an O'Madden stronghold and thought to be one of the oldest inhabitable castles in Ireland, the castle was erected in the early 13th century. Some military importance was attached to it in 1595, when Lord Deputy Sir William Russell captured it, executing its defenders by throwing them over the walls; excavations in front of the castle have uncovered bones and cannon shot. The castle and its lands were granted in the reign of Charles II to Garrett Moore, descended from Rory Oge O'Moore, the chief of ancient Leix (Laois). One of his descendants married Margaret, daughter of the 6th Earl of Clanricarde. Cloghan fell into ruin after it was abandoned in the 17th century; it was bought by the Burke family in the 1970s and has been restored to provide self-catering accommodation. Tel: 057 915 1650.

Clonmacnoise Monastery — Clonmacnoise, 5 miles (8km) north of Banagher. The site of a monastic foundation of St Ciaran beside the River Shannon, probably dating to AD 545, although the present remains date to no earlier than the 10th century. A centre of medieval learning, like many early Christian sites in the British Isles it was subjected to attack from both locals and outsiders seeking to benefit from its religious treasures. It is estimated that it may have suffered as many as 40 such incursions between the 8th and 12th centuries. The site was finally abandoned after the Reformation. The remains include two round towers, three (or four) high crosses, a cathedral and seven (or eight) early churches; the latter have been identified as Temple Finghín, Temple Connor, Temple Kelly, Temple Ciarán, Temple Melaghlin, Temple Dowling and Temple Hurpan. The 'cathedral' was built in the 10th century and extended over the next few hundred years. There is a modern visitor centre to which the high crosses have been removed for protection against the elements; copies stand in their original positions. The whole site is now in state care. Pope John Paul II made a pilgrimage here in 1979.

Clonony Castle	Clonony, 4$^1/_2$ miles (7km) northeast of Banagher. The ruin of a 16th century Norman style castle built by the McCoughlan clan on a rocky outcrop beside the River Brosna. It sits at the southeast corner of a bawn. During the 16th century it was the possession of the Bullen (Boleyn) family. It was inhabited until relatively modern times.
Derrinboy Armlets	A hoard of gold ornaments uncovered in the 1950s by Patrick McGovern while digging peat in Derrinboy Bog near Kilcormac. The items include two broad-ribbed armlets, two tress rings and a necklace made by twisting gold wire on a leather core. The hoard has been dated to 1200–1000 BC. The find is now preserved in the National Museum of Ireland, Dublin.
Doon Castle	Doon, 14 miles (23km) northwest of Tullamore. The ruin of a castle featuring a well-preserved sheela-na-gig.
Dowris Hoard	A Bronze Age hoard of items including swords, spearheads and buckets discovered at Dowris, near Fivealley, in the 1820s by two men digging potatoes. In particular there were 26 bronze trumpets/horns in the collection. Selections from the hoard are on display in the National Museum of Ireland and in the British Museum, London.
Durrow Abbey	4 miles (6km) north of Tullamore. The site of an early Christian foundation established in AD 553 by St Columba (Colmcille), and featuring grave slabs, a 9th century high cross and a holy well. In addition there is a 12th century motte and a late 18th century church believed to have been built on the site of a medieval church. The Book of Durrow, an illuminated gospel book possibly dating to the 7th century, was created on the site.
Esker Riada	A series of ancient glacial ridges extending for 120 miles (190km) across Ireland from Dublin to Galway. Because it was raised above the surrounding land, it has been used for much of its history as a highway. A notable section in Offaly links Durrow Abbey to Clonmacnoise.
Garry Castle	1 mile (1.6km) south of Banagher. The ruin of a 16th century MacCoghlan castle featuring a sheela-na-gig.
Gospels of McRegol	Produced by the monastery founded in Birr by St Brendan and named after the foundation's early 9th century abbot. It is the only surviving relic of the monastery at Birr and is now held in the Bodleian Library, Oxford.
Grand Canal	The Grand Canal extends for 82 miles (131km), connecting Dublin with Shannonbridge in Co. Offaly, and has 43 locks. Construction began in 1756, after which the canal reached Tullamore in 1798 and the Shannon in 1804. Some of the first passengers to arrive at Tullamore by boat in 1798 were soldiers on their way to meet a French force which had landed at Killala Bay. The canal proved to be of particular benefit to brewer Arthur Guinness, who opened his brewery in Dublin in the 1760s. In addition to using its waters in the brewing process the canal was used to ship raw materials to the factory and ship the beer out. The sight of Guinness barges on the Grand Canal was an iconic picture of 19th and early 20th century Ireland. The use of the canal declined with the arrival of the railways in the 1850s and the last cargo boat passed through in 1960. After being allowed to fall into disrepair, the canal has been restored since 1986 as a leisure facility.
Highest point	Arderin in the Slieve Bloom Mountains at 1725ft (527m), also the highest point of Co. Laois.
Interesting facts	**Anthony Trollope**, then a Post Office clerk, wrote his first novel in Offaly while stationed there in 1841. **Birr** was the first town in the world to be lit by electricity.
Ireland's Historic Science Centre	Birr Castle Demesne. Housed in the restored two-storey stable block of Birr Castle, designed by Mary Rosse in the 1850s, the centre celebrates the achievements of Irish scientists in fields such as astronomy, photography, engineering and horticulture, and in particular the Parsons family of Birr Castle. Displays include an illustrated timeline of astronomy, photographs and details of famous Irish scientists, scale models of the Birr Castle telescopes, and displays of engineering equipment. Tel: 057 912 0336.
Kilcormac Pietà	Kilcormac, 12 miles (19km) southwest of Tullamore. A pietà (an image of Mary holding the body of Jesus after he had been taken from the cross) measuring 5ft (1.5m) by 3ft (0.9m) and carved from a single block of oak. Believed to date to the late 16th century, it is – thanks to a remarkable set of circumstances – one of few such sculptures to survive from an era when most religious images were destroyed. It originally stood at Ballyboy but on the approach of Cromwellian troops in 1650 it was removed and is believed to have been buried 6ft (1.8m) deep in a bog to avoid destruction. It was recovered over 60 years later, having been located thanks to the deathbed instructions of the only man still alive who knew where it was buried. It was then set up in the recently rebuilt Kilcormac parish church, where it remains to this day.
Kinnitty Castle	Kinnitty, 8 miles (13km) east of Birr. A rebuilt 17th century castle on the site of a 6th century monastery founded by St Finian and a later Augustinian abbey and Norman castle. The present castle was built by William O'Carroll in 1630; after the Civil War it passed to Thomas Winter and his descendants, the Bernard family. Known at the time as Castle Bernard, it was extended in the early 19th century. The castle was burned down by Republican forces in 1922 and was rebuilt in 1928. It was in state ownership 1951–94, after which it was purchased and turned into a luxury hotel. Tel: 057 913 7318.
Kinnitty Pyramid	Kinnitty, 8 miles (13km) east of Birr. A mausoleum located in the graveyard of St Finian's Church; standing 30ft (9m) high, it was designed as a replica of the pyramid of Cheops in Egypt. Built

	1830–4 by Lt. Col. Richard Wesley Bernard, it holds the remains of five (or six) members of his family, the last interment taking place in 1907.
Leap Castle	6 miles (10km) southeast of Birr. A former stronghold of the O'Carrolls and, after the Plantation, the home of the Darby family until the 1920s. It has the reputation of being the most haunted castle in Ireland (as do one or two others!), mainly revolving around a murder in its 'Bloody Chapel' in 1532. The castle was severely damaged by a fire during the War of Independence and was left a ruin. It is in private ownership and is undergoing restoration. Tel: 057 913 1115.
Lemanaghan	$10^1/_2$ miles (17km) west of Tullamore. The scant remains of the site of a 7th century monastery founded by St Manchan.
Lough Boora Mesolithic Site	9 miles (15km) east of Banagher. The site of a Mesolithic encampment dating to 7000–6500 BC, and therefore one of the earliest known settlements in Ireland. Lough Boora was drained in the 1950s and the site was first uncovered during peat production operations. After it was excavated in the late 1970s, evidence was revealed of cooking hearths, stone tools and animal, bird and fish bones. Although now located in the centre of Ireland, in prehistoric times the settlement would have stood on the shores of a great lake which may have connected with the sea.
Lough Boora Parklands	9 miles (15km) east of Banagher. An 5000 acre (2000ha) area of cutaway bog (an area that has come out of production once all commercial peat has been removed), the restoration of which forms a pilot project for what will eventually be 2070 sq miles (800 sq km) spanning 11 counties and three provinces. In addition to the Mesolithic site, the parklands include a number of wetland areas including Finnamore's Lakes and the Turraun and Cloghan wetlands.
Nature Reserves	**Clara Bog**, $1^1/_4$ miles (2km) southwest of Clara, covers 1137 acres (460ha) and is among the few large raised Midland bogs remaining substantially intact. Established in 1987, it contains a wide variety of vegetation types and habitats and a well-developed drainage (or soak) system. **Mongan Bog**, $^1/_2$ mile (0.8km) east of Clonmacnoise, established in 1987 and covering 294 acres (119ha), is an example of a Midland raised bog with a well-developed system of pools. **Raheenmore Bog**, 7 miles (11km) northeast of Tullamore, established in 1987 and covering 400 acres (162ha), is a nationally important example of deep Midland raised bog.
Rivers	The **Brosna** rises in Lough Ennel and flows southwest through Kilbeggan, Clare, Ballycumber and Ferbane to join the Shannon at Shannon Harbour. The river is popular for fly fishing and has stocks of brown trout as well as some salmon and grilse. The **Camcor** rises in the Slieve Bloom Mountains and joins the Little Brosna at Birr. The **Little Brosna** rises in the districts around Roscrea in Co. Tipperary, flowing northwest past the town of Birr and joining the River Shannon at Meelick. It forms the boundary between Co. Offaly and Co. Tipperary.
St Manchan's Shrine	A tomb-shaped reliquary containing the relics of St Manchan, now housed in Boher Church. Believed to have been created c.1130 at Clonmacnoise, it is made of yew wood with gilt, bronze and enamelled fittings in a mixture of Irish and Viking styles. Eleven of what were originally about 50 full-length human figures remain inscribed on the box.
Seffin Stone	John's Mall, Birr. Now situated beside Birr Heritage Centre, this limestone boulder is reputed to be the *Umbilicus Hiberniae* (Navel of Ireland) referred to in the 12th century by Welsh chronicler Giraldus Cambrensis, and which once marked the centre of Ireland.
Shannon Callows	An area of water meadow covering 8500 acres (3500ha) and extending for more than 30 miles (48km) on either side of the River Shannon between Shannonbridge and Banagher. The area is renowned for its birdlife, being visited in summer by waders such as lapwing, redshank, curlew, common sandpiper and black-tailed godwit, and in winter by thousands of waterfowl including three breeds of swan. Of particular interest is the presence of the increasingly scarce corncrake. The Callows can be viewed from bridges that cross the Shannon, notably those at Shannonbridge and Banagher.
Shrah Castle	$^1/_2$ mile (0.8km) west of Tullamore. The ruin of a four-storey castle built in 1588 by John Briscoe, an officer in Elizabeth I's army.
Slieve Bloom Mountains	See Laois
Sport	
Gaelic football	**Offaly** are winners of the All-Ireland Senior Football Championship in 1971, 1972 and 1982.
hurling	**Offaly** are winners of the All-Ireland Senior Hurling Championship in 1981, 1985, 1994 and 1998.
Tullamore Dew Heritage Centre	Bury Quay, Tullamore. Tullamore Dew Irish whiskey was first distilled in Tullamore in 1829, the second part of its name deriving from the initials of an early owner, Daniel E Williams, i.e. DEW. It was marketed with the slogan 'Give every man his Dew'. Production moved to Cork when the distillery closed in 1959. The heritage centre is located on the site of the original distillery. Tel: 057 932 5015.

Some famous people born in County Offaly

Brent, George (actor) (1899–1979)	Shannonbridge
Cowen, Brian (Taoiseach of Ireland) (1960–)	Clara
Holt, Herbert (engineer) (1856–1941)	Geashill
Joly, John (physicist) (1857–1933)	Bracknagh
Mahon, Hugh (Australian politician) (1857–1931)	Killurin
Ward, Mary (artist) (1827–69)	Ferbane

Roscommon

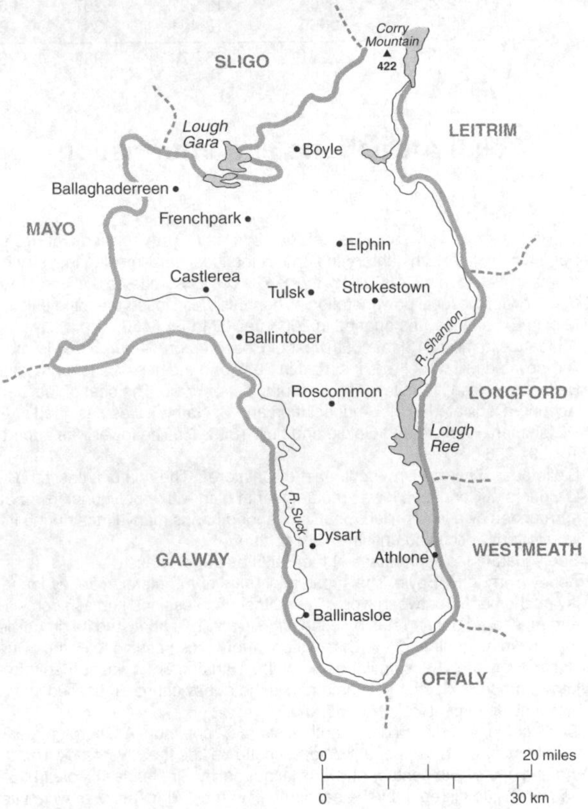
Corry Mountain
422
SLIGO
LEITRIM
Lough Gara
Boyle
Ballaghaderreen
Frenchpark
MAYO
Elphin
Castlerea
Tulsk
Strokestown
R. Shannon
Ballintober
Roscommon
LONGFORD
Lough Ree
R. Suck
Dysart
GALWAY
Athlone
WESTMEATH
Ballinasloe
OFFALY
0
20 miles
0
30 km

Roscommon is part of the province of Connacht in the west of the Republic of Ireland. Its name is derived from *ros*, meaning a forested height, and Comán, a 5th century local saint. Roscommon is bordered to the west by Mayo, to the southwest by Galway, to the southeast by Offaly, to the north by Sligo, to the northeast by Leitrim, and to the east by Longford and Westmeath, separated to a large extent by the Lough Ree part of the River Shannon. The main geographic features are the many loughs including Lough Allen, Lough Boderg, Lough Gara, Lough Key, Lough O'Flynn and Lough Ree, and much of the land is bog. Athlone is often considered the geographical centre of Ireland. The economy is largely based on agriculture and tourism.

Roscommon has been settled since Neolithic times and Rathcroghan was the home of the Kings of Connacht and possibly the legendary Queen Medb or Maeve. In the medieval period the major families were the MacDermotts, the O'Conors and the O'Kellys. The county was largely unaffected by the Anglo-Norman invasion and its lands remained native property during the 17th century. The result was that the county retained the traditional social structures and subsistence level agricultural techniques. This meant that when the potato blight hit in the 1840s the county was particularly badly affected. The population of County Roscommon fell by almost a third between 1841 and 1851, the largest single fall of any county in Ireland.

Roscommon's most famous sons and daughters are, as with much of Ireland, usually politicians or musicians, but perhaps the most celebrated are Douglas Hyde and Albert Reynolds, respectively the 1st President of Ireland and the 8th Taoiseach.

Roscommon	Population			Area	
Districts	*male*	*female*	*total*	*sq miles*	*sq km*
Athlone rural area	6340	6120	12,460	195	506
Boyle No. 1	4628	4318	8946	201	520
Castlereagh	7224	6703	13,927	257	666
Roscommon	9391	9050	18,441	331	856
Total	27,583	26,191	53,774	984	2548

Local Attractions and Information

Administrative headquarters	Courthouse, Roscommon. Tel: 090 337100.
Arigna Mining Experience	1 mile (1.6km) northwest of Derrinisky, 12 miles (19km) northeast of Boyle. Coal mining in Arigna began in the late 18th century to support the local iron smelting industry but continued after the smelters closed in the 1830s. By the 1970s the low-grade coal mined at Arigna was being mainly used to fuel the local power station. When this was closed the mine followed in 1990. The Arigna Mining Experience was opened in 2003. Tel: 071 964 6466.
Athleague Water Mill	Athleague, 8 miles (13km) southwest of Roscommon. A four-storey former water mill built c.1800. A renovated mill wheel was inserted in 2002 and the mill race is running.
Ballaghaderreen Cathedral	Ballaghaderreen, 12 miles (19km) southwest of Boyle. The seat of the Catholic Bishop of Achonry. Dedicated to the Annunciation and St Nathy, it was designed in Gothic style by Weightman, Hadfield and Goldie and built 1855–60. The tower was added in 1912. Tel: 094 986 0011.
Ballintober Castle	Ballintober, 5 miles (8km) southeast of Castlerea. The ruin of a castle built c.1300 by the O'Conors of Connacht. It was rectangular in plan with a polygonal tower at each corner and surrounded by a water-filled moat. It changed hands many times during its lifetime and was intermittently occupied until the 19th century.
Battles	See separate table for details of the Battle of Curlew Pass.
Boyle Abbey	Abbeytown Road, Boyle. The substantial ruins of a Cistercian abbey founded in the 12th century. It lay on the border between Norman and Irish possessions and as such was frequently damaged and ransacked during raids by opposing sides. The abbey and its properties were transferred to the Crown at the time of the Dissolution, afterwards passing to Patrick Cusack and then William Usher. From the 1590s until the end of the 18th century it was turned into a barracks and was known as Boyle Castle. The main ruin is the abbey church. It passed into state care in 1892 as a National Monument. Tel: 071 966 2604.
Castlecoote House and Gardens	Castlecoote, 4½ miles (7km) southwest of Roscommon. A Georgian mansion built in the late 17th century on the site of a medieval castle beside the River Suck. The original castle was built at the end of the 16th century and was 'acquired' by Sir Charles Coote in 1616, who refortified it. It had fallen into disrepair by the second half of the 17th century, at which time the present house was built within its enclosure. The house was a derelict shell By the 1990s, it was restored to its Georgian condition 1997–2003. Tel: 090 666 3794.
Castlerea Railway Museum	Main Street, Castlerea. An unusual venue for a museum, part of it actually being inside the adjacent Hell's Kitchen Bar public house. The museum was created by Sean Brown around a 1955 A55 Metropolitan Vickers diesel electric locomotive which appears to have arrived through the wall of the building into the bar. The museum's vast array of railway memorabilia includes bells, lamps, shunting poles, signal equipment, staffs, station boards and audio and visual archives. Tel: 094 962 0181.
Castlestrange Decorated Stone	Athleague, 5 miles (8km) southwest of Roscommon. An oval granite boulder measuring 2ft (0.6m) by 3ft (0.9m), decorated with incised La Tene style patterns dating to c. 500 BC. Located in the grounds of Castlestrange House, where veterinarian Aleen Cust (see Interesting facts) once practised.
Claypipe Visitor Centre	Knockcroghery, 5 miles (8km) southeast of Roscommon. The village of Knockcroghery was famous from the 17th century until the 1920s for the production of *dúidíns* or clay pipes. Production came to an abrupt end when the village was burned down during the War of Independence in 1921. The visitor centre is located on the original site of the last pipe factory and pipes are again being made using some of the surviving original moulds. Tel: 090 666 1923.
Cloghan Castle	8 miles (13km) south of Roscommon. Aka Clahane Castle. High up on the side of the ruined castle on a southeast quoinstone is a sheela-na-gig with her tongue sticking out. She also has a cap or hairpiece on her head and is very finely carved.
Clonalis House	½ mile (0.8km) northwest of Castlerea. The ancestral home of the O'Conors, kings of Connacht and providers of the last High Kings of Ireland. The land has been the property of the O'Conors since at least the 5th century, although the present house, built by Charles Owen O'Conor Don to a design by Pepys Cochrell and replacing a mid 18th century house, dates only from 1878. Clonalis houses the O'Conor coronation stone and also contains many items related to the O'Conor family history, including costumes, uniforms and the harp of Turlough O'Carolan. The house is now furnished with Sheraton and Louis XV furniture and the library contains 7000 volumes. Tel: 094 962 0014.
Cloonshanville Priory	½ mile (0.8km) east of Frenchpark, 8 miles (13km) southwest of Boyle. The ruin of a Dominican

priory said to have been founded by McDermot Roe in 1385 and located on the site of an earlier monastic foundation of St Conmitius. It passed into secular hands after the Dissolution. The remains consist mainly of an ivy-clad church tower plus some walls.

Cloontykilla Castle — $2^1/_2$ miles (4km) northeast of Boyle. The ruin of a folly built in 1839 to resemble a Norman castle, located beside Lough Key opposite Castle Island in Lough Key Forest Park. The castle is in private hands.

County Roscommon Heritage and Genealogy Centre — Church Street, Strokestown. A centre providing access to genealogical resources for visitors tracing their Roscommon roots. Tel: 071 963 3380.

Cruachan Aí Heritage Centre — Tulsk, 11 miles (18km) northwest of Roscommon. Heritage centre beside the Ogulla River opened in 1999 and sitting within a complex landscape of pre-Christian monuments including the Rathcroghan Mound and the Cave of Cruachan. The three exhibition galleries explore the history, archaeology and mythology of pre-Christian Connacht. Tel: 071 963 9268.

Derryglad Folk Museum — Curraghboy, 10 miles (16km) southeast of Roscommon. Privately owned museum with more than 4000 items recording the folk culture and rural history of the area. There is also an extensive photographic archive on display. Tel: 090 648 8192.

Dr Douglas Hyde Interpretative Centre — Frenchpark, 11 miles (18km) southwest of Boyle. The centre celebrates the life and career of Douglas Hyde (1860–1949), first President of Ireland and co-founder of Conradh Na Gaeilge (the Gaelic League), who was born at Castlerea. It is housed in the church where his father was rector and the churchyard contains the remains of the late President and other members of his family. Tel: 094 987 0016.

Donamon Castle — Donamon, 5 miles (8km) west of Roscommon. A late 13th or early 14th century castle located on the site of a previous 12th century castle. It was acquired in the late 1930s by the Divine Word Missionaries. Tel: 090 666 2222.

Drum Monastic Site — Drum, 17 miles (27km) southeast of Roscommon. The ruins of a Romanesque abbey, a medieval church and St Brigid's Well. A visitor centre was opened in 2001 by Drum Heritage Group, which restored the site 1987–9. Tel: 090 643 7128.

Drumanone Portal Tomb — $2^1/_2$ miles (4km) west of Boyle. A portal dolmen with three uprights more than 7ft (2.1m) high topped by a 14ft (4.2m) square capping stone.

Elphin Windmill — Windmill Road, Elphin, 10 miles (16km) southeast of Boyle. An 18th century working windmill. It has a thatched revolving roof with a tailpole to turn the four common sails into the wind. Built in 1730 but recorded as a ruin a century later, it was restored in 1996 and now houses a visitor centre interpreting and demonstrating the mill's workings. Tel: 071 963 5181.

Frybrook House — Elphin Street, Boyle. Georgian three-storey house built by Henry Fry in 1750 beside the Boyle River. The drawing room is noted for its examples of Georgian decorative plasterwork and an Adam fireplace. Tel: 079 63513.

Gailey Castle — 1 mile (1.6km) east of Knockcroghery, 5 miles (8km) southeast of Roscommon. The ruin of a 14th century castle built by William Boy O'Kelly overlooking Gailey Bay on Lough Ree.

Highest point — Corry Mountain, at 1385ft (422m), located west of Lough Allen on the border with Co. Leitrim.

Interesting facts — **Aleen Isabel Cust** (1868–1937) was the assistant and eventual wife of eminent Roscommon-born veterinary surgeon William Augustus Byrne. The first woman to become a veterinarian in Ireland or Britain, Aleen was admitted to the liberal New Veterinary College in Edinburgh in 1896, enrolling under the alias I A Custance to protect her mother, a member of the aristocracy who was scandalised by Aleen's veterinary ambitions. She graduated in 1900 but the licensing body, the Royal College of Veterinary Surgeons, found that it could license only 'persons' and a woman did not fit that category; as a non-person, she was therefore denied licence to practice. Aleen withdrew to Galway, where she successfully cared for farm and companion animals and was much loved by the farming community – an exception being the local Catholic priest, who was shocked that a woman should be engaged in gelding horses and urged his flock never to employ Ms Cust. Enlightenment came in 1919 when the British Parliament passed the Sex Disqualification Act, requiring the immediate registration of qualified women in the professions. But it still took the Royal College another three years to overcome its prejudice, admit Aleen Cust, and award her a licence, 22 years after she qualified!

Islands — There are six named islands in Co. Roscommon, all in Lough Key, near Rockingham Harbour: **Bullock Island**, **Castle Island** (not surprisingly the site of a ruined castle – see Rock of Lough Key), **Church Island** (the site of a ruined priory), **Drummand Island**, **Stag Island** and **Trinity Island** (see separate entry).

King House Interpretative Galleries and Museum — Main Street, Boyle. A museum and art gallery housed in King House, built by Sir Henry King in 1730. Between 1788 and 1922 it was used as a barracks by the Connaught Rangers and then by the Irish army. The house was derelict by the 1980s and was opened as a museum and art gallery in 1995 after four years of restoration. Exhibitions tell the story of the Kingdom of Connacht, the King family, the house and its military history. The house also contains the Boyle Civic Art Collection of contemporary Irish paintings and sculpture. Tel: 071 966 3242.

Lough Key Forest Park — 2 miles (3km) northeast of Boyle. Created from 860 acres (350ha) of the former Rockingham Estate and including mixed woodland, a lake and a number of islands. The Rockingham Estate was centred on Rockingham House, built by Lord Lorton in the 1810s to a design by John Nash. Destroyed by fire in 1863, it was afterwards rebuilt, but after fire again destroyed it in 1957 it was left to fall into ruin and eventually demolished. Some of the outbuildings, such as the stables and ice house, can still be seen in the park. Tel: 071 966 7037.

Loughs — **Lough Key** is popular with coarse and fly fishermen and holds stocks of bream, brown trout, perch, pike, and roach. Other loughs in Co. Roscommon include Lough Allen, Lough Boderg, Lough Gara, Lough Key, Lough O'Flynn and Lough Ree (see Longford).

MacDermot's Castle	See Rock of Lough Key
O'Carolan Heritage Park	Keadue, 9 miles (15km) northeast of Boyle. Heritage park opened in 1993 to commemorate blind harper Turlough O'Carolan (1670–1738). The O'Carolan Harp and Traditional Music Festival is held in Keadue on the first weekend of August every year. The park also features a reconstructed sweathouse, the ruins of which were found on the original site when work commenced on the park. Tel: 071 964 7204.
Old Schoolhouse Museum	Ballintubber, 5 miles (8km) southeast of Castlerea. A museum in a schoolhouse dating to the late 1920s and equipped with period furniture and equipment, with displays of school work books, readers and photographs. Tel. 094 965 5397.
Rathcroghan Mound	3 miles (5km) northwest of Tulsk, 8 miles (13km) northeast of Castlerea. A large circular flat-topped mound 300ft (90m) in diameter and between 13ft (4m) and 20ft (6m) high. Traditionally one of the places where the High Kings of Ireland were inaugurated, it is also identified with Cruachan, the capital of Connacht, reputedly the place where Queen Medb (Maeve) had her royal palace; as such it is the setting for the opening and closing of the epic poem *Táin Bó Cúailnge* (see Louth). It is a National Monument. See also Cruachan Aí Heritage Centre.
Rivers	The **Suck** is 50 miles (80km) long and is the main tributary of the River Shannon. It forms the border between the counties of Galway and Roscommon.
Rock of Lough Key	3 miles (5km) northeast of Boyle. The site of MacDermot's Castle, located on Castle Island in Lough Key. Probably built in the 12th century and besieged by Normans in 1235, the castle was in ruins by 1600. Lord Lorton built a folly castle on the site in the early 19th century; this burned down in 1930s.
Roscommon Abbey	$^1/_2$ mile (0.8km) south of Roscommon. The ruin of a Dominican friary founded by Felim O'Conor in 1253. Felim was buried here in 1265 shortly before the abbey was damaged by fire and it was also later struck by lightning. It fell into disrepair after the Dissolution and its buildings were used as a source of stone for local houses. Still visible in the remains are many effigies and carvings, including eight niches containing 15th century carved figures of gallowglasses (Scottish mercenaries).
Roscommon Castle	$^1/_4$ mile (0.4km) north of Roscommon. The ruin of a castle built in 1269 by Robert de Ufford, Lord Justice of Ireland. The original castle was sacked by Hugh O'Conor, King of Connacht, in 1280 and had to be rebuilt. It was rectangular in plan with D-shaped towers at each corner. After it was partially blown up by Cromwellian troops in 1645 the fortifications were dismantled; it was finally burned down in 1690 and left to fall into ruin.
Roscommon County Library	Abbey Street, Roscommon. Housed in the Old Infirmary, built in 1783 from an endowment of Mrs Laetitia Walcott. Used as a hospital until 1941, it was restored in 1989. Tel: 090 337271.
Roscommon County Museum	The Square, Roscommon. Local history museum charting the history of Roscommon from the 9th century to the present day. It is housed in the John Harrison Memorial Hall, a former Presbyterian church built in 1863. Exhibits include an inscribed slab from St Coman's foundation and a sheela-na-gig. Tel: 090 662 5613.
Roscommon Jail	The Square, Roscommon. The original jail was built in the early 1740s but only the façade survives. It had the distinction of having a hangwoman, Betty George ('Lady Betty'), a criminal who had her sentence for murder withdrawn on condition that she carried out the hangman's task, without fee or reward. After being used as a jail it was a lunatic asylum and a smallpox hospital. The building was demolished apart from the façade and now houses a mixture of shops, restaurants and apartments.
Sacred Heart Church	Abbey Street, Roscommon. Regarded as one of the most beautiful churches in Ireland. Designed by Walter Doolin and P J Kilgallon and built 1899–1903, it was dedicated on 18 June 1903 and retains most of its original features. Its main external feature is its 175ft (53.5m) high tower. Tel: 090 662 6298.
Shannonbridge Fort	21 miles (34km) southeast of Roscommon. The ruin of a large fort on the Roscommon/Offaly border, built in 1804 to protect the crossing of the River Shannon at Shannonbridge, Co. Offaly.
Sport	
Gaelic football	**Roscommon** were winners of the All-Ireland Senior Football Championship in 1943 and 1944.
horse racing	**Roscommon** Racecourse, Roscommon Road, Roscommon. Racing first took place in the town in 1837. Roscommon stages Flat and National Hunt racing on a right-handed oval course of $1^1/_4$ miles (2km) with a run-in of $2^1/_2$ furlongs (0.5km). Tel: 090 363494.
Strokestown Park House, Garden and Famine Museum	Strokestown, 11 miles (18km) north of Roscommon. Strokestown Park was built by Thomas Mahon MP (1701–82) and remained in the Mahon family until 1979, when it was sold while in a state of disrepair. The house was restored and opened to the public in 1987. The restored walled gardens were opened to the public in 1997 and include a croquet lawn, tennis court and summerhouse. The herbaceous border is regarded as the longest in Britain and Ireland; Georgian fruit and vegetable gardens and glasshouses have also been restored. The Famine Museum, located in the original stable yards of Strokestown Park House, is designed to balance the picture of 1840s living in Ireland portrayed by the manor house. The museum is based around the surviving estate house documentation of the mid 19th century, which spells out the devastation suffered by the mass of the population during the famine. The museum was opened in 1994 by then President of Ireland, Mary Robinson. Tel: 071 963 3013.
Tain Trail	A long distance cycling route running for 365 miles (587km) from Co. Roscommon to Co. Louth and back and retracing the route of Queen Maeve and her army on its famous Cattle Raid of Cooley, or the Tain (see Louth). It starts at Maeve Palace at Cruachan and ends at the Cooley Peninsula.
Trinity Island	$2^1/_2$ miles (4km) northeast of Boyle. An island in Lough Key on which are located the remains of the monastery of the Holy Trinity, founded for Premonstratensian monks in 1215 by Clarus

MacMailin. The ranks of canons were swelled in 1228 by the defection of monks from the Cistercian abbey of Boyle. In 1235 the island was granted protection by the Justiciar of Connacht, when he and other Anglo-Norman notables visited it to pray, prior to attacking MacDermot's Castle on Castle Island. Although the monastery was suppressed in the 16th century, the monks remained on the island until 1608 when it was confiscated by James I. The island is the burial place of Sir Conyers Clifford, commander of the English forces at the Battle of the Curlews.

Some famous people born in County Roscommon

Coleman, James (artist) (1941–)	Ballaghaderreen
Curley, James (astronomer) (1796–1889)	Athleague
Earley, Dermot (Gaelic footballer and politician) (1948–)	Roscommon
French, William Percy (songwriter and artist) (1854–1920)	Elphin
Hyde, Douglas (1st President of Ireland) (1860–1949)	Castlerea
Ireland, Patrick (artist born Brian O'Doherty) (1934–)	Roscommon
Molloy, Matt (musician) (1947–)	Ballaghaderreen
O'Conor, Roderic (artist) (1860–1940)	Castleplunket
O'Sullivan, Maureen (actress) (1911–98)	Boyle
Reynolds, Albert (8th Taoiseach of Ireland) (1932–)	Roosky

Sligo

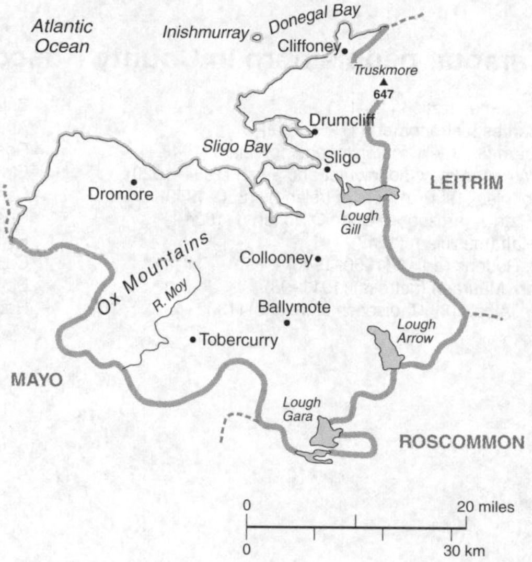
Atlantic Ocean
Inishmurray
Donegal Bay
Cliffoney
Truskmore
647
Drumcliff
Sligo Bay
Sligo
LEITRIM
Dromore
Lough Gill
Ox Mountains
Collooney
R. Moy
Ballymote
Tobercurry
Lough Arrow
MAYO
Lough Gara
ROSCOMMON
0
20 miles
0
30 km

Sligo is part of the province of Connacht in the west of Ireland and its name means 'an area abounding in shells'. The county is bordered to the west by Mayo, to the south by Roscommon and to the east by Leitrim. Its northern coast is on Donegal Bay. The county town is Sligo. The main geographical features are the long northern coastline, the Ox, Dartry and Bricklieve Mountains, and Loughs Gill and Arrow.

The county has some of the earliest megalithic structures in Ireland at the Carrowmore Megalithic Cemetery and the Carrowkeel-Keshcorran Passage Tomb complex. The Culleenamore Middens testify to the settlement of the coastline during the Mesolithic period. Christianity was proclaimed in North Sligo in the 6th century by St Molaise. Visitors from all over the world now flock to see the stone-corbelled beehive huts and monastic remains on the island of Inishmurray where this holy man founded his monastery

Sligo was invaded by the Normans during the 13th century and the town of Sligo grew up around the castle (built 1245 but demolished in 1595). Centuries of conflict and disputes between Normans and Irish followed. Sligo Town and Abbey were burned down during the 1641 uprising and there was an attempt at Plantation following the Cromwellian campaigns in Ireland. In 1798 a French expeditionary force under the command of Major General Humbert landed in Killala Bay.

Sligo Town began to grow at the beginning of the 19th century both in terms of population and economically, thanks to the brewing and linen trades. The expansion of the port was guaranteed by the arrival of the railways in 1860. However, by this time the county had already suffered from a cholera epidemic in 1832 followed by the onset of the Great Famine of the 1840s and 1850s. The result was a rapid decline in population with more than 30,000 emigrating.

Sligo's most famous sons and daughters are generally politicians or musicians, but perhaps the most celebrated are both from the acting profession: director Neil Jordan and Lola Montes, 19th century actress and courtesan. Although they were not born there, the county has close associations with both W B and Jack Yeats (born in Dublin) and also the first UK woman MP, Constance Markiewicz (née Gore-Booth, born in London).

Sligo	Population			Area	
Districts	*male*	*female*	*total*	*sq miles*	*sq km*
Boyle No. 2	2222	1943	4165	128	330
Dromore West	3343	3125	6468	152	395
Sligo Borough	8569	9,904	18,473	5	13
Sligo rural area	10,947	10,998	21,945	226	587
Tobercurry	3690	3459	7149	198	512
Total	28,771	29,429	58,200	709	1837

Local Attractions and Information

Achonry Boulder Dolmen	Achonry, 3 miles (5km) northeast of Tobercurry. A boulder dolmen consisting of three short uprights supporting a large circular capstone.
Administrative headquarters	Riverside, Sligo. Tel: 071 914 3221.
Airport	**Sligo Airport** (SLX), Strandhill. A small regional airport on Sligo Bay that operates services to Dublin and Manchester. Tel: 071 916 8280.
Ballinafad Castle	Ballinafad, 18 miles (29km) southeast of Sligo. The ruin of a late 16th fortified garrison blockhouse built to resemble a 13th century Norman castle. The four-storey rectangular keep measures 31ft (9.5m) by 25ft (8m) with three-quarter round towers at each angle. Located on the Red Earl's Road, which ran between Ballymote, Co. Sligo, and Boyle, Co. Roscommon, it was built in 1590 by Sir Richard Bingham to control a pass through the Curlew Mountains. The castle was damaged by Red Hugh O'Donnell in 1595 and was abandoned by the end of the 17th century.
Ballindoon Abbey	Ballindoon, 8 miles (13km) east of Ballymote. The ruin of a Dominican priory on the eastern shore of Lough Arrow, founded in 1507 by Thomas O'Farrell under the patronage of John MacDonagh. It was abandoned by the end of the 17th century; burials within the walls of the church are likely to have been made after it was unroofed. The church's most distinctive feature is an unusual triple-vaulted archway dividing the nave from the chancel.
Ballygilgan Nature Reserve	1 mile (1.6km) west of Carney, 5 miles (8km) northwest of Sligo. Established in 1986 and covering 72 acres (29ha) of improved grassland beside Drumcliff Bay. It supports an internationally significant population of barnacle geese.
Ballymote Abbey	Ballymote, 13 miles (21km) south of Sligo. The ruins of a Franciscan friary founded in the 1440s. The monks abandoned the friary and went into exile after the town was attacked in 1483, and the abbey was in ruins by the end of the 16th century.
Ballymote Castle	Ballymote, 13 miles (21km) south of Sligo. The ruin of an early 14th century castle built by Richard de Burgo, the Red Earl of Ulster. Ballymote fell to Rory O'Connor in 1317 and remained in Irish hands until 1584 when control passed to Sir Richard Bingham. Captured and held by the O'Donnells 1598–1602, it was surrendered to Williamite forces in 1690 and afterwards abandoned. The plan of the castle is almost square with a three-quarter round tower at each corner and D-shaped towers in the east and west curtain wall. The gatehouse is in the northern wall. The Book of Ballymote, reputedly written in the castle during the 14th century, contains Irish legends and biblical stories, versions of the Trojan Wars and a history of Alexander the Great. Tel: 071 916 1201.
Ballymote Monument	Ballymote, 13 miles (21km) south of Sligo. A monument unveiled in August 2006 in tribute to the US 'Fighting' 69th Infantry Regiment, founded in 1851 by Irish emigrants. During the early years of the American Civil War it was led by Brigadier-General Michael Corcoran (1827–63) who was born near Ballymote. He enlisted as a private in the 69th New York Militia, which became the US 69th Infantry Regiment. By 1859 he was appointed colonel of the regiment. He was captured at the First Battle of Bull Run in July 1861 but was later released in a prisoner exchange. He died from a stroke after a fall from his horse in December 1863. Designed by Fermanagh artist Philip Flanagan, the 7½ ton column is made of limestone and bronze. The inscription around the top reads 'Michael Corcoran 1827–1863' and that around the base 'New York Ballymote Creeslough Bull Run'. It was unveiled by the Mayor of New York, Michael Bloomberg.
Battles	Three battles have been fought in Sligo: the Battle of the Books, Calry Lough Gill and Collooney. See separate table for details and separate entry for the Battle of the Books.
Behy Castle	1 mile (1.6km) west of Riverstown, 5 miles (8km) northeast of Ballymote. The ruin of a castle noted for its sheela-na-gig, a red-painted figure with its hand to the right ear.
Belclare Castle	Aclare, 7 miles (11km) southwest of Tubbercurry. The ruins of a castle built by the O'Hara family.
Ben Bulben	6 miles (10km) north of Sligo. A large, flat-topped mountain 1726ft (526m) high located in the Dartry Mountains, and which inspired W B Yeats' poem 'Under Ben Bulben'.
Books, Battle of the	A battle which took place in AD 561 after St Columba (Colmcille) copied a book while a guest of St Finian. Finian claimed the copy as well as the book, but Colmcille refused. The dispute was brought to the High King of Ireland, whose edict was 'To every cow its calf and to every book its copy'. In consequence, the High King and Colmcille engaged in battle on the slopes of Ben Bulben. Aided by an angel, Colmcille won. Thousands of men were slain and the king was forced to concede the copy of the psalter to Colmcille.
Cabragh Wedge Tomb	3 miles (5km) southwest of Coolaney, 7 miles (11km) northeast of Tobercurry. A well-preserved Neolithic wedge tomb.

Cahirmore	Enniscrone, 25 miles (40km) west of Sligo. The site of a D-shaped multivallate clifftop enclosure on the east side of Killala Bay.
Carrowkeel-Keshcorran Passage Tomb Complex	2 miles (3km) south of Castlebaldwin, 6 miles (10km) southeast of Ballymote. A Neolithic passage tomb cemetery above Lough Arrow, dating to c. 3300 BC and consisting of 20 cairns (14 at Carrowkeel and six at Keshcorran). Heapstown Cairn is nearby.
Carrowmore Megalithic Cemetery	3 miles (5km) southwest of Sligo. The largest megalithic cemetery in Ireland. The tombs are located in an area of 1000 acres (405ha) in the shadow of Knocknarea. Over 60 tombs have been identified, 30 having visible traces and the oldest pre-dating the Pyramids (although their dating is uncertain). A small exhibition about the site is housed in a restored cottage.
Castle Baldwin	Castlebaldwin, 6 miles (10km) east of Ballymote. The remains of a 17th century two-storey L-plan tower house. Tel: 071 916 1201.
Cathedral of St John the Baptist	John Street, Sligo. Designed by Richard Cassels and built in the 1730s. It was here in 1863 that W B Yeats' mother and father were married. Tel: 071 916 1201.
Cathedral of the Immaculate Conception	Temple Street, Sligo. A Romanesque style cathedral designed by George Goldie. Opened on 26 July 1874, it was consecrated on 1 July 1897. Its building was inspired by Bishop Laurence Gillooly, who wished to replace the Pro Cathedral of St John's Parish Chapel. Tel: 071 916 2670.
Classiebawn Castle	$^{1}/_{2}$ mile (0.8km) south of Mullaghmore, 13 miles (21km) north of Sligo. Situated on Mullaghmore Head, the castle was completed by the 1st Lord Mount Temple in 1874 and later descended to the Mountbattens. It is now privately owned.
Clogher Castle	Monasterarden, 10 miles (16km) south of Ballymote. A relatively intact cashel enclosed by walls 14ft (4.2m) thick and 6ft (1.8m) high. Some restoration was carried out in the 19th century.
Cloghor Portal Tomb	$^{1}/_{4}$ mile (0.4km) south of Cloghboley, 7 miles (11km) northwest of Sligo. A collapsed portal dolmen. Two of the uprights still stand but the third has fallen, resulting in the collapse of the large capstone.
Court Abbey	$^{1}/_{2}$ mile (0.8km) northeast of Lavagh, $4^{1}/_{2}$ miles (7km) northeast of Tobercurry. The ruin of a Franciscan friary founded in the 15th century by the O'Hara family. The ruins are not approachable for health and safety reasons.
Creevykeel Court Tomb	1 mile (1.6km) northeast of Cliffoney, 11 miles (18km) northeast of Sligo. An impressive restored court tomb, considered to be one of the best examples of its type in Ireland. Trapezoid in shape, it encloses an oval court and a burial chamber of two compartments. The cairn is 180ft (55m) long and 82ft (25m) wide at one end; the forecourt measures 56ft (17m) by 33ft (10m). Excavations in the 1930s uncovered Neolithic pottery, a chalk ball, leaf-shaped flint arrowheads, hollow scrapers and polished stone axe heads.
Culkin's Emigration Centre	Cannaghanally, 1 mile (1.6km) southwest of Dromore West, 14 miles (23km) northwest of Tobercurry. A museum located on the site of Daniel Culkin's Shipping & Emigration Agency and telling the story of the emigration era from the mid 19th century to the 1930s. The original agency shop has been recreated as part of the museum. Tel: 096 47152.
Culleenamore Middens	$^{3}/_{4}$ mile (1.2km) south of Strandhill, 5 miles (8km) west of Sligo.The remains of Mesolithic and later middens (waste dumps) on Ballysadare Bay which reveal the local inhabitants' dependence on shellfish and fish.
Dartry Mountains	One of Co. Sligo's two main mountain ranges, situated in the north of the county.
Deerpark Court Tomb	$^{1}/_{2}$ miles (0.8km) east of Calry, 4 miles (6km) east of Sligo. Aka Magherghanrush. An impressive example of a centre court tomb dating to c. 3000 BC and located on a ridge overlooking Lough Gill. It has three double chambered galleries.
Dolly's Cottage	Strandhill, 5 miles (8km) west of Sligo. A restored two-room traditional thatched cottage furnished in its original style. It is named after its last resident, Dolly Higgins, who died in 1970. Tel: 071 916 7564.
Doorly Park	$1^{1}/_{4}$ miles (2km) east of Sligo. A park named after Bishop Edward Doorly and located alongside the Garavogue River. Tel: 071 916 1201.
Drumcliffe Church	Drumcliffe, 4 miles (6km) north of Sligo. A 19th century church built on the site of religious foundations possibly dating to the 6th century. A round tower and high cross remain from this early monastic settlement. The grave of poet W B Yeats is located in the graveyard.
Drumcliffe Tower and High Cross	Drumcliffe, 4 miles (6km) north of Sligo. The round tower and high cross are all that remains of a monastery said to have been founded by St Columba in AD 574. The monastery was sacked several times during its lifetime and seems to have been abandoned in the early 16th century. The tower is also known as the Belfry of Drumcliffe. The high cross, dating to the 10th century and standing in the grounds of Drumcliffe Church, is inscribed with several depictions of biblical events including the temptation of Adam and Eve, Cain killing Abel, and Daniel in the lions' den. Episodes from Christ's Passion are depicted on the west face.
Easky Bog	5 miles (8km) southeast of Dromore West, 10 miles (16km) northwest of Tobercurry. A nature reserve established in 1990 and covering 1500 acres (607ha) on the northern side of the Ox Mountains. It contains an extensive area of highland blanket bog and is one of the few sites in the county where all three types of blanket bog (mountain, highland and lowland) are more or less next to each other.
Heapstone Cairn	2 miles (3km) south of Castlebaldwin, 6 miles (10km) southeast of Ballymote. A very large unexcavated kerbed cairn 200ft (60m) long and 20ft (6m) high. It was originally much larger but stones have been removed over the centuries to build roads and walls.
Highest point	Truskmore in the Dartry Mountains at 2123ft (647m).
Inishmurray	An island 4 miles (6km) off the coast of Sligo and containing the ruin of a 6th century monastery reputedly founded by St Molaise. The monastery was attacked by Vikings in 795 and was subsequently moved to the mainland. The ruins include a cashel enclosing three churches, plus two corbelled huts or beehive cells. The island has been sparsely populated throughout its history,

	usually with a total population of less than 100, and was completely evacuated in 1948. The remains of 15 houses stand near the old harbour. There is an annual pilgrimage on 15 August (the Feast of the Assumption) to visit the 16 *leachta* (dry stone cairns) which may have been erected as outdoor altars in the medieval period.
Interesting facts	**Sligo** is sometimes known as Yeats Country as the great poet had such an affinity with the county. Buried in Drumcliffe Church, his tombstone carries the words of his final poem 'Under Ben Bulben'. 'Cast a cold eye on life, on death, Horseman, pass by!' The horseman in question is a ghostly rider of Sligo legend who carries the souls of the wicked off to hell. **The Battle of the Books** (see separate entry) gives us the first ruling on copyright, although Columba (Colmcille) refused to accept the ruling and left Ireland in the aftermath, sailing to Iona in Scotland where he founded his famous monastery. **Markree Castle** has a number of claims to fame. It was the home of the world's first cast-iron telescope with a 13$^1/_2$ inch (340mm) refractor lens (the largest in the world at the time). Edward Joshua Cooper (1798–1863) built the observatory at the castle in 1830 and in 1848 his assistant, Andrew Graham, discovered a minor planet, Metis, the only asteroid ever to be discovered from Ireland. 'All Things Bright and Beautiful' (words by the female hymnist Cecil Frances Alexander) was written to help explain to children the opening words of the Apostles' Creed, a Christian statement of belief. The wife of an archbishop, Mrs Alexander was known to be a generous woman who cared for the poor and opened a school for the deaf with her sister. The words 'The rich man in his castle, The poor man at his gate … The purple headed mountains, The river running by' are thought to be inspired by the view from her window while staying at Markree. The Queen's cousin, **Lord Louis Mountbatten**, and his family traditionally spent their summer holidays at Markree Castle. On 27 August 1979 Lord Mountbatten, aged 79, was killed by a bomb blast on his boat *Shadow V*, which had just set off from Mullaghmore, a small fishing village situated on a peninsula in the northwestern corner of Co. Sligo. The bomb detonated around 11.30 am; one of the earl's twin grandsons, Nicholas Knatchbull, 14, and Paul Maxwell, 15, a local employed as a boat boy, also died in the explosion.
Islands	See separate table for details of offshore islands. Lough Gill has several named islands, **Church Island** being the largest and the **Lake Isle of Innisfree** the most famous. Other islands include **Annagh Island**, **Beezies** (aka Cottage Island, Gallagher's Island), **Bernard's Island**, **Black Tom's Island**, **Cormorant Rock**, **Fairy Island**, **Monk's Island**, **St Connell's Island**, **Seal Rocks**, **Swan Island**, **Willow Island** and **Wolf Island**.
Kearns Monument	Ballymote, 13 miles (21km) south of Sligo. A monument to locally born Brother Walfrid (né Andrew Kearns) (1840–1915), an Irish Marist Brother and founder of Celtic Football Club in Glasgow.
Kevinsfort House	Strandhill Road, Sligo. A Georgian house built in 1820 by George Dodwell. Tel: 071 916 2787.
Knocklane Promontory Fort	Drumcliffe, 4 miles (6km) north of Sligo. An Iron Age promontory fort surrounded by sea on three sides and blocked off from the mainland by a double bank and ditch.
Knocknarea	4$^1/_2$ miles (7km) southwest of Sligo (I. = Mountain of the Moon). A hill 1073ft (327m) high and capped by the large cairn known as Misgaun Maeve (Maeve's Lump of Butter). Medb or Maeve was the warrior queen of Connacht in Celtic mythology. The story of part of her reign is recorded in the *Táin Bó Cúailnge* (see Louth).
Knocknashee	$^1/_2$ mile (0.8km) north of Lavagh, 4$^1/_2$ miles (7km) northeast of Tobercurry. A large hill fort whose ramparts covering 53 acres (21.5ha) enclosing cairns and hut sites. It was identified as a fort only in 1988.
Lisnalurg	2 miles (3km) north of Sligo. A large earthwork enclosure with a diameter of 500ft (150m).
Lissadell House	6 miles (10km) northwest of Sligo. A large Greek Revival style house designed by Francis Goodwin for Sir Robert Gore-Booth and built 1830–5. It was the home of Constance Markievicz (née Gore-Booth) (1868–1927) who, after being imprisoned for her part in the Easter Rising of 1916 and released in 1917, was the first woman elected to the British House of Commons, although she did not take her seat. She became Minister of Labour in the first Dáil. W B Yeats was a regular visitor to the house in the 1890s. The house is in private ownership and is being restored.
Lough Gill	2$^1/_2$ miles (4km) southeast of Sligo. A lough 6$^1/_2$ miles (10.5km) long and 2$^1/_2$ miles (4km) wide, and holding brown trout and salmon. Part of the lough is a Special Area of Conservation, designated for its variety of aquatic fauna, including three species of lamprey, and for the surrounding old oak woodlands. The island of Innisfree, near the lough's southern shore, is the subject of 'The Lake Isle of Innisfree', a famous poem by W B Yeats. See also Islands.
Markree Castle	Collooney, 9 miles (15km) southwest of Sligo. A 14th century castle formerly belonging to the McDonaghs and for 370 years the home of the Cooper family. Completely refurbished in the late 1800s, Markree is now a notable example of Irish Victorian architecture, with a Rococo style dining room and recently renovated chapel. The castle is now a country house hotel. See also Interesting facts.
Mermaid Stones	1 mile (1.6km) southwest of Enniscrone, 25 miles (40km) southwest of Sligo. Aka the Children of the Mermaid. Six stones beside a Bronze or Iron Age mound with bank and ditch. According to legend, chieftain Thady O'Dowd stole a mermaid's cloak so that she would remain in human form and marry him. This she did and bore him seven children until, upon discovering the hidden cloak, she was driven to return to her old form. She turned six of her children to stone to prevent then from stopping her and fled into the sea with the seventh. It is also said that the stones weep every time an O'Dowd dies.
Misgaun Maeve	1 mile (1.6km) southeast of Strandhill, 4$^1/_2$ miles (7km) southwest of Sligo. Aka Queen Maeve's Tomb, Queen Maeve's Lump of Butter. An unexcavated Neolithic cairn of loose limestone rocks 30ft (9m) high by 180ft (55m) wide, located on the top of Knocknarea and probably covering a passage tomb. Medb (Maeve), the legendary Queen of Connacht, is reputedly entombed in the cairn standing in full armour facing northward towards her Ulster enemies.

Model Arts and Niland Gallery	The Mall, Sligo. One of Ireland's most important centres for the visual and performing arts. Housed in a recently renovated model school built in 1862, it is the home of the Niland Art Collection which includes works by John and Jack B Yeats, Paul Henry and Nick Miller. The centre hosts festivals including the Sligo Festival of Baroque Music, the Scríobh Literary Festival and the Sligo Contemporary Music Festival. Tel: 071 914 1405.
Moygara Castle	1 mile (1.6km) south of Mullaghroe, 8 miles (13km) southeast of Ballymote. The ruins of a tower house surrounded by a square bawn with flanking angled towers at each corner. It was the chief residence of the O'Garas.
Nolans Castle	Enniscrone, 25 miles (40km) southwest of Sligo. The ruin of a two-storey 17th century fortified house located on the site of an earlier fortification known as Enniscrone Castle or O'Dowd's Castle. The earlier castle, built in the 15th century by the O'Dowd family, changed hands more than once and was probably slighted at the end of the 1641 rebellion.
Ox Mountains	One of the two main mountain ranges in Co. Sligo, situated in the south of the county. A series of low, boggy summits, their highest point is Knockalongy at 1785ft (544m).
Perch Rock	An island in Sligo Bay on which since 1821 has stood one of four Metal Men cast by Thomas Kirke in London in 1819. Another is located on a headland near Tramore, Co. Waterford, but the whereabouts of the remaining two are unknown. The Metal Man is dressed in the uniform of a petty officer in the Royal Navy; with right arm outstretched, he points to the safe channel to Sligo.
Rathlee Signal Tower	Rathlee, 5 miles (8km) northeast of Enniscrone, 22 miles (35km) west of Sligo. One of many such towers built 1804–06 in response to French invasion attempts in the late 18th century, it worked on a signalling system using a ball and flag, enabling various messages to be transmitted from station to station. The towers were abandoned by 1809 as victory at Trafalgar had greatly reduced the threat of French invasion.
Rivers	**Moy** see Mayo
Sligo Abbey	Abbey Street, Sligo. The ruins of a Dominican friary founded in the 1230s by Maurice Fitzgerald, who also founded the town of Sligo as an administrative centre. The friary was accidentally burned down, along with the town, in 1414. It was destroyed and all the friars were killed by government forces during the 1641 rebellion. Replacement friars arrived but were expelled in 1698 only to return later to repair the church. The monastic community finally left the friary in 1760. The church has a number of monumental tombs including those of the O'Conor Sligo and the O'Craian. It has been in state care since 1913. Tel: 071 914 6406.
Sligo County Museum	Stephen Street, Sligo. A local history museum based in Sligo County Library. Exhibits include local artefacts and displays relating to the two prominent families of Co. Sligo – the Yeats and the Gore-Booths – including photographs, prints and memorabilia. Tel: 071 914 1623.
Sligo Folk Park	Riverstown, 5½ miles (9km) northeast of Ballymote. Opened in 2001 and dedicated to portraying local rural life in the late 19th century, the museum is based around the restored Millview House, a farmhouse with 6 acres (2.5ha) of land built in the 1870s by George Reid, a farmer and shoemaker. The museum and exhibition hall contain a collection of rural history and agricultural artefacts, along with a recreated vllage streetscape consisting of a variety of shops and services typical in every Irish village (pub, grocer etc.). Other features include Mrs Buckley's Cottage and Farmyard. Tel: 071 916 5001.
Split Rock, The	½ mile (0.8km) east of Easky, 19 miles (31km) west of Sligo. A large boulder carried to its present position by an Ice Age glacier. According to legend, the rock was split as a result of an argument between Cúchulainn and Ferdia. It is also said that if someone dares to go through the split three times, the rock will close in on them.
Sport	
football	**Sligo Rovers** were founded in 1928, and were winners of the League of Ireland in 1937 and 1977 and of the FAI Cup in 1983 and 1994. Their home ground is The Showgrounds, Sligo.
horse racing	**Sligo Racecourse**, Cleveragh Road, was founded in the early 19th century and it hosts both National Hunt and Flat races. The right-handed oval of 1 mile (1.6km) has a run-in of 2 furlongs (0.4km) and an uphill finish. Tel: 071 83342.
Tobernault	2½ miles (4km) southeast of Sligo. A holy well dedicated to St Patrick, who traditionally visited the well, blessed it and used its waters for baptism. Pilgrims still touch a rock beside the well where St Patrick placed his hand. The waters are purported to be beneficial to those suffering from mental disorders or eye complaints. Trees at the site have been festooned with beads, rags and offerings.
Valentine's Church	Enniscrone, 25 miles (40km) southwest of Sligo. The ruin of a church built by the Rev. Thomas Valentine in 1712. A plaque erected by Bishop William Cecil in 1783 eulogises the life and works of Valentine, who died in 1765 at the age of 90. The inscription ends: 'to perpetuate the memory of this worthy man and to propose to every future incumbent a perfect model of a Parish Minister'. Unfortunately the church was ransacked and damaged during the 1798 rebellion and never rebuilt.
Valley of Diamonds	Enniscrone, 25 miles (40km) southwest of Sligo. A tall sand dune off Enniscrone's beach which stands almost like a volcanic cone. The valley inside the cone is littered with shells which sparkle in sunshine, giving it its name.
Waiting on Shore Monument	Rosses Point, 4 miles (6km) northwest of Sligo. A statue depicting a woman holding out her hands towards the sea, created by Niall Bruton and erected in 2002 in memory of local men lost at sea and the families they left behind.
W B Yeats Statue	Stephen Street, Sligo. Located outside the Ulster Bank, this modern statue shows the poet in a serpentine pose with his jacket splayed out like a cobra's hood. Sculpted by Rowan Gillespie, it was erected in 1990.
Yeats Memorial Building	Hyde Bridge, Sligo. Donated to the Yeats Society by the AIB Bank, the building is the base of The Yeats Society which has a photographic exhibition of the life and times of W B Yeats and his family. Tel: 071 914 2693.

Some famous people born in County Sligo

Egan, Kian (Westlife band member) (1980–)	Sligo
Fallon, Sean (footballer) (1922–)	Sligo
Feehily, Mark (Westlife band member) (1980–)	Sligo
Flanagan, Pauline (actress) (1925–2003)	Sligo
Fleming, Tommy (singer) (1971–)	Aclare
Higgins, Bryan (scientist) (1737–1820)	Collooney
Jordan, Neil (film director) (1950–)	Sligo
Montez, Lola (actress) (1821–61)	Grange
Scanlon, Mark (cyclist) (1980–)	Cranmore
Stokes, George Gabriel (mathematician) (1819–1903)	Skreen

Offshore Islands of County Sligo

(shipping area = Malin)

Island name	**Area**	**Nearest landmark**	**General information**
Ardboline	Atlantic	Raghly	Grass-covered with a rocky shoreline. Lies 0.6 mile (1km) from Horse Island.
Ardboline Island	Sligo Bay	Cullumore	The remains of part of a 248 ton iron steamer are lodged near the southern tip.
Black Rock	Sligo Bay	Deadman's Point	The dominating lighthouse was designed by George Halpin Sr in 1835.
Black Rock	Sligo Bay	Sligo	One of two islands of the same name in Sligo Bay.
Coney Island	Sligo Bay	Deadman's Point	aka Inishmulclohy. St Patrick apparently once sat in the Wishing Chair. Population: 3.
Conor's Island	Atlantic	Streedagh Point	At low water joined to the mainland and Dernish Island.
Crumb Rock	Donegal Bay	Mullaghmore Head	Lies 330ft (100m) north of Thumb Rock.
Dernish Island	Atlantic	Streedagh Point	The island is joined to Conor's Island by a rocky outcrop.
Green Island	Sligo Bay	Deadman's Point	A large rock outcrop $^{1}/_{3}$ mile (0.5km) up the coast from the Metal Man bay.
Horse Island	Sligo Bay	Deadman's Point	Tiny island off Yellow Strand to the northwest of Raghly Point.
Inishmulclohy	Sligo Bay	Deadman's Point	See Coney Island
Inishmurray	Atlantic	Streedagh Point	There is a lake in the middle of the island and also some monastic ruins.
Oyster Island	Sligo Bay	Deadman's Point	The lighthouse was built in 1932.
Perch Rock	Sligo Bay	Deadman's Point	See separate entry
Thumb Rock	Donegal Bay	Mullaghmore Head	Lies 330ft (100m) south of Crumb Rock.

TIPPERARY

GALWAY
OFFALY
Lough Derg
Nenagh
LAOIS
CLARE
1
Templemore
R. Suir
Thurles
Holycross
KILKENNY
Cashel
Golden
Tipperary
LIMERICK
Galtymore
919
Fethard
2
Cahir
R. Suir
Clonmel
Carrick-on-Suir
CORK
WATERFORD
Districts
1 North Tipperary
2 South Tipperary
0
20 miles
0
30 km

Tipperary is part of the province of Munster. It lies in the central south of the Republic of Ireland, and is Ireland's largest inland county. It is bordered by Laois to the northeast, Kilkenny to the east, Waterford to the southeast, Cork to the southwest, Limerick to the west, Clare to the west-north-west, Galway to the northwest and Offaly to the north.

For all government administration purposes the county is divided into North Tipperary (county town: Nenagh) and South Tipperary (county town: Clonmel). This division dates back to the Local Government (Ireland) Act 1898, the county's two 'ridings' having had separate assize courts for much longer. The use of the term 'riding' for the divisions was a historical misnomer, since the word derives from the division of an area into three parts. Other major towns in the county are Cahir (Caher), Carrick-on-Suir, Cashel, Fethard, Roscrea, Templemore, Tipperary and Thurles.

Geographical features include the Galtee, Slievenamon, Silvermine and Arra mountain ranges and the Glen of Aherlow. The centre of the county is known as 'the Golden Vale'. This is a fertile stretch of land in the basin of the River Suir, which crosses the county from north to south. The saying is that 'where Tipperary leads, Ireland follows' and this has led to its nickname of the 'Premier County'.

Tipperary is famous for its horse breeding industry and is the home of Coolmore Stud. Perhaps therefore it is fitting that one of horse racing's greatest jockeys, Mick Kinane, was born here in 1959.

The county's other great sporting tradition is in the game of hurling and its teams have regularly been champions of Ireland since the 19th century.

Tipperary	**Population**			**Area**	
Districts	*male*	*female*	*total*	*sq miles*	*sq km*
Borrisokane	3641	3,421	7,062	182	471
Carrick-on-Suir rural area	937	847	1,784	37	97
Carrick-on-Suir Town	2727	2815	5542	3	9
Cashel rural area	7522	7125	14,647	243	631
Cashel Town	1143	1260	2403	1	2
Clogheen	5788	5489	11,277	183	475
Clonmel Borough	7671	8068	15,739	5	12
Clonmel rural area	2696	2638	5334	69	179
Nenagh rural area	8826	8392	17,218	292	757
Nenagh Town	2967	3154	6121	3	8
Roscrea	3908	3873	7781	90	233
Slievardagh	2919	2643	5562	104	269
Templemore	1109	1050	2159	2	4
Thurles rural area	7165	6652	13,817	219	568
Thurles Town	3248	3604	6852	2	5
Tipperary rural area	6372	5915	12,287	224	581
Tipperary Town	2224	2322	4546	1	3
Total	70,863	69,268	140,131	1662	4304

Local Attractions and Information

Administrative headquarters	**South Tipperary**: Aras an Chontae, Clonmel. Tel: 052 34455. **North Tipperary**: Courthouse, Nenagh. Tel: 067 31771.
Annagh Castle	7 miles (11km) northwest of Nenagh. The meagre ivy-covered ruins of a tower house overlooking Lough Derg.
Ardmayle	4 miles (6km) northwest of Cashel. The ruins of two houses. One is a three-storey house, the other a small four-storey tower house.
Athassel Priory	2 miles (3km) south of Golden, 7 miles (11km) east of Tipperary. The ruin of an Augustinian priory built in 1192 by William de Burgo. At one time the largest medieval priory in Ireland, it was burned down by the O'Briens in the 14th century and abandoned. The ruin of the surrounding wall encloses 4 acres (1.2ha).
Ballybeg Castle	Littleton, 4 miles (6km) southeast of Thurles. The ruin of a four-storey tower house.
Ballyfinboy Castle	1 mile (1.6km) west of Borrisokane, 10 miles (16km) northeast of Nenagh. The ivy-covered ruin of a four-storey tower house.
Ballynahow Castle	3 miles (5km) west of Thurles. A rare example of a round tower house. Built by the Purcell family in the 16th century, it has five storeys.
Ballyvada Castle	3 miles (5km) south of Golden, 7 miles (11km) east of Tipperary. The ruin of a pre-17th century four-storey tower house.
Bishops Wood	$1^1/_2$ miles (2.5km) north of Dundrum, 7 miles (11km) northwest of Cashel. An area of coniferous forest once owned by the church and then by the Earl of Montalt. The main species are Norwegian spruce and Sitka spruce with some stands of broadleaves.
Bridewell Jail	St Michael Street, Tipperary. A restored jail housing a heritage centre and Family History Research Centre. Consisting of a central governor's house with cell blocks on either side, it is reputed to have held the father of the infamous Ned Kelly before he was deported to Australia. Tel: 062 52725.
Bridge Castle, The	Liberty Square, Thurles. A castle of indeterminate date, built to guard a crossing of the River Suir at some time between the mid 15th and mid 17th century.
Burncourt Castle	Burncourt, 8 miles (13km) southwest of Cahir. The ruin of a 17th century mansion house. It appears to have had a short lifespan, perhaps as brief as 1641–50.
Cahir Abbey	Tipperary Road, Cahir. Aka Catherdunesque. The ruin of the Augustinian Priory of St Mary, probably founded in the late 12th century.
Cahir Castle	Castle Street, Cahir. A large and well-preserved castle by the River Suir, originally built in the 12th century by Conor O'Brien. It became a Butler stronghold in 1375 and the present castle seems to date from the 15th century. Although it fell to sieges in 1599, 1647 and 1650 it is remarkably undamaged. The castle passed into state care in 1961. Tel: 052 41011.
Cahir Park	$1^1/_2$ miles (2.5km) south of Cahir. An area of mainly broadleaved woodland including beech, Spanish chestnut, oak and sycamore, located beside the River Suir and once part of the Charteris estate.
Carey's Castle	2 miles (3km) south of Clonmel. The ruin of a castle next to the River Glenary amid a mixed woodland with species including ash, beech, birch and oak.
Carrick-on-Suir Heritage Centre	Main Street, Carrick-on-Suir. A local heritage centre housed in a restored former Protestant church. Exhibits include a memorial to Thomas Butler (d.1604) plus a photographic archive. Tel: 051 640200.

Carrick-on-Suir Old Bridge	Carrick-on-Suir, 12 miles (19km) east of Clonmel. A seven-arched stone bridge built c.1447, one of the first to link South Leinster and East Munster.
Cashel Folk Village	Dominick Street, Cashel. A local history museum with reconstructions of traditional thatched village shops including a forge. Tel: 062 62525.
Cashel Heritage Centre	Main Street, Cashel. Housed in the town hall, this local heritage centre focuses on the history of Cashel, the site of an early Christian foundation and the Rock of Cashel assemblage of buildings. Exhibits include a scale model of Cashel in the 1640s and the Charters of Cashel issued by Charles II (1663) and James II (1687). Tel: 062 62511.
Cathedral of St John the Baptist	John Street, Cashel. Built 1750–83 in neoclassical style to replace the cathedral on the Rock of Cashel. A tower was added in 1812.
Cathedral of the Assumption	Cathedral Street, Thurles. The cathedral of the Archdiocese of Cashel and Emly, designed by J J McCarthy and built 1865–79. It stands on the site of three earlier churches, a 14th century Carmelite church, the 18th century Mathew Chapel, and the 'Big Chapel' completed in 1807. Unlike many of McCarthy's churches, this cathedral was designed, according to the wishes of Archbishop Patrick Leahy, in an Italianate Romanesque style modelled on that of Pisa Cathedral. Its bell tower stands 120ft (36.5m) high. It also has a free-standing baptistry and a tabernacle designed by Giacomo della Porta (1537–1603), a pupil of Michelangelo, and purchased from the Gesu church in Rome. The cathedral was extensively renovated in 1979.
Charles Kickham Statue	Kickham Place, Tipperary. A monument to Mullinahone-born writer and political agitator Charles Joseph Kickham (1828–82). Probably his best known works are *Knocknagow*, *The Irish Peasant Girl* and *Slievenamon*. He spent the years 1865–70 in Pentonville Prison.
Churches	**Donaghmore Church**, 1 mile (1.6km) west of Lisronagh, 4 miles (6km) north of Clonmel. The roofless ruin of a small nave and chancel church of indeterminate date, possibly founded by St Farranan and with a Romanesque doorway. **Holy Trinity**, Main Street, Fethard. One of the largest parish churches in Ireland, its nave dating to the early 13th century. **Kilcash Church**, 8 miles (13km) northeast of Clonmel. The ruin of a church with a Romanesque doorway. The ruin of a small church stands nearby. **Kiltinan Church**, 3 miles (5km) southeast of Fethard, 6 miles (10km) northeast of Clonmel, once had a fine example of a sheela-na-gig which was stolen in 1990. It has been replaced by a replica carving. **St Mary's**, Bolton Street, Clonmel. The site of a 13th century church believed to have been built by William de Burgo, and which was superseded in the late 14th century by a fortified church. The remains of this later much-altered church include a 27ft (8.5m) square bell tower. A tower house is now the vestry of the restored church. Tel: 052 22960. **St Mary's Famine Church**, Ikerrin Road, Thurles. A Church of Ireland church built in 1820 on the site of the town's 12th century Norman church. Since 1995 it has housed a museum recalling the years of the Great Famine, and it also contains a military museum featuring memorabilia from the mid 19th century to the present day. A Garden of Remembrance outside the church commemorates the men of Thurles who lost their lives in national and international conflicts. **St Molleran's**, Carrickbeg, 1/4 mile (0.4km) south of Carrick-on-Suir. Fragments of a 14th century Franciscan abbey incorporated in a chapel built in 1820. The friary was suppressed in the 1540s but friars returned for a short time in the 1640s before it was abandoned again. There is also a boundary wall built in the 1840s as a famine relief project. **St Paul's**, Dublin Road, Cahir. One of only two churches known to have been designed by John Nash, this Gothic style Anglican church was completed in 1818.
Clairin Well	Carrick-on-Suir, 12 miles (19km) east of Clonmel. A restored early 16th century well which was once the town's water source.
Clonmel	Clonmel (I. *Cluain Meala*) is a medium-sized town and the county seat of South Tipperary County Council, although most of the townland is situated in Co. Waterford. The Comeragh Mountains are to the south, while east of the town is Slievenamon. The River Suir flows through the town. The site of the Battle of Clonmel is in the Waterford area of Clonmel while other features, such as Clonmel racecourse, are in Tipperary.
Coalbrook Chimneys	Coalbrook, 11 miles (18km) southeast of Thurles. Tall chimneys built in the area around Coalbrook in order to extract impure air from the many coal mines opened in the area between the 17th and 19th century.
Cranagh Castle	Templetuohy, 5 miles (8m) east of Templemore, 9 miles (15km) northeast of Thurles. A circular tower house built before the 17th century which was later restored and incorporated into an 18th century house.
Croke Memorial	Liberty Square, Thurles. A memorial to Dr Thomas Croke (1823–1902), Archbishop of Cashel and Emly, and the first patron of the GAA. It was erected in 1922.
Damer House	Castle Street, Roscrea. An 18th century Queen Anne style house within the walls of Roscrea Castle. It has been restored and one room has been fitted with period furniture. Other rooms house temporary exhibitions. Tel: 050 521850.
Dromineer Castle	Dromineer, 5 miles (8km) northwest of Nenagh. The ivy-covered ruin of a castle possibly built in the 14th century and remodelled in the 15th or 16th century.
Emly Cathedral	Emly, 8 miles (13km) west of Tipperary. The site of a 6th century cathedral. Emly is believed to be one of the oldest towns in Ireland.
Farney Castle	Holycross, 4 miles (6km) soutwest of Thurles. The only round tower house in Ireland occupied as a family home. Built in 1495 by Thomas Butler, 7th Earl of Ormonde, on the site of an earlier fortification, the five-storey round tower stands 58ft (17.5m) high. It was enlarged in 1790 with a

	further tower designed by Francis Johnston. The Butlers lived in the castle until 1660 when it was acquired by the Armstrongs. It is now the home of designer Cyril Cullen. Tel: 050 443281.
Fethard Folk Farm and Transport Museum	Fethard, 8 miles (13km) north of Clonmel. A museum opened in 1983 and housed in the town's former railway station. It has more than 1000 exhibits related to rural life and in particular transport. Tel: 052 31516.
Fethard Friary	Fethard, 8 miles (13km) north of Clonmel. The ruin of an Augustinian friary founded in 1303 by Walter de Mulcote. The friary was suppressed in the 16th century but the friars returned in the 19th century and refurbished the nave of the church and part of the south aisle.
Fethard Town Wall	Fethard, 8 miles (13km) north of Clonmel. The surviving and restored town walls of Fethard, probably built in the late 14th century and extended in the 15th century, enclose 13 acres (5ha), and also feature four tower houses and a town gate.
Glen of Aherlow	4 miles (6km) south of Tipperary. The valley of the River Aherlow, an area full of early Christian sites including St Berrihert's Kyle and Toureen Peakaun.
Glengarra Wood	8 miles (13km) southwest of Cahir. An area of woodland in the foothills of the Galtee Mountains covering 1918 acres (776ha) and owned by the Lismore family from the 1650s until 1940. The woodland is mainly conifer, the main species being Sitka spruce, lodgepole pine, Norwegian spruce and Scots pine. The wood is bisected by the Burncourt River.
Gortavoher	3 miles (5km) south of Tipperary. An area of the Glen of Aherlow Nature Park overlooking the Golden Vale and which was once largely covered by an ancient oak forest.
Grallagh Castle	1¼ miles (2km) south of Horse and Jockey, 6 miles (10km) southeast of Thurles. The ruin of a 16th century four-storey tower house.
Highest point	Galtymore in the Galtee Mountains at 3015ft (919m), also the highest point of Co. Limerick.
Holy Cross Abbey	Holycross, 4 miles (6km) southwest of Thurles. The ruin of a 12th century Cistercian abbey on the bank of the River Suir. The abbey church was re-roofed in 1975 and is now used by the local parish.
Hore Abbey	¼ mile (0.4km) west of Cashel. The ruin of a Cistercian abbey founded in 1266. It was originally a Benedictine foundation but was handed to the Cistercians by Archbishop David MacCearbhaill.
Interesting facts	**John Desmond Bernal** was famous for designing the 'Mulberry' floating harbours used by Allied troops immediately after the D-Day landings in 1944. **Mitchelstown Caves** in the Galtee Mountains were discovered in 1833 by a local farmer and became the first caves in Ireland to be lit by electricity. **Ronald Reagan**'s great-grandparents came from Tipperary. Born in Ballyporeen in 1829, Michael O'Reagan and his wife Catherine (also born in 1829 in Co. Tipperary) emigrated to Illinois in 1858.
'It's a Long Way to Tipperary'	A song written by Jack Judge (1878–1938) and Harry Williams (1874–1924) in 1912. It was a staple song of World War I.
Kilcooley Abbey	1¼ miles (2km) east of Gortnahoe, 10½ miles (17km) east of Thurles. The substantial ruin of a Cistercian abbey founded in 1182 by Donal Mor O'Brien and dedicated to the Virgin Mary and St Benedict. It was almost destroyed in 1445 but was rebuilt and remodelled. The chancel holds a notable tomb-chest carved by sculptor Rory O'Tunney, dating to c.1526.
Killballyboy Wood	1¼ miles (2km) southeast of Clogheen, 8 miles (13km) southwest of Cahir. The main tree species include Scots pine, Sitka spruce and Douglas fir.
Knockagh Castle	2 miles (3km) southwest of Templemore, 8 miles (13km) northwest of Thurles. The ruin of a round tower house.
Knockgraffon Castle	½ mile (0.8km) south of Knockgraffon, 2½ miles (4km) north of Cahir. The ruin of a four-storey tower house.
Knockgraffon Motte	½ mile (0.8km) south of Knockgraffon, 2½ miles (4km) north of Cahir. A 12th century Anglo-Norman motte beside the River Suir which would once have supported a wooden fort.
Lár na Páirce	Liberty Square, Thurles. A visitor centre celebrating the history of Gaelic Games. Exhibits include sporting memorabilia and a Hall of Fame. Tel: 050 422702.
Lorrha Priory	Lorrha, 16 miles (26km) northwest of Roscrea. The ruin of a 13th century Dominican priory founded on the site of an early monastery associated with St Ruadhan. Nearby is the ruin of the 15th century St Ruadhan's Church.
Lough Derg	A lough on the River Shannon, the second largest lough in the Republic of Ireland, covering an area of 45 sq miles (118 sq km) and with a maximum depth of 118ft (36m). Parts of the lough are in Co. Clare and Co. Galway.
Loughmore Castle	Loughmore, 5 miles (8km) north of Thurles. The substantial ruin of a Purcell family tower house and adjoining mansion.
Maid of Erin	Church Street, Tipperary. A monument erected in 1907 to commemorate the Manchester Martyrs (William Allen, Michael Larkin and William Goold), executed on 23 November 1867 for their part in a successful attempt to release from custody the Fenian leaders Thomas Kelly and Timothy Deasy. A policeman was shot dead during the incident.
Main Guard	Sarsfield Street, Clonmel. Built by James Butler, 1st Duke of Ormonde, in the 1670s as the courthouse for the Palatinate of Co. Tipperary. It stands at the intersection of the four main streets of Clonmel. The ground floor loggia was converted into shops in the early 19th century. Its main features are the restored open arched loggia and its octagonal cupola. Tel: 052 27484.
Marl Bog	½ mile (0.8km) southwest of Dundrum, 7 miles (11km) northwest of Cashel. A mixed, mainly coniferous woodland of Douglas fir, Norwegian spruce and Sitka spruce, surrounding an 18 acre (7ha) man-made lake.
Mona Incha Abbey	2 miles (3km) southeast of Roscrea. The ruin of an abbey church located on what was once an island in a bog. The church has a 12th century Romanesque doorway and there are also fragments of a high cross.
Moycarky Castle	Moycarky, 4 miles (6km) southeast of Thurles. A ruined 16th century tower house, once the

residence of the Cantwell family and set within a large rectangular bawn with round flanking towers at the northeast and southwest corners. William Cantwell was listed as its proprietor in 1640.

Museum of Transport	Emmet Street, Clonmel. A private transport museum housed in the restored 19th century Richmond Mill. It has examples of many vintage and classic cars including a 1904 Clement Talbot. Also on display are motoring memorabilia. Tel: 052 29727.
Nenagh Castle	Nenagh. The ruin of an early 13th century castle built by Theobald Walter, nephew of Thomas a Becket. There were originally three large five-storey circular towers connected by a curtain wall; only one now remains.
Nenagh Friary	Abbey Street, Nenagh. A 13th century Franciscan friary of which only the ruin of the friary church remains.
Nenagh Heritage Centre	Kickham Street, Nenagh. Housed in what was originally the governor's house for Nenagh gaol. Probably built in the early 19th century, this was the hub from which radiated three cell blocks, one of which still remains. The house was later used as a school before becoming the heritage centre. The centre features a scale model of the gaol plus recreations of a school room, a drapers shop, a pub, a grocery shop and a recreated diary. There is also a museum of rural life. The centre is in addition a family history resource centre. Tel: 067 33850.
Ormond Castle	Castle Park, Carrick-on-Suir. An Elizabethan U-plan manor house built in the 1560s by Thomas Butler, 10th Earl of Ormond, and incorporating two 15th century tower houses which originally stood in two corners of a bawn. It passed into state care in 1947 and has been conserved including the restoration of the state rooms with their decorative plasterwork. Tel: 051 640787.
Redwood Bog Nature Reserve	5 miles (8km) north of Lorrha, 21 miles (34km) northeast of Nenagh. A raised bog covering 326 acres (132ha) on the southern margin of the Little Brosna flood plain at its confluence with the Shannon.
Redwood Castle	3 miles (5km) north of Lorrha, 18 miles (29km) northwest of Roscrea. Aka Egan Castle. A restored 13th century tower house acquired in the 14th century by the Egan family. Enlarged in the late 16th century, it was damaged by Cromwellian forces c.1650. It was restored in the 1970s. Tel: 087 981 8126.
Rivers	The **Nore** rises on the eastern slopes of the Devil's Bit Mountain in Co. Tipperary and flows southeastwards into Co. Laois and Co. Kilkenny, passing Durrow (Laois), Ballyragget, Bennettsbridge, Thomastown and Inistioge (all in Kilkenny) before joining the River Barrow at Waterford Harbour, just north of New Ross, Co. Wexford; its total length 87 miles (140km). Together with the Suir and the Barrow, the river is one of the trio known as The Three Sisters. The **Suir** (I. Siúr) rises on the slopes of Devil's Bit Mountain, just north of Templemore in Co. Tipperary and flows south through Loughmore, Thurles, Holycross, Golden and Knockgraffon, merging with the River Aherlow at Kilmoyler and further on with the Tar. The river turns east at the Comeragh Mountains, forming the border between Co. Waterford and Co. Kilkenny, and continues through Cahir, Clonmel and Carrick-on-Suir before reaching Waterford; its total length approximately 114 miles (184km). Here, it meets the River Barrow and the River Nore to form a wide navigable estuary that opens into the Atlantic Ocean.
Rock of Cashel	$^1/_4$ mile (0.4km) northwest of Cashel. A rocky outcrop in the Golden Vale containing a group of medieval buildings. It is believed that this site was the seat of the kings of Munster in the 4th and 5th centuries and that Brian Boru was crowned High King of Ireland here in the 11th century. The buildings include a round tower, a 13th century cathedral and a 15th century castle. The restored Hall of Vicars now houses a visitor centre.
Roscrea Castle	Castle Street, Roscrea. The castle is said to have been built by King John in 1213 but has more features of a later 13th century construction. It has a rectangular gate tower, two D-shaped towers and curtain walls. Some of the castle rooms house temporary exhibitions. Tel: 050 521850.
Roscrea Franciscan Friary	Castle Street, Roscrea. The ruin of a 15th century Franciscan friary abandoned soon after the Dissolution. The main remains consist of two walls of the chancel and the bell tower. Tel: 050 521850.
Roscrea Monastic Site	Castle Street, Roscrea. The site of a 7th century monastic foundation of St Cronan. The remains consist of a church with a 12th century Romanesque doorway and a 10th century round tower 65ft (20m) high. Tel: 050 521850.
St Berrihert's Kyle	4 miles (6km) southeast of Tipperary. An early Christian enclosure or burial site in the Glen of Aherlow featuring 72 inscribed stone slabs and crosses dating to the 7th–9th century. The site is identified with Saxon cleric St Berrihert, said to have settled in Ireland after the Synod of Whitby in AD 664.
St Dominic's Priory	Dominic Street, Cashel. The substantial ruin of a Dominican priory founded in 1243 by David O'Kelly. It was burned down and rebuilt during its lifetime as a priory but was abandoned following the Dissolution.
St Patrick's Cathedral	$^1/_4$ mile (0.4km) northwest of Cashel. The ruin of a cathedral built 1235–70 on the Rock of Cashel. The Rock cathedral was closed for worship in 1721.
St Patrick's Well	2 miles (3km) west of Clonmel. A small 17th century church next to a holy well known as St Patrick's Well. The water from the well enters a pond at the foot of a tree and the well was a site of pilgrimage.
1798 Memorial	Liberty Square, Thurles. A monument commemorating the 1798 rebellion and featuring carvings of Wolfe Tone, Lord Edward Fitzgerald and Robert Emmet. It was unveiled on St Patrick's Day 1900. The memorial is known locally as 'the stone men'.
Slate Quarries	Ahenny, 4 miles (6km) north of Carrick-on-Suir. The village of Ahenny, which grew around the slate quarries on the Kilkenny/Tipperary border, is now part ruined cottages, part lived-in village and part sculptural displays.

Sliabh na mBan	(I. = Mountain of the Women). Aka Slievenamon. The highest mountain in the South Tipperary area at 2368ft (722m).
Slieveardagh Tower	1 mile (1.6km) east of Grange, 11 miles (18km) east of Thurles, in the Slieveardagh Hills. A tower erected on the Crag by Sir William Barker on the Kilcooly estate in 1816 to mark the Duke of Wellington's victory in the Battle of Waterloo.
South Tipperary County Museum	Mick Delahunty Square, Clonmel. Local history museum charting the history of the county, housed in a purpose-built museum building with large galleries and a conservation laboratory. Tel: 052 34550.
Sport	
Gaelic football	**Semple Stadium**, Thurles, is a major GAA stadium with a capacity of 53,000 (36,000 seated). One of the largest sporting venues in Ireland, it was built in 1910 and is named for Tom Semple, captain of the Thurles 'Blues' who won All-Ireland Senior Hurling Championship medals in 1900, 1906 and 1908. The stadium was improved in the 1980s and plans for further improvements to facilities are ongoing. **Tipperary** were winners of the All-Ireland Senior Football Championship in 1889, 1895, 1900 and 1920.
horse racing	**Clonmel** Racecourse, Davis Road, Clonmel. Free racing was a regular feature at Clonmel before the course was enclosed in 1913 as Powerstown Park. Refurbished in 1998, Clonmel is a right-handed oval course of 1¼ miles (2km) with a run-in of 2¼ furlongs (0.45km) and an uphill finish, holding Both Flat and National Hunt racing. Tel: 052 72481. **Coolmore Stud**, Fethard. One of the world's most important racehorse breeders, established in 1975 by trainer Vincent O'Brien and businessman Robert Sangster, and now owned by O'Brien's son-in-law John Magnier. **Kiltinan Castle Stud**, Kiltinan Castle, Fethard, was established in 1982 by Magee and Ogden White and purchased in 1995 by Andrew and Madeleine Lloyd Webber following Magee White's death the same year. The stud has since been totally redeveloped. Tel: 052 32267. **Thurles** Racecourse, Thurles. Race meetings have been held at Thurles since the 18th century. The course is a right-handed oval of 1¼ miles (2km) with run-in of 1¼ furlongs (0.25km) and an uphill finish and stages both Flat and National Hunt racing. Tel: 050 423272. **Tipperary** Racecourse, Limerick Junction, Tipperary. The first recorded meeting was held in 1848 at the Barronstown Course and the course at Limerick Junction was first used in 1916. The name was changed to Tipperary Racecourse in 1986. Both Flat and National Hunt racing are held at the course. Tipperary is a left-handed oval of 1¼ miles (2km) with a run-in of 2¼ furlongs (0.45km). Tel: 062 51357.
hurling	**Tipperary** are winners of the All-Ireland Senior Hurling Championship in 1887, 1895, 1896, 1898, 1899, 1900, 1906, 1908, 1916, 1925, 1930, 1937, 1945, 1949, 1950, 1951, 1958, 1961, 1962, 1964, 1965, 1971, 1989, 1991 and 2001.
Toureen Peakaun	Glen of Aherlow, 4 miles (6km) northwest of Cahir. The ruin of a 12th century church on a monastic site traditionally said to have been founded by St Abban in the 5th century, and named for his successor St Beccan (Peakaun).
Twomileborris Castle	Twomileborris, 4½ miles (7km) east of Thurles. The ruin of a four-storey tower house, now part of a farm complex.

Some famous people born in County Tipperary

Bernal, John Desmond (scientist) (1901–71)	Nenagh
Carroll, John (hurling player) (1978–)	Roscrea
Clancy, (William) 'Liam' (singer) (1935–)	Carrick-on-Suir
Clancy, Patrick (singer) (1922–98)	Carrick-on-Suir
Clancy, Tom (singer) (1924–90)	Carrick-on-Suir
Doyle, Jimmy (hurling player) (1939–)	Thurles
Doyle, John (hurling player) (1930–)	Holycross
Dunne, Tommy (hurling player) (1974–)	Toomevara
Feehan, John M (author) (1916–91)	Dualla
Flynn, Bernadette (dancer) (1979–)	Nenagh
Foli, Allan James (opera singer) (1837–99)	Cahir
Keating, Michael 'Babs' (hurling player) (1944–)	Ardfinnan
Kinane, Michael (jockey) (1959–)	Killenaule
O'Leary, John (poet) (1830–1907)	Tipperary
Patterson, Frank (tenor) (1938–2000)	Clonmel
Ryan, Paddy (heavyweight boxer) (1851–1900)	Thurles
Shortt, Patt (comedian) (1966–)	Thurles
Sterne, Laurence (author) (1713–68)	Clonmel

Waterford

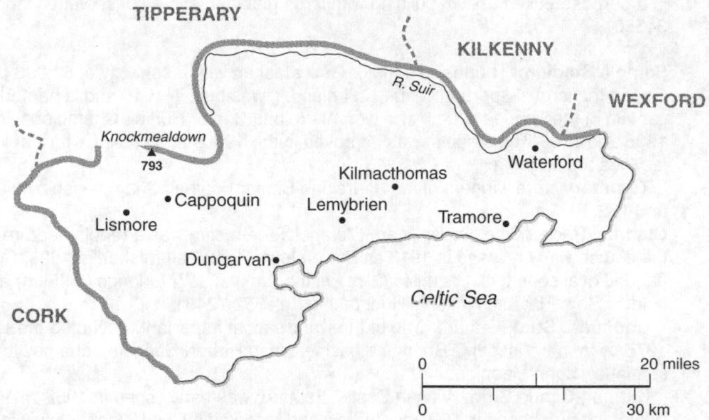
TIPPERARY
KILKENNY
R. Suir
WEXFORD
Knockmealdown
793
Waterford
Kilmacthomas
Cappoquin
Lemybrien
Lismore
Tramore
Dungarvan
Celtic Sea
CORK
0
20 miles
0
30 km

Waterford is part of the province of Munster. It lies on the southeastern coast of Ireland and is bordered by the counties of Cork to the west, Tipperary to the north, and Kilkenny and Wexford to the northeast. The southern and eastern coastline is on the Celtic Sea. County Waterford is unusual in having a bicameral local council. The county town is often considered to be the city of Waterford although the administrative headquarters are based in Dungarvan. This is because Waterford has its own city council, distinct from the rest of the county. There is a small Gaeltacht (Irish-speaking) area to the south of Dungarvan.

The area was first settled during the Mesolithic period and was later occupied by a Celtic tribe known as the Decii; the name 'The Decies' is still applied to the region. Monastic foundations were established at Lismore and Ardmore during the early Christian period and these attracted the attention of the Vikings, who established a settlement in AD 914 at what would become Waterford. An 'independent' Waterford was forced to accept the suzerainty of Diarmuid Mac Murrough, king of Leinster, in the 12th century. After Mac Murrough's expulsion and subsequent return along with what amounted to an Anglo-Norman army, Waterford fell to Richard Fitzgilbert de Clare, Earl of Pembroke (Strongbow).

Waterford has a number of contenders for most famous son/daughter. The very popular singers Val Doonican and Gilbert O'Sullivan are contenders in the entertainments field; in the sciences the honours must go to Robert Boyle, the first modern chemist, and to Ernest Walton, co-winner of the 1951 Nobel Physics Prize for his research on atomic nuclei, and in particular his 1932 achievement of 'splitting the atom'. A statesman worthy of mention is William Hobson, first Governor of New Zealand and co-author of the Treaty of Waitangi.

The settlement at **Waterford** was declared a royal city by Henry II of England in 1171 and developed as a major port. In the 15th century the city was enlarged with the building of an outer wall on the west side, much of which still stands today. Later in the century Waterford repelled two pretenders to the English throne: Lambert Simnel and Perkin Warbeck. As a result, Henry VII gave the city its motto: *Urbs Intacta Manet Waterfordia* ('Waterford remains the untaken city'). Following the Reformation, Waterford remained a Catholic city and participated from 1642 to 1649 in the Confederation of Kilkenny, an independent Catholic government. This was ended abruptly by Oliver Cromwell, who brought the country back firmly under English rule; his nephew Henry Ireton finally took Waterford in 1650 after a major siege. The River Suir flows through the city and has provided the basis for Waterford's long maritime history. In the 19th century shipbuilding was a major industry in the city. The owners of the Neptune Shipyard, the Malcomson family, built and held the largest fleet of iron steamers in the world between the mid 1850s and the late 1860s, including five transatlantic passenger liners. Today, Waterford's name is synonymous the world over with Waterford Crystal, a legacy of one of the city's most successful and enduring industries, glass making. Glass, or crystal, has been manufactured in the city since 1783.

Waterford	Population			Area	
Districts	*male*	*female*	*total*	*sq miles*	*sq km*
Carrick-on-Suir	2110	2062	4172	86	222
Clonmel	1283	1209	2492	63	164
Dungarvan rural area	4179	3941	8120	146	377
Dungarvan Town	3517	3703	7220	2	6
Kilmacthomas	3179	3014	6193	101	262
Lismore	3841	3659	7500	153	397
Waterford City	21,782	22,812	44,594	16	42
Waterford rural area	9308	9048	18,356	95	246
Youghal	1473	1426	2899	56	144
Total	50,672	50,874	101,546	718	1859

Local Attractions and Information

Abbey Road Gardens	Abbeylands, Ferrybank, Waterford. A cottage garden covering $^3/_4$ acre (0.3ha) and stocked with alpines in scree beds plus herbaceous borders. Tel: 051 851111.
Administrative headquarters	**Waterford County Council**: Civic Offices, Dungarvan. Tel: 058 22000. **Waterford City Council:** City Hall, The Mall, Waterford. Tel: 051 309900.
Airport	**Waterford Airport** (WAT), aka South East Regional Airport, serves Waterford and the southeast region. Aer Arann is currently the only carrier operating out of the airport, which operates flights to destinations in England and France. Tel: 051 875589.
Ardmore Monastic Site	Ardmore, 10 miles (16km) southwest of Dungarvan. The remains of a 5th century monastic site believed to have been founded by St Declan. The main ruins are the round tower and cathedral, both dating to the 12th century. The tower is more than 90ft (27.5m) high with a doorway 13ft (4m) above ground level; there are two ogham stones inside the cathedral. Nearby is St Declan's Oratory, traditionally the saint's resting place.
Ballynageeragh Portal Tomb	$4^1/_2$ miles (7km) west of Tramore. A late Neolithic portal dolmen dating to 2500–2000 BC. It has an oval capstone which rests on a doorstone, with a cushion stone on top of the backstone. It was excavated in the 1930s.
Ballynamona Court Cairn	1 mile (1.6km) north of Mine Head, 6 miles (10km) southeast of Dungarvan. Dating to c. 2000 BC, this is the only court cairn in the southeast of Ireland.
Ballysaggartmore Towers	2 miles (3km) west of Lismore. Two extravagant Gothic style gate towers surrounded by woodland and straddling a river. Built in 1850 by Arthur Kiely-Ussher for his wife, they were intended to be part of a larger castle project but the money ran out at this point.
Ballyscanlon Forest	1 mile (1.6km) northeast of Fenor, 3 miles (5km) northwest of Tramore. A coniferous wood overlooking Ballyscanlon Lough. The main species in the wood are lodgepole pine, Norwegian spruce and Sitka spruce.
Battles	See separate table for details of the Battle of Clonmel.
Blackfriars Abbey	Conduit Lane, Waterford. The ruin of a Dominican abbey founded in the 1220s. The buildings were put to secular use after the Dissolution and were eventually abandoned or demolished. The main feature is the square tower or belfry.
Cappoquin House and Gardens	Cappoquin, 4 miles (6km) east of Lismore. An 18th century mansion and gardens beside the River Blackwater.
Cathedral of the Most Holy Trinity	Barronstrand Street, Waterford. Ireland's oldest surviving Catholic cathedral, designed and built by John Roberts in 1793. It was refurbished in the late 1970s in line with Vatican II, with ten crystal chandeliers donated by Waterford Crystal. Tel: 051 875166.
Christ Church Cathedral	Cathedral Square, Waterford. A Church of Ireland cathedral designed by local architect John Roberts. The first church on the site was built in the 11th century; it was replaced in 1210 by the Norman Gothic cathedral, which was demolished in 1773 because it was felt to be old-fashioned. The new cathedral was complete by 1779. Roberts also designed the Catholic cathedral, and Waterford is believed to be the only city with two cathedrals designed by the same architect. Tel: 051 858958.
Clonmel	See Tipperary
Colligan Wood	4 miles (6km) northwest of Dungarvan. A mixed woodland of ash, beech, birch, larch, oak and spruce, located in the valley of the Colligan River.
Comeragh Mountains	A chain of mountains in the centre and north of the county, to the east of the Monavullagh Mountains. Their highest peak is Fauscoum at 2598ft (792m).
Copper Coast European Geopark	Designated in 2001, the Geopark runs for 15 miles (24km) along the coast from Fenor to Stradbally and is named from the 19th century copper mines at Knockmahon and Tankardstown, where the engine houses are still visible. The landscape of the area includes cliffs, coves, caves, beaches, woodland and lakes. Tel: 051 396160.
Curraghmore House and Gardens	2 miles (3km) west of Portlaw, 10 miles (16km) west of Waterford. The home of the Marquis of Waterford and his ancestors since 1170. The house is noted for its plasterwork, while the grounds feature a shell grotto and an arboretum. Tel: 051 387102.
Dane's Island	See Little Island
Dromana Gate	Villierstown, 10 miles (16km) west of Dungarvan. A unique Gothic style Hindu gate on a bridge over the River Finisk. It was built in 1830 as a wedding gift for local landlord and MP Henry Villiers-Stuart.

Dromana Wood	1/2 miles (0.8km) north of Villierstown, 10 miles (16km) west of Dungarvan. An old oak woodland on the banks of the Blackwater River, formerly part of the Villiers-Stuart estate.
Dungarvan	The administrative centre of Co. Waterford, although the city of Waterford is the de facto capital. The town's Irish name means 'Garbhan's fort', referring to St Garbhan who founded a church here in the 7th century. Dungarvan is situated at the mouth of the Colligan River, which divides the town into two parts connected by a causeway and bridge of a single arch. Both bridge and causeway were built by the Dukes of Devonshire. The neighbouring parish is called Abbeyside, where portions of an Augustinian friary founded by the McGrath family in the 4th century survive incorporated with a Roman Catholic church. In Dungarvan proper, a castle built by King John stands by the harbour.
Dungarvan Castle	See King John's Castle
Dunhill Castle	Dunhill, 5 miles (8km) west of Tramore. The ruin of a castle built in the early 13th century by the la Poer (Power) family. As its name suggests, it stands on a hilltop. The family used it as a base for attacks on Waterford and, despite defeats and executions, at least one branch of the family held on to it until it was captured, reputedly for the only time, by Cromwellian forces in 1649. The castle was passed to Sir John Cole but it was allowed to fall into disrepair.
Edmund Rice Centre	Barrack Street, Waterford. Housed in Mount Sion School, the centre celebrates the life of Edmund Ignatius Rice (1762–1844), who founded the Congregation of Christian Brothers and the Presentation Brothers, and who spent most of his life teaching or training teachers for the poor and marginalised in Ireland, and particularly Waterford. He founded the Mount Sion School in Waterford in 1802. The casket containing his remains may be seen in the chapel. Tel: 051 87439.
French Church	Greyfriars, Waterford. A Franciscan friary (Greyfriars) founded in the 1240s by Sir Hugh Purcell. It later served as a hospital and on the arrival of Huguenot refugees in Waterford in the 17th century part of the friary was converted into a church. It was in use until 1819 and is still known as the French Church.
Garter Lane Arts Centre and Theatre	O'Connell Street, Waterford. An arts centre and theatre housed in a Quaker meeting house built in 1792. Tel: 051 855038.
Gaulstown Dolmen	4 1/2 miles (7km) southwest of Waterford. A Neolithic portal tomb with six uprights and a 16ft (5m) long capstone.
Glenshelane Forest	1 mile (1.6km) northeast of Cappoquin, 4 miles (6km) northeast of Lismore. (I. *Gleann Siothlain* = Glen of the Fairies). A woodland stretching along the Glenshelane River and comprised largely of Norwegian spruce, which was planted when much of the old oak woodland was cleared, although some stands of oak remain. It is a noted bluebell wood in spring.
Harristown Passage Tomb	2 miles (3km) northwest of Dunmore East, 6 miles (10km) northeast of Tramore. A passage tomb located on a hilltop and dating to 2500–2000 BC. Only two of the capping stones remain.
Highest point	Knockmealdown at 2602ft (793m).
Interesting facts	Waterford-born **William Hobson** was the first Governor of New Zealand and co-author of the Treaty of Waitangi (which made the country a British colony and is generally considered the founding point of New Zealand as a nation). Having joined the Royal Navy in 1803, Hobson was promoted to commander in May 1824 after serving in the Napoleonic Wars and later helping to suppress piracy in the Caribbean. He arrived in the Bay of Islands on 29 January 1840 as Lieutenant-Governor of New Zealand. Upon arrival Hobson almost immediately proposed the Treaty of Waitangi, despite having a stroke midway through its drafting. In November 1840 Queen Victoria signed a royal charter allowing New Zealand to become a Crown colony separate from New South Wales. Hobson was sworn in as Governor and Commander in Chief on 3 May 1841; he suffered a second stroke and died on 10 September 1842. He was buried in Symonds Street cemetery in Auckland. Lismore-born **Robert Boyle** was a natural philosopher, chemist, physicist, inventor and scientist, noted for his work in physics and chemistry. Although his research and personal philosophy clearly has its roots in the alchemical tradition, he is largely regarded today as the first modern chemist. Among his works, *The Sceptical Chymist* is seen as a cornerstone book in the field of chemistry. Boyle is best remembered for the law named after him which states that the volume of a gas varies inversely with its pressure. As a director of the East India Company, however, he spent large sums in promoting the spread of Christianity in the East, contributing liberally to missionary societies and to the expenses of translating the Bible or portions of it into various languages. **Henry II** was the first English king to set foot in Ireland, arriving in Waterford from France in 1171 to assert his overlordship. All the Normans, along with many Irish princes, took oaths of homage to Henry, and he left after six months, granting Waterford a royal charter before he went. He never returned, but he later named his young son, the future King John, Lord of Ireland. **Henry Denny**, a butcher from the city of Waterford, invented and marketed bacon rashers in 1820. Later that century, in 1895, Quaker **W R Jacobs** invented the cream cracker at his bakery in Bridge Street, Waterford. Jacobs topped this feat in 1903 by inventing the fig roll! **Thomas Francis Meagher** became a founding member of the Young Ireland group in 1845 soon after hearing a typically rousing speech from Daniel O'Connell. Meagher formed a new repeal body, known as the Irish Confederation, and openly preached revolution. In 1848 he went to France to study revolutionary events there, returning to Ireland with the design for a new flag of Ireland, a tricolour of orange, white and green gifted by the French. The acquisition of the flag is commemorated at the 1848 Flag Monument in the Irish Parliament. The design used was similar to that of the present flag, except that orange was placed next to the staff, and the red hand of Ulster decorated the white field. This flag was first flown in public on 1 March 1848, during the Waterford by-election, when Meagher and his friends flew it from the headquarters of Meagher's Wolfe Tone Confederate Club at 33 The Mall,

Waterford. Following the incident in August 1848 known as the Young Irelander Rebellion of 1848 or the Battle of Ballingarry, Meagher was arrested, tried and convicted for sedition; due to a newly passed ex post facto law, this meant that he was sentenced to be hanged, drawn and quartered. After his trial, however, Meagher delivered his famous 'Speech From the Dock' – considered second only to Robert Emmet's pre-execution speech in the pantheon of Irish political rhetoric. Meagher's death sentence was commuted to transportation to Van Diemen's Land (Tasmania, Australia). In January 1852 he escaped to America and, after having his honour upheld by an American jury, served the Union Army with distinction as an acting major. After the war, Meagher was appointed secretary of the new Territory of Montana, and soon after arriving in the territory was designated acting governor. He is remembered for his service to Montana with a statue on the front lawn of the Capitol grounds in Helena, Montana, and with another statue in Billings. Meagher County, Montana, was also named in his honour. Meagher drowned in mysterious circumstances. Some say he was murdered, some say he took his own life; all that is known for certain is that he boarded his steamboat, the *G A Thompson* and promptly 'fell' overboard. In the 18th century Waterford Castle was the home of the formidable **Mary Frances Fitzgerald**, who dominated the social world of the time. At one stage engaged to the Duke of Wellington, she broke off the engagement to marry her first cousin, John Purcell, in 1801. An extravagant lady, she was in the habit, on her return to the family seat, of being rowed in state across the river with 24 musicians playing in the barge. Her son Edward Fitzgerald is remembered as the translator of Omar Khayyam's *Rubaiyat*. **The 3rd Marquis of Waterford** is said to have given rise to the saying 'Paint the town red' when in 1837 he and a group of friends ran riot in the Leicestershire town of Melton Mowbray, painting the town's toll-bar and several buildings red!

Island of Vryk — See Little Island

Islands — Inshore islands: although there are various rocky islets in the River Nore there are only two named islands, **Gowlaun Island** and **Harrybro Island**. Situated in Waterford City is **Little Island** in the River Suir (aka **Waterford Castle Island** or **The Island**, formerly **Dane's Island** or **Island of Vryk** – see separate entry). Offshore islands (Fastnet Sea Area): **Black Rocks**, **Falskirt Rock** (popular site for scuba diving), **The Gainers** (aka **Goat Island** – the group of tiny rock stacks are really an extension of Helvick Head at low water), **Three Mile Rock** and **Western Rock** lie southeast of Hook Head. See also Molana Abbey.

John Roberts Square — A pedestrianised area that is one of the main focal points of Waterford's modern day commercial centre. Named after the city's most celebrated architect, John Roberts (1712–96), it was formed from the junction of Barronstrand Street, Broad Street and George's Street. It is often referred to locally as Red Square, due to the red paving that was used when the area was first pedestrianised, although now it is grey-paved.

Kilclooney Wood — 4 miles (6km) northwest of Kilmacthomas, 12 miles (19km) northeast of Dungarvan. This mainly coniferous wood, comprised of species including European larch, Norwegian spruce, Sitka spruce and western hemlock, was originally part of the Curraghmore estate. Crotty's Rock and Crotty's Lake in the area attest to the tradition that the wood was the hiding place of the 19th century highwayman known as Crotty the Robber.

King John's Castle — Castle Street, Dungarvan. Aka Dungarvan Castle. Founded by King John in 1185 at the mouth of the River Colligan, one of the few royal castles in Ireland built in the 12th century. Its position enabled it to be supplied by water in the event of a siege. The castle has a shell keep, also rare in Ireland, and curtain walls. It was used as a barracks, which led to it being damaged during an IRA occupation in 1922. Restored and used as the local Garda Station until 1987, the castle is managed by Dúchas The Heritage Service. Conservation work is ongoing. Tel: 058 48144.

Knockeen Portal Tomb — $2^1/_2$ miles (4km) north of Tramore. A portal dolmen which has been built into a wall. It has two capstones, one resting on the portal stones and a second resting on the sidestones and backstone.

Lismore — The town of Lismore (I. *Lios Mor* = Great Enclosure), located on a crossing of the River Blackwater, was founded by St Mochuda, also known as St Carthage. In the 7th century, Lismore was the site of a well-known abbey. It is also home to Lismore Castle.

Lismore Castle — $^1/_4$ mile (0.4km) north of Lismore. Built in 1185 by the future King John. On his accession to the throne he gave the castle to the church and it became a bishops' palace until the late 16th century. It was the property of Sir Walter Raleigh 1589–1602; when Raleigh was imprisoned for treason he sold it to Richard Boyle, Earl of Cor, who renovated it and began turning the estate into an archetypal English lord's demesne with deer parks and ponds. Scientist Robert Boyle was born at Lismore in 1626. The castle was sacked by a force of the Catholic Confederacy in 1645. The castle is now owned by the Devonshire family, having passed in 1753 to the 4th Duke of Devonshire who had married Lady Charlotte Boyle in 1748. The 6th Duke carried out restoration and made changes to the castle and gardens between 1840 and his death in 1858 with the aid of his friend, engineer and botanist Joseph Paxton. A contemporary art gallery in the west wing was opened in 2005. Tel: 058 54424.

Lismore Castle Gardens — $^1/_4$ mile (0.4km) north of Lismore. The gardens at Lismore Castle cover 7 acres (2.8ha) within the outer defensive walls and are split between the Upper and Lower Gardens. The Upper Garden is a walled garden originally created in the early 17th century, the Lower Garden an informal planting originally laid out in the 19th century. There is a yew walk where it is said that Edmund Spenser wrote part of *The Faerie Queene* (see also Kilcolman Castle, Cork). The gardens also feature several contemporary sculptures. Tel: 058 54424.

Lismore Heritage Centre — Main Street, Lismore. Housed in the old courthouse and dedicated to the history of Lismore from its foundation in the 7th century to the present day. The exhibition galleries include a room celebrating the life and works of Lismore-born scientist Robert Boyle plus other rooms with the story of the people who helped to shape the town including Walter Raleigh, Richard Boyle and the Dukes of Devonshire. Exhibits include the 11th century Lismore Crozier. Tel: 058 54975.

Little Island — Aka Waterford Castle Island, the Island, Island of Vryk. A 310 acre (125ha) island situated in the River Suir to the east of the city of Waterford. According to tradition, a monastic settlement existed on the island sometime between the 6th and 8th century: two finds, an 8th century winged angel and the crude carving of a monk's head, dating from the 6th century and now prominently displayed over the main entrance to the castle, have lent substance to this. The island's seclusion was attractive to the monks; however, due to its strategic importance, they came under frequent attack and were eventually forced to move to safer quarters. The island then became the site of a Danish settlement, with two castles guarding the river at the north and south, and was thereafter referred to in annals as Dane's Island or the Island of Vryk. Maurice Fitzgerald, cousin of Strongbow, the English Earl of Pembroke, landed in Waterford during the Norman invasion of Ireland in 1170. During a battle he was taken prisoner by the Ossermen of Waterford and held on the island until rescued by his son-in-law to rejoin the victorious Norman army. He was rewarded for his support of the invasion by the grant of large tracts of land in Munster and Leinster, including the island on which he decided to make his home. For 800 years it thus became home to the Earls of Kildare and Ormond and the Knights of Glin and Kerry, in one of the longest unbroken stewardships on record in Ireland. **Waterford Castle** originated as a Norman keep, the first structure built by the Fitzgeralds. In the 15th century this was replaced by the tower which forms the central part of the present castle. Initially relatively modest in size, it was enlarged over the years, first in 1849 by John Fitzgerald and subsequently in 1875 and 1895 when the east and west wings were added. Built entirely of stone, they completed the main structure to such an extent that they are now indistinguishable. Until the 20th century the castle retained its original arrow slit windows, giving it a fortress-like exterior and a rather dark uncomfortable interior. During the last stage of expansion the farm buildings and stable yard were completed, enabling the island to support an entire community. Another feature added to the castle during the centuries was the rooftop gargoyles, brought from Castle Irwell in Manchester, which belonged to a female ancestor. In the 18th century the castle was the home of notable socialite Mary Frances Fitzgerald (see Interesting facts); her son Edward was the great-great-uncle of Mary Fitzgerald, the last of the family to own the castle. Mary married an Italian, Prince Caracciolo, whom she met while studying in Italy. On their return they made their home in Dublin, where she was a prominent patron of the arts; she sold the castle to the Rhodesian Igo family in 1958, thus ending the remarkable link between the Fitzgeralds and the Island. The Igos installed a 5 acre (2ha) complex of glasshouses from which they produced fruit and flowers. The chain link ferry was also commissioned at this time. Their interest in the venture and the island passed to the Farren Brothers, who concentrated on tomato growing, updating the island's roads and fencing. In 1978 the island was rented to Roger Shipsey, a Waterford pedigree dairy farmer, who later bought it outright, seeing its advantage as a disease free area thanks to its isolation. Eddie Reams, who bought the island in 1987, has developed the castle and the island into a luxury hotel and country club. Tel: 051 878203.

Master McGrath Monument — 2 miles (3km) northwest of Dungarvan. A monument erected to the greyhound Master McGrath (1866–71), winner of the Waterloo Cup in 1868, 1869 and 1871. He was buried in Lurgan. The monument was originally erected at his birthplace, Colligan Lodge, but was moved to its current position outside Dungarvan in 1933.

Molana Abbey — 11 miles (18km) southeast of Lismore. An Augustinian abbey founded in the late 12th century on the island of Molana in the River Blackwater (now joined to the mainland by a causeway built in 1806) which was the site of a 6th century monastery founded by St Macbanfaidh. The abbey is said to be the final resting place of Raymond le Gros (c. 1135–1186), a companion of Strongbow.

Monavullagh Mountains — A range of mountains in the west of the county. Their highest point is Seefin at 2379ft (725m).

Mothel Abbey — 3 miles (5km) east of Rathgormack, 12 miles (19km) northwest of Waterford. A 13th century Augustinian abbey on the site of a 6th century monastic foundation.

Mount Melleray Abbey — 3 miles (5km) north of Cappoquin, 12 miles (19km) northwest of Dungarvan. Located in the Knockmealdown Mountains and founded in 1832, this was the first monastery established in Ireland since the Reformation. It was established by 64 Irish and English monks from the Cistercian monastery of Melleray in Brittany who had been expelled by the French government. Tel: 058 54404.

Portlaw — A town built by the Quaker Malcolmson family in the mid 19th century as a model village for the workers of their cotton-spinning mills.

Portlaw Parish Church — Portlaw, 7 miles (11km) northwest of Waterford. Designed and built in 1858 by J J McCarthy (the 'Irish Pugin') overlooking the Portlaw 'model village'.

Reginald's Tower — The Quay, Waterford. A circular tower which was once part of Waterford's defences. Named after Ragnald, a 12th century Viking ruler of the city, it was originally built in the 12th or early 13th century and was enlarged in the 15th century. The oldest urban civic building in Ireland, it was at various times used as a mint, a prison and an armoury, and now houses an exhibition. Tel: 051 304220.

Rice Bridge — Road bridge over the River Suir at Merchant's Quay in Waterford. The only bridge over the Suir in the town, it was built in the 1980s on the site of the town's first bridge, constructed in 1794, and connects Waterford with the Dublin, Limerick and Rosslare roads. It is named after Edmund Rice.

Rivers — **Barrow** see Carlow; **Blackwater** see Cork; **John's River** is a small river that snakes its way through the city of Waterford before joining the River Suir at Adelphi Quay. **Nore** see Tipperary; **Suir** see Tipperary.

St Augustine's Abbey — Abbeyside, Dungarvan. The ruin of an Augustinian abbey founded in 1290 by Thomas, Lord Offaly, and abandoned after the Cromwellian siege of Dungarvan. A Catholic church now stands on the abbey's foundations and the abbey's tower still stands.

St Carthage's Cathedral — North Mall, Lismore. A Church of Ireland cathedral located on the site of a church, monastery and school founded in AD 635 by St Carthage (Carthage of Lismore) (c.555–637). As with many such monastic sites, it was subject to repeated attacks by Vikings between the 9th and 11th century. In the late 12th or early 13th century a Romanesque style cathedral was built on the site. The present cathedral dates from the 17th century, the earlier building having been burned down. A feature of the cathedral is the McGrath table tomb.

Sport

football — **Waterford United** were founded as Waterford in 1930, adopting their present name in 1982. They were winners of the League of Ireland in 1966, 1968, 1969, 1970, 1972 and 1973, and of the FAI Cup in 1937 and 1980.

horse racing — **Clonmel** Racecourse see Tipperary

Waterford and Tramore Racecourse, Graun Hill, Tramore. The 'Black Strand' course beside the sea opened in 1806 but by 1914 had been covered by water. A new course was opened by Martin Murphy in 1911 on his own land. The course and amenities have been improved since 1997. Tramore is a right-handed oval course of 1 mile (1.6km) with a 1 furlong (0.2km) uphill finish. Tel: 051 381425.

hurling — **Waterford** are winners of the All-Ireland Senior Hurling Championship in 1948 and 1959.

Stradbally Medieval Church — Stradbally, 8 miles (13km) northeast of Dungarvan. The ruin of a large fortified 13th century church, located in the grounds of St Patrick's Church of Ireland church. It was abandoned after the Reformation.

Strancally Castle — 5 miles (8km) southeast of Lismore. A castellated mansion located on the River Blackwater, close to the border with Co. Cork. Designed by James and George Pain, it was built c.1830 for John Kelly. It stands in front of the ruin of a Desmond castle containing an infamous murdering hole, used for the dispatch of those who incurred the wrath of a Desmond to the river below.

Theatre Royal — The Mall, Waterford. Housed in Waterford City Hall (see separate entry), the Theatre Royal began life as the city playhouse. It was remodelled as the Theatre Royal in 1876 with a horseshoe-shaped auditorium, and was restored and refurbished in the late 1990s. Tel: 051 874402.

Tramore — Tramore (*Tra Mhor*, 'big beach') is a seaside town on the southeast coast of Co. Waterford. A small fishing village until the arrival of the railway in 1853, the town has continually expanded since, initially as a tourist destination and latterly as a seaside suburb of the city of Waterford, 8 miles (13km) to the north. The town is situated on the northwestern corner of Tramore Bay on a hill that slopes down to the sand spit that divides the bay. Behind the spit lies the tidal lagoon known as the Cul Tra (Back Strand). Tramore has an imposing Gothic Revival Catholic Church, built 1856–71 by J J McCarthy and dominated by an asymmetrical tower and spire, on a monumental site overlooking the town. In 1816, the *Sea Horse* military transport ship, with the 2nd Battalion of the 59th Regiment of Foot, was wrecked in Tramore Bay, and 292 men and 71 women and children perished. Some time later the sea horse was adopted as the town's symbol, and was adopted as the logo for Waterford Crystal in 1955. A prominent feature of Tramore Bay is the 'Metal Man', a large cast-metal figure pointing seawards, set on top of one of three pillars. It was erected in 1823 by Lloyd's of London to warn seafarers away from dangerous shallow waters following the *Sea Horse* tragedy. Two more pillars sit on the headland opposite, Brownstown Head. Tramore has a reputation for surfing, and the T-Bay Surf Club, established in 1967, has produced national and international surfing champions. See also Sport: Horse racing.

Tramore House Gardens — Pond Road, Tramore. A $2^1/_2$ acre (1ha) garden on a sloping site surrounding Tramore House (not open to the public), a Victorian town house dating to the 1880s. There is a stream, and informal and formal elements including a long herbaceous border. Tel: 051 395555.

Waterford Castle — See Little Island

Waterford City Hall — The Mall, Waterford. Designed by local architect John Roberts and built in 1783 as the Assembly Rooms and Playhouse. After 1813 the Assembly Rooms became known as City Hall and the playhouse as the Theatre Royal. The Large Room on the first floor (originally known as the Grand Banqueting Room) has welcomed the likes of Daniel O'Connell, Charles Stewart Parnell and Edward VII. An 18th century cut-glass chandelier made by the Waterford Glass Factory and hanging in the council chambers is the oldest extant Waterford glass. It originally hung in Dublin Castle and there is a copy in the Hall of Independence in Philadelphia. Tel: 051 860856.

Waterford County Museum — St Augustine Street, Dungarvan. Local history museum which charts the history of Dungarvan and the West Waterford area. The museum was opened in the former Dungarvan Market House in the early 1980s and moved to its present site in the former town hall in 1999.

Waterford Heritage Museum — Greyfriars, Waterford. Located close to Reginald's Tower, this local history museum includes a reconstruction of the early city plus wall displays telling the story of the city. Exhibits include Viking and medieval artefacts recovered during recent excavations in the city centre. There is also a collection of royal charters and civic regalia. Tel: 051 71227.

Waterford Crystal — Kilbarry, Cork Road, Waterford. The world famous Waterford Crystal manufacturing operation was first established by George and William Penrose in 1783. The firm was bought by Ramsey, Gatchell & Barcroft in 1799 and by 1823 was a partnership involving mainly the Gatchell brothers. However, the business ceased production in 1851 and it was not until 1947 that a new glass-making factory was established in Waterford which has expanded into the large concern of today. The Waterford Crystal Gallery, established in 1997, holds the world's largest display of Waterford crystal. Tel: 051 332500.

Waterford Municipal Art Gallery	Greyfriars, Waterford. Art gallery housed in a Gothic Revival style 19th century former church which was the home to the Waterford Methodists until 1973. The Municipal Art Collection includes works by Jack B Yeats, Charles Lamb and Louis Le Brocquy. Tel: 051 860856.
Waterford Museum of Treasures	Merchant's Quay, Waterford. A museum housed in a six-floor former granary building and exploring the history of the city of Waterford with interactive presentations and artefacts. A new annexe has been constructed to act as entranceway and reception for the building and the interior retains many original structural features. Tel: 051 304500.

Some famous people born in County Waterford

Boyle, Robert (scientist) (1627–91)	Lismore Castle
Casey, Karan (singer) (1969–)	Ballyduff
Cheasty, Tom (hurling player) (1934–2007)	Ballyduff
Doonican, Val (singer) (1927–)	Waterford
Flynn, Paul (hurling player) (1974–)	Waterford
Hobson, William (first Governor of New Zealand) (1792–1842)	Waterford
Hogan, John (sculptor) (1800–58)	Tallow
Jordan, Dorothy (courtesan) (1761–1816)	Waterford
Kean, Charles (actor) (1811–68)	Waterford
Manahan, Anna (actress) (1924–2009)	Waterford
McCarthy, Thomas (poet) (1954–)	Cappoquin
Meagher, Thomas Francis (soldier) (1823–67)	Waterford
Norris, Gillian (dancer) (1978–)	Kilmacthomas
O'Sullivan, Gilbert (singer) (1946–)	Waterford
Power, Tyrone (actor) (1795–1841)	Kilmacthomas
Roberts, John (architect) (1712–96)	Waterford
Shanahan, Dan (hurler) (1977–)	Lismore
Treacy, John (athlete) (1957–)	Villierstown
Wallace, William Vincent (composer) (1812–65)	Waterford
Walton, Ernest (scientist) (1903–95)	Abbeyside

Westmeath

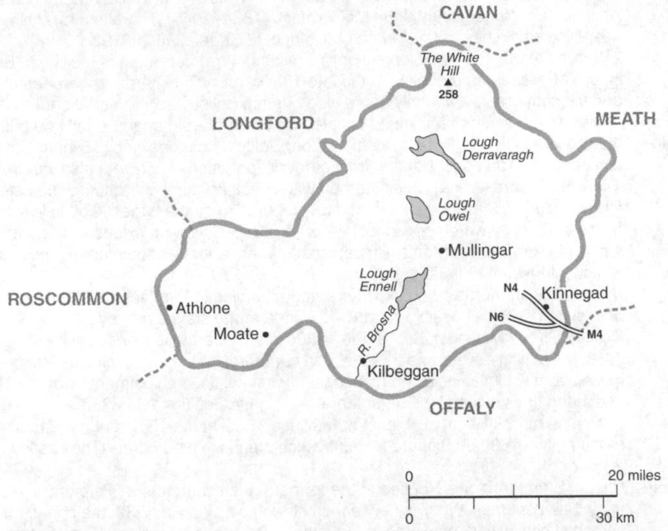
CAVAN
The White Hill
258
LONGFORD
MEATH
Lough Derravaragh
Lough Owel
Mullingar
Lough Ennell
N4
Kinnegad
ROSCOMMON
Athlone
N6
M4
Moate
R. Brosna
Kilbeggan
OFFALY
0
20 miles
0
30 km

W E S T M E A T H

Westmeath is part of the province of Leinster. It lies in the Irish Midlands and has borders with Longford to the northwest, Meath to the northeast, Offaly to the south, and Roscommon to the southwest. Its northernmost tip touches the southernmost tip of Cavan. The county was once part of the ancient province of Meath and later of County Meath, an association ended in 1543 when County Westmeath was created. Mullingar is the largest town and the county town. Athlone, on the border with Roscommon, is often considered the geographical centre of Ireland.

The county's main geographical features are its loughs, such as Lough Derravaragh, Lough Ennell, Lough Lene, Lough Owel and Lough Ree, which give Westmeath its nickname of the 'County of Lakes'. It is also famous for its cattle, pewter such as Mullingar Pewter, the canal, and the drug company Elán. Westmeath is rapidly becoming part of the outer commuter belt of Dublin.

Perhaps Westmeath's best-known natives are singer Count John McCormack, journalist and film censor Thomas Power (T P) O'Connor, Michael O'Leary, CEO of Ryanair, popular singer Joe Dolan, and Nuala Holloway, a former Miss Ireland, model and actress, now an artist and academic.

Westmeath	**Population**			**Area**	
Districts	*male*	*female*	*total*	*sq miles*	*sq km*
Athlone rural area	8125	8080	16,205	111	289
Athlone Town	3554	3800	7354	2	5
Ballymore	1088	973	2061	48	124
Coole	889	837	1726	60	155
Delvin	3286	3187	6473	119	308
Mullingar	19,018	19,021	38,039	365	944
Total	35,960	35,898	71,858	705	1825

Local Attractions and Information

Administrative headquarters	County Buildings, Mullingar. Tel: 044 40861.
An Dun Transport and Heritage Museum	Ballinahown, 7 miles (11km) southeast of Athlone. A museum with exhibits of cars and trucks from the 1920s onwards, vintage bicycles and farm machinery and transport. Tel: 090 230106.

Athlone Castle	St Peter's Square, Athlone. Built in 1210 by John de Gray, Bishop of Norwich, on the site of an earlier motte at a strategic crossing point of the River Shannon. It has a circular keep and two large drum towers. The castle was besieged twice during the Williamite Wars, once unsuccessfully in 1690 and again in 1691 when the Jacobites were forced to abandon the castle. It was remodelled in the early 19th century and served as a barracks. The visitor centre has presentations on the history of the castle, military history and local natural history, and about Athlone-born singer Count John McCormack (1884–1945). There is a local history museum in the keep. The castle has been in state care since 1970. Tel: 090 292192.
Ballinlough Castle	2½ miles (4km) south of Clonmellon, 15 miles (24km) northeast of Mullingar. Built in 1614 by Hugh O'Reilly and remodelled in the late 18th century. The gardens were restored in the 1990s and the castle is now a family home also offering holiday accommodation. Tel: 046 943 3234.
Belvedere House Gardens and Park	4 miles (6km) south of Mullingar. Located on the shore of Lough Ennell and built c.1742 as a hunting lodge/villa for Robert Rochfort, Lord Belfield, to a design by Richard Castle. The estate comprises 160 acres (65ha) of formal gardens, parkland, woodland, also incorporating the lough. There is a 7 acre (2.8ha) walled garden with specialist plant collections. The estate is dotted with follies, including the Jealous Wall which is reputed to be the largest Gothic folly in Ireland. The house and estate were opened to the public in 2000 following extensive restoration. Tel: 044 42820.
Carne Castle	1 mile (1.6km) west of Moate. Ruined castle famous for its sheela na gig, now exhibited in the National Museum of Ireland, Dublin.
Castlelost Castle	½ mile (0.8km) northwest of Rochfortbridge, 7 miles (11km) south of Mullingar. The meagre ruin of a tower house. A possibly connected ruined motte stands nearby.
Cathedral of Christ the King	College Street, Mullingar. Built in the 1930s in a modernised Renaissance style and opened in 1936. It has twin towers and a dome. The cathedral houses an ecclesiastical museum with many models and exhibits, including paintings of local saints, the vestments worn by St Oliver Plunkett and a ring once owned by Queen Marie Antoinette. Tel: 044 934 8338.
Clonyn Castle	Delvin, 12 miles (19km) northeast of Mullingar. Built in the 19th century to replace the ruined castle built in 1639 by Richard Nugent which stands in its grounds. The castle is a private residence.
Dean Crowe Theatre	Chapel Street, Athlone. Housed in the former parish church of St Peter, built in the late 18th and early 19th centuries. When a new parish church was built in 1937, the church became the parochial hall. It was renovated in the late 1950s and renamed the Dean Crowe Memorial Hall as a music, drama and community venue. The theatre was created in the late 1990s and the final phase of refurbishment was completed in 2002. Tel: 090 649 2129.
Delvin Castle	Delvin, 12 miles (19km) northeast of Mullingar. The substantial ruin of a tower house probably dating to the early 13th century. The western half of the castle, with two of its rounded turrets, still stands.
Dún Na Sí Heritage Centre	Knockdomney, 1 mile (1.6km) west of Moate, 8 miles (13km) east of Athlone. Housed in a building resembling a traditional Irish farmhouse. The attached folk park has exhibits from Ireland's rural past going back as far as prehistory. The centre also provides assistance with genealogical research. Tel: 090 648 1183.
Fore Abbey	Fore, 5 miles (8km) east of Castlepollard, 12 miles (19km) northeast of Mullingar. The extensive ruins of a Benedictine priory founded in the early 13th century near the site of an earlier monastic foundation of St Fechin of Fore. According to legend the huge lintel and its west doorway, which shows a Greek cross with a circle, was magically set in place by St Fechin himself on the strength of his prayers, a feat known locally as one of the Seven Wonders of Fore (the water that flows uphill; the monastery in a bog; the mill without a race; the water that won't boil; the tree with three branches (or the tree that won't burn); the anchorite in a stone; the stone raised by St Fechin's prayers). The priory was suppressed in the 16th century. The remains include a 13th century church. A section of the 15th century cloister was re-erected in 1912. Several Celtic crosses known as the Fore Crosses are dotted around the countryside nearby. Tel: 044 966 1780.
Highest point	The White Hill at Mullaghmeen at 846ft (258m).
Interesting facts	**Maurice James Dease** (28 September 1889–23 August 1914), from Co. Westmeath, won the first Victoria Cross to be awarded in World War I, gaining it on the first day of the first British encounter in the war. On 23 August 1914, at Mons, Belgium, Nimy Bridge was being defended by a single company of Royal Fusiliers and a machine-gun section with Lieutenant Dease in command. The gunfire was intense and casualties very heavy, but the lieutenant continued firing in spite of his severe wounds, until he was hit for the fifth time and was carried away to a place of safety where he died, aged 24. **John McCormack** was much honoured and decorated for his services to the world of music. His greatest honour came in 1928, when he received the title of count from Pope Pius XI in recognition of his work for Catholic charities. **Michael O'Leary** is one of the richest men in Ireland. Not only has he risen to be CEO of the mega-profitable Ryanair, but he is also a highly successful racehorse breeder at his Gigginstown House Stud in Co. Westmeath; in 2006, his horse War of Attrition won the Cheltenham Gold Cup, the blue riband of steeplechasing. In 2004 O'Leary purchased a hackney plate for his Mercedes-Benz to enable it to be classified as a taxi, so that he could legally make use of Dublin's bus lanes to speed his car journeys around the city! **William Wilson** was born the only son of John and Frances Wilson of Daramona House, Street. In 1871, he acquired from Sir Howard Grubb of Dublin a reflector telescope of 12in (30.5m) aperture and set it up in a dome in the garden of Daramona. With this instrument, he experimented with photography of the moon, utilising wet plates, and began his study of solar radiation using thermopiles. From 1893 onwards Wilson took a series of astronomical photographs, which at the time were of unparalleled quality. One of Wilson's main research efforts was in determining the temperature of the sun. Most of this work was done with P L Gray, the

	result of their measurements being an effective temperature of about 8000°C for the sun. After a better determination of absorption in the earth's atmosphere was made, this value was corrected to 6590°C, very close to the modern value of 6075°C. In 1978 **Joe Dolan** became the first Western pop singer to perform in the Soviet Union. **Oliver Goldsmith**'s family moved to Lissoy, a village north of Athlone, when he was two years old. Lissoy was the 'Sweet Auburn' of Goldsmith's *The Deserted Village*. A little to the northeast of the tiny hamlet is a pub called the Three Pigeons, named after the inn from *She Stoops to Conquer*. **Westmeath** is the goat capital of Ireland, with five times as many goats as Kerry.
Islands	Islands in Co. Westmeath include the following in these loughs: **Lough Derravaragh**: Clonava; **Lough Ennell**: Blind Island, Bog Island, Car Island, Chapel Island, Cherry Island, Dysart Island (aka Fort Island), Goose Island, Gosling Island, Green Island, Lady Island, Malachy's Island (aka Cormorant Island, Cro Innis), Oge Island, Rushy Island, Shan Island; **Lough Lene**: Castle Island, Nun's Island, Turgesius; **Lough Owel**: Carrickphilbin Island, Church Island, Lady's Island, Srudarra Island; **Lough Ree**: Brick Island, Carberry Island, Charlie's Island, Friar's Island, Inchturk, Nun's Island, Temple Island; **Lough Sunderlin**: Big Island, Corran Island, Green Island, Sallow Island.
Lilliput Jonathan Swift Park	7 miles (11km) southwest of Mullingar. A park on the southern shore of Lough Ennell, once part of the Boyd Rochfort estate and encompassing the townland known as Lilliput. Jonathan Swift, a regular visitor, gave its name to the country of tiny people in *Gulliver's Travels*. Tel: 044 922 6141.
Lockes Distillery Museum	Kilbeggan, 13 miles (21km) southwest of Mullingar. Believed to be the oldest licensed pot still distillery in the world. It was established in 1757 and was acquired by John Locke in 1843. Its water source was the River Brosna. It was modernised in the late 19th and early 20th centuries but ceased production in 1957. Locke's Distillery is now open as a museum of industrial archaeology showing how whiskey was produced by 'traditional' methods. Restoration of the building and machinery is ongoing. Tel: 050 632134.
Lough Derravaragh	The lough covers 2070 acres (1080ha) and is both a popular beauty spot and a mecca for angling and fly fishing. The River Inny flows into and out of the northwest end. The lough has stocks of trout, perch, roach and bream plus large specimen of pike. The lough also has a place in Irish mythology: it was here that the Children of Lir were first transformed into swans by their stepmother Aoife. The lough is a Ramsar site.
Lough Ennell	The lough covers 3460 acres (1400ha) and has large areas of shallow water, half the lake being less than (16ft) 5m deep. The Brosna River flows into the lough from the north. It has a renowned reputation for its stocks of brown trout and holds the record for Ireland's largest brown trout at 26lb 2oz, taken in 1894. The lough is a Ramsar site.
Lough Owel	A spring-fed lough with an area of 2550 acres (1032ha). It is well stocked with wild brown trout. The surrounding farmland is a popular feeding ground for greater white-fronted goose. The lough is a Ramsar site.
Lough Ree	See Longford
John McCormack Bust	Grace Road, Athlone. A bronze bust of world-famous tenor John McCormack, Located on the promenade in Athlone. The work of Cork sculptor Seamus Murphy, it was unveiled in 1970.
Moate Castle	Moate, 9 miles (15km) southeast of Athlone. A three-storey tower house built c.1550 and extended in the 18th century. It is notable for the sheela-na-gig over its rear gateway.
Moate Museum	Moate, 9 miles (15km) southeast of Athlone. Local history museum housed in the village's old courthouse and containing more than 1000 exhibits laid out in displays including a farm kitchen, church, school and jail room. Tel: 090 648 2167.
Moydrum Castle	Moydrum, 2 miles (3km) east of Athlone. The ruin of a Gothic Revival style castle designed by Richard Morrison and built in 1814 for William Handcock, 1st Baron Castlemaine. The castle was burned down by the IRA on 3 July 1921, in reprisal for the burning of local farms by the army during the Irish War of Independence. An image of the ruins of the castle features on the cover of U2's 1984 album *The Unforgettable Fire*.
Mullingar Arts Centre	Lower Mount Street, Mullingar. Opened in 1999 and housed within the refurbished Mullingar County Hall, built in 1913. Tel: 044 934 7777.
Mullingar Cathedral	See Cathedral of Christ the King
Multyfarnham Friary	Multyfarnham, 7 miles (11km) north of Mullingar. The remains of a Franciscan friary founded in 1268. The church was rebuilt in the 15th century, and despite the suppression of the monasteries there were still friars at Multyfarnham when the new church was built. All the other buildings of the foundation no longer exist. A new church was built in 1827 incorporating sections of the 15th century friary, and was renovated in 1976; its garden features statues of the Stations of the Cross. It also has stained glass art created by Richard King and commemorating the Children of Lir, portrayed by four swans wearing necklaces.
Old Walls of Athlone	Railway View, Athlone. A surviving portion of the town walls, originally built in the mid 13th century when Athlone was a fortified town.
Rivers	The **Brosna** rises in Lough Ennell and flows through Kilbeggan, Clara and Ferbane, eventually joining the Shannon at Shannon Harbour.
Sean's Bar	Main Street, Athlone. Certainly one of the three oldest and possibly the oldest pub in Ireland, with a documented history dating back to 1600. Wattle and daub construction possibly dating to the 9th century was discovered during renovations in the 1970s.
Sport	
football	**Athlone Town** were founded in 1887 and were winners of the League of Ireland in 1981 and 1983. Their home ground is Athlone Town Stadium, Lissywollen, Athlone.
horse racing	**Kilbeggan Racecourse** is Ireland's only all National Hunt racecourse. The right-handed, round course of 9 furlongs (1.8km) has a short uphill run-in of 300 yards (270m). Tel: 050 632176.

Tullynally Castle and Gardens	1 mile (1.6km) west of Castlepollard, 11 miles (18km) north of Mullingar. Tullynally (Hill of the Swan) was originally a 17th century tower house but has been greatly extended and remodelled by the Pakenham family (Earls of Longford) over the centuries into a Gothic revival castle covering 2 acres (0.8ha), making it the largest castle in Ireland. The gardens cover 30 acres (12ha) and include a lake, a grotto, formal lawns, parkland, woodland and walled gardens.
Turbotstown House	Coole, 12 miles (19km) north of Mullingar. Georgian mansion designed by Francis Johnston and built c.1810.
Tyrrelspass Castle	Tyrrellspass, 9 miles (15km) south of Mullingar. A tower house built c.1411 by the Tyrrel family and restored in the 1970s. Tel: 044 23105.
Uisneagh Hill	3 miles (5km) east of Ballymore, 12 miles (19km) southwest of Mullingar. This 590ft (180m) hill was the ancient seat of the kings of Meath and has been a gathering place throughout its history. It has several monuments including ring forts and tumuli, but its most famous feature is the Catstone or *Ail Na Mearainn* (the stone of the divisions), a boulder standing 6ft (1.8m) high and weighing 30 tonnes which is said to mark the meeting point of the Provinces of Ireland. The Hill of Uisneagh (Uisneach) is often referred to as the 'bellybutton of Ireland' as it is one of several sites claiming to be the country's central point.

Some famous people born in County Westmeath

ApIvor, Denis (composer) (1916–2004)	Collinstown
Broderick, John (author) (1924–89)	Athlone
Dolan, Joe (singer) (1939–2007)	Mullingar
Healy, Dermot (writer) (1947–)	Finnea
Holloway, Nuala (model and actress) (1957–)	Moate
Lawlor, Éammon (broadcaster) (1951–)	Delvin
MacNamara, Brinsley (writer born John Weldon) (1890–1963)	Delvin
McCormack, John (tenor) (1884–1945)	Athlone
O'Connor, T P (journalist) (1848–1929)	Athlone
O'Leary, Michael (CEO of Ryanair) (1961–)	Mullingar
O'Rourke née Lenihan, Mary (politician) (1937–)	Athlone
Stokes, George Thomas (historian) (1843–98)	Athlone

Wexford

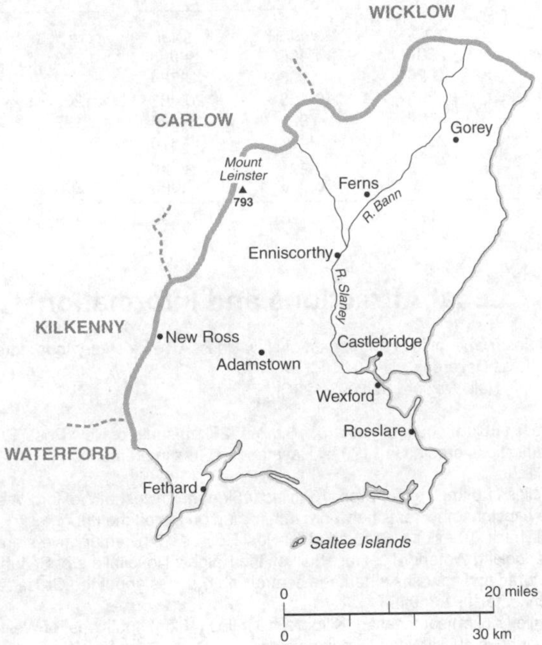
WICKLOW
CARLOW
Gorey
Mount Leinster
793
Ferns
R. Bann
Enniscorthy
R. Slaney
KILKENNY
New Ross
Adamstown
Castlebridge
Wexford
Rosslare
WATERFORD
Fethard
Saltee Islands
0
20 miles
0
30 km

Wexford is part of the province of Leinster. It is the most southeasterly of all the Irish counties and is bordered by the counties of Waterford to the southwest, Kilkenny to the west, Carlow to the northwest and Wicklow to the north. Its eastern coast is on St George's Channel, which separates the Irish Sea in the north from the Celtic Sea in the south. The county town is Wexford.

The original name of Wexford was Menapia, after a prehistoric Belgic tribe who occupied the area. The current name derives from the Viking *Waesfjord* – the harbour of the mud flats. The county was settled more than 6000 years ago. The Vikings invaded in the late 8th century and remained in control until the successful challenge of Brian Boru in 1014, founding the town of Wexford on the River Slaney c. AD 800. The Normans invaded in the 12th century and used the county as a launching pad for their invasion of the Irish hinterland. When Cromwell campaigned in Wexford in 1649 he reduced several castles before attacking the town of Wexford and its inhabitants unmercifully. A major episode in the history of the county, and indeed of Ireland, was the insurrection of 1798. The resistance to the Government was led by Father John Murphy of Boolavogue after his church and part of his village were burned down. They won a victory at Oulart Hill and for a time held most of the county before being overrun on Vinegar Hill.

Wexford has a varied geography; on the northern frontier, the Wicklow Mountains, subsiding towards the south, send spurs and offshoots into Wexford. A series of high lands begins southeast of New Ross in the west, and runs northeast toward Enniscorthy. A district running from Croghan Kinsella toward the southwest to Slieveboy is also hilly. The southeast angle of the county, namely the two baronies of Forth and Bargy, terminating in Carnsore Point, is very flat, guarded on the northwest by a small mountain knot. The rest of the county, constituting far the greater part, is a plain, diversified by ridges and isolated hills. The coast is low and mostly sandy, interrupted in a few places by fringes of rock; it is unbroken from Kilmichael Point to the Raven Point; but from here to Waterford Harbour it is indented by numerous inlets.

There are famous people associated with Wexford across many fields. In literature there are the current authors Eoin Colfer, famous for the Artemis Fowl novels, and John Banville, winner of the 2005 Booker Prize for *The Sea*; in sport there are famous hurlers such as the Rackards and Tony Doran; and as befits a coastal county, there are several naval officers of note including Sir Robert McClure and John Barry.

Wexford	**Population**			**Area**	
Districts	*male*	*female*	*total*	*sq miles*	*sq km*
Enniscorthy rural area	14,687	14,406	29,093	303	784
Enniscorthy Town	1826	1938	3764	0	1
Gorey	10,295	10,168	20,463	203	527
New Ross rural area	8102	7822	15,924	197	509
New Ross Town	2338	2472	4810	1	2
Wexford Borough	4612	4837	9449	1	2
Wexford rural area	16,310	16,783	33,093	208	540
Total	58,170	58,426	116,596	913	2365

Local Attractions and Information

Adamstown Castle	Adamstown, 9 miles (15km) east of New Ross. A 16th century four-storey tower house built by Nicholas Devereux.
Administrative headquarters	County Hall, Wexford. Tel: 053 42211.
Baginbun Bay Earthworks	1 mile (1.6km) south of Fethard, 16 miles (26km) south of New Ross. Earthworks and promontory fortifications erected in 1170 by Raymond le Gros in preparation for the Norman invasion of Ireland.
Ballybrittas Portal Tomb	1 miles (1.6km) west of Bree, 10 miles (16km) northwest of Wexford. A small portal dolmen where the capstone now rests between, rather than on top of, the uprights.
Ballyhack Castle	Ballyhack, 10 miles (16km) south of New Ross. A 15th century five-storey tower house overlooking Waterford estuary built by the Knights Hospitallers of St John. The castle has been restored and contains a heritage centre with displays about the Crusades and Norman armoured monks. Tel: 051 389468.
Ballyhealy Castle	1 mile (1.6km) southeast of Kilmore, 10 miles (16km) southwest of Wexford. A red sandstone tower house built by the Cheevers family.
Ballyteige Burrow	$1^1/_4$ miles (2km) south of Duncormick, 12 miles (19km) southwest of Wexford. A nature reserve covering 561 acres (227ha) on a long shingle spit running northwest from Kilmore Quay. The flora is rich in dune and coastal plants, including a number of rare species.
Bannow Bay	13 miles (21km) southeast of New Ross. A large estuarine site, $8^1/_2$ miles (14km) long, on the south coast of Co. Wexford. Small rivers and streams to the north and southwest flow into the bay and their sub-estuaries form part of the site. The bay contains large areas of mud and sand. Most of the estuary has been designated a Special Protection Area for its significant bird interest, particularly during the winter. Parts of the area have also been designated a wildfowl sanctuary.
Barntown Castle	3 miles (5km) west of Wexford. The ruin of a Norman castle built by the Roche family.
Battles	Four battles were fought in Co. Wexford during the Irish Insurrection (1797–8). In chronological order these were: Oulart Hill, Enniscorthy, Tubberneering and Vinegar Hill; see separate table for details of these and of the Battle of Wexford. Kildare Confey – see Kildare battles.
Bay Garden, The	Camolin, 10 miles (16km) northeast of Enniscorthy. A garden surrounding a 19th century farmhouse and featuring various themed areas including a cottage garden, a white garden and a rose garden. Tel: 053 938 3349.
Berkeley Forest House	3 miles (5km) northeast of New Ross. A Georgian house dating to 1780 and belonging to the family of philosopher George Berkeley. It houses a collection of 18th and 19th century costumes, dolls and antique toys. Tel: 051 21361.
Browne-Clayton Monument	Carrigbyrne, 7 miles (11km) southeast of New Ross. Aka Carrigbyrne Memorial. A 94ft (28.5m) high granite Corinthian column designed by Thomas Cobden and erected 1839–41 on Carrigadaggan Hill. A replica of Pompey's Column in Alexandria, Egypt, it was built by General Robert Browne-Clayton in commemoration of Sir Ralph Abercrombie, his commanding officer, who was fatally wounded during the campaign in Egypt in 1801. It is believed to be the only internally accessible Corinthian column, the staircase leading to the top giving spectacular views. The capital was severely damaged by a lightning strike on 29 December 1994 but repairs have since been effected.
Carnsore Point	7 miles (11km) south of Rosslare. Ireland's most southeasterly point. In the 1970s it was the proposed site of a nuclear power station; now it is a major area of wind generating stations, with 14 wind farms opened in 2003 by Hibernian Wind Power Ltd.
Carrickbyrne Hill	7 miles (11km) southeast of New Ross. Once part of the Jeffares Estate and a gathering point during the 1798 rebellion, this forest park covers a volcanic outcrop that stands out far above the surrounding countryside. The main species are conifers such as Douglas fir and Japanese larch.
Churches	**Church of the Assumption**, Bree, 9 miles (15km) northwest of Wexford. The first of Augustus Pugin's Irish churches. The foundation stone was laid in 1837.

St Alphonsus, Barntown, 2 miles (3km) west of Wexford. Designed by Augustus Pugin and built 1844–8, the church was dedicated to St Alphonsus in 1851.

St Iberius, Main Street, Wexford. A 19th century Venetian Renaissance style church.

St Mary's, Church Lane, New Ross. A Church of Ireland church occupying the site of the nave of St Mary's Church, built in the early 13th century by William Marshal. The chancel and transepts are in ruins.

St Michael the Archangel, Gorey, 17 miles (27km) northeast of Enniscorthy. Designed by A W Pugin and built 1839–42. It is unlike most of Pugin's other Irish churches, being in Norman style.

Clougheast Castle

¼ mile (0.4km) west of Churchtown, 6 miles (10km) south of Rosslare. A four-storey tower house probably dating to the 16th century.

Coolhull Castle

1 mile (1.6km) southeast of Carrick, 13 miles (21km) southwest of Wexford. A two-storey house owned by the Devereux family in the 17th century.

Courtown Woods

16 miles (26km) northeast of Enniscorthy. Originally part of the estate of the Stopford family. The main species are ash, beech, holly, oak, sycamore and Spanish chestnut. The Owenavorra River runs close by and empties into Courtown harbour.

Craanford Mills

Craanford, 4 miles (6km) west of Gorey, 14 miles (23km) northeast of Enniscorthy. A restored 17th century working corn-grinding mill. Tel: 055 942 8124.

Dunamore Woods

3 miles (5km) south of Enniscorthy. A forest park on the Borro River which was once part of the Beatty Estate. The tree species are mainly oak, beech, Douglas fir and Scots pine.

Dunbrody Abbey

Campile, 8 miles (13km) southwest of New Ross. A Cistercian abbey founded in 1170 and completed in the 1210s. After the Dissolution it passed into secular hands, first the Etchinghams and then by marriage to the Chichester family. It was passed into state care in 1911. A visitor centre is housed within the ruin of the neighbouring Dunbrody Castle.

Dunbrody Famine Ship

South Quay, New Ross. A full-scale replica of the *Dunbrody*, a three-masted barque built in 1845 for the Graves family of New Ross. The original ship carried thousands of Irish emigrants to North America over a period of 30 years following the Great Famine. There is a searchable database of the passenger lists plus an audio-visual presentation celebrating the lives of some of the emigrants' descendants, such as John F Kennedy, Henry Ford and Eugene O'Neill.

Duncannon Fort

Duncannon, 12 miles (19km) south of New Ross. Star-shaped fortress built in 1588 on a strategically important promontory in Waterford Harbour in anticipation of a possible attack by the Spanish Armada. Occupied by British troops until 1919 and rebuilt by the Irish Army at the outset of World War II, it now houses a maritime museum and the Cockleshell Art Centre.

Dunmain House

7 miles (11km) southeast of New Ross. Restored 17th century house, the subject of Sir Walter Scott's *Guy Mannering*. Tel: 051 562122.

Enniscorthy Castle

Castle Hill, Enniscorthy. A Norman castle originally built in 1205 beside the River Slaney and standing in the centre of the town. Striking in appearance, with three drum towers, it was remodelled in the late 16th century. The castle was once owned by Sir Henry Wallop and it is said that this man's mistreatment of his workers gave rise to the use of 'wallop' to mean to hit someone. In 1798 the town was occupied by insurgents and the castle was used as a prison. The castle was a residence until the 1950s and now houses the County Wexford Museum.

Father Murphy Centre

Boolavogue, 4 miles (6km) southeast of Ferns, 7 miles (11km) northeast of Enniscorthy. A commemorative centre housed in the restored original farmstead where Father John Murphy, the 1798 insurgent leader, lived for many years. There is a Garden of Remembrance. Tel: 053 936 6898.

Ferns Castle

Ferns, 7 miles (11km) northeast of Enniscorthy. The ruin of a castle built possibly by William Marshal in the 13th century on the site of a ringwork earth and timber 12th century Irish castle. The castle was owned 1360–1539 by the Kavanagh family; destroyed by fire in 1577, it was rebuilt in 1607 and surrendered to Cromwellian forces in 1641. Only half of the castle remains standing. Of particular interest is the Ferns Tapestry.

Ferrycarrig Castle

2 miles (3km) northwest of Wexford. The site of the first Norman castle in Ireland, originally built in 1169 by the brothers FitzGodebert de Roch in support of Robert FitzStephens. The ruin visible today is that of a 15th century tower house built by the Roches on the north side of the River Slaney to guard the ferry and the river passage.

Highest point

Mount Leinster at 2602ft (793m), part of the Blackstairs Mountains in the northwest of the county bordering Co. Carlow, and also that county's highest point.

Hook Head Lighthouse

6 miles (10km) southwest of Fethard, 19 miles (31km) south of New Ross. Thought to be one of the oldest operational lighthouses in the world. It is believed that the original lighthouse was built by William Marshal in the early 13th century in order to guide his ships into Waterford Harbour. It was automated and opened to the public in 1996. Tel: 051 397055.

Interesting facts

Jane Elgee was born in the Old Rectory, South Main Street, Wexford, in 1821. A renowned linguist, translator, folklorist, advocate of women's rights and popular poet (under the pseudonym Speranza), Jane married William Robert Wilde (knighted in 1864), the prominent Dublin eye and ear surgeon, also a writer and folklorist, in 1851. Speranza's second son, born in 1854, was none other than Oscar Fingal O'Flaherty Wills Wilde. It is no overstatement to say that Speranza's inflammatory patriotic poetry had made her a hero of Irish nationalists across the world; until his most famous works made him a household name in his own right, Oscar Wilde, as the New York newspaper *The Irish Nation* pointed out, was 'Speranza's Son'. **Sir Robert John Le Mesurier McClure** was born in North Main Street, Wexford. He entered the navy in 1824 and embarked on several Arctic exploratory expeditions. In 1848 he joined the Franklin search expedition under James Clark Ross as first lieutenant of *Enterprise*, and on his return was given the command of *Investigator* in the new search expedition (1850–4) which set out from England, sailed south on the Atlantic, rounded Cape Horn, entered the Pacific sailing north to enter the Arctic Ocean by way of Bering Strait and, sailing eastward, eventually linked up with another British expedition from the northwest. Although *Investigator* was abandoned to the pack ice in spring 1853, with McClure and his crew being rescued by the *Resolute* after a journey over the ice by sledge, he did achieve in the course of this voyage the distinction of completing (in 1850) the work connected with the discovery of a northwest passage. McClure's account of this voyage, *Discovery of the North-West Passage*, consists of excerpts of his journals from that time edited by Captain Sherard Osborn. **John Barry** was an officer in the Continental Navy during the American War of Independence and later in the United States Navy. The Wexford-born naval officer commanded *Lexington* and *Alliance.* He was seriously wounded on 29 May 1781 while in command of *Alliance* during her capture of HMS *Atalanta* and *Trepassey.* Appointed senior captain on the establishment of the US Navy, he commanded the frigate *United States* in the Quasi-War with France. He also had a hand in the establishment of the Brooklyn Navy Yard. Commodore Barry died at Strawberry Hill near Philadelphia on 13 September 1803, and was buried in St Mary's Cemetery, Philadelphia. He is acknowledged as the 'Father of the American Navy'. **Merton**, situated on the River Slaney near Adamstown, has the distinction of being the site of the first execution by guillotine. The person having this dubious honour in 1307 was one Murcod Ballagh. **Oliver Cromwell** is reputed to have coined the phrase 'by hook or by crook' when he was trying to decide whether to lay siege to Waterford by landing on the Wexford side of the harbour, at Hook Head, or at the nearby hamlet of Crooke in Waterford. **Magpies** first arrived in Ireland in 1682, blown across the sea from Wales to Wexford. **Curracloe Beach** north of Wexford was used in the filming of the opening D-Day scenes of the film *Saving Private Ryan* (1998). The idea for the *Guinness Book of Records* was reputedly formulated in the village of **Castlebridge**, to the north of Wexford harbour, in 1951. **Enniscorthy**, the largest town in Co. Wexford after Wexford itself, hosts both the annual 'Strawberry Fair' and 'Blackstairs Blues' festivals.

Irish Agricultural Museum — 3 miles (5km) southwest of Wexford. Housed in an early 19th century farm building within the grounds of Johnstown Castle. In addition to an exhibition about the Great Famine, there are also sections covering themes such as farm machinery 1750–1950, dairy farming, rural transport, rural furniture and rural crafts. Tel: 053 917 1200.

Irish National Heritage Park — 2 miles (3km) west of Wexford. A 35 acre (14ha) park containing a series of settlements that attempt to recreate the way people lived in Ireland from the Mesolithic period to the Norman invasion, including the Iron and Bronze Ages. Tel: 053 912 0733.

Islands — Islands off the coast of Co. Wexford in the Irish Sea are: **Bannow Island** (see Bannow Bay); **Brandies** (a popular site for scuba divers); **Collough Rocks** (off Great Saltee Island); **Coningbeg Rock** (submerged at high water); **Coningmore Rock** (a popular haunt of seals); **Great Saltee Island** (one of the two Saltee Islands, the other being Little Saltee Island); **Keeragh Islands** (often considered as one island but in fact two distinct islets at high water); **Little Saltee Island** (St Patrick's Bridge, an underwater landbridge, reaches out from the east of Kilmore Quay pier, in a crescent shape, all the way to Little Saltee); **Makestone Rock** (lies east of the Great Saltee Island); **Saltee Islands** (see separate entry); **Sebber's Bridge** (a shallow reef extending north from the northeast tip of Great Saltee Island); **Sigginstown Islands** (the great island is 24 acres and the little island one acre); and **Tuskar Rock** (Ireland's most southeasterly island). The inshore island of **Great Island** lies in the River Suir. **Our Lady's Island** is joined to the mainland by a causeway, so it is actually a peninsula but included by virtue of its name (see Lady's Island Castle and Lake). Although **Begerin** was formerly an island in the north of Wexford harbour, it has long since been one of the reclaimed Sloblands, but again is mentioned by virtue of its name and former status.

John F Kennedy Arboretum — 5 miles (8km) south of New Ross. An arboretum dedicated to the memory of US President John Fitzgerald Kennedy, whose antecedents were from Co. Wexford. The trees are divided into plots reflecting the species prevalent on the five continents. There are also more than 4500 shrubs. Tel: 051 388171.

Johnstown Castle Gardens — 3 miles (5km) southwest of Wexford. The grounds of this 19th century turreted castle include wild and formal gardens plus specimen trees and a lake. The former farmyard also houses the Irish Agricultural Museum. Tel: 053 917 1200.

Kennedy Homestead — Dunganstown, 4 miles (6km) southwest of New Ross. The home of Patrick Kennedy, great-grandfather of US President John F Kennedy, who emigrated to become a cooper in Boston in the United States in 1848 to escape the Great Famine. John F Kennedy visited the home on 27 June 1963. A visitor centre has memorabilia relating to Kennedy.

Killiane Castle — 1 mile (1.6km) south of Drinagh, 4 miles (6km) south of Wexford. A 15th century four-storey tower house formerly occupied by the Hay and Cheever families.

Kilmokea Country Manor and Gardens — Great Island, 2 miles (3km) west of Campile, 6 miles (10km) east of Waterford. A 7 acre (2.8ha) garden surrounding a restored Georgian house built in 1794 beside the River Barrow, and including formal walled gardens, an Italian loggia, a woodland garden and a pool. Tel: 051 388109.

Kilmore Quay Maritime Museum — Kilmore Quay, 12 miles (19km) southwest of Wexford. Housed on board the last Irish Lights vessel, the *Guillemot*, which is complete with all its cabins containing the original furniture, generations and fittings. The museum has many artefacts plus model ships, maritime paintings, and a Royal National Lifeboat Institute display covering the history of the local station. Tel: 053 912 9655.

Lady's Island Castle — 4 miles (6km) south of Rosslare. The ruin of a 15th century Augustinian priory which passed into secular hands after the Dissolution. The remains include a tower house, gatehouse and curtain wall. A tower from the outer curtain wall leans at an angle of 30 degrees from vertical. The island is connected to the mainland by a causeway and is a pilgrimage site.

Lady's Island Lake — 4 miles (6km) south of Rosslare. A shallow lagoon separated from the open sea by a shingle

	bank. The lake is home to over 1200 breeding pairs of sandwich terns and to 76 breeding pairs of the rare roseate tern.
McMurragh-Kavanagh Abbey	Ferns, 7 miles (11km) northeast of Enniscorthy. The ruin of an abbey founded in the 1150s by Dermot Mac Murrough. It stood on the site of a 6th century monastic foundation of St Maedhog which was plundered by the Vikings in 930.
Mountgarrett Castle	1 mile (1.6km) north of New Ross. The ruin of an early 15th century five-storey tower house built by Patrick Barrett, Bishop of Ferns.
National 1798 Centre	Millpark Road, Enniscorthy. A purpose-built museum opened in June 1998 by Prime Minister Bertie Ahern, and designed as a lasting memorial to those who lost their lives in the 1798 rebellion. Tel: 053 923 7596.
North Slob	$2^1/_2$ miles (4km) northeast of Wexford. One of two large mudflats beside the estuary at Wexford Harbour. See also South Slob.
Oulart Hill Memorials	1 mile (1.6km) north of Oulart, 7 miles (11km) east of Enniscorthy. A series of engraved stones located on Oulart Hill, the scene of a rebel victory during the 1798 Rebellion, and commemorating the battles of 1798 which led to the National Memorial known as *Tulach a tsolais* (Mound of Light).
Ram House Gardens	Coolgreany, 8 miles (13km) northeast of Gorey. A 2 acre (0.8ha) cottage style garden featuring a scented garden woodland, terraces, mixed borders and ponds. Tel: 040 237238.
Rathmacknee Castle	2 miles (3km) east of Murntown, 5 miles (8km) south of Wexford. A late 15th century five-storey tower house and bawn probably built by the Rossiter family.
Raven Nature Reserve	5 miles (8km) northeast of Wexford. The Raven Nature Reserve covers 589ha and is part of a well developed sand dune ecosystem, foreshore and seabed situated at the north side of the entrance to Wexford Harbour. Established in 1983, it encompasses the eastern part of the North Slob and is an important roosting area for geese and waders.
Rivers	The **Bann** rises in the southern slopes of Croghan Mountain in North Wexford on the Co. Wicklow border. The river flows south, just west of Gorey and under the R725 before taking a southwesterly course via Ferns to join up with the Slaney, north of Enniscorthy.
	Barrow see Carlow
	The **Derry** rises just south of Hacketstown, Co. Carlow, and flows southeast to Tinahely and then southwest to Shillelagh (both in Co. Wicklow), initially forming the border between Co. Wicklow and Co. Wexford, before becoming the border between Co. Wexford and Co. Carlow. The river then flows south into the River Slaney
	Slaney see Carlow
Rosslare Europort	8 miles (13km) southeast of Wexford. Formerly named Rosslare Harbour. A major passenger and freight terminal, Rosslare-Europort is located on the southeastern tip of Ireland, and is the closest point in the south of the country to the UK and continental Europe. There are regular sailings to Fishguard, Pembroke, Cherbourg, Roscoff and Le Havre. Rosslare is reputedly the sunniest town in Ireland, with a daily average of 4 hours 20 minutes of sunshine.
St Aidan's Cathedral	Cathedral Street, Enniscorthy. Designed by A W Pugin and begun in 1843. It was dedicated in 1860. The spire was completed in 1873. The church, which is Pugin's largest in Ireland, was restored in 1994.
St Edan's Cathedral	Ferns, 7 miles (11km) northeast of Enniscorthy. Located on the site of an early monastic foundation of St Aidan (Edan), the original cathedral was built in the 1230s by Bishop St John. Burned down by the O'Byrnes of Wicklow in 1575, it was rebuilt shortly afterwards; in 1817 the cathedral was enlarged and the present tower and chapter house added.
St Peter's College Chapel	Summerhill Road, Wexford. Designed by A W Pugin, the chapel contains a fine triptych altar; the Hardman stained glass in the rose window features the Talbot family coat of arms.
Saltee Islands	The two Saltee islands, Great Saltee and Little Saltee, are situated 3 miles (5km) off the south Wexford coast. Great Saltee is owned by the Neale family, who have made it into a bird sanctuary and Ireland's first bird observatory. The Saltee Islands are internationally important for breeding seabirds, especially gannets and razorbill.
Slade Castle and Harbour	Slade, 5 miles (8km) southwest of Fethard, 18 miles (29km) south of New Ross. The ruin of a late 15th or early 16th century five-storey tower house overlooking Slade Harbour built by the Laffan family. A two-storey hall was attached to the tower at a later date. The house was forfeited by the Laffans after the 1641 uprising. The hall was later used in connection with the neighbouring salt works.
South Slob	3 miles (5km) southeast of Wexford. One of two large mudflats beside of the estuary at Wexford Harbour. See also North Slob.
Sport	
football	**Wexford Youths** were founded in 2007. Their home ground is Ferrycarrig Park, Crossabeg, Wexford.
Gaelic football	**Wexford** were winners of the All-Ireland Senior Football Championship in 1893, 1915, 1916, 1917 and 1918.
horse racing	**Wexford Racecourse**, Waterford Road, Wexford. The present course dates from 1951, although the county has a very long tradition of horse breeding and racing. The course provides both Flat and National Hunt racing and is a sharp right-handed rectangular track of $1^1/_4$ miles (2km) with a run-in of just over 1 furlong (0.2km). Tel: 053 43412.
hurling	**Wexford** were winners of the All-Ireland Senior Hurling Championship in 1910, 1955, 1956, 1960, 1968 and 1996.
Taghmon Castle	Taghmon, 8 miles (13km) west of Wexford. The ruin of an early 15th century castle.
Tintern Abbey	1 mile (1.6km) northwest of Saltmills, 12 miles (19km) southeast of New Ross. A Cistercian abbey founded in the early 13th century by William Marshal. It is said that a storm took Marshal's boat as he sailed to Ireland and he vowed to found an abbey where he made landfall. Named after Tintern

	Abbey in Wales and sometimes known as Tintern of the Vow, it was occupied by the Colclough family from the 16th century until the 1960s.
Westgate Heritage Centre	Spawell Road, Wexford. Housed in the West Gate tower, the last surviving of five gate towers in the town walls of Wexford. It adjoins 12th century Selskar Abbey, built on the site of a Temple of Odin. Tel: 053 914 6506.
Wexford Arts Centre	Cornmarket, Wexford. Housed in the former market place and assembly halls, built in 1760. Tel: 053 912 3764.
Wexford County Museum	Located within Enniscorthy Castle, the museum was opened in 1962 and is dedicated to the ecclesiastical, military, maritime, agricultural and industrial history of the county, especially commemorating the risings of 1798 and 1916. Tel: 053 923 5926.
Wexford Wildfowl Reserve	2$^1/_2$ miles (4km) northeast of Wexford. Covering 479 acres (194ha) of the North Slob of Wexford harbour, the reserve is an internationally important wintering ground for migratory waterfowl species, notably Greenland white-fronted goose and brent goose. Owned jointly by the National Parks & Wildlife Service and the Irish Wildbird Conservancy.
Yola Farmstead Folk Park	Tagoate, 2 miles (3km) west of Rosslare Harbour, 7 miles (11km) south of Wexford. An 18th century themed farmstead covering 5 acres (2ha) and featuring a restored farmhouse, forge, school house, working mill and thatched cottage. Tel: 053 913 2610.

Some famous people born in County Wexford

Ahearne, Bunny (ice hockey promoter) (1900–85)	Wexford
Banville, John (author) (1945–)	Wexford
Barry, John (Father of the American Navy) (1745–1803)	Tacumshane
Bird, Wallis (musician) (1982–)	Wexford
Colfer, Eoin (author of Artemis Fowl books) (1965–)	Wexford
Corish, Brendan (politician) (1918–90)	Wexford
Doran, Tony (hurling player) (1946–)	Boolavogue
Doyle, Anne (newsreader) (1952–)	Ferns
Kennedy, Patrick (great-grandfather of JFK) (1823–58)	Dunganstown
Kent, John (premier of Newfoundland) (1805–72)	Wexford
Lacey, Bill (footballer) (1889–1969)	Enniscorthy
McClure, Robert (explorer) (1807–73)	Wexford
O'Herlihy, Dan (actor) (1919–2005)	Wexford
Rackard, Billy (hurling player) (1930–2009)	Killane
Rackard, Bobby (hurling player) (1927–96)	Killane
Rackard, Nicky (hurling player) (1922–76)	Killane
Roche, Dick (politician) (1947–)	Wexford
Rossiter, Keith (hurling player) (1984–)	Oulart
Ryan, James (politician) (1891–1970)	Taghmon
Warren, Michael (sculptor) (1950–)	Gorey

WICKLOW

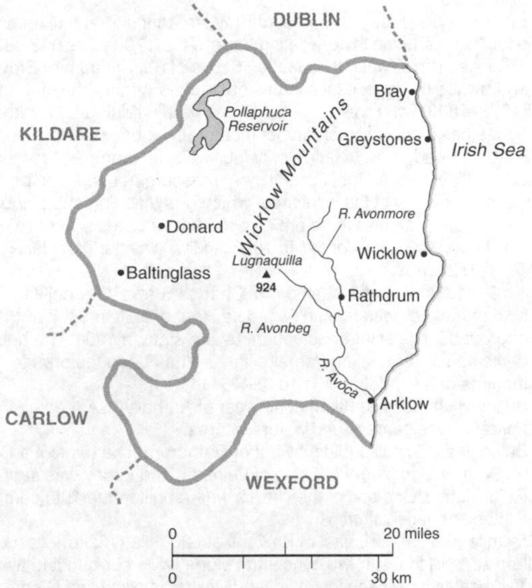
DUBLIN
KILDARE
CARLOW
WEXFORD
Irish Sea
Wicklow Mountains
Pollaphuca Reservoir
Bray
Greystones
Wicklow
Rathdrum
Arklow
Donard
Baltinglass
Lugnaquilla
924
R. Avonmore
R. Avonbeg
R. Avoca
0
20 miles
0
30 km

County Wicklow is part of the province of Leinster. It lies on the east coast of Ireland and is bordered by Wexford to the south, Carlow to the southwest, Kildare to the west and Dublin to the north. It has an eastern coastline on the Irish Sea. The county town is Wicklow. Geographically it is dominated by its coastline and the Wicklow Mountains and is known as the 'Garden of Ireland'.

A Viking presence is known at Arklow and Wicklow, where trading stations became important medieval towns in the Anglo-Norman period. When occupied by the Danes the latter town was called *Wykinglo*, from which the modern name is derived. There is much evidence of an early Christian presence in the area, including the Franciscan friary in Wicklow and the extensive monastic site of Glendalough. The religious importance of the sites declined as the Normans switched the see to Dublin. County Wicklow is sometimes known as 'the last county' as it was the last of the original counties to be established (in 1606) from land previously part of County Dublin.

The most famous son and daughter of Wicklow are undoubtedly Dame Ninette de Valois (born Edris Stannus) and Charles Stewart Parnell.

Wexford	**Population**			**Area**	
Districts	*male*	*female*	*total*	*sq miles*	*sq km*
Arklow	4896	5059	9955	3	7
Baltinglass	7464	7221	14,685	242	627
Bray	12,532	13,712	26,244	6	14
Rathdown	9175	9773	18,948	51	132
Rathdrum	15,796	15,302	31,098	352	914
Shillelagh	3480	3235	6715	130	336
Wicklow	3457	3574	7031	1	3
Total	56,800	57,876	114,676	785	2033

Local Attractions and Information

Administrative headquarters	County Offices, Wicklow. Tel: 040 420100.
Aghowle Church	4 miles (6km) west of Shillelagh, 21 miles (33km) southwest of Arklow. The ruin of a 12th century church located on the site of a 6th century monastic foundation reputedly established by St Finian of Clonard.
Agricultural Heritage Display Centre	Enniskerry, 3 miles (5km) west of Bray. An agricultural museum with a collection of period farming equipment and machinery dating back to the 1700s. Tel: 012 862423.
Altidore Castle	$1\frac{1}{4}$ miles (2km) west of Kilpedder, 6 miles (10km) south of Bray. A Georgian mansion built c.1800 and owned by direct descendants of Thomas Addis Emmet, brother of Irish patriot Robert Emmet (1778–1803), who was executed for his part in raising an ill-fated revolution in July 1803. The house has a collection of Emmet memorabilia, books and papers. Tel: 012 819186.
Ardmore Studios	Herbert Road, Bray. Ireland's only four-wall film studio, with five sound stages. Tel: 012 862971.
Arklow Maritime Museum	St Mary's Road, Arklow. Local history museum housed in a former school and focusing on the maritime history of the local area, which has a fishing and shipbuilding tradition. In addition to a photographic archive there are also models of boats built at Arklow including Sir Francis Chichester's *Gypsy Moth III*. In 1826 Arklow was the first place in Ireland to have a lifeboat station. Tel: 040 232868.
Avondale House and Gardens	1 mile (1.6km) south of Rathdrum. Charles Stewart Parnell (1846–91), president and 'uncrowned king of Ireland', was born in Avondale House, built in 1777 and surrounded by 500 acres (200ha) of grounds. The estate was bought by the state in 1904. The house now contains a museum dedicated to celebrating Parnell's life and has been restored to reflect its possible appearance at the time of his childhood. Tel: 040 446111.
Ballard Park Garden	Ballinaclash, 2 miles (3km) southwest of Rathdrum. A 4 acre (1.6ha) garden with herbaceous borders, rose gardens and water features.
Baltinglass Abbey	Baltinglass, 20 miles (32km) west of Rathdrum. The ruins of a Cistercian abbey founded in 1148 by Dermot Mac Murrough, king of Leinster. The abbey was suppressed at the time of the Reformation. One end of the church was rebuilt in the 19th century and was used for a time as a Protestant parish church.
Baltinglass Hill Fort	$\frac{1}{2}$ mile (0.8km) northeast of Baltinglass, 20 miles (32km) west of Rathdrum. Aka Rathcoran. An Iron Age hill fort with two concentric stone walls surrounding two Neolithic passage tombs.
Battles	Two battles have been fought in Co. Wicklow: Arklow and Glenmalur. See separate table for details.
Black Castle	$\frac{1}{4}$ mile (0.4km) east of Wicklow. The ruins of a 12th century castle built by the Fitzgerald family on a promontory on the northern coast of Wicklow at the mouth of the River Vartry. Built on a site previously fortified by the Vikings, it was attacked on numerous occasions and was finally destroyed by fire in the late 1640s.
Blessington Lakes	17 miles (27km) southwest of Bray. Aka Poulaphuca Reservoir. Created in 1940 by the planned flooding of the Liffey valley, the lakes are fed by the River Liffey and King River.
Bray Heritage Centre	Main Street, Bray. Local history centre housed in the town's former courthouse, built in 1841. An exhibition tells the story of Bray and there are also archaeological exhibits. Tel: 012 866796.
Billy Byrne Monument	Market Square, Wicklow. A monument depicting a 19th century pikeman and erected to commemorate the men of Wicklow who lost their lives in the revolutionary actions of 1798, 1803, 1848 and 1867.
Carnew Castle	Carnew, 15 miles (24km) southwest of Arklow. Built in the late 16th century by Sir Henry Harrington. The castle changed hands and was damaged during the 1798 rebellion but was recaptured. It was subsequently remodelled more for domesticity than defence. The castle is not open to the public.
Castleruddery Stone Circle	5 miles (8km) northeast of Baltinglass, 17 miles (27km) northwest of Rathdrum. A stone circle measuring 100ft (30.5m) in diameter and consisting of around 40 stones, mostly of granite but also including two larger quartz stones.
Dwyer-MacAllister Cottage	Derrynamuck, 6 miles (10km) east of Baltinglass, 14 miles (23km) northwest of Rathdrum. A museum in the cottage from which rebel Michael Dwyer escaped in 1799 with the help of Samuel MacAllister, who sacrificed his own life to enable the escape. The small cottage is furnished with period furniture and utensils.
Franciscan Friary	Abbey Street, Wicklow. The ruin of a Franciscan friary founded in the 13th century by the Fitzgeralds. After the monastery was suppressed in the 16th century, the building was at various times used as a courthouse and an armaments store. It is now located in the grounds of the priest's house.
Glendalough Monastic Site	6 miles (10km) northwest of Rathdrum. The extensive ruins of a religious centre located on the site of a 6th century monastery founded by St Kevin in the 'Glen of Two Lakes'. Considered to be Ireland's most sacred holy place, it includes the remains of at least seven churches, as well as high crosses and a round tower. There are two main clusters of buildings, around the Upper and Lower Lakes, plus some isolated ruins. The site is entered through the Gateway, which was set in a perimeter wall to protect the site from attack. In this area are the round tower, 100ft (30.5m) high with a door 10ft (3m) off the ground, its conical cap rebuilt in 1876 using the original stones; the **Priest's House**, a small building probably built in the 12th century as a tomb shrine, and featuring the remains of a Romanesque arch; the large church known as the **Cathedral**, actually the largest church in Glendalough, and dedicated to St Peter and St Paul. Dating to the 11th century, with many additions made later, it probably stands on the original 6th century monastery; **St Kevin's Church**, also known as St Kevin's Kitchen, a nave and chancel church possibly dating to the 12th century with a small round tower (belfry) above the west doorway; **St Kieran's Church**, a small

nave and chancel church said to have been founded by St Kevin to commemorate his friend St Kieran; and **St Mary's Church** – because this church is isolated from the main group of ruins it has been taken to be specifically for the use of women or nuns. **Trinity Church** is the ruin of one of the earliest churches in the Lower Group. A round tower stood beside it but this was blown down on 1818. Around the Upper Lake are the cave known as **St Kevin's Bed**, a small man-made cave dug into a cliff face and overlooking the Upper Lake, which it is believed St Kevin used as his sleeping quarters; **Temple-na-Skellig**, one of the oldest churches and possibly dating from the original foundation; and **Reefert Church**, a nave-and-chancel church probably dating to the 11th century, the name of which is derived from *Riogfheart*, meaning 'the burial place of kings'. The ruin of **St Saviour's Priory** stands a little aside from the other churches in a grove by the Glendassan River. Believed to have been founded by St Laurence O'Toole in 1162, it was partially reconstructed in the 19th century. There are also many crosses and memorials, including the Bresal Stone and the Market Cross in St Kevin's Church, and St Kevin's Cross. The site suffered many attacks and damage through fire and fell into decline after it was united to the See of Dublin in the 13th century, and was restored during the late 19th and early 20th centuries. Tel: 040 445352.

Graigueconna Garden — Old Connaught, 1/2 mile (0.8km) west of Bray. A plantsman's garden covering 4 acres (1.6ha) with mixed borders and climbers, originally laid out in the early 20th century by alpine gardener Lewis Meredith. The rare spotted-leaved helleborus 'Graigueconna' was discovered here. Tel: 012 822273.

Greenan Farm Museum and Maze — Greenan, 2 1/2 miles (4km) west of Rathdrum, 11 miles (18km) southwest of Wicklow. The old farmhouse dates from the 16th century and was used as a safe house during the 1798 uprising. Exhibits include weaponry and domestic utensils and furniture. The farm museum, housed in a two-storey barn, features exhibits including agricultural machinery and equipment. There is also a bottle museum with a large collection of antique 19th and early 20th century Irish bottles and jars. There are two mazes: the Greenan Maze has a Celtic design with a stream flowing through it to a pond in the middle; the Solstice Maze is set within a large stone circle of 21 stones, encircling four large standing stones which represent the seasons. Tel: 040 446000.

Halpin Memorial — Fitzwilliam Square, Wicklow. A memorial erected in 1897 to commemorate Captain Robert C Halpin (1836–94), commander of the *Great Eastern*, which laid transatlantic telegraphy cable between Valentia Island and Newfoundland in 1866.

Highest point — Lugnaquilla in the Wicklow Mountains at 3033ft (924m).

Holmsdale — Church Road, Greystones. A garden in three compartments with herbaceous plants and shrubs, alpines and ferns. Tel: 012 874270.

Holy Trinity Church — Castlemacadam, 1/2 mile (0.8km) south of Avoca, 5 miles (8km) northwest of Arklow. The church has a flagon made of local silver and presented to the old church in 1753. In this parish Cecil Frances Humphreys Alexander (1818–95) wrote many of her best-loved hymns, including 'All Things Bright and Beautiful'. Tel: 040 469117.

Humewood Castle — Kiltegan, 20 miles (32km) northwest of Arklow. A Gothic style country house built in the 1860s century for MP William Wentworth Fitzwilliam Hume Dick and recently restored to provide luxury accommodation. Tel: 059 6473215.

Interesting facts — **Roundwood** nestles among the hills of Co. Wicklow on a plateau 781ft (238m) above sea level, making it the highest village in Ireland. The village is surrounded by lakes and hills, including Vartry Lakes which can be seen from the Main Street and the spectacular Lough Dan just a few miles away. Roundwood is also known by its Gaelic name, An Tochar, which is based on the Gaelic word 'Tochar', meaning a causeway or a 'level place'. **Shillelagh** town was planned as part of the Fitzwilliam estate in the 17th century. The town, at the southern tip of the Wicklow Mountains, gave its name to the knobbled cudgel of oak or blackthorn that was once so prominent in the area. Tomnafinnoge Oak Wood remains one of the largest remaining oak forests in Ireland. **Dame Ninette de Valois** (6 June 1898–8 March 2001) has the distinction of being one of a very few people who have lived in three separate centuries. **Glenroe Farm** near Kilcoole was for 18 years (from 1983 to 2001) the principal location for the RTE soap series *Glenroe*. The series simply could not overcome the death of its favourite character, Biddy, who died in a car crash towards the end of the soap's run.

Joyce's House — Martello Terrace, Bray. The family home of writer James Joyce. The house features in *Portrait of the Artist as a Young Man*.

Killincarrig Fortified House — Kilcoole, 2 1/2 miles (4km) south of Greystones. An L-shaped tower house built in 1615. Oliver Cromwell stayed here overnight on his way to Wexford in 1649.

Killruddery House and Gardens — 1 mile (1.6km) south of Bray. The home of the Brabazon family (Earls of Meath) since 1618, the existing house was remodelled in Tudor Revival style in 1820 by architects Richard Morrison and his son William. The house was reduced in the 1950s. It is noted for its decorative plasterwork. The estate features 17th century landscape gardens, the oldest surviving formal gardens in Ireland, and a Victorian orangery. The formal gardens feature 'angles' (radiating hedges of beech and hornbeam with statuary at the centre), twin canals and a circular pond and fountain surrounded by a giant beech hedge. The Orangery was designed by William Burn in 1852, reflecting the design of the Crystal Palace in London, and has a number of classical marble statues. There is also a 'Sylvan Theatre', an outdoor performance space created using box hedging. Tel: 040 446024.

Kilmacurragh Arboretum — 3 miles (5km) east of Rathdrum. Originally planted in the 19th century and noted for its conifers. Tel: 018 570909.

Kindlestown Castle — Delgany, 1 mile (1.6km) southwest of Greystones. The ruin of a 13th century castle probably built by the Archbold family. It is believed to be one of only two hall houses with outer defences remaining in Ireland.

Knockmore Gardens — Enniskerry, $2^1/_2$ miles (4km) west of Bray. A 3 acre (1.2ha) garden established in the 19th century and surrounding a Palladian style house. Overlooking Dublin Bay, it features a rockery, kitchen garden, wild garden and ponds. The story of the garden is told in a book by Ruth Isabel Ross, *A Year of an Irish Garden*. Tel: 012 867336.

Meeting of the Waters — The name given to the confluence of the rivers Avonmore and Avonbeg near Avoca.

Mill at Avoca — $1^1/_2$ miles (2.5km) north of Avoca, 5 miles (8km) northwest of Arklow. A working family-owned handweaving mill dating to 1723. The village of Avoca was a location for the TV series *Ballykissangel*. Tel: 00 353 (0) 40 235105.

Mottee Stone — 2 miles (3km) north of Avoca, 6 miles (10km) northwest of Arklow. A huge 'erratic' boulder deposited during the Ice Age. According to local legend it was hurled by Fionn MacCumhaill from the top of Lugnaquilla Mountain. The name possibly derives from the French word *moitié* ('half'), lying as it does halfway between Wexford and Dublin.

Mount Usher Gardens — Ashford, 3 miles (5km) southwest of Wicklow. A 20 acre (8ha) garden beside the Vartry River featuring 5000 different species of plants and trees including rhododendrons, magnolias, camellias and eucryphia. Based around an old mill and designed in the 19th century in an informal, 'Robinsonian' style, the garden also has many water features. Tel: 040 440116.

Nature Reserves — **Deputy's Pass**, 1 mile (1.6km) southwest of Glenealy, 5 miles (8km) southwest of Wicklow, a 115 acre (47ha) area of previously coppiced woodland to the north of Deputy's Pass.

Glen of the Downs, 5 miles (8km) south of Bray, 146 acres (59ha) of oak woodland.

Glendalough, 6 miles (10km) northwest of Rathdrum, 388 acres (157ha) of oak woods extending from the Upper Lake to the lower slopes of Derrybawn mountain.

Glenealo Valley, 1958ha mainly of mixed heathland and peatland.

Knocksink Wood in the Glencullen River valley, 128 acres (52ha) of sessile oak and mixed woodland, including extensive areas of wet woodland.

Vale of Clara, 546 acres (221ha) of discontinuous oak wood beside the Avonmore River which has been under woodland since the Ice Age.

Parnell National Memorial Park — Rathdrum, 8 miles (13km) southwest of Wicklow. Located in Parnell's birthplace and featuring a bronze statue of Parnell.

Piper Stones — $1^1/_4$ miles (2km) southwest of Hollywood, 25 miles (40km) northwest of Wicklow. Aka Athgreany. Three standing stones remaining from what may have been a five stone circle.

Powerscourt Gardens and House — 3 miles (5km) southwest of Bray. A world-renowned garden surrounding a Palladian style mansion designed in the 1730s by Richard Cassels. The site was originally settled in the 14th century and the estate was granted to Richard Wingfield in the early 17th century. The present house was remodelled around the shell of the earlier castle and an extra storey was added in 1787. In 1961 the estate passed to the Slazenger family. The house was gutted by a fire in November 1974 which destroyed the main rooms and it remained a shell for over 20 years. A major restoration programme was begun in 1996; the house has since been re-roofed and the entrance hall and ballroom restored. The entrance hall is now home to an exhibition telling the story of the house and estate. Cassels also laid out the original gardens in the 1740s as an extensive parkland, plus gardens and terraces, but they were largely remodelled in mainly Italianate style in the mid 19th century by Daniel Robertson. Covering 47 acres (19ha), they are especially known for their specimen trees and collection of statuary. The gardens were first opened to the public in 1974, shortly before the fire of that year. The estate also contains both Ireland's highest waterfall (see Powerscourt Waterfall) and also the country's tallest tree, a Douglas fir 184ft (56m) high. Tel: 012 046000.

Powerscourt Waterfall — 3 miles (5km) south of Enniskerry. The highest waterfall in Britain and Ireland, at 398ft (121m), surrounded by woods and specimen trees. The 7th Viscount Powerscourt established a deer park here and in 1858 successfully introduced the Japanese sika deer to Ireland.

Rathgall Hill Fort — 6 miles (10km) northwest of Shillelagh, 19 miles (31km) west of Arklow. A multivallate hill fort with three concentric stone walls, probably built in the early Christian period. It is a designated National Monument.

Rivers — The **Avoca** is formed from the confluence of the rivers Avonmore ('big river') and Avonbeg ('little river'), which meet at the Meeting of the Waters (the Vale of Avoca). The Avoca flows into the Irish Sea at Arklow.

The **Dargle** rises in the Wicklow mountains and proceeds to Powerscourt Waterfall.

The **Liffey** see Dublin.

Slaney see Carlow

Russborough House — 1 mile (1.6km) southwest of Blessington, 19 miles (31km) southwest of Bray. A Palladian style house built in the early 18th century by Richard Castle for Joseph Leeson, Earl of Milltown. It has collections of fine art, furniture, tapestries, carpets, porcelain and silver. Tel: 045 865239.

St John's Church — Laragh, 6 miles (10km) northwest of Rathdrum. A Church of Ireland church founded with money raised by subscription in 1843 to build a Chapel of Ease (meaning that it was for the convenience, or ease, of the parishioners within its immediate vicinity as the nearest parish church was more than 4 miles/6km away). The church was dedicated in 1867.

Sculpture in Woodland — Ashford, 3 miles (5km) northwest of Wicklow. A collection of 16 wooden sculptures by Irish and international artists, located in Devil's Glen Wood. Tel: 012 011111.

Shekina Sculpture Garden — Glenmalure, 2 miles (3km) northwest of Greenan, 12 miles (19km) southwest of Wicklow. A garden featuring a collection of sculptures by modern Irish artists with the theme of the story of creation. Tel: 012 838711.

Sport

football — **Bray Wanderers** were formed in 1942 and were winners of the League of Ireland 1st Division in 1986, 1996, 2000 and 2002, and of the FAI Cup in 1990 and 1999. Their home ground is Carlisle Grounds, Bray.

Threecastles Castle	2 miles (3km) northeast of Blessington. The ruins of a 14th century tower house. The name derives from the existence of two other castles in the vicinity, of which no trace now remains.
Tinahely Courthouse Arts Centre	Main Street, Tinahely. Housed in the former courthouse, built in 1843. It then became a community facility before falling into disuse by the 1980s. It was restored through local efforts and the arts centre opened in 1996. Tel: 040 238529.
Valclusa Gardens	Waterfall Road, Enniskerry. A garden first laid out in the 1830s around a dower house of the Powerscourt Estate. Its specimen trees include a giant redwood, and there are collections of perennials. Tel: 012 869485.
Vale of Avoca	11 miles (18km) southwest of Wicklow. A much-loved beauty spot described by poet Thomas More in his song 'The Meeting of the Waters': 'There is not in the wide world a valley so sweet, As that vale in whose bosom the bright waters meet. Oh the last rays of feeling and life must depart, Ere the bloom of that valley shall fade from my heart.' At the southern end of the valley, in the tiny village of Woodenbridge, is Ireland's oldest hotel, established in 1608.
Victor's and Victoria's Way	Roundwood, 9 miles (15km) northwest of Wicklow. A meditation, reflection and contemplation garden covering 22 acres (9ha) and containing 14 large black granite sculptures, including seven of the Hindu deity Ganesh which were quarried and carved in India. Tel: 012 818505.
Wicklow Mountains National Park	Ireland's fourth National Park when it was established in 1991. Originally covering an area of 14 sq miles (37 sq km), it now covers 58 sq miles (150 sq km) including large areas of mountain blanket bog, oak woodland and the Upper Lake at Glendalough. Wildlife includes sika and red deer. Tel: 040 445656.
Wicklow Way	A long distance walking trail spanning 81 miles (130km) from Marlay Park, south of Dublin, to Clonegal, Co. Carlow. It skirts the Wicklow Mountains and passes through or near Enniskerry, Powerscourt, Glendalough, Glenmalure and Tinahely. Established in 1980, it is the most westerly section of the European Path E8 which, when completed, will run from Dursey Head, Cork, to Istanbul, a distance of 2750 miles (4390km).
Wicklow's Historic Gaol	Kilmantin Hill, Wicklow. Built in the early 18th century, over the years the gaol held many of the county's favourite sons who were involved in the various rebellions such as Michael Dwyer, Billy Byrne and James Napper Tandy. Closed in 1900, it was reopened in 1918 in order to house members of the Irish Republican Brotherhood and Sinn Féin, including Robert Erskine Childers. It was closed again in 1924. The gaol was restored in the 1990s, when it was opened as a visitor attraction and heritage centre. Tel: 040 461599.

Some famous people born in County Wicklow

Byrne, Shane (rugby player) (1971–)	Aughrim
Darcy, Eamonn (golfer) (1952–)	Delgany
Delany, Ron (athlete) (1935–)	Arklow
Fitzgerald, Geraldine (actress) (1913–2005)	Greystones
King, Cecil (artist) (1921–86)	Rathdrum
Marsden, William (writer and orientalist) (1754–1836)	Verval
McShane, Paul (footballer) (1986–)	Kilpeddar
Parnell, Charles Stewart (politician) (1846–91)	Avondale
Pim, Joshua (tennis player) (1869–1942)	Bray
Valois, Ninette de (ballet dancer) (1898–2001)	Blessington

Crown Dependencies and Overseas Territories

The territories of the Isle of Man, and the Bailiwicks of Jersey and Guernsey, though under the sovereignty of the British Crown, have a slightly different constitutional relationship with the United Kingdom, and are consequently classed as Crown Dependencies. Brief details of the islands are listed although the populations have not been included in the summary sheet of the 2001 National Census (2002 for Ireland). Crown Dependencies are possessions of the Crown in Right of the United Kingdom, as opposed to overseas territories or colonies of the United Kingdom. They do not form a part of the United Kingdom, being separate jurisdictions, nor do they form part of the European Union. All three Crown Dependencies are members of the British-Irish Council. From 2005, each of the three has a Chief Minister as head of government. However, as they are possessions of the British Crown they are not sovereign nations in their own right, and the UK Parliament has the ultimate ability to pass legislation affecting the islands. The Crown Dependencies, together with the United Kingdom, are collectively known as the British Islands and are therefore included in my list of islands. They are also treated as part of the United Kingdom for British nationality law purposes. However they maintain local controls over housing and employment which apply to British citizens without specified connections to that dependency (as well as to non-British citizens). Each island has its own separate international vehicle registration (GBG – Guernsey, GBJ – Jersey, GBM – Isle of Man), internet domain (.gg – Guernsey, .je – Jersey, .im – Isle of Man), and ISO 3166-2 codes (codes for the representation of names of countries and their subdivisions), first reserved on behalf of the Universal Postal Union (GGY – Guernsey, JEY – Jersey, IMN – Isle of Man) and then added officially by the International Organisation for Standardisation on 29 March 2006.

The Bailiwick of Guernsey includes the island of Guernsey, the island of Sark, the island of Alderney, Herm and other islands (see separate table). The parliament is the States of Guernsey. Within the Bailiwick of Guernsey, autonomy is exercised by Sark, a feudal (but democratising) state under the Seigneur, whose legislature is called the Chief Pleas, and by Alderney, whose legislature is also called the States, under an elected President. Guernsey issues its own coins and banknotes, which although not legal tender within the UK, are often accepted anyway.

The Bailiwick of Jersey consists of the island of Jersey and its uninhabited dependencies (see separate table). The parliament is the States of Jersey. The States of Jersey Law 2005 introduced the post of Chief Minister of Jersey, abolished the Bailiff's power of dissent to and the Lieutenant-Governor's power of veto over a resolution of the States, and established that any Order in Council or Act of the United Kingdom that it was proposed might apply to Jersey should be referred to the States in order that the States might signify their views on it. Jersey also issues its own coins and banknotes and they too are not legal tender within the UK, although they are legal tender on the Bailiwick of Guernsey (as are UK coins and notes). Jersey has its own legal and healthcare systems as well as its own separate immigration policy, with 'local status' in one bailiwick having no jurisdiction in the other. They exercise bilateral double taxation treaties. Since 1961 the bailiwicks have had separate courts of appeal, but generally the bailiff of each bailiwick has been appointed to serve on the panel of appellate judges for the other bailiwick.

The Isle of Man's Tynwald claims to be the world's oldest parliament in continuous existence, dating back to 979. (However it does not claim to be the oldest parliament, as Iceland's Althing dates back to 930.) It consists of a democratically elected House of Keys and an indirectly elected Legislative Council, which may sit separately or jointly to consider pieces of legislation; when passed into law, these are known as 'Acts of Tynwald'. Candidates often stand for election as independents, rather than being selected by political parties. There is a Council of Ministers headed by a Chief Minister. The Isle of Man issues its own coins and banknotes, which circulate freely alongside UK coinage and English and Scottish banknotes. Isle of Man Post issues its own stamps and makes significant revenue from the sale of special issues to collectors.

The British government is solely responsible for defence and international representation of the Crown Dependencies, although each island has responsibility for its own customs and immigration. Until 2001, the Home Office had responsibility for the Crown Dependencies, but this was transferred to the Lord Chancellor's Department, now replaced by the Department for Constitutional Affairs. Acts of the British Parliament do not usually apply to the Channel Islands and the Isle of Man, unless explicitly stated by an Order in Council.

The Channel Islands are part of the territory annexed by the Duchy of Normandy in 933 from the Duchy of Brittany. This territory was added to the grant of land given in settlement by the king of France in 911 to the Viking raiders who had sailed up the Seine almost to the walls of Paris. William, Duke of Normandy, claimed the title King of England in 1066 following the death of Edward the Confessor and secured the claim through the Norman conquest of England. Subsequent marriage arrangements brokered between kings of England and French nobles meant that kings of England had title to more French lands than the king of France. When the king of France asserted his feudal right of patronage, the then king of England, King John, fearing he would be imprisoned should he attend, failed to fulfil his obligation. In 1204 the title and lands of the Duchy of Normandy and his other French possessions were stripped from King John by the king of France. The Channel Islands remained loyal to the 'rightful' duke, the king of England. In retaliation King John laid claim upon the title King of France. Many subsequent English kings fought successive campaigns against the king of France. These campaigns became known as the Hundred Years' war.

British monarchs finally abandoned the claim to the French throne in 1801. At no time since or before did the Channel Islands form part of the kingdom of England, and no subsequent order was given to bring them into a union as was done subsequently between the kingdoms of Scotland and England, and with the kingdom of Ireland in 1698. Feudal responsibilities remain to the nominal duke, even though the king of England has subsequently given up claim to the title. A unique constitutional position has arisen as successive monarchs have confirmed the liberties and privileges of the Bailiwicks, often referring to the so-called Constitutions of King John, a legendary document supposed to have been granted by King John in the aftermath of 1204. Governments of the Bailiwicks have generally tried to avoid testing the limits of the unwritten constitution by avoiding conflict with British governments. Following the restoration of Charles II, who had spent part of his exile in the island of Jersey, the Channel Islands were further given the right to set their own customs duties, referred to by the Jersey Legal French term as *impôts*.

In the Isle of Man the British monarch is Lord of Mann (sic), a title variously held by Norse, Scots and English kings and nobles until it passed to the British monarch in 1765.

In addition to Crown Dependencies there are 14 British Overseas Territories which are under the sovereignty of the United Kingdom, but not considered part of the United Kingdom itself. The 14 territories are: British Antarctic Territory (capital: Rothera), South Georgia & the South Sandwich Islands (capital: King Edward Point/Grytviken), British Indian Ocean Territory (capital: Diego Garcia), Sovereign Base Areas of Akrotiri & Dhekelia (capital: Episkopi Cantonment), Pitcairn Islands (capital: Adamstown), Falkland Islands (capital: Stanley), St Helena (capital: Jamestown), Anguilla (capital: The Valley), British Virgin Islands (capital: Road Town), Cayman Islands (capital: George Town), Gibraltar (capital: Gibraltar), Montserrat (capital: Plymouth), Bermuda (capital: Hamilton), and Turks & Caicos Islands (capital: Cockburn Town). Gibraltar is the only Overseas Territory that is part of the European Union (EU).

The name 'British Overseas Territory' was introduced by the British Overseas Territories Act 2002 and replaced the name British Dependent Territory, which was introduced by the British Nationality Act 1981. Prior to that, the territories were known as colonies or Crown colonies. The Foreign and Commonwealth Office have the responsibility of looking after the interests of all Overseas Territories except the Sovereign Base Areas territory, which comes under the jurisdiction of the Ministry of Defence. Several nations dispute the UK's sovereignty in the following Overseas Territories: British Antarctic Territory (Chile and Argentina), British Indian Ocean Territory (Mauritius and Seychelles), Falkland Islands (Argentina), Gibraltar (Spain), and South Georgia & the South Sandwich Islands (Argentina). The head of state in the Overseas Territories is the British monarch, currently Queen Elizabeth II, who appoints a representative in each territory to exercise her executive power. Defence of the Overseas Territories is the responsibility of the UK.

Many of the Overseas Territories are used as military bases by the UK and its allies. **Ascension Island** (a dependency of St Helena) – RAF Ascension Island is used by both the Royal Air Force and the United States Air Force. **Bermuda** became the primary Royal Navy base in the western hemisphere following US independence. The naval establishment included an admiralty, a dockyard and a naval squadron. A considerable military garrison was built up to protect it, and Bermuda, which the British government came to see as a base, rather than as a colony, was known as the Gibraltar of the West. Canada and the USA also established bases in Bermuda during World War II, and these were maintained through the Cold War. Since 1995, the military force in Bermuda has been reduced to the local territorial battalion, the Bermuda Regiment. **British Indian Ocean Territory** – the island of Diego Garcia is home to a large naval base and airbase leased to the United States by the United Kingdom. **Falkland Islands** – British Forces Falkland Islands includes commitments from the British Army, Royal Air Force and Royal Navy. **Gibraltar** – Royal Navy dockyard, also used by NATO; RAF Gibraltar – used by RAF and NATO. The local garrison is manned by the Royal Gibraltar Regiment. **The Sovereign Base Areas of Akrotiri & Dhekelia** in Cyprus is maintained as a strategic British military base in the eastern Mediterranean Sea.

Channel Islands

(shipping area = Portland)

Island name	Area	Nearest landmark	General information
Alderney	The Swinge	Cape Hague, Normandy, France	Part of the Bailiwick of Guernsey. Third largest of the Channel Islands and first to have an airport. Area: 3.05 sq miles (7.9 sq km). Population: 2294.
Bec du Nez	English Channel	Congriere, Sark	Part of the Bailiwick of Guernsey
Brechou	English Channel	Gouliot Headland, Sark	aka Brecqhou. Part of the Bailiwick of Guernsey. Owned by the newspaper publishing tycoons Sir David and Sir Frederick Barclay (identical twins born in 1934) who also own The Ritz, London.
Bretagne Uset	English Channel	La Louge, Sark	Part of the Bailiwick of Guernsey
Burhou	The Swinge	Alderney	Part of the Bailiwick of Guernsey
Courbee du Nez	English Channel	Congriere, Sark	Part of the Bailiwick of Guernsey
Crevichon	Little Russel	Jethou	Part of the Bailiwick of Guernsey
Fort Les Homeaux Florains	English Channel	Quesnard Point, Alderney	Part of the Bailiwick of Guernsey
Fourquie	English Channel	Vallee des Goudalons, Alderney	Part of the Bailiwick of Guernsey
Galet de Jacob	English Channel	Brecqhou	Part of the Bailiwick of Guernsey
Gold Fisher Rock	Fermain Bay	Fermain Point, Guernsey	Part of the Bailiwick of Guernsey
Grande Fauconniere	English Channel	Jethou	Part of the Bailiwick of Guernsey
Grande Moie	English Channel	Point Robert, Sark	Part of the Bailiwick of Guernsey
Green Island	St Clement's Bay	Jersey	aka La Motte. Part of the Bailiwick of Jersey
Grosse Rock	The Swinge	Fort Tourgis, Alderney	Part of the Bailiwick of Guernsey
Guernsey	English Channel	Cape Hague, Normandy, France	Part of the Bailiwick of Guernsey. Known as *Sarnia* to the Romans. Victor Hugo wrote *Les Miserables* here in 1862. Area: 24.32 sq miles (63 sq km). Population: 59,710.
Guillaumesse	English Channel	Les Sept Moies, Sark	Part of the Bailiwick of Guernsey
Gull Rock	Gull Bay	St Peter, Guernsey	Part of the Bailiwick of Guernsey
Herm	English Channel	St Peter Port, Guernsey	Part of the Bailiwick of Guernsey. Geographical data includes Jethou. Herm is created from banks of shells. Area: 0.58 sq miles (1.5 sq km). Population: 97.
Herpin Rock	English Channel	Torteval, Guernsey	Part of the Bailiwick of Guernsey
Houmet des Piets	Saye Bay	Bibette Head, Alderney	Part of the Bailiwick of Guernsey
Huitriere	English Channel	La Tour, Sark	Part of the Bailiwick of Guernsey
Ile au Guerdain	Portelet Bay	Jersey	aka Janvrin's Tomb. Part of the Bailiwick of Jersey. Tidal island.
Ile de Raz	Longis Bay	Longis Common, Alderney	Part of the Bailiwick of Guernsey
Janvrin's Tomb	Portelet Bay	Jersey	See Ile au Guerdain
Jersey	English Channel	Pirou, France	Part of the Bailiwick of Jersey. Area: 45.64 sq miles (118.2 sq km). Population: 87,186.
Jethou	Little Russel	Point Sauzebourge, Herm	Part of the Bailiwick of Guernsey. The hangman's isle, where felons from Guernsey were executed.
La Capelle	L'Eree Bay	L'Eree, Guernsey	Part of the Bailiwick of Guernsey
La Grosse Rock	English Channel	Torteval, Guernsey	Part of the Bailiwick of Guernsey
La Grune	English Channel	Congriere, Sark	Part of the Bailiwick of Guernsey
La Motte	St Clement's Bay	Jersey	See Green Island
La Nache	English Channel	Vallee des Goudalons, Alderney	Part of the Bailiwick of Guernsey
Le Catioroc	L'Eree Bay	L'Eree, Guernsey	Part of the Bailiwick of Guernsey
Le Plat Houmet	Little Russel	Oyster Point, Herm	Part of the Bailiwick of Guernsey
Le Puits Jervais	The Swinge	Clos des Cables, Alderney	Part of the Bailiwick of Guernsey
Les Autelets	English Channel	Tintageu, Sark	Part of the Bailiwick of Guernsey
Les Casquets	English Channel	Alderney	Part of the Bailiwick of Guernsey. The *White Ship,* carrying Henry I's son and heir, William, was wrecked here, 25 November 1120.
Les Cretes	Belle Elizabeth	St Peter, Guernsey	Part of the Bailiwick of Guernsey
Les Dents	English Channel	Brecqhou	Part of the Bailiwick of Guernsey
Les Ecrehous	English Channel	Jersey	Part of the Bailiwick of Jersey
Les Etacs	The Swinge	Clos des Cables, Alderney	Part of the Bailiwick of Guernsey
Les Jacquets	English Channel	Le Grand Monceau, Herm	Part of the Bailiwick of Guernsey

Island name	Area	Nearest landmark	General information
Les Jumelles	The Swinge	Fort Grosnez, Alderney	Part of the Bailiwick of Guernsey
Les Kaines d'Aval	Belle Elizabeth	St Peter, Guernsey	Part of the Bailiwick of Guernsey
Les Laches	Creux Harbour	La Forge, Sark	Part of the Bailiwick of Guernsey
Les Minquiers	English Channel	Jersey	aka The Minkies. Part of the Bailiwick of Jersey
L'Etac de la Quoire	English Channel	Cachaliere, Alderney	Part of the Bailiwick of Guernsey
L'Etac de Serk	English Channel	La Sablonniere, Sark	Part of the Bailiwick of Guernsey
Lihou	Rocquaine Bay	L'Eree, Guernsey	Part of the Bailiwick of Guernsey. Advertised for sale in *The Times* in 1938 for £5. Accessible from Guernsey via Lihou Causeway at low tide.
L'Islet	English Channel	St Helier, Jersey	Part of the Bailiwick of Jersey
Minkies, The	English Channel	Jersey	See Les Minquiers
Moie de la Bretagne	English Channel	Adonis Headland, Sark	Part of the Bailiwick of Guernsey
Moie de la Fontaine	English Channel	Adonis Headland, Sark	Part of the Bailiwick of Guernsey
Moie de Port Gorey	English Channel	La Louge, Sark	Part of the Bailiwick of Guernsey
Moie du Breniere	Baleine Bay	La Sablonniere, Sark	Part of the Bailiwick of Guernsey
Moie du Gouliot	English Channel	Gouliot Headland, Sark	Part of the Bailiwick of Guernsey
Mouliere	English Channel	Frenchman's Point, Herm	Part of the Bailiwick of Guernsey
Moulinet	English Channel	Threepenny Hill, Herm	Part of the Bailiwick of Guernsey
Noire Pierre	English Channel	La Tour, Sark	Part of the Bailiwick of Guernsey
Pea Stacks	Moulin Huet Bay	Jerbourg Point, Guernsey	Part of the Bailiwick of Guernsey
Pecheressa	English Channel	Congriere, Sark	Part of the Bailiwick of Guernsey
Petite Baveuse	English Channel	Adonis Headland, Sark	Part of the Bailiwick of Guernsey
Petite Fauconniere	English Channel	Jethou	Part of the Bailiwick of Guernsey
Petite Moie	English Channel	Point Robert, Sark	Part of the Bailiwick of Guernsey
Pierre du Cours	English Channel	La Sablonniere, Sark	Part of the Bailiwick of Guernsey
Platte Rock	English Channel	Tintageu, Sark	Part of the Bailiwick of Guernsey
Queslingue	English Channel	Essex Hill, Alderney	Part of the Bailiwick of Guernsey
Rousset	English Channel	Essex Hill, Alderney	Part of the Bailiwick of Guernsey
St Aubin's	English Channel	St Helier, Jersey	Part of the Bailiwick of Jersey
Sark	English Channel	St Peter Port, Guernsey	Part of the Bailiwick of Guernsey. Motor cars are outlawed on Sark and only the Seigneur is allowed to keep a female dog on the island. Area: 2.01 sq miles (5.2 sq km). Population: 575.
Selle Roque	English Channel	Threepenny Hill, Herm	Part of the Bailiwick of Guernsey
Sercul	English Channel	La Louge, Sark	Part of the Bailiwick of Guernsey

Isle of Man and its islands

(shipping area = Irish Sea)

Island name	Area	Nearest landmark	General information
Anvil, The	Irish Sea	Cregneash	GR: SC196662
Burroo, The	Irish Sea	Calf of Man	GR: SC159645
Calf of Man	Irish Sea	Spanish Head	Area: 0.96 sq miles (2.49 sq km). GR: SC155655
Carrick, The	Irish Sea	Port St Mary	GR: SC228674
Chicken Rock	Irish Sea	Calf of Man	GR: SC143639
Conister	Irish Sea	Douglas	aka St Mary's Rock. GR: SC388755
Creg Harlot	Irish Sea	Bredda Head	GR: SC185706
Ellan Vannin	Irish Sea	St Bees Head, Cumbria	See Isle of Man
Fort Island	Irish Sea	Castletown	aka St Michael's Island. Connected to Langness by a causeway. Area: 0.02 sq miles (0.05 sq km). GR: SC295673
Kitterland	Irish Sea	Spanish Head	GR: SC170665
Lleeah-rio	Irish Sea	Castletown	GR: SC267663
Man, Isle of	Irish Sea	St Bees Head, Cumbria	Self-governing democracy at the geographical centre of the British Isles. Although it is not part of the UK, it is a British Crown Dependency. Known as Ellan Vannin (in Manx). Capital: Douglas. Area: 220.85 sq miles (572 sq km). Population: 76,315. GR: SC326847
St Mary's Rock	Irish Sea	Douglas	See Conister
St Michael's Island	Irish Sea	Castletown	See Fort Island
St Patrick's Isle	Irish Sea	Peel Head, Cumbria	Linked to Peel by a causeway. GR: SC241846
Stack, The	Irish Sea	Calf of Man	GR: SC148657
Sugarloaf, The	Irish Sea	Cregneash	GR: SC194662

Chronology of British and Irish history

AD

1 The King of the Trinovantes tribe, in southern England, Addedomarus, dies and is succeeded by Dubnovellaunus.
10 Cunobelinus (Cymbeline) rules over most of southern England from his HQ at Camulodunum (Colchester).
42 Cunobelinus, ruler of most of southern England, dies.
43 Romans invade England.
51 Caractacus, son of Cunobelinus, is captured by the Romans at Ludlow.
61 During a rebellion led by Queen Boudicca of the Iceni, the Trinovantes and Iceni tribes sack Roman Colchester, St Albans and London. Boudicca commits suicide after defeat by Suetonius Paulinus.
83 Agricola defeats the Caledonians at Mons Graupius.
84 Agricola is called back to Rome.
122 Construction of Hadrian's Wall is begun.
130 Hadrian's Wall is completed.
138 Hadrian dies and is succeeded by his recently adopted son Antoninus Pius.
139 Romans advance northwards under governor Lollius Urbicus from Hadrian's Wall to the Clyde–Forth line.
142 Construction of Antonine Wall is begun across central Scotland.
154 Brigantian revolt in Pennines put down by Governor Julius Verus, but troops withdrawn from Caledonia as a result.
155 Partial destruction by indigenous Picts of the Antonine Wall.
161 Antoninus dies and is succeeded by his adopted son Marcus Annius Verus (Marcus Aurelius).
163 Antonine Wall abandoned.
185 Mass mutiny of the Roman army in Britain eventually quelled by newly appointed governor Publius Helvius Pertinax.
197 Clodius Albinus, the British legate, revolts, but is defeated and killed by Severus at Lyons.
209 Roman legions under Severus and Caracalla march against the Caledonii, advancing as far as Aberdeen. Forts are built on Firths of Forth and Tay.
211 Emperor Septimius Severus dies at York; he is succeeded by his sons Caracalla and Geta.
216 Britannia is divided into two provinces – Upper Britain (south and west) and Lower Britain (north).
286 Roman military commander Marcus Carausius revolts and seizes Britain, declaring himself Emperor of Britain and Gaul. Construction begins on a series of forts to guard the southeastern coast (the Saxon Shore Forts).
293 Carausius murdered by Allectus, his finance minister, who seizes power in Britain.
Britannia is divided into four provinces – Britannia Prima (capital Cirencester), Britannia Secunda (York), Flavia Caesariensis (Lincoln) and Maxima Caesariensis (London).
296 Allectus defeated and killed by Constantius Chlorus in battle, possibly near Silchester (Calleva Atrebatum).
306 Constantius Chlorus dies near York. His son Constantine is proclaimed emperor
367 Picts, Scotti, Angles, Attacotti and Saxons invade Britain in a joint attack later known as the 'Barbarian Conspiracy'. **Note:** Scotti was the name given to Irish raiders by the Romans, although the Attacotti too were probably Celtic Gaels from Ireland.
369 Theodosius, a Roman general, re-establishes order in Britain.
375 The Ogham script (possibly named after the Irish god Ogma) begins to be used in Ireland, mainly on stone and wood. The 25-letter Ogham alphabet consists of a series of horizontal, vertical and diagonal lines linked together by a solid straight line.
383 Magnus Maximus mutinies against Emperor Gratian, who is assassinated. Magnus rules in Britain but begins to gradually withdraw Roman troops.
407 Roman troops depart Britain under the pretender Constantine III; Britain left to fend for itself. **Note:** Traditionally 410 is the year often given for the conclusion of the Roman occupation as it was then that Honorius officially cut all ties with Britain.
429 British, led by Bishop Germanus of Auxerre, defeat a Pictish and Saxon army, at a mountainous site near a river, of which Mold in North Wales is the traditional location. This was dubbed the 'Alleluia Victory' after Germanus ordered the troops to shout 'Alleluia' after baptising them before battle. This cry apparently caused the barbarians to flee before battle commenced!
430 Cunedda, chief of the Gododdin, moves at the Welsh King Vortigern's behest from Scotland to Gwynedd, whose royal house he thereby founds.
432 St Patrick sent as a missionary to Ireland.
441 Britain invaded by Angles, Saxons and Jutes.
446 Britain told to fend for itself when it appeals to Rome for help against barbarian invaders.
477 Sussex founded by Ælle, who lands with his sons at Selsey.
491 The South Saxons under Ælle capture Pevensey Castle.
495 Cerdic, founder of Wessex, lands near Southampton.
The British comprehensively defeat the Saxons at Mons Badonicus (this battle date is uncertain).
537 Arthur and Medrault traditionally believed to have fallen at the Battle of Camlann.
542 The Welsh monk Gildas writes *De Excidio et Conquestu Britanniae*, a history of the Roman conquest and Anglo-Saxon invasion of Britain.
547 The bubonic 'Plague of Justinian' reaches Britain.
The Angle king Ida accedes to the throne of Bernicia, in northeast England.
550 St David converts the Welsh.
560 Æthelberht I becomes King of Kent. Ceawlin becomes King of Wessex.
561 Battle of the Books ultimately results in the exile of Columcille to Iona in 563.

563 Foundation of monastery on Iona by Columcille (St Columba), one of the 'Twelve Apostles of Ireland', who proceeds to convert the Picts.
565 St Columba subdues a monster on Loch Ness, thereby making the first reference to the legendary beast.
571 Foundation of the Kingdom of East Anglia with Wuffa, son of Wehha, its first ruler.
574 Aidan (Áedán mac Gabráin), King of Dál Riata in County Antrim, Ireland, ordained King of the Argyll Scots by St Columba.
577 Celtic kings Commail, Condidan and Farinmail killed at the battle of Deorham by West Saxons under Cuthwin and Ceawlin.
592 Ceawlin of Wessex deposed by Ceol. The Bretwaldaship (overlordship) of the English peoples south of the Humber passes to Æthelbert of Kent.
593 Æthelfrith, son of Æthelric and grandson of Ida, succeeds Hussa as King of the Bernicians.
596 St Augustine dispatched by Pope Gregory to convert Britain.
597 St Augustine arrives in Kent, converts King Æthelbert and founds the Archdiocese of Canterbury.
603 Battle of Catraeth (Catterick) – Æthelfrith of Northumbria defeats a coalition of British from Lothian, north Wales and northwest England (immortalised in the Welsh poem *Y Gododdin*. **Note:** This battle is not listed elsewhere in this book as historians cannot agree either the date or the place of the battle).
604 Æthelfrith unites Bernicia and Deira (an area from the Humber to the Tees, and from the sea to the western edge of the Vale of York) to create the Kingdom of Northumbria.
611 Death of Ceolwulf of Wessex, succeeded by Cynegils.
616 Æthelbert of Kent dies; Raedwald of East Anglia becomes Bretwalda; he kills Æthelfrith of Northumbria at the River Idle in Nottinghamshire, replacing him with the exiled Edwin.
625 Death of Raedwald; Edwin of Northumbria becomes Bretwalda.
632 Edwin of Northumbria killed at Hatfield by Mercian/Welsh forces, who proceed to ravage the kingdom, which divides back into two.
634 Oswald re-establishes the Kingdom of Northumbria and becomes Bretwalda.
641 Oswald of Northumbria killed at the Battle of Maserfield (possibly near Oswestry) fighting King Penda of Mercia; he is succeeded in Bernicia by Oswy.
654 Penda of Mercia, Æthelhere of East Anglia and various other royals are killed in the Battle of the River Winwaed by Oswy of Bernicia, who re-establishes Northumbria.
657 Mercia released from Northumbrian rulership, Wulfhere son of Penda becomes King.
664 The English church adopts the Roman liturgy in preference to the Irish at the Synod of Whitby.
669 Theodore of Tarsus ordained Archbishop of Canterbury, and proceeds to reform the English Church.
670 Death of Oswiu of Northumbria, the last Bretwalda; his son Ecgfrith succeeds him.
672 The see of Canterbury given authority over the Church in England by the Synod of Hertford.
685 Ecgfrith of Northumbria falls in battle against the Picts at Nechtansmere; he is succeeded by Aldfrith.
688 Caedwalla of Wessex resigns the kingship and goes on pilgrimage to Rome, succeeded by Ine.
690 Wihtred becomes King of Kent.
692 Berhtwald becomes the first native Archbishop of Canterbury; the Irish Church accepts the authority of Rome at the Synod of Tara.
694 King Ine codifies the laws of Wessex.
709 Deaths of bishops Aldhelm of Sherborne, who converted Wessex, and St Wilfrid of Hexham.
716 Æthelbald becomes King of Mercia, succeeding Ceolred.
726 Ine of Wessex dies on pilgrimage in Rome and is succeeded by Æthelheard.
731 Bede completes his *Ecclesiastical History of the English People*.
732 A three-field system of crop rotation to help maintain a productive soil begins to be practised in Britain. The system generally consists of the rotation of rye or winter wheat, followed by spring oats or barley, then leaving the field fallow during the third stage. **Note:** The practice of growing a series of dissimilar types of crops in the same area to avoid the build up of pathogens and pests that often occurs when one species is continuously cropped, was originally invented by the Romans in Italy.
735 The Venerable Bede dies.
757 Offa succeeds Æthelbald as King of Mercia after the latter's murder.
758 King Eadbert of Northumbria abdicates to become a monk, succeeded by his son Osulf.
776 Kent gains temporary independence from Mercia as a result of winning the Battle of Otford. **Note:** The Anglo-Saxon Chronicle does not declare a victor and all that is known for certain is that King Offa of Mercia engaged the Jutes of Kent at Otford in this year.
779 Offa defeats Cynewulf of Wessex near Benson and becomes de facto ruler of England.
784 Work commences on Offa's Dyke.
787 According to the Anglo-Saxon Chronicle, the first Viking raid on England takes place near Wareham, Dorset. A group of men from Norway apparently sailed to Portland and are mistaken for merchants by a royal official, and they murder him. This event pre-dated a Viking attack on the monastery at Lindisfarne, sometimes cited as the first raid.
789 Frankish ports closed to English merchants due to a dispute between Charlemagne and Offa.
790 Irish monks sail to Iceland in skin-frame vessels.
792 Offa has King Æthelbert of East Anglia beheaded, and annexes his kingdom.
793 Lindisfarne and Jarrow sacked by the Vikings.
795 First Viking attacks in Ireland.
796 Death of Offa brings his son Ecgfrith to the throne. He dies soon after, and is succeeded by Cenwulf.
798 Revolt in Kent against Mercian rule subdued by King Cenwulf, who blinds the Kentish royal leader Eadbert and cuts off his hands.
800 The Book of Kells, an illuminated manuscript in Latin, containing the four Gospels of the New Testament together with various prefatory texts and tables, is transcribed by Celtic monks.
802 Egbert succeeds Brihtric as King of Wessex.
807 Monastery founded by Cellach of Iona at Kells.

815 Cornwall conquered by Egbert of Wessex.
819 Conchobar mac Donnchada becomes High King of Ireland.
825 Egbert of Wessex defeats Beornred of Mercia at Ellandun, near Swindon, and briefly controls all England.
Merfyn the Freckled (Merfyn Frych ap Gwriad) seizes control of Gwynedd on the death of Hywel ap Rhodri Molwynog.
839 Egbert of Wessex dies, and is succeeded by his son Æthelwulf.
843 Kenneth MacAlpin, king of Dalriada since 840, unites the Picts and Scots into a single kingdom (Alba), the forerunner of Scotland.
844 Rhodri the Great, referred to as 'King of the Britons' by the Annals of Ulster, succeeds his father, Merfyn, as king of Gwynedd.
849 Birth of Alfred the Great of Wessex, at Wantage.
851 The Vikings sack London and Canterbury, but are halted in their depredations by Æthelwulf of Wessex and his son Æthelbald at Aclea.
856 Æthelbald replaces Æthelwulf as king in Wessex, Kent, Surrey and Sussex.
858 Death of Æthelwulf of Wessex; Æthelbald becomes sole king of Wessex but grants his brother Æthelbert an under-kingship.
Donald MacAlpin, succeeds his brother as King of the Picts, and in effect King of Scotland.
860 Æthelbald of Wessex dies and is succeeded by his brother Æthelbert.
862 Constantine succeeds his uncle as King of the Picts.
865 Ivar the Boneless and his brother Halfdan arrive in England in an attempt to conquer the country.
Æthelbert of Wessex dies, succeeded by his brother Æthelred I.
870 Martyrdom of King (later St) Edmund of East Anglia at the hands of the Vikings.
871 Vikings defeated by Wessex at Ashdown, but victorious at Reading and Wilton. Vikings also thought to be victorious at the Battles of Merton and Basing although the whereabouts of the battle sites is uncertain.
Alfred succeeds Æthelred I as King of Wessex.
874 Burgred, last independent English King of Mercia, forced to abdicate by the Vikings, who replace him with their puppet Ceolwulf II.
877 Áed (of the White Flowers) succeeds his brother Constantine I as King of the Picts.
878 Alfred, after a period in hiding at Athelney, decisively defeats the Vikings at Eddington and preserves Wessex as an English kingdom.
Gregory (Giric) and Eochaid become joint rulers of the Picts. Although little is known of their history, it seems Eochaid gradually usurped more power in the kingdom.
Rhodri the Great is killed by the English under Alfred the Great and is succeeded as Welsh overlord by his son, Anarawd.
879 The Treaty of Wedmore establishes the Danelaw in parts of England: Danish laws and customs will prevail there.
886 London retaken by Alfred, who gives it, and English Mercia, to his son-in-law Æthelred.
889 Donald II succeeds his cousin Eochaid as King of Scotland.
890 Alfred the Great establishes an English navy and militia.
892 The Vikings launch another invasion attempt on England.
893 According to the Anglo-Saxon Chronicle, the Vikings are decisively defeated by Edward the Elder at Farnham, although little is known of the details of the encounter. Asser writes his life of Alfred.
896 Alfred defeats the Vikings at sea and ends their threat.
899 Alfred the Great dies, and is succeeded by his son Edward (the Elder).
900 Constantine II succeeds Donald II as King of the Picts, the area now known as Alba.
901 Edward the Elder takes the title 'King of the Angles and Saxons'.
916 Essex taken from the Vikings by Edward the Elder.
Idwal the Bald succeeds his father, Anarawd, as Welsh ruler.
918 Death of Lady Æthelflaed of the Mercians, who now acknowledge Edward the Elder as their king. Edward now controls all England south of the Humber.
919 Ragnald the Viking seizes York, making himself king.
920 Edward the Elder acknowledged as overlord by the kings of Scotland, York and Strathclyde.
921 Sitric Caoch of Dublin succeeds Ragnald as King of York.
924 Edward the Elder of Wessex and England dies; his son Athelstan is hailed king in Mercia but Wessex disputes the succession and initially hail Ælfweard, his brother, as king.
925 Athelstan crowned King of England, having finally been accepted by Wessex.
927 Sitric of York dies; he is succeeded by his brother Guthfrith who is forced to flee when Athelstan conquers York and Southern Northumbria. The kings of Scotland and Strathclyde acknowledge Athelstan as their overlord.
928 Cornwall subdued by Athelstan, who sets the River Tamar as its boundary.
934 Scotland invaded by Athelstan, whose fleet ravages the coast as far as Caithness.
937 Athelstan defeats a coalition of his foes at Brunanburh (whereabouts unknown), cementing his power in Britain.
939 Athelstan dies, and is succeeded by his half-brother Edmund (the Elder). Olaf Guthfrithsson retakes York for the Vikings.
940 Olaf of York invades the Midlands, encouraged by Archbishop Wulfstan of York. By the treaty of Leicester much of the old Danelaw is ceded to him.
941 Olaf of York dies; his cousin Olaf Sitricsson succeeds him.
942 The Five Boroughs (Leicester, Lincoln, Nottingham, Derby and Stamford) recovered by Edmund the Elder.
Hywel Dda (the Good) succeeds to the Welsh throne.
943 Constantine II of Scotland abdicates to become a monk; his son Malcolm I succeeds him.
944 Edmund the Elder recovers York, expelling Ragnald Guthfrithsson who had usurped the throne from his cousin Olaf the previous year.
946 Edmund the Elder assassinated by Leofa, an exiled thief, while celebrating St Augustine's Mass Day in Pucklechurch, South Gloucestershire; his brother Eadred succeeds him.

947 Eric Bloodaxe deposed as King of Norway by his brother Haakon I due to his violence – he flees to England where Wulfstan of York makes him king of that city.
948 Eadred ravages Northumbria in response to their crowning of Eric Bloodaxe, who is forced to flee.
949 Olaf Sitricsson is invited to return as King of York.
950 Hywel Dda, Prince of Deheubarth and Gwynedd and creator of a Welsh law code, dies; Gwynedd and Deheubarth separate, Iago becoming King of Gwynedd.
952 Eric Bloodaxe returns to York and resumes the kingship.
954 Eric Bloodaxe forced to flee from York and is killed soon after; Eadred now rules all England.
Indulf succeeds his father Malcolm as King of Scotland.
955 Eadred of England dies; his son Eadwig succeeds him.
956 St Dunstan, Abbot of Glastonbury, exiled from England after a quarrel with King Eadwig.
957 Mercia and Northumbria rebel against Eadwig and choose his younger brother Edgar as their king.
959 Eadwig of Wessex dies; his brother Edgar the Peaceable succeeds him and reunites the kingdom of England.
962 Indulf, king of the Scots, is killed fighting Vikings near Cullen, at the Battle of Bands and is succeeded by Dub, son of Malcolm I.
966 King Dub of Scotland dies; he is succeeded by his third cousin Cuilén (Culen).
967 At the Battle of Sulchoid, a Dalcassian (clan of northern Munster) army led by Mathgamain and his younger brother Brian Boru decisively defeat the Hiberno-Norse army of Limerick and loot and burn the city. **Note:** Actual events are marred by history so the battle is not included in my list.
971 Cuilén of Scotland dies, he is succeeded by his third cousin Kenneth II.
St Swithin reinterred inside Winchester Cathedral; 40 days of rain follow.
973 Edgar of England crowned king at Bath.
975 Edgar dies, and is succeeded by his son Edward.
Modern arithmetical notation introduced into Europe by the Arabs.
978 Edward (the Martyr) assassinated at Corfe, and succeeded by his half-brother Æthelred II, the Unready (ill-advised).
979 Hywel II succeeds Iago I as king of Gwynedd.
985 On the death of Hywel II, his brother Cadwallon succeeds to the throne of Gwynedd.
986 The grandson of Hywel Dda, Maredudd ap Owain of Deheubarth, invades Gwynedd, slays Cadwallon and annexes his kingdom.
991 Norsemen raid England led by Olaf Tryggveson, defeating English forces under Ealdorman Byrhtnoth at Maldon in Essex; they are paid to leave with Danegeld.
994 Sweyn of Denmark, assisted by Olaf Tryggveson, raids England, unsuccessfully besieges London and is paid off by Æthelred II. Olaf Tryggveson converts to Christianity.
995 Constantine III, son of Cuilén is proclaimed King of the Scots on the death of Kenneth II, probably killed by his own troops. Kenneth III, son of Dub, subsequently becomes King of the Scots on the death of Constantine III.
998 The king of Leinster is overthrown and replaced by Máel Mórda mac Murchada.
999 Brian Boru is victorious at the Battle of Glen Mama and takes Dublin from the Norse settlers.
On the death of Maredudd, the rule of Gwynedd returns to the original dynasty in the form of Idwal the Bald's great-grandson, Cynan I.
1002 Æthelred II marries Emma, sister of Richard II of Normandy, and orders the massacre of Danish settlers in southern England.
The Uí Néill king Máel Sechnaill mac Domnaill, abandoned by his northern kinsmen of the Cenél nEógain and Cenél Conaill, acknowledges Brian Boru as High King at Athlone.
1003 King Sweyn of Denmark raids England in revenge for the massacre of his countrymen, exacting tribute from Æthelred.
1005 Kenneth III of Scotland is killed in battle against his cousin Malcolm II, who succeeds him.
On the death of Cynan ap Hywel the throne of Gwynedd falls to Aeddan ap Blegywryd.
1007 Danegeld of £36,000 paid by Æthelred II to protect England from raids for two years.
1010 Danish forces under Thorkell the Tall defeat the East Anglians at Ringmere.
1011 Canterbury taken by the Danes, who capture Archbishop Alphege.
1012 Danegeld of £48,000 paid to the Danes, who nevertheless kill Alphege before they leave.
Thorkell the Tall defects to the English.
1013 Sweyn Forkbeard conquers England, helped by Thorkell who redefects.
Æthelred II flees to Normandy.
1014 Sweyn dies, and Æthelred returns from exile.
Brian Boru wins the Battle of Clontarf but is killed, as is his sworn enemy, Máel Mórda.
1015 Cnut invades England and Wessex submits to him.
1016 Æthelred II dies, succession disputed between his son Edmund Ironside and Cnut. Although Edmund wins a skirmish at Brentford, Cnut is ultimately victorious at Ashingdon.
Edmund allowed to reign in Wessex but dies shortly afterwards, Cnut becoming King of England.
Máel Mórda's son, Bran, becomes King of Leinster.
1017 Cnut divides England into four earldoms – Wessex, East Anglia, Mercia and Northumbria – for administrative purposes.
1018 Bran is deposed as King of Leinster and the kingship of the Uí Dúnlainge is held by the Uí Muiredaig sept.
Aeddan ap Blegywryd is defeated in battle by Llywelyn ap Seisyll and killed together with his four sons. Llywelyn becomes King of Gwynedd and of Deheubarth, and is also called King of the Britons by the Annals of Ulster.
1019 Cnut becomes King of Denmark on the death of his brother Harald II.
1020 Faroes, Shetlands and Orkneys recognise Olaf II of Norway as king.
Godwin becomes Earl of Wessex.
1021 An epidemic of St. Vitus' Dance sweeps Europe.
1023 On the death of Llywelyn I, a member of the Aberffraw dynasty, Iago ab Idwal ap Meurig, becomes ruler of Gwynedd.

1028 Cnut conquers Norway and sends his son Sweyn to rule it.
1034 Malcolm II of Scotland dies, and is succeeded by his grandson Duncan I.
1035 Cnut dies, Harthacnut succeeds him in Denmark and England, but his brother Harold seizes England for himself.
1036 Alfred, son of Æthelred II, returns to England but is murdered by Godwin of Wessex.
Harold I (Harefoot), son of Cnut, proclaimed Regent of England.
1037 Harold I proclaimed King of England.
1039 Gruffydd ap Llywelyn succeeds Iago as Prince of Gwynedd and promptly defeats an English invading force.
1040 Macbeth defeats and kills King Duncan of Scotland and assumes the crown.
Harold I dies; Harthacnut successfully claims the English crown by right of succession.
1042 Harthacnut dies; his half-brother Edward the Confessor, son of Æthelred II, is elected King.
1043 Coventry Abbey founded by Leofric of Mercia.
1048 Last Viking raid on southeast England; the raiders flee to Flanders, which is attacked by Edward the Confessor and Emperor Henry III.
1050 Robert of Jumièges becomes Archbishop of Canterbury.
1051 Earl Godwin of Wessex rebels unsuccessfully against Edward the Confessor; he and his family flee to Flanders.
1052 Earl Godwin and his family return to power in England.
Stigand uncanonically becomes Archbishop of Canterbury as Archbishop Robert is forced to flee.
1053 Godwin of Wessex dies, his son Harold succeeding him as earl.
1054 Final schism between Roman Catholic and Orthodox churches.
Macbeth defeated by Malcolm Canmore and Earl Siward of Northumbria at Dunsinane.
1055 Earl Siward of Northumbria dies and is succeeded by Tostig Godwinson, brother of the future Harold II of England.
Gruffydd ap Llywelyn claims sovereignty over the whole of Wales.
1056 The future William II of England is born. He is the third son of William I the Conqueror and Matilda of Flanders.
1057 Macbeth killed by Malcolm III Canmore at Lumphanan, but is succeeded by his stepson Lulach.
1058 Lulach killed by Malcolm III Canmore, who becomes King of Scotland.
1061 Northumbria raided by Malcolm III of Scotland.
1063 Gwynedd conquered by Earls Harold and Tostig; Prince Gruffydd killed by his own men.
1065 Westminster Abbey is consecrated.
1066 Death of Edward the Confessor causes succession dispute in England. Harold II Godwinson chosen king, defeats and kills Harald Hardrada at Stamford Bridge but is defeated and killed at Hastings by William of Normandy, who becomes king.
1068 Earls Edwin and Morcar rebel against William I, but are defeated in York.
The future Henry I of England is born at Selby, Yorkshire. He is the fourth son of William I the Conqueror and Matilda of Flanders.
1069 Northumbrians and Mercians rebel, with Danish help, against William I, but the risings are put down and William devastates Northumbria ('the harrying of the North').
1070 Sweyn II of Denmark attacks England, but is bought off by William I, who puts down the revolt of Hereward the Wake.
1081 Gruffydd ap Cynan became King of Gwynedd following the Battle of Mynydd Carn.
1082 Bishop Odo, Earl of Kent, revolts against his half-brother William I, but is stripped of his earldom and imprisoned.
1085 William I commissions the Domesday Book.
1086 The Domesday Book is compiled.
Cnut IV of Denmark dies, ending an invasion threat to England, His brother Olaf IV succeeds him.
1087 William I dies due to an injury sustained at the siege of Mantes, and is succeeded by his sons Robert in Normandy and William II Rufus in England.
1088 Bishop Odo and various Norman barons in England rebel against William II, but the revolt is crushed.
1089 Archbishop Lanfranc of Canterbury dies, but no successor is chosen, so William II can enjoy the revenues of the see.
1091 William II of England and Robert of Normandy make their peace by the Treaty of Caen.
Malcolm III of Scotland invades Northumbria, but is repulsed by William and Robert and acknowledges William as his overlord.
1092 William II takes Cumberland from the Scots and refounds Carlisle as his northwestern outpost.
1093 William II falls gravely ill and appoints St Anselm to the see of Canterbury, recovering soon after.
Malcolm III invades Northumbria again but is killed near Alnwick; his wife Margaret dies four days later. Malcolm III is succeeded by his brother Donald III Bane.
1094 Donald Bane is deposed from the Scottish throne by his nephew Duncan II, who dies after six months. Donald Bane returns to the throne.
1096 Robert of Normandy leases his duchy to William II in order to go on crusade.
The future King Stephen is born at Blois, France. He is the grandson of William I.
1097 Donald Bane of Scotland deposed with William II's help, and replaced by his nephew Edgar.
1098 Magnus III of Norway seizes the Orkneys, Hebrides and Isle of Man.
1100 William II of England dies while hunting, and is succeeded by his brother Henry I.
1101 Robert of Normandy invades England to take the throne from brother Henry, but is bought off by the Treaty of Alton.
1103 Magnus III of Norway invades Ireland, but is killed in battle; his son Eysten I succeeds him.
1106 Henry of England defeats Robert of Normandy at Tinchebrai, dispossessing Robert of his duchy and imprisoning him.
1107 King Edgar of Scotland dies, and is succeeded by his brother Alexander I.
1110 The earliest known miracle play (a medieval drama based on the Scriptures from the creation to the Second Coming and on the lives of the saints. Sometimes called mystery plays, the Passion Play is the most famous) is performed at Dunstable.
1114 Pipe Rolls (named after the 'pipe' shape formed by the rolled up parchments) are introduced by Bishop Roger of Salisbury as a means of recording Exchequer accounts.

1117 St Magnus, Earl of Orkney, murdered on the island of Egilsay on the orders of his cousin Earl Haakon.
1120 Prince William, heir and only legitimate son of Henry I, drowns in the English Channel, off the coast of Normandy, in what is known as the 'White Ship Disaster'.
1123 Rahere, a favourite courtier of King Henry I, founds St Bartholomew's Hospital, London.
1124 Alexander I of Scotland dies, succeeded by his brother David I.
1129 First Cistercian abbey founded in England, at Waverley.
Henry of Blois becomes Bishop of Winchester.
1132 Fountains Abbey founded.
1133 St Bartholomew's Fair founded in London.
The future Henry II is born at Le Mans, France. He is the son of Geoffrey V of Anjou (Geoffrey Plantagenet), and Empress Matilda.
1135 Henry I of England dies of a surfeit of lampreys; although he made his barons swear that his daughter Matilda would succeed him, his nephew Stephen of Blois engineers his own coronation as king.
1137 Gruffydd ap Cynan, Prince of Gwynedd, dies, and is succeeded by his son Owain Gwynedd.
1138 David I of Scotland invades England in support of Matilda but is defeated at the Battle of the Standard.
1139 Matilda lands at Arundel staking her claim to the English throne; anarchy breaks out in the country.
1141 Stephen of England taken prisoner after defeat at Lincoln; Matilda proclaimed queen but her high-handed behaviour alienates many, particularly in London. Stephen is released in exchange for Robert, Earl of Gloucester, and Matilda is forced back on the defensive.
1147 Matilda leaves England, her son Henry is left to carry on the fight though only 14 years old.
1150 The Black Book of Carmarthen, an anthology of ancient Welsh poetry, is compiled.
1152 Louis VII divorces Eleanor of Aquitaine, who promptly marries Henry of Anjou.
1153 David I of Scotland dies, and is succeeded by his grandson Malcolm IV.
The Treaty of Wallingford brings the English anarchy to an end by recognising Henry of Anjou as Stephen's heir.
1154 Stephen of England dies, and is succeeded by Henry, son of Geoffrey of Anjou and great-grandson of William the Conqueror as the first ruler of the House of Plantagenet; Henry now rules half of France as well as England.
On the death of Anastasius IV, Nicholas Breakspear becomes the first and only English Pope, taking the name Adrian IV.
1155 Ireland bestowed on Henry II by Pope Adrian IV. Adrian IV restores papal authority in Rome.
1157 The future Richard I of England is born at Beaumont Palace, Oxfordshire. He is the third of five sons of Henry II of England and Eleanor, Duchess of Aquitaine. Both William, Count of Poitiers and Henry the Young King, his two elder brothers, predeceased their father.
1159 Pope Adrian IV dies, and is succeeded by Alexander III.
John of Salisbury writes the *Policraticus*, a book of ethical and political philosophy and a treatise on government, most famous for attempting to define the responsibilities of kings and their relationship to their subjects.
1161 Edward the Confessor is canonised.
1162 Thomas Becket is chosen as Archbishop of Canterbury.
Danegeld – by now just a general tax – is collected in England for the final time.
1163 The Welsh rebel against Henry II, but the revolt is suppressed and Prince Rhys ap Gruffydd is imprisoned.
Henry II and Thomas Becket quarrel over the Church's status vis-à-vis the monarch.
1164 Legal rights of church and state codified by Henry II at the Council of Clarendon; Becket rejects the code and is forced to flee after he is condemned at the Council of Northampton.
1165 Malcolm IV of Scotland dies, and is succeeded by his brother William I, the Lion.
1166 The *Song of Cnut* written down by a monk of Ely.
The erection of jails in all English counties ordered by the Assize of Clarendon.
Ruaidrí mac Tairrdelbach Ua Conchobair (anglicised as Rory O'Connor) becomes the last High King of Ireland.
The future King John of England is born at Beaumont Palace, Oxfordshire. He is the youngest of five sons of King Henry II of England and Eleanor, Duchess of Aquitaine.
1167 Oxford University is created as English students are barred from attending Paris.
1169 Norman-Welsh barons land at Wexford supporting King Dermot of Leinster's efforts to regain his throne. **Note:** Prior to the invasion the Irish had their own system of law, culture and language and their own political and social structures. Following the invasion, the island continued to be governed as a single political unit, as a colony of Britain, until 1921.
1170 Henry II has his son Henry crowned joint-king (the 'Young King').
Richard Strongbow, Earl of Pembroke, takes Waterford and marries Dermot of Leinster's daughter.
Thomas Becket returns to Canterbury, but is murdered four weeks later.
Cynan ab Owain Gwynedd, an illegitimate son of Owain Gwynedd, procured the death of his father's chosen successor, Hywel (Cynan's half-brother), and ruled himself as Prince of Gwynedd.
1171 Dermot of Leinster dies, and is succeeded by his son-in-law Richard Strongbow, who is forced to accept Henry II as his overlord when Henry crosses to Ireland.
1172 Henry II receives homage from the Irish at Cashel, but his wife Eleanor raises Aquitaine against him, forcing him to seek a reconciliation with Pope Alexander at Avranches.
1173 Henry II's wife and sons revolt against him, supported by William the Lion of Scotland and Louis VII of France.
Eleanor of Aquitaine is captured and imprisoned.
Thomas Becket is canonised.
1174 Henry II does public penance for Becket's murder and subdues the revolt against him.
Dafydd ab Owain Gwynedd rules in East Gwynedd.
1175 By the Treaty of Windsor Rory O'Connor recognised as High King of Ireland under Henry II's overlordship .
1176 The first eisteddfod is held at Cardigan Castle.
Construction of the first stone London Bridge begins under the direction of Peter de Colechurch.
1180 Henry II reforms the English coinage.
1183 Henry the Young King dies.

1184 Glastonbury Abbey burns down.
1185 Prince John sent to govern Ireland, antagonises the local lords and is recalled.
1186 Rory O'Connor is usurped by his son and driven into Munster, effectively ending the agreement with Henry II, and with it the High-Kingship of Ireland.
1188 The Third Crusade is proclaimed by Henry II of England and Philip II of France.
Henry II quarrels with his son Richard and Philip II of France over his French lands and the succession.
1189 Henry II dies and is succeeded by his son Richard, whose coronation is accompanied by a massacre of Jews.
1191 Richard I conquers Cyprus from the Byzantines and sells it to the Templars, before capturing Acre. Richard marries Berengaria, first-born daughter of King Sancho VI of Navarre. The wedding is held in Limassol. Richard then leaves Cyprus and defeats Saladin at Arsuf, near Jaffa.
1192 Richard I, realising he cannot win in Palestine, makes a truce with Saladin, ending the Third Crusade. On his return home, he is captured and imprisoned by Leopold, Duke of Austria who accuses Richard of arranging the murder of his cousin Conrad of Montferrat and disrespecting his standard at Acre.
1193 Richard I is handed over to Holy Roman Emperor Henry VI, who demands ransom for his release. Prince John takes the opportunity to foment rebellion while Hubert Walter, Archbishop of Canterbury, raises the sum.
1194 Richard I is freed after the ransom is paid, returns to England briefly to put down John's rebellion and leaves the country permanently for France.
Prince Dafydd's 20 year reign as Prince of Gwynedd ends in an enforced abdication. He is succeeded by his nephew Llywelyn ap Iorwerth the Great.
1197 Prince Rhys of Deheubarth dies, and is succeeded by his son Gruffydd.
The future Alexander II of Scotland is born at Haddington, the only son of William the Lion and Ermengarde of Beaumont.
1199 Richard I dies after an injury at the siege of Chalus, he is succeeded by his brother John, although Philip II goes to war in France in support of John's nephew Arthur of Brittany.
1200 John of England and Philip II of France make peace at Le Goulet, with John confirmed in the Angevin lands in France under Philip's overlordship.
Llywelyn the Great seizes Anglesey.
1203 John murders his nephew, Arthur of Brittany, causing his French possessions to revolt.
1207 The future Henry III is born at Winchester Castle. He is the son of King John and Isabella of Angoulême.
1209 King John is excommunicated by Innocent III.
Cambridge university founded by students leaving Oxford due to town and gown clashes.
1213 King John submits to the Papacy.
1214 William the Lion of Scotland dies, succeeded by his son Alexander II.
1215 A revolt by barons in England leads to the signing under duress by King John of Magna Carta; rebel barons later capture Rochester Castle but John retakes it.
1216 Baronial revolts against King John gather force and the Dauphin Louis is invited to become king of England. John loses his baggage in the Wash and dies at Newark; he is succeeded by his son Henry III, with William Marshal, Earl of Pembroke, proclaimed Regent.
1217 William Marshal defeats baronial rebels at Lincoln; the French fleet is later defeated off Sandwich and Prince Louis sues for peace. Henry III is established as unchallenged king of England.
1219 William Marshal dies.
1220 Building commences on Salisbury Cathedral.
1222 University of Oxford establishes St George's Day, 23 April, as a national holiday in England.
1225 Magna Carta is reissued in definitive form.
1233 The Earl of Pembroke, aided by Llywelyn of Wales, leads a baronial revolt against Henry III.
1234 The Earl of Pembroke is murdered in Ireland defending his Leinster estates against royalist attacks.
Henry III and Llywelyn of Wales make peace.
1235 The Statute of Merton, allowing Lords of the Manor to enclose common land providing sufficient pasture remained for his tenants, begins the list of English Statutes. It is enacted at Merton Priory after a meeting between Henry III and his barons.
1236 The Statute of Merton is adopted in Ireland.
1239 The future Edward I is born at Westminster. He is the son of Henry III and Eleanor of Provence.
1240 Prince Llywelyn of Gwynedd dies, and is succeeded by his son Dafydd.
Richard of Cornwall and his brother-in-law Simon de Montfort lead a crusade to the Holy Land.
The future Alexander III of Scotland is born at Roxburgh, the only son of Alexander II by his second wife Marie de Coucy.
1246 Llywelyn III (ap Gruffydd) becomes the last prince of an independent Wales before its conquest by Edward I of England.
1249 Alexander II of Scotland dies, and is succeeded by his son Alexander III.
1255 Prince Llywelyn of Gwynedd ousts his brother Owen from joint-rulership of the Principality.
1257 Richard, Earl of Cornwall, the second son of King John and Isabella of Angoulême, is crowned German King (formally 'King of the Romans') in Aachen; his election is disputed by Alfonso X of Castile who becomes de facto ruler.
1258 The Provisions of Oxford establish a form of parliamentary government in England.
1263 Alexander III of Scotland defeats Haakon IV of Norway at Largs and takes the Hebrides.
1264 Civil war erupts in England between Henry III and a baronial alliance led by Simon de Montfort; de Montfort defeats and captures Henry at Lewes, becoming the de facto ruler of England.
1265 Simon de Montfort summons parliament, but is defeated and killed at Evesham by Prince Edward, who has escaped from imprisonment.
1266 The Hebrides and the Isle of Man granted to Scotland by Norway under the terms of the Treaty of Perth.
1267 Llywelyn of Gwynedd recognised as Prince of Wales by the Treaty of Montgomery, pays homage to Henry III.
1271 Prince Edward of England sails to Acre as part of the short-lived Ninth Crusade.

1272 Richard of Cornwall, King of the Romans, dies at Berkhamsted Castle, Hertfordshire.
Henry III of England dies, and is succeeded by his son Edward I, who is on crusade.
Robert the Bruce is born at Turnberry in Ayrshire, the first son of Robert de Brus, 6th Lord of Annandale, and Marjorie, Countess of Carrick, daughter of Niall, Earl of Carrick.
1275 Prince Llywelyn of Wales refuses homage to Edward I.
1277 Llywelyn of Gwynedd forced to submit to Edward I by the Treaty of Conway.
Roger Bacon imprisoned for heresy.
1282 When his younger brother David starts a rebellion against Edward I, Llywelyn of Gwynedd is forced to take part, but is killed near Builth. His brother succeeds him as Edward invades Wales.
1283 Edward I conquers Wales; Prince David III of Gwynedd is surrendered by his men and executed by Edward.
1284 Edward I settles Welsh affairs by Statute of Rhuddlan and arranges for his son Edward, the future Edward II, to be born in Caernarfon Castle.
1286 Alexander III of Scotland dies on a night ride; his heir is his granddaughter Margaret, the Maid of Norway. Historically her reign as queen is open to question as she was never crowned or indeed set foot in Scotland.
1290 Margaret of Norway dies while on board ship to Scotland; the throne is vacant. Her death sparks off the disputed succession which leads to the Wars of Scottish Independence from 1296.
Jews expelled from England by decree of Edward I.
Richard of Haldingham draws the Hereford Mappa Mundi. Measuring 5ft 3in by 4ft 5in (158cm by 133cm), Jerusalem is drawn at the centre of the circle, east is on top, showing the Garden of Eden in a circle at the edge of the world. Great Britain is drawn at the northwestern border.
1292 Edward I grants the Scottish throne to John Balliol, the son of Dervorguilla of Galloway, daughter of Alan, Lord of Galloway and granddaughter of David, Earl of Huntingdon, by her husband John, 5th Baron Balliol, Lord of Barnard Castle.
1295 A Welsh revolt collapses after defeat at Maes Moydog.
Scotland, resentful of a summons to help Edward I, forms the Auld Alliance with France.
The Model Parliament convenes at Westminster.
1296 Edward I invades Scotland, forces John Balliol to abdicate and takes the Stone of Scone, where Scottish kings are crowned, to Westminster.
1297 William Wallace leads a Scottish revolt against Edward I, defeating the English at Stirling Bridge and invading Northumberland and Cumberland.
1298 Edward I invades Scotland, defeating the Scots at Falkirk; Wallace flees abroad.
1300 Edward I invades Scotland again, but makes a truce after a Papal appeal to withdraw.
1301 Edward I makes his son, Edward, Prince of Wales.
1304 The Scottish barons submit to Edward I at St Andrews while Stirling Castle only submits after a siege.
1305 William Wallace is captured, tried and executed by the English.
1306 Robert Bruce murders John Comyn and is subsequently crowned King of Scots at Scone. The English invade Scotland and force Bruce to flee.
1307 Edward I of England dies, and is succeeded by his son Edward II, who creates Piers Gaveston Earl of Cornwall.
1308 The Templars are suppressed in England.
Parliament forces Edward II to banish Piers Gaveston, who is created Lieutenant in Ireland.
1310 Parliament forces Edward II to appoint 21 Lords Ordainers to reform the government.
1311 The English Parliament orders baronial consent to appointments by Edward II.
Robert Bruce raids Northumberland.
1312 Piers Gaveston is captured by barons and executed.
The future Edward III is born at Windsor Castle. He is the son of Edward II and Isabella of France.
1313 Perth, Roxburgh, Edinburgh and the Isle of Man taken by the Scots, who besiege Stirling Castle.
1314 Edward II invades Scotland, but is routed at Bannockburn.
1315 Edward Bruce, Robert's brother, is offered the High Kingship of Ireland; he sails to Ireland and defeats the Earl of Ulster near Connor.
1316 Edward Bruce is crowned High King of Ireland.
1318 Edward Bruce is killed at the Battle of Faughart, in Louth, Ireland.
1319 Scots raid into England, defeating an army at the Battle of Myton-in-Swaledale; a truce is subsequently made between the English and Scots.
1320 The Declaration of Arbroath asserts Scots independence and loyalty to Robert Bruce.
1321 Parliament forces Edward II to banish his close supporters Hugh Despenser and his son, but he recalls them and raises an army.
1322 Edward II defeats his cousin Thomas, Earl of Lancaster, at Boroughbridge; Lancaster is executed and Edward's opponents punished.
David Bruce is born at Dunfermline, the elder and only surviving son of Robert I of Scotland and his second wife, Elizabeth de Burgh.
1326 Queen Isabella of England and her lover Roger Mortimer invade England; Edward II is captured and the Despensers executed.
1327 Edward II is forced to abdicate in favour of his son Edward III, and is murdered eight months later in Berkeley Castle.
1328 Robert Bruce is recognised as King of the Scots by the Treaty of Northampton; Pope John XXII also recognises him.
1329 Robert Bruce dies of leprosy; he is succeeded by his son David Bruce as David II.
1330 Edward III takes control of government in England, capturing and executing Roger Mortimer.
Edward the Black Prince is born at Woodstock Palace in Oxfordshire, the eldest son of Edward III of England and Philippa of Hainault.
1332 Edward Balliol invades Scotland, defeating loyalist forces at Dupplin Moor and is crowned King, but is then defeated by loyalists and flees to England.

1333 Edward III and Edward Balliol besiege Berwick and defeat a relieving force at Halidon Hill.
The Isle of Man is seized by England.
1334 Berwick ceded to England by Edward Balliol.
David II of Scotland flees to France and loyalist revolts break out.
1337 Edward III claims the throne of France, thus precipitating the Hundred Years' War.
Edward the Black Prince is created Duke of Cornwall, the first creation of an English duke.
1338 The French initiate hostilities against England, burning Portsmouth and Southampton.
Edward III and Emperor Louis IV enter into an alliance.
1340 The English win a decisive naval victory over the French at Sluys.
John of Gaunt is born in Ghent. He is the third surviving son of Edward III of England and Philippa of Hainault.
1341 David II returns to Scotland, forcing the withdrawal of Edward Balliol.
1342 Edward III conquers most of Brittany.
1343 The Peruzzi banking house of Florence collapses as Edward III defaults on his loan repayments.
1346 The French annihilated at Crecy by English bowmen. John of Luxembourg perishes in the battle, and is succeeded by his son Charles I, who is subsequently crowned German king.
Scottish forces under David II invade England but are routed at Neville's Cross with David II taken prisoner.
1348 Edward III founds the Order of the Garter.
The Black Death enters England by the summer.
1349 The Black Death reaches Scotland and Ireland.
1351 The Statute of Labourers fixes wage rates and restricts movement of labourers in England, as a result of Black Death depopulation and the economic strain of war.
1355 The St Scholastica's Day riots in Oxford last three days with many students killed in 'town and gown' clashes.
1356 Jean II of France captured by the English at the Battle of Poitiers, where the Black Prince, Edward Prince of Wales, gains a crushing victory.
Edward Balliol, a king of Scotland in name only for more than 20 years, officially abdicates.
1357 David II of Scotland ransomed by the Treaty of Berwick.
1358 French peasants revolt in Beauvais, northern France, and are dubbed the Jacquerie after their padded surplice known as 'jacque'. The revolution is suppressed with English assistance.
1360 England and France sign the Treaty of Brétigny, which gives England territorial gains and stipulates the payment of a ransom for the French king, Jean II. When the ransom cannot be raised Jean voluntarily goes back into captivity.
1361 The Black Death reappears in England.
1362 William Langland writes *Piers Plowman*, a much-heralded Middle English allegorical narrative poem.
The Black Prince is appointed ruler of Aquitaine.
1364 Jean II of France dies in captivity in England, and is succeeded by his son Charles V.
1365 By the Statute of Praemunire the English parliament repudiates Papal overlordship of the country and forbids appeals to the Papal court.
1366 The future Henry IV is born at Bolingbroke Castle. He is the son of John of Gaunt and Blanche of Lancaster.
1367 The Black Prince invades Castile in support of Pedro the Cruel, defeating Castilian and French forces at Najera and restoring Pedro's crown.
The future Richard II is born at Bordeaux in the Principality of Aquitaine. He is the son of Edward, the Black Prince and Joan of Kent.
1369 Pedro the Cruel of Castile offends the Black Prince, who abandons him.
France declares war on England and confiscates English lands in the country.
1371 David II of Scotland dies, and is succeeded by his nephew Robert II, the first of the Stewarts. **Note:** The name Stewart derives from the political position of office similar to a governor, known as a steward. It was originally adopted as the family surname by Walter of Dundonald, 3rd High Steward of Scotland (d. 1246). In order to ensure that the Scots name was pronounced correctly Mary Stewart, Queen of Scots adopted the French spelling Stuart while living in France from 1548.
1372 The English defeated by Castilian forces at sea off La Rochelle, which falls, along with Poitou, to the French.
1375 England and France sign the Truce of Bruges – English possessions in France much reduced as a result.
1376 Edward, the Black Prince, dies.
The Good Parliament is convened, and Peter de la Mare is chosen as presiding officer (unofficial Speaker for the House of Commons).
1377 Sir Thomas Hungerford becomes the first official holder of the title Speaker of the House of Commons.
Edward III dies, and is succeeded by his grandson Richard II; John of Gaunt becomes Regent.
The French raid Sussex and Kent, burning Rye and Hastings.
David Stewart, the eldest son of Robert III and Annabella Drummond, is born.
1381 Wat Tyler and John Ball lead the Peasants' Revolt in England. Archbishop Sudbury is murdered outside the Tower by a mob but Tyler is stabbed to death by William Walworth, Mayor of London, on meeting Richard II at Smithfield. Ball is executed and the rising is suppressed.
1382 The religious reformer John Wycliffe is condemned by Archbishop William Courtenay and barred from teaching at Oxford.
1383 The Bishop of Norwich leads the 'Norwich Crusade' to Flanders in support of Pope Urban VI, but is repulsed and impeached at home by Chancellor Michael de la Pole.
1384 John Wycliffe dies.
1385 Scottish forces, aided by the French, raid Northumbria.
1386 England and Portugal sign the Treaty of Windsor, sealed by the marriage of João I with John of Gaunt's daughter Philippa.
The 'Wonderful Parliament' results in the appointment of fourteen Commissioners to oversee Royal expenditure, and the impeachment and subsequent removal of Chancellor Michael de la Pole.
1387 Geoffrey Chaucer begins *The Canterbury Tales* – a story, written in Middle English, of 29 pilgrims, and their host, Harry Bailey, who set out from the Tabard Inn, Southwark, to visit the shrine of St Thomas Becket at Canterbury

Cathedral. The pilgrims agree to tell four stories each, two on the way to Canterbury, and two on the way back. The person who tells the best story, as determined by the host, will have his supper paid for by the rest of the group.

The future Henry V is born in the tower above the gatehouse of Monmouth Castle. He is the son of Henry of Bolingbroke, later Henry IV, and sixteen-year-old Mary de Bohun.

1388 At the battle of Otterburn (Chevy Chase) the Scots under the Earl of Douglas defeat and capture Henry 'Hotspur' Percy, though Douglas himself is killed.

The 'Merciless Parliament' finds Richard II's entire Court guilty of treason. Although several of them are executed, Michael de la Pole, 1st Earl of Suffolk, Robert de Vere, Duke of Ireland, and Alexander Neville, Archbishop of York, flee the country and are sentenced in absentia.

1390 Robert II of Scotland dies, and is succeeded by his son Robert III.

1394 Richard II goes to Ireland and sets the limit of the territory later known as 'The Pale'.

The future James I of Scotland is born at Dunfermline Palace, the second son of Robert III and Annabella Drummond.

1395 Richard II receives the submission of 80 Irish chiefs and returns to England.

1396 England and France agree a 28 year truce.

1398 Richard II orders a duel to settle the dispute between John of Gaunt's son Henry Bolingbroke and the Duke of Norfolk; he then intercedes and banishes the pair.

The heir to the Scottish throne, David Stewart, is created the first Duke of Rothesay.

1399 John of Gaunt dies. Richard II confiscates the Lancastrian inheritance of Gaunt. Bolingbroke returns from exile, engineers the deposition of Richard II, and is crowned Henry IV in his stead.

1400 Richard II murdered in Pontefract Castle.

Owain Glyndŵr attacks Lord Grey of Ruthin, proclaims himself Prince of Wales and engineers a revolt against Henry IV in the Principality; he becomes the last native Welsh person to hold the title Prince of Wales.

Geoffrey Chaucer dies before completion of *The Canterbury Tales*. **Note:** Twenty-two finished, and two unfinished stories were later published but unfortunately the aforementioned prize (see entry for 1387) was not won due to Chaucer's non-completion of the text. Unless the great man had a twist intended it is likely that the completed work would have contained up to 130 stories.

1402 The Earl of Northumberland and his son Hotspur capture the Earl of Douglas at the Battle of Homildon Hill.

The English parliament issues the Penal Laws against Wales, banning the Welsh from having public assemblies, obtaining senior public office, bearing arms or buying property in English towns. Englishmen who married Welsh women also came under these laws.

The heir to the Scottish throne, David Stewart, dies in suspicious circumstances, possibly starved to death by his uncle Robert, Duke of Albany, at Falkland Palace; David's younger brother James becomes Robert III's heir.

1403 The Earl of Northumberland rebels against Henry IV but is defeated at Shrewsbury, where his son Hotspur perishes.

A Breton squadron defeats the English in the Channel and devastates Jersey, Guernsey and Plymouth while the French make a landing on the Isle of Wight.

1404 Owain Glyndŵr holds Welsh parliaments at Dolgellau, Harlech and Machynlleth, where he is officially crowned Prince of Wales.

The Unlearned Parliament (also known as the Lawless Parliament, Parliament of Dunces or the Parliamentum Indoctorum) convenes at the Great Hall of the Benedictine monastery in Coventry, Warwickshire; it is so called because Henry IV refuses to allow lawyers to stand as members.

1405 A treaty between Wales and France results in the French landing at Milford Haven and marching through Herefordshire and Worcestershire where they meet the English army ten miles from Worcester. The armies take up battle positions but after an eight-day stand-off both sides withdraw.

Richard Scrope, Archbishop of York, leads a revolt against Henry IV, but the rebellion collapses and Scrope is executed.

Owain Glyndŵr is defeated at Grosmont by John Talbot and at Usk by Henry, Prince of Wales.

1406 Robert III of Scotland sends his son James to France for safety, fearing his brother Albany, but James is captured by the English at sea and imprisoned. Robert III dies and Albany becomes Regent as James is kept captive.

English forces land in Anglesey from Ireland and gradually push the Welsh back until the resistance in Anglesey formally ends.

1408 The last threat to Henry IV in England is extinguished by the Sheriff of Yorkshire's victory at Branham Moor; the Earl of Northumberland dies in the battle.

1409 Henry, Prince of Wales, captures Harlech Castle, kills Edmund Mortimer and subdues the Welsh revolt.

1412 Owain Glyndŵr ransoms Dafydd Gam ('Crooked David'), a leading Welsh supporter of King Henry's, in Brecon, but this is the last desperate act of his revolt. This is also the last time that Owain is seen alive by his enemies although he is thought to have lived on for another four years.

1413 Henry IV of England dies, and is succeeded by his son Henry V.

1414 The 'Fire and Faggot Parliament' is held at Grey Friars Priory in Leicester and passes the Suppression of Heresy Act, aimed at suppressing the radical religious reformers known as Lollards. The Lollards, under Sir John Oldcastle, revolt against Henry V, but are suppressed.

1415 Henry V goes to war with France after the failure of marriage negotiations with Catherine of Valois, gaining a crushing victory at Agincourt.

1417 Caen falls to Henry V.

1419 John the Fearless of Burgundy is assassinated by Armagnacs supporting Dauphin Charles, driving his successor Philip the Good to an alliance with England.

1421 The future Henry VI is born at Windsor Castle. He is the son of Henry V and Catherine of Valois.

1422 Henry V dies, and is succeeded by his nine-month-old son Henry VI. Charles VI of France dies shortly after and his son Charles VII declares himself king but Henry VI is proclaimed king by Protector Bedford in the Anglo-Burgundian areas in accordance with the treaty of Troyes.

1423 James I of Scotland is freed from captivity by the Treaty of London on payment of a ransom.

1424 The English defeat Charles VII at Verneuil.
James I returns to Scotland and takes up government from his uncle Albany.
1425 James I of Scotland executes his uncle Albany and his family.
Le Mans falls to the English.
The 'Parliament of Bats', so called because members were not allowed to carry swords by the Duke of Gloucester, and so armed themselves with clubs, or bats, is convened in the great hall of Leicester Castle.
1428 English troops besiege Orleans.
1429 French lose to the English at Rouvray (Battle of the Herrings) but under the leadership of Jeanne d'Arc relieve Orleans and are victorious at Patay, where Talbot is captured.
1430 The future James II of Scotland is born at Holyrood, the son of James I of Scotland and Joan Beaufort. His elder twin, Alexander Stewart, Duke of Rothesay, died in infancy.
Jeanne d'Arc is captured by the Burgundians at Compiègne and sold to the English, who imprison her at Rouen.
1431 Jeanne d'Arc is burned as a witch at Rouen.
A Lollard conspiracy led by 'Jack Sharp' is crushed by the Duke of Gloucester.
1436 Paris falls to the French.
The Scots fail to capture Roxburgh Castle.
1437 James I of Scotland is murdered at Perth by Sir Robert Graham, who is executed for the deed. James II succeeds his father.
1440 Eton College is founded by Henry VI.
1442 Eleanor Cobham, Duchess of Gloucester, is divorced and imprisoned on charge of attempting to kill Henry VI by sorcery.
The future Edward IV is born in Rouen. He is the second son of Richard, 3rd Duke of York, and Cecily Neville.
1450 Jack Cade leads a revolt in Kent and Sussex; it fails and Cade is killed, but Henry VI is forced to flee for safety to Kenilworth for a while.
1452 James II of Scotland murders the Earl of Douglas at Stirling.
John Talbot leads an expedition to Gascony and reconquers much of it.
The future Richard III is born at Fotheringay Castle, the eighth and youngest, and fourth surviving, son of Richard Plantagenet, 3rd Duke of York.
The future James III is born at St Andrews, Fife, the son of James II of Scotland and Mary of Guelders. **Note:** There is some debate that James was born at Stirling Castle the year before.
1453 The French win a decisive victory over the English at Castillon, where Talbot dies. Gascony is reconquered and the English hold only Calais in France. The Hundred Years War is thus brought to an end.
Henry VI has a bout of insanity.
1454 Richard, Duke of York is appointed Protector during Henry VI's incapacity.
1455 Henry VI recovers his sanity and dismisses the Duke of York from the post of Protector. The Wars of the Roses begin when York and the Earl of Warwick raise an army and defeat and capture Henry VI at St Albans. York is made Constable of England but pro-Lancastrian riots break out.
1457 The future Henry VII is born at Pembroke Castle, the only son of Edmund Tudor, Earl of Richmond and Lady Margaret Beaufort.
1459 Civil War is renewed in England. The Yorkists are victorious at Blore Heath but defeated at Ludford Bridge. The Irish come out in support of the Yorkists. The 'Parliament of Devils' is subsequently held in Coventry to pass bills of attainder for high treason against the leading Yorkist nobles.
1460 Henry VI defeated and captured by the Yorkists at Northampton; Richard, Duke of York is named heir to Henry but dies at the Battle of Wakefield, where the Lancastrians are victorious. Richard's son, Edward, inherits his father's claim to the throne.
James II of Scotland dies when a cannon misfires at Roxburgh, and is succeeded by his son James III.
1461 Yorkists victorious at Mortimer's Cross, where Owen Tudor is captured and executed, but defeated at St Albans. Henry VI is released from captivity. Edward of York deposes Henry VI and crushes the Lancastrians at Towton. Henry VI and his family flee to Scotland.
1463 England, France and Burgundy sign the Truce of Hesdin, the latter two recognising Edward IV of York as King of England.
1464 Yorkists victorious at Hedgeley Moor and Hexham, and gain control of northern England.
1465 Henry VI captured in Ribblesdale and imprisoned in the Tower.
1468 James III of Scotland contracts to marry Margaret, daughter of Christian of Denmark; the Orkneys and Shetlands are pledged as security for her dowry.
1469 Rebellion develops in England against Edward IV and the power of his wife's family. Edward is imprisoned after his army deserts him at Olney, and is released with a promise to appease the rebels.
James III of Scotland marries Margaret of Denmark at Holyrood Abbey, Edinburgh.
1470 Edward IV defeats a rebel army at Empingham, but Richard Neville, 16th Earl of Warwick, and the Lancastrians reach an accord and invade, forcing Edward to flee to Burgundy. After a failed plot to crown Edward's brother, George, Duke of Clarence, Richard Neville (the kingmaker) is instrumental in restoring Henry VI to the throne.
The future Edward V is born at Westminster. He is the eldest son of Edward IV and Elizabeth Woodville.
1471 Edward IV returns to England, defeats and kills Warwick at Barnet and then decisively defeats the Lancastrians at Tewkesbury, where Edward Prince of Wales perishes.
Henry VI is murdered in the Tower.
The future James IV of Scotland is born at Stirling Castle, the son of James III and Margaret of Denmark.
1474 The Union of Constance is formed against Charles the Bold of Burgundy, who makes an anti-French alliance, via the Treaty of London, with Edward IV.
1475 Edward IV invades France but is let down by his absent ally Charles the Bold and goes on to sign a seven-year truce with Louis XI via the Treaty of Picquigny.
1476 William Caxton sets up the first printing press in Britain, at Westminster.
1477 Edward IV bans early forms of skittles and cricket due to their interference with archery practice.

1478 George, Duke of Clarence dies while imprisoned in the Tower of London. It is rumoured he drowned in a butt of Malmsey.

William Caxton publishes Geoffrey Chaucer's *Canterbury Tales*, the first book published from his Westminster press.

1483 Edward IV dies, and is succeeded by his son as Edward V, who disappears along with his brother Richard of Shrewsbury, Duke of York, in the Tower. Their uncle Richard assumes the kingship.

1485 Henry Tudor invades England against Richard III, defeats and kills him at Bosworth Field, and takes the throne as Henry VII. This effectively settles the Crown and ends the Wars of the Roses.

William Caxton publishes Thomas Malory's *Morte d'Arthur*, perhaps the best-known work of English-language Arthurian literature.

1486 Henry VII marries Elizabeth of York and unites the houses of Lancaster and York.

1487 Lambert Simnel leads revolt against Henry VII, claiming to be Edward IV's nephew, but is defeated at Stoke and sent to work in the royal kitchens.

1488 James III of Scotland is murdered after fleeing from the Battle of Sauchieburn; his son James IV succeeds him.

1489 Henry VII signs the anti-French Treaty of Redon with Brittany.

1491 Perkin Warbeck claims to be Richard, Duke of York and rallies support for his cause in France and Ireland.

The future Henry VIII is born at Greenwich Palace, the third child of Henry VII and Elizabeth of York.

1492 Henry VII invades France and is bought off by Charles VIII under the Treaty of Etaples, with compensation for Brittany's annexation and the expulsion of Warbeck.

1495 Warbeck received by James IV of Scotland.

A dry-dock is built in Portsmouth, establishing the dockyard there.

1496 Henry VII commissions John Cabot to search for new lands.

James IV invades Northumberland in support of Warbeck.

1497 John and Sebastian Cabot reach Labrador and Newfoundland.

The Cornish rebel against taxation but are defeated at Blackheath; Warbeck lands in Cornwall but is captured.

1499 Perkin Warbeck is executed.

1502 Arthur, Prince of Wales, dies at Ludlow. His brother, Henry, becomes Prince of Wales and heir to the throne.

1503 James IV of Scotland marries Margaret Tudor, daughter of Henry VII.

1509 Henry VII dies, and is succeeded by his son Henry VIII (21 April).

Henry VIII marries Catherine of Aragon, the widow of his late brother, Arthur (11 June).

1510 Sir Richard Empson and Edmund Dudley beheaded by Henry VIII for their unpopular fiscal policies under his father.

The future James V of Scotland is born at Linlithgow Palace, the son of James IV of Scotland and Margaret Tudor (sister of King Henry VIII of England).

1513 Henry VIII invades France, where he and Emperor Maximilian are successful in the Battle of Guinegatte (the Spurs).

James IV of Scotland takes advantage of the English in France to invade, but his army is routed at Flodden and James is killed, to be succeeded by his son James V.

1514 The *Henry Grace a Dieu*, the largest warship in the world, is launched in England.

Thomas Wolsey becomes Archbishop of York.

1515 Thomas Wolsey becomes a cardinal, giving him precedence over the Archbishop of Canterbury.

1516 Thomas More publishes *Utopia*, the story of a fictional island in the Atlantic Ocean, possessing a seemingly perfect socio-politico-legal system.

The future Mary I is born at Greenwich Palace.

The Royal Mail service is established although not available to the general public.

1518 Cardinal Wolsey negotiates the Peace of London between England, France, the Holy Roman Empire, Spain and the Papacy; they agree to crusade against the Turks.

1520 Henry VIII and François I meet at the Field of the Cloth of Gold near Calais.

1521 Henry VIII is awarded the title 'Defender of the Faith' by Leo X for an anti-Lutheran work.

1523 Sir Thomas More is elected Speaker of the House of Commons.

1525 Cardinal Wolsey gives Hampton Court to Henry VIII.

1526 William Tyndale completes his translation of the Bible into Early Modern English.

1527 England and France ally via the Treaty of Westminster.

Holbein paints Thomas More and his family.

1528 The King's School, Ipswich is founded by Cardinal Wolsey with money raised by dissolving 30 monasteries.

1529 Cardinal Wolsey falls from power due to his inability to secure a divorce for Henry VIII from Catherine of Aragon. Sir Thomas More replaces him as Lord Chancellor, the first layman to hold the post.

1530 Cardinal Wolsey is arrested for treason, but dies while on his way to trial.

1532 The English clergy recognise Henry VIII as Supreme Head of the Church.

Thomas Cromwell is elevated to the position of Henry VIII's chief minister.

1533 Henry VIII divorces Catherine of Aragon and marries Anne Boleyn with the sanction of Thomas Cranmer, newly appointed Archbishop of Canterbury; this leads to Henry's excommunication.

The future Elizabeth I is born at Greenwich Palace, the daughter of Henry VIII and Anne Boleyn.

1534 The Act of Supremacy marks the final break between England and Rome, confirming Henry VIII as Supreme Head of the Church of England.

1535 Thomas Cromwell is appointed Vicar-General to investigate religious houses in England.

John Fisher, Bishop of Rochester and Sir Thomas More are executed for refusing to take an oath supporting Henry VIII's acts.

1536 Protestant reformer William Tyndale is executed for heresy.

Henry VIII executes Anne Boleyn on the grounds of adultery and marries Jane Seymour.

Dissolution of the monasteries commences in earnest, leading to a rising (the Pilgrimage of Grace) under Robert Aske.

Wales is formally united with England.

1537 Robert Aske is received by Henry VIII and Cromwell, but is later executed for treason.
Jane Seymour dies after bearing the future Edward VI.

1539 The Six Articles are passed in England, reaffirming Catholic doctrine on the key issues of transubstantiation, clerical celibacy, vows of chastity, the importance of confession, permission for private masses and the reasonableness of withholding of the cup from the laity during communion.
Dissolution of the monasteries ends; the abbots of Reading, Colchester and Glastonbury are executed in the process.

1540 Henry VIII marries Anne of Cleves but quickly repudiates her. The marriage is annulled and Henry marries Catherine Howard.
Thomas Cromwell falls from grace over the Cleves marriage and is executed.

1541 Henry VIII is accepted by the Irish Parliament as King of Ireland and Head of the Irish Church.

1542 Pope Paul III establishes the Universal Inquisition to repress the Reformation.
Henry VIII executes Catherine Howard for adultery.
Mary Stewart, daughter of James V of Scotland, is born at Linlithgow Castle (8 December).
James V of Scotland raids Cumberland, but is defeated badly at Solway Moss. James dies soon after and is succeeded by his six-day-old daughter, Mary (14 December).

1543 By the Act for the Advancement of True Religion, Henry VIII restricts the reading of Bible to men and women of noble birth.
Henry VIII marries his sixth wife, Catherine Parr.

1544 Henry VIII captures Boulogne, but subsequently retires from France when his ally Charles V, and François I make peace with the Treaty of Crépy-en-Valois.

1545 The Council of Trent meets, in an attempt by the Catholic Church to establish a Counter-Reformation.
The *Mary Rose* capsizes off Portsmouth.

1546 England and France make peace with the Treaty of Ardres, by which England holds Boulogne for eight years before returning it to France.
George Wishart, a leader of the Protestant Reformation, is burnt at the stake at St Andrews on the orders of Cardinal Beaton, who is assassinated soon after.

1547 Henry VIII dies, and is succeeded by his nine-year-old son Edward VI. Edward Seymour, the eldest brother of Jane Seymour, is created 1st Duke of Somerset and Protector. As such he invades Scotland and defeats the Scots at Pinkie.
François I laughs on receiving news of Henry's death, develops a fever and dies, to be succeeded by his son Henri II.
John Knox, the leader of the Protestant Reformation, is captured at St Andrews and sent to work on a French galley.

1548 Catherine Parr, by now married to her fourth husband, Thomas Seymour, elder brother of Jane Seymour, gives birth to her only child, Mary Seymour (30 August), but dies six days later, at Sudeley Castle in Gloucestershire, from puerperal sepsis, also called childbed fever.

1549 The Protestant Book of Common Prayer is imposed in England, leading to risings in Devon and Cornwall.
Robert Kett leads a human rights revolt in Norfolk, but is defeated at Dussindale.

1550 England makes peace with France and Scotland by the Treaty of Boulogne; Boulogne is returned to France and John Knox is released from galley labour.
Cricket is first referred to in England.

1552 Edward Seymour is executed for treason.
The Second Book of Common Prayer is introduced.

1553 English explorer and navigator, Richard Chancellor, opens a trade route to Moscow via the White Sea and Archangel.
Edward VI dies, and although his Catholic half-sister Mary is the heiress presumptive to the throne Edward names the Protestant heirs of his father's sister, Mary Tudor, as his successors in a will composed on his deathbed, possibly under the persuasion of the Duke of Northumberland. Lady Jane Grey, Edward's cousin and daughter-in-law of Northumberland, becomes the Protestant Queen but reigns for just nine days before Mary is proclaimed the rightful queen and immediately attempts to reverse the Protestant Reformation.

1554 Sir Thomas Wyatt leads a revolt from Kent over Mary I's proposed marriage to Philip of Spain, but is defeated and executed. Lady Jane Grey is also executed, whilst Mary's half-sister Elizabeth is imprisoned in the Tower.

1555 John Knox returns to Scotland.
Tobacco is brought to Europe from America.
Mary I persecutes Protestants; Latimer and Ridley are burnt at the stake in Oxford.

1556 Thomas Cranmer is dismissed as Archbishop of Canterbury and burned at the stake.

1558 Calais, England's last continental possession, falls to the French.
Mary I dies, and is succeeded by her half-sister Elizabeth.
William Cecil becomes Secretary of State.
John Knox writes his *First Blast of the Trumpet Against the Monstrous Regimen(t) of Women.*

1559 The war between England, Spain and France is ended by the Treaty of Cateau-Cambrésis.
The Act of Supremacy restores the Church of England.

1560 The Treaty of Berwick is made between England and the Protestant Scottish lords against the French, whose troops are forced to return home; the Scots Parliament approves Knox's Calvinistic Confession of Faith.

1561 Flemish Calvinist refugees settle in England.
St Paul's Cathedral is damaged by fire after a lightning strike.

1563 The English establish the 39 Articles of religion, defining Anglican doctrine.
John Foxe's *Book of Martyrs* is published.
The Council of Trent comes to an end.

1564 England and France make peace by the Treaty of Troyes; in return for 220,000 crowns Elizabeth renounces claim to Calais.

1565 Mary, Queen of Scots marries her cousin Henry, Lord Darnley.
Irish chieftain Shane O'Neill of Tyrone wins a decisive battle over rival chieftain Sorley Boy MacDonnell at Glentasie. **Note:** although I have not included this battle in my separate list as its details are vague, it is thought that Sorley Boy's clan suffered hundreds of casualties with hardly one by the O'Neills.
1566 Mary, Queen of Scots' secretary, David Rizzio, is murdered at Holyrood.
James Charles Stuart, the only child of Mary, Queen of Scots, and her second husband, Henry Stuart, Lord Darnley is born at Edinburgh Castle.
Sir Thomas Gresham founds a bourse as the centre of commerce for the city.
1567 Lord Darnley is murdered at Kirk o'Field; the Earl of Bothwell, who is believed to have ordered the assassination, marries Mary, Queen of Scots. The Earl of Morton discovers the possibly fabricated Casket Letters, incriminating Bothwell and Mary; the Scots lords rebel against Mary, imprison her in Lochleven Castle and force her abdication in favour of her son James VI, with Moray as Regent.
Shane O'Neill and about 2000 clansmen engage a similar force of O'Donnells at Farsetmore. O'Neill loses more than half his men and is subsequently murdered, his head being sent to the English authorities in Dublin.
1568 Mary, Queen of Scots escapes Lochleven, raises an army, but is defeated by Moray at Langside and flees to England.
The first modern Eisteddfod is held at Caerwys.
1569 Elizabeth orders Mary, Queen of Scots' detention in Tutbury Castle and imprisons the Duke of Norfolk, who seeks to marry Mary.
Catholic earls of Northumberland and Westmorland revolt, seize Durham, but are forced to flee by Baron Hunsdon.
1570 Regent Moray is assassinated; the Earl of Lennox takes over the regency.
Elizabeth I is excommunicated.
1571 Sir Thomas Gresham's bourse is chartered as the Royal Exchange.
Regent Lennox is murdered at Stirling; the Earl of Mar replaces him.
Roberto di Ridolfi plots to free Mary, Queen of Scots and depose Elizabeth I, but the plots are exposed and fail.
1572 The Duke of Norfolk is executed for treason in assisting the Ridolfi plot.
Regent Mar dies, replaced by the Earl of Morton.
1573 Francis Walsingham is appointed Elizabeth's Secretary of State.
1576 The Theatre, England's first playhouse, is opened by Richard Burbage in Shoreditch.
1577 Francis Drake sets out on a circumnavigation of the world. His ship, originally known as the *Pelican*, is renamed the *Golden Hind* as he prepares to enter the Straits of Magellan. The move is a politic gesture, to compliment his patron, Sir Christopher Hatton, whose armorial crest is a golden hind.
1579 The Union of Arras unites the Walloons of the Netherlands while the Dutch provinces unite under the Union of Utrecht and sign a military alliance with England.
Francis Drake lands in California and claims English sovereignty over the area he calls 'New Albion'.
1580 Francis Drake becomes the first Englishman to complete a circumnavigation of the world; his first question on arriving back at Plymouth is 'Is the queen alive and well?' **Note:** Drake is estimated to have brought back bullion and jewels worth £600,000 (approximately £200m in today's terms). Queen Elizabeth was entitled to half the plunder (mainly from Spanish and Portuguese ships) and the consortium of backers returned £47 for every £1 they invested.
1581 The Jesuit Edmund Campion is arrested, tortured, tried and executed.
Francis Drake is knighted by Queen Elizabeth aboard the *Golden Hind*, at Deptford.
1582 James VI of Scotland is kidnapped by pro-English nobles at Ruthven.
1583 James VI of Scotland escapes from his captors after ten months.
Humphrey Gilbert founds a colonial settlement in Newfoundland at St Johns, but drowns on the return journey.
Plots against Elizabeth I by John Somerville and Francis Throckmorton are foiled.
1584 Walter Raleigh founds a colony on Roanoke Island, Virginia.
1585 The Netherlands are taken under English protection by the Treaty of Nonsuch and a force under the Earl of Leicester is sent to assist them.
Walter Raleigh is knighted.
1586 Sir Francis Drake raids Spanish New World colonies and rescues the survivors from the failed Roanoke settlement.
Anglo-Dutch forces defeat the Spanish at Zutphen but Sir Philip Sidney dies as a result of a wound sustained there.
Sir Anthony Babington plots against Elizabeth I, but Walsingham uncovers the plot and Babington is executed. Mary, Queen of Scots is tried for her involvement in the Babington Plot and is sentenced to death.
1587 Mary, Queen of Scots is executed at Fotheringay Castle.
Sir Francis Drake raids Cadiz, 'singeing the King of Spain's beard' and disrupting preparations for the Armada.
Sir Christopher Hatton is appointed Lord Chancellor.
1588 The Spanish Armada sails for England under the Duke of Medina Sidonia, but is defeated by the English and the weather. Although the tonnage of the two fleets is similar the Spanish lose nearly half of their 130 ships and the English none.
1589 The Reverend William Lee invents the first knitting machine, while Sir John Harington invents the Ajax, a flushing toilet.
1590 Edmund Spenser writes the first three books of *The Faerie Queene*.
William Shakespeare writes the *Henry VI* trilogy.
1591 Sir Richard Grenville dies after his ship, *Revenge*, battles a Spanish squadron single-handed for 15 hours.
1592 Trinity College, Dublin, is founded by Queen Elizabeth. It is the oldest university in Ireland.
1593 Christopher Marlowe is stabbed to death, by Ingram Friser, in Deptford during a tavern brawl.
Salisbury Cathedral's organist strikes the Dean in a fit of rage and is dismissed from his post.
Hugh O'Neill, 2nd Earl of Tyrone, enters into rebellion against Elizabeth I in Ulster, thus prompting the Nine Years' War.

1594 John Lancaster returns to Britain after sailing to the East Indies and establishes a spice trade.

1595 Spanish troops attack Cornwall, burning Penzance and Mousehole.

Sir Francis Drake and Sir John Hawkins leave Plymouth to raid Panama; Hawkins dies en route near Puerto Rico.

1596 The tomato is introduced to England.

The English sack Cadiz while Spain captures Calais.

Sir Francis Drake dies of dysentery off Panama.

1597 Philip II sends a second Armada to England, but it is scattered by storms and fails.

1599 The Globe Theatre is built in London.

The Earl of Essex is made Lord Lieutenant of Ireland, but after signing an unauthorised truce with the Earl of Tyrone returns to England and is arrested by Elizabeth I.

1600 The British East India Company is founded (31 December).

Actor Will Kempe Morris dances from London to Norwich, a distance of more than 100 miles (160km), over a period of nine separate days during February and March. He calls it his 'Nine Days Wonder'.

The future Charles I is born at Dunfermline Palace, the fourth child, and second son, of James VI of Scotland and Anne of Denmark.

Scotland adopts 1 January as the start of the Civil Year. **Note:** The rest of Great Britain still used 25 March as the beginning date until 1751, the year prior to the implementation of the Gregorian Calendar.

1601 The Earl of Essex leads a revolt against Elizabeth I, which fails and Essex is executed for treason.

A Spanish army lands in Ireland to support Tyrone's revolt.

Sir Walter Raleigh becomes MP for Cornwall, having already served as MP for Devonshire (1585) and Dorset (1597).

1602 The Spaniards in Ireland surrender to Mountjoy at Kinsale.

1603 Elizabeth I dies; her cousin twice removed, James VI of Scotland, succeeds her as James I, thus uniting the English and Scottish thrones in one person although the two kingdoms remain separate.

The Bye Plot (a conspiracy by a Catholic priest, William Watson, to kidnap King James I of England and force him to repeal anti-Catholic legislation) is revealed by English Jesuits.

Sir Walter Raleigh attempts to put Arabella Stuart on the throne rather than James (the Main Plot), and is imprisoned for treason.

Tyrone submits to Mountjoy in Ireland, where James proclaims an amnesty, thus ending the Nine Years' War.

1604 England and Spain make peace.

The Hampton Court Conference convenes to discuss religious matters, and commissions an English translation of the Bible.

1605 Robert Catesby leads a plot to assassinate James I, but the plot fails and Guy Fawkes is caught red-handed under the House of Lords.

1606 The Virginia Company is set up and 120 colonists depart London led by Captain Christopher Newport.

The Union Flag is introduced with the crosses of St George and St Andrew combined.

Guy Fawkes is hanged for his involvement in the Gunpowder Plot. He has the presence of mind to cheat the executioner by jumping from the gallows to ensure instant death rather than suffer the disembowelment which was to follow.

Shakespeare's Macbeth and King Lear are first performed.

1607 The English Parliament rejects the union of England and Scotland.

Jamestown, Virginia is founded by Christopher Newport, who returns to England leaving Captain James Smith in charge; captured by the Algonquin, Smith's life is saved by the chief's daughter Pocahontas.

Popularity at a low ebb and fearing arrest by the English, Hugh O'Neill, 2nd Earl of Tyrone and Rory O'Donnell, 1st Earl of Tyrconnell set sail for Spain from Rathmullan, a village on the shore of Lough Swilly in County Donegal, accompanied by 90 followers. This incident on 14 September is known as 'The Flight of the Earls'.

1608 Rory O'Donnell, 1st Earl of Tyrconnell, dies in Rome.

1609 James I begins settling Protestants in Ulster.

1610 The Jamestown colonists abandon their settlement, but on meeting a ship of new settlers return and try again.

1611 Henry Hudson is marooned by mutineers while searching for the Northwest Passage and is never heard of again.

The Authorised King James Version, an English translation of the Christian Bible, is published by the Church of England, having taken 54 scholars seven years to complete.

1612 Henry, Prince of Wales, dies of typhoid.

1613 The Globe Theatre burns down during a performance of Shakespeare's *Henry VIII*.

1614 The 'Addled Parliament' meets, but is dissolved after clashes with James I over finance. The second Parliament during James's reign lasts no more than two months and its name alludes to its ineffectiveness.

Pocahontas marries John Rolfe, a settler.

The Virginian colonists resist French colonial attempts in Maine and Nova Scotia.

John Napier publishes a book of logarithms.

1615 The Moluccas seized from the Portuguese by the Dutch, whilst the English defeat a Portuguese fleet off Bombay.

Lady Arabella Stuart starves herself to death in the Tower of London.

1616 Baffin Bay discovered by William Baffin.

William Shakespeare dies on his 52nd birthday.

Poet and dramatist Francis Beaumont, famous for his collaborations with John Fletcher, dies and is buried in Westminster Abbey.

Walter Raleigh is released from the Tower to search for El Dorado in Venezuela.

James I sells peerages to raise funds.

Hugh O'Neill, 2nd Earl of Tyrone (formerly The O'Neill) dies in Rome.

1617 Pocahontas is received by James I at court, but dies of smallpox soon after.

1618 Francis Bacon is made Lord Chancellor.

Sir Walter Raleigh returns from his fruitless expedition to South America, and is executed by James I for treason, to appease the Spaniards.

1619 William Harvey establishes the circulation of the blood.

John Fletcher publishes *The Maid's Tragedy*, a collaboration with the late Francis Beaumont. Set in Rhodes, the politically serious play about absolutism and tyranny is controversial because of the scene in which the king is killed in his bed by his mistress.

1620 The Pilgrim Fathers depart from Plymouth to America; the *Speedwell* is forced to turn back but the *Mayflower* arrives at Cape Cod; the settlement is called New Plymouth.

Oliver Cromwell is denounced for playing cricket.

1621 Francis Bacon is impeached by Parliament for corruption, but is pardoned by James I.

1623 The First Folio of Shakespeare's plays is published.

1625 James I and VI dies, and is succeeded by his son Charles I.

Sir William Courteen establishes a settlement on Barbados.

John Fletcher dies.

1628 George Villiers, 1st Duke of Buckingham, and favourite of the late king James I and VI, is assassinated by John Felton at Portsmouth.

1629 Charles I dissolves Parliament and assumes direct rule.

1630 Boston, Massachusetts, founded by John Winthrop.

Charles Stuart, the eldest child of King Charles I of England and Scotland and Henrietta Maria of France, is born at St James's Palace.

1632 Charles I issues a charter for the colony of Maryland under the governorship of Lord Baltimore.

The first coffee shop opens in London.

1633 James, the second son of Charles I and Henrietta Maria of France, is born at St James's Palace.

The Bishop of London, William Laud, is made Archbishop of Canterbury.

1635 The first General Post Office in England opens in Bishopsgate, London. **Note:** The Royal Mail service, first made available to the public by Charles I on 31 July, operated without stamps, postage being paid by the recipient.

1638 The Scottish Covenant is drawn up and signed, forcing Charles I to withdraw Laud's liturgy in Scotland.

Torture is abolished in England.

1639 The First Bishops' War erupts in Scotland between the Covenanters and Charles I. Peace comes by the Pacification of Berwick and Charles I grants the Scots a General Assembly and Parliament, which he dissolves at the end of the year. **Note:** The series of civil wars in England, Ireland and Scotland between 1639 and 1651 including the Bishops' Wars, the Scottish Civil War, the Irish Confederate Wars and the English Civil Wars, are often known collectively as The Wars of the Three Kingdoms.

1640 Thomas Wentworth is created Earl of Strafford.

Charles I is forced to reconvene Parliament but the 'Short Parliament' refuses to authorise any taxes and is dissolved.

The Scots revolt in the Second Bishops' War, defeating the English at Newburn.

The Great Council of Peers summoned by Charles I concludes the Treaty of Ripon, paying off the Scots, and insists on the election of Parliament. The 'Long Parliament' is duly elected.

Strafford and Laud are impeached.

1641 Strafford is executed.

The Irish Catholics revolt.

Parliament abolishes the Star Chamber.

Parliament sends the Grand remonstrance to Charles I, who is infuriated.

1642 Charles I enters the House of Commons to arrest Hampden, Pym, Holles, Haselrig and Strode for treason, but the quintet have been warned and take refuge in the City of London.

Charles flees London, rejects Parliament's 19 Propositions and raises his standard in Nottingham, triggering the Civil War.

Rupert of the Rhine defeats the Parliamentarians at Powick Bridge and Edgehill.

1643 Parliamentarians under Fairfax take Leeds.

Cromwell is victorious at Grantham, but Hampden is defeated and killed at Chalgrove Field.

Royalists are victorious at Roundway Down and take Bristol, but are defeated at Gloucester, Newbury and Winceby.

John Pym dies of cancer.

1644 John Milton writes his pamphlet *Areopagitica* on press freedom.

The Scottish Covenanters join the Civil War on the Parliamentarian side.

After a Royalist victory at Cropredy Bridge, Cromwell heavily defeats Prince Rupert at Marston Moor and takes York.

Scottish royalists under Montrose defeat the Covenanters at Tippermuir, Charles captures Fowey, while the second Battle of Newbury is indecisive.

1645 John Lilburne publicises Leveller ideas, extolling the virtues of popular sovereignty, an extended franchise, equality before the law, and religious toleration.

Archbishop Laud is executed.

Armistice talks between Charles I and Parliament fail at Uxbridge.

Montrose defeats the Covenanters at Inverlochy.

Parliament creates the New Model Army under Fairfax and Cromwell, a professionally adept national guard which decisively defeats the royalists at Naseby.

Prince Rupert surrenders Bristol, incurring his uncle's wrath.

Covenanters rout Montrose at Philiphaugh.

1646 Royalist armies in Exeter and Oxford capitulate to Parliamentarians; Charles surrenders to the Covenanters at Southwell. Held in Newcastle, Charles fails to reach agreement with Parliament and tries, but fails, to escape.

1647 George Fox founds the 'Friends of the Truth', later to become the Quakers.
The Scots hand over Charles I to Parliament in return for £400,000.
Matthew Hopkins, the 'Witchfinder General', is found guilty of witchcraft himself and hanged.
Bear-baiting and folk-dancing are banned in England.

1648 Parliament loses patience with Charles I after he makes a secret treaty with the Scots, who rebel along with the Welsh.
The Second Civil War is short-lived, Cromwell defeating the Scots at Preston; Colonel Thomas Pride purges Parliament to ensure Charles I is put on trial.
Supporters of the Kirk faction of the Covenanters march on Edinburgh to take power from the faction of the Scottish Covenanters, who made 'The Engagement' with Charles I in December 1647 while he was imprisoned in Carisbrooke Castle. **Note:** This action was known as the March of the Whiggamores (a nickname of the Kirk Party possibly deriving from the Scots for 'mare drivers'). This name was eventually shortened to Whig and was given to the 18th century political party whose origin lay in constitutional monarchism and opposition to absolute rule.

1649 Charles I is tried by Parliament and executed; Parliament abolishes the monarchy and the House of Lords, proclaiming a 'Commonwealth'.
Gerrard Winstanley, an English Protestant religious reformer and political activist, advocates a form of Christian communism. He and his followers, known as 'Diggers', take over vacant lands in Surrey, Buckinghamshire, Kent and Northamptonshire and begin cultivating the land and distributing the crops without charge to their followers.
Royalists rebel in Ireland; Cromwell sacks Drogheda and Wexford.
The Levellers and Diggers are suppressed.

1650 James Ussher, Anglican Archbishop of Armagh and Primate of All Ireland, calculates the Earth was created in 4004 BC.
James Graham, Marquess of Montrose, leads a Scottish uprising against Parliament, but is defeated at Carbisdale, betrayed by Neil McLeod and hanged.
Charles II arrives in Scotland.
Cromwell invades Scotland and is victorious at Dunbar.
The future William III is born in The Hague, the only child of stadtholder William II, Prince of Orange and Mary, Princess Royal of England.

1651 Charles II is crowned at Scone and invades England but is defeated by Cromwell at Worcester, evades capture by hiding in the Royal Oak at Boscobel House, and flees to France.
Thomas Hobbes publishes *Leviathan* and John Playford *The English Dancing Master*. Both books are among the most influential in the 17th century.

1652 Parliament publishes the reconciliatory Act of Pardon and Oblivion.
Admiral Robert Blake defeats Maarten Tromp off Dover, and England and Holland go to war, but Blake is defeated off Dungeness.

1653 The English fleet defeats the Dutch off Portland, North Foreland and Texel.
Cromwell dissolves the Long Parliament rump, and after the unsuccessful Barebones Parliament is made Lord Protector.
Izaak Walton publishes *The Compleat Angler*.

1654 The Treaty of Westminster ends the Anglo-Dutch War.

1655 The English under Vice-Admiral Penn take Jamaica from the Spanish.
Colonel Penruddock leads a rising against Cromwell in Wiltshire, which is suppressed.
Cromwell divides England into 11 districts, each governed by a major-general.

1656 Spain declares war on Britain.
A small colony of Sephardic Jews are unmasked in London, and, because of Cromwell's need of their financial assistance, are allowed to stay for the first time since Edward I's decree of 1290.

1657 Admiral Blake destroys a Spanish treasure fleet at Santa Cruz.
Cromwell rejects an offer of the crown and establishes a nominated House of Lords.

1658 An Anglo-French force defeats the Spanish at the Battle of the Dunes and England acquires Dunkirk.
The stage coach service is established in England.
Oliver Cromwell dies, his son Richard becomes Lord Protector.

1659 Richard Cromwell resigns as Lord Protector; conflict between army and Parliament leads to a state of near-anarchy. **Note:** Cromwell has an interesting place in British history. Within a year of resigning he left for France where he used the pseudonym of 'John Clarke'. He then travelled around Europe and did not return to British shores for 20 years. Although reigning for just under nine months (3 September 1658– 5 May 1659) and known as Tumbledown Dick or Queen Dick due to his indecisiveness, he lived for almost 86 years (4 October 1626–12 July 1712) and is currently, in terms of age, the longest lived ruler or former ruler of the United Kingdom.

1660 General Monck, commanding general in Scotland, leads his troops to London to call for a new Parliament, which meets and votes for the restoration of the monarchy under Charles II.
Charles makes the Declaration of Breda promising religious toleration and returns to England.
The Royal Society for the Promotion of Natural Knowledge is founded.
The future George I is born in Osnabrück, then part of the Holy Roman Empire. He is the oldest son of Ernest Augustus, Duke of Brunswick-Lüneburg, and his wife, Sophia of the Rhineland Palatinate.

1661 The Cavalier Parliament meets in England.
Tangier and Bombay are ceded to England by Portugal in a treaty of alliance.

1662 Dunkirk is sold to France by Charles II for £400,000.
France and Holland ally against England.
The Royal Society is granted a royal charter by Charles II.
The revised Prayer Book is imposed on Anglicans.
The future Mary II is born at St James's Palace, the eldest daughter of James, Duke of York (the future James II of England) and of his first wife, Lady Anne Hyde.

1663 The Theatre Royal, Drury Lane, opens with a performance of John Fletcher's *The Humorous Lieutenant*.

1664 The Conventicle Act bans unauthorised religious meetings of more than five people in England, in an attempt to suppress nonconformism.

New Amsterdam under Peter Stuyvesant surrenders to the English, who rename it New York.

1665 The Second Anglo-Dutch War opens; the Dutch are defeated off Lowestoft.

The Great Plague hits London.

The future Queen Anne is born at St James's Palace, London, the second daughter of James, Duke of York (afterwards James II), and his first wife, the Lady Anne Hyde.

1666 Holland allies with Brandenburg, Brunswick and Denmark to secure its safety, while France declares war on England.

The English and Dutch fleets meet in the inconclusive Four Days' Battle before an English victory at Orford Ness.

London is ravaged by a Great Fire starting in Pudding Lane.

1667 The Dutch sail up the Medway to Chatham, sinking several ships and taking the English flagship back to Holland.

England, Holland and France make peace by the Treaty of Breda.

The Medway debacle leads to the fall of Clarendon, and the Cabal administration under Clifford, Arlington, Buckingham, Ashley and Lauderdale is formed. **Note:** Cabal is a mnemonic for its members but the word does not derive from them.

John Milton's *Paradise Lost* is published.

1668 England, Holland and Sweden ally with the Treaty of the Hague.

John Dryden is appointed the first official Poet Laureate.

1669 Samuel Pepys ceases writing his diary.

The Royal Exchange, destroyed by the Great Fire of London, is rebuilt on the same site to a design of Edward Jerman.

1670 France and Bavaria make a defensive alliance, while Charles II makes the secret Treaty of Dover with Louis XIV, pledging anti-Dutch collaboration and conversion to Roman Catholicism at an appropriate moment.

1671 The buccaneer Henry Morgan captures Panama City, is tried for piracy but pardoned and knighted by Charles II and later becomes Deputy Governor of Jamaica.

Milton publishes *Paradise Regained* and Aphra Behn *The Forced Marriage.*

1672 An English fleet defeats the Dutch at Southwold Bay.

Charles II issues the Royal Declaration of Indulgence, which extends religious liberty to Protestant nonconformists.

1673 Parliament forces Charles II to revoke the Declaration of Indulgence. He now passes the Test Act, which states that none but persons professing the Established Church are eligible for public employment.

1674 England and Holland make peace via the Treaty of Westminster.

1675 The Royal Greenwich Observatory is founded with John Flamsteed as first Astronomer Royal.

1677 Edmund Halley returns from St Helena, having catalogued the Southern Night Sky.

James II and VII's daughter, Lady Mary, marries her first cousin, the Protestant Stadtholder, William Prince of Orange, at St James's Palace.

1678 False allegations made by Titus Oates and others of a 'Popish Plot' to kill Charles II lead to severe anti-Catholic measures.

The factional terms Whig and Tory enter use in Parliament.

John Bunyan's *The Pilgrim's Progress* is published.

1679 The Cavalier Parliament is dissolved.

Archbishop Sharp of St Andrews is murdered by Covenanters, whose rising is defeated by Monmouth at Bothwell Brig.

Henry Purcell is appointed organist of Westminster Abbey.

1681 Charles II grants Pennsylvania as a nonconformist colony to William Penn.

Bank cheques are issued for the first time in England.

1682 The Chelsea Hospital is founded.

1683 The Rye House Plot against Charles II and James, Duke of York is unmasked; Lord William Russell and Algernon Sidney are executed for their roles in the plot and the Earl of Essex commits suicide.

The future George II is born at Herrenhausen Palace, Hanover, the son of Georg Ludwig, the then Hereditary Prince of Brunswick-Lüneburg, and his wife, Sophia of Celle (George I and Sophia Dorothea).

1685 Charles II dies, and is succeeded by his brother James II, but his illegitimate son the Duke of Monmouth leads an uprising which ends in defeat at Sedgemoor. **Note:** James II and VII becomes the last Catholic monarch to reign over the Kingdoms of England, Scotland, and Ireland.

Monmouth is beheaded and Judge Jeffreys conducts the 'Bloody Assizes' against Monmouth's followers.

1687 James II proclaims the Declaration of Indulgence which effectively offers freedom of worship; he receives the Papal Nuncio.

Newton's *Principia* is published and is hailed as one of the most important scientific books to date. The three-volume work contains the statement of Newton's laws of motion forming the foundation of classical mechanics, as well as his law of universal gravitation.

1688 An heir to James II and VII is born. To forestall a Catholic succession William of Orange is invited to replace James, which he does in the 'Glorious Revolution'. James flees to exile in France. William III of England and Ireland, II of Scotland, rules jointly with his wife Mary II.

A marine insurance society is founded in Edward Lloyd's Coffee House in London.

1689 The Declaration of Rights is proclaimed in England, setting out certain constitutional requirements of the Crown to seek the consent of the people, as represented in parliament.

Louis XIV declares war on Britain while James II and VII arrives in Ireland and besieges Londonderry.

A Jacobite rising in Scotland defeats a Covenanter army at Killiecrankie before being defeated at Dunkeld.

1690 The French defeat an Anglo-Dutch fleet off Beachy Head and burn Teignmouth.

William III defeats James II at the Battle of the Boyne, forcing James back to France.

John Churchill, Earl of Marlborough, captures Cork and Kinsale from Jacobite supporters.

1691 The Irish Jacobites are defeated at Aughrim and pacified by the Treaty of Limerick.
1692 The Campbells massacre the MacDonalds at Glencoe.
Marlborough is briefly imprisoned for suspected treasonable contact with James II.
The English defeat a French invasion fleet at La Hogue, but an Anglo-Dutch army is defeated at Steenkirk.
1693 William III borrows £1m, instigating the National Debt.
Whites, the first gentlemen's club in London, is founded by Francesco Bianco in St James's Street.
1694 William Paterson leads the founding of the Bank of England, with John Houblon as its first Governor.
Mary II of England dies.
1695 William Paterson helps found the Bank of Scotland.
William III takes Namur.
Princess Anne returns to court to act as hostess for her brother-in-law William III.
1696 The Window Tax is introduced in England.
John Locke and Isaac Newton reform the coinage.
1697 France, Britain, Spain and the Holy Roman Empire make peace by the Treaty of Ryswick.
1698 Whitehall Palace is largely destroyed by fire.
1699 Henry Winstanley builds the first Eddystone Lighthouse.
1700 The Duke of Gloucester dies, leaving no direct Stuart heir after Princess Anne (James Stuart being unacceptable).
1701 Jethro Tull develops the seed drill.
Act of Settlement provides for the succession in England to pass to Electress Sophia of Hanover after Princess Anne.
War of the Spanish Succession opens; England, Holland and Savoy join Holy Roman Empire in the Grand Alliance.
1702 William III dies, succeeded in England by sister-in-law Anne while in Holland Stadtholdership is put into abeyance.
Note: At the start of Anne's reign, the Earl of Marlborough's wife, Sarah Churchill, held considerable influence over all aspects of the queen's household; the friends even continuing to correspond using the pet names Mrs Freeman (Sarah) and Mrs Morley (Anne) invented in their youth. Sarah's cousin, Abigail Masham, née Hill, gradually replaced her in the queen's favour.
The Earl of Marlborough captures Venlo, Roermond and Liége, and is raised to the Marquess of Blandford and 1st Duke of Marlborough.
The *Daily Courant* becomes London's first successful daily newspaper.
1703 Marlborough takes Cologne and Bonn.
Portugal joins the Grand Alliance and signs the Treaty of Methuen with England.
The Eddystone Lighthouse is destroyed as a great storm hits southern England.
1704 Gibraltar is captured by the English, who defeat a relieving force at Velez Malaga.
Marlborough and Eugene of Savoy heavily defeat the French at Blenheim.
Richard 'Beau' Nash becomes Master of Ceremonies at Bath.
1705 Edmund Halley predicts the return of the comet in 1758 that will bear his name.
John Erskine, 6th Earl of Mar becomes the first Secretary of State for Scotland.
1706 Marlborough defeats the French at Ramilles; Brussels, Antwerp, Ghent and Ostend quickly capitulate to him.
1707 England and Scotland formally unite with the Act of Union.
Fortnum & Mason's opens in Piccadilly.
Admiral Sir Cloudesley Shovell's squadron runs aground in the Scillies; only one man survives.
1708 Marlborough and Eugene of Savoy defeat the French at Oudenarde; Marlborough subsequently captures Lille.
Minorca captured by the British.
The East India Company and the New East India Company merge.
1709 Marlborough and Eugene of Savoy take Tournai and Mons and defeat the French at Malplaquet.
Abraham Derby develops coke-fuelled iron smelting at Coalbrookdale.
The *Tatler* is launched by Richard Steele and Joseph Addison.
1710 Stanhope is victorious at Almenara and Saragossa but is defeated and captured at Brihuega.
Handel is appointed Kapellmeister to Elector George of Hanover.
Christopher Wren completes St Paul's Cathedral.
1711 The South Sea Company is established.
Marlborough is dismissed from command and replaced by Ormonde.
Queen Anne establishes Ascot Racecourse.
Addison and Steele launch the *Spectator.*
Abigail Masham replaces Sarah Churchill as Keeper of the Privy Purse.
1712 Dudley Moore proclaims the virtues of William of Orange before a performance of Nicolas Rowe's *Tamerlane* at the Smock Alley Theatre, Dublin. Ireland's first theatre riot follows.
1714 Queen Anne dies, succeeded by her second cousin George I, as his mother Sophia had died shortly before.
The Board of Longitude promises a £20,000 reward for anybody who can discover a method of divining longitude.
1715 The Earl of Mar leads a Jacobite rising in Scotland; the Old Pretender James lands at Peterhead to support the rising, but his supporters are defeated at Sheriffmuir and Preston.
1716 The Old Pretender returns to France as the '15 Rebellion fizzles out.
1717 The Grand Lodge of the Freemasons is established at the Goose and Gridiron Tavern, Covent Garden.
1718 Edward Teach, better known as Blackbeard, is shipwrecked aboard *Queen Anne's Revenge*, which is believed to have run aground near Beaufort Inlet, North Carolina, and he is subsequently killed in a fight.
The first English bank notes are issued.
1720 The South Sea Company collapses (South Sea Bubble), as does John Law's Mississippi Company, bringing ruin to many.
1721 A regular postal service is established between London and New England.
John Aislabie, Chancellor of the Exchequer, is dismissed and imprisoned for fraud.

Robert Walpole, representing the Whigs, is appointed First Lord of the Treasury by George I, becoming the de facto first Prime Minister.

1723 Britain and Prussia sign the Treaty of Charlottenburg, arranging marriages between the two royal houses.

1725 The Treaty of Hanover allies Britain, Prussia and France against Austria and Spain.

1726 Voltaire is exiled in England.

General George Wade commences a programme of road-building in Scotland.

1727 George I dies of apoplexy, and is succeeded by his son George II.

Spain besieges Gibraltar, but does not formally declare war on Britain.

1728 Roman Catholics are disenfranchised in Ireland.

Spain abandons its siege of Gibraltar when the Convention of the Prado settles a truce with Britain.

1729 France, Britain and Spain end hostilities with the Treaty of Seville.

Charles Wesley founds the Holy Club at Oxford with his brother John and George Whitehead.

1730 Viscount Townshend improves crop husbandry with the use of turnips after leaving Walpole's government. **Note:** Charles 'Turnip' Townshend introduced the four-field crop rotation to England. The system (wheat, barley, turnips and clover) opened up a fodder crop and grazing crop, allowing livestock to be bred year-round, and increased productivity by avoiding leaving the soil uncultivated every third year. This was an improvement on the three-year rotation practised in England for 1000 years (see entry 732).

1731 John Hadley invents the reflecting quadrant, also known as the octant. The device is used to measure the altitude of the Sun or other celestial objects above the horizon at sea.

1733 James Oglethorpe establishes a colony at Savannah, founding the state of Georgia.

John Kay (born 1704) of Bury in Lancashire, invents a flying shuttle loom. The original shuttle contained a bobbin on to which the weft (crossways yarn) was wound. It was normally pushed from one side of the warp (lengthways yarn) to the other side by hand. Large looms needed two weavers to throw the shuttle. The flying shuttle was thrown by a lever that could be operated by one weaver and also greatly accelerated the speed at which weaving could be performed by allowing the shuttle carrying the weft to be passed through the warp threads more quickly.

1735 William Pitt is elected MP for Old Sarum.

John Harrison develops his marine chronometer (H1), a highly accurate time-keeping instrument that allows a navigator to accurately assess a ship's position in longitude. **Note:** The previous system of dead reckoning (estimation of current position based upon a previously determined position) was very inaccurate as it did not take into account the effect of currents or wind. By referring to Harrison's clock, when it was noon locally (i.e. the Sun was at its highest in the sky in that region) you could read, almost directly from the clock face, how far around the world you were from London. For instance, if the clock showed that it was midnight in London when it was noon locally, then you must have been half way round the world (e.g. 180 degrees of longitude) from London. The British Parliament offered a prize of £20,000 for anyone solving the problem of longitude but refused to pay Harrison as it deemed this and later models not to be of the desired accuracy. Eventually Harrison managed to gain endorsement of his H5 from George III, who attested it was accurate within a third of a second per day. In 1773 Harrison was paid £8,750 by Parliament for his achievements.

1736 Statutes against witchcraft are repealed in England.

1737 The Licensing Act orders all plays to submit to the Lord Chamberlain's censorship.

The *Belfast News Letter* is founded. **Note:** The *News Letter* is the UK's oldest surviving newspaper.

1738 John and Charles Wesley form the Methodist Society.

The future George III is born at Norfolk House, London, the grandson of King George II, and the son of Frederick, Prince of Wales, and Augusta of Saxe-Gotha.

1739 The highwayman Dick Turpin, now calling himself John Palmer, is convicted of horse-rustling and hanged at York.

England and Spain go to war (the War of Jenkins' Ear) over alleged Spanish transgressions.

Porto Bello in Panama is seized by Admiral Vernon.

1740 Admiral Vernon dilutes the Navy's rum ration, earning it the nickname grog, after Vernon's nickname 'Old Grog', attributed to his habitual wearing of a grogram coat.

'Rule, Britannia!, a British patriotic song originating from the poem 'Rule, Britannia' by James Thomson, is set to music by Thomas Arne and included in *Alfred*, a masque about Alfred the Great co-written by Thomson and David Mallet, first performed at Cliveden, country home of Frederick, Prince of Wales (1 August).

1742 Robert Walpole resigns as Prime Minister, and is replaced by Sir Spencer Compton, Earl of Wilmington.

Britain and Prussia sign the Treaty of Westminster, safeguarding Hanover.

1743 George II leads a multinational Pragmatic Army to victory over the French at Dettingen.

1744 Admiral George Anson completes a circumnavigation of the globe aboard HMS *Centurion*.

1745 The French defeat an army led by the Duke of Cumberland at Fontenoy and advance into the Austrian Netherlands.

Charles Edward Stuart lands on Eriskay, proclaiming his father king. He gains support from various Scottish clans, takes Edinburgh and is victorious at Prestonpans, but loses his nerve on reaching Derby and withdraws.

1746 The retreating Jacobites are victorious at Falkirk but are routed by Cumberland at Culloden. The Young Pretender escapes, and, helped by Flora MacDonald, reaches Skye, from where he returns to France. Cumberland severely represses the Scots, and the wearing of tartan is outlawed. The post of Secretary of State for Scotland is abolished in the Westminster parliament following the Jacobite rebellion.

Canaletto moves to England.

1747 The French defeat an Anglo-Dutch army at Laufeld.

Simon Fraser, 11th Lord Lovat, is beheaded for Jacobitism on Tower Hill. **Note:** he is the last man to be executed outside the Tower of London.

1749 Interior designer and cabinet-maker Thomas Chippendale opens a workshop in London.

Admiral Anson reforms the Royal Navy.

Author Henry Fielding and his brother John found the Bow Street Runners, London's first professional police force. Fielding also publishes *Tom Jones*, a comical tale of how a foundling came into a fortune.

1750 Thomas Gray's 'Elegy Written in a Country Churchyard' is written in Stoke Poges.

The Jockey Club is founded in the Star and Garter Coffee House, Pall Mall.

1751 Robert Clive seizes Arcot from the French.

Britain adopts January 1 as the beginning of the New Year, instead of 25 March. **Note:** Scotland had already changed in 1600.

1752 Britain adopts the Gregorian calendar system; by which time it is necessary to correct by 11 days. Wednesday, 2 September is followed by Thursday, 14 September to account for leap years.

1753 Sir Hans Sloane dies, his legacy of books and collections are used to found the British Museum and British Library.

The Marriage Act forbids unlicensed weddings in Britain.

British Prime Minister, Henry Pelham, introduces The Jewish Naturalisation Act, which allowed Jews to become naturalised by application to Parliament. **Note:** The hostility the act engendered led to its repeal in 1754.

1754 The Royal and Ancient Golf Club is founded at St Andrews, and codifies the rules of the sport.

Prolific innovator William Cookworthy discovers china clay in Cornwall and pioneers English porcelain production.

The first iron-rolling mill is built, in Fareham, Hampshire.

1755 In North America, General Braddock is killed in the Battle of the Wilderness (aka Battle of the Monongahela) as the French rout a British expedition, but the French are subsequently defeated at Lake George. **Note:** This was a precursor of the Seven Years War and is usually referred to as the French and Indian War (1754–63).

1756 John Smeaton builds a new Eddystone Lighthouse.

England and Prussia ally by the Treaty of Westminster.

Seven Years' War erupts as Prussia invades Saxony, which has allied with France, Austria, Russia and Sweden against it.

Britain declares war on France, but Montcalm drives the British from the Great Lakes.

Siraj-ud-Daula, a French ally, seizes Calcutta, imprisoning 146 Britons in a small guardroom (Black Hole of Calcutta); according to English propaganda, only 23 emerge alive the next morning.

1757 John Campbell invents the sextant.

Robert Clive recovers Calcutta and defeats Siraj-ud-Daula at Plassey.

Admiral John Byng (born 1704) is executed at Portsmouth for failing to relieve the naval base at Minorca from a French siege during the Seven Years' War. **Note:** French author Voltaire remarked in *Candide* that the English found it necessary from time to time to shoot an admiral 'pour encourager les autres' (to encourage the others).

Cumberland is routed by the French at Hastenbeck and is forced by the Convention of Klosterzeven to surrender Hanover to them.

1758 Britain promises assistance to Prussia by the Treaty of London.

Fort Duquesne is captured from the French by George Washington and John Forbes and renamed Pittsburgh.

An English army fighting for Frederick II of Prussia defeats the French at Krefeld, and Frederick crushes the Russians at Zorndorf but is defeated by the Austrians at Hochkirch.

Samuel Johnson founds *The Idler*, a series of 103 essays, all but 12 of them by Johnson himself, published in the London weekly the *Universal Chronicle*. **Note:** Among the other contributors was distinguished artist Joshua Reynolds.

The first railway is constructed, under an Act of Parliament, at Middleton, south of Leeds. **Note:** In the second half of the 18th century horse-worked tram roads proliferated in mining and quarrying districts, mostly connecting mines and quarries with canals or, particularly in the Northeast, the sea.

1759 General Wolfe defeats Montcalm on the Plains of Abraham outside Quebec; both generals die in battle. Quebec falls to the British. Admiral Hawke destroys a French squadron off Quiberon. Guadeloupe is captured by the British.

Samuel Johnson writes *Rasselas*, a novella following the travels of Rasselas, Prince of Abyssinia and his ultimate conclusion that there is no easy path to happiness for human beings.

1760 Earl Ferrers is convicted of the killing of Mr Johnson, his land-steward, and is hanged at Tyburn, the last peer to be executed in Britain.

Jeffrey Amherst, commander-in-chief of the British army in North America, captures Montreal and becomes military governor of Canada.

George II dies, and is succeeded by his grandson George III.

1761 France and Spain invade Portugal; Portugal asks for British help.

Spain and the Bourbon Italian states ally with France against Britain.

Pondicherry, the French base in southern India, falls to Sir Eyre Coote, the distinguished Irish soldier.

1762 Grenada, St Lucia, St Vincent and Martinique seized by the British under rear-admiral George Rodney.

The future George IV is born at St James's Palace, the eldest son of George III and Queen Charlotte.

John Stuart, 3rd Earl of Bute, becomes the first Scottish Prime Minister and the first Tory, breaking the dominance of the Whig Party. **Note:** The term Tory derived from Tóraidhe, originally used to refer to an Irish outlaw and later often applied to any Confederate or Royalist in arms from the time of the Glorious Revolution up until the Reform Bill of 1832 who were characterised by strong monarchist tendencies, support of the Church of England, and hostility to reform.

1763 The Treaty of Paris ends the Seven Years' War. Spain cedes Florida to Britain.

1764 James Hargreaves (born 1720), from Oswaldtwistle in Lancashire, invents the Spinning Jennifer (shortened to Jenny in 1768), a hand-powered multiple spinning machine that was the first machine to improve upon the spinning wheel, although the design was confined to producing cotton weft as it was unable to produce yarn of sufficient quality for the warp.

Sir Hector Monro defeats the Nawab of Oudh at Buxar, and takes control of Bengal.

1765 The Stamp Act imposes taxation on the American colonists, much to their disgust.

The future William IV is born at Buckingham House, the third son of George III and Queen Charlotte.

1766 The Stamp Act is repealed, but the Declaratory Act affirms the right of Parliament to tax the American colonists.

1767 Nevil Maskelyne, the Astronomer Royal, issues the first Nautical Almanac.

Robert Clive leaves India.

1768 The Royal Academy of Arts is founded, with Joshua Reynolds as its first president.

The first edition of the *Encyclopaedia Britannica* is published in Edinburgh.

1769 Richard Arkwright (born 1733) from Preston, Lancashire, develops the spinning frame, an improvement on the Spinning Jenny. A thick 'string' of cotton roving is passed between three sets of rollers, each set rotating faster than the previous one. In this way it reduces in thickness and increases in length before a strengthening twist is added by a bobbin-and-flyer mechanism. Too large to be operated by hand, the spinning frame employs the power of a water wheel, which gives the invention the name 'water frame'.

The *Morning Chronicle* is founded by William Woodfall.

James Watt patents a steam engine.

Josiah Wedgwood opens his pottery works at Etruria.

1770 Lord North replaces Grafton as Prime Minister.

All taxes, bar that on tea, on the American colonists are repealed.

An Anglo-Spanish dispute over the Falklands is resolved by French mediation.

The 'Boston Massacre', a brawl between civilians and British troops, leaves three dead.

Lt James Cook, aboard HM *Endeavour*, lands on the southeast coast of Australia and names the area Botany Bay, after the unique specimens retrieved by his botanist Joseph Banks. Cook then maps the east coast of Australia, which he names New South Wales and claims it for Great Britain.

1772 George III secures the passage of the Royal Marriages Act to control whom the royal family may marry.

Daniel Rutherford, Joseph Priestley, Henry Cavendish, and Carl Wilhelm Scheele independently discover nitrogen.

Warren Hastings becomes Governor of Bengal.

The *Morning Post* is founded by John Bell as a Conservative newspaper.

1773 Tea is thrown into the sea in the act known as the Boston Tea Party as a protest against the tea duty.

The first Stock Exchange opens in London.

James Cook enters the Antarctic Circle aboard HMS *Resolution*.

Thomas Pritchard constructs the Iron Bridge at Coalbrookdale.

Warren Hastings becomes the first Governor-General of India.

1774 The Coercive Acts against Massachusetts include closing the port of Boston.

Lord North is robbed by a highwayman at Chiswick.

Joseph Priestley publishes details of his discovery of 'dephlogisticated air' (oxygen). **Note:** The German scientist Carl Wilhelm Scheele discovered oxygen in 1772 but had not yet published his findings. French scientist Antoine-Laurent de Lavoisier also lays claim to being the first to isolate oxygen and most certainly gave the new element its name.

The Continental Congress, comprising all the America colonies bar Georgia, convenes, deciding to ban imports from and exports to Britain.

1775 Paul Revere rides to Lexington to warn of British troop movements. The American War of Independence begins. The colonists gain victories at Concord, Fort Ticonderoga and Crown Point. The Second Continental Congress convenes and John Hancock is elected its president. The British defeat the rebels at Bunker Hill, near Boston.

1776 The American colonists issue the Declaration of Independence. After defeat at Long Island and Lake Champlain they score a major victory at Trenton.

Scottish economist Adam Smith publishes *An Inquiry into the Nature and Causes of the Wealth of Nations*.

Allabaculia wins the first Doncaster St Leger (founded by Colonel Barry St Leger).

James Cook is promoted to the rank of Captain.

1777 The Americans are victorious at Princeton, Ridgefield and Bennington, but lose at Brandywine and Germantown before victory at Bemis Heights provokes Burgoyne to surrender at Saratoga.

1778 Captain Cook, aboard HMS *Resolution*, discovers and names the Sandwich Islands.

Joseph Bramah patents an improved water closet.

The British take Savannah.

1779 Samuel Crompton develops the spinning mule, a machine capable of spinning yarn suitable for use in the manufacture of muslin. **Note:** Crompton initially named his invention the Hall i' th' Wood wheel, from the name of the house in which he and his family resided.

Captain Cook is killed by natives in Hawaii.

Bridget wins the first running of The Oaks (named after the house at Epsom leased by the 12th Earl of Derby).

Warren Hastings sends British troops against the Marathas.

Spain declares war on Britain.

British troops are defeated at Baton Rouge by an augmented American army.

1780 Admiral Rodney defeats the Spanish off Cape St Vincent.

Lord George Gordon whips up anti-Catholic hysteria in London into the Gordon riots.

The Americans are defeated at Camden, but are victorious at King's Mountain.

Diomed wins the first Epsom Derby.

1781 William Herschel discovers Uranus.

Warren Hastings plunders the treasure of the Nabob of Oudh.

General Cornwallis surrenders to the Americans at Yorktown, Virginia, ending British military operations in America.

1782 Lord North resigns as Prime Minister, and is succeeded by Rockingham; on his death Shelburne replaces him, and Pitt the Younger becomes Chancellor of the Exchequer.

Admiral Rodney defeats the French at the Battle of the Saints.

The *Royal George* sinks off Portsmouth, with the loss of 800 men.

Spain captures Minorca from Britain.

1783 Shelburne resigns as Prime Minister, and is succeeded by Portland, whose government falls; Pitt the Younger becomes the Tory Prime Minister at the age of 24.

Henry Cort develops a method of puddling iron. The technique involves placing molten iron in a reverberatory furnace and stirring it with rods, which are consumed in the process.

The Treaty of Versailles recognises American Independence from Britain.

1784 The East India Company is put under government control.

John Wesley draws up his 'Deed of Declaration', providing for the continuance of the Methodist movement.

1785 The *Daily Universal Register* is founded by John Walter. **Note:** Walter renamed the newspaper *The Times* in 1788.

The Prince of Wales secretly weds Maria Fitzherbert.

Warren Hastings resigns as Governor-General of India.

Jean-Pierre Blanchard and John Jeffries cross the English Channel by balloon.

1786 Penang is ceded by the Rajah of Kedah to Britain.

Charles Cornwallis becomes commander in chief and Governor-General of India.

1787 The Marylebone Cricket Club is founded, and Thomas Lord opens his first cricket ground.

Warren Hastings is impeached by Edmund Burke.

1788 William Symington develops a workable steamboat.

The First Fleet lands convicts at Botany Bay and Sydney is founded to house them.

The trial for corruption of Warren Hastings begins.

George III suffers a bout of mental illness.

1789 George Washington is elected the first president of the United States.

A mutiny takes place, led by Fletcher Christian, on HMS *Bounty*; Christian and the mutineers settle on Pitcairn Island, Captain Bligh, set adrift, navigates across 3600 miles of ocean to Timor.

George III recovers from his illness.

1791 John Wesley dies.

The Observer is founded by W S Bourne.

Boswell's *Life of Johnson* and Tom Paine's *Rights of Man* are published.

1792 Cornwallis defeats Tipu Sultan of Mysore at Seringapatam and takes half of Mysore, paving the way towards British dominance in Southern India. He is raised to Marquess.

1793 France declares war on Britain, Holland and Spain, which join the First Coalition against France. America declares its neutrality, unable to decide which side to back. Toulon is occupied by the British, but recaptured by a force including Napoleon.

1794 Habeas Corpus (unlawful detention) is suspended in Britain.

Admiral Howe defeats the French fleet on the 'Glorious First of June', but the French have revenge at Charleroi and Fleurus.

King Kamehameha of Polynesia cedes Hawaii to George III, but the cession is not ratified.

1795 The French capture the Dutch fleet in the River Texel; Stadtholder William V is forced to flee to England and the French form the Batavian republic in the Netherlands.

Cape Town and Trincomalee are taken by the British.

Warren Hastings is acquitted.

Local magistrates meet at the Pelican Inn in Speenhamland, Berkshire and agree a means-tested sliding scale of wage supplements in order to mitigate the worst effects of rural poverty caused by the increase in grain prices.

Maynooth College, County Kildare, is established as the Roman Catholic College of St Patrick, effectively the national seminary for Ireland.

1796 Edward Jenner discovers a vaccine against smallpox.

Colombo is taken by the British, establishing British control over Ceylon.

Elba is captured by Britain.

Robbie Burns dies, aged 37.

Spain and Britain go to war.

1797 Admiral Jervis defeats the Spanish at Cape St Vincent.

Trinidad and St Lucia are taken by the British from the French.

The Royal Navy suffers mutinies at Spithead and the Nore, but defeats a Franco-Dutch fleet at Camperdown.

French troops are landed at Fishguard, but are quickly captured.

The first £1 bank notes are issued.

1798 Napoleon captures Malta en route to Egypt, where he defeats the Mamluks at the Battle of the Pyramids, but Nelson destroys his fleet at the Battle of the Nile.

Irish rebels are defeated at Vinegar Hill, while French troops landing in support are forced to surrender at Ballinamuck.

The Irish nationalist Wolfe Tone is captured, condemned, but commits suicide.

William Pitt the Younger introduces income tax in Britain.

Thomas Malthus produces his *Essay on the Principles of Population.*

Coleridge and Wordsworth publish *Lyrical Ballads.*

Marquess Cornwallis becomes Lord Lieutenant of Ireland.

1799 Napoleon invades Syria, but is repulsed by Sir Sidney Smith at Acre.

Napoleon defeats an Anglo-Turkish army at Aboukir.

Britain and Hyderabad share Mysore after Tipu Sultan is killed at Seringapatam.

The Second Coalition against France is organised by Pitt.

The Combination Act is passed, prohibiting trade unions and collective bargaining by British workers.

1800 Malta is captured by the British.

1801 Great Britain and Ireland unite and the cross of St Patrick is added to the Union Flag.

The French troops in Egypt surrender to the English.

Pitt the Younger resigns as Prime Minister over Catholic Emancipation, and is replaced by Addington.

Nelson defeats the Danish fleet at Copenhagen (after the famous incident of him turning a 'blind eye' to Parker's orders).

Surrey Iron Railway, the first 'common carrier' railway, opens from Wandsworth to quarries south of Croydon.

1802 The *Charlotte Dundas*, the world's first steamship, is built by William Symington.

Britain and France make peace via the Treaty of Amiens.

William Cobbett founds the *Political Register.*

Madame Tussaud mounts her first waxworks exhibition in London.

1803 Thomas Telford commences building the Caledonian Canal.
Henry Shrapnel develops an explosive shell.
France and Britain resume hostilities; France occupies Hanover.
Major-General Arthur Wellesley leads British troops to victory against Sindhia of Gwalior in the Second Maratha War.
1804 Addington is forced to resign by Pitt the Younger, who replaces him.
Richard Trevithick develops a steam locomotive which successfully hauls a load of 50 tons on the Pen-y-Darren tram road from Dowlais to Quakers Yard, South Wales.
1805 Francis Beaufort devises the Beaufort Scale for measuring wind speed.
Austria, Russia, Sweden and Britain form the Third Coalition against France.
Mungo Park explores the Upper Niger.
The British fleet is victorious at Trafalgar over a Franco-Spanish fleet, but Nelson is mortally wounded.
Cornwallis again becomes Governor-General of India but dies soon after.
1806 Britain occupies the Cape of Good Hope.
Pitt the Younger dies, Grenville forms a coalition; the 'Ministry of All the Talents', to replace him.
Prussia joins the Third Coalition.
Britain establishes a blockade of the European coastline; Napoleon retaliates by the Berlin Decree establishing the Continental System to bar European ports to British ships.
Wellington marries Kitty Pakenham, daughter of the 2nd Baron Longford.
1807 Slavery is prohibited in Britain.
HMS *Leopard* takes deserters from USS *Chesapeake*, enraging the Americans.
Copenhagen is bombarded by the British.
Charles and Mary Lamb's *Tales from Shakespeare* is published; Charles is guardian to his sister, who stabbed their mother during a bout of insanity.
The first official fare-paying passengers are conveyed on the Oystermouth tram road, near Swansea.
Wellington is promoted to lieutenant-general.
1808 Richard Trevithick demonstrates the locomotive *Catch-me-who-can.* **Note:** The trial was on a circular track near the later site of Euston Station in London.
1809 Sir John Moore is mortally wounded as British troops evacuate Corunna.
Wellington defeats Soult at Oporto and Jourdan at Talavera.
Britain and the Sikhs make a pact of friendship by the Treaty of Amritsar.
Canning, British foreign secretary, and Castlereagh, war minister, fight a duel on Putney Heath and resign from office.
Audiences at Covent Garden riot continuously for two months in protest at rising theatre prices.
Wizard wins the first running of the 2000 Guineas at Newmarket.
Robert Peel enters politics at the young age of 21 as MP for the Irish rotten borough of Cashel, Tipperary. **Note:** While in Ireland in 1809, Robert Peel was so impressed by the ginger breed of pig known as the 'Irish Grazer' that three years later he imported several to his Drayton Manor Estate at Tamworth and the famous Staffordshire breed was born.
1811 George III descends into madness and the Prince of Wales is declared Regent.
Luddism erupts in Nottingham. **Note:** The Luddite movement took its name from the fictive Ned Ludd, who is said to have destroyed two large stocking frames in the village of Anstey, Leicestershire in 1779. The principal objections of the movement's adherents concerned the introduction of new wide-framed automated looms that could be operated by cheap, relatively unskilled labour, resulting in the loss of jobs for many skilled textile workers.
Wellington defeats the French at Fuentes de Onoro and Albuera.
1812 Tory Prime Minister Spencer Perceval is assassinated by John Bellingham, and is succeeded by Robert Banks Jenkinson, the Earl of Liverpool.
America declares war on Britain due to trade tensions resulting from the Anglo-French conflict.
In Spain, Wellington takes Ciudad Rodrigo and Badajoz, defeats Marmont at Salamanca and enters Madrid.
Britain, Russia and Sweden ally via the Treaty of Örebro.
The first railway is established in Scotland, the Kilmarnock & Troon. **Note:** Various engineers and mechanics were at this period working on primitive steam locomotives, mostly in the Northeast.
1813 Wellington defeats Jourdan at Vittoria and crosses into France.
William Hedley builds *Puffing Billy* and *Wylam Dilly* at Wylam Colliery, Northumberland.
1814 Denmark cedes Heligoland to Britain by the Treaty of Kiel.
The White House is burned down by British troops. The Treaty of Ghent ends hostilities between Britain and America. **Note:** Although the treaty was signed on Christmas Eve it did not take effect until February 18th 1815. British casualties in the war were about 1600 killed in action and 3679 wounded. American casualties were considerably higher.
Wellington defeats the French at Toulouse. On his return to Britain he is granted a dukedom.
Thomas Young finishes translating the enchorial (demotic) text of the Rosetta Stone, and begins work on the hieroglyphic script. **Note:** The Rosetta Stone is an Ancient Egyptian artefact which was instrumental in advancing modern understanding of hieroglyphic writing. The stone is a Ptolemaic era stele with carved text made up of three translations of a single passage: two in Egyptian language scripts (hieroglyphic and Demotic) and one in classical Greek. It was created in 196 BC, discovered by the French in 1799 at Rosetta in Egypt. The stone is currently housed in the British Museum.
The Cape of Good Hope becomes a British colony.
George Stephenson builds his first locomotive, *Blucher*, at Killingworth Colliery.
Charlotte wins the first running of the 1000 Guineas at Newmarket.
1815 Napoleon returns from Elba, forcing Louis XVIII to flee to Ghent. His forces under Ney are victorious at Quatre Bras but Wellington inflicts defeat upon him at Waterloo. After surrendering to the British, he is exiled to St Helena. Louis XVIII returns, Ney is executed and Murat deposed from Naples; he is executed when trying to regain his throne.

The Corn Laws, a series of tariffs designed to support domestic British corn prices against competition from less expensive foreign imports, are passed in Britain.

Daniel O'Connell describes the Dublin Corporation ('The Corpo') as a 'beggarly corporation' and a disgruntled member, John D'Esterre, challenges him to a duel. They meet at Oughterard, County Kildare, and O'Connell mortally wounds D'Esterre.

1816 Cobbett's *Political Register* increases its radical influence after a price cut to 2d.

1817 The last major Luddite attack takes place in Loughborough.

More than 5000 'Blanketeers' march from St Peter's Field, Manchester, to lay their grievances before the Prince Regent. Most of the protesters are halted at Stockport and detained, the Habeas Corpus Act being suspended for the purpose of. **Note:** The blanketeers were so named because of the blankets they carried with them, mainly due to the cold March weather, but also to portray that many of them were weavers who were being deprived of a living.

The Scotsman is launched and becomes the first non-London newspaper to open an office in Fleet Street.

1818 James Blundell performs the first successful blood transfusion.

1819 Stamford Raffles founds the city of Singapore.

The Peterloo Massacre takes place in Manchester. The reactionary Six Acts are subsequently passed in England to suppress radical meetings and publications. **Note:** An economic crisis brought on by the cost of the Napoleonic Wars, and exacerbated by the Corn Laws and the lack of suffrage in northern England, led well-known radical orator Henry Hunt to call for a public demonstration at St Peter's Field, Manchester on 16th August. Cavalry, with their sabres drawn, charged into the 60–80,000-strong crowd resulting in the death of 11 people and hundreds more injured.

The future Queen Victoria is born at Kensington Palace, the daughter of Edward, Duke of Kent, 4th son of George III, and Victoria, daughter of Francis of Saxe-Coburg-Saalfeld.

1820 George III dies, and is succeeded by his son George IV.

The Cato Street Conspiracy to murder British Cabinet ministers is discovered and its leaders, John Brunt, William Davidson, James Ings, Arthur Thistlewood and Richard Tidd, are hanged at Newgate Prison.

1821 The *Manchester Guardian* is founded.

John Keats (b.1795), poet and 'negative capability' theorist, dies of tuberculosis.

1822 British foreign secretary Castlereagh commits suicide.

A whiskey bottle is thrown at Lord-Lieutenant Richard Wellesley while watching *She Stoops to Conquer* and *Tom Thumb* at the Theatre Royal, Dublin. The bottle misses Wellesley and lands in the box next to him but six Orangemen are arrested. The demonstration is against Wellesley's leniency towards Catholics and soon becomes known as the 'Bottle Riots'.

The Irish Constabulary Act creates the first organised Irish police force.

The *Sunday Times* is launched. **Note:** The newspaper was actually launched the previous year as the *New Observer* and then the *Independent Observer.*

Percy Bysshe Shelley (b.1792) drowns in a sudden storm while sailing back from Livorno to Lerici in his schooner, *Don Juan*. **Note** – Shelley's boat was named in honour of Byron and to complete the link between the three great romantic poets, when his body was washed ashore he was found to have a copy of Keats' poetry in his pocket.

1823 Michael Faraday succeeds in liquefying chlorine.

The *Lancet* is first published.

1824 The First Burmese War between Britain and Burma commences; Rangoon is taken by the British.

Lord Byron (b.1778) dies at Missalonghi while assisting the Greeks in their war of independence against the Ottoman Empire.

The RNLI is founded. **Note:** Founded as the National Institution for the Preservation of Life from Shipwreck, its present name was adopted in 1854, motto: Train one, save many.

The Combination Acts are repealed.

1825 The Stockton & Darlington Railway opens, hauling coal and freight by steam, but, except on the opening day, passenger traffic remains horse hauled.

Following a series of worker strikes a new Combination Act is passed, which allows labour unions but severely restricts their activity.

1826 Stamford Raffles founds the Royal Zoological Society in London.

The First Burmese War is ended by the Treaty of Yandabo.

The first steam operated railway in Scotland, the Monkland & Kirkintilloch opens near Glasgow.

Twenty-one-year-old Benjamin Disraeli brings out his first novel, *Vivian Grey*. **Note:** Disraeli initially published this novel anonymously by a 'man of fashion'. His later works included three political novels published in the 1840s, collectively known as 'The Trilogy': *Sybil, Coningsby* and *Tancred.*

1827 Count Kapodistrias is elected President of Greece as Britain, France and Russia sign the Treaty of London pledging support for the Greeks; an allied fleet crushes an Ottoman and Egyptian fleet at Navarino.

Wellington is appointed Commander-in-Chief of the British Army.

The *Standard* is founded in London with Stanley Lees Giffard its first editor.

1828 The Duke of Wellington becomes Tory Prime Minister and initially remains living at Apsley House (No. 1 London) as he considers Downing Street too small for his purposes. **Note:** Wellington was an unpopular Prime Minister at this time and the windows of his home were often smashed. Iron shutters were fitted and it was this rather than his resolute attitude which earned him the nickname 'The Iron Duke'.

Thomas Arnold becomes headmaster of Rugby School.

1829 The Catholic Relief Act is passed in Britain, allowing Catholics to have a seat in parliament. **Note:** although Wellington made a rousing speech in support of the Act, the leading campaigner was Irish lawyer and newly elected Member of Parliament Daniel O'Connell, who had won a seat in a by-election in County Clare but, as a Catholic, under British law was forbidden to take his seat in Westminster. A negative aspect of the legislation was the raising from 40 shillings to £10 the property qualification to vote, which effectively disenfranchised the Catholic peasants of Ireland.

Wellington fights a duel with the Earl of Winchelsea on Battersea Fields. Wellington fires wide and Winchelsea declines to fire but issues an apology for his accusation that Wellington had 'treacherously plotted the destruction of the Protestant constitution'.

The Metropolitan Police is founded by Robert Peel.

Promoters of the Liverpool & Manchester Railway stage a competition at Rainhill, near St Helens, offering a prize of £500 for the best and most efficient locomotive. George and Robert Stephenson's *Rocket* wins. The locomotive averaged 12 mph (19km/h) during the stringent testing; the other four finalists, *Sans Pareil, Perseverance, Novelty* and *Cycloped*, all failed to complete the trials.

The first University Boat Race takes place at Henley; Oxford gaining victory.

William Burke is hanged for his complicity in the murder of 17 people between 1827–8, their corpses being sold to the Edinburgh Medical College for dissection (28 January). His fellow Northern Irish accomplice, William Hare, walks free after being offered immunity from prosecution for confessing and agreeing to testify against Burke.

1830 George IV dies, and is succeeded by his brother William IV.

The Swing riots, caused by the introduction of threshing machines and rural unemployment, start in Kent and spread west and north. **Note:** The riots were named after the fictive Captain Swing, who signed the otherwise anonymous letters to *The Times* in this manner.

Wellington is ousted as Prime Minister after a general election, and replaced by the Whig, Earl Grey.

The Liverpool & Manchester Railway opens, the first steam operated 'main line'. Canterbury & Whitstable Railway also opens, the first steam railway in southern England.

Peel becomes MP for Tamworth.

1831 The defeat of Gray's Reform Bill in the Lords causes anti-clerical agitation.

The Dundee & Newtyle opens, the first railway north of the Tay.

Michael Faraday invents the dynamo.

The Tithe War begins in Ireland. **Note:** for five years there was sporadic outbursts of violence stemming from Catholic resistance to the statutory obligation to pay tithes for the upkeep of the Anglican Church of Ireland. Three-quarters of the population were Catholic and resented paying ten per cent of their income to a minority church, albeit the official one. Following the Rathcormac massacre in County Cork, when armed Irish Constabulary and military reportedly killed 17 locals and wounded at least 30 more, a reduced tithe became payable.

1832 The First Reform Act is passed, doubling the franchise. **Note:** The Representation of the People Act, as it was commonly known, granted seats in the Commons to large cities that had emerged during the Industrial Revolution, and took away seats from the 'rotten boroughs' – those with very small populations but exerting undue influence, Old Sarum in Wiltshire being a good example; with its three houses and seven voters it was still entitled to elect two MPs.

William Gladstone is elected to Parliament as the Conservative MP for Newark.

1833 Britain annexes the Falkland Islands.

Slavery is abolished in the British Empire.

Work commences on both the London & Birmingham, and Grand Junction Railways, to link the capital with the industrial north.

1834 To protect their constitutions, Portugal and Spain form a Quadruple Alliance with France and Britain.

For forming a trade union, six Dorset men, James Brine, James Hammett, James Loveless, Thomas Standfield, John Standfield and their leader George Loveless, known as the Tolpuddle Martyrs, are arrested and transported to Australia.

Fire destroys the Houses of Parliament.

The first railway in Ireland, the Dublin & Kingstown, is founded.

Robert Peel becomes Prime Minister representing the Tory Party. **Note:** In 1834 Peel issued the Tamworth Manifesto, which is widely credited by historians as having laid down the principles upon which the modern British Conservative Party is based.

1835 Peel's ministry resigns after being repeatedly defeated on various bills by the Whigs and Daniel O'Connell's Irish Radical members.

Isambard Kingdom Brunel's Great Western Railway is authorised.

1836 The first railway in London, the London & Greenwich, opens for passengers. Construction of the South Eastern Railway from London to Dover is authorised by Parliament.

1837 William IV dies, and is succeeded by his niece Victoria in England and his brother Ernst Augustus, Duke of Cumberland, in Hanover, who promptly cancels the constitution of 1833 there. Buckingham Palace becomes the official residence of the British monarch.

Brunel launches the *Great Western.*

Births, marriages and deaths are officially registered in England and Wales.

Isaac Pitman develops shorthand.

The Grand Junction Railway is opened, linking Liverpool and Manchester with Birmingham.

French Canadians revolt against British rule.

1838 The First Afghan War begins; the British capture Kabul and imprison the Emir Dost Muhammed.

The 'People's Charter' is published. **Note:** Chartism was a movement for political and social reform which flourished 1838–48. The six main aims of the movement were: suffrage for all men age 21 and over, equal-sized electoral districts, voting by secret ballot, an end to the need for a property qualification for Parliament, payment for MPs and Annual election of Parliament.

Richard Cobden establishes the Anti-Corn Law League.

Grace Darling assists in the rescue from the wreck of the *Forfarshire.*

The London & Birmingham Railway opens throughout, connecting Euston with the Grand Junction Railway at Birmingham. The first section of Brunel's Great Western Railway opens from Paddington to Maidenhead. First section of the London & Southampton railway opens, Nine Elms to Woking. Newcastle & Carlisle Railway opens, the first railway to cross England from coast to coast. **Note:** Brunel's GWR was built to a track gauge of 7ft $^1/_2$in (2.14m). Over the next few years the question of a national railway gauge was hotly debated, but it was a foregone conclusion that 4ft $8^{1}/_{2}$in (1.43m) would become the national, indeed the world, standard, in view of the overwhelming preponderance of pre-existing mileage of this gauge. The late 1830s saw a huge boom in the promotion of railway schemes throughout the British Isles, too numerous to mention individually, resulting in a recognisable national network being in place by 1845.

1839 The Rebecca Riots against the Poor Law Amendment Act take place in Wales (rioters disguise themselves as women).

Following the resignation of Lord Melbourne, Robert Peel is offered the opportunity of forming a Tory government but is concerned at Queen Victoria's allegiance to the Whig Party. Peel offers to accept the invitation on the condition that the Queen dismisses her Whig-appointed ladies of the bedchamber. The Queen refuses to accept the condition.

The railway system develops via the opening of the first section of the Midland Counties Railway, Derby to Trent Junction. The Ulster Railway, Belfast to Lisburn and the London & Croydon Railway also open. George Bradshaw publishes *Bradshaw's Guide*, the first national railway timetable, the cloth-bound book costing 6d.

Chinese attempts to stop the importation of opium lead to the Opium War with Britain.

The first Grand National is run at Aintree, won by the aptly named Lottery. **Note:** Two years previously a horse named The Duke won the steeplechase sometimes considered the first 'National', although this race took place at Maghull.

1840 Britain, Austria, Prussia and Russia ally against Mehmet Ali of Egypt via the Treaty of London; after Beirut and Acre are captured, Mehmet agrees to return Syria to Ottoman rule.

Rowland Hill introduces the Penny Post, whereby delivery to anywhere in the UK is available for a single pre-paid rate of 1d. Soon after its introduction an adhesive stamp, the Penny Black, is issued as the means of prepayment and Britain becomes the first nation to use postage stamps.

The Midland Counties Railway is completed, connecting Derby and Rugby. North Midland Railway opens, connecting Derby and Leeds. York & North Midland Railway opens, giving York rail connection with London, via Rugby. All the developments were part of the huge speculative empire of George Hudson of York, the so-called 'Railway King'.

Later in the year the London & Southampton Railway opens throughout. Great Western Railway reaches Swindon, and opens between Bristol and Bath. In Scotland, Glasgow and Ardrossan are connected by rail. A London connection is provided by steamship to Liverpool and rail from there.

The Maoris cede sovereignty of New Zealand to England via the Treaty of Waitangi.

The Repeal Association is set up by Daniel O'Connell at the Corn Exchange, Dublin, its intentions to campaign for the repeal of the Act of Union 1800 between the kingdoms of Great Britain and Ireland.

Gladstone begins to walk the streets of London attempting to rehabilitate prostitutes.

1841 Hong Kong is taken by the British.

Robert Peel begins his second administration as Conservative Prime Minister. **Note:** Although George Canning first used the term 'Conservative' in the 1820s and it was suggested as a title for the party by John Wilson Croker in the 1830s, it was only officially adopted after the announcement of the Tamworth Manifesto to fight the election of 1835. Peel is therefore acknowledged as the founder of the Conservative party and the first Conservative Prime Minister.

The Great Western Railway is complete from Paddington to Bristol. London & Brighton railway opens. Great North of England Railway connects York and Darlington. Manchester & Leeds Railway opens, the first line to cross the Pennines. Edinburgh & Glasgow Railway opens. First fully recorded multi-death railway accident when a GWR train runs into a landslip in Sonning Cutting, east of Reading.

The first issue of *Punch* is published.

Thomas Cook arranges his first excursion, a group of 570 temperance campaigners from Leicester railway station to a rally in Loughborough, eleven miles away, at a cost of one shilling per traveller.

The future Edward VII is born at Buckingham Palace, the eldest son of Queen Victoria and Prince Albert.

1842 The Treaty of Nanking ends the Opium War; Hong Kong is officially ceded to Britain.

British troops in Afghanistan are massacred, resulting in withdrawal.

A Railway Clearing House is set up in London to handle inter-company revenue accounts, and also to bring about uniformity in such matters as rolling stock coupling arrangements.

The second Chartist petition is rejected.

The Nation, a new Irish nationalist newspaper, is founded.

1843 Muslim rulers of the region of Sindh, make hostile demonstrations against the British government after the termination of the First Anglo-Afghan War. Sindh is subjugated by General Charles Napier.

Robert Peel is the target of a failed assassination attempt; a criminally insane Scottish woodsman named Daniel M'Naghten stalks him for several days before accidentally killing Peel's personal secretary Edward Drummond instead.

Grand Junction Railway moves its locomotive workshops from Edge Hill, Liverpool, to a greenfield site near Crewe Hall, in Cheshire, virtually founding the modern town of Crewe. Great Western Railway establishes workshops at Swindon, expanding the old town dramatically.

The Thames Tunnel opens, the first underwater tunnel in the world.

Brunel launches the *Great Britain*.

The *Economist* is founded by James Wilson with help from the Anti-Corn Law League. **Note:** Wilson's son-in-law Walter Bagehot later became the editor of this newspaper.

The world's first rugby football club is founded at Guy's Hospital.

The *News of the World* is founded by John Browne Bell.

1844 The Co-operative movement is founded in Rochdale.

The Factory Act fixes maximum workdays of six and a half hours for children, 12 hours for women.

George Williams founds the YMCA in London, its aims to replace life on the streets with prayer and Bible study but showing no allegiance to any one Christian denomination.

South Eastern Railway reaches Dover, connecting at Folkestone with cross-Channel steamships. Midland

Railway company is formed by amalgamation of the Midland Counties, North Midland, and other railways, consolidating George Hudson's financial stranglehold. Construction begins of the North British Railway from Edinburgh to Berwick. Hudson promotes the Newcastle & Berwick to connect with it. The so-called 'Railway Mania', a frenzy of speculation in railway shares almost comparable to the 'South Sea Bubble' of 1711–20, begins. **Note:** The discovery of grave financial irregularities in the Hudson empire, e.g. the financing of inflated dividends to shareholders from capital, led to the collapse of the 'Railway Mania' in 1846–7. Many speculators and ordinary investors were ruined, and Hudson fled abroad, eventually dying in penury in 1871. Despite the severe damage to public confidence resulting from this financial disaster, by 1850 railways had proved themselves to be absolutely indispensable to the industrial and commercial life of Great Britain, as well as bringing untold benefits in terms of social mobility and quality of life. Railway construction continued unabated for the rest of the 19th century, until the network, still owned and operated by over 100 separate companies, reached from Penzance in Cornwall to Thurso in the remote north of Scotland.

Bank note issue is regulated in Britain by the Bank Charter Act.

1845 The Irish famine begins as the potato crop fails. **Note:** As a result of the fungal disease *Phytophthora infestans*, commonly known as blight, a huge increase in emigration, particularly to the USA, took place. The population fell from 8.5 million in 1845 to just under 6.5 million in 1851, the loss being about half and half through death and emigration.

Henry Newman, a major figure in the Oxford Movement, converts from Anglicanism to Catholicism.

Sir John Franklin sets out with the *Erebus* and *Terror* to find the Northwest Passage.

British incursions in the Punjab and Kashmir cause the Anglo-Sikh War.

Gladstone resigns temporarily from Robert Peel's government over the issue of an increased grant to the Maynooth Seminary for training Catholic priests but returns later in the year as Colonial Secretary.

1846 Peel repeals the Corn Laws, fatally splitting his party and forcing him to resign as PM; Lord John Russell replaces him.

The Anglo-Sikh War is ended by the Treaty of Lahore.

Charles Dickens founds the *Daily News* as a rival newspaper to the *Morning Chronicle*.

1847 The Irish Confederation, a nationalist independence movement, is formed at the Rotunda, Dublin. It is established by members of the Young Ireland movement who had themselves seceded from Daniel O'Connell's Repeal Association. **Note:** Although the term 'Young Ireland' was actually coined by the English press, it was Daniel O'Connell who popularised the name by referring to the young men of *The Nation* newspaper as 'Young Irelanders'.

Four months after the formation of the Irish Confederation Daniel O'Connell dies in Genoa, Italy while on a pilgrimage to Rome at the age of 71. According to his dying wish, his heart was buried in Rome and the remainder of his body in Glasnevin Cemetery, Dublin. **Note:** Daniel O'Connell is known in Ireland as 'The Liberator' or 'The Great Emancipator' for his success in achieving Catholic Emancipation. He stands alongside any of the great statesmen of the 19th century and the main streets of Dublin and Limerick are named in his honour, both adorned by statues of one of Ireland's greatest nationalists.

1848 The third Chartist petition is presented amid a meeting which collapses in farce, and is rejected. **Note:** The third petition was organised by Feargus O'Connor, the leader of the Physical Force Chartists. At the meeting held at Kennington Common on 10th April, O'Connor told the crowd that the petition contained 5,706,000 signatures. However, when it was examined by MPs it contained only 1,975,496 names, many of which, such as those of well-known opponents of parliamentary reform, Queen Victoria, Sir Robert Peel and the Duke of Wellington, were clear forgeries. Despite the climate of political unrest, Britain is one of few European nations not to suffer major riots in 1848, a year given the name 'Year of Revolution'.

The Second Anglo-Sikh War breaks out.

The Pre-Raphaelite Brotherhood, a group of English painters, poets and critics, is founded by Dante Gabriel Rossetti, William Michael Rossetti, James Collinson, John Everett Millais, Frederic George Stephens, Thomas Woolner and William Holman Hunt; their aim is to return to the abundant detail, intense colours and complex compositions of Quattrocento Italian and Flemish art.

The Sikhs are defeated by the British at Chillianwalla and forced to surrender at Rawalpindi; the Punjab is annexed by Britain.

Gladstone founds the Church Penitentiary Association for the Reclamation of Fallen Women.

1850 Palmerston blockades Piraeus over the Don Pacifico Affair, forcing to Greeks to comply with his wishes, but is censured in parliament. **Note:** Don Pacifico was a Portuguese Jew born in Gibraltar, a British possession. In 1847 his home in Athens was vandalised by an antisemitic mob, which included the sons of a government minister, while the police looked on and took no action. After he unsuccessfully appealed to the Greek government for compensation for his losses, he brought the matter to the attention of the British government in 1848.

Sir Robert Peel is thrown from his horse while riding up Constitution Hill in London; he dies three days later at the age of 62. **Note:** His Peelite followers, led by Lord Aberdeen and William Gladstone, went on to fuse with the Whigs as the Liberal Party.

1851 The Royal Yacht Squadron's first regatta around the Isle of Wight is held and won by the 101ft 3in (30.86m) schooner-yacht *America*, owned by a syndicate that represented the New York Yacht Club. **Note:** The Cup subsequently became known as the 'One Hundred Guineas Cup' but eventually became officially known as the America's Cup, affectionately called the 'Auld Mug' by the sailing community.

The Great Exhibition, the first in a series of World's Fair exhibitions of culture and industry, is held in Hyde Park.

1852 The Second Burmese War breaks out between Britain and Burma.

The pillar box is introduced as a catchment for the sending of mail. The first boxes are olive green; on the advice of Anthony Trollope, novelist and Surveyor for the Western District, they are placed in David Place, New Street, Cheapside and St Clement's Road, all in St Helier, Jersey.

Wellington dies at Walmer Castle, his honorary residence as Lord Warden of the Cinque Ports.

1853 Pegu is taken by Britain as the Second Burmese War ends.

The first pillar box in mainland Britain is erected in Botchergate, Carlisle.

1854 Britain and France declare war on Russia in support of Turkey and are victorious at the Alma, Balaklava (where the Charge of the Light Brigade takes place), and Inkerman, before besieging Sebastopol.

America makes the Treaty of Kanagawa with Japan over trade and the Elgin Treaty with Britain over Canadian trade.

The Convention of Bloemfontein leaves the Orange Free State free for the Boers and withdraws the British south of the Orange River.

1855 Aberdeen resigns as Prime Minister over the conduct of the war, and is replaced by Palmerston.

Sebastopol falls to the allied armies.

Britain and Afghanistan sign the anti-Persian Treaty of Peshawar.

Pillar boxes are introduced in London.

The *Daily Telegraph* is first published.

1856 Henry Bessemer introduces his steel-making converter.

The Victoria Cross is instituted.

Britain annexes Oudh and establishes Natal as a Crown Colony.

The Crimean War is ended by the Treaty of Paris; the integrity of the Ottoman Empire is recognised and the Black Sea demilitarised.

The Chinese board the *Arrow* off Canton over suspected piracy; British ships bombard Canton in response.

The Department of Education is set up in England.

1857 The Sepoys in Meerut revolt, sparking a general Indian Mutiny; the inhabitants of Cawnpore are massacred and Lucknow besieged for six months.

Further Chinese insults on British and French nationals lead to the occupation of Canton.

Britain forces Afghani independence on the Persians by the Treaty of Paris.

1858 Anglo-Chinese hostilities are ended by the Treaty of Tianjin (Tientsin).

The Indian Mutiny is suppressed; the East India Company is wound up and its powers transferred to the British crown.

1859 Henry John Temple, the Viscount Palmerston forms a new mixed government with Radicals included, and Gladstone joins the government as Chancellor of the Exchequer to become part of the new Liberal Party.

Darwin publishes *The Origin of Species*.

The *Irish Times* is launched in Dublin.

The *Standard* becomes an evening newspaper and is renamed the *Evening Standard*.

1860 Richard Cobden negotiates an Anglo-French trade treaty.

Anglo-French forces bombard Sinho, occupy the Tagu (Taku) forts, defeat the Chinese army at Ba Lizhao (Pa-li-chiao) and burn the Summer Palace in Peking in retaliation for Chinese treaty breaches and cruelty to captives; the Treaty of Peking forces further concessions on the Chinese.

Scottish golfer Willie Park Sr wins the Challenge Belt as the first winner of the Open Golf Championship at Prestwick.

The London Trades Council is formed.

1861 Prince Albert dies of typhoid fever.

With the commissioning into the Royal Navy of the iron-hulled HMS *Warrior*, all other naval vessels are rendered effectively obsolete.

1862 Napoleon III sends French troops to establish a Catholic Empire in Mexico, forcing the withdrawal of British and Spanish troops; the French are heavily defeated at Puebla.

1863 The Greeks elect Prince Alfred of Britain as their new king, but he is forced to reject the position; William of Denmark is elected instead, taking the title George I.

The English Football Association is founded in the Freemasons' Tavern on Long Acre, London.

The first underground railway, from Farringdon Street to Paddington, is opened.

1865 William Booth founds the Christian Revival Society in London's East End. **Note:** The pro-active Christian association started the first soup kitchens for the poor and needy. In 1878 it became the Salvation Army.

British illustrator Edward Whymper becomes the first man to climb the Matterhorn.

Joseph Lister's use of carbolic acid founds modern antiseptic surgery.

Lord Palmerston dies in office, and is succeeded as Prime Minister by Lord John Russell.

The future George V is born at Marlborough House, London, the second son of the Prince of Wales (later Edward VII) and the Princess of Wales (later Queen Alexandra).

The Locomotive Act 1865 introduces speed limits of 2 mph and 4 mph (Red Flag Act).

1866 The United Kingdom Alliance of Organised Trades, representing over 200,000 trade unionists, is founded in Sheffield.

1867 The Second Reform Act doubles the British electorate.

The Queensberry Rules on boxing are drawn up.

1868 The first Trades Union Congress meets in the Manchester Mechanics' Institute. **Note:** Initially the Congress was set up as a northern rival of the southern-based London Trades Council but gradually became the national voice of the unions and also formalised its role as the 'General Staff of the Labour Movement', initiating the Labour Representation Committee, the forerunner of the Labour Party. In 2009 there are 58 affiliated unions with a total of around 6.5 million members, approximately half of whom are represented by the two largest unions, Unite (a British and Irish trade union formed on 1 May 2007 by the merger of Amicus and the Transport and General Workers' Union) and UNISON (formed in 1993 from the amalgamation of three previous public sector trade unions, the National and Local Government Officers' Association (NALGO), the National Union of Public Employees (NUPE) and the Confederation of Health Service Employees (COHSE). UNISON currently has over 1.3 million members and since 1 January 2001 its general secretary has been Dave Prentis. Unite is the largest union in Britain and Ireland and currently has two Joint General Secretaries, Derek Simpson and Tony Woodley. The General Secretary of the TUC has been Brendan Barber since June 2003.

The last fully public hanging in England takes place – that of Michael Barrett at Newgate for the Fenian bombing at Clerkenwell which killed and maimed several people. **Note:** Three days later on 29 May Parliament passed the

Capital Punishment (Amendment) Act, ending public hanging as such, and requiring executions to be carried out behind prison walls. The last woman to be hanged in public, two months before Barrett, was Frances Kidder at Maidstone Prison.

Conservative MP Benjamin Disraeli becomes Prime Minister on the resignation of Lord Derby in February, to become the first British Prime Minister of Jewish heritage. He makes his famous statement 'I have climbed to the top of the greasy pole'; however in December he is defeated in a general election by the Liberal leader William Gladstone, who replaces him.

1869 The clipper *Cutty Sark* is built at Dumbarton, Scotland.

1871 The Church of Ireland is disestablished by the Liberal government under William Gladstone. **Note:** The Roman Catholic Church was, and still is, by far the largest tradition in Ireland although the Church of Ireland remains an Anglican communion considering itself to be both Catholic and Reformed.

Britain and America settle differences by the Treaty of Washington.

Stanley meets Livingstone at Ujiji (now in Tanzania).

The Rugby Football Union is founded.

Sir John Lubbock, Liberal Party Member of Parliament for Maidstone, introduces the Bank Holidays Act. **Note:** As at 2009, England and Wales have eight bank holidays: New Year's Day, Good Friday, Easter Monday, May Day (first Monday), Spring Bank Holiday (last Monday in May), Summer Bank Holiday (last Monday in August), Christmas Day and Boxing Day. Scotland has nine bank holidays: New Year's Day, 2 January, Good Friday, May Day (first Monday), Spring Bank Holiday (last Monday in May), Summer Bank Holiday (first Monday in August), St Andrew's Day, Christmas Day and Boxing Day. Northern Ireland has ten bank holidays: New Year's Day, St Patrick's Day, Good Friday, Easter Monday, May Day (first Monday), Spring Bank Holiday (last Monday in May), Orangemen's Day (12 July), Summer Bank Holiday (last Monday in August), Christmas Day and Boxing Day. The Republic of Ireland has nine bank holidays: New Year's Day, St Patrick's Day, Easter Monday, Labour Day (first Monday in May), June Bank Holiday (first Monday), Summer Bank Holiday (first Monday in August), October Bank Holiday (last Monday), Christmas Day and Boxing Day.

1872 Wanderers beat the Royal Engineers 1–0 at the Kennington Oval, to win the first FA Cup final. The scorer of the goal, Morton Betts, plays under the pseudonym A H Chequer, as he is a former member of the Harrow Chequers Club.

The secret ballot is introduced in Britain.

1873 The Claret Jug, officially called the Golf Champion Trophy, is first presented to the winner of the Open, Tom Kidd of Scotland, although the first name on it is the previous year's winner fellow Scot Tom Morris Jr.

Major Walter Clopton Wingfield of Nantclwyd, Llanelidon, north Wales, patents the game of Sphairistike (lawn tennis).

1874 Fiji is annexed by Britain who immediately brings over Indian contract labourers.

Disraeli defeats William Gladstone in the general election to become Prime Minister.

Pillar boxes in the UK are standardised as bright red in colour as pedestrians have had a tendency to walk into the green ones. **Note:** Following Irish independence in 1922, existing British pillar boxes were retained but painted green.

1875 Matthew Webb becomes the first person to swim the English Channel.

Disraeli arranges the purchase of shares in the Suez Canal.

Sir Joseph Bazalgette completes the London sewerage system.

The MCC codifies the rules of lawn tennis.

1876 Alexander Graham Bell patents the telephone.

Queen Victoria is proclaimed Empress of India. **Note:** She is officially inaugurated in January 1877.

Disraeli is raised to the peerage as the 1st Earl of Beaconsfield.

1877 Russia declares war on Turkey and takes Kars and Plevna. Britain warns Russia off taking Constantinople.

Australia beats England in the first cricket Test match.

The first Lawn Tennis Championships are held at the All England Croquet Club, Wimbledon. Surrey county cricketer Spencer Gore wins the Gentlemen's Singles.

1879 The Irish Land League is founded.

Britain goes to war with the Zulus, who massacre the British at Isandlwana but are held at Rorke's Drift and defeated at Ulundi. Their king Cetewayo is captured and deported and the Zulu wars end.

Britain occupies the Khyber Pass by the Treaty of Gandamak with Afghanistan and invades when the legation in Kabul is massacred, taking the city and deposing Emir Yakub.

The Tay Bridge collapses in a storm.

1880 Andrew Carnegie presents Dunfermline with a free library.

Gladstone defeats Disraeli in the general election.

Captain Charles Cunningham Boycott, a Norfolk-born land agent, is ostracised by his tenants as part of a campaign for the 'Three Fs' (fair rent, fixity of tenure and free sale). Local shops in the Lough Mask area of County Mayo where he lives, refuse to serve him and local residents refuse to speak to him. **Note:** Boycott's name later became immortalised by the creation of the verb to boycott, meaning 'to ostracise'.

1881 Boers repulse the British at Laing's Neck and defeat them at Majuba Hill; peace is made via the Treaty of Pretoria which recognises an independent Transvaal as the South African Republic.

The last flogging of a British soldier takes place.

The *People* is founded as a newspaper to aid the Conservative cause.

1882 The Hague Convention establishes a three-mile limit for territorial waters.

The Fenians assassinate two British ministers in Phoenix Park, Dublin.

Nationalist riots in Egypt led by Arabi Pasha lead to the British fleet bombarding Alexandria; Sir Garnet Wolseley defeats Arabi at Tel-el-Kebir and occupies Cairo.

Michael Cusack founds the Dublin Hurling Club.

1883 Khedive Tewfik appoints a British agent to assist his government; Evelyn Baring takes up the post.

The Mahdi stirs up a revolt in Sudan and defeats an Anglo-Egyptian army at El Obeid.

1884 The Third Reform Act is passed in Britain, again increasing the electorate.

The Fabian Society is established, its aims to advance the principles of social democracy via gradualist and reformist, rather than revolutionary means. **Note:** The group, which favoured gradual incremental change rather than revolutionary change, was named – at the suggestion of English author Frank Podmore – in honour of the Roman general Quintus Fabius Maximus (nicknamed 'Cunctator', meaning 'the Delayer').

General Gordon reaches Khartoum intent on evacuating the city but decides to stay and take siege.

The Gaelic Athletic Association (Cumann Lúthchleas Gael) is founded by Michael Cusack on Saturday, 1 November, at the Hayes Hotel, Thurles, County Tipperary. **Note:** The original intention was to resurrect the ancient Tailteann Games, the oldest sporting event in the world, held in Ireland in honour of Queen Tailtiu between 1829 BC and AD 1180. The high-profile games of hurling and Gaelic football soon became dominant, although the Tailteann Games were held by the GAA at Croke Park in 1924, 1928 and 1932, and were open to all people of Irish birth or ancestry.

1885 Wolseley defeats the Madhi's followers at Abu Klea but reaches Khartoum two days after its fall and Gordon's death. Wolseley is forced to withdraw and the news helps contribute to the fall of Gladstone's government.

Robert Arthur Talbot Cecil, Marquis of Salisbury, replaces Gladstone as Prime Minister.

The British parliament reintroduces the post of Secretary of State for Scotland; Charles Henry Gordon-Lennox, 6th Duke of Richmond, 6th Duke of Lennox and 1st Duke of Gordon becomes the first incumbent.

1886 Gladstone becomes Prime Minister for the third time. His conversion to Irish Home Rule splits the Liberals; Joseph Chamberlain leads the Liberal Unionists into partnership with the Conservatives and the Marquis of Salisbury forms his second administration.

Randolph Churchill resigns as Chancellor in a fit of pique and destroys his political career in the process.

1887 The First Colonial Conference opens in London.

Zululand is annexed by Britain.

Limerick defeat Louth in the first GAA All-Ireland Senior Football Championship, at Clonskeagh. **Note:** Croke Park has been the venue for the championships since 1914 and since 1928 the winners have been presented with the Sam MacGuire Trophy, named in honour of a former influential player. The first All-Ireland Hurling Senior Championship also sanctioned by the GAA took place in 1887 and since 1921 the winners (Limerick in that year) have received the Liam McCarthy Cup in honour of one of its founding members.

A game of shinty is played between Glenurquhart Shinty Club and Strathglass Shinty Club in Inverness. **Note:** Attended by a huge crowd, this match was a major milestone in developing a set of common rules.

1888 The Jack the Ripper murders take place in London. **Note:** Marie Jeanette Kelly, a 25-year-old Irish prostitute, was the last of the five certain victims.

The world's first-ever moving film, of a horse-drawn tram on Leeds Bridge, Yorkshire, was photographed by Louis Le Prince.

Lord Randolph Churchill's horse L'Abbesse de Jouarre wins the Epsom Oaks.

The *Financial Times* is founded in London. **Note:** The pink edition was adopted in 1893.

1889 The Regulation of Railways Act legislates for an infallible code of requirements which forms the basis of safe railway working.

1890 Heligoland is exchanged for the German colonies of Zanzibar and Pemba by Britain.

The Forth Railway Bridge opens.

The first electric 'tube' is introduced, connecting the City with Stockwell.

Surrey win the inaugural English County Cricket Championship.

1892 Gladstone forms his fourth administration at the age of 82 after victory in the general election.

Brunel's Broad Gauge finally disappears from the Great Western.

1893 The Matabele rise against the British South Africa Company, but Jameson crushes the revolt and takes Bulawayo, forcing King Lobengula into exile.

HMS *Victoria* sinks off Tripoli after being rammed by HMS *Camperdown* during manoeuvres. **Note:** 358 crew died, including the commander of the British Mediterranean Fleet, Vice-Admiral Sir George Tryon. One of the survivors however was second-in-command, John Jellicoe, later commander-in-chief of the British Grand Fleet at the Battle of Jutland.

The Independent Labour Party is founded in Bradford. James Keir Hardie becomes its first chairman.

The Gaelic League (Conradh na Gaeilge) is founded in Dublin by Douglas Hyde 'for the purpose of keeping the Irish language spoken in Ireland'.

1894 The Manchester Ship Canal is opened.

Gladstone resigns from office, replaced as Prime Minister by Archibald Philip Primrose, Earl of Rosebery.

Uganda becomes a British protectorate.

The future Edward VIII is born at White Lodge, Richmond, the eldest son of the Duke of York (later George V), and the Duchess of York (later Queen Mary of Teck).

1895 The future George VI is born at Sandringham House, Norfolk, the second son of the Duke and Duchess of York.

The British South Africa Company's land south of the Zambesi is renamed Rhodesia.

The so-called Jameson Raid on Paul Kruger's Transvaal Republic begins on 29 December, carried out by British colonial statesman Leander Starr Jameson and his Rhodesian and Bechuanaland policemen.

The Marquis of Salisbury replaces the Earl of Rosebery as Prime Minister and forms his third administration.

The *Daily Record* is founded in Glasgow.

1896 Jameson is captured by the Boers at Doorn Kop. Kaiser Wilhelm sends the Kruger Telegram on 3 January, congratulating the president of the Transvaal on repelling the Jameson Raid, thus inflaming Anglo-German relations. **Note:** Although Jameson's raid was abortive he was lionised in Britain, Joseph Chamberlain, British colonial secretary, bearing the brunt of criticism for his clandestine involvement. Jameson was later immortalised in Rudyard Kipling's poem 'If', which was based on his character and fortitude.

Kitchener leads an Anglo-Egyptian force into the Sudan.

The first prosecution for speeding and first recorded road death occur in Britain.

The *Daily Mail* is founded by Alfred Harmsworth, Lord Northcliffe.

1898 Kitchener defeats the Sudanese at Omdurman, retakes Khartoum and advances to Fashoda where he discovers a French force which is ordered to withdraw after the British government protests to the French.

1899 Transvaal declares war on Britain; the Orange Free State allies with Transvaal.

The Boers besiege Kimberley, Mafeking and Ladysmith and are victorious at Stormberg, Magersfontein and Colenso.

1900 The Boers are victorious at Spion Kop, but Kimberley, Ladysmith and Mafeking are relieved and Bloemfontein, Johannesburg and Pretoria are taken by the British, who annex the Orange Free State and Transvaal.

Heavily influenced by postwar sentiment, the Conservative government of Lord Salisbury is returned to office with an increased majority over the Liberal Party. **Note:** This was dubbed the 'khaki election' after the colour of the military uniform of the British army during the Boer War. The term was also used to describe the elections of 1918 and 1945.

The Labour Representation Committee is established, with Ramsay MacDonald as secretary.

The *Daily Express* is founded by C Arthur Pearson.

1901 Queen Victoria dies, and is succeeded by her son Edward VII.

Designed by John Philip Holland and built at Vickers Maxim shipyard, Barrow-in-Furness, the first British submarine commissioned by the Royal Navy, *Holland I*, is launched.

Marconi, who is in Newfoundland, receives a wireless message from Cornwall.

The Boers begin guerilla warfare against the British.

Lloyds underwriters issue the first motor insurance policy.

1902 Britain allies with Japan.

The Treaty of Vereeniging ends the Boer War with British sovereignty established.

Arthur Balfour replaces the Marquis of Salisbury as Prime Minister.

The Order of Merit is established.

Newgate prison in London is closed. Male inmates are transferred to Pentonville prison and female ones to Holloway prison.

1903 Newgate is pulled down and replaced by the Central Criminal Court, the Old Bailey.

The Bank Holiday (Ireland) Act adds 17 March, St Patrick's Day, as an Irish bank holiday.

The *Daily Mirror* is founded by Alfred Harmsworth, Lord Northcliffe, as a newspaper for women.

Sir William 'Randal' Cremer becomes the first British-born winner of a Nobel Prize (Peace) for his work in international arbitration.

Driving licences are introduced at a cost of five shillings and are renewable every three months from the post office. Vehicle registration marks are also introduced and the speed limit is raised to 20 mph.

1904 The wireless distress signal CQD is adopted.

The Russian fleet attacks Hull trawlers off the Dogger Bank, mistaking them for Japanese warships; the French mediate between Britain and Russia and the matter is resolved.

Britain and France ally via the 'Entente Cordiale'.

The British enter Tibet, by imposing the Treaty of Lhasa; they aim to safeguard it from Russian penetration.

GWR locomotive No.3440 *City of Truro* is credited with a speed of 102.3 mph (164.6 km/h), descending Wellington Bank, Somerset with a special mail train. The flawed timing mechanism negates the performance for record purposes.

The Rolls-Royce motor company is founded.

The Abbey Theatre, Dublin is founded.

1905 The Conservative Party splits over tariff reform; Balfour resigns as PM as a result and Henry Campbell-Bannerman replaces him.

Sinn Féin is founded by Arthur Griffith on 28 November at the Rotunda, Dublin. **Note:** The name of the new republican political party, translating from Gaelic as 'we ourselves', was suggested to Griffith by Gaelic League (Conradh na Gaeilge) activist, Máire de Buitléir. The party's first president was Edward Martyn.

The *Irish Independent* is launched in Dublin.

1906 HMS *Dreadnought* is launched in Britain, making all other warships outdated and precipitating a naval arms race.

The Liberals gain a landslide victory in the general election.

1907 Britain and Russia reach an entente, forming the Triple Entente with France as a counterweight to the Triple Alliance of Germany, Italy and Austria-Hungary.

Riots break out at the first performance of J M Synge's *Playboy of the Western World* at the National Theatre, Dublin on 26 January and continue throughout the first week's performances. A mixture of strong language, sexuality and negative depicting of Irish peasantry contributed to the problem.

The National Library of Wales is established by royal charter. **Note:** In 1912 it became one of six British libraries entitled to claim a copy of all books, pamphlets or maps published in the British Isles.

Automobile Association patrols are introduced to warn members of police speed traps.

1908 The National Insurance Act is passed and is regarded as one of the foundations of modern social welfare in the United Kingdom.

American-born kite aviator Samuel Franklin Cody, performs the first powered flight in Britain. The flight, in the self-built British Army *Aeroplane No.1*, lasts only 27 seconds and it crashes on landing.

Herbert Henry Asquith replaces Henry Campbell-Bannerman as Prime Minister.

1909 The House of Lords rejects Lloyd-George's 'People's Budget', causing a constitutional crisis. Asquith calls a general election.

The *Daily Sketch* is founded in London. **Note:** The newspaper was merged into the *Daily Mail* in 1971.

1910 Liberals and Tories tie in the general election; Asquith's government depends on Labour and Irish Nationalist votes but a second election produces another hung parliament.

Edward VII dies, and is succeeded by his son George V who inherits a constitutional crisis.

1911 Electric escalators are installed for the first time at Earl's Court Station.

The Parliament Bill is passed by the Lords, under duress, settling the constitutional crisis.

The first British Airmail service begins.

The *Daily Herald* is founded. **Note:** The newspaper was merged into the *Sun* in 1964.

The Royal Flying Corps and Royal Naval Air Service are formed.

1912 RMS *Titanic* sinks on its maiden voyage, with the loss of 1517 lives. It becomes the first ship to use the newly adopted SOS distress signal (15 April).

British Royal Naval officer Robert Falcon Scott leads the Terra Nova expedition to the South Pole and reaches his destination on 17 January only to find that he has been preceded by Roald Amundsen's Norwegian party. On the return journey Scott and his four comrades, Edward Wilson, H R Bowers, Lawrence Oates and Edgar Evans, all perish; the final words of an ailing and despondent Oates before leaving his tent for the last time are 'I am just going outside and may be some time'.

1913 Suffragette Emily Davison throws herself under the King's horse at the Derby.

Holland I sinks and is lost about a mile and a half off Eddystone lighthouse while under tow to the scrapyard following decommissioning.

1914 Archduke Franz Ferdinand of Austria is assassinated by a Serb extremist in Sarajevo. Austria seeks to punish Serbia, but merely succeeds in dragging most of Europe into World War I. The British Expeditionary Force lands to support the French.

The First Battle of Ypres is a bloody draw and the trench system of warfare emerges on the Western Front.

The British fleet is defeated by the Germans at Coronel but victorious at the Falkland Islands.

HMS *Ark Royal* becomes the world's first aircraft carrier.

Ireland is pushed to the brink of civil war over Home Rule, but the onset of war diverts attention away from the crisis.

The *Post Sunday Special* is founded in Glasgow. **Note:** As the *Sunday Post* it became Scotland's leading Sunday newspaper.

1915 The British attempt to surprise Turkey at Gallipoli, but are repulsed.

A German U-Boat sinks the *Lusitania*, causing international outrage.

Edith Cavell is shot after accusations that she helped Allied soldiers escape from Brussels.

Sir William Henry Bragg uniquely shares the Nobel Prize in Physics with his son, William Lawrence Bragg, for their X-ray analysis of crystal structure.

The *Sunday Pictorial* is launched by Harold Harmsworth.

1916 Irish republicans stage the Easter Rising in Dublin, but the coup fails and the leaders are executed.

The British and German fleets fight the Battle of Jutland, which proves indecisive but the German fleet withdraws to Kiel and remains there.

Allied troops mount a major offensive on the Somme, which gains them some ground after five months of bloody battle.

David Lloyd George replaces Asquith as Prime Minister.

1917 The Orders of the Companions of Honour and of the British Empire are established.

The Balfour Declaration over a Jewish homeland in Palestine is issued.

America, Cuba and China enter the War on the Allied side.

The Allies are victorious at Arras and Passchendaele, although with much loss of life at the latter.

The Sopwith Camel goes into service with the Royal Flying Corps in July and the Vickers Vimy makes its first flight in November.

Tanks are used for the first time with any effect at Cambrai.

1918 Allied forces remove the Turks from the Middle East.

A German offensive is successful on the Western Front, but the Allies regroup and push them back, being victorious at the Marne and Amiens.

The Royal Flying Corps and Royal Naval Air Service combine to create the Royal Air Force.

An armistice is signed ending action in World War I.

In Britain, a Representation of the People Act gives the vote to all men over 21 and all women over 30.

The Irish general election (part of the UK general election at this time) sees the overwhelming defeat of the moderate nationalist Irish Parliamentary Party (IPP), which had dominated the Irish political landscape since the 1880s, and a landslide victory for the radical Sinn Féin party, which had never previously enjoyed such significant electoral success. London-born Constance Georgine, Countess Markiewicz née Gore-Booth is elected for the constituency of Dublin St Patrick's as one of 73 Sinn Féin MPs. This makes her the first woman elected to the British House of Commons. However, in line with Sinn Féin abstensionist policy, she would not take her seat in the House of Commons.

The *Sunday Express* is launched by Lord Beaverbrook.

1919 In India, British troops kill 379 demonstrators in the Amritsar Massacre.

American-born Nancy Witcher, Viscountess Astor née Langhorne becomes the first woman to take her seat as a serving MP representing Plymouth Sutton.

The Allies convene in Paris to settle the world map after World War I; the treaties of Versailles with Germany, Saint-Germain with Austria and Neuilly with Bulgaria are imposed.

The League of Nations is founded.

Irish republicans begin guerilla war against continued British rule, thus beginning the Irish War of Independence.

British aviators Alcock and Brown become the first men to fly the Atlantic non-stop (see the Derrygimlagh bog entry in Galway).

1920 Twelve people, commonly referred to as the 'Cairo Gang' and including British Army officers, Royal Irish Constabulary officers and a civilian informant, are assassinated on the morning of 21 November by the IRA in a planned series of simultaneous early morning strikes engineered by Michael Collins. Later that afternoon, British forces open fire on the crowd at a Gaelic football match at Croke Park, Dublin, killing 14 civilians, including the captain of the Tipperary football team, Michael Hogan. The same evening there are scattered shootings in the city streets, and three Irish prisoners in Dublin Castle are killed by their British captors under suspicious circumstances. The day is referred to as 'Bloody Sunday'.

1921 The partition of Ireland between the northeastern six counties and the rest of Ireland takes place on 3 May under a British parliamentary act – the Government of Ireland Act 1920. The consent of the Irish people is neither sought nor freely given. Britain and Irish republicans reach an accord; Northern Ireland is granted its own parliament with Sir James Craig as Prime Minister. Irish Teachta Dála (members of the Irish parliament) and Senators are required to take an oath of allegiance, in order to take their seats in Dáil Éireann (the Chamber of Deputies) and Seanad Éireann (the Irish Senate). **Note:** Although the oath was sworn as an allegiance to uphold the Constitution of the Irish Free State, the additional wording 'and that I will be faithful to H M King George V, his heirs and successors' was seen by the Irish people as an allegiance to the British king.

1922 The IRA declares civil war against the government in Dublin and assassinates Michael Collins on 22 August. The Irish Free State is established on 6 December; however, the Parliament of Northern Ireland exercises its right to opt out of the new Dominion the following day. The Royal Irish Constabulary is disbanded and replaced by two new police forces, the Garda Síochána (Guardians of the Peace) patrolling the Irish Free State and the Royal Ulster Constabulary patrolling Northern Ireland, which remains in the United Kingdom. **Note:** The RUC was replaced after the Good Friday Agreement of 1998 by the Police Service of Northern Ireland.

The BBC begins its radio broadcasts.

Howard Carter opens Tutankhamun's tomb.

The Conservatives withdraw from the coalition government, bringing down Lloyd George. Bonar Law becomes Prime Minister.

1923 W B Yeats becomes the first Irish Nobel Laureate (Literature).

The Railways Act 1921 comes into effect on 1 January, effectively forcing the amalgamation of the 123 separate companies, subject to the Act, into four great companies, the London & North Eastern Railway, the London, Midland & Scottish Railway and the Southern Railway, while the Great Western, apart from absorbing the smaller Welsh companies and other odds and ends within its territory, carries on much as before. **Note:** This Act is universally referred to as 'The Grouping'. A similar amalgamation took place in 1925 in post-partition Ireland, where all railways lying wholly within the Republic were incorporated into the Great Southern Railway, later CIE.

1924 After a general election produces a hung parliament, Ramsay MacDonald forms the first Labour government in Britain; he is defeated by Stanley Baldwin in a subsequent election, in which the Conservatives are helped by the forged Zinoviev Letter.

Red Splash wins the first running of the Cheltenham Gold Cup.

1925 Plaid Genedlaethol Cymru (National Party of Wales) is founded on 5 August by members of Byddin Ymreolwyr Cymru (The Welsh Home Rule Army) and Y Mudiad Cymreig (The Welsh Movement), its main aim to promote Welsh as the nation's first language. **Note:** By 1932 the main aim of Plaid Cymru was for home rule.

The Dublin Metropolitan Police Force is disbanded and incorporated into the Garda Síochána.

George Bernard Shaw wins the Nobel Prize for Literature.

1926 The General Strike, in support of the miners, is called in Britain, but fails to achieve much.

Fianna Fáil is founded in the La Scala Theatre, O'Connell Street, Dublin. The Republican Party's principal aim is for the unity of the island and a commitment to the historic principles of European republican philosophy, namely liberty, equality and fraternity. **Note:** Fianna Fáil is traditionally translated into English as Soldiers of Destiny, although a literal translation is Soldiers of Fál, a pre-Christian personification of Ireland.

John Logie Baird develops television.

The future Queen Elizabeth II is born at 17 Bruton Street, Mayfair, the first child of Prince Albert, Duke of York, and Elizabeth, Duchess of York.

Riots break out at Dublin's Abbey Theatre during a performance of Sean O'Casey's play *The Plough and The Stars*, because of the play's anti-heroic treatment of the 1916 Easter Rising. The theatre's founder, W B Yeats, stands up in front of the audience to begin a speech 'You have disgraced yourselves again . . .' and quickly feels the leather of a flying boot around his head.

1927 The Irish pound comes into existence as a separate currency from the British pound, although the terms of the Irish Currency Act oblige the Irish currency commissioners to redeem Irish pounds on a fixed 1:1 basis.

Blaris wins the first running of the Champion Hurdle at Cheltenham.

Entry Badge wins the first English Greyhound Derby at the White City.

USA beat Great Britain in the inaugural Ryder Cup gold competition.

1928 Scottish biologist and pharmacologist Alexander Fleming discovers penicillin, the world's first antibiotic. **Note:** Fleming shared the Nobel Prize in Physiology or Medicine in 1945 for this discovery.

In Britain, all women receive the vote.

The Gresley Pacific No. 4472 *Flying Scotsman* achieves the first scientifically authenticated 100mph (160km/h) on a British railway.

1929 Labour wins a general election for the first time and Ramsay MacDonald returns to office as Prime Minister.

Traffic lights are standardised by the Ministry of Transport. As on the railways, red signals stop and green go; however an amber light warns of a coming change.

1930 The Youth Hostels Association is founded.

Amy Johnson makes the first solo flight to Australia by a woman.

The *R101* airship crashes and burns.

Her Royal Highness Princess Margaret Rose of York is born on 21 August at Glamis Castle, Angus.

1931 Oswald Mosley leaves the Labour Party and forms the short-lived New Party.

Ramsay MacDonald forms a National Government to deal with the deteriorating economic situation, but the Labour Party mostly splits from him.

The Invergordon Mutiny over pay cuts occurs.

The Statute of Westminster defines dominion statutes and creates the Commonwealth.

The first edition of the Highway Code is published, with a price of 1d.

1932 The First Fianna Fáil government, led by Eamon de Valera, is elected. The controversial Irish Oath of Allegiance is abolished.

Iraq ceases to be a British mandate.

Mosley founds the British Union of Fascists.

John Galsworthy wins the Nobel Prize for Literature.

1933 Fine Gael (Family of the Irish) is founded following the merger of its parent party Cumann na nGaedhael, the Centre Party and the Army Comrades Association, popularly known as the 'Blueshirts'.

The England cricket team come in for severe criticism following skipper Douglas Jardine's 'leg theory' restricting scoring strokes for opposition batsmen. The Australian tour is dubbed the 'Bodyline' series after England's victory in the third Test at Adelaide where several Australian cricketers were hit by bouncers from Harold Larwood.

1934 The Scottish National Party (G. Pàrtaidh Nàiseanta na h-Alba) is formed from the merger of the National Party of Scotland and the Scottish Party; its aim is to achieve Scottish independence.

Cats' eyes, an innovative method of lighting the way along roads in the dark, are patented by Percy Shaw. **Note:** Within a year Halifax-born Percy Shaw (1890–1976) could witness his invention on numerous highways throughout Britain.

1935 Alcoholics Anonymous is established.

British scientist Sir James Chadwick is awarded the Nobel Prize for Physics for his discovery of the neutron.

Stanley Baldwin replaces Ramsay MacDonald as Prime Minister.

The United Kingdom driving test is introduced by Transport Minister Isaac Leslie Hore-Belisha, as enacted in the Road Traffic Act 1934. **Note:** Originally the test was voluntary, Mr J Beene becoming the first person to pass, at a cost of 7s 6d, although by 1 June it was made compulsory for all licence-holders who started driving on or after 1 April 1934. In the first year approximately 246,000 candidates applied and the pass rate was 63 per cent.

1936 George V dies. His son Edward VIII succeeds him but abdicates in favour of his brother George VI after falling in love with Wallis Simpson.

The Supermarine Spitfire, designed by R J Mitchell, makes its first flight piloted by Mutt Summers.

The Crystal Palace, designed by Joseph Paxton for the Great Exhibition, and now situated at Sydenham, burns down.

Television broadcasts start in Britain, from Alexandra Palace. **Note:** Although a regular service by the BBC began in 1936, experimental broadcasts started in 1932.

Two hundred marchers, including local MP Ellen Wilkinson, known as 'Red Ellen', walk from the town of Jarrow to London to protest against unemployment and poverty in the North East; no direct remedial action is taken although they are given £1 each to catch the train back from London.

Daphne Watson from Ferndown in Dorset becomes Britain's first air hostess.

Aer Loingeas (Aer Lingus = Air Fleet) is founded in Dublin. Its first service, using a six-seater De Havilland 84 Dragon (registration EI-ABI) biplane named *Iolar* (Eagle), begins between Baldonnel Airfield in Dublin and Whitchurch in Bristol, England. **Note:** By 1959 Aer Lingus had established itself as the national airline of Ireland.

1937 The British monarch is replaced as head of state of the Irish Free State by an elected president. Under the new constitution the Irish Free State's name is changed to Éire (Ireland).

The Peel Commission on Palestine proposes partition into Arab and Jewish states with a British mandate for Jerusalem and Bethlehem.

The *Morning Post* is merged into the *Daily Telegraph*.

Neville Chamberlain replaces Stanley Baldwin as British Prime Minister.

1938 Britain drops the Peel proposals on Palestine, prompting terrorist attacks in the area.

The Spitfire goes into RAF service.

The Sudeten Germans demand secession from Czechoslovakia; Britain and France appease Hitler at Munich and allow this, to much public disgust.

Arabs seize Bethlehem and Jerusalem, but the British retake them.

During a series of scientific tests to ascertain the upper limits of the performance of the vacuum brake, the brand-new A4 Pacific No. 4468 *Mallard*, hauling a train which includes the LNER's dynamometer car, which is fitted with apparatus to monitor all aspects of the locomotive's performance, is given her head on the long downhill stretch from Stoke summit towards Peterborough, and reaches a speed of 126.3 mph (203.3 km/h), a record for steam traction. **Note:** This record can be expected to stand for all time unless a steam train is designed specifically to improve the record.

1939 After Poland is invaded by Germany and Russia, Britain declares war on Germany on 3 September. Conscription is introduced for able-bodied men over 18 not working down the mines or in armament or aircraft factories or shipbuilding yards. The British Royal Navy battleship HMS *Royal Oak* is torpedoed by the German submarine U-47 while anchored at Scapa Flow, Orkney, with the loss of 833 lives.

1940 Allied troops are evacuated at Dunkirk.

Italy declares war on Britain and France.

The British destroy the French fleet at Mers-el-Kebir to prevent it falling into Vichy hands.

A German aerial assault on Britain is repulsed (the Battle of Britain).

Winston Churchill replaces Chamberlain as Prime Minister.

The Home Guard is founded.

1941 British troops help the Abyssinians expel the Italians; Haile Selassie is restored to his throne.

Iran is invaded by Britain and Russia; Reza Shah abdicates in favour of his pro-Allied son Muhammad Reza.

Adolf Hitler's deputy, Rudolf Hess, parachutes over Renfrewshire, Scotland and lands (breaking his ankle) at Floors Farm near Eaglesham, where he is soon arrested (10 May).

1942 Rudolf Hess is imprisoned in the Tower of London for four days. **Note:** RAF Wing Commander George Salaman was placed in the same cell as Hess, acting undercover as a Luftwaffe officer. Although acting covertly as a spy, Salaman remains the last Englishman to be locked in the Tower.

General Bernard Montgomery and the Eighth Army are successful at El Alamein.

1943 The Allies drive the Germans from North Africa and cross into Sicily and Italy.

The first British jet fighter, the Gloster Meteor, makes its maiden flight.

Churchill, Roosevelt and De Gaulle meet at Casablanca in January to discuss war plans and Churchill, Stalin and Roosevelt hold a similar meeting at Teheran in November.

1944 The Allies land at Anzio and take Rome.

The D-Day landings provide the springboard for the reconquest of France.

North Burma is retaken by the British.

1945 Burma is recaptured by the British.
Germany surrenders to the Allies.
Churchill, Truman and Stalin meet at Potsdam to consider the future.
Attlee replaces Churchill after a Labour landslide at the general election.
The SNP wins its first parliamentary seat, at the Motherwell by-election in April, but Dr Robert McIntyre MP loses the seat at the general election three months later.

1946 The United Nations convenes in London, as the League of Nations is formally wound up.
Irish-American traitor William Joyce, better known as 'Lord Haw Haw', is hanged for high treason. **Note:** His was the last execution for this offence.

1947 The Palestine question is passed to the United Nations for resolution after British partition proposals are rejected there.
India, Pakistan and Burma become independent states.
The coal-mining industry is nationalised.

1948 The British leave Palestine once their mandate expires.
The National Health Service is established by minister of Health, Aneurin Bevan. **Note:** In Northern Ireland the service is referred to as Health and Social Care (HSC).
The railways are nationalised on 1 January and electricity on 1 April, establishing a British Electricity Authority and 15 Area Electricity Boards.

1949 The Republic of Ireland becomes an independent state without the Commonwealth.
National Service is introduced for men between the ages of 18 and 26. **Note:** The term was initially for 18 months but increased to two years in 1950.
The British De Havilland Comet, the world's first jet airliner, makes its maiden flight in July.
The Gas Act 1948 is implemented in May. **Note:** The act nationalised the UK gas industry and 1062 privately owned and municipal gas companies were merged into 12 Area Gas Boards, each a separate body with its own management structure.

1950 The world's worst air crash occurs on 12 March; 80 are killed when an Avro Tudor carrying rugby fans crashes in a field near Cardiff.
Bertrand Russell wins the Nobel Prize for Literature.

1951 The spies Burgess and Maclean flee to Moscow.
A general election makes Churchill Prime Minister for the second time.
Englishman John Cockroft and Ernest Walton, from Abbeyside, County Waterford, are jointly awarded the Nobel Prize for Physics for their atomic nuclei research at Cambridge University.

1952 George VI dies, and is succeeded by his daughter Elizabeth II.
Jomo Kenyatta heads the Mau Mau resistance to drive the British from Kenya.
Britain tests an atomic bomb in the Monte Bello islands, off the northwest coast of Australia.

1953 Hillary and Tensing achieve the first successful ascent of Mount Everest.
Winston Churchill is knighted and later in the year wins the Nobel Prize for Literature.

1954 Roger Bannister runs the first four-minute mile at Iffley Road, Oxford.
Rationing ends on 4 July with meat the final product to regain unrestricted sale.

1955 Churchill resigns as Prime Minister, and is replaced by Anthony Eden.
Ruth Ellis is hanged at London's Holloway Prison for the murder of David Blakely. **Note:** Ellis was the fifteenth and last woman to be executed in Great Britain in the 20th century.
Cardiff is chosen as the capital of Wales.
The Independent Television Authority provides a second British station, ITV, also known as Channel 3, to compete with the BBC.

1956 Nasser nationalises the Suez Canal.
Israel invades the Sinai, encouraged by Britain and France who send troops to the Suez Canal to 'protect' it. Under international pressure, they withdraw when UN forces arrive.
Premium Bonds are introduced by Chancellor of the Exchequer Harold Macmillan.

1957 Eden resigns as Prime Minister after the Suez fiasco, and is succeeded by Macmillan. During a Conservative rally in Bradford, Macmillan utters the immortal words 'Let us be frank about it. Most of our people have never had it so good.'
Britain tests its first hydrogen bomb in the Pacific.

1958 Frederick Sanger wins the Nobel Prize for Chemistry for his determination of the structure of the insulin molecule.

1959 Singapore gains independence under Prime Minister Lee Kuan Yew.
Several of the so-called 'Busby Babes' are killed following an air crash on a snow-covered Munich runway.
Eamon de Valera resigns as leader of Fianna Fáil and is replaced by Seán Lemass TD.
The *Manchester Guardian* becomes a national newspaper and is renamed the *Guardian*.

1960 The farthing, last minted in 1956, ceases to be legal tender.
Princess Margaret marries the photographer Antony Armstrong-Jones at Westminster Abbey (6 May).
MOT testing is introduced for cars over ten years old.
National Service is abolished. **Note:** The last recruits passed out in 1962.

1961 South Africa leaves the Commonwealth.
Antony Armstrong-Jones is created Earl of Snowdon and Viscount Linley of Nymans in the County of Sussex.
RTÉ One (Irish: RTÉ a hAon) is launched and operated by Irish state broadcaster Radio Telefís Éireann.
The *Sunday Telegraph* is launched.

1962 Harold Macmillan sacks seven members of his cabinet on 27 November. **Note:** Jeremy Thorpe said of this 'Night of the Long Knives': 'Greater love hath no man than this, that he lay down his friends for his life.'
The world's first hovercraft passenger service began across the estuary of the River Dee between Rhyl and Wallasey.
A smallpox outbreak in Yorkshire kills several people.
Stirling Moss sustains serious head injuries after crashing at Goodwood in a Lotus.

The *Sunday Times* becomes the first newspaper to publish a colour supplement.

1963 A nuclear test ban treaty is signed by the US, USSR and Britain.

Kim Philby flees to Moscow after his espionage activities are uncovered.

A £2.6m train robbery is carried out in Buckinghamshire.

The Profumo crisis develops in Britain, weakening Macmillan's government.

Macmillan resigns through ill health, and is replaced by Alec Douglas-Home.

Doctor Beeching's report initiates harsh cuts in the British railway system.

Twenty-one-year-old Henry Burnett is executed at Craiginches Prison in Aberdeen for the murder of seaman Thomas Guyan. **Note:** This was the last hanging in Scotland.

Henry Cooper knocks down Cassius Clay in the fourth round of their heavyweight clash at Wembley but Clay recovers and stops Cooper in the fifth.

The *Sunday Pictorial* is relaunched as the *Sunday Mirror.*

1964 Peter Anthony Allen (at Walton Prison Liverpool) and Gwynne Owen Evans – real name John Robson Walby – (at Strangeways Prison Manchester) are hanged simultaneously at 8 am. **Note:** These executions were the last in Britain before Parliament agreed to abolish capital punishment for an experimental period of five years. At the end of the period, 18 December 1969, Parliament confirmed its decision although hanging was still retained as a punishment for treason and piracy unyil 1998.

The *Sun* newspaper is launched. **Note:** The first tabloid edition appeared on 17 November 1969, featuring the paper's first 'Page Three' girl, Ulla Lindstrom.

Harold Wilson replaces Douglas-Home as Prime Minister.

The Labour government creates a Secretary of State for Wales; James Griffiths becomes the first incumbent.

Britain's third television station is launched, BBC 2.

1965 Rhodesia declares independence from Britain; sanctions are imposed on it as an illegal state.

1966 Harold Wilson and Ian Smith discuss the Rhodesia affair on HMS *Tiger*, but the talks come to nothing.

Gwynfor Evans gains the first-ever seat in Parliament for Plaid Cymru when he wins the Carmarthen by-election in July.

England win the football World Cup, defeating West Germany 4–2.

144 people, 116 of them children, are killed when a tip of coal waste slides onto the village of Aberfan in South Wales.

1967 Winnie Ewing gains victory for the Scottish National Party in the Hamilton by-election to elevate Scottish independence and devolution to the top of the agenda in Scottish politics.

Colour television begins in Britain.

The Ministry of Transport introduces drink drive limits, compulsory fitting of front seat belts in new cars and MOT tests for cars over three years old.

Merched y Wawr (Daughters of the Dawn), an organisation for women similar to the Women's Institute, is established in Wales; its activities are conducted through the medium of Welsh.

1968 As part of future plans for Britain to decimalise its currency, 5p and 10p coins are introduced in April, and are the same size, composition and value as the shillings and florins they replace.

1969 Civil unrest in Northern Ireland spills over into fighting and terrorism; troops are sent to maintain order. The 'Provisional Army Council' is formed in December, when an IRA Convention votes to recognise the Parliaments of Northern Ireland, the Republic of Ireland and the United Kingdom.

Irish writer Samuel Beckett is awarded the Nobel Prize for Literature.

The old halfpenny (31 July) and half-crown (31 December) are withdrawn from circulation while the 50p piece is introduced in October.

In February, the Boeing 747 makes its maiden flight and in April the first UK-built Concorde flies from Filton in Bristol to RAF Fairford in Gloucestershire, piloted by Brian Trubshaw.

1970 After the Annual Conference (Ard Fheis) of Sinn Féin in January, the party is split between Republicans willing to campaign for home rule by peaceful means and those who feel a militant approach is justifiable and necessary. The Provisional IRA develops from the Provisional Army Council with its political wing, renamed Provisional Sinn Féin. Cathal Goulding now becomes chief of staff of the Official IRA; its political wing renamed Official Sinn Féin.

The ten-shilling note is withdrawn in November.

The *Irish Post* is founded by Breandán Mac Lua and Tony Beatty as a newspaper for the Irish community in Britain.

Ted Heath replaces Harold Wilson as Prime Minister.

1971 The new $^1/_2$p, 1p and 2p coins are introduced on 15 February to give Britain and Ireland a totally decimalised currency; the transition day is referred to as D-Day. In August the old penny (1d) and threepenny bits (3d) are withdrawn from circulation.

Internment without trial is introduced in Northern Ireland, British troops rounding up hundreds of nationalists (and a handful of loyalists) in dawn raids.

1972 Twenty-seven civil rights protesters are shot by members of the 1st Battalion of the British Parachute Regiment during a Northern Ireland Civil Rights Association march in the Bogside area of Londonderry. Thirteen people, including seven teenagers, die. The events of 30 January are dubbed 'Bloody Sunday'. **Note:** The death of another person $4^1/_2$ months later has been attributed to the injuries he received on the day. Three weeks after Bloody Sunday the Official IRA launched its first attack in England when it detonated a bomb hidden in a Ford Cortina positioned outside the officers' mess of the Parachute Regiment, killing seven civilians. The attack led to severe criticism as none of the intended targets were present and one of the victims was an Irish Roman Catholic priest. A ceasefire was agreed in June although the larger, and more militant, Provisional IRA continued to attack targets in Britain. In November Noel Jenkinson was convicted of the murders. Direct rule from London was imposed in Northern Ireland for the next 27 years.

The Conservative government in Westminster creates a Secretary of State for Northern Ireland; William Whitelaw becomes the first incumbent.

The British Airways Board takes over BOAC, BEA and their subsidiaries.

1973 Britain, Ireland and Denmark join the EEC.

The Cod War between Britain and Iceland develops.

A coal strike in Britain forces the government to declare a three-day working week.

Crash helmets for motorcyclists become compulsory.

Princess Anne and Mark Phillips are married at Westminster Abbey.

1974 IRA volunteer Michael Gaughan dies on hunger strike in an English Prison.

Harold Wilson beats Heath in a general election to form his second administration.

British scientists Sir Martin Ryle and Antony Hewish are awarded the Nobel Prize for Physics for their work in radio astronomy.

1976 The British Aircraft Corporation's Concorde, piloted by Captain Norman Todd, makes its first commercial flight on 21 January, from London to Bahrain.

Harold Wilson resigns as Prime Minister and is succeeded by James Callaghan.

Ireland introduces its own Irish Mint, a division of the Central Bank of Ireland, which is located in Sandyford, Dún Laoghaire-Rathdown.

1977 Freddie Laker launches his Skytrain service from London to New York.

1978 Princess Margaret and Lord Snowdon divorce.

RTÉ Two (Irish: RTÉ a Dó) is launched as Ireland's second terrestrial television station.

The *Daily Star* is founded by United Newspapers (Express Group).

1979 Margaret Thatcher comes to power in Britain as the first female Prime Minister.

Charles J Haughey succeeds Jack Lynch as Taoiseach and Leader of Fianna Fáil.

Lord Mountbatten is assassinated by the IRA.

Irish obligations to the European Monetary System force them to break the historic link with sterling and implement an exchange rate.

1980 The SAS retake the Iranian Embassy in London, which had been taken by opponents of the Islamic regime.

Gloucestershire-born Frederick Sanger wins his second Nobel Prize for Chemistry for his research into the chemical analysis of DNA structure.

The old sixpence (6d), worth exactly $2^1/_2$p, is officially withdrawn from circulation.

Michael Foot replaces James Callaghan as leader of the Labour Party.

1981 Bobby Sands, an Irish Provisional Irish Republican Army volunteer and MP for Fermanagh and South Tyrone in the UK Parliament, dies while on hunger strike at HM Prison Maze (also known as Long Kesh).

Prince Charles and Lady Diana Spencer are married at St Paul's Cathedral.

1982 Argentina invades the Falklands, but Britain sends a task force and retakes them; the military junta in Argentina falls as a result of this defeat.

The *Mary Rose* is raised by a team led by the Royal Engineers, and put upright in a dry dock with a temperature of 2–6°C and a relative humidity of 95 per cent.

The word 'new' in 'new penny' or 'new pence' is removed from the inscriptions on British coins. A new 20p coin is now introduced.

Holland 1, the Royal Navy submarine lost in 1913, is raised and after preservation is displayed in open air at the Royal Navy Submarine Museum, Gosport.

A fourth television station is launched in Britain, Channel 4.

The *Mail on Sunday* is launched.

1983 Legislation is introduced to make wearing of front seat belts compulsory.

British novelist William Golding is awarded the Nobel Prize for Literature.

Neil Kinnock replaces Michael Foot as leader of the Labour Party.

1984 Britain agrees to hand Hong Kong back to China in 1997 on the expiration of the lease on the New Territories.

The office of Minister for Posts and Telegraphs, established in 1924, is abolished in Ireland. The Department of Posts & Telegraphs (P&T) is now split between An Post, the State-owned provider of postal services, and Telecom Éireann.

York Minster catches fire shortly after the modernist David Jenkins is enthroned as Bishop of Durham.

The new $^1/_2$p is withdrawn from circulation.

1985 RMS *Titanic* is located at a depth of $2^1/_2$ miles (4km), slightly more than 370 miles (595km) southeast of Mistaken Point, Newfoundland, the stern section lying 1970ft (600m) from the bow section and facing in the opposite direction.

Two football-related incidents in May devastate the game. On 11 May a fire in the main stand at Bradford City kills at least 52 people and on 29 May rampaging Liverpool fans crush Italian and Belgian supporters at the Heysel Stadium, causing 39 deaths.

1986 The London Stock Exchange is computerised in the 'big bang'.

Two national newspapers are established this year: *Today*, founded by Eddie Shah, launched on 4 March, and the *Independent*, launched on 7 October. **Note:** *Today* ceased publication on 16 November 1995.

1987 Terry Waite is taken hostage in Lebanon while seeking to free others.

The *Herald of Free Enterprise* capsizes outside Zeebrugge.

A great storm crosses southern England, causing severe damage.

An escalator catches fire at King's Cross; 31 die in the ensuing conflagration.

1988 A terrorist bomb brings down a Pan-Am 747 over Lockerbie in Scotland.

Scotland on Sunday is launched as a sister paper to the *Scotsman*.

1989 Seat belt laws are applied to rear seat child passengers.

On 12 July, the Abbey National Building Society becomes the first UK building society to demutualise and become a public limited company – Abbey National plc.

1990 The premiership of Mrs Thatcher collapses; John Major is elected to replace her.

Mary Therese Winifred Robinson (Irish: Máire Mhic Róibín), born 21 May 1944, becomes the seventh, and first female, President of Ireland. As an Independent candidate nominated by the Labour Party, the Workers Party of

Ireland and independent senators, Robinson also becomes the first elected president in the office's history not to have the support of Fianna Fáil.
A smaller 5p coin is introduced into Britain.
The *Independent on Sunday* is launched.

1991 Rear seat belt laws are applied to all rear seat passengers.

1992 Following Labour's fourth successive defeat at a general election, Neil Kinnock resigns as leader and John Smith is elected Labour leader.
Albert Reynolds succeeds Charles Haughey as Taoiseach and leader of Fianna Fáil.
The first fixed site speed cameras are introduced on Britain's roads.
A smaller 10p coin is introduced into Britain.
In March it is announced that the Queen's second son, Prince Andrew, will separate from his wife Sarah; in April, the Queen's daughter, Princess Anne, divorces her husband Captain Mark Phillips; in November one of the Queen's homes, Windsor Castle, catches fire and in December the separation of Prince Charles and his wife Diana is announced. The Queen consequently dubs 1992 her 'annus horribilis'.

1993 The Isle of Man abolish the use of the birch as a legal method of corporal punishment. **Note:** The last birching on the island was in 1976 and subsequent sentences were commuted, the European Court of Human rights condemning the use of the birch as 'cruel and unusual'.
The Conservative government passes the Welsh Language Act and sets up the Welsh Language Board to promote the use of Welsh. It also gives Welsh speakers the right to speak Welsh in court proceedings under all circumstances, and obliges all organisations in the public sector providing services to the Welsh public to treat Welsh and English on an equal basis.

1994 John Smith dies of a heart attack (12 May) and Margaret Beckett becomes temporary leader of the Labour Party. Tony Blair subsequently becomes leader in July.
Bertie Ahern succeeds Albert Reynolds as Taoiseach and leader of Fianna Fáil. The IRA call a historic ceasefire.

1995 The first Boeing 777 begins operations at Heathrow (United Airlines).
Irish poet Seamus Heaney is awarded the Nobel Prize for Literature.

1996 A separate written theory test is introduced into the UK driving test, replacing questions asked about the Highway Code (1 July).

1997 Diana, Princess of Wales, is killed in a car crash.
Mary Patricia McAleese (Irish: Máire Pádraigín Bean Mhic Ghiolla Íosa), born 27 June 1951, becomes the eighth, and second female, President of Ireland, replacing Mary Robinson. The Belfast-born Fianna Fáil representative is the first President to come from Northern Ireland.
Labour win a landslide victory in the general election. Tony Blair becomes Prime Minister. William Hague replaces John Major as leader of the Conservative Party.
British Gas is demerged to form separate companies and is rebranded as Centrica.
A fifth terrestrial television channel is launched in Great Britain, Channel 5. **Note:** the station rebranded itself as Five in 2002.
A smaller 50p coin is introduced into Britain.

1998 Irish and UK governments sign the Good Friday Agreement in Belfast on 10 April. **Note:** The peace agreement's main provisions included the establishment of a Northern Ireland Assembly with devolved legislative powers; a commitment by all parties to use 'exclusively peaceful and democratic means'; and abolition of the Republic of Ireland's territorial claim to Northern Ireland.
On 31 December the exchange rate between the Irish pound and its new currency of the euro became fixed at 1 = IR£0.787564. At the same time the exchange rate between pounds and euros became GB£1 = 1.42210, making GB£1 = IR£1.12. By the same token, GB£1 is now worth about IR£1.287.

1999 As a result of the Good Friday Agreement, a new coalition government is formed, with the British government formally transferring governing power to the Northern Irish parliament. David Trimble, the Protestant leader of the Ulster Unionist Party (UUP) and winner of the 1998 Nobel Peace Prize, becomes First Minister. **Note:** The parliament comprises 108 members who are known as Members of the Legislative Assembly, or MLAs. The government has been suspended four times since then, the longest suspension being from 14 October 2002 until 7 May 2007.
The first meeting of the new Scottish Parliament takes place on 12 May and on 1 July power is transferred from Westminster to the new Parliament, informally referred to as 'Holyrood'. Donald Dewar becomes First Minister of Scotland. **Note:** The Scottish Parliament currently has 129 members, known as Members of the Scottish Parliament (MSPs). Members are elected for four-year terms.
The first meeting of the National Assembly for Wales (Welsh: Cynulliad Cenedlaethol Cymru) takes place on 12 May. Alun Michael becomes First Minister for Wales. **Note:** The Assembly comprises 60 members, who are known as Assembly Members, or AMs (Welsh: Aelod y Cynulliad), elected for four-year terms.
The Australian people vote to 're-elect' the Queen as their head of state.
Cardinal Basil Hume, Archbishop of Westminster, dies.
Telecom Éireann, the leading Irish telecommunications provider, is privatised and rebranded as Eircom.

2000 Following the resignation of Alun Michael, Labour Party MP Rhodri Morgan becomes First Minister for Wales (17 February).
Donald Dewar dies and is replaced as First Minister of Scotland by Henry McLeish (27 October).

2001 Henry McLeish resigns as First Minister of Scotland and is replaced by Jack McConnell (22 November).

2002 On 1 January Ireland adopts the euro as its new currency; on 9 February the Irish pound is withdrawn from circulation.
Princess Margaret dies (9 February); her mother, Her Majesty Queen Elizabeth the Queen Mother, dies, aged 101, soon after (31 March).
In a BBC poll of the '100 Greatest Britons', Sir Winston Churchill is named the winner (22 August).
The British government again assumes direct rule of Northern Ireland, after the Unionists threaten to quit the Northern Ireland Assembly in protest of suspected spying activity by the IRA (14 October).

2003 Iain Duncan Smith loses a confidence vote by 75 votes to 90 in October and is forced to resign as leader of the Conservative Party. Michael Howard becomes temporary leader in November.

Concorde ends its 27 years of passenger flight.

2004 Ireland becomes the first country in Europe to impose an outright ban on smoking in public places (12 April).

2005 The Health Service Executive (HSE) is introduced in Ireland, replacing the ten regional Health Boards (1 January).

Twenty-eight-year-old Ellen MacArthur completes a non-stop circumnavigation in 71 days 14 hours 18 minutes and 33 seconds, to smash the record for sailing non-stop around the world by more than a day in her 75ft (23m) long trimaran *B & Q* (7 February).

The Prince of Wales marries Camilla Parker Bowles in a civil wedding at Windsor's Guildhall (9 April).

The IRA announces it will unequivocally relinquish violence, give up its arms, and pursue its aims exclusively through political means (28 July).

Dolores McNamara, a mother of six from Garryowen, near Limerick, collects almost £80m on the Euromillions lottery (4 August).

Harold Pinter, the playwright and poet, is awarded the Nobel Prize for Literature (13 October).

Thousands of pubs and clubs in England and Wales take advantage of new licensing laws whereby every business selling hot food after 11pm, serving alcohol or putting on public entertainment is no longer required to obtain a new licence to do so (24 November).

David Cameron, 39, defeats David Davis by 134,446 votes to 64,398 in a postal ballot of party members to decide the Conservative Party leadership (6 December).

2006 £53 million is estimated to have been stolen from a security depot in Tonbridge, Kent, during Britain's biggest-ever armed robbery (22 February).

Smoking is banned in pubs, clubs and cafes in Scotland, the first such action in the United Kingdom (26 March). **Note:** Similar action is later taken in the other UK countries – Wales (2 April 2007), Northern Ireland (30 April 2007) and England (1 July 2007).

A 62-year-old woman, Dr Patricia Rashbrook, becomes Britain's oldest mother after giving birth to a 6lb 10oz son, JJ, following IVF treatment at the Royal Sussex County Hospital in Brighton (7 July).

The Independent Monitoring Commission (IMC) announces that the IRA has committed itself to a 'political path' and is not 'now engaged in terrorism' and 'has disbanded "military" structures'. Dublin and London increase pressure on the DUP to agree to share power with Sinn Féin (4 October).

2007 Following the multi-party talks, held in St Andrews, Fife, 11–13 October 2006, between the two governments and all the major parties in Northern Ireland, including the Democratic Unionist Party (DUP) and Sinn Féin, the Northern Ireland Assembly is restored (8 May).

Alex Salmond replaces Jack McConnell as First Minister of Scotland following the SNP's narrow victory over the Scottish Labour Party 47 seats to 46 (16 May).

Tony Blair stands down as Prime Minister and MP for Sedgefield to become a Middle East peace envoy. Gordon Brown replaces him as Prime Minister (27 June).

Queen Elizabeth II becomes Britain's oldest monarch, overtaking her great-great-grandmother, Queen Victoria, who died in 1901 aged 81 years and 243 days (20 December).

2008 British Chancellor of the Exchequer Alistair Darling announces the first nationalisation of a sizeable British bank in a quarter of a century as he places Northern Rock into public ownership in what he calls a 'temporary measure' (17 February).

Boris Johnson, 43, the Tory MP for Henley, polls 1,168,738 votes to Ken Livingstone's 1,028,966 to become the new Mayor of London (1 May).

Brian Cowen succeeds Bertie Ahern as Taoiseach and leader of Fianna Fáil (6 May).

The Queen bids farewell to the *QE2*, in Southampton, before it sets sail for its new life as a hotel in Dubai (2 June).

Ireland rejects the Lisbon Treaty with 53.4 per cent of voters declaring dissatisfaction at increased European Union integration (13 June).

The Church of England votes to allow the consecration of women bishops (7 July).

The Republic of Ireland, whose economy was nicknamed the Celtic Tiger during the boom years, becomes the first country using the euro to fall into recession (25 September). **Note:** The technical definition of recession is when a nation's economy shrinks for a second successive quarter.

2009 Two sappers from 38 Regiment Royal Engineers become the first soldiers to be killed in Northern Ireland for 12 years. The soldiers are gunned down outside the Massereene Barracks in Antrim. The Real IRA splinter group claim responsibility for the attack (7 March).

A policeman is shot and killed in Craigavon, south of Belfast, 32 miles (51km) from the Massereene Barracks (9 March).

MAJOR BATTLES ON BRITISH AND IRISH SOIL

Name, county and nearest grid reference	Conflict	Protagonists		Date	Details
Aberdeen (Aberdeen City, Grampian, NJ9305)	English Civil War (1st) (1642–6)	Royalists (James Graham, Marquess of Montrose)	Covenanters (Lord Burleigh)	13 September 1644	Royalist victory. Aberdeen sacked. Aka Justice Mills.
Adwalton Moor (West Yorkshire, SE2228)	English Civil War (1st) (1642–6)	Royalists (Earl of Newcastle)	Parliamentarians (Fernando Fairfax)	30 June 1643	Royalist victory. Parliamentarians foiled in attempt to prevent siege of Bradford. Parliamentarians in the North moved to secure help from the Scottish. Aka Adderton or Atherton Moor.
Alford (Aberdeenshire, Grampian, NJ5716)	English Civil War (1st) (1642–6)	Royalists (James Graham, Marquess of Montrose)	Covenanters (William Baillie/Earl Balcarres)	2 July 1645	Royalist victory. Covenanter army destroyed.
Alnwick (I) (Northumberland, NU1914)	Anglo-Scottish Wars: Scottish Raids (1093)	English (Richard Mowbray, Earl of Northumberland)	Scottish (Malcolm III Canmore)	13 November 1093	English victory. Malcolm Canmore and his eldest son Prince Edward both killed in surprise attack.
Alnwick (II) (Northumberland, NU1813)	Alliance against Henry II (1173–4)	English (Ranulf de Glanville)	Scottish (William I, The Lion)	13 July 1174	English victory. William captured and imprisoned in Falaise, Normandy until he agreed to the Treaty of Falaise.
Ancrum Moor (Scottish Borders, ST6127)	Anglo-Scottish Wars: The Rough Wooing (1545)	English (Sir Ralph Evers/ Sir Bryan Latoun)	Scottish (Archibald Douglas, Earl of Angus)	27 February 1545	Scottish victory. English marauding during the 'Rough Wooing'. Evers and Latoun killed.
Antrim (Antrim)	Irish Insurrection (1797–8)	Irish (Henry Joy McCracken)	Government (Clavering/ James Durham)	7 June 1798	Government victory. Insurgent attempt to capture Antrim beaten off and rebels dispersed. General amnesty issued saw the insurrection end in eastern Ulster. McCracken hanged.
Arklow (Wicklow)	Irish Insurrection (1797–8)	Irish (Anthony Perry/ Father Michael Murphy)	Government (Francis Needham)	9 June 1798	Government victory. Insurgents' attempt to capture Arklow failed; insurrection began to stutter.
Ashdown (Berkshire, SU5381, site disputed)	Viking invasions of England (796–991)	West Saxons (Aethelred I/ Alfred)	Vikings (Halfdan I/ Bagsecg)	8 January 871	West Saxon victory. Battle fought on Ridgeway Path. Danes retreated and Bagsecg killed.
Ashingdon (Essex, TQ8793)	Danish invasion of England (1016)	Saxons (Edmund Ironside)	Danes (Cnut)	18 October 1016	Danish victory. Edmund and Cnut concluded a peace treaty. Edmund died a month later leaving Cnut as sole king. Also spelled Assandun(e), Ashdon, Ashington or Assingdon.
Athenry (Galway)	Bruce invasion of Ireland (1315–18)	Irish (Felim O'Connor, King of Connaught)	Anglo-Irish (William de Burgh, Earl of Ulster)	10 August 1316	Anglo-Irish victory. Attempt by the Irish to regain control of Connaught thwarted. Many Irish chieftains slain including O'Connor.
Aughrim (Galway)	Jacobite Rising (1st) (1689–91)	Government (Godert de Ginkel)	Jacobites (Earl of Lucan/ Marquis de Saint-Ruth)	12 July 1691	Government victory. Bloodiest battle on Irish soil with over 7000 killed including Saint-Ruth. Jacobite army destroyed and Limerick captured. Treaty of Limerick followed.

Name, county and nearest grid reference	Conflict	Protagonists		Date	Details
Auldearn (Highland, NH916554)	English Civil War (1st) (1642–6)	Royalists (James Graham, Marquess of Montrose)	Covenanters (Sir John Urry)	9 May 1645	Royalist victory. Royalist MacDonalds helped to overcome Covenanter Campbells.
Ballina (Mayo)	Irish Insurrection (1797–8)	Irish/French	Government (Sir Thomas Chapman)	24 August 1798	French victory. Small French force defeated Ballina garrison.
Ballinamuck (Longford)	Irish Insurrection (1797–8)	Irish/French (General Joseph Humbert)	Government (Gerard Lake/ Robert Crauford)	8 September 1798	Government victory. Small French force belatedly sent in an attempt to support the rebellion was trapped after victory at Castlebar. General Humbert captured.
Ballynahinch (Down)	Irish Insurrection (1797–8)	Irish (Henry Monro)	Government (George Nugent)	12–13 June 1798	Government victory. Second northern rebellion defeated. Monro, a tailor, hanged outside his shop in Lisburn.
Bannockburn (Stirlingshire, NS8191)	Anglo-Scottish Wars: Scottish Wars of Independence (1286–1388)	English (Edward II)	Scottish (Robert the Bruce)	23–24 June 1314	Scottish victory. Smaller Scottish force defeated English army attempting to reach Stirling Castle. Robert the Bruce confirmed as king of Scotland.
Barnet (Hertfordshire, TQ2497)	Wars of the Roses (1455–87)	Lancastrians (Richard Neville, Earl of Warwick)	Yorkists (Edward IV)	14 April 1471	Yorkist victory. Warwick killed. Confusing battle fought in thick mist. Lancastrians killed in friendly fire incident led to calls of treachery and the rout of the Lancastrian army.
Basing House (Hampshire, SU662526)	English Civil War (1st) (1642–6)	Royalists (John Paulet, Marquis of Winchester)	Parliamentarians (Oliver Cromwell)	14 October 1645	Parliamentarian victory. After a defence lasting much of the war, Basing House, which housed many Royalist fugitives, was overwhelmed by Cromwell's artillery train. The house was ransacked, razed to the ground and many civilians put to the sword.
Benburb (Tyrone)	Irish Confederate War/ Eleven Years' War (1641–53)	Irish Confederates (Owen Roe O'Neill)	Covenanters (Robert Munro)	5 June 1646	Irish victory. Scottish Covenanter army destroyed by Irish Confederate army. Only Gaelic Irish field victory.
Berwick-upon-Tweed (Northumberland, NT9952)	Anglo-Scottish Wars: Scottish Wars of Independence (1286–1388)	English (Edward I)	Scottish (Sir William Douglas)	30 March 1296	English victory. Edward massacred the citizens of Berwick (up to 20,000 died).
Blore Heath (Staffordshire, SJ7135)	Wars of the Roses (1455–87)	Lancastrians (James Touchet, Lord Audley)	Yorkists (Richard Neville, Earl of Salisbury)	23 September 1459	Yorkist victory. Audley killed and larger Lancastrian army routed.
Boldon Hill (South Tyne & Wear, NZ3560)	English Civil War (1st) (1642–6)	Royalists (William Cavendish, Earl of Newcastle)	Scottish (Alexander Leslie, Earl of Leven)	24 March 1644	Inconclusive. A Scottish army invaded England under the terms of The Solemn League and Covenant of 1643. After this clash the Scots moved into Sunderland and the Royalists into Durham. The armies were to clash again at Marston Moor.
Books, The (Sligo)	Irish Clan Wars	O'Neills	O'Donnells	561	See Sligo. Aka Cul Dreimhne
Boroughbridge (North Yorkshire, SE3967)	English Baronial Wars: Anti-Despenser Alliance (1321–2)	Royal Army (Andrew Harcla, Sheriff of Carlisle)	Barons (Earl of Lancaster/ Earl of Hereford)	16 March 1322	Royal army victory. Lancaster captured and executed by order of Edward II. Hereford killed by a pikeman skewering him from below as he crossed the bridge.
Bosworth Field (Leicestershire, SK3899)	Wars of the Roses (1455–87)	Lancastrians	Yorkists	22 August 1485	See Leicestershire

Name, county and nearest grid reference	Conflict	Protagonists		Date	Details
Bothwell Bridge (South Lanarksihre, Strathclyde, NS7157)	Western Rebellion/ Covenanter Rising (1679)	Government (James Scott, Duke of Monmouth)	Covenanters (Robert Hamilton)	22 June 1679	Government victory. Fought at Hamilton on the outskirts of Glasgow, which the rebels had previously occupied. Covenanters routed and the rising crushed.
Boyne (Meath)	Jacobite Rising (1st) (1689–91)	Government (William III/ Friedrich Herman, Count Schomberg)	Jacobites (James II/Antoine de Caumont, Comte de Lauzun)	1 July 1690	Williamite victory. Probably largest and most significant battle fought on Irish soil. Jacobites, with French aid in finance and personnel, defeated. James fled to exile in France.
Braddock Down (Cornwall and the Scilly Isles, SX177631)	English Civil War (1st) (1642–6)	Royalists (Sir Ralph Hopton)	Parliamentarians (William Ruthin)	19 January 1643	Royalist victory. Helped establish Royalist control of Cornwall.
Bramham Moor (West Yorkshire, SE4341)	English Baronial Wars: Percy Rebellions (1403 and 1408)	Royal Army (Sir Thomas Rokeby, Sheriff of York)	Rebels (Henry Percy, Earl of Northumberland)	19 February 1408	Royal army victory. Rebel army routed and Northumberland killed. Henry IV position secured.
Brentford (London, TQ177177)	English Civil War (1st) (1642–6)	Royalists (Patrick Ruthven, Lord Forth)	Parliamentarians (Robert Devereux, Earl of Essex)	12 November 1642	Royalist victory. Royalist advance on London held up to allow Parliamentary reinforcements to arrive.
Bridge of Dee (Aberdeenshire, Grampian, NJ9203)	First Bishops' War (1639)	Royalists (James Gordon, Viscount Aboyne)	Covenanters (James Graham, Earl of Montrose)	18–19 June 1639	Covenanters claimed the bridge after an artillery bombardment brought down the gatehouse turret defended by the Royalists.
Bristol (Bristol, ST5872)	English Civil War (1st) (1642–6)	Royalists (Prince Rupert/ Prince Maurice)	Parliamentarians (Nathaniel Fiennes)	26 July 1643	Royalist victory. Royalists forced a breach and after some street fighting Fiennes accepted surrender terms and marched away. The fall of Bristol gave the King a much needed major port.
Broad Street (Berkshire)	Glorious Revolution (1688)	Jacobites (James II, Patrick Sarsfield)	Williamites (William of Orange)	9 December 1688	See Second Battle of Reading
Brunanburh (site unknown)	Viking invasions of England (796–991)	Saxons (Athelstan)	Norse, Scots and Irish Allies (Olaf Guthfrithsson/ Constantine II)	937	Saxon victory. Alliance of Norse, Scots and Irish decisively defeated. Confirmed England as the power in the British Isles with governance in the south. Aka Bruneswald, Wendune.
Calry Lough Gill (Sligo)	Irish Clan Wars	O'Conors (Rory, son of Cathal O'Conor)	O'Rourkes	1346	O'Connor victory. O'Rourke routed and his gallowglasses, Mac Buirrce and Mac Neill Cam, slain. O'Rourke pursued by O'Conor and the Clann-Donough and killed by Mulrony Mac Donough.
Cannington (Somerset)	Viking invasions of England (796–991)	Saxons (Ealdorman Odda)	Vikings (Ubbe Ragnarsson)	878	Odda and the English forces killed Ubbe and also captured a Danish War banner called '*Hrefn*' or The Raven.
Carbisdale (Highland, NH5694)	English Civil War (3rd) (1650–1)	Royalists (James Graham, Marquess of Montrose)	Covenanters (Archibald Strachan)	27 April 1650	Covenanter victory. Montrose landed at John o'Groats on 12 April with a small force recruited in Denmark and the Orkneys, but was surprised and defeated by a mobile Covenanter army. Montrose captured and executed after the battle.

MAJOR BATTLES ON BRITISH AND IRISH SOIL

Name, county and nearest grid reference	Conflict	Protagonists		Date	Details
Carham (Northumberland, NT8338)	British wars (410–1018)	Northumbrians (Earl Uhtred)	Scottish (Malcolm II)	1018	Scottish victory. Established the England/Scotland border on the Tweed.
Castlebar (Mayo)	Irish Insurrection (1797–8)	Irish/French (Joseph Humbert)	Government (Gerard Lake)	27 August 1798	French/Irish victory. A small French force defeated a larger British force. This humiliating defeat is known as 'the races of Castlebar'. Republic of Connacht proclaimed.
Cefn Carnedd (Powys or Shropshire)	Roman conquest of Britain (43–410)	British Tribes (Caractacus)	Romans (Ostorius Scapula)	AD 51	Roman victory. Caractacus (Caradog) fled north before being captured.
Chalgrove Field (Oxfordshire, SU645978)	English Civil War (1st) (1642–6)	Royalists (Prince Rupert)	Parliamentarians (Sir Philip Stapleton/John Hampden)	18 June 1643	Royalist victory. John Hampden killed when Rupert ambushed a Parliamentarian column.
Chippenham (Wiltshire, ST9173)	Viking invasions of England (796–991)	English (Alfred the Great)	Danes (Guthrum)	January 878	Danish victory. Alfred forced to flee and hide out in Athelney by surprise attack shortly after Twelfth Night 878.
Cheriton (Hampshire, SU598294)	English Civil War (1st) (1642–6)	Royalists (Patrick Ruthven, Lord Forth)	Parliamentarians (Sir William Waller)	29 March 1644	Parliamentary victory. Royalists forced back on the defensive. Aka Alresford.
Clashacrow (Kilkenny)	Norman invasion of Ireland (1169–1333)	Irish (Donal MacGillapatrick of Ossory)	Normans/Irish (Robert Fitzstephen/Dermot MacMurrough)	1169	Norman/Irish victory. Normans supported Dermot MacMurrcugh on a raid into Ossory.
Clifton (Cumbria, NY5325)	Jacobite Rising (3rd)/ The Forty-Five (1745–6)	Government (William, Duke of Cumberland	Jacobites (Lord George Murray)	18 December 1745	Jacobite victory. Claimed as the last battle fought on English scil. The Jacobite army had reached Derby on its invasion of England but had turned back on 6 December. The fight at Clifton was a rearguard action by the retreating army. Also known as Clifton Moor.
Clonmel (Waterford)	Irish Confederate War (1641–53)	Irish (Hugh Dubh 'Black Hugh' O'Neill)	Parliamentarians (Oliver Cromwell)	18 May 1650	Parliamentary victory. Culmination of a siege. O'Neill successfully defended a breach in the walls, with large losses for Cromwell's forces, then withdrawing without Cromwell's knowledge. Town surrendered without further loss of life.
Clontarf (Dublin City)	Viking invasion of Ireland (877–1014)	Irish/Munster (Brian Boru/ Murchad)	Vikings/Leinster (Sigtrygg/ Maelmorda)	23 April 1014	Irish/Munster victory. Fought on Good Friday. Irish victorious even though Brian Boru and his son Murchad killed. Viking threat to Ireland ended.
Clontibret (Monaghan)	Nine Years' War (1593–1603)	English (Henry Bagenal)	Irish (Hugh O'Neill, Earl of Tyrone)	27 May 1595	Irish victory. English ambushed while trying to reach Monaghan.
Clyst St Mary (Devon, SX9791)	Prayer Book Rebellion/ Western Rebellion (1549)	Royal Army (Lord John Russell/William Grey, Lord de Wilton)	Rebels	4–5 August 1549	Royal army victory. Royal forces eventually broke siege of Exeter in a two-day action which scattered the rebels. They made a last stand at Stampford Courtenay (Devon, SS9301) on 18 August 1549.

Name, county and nearest grid reference	Conflict	Protagonists		Date	Details
Collooney (Sligo)	Irish Insurrection (1797–8)	Irish/French (Joseph Humbert)	Government (Vereker)	5 September 1798	French victory. Small French force defeated garrison of Sligo Town.
Confey (Kildare)	Viking Raids	Irish	Vikings	c.915–917	See Kildare
Corrichie (Aberdeenshire, Grampian, NJ6902)	Huntly's Revolt (1562)	Royal Army (James Stewart, Earl of Moray)	Rebels (George Gordon, Earl of Huntly)	28 October 1562	Royal army victory. Rebellion against Mary Queen of Scots, who had given her half-brother James Stewart the Earlship of Moray, which Gordon coveted. Rebels marched on Aberdeen but were roundly defeated. Gordon died from stroke or heart attack on the battlefield while trying to surrender. His embalmed corpse brought before the Scottish Parliament and tried for treason.
Cropredy Bridge (Oxfordshire, SP477460)	English Civil War (1st) (1642–6)	Royalists (Charles I)	Parliamentarians (Sir William Waller)	29 June 1644	Royalist victory. Waller's army was dispersed.
Crug Mawr (Ceredigion, Dyfed, SN2047)	Norman/English conquest of Wales (1066–1295)	Welsh (Owain Gwynedd/ Gruffydd ap Rhys)	Normans (Stephen, Constable of Cardigan)	October 1136	Welsh victory. Cardigan captured by the Welsh and Ceredigion annexed by Gwynedd.
Culblean (Aberdeenshire, Grampian, NO4199)	Anglo-Scottish Wars: Scottish Wars of Independence (1286–1388)	Royal Army (Sir Andrew Moray)	Scottish Claimant Army (David Strathbogie)	30 November 1335	Royal Army victory. Strathbogie killed, a blow to the claims of Edward Balliol.
Culloden (Highland, NH7345)	Jacobite Rising (3rd)/ The Forty-Five (1745–6)	Government (Duke of Cumberland)	Jacobites (Prince Charles Edward Stewart)	16 April 1746	Government victory. Complete defeat of the Jacobite army and the end of the rebellion. Also known as Drummossie Moor.
Curlew Pass (Roscommon)	Nine Years' War (1593–1603)	English (Henry Bagenal)	Irish (Hugh O'Neill, Earl of Tyrone)	15 August 1599	Irish victory. English ambushed en route from Athlone to relieve Collooney Castle and routed. Clifford killed. Battlefield is marked by a sculpture by Maurice Harron called *The Gaelic Chieftain*, unveiled in 1999.
Cymerau (Carmarthen-shire, Dyfed, SN5020)	Norman/English conquest of Wales (1066–1295)	English (Stephen Bauzan)	Welsh (Maredudd ap Owain)	2 June 1257	Welsh victory. English raiding expedition slaughtered while still in marching order.
Degsastan (Scottish Borders, NY5697 possible site)	British wars (410–1018)	Bernicia (Aethelfrith)	Picts (Aedan of Dalradia)	603	Bernician victory. Aethelfrith went on to establish Northumbria as the union of Bernicia and Deira. Aka Dawston Rigg.
Deorham (Gloucestershire, ST7476 possible site)	British wars (410–1018)	British (Commail/ Condidan/Farinmail)	West Saxons (Cuthwin/ Ceawlin)	577	West Saxon victory. Commail, Condidan and Farinmail killed followed by capture of Bath, Cirencester and Gloucester. Aka Dyrham.
Deptford Bridge (London, TQ 36 77)	Cornish Rebellion of 1497	Rebels from Cornwall (Michael An Gof)	Royal troops led (Giles, Lord Daubeney)	17 June 1497	Royal victory. See entry in Cornwall under Cornish Rebellion. Also known as Blackheath.
Diamond (Armagh)	Sectarian conflicts	Catholic faction known as the Defenders	Protestant faction known as the Peep O'Day Boys	21 September 1795	See Armagh
Downpatrick (Down)	Norman invasion of Ireland (1169–1333)	Irish (Rory MacDonleavy)	Normans (John de Courcy)	1177	Norman victory. De Courcy led a private raid and secured the Kingdom of Ulaid which became the basis for Ulster.

MAJOR BATTLES ON BRITISH AND IRISH SOIL

Name, county and nearest grid reference	Conflict	Protagonists		Date	Details
Drogheda (Louth)	Irish Confederate War (1641–53)	Royalists (Sir George Aston)	Parliamentarians (Oliver Cromwell)	11 September 1649	See Louth
Drumclog (Strathclyde, NS6239)	Western Rebellion/ Covenanter Rising (1679)	Government (John Graham of Claverhouse)	Covenanters (Robert Hamilton/William Cleland)	1 June 1679	Rising based around the assassins of James Sharp, Archbishop of St Andrews. The smaller government force was routed.
Drumderg (Down)	Norman invasion of Ireland (1169–1333)	Irish (Brian O'Neill)	Normans (Roger le Taylleur)	12 May 1260	Norman victory. O'Neill, who styled himself 'King of the Irish of Ireland', killed in a clash with the citizens of Down.
Dublin (I) (Dublin City)	Norman invasion of Ireland (1169–1333)	Irish (Rory O'Connor)	Norman (Richard Fitz-Gilbert de Clare, Earl Strongbow)	1 September 1171	Norman victory. Normans besieged in Dublin by High King O'Connor but sallied out and attacked the Irish camp, provoking a rout.
Dublin (II) (Dublin City)	Easter Rising (1916)	Irish	Government	24–29 April 1916	See Dublin entry for Easter Rising.
Dunbar (I) (East Lothian NT6776)	Anglo-Scottish Wars: Scottish Wars of Independence (1286–1388)	English (John de Warenne, Earl of Surrey)	Scottish (John Balliol)	27 April 1296	English victory. Scottish army routed; Balliol effectively ceded the Scottish crown to Edward I.
Dunbar (II) (East Lothian NT6976)	English Civil War (3rd) (1650–1)	Royalists (David Leslie)	Commonwealth (Oliver Cromwell)	3 September 1650	Commonwealth victory. Royalist/Covenanter army destroyed and Cromwell took Edinburgh. Aka the Race or Drove of Dunbar.
Dunboy (Cork)	Tyrone's Rebellion (1593–1603)	English	Irish/Spanish	5–18 June 1602	See Cork
Dungan's Hill (Meath)	Irish Confederate War (1641–3)	Irish Confederates (Thomas Preston)	Parliamentarians (Michael Jones)	8 August 1647	Parliamentarian victory. Irish Confederate Army of Leinster destroyed.
Dungeness (Kent)	First Anglo-Dutch War (1652-1654)	English (Robert Blake)	United Provinces (Maarten Tromp)	10 December 1652	Dutch victory. Legend says that Tromp attached a broom to his mast as a sign that he had swept the sea clean of his enemies.
Dunkeld (Perth and Kinross, NO0242)	Jacobite Rising (1st) (1689–91)	Government (William Cleland)	Jacobites (Alexander Cannon)	21 August 1689	Government victory. Small government force held off the attack of a much larger body of clansmen. Cleland killed. Highlanders dispersed to their homes during the autumn.
Dunsinane Hill (Perth and Kinross, NO2131)	Scottish Dynastic Wars (1054–7)	Royal Army (Macbeth)	Scottish Claimant Army (Siward, Earl of Northumberland/Malcolm Canmore)	27 July 1054	Scottish Claimant victory. English aid for King Duncan's son Malcolm Canmore ('Bighead'). Macbeth remained king until killed at the battle of Lumphanan in 1057.
Dupplin Moor (Perth and Kinross, NO0219 possible site)	Anglo-Scottish Wars: Scottish Wars of Independence (1286–1388)	Royal Army (Earl of Mar)	Scottish Claimant Army (Edward Balliol)	11 August 1332	Scottish claimant victory. Earl of Mar killed. With English help Edward Balliol was crowned at Scone on 24 September 1332 but his reign was short-lived.

Name, county and nearest grid reference	Conflict	Protagonists		Date	Details
Dussindale (Norfolk, unknown site near Norwich)	Kett's Rebellion (1549)	Royal Army (John Dudley, Earl of Warwick)	Rebels (Robert Kett)	27 August 1549	Royal army victory. A rebellion in the South East and East Anglia against misgovernment by the Somerset regime which eventually centred on Mousehold Heath, near Norwich. The ill-equipped rebels were smashed by Warwick's army. Warwick replaced Somerset as head of Council.
Dysert O'Dea (Clare)	Bruce invasion of Ireland (1315–18)	Irish (Murtough O'Brien)	Anglo-Irish (Richard de Clare)	10 May 1318	Irish victory. Anglo-Irish caught in an ambush while chasing a raiding party.
Edgcote (Northampton-SP517461)	Wars of the Roses (1455–87)	Yorkists (William Herbert, Earl of Pembroke)	Lancastrians (Robin of Redesdale)	26 July 1469	Lancastrian victory. Pembroke captured and executed on orders of Earl of Warwick. Aka Danes Moor.
Edgehill (Warwickshire, SP359493)	English Civil War (1st) (1642–6)	Royalists (Charles I)	Parliamentarians (Robert Devereux, Earl of Essex)	23 October 1642	Royalist victory. Narrow victory for Royalists opening the road to London where they were turned back at Turnham Green. Also known as Kineton Fight. Edgehill was the first full battle of the war.
Edington (Wiltshire, ST9252 possible site)	Viking invasions of England (796–991)	English (Alfred the Great)	Vikings (Guthrum)	May 878	English victory. Guthrum became a Christian and withdrew from Wessex. Aka Ethandun(e).
Ellendun (Wiltshire, SU1083)	British wars (410–1018)	West Saxons (Egbert)	Mercia (Beornwulf)	825	West Saxon victory. End of Mercian supremacy. Egbert expanded Wessex to include Kent and briefly held sway in all the Kingdoms.
Empingham (Rutland, SK9711)	Wars of the Roses (1455–87)	Lancastrians (Sir Robert Welles)	Yorkists (Edward IV)	12 March 1470	Yorkist victory. Also known as Losecoat Field because Warwick's troops discarded their coats so as to avoid being identified (although this may be apocryphal).
Enniscorthy (Wexford)	Irish Insurrection (1797–8)	Irish (Fr John Murphy/ Edward Roche)	Government (William Snowe)	28 May 1798	Irish victory. Irish gained town of Enniscorthy after a short action. The insurgents went on to claim most of Co. Wexford except New Ross.
Evesham (Worcestershire, SP039455)	English Baronial War (1264–5)	Royal Army (Prince Edward)	Barons (Simon de Montfort)	4 August 1265	Royal army victory. Simon de Montfort killed and Baronial Army destroyed.
Falkirk (I) (Falkirk NS9179 possible site)	Anglo-Scottish Wars: Scottish Wars of Independence (1286–1388)	England (Edward I)	Scotland (William Wallace)	22 July 1298	English victory. First major battle decided by the longbow. Wallace escaped but was later captured and hanged, drawn and quartered.
Falkirk (II) (Falkirk NS8679)	Jacobite Rising (3rd)/ The Forty-Five (1745–6)	Government (Henry Hawley)	Jacobites (Prince Charles Edward Stewart/Lord George Murray)	17 January 1746	Jacobite victory. A short engagement ending with Hawley's defeat. He took 'revenge' by hanging some of his own men ('Hangman' Hawley). The Jacobites continued to withdraw into the Highlands.
Farsetmore (Donegal)	Irish Clan Wars	O'Neills of Tyrone (Shane O'Neill)	O'Donnells of Tyrconnell (Hugh O'Donnell)	8 May 1567	O'Donnell victory. Hugh O'Donnell's horsemen harassed O'Neill as his men were fording the River Swilly just north of Letterkenny and won a decisive battle.

MAJOR BATTLES ON BRITISH AND IRISH SOIL

Name, county and nearest grid reference	Conflict	Protagonists		Date	Details
Faughart (Louth)	Bruce invasion of Ireland (1315–18)	Scottish (Edward Bruce)	Anglo-Normans (John Bermingham)	14 October 1318	Anglo-Norman victory. Bruce, younger brother of Robert and king of Ireland since 1 May 1316, killed.
Fenny Bridges (Devon, SY1198)	Prayer Book Rebellion/ Western Rebellion (1549)	Royal Army (Lord John Russell)	Rebels (Robert Smyth)	28 July 1549	Royal army victory. Rebels besieging Exeter. Rebellion led by Cornishmen objecting to the new English liturgy.
Ferrybridge (Yorkshire, SE4824)	Wars of the Roses (1455–87)	Lancastrians (Lord John Clifford)	Yorkists (Edward IV)	28 March 1461	Yorkist victory. Delaying battle before Towton with Lancastrians defending a crossing of the River Aire. Clifton killed.
Fishguard (Pembrokeshire, Dyfed, SM9437)	Irish Insurrection (1797–8)	French (William Tate)	Government (John Campbell, Lord Cawdor)	24 February 1797	Government victory. Tate was an American charged by the French with burning Bristol, Liverpool and Chester as part of a strategy to incite rebellion among the Welsh and Irish. He and his force surrendered shortly after landing near Fishguard. This is the only battle honour issued (to the Pembroke Yeomanry) for an action in the UK. This was the last invasion of mainland Britain.
Flodden Field (Northumberland, NT8937)	Anglo-Scottish Wars: Scottish raids (1513)	English (Thomas Howard, Earl of Surrey)	Scottish (James IV)	9 September 1513	English victory. James IV killed. Scottish army destroyed. Aka Branxton Field.
Ford of the Biscuits (Fermanagh)	Tyrone's Rebellion/Nine Years' War (1593–1603)	English (Henry Duke/ Edward Herbert)	Irish (Hugh Maguire/ Hugh Roe O'Donnell)	7 August 1594	Irish victory. Rebels ambushed supply column on its way to Enniskillen which spilled its provisions into the river, hence the name. Aka Drumane Ford.
Fornham (Suffolk, TL8368)	Alliance against Henry II (1173–4)	Royal Army (Richard de Lucy/Humphrey de Bohun)	Rebels (Robert, Earl of Leicester)	17 October 1173	Royal Army victory. Supporters of Princes Richard and John defeated and routed. Earl of Leicester captured.
Gainsborough (Lincolnshire, SK8287)	English Civil War (1st) (1642–6)	Royalists (William Cavendish, Earl of Newcastle/Charles Cavendish)	Parliamentarians (Sir John Meldrum/Oliver Cromwell)	28 July 1643	Inconclusive. Parliamentary force attempting to relieve a raiding party trapped in Gainsborough. Charles Cavendish killed but Royalists went on to take Lincoln.
Gate Fulford (North Yorkshire, SE611489)	Norwegian invasion of England (1066)	English (Earl Edwin/Earl Morcar)	Vikings (Harald Hardrada/ Tostig)	20 September 1066	Norwegian victory. The defeat of the Northern Earls Edwin and Morcar left York open for Harald and meant Harold II had to march North instead of waiting for the Norman invasion.
Gladsmuir see Prestonpans					
Glenlivet (Moray, Grampian, NJ2429)	Scottish Wars: anti-Catholic suppression (1594)	Catholics (Francis Hay, Earl Errol/George Gordon, Earl Huntley)	Protestants (Archibald Graham, Earl of Argyll)	3 October 1594	Catholic victory. Despite victory the Catholic earls were forced to flee into exile. Also known as Allt a' Choileachain.
Glenmalur (Wicklow)	Desmond Rebellion (1579–83)	English (Arthur Grey, Lord de Wilton)	Irish (Feagh MacHugh O'Byrne)	25 August 1580	Irish victory. Grey ambushed and defeated after chasing rebels into their stronghold in Wicklow Mountains.
Glen Mama (Dublin)	Viking invasion of Ireland (877–1014)	Vikings (Sigtrygg Silkbeard and hiscousin Máel Mórda)	Munster (Brian Boru)	999	Brian Boru gained victory and looted and burned the Viking-held city of Dublin.

Name, county and nearest grid reference	Conflict	Protagonists		Date	Details
Glenshiel (Highland, NG9913)	Jacobite Rising/The Nineteen/The Little Rising (1719)	Government (Joseph Wightman)	Jacobites/Spanish (William Murray, Marquess of Tullibardine/George Keith, Earl Marischal)	10 June 1719	Government victory. A failed Spanish-backed attempt in April 1719 to raise the Western clans with 300 Spanish troops and the hereditary earl marischal of Scotland at Loch Alsh. Campaign a farce and ended with defeat and the capture of the Spanish.
Halidon Hill (Northumberland, NT9655)	Anglo-Scottish Wars: Scottish Wars of Independence (1286–1388)	English (Edward III)	Scottish (Sir Archibald Douglas)	19 July 1333	English victory. Scots army destroyed. Douglas killed. Edward put Edward Balliol back on the Scottish throne and young David II fled to France before returning in 1336.
Harlaw (Aberdeenshire, Grampian, NJ7524)	Scottish Wars: territorial dispute (1411)	Highlanders (Donald, Lord of the Isles)	Lowlanders (Alexander Stewart, Earl of Mar)	24 July 1411	Inconclusive. Fought over securing the Earldom of Ross for the Scottish crown. Known as Red Harlaw because of the amount of blood spilled.
Hastings (East Sussex, TQ750157)	Norman Conquest of England (1066)	English (Harold II)	Normans (William, Duke of Normandy)	14 October 1066	Norman victory. King Harold killed. William luckily shades a day long battle and wins the whole of England as his prize. Aka Senlac Hill.
Hatfield Chase (Nottinghamshire, SK5669)	British wars (410–1018)	Northumbria (Edwin)	Mercia (Penda/ Cadwallon of Gwynedd)	12 October 632	Mercian victory. Edwin and two sons killed and army destroyed. Power struggle ensued in Northumbria. Aka Haethfelth.
Heavenfield (Northumberland, NY9056 possible site)	British wars (410–1018)	Northumbria (St Oswald)	Welsh (Cadwallon of Gwynedd)	c 633	Northumbrian victory. Cadwallon trying to build on victory at Hatfield Chase. Cadwallon killed. Decisive victory enabled Oswald to reunite Northumbria under his rule. Battle so-called because Oswald raised a cross and prayed on the battlefield. Aka Hefenfelth, Denisesburna.
Hedgeley Moor (Northumberland, NU0420)	Wars of the Roses (1455–87)	Lancastrians (Henry Beaufort, Duke of Somerset/Sir Ralph Percy)	Yorkists (John Neville, Marquess of Montagu)	25 April 1464	Yorkist victory. Sir Ralph Percy killed. Lancastrian attempt to disrupt Anglo-Scottish peace negotiations.
Hereford (Herefordshire, unknown site)	Anglo-Welsh Wars: Welsh raid (1055)	English (Ralph, Earl of Hereford)	Welsh (Gruffudd ap Llywelyn/Aelfgar)	24 October 1055	Welsh victory. English army defeated by a Welsh army aided by the exiled English Earl Aelfgar of East Anglia. Hereford burned to the ground.
Hexham (Northumberland, NY9662)	Wars of the Roses (1455–1487)	Lancastrians (Henry Beaufort, Duke of Somerset)	Yorkists (John Neville, Marquess of Montagu)	15 May 1464	Yorkist victory. Somerset executed after battle in which all his army was either killed, captured or dispersed.
Highnam (Gloucestershire, SO7919)	English Civil War (1st) (1642–6)	Royalists (Sir Jerome Brett)	Parliamentarians (Sir William Waller)	24 March 1643	Parliamentarian victory. Royalist army raised in Wales destroyed.
Homildon Hill (Northumberland, NT9628)	Anglo-Scottish Wars: Scottish raids (1402)	English (Henry Percy, Earl of Northumberland)	Scottish (Archibald, Earl of Douglas)	14 September 1402	English victory. Douglas captured. A disagreement over ransoms led to a dispute between Percy and Henry IV which culminated in the Battle of Shrewsbury. The battle is mentioned at the beginning of Shakespeare's *Henry IV Part I*. Aka Humbleton Hill.

Name, county and nearest grid reference	Conflict	Protagonists		Date	Details
Hopton Heath (Staffordshire, SJ956264)	English Civil War (1st) (1642–6)	Royalists (Spencer Compton, Earl of Northampton)	Parliamentarians (Sir John Gell)	19 March 1643	Inconclusive. Rival armies converging on Stafford. Earl of Northampton killed.
Inverkeithing (Fife, NT1182)	English Civil War (3rd) (1650–1)	Royalists (James Holborne/ John Browne)	Commonwealth (John Lambert)	20 July 1651	Commonwealth victory. Royalist army destroyed. The battle site is close to the North Queensferry approach to the Forth Road Bridge but is covered by urban development.
Inverlochy (I) (Highland, NN1275)	Scottish Wars: territorial dispute 1431	Royal Army (Earl of Mar)	Clan Donald (Donald Balloch)	September 1431	Victory for Clan Donald. It gained the release of Alexander, Earl of Ross, who was being held by James IV.
Inverlochy (II) (Highland, NN1275)	English Civil War (1st) (1642–6)	Royalists (James Graham, Marquess of Montrose)	Covenanters (Sir Duncan Campbell)	2 February 1645	Royalist victory. Covenanter army routed and Duncan Campbell killed and Clan Campbell leadership severely depleted.
Inverurie (Aberdeenshire, Grampian, NJ7926)	Scottish Dynastic Wars (1308)	Bruces (Robert the Bruce)	Comyns (John Comyn, Earl of Buchan)	23 May 1308	Bruce victory. Cemented Bruce's position and enabled him to reward his supporters with the confiscated estates of his enemies.
Julianstown (Meath)	Irish Rising (1641)	English (Sir Patrick Wemyss)	Irish (Phelim O'Neill)	29 November 1641	Irish victory. English column marching to relieve Drogheda destroyed, encouraging spread of the rebellion and formation of Confederation of Ireland (Kilkenny), supported by both Catholic Irish and Old English of the Pale.
Kilkenny (Kilkenny)	Irish Confederate War/ Eleven Years' War (1641–53)	Irish (Sir Walter Butler)	Parliamentarians (Oliver Cromwell)	27 March 1650	Parliamentarian victory. Kilkenny surrendered to Cromwell after he was paid £2000 compensation for his troops not being allowed to plunder it.
Killala (Mayo)	Irish Insurrection (1797–8)	Irish/French (Jean Sarrazin)	Government	22 August 1798	Irish/French victory. Local support of the invasion/uprising encouraged.
Killiecrankie (Perth and Kinross, NN9063)	Jacobite Rising (1st) (1689–91)	Government (Hugh MacKay)	Jacobites (John Graham of Claverhouse, Viscount Dundee)	27 July 1689	Jacobite victory. Government army destroyed but Graham (Bonnie Dundee or Bluidy Clavers) killed, seriously harming Jacobite cause.
Kilrush (Kildare)	Irish Confederate War (1641–53)	Irish (Hugh MacPhelim O'Byrne)	Parliamentarians (James Butler, Marquess of Ormond)	15 April 1642	Parliamentarian victory. Irish army routed. Aka Cnocaterife.
Kilsyth (Strathclyde, NS7478)	English Civil War (1st) (1642–6)	Royalists (James Graham, Marquess of Montrose)	Covenanters (William Baillie)	15 August 1645	Royalist victory. Covenanter force destroyed but Montrose now had the only Royalist field army in Britain.
Kinsale (Cork)	Tyrone's Rebellion (1593–1603)	English (Charles Blount, Lord Mountjoy)	Irish/Spanish (Hugh O'Neill, Earl of Tyrone)	24 December 1601	English victory. Irish army tried to relieve a Spanish garrison in Kinsale. See also Cork.

Name, county and nearest grid reference	Conflict	Protagonists		Date	Details
Knocknaclashy (Cork)	Irish Confederate War/ Eleven Years' War (1641–53)	Irish (Donagh MacCarthy, Viscount Muskerry(	Parliamentarians (Roger Boyle, Lord Broghill)	25 July 1651	Parliamentarian victory. The Irish failed to relieve Limerick, which capitulated shortly thereafter. This was the final field battle of the Irish Confederate War.
Knocknanuss (Cork)	Irish Confederate War/ Eleven Years' War (1641–53)	Irish Confederates (Viscount Taafe/ Alasdair MacColla MacDonnell)	Parliamentarians (Murrough O'Brien, Earl Inchiquin)	13 November 1647	Parliamentarian victory. Having massacred the garrison on the Rock of Cashel, Murrough O'Brien routed Irish forces of the Confederate Army of Munster at Knocknanuss. Alasdair MacColla MacDonnell killed.
Langport (Somerset, ST441276)	English Civil War (1st) (1642–6)	Royalists (Lord George Goring)	Parliamentarians (Sir Thomas Fairfax)	10 July 1645	Parliamentarian victory. Last significant Royalist field army defeated. Bridgwater fell and Royalist garrisons in the West isolated.
Langside (Strathclyde, NS5761)	Scottish Dynastic Wars (1568)	Marians (Archibald Campbell, Earl of Argyll/ Mary Queen of Scots)	Anti-Marians (James Stewart, Earl of Moray)	13 May 1568	Anti-Marian victory. Mary Queen of Scots, having escaped from Loch Leven Castle, forced to flee to England and into further imprisonment. The battlefield is in a suburb of Glasgow.
Lansdown Hill (Somerset, ST721703)	English Civil War (1st) (1642–6)	Royalists (Sir Ralph Hopton/Prince Maurice)	Parliamentarians (Sir William Waller)	5 July 1643	Inconclusive. Royalists suffered heavy losses but Parliamentarians left the field. Hopton was injured in an explosion of ammunition after the battle.
Largs (Strathclyde, NS2059)	Scottish Wars: Norwegian War (1263)	Scottish (Alexander III)	Vikings (Haakon IV of Norway)	2 October 1263	Scottish victory. Hebrides and Isle of Man eventually ceded to Scotland in 1566.
Lewes (East Sussex, TQ3911)	English Baronial War (1264–5)	Royal Army (Henry III)	Barons (Simon de Montfort)	14 May 1264	Baronial victory. Henry captured and controlled by Barons for a year until Evesham.
Limerick (Limerick)	Irish Confederate War (1641–53)	Irish (Hugh Dubh 'Black Hugh' O'Neill)	Parliamentarians (Henry Ireton)	27 October 1651	Parliamentarian victory. Limerick surrendered after a protracted siege. O'Neill sent to London and imprisoned in the Tower of London. Ireton fell ill and died in Limerick on 26 November 1651.
Lincoln (I) (Lincolnshire, SK9671)	English Civil War/Stephen and Matilda (1135–54)	Royal Army (King Stephen/William of Ypres)	Angevin Claimants (Robert, Earl of Gloucester/ Ranulf, Earl of Chester)	2 February 1141	Angevin claimant victory. Stephen's army attacked by Matilda's supporters led by Gloucester as he was trying to capture Lincoln which was being held by Earl Ranulf's wife. Stephen was captured and taken to Bristol.
Lincoln (II) (Lincolnshire, SK9771)	English Baronial War (1216–17)	Royal Army (William Marshal)	Barons/French (Comte de Perche)	20 May 1217	Royal army victory. Barons in support of Louis, Dauphin of France's (future Louis VIII) claim to the English throne against Henry III. Louis had actually been invited to replace King John (d. 1216) and continued to press his claim. Caught besieging the Royal castle at Lincoln, de Perche was killed and the Baronial army driven off.
Liscarroll (Cork)	Irish Confederate War/ Eleven Years' War (1641–53)	English (Murrough O'Brien, Earl Inchiquinn)	Irish (Garret Barry)	3 September 1642	English victory. Cork secured as an English stronghold.

Name, county and nearest grid reference	Conflict	Protagonists		Date	Details
Londonderry (Londonderry)	Jacobite Rising (1st) (1689–91)	Government (Percy Kirke/ John Leake)	Jacobites (Conrad, Count of Rosen/Richard Hamilton)	28 July 1689	Government victory. Londonderry closed its gates against the Earl of Antrim in December 1688. James II arrived before its walls on 17 April 1689 and a 105 day siege and blockade ensued. On 28 July government supply ships broke the defensive boom across the River Foyle and resupplied the city. The siege was broken and the Jacobites had quit the scene by 1 August 1689.
Lostwithiel (Cornwall and the Scilly Isles, SX1054)	English Civil War (1st) (1642–6)	Royalists (Charles I/Prince Maurice)	Parliamentarians (Robert Devereux, Earl of Essex)	21 August–2 September 1644	Royalist victory. Two separate battles which ended with the surrender of the Parliamentary army and maintained Royalist supremacy in the South West.
Loudoun Hill (Strathclyde, NS6137)	Anglo-Scottish Wars: Scottish Wars of Independence (1286–1388)	English (Aymer de Valence, Earl of Pembroke)	Scottish (Robert the Bruce)	10 May 1307	Scottish victory.
Lowestoft (Suffolk)	Second Anglo-Dutch War (1665–7)	England (James Stuart, Duke of York)	Dutch (Jacob van Wassenaer Obdam)	13 June 1665	A Dutch fleet of 103 ships attacked an English fleet of 109, forty miles east of the port of Lowestoft. HMS *Great Charity* was lost but so were 17 Dutch ships. It remains the worst naval defeat in Dutch history.
Ludford Bridge (Shropshire SO5173)	Wars of the Roses (1455–87)	Lancastrians (Henry VI/ Margaret of Anjou)	Yorkists (Richard, Duke of York)	12 October 1459	Lancastrian victory. Yorkist troops refused to fight against the King in the field and the Yorkist army withdrew without a fight. The Duke of York eventually fled to Dublin and the Nevilles with Edward, Earl of March to Calais.
Ludgate Hill (London, TQ3181)	Wyatt's Rebellion (1554)	Royal Army (William Herbert, Earl of Pembroke)	Rebels (Sir Thomas Wyatt)	7 February 1554	Royal army victory. Rebellion against Catholic Mary I and her marriage to Philip II of Spain. Wyatt advanced on London and was cornered by the Royal army in Fleet Street and forced to surrender. Wyatt was executed 11 April 1554.
Lumphanan (Aberdeenshire, Grampian, NJ5703)	Scottish Dynastic Wars (1054–7)	Royal Army (Macbeth)	Scottish Claimant Army (Malcolm Canmore)	15 August 1057	Scottish claimant victory. Macbeth killed and Malcolm Canmore became King of Scotland as Malcolm III.
Maes Madog (Powys)	Norman/English conquest of Wales (1066–1295)	English (William Beauchamp, Earl of Warwick)	Welsh (Madog ap Llywelyn)	5 March 1295	English victory. Welsh revolt over army conscription suppressed.
Maldon (Essex, TL867055)	Viking invasions of England (796–991)	East Saxons (Earl Brithnoth)	Vikings (Olaf Trygvasson/ Svein Forkbeard)	10 August 991	Viking victory. Fought on Northey Island. Earl Brithnoth killed along with his retainers. The battle is recorded in the epic poem *The Battle of Maldon*.
Mancetter (Warwickshire, possible site)	Roman conquest of Britain (43–410)	Romans (Suetonius Paulinus)	British Tribes (Boudicca)	AD 61	Roman victory. Boudicca commits suicide. End of rebellion. Other possible locations for this battle are Paulerspury near Towcester or Wroxeter.
Marshall's Elm (Somerset, ST483363)	English Civil War (1st) (1642–6)	Royalists (Sir John Stawell)	Parliamentarians (John Pyne MP)	4 August 1642	Royalist victory. 27 were killed and 60 taken prisoner.

Name, county and nearest grid reference	Conflict	Protagonists		Date	Details
Marston Moor (Yorkshire, SE491522)	English Civil War (1st) (1642–6)	Royalists (Prince Rupert/ William Cavendish, Marquess of Newcastle)	Parliamentarians (Alexander Leslie, Earl of Leven/Fernando Fairfax)	2 July 1644	Parliamentarian victory. Largest battle fought on English soil post Roman times with at least 46,000 combatants. Probably the most decisive battle of the Civil War. Royalist cause in the North destroyed with York surrendering on 16 July.
Maserfield (Shropshire, SJ2929 possible site)	British wars (410–1018)	Northumbria (St Oswald)	Mercia (Penda)	5 August 641	Mercian victory. Oswald killed and dismembered, his limbs and head stuck on poles by his pagan enemies. Battle possibly took place near Oswestry (Oswald's Tree) and Oswald became a Christian martyr.
Medway (Kent, TQ6973)	Roman conquest of Britain (43–410)	Romans (Aulus Plautius)	British tribes (Caractacus/ Togodumnus)	AD 43	Roman victory. British tribes under Caractacus and Togodumnus defeated. Probably fought in the vicinity of Rochester.
Methven (Perth and Kinross, NO0226)	Anglo-Scottish Wars: Scottish Wars of Independence (1286–1388)	English (Aymer de Valence, Earl of Pembroke)	Scottish (Robert the Bruce)	19 June 1306	English victory. Scots army destroyed in surprise attack.
Mondynes (Aberdeenshire, Grampian, NO7879)	Scottish Dynastic Wars (1094)	Royal Army (Duncan II)	Scottish Claimant Army (Princes Edmund and Duncan)	12 November 1094	Scottish claimant victory. Duncan II killed and Donald Bain regained the kingship which he had lost in May 1094. He had himself siezed the Scottish throne on 13 November 1093 on the death of Malcolm Canmore III.
Mons Badonicus (Wiltshire, SU2079 possible site)	British wars (410–1018)	British	Saxons	c 495	British victory. A significant battle but with little evidence as to precise date and location. A likely site is Liddington Hill, near Swindon. Aka Mount Badon.
Mons Graupius (Aberdeenshire, Grampian, NJ6825 possible site)	Roman conquest of Britain (43–410)	Romans (Gnaeus Julius Agricola)	Caledonians (Calgacus)	AD 83	Roman victory. Marked furthest extent of Roman penetration into Scotland.
Montgomery (Powys)	English Civil War (1st) (1642–6)	Royalists (Lord Byron)	Parliamentarians (Sir John Meldrum/Sir William Brereton)	18 September 1644	Parliamentarian victory. A Parliamentary force had captured Montgomery and was itself besieged in turn. A relieving force routed the Royalist army and gave Parliament control of North Wales.
Mortimer's Cross (Herefordshire, SO427627)	Wars of the Roses (1455–87)	Lancastrians (Jasper Tudor, Earl of Pembroke/ Jasper Butler, Earl of Wiltshire)	Yorkists (Edward, Earl of March)	2 February 1461	Yorkist victory. Lancastrian army destroyed. Owen Tudor, father of the Earl of Pembroke, captured and executed.
Mortlach (Moray, Grampian, NJ3239)	Viking Invasion of Scotland (1005)	Scottish (Malcolm II)	Vikings (Sigurd the Stout)	1005	Scottish victory. Battle fought near Dufftown and Balvenie Castle.
Moyry Pass (Armagh)	Tyrone's Rebellion/ Nine Years' War (1593–1603)	English (Charles Blount, Lord Mountjoy)	Irish (Hugh O'Neill, Earl of Tyrone)	20 September–6 October 1600	Result inconclusive. Mountjoy tried to force the pass but eventually had to admit defeat. O'Neill then quit the position for fear of it being turned.

MAJOR BATTLES ON BRITISH AND IRISH SOIL

Name, county and nearest grid reference	Conflict	Protagonists		Date	Details
Mynydd Carn (unknown – possible site Pembrokeshire, Dyfed, SN1131)	Welsh Dynastic Wars (1081)	Gwynedd and Deheubarth Encumbents (Trahaearn ap Caradog/Caradog ap Gruffydd)	Gwynedd and Deheubarth Claimants (Gruffydd ap Cynan/Rhys ap Tewdwr)	1081	Victory for the Gwynedd Claimants. Both Trahaearn ap Caradog and Caradog ap Gruffydd were killed. Rhys ap Tewdwr regained Deheubarth and Gruffydd ap Cynan became king of Gwynedd.
Myton-on-Swale (North Yorkshire, SE428675)	Anglo-Scottish Wars: Scottish Wars of Independence (1286–1388)	English (William Melton, Archbishop of York)	Scottish (James Douglas/ Earl of Moray)	20 September 1319	Scottish victory. English force attempting to prevent the Scots from raising the siege of Berwick defeated. Also known as The Chapter of Myton or the White Battle after the 300 English priests killed.
Nantwich (Cheshire, SJ635536)	English Civil War (1st) (1642–6)	Royalists (John, Lord Byron)	Parliamentarians (Sir Thomas Fairfax)	25 January 1644	Parliamentary victory. Nantwich relieved and Cheshire and Lancashire fell to Parliament.
Naseby (Northamptonshire, SP684799)	English Civil War (1st) (1642–6)	Royalists (Charles I/ Prince Rupert)	Parliamentarians (Sir Thomas Fairfax/Oliver Cromwell)	14 June 1645	Parliamentarian victory. Main Royalist field army destroyed by New Model Army. Royalist cause dealt a fatal blow. The site is marked by a commemorative plaque and obelisk.
Nechtanesmere (Angus, NO5149)	British wars (410–1018)	Northumbria (Ecgfrith)	Picts (Bridei III)	20 May 685	Pictish victory. Ecgfrith killed. Decisive victory for Picts forced Northumbrians out of Scotland. On the 1300th anniversary of the battle in 1985 a cairn was erected outside the parish church in commemoration. Aka Dunnichen Moss.
Neville's Cross (Durham, NZ260424)	Anglo-Scottish Wars: Scottish Wars of Independence (1286–1388)	English (Lord Ralph Neville of Raby/Lord Henry Percy)	Scottish (David II)	17 October 1346	English victory. Scottish army destroyed. David II captured and put into the Tower of London until ransomed in 1356.
Newark (Nottinghamshire, SK8154)	English Civil War (1st) (1642–6)	Royalists (Prince Rupert)	Parliamentarians (Sir John Meldrum)	21 March 1644	Royalist victory. Rupert attacked Meldrum, who was investing Newark and forced his surrender. Newark remained in Royalist hands until the end of the war.
Newburn Ford (Tyne & Wear, NZ163650)	Second Bishops' War (1640)	English (Edward, Viscount Conway)	Scottish (Sir Alexander Leslie)	28 August 1640	Scottish victory. English fled and Newcastle captured. Charles I recalled Parliament to call for more funds, which was the first step towards Civil War.
Newbury (I) (Berkshire, SU454662)	English Civil War (1st) (1642–6)	Royalists (Charles I/ Prince Rupert)	Parliamentarians (Robert Devereux, Earl of Essex)	20 September 1643	Inconclusive. Parliament celebrated a victory as the Royalist forces quit the field during the night after the battle.
Newbury (II) (Berkshire, SU4568)	English Civil War (1st) (1642–6)	Royalists (Charles I/ Prince Maurice)	Parliamentarians (Sir William Waller/Edward Montagu, Earl of Manchester)	27 October 1644	Inconclusive. Charles withdrew towards Bath before going into winter quarters.
Newtonbutler (Fermanagh)	Jacobite Rising (1st) (1689–91)	Government (William Wolseley/William Berry)	Jacobites (Justin MacCarthy, Viscount Mountcashel/Anthony Hamilton)	31 July 1689	Government victory. Jacobite attack on Crom Castle near Enniskillen driven off and pursued until the Jacobite force was destroyed. Mountcashel taken prisoner.

Name, county and nearest grid reference	Conflict	Protagonists		Date	Details
Northallerton (North Yorkshire, SE362979)	English Civil War/Stephen and Matilda (1135–54)	English (Thurstan, Archbishop of York/Walter Espec, Sheriff of Yorkshire)	Scottish (David I)	22 August 1138	English victory. David supported Empress Matilda's claim to the English throne. Aka Battle of the Standard. The battle takes its name from a wagon in centre of English line which supported a ship's mast hung with the banners of the local saints (St Peter of York, St John of Beverly, St Cuthbert of Durham and St Wilfred of Ripon) and topped with a silver communion cup.
Northampton (I) (Northamptonshire, SP763594)	English Baronial War (1264–5)	Royal Army (Henry III)	Barons (Simon De Montfort)	6 April 1264	De Montfort's supporters were holed in at Northampton Castle. De Montfort mounted a rear-guard rescue attempt but the castle fell and De Montfort's son (another Simon) was captured by the King's forces.
Northampton (II) (Northamptonshire, SP763594)	Wars of the Roses (1455–87)	Lancastrians (Henry Stafford, Duke of Buckingham/Lord John Grey of Ruthin)	Yorkists (Edward, Earl of March/Richard Earl of Warwick)	10 July 1460	Yorkist victory. The Earls of March and Warwick returned from Calais, where they had fled after Ludford Bridge. Lancastrians betrayed by Lord Grey of Ruthin. Buckingham killed. Henry VI recaptured by Yorkists.
Orewin Bridge (Powys)	Norman/English conquest of Wales (1066–1295)	Welsh (Llewelyn ap Gruffydd)	English (Edmund Mortimer/John Giffard)	11 December 1282	Norman victory. Fought at Climeri nr Builth Wells. Llewelyn ap Gruffydd killed, allowing Edward I to bring Welsh independence to an end. Aka Irfon Bridge.
Otterburn (Northumberland, NY8793)	Anglo-Scottish Wars: Scottish Wars of Independence (1286–1388)	English (Henry Percy 'Hotspur')	Scottish (James, Earl of Douglas)	19 August 1388	Scottish victory. Percy captured. Douglas killed. Scottish raiding party returned to Scotland and a truce was signed in 1389. Aka Chevy Chase.
Oulart Hill (Wexford)	Irish Insurrection (1797–8)	Irish (Fr John Murphy/Edward Roche)	Government (Foote)	27 May 1798	Irish victory. Attempted militia attack on rebel camp ambushed and routed. The rebellion gained momentum and this action was followed the next day by the Battle of Enniscorthy.
Philiphaugh (Borders NT4528)	English Civil War (1st) (1642–6)	Royalists (James Graham, Marquess of Montrose)	Covenanters (David Leslie)	13 September 1645	Covenanter victory. Royalists surprised in an early morning attack and forced to surrender. Montrose rallied the remnants of his army but after Charles I's surrender to the Scots he fled abroad.
Pilleth (Powys)	Glyndŵr Rebellion (1400–16)	English (Sir Edmund Mortimer)	Welsh (Owain Glyndŵr)	22 June 1402	Welsh victory. Owain Glyndŵr proclaimed Prince of Wales in September 1400. Mortimer captured.
Piltown (Kilkenny)	Wars of the Roses (1455–87)	Lancastrians (Sir Edmund MacRichard Butler)	Yorkists (Thomas Fitzgerald, Earl of Desmond)	14 August 1462	Yorkist victory. Rare Roses battle in Ireland. Sir Edmund Butler captured.
Pinkiecleugh (East Lothian, NT3671)	Anglo-Scottish Wars: English invasion (1547)	English (Edward Seymour, Duke of Somerset)	Scottish (James Hamilton, Earl of Arran)	10 September 1547	English victory. Scottish army destroyed, the defeat being known as 'Black Saturday'. Aka Pinkie, Inveresk, Falside, Musselburgh.
Powick Bridge (Worcestershire, SO835524)	English Civil War (1st) (1642–6)	Royalists (Prince Rupert)	Parliamentarians (John Brown/Nathaniel Fiennes)	23 September 1642	Royalist victory. First serious action of the English Civil War. Aka Wick Field.

Name, county and nearest grid reference	Conflict	Protagonists		Date	Details
Preston (I) (Lancashire, SD5530)	English Civil War (2nd) (1648)	Royalists (James Hamilton, Duke of Hamilton/William Baillie)	Parliamentarians (Oliver Cromwell/John Lambert)	17 August 1648	Parliamentarian victory. Royalist and Scottish armies routed.
Preston (II) (Lancashire, SD5429)	Jacobite Rising (2nd)/ The Fifteen (1715)	Government (Sir Charles Wills/George Carpenter)	Jacobites (Thomas Forster/James Radcliffe, Earl of Derwentwater)	12–14 November 1715	Government victory. Forster out-manoeuvred and forced to surrender with most of his men. Radcliffe executed.
Prestonpans (East Lothian, NT4074)	Jacobite Rising (3rd)/ The Forty-Five (1745–6)	Government (Sir John Cope)	Jacobites (Prince Charles Edward Stewart/Lord George Murray)	21 September 1745	Jacobite victory. The Young Pretender, Prince Charles Edward Stewart, landed at Arisaig on 25 July 1745, reached Edinburgh in September and began march on London. The first action, a ten minute engagement, ended in the destruction of Cope's force. Aka Gladsmuir.
Radcot Bridge (Oxfordshire, SU2899)	English Baronial Wars: Lords Appellant War (1387)	Royal Army (Robert de Vere, Marquess of Dublin)	Baronial Army (Henry Bolingbroke, Earl of Derby/ Thomas, Duke of Gloucester)	20 December 1387	Baronial victory. De Vere fled to France. The Lords Appellant forced Richard II to call The Merciless Parliament in February 1388.
Rathmines (Dublin City)	Irish Confederate War/ Eleven Years' War 1641–53)	Irish/Royalists (James Butler, Marquess of Ormonde)	Parliamentarians (Michael Jones)	2 August 1649	Parliamentarian victory. Combined Irish and English Royalist army routed. Fought in what are now the suburbs of Dublin on Baggot Street at Baggotrath Castle. The victory facilitated the arrival of Oliver Cromwell in Ireland. Aka Baggot Rath.
Reading (I) (Berkshire, SU7173 possible site)	Viking Invasions of England (796–991)	West Saxons (Aethelred I/ Alfred/Aethelwulf)	Vikings (Halfdan I/ Bagsecg)	4 January 871	Viking victory. The Saxons assaulted Viking defences on the Thames. Aethelwulf killed and the Saxons retreated towards Ashdown.
Reading (II) (Berkshire, SU7173)	The Glorious Revolution (1688)	Jacobites (Patrick Sarsfield, Earl of Lucan)	Williamites (William of Orange)	9 December 1688	Decisive Williamite victory. James fled to France. Aka Broad Street.
Redeswire Raid (Northumberland, NT 70 06)	Border Wars: Scottish raid (1575)	English (Sir John Forster)	Scottish (Sir John Carmichael)	7 July 1575	Scottish victory. The last such clash before the union under James VI and I.
River Idle (Nottinghamshire, SK7117)	British Wars (410–1018)	Northumbria (Aethelfrith)	East Angles (Raedwald)	616	Raedwald slew Aethelfrith and established Edwin as king of Northumbria.
Roslin (Midlothian, NT2763)	Anglo-Scottish Wars: Scottish Wars of Independence (1286–1388)	English (Sir John Segrave)	Scottish (John 'Red' Comyn/Sinclair Fraser)	24 February 1303	Scottish victory. Scottish army outnumbered 3 to 1.
Roundway Down (Wiltshire, SU0264)	English Civil War (1st) (1642–6)	Royalists (Lord Henry Wilmot/Sir Ralph Hopton)	Parliamentarians (Sir William Waller/Sir Arthur Hesilrige)	13 July 1643	Royalist victory. Relief force trying to lift siege of Devizes succeeded in driving off Parliamentary army. The battle is nicknamed Runaway Down after the headlong flight of the Parliamentarian cavalry over a steep descent. Victory enabled the Royalist army to move on Bristol.

Name, county and nearest grid reference	Conflict	Protagonists		Date	Details
Rowton Heath (Cheshire, SJ456630)	English Civil War (1st) (1642–6)	Royalists (Charles I/Sir Marmaduke Langdale)	Parliamentarians (Sydenham Poyntz/ Michael Jones)	24 September 1645	Parliamentarian victory. Charles watched the defeat from the walls of Chester. Royalist hopes of combining with Montrose dashed (unbeknown to them he had already been defeated at Philiphaugh).
Rullion Green (Midlothian, NT2262)	Pentland Hills Rising (1666)	Royalists (Sir Thomas Dalyell/William Drummond)	Covenanters (James Wallace)	23 November 1666	Royalist victory. Covenanters rebelling against the regime's support for episcopacy marched on Edinburgh. They were met by a much larger government force and defeated.
St Albans (I) (Hertford-shire, TL1407)	Wars of the Roses (1455–87)	Lancastrians (Henry VI/ Edmund Beaumont, Duke of Somerset)	Yorkists (Richard, Duke of York)	22 May 1455	Yorkist victory. First major battle of the Wars of the Roses and fought in the streets of the town. Henry VI captured. Somerset killed. Richard of York declared Constable of England.
St Albans (II) (Hertford-shire, TL1508)	Wars of the Roses (1455–87)	Lancastrians (Margaret of Anjou/Sir Andrew Trollope)	Yorkists (Richard Neville, Earl of Warwick)	17 February 1461	Lancastrian victory. Henry VI released from captivity. Edward of York marched to London and was proclaimed Edward IV.
St Fagans (South Glamorgan, ST1077)	English Civil War (2nd) (1648)	Royalists (Rowland Laugharne/John Poyer)	Parliamentarians (Thomas Horton)	8 May 1648	Parliamentarian victory. Discontented Parliamentarians who had turned Royalist moved against Cardiff but were routed. John Poyer executed.
Sauchieburn (Stirlingshire, NS8384)	Scottish Dynastic Wars (1488)	Royal Army (James III)	Baronial Army (James, Duke of Rothesay)	11 June 1488	Baronial Army victory. Barons supported James' son – James, Duke of Rothesay, the future James IV. James III escaped but was murdered during his flight.
Scarrifholis (Donegal)	Irish Confederate War/ Eleven Years' War (1641–53)	Irish/Royalists (Heber MacMahon, Bishop of Clogher)	Parliamentarians (Sir Charles Coote)	21 June 1650	Ulster army destroyed with losses amounting to two-thirds of its strength of 3000, no quarter being given. Bishop Macmahon subsequently captured and executed. Aka Letterkenny.
Seacroft Moor (West Yorkshire, SE346360)	English Civil War (1st) (1642–6)	Royalists (Lord George Goring)	Parliamentarians (Sir Thomas Fairfax)	30 March 1643	Royalist victory. Parliamentarian infantry attacked on the march by Royalist cavalry.
Sedgemoor (Somerset, ST351356)	Monmouth Rebellion (1685)	Government (Louis Duras, Earl of Feversham/John Churchill)	Rebels (James Scott, Duke of Monmouth)	6 July 1685	See Somerset
Selby (North Yorkshire, SE6132)	English Civil War (1st) (1642–6)	Royalists (Sir John Bellasis)	Parliamentarians (Fernando Fairfax/Sir Thomas Fairfax)	11 April 1644	Parliamentarian victory. Royalist forces defending Selby scattered.
Sevenoaks (Kent, TQ5353)	Cade's Rebellion (1450)	Royal Army (Sir Humphrey Stafford)	Rebels (Jack Cade)	18 June 1450	Rebel victory. Cade's rebels defeated a royal army and marched on to London. Aka Solefield.
Sheriffmuir (Stirlingshire, NN8101)	Jacobite Rising (2nd)/ The Fifteen (1715)	Government (John Campbell, Duke of Argyll)	Jacobites (John Erskine, Earl of Mar)	13 November 1715	Inconclusive. Mar needed a victory to gain local support but failed to achieve this and the rebellion in Scotland ended. The Old Pretender, Prince James Edward Stewart, arrived in December 1716 and remained in Scotland for six weeks before returning to France.

Name, county and nearest grid reference	Conflict	Protagonists		Date	Details
Shrewsbury (Shropshire, SJ505173)	English Baronial Wars: Percy Rebellions (1403 and 1408)	Royal Army (Henry IV/ Henry, Prince of Wales)	Rebels (Henry Percy, 'Hotspur'/ Archibald, Earl of Douglas)	21 July 1403	Royal army victory. Rebel army besieging Shrewsbury, being held by 14 year old Prince Henry. Hotspur killed, Douglas captured (again) and rebellion suppressed.
Smerwick (Kerry)	Desmond Rebellion (1579–83)	English (Arthur Grey, Lord de Wilton)	Irish/Italians (Sebastiano di San Guiseppi)	7–10 November 1580	English victory. Papal troops landed and entrenched at Smerwick in support of Desmond, who failed to send promised troops. Garrison of 600 surrendered but was put to the sword by de Wilton.
Sole Bay (Suffolk)	Third Anglo-Dutch War (1672–4)	United Provinces (Netherlands) (Michiel de Ruyter, Adriaen Banckert, Willem Joseph van Ghent)	Anglo-French (James Stuart, Edward Montagu the 1st Earl of Sandwich, Jean II d'Estrées)	7 June 1672	A fleet of 75 Dutch ships surprised a joint Anglo-French fleet of 93 at anchor in Sole Bay, off the Suffolk coast. Flagship of Admiral Lord Sandwich, HMS *Royal James*, sunk; Sandwich himself drowned trying to escape. Tactical draw but Dutch strategic victory.
Solway Moss (Cumbria, NY383677)	Anglo-Scottish Wars: Scottish raid (1542)	English (Sir Thomas Wharton)	Scottish (Oliver Sinclair/ Robert, Lord Maxwell)	24 November 1542	English victory. The news of the defeat is said to have hastened the death of the already ill James V.
Stainmoor (Durham, NY9012 possible site)	Viking invasions of England (796–991)	Northumbrians (Maccus)	Vikings (Eric Bloodaxe)	954	Northumbrian victory. Eric Bloodaxe, last Viking king of York, killed. England unified.
Stamford Bridge (East Riding of Yorkshire, SE720551)	Norwegian invasion of England (1066)	English (Harold II)	Vikings (Harald Hardrada/ Tostig)	25 September 1066	English victory. Harald Hardrada and Earl Tostig killed. Norwegians fled never to return. Harold learned of Norman invasion in aftermath of battle.
Stirling Bridge (Stirling-shire, NS8095)	Anglo-Scottish Wars: Scottish Wars of Independence (1286–1388)	English (John Warenne, Earl of Surrey/Hugh Cressingham)	Scottish (William Wallace/ Andrew Moray)	11 September 1297	Scottish victory. Vanguard of English army destroyed after crossing the bridge. Cressingham killed. Moray died from wounds. Wallace made Guardian of Scotland. Aka Cambuskenneth.
Stockbridge (Hampshire, SU3535)	English Civil War/Stephen and Matilda (1135–54)	Royal Army (William of Ypres/Henry of Blois)	Angevin Claimants (Robert, Earl of Gloucester)	14 September 1141	Royal army victory. Matilda's attempt to capture Henry of Blois, Bishop of Winchester (brother of King Stephen) led to the siege of Winchester (1 August–14 September 1141). The besiegers were themselves then surrounded by Royalist forces, and were attacked and routed while retreating. Gloucester captured.
Stoke Field (Nottingham-shire, SK740490)	Wars of the Roses (1455–87)	Lancastrians (Henry VII /John de Vere, Earl of Oxford)	Yorkists (John de la Pole, Earl of Lincoln/Francis, Lord Lovell/Martin Schwarz)	16 June 1487	Lancastrian victory. Lincoln and Schwarz killed. In support of the pretender Lambert Simnel who was captured and put to work in the Royal kitchens. Last major action of the Wars of the Roses.
Stow-on-the-Wold (Gloucestershire, SP191272)	English Civil War (1st) (1642–6)	Royalists (Jacob, Lord Astley)	Parliamentarians (Thomas Morgan/Sir William Brereton)	21 March 1646	Parliamentarian victory. Last battle of the 1st Civil War. Astley captured in Stow-on-the-Wold market square.

Name, county and nearest grid reference	Conflict	Protagonists		Date	Details
Stratton (Cornwall and the Scilly Isles, SS227071)	English Civil War (1st) (1642–6)	Royalists (Sir Ralph Hopton)	Parliamentarians (Henry Grey, Earl of Stamford)	16 May 1643	Royalist victory. Following an embarrassing defeat at Sourton Down (Devon, SX5491) on 25 April 1643, Royalist army defeated an army twice its size and secured Cornwall for the Royalist cause. Aka Stamford Hill.
Tewkesbury (Gloucester-shire, SO890316)	Wars of the Roses (1455–87)	Lancastrians (Margaret of Anjou/Henry Beaufort, Duke of Somerset)	Yorkists (Edward IV/ Richard, Duke of Gloucester)	4 May 1471	Yorkist victory. Somerset and Edward, Prince of Wales killed. Queen Margaret and Henry VI captured, later dying in captivity.
Tippermuir (Perth and Kinross, NO0623)	English Civil War (1st) (1642–6)	Royalists (James Graham, Marquess of Montrose)	Covenanters (Lord Elcho)	1 September 1644	Royalist victory. Covenanter army destroyed. Montrose occupied Perth. The first battle of Montrose's campaign. Aka Tibbermore.
Torfnes (Moray, Grampian, NJ1069)	Scottish Wars: Viking War (1040)	Scots (Duncan I)	Vikings (Thorfinn Sigurdsson, Jarl of the Orkneys)	14 August 1040	Viking victory. Duncan killed by Macbeth in aftermath of the battle.
Torrington (Devon)	English Civil War (1st) (1642–6)	Royalists (Lord Hopton)	Parliamentarians (Sir Thomas Fairfax)	16 February 1646	Fairfax, and his second in command Oliver Cromwell of the New Model Army, defeated Lord Hopton and his men, marking the end of Royalist resistance in the West Country.
Towton (North Yorkshire, SE4737)	Wars of the Roses (1455–87)	Lancastrians (Henry Beaufort, Duke of Somerset/Henry Percy, Earl of Northumberland)	Yorkists (Edward IV/ Richard Neville, Earl of Warwick)	29 March 1461	Yorkist victory. Possibly bloodiest battle fought on English soil with up to 28,000 killed. Henry Percy killed. An all-day fight during a blizzard on Palm Sunday, hence the alternative name of Palm Sunday Field.
Tubberneering (Wexford)	Irish Insurrection (1797–8)	Irish (Fr Philip Roche/ Edward Roche)	Government (William Loftus/Lambert Walpole)	4 June 1798	Irish victory. Rebels ambushed an attacking force, Walpole killed. Rebels' attempt to capture New Ross was repelled on 5 June 1798. Aka The Gorey Races.
Turnham Green (London, TQ2077)	English Civil War (1st) (1642–6)	Royalists (Charles I)	Parliamentarians (Robert Devereux, Earl of Essex)	13 November 1642	Parliamentarian victory. Royalist advance on London turned back by the London Trained Bands.
Vinegar Hill (Wexford)	Irish Insurrection (1797–8)	Irish (Fr John Murphy/ Edward Roche)	Government (Gerard Lake)	21 June 1798	Government victory. Irish routed, their camp on Vinegar Hill destroyed and the rebellion in Co. Wexford effectively ended.
Wakefield (West Yorkshire, SE3318)	Wars of the Roses (1455–87)	Lancastrians (Henry Beaufort, Duke of Somerset/Henry Percy, Earl of Northumberland)	Yorkists (Richard, Duke of York/Richard Neville, Earl of Salisbury)	30–31 December 1460	Lancastrian victory. Richard of York and son Edmund killed. Salisbury executed. Lancastrians marched on London (to St Albans).
Wexford (Wexford)	Irish Confederate War/ Eleven Years' War (1641–53)	Royalists (David Synnott)	Parliamentarians (Oliver Cromwell)	11 October 1649	Parliamentarian victory. Wexford Castle betrayed to Cromwell, the town stormed and the defenders slaughtered. Many civilians drowned in the River Slaney while trying to escape.

MAJOR BATTLES ON BRITISH AND IRISH SOIL

Name, county and nearest grid reference	Conflict	Protagonists		Date	Details
Wigan Lane (Greater Manchester, SD5806)	English Civil War (3rd) (1650–1)	Royalists (James Stanley, Earl of Derby/Sir Thomas Tyldesley)	Parliamentarians (Robert Lilburne)	25 August 1651	Parliamentarian victory. Royalist rising in support of Charles II's invasion of England with Scottish help. Royalist supporters routed and Tyldesley killed.
Wilton (Wiltshire, site unknown but near Salisbury)	Viking invasions of England (796–991)	West Saxon (Alfred)	Vikings (Halfdan I)	May 871	Viking victory. Halfdan bought off and withdrew to London.
Winceby (Lincolnshire, TF317684)	English Civil War (1st) (1642–6)	Royalists (Sir William Widdrington)	Parliamentarians (Edward Montagu, Earl of Manchester/Sir Thomas Fairfax/Oliver Cromwell)	11 October 1643	Parliamentarian victory. Royalists attempting to relieve Old Bolingbroke Castle. Lincolnshire secured for Parliament. Aka Horncastle Fight.
Winwaed (West Yorkshire, SE4317 possible site)	British wars (410–1018)	Northumbria (Oswy)	Mercia (Penda)	15 November 654	Northumbrian victory. Penda killed and army destroyed after being deserted by his allies including Cadfael of Gwynedd, known as 'Battle Shirker'.
Winwick (Cheshire, SJ5993)	English Civil War (2nd) (1648)	Royalists (James Hamilton, Duke of Hamilton)	Parliamentarians (Oliver Cromwell/John Lambert)	19 August 1648	Parliamentarian victory. Following the defeat at Preston the retreating Scottish army was caught and destroyed by Cromwell. Hamilton captured and executed in 1649.
Worcester (Worcestershire, SO854528)	English Civil War (3rd) (1650–1)	Mainly Scottish Royalists (Charles II/David Leslie)	Commonwealth (Oliver Cromwell)	3 September 1651	Commonwealth victory. Charles II forced to flee into exile. Final battle of the Civil Wars, fought on the same ground as the first at Powick Bridge in 1642.
Yellow Ford (Armagh)	Tyrone's Rebellion/Nine Years' War (1593–1603)	English (Henry Bagenal)	Irish (Hugh O'Neill, Earl of Tyrone/Hugh Roe O'Donnell)	14 August 1598	Irish victory. Irish ambushed a column going to the relief of Blackwater Fort and destroyed the English army. Henry Bagenal killed. Biggest defeat of English arms on Irish soil.
York (York, SE6051)	Viking invasions of England (796–991)	Northumbria (Aelle/Osbert)	Vikings (Ivar the Boneless)	21–23 March 867	Viking victory. Both King Aelle and King Osbert killed and York sacked.

British and Irish Cities

City status in Britain and Ireland has historically been granted by the British monarch to a select group of communities the status of which is not based on any particular criteria, although in England and Wales it was traditionally conferred on towns with diocesan cathedrals. Gradually this system was changed and in 1889 Birmingham became the first city created without having a cathedral church. The presence of a cathedral in a Scottish town before the Reformation often led to its recognition as a city; however, Dornoch for instance, has never generally been called a city despite having had a pre-Reformation cathedral. City status in Ireland tended historically to be granted by royal charter and there are many towns in Ireland with Church of Ireland cathedrals which have never been called cities. Conversely, the seat of the Primate of All Ireland, Armagh, was considered a city despite its never having been granted a charter. In fact the only historic city with a charter in present-day Northern Ireland is Derry, which was renamed 'Londonderry' by its city charter.

Although city status is generally conferred by letters patent and not by a royal charter there are some cities in England and Wales that predate the historical monarchy, and have been regarded as cities since 'time immemorial' (legally the end of the reign of Henry II in 1189). The status of royal burgh was, in terms of privileges, more relevant in Scotland than the status of city. The two largest royal burghs, Glasgow and Edinburgh, have in fact never officially been designated as cities by letters patent so are also exceptions to the rule. The holding of city status brings no particular benefits other than the right to be called a city.

All cities have to be reissued with letters patent reconfirming city status following local government reorganisation where the original city has been abolished. This process was followed by a number of cities since 1974, and the status of York and Hereford was confirmed in both 1974 and again in the 1990s. Failure to do so leads to the loss of city status, as happened at Rochester in 1998 and also previously in St David's and Armagh, although both of these have since regained city status. There are currently 72 officially designated cities in Britain and Ireland, of which eight have been created since 2000 in competitions to celebrate the new millennium and Queen Elizabeth II's Golden Jubilee. Interestingly, London is not officially a city although it does contain two cities (City of London and City of Westminster).

English cities	Created
Bath	1590
Birmingham	1889
Bradford	1897
Brighton & Hove	2000
Bristol	1373
Cambridge	1951
Canterbury	1189
Carlisle	1189
Chester	1541
Chichester	1189
Coventry	1345
Derby	1977
Durham	1189
Ely	1189
Exeter	1189
Gloucester	1541
Hereford	1189
Kingston upon Hull	1897
Lancaster	1937
Leeds	1893
Leicester	1919
Lichfield	1553
Lincoln	1189
Liverpool	1880
City of London	1189
Manchester	1853

English cities	Created
Newcastle upon Tyne	1882
Norwich	1195
Nottingham	1897
Oxford	1542
Peterborough	1541
Plymouth	1928
Portsmouth	1926
Preston	2002
Ripon	1836
Salford	1926
Salisbury	1189
Sheffield	1893
Southampton	1964
St Albans	1877
Stoke-on-Trent	1925
Sunderland	1992
Truro	1877
Wakefield	1888
Wells	1205
Westminster	1540
Winchester	1189
Wolverhampton	2000
Worcester	1189
York	1189

Scottish cities	Created
Aberdeen	1891
Dundee	1889
Edinburgh	1329
Glasgow	1451
Inverness	2000
Stirling	2002

Welsh cities	Created
Bangor	1189
Cardiff	1905
Newport	2002
St David's	1994
Swansea	1969

Northern Irish cities	Created
Armagh	1995
Belfast	1888
Derry/Londonderry	1613
Lisburn	2002
Newry	2002

Irish cities	Created
Cork	1185
Dublin	1171
Galway	1484
Kilkenny	1609
Limerick	1197
Waterford	1171

County Flowers

Plantlife International launched a County Flowers campaign in 2002 asking members of the public to nominate a wild flower emblem for their designated areas. The English bluebell topped the poll but was so far ahead of the competition that it was excluded as a choice. In addition to the present counties of England, the poll also included the traditional counties of Scotland, Wales and Northern Ireland (some of which are now unitary authorities). Several of the old English counties were also covered, as were a number of major conurbations. A total of 50,000 people voted and the results were as follows.

ENGLAND

Bedfordshire	**Bee orchid** (*Ophrys apifera*). The mauve orchids, which mimic a bumblebee, are seen in disused quarries, on roadsides, even on waste ground in towns.
Berkshire	**Summer snowflake** (*Leucojum aestivum*). Because they grow beside the River Loddon, the tall-stemmed plants with drooping white flowers are known in the county as Loddon lilies.
Birmingham	**Foxglove** (*Digitalis purpurea*). The tall purple flowers are found in parks and on industrial wastelands. Tellingly perhaps, William Withering, discoverer of the heart drug digitalis, which was derived from the foxglove, was chief physician of Birmingham General Hospital from 1775.
Bristol	**Maltese-cross** (*Lychnis chalcedonica*). Introduced to Britain in the 16th century. The delicate red petals can be seen in waste ground and on roadsides. It is known as the Flower of Bristol.
Buckinghamshire	**Chiltern gentian** (*Gentianella germanica*). Grows on the chalk downs of Buckinghamshire and flowers in the late summer.
Cambridgeshire	**Pasqueflower** (*Pulsatilla vulgaris*). Has been a famous Cambridgeshire flower since its discovery on the Gog Magog Hills by John Ray in 1660. According to legend, the fluffy-stemmed purple plants grow on the graves of Viking warriors.
Cheshire	**Cuckooflower** (*Cardamine pratensis*). Also known as 'milkmaids'. It is a delicate flower of wet meadows and pond margins, befitting a county with more ponds than any other.
Cornwall	**Cornish heath** (*Erica vagans*). The lilac blooms are found in late summer on the moors of the Lizard, the only part of Britain where this shrub is found.
Cumbria	**Grass-of-Parnassus** (*Parnassia palustris*). The tallish white-petalled flowers appear on the county arms. Legend has it that the cattle of the gods of Mount Parnassus fed on the plant, and so it was given honorary status as a grass.
Derbyshire	**Jacob's ladder** (*Polemonium caeruleum*). The bright blue flowers and delicate ladder-shaped leaves of the wild plant are common in the Peak District and Yorkshire Dales.
Devon	**Primrose** (*Primula vulgaris*). The yellowy-white flowers have a strong presence in Devon's high-banked scenic country lanes. Local paper-makers used to present little bunches to their customers to provide a 'breath of Devon'.
Dorset	**Dorset heath** (*Erica ciliaris*). This tall crimson heather is a defining species of Dorset's heathland and bogs.
Durham	**Spring gentian** (*Gentiana verna*). Even if Upper Teesdale had no other plant, botanical diehards would flock there to see this deep-blue five-petalled favourite.
Essex	**Common poppy** (*Papaver rhoeas*). The unmistakable blood-red flowers still adorn cornfields in the county, though they are just as common on disturbed ground, especially on the chalk. The traditional county flower of Essex is the cowslip, locally known as the paigle or peggle, and frequently mentioned in the writings of Essex bucolic authors such as Samuel Bensusan and C H Warren.
Gloucestershire	**Wild daffodil** (*Narcissus pseudonarcissus*). The county's golden triangle around the villages of Newent and Dymock is famous for its wild daffodils or Lent lilies. A 10 mile (16km) footpath known as 'The Daffodil Way' runs through the heart of Gloucestershire.
Hampshire	**Dog-rose** (*Rosa canina*). Hampshire is rich in hedgerow roses and the lilac-petalled flower has long been the county's emblem.
Herefordshire	**Mistletoe** (*Viscum album*). In Hereford, mistletoe grows on apple trees and hawthorns, from which it can be harvested as a winter crop.
Hertfordshire	**Pasqueflower** (*Pulsatilla vulgaris*). To be seen in abundance on the limestone hillsides, this popular flower was chosen by Cambridgeshire folk too.
Huntingdonshire	**Water-violet** (*Hottonia palustris*). No longer a county in name but considered as such for the survey. The dainty five-petalled lilac flowers are hardier than they appear and can survive summer droughts.
Isle of Man	**Fuchsia** (*Fuchsia magellanica*). On the island this exotic plant with its red shrimp-like blossom grows unusually tall.
Isle of Wight	**Pyramidal orchid** (*Anacamptis pyramidalis*). The cone-shaped lilac plant abounds on the undercliff and across the island's hog's-back of chalk in June.
Isles of Scilly	**Thrift** (*Armeria maritima*). Part of the county of Cornwall but with its own flower. The lilac-coloured thrift can be seen on rocks and sea cliffs. The pre-decimal threepenny bit used to have a depiction of thrift on the reverse.
Kent	**Hop** (*Humulus lupulus*). The pale green and white plants are unobtrusive climbers in hedgerows and thickets.

Lancashire	**Red rose** (*Rosa species*). The Red Rose county since the Middle Ages, when the House of Lancaster adopted it as its heraldic badge. The true red rose of Lancashire is supposedly the red rose of the Mediterranean (*Rosa gallica*).
Leeds	**Bilberry** (*Vaccinium myrtillus*). The bulbous purple berries are a symbol of the open air of the hills, especially around Bradford and Leeds.
Leicestershire	**Foxglove** (*Digitalis purpurea*). The foxglove helps to define Leicestershire's uplands, the woods and bracken swards of Charnwood Forest, but is scarce in the agricultural east of the county. Birmingham also chose the foxglove.
Lincolnshire	**Common dog-violet** (*Viola riviniana*). Carpets the great limewoods of Bardney Forest near Lincoln. The term 'dog' denotes its lack of scent and is contrasted to 'sweet' violet.
Liverpool	**Sea-holly** (*Eryngium maritimum*). The powder-blue cone-shaped flowers emerge in July, protected by prickly, wax-covered leaves.
London	**Rosebay willowherb** (*Epilobium angustifolium*). The tall purple flowers mingle with buddleias and Michaelmas daisies on railway banks, walls and waste ground.
Manchester	**Common cotton-grass** (*Eriophorum angustifolium*). The white hairy plumes are an emblem of their boggy habitat and the wide open spaces.
Middlesex	**Wood anemone** (*Anemone nemorosa*). The long-stemmed pale-blue unsymmetrical flowers are seen in woods and hedgebanks.
Newcastle upon Tyne	**Monkeyflower** (*Mimulus guttatus*). From midsummer, the banks and shingles of the Tyne are bright with the yellowy-orange, red-spotted 'monkey faces' more common in rural Northumberland.
Norfolk	**Common poppy** (*Papaver rhoeas)*. The county's original choice was Alexanders (*Smyrnium olusatrum*) but natives demanded a re-vote and out of five possible alternatives the poppy won. North Norfolk has long been known as 'poppyland'. Essex also chose the poppy as its county flower.
Northamptonshire	**Cowslip** (*Primula veris*). Frequently seen on road verges, quarries and railway banks, the tubular-budded long-stemmed flowers adorned with beautiful orange-yellow petals were chosen by three English counties.
Northumberland	**Bloody crane's-bill** (*Geranium sanguineum*). The vivid magenta flowers adorn coastal cliffs and dunes and spread inland on the rocks of the Whin Sill.
Nottingham	**Nottingham catchfly** (*Silene nutans*). The spider-like flowers were once seen on the walls of the castle but since renovation are not to be found anywhere in Nottingham.
Nottinghamshire	**Autumn crocus** (*Crocus nudiflorus*). The tightly petalled purple flower used to adorn the meadows of the Trent and the blooms were sold at Nottingham market.
Oxfordshire	**Snake's-head fritillary** (*Fritillaria meleagris*). Some of the best-known fritillary fields are in Oxfordshire, along the flood-meadows of the Thames, the purple bells bowing on their snakey stalks.
Rutland	**Clustered bellflower** (*Campanula glomerata*). The familiar rich-blue flowers of the southern limestone are scarce in Rutland and therefore highly regarded.
Sheffield	**Wood crane's-bill** (*Geranium sylvaticum*). A much-loved flower of old hay-meadows and damp, open woods near Sheffield, with its distinctive flowers the colour of runny blue ink.
Shropshire	**Round-leaved sundew** *(Drosera rotundifolia*). This crimson-leaved carnivore, which uses glues and acids to trap and devour careless insects, is a bog plant.
Somerset	**Cheddar pink** (*Dianthus gratianopolitanus*). Discovered on 'Chidderoks' 300 years ago, it grows in several places in the Mendip Hills but nowhere more profusely than the original site at Cheddar Gorge.
Staffordshire	**Heather** (*Calluna vulgaris*). Traditionally a Scottish flower but Staffordshire is proud of its heather moors, blooming purple beyond the Potteries and manufacturing towns.
Suffolk	**Oxlip** (*Primula elatior*). The signature flower of well-established woods on the East Anglian boulder clay. The apricot scents of the drooping yellow blooms made this a popular choice.
Surrey	**Cowslip** (*Primula veris*). In Surrey, cowslips grow in contrasting places – dry chalk downs and damp meadows. One of three English counties to select the cowslip as their designated flower.
Sussex	**Round-headed rampion** (*Phyteuma orbiculare*). East and West Sussex are considered one county in the survey. Known as the Pride of Sussex, the sharp-blue flowers are common on the South Downs and bear resemblance to a many-tentacled jellyfish ready for its prey.
Warwickshire	**Honeysuckle** (*Lonicera periclymenum*). Honeysuckle is Shakespeare's 'woodbine', mentioned in *A Midsummer Night's Dream*, a play thought to have been set in the Forest of Arden.
Westmorland	**Alpine forget-me-not** *(Myosotis alpestris*). The blue flowers of this prettiest of forget-me-nots are confined in England to a few limestone hilltops in the North Pennines.
Wiltshire	**Burnt orchid** (*Orchis ustulata*). This dwarf orchid belongs to the chalky core of Wiltshire, its white cone-shaped bloom turning pink and then dark red at the top.
Worcestershire	**Cowslip** (*Primula veris)*. In parts of the county there are still small cowslip meadows hidden behind tall hedges. Locals call them 'cowslups'. One of three English counties to choose the cowslip as their preferred flower.
Yorkshire	**Harebell** (*Campanula rotundifolia*). For the purposes of the survey Yorkshire was considered as a single county. It may appear surprising that the white rose was not chosen but the blue and white blossoms of the harebell match the native folk for toughness and resilience, making it a perfect choice.

SCOTLAND

Aberdeenshire	**Bearberry** (*Arctostaphylos uva-ursi*). This red-berried trailing shrub is widespread at beautiful sites like the Muir of Dinnet.
Angus/Forfarshire	**Alpine catchfly** (*Lychnis alpina*). A single, remote hilltop of Angus boasts almost the whole British population of this pink alpine, although there are small areas of Cumbria where it is also seen.
Argyll	**Foxglove** (*Digitalis purpurea*). Seen on roadside banks in the mild, humid climate, foxgloves look bigger and redder than those seen further south. Birmingham and Leicestershire also chose the foxglove.
Ayrshire	**Green-winged orchid** (*Orchis morio*). Varying from pink-purple to almost white, the upper petals are marked with dark veins and often suffused green. Although this beautiful flower is seen throughout the British Isles it is in fact rare in Ayrshire.
Banffshire	**Dark-red helleborine** (*Epipactis atrorubens*). This rare and beautiful wild red orchid is a special plant of old Banff.
Berwickshire	**Rock-rose** (*Helianthemum nummularium*). The five-petalled 'solflowers' form spectacular golden banks on some coastal cliffs in early summer.
Bute	**Thrift** (*Armeria maritima*). At its brightest and best on the rocky headlands and islands of the west coast, Bute shares the love of the thrift with the Isles of Scilly.
Caithness	**Scots primrose** (*Primula scotica*). Scots primrose grows on coastal promontories on the north coast including the most northerly point of mainland Britain, Dunnet Head. The rich-purple flower is native to Orkney and Pentland Firth but is found nowhere else.
Clackmannanshire	**Opposite-leaved golden saxifrage** (*Chrysosplenium oppositifolium*). Creeping plant characteristic of the shaded, wooded glens.
Cromarty	**Spring cinquefoil** (*Potentilla species*). This pretty five-petalled golden trailing flower reaches its northern limit on the sea-cliffs.
Dumfriesshire	**Harebell** (*Campanula rotundifolia*). The true bluebell of Scotland, aka the 'cuckoo's shoe'. Also chosen by Yorkshire.
Dunbartonshire	**Lesser water-plantain** (*Baldellia ranunculoides*). This pale pink-flowered aquatic brightens a few bays and shores of Loch Lomond, Scotland's first National Park.
East Lothian and Haddingtonshire	**Viper's-bugloss** (*Echium vulgare*). A rich blue and black flower found on dry banks and dunes.
Edinburgh	**Sticky catchfly** (*Lychnis viscaria*). The pale purple flower has grown on rocks in Holyrood Park for at least 400 years.
Fife	**Coralroot orchid** (*Corallorrhiza trifida*). This pale yellow claw-fingered flower grows in quarries and disused railway lines.
Glasgow	**Broom** (*Cytisus scoparius*). The pale orange-brown vanilla-scented flowers brighten many braes and railway lines.
Inverness-shire	**Twinflower** (*Linnaea borealis*). A shy species that creeps over the shady floor of mossy pinewoods, its drooping bell-shaped flowers hiding their inner beauty.
Kinross	**Holy-grass** (*Hierochloe odorata*). This delicate, scented grass grows on the banks of Loch Leven, the castle on a small island in the loch being the prison for a year of Mary, Queen of Scots.
Kirkcudbright	**Bog-rosemary** (*Andromeda polifolia).* The delicate bulbous pink flowers are a particular feature of the much-reduced bogs of Galloway.
Lanarkshire	**Dune helleborine** (*Epipactis leptochila*). The county's coal 'bings' are home to two exotic orchids: the narrow-lipped or dune helleborine and Young's helleborine.
Moray	**One-flowered wintergreen** (*Moneses uniflora*). This star-shaped white plant needs mossy hollows in undisturbed pinewoods. Aka St Olaf's candle stick.
Nairn	**Chickweed wintergreen** (*Trientalis europaea*). This six-petalled white flower is not a true wintergreen but, surprisingly, a relative of the primrose.
Orkney	**Alpine bearberry** (*Arctostaphylos alpinus*). The black berries amid lightly veined leaves that turn red in autumn are in evidence on the path to the Old Man of Hoy rock stack.
Peebles	**Cloudberry** (*Rubus chamaemorus*). A miniature bramble of high places. The four-petalled, large white flowers with marmalade berries are hard to find but can be seen on the Pentland Hills.
Perthshire	**Alpine gentian** (*Gentiana nivalis*). This sweet 'gentian of the snows' is among the gems of Ben Lawers, the highest of the Perthshire hills.
Renfrewshire	**Bogbean** (*Menyanthes trifoliata*). A plant of dark, moorland waters, the bogbean's feathery flowers are somewhat like an azalea.
Ross	**Bog asphodel** (*Narthecium ossifragum*). The golden spires of bog asphodel light up dark, peaty places after midsummer.
Roxburghshire	**Maiden pink** (*Dianthus deltoides*). Purple five-petalled scentless flower inhabiting dry banks and hill pastures.
Selkirkshire	**Mountain pansy** (*Viola lutea*). Largest of the native pansies, a flower of upland pastures, sheep and trout becks.
Shetland	**Shetland mouse-ear** (*Cerastium nigrescens*). The white ten-petalled flower is entirely confined to the island of Unst.
Stirlingshire	**Scottish dock** (*Rumex aquaticus*). Confined to the banks of Loch Lomond, the towering russet spires are sometimes called the Loch Lomond dock.

Sutherland	**Grass-of-Parnassus** (*Parnassia palustris*). Increasingly scarce elsewhere, this flower of wet flushes and hollows is still fairly common here. Also chosen by Cumbria.
West Lothian and Linlithgowshire	**Common spotted-orchid** (*Dactylorhiza fuchsii*). The lilac spikes and red spotted leaves of this flower enliven many wild places in West Lothian.
Western Isles	**Hebridean spotted-orchid** (*Dactylorhiza fuchsii* subspecies *hebridensis*). Believed to be a low-growing form of the much more widespread common spotted-orchid, although more conical in shape and a richer lilac in colour.
Wigtownshire	**Yellow iris** (*Iris pseudacorus*). Known locally as 'segg' or 'sword-grass', a reference to the remarkable blade-like leaves. The flagging appearance belies a hardiness demanded by its habitat of wet fields and marshes.

WALES

Anglesey/Sir Fon	**Spotted rock-rose** (*Tuberaria guttata*). Yellow five-petalled flower with distinct crimson spots near the base of each petal. Predominant on Anglesey's Holy Island.
Brecknockshire/ Sir Frycheiniog	**Cuckooflower** (*Cardamine pratensis*). The delicate tall-stemmed lilac flowers appear in the meadows of Brecknock when the cuckoo returns in mid-April.
Caernarvonshire/ Sir Gaernarfon	**Snowdon lily** (*Lloydia serotina*). The pride of Wales, unlike most alpines, blooms alone, and often out of reach, in rock crevices.
Cardiff/Caerdydd	**Wild leek** (*Allium ampeloprasum*). The lilac globes of the flowering wild leek were used to identify Welsh soldiers in battle against the English. The traditional emblem of Wales.
Cardiganshire/ Ceredigion	**Bog-rosemary** (*Andromeda polifolia*). A speciality of mid-west Wales, with delicate pink bells and rosemary-like foliage. Also chosen by Kirkcudbright.
Carmarthenshire/ Sir Gaerfyddin	**Whorled caraway** (*Carum verticillatum*). Found on rough pasture, its frothy blossom symbolises the battle between conservation and intensive agriculture.
Denbighshire/ Sir Ddinbych	**Limestone woundwort** (*Stachys alpina*). Grows among rocks by roadsides and is seen only in Denbigh and Gloucestershire.
Flintshire/Sir Fflint	**Bell heather** (*Erica cinerea*). Bell heather announces the brief blaze of colour that lights up the moors at the end of summer.
Glamorgan/Morgannwg	**Yellow whitlow-grass** (*Draba aizoides*). Confined to cliffs and old walls on the Gower, this tiny cress flowers in the early spring.
Merioneth/Merionnydd	**Welsh poppy** (*Meconopsis cambrica*). The bright yellow Welsh poppy is a native of rocky gullies and stream sides in Merioneth.
Monmouthshire/ Sir Fynwy	**Foxglove** (*Digitalis purpurea*). The foxglove is a common wayside flower in Gwent. Also chosen by Argyll, Birmingham and Leicestershire.
Montgomeryshire/ Sir Drefaldwyn	**Spiked speedwell** (*Veronica spicata*). The tall deep blue spikes of this rock plant are one of the celebrated rarities of Craig Breidden.
Pembrokeshire	**Thrift** (*Armeria maritima*). Thrift brightens up the county's coastline of headlands, rock arches and bays in May. Also chosen by the Isles of Scilly and Bute.
Radnorshire/ Sir Faesyfed	**Radnor Lily** (*Gagea bohemica*). Aka 'early-star-of-Bethlehem' and sometimes flowering as early as midwinter.

NORTHERN IRELAND

Antrim	**Harebell** (*Campanula rotundifolia*). Known as the 'goblin's thimble' in Co. Antrim; legend has it that you pick it at your peril. Also chosen by Dumfriesshire and Yorkshire.
Armagh	**Cowbane** (*Cicula virosa*). As its name implies, it is poisonous to cattle and is consequently slowly being eradicated.
Belfast	**Gorse** (*Ulex europaeus*). The bright yellow, sweetly scented flowers are ever-present in heathland, waste ground, banks and coastal regions.
Derry	**Purple saxifrage** (*Saxifraga oppositifolia*). Inhabits cliff edges and rocks, flowering in early spring, often amid lying snow.
Down	**Spring squill** (*Scilla verna*). The lilac petals of the squill inhabit coastal grasslands and cliffs.
Fermanagh	**Globeflower** (*Trollius europaeus*). The distinctive golden puffballs adorn the lake margins of west Fermanagh.
Tyrone	**Bog-rosemary** (*Andromeda polifolia*) One of the special plants of the central Irish peat bogs. Also chosen by Kirkcudbright and Cardiganshire.

Longest and Highest

Some general geographical information about Britain and Ireland (the right-hand column shows the section where further details can be found).

10 longest rivers of Britain and Ireland

	miles	km	
Shannon	240	384	Clare
Severn	220	352	Powys
Thames	215	346	London
Trent	170	272	Nottinghamshire
Great Ouse	150	240	Bedfordshire
Wye	130	208	Gwent
Tay	117	187	Tayside
Spey	107	171	Grampian
Blackwater	104	167	Cork
Clyde	98	157	Strathclyde

Note: The River Swale, a major tributary of the River Ure, and the Ure itself both meet and continue as the Yorkshire Ouse. The longest combined length of the Swale and Ouse is approximately 114 miles (182km) although these are usually considered as distinct rivers. The River Nene (see Cambridgeshire attractions) is currently 91 miles (146km) in length although the old middle level course detouring to March midway between Peterborough and Wisbech added approximately 11 miles (18km) to its length.

Longest rivers by country

	miles	km		
Shannon	240	384	Clare	Ireland
Thames	215	346	London	England
Tay	117	187	Tayside	Scotland
Bann	76	122	Down	Northern Ireland
Towy	65	104	Dyfed	Wales

Note: The five rivers mentioned above are the longest rivers completely within their respective countries. The River Severn is the longest river in Wales, but as it flows into England it is excluded from this table.

Highest mountains

	feet	metres	
Ben Nevis	4406	1344	Highland
Snowdon	3560	1085	Gwynedd
Carrantuohill	3414	1041	Kerry
Scafell Pike	3208	978	Cumbria
Slieve Donard	2707	850	Down

Largest islands

	sq miles	sq km	
Anglesey	274.52	711	Gwynedd
Isle of Wight	146.83	380.28	Hampshire
Achill Island	60	155.4	Mayo
Rathlin Island	12.9	33.44	Antrim
Lewis and Harris	838.56	2171.86	Western Isles

Note: The largest island of Great Britain and Ireland is Great Britain itself, the eighth largest in the world (if the continent of Australia is excluded). The second largest island is quite obviously the island of Ireland. The list of largest islands of each of the five home countries is by area and not population. The Isle of Wight has by far the largest population (132,731 as at 2001 Census) while Northern Ireland's largest island has only a population of about 100. It should also be noted that these areas are not the five largest in Britain and Ireland, nor are the mountains or lakes. There are for instance hundreds of mountains in Scotland higher than Slieve Donard and more than 50 higher than Snowdon.

Largest lakes

	sq miles	sq km	
Lough Neagh	147.39	381.73	Armagh
Lough Corrib	77.22	200	Galway
Loch Lomond	27.46	71.12	Strathclyde
Windermere	5.69	14.74	Cumbria
Vyrnwy	1.75	4.53	Powys

Deepest lakes

	feet	metres	
Morar	1017	310	Highland
Wastwater	260	79	Cumbria
Muckross	230	70	Kerry
Lower Lough Erne	200	61	Fermanagh
Bala	125	38	Gwynedd

Population Summary

English County Councils

		Population			Area	
County	*County town*	*male*	*female*	*total*	*sq miles*	*sq km*
Buckinghamshire	Aylesbury	234,739	244,287	479,026	604	1565
Cambridgeshire	Cambridge	273,645	279,013	552,658	1176	3046
Cumbria	Carlisle	237,915	249,692	487,607	2613	6768
Derbyshire	Matlock	360,839	373,746	734,585	983	2547
Devon	Exeter	340,013	364,480	704,493	2534	6564
Dorset	Dorchester	188,780	202,200	390,980	981	2542
East Sussex	Lewes	232,952	259,372	492,324	660	1709
Essex	Chelmsford	640,193	670,642	1,310,835	1338	3465
Gloucestershire	Gloucester	275,513	289,046	564,559	1024	2653
Hampshire	Winchester	608,043	632,060	1,240,103	1420	3679
Hertfordshire	Hertford	505,059	528,918	1,033,977	634	1643
Kent	Maidstone	643,886	685,832	1,329,718	1368	3544
Lancashire	Preston	550,533	584,441	1,134,974	1121	2903
Leicestershire	Leicester	301,268	308,310	609,578	804	2083
Lincolnshire	Lincoln	316,584	330,061	646,645	2286	5921
Norfolk	Norwich	387,827	408,901	796,728	2074	5371
North Yorkshire	Northallerton	277,677	291,983	569,660	3103	8038
Northamptonshire	Northampton	310,744	318,932	629,676	913	2364
Nottinghamshire	Nottingham	366,118	382,392	748,510	805	2085
Oxfordshire	Oxford	299,257	306,231	605,488	1006	2605
Somerset	Taunton	241,960	256,133	498,093	1332	3451
Staffordshire	Stafford	396,160	410,584	806,744	1012	2620
Suffolk	Ipswich	327,900	340,653	668,553	1468	3801
Surrey	Kingston upon Thames	516,525	542,490	1,059,015	642	1663
Warwickshire	Warwick	248,267	257,593	505,860	763	1975
West Sussex	Chichester	360,604	393,010	753,614	769	1991
Worcestershire	Worcester	265,887	276,220	542,107	672	1741
		9,708,888	10,187,222	19,896,110	34,105	88,337

Unitary Authorities

Metropolitan Authorities

Authority	*Headquarters*	Population *male*	*female*	*total*	Area *sq miles*	*sq km*
Barnsley	Barnsley	106,096	111,967	218,063	127	329
Birmingham	Birmingham	473,266	503,821	977,087	103	268
Bolton	Bolton	127,101	133,936	261,037	54	140
Bradford	Bradford	225,133	242,532	467,665	141	366
Bury	Bury	87,942	92,666	180,608	38	99
Calderdale	Halifax	93,013	99,392	192,405	141	364
Coventry	Coventry	149,115	151,733	300,848	38	99
Doncaster	Doncaster	140,114	146,752	286,866	219	568
Dudley	Dudley	149,714	155,441	305,155	38	98
Gateshead	Gateshead	92,408	98,743	191,151	55	142
Kirklees	Huddersfield	188,832	199,735	388,567	158	409
Knowsley	Huyton	71,064	79,395	150,459	33	86
Leeds	Leeds	345,754	369,648	715,402	213	552
Liverpool	Liverpool	209,805	229,668	439,473	43	112
Manchester	Manchester	191,570	201,249	392,819	45	116
Newcastle-upon-Tyne	Newcastle-upon-Tyne	125,473	134,063	259,536	44	113
North Tyneside	North Shields	91,707	99,952	191,659	32	82
Oldham	Oldham	105,036	112,237	217,273	55	142
Rochdale	Rochdale	99,705	105,652	205,357	61	158
Rotherham	Rotherham	120,691	127,484	248,175	111	287
St Helens	St Helens	85,714	91,129	176,843	53	136
Salford	Swinton	106,191	109,912	216,103	38	97
Sandwell	West Bromwich	136,497	146,407	282,904	33	86
Sefton	Southport	133,489	149,469	282,958	59	153
Sheffield	Sheffield	250,630	262,604	513,234	142	368
Solihull	Solihull	96,683	102,834	199,517	69	178
South Tyneside	South Shields	74,073	78,712	152,785	25	64
Stockport	Stockport	137,268	147,260	284,528	49	126
Sunderland	Sunderland	136,625	144,182	280,807	53	137
Tameside	Ashton-under-Lyme	103,347	109,696	213,043	40	103
Trafford	Stretford	102,161	107,984	210,145	41	106
Wakefield	Wakefield	153,210	161,962	315,172	131	339
Walsall	Walsall	123,189	130,310	253,499	40	104
Wigan	Wigan	147,856	153,559	301,415	73	188
Wirral	Wallasey	147,182	165,111	312,293	61	157
Wolverhampton	Wolverhampton	115,858	120,724	236,582	27	69
		5,243,512	5,577,921	10,821,433	2680	6941

Non-Metropolitan Authorities

		Population			Area	
Authority	*Headquarters*	*male*	*female*	*total*	*sq miles*	*sq km*
Bath & North East Somerset	Bath	82,143	86,897	169,040	134	346
Bedford	Bedford	73,066	74,845	147,911	184	476
Blackburn with Darwen	Blackburn	67,309	70,161	137,470	53	137
Blackpool	Blackpool	68,742	73,541	142,283	13	35
Bournemouth	Bournemouth	78,434	85,010	163,444	18	46
Bracknell Forest	Bracknell	54,879	54,738	109,617	42	109
Brighton & Hove	Brighton	119,897	127,920	247,817	32	83
Bristol	Bristol	185,660	194,955	380,615	42	110
Central Bedfordshire	Chicksands	116098	117563	233661	276	716
Cheshire East	Sandbach	171,376	180,441	351,817	450	1166
Cheshire West & Chester	Chester	156,636	165,335	321,971	354	916
Cornwall	Truro	241,415	257,699	499,114	1369	3547
Darlington	Darlington	46,960	50,878	97,838	76	197
Derby	Derby	108,240	113,468	221,708	30	78
Durham	.Durham	239,908	253,562	493,470	860	2227
East Riding of Yorkshire	Beverley	153,049	161,064	314,113	930	2408
Halton	Widnes	57,135	61,073	118,208	31	79
Hartlepool	Hartlepool	42,560	46,051	88,611	36	94
Herefordshire	Hereford	85,350	89,521	174,871	842	2180
Isle of Wight	Newport	63,697	69,034	132,731	147	380
Isles of Scilly	Hugh Town	1,072	1,081	2,153	6	16
Kingston upon Hull	Kingston upon Hull	119,131	124,458	243,589	28	71
Leicester	Leicester	134,782	145,139	279,921	28	73
Luton	Luton	92,119	92,252	184,371	17	43
Medway Towns	Rochester	122,896	126,592	249,488	74	192
Middlesborough	Middlesborough	64,694	70,161	134,855	21	54
Milton Keynes	Milton Keynes	102,844	104,213	207,057	119	309
North East Lincolnshire	Grimsby	76,706	81,273	157,979	74	192
North Lincolnshire	Brigg	74,771	78,078	152,849	327	846
North Somerset	Weston-super-Mare	91,632	96,932	188,564	144	374
Northumberland	Morpeth	149,953	157,237	307,190	1936	5013
Nottingham	Nottingham	132,530	134,458	266,988	29	75
Peterborough	Peterborough	76,010	80,051	156,061	132	343
Plymouth	Plymouth	117,571	123,149	240,720	31	80
Poole	Poole	66,055	72,233	138,288	25	65
Portsmouth	Portsmouth	92,042	94,659	186,701	15	40
Reading	Reading	72,076	71,020	143,096	15	40
Redcar & Cleveland	Redcar	67,095	72,037	139,132	95	245
Rutland	Oakham	17,753	16,810	34,563	147	382
Shropshire	Shrewsbury	140,108	143,065	283,173	1234	3197
Slough	Slough	59,318	59,749	119,067	13	33
South Gloucestershire	Thornbury	121,441	124,200	245,641	192	497
Southampton	Southampton	108,784	108,661	217,445	19	50
Southend-on-Sea	Southend	76,749	83,508	160,257	16	42
Stockton-on-Tees	Stockton-on-Tees	87,123	91,285	178,408	79	204
Stoke-on-Trent	Stoke-on-Trent	117,158	123,478	240,636	36	93
Swindon	Swindon	89,560	90,491	180,051	89	230
Telford & Wrekin	Telford	77,859	80,466	158,325	112	290
Thurrock	Grays	69,669	73,459	143,128	63	163
Torbay	Torquay	61,773	67,933	129,706	24	63
Warrington	Warrington	93,877	97,203	191,080	70	181
West Berkshire	Newbury	71,703	72,780	144,483	272	704
Wiltshire	Trowbridge	213,393	219,580	432,973	1256	3255
Windsor & Maidenhead	Maidenhead	65,895	67,731	133,626	76	197
Wokingham	Wokingham	75,118	75,111	150,229	69	179
York	York	87,137	93,957	181,094	105	272
		5,500,951	5,748,246	11,249,197	12,911	33,433

London Boroughs

		Population			Area	
Authority	*Headquarters*	*male*	*female*	*total*	*sq miles*	*sq km*
Barking & Dagenham	Dagenham	78,068	85,876	163,944	14	36
Barnet	Hendon	149,781	164,783	314,564	33	87
Bexley	Bexleyheath	105,148	113,159	218,307	23	61
Brent	Wembley	127,806	135,658	263,464	17	43
Bromley	Bromley	141,785	153,747	295,532	58	150
Camden	Camden	95,398	102,622	198,020	8	22
City of London	Guildhall, London	3832	3353	7,185	1	3
Croydon	Croydon	159,111	171,476	330,587	33	87
Ealing	Ealing	147,563	153,385	300,948	21	56
Enfield	Enfield	130,706	142,853	273,559	31	81
Greenwich	Woolwich	102,777	111,626	214,403	18	47
Hackney	Hackney	97,003	105,821	202,824	7	19
Hammersmith & Fulham	Hammersmith	78,993	86,249	165,242	6	16
Haringey	Wood Green	103,666	112,841	216,507	11	30
Harrow	Harrow	99,953	106,861	206,814	19	50
Havering	Romford	107,957	116,291	224,248	43	112
Hillingdon	Uxbridge	117,461	125,545	243,006	45	116
Hounslow	Hounslow	104,239	108,102	212,341	22	56
Islington	Islington	84,229	91,568	175,797	6	15
Kensington & Chelsea	Kensington	75,959	82,960	158,919	5	12
Kingston upon Thames	Kingston upon Thames	71,987	75,286	147,273	14	37
Lambeth	Lambeth	131,152	135,017	266,169	10	27
Lewisham	Catford	119,979	128,943	248,922	14	35
Merton	Morden	91,514	96,394	187,908	15	38
Newham	East Ham	119,872	124,019	243,891	14	36
Redbridge	Ilford	115,849	122,786	238,635	22	56
Richmond upon Thames	Twickenham	83,338	88,997	172,335	22	57
Southwark	Southwark	119,817	125,049	244,866	11	29
Sutton	Sutton	86,878	92,890	179,768	17	44
Tower Hamlets	Tower Hamlets	98,178	97,928	196,106	8	20
Waltham Forest	Walthamstow	106,245	112,096	218,341	15	39
Wandsworth	Wandsworth	123,742	136,638	260,380	13	34
Westminster	Westminster	88,807	92,479	181,286	8	21
		3,468,793	3,703,298	7,172,091	607	1572

Scottish Districts

		Population			Area	
District Council	*Headquarters*	*male*	*female*	*total*	*sq miles*	*sq km*
Aberdeen City	Aberdeen	103,818	108,307	212,125	72	186
Aberdeenshire	Aberdeen	112,470	114,401	226,871	2437	6313
Angus	Forfar	52,458	55,942	108,400	842	2182
Argyll and Bute	Argyll	44,877	46,429	91,306	2668	6909
Clackmannanshire	Alloa	23,234	24,843	48,077	61	159
Comhairlenan Eilean Siar	Stornoway	13,082	13,420	26,502	1186	3071
Dumfries and Galloway	Dumfries	71,303	76,462	147,765	2481	6426
Dundee	Dundee	69,140	76,523	145,663	23	60
East Ayrshire	Kilmarnock	57,842	62,393	120,235	487	1262
East Dunbartonshire	Glasgow	52,014	56,229	108,243	68	175
East Lothian	Haddington	42,963	47,125	90,088	262	679
East Renfrewshire	Glasgow	42,583	46,728	89,311	67	174
Edinburgh City	Edinburgh	214,711	233,913	448,624	102	264
Falkirk	Falkirk	70,016	75,175	145,191	115	297
Fife	Glenrothes	167,628	181,801	349,429	512	1325
Glasgow City	Glasgow	272,309	305,560	577,869	68	175
Highland	Inverness	102,297	106,617	208,914	9907	25,659
Inverclyde	Greenock	40,098	44,105	84,203	62	160
Midlothian	Dalkeith	38,670	42,271	80,941	137	354
Moray	Elgin	43,447	43,493	86,940	864	2238
North Ayrshire	Irvine	64,238	71,579	135,817	342	885
North Lanarkshire	Motherwell	153,966	167,101	321,067	181	470
Orkney Islands	Kirkwall	9,497	9,748	19,245	382	990
Perth and Kinrosshire	Perth	65,172	69,777	134,949	2041	5286
Renfrewshire	Paisley	82,525	90,342	172,867	101	261
Scottish Borders	Newton St Boswells	51,361	55,403	106,764	1827	4732
Shetland Islands	Lerwick	11,071	10,917	21,988	566	1466
South Ayrshire	Ayr	53,406	58,691	112,097	472	1222
South Lanarkshire	Hamilton	144,206	158,010	302,216	684	1772
Stirling	Stirling	41,194	45,018	86,212	844	2187
West Dunbartonshire	Dumbarton	44,197	49,181	93,378	61	159
West Lothian	Livingston	76,701	82,013	158,714	165	427
		2,432,494	2,629,517	5,062,011	30,087	77,925

Irish County Councils

		Population			Area	
District Council	*Headquarters*	*male*	*female*	*total*	*sq miles*	*sq km*
Carlow	Carlow	23,403	22,611	46,014	347	898
Cavan	Cavan	29,015	27,531	56,546	746	1932
Clare	Ennis	52,063	51,214	103,277	1329	3442
Cork	Cork	222,317	225,512	447,829	2899	7508
Donegal	Lifford	69,016	68,559	137,575	1876	4860
Dublin	Dublin	544,075	578,746	1,122,821	355	921
Galway	Galway	104,367	104,710	209,077	2375	6151
Kerry	Tralee	66,572	65,955	132,527	1828	4735
Kildare	Naas	82,735	81,209	163,944	654	1694
Kilkenny	Kilkenny	40,540	39,799	80,339	800	2072
Laoi(ghi)s	Portlaoise	30,131	28,643	58,774	664	1719
Leitrim	Carrick-on-Shannon	13,324	12,475	25,799	613	1589
Limerick	Limerick	87,631	87,673	175,304	1066	2760
Longford	Longford	15,794	15,274	31,068	421	1091
Louth	Dundalk	50,489	51,332	101,821	321	832
Mayo	Castlebar	59,149	58,297	117,446	2158	5588
Meath	Navan	67,733	66,272	134,005	901	2335
Monaghan	Monaghan	26,806	25,787	52,593	500	1296
Offaly	Tullamore	32,185	31,478	63,663	768	1990
Roscommon	Roscommon	27,583	26,191	53,774	984	2548
Sligo	Sligo	28,771	29,429	58,200	709	1837
Tipperary	Clonmel	70,863	69,268	140,131	1662	4304
Waterford	Dungarvan	50,672	50,874	101,546	718	1859
Westmeath	Mullingar	35,960	35,898	71,858	705	1825
Wexford	Wexford	58,170	58,426	116,596	913	2365
Wicklow	Wicklow	56,800	57,876	114,676	785	2033
		1,946,164	1,971,039	3,917,203	27,096	70,184

Welsh Districts

District Council	Headquarters	Population male	female	total	Area sq miles	sq km
Anglesey, Isle of	Anglesey	32,348	34,481	66,829	275	711
Blaenau Gwent	Ebbw Vale	33,969	36,095	70,064	42	109
Bridgend	Bridgend	62,506	66,139	128,645	97	251
Caerphilly	Ystrad Mynach	82,594	86,925	169,519	107	277
Cardiff	Cardiff	145,761	159,592	305,353	54	139
Carmarthenshire	Carmarthen	83,171	89,671	172,842	915	2371
Ceredigion	Aberystwyth	36,546	38,395	74,941	693	1794
Conwy	Conwy	52,161	57,435	109,596	435	1126
Denbighshire	Ruthin	44,544	48,521	93,065	323	837
Flintshire	Mold	72,894	75,700	148,594	169	438
Gwynedd	Caernarfon	56,029	60,814	116,843	979	2535
Merthyr Tydfil	Merthyr Tydfil	26,929	29,052	55,981	43	111
Monmouthshire	Cwmbran	41,448	43,437	84,885	328	849
Neath Port Talbot	Port Talbot	64,968	69,500	134,468	170	441
Newport	Newport	65,764	71,247	137,011	73	190
Pembrokeshire	Haverfordwest	55,033	59,098	114,131	622	1610
Powys	Llandrindod Wells	62,493	63,861	126,354	2000	5181
Rhondda Cynon Taff	Cardiff	112,457	119,489	231,946	164	424
Swansea	Swansea	108,075	115,226	223,301	146	378
Torfaen	Pontypool	44,014	46,935	90,949	49	126
Vale of Glamorgan	Barry	57,356	61,936	119,292	128	331
Wrexham	Wrexham	62,722	65,754	128,476	195	504
		1,403,782	1,499,303	2,903,085	8005	20,733

Northern Ireland Districts

District Council	Headquarters	Population male	female	total	Area sq miles	sq km
Antrim	Antrim	24,242	24,124	48,366	223	577
Ards	Newtownards	35,759	37,485	73,244	145	376
Armagh	Armagh	26,923	27,340	54,263	259	671
Ballymena	Ballymena	28,571	30,039	58,610	244	632
Ballymoney	Ballymoney	13,323	13,571	26,894	161	418
Banbridge	Banbridge	20,705	20,687	41,392	175	453
Belfast	Belfast	129,778	147,613	277,391	44	115
Carrickfergus	Carrickfergus	18,239	19,420	37,659	32	82
Castlereagh	Castlereagh	31,669	34,819	66,488	33	85
Coleraine	Coleraine	26,877	29,438	56,315	188	486
Cookstown	Cookstown	16,188	16,393	32,581	240	622
Craigavon	Craigavon	39,753	40,918	80,671	146	378
Derry	Londonderry	51,137	53,929	105,066	149	387
Down	Downpatrick	31,622	32,206	63,828	250	647
Dungannon	Dungannon	23,624	24,111	47,735	303	784
Fermanagh	Enniskillen	28,818	28,709	57,527	724	1876
Larne	Larne	15,125	15,707	30,832	130	336
Limavady	Limavady	16,497	15,925	32,422	226	586
Lisburn	Lisburn	52,979	55,715	108,694	173	447
Magherafelt	Magherafelt	20,041	19,739	39,780	221	573
Moyle	Ballycastle	7,831	8,102	15,933	185	480
Newry & Mourne	Newry	43,095	43,963	87,058	348	902
Newtownabbey	Newtownabbey	38,661	41,334	79,995	58	151
North Down	Bangor	36,821	39,502	76,323	31	81
Omagh	Omagh	24,038	23,914	47,952	436	1130
Strabane	Strabane	19,133	19,115	38,248	333	862
		821,449	863,818	1,685,267	5458	14,137

Population summary as per Census

	Population			Area	
	male	*female*	*total*	*sq miles*	*sq km*
England					
Counties	9,708,888	10,187,222	19,896,110	34,105	88337
Metropolitan Authorities	5,243,512	5,577,921	10,821,433	2680	6941
Non-Metropolitan Authorities	5,500,951	5,748,246	11,249,197	12,911	33,433
London	3,468,793	3,703,298	7,172,091	607	1572
England total	23,922,144	25,216,687	49,138,831	50,303	130,283
Scotland	2,432,494	2,629,517	5,062,011	30,087	77,925
Wales	1,403,782	1,499,303	2,903,085	8005	20,733
Great Britain	27,758,420	29,345,507	57,103,927	88,395	228,941
Northern Ireland	821,449	863,818	1,685,267	5458	14,137
United Kingdom	28,579,869	30,209,325	58,789,194	93,853	243,078
Ireland	1,946,164	1,971,039	3,917,203	27,096	70,184
British (and Irish) Isles	30,526,033	32,180,364	62,706,397	120,949	313,262

Population summary as per *A to Z of Britain and Ireland*

	Population			Area	
	male	*female*	*total*	*sq miles*	*sq km*
Bedfordshire	281,283	284,660	565,943	477	1235
Berkshire	398,989	401,129	800,118	487	1262
Buckinghamshire	337,583	348,500	686,083	724	1874
Cambridgeshire	349,655	359,064	708,719	1308	3389
Cheshire	479,024	504,052	983,076	905	2342
Cornwall (and Isles of Scilly)	242,487	258,780	501,267	1375	3563
Cumbria	237,915	249,692	487,607	2613	6768
Derbyshire	469,079	487,214	956,293	1013	2625
Devon	519,357	555,562	1,074,919	2590	6707
Dorset	333,269	359,443	692,712	1024	2651
Durham	371,104	394,382	765,486	1011	2620
Essex	786,611	827,609	1,614,220	1417	3670
Gloucestershire	396,954	413,246	810,200	1216	3150
Greater Manchester	1,208,177	1,274,151	2,482,328	495	1280
Hampshire (and the Isle of Wight)	872,566	904,414	1,776,980	1602	4148
Herefordshire	85,350	89,521	174,871	842	2180
Hertfordshire	505,059	528,918	1,033,977	634	1643
Kent	766,782	812,424	1,579,206	1443	3735
Lancashire	686,584	728,143	1,414,727	1185	3075
Leicestershire	453,803	470,259	924,062	980	2538
Lincolnshire	468,061	489,412	957,473	2687	6959
London	3,468,793	3,703,298	7,172,091	607	1572
Merseyside	647,254	714,772	1,362,026	249	644
Norfolk	387,827	408,901	796,728	2073	5371
Northamptonshire	310,744	318,932	629,676	913	2364
Northumberland	149,953	157,237	307,190	1936	5013
Nottinghamshire	498,648	516,850	1,015,498	833	2160
Oxfordshire	299,257	306,231	605,488	1006	2606
Shropshire	217,967	223,531	441,498	1346	3487
Somerset	601,395	634,917	1,236,312	1653	4281
Staffordshire	513,318	534,062	1,047,380	1046	2713
Suffolk	327,900	340,653	668,553	1468	3801
Surrey	516,525	542,490	1,059,015	642	1663
Sussex (East)	352,849	387,292	740,141	692	1791
Sussex (West)	360,604	393,010	753,614	769	1990
Tyne & Wear	520,286	555,652	1,075,938	209	538
Warwickshire	248,267	257,593	505,860	763	1975
West Midlands	1,244,322	1,311,270	2,555,592	348	902
Wiltshire	302,953	310,071	613,024	1345	3485
Worcestershire	265,887	276,220	542,107	672	1741

Population				Area	
	male	female	total	sq miles	sq km
Yorkshire (East)	272,180	285,522	557,702	958	2479
Yorkshire (North)	542,050	575,532	1,117,582	3364	8711
Yorkshire (South)	617,531	648,807	1,266,338	599	1552
Yorkshire (West)	1,005,942	1,073,269	2,079,211	784	2030
England Total	23,922,144	25,216,687	49,138,831	50,303	130,283
Scottish Borders	51,361	55,403	106,764	1827	4732
Central	134,444	145,036	279,480	1020	2643
Dumfries & Galloway	71,303	76,462	147,765	2481	6426
Fife	167,628	181,801	349,429	512	1325
Grampian	259,735	266,201	525,936	3373	8737
Highland	102,297	106,617	208,914	9907	25,659
Lothian	373,045	405,322	778,367	666	1724
Orkney Islands	9,497	9,748	19,245	382	990
Shetland Islands	11,071	10,917	21,988	566	1466
Strathclyde	1,052,261	1,156,348	2,208,609	5261	13,624
Tayside	186,770	202,242	389,012	2906	7528
Western Isles	13,082	13,420	26,502	1186	3071
Scotland Total	2,432,494	2,629,517	5,062,011	30,087	77,925
Clwyd	232,321	247,410	479,731	1122	2905
Dyfed	174,750	187,164	361,914	2230	5775
Gwent	267,789	284,639	552,428	599	1551
Gwynedd	88,377	95,295	183,672	1254	3246
Mid Glamorgan	201,892	214,680	416,572	304	786
Powys	62,493	63,861	126,354	2000	5181
South Glamorgan	203,117	221,528	424,645	182	470
West Glamorgan	173,043	184,726	357,769	316	819
Wales Total	1,403,782	1,499,303	2,903,085	8007	20,733
Antrim	328,749	355,625	68,4374	1250	3238
Armagh	109,771	112,221	221,992	753	1951
(London) Derry	114,552	119,031	233,583	784	2032
Down	156,576	164,699	321,275	634	1642
Fermanagh	28,818	28,709	57,527	724	1876
Tyrone	82,983	83,533	166,516	1312	3398
Northern Ireland Total	821,449	863,818	1,685,267	5457	14137
Carlow	23,403	22,611	46,014	347	898
Cavan	29,015	27,531	56,546	746	1932
Clare	52,063	51,214	103,277	1329	3442
Cork	222,317	225,512	447,829	2899	7508
Donegal	69,016	68,559	137,575	1876	4860
Dublin	544,075	578,746	1,122,821	355	921
Galway	104,367	104,710	209,077	2375	6151
Kerry	66,572	65,955	132,527	1828	4735
Kildare	82,735	81,209	163,944	654	1694
Kilkenny	40,540	39,799	80,339	800	2072
Laois	30,131	28,643	58,774	664	1719
Leitrim	13,324	12,475	25,799	613	1589
Limerick	87,631	87,673	175,304	1066	2760
Longford	15,794	15,274	31,068	421	1091
Louth	50,489	51,332	101,821	321	832
Mayo	59,149	58,297	117,446	2158	5588
Meath	67,733	66,272	134,005	901	2335
Monaghan	26,806	25,787	52,593	500	1296
Offaly	32,185	31,478	63,663	768	1990
Roscommon	27,583	26,191	53,774	984	2548
Sligo	28,771	29,429	58,200	709	1837
Tipperary	70,863	69,268	140,131	1662	4304
Waterford	50,672	50,874	101,546	718	1859
Westmeath	35,960	35,898	71,858	705	1825
Wexford	58,170	58,426	116,596	913	2365
Wicklow	56,800	57,876	114,676	785	2033
Ireland Total	1,946,164	1,971,039	3,917,203	27,097	70,184

Note: There are slight rounding differences in one or two of the mileage conversions.

Acknowledgements

I would like to thank the following people for their help in the compilation of this work: Kevin Ashman, for casting a knowledgeable eye over his home county of Hampshire; Ruth Benjamin, for supplying her considerable literary and computer skills to aid completion; Mark Bytheway, for supplying valuable research data for Scotland and Ireland; the Caroline Davidson Literary Agency, for her expertise and advice given me in the formation stage of the project; Gavin Fuller, for filling in gaps in my castles directory; Steve Gove, for not only scribing much of the Sussex section but also for undertaking the daunting prospect of editing the whole book!; Stephen Guise (and latterly Iain Hunt and Tim Whiting), my publishers of the past few years, for their unerring support and endeavours in coordinating the mammoth task of guiding this book to publication; Chris Hughes, for his input on railways; June Humphries, for paginating the original script; Will Jones for administering my website; Phil Lewis, for putting me in touch with his lovely secretary who ensured I made my copy deadline; Brian O'Connor, for giving expert information on some of the Irish islands; Diane Penny, the aforementioned secretary, for printing and sorting the text for presentation to Little, Brown; Alan Samson, my original publisher, for initiating the concept of the A to Z series and for having the belief in me to bring that concept to fruition; and finally, Barry Simmons, Geoff Thomas and Tim Westcott for detailing many of the attractions of Surrey, Lancashire and Wiltshire respectively. I must also give a special thank you to Eric Kilby who helped me in so many areas, seeking out obscure islands, offering valuable assistance in the battles section and supplying me with a plethora of information on all the Celtic nations. When spirits were low and on days when my labour of love seemed more like a Sisyphean chore, Eric would invariably send me something to ease my burden and make me believe I could achieve my goals. Geoff and Eric were also employed as what I refer to as proofreaders plus.

Many of my friends listed above will be instantly recognisable as household names in the world of quiz, including British, European and World Quiz Champions, *Brains of Britain*, *Eggheads*, *Fifteen-to-One* champions and *Mastermind* champions of the distant, and in Geoff's case the not too distant past. Four more friends and past contributors I would like to mention, although they are no longer with us, are Eric Carden, Jeremy Beadle MBE, Craig Scott and Magnus Magnusson KBE. Eric was a quiet man but a very knowledgeable one. He helped me behind the scenes in the foundation of the British Quiz Association, proofed quizzes for me and input a lot of data when I reluctantly became computerised and had the task of transferring my loose-leaf pages to Lotus spreadsheets. Eric also has the distinction of being one of few quiz players to have ever beaten the mighty Kevin Ashman in a televised quiz. Jeremy let me loose on his vast library as and when the desire took me and he also ensured I was privy to every conceivable publication however tenuously linked to Britain and Ireland, often arranging for books to be sent to me via online book clubs. Craig was a big burly American with a heart and brain to match his size. He was the former editor of the Mastermind Club in-house magazine *Pass*, and he was also the president of the club at the time of his premature death. When I think of Craig I think Bill Bryson, another American Anglophile hewn from the same block. Magnus requires no introduction from me and his rich body of work both in print and on film, as well as his status as an ambassador for his native Iceland and much-loved home of Scotland, will ensure his lasting legacy as one of these islands' favourite sons. It was Magnus that first introduced me to publisher Alan Samson, who himself was a Mastermind contender way back in 1985. Both Craig and Magnus offered me valuable advice on their adopted country of Scotland.

One final acknowledgement I must make is to my much-loved family; Douglas, my father, brothers Mike, Kevin, Gary and Shaun, sister June, and our sainted mother, Elizabeth. It is to them I dedicate this work.